MW00773525

YOUR WORD IS A LAMP TO MY FEET AND A LIGHT FOR MY PATH. PS 119:105

PRESENTED

TO

BY

ON

YOU KNIT ME TOGETHER IN MY MOTHER'S WOMB. PS 139:13

BIRTHS

NAME

BORN TO DATE

NAME

BORN TO DATE

NAME

BORN TO DATE

NAME

BORN TO DATE

NAME

BORN TO DATE

NAME

BORN TO DATE

NAME

BORN TO DATE

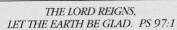

THE LORD REIGNS,
LET THE EARTH BE GLAD. PS 97:1

SPECIAL EVENTS

EVENT

PLACE DATE

EVENT

PLACE DATE

EVENT

PLACE DATE

EVENT

PLACE DATE

EVENT

PLACE DATE

EVENT

PLACE DATE

A MAN WILL… BE UNITED TO HIS WIFE, AND THEY WILL BECOME ONE FLESH. GE 2:24

THIS CERTIFIES THAT

____

and

____

were united in

HOLY MATRIMONY

on ______________________ *the* ______________

day of ______________________ *A.D.* ______________

at ______________________________

in accordance with the laws of ______________________________

Officiating ______________________________

Witness ______________________________

Witness ______________________________

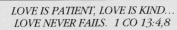

LOVE IS PATIENT, LOVE IS KIND...
LOVE NEVER FAILS. 1 CO 13:4,8

MARRIAGES

HUSBAND

WIFE

PLACE DATE

HUSBAND

WIFE

PLACE DATE

HUSBAND

WIFE

PLACE DATE

HUSBAND

WIFE

PLACE DATE

HUSBAND

WIFE

PLACE DATE

HUSBAND

WIFE

PLACE DATE

BLESSED IS THE MAN
WHO FEARS THE LORD. PS 112:1

HUSBAND'S FAMILY TREE

NAME

BIRTHPLACE DATE

BROTHERS AND SISTERS

PARENTS

FATHER

NAME

BIRTHPLACE DATE

MOTHER

NAME

BIRTHPLACE DATE

GRANDPARENTS

PATERNAL

GRANDFATHER

BIRTHPLACE DATE

GRANDMOTHER

BIRTHPLACE DATE

MATERNAL

GRANDFATHER

BIRTHPLACE DATE

GRANDMOTHER

BIRTHPLACE DATE

GREAT-GRANDPARENTS

PATERNAL

GRANDFATHER'S FATHER

BIRTHPLACE DATE

GRANDFATHER'S MOTHER

BIRTHPLACE DATE

GRANDMOTHER'S FATHER

BIRTHPLACE DATE

GRANDMOTHER'S MOTHER

BIRTHPLACE DATE

MATERNAL

GRANDFATHER'S FATHER

BIRTHPLACE DATE

GRANDFATHER'S MOTHER

BIRTHPLACE DATE

GRANDMOTHER'S FATHER

BIRTHPLACE DATE

GRANDMOTHER'S MOTHER

BIRTHPLACE DATE

A WOMAN WHO FEARS THE LORD IS TO BE PRAISED. PR 31:30

WIFE'S FAMILY TREE

NAME

BIRTHPLACE DATE

BROTHERS AND SISTERS

PARENTS

FATHER

NAME

BIRTHPLACE DATE

MOTHER

NAME

BIRTHPLACE DATE

GRANDPARENTS

PATERNAL

GRANDFATHER

BIRTHPLACE DATE

GRANDMOTHER

BIRTHPLACE DATE

MATERNAL

GRANDFATHER

BIRTHPLACE DATE

GRANDMOTHER

BIRTHPLACE DATE

GREAT-GRANDPARENTS

PATERNAL

GRANDFATHER'S FATHER

BIRTHPLACE DATE

GRANDFATHER'S MOTHER

BIRTHPLACE DATE

GRANDMOTHER'S FATHER

BIRTHPLACE DATE

GRANDMOTHER'S MOTHER

BIRTHPLACE DATE

MATERNAL

GRANDFATHER'S FATHER

BIRTHPLACE DATE

GRANDFATHER'S MOTHER

BIRTHPLACE DATE

GRANDMOTHER'S FATHER

BIRTHPLACE DATE

GRANDMOTHER'S MOTHER

BIRTHPLACE DATE

FOR TO ME, TO LIVE IS CHRIST AND TO DIE IS GAIN. PHP 1:21

DEATHS

NAME

DATE

NAME

DATE

NAME

DATE

NAME

DATE

NAME

DATE

NAME

DATE

NAME

DATE

THE FULL LIFE STUDY BIBLE

THE FULL LIFE STUDY BIBLE

NEW INTERNATIONAL VERSION

General Editor
DONALD C. STAMPS

Associate Editor
J. WESLEY ADAMS

ZONDERVAN PUBLISHING HOUSE
GRAND RAPIDS, MICHIGAN 49530, U.S.A.

Library of Congress Catalog Card Number 92–060910

Published by Zondervan Publishing House
Grand Rapids, Michigan 49530, U.S.A.
http://www.zondervan.com

98 99 00 01 02 9 8 7 6

RRD-C

You will be pleased to know that a portion of the purchase price of your new NIV Bible has been provided to International Bible Society to help spread the gospel of Jesus Christ around the world!

The Full Life Study Bible

General Editor

Donald C. Stamps, M.A., M. Div.

Writer of study notes and articles

Associate Editor

J. Wesley Adams, Ph.D.

Writer of introductions to books of the Bible

Editorial Committee

Stanley M. Horton, Th.D., Chairman

William W. Menzies, Ph.D., Co-chairman

French Arrington, Ph.D.

Robert Shank, A.B., D.H.L.

Roger Stronstad, M.C.S.

Richard Waters, D.Min.

Bishop Roy L. H. Winbush, M.Div., D.D.

Zondervan Editors

Verlyn D. Verbrugge, Ph.D.

Dirk R. Buursma, M.Div.

Dedication

On November 7, 1991, after a year-long struggle with cancer, Donald C. Stamps went to be with his Lord and Savior (Philippians 1:21,23). Though he did not live to see the complete Full Life Study Bible published, he did persevere to finish writing the notes. We gratefully acknowledge that his vision, his love for God and the Word, his zeal for truth and righteousness, and his persevering faith enabled God to use him in a crucial way for the realization of this Study Bible. Thus we dedicate in his memory this edition of God's Word to the glory of God and the advancement of His kingdom, righteousness and truth throughout the world.

Table of Contents

Contents: Articles

Contents: Maps and Charts

Abbreviations

BOOKS OF THE BIBLE

Genesis	Ge
Exodus	Ex
Leviticus	Lev
Numbers	Nu
Deuteronomy	Dt
Joshua	Jos
Judges	Jdg
Ruth	Ru
1 Samuel	1Sa
2 Samuel	2Sa
1 Kings	1Ki
2 Kings	2Ki
1 Chronicles	1Ch
2 Chronicles	2Ch
Ezra	Ezr
Nehemiah	Ne
Esther	Est
Job	Job
Psalms	Ps
Proverbs	Pr
Ecclesiastes	Ecc
Song of Songs	SS
Isaiah	Isa
Jeremiah	Jer
Lamentations	La
Ezekiel	Eze
Daniel	Da
Hosea	Hos
Joel	Joel
Amos	Am
Obadiah	Ob
Jonah	Jnh
Micah	Mic
Nahum	Na
Habakkuk	Hab
Zephaniah	Zep
Haggai	Hag
Zechariah	Zec
Malachi	Mal
Matthew	Mt
Mark	Mk
Luke	Lk
John	Jn
Acts	Ac
Romans	Ro
1 Corinthians	1Co
2 Corinthians	2Co
Galatians	Gal
Ephesians	Eph
Philippians	Php
Colossians	Col
1 Thessalonians	1Th
2 Thessalonians	2Th
1 Timothy	1Ti
2 Timothy	2Ti
Titus	Tit
Philemon	Phm
Hebrews	Heb
James	Jas
1 Peter	1Pe
2 Peter	2Pe
1 John	1Jn
2 John	2Jn
3 John	3Jn
Jude	Jude
Revelation	Rev

GENERAL

i.e.	that is
e.g.	for example
ch., chs.	chapter(s)
v., vv.	verse(s)
etc.	and so forth
c.	about (with dates)
f., ff.	and the following verse(s)
Gk	Greek
Heb	Hebrew

The Full Life Study Bible

Author's Preface

The vision, call and urgency from God for this study Bible came to me while serving as a missionary in Brazil. I realized how much Christian workers needed a Bible that would give them direction in their thinking and preaching. Thus, ten years ago I began writing the notes and articles for this work. Later, when I came back to the United States for a short period of time, I discovered a similar desire among both pastors and lay people for a study Bible with notes that have a Pentecostal emphasis.

During the past number of years I have written with an increasing assurance that the Holy Spirit is not confined to the pages of Scripture, but that he wants to act today as he did in Bible times. The Spirit has come to remain personally with God's people, and his abiding presence is to be manifested in righteousness and power (Mt 6:33; Ro 14:17; 1Co 2:4; 4:20; Heb 1:8). In and through the church, God's Spirit desires to work in the same manner as he did in the earthly ministry of Jesus and continued to do in the apostolic church of the first century.

This study Bible is called *The Full Life Study Bible*. It has been so named because it is founded on three fundamental convictions:

(1) The original revelation of Christ and the apostles as recorded in the Bible is fully inspired by the Holy Spirit; along with the OT, it is God's inerrant and infallible truth and the ultimate authority for the church of Christ today. All believers throughout history are dependent on the words and teachings of Biblical revelation for determining God's standard of truth and practice. In other words, we must view the NT message, standards and experience as God's preeminent pattern for the church, valid for all times.

(2) It is the task of every generation of believers not only to accept the NT as God's inspired Word, but also to sincerely seek to reproduce in their personal lives and congregations the same faith, devotion and power demonstrated in and through the faithful members of the early church. I am persuaded that the full life in the Spirit as promised by Christ and experienced by NT believers is still available for God's people today (Jn 10:10; 17:20; Ac 2:38-39; Eph 3:20-21; 4:11-13). It is the divine inheritance of all God's children to receive the fullness of Christ in the original power of the Holy Spirit.

(3) The church will fully experience the original kingdom power and life in the Holy Spirit only as it seeks with all its heart the righteousness and holiness set forth by God in the NT as his standard and will for all believers (2Co 6:14-18). Kingdom power and kingdom righteousness go together; they cannot be separated. Jesus states that we must seek both God's "kingdom and his righteousness" (Mt 6:33). The apostle Paul states that God's kingdom consists of both "power" (1Co 4:20) and "righteousness" (Ro 14:17). Thus the way to the fullness of God's kingdom with all its redemptive power is found in sincere faith in and devotion to the Lord Jesus Christ and in a separation from all unrighteousness that offends both God and the Holy Spirit whom he has poured out (Ac 2:17,38-40).

In summary, the major purpose of this study Bible is to lead you, the reader, to an abiding faith in holy Scripture, and especially a deeper faith in the NT's apostolic message that will lead you to a greater expectancy for a NT experience made possible by the fullness of Christ living in the church (Eph 4:13) and by the fullness of the Holy Spirit living in the believer (Ac 2:4; 4:31).

We sincerely hope and pray that all readers will earnestly seek the NT church's devotion to God, its longing for the nearness of the risen Christ, its unshakeable trust in and love for God's Word, its zeal for truth and righteousness, its mutual care for other believers, its compassion for the lost, its dedication to a life of fervent prayer, its passion for holiness, its fullness in the Spirit, its manifestation of spiritual gifts, its urgency to preach the gospel to all nations, and its hope for the imminent return of our Lord and Savior Jesus Christ.

I gratefully acknowledge that I owe a great debt to those who served on the Editorial Committee for this study Bible. Their evaluations and suggestions have been invaluable. They gave of themselves and sacrificially took time from their own tasks to help in this work. What will be accomplished in God's kingdom through this work is in no small measure due to their help in the Lord. Also, I have benefited from the learning and labor of godly writers past and present who have produced a vast amount of literature and commentaries on the holy Scriptures. I have thankfully entered into their research and expertise and have reaped where they have sown.

Throughout these years of labor I have felt a profound sense of weakness and unworthiness to expound on God's holy Word. Many times I have been driven to my knees in need of special grace and help. I can testify that God, who is rich in mercy and whose grace is sufficient, has sustained me by his Spirit. Through all the long days and hours his Word has spoken to my heart. My desire for a full manifestation of Biblical Christianity has deepened and developed into an intense longing that is surpassed only by my longing for that day of the appearing of our Lord and Savior. With thanks to God—the Father, the Son and the Holy Spirit—for the privilege of laboring in the Scriptures, I send forth this work unto him who loves us and gave himself for us so that we may have life and have it to the full (John 10:10).

Donald C. Stamps
November, 1991

Note: The author's and editor's royalties from *The Full Life Study Bible* will go entirely to missions for the translating and printing of additional copies of *The Full Life Study Bible* in foreign languages.

How to Use The Full Life Study Bible

The Full Life Study Bible is designed to help you gain a more thorough understanding of the truths of God's Word, whereby you may grow in love, purity and faith toward the Lord Jesus Christ (1Ti 1:5). The special features and study helps of *The Full Life Study Bible* are the following:

Sectional headings

The entire Bible contains sectional headings within the Bible text in order to help you more easily understand the subject and content of each section. NOTE: the standard New International Version sectional headings have been altered for this particular edition of the NIV. When two or more passages of Scripture are nearly identical or deal with the same event, this "parallel" is noted at the sectional headings for those passages. Identical or nearly identical passages are noted with *"pp."* Similar passages—those not dealing with the same event—are noted with *"Ref."*

Cross-reference system

The center-column cross-reference system is designed to help you connect one text of the Bible with others that have a similar theme. By using this system, difficult or obscure passages are clarified by Scripture itself. Cross references are indicated by raised light italic letters. A corresponding letter in the center column under the designated verse is followed by a list of appropriate Scripture verses.

When a single word is addressed by both text notes and cross references, the bold NIV text-note letter comes first. The cross references normally appear in the center column and, when necessary, continue at the bottom of the right-hand column preceding the NIV text notes.

The NIV cross-reference system resembles a series of interlocking chains with many links. The head, or organizing, link in each concept chain is indicated by the letter "S" (short for "see"). The appearance of a head link in a list of references usually signals another list of references that will cover a slightly different aspect of the concept or word being studied.

The lists of references are in Biblical order with one exception: If reference is made to a verse within the same chapter, that verse (indicated by "ver") is listed first. If an Old Testament verse is quoted in the New Testament, the New Testament reference is marked with an asterisk (*).

Study Notes

The study notes at the bottom of nearly every page are written from a Pentecostal perspective and with the belief that the full message, standard and experience testified to by Christ and the apostles are forever valid and available for his people today.

The study notes fall into five classes:

(1) Expositional. The notes explain the meaning of words and phrases of many important passages in the Word of God.

(2) Theological. The notes define and explain the great doctrines and truths of the Bible, summarizing the Bible's teachings about baptism, forgiveness, perseverance, repentance, salvation, sanctification, etc.

(3) Devotional. The notes emphasize the importance of maintaining an intimate and devoted relationship with God—the Father, the Son and the Holy Spirit—through faith, obedience, prayer and the many means of grace.

(4) Ethical. The notes direct you to unreservedly commit yourself to God's kingdom and his righteousness. They emphasize the importance of Biblical principles of self-denial, godly conduct, following Christ, separation from sin, discernment of good and evil, and obligation to God and others.

(5) Practical. The notes present useful information on the believer's daily walk. They contain practical instruction about healing, the baptism in the Spirit, bringing up godly children, spiritual warfare, overcoming worry, resisting temptations, etc.

The study notes provide extensive Scripture references (usually in parentheses) that confirm comments made in the notes and help you in further in-depth Bible study. If the Scripture reference in parentheses is from the same chapter, it will normally appear first in the list, with the symbol "v." or "vv." Next will come Scripture references from the same book, usually without mention of the book's name. Last in the parentheses are passages from other Bible books, given in Bible book order. In many cases, other notes and articles are also cross-referenced.

Articles

The articles deal with important subjects more comprehensively than do the notes. They usually appear in close proximity to one of the major texts related to the subject of the article. For a complete list of the articles, see the Table of Contents for Articles on p. viii.

The articles, like the study notes, provide extensive Biblical references in parentheses. In the articles, the name of each Bible book, in Bible book order, is usually given for each reference. If there is no book mentioned before a Scripture reference, it means that that reference is found in the same book as the previous reference.

Introductions

Each book of the Bible has an introduction, which includes (1) an outline of the book; (2) an explanation of the book's background and historical setting, including information about the author, circumstances and date of writing; (3) a statement about the original purpose of the book; (4) a survey of its contents; (5) a list of the book's special features and emphases; and (6) a suggested reading plan for covering the entire Bible in two years (one year for the OT and one year for the NT). Careful reading of the introductions will help you understand each book and its applications more fully. At the end of each introduction, space is provided for you to write personal notes on that book.

Themefinders™

On many pages of this Bible you will see one of twelve symbols in the margin, next to a vertical line. Each of these symbols represents a specific theme of importance in the Pentecostal tradition. They are:

— Baptized in/Filled with the Holy Spirit (begin at Exodus 31:1-6)

— Gifts of the Holy Spirit (begin at Exodus 35:30-35)

— Fruit of the Holy Spirit (begin at Genesis 50:19-21)

— Healing (begin at Genesis 20:17-18)

— Faith that moves mountains (begin at Genesis 15:3-6)

— Witnessing (begin at Exodus 10:1-2)

— Salvation (begin at Genesis 12:1-3)

— Second Coming (begin at Psalm 98:8-9)

— Victory over Satan and demons (begin at Genesis 3:15)

— Overcoming the world and worldliness (begin at Genesis 19:15-26)

— Praise (begin at Exodus 15:1-21)

— Walking in obedience and righteousness (begin at Genesis 5:22)

The symbol informs you which theme is contained in accompanying verses; at the bottom of each vertical line is a Bible text, directing you to the next text on that particular theme.

Charts

The Full Life Study Bible contains various charts that will help you at a glance to learn more about the Bible and its teachings, on such topics as the ministry of Jesus, the kingdom of God versus the kingdom of Satan, the last days of history, the gifts of the Holy Spirit, etc. See the Table of Contents for Maps and Charts on p. ix for a list of these charts.

Maps

A number of maps have been included within the Bible text to help you understand where the events written about in the Bible occurred. See the Table of Contents for Maps and Charts on p. ix for a list of these maps. At the back of this book are 16 full-color maps.

Subject Index

The subject index directs you to the most important notes and articles on the many topics and great doctrines of Scripture. Under each entry in this index, you will find texts of the Bible that have notes on that particular subject; next to the text is the page number on which that note is found. Articles and introductions are also included in this index.

Themefinder™ Index

The Themefinder Index at the back of this Bible lists the Scripture passages assigned to the 12 key themes described earlier in the Themefinder section. Under each pertinent Themefinder you will find the passages in the order in which they are linked.

Reading Plan

The Reading Plan outlined in the back gives you the flexibility of choosing a method of reading through the Bible either in one year or in two years. The reading plan found at the end of each book introduction follows the two-year design, listing Old Testament readings for one year and New Testament readings for the second year.

Concordance

A concordance, compiled and edited by John R. Kohlenberger III and Edward W. Goodrick, is included to help you find Bible verses quickly and easily. By looking up key words in a Bible verse, you can find a verse for which you remember a word or two but not its location. For example, if you wanted to find out where the Bible says that the Word of God is "sharper than any double-edged sword," you could look up either "sharper," "double-edged" or "sword" in the concordance and find that the verse is located at Heb 4:12.

We trust that you will receive a rich blessing from using *The Full Life Study Bible.* It is our prayer that your knowledge of God's Word, your experience of the presence and power of the Holy Spirit, and your daily walk with Christ in truth and righteousness will increase through your use of this book.

Preface

THE NEW INTERNATIONAL VERSION is a completely new translation of the Holy Bible made by over a hundred scholars working directly from the best available Hebrew, Aramaic and Greek texts. It had its beginning in 1965 when, after several years of exploratory study by committees from the Christian Reformed Church and the National Association of Evangelicals, a group of scholars met at Palos Heights, Illinois, and concurred in the need for a new translation of the Bible in contemporary English. This group, though not made up of official church representatives, was transdenominational. Its conclusion was endorsed by a large number of leaders from many denominations who met in Chicago in 1966.

Responsibility for the new version was delegated by the Palos Heights group to a self-governing body of fifteen, the Committee on Bible Translation, composed for the most part of biblical scholars from colleges, universities and seminaries. In 1967 the New York Bible Society (now the International Bible Society) generously undertook the financial sponsorship of the project—a sponsorship that made it possible to enlist the help of many distinguished scholars. The fact that participants from the United States, Great Britain, Canada, Australia and New Zealand worked together gave the project its international scope. That they were from many denominations—including Anglican, Assemblies of God, Baptist, Brethren, Christian Reformed, Church of Christ, Evangelical Free, Lutheran, Mennonite, Methodist, Nazarene, Presbyterian, Wesleyan and other churches—helped to safeguard the translation from sectarian bias.

How it was made helps to give the New International Version its distinctiveness. The translation of each book was assigned to a team of scholars. Next, one of the Intermediate Editorial Committees revised the initial translation, with constant reference to the Hebrew, Aramaic or Greek. Their work then went to one of the General Editorial Committees, which checked it in detail and made another thorough revision. This revision in turn was carefully reviewed by the Committee on Bible Translation, which made further changes and then released the final version for publication. In this way the entire Bible underwent three revisions, during each of which the translation was examined for its faithfulness to the original languages and for its English style. All this involved many thousands of hours of research and discussion regarding the meaning of the texts and the precise way of putting them into English. It may well be that no other translation has been made by a more thorough process of review and revision from committee to committee than this one.

From the beginning of the project, the Committee on Bible Translation held to certain goals for the New International Version: that it would be an accurate translation and one that would have clarity and literary quality and so prove suitable for public and private reading, teaching, preaching, memorizing and liturgical use. The Committee also sought to preserve some measure of continuity with the long tradition of translating the Scriptures into English.

In working toward these goals, the translators were united in their commitment to the authority and infallibility of the Bible as God's Word in written form. They believe that it contains the divine answer to the deepest needs of humanity, that it sheds unique light on our path in a dark world, and that it sets forth the way to our eternal well-being.

The first concern of the translators has been the accuracy of the translation and its fidelity to the thought of the biblical writers. They have weighed the significance of the lexical and grammatical details of the Hebrew, Aramaic and Greek texts. At the same time, they have striven for more than a word-for-word translation. Because thought patterns and syntax differ from language to language, faithful communication of the meaning of the writers of the Bible demands frequent modifications in sentence structure and constant regard for the contextual meanings of words.

A sensitive feeling for style does not always accompany scholarship. Accordingly the Committee on Bible Translation submitted the developing version to a number of stylistic consultants. Two of them read every book of both Old and New Testaments twice—once before and once after the last major revision—and made invaluable suggestions. Samples of the translation were tested for clarity and ease of reading by various kinds of people—young and old, highly educated and less well educated, ministers and laymen.

Concern for clear and natural English—that the New International Version should be idiomatic but not idiosyncratic, contemporary but not dated—motivated the translators and consultants. At the same time, they tried to reflect the differing styles of the biblical writers. In view of the international use of English, the translators sought to avoid obvious Americanisms on the one hand and obvious Anglicisms on the other. A British edition reflects the comparatively few differences of significant idiom and of spelling.

As for the traditional pronouns "thou," "thee" and "thine" in reference to the Deity, the translators judged that to use these archaisms (along with the old verb forms such as "doest," "wouldest" and "hadst") would violate accuracy in translation. Neither Hebrew, Aramaic nor Greek uses special pronouns for the persons of the Godhead. A present-day translation is not enhanced by forms that in the time of the King James Version were used in everyday speech, whether referring to God or man.

For the Old Testament the standard Hebrew text, the Masoretic Text as published in the latest editions of *Biblia Hebraica,* was used throughout. The Dead Sea Scrolls contain material bearing on an earlier stage of the Hebrew text. They were consulted, as were the Samaritan Pentateuch and the ancient scribal traditions relating to textual changes. Sometimes a variant Hebrew reading in the margin of the Masoretic Text was followed instead of the text itself. Such instances, being variants within the Masoretic tradition, are not specified by footnotes. In rare cases, words in the consonantal text were divided differently from the way they appear in the Masoretic Text. Footnotes indicate this. The translators also consulted the more important early versions—the Septuagint; Aquila, Symmachus and Theodotion; the Vulgate; the Syriac Peshitta; the Targums; and for the Psalms the *Juxta Hebraica* of Jerome. Readings from these versions were occasionally followed where the Masoretic Text seemed doubtful and where accepted principles of textual criticism showed that one or more of these textual witnesses appeared to provide the correct reading. Such instances are footnoted. Sometimes vowel letters and vowel signs did not, in the judgment of the translators, represent the correct vowels for the original consonantal text. Accordingly some words were read with a different set of vowels. These instances are usually not indicated by footnotes.

The Greek text used in translating the New Testament was an eclectic one. No other piece of ancient literature has such an abundance of manuscript witnesses as does the New Testament. Where existing manuscripts differ, the translators made their choice of readings according to accepted principles of New Testament textual criticism. Footnotes call attention to places where there was uncertainty about what the original text was. The best current printed texts of the Greek New Testament were used.

There is a sense in which the work of translation is never wholly finished. This applies to all great literature and uniquely so to the Bible. In 1973 the New Testament in the New International Version was published. Since then, suggestions for corrections and revisions have been received from various sources. The Committee on Bible Translation carefully considered the suggestions and adopted a number of them. These were incorporated in the first printing of the entire Bible in 1978. Additional revisions were made by the Committee on Bible Translation in 1983 and appear in printings after that date.

As in other ancient documents, the precise meaning of the biblical texts is sometimes uncertain. This is more often the case with the Hebrew and Aramaic texts than with the Greek text. Although archaeological and linguistic discoveries in this century aid in understanding difficult passages, some uncertainties remain. The more significant of these have been called to the reader's attention in the footnotes.

In regard to the divine name *YHWH,* commonly referred to as the *Tetragrammaton,* the translators adopted the device used in most English versions of rendering that name as "LORD" in capital letters to distinguish it from *Adonai,* another Hebrew word rendered "Lord," for which small letters are used. Wherever the two names stand together in the Old Testament as a compound name of God, they are rendered "Sovereign LORD."

Because for most readers today the phrases "the LORD of hosts" and "God of hosts" have little meaning, this version renders them "the LORD Almighty" and "God Almighty." These renderings convey the sense of the Hebrew, namely, "he who is sovereign over all the 'hosts' (powers) in heaven and on earth, especially over the 'hosts' (armies) of Israel." For readers unacquainted with Hebrew this does not make clear the distinction between *Sabaoth* ("hosts" or "Almighty") and *Shaddai* (which can also be translated "Almighty"), but the latter occurs infrequently and is always footnoted. When *Adonai* and *YHWH Sabaoth* occur together, they are rendered "the Lord, the LORD Almighty."

As for other proper nouns, the familiar spellings of the King James Version are generally retained. Names traditionally spelled with "ch," except where it is final, are usually spelled in this translation with "k" or "c," since the biblical languages do not have the sound that "ch" frequently indicates in English—for example, in *chant.* For well-known names such as Zechariah, however, the traditional spelling has been retained. Variation in the spelling of names in the original languages has usually not been indicated. Where a person or place has two or more different names in the Hebrew, Aramaic or Greek texts, the more familiar one has generally been used, with footnotes where needed.

To achieve clarity the translators sometimes supplied words not in the original texts but required by the context. If there was uncertainty about such material, it is enclosed in brackets. Also for the sake of clarity or style, nouns, including some proper nouns, are sometimes substituted for pronouns, and vice versa. And though the Hebrew writers often shifted back and forth between first, second and third personal pronouns without change of antecedent, this translation often makes them uniform, in accordance with English style and without the use of footnotes.

Poetical passages are printed as poetry, that is, with indentation of lines and with separate stanzas. These are generally designed to reflect the structure of Hebrew poetry. This poetry is normally characterized by parallelism in balanced lines. Most of the poetry in the Bible is in the Old Testament, and scholars differ regarding the scansion of Hebrew lines. The translators determined the stanza divisions for the most part by analysis of the subject matter. The stanzas therefore serve as poetic paragraphs.

As an aid to the reader, italicized sectional headings are inserted in most of the books. They are not to be regarded as part of the NIV text, are not for oral reading, and are not intended to dictate the interpretation of the sections they head.

The footnotes in this version are of several kinds, most of which need no explanation. Those giving alternative translations begin with "Or" and generally introduce the alternative with the last word preceding it in the text, except when it is a single-word alternative; in poetry quoted in a footnote a slant mark indicates a line division. Footnotes introduced by "Or" do not have uniform significance. In some cases two possible translations were considered to have about equal validity. In other cases, though the translators were convinced that the translation in the text was correct, they judged that another interpretation was possible and of sufficient importance to be represented in a footnote.

In the New Testament, footnotes that refer to uncertainty regarding the original text are introduced by "Some manuscripts" or similar expressions. In the Old Testament, evidence for the reading chosen is given first and evidence for the alternative is added after a semicolon (for example: Septuagint; Hebrew *father*). In such notes the term "Hebrew" refers to the Masoretic Text.

It should be noted that minerals, flora and fauna, architectural details, articles of clothing and jewelry, musical instruments and other articles cannot always be identified with precision. Also measures of capacity in the biblical period are particularly uncertain (see the table of weights and measures following the text).

Like all translations of the Bible, made as they are by imperfect man, this one undoubtedly falls short of its goals. Yet we are grateful to God for the extent to which he has enabled us to realize these goals and for the strength he has given us and our colleagues to complete our task. We offer this version of the Bible to him in whose name and for whose glory it has been made. We pray that it will lead many into a better understanding of the Holy Scriptures and a fuller knowledge of Jesus Christ the incarnate Word, of whom the Scriptures so faithfully testify.

The Committee on Bible Translation

June 1978
(Revised August 1983)

Names of the translators and editors may be secured
from the International Bible Society,
translation sponsors of the New International Version,
P.O. Box 62970, Colorado Springs, Colorado 80962-2970 U.S.A.

THE OLD TESTAMENT

GENESIS

Outline

I. The Beginnings of Human History (1:1—11:26)
  A. Origin of the Universe and Life (1:1—2:25)
    1. Summary of all Creation (1:1—2:4)
    2. Expanded Creation Account of Adam and Eve (2:5–25)
  B. Origin of Sin (3:1–24)
    1. Temptation and the Fall (3:1–6)
    2. Consequences of the Fall (3:7–24)
  C. Origins of Civilization (4:1—5:32)
    1. Cain: Pagan Culture (4:1–24)
    2. Seth: A Righteous Remnant (4:25–26)
    3. Genealogical History of Pre-flood Patriarchs (5:1–32)
  D. The Great Flood: God's Judgment on Primeval Civilization (6:1—8:19)
    1. Universal Depravity (6:1–8,11–12)
    2. Noah: Preparation to Save a Righteous Remnant (6:9–22)
    3. Final Instructions and the Flood (7:1—8:19)
  E. Humanity's New Beginning (8:20—11:26)
    1. The Posterity of Noah (8:20—10:32, especially Shem, 11:10–26)
    2. The Tower of Babel (11:1–9)
    3. Genealogical Links Between Shem and Abraham (11:10–26)

II. The Beginnings of the Hebrew People (11:27—50:26)
  A. Abraham (11:27—25:18)
    1. Abram's Family Background (11:27–32)
    2. Abram's Call and Journey of Faith (12:1—14:24)
    3. God's Formal Covenant with Abram (15:1–21)
    4. Hagar and Ishmael (16:1–16)
    5. Abrahamic Covenant Sealed by a New Name and Circumcision (17:1–27)
    6. Abraham's Promise and Lot's Tragedy (18:1—19:38)
    7. Abraham and Abimelech (20:1–18)
    8. Abraham and Isaac, the Son of Promise (21:1—24:67)
    9. The Posterity of Abraham (25:1–18)
  B. Isaac (25:19—28:9)
    1. Birth of Esau and Jacob (25:19–26)
    2. Esau Selling his Birthright to Jacob (25:27–34)
    3. Isaac, Rebekah and Abimelech II (26:1–17)
    4. Dispute about Wells and the Move to Beersheba (26:18–33)
    5. The Patriarchal Blessing (26:34—28:9)
  C. Jacob (28:10—37:2a)
    1. Jacob's Dream and Journey (28:10–22)
    2. Jacob with Laban in Haran (29:1—31:55)
    3. Jacob and Esau Reconciled (32:1—33:17)
    4. Jacob's Return to the Promised Land (33:18—35:20)
    5. The Posterity of Jacob and Esau (35:21—37:2a)
  D. Joseph (37:2b—50:26)
    1. Joseph and his Brothers in Canaan (37:2b–36)

2. Judah and Tamar (38:1–30)
3. Joseph's Testing and Promotion in Egypt (39:1—41:57)
4. Joseph and his Brothers in Egypt (42:1—45:28)
5. Joseph's Father and Brothers Settle in Egypt (46:1—47:26)
6. Jacob's Last Days, Final Prophecies and Death (47:27—50:14)
7. The Joseph Summary (50:15–26)

Author: Moses

Theme: Beginnings

Date of Writing: c. 1445–1405 B.C.

Background

Genesis appropriately stands as the first book of the OT and serves as an essential introduction to the whole Bible. The book's title in Hebrew is derived from the first word of the book, *bereshith* ("in the beginning"). "Genesis," the title in our English Bible, is the Greek translation of the Hebrew title and means "the origin, source, creation or beginning of something." Genesis is "the book of beginnings."

The author of Genesis is nowhere designated in the book itself. The testimony of the rest of the Bible, however, is that Moses was the author of the entire Pentateuch (i.e., the first five OT books) and thus of Genesis (e.g., 1Ki 2:3; 2Ki 14:6; Ezr 6:18; Ne 13:1; Da 9:11–13; Mal 4:4; Mk 12:26; Lk 16:29,31; Jn 7:19–23; Ac 26:22; 1Co 9:9; 2Co 3:15). Also, ancient Jewish writers and the early church fathers unanimously testify that Moses was the author/editor of Genesis. Insofar as the entire history of Genesis antedates Moses' life, his role in writing Genesis was largely to integrate, under the inspiration of the Holy Spirit, all the available written and oral records from Adam to the death of Joseph that are now preserved in Genesis. Perhaps an indication of the historical records used by Moses when writing Genesis is found in the 11 occurrences of the phrase, "this is the account of" (Heb *'elleh toledoth*), which also may be translated as "these are the histories by" (see 2:4; 5:1; 6:9; 10:1; 11:10,27; 25:12,19; 36:1,9; 37:2).

Genesis accurately records creation, the beginnings of human history, and the origin of the Hebrew people and God's covenant with them through Abraham and the other patriarchs. Its historical reliability as inspired Scripture is certified in the NT by the Lord Jesus (Mt 19:4–6; 24:37–39; Lk 11:51; 17:26–32; Jn 7:21–23; 8:56–58) and by the apostles (Ro 4; 1Co 15:21–22,45–47; 2Co 11:3; Gal 3:8; 4:22–24,28; 1Ti 2:13–14; Heb 11:4–22; 2Pe 3:4–6; Jude 7,11). Its historicity continues to be confirmed by modern archaeological discoveries. Moses was remarkably prepared by education (Ac 7:22) and by God to write this unique first book of the Bible.

Purpose

Genesis provides an essential foundation for the remainder of the Pentateuch and all subsequent Biblical revelation. It preserves the only trustworthy record about the beginnings of the universe, humankind, marriage, sin, cities, languages, nations, Israel and redemptive history. It was written in accordance with God's purpose to give his covenant people in both the OT and NT a foundational understanding of himself, creation, the human race, the fall, death, judgment, covenant and the promise of redemption through the offspring of Abraham.

Survey

Genesis divides naturally into two major parts. (A) Chs. 1—11 provide an overview of human beginnings from Adam to Abraham and focus on five epochal events. (1) Creation: God created all things, including Adam and Eve whom he placed in the Garden of Eden (chs. 1—2). (2) The Fall: Adam and Eve by their transgression introduced the curse of sin and death into human history (ch. 3). (3) Cain and Abel: This tragedy set in motion the two basic streams of history: humanistic civilization and a redemptive remnant (chs. 4—5).

(4) The Great Flood: The ancient world had become so evil by the time of Noah's generation that God destroyed it by a universal flood, sparing only righteous Noah and his family as a remnant (chs. 6—10). (5) Tower of Babel: When the post-flood world unified in idolatry and rebellion, God dispersed it by fragmenting language and culture and by scattering the human race throughout the earth (ch. 11).

(B) Chs. 12—50 record the beginnings of the Hebrew people and focus on God's ongoing redemptive purpose through the lives of Israel's four great patriarchs—Abraham, Isaac, Jacob and Joseph. God's call of Abraham (ch. 12) and his covenantal dealings with him and his descendants form the pivotal beginning of the outworking of God's purpose concerning a Redeemer and redemption in history. Genesis concludes with Joseph's death and the impending bondage of Israel in Egypt.

Special Features

Seven major features characterize Genesis. (1) It was the first book of the Bible written (with the possible exception of Job), and it records the beginning of human history, sin, the Hebrew people and redemption. (2) The history in Genesis spans a larger period of time than the rest of the Bible combined, beginning with the first human couple, broadening to pre-flood world history, and then narrowing to Hebrew history as the redemptive stream that is traced throughout the remainder of the OT. (3) Genesis reveals that the material universe and life on earth are distinctly God's work and not an independent process of nature. Fifty times in chs. 1—2 God is the subject of verbs showing what he did as Creator. (4) Genesis is a book of firsts—recording the first marriage, first family, first birth, first sin, first murder, first polygamist, first musical instruments, first promise of redemption, and the like. (5) God's covenant with Abraham, which began with his call (12:1–3), was made formal in ch. 15 and was ratified in ch. 17, is central to all of Scripture. (6) Genesis alone explains the origin of the twelve tribes of Israel. (7) It reveals how Abraham's descendants ended up in Egypt (for 430 years) and thus sets the stage for the exodus, the central redemptive event in the OT.

New Testament Fulfillment

Genesis reveals the prophetic history of redemption and a Redeemer as coming through the offspring of the woman (3:15), through the line of Seth (4:25–26), through the line of Shem (9:26–27) and through the descendants of Abraham (12:3). The NT applies 12:3 directly to God's provision of redemption in Jesus Christ (Gal 3:16,29). Numerous persons and events from Genesis are mentioned in the NT in relation to faith and righteousness (e.g., Ro 4; Heb 11:1–22), God's judgment (e.g., Lk 17:26–29,32; 2Pe 3:6; Jude 7,11a) and the person of Christ (e.g., Mt 1:1; Jn 8:58; Heb 7).

Reading Genesis

In order to read the entire Old Testament in one year, the book of Genesis should be read in 21 days, according to the following schedule: ☐ 1–2 ☐ 3–5 ☐ 6–8 ☐ 9–11 ☐ 12–14 ☐ 15–17 ☐ 18–19 ☐ 20–22 ☐ 23–24 ☐ 25–26 ☐ 27–28 ☐ 29–30 ☐ 31–33 ☐ 34–35 ☐ 36–37 ☐ 38–39 ☐ 40–41 ☐ 42–43 ☐ 44–45 ☐ 46–48 ☐ 49–50

NOTES

The Beginning

1 In the beginning[a] God created[b] the heavens[c] and the
earth.[d] **2**Now the earth was[a]
formless[e] and empty,[f] darkness was over the surface of the
deep,[g] and the Spirit of God[h]
was hovering[i] over the waters.
3And God said,[j] "Let there be light,"
and there was light.[k] **4**God saw
that the light was good,[l] and
he separated the light from the
darkness.[m] **5**God called[n] the
light "day," and the darkness he
called "night."[o] And there was
evening, and there was morning[p]—the first day.
6And God said,[q] "Let there be an expanse[r] between the waters[s]
to separate water from water."
7So God made the expanse and
separated the water under the
expanse from the water above
it.[t] And it was so.[u] **8**God
called[v] the expanse "sky."[w]
And there was evening, and
there was morning[x]—the second day.
9And God said, "Let the water under
the sky be gathered to one
place,[y] and let dry ground[z]
appear." And it was so.[a] **10**God
called[b] the dry ground "land,"
and the gathered waters[c] he
called "seas."[d] And God saw
that it was good.[e]
11Then God said, "Let the
land produce vegetation:[f]
seed-bearing plants and trees
on the land that bear fruit with

1:1 [a]Ps 102:25; Pr 8:23; Isa 40:21; 41:4,26; Jn 1:1-2 [b]ver 21,27; Ge 2:3 [c]ver 6; Ne 9:6; Job 9:8; 37:18; Ps 96:5; 104:2; 115:15; 121:2; 136:5; Isa 40:22; 42:5; 51:13; Jer 10:12; 51:15 [d]Ge 14:19; 2Ki 19:15; Ne 9:6; Job 38:4; Ps 90:2; 136:6; 146:6; Isa 37:16; 40:28; 42:5; 44:24; 45:12,18; Jer 27:5; 32:17; Ac 14:15; 17:24; Eph 3:9; Col 1:16; Heb 3:4; 11:3; Rev 4:11; 10:6 **1:2** [e]Isa 23:1; 24:10; 27:10; 32:14; 34:11 [f]Isa 45:18; Jer 4:23 [g]Ge 8:2; Job 7:12; 26:8; 38:9; Ps 36:6; 42:7; 104:6; 107:24; Pr 30:4 [h]Ge 2:7; Job 33:4; Ps 104:30; Isa 32:15 [i]Dt 32:11; Isa 31:5 **1:3** [j]ver 6; Ps 33:6,9; 148:5; Heb 11:3 [k]2Co 4:6*; 1Jn 1:5-7 **1:4** [l]ver 10,12,18,21,25,31; Ps 104:31; 119:68; Jer 31:35 [m]ver 14; Ex 10:21-23; Job 26:10; 38:19; Ps 18:28; 104:20; 105:28; Isa 42:16; 45:7 **1:5** [n]ver 8,10; Ge 2:19,23 [o]Ps 74:16 [p]ver 8,13,19,23, 31 **1:6** [q]S ver 3 [r]S ver 1; Isa 44:24; 2Pe 3:5 [s]ver 9; Ps 24:2; 136:6 **1:7** [t]Ge 7:11; Job 26:10; 38:8-11,16; Ps 68:33; 148:4; Pr 8:28 [u]ver 9,11,15,24 **1:8** [v]S ver 5 [w]Job 9:8; 37:18; Ps 19:1; 104:2; Isa 40:22; 44:24; 45:12; Jer 10:12; Zec 12:1 [x]S ver 5 **1:9** [y]Job 38:8-11; Ps 33:7; 104:6-9; Pr 8:29; Jer 5:22; 2Pe 3:5 [z]Ps 95:5; Jnh 1:9; Hag 2:6 [a]S ver 7 **1:10** [b]S ver 5 [c]Ps 33:7 [d]Job 38:8; Ps 90:2; 95:5 [e]S ver 4 **1:11** [f] Ps 65:9-13; 104:14

[a] *2* Or possibly *became*

1:1 IN THE BEGINNING GOD CREATED. "In the beginning" here is emphatic and draws attention to the fact of a real beginning. Other ancient religions, when speaking of creation, indicate that it came about out of something that was already there. They see history as occurring forever in cycles. The Bible looks at history in a linear way, with a God-given goal. God had a plan in creation, and he will carry it out. For comments on God and his role as Creator, see article on CREATION, p. 6.

Several implications flow from the truth contained in the first verse of the Bible. (1) Since God is the source of all that exists, human beings and nature are not self-existent, but owe their being and continuance to him. (2) All existence and life is good if it is related rightly to God and dependent on him. (3) All life and creation can be eternally meaningful and purposeful. (4) God has sovereign rights over all creation by virtue of being its Creator. In a fallen world, he lays claim to those rights through redemption (Ex 6:6; 15:13; Dt 21:8; Lk 1:68; Ro 3:24; Gal 3:13; 1Pe 1:18).

1:2 EARTH WAS FORMLESS AND EMPTY. This verse describes both the process God used in creating and the role of the Holy Spirit in creation (see article on CREATION, p. 6).

1:3 LET THERE BE LIGHT. The Hebrew word for "light" is *'or*, referring to the initial waves of light energy coming upon the earth. Later God placed "lights" (Heb *ma'or*, literally, light-bearers, v. 14) in the heavens as permanent generators and reflectors of light waves. The primary purpose of these light-bearers was to serve as signs to mark seasons, and days and years (vv. 5,14). For comments about the role of God's word or speech in creation, see article on CREATION, p. 6.

1:5 THERE WAS EVENING, AND THERE WAS MORNING—THE FIRST DAY. This designation is repeated six times in this chapter (vv. 5,8,13,19,23,31). The Hebrew word for day is *yom*. It normally means a twenty-four hour day (cf. 7:17; Mt 17:1), or the daylight portion of the twenty-four hours ("day" as distinct from "night"). But it also can refer to a time period of undetermined length (e.g., "harvest time," Pr 25:13). Many believe the creation days were twenty-four hour days because they are described as consisting of an "evening" and "morning" (v. 5; cf. Ex 20:11). Others believe that "evening" and "morning" simply mean that a particular evening brought an end to that step of creation and the next morning brought a new beginning.

1:7 THE EXPANSE. The "expanse" refers to the atmosphere between the water on earth and the clouds above.

1:10 IT WAS GOOD. Seven times God states that what he created was "good" (vv. 4, 10,12,18,21,25,31). Each part of God's creation completely fulfilled his will and intended purpose. God created the world to reflect his glory and to be a place where humankind could share in his joy and life. Notice how God created according to a plan and order:

Day 1	light	bringing order to creation
Day 2	expanse	
Day 3	dry ground	
Day 4	light-bearers	
Day 5	fish and birds	giving life to creation
Day 6	animals and humans	
Day 7	rest	creation is complete and good

CREATION

Ge 1:1 "In the beginning God created the heavens and the earth."

THE GOD OF CREATION. (1) God is revealed in the Bible as an infinite, eternal, self-existent Being who is the First Cause of all that is. Never was there a moment when God did not exist. As Moses affirms, "Before the mountains were born or you brought forth the earth and the world, from everlasting to everlasting you are God" (Ps 90:2). In other words, God existed eternally and infinitely before creating the finite universe. He is above, independent of and prior to all that has been created in heaven and on earth (see 1Ti 6:16, note; cf. Col 1:16).

(2) God is revealed as a personal Being who created Adam and Eve "in his own image" (Ge 1:27; see 1:26, note). Because Adam and Eve were created in God's image, they could respond to and have fellowship with God in a loving and personal way.

(3) God is also revealed as a moral Being who created everything good and therefore without sin. After God had finished creating and was surveying what he had made, he observed that it was "very good" (Ge 1:31). Since Adam and Eve were created in God's image and likeness, they were also without sin (see Ge 1:26, note). Sin entered human existence when Eve was tempted by the serpent, or Satan (Ge 3; cf. Ro 5:12; Rev 12:9).

THE ACTIVITY OF CREATION. (1) God created all things in "the heavens and the earth" (Ge 1:1; cf. Isa 40:28; 42:5; 45:18; Mk 13:19; Eph 3:9; Col 1:16; Heb 1:2; Rev 10:6). The word "created" (Heb *bara'*) is used exclusively of an activity that only God can do. It means that at a specific moment God called into existence matter and substance that had no prior existence (see Ge 1:3, note).

(2) The Bible describes God's creation as formless, empty and covered with darkness (Ge 1:2). At that time the universe and the world did not have the ordered form it has now. It was empty, barren of all living creatures and void of all light. After this initial stage, God created light to dispel the darkness (Ge 1:3–5), gave form to the universe (Ge 1:6–13) and filled the earth with living things (Ge 1:20–28).

(3) The method God used in creation was the power of his word. Over and over it is stated, "And God said . . ." (Ge 1:3,6,9,11,14,20,24,26). In other words, God spoke the heavens and the earth into being; before God's creative word went forth, they had no prior existence (cf. Ps 33:6,9; 148:5; Isa 48:13; Ro 4:17; Heb 11:3).

(4) The entire Trinity, not just the Father, had a role in creation. (a) The Son himself is the powerful Word through whom God created all things. In the prologue to John's Gospel, Christ is revealed as the eternal Word of God (Jn 1:1). "Through him all things were made; without him nothing was made that has been made" (Jn 1:3). Likewise, the apostle Paul affirms that by Christ "all things were created: things in heaven and on earth, visible and invisible . . . all things were created by him and for him" (Col 1:16). Finally, the author of the letter to the Hebrews asserts emphatically that by his Son, God made the universe (Heb 1:2).

(b) Likewise, the Holy Spirit had an active role in the work of creation. He is pictured as "hovering" over the creation, preserving and preparing it for God's further creative activity. The Hebrew word for "Spirit" (*ruah*) may also be translated as "wind" and "breath." Thus, the psalmist affirms the role of the Spirit when he states: "By the word of the LORD were the heavens made, their starry host by the breath [*ruah*] of his mouth" (Ps 33:6). Also, the Holy Spirit continues to be involved in sustaining creation (Job 33:4; Ps 104:30).

THE PURPOSE AND GOAL OF CREATION. God had specific reasons for creating the world. (1) God created the heavens and the earth as a manifestation of his glory, majesty and power. David says, "The heavens declare the glory of God; the skies proclaim the work of his hands" (Ps 19:1; cf. Ps 8:1). By looking at the entire created cosmos—from the immense expanse of the created universe to the beauty and order of nature—we cannot help but stand in awe of the majesty of the Lord God, our Creator.

(2) God created the heavens and the earth in order to receive back the glory and honor due him. All the elements of nature—e.g., sun and moon, trees of the forest, rain and snow, rivers and streams, hills and mountains, animals and birds—shout out praise to the God who made them (Ps 98:7–8; 148:1–10; Isa 55:12). How much more God desires and expects to receive glory and praise from human beings!

(3) God created the earth in order to provide a place where his purpose and goals for humankind might be fulfilled. (a) God created Adam and Eve in his own image so that he could have a loving, personal relationship for all eternity. God designed humankind as a triune being (body, soul, spirit), possessing mind, emotion and will with which they can respond to him freely as Lord and worship and serve him out of faith, loyalty and gratitude. (b) God so desired this intimate relationship with the human race that, when Satan succeeded in tempting Adam and Eve to rebel against and disobey God's command, he promised to send a Savior to redeem humankind from sin's consequences (see Ge 3:15, note). In this way God would have a people for his own possession who would enjoy him, glorify him, and live in righteousness and holiness before him (Isa 60:21; 61:1–3; Eph 1:11–12; 1Pe 2:9). (c) The culmination of God's purpose in creation is recorded in the book of Revelation, where John describes the end of history with these words: "He will live with them. They will be his people, and God himself will be with them and be their God" (Rev 21:3).

CREATION AND EVOLUTION. Evolution is the predominant view regarding the origin of life and the universe proposed in the scientific and educational community of the contemporary world. Bible-believing Christians should consider these four observations about evolution.

(1) Evolution is a *naturalistic effort* to account for the origin and development of the universe. This view begins with the assumption that there is no personal, divine Creator who made and fashioned the world; rather, everything came into existence by a series of chance happenings that occurred over billions of years. Proponents of evolution claim to have scientific data that support their hypothesis.

(2) The teaching of evolution is *not truly scientific*. According to the scientific method, all conclusions must be based on indisputable evidence gathered from experiments that can be duplicated in any laboratory. However, no experiments have been or can be devised to test and substantiate theories about the origin of matter from some supposed "big bang" beginning or about the gradual development of living beings from their simplest to their most complex form. Consequently, evolution is a hypothesis without scientific "evidence"; therefore, to accept it one must have faith in a human theory. The faith of God's people, in contrast, is in the Lord and in his inspired revelation, which states that he is the One who made all things out of nothing (Heb 11:3).

(3) It is undeniable that change and development within various species of living things occur. For example, some varieties of species are becoming extinct; on the other hand, we occasionally see new strains forming within species. But there is no evidence, not even in the geologic record, which supports the theory that one kind of living thing ever evolved from another kind. Rather, existing evidence supports the Bible's declaration that God created each living creature "according to its kind" (Ge 1:21,24–25).

(4) Bible-believing Christians must also reject the theory called *theistic evolution*. This theory adopts most of the conclusions of naturalistic evolution, adding only that God started the evolutionary process. Such a theory denies the Biblical revelation that ascribes to God an active role in *all* aspects of creation. For example, every main verb in Ge 1 has God as its subject, except for Ge 1:12 (which fulfills the command of God in v. 11) and the recurring phrase "there was evening, and there was morning." God is not a passive supervisor of an evolutionary process; rather, he is the active Creator of all things (cf. Col 1:16).

seed in it, according to their
various kinds.[g]" And it was
so.[h] 12The land produced vegetation: plants bearing seed according to their kinds[i] and
trees bearing fruit with seed in
it according to their kinds. And
God saw that it was good.[j]
13And there was evening, and
there was morning[k]—the third
day.
14And God said, "Let there be lights[l]
in the expanse of the sky to separate the day from the night,[m]
and let them serve as signs[n] to
mark seasons[o] and days and
years,[p] 15and let them be
lights in the expanse of the sky
to give light on the earth." And
it was so.[q] 16God made two
great lights—the greater
light[r] to govern[s] the day and
the lesser light to govern[t] the
night.[u] He also made the
stars.[v] 17God set them in the
expanse of the sky to give light
on the earth, 18to govern the
day and the night,[w] and to separate light from darkness. And
God saw that it was good.[x]
19And there was evening, and
there was morning[y]—the
fourth day.
20And God said, "Let the water teem
with living creatures,[z] and let
birds fly above the earth across
the expanse of the sky."[a] 21So
God created[b] the great creatures of the sea[c] and every living and moving thing with
which the water teems,[d] according to their kinds, and every winged bird according to its
kind.[e] And God saw that it was
good.[f] 22God blessed them and
said, "Be fruitful and increase in
number and fill the water in the
seas, and let the birds increase
on the earth."[g] 23And there
was evening, and there was
morning[h]—the fifth day.
24And God said, "Let the land produce
living creatures[i] according to
their kinds:[j] livestock, creatures that move along the
ground, and wild animals, each
according to its kind." And it
was so.[k] 25God made the wild
animals[l] according to their
kinds, the livestock according
to their kinds, and all the creatures that move along the
ground according to their
kinds.[m] And God saw that it
was good.[n]
26Then God said, "Let us[o]

1:11 [g]ver 12,21, 24,25; Ge 2:5; 6:20; 7:14; Lev 11:14,19,22; Dt 14:13,18; 1Co 15:38 [h]S ver 7 **1:12** [i]S ver 11 [j]S ver 4 **1:13** [k]S ver 5 **1:14** [l]Ps 74:16; 136:7 [m]S ver 4 [n]Jer 10:2 [o]Ps 104:19 [p]Ge 8:22; Jer 31:35-36; 33:20,25 **1:15** [q]S ver 7 **1:16** [r]Dt 17:3; Job 31:26; Jer 43:13; Eze 8:16 [s]Ps 136:8 [t]Ps 136:9 [u]Job 38:33; Ps 74:16; 104:19; Jer 31:35; Jas 1:17 [v]Dt 4:19; Job 9:9; 38:7,31-32; Ps 8:3; 33:6; Ecc 12:2; Isa 40:26; Jer 8:2; Am 5:8 **1:18** [w]Jer 33:20, 25 [x]S ver 4 **1:19** [y]S ver 5 **1:20** [z]Ps 146:6 [a]Ge 2:19 **1:21** [b]S ver 1 [c]Job 3:8; 7:12; Ps 74:13; 148:7; Isa 27:1; Eze 32:2 [d]Ps 104:25-26 [e]S ver 11 [f]S ver 4 **1:22** [g]ver 28; Ge 8:17; 9:1,7,19; 47:27; Lev 26:9; Eze 36:11 **1:23** [h]S ver 5 **1:24** [i]Ge 2:19 [j]S ver 11 [k]S ver 7 **1:25** [l]Ge 7:21-22; Jer 27:5 [m]S ver 11 [n]S ver 4 **1:26** [o]Ge 3:5,22; 11:7; Ps 100:3; Isa 6:8

1:14 SERVE AS SIGNS. God intended that the sun, moon and stars serve as signs that point to him as well as mark the advancing days, seasons and years. Astrology has twisted these intended purposes for the stars by proposing the false theory that the stars and planets guide peoples' lives.

1:22 GOD BLESSED THEM. God blessed living creatures and declared nature and animals to be good (vv. 12,21–22). (1) God delighted in his work and valued it for itself. Likewise, believers should regard nature and its beauty and its animals as good, something to be enjoyed, and of immense value. (2) Although nature is now marred by sin, it still has great value as an expression of God's glory and love for humankind (cf. Ps 19:1). Believers should pray for the complete liberation of creation from its bondage to sin and decay (Ro 8:21; Rev 21:1).

1:26 GOD SAID, LET US. This expression contains an early implication of the triune God. The use of the plural "us" suggests that God has a certain plurality (cf. Ps 2:7; Isa 48:16). Revelation of the tri-unity of God does not become clear, however, until the NT (see Mt 3:17, note; Mk 1:11, note).

1:26 LET US MAKE MAN. In vv. 26–28 we read about the creation of human beings; 2:4–25 gives more specific details about their creation and environment. These two accounts are complementary and teach several things. (1) Both man and woman were a special creation of God, not a product of evolution (v. 27; Mt 19:4; Mk 10:6).

(2) Man and woman were both created in the "image" and "likeness" of God. On the basis of this image, they could respond to and have fellowship with God and uniquely reflect his love, glory and holiness. They were to do so by knowing God and obeying him (2:15–17). (a) They possessed a *moral* likeness to God, for they were sinless and holy, possessing wisdom, a heart of love and the will to do the right (cf. Eph 4:24). They lived in a personal fellowship with God that involved moral obedience (2:16–17) and intimate communion. When Adam and Eve sinned, their moral likeness to God was corrupted (6:5). In redemption believers must be renewed to the original moral likeness (cf. Eph 4:22–24; Col 3:10). (b) Adam and Eve possessed a *natural* likeness to God. They were created personal beings with spirit, mind, emotions, self-consciousness and power of choice (2:19–20; 3:6–7; 9:6). (c) In some sense man and woman's *physical* makeup is in God's image in a way not true of animals. God gave to human beings the image in which he was to appear visibly to them (18:1–2)

make man[p] in our image,[q] in
our likeness,[r] and let them
rule[s] over the fish of the sea
and the birds of the air,[t] over
the livestock, over all the
earth,[b] and over all the creatures that move along the
ground."

27So God created[u] man[v] in his
own image,[w]
in the image of God[x] he created
him;
male and female[y] he created
them.[z]

28God blessed them and said
to them,[a] "Be fruitful and increase in number;[b] fill the
earth[c] and subdue it. Rule
over[d] the fish of the sea and
the birds of the air and over every living creature that moves
on the ground.[e]"
29Then God said, "I give you
every seed-bearing plant on the
face of the whole earth and every tree that has fruit with seed
in it. They will be yours for
food.[f] 30And to all the beasts
of the earth and all the birds of
the air and all the creatures that
move on the ground—every-
thing that has the breath of
life[g] in it—I give every green
plant for food.[h]" And it was so.
31God saw all that he had
made,[i] and it was very good.[j]
And there was evening, and
there was morning[k]—the
sixth day.

2 Thus the heavens and the
earth were completed in all
their vast array.[l]

2By the seventh day[m] God had finished the work he had been doing; so on the seventh day he
rested[c] from all his work.[n]
3And God blessed the seventh
day and made it holy,[o] because
on it he rested[p] from all the
work of creating[q] that he had
done.

Adam and Eve

4This is the account[r] of the heav-

1:26 [p] Isa 45:18 [q] ver 27; Ge 5:3; 9:6; Ps 8:5; 82:6; 89:6; 1Co 11:7; 2Co 4:4; Col 1:15; 3:10; Jas 3:9 [r] Ac 17:28-29 [s] Ge 9:2; Ps 8:6-8 [t] Ps 8:8 **1:27** [u] S ver 1 [v] Ge 2:7; Ps 103:14; 119:73 [w] S ver 26 [x] Ge 5:1 [y] Ge 5:2; Mt 19:4*; Mk 10:6*; Gal 3:28 [z] Dt 4:32 **1:28** [a] Ge 33:5; Jos 24:3; Ps 113:9; 127:3,5 [b] S Ge 17:6 [c] S ver 22; Ge 6:1; Ac 17:26 [d] ver 26; Ps 115:16 [e] Ps 8:6-8 **1:29** [f] Ge 9:3; Dt 12:15; Ps 104:14; 1Ti 4:3 **1:30** [g] Ge 2:7; 7:22 [h] Job 38:41; Ps 78:25; 104:14, 27; 111:5; 136:25; 145:15; 147:9 **1:31** [i] Ps 104:24; 136:5; Pr 3:19; Jer 10:12 [j] S ver 4; 1Ti 4:4 [k] S ver 5 **2:1** [l] Dt 4:19; 17:3; 2Ki 17:16; 21:3; Ps 104:2; Isa 44:24; 45:12; 48:13; 51:13 **2:2** [m] Dt 5:14 [n] ver 2-3; Ex 20:11; 31:17; 34:21; Jn 5:17; Heb 4:4* **2:3** [o] Ex 16:23; 20:10; 23:12; 31:15; 35:2; Lev 23:3; Ne 9:14; Isa 58:13; Jer 17:22 [p] Ps 95:11; Heb 4:1-11 [q] S Ge 1:1 **2:4** [r] Ge 5:1; 6:9; 10:1; 11:10,27; 25:12,19; 36:1,9; 37:2

[b] *26* Hebrew; Syriac *all the wild animals*
[c] *2* Or *ceased*; also in verse 3

---

and the form that his Son would one day assume (Lk 1:35; Php 2:7; Heb 10:5).

(3) That human beings were made in the image of God does not mean they are divine. They have been created on a lower order and are dependent on God (Ps 8:5).

(4) All human life is derived initially from Adam and Eve (Ge 3:20; Ro 5:12).

1:28 BE FRUITFUL AND INCREASE. Man and woman were charged with being fruitful and ruling over the earth and animal kingdom. (1) They were created to form family relationships. This stated purpose of God in creation indicates that he considers a godly family and the raising of children of utmost priority in the world (see Eph 5:21, note; Tit 2:4–5, note; see article on PARENTS AND CHILDREN, p. 1854).

(2) God expected them to consecrate all things in the earth to him and to manage it in a God-glorifying way, fulfilling the divine purpose (cf. Ps 8:6–8; Heb 2:7–9).

(3) The future of the earth was placed under their dominion. When they sinned, they brought ruin, futility and suffering to God's creation (cf. 3:14–24; Ro 8:19–22).

(4) It is the work of Jesus Christ alone to restore the earth to its perfect place and function at his coming at the end of this age (Ro 8:19–25; 1Co 15:24–28; Heb 2:5–8; see Rev 21:1, note).

2:3 GOD BLESSED THE SEVENTH DAY. God blessed the seventh day (i.e., Sabbath) and designated it both as a sacred and special day of rest and as a memorial to the completion of all his created work. God later made the Sabbath a day of blessing for his faithful people (Ex 20:8). He designed it as a day of rest, service and communion with him (Ex 16:29; 31:12–17; see Mt 12:1, note).

2:4 THE ACCOUNT. This second account of creation (2:4–25) is not contradictory to 1:1—2:3. It explains in greater detail the creation of man and woman, their environment and their probation. Ch. 2 gives details in a topical fashion, whereas ch. 1 gives the chronological order.

2:4 THE LORD GOD. Another name for God is introduced in 2:4, the name "LORD" (Heb *YHWH*, "Yahweh"). Whereas *Elohim* (e.g., 1:1) is the general name for God, emphasizing his greatness and power (see article on CREATION, p. 6), "LORD" is the personal and covenant name by which God reveals himself to his own people. Inherent in the revelation of God's covenant name is his loving-kindness, his redemptive concern for the human race, and his nearness to and faithful presence with his people. This personal name is used in situations where he is seen in direct relationship to his people or to nature. Where the words "LORD God" are coupled together, they point to God as the all-powerful Creator who has entered into a caring covenant relationship with humankind (see vv. 9–25; Ex 6:6; Lev 11:44–45; Isa 53:1,5–6; see Ex 3:14, note).

ens and the earth when they were created.[s]

When the LORD God made the earth
and the heavens— 5and no shrub of
the field had yet appeared on the
earth[d] and no plant of the field had yet
sprung up,[t] for the LORD God had not
sent rain on the earth[d][u] and there
was no man to work the ground, 6but
streams[e] came up from the earth and
watered the whole surface of the
ground— 7the LORD God formed[v] the
man[f][w] from the dust[x] of the
ground[y] and breathed into his nostrils
the breath[z] of life,[a] and the man became a living being.[b]

8Now the LORD God had planted a
garden in the east, in Eden;[c] and
there he put the man he had formed.
9And the LORD God made all kinds of
trees grow out of the ground—trees[d]
that were pleasing to the eye and good
for food. In the middle of the garden
were the tree of life[e] and the tree of
the knowledge of good and evil.[f]

10A river[g] watering the garden
flowed from Eden;[h] from there it was
separated into four headwaters. 11The
name of the first is the Pishon; it winds
through the entire land of Havilah,[i]
where there is gold. 12(The gold of that
land is good; aromatic resin[g][j] and
onyx are also there.) 13The name of the
second river is the Gihon; it winds
through the entire land of Cush.[h]
14The name of the third river is the Tigris;[k] it runs along the east side of
Asshur. And the fourth river is the Euphrates.[l]

15The LORD God took the man and
put him in the Garden of Eden[m] to
work it and take care of it. 16And the
LORD God commanded the man, "You
are free to eat from any tree in the garden;[n] 17but you must not eat from the
tree of the knowledge of good and
evil,[o] for when you eat of it you will
surely die."[p]

18The LORD God said, "It is not good
for the man to be alone. I will make a
helper suitable for him."[q]

2:4 [s]Ge 1:1; Job 38:8-11 **2:5** [t]Ge 1:11 [u]Job 38:28; Ps 65:9-10; Jer 10:13 **2:7** [v]Isa 29:16; 43:1,21; 44:2 [w]S Ge 1:27 [x]Ge 3:19; 18:27; Job 4:19; 10:9; 17:16; 34:15; Ps 90:3; Ecc 3:20; 12:7 [y]Ge 3:23; 4:2; Ps 103:14; Jer 18:6; 1Co 15:47 [z]S Ge 1:2; Job 27:3; Isa 2:22 [a]S Ge 1:30; Isa 42:5; Ac 17:25 [b]Job 12:10; 32:8; 33:4; 34:14; Ps 104:29; Isa 57:16; Eze 37:5; 1Co 15:45* **2:8** [c]ver 10,15; Ge 3:23,24; 4:16; 13:10; Isa 51:3; Eze 28:13; 31:9, 16; 36:35; Joel 2:3 **2:9** [d]Eze 31:8 [e]Ge 3:22,24; Pr 3:18; 11:30; S Rev 2:7 [f]Eze 47:12 **2:10** [g]Nu 24:6; Ps 46:4; Eze 47:5 [h]S ver 8 **2:11** [i]Ge 10:7; 25:18 **2:12** [j]Nu 11:7 **2:14** [k]Ge 41:1; Da 10:4 [l]Ge 15:18; 31:21; Ex 23:31; Nu 22:5; Dt 1:7; 11:24; Jos 1:4; 2Sa 8:3; 1Ki 4:21; 2Ki 23:29; 24:7; 1Ch 5:9; 18:3; 2Ch 35:20; Jer 13:4; 46:2; 51:63; S Rev 9:14 **2:15** [m]S ver 8 **2:16** [n]Ge 3:1-2 **2:17** [o]Ge 3:11, 17 [p]Ge 3:1,3; 5:5; 9:29; Dt 30:15,19; Jer 42:16; Eze 3:18; S Ro 5:12; S 6:23 **2:18** [q]Pr 31:11; 1Co 11:9; 1Ti 2:13

d *5* Or *land*; also in verse 6 **e** *6* Or *mist*
f *7* The Hebrew for *man (adam)* sounds like and may be related to the Hebrew for *ground (adamah)*; it is also the name *Adam* (see Gen. 2:20). **g** *12* Or *good; pearls* **h** *13* Possibly southeast Mesopotamia

2:7 A LIVING BEING. The giving of life to human beings is described as the result of a special act of God in distinction from the creation of all other living things. God specifically imparted life and breath to the first man, indicating that human life stands higher and in a different category from all other forms of life and that there is a unique relationship of divine life to human life (cf. Ge 1:26–27). God is the ultimate source of human life.

2:8 GARDEN IN THE EAST, IN EDEN. The garden was located near the Tigris and Euphrates flood plain (see v. 14). Some believe it was located in what is now known as southern Iraq; others maintain that there is not sufficient data given in the Biblical account (vv. 10–14) to determine a specific location.

2:9 TREE OF LIFE. Two trees in the garden had special importance. (1) The "tree of life" was probably intended to make physical death impossible. It is related to eternal life in 3:22 (cf. Rev 2:7). God's people will have access to the tree of life in the new heaven and new earth (Rev 2:7; 22:2). (2) The "tree of the knowledge of good and evil" was designed to test Adam's faith and obedience to God and his word (see v. 16, note). God created humans as moral beings with the ability to choose freely to love and obey their Creator, or to disobey him and rebel against his will.

2:15 PUT HIM IN THE GARDEN OF EDEN. At this time Adam as the first man was holy, free from sin, and in perfect communion with God. Adam was the pinnacle of God's creation and was given the responsibility of working under the direction of God in caring for his creation. This harmonious relationship between God and the human race was lost because of Adam and Eve's disobedience (3:6,14–19).

2:16 THE LORD GOD COMMANDED THE MAN. From the very beginning of history the human race has been bound to God through belief in and obedience to his word as absolute truth. (1) Life through faith and obedience is presented as the governing principle in Adam's relationship to God in Eden. Adam was warned that he would die if he transgressed God's will and partook of the tree of the knowledge of good and evil (v. 17). This threat of death had to be accepted by faith based on what God said, since Adam had not yet seen human death.

(2) God's command (vv. 16–17) was given to Adam as a moral test. It placed before him a conscious, deliberate choice to believe and obey, or to disbelieve and disobey his Creator's will.

(3) As long as Adam believed God's word and obeyed, he would continue in eternal life and in blessed fellowship with God (see article on FAITH AND GRACE, p. 1720). If he sinned by disobeying, he would reap moral disaster and a harvest of death (v. 17).

2:18 HELPER SUITABLE FOR HIM. Woman was created to be a loving companion for man and a helper for him. As such she was to share his

19 Now the LORD God had formed out
of the ground all the beasts of the
field[r] and all the birds of the air.[s] He
brought them to the man to see what
he would name them; and whatever the
man called[t] each living creature,[u]
that was its name. 20 So the man gave
names to all the livestock, the birds of
the air and all the beasts of the field.
But for Adam[i] no suitable helper[v]
was found. 21 So the LORD God caused
the man to fall into a deep sleep;[w] and
while he was sleeping, he took one of
the man's ribs[j] and closed up the
place with flesh. 22 Then the LORD God
made a woman from the rib[k][x] he had
taken out of the man, and he brought
her to the man.
23 The man said,

"This is now bone of my bones
and flesh of my flesh;[y]
she shall be called[z] 'woman,[l]'
for she was taken out of man.[a]"

24 For this reason a man will leave his
father and mother and be united[b] to
his wife, and they will become one
flesh.[c]
25 The man and his wife were both
naked,[d] and they felt no shame.

2:19 [r] Ps 8:7 [s] S Ge 1:20 [t] S Ge 1:5 [u] Ge 1:24
2:20 [v] Ge 3:20; 4:1
2:21 [w] Ge 15:12; 1Sa 26:12; Job 33:15
2:22 [x] 1Co 11:8,9, 12; 1Ti 2:13
2:23 [y] Ge 29:14; Eph 5:28-30 [z] S Ge 1:5 [a] 1Co 11:8
2:24 [b] Mal 2:15 [c] Mt 19:5*; Mk 10:7-8*; 1Co 6:16*; Eph 5:31*
2:25 [d] Ge 3:7, 10-11; Isa 47:3; La 1:8
3:1 [e] Job 1:7; 2:2; 2Co 11:3; Rev 12:9; 20:2 [f] S Ge 2:17
3:2 [g] Ge 2:16
3:3 [h] S Ge 2:17
3:4 [i] S Jn 8:44; 2Co 11:3
3:5 [j] S Ge 1:26; 14:18,19; Ps 7:8; Isa 14:14; Eze 28:2

The Fall of Man

3 Now the serpent[e] was more crafty
than any of the wild animals the
LORD God had made. He said to the
woman, "Did God really say, 'You must
not eat from any tree in the garden'?[f]"
2 The woman said to the serpent,
"We may eat fruit from the trees in the
garden,[g] 3 but God did say, 'You must
not eat fruit from the tree that is in the
middle of the garden, and you must not
touch it, or you will die.' "[h]
4 "You will not surely die," the serpent said to the woman.[i] 5 "For God
knows that when you eat of it your eyes
will be opened, and you will be like
God,[j] knowing good and evil."
6 When the woman saw that the fruit

[i] 20 Or *the man* [j] 21 Or *took part of the man's side* [k] 22 Or *part* [l] 23 The Hebrew for *woman* sounds like the Hebrew for *man.*

responsibility and cooperate with him in fulfilling God's purpose for his life and the life of their family (see Eph 5:22, note; see Ps 33:20; 70:5; 115:9, where the term "help" is also used to describe God).

2:24 LEAVE HIS FATHER AND MOTHER. God in the beginning ordained marriage and the family unit as the first and most important institution on earth (see 1:28, note). God's plan for marriage consists of one male and one female who become "one flesh" (i.e., united physically and spiritually). This instruction excludes adultery, polygamy, homosexuality, immoral living and unscriptural divorce (Mk 10:7–9; see Mt 19:9, note).

3:1 THE SERPENT. In this episode the serpent attacked God through God's creation. He stated that what God had said to Adam was not true (vv. 3–4); he ultimately caused God to curse his creation, including the human race whom God had made in his image (vv. 16–19). The "serpent" is later identified with Satan, or the devil (cf. Rev 12:9; 20:2). Satan evidently took control of the serpent and used it as an instrument in his work of temptation (cf. 2Co 11:3,14; Rev 20:2; see Mt 4:10, note on Satan).

3:4 YOU WILL NOT SURELY DIE. The human race is bound to God by faith in his word as absolute truth (see 2:16, note). (1) Because he knew this, Satan sought to destroy the woman's faith in what God had said by raising doubts about that word. Satan suggested that God did not really mean what he said (cf. 2:16–17). In other words, the first lie proposed by Satan was a form of antinomianism, denying the judgment of death for sin and apostasy.

(2) One of the basic sins of humankind is unbelief in God's word. It is believing that somehow God does not really mean what he says about salvation, righteousness, sin, judgment and death. Satan's most persistent lie is that unrepentant, deliberate sin and rebellion against God will not necessarily bring separation from God and eternal condemnation (see 1Co 6:9, note; Gal 5:21, note; 1Jn 2:4, note).

3:5 YOU WILL BE LIKE GOD. Satan, from the beginning of the human race, has tempted humans to believe that they can be like God and decide for themselves what is good and what is evil. (1) Humanity, in seeking to be "like God," became independent from God Almighty and as such became a false god (see v. 22, note; Jn 10:34, note). Humans now seek to gain moral knowledge and ethical discernment from their own minds and desire independence from God's word. Nevertheless, only God has the right to determine what is good and evil. (2) Scripture declares that all who seek to be gods "will perish from the earth and from under the heavens" (Jer 10:10–11). This will also be the fate of the antichrist, who will proclaim himself "to be God" (2Th 2:4).

3:6 WHEN THE WOMAN SAW . . . SHE TOOK. See Mt 4:1–11, note on how to overcome temptation.

3:6 THE WOMAN . . . ATE IT . . . HER HUSBAND . . . WITH HER. When Adam and Eve sinned, moral and spiritual death came immediately (cf. 2:17), while physical death came later (5:5). (1) God had said, "when you eat of it you will surely die" (2:17). Thus spiritual and moral death occurred at once when they sinned (cf. Jn 17:3, note). Moral death consisted in the death of God's life in them and their nature becoming sinful; spiritual

of the tree was good for food and pleasing to the eye, and also desirable[k] for
gaining wisdom, she took some and ate
it. She also gave some to her husband,[l] who was with her, and he ate
it.[m] **7**Then the eyes of both of them
were opened, and they realized they
were naked;[n] so they sewed fig leaves
together and made coverings for themselves.[o]

8Then the man and his wife heard
the sound of the LORD God as he was
walking[p] in the garden in the cool of
the day, and they hid[q] from the LORD
God among the trees of the garden.
9But the LORD God called to the man,
"Where are you?"[r]

10He answered, "I heard you in the
garden, and I was afraid[s] because I
was naked;[t] so I hid."

11And he said, "Who told you that
you were naked?[u] Have you eaten
from the tree that I commanded you
not to eat from?[v]"

12The man said, "The woman you
put here with me[w]—she gave me
some fruit from the tree, and I ate it."

13Then the LORD God said to the
woman, "What is this you have done?"

The woman said, "The serpent deceived me,[x] and I ate."

14So the LORD God said to the serpent, "Because you have done this,

"Cursed[y] are you above all the
livestock
and all the wild animals!
You will crawl on your belly
and you will eat dust[z]
all the days of your life.
15And I will put enmity
between you and the woman,
and between your offspring[m][a]
and hers;[b]
he will crush[n] your head,[c]
and you will strike his heel."

3:6 [k]Jas 1:14-15; 1Jn 2:16 [l]Nu 30:7-8; Jer 44:15,19,24 [m]2Co 11:3; 1Ti 2:14
3:7 [n]Ge 2:25 [o]ver 21
3:8 [p]Lev 26:12; Dt 23:14 [q]Job 13:16; 23:7; 31:33; 34:22,23; Ps 5:5; 139:7-12; Isa 29:15; Jer 16:17; 23:24; 49:10; Rev 6:15-16
3:9 [r]Ge 4:9; 16:8; 18:9; 1Ki 19:9,13
3:10 [s]Ex 19:16; 20:18; Dt 5:5; 1Sa 12:18 [t]Ge 2:25
3:11 [u]Ge 2:25 [v]S Ge 2:17
3:12 [w]Ge 2:22
3:13 [x]Ro 7:11; 2Co 11:3; 1Ti 2:14
3:14 [y]Dt 28:15-20 [z]Ps 72:9; Isa 49:23; 65:25; Mic 7:17
3:15 [a]Jn 8:44; Ac 13:10; 1Jn 3:8 [b]Ge 16:11; Jdg 13:5; Isa 7:14; 8:3; 9:6; Mt 1:23; Lk 1:31; Gal 4:4; Rev 12:17 [c]Ro 16:20; Heb 2:14

[m]*15* Or *seed* [n]*15* Or *strike*

death meant that their former relationship to God was destroyed. Since the sin of Adam and Eve, every person born comes into the world with a sinful nature (Ro 8:5–8). This corruption of human nature involves the innate desire to go one's own selfish way without concern for God or others, and it is passed on to all human beings (5:3; 6:5; 8:21; see Ro 3:10–18, note; Eph 2:3).

(2) Note, however, that nowhere does Scripture teach that all sinned when Adam sinned or that his guilt was imputed to the whole human race (see Ro 5:12, note). The Bible does teach that Adam introduced the law of sin and death to the whole human race (cf. Ro 5:12; 8:2; 1Co 15:21–22).

3:7 THEY REALIZED THEY WERE NAKED. When Adam and Eve lived in moral innocence (i.e., before the fall), nakedness was not wrong nor did it bring a feeling of shame (2:25). However, after they sinned, the awareness of nakedness became associated with sin and the fallen, depraved condition of humankind. Because of the evil that nakedness would cause in the world, God himself made garments and clothed Adam and Eve (v. 21), and now he commands all people to dress modestly (see 1Ti 2:9, note).

3:8 THEY HID. The guilt and consciousness of sin caused Adam and Eve to shun God. They felt afraid and uncomfortable in his presence, knowing that they were sinful and under his displeasure. In this condition they found it impossible to draw near to him with confidence (see Ac 23:1, note; 24:16, note). In our sinful condition, we too are like Adam and Eve. However, God has provided us a way to cleanse our guilty conscience, free us from sin, and restore us to his fellowship—the "way" called Jesus Christ (Jn 14:6). Through the redemption God provided in his Son, we can draw near to him in order to receive his love, mercy, grace and help in time of need (see Heb 4:16, note; 7:25, note).

3:13 THE SERPENT DECEIVED ME. Satan caused the downfall of the human race through deception. This is one of his chief methods for leading people away from God's way and truth. (1) The Bible teaches that Satan deceives and blinds the minds of the unbelieving of this world in order that they may not understand the gospel (see 2Co 4:4, note). (2) According to Paul, it is through Satan's deception that some within the church will believe they can live immoral lives and still inherit God's kingdom (see 1Co 6:9, note; Gal 5:21, note). (3) Deception will be Satan's chief means of leading many into rebellion against God at history's end (2Th 2:8–12; Rev 20:8). (4) All Christians must be prepared for, and committed to, a continuous life-and-death struggle against the deception of Satan as it relates to their personal lives, marriages, families, schools, churches and work (see Mt 24:4,11,24; Eph 6:11, note).

3:15 HE WILL CRUSH YOUR HEAD, AND YOU WILL STRIKE HIS HEEL. This verse contains the first implicit promise of God's plan of redemption for the world. It predicts the ultimate victory for humankind and God over Satan and evil by prophesying of a spiritual conflict between the offspring of the woman (i.e., the Lord Jesus Christ) and the offspring of the serpent (i.e., Satan and his followers; see v. 1, note). God promised here that Christ would be born of a woman (cf. Isa 7:14) and would be "struck" through his crucifixion. Yet, he would rise from the dead to completely destroy (i.e., "crush") Satan, sin and death for the sake of the salvation of the human race (cf. Isa 53:5; Mt 1:20–23; Jn 12:31; Ac 26:18; Ro 5:18–19; 16:20; 1Jn 3:8; Rev 20:10).

16To the woman he said,

"I will greatly increase your pains
in childbearing;
with pain you will give birth to
children.[d]
Your desire will be for your
husband,
and he will rule over you.[e]"

17To Adam he said, "Because you
listened to your wife and ate from the
tree about which I commanded you,
'You must not eat of it,'[f]

"Cursed[g] is the ground[h] because
of you;
through painful toil[i] you will
eat of it
all the days of your life.[j]
18It will produce thorns and
thistles[k] for you,
and you will eat the plants of
the field.[l]
19By the sweat of your brow[m]
you will eat your food[n]
until you return to the ground,
since from it you were taken;
for dust you are
and to dust you will return."[o]

20Adam[o] named his wife Eve,[p][p]
because she would become the mother
of all the living.

21The LORD God made garments of
skin for Adam and his wife and clothed
them.[q] **22**And the LORD God said, "The
man has now become like one of us,[r]
knowing good and evil. He must not be
allowed to reach out his hand and take
also from the tree of life[s] and eat, and
live forever." **23**So the LORD God banished him from the Garden of Eden[t] to
work the ground[u] from which he had
been taken. **24**After he drove the man
out, he placed on the east side[q] of the
Garden of Eden[v] cherubim[w] and a
flaming sword[x] flashing back and
forth to guard the way to the tree of
life.[y]

Cain and Abel

4 Adam[o] lay with his wife[z] Eve,[a]
and she became pregnant and gave
birth to Cain.[r][b] She said, "With the
help of the LORD I have brought forth[s]
a man." **2**Later she gave birth to his
brother Abel.[c]

Now Abel kept flocks, and Cain
worked the soil.[d] **3**In the course of
time Cain brought some of the fruits of
the soil as an offering[e] to the LORD.[f]

3:16 [d]Ps 48:5-6; Isa 13:8; 21:3; 26:17; Jer 4:31; 6:24; Mic 4:9; 1Ti 2:15 [e]1Co 11:3; Eph 5:22 **3:17** [f]S Ge 2:17 [g]Ge 5:29; Nu 35:33; Ps 106:39; Isa 24:5; Jer 3:1; Ro 8:20-22 [h]Ge 6:13; 8:21; Isa 54:9 [i]Ge 29:32; 31:42; Ex 3:7; Ps 66:11; 127:2; Ecc 1:13 [j]Ge 47:9; Job 5:7; 7:1; 14:1; Ecc 2:23; Jer 20:18 **3:18** [k]Job 31:40; Isa 5:6; Heb 6:8 [l]Ps 104:14 **3:19** [m]Ps 104:23 [n]Ge 14:18; Dt 8:3, 9; 23:4; Ru 1:6; 2:14; 2Th 3:10 [o]S Ge 2:7; S Job 7:21; S Ps 146:4; 1Co 15:47; Heb 9:27 **3:20** [p]S Ge 2:20; 2Co 11:3; 1Ti 2:13 **3:21** [q]S ver 7 **3:22** [r]S Ge 1:26 [s]S Ge 2:9; S Rev 2:7 **3:23** [t]S Ge 2:8 [u]S Ge 2:7 **3:24** [v]S Ge 2:8 [w]Ex 25:18-22; 1Sa 4:4; 2Sa 6:2; 22:11; 1Ki 6:27; 8:6; 2Ki 19:15; 2Ch 5:8; Ps 18:10; 80:1; 99:1; Isa 37:16; Eze 10:1; 28:16

[x]Job 40:19; Ps 104:4; Isa 27:1 [y]S Ge 2:9 **4:1** [z]ver 17,25 [a]S Ge 2:20 [b]Heb 11:4; 1Jn 3:12; Jude 1:11 **4:2** [c]Mt 23:35; Lk 11:51; Heb 11:4; 12:24 [d]S Ge 2:7 **4:3** [e]Lev 2:1-2; Isa 43:23; Jer 41:5 [f]Nu 18:12

[o] *20,1* Or *The man* [p] *20 Eve* probably means *living.* [q] *24* Or *placed in front* [r] *1 Cain* sounds like the Hebrew for *brought forth* or *acquired.* [s] *1* Or *have acquired*

3:16–19 I WILL GREATLY INCREASE YOUR PAINS. The punishment placed on man and woman (vv. 16–19), as well as the effect of sin on nature, were meant to remind humankind of the terrible consequences of sin and cause them to depend on God in faith and obedience. God intended the present condition of the human race on earth to be redemptive. (1) Eve's attempt to liberate herself from God and act independently from her husband would be counteracted by a strong desire for her husband. Her deep attraction towards Adam and his headship over her would bring trouble and suffering along with joy and blessing (cf. 1:26–27; 1Co 11:7–9; Eph 5:22–25; 1Ti 2:11–14). (2) Because of God's curse on nature, Adam and Eve would experience physical hardships, toil, struggle, and eventually death for themselves and all their offspring.

3:20 NAMED HIS WIFE EVE. Adam called his wife "Eve," meaning "living," because she was the first mother of all humanity of all generations.

3:22 TO KNOW GOOD AND EVIL. Adam and Eve had attempted to set themselves up as God's equal and to determine their own standards (see v. 5, note). Through their fall, human beings became to some extent independent of God and began to distinguish for themselves between good and evil. (1) In this world, imperfect and perverted human judgment often decides what is good or evil. This was never God's will, for he intended us to know only good in dependence on him and his word. (2) All who confess Christ as Lord return to God's original purpose for humankind. They rely on God's word to determine what is good.

3:24 HE DROVE THE MAN OUT. Adam's perfect relationship to God had been lost. He was now driven out of the garden, and a life of dependence on God in the midst of trials began. In addition, Satan in some sense gained power over the world through the fall of Adam and Eve, for the NT speaks of Satan as being "the prince of this world" (Jn 14:30; cf. 2Co 4:4; 1Jn 5:19). However, God loved the human race so much that he determined to conquer Satan by reconciling them and the world to himself at the cost of his Son's life (see v. 15, note; cf. Jn 3:16; Rev 21:1–8).

4:1 ADAM LAY WITH HIS WIFE. The Hebrew word *yada'* ("to know"), here translated "lay with," is commonly used in the Bible for marital and sexual intimacy. Note that when Eve gave birth to her son, she gave sincere praise to the Lord for the child. She was seeking to be rightly related to God in thankfulness for his love, forgiveness and help.

4:3–5 AN OFFERING TO THE LORD. The Lord accepted Abel's offering because he came before God in true faith and dedication to righteous-

4But Abel brought fat portions[g] from
some of the firstborn of his flock.[h]
The LORD looked with favor on Abel and
his offering,[i] 5but on Cain and his offering he did not look with favor. So
Cain was very angry, and his face was
downcast.
6Then the LORD said to Cain, "Why
are you angry?[j] Why is your face
downcast? 7If you do what is right, will
you not be accepted? But if you do not
do what is right, sin is crouching at
your door;[k] it desires to have you, but
you must master it.[l]"
8Now Cain said to his brother Abel,
"Let's go out to the field."[t] And while
they were in the field, Cain attacked
his brother Abel and killed him.[m]
9Then the LORD said to Cain, "Where
is your brother Abel?"[n]
"I don't know,[o]" he replied. "Am I
my brother's keeper?"
10The LORD said, "What have you
done? Listen! Your brother's blood
cries out to me from the ground.[p]
11Now you are under a curse[q] and
driven from the ground, which opened
its mouth to receive your brother's
blood from your hand. 12When you
work the ground, it will no longer yield
its crops for you.[r] You will be a restless wanderer[s] on the earth.[t]"
13Cain said to the LORD, "My punishment is more than I can bear. 14Today
you are driving me from the land, and
I will be hidden from your presence;[u]
I will be a restless wanderer on the
earth,[v] and whoever finds me will kill
me."[w]
15But the LORD said to him, "Not
so[u]; if anyone kills Cain[x], he will suffer vengeance[y] seven times over.[z]"
Then the LORD put a mark on Cain so
that no one who found him would kill
him. 16So Cain went out from the
LORD's presence[a] and lived in the land
of Nod,[v] east of Eden.[b]
17Cain lay with his wife,[c] and she
became pregnant and gave birth to
Enoch. Cain was then building a city,[d]
and he named it after his son[e] Enoch.
18To Enoch was born Irad, and Irad
was the father of Mehujael, and Mehujael was the father of Methushael, and
Methushael was the father of Lamech.
19Lamech married[f] two women,[g]
one named Adah and the other Zillah.

4:4 [g] Lev 3:16; 2Ch 29:35 [h] Ex 13:2,12; Dt 15:19 [i] Heb 11:4 **4:6** [j] Jnh 4:4 **4:7** [k] Ge 44:16; Nu 32:23; Isa 59:12 [l] Job 11:15; 22:27; Ps 27:3; 46:2; S Ro 6:16 **4:8** [m] Mt 23:35; Lk 11:51; 1Jn 3:12; Jude 1:11 **4:9** [n] S Ge 3:9 [o] S Jn 8:44 **4:10** [p] Ge 9:5; 37:20,26; Ex 21:12; Nu 35:33; Dt 21:7, 9; 2Sa 4:11; Job 16:18; 24:2; 31:38; Ps 9:12; 106:38; Heb 12:24; Rev 6:9-10 **4:11** [q] Dt 11:28; 2Ki 2:24 **4:12** [r] Dt 28:15-24 [s] Ps 37:25; 59:15; 109:10 [t] ver 14 **4:14** [u] 2Ki 17:18; Ps 51:11; 139:7-12; Jer 7:15; 52:3 [v] ver 12; Dt 28:64-67 [w] Ge 9:6; Ex 21:12,14; Lev 24:17; Nu 35:19,21,27, 33; 1Ki 2:32; 2Ki 11:16 **4:15** [x] Eze 9:4,6 [y] Ex 21:20 [z] ver 24; Lev 26:21; Ps 79:12 **4:16** [a] Jude 1:11 [b] S Ge 2:8 **4:17** [c] S ver 1 [d] Ps 55:9 [e] Ps 49:11 **4:19** [f] Ge 6:2 [g] Ge 29:28; Dt 21:15; Ru 4:11; 1Sa 1:2

[t] *8* Samaritan Pentateuch, Septuagint, Vulgate and Syriac; Masoretic Text does not have *"Let's go out to the field."* [u] *15* Septuagint, Vulgate and Syriac; Hebrew *Very well* [v] *16* *Nod* means *wandering* (see verses 12 and 14).

ness (cf. Heb 11:4; 1Jn 3:12; cf. Jn 4:23–24). Cain's offering was rejected because he lacked a sincerely obedient faith and because his deeds were evil (vv. 6–7; 1Jn 3:12). God takes pleasure in our offerings and thanksgivings only when we are striving to live a righteous life according to his will (see Dt 6:5, note).

4:7 IT DESIRES TO HAVE YOU. God pictures sin as a tempting force or power that, like a wild beast or demon, is ready to attack and to devour. Yet God also gives to human beings the capacity to overcome and resist sin by submitting to his word, with the assistance of his grace. It is their choice whether they will yield to sin or will conquer it (cf. Ro 6).

4:10 YOUR BROTHER'S BLOOD CRIES OUT TO ME. The death of Abel and God's concern for him show that throughout the ages God cares for all who suffer because of their commitment to righteousness. Their suffering is known to God, and he will one day act on their behalf to render justice and destroy all evil (cf. Heb 12:24).

4:11 NOW YOU ARE UNDER A CURSE. Cain was cursed by God in the sense that God would no longer bless his efforts to gain his living from the ground (cf. vv. 2–3). Evidently Cain did not humble himself in godly sorrow and repentance, for he separated himself from the Lord and sought to live without God's help (v. 16).

4:15 A MARK ON CAIN. This should probably be understood in the sense of a sign given to Cain to assure him of God's promise. The death penalty was not carried out on Cain. Capital punishment came later when the wickedness and violence of humankind became very great on the earth (6:5–7,11; 9:6).

4:16 CAIN WENT OUT FROM THE LORD'S PRESENCE. Cain and his descendants were the pioneers of God-estranged human civilization. A basic motivation in all humanistic societies is the attempt to overcome the curse, find pleasure and regain "paradise" without submission to God. In other words, the world's system is founded on the principle of self-redemption for the human race in its revolt against God (see 1Jn 5:19, note).

4:17 CAIN . . . HIS WIFE. Adam and Eve had other sons and daughters (5:4). Therefore, Cain must have married one of his sisters. Such a relationship was necessary in the beginning. Later, because the results of the fall increased and interfamily marriages multiplied the biological weaknesses in the children, this type of marriage was forbidden (Lev 18:6,9).

4:19 MARRIED TWO WOMEN. Lamech was the first to reject God's ordained principle of monogamy (2:21–24). Inherited depravity was progressively revealing itself in the home and family.

20 Adah gave birth to Jabal; he was the
father of those who live in tents and
raise livestock. 21 His brother's name
was Jubal; he was the father of all who
play the harp[h] and flute.[i] 22 Zillah
also had a son, Tubal-Cain, who
forged[j] all kinds of tools out of[w]
bronze and iron. Tubal-Cain's sister
was Naamah.
23 Lamech said to his wives,

"Adah and Zillah, listen to me;
wives of Lamech, hear my
words.
I have killed[x][k] a man for
wounding me,
a young man for injuring me.
24 If Cain is avenged[l] seven times,[m]
then Lamech seventy-seven
times.[n]"

25 Adam lay with his wife[o] again,
and she gave birth to a son and named
him Seth,[y][p] saying, "God has granted me another child in place of Abel,
since Cain killed him."[q] 26 Seth also
had a son, and he named him Enosh.[r]
At that time men began to call on[z]
the name of the LORD.[s]

From Adam to Noah

5 This is the written account[t] of
Adam's line.[u]

When God created man, he made
him in the likeness of God.[v] 2 He created them[w] male and female[x] and
blessed them. And when they were created, he called them "man.[a]"
3 When Adam had lived 130 years, he
had a son in his own likeness, in his
own image;[y] and he named him
Seth.[z] 4 After Seth was born, Adam
lived 800 years and had other sons and
daughters. 5 Altogether, Adam lived
930 years, and then he died.[a]
6 When Seth had lived 105 years, he
became the father[b] of Enosh.[b] 7 And
after he became the father of Enosh,
Seth lived 807 years and had other
sons and daughters. 8 Altogether, Seth
lived 912 years, and then he died.
9 When Enosh had lived 90 years, he
became the father of Kenan.[c] 10 And
after he became the father of Kenan,
Enosh lived 815 years and had other
sons and daughters. 11 Altogether,
Enosh lived 905 years, and then he
died.
12 When Kenan had lived 70 years,
he became the father of Mahalalel.[d]
13 And after he became the father of
Mahalalel, Kenan lived 840 years and
had other sons and daughters. 14 Altogether, Kenan lived 910 years, and
then he died.
15 When Mahalalel had lived 65
years, he became the father of Jared.[e]
16 And after he became the father of Jared, Mahalalel lived 830 years and had
other sons and daughters. 17 Altogether, Mahalalel lived 895 years, and then
he died.

4:21 [h] Ge 31:27; Ex 15:20; 1Sa 16:16; 1Ch 25:3; Ps 33:2; 43:4; Isa 16:11; Da 3:5 [i] Job 21:12; 30:31; Ps 150:4 **4:22** [j] Ex 35:35; 1Sa 13:19; 2Ki 24:14 **4:23** [k] Ge 9:5-6; Ex 20:13; 21:12; 23:7; Lev 19:18; 24:17; Dt 27:24; 32:35 **4:24** [l] Dt 32:35; 2Ki 9:7; Ps 18:47; 94:1; Isa 35:4; Jer 51:56; Na 1:2 [m] S ver 15 [n] Mt 18:22 **4:25** [o] ver 1 [p] Ge 5:3; 1Ch 1:1 [q] ver 8 **4:26** [r] Ge 5:6; 1Ch 1:1; Lk 3:38 [s] Ge 12:8; 13:4; 21:33; 22:9; 26:25; 33:20; 35:1; Ex 17:15; 1Ki 18:24; Ps 116:17; Joel 2:32; Zep 3:9; S Ac 2:21 **5:1** [t] S Ge 2:4 [u] 1Ch 1:1 [v] S Ge 1:27; Col 3:10 **5:2** [w] Ge 1:28 [x] S Ge 1:27; Mt 19:4; Mk 10:6; Gal 3:28 **5:3** [y] S Ge 1:26; 1Co 15:49 [z] S Ge 4:25; Lk 3:38 **5:5** [a] S Ge 2:17; Heb 9:27 **5:6** [b] S Ge 4:26; Lk 3:38 **5:9** [c] 1Ch 1:2; Lk 3:37 **5:12** [d] 1Ch 1:2; Lk 3:37 **5:15** [e] 1Ch 1:2; Lk 3:37

[w] 22 Or *who instructed all who work in* [x] 23 Or *I will kill* [y] 25 *Seth* probably means *granted.* [z] 26 Or *to proclaim* [a] 2 Hebrew *adam* [b] 6 *Father* may mean *ancestor*; also in verses 7-26.

4:26 CALL ON THE NAME OF THE LORD. Under the encouragement of Enosh, public prayer and worship began (see 2Sa 6:2; 1Ch 13:6; Ps 79:6; Jer 10:25, where calling on the name of the Lord refers to public worship). The ungodly family of Cain developed and centered their lives around the secular arts and business, establishing a way of self-reliance. The family of Seth, in contrast, called "on the name of the LORD" in order to express their dependence on him. Thus, two fundamentally different family groups were developing on the earth—the godly and the ungodly.

5:1 WRITTEN ACCOUNT OF ADAM'S LINE. This chapter gives a list of Adam's descendants down to the flood. These names reflect the godly line who stood for God in an increasingly corrupt age (see ch. 6). (1) Heb 11 selects two individuals (Abel and Enoch) for special mention from this period as those who pleased God by their faith (Heb 11:4–5). These two were among the remnant, the faithful few who refused to go the way of Cain. By the time of the flood the hearts of nearly everyone were evil; only eight individuals remained who were saved (6:5,11,18; 7:1,7; 1Pe 3:20).

(2) There will always be some, at times only a few, who will worship God, remain faithful to him, obey his word and wait for his promises. These people will be a minority (Mt 7:13–14). Yet God marks their names as he did the people in this chapter. Today, if we feel we are standing alone in our faith in God and our response to his word, we must remember we are really never alone. God still has his thousands throughout the earth who remain faithful to him and his cause (cf. 1Ki 19:18).

5:5 ADAM LIVED 930 YEARS. The reason that humankind lived a great number of years may be because sin had only just begun to work its corrupting influence on the environment and on people's physical bodies. By Abraham's time life expectancy had fallen to less than two hundred years.

5:6 SETH ... FATHER OF ENOSH. "Father" may mean "ancestor" (see NIV text note). Thus these genealogies, like other genealogies in the Bible, were not intended to name every individual in the line.

18When Jared had lived 162 years,
he became the father of Enoch.[f]
19And after he became the father of
Enoch, Jared lived 800 years and had
other sons and daughters. 20Altogeth-
er, Jared lived 962 years, and then he
died.
21When Enoch had lived 65 years,
he became the father of Methuselah.[g]
22And after he became the father of
Methuselah, Enoch walked with God[h]
300 years and had other sons and
daughters. 23Altogether, Enoch lived
365 years. 24Enoch walked with
God;[i] then he was no more, because
God took him away.[j]
25When Methuselah had lived 187
years, he became the father of Lamech.[k] 26And after he became the father of Lamech, Methuselah lived 782
years and had other sons and daughters. 27Altogether, Methuselah lived
969 years, and then he died.
28When Lamech had lived 182
years, he had a son. 29He named him
Noah[c][l] and said, "He will comfort us
in the labor and painful toil of our
hands caused by the ground the LORD
has cursed.[m]" 30After Noah was born,
Lamech lived 595 years and had other
sons and daughters. 31Altogether,
Lamech lived 777 years, and then he
died.
32After Noah was 500 years old,[n]
he became the father of Shem,[o] Ham
and Japheth.[p]

Ge 6:9-10

The Flood

6 When men began to increase in
number on the earth[q] and daughters were born to them, 2the sons of
God[r] saw that the daughters of men[s]
were beautiful,[t] and they married[u]
any of them they chose. 3Then the LORD
said, "My Spirit[v] will not contend
with[d] man forever,[w] for he is mortal[e];[x] his days will be a hundred and
twenty years."
4The Nephilim[y] were on the earth
in those days—and also afterward—
when the sons of God went to the
daughters of men[z] and had children
by them. They were the heroes of old,
men of renown.[a]
5The LORD saw how great man's
wickedness on the earth had become,[b] and that every inclination of
the thoughts of his heart was only evil

5:18 [f]1Ch 1:3; Lk 3:37; Jude 1:14 **5:21** [g]1Ch 1:3; Lk 3:37 **5:22** [h]ver 24; Ge 6:9; 17:1; 24:40; 48:15; 2Ki 20:3; Ps 116:9; Mic 6:8; Mal 2:6 **5:24** [i]S ver 22 [j]2Ki 2:1,11; Ps 49:15; 73:24; 89:48; Heb 11:5 **5:25** [k]1Ch 1:3; Lk 3:36 **5:29** [l]1Ch 1:3; Lk 3:36 [m]S Ge 3:17; Ro 8:20 **5:32** [n]Ge 7:6,11; 8:13 [o]Lk 3:36 [p]Ge 6:10; 9:18; 10:1; 1Ch 1:4; Isa 65:20 **6:1** [q]S Ge 1:28 **6:2** [r]Job 1:6 *fn*; 2:1 *fn* [s]ver 4 [t]Dt 21:11 [u]S Ge 4:19 **6:3** [v]Job 34:14; Gal 5:16-17 [w]Isa 57:16; 1Pe 3:20 [x]Job 10:9; Ps 78:39; 103:14; Isa 40:6 **6:4** [y]Nu 13:33 [z]ver 2 [a]Ge 11:4 **6:5** [b]Ge 38:7; Job 34:26; Jer 1:16; 44:5; Eze 3:19

[c] *29 Noah* sounds like the Hebrew for *comfort.* [d] *3* Or *My spirit will not remain in* [e] *3* Or *corrupt*

5:22 ENOCH WALKED WITH GOD. Enoch undoubtedly excelled in godliness. Notice what the Bible says about him. (1) He "walked with God" (vv. 22,24)—i.e., he lived by faith in God, trusted in his word and promises (Heb 11:5–6), made every effort to live a holy life (cf. 1Jn 1:5–7) and embraced God's ways (cf. Am 3:3), while standing firm against his generation's ungodliness (Jude 14–15).

(2) Enoch was a preacher of righteousness who denounced sin and the unrighteous lifestyle of his generation. Jude 14–15 tell us that Enoch cried out against ungodliness and immorality by warning people of God's coming in judgment to punish men and women for their ungodly deeds: "Enoch, the seventh from Adam, prophesied about these men: See, the Lord is coming with thousands upon thousands of his holy ones to judge everyone, and to convict all the ungodly of all the ungodly acts they have done in the ungodly way, and of all the harsh words ungodly sinners have spoken against him."

(3) Enoch pleased God (Heb 11:5). His life, message and godliness so pleased God that God honored him by taking him away from the earth to be in his presence forever without experiencing death.

Believers today should ponder Enoch's life as an example, for we too live in an evil and ungodly generation. Do we walk with God, live in true holiness, denounce sin and warn people to flee the coming wrath (Ac 3:19–20; 1Th 1:10)? Do we wait for Christ's return to take us away from this earth to be with him forever (1Th 4:16–17)?

5:24 GOD TOOK HIM. Enoch's entrance into heaven without experiencing death implies that righteous men and women before Abraham's time possessed a hope for future life with God (Heb 11:5; cf. Job 19:25–26; 2Ki 2:10–11).

6:2 THE SONS OF GOD. The "sons of God" most likely refer to men who were descendants of the godly line of Seth (cf. Dt 14:1; 32:5; Ps 73:15; Hos 1:10); they began to intermarry with the "daughters of men," i.e., women from the ungodly family of Cain (see 4:16, note). The theory that the "sons of God" were angels is less likely in view of Jesus' words that angels do not marry (Mt 22:30; Mk 12:25). This union of the godly with the unrighteous led to "wickedness" (v. 5), i.e., the godly became preoccupied with evil. As a result the earth became corrupt and filled with violence (vv. 11–13; see article on SPIRITUAL SEPARATION FOR BELIEVERS, p. 1794).

6:5 HOW GREAT MAN'S WICKEDNESS. In Noah's day the character of human sin was blatantly manifested in two primary ways: sexual lust (v. 2) and violence (v. 11). Human depravity has not changed; it is still through lust and violence that evil finds unrestrained expression. Today immorality, ungodliness, pornography and violence dominate our societies (see Mt 24:37–39; Ro 1:32, note).

all the time.[c] **6**The LORD was grieved[d]
that he had made man on the earth,
and his heart was filled with pain. **7**So
the LORD said, "I will wipe mankind,
whom I have created, from the face of
the earth[e]—men and animals, and
creatures that move along the ground,
and birds of the air—for I am grieved
that I have made them.[f]" **8**But Noah[g]
found favor in the eyes of the LORD.[h]

9This is the account[i] of Noah.

Noah was a righteous man, blameless[j] among the people of his time,[k]
and he walked with God.[l] **10**Noah had
three sons: Shem,[m] Ham and Ja-
-2 pheth.[n]
11Now the earth was corrupt[o] in
God's sight and was full of violence.[p]
12God saw how corrupt[q] the earth had
become, for all the people on earth had
corrupted their ways.[r] **13**So God said
to Noah, "I am going to put an end to
all people, for the earth is filled with
violence because of them. I am surely
going to destroy[s] both them and the
earth.[t] **14**So make yourself an ark of
cypress[f] wood;[u] make rooms in it
and coat it with pitch[v] inside and out.
15This is how you are to build it: The
ark is to be 450 feet long, 75 feet wide
and 45 feet high.[g] **16**Make a roof for
it and finish[h] the ark to within 18
inches[i] of the top. Put a door in the
side of the ark and make lower, middle
and upper decks. **17**I am going to bring
floodwaters[w] on the earth to destroy
all life under the heavens, every creature that has the breath of life in it.
Everything on earth will perish.[x]
18But I will establish my covenant with
you,[y] and you will enter the ark[z]—
you and your sons and your wife and

6:5 [c]Ge 8:21; Ps 14:1-3 **6:6** [d]Ex 32:14; 1Sa 15:11,35; 2Sa 24:16; 1Ch 21:15; Isa 63:10; Jer 18:7-10; Eph 4:30 **6:7** [e]Eze 33:28; Zep 1:2,18 [f]ver 17; Ge 7:4,21; Dt 28:63; 29:20 **6:8** [g]Eze 14:14 [h]Ge 19:19; 39:4; Ex 33:12,13,17; 34:9; Nu 11:15; Ru 2:2; Lk 1:30; Ac 7:46 **6:9** [i]S Ge 2:4 [j]Ge 17:1; Dt 18:13; 2Sa 22:24; Job 1:1; 4:6; 9:21; 12:4; 31:6; Ps 15:2; 18:23; 19:13; 37:37; Pr 2:7 [k]Ge 7:1; Ps 37:39; Jer 15:1; Eze 14:14,20; Da 10:11; S Lk 1:6; Heb 11:7; 2Pe 2:5 [l]S Ge 5:22 **6:10** [m]Lk 3:36 [n]S Ge 5:32 **6:11** [o]Dt 31:29; Jdg 2:19 [p]Ps 7:9; 73:6; Eze 7:23; 8:17; 28:16; Mal 2:16 **6:12** [q]Ex 32:7; Dt 4:16; 9:12,24 [r]Ps 14:1-3

6:13 [s]Dt 28:63; 2Ki 8:19; Ezr 9:14; Jer 44:11 [t]ver 17; Ge 7:4,21-23; Job 34:15; Isa 5:6; 24:1-3; Jer 44:27; Eze 7:2-3 **6:14** [u]Heb 11:7; 1Pe 3:20 [v]Ex 2:3 **6:17** [w]Ps 29:10 [x]S ver 7,S 13; 2Pe 2:5 **6:18** [y]Ge 9:9-16; 17:7; 19:12; Ex 6:4; 34:10,27; Dt 29:13,14-15; Ps 25:10; 74:20; 106:45; Isa 55:3; Jer 32:40; Eze 16:60; Hag 2:5; 1Pe 3:20 [z]Ge 7:1,7,13

[f] *14* The meaning of the Hebrew for this word is uncertain. [g] *15* Hebrew *300 cubits long, 50 cubits wide and 30 cubits high* (about 140 meters long, 23 meters wide and 13.5 meters high) [h] *16* Or *Make an opening for light by finishing* [i] *16* Hebrew *a cubit* (about 0.5 meter)

6:6 THE LORD WAS GRIEVED. God is revealed in these early chapters of the Bible as a God who deals with people personally and is capable of emotion, disappointment and reaction against the willful sin and rebellion of humankind. (1) The word "grieved" indicates that because of the tragic sin of the human race, God's disposition was changed towards them; his attitude of mercy and patience turned to one of judgment.

(2) Although God's existence, character and ultimate purposes remain changeless (1Sa 15:29; Jas 1:17), he remains open and responsive in his dealings with humans. God does alter his feelings, attitudes, actions and mind in accordance with a changing response to his will (cf. Ex 32:14; 2Sa 24:16; Jer 18:7,8; 26:3,13,19; Eze 18; Jnh 3:10).

(3) This revelation of God as a God who can feel regret and grief makes clear that God exists in a personal and intimate relationship to his creation. He possesses an intense love for human beings and a divine attentiveness to the plight of the human race (Ps 139:7–18).

6:9 NOAH WAS A RIGHTEOUS MAN, BLAMELESS AMONG THE PEOPLE. Amidst the widespread wickedness and evil of those days (v. 5), God found in Noah one man who still sought communion with him and who was a righteous man. (1) "Blameless among the people of his time" indicates that he kept himself separate from the moral evil of the society around him. Because he was a righteous man who feared God and set his face against popular public opinion and conduct, Noah found favor with God (v. 8; 7:1; Heb 11:7; 2Pe 2:5).

(2) This righteousness in Noah's life came by God's grace, through Noah's faith and walk with God (v. 9). Salvation in the NT era must be found in exactly the same way, namely, by God's mercy and grace received through a faith so vital that it results in a sincere effort to walk with God and remain separated from a perverse generation (v. 22; 7:5,9,16). Heb 11:7 states that Noah "became heir of the righteousness that comes by faith."

(3) The NT also states that Noah was a preacher of righteousness (2Pe 2:5). In this he is an example of what preachers ought to be.

6:14 AN ARK. The Hebrew word "ark" means a vessel for floating and occurs only here and in Ex 2:3,5 (where it is used of the basket in which the baby Moses was placed). It resembled a barge, but not necessarily with square corners. Its carrying capacity was equal to more than 300 railroad stock cars. It is calculated that the ark could hold some 7,000 kinds of animals. Heb 11:7 suggests that the ark is a type of Christ, the one who is the means of the believer's salvation from judgment and death (cf. 1Pe 3:20–21).

6:18 I WILL ESTABLISH MY COVENANT WITH YOU. Through his covenant, God promised Noah that he would be saved from the judgment to be meted out through the flood. Noah responded to God's covenant by believing in him and his word (v. 13; Heb 11:7). His faith was demonstrated in his response of "holy fear" (Heb 11:7) and his actions of preparing and entering the ark (v. 22; 7:7; see 1Pe 3:21, note; see article on GOD'S COVENANT WITH ABRAHAM, ISAAC AND JACOB, p. 46).

your sons' wives with you. 19You are to
bring into the ark two of all living creatures, male and female, to keep them
alive with you.[a] 20Two[b] of every kind
of bird, of every kind of animal and of
every kind[c] of creature that moves
along the ground will come to you to be
kept alive.[d] 21You are to take every
kind of food that is to be eaten and
store it away as food for you and for
them."

22Noah did everything just as God
commanded him.[e]

7 The LORD then said to Noah, "Go
into the ark, you and your whole
family,[f] because I have found you
righteous[g] in this generation. 2Take
with you seven[j] of every kind of
clean[h] animal, a male and its mate,
and two of every kind of unclean animal, a male and its mate, 3and also
seven of every kind of bird, male and
female, to keep their various kinds
alive[i] throughout the earth. 4Seven
days from now I will send rain[j] on the
earth[k] for forty days[l] and forty
nights,[m] and I will wipe from the face
of the earth every living creature I have
made.[n]"

5And Noah did all that the LORD commanded him.[o]

6Noah was six hundred years old[p]
when the floodwaters came on the
earth. 7And Noah and his sons and his
wife and his sons' wives entered the
ark[q] to escape the waters of the flood.
8Pairs of clean and unclean[r] animals,
of birds and of all creatures that move
along the ground, 9male and female,
came to Noah and entered the ark, as
God had commanded Noah.[s] 10And after the seven days[t] the floodwaters
came on the earth.

11In the six hundredth year of
Noah's life,[u] on the seventeenth day
of the second month[v]—on that day all
the springs of the great deep[w] burst
forth, and the floodgates of the heavens[x] were opened. 12And rain fell on
the earth forty days and forty nights.[y]

13On that very day Noah and his
sons,[z] Shem, Ham and Japheth, together with his wife and the wives of
his three sons, entered the ark.[a]
14They had with them every wild animal according to its kind, all livestock
according to their kinds, every creature that moves along the ground according to its kind and every bird according to its kind,[b] everything with
wings. 15Pairs of all creatures that
have the breath of life in them came to
Noah and entered the ark.[c] 16The animals going in were male and female of
every living thing, as God had commanded Noah.[d] Then the LORD shut
him in.

17For forty days[e] the flood kept
coming on the earth, and as the waters
increased they lifted the ark high
above the earth. 18The waters rose and
increased greatly on the earth, and the
ark floated on the surface of the water.
19They rose greatly on the earth, and
all the high mountains under the entire
heavens were covered.[f] 20The waters
rose and covered the mountains to a

6:19 [a] Ge 7:15
6:20 [b] Ge 7:15 [c] S Ge 1:11 [d] Ge 7:3
6:22 [e] Ge 7:5,9, 16; Ex 7:6; 39:43; 40:16,19,21,23,25, 27,29,32
7:1 [f] S Ge 6:18; Mt 24:38; Lk 17:26-27; Heb 11:7; 1Pe 3:20; 2Pe 2:5 [g] Ge 6:9; Eze 14:14
7:2 [h] ver 8; Ge 8:20; Lev 10:10; 11:1-47; Dt 14:3-20; Eze 44:23; Hag 2:12; Ac 10:14-15
7:3 [i] Ge 6:20
7:4 [j] Ge 8:2 [k] 1Ki 13:34; Jer 28:16 [l] Nu 13:25; Dt 9:9; 1Sa 17:16; 1Ki 19:8 [m] ver 12, 17; Ex 24:18; 32:1; 34:28; Dt 9:9,11,18,25; 10:10; Job 37:6, 13; Mt 4:2 [n] S Ge 6:7,13
7:5 [o] S Ge 6:22
7:6 [p] S Ge 5:32
7:7 [q] S Ge 6:18
7:8 [r] S ver 2
7:9 [s] S Ge 6:22
7:10 [t] S ver 4
7:11 [u] S Ge 5:32 [v] Ge 8:4,14 [w] S Ge 1:7; Job 28:11; Ps 36:6; 42:7; Pr 8:24; Isa 51:10; Eze 26:19 [x] Ge 8:2; 2Ki 7:2; Ps 78:23; Isa 24:18; Mal 3:10
7:12 [y] S ver 4; S 1Sa 12:17; S Job 28:26
7:13 [z] Ge 8:16; 1Pe 3:20; 2Pe 2:5 [a] S Ge 6:18
7:14 [b] S Ge 1:11
7:15 [c] ver 8-9; Ge 6:19
7:16 [d] S Ge 6:22 7:17 [e] S ver 4 7:19 [f] Ps 104:6

[j] 2 Or *seven pairs*; also in verse 3

7:6 THE FLOODWATERS CAME ON THE EARTH. The flood was God's universal judgment on an ungodly and unrepentant world. The apostle Peter refers to the flood to remind his readers that God will again judge the whole world at the end of time, this time by fire (2Pe 3:10). That judgment will involve the outpouring of God's wrath on the ungodly in a way unequaled in history (Mt 24:21; see article on THE GREAT TRIBULATION, p. 1456). God calls believers today, as he called Noah of old, to warn the unsaved about this terrible day and to urge them to repent of their sins, turn to God through Christ and be saved.

7:11–12 THE GREAT DEEP BURST FORTH. Two cataclysmic events precipitated the flood: the eruption of great reservoirs of subterranean waters, perhaps caused by earthquakes with subsequent great tidal waves from the oceans, and torrential rains that fell on the earth for forty days (v. 12). (1) Thus, all living creatures outside the ark who normally lived on dry land died, both human and animal life (vv. 21–22; Mt 24:37–39; 1Pe 3:20; 2Pe 2:5).

(2) Water rose to such height that it covered "all the high mountains under the entire heavens" (vv. 19–20); i.e., the entire earth was covered with water. This indicates a universal flood and not simply a local one confined to a small portion of earth (cf. 2Pe 3:6). The water began to recede only after 150 days (v. 24). Noah's ark finally came to rest on one of the mountains of Ararat (Armenia), 500 miles from where it started (8:4).

(3) The earth dried up, and Noah left the ark 377 days after the flood began (8:13–14).

(4) The apostle Peter states that the pre-flood world was "destroyed" (2Pe 3:6). This suggests that due to the enormous topographical upheaval, the pre-flood earth changed radically, both physically and geologically, into the earth that now exists.

depth of more than twenty feet.[k,l] [g]
21Every living thing that moved on the
earth perished—birds, livestock, wild
animals, all the creatures that swarm
over the earth, and all mankind.[h]
22Everything on dry land that had the
breath of life[i] in its nostrils died.
23Every living thing on the face of the
earth was wiped out; men and animals
and the creatures that move along the
ground and the birds of the air were
wiped from the earth.[j] Only Noah was
left, and those with him in the ark.[k]
24The waters flooded the earth for a
hundred and fifty days.[l]

8 But God remembered[m] Noah and
all the wild animals and the livestock that were with him in the ark,
and he sent a wind over the earth,[n]
and the waters receded. **2**Now the
springs of the deep and the floodgates
of the heavens[o] had been closed, and
the rain[p] had stopped falling from the
sky. **3**The water receded steadily from
the earth. At the end of the hundred
and fifty days[q] the water had gone
down, **4**and on the seventeenth day of
the seventh month[r] the ark came to
rest on the mountains[s] of Ararat.[t]
5The waters continued to recede until
the tenth month, and on the first day of
the tenth month the tops of the mountains became visible.
6After forty days[u] Noah opened the
window he had made in the ark **7**and
sent out a raven,[v] and it kept flying
back and forth until the water had
dried up from the earth.[w] **8**Then he
sent out a dove[x] to see if the water
had receded from the surface of the
ground. **9**But the dove could find no
place to set its feet because there was
water over all the surface of the earth;
so it returned to Noah in the ark. He
reached out his hand and took the dove
and brought it back to himself in the
ark. **10**He waited seven more days and
again sent out the dove from the ark.
11When the dove returned to him in the
evening, there in its beak was a freshly
plucked olive leaf! Then Noah knew
that the water had receded from the
earth.[y] **12**He waited seven more days
and sent the dove out again, but this
time it did not return to him.
13By the first day of the first month
of Noah's six hundred and first year,[z]
the water had dried up from the earth.
Noah then removed the covering from
the ark and saw that the surface of the
ground was dry. **14**By the twenty-seventh day of the second month[a] the
earth was completely dry.
15Then God said to Noah, **16**"Come
out of the ark, you and your wife and
your sons and their wives.[b] **17**Bring
out every kind of living creature that is
with you—the birds, the animals, and
all the creatures that move along the
ground—so they can multiply on the
earth and be fruitful and increase in
number upon it."[c]
18So Noah came out, together with
his sons and his wife and his sons'
wives.[d] **19**All the animals and all the
creatures that move along the ground
and all the birds—everything that
moves on the earth—came out of the
ark, one kind after another.
20Then Noah built an altar to the
LORD[e] and, taking some of all the
clean animals and clean[f] birds, he
sacrificed burnt offerings[g] on it.
21The LORD smelled the pleasing aro-

7:20 [g] Ge 8:4-5; 2Pe 3:6
7:21 [h] S Ge 6:7, 13; 2Pe 3:6
7:22 [i] S Ge 1:30
7:23 [j] Job 14:19; 21:18; 22:11,16; Ps 90:5; Isa 28:2; Mt 24:39; Lk 17:27; 1Pe 3:20; 2Pe 2:5 [k] Heb 11:7
7:24 [l] Ge 8:3; Job 12:15
8:1 [m] Ge 9:15; 19:29; 21:1; 30:22; Ex 2:24; Nu 10:9; Ru 4:13; 1Sa 1:11,19; 2Ki 20:3; 1Ch 16:15; Ne 1:8; 5:19; 13:14,22,31; Job 14:13; Ps 105:42; 106:4; Lk 1:54,72 [n] Ex 14:21; Jos 2:10; 3:16; Job 12:15; Ps 66:6; Isa 11:15; 44:27; Na 1:4
8:2 [o] S Ge 7:11 [p] S Ge 7:4
8:3 [q] S Ge 7:24
8:4 [r] S Ge 7:11 [s] Ge 7:20 [t] 2Ki 19:37; Jer 51:27
8:6 [u] Ge 7:12
8:7 [v] Lev 11:15; Dt 14:14; 1Ki 17:4,6; Job 38:41; Ps 147:9; Pr 30:17; Isa 34:11; Lk 12:24 [w] ver 11
8:8 [x] Job 30:31; Ps 55:6; 74:19; SS 2:12,14; Isa 38:14; 59:11; 60:8; Jer 48:28; Eze 7:16; Hos 7:11; 11:11; Na 2:7; Mt 3:16; 10:16; Jn 1:32
8:11 [y] ver 7
8:13 [z] S Ge 5:32
8:14 [a] S Ge 7:11
8:16 [b] S Ge 7:13
8:17 [c] S Ge 1:22
8:18 [d] 1Pe 3:20; 2Pe 2:5
8:20 [e] Ge 12:7-8; 13:18; 22:9; 26:25; 33:20; 35:7; Ex 17:15; 24:4 [f] S Ge 7:8 [g] Ge 22:2,13; Ex 10:25; 20:24; 40:29; Lev 1:3; 4:29; 6:8-13; Nu 6:11; Jdg 6:26; 11:31; 1Sa 20:29; Job 1:5; 42:8

[k] *20* Hebrew *fifteen cubits* (about 6.9 meters)
[l] *20* Or *rose more than twenty feet, and the mountains were covered*

7:23 EVERY LIVING THING . . . WAS WIPED OUT . . . ONLY NOAH WAS LEFT. The flood story tells of both judgment and salvation. (1) The flood with its total destruction of all human life outside the ark was necessary in order to blot out the extreme moral corruption of men and women and to give the human race a new chance for fellowship with God. (2) The apostle Peter states that Christian baptism corresponds to Noah's salvation through the floodwaters (see 1Pe 3:21, note).

8:1 BUT GOD REMEMBERED NOAH. Noah had not heard from God for 150 days (cf. 7:24). His faith was being tested, for he had no idea when the waters would subside or when God would intervene again. Then God acted out of concern and love for Noah and his family. God's dealings with Noah are recorded to give all God's faithful people hope and trust in his ways. If God has not acted in your life for a long time, you can be confident he will act again and show his loving care toward you. At the present time your task is to draw near to the Lord and continue in faithful obedience to his word and Spirit (Pr 3:5–6; 16:3; Php 2:13).

8:21 HEART IS EVIL FROM CHILDHOOD. The Lord states the truth about the corruption and depravity of human nature. The tendency toward evil is innate in a person from birth and is expressed early in childhood or youth (see Ro 3:10–18, note).

ma[h] and said in his heart: "Never
again will I curse the ground[i] because
of man, even though[m] every inclination of his heart is evil from childhood.[j] And never again will I destroy[k] all living creatures,[l] as I have
done.

22"As long as the earth endures,
seedtime and harvest,[m]
cold and heat,
summer and winter,[n]
day and night
will never cease."[o]

God's Covenant With Noah

9 Then God blessed Noah and his
sons, saying to them, "Be fruitful
and increase in number and fill the
earth.[p] 2The fear and dread of you will
fall upon all the beasts of the earth and
all the birds of the air, upon every creature that moves along the ground, and
upon all the fish of the sea; they are
given into your hands.[q] 3Everything
that lives and moves will be food for
you.[r] Just as I gave you the green
plants, I now give you everything.[s]

4"But you must not eat meat that
has its lifeblood still in it.[t] 5And for
your lifeblood I will surely demand an
accounting.[u] I will demand an accounting from every animal.[v] And
from each man, too, I will demand an
accounting for the life of his fellow
man.[w]

6"Whoever sheds the blood of man,
by man shall his blood be
shed;[x]
for in the image of God[y]
has God made man.

7As for you, be fruitful and increase in
number; multiply on the earth and increase upon it."[z]

8Then God said to Noah and to his
sons with him: 9"I now establish my
covenant with you[a] and with your
descendants after you 10and with every living creature that was with you—
the birds, the livestock and all the wild
animals, all those that came out of the
ark with you—every living creature on
earth. 11I establish my covenant[b]
with you:[c] Never again will all life be
cut off by the waters of a flood; never
again will there be a flood to destroy
the earth.[d]"

12And God said, "This is the sign of
the covenant[e] I am making between
me and you and every living creature
with you, a covenant for all generations to come:[f] 13I have set my rainbow[g] in the clouds, and it will be the
sign of the covenant between me and
the earth. 14Whenever I bring clouds
over the earth and the rainbow[h] appears in the clouds, 15I will remember
my covenant[i] between me and you
and all living creatures of every kind.
Never again will the waters become a
flood to destroy all life.[j] 16Whenever
the rainbow[k] appears in the clouds, I
will see it and remember the everlasting covenant[l] between God and all living creatures of every kind on the
earth."

17So God said to Noah, "This is the
sign of the covenant[m] I have established between me and all life on the
earth."

The Sons of Noah

18The sons of Noah who came out of
the ark were Shem, Ham and Japheth.[n] (Ham was the father of Canaan.)[o] 19These were the three sons
of Noah,[p] and from them came the
people who were scattered over the
earth.[q]

8:21 [h]Ex 29:18, 25; Lev 1:9,13; 2:9; 4:31; Nu 15:3,7; 2Co 2:15 [i]S Ge 3:17 [j]Ge 6:5; Ps 51:5; Jer 17:9; Mt 15:19; Ro 1:21 [k]Jer 44:11 [l]Ge 9:11,15; Isa 54:9 **8:22** [m]Jos 3:15; Ps 67:6; Jer 5:24 [n]Ps 74:17; Zec 14:8 [o]S Ge 1:14 **9:1** [p]S Ge 1:22 **9:2** [q]S Ge 1:26 **9:3** [r]S Ge 1:29 [s]S Ac 10:15; Col 2:16 **9:4** [t]Lev 3:17; 7:26; 17:10-14; 19:26; Dt 12:16, 23-25; 15:23; 1Sa 14:33; Eze 33:25; Ac 15:20,29 **9:5** [u]Ge 42:22; 50:15; 1Ki 2:32; 2Ch 24:22; Ps 9:12 [v]Ex 21:28-32 [w]Ge 4:10 **9:6** [x]S Ge 4:14; S Jdg 9:24; S Mt 26:52 [y]S Ge 1:26 **9:7** [z]S Ge 1:22 **9:9** [a]ver 11; S Ge 6:18

9:11 [b]ver 16; Isa 24:5; 33:8; Hos 6:7 [c]S ver 9 [d]S Ge 8:21 **9:12** [e]ver 17; Ge 17:11 [f]Ge 17:12; Ex 12:14; Lev 3:17; 6:18; 17:7; Nu 10:8 **9:13** [g]ver 14; Eze 1:28; Rev 4:3; 10:1 **9:14** [h]S ver 13 **9:15** [i]S Ge 8:1; Ex 2:24; 6:5; 34:10; Lev 26:42, 45; Dt 7:9; Ps 89:34; 103:18; 105:8; 106:45; Eze 16:60 [j]S Ge 8:21 **9:16** [k]ver 13 [l]S ver 11; Ge 17:7, 13,19; 2Sa 7:13; 23:5; Ps 105:9-10; Isa 9:7; 54:10; 55:3; 59:21; 61:8; Jer 31:31-34; 32:40; 33:21; Eze 16:60; 37:26; S Heb 13:20 **9:17** [m]S ver 12 **9:18** [n]S Ge 5:32; Lk 3:36 [o]ver 25-27; Ge 10:6,15 **9:19** [p]Ge 5:32 [q]S Ge 1:22; 10:32; 11:4,8,9

[m]21 Or *man, for*

9:6 WHOEVER SHEDS THE BLOOD OF MAN, BY MAN SHALL HIS BLOOD BE SHED. Because of the desire for violence and bloodshed that arises within the human heart (cf. 6:11; 8:21), God sought to guard the sanctity of human life by restraining murder in society. He did this in two ways: (1) By emphasizing that humans have been created in his image (1:26) and that their lives are sacred in his sight; (2) by instituting capital punishment, commanding that every murderer be punished with death (cf. Ex 21:12,14; 22:2; Nu 35:6–34; Dt 19:1–13; see Ro 13:4, note). The authority of governments to use the "sword" for capital punishment is reaffirmed in the NT (Ac 25:11; Ro 13:4; cf. Mt 26:52).

9:9–17 I NOW ESTABLISH MY COVENANT. These verses speak of God's covenant with humanity and nature, in which he promised never again to destroy the earth and all living creatures with a flood (vv. 11,15).

9:13 MY RAINBOW IN THE CLOUDS. The rainbow was God's sign and ongoing reminder of his promise never again to destroy all inhabitants on the earth by a flood. The rainbow should remind us of God's mercy and his faithfulness to his word.

[20]Noah, a man of the soil, proceeded[n] to plant a vineyard. [21]When he
drank some of its wine,[r] he became
drunk and lay uncovered inside his
tent. [22]Ham, the father of Canaan, saw
his father's nakedness[s] and told his
two brothers outside. [23]But Shem and
Japheth took a garment and laid it
across their shoulders; then they
walked in backward and covered their
father's nakedness. Their faces were
turned the other way so that they
would not see their father's nakedness.
[24]When Noah awoke from his wine
and found out what his youngest son
had done to him, [25]he said,

"Cursed[t] be Canaan![u]
The lowest of slaves
will he be to his brothers.[v]"

[26]He also said,

"Blessed be the LORD, the God of
Shem![w]
May Canaan be the slave[x] of
Shem.[o]
[27]May God extend the territory of
Japheth[p];[y]
may Japheth live in the tents of
Shem,[z]
and may Canaan be his[q] slave."

[28]After the flood Noah lived 350
years. [29]Altogether, Noah lived 950
years, and then he died.[a]

9:21 [r]Ge 19:35
9:22 [s]Hab 2:15
9:25 [t]Ge 27:12
[u]ver 18; Ex 20:5; Ps 79:8; Isa 14:21; Jer 31:29; 32:18
[v]Ge 25:23; 27:29, 37,40; 37:10; 49:8; Nu 24:18; Jos 9:23
9:26 [w]Ge 14:20; Ex 18:10; Ps 7:17
[x]1Ki 9:21
9:27 [y]Ge 10:2-5
[z]Eph 2:13-14; 3:6
9:29 [a]S Ge 2:17
10:1 [b]Ge 2:4
[c]S Ge 5:32
[d]ver 32; 1Ch 1:4
10:2 [e]Eze 38:6
[f]Eze 38:2; 39:6; Rev 20:8
[g]Eze 27:19
[h]Isa 66:19; Eze 27:13; 32:26
[i]Eze 39:1
10:3 [j]Jer 51:27
[k]Eze 27:14; 38:6
10:4 [l]Eze 27:7
[m]Ps 48:7; 72:10; Isa 2:16; 23:1,6, 10,14; 60:9; 66:19; Jer 10:9; Eze 27:12,25; 38:13; Jnh 1:3
[n]Nu 24:24; Isa 23:12; Jer 2:10; Eze 27:6; Da 11:30
10:5 [o]Ge 9:27

The Table of Nations

10 This is the account[b] of Shem,
Ham and Japheth,[c] Noah's
sons,[d] who themselves had sons after
the flood.

The Japhethites

10:2–5pp — 1Ch 1:5–7

[2]The sons[r] of Japheth:
Gomer,[e] Magog,[f] Madai, Javan,[g] Tubal,[h] Meshech[i] and
Tiras.
[3]The sons of Gomer:
Ashkenaz,[j] Riphath and Togarmah.[k]
[4]The sons of Javan:
Elishah,[l] Tarshish,[m] the Kittim[n] and the Rodanim.[s]
[5](From these the maritime peoples spread out into their territories by their clans within
their nations, each with its own
language.)[o]

The Hamites

10:6–20pp — 1Ch 1:8–16

[6]The sons of Ham:

[n] *20* Or *soil, was the first* [o] *26* Or *be his slave* [p] *27* *Japheth* sounds like the Hebrew for *extend.* [q] *27* Or *their* [r] *2* *Sons* may mean *descendants* or *successors* or *nations;* also in verses 3, 4, 6, 7, 20-23, 29 and 31.
[s] *4* Some manuscripts of the Masoretic Text and Samaritan Pentateuch (see also Septuagint and 1 Chron. 1:7); most manuscripts of the Masoretic Text *Dodanim*

9:21 DRANK SOME OF ITS WINE, HE BECAME DRUNK. This first mention of wine in Scripture is connected with drunkenness, sin, shame and a curse (vv. 21–25). Because of the accompanying evils of intoxicating beverages, God has made total abstinence the high standard for his people (cf. Lev 10:9; Jdg 13:4–7; Pr 31:4; see Nu 6:3; Pr 23:31, note; 1Th 5:6, note; Tit 2:2, note; see articles on WINE IN THE OLD TESTAMENT, p. 204, and WINE IN NEW TESTAMENT TIMES (1) and (2), p. 1534 and p. 1586).

9:22 HAM. Ham's sin consisted in his failure to honor and respect his father; rather than covering Noah, he exposed his shameful condition.

9:25 CURSED BE CANAAN. When Noah learned of Ham's shameful action, he pronounced a curse on Ham's son Canaan (though not on Ham himself). (1) Perhaps Canaan was in some way involved in Ham's sin or possessed the same character faults of his father. The curse indicated that Canaan's descendants (who were not black) would be oppressed and under the control of other nations. In contrast, Shem and Japheth's descendants would be blessed by God (vv. 26–27). (2) This prophecy of Noah was conditional for all concerned. Any descendants of Canaan who turned to God would also receive the blessings bestowed on Shem (Jos 6:22–25; Heb 11:31), while any descendants of Shem and Japheth who departed from God would experience the curse bestowed on Canaan (cf. Jer 18:7–10).

10:1 THE ACCOUNT OF SHEM, HAM AND JAPHETH. The purpose of ch. 10 was to reveal how all the nations and people of the earth stemmed from Noah and his sons after the flood (v. 32).

10:2–5 THE SONS OF JAPHETH. These verses list the descendants of Japheth, who went north and settled around the coast lands of the Black and Caspian Seas. They became the progenitors of the Medes and Greeks, as well as the Caucasian races of Europe and Asia.

10:6–20 THE SONS OF HAM. These verses list the descendants of Ham, who settled in southern Arabia, southern Egypt, the east shore of the Mediterranean, and north coast of Africa. Canaan's descendants (vv. 15–19) settled in a territory that was given the name of Canaan, a territory that was later to become the home of the Jewish people.

Cush,[p] Mizraim,[t] Put[q] and
Canaan.[r]
7The sons of Cush:
Seba,[s] Havilah,[t] Sabtah, Ra-
amah[u] and Sabteca.
The sons of Raamah:
Sheba[v] and Dedan.[w]

8Cush was the father[u] of Nimrod,[x]
who grew to be a mighty warrior on the
earth. **9**He was a mighty[y] hunter[z] before the LORD; that is why it is said,
"Like Nimrod, a mighty hunter before
the LORD." **10**The first centers of his
kingdom were Babylon,[a] Erech,[b] Akkad and Calneh,[c] in[v] Shinar.[w][d]
11From that land he went to Assyria,[e]
where he built Nineveh,[f] Rehoboth
Ir,[x] Calah **12**and Resen, which is between Nineveh and Calah; that is the
great city.

13Mizraim was the father of
the Ludites, Anamites, Lehabites, Naphtuhites, **14**Pathru-
sites, Casluhites (from whom
the Philistines[g] came) and
Caphtorites.[h]
15Canaan[i] was the father of
Sidon[j] his firstborn,[y][k] and
of the Hittites,[l] **16**Jebusites,[m]
Amorites,[n] Girgashites,[o]
17Hivites,[p] Arkites, Sinites,
18Arvadites,[q] Zemarites and
Hamathites.[r]

Later the Canaanite[s] clans scattered **19**and the borders of Canaan[t]
reached from Sidon[u] toward Gerar[v]
as far as Gaza,[w] and then toward Sod-

10:6 [p] 2Ki 19:9; 2Ch 12:3; 16:8; Isa 11:11; 18:1; 20:3; 43:3; Jer 46:9; Eze 30:4, 9; 38:5; Na 3:9; Zep 2:12; 3:10 [q] Eze 27:10; 38:5 [r] S Ge 9:18 **10:7** [s] Isa 43:3 [t] S Ge 2:11 [u] Eze 27:22 [v] Ge 25:3; 1Ki 10:1; 2Ch 9:1; Job 1:15; 6:19; 16:11; Ps 72:10, 15; Isa 60:6; Jer 6:20; Eze 27:22; 38:13; Joel 3:8 [w] 1Ch 1:32; Isa 21:13; Jer 25:23-24; 49:8; Eze 27:15,20; 38:13 **10:8** [x] Mic 5:6 **10:9** [y] 2Ch 14:9; 16:8; Isa 18:2 [z] Ge 25:27; 27:3 **10:10** [a] Ge 11:9; 2Ch 36:17; Isa 13:1; 47:1; Jer 21:2; 25:12; 50:1 [b] Ezr 4:9 [c] Isa 10:9; Am 6:2 [d] Ge 11:2; 14:1; Zec 5:11 **10:11** [e] Ps 83:8; Mic 5:6 [f] 2Ki 19:36; Isa 37:37; Jnh 1:2; 3:2,3; 4:11; Na 1:1; Zep 2:13

10:14 [g] Ge 21:32, 34; 26:1,8;Jos 13:2; Jdg 3:3;Isa 14:31; Jer 47:1,4; Am 9:7 [h] Dt 2:23; 1Ch 1:12 **10:15** [i] S Ge 9:18 [j] ver 19; Jos 11:8; Jdg 10:6; Isa 23:2,4; Jer 25:22; 27:3; 47:4; Eze 28:21; 32:30; Joel 3:4; Zec 9:2 [k] Ex 4:22; Nu 1:20; 3:2; 18:15; 26:5; 33:4 [l] Ge 15:20; 23:3,20; 25:10; 26:34; 27:46; 49:32; Nu 13:29; Jos 1:4; 1Sa 26:6; Eze 16:3 **10:16** [m] Jdg 19:10; 1Ch 11:4; Ezr 9:1 [n] Ex 3:8; Nu 13:29; 21:13; 32:39; Dt 1:4; Jos 2:10; 2Ch 8:7 [o] Ge 15:18-21; Dt 7:1 **10:17** [p] Ge 34:2; 36:2; Ex 3:8; Dt 7:1; Jdg 3:3 **10:18** [q] Eze 27:8 [r] 1Ch 18:3 [s] Ge 12:6; 13:7; 50:11; Ex 13:11; Nu 13:29; 14:25; 21:3; 33:40; Dt 1:7; Jdg 1:1 **10:19** [t] Ge 11:31; 12:1; 13:12; 17:8; 24:3; 26:34; 27:46; 28:1,6,8; 31:18; 35:6; 37:1; Lev 25:38 [u] S ver 15; Ge 49:13; Jos 19:28; Jdg 1:31; 18:28; 2Sa 24:6 [v] 2Ch 14:13 [w] Dt 2:23; Jos 10:41; 11:22; 15:47; Jdg 1:18; 6:4; 16:1,21; 1Sa 6:17; Jer 25:20; 47:1; Am 1:6; Zep 2:4

[t] *6* That is, Egypt; also in verse 13
[u] *8* *Father* may mean *ancestor* or *predecessor* or *founder*; also in verses 13, 15, 24 and 26.
[v] *10* Or *Erech and Akkad—all of them in*
[w] *10* That is, Babylonia
[x] *11* Or *Nineveh with its city squares*
[y] *15* Or *of the Sidonians, the foremost*

TABLE OF NATIONS

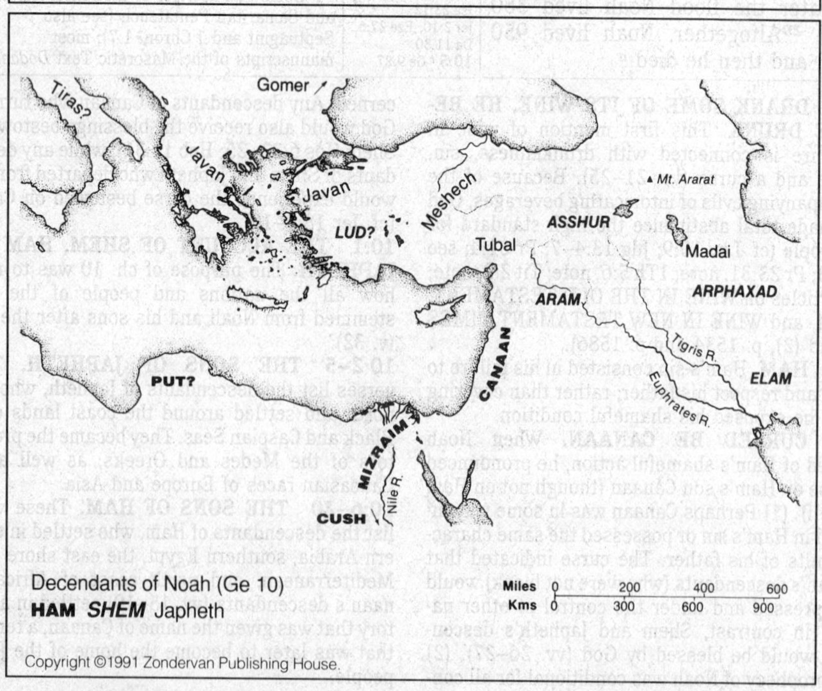

Decendants of Noah (Ge 10)
HAM ***SHEM*** Japheth

om, Gomorrah, Admah and Zeboiim,[x]
as far as Lasha.
20These are the sons of Ham by their
clans and languages, in their territories and nations.

The Semites

10:21–31pp — Ge 11:10–27; 1Ch 1:17–27

21Sons were also born to Shem,
whose older brother was[z] Japheth;
Shem was the ancestor of all the sons
of Eber.[y]
22The sons of Shem:
Elam,[z] Asshur,[a] Arphaxad,[b]
Lud and Aram.[c]
23The sons of Aram:
Uz,[d] Hul, Gether and Meshech.[a]
24Arphaxad was the father of[b]
Shelah,
and Shelah the father of
Eber.[e]
25Two sons were born to Eber:
One was named Peleg,[c] because in his time the earth was
divided; his brother was named
Joktan.
26Joktan was the father of
Almodad, Sheleph, Hazarmaveth, Jerah, 27Hadoram,
Uzal,[f] Diklah, 28Obal, Abimael, Sheba,[g] 29Ophir,[h] Havilah
and Jobab. All these were sons
of Joktan.
30The region where they lived
stretched from Mesha toward Sephar,
in the eastern hill country.
31These are the sons of Shem by
their clans and languages, in their territories and nations.

32These are the clans of Noah's
sons,[i] according to their lines of descent, within their nations. From these
the nations spread out over the earth[j]
after the flood.

10:19 [x] Ge 14:2; Dt 29:23
10:21 [y] ver 24; Nu 24:24
10:22 [z] Ge 14:1; Isa 11:11; 21:2; Jer 25:25; 49:34; Eze 32:24; Da 8:2 [a] Nu 24:22,24; Eze 27:23 [b] Lk 3:36 [c] Jdg 3:10; 1Ki 11:25; 19:15; 20:34; 22:31; 2Ki 5:1; 8:7
10:23 [d] Ge 22:21; Job 1:1; Jer 25:20; La 4:21
10:24 [e] S ver 21; Lk 3:35
10:27 [f] Eze 27:19
10:28 [g] 1Ki 10:1; Job 6:19; Ps 72:10,15; Isa 60:6; Eze 27:22
10:29 [h] 1Ki 9:28; 10:11; 1Ch 29:4; Job 22:24; 28:16; Ps 45:9; Isa 13:12
10:32 [i] S ver 1 [j] S Ge 9:19

11:1 [k] ver 6
11:2 [l] S Ge 10:10
11:3 [m] Ex 1:14; 5:7; Jer 43:9 [n] Isa 9:10; Am 5:11 [o] Ge 14:10
11:4 [p] Dt 1:28; 6:10; 9:1; Job 20:6; Jer 51:53 [q] Ge 6:4 [r] Dt 30:3; 1Ki 22:17; Est 3:8; Ps 44:11; Jer 31:10; 40:15; Eze 6:8; Joel 3:2 [s] S Ge 9:19; Dt 4:27
11:5 [t] ver 7; Ge 18:21; Ex 3:8; 19:11,18,20; Ps 18:9; 144:5
11:6 [u] S ver 1
11:7 [v] S Ge 1:26 [w] S ver 5 [x] Ge 42:23; Dt 28:49; Isa 28:11; 33:19; Jer 5:15; 1Co 14:2, 11
11:8 [y] S Ge 9:19; Dt 32:8; S Lk 1:51
11:9 [z] S Ge 10:10 [a] Ps 55:9 [b] Ac 2:5-11 [c] Isa 2:10,21; 13:14; 24:1
11:10 [d] S Ge 2:4

The Tower of Babel

11 Now the whole world had one
language[k] and a common
speech. 2As men moved eastward,[d]
they found a plain in Shinar[e][l] and
settled there.
3They said to each other, "Come,
let's make bricks[m] and bake them
thoroughly." They used brick instead
of stone,[n] and tar[o] for mortar. 4Then
they said, "Come, let us build ourselves
a city, with a tower that reaches to the
heavens,[p] so that we may make a
name[q] for ourselves and not be scattered[r] over the face of the whole
earth."[s]
5But the LORD came down[t] to see
the city and the tower that the men
were building. 6The LORD said, "If as
one people speaking the same language[u] they have begun to do this,
then nothing they plan to do will be impossible for them. 7Come, let us[v] go
down[w] and confuse their language so
they will not understand each other."[x]
8So the LORD scattered them from
there over all the earth,[y] and they
stopped building the city. 9That is why
it was called Babel[f][z]—because
there the LORD confused the language[a] of the whole world.[b] From
there the LORD scattered[c] them over
the face of the whole earth.

From Shem to Abram

11:10–27pp — Ge 10:21–31; 1Ch 1:17–27

10This is the account[d] of Shem.

Two years after the flood, when
Shem was 100 years old, he became

[z] *21* Or *Shem, the older brother of* [a] *23* See Septuagint and 1 Chron. 1:17; Hebrew *Mash* [b] *24* Hebrew; Septuagint *father of Cainan, and Cainan was the father of* [c] *25 Peleg* means *division.* [d] *2* Or *from the east*; or *in the east* [e] *2* That is, Babylonia [f] *9* That is, Babylon; *Babel* sounds like the Hebrew for *confused.*

10:21–31 BORN TO SHEM. These verses list the descendants of Shem, who settled in Arabia and the Middle East valley. They include Jews, Assyrians, Syrians and Elamites.

11:2 A PLAIN IN SHINAR. Shinar is the OT name for the territory of ancient Sumer and later of Babylonia or Mesopotamia.

11:4 LET US BUILD ... THAT WE MAY MAKE A NAME. The sin of the people in the land of Shinar was the desire to dominate the world and their own destiny apart from God through man-centered organizational unity, power and great accomplishments. This purpose was based on pride and rebellion against God. God destroyed this effort by multiplying languages so that some could no longer communicate with others (v. 7). This explains the diversity of race and language in the world. At this time the human race turned from God to idolatry, sorcery and astrology (cf. Isa 47:12; see Ex 22:18, note; Dt 18:10, note). The spiritual condition of humans is described in Ro 1:21–28. As a result, God gave them up to the sinful desires of their own hearts (Ro 1:24,26,28), and he turned to Abram to begin a way of salvation for humanity (see v. 31, note).

the father[g] of Arphaxad.[e] **11**And after he became the father of Arphaxad,
Shem lived 500 years and had other
sons and daughters.
12When Arphaxad had lived 35
years, he became the father of Shelah.[f] **13**And after he became the father of Shelah, Arphaxad lived 403
years and had other sons and daughters.[h]
14When Shelah had lived 30 years,
he became the father of Eber.[g] **15**And
after he became the father of Eber,
Shelah lived 403 years and had other
sons and daughters.
16When Eber had lived 34 years, he
became the father of Peleg.[h] **17**And after he became the father of Peleg, Eber
lived 430 years and had other sons and
daughters.
18When Peleg had lived 30 years, he
became the father of Reu.[i] **19**And after he became the father of Reu, Peleg
lived 209 years and had other sons and
daughters.
20When Reu had lived 32 years, he
became the father of Serug.[j] **21**And
after he became the father of Serug,
Reu lived 207 years and had other sons
and daughters.
22When Serug had lived 30 years, he
became the father of Nahor.[k] **23**And
after he became the father of Nahor,
Serug lived 200 years and had other
sons and daughters.
24When Nahor had lived 29 years, he
became the father of Terah.[l] **25**And
after he became the father of Terah,
Nahor lived 119 years and had other
sons and daughters.
26After Terah had lived 70 years, he
became the father of Abram,[m] Nahor[n]
and Haran.[o]

27This is the account[p] of Terah.

Terah became the father of Abram,
Nahor[q] and Haran. And Haran became the father of Lot.[r] **28**While his
father Terah was still alive, Haran died
in Ur of the Chaldeans,[s] in the land of
his birth. **29**Abram and Nahor[t] both
married. The name of Abram's wife
was Sarai,[u] and the name of Nahor's
wife was Milcah;[v] she was the daughter of Haran, the father of both Milcah
and Iscah. **30**Now Sarai was barren;
she had no children.[w]
31Terah took his son Abram, his
grandson Lot[x] son of Haran, and his
daughter-in-law[y] Sarai, the wife of
his son Abram, and together they set
out from Ur of the Chaldeans[z] to go to
Canaan.[a] But when they came to
Haran,[b] they settled there.
32Terah[c] lived 205 years, and he
died in Haran.

The Call of Abram

12 The LORD had said to Abram,
"Leave your country, your people and your father's household[d] and
go to the land[e] I will show you.[f]

2"I will make you into a great
    nation[g]
  and I will bless you;[h]
I will make your name great,
  and you will be a blessing.[i]
3I will bless those who bless you,

11:10 [e]Lk 3:36
11:12 [f]Lk 3:35
11:14 [g]Lk 3:35
11:16 [h]Lk 3:35
11:18 [i]Lk 3:35
11:20 [j]Lk 3:35
11:22 [k]Lk 3:34
11:24 [l]Lk 3:34
11:26 [m]Lk 3:34
[n]Jos 24:2
[o]2Ki 19:12;
Isa 37:12;
Eze 27:23
11:27 [p]S Ge 2:4
[q]ver 29; Ge 31:53
[r]ver 31; Ge 12:4;
13:1,5,8,12;
14:12; 19:1;
Lk 17:28; 2Pe 2:7
11:28 [s]ver 31;
Ge 15:7; Ne 9:7;
Job 1:17; 16:11;
Eze 23:23; Ac 7:4
11:29 [t]S ver 27,
31; Ge 22:20,23;
24:10,15,24; 29:5
[u]Ge 12:5,11; 16:1;
17:15 [v]Ge 22:20
11:30 [w]Ge 16:1;
18:11; 25:21;
29:31; 30:1,22;
Jdg 13:2; 1Sa 1:5;
Ps 113:9; Lk 1:7,
36
11:31 [x]S ver 27
[y]Ge 38:11;
Lev 18:15; 20:12;
Ru 1:6,22; 2:20;
4:15; 1Sa 4:19;
1Ch 2:4;
Eze 22:11; Mic 7:6
[z]S ver 28
[a]S Ge 10:19
[b]S ver 29;
Ge 12:4; 27:43;
28:5,10; 29:4;
2Ki 19:12;
Eze 27:23
11:32 [c]Jos 24:2
12:1 [d]Ge 20:13;
24:4,27,40
[e]S Ge 10:19
[f]Ge 15:7; 26:2;
Jos 24:3; Ac 7:3*;
Heb 11:8
12:2 [g]Ge 13:16;
15:5; 17:2,4;
18:18; 22:17;
26:4; 28:3,14;
32:12; 35:11;
41:49; 46:3;
47:27; 48:4,16,19;
Ex 1:7; 5:5;
32:13; Dt 1:10;
10:22; 13:17;
26:5; Jos 11:4;
24:3; 2Sa 17:11;
1Ki 3:8; 4:20;
1Ch 27:23;
2Ch 1:9; Ne 9:23;
Ps 107:38; Isa 6:13; 10:22; 48:19; 51:2; 54:3; 60:22;
Jer 33:22; Mic 4:7 [h]Ge 24:1,35; 25:11; 26:3; 28:4;
Ex 20:24; Nu 22:12; 23:8,20; 24:9; Ps 67:6; 115:12;
Isa 44:3; 61:9; 65:23; Mal 3:12 [i]Ge 22:18; Isa 19:24;
Jer 4:2; Hag 2:19; Zec 8:13

[g]*10 Father* may mean *ancestor*; also in verses 11-25. [h]*12,13* Hebrew; Septuagint (see also Luke 3:35, 36 and note at Gen. 10:24) *35 years, he became the father of Cainan.* [13]*And after he became the father of Cainan, Arphaxad lived 430 years and had other sons and daughters, and then he died. When Cainan had lived 130 years, he became the father of Shelah. And after he became the father of Shelah, Cainan lived 330 years and had other sons and daughters*

11:28 UR OF THE CHALDEANS. This ancient city was located about one hundred miles southeast of Babylon near the Euphrates River, in what is now known as Iraq. The moon god "Sin" was the patron god of this city.

11:31 HIS SON ABRAM. With v. 27 the Bible begins the history of a single family chosen by God in order to bring redemption to the human race. The head of that family was Abram (later changed to Abraham, see 17:5), who lived approximately 2100 B.C. In Ac 7:2–3 Stephen stated that God first appeared to Abram in the land of the Chaldeans before he lived in Haran (cf. 15:7; Ne 9:7). God's call to Abram was probably the motivating factor in his father Terah's move to Haran (see article on THE CALL OF ABRAHAM, p. 25). Abram, who became the father of the Jewish nation, was from the line of Shem (11:10).

12:1 LEAVE YOUR COUNTRY. Abram was not told at this time where God would lead him (Heb 11:8). Instead he had to journey under direct guidance from the Lord.

12:3 ALL PEOPLES ON EARTH WILL BE BLESSED THROUGH YOU. This is the second prophecy in Scripture concerning the coming of Jesus Christ (cf. 3:15, note). (1) It speaks of a spiritual blessing that would come through a descendant of Abraham. Paul states that this blessing

THE CALL OF ABRAHAM

Ge 12:1–3 "The LORD had said to Abram, "Leave your country, your people and your father's household and go to the land I will show you. I will make you into a great nation and I will bless you; I will make your name great, and you will be a blessing. I will bless those who bless you, and whoever curses you I will curse; and all peoples on earth will be blessed through you.' "

The call of Abram (later named Abraham, see Ge 17:5) as recorded in Ge 12 begins a new chapter in the OT revelation of God's purpose to redeem and save humanity. God intended to have a man who would know and serve him with devoted faith. From this man would come a family who would know, teach and keep the ways of the Lord (see Ge 18:19, note). From this family would come a chosen nation of people who would be separated from the ungodly ways of other nations to do God's will. From this nation would come Jesus Christ, the Savior of the world, the promised offspring of the woman (see Ge 3:15, note; Gal 3:8,16,18). Several important principles can be deduced from Abraham's call.

(1) Abraham's call involved separating himself from his country, his people and his household (Ge 12:1) in order to become an alien and stranger on earth (Heb 11:13). In Abraham God was establishing the important principle that his people were to separate themselves from all that hinders his purpose for their lives (see articles on SPIRITUAL SEPARATION FOR BELIEVERS, p. 1794, and THE CHRISTIAN'S RELATIONSHIP TO THE WORLD, p. 1976).

(2) God promised Abraham a land, a great nation through his descendants, and a blessing that would affect all the nations of the earth (Ge 12:2–3). The NT clearly teaches that the last element of this promise is being fulfilled in the missionary proclamation of the gospel of Christ (Ac 3:25; Gal 3:8).

(3) Moreover, Abraham's call involved not only an earthly land, but also a heavenly one. His vision came to encompass an ultimate home no longer on earth but in heaven, and a city whose architect and builder was God himself. Abraham henceforth desired and sought a heavenly country where he would live forever with his God in righteousness, joy and peace (see Heb 11:9–10,14–16; cf. Rev 21:1–4; 22:1–5). Until then he would be an alien and stranger on earth (Heb 11:9,13).

(4) The call of Abraham contained not only promises, but also obligations. God required both obedience from Abraham and personal commitment to him as Lord in order to receive what was promised. Obedience and commitment entailed: (a) trust in God's word, even when the realization of the promises appeared humanly impossible (Ge 15:1–6; 18:10–14), (b) obedience to God's command to leave his home (Ge 12:4; Heb 11:8), and (c) a sincere endeavor to live a righteous life (Ge 17:1–2).

(5) God's promise to and blessing on Abraham extend not only to his physical descendants (i.e., believing Jews), but also to all who in true faith (Ge 12:3) embrace and follow Jesus Christ, the true "seed" of Abraham (see Gal 3:14,16). All who possess faith like Abraham's are "children of Abraham" (Gal 3:7) and are blessed along with him (Gal 3:9). They become Abraham's offspring, heirs according to the promise (Gal 3:29), which includes receiving by faith "the promise of the Spirit" in Christ Jesus (see Gal 3:14, note).

(6) Because Abraham possessed a faith in God that expressed itself in obedience, he is declared a foremost example of true saving faith (cf. Ge 15:6; Ro 4:1–5,16–24; Gal 3:6–9; Heb 11:8–19; Jas 2:21–23; see Ge 15:6, note). Biblically, any profession of faith in Jesus Christ as Savior that does not involve obedience to him as Lord is not the kind of faith Abraham possessed and thus is not true saving faith (see Jn 3:36, note; see article on FAITH AND GRACE, p. 1720).

and whoever curses you I will
curse;[j]
Ex 12:29-42 and all peoples on earth
will be blessed through you.[k]"

4So Abram left, as the LORD had told
him; and Lot[l] went with him. Abram
was seventy-five years old[m] when he
set out from Haran.[n] 5He took his wife
Sarai,[o] his nephew Lot, all the possessions they had accumulated[p] and the
people[q] they had acquired in Haran,
and they set out for the land of Canaan,[r] and they arrived there.

6Abram traveled through the land[s]
as far as the site of the great tree of
Moreh[t] at Shechem.[u] At that time
the Canaanites[v] were in the land.
7The LORD appeared to Abram[w] and
said, "To your offspring[i] I will give
this land.[x]"[y] So he built an altar
there to the LORD,[z] who had appeared
to him.

8From there he went on toward the
hills east of Bethel[a] and pitched his
tent,[b] with Bethel on the west and
Ai[c] on the east. There he built an altar
to the LORD and called on the name of
the LORD.[d] 9Then Abram set out and
continued toward the Negev.[e]

Abram in Egypt

12:10–20Ref — Ge 20:1–18; 26:1–11

10Now there was a famine in the
land,[f] and Abram went down to Egypt
to live there for a while because the
famine was severe.[g] 11As he was
about to enter Egypt, he said to his
wife Sarai,[h] "I know what a beautiful
woman[i] you are. 12When the Egyptians see you, they will say, 'This is his
wife.' Then they will kill me but will let
you live. 13Say you are my sister,[j] so
that I will be treated well for your sake
and my life will be spared because of
you."

14When Abram came to Egypt, the
Egyptians saw that she was a very
beautiful woman.[k] 15And when Phar-

12:3 [j] Ge 27:29; Ex 23:22; Nu 24:9; Dt 30:7 [k] Ge 15:5; 18:18; 22:18; 26:4; 28:4,14; Dt 9:5; Ps 72:17; Isa 19:25; Ac 3:25; Gal 3:8* **12:4** [l] S Ge 11:27 [m] Ge 16:3,16; 17:1,17,24; 21:5 [n] S Ge 11:31 **12:5** [o] S Ge 11:29 [p] ver 16; Ge 13:2, 6; 31:18; 46:6 [q] Ge 14:14; 15:3; 17:23; Ecc 2:7 [r] Ge 11:31; 16:3; Heb 11:8 **12:6** [s] Heb 11:9 [t] Ge 35:4; Dt 11:30; Jos 24:26; Jdg 7:1; 9:6 [u] Ge 33:18; 37:12; Jos 17:7; 20:7; 24:1; Jdg 8:31; 21:19; 1Ki 12:1; Ps 60:6; 108:7 [v] S Ge 10:18 **12:7** [w] Ge 17:1; 18:1; 26:2; 35:1; Ex 6:3; Ac 7:2 [x] Ex 3:8; Nu 10:29; Dt 30:5; Heb 11:8 [y] Ge 13:15,17; 15:18; 17:8; 23:18; 24:7; 26:3-4; 28:13; 35:12; 48:4; 50:24; Ex 6:4,8; 13:5,11; 32:13; 33:1; Nu 11:12; Dt 1:8; 2:31; 9:5; 11:9; 34:4; 2Ki 25:21; 1Ch 16:16; 2Ch 20:7; Ps 105:9-11; Jer 25:5; Eze 47:14; Ac 7:5; Ro 4:13; Gal 3:16* [z] S Ge 8:20; 13:4 **12:8** [a] Ge 13:3; 28:11,19; 35:1,8,15; Jos 7:2; 8:9; 1Sa 7:16; 1Ki 12:29; Hos 12:4; Am 3:14; 4:4 [b] Ge 26:25; 33:19; Heb 11:9 [c] Jos 7:2; 12:9; Ezr 2:28; Ne 7:32; Jer 49:3 [d] S Ge 4:26; S 8:20 **12:9** [e] Ge 13:1,3; 20:1; 24:62; Nu 13:17; 33:40; Dt 34:3; Jos 10:40 **12:10** [f] Ge 41:27,57; 42:5; 43:1; 47:4,13; Ru 1:1; 2Sa 21:1; 2Ki 8:1; Ps 105:19 [g] Ge 41:30,54,56; 47:20; Ps 105:16 **12:11** [h] S Ge 11:29 [i] ver 14; Ge 24:16; 26:7; 29:17; 39:6 **12:13** [j] Ge 20:2; 26:7 **12:14** [k] S ver 11

i 7 Or *seed*

refers to the gospel of Christ offered to all the nations (cf. Gal 3:8,16). (2) God's promise to Abram reveals that from the very beginning the purpose of the gospel was to bless all the nations with salvation and goodness. God is now accomplishing this purpose through Jesus Christ and his faithful people who share his burden by sending out preachers who proclaim the gospel to all peoples on earth. This verse serves as a foundation for mission work throughout the world (see article on THE CALL OF ABRAHAM, p. 25).

12:4 ABRAM LEFT, AS THE LORD HAD TOLD HIM. The narrative from the very beginning emphasizes the truth that obedience to God is essential to a saving relationship with him. (1) Abram obeyed the word of the Lord. His obedience included leaving his home and country and trusting in God's care, guidance and promises (see v. 1, note; Jas 2:17, note; 1Jn 2:4, note). (2) Like Abram, all believers in Christ are called to leave their "country . . . people and . . . father's household" (12:1) to follow Jesus in the sense of seeking "a better country—a heavenly one" (Heb 11:16; see article on THE CALL OF ABRAHAM, p. 25).

12:7 THE LORD APPEARED TO ABRAM. This is the first time Scripture explicitly states that God "appeared" to someone, though it is reasonable to assume that God had already appeared to Adam and others (cf. 2:15–16,22; 3:8). That this appearance was an objective, visible manifestation of God in the likeness of a human being is indicated in 18:1–3,9–33; (cf. Ex 33:18–23). Visible appearances of the Lord are called "theophanies"—i.e., God-manifestations (see Ex 3:2, note). The land that God promised to give to Abram was the land of Canaan (the ancient name for Palestine), along the southeast coast of the Mediterranean Sea.

12:10 A FAMINE IN THE LAND. Obedience to God does not mean that we will never encounter serious problems and trials. (1) Abram had barely arrived at his destination when he faced bitter disappointment. His problems included a barren wife (11:30), separation from his family (12:1), and a famine that was bringing him to starvation and driving him from the land. (2) As Abram's example teaches, believers who are seeking to serve God and obey his word must not think it strange if they encounter great obstacles, hardships and problems. It is often God's way with those whom he has called to obey him. In such cases we must go forward with obedience and trust that God is still working on our behalf to accomplish his purpose (see Mt 2:13, note).

12:13 SAY YOU ARE MY SISTER. Abram's trust in God momentarily failed, resulting in sinful deception and in shameful deportation from Egypt (12:19—13:1). These verses show how honest God's Word is regarding the saints. Although Abram repented, his moral failure was not covered up. Such failure solemnly reminds all believers to look not at circumstances but at the promises and faithfulness of God. Abram's failure also encourages us in that it reveals how God in mercy worked to bring Abram back into his will and purpose.

aoh's officials saw her, they praised
her to Pharaoh, and she was taken into
his palace. 16He treated Abram well for
her sake, and Abram acquired sheep
and cattle, male and female donkeys,
menservants and maidservants, and
camels.[l]
17But the LORD inflicted[m] serious
diseases on Pharaoh and his household[n] because of Abram's wife Sarai.
18So Pharaoh summoned Abram.
"What have you done to me?"[o] he
said. "Why didn't you tell me she was
your wife?[p] 19Why did you say, 'She is
my sister,'[q] so that I took her to be my
wife? Now then, here is your wife. Take
her and go!" 20Then Pharaoh gave orders about Abram to his men, and they
sent him on his way, with his wife and
everything he had.

Abram and Lot Separate

13 So Abram went up from
Egypt[r] to the Negev,[s] with
his wife and everything he had, and
Lot[t] went with him. 2Abram had become very wealthy[u] in livestock[v] and
in silver and gold.
3From the Negev[w] he went from
place to place until he came to Bethel,[x] to the place between Bethel and
Ai[y] where his tent had been earlier
4and where he had first built an altar.[z] There Abram called on the name
of the LORD.[a]
5Now Lot,[b] who was moving about
with Abram, also had flocks and herds
and tents. 6But the land could not support them while they stayed together,
for their possessions were so great
that they were not able to stay together.[c] 7And quarreling[d] arose between
Abram's herdsmen and the herdsmen
of Lot. The Canaanites[e] and Perizzites[f] were also living in the land[g] at
that time.
8So Abram said to Lot,[h] "Let's not
have any quarreling between you and
me,[i] or between your herdsmen and
mine, for we are brothers.[j] 9Is not the
whole land before you? Let's part company. If you go to the left, I'll go to the
right; if you go to the right, I'll go to the
left."[k]
10Lot looked up and saw that the
whole plain[l] of the Jordan[m] was well
watered, like the garden of the LORD,[n]
like the land of Egypt,[o] toward
Zoar.[p] (This was before the LORD destroyed Sodom[q] and Gomorrah.)[r]
11So Lot chose for himself the whole
plain of the Jordan and set out toward
the east. The two men parted company: 12Abram lived in the land of Canaan,[s] while Lot[t] lived among the
cities of the plain[u] and pitched his
tents near Sodom.[v] 13Now the men of
Sodom[w] were wicked and were sinning greatly against the LORD.[x]
14The LORD said to Abram after Lot
had parted from him, "Lift up your eyes
from where you are and look north and
south, east and west.[y] 15All the land
that you see I will give to you and your
offspring[j] forever.[z] 16I will make
your offspring like the dust of the
earth, so that if anyone could count the
dust, then your offspring could be
counted.[a] 17Go, walk through the
length and breadth of the land,[b] for I
am giving it to you."[c]
18So Abram moved his tents and
went to live near the great trees of
Mamre[d] at Hebron,[e] where he built
an altar to the LORD.[f]

12:16 [l] S ver 5; Ge 24:35; 26:14; 30:43; 32:5; 34:23; 47:17; Job 1:3; 31:25 **12:17** [m] 2Ki 15:5; Job 30:11; Isa 53:4,10 [n] 1Ch 16:21; Ps 105:14 **12:18** [o] Ge 20:9; 26:10; 29:25; 31:26; 44:15 [p] Isa 43:27; 51:2; Eze 16:3 **12:19** [q] Ge 20:5; 26:9 **13:1** [r] Ge 45:25 [s] S Ge 12:9 [t] S Ge 11:27 **13:2** [u] S Ge 12:5; 26:13; Pr 10:22 [v] Ge 32:15; Job 1:3; 42:12 **13:3** [w] S Ge 12:9 [x] S Ge 12:8 [y] Jos 7:2 **13:4** [z] S Ge 12:7 [a] S Ge 4:26 **13:5** [b] S Ge 11:27 **13:6** [c] S Ge 12:5; 33:9; 36:7 **13:7** [d] Ge 26:20, 21; Nu 20:3 [e] S Ge 10:18 [f] Ge 15:20; 34:30; Ex 3:8; Jdg 1:4 [g] Ge 12:6; 34:30 **13:8** [h] S Ge 11:27 [i] Pr 15:18; 20:3 [j] Ge 19:9; Ex 2:14; Nu 16:13; Ps 133:1 **13:9** [k] Ge 20:15; 34:10; 47:6; Jer 40:4 **13:10** [l] 1Ki 7:46; 2Ch 4:17 [m] Nu 13:29; 33:48 [n] Ge 2:8-10; Isa 51:3; Eze 31:8-9 [o] Ge 46:7 [p] Ge 14:2; 19:22, 30; Dt 34:3; Isa 15:5; Jer 48:34 [q] Dt 29:23; Job 39:6; Ps 107:34; Jer 4:26 [r] Ge 14:8; 19:17-29 **13:12** [s] S Ge 10:19 [t] S Ge 11:27 [u] S ver 10; Ge 19:17,25,29 [v] Ge 14:12 **13:13** [w] Ge 19:4; Isa 1:10; 3:9 [x] Ge 18:20; 19:5; 20:6; 39:9; Nu 32:23; 1Sa 12:23; 2Sa 12:13; Ps 51:4; Eze 16:49-50; 2Pe 2:8 **13:14** [y] Ge 28:14; 32:12; 48:16; Dt 3:27; 13:17; Isa 54:3 **13:15** [z] S Ge 12:7; Gal 3:16* **13:16** [a] S Ge 12:2; 16:10; 17:20; 21:13,18; 25:16; Nu 23:10 **13:17** [b] ver 15; Nu 13:17-25 [c] S Ge 12:7; 15:7 **13:18** [d] Ge 14:13,24; 18:1; 23:17,19; 25:9; 49:30; 50:13 [e] Ge 23:2; 35:27; 37:14; Nu 13:22; Jos 10:3,36; Jdg 1:10; 1Sa 30:31; 2Sa 2:1,3,11; 1Ch 11:1 [f] S Ge 8:20

j15 Or *seed*; also in verse 16

13:10 LOT LOOKED UP AND SAW. Scripture states that "the LORD does not look at the things man looks at" (1Sa 16:7). Lot saw only the well-watered valley. God saw the people of Sodom who were "wicked and were sinning greatly" (v. 13). Lot's failure to discern and oppose evil brought death and tragedy to his family (see next note).

13:12 PITCHED HIS TENTS NEAR SODOM. Lot's great failure was that he loved personal gain more than he hated Sodom's wickedness (vv. 10–13). (1) If he had loved righteousness sufficiently (see Heb 1:9, note), it would have caused him to remain separate from the wicked ways of sinful people. Instead he tolerated evil and chose to live in wicked Sodom (v. 13). Perhaps he reasoned that the material and cultural advantages, and the enticing pleasures of Sodom, outweighed the dangers, and that he was strong enough spiritually to remain faithful to God. Thus, he exposed himself and his family to the immorality and ungodliness of Sodom, only to learn the bitter lesson that his family was not strong enough to resist its evil influences (see 19:24–26,30–38). (2) Parents must be careful not to place themselves or their children in any "Sodom," lest they come to spiritual ruin as did the family of Lot.

Abram Rescues Lot

14 At this time Amraphel king of
Shinar,[k][g] Arioch king of Ellasar, Kedorlaomer[h] king of Elam[i] and
Tidal king of Goiim [2]went to war
against Bera king of Sodom, Birsha
king of Gomorrah, Shinab king of Admah, Shemeber king of Zeboiim,[j] and
the king of Bela (that is, Zoar).[k] [3]All
these latter kings joined forces in the
Valley of Siddim[l] (the Salt Sea[l][m]).
[4]For twelve years they had been subject to Kedorlaomer,[n] but in the thirteenth year they rebelled.
[5]In the fourteenth year, Kedorlaomer[o] and the kings allied with him
went out and defeated the Rephaites[p]
in Ashteroth Karnaim, the Zuzites in
Ham, the Emites[q] in Shaveh Kiriathaim [6]and the Horites[r] in the hill country of Seir,[s] as far as El Paran[t] near
the desert. [7]Then they turned back and
went to En Mishpat (that is, Kadesh),[u] and they conquered the whole
territory of the Amalekites,[v] as well
as the Amorites[w] who were living in
Hazazon Tamar.[x]
[8]Then the king of Sodom, the king of
Gomorrah,[y] the king of Admah, the
king of Zeboiim[z] and the king of Bela
(that is, Zoar)[a] marched out and drew
up their battle lines in the Valley of
Siddim[b] [9]against Kedorlaomer[c] king
of Elam,[d] Tidal king of Goiim, Amraphel king of Shinar and Arioch king of
Ellasar—four kings against five.
[10]Now the Valley of Siddim[e] was full
of tar[f] pits, and when the kings of
Sodom and Gomorrah[g] fled, some of
the men fell into them and the rest fled
to the hills.[h] [11]The four kings seized
all the goods[i] of Sodom and Gomorrah and all their food; then they went
away. [12]They also carried off Abram's
nephew Lot[j] and his possessions,
since he was living in Sodom.
[13]One who had escaped came and
reported this to Abram the Hebrew.[k]
Now Abram was living near the great
trees of Mamre[l] the Amorite, a brother[m] of Eshcol[m] and Aner, all of whom
were allied with Abram. [14]When
Abram heard that his relative[n] had
been taken captive, he called out the
318 trained[o] men born in his household[p] and went in pursuit as far as
Dan.[q] [15]During the night Abram divided his men[r] to attack them and he
routed them, pursuing them as far as
Hobah, north of Damascus.[s] [16]He recovered[t] all the goods[u] and brought
back his relative Lot and his possessions, together with the women and
the other people.
[17]After Abram returned from defeating Kedorlaomer[v] and the kings allied
with him, the king of Sodom[w] came
out to meet him in the Valley of Shaveh
(that is, the King's Valley).[x]
[18]Then Melchizedek[y] king of Salem[n][z] brought out bread[a] and
wine.[b] He was priest of God Most
High,[c] [19]and he blessed Abram,[d]
saying,

"Blessed be Abram by God Most
High,[e]
Creator[o] of heaven and earth.[f]
[20]And blessed be[p] God Most
High,[g]
who delivered your enemies into
your hand."

14:1 [g]S Ge 10:10 [h]ver 4,9,17 [i]S Ge 10:22 **14:2** [j]S Ge 10:19 [k]S Ge 13:10 **14:3** [l]ver 8,10 [m]Nu 34:3,12; Dt 3:17; Jos 3:16; 12:3; 15:2,5; 18:19 **14:4** [n]S ver 1 **14:5** [o]S ver 1 [p]Ge 15:20; Dt 2:11,20; 3:11, 13; Jos 12:4; 13:12; 17:15; 1Ch 20:4 [q]Dt 2:10 **14:6** [r]Ge 36:20; Dt 2:12,22 [s]Ge 32:3; 33:14, 16; 36:8; Dt 1:2; 2:1,5,22; Jos 11:17; 24:4; 1Ch 4:42; Isa 34:5; Eze 25:8; 35:2; Am 1:6 [t]Ge 21:21; Nu 10:12; 12:16; 13:3,26; Hab 3:3 **14:7** [u]Ge 16:14; 20:1; Nu 13:26; 20:1; 32:8; Dt 1:2; Jos 10:41; Jdg 11:16; Ps 29:8 [v]Ex 17:8; Nu 13:29; 14:25; 24:20; Dt 25:17; Jdg 3:13; 6:3; 10:12; 12:15; 1Sa 14:48; 15:2; 28:18; 2Sa 1:1; 1Ch 4:43; Ps 83:7 [w]Nu 13:29; Dt 1:4; Jos 2:10; 13:4 [x]2Ch 20:2; Eze 48:28 **14:8** [y]S Ge 13:10 [z]Dt 29:23; Hos 11:8 [a]S Ge 13:10 [b]S ver 3 **14:9** [c]S ver 1 [d]S Ge 10:22 **14:10** [e]S ver 3 [f]Ge 11:3 [g]ver 17, 21 [h]Ge 19:17,30; Jos 2:16; Ps 11:1 **14:11** [i]ver 16,21 **14:12** [j]S Ge 11:27 **14:13** [k]Ge 37:28; 39:14,17; 40:15; 41:12; 43:32; Ex 3:18; 1Sa 4:6; 14:11 [l]ver 24; S Ge 13:18 [m]Nu 13:23; 32:9; Dt 1:24 **14:14** [n]ver 12 [o]Dt 4:9; Pr 22:6 [p]S Ge 12:5 [q]Dt 34:1; Jdg 18:29; 1Ki 15:20 **14:15** [r]Jdg 7:16 [s]Ge 15:2; 2Sa 8:5; 1Ki 20:34; 2Ki 16:9; Isa 7:8; 8:4; 10:9; 17:1; Jer 49:23,27; Eze 27:18; Am 1:3-5 **14:16** [t]1Sa 30:8,18 [u]S ver 11 **14:17** [v]S ver 1 [w]S ver 10 [x]2Sa 18:18 **14:18** [y]Ps 110:4; Heb 5:6; 7:17,21 [z]Ps 76:2; Heb 7:2 [a]S Ge 3:19 [b]Jdg 9:13; 19:19; Est 1:10; Ps 104:15; Pr 31:6; Ecc 10:19; SS 1:2 [c]ver 22; Ps 7:8,17; Da 7:27 **14:19** [d]Heb 7:6 [e]ver 18 [f]ver 22; S Ge 1:1; 24:3; Jos 2:11; Ps 148:5; Mt 11:25 **14:20** [g]S Ge 9:26; S 24:27

k *1* That is, Babylonia; also in verse 9
l *3* That is, the Dead Sea **m** *13* Or *a relative*; or *an ally* **n** *18* That is, Jerusalem
o *19* Or *Possessor*; also in verse 22 **p** *20* Or *And praise be to*

14:13 ABRAM THE HEBREW. The term "Hebrew" may have initially referred to any people who wandered from place to place, crossing over lands as nomads; it later came to refer specifically to Abraham and his descendants (cf. Ex 3:18; 5:3).

14:14 CALLED OUT THE 318 TRAINED MEN. Abram was not a solitary nomad but a wealthy leader of a large clan. His 318 trained men shows that he probably had a total company of about one thousand.

14:18 MELCHIZEDEK KING OF SALEM. Melchizedek (meaning "king of righteousness") was both "king of Salem" (possibly ancient Jerusalem) and "priest of God Most High." He served the one true God, as did Abram. Melchizedek was a Canaanite, and thus, like Job, an example of a godly non-Israelite. Melchizedek is a type or figure of the royalty and eternal priesthood of Jesus Christ (cf. Ps 110:4; see Heb 7:1,3, notes).

14:20 GAVE HIM A TENTH OF EVERYTHING. Abram gave Melchizedek a tenth of the spoils he had recovered (cf. Heb 7:4) in gratitude for God's help and grace. This is the first time tithing is mentioned in the Bible.

Then Abram gave him a tenth of everything.[h]
21The king of Sodom[i] said to
Abram, "Give me the people and keep
the goods[j] for yourself."
22But Abram said to the king of Sodom,[k] "I have raised my hand[l] to the
LORD, God Most High,[m] Creator of
heaven and earth,[n] and have taken an
oath **23**that I will accept nothing belonging to you,[o] not even a thread or
the thong of a sandal, so that you will
never be able to say, 'I made Abram
rich.' **24**I will accept nothing but what
my men have eaten and the share that
belongs to the men who went with
me—to Aner, Eshcol and Mamre.[p]
Let them have their share."

God's Covenant With Abram

15 After this, the word of the LORD
came to Abram[q] in a vision:[r]

"Do not be afraid,[s] Abram.
I am your shield,[q][t]
your very great reward.[r][u]"

2But Abram said, "O Sovereign
LORD,[v] what can you give me since I
remain childless[w] and the one who
will inherit[s] my estate is Eliezer of
Damascus?[x]" **3**And Abram said, "You
have given me no children; so a servant[y] in my household[z] will be my
heir."
4Then the word of the LORD came to
him: "This man will not be your heir,
but a son coming from your own body
will be your heir.[a]" **5**He took him outside and said, "Look up at the heavens
and count the stars[b]—if indeed you
can count them." Then he said to him,
"So shall your offspring be."[c]
6Abram believed the LORD, and he
credited it to him as righteousness.[d] Ge 22:1-14
7He also said to him, "I am the LORD,
who brought you out[e] of Ur of the
Chaldeans[f] to give you this land to
take possession of it."[g]
8But Abram said, "O Sovereign
LORD,[h] how can I know[i] that I will
gain possession of it?"[j]
9So the LORD said to him, "Bring me
a heifer,[k] a goat and a ram, each three
years old,[l] along with a dove and a
young pigeon.[m]"
10Abram brought all these to him,
cut them in two and arranged the
halves opposite each other;[n] the
birds, however, he did not cut in half.[o]
11Then birds of prey came down on the
carcasses,[p] but Abram drove them
away.
12As the sun was setting, Abram fell
into a deep sleep,[q] and a thick and
dreadful darkness came over him.

14:20 [h] Ge 28:22; Dt 14:22; 26:12; Lk 18:12; Heb 7:4 **14:21** [i] S ver 10 [j] S ver 11 **14:22** [k] S ver 10 [l] Ex 6:8; Nu 14:30; Dt 32:40; Ne 9:15; Eze 20:5; Da 12:7; Rev 10:5-6 [m] S ver 18 [n] S ver 19 **14:23** [o] 1Sa 15:3, 19; 2Ki 5:16; Est 8:11; 9:10,15 **14:24** [p] S Ge 13:18 **15:1** [q] 1Sa 15:10; 2Sa 7:4; 1Ki 6:11; 12:22; Jer 1:13; Eze 3:16; Da 10:1 [r] Ge 46:2; Nu 12:6; 24:4; Ru 1:20; Job 33:15 [s] Ge 21:17; 26:24; 46:3; Ex 14:13; 20:20; 2Ki 6:16; 2Ch 20:15,17; Ps 27:1; Isa 7:4; 41:10,13-14; 43:1, 5; Jer 1:8; Hag 2:5 [t] Dt 33:29; 2Sa 22:3,31; Ps 3:3; 5:12; 18:2; 28:7; 33:20; 84:11; 119:114; 144:2; Pr 2:7; 30:5 [u] Ps 18:20; 37:25; 58:11; Isa 3:10 **15:2** [v] ver 8; Isa 49:22; Jer 44:26; Eze 5:11; 16:48 [w] Ac 7:5 [x] S Ge 14:15 **15:3** [y] Ge 24:2,34 [z] S Ge 12:5 **15:4** [a] Gal 4:28 **15:5** [b] Job 11:8; 35:5; Ps 8:3; 147:4; Jer 33:22 [c] S Ge 12:2; S Jer 30:19; Ro 4:18*; Heb 11:12

15:6 [d] Ps 106:31; Ro 4:3*,20-24*; Gal 3:6*; Jas 2:23* **15:7** [e] Ge 12:1; Ex 20:2; Ac 7:3; Heb 11:8 [f] S Ge 11:28; Ac 7:4 [g] S Ge 13:17; 17:8; 28:4; 35:12; 48:4; Ex 6:8; Dt 9:5 **15:8** [h] S ver 2 [i] Lk 1:18 [j] Dt 12:20; 19:8 **15:9** [k] Nu 19:2; Dt 21:3; Hos 4:16; Am 4:1 [l] 1Sa 1:24 [m] Lev 1:14; 5:7,11; 12:8 **15:10** [n] ver 17; Jer 34:18 [o] Lev 1:17; 5:8 **15:11** [p] Dt 28:26; Jer 7:33 **15:12** [q] S Ge 2:21

[q] *1* Or *sovereign* [r] *1* Or *shield; / your reward will be very great* [s] *2* The meaning of the Hebrew for this phrase is uncertain.

14:23 I WILL ACCEPT NOTHING BELONGING TO YOU. Abram's refusal to take the riches of the Canaanites reveals his dependence on God and on God's blessing alone (v. 19; see Mt 14:19, note).

15:1 YOUR SHIELD, YOUR VERY GREAT REWARD. After his battle with the kings, Abram became troubled and fearful. Thus God reassured him in a vision that he was Abram's shield and reward. Abram responded to these comforting words by recalling that he had no children and thus no heir (v. 2), so he suggested that he adopt one of his servants to become his heir. God rejected the idea, promising Abram that he would father a son with his barren wife Sarai (cf. 11:30) and have countless descendants. The incredible thing—and Abram's greatness—is that he believed God. It is this faith in God that was credited to him as righteousness (see next note).

15:6 HE BELIEVED . . . HE CREDITED IT TO HIM AS RIGHTEOUSNESS. For the first time faith and righteousness are mentioned together in Scripture. (1) In the OT, faith had a twofold designation: (a) "trust in" or "reliance on," and (b) "fidelity to" or "faithfulness." Thus, "believe" (Heb *'aman*) means to persevere in trust and belief by manifesting an obedient faithfulness. This was the kind of faith Abram possessed. His heart was turned toward God in an enduring trust, obedience and submission.

(2) God saw Abram's heart-attitude of faith and credited it to him as righteousness. The term "righteousness" means being in a right relationship to God and his will (cf. 6:9; Job 15:14–16). Furthermore, God entered into covenant fellowship with Abram, whereby Abram received God as his shield and reward (v. 1), many offspring (v. 5), and the promise of the land (v. 7; see article on GOD'S COVENANT WITH ABRAHAM, ISAAC AND JACOB, p. 46).

(3) Under the new covenant, God's blessing, a right relationship with him and fellowship with him also come through faith. This is a foundational truth in the NT (Ro 4:3; Gal 3:6; Jas 2:23; see article on FAITH AND GRACE, p. 1720). As such Abraham is the "father of all who believe" (Ro 4:11).

13Then the LORD said to him, "Know for
certain that your descendants will be
strangers in a country not their own,
and they will be enslaved[r] and mistreated four hundred years.[s] **14**But I
will punish the nation they serve as
slaves, and afterward they will come
out[t] with great possessions.[u] **15**You,
however, will go to your fathers[v] in
peace and be buried at a good old
age.[w] **16**In the fourth generation[x]
your descendants will come back
here,[y] for the sin of the Amorites[z]
has not yet reached its full measure."

17When the sun had set and darkness had fallen, a smoking firepot with
a blazing torch[a] appeared and passed
between the pieces.[b] **18**On that day
the LORD made a covenant with
Abram[c] and said, "To your descendants I give this land,[d] from the river[t] of Egypt[e] to the great river, the
Euphrates[f]— **19**the land of the Kenites,[g] Kenizzites, Kadmonites, **20**Hittites,[h] Perizzites,[i] Rephaites,[j]
21Amorites, Canaanites, Girgashites
and Jebusites."[k]

Hagar and Ishmael

16 Now Sarai,[l] Abram's wife, had
borne him no children.[m] But
she had an Egyptian maidservant[n]
named Hagar;[o] **2**so she said to Abram,
"The LORD has kept me from having
children.[p] Go, sleep with my maidservant; perhaps I can build a family
through her."[q]

Abram agreed to what Sarai said.
3So after Abram had been living in Canaan[r] ten years,[s] Sarai his wife took
her Egyptian maidservant Hagar and
gave her to her husband to be his wife.
4He slept with Hagar,[t] and she conceived.

When she knew she was pregnant,
she began to despise her mistress.[u]
5Then Sarai said to Abram, "You are
responsible for the wrong I am suffering. I put my servant in your arms, and
now that she knows she is pregnant,
she despises me. May the LORD judge
between you and me."[v]

6"Your servant is in your hands,[w]"
Abram said. "Do with her whatever you
think best." Then Sarai mistreated[x]
Hagar; so she fled from her.

7The angel of the LORD[y] found Hagar near a spring[z] in the desert; it was
the spring that is beside the road to
Shur.[a] **8**And he said, "Hagar,[b] servant of Sarai, where have you come
from, and where are you going?"[c]

"I'm running away from my mistress
Sarai," she answered.

9Then the angel of the LORD told her,
"Go back to your mistress and submit
to her." **10**The angel added, "I will so
increase your descendants that they
will be too numerous to count."[d]

15:13 [r]Ex 1:11; 3:7; 5:6,10-14,18; 6:5; Dt 5:15; Job 3:18 [s]ver 16; Ex 12:40; Nu 20:15; Ac 7:6, 17; Gal 3:17 **15:14** [t]Ge 50:24; Ex 3:8; 6:6-8; 12:25; Nu 10:29; Jos 1:2; Ac 7:7* [u]Ex 12:32-38 **15:15** [v]Ge 47:30; 49:29; Dt 31:16; 2Sa 7:12; 1Ki 1:21; Ps 49:19 [w]Ge 25:8; 35:29; Ex 23:26; Dt 34:7; Jos 14:11; Jdg 8:32; 1Ch 29:28; Job 5:26; 21:23; 42:17; Ps 91:16; Pr 3:16; 9:11; Isa 65:20 **15:16** [x]S ver 13; Ex 12:40 [y]Ge 28:15; 46:4; 48:21; 50:24; Ex 3:8,17 [z]Lev 18:28; Jos 13:4; Jdg 10:11; 1Ki 21:26; 2Ki 16:3; 21:11; Eze 16:3 **15:17** [a]Jdg 7:16, 20; 15:4,5 [b]S ver 10 **15:18** [c]Ge 17:2, 4,7; Ex 6:4; 34:10, 27; 1Ch 16:16; Ps 105:9 [d]S Ge 12:7 [e]Nu 34:5; Jos 15:4,47; 1Ki 8:65; 2Ki 24:7; 2Ch 7:8; Isa 27:12; Jer 37:5; 46:2; La 4:17; Eze 30:22; 47:19 [f]S Ge 2:14 **15:19** [g]Nu 24:21; Jdg 1:16; 4:11,17; 5:24; 1Sa 15:6; 27:10; 30:29; 1Ch 2:55 **15:20** [h]S Ge 10:15; S Dt 7:1 [i]S Ge 13:7 [j]S Ge 14:5 **15:21** [k]S Ge 10:16; Jos 3:10; 24:11; Ne 9:8 **16:1** [l]S Ge 11:29 [m]S Ge 11:30; Lk 1:7,36; Gal 4:24-25 [n]Ge 21:9; 24:61; 29:24,29; 31:33; 46:18 [o]ver 3-4,8,15; Ge 21:14; 25:12 **16:2** [p]Ge 29:31; 30:2 [q]Ge 19:32; 30:3-4, 9-10 **16:3** [r]S Ge 12:5 [s]S Ge 12:4 **16:4** [t]S ver 1 [u]Ge 30:1; 1Sa 1:6 **16:5** [v]Ge 31:53; Ex 5:21; Jdg 11:27; 1Sa 24:12, 15; 26:10,23; Ps 50:6; 75:7 **16:6** [w]Jos 9:25 [x]Ge 31:50 **16:7** [y]ver 11; Ge 21:17; 22:11,15; 24:7,40; 31:11; 48:16; Ex 3:2; 14:19; 23:20,23; 32:34; 33:2; Nu 22:22; Jdg 2:1; 6:11; 13:3; 2Sa 24:16; 1Ki 19:5; 2Ki 1:3; 19:35; Ps 34:7; Zec 1:11; S Ac 5:19 [z]ver 14; Ge 21:19 [a]Ge 20:1; 25:18; Ex 15:22; 1Sa 15:7; 27:8 **16:8** [b]S ver 1 [c]S Ge 3:9 **16:10** [d]S Ge 13:16

[t] *18* Or *Wadi*

15:13 A COUNTRY NOT THEIR OWN. God told Abram that his descendants would go into Egypt and be oppressed for four hundred years. This figure is a round number for the actual 430 years (cf. Ex 12:40).

15:18 THE LORD MADE A COVENANT WITH ABRAM. The making of a covenant is described in vv. 9–17. (1) It consisted in taking slaughtered animals, cutting them in half, and the halves separated and placed opposite each other (v. 10). After this the two parties entering into the agreement would walk between the two halves of the slain animal, symbolizing that if they did not keep the promises of the covenant, they would perish just like the slain animals (v. 17; cf. Jer 34:18). The "smoking firepot with a blazing torch" represented God's presence (v. 17; cf. Ex 3:2; 14:24).

(2) Note that although a covenant usually established responsibilities for both parties (cf. 17:9–14), in this instance only God passed between the pieces of the animal (v. 17). God alone established the promises and obligations of the covenant; Abram had only to accept them in obedient faith (see 17:2, note).

16:2 THE LORD HAS KEPT ME FROM HAVING CHILDREN. It was customary among the people of Mesopotamia for a barren wife to have her handmaid bear children. Such children were considered as belonging to the wife. (1) Regardless of this custom, Abram and Sarai's attempt to provide a way for God to bring a child into the family through Abram's union with Hagar was not God's way (cf. 2:24). (2) The NT likens Hagar's son to the product of human effort—"in the ordinary way" and not "by the power of the Spirit" (Gal 4:29). In other words, it is never right to attempt to accomplish God's purpose in ways not according to the Spirit, patient hope and fervent prayer.

16:7 THE ANGEL OF THE LORD. As this story progresses, the "angel of the LORD" is revealed to be God himself speaking to Hagar (v. 13; cf. 18:1; Jdg 6:12,14).

11The angel of the LORD[e] also said
to her:

"You are now with child
and you will have a son.[f]
You shall name him[g] Ishmael,[u][h]
for the LORD has heard of your
misery.[i]
12He will be a wild donkey[j] of a
man;
his hand will be against
everyone
and everyone's hand against
him,
and he will live in hostility
toward[v] all his brothers.[k]"

13She gave this name to the LORD
who spoke to her: "You are the God
who sees me,[l]" for she said, "I have
now seen[w] the One who sees me."[m]
14That is why the well[n] was called
Beer Lahai Roi[x];[o] it is still there, between Kadesh[p] and Bered.
15So Hagar[q] bore Abram a son,[r]
and Abram gave the name Ishmael[s] to
the son she had borne. 16Abram was
eighty-six years old[t] when Hagar bore
him Ishmael.

The Covenant of Circumcision

17 When Abram was ninety-nine
years old,[u] the LORD appeared
to him[v] and said, "I am God Almighty[y];[w] walk before me and be
blameless.[x] 2I will confirm my covenant between me and you[y] and will
greatly increase your numbers."[z] Ge 26:2-6
3Abram fell facedown,[a] and God
said to him, 4"As for me, this is my covenant with you:[b] You will be the father
of many nations.[c] 5No longer will you
be called Abram[z]; your name will be
Abraham,[a][d] for I have made you a father of many nations.[e] 6I will make
you very fruitful;[f] I will make nations
of you, and kings will come from you.[g]
7I will establish my covenant[h][i] as an
everlasting covenant[j][k] between me
and you and your descendants after
you for the generations to come, to be

16:11 [e]S ver 7; S Ac 5:19 [f]S Ge 3:15 [g]Ge 12:2-3; 18:19; Ne 9:7; Isa 44:1; Am 3:2; Mt 1:21; Lk 1:13,31 [h]Ge 17:19; 21:3; 37:25,28; 39:1; Jdg 8:24 [i]Ge 29:32; 31:42; Ex 2:24; 3:7,9; 4:31; Nu 20:16; Dt 26:7; 1Sa 9:16 **16:12** [j]Job 6:5; 11:12; 24:5; 39:5; Ps 104:11; Jer 2:24; Hos 8:9 [k]Ge 25:18 **16:13** [l]Ps 139:1-12 [m]Ge 32:30; 33:10; Ex 24:10; 33:20, 23; Nu 12:8; Jdg 6:22; 13:22; Isa 6:5 **16:14** [n]S ver 7 [o]Ge 24:62; 25:11 [p]S Ge 14:7 **16:15** [q]S ver 1 [r]Ge 21:9; Gal 4:22 [s]Ge 17:18; 25:12; 28:9 **16:16** [t]S Ge 12:4 **17:1** [u]S Ge 12:4 [v]S Ge 12:7 [w]Ge 28:3; 35:11; 43:14; 48:3; 49:25; Ex 6:3; Ru 1:20; Job 5:17; 6:4,14; 22:21; 33:19; 36:16; Isa 13:6; Joel 1:15; Mic 6:9 [x]S Ge 5:22; 20:5; Dt 18:13; 1Ki 3:6; 9:4; Job 1:1; Ps 15:2; 18:23; 78:72; 101:2 **17:2** [y]S Ge 15:18; S 22:16-18 [z]S Ge 12:2 **17:3** [a]ver 17; Ge 18:2; 19:1; 33:3; Ex 18:7; Nu 14:5; Jos 5:14; 7:6; Jdg 13:20; Eze 1:28; 3:23 **17:4** [b]S Ge 15:18 [c]ver 16; S Ge 12:2; 25:23 **17:5** [d]ver 15; Ge 32:28; 35:10; 37:3,13; 43:6; 46:2; 1Ki 18:31; 2Ki 17:34; 1Ch 1:34; Ne 9:7; Isa 48:1; S Jn 1:42 [e]Ro 4:17* **17:6** [f]Ge 1:28; 22:17; 26:22; 28:3; 35:11; 41:52; 47:27; 48:4; 49:22; Lev 26:9; Dt 7:13 [g]ver 16,19; Ge 18:10; 21:1; 36:31; Isa 51:2; Mt 1:6 **17:7** [h]S Ge 15:18; Lev 26:9,15 [i]S Ge 6:18 [j]S Heb 13:20 [k]S Ge 9:16

[u]*11 Ishmael* means *God hears.* [v]*12* Or *live to the east / of* [w]*13* Or *seen the back of* [x]*14 Beer Lahai Roi* means *well of the Living One who sees me.* [y]*1* Hebrew *El-Shaddai* [z]*5 Abram* means *exalted father.* [a]*5 Abraham* means *father of many.*

16:11 ISHMAEL. The name "Ishmael" means "God hears" and signifies that God saw and responded to Abram and Sarai's unjust treatment of Hagar. That name is a judgment against Abram, revealing that God hates any injustice within his community. That God will punish a person because of wrong done toward those within the church is emphasized in the NT (see Col 3:25, note).

16:12 AGAINST EVERYONE. Ishmael, along with his descendants, would be a man of conflict, power and courage. His desire for conflict could be used in a struggle for God or against God. The choice would be his.

17:1 NINETY-NINE YEARS OLD. Abram was now ninety-nine years old and Sarai long past the age of having children. But thirteen years after Ishmael's birth and twenty-four years after God's original promise, the Lord appeared to Abram with a message and a demand. (1) God revealed himself as "God Almighty" (Heb *El Shaddai*), meaning that he was all-powerful and that nothing was impossible with him. As God Almighty, he could fulfill his promises when no natural way seemed to exist to fulfill them. Thus, God would bring Abram's promised son into the world by a miracle (cf. vv. 15–19; 35:11; Isa 13:6; Ro 4:19; Heb 11:12).

(2) God demanded that Abram walk before him and be "perfect" (i.e., wholly dedicated to performing his will). Just as Abram's faith was necessary to receive God's covenant, so a sincere effort to please God was required for the continuation of God's covenant blessings (cf. 22:16–18). Abram's faith had to be accompanied by obedience (see Ro 1:5), or he would disqualify himself from participation in God's eternal purposes (see article on GOD'S COVENANT WITH ABRAHAM, ISAAC AND JACOB, p. 46). In other words, God's promises and miracles will only occur when his people seek to live blameless lives and keep their hearts turned toward him (cf. 5:24; 6:9; Dt 13:4; see Mt 17:20, note).

17:2 MY COVENANT. God had earlier covenanted to give Abram the promised land (ch. 15); now he renewed that promise by stating that from Abram would come many nations and kings (v. 6), that the Lord would be God of his descendants, and that Sarai, his wife, would bear a son and be the mother of nations and kings (vv. 15–16). Abram and his descendants would see the fulfillment of the covenant as they bound themselves to God and the obligations of the covenant (vv. 9–14; see 15:6, note).

17:5 ABRAM . . . ABRAHAM. Abram means "exalted father"; Abraham means "father of many" (see next note; cf. Ne 9:7; Ro 4:17). A new relationship with God often required a new name to signify that new relationship.

17:7 TO BE YOUR GOD. The very essence and reality of the Abrahamic covenant was God giving himself to Abraham and his descendants (vv. 7–8).

your God[l] and the God of your descendants after you.[m] **8**The whole land of
Canaan,[n] where you are now an
alien,[o] I will give as an everlasting
possession to you and your descendants after you;[p] and I will be their
God.[q]"
9Then God said to Abraham, "As for
you, you must keep my covenant,[r]
you and your descendants after you for
the generations to come.[s] **10**This is
my covenant with you and your descendants after you, the covenant you are
to keep: Every male among you shall
be circumcised.[t] **11**You are to undergo
circumcision,[u] and it will be the sign
of the covenant[v] between me and you.
12For the generations to come[w] every
male among you who is eight days old
must be circumcised,[x] including those
born in your household or bought with
money from a foreigner—those who
are not your offspring. **13**Whether born
in your household or bought with your
money, they must be circumcised.[y]
My covenant in your flesh is to be an
everlasting covenant.[z] **14**Any uncircumcised male, who has not been circumcised[a] in the flesh, will be cut off
from his people;[b] he has broken my
covenant.[c]"
15God also said to Abraham, "As for
Sarai[d] your wife, you are no longer to
call her Sarai; her name will be Sarah.[e] **16**I will bless her and will surely
give you a son by her.[f] I will bless her
so that she will be the mother of nations;[g] kings of peoples will come
from her."
17Abraham fell facedown;[h] he
laughed[i] and said to himself, "Will a
son be born to a man a hundred years
old?[j] Will Sarah bear a child at the
age of ninety?"[k] **18**And Abraham said
to God, "If only Ishmael[l] might live
under your blessing!"[m]
19Then God said, "Yes, but your wife
Sarah will bear you a son,[n] and you
will call him Isaac.[b][o] I will establish
my covenant with him[p] as an everlasting covenant[q] for his descendants after him. **20**And as for Ishmael, I have
heard you: I will surely bless him; I will
make him fruitful and will greatly increase his numbers.[r] He will be the
father of twelve rulers,[s] and I will
make him into a great nation.[t] **21**But
my covenant[u] I will establish with
Isaac, whom Sarah will bear to you[v]
by this time next year."[w] **22**When he
had finished speaking with Abraham,
God went up from him.[x]
23On that very day Abraham took his
son Ishmael and all those born in his
household[y] or bought with his money,
every male in his household, and circumcised them, as God told him.[z]
24Abraham was ninety-nine years
old[a] when he was circumcised,[b]
25and his son Ishmael[c] was thirteen;
26Abraham and his son Ishmael were
both circumcised on that same day.
27And every male in Abraham's household[d], including those born in his

17:7 [l] Ex 6:7; 20:2; 29:45,46; Lev 11:44-45; 18:2; 22:33; 25:38; 26:12,45; Nu 15:41; Dt 4:20; 7:6,21; 29:13; 2Sa 7:24; Jer 14:9; Rev 21:7 [m] Ro 9:8; Gal 3:16 **17:8** [n] S Ge 10:19 [o] Ge 23:4; 28:4; 35:27; 37:1; Ex 6:4; 1Ch 29:15 [p] S Ge 12:7; S 15:7 [q] S ver 7; Jer 31:1 **17:9** [r] Ge 22:18; Ex 19:5; Dt 5:2 [s] Ge 18:19 **17:10** [t] ver 23; Ge 21:4; Lev 12:3; Jos 5:2,5,7; Jn 7:22; Ac 7:8; Ro 4:11 **17:11** [u] Ex 12:48; Dt 10:16 [v] S Ge 9:12; Ro 4:11 **17:12** [w] S Ge 9:12 [x] Ge 21:4; Lev 12:3; Jos 5:2; S Lk 1:59 **17:13** [y] Ex 12:44, 48 [z] S Ge 9:16 **17:14** [a] ver 23 [b] Ex 4:24-26; 12:15,19; 30:33; Lev 7:20,25; 17:4; 18:29; 19:8; 20:17; Nu 9:13; 15:30; 19:13; Dt 17:12; Jos 5:2-8; Job 38:15; Ps 37:28 [c] Eze 44:7 **17:15** [d] S Ge 11:29 [e] S ver 5 **17:16** [f] S ver 6; S Isa 29:22 [g] S ver 4; Ge 24:60; Gal 4:31 **17:17** [h] S ver 3 [i] Ge 18:12; 21:6 [j] S Ge 12:4 [k] Ge 18:11,13; 21:7; 24:1,36; Jer 20:15; Lk 1:18; Ro 4:19; Gal 4:23; Heb 11:11

17:18 [l] S Ge 16:15 [m] Ge 21:11 **17:19** [n] S ver 6,21; Ge 18:14; 21:2; 1Sa 1:20 [o] S Ge 16:11; Mt 1:21; Lk 1:13,31 [p] Ge 26:3; 50:24; Ex 13:11; Dt 1:8 [q] S Ge 9:16; S Gal 3:16 **17:20** [r] S Ge 13:16 [s] Ge 25:12-16 [t] Ge 25:18; 48:19 **17:21** [u] Ex 34:10 [v] S ver 19 [w] Ge 18:10,14 **17:22** [x] Ge 18:33; 35:13; Nu 12:9 **17:23** [y] S Ge 12:5 [z] S ver 10,S 14 **17:24** [a] S Ge 12:4 [b] Ro 4:11 **17:25** [c] Ge 16:16 **17:27** [d] Ge 14:14

[b] *19 Isaac* means *he laughs.*

God's promise "to be your God" is the greatest promise in Scripture. It is the first and fundamental promise on which all other promises rest. It means that God unreservedly binds himself to his faithful people to be their God, their shield and their reward (cf. 15:1, note). It also means that God's grace, pardon, promises, protection, guidance, goodness, help and blessing are given to them in love (cf. Jer 11:4; 24:7; 30:22; 32:38; Eze 11:20; 36:28; Zec 8:8). All Christians inherit this same promise through faith in Christ (Gal 3:16).

17:8 EVERLASTING POSSESSION. Abraham and his physical descendants were promised the land of Canaan (12:7; 13:15; 15:7,18–21). The covenant was "everlasting" from God's point of view. It could be broken only by Abraham's descendants (Isa 24:5; Jer 31:32), so that possession of the land was conditional on obedience to God (v. 9, see v. 1, note; see article on GOD'S COVENANT WITH ABRAHAM, ISAAC AND JACOB, p. 46).

17:11 CIRCUMCISION. Circumcision was to be a sign and seal of God's covenant with Abraham and his offspring. (1) It was a sign or mark that they had accepted God's covenant and God himself as their Lord. (2) It was a seal of the righteousness they had by faith (15:6; Ro 4:11). (3) It was to remind the people of God's promises to them and their own personal covenant obligations.

17:15 SARAH. Sarah means "princess" and points to her place as "the mother of nations" and kings (v. 16).

17:17 LAUGHED. Abraham probably experienced a temporary measure of disbelief (cf. 18:12). We should understand that even people of great faith may at times undergo momentary periods of doubt. When this occurs in our lives, we must nevertheless press on in obedience, calling on God to renew our faith.

household or bought from a foreigner,
was circumcised with him.

The Three Visitors

18 The LORD appeared to Abraham[e] near the great trees of
Mamre[f] while he was sitting at the
entrance to his tent[g] in the heat of the
day. 2Abraham looked up[h] and saw
three men[i] standing nearby. When he
saw them, he hurried from the entrance of his tent to meet them and
bowed low to the ground.[j]
3He said, "If I have found favor in
your eyes,[k] my lord,[c] do not pass
your servant[l] by. 4Let a little water be
brought, and then you may all wash
your feet[m] and rest under this tree.
5Let me get you something to eat,[n] so
you can be refreshed and then go on
your way—now that you have come to
your servant."

"Very well," they answered, "do as
you say."
6So Abraham hurried into the tent to
Sarah. "Quick," he said, "get three
seahs[d] of fine flour and knead it and
bake some bread."[o]
7Then he ran to the herd and selected a choice, tender calf[p] and gave it to
a servant, who hurried to prepare it.
8He then brought some curds[q] and
milk[r] and the calf that had been prepared, and set these before them.[s]
While they ate, he stood near them under a tree.
9"Where is your wife Sarah?"[t] they
asked him.

"There, in the tent,[u]" he said.
10Then the LORD[e] said, "I will surely
return to you about this time next
year,[v] and Sarah your wife will have
a son."[w]

Now Sarah was listening at the entrance to the tent, which was behind
him. 11Abraham and Sarah were already old and well advanced in
years,[x] and Sarah was past the age of
childbearing.[y] 12So Sarah laughed[z]
to herself as she thought, "After I am
worn out and my master[f][a] is old, will
I now have this pleasure?"
13Then the LORD said to Abraham,
"Why did Sarah laugh and say, 'Will I
really have a child, now that I am
old?'[b] 14Is anything too hard for the
LORD?[c] I will return to you at the appointed time next year[d] and Sarah
will have a son."[e]
15Sarah was afraid, so she lied and
said, "I did not laugh."

But he said, "Yes, you did laugh."

Abraham Pleads for Sodom

16When the men[f] got up to leave,
they looked down toward Sodom, and
Abraham walked along with them to
see them on their way. 17Then the LORD
said, "Shall I hide from Abraham[g]
what I am about to do?[h] 18Abraham
will surely become a great and powerful nation,[i] and all nations on earth
will be blessed through him. 19For I
have chosen him[j], so that he will direct his children[k] and his household
after him to keep the way of the LORD[l]
by doing what is right and just,[m] so
that the LORD will bring about for Abraham what he has promised him."[n]
20Then the LORD said, "The outcry
against Sodom[o] and Gomorrah is so
great[p] and their sin so grievous[q]
21that I will go down[r] and see if what
they have done is as bad as the outcry
that has reached me. If not, I will
know."
22The men[s] turned away and went

18:1 [e]S Ge 12:7; Ac 7:2 [f]S Ge 13:18 [g]Ge 19:1; 23:10, 18; 34:20,24; Ru 4:1; Ps 69:12; Heb 11:9 **18:2** [h]Ge 24:63 [i]ver 16,22; Ge 19:1,10; 32:24; Jos 5:13; Jdg 13:6-11; Hos 12:3-4; Heb 13:2 [j]S Ge 17:3; S 43:28 **18:3** [k]Ge 19:19; 39:4; Ru 2:2,10, 13; 1Sa 1:18; Est 2:15 [l]Ge 32:4, 18,20; 33:5 **18:4** [m]Ge 19:2; 24:32; 43:24; Jdg 19:21; 2Sa 11:8; S Lk 7:44 **18:5** [n]Jdg 13:15; 19:5 **18:6** [o]Ge 19:3; 2Sa 13:8 **18:7** [p]1Sa 28:24; Lk 15:23 **18:8** [q]Isa 7:15,22 [r]Jdg 4:19; 5:25 [s]Jdg 6:19 **18:9** [t]S Ge 3:9 [u]Ge 24:67; Heb 11:9 **18:10** [v]S Ge 17:21; 21:2; 2Ki 4:16 [w]S Ge 17:6; Ro 9:9* **18:11** [x]S Ge 17:17; Lk 1:18 [y]S Ge 11:30; Ro 4:19; Heb 11:11-12 **18:12** [z]S Ge 17:17 [a]1Pe 3:6 **18:13** [b]S Ge 17:17 **18:14** [c]Job 42:2; Isa 40:29; 50:2; 51:9; Jer 32:17,27; S Mt 19:26; Ro 4:21 [d]S ver 10 [e]S Ge 17:19; Ro 9:9*; Gal 4:23 **18:16** [f]S ver 2 **18:17** [g]Am 3:7 [h]Ge 19:24; Job 1:16; Ps 107:34 **18:18** [i]S Ge 12:2; Gal 3:8* **18:19** [j]Ge 17:9 [k]Dt 4:9-10; 6:7 [l]Jos 24:15; Eph 6:4 [m]Ge 22:12,18; 26:5; 2Sa 8:15; Ps 17:2; 99:4; Jer 23:5 [n]S Ge 16:11; S Isa 14:1 **18:20** [o]Isa 1:10; Jer 23:14; Eze 16:46 [p]Ge 19:13 [q]S Ge 13:13 **18:21** [r]S Ge 11:5 **18:22** [s]S ver 2

[c]*3* Or *O Lord* [d]*6* That is, probably about 20 quarts (about 22 liters) [e]*10* Hebrew *Then he* [f]*12* Or *husband*

18:2 THREE MEN. One of the three men was most likely a manifestation of God in human form and the other two were angels appearing as men. Abraham may not have initially recognized the visitors as God and angels.

18:14 IS ANYTHING TOO HARD FOR THE LORD? God wants us to understand that he has the power to accomplish what he has promised. Jesus emphasized this truth when he said, "with God all things are possible" (Mt 19:26).

18:19 HE WILL DIRECT HIS CHILDREN . . . KEEP THE WAY OF THE LORD. Essential in the calling of Abraham was God's purpose that he be a spiritual leader at home and teach his children the way of the Lord. With the call of Abraham, God established the father as the one responsible to train his children to "keep the way of the LORD by doing what is right and just" (see Dt 6:7, note; see article on PARENTS AND CHILDREN, p. 1854).

18:20 THEIR SIN IS SO GRIEVOUS. God does not overlook sin; he sees every evil, injustice and immorality that are committed (cf. 4:10; Ps 34:17; Jas 5:4). At the right time, if there is no repentance from sin, God will judge and condemn. The very nature of God requires that wickedness be punished.

toward Sodom,[t] but Abraham remained standing before the LORD.[g][u]
23 Then Abraham approached him and
said: "Will you sweep away the righteous with the wicked?[v] 24 What if
there are fifty righteous people in the
city? Will you really sweep it away and
not spare[h] the place for the sake of
the fifty righteous people in it?[w] 25 Far
be it from you to do such a thing[x]—to
kill the righteous with the wicked,
treating the righteous[y] and the wicked alike.[z] Far be it from you! Will not
the Judge[i][a] of all the earth do
right?"[b]

26 The LORD said, "If I find fifty righteous people in the city of Sodom, I will
spare the whole place for their sake.[c]"

27 Then Abraham spoke up again:
"Now that I have been so bold as to
speak to the Lord, though I am nothing
but dust and ashes,[d] 28 what if the
number of the righteous is five less
than fifty? Will you destroy the whole
city because of five people?"

"If I find forty-five there," he said, "I
will not destroy it."

29 Once again he spoke to him,
"What if only forty are found there?"

He said, "For the sake of forty, I will
not do it."

30 Then he said, "May the Lord not
be angry,[e] but let me speak. What if
only thirty can be found there?"

He answered, "I will not do it if I find
thirty there."

31 Abraham said, "Now that I have
been so bold as to speak to the Lord,
what if only twenty can be found
there?"

He said, "For the sake of twenty, I
will not destroy it."

32 Then he said, "May the Lord not
be angry, but let me speak just once
more.[f] What if only ten can be found
there?"

He answered, "For the sake of ten,[g]
I will not destroy it."

33 When the LORD had finished speaking[h] with Abraham, he left,[i] and
Abraham returned home.[j]

Sodom and Gomorrah Destroyed

19 The two angels[k] arrived at
Sodom[l] in the evening, and
Lot[m] was sitting in the gateway of the
city.[n] When he saw them, he got up to
meet them and bowed down with his
face to the ground.[o] 2 "My lords," he
said, "please turn aside to your servant's house. You can wash your feet[p]
and spend the night and then go on
your way early in the morning."

"No," they answered, "we will spend
the night in the square."[q]

3 But he insisted[r] so strongly that
they did go with him and entered his
house.[s] He prepared a meal for them,
baking bread without yeast,[t] and they
ate.[u] 4 Before they had gone to bed, all
the men from every part of the city of
Sodom[v]—both young and old—surrounded the house. 5 They called to
Lot, "Where are the men who came to
you tonight? Bring them out to us so
that we can have sex with them."[w]

6 Lot went outside to meet them[x]
and shut the door behind him 7 and
said, "No, my friends. Don't do this
wicked thing. 8 Look, I have two daughters who have never slept with a man.

18:22 [t] Ge 19:1 [u] ver 1; Ge 19:27 **18:23** [v] Ex 23:7; Lev 4:3,22,27; Nu 16:22; Dt 27:25; 2Sa 24:17; Ps 11:4-7; 94:21; Eze 18:4; 2Pe 2:9 **18:24** [w] ver 26; Jer 5:1 **18:25** [x] Ge 44:7, 17; Dt 32:4; Job 8:3-7; 34:10 [y] Isa 5:20; Am 5:15; Mal 2:17; 3:18 [z] Dt 1:16-17 [a] Jdg 11:27; Job 9:15; Ps 7:11; 94:2; Heb 12:23 [b] Ge 20:4; Dt 32:4; 2Ch 19:7; Ezr 9:15; Ne 9:33; Job 8:3,20; 34:10; 36:23; Ps 58:11; 75:7; 94:2; 119:137; Isa 3:10-11; Eze 18:25; Da 4:37; 9:14; Mal 2:17; Ro 3:6 **18:26** [c] S ver 24 **18:27** [d] S Ge 2:7; S Job 2:8 **18:30** [e] ver 32; Ge 44:18; Ex 32:22 **18:32** [f] S ver 30; Jdg 6:39 [g] Jer 5:1 **18:33** [h] Ex 31:18 [i] S Ge 17:22 [j] Ge 31:55 **19:1** [k] S Ge 18:2; Heb 13:2 [l] Ge 18:22 [m] S Ge 11:27 [n] S Ge 18:1 [o] S Ge 17:3; 48:12; Ru 2:10; 1Sa 25:23; 2Sa 14:33; 2Ki 2:15 **19:2** [p] S Ge 18:4; Lk 7:44 [q] Jdg 19:15,20 **19:3** [r] Ge 33:11 [s] Job 31:32 [t] Ex 12:39 [u] S Ge 18:6 **19:4** [v] S Ge 13:13 **19:5** [w] S Ge 13:13; Lev 18:22; Dt 23:18; Jdg 19:22; Ro 1:24-27 **19:6** [x] Jdg 19:23

[g] 22 Masoretic Text; an ancient Hebrew scribal tradition *but the LORD remained standing before Abraham* [h] 24 Or *forgive*; also in verse 26 [i] 25 Or *Ruler*

18:22 ABRAHAM REMAINED STANDING BEFORE THE LORD. Out of concern for Lot and his relatives, Abraham prayed that God would not destroy the cities (vv. 22–33). God answered Abraham's prayer, though not in the way Abraham expected. God did not sweep away the righteous with the wicked. He saved the righteous, yet destroyed the guilty. In the day of God's future wrath that is coming on the world (see 1Th 5:2, note; 2Th 2:2, note), God has promised to rescue the righteous (see Lk 21:36, note; Rev 3:10, note; see article on THE RAPTURE, p. 1864).

19:1 LOT WAS SITTING IN THE GATEWAY. Although Lot was distressed by the filthy deeds he saw and heard (2Pe 2:7–8), he still was willing to tolerate the wickedness of Sodom for the social and material advantages (see 13:12, note). This compromise brought tragedy to his family (v. 24). Likewise, believers today who expose their families to ungodly environments and evil influences for social or material gain are setting themselves up for family tragedies.

19:5 HAVE SEX WITH THEM. The men of the city wanted to sexually abuse the male strangers. It is from this incident that the word "sodomy" gains its meaning; it primarily refers to homosexuality and homosexual lust. Sodomy is severely condemned in the Bible (Lev 20:13; Dt 23:17; 1Co 6:9; 1Ti 1:8–10; see Ro 1:27, note).

19:8 I HAVE TWO DAUGHTERS. It is difficult to believe that Lot was truly willing to allow his two daughters to be defiled and abused by a mob of sexual perverts merely in order to protect two men he had never met. It may have been that in

Let me bring them out to you, and you can do what you like with them. But don't do anything to these men, for they have come under the protection of my roof."[y]

9"Get out of our way," they replied. And they said, "This fellow came here as an alien,[z] and now he wants to play the judge![a] We'll treat you worse than them." They kept bringing pressure on Lot and moved forward to break down the door.

10But the men[b] inside reached out and pulled Lot back into the house and shut the door. **11**Then they struck the men who were at the door of the house, young and old, with blindness[c] so that they could not find the door.

12The two men said to Lot, "Do you have anyone else here—sons-in-law, sons or daughters, or anyone else in the city who belongs to you?[d] Get them out of here, **13**because we[e] are going to destroy this place. The outcry to the LORD against its people is so great[f] that he has sent us to destroy it."[g]

14So Lot went out and spoke to his sons-in-law, who were pledged to marry[j] his daughters. He said, "Hurry and get out of this place, because the LORD is about to destroy the city![h]" But his sons-in-law thought he was joking.[i]

15With the coming of dawn, the angels urged Lot, saying, "Hurry! Take your wife and your two daughters who are here, or you will be swept away[j] when the city is punished.[k]"

16When he hesitated, the men grasped his hand and the hands of his wife and of his two daughters[l] and led them safely out of the city, for the LORD was merciful to them.[m] **17**As soon as they had brought them out, one of them said, "Flee for your lives![n] Don't look back,[o] and don't stop anywhere in the plain![p] Flee to the mountains[q] or you will be swept away!"

18But Lot said to them, "No, my lords,[k] please! **19**Your[l] servant has found favor in your[l] eyes,[r] and you[l] have shown great kindness[s] to me in sparing my life. But I can't flee to the mountains;[t] this disaster will overtake me, and I'll die. **20**Look, here is a town near enough to run to, and it is small. Let me flee to it—it is very small, isn't it? Then my life will be spared."

21He said to him, "Very well, I will grant this request[u] too; I will not overthrow the town you speak of. **22**But flee there quickly, because I cannot do anything until you reach it." (That is why the town was called Zoar.[m][v])

23By the time Lot reached Zoar,[w] the sun had risen over the land. **24**Then the LORD rained down burning sulfur[x] on Sodom and Gomorrah[y]—from the LORD out of the heavens.[z] **25**Thus he overthrew those cities[a] and the entire plain,[b] including all those living in the cities—and also the vegetation in the land.[c] **26**But Lot's wife looked back,[d] and she became a pillar of salt.[e]

Ex 23:23-24

27Early the next morning Abraham got up and returned to the place where he had stood before the LORD.[f] **28**He looked down toward Sodom and Gomorrah, toward all the land of the plain, and he saw dense smoke rising from the land, like smoke from a furnace.[g]

29So when God destroyed the cities of the plain,[h] he remembered[i] Abraham, and he brought Lot out of the catastrophe[j] that overthrew the cities where Lot had lived.[k]

19:8 [y]Jdg 19:24; 2Pe 2:7-8 **19:9** [z]Ge 23:4 [a]S Ge 13:8; Ac 7:27 **19:10** [b]S Ge 18:2 **19:11** [c]Dt 28:28-29; 2Ki 6:18; Ac 13:11 **19:12** [d]S Ge 6:18 **19:13** [e]Ex 12:29; 2Sa 24:16; 2Ki 19:35; 1Ch 21:12; 2Ch 32:21 [f]Ge 18:20 [g]1Ch 21:15; Ps 78:49; Jer 21:12; 25:18; 44:22; 51:45 **19:14** [h]Nu 16:21; Rev 18:4 [i]Ex 9:21; 1Ki 13:18; Jer 5:12; 43:2; Lk 17:28 **19:15** [j]Nu 16:26; Job 21:18; Ps 58:9; 73:19; 90:5 [k]Rev 18:4 **19:16** [l]2Pe 2:7 [m]Ex 34:6; Ps 33:18-19 **19:17** [n]1Ki 19:3; Jer 48:6 [o]ver 26 [p]S Ge 13:12 [q]S ver 19; S Ge 14:10; Mt 24:16 **19:19** [r]S Ge 6:8; S 18:3 [s]Ge 24:12; 39:21; 40:14; 47:29; Ru 1:8; 2:20; 3:10 [t]S ver 17,30 **19:21** [u]1Sa 25:35; 2Sa 14:8; Job 42:9 **19:22** [v]S Ge 13:10 **19:23** [w]S Ge 13:10 **19:24** [x]Job 18:15; Ps 11:6; Isa 30:33; 34:9; Eze 38:22 [y]Dt 29:23; Isa 1:9; 13:19; Jer 49:18; 50:40; Am 4:11 [z]S Ge 18:17; S Lev 10:2; S Mt 10:15; Lk 17:29 **19:25** [a]S ver 24; Eze 26:16; Zep 3:8; Hag 2:22 [b]S Ge 13:12 [c]Ps 107:34; Isa 1:10; Jer 20:16; 23:14; La 4:6; Eze 16:48 **19:26** [d]S ver 17 [e]Lk 17:32 **19:27** [f]Ge 18:22 **19:28** [g]Ge 15:17; Ex 19:18; Rev 9:2; 18:9 **19:29** [h]S Ge 13:12 [i]S Ge 8:1 [j]2Pe 2:7 [k]Ge 14:12; Eze 14:16

[j]*14* Or *were married to* [k]*18* Or *No, Lord*; or *No, my lord* [l]*19* The Hebrew is singular. [m]*22* *Zoar* means *small.*

desperation he was stalling for time, believing that his friends in the city would not allow the others to brutalize him or his family.

19:26 LOT'S WIFE LOOKED BACK, AND SHE BECAME A PILLAR OF SALT. Lot's wife did not take the angel's specific command seriously (v. 17), and she was struck dead. Evidently her heart was still clinging to the pleasures of Sodom. Jesus warns believers to "remember Lot's wife!" (Lk 17:32), meaning that those whose hearts are attached to the world's present corrupt system will not be spared God's wrath and the destruction that is coming upon the ungodly (cf. Eze 3:20; Ro 8:13; Heb 4:1; see articles on PERSONAL APOSTASY, p. 1918, and THE CHRISTIAN'S RELATIONSHIP TO THE WORLD, p. 1976).

19:28 SMOKE FROM A FURNACE. The apostle Peter states that the destruction of Sodom and Gomorrah is an example of what is going to happen to all the ungodly (2Pe 2:6,9). The NT warns that the final day of God's wrath is approaching (see article on THE GREAT TRIBULATION, p. 1456).

Lot and His Daughters

30Lot and his two daughters left
Zoar[l] and settled in the mountains,[m]
for he was afraid to stay in Zoar. He
and his two daughters lived in a cave.
31One day the older daughter said to
the younger, "Our father is old, and
there is no man around here to lie with
us, as is the custom all over the earth.
32Let's get our father to drink wine and
then lie with him and preserve our family line[n] through our father."[o]

33That night they got their father to
drink wine, and the older daughter
went in and lay with him. He was not
aware of it when she lay down or when
she got up.[p]

34The next day the older daughter
said to the younger, "Last night I lay
with my father. Let's get him to drink
wine again tonight, and you go in and
lie with him so we can preserve our
family line through our father."[q] 35So
they got their father to drink wine[r]
that night also, and the younger daughter went and lay with him. Again he
was not aware of it when she lay down
or when she got up.[s]

36So both of Lot's daughters became
pregnant by their father.[t] 37The older
daughter had a son, and she named
him Moab[n];[u] he is the father of the
Moabites[v] of today. 38The younger
daughter also had a son, and she
named him Ben-Ammi[o]; he is the father of the Ammonites[w] of today.

Abraham and Abimelech

20:1–18Ref — Ge 12:10–20; 26:1–11

20 Now Abraham moved on from
there[x] into the region of the
Negev[y] and lived between Kadesh[z]
and Shur.[a] For a while[b] he stayed in
Gerar,[c] 2and there Abraham said of
his wife Sarah, "She is my sister.[d]"
Then Abimelech[e] king of Gerar sent
for Sarah and took her.[f]

3But God came to Abimelech[g] in a
dream[h] one night and said to him,
"You are as good as dead[i] because of
the woman you have taken; she is a
married woman."[j]

4Now Abimelech had not gone near
her, so he said, "Lord, will you destroy
an innocent nation?[k] 5Did he not say
to me, 'She is my sister,[l]' and didn't
she also say, 'He is my brother'? I have
done this with a clear conscience[m] and
clean hands.[n]"

6Then God said to him in the dream,
"Yes, I know you did this with a clear
conscience, and so I have kept[o] you
from sinning against me.[p] That is why
I did not let you touch her. 7Now return
the man's wife, for he is a prophet,[q]
and he will pray for you[r] and you will
live. But if you do not return her, you
may be sure that you and all yours will
die."[s]

8Early the next morning Abimelech
summoned all his officials, and when
he told them all that had happened,
they were very much afraid. 9Then
Abimelech called Abraham in and said,
"What have you done to us? How have
I wronged you that you have brought
such great guilt upon me and my kingdom? You have done things to me that
should not be done.[t]" 10And Abimelech asked Abraham, "What was your
reason for doing this?"

11Abraham replied, "I said to myself, 'There is surely no fear of God[u]
in this place, and they will kill me because of my wife.'[v] 12Besides, she
really is my sister,[w] the daughter of
my father though not of my mother;
and she became my wife. 13And when

19:30 [l]ver 22; S Ge 13:10 [m]S ver 19; S Ge 14:10 **19:32** [n]S Ge 16:2 [o]ver 34,36; Ge 38:18 **19:33** [p]ver 35 **19:34** [q]S ver 32 **19:35** [r]Ge 9:21 [s]ver 33 **19:36** [t]S ver 32 **19:37** [u]Ge 36:35; Ex 15:15; Nu 25:1; Isa 15:1; 25:10; Jer 25:21; 48:1; Eze 25:8; Zep 2:9 [v]Nu 22:4; 24:17; Dt 2:9; Jdg 3:28; Ru 1:4,22; 1Sa 14:47; 22:3-4; 2Sa 8:2; 2Ki 1:1; 3:4; Ezr 9:1; Ps 108:9; Jer 48:1 **19:38** [w]Nu 21:24; Dt 2:19; 23:3; Jos 12:2; Jdg 3:13; 10:6,7; 1Sa 11:1-11; 14:47; 1Ch 19:1; 2Ch 20:23; 26:8; 27:5; Ne 2:19; 4:3; Jer 25:21; 40:14; 49:1; Eze 21:28; 25:2; Am 1:13 **20:1** [x]Ge 18:1 [y]S Ge 12:9 [z]S Ge 14:7 [a]S Ge 16:7 [b]Ge 26:3 [c]Ge 26:1,6,17 **20:2** [d]ver 12; S Ge 12:13 [e]ver 14; Ge 21:22; 26:1 [f]S Ge 12:15

20:3 [g]Nu 22:9,20 [h]Ge 28:12; 31:10, 24; 37:5,9; 40:5; 41:1; Nu 12:6; Dt 13:1; Job 33:15; Da 2:1; 4:5 [i]Ex 10:7; 12:33; Ps 105:38 [j]ver 7; Ge 26:11; 1Ch 16:21; Ps 105:14 **20:4** [k]S Ge 18:25 **20:5** [l]S Ge 12:19 [m]S Ge 17:1 [n]Ps 7:8; 25:21; 26:6; 41:12 **20:6** [o]1Sa 25:26, 34 [p]S Ge 13:13; Ps 41:4; 51:4 **20:7** [q]Dt 18:18; 34:10; 2Ki 3:11; 5:3; 1Ch 16:22; Ps 105:15 [r]ver 17; Ex 8:8; Nu 11:2; 12:13; 1Sa 7:5; 1Ki 13:6; Job 42:8; Jer 18:20; 37:3; 42:2 [s]S ver 3; S Ps 9:5 **20:9** [t]S Ge 12:18; 34:7 **20:11** [u]Ge 42:18; Ne 5:15; Job 31:23; Ps 36:1; Pr 16:6 [v]S Ge 12:12; 31:31 **20:12** [w]S Ge 12:13

[n] *37 Moab* sounds like the Hebrew for *from father.* [o] *38 Ben-Ammi* means *son of my people.*

19:33 THEY GOT THEIR FATHER TO DRINK WINE. Lot's daughters were guilty of the sin of incest and Lot the sin of drunkenness. (1) Evidently, the girls' close association with the ungodly Sodomites, tolerated by their father (v. 14), had caused them to adopt low moral standards for their lives. Because of Lot's toleration of the ungodly, he lost his family and his descendants became pagans. (2) Lot remains an example of a believing father whose faith and commitment were enough to save himself, but not enough to save his family. He learned too late that the true way of faith is to teach one's family to stand apart and "not love the world" (1Jn 2:15,17; see 2Co 6:14, note).

20:2 SAID OF HIS WIFE SARAH, SHE IS MY SISTER. Once again Abraham's faith failed and he jeopardized God's plan for Sarah. God intervened in order to preserve Sarah's participation in the history of redemption as the mother of the covenant people (vv. 3–7). God in his grace will at times deliver his normally faithful children from situations that are the result of their failure in faith and obedience.

God had me wander[x] from my father's
household,[y] I said to her, 'This is how
you can show your love to me: Everywhere we go, say of me, "He is my
brother." ' "
14Then Abimelech[z] brought sheep
and cattle and male and female slaves
and gave them to Abraham,[a] and he
returned Sarah his wife to him. **15**And
Abimelech said, "My land is before
you; live wherever you like."[b]
16To Sarah he said, "I am giving
your brother a thousand shekels[p] of
silver. This is to cover the offense
against you before all who are with
you; you are completely vindicated."
17Then Abraham prayed to God,[c]
and God healed Abimelech, his wife
and his slave girls so they could have
children again, **18**for the LORD had
closed up every womb in Abimelech's
household because of Abraham's wife
Sarah.[d]

The Birth of Isaac

21 Now the LORD was gracious to
Sarah[e] as he had said, and the
LORD did for Sarah what he had promised.[f] **2**Sarah became pregnant and
bore a son[g] to Abraham in his old
age,[h] at the very time God had promised him.[i] **3**Abraham gave the name
Isaac[q][j] to the son Sarah bore him.
4When his son Isaac was eight days
old, Abraham circumcised him,[k] as
God commanded him. **5**Abraham was a
hundred years old[l] when his son
Isaac was born to him.
6Sarah said, "God has brought me
laughter,[m] and everyone who hears
about this will laugh with me." **7**And
she added, "Who would have said to
Abraham that Sarah would nurse children? Yet I have borne him a son in his
old age."[n]

Hagar and Ishmael Sent Away

8The child grew and was weaned,[o]
and on the day Isaac was weaned Abraham held a great feast. **9**But Sarah saw
that the son whom Hagar the Egyptian
had borne to Abraham[p] was mocking,[q] **10**and she said to Abraham, "Get
rid of that slave woman[r] and her son,
for that slave woman's son will never
share in the inheritance with my son
Isaac."[s]
11The matter distressed Abraham
greatly because it concerned his son.[t]
12But God said to him, "Do not be so
distressed about the boy and your
maidservant. Listen to whatever Sarah
tells you, because it is through Isaac
that your offspring[r] will be reckoned.[u] **13**I will make the son of the
maidservant into a nation[v] also, because he is your offspring."
14Early the next morning Abraham
took some food and a skin of water and
gave them to Hagar.[w] He set them on
her shoulders and then sent her off
with the boy. She went on her way and
wandered in the desert of Beersheba.[x]
15When the water in the skin was
gone, she put the boy under one of the
bushes. **16**Then she went off and sat
down nearby, about a bowshot away,
for she thought, "I cannot watch the
boy die." And as she sat there nearby,
she[s] began to sob.[y]
17God heard the boy crying,[z] and
the angel of God[a] called to Hagar from
heaven[b] and said to her, "What is the
matter, Hagar? Do not be afraid;[c] God
has heard the boy crying as he lies
there. **18**Lift the boy up and take him by
the hand, for I will make him into a
great nation.[d]"
19Then God opened her eyes[e] and
she saw a well of water.[f] So she went
and filled the skin with water and gave
the boy a drink.
20God was with the boy[g] as he grew
up. He lived in the desert and became
an archer. **21**While he was living in the
Desert of Paran,[h] his mother got a
wife for him[i] from Egypt.

20:13 [x]Dt 26:5; 1Ch 16:20; Isa 30:28; 63:17 [y]S Ge 12:1 **20:14** [z]S ver 2 [a]Ge 12:16 **20:15** [b]Ge 13:9; S 45:18 **20:17** [c]S ver 7; Job 42:9 **20:18** [d]Ge 12:17 **21:1** [e]1Sa 2:21 [f]S Ge 8:1; S 17:16,21; 18:14; Gal 4:23; Heb 11:11 **21:2** [g]S Ge 17:19; S 30:6 [h]Gal 4:22; Heb 11:11 [i]S Ge 18:10 **21:3** [j]S Ge 16:11; S 17:19; Jos 24:3 **21:4** [k]Ge 17:10, 12; Ac 7:8 **21:5** [l]S Ge 12:4; Heb 6:15 **21:6** [m]Ge 17:17; Job 8:21; Ps 126:2; Isa 12:6; 35:2; 44:23; 52:9; 54:1 **21:7** [n]S Ge 17:17 **21:8** [o]1Sa 1:23

21:9 [p]S Ge 16:15 [q]Ge 39:14; Gal 4:29 **21:10** [r]Ge 39:17 [s]Ge 25:6; Gal 4:30* **21:11** [t]Ge 17:18 **21:12** [u]Mt 1:2; Ro 9:7*; Heb 11:18* **21:13** [v]ver 18; S Ge 13:16 **21:14** [w]S Ge 16:1 [x]ver 31,32; Ge 22:19; 26:33; 28:10; 46:1,5; Jos 15:28; 19:2; Jdg 20:1; 1Sa 3:20; 1Ch 4:28; Ne 11:27 **21:16** [y]Jer 6:26; Am 8:10; Zec 12:10 **21:17** [z]Ex 3:7; Nu 20:16; Dt 26:7; Ps 6:8 [a]S Ge 16:7 [b]Ge 22:11,15 [c]S Ge 15:1 **21:18** [d]ver 13; S Ge 17:20 **21:19** [e]Nu 22:31 [f]S Ge 16:7 **21:20** [g]Ge 26:3, 24; 28:15; 39:2, 21,23; Lk 1:66 **21:21** [h]S Ge 14:6 [i]Ge 24:4,38; 28:2; 34:4,8; Jdg 14:2

p *16* That is, about 25 pounds (about 11.5 kilograms) **q** *3* Isaac means *he laughs.* **r** *12* Or *seed* **s** *16* Hebrew; Septuagint *the child*

21:5 HIS SON ISAAC WAS BORN. Isaac, the son of promise, was finally born to Abraham and Sarah. Through Isaac God would continue his covenant with Abraham (v. 12; 17:19). Twenty-five years had passed before God's promise to Abraham was fulfilled (cf. 12:4). "The LORD is good to those whose hope is in him" (La 3:25); in his own time he faithfully brings his promises to pass.

21:17 GOD HAS HEARD. God knew it was best that Hagar and Ishmael leave Abraham. Nevertheless, God did not forsake those two, for they remained in his presence and under his care (vv. 17–21). God had a purpose for Ishmael, paralleling his purpose for Isaac, namely, that he would "make him into a great nation" (v. 18).

The Treaty at Beersheba

22At that time Abimelech[j] and Phicol the commander of his forces[k] said
to Abraham, "God is with you in everything you do.[l] 23Now swear[m] to me
here before God that you will not deal
falsely with me or my children or my
descendants.[n] Show to me and the
country where you are living as an
alien the same kindness I have shown
to you."[o]
24Abraham said, "I swear it."
25Then Abraham complained to
Abimelech about a well of water that
Abimelech's servants had seized.[p]
26But Abimelech said, "I don't know
who has done this. You did not tell me,
and I heard about it only today."
27So Abraham brought sheep and
cattle and gave them to Abimelech,
and the two men made a treaty.[q]
28Abraham set apart seven ewe lambs
from the flock, 29and Abimelech asked
Abraham, "What is the meaning of
these seven ewe lambs you have set
apart by themselves?"
30He replied, "Accept these seven
lambs from my hand as a witness[r]
that I dug this well.[s]"
31So that place was called Beersheba,[t][t] because the two men swore an
oath[u] there.
32After the treaty[v] had been made
at Beersheba,[w] Abimelech and Phicol
the commander of his forces[x] returned to the land of the Philistines.[y]
33Abraham planted a tamarisk tree[z]
in Beersheba, and there he called upon
the name of the LORD,[a] the Eternal
God.[b] 34And Abraham stayed in the
land of the Philistines[c] for a long
time.

Abraham Tested

22 Some time later God tested[d]
Abraham. He said to him,
"Abraham!"
"Here I am,"[e] he replied.
2Then God said, "Take your son[f],
your only son, Isaac, whom you love,
and go to the region of Moriah.[g] Sacrifice him there as a burnt offering[h] on
one of the mountains I will tell you
about.[i]"
3Early the next morning[j] Abraham
got up and saddled his donkey. He took
with him two of his servants and his
son Isaac. When he had cut enough
wood for the burnt offering, he set out
for the place God had told him about.
4On the third day Abraham looked up
and saw the place in the distance. 5He
said to his servants, "Stay here with
the donkey while I and the boy go over
there. We will worship and then we will
come back to you.[k]"
6Abraham took the wood for the
burnt offering and placed it on his son
Isaac,[l] and he himself carried the fire
and the knife.[m] As the two of them
went on together, 7Isaac spoke up and
said to his father Abraham, "Father?"
"Yes, my son?" Abraham replied.

21:22 [j]S Ge 20:2 [k]ver 32; Ge 26:26 [l]ver 23; Ge 26:28; 28:15; 31:3,5,42; 39:2,3; 1Sa 3:19; 16:18; 2Ch 1:1; Ps 46:7; Isa 7:14; 8:8,10; 41:10; 43:5 **21:23** [m]ver 31; Ge 25:33; 26:31; 31:53; Jos 2:12; 1Ki 2:8 [n]1Sa 24:21 [o]S ver 22; Jos 2:12 **21:25** [p]Ge 26:15, 18,20-22 **21:27** [q]ver 31,32; Ge 26:28,31; 31:44,53 **21:30** [r]Ge 31:44, 47,48,50,52; Jos 22:27,28,34; 24:27; Isa 19:20; Mal 2:14 [s]ver 25; Ge 26:25,32 **21:31** [t]S ver 14 [u]S ver 23,S 27 **21:32** [v]S ver 27 [w]S ver 14 [x]S ver 22 [y]S Ge 10:14 **21:33** [z]1Sa 22:6; 31:13 [a]S Ge 4:26 [b]Ex 15:18; Dt 32:40; 33:27; Job 36:26; Ps 10:16; 45:6; 90:2; 93:2; 102:24; 103:19; 146:10; Isa 40:28; Jer 10:10; Hab 1:12; 3:6; Heb 13:8 **21:34** [c]S Ge 10:14 **22:1** [d]Ex 15:25; 16:4; 20:20; Dt 8:2,16; 13:3; Jdg 2:22; 3:1; 2Ch 32:31; Ps 66:10; Heb 11:17; Jas 1:12-13 [e]ver 11; Ge 31:11; 46:2; 1Sa 3:4,6,8; Isa 6:8 **22:2** [f]ver 12,16; Jn 3:16; Heb 11:17; 1Jn 4:9 [g]2Ch 3:1 [h]S Ge 8:20 [i]ver 9 **22:3** [j]Jos 8:10 **22:5** [k]Ex 24:14 **22:6** [l]Jn 19:17 [m]ver 10; Jdg 19:29

t31 *Beersheba* can mean *well of seven* or *well of the oath.*

22:1 GOD TESTED ABRAHAM. Abraham's faith in and commitment to God were tested to the maximum. God commanded him to do something completely contrary to common sense and to his fatherly love and lifelong hope (v. 2). In the Abraham story, we read of three great tests of his faith: (1) the call to separate himself from his people and country (12:1) and to go forth, not knowing where he was going (cf. Heb 11:8); (2) the requirement to trust God for the promise of the covenant without seeing the fulfillment of that promise for twenty-five years (12:1–3; 15:6,8; 18:9–14; Heb 11:8–13); (3) the command that he offer up Isaac, the promised son (ch. 22). In a manner similar to Abraham, the true faith of all believers will be tested.

22:2 TAKE YOUR SON. Abraham was commanded to sacrifice his son Isaac. (1) The central issue lay in two areas that illustrate God's measure in dealing with all believers. (a) Was Abraham's love for God greater than his love for others, even his beloved son? (b) Was Abraham's hope of the fulfillment of the promise still in God, or did he now hope in something else, i.e., in Isaac? (2) Through this test God forced Abraham to face these questions and to make clear whether he indeed feared God with all his heart (v. 12). (3) God did not really desire Isaac's physical death (cf. vv. 12–13), for he later condemned human sacrifice as a terrible sin (Lev 20:1–5). But he did want to test Abraham's commitment.

22:5 I AND THE BOY . . . WILL COME BACK. Abraham's statement that he and Isaac would return from the sacrifice was a testimony to his faith and conviction that God's promises concerning Isaac would be fulfilled (i.e., "it is through Isaac that your offspring will be reckoned" 21:12). In this story, Isaac is a type of Christ: (1) in his giving himself to his father for a sacrifice unto death (v. 16; cf. Jn 10:17–18), and (2) in his being saved from death, an act that corresponds to Christ's resurrection (v. 12; see Heb 11:17–19).

"The fire and wood are here," Isaac
said, "but where is the lamb[n] for the
burnt offering?"
8Abraham answered, "God himself
will provide[o] the lamb[p] for the burnt
offering, my son." And the two of them
went on together.
9When they reached the place God
had told him about,[q] Abraham built an
altar[r] there and arranged the wood[s]
on it. He bound his son Isaac and laid
him on the altar,[t] on top of the wood.
10Then he reached out his hand and
took the knife[u] to slay his son.[v]
11But the angel of the LORD[w] called out
to him from heaven,[x] "Abraham!
Abraham!"[y]
"Here I am,"[z] he replied.
12"Do not lay a hand on the boy," he
said. "Do not do anything to him. Now
I know that you fear God,[a] because
you have not withheld from me your
son, your only son.[b]"
13Abraham looked up and there in a
thicket he saw a ram[u] caught by its
horns.[c] He went over and took the
ram and sacrificed it as a burnt offering
instead of his son.[d] **14**So Abraham
called[e] that place The LORD[f] Will
Provide. And to this day it is said, "On
the mountain of the LORD it will be provided.[g]"
15The angel of the LORD[h] called to
Abraham from heaven[i] a second time
16and said, "I swear by myself,[j] declares the LORD, that because you have
done this and have not withheld your
son, your only son,[k] **17**I will surely
bless you[l] and make your descendants[m] as numerous as the stars in
the sky[n] and as the sand on the seashore.[o] Your descendants will take
possession of the cities of their enemies,[p] **18**and through your offspring[v]
all nations on earth will be blessed,[q]
because you have obeyed me."[r]
19Then Abraham returned to his servants, and they set off together for Beersheba.[s] And Abraham stayed in Beersheba.

Ex 17:8-13

22:7 [n] Ex 29:38-42; Lev 1:10; Rev 13:8 **22:8** [o] ver 14 [p] ver 13; S Jn 1:29 **22:9** [q] ver 2 [r] S Ge 4:26; S 8:20 [s] Lev 1:7; 1Ki 18:33 [t] Heb 11:17-19; Jas 2:21 **22:10** [u] S ver 6 [v] ver 3; S Ge 18:19 **22:11** [w] S Ge 16:7 [x] S Ge 21:17 [y] Ge 46:2 [z] S ver 1 **22:12** [a] S Ge 18:19; 42:18; Ex 18:21; 1Sa 15:22; Job 1:1; 37:24; Pr 8:13; Jas 2:21-22 [b] S ver 2; Jn 3:16; 1Jn 4:9 **22:13** [c] S ver 8 [d] S Ge 8:20; Ro 8:32 **22:14** [e] Ex 17:15; Jdg 6:24 [f] Isa 30:29 [g] ver 8 **22:15** [h] S Ge 16:7 [i] S Ge 21:17 **22:16** [j] Ex 13:11; 32:13; 33:1; Isa 45:23; 62:8; Jer 22:5; 44:26; 49:13; 51:14; Am 6:8; Lk 1:73; Heb 6:13 [k] S ver 2 **22:17** [l] S Ge 12:2 [m] Heb 6:14* [n] S Ge 15:5; Ex 32:13; Dt 7:7; 28:62 [o] S Ge 12:2; S 26:24; Hos 1:10; Ro 9:27; Heb 11:12 [p] Ge 24:60; Est 9:2 **22:18** [q] S Ge 12:2, 3; Ac 3:25*; Gal 3:8* [r] S ver 10; Ge 17:2,9; Ps 105:9 **22:19** [s] Ge 21:14; 26:23; 28:10

[u] *13* Many manuscripts of the Masoretic Text, Samaritan Pentateuch, Septuagint and Syriac; most manuscripts of the Masoretic Text *a ram behind ⌞him⌟* [v] *18* Or *seed*

22:8 GOD HIMSELF WILL PROVIDE. "God himself will provide" ("Yahweh-yireh," v. 14) is prophetic and points to God providing a substitute sacrifice, a ram (v. 13). The ultimate fulfillment of Abraham's statement is found in God providing his one and only Son as an atoning sacrifice at Golgotha for the redemption of humankind. Thus, the heavenly Father himself did what he had asked Abraham to do (Jn 3:16; Ro 3:24–25; 8:32).

22:9 BOUND HIS SON ISAAC. Isaac was probably a young adult who was well able to resist his father, had he so desired. But in complete submission to God and obedience to his father, he allowed himself to be bound and laid on the altar, just as Jesus voluntarily went to the cross.

22:10 HE REACHED OUT HIS HAND. Scripture states that Abraham was "considered righteous for what he did when he offered his son Isaac on the altar" (Jas 2:21). Abraham's faith manifested itself in sincere obedience to God (see 15:6, note). The hidden life of true saving faith will inevitably become a manifested life of obedience (see Ro 1:5, note; 2:7, note; Jas 2:21, note; see article on FAITH AND GRACE, p. 1720).

22:12 NOW I KNOW THAT YOU FEAR GOD. As Abraham began to perform the sacrifice (v. 10), God saw that he had made the ultimate surrender in his heart. The Lord now knew that Abraham was a God-fearing man whose chief concern was to do God's will.

22:14 YAHWEH-YIREH. This name means "the LORD will provide." From God's test of Abraham we learn that: (1) God sometimes tests the faith of his children (cf. 1Pe 1:6–7; Heb 11:35, note). Testing must be considered an honor in God's kingdom (1Pe 4:12–14).

(2) God may be trusted to provide his presence, grace, and all that is necessary for any circumstance that lies within his will (Ps 46:1–3; 2Co 9:8; 12:9; Eph 3:20).

(3) God often works his redemptive purpose through the death of a vision; i.e., he may allow things to happen in our lives that seem to destroy our hopes and dreams (17:15–17; 22:1–12; 37:5–7,28; Mk 14:43–50; 15:25,37).

(4) After a trial of faith, God will confirm, strengthen, establish and reward the believer (vv. 16–18; 1Pe 5:10).

(5) The way to find true life in God is through the willingness to sacrifice all that God requires (cf. Mt 10:37–39; 16:24–25; Jn 12:25).

(6) After a test of suffering and faith, the outcome of all the Lord's dealings toward the believer is "full of compassion and mercy" (Jas 5:11).

22:18 BECAUSE YOU HAVE OBEYED ME. Because of Abraham's sincere, heartfelt obedience, demonstrated by his willingness to sacrifice his son, Abraham was told that God would continue his covenant promise with him (see article on GOD'S COVENANT WITH ABRAHAM, ISAAC AND JACOB, p. 46). The "offspring" that would bless the nations ultimately refers to Christ Jesus (Gal 3:8,16,18; see article on THE CALL OF ABRAHAM, p. 25).

Nahor's Sons

20Some time later Abraham was
told, "Milcah is also a mother; she has
borne sons to your brother Nahor:[t]
21Uz[u] the firstborn, Buz[v] his brother,
Kemuel (the father of Aram), **22**Kesed,
Hazo, Pildash, Jidlaph and Bethuel.[w]"
23Bethuel became the father of Rebekah.[x] Milcah bore these eight sons to
Abraham's brother Nahor.[y] **24**His concubine,[z] whose name was Reumah,
also had sons: Tebah, Gaham, Tahash
and Maacah.

The Death of Sarah

23 Sarah lived to be a hundred and
twenty-seven years old. **2**She
died at Kiriath Arba[a] (that is, Hebron)[b] in the land of Canaan, and
Abraham went to mourn for Sarah and
to weep over her.[c]

3Then Abraham rose from beside his
dead wife and spoke to the Hit-
tites.[w][d] He said, **4**"I am an alien and
a stranger[e] among you. Sell me some
property for a burial site here so I can
bury my dead.[f]"

5The Hittites replied to Abraham,
6"Sir, listen to us. You are a mighty
prince[g] among us. Bury your dead in
the choicest of our tombs. None of us
will refuse you his tomb for burying
your dead."

7Then Abraham rose and bowed
down before the people of the land, the
Hittites. **8**He said to them, "If you are
willing to let me bury my dead, then
listen to me and intercede with Ephron
son of Zohar[h] on my behalf **9**so he will
sell me the cave of Machpelah,[i] which
belongs to him and is at the end of his
field. Ask him to sell it to me for the
full price as a burial site among you."

10Ephron the Hittite was sitting
among his people and he replied to
Abraham in the hearing of all the Hittites[j] who had come to the gate[k] of
his city. **11**"No, my lord," he said. "Listen to me; I give[x][l] you the field, and
I give[x] you the cave that is in it. I
give[x] it to you in the presence of my
people. Bury your dead."

12Again Abraham bowed down before the people of the land **13**and he
said to Ephron in their hearing, "Listen
to me, if you will. I will pay the price
of the field. Accept it from me so I can
bury my dead there."

14Ephron answered Abraham,
15"Listen to me, my lord; the land is
worth four hundred shekels[y] of silver,[m] but what is that between me and
you? Bury your dead."

16Abraham agreed to Ephron's
terms and weighed out for him the
price he had named in the hearing of
the Hittites: four hundred shekels of
silver,[n] according to the weight current among the merchants.[o]

17So Ephron's field in Machpelah[p]
near Mamre[q]—both the field and the
cave in it, and all the trees within the
borders of the field—was deeded **18**to
Abraham as his property[r] in the presence of all the Hittites[s] who had come
to the gate[t] of the city. **19**Afterward
Abraham buried his wife Sarah in the
cave in the field of Machpelah[u] near
Mamre (which is at Hebron[v]) in the
land of Canaan.[w] **20**So the field and
the cave in it were deeded[x] to Abraham by the Hittites as a burial site.[y]

Isaac and Rebekah

24 Abraham was now old and well
advanced in years,[z] and the
LORD had blessed[a] him in every way.[b]
2He said to the chief[z] servant[c] in his
household, the one in charge of all that
he had,[d] "Put your hand under my
thigh.[e] **3**I want you to swear[f] by the
LORD, the God of heaven[g] and the God

[w] *3* Or *the sons of Heth*; also in verses 5, 7, 10, 16, 18 and 20 [x] *11* Or *sell* [y] *15* That is, about 10 pounds (about 4.5 kilograms)
[z] *2* Or *oldest*

22:20 [t]S Ge 11:29
22:21 [u]S Ge 10:23 [v]Job 32:2; Jer 25:23
22:22 [w]Ge 24:15, 47; 25:20
22:23 [x]Ge 24:15 [y]S Ge 11:29
22:24 [z]Ge 25:6; 35:22; 36:12; Jdg 8:31; 2Sa 3:7; 1Ki 2:22; 11:3; 1Ch 1:32; SS 6:8
23:2 [a]Jos 14:15; 15:13; 20:7; 21:11 [b]ver 19; S Ge 13:18 [c]Ge 24:67
23:3 [d]S Ge 10:15
23:4 [e]S Ge 17:8; 19:9; Ex 2:22; Lev 25:23; Ps 39:12; 105:12; 119:19; Heb 11:9, 13 [f]Ge 49:30; Ac 7:16
23:6 [g]Ge 14:14-16; 24:35
23:8 [h]Ge 25:9
23:9 [i]ver 17,19; Ge 25:9; 47:30; 49:30; 50:13
23:10 [j]ver 18 [k]S Ge 18:1; Dt 22:15; 25:7; Jos 20:4; Ru 4:11; 2Sa 15:2; 2Ki 15:35; Ps 127:5; Pr 31:23; Jer 26:10; 36:10
23:11 [l]2Sa 24:23
23:15 [m]Eze 45:12
23:16 [n]2Sa 24:24; Jer 32:9; Zec 11:12 [o]2Sa 14:26
23:17 [p]S ver 9 [q]S Ge 13:18
23:18 [r]S Ge 12:7 [s]ver 10 [t]S Ge 18:1
23:19 [u]S ver 9 [v]S Ge 13:18; Jos 14:13; 1Ch 29:27 [w]Ge 49:31
23:20 [x]Jer 32:10 [y]S Ge 10:15; 35:29; 47:30; 49:30; 50:5,13
24:1 [z]S Ge 17:17; Jos 23:1 [a]Ge 12:2; Gal 3:9 [b]ver 35
24:2 [c]S Ge 15:3 [d]Ge 39:4-6 [e]ver 9; Ge 47:29
24:3 [f]Ge 47:31; 50:25 [g]ver 7

23:20 THE FIELD ... AS A BURIAL SITE. Scripture reveals that the only piece of land in Canaan that Abraham ever possessed in fulfillment of God's promise was a grave (Heb 11:8–9). His descendants did not begin to possess the promised land until the time of Joshua. This fact points to the life of faith that waits till the end of life for the full reward of one's trust in God (Heb 11:13). Believers, like Abraham, must not set their hearts ultimately on things of this earth, but must desire a heavenly country where God "has prepared a city for them" (Heb 11:16; see 11:10, note).

24:3 NOT GET A WIFE. Abraham knew that God had called him and his descendants to live a life separated from the people around him (see article on THE CALL OF ABRAHAM, p. 25). Their separation was God's method of preserving a holy people for himself. For this reason Isaac was not permitted to marry a Canaanite woman or to return to the land from where Abraham came (vv. 3,5; see article on SPIRITUAL SEPARATION FOR BELIEVERS, p. 1794).

of earth,[h] that you will not get a wife
for my son[i] from the daughters of the
Canaanites,[j] among whom I am living,[k] **4**but will go to my country and
my own relatives[l] and get a wife for
my son Isaac.[m]"
5The servant asked him, "What if
the woman is unwilling to come back
with me to this land?[n] Shall I then
take your son back to the country you
came from?[o]"
6"Make sure that you do not take my
son back there,"[p] Abraham said.
7"The LORD, the God of heaven,[q] who
brought me out of my father's household and my native land[r] and who
spoke to me and promised me on oath,
saying, 'To your offspring[a][s] I will
give this land'[t]—he will send his angel before you[u] so that you can get a
wife for my son from there. **8**If the
woman is unwilling to come back with
you, then you will be released from this
oath[v] of mine. Only do not take my
son back there."[w] **9**So the servant put
his hand under the thigh[x] of his master[y] Abraham and swore an oath to
him concerning this matter.
10Then the servant took ten of his
master's camels[z] and left, taking with
him all kinds of good things[a] from his
master. He set out for Aram Naharaim[b][b] and made his way to the town
of Nahor.[c] **11**He had the camels kneel
down near the well[d] outside the town;
it was toward evening, the time the
women go out to draw water.[e]
12Then he prayed, "O LORD, God of
my master Abraham,[f] give me success[g] today, and show kindness[h] to
my master Abraham. **13**See, I am
standing beside this spring, and the
daughters of the townspeople are coming out to draw water.[i] **14**May it be
that when I say to a girl, 'Please let
down your jar that I may have a drink,'
and she says, 'Drink,[j] and I'll water
your camels too'[k]—let her be the one
you have chosen for your servant
Isaac.[l] By this I will know[m] that you
have shown kindness to my master."

24:3 [h] S Ge 14:19; S Nu 20:14 [i] Dt 7:3; 2Co 6:14-17 [j] S Ge 10:15-19 [k] ver 37 **24:4** [l] S Ge 12:1; Jdg 14:3 [m] S ver 29; S Ge 21:21 **24:5** [n] ver 39 [o] Heb 11:15 **24:6** [p] ver 8 **24:7** [q] ver 3 [r] Ge 12:1 [s] Ro 4:13; Gal 3:16* [t] S Ge 12:7 [u] S Ge 16:7 **24:8** [v] ver 41; Jos 2:12,17,20; 9:20 [w] S ver 6 **24:9** [x] S ver 2 [y] Ge 32:4; 33:8 **24:10** [z] ver 19; 1Ki 10:2; 1Ch 12:40; Isa 30:6 [a] ver 22, 30,47,53; Ge 43:11; 45:23 [b] Nu 23:7; Dt 23:4; Jdg 3:8 [c] S Ge 11:29 **24:11** [d] Ex 2:15 [e] ver 13; Ge 29:2, 9-10; Ex 2:16; 1Sa 9:11; Jn 4:7 **24:12** [f] ver 27,42, 48; Ge 26:24; 28:13; 31:42,53; 32:9; 43:23; 46:3; Ex 3:6,15,16; 4:5; 1Ki 18:36; Ps 75:9; 94:7 [g] ver 21,40,51,56; Ge 27:20; Ne 1:11 [h] S Ge 19:19; Jos 2:12; Job 10:12 **24:13** [i] S ver 11, 43; Ge 29:8 **24:14** [j] ver 18,46 [k] ver 19 [l] ver 44 [m] Jos 2:12; Jdg 6:17,37; 1Sa 14:10; 1Ki 13:3; Ps 86:17; Isa 38:7; Jer 44:29

24:15 [n] ver 45 [o] S Ge 22:23 [p] S Ge 22:22 [q] S Ge 11:29 [r] S Ge 11:29 **24:16** [s] S Ge 12:11 [t] Dt 22:15-21 **24:17** [u] ver 45; 1Ki 17:10; Jn 4:7 **24:18** [v] S ver 14 **24:19** [w] S ver 10 [x] ver 14 **24:20** [y] ver 46 **24:21** [z] S ver 12 **24:22** [a] ver 47; Ge 41:42;

15Before he had finished praying,[n]
Rebekah[o] came out with her jar on
her shoulder. She was the daughter of
Bethuel[p] son of Milcah,[q] who was
the wife of Abraham's brother Nahor.[r]
16The girl was very beautiful,[s] a virgin;[t] no man had ever lain with her.
She went down to the spring, filled her
jar and came up again.
17The servant hurried to meet her
and said, "Please give me a little water
from your jar."[u]
18"Drink,[v] my lord," she said, and
quickly lowered the jar to her hands
and gave him a drink.
19After she had given him a drink,
she said, "I'll draw water for your camels[w] too,[x] until they have finished
drinking." **20**So she quickly emptied
her jar into the trough, ran back to the
well to draw more water, and drew
enough for all his camels.[y] **21**Without
saying a word, the man watched her
closely to learn whether or not the
LORD had made his journey successful.[z]
22When the camels had finished
drinking, the man took out a gold nose
ring[a] weighing a beka[c] and two gold
bracelets[b] weighing ten shekels.[d]
23Then he asked, "Whose daughter are
you?[c] Please tell me, is there room in
your father's house for us to spend the
night?[d]"
24She answered him, "I am the
daughter of Bethuel, the son that Milcah bore to Nahor.[e]" **25**And she added,
"We have plenty of straw and fodder,[f]
as well as room for you to spend the
night."
26Then the man bowed down
and worshiped the LORD,[g] **27**saying,

Isa 3:21; Eze 16:11-12 [b] S ver 10 **24:23** [c] ver 47 [d] Jdg 19:15; 20:4 **24:24** [e] ver 29,47; S Ge 11:29 **24:25** [f] ver 32; Jdg 19:19 **24:26** [g] ver 48,52; Ex 4:31; 12:27; 1Ch 29:20; 2Ch 20:18

[a] *7* Or *seed* [b] *10* That is, Northwest Mesopotamia [c] *22* That is, about 1/5 ounce (about 5.5 grams) [d] *22* That is, about 4 ounces (about 110 grams)

24:12 HE PRAYED, O LORD. Abraham's servant (probably Eliezer, 15:2) was a devout man who sought the Lord through prayer. This narrative indicates that each step of his journey was marked by asking God for his blessing and guidance (cf. 1Th 5:17). Notice also that after Rebekah responded favorably, he immediately praised God (vv. 26–27). The servant's prayer and his faith in God reveal that Abraham's obedient faith was not merely private; it was active also in the lives of other members of his household.

24:14 I'LL WATER YOUR CAMELS TOO. Abraham's servant asked for a sign from God as to which girl God had chosen. Watering camels would be a difficult and laborious task. Any young woman who would voluntarily agree to such a task would be demonstrating an inner spirit of submission, helpfulness and willingness to serve.

"Praise be to the LORD,[h] the God of my
master Abraham,[i] who has not abandoned his kindness and faithfulness[j]
to my master. As for me, the LORD has
led me on the journey[k] to the house of
my master's relatives."[l]
28The girl ran and told her mother's
household about these things.[m] **29**Now
Rebekah had a brother named La-
ban,[n] and he hurried out to the man at
the spring. **30**As soon as he had seen
the nose ring, and the bracelets on his
sister's arms,[o] and had heard Rebekah tell what the man said to her, he
went out to the man and found him
standing by the camels near the
spring. **31**"Come, you who are blessed
by the LORD,"[p] he said. "Why are you
standing out here? I have prepared the
house and a place for the camels."
32So the man went to the house, and
the camels were unloaded. Straw and
fodder[q] were brought for the camels,
and water for him and his men to wash
their feet.[r] **33**Then food was set before him, but he said, "I will not eat
until I have told you what I have to
say."
"Then tell us," ⌊Laban⌋ said.
34So he said, "I am Abraham's servant.[s] **35**The LORD has blessed[t] my
master abundantly,[u] and he has become wealthy.[v] He has given him
sheep and cattle, silver and gold, menservants and maidservants, and camels and donkeys.[w] **36**My master's wife
Sarah has borne him a son in her[e] old
age,[x] and he has given him everything
he owns.[y] **37**And my master made me
swear an oath,[z] and said, 'You must
not get a wife for my son from the
daughters of the Canaanites, in whose
land I live,[a] **38**but go to my father's
family and to my own clan, and get a
wife for my son.'[b]
39"Then I asked my master, 'What if
the woman will not come back with
me?'[c]
40"He replied, 'The LORD, before
whom I have walked,[d] will send his
angel with you[e] and make your journey a success,[f] so that you can get a
wife for my son from my own clan and
from my father's family.[g] **41**Then,
when you go to my clan, you will be
released from my oath even if they refuse to give her to you—you will be
released from my oath.'
42"When I came to the spring today,
I said, 'O LORD, God of my master Abraham, if you will, please grant success[i]
to the journey on which I have come.
43See, I am standing beside this
spring;[j] if a maiden[k] comes out to
draw water and I say to her, "Please let
me drink a little water from your
jar,"[l] **44**and if she says to me, "Drink,
and I'll draw water for your camels
too," let her be the one the LORD has
chosen for my master's son.'[m]
45"Before I finished praying in my
heart,[n] Rebekah came out, with her
jar on her shoulder.[o] She went down
to the spring and drew water, and I
said to her, 'Please give me a drink.'[p]
46"She quickly lowered her jar from
her shoulder and said, 'Drink, and I'll
water your camels too.'[q] So I drank,
and she watered the camels also.[r]
47"I asked her, 'Whose daughter are
you?'[s]
"She said, 'The daughter of Bethuel[t] son of Nahor, whom Milcah bore to
him.'[u]
"Then I put the ring in her nose[v]
and the bracelets on her arms,[w] **48**and
I bowed down and worshiped the
LORD.[x] I praised the LORD, the God of
my master Abraham,[y] who had led me
on the right road to get the granddaughter of my master's brother for his
son.[z] **49**Now if you will show kindness
and faithfulness[a] to my master, tell
me; and if not, tell me, so I may know
which way to turn."
50Laban and Bethuel[b] answered,
"This is from the LORD;[c] we can say

24:27 [h] Ge 14:20; Ex 18:10; Ru 4:14; 1Sa 25:32; 2Sa 18:28; 1Ki 1:48; 8:56; Ps 28:6; 41:13; 68:19; 106:48; Lk 1:68 [i] S ver 12 [j] ver 49; Ge 32:10; 47:29; Jos 2:14; Ps 98:3 [k] ver 21 [l] S ver 12,48; S Ge 12:1
24:28 [m] Ge 29:12
24:29 [n] ver 4; Ge 25:20; 27:43; 28:2,5; 29:5,12,13
24:30 [o] S ver 10; Eze 23:42
24:31 [p] Ge 26:29; Ps 115:15
24:32 [q] S ver 25 [r] S Ge 18:4
24:34 [s] S Ge 15:3
24:35 [t] S Ge 12:2 [u] ver 1 [v] S Ge 23:6 [w] S Ge 12:16
24:36 [x] S Ge 17:17 [y] Ge 25:5; 26:14
24:37 [z] Ge 50:5, 25 [a] ver 3
24:38 [b] S Ge 21:21
24:39 [c] S ver 5
24:40 [d] S Ge 5:22 [e] S Ge 16:7 [f] S ver 12 [g] S Ge 12:1
24:41 [h] S ver 8
24:42 [i] S ver 12
24:43 [j] S ver 13 [k] Pr 30:19; Isa 7:14 [l] S ver 14
24:44 [m] ver 14
24:45 [n] 1Sa 1:13 [o] ver 15 [p] S ver 17; Jn 4:7
24:46 [q] ver 18-19 [r] ver 20
24:47 [s] ver 23 [t] S Ge 22:22 [u] S ver 24 [v] S ver 22 [w] S ver 10; Isa 3:19; Eze 16:11-12
24:48 [x] S ver 26 [y] S ver 12 [z] S ver 27
24:49 [a] S ver 27
24:50 [b] Ge 22:22 [c] Ps 118:23

[e] *36* Or *his*

24:27 THE LORD HAS LED ME. Because the servant had devoutly sought the Lord, the Lord guided him along the way. This accords with Scripture's teaching that "if the LORD delights in a man's way, he makes his steps firm" (Ps 37:23). Again, "in all your ways acknowledge him, and he will make your paths straight" (Pr 3:6). In a similar manner, all believers should expect God to faithfully guide them as he did Abraham's servant (see v. 40, note; cf. Jn 7:17; Ro 12:2).

24:40 WILL SEND HIS ANGEL WITH YOU AND MAKE YOUR JOURNEY A SUCCESS. This verse reveals one of the ways that God protects his children and guides them on their way. He may send angels to operate behind the scenes to make their way successful. Heb 1:14 states that angels are "ministering spirits sent to serve those who will inherit salvation" (see Mt 18:10, note; see article on ANGELS AND THE ANGEL OF THE LORD, p. 340).

nothing to you one way or the other.[d]
51Here is Rebekah; take her and go,
and let her become the wife of your
master's son, as the LORD has directed.[e]"
52When Abraham's servant heard
what they said, he bowed down to the
ground before the LORD.[f] 53Then the
servant brought out gold and silver
jewelry and articles of clothing[g] and
gave them to Rebekah; he also gave
costly gifts[h] to her brother and to her
mother. 54Then he and the men who
were with him ate and drank and spent
the night there.
When they got up the next morning,
he said, "Send me on my way[i] to my
master."
55But her brother and her mother replied, "Let the girl remain with us ten
days or so;[j] then you[f] may go."
56But he said to them, "Do not detain me, now that the LORD has granted
success[k] to my journey. Send me on
my way[l] so I may go to my master."
57Then they said, "Let's call the girl
and ask her about it."[m] 58So they
called Rebekah and asked her, "Will
you go with this man?"
"I will go,"[n] she said.
59So they sent their sister Rebekah
on her way,[o] along with her nurse[p]
and Abraham's servant and his men.
60And they blessed[q] Rebekah and
said to her,

"Our sister, may you increase
to thousands upon thousands;[r]
may your offspring possess
the gates of their enemies."[s]

61Then Rebekah and her maids[t]
got ready and mounted their camels
and went back with the man. So the
servant took Rebekah and left.
62Now Isaac had come from Beer Lahai Roi,[u] for he was living in the Negev.[v] 63He went out to the field one
evening to meditate,[g][w] and as he
looked up,[x] he saw camels approaching. 64Rebekah also looked up and saw
Isaac. She got down from her camel[y]
65and asked the servant, "Who is that
man in the field coming to meet us?"
"He is my master," the servant answered. So she took her veil[z] and covered herself.
66Then the servant told Isaac all he
had done. 67Isaac brought her into the
tent[a] of his mother Sarah,[b] and he
married Rebekah.[c] So she became his
wife, and he loved her;[d] and Isaac was
comforted after his mother's death.[e]

The Death of Abraham

25:1-4pp — 1Ch 1:32-33

25 Abraham took[h] another wife,
whose name was Keturah. 2She
bore him Zimran,[f] Jokshan, Medan,
Midian,[g] Ishbak and Shuah.[h] 3Jok-
shan was the father of Sheba[i] and Dedan;[j] the descendants of Dedan were
the Asshurites, the Letushites and the
Leummites. 4The sons of Midian were
Ephah,[k] Epher, Hanoch, Abida and
Eldaah. All these were descendants of
Keturah.
5Abraham left everything he owned
to Isaac.[l] 6But while he was still living, he gave gifts to the sons of his concubines[m] and sent them away from his
son Isaac[n] to the land of the east.[o]
7Altogether, Abraham lived a hundred and seventy-five years.[p] 8Then
Abraham breathed his last and died at
a good old age,[q] an old man and full
of years; and he was gathered to his
people.[r] 9His sons Isaac and Ishmael
buried him[s] in the cave of Machpelah[t] near Mamre,[u] in the field of
Ephron[v] son of Zohar the Hittite,[w]
10the field Abraham had bought from

24:50 [d]Ge 31:7, 24,29,42; 48:16 **24:51** [e]S ver 12 **24:52** [f]S ver 26 **24:53** [g]Ge 45:22; Ex 3:22; 12:35; 2Ki 5:5 [h]S ver 10, 22 **24:54** [i]ver 56,59; Ge 30:25 **24:55** [j]Jdg 19:4 **24:56** [k]S ver 12 [l]S ver 54 **24:57** [m]Jdg 19:3 **24:58** [n]Ru 1:16 **24:59** [o]S ver 54 [p]Ge 35:8 **24:60** [q]Ge 27:4, 19; 28:1; 31:55; 48:9,15,20; Jos 22:6 [r]S Ge 17:16 [s]Ge 22:17; Ps 127:5; Pr 27:11 **24:61** [t]S Ge 16:1; 30:3; 46:25 **24:62** [u]S Ge 16:14 [v]S Ge 12:9 **24:63** [w]Jos 1:8; Ps 1:2; 77:12; 119:15,27,48,97, 148; 143:5; 145:5 [x]Ge 18:2

24:64 [y]Ge 31:17, 34; 1Sa 30:17 **24:65** [z]Ge 38:14; SS 1:7; 4:1,3; 6:7; Isa 47:2 **24:67** [a]Ge 31:33 [b]S Ge 18:9 [c]Ge 25:20; 49:31 [d]Ge 29:18,20; 34:3; Jdg 16:4 [e]Ge 23:1-2 **25:2** [f]Jer 25:25 [g]Ge 36:35; 37:28, 36; Ex 2:15; Nu 22:4; 25:6,18; 31:2; Jos 13:21; Jdg 6:1,3; 7:1; 8:1, 22,24; 9:17; 1Ki 11:18; Ps 83:9; Isa 9:4; 10:26; 60:6; Hab 3:7 [h]Job 2:11; 8:1 **25:3** [i]S Ge 10:7 [j]S Ge 10:7 **25:4** [k]Isa 60:6 **25:5** [l]S Ge 24:36 **25:6** [m]S Ge 22:24 [n]S Ge 21:10,14 [o]Ge 29:1; Jdg 6:3, 33; 1Ki 4:30; Job 1:3; Eze 25:4 **25:7** [p]ver 26; Ge 12:4; 35:28; 47:9,28; 50:22,26; Job 42:16 **25:8** [q]S Ge 15:15 [r]ver 17; Ge 35:29; 49:29,33; Nu 20:24; 31:2; Dt 31:14; 32:50; 34:5 **25:9** [s]Ge 35:29; 47:30; 49:31 [t]S Ge 23:9 [u]S Ge 13:18 [v]Ge 23:8 [w]Ge 49:29; 50:13

[f]*55* Or *she* [g]*63* The meaning of the Hebrew for this word is uncertain. [h]*1* Or *had taken*

25:5 ABRAHAM LEFT EVERYTHING HE OWNED TO ISAAC. Abraham's last act was to ensure that God's covenant promise would pass on to Isaac. His concern and action provide an example to all family and church leaders, who must do all they can to ensure that the full reality of the believer's fellowship with God in truth, purity, power and blessing is passed on to the next generation. To allow God's people to drift gradually into worldliness and away from God's way is the ultimate failure in spiritual leadership (see Eph 4:11-13; see article on THE MINISTRY GIFTS OF THE CHURCH, p. 1830).

25:6 GIFTS. Most likely the gifts were an adequate inheritance for each one to establish his own flocks and herds.

25:6 CONCUBINES. See 29:28, note.

25:8 THEN ABRAHAM . . . WAS GATHERED TO HIS PEOPLE. This OT expression signifies more than mere burial; it refers to life with one's people after death (cf. 15:15; 47:30; 2Sa 12:23; Mt 22:31-32; Heb 11:13-16).

the Hittites.[i][x] There Abraham was
buried with his wife Sarah. 11After
Abraham's death, God blessed his son
Isaac,[y] who then lived near Beer Lahai Roi.[z]

Ishmael's Sons

25:12–16pp — 1Ch 1:29–31

12This is the account[a] of Abraham's son Ishmael, whom Sarah's
maidservant, Hagar[b] the Egyptian,
bore to Abraham.[c]

13These are the names of the sons of
Ishmael, listed in the order of their
birth: Nebaioth[d] the firstborn of Ishmael, Kedar,[e] Adbeel, Mibsam,
14Mishma, Dumah,[f] Massa, 15Hadad,
Tema,[g] Jetur,[h] Naphish and Kedemah. 16These were the sons of Ishmael, and these are the names of the
twelve tribal rulers[i] according to
their settlements and camps.[j] 17Alto-
gether, Ishmael lived a hundred and
thirty-seven years. He breathed his
last and died, and he was gathered to
his people.[k] 18His descendants[l] settled in the area from Havilah to Shur,[m]
near the border of Egypt, as you go toward Asshur. And they lived in hostility toward[j] all their brothers.[n]

Jacob and Esau

19This is the account[o] of Abraham's son Isaac.

Abraham became the father of Isaac,
20and Isaac was forty years old[p] when
he married Rebekah[q] daughter of Bethuel[r] the Aramean from Paddan
Aram[k][s] and sister of Laban[t] the Aramean.[u]
21Isaac prayed to the LORD on behalf
of his wife, because she was barren.[v]
The LORD answered his prayer,[w] and
his wife Rebekah became pregnant.
22The babies jostled each other within
her, and she said, "Why is this happening to me?" So she went to inquire of
the LORD.[x]
23The LORD said to her,

"Two nations[y] are in your womb,
and two peoples from within you
will be separated;
one people will be stronger than
the other,
and the older will serve the
younger.[z]"

24When the time came for her to give
birth,[a] there were twin boys in her
womb.[b] 25The first to come out was
red,[c] and his whole body was like a
hairy garment;[d] so they named him
Esau.[l][e] 26After this, his brother
came out,[f] with his hand grasping
Esau's heel;[g] so he was named Jacob.[m][h] Isaac was sixty years old[i]
when Rebekah gave birth to them.
27The boys grew up, and Esau became a skillful hunter,[j] a man of the
open country,[k] while Jacob was a quiet man, staying among the tents.
28Isaac, who had a taste for wild
game,[l] loved Esau, but Rebekah
loved Jacob.[m]

25:10 [x]S Ge 10:15 **25:11** [y]S Ge 12:2 [z]S Ge 16:14 **25:12** [a]S Ge 2:4 [b]S Ge 16:1 [c]S Ge 17:20; 21:18 **25:13** [d]Ge 28:9; 36:3 [e]Ps 120:5; SS 1:5; Isa 21:16; 42:11; 60:7; Jer 2:10; 49:28; Eze 27:21 **25:14** [f]Jos 15:52; Isa 21:11; Ob 1:1 **25:15** [g]Job 6:19; Isa 21:14; Jer 25:23 [h]1Ch 5:19 **25:16** [i]Ge 17:20 [j]S Ge 13:16; Ps 83:6 **25:17** [k]S ver 8 **25:18** [l]S Ge 17:20; 21:18 [m]S Ge 16:7 [n]Ge 16:12 **25:19** [o]S Ge 2:4 **25:20** [p]ver 26; Ge 26:34; 35:28 [q]S Ge 24:67 [r]S Ge 22:22 [s]Ge 28:2,5,6; 30:20; 31:18; 33:18; 35:9,26; 46:15; 48:7 [t]S Ge 24:29 [u]Ge 31:20,24; Dt 26:5 **25:21** [v]S Ge 11:30 [w]Ge 30:17,22; 1Sa 1:17,23; 1Ch 5:20; 2Ch 33:13; Ezr 8:23; Ps 127:3 **25:22** [x]Ex 18:15; 28:30; 33:7; Lev 24:12; Nu 9:6-8; 27:5,21; Dt 17:9; Jdg 18:5; 1Sa 9:9; 10:22; 14:36; 22:10; 1Ki 22:8; 2Ki 3:11; 22:13; Isa 30:2; Jer 21:2; 37:7,17; Eze 14:7; 20:1,3 **25:23** [y]S Ge 17:4 [z]S Ge 9:25; 48:14, 19; Ro 9:11-12* **25:24** [a]Lk 1:57; 2:6 [b]Ge 38:27 **25:25** [c]1Sa 16:12 [d]Ge 27:11 [e]Ge 27:1,15 **25:26** [f]Ge 38:29 [g]Hos 12:3 [h]Ge 27:36; 32:27; Dt 23:7; Jos 24:4; Ob 1:10,12 [i]S ver 7, S 20 **25:27** [j]S Ge 10:9 [k]ver 29; Ge 27:3,5 **25:28** [l]Ge 27: 3,4,9,14,19 [m]Ge 27:6; 37:3

[i]*10* Or *the sons of Heth* [j]*18* Or *lived to the east of* [k]*20* That is, Northwest Mesopotamia [l]*25 Esau* may mean *hairy*; he was also called Edom, which means *red.* [m]*26 Jacob* means *he grasps the heel* (figuratively, *he deceives*).

25:17 ISHMAEL ... WAS GATHERED TO HIS PEOPLE. This statement suggests that Ishmael trusted in God and received the spiritual inheritance of his father and of all who die in faith (cf. previous note).

25:21 ISAAC PRAYED TO THE LORD. Rebekah, like Sarah, was barren for many years, and Isaac had to ask the Lord for the next child of promise from whose seed the Redeemer eventually would be born. In this way God emphasizes the spiritual principle that redemption, spiritual inheritance and the fulfillment of the covenant are not realized through natural means, but through God's action and grace in response to prayer and seeking God. In other words, prayer is the means by which God chooses to grant his promises and blessings.

25:23 TWO NATIONS. The two nations are the Israelites (Jacob's descendants) and the Edomites (Esau's descendants). Hostility and conflict long characterized the relationship between these two nations (e.g., Nu 20:14–21; 2Sa 8:14; Ps 137:7).

25:23 OLDER WILL SERVE THE YOUNGER. It was customary that the younger son would serve the older. In this case, however, God reversed the pattern. This illustrates the principle that one's place in God's redemptive purpose is not determined by natural development but by God's grace and will (cf. 48:13ff; 1Sa 16:1; Ro 9:11–12).

25:26 ISAAC WAS SIXTY YEARS OLD. Because Rebekah was barren, Isaac and Rebekah had to wait twenty years for the promised offspring (cf. v. 20). The fulfillment of God's purposes in their lives came through prayer and the endurance of faith (see v. 21, note).

29Once when Jacob was cooking
some stew,[n] Esau came in from the
open country,[o] famished. **30**He said to
Jacob, "Quick, let me have some of that
red stew![p] I'm famished!" (That is
why he was also called Edom.[n])[q]
31Jacob replied, "First sell me your
birthright.[r]"
32"Look, I am about to die," Esau
said. "What good is the birthright to
me?"
33But Jacob said, "Swear[s] to me
first." So he swore an oath to him, selling his birthright[t] to Jacob.
34Then Jacob gave Esau some bread
and some lentil stew.[u] He ate and
drank, and then got up and left.
So Esau despised his birthright.

Isaac and Abimelech

26:1–11Ref — Ge 12:10–20; 20:1–18

26 Now there was a famine in the
land[v]—besides the earlier
famine of Abraham's time—and Isaac
went to Abimelech king of the Philistines[w] in Gerar.[x] **2**The LORD appeared[y] to Isaac and said, "Do not go
down to Egypt;[z] live in the land where
I tell you to live.[a] **3**Stay in this land for
a while,[b] and I will be with you[c] and
will bless you.[d] For to you and your
descendants I will give all these
lands[e] and will confirm the oath I
swore to your father Abraham.[f] **4**I will
make your descendants[g] as numerous
as the stars in the sky[h] and will give
them all these lands,[i] and through
your offspring[o] all nations on earth
will be blessed,[j] **5**because Abraham
obeyed me[k] and kept my requirements, my commands, my decrees[l]
and my laws.[m]" **6**So Isaac stayed in
Gerar.[n]
7When the men of that place asked
him about his wife, he said, "She is my
sister,[o]" because he was afraid to say,
"She is my wife." He thought, "The
men of this place might kill me on account of Rebekah, because she is beautiful."
8When Isaac had been there a long
time, Abimelech king of the Philistines[p] looked down from a window
and saw Isaac caressing his wife Rebekah. **9**So Abimelech summoned
Isaac and said, "She is really your wife!
Why did you say, 'She is my sister'?[q]"
Isaac answered him, "Because I
thought I might lose my life on account
of her."
10Then Abimelech said, "What is
this you have done to us?[r] One of the
men might well have slept with your
wife, and you would have brought guilt
upon us."
11So Abimelech gave orders to all
the people: "Anyone who molests[s]
this man or his wife shall surely be put
to death."[t]
12Isaac planted crops in that land
and the same year reaped a hundred-
fold,[u] because the LORD blessed
him.[v] **13**The man became rich, and his
wealth continued to grow until he became very wealthy.[w] **14**He had so
many flocks and herds and servants[x]
that the Philistines envied him.[y] **15**So

Ex 19:3-6

25:29 [n] 2Ki 4:38-40 [o] S ver 27
25:30 [p] ver 34 [q] Ge 32:3; 36:1,8, 8-9,19; Nu 20:14; Dt 23:7; Ps 137:7; Jer 25:21; 40:11; 49:7
25:31 [r] Dt 21:16-17; 1Ch 5:1-2
25:33 [s] S Ge 21:23; S 47:31 [t] Ge 27:36; Heb 12:16
25:34 [u] ver 30
26:1 [v] S Ge 12:10; S Dt 32:24 [w] S Ge 10:14; Jdg 10:6 [x] S Ge 20:1
26:2 [y] S Ge 12:7 [z] Ge 46:3 [a] S Ge 12:1
26:3 [b] Ge 20:1 [c] S Ge 21:20; 27:45; 31:3,5; 32:9; 35:3; 48:21; Ex 3:12; 33:14-16; Nu 23:21; Dt 31:23; Jos 1:5; Isa 43:2; Jer 1:8, 19; Hag 1:13 [d] ver 12; S Ge 12:2 [e] S Ge 12:7; Ac 7:5 [f] S Ge 17:19
26:4 [g] ver 24; Ge 48:4 [h] S Ge 12:2; S Nu 10:36 [i] S Ge 12:7 [j] S Ge 12:3; Ac 3:25*; Gal 3:8
26:5 [k] S Ge 18:19 [l] Ps 119:80,112; Eze 18:21 [m] Lev 18:4,5,26; 19:19,37; 20:8,22; 25:18; 26:3; Nu 15:40; Dt 4:40; 6:2; 11:1; 1Ki 2:3
26:6 [n] S Ge 20:1
26:7 [o] S Ge 12:13
26:8 [p] S Ge 10:14
26:9 [q] S Ge 12:19
26:10 [r] S Ge 12:18
26:11 [s] 1Sa 24:6; 26:9; Ps 105:15 [t] S Ge 20:3
26:12 [u] Mt 13:8 [v] S ver 3 **26:13** [w] S Ge 13:2; S Dt 8:18
26:14 [x] S Ge 12:16; S 24:36; 32:23 [y] Ge 37:11

[n] *30 Edom* means *red.* [o] *4* Or *seed*

25:31 BIRTHRIGHT. The birthright (i.e., the inheritance of the firstborn) consisted of: (1) leadership in worship and headship in the family; (2) a double portion of the inheritance (at least in later times, cf. Dt 21:17); and (3) the title to the covenant blessing that God had promised to Abraham. That Esau sold his birthright reveals how little value he placed on God's blessings and covenant promises. He foolishly chose to trade future long-range blessings for present momentary pleasures. Thus, he "despised his birthright" (v. 34; cf. Heb 12:16). Jacob, on the other hand, desired the spiritual blessings of the future, and from him came the twelve tribes of Israel.

26:3–4 I WILL BE WITH YOU. God appeared to Isaac and passed on to him the promises made with Abraham (12:1–3,7; 13:14–18; 15; 17:1–8, 15–22; 22:15–18). Like his father, Isaac had to learn to live by God's promises. An important part of the covenant promise was the personal relationship with God described in the words, "I will be with you" (v. 24; see 17:7, note; see article on GOD'S COVENANT WITH ABRAHAM, ISAAC AND JACOB, p. 46).

26:5 BECAUSE ABRAHAM OBEYED. God lifted up Abraham as a model of the obedience that comes from faith (cf. Ro 1:5; 16:26). Abraham had made a sincere effort to keep the Lord's laws and commands. Because of this, God blessed him. Isaac and all believers must emulate Abraham's faith and obedience if they hope to participate in God's covenant promises and salvation (cf. Lev 26:14–15,46; Dt 11:1).

26:12 THE LORD BLESSED HIM. In the OT, wealth was sometimes given as a reward for faithfulness. In the NT, by contrast, wealth is usually viewed as a potential hindrance to spiritual life and commitment to God (see 3Jn 2, note; see article on RICHES AND POVERTY, p. 1562).

GOD'S COVENANT WITH ABRAHAM, ISAAC AND JACOB

***Ge 26:3–5** "Stay in this land for a while, and I will be with you and will bless you. For to you and to your descendants I will give all these lands and will confirm the oath I swore to your father Abraham. I will make your descendants as numerous as the stars in the sky and will give them all these lands, and through your offspring all nations on earth will be blessed, because Abraham obeyed me and kept my requirements, my commands, my decrees and my laws."*

THE NATURE OF A COVENANT. God's relationship with his people is described throughout the Bible in terms of "covenant." The word first occurs in Ge 6:18 and extends into the NT, where God made a new covenant with humankind in Jesus Christ (see article on THE OLD COVENANT AND THE NEW COVENANT, p. 1926). By understanding God's covenant with the patriarchs (Abraham, Isaac and Jacob), we learn about how God wants us to live in our covenantal relationship with him.

(1) God's special covenant name as revealed in the Bible is *Yahweh* (translated as "LORD"; see Ge 2:4, note; Ex 3:14, note). Inherent in this covenant name is God's lovingkindness, his redemptive concern for the human race, his faithful presence with his people, and his desire to be in fellowship with them and to be their Lord.

(2) The fundamental promise of the covenant is the Lord's promise "to be your God and the God of your descendants after you" (see Ge 17:7, note). On this promise rest all the other promises that are a part of the covenant. It means that God firmly binds himself to his faithful people to be their God, and that his grace, protection, goodness and blessing are given to them in love (cf. Jer 11:4; 24:7; 30:22; 32:38; Eze 11:20; 36:28; Zec 8:8).

(3) The ultimate goal of God's covenant with humankind was to bring salvation, not just to one nation (Israel), but to the whole human race. Already with Abraham God promised that in him "all peoples on earth" would be blessed (Ge 12:3; 18:18; 22:18; cf. 26:4). God extended his covenant grace to the nation of Israel in order that they might be "a light for the Gentiles" (Isa 49:6; cf. 42:6). This covenant was fulfilled through the coming of the Lord Jesus Christ as Redeemer, when Christians began to spread the message of the gospel throughout the world (see Lk 2:32; Ac 13:46–47; Gal 3:8–14).

(4) In the various covenantal arrangements that God made with humans throughout Scripture, two principles are operative: (a) God alone established the promises and obligations of his covenant, and (b) human beings were expected to accept them in obedient faith. On some occasions God outlined fully ahead of time the promises and responsibilities for both parties (see article on GOD'S COVENANT WITH THE ISRAELITES, p. 290); at no time, however, were people in a situation where they could bargain with God about the stipulations of the covenant.

GOD'S COVENANT WITH ABRAHAM. (1) When God entered into covenant fellowship with Abraham (see Ge 15), he explicitly offered several promises: God as Abraham's shield and reward (Ge 15:1), many descendants (Ge 15:5) and the land of Canaan as his inheritance (Ge 15:7; see Ge 15:6, note; 17:8, note; cf. also 12:1–3; see article on THE CALL OF ABRAHAM, p. 25).

(2) God called on Abraham to respond in faith to these promises, to accept them and to trust in God as his Lord. Because he did so, Abraham was accepted by God as righteous (Ge 15:6) and was confirmed in a personal relationship with him.

(3) Not only was faith necessary to receive the covenant initially, but God also required that if covenant blessings were to continue, Abraham had to make a sincere effort to please him through an obedient life. (a) God demanded that Abraham walk before him and "be blameless" (see Ge 17:1, note). In other words, if his faith were not accompanied

by obedience (cf. Ro 1:5), Abraham would disqualify himself from participation in God's eternal purposes. (b) In one specific instance, God tested Abraham by commanding him to sacrifice his son Isaac (Ge 22:1–2). Abraham passed the test, and consequently God promised to continue his covenant with him (see Ge 22:18, note). (c) God specifically informed Isaac that the blessings of the covenant were still valid and would be passed on to him, *because* Abraham had obeyed him and kept his commands (Ge 26:4–5).

(4) God specifically commanded Abraham and his descendants to see to it that every male child born in his household be circumcised (Ge 17:9–13). The Lord went on to stipulate that any male who was not circumcised would be cut off from God's people (Ge 17:14), for he had broken the covenant. In other words, refusal to obey God would lead to the removal of covenant blessings.

(5) God's covenant with Abraham was called an "everlasting covenant" (Ge 17:7). God intended that the covenant be a permanent arrangement. However, it could be broken by Abraham's descendants, so that God would no longer be bound to his promises. For example, his promise that the land of Canaan would be an everlasting possession for Abraham and his descendants (Ge 17:8) was broken by Israel's apostasy and Judah's unfaithfulness and their refusal to obey God's law (Isa 24:5; Jer 31:32); thus Israel was carried away into exile in Assyria (2Ki 17), while Judah was later carried away captive to Babylon (see 2Ki 25; 2Ch 36; Jer 11:1–17; Eze 17:16–21).

GOD'S COVENANT WITH ISAAC. (1) God sought to establish the Abrahamic covenant with each succeeding generation, beginning with Abraham's son Isaac (see Ge 17:21). In other words, it was not enough that Isaac had Abraham as his father; he too had to accept God's promises by faith. Only then would God say, "I am with you; I will bless you and will increase the number of your descendants" (Ge 26:24).

(2) For the first twenty years of their marriage, Isaac and Rebekah had no children (cf. Ge 25:20,26). Rebekah's womb was not opened until Isaac earnestly prayed to the Lord for his wife to conceive (Ge 25:21). This answered prayer demonstrates that the covenant's fulfillment is not realized through natural means, but only by God's gracious action in response to prayer and seeking him (see Ge 25:21, note).

(3) Isaac also had to be obedient in order to continue receiving the covenant blessings. When a famine struck the land of Canaan, for example, God told Isaac not to go down to Egypt but to remain where he was. If he obeyed God, God promised to "confirm the oath I swore to your father Abraham" (Ge 26:3; see 26:5, note).

GOD'S COVENANT WITH JACOB. (1) Isaac and Rebekah had two children, Esau and Jacob. Normally one would expect the blessings of the covenant to be passed on through the firstborn, i.e., Esau. But God revealed to Rebekah that her older twin would serve the younger, and Esau himself despised his birthright (see Ge 25:31, note). Furthermore, he showed indifference to the righteous standards of his parents by marrying two women who were not followers of the true God. In summary, Esau showed no interest in God's covenant blessings. Consequently, Jacob, who did desire the spiritual blessings of the future, received the promises rather than Esau (Ge 28:13–15).

(2) As with Abraham and Isaac, the covenant with Jacob required the "obedience that comes from faith" (Ro 1:5) for its continuance. For much of his life, this patriarch depended on his own ingenuity to survive and succeed. It was not until Jacob finally obeyed the Lord's command and will (Ge 31:13) to leave Haran and return to the promised land of Canaan, and more specifically, to go to Bethel (Ge 35:1–7), that God renewed with him the covenant promises made to Abraham (Ge 35:9–13).

For more on covenant, see article on GOD'S COVENANT WITH THE ISRAELITES, p. 290.

all the wells[z] that his father's servants had dug in the time of his father
Abraham, the Philistines stopped up,[a]
filling them with earth.
16 Then Abimelech said to Isaac,
"Move away from us;[b] you have become too powerful for us.[c]"
17 So Isaac moved away from there
and encamped in the Valley of Gerar[d]
and settled there. 18 Isaac reopened the
wells[e] that had been dug in the time
of his father Abraham, which the Philistines had stopped up after Abraham
died, and he gave them the same
names his father had given them.
19 Isaac's servants dug in the valley
and discovered a well of fresh water
there. 20 But the herdsmen of Gerar
quarreled[f] with Isaac's herdsmen and
said, "The water is ours!"[g] So he
named the well Esek,[p] because they
disputed with him. 21 Then they dug another well, but they quarreled[h] over
that one also; so he named it Sitnah.[q]
22 He moved on from there and dug another well, and no one quarreled over
it. He named it Rehoboth,[r][i] saying,
"Now the LORD has given us room[j] and
we will flourish[k] in the land."
23 From there he went up to Beersheba.[l] 24 That night the LORD appeared
to him and said, "I am the God of your
father Abraham.[m] Do not be afraid,[n]
for I am with you;[o] I will bless you and
will increase the number of your
descendants[p] for the sake of my servant Abraham."[q]
25 Isaac built an altar[r] there and
called on the name of the LORD.[s] There
he pitched his tent, and there his servants dug a well.[t]
26 Meanwhile, Abimelech had come
to him from Gerar, with Ahuzzath his
personal adviser and Phicol the commander of his forces.[u] 27 Isaac asked
them, "Why have you come to me, since
you were hostile to me and sent me
away?[v]"

26:15 [z] S Ge 21:30 [a] S Ge 21:25 **26:16** [b] ver 27; Jdg 11:7 [c] Ex 1:9; Ps 105:24-25 **26:17** [d] S Ge 20:1 **26:18** [e] S Ge 21:30 **26:20** [f] S Ge 13:7 [g] Ge 21:25 **26:21** [h] S Ge 13:7 **26:22** [i] Ge 36:37 [j] Ps 18:19; Isa 33:20; 54:2; Am 9:11 [k] S Ge 17:6 **26:23** [l] S Ge 22:19 **26:24** [m] S Ge 24:12 [n] S Ge 15:1; S Jos 8:1 [o] S Ge 21:20 [p] S ver 4 [q] ver 4; Ge 17:7; S 22:17; 28:14; 30:27; 39:5; Dt 13:17 **26:25** [r] S Ge 8:20 [s] S Ge 4:26; S Ac 2:21 [t] S Ge 21:30 **26:26** [u] S Ge 21:22 **26:27** [v] S ver 16 **26:28** [w] S Ge 21:22 [x] S Ge 21:27; Jos 9:6 **26:29** [y] Ge 31:29, 52 [z] S Ge 24:31 **26:30** [a] Ge 31:54; Ex 18:12; 24:11; 1Sa 20:27 **26:31** [b] S Ge 21:23,27 **26:32** [c] S Ge 21:30 **26:33** [d] S Ge 21:14 **26:34** [e] S Ge 25:20 [f] S Ge 10:15; 28:9; 36:2; Jos 3:10; 1Sa 26:6; 1Ki 10:29 **26:35** [g] Ge 27:46; 28:8; Job 7:16 **27:1** [h] Ge 48:10; Dt 34:7; 1Sa 3:2 [i] S Ge 25:25 **27:2** [j] Ge 47:29; 1Ki 2:1 **27:3** [k] S Ge 25:27 **27:4** [l] S Ge 25:28

28 They answered, "We saw clearly
that the LORD was with you;[w] so we
said, 'There ought to be a sworn agreement between us'—between us and
you. Let us make a treaty[x] with you
29 that you will do us no harm,[y] just as
we did not molest you but always treated you well and sent you away in
peace. And now you are blessed by the
LORD."[z]
30 Isaac then made a feast[a] for
them, and they ate and drank. 31 Early
the next morning the men swore an
oath[b] to each other. Then Isaac sent
them on their way, and they left him in
peace.
32 That day Isaac's servants came
and told him about the well[c] they had
dug. They said, "We've found water!"
33 He called it Shibah,[s] and to this day
the name of the town has been Beersheba.[t][d]
34 When Esau was forty years old,[e]
he married Judith daughter of Beeri the
Hittite, and also Basemath daughter of
Elon the Hittite.[f] 35 They were a
source of grief to Isaac and Rebekah.[g]

Jacob Gets Isaac's Blessing

27 When Isaac was old and his
eyes were so weak that he
could no longer see,[h] he called for
Esau his older son[i] and said to him,
"My son."
"Here I am," he answered.
2 Isaac said, "I am now an old man
and don't know the day of my death.[j]
3 Now then, get your weapons—your
quiver and bow—and go out to the
open country[k] to hunt some wild
game for me. 4 Prepare me the kind of
tasty food I like[l] and bring it to me to

[p] 20 *Esek* means *dispute.* [q] 21 *Sitnah* means *opposition.* [r] 22 *Rehoboth* means *room.*
[s] 33 *Shibah* can mean *oath* or *seven.*
[t] 33 *Beersheba* can mean *well of the oath* or *well of seven.*

26:35 A SOURCE OF GRIEF TO ISAAC AND REBEKAH. Esau was indifferent to the righteous standards of his parents, for he married two women who were not followers of the true God. This action also demonstrated his lack of interest in God's covenant blessing.

27:1 WHEN ISAAC WAS OLD. Ch. 27 portrays Isaac and his family pursuing God's blessing in an unrighteous way. Isaac's personal preference for Esau, contrary to God's will, and deceptive manipulation by Rebekah and Jacob took preeminence over the spiritual good of God's covenant. Whenever God's work is undertaken in unrighteous ways, damage is done to God's purpose and to all those involved.

27:4 I MAY GIVE YOU MY BLESSING. The birthright blessing and the father's oral declaration were legally binding in ancient Near Eastern law (cf. 49:28–33). Isaac appeared to have forgotten or ignored God's word that Esau would serve Jacob, the younger (25:23). He also disregarded the fact that Esau had married two pagan women (cf. 26:34–35). Furthermore, Isaac made no attempt to seek or consider God's will in the matter.

eat, so that I may give you my blessing[m] before I die."[n]
5 Now Rebekah was listening as
Isaac spoke to his son Esau. When
Esau left for the open country[o] to
hunt game and bring it back, 6 Rebekah
said to her son Jacob,[p] "Look, I overheard your father say to your brother
Esau, 7 'Bring me some game and prepare me some tasty food to eat, so that
I may give you my blessing in the presence of the LORD before I die.'[q] 8 Now,
my son, listen carefully and do what I
tell you:[r] 9 Go out to the flock and
bring me two choice young goats,[s] so
I can prepare some tasty food for your
father, just the way he likes it.[t]
10 Then take it to your father to eat, so
that he may give you his blessing[u] before he dies."
11 Jacob said to Rebekah his mother,
"But my brother Esau is a hairy man,[v]
and I'm a man with smooth skin.
12 What if my father touches me?[w] I
would appear to be tricking him and
would bring down a curse[x] on myself
rather than a blessing."
13 His mother said to him, "My son,
let the curse fall on me.[y] Just do what
I say;[z] go and get them for me."
14 So he went and got them and
brought them to his mother, and she
prepared some tasty food, just the way
his father liked it.[a] 15 Then Rebekah
took the best clothes[b] of Esau her older son,[c] which she had in the house,
and put them on her younger son Jacob. 16 She also covered his hands and
the smooth part of his neck with the
goatskins.[d] 17 Then she handed to her
son Jacob the tasty food and the bread
she had made.
18 He went to his father and said,
"My father."
"Yes, my son," he answered. "Who is
it?"[e]
19 Jacob said to his father, "I am
Esau your firstborn.[f] I have done as
you told me. Please sit up and eat some
of my game[g] so that you may give me
your blessing."[h]
20 Isaac asked his son, "How did you
find it so quickly, my son?"
"The LORD your God gave me success,[i]" he replied.
21 Then Isaac said to Jacob, "Come
near so I can touch you,[j] my son, to
know whether you really are my son
Esau or not."
22 Jacob went close to his father
Isaac,[k] who touched[l] him and said,
"The voice is the voice of Jacob, but the
hands are the hands of Esau." 23 He did
not recognize him, for his hands were
hairy like those of his brother Esau;[m]
so he blessed him. 24 "Are you really
my son Esau?" he asked.
"I am," he replied.
25 Then he said, "My son, bring me
some of your game to eat, so that I may
give you my blessing."[n]
Jacob brought it to him and he ate;
and he brought some wine and he
drank. 26 Then his father Isaac said to
him, "Come here, my son, and kiss
me."
27 So he went to him and kissed[o]
him[p]. When Isaac caught the smell of
his clothes,[q] he blessed him and said,

"Ah, the smell of my son
is like the smell of a field
that the LORD has blessed.[r]
28 May God give you of heaven's
dew[s]
and of earth's richness[t]—
an abundance of grain[u] and
new wine.[v]
29 May nations serve you
and peoples bow down to you.[w]
Be lord over your brothers,
and may the sons of your
mother bow down to you.[x]
May those who curse you be
cursed

27:4 [m] ver 10,25, 31; S Ge 24:60; 49:28; Dt 33:1; Heb 11:20 [n] ver 7
27:5 [o] S Ge 25:27
27:6 [p] S Ge 25:28
27:7 [q] ver 4
27:8 [r] ver 13,43
27:9 [s] 1Sa 16:20 [t] S Ge 25:28
27:10 [u] S ver 4
27:11 [v] Ge 25:25
27:12 [w] ver 22 [x] S Ge 9:25
27:13 [y] Mt 27:25 [z] S ver 8
27:14 [a] S Ge 25:28
27:15 [b] ver 27; SS 4:11 [c] S Ge 25:25
27:16 [d] ver 22-23
27:18 [e] ver 32
27:19 [f] ver 32 [g] S Ge 25:28 [h] S ver 4
27:20 [i] S Ge 24:12
27:21 [j] ver 12
27:22 [k] Ge 45:4 [l] ver 12
27:23 [m] ver 16
27:25 [n] S ver 4
27:27 [o] Ge 31:28, 55; 33:4; 48:10; Ex 4:27; 18:7; Ru 1:9; 1Sa 20:41; 2Sa 14:33; 19:39 [p] Heb 11:20 [q] S ver 15 [r] Ps 65:9-13
27:28 [s] Dt 33:13; 2Sa 1:21; Job 18:16; 29:19; Pr 3:20; Isa 26:19; Hos 14:5; Hag 1:10; Zec 8:12 [t] ver 39; Ge 49:25; Lev 26:20; Dt 33:13 [u] Ps 65:9; 72:16 [v] ver 37; Nu 18:12; Dt 7:13; 33:28; 2Ki 18:32; Ps 4:7; Isa 36:17; Jer 31:12; 40:10
27:29 [w] 2Sa 8:14; Ps 68:31; 72:11; Isa 19:21,23; 27:13; 45:14,23; 49:7,23; 60:12,14; 66:23; Jer 12:17; Da 2:44; Zec 14:17-18 [x] S Ge 9:25; S 25:23; S 37:7

27:6–17 REBEKAH SAID TO HER SON JACOB. Rebekah and Jacob sought to fulfill God's covenant purposes through deception and manipulation. They had lost sight of the basic reason for God's blessing—to bring about a godly and just people who walked with God in faith and obedience. Rebekah suffered greatly for her deceitful scheme, for Jacob had to flee, and she never saw her son again (v. 43; 28:5).

27:19 JACOB SAID TO HIS FATHER. If only Jacob had trusted God and committed his way to the Lord, he would have gained the blessing in God's own time. Yet he lied twice to obtain the blessing in his own way (vv. 19–20). (1) He got what he wanted, yet it cost him dearly. He had to flee for his life and give up his possessions and the comforts of home. He reaped deceitful treatment himself (29:20–25; 31:7; 37:32–36) and lived many years in exile (31:41). All his life he had one misfortune after another until he finally stated: "My years have been few and difficult" (47:9). (2) Jacob's actions and experiences should be pondered by all who misrepresent facts and deceive others in the work of God's kingdom. Spiritual success must be gained by righteous means, not by manipulation and deception.

and those who bless you be
blessed.[y]"

30After Isaac finished blessing him
and Jacob had scarcely left his father's
presence, his brother Esau came in
from hunting. **31**He too prepared some
tasty food and brought it to his father.
Then he said to him, "My father, sit up
and eat some of my game, so that you
may give me your blessing."[z]
32His father Isaac asked him, "Who
are you?"[a]

"I am your son," he answered, "your
firstborn, Esau.[b]"

33Isaac trembled violently and said,
"Who was it, then, that hunted game
and brought it to me?[c] I ate it just before you came and I blessed him—and
indeed he will be blessed![d]"

34When Esau heard his father's
words, he burst out with a loud and bitter cry[e] and said to his father,
"Bless[f] me—me too, my father!"

35But he said, "Your brother came
deceitfully[g] and took your blessing."[h]

36Esau said, "Isn't he rightly named
Jacob[u]?[i] He has deceived[j] me these
two times: He took my birthright,[k]
and now he's taken my blessing!"[l]
Then he asked, "Haven't you reserved
any blessing for me?"

37Isaac answered Esau, "I have
made him lord over you and have made
all his relatives his servants, and I
have sustained him with grain and new
wine.[m] So what can I possibly do for
you, my son?"

38Esau said to his father, "Do you
have only one blessing, my father?
Bless me too, my father!" Then Esau
wept aloud.[n]

39His father Isaac answered him,[o]

"Your dwelling will be
away from the earth's richness,
away from the dew[p] of heaven
above.[q]
40You will live by the sword
and you will serve[r] your
brother.[s]
But when you grow restless,
you will throw his yoke
from off your neck.[t]"

Jacob Flees to Laban

41Esau held a grudge[u] against Jacob[v] because of the blessing his father had given him. He said to himself,
"The days of mourning[w] for my father
are near; then I will kill[x] my brother
Jacob."[y]

42When Rebekah was told what her
older son Esau[z] had said, she sent for
her younger son Jacob and said to him,
"Your brother Esau is consoling himself with the thought of killing you.[a]
43Now then, my son, do what I say:[b]
Flee at once to my brother Laban[c] in
Haran.[d] **44**Stay with him for a while[e]
until your brother's fury subsides.
45When your brother is no longer angry
with you and forgets what you did to
him,[f] I'll send word for you to come
back from there.[g] Why should I lose
both of you in one day?"

46Then Rebekah said to Isaac, "I'm
disgusted with living because of these
Hittite[h] women. If Jacob takes a wife
from among the women of this land,[i]
from Hittite women like these, my life
will not be worth living."[j]

28 So Isaac called for Jacob and
blessed[v][k] him and commanded him: "Do not marry a Canaanite
woman.[l] **2**Go at once to Paddan
Aram,[w][m] to the house of your mother's father Bethuel.[n] Take a wife for
yourself there, from among the daughters of Laban, your mother's brother.[o]
3May God Almighty[x][p] bless[q] you
and make you fruitful[r] and increase
your numbers[s] until you become a
community of peoples. **4**May he give
you and your descendants the blessing
given to Abraham,[t] so that you may
take possession of the land[u] where

27:29 [y] ver 33; Ge 12:3
27:31 [z] S ver 4
27:32 [a] ver 18 [b] ver 19
27:33 [c] ver 35 [d] S ver 29
27:34 [e] Heb 12:17 [f] Ex 12:32
27:35 [g] Jer 9:4; 12:6 [h] ver 19,45
27:36 [i] S Ge 25:26 [j] Ge 29:25; 31:20, 26; 34:13; 1Sa 28:12 [k] S Ge 25:33 [l] Heb 12:16-17
27:37 [m] S ver 28; Dt 16:13; Ezr 6:9; Isa 16:10; Jer 40:12
27:38 [n] Ge 29:11; Nu 14:1; Jdg 2:4; 21:2; Ru 1:9; 1Sa 11:4; 30:4; Heb 12:17
27:39 [o] Heb 11:20 [p] ver 28 [q] Ge 36:6
27:40 [r] 2Sa 8:14 [s] S Ge 9:25 [t] 2Ki 8:20-22
27:41 [u] Ge 37:4; 49:23; 50:15; 1Sa 17:28 [v] Ge 31:17; 32:11; Hos 10:14 [w] Ge 50:4,10; Nu 20:29 [x] ver 42 [y] Ob 1:10
27:42 [z] Ge 32:3, 11; 33:4 [a] ver 41
27:43 [b] S ver 8 [c] S Ge 24:29 [d] S Ge 11:31
27:44 [e] Ge 31:38, 41
27:45 [f] S ver 35 [g] S Ge 26:3
27:46 [h] S Ge 10:15 [i] S Ge 10:15-19 [j] S Ge 26:35; S Job 7:7
28:1 [k] S Ge 24:60 [l] Ge 24:3
28:2 [m] S Ge 25:20 [n] S Ge 25:20 [o] S Ge 21:21; S 24:29
28:3 [p] S Ge 17:1 [q] Ge 48:16; Nu 6:24; Ru 2:4; Ps 129:8; 134:3; Jer 31:23 [r] S Ge 17:6 [s] S Ge 12:2
28:4 [t] S Ge 12:2,3 [u] S Ge 15:7

[u] *36 Jacob* means *he grasps the heel* (figuratively, *he deceives*). [v] *1* Or *greeted* [w] *2* That is, Northwest Mesopotamia; also in verses 5, 6 and 7 [x] *3* Hebrew *El-Shaddai*

27:38 ESAU WEPT ALOUD. According to Heb 12:16–17, Esau lost his blessing because he was a godless person who had despised the sacredness of the blessing (cf. 25:31–34). Now he changed his mind and sought the blessing with tears, yet his tears were tears of disappointment and anger, not of sorrow for his own sinful choices. Esau's experience warns us about wrong choices in life that bring terrible consequences that cannot be undone (see 2Sa 12:7–14).

28:4 THE BLESSING GIVEN TO ABRAHAM. The blessing given to Abraham is the land: "so that you may take possession of the land . . . God gave to Abraham." Note that when Paul applies this to NT believers ("Abraham's seed," Gal 3:29), he does so concerning spiritual rather than material blessings—specifically, the promise of the Spirit through faith (Gal 3:14).

you now live as an alien,[v] the land
God gave to Abraham." **5**Then Isaac
sent Jacob on his way,[w] and he went
to Paddan Aram,[x] to Laban son of Bethuel the Aramean,[y] the brother of
Rebekah,[z] who was the mother of Jacob and Esau.
6Now Esau learned that Isaac had
blessed Jacob and had sent him to Paddan Aram to take a wife from there,
and that when he blessed him he commanded him, "Do not marry a Canaanite woman,"[a] **7**and that Jacob had
obeyed his father and mother and had
gone to Paddan Aram. **8**Esau then realized how displeasing the Canaanite
women[b] were to his father Isaac;[c]
9so he went to Ishmael[d] and married
Mahalath, the sister of Nebaioth[e] and
daughter of Ishmael son of Abraham,
in addition to the wives he already
had.[f]

Jacob's Dream at Bethel

10Jacob left Beersheba[g] and set out
for Haran.[h] **11**When he reached a certain place,[i] he stopped for the night
because the sun had set. Taking one of
the stones there, he put it under his
head[j] and lay down to sleep. **12**He had
a dream[k] in which he saw a stairway[y] resting on the earth, with its top
reaching to heaven, and the angels of
God were ascending and descending on
it.[l] **13**There above it[z] stood the
LORD,[m] and he said: "I am the LORD, the
God of your father Abraham and the
God of Isaac.[n] I will give you and your
descendants the land[o] on which you
are lying.[p] **14**Your descendants will be
like the dust of the earth, and you[q]
will spread out to the west and to the
east, to the north and to the south.[r]
All peoples on earth will be blessed
through you and your offspring.[s] **15**I
am with you[t] and will watch over
you[u][v] wherever you go,[w] and I will
bring you back to this land.[x] I will not
leave you[y] until I have done what I
have promised you.[z]"[a]
16When Jacob awoke from his
sleep,[b] he thought, "Surely the LORD is
in this place, and I was not aware of it."
17He was afraid and said, "How awesome is this place![c] This is none other
than the house of God;[d] this is the
gate of heaven."
18Early the next morning Jacob took
the stone he had placed under his
head[e] and set it up as a pillar[f] and
poured oil on top of it.[g] **19**He called
that place Bethel,[a][h] though the city
used to be called Luz.[i]
20Then Jacob made a vow,[j] saying,
"If God will be with me and will watch
over me[k] on this journey I am taking
and will give me food to eat and clothes
to wear[l] **21**so that I return safely[m] to
my father's house,[n] then the LORD[b]
will be my God[o] **22**and[c] this stone
that I have set up as a pillar[p] will be
God's house,[q] and of all that you give
me I will give you a tenth.[r]"

Jacob Arrives in Paddan Aram

29 Then Jacob continued on his
journey and came to the land of
the eastern peoples.[s] **2**There he saw
a well in the field, with three flocks of
sheep lying near it because the flocks
were watered from that well.[t] The
stone[u] over the mouth of the well was
large. **3**When all the flocks were gathered there, the shepherds would roll
the stone[v] away from the well's
mouth and water the sheep.[w] Then
they would return the stone to its place
over the mouth of the well.
4Jacob asked the shepherds, "My
brothers, where are you from?"[x]
"We're from Haran,[y]" they replied.
5He said to them, "Do you know Laban, Nahor's grandson?"[z]

28:4 [v]S Ge 17:8 **28:5** [w]S Ge 11:31 [x]Hos 12:12 [y]S Ge 25:20 [z]S Ge 24:29 **28:6** [a]S ver 1 **28:8** [b]S Ge 10:15-19 [c]S Ge 26:35 **28:9** [d]S Ge 16:15 [e]S Ge 25:13 [f]S Ge 26:34 **28:10** [g]S Ge 21:14 [h]S Ge 11:31 **28:11** [i]S Ge 12:8 [j]ver 18 **28:12** [k]S Ge 20:3; 37:19 [l]Jn 1:51 **28:13** [m]S Ge 12:7; 35:7, 9; 48:3 [n]S Ge 24:12; 48:16; 49:25; 50:17 [o]S Ge 12:7 [p]Ge 46:4; 48:21 **28:14** [q]Ge 26:4 [r]S Ge 12:2; S 13:14; S 26:24 [s]S Ge 12:3; Ac 3:25; Gal 3:8 **28:15** [t]S Ge 21:20 [u]Ps 121:5,7-8 [v]ver 20 [w]ver 22; Ge 35:3 [x]ver 21; S Ge 15:16; 30:25; 31:30 [y]Dt 31:6,8; Jos 1:5; Ne 4:14; Ps 9:10 [z]Lev 26:42 [a]Ps 105:10

28:16 [b]1Ki 3:15; Jer 31:26 **28:17** [c]Ex 3:5; 19:21; Jos 5:15; Ps 68:24,35 [d]ver 22; Ge 32:2; 1Ch 22:1; 2Ch 3:1 **28:18** [e]ver 11 [f]ver 22; Ge 31:13, 45,51; 35:14; Ex 24:4; Jos 24:26,27; Isa 19:19 [g]Lev 8:11; Jos 4:9 **28:19** [h]S Ge 12:8 [i]Ge 35:6; 48:3; Jos 16:2; 18:13; Jdg 1:23,26 **28:20** [j]Ge 31:13; Lev 7:16; 22:18; 23:38; 27:2,9; Nu 6:2; 15:3; Dt 12:6; Jdg 11:30; 1Sa 1:21; 2Sa 15:8 [k]S ver 15 [l]1Ti 6:8 **28:21** [m]Jdg 11:31 [n]S ver 15 [o]Ex 15:2; Dt 26:17; Jos 24:18; Ps 48:14; 118:28 **28:22** [p]S ver 18; 1Sa 7:12 [q]S ver 17 [r]S Ge 14:20; S Nu 18:21; Lk 18:12 **29:1** [s]S Ge 25:6 **29:2** [t]S Ge 24:11 [u]ver 3,8,10 **29:3** [v]S ver 2 [w]ver 8 **29:4** [x]Ge 42:7; Jdg 19:17 [y]S Ge 11:31 **29:5** [z]S Ge 11:29

[y]*12* Or *ladder* [z]*13* Or *There beside him*
[a]*19* *Bethel* means *house of God.*
[b]*20,21* Or *Since God . . . father's house, the LORD*
[c]*21,22* Or *house, and the LORD will be my God, 22then*

28:12 THE ANGELS OF GOD. The vision of the angels suggests that they played an important part in God's protection and guidance of his people. Under the new covenant, angels are also active in the lives of believers (see 24:40, note).

28:13–15 ABOVE IT STOOD THE LORD. God came to Jacob with the message that the blessing promised to Abraham would be carried on through him (cf. 12:3; 13:14–17). With this blessing came the promise of God's presence, guidance and protection.

28:19 BETHEL. "Bethel" means "house of God" and may represent any place where God is present in a very special sense.

29:5 LABAN. Laban was Jacob's uncle. Jacob was looking for his mother's family near Haran (v. 10; cf. 24:15,50).

"Yes, we know him," they answered.
6Then Jacob asked them, "Is he
well?"
"Yes, he is," they said, "and here
comes his daughter Rachel[a] with the
sheep.[b]"
7"Look," he said, "the sun is still
high; it is not time for the flocks to be
gathered. Water the sheep and take
them back to pasture."
8"We can't," they replied, "until all
the flocks are gathered and the stone[c]
has been rolled away from the mouth
of the well. Then we will water[d] the
sheep."
9While he was still talking with
them, Rachel came with her father's
sheep,[e] for she was a shepherdess.
10When Jacob saw Rachel[f] daughter
of Laban, his mother's brother, and Laban's sheep, he went over and rolled
the stone[g] away from the mouth of the
well and watered[h] his uncle's
sheep.[i] 11Then Jacob kissed[j] Rachel
and began to weep aloud.[k] 12He had
told Rachel that he was a relative[l] of
her father and a son of Rebekah.[m] So
she ran and told her father.[n]
13As soon as Laban[o] heard the
news about Jacob, his sister's son, he
hurried to meet him. He embraced
him[p] and kissed him and brought him
to his home, and there Jacob told him
all these things. 14Then Laban said to
him, "You are my own flesh and
blood."[q]

Jacob Marries Leah and Rachel

After Jacob had stayed with him for
a whole month, 15Laban said to him,
"Just because you are a relative[r] of
mine, should you work for me for nothing? Tell me what your wages[s] should
be."
16Now Laban had two daughters;
the name of the older was Leah,[t] and
the name of the younger was Rachel.[u]
17Leah had weak[d] eyes, but Rachel[v]
was lovely in form, and beautiful.[w]
18Jacob was in love with Rachel[x] and
said, "I'll work for you seven years in
return for your younger daughter Rachel."[y]
19Laban said, "It's better that I give
her to you than to some other man.
Stay here with me." 20So Jacob served
seven years to get Rachel,[z] but they
seemed like only a few days to him because of his love for her.[a]
21Then Jacob said to Laban, "Give
me my wife. My time is completed, and
I want to lie with her.[b]"
22So Laban brought together all the
people of the place and gave a feast.[c]
23But when evening came, he took his
daughter Leah[d] and gave her to Jacob,
and Jacob lay with her. 24And Laban
gave his servant girl Zilpah[e] to his
daughter as her maidservant.[f]
25When morning came, there was
Leah! So Jacob said to Laban, "What is
this you have done to me?[g] I served
you for Rachel, didn't I? Why have you
deceived me?[h]"
26Laban replied, "It is not our custom here to give the younger daughter
in marriage before the older one.[i]
27Finish this daughter's bridal week;[j]
then we will give you the younger one
also, in return for another seven years
of work.[k]"
28And Jacob did so. He finished the
week with Leah, and then Laban gave
him his daughter Rachel to be his
wife.[l] 29Laban gave his servant girl
Bilhah[m] to his daughter Rachel as her
maidservant.[n] 30Jacob lay with Rachel also, and he loved Rachel more
than Leah.[o] And he worked for Laban
another seven years.[p]

29:6 [a]Ge 30:22-24; 35:16; 46:19,22 [b]Ex 2:16 **29:8** [c]S ver 2 [d]S Ge 24:13 **29:9** [e]Ex 2:16 **29:10** [f]ver 16 [g]S ver 2 [h]S Ge 24:11 [i]ver 3; Ex 2:17 **29:11** [j]ver 13 [k]Ge 33:4; 42:24; 43:30; 45:2,14-15; 46:29; 50:1,17; Ru 1:9 **29:12** [l]ver 15 [m]S Ge 24:29 [n]Ge 24:28 **29:13** [o]S Ge 24:29 [p]Ge 33:4; 45:14-15,14; 48:10; Ex 4:27; 18:7; Lk 15:20 **29:14** [q]Ge 2:23; 37:27; Jdg 9:2; 2Sa 5:1; 19:12-13; 20:1; Ne 5:5; Isa 58:7 **29:15** [r]ver 12 [s]Ge 30:28,32; 31:7,41 **29:16** [t]ver 17,23, 28,30; Ge 30:9; 35:23; 47:30; 49:31; Ru 4:11 [u]ver 9-10 **29:17** [v]S ver 16 [w]S Ge 12:11 **29:18** [x]S Ge 24:67 [y]ver 20,27,30; Ge 30:26; Hos 12:12 **29:20** [z]S ver 18; Ge 31:15 [a]SS 8:7; Hos 12:12 **29:21** [b]Jdg 15:1 **29:22** [c]Jdg 14:10; Isa 25:6; Jn 2:1-2 **29:23** [d]S ver 16 **29:24** [e]Ge 30:9 [f]S Ge 16:1 **29:25** [g]S Ge 12:18 [h]S Ge 27:36 **29:26** [i]Jdg 15:2; 1Sa 14:49; 18:17, 20; 2Sa 6:23 **29:27** [j]Jdg 14:12 [k]S ver 18; Ge 31:41 **29:28** [l]S ver 16; S Ge 4:19 **29:29** [m]Ge 30:3; 35:22; 49:4; Dt 22:30; 1Ch 5:1 [n]S Ge 16:1 **29:30** [o]S ver 16 [p]S ver 20

[d]17 Or *delicate*

29:25 WHY HAVE YOU DECEIVED ME? Perhaps God allowed Jacob to be deceived by Laban and Leah in order to chastise him and to make him aware of the evil and hurt that he caused when he deceived his own father and brother (cf. ch. 27). We must understand that although God forgives us for a certain sin and restores us to his favor, he may at the same time discipline us for that sin (see 2Sa 12:7–14). God's principle remains: "Do not be deceived . . . A man reaps what he sows" (Gal 6:7; cf. Pr 22:8; Hos 8:7; 10:12–13).

29:28 LABAN GAVE HIM HIS DAUGHTER RACHEL TO BE HIS WIFE. Jacob's marriage to two sisters conflicted with God's creation ordinance that marriage should consist of only one man and one woman (see 2:24, note; cf. Ex 20:17; Dt 5:21). Later, in the Mosaic Law, God specifically forbade Jacob's type of marriage (Lev 18:18). The NT revelation regards monogamy (one wife and one husband) as the only rightful form of marriage (Mt 19:4–6; Mk 10:4–9). God may have tolerated polygamy in the OT because the people lacked a full understanding of God's will regarding marriage and because their hearts were hard. Polygamy's evil effects are described in v. 30; 30:1; 35:22; 1Ki 11:1–12.

Jacob's Children

31When the LORD saw that Leah was
not loved,[q] he opened her womb,[r]
but Rachel was barren. **32**Leah became
pregnant and gave birth to a son.[s] She
named him Reuben,[e][t] for she said,
"It is because the LORD has seen my
misery.[u] Surely my husband will love
me now."
33She conceived again, and when
she gave birth to a son she said, "Because the LORD heard that I am not
loved,[v] he gave me this one too." So
she named him Simeon.[f][w]
34Again she conceived, and when
she gave birth to a son she said, "Now
at last my husband will become attached to me,[x] because I have borne
him three sons." So he was named
Levi.[g][y]
35She conceived again, and when
she gave birth to a son she said, "This
time I will praise the LORD." So she
named him Judah.[h][z] Then she
stopped having children.[a]
30 When Rachel saw that she was
not bearing Jacob any chil-
dren,[b] she became jealous of her sister.[c] So she said to Jacob, "Give me
children, or I'll die!"
2Jacob became angry with her and
said, "Am I in the place of God,[d] who
has kept you from having children?"[e]
3Then she said, "Here is Bilhah,[f]
my maidservant.[g] Sleep with her so
that she can bear children for me and
that through her I too can build a family."[h]
4So she gave him her servant Bilhah
as a wife.[i] Jacob slept with her,[j]
5and she became pregnant and bore
him a son. **6**Then Rachel said, "God
has vindicated me;[k] he has listened to
my plea and given me a son."[l]
Because of this she named him
Dan.[i][m]
7Rachel's servant Bilhah[n] conceived again and bore Jacob a second
son. **8**Then Rachel said, "I have had a
great struggle with my sister, and I
have won."[o] So she named him Naphtali.[j][p]
9When Leah[q] saw that she had
stopped having children,[r] she took
her maidservant Zilpah[s] and gave her
to Jacob as a wife.[t] **10**Leah's servant
Zilpah[u] bore Jacob a son. **11**Then Leah
said, "What good fortune!"[k] So she
named him Gad.[l][v]
12Leah's servant Zilpah bore Jacob a
second son. **13**Then Leah said, "How
happy I am! The women will call me[w]
happy."[x] So she named him Asher.[m][y]
14During wheat harvest,[z] Reuben
went out into the fields and found some
mandrake plants,[a] which he brought
to his mother Leah. Rachel said to
Leah, "Please give me some of your
son's mandrakes."
15But she said to her, "Wasn't it
enough[b] that you took away my husband? Will you take my son's mandrakes too?"
"Very well," Rachel said, "he can
sleep with you tonight in return for
your son's mandrakes."[c]
16So when Jacob came in from the
fields that evening, Leah went out to
meet him. "You must sleep with me,"
she said. "I have hired you with my
son's mandrakes."[d] So he slept with
her that night.
17God listened to Leah,[e] and she
became pregnant and bore Jacob a fifth
son. **18**Then Leah said, "God has re-

29:31 [q] ver 33; Dt 21:15-17 [r] S Ge 11:30; S 16:2; Ru 4:13; 1Sa 1:19; Ps 127:3 **29:32** [s] Ge 30:23; Ru 4:13; 1Sa 1:20 [t] Ge 37:21; 46:8; 48:5,14; 49:3; Ex 6:14; Nu 1:5, 20; 26:5; Dt 33:6; Jos 4:12; 1Ch 5:1, 3 [u] S Ge 16:11 **29:33** [v] S ver 31 [w] Ge 34:25; 46:10; 48:5; 49:5; Ex 6:15; Nu 1:6, 22; 34:20; 1Ch 4:24; Eze 48:24 **29:34** [x] Ge 30:20; 1Sa 1:2-4 [y] Ge 34:25; 46:11; 49:5-7; Ex 2:1; 6:16,19; Nu 1:47; 3:17-20; 26:57; Dt 33:8; 1Ch 6:1, 16; 23:6-24,13-14 **29:35** [z] Ge 35:23; 37:26; 38:1; 43:8; 44:14,18; 46:12; 49:8; 1Ch 2:3; 4:1; Isa 48:1; Mt 1:2-3 [a] Ge 30:9 **30:1** [b] S Ge 11:30; Isa 49:21; 54:1 [c] S Ge 16:4; Lev 18:18 **30:2** [d] Ge 50:19; Dt 32:35; 2Ki 5:7 [e] S Ge 16:2 **30:3** [f] ver 7; S Ge 29:29 [g] S Ge 24:61 [h] Ge 16:2 **30:4** [i] ver 9,18 [j] Ge 16:3-4 **30:6** [k] Ps 35:24; 43:1 [l] ver 23; Ge 21:2; Ru 4:13; 1Sa 1:20 [m] Ge 46:23; 49:16-17; Nu 26:42-43; Jos 19:40-48; Jdg 1:34; 13:2; 18:2; Jer 4:15; 8:16; Eze 48:1 **30:7** [n] S ver 3 **30:8** [o] Ge 32:28; Hos 12:3-4 [p] Ge 35:25; 46:24; 49:21; Nu 1:42; 26:48; Dt 33:23; Jdg 4:6; 5:18; 1Ch 7:13 **30:9** [q] S Ge 29:16 [r] Ge 29:35 [s] Ge 29:24 [t] S ver 4 **30:10** [u] Ge 46:18 **30:11** [v] Ge 35:26; 46:16; 49:19; Ex 1:4; Nu 1:24; 26:18; Jos 4:12; 1Ch 5:11; 12:8; Jer 49:1

30:13 [w] Ps 127:3 [x] Ru 4:14; Ps 127:4-5; Lk 1:48 [y] Ge 35:26; 46:17; 49:20; Nu 1:40; 26:47; Dt 33:24; Jos 19:24-31; 1Ch 7:30-31 **30:14** [z] Ex 34:22; Jdg 15:1; Ru 2:23; 1Sa 6:13; 12:17 [a] ver 15,16; SS 7:13 **30:15** [b] Nu 16:9,13; Isa 7:13; Eze 34:18 [c] Ge 38:16; Eze 16:33; Hos 9:1 **30:16** [d] S ver 14 **30:17** [e] S Ge 25:21

[e] *32 Reuben* sounds like the Hebrew for *he has seen my misery*; the name means *see, a son.*
[f] *33 Simeon* probably means *one who hears.*
[g] *34 Levi* sounds like and may be derived from the Hebrew for *attached.*
[h] *35 Judah* sounds like and may be derived from the Hebrew for *praise.*
[i] *6 Dan* here means *he has vindicated.*
[j] *8 Naphtali* means *my struggle.*
[k] *11* Or *"A troop is coming!"*
[l] *11 Gad* can mean *good fortune* or *a troop.*
[m] *13 Asher* means *happy.*

29:31 THE LORD SAW THAT LEAH WAS NOT LOVED. God allowed Leah to have a child. From her was born Judah, and from Judah's line was born the Christ (Mt 1:3,16). Often God takes the side of those who are oppressed or treated wrongfully (cf. Ps 9:18; 22:24; Lk 4:18). Injustice is intolerable to God, especially among his covenant people (see Col 3:25, note).

30:1–24 GIVE ME CHILDREN. These verses record the forming of the family of Jacob, the founders of the tribes of Israel. The narrative shows that God worked to accomplish his ultimate purpose in spite of weaknesses, struggles and blemishes in Jacob's family.

30:1 OR I'LL DIE! In the ancient Near East, a childless woman was looked on with disdain (cf. 16:2; 30:2); thus, Rachel's despairing comment.

warded me for giving my maidservant
to my husband."[f] So she named him
Issachar.[n][g]
19Leah conceived again and bore Jacob a sixth son. 20Then Leah said,
"God has presented me with a precious
gift. This time my husband will treat
me with honor,[h] because I have borne
him six sons." So she named him Zebulun.[o][i]
21Some time later she gave birth to
a daughter and named her Dinah.[j]
22Then God remembered Rachel;[k]
he listened to her[l] and opened her
womb.[m] 23She became pregnant and
gave birth to a son[n] and said, "God
has taken away my disgrace."[o] 24She
named him Joseph,[p][p] and said, "May
the LORD add to me another son."[q]

Jacob's Flocks Increase

25After Rachel gave birth to Joseph,
Jacob said to Laban, "Send me on my
way[r] so I can go back to my own
homeland.[s] 26Give me my wives and
children, for whom I have served
you,[t] and I will be on my way. You
know how much work I've done for
you."
27But Laban said to him, "If I have
found favor in your eyes,[u] please stay.
I have learned by divination[v] that[q]
the LORD has blessed me because of
you."[w] 28He added, "Name your
wages,[x] and I will pay them."
29Jacob said to him, "You know how
I have worked for you[y] and how your
livestock has fared under my care.[z]
30The little you had before I came has
increased greatly, and the LORD has
blessed you wherever I have been.[a]
But now, when may I do something for
my own household?[b]"
31"What shall I give you?" he asked.
"Don't give me anything," Jacob replied. "But if you will do this one thing
for me, I will go on tending your flocks
and watching over them: 32Let me go
through all your flocks today and remove from them every speckled or
spotted sheep, every dark-colored
lamb and every spotted or speckled
goat.[c] They will be my wages.[d]
33And my honesty will testify for me in
the future, whenever you check on the
wages you have paid me. Any goat in
my possession that is not speckled or
spotted, or any lamb that is not dark-
colored,[e] will be considered stolen.[f]"
34"Agreed," said Laban. "Let it be as
you have said." 35That same day he removed all the male goats that were
streaked or spotted, and all the speckled or spotted female goats (all that
had white on them) and all the dark-
colored lambs,[g] and he placed them in
the care of his sons.[h] 36Then he put
a three-day journey[i] between himself
and Jacob, while Jacob continued to
tend the rest of Laban's flocks.
37Jacob, however, took fresh-cut
branches from poplar, almond[j] and
plane trees[k] and made white stripes
on them by peeling the bark and exposing the white inner wood of the
branches.[l] 38Then he placed the
peeled branches[m] in all the watering
troughs,[n] so that they would be directly in front of the flocks when they
came to drink. When the flocks were in
heat[o] and came to drink, 39they mated in front of the branches.[p] And they
bore young that were streaked or
speckled or spotted.[q] 40Jacob set
apart the young of the flock by themselves, but made the rest face the
streaked and dark-colored animals[r]
that belonged to Laban. Thus he made
separate flocks for himself and did not
put them with Laban's animals.
41Whenever the stronger females were
in heat,[s] Jacob would place the
branches in the troughs in front of the
animals so they would mate near the
branches,[t] 42but if the animals were
weak, he would not place them there.
So the weak animals went to Laban
and the strong ones to Jacob.[u] 43In
this way the man grew exceedingly
prosperous and came to own large

30:18 [f]S ver 4 [g]Ge 46:13; 49:14; Nu 1:8,28,29; 26:25; Dt 27:12; 33:18; Jos 17:10; 19:17; 21:6,28; Jdg 5:15; 10:1; 1Ch 7:1
30:20 [h]S Ge 29:34; 1Pe 3:7 [i]Ge 35:23; 46:14; 49:13; Nu 1:30; 26:27; 34:25; Dt 33:18; Jdg 5:18
30:21 [j]Ge 34:1; 46:15
30:22 [k]S Ge 8:1 [l]S Ge 25:21 [m]S Ge 11:30
30:23 [n]S ver 6; S Ge 29:32 [o]Isa 4:1; 25:8; 45:17; 54:4; Lk 1:25
30:24 [p]S Ge 29:6; 32:22; 33:2,7; 35:24; 37:2; 39:1; 49:22-26; Dt 33:13 [q]Ge 35:17; 1Sa 4:20
30:25 [r]S Ge 24:54 [s]S Ge 28:15
30:26 [t]S Ge 29:18
30:27 [u]Ge 33:10; 50:4; Est 2:15 [v]Ge 44:5,15; Lev 19:26; Nu 22:7; 23:23; 24:1; Jos 13:22; 2Ki 17:17; Jer 27:9 [w]ver 30; S Ge 26:24; 31:38; Dt 28:11; 2Sa 6:11
30:28 [x]S Ge 29:15
30:29 [y]Ge 31:6 [z]Ge 31:38-40
30:30 [a]S ver 27 [b]1Ti 5:8
30:32 [c]ver 33,35, 39,40; Ge 31:8,12 [d]S Ge 29:15
30:33 [e]S ver 32 [f]Ge 31:39
30:35 [g]S ver 32 [h]Ge 31:1
30:36 [i]Ge 31:22; Ex 3:18; 5:3; 8:27
30:37 [j]Jer 1:11 [k]Eze 31:8 [l]ver 38, 41
30:38 [m]S ver 37 [n]Ex 2:16 [o]ver 41; Jer 2:24
30:39 [p]ver 41 [q]S ver 32
30:40 [r]S ver 32
30:41 [s]S ver 38 [t]S ver 37
30:42 [u]Ge 31:1, 9,16,43

[n] *18 Issachar* sounds like the Hebrew for *reward.* [o] *20 Zebulun* probably means *honor.* [p] *24 Joseph* means *may he add.* [q] *27* Or possibly *have become rich and*

30:18 GOD HAS REWARDED ME. Leah's declaration that God had rewarded her for giving her maidservant to Jacob reflects her own feeling about the matter, not necessarily God's. The narrative here only tells us what Leah said. God tolerated this situation for a time and worked through the kind of marriages into which Jacob entered (see 29:28, note).

30:39 BORE YOUNG THAT WERE STREAKED OR SPECKLED OR SPOTTED. The breeding process of the flocks was influenced not by the branches but by the intervention of God. Jacob himself acknowledged God's work in increasing his flock (31:7–9).

flocks, and maidservants and menservants, and camels and donkeys.[v]

Jacob Flees From Laban

31 Jacob heard that Laban's
sons[w] were saying, "Jacob has
taken everything our father owned and
has gained all this wealth from what
belonged to our father."[x] 2 And Jacob
noticed that Laban's attitude toward
him was not what it had been.[y]
3 Then the LORD said to Jacob, "Go
back[z] to the land of your fathers and
to your relatives, and I will be with
you."[a]
4 So Jacob sent word to Rachel and
Leah to come out to the fields where
his flocks were. 5 He said to them, "I
see that your father[b]'s attitude toward me is not what it was before,[c]
but the God of my father has been with
me.[d] 6 You know that I've worked for
your father with all my strength,[e] 7 yet
your father has cheated[f] me by
changing my wages[g] ten times.[h]
However, God has not allowed him to
harm me.[i] 8 If he said, 'The speckled
ones will be your wages,' then all the
flocks gave birth to speckled young;
and if he said, 'The streaked ones will
be your wages,'[j] then all the flocks
bore streaked young. 9 So God has tak-
en away your father's livestock[k] and
has given them to me.[l]
10 "In breeding season I once had a
dream[m] in which I looked up and saw
that the male goats mating with the
flock were streaked, speckled or spotted. 11 The angel of God[n] said to me in
the dream,[o] 'Jacob.' I answered, 'Here
I am.'[p] 12 And he said, 'Look up and
see that all the male goats mating with
the flock are streaked, speckled or
spotted,[q] for I have seen all that Laban has been doing to you.[r] 13 I am the
God of Bethel,[s] where you anointed a
pillar[t] and where you made a vow[u] to
me. Now leave this land at once and go
back to your native land.[v]' "
14 Then Rachel and Leah replied,
"Do we still have any share[w] in the
inheritance of our father's estate?
15 Does he not regard us as foreigners?[x] Not only has he sold us, but he
has used up what was paid for us.[y]
16 Surely all the wealth that God took
away from our father belongs to us and
our children.[z] So do whatever God
has told you."
17 Then Jacob put his children and
his wives[a] on camels,[b] 18 and he
drove all his livestock ahead of him,
along with all the goods he had accumulated[c] in Paddan Aram,[r][d] to go
to his father Isaac[e] in the land of Canaan.[f]
19 When Laban had gone to shear his
sheep,[g] Rachel stole her father's
household gods.[h] 20 Moreover, Jacob
deceived[i] Laban the Aramean[j] by
not telling him he was running away.[k]
21 So he fled[l] with all he had, and
crossing the River,[s][m] he headed for
the hill country of Gilead.[n]

Laban Pursues Jacob

22 On the third day[o] Laban was told
that Jacob had fled.[p] 23 Taking his relatives[q] with him[r], he pursued Jacob
for seven days and caught up with him
in the hill country of Gilead.[s] 24 Then
God came to Laban the Aramean[t] in
a dream at night and said to him,[u] "Be
careful not to say anything to Jacob,
either good or bad."[v]
25 Jacob had pitched his tent in the
hill country of Gilead[w] when Laban
overtook him, and Laban and his relatives camped there too. 26 Then Laban
said to Jacob, "What have you done?[x]
You've deceived me,[y] and you've carried off my daughters like captives in
war.[z] 27 Why did you run off secretly
and deceive me? Why didn't you tell
me,[a] so I could send you away with
joy and singing to the music of tambourines[b] and harps?[c] 28 You didn't even

30:43 [v]S Ge 12:16 **31:1** [w]Ge 30:35 [x]S Ge 30:42 **31:2** [y]ver 5 **31:3** [z]ver 13; Ge 32:9; Dt 30:3; Isa 10:21; 35:10; Jer 30:3; 42:12 [a]S Ge 21:22; S 26:3 **31:5** [b]ver 29,42, 53; Ge 43:23; Da 2:23 [c]ver 2 [d]S Ge 21:22; S 26:3 **31:6** [e]Ge 30:29 **31:7** [f]Lev 6:2; Am 8:5 [g]S Ge 29:15 [h]ver 41; Nu 14:22; Job 19:3 [i]ver 52; S Ge 24:50 **31:8** [j]S Ge 30:32 **31:9** [k]Job 39:2; Eze 31:6 [l]S Ge 30:42 **31:10** [m]S Ge 20:3 **31:11** [n]S Ge 16:7 [o]S Ge 20:3 [p]S Ge 22:1; S Ex 3:4 **31:12** [q]S Ge 30:32 [r]Ex 3:7 **31:13** [s]Ge 28:10-22 [t]S Ge 28:18 [u]S Ge 28:20 [v]S ver 3 **31:14** [w]2Sa 20:1; 1Ki 12:16 **31:15** [x]Dt 15:3; 23:20; Ru 2:10; 2Sa 15:19; 1Ki 8:41; Ob 1:11 [y]S Ge 29:20 **31:16** [z]S Ge 30:42 **31:17** [a]S Ge 27:41 [b]S Ge 24:63-64 **31:18** [c]S Ge 12:5 [d]S Ge 25:20 [e]Ge 35:27 [f]S Ge 10:19 **31:19** [g]Ge 38:12, 13; 1Sa 25:2,4,7; 2Sa 13:23 [h]ver 30,32,34-35; Ge 35:2; Jos 24:14; Jdg 17:5; 18:14, 17,24,30; 1Sa 7:3; 19:13; 2Ki 23:24; Hos 3:4 **31:20** [i]S Ge 27:36 [j]S Ge 25:20 [k]ver 27 **31:21** [l]ver 22; Ex 2:15; 14:5; 1Ki 18:46; 19:3; Jer 26:21 [m]S Ge 2:14 [n]ver 23,25; Ge 37:25; Nu 26:30; 32:1; Dt 3:10; Jos 12:2; Jer 22:6 **31:22** [o]S Ge 30:36 [p]S ver 21 **31:23** [q]ver 37 [r]Ex 14:9 [s]S ver 21 **31:24** [t]S Ge 25:20 [u]S Ge 20:3 [v]S Ge 24:50 **31:25** [w]S ver 21 **31:26** [x]S Ge 12:18 [y]S Ge 27:36 [z]Ge 34:29; 1Sa 30:2-3 **31:27** [a]ver 20 [b]Ex 15:20; Jdg 11:34; 1Sa 10:5; 2Sa 6:5; Ps 68:25; Isa 24:8; Jer 31:4 [c]S Ge 4:21

[r] *18* That is, Northwest Mesopotamia
[s] *21* That is, the Euphrates

31:19 RACHEL STOLE HER FATHER'S HOUSEHOLD GODS. Rachel stole the household gods and then lied in order to keep them (vv. 34–35). Archaeological discoveries in that area show that the possession of those idols were thought to guarantee a double portion of the inheritance when the father died. Rachel and Leah felt cheated out of any inheritance (v. 15). Thus, Rachel took the idols, not for purposes of worship but for financial gain. They did her no good, however, for Jacob later ordered his household to get rid of all the idols and symbols of foreign gods, which Jacob then buried before setting out for Bethel (35:2–4; see 35:2, note).

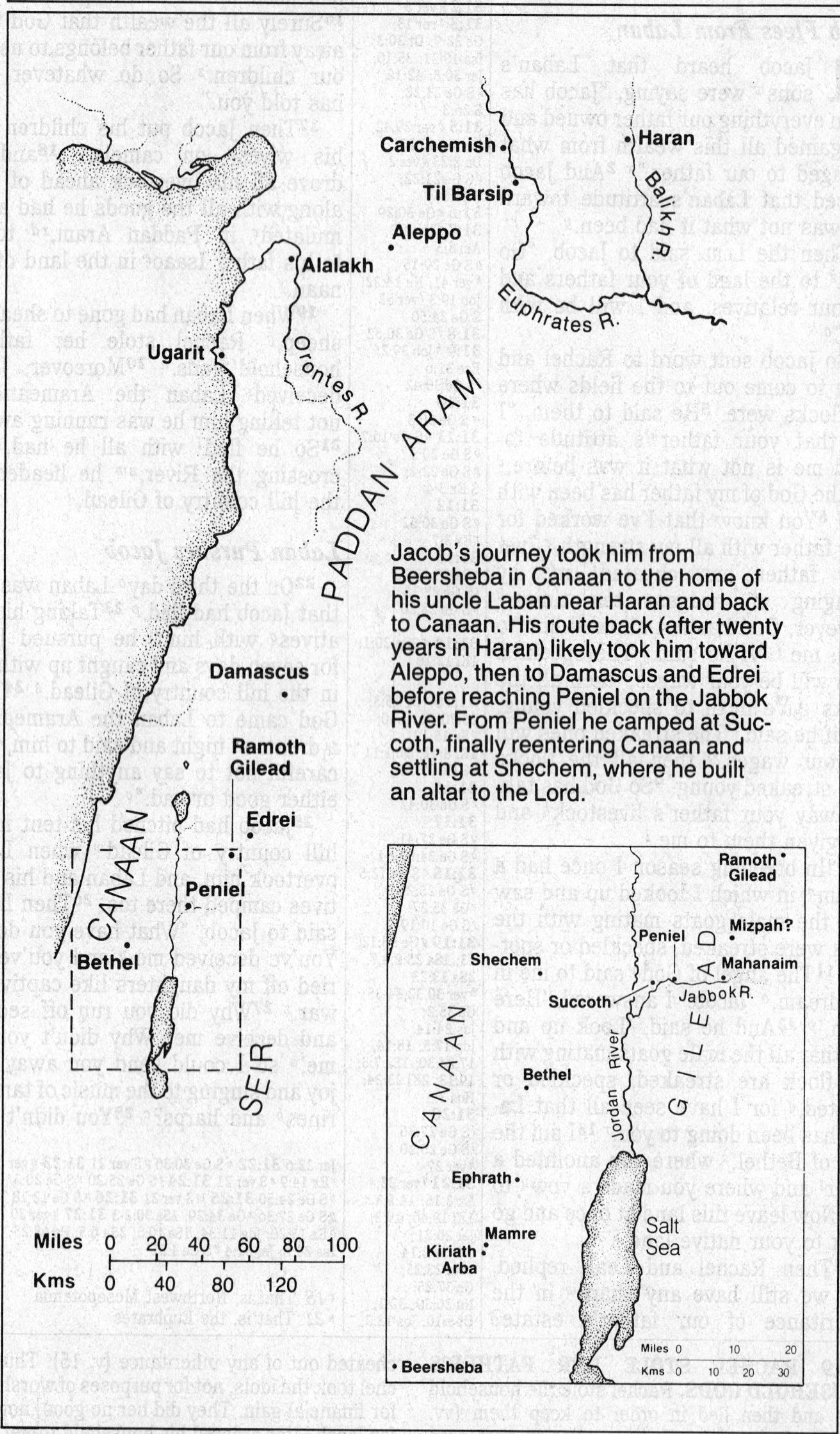

Jacob's journey took him from Beersheba in Canaan to the home of his uncle Laban near Haran and back to Canaan. His route back (after twenty years in Haran) likely took him toward Aleppo, then to Damascus and Edrei before reaching Peniel on the Jabbok River. From Peniel he camped at Succoth, finally reentering Canaan and settling at Shechem, where he built an altar to the Lord.

let me kiss my grandchildren and my
daughters good-by.[d] You have done a
foolish thing. **29**I have the power to
harm you;[e] but last night the God of
your father[f] said to me, 'Be careful
not to say anything to Jacob, either
good or bad.'[g] **30**Now you have gone
off because you longed to return to
your father's house.[h] But why did you
steal[i] my gods?[j]"

31Jacob answered Laban, "I was
afraid, because I thought you would
take your daughters away from me by
force.[k] **32**But if you find anyone who
has your gods, he shall not live.[l] In
the presence of our relatives, see for
yourself whether there is anything of
yours here with me; and if so, take it."
Now Jacob did not know that Rachel
had stolen the gods.[m]

33So Laban went into Jacob's tent
and into Leah's tent[n] and into the tent
of the two maidservants,[o] but he
found nothing.[p] After he came out of
Leah's tent, he entered Rachel's tent.
34Now Rachel had taken the household
gods[q] and put them inside her camel's
saddle[r] and was sitting on them. Laban searched[s] through everything in
the tent but found nothing.

35Rachel said to her father, "Don't
be angry, my lord, that I cannot stand
up in your presence;[t] I'm having my
period.[u]" So he searched but could not
find the household gods.[v]

36Jacob was angry and took Laban
to task. "What is my crime?" he asked
Laban. "What sin have I committed[w]
that you hunt me down?[x] **37**Now that
you have searched through all my
goods, what have you found that belongs to your household?[y] Put it here
in front of your relatives[z] and mine,
and let them judge between the two of
us.[a]

38"I have been with you for twenty
years now.[b] Your sheep and goats
have not miscarried,[c] nor have I eaten
rams from your flocks. **39**I did not bring
you animals torn by wild beasts; I bore
the loss myself. And you demanded
payment from me for whatever was
stolen[d] by day or night.[e] **40**This was
my situation: The heat consumed me in
the daytime and the cold at night, and
sleep fled from my eyes.[f] **41**It was like
this for the twenty years[g] I was in
your household. I worked for you fourteen years for your two daughters[h]
and six years for your flocks,[i] and you
changed my wages[j] ten times.[k] **42**If
the God of my father,[l] the God of
Abraham[m] and the Fear of Isaac,[n]
had not been with me,[o] you would
surely have sent me away empty-handed. But God has seen my hardship and
the toil of my hands,[p] and last night
he rebuked you.[q]"

43Laban answered Jacob, "The wom-
en are my daughters, the children are
my children, and the flocks are my
flocks.[r] All you see is mine. Yet what
can I do today about these daughters
of mine, or about the children they
have borne? **44**Come now, let's make a
covenant,[s] you and I, and let it serve
as a witness between us."[t]

45So Jacob took a stone and set it up
as a pillar.[u] **46**He said to his relatives,
"Gather some stones." So they took
stones and piled them in a heap,[v] and
they ate there by the heap. **47**Laban
called it Jegar Sahadutha,[t] and Jacob
called it Galeed.[u][w]

48Laban said, "This heap[x] is a witness between you and me today."[y]
That is why it was called Galeed. **49**It
was also called Mizpah,[v][z] because
he said, "May the LORD keep watch between you and me when we are away
from each other. **50**If you mistreat[a]
my daughters or if you take any wives
besides my daughters, even though no
one is with us, remember that God is a
witness[b] between you and me."[c]

51Laban also said to Jacob, "Here is
this heap,[d] and here is this pillar[e] I
have set up between you and me.
52This heap is a witness, and this pillar
is a witness,[f] that I will not go past
this heap to your side to harm you and
that you will not go past this heap[g]
and pillar to my side to harm me.[h]
53May the God of Abraham[i] and the
God of Nahor,[j] the God of their father,
judge between us."[k]

So Jacob took an oath[l] in the name
of the Fear of his father Isaac.[m] **54**He
offered a sacrifice[n] there in the hill
country and invited his relatives to a
meal.[o] After they had eaten, they
spent the night there.

55Early the next morning Laban

31:28 [d] ver 55; S Ge 27:27; Ru 1:14; Ac 20:37
31:29 [e] S ver 7; S Ge 26:29 [f] S ver 5 [g] S Ge 24:50
31:30 [h] S Ge 28:15; Job 29:2 [i] Ge 44:8 [j] S ver 19
31:31 [k] S Ge 20:11
31:32 [l] Ge 44:9 [m] S ver 19
31:33 [n] Ge 24:67 [o] S Ge 16:1 [p] ver 37
31:34 [q] S ver 19 [r] S Ge 24:63-64 [s] ver 37; Ge 44:12
31:35 [t] Ex 20:12; Lev 19:3,32; Dt 21:18; 27:16; Jer 35:18 [u] Lev 15:19-23 [v] ver 19
31:36 [w] 1Sa 19:5; 20:32 [x] 1Sa 23:23; 24:11
31:37 [y] ver 33 [z] ver 23 [a] Dt 1:16; 16:18
31:38 [b] S Ge 27:44 [c] S Ge 30:27
31:39 [d] Ge 30:33 [e] Ex 22:13
31:40 [f] Ps 132:4; 2Co 11:27
31:41 [g] S Ge 27:44 [h] Ge 29:30 [i] S Ge 30:32 [j] S Ge 29:15 [k] S ver 7
31:42 [l] S ver 5; S Ex 3:15 [m] S Ge 24:12 [n] ver 53; Ge 46:1 [o] S Ge 21:22; Ps 124:1-2 [p] S Ge 3:17 [q] S Ge 24:50
31:43 [r] Ge 30:32, 42
31:44 [s] S Ge 21:27 [t] S Ge 21:30
31:45 [u] S Ge 28:18
31:46 [v] ver 48,51, 52
31:47 [w] S Ge 21:30
31:48 [x] S ver 46 [y] S Ge 21:30; Jer 29:23; 42:5
31:49 [z] Jos 11:3; Jdg 10:17; 11:29
31:50 [a] Ge 16:6 [b] Dt 31:19; Jos 24:27; Jdg 11:10; 1Sa 12:5; 20:14, 23,42; Job 16:19; Jer 29:23; 42:5; Mic 1:2 [c] S Ge 21:30; S Dt 4:26; S Jer 7:11
31:51 [d] S ver 46 [e] S Ge 28:18
31:52 [f] S Ge 21:30 [g] S ver 46 [h] S ver 7; S Ge 26:29
31:53 [i] S Ge 24:12 [j] S Ge 11:27 [k] S Ge 16:5 [l] S Ge 21:23,27 [m] S ver 42
31:54 [n] Ge 46:1; Ex 24:5; Lev 3:1 [o] S Ge 26:30

[t] *47* The Aramaic *Jegar Sahadutha* means *witness heap.* [u] *47* The Hebrew *Galeed* means *witness heap.* [v] *49* *Mizpah* means *watchtower.*

kissed his grandchildren and his
daughters[p] and blessed[q] them. Then
he left and returned home.[r]

Jacob Prepares to Meet Esau

32 Jacob also went on his way, and
the angels of God[s] met him.
2When Jacob saw them, he said, "This
is the camp of God!"[t] So he named
that place Mahanaim.[w][u]
3Jacob sent messengers[v] ahead of
him to his brother Esau[w] in the land
of Seir,[x] the country of Edom.[y] **4**He
instructed them: "This is what you are
to say to my master[z] Esau: 'Your servant[a] Jacob says, I have been staying
with Laban[b] and have remained there
till now. **5**I have cattle and donkeys,
sheep and goats, menservants and
maidservants.[c] Now I am sending this
message to my lord,[d] that I may find
favor in your eyes.[e]' "
6When the messengers returned to
Jacob, they said, "We went to your
brother Esau, and now he is coming to
meet you, and four hundred men are
with him."[f]
7In great fear[g] and distress[h] Jacob
divided the people who were with him
into two groups,[x][i] and the flocks and
herds and camels as well. **8**He thought,
"If Esau comes and attacks one
group,[y] the group[y] that is left may
escape."
9Then Jacob prayed, "O God of my
father Abraham,[j] God of my father
Isaac,[k] O LORD, who said to me, 'Go
back to your country and your relatives, and I will make you prosper,'[l]
10I am unworthy of all the kindness
and faithfulness[m] you have shown
your servant. I had only my staff[n]
when I crossed this Jordan, but now I
have become two groups.[o] **11**Save me,
I pray, from the hand of my brother
Esau, for I am afraid[p] he will come
and attack me,[q] and also the mothers
with their children.[r] **12**But you have
said, 'I will surely make you prosper
and will make your descendants like
the sand[s] of the sea, which cannot be
counted.[t]' "
13He spent the night there, and from
what he had with him he selected a
gift[u] for his brother Esau: **14**two hundred female goats and twenty male
goats, two hundred ewes and twenty
rams,[v] **15**thirty female camels with
their young, forty cows and ten bulls,
and twenty female donkeys and ten
male donkeys.[w] **16**He put them in the
care of his servants, each herd by itself, and said to his servants, "Go
ahead of me, and keep some space between the herds."[x]
17He instructed the one in the lead:
"When my brother Esau meets you and
asks, 'To whom do you belong, and
where are you going, and who owns all
these animals in front of you?' **18**then
you are to say, 'They belong to your
servant[y] Jacob. They are a gift[z] sent
to my lord Esau, and he is coming behind us.' "
19He also instructed the second, the
third and all the others who followed
the herds: "You are to say the same
thing to Esau when you meet him.
20And be sure to say, 'Your servant[a]
Jacob is coming behind us.' " For he
thought, "I will pacify him with these
gifts[b] I am sending on ahead;[c] later,
when I see him, perhaps he will receive
me."[d] **21**So Jacob's gifts[e] went on
ahead of him, but he himself spent the
night in the camp.

Jacob Wrestles With God

22That night Jacob got up and took
his two wives, his two maidservants
and his eleven sons[f] and crossed the
ford of the Jabbok.[g] **23**After he had

31:55 p S ver 28; Ru 1:9 q S Ge 24:60; S Ex 39:43 r Ge 18:33 **32:1** s S Ge 16:11; 2Ki 6:16-17; 1Ch 21:15; Ps 34:7; 35:5; 91:11; Da 6:22 **32:2** t S Ge 28:17 u Jos 13:26,30; 21:38; 2Sa 2:8,29; 17:24; 19:32; 1Ki 2:8; 4:14; 1Ch 6:80 **32:3** v Nu 21:21; Jdg 11:17 w S Ge 27:41-42 x S Ge 14:6; S Nu 24:18 y S Ge 25:30; S 36:16 **32:4** z S Ge 24:9 a S Ge 18:3 b Ge 31:41 **32:5** c S Ge 12:16 d S Ge 24:9 e Ge 33:8,10,15; 34:11; 47:25,29; 50:4; Ru 2:13 **32:6** f Ge 33:1 **32:7** g ver 11 h Ge 35:3; Ps 4:1; 77:2; 107:6 i ver 10; Ge 33:1 **32:9** j S Ge 24:12 k S Ge 28:13 l S Ge 26:3; 31:13 **32:10** m S Ge 24:27 n Ge 38:18; 47:31; Nu 17:2 o S ver 7 **32:11** p S ver 7 q Ge 43:18; Ps 59:2 r S Ge 27:41 **32:12** s S Ge 22:17; 1Ki 4:20,29 t S Ge 12:2; S 13:14; Hos 1:10; Ro 9:27 **32:13** u ver 13-15,18,20, 21; Ge 33:10; 43:11,15,25,26; 1Sa 16:20; Pr 18:16; 21:14 **32:14** v Nu 7:88 **32:15** w S Ge 13:2; 42:26; 45:23 **32:16** x Ge 33:8 **32:18** y S Ge 18:3 z S ver 13 **32:20** a S Ge 18:3 b S ver 13; 1Sa 9:7; 2Ki 8:8; Jer 40:5 c 1Sa 25:19 d Ge 33:10; Ex 28:38; Lev 1:4; Mal 1:8 **32:21** e S ver 13 **32:22** f S Ge 30:24 g Nu 21:24; Dt 2:37; 3:16; Jos 12:2

w *2 Mahanaim* means *two camps.* x *7* Or *camps*; also in verse 10 y *8* Or *camp*

32:1 THE ANGELS OF GOD MET HIM. Jacob had obeyed God's instruction by leaving Laban and returning to the land of Canaan (31:13), the region where his hostile brother Esau lived. God sent angels to assure Jacob of his continued presence and protection.

32:9 O GOD OF MY FATHER. Jacob was fearful and distressed as he approached Esau's territory. Would he and his family suffer violence at Esau's hand because of Jacob's deception more than twenty years earlier? In that situation Jacob prayed to God for help. His prayer is a pattern for all believers who find themselves in life-threatening circumstances. (1) Jacob reminded God of his promise of protection for those who follow God's will (v. 9); (2) in awareness of his unworthiness, he expressed his gratitude for God's past blessing and help (v. 10); (3) he prayed for God's deliverance (v. 11); and (4) he stated the ultimate reason for requesting God's protection, i.e., to fulfill God's covenant purpose in his life (v. 12).

sent them across the stream, he sent
over all his possessions.[h] **24**So Jacob
was left alone,[i] and a man[j] wrestled
with him till daybreak. **25**When the
man saw that he could not overpower
him, he touched the socket of Jacob's
hip[k] so that his hip was wrenched as
he wrestled with the man. **26**Then the
man said, "Let me go, for it is daybreak."

But Jacob replied, "I will not let you
go unless you bless me."[l]

27The man asked him, "What is your
name?"

"Jacob,"[m] he answered.

28Then the man said, "Your name[n]
will no longer be Jacob, but Israel,[z][o]
because you have struggled with God
and with men and have overcome."[p]

29Jacob said, "Please tell me your
name."[q]

But he replied, "Why do you ask my
name?"[r] Then he blessed[s] him there.

30So Jacob called the place Peniel,[a]
saying, "It is because I saw God face to
face,[t] and yet my life was spared."

31The sun rose above him as he
passed Peniel,[b][u] and he was limping
because of his hip. **32**Therefore to this
day the Israelites do not eat the tendon
attached to the socket of the hip,[v] because the socket of Jacob's hip was
touched near the tendon.

Jacob Meets Esau

33 Jacob looked up and there was
Esau, coming with his four hundred men;[w] so he divided the children
among Leah, Rachel and the two maidservants.[x] **2**He put the maidservants
and their children[y] in front, Leah and
her children next, and Rachel and Joseph[z] in the rear. **3**He himself went on
ahead and bowed down to the ground[a]
seven times[b] as he approached his
brother.

4But Esau[c] ran to meet Jacob and
embraced him; he threw his arms
around his neck and kissed him.[d] And
they wept.[e] **5**Then Esau looked up
and saw the women and children. "Who
are these with you?" he asked.

Jacob answered, "They are the children God has graciously given your
servant.[f]"

6Then the maidservants and their
children[g] approached and bowed
down.[h] **7**Next, Leah and her children[i] came and bowed down.[j] Last
of all came Joseph and Rachel,[k] and
they too bowed down.

8Esau asked, "What do you mean by
all these droves I met?"[l]

"To find favor in your eyes, my
lord,"[m] he said.

9But Esau said, "I already have plenty,[n] my brother. Keep what you have
for yourself."

10"No, please!" said Jacob. "If I have
found favor in your eyes,[o] accept this
gift[p] from me. For to see your face is
like seeing the face of God,[q] now that
you have received me favorably.[r]
11Please accept the present[s] that was
brought to you, for God has been gracious to me[t] and I have all I need."[u]

32:23 [h]S Ge 26:14
32:24 [i]Da 10:8 [j]S Ge 18:2
32:25 [k]ver 32
32:26 [l]Hos 12:4
32:27 [m]S Ge 25:26
32:28 [n]Isa 1:26; 56:5; 60:14; 62:2, 4,12; 65:15 [o]S Ge 17:5 [p]S Ge 30:8
32:29 [q]Ex 3:13; 6:3; Jdg 13:17 [r]Jdg 13:18 [s]Ge 25:11; 35:9; 48:3
32:30 [t]S Ge 16:13; 1Co 13:12
32:31 [u]Jdg 8:9
32:32 [v]ver 25
33:1 [w]S Ge 32:6 [x]S Ge 32:7
33:2 [y]ver 6 [z]S Ge 30:24
33:3 [a]ver 6,7; S Ge 17:3; 37:7-10; 42:6; 43:26; 44:14; 48:12; 1Sa 20:41 [b]2Ki 5:10,14
33:4 [c]S Ge 27:41-42 [d]S Ge 29:11; Lk 15:20 [e]S Ge 27:27
33:5 [f]S Ge 18:3; Ge 48:9; Ps 127:3; Isa 8:18
33:6 [g]ver 2 [h]S ver 3
33:7 [i]ver 2 [j]S ver 3 [k]S Ge 30:24
33:8 [l]Ge 32:14-16 [m]S Ge 24:9; S 32:5
33:9 [n]ver 11; S Ge 13:6
33:10 [o]S Ge 30:27; S 32:5 [p]S Ge 32:13 [q]S Ge 16:13 [r]S Ge 32:20
33:11 [s]1Sa 25:27; 30:26 [t]Ge 30:43 [u]S ver 9

[z] *28 Israel* means *he struggles with God.*
[a] *30 Peniel* means *face of God.* [b] *31* Hebrew *Penuel,* a variant of *Peniel*

32:24 A MAN WRESTLED WITH HIM. The man who wrestled with Jacob was probably the "angel of the LORD" (see 16:7ff; 21:17; 22:11; 31:11; Hos 12:4), who is often identified with God himself (cf. vv. 28,30; Jdg 6:12–14,22; see Ex 3:2, note). As Jacob desperately wrestled with God for the promised blessing, God allowed him to prevail (v. 28); but God disabled Jacob's hip (v. 25) as a reminder that Jacob must no longer walk in his own strength but must rely entirely on God and walk in dependence on him (vv. 30–32).

32:28 YOUR NAME . . . ISRAEL. The name Jacob, which implied a crafty deceiver, was now changed to "Israel," which means "he struggles with God" (see next note). Followers of Christ are sometimes called the "Israel of God" (Gal 6:16)—i.e., the God-strugglers. God does not want his people to be passive but to earnestly seek him for his blessing and grace (Mt 5:6; 6:33; 7:7–8; 11:12; Lk 11:5–10).

32:29 HE BLESSED HIM THERE. Jacob's night of wrestling with God resulted in God's blessing on his life. (1) From then on, he knew that his life and well-being were dependent not on his own devices but on God's help, guidance and blessing. Later God reminded the descendants of Israel of this truth: "Not by might nor by power, but by my Spirit, says the LORD Almighty" (Zec 4:6). (2) Victory and blessing in the lives of all of God's people come the same way. While we may not wrestle physically with God, we can seek him earnestly and persistently in prayer (Lk 11:5–10), confess our sin and ask his forgiveness (Lk 11:4), hunger and thirst for his kingdom and his intimate presence (Lk 11:2), desire the reality and power of the Holy Spirit (Ac 1:8; 2:4), and pursue a life of true faith and righteousness (Mt 6:30–33).

33:4 ESAU . . . KISSED HIM. AND THEY WEPT. God had dealt with Esau and placed within him the desire for reconciliation with his brother. Esau's friendly attitude was God's answer to Jacob's prayer (32:11).

And because Jacob insisted,[v] Esau accepted it.
[12]Then Esau said, "Let us be on our
way; I'll accompany you."
[13]But Jacob said to him, "My lord[w]
knows that the children are tender and
that I must care for the ewes and cows
that are nursing their young.[x] If they
are driven hard just one day, all the
animals will die. [14]So let my lord go on
ahead of his servant, while I move
along slowly at the pace of the
droves[y] before me and that of the children, until I come to my lord in Seir.[z]"
[15]Esau said, "Then let me leave
some of my men with you."
"But why do that?" Jacob asked.
"Just let me find favor in the eyes of my
lord."[a]
[16]So that day Esau started on his
way back to Seir.[b] [17]Jacob, however,
went to Succoth,[c] where he built a
place for himself and made shelters for
his livestock. That is why the place is
called Succoth.[c]
[18]After Jacob came from Paddan
Aram,[d][d] he arrived safely at the[e]
city of Shechem[e] in Canaan and
camped within sight of the city. [19]For
a hundred pieces of silver,[f] he bought
from the sons of Hamor,[f] the father of
Shechem,[g] the plot of ground[h] where
he pitched his tent.[i] [20]There he set
up an altar[j] and called it El Elohe
Israel.[g]

Dinah and the Shechemites

34 Now Dinah,[k] the daughter
Leah had borne to Jacob, went
out to visit the women of the land.
[2]When Shechem[l] son of Hamor[m] the
Hivite,[n] the ruler of that area, saw
her, he took her and violated her.[o]
[3]His heart was drawn to Dinah[p]
daughter of Jacob,[q] and he loved[r] the
girl and spoke tenderly[s] to her. [4]And
Shechem said to his father Hamor,
"Get me this girl as my wife."[t]
[5]When Jacob heard that his daughter
Dinah had been defiled,[u] his sons
were in the fields with his livestock; so
he kept quiet about it until they came
home.
[6]Then Shechem's father Hamor
went out to talk with Jacob.[v] [7]Now Jacob's sons had come in from the fields
as soon as they heard what had happened. They were filled with grief[w]
and fury,[x] because Shechem had done
a disgraceful thing in[h] Israel[y] by lying with Jacob's daughter—a thing
that should not be done.[z]
[8]But Hamor said to them, "My son
Shechem has his heart set on your
daughter. Please give her to him as his
wife.[a] [9]Intermarry with us; give us
your daughters and take our daughters
for yourselves.[b] [10]You can settle
among us;[c] the land is open to you.[d]
Live in it, trade[i] in it,[e] and acquire
property in it.[f]"
[11]Then Shechem said to Dinah's father and brothers, "Let me find favor in
your eyes,[g] and I will give you whatever you ask. [12]Make the price for the
bride[h] and the gift I am to bring as
great as you like, and I'll pay whatever
you ask me. Only give me the girl as my
wife."
[13]Because their sister Dinah had
been defiled,[i] Jacob's sons replied de-

33:11 v Ge 19:3
33:13 w ver 8 x Isa 40:11; Jer 31:8
33:14 y Ex 12:38 z S Ge 14:6
33:15 a S Ge 32:5
33:16 b S Ge 14:6
33:17 c Jos 13:27; Jdg 8:5,6,8,14, 14-16,15,16; 1Ki 7:46; 2Ch 4:17; Ps 60:6; 108:7
33:18 d S Ge 25:20 e S Ge 12:6
33:19 f Ge 34:2; Jdg 9:28; Ac 7:16 g Ge 34:2; Jos 24:32 h Ge 34:10,16,21; 47:27; Jn 4:5 i S Ge 12:8
33:20 j S Ge 4:26; S 8:20
34:1 k S Ge 30:21
34:2 l S Ge 33:19 m S Ge 33:19 n S Ge 10:17 o Dt 21:14; 2Sa 13:14
34:3 p ver 26 q ver 19 r S Ge 24:67 s Ge 50:21; Isa 14:1; 40:2
34:4 t S Ge 21:21
34:5 u ver 2,13, 27; Ge 35:22; 49:4; Dt 27:20; 33:6; 1Ch 5:1
34:6 v Jdg 14:2-5
34:7 w 1Co 5:2 x Ge 39:19; 49:6-7; 2Sa 12:5; 13:21; Est 7:7; Pr 6:34 y Dt 22:21; Jdg 19:23; 20:6; 2Sa 13:12; Jer 29:23 z S Ge 20:9
34:8 a S Ge 21:21; Dt 21:11
34:9 b ver 16,21; Dt 7:3; Jos 23:12
34:10 c ver 23; Ge 46:34; 47:6,27 d S Ge 13:9 e Ge 42:34 f S Ge 33:19
34:11 g S Ge 32:5
34:12 h Ex 22:16; Dt 22:29; 1Sa 18:25
34:13 i S ver 5

c *17 Succoth* means *shelters.* d *18* That is, Northwest Mesopotamia e *18* Or *arrived at Shalem, a* f *19* Hebrew *hundred kesitahs*; a kesitah was a unit of money of unknown weight and value. g *20 El Elohe Israel* can mean *God, the God of Israel* or *mighty is the God of Israel.* h *7* Or *against* i *10* Or *move about freely*; also in verse 21

34:1 DINAH ... THE WOMEN OF THE LAND. Jacob settled near the pagan city of Shechem rather than the home of his father Isaac, where God had commanded him to go (cf. 31:13; 35:1). He later bitterly regretted his choice. Only after the tragic incident involving Dinah did Jacob finally go to Bethel and destroy all the foreign gods in his home (see next note; 35:2, note).

34:2 HE TOOK HER AND VIOLATED HER. Both Dinah and her parents were at fault. (1) Jacob failed by choosing to live in close association with evil and immoral people, just as Lot had done (cf. 13:12–13). He failed to establish correct boundaries and rules for his children concerning their interaction with unbelievers and to supervise his children properly. For her part, Dinah appears to have been seeking companionship with the ungodly "women of the land." The end result was tragedy, hurt and shame for Jacob, his daughter and his family.

(2) Parents who fail to maintain a strict separation of their family from evil companions put their children in a place of temptation and compromise, along with potential shame and disaster (see article on PARENTS AND CHILDREN, p. 1854).

34:7 JACOB'S SONS ... WERE FILLED WITH GRIEF. The sons of Jacob were justifiably angry about the sexual violation of their sister, and they knew that such a disgraceful deed could not be tolerated. They sinned, however, by retaliating in an excessive, unjust and ruthless manner.

ceitfully[j] as they spoke to Shechem
and his father Hamor. 14 They said to
them, "We can't do such a thing; we
can't give our sister to a man who is
not circumcised.[k] That would be a disgrace to us. 15 We will give our consent
to you on one condition[l] only: that
you become like us by circumcising all
your males.[m] 16 Then we will give you
our daughters and take your daughters
for ourselves.[n] We'll settle among you
and become one people with you.[o]
17 But if you will not agree to be circumcised, we'll take our sister[j] and go."

18 Their proposal seemed good to
Hamor and his son Shechem. 19 The
young man, who was the most honored[p] of all his father's household,
lost no time in doing what they said,
because he was delighted with Jacob's
daughter.[q] 20 So Hamor and his son
Shechem went to the gate of their
city[r] to speak to their fellow townsmen. 21 "These men are friendly toward
us," they said. "Let them live in our
land and trade in it;[s] the land has
plenty of room for them. We can marry
their daughters and they can marry
ours.[t] 22 But the men will consent to
live with us as one people only on the
condition that our males be circumcised,[u] as they themselves are.
23 Won't their livestock, their property
and all their other animals become
ours?[v] So let us give our consent to
them, and they will settle among us.[w]"

24 All the men who went out of the
city gate[x] agreed with Hamor and his
son Shechem, and every male in the
city was circumcised.

25 Three days later, while all of them
were still in pain,[y] two of Jacob's
sons, Simeon[z] and Levi,[a] Dinah's
brothers, took their swords[b] and attacked the unsuspecting city,[c] killing
every male.[d] 26 They put Hamor and
his son Shechem to the sword[e] and
took Dinah[f] from Shechem's house
and left. 27 The sons of Jacob came
upon the dead bodies and looted the
city[g] where[k] their sister had been defiled.[h] 28 They seized their flocks and
herds and donkeys[i] and everything
else of theirs in the city and out in the
fields.[j] 29 They carried off all their
wealth and all their women and children,[k] taking as plunder[l] everything
in the houses.[m]

30 Then Jacob said to Simeon and
Levi, "You have brought trouble[n] on
me by making me a stench[o] to the Canaanites and Perizzites, the people living in this land.[p] We are few in number,[q] and if they join forces against
me and attack me, I and my household
will be destroyed."

31 But they replied, "Should he have
treated our sister like a prostitute?[r]"

Jacob Returns to Bethel

35 Then God said to Jacob, "Go up
to Bethel[s] and settle there,
and build an altar[t] there to God,[u]
who appeared to you[v] when you were
fleeing from your brother Esau."[w]

2 So Jacob said to his household[x]
and to all who were with him, "Get rid
of the foreign gods[y] you have with
you, and purify yourselves and change
your clothes.[z] 3 Then come, let us go
up to Bethel, where I will build an altar
to God,[a] who answered me in the day
of my distress[b] and who has been with
me wherever I have gone.[c]" 4 So they
gave Jacob all the foreign gods they
had and the rings in their ears,[d] and
Jacob buried them under the oak[e] at

34:13 [j] S Ge 27:36
34:14 [k] Ge 17:14; Jdg 14:3; 1Sa 31:4; Isa 52:1
34:15 [l] 1Sa 11:2 [m] ver 22; Ex 12:48
34:16 [n] S ver 9 [o] S Ge 33:19
34:19 [p] Ge 49:3; 1Ch 11:21 [q] ver 3
34:20 [r] S Ge 18:1
34:21 [s] S Ge 33:19 [t] S ver 9
34:22 [u] S ver 15
34:23 [v] ver 28; S Ge 12:16 [w] S ver 10
34:24 [x] S Ge 18:1
34:25 [y] Jos 5:8 [z] S Ge 29:33 [a] S Ge 29:34 [b] Ge 49:5; Mal 2:16 [c] Jdg 18:7,10,27; Eze 38:11 [d] Ge 49:7
34:26 [e] S ver 7; Ge 48:22 [f] ver 3
34:27 [g] 2Ki 21:14 [h] S ver 5
34:28 [i] Ge 43:18 [j] S ver 23
34:29 [k] S Ge 31:26 [l] Nu 14:3; 31:9,53; Dt 2:35; Jos 7:21 [m] 2Ki 8:12; Isa 13:16; La 5:11; Am 1:13; Zec 14:2
34:30 [n] Ge 43:6; Ex 5:23; Nu 11:11 [o] Ex 5:21; 6:9; 1Sa 13:4; 27:12; 2Sa 10:6; 1Ch 19:6 [p] S Ge 13:7 [q] Ge 35:26; 46:27; Ex 1:5; Dt 10:22; 26:5; 1Ch 16:19; Ps 105:12
34:31 [r] ver 2
35:1 [s] S Ge 12:8 [t] S Ge 4:26; 8:20 [u] ver 3 [v] S Ge 12:7 [w] ver 7; Ge 27:43
35:2 [x] Ge 18:19; Jos 24:15 [y] S Ge 31:19; S Jos 24:14 [z] Ex 19:10,14; Nu 8:7,21; 19:19
35:3 [a] ver 1 [b] S Ge 32:7; S Jdg 2:15 [c] S Ge 26:3
35:4 [d] S Ge 24:22; Ex 32:3; 35:22; Jdg 8:24; Pr 25:12 [e] ver 8

[j] 17 Hebrew *daughter* [k] 27 Or *because*

34:15 CIRCUMCISING ALL YOUR MALES. Jacob's sons wrongfully used the sign of their covenant relationship with God in a deceptive manner.

34:25 SIMEON AND LEVI . . . ATTACKED THE UNSUSPECTING CITY. Simeon and Levi not only killed the males of the city, but also looted the city and captured the women and children. This cruel action resulted in Simeon and Levi losing the leadership of the nation. God distinguishes between justifiable war and ruthless cruelty (see 49:5–7).

35:2 GET RID OF THE FOREIGN GODS. After the terrible events of ch. 34, God directed Jacob's family to go to Bethel in order to bring them into closer obedience to his word. Jacob, realizing the depth of spiritual deterioration in his family, commanded all the members of his household to "get rid of the foreign gods you have with you." This spiritual renewal in the life of Jacob's family consisted in: (1) removing from their home everything that offended God (v. 2); (2) committing themselves to personal holiness (v. 2); (3) renewing vows to God in devotion and worship (v. 7; 28:20–22); (4) entering fellowship with God (v. 9); (5) and leading lives based on God's word (vv. 10–15) and spiritual sacrifice (v. 14). Because of Jacob's renewal, he again experienced God's protection, presence, revelation and blessing (vv. 5, 9–13).

Shechem.[f] 5Then they set out, and
the terror of God[g] fell upon the towns
all around them so that no one pursued
them.[h]
6Jacob and all the people with him
came to Luz[i] (that is, Bethel) in the
land of Canaan.[j] 7There he built an
altar,[k] and he called the place El
Bethel,[1][l] because it was there that
God revealed himself to him[m] when he
was fleeing from his brother.[n]
8Now Deborah, Rebekah's nurse,[o]
died and was buried under the oak[p]
below Bethel.[q] So it was named Allon
Bacuth.[m]
9After Jacob returned from Paddan
Aram,[n][r] God appeared to him again
and blessed him.[s] 10God said to him,
"Your name is Jacob,[o] but you will no
longer be called Jacob; your name will
be Israel.[p]"[t] So he named him Israel.
11And God said to him, "I am God
Almighty[q];[u] be fruitful and increase
in number.[v] A nation[w] and a community of nations will come from you, and
kings will come from your body.[x]
12The land I gave to Abraham and
Isaac I also give to you, and I will give
this land to your descendants after
you.[y]"[z] 13Then God went up from
him[a] at the place where he had talked
with him.
14Jacob set up a stone pillar[b] at the
place where God had talked with him,
and he poured out a drink offering[c] on
it; he also poured oil on it.[d] 15Jacob
called the place where God had talked
with him Bethel.[r][e]

The Deaths of Rachel and Isaac

35:23–26pp — 1Ch 2:1–2

16Then they moved on from Bethel.
While they were still some distance
from Ephrath,[f] Rachel[g] began to
give birth and had great difficulty.
17And as she was having great difficulty in childbirth, the midwife[h] said to
her, "Don't be afraid, for you have another son."[i] 18As she breathed her
last—for she was dying—she named
her son Ben-Oni.[s][j] But his father
named him Benjamin.[t][k]
19So Rachel died and was buried on
the way to Ephrath[l] (that is, Bethlehem[m]). 20Over her tomb Jacob set up
a pillar, and to this day[n] that pillar
marks Rachel's tomb.[o]
21Israel moved on again and pitched
his tent beyond Migdal Eder.[p] 22While
Israel was living in that region, Reuben went in and slept with his father's
concubine[q] Bilhah,[r] and Israel heard
of it.

Jacob had twelve sons:
23The sons of Leah:[s]
Reuben the firstborn[t] of Jacob,
Simeon, Levi, Judah,[u] Issachar and Zebulun.[v]
24The sons of Rachel:
Joseph[w] and Benjamin.[x]
25The sons of Rachel's maidservant Bilhah:[y]
Dan and Naphtali.[z]
26The sons of Leah's maidservant Zilpah:[a]
Gad[b] and Asher.[c]
These were the sons of Jacob,[d] who
were born to him in Paddan Aram.[e]
27Jacob came home to his father
Isaac[f] in Mamre,[g] near Kiriath
Arba[h] (that is, Hebron),[i] where
Abraham and Isaac had stayed.[j]
28Isaac lived a hundred and eighty

35:4 [f]S Ge 12:6 35:5 [g]Ex 15:16; 23:27; Dt 2:25; Jos 2:9; 1Sa 7:10; 13:7; 14:15; 2Ch 14:14; 17:10; 20:29; Ps 9:20; Isa 19:17; Zec 14:13 [h]Ps 105:14 35:6 [i]S Ge 28:19 [j]S Ge 10:19 35:7 [k]S Ge 8:20 [l]Ge 28:19 [m]S Ge 28:13 [n]S ver 1 35:8 [o]Ge 24:59 [p]ver 4 [q]S Ge 12:8; 1Sa 10:3 35:9 [r]S Ge 25:20 [s]S Ge 28:13; S 32:29 35:10 [t]S Ge 17:5 35:11 [u]S Ge 17:1 [v]S Ge 12:2 [w]S Ge 12:2 [x]S Ge 17:6 35:12 [y]S Ge 28:13 [z]S Ge 12:7; S 15:7 35:13 [a]S Ge 17:22 35:14 [b]S Ge 28:22 [c]Ex 29:40; Lev 23:13; Nu 6:15,17; 15:5; 28:7,14; 2Sa 23:16; 2Ch 29:35 [d]S Ge 28:18 35:15 [e]S Ge 12:8 35:16 [f]ver 19; Ge 48:7; Ru 1:2; 4:11; 1Sa 17:12; Mic 5:2 [g]S Ge 29:6 35:17 [h]Ge 38:28; Ex 1:15 [i]S Ge 30:24 35:18 [j]1Sa 4:21; 14:3 [k]ver 24; Ge 42:4; 43:16,29; 45:12,14; 49:27; Nu 1:36; Dt 33:12 35:19 [l]S ver 16 [m]Ge 48:7; Jos 19:15; Jdg 12:8; 17:7; 19:1,18; Ru 1:1, 19; 1Sa 17:12; Mic 5:2 35:20 [n]Jos 4:9; 7:26; 8:28; 10:27; 1Sa 6:18 [o]1Sa 10:2 35:21 [p]Jos 15:21 35:22 [q]S Ge 22:24 [r]S Ge 29:29; S 34:5; S Lev 18:8 35:23 [s]S Ge 29:16 [t]Ge 43:33; 46:8 [u]S Ge 29:35 [v]S Ge 30:20 35:24 [w]S Ge 30:24 [x]S ver 18 35:25 [y]Ge 37:2 [z]S Ge 30:8 35:26 [a]Ge 37:2 [b]S Ge 30:11 [c]S Ge 30:13 [d]S Ge 34:30; 46:8; Ex 1:1-4 [e]S Ge 25:20 35:27 [f]Ge 31:18 [g]S Ge 13:18 [h]Ge 23:2; Jos 15:54; Jdg 1:10; Ne 11:25 [i]S Ge 13:18 [j]S Ge 17:8

[l]7 *El Bethel* means *God of Bethel.* [m]8 *Allon Bacuth* means *oak of weeping.* [n]9 That is, Northwest Mesopotamia; also in verse 26 [o]10 *Jacob* means *he grasps the heel* (figuratively, *he deceives*). [p]10 *Israel* means *he struggles with God.* [q]11 Hebrew *El-Shaddai* [r]15 *Bethel* means *house of God.* [s]18 *Ben-Oni* means *son of my trouble.* [t]18 *Benjamin* means *son of my right hand.*

35:9–13 GOD APPEARED TO HIM AGAIN. Now that Jacob was finally back in the land of promise and allied with God's will, the covenant promise made to Abraham (17:1–8) was renewed (see article on GOD'S COVENANT WITH ABRAHAM, ISAAC AND JACOB, p. 46).

35:18 NAMED HER SON BEN-ONI . . . FATHER NAMED HIM BENJAMIN. Leah and Rachel named all of Jacob's children. However, to go by the name Ben-Oni ("son of my trouble") would have put a terrible burden of guilt on the boy, for it would make him think he was responsible for his mother's death. Jacob changed his name to the honorable name of Benjamin, "son of my right hand," showing that he was happy to have Benjamin as his son even though Rachel was gone. Children need to be protected from guilt for trouble that comes through no fault of their own.

35:22 REUBEN. Because of Reuben's sexual immorality, his rights as the firstborn were taken away from him. He lost his inheritance and place of leadership forever (see 49:3–4; 1Ch 5:1).

years.[k] 29Then he breathed his last
and died and was gathered to his people,[l] old and full of years.[m] And his
sons Esau and Jacob buried him.[n]

Esau's Descendants

36:10–14pp — 1Ch 1:35–37
36:20–28pp — 1Ch 1:38–42

36 This is the account[o] of Esau
(that is, Edom).[p]

2Esau took his wives from the
women of Canaan:[q] Adah daughter of Elon the Hittite,[r] and Oholibamah[s] daughter of Anah[t] and
granddaughter of Zibeon the
Hivite[u]— 3also Basemath[v]
daughter of Ishmael and sister of
Nebaioth.[w]
4Adah bore Eliphaz to Esau,
Basemath bore Reuel,[x] 5and
Oholibamah bore Jeush, Jalam
and Korah.[y] These were the sons
of Esau, who were born to him in
Canaan.
6Esau took his wives and sons
and daughters and all the members of his household, as well as
his livestock and all his other animals and all the goods he had acquired in Canaan,[z] and moved to
a land some distance from his
brother Jacob.[a] 7Their possessions were too great for them to
remain together; the land where
they were staying could not support them both because of their
livestock.[b] 8So Esau[c] (that is,
Edom)[d] settled in the hill country of Seir.[e]

9This is the account[f] of Esau the
father of the Edomites[g] in the hill
country of Seir.

10These are the names of Esau's
sons:
Eliphaz, the son of Esau's wife
Adah, and Reuel, the son of
Esau's wife Basemath.[h]
11The sons of Eliphaz:[i]
Teman,[j] Omar, Zepho, Gatam
and Kenaz.[k]
12Esau's son Eliphaz also had a
concubine[l] named Timna,
who bore him Amalek.[m] These
were grandsons of Esau's wife
Adah.[n]
13The sons of Reuel:
Nahath, Zerah, Shammah and
Mizzah. These were grandsons
of Esau's wife Basemath.[o]
14The sons of Esau's wife Oholibamah[p] daughter of Anah and
granddaughter of Zibeon, whom
she bore to Esau:
Jeush, Jalam and Korah.[q]

15These were the chiefs[r] among
Esau's descendants:
The sons of Eliphaz the firstborn
of Esau:
Chiefs Teman,[s] Omar, Zepho,
Kenaz,[t] 16Korah,[u] Gatam
and Amalek. These were the
chiefs descended from Eliphaz[u] in Edom;[v] they were
grandsons of Adah.[w]
17The sons of Esau's son Reuel:[x]
Chiefs Nahath, Zerah, Shammah and Mizzah. These were
the chiefs descended from Reuel in Edom; they were grandsons of Esau's wife Base-
math.[y]
18The sons of Esau's wife Oholibamah:[z]
Chiefs Jeush, Jalam and Korah.[a] These were the chiefs
descended from Esau's wife
Oholibamah daughter of Anah.
19These were the sons of Esau[b]
(that is, Edom),[c] and these were their
chiefs.[d]

20These were the sons of Seir the
Horite,[e] who were living in the region:
Lotan, Shobal, Zibeon, Anah,[f]
21Dishon, Ezer and Dishan.
These sons of Seir in Edom
were Horite chiefs.[g]
22The sons of Lotan:
Hori and Homam.[v] Timna was
Lotan's sister.
23The sons of Shobal:
Alvan, Manahath, Ebal, Shepho and Onam.
24The sons of Zibeon:[h]

35:28 [k]S Ge 25:7,20 **35:29** [l]S Ge 25:8 [m]S Ge 15:15 [n]S Ge 23:20; S 25:9 **36:1** [o]S Ge 2:4 [p]S Ge 25:30 **36:2** [q]Ge 28:8-9 [r]Ge 26:34 [s]ver 14, 18 [t]ver 25; 1Ch 1:40 [u]ver 24; S Ge 10:17; 1Ch 1:40 **36:3** [v]ver 4,10, 13,17 [w]S Ge 25:13 **36:4** [x]S ver 3; 1Ch 1:35 **36:5** [y]ver 14,18; 1Ch 1:35 **36:6** [z]Ge 12:5 [a]Ge 27:39 **36:7** [b]S Ge 13:6 **36:8** [c]Dt 2:4 [d]S Ge 25:30 [e]S Ge 14:6 **36:9** [f]S Ge 2:4 [g]ver 1,43 **36:10** [h]S ver 3 **36:11** [i]ver 15-16; 1Ch 1:45; Job 2:11; 4:1 [j]Jer 49:7,20; Eze 25:13; Am 1:12; Ob 1:9; Hab 3:3 [k]ver 15 **36:12** [l]S Ge 22:24 [m]Ex 17:8,16; Nu 24:20; Dt 25:17,19; 1Sa 15:2; 27:8 [n]ver 16 **36:13** [o]S ver 3 **36:14** [p]S ver 2 [q]S ver 5 **36:15** [r]ver 19,40; Ex 15:15 [s]Job 2:11; Jer 49:7; Eze 25:13; Am 1:12; Hab 3:3 [t]S ver 11 **36:16** [u]S ver 11 [v]Ge 32:3; Ex 15:15; Nu 20:14; 33:37 [w]ver 12 **36:17** [x]1Ch 1:37 [y]S ver 3 **36:18** [z]S ver 2 [a]S ver 5 **36:19** [b]1Ch 1:35 [c]S Ge 25:30 [d]S ver 15 **36:20** [e]S Ge 14:6 [f]ver 29 **36:21** [g]ver 30 **36:24** [h]S ver 2

[u] *16* Masoretic Text; Samaritan Pentateuch (see also Gen. 36:11 and 1 Chron. 1:36) does not have *Korah.* [v] *22* Hebrew *Hemam,* a variant of *Homam* (see 1 Chron. 1:39)

36:6–7 ESAU . . . POSSESSIONS. In many ways Esau prospered materially, yet he did not prosper spiritually. His life was characterized by little regard for spiritual things (25:34; 26:34–35; 36:2). Consequently, the nation he founded (Edom) was ungodly, and it became a special object of God's wrath (see Isa 11:14; Am 9:12; Ob 1–4).

Aiah and Anah. This is the
Anah who discovered the hot
springs[w][i] in the desert while
he was grazing the donkeys[j]
of his father Zibeon.
25 The children of Anah:[k]
Dishon and Oholibamah[l]
daughter of Anah.
26 The sons of Dishon[x]:
Hemdan, Eshban, Ithran and
Keran.
27 The sons of Ezer:
Bilhan, Zaavan and Akan.
28 The sons of Dishan:
Uz and Aran.
29 These were the Horite chiefs:
Lotan, Shobal, Zibeon, Anah,[m]
30 Dishon, Ezer and Dishan.
These were the Horite chiefs,[n]
according to their divisions, in
the land of Seir.

The Rulers of Edom

36:31–43pp — 1Ch 1:43–54

31 These were the kings who reigned
in Edom before any Israelite king[o]
reigned[y]:
32 Bela son of Beor became king
of Edom. His city was named
Dinhabah.
33 When Bela died, Jobab son of Zerah from Bozrah[p] succeeded
him as king.
34 When Jobab died, Husham from
the land of the Temanites[q]
succeeded him as king.
35 When Husham died, Hadad son of
Bedad, who defeated Midian[r]
in the country of Moab,[s] succeeded him as king. His city
was named Avith.
36 When Hadad died, Samlah from
Masrekah succeeded him as
king.
37 When Samlah died, Shaul from
Rehoboth[t] on the river[z] succeeded him as king.
38 When Shaul died, Baal-Hanan son
of Acbor succeeded him as
king.

36:24 [i] Jos 15:19 [j] Job 1:14
36:25 [k] S ver 2 [l] S ver 2
36:29 [m] ver 20
36:30 [n] ver 21
36:31 [o] S Ge 17:6
36:33 [p] Isa 34:6; 63:1; Jer 49:13,22
36:34 [q] Jer 49:7; Eze 25:13; Ob 1:9
36:35 [r] S Ge 25:2 [s] S Ge 19:37; Nu 21:11; 22:1; Dt 1:5; Jdg 3:30; Ru 1:1,6
36:37 [t] Ge 26:22
36:40 [u] S ver 15
36:43 [v] S ver 9
37:1 [w] S Ge 17:8 [x] S Ge 10:19
37:2 [y] S Ge 2:4 [z] S Ge 30:24 [a] Ge 41:46; 2Sa 5:4 [b] Ge 46:32; 1Sa 16:11; 17:15; Ps 78:71; Am 7:15 [c] Ge 35:25 [d] Ge 35:26 [e] 1Sa 2:24
37:3 [f] S Ge 17:5 [g] S Ge 25:28 [h] Ge 43:27; 44:20 [i] ver 23,31,32; 2Sa 13:18-19 [j] Ge 43:34; 45:22; 1Sa 1:4-5; Est 2:9

39 When Baal-Hanan son of Acbor
died, Hadad[a] succeeded him
as king. His city was named
Pau, and his wife's name was
Mehetabel daughter of Matred,
the daughter of Me-Zahab.

40 These were the chiefs[u] descended from Esau, by name, according to
their clans and regions:
Timna, Alvah, Jetheth, 41 Oholibamah, Elah, Pinon, 42 Kenaz,
Teman, Mibzar, 43 Magdiel and
Iram. These were the chiefs of
Edom, according to their settlements in the land they occupied.

This was Esau the father of the
Edomites.[v]

Joseph's Dreams

37 Jacob lived in the land where
his father had stayed,[w] the
land of Canaan.[x]

2 This is the account[y] of Jacob.

Joseph,[z] a young man of seventeen,[a] was tending the flocks[b] with
his brothers, the sons of Bilhah[c] and
the sons of Zilpah,[d] his father's wives,
and he brought their father a bad report[e] about them.
3 Now Israel[f] loved Joseph more
than any of his other sons,[g] because
he had been born to him in his old
age;[h] and he made a richly ornamented[b] robe[i] for him.[j] 4 When his brothers saw that their father loved him
more than any of them, they hated

[w] 24 Vulgate; Syriac *discovered water;* the meaning of the Hebrew for this word is uncertain. [x] 26 Hebrew *Dishan,* a variant of *Dishon* [y] 31 Or *before an Israelite king reigned over them* [z] 37 Possibly the Euphrates [a] 39 Many manuscripts of the Masoretic Text, Samaritan Pentateuch and Syriac (see also 1 Chron. 1:50); most manuscripts of the Masoretic Text *Hadar* [b] 3 The meaning of the Hebrew for *richly ornamented* is uncertain; also in verses 23 and 32.

37:2 JOSEPH. The story of Joseph reveals how Jacob's descendants became a nation that lived in Egypt. This section of Genesis not only prepares us for the narrative of the exodus; it also highlights the loyalty that Joseph showed toward his God and the many ways by which God protected and directed his life for the good of others. Joseph's story emphasizes the truth that though the righteous may suffer in an evil and unjust world, ultimately God's purpose for the righteous will triumph.

37:3 A RICHLY ORNAMENTED ROBE. The richly ornamented robe that Joseph received from his father presented a marked contrast to the plainer tunics worn by his brothers. It represented a position of special favoritism and honor with his father.

him[k] and could not speak a kind word
to him.
5Joseph had a dream,[l] and when he
told it to his brothers,[m] they hated him
all the more.[n] **6**He said to them, "Listen to this dream I had: **7**We were binding sheaves[o] of grain out in the field
when suddenly my sheaf rose and
stood upright, while your sheaves
gathered around mine and bowed down
to it."[p]
8His brothers said to him, "Do you
intend to reign over us? Will you actually rule us?"[q] And they hated him all
the more[r] because of his dream and
what he had said.
9Then he had another dream,[s] and
he told it to his brothers. "Listen," he
said, "I had another dream, and this
time the sun and moon and eleven
stars[t] were bowing down to me."[u]
10When he told his father as well as
his brothers,[v] his father rebuked[w]
him and said, "What is this dream you
had? Will your mother and I and your
brothers actually come and bow down
to the ground before you?"[x] **11**His
brothers were jealous of him,[y] but his
father kept the matter in mind.[z]

Joseph Sold by His Brothers

12Now his brothers had gone to
graze their father's flocks near Shechem,[a] **13**and Israel[b] said to Joseph,
"As you know, your brothers are grazing the flocks near Shechem.[c] Come,
I am going to send you to them."
"Very well," he replied.
14So he said to him, "Go and see if
all is well with your brothers[d] and
with the flocks, and bring word back to
me." Then he sent him off from the Valley of Hebron.[e]
When Joseph arrived at Shechem,
15a man found him wandering around
in the fields and asked him, "What are
you looking for?"
16He replied, "I'm looking for my
brothers. Can you tell me where they
are grazing their flocks?"
17"They have moved on from here,"
the man answered. "I heard them say,
'Let's go to Dothan.[f]' "
So Joseph went after his brothers
and found them near Dothan. **18**But
they saw him in the distance, and before he reached them, they plotted to
kill him.[g]
19"Here comes that dreamer![h]"
they said to each other. **20**"Come now,
let's kill him and throw him into one of
these cisterns[i] and say that a ferocious animal[j] devoured him.[k] Then
we'll see what comes of his dreams."[l]
21When Reuben[m] heard this, he
tried to rescue him from their hands.
"Let's not take his life," he said.[n]
22"Don't shed any blood. Throw him
into this cistern[o] here in the desert,
but don't lay a hand on him." Reuben
said this to rescue him from them and
take him back to his father.[p]
23So when Joseph came to his brothers, they stripped him of his robe—the
richly ornamented robe[q] he was wearing— **24**and they took him and threw
him into the cistern.[r] Now the cistern
was empty; there was no water in it.
25As they sat down to eat their meal,
they looked up and saw a caravan of
Ishmaelites[s] coming from Gilead.[t]
Their camels were loaded with spices,
balm[u] and myrrh,[v] and they were on
their way to take them down to
Egypt.[w]
26Judah[x] said to his brothers,
"What will we gain if we kill our brother and cover up his blood?[y] **27**Come,
let's sell him to the Ishmaelites and
not lay our hands on him; after all, he
is our brother,[z] our own flesh and
blood.[a]" His brothers agreed.

37:4 [k]S ver 24; S Ge 27:41; Ac 7:9 **37:5** [l]S Ge 20:3; S 28:12 [m]ver 10 [n]ver 8 **37:7** [o]Ru 2:7,15 [p]ver 9,10; Ge 27:29; 42:6,9; 43:26,28; 44:14; 50:18; 2Sa 1:2; 9:6 **37:8** [q]Ge 41:44; 42:10; 44:16,18; 48:22; 49:26; Dt 33:16 [r]ver 5 **37:9** [s]S ver 7; Ge 28:12 [t]Rev 12:1 [u]Dt 4:19; 17:3 **37:10** [v]ver 5 [w]Ru 2:16; Ps 9:5; 68:30; 106:9; 119:21; Isa 17:13; 54:9; Zec 3:2 [x]S ver 7; S Ge 9:25; S 33:3 **37:11** [y]Ge 26:14; Ac 7:9 [z]Lk 2:19, 51 **37:12** [a]S Ge 12:6 **37:13** [b]S Ge 17:5 [c]Ge 33:19 **37:14** [d]1Sa 17:18 [e]S Ge 13:18 **37:17** [f]2Ki 6:13 **37:18** [g]1Sa 19:1; 2Ch 24:21; Ps 31:13,20; 37:12,32; S Mt 12:14; Mk 14:1; Ac 23:12 **37:19** [h]S Ge 28:12 **37:20** [i]ver 22; Jer 38:6,9 [j]ver 33; Lev 26:6,22; Dt 32:24; 2Ki 17:25; Eze 34:25 [k]ver 31-33; S Ge 4:10 [l]Ge 50:20 **37:21** [m]S Ge 29:32 [n]Ge 42:22 **37:22** [o]S ver 20 [p]ver 29-30 **37:23** [q]ver 3 **37:24** [r]S ver 4; Ge 49:23; Jer 38:6; 41:7; Eze 22:27 **37:25** [s]S Ge 16:11 [t]S Ge 31:21; S SS 4:1 [u]Jer 8:22; 22:6; 46:11 [v]Ge 43:11; Ex 30:23; Ps 45:8; Pr 7:17; SS 1:13; Mt 2:11 [w]ver 28; Ge 39:1; Ps 105:17 **37:26** [x]S Ge 29:35 [y]S Ge 4:10 **37:27** [z]Ge 42:21 [a]S Ge 29:14

37:5 A DREAM. God sometimes reveals his will to us through prophetic dreams (cf. 28:10–17; Nu 12:6–8; Da 7; Mt 1:20–24). Today, under the new covenant, God may still speak to us through dreams (cf. Ac 2:17), although his primary revelation and guidance come through Scripture (Jn 15:7; 1Ti 4:6; Jas 1:21) and the indwelling Holy Spirit (Ro 8:1–17; Gal 5:16–25).

37:6 LISTEN TO THIS DREAM. Joseph showed insensitivity and immaturity in telling his brothers his dream. The dream's purpose was to provide revelation and faith for his difficult future, not to give him an occasion to exalt himself over his brothers. God may have chosen Joseph for the task of protecting Jacob's family in Egypt because his moral standards and dedication to God and his laws were clearly superior to those of his brothers (see 2Ti 2:20–21).

37:7 BOWED DOWN TO IT. Later this dream was literally fulfilled (42:6; 43:26; 44:14).

37:21 REUBEN. Reuben was Jacob's firstborn and as such was supposed to be the leader of the brothers. However, after his immorality with Bilhah (see 35:22, note), he forever lost his effective spiritual leadership and could not influence his brothers sufficiently (vv. 22–29; cf. 42:37–38).

28So when the Midianite[b] merchants came by, his brothers pulled Joseph up out of the cistern[c] and sold[d]
him for twenty shekels[c] of silver[e] to
the Ishmaelites,[f] who took him to
Egypt.[g]
29When Reuben returned to the cistern and saw that Joseph was not
there, he tore his clothes.[h] 30He went
back to his brothers and said, "The boy
isn't there! Where can I turn now?"[i]
31Then they got Joseph's robe,[j]
slaughtered a goat and dipped the robe
in the blood.[k] 32They took the ornamented robe[l] back to their father and
said, "We found this. Examine it to see
whether it is your son's robe."
33He recognized it and said, "It is my
son's robe! Some ferocious animal[m]
has devoured him. Joseph has surely
been torn to pieces."[n]
34Then Jacob tore his clothes,[o] put
on sackcloth[p] and mourned for his
son many days.[q] 35All his sons and
daughters came to comfort him,[r] but
he refused to be comforted.[s] "No," he
said, "in mourning will I go down to the
grave[d][t] to my son.[u]" So his father
wept for him.
36Meanwhile, the Midianites[e][v]
sold Joseph[w] in Egypt to Potiphar, one
of Pharaoh's officials, the captain of
the guard.[x]

Judah and Tamar

38 At that time, Judah[y] left his
brothers and went down to stay
with a man of Adullam[z] named Hi-
rah.[a] 2There Judah met the daughter
of a Canaanite man named Shua.[b] He
married her and lay with her; 3she became pregnant and gave birth to a son,
who was named Er.[c] 4She conceived
again and gave birth to a son and
named him Onan.[d] 5She gave birth to
still another son and named him Shelah.[e] It was at Kezib that she gave
birth to him.
6Judah got a wife for Er, his firstborn, and her name was Tamar.[f] 7But
Er, Judah's firstborn, was wicked in
the LORD's sight;[g] so the LORD put him
to death.[h]
8Then Judah said to Onan, "Lie with
your brother's wife and fulfill your duty
to her as a brother-in-law to produce
offspring for your brother."[i] 9But
Onan knew that the offspring would
not be his; so whenever he lay with his
brother's wife, he spilled his semen on
the ground to keep from producing offspring for his brother. 10What he did
was wicked in the LORD's sight; so he
put him to death also.[j]
11Judah then said to his daughter-in-
law[k] Tamar,[l] "Live as a widow in
your father's house[m] until my son She-

37:28 [b] S Ge 25:2 [c] Jer 38:13 [d] Ex 21:16 [e] Lev 27:5; Mt 26:15 [f] S Ge 16:11 [g] ver 36; Ge 39:1; 45:4-5; Ps 105:17; Jer 12:6; Ac 7:9 **37:29** [h] ver 34; Ge 44:13; Nu 14:6; Jos 7:6; 2Sa 1:11; 2Ki 2:12; 5:7; 11:14; 22:11; Job 1:20; 2:12; Isa 36:22; 37:1; Jer 36:24; 41:5; Joel 2:13 **37:30** [i] ver 22 **37:31** [j] S ver 3 [k] Rev 19:13 **37:32** [l] S ver 3 **37:33** [m] S ver 20 [n] Ge 42:13,38; 44:20,28 **37:34** [o] S ver 29 [p] 2Sa 3:31; 1Ki 20:31; 21:27; 2Ki 6:30; 19:1,2; Job 16:15; Ps 69:11; Isa 3:24; 15:3; 22:12; 32:11; 37:1; Jer 48:37; 49:3; Joel 1:13 [q] Ge 50:3,10,11; Nu 20:29; Dt 34:8 **37:35** [r] Job 2:11; 15:11; 16:5; 42:11 [s] 2Sa 12:17; Ps 77:2; Jer 31:15 [t] Ge 42:38; 44:22, 29,31 [u] 2Sa 12:23 **37:36** [v] S Ge 25:2 [w] S ver 28 [x] Ge 39:1; 40:3; 41:10,12; 1Sa 22:14 **38:1** [y] S Ge 29:35 [z] Jos 12:15; 15:35; 1Sa 22:1; 2Sa 23:13; 2Ch 11:7 [a] ver 12,20 **38:2** [b] ver 12; 1Ch 2:3 **38:3** [c] ver 6; Ge 46:12; Nu 26:19 **38:4** [d] ver 8,9; Ge 46:12; Nu 26:19 **38:5** [e] Nu 26:20 **38:6** [f] ver 11,13 **38:7** [g] S Ge 6:5 [h] ver 10; Ge 46:12; Lev 10:1-2; 1Ch 2:3 **38:8** [i] Dt 25:5-6; Ru 4:5; Mt 22:24-28 **38:10** [j] S ver 7; Dt 25:7-10 **38:11** [k] S Ge 11:31 [l] S ver 6 [m] Ru 1:8

c *28* That is, about 8 ounces (about 0.2 kilogram) d *35* Hebrew *Sheol*
e *36* Samaritan Pentateuch, Septuagint, Vulgate and Syriac (see also verse 28); Masoretic Text *Medanites*

37:28 TOOK HIM TO EGYPT. Though Joseph was treated cruelly by his brothers and sold into slavery, yet in all this God used the evil action of humans to work out his will in Joseph's life (see article on THE PROVIDENCE OF GOD, p. 78).

37:35 DOWN TO THE GRAVE. The word "grave" here is the Hebrew word *Sheol* (see Ps 16:10, note, for comments on this important word).

38:2 DAUGHTER OF A CANAANITE. Scripture records this shameful story of Judah for at least four reasons. (1) It exposes the loose morals of that day against which Joseph's purity stands out in sharp contrast. Notice the contrast between "Judah . . . went down" (of his own accord, v. 1) and "Joseph had been taken down" (39:1). (2) It shows why it was necessary for Israel's (Jacob's) family to leave Canaan and go to Egypt. If Jacob had remained among the Canaanites, his descendants would have lost their identity through mixed marriages (see vv. 1–2). In Egypt Jacob's descendants were segregated from the Egyptians and thereby were able to become a distinctly separate people devoted only to God (see note on 46:34). (3) It illustrates that the sins of everyone, even prominent people in God's redemptive plan, will ultimately be exposed (see article on THE JUDGMENT OF BELIEVERS, p. 1791). (4) It shows that leadership of God's people goes to those who are morally pure. Joseph was faithful to God and his laws, while Judah failed. The same standard applies in the NT for those appointed to spiritual leadership (see article on MORAL QUALIFICATIONS FOR OVERSEERS, p. 1882).

38:6 TAMAR. When Tamar's husband died (v. 7), she was left a childless widow. She longed for a child by which to carry on her family name and to produce offspring (v. 8).

38:9 ONAN. Ancient laws of the Near East required that a brother should marry his brother's widow if she had no children and thus produce a child in the name of his deceased brother (v. 8; Dt 25:5–10). Onan's sin was his refusal to fulfill this responsibility. God took his life because he would not give Tamar a son (v. 10).

lah[n] grows up."[o] For he thought, "He
may die too, just like his brothers." So
Tamar went to live in her father's
house.
12After a long time Judah's wife, the
daughter of Shua,[p] died. When Judah
had recovered from his grief, he went
up to Timnah,[q] to the men who were
shearing his sheep,[r] and his friend Hi-
rah the Adullamite[s] went with him.
13When Tamar[t] was told, "Your father-in-law is on his way to Timnah to
shear his sheep,"[u] 14she took off her
widow's clothes,[v] covered herself
with a veil[w] to disguise herself, and
then sat down[x] at the entrance to
Enaim, which is on the road to Timnah.[y] For she saw that, though Shelah[z] had now grown up, she had not
been given to him as his wife.
15When Judah saw her, he thought
she was a prostitute,[a] for she had covered her face. 16Not realizing[b] that
she was his daughter-in-law,[c] he went
over to her by the roadside and said,
"Come now, let me sleep with you."[d]
"And what will you give me to sleep
with you?"[e] she asked.
17"I'll send you a young goat[f] from
my flock," he said.
"Will you give me something as a
pledge[g] until you send it?" she asked.
18He said, "What pledge should I
give you?"
"Your seal[h] and its cord, and the
staff[i] in your hand," she answered. So
he gave them to her and slept with her,
and she became pregnant by him.[j]
19After she left, she took off her veil
and put on her widow's clothes[k]
again.
20Meanwhile Judah sent the young
goat by his friend the Adullamite[l] in
order to get his pledge[m] back from the
woman, but he did not find her. 21He
asked the men who lived there, "Where
is the shrine prostitute[n] who was beside the road at Enaim?"
"There hasn't been any shrine prostitute here," they said.
22So he went back to Judah and said,
"I didn't find her. Besides, the men
who lived there said, 'There hasn't
been any shrine prostitute here.'"
23Then Judah said, "Let her keep
what she has,[o] or we will become a
laughingstock.[p] After all, I did send
her this young goat, but you didn't find
her."
24About three months later Judah
was told, "Your daughter-in-law Tamar
is guilty of prostitution, and as a result
she is now pregnant."
Judah said, "Bring her out and have
her burned to death!"[q]
25As she was being brought out, she
sent a message to her father-in-law. "I
am pregnant by the man who owns
these," she said. And she added, "See
if you recognize whose seal and cord
and staff these are."[r]
26Judah recognized them and said,
"She is more righteous than I,[s] since
I wouldn't give her to my son Shelah.[t]" And he did not sleep with her
again.
27When the time came for her to give
birth, there were twin boys in her
womb.[u] 28As she was giving birth, one
of them put out his hand; so the midwife[v] took a scarlet thread and tied it
on his wrist[w] and said, "This one came
out first." 29But when he drew back his
hand, his brother came out,[x] and she
said, "So this is how you have broken
out!" And he was named Perez.[f][y]
30Then his brother, who had the scarlet thread on his wrist,[z] came out and
he was given the name Zerah.[g][a]

Joseph and Potiphar's Wife

39 Now Joseph[b] had been taken
down to Egypt. Potiphar, an
Egyptian who was one of Pharaoh's officials, the captain of the guard,[c]
bought him from the Ishmaelites who
had taken him there.[d]

38:11 [n]ver 14,26 [o]Ru 1:13 **38:12** [p]S ver 2 [q]ver 14; Jos 15:10,57; 19:43; Jdg 14:1,2; 2Ch 28:18 [r]S Ge 31:19 [s]S ver 1 **38:13** [t]S ver 6 [u]S Ge 31:19 **38:14** [v]ver 19 [w]S Ge 24:65 [x]Jer 3:2 [y]S ver 12 [z]S ver 11 **38:15** [a]Jdg 11:1; 16:1 **38:16** [b]Ge 42:23 [c]Lev 18:15; 20:12; Ru 1:6 [d]Ge 39:7, 12; 2Sa 13:11 [e]S Ge 30:15 **38:17** [f]Jdg 15:1 [g]ver 20 **38:18** [h]ver 25; 1Ki 21:8; Est 3:12; 8:8; SS 8:6; Isa 49:16; Jer 22:24; Hag 2:23; 2Co 1:22; Eph 1:13 [i]S Ge 32:10; S Ex 4:2 [j]S Ge 19:32 **38:19** [k]ver 14 **38:20** [l]S ver 1 [m]ver 17 **38:21** [n]S Ge 19:5; Lev 19:29; Dt 22:21; 23:17; 2Ki 23:7; Hos 4:14 **38:23** [o]ver 18 [p]Ex 32:25; Job 12:4; Jer 20:7; La 3:14 **38:24** [q]Lev 20:10,14; 21:9; Dt 22:21,22; Jos 7:25; Jdg 15:6; 1Sa 31:12; Job 31:11,28; Eze 16:38 **38:25** [r]S ver 18 **38:26** [s]1Sa 24:17 [t]S ver 11 **38:27** [u]Ge 25:24 **38:28** [v]S Ge 35:17 [w]ver 30 **38:29** [x]Ge 25:26 [y]Ge 46:12; Nu 26:20,21; Ru 4:12,18; 2Sa 5:20; 6:8; 1Ch 2:4; 9:4; Isa 28:21; Mt 1:3 **38:30** [z]ver 28 [a]Ge 46:12; 1Ch 2:4; Ne 11:24 **39:1** [b]S Ge 30:24 [c]S Ge 37:36 [d]S Ge 37:25

[f]29 *Perez* means *breaking out.* [g]30 *Zerah* can mean *scarlet* or *brightness.*

38:15 THOUGHT SHE WAS A PROSTITUTE. Although Tamar was wrong in her action, Judah was the greater sinner whose conduct was hypocritical and corrupt (v. 26). In the time before Jesus came, God overlooked some human ignorance and sin until full redemption was made available in Christ (see Ac 17:30).

39:1 JOSEPH HAD BEEN TAKEN DOWN TO EGYPT. Joseph was taken to Egypt approximately 1900 B.C. This would have been about two hundred years after the call of Abraham (12:1–3). Joseph faced three great tests in Egypt: the test of personal purity, a test that often comes to young people away from home; the test of the opportunity for revenge, a test that often comes to people who have been mistreated; and the test of facing death. In each case he overcame the test through his trust in God and his promises.

2The LORD was with Joseph[e] and he
prospered, and he lived in the house of
his Egyptian master. **3**When his master
saw that the LORD was with him[f] and
that the LORD gave him success in everything he did,[g] **4**Joseph found favor
in his eyes[h] and became his attendant. Potiphar put him in charge of his
household,[i] and he entrusted to his
care everything he owned.[j] **5**From the
time he put him in charge of his household and of all that he owned, the LORD
blessed the household[k] of the Egyptian because of Joseph.[l] The blessing
of the LORD was on everything Potiphar
had, both in the house and in the
field.[m] **6**So he left in Joseph's care everything he had;[n] with Joseph in
charge, he did not concern himself with
anything except the food he ate.

Now Joseph was well-built and handsome,[o] **7**and after a while his master's
wife took notice of Joseph and said,
"Come to bed with me!"[p]

8But he refused.[q] "With me in
charge," he told her, "my master does
not concern himself with anything in
the house; everything he owns he has
entrusted to my care.[r] **9**No one is
greater in this house than I am.[s] My
master has withheld nothing from me
except you, because you are his wife.
How then could I do such a wicked
thing and sin against God?"[t] **10**And
though she spoke to Joseph day after
day, he refused[u] to go to bed with her
or even be with her.

11One day he went into the house to
attend to his duties,[v] and none of the
household servants[w] was inside.
12She caught him by his cloak[x] and
said, "Come to bed with me!"[y] But he
left his cloak in her hand and ran out
of the house.[z]

13When she saw that he had left his
cloak in her hand and had run out of
the house, **14**she called her household
servants.[a] "Look," she said to them,
"this Hebrew[b] has been brought to us
to make sport of us![c] He came in here
to sleep with me, but I screamed.[d]
15When he heard me scream for help,
he left his cloak beside me and ran out
of the house."[e]

16She kept his cloak beside her until
his master came home. **17**Then she told
him this story:[f] "That Hebrew[g]
slave[h] you brought us came to me
to make sport of me. **18**But as soon
as I screamed for help, he left his
cloak beside me and ran out of the
house."

19When his master heard the story
his wife told him, saying, "This is how
your slave treated me," he burned with
anger.[i] **20**Joseph's master took him
and put him in prison,[j] the place
where the king's prisoners were confined.

But while Joseph was there in the
prison, **21**the LORD was with him;[k] he
showed him kindness[l] and granted
him favor in the eyes of the prison warden.[m] **22**So the warden put Joseph in
charge of all those held in the prison,
and he was made responsible for all
that was done there.[n] **23**The warden
paid no attention to anything under Joseph's[o] care, because the LORD was
with Joseph and gave him success in
whatever he did.[p]

39:2 [e]S Ge 21:20, 22; Jos 1:5; 6:27; Jdg 1:19; 1Sa 18:14; Ac 7:9 **39:3** [f]S Ge 21:22 [g]ver 23; 1Sa 18:14; 2Ki 18:7; 2Ch 20:20; Ps 1:3; 128:2; Isa 33:6 **39:4** [h]S Ge 6:8; S 18:3 [i]Ge 47:6; 1Ki 11:28; Pr 22:29 [j]ver 8, 22; Ge 40:4; 42:37 **39:5** [k]2Sa 6:11 [l]S Ge 26:24 [m]Dt 28:3; Ps 128:4 **39:6** [n]Ge 24:2 [o]S Ge 12:11; Ex 2:2; 1Sa 9:2; 16:12; 17:42; Est 2:7; Da 1:4 **39:7** [p]S Ge 38:16; Pr 7:15-18 **39:8** [q]Pr 6:23-24 [r]S ver 4 **39:9** [s]Ge 41:33, 40 [t]S Ge 13:13; S Nu 22:34 **39:10** [u]Est 3:4 **39:11** [v]Ex 18:20; Dt 1:18 [w]ver 14 **39:12** [x]2Sa 13:11; Pr 7:13 [y]S Ge 38:16 [z]ver 15; Pr 5:8; 2Ti 2:22 **39:14** [a]ver 11 [b]S Ge 14:13 [c]S Ge 21:9 [d]Dt 22:24,27 **39:15** [e]S ver 12 **39:17** [f]Ex 20:16; 23:1,7; Dt 5:20; Ps 101:5 [g]S Ge 14:13 [h]Ge 21:10 **39:19** [i]S Ge 34:7; S Est 1:12 **39:20** [j]Ge 40:3; 41:10; Ps 105:18 **39:21** [k]S Ge 21:20 [l]S Ge 19:19 [m]Ex 3:21; 11:3; 12:36; Est 2:9; Ps 106:46; Pr 16:7; Da 1:9 **39:22** [n]S ver 4 **39:23** [o]S Ge 21:20; S Nu 14:43 [p]S ver 3

39:2 THE LORD WAS WITH JOSEPH. Scripture is clear that Joseph's separation from his people was under God's direction. God was working through Joseph and Joseph's circumstances to preserve Israel's family and unite them again according to his promise (cf. 45:5–15; 50:17–20,24; see article on THE PROVIDENCE OF GOD, p. 78).

39:9 SIN AGAINST GOD. All sin, including sin against the integrity of marriage (i.e., adultery), is fundamentally a sin against God (cf. Ps 51:4). King David later learned this the hard way through God's continued judgment on his life and on his home (see Ex 20:14, note).

39:12 HE . . . RAN. Joseph, both out of faithfulness to his God and loyalty to Potiphar, continued to resist sin (cf. Pr 7:6–27). He was victorious over the temptation because he had previously made up his mind to remain obedient to his Lord and not to sin (v. 9). Believers under the new covenant emerge victorious over temptation the same way. We must make a firm and determined decision not to sin against God. Given this purpose, there can be no room for evasion, exception or compromise.

39:20 PUT HIM IN PRISON. Victory over temptation and faithfulness to God do not always result in immediate reward. Joseph suffered because of his righteousness. Christ speaks of his followers also being persecuted because of righteousness (Mt 5:10) and reminds us that such people will be considered blessed and will receive a great reward in heaven (Mt 5:11–12).

39:21 THE LORD WAS WITH HIM. Four times in ch. 39 it is said that "the LORD was with Joseph" (vv. 2,3,21,23). Because Joseph honored God, God honored him. Those who fear God and acknowledge him in all their ways have the promise that God will make all their paths straight (Pr 3:5–7).

The Cupbearer and the Baker

40 Some time later, the cupbearer[q] and the baker[r] of the king
of Egypt offended their master, the
king of Egypt. **2**Pharaoh was angry[s]
with his two officials,[t] the chief cupbearer and the chief baker, **3**and put
them in custody in the house of the
captain of the guard,[u] in the same
prison where Joseph was confined.
4The captain of the guard[v] assigned
them to Joseph,[w] and he attended
them.

After they had been in custody[x] for
some time, **5**each of the two men—the
cupbearer and the baker of the king of
Egypt, who were being held in prison—had a dream[y] the same night,
and each dream had a meaning of its
own.[z]

6When Joseph came to them the next
morning, he saw that they were dejected. **7**So he asked Pharaoh's officials
who were in custody[a] with him in his
master's house, "Why are your faces so
sad today?"[b]

8"We both had dreams," they answered, "but there is no one to interpret them."[c]

Then Joseph said to them, "Do not
interpretations belong to God?[d] Tell
me your dreams."

9So the chief cupbearer[e] told Joseph his dream. He said to him, "In my
dream I saw a vine in front of me, **10**and
on the vine were three branches. As
soon as it budded, it blossomed,[f] and
its clusters ripened into grapes.
11Pharaoh's cup was in my hand, and
I took the grapes, squeezed them into
Pharaoh's cup and put the cup in his
hand."

12"This is what it means,[g]" Joseph
said to him. "The three branches are
three days.[h] **13**Within three days[i]
Pharaoh will lift up your head[j] and
restore you to your position, and you
will put Pharaoh's cup in his hand, just
as you used to do when you were his
cupbearer.[k] **14**But when all goes well
with you, remember me[l] and show me
kindness;[m] mention me to Pharaoh[n]
and get me out of this prison. **15**For I
was forcibly carried off from the land of
the Hebrews,[o] and even here I have
done nothing to deserve being put in a
dungeon."[p]

16When the chief baker[q] saw that
Joseph had given a favorable interpretation,[r] he said to Joseph, "I too had
a dream: On my head were three baskets[s] of bread.[h] **17**In the top basket
were all kinds of baked goods for Pharaoh, but the birds were eating them out
of the basket on my head."

18"This is what it means," Joseph
said. "The three baskets are three
days.[t] **19**Within three days[u] Pharaoh
will lift off your head[v] and hang you
on a tree.[i][w] And the birds will eat
away your flesh."[x]

20Now the third day[y] was Pharaoh's birthday,[z] and he gave a feast
for all his officials.[a] He lifted up the
heads of the chief cupbearer and the
chief baker[b] in the presence of his officials: **21**He restored the chief cupbearer[c] to his position,[d] so that he
once again put the cup into Pharaoh's
hand,[e] **22**but he hanged[j] the chief
baker,[f] just as Joseph had said to
them in his interpretation.[g]

23The chief cupbearer, however, did
not remember Joseph; he forgot him.[h]

Pharaoh's Dreams

41 When two full years had
passed, Pharaoh had a
dream:[i] He was standing by the
Nile,[j] **2**when out of the river there
came up seven cows, sleek and fat,[k]
and they grazed among the reeds.[l]
3After them, seven other cows, ugly
and gaunt, came up out of the Nile and

40:1 q ver 9,13, 21; Ne 1:11 r ver 16,20
40:2 s Pr 16:14, 15; 19:12 t Ge 41:10; Est 2:21
40:3 u S Ge 37:36; S 39:20
40:4 v S Ge 37:36 w S Ge 39:4 x ver 7; Ge 42:17
40:5 y S Ge 20:3 z Ge 41:11
40:7 a S ver 4 b Ne 2:2
40:8 c Ge 41:8,15 d Ge 41:16,25,28, 32; Dt 29:29; Da 2:22,28,47
40:9 e S ver 1
40:10 f Isa 27:6; 35:1-2; Hos 14:7
40:12 g ver 16; Ge 41:12,15,25; Da 2:36; 4:19 h ver 18
40:13 i ver 19,20; Jos 1:11; 3:2; Ezr 8:32; Ne 2:11 j ver 19
k S ver 1
40:14 l 1Sa 25:31; Lk 23:42 m S Ge 19:19; 1Sa 20:14,42; 2Sa 9:1; 1Ki 2:7 n ver 23; Ge 41:9; Ecc 9:15
40:15 o S Ge 14:13 p Ge 39:20; Job 13:27
40:16 q S ver 1 r S ver 12 s Am 8:1-2
40:18 t ver 12
40:19 u ver 13 v S ver 13 w ver 22; Dt 21:22-23; Est 2:23; 7:10 x Dt 28:26; 1Sa 17:44; 2Sa 21:10; 1Ki 14:11; 16:4; 21:24; Eze 39:4
40:20 y S ver 13 z Mt 14:6-10 a Est 2:18; Mk 6:21 b S ver 1
40:21 c S ver 1 d 2Ki 25:27; Jer 52:31 e ver 13
40:22 f S ver 19 g Ge 41:13; Ps 105:19
40:23 h S ver 14; S Ecc 1:11
41:1 i S Ge 20:3 j ver 17; S Ge 2:14; Ex 1:22; 2:5; 7:15
41:2 k ver 26; Jer 5:28
l ver 18; Ex 2:3; Job 40:21; Isa 19:6

h 16 Or *three wicker baskets* i 19 Or *and impale you on a pole* j 22 Or *impaled*

40:1 SOME TIME LATER. Joseph maintained his faith in God while being unjustly confined to prison for at least two years. His interpretations of Pharaoh's dreams through God's revelation provided the opportunity for his later release and ascendancy in authority. This narrative emphasizes that although God does not cause all things that happen (see 39:7–23), he nevertheless can use adverse circumstances to work in all things for the good of those who love him (see Ro 8:28, note).

40:2 PHARAOH. This was the general term used for all the kings of Egypt. It was commonly attached to the monarch's name.

41:1 WHEN TWO FULL YEARS HAD PASSED, PHARAOH HAD A DREAM. Ch. 41 shows God working in the lives of Pharaoh and Joseph in order to control the destinies of the nations and to provide a place for his chosen people. All nations are subject to God's interventions and direct control.

stood beside those on the riverbank.
4And the cows that were ugly and
gaunt ate up the seven sleek, fat cows.
Then Pharaoh woke up.[m]
5He fell asleep again and had a second dream: Seven heads of grain,[n]
healthy and good, were growing on a
single stalk. 6After them, seven other
heads of grain sprouted—thin and
scorched by the east wind.[o] 7The thin
heads of grain swallowed up the seven
healthy, full heads. Then Pharaoh
woke up;[p] it had been a dream.
8In the morning his mind was troubled,[q] so he sent for all the magicians[r] and wise men of Egypt. Pharaoh told them his dreams, but no one
could interpret them for him.[s]
9Then the chief cupbearer said to
Pharaoh, "Today I am reminded of my
shortcomings.[t] 10Pharaoh was once
angry with his servants,[u] and he imprisoned me and the chief baker in the
house of the captain of the guard.[v]
11Each of us had a dream the same
night, and each dream had a meaning
of its own.[w] 12Now a young Hebrew[x]
was there with us, a servant of the captain of the guard.[y] We told him our
dreams, and he interpreted them for
us, giving each man the interpretation
of his dream.[z] 13And things turned
out exactly as he interpreted them to
us: I was restored to my position, and
the other man was hanged.[k][a]"
14So Pharaoh sent for Joseph, and
he was quickly brought from the dungeon.[b] When he had shaved[c] and
changed his clothes,[d] he came before
Pharaoh.
15Pharaoh said to Joseph, "I had a
dream, and no one can interpret it.[e]
But I have heard it said of you that
when you hear a dream you can interpret it."[f]
16"I cannot do it," Joseph replied to
Pharaoh, "but God will give Pharaoh
the answer he desires."[g]
17Then Pharaoh said to Joseph, "In
my dream I was standing on the bank
of the Nile,[h] 18when out of the river
there came up seven cows, fat and
sleek, and they grazed among the
reeds.[i] 19After them, seven other
cows came up—scrawny and very ugly
and lean. I had never seen such ugly
cows in all the land of Egypt. 20The
lean, ugly cows ate up the seven fat
cows that came up first. 21But even after they ate them, no one could tell that
they had done so; they looked just as
ugly as before. Then I woke up.
22"In my dreams I also saw seven
heads of grain, full and good, growing
on a single stalk. 23After them, seven
other heads sprouted—withered and
thin and scorched by the east wind.
24The thin heads of grain swallowed up
the seven good heads. I told this to the
magicians, but none could explain it to
me.[j]"
25Then Joseph said to Pharaoh, "The
dreams of Pharaoh are one and the
same.[k] God has revealed to Pharaoh
what he is about to do.[l] 26The seven
good cows[m] are seven years, and the
seven good heads of grain are seven
years; it is one and the same dream.
27The seven lean, ugly cows that came
up afterward are seven years, and so
are the seven worthless heads of grain
scorched by the east wind: They are
seven years of famine.[n]
28"It is just as I said to Pharaoh:
God has shown Pharaoh what he is
about to do.[o] 29Seven years of great
abundance[p] are coming throughout
the land of Egypt, 30but seven years of
famine[q] will follow them. Then all the
abundance in Egypt will be forgotten,
and the famine will ravage the land.[r]
31The abundance in the land will not be
remembered, because the famine that
follows it will be so severe. 32The reason the dream was given to Pharaoh in
two forms is that the matter has been
firmly decided[s] by God, and God will
do it soon.[t]
33"And now let Pharaoh look for a

41:4 [m]ver 7
41:5 [n]Jos 13:3; 2Ki 4:42; 1Ch 13:5; Isa 23:3; Jer 2:18
41:6 [o]Ex 10:13; 14:21; Job 6:26; 11:2; 15:2; Ps 11:6; 48:7; Isa 11:15; 27:8; Jer 4:11; 18:17; Eze 19:12; 27:26; Hos 12:1; 13:15; Jnh 4:8
41:7 [p]ver 4
41:8 [q]Job 7:14; Da 2:1,3; 4:5,19 [r]Ex 7:11,22; Da 1:20; 2:2,27; 4:7; 5:7 [s]ver 24; S Ge 40:8; Da 4:18
41:9 [t]S Ge 40:14
41:10 [u]S Ge 40:2 [v]S Ge 37:36; S 39:20
41:11 [w]Ge 40:5
41:12 [x]S Ge 14:13; 39:17 [y]S Ge 37:36; 40:4 [z]S Ge 40:12
41:13 [a]S Ge 40:22
41:14 [b]Ps 105:20 [c]Isa 18:2,7 [d]S Ge 35:2; 45:22; Ru 3:3; 2Sa 12:20
41:15 [e]S Ge 40:8 [f]S Ge 40:12; Da 4:18; 5:16
41:16 [g]S Ge 40:8
41:17 [h]S ver 1
41:18 [i]S ver 2
41:24 [j]S ver 8
41:25 [k]S Ge 40:12 [l]S Ge 40:8; Isa 46:11; Da 2:45
41:26 [m]S ver 2
41:27 [n]S Ge 12:10
41:28 [o]S Ge 40:8
41:29 [p]ver 47
41:30 [q]ver 54; Ge 45:6,11; 47:13; Ps 105:16 [r]ver 56; S Ge 12:10
41:32 [s]Da 2:5 [t]S Ge 40:8

[k]13 Or *impaled*

41:8 THE MAGICIANS OF EGYPT. Magicians (people who practiced magic arts) were common in Egypt (cf. Ex 7:11; 8:7,18–19; 9:11). Magic arts consisted in practicing divination or sorcery (i.e., attempting to discover hidden knowledge by means of spirits), trying to discover the future through interpreting omens, and attempting to control the course of nature, humans or circumstances with the aid of supernatural powers or spirits. The Mosaic Law strictly condemned all contact with magic arts (Dt 18:9–14), as does the NT (Ac 19:17–20; Rev 9:20–21; 22:15).

41:16 GOD WILL GIVE PHARAOH THE ANSWER. Joseph insisted that his God would give the interpretation of Pharaoh's dream. His outspoken faith in the Lord God could have cost him his life in the presence of an Egyptian king who was himself considered to be a god.

discerning and wise man[u] and put him
in charge of the land of Egypt.[v] **34**Let
Pharaoh appoint commissioners[w]
over the land to take a fifth[x] of the
harvest of Egypt during the seven
years of abundance.[y] **35**They should
collect all the food of these good years
that are coming and store up the grain
under the authority of Pharaoh, to be
kept in the cities for food.[z] **36**This
food should be held in reserve for the
country, to be used during the seven
years of famine that will come upon
Egypt,[a] so that the country may not
be ruined by the famine."

37The plan seemed good to Pharaoh
and to all his officials.[b] **38**So Pharaoh
asked them, "Can we find anyone like
this man, one in whom is the spirit of
God[l]?"[c]

39Then Pharaoh said to Joseph,
"Since God has made all this known to
you,[d] there is no one so discerning
and wise as you.[e] **40**You shall be in
charge of my palace,[f] and all my people are to submit to your orders.[g] Only
with respect to the throne will I be
greater than you.[h]"

Joseph in Charge of Egypt

41So Pharaoh said to Joseph, "I hereby put you in charge of the whole land
of Egypt."[i] **42**Then Pharaoh took his
signet ring[j] from his finger and put it
on Joseph's finger. He dressed him in
robes[k] of fine linen[l] and put a gold
chain around his neck.[m] **43**He had him
ride in a chariot[n] as his second-in-
command,[m][o] and men shouted before
him, "Make way[n]!"[p] Thus he put him
in charge of the whole land of Egypt.[q]

44Then Pharaoh said to Joseph, "I
am Pharaoh, but without your word no
one will lift hand or foot in all Egypt."[r]
45Pharaoh gave Joseph[s] the name
Zaphenath-Paneah and gave him Asenath daughter of Potiphera, priest[t] of
On,[o][u] to be his wife.[v] And Joseph
went throughout the land of Egypt.

46Joseph was thirty years old[w]
when he entered the service[x] of Pharaoh king of Egypt. And Joseph went out
from Pharaoh's presence and traveled
throughout Egypt. **47**During the seven
years of abundance[y] the land produced plentifully. **48**Joseph collected
all the food produced in those seven
years of abundance in Egypt and
stored it in the cities.[z] In each city he
put the food grown in the fields surrounding it. **49**Joseph stored up huge
quantities of grain, like the sand of the
sea;[a] it was so much that he stopped
keeping records because it was beyond
measure.

50Before the years of famine came,
two sons were born to Joseph by Asenath daughter of Potiphera, priest of
On.[b] **51**Joseph named his firstborn[c]
Manasseh[p][d] and said, "It is because
God has made me forget all my trouble
and all my father's household." **52**The
second son he named Ephraim[q][e] and
said, "It is because God has made me
fruitful[f] in the land of my suffering."

53The seven years of abundance in
Egypt came to an end, **54**and the seven
years of famine[g] began,[h] just as Joseph had said. There was famine in all
the other lands, but in the whole land
of Egypt there was food. **55**When all
Egypt began to feel the famine,[i] the
people cried to Pharaoh for food. Then
Pharaoh told all the Egyptians, "Go to
Joseph and do what he tells you."[j]

56When the famine had spread over
the whole country, Joseph opened the
storehouses and sold grain to the
Egyptians,[k] for the famine[l] was severe throughout Egypt.[m] **57**And all the
countries came to Egypt to buy grain
from Joseph,[n] because the famine was
severe in all the world.[o]

Joseph's Brothers Go to Egypt

42 When Jacob learned that there
was grain in Egypt,[p] he said to
his sons, "Why do you just keep look-

41:33 [u] ver 39 [v] S Ge 39:9 **41:34** [w] Est 2:3 [x] Ge 47:24,26; 1Sa 8:15 [y] ver 48; Ge 47:14 **41:35** [z] ver 48 **41:36** [a] ver 56; Ge 42:6; 47:14 **41:37** [b] Ge 45:16; Est 2:4; Isa 19:11 **41:38** [c] Nu 27:18; Dt 34:9; Da 2:11; 4:8,8-9,18; 5:11, 14 **41:39** [d] Da 2:11; 5:11 [e] ver 33 **41:40** [f] 1Ki 4:6; 2Ki 15:5; Isa 22:15; 36:3 [g] S Ge 39:9; Ps 105:21-22; Ac 7:10 [h] Est 10:3 **41:41** [i] ver 43,55; Ge 42:6; 45:8,13, 26; Est 8:2; Jer 40:7; Da 6:3 **41:42** [j] S Ge 24:22; Est 3:10; 8:2,8 [k] 1Sa 17:38; 18:4; 1Ki 19:19; Est 6:8,11; Da 5:29; Zec 3:4 [l] Ex 25:4; Est 8:15; Da 5:29 [m] Ps 73:6; SS 4:9; Isa 3:18; Eze 16:11; Da 5:7, 16,29 **41:43** [n] Ge 46:29; 50:9; Isa 2:7; 22:18 [o] Est 10:3 [p] Est 6:9 [q] S ver 41 **41:44** [r] S Ge 37:8; Est 10:2; Ps 105:22 **41:45** [s] Est 2:7 [t] Ex 2:16 [u] Eze 30:17 [v] ver 50; Ge 46:20, 27 **41:46** [w] S Ge 37:2 [x] 1Sa 8:11; 16:21; Pr 22:29; Da 1:19 **41:47** [y] ver 29 **41:48** [z] S ver 34 **41:49** [a] S Ge 12:2 **41:50** [b] S ver 45 **41:51** [c] Ge 48:14, 18,20; 49:3 [d] Ge 46:20; 48:1; 50:23; Nu 1:34; Dt 33:17; Jos 4:12; 17:1; 1Ch 7:14 **41:52** [e] Ge 46:20; 48:1,5; 50:23; Nu 1:32; 26:28; Dt 33:17; Jos 14:4; Jdg 5:14; 1Ch 7:20; 2Ch 30:1; Ps 60:7; Jer 7:15; Ob 1:19 [f] S Ge 17:6 **41:54** [g] S Ge 12:10 [h] Ac 7:11 **41:55** [i] Dt 32:24; 2Ch 20:9; Isa 51:19; Jer 5:12; 27:8; 42:16; 44:27 [j] S ver 41; Jn 2:5

41:56 [k] S ver 36 [l] S Ge 12:10 [m] S ver 30 **41:57** [n] Ge 42:5; 47:15 [o] S Ge 12:10 **42:1** [p] Ac 7:12

[l] 38 Or *of the gods* [m] 43 Or *in the chariot of his second-in-command*; or *in his second chariot* [n] 43 Or *Bow down* [o] 45 That is, Heliopolis; also in verse 50 [p] 51 *Manasseh* sounds like and may be derived from the Hebrew for *forget.* [q] 52 *Ephraim* sounds like the Hebrew for *twice fruitful.*

41:46 JOSEPH WAS THIRTY YEARS OLD. Joseph was seventeen years old when he was sold into slavery by his brothers (37:2). He spent thirteen years as a slave and at least three of those years were spent in prison. When God exalted him to a position of honor and rulership at age thirty, Joseph continued to be faithful to his God. This commitment to God is signified in the Hebrew names of his two sons (vv. 50–52).

ing at each other?" **2**He continued, "I
have heard that there is grain in Egypt.
Go down there and buy some for us,[q]
so that we may live and not die."[r]
3Then ten of Joseph's brothers went
down to buy grain[s] from Egypt. **4**But
Jacob did not send Benjamin,[t] Joseph's brother, with the others, because he was afraid that harm might
come to him.[u] **5**So Israel's sons were
among those who went to buy grain,[v]
for the famine was in the land of Canaan[w] also.[x]
6Now Joseph was the governor of the
land,[y] the one who sold grain to all its
people.[z] So when Joseph's brothers
arrived, they bowed down to him with
their faces to the ground.[a] **7**As soon
as Joseph saw his brothers, he recognized them, but he pretended to be a
stranger and spoke harshly to them.[b]
"Where do you come from?"[c] he
asked.
"From the land of Canaan," they replied, "to buy food."
8Although Joseph recognized his
brothers, they did not recognize him.[d]
9Then he remembered his dreams[e]
about them and said to them, "You are
spies![f] You have come to see where
our land is unprotected."[g]
10"No, my lord,[h]" they answered.
"Your servants have come to buy
food.[i] **11**We are all the sons of one
man. Your servants[j] are honest
men,[k] not spies.[l]"
12"No!" he said to them. "You have
come to see where our land is unprotected."[m]
13But they replied, "Your servants[n]
were twelve brothers, the sons of one
man, who lives in the land of Canaan.[o]
The youngest is now with our father,
and one is no more."[p]
14Joseph said to them, "It is just as
I told you: You are spies![q] **15**And this
is how you will be tested: As surely as
Pharaoh lives,[r] you will not leave this
place unless your youngest brother
comes here.[s] **16**Send one of your number to get your brother;[t] the rest of
you will be kept in prison,[u] so that
your words may be tested to see if you
are telling the truth.[v] If you are not,
then as surely as Pharaoh lives, you
are spies![w]" **17**And he put them all in
custody[x] for three days.
18On the third day, Joseph said to
them, "Do this and you will live, for I
fear God:[y] **19**If you are honest men,[z]
let one of your brothers stay here in
prison,[a] while the rest of you go and
take grain back for your starving
households.[b] **20**But you must bring
your youngest brother to me,[c] so that
your words may be verified and that
you may not die." This they proceeded
to do.
21They said to one another, "Surely
we are being punished because of our
brother.[d] We saw how distressed he
was when he pleaded with us for his
life, but we would not listen; that's why
this distress[e] has come upon us."
22Reuben replied, "Didn't I tell you
not to sin against the boy?[f] But you
wouldn't listen! Now we must give an
accounting[g] for his blood."[h] **23**They
did not realize[i] that Joseph could understand them,[j] since he was using
an interpreter.
24He turned away from them and began to weep,[k] but then turned back
and spoke to them again. He had Simeon taken from them and bound before
their eyes.[l]
25Joseph gave orders to fill their
bags with grain,[m] to put each man's
silver back in his sack,[n] and to give
them provisions[o] for their journey.[p]
After this was done for them, **26**they

42:2 [q] Ge 43:2,4; 44:25 [r] ver 19,33; Ge 43:8; 47:19; Ps 33:18-19
42:3 [s] ver 10; Ge 43:20
42:4 [t] S Ge 35:18 [u] ver 38
42:5 [v] S Ge 41:57 [w] ver 13,29; Ge 31:18; 45:17 [x] S Ge 12:10; S Dt 32:24; Ac 7:11
42:6 [y] S Ge 41:41; S Ne 5:14 [z] S Ge 41:36 [a] S Ge 33:3
42:7 [b] ver 30 [c] S Ge 29:4
42:8 [d] Ge 37:2
42:9 [e] S Ge 37:7 [f] ver 14,16,30; Dt 1:22; Jos 2:1; 6:22 [g] ver 12
42:10 [h] S Ge 37:8 [i] S ver 3
42:11 [j] ver 13; Ge 44:7,9,16,19, 21,31; 46:34; 47:3 [k] ver 15,16,19,20, 34 [l] ver 31
42:12 [m] ver 9
42:13 [n] S ver 11 [o] S ver 5; Ge 46:31; 47:1 [p] ver 24,32,36; S Ge 37:30,33; 43:7,29,33; 44:8; Jer 31:15
42:14 [q] S ver 9
42:15 [r] 1Sa 17:55 [s] S ver 11; Ge 43:3,5,7; 44:21,23
42:16 [t] ver 15 [u] ver 19 [v] S ver 11 [w] S ver 9
42:17 [x] S Ge 40:4
42:18 [y] S Ge 20:11; S 22:12; Lev 19:14; 25:43; 2Sa 23:3
42:19 [z] S ver 11 [a] ver 16 [b] S ver 2
42:20 [c] S ver 15
42:21 [d] Ge 37:26-28 [e] Ge 45:5
42:22 [f] Ge 37:21-22 [g] S Ge 9:5 [h] Ge 45:24
42:23 [i] Ge 38:16 [j] S Ge 11:7
42:24 [k] S Ge 29:11 [l] S ver 13; Ge 43:14,23
42:25 [m] Ge 43:2 [n] ver 27,35; Ge 43:12,18,21; 44:1,8 [o] Jer 40:5 [p] Ge 45:21,23

42:4 BENJAMIN. Benjamin was one of Rachel's two sons and thus a full brother of Joseph. Having already lost one son of Rachel, Jacob carefully protected Benjamin by keeping him safely at home.

42:8 JOSEPH RECOGNIZED HIS BROTHERS. Joseph concealed his identity until he determined whether his brothers would show sorrow for what they had done to him and to his father years ago (ch. 37).

42:9 YOU ARE SPIES! While Joseph recognized his brothers and knew that they were not spies, he tested them in order to determine if they had changed in character and had come to a point of remorse over the evil they had done to him and to his father Jacob.

42:21 WE ARE BEING PUNISHED. The brothers were brought to a realization of their guilt for their unmerciful treatment of Joseph twenty years earlier (37:2; 41:46,53–54). They saw that God was justly punishing them for their crime (vv. 21–22). Often when we have concealed sin in our lives, God will work in order to open our consciences to our guilt. We can either harden our hearts or humble ourselves before God, confess our sin and resolve to act righteously.

loaded their grain on their donkeys[q]
and left.
27At the place where they stopped
for the night one of them opened his
sack to get feed for his donkey,[r] and
he saw his silver in the mouth of his
sack.[s] **28**"My silver has been returned," he said to his brothers. "Here
it is in my sack."
Their hearts sank[t] and they turned
to each other trembling[u] and said,
"What is this that God has done to
us?"[v]
29When they came to their father Jacob in the land of Canaan,[w] they told
him all that had happened to them.[x]
They said, **30**"The man who is lord over
the land spoke harshly to us[y] and
treated us as though we were spying
on the land.[z] **31**But we said to him,
'We are honest men; we are not
spies.[a] **32**We were twelve brothers,
sons of one father. One is no more, and
the youngest is now with our father in
Canaan.'[b]
33"Then the man who is lord over
the land said to us, 'This is how I will
know whether you are honest men:
Leave one of your brothers here with
me, and take food for your starving
households and go.[c] **34**But bring your
youngest brother to me so I will know
that you are not spies but honest
men.[d] Then I will give your brother
back to you,[e] and you can trade[r] in
the land.[f]' "
35As they were emptying their
sacks, there in each man's sack was
his pouch of silver![g] When they and
their father saw the money pouches,
they were frightened.[h] **36**Their father
Jacob said to them, "You have deprived
me of my children. Joseph is no more
and Simeon is no more,[i] and now you
want to take Benjamin.[j] Everything is
against me![k]"
37Then Reuben said to his father,
"You may put both of my sons to death
if I do not bring him back to you. Entrust him to my care,[l] and I will bring
him back."[m]
38But Jacob said, "My son will not go
down there with you; his brother is
dead[n] and he is the only one left. If
harm comes to him[o] on the journey
you are taking, you will bring my gray
head down to the grave[s][p] in sorrow.[q]"

The Second Journey to Egypt

43 Now the famine was still severe
in the land.[r] **2**So when they
had eaten all the grain they had
brought from Egypt,[s] their father said
to them, "Go back and buy us a little
more food."[t]
3But Judah[u] said to him, "The man
warned us solemnly, 'You will not see
my face again unless your brother is
with you.'[v] **4**If you will send our brother along with us, we will go down and
buy food for you.[w] **5**But if you will not
send him, we will not go down, because
the man said to us, 'You will not see my
face again unless your brother is with
you.[x]' "
6Israel[y] asked, "Why did you bring
this trouble[z] on me by telling the man
you had another brother?"
7They replied, "The man questioned
us closely about ourselves and our
family. 'Is your father still living?'[a] he
asked us. 'Do you have another brother?'[b] We simply answered his questions. How were we to know he would
say, 'Bring your brother down
here'?"[c]
8Then Judah[d] said to Israel[e] his
father, "Send the boy along with me
and we will go at once, so that we and
you and our children may live and not
die.[f] **9**I myself will guarantee his safety; you can hold me personally responsible for him.[g] If I do not bring him
back to you and set him here before
you, I will bear the blame[h] before you
all my life.[i] **10**As it is, if we had not
delayed,[j] we could have gone and returned twice."
11Then their father Israel[k] said to
them, "If it must be, then do this: Put
some of the best products[l] of the land
in your bags and take them down to the
man as a gift[m]—a little balm[n] and a
little honey, some spices[o] and
myrrh,[p] some pistachio nuts and al-

42:26 [q]S Ge 32:15; 44:13; 45:17; 1Sa 25:18; Isa 30:6
42:27 [r]Jdg 19:19; Job 39:9; Isa 1:3 [s]S ver 25
42:28 [t]Jos 2:11; 5:1; 7:5 [u]Mk 5:33 [v]Ge 43:23
42:29 [w]S ver 5 [x]Ge 44:24
42:30 [y]ver 7 [z]S ver 9
42:31 [a]ver 11
42:32 [b]S ver 13
42:33 [c]S ver 2
42:34 [d]S ver 11 [e]S ver 24 [f]Ge 34:10
42:35 [g]S ver 25 [h]Ge 43:18
42:36 [i]S ver 13 [j]S ver 24 [k]Job 3:25; Pr 10:24; Ro 8:31
42:37 [l]S Ge 39:4 [m]Ge 43:9; 44:32
42:38 [n] Ge 37:33 [o]ver 4 [p]S Ge 37:35 [q]Ge 44:29,34; 48:7
43:1 [r]S Ge 12:10
43:2 [s]Ge 42:25 [t]S Ge 42:2
43:3 [u]ver 8; Ge 44:14,18; 46:28 [v]S Ge 42:15
43:4 [w]S Ge 42:2
43:5 [x]S Ge 42:15; 44:26; 2Sa 3:13
43:6 [y]ver 8,11; S Ge 17:5 [z]S Ge 34:30
43:7 [a]ver 27; Ge 45:3 [b]S Ge 42:13; 44:19 [c]S Ge 42:15
43:8 [d]S ver 3; S Ge 29:35 [e]S ver 6 [f]S Ge 42:2; Ps 33:18-19
43:9 [g]1Sa 23:20 [h]Ge 44:10,17 [i]S Ge 42:37; Phm 1:18-19
43:10 [j]Ge 45:9
43:11 [k]S ver 6 [l]S Ge 24:10 [m]S Ge 32:13 [n]S Ge 37:25; Eze 27:17 [o]Ex 30:23; 1Ki 10:2; Eze 27:22 [p]S Ge 37:25

[r]34 Or *move about freely* [s]38 Hebrew *Sheol*

42:37 PUT BOTH OF MY SONS TO DEATH. Vv. 29–38 show that Joseph's brothers had changed for the better. Reuben, for example, was willing to give up his own sons rather than bring any more sorrow on his father.

43:9 I WILL BEAR THE BLAME. Like Reuben (42:37), Judah willingly accepted responsibility for his brother Benjamin. He offered to accept lasting disgrace and blame should Benjamin not come back safely.

monds. **12**Take double the amount[q] of
silver with you, for you must return the
silver that was put back into the
mouths of your sacks.[r] Perhaps it
was a mistake. **13**Take your brother
also and go back to the man at once.[s]
14And may God Almighty[t]t grant
you mercy[u] before the man so that he
will let your other brother and Benjamin come back with you.[v] As for me,
if I am bereaved, I am bereaved."[w]

15So the men took the gifts and double the amount of silver,[x] and Benjamin also. They hurried[y] down to
Egypt and presented themselves[z] to
Joseph. **16**When Joseph saw Benjamin[a] with them, he said to the steward of his house,[b] "Take these men to
my house, slaughter an animal and
prepare dinner;[c] they are to eat with
me at noon."

17The man did as Joseph told him
and took the men to Joseph's house.[d]
18Now the men were frightened[e]
when they were taken to his house.[f]
They thought, "We were brought here
because of the silver that was put back
into our sacks[g] the first time. He
wants to attack us[h] and overpower us
and seize us as slaves[i] and take our
donkeys.[j]"

19So they went up to Joseph's steward[k] and spoke to him at the entrance
to the house. **20**"Please, sir," they said,
"we came down here the first time to
buy food.[l] **21**But at the place where
we stopped for the night we opened our
sacks and each of us found his silver—
the exact weight—in the mouth of
his sack. So we have brought it back
with us.[m] **22**We have also brought
additional silver with us to buy food.
We don't know who put our silver in
our sacks."

23"It's all right," he said. "Don't be
afraid. Your God, the God of your father,[n] has given you treasure in your
sacks;[o] I received your silver." Then
he brought Simeon out to them.[p]

24The steward took the men into Joseph's house,[q] gave them water to
wash their feet[r] and provided fodder
for their donkeys. **25**They prepared
their gifts[s] for Joseph's arrival at
noon,[t] because they had heard that
they were to eat there.

26When Joseph came home,[u] they
presented to him the gifts[v] they had
brought into the house, and they
bowed down before him to the
ground.[w] **27**He asked them how they
were, and then he said, "How is your
aged father[x] you told me about? Is he
still living?"[y]

28They replied, "Your servant our father[z] is still alive and well." And they
bowed low[a] to pay him honor.[b]

29As he looked about and saw his
brother Benjamin, his own mother's
son,[c] he asked, "Is this your youngest
brother, the one you told me about?"[d]
And he said, "God be gracious to you,[e]
my son." **30**Deeply moved[f] at the
sight of his brother, Joseph hurried out
and looked for a place to weep. He
went into his private room and wept[g]
there.

31After he had washed his face, he
came out and, controlling himself,[h]
said, "Serve the food."[i]

32They served him by himself, the
brothers by themselves, and the Egyptians who ate with him by themselves,
because Egyptians could not eat with
Hebrews,[j] for that is detestable to
Egyptians.[k] **33**The men had been seated before him in the order of their ages,
from the firstborn[l] to the youngest;[m]
and they looked at each other in astonishment. **34**When portions were served
to them from Joseph's table, Benjamin's portion was five times as much
as anyone else's.[n] So they feasted[o]
and drank freely with him.

A Silver Cup in a Sack

44 Now Joseph gave these instructions to the steward of his
house:[p] "Fill the men's sacks with as
much food as they can carry, and put
each man's silver in the mouth of his
sack.[q] **2**Then put my cup,[r] the silver
one,[s] in the mouth of the youngest
one's sack, along with the silver for his
grain." And he did as Joseph said.

43:12 [q] ver 15; Ex 22:4,7; Pr 6:31 [r] S Ge 42:25
43:13 [s] ver 3
43:14 [t] S Ge 17:1 [u] Dt 13:17; Ps 25:6 [v] S Ge 42:24 [w] 2Sa 18:33; Est 4:16
43:15 [x] ver 12 [y] Ge 45:9,13 [z] Ge 47:2,7; Mt 2:11
43:16 [a] S Ge 35:18 [b] ver 17,24,26; Ge 44:1,4,12; 2Sa 19:17; Isa 22:15 [c] ver 31; Lk 15:23
43:17 [d] S ver 16
43:18 [e] Ge 42:35 [f] Ge 44:14 [g] S Ge 42:25 [h] S Ge 32:11 [i] Ge 44:9,16,33; 50:18 [j] Ge 34:28
43:19 [k] ver 16
43:20 [l] S Ge 42:3
43:21 [m] S ver 15; S Ge 42:25
43:23 [n] S Ge 24:12; S 31:5; Ex 3:6 [o] Ge 42:28 [p] S Ge 42:24
43:24 [q] S ver 16 [r] S Ge 18:4
43:25 [s] S Ge 32:13 [t] ver 16
43:26 [u] S ver 16 [v] S Ge 32:13; Mt 2:11 [w] S Ge 33:3
43:27 [x] S Ge 37:3 [y] S ver 7
43:28 [z] Ge 44:24, 27,30 [a] Ge 18:2; Ex 18:7 [b] S Ge 37:7
43:29 [c] S Ge 35:18 [d] S Ge 42:13 [e] Nu 6:25; Ps 67:1; 119:58; Isa 30:18-19; 33:2
43:30 [f] Jn 11:33, 38 [g] S Ge 29:11
43:31 [h] Ge 45:1; Isa 30:18; 42:14; 63:15; 64:12 [i] S ver 16
43:32 [j] S Ge 14:13; Gal 2:12 [k] Ge 46:34; Ex 8:26
43:33 [l] S Ge 35:23 [m] S Ge 42:13; 44:12
43:34 [n] S Ge 37:3; S 2Ki 25:30 [o] Lk 15:23
44:1 [p] S Ge 43:16 [q] S Ge 42:25
44:2 [r] ver 5,10, 12,16 [s] ver 8

t14 Hebrew *El-Shaddai*

43:14 IF I AM BEREAVED. When Israel saw that he could do nothing to change his terrible circumstances, the only thing he could do was place his sons into God's hands, pray for mercy and prepare himself for the worst. He was willing to accept God's will even if it meant bereavement and suffering. As things turned out, however, he ended his life rejoicing in God and trusting the One who had guided him all his life.

3As morning dawned, the men were
sent on their way with their donkeys.[t]
4They had not gone far from the city
when Joseph said to his steward,[u] "Go
after those men at once, and when you
catch up with them, say to them, 'Why
have you repaid good with evil?[v]
5Isn't this the cup[w] my master drinks
from and also uses for divination?[x]
This is a wicked thing you have
done.'"
6When he caught up with them, he
repeated these words to them. **7**But
they said to him, "Why does my lord
say such things? Far be it from your
servants[y] to do anything like that![z]
8We even brought back to you from the
land of Canaan[a] the silver[b] we found
inside the mouths of our sacks.[c] So
why would we steal[d] silver or gold
from your master's house? **9**If any of
your servants[e] is found to have it, he
will die;[f] and the rest of us will become my lord's slaves.[g]"
10"Very well, then," he said, "let it
be as you say. Whoever is found to
have it[h] will become my slave;[i] the
rest of you will be free from blame."[j]
11Each of them quickly lowered his
sack to the ground and opened it.
12Then the steward[k] proceeded to
search,[l] beginning with the oldest
and ending with the youngest.[m] And
the cup was found in Benjamin's
sack.[n] **13**At this, they tore their
clothes.[o] Then they all loaded their
donkeys[p] and returned to the city.
14Joseph was still in the house[q]
when Judah[r] and his brothers came
in, and they threw themselves to the
ground before him.[s] **15**Joseph said to
them, "What is this you have done?[t]
Don't you know that a man like me can
find things out by divination?[u]"
16"What can we say to my lord?[v]"
Judah[w] replied. "What can we say?
How can we prove our innocence?[x]
God has uncovered your servants'[y]
guilt. We are now my lord's slaves[z]—
we ourselves and the one who was
found to have the cup.[a]"
17But Joseph said, "Far be it from me
to do such a thing![b] Only the man who
was found to have the cup will become
my slave.[c] The rest of you, go back to
your father in peace."[d]
18Then Judah[e] went up to him and
said: "Please, my lord,[f] let your servant speak a word to my lord. Do not
be angry[g] with your servant, though
you are equal to Pharaoh himself.
19My lord asked his servants,[h] 'Do
you have a father or a brother?'[i]
20And we answered, 'We have an aged
father, and there is a young son born
to him in his old age.[j] His brother is
dead,[k] and he is the only one of his
mother's sons left, and his father loves
him.'[l]
21"Then you said to your servants,[m]
'Bring him down to me so I can see him
for myself.'[n] **22**And we said to my
lord,[o] 'The boy cannot leave his father; if he leaves him, his father will
die.'[p] **23**But you told your servants,
'Unless your youngest brother comes
down with you, you will not see my face
again.'[q] **24**When we went back to your
servant my father,[r] we told him what
my lord[s] had said.[t]
25"Then our father said, 'Go back
and buy a little more food.'[u] **26**But we
said, 'We cannot go down. Only if our
youngest brother is with us will we go.
We cannot see the man's face unless
our youngest brother is with us.'[v]
27"Your servant my father[w] said to
us, 'You know that my wife bore me

44:3 [t] Jdg 19:9 **44:4** [u] S Ge 43:16 [v] Ps 35:12; 38:20; 109:5; Pr 17:13; Jer 18:20 **44:5** [w] S ver 2 [x] S Ge 30:27; Dt 18:10-14 **44:7** [y] S Ge 42:11 [z] S Ge 18:25 **44:8** [a] S Ge 42:13 [b] ver 2 [c] S Ge 42:25; S 43:15 [d] Ge 31:30 **44:9** [e] S Ge 42:11 [f] Ge 31:32 [g] S ver 10; S Ge 43:18 **44:10** [h] S ver 2 [i] ver 9,17,33 [j] S Ge 43:9 **44:12** [k] S Ge 43:16 [l] S Ge 31:34 [m] S Ge 43:33 [n] ver 2 **44:13** [o] S Ge 37:29 [p] S Ge 42:26 **44:14** [q] Ge 43:18 [r] ver 16; S Ge 29:35; S 43:3 [s] S Ge 33:3 **44:15** [t] S Ge 12:18 [u] S Ge 30:27 **44:16** [v] ver 22,24; S Ge 37:8 [w] S ver 14 [x] Ps 26:6; 73:13 [y] S Ge 42:11 [z] S Ge 43:18 [a] S ver 2 **44:17** [b] S Ge 18:25 [c] S ver 10 [d] S Ge 43:9 **44:18** [e] S Ge 29:35 [f] S ver 16 [g] S Ge 18:30 **44:19** [h] S Ge 42:11 [i] S Ge 43:7 **44:20** [j] S Ge 37:3 [k] S Ge 37:33 [l] S Ge 42:13 **44:21** [m] S Ge 42:11 [n] S Ge 42:15 **44:22** [o] S ver 16 [p] S Ge 37:35 **44:23** [q] S Ge 42:15; S 43:5 **44:24** [r] S Ge 43:28 [s] S ver 16 [t] Ge 42:29

44:25 [u] S Ge 42:2 **44:26** [v] S Ge 43:5 **44:27** [w] S Ge 43:28

44:5 USES FOR DIVINATION. Surely Joseph did not practice divination, which was forbidden by God. There are two possible explanations for its mention here. (1) The Hebrew term for "divination" can also be rendered "be sure to notice." Thus the reading would mean that Joseph would be sure to notice that the cup was gone. (2) It could also be that Joseph was merely adapting to the image that the brothers would have had of him as an Egyptian leader (cf. v. 15).

44:13 TORE THEIR CLOTHES. This was a clear sign of great grief and distress. The brothers could have gone on without Benjamin, but their determination to return and face the consequences with him revealed that their character had indeed changed and that they were truly concerned about their brother and father (cf. vv. 18–34).

44:15 FIND THINGS OUT BY DIVINATION. See v. 5, note.

44:18–34 JUDAH WENT UP TO HIM. That Joseph's brothers had experienced a great change of attitude since they sold Joseph into Egypt is seen not only in all the brothers' willingness to suffer as slaves for Benjamin's sake (vv. 13–16), but especially in Judah's plea for Benjamin (vv. 18–34). They were now ready to bear the blame for their past evil and to pay any price to save Benjamin and prevent overwhelming grief to their father (vv. 16, 32–33).

two sons.[x] **28**One of them went away
from me, and I said, "He has surely
been torn to pieces."[y] And I have not
seen him since.[z] **29**If you take this one
from me too and harm comes to him,
you will bring my gray head down to
the grave[u][a] in misery.'[b]

30"So now, if the boy is not with us
when I go back to your servant my father[c] and if my father, whose life is
closely bound up with the boy's life,[d]
31sees that the boy isn't there, he will
die.[e] Your servants[f] will bring the
gray head of our father down to the
grave[g] in sorrow. **32**Your servant
guaranteed the boy's safety to my father. I said, 'If I do not bring him back
to you, I will bear the blame before you,
my father, all my life!'[h]

33"Now then, please let your servant
remain here as my lord's slave[i] in
place of the boy,[j] and let the boy return with his brothers. **34**How can I go
back to my father if the boy is not with
me? No! Do not let me see the misery[k]
that would come upon my father."[l]

Joseph Makes Himself Known

45 Then Joseph could no longer
control himself[m] before all his
attendants, and he cried out, "Have everyone leave my presence!"[n] So there
was no one with Joseph when he made
himself known to his brothers. **2**And he
wept[o] so loudly that the Egyptians
heard him, and Pharaoh's household
heard about it.[p]

3Joseph said to his brothers, "I am
Joseph! Is my father still living?"[q] But
his brothers were not able to answer
him,[r] because they were terrified at
his presence.[s]

4Then Joseph said to his brothers,
"Come close to me."[t] When they had
done so, he said, "I am your brother
Joseph, the one you sold into Egypt![u]
5And now, do not be distressed[v] and
do not be angry with yourselves for
selling me here,[w] because it was to
save lives that God sent me ahead of
you.[x] **6**For two years now there has
been famine[y] in the land, and for the
next five years there will not be plowing and reaping. **7**But God sent me
ahead of you to preserve for you a remnant[z] on earth and to save your lives
by a great deliverance.[v][a]

8"So then, it was not you who sent
me here, but God.[b] He made me father[c] to Pharaoh, lord of his entire
household and ruler of all Egypt.[d]
9Now hurry[e] back to my father and
say to him, 'This is what your son Joseph says: God has made me lord of all
Egypt. Come down to me; don't de-
lay.[f] **10**You shall live in the region of
Goshen[g] and be near me—you, your
children and grandchildren, your
flocks and herds, and all you have.[h]
11I will provide for you there,[i] because five years of famine[j] are still to
come. Otherwise you and your household and all who belong to you will become destitute.'[k]

12"You can see for yourselves, and
so can my brother Benjamin,[l] that it
is really I who am speaking to you.[m]
13Tell my father about all the honor ac-
corded me in Egypt[n] and about everything you have seen. And bring my father down here quickly.[o]"

14Then he threw his arms around his
brother Benjamin and wept, and Benjamin[p] embraced him,[q] weeping.
15And he kissed[r] all his brothers and
wept over them.[s] Afterward his brothers talked with him.[t]

16When the news reached Pharaoh's
palace that Joseph's brothers had
come,[u] Pharaoh and all his officials[v]
were pleased.[w] **17**Pharaoh said to Joseph, "Tell your brothers, 'Do this:
Load your animals[x] and return to the
land of Canaan,[y] **18**and bring your fa-

44:27 [x]Ge 46:19 **44:28** [y]S Ge 37:33 [z]Ge 45:26,28; 46:30; 48:11 **44:29** [a]S Ge 37:35 [b]S Ge 42:38 **44:30** [c]S Ge 43:28 [d]1Sa 18:1; 2Sa 1:26 **44:31** [e]S ver 22 [f]S Ge 42:11 [g]S Ge 37:35 **44:32** [h]S Ge 42:37 **44:33** [i]S ver 10; S Ge 43:18 [j]Jn 15:13 **44:34** [k]S Ge 42:38 [l]Est 8:6 **45:1** [m]S Ge 43:31 [n]2Sa 13:9 **45:2** [o]S Ge 29:11 [p]ver 16; Ac 7:13 **45:3** [q]S Ge 43:7 [r]ver 15 [s]S Ge 44:20; Job 21:6; 23:15; Mt 17:6; Mk 6:49-50 **45:4** [t]Ge 27:21-22 [u]Ge 37:28 **45:5** [v]Ge 42:21 [w]Ge 42:22 [x]ver 7-8; Ge 50:20; Job 10:12; Ps 105:17 **45:6** [y]S Ge 41:30 **45:7** [z]2Ki 19:4, 30,31; Ezr 9:8,13; Isa 1:9; 10:20,21; 11:11,16; 46:3; Jer 6:9; 42:2; 50:20; Mic 4:7; 5:7; Zep 2:7 [a]S ver 5; Ge 49:18; Ex 15:2; 1Sa 14:45; 2Ki 13:5; Est 4:14; Isa 25:9; Mic 7:7 **45:8** [b]ver 5 [c]Jdg 17:10; 2Ki 6:21; 13:14 [d]S Ge 41:41 **45:9** [e]S Ge 43:15 [f]Ge 43:10; Ac 7:14 **45:10** [g]Ge 46:28, 34; 47:1,11,27; 50:8; Ex 8:22; 9:26; 10:24; 47:1 [h]Ge 46:6-7 **45:11** [i]Ge 47:12; 50:21 [j]S Ge 41:30 [k]Ps 102:17 **45:12** [l]S Ge 35:18 [m]Mk 6:50 **45:13** [n]S Ge 41:41 [o]S Ge 43:15; Ac 7:14 **45:14** [p]S Ge 35:18 [q]S Ge 29:13 **45:15** [r]S Ge 29:11; Lk 15:20 [s]S Ge 29:11,13; S 46:4 [t]ver 3 **45:16** [u]S ver 2; Ac 7:13 [v]Ge 50:7 [w]S Ge 41:37 **45:17** [x]S Ge 42:26 [y]S Ge 42:5

[u]*29* Hebrew *Sheol*; also in verse 31 [v]*7* Or *save you as a great band of survivors*

45:5 GOD SENT ME. Joseph reveals that many times God overrules the evil actions of humans in order to carry out his will (cf. 50:20; see article on THE PROVIDENCE OF GOD, p. 78).

45:7 TO PRESERVE FOR YOU A REMNANT. God worked through Joseph to preserve the covenant people through whom would come the Christ. It should be noted that even though the Christ would come through Judah's descendant and not Joseph's, God used Joseph to keep the line of Christ alive. Joseph, therefore, was a spiritual ancestor of Christ, something far more important than being a physical ancestor (see Ro 4:12–16).

45:10 THE REGION OF GOSHEN. Located about forty miles from present-day Cairo, Goshen was situated in the delta of the Nile and was separated from the main centers of Egyptian life. There the Israelites would live in isolation from the Egyptians and develop into a nation.

ther and your families back to me. I
will give you the best of the land of
Egypt[z] and you can enjoy the fat of
the land.'[a]
19"You are also directed to tell them,
'Do this: Take some carts[b] from
Egypt for your children and your wives,
and get your father and come. 20Never
mind about your belongings,[c] because
the best of all Egypt[d] will be yours.' "
21So the sons of Israel did this. Joseph gave them carts,[e] as Pharaoh
had commanded, and he also gave
them provisions for their journey.[f]
22To each of them he gave new clothing,[g] but to Benjamin he gave three
hundred shekels[w] of silver and five
sets of clothes.[h] 23And this is what he
sent to his father: ten donkeys[i] loaded with the best things[j] of Egypt, and
ten female donkeys loaded with grain
and bread and other provisions for his
journey.[k] 24Then he sent his brothers
away, and as they were leaving he
said to them, "Don't quarrel on the
way!"[l]
25So they went up out of Egypt[m]
and came to their father Jacob in the
land of Canaan.[n] 26They told him, "Joseph is still alive! In fact, he is ruler of
all Egypt."[o] Jacob was stunned; he did
not believe them.[p] 27But when they
told him everything Joseph had said to
them, and when he saw the carts[q] Joseph had sent to carry him back, the
spirit of their father Jacob revived.
28And Israel said, "I'm convinced![r]
My son Joseph is still alive. I will go
and see him before I die."[s]

Jacob Goes to Egypt

46 So Israel[t] set out with all that
was his, and when he reached
Beersheba,[u] he offered sacrifices[v] to
the God of his father Isaac.[w]
2And God spoke to Israel[x] in a vision at night[y] and said, "Jacob! Jacob!"
"Here I am,"[z] he replied.
3"I am God, the God of your father,"[a] he said. "Do not be afraid[b] to
go down to Egypt,[c] for I will make you
into a great nation[d] there.[e] 4I will go
down to Egypt with you, and I will
surely bring you back again.[f] And Joseph's own hand will close your
eyes.[g]"
5Then Jacob left Beersheba,[h] and
Israel's[i] sons took their father Jacob
and their children and their wives in
the carts[j] that Pharaoh had sent to
transport him. 6They also took with
them their livestock and the possessions[k] they had acquired[l] in Canaan,
and Jacob and all his offspring went to
Egypt.[m] 7He took with him to Egypt[n]
his sons and grandsons and his daughters and granddaughters—all his offspring.[o]

8These are the names of the sons of
Israel[p] (Jacob and his descendants)
who went to Egypt:

Reuben the firstborn[q] of Jacob.
9The sons of Reuben:[r]
Hanoch, Pallu,[s] Hezron and
Carmi.[t]
10The sons of Simeon:[u]
Jemuel,[v] Jamin, Ohad, Jakin,
Zohar[w] and Shaul the son of a
Canaanite woman.
11The sons of Levi:[x]
Gershon,[y] Kohath[z] and Me-
rari.[a]
12The sons of Judah:[b]
Er,[c] Onan,[d] Shelah, Perez[e]

45:18 [z] ver 20; Ge 20:15; 46:34; 47:6,11,27; Jer 40:4 [a] Ezr 9:12; Ps 37:19; Isa 1:19 **45:19** [b] ver 21,27; Ge 46:5; Nu 7:3-8 **45:20** [c] Ge 46:6, 32 [d] S ver 18 **45:21** [e] S ver 19 [f] S Ge 42:25 **45:22** [g] S Ge 24:53 [h] S Ge 37:3; S 41:14; Jdg 14:12,13; 2Ki 5:22 **45:23** [i] S Ge 42:26 [j] S Ge 24:10 [k] S Ge 42:25 **45:24** [l] Ge 42:21-22 **45:25** [m] Ge 13:1 [n] Ge 42:29 **45:26** [o] S Ge 41:41 [p] S Ge 44:28; 1Ki 10:7 **45:27** [q] S ver 19 **45:28** [r] Lk 16:31 [s] S Ge 44:28 **46:1** [t] ver 5 [u] S Ge 21:14 [v] S Ge 31:54 [w] S Ge 31:42 **46:2** [x] S Ge 17:5 [y] S Ge 15:1 [z] S Ge 22:1 **46:3** [a] S Ge 28:13 [b] S Ge 15:1 [c] Ge 26:2 [d] S Ge 12:2 [e] Ex 1:7 **46:4** [f] S Ge 15:16; S 28:13 [g] ver 29; Ge 45:14-15; 50:1 **46:5** [h] S Ge 21:14 [i] ver 1 [j] S Ge 45:19 **46:6** [k] S Ge 45:20 [l] S Ge 12:5 [m] Nu 20:15; Dt 26:5; Jos 24:4; Ps 105:23; Isa 52:4; Ac 7:15 **46:7** [n] Ge 13:10 [o] ver 6; Ge 45:10 **46:8** [p] S Ge 35:26; Ex 1:1; Nu 26:4 [q] S Ge 29:32 **46:9** [r] Ex 6:14; Nu 1:20; 26:7; 1Ch 5:3 [s] Nu 26:5; 1Ch 5:3 [t] Nu 26:6 **46:10** [u] S Ge 29:33; Nu 26:14 [v] Ex 6:15; Nu 26:12 [w] Nu 26:13 **46:11** [x] S Ge 29:34; S Nu 3:17 [y] Ex 6:16; Nu 3:21; 4:38 [z] Ex 6:16; Nu 3:27; 1Ch 23:12 [a] Ex 6:19; Nu 3:20,33; 4:29; 26:57; 1Ch 6:19 **46:12** [b] S Ge 29:35 [c] S Ge 38:3 [d] S Ge 38:4 [e] S Ge 38:29

[w] *22* That is, about 7 1/2 pounds (about 3.5 kilograms)

46:1 SO ISRAEL SET OUT. Israel (Jacob) and his family migrated to Egypt. (1) The resettlement of God's people was the direct consequence of the severe famine that God had brought on the world (47:13). God literally forced Israel to move to Egypt by his sovereign control (cf. 15:13–14). In that land God's chosen people would multiply and become a great nation, and from there they would return to Canaan (cf. 50:24). (2) In response to the Egyptians' demand (cf. 43:32; 46:34), the children of Israel lived in isolation in the region of Goshen. There they would remain separated, a people set apart for God, looking for the day of their return to the promised fatherland in Canaan where they would assume their role in God's redemptive plan (see article on THE CALL OF ABRAHAM, p. 25).

46:3 I AM GOD . . . DO NOT BE AFRAID. God once again promised to be with Jacob and his family, reiterating the promise that Jacob's descendants would become a great nation and that they would return to the land of Canaan. We all need God's reassurances of his love, care and presence as we live on this earth and experience the difficulties and decisions that are inevitable in this fallen world. If you are sincerely trying to follow the Lord, you have the right to ask God for a reaffirmation of his love for you and his guidance in your life (cf. Jn 1:12–13).

THE PROVIDENCE OF GOD

Ge 45:5 "Do not be distressed and do not be angry with yourselves for selling me here, because it was to save lives that God sent me ahead of you."

After the Lord God created the heavens and the earth (Ge 1:1), he did not abandon the world to run on its own. Rather, he continues to be involved in the lives of his people and in the care of his creation. God is not like a master clockmaker who fashioned the world, wound it up, and is now letting it slowly unwind on its own; instead, he is the loving Father who cares for what he has made. God's continual care for his creation and his people is called, in doctrinal terms, his providence.

ASPECTS OF PROVIDENCE. There are at least three aspects to God's providence. (1) *Preservation*. By his power God preserves the world he has created. David's confession is clear: "Your righteousness is like the mighty mountains, your justice like the great deep. O LORD, you preserve both man and beast" (Ps 36:6). God's preserving power is accomplished through his Son Jesus Christ, as Paul testifies in Col 1:17: Christ "is before all things, and in him all things hold together." By the power of Christ even the very smallest particles of life are held together.

(2) *Provision*. Not only does God preserve the world that he created, but he also provides for the needs of his creatures. When God created the world, he created the seasons (Ge 1:14) and gave food for humans and animals (Ge 1:29–30). After the flood had destroyed the earth, God renewed this promise of provision with these words: "As long as the earth endures, seedtime and harvest, cold and heat, summer and winter, day and night will never cease" (Ge 8:22). Several of the psalms testify to God's goodness in providing for all of his creatures (e.g., Ps 104; 145). God himself revealed his creative and caring power to Job (Job 38—41), and Jesus asserted in no uncertain terms that God provides for the birds of the air and the lilies of the field (Mt 6:26–30; 10:29). His care not only involves the physical needs of humankind but also the spiritual needs (cf. Jn 3:16–17). The Bible reveals that God manifests a special love and care for his own people, each of whom he values (e.g., Ps 91; see Mt 10:31, note). Paul writes unequivocally to believers in Philippi, "My God will meet all your needs according to his glorious riches in Christ Jesus" (Php 4:19, see note). According to the apostle John, God wants his people to "enjoy good health" and have all go well with them (see 3Jn 2, note).

(3) *Government*. In addition to God's preservation of and provision for his creation, he also rules the world. Since God is sovereign, the events of history happen under his permissive will and oversight; at times he directly intervenes according to his redemptive purpose (see article on THE WILL OF GOD, p. 1056). Nevertheless, until God consummates history, he has limited his supreme power and rule in this world. Scripture states that Satan is "the god of this age" (2Co 4:4) and exercises considerable control in this present evil age (see 1Jn 5:19, note; cf. Lk 13:16; Gal 1:4; Eph 6:12; Heb 2:14). In other words, the world is not now submissive to God's ruling power, but is in rebellion against him and enslaved to Satan. Note, however, that this self-limitation on God's part is only temporary; at the time he has determined by his wisdom, he will destroy Satan and all the armies of evil (Rev 19—20).

GOD'S PROVIDENCE AND HUMAN SUFFERING. Biblical revelation shows God's providence to be not an abstract doctrine but one that concerns everyday living in an evil and fallen world. (1) Everyone experiences suffering at times in his or her life and inevitably asks the question, "Why?" (cf. Job 7:17–21; Ps 10:1; 22:1; 74:11–12; Jer 14:8–9,19); such experiences raise the problem of evil and its place in God's plan.

(2) God allows humans to experience the consequences of the sin that entered into the world through the fall of Adam and Eve. Joseph, for example, suffered much because of his brothers' jealousy and cruelty. He was sold by his brothers into slavery and

became Potiphar's slave in Egypt (Ge 37; 39). While living a God-fearing life in Egypt, he was unjustly charged with immorality, thrown into prison (Ge 39) and kept there for well over two years (cf. Ge 40:1—41:14). God may allow suffering because of the evil actions of fellow humans, even though he can supersede such deeds so as to work out his will. According to Joseph's testimony, God was working through the sins of his brothers in order to preserve life (Ge 45:5; 50:20).

(3) Not only do we suffer from the consequences of others' sins, but we also experience the consequences of our own sinful actions. For example, the sin of immorality and adultery often results in the breakdown of one's marriage and family. The sin of unchecked anger against another person can lead to serious injury or even the death of one or both of those involved. The sin of greed may result in a prison sentence for someone who has stolen or embezzled.

(4) Suffering also occurs in the world because Satan, the god of this age, is permitted to do his work by blinding the minds of unbelievers and controlling their lives (2Co 4:4; Eph 2:1–3). The NT is filled with examples of people who experienced suffering because of demons who tormented them with mental affliction (e.g., Mk 5:1–14) or with physical ailments (Mt 9:32–33; 12:22; Mk 9:14–22; Lk 13:11,16; see article on POWER OVER SATAN AND DEMONS, p. 1484).

To say that God allows suffering does not mean that God causes the evil that happens to us in this world, or that he personally decrees all of life's tragedies. God is never the instigator of evil or ungodliness (Jas 1:13). Nevertheless, he does at times permit it, direct it and overrule it in order to carry out his will, to accomplish his redemptive purpose, and in all things to work for the good of those faithful to him (see Mt 2:13, note; Ro 8:28, note; see article on THE SUFFERING OF THE RIGHTEOUS, p. 710).

OUR RELATIONSHIP TO GOD'S PROVIDENCE. In order for us to experience God's providential care in our lives, the Bible reveals that we have certain responsibilities. (1) We must obey God and his revealed will. With Joseph, for example, it is clear that because Joseph honored God by his life of obedience, God honored him by being with him (see Ge 39:2–3,21,23). Likewise, in order for Jesus himself to experience God's protective care in the face of King Herod's murderous intent, Jesus' parents had to obey God and flee to Egypt (see Mt 2:13, note). Those who fear God and acknowledge him in all their ways have the promise that God will make their paths straight (Pr 3:5–7).

(2) In his providence, God directs the affairs of the church and of each of us as his servants. We must constantly be in tune with God's will for our lives as we serve him and minister to other people in his name (cf. Ac 18:9–10; 23:11; 26:15–18; 27:22–24).

(3) We must love God and submit to him by faith in Christ if we want him in all things to work for our good (see Ro 8:28, note).

(4) In order to experience God's care in the midst of affliction, we must call out to him in persistent prayer and faith. Through prayer and trust we experience God's peace (Php 4:6–7), we receive strength from the Lord (Eph 3:16; Php 4:13), and we receive God's mercy, grace and help in time of need (Heb 4:16; see Php 4:6, note). Such prayers of faith may be either on our own behalf or on behalf of others (see Ro 15:30–32; Col 4:3, note; see article on INTERCESSION, p. 1268).

and Zerah[f] (but Er and Onan
had died in the land of Canaan).[g]
The sons of Perez:[h]
Hezron and Hamul.[i]
13The sons of Issachar:[j]
Tola, Puah,[x][k] Jashub[y][l] and
Shimron.
14The sons of Zebulun:[m]
Sered, Elon and Jahleel.
15These were the sons Leah bore to
Jacob in Paddan Aram,[z][n] besides his
daughter Dinah.[o] These sons and
daughters of his were thirty-three in
all.

16The sons of Gad:[p]
Zephon,[a][q] Haggi, Shuni, Ez-
bon, Eri, Arodi and Areli.
17The sons of Asher:[r]
Imnah, Ishvah, Ishvi and
Beriah.
Their sister was Serah.
The sons of Beriah:
Heber and Malkiel.
18These were the children born to
Jacob by Zilpah,[s] whom Laban had
given to his daughter Leah[t]—sixteen
in all.

19The sons of Jacob's wife Rachel:[u]
Joseph and Benjamin.[v] 20In
Egypt, Manasseh[w] and Ephraim[x] were born to Joseph[y] by
Asenath daughter of Potiphera,
priest of On.[b][z]
21The sons of Benjamin:[a]
Bela, Beker, Ashbel, Gera, Naaman, Ehi, Rosh, Muppim,
Huppim and Ard.[b]
22These were the sons of Rachel[c]
who were born to Jacob—fourteen in
all.
23The son of Dan:[d]
Hushim.[e]
24The sons of Naphtali:[f]
Jahziel, Guni, Jezer and Shillem.
25These were the sons born to Jacob
by Bilhah,[g] whom Laban had given to
his daughter Rachel[h]—seven in all.

26All those who went to Egypt with
Jacob—those who were his direct
descendants, not counting his sons'
wives—numbered sixty-six persons.[i]
27With the two sons[c] who had been
born to Joseph in Egypt,[j] the members of Jacob's family, which went to
Egypt, were seventy[d] in all.[k]

28Now Jacob sent Judah[l] ahead of
him to Joseph to get directions to Goshen.[m] When they arrived in the region of Goshen, 29Joseph had his chariot[n] made ready and went to Goshen to
meet his father Israel.[o] As soon as Joseph appeared before him, he threw his
arms around his father[e] and wept[p]
for a long time.[q]

30Israel[r] said to Joseph, "Now I am
ready to die, since I have seen for myself that you are still alive."[s]

31Then Joseph said to his brothers
and to his father's household, "I will go
up and speak to Pharaoh and will say
to him, 'My brothers and my father's
household, who were living in the land
of Canaan,[t] have come to me.[u] 32The
men are shepherds;[v] they tend livestock,[w] and they have brought along
their flocks and herds and everything
they own.'[x] 33When Pharaoh calls you
in and asks, 'What is your occupation?'[y] 34you should answer, 'Your
servants[z] have tended livestock from
our boyhood on, just as our fathers
did.'[a] Then you will be allowed to settle[b] in the region of Goshen,[c] for all
shepherds are detestable to the Egyptians.[d]"

47 Joseph went and told Pharaoh,
"My father and brothers, with
their flocks and herds and everything
they own, have come from the land of

46:12 [f]S Ge 38:30 [g]S Ge 38:7; Nu 26:19 [h]1Ch 2:5; Mt 1:3 [i]Nu 26:21
46:13 [j]S Ge 30:18 [k]Nu 26:23; Jdg 10:1; 1Ch 7:1 [l]Nu 26:24
46:14 [m]S Ge 30:20
46:15 [n]S Ge 25:20; 29:31-35 [o]S Ge 30:21
46:16 [p]S Ge 30:11; S Nu 1:25 [q]Nu 26:15
46:17 [r]S Ge 30:13
46:18 [s]Ge 30:10 [t]S Ge 16:1
46:19 [u]S Ge 29:6 [v]Ge 44:27
46:20 [w]S Ge 41:51 [x]S Ge 41:52 [y]Nu 26:28-37 [z]S Ge 41:45
46:21 [a]Nu 26:38-41; 1Ch 7:6-12; 8:1 [b]Nu 26:40; 1Ch 8:3
46:22 [c]S Ge 29:6
46:23 [d]S Ge 30:6 [e]Nu 26:42
46:24 [f]S Ge 30:8
46:25 [g]Ge 30:8 [h]S Ge 24:61
46:26 [i]ver 5-7; Ex 1:5; Dt 10:22
46:27 [j]S Ge 41:45 [k]S Ge 34:30; Ac 7:14
46:28 [l]S Ge 43:3 [m]S Ge 45:10
46:29 [n]S Ge 41:43 [o]ver 1,30; S Ge 32:28; 47:29, 31 [p]S Ge 29:11 [q]S ver 4; Lk 15:20
46:30 [r]S ver 29 [s]S Ge 44:28
46:31 [t]S Ge 42:13 [u]S Ge 45:10
46:32 [v]Ge 47:3 [w]S Ge 37:2 [x]S Ge 45:20
46:33 [y]Ge 47:3
46:34 [z]S Ge 42:11 [a]Ge 47:3 [b]S Ge 34:10 [c]S Ge 45:10 [d]S Ge 43:32

x *13* Samaritan Pentateuch and Syriac (see also 1 Chron. 7:1); Masoretic Text *Puvah*
y *13* Samaritan Pentateuch and some Septuagint manuscripts (see also Num. 26:24 and 1 Chron. 7:1); Masoretic Text *Iob*
z *15* That is, Northwest Mesopotamia
a *16* Samaritan Pentateuch and Septuagint (see also Num. 26:15); Masoretic Text *Ziphion*
b *20* That is, Heliopolis
c *27* Hebrew; Septuagint *the nine children*
d *27* Hebrew (see also Exodus 1:5 and footnote); Septuagint (see also Acts 7:14) *seventy-five*
e *29* Hebrew *around him*

46:26 SIXTY-SIX PERSONS. The sixty-six persons are those who traveled *with* Jacob to Egypt. The seventy of v. 27 included Joseph, his two sons and Jacob. Ac 7:14 gives the number of persons as seventy-five, thus including Joseph's grandchildren.

46:34 SHEPHERDS ARE DETESTABLE. The primary occupation of Jacob's family was tending livestock. Traditionally the Egyptians had a strong disdain for shepherds. This animosity helped the Israelites to remain separated from the Egyptians and their ways (cf. 43:32; see 45:10, note).

Canaan[e] and are now in Goshen."[f]
2He chose five of his brothers and presented them[g] before Pharaoh.
3Pharaoh asked the brothers, "What
is your occupation?"[h]
"Your servants[i] are shepherds,[j]"
they replied to Pharaoh, "just as our
fathers were." 4They also said to him,
"We have come to live here awhile,[k]
because the famine is severe in Canaan[l] and your servants' flocks have
no pasture.[m] So now, please let your
servants settle in Goshen."[n]
5Pharaoh said to Joseph, "Your father and your brothers have come to
you, 6and the land of Egypt is before
you; settle[o] your father and your
brothers in the best part of the land.[p]
Let them live in Goshen. And if you
know of any among them with special
ability,[q] put them in charge of my own
livestock.[r]"
7Then Joseph brought his father Jacob in and presented him[s] before
Pharaoh. After Jacob blessed[f] Pharaoh,[t] 8Pharaoh asked him, "How old
are you?"
9And Jacob said to Pharaoh, "The
years of my pilgrimage are a hundred
and thirty.[u] My years have been few
and difficult,[v] and they do not equal
the years of the pilgrimage of my fathers.[w]" 10Then Jacob blessed[g] Pharaoh[x] and went out from his presence.
11So Joseph settled his father and
his brothers in Egypt and gave them
property in the best part of the land,[y]
the district of Rameses,[z] as Pharaoh
directed. 12Joseph also provided his father and his brothers and all his father's household with food, according
to the number of their children.[a]

Joseph and the Famine

13There was no food, however, in the
whole region because the famine was
severe; both Egypt and Canaan wasted
away because of the famine.[b] 14Jo-
seph collected all the money that was
to be found in Egypt and Canaan in
payment for the grain they were buying,[c] and he brought it to Pharaoh's
palace.[d] 15When the money of the
people of Egypt and Canaan was
gone,[e] all Egypt came to Joseph[f] and
said, "Give us food. Why should we die
before your eyes?[g] Our money is used
up."
16"Then bring your livestock,[h]"
said Joseph. "I will sell you food in exchange for your livestock, since your
money is gone.[i]" 17So they brought
their livestock to Joseph, and he gave
them food in exchange for their
horses,[j] their sheep and goats, their
cattle and donkeys.[k] And he brought
them through that year with food in exchange for all their livestock.
18When that year was over, they
came to him the following year and
said, "We cannot hide from our lord the
fact that since our money is gone[l] and
our livestock belongs to you,[m] there is
nothing left for our lord except our bodies and our land. 19Why should we perish before your eyes[n]—we and our
land as well? Buy us and our land in
exchange for food,[o] and we with our
land will be in bondage to Pharaoh.[p]
Give us seed so that we may live and
not die,[q] and that the land may not
become desolate."
20So Joseph bought all the land in
Egypt for Pharaoh. The Egyptians, one
and all, sold their fields, because the
famine was too severe[r] for them. The
land became Pharaoh's, 21and Joseph
reduced the people to servitude,[h][s]
from one end of Egypt to the other.
22However, he did not buy the land of
the priests,[t] because they received a
regular allotment from Pharaoh and
had food enough from the allotment[u]
Pharaoh gave them. That is why they
did not sell their land.
23Joseph said to the people, "Now
that I have bought you and your land
today for Pharaoh, here is seed[v] for
you so you can plant the ground.[w]
24But when the crop comes in, give a
fifth[x] of it to Pharaoh. The other four-

47:1 [e]S Ge 42:13 [f]S Ge 46:31 **47:2** [g]S Ge 43:15 **47:3** [h]Ge 46:33 [i]S Ge 42:11 [j]Ge 46:32 **47:4** [k]Ru 1:1 [l]S Ge 12:10 [m]1Ki 18:5; Jer 14:5-6; Joel 1:18 [n]Ge 46:34 **47:6** [o]S Ge 34:10 [p]S Ge 13:9; S 45:18 [q]Ex 18:21,25; Dt 1:13,15; 2Ch 19:5; Ps 15:2 [r]S Ge 39:4 **47:7** [s]S Ge 43:15 [t]ver 10; 2Sa 14:22; 19:39; 1Ki 8:66 **47:9** [u]S Ge 25:7 [v]S Ge 3:17; Ps 39:4; 89:47 [w]Job 8:9; Ps 39:12 **47:10** [x]S ver 7 **47:11** [y]S Ge 45:10,18 [z]Ex 1:11; 12:37; Nu 33:3,5 **47:12** [a]S Ge 45:11 **47:13** [b]S Ge 12:10; S 41:30 **47:14** [c]S Ge 41:36 [d]S Ge 41:34; Ex 7:23; 8:24; Jer 43:9

47:15 [e]ver 16,18 [f]S Ge 41:57 [g]ver 19; Ex 16:3 **47:16** [h]ver 18,19 [i]ver 15 **47:17** [j]Ex 14:9 [k]S Ge 12:16 **47:18** [l]S ver 15 [m]S ver 16 **47:19** [n]S ver 15 [o]S ver 16 [p]ver 21, 25 [q]S Ge 42:2 **47:20** [r]S Ge 12:10 **47:21** [s]S ver 19 **47:22** [t]ver 26 [u]Dt 14:28-29 **47:23** [v]Isa 55:10; 61:11 [w]Ne 5:3 **47:24** [x]S Ge 41:34

[f]*7* Or *greeted* [g]*10* Or *said farewell to*
[h]*21* Samaritan Pentateuch and Septuagint (see also Vulgate); Masoretic Text *and he moved the people into the cities*

47:9 MY PILGRIMAGE. Jacob referred to his life and that of his fathers as a pilgrimage. (1) As a stranger and a pilgrim in the land, he trusted God for possession of the promised land. Thus it was by faith that he lived. Along with Abraham and Isaac, he died without receiving the promises; his ultimate goal was a better country, a heavenly one (see Heb 11:8–16). (2) All believers are likewise pilgrims and strangers on earth, living by faith and looking for a heavenly city "with foundations, whose architect and builder is God" (see Heb 11:10–13, notes).

fifths you may keep as seed for the
fields and as food for yourselves and
your households and your children."
25"You have saved our lives," they
said. "May we find favor in the eyes of
our lord;[y] we will be in bondage to
Pharaoh."[z]
26So Joseph established it as a law
concerning land in Egypt—still in
force today—that a fifth[a] of the produce belongs to Pharaoh. It was only
the land of the priests that did not become Pharaoh's.[b]
27Now the Israelites settled in Egypt
in the region of Goshen.[c] They acquired property there[d] and were fruitful and increased greatly in number.[e]
28Jacob lived in Egypt[f] seventeen
years, and the years of his life were a
hundred and forty-seven.[g] 29When the
time drew near for Israel[h] to die,[i] he
called for his son Joseph and said to
him, "If I have found favor in your
eyes,[j] put your hand under my
thigh[k] and promise that you will show
me kindness[l] and faithfulness.[m] Do
not bury me in Egypt, 30but when I rest
with my fathers,[n] carry me out of
Egypt and bury me where they are buried."[o]
"I will do as you say," he said.
31"Swear to me,"[p] he said. Then Joseph swore to him,[q] and Israel[r] worshiped as he leaned on the top of his
staff.[i][s]

Manasseh and Ephraim

48 Some time later Joseph was
told, "Your father is ill." So he
took his two sons Manasseh and
Ephraim[t] along with him. 2When Jacob was told, "Your son Joseph has
come to you," Israel[u] rallied his
strength and sat up on the bed.
3Jacob said to Joseph, "God Almighty[j][v] appeared to me at Luz[w] in
the land of Canaan, and there he
blessed me[x] 4and said to me, 'I am
going to make you fruitful and will increase your numbers.[y] I will make
you a community of peoples, and I will
give this land[z] as an everlasting pos-

47:25 [y]S Ge 32:5 [z]S ver 19
47:26 [a]S Ge 41:34 [b]ver 22
47:27 [c]S Ge 45:10,18 [d]S Ge 33:19 [e]S Ge 1:22; S 12:2; S 17:6
47:28 [f]Ps 105:23 [g]S Ge 25:7
47:29 [h]S Ge 46:29 [i]S Ge 27:2 [j]S Ge 32:5 [k]S Ge 24:2 [l]S Ge 19:19 [m]S Ge 24:27; Jdg 1:24; 2Sa 2:6
47:30 [n]S Ge 15:15 [o]S Ge 23:20; S 25:9; S 29:16; 50:25; Ex 13:19; Jos 24:32; Ac 7:15-16
47:31 [p]Ge 21:23; Jos 2:20; Jdg 15:12; 1Sa 24:21; 30:15 [q]S Ge 24:3 [r]S Ge 46:29 [s]S Ge 32:10; Heb 11:21 fn 1Ki 1:47
48:1 [t]S Ge 41:52; Heb 11:21
48:2 [u]ver 8,9,11, 14,20
48:3 [v]S Ge 17:1 [w]S Ge 28:19 [x]S Ge 28:13; S 32:29
48:4 [y]S Ge 12:2; S 17:6 [z]S Ge 12:7; S 28:13

[a]S Ge 15:7
48:5 [b]S Ge 41:50-52 [c]1Ch 5:1 [d]S Ge 29:32 [e]S Ge 29:33
48:7 [f]S Ge 25:20 [g]S Ge 42:38 [h]Ge 35:19; Ru 1:2; 1Sa 16:4
48:8 [i]S ver 2 [j]ver 10
48:9 [k]S Ge 33:5 [l]S Ge 24:60
48:10 [m]S Ge 27:1 [n]S Ge 27:27 [o]S Ge 29:13
48:11 [p]S ver 2 [q]S Ge 44:28 [r]Ge 50:23; Job 42:16; Ps 103:17; 128:6
48:12 [s]Ge 50:23; Job 3:12 [t]S Ge 19:1; S 33:3; 37:10
48:13 [u]Ps 16:8; 73:23; 110:1; Mt 25:33
48:14 [v]S ver 2 [w]ver 17,18

session to your descendants after
you.'[a]
5"Now then, your two sons born to
you in Egypt[b] before I came to you
here will be reckoned as mine; Ephraim and Manasseh will be mine,[c] just
as Reuben[d] and Simeon[e] are mine.
6Any children born to you after them
will be yours; in the territory they inherit they will be reckoned under the
names of their brothers. 7As I was returning from Paddan,[k][f] to my sorrow[g] Rachel died in the land of Canaan while we were still on the way, a
little distance from Ephrath. So I buried her there beside the road to Ephrath" (that is, Bethlehem).[h]
8When Israel[i] saw the sons of Joseph,[j] he asked, "Who are these?"
9"They are the sons God has given
me here,"[k] Joseph said to his father.
Then Israel said, "Bring them to me
so I may bless[l] them."
10Now Israel's eyes were failing because of old age, and he could hardly
see.[m] So Joseph brought his sons close
to him, and his father kissed them[n]
and embraced them.[o]
11Israel[p] said to Joseph, "I never
expected to see your face again,[q] and
now God has allowed me to see your
children too."[r]
12Then Joseph removed them from
Israel's knees[s] and bowed down with
his face to the ground.[t] 13And Joseph
took both of them, Ephraim on his right
toward Israel's left hand and Manasseh on his left toward Israel's right
hand,[u] and brought them close to him.
14But Israel[v] reached out his right
hand and put it on Ephraim's head,[w]
though he was the younger,[x] and
crossing his arms, he put his left hand
on Manasseh's head, even though Manasseh was the firstborn.[y]

[x]S Ge 25:23 [y]S Ge 29:32; S 41:51

[i]31 Or *Israel bowed down at the head of his bed*
[j]3 Hebrew *El-Shaddai* [k]7 That is, Northwest Mesopotamia

47:30 CARRY ME OUT OF EGYPT. Jacob was about to die without receiving the promise, but by faith in God he looked forward to the day when God would lead the people back to Canaan (see 46:3, note). With this in mind, he requested to be laid to rest in the burial place of his family (cf. Heb 11:22).

48:5 WILL BE RECKONED AS MINE. Jacob considered Joseph's two sons as his own, thus guaranteeing Joseph a double portion of the inheritance. Ephraim and Manasseh were thus to have equal rights and status with Jacob's other sons, such as Reuben and Simeon. The descendants of Ephraim and Manasseh each became a full tribe.

15Then he blessed[z] Joseph and
said,

"May the God before whom my
fathers
Abraham and Isaac walked,[a]
the God who has been my
shepherd[b]
all my life to this day,
16the Angel[c] who has delivered me
from all harm[d]
—may he bless[e] these boys.[f]
May they be called by my name
and the names of my fathers
Abraham and Isaac,[g]
and may they increase greatly
upon the earth."[h]

17When Joseph saw his father placing
his right hand[i] on Ephraim's
head[j] he was displeased; so he took
hold of his father's hand to move it
from Ephraim's head to Manasseh's
head. 18Joseph said to him, "No, my father,
this one is the firstborn; put your
right hand on his head."[k]

19But his father refused and said, "I
know, my son, I know. He too will become
a people, and he too will become
great.[l] Nevertheless, his younger
brother will be greater than he,[m] and
his descendants will become a group of
nations.[n]" 20He blessed[o] them that
day[p] and said,

"In your[1] name will Israel[q]
pronounce this blessing:[r]
'May God make you like
Ephraim[s] and
Manasseh.[t]' "

So he put Ephraim ahead of Manasseh.
21Then Israel said to Joseph, "I am
about to die, but God will be with
you[m][u] and take you[m] back to the
land of your[m] fathers.[v] 22And to you,
as one who is over your brothers,[w] I
give the ridge of land[n][x] I took from
the Amorites with my sword[y] and my
bow."

48:15 [z]S Ge 24:60 [a]S Ge 5:22 [b]Ge 49:24; 2Sa 5:2; Ps 23:1; 80:1; Isa 40:11; Jer 23:4 **48:16** [c]S Ge 16:7 [d]S Ge 24:50; 2Sa 4:9; Ps 71:4; Jer 15:21; Da 3:17 [e]S Ge 28:3 [f]1Ch 5:1; Eze 47:13; Heb 11:21 [g]S Ge 28:13 [h]S Ge 12:2; S 13:14 **48:17** [i]ver 13 [j]S ver 14 **48:18** [k]S ver 14 **48:19** [l]Ge 17:20 [m]S Ge 25:23 [n]S Ge 12:2 **48:20** [o]S Ge 24:60 [p]Heb 11:21 [q]S ver 2 [r]Lev 9:22; Nu 6:23; Dt 10:8; 21:5 [s]Nu 2:18; Jer 31:9 [t]S Ge 41:51; Nu 2:20; 10:23; Ru 4:11 **48:21** [u]S Ge 26:3 [v]S Ge 15:16; S 28:13; Dt 30:3; Ps 126:1; Jer 29:14; Eze 34:13 **48:22** [w]Ge 37:8 [x]Jos 24:32; Jn 4:5 [y]S Ge 34:26 **49:1** [z]Nu 24:14; Dt 31:29; Jer 23:20; Da 2:28,45 **49:2** [a]Jos 24:1 [b]ver 16,28; Ps 34:11 **49:3** [c]S Ge 29:32; S 41:51 [d]Dt 21:17; Ps 78:51; 105:36 [e]S Ge 34:19 **49:4** [f]Isa 57:20; Jer 49:23 [g]S Ge 29:29; S 34:5

Jacob Blesses His Sons

49:1–28Ref — Dt 33:1–29

49 Then Jacob called for his sons
and said: "Gather around so I
can tell you what will happen to you in
days to come.[z]

2"Assemble[a] and listen, sons of
Jacob;
listen to your father Israel.[b]

3"Reuben, you are my firstborn,[c]
my might, the first sign of my
strength,[d]
excelling in honor,[e] excelling in
power.
4Turbulent as the waters,[f] you will
no longer excel,
for you went up onto your
father's bed,
onto my couch and defiled it.[g]

5"Simeon[h] and Levi[i] are
brothers—
their swords[o] are weapons of
violence.[j]

49:5 [h]S Ge 29:33 [i]Ge 29:34 [j]S Ge 34:25; S Pr 4:17

[1]*20* The Hebrew is singular. [m]*21* The Hebrew is plural. [n]*22* Or *And to you I give one portion more than to your brothers—the portion* [o]*5* The meaning of the Hebrew for this word is uncertain.

48:15 WHO HAS BEEN MY SHEPHERD ALL MY LIFE. Jacob left his children with an example of persevering faith in God and a testimony that God had shepherded him his entire life, delivering him from all harm. The book of Hebrews points to Jacob's act of blessing Ephraim and Manasseh as the ultimate proof of his sincere faith in God (Heb 11:21). The greatest thing a father can pass on to his children is his faith in and commitment to God and his ways. There is no legacy greater than this.

48:19 HIS YOUNGER BROTHER WILL BE GREATER. Note that numerous times in OT history God chose the younger son over the older. He chose Isaac instead of Ishmael (21:12), Jacob instead of Esau (25:23), Joseph instead of Reuben (vv. 21–22; 49:3–4), Ephraim instead of Manasseh (vv. 14–20), Gideon over his brothers (Jdg 6:11–16), and David over his brothers (1Sa 16). This emphasizes that what is first among humans is not necessarily first with God. God chooses people on the basis of their sincerity, purity and love, not their position in their family (see Mt 19:30, note; Mt 20:26, note; 1Co 1:27–28; Jas 2:5).

49:1 JACOB CALLED FOR HIS SONS. As Jacob's life drew to an end, he gathered together his sons and prophesied about their lives and their future in God's purpose of redemption. The blessings and the curses of this chapter are conditional on the descendants' relationship with God (see v. 7, note).

49:4 YOU WILL NO LONGER EXCEL. Reuben was Jacob's firstborn. As such he was entitled to the birthright and the first place of leadership, honor and power. Instead, his place as leader was taken from him because of his sexual immorality with his father's wife (35:22; Dt 27:20). In other words, failure in character, manifested by serious sinful actions, may remove one forever from a position of leadership (see article on MORAL QUALIFICATIONS FOR OVERSEERS, p. 1882).

6Let me not enter their council,
let me not join their assembly,[k]
for they have killed men in their anger[l]
and hamstrung[m] oxen as they pleased.
7Cursed be their anger, so fierce,
and their fury,[n] so cruel![o]
I will scatter them in Jacob
and disperse them in Israel.[p]

8"Judah,[p][q] your brothers will praise you;
your hand will be on the neck[r]
of your enemies;
your father's sons will bow down to you.[s]
9You are a lion[t]'s cub,[u]
O Judah;[v]
you return from the prey,[w] my son.
Like a lion he crouches and lies down,
like a lioness—who dares to rouse him?
10The scepter will not depart from Judah,[x]
nor the ruler's staff from between his feet,
until he comes to whom it belongs[q][y]
and the obedience of the nations is his.[z]
11He will tether his donkey[a] to a vine,
his colt to the choicest branch;[b]
he will wash his garments in wine,
his robes in the blood of grapes.[c]
12His eyes will be darker than wine,
his teeth whiter than milk.[r][d]

13"Zebulun[e] will live by the seashore
and become a haven for ships;
his border will extend toward Sidon.[f]

14"Issachar[g] is a rawboned[s] donkey
lying down between two saddlebags.[t][h]
15When he sees how good is his resting place
and how pleasant is his land,[i]
he will bend his shoulder to the burden[j]
and submit to forced labor.[k]

16"Dan[u][l] will provide justice for his people
as one of the tribes of Israel.[m]
17Dan[n] will be a serpent by the roadside,
a viper along the path,[o]
that bites the horse's heels[p]
so that its rider tumbles backward.

18"I look for your deliverance,[q]
O LORD.[r]

19"Gad[v][s] will be attacked by a band of raiders,
but he will attack them at their heels.[t]

20"Asher's[u] food will be rich;[v]
he will provide delicacies fit for a king.[w]

21"Naphtali[x] is a doe set free

49:6 [k] Ps 1:1; Pr 1:15; Eph 5:11 [l] S Ge 34:26 [m] Jos 11:6,9; 2Sa 8:4; 1Ch 18:4 **49:7** [n] Ge 34:7 [o] Ge 34:25 [p] Jos 19:1,9; 21:1-42 **49:8** [q] S Ge 29:35 [r] Dt 28:48 [s] S Ge 9:25; 1Ch 5:2 **49:9** [t] Nu 24:9; Ps 7:2; 10:9; Eze 19:5; Mic 5:8 [u] Eze 19:2 [v] Rev 5:5 [w] ver 27; Nu 23:24; Job 38:39; Ps 17:12; 22:13; 104:21 **49:10** [x] Nu 24:17, 19; Jdg 1:1-2; 20:18; 1Ch 5:2; 28:4; Ps 60:7; 108:8 [y] Eze 21:27 [z] Ps 2:9; 72:8-11; 98:3; 110:2; Isa 2:4; 26:18; 42:1,4; 45:22; 48:20; 49:6; 51:5 **49:11** [a] Jdg 5:10; 10:4; Zec 9:9 [b] Dt 8:8; 2Ki 18:32 [c] Dt 32:14; Isa 63:2 **49:12** [d] SS 5:12 **49:13** [e] S Ge 30:20 [f] S Ge 10:19 **49:14** [g] S Ge 30:18 [h] Jdg 5:16; Ps 68:13 **49:15** [i] Jos 19:17-23 [j] Eze 29:18 [k] 1Ki 4:6; 5:13; 9:21; Isa 14:2; 31:8 **49:16** [l] Ge 30:6 [m] S ver 2 **49:17** [n] Jdg 18:27 [o] Jer 8:17; Am 9:3 [p] ver 19 **49:18** [q] S Ge 45:7; Ps 40:1-3 [r] Ps 119:166,174 **49:19** [s] S Ge 30:11 [t] ver 17 **49:20** [u] S Ge 30:13 [v] Isa 25:6 [w] Job 29:6 **49:21** [x] S Ge 30:8

[p] 8 *Judah* sounds like and may be derived from the Hebrew for *praise.* [q] 10 Or *until Shiloh comes*; or *until he comes to whom tribute belongs* [r] 12 Or *will be dull from wine, / his teeth white from milk* [s] 14 Or *strong* [t] 14 Or *campfires* [u] 16 *Dan* here means *he provides justice.* [v] 19 *Gad* can mean *attack* and *band of raiders.*

49:7 CURSED BE THEIR ANGER. Jacob's curse on Simeon and Levi (vv. 5–7) was of a conditional nature, as were all the blessings and curses of this chapter. Because of the stand for God taken by the Levites (i.e., the family of Levi) at the scene of the golden calf, the curse spoken here was removed and a blessing and honorable place were given them (Ex 32:26–29; Lev 25:32–33; Dt 10:8; 33:8–11)—showing that the curses on a father and his family can be broken and removed by the repentance and faith of his children (Lev 26:39–42; 2Ch 30:7–9; Jer 31:29–30; Eze 18:1–9).

49:10 UNTIL HE COMES TO WHOM IT BELONGS. The blessing conferred on Judah (vv. 8–12) indicates that he was given the rights of the firstborn, and thus the blessing promised to Abraham (12:1–3). The essence of this promise was that all nations would be blessed through him by the "offspring" of the woman (see 3:15, note; see article on THE CALL OF ABRAHAM, p. 25). (1) Judah was told that his descendants would live in a position of general superiority to his brothers "until he comes to whom it belongs" (vv. 8–10). This was partially fulfilled in that the royal line of Israel was the line of King David, a descendant of Judah. (2) "He comes to whom it belongs" (cf. Eze 21:27) ultimately refers to the coming Messiah, Jesus Christ, who came through the tribe of Judah (Rev 5:5). Jacob prophesied that all people would obey him (v. 10; Rev 19:15), and that he would bring great spiritual blessing (vv. 11–12).

that bears beautiful fawns.[w][y]

22"Joseph[z] is a fruitful vine,[a]
a fruitful vine near a spring,
whose branches[b] climb over a
wall.[x]
23With bitterness archers attacked
him;[c]
they shot at him with hostility.[d]
24But his bow remained steady,[e]
his strong arms[f] stayed[y]
limber,
because of the hand of the Mighty
One of Jacob,[g]
because of the Shepherd,[h] the
Rock of Israel,[i]
25because of your father's God,[j]
who helps[k] you,
because of the Almighty,[z][l]
who blesses you
with blessings of the heavens
above,
blessings of the deep that lies
below,[m]
blessings of the breast[n] and
womb.[o]
26Your father's blessings are greater
than the blessings of the ancient
mountains,
than[a] the bounty of the age-old
hills.[p]
Let all these rest on the head of
Joseph,[q]
on the brow of the prince
among[b] his brothers.[r]

27"Benjamin[s] is a ravenous wolf;[t]
in the morning he devours the
prey,[u]
in the evening he divides the
plunder."[v]

28All these are the twelve tribes of
Israel,[w] and this is what their father
said to them when he blessed them,
giving each the blessing[x] appropriate
to him.

The Death of Jacob

29Then he gave them these instructions:[y] "I am about to be gathered to
my people.[z] Bury me with my fathers[a] in the cave in the field of
Ephron the Hittite,[b] 30the cave in the
field of Machpelah,[c] near Mamre[d] in
Canaan, which Abraham bought as a
burial place[e] from Ephron the Hittite,
along with the field.[f] 31There Abraham[g] and his wife Sarah[h] were buried, there Isaac and his wife Rebekah[i] were buried, and there I buried
Leah.[j] 32The field and the cave in it
were bought from the Hittites.[c][k]"

33When Jacob had finished giving instructions to his sons, he drew his feet
up into the bed, breathed his last and
was gathered to his people.[l]

50 Joseph threw himself upon his
father and wept over him and
kissed him.[m] 2Then Joseph directed
the physicians in his service to embalm
his father Israel. So the physicians em-
balmed him,[n] 3taking a full forty days,
for that was the time required for em-
balming. And the Egyptians mourned
for him seventy days.[o]

4When the days of mourning[p] had
passed, Joseph said to Pharaoh's
court,[q] "If I have found favor in your
eyes,[r] speak to Pharaoh for me. Tell
him, 5'My father made me swear an
oath[s] and said, "I am about to die;[t]
bury me in the tomb I dug for myself[u]
in the land of Canaan."[v] Now let me go
up and bury my father;[w] then I will
return.' "

6Pharaoh said, "Go up and bury your
father, as he made you swear to do."

49:21 [y]Job 39:1 **49:22** [z]S Ge 30:24 [a]S Ge 17:6; Ps 128:3; Eze 19:10 [b]Ps 80:10 **49:23** [c]1Ch 10:3 [d]S Ge 27:41; S 37:24 **49:24** [e]Job 29:20 [f]Ps 18:34; Isa 63:12 [g]Ps 132:2,5; Isa 1:24; 10:34; 49:26; 60:16 [h]S Ge 48:15 [i]Dt 32:4,15,18,31; 1Sa 2:2; 2Sa 22:32; Ps 18:2,31; 19:14; 78:35; 89:26; 144:1; Isa 17:10; 26:4; 30:29; 44:8; Hab 1:12 **49:25** [j]S Ge 28:13 [k]Ex 18:4; Ps 27:9 [l]S Ge 17:1 [m]S Ge 27:28 [n]Isa 66:11 [o]Dt 7:13; 28:4; Ps 107:38; Pr 10:22 **49:26** [p]Hab 3:6 [q]1Ch 5:1; Eze 47:13 [r]S Ge 37:8 **49:27** [s]S Ge 35:18; Jdg 20:12-13 [t]Hab 1:8; Zep 3:3 [u]S ver 9 [v]Nu 31:11; Dt 2:35; Jos 7:21; 8:2; 22:8; Jdg 8:24 **49:28** [w]S ver 2 [x]S Ge 27:4 **49:29** [y]Ge 50:16 [z]S Ge 25:8 [a]S Ge 15:15; 50:25; 2Sa 2:32; 19:37 [b]S Ge 25:9 **49:30** [c]S Ge 23:9 [d]S Ge 13:18 [e]S Ge 23:4 [f]S Ge 23:20 **49:31** [g]Ge 25:9 [h]Ge 23:19 [i]S Ge 24:67 [j]S Ge 23:20; S 29:16 **49:32** [k]S Ge 10:15 **49:33** [l]S Ge 25:8; Ac 7:15 **50:1** [m]S Ge 29:11; S 46:4 **50:2** [n]ver 26; 2Ch 16:14; Mt 26:12; Mk 16:1; Jn 19:39-40 **50:3** [o]S Ge 37:34; S Dt 1:3 **50:4** [p]S Ge 27:41 [q]ver 7 [r]S Ge 30:27; S 32:5 **50:5** [s]S Ge 24:37 [t]ver 24 [u]2Sa 18:18; 2Ch 16:14; Isa 22:16; Mt 27:60 [v]Ge 47:31 [w]Mt 8:21

[w]21 Or *free; / he utters beautiful words* [x]22 Or *Joseph is a wild colt, / a wild colt near a spring, / a wild donkey on a terraced hill* [y]23,24 Or *archers will attack . . . will shoot . . . will remain . . . will stay* [z]25 Hebrew *Shaddai* [a]26 Or *of my progenitors, / as great as* [b]26 Or *the one separated from* [c]32 Or *the sons of Heth*

50:1 WEPT OVER HIM. Joseph's reaction to his father's death is a model for all believers who experience the death of a Christian loved one. (1) Sincere grief. Joseph wept and entered into a long period of mourning, consisting of seventy days and then several more weeks as he carried Jacob's remains back to Canaan for the burial (vv. 1–4,7–14). It is not abnormal or wrong to grieve weeks or even months over the death of someone very close to us.

(2) Care in preparing for burial (v. 2). Joseph wanted to honor his father's memory in a right and decent way.

(3) Fulfilling last wishes. Joseph honored the promises he made to his father (vv. 5,12–13). Promises made in faith and based on God's will must be carried out after the death of a loved one.

(4) Faithful testimony. Joseph testified to his faith in God's promises by carrying his father back to the promised land of Canaan and laying him in the tomb of Abraham, Isaac and the others (cf. 1Th 4:13,18; see Php 1:21, note).

7So Joseph went up to bury his father. All Pharaoh's officials[x] accompanied him—the dignitaries of his
court[y] and all the dignitaries of
Egypt— 8besides all the members of
Joseph's household and his brothers
and those belonging to his father's
household.[z] Only their children and
their flocks and herds were left in Goshen.[a] 9Chariots[b] and horsemen[d]
also went up with him. It was a very
large company.
10When they reached the threshing
floor[c] of Atad, near the Jordan, they
lamented loudly and bitterly;[d] and
there Joseph observed a seven-day period[e] of mourning[f] for his father.[g]
11When the Canaanites[h] who lived
there saw the mourning at the threshing floor of Atad, they said, "The Egyptians are holding a solemn ceremony of
mourning."[i] That is why that place
near the Jordan is called Abel Mizraim.[e]
12So Jacob's sons did as he had commanded them:[j] 13They carried him to
the land of Canaan and buried him in
the cave in the field of Machpelah,[k]
near Mamre,[l] which Abraham had
bought as a burial place from Ephron
the Hittite,[m] along with the field.[n]
14After burying his father, Joseph returned to Egypt, together with his
brothers and all the others who had
gone with him to bury his father.[o]

Joseph Reassures His Brothers

15When Joseph's brothers saw that
their father was dead, they said, "What
if Joseph holds a grudge[p] against us
and pays us back for all the wrongs we
did to him?"[q] 16So they sent word to
Joseph, saying, "Your father left these
instructions[r] before he died: 17'This
is what you are to say to Joseph: I ask
you to forgive your brothers the sins[s]
and the wrongs they committed in
treating you so badly.'[t] Now please
forgive the sins of the servants of the
God of your father.[u]" When their message came to him, Joseph wept.[v]
18His brothers then came and threw
themselves down before him.[w] "We
are your slaves,"[x] they said.
19But Joseph said to them, "Don't be
afraid. Am I in the place of God?[y]
20You intended to harm me,[z] but God
intended[a] it for good[b] to accomplish
what is now being done, the saving of
many lives.[c] 21So then, don't be
afraid. I will provide for you and your
children.[d]" And he reassured them
and spoke kindly[e] to them.

The Death of Joseph

22Joseph stayed in Egypt, along with
all his father's family. He lived a hundred and ten years[f] 23and saw the
third generation[g] of Ephraim's[h] children.[i] Also the children of Makir[j]
son of Manasseh[k] were placed at birth
on Joseph's knees.[f]
24Then Joseph said to his brothers,
"I am about to die.[m] But God will surely come to your aid[n] and take you up
out of this land to the land[o] he promised on oath to Abraham,[p] Isaac[q]
and Jacob."[r] 25And Joseph made the
sons of Israel swear an oath[s] and
said, "God will surely come to your aid,
and then you must carry my bones[t] up
from this place."[u]
26So Joseph died[v] at the age of a
hundred and ten.[w] And after they em-
balmed him,[x] he was placed in a coffin
in Egypt.

50:7 [x]Ge 45:16 [y]ver 4 **50:8** [z]ver 14 [a]S Ge 45:10 **50:9** [b]S Ge 41:43 **50:10** [c]Nu 15:20; Ru 3:2; 2Sa 24:18; 1Ki 22:10 [d]2Sa 1:17; 3:33; 2Ch 35:25; Eze 32:16; Ac 8:2 [e]1Sa 31:13; Job 2:13; Eze 3:15 [f]S Ge 27:41; S Lev 10:6 [g]S Ge 37:34 **50:11** [h]S Ge 10:18 [i]S Ge 37:34 **50:12** [j]Ge 49:29 **50:13** [k]S Ge 23:9 [l]S Ge 13:18 [m]S Ge 25:9 [n]S Ge 23:20 **50:14** [o]ver 8 **50:15** [p]S Ge 27:41 [q]ver 17; S Ge 9:5; 37:28; Zep 3:11; 1Pe 3:9 **50:16** [r]Ge 49:29 **50:17** [s]S Mt 6:14 [t]S ver 15 [u]S Ge 28:13 [v]S Ge 29:11 **50:18** [w]S Ge 37:7 [x]S Ge 43:18 **50:19** [y]S Ge 30:2; S Ex 32:34; Ro 12:19; Heb 10:30 **50:20** [z]Ge 37:20 [a]Isa 10:7; Mic 4:11-12 [b]Ro 8:28 [c]S Ge 45:5; Est 4:14 **50:21** [d]S Ge 45:11 [e]S Ge 34:3; Eph 4:32 **50:22** [f]S Ge 25:7; Jos 24:29 **50:23** [g]Job 42:16 [h]S Ge 41:52 [i]S Ge 48:11 [j]Nu 26:29; 27:1; 32:39,40; 36:1; Dt 3:15; Jos 13:31; 17:1; Jdg 5:14 [k]S Ge 41:51 [l]S Ge 48:12 **50:24** [m]ver 5 [n]Ru 1:6; Ps 35:2; 106:4; Isa 38:14 [o]S Ge 15:14 [p]S Ge 13:17 [q]S Ge 17:19 [r]S Ge 12:7; S 15:16 **50:25** [s]S Ge 24:37 [t]S Ge 49:29 [u]S Ge 47:29-30; Heb 11:22 **50:26** [v]Ex 1:6 [w]S Ge 25:7 [x]S ver 2

[d] *9* Or *charioteers* [e] *11 Abel Mizraim* means *mourning of the Egyptians.* [f] *23* That is, were counted as his

50:20 GOD INTENDED IT FOR GOOD. See article on THE PROVIDENCE OF GOD, p. 78.

50:25 CARRY MY BONES UP. Joseph's enduring faith was in God's promise that Canaan would be his people's homeland (13:12–15; 26:3; 28:13). Thus he requested that his bones be taken to the land of promise. Four hundred years later, when the Israelites left Egypt to go to Canaan, they took Joseph's bones with them (Ex 13:19; Jos 24:32; cf. Heb 11:22). Likewise, all believers know that their future lies not in this present world, but in another land, a heavenly country, where they will live forever with God and enjoy his eternal presence and blessings (Heb 11:8–16; Rev 21:1–4).

EXODUS

Outline

I. Oppression of the Hebrews in Egypt (1:1—11:10)
   A. Burden of the Oppressed (1:1–22)
   B. Preparation of the Deliverer (2:1—4:31)
      1. Moses' Birth and First Forty Years (2:1–15a)
      2. Moses' Exile and Second Forty Years (2:15b-25)
      3. Moses' Call and Return to Egypt (3:1—4:31)
   C. Struggle with the Oppressor (5:1—11:10)
      1. The Request: "Let My People Go" (5:1–3)
      2. The Response: Tyrannical Persecution (5:4–21)
      3. The Reassurance: The Lord Will Manifest His Lordship (5:22—7:13)
      4. The Recourse: The Ten Plagues (7:14—11:10)
II. Deliverance of the Hebrews from Egypt (12:1—15:21)
   A. The Passover Deliverance: Redemption by Blood (12:1—13:16)
   B. The Red Sea Deliverance: Redemption by Power (13:17—14:31)
   C. The Songs of Deliverance: Praise to the Redeemer (15:1–21)
III. Education of the Hebrews En Route to Mount Sinai (15:22—18:27)
   A. The Test of Adversity and Providential Care (15:22—17:16)
      1. The First Test: Bitter Water at Marah (15:22–27)
      2. The Hunger Test: Provision of Quail and Manna (16:1–36)
      3. The Thirst Test: Water at Rephidim (17:1–7)
      4. The Conflict Test: Battle with Amalek (17:8–16)
   B. The Wise Counsel of Jethro (18:1–27)
IV. Covenant with the Hebrews at Mount Sinai (19:1—24:18)
   A. Preparatory Instructions to Moses (19:1—25)
   B. The Ten Commandments: Foundation for Covenant Life (20:1–17)
   C. Ordinances Guarding the Covenant Relationship (20:18—23:19)
   D. Promises Regarding the Promised Land (23:20–33)
   E. Ratification of the Covenant (24:1–18)
V. Worship by the Hebrews Delineated at Mount Sinai (25:1—40:38)
   A. Instructions Concerning the Tabernacle (25:1—27:21)
   B. Instructions Concerning the Priest (28:1—31:18)
   C. The Sin of Idolatry (32:1—34:35)
   D. The Implementation of the Divine Instructions (35:1—40:38)

Author: Moses

Theme: Redemption

Date of Writing: c. 1445–1405 B.C.

Background

Exodus continues the narrative begun in Genesis. The book's title, derived from the Greek word *exodos* (the title used in the Septuagint, i.e., the Greek translation of the OT), means "exit" or "departure." It refers to God's mighty deliverance of the Israelites from slavery in Egypt and their departure from that land as the people of God.

Two issues related to Exodus's background have involved major controversy: the date of Israel's exodus from Egypt and the authorship of the book. (1) Two different dates for the exodus have been proposed by scholars. (a) An "early date" (also referred to as the Biblical date) is derived from 1Ki 6:1, which states that it occurred 480 years before "the fourth year of Solomon's reign"; this dates the exodus c. 1445 B.C. Also, in Jdg 11:26, Jephthah (c. 1100 B.C.) declared that Israel had occupied their land for 300 years, which would date the conquest at approximately 1400 B.C. This chronology for the exodus, the conquest and the period of the judges fits well with the datable history of Israel's first three kings (Saul, David and Solomon). (b) A "late date" for the exodus (c. 1290) is proposed by liberal critics of the Bible, based on certain assumptions about Egyptian rulers and on a 13th-century B.C. archaeological dating for the destruction of Canaanite cities during the conquest.

(2) There is also disagreement between conservative and liberal Biblical scholars over the Mosaic authorship of the book of Exodus. (a) Modern interpreters often view the book as a composite work by various editors, completed at a much later time in Israel's history than the time of Moses (called the JEDP theory). (b) However, Jewish tradition from the time of Joshua onward (Jos 8:31–35), plus the testimony of Jesus (cf. Mk 12:26), early Christianity and contemporary conservative scholarship, all attribute the book's origin to Moses (see the introduction to Deuteronomy). Furthermore, internal evidence supports Moses' authorship. Numerous details in Exodus indicate that the author was an eyewitness of the recorded events (e.g., 2:12; 9:31–32; 15:27); also, portions of the book itself testify to Moses' direct involvement in its writing (e.g., 17:14; 24:4; 34:27).

Purpose

Exodus was written to provide an enduring record of the historical and redemptive acts of God whereby Israel was delivered from Egypt, established as his chosen nation and given the written revelation about his covenant with her. Also, it was written as a supremely important link in God's overall progressive self-revelation that culminated in the person of Jesus Christ and in the NT.

Survey

The book of Exodus begins with Jacob's descendants suffering oppression, slavery and infanticide in Egypt; the book ends with God's presence, power and glory manifested (i.e., tabernacling) in the midst of his liberated people in the desert. Exodus divides into three major sections. (A) Chs. 1—14 reveal *Israel in Egypt* suffering oppression under a king who did not know about Joseph, and God redeeming Israel "with an outstretched arm and with mighty acts of judgment" (6:6). Among the monumental events in this part of Israel's history are: (1) Moses' birth, preservation and preparation (ch. 2); (2) Moses' call at the burning bush (chs. 3—4); (3) the ten plagues (chs. 7—12); (4) the Passover (ch. 12); and (5) the Red Sea crossing (chs. 13—14). Israel's exodus from Egypt is viewed throughout the OT as the greatest experience of redemption in the old covenant. (B) Chs. 16—18 describe *Israel in the desert* en route to Mount Sinai. God guided his redeemed people by a pillar of fire and cloud and provided manna, quail and water, while training them to walk by faith and obedience. (C) Chs. 19—40 record *Israel at Mount Sinai* receiving revelation involving (1) the covenant (ch. 19), (2) the Ten Commandments (ch. 20), and (3) the tabernacle and priesthood (chs. 25—31). The book concludes with the completion of the tabernacle and God's glory filling it (ch. 40).

Special Features

Five major features characterize Exodus. (1) It records the historical circumstances of Israel's birth as a nation. (2) It contains, in the Ten Commandments (ch. 20), God's summary of his moral law and righteous requirements for his people, and thus provides a foundation for Biblical ethics and morals in subsequent revelation. (3) It is the foremost OT book describing the nature of God's redemptive grace and power in action. In OT terms, Exodus describes the supernatural character of God's deliverance of his people from the peril and bondage of sin, Satan and the world. (4) The entire book is permeated with a majestic revelation of God as (a) glorious in attributes (truthful, merciful, faithful, holy and omnipotent); (b) Lord over history and powerful kings; (c) Redeemer who enters into covenant with the redeemed; (d) just and righteous as revealed in his moral law and judgments; and (e) worthy of devout worship as the transcendent God who descends to "tabernacle" with his people. (5) Exodus emphasizes the how, what and why of the true worship that should necessarily follow God's redemption of his people.

New Testament Fulfillment

Throughout Exodus there is a foreshadowing of the redemption that is offered under the new covenant. The first Passover, the Red Sea crossing and the giving of the Law at Mount Sinai are to the old covenant what Jesus' death, resurrection and the giving of the Holy Spirit at Pentecost are to the new covenant. Types in Exodus that foreshadow Christ and redemption in the NT are (1) Moses, (2) the Passover, (3) the Red Sea crossing, (4) manna, (5) the rock and water, (6) the tabernacle and (7) the high priest. The absolute moral demands of the Ten Commandments are repeated in the NT as requirements for new covenant believers.

Reading Exodus

In order to read the entire Old Testament in one year, the book of Exodus should be read in 21 days, according to the following schedule: □ 1–2 □ 3–5 □ 6–7 □ 8–9 □ 10–12 □ 13–14 □ 15 □ 16–17 □ 18–19 □ 20–21 □ 22–23 □ 24–25 □ 26–27 □ 28 □ 29–30 □ 31 □ 32–33 □ 34–35 □ 36–37 □ 38–39 □ 40

NOTES

The Israelites Oppressed

1 These are the names of the sons of
Israel[a] who went to Egypt with
Jacob, each with his family: **2**Reuben,
Simeon, Levi and Judah; **3**Issachar,
Zebulun and Benjamin; **4**Dan and
Naphtali; Gad and Asher.[b] **5**The
descendants of Jacob numbered seven-
ty[a] in all;[c] Joseph was already in
Egypt.

6Now Joseph and all his brothers and
all that generation died,[d] **7**but the Israelites were fruitful and multiplied
greatly and became exceedingly numerous,[e] so that the land was filled
with them.

8Then a new king, who did not know
about Joseph, came to power in
Egypt.[f] **9**"Look," he said to his people, "the Israelites have become much
too numerous[g] for us.[h] **10**Come, we
must deal shrewdly[i] with them or
they will become even more numerous
and, if war breaks out, will join our enemies, fight against us and leave the
country."[j]

11So they put slave masters[k] over
them to oppress them with forced labor,[l] and they built Pithom and Rameses[m] as store cities[n] for Pharaoh.
12But the more they were oppressed,
the more they multiplied and spread;
so the Egyptians came to dread the Israelites **13**and worked them ruthlessly.[o] **14**They made their lives bitter
with hard labor[p] in brick[q] and mortar
and with all kinds of work in the fields;
in all their hard labor the Egyptians
used them ruthlessly.[r]

15The king of Egypt said to the Hebrew midwives,[s] whose names were
Shiphrah and Puah, **16**"When you help
the Hebrew women in childbirth and
observe them on the delivery stool, if it
is a boy, kill him; but if it is a girl, let
her live."[t] **17**The midwives, however,
feared[u] God and did not do what the
king of Egypt had told them to do;[v]
they let the boys live. **18**Then the king
of Egypt summoned the midwives and
asked them, "Why have you done this?
Why have you let the boys live?"

19The midwives answered Pharaoh,
"Hebrew women are not like Egyptian
women; they are vigorous and give
birth before the midwives arrive."[w]

20So God was kind to the midwives[x] and the people increased and
became even more numerous. **21**And
because the midwives feared[y] God, he
gave them families[z] of their own.

22Then Pharaoh gave this order to
all his people: "Every boy that is born[b]
you must throw into the Nile,[a] but let
every girl live."[b]

The Birth of Moses

2 Now a man of the house of Levi[c]
married a Levite woman,[d] **2**and
she became pregnant and gave birth to
a son. When she saw that he was a
fine[e] child, she hid him for three

1:1 [a] S Ge 46:8 **1:4** [b] Ge 35:22-26; Nu 1:20-43 **1:5** [c] S Ge 46:26 **1:6** [d] Ge 50:26; Ac 7:15 **1:7** [e] ver 9; S Ge 12:2; Dt 7:13; Eze 16:7 **1:8** [f] Jer 43:11; 46:2 **1:9** [g] S ver 7 [h] S Ge 26:16 **1:10** [i] Ge 15:13; Ex 3:7; 18:11; Ps 64:2; 71:10; 83:3; Isa 53:3 [j] Ps 105:24-25; Ac 7:17-19 **1:11** [k] Ex 3:7; 5:10,13,14 [l] S Ge 15:13; Ex 2:11; 5:4; 6:6-7; Jos 9:27; 1Ki 9:21; 1Ch 22:2; Isa 60:10 [m] S Ge 47:11 [n] 1Ki 9:19; 2Ch 8:4 **1:13** [o] ver 14; Ge 15:13-14; Ex 5:21; 16:3; Lev 25:43,46,53; Dt 4:20; 26:6; 1Ki 8:51; Ps 129:1; Isa 30:6; 48:10; Jer 11:4 **1:14** [p] Dt 26:6; Ezr 9:9; Isa 14:3 [q] S Ge 11:3 [r] Ex 2:23; 3:9; Nu 20:15; 1Sa 10:18; 2Ki 13:4; Ps 66:11; 81:6; Ac 7:19

1:15 [s] S Ge 35:17 **1:16** [t] ver 22 **1:17** [u] ver 21; Pr 16:6 [v] 1Sa 22:17; Da 3:16-18; Ac 4:18-20; 5:29 **1:19** [w] Lev 19:11; Jos 2:4-6; 1Sa 19:14; 2Sa 17:20 **1:20** [x] Pr 11:18; 22:8; Ecc 8:12; Isa 3:10; Heb 6:10 **1:21** [y] S ver 17 [z] 1Sa 2:35; 2Sa 7:11,27-29; 1Ki 11:38; 14:10 **1:22** [a] S Ge 41:1 [b] ver 16; Ac 7:19 **2:1** [c] S Ge 29:34 [d] ver 2; Ex 6:20; Nu 26:59 **2:2** [e] S Ge 39:6

[a] *5* Masoretic Text (see also Gen. 46:27); Dead Sea Scrolls and Septuagint (see also Acts 7:14 and note at Gen. 46:27) *seventy-five*
[b] *22* Masoretic Text; Samaritan Pentateuch, Septuagint and Targums *born to the Hebrews*

1:1 THE SONS OF ISRAEL. Israel, the father of the sons listed in vv. 2–6, is also called "Jacob" (see Ge 32:28, note). His descendants became known as Israelites.

1:7 MULTIPLIED GREATLY. The Israelites multiplied greatly according to the promises God made to Abraham, Isaac and Jacob (Ge 12:2; 17:2, 6; 22:17; 48:4; cf. Ac 7:17), growing to such an extent that when they left Egypt they numbered about 600,000 men, besides women and children (12:37). God's prediction of oppression was also fulfilled (cf. v. 11; Ge 15:13).

1:8 WHO DID NOT KNOW ABOUT JOSEPH. The book of Exodus continues the story of God's dealing with the children of Israel that began in Genesis. (1) The time gap between Joseph's death (Ge 50:26) and the beginning of Israel's persecution by the Egyptians (cf. v. 11) was approximately 220 years. (2) If the date of the exodus is set at around 1440 B.C., then the pharaoh "who did not know about Joseph" would probably be Thutmose I (1539–1514 B.C.) (see Ac 7:18); the pharaoh of the exodus would be Amenhotep II (1447–1421 B.C.). The total time of the Israelites' stay in Egypt was 430 years (Ex 12:40).

1:11 SLAVE MASTERS OVER THEM TO OPPRESS THEM. God permitted and used the oppression of Israel in order to separate them from the idolatry and the immoral ways of Egypt, and to prepare them for their miraculous deliverance and their faith-relationship with him (cf. Jos 24:14; Eze 23:8).

2:2 A SON. The "son" referred to is Moses (cf. v. 10). His birth, his escape from death, and all the events of his youth were under God's direction in order that he might deliver Israel from bondage. All believers need to know that God also works in their lives, using appropriate means to accomplish his will (see Mt 2:13, note; Ro 8:28, note).

months.[f] 3But when she could hide
him no longer, she got a papyrus[g] basket for him and coated it with tar and
pitch.[h] Then she placed the child in it
and put it among the reeds[i] along the
bank of the Nile. 4His sister[j] stood at
a distance to see what would happen to
him.
5Then Pharaoh's daughter went
down to the Nile to bathe, and her attendants were walking along the river
bank.[k] She saw the basket among the
reeds and sent her slave girl to get it.
6She opened it and saw the baby. He
was crying, and she felt sorry for him.
"This is one of the Hebrew babies," she
said.
7Then his sister asked Pharaoh's
daughter, "Shall I go and get one of the
Hebrew women to nurse the baby for
you?"
8"Yes, go," she answered. And the
girl went and got the baby's mother.
9Pharaoh's daughter said to her, "Take
this baby and nurse him for me, and I
will pay you." So the woman took the
baby and nursed him. 10When the child
grew older, she took him to Pharaoh's
daughter and he became her son. She
named[l] him Moses,[c] saying, "I
drew[m] him out of the water."

Moses Flees to Midian

11One day, after Moses had grown
up, he went out to where his own people[n] were and watched them at their
hard labor.[o] He saw an Egyptian beating a Hebrew, one of his own people.
12Glancing this way and that and seeing no one, he killed the Egyptian and
hid him in the sand. 13The next day he
went out and saw two Hebrews fighting. He asked the one in the wrong,

2:2 [f]Heb 11:23
2:3 [g]Isa 18:2
[h]Ge 6:14
[i]S Ge 41:2;
S Job 8:11;
Ac 7:21
2:4 [j]Ex 15:20
2:5 [k]Ex 7:15;
8:20
2:10 [l]1Sa 1:20
[m]2Sa 22:17
2:11 [n]Ac 7:23;
Heb 11:24-26
[o]S Ex 1:11
2:13 [p]Ac 7:26
2:14 [q]S Ge 13:8;
Ac 7:27*
2:15 [r]Ex 4:19
[s]S Ge 31:21
[t]Heb 11:27
2:16 [u]Ex 3:1;
18:1 [v]S Ge 24:11
[w]S Ge 30:38
2:17 [x]1Sa 30:8;
Ps 31:2
[y]S Ge 29:10
2:18 [z]Ex 3:1;
4:18; 18:1,5,12;
Nu 10:29
2:20 [a]Ge 18:2-5
2:21 [b]Ex 4:25;
18:2; Nu 12:1
2:22 [c]Jdg 18:30
[d]S Ge 23:4;
Heb 11:13
2:23 [e]Ac 7:30
[f]Ex 4:19
[g]S Ex 1:14
[h]ver 24; Ex 3:7,9;
6:5; Nu 20:15-16;
Dt 26:7; Jdg 2:18;
1Sa 12:8; Ps 5:2;
18:6; 39:12; 81:7;
102:1; Jas 5:4

"Why are you hitting your fellow Hebrew?"[p]
14The man said, "Who made you ruler and judge over us?[q] Are you thinking of killing me as you killed the Egyptian?" Then Moses was afraid and
thought, "What I did must have become known."
15When Pharaoh heard of this, he
tried to kill[r] Moses, but Moses fled[s]
from Pharaoh and went to live in Midian,[t] where he sat down by a well.
16Now a priest of Midian[u] had seven
daughters, and they came to draw water[v] and fill the troughs[w] to water
their father's flock. 17Some shepherds
came along and drove them away, but
Moses got up and came to their rescue[x] and watered their flock.[y]
18When the girls returned to Reuel[z] their father, he asked them, "Why
have you returned so early today?"
19They answered, "An Egyptian rescued us from the shepherds. He even
drew water for us and watered the
flock."
20"And where is he?" he asked his
daughters. "Why did you leave him? Invite him to have something to eat."[a]
21Moses agreed to stay with the
man, who gave his daughter Zipporah[b] to Moses in marriage. 22Zippo-
rah gave birth to a son, and Moses
named him Gershom,[d][c] saying, "I
have become an alien[d] in a foreign
land."
23During that long period,[e] the
king of Egypt died.[f] The Israelites
groaned in their slavery[g] and cried
out, and their cry[h] for help because of

[c] *10 Moses* sounds like the Hebrew for *draw out.* [d] *22 Gershom* sounds like the Hebrew for *an alien there.*

2:6 HEBREW BABIES. See Ge 14:13, note.

2:11 MOSES. Moses' ministry in some ways foreshadows the ministry of Jesus Christ. (1) An attempt was made to kill both Moses and Jesus as infants (1:16; Mt 2:13). (2) Both Moses and Christ ministered as prophet (Dt 18:15,18; Ac 3:22; 7:37), priest (Ps 99:6; Heb 7:24), king (Dt 33:4–5) and shepherd (Ex 3:1; Jn 10:11–14). (3) They both suffered with God's people (Tit 2:14; Heb 11:25–26), delivered the people from slavery (Ac 7:35) and brought in a covenant (19:5; 34:10; Heb 8:5–13).

2:12 KILLED THE EGYPTIAN. Moses' willingness to identify with God's people and to defend the Hebrews who were being oppressed demonstrated his faith in God. Moses rejected sin's passing pleasures for the honor of suffering for God and with God's people (cf. Ac 7:23–29; Heb 11:24–29).

2:15 MIDIAN. The Midianites, descendants of Abraham through Keturah, lived south and southeast of Canaan. Moses remained in Midian for forty years (cf. 7:7; Ac 7:23,30), where God prepared him for his future task in this same region—the Desert of Sinai. God did important work in his life in the desert (see article on THE PROVIDENCE OF GOD, p. 78).

2:23 THEIR CRY . . . WENT UP TO GOD. After many years of oppression, the people of Israel began to cry to God for help. When they turned to the Lord, he turned to them (vv. 23–25). Until this time many had been worshiping the gods of Egypt and had probably been calling on them for help and deliverance (see Jos 24:14; Eze 20:5–10).

their slavery went up to God. 24God
heard their groaning and he remembered[i] his covenant[j] with Abraham,
with Isaac and with Jacob. 25So God
looked on the Israelites and was concerned[k] about them.

Moses and the Burning Bush

3 Now Moses was tending the flock
of Jethro[l] his father-in-law, the
priest of Midian,[m] and he led the flock
to the far side of the desert and came
to Horeb,[n] the mountain[o] of God.
2There the angel of the LORD[p] appeared to him in flames of fire[q] from
within a bush.[r] Moses saw that
though the bush was on fire it did not
burn up. 3So Moses thought, "I will go
over and see this strange sight—why
the bush does not burn up."
4When the LORD saw that he had
gone over to look, God called[s] to him
from within the bush,[t] "Moses! Moses!"
And Moses said, "Here I am."[u]
5"Do not come any closer,"[v] God
said. "Take off your sandals, for the
place where you are standing is holy
ground."[w] 6Then he said, "I am the
God of your father, the God of Abraham, the God of Isaac and the God of
Jacob."[x] At this, Moses hid[y] his face,
because he was afraid to look at God.[z]
7The LORD said, "I have indeed
seen[a] the misery[b] of my people in
Egypt. I have heard them crying out
because of their slave drivers, and I am
concerned[c] about their suffering.[d]
8So I have come down[e] to rescue
them from the hand of the Egyptians
and to bring them up out of that land
into a good and spacious land,[f] a land
flowing with milk and honey[g]—the
home of the Canaanites, Hittites, Amorites, Perizzites, Hivites[h] and Jebusites.[i] 9And now the cry of the Israelites has reached me, and I have seen
the way the Egyptians are oppressing[j] them. 10So now, go. I am sending[k] you to Pharaoh to bring my people the Israelites out of Egypt."[l]
11But Moses said to God, "Who am
I,[m] that I should go to Pharaoh and
bring the Israelites out of Egypt?"
12And God said, "I will be with
you.[n] And this will be the sign[o] to
you that it is I who have sent you:
When you have brought the people out
of Egypt, you[e] will worship God on
this mountain.[p]"
13Moses said to God, "Suppose I go
to the Israelites and say to them, 'The
God of your fathers has sent me to
you,' and they ask me, 'What is his
name?'[q] Then what shall I tell them?"
14God said to Moses, "I AM WHO I

2:24 [i]S Ge 8:1 [j]S Ge 9:15; 15:15; 17:4; 22:16-18; 26:3; 28:13-15; Ex 32:13; 2Ki 13:23; Ps 105:10,42; Jer 14:21 **2:25** [k]Ex 3:7; 4:31; Lk 1:25 **3:1** [l]S Ex 2:18; Jdg 1:16 [m]S Ex 2:16 [n]ver 12; Ex 17:6; 19:1-11,5; 33:6; Dt 1:2,6; 4:10; 5:2; 29:1; 1Ki 19:8; Mal 4:4 [o]Ex 4:27; 18:5; 24:13; Dt 4:11,15 **3:2** [p]S Ge 16:7; S Ex 12:23; S Ac 5:19 [q]Ex 19:18; 1Ki 19:12 [r]ver 4; Ex 2:2-6; Dt 33:16; Mk 12:26; Lk 20:37; Ac 7:30 **3:4** [s]Ex 19:3; Lev 1:1 [t]Ex 4:5 [u]Ge 31:11; 1Sa 3:4; Isa 6:8 **3:5** [v]Jer 30:21 [w]S Ge 28:17; Ac 7:33* **3:6** [x]S Ge 24:12; S Ex 4:5; Mt 22:32*; Mk 12:26*; Lk 20:37*; Ac 3:13; 7:32* [y]1Ki 19:13 [z]Ex 24:11; 33:20; Jdg 13:22; Job 13:11; 23:16; 30:15; Isa 6:5 **3:7** [a]1Sa 9:16 [b]ver 16; S Ge 16:11; 1Sa 1:11; Ne 9:9; Ps 106:44 [c]S Ex 2:25; Ac 7:34* [d]S Ex 1:10 **3:8** [e]S Ge 11:5; Ac 7:34* [f]S Ge 12:7; S 15:14 [g]ver 17; Ex 13:5; 33:3; Lev 20:24; Nu 13:27; Dt 1:25; 6:3; 8:7-9; 11:9; 26:9; 27:3; Jos 5:6; Jer 11:5; 32:22; Eze 20:6 [h]Jos 11:3; Jdg 3:3; 2Sa 24:7 [i]S Ge 15:18-21; Ezr 9:1 **3:9** [j]S Ex 1:14; S Nu 10:9 **3:10** [k]Ex 4:12; Jos 24:5; 1Sa 12:8; Ps 105:26; Ac 7:34* [l]Ex 6:13,26; 12:41,51; 20:2; Dt 4:20; 1Sa 12:6; 1Ki 8:16; Mic 6:4 **3:11** [m]Ex 4:10; 6:12,30; Jdg 6:15; 1Sa 9:21; 15:17; 18:18; 2Sa 7:18; 2Ch 2:6; Isa 6:5; Jer 1:6 **3:12** [n]S Ge 26:3; S Ex 14:22; Ro 8:31 [o]Nu 26:10; Jos 2:12; Jdg 6:17; Ps 86:17; Isa 7:14; 8:18; 20:3; Jer 44:29 [p]S ver 1; Ac 7:7 **3:13** [q]S Ge 32:29

[e] *12* The Hebrew is plural.

3:1 MOSES WAS TENDING THE FLOCK. Mere human education in Pharaoh's court was inadequate to equip Moses for God's work. Solitude with God and forty years of training and hardship tending sheep in the desert were also needed to prepare him for his future task of shepherding Israel through the desert (cf. 1Co 2:14).

3:2 THE ANGEL OF THE LORD. The "angel of the LORD" is the Lord himself (vv. 4–6). God also appeared to Abraham as the "angel of the LORD" (Ge 22:11; see article on ANGELS AND THE ANGEL OF THE LORD, p. 340).

3:5 HOLY GROUND. God's initial revelation to Moses was of his holiness. Holiness means separation from sin and all evil, and commitment to righteousness. Moses, as God's servant, had to remember constantly that the God whom he served was holy—so holy that for a human to look fully at him would bring death (v. 6; 19:21; Isa 6:1–7; 1Ti 6:16; see article on SANCTIFICATION, p. 1956). God's initial revelation to Abraham was of his great power; here to Moses it was of his holiness. This illustrates the principle of progressive revelation (cf. Ex 6:1–6; Heb 1:1–2).

3:7 SEEN THE MISERY OF MY PEOPLE. Just as God was concerned about the misery of his people in Egypt, he is aware of the distress of all his people. He hears the cry of those who are troubled and oppressed. In such times God's people must cry out to him that he might mercifully intervene in their behalf. Whether our oppression comes from circumstances, people, Satan, sin or the world, God's comfort, grace and help are more than sufficient to meet all our needs (see Ro 8:32). In God's time he will rescue us (cf. Ge 15:13).

3:8 MILK AND HONEY. This is a proverbial statement picturing agricultural abundance. The honey included honey from grapes or dates as well as from bees; the juice was boiled down to produce a thick syrup.

3:12 I WILL BE WITH YOU. See next note for the significance of God's name "I AM WHO I AM" as it relates to his presence with his people.

3:14 I AM WHO I AM. The Lord gave himself the personal name "I AM WHO I AM" (from this is derived the Heb *Yahweh*), a Hebrew phrase that

AM.[f] This is what you are to say to
the Israelites: 'I AM[r] has sent me to
you.' "
15God also said to Moses, "Say to
the Israelites, 'The LORD,[g] the God of
your fathers[s]—the God of Abraham,
the God of Isaac and the God of Jacob[t]—has sent me to you.' This is my
name[u] forever, the name by which I
am to be remembered from generation
to generation.[v]
16"Go, assemble the elders[w] of Israel and say to them, 'The LORD, the God
of your fathers—the God of Abraham,
Isaac and Jacob[x]—appeared to me
and said: I have watched over you and
have seen[y] what has been done to you
in Egypt. **17**And I have promised to
bring you up out of your misery in
Egypt[z] into the land of the Canaanites, Hittites, Amorites, Perizzites, Hivites and Jebusites—a land flowing
with milk and honey.'[a]
18"The elders of Israel will listen[b]
to you. Then you and the elders are to
go to the king of Egypt and say to him,
'The LORD, the God of the Hebrews,[c]
has met[d] with us. Let us take a three-
day journey[e] into the desert to offer
sacrifices[f] to the LORD our God.' **19**But
I know that the king of Egypt will not
let you go unless a mighty hand[g] compels him. **20**So I will stretch out my
hand[h] and strike the Egyptians with
all the wonders[i] that I will perform
among them. After that, he will let you
go.[j]
21"And I will make the Egyptians favorably disposed[k] toward this people,
so that when you leave you will not go
empty-handed.[l] **22**Every woman is to
ask her neighbor and any woman living
in her house for articles of silver[m] and
gold[n] and for clothing, which you will
put on your sons and daughters. And
so you will plunder[o] the Egyptians."[p]

Signs for Moses

4 Moses answered, "What if they do
not believe me or listen[q] to me
and say, 'The LORD did not appear to
you'?"
2Then the LORD said to him, "What is
that in your hand?"
"A staff,"[r] he replied.
3The LORD said, "Throw it on the
ground."
Moses threw it on the ground and it
became a snake,[s] and he ran from it.
4Then the LORD said to him, "Reach out
your hand and take it by the tail." So
Moses reached out and took hold of the
snake and it turned back into a staff in
his hand. **5**"This," said the LORD, "is so
that they may believe[t] that the LORD,
the God of their fathers—the God of
Abraham, the God of Isaac and the God
of Jacob—has appeared to you."
6Then the LORD said, "Put your hand
inside your cloak." So Moses put his
hand into his cloak, and when he took
it out, it was leprous,[h] like snow.[u]
7"Now put it back into your cloak,"
he said. So Moses put his hand back
into his cloak, and when he took it out,
it was restored,[v] like the rest of his
flesh.

3:14 [r]Ex 6:2-3; Jn 8:58; Heb 13:8; Rev 1:8; 4:8 **3:15** [s]Ge 31:42; Da 2:23 [t]S Ge 24:12 [u]Ex 6:3,7; 15:3; 23:21; 34:5-7; Lev 24:11; Dt 28:58; Ps 30:4; 83:18; 96:2; 97:12; 135:13; 145:21; Isa 42:8; Jer 16:21; 33:2; Hos 12:5 [v]Ps 45:17; 72:17; 102:12 **3:16** [w]Ex 4:29; 17:5; Lev 4:15; Nu 11:16; 16:25; Dt 5:23; 19:12; Jdg 8:14; Ru 4:2; Pr 31:23; Eze 8:11 [x]S Ge 24:12 [y]Ex 4:31; 2Ki 19:16; 2Ch 6:20; Ps 33:18; 66:7 **3:17** [z]S Ge 15:16; 46:4; Ex 6:6 [a]S ver 8 **3:18** [b]Ex 4:1,8, 31; 6:12,30 [c]S Ge 14:13 [d]Nu 23:4,16 [e]S Ge 30:36 [f]Ex 4:23; 5:1,3; 6:11; 7:16; 8:20, 27; 9:13; 10:9,26 **3:19** [g]Ex 4:21; 6:6; 7:3; 10:1; 11:9; Dt 4:34; 2Ch 6:32 **3:20** [h]Ex 6:1,6; 7:4-5; 9:15; 13:3, 9,14,16; 15:6,12; Dt 4:34,37; 5:15; 7:8; 26:8; 2Ki 17:36; 2Ch 6:32; Ps 118:15-16; 136:12; Isa 41:10; 63:12; Jer 21:5; 51:25; Da 9:15 [i]Ex 4:21; 7:3; 11:9,10; 15:11; 34:10; Nu 14:11; Dt 3:24; 4:34; 6:22; Ne 9:10; Ps 71:19; 72:18; 77:14; 78:43; 86:10; 105:27; 106:22; 135:9; 136:4; Jer 32:20; Mic 7:15; Ac 7:36 [j]Ex 11:1; 12:31-33 **3:21** [k]S Ge 39:21 [l]Ex 11:2; 2Ch 30:9; Ne 1:11; Ps 105:37; 106:46; Jer 42:12 **3:22** [m]Job 27:16-17 [n]Ex 11:2; 12:35; Ezr 1:4,6; 7:16; Ps 105:37 [o]S Ge 15:14; Eze 39:10 [p]Eze 29:10 **4:1** [q]S Ex 3:18 **4:2** [r]ver 17,20; Ge 38:18; Ex 7:19; 8:5,16; 14:16,21; 17:5-6,9; Nu 17:2; 20:8; Jos 8:18; Jdg 6:21; 1Sa 14:27; 2Ki 4:29 **4:3** [s]Ex 7:8-12,15 **4:5** [t]ver 31; S Ex 3:6; 14:31; 19:9 **4:6** [u]Lev 13:2,11; Nu 12:10; Dt 24:9; 2Ki 5:1,27; 2Ch 26:21 **4:7** [v]2Ki 5:14; Mt 8:3; Lk 17:12-14

[f]*14* Or *I WILL BE WHAT I WILL BE* [g]*15* The Hebrew for *LORD* sounds like and may be derived from the Hebrew for *I AM* in verse 14. [h]*6* The Hebrew word was used for various diseases affecting the skin—not necessarily leprosy.

indicates action. God was in effect saying to Moses, "I wish to be known as the God who is present and active." (1) Inherent in the name *Yahweh* is the promise of the living presence of God himself day by day with his people (cf. v. 12; see Ge 2:4, note). It expresses his faithful love and care and his desire to redeem his people and live in fellowship with them. This corresponds with the fundamental promise of the covenant, "to be your God" (see Ge 17:7, note; Ps 46). The Lord states that this will be his name forever (v. 15). (2) It is significant that when Jesus Christ was born, he was called Immanuel, meaning "God with us" (Mt 1:23). He also called himself by the name "I am" (Jn 8:58).

3:22 ASK . . . PLUNDER THE EGYPTIANS. The Israelites had been invited into Goshen and were made slaves unfairly. They deserved back wages, but they were not supposed to take anything by force. God would give the Egyptians a favorable disposition so when the Israelites asked for silver, gold and clothing, the Egyptians would give to them abundantly. Thus, instead of sneaking out of Egypt like runaway slaves, they would be able to go out triumphantly, like a victorious army carrying the fruits of victory.

4:2–3 STAFF . . . BECAME A SNAKE. Miraculous signs served the purpose of confirming the message and ministry of Moses (vv. 1–9). The manifestation of such signs is also God's intention for his people under the new covenant (see article on SIGNS OF BELIEVERS, p. 1513).

8Then the LORD said, "If they do not believe[w] you or pay attention to the first miraculous sign,[x] they may believe the second. 9But if they do not believe these two signs or listen to you, take some water from the Nile and pour it on the dry ground. The water you take from the river will become blood[y] on the ground."

10Moses said to the LORD, "O Lord, I have never been eloquent, neither in the past nor since you have spoken to your servant. I am slow of speech and tongue."[z]

11The LORD said to him, "Who gave man his mouth? Who makes him deaf or mute?[a] Who gives him sight or makes him blind?[b] Is it not I, the LORD? 12Now go;[c] I will help you speak and will teach you what to say."[d]

13But Moses said, "O Lord, please send someone else to do it."[e]

14Then the LORD's anger burned[f] against Moses and he said, "What about your brother, Aaron the Levite? I know he can speak well. He is already on his way to meet[g] you, and his heart will be glad when he sees you. 15You shall speak to him and put words in his mouth;[h] I will help both of you speak and will teach you what to do. 16He will speak to the people for you, and it will be as if he were your mouth[i] and as if you were God to him.[j] 17But take this staff[k] in your hand[l] so you can perform miraculous signs[m] with it."

Moses Returns to Egypt

18Then Moses went back to Jethro his father-in-law and said to him, "Let me go back to my own people in Egypt to see if any of them are still alive."

Jethro said, "Go, and I wish you well."

19Now the LORD had said to Moses in Midian, "Go back to Egypt, for all the men who wanted to kill[n] you are dead.[o]" 20So Moses took his wife and sons,[p] put them on a donkey and started back to Egypt. And he took the staff[q] of God in his hand.

21The LORD said to Moses, "When you return to Egypt, see that you perform before Pharaoh all the wonders[r] I have given you the power to do. But I will harden his heart[s] so that he will not let the people go.[t] 22Then say to Pharaoh, 'This is what the LORD says: Israel is my firstborn son,[u] 23and I told you, "Let my son go,[v] so he may worship[w] me." But you refused to let him go; so I will kill your firstborn son.'"[x]

24At a lodging place on the way, the LORD met ⌊Moses⌋[i] and was about to kill[y] him. 25But Zipporah[z] took a flint knife, cut off her son's foreskin[a] and touched ⌊Moses'⌋ feet with it.[j] "Surely you are a bridegroom of blood to me," she said. 26So the LORD let him alone. (At that time she said "bridegroom of blood," referring to circumcision.)

27The LORD said to Aaron, "Go into the desert to meet Moses." So he met Moses at the mountain[b] of God and

4:8 [w]S Ex 3:18 [x]ver 30; Jdg 6:17; 1Ki 13:3; Isa 7:14; Jer 44:29 **4:9** [y]Ex 7:17-21 **4:10** [z]S Ex 3:11 **4:11** [a]Lk 1:20,64 [b]Ps 94:9; 146:8; Mt 11:5; Jn 10:21 **4:12** [c]S Ex 3:10 [d]ver 15-16; Nu 23:5; Dt 18:15, 18; Isa 50:4; 51:16; Jer 1:9; Mt 10:19-20; Mk 13:11; S Lk 12:12 **4:13** [e]Jnh 1:1-3 **4:14** [f]Nu 11:1,10, 33; 12:9; 16:15; 22:22; 24:10; 32:13; Dt 7:25; Jos 7:1; Job 17:8 [g]ver 27; 1Sa 10:2-5 **4:15** [h]ver 30; Nu 23:5,12,16; Dt 18:18; Jos 1:8; Isa 51:16; 59:21; Jer 1:9; 31:33 **4:16** [i]Ex 7:1-2; Jer 15:19; 36:6 [j]Nu 33:1; Ps 77:20; 105:26; Mic 6:4 **4:17** [k]S ver 2 [l]ver 20; Ex 17:9 [m]Ex 7:9-21; 8:5, 16; 9:22; 10:12-15,21-23; 14:15-18,26; Nu 14:11; Dt 4:34; Ps 74:9; 78:43; 105:27 **4:19** [n]Ex 2:15 [o]Ex 2:23; Mt 2:20 **4:20** [p]Ex 2:22; 18:3; Ac 7:29 [q]S ver 2 **4:21** [r]S Ex 3:19, 20 [s]Ex 7:3,13; 8:15; 9:12,35; 10:1,20,27; 11:10; 14:4,8; Dt 2:30; Jos 11:20; 1Sa 6:6; Ps 105:25; Isa 6:10; 63:17; Jn 12:40; Ro 9:18 [t]Ex 8:32; 9:17 **4:22** [u]S Ge 10:15; Dt 32:6; Isa 9:6; 63:16; 64:8; Jer 3:19; 31:9; Hos 11:1; Mal 2:10; Ro 9:4; 2Co 6:18 **4:23** [v]Ex 5:1; 7:16 [w]S Ex 3:18 [x]Ge 49:3; Ex 11:5; 12:12,29; Nu 8:17; 33:4; Ps 78:51; 105:36; 135:8; 136:10 **4:24** [y]Nu 22:22 **4:25** [z]S Ex 2:21 [a]Ge 17:14; Jos 5:2,3 **4:27** [b]S Ex 3:1

[i]*24* Or ⌊*Moses' son*⌋; Hebrew *him* [j]*25* Or *and drew near* ⌊*Moses'*⌋ *feet*

4:10 I AM SLOW OF SPEECH. In his reluctance to accept God's calling, Moses pointed out his limitation in speaking; God promised to give him help and power (vv. 11–17). When God calls us to a task, he will furnish the means and ability to fulfill that task (cf. 2Co 3:5–6; 4:11–12).

4:11 WHO MAKES HIM . . . BLIND? God has the power to make someone deaf or blind, or to heal the deaf or blind. It does not mean that every person who is mute, deaf or blind has become so due to the direct desire, decision and act of God. Such conditions, as with all disease and sickness, are originally the result of Satan's activity and sin's entrance into the world through Adam (Ge 3:1–24); they do not necessarily occur because the individual affected has sinned (see Jn 9:2–3; see article on DIVINE HEALING, p. 1420).

4:21 I WILL HARDEN HIS HEART. See Ex 7:3, note.

4:22 ISRAEL . . . MY FIRSTBORN. "Firstborn" indicates a special love and relationship with God. God claimed Israel as his son—his firstborn. Later in a narrowing of the sonship theme, God claimed the Davidic dynasty as his son (2Sa 7:14; Ps 2:7), and still later, in a further narrowing, he claimed Jesus as his Son—his firstborn (Lk 1:35; 3:22; Heb 1:5–13).

4:24 THE LORD . . . WAS ABOUT TO KILL HIM. Moses had neglected to perform the covenant sign of circumcision in the case of his own son. This was seen as a clear sign of disobedience on the part of Moses and his wife (vv. 24–25; see Ge 17:11, note). Evidently God afflicted Moses with a potentially fatal illness until he had his son circumcised. This incident demonstrates that God's election of an individual continues only as long as he or she remains obedient (see 2Pe 1:10, note).

kissed[c] him. **28**Then Moses told Aaron everything the LORD had sent him to
say, and also about all the miraculous
signs he had commanded him to perform.
29Moses and Aaron brought together all the elders[d] of the Israelites,
30and Aaron told them everything the
LORD had said to Moses. He also performed the signs[e] before the people,
31and they believed.[f] And when they
heard that the LORD was concerned[g]
about them and had seen their misery,[h] they bowed down and worshiped.[i]

Bricks Without Straw

5 Afterward Moses and Aaron went
to Pharaoh and said, "This is what
the LORD, the God of Israel, says: 'Let
my people go,[j] so that they may hold
a festival[k] to me in the desert.' "
2Pharaoh said, "Who is the LORD,[l]
that I should obey him and let Israel
go? I do not know the LORD and I will
not let Israel go."[m]
3Then they said, "The God of the Hebrews has met with us. Now let us take
a three-day journey[n] into the desert to
offer sacrifices to the LORD our God, or
he may strike us with plagues[o] or
with the sword."
4But the king of Egypt said, "Moses
and Aaron, why are you taking the people away from their labor?[p] Get back
to your work!" **5**Then Pharaoh said,
"Look, the people of the land are now
numerous,[q] and you are stopping
them from working."
6That same day Pharaoh gave this
order to the slave drivers[r] and foremen in charge of the people: **7**"You are
no longer to supply the people with
straw for making bricks;[s] let them go
and gather their own straw. **8**But require them to make the same number
of bricks as before; don't reduce the
quota.[t] They are lazy;[u] that is why
they are crying out, 'Let us go and sacrifice to our God.'[v] **9**Make the work
harder for the men so that they keep
working and pay no attention to lies."
10Then the slave drivers[w] and the
foremen went out and said to the people, "This is what Pharaoh says: 'I will
not give you any more straw. **11**Go and
get your own straw wherever you can
find it, but your work will not be reduced[x] at all.' " **12**So the people scattered all over Egypt to gather stubble
to use for straw. **13**The slave drivers
kept pressing them, saying, "Complete
the work required of you for each day,
just as when you had straw." **14**The Israelite foremen appointed by Pharaoh's slave drivers were beaten[y] and
were asked, "Why didn't you meet your
quota of bricks yesterday or today, as
before?"
15Then the Israelite foremen went
and appealed to Pharaoh: "Why have
you treated your servants this way?
16Your servants are given no straw, yet
we are told, 'Make bricks!' Your servants are being beaten, but the fault is
with your own people."
17Pharaoh said, "Lazy, that's what
you are—lazy![z] That is why you keep
saying, 'Let us go and sacrifice to the
LORD.' **18**Now get to work.[a] You will
not be given any straw, yet you must
produce your full quota of bricks."
19The Israelite foremen realized
they were in trouble when they were
told, "You are not to reduce the number
of bricks required of you for each day."
20When they left Pharaoh, they found
Moses and Aaron waiting to meet
them, **21**and they said, "May the LORD
look upon you and judge[b] you! You
have made us a stench[c] to Pharaoh
and his officials and have put a
sword[d] in their hand to kill us."[e]

God Promises Deliverance

22Moses returned to the LORD and
said, "O Lord, why have you brought
trouble upon this people?[f] Is this why

4:27 [c]S Ge 27:27; S 29:13 **4:29** [d]S Ex 3:16 **4:30** [e]S ver 8 **4:31** [f]S Ex 3:18 [g]S Ex 2:25 [h]S Ge 16:11 [i]S Ge 24:26 **5:1** [j]S Ex 4:23 [k]S Ex 3:18 **5:2** [l]Jdg 2:10; Job 21:15; Mal 3:14 [m]Ex 3:19 **5:3** [n]S Ge 30:36 [o]Lev 26:25; Nu 14:12; Dt 28:21; 2Sa 24:13 **5:4** [p]S Ex 1:11; 6:6-7 **5:5** [q]S Ge 12:2 **5:6** [r]S Ge 15:13 **5:7** [s]S Ge 11:3 **5:8** [t]ver 14,18 [u]ver 17 [v]Ex 10:11 **5:10** [w]ver 13; Ex 1:11 **5:11** [x]ver 19 **5:14** [y]ver 16; Isa 10:24 **5:17** [z]ver 8 **5:18** [a]S Ge 15:13 **5:21** [b]S Ge 16:5 [c]S Ge 34:30 [d]Ex 16:3; Nu 14:3; 20:3 [e]S Ex 1:13; S 14:11 **5:22** [f]Nu 11:11; Dt 1:12; Jos 7:7

5:1 THIS IS WHAT THE LORD, THE GOD OF ISRAEL, SAYS. The narrative of the exodus is basically a conflict between two gods: the Lord and Pharaoh, who in Egyptian religion was believed to be an incarnation of the sun god Re. Pharaoh questioned the power of the God of Israel (v. 2); after all, Pharaoh had enslaved Israel and therefore had to be more powerful than Israel's God. The ten plagues were the Lord's method of demonstrating to his people that he was more powerful than any or all Egyptian gods; the Nile, the sun and frogs, for example, were all Egyptian deities.

5:22 IS THIS WHY YOU SENT ME? Moses either ignored or forgot what God had told him earlier about Pharaoh's responses (3:19–20; 4:21). He was disappointed because his obedience to God was bringing trouble and not immediate success. Often believers under the new covenant forget that God's Word says that "we must go through many hardships to enter the kingdom of God" (Ac 14:22; cf. Jn 16:33; 1Th 3:3; 2Ti 3:12).

you sent me? **23**Ever since I went to
Pharaoh to speak in your name, he has
brought trouble upon this people, and
you have not rescued[g] your people at
all."

6 Then the LORD said to Moses, "Now
you will see what I will do to Pharaoh: Because of my mighty hand[h] he
will let them go;[i] because of my
mighty hand he will drive them out of
his country."[j]

2God also said to Moses, "I am the
LORD.[k] **3**I appeared to Abraham, to
Isaac and to Jacob as God Almighty,[k][l] but by my name[m] the
LORD[l][n] I did not make myself known
to them.[m] **4**I also established my covenant[o] with them to give them the
land[p] of Canaan, where they lived as
aliens.[q] **5**Moreover, I have heard the
groaning[r] of the Israelites, whom the
Egyptians are enslaving, and I have remembered my covenant.[s]

6"Therefore, say to the Israelites: 'I
am the LORD, and I will bring you out
from under the yoke of the Egyptians.[t] I will free you from being
slaves to them, and I will redeem[u] you
with an outstretched arm[v] and with
mighty acts of judgment.[w] **7**I will take
you as my own people, and I will be
your God.[x] Then you will know[y] that
I am the LORD your God, who brought
you out from under the yoke of the
Egyptians. **8**And I will bring you to the
land[z] I swore[a] with uplifted hand[b]
to give to Abraham, to Isaac and to Jacob.[c] I will give it to you as a possession. I am the LORD.'"[d]

9Moses reported this to the Israelites, but they did not listen to him because of their discouragement and cruel bondage.[e]

10Then the LORD said to Moses,
11"Go, tell[f] Pharaoh king of Egypt to
let the Israelites go out of his country."[g]

5:23 [g]Jer 4:10; 20:7; Eze 14:9 **6:1** [h]S Ex 3:20; S Dt 5:15 [i]S Ex 3:20 [j]Ex 11:1; 12:31, 33,39 **6:2** [k]ver 6,7,8,29; Ex 3:14,15; 7:5, 17; 8:22; 10:2; 12:12; 14:4,18; 16:12; Lev 11:44; 18:21; 20:7; Isa 25:3; 41:20; 43:11; 49:23; 60:16; Eze 13:9; 25:17; 36:38; 37:6,13; Joel 2:27 **6:3** [l]S Ge 17:1 [m]S Ex 3:15; 2Sa 7:26; Ps 48:10; 61:5; 68:4; 83:18; 99:3; Isa 52:6 [n]Ex 3:14; Jn 8:58 **6:4** [o]S Ge 6:18; S 15:18 [p]S Ge 12:7; Ac 7:5; Ro 4:13; Gal 3:16; Heb 11:8-10 [q]S Ge 17:8 **6:5** [r]S Ex 2:23; Ac 7:34 [s]S Ge 9:15 **6:6** [t]ver 7; Ex 3:8; 12:17,51; 16:1,6; 18:1; 19:1; 20:2; 29:46; Lev 22:33; 26:13; Dt 6:12; Ps 81:10; 136:11; Jer 2:6; Hos 13:4; Am 2:10; Mic 6:4 [u]Ex 15:13; Dt 7:8; 9:26; 1Ch 17:21; Job 19:25; Ps 19:14; 34:22; 74:2; 77:15; 107:2; Isa 29:22; 35:9; 43:1; 44:23; 48:20; Jer 15:21; 31:11; 50:34 [v]S Ex 3:19,20; S Jer 32:21; Ac 13:17 [w]Ex 3:20; Ps 9:16; 105:27 **6:7** [x]S Ge 17:7; S Ex 34:9; Eze 11:19-20; Ro 9:4 [y]S ver 2; 1Ki 20:13,28; Isa 43:10; 48:7; Eze 39:6; Joel 3:17 **6:8** [z]S Ge 12:7; Ex 3:8 [a]Jer 11:5; Eze 20:6 [b]S Ge 14:22; Rev 10:5-6 [c]Ps 136:21-22 [d]Lev 18:21 **6:9** [e]S Ge 34:30; Ex 2:23 **6:11** [f]ver 29 [g]S Ex 3:18

k3 Hebrew *El-Shaddai* **l**3 See note at Exodus 3:15. **m**3 Or *Almighty, and by my name the LORD did I not let myself be known to them?*

5:23 YOU HAVE NOT RESCUED YOUR PEOPLE AT ALL. The fulfilling of God's promise of deliverance seemed more unlikely than ever, for the situation was becoming worse rather than better (v. 21). (1) Through these disheartening circumstances, God wanted to teach the people that his deliverance and miraculous power are often preceded by unfavorable conditions and great difficulties that give little reason for hope. (2) Through times of disappointment, the believer must continue to walk by faith in God and his word, trusting God to work out his will in his own time (see Ro 8:28, note; see article on THE PROVIDENCE OF GOD, p. 78).

6:3 BY MY NAME THE LORD I DID NOT MAKE MYSELF KNOWN TO THEM. The Lord did not make himself known to Abraham, Isaac and Jacob by the name "LORD" (Heb *Yahweh*, see Ge 2:4, note). (1) This does not mean that the patriarchs were not acquainted with the name, but only that they did not receive the full revelation of the meaning of that name (see 3:14, note). They had indeed used and heard God's name as *Yahweh*, but they had known him in their experience more as "God Almighty," a name that emphasizes his power to perform or fulfill what he has promised (see Ge 17:1, note). (2) *Yahweh* is his covenant-keeping name, especially centered on redemption (cf. v. 6). Abraham did not live to see the covenant of Ge 15 fulfilled, but he did experience God's power.

6:7 I WILL TAKE YOU AS MY OWN PEOPLE, AND I WILL BE YOUR GOD. Vv. 6–7 declare the essential meaning and purpose of the exodus and the making of the covenant at Sinai (19:5): the Lord promised to redeem Israel from bondage (v. 6), adopt them as his people (v. 7) and be their God (v. 7); they in return would promise to do the will of their Redeemer (chs. 19–23). (1) These verses emphasize that Israel was helplessly held in bondage by a force they could not hope to overcome. Only by the Lord their God could they be freed (vv. 5–6). Because of God's covenant with the patriarchs and his love for his people, he would indeed deliver them (vv. 6–8; Dt 7:7–8).

(2) God's redemption of Israel from Egypt served as a major basis for the transfer of ownership of Israel to himself. Israel was God's by creation and election (4:22), and now by redemption.

(3) Historically the redemption of Israel out of Egypt anticipates the greater redemption of the sinful human race through Jesus' death on the cross. All believers are redeemed by Christ from the power of Satan, sin and the world. They now belong to him and can trust in his love and promises (see article on BIBLICAL WORDS FOR SALVATION, p. 1710).

6:9 THEY DID NOT LISTEN TO HIM. God did not bring Israel out of Egypt because they had great faith, but because of his grace and his faithfulness to his promises (Ge 17:1–8; 50:24). In the beginning their faith was weak, but through the ten plagues, by which God revealed himself and his power and concern for Israel, he built up their faith until they were able to trust him in obedience (Ex 12:28). In other words, God delivered them by grace through faith.

12 But Moses said to the LORD, "If the Israelites will not listen[h] to me, why would Pharaoh listen to me, since I speak with faltering lips[n]?"[i]

Family Record of Moses and Aaron

13 Now the LORD spoke to Moses and Aaron about the Israelites and Pharaoh king of Egypt, and he commanded them to bring the Israelites out of Egypt.[j]

14 These were the heads of their families[o]:[k]

The sons of Reuben[l] the firstborn son of Israel were Hanoch and Pallu, Hezron and Carmi. These were the clans of Reuben.

15 The sons of Simeon[m] were Jemuel, Jamin, Ohad, Jakin, Zohar and Shaul the son of a Canaanite woman. These were the clans of Simeon.

16 These were the names of the sons of Levi[n] according to their records: Gershon,[o] Kohath and Merari.[p] Levi lived 137 years.

17 The sons of Gershon, by clans, were Libni and Shimei.[q]

18 The sons of Kohath[r] were Amram, Izhar, Hebron and Uzziel.[s] Kohath lived 133 years.

19 The sons of Merari were Mahli and Mushi.[t]

These were the clans of Levi according to their records.

20 Amram[u] married his father's sister Jochebed, who bore him Aaron and Moses.[v] Amram lived 137 years.

21 The sons of Izhar[w] were Korah, Nepheg and Zicri.

22 The sons of Uzziel were Mishael, Elzaphan[x] and Sithri.

23 Aaron married Elisheba, daughter of Amminadab[y] and sister of Nahshon,[z] and she bore him Nadab and Abihu,[a] Eleazar[b] and Ithamar.[c]

24 The sons of Korah[d] were Assir, Elkanah and Abiasaph. These were the Korahite clans.

25 Eleazar son of Aaron married one of the daughters of Putiel, and she bore him Phinehas.[e]

These were the heads of the Levite families, clan by clan.

26 It was this same Aaron and Moses to whom the LORD said, "Bring the Israelites out of Egypt[f] by their divisions."[g] 27 They were the ones who spoke to Pharaoh[h] king of Egypt about bringing the Israelites out of Egypt. It was the same Moses and Aaron.[i]

Aaron to Speak for Moses

28 Now when the LORD spoke to Moses in Egypt, 29 he said to him, "I am the LORD.[j] Tell Pharaoh king of Egypt everything I tell you."

30 But Moses said to the LORD, "Since I speak with faltering lips,[k] why would Pharaoh listen to me?"

7 Then the LORD said to Moses, "See, I have made you like God[l] to Pharaoh, and your brother Aaron will be your prophet.[m] 2 You are to say everything I command you, and your brother Aaron is to tell Pharaoh to let the Israelites go out of his country. 3 But I will harden Pharaoh's heart,[n] and though I multiply my miraculous signs and wonders[o] in Egypt, 4 he will not listen[p] to you. Then I will lay my hand on Egypt and with mighty acts of judgment[q] I will bring out my divisions,[r] my people the Israelites. 5 And the Egyptians will know that I am the LORD[s] when I stretch out my hand[t] against Egypt and bring the Israelites out of it."

6 Moses and Aaron did just as the LORD commanded[u] them. 7 Moses was

6:12 [h] S Ex 3:18 [i] Ex 4:10
6:13 [j] S Ex 3:10
6:14 [k] Ex 13:3; Nu 1:1; 26:4 [l] S Ge 29:32
6:15 [m] S Ge 29:33
6:16 [n] S Ge 29:34 [o] S Ge 46:11 [p] Nu 3:17; Jos 21:7; 1Ch 6:1, 16
6:17 [q] Nu 3:18; 1Ch 6:17
6:18 [r] Nu 3:27; 1Ch 23:12 [s] Nu 3:19; 1Ch 6:2, 18
6:19 [t] Nu 3:20,33; 1Ch 6:19; 23:21
6:20 [u] 1Ch 23:13 [v] Ex 2:1-2; Nu 26:59
6:21 [w] 1Ch 6:38
6:22 [x] Lev 10:4; Nu 3:30; 1Ch 15:8; 2Ch 29:13
6:23 [y] Ru 4:19, 20; 1Ch 2:10 [z] Nu 1:7; 2:3; Mt 1:4 [a] Ex 24:1; 28:1; Lev 10:1 [b] Lev 10:6; Nu 3:2, 32; 16:37,39; Dt 10:6; Jos 14:1 [c] Ex 28:1; Lev 10:12,16; Nu 3:2; 4:28; 26:60; 1Ch 6:3; 24:1
6:24 [d] ver 21; Nu 16:1; 1Ch 6:22, 37
6:25 [e] Nu 25:7,11; 31:6; Jos 24:33; Ps 106:30
6:26 [f] S Ex 3:10 [g] Ex 7:4; 12:17,41, 51
6:27 [h] Ex 5:1 [i] Nu 3:1; Ps 77:20
6:29 [j] S ver 2
6:30 [k] S Ex 3:11
7:1 [l] S Ex 4:16 [m] Ex 4:15; Ac 14:12
7:3 [n] S Ex 4:21; Ro 9:18 [o] S Ex 3:20; S 10:1; Ac 7:36
7:4 [p] ver 13,16, 22; Ex 8:15,19; 9:12; 11:9 [q] S Ex 3:20; Ac 7:36 [r] S Ex 6:26
7:5 [s] S Ex 6:2 [t] Ex 3:20; Ps 138:7; Eze 6:14; 25:13
7:6 [u] ver 2,10,20; Ge 6:22

[n] 12 Hebrew *I am uncircumcised of lips*; also in verse 30 [o] 14 The Hebrew for *families* here and in verse 25 refers to units larger than clans.

7:3 I WILL HARDEN PHARAOH'S HEART. God hardened Pharaoh's heart as punishment because his heart was already hard and opposed to God (cf. 5:2; 7:13–14,22; 8:15,19,32; 9:7). (1) In adding to the hardness of Pharaoh's heart, God was acting on a divine principle that applies to all the unrepentant. When a person persists in rebellion against God and his word, God finally ordains that the heart be hardened (see Ro 9:18, note). This principle is seen in God giving people up to their sinful desires (see Ro 1:24, note) and in his sending a delusion on those who refuse to love the truth of his word (see 2Th 2:10, note). (2) Notice that the judgments of the early plagues softened Pharaoh's heart a little. When God removed each plague, his heart was hardened again, i.e., Pharaoh hardened his own heart whenever God showed mercy (e.g., 8:8–15).

eighty years old[v] and Aaron eighty-
three when they spoke to Pharaoh.

Aaron's Staff Becomes a Snake

8The LORD said to Moses and Aaron,
9"When Pharaoh says to you, 'Perform
a miracle,[w]' then say to Aaron, 'Take
your staff and throw it down before
Pharaoh,' and it will become a
snake."[x]
10So Moses and Aaron went to Pharaoh and did just as the LORD commanded. Aaron threw his staff down in front
of Pharaoh and his officials, and it became a snake. 11Pharaoh then summoned wise men and sorcerers,[y] and
the Egyptian magicians[z] also did the
same things by their secret arts:[a]
12Each one threw down his staff and it
Jdg 6:25-32 became a snake. But Aaron's staff
swallowed up their staffs. 13Yet Pharaoh's heart[b] became hard and he
would not listen[c] to them, just as the
LORD had said.

The Plague of Blood

14Then the LORD said to Moses,
"Pharaoh's heart is unyielding;[d] he
refuses to let the people go. 15Go to
Pharaoh in the morning as he goes out
to the water.[e] Wait on the bank of the
Nile[f] to meet him, and take in your
hand the staff that was changed into a
snake. 16Then say to him, 'The LORD,
the God of the Hebrews, has sent me to
say to you: Let my people go, so that
they may worship[g] me in the desert.
But until now you have not listened.[h]
17This is what the LORD says: By this
you will know that I am the LORD:[i]
With the staff that is in my hand I will
strike the water of the Nile, and it will

7:7 [v]Dt 31:2; 34:7; Ac 7:23,30
7:9 [w]Dt 6:22; 2Ki 19:29; Ps 78:43; 86:17; 105:27; 135:9; Isa 7:11; 37:30; 38:7-8; 55:13; S Jn 2:11 [x]Ex 4:2-5
7:11 [y]Ex 22:18; Dt 18:10; 1Sa 6:2; 2Ki 21:6; Isa 2:6; 47:12; Jer 27:9; Mal 3:5 [z]S Ge 41:8; 2Ti 3:8 [a]ver 22; Ex 8:7,18; S Mt 24:24
7:13 [b]S Ex 4:21 [c]S ver 4
7:14 [d]ver 22; Ex 8:15,32; 9:7; 10:1,20,27
7:15 [e]Ex 8:20 [f]S Ge 41:1
7:16 [g]S Ex 3:18 [h]S ver 4
7:17 [i]S Ex 6:2; 14:25 [j]ver 19-21; Ex 4:9; Rev 11:6; 16:4
7:18 [k]Isa 19:6 [l]ver 21,24; Ps 78:44
7:19 [m]S Ex 4:2 [n]Ex 14:21; 2Ki 5:11
7:20 [o]S ver 6 [p]Ex 17:5 [q]Ps 78:44; 105:29; 114:3; Hab 3:8
7:22 [r]S Ge 41:8 [s]S ver 11; S Mt 24:24 [t]ver 13,S 14; Ex 8:19; Ps 105:28
7:24 [u]S ver 18
8:1 [v]Ex 3:12,18; 4:23; 5:1; 9:1

be changed into blood.[j] 18The fish in
the Nile will die, and the river will
stink;[k] the Egyptians will not be able
to drink its water.' "[l]
19The LORD said to Moses, "Tell Aaron, 'Take your staff[m] and stretch out
your hand[n] over the waters of
Egypt—over the streams and canals,
over the ponds and all the reservoirs'—and they will turn to blood.
Blood will be everywhere in Egypt,
even in the wooden buckets and stone
jars."
20Moses and Aaron did just as the
LORD had commanded.[o] He raised his
staff in the presence of Pharaoh and
his officials and struck the water of the
Nile,[p] and all the water was changed
into blood.[q] 21The fish in the Nile
died, and the river smelled so bad that
the Egyptians could not drink its water. Blood was everywhere in Egypt.
22But the Egyptian magicians[r] did
the same things by their secret arts,[s]
and Pharaoh's heart[t] became hard;
he would not listen to Moses and Aaron, just as the LORD had said. 23In-
stead, he turned and went into his palace, and did not take even this to heart.
24And all the Egyptians dug along the
Nile to get drinking water[u], because
they could not drink the water of the
river.

The Plague of Frogs

25Seven days passed after the LORD
8 struck the Nile. 1Then the LORD
said to Moses, "Go to Pharaoh and
say to him, 'This is what the LORD says:
Let my people go, so that they may
worship[v] me. 2If you refuse to let
them go, I will plague your whole coun-

7:12 IT BECAME A SNAKE. (1) The magicians' staffs also turned into snakes, an act accomplished by demonic power. Egypt was fully addicted to magic, occultism, spiritism and sorcery as their religion. By Aaron's staff swallowing up their staffs, however, the God of Israel was demonstrating that his power was greater than the power of the gods of Egypt. (2) In the final days of this age, before Christ's return, Satan will display miracles through false ministers within the visible church and through the antichrist (cf. 2Ti 3:8; see articles on THE GREAT TRIBULATION, p. 1456, and THE AGE OF THE ANTICHRIST, p. 1872). Believers must not assume, therefore, that miraculous occurrences are always evidence that the Lord is working (see Rev 16:14, note; 19:20, note).

7:20 HE . . . STRUCK THE WATER. The ten miraculous plagues against Egypt (7:20; 8:2,16, 21; 9:3,9,18; 10:4,21; 11:5) had several purposes. (1) They were signs and wonders to show Egypt, as well as Israel, that the Lord is God above all gods and human beings (v. 5; 9:14–15; 10:2; 15:11), and to exalt God's name "in all the earth" (9:16).

(2) They were performed to establish Israel's faith and to convince them of God's power, love and supremacy. Israel was hereafter to tell their children about these events in order that they might serve the Lord as God (6:7; 10:2; 12:42).

(3) They demonstrated God's power over the gods of Egypt and all the forces of evil on behalf of his people (12:12; see previous note).

(4) They were divine judgments on Egypt and her gods in order to compel Pharaoh to let God's people go (8:2,21; 11:1; 12:31–33; cf. Nu 33:4).

8:2 FROGS. In ancient Egypt frogs represented gods, and were considered sacred. The Lord,

try with frogs.[w] 3The Nile will teem
with frogs. They will come up into your
palace and your bedroom and onto your
bed, into the houses of your officials
and on your people,[x] and into your ovens and kneading troughs.[y] 4The
frogs will go up on you and your people
and all your officials.' "
5Then the LORD said to Moses, "Tell
Aaron, 'Stretch out your hand with
your staff[z] over the streams and canals and ponds, and make frogs[a]
come up on the land of Egypt.' "
6So Aaron stretched out his hand
over the waters of Egypt, and the
frogs[b] came up and covered the land.
7But the magicians did the same things
by their secret arts;[c] they also made
frogs come up on the land of Egypt.
8Pharaoh summoned Moses and
Aaron and said, "Pray[d] to the LORD to
take the frogs away from me and my
people, and I will let your people go to
offer sacrifices[e] to the LORD."
9Moses said to Pharaoh, "I leave to
you the honor of setting the time[f] for
me to pray for you and your officials
and your people that you and your
houses may be rid of the frogs, except
for those that remain in the Nile."
10"Tomorrow," Pharaoh said.
Moses replied, "It will be as you say,
so that you may know there is no one
like the LORD our God.[g] 11The frogs
will leave you and your houses, your
officials and your people; they will remain only in the Nile."
12After Moses and Aaron left Pharaoh, Moses cried out to the LORD about
the frogs he had brought on Pharaoh.
13And the LORD did what Moses
asked.[h] The frogs died in the houses,
in the courtyards and in the fields.
14They were piled into heaps, and the
land reeked of them. 15But when Pharaoh saw that there was relief,[i] he
hardened his heart[j] and would not listen to Moses and Aaron, just as the
LORD had said.

The Plague of Gnats

16Then the LORD said to Moses, "Tell
Aaron, 'Stretch out your staff[k] and
strike the dust of the ground,' and
throughout the land of Egypt the dust
will become gnats." 17They did this,
and when Aaron stretched out his hand
with the staff and struck the dust of
the ground, gnats[l] came upon men
and animals. All the dust throughout
the land of Egypt became gnats. 18But
when the magicians[m] tried to produce
gnats by their secret arts,[n] they could
not. And the gnats were on men and
animals.
19The magicians said to Pharaoh,
"This is the finger[o] of God." But Pharaoh's heart[p] was hard and he would
not listen,[q] just as the LORD had said.

The Plague of Flies

20Then the LORD said to Moses, "Get
up early in the morning[r] and confront
Pharaoh as he goes to the water and
say to him, 'This is what the LORD says:
Let my people go, so that they may
worship[s] me. 21If you do not let my
people go, I will send swarms of flies
on you and your officials, on your people and into your houses. The houses
of the Egyptians will be full of flies, and
even the ground where they are.
22" 'But on that day I will deal differently with the land of Goshen,[t] where
my people live;[u] no swarms of flies
will be there, so that you will know[v]
that I, the LORD, am in this land. 23I will
make a distinction[p] between my people and your people.[w] This miraculous
sign will occur tomorrow.' "
24And the LORD did this. Dense
swarms of flies poured into Pharaoh's
palace and into the houses of his officials, and throughout Egypt the land
was ruined by the flies.[x]
25Then Pharaoh summoned[y] Moses and Aaron and said, "Go, sacrifice
to your God here in the land."
26But Moses said, "That would not
be right. The sacrifices we offer the
LORD our God would be detestable to
the Egyptians.[z] And if we offer sacrifices that are detestable in their eyes,
will they not stone us? 27We must take
a three-day journey[a] into the desert to
offer sacrifices[b] to the LORD our God,
as he commands us."
28Pharaoh said, "I will let you go to
offer sacrifices to the LORD your God in

8:2 [w]Ps 78:45; 105:30; Rev 16:13
8:3 [x]Ex 10:6 [y]Ex 12:34
8:5 [z]S Ex 4:2; 7:9-20; 9:23; 10:13,21-22; 14:27 [a]S Ex 4:17
8:6 [b]Ps 78:45; 105:30
8:7 [c]S Ex 7:11; S Mt 24:24
8:8 [d]ver 28; Ex 9:28; 10:17; Nu 21:7; 1Sa 12:19; 1Ki 13:6; Jer 42:2; Ac 8:24 [e]ver 25; Ex 10:8,24; 12:31
8:9 [f]Ex 9:5
8:10 [g]Ex 9:14; 15:11; Dt 3:24; 4:35; 33:26; 2Sa 7:22; 1Ki 8:23; 1Ch 17:20; 2Ch 6:14; Ps 71:19; 86:8; 89:6; 113:5; Isa 40:18; 42:8; 46:9; Jer 10:6; 49:19; Mic 7:18
8:13 [h]Jas 5:16-18
8:15 [i]Ecc 8:11 [j]S Ex 7:14
8:16 [k]S Ex 4:2
8:17 [l]Ps 105:31
8:18 [m]Ex 9:11; Da 5:8 [n]S Ex 7:11
8:19 [o]Ex 7:5; 10:7; 12:33; 31:18; 1Sa 6:9; Ne 9:6; Ps 8:3; 33:6; Lk 11:20 [p]S Ex 7:22 [q]S Ex 7:4
8:20 [r]Ex 7:15; 9:13 [s]S Ex 3:18
8:22 [t]S Ge 45:10 [u]Ex 9:4,6,26; 10:23; 11:7; 12:13; 19:5; Dt 4:20; 7:6; 14:2; 26:18; 1Ki 8:36; Job 36:11; Ps 33:12; 135:4; Mal 3:17 [v]Ex 7:5; 9:29
8:23 [w]Ex 9:4,6; 10:23; 11:7; 12:13,23,27
8:24 [x]Ps 78:45; 105:31
8:25 [y]ver 8; Ex 9:27; 10:16; 12:31
8:26 [z]S Ge 43:32
8:27 [a]S Ge 30:36 [b]S Ex 3:18

p 23 Septuagint and Vulgate; Hebrew *will put a deliverance*

through this plague, was attacking Egypt's gods in order to show that his power was far superior to all the supernatural powers of Egypt.

8:18–19 THIS IS THE FINGER OF GOD. By this saying, the Egyptian magicians were admitting that God's power was far superior to theirs.

the desert, but you must not go very
far. Now pray[c] for me."
29Moses answered, "As soon as I
leave you, I will pray to the LORD, and
tomorrow the flies will leave Pharaoh
and his officials and his people. Only be
sure that Pharaoh does not act deceitfully[d] again by not letting the people
go to offer sacrifices to the LORD."
30Then Moses left Pharaoh and
prayed to the LORD,[e] 31and the LORD
did what Moses asked: The flies left
Pharaoh and his officials and his people; not a fly remained. 32But this time
also Pharaoh hardened his heart[f] and
would not let the people go.

The Plague on Livestock

9 Then the LORD said to Moses, "Go
to Pharaoh and say to him, 'This is
what the LORD, the God of the Hebrews,
says: "Let my people go, so that they
may worship[g] me." 2If you refuse to
let them go and continue to hold them
back, 3the hand[h] of the LORD will bring
a terrible plague[i] on your livestock in
the field—on your horses and donkeys
and camels and on your cattle and
sheep and goats. 4But the LORD will
make a distinction between the livestock of Israel and that of Egypt,[j] so
that no animal belonging to the Israelites will die.' "
5The LORD set a time and said, "Tomorrow the LORD will do this in the
land." 6And the next day the LORD did
it: All the livestock[k] of the Egyptians
died,[l] but not one animal belonging to
the Israelites died. 7Pharaoh sent men
to investigate and found that not even
one of the animals of the Israelites had
died. Yet his heart[m] was unyielding
and he would not let the people go.[n]

The Plague of Boils

8Then the LORD said to Moses and
Aaron, "Take handfuls of soot from a
furnace and have Moses toss it into the
air in the presence of Pharaoh. 9It will
become fine dust over the whole land
of Egypt, and festering boils[o] will
break out on men and animals throughout the land."
10So they took soot from a furnace
and stood before Pharaoh. Moses
tossed it into the air, and festering
boils broke out on men and animals.
11The magicians[p] could not stand before Moses because of the boils that
were on them and on all the Egyptians.
12But the LORD hardened Pharaoh's
heart[q] and he would not listen[r] to
Moses and Aaron, just as the LORD had
said to Moses.

The Plague of Hail

13Then the LORD said to Moses, "Get
up early in the morning, confront Pharaoh and say to him, 'This is what the
LORD, the God of the Hebrews, says:
Let my people go, so that they may
worship[s] me, 14or this time I will send
the full force of my plagues against you
and against your officials and your people, so you may know[t] that there is no
one like[u] me in all the earth. 15For by
now I could have stretched out my
hand and struck you and your people[v]
with a plague that would have wiped
you off the earth. 16But I have raised
you up[q] for this very purpose,[w] that
I might show you my power[x] and that
my name might be proclaimed in all the
earth. 17You still set yourself against
my people and will not let them go.
18Therefore, at this time tomorrow I
will send the worst hailstorm[y] that
has ever fallen on Egypt, from the day
it was founded till now.[z] 19Give an order now to bring your livestock and everything you have in the field to a place
of shelter, because the hail will fall on
every man and animal that has not
been brought in and is still out in the
field, and they will die.' "
20Those officials of Pharaoh who
feared[a] the word of the LORD hurried
to bring their slaves and their livestock

8:28 [c]S ver 8; S Jer 37:3; Ac 8:24
8:29 [d]ver 15; Ex 9:30; 10:11; Isa 26:10
8:30 [e]ver 12; Ex 9:33; 10:18
8:32 [f]S Ex 7:14
9:1 [g]S Ex 8:1
9:3 [h]Ex 7:4; 1Sa 5:6; Job 13:21; Ps 32:4; 39:10; Ac 13:11 [i]Lev 26:25; Ps 78:50; Am 4:10
9:4 [j]ver 26; S Ex 8:23
9:6 [k]ver 19-21; Ex 11:5; 12:29 [l]Ps 78:48-50
9:7 [m]S Ex 7:22 [n]Ex 7:14; 8:32
9:9 [o]Lev 13:18, 19; Dt 28:27,35; 2Ki 20:7; Job 2:7; Isa 38:21; Rev 16:2
9:11 [p]S Ex 8:18
9:12 [q]S Ex 4:21 [r]S Ex 7:4
9:13 [s]S Ex 3:18
9:14 [t]S Ex 8:10 [u]Ex 15:11; 1Sa 2:2; 2Sa 7:22; 1Ki 8:23; 1Ch 17:20; Ps 35:10; 71:19; 86:8; 89:6; Isa 46:9; Jer 10:6; Mic 7:18
9:15 [v]Ex 3:20
9:16 [w]Pr 16:4 [x]Ex 14:4,17,31; Ps 20:6; 25:11; 68:28; 71:18; 106:8; 109:21; Ro 9:17*
9:18 [y]ver 23; Jos 10:11; Ps 78:47-48; 105:32; 148:8; Isa 30:30; Eze 38:22; Hag 2:17 [z]ver 24; Ex 10:6
9:20 [a]Pr 13:13

[q]16 Or *have spared you*

9:3 YOUR CATTLE. The Egyptians worshiped bulls and other animals. They believed that gods revealed themselves through these animals and were the Egyptians' protectors. Thus, the plague on the livestock was again a direct attack on the polytheism and idolatry of the Egyptians (cf. 20:4–6; 32).

9:6 LIVESTOCK OF THE EGYPTIANS. Livestock that were brought to shelter evidently were not killed (cf. v. 3,19; 11:5; 12:29; 13:15).

9:15–16 I HAVE RAISED YOU UP FOR THIS VERY PURPOSE. Pharaoh deserved to be cut off when he first said, "Who is the LORD, that I should obey him" (5:2). Instead of destroying him, however, God permitted him to experience plague after plague so he would know that God has power and that not only he but the entire world would witness God's power.

inside. **21**But those who ignored[b] the word of the LORD left their slaves and livestock in the field.

22Then the LORD said to Moses, "Stretch out your hand toward the sky so that hail will fall all over Egypt—on men and animals and on everything growing in the fields of Egypt." **23**When Moses stretched out his staff toward the sky, the LORD sent thunder[c] and hail,[d] and lightning flashed down to the ground. So the LORD rained hail on the land of Egypt; **24**hail fell and lightning flashed back and forth. It was the worst storm in all the land of Egypt since it had become a nation.[e] **25**Throughout Egypt hail struck everything in the fields—both men and animals; it beat down everything growing in the fields and stripped every tree.[f] **26**The only place it did not hail was the land of Goshen,[g] where the Israelites were.[h]

27Then Pharaoh summoned Moses and Aaron. "This time I have sinned,"[i] he said to them. "The LORD is in the right,[j] and I and my people are in the wrong. **28**Pray[k] to the LORD, for we have had enough thunder and hail. I will let you go;[l] you don't have to stay any longer."

29Moses replied, "When I have gone out of the city, I will spread out my hands[m] in prayer to the LORD. The thunder will stop and there will be no more hail, so you may know that the earth[n] is the LORD's. **30**But I know that you and your officials still do not fear[o] the LORD God."

31(The flax and barley[p] were destroyed, since the barley had headed and the flax was in bloom. **32**The wheat and spelt,[q] however, were not destroyed, because they ripen later.)

33Then Moses left Pharaoh and went out of the city. He spread out his hands toward the LORD; the thunder and hail stopped, and the rain no longer poured down on the land. **34**When Pharaoh saw that the rain and hail and thunder had stopped, he sinned again: He and his officials hardened their hearts. **35**So Pharaoh's heart[r] was hard and he would not let the Israelites go, just as the LORD had said through Moses.

The Plague of Locusts

10 Then the LORD said to Moses, "Go to Pharaoh, for I have hardened his heart[s] and the hearts of his officials so that I may perform these miraculous signs[t] of mine among them **2**that you may tell your children[u] and grandchildren how I dealt harshly[v] with the Egyptians and how I performed my signs among them, and that you may know that I am the LORD."[w] Nu 10:29

3So Moses and Aaron went to Pharaoh and said to him, "This is what the LORD, the God of the Hebrews, says: 'How long will you refuse to humble[x] yourself before me? Let my people go, so that they may worship me. **4**If you refuse[y] to let them go, I will bring locusts[z] into your country tomorrow. **5**They will cover the face of the ground so that it cannot be seen. They will devour what little you have left[a] after the hail, including every tree that is growing in your fields.[b] **6**They will fill your houses[c] and those of all your officials and all the Egyptians—something neither your fathers nor your forefathers have ever seen from the day they settled in this land till now.'"[d] Then Moses turned and left Pharaoh.

7Pharaoh's officials said to him, "How long will this man be a snare[e] to us? Let the people go, so that they may worship the LORD their God. Do you not yet realize that Egypt is ruined?"[f]

8Then Moses and Aaron were brought back to Pharaoh. "Go, worship[g] the LORD your God," he said. "But just who will be going?"

9Moses answered, "We will go with our young and old, with our sons and

9:21 [b]S Ge 19:14; Eze 33:4-5
9:23 [c]Ex 20:18; 1Sa 7:10; 12:17; Ps 18:13; 29:3; 68:33; 77:17; 104:7 [d]S ver 18; Rev 8:7; 16:21
9:24 [e]S ver 18
9:25 [f]Ps 105:32-33; Eze 13:13
9:26 [g]S ver 4; Isa 32:18-20 [h]Ex 10:23; 11:7; 12:13; Am 4:7
9:27 [i]ver 34; Ex 10:16; Nu 14:40; Dt 1:41; Jos 7:11; Jdg 10:10; 1Sa 15:24; 24:17; 26:21 [j]Ps 11:7; 116:5; 119:137; 129:4; 145:17; Jer 12:1; La 1:18
9:28 [k]Ex 8:8; Ac 8:24 [l]S Ex 8:8
9:29 [m]ver 33; 1Ki 8:22,38; Job 11:13; Ps 77:2; 88:9; 143:6; Isa 1:15 [n]Ex 19:5; Job 41:11; Ps 24:1; 50:12; 1Co 10:26
9:30 [o]S Ex 8:29
9:31 [p]Dt 8:8; Ru 1:22; 2:23; 2Sa 14:30; 17:28; Isa 28:25; Eze 4:9; Joel 1:11
9:32 [q]Isa 28:25
9:35 [r]S Ex 4:21
10:1 [s]S Ex 4:21 [t]S Ex 3:19; S 7:3; Jos 24:17; Ne 9:10; Ps 74:9; 105:26-36
10:2 [u]Ex 12:26-27; 13:8,14; Dt 4:9; 6:20; 32:7; Jos 4:6; Ps 44:1; 71:18; 78:4,5; Joel 1:3 [v]1Sa 6:6 [w]S Ex 6:2
10:3 [x]1Ki 21:29; 2Ki 22:19; 2Ch 7:14; 12:7; 33:23; 34:27; Job 42:6; Isa 58:3; Da 5:22; Jas 4:10; 1Pe 5:6
10:4 [y]Ex 8:2; 9:2 [z]Dt 28:38; Ps 105:34; Pr 30:27; Joel 1:4; Rev 9:3
10:5 [a]Ex 9:32; Joel 1:4 [b]ver 15
10:6 [c]Joel 2:9 [d]S Ex 9:18
10:7 [e]Ex 23:33; 34:12; Dt 7:16; 12:30; 20:18; Jos 23:13; Jdg 2:3; 8:27; 16:5; 1Sa 18:21; Ps 106:36; Ecc 7:26 [f]S Ge 20:3; S Ex 8:19
10:8 [g]S Ex 8:8

10:2 YOU MAY TELL YOUR CHILDREN. God showed great concern that the children in Israel would come to know who he was and would accept him as their God in faith and obedience. God chose Abraham with the purpose that he should teach his children to keep the way of the Lord (see Ge 18:19, note). Later he commanded the Israelites to be diligent in teaching their children the words of the Lord (see Dt 6:7, note). God knew that if his people failed in this solemn duty, the next generation would turn from him and his righteous ways.

10:9 A FESTIVAL. The request to be allowed to make a three-day journey to worship the Lord was sincere. But it was also given without any assurance that the Israelites would return. Pharaoh seemed to have realized this (vv. 11,24).

daughters, and with our flocks and
herds, because we are to celebrate a
festival[h] to the LORD."
10Pharaoh said, "The LORD be with
you—if I let you go, along with your
women and children! Clearly you are
bent on evil.[r] 11No! Have only the men
go; and worship the LORD, since that's
what you have been asking for." Then
Moses and Aaron were driven out of
Pharaoh's presence.
12And the LORD said to Moses,
"Stretch out your hand[i] over Egypt so
that locusts will swarm over the land
and devour everything growing in the
fields, everything left by the hail."
13So Moses stretched out his staff[j]
over Egypt, and the LORD made an east
wind blow across the land all that day
and all that night. By morning the wind
had brought the locusts;[k] 14they invaded all Egypt and settled down in every area of the country in great numbers. Never before had there been such
a plague of locusts,[l] nor will there
ever be again. 15They covered all the
ground until it was black. They devoured[m] all that was left after the
hail—everything growing in the fields
and the fruit on the trees. Nothing
green remained on tree or plant in all
the land of Egypt.
16Pharaoh quickly summoned[n] Moses and Aaron and said, "I have
sinned[o] against the LORD your God
and against you. 17Now forgive[p] my
sin once more and pray[q] to the LORD
your God to take this deadly plague
away from me."
18Moses then left Pharaoh and
prayed to the LORD.[r] 19And the LORD
changed the wind to a very strong west
wind, which caught up the locusts and
carried them into the Red Sea.[s] Not a
locust was left anywhere in Egypt.
20But the LORD hardened Pharaoh's
heart,[s] and he would not let the Israelites go.

The Plague of Darkness

21Then the LORD said to Moses,
"Stretch out your hand toward the sky
so that darkness[t] will spread over
Egypt—darkness that can be felt."
22So Moses stretched out his hand toward the sky, and total darkness[u]
covered all Egypt for three days. 23No
one could see anyone else or leave his
place for three days. Yet all the Israelites had light in the places where they
lived.[v]
24Then Pharaoh summoned Moses
and said, "Go,[w] worship the LORD.
Even your women and children[x] may
go with you; only leave your flocks and
herds behind."[y]
25But Moses said, "You must allow
us to have sacrifices and burnt offerings[z] to present to the LORD our God.
26Our livestock too must go with us;
not a hoof is to be left behind. We have
to use some of them in worshiping the
LORD our God, and until we get there we
will not know what we are to use to
worship the LORD."
27But the LORD hardened Pharaoh's
heart,[a] and he was not willing to let
them go. 28Pharaoh said to Moses,
"Get out of my sight! Make sure you do
not appear before me again! The day
you see my face you will die."
29"Just as you say," Moses replied,
"I will never appear[b] before you
again."

The Plague on the Firstborn

11 Now the LORD had said to Moses, "I will bring one more
plague on Pharaoh and on Egypt. After
that, he will let you go[c] from here, and
when he does, he will drive you out
completely.[d] 2Tell the people that
men and women alike are to ask their
neighbors for articles of silver and
gold."[e] 3(The LORD made the Egyptians favorably disposed[f] toward the
people, and Moses himself was highly
regarded[g] in Egypt by Pharaoh's officials and by the people.)
4So Moses said, "This is what the
LORD says: 'About midnight[h] I will go
throughout Egypt.[i] 5Every firstborn[j] son in Egypt will die, from the
firstborn son of Pharaoh, who sits on

10:9 [h]S Ex 3:18 **10:12** [i]Ex 7:19 **10:13** [j]ver 21-22; Ex 4:17; 8:5,17; 9:23; 14:15-16, 26-27; 17:5; Nu 20:8 [k]ver 4; 1Ki 8:37; Ps 78:46; 105:34; Am 4:9; Na 3:16 **10:14** [l]Dt 28:38; Ps 78:46; Isa 33:4; Joel 1:4; 2:1-11,25; Am 4:9 **10:15** [m]Dt 28:38; Ps 105:34-35; Joel 1:4; Am 7:2; Mal 3:11 **10:16** [n]S Ex 8:25 [o]S Ex 9:27 **10:17** [p]1Sa 15:25 [q]S Ex 8:8 **10:18** [r]S Ex 8:30 **10:20** [s]S Ex 4:21 **10:21** [t]Dt 28:29 **10:22** [u]Ps 105:28; Isa 13:10; 45:7; 50:3; Rev 16:10 **10:23** [v]S Ex 8:22; Am 4:7 **10:24** [w]S Ex 8:8 [x]ver 8-10 [y]S Ge 45:10 **10:25** [z]S Ge 8:20; S Ex 18:12 **10:27** [a]S Ex 4:21 **10:29** [b]Ex 11:8; Heb 11:27 **11:1** [c]S Ex 3:20 [d]S Ex 6:1 **11:2** [e]S Ex 3:21, 22 **11:3** [f]S Ge 39:21 [g]Dt 34:11; 2Sa 7:9; 8:13; 22:44; 23:1; Est 9:4; Ps 89:27 **11:4** [h]Ex 12:29; Job 34:20 [i]Ex 12:23; Ps 81:5 **11:5** [j]S Ex 4:23

[r] *10* Or *Be careful, trouble is in store for you!*
[s] *19* Hebrew *Yam Suph*; that is, Sea of Reeds

11:5 FIRSTBORN . . . WILL DIE. God himself would bring the final judgment on the Egyptians: the firstborn son of every family would die. This would be a terrible blow to the Egyptians because the firstborn normally carried on the family's hopes and ambitions. God's judgment was his just recompense because of the Egyptians' wickedness. Their cruelty to the Hebrews and the drowning of the male babies were in themselves a persecution of God's "firstborn" (4:22). The Egyptians were reaping what they had sown.

the throne, to the firstborn son of the
slave girl, who is at her hand mill,[k]
and all the firstborn of the cattle as
well. **6**There will be loud wailing[l]
throughout Egypt—worse than there
has ever been or ever will be again.
7But among the Israelites not a dog
will bark at any man or animal.' Then
you will know that the LORD makes a
distinction[m] between Egypt and Israel. **8**All these officials of yours will
come to me, bowing down before me
and saying, 'Go,[n] you and all the people who follow you!' After that I will
leave."[o] Then Moses, hot with anger,
left Pharaoh.

9The LORD had said to Moses, "Pharaoh will refuse to listen[p] to you—so
that my wonders[q] may be multiplied
in Egypt." **10**Moses and Aaron performed all these wonders before Pharaoh, but the LORD hardened Pharaoh's
heart,[r] and he would not let the Israelites go out of his country.

The Passover

12:14–20pp — Lev 23:4–8; Nu 28:16–25; Dt 16:1–8

12 The LORD said to Moses and
Aaron in Egypt, **2**"This month
is to be for you the first month,[s] the
first month of your year. **3**Tell the
whole community of Israel that on the
tenth day of this month each man is to
take a lamb[t][t] for his family, one for
each household.[u] **4**If any household is
too small for a whole lamb, they must
share one with their nearest neighbor,
having taken into account the number
of people there are. You are to determine the amount of lamb needed in accordance with what each person will
eat. **5**The animals you choose must be
year-old males without defect,[v] and
you may take them from the sheep or
the goats. **6**Take care of them until the
fourteenth day of the month,[w] when
all the people of the community of Israel must slaughter them at twilight.[x]
7Then they are to take some of the
blood[y] and put it on the sides and tops
of the doorframes of the houses where
they eat the lambs. **8**That same night[z]
they are to eat the meat roasted[a] over
the fire, along with bitter herbs,[b] and
bread made without yeast.[c] **9**Do not
eat the meat raw or cooked in water,
but roast it over the fire—head, legs
and inner parts.[d] **10**Do not leave any
of it till morning;[e] if some is left till
morning, you must burn it. **11**This is
how you are to eat it: with your cloak
tucked into your belt, your sandals on
your feet and your staff in your hand.
Eat it in haste;[f] it is the LORD's Passover.[g]

12"On that same night I will pass
through[h] Egypt and strike down[i] every firstborn[j]—both men and animals—and I will bring judgment on all
the gods[k] of Egypt. I am the LORD.[l]
13The blood will be a sign for you on
the houses where you are; and when I
see the blood, I will pass over[m] you.
No destructive plague will touch you
when I strike Egypt.[n]

14"This is a day you are to commemorate;[o] for the generations to come
you shall celebrate it as a festival to

11:5 [k]Isa 47:2 **11:6** [l]Ex 12:30; Pr 21:13; Am 5:17 **11:7** [m]S Ex 8:22 **11:8** [n]Ex 12:31-33 [o]Heb 11:27 **11:9** [p]S Ex 7:4 [q]S Ex 3:20 **11:10** [r]S Ex 4:21; Ro 2:5 **12:2** [s]ver 18; Ex 13:4; 23:15; 34:18; 40:2; Dt 16:1 **12:3** [t]Mk 14:12; 1Co 5:7 [u]ver 21 **12:5** [v]Ex 29:1; Lev 1:3; 3:1; 4:3; 22:18-21; 23:12; Nu 6:14; 15:8; 28:3; Dt 15:21; 17:1; Heb 9:14; 1Pe 1:19 **12:6** [w]ver 19; Lev 23:5; Nu 9:1-3,5,11; Jos 5:10; 2Ch 30:2 [x]Ex 16:12; Dt 16:4,6 **12:7** [y]ver 13,23; Eze 9:6 **12:8** [z]ver 10; Ex 16:19; 23:18; 34:25; Lev 7:15; Nu 9:12 [a]Dt 16:7; 2Ch 35:13 [b]Nu 9:11 [c]ver 19-20; Ex 13:3; Dt 16:3-4; 1Co 5:8 **12:9** [d]Ex 29:13, 17,22; Lev 3:3 **12:10** [e]S ver 8; Ex 13:7; 29:34; Lev 22:30; Dt 16:4 **12:11** [f]ver 33; Dt 16:3; Isa 48:20; 52:12 [g]ver 13,21,27,43; Lev 23:5; Nu 9:2, 4; 28:16; Dt 16:1; Jos 5:10; 2Ki 23:21,23; 2Ch 30:1; Ezr 6:19; Isa 31:5; Eze 45:21 **12:12** [h]Am 5:17 [i]Isa 10:33; 31:8; 37:36 [j]ver 29; S Ex 4:23; 13:15 [k]Ex 15:11; 18:11; Nu 33:4; 2Ch 2:5; Ps 95:3; 97:9; 135:5; Isa 19:1; Jer 43:12; 44:8 [l]S Ex 6:2 **12:13** [m]S ver 11,23; Heb 11:28 [n]S Ex 8:23 **12:14** [o]Ex 13:9; 23:14; 32:5

[t]*3* The Hebrew word can mean *lamb* or *kid*; also in verse 4.

12:2 THE FIRST MONTH OF YOUR YEAR. Ch. 12 describes the Feast of the Passover (vv. 1–14,21–28) and the Feast of Unleavened Bread (vv. 15–20). These celebrations were based on the historical events of the first Passover at the time of the exodus (chs. 12–14). Because the Passover marked a new beginning for Israel, the month in which it occurred (March-April in our calendar) became "the first month" of a new year for the nation—intended to remind the people that their very existence as God's people was the result of their deliverance from Egypt by his mighty redemptive acts.

12:7 THEY ARE TO TAKE SOME OF THE BLOOD. The Passover lamb and its blood point to Jesus Christ and his shed blood as "the Lamb of God, who takes away the sin of the world" (Jn 1:29, 36; cf. Isa 53:7; Ac 8:32–35; 1Co 5:7; Rev 13:8; see article on THE PASSOVER, p. 104).

12:8 BITTER HERBS, AND BREAD MADE WITHOUT YEAST. For the symbolism of the unleavened bread, see article on THE PASSOVER, p. 104. The "bitter herbs" would bring to mind the bitter time of their slavery in Egypt (cf. Ro 6:21).

12:11 YOUR CLOAK TUCKED INTO YOUR BELT, YOUR SANDALS ON YOUR FEET. This imagery points to the need for decisive and immediate obedience from God's people.

12:14 A LASTING ORDINANCE. The Passover feast was supposed to be an annual festival. Regular participation in the Lord's Supper for the NT Christian continues the prophetic significance of the Passover (see Mt 26:26, note; 1Co 11:24–25, note; cf. 1Co 5:7–8; see article on THE PASSOVER, p. 104).

THE PASSOVER

Ex 12:11 "This is how you are to eat it: with your cloak tucked into your belt, your sandals on your feet and your staff in your hand. Eat it in haste; it is the LORD's Passover."

HISTORICAL BACKGROUND. Since the time of Israel's departure out of Egypt about 1445 B.C., the Hebrew people (later called Jews) have been celebrating the Passover each year in the spring (generally near the time of Good Friday and Easter).

After more than four hundred years of bondage in Egypt, God determined to deliver the descendants of Abraham, Isaac and Jacob from slavery. He raised up Moses and commissioned him to be the leader of the exodus (Ex 3—4). In obedience to God's call, Moses confronted Pharaoh with God's mandate: "Let my people go." To impress on him the seriousness of this message from the Lord, Moses, by God's power, called down plagues as judgments on Egypt. During several of these, Pharaoh agreed to let the Israelites go, but then reneged on his decision once the plague was lifted. The time came for the tenth and final plague, the one that would give the Egyptians no other choice than to drive the Israelites out. God sent a destroying angel throughout the land of Egypt to strike down "every firstborn—both men and animals" (Ex 12:12).

Since the Israelites were also living in Egypt, how could they escape the destroying angel? The Lord gave a specific command to his people; to obey it would bring his protection to each Hebrew family and firstborn son. Each family was to take a year-old male lamb without defect and kill it at twilight on the fourteenth day of the month Abib; smaller households could share a single lamb (Ex 12:4). Some of the blood of the slain lamb was to be sprinkled on the two sides and on the top of the doorframes of their homes. When the destroyer went through the land, he would *pass over* those homes that had the blood sprinkled on them (thus the term *Passover*, from Heb *pesah*, meaning "to jump past," "to pass over" or "to spare"). Thus by the blood of the slain lamb, the Israelites were spared the judgment of death that came to all Egyptian firstborn. God commanded the sign of the blood not because he couldn't otherwise distinguish the Israelites from the Egyptians, but because he wanted to teach his people the importance of obedience and of blood redemption, thus preparing for "the Lamb of God," who centuries later would take away the sin of the world (Jn 1:29).

On that particular night the Israelites were supposed to be dressed and ready to leave (Ex 12:11). They were commanded to roast, not boil, the lamb and to prepare bitter herbs and bread made without yeast. As night approached, they would then be ready to eat the food and depart in haste when the Egyptians came and begged them to leave their country. Everything happened as the Lord had spoken (Ex 12:29–36).

THE PASSOVER IN ISRAELITE/JEWISH HISTORY. From that moment in history, God's people celebrated the Passover every spring, in response to his command that the Passover be "a lasting ordinance" (Ex 12:14). It was, however, a memorial sacrifice. Only the initial sacrifice in Egypt was an effective sacrifice. Before the temple was built, each Passover the Israelites gathered in households, killed a lamb, removed all yeast from their homes and ate bitter herbs. More important, they retold the story of the miraculous exodus of their ancestors from the land of Egypt and from slavery to the pharaoh. Thus from generation to generation, the Hebrew people remembered God's redemption and their deliverance from Egypt (see Ex 12:26, note). Once the temple was built, God commanded that the Passover celebration and the killing of the lamb take place in Jerusalem (cf. Dt 16:1–6). The OT records several times in which an especially significant Passover was celebrated in the holy city (e.g., 2Ki 23:21–23; 2Ch 30:1–20; 35:1–19; Ezr 6:19–22).

The Passover was likewise observed by the Jews in NT times. The only incident from Jesus' boyhood recorded in Scripture occurred when his parents took him to Jerusalem at twelve years old to celebrate the Passover (Lk 2:41–50). Later in life, Jesus regularly went to Jerusalem for the Passover (e.g., Jn 2:13). The last supper that Jesus ate with his disciples in Jerusalem, shortly before going to the cross, was a Passover meal (see Mt 26:1–2,17–29). Jesus himself was crucified on the Passover, as *the* Passover Lamb (cf. 1Co 5:7) who delivers from sin and death all who believe.

Jews today still celebrate the Passover, though its nature has changed somewhat. Since there is no longer a temple in Jerusalem where a lamb can be slain in obedience to Dt 16:1–6, the contemporary Jewish feast (called the *Seder*) is no longer celebrated with a sacrificed lamb. But families still gather together, all yeast is ceremonially removed from Jewish homes, and the story of the exodus from Egypt is retold by the father of the household.

THE PASSOVER AND JESUS CHRIST. For Christians, the Passover contains rich prophetic symbolism that points forward to Jesus Christ. The NT explicitly teaches that the Jewish feasts are "a shadow of the things that were to come" (Col 2:16–17; Heb 10:1), i.e., redemption through the blood of Jesus Christ. Note the following in Ex 12 that remind us of our Savior and his will for us. (1) The heart and soul of the Passover event was God's saving grace. God brought the Israelites out of Egypt not because they were such a worthy people but because he loved them and because he was faithful to his covenant (see Dt 7:7–10). Similarly, the salvation we receive from Christ comes to us through God's amazing grace (see Eph 2:8–10; Tit 3:4–5).

(2) The purpose of the blood applied on the doorframes was to save the firstborn son of each family from death; this blood points to Christ's shedding of blood on the cross in order to save us from death and from God's wrath against sin (Ex 12:13,23,27; Heb 9:22).

(3) The Passover lamb was a "sacrifice" (Ex 12:27) that functioned as a substitute for the firstborn; this sacrifice points to Christ's death as a substitution for the believer's death (see Ro 3:25, note). Paul explicitly calls Christ our Passover lamb who was sacrificed for us (1Co 5:7).

(4) The male lamb marked for death had to be "without defect" (Ex 12:5); the lamb prefigures the sinlessness of Christ, the perfect Son of God (cf. Jn 8:46; Heb 4:15).

(5) The eating of the lamb represented the identification of the Israelite community with the lamb's death, a death that saved them from physical death. Similarly, taking the Lord's Supper represents our participation in Christ's death, a death that saves us from spiritual death (1Co 10:16–17; 11:24–26). As in the case of the Passover, only the initial sacrifice, his death on the cross, was an effective sacrifice. We observe the Lord's Supper as a memorial, "in remembrance" of him (1Co 11:24).

(6) The sprinkling of the blood on the doorframes was done in obedient faith (Ex 12:28; cf. Heb 11:28); this response of faith brought about redemption through the blood (Ex 12:7,13). Salvation through Christ's blood is obtained only through "the obedience that comes from faith" (Ro 1:5; cf. 16:26).

(7) The Passover lamb was to be eaten along with unleavened bread (Ex 12:8). Since yeast in the Bible usually represents sin and corruption (see Ex 13:7, note; Mt 16:6, note; Mk 8:15, note), this unleavened bread represented the separation of the redeemed Israelites from Egypt, i.e., from the world and from sin (see Ex 12:15, note). Similarly, God's redeemed people are called to separate themselves from the sinful world and to dedicate themselves to God alone (see articles on SPIRITUAL SEPARATION FOR BELIEVERS, p. 1794, and THE CHRISTIAN'S RELATIONSHIP TO THE WORLD, p. 1976).

the LORD—a lasting ordinance.[p] **15**For
seven days you are to eat bread made
without yeast.[q] On the first day remove the yeast from your houses, for
whoever eats anything with yeast in it
from the first day through the seventh
must be cut off[r] from Israel. **16**On the
first day hold a sacred assembly, and
another one on the seventh day. Do no
work[s] at all on these days, except to
prepare food for everyone to eat—that
is all you may do.
17"Celebrate the Feast of Unleavened Bread,[t] because it was on this
very day that I brought your divisions
out of Egypt.[u] Celebrate this day as a
lasting ordinance for the generations
to come.[v] **18**In the first month[w] you
are to eat bread made without yeast,
from the evening of the fourteenth day
until the evening of the twenty-first
day. **19**For seven days no yeast is to be
found in your houses. And whoever
eats anything with yeast in it must be
cut off[x] from the community of Israel,
whether he is an alien[y] or native-born.
20Eat nothing made with yeast. Wherever you live,[z] you must eat unleavened bread."[a]
21Then Moses summoned all the elders of Israel and said to them, "Go at
once and select the animals for your
families and slaughter the Passover[b]
lamb. **22**Take a bunch of hyssop,[c] dip
it into the blood in the basin and put
some of the blood[d] on the top and on
both sides of the doorframe. Not one of
you shall go out the door of his house
until morning. **23**When the LORD goes
through the land to strike[e] down the
Egyptians, he will see the blood[f] on
the top and sides of the doorframe and
will pass over[g] that doorway, and he
will not permit the destroyer[h] to enter
your houses and strike you down.
24"Obey these instructions as a lasting ordinance[i] for you and your
descendants. **25**When you enter the
land[j] that the LORD will give you as he
promised, observe this ceremony.
26And when your children[k] ask you,
'What does this ceremony mean to
you?' **27**then tell them, 'It is the Passover[l] sacrifice to the LORD, who
passed over the houses of the Israelites in Egypt and spared our homes
when he struck down the Egyptians.' "[m] Then the people bowed
down and worshiped.[n] **28**The Israelites did just what the LORD commanded[o] Moses and Aaron.
29At midnight[p] the LORD[q] struck
down all the firstborn[r] in Egypt, from
the firstborn of Pharaoh, who sat on
the throne, to the firstborn of the prisoner, who was in the dungeon, and the
firstborn of all the livestock[s] as well.
30Pharaoh and all his officials and all
the Egyptians got up during the night,
and there was loud wailing[t] in Egypt,
for there was not a house without
someone dead.

12:14 [p] ver 17, 24; Ex 13:5,10; 27:21; Lev 3:17; 10:9; 16:29; 17:7; 23:14; 24:3; Nu 18:23
12:15 [q] Ex 13:6-7; 23:15; 34:18; Lev 23:6; Nu 28:17; Dt 16:3; 1Co 5:7 [r] S Ge 17:14
12:16 [s] Nu 29:35
12:17 [t] Ex 23:15; 34:18; Dt 16:16; 2Ch 8:13; 30:21; Ezr 6:22; Mt 26:17; Lk 22:1; Ac 12:3 [u] ver 41; S Ex 6:6,26; 13:3; Lev 19:36 [v] Lev 3:17
12:18 [w] S ver 2
12:19 [x] S Ge 17:14 [y] Nu 9:14; 15:14; 35:15; Dt 1:16; Jos 8:33
12:20 [z] Lev 3:17; Nu 35:29; Eze 6:6 [a] Ex 13:6
12:21 [b] S ver 11; Mk 14:12-16
12:22 [c] Lev 14:4, 6; Nu 19:18; Ps 51:7 [d] Heb 11:28
12:23 [e] Isa 19:22 [f] S ver 7; Rev 7:3 [g] S ver 13 [h] S Ge 16:7; Isa 37:36; Jer 6:26; 48:8; 1Co 10:10; Heb 11:28
12:24 [i] S ver 14
12:25 [j] S Ge 15:14; Ex 3:17
12:26 [k] Ex 10:2
12:27 [l] S ver 11 [m] S Ex 8:23 [n] S Ge 24:26
12:28 [o] ver 50
12:29 [p] S Ex 11:4 [q] S Ge 19:13 [r] S Ex 4:23 [s] S Ex 9:6
12:30 [t] S Ex 11:6

12:15 MUST BE CUT OFF FROM ISRAEL. Willful, deliberate rejection of God's instruction resulted in divine judgment (see also v. 19). The guilty person was removed from the covenant people by death (e.g., 31:14) or expulsion. Likewise, under the new covenant, those who reject the lordship of Christ and choose to eat the yeast of sin are excluded from grace and salvation in Christ (see article on PERSONAL APOSTASY, p. 1918).

12:17 THE FEAST OF UNLEAVENED BREAD. Vv. 15–20 describe the Feast of Unleavened Bread Israel was to observe after they entered Canaan. This feast represented the consecration of God's people, based on their redemption from Egypt. In this context yeast, an agent that causes fermentation, symbolized sin, and unleavened bread symbolized repentance, repudiation of sin and consecration to God (see 13:7, note).

(1) All yeast (i.e., worldly corruption and sin) had to be removed from the Israelites' houses, implying that their lives and homes as believers had to be set apart for God (vv. 15–16) because of what God had done for them (13:8–9). The NT establishes a link between this Feast of the Unleavened Bread and believers purging out "malice and wickedness" and living in "sincerity and truth" (1Co 5:6–8).

(2) Failure to turn from sin in true faith toward God resulted in divine judgment, i.e., being cut off from God's covenant of promise and salvation (see previous note).

(3) The Passover meal signaled the beginning of the Feast of Unleavened Bread (vv. 6,18–19), foreshadowing the importance of faith in and obedience to the sacrificial Lamb. Believers committed themselves to repentance and to lives lived for God in humble gratitude.

12:19 NO YEAST IS TO BE FOUND IN YOUR HOUSES. See 13:7, note.

12:26 WHAT DOES THIS CEREMONY MEAN TO YOU? Parents were expected to use the Passover to teach their children the truth of how God had redeemed them from slavery and sin and made them a special people under his care and rule. Likewise, the Lord's Supper, the NT believers' "Passover," is designed to remind us of salvation in Christ and our redemption from sin and satanic bondage (see 1Co 11:24–25, note).

The Exodus

31During the night Pharaoh summoned Moses and Aaron and said, "Up! Leave my people, you and the Israelites! Go, worship[u] the LORD as you have requested. 32Take your flocks and herds,[v] as you have said, and go. And also bless[w] me."

33The Egyptians urged the people to hurry[x] and leave[y] the country. "For otherwise," they said, "we will all die!"[z] 34So the people took their dough before the yeast was added, and carried it on their shoulders in kneading troughs[a] wrapped in clothing. 35The Israelites did as Moses instructed and asked the Egyptians for articles of silver and gold[b] and for clothing.[c] 36The LORD had made the Egyptians favorably disposed[d] toward the people, and they gave them what they asked for; so they plundered[e] the Egyptians.

37The Israelites journeyed from Rameses[f] to Succoth.[g] There were about six hundred thousand men[h] on foot, besides women and children. 38Many other people[i] went up with them, as well as large droves of livestock, both flocks and herds. 39With the dough they had brought from Egypt, they baked cakes of unleavened bread. The dough was without yeast because they had been driven out[j] of Egypt and did not have time to prepare food for themselves.

40Now the length of time the Israelite people lived in Egypt[u] was 430 years.[k] 41At the end of the 430 years, to the very day, all the LORD's divisions[l] left Egypt.[m] 42Because the LORD kept vigil that night to bring them out of Egypt, on this night all the Israelites are to keep vigil to honor the LORD for the generations to come.[n]

Passover Restrictions

43The LORD said to Moses and Aaron, "These are the regulations for the Passover:[o]

"No foreigner[p] is to eat of it. 44Any slave you have bought may eat of it after you have circumcised[q] him, 45but a temporary resident and a hired worker[r] may not eat of it.

46"It must be eaten inside one house; take none of the meat outside the house. Do not break any of the bones.[s] 47The whole community of Israel must celebrate it.

48"An alien living among you who wants to celebrate the LORD's Passover must have all the males in his household circumcised; then he may take part like one born in the land.[t] No uncircumcised[u] male may eat of it. 49The same law applies to the native-born and to the alien[v] living among you."

50All the Israelites did just what the LORD had commanded[w] Moses and Aaron. 51And on that very day the LORD brought the Israelites out of Egypt[x] by their divisions.[y]

Consecration of the Firstborn

13 The LORD said to Moses, 2"Consecrate to me every firstborn male.[z] The first offspring of every womb among the Israelites belongs to me, whether man or animal."

3Then Moses said to the people, "Commemorate this day, the day you came out of Egypt,[a] out of the land of slavery, because the LORD brought you out of it with a mighty hand.[b] Eat nothing containing yeast.[c] 4Today, in the month of Abib,[d] you are leaving. 5When the LORD brings you into the land of the Canaanites,[e] Hittites, Amorites, Hivites and Jebusites[f]—the land he swore to your forefathers to give you, a land flowing with milk and honey[g]—you are to observe this ceremony[h] in this month: 6For seven days eat bread made without yeast and on the seventh day hold a festival[i] to the LORD. 7Eat unleavened bread during those seven days; nothing with yeast in

12:31 [u] S Ex 8:8
12:32 [v] Ex 10:9, 26 [w] Ge 27:34
12:33 [x] S ver 11 [y] S Ex 6:1; 1Sa 6:6 [z] S Ge 20:3; S Ex 8:19
12:34 [a] Ex 8:3
12:35 [b] S Ex 3:22 [c] S Ge 24:53
12:36 [d] S Ge 39:21 [e] S Ex 3:22
12:37 [f] S Ge 47:11 [g] Ex 13:20; Nu 33:3-5 [h] Ge 12:2; Ex 38:26; Nu 1:46; 2:32; 11:13,21; 26:51
12:38 [i] Nu 11:4; Jos 8:35
12:39 [j] Ex 3:20; 11:1
12:40 [k] Ge 15:13; Ac 7:6; Gal 3:17
12:41 [l] S Ex 6:26 [m] S Ex 3:10
12:42 [n] Ex 13:10; Lev 3:17; Nu 9:3; Dt 16:1,6
12:43 [o] S ver 11 [p] ver 48; Nu 9:14; 15:14; 2Ch 6:32-33; Isa 14:1; 56:3,6; 60:10
12:44 [q] S Ge 17:12-13
12:45 [r] Lev 22:10
12:46 [s] Nu 9:12; Ps 22:14; 34:20; 51:8; Pr 17:22; Jn 19:36*
12:48 [t] ver 49; Lev 19:18,34; 24:22; Nu 9:14; 10:32 [u] Eze 44:7
12:49 [v] Lev 24:22; Nu 15:15-16,29; Dt 1:16
12:50 [w] ver 28
12:51 [x] S Ex 3:10; S 6:6 [y] S Ex 6:26
13:2 [z] ver 12,13, 15; Ex 22:29; 34:20; Lev 27:26; Nu 3:13; 8:17; 18:15; Dt 15:19; Ne 10:36; Lk 2:23*
13:3 [a] ver 14; Ex 7:4; Lev 26:13; Nu 1:1; 9:1; 22:5; 26:4; Dt 4:45; 5:6; Ps 81:10; 114:1 [b] S Ex 3:20 [c] S Ex 12:8
13:4 [d] S Ex 12:2
13:5 [e] ver 11 [f] S Ex 3:8 [g] S Ex 3:8 [h] Ex 12:25-26
13:6 [i] S Ex 12:15-20

[u] 40 Masoretic Text; Samaritan Pentateuch and Septuagint *Egypt and Canaan*

13:2 CONSECRATE TO ME EVERY FIRSTBORN MALE. Because God had saved all Israelite firstborn and rescued the Israelites from the Egyptians, he now considered them his property. (1) The nation was commanded to acknowledge this by dedicating their firstborn for service to God. Later this obligation was transferred to the Levites as the people's representatives. However, the people were to "redeem" (or "buy back") such children by paying a price (v. 13; cf. Nu 3:11–13,50–51; 18:16). (2) This act reminded the Israelites that God had redeemed them from slavery and bondage in Egypt and that they belonged to him. Joseph and Mary presented Jesus as their firstborn in obedience to this law (Lk 2:22–23).

13:7 NOTHING WITH YEAST IN IT IS TO BE

it is to be seen among you, nor shall
any yeast be seen anywhere within
your borders. 8On that day tell your
son,[j] 'I do this because of what the
LORD did for me when I came out of
Egypt.' 9This observance will be for
you like a sign on your hand[k] and a
reminder on your forehead[l] that the
law of the LORD is to be on your lips. For
the LORD brought you out of Egypt with
his mighty hand.[m] 10You must keep
this ordinance[n] at the appointed
time[o] year after year.

11"After the LORD brings you into the
land of the Canaanites[p] and gives it to
you, as he promised on oath[q] to you
and your forefathers,[r] 12you are to
give over to the LORD the first offspring
of every womb. All the firstborn males
of your livestock belong to the LORD.[s]
13Redeem with a lamb every firstborn
donkey,[t] but if you do not redeem it,
break its neck.[u] Redeem[v] every firstborn among your sons.[w]

14"In days to come, when your son[x]
asks you, 'What does this mean?' say
to him, 'With a mighty hand the LORD
brought us out of Egypt, out of the land
of slavery.[y] 15When Pharaoh stubbornly refused to let us go, the LORD
killed every firstborn in Egypt, both
man and animal. This is why I sacrifice
to the LORD the first male offspring of
every womb and redeem each of my
firstborn sons.'[z] 16And it will be like
a sign on your hand and a symbol on
your forehead[a] that the LORD brought
us out of Egypt with his mighty hand."

Crossing the Sea

17When Pharaoh let the people go,
God did not lead them on the road
through the Philistine country, though
that was shorter. For God said, "If they
face war, they might change their
minds and return to Egypt."[b] 18So
God led[c] the people around by the
desert road toward the Red Sea.[v] The
Israelites went up out of Egypt armed
for battle.[d]

19Moses took the bones of Joseph[e]
with him because Joseph had made the
sons of Israel swear an oath. He had
said, "God will surely come to your aid,
and then you must carry my bones up
with you from this place."[w][f]

20After leaving Succoth[g] they
camped at Etham on the edge of the
desert.[h] 21By day the LORD went
ahead[i] of them in a pillar of cloud[j]
to guide them on their way and by night
in a pillar of fire to give them light, so
that they could travel by day or night.
22Neither the pillar of cloud by day nor
the pillar of fire by night left[k] its place
in front of the people.

14 Then the LORD said to Moses,
2"Tell the Israelites to turn
back and encamp near Pi Hahiroth, between Migdol[l] and the sea. They are
to encamp by the sea, directly opposite
Baal Zephon.[m] 3Pharaoh will think,
'The Israelites are wandering around
the land in confusion, hemmed in by
the desert.' 4And I will harden Pharaoh's heart,[n] and he will pursue
them.[o] But I will gain glory[p] for myself through Pharaoh and all his army,
and the Egyptians will know that I am
the LORD."[q] So the Israelites did this.
5When the king of Egypt was told

13:8 [j]S Ex 10:2; Ps 78:5-6
13:9 [k]Isa 44:5 [l]ver 16; Dt 6:8; 11:18; Pr 3:3; Mt 23:5 [m]S Ex 3:20
13:10 [n]S Ex 12:14 [o]Ps 75:2; 102:13
13:11 [p]S ver 5 [q]S Ge 22:16; Dt 1:8 [r]S Ge 12:7; S 17:19; Ps 105:42-45
13:12 [s]S Ge 4:4; Lev 27:26; Nu 3:13; 18:15,17; Lk 2:23*
13:13 [t]ver 15; Lev 27:11 [u]Ex 34:20; Isa 66:3 [v]Nu 3:46-47 [w]Nu 18:15
13:14 [x]S Ex 10:2 [y]Ex 20:2; Dt 7:8; 28:68
13:15 [z]S ver 2
13:16 [a]S ver 9
13:17 [b]Ex 14:11; Nu 14:1-4; Dt 17:16; Hos 11:5
13:18 [c]Ex 15:22; Ps 136:16; Eze 20:10 [d]Jos 1:14; 4:13
13:19 [e]Jos 24:32; Ac 7:16; Heb 11:22 [f]S Ge 47:29-30
13:20 [g]S Ex 12:37 [h]Nu 33:6
13:21 [i]Ex 32:1; 33:14; Dt 2:7; 31:8; Jdg 4:14; 5:4; Ps 68:7; 77:20; Jer 2:2; Hab 3:13 [j]Ex 14:19,24; 24:16; 33:9-10; 34:5; 40:38; Nu 9:16; 12:5; 14:14; Dt 1:33; Ne 9:12,19; Ps 78:14; 99:7; 105:39; Isa 4:5; 1Co 10:1
13:22 [k]Ne 9:19
14:2 [l]Nu 33:7; Jer 44:1; Eze 29:10 [m]ver 9
14:4 [n]S Ex 4:21 [o]ver 8,17,23; Ps 71:11 [p]S Ex 9:16; Ro 9:17,22-23 [q]S Ex 6:2; Eze 32:15

[v]*18* Hebrew *Yam Suph*; that is, Sea of Reeds
[w]*19* See Gen. 50:25.

SEEN. During the week of the Passover, yeast (Heb *se'or*, i.e., any yeastlike substance capable of producing fermentation in dough or a liquid) and anything leavened (Heb *hamets*, i.e., anything that had undergone fermentation or anything with yeast in it) was to be removed from the homes of the Israelites (cf. 12:15,19). In 13:7 *hamets* is translated "anything with yeast in it"; however, the literal meaning of the word is "fermented thing." All foods of the Passover were to conform to this divine ordinance concerning yeast or fermentation (see article on THE PASSOVER, p. 104). The principal reason for this prohibition is most likely found in the Biblical teaching that regards fermentation and fermented things as symbolizing corruption, evil and moral impurity (see Mt 16:6, note; Mk 8:15, note; 1Co 5:6–8).

(2) Note also that the Law of Moses did not require wine, either fermented or unfermented, to be used during the Passover week. However, for any wine or food that was used, it had to conform to this rule of no yeast or fermentation (12:20). Insofar as this event looked forward to the perfect blood sacrifice of Christ (see article on THE PASSOVER, p. 104), it is understandable that there was to be no corruption in that which represented his blood (cf. 34:25; Lev 2:11; 6:17; 1Co 5:7–8; see Lk 22:18, note; see article on WINE IN NEW TESTAMENT TIMES (1), p. 1534).

13:21 A PILLAR OF CLOUD. God placed the pillars of cloud and fire as proof of his presence, love and care for Israel (cf. 40:38; Nu 9:15–23; 14:14; Dt 1:33; 1Co 10:1). The cloud and the fire were present with them until they reached the promised land forty years later.

that the people had fled,[r] Pharaoh
and his officials changed their minds[s]
about them and said, "What have we
done? We have let the Israelites go and
have lost their services!" 6So he had
his chariot made ready and took his
army with him. 7He took six hundred of
the best chariots,[t] along with all the
other chariots of Egypt, with officers
over all of them. 8The LORD hardened
the heart[u] of Pharaoh king of Egypt,
so that he pursued the Israelites, who
were marching out boldly.[v] 9The
Egyptians—all Pharaoh's horses[w]
and chariots, horsemen[x] and
troops[x]—pursued the Israelites and
overtook[y] them as they camped by the
sea near Pi Hahiroth, opposite Baal Zephon.[z]
10As Pharaoh approached, the Israelites looked up, and there were the
Egyptians, marching after them. They
were terrified and cried[a] out to the
LORD. 11They said to Moses, "Was it because there were no graves in Egypt
that you brought us to the desert to
die?[b] What have you done to us by
bringing us out of Egypt? 12Didn't
we say to you in Egypt, 'Leave us
alone; let us serve the Egyptians'? It
would have been better for us to
serve the Egyptians than to die in
the desert!"[c]
13Moses answered the people, "Do
not be afraid.[d] Stand firm and you will
see[e] the deliverance the LORD will
bring you today. The Egyptians you see
today you will never see[f] again. 14The

14:5 [r]S Ge 31:21 [s]Ps 105:25
14:7 [t]Ex 15:4
14:8 [u]S Ex 11:10 [v]Nu 33:3; Ac 13:17
14:9 [w]Ge 47:17 [x]ver 6-7,25; Jos 24:6; Isa 43:17 [y]Ex 15:9 [z]ver 2
14:10 [a]Ex 15:25; Jos 24:7; Ne 9:9; Ps 5:2; 34:17; 50:15; 107:6,28
14:11 [b]S Ex 5:21; 16:3; 17:3; Nu 11:1; 14:22; 20:4; 21:5; Dt 9:7
14:12 [c]S Ex 5:21; 15:24; 17:2; Ps 106:7-8
14:13 [d]S Ge 15:1 [e]1Sa 12:16; 2Ch 20:17 [f]ver 30

x9 Or *charioteers*; also in verses 17, 18, 23, 26 and 28

THE EXODUS

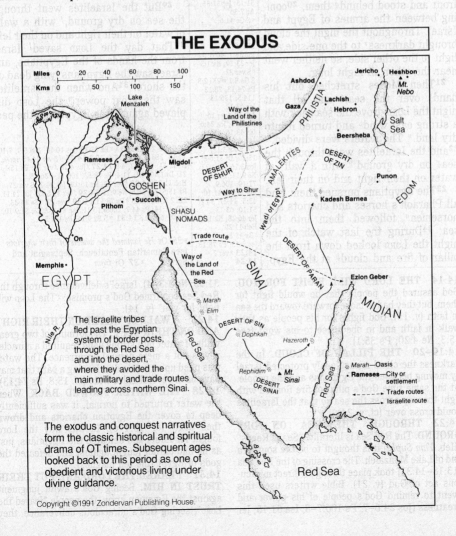

Miles 0 20 40 60 80 100
Kms 0 50 100 150

Lake Menzaleh · Way of the Land of the Philistines · Jericho · Heshbon · Mt. Nebo · Ashdod · PHILISTIA · Lachish · Gaza · Hebron · Salt Sea · Beersheba · Rameses · Migdol · DESERT OF SHUR · AMALEKITES · DESERT OF ZIN · GOSHEN · Punon · Way to Shur · Wadi of Egypt · EDOM · Succoth · Pithom · Kadesh Barnea · SHASU NOMADS · On · Trade route · DESERT OF PARAN · Memphis · Way of the Land of the Red Sea · SINAI · EGYPT · Ezion Geber · Marah · Elim · MIDIAN · Nile R. · DESERT OF SIN · Dophkah · Red Sea · Hazeroth · Rephidim · Mt. Sinai · DESERT OF SINAI · Red Sea · Red Sea

Marah—Oasis
Rameses—City or settlement
Trade routes
Israelite route

The Israelite tribes fled past the Egyptian system of border posts, through the Red Sea and into the desert, where they avoided the main military and trade routes leading across northern Sinai.

The exodus and conquest narratives form the classic historical and spiritual drama of OT times. Subsequent ages looked back to this period as one of obedient and victorious living under divine guidance.

Lev 16:15-22

LORD will fight[g] for you; you need only
to be still."[h]
15Then the LORD said to Moses,
"Why are you crying out to me?[i] Tell
the Israelites to move on. 16Raise your
staff[j] and stretch out your hand over
the sea to divide the water[k] so that
the Israelites can go through the sea
on dry ground. 17I will harden the
hearts[l] of the Egyptians so that they
will go in after them.[m] And I will gain
glory through Pharaoh and all his
army, through his chariots and his
horsemen. 18The Egyptians will know
that I am the LORD[n] when I gain glory
through Pharaoh, his chariots and his
horsemen."
19Then the angel of God,[o] who had
been traveling in front of Israel's army,
withdrew and went behind them. The
pillar of cloud[p] also moved from in
front and stood behind[q] them, 20com-
ing between the armies of Egypt and
Israel. Throughout the night the cloud
brought darkness[r] to the one side and
light to the other side; so neither went
near the other all night long.
21Then Moses stretched out his
hands[s] over the sea,[t] and all that
night the LORD drove the sea back with
a strong east wind[u] and turned it into
dry land.[v] The waters were divided,[w]
22and the Israelites went through the
sea[x] on dry ground,[y] with a wall[z] of
water on their right and on their left.
23The Egyptians pursued them, and
all Pharaoh's horses and chariots and
horsemen[a] followed them into the
sea. 24During the last watch of the
night the LORD looked down from the
pillar of fire and cloud[b] at the Egyptian army and threw it into confusion.[c] 25He made the wheels of their
chariots come off[y] so that they had
difficulty driving. And the Egyptians
said, "Let's get away from the Israelites! The LORD is fighting[d] for them
against Egypt."[e]
26Then the LORD said to Moses,
"Stretch out your hand over the sea so
that the waters may flow back over the
Egyptians and their chariots and
horsemen." 27Moses stretched out his
hand over the sea, and at daybreak the
sea went back to its place.[f] The Egyptians were fleeing toward[z] it, and the
LORD swept them into the sea.[g] 28The
water flowed back and covered the
chariots and horsemen—the entire
army of Pharaoh that had followed the
Israelites into the sea.[h] Not one of
them survived.[i]
29But the Israelites went through
the sea on dry ground,[j] with a wall[k]
of water on their right and on their left.
30That day the LORD saved[l] Israel
from the hands of the Egyptians, and
Israel saw the Egyptians lying dead on
the shore. 31And when the Israelites
saw the great power[m] the LORD displayed against the Egyptians, the peo-

14:14 [g]ver 25; Ex 15:3; Dt 1:30; 3:22; 20:4; Jos 10:14; 23:3, 10; 2Sa 5:24; 2Ch 20:29; Ne 4:20; Ps 24:8; 35:1; Isa 42:13; Jer 41:12 [h]1Sa 12:16; Ps 37:7; 46:10; 116:7; Isa 28:12; 30:15; Zec 2:13 **14:15** [i]Jos 7:10 **14:16** [j]S Ex 4:2 [k]ver 27; Isa 10:26 **14:17** [l]Ex 4:21 [m]S ver 4 **14:18** [n]S Ex 6:2; Eze 32:15 **14:19** [o]S Ge 16:7; Isa 63:9 [p]S Ex 13:21; 1Co 10:1 [q]Isa 26:7; 42:16; 49:10; 52:12; 58:8 **14:20** [r]Jos 24:7 **14:21** [s]S Ex 7:19 [t]S Ex 4:2; Job 26:12; Isa 14:27; 23:11; 51:15; Jer 31:35; Ac 7:36 [u]S Ge 41:6; Ex 15:8; 2Sa 22:16; 1Ki 19:11; Job 38:1; 40:6; Jer 23:19; Na 1:3 [v]S ver 22; S Ge 8:1 [w]2Ki 2:8; Ps 74:13; 78:13; 114:5; 136:13; Isa 63:12 **14:22** [x]ver 16; Nu 33:8; Jos 24:6; Isa 43:16; 63:11; 1Co 10:1 [y]ver 21, 29; S Ex 3:12; 15:19; Dt 31:6-8; Jos 3:16,17; 4:22; Ne 9:11; Ps 66:6; 77:19; 106:9; Isa 11:15; 41:10; 43:5; 44:27; 50:2; 51:10; 63:13; Jer 46:28; Na 1:4; Heb 11:29 [z]Ex 15:8; Jos 3:13; Ps 78:13 **14:23** [a]ver 7 **14:24** [b]S Ex 13:21; 1Co 10:1 [c]Ex 23:27; Jos 10:10; 1Sa 5:9; 7:10; 14:15; 2Sa 5:24; 2Ki 7:6; 19:7 **14:25** [d]S ver 14 [e]S ver 9; Dt 32:31; 1Sa 2:2; 4:8 **14:27** [f]Jos 4:18 [g]ver 28; Ex 15:1, 21; Dt 1:40; 2:1; 11:4; Ps 78:53; 106:11; 136:15; Heb 11:29 **14:28** [h]ver 23; Ex 15:19; Jos 24:7 [i]S ver 27; Ex 15:5; Jdg 4:16; Ne 9:11 **14:29** [j]ver 21,S 22; Jos 24:11; 2Ki 2:8; Ps 74:15 [k]Ps 78:13 **14:30** [l]ver 29; 1Sa 14:23; 1Ch 11:14; Ps 44:7; 106:8,10,21; Isa 43:3; 50:2; 51:9-10; 60:16; 63:8,11 **14:31** [m]S Ex 9:16; Ps 147:5

[y]*25* Or *He jammed the wheels of their chariots* (see Samaritan Pentateuch, Septuagint and Syriac) [z]*27* Or *from*

14:14 THE LORD WILL FIGHT FOR YOU. God assured the people that he would fight for them, but they had to move forward toward the sea in faith (v. 15). God fights for his people as they walk in faith and in obedience to his word (see 15:3; Ne 4:20; Ps 35:1).

14:19–20 THE PILLAR OF CLOUD. In the darkness the cloud miraculously protected Israel by moving between the Egyptians and the people. At the same time God's pillar of fire flooded with light the way across the sea so that the Israelites could cross over (cf. v. 24).

14:22 THROUGH THE SEA ON DRY GROUND. The Red Sea is literally, "Sea of Reeds" (Heb. *Yam Suph*); it is thought to be the southern end of Lake Menzaleh. The crossing of the Red Sea (13:18–14:31) took place through a direct miraculous act of God (v. 21). Bible writers used this event to remind God's people of his power and greatness (Jos 24:6–7; Ps 106:7–8; Isa 51:15; Jer 31:35; Na 1:3–4). Israel's deliverance through the Red Sea confirmed God's promise: "The LORD will fight for you" (v. 14).

14:22 A WALL OF WATER ON THEIR RIGHT AND ON THEIR LEFT. The forming of two great walls of water by a strong wind required a miracle; it was not a mere natural occurrence. The water was piled up on both sides, leaving a path that may have been several miles wide (cf. 15:8; Ps 74:13).

14:28 THE WATER FLOWED BACK. When the water returned to normal, it was sufficiently deep to cover the Egyptian chariots and drown their army (cf. 15:4–6). In this way the Lord fought for Israel and defeated the Egyptians, just as he had earlier fought against and defeated the gods of Egypt (the ten plagues).

14:31 FEARED THE LORD AND PUT THEIR TRUST IN HIM. Seeing God's awful judgment against the Egyptian army, the people "feared the LORD"; seeing God's miraculous deliverance, they

ple feared[n] the LORD and put their trust[o] in him and in Moses his servant.

The Song of Moses and Miriam

15 Then Moses and the Israelites sang this song[p] to the LORD:

"I will sing[q] to the LORD,
for he is highly exalted.
The horse and its rider[r]
he has hurled into the sea.[s]
2The LORD is my strength[t] and my
song;
he has become my salvation.[u]
He is my God,[v] and I will praise
him,
my father's God, and I will
exalt[w] him.
3The LORD is a warrior;[x]
the LORD is his name.[y]
4Pharaoh's chariots and his army[z]
he has hurled into the sea.
The best of Pharaoh's officers
are drowned in the Red Sea.[a]
5The deep waters[a] have covered
them;
they sank to the depths like a
stone.[b]
6"Your right hand,[c] O LORD,
was majestic in power.
Your right hand,[d] O LORD,
shattered[e] the enemy.
7In the greatness of your majesty[f]
you threw down those who
opposed you.
You unleashed your burning
anger;[g]
it consumed[h] them like stubble.
8By the blast of your nostrils[i]
the waters piled up.[j]
The surging waters stood firm like
a wall;[k]
the deep waters congealed in the
heart of the sea.[l]
9"The enemy boasted,
'I will pursue,[m] I will overtake
them.
I will divide the spoils;[n]
I will gorge myself on them.
I will draw my sword
and my hand will destroy them.'
10But you blew with your breath,[o]
and the sea covered them.
They sank like lead
in the mighty waters.[p]
11"Who among the gods is like
you,[q] O LORD?
Who is like you—
majestic in holiness,[r]
awesome in glory,[s]
working wonders?[t]
12You stretched out[u] your right
hand
and the earth swallowed them.[v]
13"In your unfailing love you will
lead[w]
the people you have redeemed.[x]
In your strength you will guide
them
to your holy dwelling.[y]
14The nations will hear and
tremble;[z]
anguish[a] will grip the people of
Philistia.[b]
15The chiefs[c] of Edom[d] will be
terrified,
the leaders of Moab will be
seized with trembling,[e]
the people[b] of Canaan will melt[f]
away;
16 terror[g] and dread will fall upon
them.
By the power of your arm
they will be as still as a
stone[h]—
until your people pass by, O LORD,
until the people you bought[c][i]
pass by.[j]

14:31 [n]Ex 20:18; Dt 31:13; Jos 4:24; 1Sa 12:18; Ps 76:7; 112:1 [o]S Ex 4:5; Ps 22:4; 40:3; 106:12; Jn 2:11; 11:45 **15:1** [p]Nu 21:17; Jdg 5:1; 2Sa 22:1; 1Ch 16:9; Job 36:24; Ps 59:16; 105:2; Rev 15:3 [q]Jdg 5:3; Ps 13:6; 21:13; 27:6; 61:8; 104:33; 106:12; Isa 12:5,6; 42:10; 44:23 [r]Dt 11:4; Ps 76:6; Jer 51:21 [s]S Ex 14:27 **15:2** [t]Ps 18:1; 59:17 [u]S Ge 45:7; Ex 14:13; Ps 18:2, 46; 25:5; 27:1; 62:2; 118:14; Isa 12:2; 33:2; Jnh 2:9; Hab 3:18 [v]S Ge 28:21 [w]Dt 10:21; 2Sa 22:47; Ps 22:3; 30:1; 34:3; 35:27; 99:5; 103:19; 107:32; 108:5; 109:1; 118:28; 145:11; 148:14; Isa 24:15; 25:1; Jer 17:14; Da 4:37 **15:3** [x]S Ex 14:14; Rev 19:11 [y]S Ex 3:15 **15:4** [z]Ex 14:6-7; Jer 51:21 **15:5** [a]S Ex 14:28 [b]ver 10; Ne 9:11 **15:6** [c]Ps 16:11; 17:7; 21:8; 63:8; 74:11; 77:10; 89:13; 98:1; 118:15; 138:7 [d]S Ex 3:20; S Job 40:14 [e]Nu 24:8; 1Sa 2:10; Ps 2:9 **15:7** [f]Dt 33:26; Ps 150:2 [g]Ps 2:5; 78:49-50; Jer 12:13; 25:38 [h]Ex 24:17; Dt 4:24; 9:3; Ps 18:8; 59:13; Heb 12:29 **15:8** [i]S Ex 14:21; Ps 18:15 [j]Jos 3:13; Ps 78:13; Isa 43:16 [k]S Ex 14:22 [l]Ps 46:2 **15:9** [m]Ex 14:5-9; Dt 28:45; Ps 7:5; La 1:3 [n]Jdg 5:30; Isa 9:3; 53:12; Lk 11:22 **15:10** [o]Job 4:9; 15:30; Isa 11:4; 30:33; 40:7 [p]ver 5; Ne 9:11; Ps 29:3; 32:6; 77:19 **15:11** [q]S Ex 8:10; Ps 77:13; S Isa 46:5 [r]Lev 19:2; 1Sa 2:2; 1Ch 16:29; Ps 99:3; 110:3; Isa 6:3; Rev 4:8 [s]S Ex 14:4; Ps 4:2; 8:1; 26:8; Isa 35:2; 40:5 [t]S Ex 3:20 **15:12** [u]S Ex 7:5 [v]Nu 16:32; 26:10; Dt 11:6; Ps 106:17 **15:13** [w]Ne 9:12; Ps 77:20 [x]S Ex 6:6; Job 33:28; Ps 71:23; 106:10; Isa 1:27; 41:14; 43:14; 44:22-24; 51:10; 63:9; Tit 2:14 [y]ver 17; Ps 68:16; 76:2; 78:54 **15:14** [z]ver 16; Ex 23:27; Dt 2:25; Jos 2:9; 5:1; 9:24; 1Sa 4:7; Est 8:17; Ps 48:6; 96:9; 99:1; 114:7; Eze 38:20 [a]Isa 13:8 [b]Ps 83:7 **15:15** [c]S Ge 36:15 [d]Dt 2:4 [e]Nu 22:3; Ps 114:7 [f]Jos 2:9,24 **15:16** [g]S ver 14; S Ge 35:5 [h]1Sa 25:37 [i]Ps 74:2; 2Pe 2:1 [j]Dt 2:4

[a] *4* Hebrew *Yam Suph*; that is, Sea of Reeds; also in verse 22 [b] *15* Or *rulers* [c] *16* Or *created*

"put their trust in him." When we receive a true revelation of God's majesty and his judgment against sin, we will follow him in faith while growing in the fear of God.

15:1–18 THEN MOSES . . . SANG THIS SONG. This song celebrates God's victory at the Red Sea over Egyptian powers. It is a hymn of praise and thanksgiving to God for his majesty, military might and faithfulness to his people. The deliverance out of Egypt foreshadows and prophesies the victory of God's people over Satan and the antichrist during the last days; so it is that one of the songs of the redeemed is called the "song of Moses" (Rev 15:3).

17You will bring[k] them in and
plant[l] them
on the mountain[m] of your
inheritance—
the place, O LORD, you made for
your dwelling,[n]
the sanctuary,[o] O Lord, your
hands established.
18The LORD will reign
for ever and ever."[p]

19When Pharaoh's horses, chariots
and horsemen[d] went into the sea,[q]
the LORD brought the waters of the sea
back over them, but the Israelites
walked through the sea on dry
ground.[r] 20Then Miriam[s] the prophetess,[t] Aaron's sister, took a tambourine in her hand, and all the women followed her, with tambourines[u] and
dancing.[v] 21Miriam sang[w] to them:

"Sing to the LORD,
for he is highly exalted.
The horse and its rider[x]
Dt 8:10 he has hurled into the sea."[y]

The Waters of Marah and Elim

22Then Moses led Israel from the
Red Sea and they went into the
Desert[z] of Shur.[a] For three days they
traveled in the desert without finding
water.[b] 23When they came to Marah,
they could not drink its water because
it was bitter. (That is why the place is
called Marah.[e][c]) 24So the people
grumbled[d] against Moses, saying,
"What are we to drink?"[e]
25Then Moses cried out[f] to the
LORD, and the LORD showed him a piece
of wood. He threw[g] it into the water,
and the water became sweet.

There the LORD made a decree and a
law for them, and there he tested[h]
them. 26He said, "If you listen carefully
to the voice of the LORD your God and
do what is right in his eyes, if you pay
attention to his commands and keep[i]
all his decrees,[j] I will not bring on you
any of the diseases[k] I brought on the
Egyptians, for I am the LORD, who
heals[l] you."
27Then they came to Elim, where
there were twelve springs and seventy
palm trees, and they camped[m] there
near the water.

Manna and Quail

16 The whole Israelite community
set out from Elim and came to
the Desert of Sin,[n] which is between
Elim and Sinai, on the fifteenth day of
the second month after they had come
out of Egypt.[o] 2In the desert the
whole community grumbled[p] against
Moses and Aaron. 3The Israelites said
to them, "If only we had died by the
LORD's hand in Egypt![q] There we sat
around pots of meat and ate all the
food[r] we wanted, but you have
brought us out into this desert to
starve this entire assembly to
death."[s]
4Then the LORD said to Moses, "I will

15:17 [k] Ex 23:20; 32:34; 33:12 [l] 2Sa 7:10; Ps 44:2; 80:8,15; Isa 5:2; 60:21; Jer 2:21; 11:17; 24:6; Am 9:15 [m] Dt 33:19; Ps 2:6; 3:4; 15:1; 78:54, 68; 133:3; Da 9:16; Joel 2:1; Ob 1:16; Zep 3:11 [n] S ver 13; Ps 132:13-14 [o] Ps 78:69; 114:2 **15:18** [p] S Ge 21:33; Ps 9:7; 29:10; 55:19; 66:7; 80:1; 102:12; 145:13; La 5:19 **15:19** [q] S Ex 14:28 [r] S Ex 14:22 **15:20** [s] ver 21; Ex 2:4; Nu 12:1; 20:1; 26:59; 1Ch 4:17; 6:3 [t] Jdg 4:4; 2Ki 22:14; 2Ch 34:22; Ne 6:14; Isa 8:3; Eze 13:17 [u] S Ge 31:27; 1Sa 18:6; Ps 81:2; Isa 30:32 [v] S Ge 4:21; Jdg 11:34; 21:21; 1Sa 18:6; 2Sa 6:5, 14,16; Ps 30:11; 149:3; 150:4; SS 6:13; Jer 31:4, 13 **15:21** [w] 1Sa 18:7 [x] Am 2:15; Hag 2:22 [y] S Ex 14:27 **15:22** [z] Ps 78:52 [a] S Ge 16:7 [b] Ex 17:1,3; Nu 20:2,5; 33:14; Ps 107:5 **15:23** [c] Nu 33:8; Ru 1:20 **15:24** [d] S Ex 14:12; 16:2; 7:3; Nu 14:2; Jos 9:18; Ps 78:18,42; 106:13,25; Eze 16:43 [e] Mt 6:31 **15:25** [f] S Ex 14:10 [g] 2Ki 2:21; 4:41; 6:6 [h] S Ge 22:1; Jdg 3:4; Job 23:10; Ps 81:7; Isa 48:10 **15:26** [i] Ex 23:22; Dt 11:13; 15:5; 28:1; Jer 11:6 [j] Ex 19:5-6; 20:2-17; Dt 7:12 [k] Dt 7:15; 28:27,58-60; 32:39; 1Sa 5:6; Ps 30:2; 41:3-4; 103:3 [l] Ex 23:25-26; 2Ki 20:5; Ps 25:11; 103:3; 107:20; Jer 30:17; Hos 11:3 **15:27** [m] Nu 33:9 **16:1** [n] Ex 17:1; Nu 33:11,12 [o] S Ex 6:6; 12:1-2 **16:2** [p] S Ex 15:24; 1Co 10:10 **16:3** [q] Ex 17:3; Nu 14:2; 20:3 [r] Nu 11:4,34; Dt 12:20; Ps 78:18; 106:14; Jer 44:17 [s] S Ge 47:15; Dt 8:3

[d] *19* Or *charioteers* [e] *23* *Marah* means *bitter.*

15:20 PROPHETESS. Miriam is called a "prophetess" because she moved in the Spirit of prophecy and spoke a message from God to the people (see Nu 12:2,6; cf. Jdg 4:4; 2Ki 22:14; Isa 8:3; Lk 2:36; see article on THE PROPHET IN THE OLD TESTAMENT, p. 986).

15:26 I AM THE LORD, WHO HEALS YOU. If the Israelites earnestly listened to and obeyed God, he would permit none of the diseases or plagues he brought on the Egyptians to afflict them. This promise shows that God desires to heal his people rather than to inflict illness and disease on them (see also 23:25; Dt 7:15; Ps 103:3; 107:20; Eze 18:23,32; 33:11). For God's promise of healing under the new covenant, see the article on DIVINE HEALING, p. 1420.

16:2 GRUMBLED AGAINST MOSES. The Israelites grumbled against Moses and God for the third time (cf. 14:10–12; 15:24). In spite of all that God had done for them, they were quick to lose faith in his goodness, his wisdom and his will for their lives (also see 17:3; Nu 14:2; 16:11,41). Paul warns NT believers not to follow Israel's example (1Co 10:10). When serious problems arise, instead of accusing God of neglect and unfaithfulness, we should commit our way to him and humbly ask for help in resolving the problem, trusting him to act on our behalf.

16:4 BREAD FROM HEAVEN. This "bread from heaven" is called "manna" (v. 15). It was a special food miraculously sent from God to feed the people after the exodus from Egypt. It was a white substance that resembled frost, took the form of thin flakes, and tasted like honey (v. 14,31; Nu 11:9). The supply of manna ceased when the Israelites entered the promised land and other food became available (Jos 5:12). Manna was a type or foreshadowing of Jesus Christ, who as "the true bread from heaven" (Jn 6:32; cf. Rev 2:17) gives eternal life (Jn 6:33,51,58).

rain down bread from heaven[t] for you.
The people are to go out each day and
gather enough for that day. In this way
I will test[u] them and see whether they
will follow my instructions. 5On the
sixth day they are to prepare what they
bring in, and that is to be twice[v] as
much as they gather on the other
days."
6So Moses and Aaron said to all the
Israelites, "In the evening you will
know that it was the LORD who brought
you out of Egypt,[w] 7and in the morning you will see the glory[x] of the LORD,
because he has heard your grumbling[y] against him. Who are we, that
you should grumble against us?"[z]
8Moses also said, "You will know that
it was the LORD when he gives you meat
to eat in the evening and all the bread
you want in the morning, because he
has heard your grumbling[a] against
him. Who are we? You are not grumbling against us, but against the
LORD."[b]
9Then Moses told Aaron, "Say to the
entire Israelite community, 'Come before the LORD, for he has heard your
grumbling.' "
10While Aaron was speaking to the
whole Israelite community, they
looked toward the desert, and there
was the glory[c] of the LORD appearing
in the cloud.[d]
11The LORD said to Moses, 12"I have
heard the grumbling[e] of the Israelites. Tell them, 'At twilight you will eat
meat, and in the morning you will be
filled with bread. Then you will know
that I am the LORD your God.' "[f]
13That evening quail[g] came and
covered the camp, and in the morning
there was a layer of dew[h] around the
camp. 14When the dew was gone, thin
flakes like frost[i] on the ground appeared on the desert floor. 15When the
Israelites saw it, they said to each other, "What is it?" For they did not
know[j] what it was.
Moses said to them, "It is the
bread[k] the LORD has given you to eat.
16This is what the LORD has commanded: 'Each one is to gather as much as
he needs. Take an omer[f][l] for each
person you have in your tent.' "
17The Israelites did as they were
told; some gathered much, some little.
18And when they measured it by the
omer, he who gathered much did not
have too much, and he who gathered
little did not have too little.[m] Each one
gathered as much as he needed.
19Then Moses said to them, "No one
is to keep any of it until morning."[n]
20However, some of them paid no attention to Moses; they kept part of it
until morning, but it was full of maggots and began to smell.[o] So Moses
was angry[p] with them.
21Each morning everyone gathered
as much as he needed, and when the
sun grew hot, it melted away. 22On the
sixth day, they gathered twice[q] as
much—two omers[g] for each person—
and the leaders of the community[r]
came and reported this to Moses. 23He
said to them, "This is what the LORD
commanded: 'Tomorrow is to be a day
of rest, a holy Sabbath[s] to the LORD.
So bake what you want to bake and boil
what you want to boil. Save whatever
is left and keep it until morning.' "
24So they saved it until morning, as
Moses commanded, and it did not stink
or get maggots in it. 25"Eat it today,"
Moses said, "because today is a Sabbath to the LORD. You will not find any
of it on the ground today. 26Six days
you are to gather it, but on the seventh
day, the Sabbath,[t] there will not be
any."
27Nevertheless, some of the people
went out on the seventh day to gather
it, but they found none. 28Then the
LORD said to Moses, "How long will
you[h] refuse to keep my commands[u]
and my instructions? 29Bear in mind
that the LORD has given you the Sabbath; that is why on the sixth day he
gives you bread for two days. Everyone
is to stay where he is on the seventh

16:4 [t] ver 14-15; Dt 8:3; Ne 9:15; Ps 78:24; 105:40; S Jn 6:31* [u] S Ge 22:1
16:5 [v] ver 22; Lev 25:21
16:6 [w] S Ex 6:6
16:7 [x] ver 10; Ex 24:16; 29:43; 33:18,22; 40:34; Lev 9:6; Nu 16:19, 42; Dt 5:24; 1Ki 8:11; Ps 63:2; Isa 6:3; 35:2; 40:5; 44:23; 60:1; 66:18; Eze 1:28; 10:4; 43:5; Hab 2:14; Hag 2:7; Jn 11:40 [y] ver 12; Nu 11:1, 18; 14:2,27,28; 17:5 [z] Nu 16:11
16:8 [a] ver 7 [b] Nu 23:21; Dt 33:5; Jdg 8:23; 1Sa 8:7; 12:12; S Mt 10:40; Ro 13:2; 1Th 4:8
16:10 [c] S ver 7; Jn 11:4 [d] Ex 13:21; 40:34-35; 1Ki 8:10; 2Ch 7:1; Eze 10:4
16:12 [e] S ver 7 [f] S Ex 6:2; S 20:2
16:13 [g] Nu 11:31; Ps 78:27-28; 105:40; 106:15 [h] Nu 11:9
16:14 [i] ver 31; Nu 11:7-9; Dt 8:3, 16; Ps 105:40
16:15 [j] Dt 8:16 [k] S ver 4; Ne 9:20; S Jn 6:31
16:16 [l] ver 32,36
16:18 [m] 2Co 8:15*
16:19 [n] ver 23; Ex 12:10
16:20 [o] ver 24 [p] Ex 32:19
16:22 [q] S ver 5 [r] Ex 34:31
16:23 [s] S Ge 2:3; S Ex 20:8; Dt 5:13-14
16:26 [t] ver 23
16:28 [u] Jos 9:14; Ps 78:10; 106:13; 107:11; 119:1; Jer 32:23

[f] *16* That is, probably about 2 quarts (about 2 liters); also in verses 18, 32, 33 and 36
[g] *22* That is, probably about 4 quarts (about 4.5 liters)
[h] *28* The Hebrew is plural.

16:4 IN THIS WAY I WILL TEST THEM. The people were given exact instructions about the bread from heaven in order to test their willingness to trust and obey God (cf. Dt 8:2–3). In the same way God sometimes orders the circumstances of our lives to test our faith and loyalty to him.

16:21 EACH MORNING. God gave orders to gather only enough for each day in order to teach the people that their daily existence depended exclusively on his gift (cf. Mt 6:11).

day; no one is to go out." 30So the people rested on the seventh day.
31The people of Israel called the
bread manna.[i][v] It was white like coriander seed and tasted like wafers
made with honey. 32Moses said, "This
is what the LORD has commanded:
'Take an omer of manna and keep it for
the generations to come, so they can
see the bread I gave you to eat in the
desert when I brought you out of
Egypt.'"
33So Moses said to Aaron, "Take a
jar and put an omer of manna[w] in it.
Then place it before the LORD to be kept
for the generations to come."
34As the LORD commanded Moses,
Aaron put the manna in front of the
Testimony,[x] that it might be kept.
35The Israelites ate manna[y] forty
years,[z] until they came to a land that
was settled; they ate manna until they
reached the border of Canaan.[a]
36(An omer[b] is one tenth of an
ephah.)[c]

Water From the Rock

17 The whole Israelite community
set out from the Desert of
Sin,[d] traveling from place to place as
the LORD commanded. They camped at
Rephidim,[e] but there was no water[f]
for the people to drink. 2So they quarreled with Moses and said, "Give us
water[g] to drink."[h]
Moses replied, "Why do you quarrel
with me? Why do you put the LORD to
the test?"[i]
3But the people were thirsty[j] for
water there, and they grumbled[k]
against Moses. They said, "Why did
you bring us up out of Egypt to make
us and our children and livestock die[l]
of thirst?"
4Then Moses cried out to the LORD,
"What am I to do with these people?
They are almost ready to stone[m] me."
5The LORD answered Moses, "Walk
on ahead of the people. Take with you
some of the elders of Israel and take in
your hand the staff[n] with which you
struck the Nile,[o] and go. 6I will stand
there before you by the rock at Horeb.[p] Strike[q] the rock, and water[r]
will come out of it for the people to
drink." So Moses did this in the sight
of the elders of Israel. 7And he called
the place Massah[j][s] and Meribah[k][t]
because the Israelites quarreled and
because they tested the LORD saying,
"Is the LORD among us or not?"

The Amalekites Defeated

8The Amalekites[u] came and attacked the Israelites at Rephidim.[v]
9Moses said to Joshua,[w] "Choose
some of our men and go out to fight the
Amalekites. Tomorrow I will stand on
top of the hill with the staff[x] of God in
my hands."
10So Joshua fought the Amalekites
as Moses had ordered, and Moses, Aaron and Hur[y] went to the top of the hill.
11As long as Moses held up his hands,
the Israelites were winning,[z] but

16:31 [v]S ver 14 **16:33** [w]Heb 9:4; Rev 2:17 **16:34** [x]Ex 25:16, 21,22; 27:21; 31:18; 40:20; Lev 16:13; Nu 1:50; 7:89; 10:11; 17:4,10; Dt 10:2; 1Ki 8:9; 2Ch 5:10 **16:35** [y]Jn 6:31, 49 [z]Nu 14:33; 33:38; Dt 1:3; 2:7; 8:2-4; Jos 5:6; Jdg 3:11; Ne 9:21; Ps 95:10; Am 5:25 [a]Jos 5:12 **16:36** [b]S ver 16 [c]Lev 5:11; 6:20; Nu 5:15; 15:4; 28:5 **17:1** [d]S Ex 16:1 [e]ver 8; Ex 19:2; Nu 33:15 [f]Nu 20:5; 21:5; 33:14 **17:2** [g]Nu 20:2; 33:14; Ps 107:5 [h]S Ex 14:12 [i]Dt 6:16; Ps 78:18,41; 106:14; Mt 4:7; 1Co 10:9 **17:3** [j]S Ex 15:22 [k]S Ex 15:24 [l]S Ex 14:11 **17:4** [m]Nu 14:10; 1Sa 30:6; S Jn 8:59 **17:5** [n]S Ex 4:2; S 10:12-13 [o]Ex 7:20 **17:6** [p]S Ex 3:1 [q]Nu 20:8 [r]Nu 20:11; Dt 8:15; Jdg 15:19; 2Ki 3:20; Ne 9:15; Ps 74:15; 78:15-16; 105:41; 107:35; 114:8; Isa 30:25; 35:6; 43:19; 48:21; 1Co 10:4 **17:7** [s]Dt 6:16; 9:22; 33:8; Ps 95:8 [t]Nu 20:13,24; 27:14; Ps 81:7; 106:32 **17:8** [u]S Ge 36:12 [v]S ver 1 **17:9** [w]Ex 24:13; 32:17; 33:11; Nu 11:28; 27:22; Dt 1:38; Jos 1:1; Ac 7:45 [x]S Ex 4:17 **17:10** [y]ver 10-12; Ex 24:14; 31:2 **17:11** [z]Jas 5:16

[i] *31 Manna* means *What is it?* (see verse 15).
[j] *7 Massah* means *testing.* [k] *7 Meribah* means *quarreling.*

16:30 RESTED ON THE SEVENTH DAY. Through his instructions regarding the seventh day (vv. 22–30), God wanted to emphasize that his people were to respond by resting, just as he rested on the seventh day of creation (Ge 2:1–4). God knew, from the very beginning, that if his people failed to observe the Sabbath, they would deplete both their physical and spiritual strength by continual earthly worries and pursuits; this failure would result in spiritual, godly concerns being relegated to a place of least importance in their lives (see Mt 12:1, note; Lk 6:2–10, note).

17:6 STRIKE THE ROCK. In the NT, this rock is identified with Jesus Christ, the spring of living water (1Co 10:4). As the rock was struck, so was Christ smitten by death on the cross (Isa 53:5). As Christ was the source of blessing for Israel, he is the source of blessing and the giver of the Holy Spirit for the church (cf. Ps 105:41–12; Isa 53:4–5; Jn 7:37–38; 20:22; Ac 2:1–4).

17:9 JOSHUA. The man chosen to succeed Moses as leader of Israel makes his first appearance here in the Biblical narrative. Joshua means "the LORD saves," or "Yahweh is Savior"; the Greek form of the name is "Jesus" (see Mt 1:21, note). Appropriately enough, the man who would later conquer Canaan appears first in a military role. God was providentially preparing him for his later wars against the Canaanites.

17:11 MOSES HELD UP HIS HANDS. By holding up his hands to the Lord, Moses reveals his dependence on and faith in God. (1) Israel's strength and victory lay only in a continuous approach to God in prayer, faith and obedience. When Moses' prayer ceased, the flow of divine power to God's people ceased (cf. Heb 7:25, note). (2) This divine principle continues to operate under the new covenant. If we fail to call on God daily in prayer, then the divine life, protection, blessing and grace will begin to stop flowing toward us. Our

whenever he lowered his hands, the
Amalekites were winning. 12When Moses' hands grew tired, they took a
stone and put it under him and he sat
on it. Aaron and Hur held his hands
up—one on one side, one on the other—so that his hands remained steady
till sunset.[a] 13So Joshua overcame
the Amalekite[b] army with the sword.
14Then the LORD said to Moses,
"Write[c] this on a scroll as something
to be remembered and make sure that
Joshua hears it, because I will completely blot out[d] the memory of Amalek[e] from under heaven."
15Moses built an altar[f] and
called[g] it The LORD is my Banner.
16He said, "For hands were lifted up to
the throne of the LORD. The[1] LORD will
be at war against the Amalekites[h]
from generation to generation."[i]

Jethro Visits Moses

18 Now Jethro,[j] the priest of Midian[k] and father-in-law of Moses, heard of everything God had done
for Moses and for his people Israel,
and how the LORD had brought Israel
out of Egypt.[l]
2After Moses had sent away his wife
Zipporah,[m] his father-in-law Jethro received her 3and her two sons.[n] One
son was named Gershom,[m] for Moses
said, "I have become an alien in a foreign land";[o] 4and the other was
named Eliezer,[n][p] for he said, "My father's God was my helper;[q] he saved
me from the sword of Pharaoh."
5Jethro, Moses' father-in-law, together with Moses' sons and wife,
came to him in the desert, where he
was camped near the mountain[r] of
God. 6Jethro had sent word to him, "I,
your father-in-law Jethro, am coming to
you with your wife and her two sons."
7So Moses went out to meet his father-in-law and bowed down[s] and
kissed[t] him. They greeted each other
and then went into the tent. 8Moses
told his father-in-law about everything
the LORD had done to Pharaoh and the
Egyptians for Israel's sake and about
all the hardships[u] they had met along
the way and how the LORD had saved[v]
them.
9Jethro was delighted to hear about
all the good things[w] the LORD had done
for Israel in rescuing them from the
hand of the Egyptians. 10He said,
"Praise be to the LORD,[x] who rescued
you from the hand of the Egyptians and
of Pharaoh, and who rescued the people from the hand of the Egyptians.
11Now I know that the LORD is greater
than all other gods,[y] for he did this to
those who had treated Israel arrogantly."[z] 12Then Jethro, Moses' father-in-
law,[a] brought a burnt offering[b] and
other sacrifices[c] to God, and Aaron
came with all the elders of Israel to eat
bread[d] with Moses' father-in-law in
the presence[e] of God.
13The next day Moses took his seat
to serve as judge for the people, and
they stood around him from morning
till evening. 14When his father-in-law
saw all that Moses was doing for the
people, he said, "What is this you are
doing for the people? Why do you alone
sit as judge, while all these people
stand around you from morning till
evening?"
15Moses answered him, "Because
the people come to me to seek God's
will.[f] 16Whenever they have a dispute,[g] it is brought to me, and I decide
between the parties and inform them of
God's decrees and laws."[h]
17Moses' father-in-law replied,
"What you are doing is not good. 18You
and these people who come to you will
only wear yourselves out. The work is
too heavy for you; you cannot handle it
alone.[i] 19Listen now to me and I will
give you some advice, and may God be
with you.[j] You must be the people's
representative before God and bring

17:12 [a] Jos 8:26 **17:13** [b] ver 8 **17:14** [c] Ex 24:4; 34:27; Nu 33:2; Dt 31:9; Job 19:23; Isa 30:8; Jer 36:2; 45:1; 51:60 [d] Ex 32:33; Dt 29:20; Job 18:17; Ps 9:5; 34:16; 109:15; Eze 18:4 [e] ver 13; S Ge 36:12; Nu 24:7; Jdg 3:13; 1Sa 30:17-18; Ps 83:7 **17:15** [f] S Ge 8:20 [g] S Ge 22:14 **17:16** [h] Nu 24:7; 1Sa 15:8,32; 1Ch 4:43; Est 3:1; 8:3; 9:24 [i] Est 9:5 **18:1** [j] S Ex 2:18 [k] S Ex 2:16 [l] S Ex 6:6 **18:2** [m] S Ex 2:21 **18:3** [n] S Ex 4:20; Ac 7:29 [o] Ex 2:22 **18:4** [p] 1Ch 23:15 [q] S Ge 49:25; S Dt 33:29 **18:5** [r] S Ex 3:1 **18:7** [s] S Ge 17:3; S 43:28 [t] S Ge 29:13 **18:8** [u] Nu 20:14; Ne 9:32 [v] Ex 15:6, 16; Ps 81:7 **18:9** [w] Jos 21:45; 1Ki 8:66; Ne 9:25; Ps 145:7; Isa 63:7 **18:10** [x] S Ge 9:26; S 24:27 **18:11** [y] S Ex 12:12; S 1Ch 16:25 [z] S Ex 1:10; S Lk 1:51 **18:12** [a] S Ex 3:1 [b] Ex 10:25; 20:24; Lev 1:2-9 [c] Ge 31:54; Ex 24:5 [d] S Ge 26:30 [e] Dt 12:7 **18:15** [f] S ver 19; S Ge 25:22 **18:16** [g] Ex 24:14 [h] ver 15; Lev 24:12; Nu 15:34; Dt 1:17; 2Ch 19:7; Pr 24:23; Mal 2:9 **18:18** [i] Nu 11:11, 14,17; Dt 1:9,12 **18:19** [j] Ex 3:12

[1] 16 Or *"Because a hand was against the throne of the LORD, the* [m] 3 *Gershom* sounds like the Hebrew for *an alien there.* [n] 4 *Eliezer* means *my God is helper.*

only hope of victory lies in continually approaching the throne of grace through Christ, that we might receive God's power and grace to help us in times of need (Heb 4:16; 7:25; see Mt 7:7–8, note).

18:2 JETHRO RECEIVED HER. Moses may have sent his wife Zipporah and his two sons back to Jethro during the time of his conflict with Pharaoh.

18:11 NOW I KNOW THAT THE LORD IS GREATER. The word "know" frequently occurs in the book of Exodus. Moses and the Israelites needed to know who God was and to understand his great power. These manifestations of God's power and deliverance became a witness to Jethro so he could say, "Now I know," and could then join in worshiping the Lord. These things are recorded so that we too may come to know and worship the one true God.

their disputes[k] to him. 20Teach them
the decrees and laws,[l] and show them
the way to live[m] and the duties they
are to perform.[n] 21But select capable
men[o] from all the people—men who
fear[p] God, trustworthy men who hate
dishonest gain[q]—and appoint them
as officials[r] over thousands, hundreds, fifties and tens. 22Have them
serve as judges for the people at all
times, but have them bring every difficult case[s] to you; the simple cases
they can decide themselves. That will
make your load lighter, because they
will share[t] it with you. 23If you do this
and God so commands, you will be able
to stand the strain, and all these people will go home satisfied."
24Moses listened to his father-in-law
and did everything he said. 25He chose
capable men from all Israel and made
them leaders[u] of the people, officials
over thousands, hundreds, fifties and
tens.[v] 26They served as judges[w] for
the people at all times. The difficult
cases[x] they brought to Moses, but the
simple ones they decided themselves.[y]
27Then Moses sent his father-in-law
on his way, and Jethro returned to his
own country.[z]

18:19 [k]ver 15; Nu 27:5 **18:20** [l]Dt 4:1,5; 5:1; Ps 119:12,26, 68 [m]Ps 143:8 [n]S Ge 39:11 **18:21** [o]S Ge 47:6; Ac 6:3 [p]S Ge 22:12 [q]Ex 23:8; Dt 16:19; 1Sa 12:3; Ps 15:5; Pr 17:23; 28:8; Ecc 7:7; Eze 18:8; 22:12 [r]Nu 1:16; 7:2; 10:4; Dt 16:18; Ezr 7:25 **18:22** [s]Lev 24:11; Dt 1:17-18 [t]Nu 11:17; Dt 1:9 **18:25** [u]Nu 1:16; 7:2; 11:16; Dt 16:18 [v]Dt 1:13-15 **18:26** [w]Dt 16:18; 2Ch 19:5; Ezr 7:25 [x]Dt 1:17 [y]ver 22 **18:27** [z]Nu 10:29-30

19:1 [a]S Ex 6:6 [b]Nu 1:1; 3:14; 33:15 **19:2** [c]S Ex 17:1 [d]S ver 17; S Ex 3:1; Dt 5:2-4 **19:3** [e]Ex 20:21 [f]S Ex 3:4; S 25:22; Ac 7:38 **19:4** [g]Dt 29:2; Jos 24:7 [h]Dt 32:11; Ps 103:5; Isa 40:31; Jer 4:13; 48:40; Rev 12:14 [i]Dt 33:12;

At Mount Sinai

19 In the third month after the Israelites left Egypt[a]—on the
very day—they came to the Desert of
Sinai.[b] 2After they set out from Rephidim,[c] they entered the Desert of Sinai,
and Israel camped there in the desert
in front of the mountain.[d]
3Then Moses went up to God,[e] and
the LORD called[f] to him from the
mountain and said, "This is what you
are to say to the house of Jacob and
what you are to tell the people of Israel: 4'You yourselves have seen what I
did to Egypt,[g] and how I carried you
on eagles' wings[h] and brought you to
myself.[i] 5Now if you obey me fully[j]
and keep my covenant,[k] then out of all
nations you will be my treasured possession.[l] Although the whole earth[m]
is mine, 6you[o] will be for me a kingdom of priests[n] and a holy nation.'[o]
These are the words you are to speak
to the Israelites."

Isa 31:5; Eze 16:6 **19:5** [j]Ex 15:26; Dt 6:3; Ps 78:10; Jer 7:23 [k]S Ge 17:9; S Ex 3:1 [l]S Ex 8:22; S 34:9; S Dt 8:1; S Tit 2:14 [m]S Ex 9:29; 1Co 10:26 **19:6** [n]Isa 61:6; 66:21; S 1Pe 2:5 [o]Ge 18:19; Lev 11:44-45; Dt 4:37; 7:6; 26:19; 28:9; 29:13; 33:3; Isa 4:3; 62:12; Jer 2:3; Am 3:2

[o] 5,6 Or *possession, for the whole earth is mine.* 6*You*

18:21 SELECT CAPABLE MEN. Jethro's counsel that Moses delegate authority to godly men in order to do God's work more efficiently still applies today. Several qualifications for leaders of God's people are mentioned in this verse: they must be (1) capable people, (2) people who fear God, (3) people instructed in truth and strongly committed to it, and (4) people who hate dishonest gain, and are thus free from covetousness and the love of money.

19:1 THE DESERT OF SINAI. Ch. 19 records the establishment of God's covenant with the people of Israel at Mount Sinai. That covenant is an extension of the covenant with Abraham and his descendants (see Ge 15:6,18, notes; 17:7, note; 22:18, note). (1) This covenant was based on Israel's prior reconciliation to God and their ongoing fellowship with him. It defined the conditions by which Israel would remain God's treasured possession, continue in his blessing and carry out his will for the nation (see Ge 12:2–3; 26:4).

(2) God intended that Israel be a unique people, chosen and set apart to him for this purpose. The people were to respond in obedience and gratitude to God by seeking to keep the commandments and by offering the prescribed sacrifices of God's covenant. As a result, they would remain God's special people (cf. Am 3:2; 9:7)—a kingdom of priests who were holy and pure (see v. 6, note; see article on GOD'S COVENANT WITH THE ISRAELITES, p. 290).

19:4 I CARRIED YOU ON EAGLES' WINGS. As the mother eagle catches her young on her wings to keep them from crashing while learning to fly, so God was caring for Israel and bringing her not just to Sinai, but to himself (cf. Dt 32:11; Isa 43:1–4). This expression demonstrates God's love for Israel and serves as the basis for their obedience and covenant obligation to him (see next note).

19:5 IF YOU OBEY ME FULLY. Israel's continued election as the people of God was conditioned on their obedience to him as their Lord; this is indicated in the "if . . . then" construction of this verse. And God expected this obedience, so essential in fulfilling his future purposes for them (vv. 5–6), to come from hearts of gratitude responding to his love and care demonstrated especially in their redemption from Egypt (see previous note; see Dt 6:5). Similarly, the principle of obedience is an essential element in our relationship with Christ under the new covenant (see Jn 8:31; 14:21; Ro 4:12; Heb 3:7–19).

19:5 MY TREASURED POSSESSION. Israel was to be God's own special treasure (cf. Dt 4:10; Am 3:2; 9:7). Even though all nations are accountable to God because he is their Creator, Israel was to have a unique relationship to God because he was their Redeemer. This purpose for Israel foreshadowed God's purpose for the church (1Co 3:16; Tit 2:14; 1Pe 2:5,9).

19:6 A KINGDOM OF PRIESTS AND A HOLY

7So Moses went back and summoned the elders[p] of the people and
set before them all the words the LORD
had commanded him to speak.[q] 8The
people all responded together, "We will
do everything the LORD has said."[r] So
Moses brought their answer back to
the LORD.
9The LORD said to Moses, "I am going to come to you in a dense cloud,[s]
so that the people will hear me speaking[t] with you and will always put
their trust[u] in you." Then Moses told
the LORD what the people had said.
10And the LORD said to Moses, "Go to
the people and consecrate[v] them today and tomorrow. Have them wash
their clothes[w] 11and be ready by the
third day,[x] because on that day the
LORD will come down[y] on Mount Sinai[z] in the sight of all the people.
12Put limits[a] for the people around
the mountain and tell them, 'Be careful
that you do not go up the mountain or
touch the foot of it. Whoever touches
the mountain shall surely be put to
death. 13He shall surely be stoned[b] or
shot with arrows; not a hand is to be
laid on him. Whether man or animal, he
shall not be permitted to live.' Only
when the ram's horn[c] sounds a long
blast may they go up to the mountain."[d]
14After Moses had gone down the
mountain to the people, he consecrated them, and they washed their
clothes.[e] 15Then he said to the people, "Prepare yourselves for the third
day. Abstain[f] from sexual relations."
16On the morning of the third day
there was thunder[g] and lightning,
with a thick cloud[h] over the mountain,
and a very loud trumpet blast.[i] Everyone in the camp trembled.[j] 17Then
Moses led the people out of the camp
to meet with God, and they stood at the
foot of the mountain.[k] 18Mount Sinai
was covered with smoke,[l] because
the LORD descended on it in fire.[m] The
smoke billowed up from it like smoke
from a furnace,[n] the whole mountain[p] trembled[o] violently, 19and the
sound of the trumpet grew louder and
louder. Then Moses spoke and the
voice[p] of God answered[q] him.[q]
20The LORD descended to the top of
Mount Sinai[r] and called Moses to the
top of the mountain. So Moses went up
21and the LORD said to him, "Go down
and warn the people so they do not
force their way through to see[s] the
LORD and many of them perish.[t]
22Even the priests, who approach[u]
the LORD, must consecrate[v] themselves, or the LORD will break out
against them."[w]
23Moses said to the LORD, "The people cannot come up Mount Sinai,[x] because you yourself warned us, 'Put limits[y] around the mountain and set it
apart as holy.'"
24The LORD replied, "Go down and
bring Aaron[z] up with you. But the
priests and the people must not force
their way through to come up to the
LORD, or he will break out against
them."[a]
25So Moses went down to the people
and told them.

The Ten Commandments

20:1-17pp — Dt 5:6-21

20 And God spoke[b] all these
words:[c]

19:7 [p] Ex 18:12; Lev 4:15; 9:1; Nu 16:25 [q] Ex 4:30; 1Sa 8:10 **19:8** [r] Ex 24:3,7; Dt 5:27; 26:17 **19:9** [s] ver 16; Ex 20:21; 24:15-16; 33:9; 34:5; Dt 4:11; 2Sa 22:10,12; 2Ch 6:1; Ps 18:11; 97:2; 99:7; Mt 17:5 [t] Dt 4:12, 36; Jn 12:29-30 [u] S Ex 4:5 **19:10** [v] ver 14,22; Lev 11:44; Nu 11:18; 1Sa 16:5; Joel 2:16; Heb 10:22 [w] S Ge 35:2; Rev 22:14 **19:11** [x] ver 16 [y] S Ge 11:5 [z] ver 3, 20; S Ex 3:1; 24:16; 31:18; 34:2,4,29,32; Lev 7:38; 26:46; 27:34; Nu 3:1; Dt 10:5; Ne 9:13; Gal 4:24-25 **19:12** [a] ver 23 **19:13** [b] Heb 12:20* [c] Jos 6:4; 1Ch 15:28; Ps 81:3; 98:6 [d] ver 21; Ex 34:3 **19:14** [e] S Ge 35:2 **19:15** [f] 1Sa 21:4; 1Co 7:5 **19:16** [g] 1Sa 2:10; Isa 29:6 [h] S ver 9 [i] Heb 12:18-19; Rev 4:1 [j] S Ge 3:10; 1Sa 13:7; 14:15; 28:5; Ps 99:1; Heb 12:21 **19:17** [k] S ver 2; Dt 4:11 **19:18** [l] Ex 20:18; Ps 104:32; Isa 6:4; Rev 15:8 [m] S Ex 3:2; 24:17; Lev 9:24; Dt 4:11, 24,33,36; 5:4; 9:3; 1Ki 18:24,38; 1Ch 21:26; 2Ch 7:1; Ps 18:8; Heb 12:18 [n] S Ge 19:28; Rev 9:2 [o] Jdg 5:5; 2Sa 22:8; Ps 18:7; 68:8; Isa 2:19; 5:25; 41:15; 64:1; Jer 4:24; 10:10; Mic 1:4; Na 1:5; Hab 3:6,10; Hag 2:6 **19:19** [p] S ver 9; Dt 4:33; Ne 9:13 [q] Ps 81:7 **19:20** [r] S ver 11 **19:21** [s] Ex 24:10-11; Nu 4:20; 1Sa 6:19 [t] S ver 13 **19:22** [u] Lev 10:3 [v] 1Sa 16:5; 2Ch 29:5; Joel 2:16 [w] ver 24; 2Sa 6:7 **19:23** [x] ver 11 [y] ver 12 **19:24** [z] Ex 24:1, 9 [a] ver 22 **20:1** [b] Dt 10:4 [c] Ne 9:13; Ps 119:9; 147:19; Mal 4:4

[p] 18 Most Hebrew manuscripts; a few Hebrew manuscripts and Septuagint *all the people*
[q] 19 Or *and God answered him with thunder*

NATION. As part of God's purpose for the Israelites in bringing them out of Egypt, they were to be a "kingdom of priests" (i.e., set apart and consecrated for God's service) and a "holy nation." Likewise, believers under the new covenant must be a kingdom of priests (1Pe 2:5–9; Rev 1:6; 5:10; 20:6) and a holy people, i.e., a people separated from the world's ungodly ways and walking in God's righteous ways and holy will (see Ac 9:13, note on the meaning of saint; see article on SANCTIFICATION, p. 1956).

19:16 THUNDER AND LIGHTNING. The awesome manifestations that accompanied God's visitation had several goals: (1) to demonstrate God's holiness, power and transcendence (v. 9); (2) to instill faith in God and establish the authority of his servant, Moses (v. 9); (3) to establish the fear of God in the hearts of the people so that they might not sin (v. 16; 20:20; cf. Heb 12:18–21); and (4) to impress upon the people that judgment and death would be the result of willful disobedience to God (vv. 12–25; cf. Heb 10:26–31).

20:1 AND GOD SPOKE ALL THESE WORDS. For general comments on the place of God's law in the OT, see article on THE OLD TESTAMENT LAW, p. 118.

THE OLD TESTAMENT LAW

***Ex 20:1–2** "And God spoke all these words: I am the* Lord *your God, who brought you out of Egypt, out of the land of slavery."*

Receiving God's law through their leader, Moses, was one of the most important aspects of the Israelites' experience at Mount Sinai. The Mosaic Law (Heb *torah*, meaning "teaching") can be divided into three categories: (a) the moral law, dealing with God's rules for holy living (Ex 20:1–17); (b) the civil law, dealing with Israel's legal and social life as a nation (Ex 21:1—23:33); and (c) the ceremonial law, dealing with the form and ritual of Israel's worship of the Lord, including the sacrificial system (Ex 24:12–31:18). Note the following regarding the nature and function of the OT law.

(1) The law was given in connection with the covenant that God made with his people; it set forth the covenant stipulations they were expected to obey in loyalty to the Lord God to whom they belonged. The Israelites formally accepted these covenant obligations (Ex 24:1–8; see article on GOD'S COVENANT WITH THE ISRAELITES, p. 290).

(2) Israel's obedience to the law was to be grounded in God's saving mercy and in his deliverance of the people (Ex 19:4). Note that the law was given after they had been saved by the blood of the Passover lamb and redeemed from slavery (Ex 20:2), and while they were living as pilgrims on the earth by God's grace (Ex 19:4).

(3) The law revealed God's will for his people's behavior (Ex 19:4–6; 20:1–17; 21:1—24:8) and prescribed blood sacrifices to atone for their sin (Lev 1:5; 16:33). The law was not designed as a way to obtain salvation for the unsaved; the people to whom it was given were already in a saved relationship with God (Ex 20:2). Rather, through the law they learned how God wanted them to live righteously toward both their Redeemer and their neighbor. The Israelites were expected to obey the law by God's grace in order to maintain and celebrate their faith relationship with him (Dt 28:1–2; 30:15–20).

(4) In both the OT and NT, a committed trust in God and his word (Ge 15:6) and a heartfelt love for him (Dt 6:5) formed the foundation for keeping God's commandments. Israel failed exactly at this point, for they often did not make believing in God, loving him with all their heart and desiring to walk in his ways their motive for fulfilling the law. Paul states that Israel did not attain the righteousness that the law intended because "they pursued it not by faith" (Ro 9:32).

(5) The law emphasized the eternal truth that obedience to God from a heart of love (see Ge 2:9, note; Dt 6:5, note) would result in a full life and in rich blessings from the Lord (cf. Ge 2:16, note; Dt 4:1,40; 5:33; 8:1; Ps 119:45; Ro 8:13; 1Jn 1:7).

(6) The law expressed God's nature and disposition, i.e., his love, goodness, justice, and hatred of evil. Israelite believers were expected to keep God's moral law because they had been created in his image (Lev 19:2).

(7) Salvation in the OT was never based on perfection in keeping all the commandments. Inherent in Israel's relationship with God was the sacrificial system that provided forgiveness for those who transgressed the commandment but who sincerely returned in repentance and faith to God's mercy and provision of blood atonement.

(8) The OT law and covenant were not complete, nor were they intended to be permanent. The law acted as a temporary guardian for God's people until Christ came (Gal 3:22–26). The old covenant has now been replaced by the new covenant, in which God has disclosed fully his plan of salvation through Jesus Christ (Ro 3:24–26; see Gal 3:19, note, for more on the nature and function of OT law).

(9) The law was given by God and added to the promise "because of transgressions" (Gal 3:19); i.e., it was designed (a) to regulate conduct, (b) to define what sin was, (c) to show Israel their inherent tendency to violate God's will and do evil, and (d) to awaken their sense of need for God's mercy, grace and redemption (cf. Ro 3:20; 5:20; 8:2).

2 "I am the LORD your God,[d]
who brought you out[e] of
Egypt,[f] out of the land of
slavery.[g]
3 "You shall have no other gods before[r] me.[h]
4 "You shall not make for yourself
an idol[i] in the form of anything in heaven above or on
the earth beneath or in the
waters below. 5 You shall not
bow down to them or wor-
ship[j] them; for I, the LORD
your God, am a jealous
God,[k] punishing the children for the sin of the fathers[l] to the third and
fourth generation[m] of those
who hate me, 6 but showing
love to a thousand[n] ⌊genera-
tions⌋ of those who love me
and keep my command-
ments.
7 "You shall not misuse the name of
the LORD your God, for the
LORD will not hold anyone

20:2 [d] S Ge 17:7; Ex 16:12; Lev 19:2; 20:7; Isa 43:3; Eze 20:19 [e] S Ge 15:7 [f] S Ex 6:6 [g] Ex 13:3; Eze 20:6 **20:3** [h] ver 23; Ex 34:14; Dt 6:14; 13:10; 2Ki 17:35; Ps 44:20; 81:9; Jer 1:16; 7:6,9; 11:13; 19:4; 25:6; 35:15 **20:4** [i] ver 5,23; Ex 32:8; 34:17; Lev 19:4; 26:1; Dt 4:15-19,23; 27:15; 2Sa 7:22; 1Ki 14:9; 2Ki 17:12; Isa 40:19; 42:8; 44:9 **20:5** [j] Ex 23:13, 24; Jos 23:7; Jdg 6:10; 2Ki 17:35; Isa 44:15,17,19; 46:6 [k] Ex 34:14; Dt 4:24; Jos 24:19; Na 1:2 [l] S Ge 9:25; S Lev 26:39 [m] Ex 34:7; Nu 14:18; Jer 32:18 **20:6** [n] Ex 34:7; Nu 14:18; Dt 7:9; Jer 32:18; Lk 1:50; Ro 11:28

[r] 3 Or *besides*

20:2 THE TEN COMMANDMENTS. The Ten Commandments, recorded here (cf. Dt 5:6–21), were written by God himself on two stone tablets and given to Moses and the Israelites (31:18; 32:16; Dt 4:13; 10:4). Keeping the commandments provided a way for Israel to respond righteously to God in gratitude for their deliverance out of Egypt; at the same time, such obedience was required in order to remain in the promised land (Dt 4:1,14; see article on THE OLD TESTAMENT LAW, p. 118).

(1) The Ten Commandments summarize God's moral law for Israel and describe their obligations both to God and others. Christ and the apostles affirm that, as valid expressions of God's holy will, the commandments remain obligatory for NT believers (Mt 22:37–39; Mk 12:28–34; Lk 10:27; Ro 13:9; Gal 5:14; cf. Lev 19:18; Dt 6:5; 10:12; 30:6). According to these NT passages, the Ten Commandments are summed up by love for God and love for one's neighbor; obeying them is not only a matter of obeying external rules but also requires action from the heart (see Dt 6:5, note). Thus the law demands an inner spiritual righteousness that is expressed in outward justice and holiness.

(2) The OT civil and ceremonial commandments that governed Israel's worship and social life (see article on THE OLD TESTAMENT LAW, p. 118) are no longer binding on the NT believer. They were types and shadows of better things to come; they have been fulfilled in Jesus Christ (Heb 10:1; cf. Mt 7:12; 22:37–40; Ro 13:8; Gal 5:14; 6:2). These laws do, however, contain wisdom and spiritual principles applicable to all generations (see Mt 5:17, note).

20:3 YOU SHALL HAVE NO OTHER GODS BEFORE ME. This command prohibited the polytheism that characterized all the religions of the ancient Near East. Israel was not to worship or call on any of the gods of other nations, but was commanded to fear the Lord and serve only him (cf. Dt 32:39; Jos 24:14–15).

When applied to NT believers, this commandment means at least three things: (1) Believers' worship must be directed to God alone. There may be no worshiping, praying to, or seeking guidance and help from any "other gods," any spirits, or the dead (cf. Lev 17:7; Dt 6:4; 32:17; Ps 106:37; 1Co 10:19–20). The first commandment is especially directed against the worship of spirits (i.e., demons) through spiritism, divination and other forms of idolatry (cf. Dt 18:9–22). (2) Believers must be totally consecrated to God. Only God through his revealed will and inspired Word may guide their lives (Mt 4:4; see article on THE INSPIRATION AND AUTHORITY OF SCRIPTURE, p. 1898). (3) Believers must have as their purpose in life to seek and love God with their whole heart, soul and strength, relying on him to provide that which is good for their lives (Dt 6:5; Ps 119:2; Mt 6:33; Php 3:8; see Mt 22:37, note; Col 3:5, note).

20:4 AN IDOL IN THE FORM OF ANYTHING. The prohibition against the worship of other gods required that no image be made of them (cf. Dt 4:19,23–28), nor could anyone make an image of the Lord God himself. He is too great to be represented by anything made by human hands. As applied to believers in Christ, the second commandment forbids making images of God or creatures for the purpose of worship, prayer or any sort of spiritual help (cf. Dt 4:15–16). The principle behind this command applies equally to all three persons of the Trinity. (1) It is impossible for any image or picture of God to truly represent God's personal glory and character (cf. Isa 40:18). (2) God is so transcendent, so holy and unsearchable, that any image of him dishonors him and detracts from his true nature and from what he has revealed about himself (cf. 32:1–6). (3) The believer's concepts of God must not be based on images or pictures of him, but on God's Word and on his revelation in the person and work of Jesus Christ (cf. Jn 17:3).

20:5 THE CHILDREN. See 34:7, note.

20:7 NOT MISUSE THE NAME OF THE LORD. Misusing God's name included making a false promise by it (Lev 19:12; cf. Mt 5:33–37), pronouncing it insincerely or thoughtlessly, or cursing and blaspheming (Lev 24:10–16). God's name must be hallowed, honored and respected as profoundly sacred, and it may be used only in a holy manner (see Mt 6:9, note).

guiltless who misuses his
name.[o]
8"Remember the Sabbath[p] day by
keeping it holy. 9Six days
you shall labor and do all
your work,[q] 10but the seventh day is a Sabbath[r] to
the LORD your God. On it you
shall not do any work, neither you, nor your son or
daughter, nor your manservant or maidservant, nor
your animals, nor the alien
within your gates. 11For in
six days the LORD made the
heavens and the earth,[s] the
sea, and all that is in them,
but he rested[t] on the seventh day.[u] Therefore the
LORD blessed the Sabbath
day and made it holy.
12"Honor your father and your
mother,[v] so that you may
live long[w] in the land[x] the
LORD your God is giving you.
13"You shall not murder.[y]
14"You shall not commit adultery.[z]
15"You shall not steal.[a]
16"You shall not give false testimo-

20:7 [o] Ex 22:28; Lev 18:21; 19:12; 22:2; 24:11,16; Dt 6:13; 10:20; Job 2:5,9; Ps 63:11; Isa 8:21; Eze 20:39; 39:7; S Mt 5:33 **20:8** [p] S Ex 16:23; 31:13-16; 35:3; Lev 19:3,30; 26:2; Isa 56:2; Jer 17:21-27; Eze 22:8 **20:9** [q] Ex 23:12; 31:13-17; 34:21; 35:2-3; Lev 23:3; Lk 13:14 **20:10** [r] S Ge 2:3; Ex 31:14; Lev 23:38; Nu 28:9; Isa 56:2; Eze 20:12,20 **20:11** [s] Ge 1:3-2:1 [t] S Ge 2:2 [u] Ex 31:17; Heb 4:4 **20:12** [v] S Ge 31:35; S Dt 5:16; Mt 15:4*; 19:19*; Mk 7:10*; 10:19*; Lk 18:20*; Eph 6:2 [w] Dt 6:2; Eph 6:3 [x] Dt 11:9; 25:15; Jer 35:7 **20:13** [y] S Ge 4:23; Mt 5:21*; 19:18*; Mk 10:19*; Lk 18:20*; Ro 13:9*; Jas 2:11* **20:14** [z] Lev 18:20; 20:10; Nu 5:12,13,29; Pr 6:29,32; Mt 5:27*; 19:18*; Mk 10:19*; Lk 18:20*; Ro 13:9*; Jas 2:11* **20:15** [a] Lev 19:11,13; Eze 18:7; Mt 19:18*; Mk 10:19*; Lk 18:20*; Ro 13:9*

20:8 REMEMBER THE SABBATH DAY. The OT Sabbath was the seventh day of the week. To keep that day holy meant setting it apart as different from other days by ceasing one's labor in order to rest, serve God and concentrate on the things concerning eternity, spiritual life and God's honor (vv. 9–11; cf. Ge 2:2–3; Isa 58:13–14). (1) The Israelites were expected to model their conduct after God's work in creation (v. 11; Ge 2:2–3). (2) The Sabbath was a sign that they belonged to God (31:13). (3) It reminded them of their deliverance from slavery in Egypt (Dt 5:15; see Mt 12:1, note).

20:12 HONOR YOUR FATHER AND YOUR MOTHER. This commandment includes all necessary acts of kindness, material support, respect and obedience to one's parents (Eph 6:1–3; Col 3:20). It prohibits unkind words and injurious acts. (1) In 21:15,17, God required the death penalty for any person who hit or cursed father or mother. This shows how much importance God placed on respect for parents (see Eph 6:1, note). (2) Related to this commandment is the reciprocal duty of the father and mother to love their children and teach them the fear of the Lord and the ways of God (Dt 4:9; 6:6–7; Eph 6:4).

20:13 YOU SHALL NOT COMMIT MURDER. The sixth commandment forbids willful murder, i.e., the unauthorized or unlawful taking of life (see Mt 5:22, note). God prescribed the death penalty for violating this commandment (see Ge 9:6, note). The NT condemns not only murder, but also hate, which prompts one to desire the death of another (1 Jn 3:15), and any other ungodly action or influence that causes the spiritual death of another (see Mt 5:21, note; 18:6, note).

20:14 YOU SHALL NOT COMMIT ADULTERY. This seventh commandment prohibiting adultery (cf. Lev 20:10; Dt 22:22) encompasses immorality and all sexual sins (Mt 5:27–32; 1Co 6:13–20). Adultery (i.e., unfaithfulness to one's spouse) is so abominable in God's sight that the Bible everywhere condemns its practice. About adultery the Bible teaches the following: (1) It transgresses God's moral law as expressed in the Ten Commandments.

(2) In the OT law, it was punishable by death (Lev 20:10; Dt 22:22).

(3) It brings permanent and serious consequences (2Sa 11:1–17; 12:14; Jer 23:10–11; 1Co 6:16–18); the one committing adultery will bear shame for the rest of his or her life (Pr 6:32–33).

(4) Adultery is an especially heinous sin when committed by leaders of God's people. If and when they commit this sin, it is equivalent to despising God's word and the Lord himself (2Sa 12:9–10). By marital unfaithfulness professed believers disqualify themselves from being chosen for or continuing in church leadership (see article on MORAL QUALIFICATIONS FOR OVERSEERS, p. 1882). Note how in the OT, adultery filled the land because of the influence of godless prophets and priests (Jer 23:10–14; 29:23).

(5) Adultery and promiscuous sex among the leaders and members of God's people are typically the result of prior spiritual adultery, i.e., unfaithfulness to God (Hos 4:13–14; 9:1; see article on PERSONAL APOSTASY, p. 1918).

(6) Adultery begins as a desire in the heart before it is expressed as a physical act. Lust is clearly regarded as sin in the Bible (Job 31:1,7; see Mt 5:28, note).

(7) Adultery is a sin of such magnitude and consequence that it gives the innocent person the right to end the marriage by divorce (see Mt 19:9, note; Mk 10:11, note).

(8) Sexual immorality within the church must be disciplined and can never be tolerated (1Co 5:1–13).

(9) Unrepentant adulterers have no inheritance in God's kingdom, i.e., they are separated from the life and salvation of God (1Co 6:9; Gal 5:19–21).

(10) Adultery and prostitution are terms used to describe the apostate church and the abominations it produces (Rev 17:1–5; see Rev 17:1, note).

20:15 YOU SHALL NOT STEAL. This commandment prohibits stealing money or anything belonging to another. Cheating is also a form of stealing (2Co 8:21). The eighth commandment demands honesty in all our dealings with people.

20:16 NOT GIVE FALSE TESTIMONY. The

ny[b] against your neighbor.[c]
17"You shall not covet[d] your neighbor's house. You shall not covet your neighbor's wife, or his manservant or maidservant, his ox or donkey, or anything that belongs to your neighbor."

18When the people saw the thunder
and lightning and heard the trumpet[e]
and saw the mountain in smoke,[f] they
trembled with fear.[g] They stayed at a
distance 19and said to Moses, "Speak
to us yourself and we will listen. But do
not have God speak[h] to us or we will
die."[i]
20Moses said to the people, "Do not
be afraid.[j] God has come to test[k]
you, so that the fear[l] of God will be
with you to keep you from sinning."[m]
21The people remained at a distance, while Moses approached the thick darkness[n] where God was.

Idols and Altars

22Then the LORD said to Moses, "Tell
the Israelites this: 'You have seen for
yourselves that I have spoken to you
from heaven:[o] 23Do not make any
gods to be alongside me;[p] do not
make for yourselves gods of silver or
gods of gold.[q]
24" 'Make an altar[r] of earth for me
and sacrifice on it your burnt offerings[s] and fellowship offerings,[s] your

20:16 [b]Lev 19:11; Jer 9:3,5 [c]Ex 23:1, 7; Lev 19:18; Ps 50:20; 101:5; 119:29; Mt 19:18*; Mk 10:19; Lk 3:14*; 18:20* **20:17** [d]Lk 12:15; Ro 7:7*; 13:9*; Eph 5:3; Heb 13:5 **20:18** [e]Ex 19:16-19; Dt 4:36; Isa 58:1; Jer 6:17; Eze 33:3; Heb 12:18-19; Rev 1:10 [f]S Ex 19:18 [g]S Ge 3:10; S Ex 14:31; S 19:16 **20:19** [h]Job 37:4, 5; 40:9; Ps 29:3-4 [i]Dt 5:5,23-27; 18:16; Gal 3:19 **20:20** [j]S Ge 15:1 [k]S Ge 22:1 [l]Dt 4:10; 6:2,24; 10:12; Ps 111:10; 128:1; Pr 1:7; Ecc 12:13; Isa 8:13 [m]Job 1:8; 2:3; 28:28; Pr 3:7; 8:13; 14:16; 16:6 **20:21** [n]S Ex 19:9; Dt 5:22; Ps 18:9; 68:4; 97:2; Isa 19:1 **20:22** [o]Dt 5:24, 26; Ne 9:13 **20:23** [p]S ver 3 [q]Ex 22:20; 32:4,8, 31; 34:17; Dt 29:17-18; Ne 9:18 **20:24** [r]Ex 27:1; 40:29; Nu 16:38; Dt 27:5; Jos 8:30; 2Ki 16:14; 2Ch 4:1; Ezr 3:2; Eze 43:13 [s]S Ge 8:20; S Ex 18:12 [t]Dt 12:5; 16:6,11;

sheep and goats and your cattle. Wherever I cause my name[t] to be honored,
I will come to you and bless[u] you. 25If
you make an altar of stones for me, do
not build it with dressed stones, for
you will defile it if you use a tool[v] on
it. 26And do not go up to my altar on
steps, lest your nakedness[w] be exposed on it.'

21

"These are the laws[x] you are to set before them:

Hebrew Servants

21:2–6pp — Dt 15:12–18
21:2–11Ref — Lev 25:39–55

2"If you buy a Hebrew servant,[y] he
is to serve you for six years. But in the
seventh year, he shall go free,[z] without paying anything. 3If he comes
alone, he is to go free alone; but if he
has a wife when he comes, she is to go
with him. 4If his master gives him a
wife and she bears him sons or daughters, the woman and her children shall
belong to her master, and only the man
shall go free.
5"But if the servant declares, 'I love
my master and my wife and children
and do not want to go free,'[a] 6then his
master must take him before the

26:2; 1Ki 9:3; 2Ki 21:4,7; 2Ch 6:6; 12:13; Ezr 6:12 [u]S Ge 12:2; 22:17 **20:25** [v]Jos 8:31; 1Ki 6:7 **20:26** [w]Eze 43:17 **21:1** [x]Ex 24:3; 34:32; Dt 4:14; 6:1 **21:2** [y]Ex 22:3 [z]ver 7; Jer 34:8,14 **21:5** [a]Dt 15:16

[s]*24* Traditionally *peace offerings*

ninth commandment protects the name and reputation of other persons. No one may make false statements about anyone's character or actions. We must speak about all people in a fair and just manner (cf. Lev 19:16; see Jn 8:44, note; 2Co 12:20, note). This commandment also encompasses lying in general (cf. Lev 6:2–3; Pr 14:5; Col 3:9).

20:17 YOU SHALL NOT COVET. (1) This commandment goes beyond the external sin of word or deed to condemn evil motives and desires. Coveting involves the desire or lust for all that is wrong or belongs to another person. Paul claims that this commandment reveals the depth of human sinfulness (Ro 7:7–13). (2) This law, as well as the others, exposes the depravity of men and women and calls for them to seek grace and moral power from God (cf. Lk 12:15–21; Ro 7:24–25; Eph 5:3). Only by the regenerative power of the Holy Spirit can one live a life pleasing to God (see Ro 8:2, note).

20:20 DO NOT BE AFRAID. The sights and sounds at Sinai caused the Israelites to become afraid and to back off to the opposite side of the valley. Moses told them to stop being afraid with cowardly fear. God was using this display of power to inspire in them a godly fear and reverence that would help keep them from sinning.

21:1 THESE ARE THE LAWS. This next section (20:22—23:33) contains "the Book of the Covenant" (24:7), i.e, the laws for the nation of Israel that governed its society and worship. These laws, mostly civil in nature, were applicable only to Israel, her religion, and the conditions and environment existing in that period. However, the principles embodied in these laws—values like reverence for life and commitment to justice and fairness—are eternally valid.

21:2 A HEBREW SERVANT. Although God did not immediately abolish such evils as slavery or polygamy in Israel, he did regulate them in order to make them more humane (cf. Lev 25:39–40; Dt 15:12–18). On the one hand, these practices were not God's ideal. On the other hand, he permitted them for a time because of the hardness of human hearts (cf. Mt 19:8; see Ge 29:28, note). Furthermore, God's laws concerning slavery were much more humane than the customs of the nations surrounding them. In the NT, however, God expressed an even higher standard (see Jn 13:34, note; Col 3:22, note).

judges.[t][b] He shall take him to the door or the doorpost and pierce[c] his ear with an awl. Then he will be his servant for life.[d]

7 "If a man sells his daughter as a servant, she is not to go free as menservants do. 8 If she does not please the master who has selected her for himself,[u] he must let her be redeemed. He has no right to sell her to foreigners, because he has broken faith with her. 9 If he selects her for his son, he must grant her the rights of a daughter. 10 If he marries another woman, he must not deprive the first one of her food, clothing and marital rights.[e] 11 If he does not provide her with these three things, she is to go free, without any payment of money.

Personal Injuries

12 "Anyone who strikes a man and kills him shall surely be put to death.[f] 13 However, if he does not do it intentionally, but God lets it happen, he is to flee to a place[g] I will designate. 14 But if a man schemes and kills another man deliberately,[h] take him away from my altar and put him to death.[i]

15 "Anyone who attacks[v] his father or his mother must be put to death.

16 "Anyone who kidnaps another and either sells[j] him or still has him when he is caught must be put to death.[k]

17 "Anyone who curses his father or mother must be put to death.[l]

18 "If men quarrel and one hits the other with a stone or with his fist[w] and he does not die but is confined to bed, 19 the one who struck the blow will not be held responsible if the other gets up and walks around outside with his staff; however, he must pay the injured man for the loss of his time and see that he is completely healed.

20 "If a man beats his male or female slave with a rod and the slave dies as a direct result, he must be punished, 21 but he is not to be punished if the slave gets up after a day or two, since the slave is his property.[m]

22 "If men who are fighting hit a pregnant woman and she gives birth prematurely[x] but there is no serious injury, the offender must be fined whatever the woman's husband demands[n] and the court allows. 23 But if there is serious injury, you are to take life for life,[o] 24 eye for eye, tooth for tooth,[p] hand for hand, foot for foot, 25 burn for burn, wound for wound, bruise for bruise.

26 "If a man hits a manservant or maidservant in the eye and destroys it, he must let the servant go free to compensate for the eye. 27 And if he knocks out the tooth of a manservant or maidservant, he must let the servant go free to compensate for the tooth.

28 "If a bull gores a man or a woman to death, the bull must be stoned to death,[q] and its meat must not be eaten. But the owner of the bull will not be held responsible. 29 If, however, the bull has had the habit of goring and the owner has been warned but has not kept it penned up[r] and it kills a man or woman, the bull must be stoned and the owner also must be put to death. 30 However, if payment is demanded of him, he may redeem his life by paying whatever is demanded.[s] 31 This law also applies if the bull gores a son or daughter. 32 If the bull gores a male or female slave, the owner must pay thir-

21:6 [b] Ex 22:8-9; Dt 17:9; 19:17; 25:1 [c] Ps 40:6 [d] Job 39:9; 41:4 **21:10** [e] 1Co 7:3-5 **21:12** [f] ver 15,17; S Ge 4:14,23; Ex 31:15; Lev 20:9,10; 24:16; 27:29; Nu 1:51; 35:16, 30-31; Dt 13:5; 19:11; 22:22; 27:16; Job 31:11; Pr 20:20; S Mt 26:52 **21:13** [g] Nu 35:10-34; Dt 4:42; 19:2-13; Jos 20:9 **21:14** [h] Ge 4:8; Nu 35:20; 2Sa 3:27; 20:10; Heb 10:26 [i] Dt 19:11-12; 1Ki 2:28-34 **21:16** [j] Ge 37:28 [k] Ex 22:4; Dt 24:7 **21:17** [l] S ver 12; S Dt 5:16; Mt 15:4*; Mk 7:10* **21:21** [m] Lev 25:44-46 **21:22** [n] ver 30 **21:23** [o] Lev 24:19; Dt 19:21 **21:24** [p] S ver 23; Mt 5:38* **21:28** [q] ver 32; Ge 9:5 **21:29** [r] ver 36 **21:30** [s] ver 22

[t] 6 Or *before God* [u] 8 Or *master so that he does not choose her* [v] 15 Or *kills* [w] 18 Or *with a tool* [x] 22 Or *she has a miscarriage*

21:12–17 SURELY BE PUT TO DEATH. These verses list four crimes to which God assigned the death penalty: premeditated murder (vv. 12,14), inflicting physical harm on parents (v. 15), kidnapping (v. 16) and verbal cursing of parents (v. 17). This punishment indicates the importance God put on proper interpersonal relationships (murder and kidnapping) and proper family relationships (treatment of parents).

21:22–23 SHE GIVES BIRTH PREMATURELY. In addition to the protection of living persons, God required the protection of unborn children. (1) V. 21 refers to a woman giving birth prematurely because of violence done to her. If birth took place, the one causing the premature birth had to pay a fine.

(2) If there was serious injury to the mother or the child, then the offending party had to pay according to the law of retaliation. Note that if death resulted to the mother or the child, then the perpetrator was found guilty of murder and had to pay with his life (v. 23). In other words, the unborn child is viewed here as a human being; the fetus's death is considered murder.

(3) Note that this is the only instance in the law where accidental manslaughter called for the death penalty (cf. Dt 19:4–10). The principle is clear — God seeks to protect those who are least able to protect themselves (i.e., the unborn).

ty shekels[y][t] of silver to the master of
the slave, and the bull must be stoned.
33 "If a man uncovers a pit[u] or digs
one and fails to cover it and an ox or
a donkey falls into it, 34 the owner of
the pit must pay for the loss; he must
pay its owner, and the dead animal will
be his.
35 "If a man's bull injures the bull of
another and it dies, they are to sell the
live one and divide both the money and
the dead animal equally. 36 However, if
it was known that the bull had the habit of goring, yet the owner did not keep
it penned up,[v] the owner must pay,
animal for animal, and the dead animal
will be his.

Protection of Property

22 "If a man steals an ox or a
sheep and slaughters it or sells
it, he must pay back[w] five head of cattle for the ox and four sheep for the
sheep.
2 "If a thief is caught breaking in[x]
and is struck so that he dies, the defender is not guilty of bloodshed;[y]
3 but if it happens[z] after sunrise, he is
guilty of bloodshed.
"A thief must certainly make restitution,[z] but if he has nothing, he must
be sold[a] to pay for his theft.
4 "If the stolen animal is found alive
in his possession[b]—whether ox or
donkey or sheep—he must pay back
double.[c]
5 "If a man grazes his livestock in a
field or vineyard and lets them stray
and they graze in another man's field,
he must make restitution[d] from the
best of his own field or vineyard.
6 "If a fire breaks out and spreads
into thornbushes so that it burns
shocks[e] of grain or standing grain or
the whole field, the one who started
the fire must make restitution.[f]
7 "If a man gives his neighbor silver
or goods for safekeeping[g] and they
are stolen from the neighbor's house,
the thief, if he is caught, must pay back
double.[h] 8 But if the thief is not found,
the owner of the house must appear before the judges[a][i] to determine
whether he has laid his hands on the
other man's property. 9 In all cases of
illegal possession of an ox, a donkey,
a sheep, a garment, or any other lost
property about which somebody says,
'This is mine,' both parties are to bring
their cases before the judges.[j] The
one whom the judges declare[b] guilty
must pay back double to his neighbor.
10 "If a man gives a donkey, an ox, a
sheep or any other animal to his neighbor for safekeeping[k] and it dies or is
injured or is taken away while no one
is looking, 11 the issue between them
will be settled by the taking of an
oath[l] before the LORD that the neighbor did not lay hands on the other person's property. The owner is to accept
this, and no restitution is required.
12 But if the animal was stolen from the
neighbor, he must make restitution[m]
to the owner. 13 If it was torn to pieces
by a wild animal, he shall bring in the
remains as evidence and he will not be
required to pay for the torn animal.[n]
14 "If a man borrows an animal from
his neighbor and it is injured or dies
while the owner is not present, he must
make restitution.[o] 15 But if the owner
is with the animal, the borrower will
not have to pay. If the animal was
hired, the money paid for the hire covers the loss.[p]

Social Responsibility

16 "If a man seduces a virgin[q] who
is not pledged to be married and sleeps
with her, he must pay the bride-
price,[r] and she shall be his wife. 17 If
her father absolutely refuses to give
her to him, he must still pay the bride-
price for virgins.
18 "Do not allow a sorceress[s] to
live.
19 "Anyone who has sexual relations
with an animal[t] must be put to death.
20 "Whoever sacrifices to any god[u]
other than the LORD must be destroyed.[c][v]
21 "Do not mistreat an alien[w] or op-

21:32 [t] Ge 37:28; Zec 11:12-13; Mt 26:15; 27:3,9
21:33 [u] Lk 14:5
21:36 [v] ver 29
22:1 [w] Lev 6:1-7; 2Sa 12:6; Pr 6:31; S Lk 19:8
22:2 [x] Job 24:16; Jer 2:34; Hos 7:1; Mt 6:19-20; 24:43 [y] Nu 35:27
22:3 [z] ver 1 [a] S Ex 21:2; S Mt 18:25
22:4 [b] 1Sa 12:5 [c] S Ge 43:12
22:5 [d] ver 1
22:6 [e] Jdg 15:5 [f] ver 1
22:7 [g] ver 10; Lev 6:2 [h] S Ge 43:12
22:8 [i] S Ex 21:6
22:9 [j] ver 8; Dt 25:1
22:10 [k] S ver 7
22:11 [l] Lev 6:3; 1Ki 8:31; 2Ch 6:22; Heb 6:16
22:12 [m] ver 1
22:13 [n] Ge 31:39
22:14 [o] ver 1
22:15 [p] Lev 19:13; Job 17:5
22:16 [q] Dt 22:28 [r] S Ge 34:12
22:18 [s] S Ex 7:11; Lev 19:26,31; 20:27; Dt 18:11; 1Sa 28:3; 2Ch 33:6; Isa 57:3
22:19 [t] Lev 18:23; 20:15; Dt 27:21
22:20 [u] S Ex 20:23; 34:15; Lev 17:7; Nu 25:2; Dt 32:17; Ps 106:37 [v] Lev 27:29; Dt 13:5; 17:2-5; 18:20; 1Ki 18:40; 19:1; 2Ki 10:25; 23:20; 2Ch 15:13
22:21 [w] Ex 23:9; Lev 19:33; 24:22; Nu 15:14; Dt 1:16; 24:17; Eze 22:29

[y] *32* That is, about 12 ounces (about 0.3 kilogram) [z] *3* Or *if he strikes him* [a] *8* Or *before God*; also in verse 9 [b] *9* Or *whom God declares* [c] *20* The Hebrew term refers to the irrevocable giving over of things or persons to the LORD, often by totally destroying them.

22:18 A SORCERESS. A sorceress was a woman who practiced witchcraft and occultism, e.g., divination, sorcery, contact with the dead (see Ac 19:19, note; Rev 9:21, note). To seek power or guidance from the supernatural realm of the dead or through demonic activity was, and is, an abomination to God (cf. Lev 19:31; 20:27; Dt 18:9–12; 1Sa 28:7; Mal 3:5).

press him, for you were aliens[x] in
Egypt.
22"Do not take advantage of a widow
or an orphan.[y] **23**If you do and they
cry out[z] to me, I will certainly hear
their cry.[a] **24**My anger will be
aroused, and I will kill you with the
sword; your wives will become widows
and your children fatherless.[b]
25"If you lend money to one of my
people among you who is needy, do not
be like a moneylender; charge him no
interest.[d][c] **26**If you take your neighbor's cloak as a pledge,[d] return it to
him by sunset, **27**because his cloak is
the only covering he has for his body.
What else will he sleep in?[e] When he
cries out to me, I will hear, for I am
compassionate.[f]
28"Do not blaspheme God[e][g] or
curse[h] the ruler of your people.[i]
29"Do not hold back offerings[j] from
your granaries or your vats.[f]
"You must give me the firstborn of
your sons.[k] **30**Do the same with your
cattle and your sheep.[l] Let them stay
with their mothers for seven days, but
give them to me on the eighth day.[m]
31"You are to be my holy people.[n]
So do not eat the meat of an animal
torn by wild beasts;[o] throw it to the
dogs.

Laws of Justice and Mercy

23 "Do not spread false reports.[p]
Do not help a wicked man by
being a malicious witness.[q]
2"Do not follow the crowd in doing
wrong. When you give testimony in a
lawsuit, do not pervert justice[r] by siding with the crowd,[s] **3**and do not show
favoritism[t] to a poor man in his lawsuit.
4"If you come across your enemy's[u]
ox or donkey wandering off, be sure to
take it back to him.[v] **5**If you see the
donkey[w] of someone who hates you
fallen down under its load, do not leave
it there; be sure you help him with it.
6"Do not deny justice[x] to your poor
people in their lawsuits. **7**Have nothing
to do with a false charge[y] and do not
put an innocent[z] or honest person to
death,[a] for I will not acquit the
guilty.[b]
8"Do not accept a bribe,[c] for a bribe
blinds those who see and twists the
words of the righteous.
9"Do not oppress an alien;[d] you
yourselves know how it feels to be
aliens, because you were aliens in
Egypt.

Sabbath Laws

10"For six years you are to sow your
fields and harvest the crops, **11**but during the seventh year let the land lie unplowed and unused.[e] Then the poor
among your people may get food from
it, and the wild animals may eat what
they leave. Do the same with your vineyard and your olive grove.
12"Six days do your work,[f] but on
the seventh day do not work, so that
your ox and your donkey may rest and
the slave born in your household, and
the alien as well, may be refreshed.[g]
13"Be careful[h] to do everything I
have said to you. Do not invoke the
names of other gods;[i] do not let them
be heard on your lips.[j]

The Three Annual Festivals

14"Three times[k] a year you are to
celebrate a festival to me.
15"Celebrate the Feast of Unleavened Bread;[l] for seven days eat bread
made without yeast, as I commanded
you. Do this at the appointed time in

22:21 [x]Dt 10:19; 27:19; Zec 7:10; Mal 3:5 **22:22** [y]ver 26; Dt 10:18; 24:6,10, 12,17; Job 22:6,9; 24:3,21; Ps 68:5; 146:9; Pr 23:10; Isa 1:17; Jer 7:5,6; 21:12; 22:3; Eze 18:5-9,12; Zec 7:9-10; Mal 3:5; Jas 1:27 **22:23** [z]Lk 18:7 [a]Dt 10:18; 15:9; 24:15; Job 34:28; 35:9; Ps 10:14,17; 12:5; 18:6; 34:15; Jas 5:4 **22:24** [b]Ps 69:24; 109:9; La 5:3 **22:25** [c]Lev 25:35-37; Dt 15:7-11; 23:20; Ne 5:7,10; Ps 15:5; Eze 18:8 **22:26** [d]S ver 22; Pr 20:16; Eze 33:15; Am 2:8 **22:27** [e]Dt 24:13, 17; Job 22:6; 24:7; 29:11; 31:19-20; Eze 18:12,16 [f]Ex 34:6; Dt 4:31; 2Ch 30:9; Ne 9:17; Ps 99:8; 103:8; 116:5; 145:8; Joel 2:13; Jnh 4:2 **22:28** [g]S Ex 20:7 [h]2Sa 16:5,9; 19:21; 1Ki 21:10; 2Ki 2:23; Ps 102:8 [i]Ecc 10:20; Ac 23:5* **22:29** [j]Ex 23:15, 16,19; 34:20,26; Lev 19:24; 23:10; Nu 18:13; 28:26; Dt 18:4; 26:2,10; 1Sa 6:3; Ne 10:35; Pr 3:9; Mal 3:10 [k]S Ex 13:2; Nu 8:16-17; Lk 2:23 **22:30** [l]Ex 34:19; Dt 15:19 [m]Ge 17:12; Lev 12:3; 22:27 **22:31** [n]Ex 19:6; Lev 19:2; 22:31; Ezr 9:2 [o]Lev 7:24; 17:15; 22:8; Dt 14:21; Eze 4:14; 44:31 **23:1** [p]S Ge 39:17; Mt 19:18; Lk 3:14 [q]S Ex 20:16; Dt 5:20; 19:16-21; Ps 27:12; 35:11; Pr 19:5; Ac 6:11 **23:2** [r]ver 3,6,9; Lev 19:15,33; Dt 1:17; 16:19; 24:17; 27:19; 1Sa 8:3 [s]Job 31:34 **23:3** [t]Dt 1:17 **23:4** [u]Ro 12:20 [v]Lev 6:3; 19:11; Dt 22:1-3 **23:5** [w]Dt 22:4 **23:6** [x]S ver 2; Dt 23:16; Pr 22:22 **23:7** [y]S Ex 20:16; S Eph 4:25 [z]Mt 27:4 [a]S Ge 18:23 [b]Ex 34:7; Dt 19:18; 25:1 **23:8** [c]S Ex 18:21; Lev 19:15; Dt 10:17; 27:25; Job 15:34; 36:18; Ps 26:10; Pr 6:35; 15:27; 17:8; Isa 1:23; 5:23; Mic 3:11; 7:3 **23:9** [d]S ver 2; S Ex 22:21; Lev 19:33-34; Eze 22:7 **23:11** [e]Lev 25:1-7; Ne 10:31 **23:12** [f]S Ex 20:9; Lk 13:14 [g]Ge 2:2-3 **23:13** [h]Dt 4:9,23; 1Ti 4:16 [i]ver 32; Dt 12:3; Jos 23:7; Ps 16:4; Zec 13:2 [j]Dt 18:20; Jos 23:7; Ps 16:4; Hos 2:17 **23:14** [k]ver 17; S Ex 12:14; 34:23,24; Dt 16:16; 1Ki 9:25; 2Ch 8:13; Eze 46:9 **23:15** [l]S Ex 12:17; Mt 26:17; Lk 22:1; Ac 12:3

[d] 25 Or *excessive interest* [e] 28 Or *Do not revile the judges* [f] 29 The meaning of the Hebrew for this phrase is uncertain.

22:22–24 WIDOW OR AN ORPHAN. The regulations in vv. 22–27 reveal that God was deeply concerned about the hardships of the widow, the poor and the disadvantaged, and he was moved with compassion for them (cf. Dt 24:6,12–13; Job 22:6; 24:7; Eze 18:12,16; see Mk 6:34, note; 8:2, note; Lk 2:36–37, note; 7:13, note; see article on THE CARE OF THE POOR AND NEEDY, p. 1316).

22:25 IF YOU LEND MONEY. God prohibited the charging of interest for loans to the needy to supply their basic needs (cf. Lev 25:25,35,39,47). God wanted to prevent the poor from being exploited by the rich. This law did not, however, forbid loaning money for reasonable interest to non-Israelites for commercial purposes (cf. Dt 23:19–20; Hab 2:6; Mt 25:27; Lk 19:23).

23:15 FEAST OF UNLEAVENED BREAD. See 12:17, note.

HEBREW CALENDAR AND SELECTED EVENTS

Sacred Sequence Begins	Hebrew Name	Modern Equivalent	Biblical References	Agriculture	Feasts
1	**Abib; Nisan**	March-April	Ex 12:2; 13:4; 23:15; 34:18; Dt 16:1; Ne 2:1; Est 3:7	Spring (later) rains; barley and flax harvest begins	Passover; Unleavened Bread; Firstfruits
2	**Ziv (Iyyar)***	April-May	1 Ki 6:1,37	Barley havest; dry season begins	
3	**Sivan**	May-June	Est 8:9	Wheat harvest	Pentecost (Weeks)
4	**(Tammuz)***	June-July		Tending vines	
5	**(Ab)***	July-August		Ripening of grapes, figs and olives	
6	**Elul**	August-September	Ne 6:15	Processing grapes, figs and olives	
7	**Ethanim (Tishri)***	September-October	1 Ki 8:2	Autumn (early) rains begin; plowing	Trumpets; Atonement; Tabernacles (Booths)
8	**Bul (Marcheshvan)***	October-November	1 Ki 6:38	Sowing of wheat and barley	
9	**Kislev**	November-December	Ne 1:1, Zec 7:1	Winter rains begin (snow in some areas)	Hanukkah ("Dedication")
10	**Tebeth**	December-January	Est 2:16		
11	**Shebat**	January-February	Zec 1:7		
12	**Adar**	February-March	Ezr 6:15; Est 3:7,13; 8:12; 9:1,15,17,19,21	Almond trees bloom; citrus fruit harvest	Purim
		(Adar Sheni)* **Second Adar**	This intercalary month was added about every three years so the lunar calendar would correspond to the solar year.		

* Names in parentheses are not in the Bible

the month of Abib,[m] for in that month
you came out of Egypt.
"No one is to appear before me empty-handed.[n]
16"Celebrate the Feast of Harvest[o]
with the firstfruits[p] of the crops you
sow in your field.
"Celebrate the Feast of Ingathering[q] at the end of the year, when you
gather in your crops from the field.[r]
17"Three times[s] a year all the men
are to appear before the Sovereign
LORD.
18"Do not offer the blood of a sacrifice to me along with anything containing yeast.[t]
"The fat of my festival offerings
must not be kept until morning.[u]
19"Bring the best of the firstfruits[v]
of your soil to the house of the LORD
your God.
"Do not cook a young goat in its
mother's milk.[w]

God's Angel to Prepare the Way

20"See, I am sending an angel[x]
ahead of you to guard you along the
way and to bring you to the place I have
prepared.[y] 21Pay attention to him and
listen[z] to what he says. Do not rebel
against him; he will not forgive[a] your
rebellion,[b] since my Name[c] is in him.
22If you listen carefully to what he says
and do[d] all that I say, I will be an enemy[e] to your enemies and will oppose
those who oppose you. 23My angel will
go ahead of you and bring you into the
land of the Amorites, Hittites, Perizzites, Canaanites, Hivites and Jebusites,[f] and I will wipe them out. 24Do
not bow down before their gods or worship[g] them or follow their practices.[h]
You must demolish[i] them and break
their sacred stones[j] to pieces. 25Wor-
ship the LORD your God,[k] and his
blessing[l] will be on your food and water. I will take away sickness[m] from
among you, 26and none will miscarry
or be barren[n] in your land. I will give
you a full life span.[o]
27"I will send my terror[p] ahead of
you and throw into confusion[q] every
nation you encounter. I will make all
your enemies turn their backs and
run.[r] 28I will send the hornet[s] ahead
of you to drive the Hivites, Canaanites
and Hittites[t] out of your way. 29But I
will not drive them out in a single year,
because the land would become desolate and the wild animals[u] too numerous for you. 30Little by little I will drive
them out before you, until you have increased enough to take possession[v]
of the land.
31"I will establish your borders from
the Red Sea[g] to the Sea of the Philistines,[h] and from the desert to the River.[i][w] I will hand over to you the people who live in the land and you will
drive them out[x] before you. 32Do not
make a covenant[y] with them or with
their gods. 33Do not let them live in
your land, or they will cause you to sin
against me, because the worship of
their gods will certainly be a snare[z] to
you."

23:15 [m]S Ex 12:2 [n]S Ex 22:29 **23:16** [o]Lev 23:15-21; Nu 28:26; Dt 16:9; 2Ch 8:13 [p]S Ex 22:29; S 34:22 [q]Ex 34:22; Lev 23:34,42; Dt 16:16; 31:10; Ezr 3:4; Ne 8:14; Zec 14:16 [r]Lev 23:39; Dt 16:13; Jer 40:10 **23:17** [s]S ver 14 **23:18** [t]Ex 34:25; Lev 2:11 [u]S Ex 12:8 **23:19** [v]S Ex 22:29; S 34:22; S Nu 18:12 [w]Ex 34:26; Dt 14:21 **23:20** [x]S Ge 16:7 [y]Ex 15:17 **23:21** [z]Dt 18:19; Jer 13:15 [a]Dt 29:20; 2Ki 24:4; La 1:17 [b]Nu 17:10; Dt 9:7; 31:27; Jos 24:19; Ps 25:7; 78:8,40, 56; 106:33; 107:11; 1Jn 5:16 [c]S Ex 3:15 **23:22** [d]S Ex 15:26 [e]S Ge 12:3; Isa 41:11; Jer 30:20 **23:23** [f]Nu 13:29; 21:21; Jos 3:10; 24:8,11; Ezr 9:1; Ps 135:11 **23:24** [g]S Ex 20:5 [h]Lev 18:3; 20:23; Dt 9:4; 12:30-31; Jer 10:2 [i]Ex 34:13; Nu 33:52; Dt 7:5; 12:3; Jdg 2:2; 2Ki 18:4; 23:14 [j]Lev 26:1; Dt 16:22; 1Ki 14:23; 2Ki 3:2; 10:26; 17:10; 2Ch 14:3; Isa 27:9 **23:25** [k]Mt 4:10 [l]Lev 26:3-13; Dt 7:12-15; 28:1-14 [m]S Ex 15:26 **23:26** [n]Lev 26:3-4; Dt 7:14; 28:4; Mal 3:11 [o]S Ge 15:15; Dt 4:1,40; 32:47; Ps 90:10 **23:27** [p]S Ge 35:5; S Ex 15:14 [q]S Ex 14:24; Dt 7:23 [r]2Sa 22:41; Ps 18:40; 21:12 **23:28** [s]Dt 7:20; Jos 24:12 [t]Ex 33:2; 34:11,24; Nu 13:29; Dt 4:38; 11:23; 18:12; Jos 3:10; 24:11; Ps 78:55 **23:29** [u]Dt 7:22 **23:30** [v]Jos 23:5 **23:31** [w]S Ge 2:14; Dt 34:2; Ezr 4:20 [x]Dt 7:24; 9:3; Jos 21:44; 24:12,18; Ps 80:8 **23:32** [y]S Ge 26:28; Ex 34:12; Dt 7:2; Jos 9:7; Jdg 2:2; 1Sa 11:1; 1Ki 15:19; 20:34; Eze 17:13 **23:33** [z]S Ex 10:7

[g]*31* Hebrew *Yam Suph*; that is, Sea of Reeds [h]*31* That is, the Mediterranean [i]*31* That is, the Euphrates

23:16 THE FEAST OF HARVEST. This is also called the "Feast of Weeks" (34:22) or the "day of Pentecost" (Ac 2:1; 20:16; see Lev 23:15, note).

23:16 THE FEAST OF INGATHERING. This is also called the "Feast of Tabernacles" or "Booths" (see Lev 23:34).

23:20 AN ANGEL. This was probably "the angel of the LORD" (see 3:2, note).

23:24 FOLLOW THEIR PRACTICES. God commanded his people not to adopt the religions or to conform to the morals of the societies around them. Israel failed to observe fully this requirement; as a result they were not protected by the Lord (vv. 20–23). Under the new covenant, believers who conform to the ways of the world will also forfeit the promises and protection of God (see v. 25). We cannot have God's blessings and presence and at the same time participate in the sinful ways of the world (see 2Co 6:16–18; see article on SPIRITUAL SEPARATION FOR BELIEVERS, p. 1794).

23:25–26 TAKE AWAY SICKNESS. God connected the removal of sickness from among his people with their wholehearted devotion to him and their separation from the ungodly influences around them. We should not conclude, however, that the sickness of an individual necessarily indicates he or she has conformed to the wicked ways of society. This passage does suggest that the worldliness of God's people as a whole will cause God to withdraw a portion of his blessing and power from them, thus affecting even the righteous among God's people (cf. 1Co 12:26).

The Covenant Confirmed

24 Then he said to Moses, "Come
up to the LORD, you and Aar-
on,[a] Nadab and Abihu,[b] and seventy
of the elders[c] of Israel. You are to
worship at a distance, **2**but Moses
alone is to approach[d] the LORD; the
others must not come near. And the
people may not come up with him."
3When Moses went and told the people all the LORD's words and laws,[e]
they responded with one voice, "Everything the LORD has said we will do."[f]
4Moses then wrote[g] down everything
the LORD had said.
He got up early the next morning
and built an altar[h] at the foot of the
mountain and set up twelve stone pillars[i] representing the twelve tribes of
Israel. **5**Then he sent young Israelite
men, and they offered burnt offerings[j]
and sacrificed young bulls as fellowship offerings[jk] to the LORD. **6**Moses[l] took half of the blood[m] and put
it in bowls, and the other half he sprinkled[n] on the altar. **7**Then he took the
Book of the Covenant[o] and read it to
the people. They responded, "We will
do everything the LORD has said; we
will obey."[p]
8Moses then took the blood, sprinkled it on the people[q] and said, "This
is the blood of the covenant[r] that the
LORD has made with you in accordance
with all these words."
9Moses and Aaron, Nadab and Abihu, and the seventy elders[s] of Israel
went up **10**and saw[t] the God of Israel.
Under his feet was something like a
pavement made of sapphire,[ku] clear
as the sky[v] itself. **11**But God did not
raise his hand against these leaders of
the Israelites; they saw[w] God, and
they ate and drank.[x]
12The LORD said to Moses, "Come up
to me on the mountain and stay here,
and I will give you the tablets of
stone,[y] with the law and commands I
have written for their instruction."
13Then Moses set out with Joshua[z]
his aide, and Moses went up on the
mountain[a] of God. **14**He said to the elders, "Wait here for us until we come
back to you. Aaron and Hur[b] are with
you, and anyone involved in a dispute[c] can go to them."
15When Moses went up on the
mountain, the cloud[d] covered it,
16and the glory[e] of the LORD settled on
Mount Sinai.[f] For six days the cloud
covered the mountain, and on the seventh day the LORD called to Moses from
within the cloud.[g] **17**To the Israelites
the glory of the LORD looked like a consuming fire[h] on top of the mountain.
18Then Moses entered the cloud as he
went on up the mountain. And he
stayed on the mountain forty[i] days
and forty nights.[j]

Offerings for the Tabernacle

25:1–7pp — Ex 35:4–9

25 The LORD said to Moses, **2**"Tell
the Israelites to bring me an offering. You are to receive the offering

24:1 [a]S Ex 19:24 [b]S Ex 6:23 [c]ver 9; Nu 11:16 **24:2** [d]Nu 12:6-8 **24:3** [e]S Ex 21:1; Gal 3:19 [f]S Ex 19:8; Jos 24:24 **24:4** [g]S Ex 17:14 [h]S Ge 8:20 [i]S Ge 28:18; S Dt 27:2 **24:5** [j]Lev 1:3 [k]S Ge 31:54 **24:6** [l]Ex 14:15; 32:31; Ps 99:6 [m]Heb 9:18 [n]Lev 1:11; 3:2,8, 13; 5:9; Mt 26:28 **24:7** [o]2Ki 23:2, 21; Heb 9:19 [p]Ex 19:8; Jer 40:3; 42:6,21; 43:2 **24:8** [q]Heb 9:19; 1Pe 1:2 [r]Lev 26:3; Dt 5:2-3; Jos 24:25; 2Ki 11:17; Jer 11:4,8; 31:32; 34:13; Zec 9:11; S Mt 26:28; S Lk 22:20; Heb 9:20* **24:9** [s]S ver 1 **24:10** [t]S Ge 16:13; Nu 12:6; Isa 6:1; Eze 1:1; 8:3; 40:2; S Jn 1:18 [u]Job 28:16; Isa 54:11; Eze 1:26; 10:1 [v]Rev 4:3 **24:11** [w]S ver 10; S Ex 3:6; S 19:21 [x]Eze 44:3; Mt 26:29 **24:12** [y]Ex 31:18; 32:15-16; 34:1,28, 29; Dt 4:13; 5:22; 8:3; 9:9,10,11; 10:4; 2Co 3:3 **24:13** [z]S Ex 17:9 [a]S Ex 3:1 **24:14** [b]S Ex 17:10 [c]Ex 18:16 **24:15** [d]S Ex 19:9; Mt 17:5 **24:16** [e]S Ex 16:7; Lev 9:23; Nu 14:10; 1Sa 4:21,22; Eze 8:4; 11:22 [f]S Ex 19:11 [g]Ps 99:7 **24:17** [h]S Ex 15:7; S 19:18; Heb 12:18,29 **24:18** [i]1Ki 19:8 [j]S Ge 7:4; Mt 4:2

[j]5 Traditionally *peace offerings* [k]10 Or *lapis lazuli*

24:8 THE BLOOD OF THE COVENANT. The covenant was sealed with Israel through the sprinkling of blood, indicating that atoning sacrifices were necessary to maintain their relationship with God. (1) The blood signified cleansing and forgiveness made possible by means of a life sacrificed to God; such sacrifices opened the way to reconciliation with God and the people's obedience that comes from faith (cf. Ro 1:5; Heb 9:19–20).

(2) The ultimate significance of "the blood of the covenant" was realized when Christ shed his blood on the cross and established the new covenant (cf. Mk 14:24; Heb 9:11–18). His sacrificial death cleanses believers from sin as they seek to walk in the way of holiness (1Jn 1:7—2:2).

(3) Obedience and blood (vv. 7–8) must always be joined together to validate God's acceptance of his people and their consecration to him. Only after the people pledged to obey God through the atoning blood could they participate in the covenant blessings (see article on GOD'S COVENANT WITH THE ISRAELITES, p. 290). In a similar vein, the apostle Peter states that we are chosen "for obedience to Jesus Christ and sprinkling by his blood" (1Pe 1:2).

24:11 SAW GOD, AND THEY ATE AND DRANK. We are not told in what manner God revealed himself. We do know that he did not show himself fully, since no human can see God's full glory and live (see 33:18–23). God's appearance and the accompanying meal signified that after atonement had been made and the people had consecrated themselves to the Lord, then fellowship with him was possible; this is a NT principle as well (cf. Mt 26:28; Heb 12:18–24).

24:16–17 THE GLORY OF THE LORD. The Lord's glory is revealed in a brilliant manifestation of light emanating from God's being (see 40:34, note; cf. 1Ti 6:16).

for me from each man whose heart
prompts[k] him to give. 3 These are the
offerings you are to receive from them:
gold, silver and bronze; 4 blue, purple
and scarlet yarn[l] and fine linen; goat
hair; 5 ram skins dyed red and hides of
sea cows[l];[m] acacia wood;[n] 6 olive
oil[o] for the light; spices for the anointing oil and for the fragrant incense;[p]
7 and onyx stones and other gems to be
mounted on the ephod[q] and breastpiece.[r]
8 "Then have them make a sanctuary[s] for me, and I will dwell[t] among
them. 9 Make this tabernacle and all its
furnishings exactly like the pattern[u] I
will show you.

The Ark

25:10–20pp — Ex 37:1–9

10 "Have them make a chest[v] of acacia wood—two and a half cubits long,
a cubit and a half wide, and a cubit and
a half high.[m] 11 Overlay[w] it with pure
gold, both inside and out, and make a
gold molding around it. 12 Cast four
gold rings for it and fasten them to its
four feet, with two rings[x] on one side
and two rings on the other. 13 Then
make poles of acacia wood and overlay
them with gold.[y] 14 Insert the poles[z]
into the rings on the sides of the chest
to carry it. 15 The poles are to remain
in the rings of this ark; they are not to
be removed.[a] 16 Then put in the ark
the Testimony,[b] which I will give you.
17 "Make an atonement cover[n][c] of
pure gold—two and a half cubits long
and a cubit and a half wide.[o] 18 And
make two cherubim[d] out of hammered
gold at the ends of the cover. 19 Make
one cherub on one end and the second
cherub on the other; make the cherubim of one piece with the cover, at the
two ends. 20 The cherubim[e] are to
have their wings spread upward, overshadowing[f] the cover with them. The
cherubim are to face each other, look-

25:2 [k] Ex 35:21, 22,26,27,29; 36:2; 2Ki 12:4; 1Ch 29:5,7,9; 2Ch 24:10; 29:31; Ezr 2:68; Ne 7:70-72; 2Co 8:11-12; 9:7 **25:4** [l] Ex 28:4-8 **25:5** [m] Nu 4:6,10 [n] Dt 10:3 **25:6** [o] Ex 27:20; 30:22-32; 35:28; 39:37; Nu 4:16 [p] Ex 30:1,7,35; 31:11; 35:28; Lev 16:12; Nu 4:16; 7:14; 2Ch 13:11 **25:7** [q] Ex 28:4, 6-14; 29:5; Jdg 8:27; Hos 3:4 [r] Lev 8:8 **25:8** [s] Ex 36:1-5; Lev 4:6; 10:4,7; 21:12,23; Nu 3:28; Heb 9:1-2 [t] Ex 29:45; Lev 26:11-12; Nu 5:3; Dt 12:11; 1Ki 6:13; Zec 2:10; 2Co 6:16 **25:9** [u] ver 40; Ex 26:30; 27:8; 31:11; 39:32,42, 43; Nu 8:4; 1Ch 28:11,19; Ac 7:44; Heb 8:5 **25:10** [v] Dt 10:1-5; 1Ki 6:19; Heb 9:4 **25:11** [w] ver 24; Ex 30:3 **25:12** [x] ver 26; Ex 30:4 **25:13** [y] ver 28; Ex 27:6; 30:5; 37:28 **25:14** [z] Ex 27:7; 40:20; 1Ch 15:15 **25:15** [a] 1Ki 8:8 **25:16** [b] S Ex 16:34; Heb 9:4 **25:17** [c] ver 21; Lev 16:13; Ro 3:25 **25:18** [d] Ex 26:1,31; 36:35; 1Ki 6:23,27; 8:6; 2Ch 3:10-13; Heb 9:5 **25:20** [e] S Ge 3:24 [f] Ex 37:9; 1Ki 8:7; 1Ch 28:18; Heb 9:5

[l] *5* That is, dugongs [m] *10* That is, about 3 3/4 feet (about 1.1 meters) long and 2 1/4 feet (about 0.7 meter) wide and high
[n] *17* Traditionally *a mercy seat* [o] *17* That is, about 3 3/4 feet (about 1.1 meters) long and 2 1/4 feet (about 0.7 meter) wide

25:9 THIS TABERNACLE. In ch. 25, God gives his instruction concerning the tabernacle. The historical, spiritual and typological significance of the tabernacle must be based on what the Bible says about it. (1) The tabernacle was a "sanctuary" (v. 8), a place set apart for the Lord to dwell among and meet with his people (v. 22; 29:45–46; Nu 5:3; Eze 43:7,9). God's glory was over the tabernacle day and night. When God's glory moved, Israel had to move. God guided them in this manner while they were in the desert (40:36–38; Nu 9:15–16).

(2) It was a "tabernacle of the Testimony" (38:21), i.e., it contained the Ten Commandments (see next note). The Ten Commandments were a constant reminder of God's holiness and his demands. Our relationship to God can never be separated from our obedience to his law.

(3) It was the place where God provided forgiveness of sins through a blood sacrifice (29:10–14). Thus it pointed to the ultimate sacrifice of Christ on the cross for the sins of the human race (see Heb 8:1–2; 9:11–14).

(4) It pointed to heaven, i.e., to a heavenly tabernacle where Christ, our eternal high priest, lives forever to pray for us (Heb 9:11–12,24–28).

(5) It pointed toward God's final redemption when a new heaven and new earth will come, i.e., "the dwelling [lit. tabernacle] of God is with men, and he will live with them. They will be his people, and God himself will be with them" (Rev 21:3).

25:10 CHEST. This chest was the ark containing the Ten Commandments (cf. vv. 16,22), a jar of manna (16:33–34), and Aaron's staff (Nu 17:10; Heb 9:4). It was topped by a lid called the "atonement cover" (v. 17). Fixed at both ends of the atonement cover were two carved, winged cherubim (see v. 18, note). The ark was placed in the Most Holy Place of the tabernacle (26:34) and represented the throne of God, before which the high priest stood once a year on the Day of Atonement to sprinkle blood on the atonement cover to atone for the people's unintentional sins during the previous year (see article on THE DAY OF ATONEMENT, p. 174).

25:16 THE TESTIMONY. This "Testimony" was the two stone tablets on which were inscribed the Ten Commandments Moses received on the mountain (31:18).

25:17 ATONEMENT COVER. The atonement cover was the lid for the ark. On it the high priest sprinkled the shed blood of the sacrificial offering to make atonement for sins. This act was symbolic of God's forgiving mercy (Lev 16:14–15; 17:11; see Ro 3:25, note). Thus the atonement cover and the blood foreshadowed the forgiveness available to sinful people through Christ's atoning sacrifice (Ro 3:21–25; Heb 4:14–16; 7:26).

25:18 TWO CHERUBIM. These were carvings of the angelic beings who hover around God's throne in heaven (cf. Heb 8:5; Rev 4:6,8). They symbolized God's presence and kingship among his people on earth (1Sa 4:4; 2Sa 6:2; 2Ki 19:15). Their placement on the ark testified to the truth that God would remain among his people only as long as blood sacrifice was made and the people strove to keep God's commandments.

ing toward the cover. 21 Place the cover
on top of the ark[g] and put in the ark
the Testimony,[h] which I will give you.
22 There, above the cover between the
two cherubim[i] that are over the ark of
the Testimony, I will meet[j] with you
and give you all my commands for the
Israelites.[k]

The Table

25:23–29pp — Ex 37:10–16

23 "Make a table[l] of acacia wood—
two cubits long, a cubit wide and a cubit and a half high.[p] 24 Overlay it with
pure gold and make a gold molding
around it. 25 Also make around it a rim
a handbreadth[q] wide and put a gold
molding on the rim. 26 Make four gold
rings for the table and fasten them to
the four corners, where the four legs
are. 27 The rings are to be close to the
rim to hold the poles used in carrying
the table. 28 Make the poles of acacia
wood, overlay them with gold[m] and
carry the table with them. 29 And make
its plates and dishes of pure gold, as
well as its pitchers and bowls for the
pouring out of offerings.[n] 30 Put the
bread of the Presence[o] on this table to
be before me at all times.

The Lampstand

25:31–39pp — Ex 37:17–24

31 "Make a lampstand[p] of pure gold
and hammer it out, base and shaft; its
flowerlike cups, buds and blossoms
shall be of one piece with it. 32 Six
branches are to extend from the sides
of the lampstand—three on one side
and three on the other. 33 Three cups
shaped like almond flowers with buds
and blossoms are to be on one branch,
three on the next branch, and the same
for all six branches extending from the
lampstand. 34 And on the lampstand
there are to be four cups shaped like
almond flowers with buds and blossoms. 35 One bud shall be under the
first pair of branches extending from
the lampstand, a second bud under the
second pair, and a third bud under the
third pair—six branches in all. 36 The
buds and branches shall all be of one
piece with the lampstand, hammered
out of pure gold.[q]
37 "Then make its seven lamps[r] and
set them up on it so that they light the
space in front of it. 38 Its wick trimmers
and trays[s] are to be of pure gold. 39 A
talent[r] of pure gold is to be used for
the lampstand and all these accessories. 40 See that you make them according to the pattern[t] shown you on the
mountain.

The Tabernacle

26:1–37pp — Ex 36:8–38

26 "Make the tabernacle[u] with
ten curtains of finely twisted
linen and blue, purple and scarlet yarn,
with cherubim[v] worked into them by
a skilled craftsman. 2 All the curtains
are to be the same size[w]—twenty-
eight cubits long and four cubits
wide.[s] 3 Join five of the curtains together, and do the same with the other
five. 4 Make loops of blue material
along the edge of the end curtain in one
set, and do the same with the end curtain in the other set. 5 Make fifty loops
on one curtain and fifty loops on the
end curtain of the other set, with the
loops opposite each other. 6 Then make
fifty gold clasps and use them to fasten
the curtains together so that the tabernacle is a unit.[x]
7 "Make curtains of goat hair for the
tent over the tabernacle—eleven altogether. 8 All eleven curtains are to be
the same size[y]—thirty cubits long
and four cubits wide.[t] 9 Join five of the

25:21 [g] ver 10-15; Ex 26:34; 40:20; Dt 10:5 [h] S Ex 16:34; Heb 9:4
25:22 [i] Nu 7:89; 1Sa 4:4; 2Sa 6:2; 22:11; 2Ki 19:15; 1Ch 13:6; 28:18; Ps 18:10; 80:1; 99:1; Isa 37:16 [j] S Ex 19:3; 29:42; 30:6,36; Lev 1:1; 16:2; Nu 17:4 [k] Jer 3:16
25:23 [l] ver 30; Ex 26:35; 40:4,22; Lev 24:6; Nu 3:31; 1Ki 7:48; 1Ch 28:16; 2Ch 4:8,19; Eze 41:22; 44:16; Heb 9:2
25:28 [m] S ver 13
25:29 [n] Nu 4:7
25:30 [o] Ex 35:13; 39:36; 40:4,23; Lev 24:5-9; Nu 4:7; 1Sa 21:4-6; 1Ki 7:48; 1Ch 23:29
25:31 [p] Ex 26:35; 31:8; 35:14; 39:37; 40:4,24; Lev 24:4; Nu 3:31; 1Ki 7:49; 2Ch 4:7; Zec 4:2; Heb 9:2; Rev 1:12
25:36 [q] ver 18; Nu 8:4
25:37 [r] Ex 27:21; 30:8; Lev 24:3-4; Nu 8:2; 1Sa 3:3; 2Ch 13:11
25:38 [s] S ver 37; Nu 4:9
25:40 [t] S ver 9; Ac 7:44; Heb 8:5*
26:1 [u] Ex 29:42; 40:2; Lev 8:10; Nu 1:50; Jos 22:19,29; 2Sa 7:2; 1Ki 1:39; Ac 7:44; Heb 8:2, 5; 13:10; S Rev 21:3 [v] S Ex 25:18
26:2 [w] ver 8
26:6 [x] ver 11
26:8 [y] ver 2

[p] *23* That is, about 3 feet (about 0.9 meter) long and 1 1/2 feet (about 0.5 meter) wide and 2 1/4 feet (about 0.7 meter) high [q] *25* That is, about 3 inches (about 8 centimeters) [r] *39* That is, about 75 pounds (about 34 kilograms) [s] *2* That is, about 42 feet (about 12.5 meters) long and 6 feet (about 1.8 meters) wide [t] *8* That is, about 45 feet (about 13.5 meters) long and 6 feet (about 1.8 meters) wide

25:30 THE BREAD OF THE PRESENCE. The bread placed on the table represented the Lord's presence that sustained Israel in all of life (cf. Lev 24:5–9; Isa 63:9). It points to Christ, the bread of life (see 16:4, note; Mt 26:26–29; 1Co 10:16).

25:31 LAMPSTAND. This lampstand held seven oil lamps and furnished light in the tabernacle. The burning lamps represented God's light or presence in the midst of the camp (Jer 25:10; cf. Rev 21:22—22:6).

26:1 FINELY TWISTED LINEN. Exact instructions were given for building the tabernacle. It had to be constructed according to God's pattern because it was his house and he was the designer (cf. 25:9). Salvation and communion with God are possible only on his terms and according to his pattern and revelation (see Mt 5:17, note; Ac 7:44, note).

curtains together into one set and the
other six into another set. Fold the
sixth curtain double at the front of the
tent. **10**Make fifty loops along the edge
of the end curtain in one set and also
along the edge of the end curtain in the
other set. **11**Then make fifty bronze
clasps and put them in the loops to fasten the tent together as a unit.[z] **12**As
for the additional length of the tent
curtains, the half curtain that is left
over is to hang down at the rear of the
tabernacle. **13**The tent curtains will be
a cubit[u] longer on both sides; what is
left will hang over the sides of the tabernacle so as to cover it. **14**Make for
the tent a covering[a] of ram skins dyed
red, and over that a covering of hides
of sea cows.[v][b]

15"Make upright frames of acacia
wood for the tabernacle. **16**Each frame
is to be ten cubits long and a cubit and
a half wide,[w] **17**with two projections
set parallel to each other. Make all the
frames of the tabernacle in this way.
18Make twenty frames for the south
side of the tabernacle **19**and make forty
silver bases[c] to go under them—two
bases for each frame, one under each
projection. **20**For the other side, the
north side of the tabernacle, make
twenty frames **21**and forty silver bases[d]—two under each frame. **22**Make
six frames for the far end, that is, the
west end of the tabernacle, **23**and make
two frames for the corners at the far
end. **24**At these two corners they must
be double from the bottom all the way
to the top, and fitted into a single ring;
both shall be like that. **25**So there will
be eight frames and sixteen silver bases—two under each frame.

26"Also make crossbars of acacia
wood: five for the frames on one side of
the tabernacle, **27**five for those on the
other side, and five for the frames on
the west, at the far end of the tabernacle. **28**The center crossbar is to extend
from end to end at the middle of the
frames. **29**Overlay the frames with gold
and make gold rings to hold the crossbars. Also overlay the crossbars with
gold.

30"Set up the tabernacle[e] according to the plan[f] shown you on the
mountain.

31"Make a curtain[g] of blue, purple
and scarlet yarn and finely twisted lin-
en, with cherubim[h] worked into it by
a skilled craftsman. **32**Hang it with
gold hooks on four posts of acacia
wood overlaid with gold and standing
on four silver bases.[i] **33**Hang the curtain from the clasps and place the ark
of the Testimony behind the curtain.[j]
The curtain will separate the Holy
Place from the Most Holy Place.[k]
34Put the atonement cover[l] on the
ark of the Testimony in the Most Holy
Place. **35**Place the table[m] outside the
curtain on the north side of the tabernacle and put the lampstand[n] opposite it on the south side.

36"For the entrance to the tent make
a curtain[o] of blue, purple and scarlet
yarn and finely twisted linen—the
work of an embroiderer.[p] **37**Make gold
hooks for this curtain and five posts of
acacia wood overlaid with gold. And
cast five bronze bases for them.

The Altar of Burnt Offering

27:1–8pp — Ex 38:1–7

27 "Build an altar[q] of acacia
wood, three cubits[x] high; it is

26:11 [z] ver 6 **26:14** [a] Nu 3:25 [b] Nu 4:25 **26:19** [c] ver 21,25, 32; Ex 38:27 **26:21** [d] S ver 19 **26:30** [e] Ex 40:2; Nu 9:15 [f] S Ex 25:9 **26:31** [g] Nu 4:5; 2Ch 3:14; Mt 27:51; Lk 23:45; Heb 9:3 [h] S Ex 25:18 **26:32** [i] S ver 19 **26:33** [j] Ex 27:21; 35:12; 40:3,21; Lev 16:2; Nu 3:31; 4:5; 2Ch 3:14 [k] Lev 16:2,16; 1Ki 6:16; 7:50; 8:6; 2Ch 3:8; 5:7; Eze 41:4; Heb 9:2-3 **26:34** [l] Ex 25:21; 30:6; 37:6; Lev 16:2; Heb 9:5 **26:35** [m] S Ex 25:23; Heb 9:2 [n] S Ex 25:31 **26:36** [o] Ex 35:15; 40:5,28 [p] Ps 45:14; Eze 16:10; 26:16; 27:7 **27:1** [q] S Ex 20:24; S 40:6; S 1Ki 8:64

[u] *13* That is, about 1 1/2 feet (about 0.5 meter) [v] *14* That is, dugongs [w] *16* That is, about 15 feet (about 4.5 meters) long and 2 1/4 feet (about 0.7 meter) wide [x] *1* That is, about 4 1/2 feet (about 1.3 meters)

26:33 THE CURTAIN. A curtain separated the Holy Place (i.e., the place where the priest prayed and gave thanks on behalf of the people) from the Most Holy Place (i.e., God's dwelling place). The curtain pictured the solemn truth that humans could not freely approach God because of their sinful condition. (1) Access to the Most Holy Place was severely restricted. The high priest could enter only one day each year to represent the people, and then only if he brought with him the blood of an atoning sacrifice (cf. 30:10; Lev 16:12ff; Heb 9:6–8). The way for all God's people to enter freely into God's presence had not yet been provided (Heb 9:8).

(2) The only way to have perfect access to God would be by tearing the curtain and removing the existing order of the tabernacle. This Jesus Christ did by shedding his blood on the cross. His body represented the curtain that at the time of his death was torn (Mt 27:51; Col 1:20–22; Heb 10:20). Now every believer may "enter the Most Holy Place by the blood of Jesus" (Heb 10:19).

27:1 AN ALTAR. The altar, also called the "altar of burnt offering" (cf. 30:28; 31:9; Lev 4:7, 10,18), was used for the sacrifice of animals in order to make atonement (i.e., cover sin and provide forgiveness, see article on THE DAY OF ATONEMENT, p. 174). The blood of the sacrificial animal was put on the horns of the altar and poured out at its base (cf. 29:12; Lev 4:7,

THE TABERNACLE

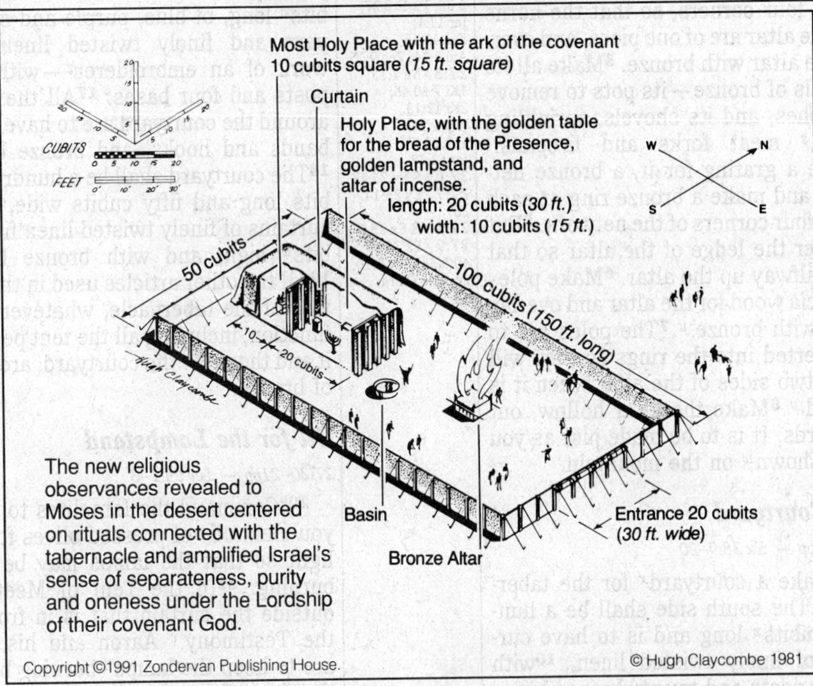

TABERNACLE FURNISHINGS

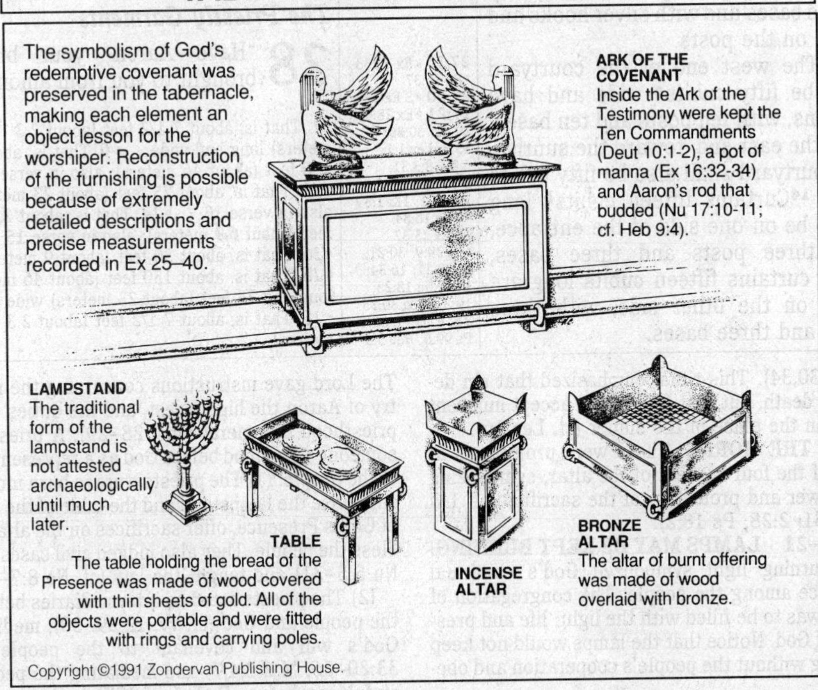

to be square, five cubits long and five cubits wide.[y] 2Make a horn[r] at each of the four corners, so that the horns and the altar are of one piece, and overlay the altar with bronze. 3Make all its utensils of bronze—its pots to remove the ashes, and its shovels, sprinkling bowls,[s] meat forks and firepans.[t] 4Make a grating for it, a bronze network, and make a bronze ring at each of the four corners of the network. 5Put it under the ledge of the altar so that it is halfway up the altar. 6Make poles of acacia wood for the altar and overlay them with bronze.[u] 7The poles are to be inserted into the rings so they will be on two sides of the altar when it is carried.[v] 8Make the altar hollow, out of boards. It is to be made just as you were shown[w] on the mountain.

The Courtyard

27:9–19pp — Ex 38:9–20

9"Make a courtyard[x] for the tabernacle. The south side shall be a hundred cubits[z] long and is to have curtains of finely twisted linen, 10with twenty posts and twenty bronze bases and with silver hooks and bands on the posts. 11The north side shall also be a hundred cubits long and is to have curtains, with twenty posts and twenty bronze bases and with silver hooks and bands on the posts.

12"The west end of the courtyard shall be fifty cubits[a] wide and have curtains, with ten posts and ten bases. 13On the east end, toward the sunrise, the courtyard shall also be fifty cubits wide. 14Curtains fifteen cubits[b] long are to be on one side of the entrance, with three posts and three bases, 15and curtains fifteen cubits long are to be on the other side, with three posts and three bases.

16"For the entrance to the courtyard, provide a curtain[y] twenty cubits[c] long, of blue, purple and scarlet yarn and finely twisted linen—the work of an embroiderer[z]—with four posts and four bases. 17All the posts around the courtyard are to have silver bands and hooks, and bronze bases. 18The courtyard shall be a hundred cubits long and fifty cubits wide,[d] with curtains of finely twisted linen five cubits[e] high, and with bronze bases. 19All the other articles used in the service of the tabernacle, whatever their function, including all the tent pegs for it and those for the courtyard, are to be of bronze.

Oil for the Lampstand

27:20–21pp — Lev 24:1–3

20"Command the Israelites to bring you clear oil[a] of pressed olives for the light so that the lamps may be kept burning. 21In the Tent of Meeting,[b] outside the curtain that is in front of the Testimony,[c] Aaron and his sons are to keep the lamps[d] burning before the LORD from evening till morning. This is to be a lasting ordinance[e] among the Israelites for the generations to come.

The Priestly Garments

28 "Have Aaron[f] your brother brought to you from among the

27:2 [r] Ex 29:12; 30:2; 37:25; Lev 4:7; 1Ki 1:50; 2:28; Ps 118:27; Jer 17:1; Eze 43:15; Am 3:14; Zec 9:15 **27:3** [s] Nu 7:13; 1Ki 7:40,45; 2Ki 12:13 [t] Nu 4:14; 1Ch 28:17; Jer 52:18 **27:6** [u] S Ex 25:13 **27:7** [v] Ex 25:14, 28 **27:8** [w] S Ex 25:9 **27:9** [x] Ex 35:17; 40:8,33; Lev 6:16, 26; Eze 40:14; 42:1

27:16 [y] Ex 40:33 [z] Ex 36:37 **27:20** [a] S Ex 25:6 **27:21** [b] Ex 28:43; 29:42; 30:36; 33:7; Lev 1:1; 6:26; 8:3,31; Nu 1:1; 31:54; Jos 18:1; 1Ki 1:39 [c] S Ex 16:34 [d] S Ex 25:37 [e] Ex 29:9; 30:21; Lev 3:17; 16:34; 17:7; Nu 18:23; 19:21; 1Sa 30:25 **28:1** [f] Lev 8:30; Ps 99:6; Heb 5:4

[y] *1* That is, about 7 1/2 feet (about 2.3 meters) long and wide [z] *9* That is, about 150 feet (about 46 meters); also in verse 11 [a] *12* That is, about 75 feet (about 23 meters); also in verse 13 [b] *14* That is, about 22 1/2 feet (about 6.9 meters); also in verse 15 [c] *16* That is, about 30 feet (about 9 meters) [d] *18* That is, about 150 feet (about 46 meters) long and 75 feet (about 23 meters) wide [e] *18* That is, about 7 1/2 feet (about 2.3 meters)

18,25,30,34). This ritual emphasized that sin deserves death, but that God would accept innocent blood in the place of the sinner (cf. Lev 16).

27:2 THE HORNS. These were projections at each of the four corners of the altar, symbolizing the power and protection of the sacrifice (cf. 1Ki 1:50–51; 2:28; Ps 18:2).

27:20–21 LAMPS MAY BE KEPT BURNING. The burning light symbolized God's continual presence among the people. The congregation of Israel was to be filled with the light, life and presence of God. Notice that the lamps would not keep burning without the people's cooperation and obedience.

28:1 AARON . . . SERVE ME AS PRIESTS. The Lord gave instructions concerning the ministry of Aaron the high priest, and the duties of the priesthood in general (chs. 28–29). A priest was someone who stood before God as a representative of the people. (1) The priests were to burn incense, supervise the lampstand and the table of the bread of God's Presence, offer sacrifices on the altar and bless the people. They also judged civil cases (e.g., Nu 5:5–31) and taught the law (cf. Ne 8:7–8).

(2) The priests acted as intermediaries between the people and God (cf. vv. 12,29–30), mediating God's will and covenant to the people (Jer 33:20–26; Mal 2:4,7) and mediating the people's sinfulness before God. In fulfilling these tasks, they made atonement for the people's sin and their

Israelites, along with his sons Nadab
and Abihu,[g] Eleazar and Ithamar,[h]
so they may serve me as priests.[i]
2Make sacred garments[j] for your
brother Aaron, to give him dignity and
honor.[k] **3**Tell all the skilled men[l] to
whom I have given wisdom[m] in such
matters that they are to make garments for Aaron, for his consecration,
so he may serve me as priest. **4**These
are the garments they are to make: a
breastpiece,[n] an ephod,[o] a robe,[p] a
woven tunic,[q] a turban[r] and a sash.
They are to make these sacred garments for your brother Aaron and his
sons, so they may serve me as priests.
5Have them use gold, and blue, purple
and scarlet yarn, and fine linen.[s]

The Ephod

28:6–14pp — Ex 39:2–7

6"Make the ephod[t] of gold, and of
blue, purple and scarlet yarn, and of
finely twisted linen—the work of a
skilled craftsman. **7**It is to have two
shoulder pieces attached to two of its
corners, so it can be fastened. **8**Its
skillfully woven waistband[u] is to be
like it—of one piece with the ephod
and made with gold, and with blue, purple and scarlet yarn, and with finely
twisted linen.

9"Take two onyx stones and engrave[v] on them the names of the sons
of Israel **10**in the order of their birth—
six names on one stone and the remaining six on the other. **11**Engrave
the names of the sons of Israel on the
two stones the way a gem cutter en-
graves a seal. Then mount the stones
in gold filigree settings **12**and fasten
them on the shoulder pieces of the
ephod as memorial stones for the sons
of Israel. Aaron is to bear the names on
his shoulders[w] as a memorial[x] before
the LORD. **13**Make gold filigree settings
14and two braided chains of pure gold,
like a rope, and attach the chains to the
settings.

The Breastpiece

28:15–28pp — Ex 39:8–21

15"Fashion a breastpiece[y] for making decisions—the work of a skilled
craftsman. Make it like the ephod: of
gold, and of blue, purple and scarlet
yarn, and of finely twisted linen. **16**It is
to be square—a span[f] long and a
span wide—and folded double. **17**Then
mount four rows of precious stones[z]
on it. In the first row there shall be a
ruby, a topaz and a beryl; **18**in the second row a turquoise, a sapphire[g] and
an emerald; **19**in the third row a jacinth, an agate and an amethyst; **20**in
the fourth row a chrysolite,[a] an onyx
and a jasper.[h] Mount them in gold filigree settings. **21**There are to be twelve
stones, one for each of the names of
the sons of Israel,[b] each engraved like
a seal with the name of one of the
twelve tribes.[c]

22"For the breastpiece make braided
chains of pure gold, like a rope.
23Make two gold rings for it and fasten
them to two corners of the breastpiece.
24Fasten the two gold chains to the
rings at the corners of the breastpiece,
25and the other ends of the chains to
the two settings, attaching them to the
shoulder pieces of the ephod at the
front. **26**Make two gold rings and attach them to the other two corners of
the breastpiece on the inside edge next
to the ephod. **27**Make two more gold
rings and attach them to the bottom of
the shoulder pieces on the front of the
ephod, close to the seam just above the
waistband of the ephod. **28**The rings of
the breastpiece are to be tied to the
rings of the ephod with blue cord, connecting it to the waistband, so that the
breastpiece will not swing out from the
ephod.

29"Whenever Aaron enters the Holy

28:1 [g] S Ex 6:23; 24:9 [h] S Ex 6:23 [i] Lev 8:2; 21:1; Nu 18:1-7; Dt 18:5; 1Sa 2:28; Heb 5:1
28:2 [j] Ex 29:5,29; 31:10; 35:19; 39:1; Lev 8:7-9, 30; 16:32; Nu 20:26-28 [k] ver 40
28:3 [l] Ex 31:6; 35:10,25,35; 36:1 [m] Ex 31:3; Dt 34:9; Isa 11:2; 1Co 12:8; S Eph 1:17
28:4 [n] ver 15-30 [o] S Ex 25:7 [p] ver 31-35 [q] ver 39; Lev 10:5 [r] ver 37
28:5 [s] S Ex 25:4
28:6 [t] S Ex 25:7
28:8 [u] Ex 29:5
28:9 [v] SS 8:6; Isa 49:16; Hag 2:23
28:12 [w] Dt 33:12; Job 31:36 [x] ver 29; Ex 30:16; Nu 10:10; 31:54; Jos 4:7; Zec 6:14
28:15 [y] S Ex 25:7
28:17 [z] Eze 28:13; Rev 21:19-20
28:20 [a] Eze 1:16; 10:9; Da 10:6
28:21 [b] Jos 4:8 [c] Rev 21:12

[f] *16* That is, about 9 inches (about 22 centimeters) [g] *18* Or *lapis lazuli*
[h] *20* The precise identification of some of these precious stones is uncertain.

own sin (29:33; Heb 9:6–8) and testified concerning God's holiness (v. 38; Nu 18:1).

(3) For NT believers Jesus is the priest of God's people. He initiated the new covenant through his death (Heb 9:15–22) and offered himself as the perfect sacrifice (Heb 9:23–28). He sympathizes with our weaknesses (Heb 4:15), appears in God's presence on our behalf (Heb 9:24), brings our salvation to completion (Heb 10:14) and makes it possible for us to draw near to God the Father (Heb 4:16; 6:19–20; 7:25; 10:19–22).

28:4 A BREASTPIECE. This was a square on which were placed twelve small precious stones in four horizontal rows of three stones each; on these stones the names of the twelve sons of Israel were engraved (vv. 15–21,29–30).

28:6 EPHOD. The ephod was a loose-fitting, sleeveless garment extending to the knees; it was worn like an apron over the priest's robe (vv. 6–20; 39:1–21).

Place,[d] he will bear the names of the
sons of Israel over his heart on the
breastpiece of decision as a continuing
memorial before the LORD. **30**Also put
the Urim and the Thummim[e] in the
breastpiece, so they may be over Aaron's heart whenever he enters the
presence of the LORD. Thus Aaron will
always bear the means of making decisions for the Israelites over his heart
before the LORD.

Other Priestly Garments

28:31–43pp — Ex 39:22–31

31"Make the robe of the ephod entirely of blue cloth, **32**with an opening
for the head in its center. There shall
be a woven edge like a collar[i] around
this opening, so that it will not tear.
33Make pomegranates[f] of blue, purple and scarlet yarn around the hem of
the robe, with gold bells between them.
34The gold bells and the pomegranates
are to alternate around the hem of the
robe. **35**Aaron must wear it when he
ministers. The sound of the bells will
be heard when he enters the Holy
Place before the LORD and when he
comes out, so that he will not die.
36"Make a plate[g] of pure gold and
engrave on it as on a seal: HOLY TO THE
LORD.[h] **37**Fasten a blue cord to it to
attach it to the turban; it is to be on the
front of the turban. **38**It will be on Aaron's forehead, and he will bear the
guilt[i] involved in the sacred gifts the
Israelites consecrate, whatever their
gifts may be. It will be on Aaron's forehead continually so that they will be
acceptable[j] to the LORD.
39"Weave the tunic[k] of fine linen
and make the turban[l] of fine linen.
The sash is to be the work of an embroiderer. **40**Make tunics, sashes and
headbands for Aaron's sons,[m] to give
them dignity and honor.[n] **41**After you
put these clothes[o] on your brother
Aaron and his sons, anoint[p] and ordain them. Consecrate them so they
may serve me as priests.[q]

28:29 [d]ver 43 **28:30** [e]Lev 8:8; Nu 27:21; Dt 33:8; 1Sa 28:6; Ezr 2:63; Ne 7:65 **28:33** [f]Nu 13:23; 1Sa 14:2; 1Ki 7:18; SS 4:3; Jer 52:22; Joel 1:12; Hag 2:19 **28:36** [g]ver 37; Ex 29:6; Lev 8:9 [h]Zec 14:20 **28:38** [i]Lev 5:1; 10:17; 16:22; 22:9,16; Nu 18:1; Isa 53:5,6,11; Eze 4:4-6; Heb 9:28; 1Pe 2:24 [j]S Ge 32:20; Lev 22:20,27; 23:11; Isa 56:7 **28:39** [k]ver 4 [l]Ex 29:6; Lev 16:4; Eze 24:17,23; 44:18 **28:40** [m]ver 4; Ex 29:8-9; 39:41; 40:14; Lev 8:13 [n]ver 2 **28:41** [o]Ex 40:13 [p]Ex 29:7; Lev 6:20; 10:7; 21:12; Nu 35:25 [q]Ex 29:7-9; 30:30; 40:15; Lev 4:3; 6:22; 8:1-36; Nu 3:3; Heb 7:28

28:42 [r]Lev 6:10; 16:4,23; Eze 44:18 **28:43** [s]S Ex 27:21 [t]ver 29 [u]Ex 30:20, 21; Lev 16:13; 22:9; Nu 1:51; 4:15,20; 18:22 [v]S Ex 27:21 **29:1** [w]ver 21,44; Lev 20:7; Jos 3:5; 1Ch 15:12 [x]Eze 43:23 **29:2** [y]ver 23; Lev 2:1,4; 6:19-23; Nu 6:15 **29:3** [z]ver 15,19 **29:4** [a]Ex 40:12; Lev 14:8; 16:4; Heb 10:22 **29:5** [b]S Ex 28:2 [c]Ex 28:8 **29:6** [d]Ex 28:39; Isa 3:23; Zec 3:5 [e]S Ex 28:36 **29:7** [f]ver 21; S Ex 28:41; 30:25, 30,31; 37:29; 40:9; Lev 21:10; 1Sa 10:1; 1Ki 1:39; Ps 89:20; 133:2; 141:5 **29:8** [g]S Ex 28:4;

42"Make linen undergarments[r] as a
covering for the body, reaching from
the waist to the thigh. **43**Aaron and his
sons must wear them whenever they
enter the Tent of Meeting[s] or approach the altar to minister in the Holy
Place,[t] so that they will not incur
guilt and die.[u]
"This is to be a lasting ordinance[v]
for Aaron and his descendants.

Consecration of the Priests

29:1–37pp — Lev 8:1–36

29 "This is what you are to do to
consecrate[w] them, so they may
serve me as priests: Take a young bull
and two rams without defect.[x] **2**And
from fine wheat flour, without yeast,
make bread, and cakes mixed with oil,
and wafers spread with oil.[y] **3**Put
them in a basket and present them in
it—along with the bull and the two
rams.[z] **4**Then bring Aaron and his
sons to the entrance to the Tent of
Meeting and wash them with water.[a]
5Take the garments[b] and dress Aaron
with the tunic, the robe of the ephod,
the ephod itself and the breastpiece.
Fasten the ephod on him by its skillfully woven waistband.[c] **6**Put the turban[d] on his head and attach the sacred diadem[e] to the turban. **7**Take the
anointing oil[f] and anoint him by pouring it on his head. **8**Bring his sons and
dress them in tunics[g] **9**and put headbands on them. Then tie sashes on Aaron and his sons.[j][h] The priesthood is
theirs by a lasting ordinance.[i] In this
way you shall ordain Aaron and his
sons.
10"Bring the bull to the front of the
Tent of Meeting, and Aaron and his
sons shall lay their hands on its

Lev 16:4 **29:9** [h]Ex 28:40 [i]S Ex 27:21; 40:15; Nu 3:10; 18:7; 25:13; Dt 18:5; Jdg 17:5; 1Sa 2:30; 1Ki 12:31

[i]*32* The meaning of the Hebrew for this word is uncertain. [j]*9* Hebrew; Septuagint *on them*

28:29 BEAR THE NAMES OF THE SONS OF ISRAEL. As high priest, Aaron represented the people before the Lord when he entered the Holy Place (vv. 12,29). In doing so, he foreshadowed Jesus our High Priest, who entered heaven to appear in his Father's presence as our representative (Heb 9:24; see article on CHRIST IN THE OLD TESTAMENT, p. 518).

28:30 THE URIM AND THE THUMMIM. Scripture does not explain what is meant by the Urim and the Thummim. The literal meaning may be "lights" and "perfections," or "curses" and "perfections." They were probably used for casting lots to receive a "yes" or "no" answer in order to determine God's will in particular cases (cf. Lev 8:8; Nu 27:21; Dt 33:8; 1Sa 28:6).

29:4 WASH THEM WITH WATER. The ceremonial washing with water symbolized the purity that was to characterize the priests.

29:10 THE BULL. When the priests laid their

head.[j] **11**Slaughter it in the LORD's
presence[k] at the entrance to the Tent
of Meeting. **12**Take some of the bull's
blood and put it on the horns[l] of the
altar with your finger, and pour out the
rest of it at the base of the altar.[m]
13Then take all the fat[n] around the
inner parts,[o] the covering of the liver,
and both kidneys with the fat on them,
and burn them on the altar. **14**But burn
the bull's flesh and its hide and its offal[p] outside the camp.[q] It is a sin offering.
15"Take one of the rams,[r] and Aaron and his sons shall lay their hands on
its head.[s] **16**Slaughter it and take the
blood and sprinkle it against the altar
on all sides. **17**Cut the ram into pieces
and wash[t] the inner parts and the
legs, putting them with the head and
the other pieces. **18**Then burn the entire ram on the altar. It is a burnt offering to the LORD, a pleasing aroma,[u] an
offering made to the LORD by fire.
19"Take the other ram,[v] and Aaron
and his sons shall lay their hands on its
head.[w] **20**Slaughter it, take some of its
blood and put it on the lobes of the
right ears of Aaron and his sons, on the
thumbs of their right hands, and on
the big toes of their right feet.[x] Then
sprinkle blood against the altar on all
sides.[y] **21**And take some of the
blood[z] on the altar and some of the
anointing oil[a] and sprinkle it on Aaron and his garments and on his sons
and their garments. Then he and his
sons and their garments will be consecrated.[b]
22"Take from this ram the fat,[c] the
fat tail, the fat around the inner parts,
the covering of the liver, both kidneys
with the fat on them, and the right
thigh. (This is the ram for the ordination.) **23**From the basket of bread made
without yeast, which is before the
LORD, take a loaf, and a cake made with
oil, and a wafer. **24**Put all these in the
hands of Aaron and his sons and wave
them before the LORD as a wave offering.[d] **25**Then take them from their
hands and burn them on the altar along
with the burnt offering for a pleasing
aroma to the LORD, an offering made to
the LORD by fire.[e] **26**After you take the
breast of the ram for Aaron's ordination, wave it before the LORD as a wave
offering, and it will be your share.[f]
27"Consecrate those parts of the ordination ram that belong to Aaron and
his sons:[g] the breast that was waved
and the thigh that was presented.
28This is always to be the regular
share from the Israelites for Aaron and
his sons. It is the contribution the Israelites are to make to the LORD from
their fellowship offerings.[k][h]
29"Aaron's sacred garments[i] will
belong to his descendants so that they
can be anointed and ordained in
them.[j] **30**The son[k] who succeeds him
as priest and comes to the Tent of
Meeting to minister in the Holy Place
is to wear them seven days.
31"Take the ram[l] for the ordination
and cook the meat in a sacred place.[m]
32At the entrance to the Tent of Meeting, Aaron and his sons are to eat the
meat of the ram and the bread[n] that
is in the basket. **33**They are to eat these
offerings by which atonement was
made for their ordination and consecration. But no one else may eat[o]
them, because they are sacred. **34**And
if any of the meat of the ordination ram
or any bread is left over till morning,[p]
burn it up. It must not be eaten, because it is sacred.
35"Do for Aaron and his sons everything I have commanded you, taking
seven days to ordain them. **36**Sacrifice
a bull each day[q] as a sin offering to
make atonement[r]. Purify the altar by
making atonement for it, and anoint it
to consecrate[s] it. **37**For seven days
make atonement for the altar and consecrate it. Then the altar will be most
holy, and whatever touches it will be
holy.[t]
38"This is what you are to offer on
the altar regularly each day:[u] two
lambs a year old. **39**Offer one in the
morning and the other at twilight.[v]
40With the first lamb offer a tenth of an

29:10 [j] ver 19; Lev 1:4; 4:15; 16:21; Nu 8:12 **29:11** [k] Lev 1:5, 11; 4:24; 6:16,25; 14:13 **29:12** [l] S Ex 27:2 [m] Lev 4:7; 9:9 **29:13** [n] ver 22; Lev 1:8; 3:3,5,9; 4:10; 6:12; 7:3,5, 31; 9:10; Nu 18:17; 1Sa 2:15; 1Ki 8:64; 2Ch 7:7; 29:35; 35:14; Isa 43:24; Eze 44:15 [o] S Ex 12:9 **29:14** [p] Na 3:6; Mal 2:3 [q] Lev 4:12,21; 16:27; Nu 19:3-5; Heb 13:11 **29:15** [r] S ver 3 [s] ver 10; Lev 3:2; 2Ch 29:23 **29:17** [t] Lev 1:9, 13 **29:18** [u] S Ge 8:21; 2Co 2:15 **29:19** [v] S ver 3 [w] S ver 10 **29:20** [x] Lev 14:14,25 [y] ver 16; Lev 1:5, 11; 3:2 **29:21** [z] Heb 9:22 [a] S ver 7 [b] S ver 1 **29:22** [c] S ver 13 **29:24** [d] Lev 7:30; 9:21; 10:15; 14:12; 23:11,20; Nu 6:20; 8:11,13, 15 **29:25** [e] ver 18 **29:26** [f] Lev 7:31-34 **29:27** [g] Ex 22:29; Lev 7:31,34; Nu 18:11,12; Dt 18:3 **29:28** [h] ver 22-27; Lev 7:30,34; 10:15 **29:29** [i] S Ex 28:2; S Lev 16:4 [j] Nu 20:28 **29:30** [k] Lev 6:22; Nu 3:3; 20:28 **29:31** [l] Lev 7:37; 2Ch 13:9 [m] Lev 10:14; Nu 19:9; Eze 42:13 **29:32** [n] Mt 12:4 **29:33** [o] Lev 22:10,13 **29:34** [p] S Ex 12:10 **29:36** [q] Heb 10:11 [r] ver 33,37; Ex 30:10; Lev 1:4; 4:20; 16:16; Nu 6:11; 8:12,19; 16:46; 25:13; 2Ch 29:24 [s] Ex 40:10; Nu 7:10 **29:37** [t] Ex 30:28-29; 40:10; Eze 43:25; Mt 23:19 **29:38** [u] Lev 23:2; Nu 28:3-8; 1Ch 16:40; 2Ch 8:13; Eze 46:13-15; Da 12:11 **29:39** [v] Nu 28:4,8; 1Ki 18:36; 2Ch 13:11; Ezr 3:3; Ps 141:2; Da 9:21

[k] *28* Traditionally *peace offerings*

hands on the bull's head, they symbolized identification with the animal and perhaps the transfer of the people's sins to the animal. Thus, the bull became a substitutionary sacrifice that died because of the people's sins (v. 14). This ceremony points to the substitutionary sacrifice of Christ, who became our sin offering (cf. Isa 53:5; Gal 3:13; Heb 13:11–13).

ephah[l] of fine flour mixed with a quarter of a hin[m] of oil[w] from pressed olives, and a quarter of a hin of wine as a drink offering.[x] 41Sacrifice the other lamb at twilight[y] with the same grain offering[z] and its drink offering as in the morning—a pleasing aroma, an offering made to the LORD by fire.

42"For the generations to come[a] this burnt offering is to be made regularly[b] at the entrance to the Tent of Meeting[c] before the LORD. There I will meet you and speak to you;[d] 43there also I will meet with the Israelites, and the place will be consecrated by my glory.[e]

44"So I will consecrate the Tent of Meeting and the altar and will consecrate Aaron and his sons to serve me as priests.[f] 45Then I will dwell[g] among the Israelites and be their God.[h] 46They will know that I am the LORD their God, who brought them out of Egypt[i] so that I might dwell among them. I am the LORD their God.[j]

The Altar of Incense

30:1–5pp — Ex 37:25–28

30 "Make an altar[k] of acacia wood for burning incense.[l] 2It is to be square, a cubit long and a cubit wide, and two cubits high[n]—its horns[m] of one piece with it. 3Overlay the top and all the sides and the horns with pure gold, and make a gold molding around it.[n] 4Make two gold rings[o] for the altar below the molding—two on opposite sides—to hold the poles used to carry it. 5Make the poles of acacia wood and overlay them with gold.[p] 6Put the altar in front of the curtain that is before the ark of the Testimony—before the atonement cover[q] that is over the Testimony—where I will meet with you.

7"Aaron must burn fragrant incense[r] on the altar every morning when he tends the lamps. 8He must burn incense again when he lights the lamps at twilight so incense will burn regularly before the LORD for the generations to come.[s] 9Do not offer on this altar any other incense[t] or any burnt offering or grain offering, and do not pour a drink offering on it. 10Once a year[u] Aaron shall make atonement[v] on its horns. This annual atonement must be made with the blood of the atoning sin offering[w] for the generations to come.[x] It is most holy to the LORD."

Atonement Money

11Then the LORD said to Moses, 12"When you take a census[y] of the Israelites to count them, each one must pay the LORD a ransom[z] for his life at the time he is counted. Then no plague[a] will come on them when you number them. 13Each one who crosses over to those already counted is to give a half shekel,[o] according to the sanctuary shekel,[b] which weighs twenty gerahs. This half shekel is an offering to the LORD. 14All who cross over, those twenty years old or more,[c] are to give an offering to the LORD. 15The rich are not to give more than a half shekel and the poor are not to give less[d] when you make the offering to the LORD to atone for your lives. 16Receive the atonement[e] money from the Israelites and use it for the service of the Tent of Meeting.[f] It will be a memorial[g] for the Israelites before the LORD, making atonement for your lives."

Basin for Washing

17Then the LORD said to Moses, 18"Make a bronze basin,[h] with its bronze stand, for washing. Place it between the Tent of Meeting and the altar, and put water in it. 19Aaron and

29:40 [w]Ex 30:24; Nu 15:4; 28:5 [x]S Ge 35:14; Lev 23:37; 2Ki 16:13 **29:41** [y]1Ki 18:29,36; 2Ki 3:20; 16:15; Ezr 9:4,5; Ps 141:2; Da 9:21 [z]Lev 2:1; 5:13; 10:12; Nu 4:16; 6:17; 1Ki 8:64; Isa 43:23 **29:42** [a]Ex 30:8, 10,21,31; 31:13 [b]Eze 46:15 [c]S Ex 26:1; S 27:21 [d]ver 43; Ex 25:22; 33:9,11; Nu 7:89 **29:43** [e]Ex 33:18; 40:34; Lev 9:6; 1Ki 8:11; 2Ch 5:14; 7:2; Ps 26:8; 85:9; Eze 1:28; 43:5; Hag 1:8; 2:7 **29:44** [f]S ver 1 **29:45** [g]S Ex 25:8; Nu 35:34; Jn 14:17; S Ro 8:10 [h]S Ge 17:7; 2Co 6:16 **29:46** [i]S Ex 6:6; 19:4-6; Dt 5:6; Ps 114:1; Hag 2:5 [j]S Ge 17:7 **30:1** [k]Ex 40:5,26; Nu 4:11; 1Ki 6:20; Eze 41:22 [l]S Ex 25:6; 37:29; Lk 1:11; Heb 9:4; Rev 8:3 **30:2** [m]S Ex 27:2; Rev 9:13 **30:3** [n]S Ex 25:11 **30:4** [o]S Ex 25:12 **30:5** [p]S Ex 25:13 **30:6** [q]Ex 25:22; S 26:34 **30:7** [r]S Ex 25:6; 40:27; Nu 3:10; Dt 33:10; 1Sa 2:28; 1Ch 6:49; 2Ch 2:4; 26:18; 29:7 **30:8** [s]S Ex 25:37; S 29:42 **30:9** [t]Lev 10:1; Nu 16:7,40 **30:10** [u]Lev 16:2 [v]Lev 9:7; 16:18-19,30; 23:27,28; 25:9 [w]Ex 29:14; Lev 4:3; 6:25; 7:7; 8:2,14; Nu 6:11 [x]S Ex 29:42 **30:12** [y]Ex 38:25; Nu 1:2,49; 4:2,29; 14:29; 26:2; 31:26; 2Sa 24:1; 2Ki 12:4 [z]Ex 38:26; Nu 31:50; S Mt 20:28 [a]Nu 14:12; Dt 28:58-61; 2Sa 24:13; 1Ki 8:37 **30:13** [b]ver 24; Ex 38:24,26; Lev 5:15; 27:3,25; Nu 3:47; 7:13; 18:16; Eze 4:10; 45:12; Mt 17:24 **30:14** [c]Ex 38:26; Nu 1:3,18; 14:29; 26:2; 32:11; 2Ch 25:5 **30:15** [d]Pr 22:2; Eph 6:9 **30:16** [e]ver 12 [f]Ex 38:25-28; 2Ch 24:5 [g]Nu 31:54 **30:18** [h]Ex 31:9; 35:16; 38:8; 39:39; 40:7,30; 1Ki 7:38; 2Ch 4:6

[l] *40* That is, probably about 2 quarts (about 2 liters) [m] *40* That is, probably about 1 quart (about 1 liter) [n] *2* That is, about 1 1/2 feet (about 0.5 meter) long and wide and about 3 feet (about 0.9 meter) high [o] *13* That is, about 1/5 ounce (about 6 grams); also in verse 15

30:1 FOR BURNING INCENSE. The burning incense symbolized the continual worship and prayers of God's people (v. 8; Ps 141; Lk 1:10; Rev 8:3–4; see Rev 5:8, note). The altar for burning incense could be desecrated (v. 9), indicating that prayer that was not offered to the glory of God or with hearts committed to holiness was, and is, unacceptable to the Lord (cf. Ps 66:18–19; Isa 1:15–16).

30:10 ATONEMENT. For comments on atonement and how it points to Jesus Christ and the new covenant, see article on THE DAY OF ATONEMENT, p. 174.

his sons are to wash their hands and
feet[i] with water[j] from it. 20Whenev-
er they enter the Tent of Meeting, they
shall wash with water so that they will
not die.[k] Also, when they approach
the altar to minister by presenting an
offering made to the LORD by fire,
21they shall wash their hands and feet
so that they will not die. This is to be
a lasting ordinance[l] for Aaron and his
descendants for the generations to
come."[m]

Anointing Oil

22Then the LORD said to Moses,
23"Take the following fine spices:[n]
500 shekels[p] of liquid myrrh,[o] half
as much (that is, 250 shekels) of fragrant cinnamon,[p] 250 shekels of fragrant cane,[q] 24500 shekels[r] of cassia[s]—all according to the sanctuary
shekel—and a hin[q] of olive oil.
25Make these into a sacred anointing
oil, a fragrant blend, the work of a perfumer.[t] It will be the sacred anointing
oil.[u] 26Then use it to anoint[v] the
Tent of Meeting, the ark of the Testimony, 27the table and all its articles,
the lampstand and its accessories, the
altar of incense, 28the altar of burnt offering and all its utensils, and the basin with its stand. 29You shall consecrate them[w] so they will be most holy,
and whatever touches them will be
holy.[x]
30"Anoint Aaron and his sons and
consecrate[y] them so they may serve
me as priests.[z] 31Say to the Israelites, 'This is to be my sacred anointing
oil[a] for the generations to come.[b]
32Do not pour it on men's bodies and
do not make any oil with the same formula. It is sacred, and you are to consider it sacred.[c] 33Whoever makes
perfume like it and whoever puts it on
anyone other than a priest must be cut
off[d] from his people.' "

Incense

34Then the LORD said to Moses,
"Take fragrant spices[e]—gum resin,
onycha and galbanum—and pure
frankincense, all in equal amounts,
35and make a fragrant blend of incense,[f] the work of a perfumer.[g] It is
to be salted and pure and sacred.
36Grind some of it to powder and place
it in front of the Testimony in the Tent
of Meeting, where I will meet[h] with
you. It shall be most holy[i] to you.
37Do not make any incense with this
formula for yourselves; consider it
holy[j] to the LORD. 38Whoever makes
any like it to enjoy its fragrance must
be cut off[k] from his people."

30:19 [i]Ex 40:31-32; Jn 13:10 [j]Ex 29:4; 40:12; Lev 8:6; Ps 26:6; Heb 10:22 **30:20** [k]S Ex 28:43 **30:21** [l]S Ex 27:21 [m]Ex 29:42 **30:23** [n]S Ge 43:11 [o]S Ge 37:25 [p]Pr 7:17; SS 4:14 [q]SS 4:14; Isa 43:24; Jer 6:20 **30:24** [r]S ver 13 [s]Ps 45:8; Eze 27:19 **30:25** [t]ver 35; Ex 37:29; 1Ch 9:30 [u]S Ex 29:7; S 1Sa 9:16 **30:26** [v]Ex 40:9; Lev 8:10; Nu 7:1 **30:29** [w]Lev 8:10-11 [x]Ex 29:37; Lev 6:18,27; Mt 23:17 **30:30** [y]Ex 29:7; Lev 8:2,12,30; 10:7; 16:32; 21:10,12; 1Ch 15:12; Ps 133:2 [z]S Ex 28:41 **30:31** [a]S Ex 29:7 [b]S Ex 29:42 **30:32** [c]ver 25,37 **30:33** [d]ver 38; S Ge 17:14 **30:34** [e]SS 3:6 **30:35** [f]S Ex 25:6 [g]S ver 25 **30:36** [h]S Ex 25:22 [i]ver 32; Ex 29:37; Lev 2:3 **30:37** [j]S ver 32 **30:38** [k]S ver 33 **31:2** [l]Ex 36:1,2; 37:1; 38:22; 1Ch 2:20; 2Ch 1:5 [m]S Ex 17:10 **31:3** [n]S Ex 28:3 [o]1Ki 7:14; 1Co 12:4 **31:6** [p]Ex 36:1,2; 38:23 [q]1Ki 7:14; 2Ch 2:14 [r]S Ex 28:3 **31:7** [s]Ex 36:8-38 [t]Ex 37:1-5 [u]Ex 37:6; 40:20 **31:8** [v]Ex 37:10-16 [w]Ex 37:17-24; Lev 24:4 [x]Ex 37:25-28 **31:9** [y]Ex 38:3; Nu 4:14 [z]S Ex 30:18 **31:10** [a]S Ex 28:2 **31:11** [b]Ex 30:22-32; 37:29 [c]S Ex 25:6 [d]S Ex 25:9 **31:13** [e]S Ex 20:8 [f]ver 17; Isa 56:4; Eze 20:12,20 [g]S Ex 29:42

Bezalel and Oholiab

31:2-6pp — Ex 35:30-35

31 Then the LORD said to Moses,
2"See, I have chosen Bezalel[l]
son of Uri, the son of Hur,[m] of the tribe
of Judah, 3and I have filled him with
the Spirit of God, with skill, ability and
knowledge[n] in all kinds of crafts[o]—
4to make artistic designs for work in
gold, silver and bronze, 5to cut and set
stones, to work in wood, and to engage
in all kinds of craftsmanship. 6More-
over, I have appointed Oholiab[p] son of
Ahisamach, of the tribe of Dan,[q] to
help him. Also I have given skill to all
the craftsmen[r] to make everything I
have commanded you: 7the Tent of Nu 27:18
Meeting,[s] the ark of the Testimony[t]
with the atonement cover[u] on it, and
all the other furnishings of the tent—
8the table[v] and its articles, the pure
gold lampstand[w] and all its accessories, the altar of incense,[x] 9the altar
of burnt offering[y] and all its utensils,
the basin[z] with its stand— 10and also
the woven garments[a], both the sacred
garments for Aaron the priest and the
garments for his sons when they serve
as priests, 11and the anointing oil[b]
and fragrant incense[c] for the Holy
Place. They are to make them just as
I commanded[d] you."

The Sabbath

12Then the LORD said to Moses,
13"Say to the Israelites, 'You must observe my Sabbaths.[e] This will be a
sign[f] between me and you for the generations to come,[g] so you may know

p 23 That is, about 12 1/2 pounds (about 6 kilograms) q 24 That is, probably about 4 quarts (about 4 liters)

31:3 FILLED HIM WITH THE SPIRIT OF GOD. The idea of "being filled with the Spirit of God" here means spiritual equipping and enabling for special service to God. It is appropriate under the new covenant to pray that the Spirit will give us both physical skills and spiritual gifts to fulfill God's will for our lives (see article on SPIRITUAL GIFTS FOR BELIEVERS, p. 1770).

that I am the LORD, who makes you
holy.[r][h]
14 " 'Observe the Sabbath, because it
is holy to you. Anyone who desecrates
it must be put to death;[i] whoever
does any work on that day must be cut
off from his people. 15 For six days,
work[j] is to be done, but the seventh
day is a Sabbath of rest,[k] holy to the
LORD. Whoever does any work on the
Sabbath day must be put to death.
16 The Israelites are to observe the
Sabbath,[l] celebrating it for the generations to come as a lasting covenant.
17 It will be a sign[m] between me and
the Israelites forever, for in six days
the LORD made the heavens and the
earth, and on the seventh day he abstained from work and rested.[n]' "[o]
18 When the LORD finished speaking
to Moses on Mount Sinai,[p] he gave
him the two tablets of the Testimony,
the tablets of stone[q] inscribed by the
finger of God.[r]

The Golden Calf

32 When the people saw that Moses was so long in coming down
from the mountain,[s] they gathered
around Aaron and said, "Come, make
us gods[s] who will go before[t] us. As
for this fellow Moses who brought us
up out of Egypt, we don't know what
has happened to him."[u]
2 Aaron answered them, "Take off
the gold earrings[v] that your wives,
your sons and your daughters are
wearing, and bring them to me." 3 So all
the people took off their earrings and
brought them to Aaron. 4 He took what
they handed him and made it into an
idol[w] cast in the shape of a calf,[x]
fashioning it with a tool. Then they
said, "These are your gods,[t][y] O Israel, who brought you up out of Egypt."[z]
5 When Aaron saw this, he built an
altar in front of the calf and announced, "Tomorrow there will be a
festival[a] to the LORD." 6 So the next
day the people rose early and sacrificed burnt offerings and presented fellowship offerings.[u][b] Afterward they
sat down to eat and drink[c] and got up
to indulge in revelry.[d]
7 Then the LORD said to Moses, "Go
down, because your people, whom you
brought up out of Egypt,[e] have become corrupt.[f] 8 They have been quick
to turn away[g] from what I commanded them and have made themselves an
idol[h] cast in the shape of a calf.[i]
They have bowed down to it and sacrificed[j] to it and have said, 'These are
your gods, O Israel, who brought you
up out of Egypt.'[k]
9 "I have seen these people," the
LORD said to Moses, "and they are a
stiff-necked[l] people. 10 Now leave me
alone[m] so that my anger may burn
against them and that I may destroy[n]
them. Then I will make you into a great
nation."[o]
11 But Moses sought the favor[p] of
the LORD his God. "O LORD," he said,

31:13 [h] Lev 11:44; 20:8; 21:8; Eze 37:28 **31:14** [i] Ex 35:2; Nu 15:32-36 **31:15** [j] S Ex 20:8-11; 35:2; Lev 16:29; 23:3; Nu 29:7 [k] S Ge 2:3 **31:16** [l] S Ex 20:8 **31:17** [m] S ver 13 [n] S Ge 2:2-3 [o] S Ge 2:2; S Ex 20:9; Isa 56:2; 58:13; 66:23; Jer 17:21-22; Eze 20:12,20 **31:18** [p] S Ex 19:11 [q] S Ex 24:12; 2Co 3:3; Heb 9:4 [r] Ex 32:15-16; 34:1,28; Dt 4:13; 9:10 **32:1** [s] S Ge 7:4; Dt 9:9-12 [t] S Ex 13:21 [u] ver 23; Ac 7:40* **32:2** [v] Jdg 8:24-27 **32:4** [w] S Ex 20:23; Jdg 17:3-4; Isa 30:22 [x] ver 8, 24,35; Dt 9:16; Ne 9:18; Ps 106:19; Ac 7:41 [y] Ex 20:23; Isa 42:17 [z] 1Ki 12:28; 14:9; 2Ki 10:29; 17:16; 2Ch 13:8; Hos 8:6; 10:5 **32:5** [a] Lev 23:2, 37; 2Ki 10:20; Joel 2:15 **32:6** [b] Ex 20:24; 34:15; Lev 3:1; 4:10; 6:12; 9:4; 22:21; Nu 6:14; 25:2; Dt 27:7; Jdg 20:26; Eze 43:27; Ac 7:41 [c] Jdg 19:4; Ru 3:3; 1Sa 1:9; 2Sa 11:11; 1Ki 13:23; 18:42; Ne 8:12; Job 1:4; Ecc 5:18; 8:15; Jer 16:8 [d] ver 17-19; 1Co 10:7* **32:7** [e] ver 4,11; Ex 33:1 [f] S Ge 6:11-12; Eze 20:8 **32:8** [g] Jer 7:26; 16:12; Mal 2:8; 3:7 [h] S Ex 20:4 [i] S ver 4 [j] Ex 22:20 [k] 1Ki 12:28; Eze 23:8 **32:9** [l] Ex 33:3,5; 34:9; Dt 9:6,13; 10:16; 31:27; Jdg 2:19; 2Ki 17:14; 2Ch 30:8; 36:13; Ne 9:16; Ps 78:8; Pr 29:1; Isa 46:12; 48:4; Jer 7:26; Eze 2:4; Hos 4:16; Ac 7:51 **32:10** [m] 1Sa 2:25; Jer 7:16; 11:14; 14:11 [n] Ex 22:24; 33:3,5; Nu 16:21,45; Dt 9:14,19; Ps 106:23; Jer 14:12; Eze 20:13 [o] Nu 14:12; Dt 9:14 **32:11** [p] Dt 9:18; 2Sa 21:1; 2Ch 15:2; Ps 9:10; 34:4; 106:23; Isa 9:13; Jer 15:1

[r] *13* Or *who sanctifies you*; or *who sets you apart as holy* [s] *1* Or *a god*; also in verses 23 and 31 [t] *4* Or *This is your god*; also in verse 8 [u] *6* Traditionally *peace offerings*

32:4 CAST IN THE SHAPE OF A CALF. As a leader, Aaron seriously compromised God's standard in order to please the people he served. He gave in to the godless pressure of the Israelites and violated the second commandment (20:4–5). Only Moses' intercession saved him from God's wrath and from death (Dt 9:20).

32:6 GOT UP TO INDULGE IN REVELRY. The people began to indulge in sensuous dancing and sexual immorality. V. 25 says that they were "running wild," suggesting that they may have been naked. Thus, the sin of the Israelites may have involved exploring others' nakedness for sexual play and pleasure, something strictly forbidden in God's law (Lev 18:6–30; 20:11,17,19–21; see article on STANDARDS OF SEXUAL MORALITY, p. 1936).

32:10 DESTROY THEM. Because of the people's apostasy and sin, God declared his intention to destroy them and raise up another nation through Moses.

32:11 MOSES SOUGHT THE FAVOR OF THE LORD. Moses' intercession for the people of Israel (vv. 11–14) reveals that God answers the prayers of his faithful servants and allows them to share in his redemptive purposes and decisions. (1) God clearly desired to destroy the rebellious people (v. 10). Yet Moses, acting as a mediator between the Lord and the people, earnestly interceded in order to turn away God's wrath and change his stated intention.

(2) Because of Moses' intense prayer, the Lord relented (v. 14; see Jas 5:16, note; see article on INTERCESSION, p. 1268).

(3) The great truth emphasized here is that God makes his servants co-workers with him (1Co 3:9).

"why should your anger burn against
your people, whom you brought out of
Egypt with great power and a mighty
hand?[q] **12**Why should the Egyptians
say, 'It was with evil intent that he
brought them out, to kill them in the
mountains and to wipe them off the
face of the earth'?[r] Turn from your
fierce anger; relent and do not bring
disaster[s] on your people. **13**Remember[t] your servants Abraham, Isaac
and Israel, to whom you swore by your
own self:[u] 'I will make your descendants as numerous as the stars[v] in
the sky and I will give your descendants all this land[w] I promised them,
and it will be their inheritance forever.' " **14**Then the LORD relented[x] and
did not bring on his people the disaster
he had threatened.

15Moses turned and went down the
mountain with the two tablets of the
Testimony[y] in his hands.[z] They were
inscribed[a] on both sides, front and
back. **16**The tablets were the work of
God; the writing was the writing of
God, engraved on the tablets.[b]

17When Joshua[c] heard the noise of
the people shouting, he said to Moses,
"There is the sound of war in the
camp."

18Moses replied:

"It is not the sound of victory,
it is not the sound of defeat;
it is the sound of singing that I
hear."

19When Moses approached the camp
and saw the calf[d] and the dancing,[e]
his anger burned[f] and he threw the
tablets out of his hands, breaking them
to pieces[g] at the foot of the mountain.
20And he took the calf they had made
and burned[h] it in the fire; then he
ground it to powder,[i] scattered it on
the water[j] and made the Israelites
drink it.

21He said to Aaron, "What did these
people do to you, that you led them into
such great sin?"

22"Do not be angry,[k] my lord," Aaron answered. "You know how prone
these people are to evil.[l] **23**They said
to me, 'Make us gods who will go before us. As for this fellow Moses who
brought us up out of Egypt, we don't
know what has happened to him.'[m]
24So I told them, 'Whoever has any
gold jewelry, take it off.' Then they
gave me the gold, and I threw it into
the fire, and out came this calf!"[n]

25Moses saw that the people were
running wild and that Aaron had let
them get out of control and so become
a laughingstock[o] to their enemies.
26So he stood at the entrance to the
camp and said, "Whoever is for the
LORD, come to me." And all the Levites
rallied to him.

27Then he said to them, "This is
what the LORD, the God of Israel, says:
'Each man strap a sword to his side. Go
back and forth through the camp from
one end to the other, each killing his
brother and friend and neighbor.' "[p]
28The Levites did as Moses commanded, and that day about three thousand
of the people died. **29**Then Moses said,
"You have been set apart to the LORD
today, for you were against your own

32:11 [q]ver 13; Dt 9:26; 1Sa 7:9; Ne 1:10; Ps 136:12
32:12 [r]Nu 14:13-16; Dt 9:28 [s]ver 14; Ex 33:13
32:13 [t]S Ex 2:24; 33:13 [u]S Ge 22:16; Heb 6:13 [v]Ge 15:5; 22:17 [w]S Ge 12:7
32:14 [x]Dt 9:19; 1Sa 15:11; 2Sa 24:16; 1Ki 21:29; 1Ch 21:15; Ps 106:45; Jer 18:8; 26:3,19; Am 7:3,6; Jnh 3:10
32:15 [y]Ex 31:18; Heb 9:4 [z]S Ex 19:18; 34:4, 29; Dt 9:15 [a]2Co 3:3
32:16 [b]S Ex 24:12
32:17 [c]S Ex 17:9
32:19 [d]Dt 9:16 [e]ver 6; 1Co 10:7 [f]Ezr 9:3; Ps 119:53,158
[g]Ex 34:1; Dt 9:17
32:20 [h]Dt 7:25; 12:3; Jos 7:1; 2Ki 23:6; 1Ch 14:12 [i]2Ch 34:7; Mic 1:7 [j]Dt 9:21
32:22 [k]S Ge 18:30 [l]Dt 9:24; 28:20; 2Ki 21:15; Ezr 9:13; Ne 9:28; Jer 4:4; 44:3; Eze 6:9
32:23 [m]S ver 1; Ac 7:40
32:24 [n]S ver 4
32:25 [o]S Ge 38:23
32:27 [p]Nu 25:3, 5; Dt 33:9; Eze 9:5

He appoints them mediators and intercessors for the lost (see Ro 9:2, note), and in some measure the fate of the perishing is in their hands (see Mt 9:38, note). Thus, God has ordained that the sincere intercession of a righteous person may move him to change his temporal will and bring redemption instead of judgment (cf. Eze 22:30). Prayer does indeed change things (cf. Ps 106:44–45; Jer 18:8; 26:3,13,19; Am 7:2–6; Jnh 3:10; see article on INTERCESSION, p. 1268).

(4) God does not disregard the intercession of a faithful servant as long as hope for redemption remains. Intercession will be rejected by God only when sin has reached its limit (cf. Jer 15:1; Eze 14:14,16).

(5) It is an unfathomable mystery that God should be persuaded by the intercession of fallible human beings to alter his announced course of action and turn from wrath to mercy. God is not an implacable deity or a God of inflexible fate, but a personal God who delights to be moved by the love, faith and prayers of his faithful people (see article on THE PROVIDENCE OF GOD, p. 78).

32:14 RELENTED. God does not change his mind the same way a human being does, for he is totally free from fickleness and sin.

32:19 BREAKING THEM TO PIECES. Moses did not shatter the tablets of stone because of uncontrolled passion, but because of a righteous indignation against sin (cf. vv. 10,34–35). Christ too manifested godly anger against sin (Jn 2:15; 11:33, note). Such anger will be demonstrated by all who have a genuine concern for God's glory and holiness and for human suffering.

32:26 WHOEVER IS FOR THE LORD. Moses' call for loyalty to God reflects the principle that in the midst of spiritual decline and rebellion, the only path for the faithful is the one marked out by decisive obedience to God's law and clear separation from apostasy (see Rev 18:4, note; cf. Jos 24:15; 1Ki 18:21; see article on PERSONAL APOSTASY, p. 1918).

sons and brothers, and he has blessed
you this day."
30The next day Moses said to the
people, "You have committed a great
sin.[q] But now I will go up to the LORD;
perhaps I can make atonement[r] for
your sin."
31So Moses went back to the LORD
and said, "Oh, what a great sin these
people have committed![s] They have
made themselves gods of gold.[t] 32But
now, please forgive their sin[u]—but if
not, then blot me[v] out of the book[w]
you have written."
33The LORD replied to Moses, "Whoever has sinned against me I will blot
out[x] of my book. 34Now go, lead[y] the
people to the place[z] I spoke of, and
my angel[a] will go before you. However, when the time comes for me to punish,[b] I will punish them for their sin."
35And the LORD struck the people
with a plague because of what they did
with the calf[c] Aaron had made.

33 Then the LORD said to Moses,
"Leave this place, you and the
people you brought up out of Egypt,
and go up to the land I promised on
oath[d] to Abraham, Isaac and Jacob,
saying, 'I will give it to your descendants.'[e] 2I will send an angel[f] before
you and drive out the Canaanites, Amorites, Hittites, Perizzites, Hivites and
Jebusites.[g] 3Go up to the land flowing
with milk and honey.[h] But I will not
go with you, because you are a stiff-
necked[i] people and I might destroy[j]
you on the way."
4When the people heard these dis-
tressing words, they began to mourn[k]
and no one put on any ornaments. 5For
the LORD had said to Moses, "Tell the
Israelites, 'You are a stiff-necked people.[l] If I were to go with you even for
a moment, I might destroy[m] you. Now
take off your ornaments and I will decide what to do with you.' " 6So the Israelites stripped off their ornaments at
Mount Horeb.[n]

The Tent of Meeting

7Now Moses used to take a tent and
pitch it outside the camp some distance away, calling it the "tent of meeting."[o] Anyone inquiring[p] of the LORD
would go to the tent of meeting outside
the camp. 8And whenever Moses went
out to the tent, all the people rose and
stood at the entrances to their tents,[q]
watching Moses until he entered the
tent. 9As Moses went into the tent, the
pillar of cloud[r] would come down and
stay at the entrance, while the LORD
spoke[s] with Moses. 10Whenever the
people saw the pillar of cloud standing
at the entrance to the tent, they all
stood and worshiped, each at the entrance to his tent.[t] 11The LORD would
speak to Moses face to face,[u] as a

32:30 [q] 1Sa 12:20; Ps 25:11; 85:2 [r] Lev 1:4; 4:20,26; 5:6,10,13; 6:7 **32:31** [s] S Ex 34:9; Dt 9:18 [t] S Ex 20:23 **32:32** [u] Nu 14:19 [v] Ro 9:3 [w] Ps 69:28; Eze 13:9; Da 7:10; 12:1; Mal 3:16; S Lk 10:20 **32:33** [x] S Ex 17:14; S Job 21:20; Rev 3:5 **32:34** [y] S Ex 15:17 [z] Ex 3:17 [a] S Ex 14:19 [b] S Ge 50:19; Dt 32:35; Ps 89:32; 94:23; 99:8; 109:20; Isa 27:1; Jer 5:9; 11:22; 23:2; 44:13,29; Hos 12:2; Ro 2:5-6 **32:35** [c] S ver 4 **33:1** [d] S Ex 13:11; S Nu 14:23; Heb 6:13 [e] S Ge 12:7 **33:2** [f] S Ex 14:19 [g] S Ex 23:28 **33:3** [h] S Ex 3:8 [i] Ex 32:9; Ac 7:51 [j] S Ex 32:10 **33:4** [k] Nu 14:39; Ezr 9:3; Est 4:1; Ps 119:53 **33:5** [l] S Ex 32:9 [m] S Ex 32:10 **33:6** [n] S Ex 3:1 **33:7** [o] S Ex 27:21 [p] S Ge 25:22; S 1Ki 22:5 **33:8** [q] ver 10; Nu 16:27 **33:9** [r] Ex 13:21; S 19:9; Dt 31:15; 1Co 10:1 [s] S Ex 29:42; 31:18; Ps 99:7 **33:10** [t] S ver 8 **33:11** [u] Nu 12:8; Dt 5:4; 34:10

32:29 HAS BLESSED YOU. Because the children of Levi remained faithful to the Lord, they turned the curse that had been pronounced upon them (Ge 49:7) into a blessing (cf. Nu 3). They were appointed to care for the tabernacle and to assist the priests (Nu 1:47–53; 3:5–9,12,41,45; 4:2–3). God's curses and blessings are often conditioned on one's actions and can be reversed by repentance and obedience.

32:32 FORGIVE THEIR SIN. Moses' love for the sinful people (cf. Ro 9:3) points to the love of a greater mediator, Christ Jesus, who "made intercession for the transgressors" (Isa 53:12; Ro 8:34; see Mt 26:39, note; 1Ti 2:5, note; Heb 7:25, note).

33:3 I WILL NOT GO WITH YOU. Because of Israel's sin, God stated that an angel would take his place on the way to the promised land (vv. 1–3). However, Moses, not wanting to accept this decision, once again interceded with God (vv. 12–14), as he had just done (32:11–13,31–32). Notice the sequence of events that took place in regard to Israel's sin with the golden calf (32:1–6), Moses' perseverance in prayer and God's revelation to him. (1) God intended to destroy the people (32:10). Moses' intercession (32:11–13) provided a basis for God to change his course of action and not fulfill his threat to destroy the people (32:14; see 32:11, note). (2) God then decided to allow the people to go into Canaan, but led only by Moses and an angel (32:34). God clearly and sincerely stated that he himself would not go with them (33:3). (3) After more prayer (33:12–13) the Lord changed his plan, responded to Moses' petition, and agreed that his Presence would accompany them (vv. 14–17; see article on INTERCESSION, p. 1268).

God's response to Moses' intercession reveals something of his ways (cf. v. 13) with his people. Not every decision of God is absolutely fixed and irrevocable. Rather, he is a God who responds to his people (see 32:11, note); at times he changes his declared course of action when his people sincerely call on him and commit themselves to him and his will. God always remains free to change his declared judgment in order to show love and mercy (cf. Jnh 3).

33:11 HIS FRIEND. God considered Moses to be a close friend with whom he could talk face to face. This special relationship was partly due to

man speaks with his friend. Then Moses would return to the camp, but his
young aide Joshua[v] son of Nun did not
leave the tent.

Moses and the Glory of the LORD

12 Moses said to the LORD, "You have
been telling me, 'Lead these people,'[w]
but you have not let me know whom
you will send with me. You have said,
'I know you by name[x] and you have
found favor[y] with me.' 13 If you are
pleased with me, teach me your ways[z]
so I may know you and continue to find
favor with you. Remember that this nation is your people."[a]
14 The LORD replied, "My Presence[b]
will go with you, and I will give you
rest."[c]
15 Then Moses said to him, "If your
Presence[d] does not go with us, do not
send us up from here. 16 How will anyone know that you are pleased with me
and with your people unless you go
with us?[e] What else will distinguish
me and your people from all the other
people on the face of the earth?"[f]
17 And the LORD said to Moses, "I will
do the very thing you have asked,[g] because I am pleased with you and I
know you by name."[h]
18 Then Moses said, "Now show me
your glory."[i]
19 And the LORD said, "I will cause all
my goodness to pass[j] in front of you,
and I will proclaim my name,[k] the
LORD, in your presence. I will have mercy on whom I will have mercy, and I
will have compassion on whom I will
have compassion.[l] 20 But," he said,
"you cannot see my face, for no one
may see[m] me and live."
21 Then the LORD said, "There is a
place near me where you may stand on
a rock. 22 When my glory passes by, I
will put you in a cleft in the rock[n] and
cover you with my hand[o] until I have
passed by. 23 Then I will remove my
hand and you will see my back; but my
face must not be seen."

The New Stone Tablets

34 The LORD said to Moses, "Chisel
out two stone tablets like the
first ones,[p] and I will write on them
the words that were on the first tablets,[q] which you broke.[r] 2 Be ready in
the morning, and then come up on
Mount Sinai.[s] Present yourself to me
there on top of the mountain. 3 No one
is to come with you or be seen anywhere on the mountain;[t] not even the
flocks and herds may graze in front of
the mountain."
4 So Moses chiseled[u] out two stone
tablets like the first ones and went up
Mount Sinai early in the morning, as
the LORD had commanded him; and he
carried the two stone tablets in his
hands.[v] 5 Then the LORD came down in
the cloud[w] and stood there with him
and proclaimed his name, the LORD.[x]
6 And he passed in front of Moses, proclaiming, "The LORD, the LORD, the compassionate[y] and gracious God, slow to
anger,[z] abounding in love[a] and faith-

33:11 [v] S Ex 17:9 **33:12** [w] Ex 3:10; S 15:17 [x] ver 17; Isa 43:1; 45:3; 49:1; Jn 10:14-15; 2Ti 2:19 [y] S Ge 6:8 **33:13** [z] Ps 25:4; 27:11; 51:13; 86:11; 103:7; 143:8 [a] Ex 3:7; Dt 9:26,29; Ps 77:15 **33:14** [b] S Ex 13:21; Dt 4:37; Isa 63:9; Hag 1:13; 2:4 [c] Dt 12:9,10; 25:19; Jos 1:13; 11:23; 21:44; 22:4; 23:1; 1Ki 8:56; Isa 63:14; Jer 31:2; Mt 11:28; Heb 4:1-11 **33:15** [d] ver 3; Ex 34:9; 2Ki 13:23; 17:18; 23:27; 24:20; Ps 51:11; 80:3,7, 19; Jer 7:15; 52:3 **33:16** [e] Ex 34:5; 40:34,35; Nu 9:15; 14:14 [f] Ex 34:10; Lev 20:24,26; Nu 23:9; Dt 4:7, 32,34; 32:9; 33:28 **33:17** [g] Ex 34:28; Dt 9:18,25; 10:10; Jas 5:16 [h] S Ge 6:8 **33:18** [i] S Ex 16:7; Jn 1:14; 12:41; 1Ti 6:16; Rev 15:8 **33:19** [j] 1Ki 19:11 [k] Ex 6:3; 34:5-7 [l] Ro 9:15* **33:20** [m] S Ge 16:13; S Ex 3:6; S Dt 5:26; S Jn 1:18 **33:22** [n] Ge 49:24; 1Ki 19:9; Ps 27:5; 31:20; 62:7; 91:1; Isa 2:21; Jer 4:29 [o] Ps 91:4; Isa 49:2; 51:16 **34:1** [p] S Ex 24:12 [q] Dt 10:2,4 [r] S Ex 32:19 **34:2** [s] S Ex 19:11

34:3 [t] S Ex 19:13 **34:4** [u] Dt 10:3 [v] S Ex 32:15 **34:5** [w] S Ex 13:21; S 19:9 [x] Ex 6:3; 33:19 **34:6** [y] S Ex 22:27; S Nu 14:20; S Ps 86:15 [z] Nu 14:18; Ps 78:38; Jer 15:15; Ro 2:4 [a] S Ge 19:16

---

the fact that Moses was sincerely devoted to God and to his cause, desires and purposes. Moses was one with the Spirit of God to such an extent that he shared the very feelings of God, suffering when he suffered and grieving when he grieved at sin (cf. 32:19). Every believer should, through prayer, seek to know God's ways and to grow into such a profound union with him and his purposes that he or she is indeed God's friend.

33:11 JOSHUA ... DID NOT LEAVE THE TENT. Joshua not only faithfully served Moses, God's anointed, but he also diligently developed a personal communion with God. From his youth, he learned to spend time with the Lord. Such devotion prepared him to become Moses' successor.

33:12 MOSES SAID. Through Moses' prayer, God relented, changed his resolve (cf. v. 3) and agreed to go with Moses and the people (v. 14, see v. 3, note).

33:13 TEACH ME YOUR WAYS. All God's children should fervently pray to know his ways, i.e., his heart, purpose, wisdom, holy principles, and even his suffering; in so doing we come to know God himself.

33:17 I AM PLEASED WITH YOU. God answered Moses' prayer because he respected him, considered him a friend, and was pleased with him. Moses found favor because, even though Aaron and the nation disobeyed God, he remained loyal to the Lord and mediated between the Lord and Israel.

34:6–7 THE LORD, THE COMPASSIONATE AND GRACIOUS GOD. For comments on God's name as "LORD" (i.e., *Yahweh*), see Ge 2:4, note; Ex 3:14, note. Here God gives further light on the meaning of that name and on his innermost nature. The Lord is a God whose compassion, kindness and forgiveness are united with truth, holiness and justice. The fact that God is gracious and compassionate shows that he will not punish anyone unless and until his long-suffering love is rejected and despised.

fulness,[b] 7maintaining love to thousands,[c] and forgiving wickedness, rebellion and sin.[d] Yet he does not leave the guilty unpunished;[e] he punishes the children and their children for the sin of the fathers to the third and fourth generation."[f]

8Moses bowed to the ground at once and worshiped. 9"O Lord, if I have found favor[g] in your eyes," he said, "then let the Lord go with us.[h] Although this is a stiff-necked[i] people, forgive our wickedness and our sin,[j] and take us as your inheritance."[k]

10Then the LORD said: "I am making a covenant[l] with you. Before all your people I will do wonders[m] never before done in any nation in all the world.[n] The people you live among will see how awesome is the work that I, the LORD, will do for you. 11Obey what I command[o] you today. I will drive out before you the Amorites, Canaanites, Hittites, Perizzites, Hivites and Jebusites.[p] 12Be careful not to make a treaty[q] with those who live in the land where you are going, or they will be a snare[r] among you. 13Break down their altars, smash their sacred stones and cut down their Asherah poles.[v][s] 14Do not worship any other god,[t] for the LORD, whose name[u] is Jealous, is a jealous God.[v]

15"Be careful not to make a treaty[w] with those who live in the land; for when they prostitute[x] themselves to their gods and sacrifice to them, they will invite you and you will eat their sacrifices.[y] 16And when you choose some of their daughters as wives[z] for your sons and those daughters prostitute themselves to their gods,[a] they will lead your sons to do the same.

17"Do not make cast idols.[b]

18"Celebrate the Feast of Unleavened Bread.[c] For seven days eat bread made without yeast,[d] as I commanded you. Do this at the appointed time in the month of Abib,[e] for in that month you came out of Egypt.

19"The first offspring[f] of every womb belongs to me, including all the firstborn males of your livestock, whether from herd or flock. 20Redeem the firstborn donkey with a lamb, but if you do not redeem it, break its neck.[g] Redeem all your firstborn sons.[h]

"No one is to appear before me empty-handed.[i]

21"Six days you shall labor, but on the seventh day you shall rest;[j] even during the plowing season and harvest[k] you must rest.

22"Celebrate the Feast of Weeks with the firstfruits[l] of the wheat harvest, and the Feast of Ingathering[m] at the turn of the year.[w] 23Three times[n] a year all your men are to appear before the Sovereign LORD, the God of Israel. 24I will drive out nations[o] before you and enlarge your territory,[p] and no one will covet your land when you go up three times each year to appear before the LORD your God.

25"Do not offer the blood of a sacrifice to me along with anything containing yeast,[q] and do not let any of the sacrifice from the Passover Feast remain until morning.[r]

26"Bring the best of the firstfruits[s] of your soil to the house of the LORD your God.

"Do not cook a young goat in its mother's milk."[t]

27Then the LORD said to Moses, "Write[u] down these words, for in accordance with these words I have made a covenant[v] with you and with Israel." 28Moses was there with the LORD forty days and forty nights[w] without eating bread or drinking water.[x] And he wrote on the tablets[y] the

34:6 [b]Ps 61:7; 108:4; 115:1; 138:2; 143:1; La 3:23; Jas 5:11 **34:7** [c]S Ex 20:6; Dt 5:10 [d]1Ki 8:30; Ps 86:5; 103:3; 130:4,8; Isa 43:25; Da 9:9; 1Jn 1:9 [e]Ex 23:7; Jos 24:19; Job 7:20-21; 9:28; 10:14; Mic 6:1-16; Na 1:3 [f]S Ex 20:5 **34:9** [g]Ex 33:13; Nu 11:15 [h]S Ex 33:15 [i]Ex 32:9 [j]Nu 14:19; 1Ki 8:30; 2Ch 6:21; Ps 19:12; 25:11; Jer 33:8; Hos 14:2 [k]S Ex 6:7; 19:5; Dt 4:20; 7:6; 9:26, 29; 14:2; 26:18; 32:9; 1Sa 10:1; 2Sa 14:16; 1Ki 8:51,53; Ps 28:9; 33:12; 74:2; 79:1; 94:14; 106:5,40; Isa 19:25; 63:17; Jer 10:16; 51:19; Mic 7:18; Zec 2:12 **34:10** [l]S Ge 6:18; S 9:15; S 15:18; Dt 5:2-3 [m]S Ex 3:20 [n]S Ex 33:16 **34:11** [o]Dt 6:25; Jos 11:15 [p]S Ex 23:28 **34:12** [q]Jdg 2:2 [r]S Ex 10:7 **34:13** [s]S Ex 23:24; Nu 33:52; Dt 7:5; 12:3; Jdg 6:26; 1Ki 15:13; 2Ch 15:16; 17:6; 34:3-4; Mic 5:14 **34:14** [t]S Ex 20:3 [u]Isa 9:6 [v]S Ex 20:5 **34:15** [w]ver 12; Dt 23:6; Ezr 9:12 [x]Ex 22:20; 32:8; Dt 31:16; Jdg 2:17; 2Ki 17:8; 1Ch 5:25; 2Ch 11:15; Am 2:4 [y]S Ex 32:6; 1Co 8:4 **34:16** [z]Dt 7:3; 17:17; Jos 23:12; Jdg 3:6; 14:3; 1Ki 11:1,2; 16:31; Ezr 9:2; 10:3; Ne 10:30; 13:25, 26 [a]Dt 7:4; 12:31; 20:18; 1Ki 11:4; 2Ki 21:3-15; Ps 106:34-41; Mal 2:11 **34:17** [b]S Ex 20:4 **34:18** [c]S Ex 12:17; Mt 26:17; Lk 22:1; Ac 12:3 [d]S Ex 12:15 [e]S Ex 12:2 **34:19** [f]Ex 13:2 **34:20** [g]S Ex 13:13 [h]S Ex 13:2 [i]S Ex 22:29; Dt 16:16; Eze 46:9 **34:21** [j]Ge 2:2-3 [k]Ne 13:15; Isa 56:2; 58:13 **34:22** [l]ver 26; Ex 23:19; Lev 2:12,14; 7:13; 23:10,17; Nu 28:26 [m]S Ex 23:16 **34:23** [n]S Ex 23:14 **34:24** [o]S Ex 23:28 [p]Dt 12:20; 19:8; Job 12:23 **34:25** [q]S Ex 23:18 [r]S Ex 12:8 **34:26** [s]S Ex 22:29; S Nu 18:12 [t]S Ex 23:19 **34:27** [u]S Ex 17:14 [v]S Ge 6:18; S 15:18 **34:28** [w]S Ge 7:4; Mt 4:2; Lk 4:2 [x]Dt 9:9,18; Ezr 10:6 [y]ver 1; Ex 31:18

[v] *13* That is, symbols of the goddess Asherah
[w] *22* That is, in the fall

34:7 CHILDREN FOR THE SIN OF THE FATHERS. Parents should take note that their sins, spiritual neglect or failure to separate themselves from the ungodliness of the world can have tragic consequences for their children. Children suffer for the sins of the parents in the sense that they generally follow their parents along the path of temptation or spiritual compromise, thereby adopting evil habits and attitudes that will lead them away from God and toward destruction.

34:28 FORTY DAYS. Moses was sustained supernaturally by God during his forty-day fast in which he did not eat food or drink water. Biblically and physiologically, a fast that includes abstinence from water should be no longer than three days (see Mt 6:16, note).

words of the covenant—the Ten Commandments.[z]

The Radiant Face of Moses

29When Moses came down from Mount Sinai[a] with the two tablets of the Testimony in his hands,[b] he was not aware that his face was radiant[c] because he had spoken with the LORD. 30When Aaron and all the Israelites saw Moses, his face was radiant, and they were afraid to come near him. 31But Moses called to them; so Aaron and all the leaders of the community[d] came back to him, and he spoke to them. 32Afterward all the Israelites came near him, and he gave them all the commands[e] the LORD had given him on Mount Sinai.

33When Moses finished speaking to them, he put a veil[f] over his face. 34But whenever he entered the LORD's presence to speak with him, he removed the veil until he came out. And when he came out and told the Israelites what he had been commanded, 35they saw that his face was radiant.[g] Then Moses would put the veil back over his face until he went in to speak with the LORD.

Sabbath Regulations

35 Moses assembled the whole Israelite community and said to them, "These are the things the LORD has commanded[h] you to do: 2For six days, work is to be done, but the seventh day shall be your holy day, a Sabbath[i] of rest to the LORD. Whoever does any work on it must be put to death.[j] 3Do not light a fire in any of your dwellings on the Sabbath day.[k]"

Materials for the Tabernacle

35:4–9pp — Ex 25:1–7
35:10–19pp — Ex 39:32–41

4Moses said to the whole Israelite community, "This is what the LORD has commanded: 5From what you have, take an offering for the LORD. Everyone who is willing is to bring to the LORD an offering of gold, silver and bronze; 6blue, purple and scarlet yarn and fine linen; goat hair; 7ram skins dyed red and hides of sea cows[x]; acacia wood; 8olive oil[l] for the light; spices for the anointing oil and for the fragrant incense; 9and onyx stones and other gems to be mounted on the ephod and breastpiece.

10"All who are skilled among you are to come and make everything the LORD has commanded:[m] 11the tabernacle[n] with its tent and its covering, clasps, frames, crossbars, posts and bases; 12the ark[o] with its poles and the atonement cover and the curtain[p] that shields it; 13the table[q] with its poles and all its articles and the bread of the Presence; 14the lampstand[r] that is for light with its accessories, lamps and oil for the light; 15the altar[s] of incense with its poles, the anointing oil[t] and the fragrant incense;[u] the curtain for the doorway at the entrance to the tabernacle;[v] 16the altar[w] of burnt offering with its bronze grating, its poles and all its utensils; the bronze basin[x] with its stand; 17the curtains of the courtyard with its posts and bases, and the curtain for the entrance to the courtyard;[y] 18the tent pegs[z] for the tabernacle and for the courtyard, and their ropes; 19the woven garments worn for ministering in the sanctuary—both the sacred garments[a] for Aaron the priest and the garments for his sons when they serve as priests."

20Then the whole Israelite community withdrew from Moses' presence, 21and everyone who was willing and whose heart moved him came and brought an offering to the LORD for the work on the Tent of Meeting, for all its service, and for the sacred garments. 22All who were willing, men and women alike, came and brought gold jewelry of all kinds: brooches, earrings, rings and ornaments. They all presented their gold as a wave offering to the LORD. 23Everyone who had blue, purple or scarlet yarn[b] or fine linen, or goat hair, ram skins dyed red or hides of sea cows brought them. 24Those presenting an offering of silver or bronze brought it as an offering to the LORD, and everyone who had acacia wood for

34:28 [z] Dt 4:13; 10:4
34:29 [a] S Ex 19:11 [b] S Ex 32:15 [c] ver 35; Ps 34:5; Isa 60:5; Mt 17:2; 2Co 3:7,13
34:31 [d] Ex 16:22
34:32 [e] S Ex 21:1; 35:1,4
34:33 [f] 2Co 3:13
34:35 [g] S ver 29
35:1 [h] S Ex 34:32
35:2 [i] S Ge 2:3; Ex 34:21; Dt 5:13-14 [j] S Ex 31:14
35:3 [k] Ex 16:23
35:8 [l] S Ex 25:6
35:10 [m] Ex 31:6; 39:43
35:11 [n] Ex 26:1-37; 36:8-38
35:12 [o] Ex 25:10-22; 37:1-9 [p] S Ex 26:33
35:13 [q] Ex 25:23-30; 37:10-16
35:14 [r] S Ex 25:31
35:15 [s] Ex 30:1-6; 37:25-28 [t] Ex 30:25 [u] Ex 30:34-38 [v] S Ex 26:36
35:16 [w] Ex 27:1-8; 38:1-7 [x] S Ex 30:18
35:17 [y] S Ex 27:9; 38:9-20
35:18 [z] Ex 27:19; 38:20
35:19 [a] S Ex 28:2
35:23 [b] Ex 39:1

[x] 7 That is, dugongs; also in verse 23

35:1—40:38 THINGS ... COMMANDED. These chapters repeat in general the material of chs. 25—31, except that here the instructions given to Moses for the tabernacle are carried out. This section is included to emphasize how crucial it is that God's people take his instructions with utmost seriousness and obey them diligently.

any part of the work brought it. 25Every skilled woman[c] spun with her hands and brought what she had spun—blue, purple or scarlet yarn or fine linen. 26And all the women who were willing and had the skill spun the goat hair. 27The leaders[d] brought onyx stones and other gems[e] to be mounted on the ephod and breastpiece. 28They also brought spices and olive oil for the light and for the anointing oil and for the fragrant incense.[f] 29All the Israelite men and women who were willing[g] brought to the LORD freewill offerings[h] for all the work the LORD through Moses had commanded them to do.

Bezalel and Oholiab

35:30–35pp — Ex 31:2-6

30Then Moses said to the Israelites, "See, the LORD has chosen Bezalel son of Uri, the son of Hur, of the tribe of Judah, 31and he has filled him with the Spirit of God, with skill, ability and knowledge in all kinds of crafts[i]— 32to make artistic designs for work in gold, silver and bronze, 33to cut and set stones, to work in wood and to engage in all kinds of artistic craftsmanship. 34And he has given both him and Oholiab[j] son of Ahisamach, of the tribe of Dan, the ability to teach[k] others. 35He has filled them with skill to do all kinds of work[l] as craftsmen, designers, embroiderers in blue, purple and scarlet yarn and fine linen, and weavers—all of them master craftsmen and designers.

Nu 11:24-29

36 1So Bezalel, Oholiab and every skilled person[m] to whom the LORD has given skill and ability to know how to carry out all the work of constructing the sanctuary[n] are to do the work just as the Lord has commanded."

2Then Moses summoned Bezalel[o] and Oholiab[p] and every skilled person to whom the LORD had given ability and who was willing[q] to come and do the work. 3They received from Moses all the offerings[r] the Israelites had brought to carry out the work of constructing the sanctuary. And the people continued to bring freewill offerings morning after morning. 4So all the skilled craftsmen who were doing all the work on the sanctuary left their work 5and said to Moses, "The people are bringing more than enough[s] for doing the work the LORD commanded to be done."

6Then Moses gave an order and they sent this word throughout the camp: "No man or woman is to make anything else as an offering for the sanctuary." And so the people were restrained from bringing more, 7because what they already had was more[t] than enough to do all the work.

The Tabernacle

36:8–38pp — Ex 26:1-37

8All the skilled men among the workmen made the tabernacle with ten curtains of finely twisted linen and blue, purple and scarlet yarn, with cherubim worked into them by a skilled craftsman. 9All the curtains were the same size—twenty-eight cubits long and four cubits wide.[y] 10They joined five of the curtains together and did the same with the other five. 11Then they made loops of blue material along the edge of the end curtain in one set, and the same was done with the end curtain in the other set. 12They also made fifty loops on one curtain and fifty loops on the end curtain of the other set, with the loops opposite each other. 13Then they made fifty gold clasps and used them to fasten the two sets of curtains together so that the tabernacle was a unit.[u]

14They made curtains of goat hair for the tent over the tabernacle—eleven altogether. 15All eleven curtains were the same size—thirty cubits long and four cubits wide.[z] 16They joined five of the curtains into one set and the other six into another set. 17Then they made fifty loops along the edge of the end curtain in one set and also along the edge of the end curtain in the other set. 18They made fifty bronze clasps to fasten the tent together as a unit.[v] 19Then they made for the tent a covering of ram skins dyed red, and over that a covering of hides of sea cows.[a]

20They made upright frames of acacia wood for the tabernacle. 21Each frame was ten cubits long and a cubit and a half wide,[b] 22with two projec-

35:25 [c] S Ex 28:3 **35:27** [d] S Ex 25:2; 1Ch 29:6 [e] 1Ch 29:8 **35:28** [f] S Ex 25:6 **35:29** [g] S Ex 25:2 [h] ver 4-9; Ex 25:1-7; 36:3; 2Ki 12:4 **35:31** [i] ver 35; 2Ch 2:7,14 **35:34** [j] S Ex 31:6 [k] 2Ch 2:14 **35:35** [l] ver 31 **36:1** [m] S Ex 28:3 [n] Ex 25:8 **36:2** [o] S Ex 31:2 [p] S Ex 31:6 [q] S Ex 25:2 **36:3** [r] S Ex 35:29 **36:5** [s] 2Ch 24:14; 31:10; 2Co 8:2-3

36:7 [t] 1Ki 7:47 **36:13** [u] ver 18 **36:18** [v] ver 13

[y] *9* That is, about 42 feet (about 12.5 meters) long and 6 feet (about 1.8 meters) wide
[z] *15* That is, about 45 feet (about 13.5 meters) long and 6 feet (about 1.8 meters) wide
[a] *19* That is, dugongs
[b] *21* That is, about 15 feet (about 4.5 meters) long and 2 1/4 feet (about 0.7 meter) wide

tions set parallel to each other. They
made all the frames of the tabernacle
in this way. 23 They made twenty
frames for the south side of the tabernacle 24 and made forty silver bases to
go under them—two bases for each
frame, one under each projection.
25 For the other side, the north side of
the tabernacle, they made twenty
frames 26 and forty silver bases—two
under each frame. 27 They made six
frames for the far end, that is, the west
end of the tabernacle, 28 and two
frames were made for the corners of
the tabernacle at the far end. 29 At
these two corners the frames were
double from the bottom all the way to
the top and fitted into a single ring;
both were made alike. 30 So there were
eight frames and sixteen silver bases—two under each frame.
31 They also made crossbars of acacia wood: five for the frames on one
side of the tabernacle, 32 five for those
on the other side, and five for the
frames on the west, at the far end of
the tabernacle. 33 They made the center crossbar so that it extended from
end to end at the middle of the frames.
34 They overlaid the frames with gold
and made gold rings to hold the crossbars. They also overlaid the crossbars
with gold.
35 They made the curtain[w] of blue,
purple and scarlet yarn and finely
twisted linen, with cherubim worked
into it by a skilled craftsman. 36 They
made four posts of acacia wood for it
and overlaid them with gold. They
made gold hooks for them and cast
their four silver bases. 37 For the entrance to the tent they made a curtain
of blue, purple and scarlet yarn and
finely twisted linen—the work of an
embroiderer;[x] 38 and they made five
posts with hooks for them. They overlaid the tops of the posts and their
bands with gold and made their five
bases of bronze.

The Ark

37:1–9pp — Ex 25:10–20

37 Bezalel[y] made the ark[z] of
acacia wood—two and a half
cubits long, a cubit and a half wide, and
a cubit and a half high.[c] 2 He overlaid
it with pure gold,[a] both inside and out,
and made a gold molding around it.
3 He cast four gold rings for it and fastened them to its four feet, with two
rings on one side and two rings on the
other. 4 Then he made poles of acacia
wood and overlaid them with gold.
5 And he inserted the poles into the
rings on the sides of the ark to carry it.
6 He made the atonement cover[b] of
pure gold—two and a half cubits long
and a cubit and a half wide.[d] 7 Then he
made two cherubim[c] out of hammered
gold at the ends of the cover. 8 He made
one cherub on one end and the second
cherub on the other; at the two ends he
made them of one piece with the cover.
9 The cherubim had their wings spread
upward, overshadowing[d] the cover
with them. The cherubim faced each
other, looking toward the cover.[e]

The Table

37:10–16pp — Ex 25:23–29

10 They[e] made the table[f] of acacia
wood—two cubits long, a cubit wide,
and a cubit and a half high.[f] 11 Then
they overlaid it with pure gold[g] and
made a gold molding around it. 12 They
also made around it a rim a handbreadth[g] wide and put a gold molding
on the rim. 13 They cast four gold rings
for the table and fastened them to the
four corners, where the four legs were.
14 The rings[h] were put close to the rim
to hold the poles used in carrying the
table. 15 The poles for carrying the table were made of acacia wood and were
overlaid with gold. 16 And they made
from pure gold the articles for the table—its plates and dishes and bowls
and its pitchers for the pouring out of
drink offerings.

The Lampstand

37:17–24pp — Ex 25:31–39

17 They made the lampstand[i] of
pure gold and hammered it out, base
and shaft; its flowerlike cups, buds and
blossoms were of one piece with it.
18 Six branches extended from the
sides of the lampstand—three on one
side and three on the other. 19 Three

36:35 [w] Ex 39:38
36:37 [x] Ex 27:16
37:1 [y] S Ex 31:2 [z] Ex 30:6; 39:35; Dt 10:3
37:2 [a] ver 11,26
37:6 [b] S Ex 26:34; S 31:7; Heb 9:5
37:7 [c] Eze 41:18
37:9 [d] Heb 9:5 [e] Dt 10:3
37:10 [f] Heb 9:2
37:11 [g] S ver 2
37:14 [h] ver 27
37:17 [i] Heb 9:2; Rev 1:12

[c] *1* That is, about 3 3/4 feet (about 1.1 meters) long and 2 1/4 feet (about 0.7 meter) wide and high [d] *6* That is, about 3 3/4 feet (about 1.1 meters) long and 2 1/4 feet (about 0.7 meter) wide [e] *10* Or *He*; also in verses 11-29 [f] *10* That is, about 3 feet (about 0.9 meter) long, 1 1/2 feet (about 0.5 meter) wide, and 2 1/4 feet (about 0.7 meter) high
[g] *12* That is, about 3 inches (about 8 centimeters)

cups shaped like almond flowers with buds and blossoms were on one branch, three on the next branch and the same for all six branches extending from the lampstand. **20**And on the lampstand were four cups shaped like almond flowers with buds and blossoms. **21**One bud was under the first pair of branches extending from the lampstand, a second bud under the second pair, and a third bud under the third pair—six branches in all. **22**The buds and the branches were all of one piece with the lampstand, hammered out of pure gold.[j]

23They made its seven lamps,[k] as well as its wick trimmers and trays, of pure gold. **24**They made the lampstand and all its accessories from one talent[h] of pure gold.

The Altar of Incense

37:25–28pp — Ex 30:1–5

25They made the altar of incense[l] out of acacia wood. It was square, a cubit long and a cubit wide, and two cubits high[i]—its horns[m] of one piece with it. **26**They overlaid the top and all the sides and the horns with pure gold, and made a gold molding around it. **27**They made two gold rings[n] below the molding—two on opposite sides—to hold the poles used to carry it. **28**They made the poles of acacia wood and overlaid them with gold.[o]

29They also made the sacred anointing oil[p] and the pure, fragrant incense[q]—the work of a perfumer.

The Altar of Burnt Offering

38:1–7pp — Ex 27:1–8

38 They[j] built the altar of burnt offering of acacia wood, three cubits[k] high; it was square, five cubits long and five cubits wide.[l] **2**They made a horn at each of the four corners, so that the horns and the altar were of one piece, and they overlaid the altar with bronze.[r] **3**They made all its utensils[s] of bronze—its pots, shovels, sprinkling bowls, meat forks and firepans. **4**They made a grating for the altar, a bronze network, to be under its ledge, halfway up the altar. **5**They cast bronze rings to hold the poles for the four corners of the bronze grating. **6**They made the poles of acacia wood and overlaid them with bronze. **7**They inserted the poles into the rings so they would be on the sides of the altar for carrying it. They made it hollow, out of boards.

Basin for Washing

8They made the bronze basin[t] and its bronze stand from the mirrors of the women[u] who served at the entrance to the Tent of Meeting.

The Courtyard

38:9–20pp — Ex 27:9–19

9Next they made the courtyard. The south side was a hundred cubits[m] long and had curtains of finely twisted linen, **10**with twenty posts and twenty bronze bases, and with silver hooks and bands on the posts. **11**The north side was also a hundred cubits long and had twenty posts and twenty bronze bases, with silver hooks and bands on the posts.

12The west end was fifty cubits[n] wide and had curtains, with ten posts and ten bases, with silver hooks and bands on the posts. **13**The east end, toward the sunrise, was also fifty cubits wide. **14**Curtains fifteen cubits[o] long were on one side of the entrance, with three posts and three bases, **15**and curtains fifteen cubits long were on the other side of the entrance to the courtyard, with three posts and three bases. **16**All the curtains around the courtyard were of finely twisted linen. **17**The bases for the posts were bronze. The hooks and bands on the posts were silver, and their tops were overlaid with silver; so all the posts of the courtyard had silver bands.

18The curtain for the entrance to the courtyard was of blue, purple and scarlet yarn and finely twisted linen—the work of an embroiderer. It was twenty cubits[p] long and, like the curtains of the courtyard, five cubits[q] high, **19**with four posts and four bronze bases. Their hooks and bands were silver,

37:22 [j] ver 17; Nu 8:4 **37:23** [k] Ex 40:4, 25 **37:25** [l] Ex 30:34-36; Lk 1:11; Heb 9:4; Rev 8:3 [m] S Ex 27:2; Rev 9:13 **37:27** [n] ver 14 **37:28** [o] S Ex 25:13 **37:29** [p] S Ex 31:11 [q] Ex 30:1,25; 39:38 **38:2** [r] 2Ch 1:5 **38:3** [s] S Ex 31:9 **38:8** [t] S Ex 30:18; S 40:7 [u] Dt 23:17; 1Sa 2:22; 1Ki 14:24

[h] *24* That is, about 75 pounds (about 34 kilograms) [i] *25* That is, about 1 1/2 feet (about 0.5 meter) long and wide, and about 3 feet (about 0.9 meter) high [j] *1* Or *He*; also in verses 2-9 [k] *1* That is, about 4 1/2 feet (about 1.3 meters) [l] *1* That is, about 7 1/2 feet (about 2.3 meters) long and wide
[m] *9* That is, about 150 feet (about 46 meters)
[n] *12* That is, about 75 feet (about 23 meters)
[o] *14* That is, about 22 1/2 feet (about 6.9 meters) [p] *18* That is, about 30 feet (about 9 meters) [q] *18* That is, about 7 1/2 feet (about 2.3 meters)

and their tops were overlaid with silver. **20**All the tent pegs[v] of the tabernacle and of the surrounding courtyard
were bronze.

The Materials Used

21These are the amounts of the materials used for the tabernacle, the tabernacle of the Testimony,[w] which
were recorded at Moses' command by
the Levites under the direction of Ithamar[x] son of Aaron, the priest. **22**(Bezalel[y] son of Uri, the son of Hur, of the
tribe of Judah, made everything the
LORD commanded Moses; **23**with him
was Oholiab[z] son of Ahisamach, of
the tribe of Dan—a craftsman and designer, and an embroiderer in blue,
purple and scarlet yarn and fine linen.)
24The total amount of the gold from the
wave offering used for all the work on
the sanctuary[a] was 29 talents and
730 shekels,[r] according to the sanctuary shekel.[b]

25The silver obtained from those of
the community who were counted in
the census[c] was 100 talents and
1,775 shekels,[s] according to the sanctuary shekel— **26**one beka per person,[d] that is, half a shekel,[t] according to the sanctuary shekel,[e] from
everyone who had crossed over to
those counted, twenty years old or
more,[f] a total of 603,550 men.[g]
27The 100 talents[u] of silver were used
to cast the bases[h] for the sanctuary
and for the curtain—100 bases from
the 100 talents, one talent for each
base. **28**They used the 1,775 shekels[v]
to make the hooks for the posts, to
overlay the tops of the posts, and to
make their bands.

29The bronze from the wave offering
was 70 talents and 2,400 shekels.[w]
30They used it to make the bases for
the entrance to the Tent of Meeting,
the bronze altar with its bronze grating
and all its utensils, **31**the bases for the
surrounding courtyard and those for
its entrance and all the tent pegs for
the tabernacle and those for the surrounding courtyard.

The Priestly Garments

39 From the blue, purple and scarlet yarn[i] they made woven
garments for ministering in the sanctuary.[j] They also made sacred garments[k] for Aaron, as the LORD commanded Moses.

The Ephod

39:2–7pp — Ex 28:6–14

2They[x] made the ephod of gold, and
of blue, purple and scarlet yarn, and of
finely twisted linen. **3**They hammered
out thin sheets of gold and cut strands
to be worked into the blue, purple and
scarlet yarn and fine linen—the work
of a skilled craftsman. **4**They made
shoulder pieces for the ephod, which
were attached to two of its corners, so
it could be fastened. **5**Its skillfully woven waistband was like it—of one
piece with the ephod and made with
gold, and with blue, purple and scarlet
yarn, and with finely twisted linen, as
the LORD commanded Moses.

6They mounted the onyx stones in
gold filigree settings and engraved
them like a seal with the names of the
sons of Israel. **7**Then they fastened
them on the shoulder pieces of the
ephod as memorial[l] stones for the
sons of Israel, as the LORD commanded
Moses.

The Breastpiece

39:8–21pp — Ex 28:15–28

8They fashioned the breastpiece[m]—the work of a skilled craftsman. They made it like the ephod: of
gold, and of blue, purple and scarlet
yarn, and of finely twisted linen. **9**It
was square—a span[y] long and a span
wide—and folded double. **10**Then they
mounted four rows of precious stones
on it. In the first row there was a ruby,
a topaz and a beryl; **11**in the second
row a turquoise, a sapphire[z] and an
emerald; **12**in the third row a jacinth,
an agate and an amethyst; **13**in the
fourth row a chrysolite, an onyx and a
jasper.[a] They were mounted in gold
filigree settings. **14**There were twelve
stones, one for each of the names of
the sons of Israel, each engraved like

38:20 [v]S Ex 35:18
38:21 [w]Nu 1:50, 53; 8:24; 9:15; 10:11; 17:7; 1Ch 23:32; 2Ch 24:6; Ac 7:44; Rev 15:5 [x]Nu 4:28,33
38:22 [y]S Ex 31:2
38:23 [z]S Ex 31:6
38:24 [a]S Ex 30:16 [b]S Ex 30:13
38:25 [c]S Ex 30:12
38:26 [d]S Ex 30:12 [e]S Ex 30:13 [f]S Ex 30:14 [g]S Ex 12:37
38:27 [h]S Ex 26:19
39:1 [i]Ex 35:23 [j]Ex 35:19 [k]ver 41; Ex 28:2
39:7 [l]Lev 24:7; Jos 4:7
39:8 [m]Lev 8:8

[r] *24* The weight of the gold was a little over one ton (about 1 metric ton). [s] *25* The weight of the silver was a little over 3 3/4 tons (about 3.4 metric tons). [t] *26* That is, about 1/5 ounce (about 5.5 grams) [u] *27* That is, about 3 3/4 tons (about 3.4 metric tons) [v] *28* That is, about 45 pounds (about 20 kilograms) [w] *29* The weight of the bronze was about 2 1/2 tons (about 2.4 metric tons). [x] *2* Or *He*; also in verses 7, 8 and 22 [y] *9* That is, about 9 inches (about 22 centimeters) [z] *11* Or *lapis lazuli* [a] *13* The precise identification of some of these precious stones is uncertain.

a seal with the name of one of the
twelve tribes.[n]
15 For the breastpiece they made
braided chains of pure gold, like a rope.
16 They made two gold filigree settings
and two gold rings, and fastened the
rings to two of the corners of the
breastpiece. 17 They fastened the two
gold chains to the rings at the corners
of the breastpiece, 18 and the other
ends of the chains to the two settings,
attaching them to the shoulder pieces
of the ephod at the front. 19 They made
two gold rings and attached them to
the other two corners of the breastpiece on the inside edge next to the
ephod. 20 Then they made two more
gold rings and attached them to the
bottom of the shoulder pieces on the
front of the ephod, close to the seam
just above the waistband of the ephod.
21 They tied the rings of the breastpiece
to the rings of the ephod with blue
cord, connecting it to the waistband so
that the breastpiece would not swing
out from the ephod—as the LORD commanded Moses.

Other Priestly Garments

39:22–31pp — Ex 28:31–43

22 They made the robe of the ephod
entirely of blue cloth—the work of a
weaver— 23 with an opening in the center of the robe like the opening of a
collar,[b] and a band around this opening, so that it would not tear. 24 They
made pomegranates of blue, purple
and scarlet yarn and finely twisted lin-
en around the hem of the robe. 25 And
they made bells of pure gold and attached them around the hem between
the pomegranates. 26 The bells and
pomegranates alternated around the
hem of the robe to be worn for ministering, as the LORD commanded Moses.
27 For Aaron and his sons, they made
tunics of fine linen[o]—the work of a
weaver— 28 and the turban[p] of fine
linen, the linen headbands and the undergarments of finely twisted linen.
29 The sash was of finely twisted linen
and blue, purple and scarlet yarn—the
work of an embroiderer—as the LORD
commanded Moses.
30 They made the plate, the sacred
diadem, out of pure gold and engraved
on it, like an inscription on a seal: HOLY
TO THE LORD.[q] 31 Then they fastened a
blue cord to it to attach it to the turban,[r] as the LORD commanded Moses.

Moses Inspects the Tabernacle

39:32–41pp — Ex 35:10–19

32 So all the work on the tabernacle,
the Tent of Meeting, was completed.
The Israelites did everything just as
the LORD commanded Moses.[s] 33 Then
they brought the tabernacle[t] to Moses: the tent and all its furnishings, its
clasps, frames, crossbars, posts and
bases; 34 the covering of ram skins
dyed red, the covering of hides of sea
cows[c] and the shielding curtain; 35 the
ark of the Testimony[u] with its poles
and the atonement cover; 36 the table[v]
with all its articles and the bread of the
Presence;[w] 37 the pure gold lampstand[x] with its row of lamps and all its
accessories,[y] and the oil[z] for the
light; 38 the gold altar,[a] the anointing
oil,[b] the fragrant incense,[c] and the
curtain[d] for the entrance to the tent;
39 the bronze altar[e] with its bronze
grating, its poles and all its utensils;
the basin[f] with its stand; 40 the curtains of the courtyard with its posts
and bases, and the curtain for the entrance to the courtyard;[g] the ropes
and tent pegs for the courtyard; all the
furnishings for the tabernacle, the
Tent of Meeting; 41 and the woven garments[h] worn for ministering in the
sanctuary, both the sacred garments
for Aaron the priest and the garments
for his sons when serving as priests.
42 The Israelites had done all the
work just as the LORD had commanded
Moses.[i] 43 Moses inspected the work
and saw that they had done it just as
the LORD had commanded.[j] So Moses
blessed[k] them.

Setting Up the Tabernacle

40 Then the LORD said to Moses:
2 "Set up[l] the tabernacle, the
Tent of Meeting,[m] on the first day of
the first month.[n] 3 Place the ark[o] of
the Testimony in it and shield the ark
with the curtain. 4 Bring in the table[p]
and set out what belongs on it.[q] Then
bring in the lampstand[r] and set up its
lamps. 5 Place the gold altar[s] of incense in front of the ark of the Testimony and put the curtain at the entrance
to the tabernacle.

39:14 [n] Rev 21:12 **39:27** [o] Lev 6:10; 8:2 **39:28** [p] ver 31; S Ex 28:4; Lev 8:9; Isa 61:10 **39:30** [q] Isa 23:18; Zec 14:20 **39:31** [r] S ver 28 **39:32** [s] S Ex 25:9 **39:33** [t] Ex 25:8-40; 36:8-38 **39:35** [u] S Ex 37:1 **39:36** [v] Ex 25:23-30; 37:10-16 [w] S Ex 25:30 **39:37** [x] S Ex 25:31 [y] Ex 25:31-39 [z] S Ex 25:6 **39:38** [a] Ex 30:1-10 [b] Ex 30:22-32; 37:29 [c] Ex 30:34-38; S 37:29 [d] S Ex 36:35 **39:39** [e] Ex 27:1-8; 38:1-7 [f] S Ex 30:18 **39:40** [g] Ex 27:9-19; 38:9-20 **39:41** [h] S ver 1 **39:42** [i] S Ex 25:9 **39:43** [j] S Ex 25:9; S 35:10 [k] Ge 31:55; Lev 9:22,23; Nu 6:23-27; Dt 21:5; 26:15; 2Sa 6:18; 1Ki 8:14,55; 1Ch 16:2; 2Ch 30:27 **40:2** [l] S Ex 26:30 [m] ver 34,35; Lev 1:1; 3:2; 6:26; 9:23; 16:16; Nu 1:1; 7:89; 11:16; 17:4; 20:6; Jos 18:1; 19:51; Jer 7:12 [n] ver 17; S Ex 12:2; Nu 9:1 **40:3** [o] S Ex 26:33 **40:4** [p] S Ex 25:23 [q] S Ex 25:30 [r] S Ex 25:31 **40:5** [s] S Ex 30:1

[b] *23* The meaning of the Hebrew for this word is uncertain. [c] *34* That is, dugongs

6"Place the altar[t] of burnt offering
in front of the entrance to the tabernacle, the Tent of Meeting; 7place the basin[u] between the Tent of Meeting and
the altar and put water in it. 8Set up
the courtyard[v] around it and put the
curtain at the entrance to the courtyard.
9"Take the anointing oil and
anoint[w] the tabernacle and everything
in it; consecrate it and all its furnishings,[x] and it will be holy. 10Then
anoint the altar of burnt offering and
all its utensils; consecrate[y] the altar,
and it will be most holy. 11Anoint the
basin and its stand and consecrate
them.
12"Bring Aaron and his sons to the
entrance to the Tent of Meeting[z] and
wash them with water.[a] 13Then dress
Aaron in the sacred garments,[b] anoint
him and consecrate[c] him so he may
serve me as priest. 14Bring his sons
and dress them in tunics.[d] 15Anoint
them just as you anointed their father,
so they may serve me as priests. Their
anointing will be to a priesthood that
will continue for all generations to
come.[e]" 16Moses did everything just
as the LORD commanded[f] him.
17So the tabernacle[g] was set up on
the first day of the first month[h] in the
second year. 18When Moses[i] set up
the tabernacle, he put the bases in
place, erected the frames,[j] inserted
the crossbars and set up the posts.
19Then he spread the tent over the tabernacle and put the covering[k] over
the tent, as the LORD commanded[l]
him.
20He took the Testimony[m] and
placed it in the ark,[n] attached the
poles to the ark and put the atonement
cover[o] over it. 21Then he brought the
ark into the tabernacle and hung the
shielding curtain[p] and shielded the
ark of the Testimony, as the LORD commanded[q] him.
22Moses placed the table[r] in the
Tent of Meeting on the north side of
the tabernacle outside the curtain
23and set out the bread[s] on it before
the LORD, as the LORD commanded[t]
him.
24He placed the lampstand[u] in the
Tent of Meeting opposite the table on
the south side of the tabernacle 25and
set up the lamps[v] before the LORD, as
the LORD commanded[w] him.
26Moses placed the gold altar[x] in
the Tent of Meeting in front of the curtain 27and burned fragrant incense on
it, as the LORD commanded[y] him.
28Then he put up the curtain[z] at the
entrance to the tabernacle.
29He set the altar[a] of burnt offering
near the entrance to the tabernacle,
the Tent of Meeting, and offered on it
burnt offerings and grain offerings,[b]
as the LORD commanded[c] him.
30He placed the basin[d] between the
Tent of Meeting and the altar and put
water in it for washing, 31and Moses
and Aaron and his sons used it to
wash[e] their hands and feet. 32They
washed whenever they entered the
Tent of Meeting or approached the altar,[f] as the LORD commanded[g] Moses.
33Then Moses set up the courtyard[h] around the tabernacle and altar
and put up the curtain[i] at the entrance to the courtyard. And so Moses
finished the work.

The Glory of the LORD

34Then the cloud[j] covered the Tent
of Meeting, and the glory[k] of the LORD
filled the tabernacle. 35Moses could
not enter the Tent of Meeting because
the cloud had settled upon it, and the
glory[l] of the LORD filled the tabernacle.[m]
36In all the travels of the Israelites,
whenever the cloud lifted from above
the tabernacle, they would set out;[n]
37but if the cloud did not lift, they did
not set out—until the day it lifted.
38So the cloud[o] of the LORD was over
the tabernacle by day, and fire was in
the cloud by night, in the sight of all
the house of Israel during all their travels.

40:6 [t] S Ex 27:1; 2Ki 16:14; 2Ch 4:1 **40:7** [u] Ex 30:18 **40:8** [v] S Ex 27:9 **40:9** [w] S Ex 30:26 [x] Nu 7:1 **40:10** [y] S Ex 29:36 **40:12** [z] Nu 8:9 [a] S Ex 29:4; S 30:19 **40:13** [b] S Ex 28:41 [c] Lev 8:12 **40:14** [d] S Ex 28:40; Lev 10:5 **40:15** [e] S Ex 29:9 **40:16** [f] S Ge 6:22 **40:17** [g] Nu 7:1 [h] S ver 2 **40:18** [i] 2Ch 1:3 [j] Ex 36:20-34 **40:19** [k] Ex 36:19 [l] S Ge 6:22 **40:20** [m] S Ex 16:34; Heb 9:4 [n] S Ex 25:21 [o] Ex 25:17-22; S 26:34; S 31:7 **40:21** [p] S Ex 26:33 [q] S Ge 6:22 **40:22** [r] S Ex 25:23 **40:23** [s] S Ex 25:30; Lev 24:5-8 [t] S Ge 6:22 **40:24** [u] S Ex 25:31 **40:25** [v] S Ex 37:23 [w] S Ge 6:22 **40:26** [x] S Ex 30:1 **40:27** [y] S Ge 6:22 **40:28** [z] S Ex 26:36 **40:29** [a] S Ex 20:24 [b] Ex 29:38-42 [c] S Ge 6:22 **40:30** [d] S ver 7; S Ex 30:18 **40:31** [e] Ex 30:19-21 **40:32** [f] Ex 30:20 [g] S Ge 6:22 **40:33** [h] S Ex 27:9; 38:9-20 [i] Ex 27:16 **40:34** [j] Ex 19:16; Lev 16:2; Nu 9:15-23; 1Ki 8:12; 2Ch 5:13; Isa 6:4; Eze 10:4 [k] S Ex 16:7; Jn 1:14; 12:41; Rev 15:8 **40:35** [l] S Ex 16:10 [m] 1Ki 8:11; 2Ch 5:13-14; 7:2 **40:36** [n] Nu 9:17-23; 10:13 **40:38** [o] S Ex 13:21; 1Co 10:1

40:34 THE GLORY OF THE LORD. The book of Exodus ends with the glory of the Lord filling the tabernacle. (1) This manifestation foreshadows the Lord's dwelling in and among his people through the true church (cf. 1Co 3:16; Eph 2:18–22). It further foreshadows God's future dwelling among all his faithful saints in the new heaven and new earth (Rev 21:3).

(2) The "glory of the LORD" is sometimes referred to as the "Shekinah" glory (see article on THE GLORY OF GOD, p. 1192).

LEVITICUS

Outline

I. The Way of Access to God: Atonement (1:1—16:34)
  A. Through Sacrifices (1:1–7:38)
    1. The Burnt Offering (1:1–17)
    2. The Grain Offering (2:1–16)
    3. The Fellowship Offering (3:1–17)
    4. The Sin Offering for Unintentional Sins (4:1—5:13)
    5. The Guilt Offering (5:14—6:7)
    6. The Continual Burnt Offering and Offerings of Priests (6:8–23)
    7. The Disposition of the Victim in a Sin Offering, Guilt Offering and Fellowship Offering (6:24—7:27)
    8. The Wave Offering and Summary of the Offerings (7:28–38)
  B. Through Priestly Intercession (8:1—10:20)
  C. Through Purification Laws (11:1—15:33)
  D. Through the Annual Day of Atonement (16:1–34)
II. The Way of Living Before God: Holiness (17:1—27:34)
  A. Through Revelation About the Blood (17:1–16)
  B. Through Moral Standards (18:1—22:33)
  C. Through Regular Worship (23:1—24:23)
  D. Through Reparation Laws, Obedience and Consecration (25:1—27:34)

Author: Moses

Theme: Holiness

Date of Writing: 1445–1405 B.C.

Background

Leviticus is closely related to the book of Exodus. Exodus records how the Israelites were delivered from Egypt, received God's law and built the tabernacle according to God's pattern; it concludes with the Holy One coming to indwell the newly constructed tabernacle (Ex 40:34). Leviticus contains God's instruction given to Moses during the two months between the completion of the tabernacle (Ex 40:17) and Israel's departure from Mount Sinai (Nu 10:11). The title "Leviticus" is derived not from the Hebrew Bible, but from the Greek and Latin versions. This title might lead some to believe that the book concerns only the Levitical priests; this is not the case, however, for much of the book relates to all of Israel.

Leviticus is the third book of Moses. More than 50 times it affirms that its contents are God's direct words and revelation to Moses for Israel, which Moses subsequently preserved in written form. Jesus refers to a passage in Leviticus and attributes it to Moses (Mk 1:44). The apostle Paul refers to a passage in this book by saying, "Moses describes . . ." (Ro 10:5). Critics who attribute Leviticus to a much later priestly editor do so by rejecting the integrity of Biblical testimony (see the introduction to Exodus).

Purpose

Leviticus was written to instruct the Israelites and their priestly mediators about their access to God by means of atoning blood and to make clear God's standard of holy living for his chosen people.

Survey

Leviticus preeminently involves two important themes: atonement and holiness. (A) Chs. 1—16 contain God's provision for redemption from sin and from the alienation between God and humankind that has resulted from sin. Variations of the verb "to make atonement" (Heb *kaphar*) occur some 48 times in Leviticus; the noun "atonement" occurs three times. The basic meaning of the verb is "to cover, to make a covering." The OT blood sacrifices (chs. 1—7) were temporary blood coverings for sin (cf. Heb 10:4) until such time as Jesus Christ would die as the perfect sacrifice to take away the sin of the world (cf. Jn 1:29; Ro 3:25; Heb 10:11–12). The Levitical priests (chs. 8—10) foreshadow Christ's ministry of mediation, while the annual Day of Atonement (ch. 16) foreshadows the crucifixion.

(B) Chs. 17—27 present a series of practical standards by which God called his people to purity and holy living. God's recurring command is, "Be holy because I, the LORD your God, am holy" (e.g., 19:2; 20:7,26). The Hebrew words for "holy" occur over 100 times, and when applied to humans denote lives of purity and obedience. Holiness is expressed in ceremony (ch. 17) and worship (chs. 23—25), but especially in issues of daily living (chs. 18—22). Leviticus ends with an exhortation by Moses (ch. 26) and instruction concerning certain special vows (ch. 27).

Special Features

Four major emphases characterize Leviticus. (1) Revelation as a direct word from God is emphasized more in Leviticus than in any other Bible book. No less than 38 times it is explicitly stated that the Lord spoke to Moses. (2) Instruction concerning the sacrificial system and substitutionary atonement is given in minute detail in this book. (3) Ch. 16 is the foremost chapter in the Bible describing the Day of Atonement. (4) Leviticus stresses the theme that the people of Israel were to fulfill their priestly calling through lives of spiritual and moral purity, separation from other nations, and obedience to God.

New Testament Fulfillment

Because of the twofold emphasis on blood atonement and holiness, this book has enduring relevance for believers under the new covenant. The NT teaches that the atoning blood of sacrificial animals, prominent in Leviticus, was "a shadow of the good things that are coming" (Heb 10:1) and pointed to Christ's once-for-all-time sacrifice for sin (Heb 9:12). The command to be holy can be fully realized through the precious blood of Christ in the new covenant believer, whose calling is to be holy in all areas of life (1Pe 1:15). The second great commandment as stated by Jesus was derived from Lev 19:18, "Love your neighbor as yourself" (Mt 22:39).

Reading Leviticus

In order to read the entire Old Testament in one year, the book of Leviticus should be read in 14 days, according to the following schedule: ☐ 1–3 ☐ 4–5 ☐ 6–7 ☐ 8 ☐ 9–10 ☐ 11–12 ☐ 13–14 ☐ 15 ☐ 16–18 ☐ 19–21 ☐ 22–23 ☐ 24 ☐ 25 ☐ 26–27

NOTES

The Burnt Offering

1 The LORD called to Moses[a] and
spoke to him from the Tent of
Meeting.[b] He said, 2"Speak to the Israelites and say to them: 'When any of
you brings an offering to the LORD,[c]
bring as your offering an animal from
either the herd or the flock.[d]

3" 'If the offering is a burnt offering[e] from the herd,[f] he is to offer a
male without defect.[g] He must
present it at the entrance to the Tent[h]
of Meeting so that it[a] will be acceptable[i] to the LORD. 4He is to lay his
hand on the head[j] of the burnt offering,[k] and it will be accepted[l] on his
behalf to make atonement[m] for him.
5He is to slaughter[n] the young bull[o]
before the LORD, and then Aaron's
sons[p] the priests shall bring the blood
and sprinkle it against the altar on all
sides[q] at the entrance to the Tent of
Meeting. 6He is to skin[r] the burnt offering and cut it into pieces.[s] 7The
sons of Aaron the priest are to put fire
on the altar and arrange wood[t] on the
fire. 8Then Aaron's sons the priests
shall arrange the pieces, including the
head and the fat,[u] on the burning
wood[v] that is on the altar. 9He is to
wash the inner parts and the legs with
water,[w] and the priest is to burn all of
it[x] on the altar.[y] It is a burnt offering,[z] an offering made by fire,[a] an
aroma pleasing to the LORD.[b]

10" 'If the offering is a burnt offering
from the flock, from either the sheep[c]
or the goats,[d] he is to offer a male
without defect. 11He is to slaughter it
at the north side of the altar[e] before
the LORD, and Aaron's sons the priests
shall sprinkle its blood against the altar on all sides.[f] 12He is to cut it into
pieces, and the priest shall arrange
them, including the head and the fat,[g]
on the burning wood that is on the altar. 13He is to wash the inner parts and
the legs with water,[h] and the priest is
to bring all of it and burn it[i] on the
altar.[j] It is a burnt offering,[k] an offering made by fire, an aroma pleasing
to the LORD.

14" 'If the offering to the LORD is a
burnt offering of birds, he is to offer a

1:1 [a]S Ex 3:4; S 25:22 [b]S Ex 27:21; S 40:2 **1:2** [c]Lev 7:16,38; 22:21; 23:38; 27:9 [d]Lev 22:18-19; Nu 15:3 **1:3** [e]S Ge 8:20 [f]ver 10; Lev 22:27; Ezr 8:35; Mal 1:8 [g]S ver 5; S Ex 12:5; S Lev 22:19,20; Heb 9:14; 1Pe 1:19 [h]Lev 6:25; 17:9; Nu 6:16; Dt 12:5-6,11 [i]Isa 58:5 **1:4** [j]S Ex 29:10, 15 [k]ver 3; Lev 4:29; 6:25; Eze 45:15 [l]S Ge 32:20 [m]S Ex 29:36; S 32:30 **1:5** [n]Ex 29:11; Lev 3:2,8 [o]S ver 3; Ex 29:1; Nu 15:8; Dt 18:3; Ps 50:9; 69:31 [p]Lev 8:2; 10:6; 21:1 [q]S Ex 29:20; Heb 12:24; 1Pe 1:2 **1:6** [r]Lev 7:8 [s]Ex 29:17 **1:7** [t]ver 17; S Ge 22:9; Lev 3:5; 6:12 **1:8** [u]ver 12; S Ex 29:13; Lev 8:20 [v]Lev 9:13 **1:9** [w]S Ex 29:17 [x]Lev 6:22 [y]ver 13; Ex 29:18; Lev 9:14 [z]ver 3 [a]Lev 23:8, 25,36; Nu 28:6,19 [b]ver 13; Ge 8:21; Lev 2:2; 3:5,16; 17:6; Nu 18:17; 28:11-13; Eph 5:2 **1:10** [c]S Ge 22:7 [d]S ver 3; Ex 12:5; Lev 3:12; 4:23,28; 5:6; Nu 15:11 **1:11** [e]S Ex 29:11 [f]S Ex 29:20 **1:12** [g]S ver 8 **1:13** [h]S Ex 29:17 [i]Lev 6:22 [j]S ver 9 [k]Dt 12:27

[a] *3* Or *he*

1:2 BRINGS AN OFFERING. The noun "offering" (Heb *corban*) is related to the verb that means "to draw near." Therefore, an offering was a gift that Israelite believers brought near to God in order to approach God and enjoy his fellowship and blessing (cf. Ps 73:28). (1) Five offerings are described in chs. 1–7: the burnt offering (1:3–17), the grain offering (2:1–16), the fellowship offering (3:1–17), the sin offering (ch. 4) and the guilt offering (5:14—6:7; 7:1–7).

(2) Worshipers presented offerings to express thanksgiving and faith, renew fellowship, deepen their dedication to the Lord, or ask for forgiveness. Offerings were in a real sense "enacted" prayers (cf. Ps 116:17; Hos 14:2; Heb 13:15).

(3) In many cases, an offering involved a sacrifice, i.e., an animal's life was taken (see 9:8, note).

(4) These offerings taught Israel that: (a) humans are basically sinful beings whose sins merit death; (b) without the shedding of blood there is no forgiveness (17:11; Heb 9:22); (c) atonement for sin must be made by substitution (v. 4; 17:11); (d) God's holiness must regulate and direct every area of human life (cf. 10:3); and (e) God desires to be gracious, to forgive, and to have fellowship with men and women (Ex 34:6–7).

(5) In order to make the offering acceptable to God, there had to be genuine heartfelt repentance and a sincere commitment to walk in goodness and righteousness (23:27–29; Isa 1:11–17; Mic 6:6–8).

1:3 BURNT OFFERING. The Hebrew term for burnt offering means "that which goes up" to God. The entire offering was burned up, signifying that complete consecration to God was essential to true worship. At the same time, forgiveness was involved (v. 4), emphasizing that before worshipers could devote themselves to God, they had to be cleansed from sin (cf. Mt 5:23–24). According to the writer of Hebrews, Jesus is the ultimate fulfillment of the burnt offering (Heb 10:5–10).

1:4 LAY HIS HAND ON. An Israelite sacrificing an animal leaned on the animal, signfying that he was identifying himself with the animal as it stood in his place. This act expressed the idea of substitution (cf. 16:21–22; 24:14). When the animal died, it was as if the person who brought it also died, yet remained alive to serve God. Similarly, Christians entrust themselves to Christ and become one with him in his death (Ro 6:3–11; cf. 2Co 5:21; Heb 9:14). They are thus called on to live as people risen from the dead and to present themselves as living sacrifices to God (Ro 12:1; Heb 13:15).

1:5 SLAUGHTER THE YOUNG BULL. See 9:8, note.

1:9 AROMA PLEASING TO THE LORD. God was well pleased with the person's sacrifice given in obedient faith. Paul applied this imagery both to the offering of Christ (Eph 5:2) and to the good deeds of believers (Php 4:18; cf. Heb 13:16).

dove or a young pigeon.[l] **15**The priest shall bring it to the altar, wring off the head[m] and burn it on the altar; its blood shall be drained out on the side of the altar.[n] **16**He is to remove the crop with its contents[b] and throw it to the east side of the altar, where the ashes[o] are. **17**He shall tear it open by the wings, not severing it completely,[p] and then the priest shall burn it on the wood[q] that is on the fire on the altar. It is a burnt offering, an offering made by fire, an aroma pleasing to the LORD.

The Grain Offering

2 " 'When someone brings a grain offering[r] to the LORD, his offering is to be of fine flour.[s] He is to pour oil[t] on it,[u] put incense on it[v] **2**and take it to Aaron's sons the priests. The priest shall take a handful of the fine flour[w] and oil, together with all the incense,[x] and burn this as a memorial portion[y] on the altar, an offering made by fire,[z] an aroma pleasing to the LORD.[a] **3**The rest of the grain offering belongs to Aaron and his sons;[b] it is a most holy[c] part of the offerings made to the LORD by fire.

4" 'If you bring a grain offering baked in an oven,[d] it is to consist of fine flour: cakes made without yeast and mixed with oil, or[c] wafers[e] made without yeast and spread with oil.[f] **5**If your grain offering is prepared on a griddle,[g] it is to be made of fine flour mixed with oil, and without yeast. **6**Crumble it and pour oil on it; it is a grain offering. **7**If your grain offering is cooked in a pan,[h] it is to be made of fine flour and oil. **8**Bring the grain offering made of these things to the LORD; present it to the priest, who shall take it to the altar. **9**He shall take out the memorial portion[i] from the grain offering and burn it on the altar as an offering made by fire, an aroma pleasing to the LORD.[j] **10**The rest of the grain offering belongs to Aaron and his sons;[k] it is a most holy part of the offerings made to the LORD by fire.[l]

11" 'Every grain offering you bring to the LORD must be made without yeast,[m] for you are not to burn any yeast or honey in an offering made to the LORD by fire. **12**You may bring them to the LORD as an offering of the firstfruits,[n] but they are not to be offered on the altar as a pleasing aroma. **13**Season all your grain offerings with salt.[o] Do not leave the salt of the covenant[p] of your God out of your grain offerings; add salt to all your offerings.

14" 'If you bring a grain offering of firstfruits[q] to the LORD, offer crushed heads of new grain roasted in the fire. **15**Put oil and incense[r] on it; it is a grain offering. **16**The priest shall burn the memorial portion[s] of the crushed grain and the oil, together with all the incense,[t] as an offering made to the LORD by fire.[u]

The Fellowship Offering

3 " 'If someone's offering is a fellowship offering,[d][v] and he offers an animal from the herd, whether male or female, he is to present before the LORD an animal without defect.[w] **2**He is to lay his hand on the head[x] of his offering and slaughter it[y] at the entrance to the Tent of Meeting.[z] Then Aaron's sons the priests shall sprinkle[a] the blood against the altar[b] on all sides.[c] **3**From the fellowship offering he is to bring a sacrifice made to the LORD by fire: all the fat[d] that covers the inner parts[e] or is connected to them, **4**both kidneys[f] with the fat on them near the

1:14 [l] S Ge 15:9; Lk 2:24 **1:15** [m] Lev 5:8 [n] Lev 5:9 **1:16** [o] Lev 4:12; 6:10; Nu 4:13 **1:17** [p] S Ge 15:10 [q] S ver 7 **2:1** [r] S Ex 29:41; Lev 6:14-18 [s] Ex 29:2,40; Lev 5:11 [t] Nu 15:4; 28:5 [u] S Ex 29:2; Lev 7:12 [v] ver 2, 15,16; Lev 24:7; Ne 13:9; Isa 43:23 **2:2** [w] Lev 5:11 [x] Lev 6:15; Isa 1:13; 65:3; 66:3 [y] ver 9,16; Lev 5:12; 6:15; 24:7; Nu 5:26; 18:8; Ps 16:5; 73:26; Isa 53:12 [z] ver 16 [a] S Lev 1:9 **2:3** [b] ver 10; Lev 6:16; 10:12, 13 [c] S Ex 30:36 **2:4** [d] Lev 7:9; 26:26 [e] Lev 7:12; 8:26 [f] S Ex 29:2 **2:5** [g] Lev 6:21; 7:9; Eze 4:3 **2:7** [h] Lev 7:9 **2:9** [i] S ver 2 [j] S Ge 8:21 **2:10** [k] ver 3 [l] Ezr 2:63 **2:11** [m] S Ex 23:18; Lev 6:16 **2:12** [n] S Ex 34:22 **2:13** [o] Mk 9:49 [p] Nu 18:19; 2Ch 13:5; Eze 43:24 **2:14** [q] S Ex 34:22; Nu 15:20; Dt 16:13; 26:2; Ru 3:2 **2:15** [r] S ver 1 **2:16** [s] S ver 2 [t] S ver 1 [u] Nu 4:16; Jer 14:12 **3:1** [v] S ver 6; S Ex 32:6; Lev 7:11-34; S 17:5 [w] S Ex 12:5 **3:2** [x] S Ex 29:15; Nu 8:10 [y] S Lev 1:5 [z] S Ex 40:2 [a] S Ex 24:6 [b] Lev 17:6; Nu 18:17 [c] S Ex 29:20 **3:3** [d] S Ex 29:13 [e] S Ex 12:9 **3:4** [f] ver 10; Ex 29:13; Lev 4:9

[b] *16* Or *crop and the feathers*; the meaning of the Hebrew for this word is uncertain.
[c] *4* Or *and* [d] *1* Traditionally *peace offering*; also in verses 3, 6 and 9

2:1 GRAIN OFFERING. The grain offering was a gift presented to God as an act of worship, symbolizing the dedication to God of the fruit of a person's labor. It implied that all human work should be done for the Lord and that one's daily food should be received with thanksgiving to him (cf. 1Co 10:31; see Col 3:23, note).

2:11 NOT . . . ANY YEAST OR HONEY. Yeast and honey were forbidden on the altar because they were used to aid fermentation. Fermentation, which involves change, decomposition or decay, often symbolized evil (see Ex 13:7, Mk 8:15, note).

3:1 FELLOWSHIP OFFERING. The fellowship offering was brought before God in order to have fellowship with him, to express thanksgiving (7:12–16; 22:29) or to make a vow (7:16). (1) For the offerer, it involved commitment to the covenant and celebrated peace and reconciliation between God and the worshiper. (2) This offering points forward to the peace and fellowship that believers have with God and other believers on the basis of Christ's death on the cross (cf. Col 1:20; 1Jn 1:3), and then to the final communion when we will all sit down with God in his kingdom (Ps 22:26; Lk 14:15; Rev 19:6–10).

loins, and the covering of the liver,
which he will remove with the kidneys.
5 Then Aaron's sons[g] are to burn it on
the altar[h] on top of the burnt offering[i] that is on the burning wood,[j] as
an offering made by fire, an aroma
pleasing to the LORD.[k]
6 " 'If he offers an animal from the
flock as a fellowship offering[l] to the
LORD, he is to offer a male or female
without defect. 7 If he offers a lamb,[m]
he is to present it before the LORD.[n]
8 He is to lay his hand on the head of his
offering and slaughter it[o] in front of
the Tent of Meeting. Then Aaron's
sons shall sprinkle its blood against
the altar on all sides. 9 From the fellowship offering he is to bring a sacrifice[p]
made to the LORD by fire: its fat, the
entire fat tail cut off close to the backbone, all the fat that covers the inner
parts or is connected to them, 10 both
kidneys with the fat on them near the
loins, and the covering of the liver,
which he will remove with the kidneys.
11 The priest shall burn them on the altar[q] as food,[r] an offering made to the
LORD by fire.[s]
12 " 'If his offering is a goat,[t] he is
to present it before the LORD. 13 He is to
lay his hand on its head and slaughter
it in front of the Tent of Meeting. Then
Aaron's sons shall sprinkle[u] its blood
against the altar on all sides.[v] 14 From
what he offers he is to make this offering to the LORD by fire: all the fat
that covers the inner parts or is connected to them, 15 both kidneys with
the fat on them near the loins, and
the covering of the liver, which he
will remove with the kidneys.[w] 16 The
priest shall burn them on the altar[x]
as food,[y] an offering made by fire,
a pleasing aroma.[z] All the fat[a] is the
LORD's.[b]

3:5 [g] Lev 7:29-34 [h] ver 11,16 [i] Ex 29:13,38-42; Nu 28:3-10 [j] S Lev 1:7 [k] S Lev 1:9
3:6 [l] S ver 1; Lev 22:21; Nu 15:3,8
3:7 [m] Lev 17:3; Nu 15:5; 28:5,7,8 [n] Lev 17:8-9; 1Ki 8:62
3:8 [o] S Lev 1:5
3:9 [p] Isa 34:6; Jer 46:10; Eze 39:19; Zep 1:7
3:11 [q] S ver 5 [r] ver 16; Lev 21:6, 17; Nu 28:2 [s] Lev 9:18
3:12 [t] S Lev 1:10; S 4:3
3:13 [u] S Ex 24:6 [v] Lev 1:5
3:15 [w] Lev 7:4
3:16 [x] S ver 5; Lev 7:31 [y] S ver 11 [z] S Lev 1:9 [a] S Ge 4:4 [b] 1Sa 2:16
3:17 [c] S Ex 12:14; S 27:21 [d] S Ge 9:12 [e] S Ex 12:20 [f] Ge 9:4; Lev 7:25-26; 17:10-16; Dt 12:16; Ac 15:20
4:2 [g] ver 13,27; Lev 5:15-18; 22:14; Nu 15:24-29; 35:11-15; Jos 20:3,9; Heb 9:7 [h] ver 22; Nu 15:22
4:3 [i] S Ex 28:41 [j] S Ge 18:23 [k] ver 14; Lev 3:12; 8:14; 10:16; 16:3, 5; Nu 15:27; Ps 66:15; Eze 43:19,23 [l] S Ex 12:5 [m] S ver 24; S Ex 30:10; Lev 5:6-13; 9:2-22; Heb 9:13-14 [n] ver 32
4:4 [o] ver 15,24; Lev 1:3; Nu 8:12
4:5 [p] ver 16; Lev 16:14
4:6 [q] Ex 24:8 [r] ver 17; Lev 16:14,19

17 " 'This is a lasting ordinance[c] for
the generations to come,[d] wherever
you live:[e] You must not eat any fat or
any blood.[f] ' "

The Sin Offering

4 The LORD said to Moses, 2 "Say to
the Israelites: 'When anyone sins
unintentionally[g] and does what is forbidden in any of the LORD's commands[h]—

3 " 'If the anointed priest[i] sins,[j]
bringing guilt on the people, he must
bring to the LORD a young bull[k] without defect[l] as a sin offering[m] for the
sin he has committed.[n] 4 He is to
present the bull at the entrance to the
Tent of Meeting before the LORD.[o] He
is to lay his hand on its head and
slaughter it before the LORD. 5 Then the
anointed priest shall take some of the
bull's blood[p] and carry it into the Tent
of Meeting. 6 He is to dip his finger into
the blood and sprinkle[q] some of it sev-
en times before the LORD,[r] in front of
the curtain of the sanctuary.[s] 7 The
priest shall then put some of the blood
on the horns[t] of the altar of fragrant
incense that is before the LORD in the
Tent of Meeting. The rest of the bull's
blood he shall pour out at the base of
the altar[u] of burnt offering[v] at the
entrance to the Tent of Meeting. 8 He
shall remove all the fat[w] from the bull
of the sin offering—the fat that covers
the inner parts or is connected to them,
9 both kidneys with the fat on them
near the loins, and the covering of the
liver, which he will remove with the
kidneys[x]— 10 just as the fat is re-

[s] S Ex 25:8 **4:7** [t] S Ex 27:2 [u] ver 34; S Ex 29:12; Lev 8:15 [v] ver 18,30; Lev 5:9; 9:9; 16:18 **4:8** [w] ver 19 **4:9** [x] S Lev 3:4

3:17 ANY FAT OR ANY BLOOD. Fat and blood are both vital to life (see 17:11, note). Thus, they represent the life of the sacrificial victim, a life that belonged only to God (cf. v. 16).

4:3 SIN OFFERING. God required a sin offering in order that those who sinned in ignorance, in weakness or unintentionally (v. 2) could receive forgiveness. Deliberately defiant sins, on the other hand, were to be punished by death (Nu 15:30–31; Heb 10:28). A guilt offering (similar to the sin offering) was used for those who were guilty of a sin or injury for which full restitution could be made (6:2–6; see 5:15, note); sin offerings were necessary for ritual cleansing as well (12:6–8; 14:13–17; Nu 6:11).

(1) The sin offering foreshadows Christ's atoning death and his bearing the punishment of our sins. His death, however, was infinitely more perfect than the OT sin offering in that it provided a single atonement for *all* sin (Isa 53; 2Co 5:21; Eph 1:7; Heb 9:11–12; see article on THE DAY OF ATONEMENT, p. 174). (2) We as NT believers continually need Christ's atoning blood to cover mistakes, weaknesses and unintentional failings that flow from the frailty of human nature (Ps 19:12). Sins coming from a rebellious disposition against God and his word, however, will bring us under judgment and spiritual death unless we confess them and repent through renewed faith in Christ's atonement (Heb 2:3; 10:26,31; 2Pe 2:20–21).

OLD TESTAMENT SACRIFICES

Sacrifice	OT References	Elements	Purpose
BURNT OFFERING	Lev 1; 6:8-13; 8:18-21; 16:24	Bull, ram or male bird (dove or young pigeon for poor); wholly consumed; no defect	Voluntary act of worship; atonement for unintentional sin in general; expression of devotion, commitment and complete surrender to God
GRAIN OFFERING	Lev 2; 6:14-23	Grain, fine flour, olive oil, incense, baked bread (cakes or wafers), salt; no yeast or honey; accompanied burnt offering and fellowship offering (along with drink offering)	Voluntary act of worship; recognition of God's goodness and provisions; devotion to God
FELLOWSHIP OFFERING	Lev 3; 7:11-34	Any animal without defect from herd or flock; variety of breads	Voluntary act of worship; thanksgiving and fellowship (it included a communal meal)
SIN OFFERING	Lev 4:1-5:13; 6:24-30; 8:14-17; 16:3-22	1. Young bull: for high priest and congregation 2. Male goat: for leader 3. Female goat or lamb: for common person 4. Dove or pigeon: for the poor 5. Tenth of an ephah of fine flour: for the very poor	Mandatory atonement for specific unintentional sin; confession of sin; forgiveness of sin; cleansing from defilement
GUILT OFFERING	Lev 5:14-6:7; 7:1-6	Ram or lamb	Mandatory atonement for unintentional sin requiring restitution; cleansing from defilement; make restitution; pay 20% fine

When more than one kind of offering was presented (as in Nu 7:16, 17), the procedure was usually as follows: (1) sin offering or guilt offering, (2) burnt offering, (3) fellowship offering and grain offering (along with a drink offering). This sequence furnishes part of the spiritual significance of the sacrificial system. First, sin had to be dealt with (sin offering or guilt offering). Second, the worshiper committed himself completely to God (burnt offering and grain offering). Third, fellowship or communion between the Lord, the priest and the worshiper (fellowship offering) was established.

moved from the ox[e][y] sacrificed as a
fellowship offering.[f][z] Then the
priest shall burn them on the altar of
burnt offering.[a] **11**But the hide of the
bull and all its flesh, as well as the
head and legs, the inner parts and offal[b]— **12**that is, all the rest of the
bull—he must take outside the camp[c]
to a place ceremonially clean,[d] where
the ashes[e] are thrown, and burn it[f]
in a wood fire on the ash heap.[g]

13“ ‘If the whole Israelite community sins unintentionally[h] and does
what is forbidden in any of the LORD’s
commands, even though the community is unaware of the matter, they are
guilty. **14**When they become aware of
the sin they committed, the assembly
must bring a young bull[i] as a sin offering[j] and present it before the Tent
of Meeting. **15**The elders[k] of the community are to lay their hands[l] on the
bull’s head[m] before the LORD, and the
bull shall be slaughtered before the
LORD.[n] **16**Then the anointed priest is
to take some of the bull’s blood[o] into
the Tent of Meeting. **17**He shall dip his
finger into the blood and sprinkle[p] it
before the LORD[q] seven times in front
of the curtain. **18**He is to put some of
the blood[r] on the horns of the altar
that is before the LORD[s] in the Tent of
Meeting. The rest of the blood he shall
pour out at the base of the altar[t] of
burnt offering at the entrance to the
Tent of Meeting. **19**He shall remove all
the fat[u] from it and burn it on the altar,[v] **20**and do with this bull just as he
did with the bull for the sin offering. In
this way the priest will make atonement[w] for them, and they will be forgiven.[x] **21**Then he shall take the bull
outside the camp[y] and burn it as he
burned the first bull. This is the sin offering for the community.[z]

22“ ‘When a leader[a] sins unintentionally[b] and does what is forbidden
in any of the commands of the LORD his
God, he is guilty. **23**When he is made
aware of the sin he committed, he must
bring as his offering a male goat[c]
without defect. **24**He is to lay his hand
on the goat’s head and slaughter it at
the place where the burnt offering is
slaughtered before the LORD.[d] It is a
sin offering.[e] **25**Then the priest shall
take some of the blood of the sin offering with his finger and put it on the
horns of the altar[f] of burnt offering
and pour out the rest of the blood at the
base of the altar.[g] **26**He shall burn all
the fat on the altar as he burned the
fat of the fellowship offering. In this
way the priest will make atonement[h]
for the man’s sin, and he will be forgiven.[i]

27“ ‘If a member of the community
sins unintentionally[j] and does what is
forbidden in any of the LORD’s commands, he is guilty. **28**When he is made
aware of the sin he committed, he must
bring as his offering[k] for the sin he
committed a female goat[l] without defect. **29**He is to lay his hand on the
head[m] of the sin offering[n] and slaughter it at the place of the burnt offering.[o] **30**Then the priest is to take some
of the blood with his finger and put it
on the horns of the altar of burnt offering[p] and pour out the rest of the blood
at the base of the altar. **31**He shall remove all the fat, just as the fat is removed from the fellowship offering,
and the priest shall burn it on the altar[q] as an aroma pleasing to the
LORD.[r] In this way the priest will make
atonement[s] for him, and he will be forgiven.[t]

32“ ‘If he brings a lamb[u] as his sin
offering, he is to bring a female without
defect.[v] **33**He is to lay his hand on its
head and slaughter it[w] for a sin offering[x] at the place where the burnt offering is slaughtered.[y] **34**Then the
priest shall take some of the blood of
the sin offering with his finger and put
it on the horns of the altar of burnt offering and pour out the rest of the
blood at the base of the altar.[z] **35**He
shall remove all the fat, just as the fat

4:10 [y] Lev 9:4 [z] S Ex 32:6 [a] S Ex 29:13 **4:11** [b] Ex 29:14; Lev 8:17; 9:11; Nu 19:5 **4:12** [c] S Ex 29:14; Lev 8:17; 9:11; Heb 13:11 [d] Lev 6:11; 10:14; Nu 19:9 [e] S Lev 1:16 [f] Lev 6:30 [g] Lev 16:3 **4:13** [h] S ver 2 **4:14** [i] S ver 3 [j] Nu 15:24 **4:15** [k] S Ex 3:16; S 19:7 [l] 2Ch 29:23 [m] S Ex 29:10; Lev 8:14,22; Nu 8:10 [n] S ver 4 **4:16** [o] S ver 5 **4:17** [p] Nu 19:4,18 [q] S ver 6 **4:18** [r] Lev 8:15; 17:6; 2Ch 29:22 [s] ver 7; Lev 6:30; 10:18 [t] Lev 5:9 **4:19** [u] ver 8 [v] ver 26 **4:20** [w] S Ex 29:36; S 32:30; S Ro 3:25; Heb 10:10-12 [x] ver 26,31,35; Nu 15:25 **4:21** [y] S ver 12 [z] Lev 16:5,15; 2Ch 29:21 **4:22** [a] Nu 31:13 [b] ver 2 **4:23** [c] S ver 3; S Lev 1:10

4:24 [d] S ver 4 [e] S ver 3; Lev 6:25 **4:25** [f] Lev 16:18; Eze 43:20,22 [g] Lev 9:9 **4:26** [h] S Ex 32:30 [i] Lev 5:10; 12:8 **4:27** [j] S ver 2 **4:28** [k] Lev 5:6; Eze 40:39; 44:27 [l] S ver 3; S Lev 1:10 **4:29** [m] ver 4,24 [n] S Lev 1:4 [o] S Ge 8:20 **4:30** [p] S ver 7 **4:31** [q] ver 35 [r] S Ge 8:21 [s] Lev 1:4 [t] S ver 20 **4:32** [u] Ex 29:38; Lev 9:3; 14:10 [v] Lev 1:3 **4:33** [w] Lev 1:5 [x] Lev 1:4 [y] ver 29 **4:34** [z] S ver 7

[e] *10* The Hebrew word can include both male and female. [f] *10* Traditionally *peace offering*; also in verses 26, 31 and 35

4:12 OUTSIDE THE CAMP. The burning of the sacrificial animal “outside the camp” was to symbolize sin’s complete removal. The NT relates this to the suffering of Jesus outside the gate (i.e., outside Jerusalem) in order to sanctify his people through his own blood (cf. Jn 19:17–18; Heb 13:11–15). The Christian is also called on to “go to him outside the camp” (i.e., to leave behind the sinful pleasures of this world) to look for a heavenly city and to offer the sacrifice of praise and thanksgiving to God (see Heb 13:13, note).

is removed from the lamb of the fellowship offering, and the priest shall burn
it on the altar[a] on top of the offerings
made to the LORD by fire. In this way
the priest will make atonement for him
for the sin he has committed, and he
will be forgiven.

5 " 'If a person sins because he does
not speak up when he hears a public charge to testify[b] regarding something he has seen or learned about, he
will be held responsible.[c]
2" 'Or if a person touches anything
ceremonially unclean—whether the
carcasses of unclean wild animals or of
unclean livestock or of unclean creatures that move along the ground[d]—
even though he is unaware of it, he has
become unclean[e] and is guilty.
3" 'Or if he touches human uncleanness[f]—anything that would make
him unclean[g]—even though he is unaware of it, when he learns of it he will
be guilty.
4" 'Or if a person thoughtlessly
takes an oath[h] to do anything, whether good or evil[i]—in any matter one
might carelessly swear about—even
though he is unaware of it, in any case
when he learns of it he will be guilty.
5" 'When anyone is guilty in any of
these ways, he must confess[j] in what
way he has sinned 6and, as a penalty
for the sin he has committed, he must
bring to the LORD a female lamb or
goat[k] from the flock as a sin offering;[l] and the priest shall make atonement[m] for him for his sin.
7" 'If he cannot afford[n] a lamb,[o] he
is to bring two doves or two young pigeons[p] to the LORD as a penalty for his
sin—one for a sin offering and the other for a burnt offering. 8He is to bring
them to the priest, who shall first offer
the one for the sin offering. He is to
wring its head from its neck,[q] not severing it completely,[r] 9and is to sprinkle[s] some of the blood of the sin offering against the side of the altar;[t] the
rest of the blood must be drained out
at the base of the altar.[u] It is a sin
offering. 10The priest shall then offer
the other as a burnt offering in the prescribed way[v] and make atonement[w]
for him for the sin he has committed,
and he will be forgiven.[x]
11" 'If, however, he cannot afford[y]
two doves or two young pigeons,[z] he
is to bring as an offering for his sin a
tenth of an ephah[g][a] of fine flour[b] for
a sin offering. He must not put oil or
incense on it, because it is a sin offering. 12He is to bring it to the priest,
who shall take a handful of it as a memorial portion[c] and burn it on the altar[d] on top of the offerings made to
the LORD by fire. It is a sin offering. 13In
this way the priest will make atonement[e] for him for any of these sins he
has committed, and he will be forgiven.
The rest of the offering will belong to
the priest,[f] as in the case of the grain
offering.[g]' "

The Guilt Offering

14The LORD said to Moses: 15"When
a person commits a violation and sins
unintentionally[h] in regard to any of
the LORD's holy things, he is to bring to
the LORD as a penalty[i] a ram[j] from
the flock, one without defect and of the
proper value in silver, according to the

4:35 [a]ver 31 **5:1** [b]Pr 29:24; Mt 26:63 [c]ver 17; S Ex 28:38; Lev 7:18; 17:16; 19:8; 20:17; 24:15; Nu 5:31; 9:13; 15:31; 19:20; 30:15 **5:2** [d]Lev 11:11, 24-40; Dt 14:8; Isa 52:11 [e]ver 3; Lev 7:21; 11:8,24; 13:45; Nu 19:22; Job 15:16; Ps 51:5; Isa 6:5; 64:6; Eze 36:17; Hag 2:13 **5:3** [f]Nu 19:11-16 [g]Lev 7:20; 11:25; 14:19; 21:1; Nu 5:2; 9:6; 19:7; Eze 44:25 **5:4** [h]Nu 30:6,8 [i]Isa 41:23 **5:5** [j]Lev 16:21; 26:40; Nu 5:7; Jos 7:19; 1Ki 8:47; Pr 28:13 **5:6** [k]S Lev 1:10; S 4:3 [l]S Lev 4:28 [m]S Ex 32:30 **5:7** [n]ver 11; Lev 12:8; 14:21; 27:8 [o]Lev 12:8; 14:22,30 [p]S Ge 15:9; Nu 6:10

5:8 [q]Lev 1:15 [r]Lev 1:17 **5:9** [s]S Ex 24:6 [t]Lev 1:15 [u]S Lev 4:7 **5:10** [v]Lev 1:14-17; 1Ch 15:13 [w]S Ex 32:30 [x]S Lev 4:26 **5:11** [y]S ver 7 [z]S Ge 15:9 [a]S Ex 16:36 [b]S Lev 2:1 **5:12** [c]S Lev 2:2 [d]Lev 2:9 **5:13** [e]S Ex 32:30 [f]Lev 2:3 [g]S Ex 29:41 **5:15** [h]S Lev 4:2 [i]Lev 22:14 [j]S Ex 29:3; Lev 6:6; Nu 5:8; 6:14; 15:6; 28:11

[g] *11* That is, probably about 2 quarts (about 2 liters)

5:5 HE MUST CONFESS. To confess sin is to admit to God that we have sinned and that our thoughts, words and deeds were wrong. Confession is required by God for forgiveness (Hos 5:15; 1Jn 1:9) and must always be accompanied by turning away from confessed sin (Pr 28:13; Da 9:3–19; Mk 1:5), praying for forgiveness (Ps 38:18; 51:1) and humbling oneself under God's judgment (Ne 9:33). See Lk 15:11–24 for an example of genuine confession and forgiveness in the story of the lost son (cf. Ac 19:18; Jas 5:16).

5:11 FINE FLOUR FOR A SIN OFFERING. The shedding of blood in the sin offering was important in that it pointed ahead to Jesus' death and the shedding of his blood on the cross for our sins. But what about those who were so poor that they could not afford a goat or a lamb for an offering? God also wanted them to confess their sins, bring an offering and seek his forgiveness. Thus he provided that such people could bring doves or young pigeons in the place of goats or lambs. If they were too poor even for that, they could bring a little fine flour and God would accept that as a sin offering (cf. "nearly" in Heb 9:22; see also Heb 10:1–10). Note that Christ's sacrifice on the cross is the only sacrifice that can really take away sin (Heb 10:4,12,14).

5:15 GUILT OFFERING. The guilt offering was required when someone intentionally or unintentionally disregarded the property rights of another person (cf. 5:14—6:7; Jos 7:1; 22:20). This offering was also necessary when any of the Lord's commands was unintentionally broken (v. 17). An offering had to be brought along with restitution for the wrong done, plus a twenty percent fine (v. 16; 6:5).

sanctuary shekel.[h][k] It is a guilt offering.[l] 16He must make restitution[m]
for what he has failed to do in regard
to the holy things, add a fifth of the
value[n] to that and give it all to the
priest, who will make atonement for
him with the ram as a guilt offering,
and he will be forgiven.
17"If a person sins and does what is
forbidden in any of the LORD's commands, even though he does not know
it,[o] he is guilty and will be held responsible.[p] 18He is to bring to the
priest as a guilt offering[q] a ram from
the flock, one without defect and of the
proper value. In this way the priest will
make atonement for him for the wrong
he has committed unintentionally, and
he will be forgiven.[r] 19It is a guilt offering; he has been guilty of[i] wrongdoing against the LORD."[s]

6 The LORD said to Moses: 2"If anyone sins and is unfaithful to the
LORD[t] by deceiving his neighbor[u]
about something entrusted to him or
left in his care[v] or stolen, or if he
cheats[w] him, 3or if he finds lost property and lies about it,[x] or if he swears
falsely,[y] or if he commits any such sin
that people may do— 4when he thus
sins and becomes guilty, he must return[z] what he has stolen or taken by
extortion, or what was entrusted to
him, or the lost property he found, 5or
whatever it was he swore falsely about.
He must make restitution[a] in full, add
a fifth of the value to it and give it all
to the owner on the day he presents his
guilt offering.[b] 6And as a penalty he
must bring to the priest, that is, to the
LORD, his guilt offering,[c] a ram from
the flock, one without defect and of the
proper value.[d] 7In this way the priest
will make atonement[e] for him before
the LORD, and he will be forgiven for
any of these things he did that made
him guilty."

The Burnt Offering

8The LORD said to Moses: 9"Give
Aaron and his sons this command:
'These are the regulations for the
burnt offering[f]: The burnt offering is
to remain on the altar hearth throughout the night, till morning, and the fire
must be kept burning on the altar.[g]
10The priest shall then put on his linen
clothes,[h] with linen undergarments
next to his body,[i] and shall remove
the ashes[j] of the burnt offering that

5:15 [k]S Ex 30:13 [l]ver 16,18; Lev 6:5,6; 7:1,7; 14:12-17; 19:21, 22; Nu 6:12; 18:9; 1Sa 6:3; Ezr 10:19; Isa 53:10 **5:16** [m]Lev 6:4 [n]ver 15; Lev 27:13; Nu 5:7 **5:17** [o]ver 15 [p]S ver 1 **5:18** [q]Lev 6:6; 14:12 [r]S ver 15 **5:19** [s]2Ki 12:16 **6:2** [t]Nu 5:6; Ps 73:27; Ac 5:4; Col 3:9 [u]Lev 19:11; Jer 9:4,5 [v]S Ex 22:7 [w]S Ge 31:7 **6:3** [x]S Ex 23:4 [y]S Ex 22:11 **6:4** [z]Lev 5:16; Eze 33:15; S Lk 19:8 **6:5** [a]Nu 5:7 [b]S Lev 5:15 **6:6** [c]S Lev 5:15 [d]Nu 5:8 **6:7** [e]S Ex 32:30 **6:9** [f]Lev 7:37 [g]ver 12 **6:10** [h]S Ex 39:27 [i]Ex 28:39-42,43; 39:28 [j]S Lev 1:16

6:11 [k]S Lev 4:12 **6:12** [l]S Lev 1:7 [m]S Ex 29:13 [n]S Ex 32:6 **6:14** [o]S Lev 2:1; Nu 6:15; 15:4; 28:13 **6:15** [p]S Lev 2:1 [q]Lev 2:9 [r]S Lev 2:2 **6:16** [s]S Lev 2:3 [t]Eze 44:29 [u]S Lev 2:11 [v]ver 26; S Ex 29:11; Lev 10:13; 16:24; 24:9; Nu 18:10 [w]S Ex 27:9 [x]Ex 29:31; Lev 8:31 **6:17** [y]Nu 5:9 [z]Ex 29:28; Lev 7:7; 10:16-18 [a]ver 29; Ex 40:10; Lev 10:12; 21:22; 24:9; Nu 18:9,10 **6:18** [b]ver 29; Lev 2:3; 7:6; Nu 18:9-10 [c]Nu 5:9 [d]S Ge 9:12 [e]S Ex 30:29 **6:20** [f]S Ex 28:41 [g]S Ex 16:36 [h]Nu 5:15; 28:5 [i]Ex 29:2; Lev 23:13; Nu 4:16 **6:21** [j]Lev 2:5 **6:22** [k]S Ex 28:41; S 29:30 [l]S Lev 1:9

the fire has consumed on the altar and
place them beside the altar. 11Then he
is to take off these clothes and put on
others, and carry the ashes outside the
camp to a place that is ceremonially
clean.[k] 12The fire on the altar must be
kept burning; it must not go out. Every
morning the priest is to add firewood[l]
and arrange the burnt offering on the
fire and burn the fat[m] of the fellowship
offerings[j][n] on it. 13The fire must be
kept burning on the altar continuously;
it must not go out.

The Grain Offering

14" 'These are the regulations for
the grain offering:[o] Aaron's sons are
to bring it before the LORD, in front of
the altar. 15The priest is to take a
handful of fine flour and oil, together
with all the incense[p] on the grain offering,[q] and burn the memorial portion[r] on the altar as an aroma pleasing to the LORD. 16Aaron and his sons[s]
shall eat the rest[t] of it, but it is to be
eaten without yeast[u] in a holy
place;[v] they are to eat it in the courtyard[w] of the Tent of Meeting.[x] 17It
must not be baked with yeast; I have
given it as their share[y] of the offerings made to me by fire.[z] Like the sin
offering and the guilt offering, it is
most holy.[a] 18Any male descendant of
Aaron may eat it.[b] It is his regular
share[c] of the offerings made to the
LORD by fire for the generations to
come.[d] Whatever touches them will
become holy.[k][e] ' "
19The LORD also said to Moses,
20"This is the offering Aaron and his
sons are to bring to the LORD on the day
he[l] is anointed:[f] a tenth of an
ephah[m][g] of fine flour[h] as a regular
grain offering,[i] half of it in the morning and half in the evening. 21Prepare
it with oil on a griddle;[j] bring it well-
mixed and present the grain offering
broken[n] in pieces as an aroma pleasing to the LORD. 22The son who is to
succeed him as anointed priest[k] shall
prepare it. It is the LORD's regular
share and is to be burned completely.[l]

h *15* That is, about 2/5 ounce (about 11.5 grams) **i** *19* Or *has made full expiation for his* **j** *12* Traditionally *peace offerings* **k** *18* Or *Whoever touches them must be holy*; similarly in verse 27 **l** *20* Or *each* **m** *20* That is, probably about 2 quarts (about 2 liters) **n** *21* The meaning of the Hebrew for this word is uncertain.

23Every grain offering of a priest shall
be burned completely; it must not be
eaten."

The Sin Offering

24The LORD said to Moses, 25"Say to
Aaron and his sons: 'These are the regulations for the sin offering:[m] The sin
offering is to be slaughtered before the
LORD[n] in the place[o] the burnt offering
is slaughtered; it is most holy. 26The
priest who offers it shall eat it; it is to
be eaten in a holy place,[p] in the courtyard[q] of the Tent of Meeting.[r]
27Whatever touches any of the flesh
will become holy,[s] and if any of the
blood is spattered on a garment, you
must wash it in a holy place. 28The clay
pot[t] the meat is cooked in must be
broken; but if it is cooked in a bronze
pot, the pot is to be scoured and rinsed
with water. 29Any male in a priest's
family may eat it;[u] it is most holy.[v]
30But any sin offering whose blood is
brought into the Tent of Meeting to
make atonement[w] in the Holy Place[x]
must not be eaten; it must be burned.[y]

The Guilt Offering

7 "'These are the regulations for the
guilt offering,[z] which is most
holy: 2The guilt offering is to be
slaughtered in the place where the
burnt offering is slaughtered, and its
blood is to be sprinkled against the altar on all sides. 3All its fat[a] shall be
offered: the fat tail and the fat that covers the inner parts, 4both kidneys with
the fat on them near the loins, and the
covering of the liver, which is to be removed with the kidneys.[b] 5The priest
shall burn them on the altar[c] as an
offering made to the LORD by fire. It is
a guilt offering. 6Any male in a priest's
family may eat it,[d] but it must be eat-
en in a holy place; it is most holy.[e]
7"'The same law applies to both the
sin offering[f] and the guilt offering:[g]
They belong to the priest[h] who makes
atonement with them.[i] 8The priest
who offers a burnt offering for anyone
may keep its hide[j] for himself. 9Every
grain offering baked in an oven[k] or
cooked in a pan[l] or on a griddle[m] belongs to the priest who offers it, 10and
every grain offering, whether mixed
with oil or dry, belongs equally to all
the sons of Aaron.

The Fellowship Offering

11"'These are the regulations for
the fellowship offering[o] a person may
present to the LORD:
12"'If he offers it as an expression of
thankfulness, then along with this
thank offering[n] he is to offer cakes[o]
of bread made without yeast[p] and
mixed with oil, wafers[q] made without
yeast and spread with oil,[r] and cakes
of fine flour well-kneaded and mixed
with oil. 13Along with his fellowship offering of thanksgiving[s] he is to
present an offering with cakes of bread
made with yeast.[t] 14He is to bring one
of each kind as an offering, a contribution to the LORD; it belongs to the priest
who sprinkles the blood of the fellowship offerings. 15The meat of his fellowship offering of thanksgiving must
be eaten on the day it is offered; he
must leave none of it till morning.[u]
16"'If, however, his offering is the
result of a vow[v] or is a freewill offering,[w] the sacrifice shall be eaten on
the day he offers it, but anything left
over may be eaten on the next day.[x]
17Any meat of the sacrifice left over till
the third day must be burned up.[y] 18If
any meat of the fellowship offering[z] is
eaten on the third day, it will not be
accepted.[a] It will not be credited[b] to
the one who offered it, for it is impure;
the person who eats any of it will be
held responsible.[c]
19"'Meat that touches anything ceremonially unclean must not be eaten;
it must be burned up. As for other
meat, anyone ceremonially clean may
eat it. 20But if anyone who is unclean[d]
eats any meat of the fellowship offering belonging to the LORD, that person

[o] *11* Traditionally *peace offering*; also in verses 13-37

6:25 [m] S Ex 30:10; S Lev 4:24 [n] S Lev 1:3 [o] S Ex 29:11 **6:26** [p] S ver 16 [q] S Ex 27:9 [r] S Ex 27:21; S 40:2 **6:27** [s] S Ex 29:37; Lev 10:10; Eze 44:19; 46:20; Hag 2:12 **6:28** [t] Lev 11:33; 15:12; Nu 19:15 **6:29** [u] S ver 18 [v] S ver 17; Eze 42:13 **6:30** [w] Eze 45:15 [x] S Lev 4:18 [y] Lev 4:12 **7:1** [z] S Lev 5:15; Eze 40:39 **7:3** [a] S Ex 29:13 **7:4** [b] Lev 3:15 **7:5** [c] S Ex 29:13 **7:6** [d] S Lev 6:18 [e] Eze 42:13 **7:7** [f] S Ex 30:10 [g] S Lev 5:15 [h] ver 6; Lev 2:3; 6:17,26; 14:13; 2Ki 12:16; 1Co 9:13; 10:18 [i] Nu 5:8 **7:8** [j] Lev 1:6 **7:9** [k] S Lev 2:4 [l] Lev 2:7 [m] S Lev 2:5 **7:12** [n] ver 13,15; Lev 22:29; Ps 50:14; 54:6; 107:22; 116:17; Jer 33:11 [o] Jer 44:19 [p] Nu 6:19 [q] S Lev 2:4 [r] S Lev 2:1 **7:13** [s] S ver 12; S Ex 34:22 [t] Lev 23:17; Am 4:5 **7:15** [u] S Ex 12:10 **7:16** [v] S Ge 28:20; S Lev 1:2; Dt 23:21-23 [w] Ex 35:29; Lev 22:18,21; 23:38; Nu 15:3; 29:39; Dt 12:6; Ps 54:6; Eze 46:12 [x] Lev 19:5-8 **7:17** [y] Ex 12:10; Lev 19:6 **7:18** [z] 2Ch 33:16 [a] Lev 19:7 [b] Nu 18:27 [c] S Lev 5:1 **7:20** [d] S Lev 5:3

7:2 AGAINST THE ALTAR. In the OT, ritualized forms of worship were a means of communication between God and his people. They were dramatized prayers expressing the people's repentance and their pleas for forgiveness and reconciliation. They also communicated the Israelites' gratitude and dedication to God. On God's part they were dramatized divine promises, warnings and teachings that revealed God's attitude toward his people and what he expected from them (see 1:2, note).

7:13 BREAD MADE WITH YEAST. Bread made with yeast could be presented with the fellowship offering because it was not placed on the altar (cf. 2:11, note).

7:20 UNCLEAN . . . MUST BE CUT OFF. Per-

must be cut off from his people.[e] 21If
anyone touches something unclean[f]—whether human uncleanness
or an unclean animal or any unclean,
detestable thing—and then eats any of
the meat of the fellowship offering belonging to the LORD, that person must
be cut off from his people.' "

Eating Fat and Blood Forbidden

22The LORD said to Moses, 23"Say to
the Israelites: 'Do not eat any of the fat
of cattle, sheep or goats.[g] 24The fat of
an animal found dead or torn by wild
animals[h] may be used for any other
purpose, but you must not eat it.
25Anyone who eats the fat of an animal
from which an offering by fire may be[p]
made to the LORD must be cut off from
his people. 26And wherever you live,
you must not eat the blood[i] of any
bird or animal. 27If anyone eats
blood,[j] that person must be cut off
from his people.' "

The Priests' Share

28The LORD said to Moses, 29"Say to
the Israelites: 'Anyone who brings a
fellowship offering to the LORD is to
bring part of it as his sacrifice to the
LORD. 30With his own hands he is to
bring the offering made to the LORD by
fire; he is to bring the fat, together with
the breast, and wave the breast before
the LORD as a wave offering.[k] 31The
priest shall burn the fat on the altar,[l]
but the breast belongs to Aaron and his
sons.[m] 32You are to give the right
thigh of your fellowship offerings to
the priest as a contribution.[n] 33The
son of Aaron who offers the blood and
the fat of the fellowship offering shall
have the right thigh as his share.
34From the fellowship offerings of the
Israelites, I have taken the breast that
is waved and the thigh[o] that is presented and have given them to Aaron
the priest and his sons[p] as their regular share from the Israelites.' "

35This is the portion of the offerings
made to the LORD by fire that were allotted to Aaron and his sons on the day
they were presented to serve the LORD
as priests. 36On the day they were
anointed,[q] the LORD commanded that
the Israelites give this to them as their
regular share for the generations to
come.

37These, then, are the regulations
for the burnt offering,[r] the grain offering,[s] the sin offering, the guilt offering, the ordination offering[t] and the
fellowship offering, 38which the LORD
gave Moses[u] on Mount Sinai[v] on the
day he commanded the Israelites to
bring their offerings to the LORD,[w] in
the Desert of Sinai.

The Ordination of Aaron and His Sons

8:1-36pp — Ex 29:1-37

8 The LORD said to Moses, 2"Bring
Aaron and his sons,[x] their garments,[y] the anointing oil,[z] the bull
for the sin offering,[a] the two rams[b]
and the basket containing bread made
without yeast,[c] 3and gather the entire
assembly[d] at the entrance to the Tent
of Meeting." 4Moses did as the LORD

7:20 [e]S Ge 17:14; Lev 22:3-7 **7:21** [f]S Lev 5:2 **7:23** [g]Lev 17:13-14; Dt 14:4 **7:24** [h]S Ex 22:31 **7:26** [i]S Ge 9:4 **7:27** [j]S Ge 9:4 **7:30** [k]S Ex 29:24 **7:31** [l]S Ex 29:13 [m]S Ex 29:27 **7:32** [n]Ex 29:27; Lev 10:14,15; Nu 5:9; 6:20; 18:18 **7:34** [o]Ex 29:22; Lev 10:15; Nu 6:20; 1Sa 9:24 [p]S Ex 29:27 **7:36** [q]Lev 8:12, 30 **7:37** [r]Lev 6:9 [s]Lev 6:14 [t]S Ex 29:31 **7:38** [u]Lev 26:46; Nu 36:13; Dt 4:5; 29:1 [v]S Ex 19:11 [w]S Lev 1:2 **8:2** [x]S Ex 28:1; S Lev 1:5 [y]Ex 28:2,4,43; S 39:27 [z]Ex 30:23-25,30 [a]S Ex 30:10 [b]ver 18,22 [c]Ex 29:2-3 **8:3** [d]Nu 8:9

[p]25 Or *fire is*

sons who were ceremonially unclean and yet participated in the sacrifices and offerings were subject to God's severe judgment. This rule was designed to teach how great an abomination it was for a person to claim to be in a covenantal relationship with God, yet deliberately and knowingly to cling to sin. See 1Co 11:27–30, where Paul warns that all who partake of the Lord's Supper in an unworthy manner will experience God's wrath and judgment.

7:30 WAVE OFFERING. The "wave offering" was the priests' portion of the fellowship offering. It was waved toward the sanctuary as a sign of dedication to God and then waved toward the offerer or priest, indicating that the Lord was now putting the offering at his or her disposal.

8:2 AARON AND HIS SONS. Ch. 8 describes the ordination of Aaron and his sons to the priesthood. In the OT the worshiper who approached God needed not only an offering (chs. 1–7) but also the mediation of a priest (cf. 1Ti 2:5). The Levitical priesthood described here finds its fulfillment in Jesus Christ, the believer's high priest (Heb 2:17). (1) A priest was appointed on behalf of people as a mediator between God and humans (Heb 5:1). His purpose was to help men and women draw near to God and to bring them to forgiveness and salvation (Heb 7:24–25; 10:14).

(2) The priest brought people near to God by offering gifts and sacrifices for sin and by teaching God's law (Dt 33:8–10; Heb 5:1; 8:3; 9:7,13).

(3) Under the new covenant the priestly office is no longer needed; the NT includes no priestly ministry among the ministry gifts of believers (cf. Eph 4:11). Jesus Christ is now the high priest of the new covenant (Heb 9:15–22), replacing the imperfect OT priesthood. He is a perfect priest "forever" (cf. 1Ti 2:5; Heb 7:25; 9:23–28; see 2:17, note; see article on THE OLD COVENANT AND THE NEW COVENANT, p. 1926).

commanded him, and the assembly
gathered at the entrance to the Tent of
Meeting.
5Moses said to the assembly, "This
is what the LORD has commanded to be
done.[e]" **6**Then Moses brought Aaron
and his sons forward and washed them
with water.[f] **7**He put the tunic on Aaron, tied the sash around him, clothed
him with the robe and put the ephod on
him. He also tied the ephod to him by
its skillfully woven waistband; so it
was fastened on him.[g] **8**He placed the
breastpiece[h] on him and put the Urim
and Thummim[i] in the breastpiece.
9Then he placed the turban[j] on Aaron's head and set the gold plate, the
sacred diadem,[k] on the front of it, as
the LORD commanded Moses.[l]
10Then Moses took the anointing
oil[m] and anointed[n] the tabernacle[o]
and everything in it, and so consecrated them. **11**He sprinkled some of the oil
on the altar seven times, anointing the
altar and all its utensils and the basin
with its stand, to consecrate them.[p]
12He poured some of the anointing oil
on Aaron's head and anointed[q] him to
consecrate him.[r] **13**Then he brought
Aaron's sons[s] forward, put tunics[t]
on them, tied sashes around them and
put headbands on them, as the LORD
commanded Moses.[u]
14He then presented the bull[v] for
the sin offering,[w] and Aaron and his
sons laid their hands on its head.[x]
15Moses slaughtered the bull and took
some of the blood,[y] and with his finger
he put it on all the horns of the altar[z]
to purify the altar.[a] He poured out the
rest of the blood at the base of the altar. So he consecrated it to make
atonement for it.[b] **16**Moses also took
all the fat around the inner parts, the
covering of the liver, and both kidneys
and their fat, and burned it on the altar.
17But the bull with its hide and its flesh
and its offal[c] he burned up outside the
camp,[d] as the LORD commanded Moses.
18He then presented the ram[e] for
the burnt offering, and Aaron and his
sons laid their hands on its head.
19Then Moses slaughtered the ram
and sprinkled the blood against the altar on all sides. **20**He cut the ram into
pieces and burned the head, the pieces
and the fat.[f] **21**He washed the inner
parts and the legs with water and
burned the whole ram on the altar as
a burnt offering, a pleasing aroma, an
offering made to the LORD by fire, as the
LORD commanded Moses.
22He then presented the other ram,
the ram for the ordination,[g] and Aaron and his sons laid their hands on its
head.[h] **23**Moses slaughtered the ram
and took some of its blood and put it on
the lobe of Aaron's right ear, on the
thumb of his right hand and on the big
toe of his right foot.[i] **24**Moses also
brought Aaron's sons forward and put
some of the blood on the lobes of their
right ears, on the thumbs of their right
hands and on the big toes of their right
feet. Then he sprinkled blood against
the altar on all sides.[j] **25**He took the
fat[k], the fat tail, all the fat around the
inner parts, the covering of the liver,
both kidneys and their fat and the right
thigh. **26**Then from the basket of bread
made without yeast, which was before
the LORD, he took a cake of bread, and
one made with oil, and a wafer;[l] he
put these on the fat portions and on the
right thigh. **27**He put all these in the
hands of Aaron and his sons and waved
them before the LORD[m] as a wave offering. **28**Then Moses took them from
their hands and burned them on the altar on top of the burnt offering as an
ordination offering, a pleasing aroma,
an offering made to the LORD by fire.
29He also took the breast—Moses'
share of the ordination ram[n]—and
waved it before the LORD as a wave offering, as the LORD commanded Moses.
30Then Moses[o] took some of the
anointing oil and some of the blood
from the altar and sprinkled them on
Aaron and his garments[p] and on his
sons and their garments. So he consecrated[q] Aaron and his garments and
his sons and their garments.
31Moses then said to Aaron and his
sons, "Cook the meat at the entrance
to the Tent of Meeting[r] and eat it
there with the bread from the basket of
ordination offerings, as I commanded,
saying,[q] 'Aaron and his sons are to
eat it.' **32**Then burn up the rest of the
meat and the bread. **33**Do not leave the
entrance to the Tent of Meeting for
seven days, until the days of your ordination are completed, for your ordination will last seven days.[s] **34**What has
been done today was commanded by
the LORD[t] to make atonement for you.

8:5 [e] Ex 29:1
8:6 [f] S Ex 29:4; S 30:19; S Ac 22:16
8:7 [g] Ex 28:4
8:8 [h] S Ex 25:7 [i] S Ex 28:30
8:9 [j] S Ex 39:28 [k] S Ex 28:36 [l] S Ex 28:2; Lev 21:10
8:10 [m] ver 2 [n] S Ex 30:26 [o] S Ex 26:1
8:11 [p] S Ex 30:29
8:12 [q] S Lev 7:36 [r] S Ex 30:30
8:13 [s] S Ex 28:40 [t] S Ex 28:4,39; 39:27 [u] Lev 21:10
8:14 [v] S Lev 4:3 [w] S Ex 30:10 [x] S Lev 4:15
8:15 [y] S Lev 4:18 [z] S Lev 4:7 [a] Heb 9:22 [b] Eze 43:20
8:17 [c] S Lev 4:11 [d] S Lev 4:12
8:18 [e] S ver 2
8:20 [f] S Lev 1:8
8:22 [g] S ver 2 [h] S Lev 4:15
8:23 [i] Lev 14:14, 25
8:24 [j] Heb 9:18-22
8:25 [k] Lev 3:3-5
8:26 [l] S Lev 2:4
8:27 [m] Nu 5:25
8:29 [n] Lev 7:31-34
8:30 [o] S Ex 28:1 [p] S Ex 28:2 [q] S Lev 7:36
8:31 [r] S Lev 6:16
8:33 [s] Lev 14:8; 15:13,28; Nu 19:11; Eze 43:25
8:34 [t] Heb 7:16

[q] *31* Or *I was commanded:*

35You must stay at the entrance to the Tent of Meeting day and night for seven days and do what the LORD requires,[u] so you will not die; for that is what I have been commanded." 36So Aaron and his sons did everything the LORD commanded through Moses.

The Priests Begin Their Ministry

9 On the eighth day[v] Moses summoned Aaron and his sons and the elders[w] of Israel. 2He said to Aaron, "Take a bull calf for your sin offering and a ram for your burnt offering, both without defect, and present them before the LORD. 3Then say to the Israelites: 'Take a male goat[x] for a sin offering,[y] a calf[z] and a lamb[a]—both a year old and without defect—for a burnt offering, 4and an ox[r][b] and a ram for a fellowship offering[s][c] to sacrifice before the LORD, together with a grain offering mixed with oil. For today the LORD will appear to you.[d]' "

5They took the things Moses commanded to the front of the Tent of Meeting, and the entire assembly came near and stood before the LORD. 6Then Moses said, "This is what the LORD has commanded you to do, so that the glory of the LORD[e] may appear to you."

7Moses said to Aaron, "Come to the altar and sacrifice your sin offering and your burnt offering and make atonement for yourself and the people;[f] sacrifice the offering that is for the people and make atonement for them, as the LORD has commanded.[g]"

8So Aaron came to the altar and slaughtered the calf as a sin offering[h] for himself. 9His sons brought the blood to him,[i] and he dipped his finger into the blood and put it on the horns of the altar; the rest of the blood he poured out at the base of the altar.[j][k] 10On the altar he burned the fat, the kidneys and the covering of the liver from the sin offering, as the LORD commanded Moses; 11the flesh and the hide[l] he burned up outside the camp.[m]

12Then he slaughtered the burnt offering.[n] His sons handed him the blood,[o] and he sprinkled it against the altar on all sides. 13They handed him the burnt offering piece by piece, including the head, and he burned them on the altar.[p] 14He washed the inner parts and the legs and burned them on top of the burnt offering on the altar.[q]

15Aaron then brought the offering that was for the people.[r] He took the goat for the people's sin offering and slaughtered it and offered it for a sin offering as he did with the first one.

16He brought the burnt offering and offered it in the prescribed way.[s] 17He also brought the grain offering, took a handful of it and burned it on the altar in addition to the morning's burnt offering.[t]

18He slaughtered the ox and the ram as the fellowship offering for the people.[u] His sons handed him the blood, and he sprinkled it against the altar on all sides. 19But the fat portions of the ox and the ram—the fat tail, the layer of fat, the kidneys and the covering of the liver— 20these they laid on the breasts, and then Aaron burned the fat on the altar. 21Aaron waved the breasts and the right thigh before the LORD as a wave offering,[v] as Moses commanded.

22Then Aaron lifted his hands to-

8:35 [u]Lev 18:30; 22:9; Nu 3:7; 9:19; Dt 11:1; 1Ki 2:3; Eze 48:11; Zec 3:7
9:1 [v]Eze 43:27 [w]S Lev 4:15
9:3 [x]S Lev 4:3 [y]ver 15; Lev 10:16 [z]ver 8 [a]S Lev 4:32
9:4 [b]Lev 4:10 [c]S Ex 32:6 [d]Ex 29:43
9:6 [e]S Ex 16:7
9:7 [f]Lev 16:6 [g]S Ex 30:10; Heb 5:1,3; 7:27
9:8 [h]Lev 4:1-12; 10:19
9:9 [i]ver 12,18 [j]S Ex 29:12 [k]Eze 43:20
9:11 [l]S Lev 4:11 [m]S Lev 4:12
9:12 [n]Lev 10:19 [o]S ver 9
9:13 [p]S Lev 1:8
9:14 [q]S Lev 1:9
9:15 [r]Lev 4:27-31
9:16 [s]Lev 1:1-13
9:17 [t]Lev 3:5
9:18 [u]Lev 3:1-11
9:21 [v]S Ex 29:24, 26

[r]*4* The Hebrew word can include both male and female; also in verses 18 and 19.
[s]*4* Traditionally *peace offering*; also in verses 18 and 22

9:8 SLAUGHTERED THE CALF. God instituted animal sacrifice as an ordinance whereby sinners might draw near to him in repentance and faith and so experience his forgiveness, salvation and fellowship. (1) The offering of the animal was an object lesson, pointing to the principle of vicarious sacrifice and substitutionary atonement. The life of the innocent animal was offered in the place of the sinful and guilty worshiper (see 1:4, note).

(2) The sacrifice expressed a person's repentance and constituted both a confession of sin and a recognition of the need for cleansing and redemption (16:30–34; see 1:2, note).

(3) When a sacrifice was made in faith and obedience, God was pleased with the act of the worshiper and so imparted to that individual the desired grace and forgiveness (4:3,20; 5:15–16).

(4) The sacrifice provided atonement through a "covering up" of sin (see article on THE DAY OF ATONEMENT, p. 174).

(5) Note that from the NT perspective, animal sacrifices were imperfect in that they could not bring the worshiper into the state of mature faith and obedience that is now available under the new covenant (Heb 10:1–4). The ordinance served as a shadow or a preliminary sketch of the "one sacrifice for sins" for all time that was provided when Jesus Christ offered his body once for all (Heb 10:12).

ward the people and blessed them.[w]
And having sacrificed the sin offering,
the burnt offering and the fellowship
offering, he stepped down.
23Moses and Aaron then went into
the Tent of Meeting.[x] When they
came out, they blessed the people; and
the glory of the LORD[y] appeared to all
the people. **24**Fire[z] came out from the
presence of the LORD and consumed the
burnt offering and the fat portions on
the altar. And when all the people saw
it, they shouted for joy and fell facedown.[a]

The Death of Nadab and Abihu

10 Aaron's sons Nadab and Abihu[b] took their censers,[c] put
fire in them[d] and added incense;[e]
and they offered unauthorized fire before the LORD,[f] contrary to his command.[g] **2**So fire came out[h] from the
presence of the LORD and consumed
them,[i] and they died before the
LORD.[j] **3**Moses then said to Aaron,
"This is what the LORD spoke of when
he said:

" 'Among those who approach me[k]
I will show myself holy;[l]
in the sight of all the people
I will be honored.[m]' "

Aaron remained silent.
4Moses summoned Mishael and Elzaphan,[n] sons of Aaron's uncle Uzziel,[o] and said to them, "Come here;
carry your cousins outside the camp,[p]
away from the front of the sanctuary.[q]" **5**So they came and carried
them, still in their tunics,[r] outside the
camp, as Moses ordered.
6Then Moses said to Aaron and his
sons Eleazar and Ithamar,[s] "Do not
let your hair become unkempt,[t][t] and
do not tear your clothes,[u] or you will
die and the LORD will be angry with the
whole community.[v] But your relatives, all the house of Israel, may
mourn[w] for those the LORD has destroyed by fire. **7**Do not leave the entrance to the Tent of Meeting[x] or you
will die, because the LORD's anointing
oil[y] is on you." So they did as Moses
said.
8Then the LORD said to Aaron, **9**"You
and your sons are not to drink wine[z]
or other fermented drink[a] whenever
you go into the Tent of Meeting, or you
will die. This is a lasting ordinance[b]
for the generations to come. **10**You
must distinguish between the holy and
the common, between the unclean and
the clean,[c] **11**and you must teach[d]
the Israelites all the decrees the LORD
has given them through Moses.[e]"
12Moses said to Aaron and his remaining sons, Eleazar and Ithamar,
"Take the grain offering[f] left over
from the offerings made to the LORD by
fire and eat it prepared without yeast

9:22 [w]S Ge 48:20; S Ex 39:43; Lk 24:50 **9:23** [x]S Ex 40:2 [y]S Ex 24:16 **9:24** [z]S Ex 19:18; Jdg 6:21; 13:20 [a]1Ki 18:39 **10:1** [b]Ex 6:23; 24:1; 28:1; Nu 3:2-4; 26:61; 1Ch 6:3 [c]Nu 16:46; 1Ki 7:50; 2Ki 25:15; 2Ch 4:22; Jer 52:19; Eze 8:11 [d]Lev 16:12; Nu 16:7,18; Isa 6:6 [e]S Ex 30:9 [f]ver 2; Lev 16:1 [g]Ex 30:9 **10:2** [h]Ps 106:18 [i]Nu 11:1; 16:35; Ps 2:12; 50:3; Isa 29:6 [j]S Ge 19:24; S 38:7; Nu 16:35; 1Ch 24:2; Job 1:16 **10:3** [k]Ex 19:22 [l]Ex 30:29; Lev 21:6; 22:32; Nu 16:5; 20:13; Isa 5:16; Eze 28:22; 38:16 [m]Ex 14:4; Isa 44:23; 49:3; 55:5; 60:21 **10:4** [n]S Ex 6:22 [o]Ex 6:18 [p]Ac 5:6, 9,10 [q]S Ex 25:8 **10:5** [r]S Lev 8:13 **10:6** [s]S Ex 6:23 [t]Lev 13:45; 21:10; Nu 5:18 [u]Jer 41:5; S Mk 14:63 [v]Nu 1:53; 16:22; Jos 7:1; 22:18 [w]Ge 50:3,10; Nu 20:29; 1Sa 25:1 **10:7** [x]S Ex 25:8 [y]S Ex 28:41 **10:9** [z]Ge 9:21; Ex 29:40; Lev 23:13; Nu 15:5; Dt 28:39; Isa 5:22; 22:13; 28:1; 29:9; 56:12; Jer 35:6; Hos 4:11; Hab 2:15-16 [a]Nu 6:3; 28:7; Dt 14:26; 29:6; Jdg 13:4; Pr 20:1; 23:29-35; 31:4-7; Isa 28:7; Eze 44:21; Mic 2:11; Lk 1:15; S Eph 5:18; 1Ti 3:3; Tit 1:7 [b]S Ex 12:14 **10:10** [c]S Ge 7:2; S Lev 6:27; 14:57; 20:25; Eze 22:26 **10:11** [d]2Ch 15:3; 17:7; Ezr 7:25; Ne 8:7; Mal 2:7 [e]Dt 17:10,11; 24:8; 25:1; 33:10; Pr 4:27; Hag 2:11; Mal 2:7 **10:12** [f]S Ex 29:41

[t]6 Or *Do not uncover your heads*

10:1 UNAUTHORIZED FIRE. Nadab and Abihu put into their censers (i.e., fire pans) coals of fire from an unauthorized source (cf. Ex 30:7–9); note also that the offering of incense on the altar was to be done only by the high priest (Ex 30:7–9). Some interpreters have suggested that Nadab and Abihu sinned while under the influence of alcohol (see vv. 9–10).

10:2 FIRE . . . CONSUMED THEM. Nadab and Abihu were killed because, as priests, they defiantly rebelled against God and his law and thus profaned the holy place (v. 3). (1) They had been explicitly forbidden to offer "unauthorized fire" before the Lord (see previous note; cf. Ex 30:9–10). By their act those who were supposed to teach God's law refused to take God's commandments seriously. While professing to be holy ministers of God, they really were serving their own desires, and there was no fear of God in their lives.

(2) These two men were leaders of God's people. When God's ministers commit blatant sin, it does great damage to God and his redemptive purposes on earth. Their transgressions defile the church and all God's people and bring dishonor to him. For this reason the Bible teaches that only those who have demonstrated a Christian life of perseverance in loyalty to God and his word may be appointed as overseers of God's people (see 1Ti 3:1–7; see article on MORAL QUALIFICATIONS FOR OVERSEERS, p. 1882).

10:9 NOT TO DRINK WINE. Abstinence from intoxicating wine was required of all priests when performing their religious duties. (1) They were expected to be holy instruments before God and the people whom they were to teach soberly God's ways (vv. 10–11; see Eph 5:18, notes). (2) The violation of this ordinance about abstinence was serious enough to incur the penalty of death. The point is clear — God considered any amount of intoxicating drink incompatible with his highest standards of godliness and with wise discernment and sensitivity to the leadership of the Holy Spirit (see Pr 23:29–35; 1Ti 3:3, note; Tit 2:2, note).

beside the altar,[g] for it is most holy.
13Eat it in a holy place,[h] because it is
your share and your sons' share of the
offerings made to the LORD by fire; for
so I have been commanded.[i] 14But
you and your sons and your daughters
may eat the breast[j] that was waved
and the thigh that was presented. Eat
them in a ceremonially clean place;[k]
they have been given to you and your
children as your share of the Israelites'
fellowship offerings.[u] 15The thigh[l]
that was presented and the breast that
was waved must be brought with the
fat portions of the offerings made by
fire, to be waved before the LORD as a
wave offering.[m] This will be the regular share for you and your children, as
the LORD has commanded."

16When Moses inquired about the
goat of the sin offering[n] and found
that it had been burned up, he was angry with Eleazar and Ithamar, Aaron's
remaining sons, and asked, 17"Why
didn't you eat the sin offering[o] in the
sanctuary area? It is most holy; it was
given to you to take away the guilt[p] of
the community by making atonement
for them before the LORD. 18Since its
blood was not taken into the Holy
Place,[q] you should have eaten the
goat in the sanctuary area, as I commanded.[r]"

19Aaron replied to Moses, "Today
they sacrificed their sin offering and
their burnt offering[s] before the LORD,
but such things as this have happened
to me. Would the LORD have been
pleased if I had eaten the sin offering
today?" 20When Moses heard this, he
was satisfied.

Clean and Unclean Food

11:1–23pp — Dt 14:3–20

11 The LORD said to Moses and
Aaron, 2"Say to the Israelites:
'Of all the animals that live on land,
these are the ones you may eat:[t] 3You
may eat any animal that has a split
hoof completely divided and that
chews the cud.

4" 'There are some that only chew
the cud or only have a split hoof, but
you must not eat them.[u] The camel,
though it chews the cud, does not have
a split hoof; it is ceremonially unclean
for you. 5The coney,[v] though it chews
the cud, does not have a split hoof; it
is unclean for you. 6The rabbit, though
it chews the cud, does not have a split
hoof; it is unclean for you. 7And the
pig,[v] though it has a split hoof completely divided, does not chew the cud;
it is unclean for you. 8You must not eat
their meat or touch their carcasses;
they are unclean for you.[w]

9" 'Of all the creatures living in the
water of the seas and the streams, you
may eat any that have fins and scales.
10But all creatures in the seas or
streams that do not have fins and
scales—whether among all the
swarming things or among all the other living creatures in the water—you
are to detest.[x] 11And since you are to
detest them, you must not eat their
meat and you must detest their carcasses.[y] 12Anything living in the water that does not have fins and scales
is to be detestable to you.[z]

13" 'These are the birds you are to
detest and not eat because they are detestable: the eagle, the vulture, the
black vulture, 14the red kite, any
kind[a] of black kite, 15any kind of raven,[b] 16the horned owl, the screech
owl, the gull, any kind of hawk, 17the
little owl, the cormorant, the great owl,
18the white owl,[c] the desert owl, the
osprey, 19the stork,[d] any kind[e] of
heron, the hoopoe and the bat.[w][f]

20" 'All flying insects that walk on
all fours are to be detestable to you.[g]
21There are, however, some winged
creatures that walk on all fours that
you may eat: those that have jointed
legs for hopping on the ground. 22Of
these you may eat any kind of locust,[h]
katydid, cricket or grasshopper. 23But
all other winged creatures that have
four legs you are to detest.

24" 'You will make yourselves unclean by these;[i] whoever touches
their carcasses will be unclean till evening.[j] 25Whoever picks up one of
their carcasses must wash his
clothes,[k] and he will be unclean till
evening.[l]

26" 'Every animal that has a split
hoof not completely divided or that
does not chew the cud is unclean for
you; whoever touches ⌞the carcass of⌟
any of them will be unclean. 27Of all
the animals that walk on all fours,

10:12 [g] Lev 6:14-18
10:13 [h] S Lev 6:16 [i] Eze 42:13
10:14 [j] Nu 5:9 [k] S Ex 29:31; S Lev 4:12
10:15 [l] S Lev 7:34 [m] S Ex 29:28
10:16 [n] S Lev 9:3
10:17 [o] Lev 6:24-30; Eze 42:13 [p] S Ex 28:38
10:18 [q] S Lev 4:18; 6:26 [r] S Lev 6:17
10:19 [s] Lev 9:12
11:2 [t] Ac 10:12-14
11:4 [u] Ac 10:14
11:7 [v] Isa 65:4; 66:3,17
11:8 [w] S Lev 5:2; Heb 9:10
11:10 [x] ver 12
11:11 [y] S Lev 5:2
11:12 [z] ver 10
11:14 [a] S Ge 1:11
11:15 [b] S Ge 8:7
11:18 [c] Isa 13:21; 14:23; 34:11,13; Zep 2:14
11:19 [d] Zec 5:9 [e] S Ge 1:11 [f] Isa 2:20
11:20 [g] Ac 10:14
11:22 [h] Mt 3:4; Mk 1:6
11:24 [i] S Lev 5:2 [j] ver 27-40; Lev 13:3; 14:46; 15:5; 22:6; Nu 19:7,19
11:25 [k] ver 28; S Ex 19:10; Lev 13:6; 14:8,47; 15:5; 16:26; Nu 8:7; 19:7 [l] Lev 13:34; Nu 19:8; 31:24

[u] *14* Traditionally *peace offerings* [v] *5* That is, the hyrax or rock badger [w] *19* The precise identification of some of the birds, insects and animals in this chapter is uncertain.

those that walk on their paws are unclean for you; whoever touches their
carcasses will be unclean till evening.
28Anyone who picks up their carcasses
must wash his clothes, and he will be
unclean till evening.[m] They are unclean for you.
29" 'Of the animals that move about
on the ground, these are unclean for
you:[n] the weasel, the rat,[o] any kind
of great lizard, **30**the gecko, the moni-
tor lizard, the wall lizard, the skink and
the chameleon. **31**Of all those that
move along the ground, these are unclean for you. Whoever touches them
when they are dead will be unclean till
evening. **32**When one of them dies and
falls on something, that article, whatever its use, will be unclean, whether
it is made of wood, cloth, hide or sackcloth.[p] Put it in water; it will be unclean till evening, and then it will be
clean. **33**If one of them falls into a clay
pot, everything in it will be unclean,
and you must break the pot.[q] **34**Any
food that could be eaten but has water
on it from such a pot is unclean, and
any liquid that could be drunk from it
is unclean. **35**Anything that one of their
carcasses falls on becomes unclean; an
oven or cooking pot must be broken up.
They are unclean, and you are to regard them as unclean. **36**A spring, however, or a cistern for collecting water
remains clean, but anyone who
touches one of these carcasses is unclean. **37**If a carcass falls on any seeds
that are to be planted, they remain
clean. **38**But if water has been put on
the seed and a carcass falls on it, it is
unclean for you.

11:28 [m] Heb 9:10
11:29 [n] ver 41 [o] Isa 66:17
11:32 [p] Lev 15:12; Nu 19:18; 31:20
11:33 [q] S Lev 6:28
11:39 [r] Lev 17:15; 22:8; Dt 14:21; Eze 4:14; 44:31 [s] ver 40; Lev 22:4; Nu 19:11
11:40 [t] S ver 39 [u] ver 25; Lev 14:8; 17:15; 22:8; Eze 44:31; Heb 9:10
11:43 [v] ver 44; Lev 20:25; 22:5
11:44 [w] S Ex 6:2, 7; 20:2; Isa 43:3; 51:15; Eze 20:5 [x] S Ex 19:10; Lev 20:7; Nu 15:40; Jos 3:5; 7:13; 1Ch 15:12; 2Ch 29:5; 35:6 [y] S Ex 22:31; S Dt 14:2 [z] S Ex 31:13; Lev 19:2; 20:7; Jos 24:19; 1Sa 2:2; Job 6:10; Ps 99:3; Eph 1:4; 1Th 4:7; 1Pe 1:15, 16* [a] S ver 43
11:45 [b] Lev 25:38,55 [c] S Ge 17:7 [d] S Ex 19:6; 1Pe 1:16*
11:47 [e] Lev 10:10

39" 'If an animal that you are allowed to eat dies,[r] anyone who
touches the carcass[s] will be unclean
till evening. **40**Anyone who eats some
of the carcass[t] must wash his clothes,
and he will be unclean till evening.[u]
Anyone who picks up the carcass must
wash his clothes, and he will be unclean till evening.
41" 'Every creature that moves
about on the ground is detestable; it is
not to be eaten. **42**You are not to eat
any creature that moves about on the
ground, whether it moves on its belly
or walks on all fours or on many feet;
it is detestable. **43**Do not defile yourselves by any of these creatures.[v] Do
not make yourselves unclean by means
of them or be made unclean by them.
44I am the LORD your God;[w] consecrate
yourselves[x] and be holy,[y] because I
am holy.[z] Do not make yourselves unclean by any creature that moves about
on the ground.[a] **45**I am the LORD who
brought you up out of Egypt[b] to be
your God;[c] therefore be holy, because
I am holy.[d]
46" 'These are the regulations concerning animals, birds, every living
thing that moves in the water and every creature that moves about on the
ground. **47**You must distinguish between the unclean and the clean, between living creatures that may be eat-
en and those that may not be
eaten.[e] ' "

Purification After Childbirth

12 The LORD said to Moses, **2**"Say
to the Israelites: 'A woman who
becomes pregnant and gives birth to a

11:44 BE HOLY. The instructions concerning clean and unclean (i.e., proper and improper) food (ch. 11) were given apparently for health reasons, but also as standards to help Israel remain a people separated from the ungodly society around them (cf. Dt 14:1–2). These dietary instructions are no longer binding on NT believers, for Christ fulfilled their significance and purpose (cf. Mt 5:17; 15:1–20; Ac 10:14–15; Col 2:16; 1Ti 4:3). However, the principles embodied in those instructions are still valid today.

(1) Christians today must distinguish themselves from their surrounding society by eating, drinking and dressing so as to honor God with their bodies (cf. 1Co 6:20; 10:31), and by rejecting all unholy social customs of unbelievers. They must be "holy in all [they] do" (1Pe 1:15).

(2) The detailed emphasis on ceremonial cleanliness highlighted the necessity of moral separation of God's people in thought and deed from the surrounding world (Ex 19:6; 2Co 7:1; see article on SPIRITUAL SEPARATION FOR BELIEVERS, p. 1794). All aspects of life must be regulated by God's will (1Co 10:31).

12:2 GIVES BIRTH TO A SON. Parenthood is God's will for men and women and can be one of the greatest joys of life (Ge 1:28; 9:1; Ps 127:3; 128:3). However, the discharges associated with childbirth had to be treated as unclean (15:16–19; Ex 19:15; see next note) and symbolized the results of humanity's fall (see Ge 3:15, note). (1) Children are now born with a sinful nature (see 1Jn 1:8, note). The psalmist's words apply here: "Surely I was sinful at birth, sinful from the time my mother conceived me" (Ps 51:5). (2) Children also face the reality of physical death (Ge 2:16–17; 5:3) and the possibility of eternal death unless they accept Christ's redemption. Death was never God's intention or perfect will for humans. The uncleanness associated with childbearing expresses the

son will be ceremonially unclean for
seven days, just as she is unclean during her monthly period.[f] **3**On the
eighth day[g] the boy is to be circumcised.[h] **4**Then the woman must wait
thirty-three days to be purified from
her bleeding. She must not touch anything sacred or go to the sanctuary until the days of her purification are over.
5If she gives birth to a daughter, for
two weeks the woman will be unclean,
as during her period. Then she must
wait sixty-six days to be purified from
her bleeding.

6" 'When the days of her purification
for a son or daughter are over,[i] she is
to bring to the priest at the entrance to
the Tent of Meeting a year-old lamb[j]
for a burnt offering and a young pigeon
or a dove for a sin offering.[k] **7**He shall
offer them before the LORD to make
atonement for her, and then she will be
ceremonially clean from her flow of
blood.

" 'These are the regulations for the
woman who gives birth to a boy or a
girl. **8**If she cannot afford a lamb, she
is to bring two doves or two young pigeons,[l] one for a burnt offering and
the other for a sin offering.[m] In this
way the priest will make atonement for
her, and she will be clean.[n]' "

Regulations About Infectious Skin Diseases

13 The LORD said to Moses and
Aaron, **2**"When anyone has a
swelling[o] or a rash or a bright spot[p]
on his skin that may become an infectious skin disease,[x][q] he must be
brought to Aaron the priest[r] or to one
of his sons[y] who is a priest. **3**The
priest is to examine the sore on his
skin, and if the hair in the sore has
turned white and the sore appears to
be more than skin deep,[z] it is an infectious skin disease. When the priest examines him, he shall pronounce him
ceremonially unclean.[s] **4**If the spot[t]
on his skin is white but does not appear
to be more than skin deep and the hair
in it has not turned white, the priest is
to put the infected person in isolation
for seven days.[u] **5**On the seventh
day[v] the priest is to examine him,[w]
and if he sees that the sore is unchanged and has not spread in the
skin, he is to keep him in isolation another seven days. **6**On the seventh day
the priest is to examine him again, and
if the sore has faded and has not
spread in the skin, the priest shall pronounce him clean;[x] it is only a rash.
The man must wash his clothes,[y] and
he will be clean.[z] **7**But if the rash does
spread in his skin after he has shown
himself to the priest to be pronounced
clean, he must appear before the priest
again.[a] **8**The priest is to examine him,
and if the rash has spread in the skin,
he shall pronounce him unclean; it is
an infectious disease.

9"When anyone has an infectious
skin disease, he must be brought to the
priest. **10**The priest is to examine him,
and if there is a white swelling in the
skin that has turned the hair white and
if there is raw flesh in the swelling, **11**it
is a chronic skin disease[b] and the
priest shall pronounce him unclean. He
is not to put him in isolation, because
he is already unclean.

12"If the disease breaks out all over
his skin and, so far as the priest can
see, it covers all the skin of the infected person from head to foot, **13**the
priest is to examine him, and if the disease has covered his whole body, he
shall pronounce that person clean.
Since it has all turned white, he is
clean. **14**But whenever raw flesh appears on him, he will be unclean.
15When the priest sees the raw flesh,
he shall pronounce him unclean. The
raw flesh is unclean; he has an infec-

12:2 [f]Lev 15:19; 18:19; Isa 64:6; Eze 18:6; 22:10; 36:17 **12:3** [g]S Ex 22:30 [h]S Ge 17:10; S Lk 1:59 **12:6** [i]Lk 2:22 [j]Ex 29:38; Lev 23:12; Nu 6:12,14; 7:15 [k]Lev 5:7 **12:8** [l]S Ge 15:9; Lev 14:22 [m]Lev 5:7; Lk 2:22-24* [n]S Lev 4:26 **13:2** [o]ver 10,19, 28,43 [p]ver 4,38, 39; Lev 14:56 [q]ver 3,9,15; S Ex 4:6; Lev 14:3,32; Nu 5:2; Dt 24:8 [r]Dt 24:8 **13:3** [s]ver 8,11, 20,30; Lev 21:1; Nu 9:6 **13:4** [t]S ver 2 [u]ver 5,21,26,33, 46; Lev 14:38; Nu 12:14,15; Dt 24:9 **13:5** [v]Lev 14:9 [w]ver 27,32,34,51 **13:6** [x]ver 13,17, 23,28,34; Mt 8:3; Lk 5:12-14 [y]S Lev 11:25 [z]Lev 11:25; 14:8, 9,20,48; 15:8; Nu 8:7 **13:7** [a]Lk 5:14 **13:11** [b]S Ex 4:6; S Lev 14:8; S Nu 12:10; Mt 8:2

[x]*2* Traditionally *leprosy*; the Hebrew word was used for various diseases affecting the skin—not necessarily leprosy; also elsewhere in this chapter. [y]*2* Or *descendants* [z]*3* Or *be lower than the rest of the skin*; also elsewhere in this chapter

truth that the newborn child needs a Savior. (3) Christian parents, knowing the sinful tendencies with which their children are born, should pray earnestly that their children might accept Christ as Lord and be born again, regenerated by the Holy Spirit (see articles on REGENERATION, p. 1589, and PARENTS AND CHILDREN, p. 1854).

13:3 PRONOUNCE HIM CEREMONIALLY UNCLEAN. Uncleanness here must be equated with whatever did not accord with God's will and holiness. It could be caused by that which was associated with parenthood (see previous note), sickness (chs. 13—14; Nu 5:2; 12:10–14) or death (Nu 5:2; 31:19; 35:33). All these things deviate from the perfection God intended at creation. In other words, the laws of uncleanness constantly reminded the people of the devastating results of their sin.

tious disease.[c] 16Should the raw flesh
change and turn white, he must go to
the priest. 17The priest is to examine
him, and if the sores have turned
white, the priest shall pronounce the
infected person clean;[d] then he will be
clean.
18"When someone has a boil[e] on his
skin and it heals, 19and in the place
where the boil was, a white swelling or
reddish-white[f] spot[g] appears, he
must present himself to the priest.
20The priest is to examine it, and if it
appears to be more than skin deep and
the hair in it has turned white, the
priest shall pronounce him unclean. It
is an infectious skin disease[h] that has
broken out where the boil was. 21But
if, when the priest examines it, there is
no white hair in it and it is not more
than skin deep and has faded, then the
priest is to put him in isolation for sev-
en days. 22If it is spreading in the skin,
the priest shall pronounce him unclean; it is infectious. 23But if the spot
is unchanged and has not spread, it is
only a scar from the boil, and the priest
shall pronounce him clean.[i]
24"When someone has a burn on his
skin and a reddish-white or white spot
appears in the raw flesh of the burn,
25the priest is to examine the spot, and
if the hair in it has turned white, and
it appears to be more than skin deep,
it is an infectious disease that has broken out in the burn. The priest shall
pronounce him unclean; it is an infectious skin disease.[j] 26But if the priest
examines it and there is no white hair
in the spot and if it is not more than
skin deep and has faded, then the
priest is to put him in isolation for sev-
en days.[k] 27On the seventh day the
priest is to examine him,[l] and if it is
spreading in the skin, the priest shall
pronounce him unclean; it is an infectious skin disease. 28If, however, the
spot is unchanged and has not spread
in the skin but has faded, it is a swelling from the burn, and the priest shall
pronounce him clean; it is only a scar
from the burn.[m]
29"If a man or woman has a sore on
the head[n] or on the chin, 30the priest
is to examine the sore, and if it appears
to be more than skin deep and the hair
in it is yellow and thin, the priest shall
pronounce that person unclean; it is an
itch, an infectious disease of the head
or chin. 31But if, when the priest examines this kind of sore, it does not seem
to be more than skin deep and there is
no black hair in it, then the priest is to
put the infected person in isolation for
seven days.[o] 32On the seventh day the
priest is to examine the sore,[p] and if
the itch has not spread and there is no
yellow hair in it and it does not appear
to be more than skin deep, 33he must
be shaved except for the diseased area,
and the priest is to keep him in isolation another seven days. 34On the seventh day the priest is to examine the
itch,[q] and if it has not spread in the
skin and appears to be no more than
skin deep, the priest shall pronounce
him clean. He must wash his clothes,
and he will be clean.[r] 35But if the itch
does spread in the skin after he is pronounced clean, 36the priest is to examine him, and if the itch has spread in
the skin, the priest does not need to
look for yellow hair; the person is unclean.[s] 37If, however, in his judgment
it is unchanged and black hair has
grown in it, the itch is healed. He is
clean, and the priest shall pronounce
him clean.
38"When a man or woman has white
spots on the skin, 39the priest is to examine them, and if the spots are dull
white, it is a harmless rash that has
broken out on the skin; that person is
clean.
40"When a man has lost his hair and
is bald,[t] he is clean. 41If he has lost
his hair from the front of his scalp and
has a bald forehead, he is clean. 42But
if he has a reddish-white sore on his
bald head or forehead, it is an infectious disease breaking out on his head
or forehead. 43The priest is to examine
him, and if the swollen sore on his head
or forehead is reddish-white like an infectious skin disease, 44the man is diseased and is unclean. The priest shall
pronounce him unclean because of the
sore on his head.
45"The person with such an infectious disease must wear torn
clothes,[u] let his hair be unkempt,[a]
cover the lower part of his face[v] and
cry out, 'Unclean! Unclean!'[w] 46As
long as he has the infection he remains
unclean. He must live alone; he must
live outside the camp.[x]

13:15 [c] S ver 2
13:17 [d] S ver 6
13:18 [e] S Ex 9:9
13:19 [f] ver 24,42; Lev 14:37 [g] S ver 2
13:20 [h] ver 2
13:23 [i] S ver 6
13:25 [j] ver 11
13:26 [k] S ver 4
13:27 [l] S ver 5
13:28 [m] S ver 2
13:29 [n] ver 43,44
13:31 [o] ver 4
13:32 [p] S ver 5
13:34 [q] S ver 5 [r] S Lev 11:25
13:36 [s] ver 30
13:40 [t] Lev 21:5; 2Ki 2:23; Isa 3:24; 15:2; 22:12; Eze 27:31; 29:18; Am 8:10; Mic 1:16
13:45 [u] S Lev 10:6 [v] Eze 24:17,22; Mic 3:7 [w] S Lev 5:2; La 4:15; Lk 17:12
13:46 [x] Nu 5:1-4; 12:14; 2Ki 7:3; 15:5

[a] 45 Or *clothes, uncover his head*

Regulations About Mildew

47"If any clothing is contaminated
with mildew—any woolen or linen
clothing, 48any woven or knitted material of linen or wool, any leather or
anything made of leather— 49and if
the contamination in the clothing, or
leather, or woven or knitted material,
or any leather article, is greenish or
reddish, it is a spreading mildew and
must be shown to the priest.[y] 50The
priest is to examine the mildew[z] and
isolate the affected article for seven
days. 51On the seventh day he is to examine it,[a] and if the mildew has
spread in the clothing, or the woven or
knitted material, or the leather, whatever its use, it is a destructive mildew;
the article is unclean.[b] 52He must
burn up the clothing, or the woven or
knitted material of wool or linen, or
any leather article that has the contamination in it, because the mildew
is destructive; the article must be
burned up.[c]

53"But if, when the priest examines
it, the mildew has not spread in the
clothing, or the woven or knitted material, or the leather article, 54he shall
order that the contaminated article be
washed. Then he is to isolate it for another seven days. 55After the affected
article has been washed, the priest is
to examine it, and if the mildew has not
changed its appearance, even though it
has not spread, it is unclean. Burn it
with fire, whether the mildew has affected one side or the other. 56If, when
the priest examines it, the mildew has
faded after the article has been
washed, he is to tear the contaminated
part out of the clothing, or the leather,
or the woven or knitted material. 57But
if it reappears in the clothing, or in
the woven or knitted material, or in
the leather article, it is spreading,
and whatever has the mildew must
be burned with fire. 58The clothing,
or the woven or knitted material,
or any leather article that has been
washed and is rid of the mildew,
must be washed again, and it will be
clean."

59These are the regulations concerning contamination by mildew in
woolen or linen clothing, woven or
knitted material, or any leather article, for pronouncing them clean or unclean.

Cleansing From Infectious Skin Diseases

14 The LORD said to Moses,
2"These are the regulations for
the diseased person at the time of his
ceremonial cleansing, when he is
brought to the priest:[d] 3The priest is
to go outside the camp and examine
him.[e] If the person has been healed of
his infectious skin disease,[b][f] 4the
priest shall order that two live clean
birds and some cedar wood, scarlet
yarn and hyssop[g] be brought for the
one to be cleansed.[h] 5Then the priest
shall order that one of the birds be
killed over fresh water in a clay pot.[i]
6He is then to take the live bird and dip
it, together with the cedar wood, the
scarlet yarn and the hyssop, into the
blood of the bird that was killed over
the fresh water.[j] 7Seven times[k] he
shall sprinkle[l] the one to be cleansed
of the infectious disease and pronounce him clean. Then he is to release
the live bird in the open fields.[m]

8"The person to be cleansed must
wash his clothes,[n] shave off all his
hair and bathe with water;[o] then he
will be ceremonially clean.[p] After this
he may come into the camp,[q] but he
must stay outside his tent for seven
days. 9On the seventh day[r] he must
shave off all his hair;[s] he must shave
his head, his beard, his eyebrows and
the rest of his hair. He must wash his
clothes and bathe himself with water,
and he will be clean.[t]

10"On the eighth day[u] he must
bring two male lambs and one ewe
lamb[v] a year old, each without defect,
along with three-tenths of an
ephah[c][w] of fine flour mixed with oil
for a grain offering,[x] and one log[d] of
oil.[y] 11The priest who pronounces
him clean shall present[z] both the one
to be cleansed and his offerings before
the LORD at the entrance to the Tent of
Meeting.[a]

12"Then the priest is to take one of
the male lambs and offer it as a guilt
offering,[b] along with the log of oil; he
shall wave them before the LORD as a

b *3* Traditionally *leprosy*; the Hebrew word was used for various diseases affecting the skin—not necessarily leprosy; also elsewhere in this chapter. **c** *10* That is, probably about 6 quarts (about 6.5 liters) **d** *10* That is, probably about 2/3 pint (about 0.3 liter); also in verses 12, 15, 21 and 24

13:49 [y]Mk 1:44
13:50 [z]Eze 44:23
13:51 [a]S ver 5 [b]Lev 14:44
13:52 [c]ver 55,57

14:2 [d]Lev 13:57; Dt 24:8; Mt 8:2-4; Mk 1:40-44; Lk 5:12-14; 17:14
14:3 [e]Lev 13:46 [f]S Lev 13:2
14:4 [g]S Ex 12:22 [h]ver 6,49,51,52; Nu 19:6; Ps 51:7
14:5 [i]ver 50
14:6 [j]S ver 4
14:7 [k]ver 51 [l]2Ki 5:10,14; Isa 52:15; Eze 36:25 [m]ver 53
14:8 [n]S Lev 11:25 [o]ver 9; S Ex 29:4; Lev 15:5; 17:15; 22:6; Nu 19:7,8 [p]ver 20 [q]S Lev 13:11; Nu 5:2,3; 12:14,15; 19:20; 31:24; 2Ch 26:21
14:9 [r]S Lev 13:5 [s]Nu 6:9; Dt 21:12 [t]S Lev 13:6
14:10 [u]Nu 6:10; Mt 8:4; Mk 1:44; Lk 5:14 [v]S Lev 4:32 [w]Nu 15:9; 28:20 [x]Lev 2:1 [y]ver 12,15,21,24
14:11 [z]Nu 6:16 [a]Nu 6:10
14:12 [b]S Lev 5:18

wave offering.[c] 13He is to slaughter
the lamb in the holy place[d] where the
sin offering and the burnt offering are
slaughtered. Like the sin offering, the
guilt offering belongs to the priest;[e] it
is most holy. 14The priest is to take
some of the blood of the guilt offering
and put it on the lobe of the right ear
of the one to be cleansed, on the thumb
of his right hand and on the big toe of
his right foot.[f] 15The priest shall then
take some of the log of oil, pour it in the
palm of his own left hand,[g] 16dip his
right forefinger into the oil in his palm,
and with his finger sprinkle some of it
before the LORD seven times.[h] 17The
priest is to put some of the oil remaining in his palm on the lobe of the right
ear of the one to be cleansed, on the
thumb of his right hand and on the big
toe of his right foot, on top of the blood
of the guilt offering.[i] 18The rest of the
oil in his palm the priest shall put on
the head of the one to be cleansed[j]
and make atonement for him before the
LORD.

19"Then the priest is to sacrifice the
sin offering and make atonement for
the one to be cleansed from his uncleanness.[k] After that, the priest
shall slaughter the burnt offering
20and offer it on the altar, together
with the grain offering, and make
atonement for him,[l] and he will be
clean.[m]

21"If, however, he is poor[n] and cannot afford these,[o] he must take one
male lamb as a guilt offering to be
waved to make atonement for him, together with a tenth of an ephah[e] of
fine flour mixed with oil for a grain offering, a log of oil, 22and two doves or
two young pigeons,[p] which he can afford, one for a sin offering and the other for a burnt offering.[q]

23"On the eighth day he must bring
them for his cleansing to the priest at
the entrance to the Tent of Meeting,[r]
before the LORD.[s] 24The priest is to
take the lamb for the guilt offering,[t]
together with the log of oil,[u] and wave
them before the LORD as a wave offering.[v] 25He shall slaughter the lamb
for the guilt offering and take some of
its blood and put it on the lobe of the
right ear of the one to be cleansed, on
the thumb of his right hand and on the
big toe of his right foot.[w] 26The priest
is to pour some of the oil into the palm
of his own left hand,[x] 27and with his

14:12 [c]S Ex 29:24
14:13 [d]S Ex 29:11 [e]Lev 6:24-30; S 7:7
14:14 [f]S Ex 29:20
14:15 [g]ver 26
14:16 [h]ver 27
14:17 [i]ver 28
14:18 [j]ver 31; Lev 15:15
14:19 [k]ver 31; S Lev 5:3; 15:15
14:20 [l]Lev 15:30 [m]ver 8
14:21 [n]S Lev 5:7 [o]ver 22,32
14:22 [p]S Lev 5:7 [q]Lev 15:30
14:23 [r]Lev 15:14,29 [s]S ver 10,11
14:24 [t]Nu 6:14 [u]S ver 10 [v]ver 12
14:25 [w]S Ex 29:20
14:26 [x]ver 15
14:29 [y]ver 18
14:30 [z]S Lev 5:7
14:31 [a]ver 22; Lev 5:7; 15:15,30 [b]S ver 18,19
14:32 [c]S Lev 13:2 [d]S ver 21
14:34 [e]Ge 12:5; Ex 6:4; Nu 13:2 [f]Ge 17:8; 48:4; Nu 27:12; 32:22; Dt 3:27; 7:1; 32:49
14:37 [g]S Lev 13:19
14:38 [h]S Lev 13:4
14:39 [i]Lev 13:5
14:40 [j]ver 45

right forefinger sprinkle some of the oil
from his palm seven times before the
LORD. 28Some of the oil in his palm he
is to put on the same places he put the
blood of the guilt offering—on the lobe
of the right ear of the one to be
cleansed, on the thumb of his right
hand and on the big toe of his right
foot. 29The rest of the oil in his palm
the priest shall put on the head of the
one to be cleansed, to make atonement
for him before the LORD.[y] 30Then he
shall sacrifice the doves or the young
pigeons, which the person can afford,[z] 31one[f] as a sin offering and the
other as a burnt offering,[a] together
with the grain offering. In this way the
priest will make atonement before the
LORD on behalf of the one to be
cleansed.[b]"

32These are the regulations for anyone who has an infectious skin disease[c] and who cannot afford the regular offerings[d] for his cleansing.

Cleansing From Mildew

33The LORD said to Moses and Aaron, 34"When you enter the land of Canaan,[e] which I am giving you as your
possession,[f] and I put a spreading
mildew in a house in that land, 35the
owner of the house must go and tell the
priest, 'I have seen something that
looks like mildew in my house.' 36The
priest is to order the house to be emptied before he goes in to examine the
mildew, so that nothing in the house
will be pronounced unclean. After this
the priest is to go in and inspect the
house. 37He is to examine the mildew
on the walls, and if it has greenish or
reddish[g] depressions that appear to
be deeper than the surface of the wall,
38the priest shall go out the doorway of
the house and close it up for seven
days.[h] 39On the seventh day[i] the
priest shall return to inspect the
house. If the mildew has spread on the
walls, 40he is to order that the contaminated stones be torn out and thrown
into an unclean place outside the
town.[j] 41He must have all the inside
walls of the house scraped and the material that is scraped off dumped into
an unclean place outside the town.
42Then they are to take other stones to

[e] *21* That is, probably about 2 quarts (about 2 liters) [f] *31* Septuagint and Syriac; Hebrew *31such as the person can afford, one*

replace these and take new clay and
plaster the house.

43"If the mildew reappears in the
house after the stones have been torn
out and the house scraped and plastered, **44**the priest is to go and examine
it and, if the mildew has spread in the
house, it is a destructive mildew; the
house is unclean.[k] **45**It must be torn
down—its stones, timbers and all the
plaster—and taken out of the town to
an unclean place.

46"Anyone who goes into the house
while it is closed up will be unclean till
evening.[l] **47**Anyone who sleeps or
eats in the house must wash his
clothes.[m]

48"But if the priest comes to examine it and the mildew has not spread
after the house has been plastered, he
shall pronounce the house clean,[n] because the mildew is gone. **49**To purify
the house he is to take two birds and
some cedar wood, scarlet yarn and hyssop.[o] **50**He shall kill one of the birds
over fresh water in a clay pot.[p] **51**Then
he is to take the cedar wood, the hyssop,[q] the scarlet yarn and the live
bird, dip them into the blood of the
dead bird and the fresh water, and
sprinkle the house seven times.[r] **52**He
shall purify the house with the bird's
blood, the fresh water, the live bird, the
cedar wood, the hyssop and the scarlet
yarn. **53**Then he is to release the live
bird in the open fields[s] outside the
town. In this way he will make atonement for the house, and it will be
clean.[t]"

54These are the regulations for any
infectious skin disease,[u] for an itch,
55for mildew[v] in clothing or in a
house, **56**and for a swelling, a rash or
a bright spot,[w] **57**to determine when
something is clean or unclean.

These are the regulations for infectious skin diseases and mildew.[x]

Discharges Causing Uncleanness

15 The Lord said to Moses and
Aaron, **2**"Speak to the Israelites and say to them: 'When any man
has a bodily discharge,[y] the discharge
is unclean. **3**Whether it continues flowing from his body or is blocked, it will
make him unclean. This is how his discharge will bring about uncleanness:

4" 'Any bed the man with a discharge lies on will be unclean, and anything he sits on will be unclean. **5**Anyone who touches his bed must wash his
clothes[z] and bathe with water,[a] and
he will be unclean till evening.[b] **6**Whoever sits on anything that the man with
a discharge sat on must wash his
clothes and bathe with water, and he
will be unclean till evening.

7" 'Whoever touches the man[c] who
has a discharge[d] must wash his
clothes and bathe with water, and he
will be unclean till evening.

8" 'If the man with the discharge
spits[e] on someone who is clean, that
person must wash his clothes and
bathe with water, and he will be unclean till evening.

9" 'Everything the man sits on when
riding will be unclean, **10**and whoever
touches any of the things that were under him will be unclean till evening;
whoever picks up those things[f] must
wash his clothes and bathe with water,
and he will be unclean till evening.

11" 'Anyone the man with a discharge touches without rinsing his
hands with water must wash his
clothes and bathe with water, and he
will be unclean till evening.

12" 'A clay pot[g] that the man
touches must be broken, and any
wooden article[h] is to be rinsed with
water.

13" 'When a man is cleansed from
his discharge, he is to count off seven
days[i] for his ceremonial cleansing; he
must wash his clothes and bathe himself with fresh water, and he will be
clean.[j] **14**On the eighth day he must
take two doves or two young pigeons[k]
and come before the Lord to the entrance to the Tent of Meeting and give
them to the priest. **15**The priest is to
sacrifice them, the one for a sin offering[l] and the other for a burnt offering.[m] In this way he will make atonement before the Lord for the man
because of his discharge.[n]

16" 'When a man has an emission of

14:44 [k] Lev 13:51
14:46 [l] S Lev 11:24
14:47 [m] S Lev 11:25
14:48 [n] S Lev 13:6
14:49 [o] ver 4; 1Ki 4:33
14:50 [p] ver 5
14:51 [q] ver 6; Ps 51:7 [r] S ver 4,7
14:53 [s] S ver 7 [t] ver 20
14:54 [u] Lev 13:2
14:55 [v] Lev 13:47-52
14:56 [w] Lev 13:2
14:57 [x] S Lev 10:10
15:2 [y] ver 16,32; Lev 22:4; Nu 5:2; 2Sa 3:29; Mt 9:20
15:5 [z] S Lev 11:25 [a] Lev 14:8 [b] S Lev 11:24
15:7 [c] ver 19; Lev 22:5 [d] ver 16; Lev 22:4
15:8 [e] Nu 12:14
15:10 [f] Nu 19:10
15:12 [g] S Lev 6:28 [h] S Lev 11:32
15:13 [i] S Lev 8:33 [j] ver 5
15:14 [k] Lev 14:22
15:15 [l] Lev 5:7 [m] Lev 14:31 [n] S Lev 14:18,19

15:5 WASH HIS CLOTHES AND BATHE. Chs. 11—15 show God's concern over the physical health and well-being of his people. The ancient people around them knew nothing about hygiene, sanitation, the importance of washing or the prevention of infectious diseases, nor did they care adequately for the poor and the sick. God's laws promoted concern for these things and encouraged the people to treat their lives and their God as holy.

semen,[o] he must bathe his whole body
with water, and he will be unclean till
evening.[p] **17**Any clothing or leather
that has semen on it must be washed
with water, and it will be unclean till
evening. **18**When a man lies with a
woman and there is an emission
of semen,[q] both must bathe with
water, and they will be unclean till
evening.

19" 'When a woman has her regular
flow of blood, the impurity of her
monthly period[r] will last seven days,
and anyone who touches her will be unclean till evening.

20" 'Anything she lies on during her
period will be unclean, and anything
she sits on will be unclean. **21**Whoever
touches her bed must wash his clothes
and bathe with water, and he will be
unclean till evening.[s] **22**Whoever
touches anything she sits on must
wash his clothes and bathe with water,
and he will be unclean till evening.
23Whether it is the bed or anything she
was sitting on, when anyone touches
it, he will be unclean till evening.

24" 'If a man lies with her and her
monthly flow[t] touches him, he will be
unclean for seven days; any bed he lies
on will be unclean.

25" 'When a woman has a discharge
of blood for many days at a time other
than her monthly period[u] or has a discharge that continues beyond her period, she will be unclean as long as she
has the discharge, just as in the days
of her period. **26**Any bed she lies on
while her discharge continues will be
unclean, as is her bed during her
monthly period, and anything she sits
on will be unclean, as during her period. **27**Whoever touches them will be
unclean; he must wash his clothes and
bathe with water, and he will be unclean till evening.

28" 'When she is cleansed from her
discharge, she must count off seven
days, and after that she will be ceremonially clean. **29**On the eighth day
she must take two doves or two young
pigeons[v] and bring them to the priest
at the entrance to the Tent of Meeting.
30The priest is to sacrifice one for a sin
offering and the other for a burnt offering. In this way he will make atonement for her before the LORD for the uncleanness of her discharge.[w]

31" 'You must keep the Israelites
separate from things that make them
unclean, so they will not die in their
uncleanness for defiling my dwelling
place,[g][x] which is among them.' "

32These are the regulations for a
man with a discharge, for anyone made
unclean by an emission of semen,[y]
33for a woman in her monthly period,
for a man or a woman with a discharge,
and for a man who lies with a woman
who is ceremonially unclean.[z]

The Day of Atonement

16:2–34pp — Lev 23:26–32; Nu 29:7–11

16 The LORD spoke to Moses after
the death of the two sons of
Aaron who died when they approached
the LORD.[a] **2**The LORD said to Moses:
"Tell your brother Aaron not to come
whenever he chooses[b] into the Most
Holy Place[c] behind the curtain[d] in
front of the atonement cover[e] on the
ark, or else he will die, because I appear[f] in the cloud[g] over the atonement cover.

3"This is how Aaron is to enter the
sanctuary area:[h] with a young bull[i]
for a sin offering and a ram for a burnt
offering.[j] **4**He is to put on the sacred
linen tunic,[k] with linen undergarments next to his body; he is to tie the
linen sash around him and put on the
linen turban.[l] These are sacred garments;[m] so he must bathe himself
with water[n] before he puts them on.[o]
5From the Israelite community[p] he is
to take two male goats[q] for a sin offering and a ram for a burnt offering.

6"Aaron is to offer the bull for his
own sin offering to make atonement for
himself and his household.[r] **7**Then he
is to take the two goats and present
them before the LORD at the entrance to
the Tent of Meeting. **8**He is to cast
lots[s] for the two goats—one lot for
the LORD and the other for the scapegoat.[h][t] **9**Aaron shall bring the goat
whose lot falls to the LORD and sacrifice
it for a sin offering. **10**But the goat cho-

15:16 [o] S ver 2; Dt 23:10 [p] ver 5; Dt 23:11
15:18 [q] 1Sa 21:4
15:19 [r] S ver 24
15:21 [s] ver 27
15:24 [t] ver 19; Lev 12:2; 18:19; 20:18; Eze 18:6
15:25 [u] Mt 9:20; Mk 5:25; Lk 8:43
15:29 [v] Lev 14:22
15:30 [w] Lev 5:10; 14:20,31; 18:19; 2Sa 11:4; Mk 5:25; Lk 8:43
15:31 [x] Lev 20:3; Nu 5:3; 19:13,20; 2Sa 15:25; 2Ki 21:7; Ps 33:14; 74:7; 76:2; Eze 5:11; 23:38
15:32 [y] S ver 2
15:33 [z] ver 19,24, 25
16:1 [a] S Lev 10:1
16:2 [b] Ex 30:10; Heb 9:7 [c] S Ex 26:33; Heb 9:25; 10:19 [d] S Ex 26:33; Heb 6:19 [e] S Ex 26:34 [f] S Ex 25:22 [g] S Ex 40:34; S 2Sa 22:10
16:3 [h] ver 6; Lev 4:1-12; Heb 9:24,25 [i] S Lev 4:3 [j] ver 5
16:4 [k] S Lev 8:13 [l] S Ex 28:39 [m] ver 32; S Ex 28:42; 29:29, 30; Lev 21:10; Nu 20:26,28 [n] S Ex 29:4; Heb 10:22 [o] Eze 9:2; 44:17-18
16:5 [p] S Lev 4:13-21 [q] ver 20; S Lev 4:3; 2Ch 29:23; Ps 50:9
16:6 [r] Lev 9:7; Heb 7:27; 9:7,12
16:8 [s] Nu 26:55, 56; 33:54; 34:13; Jos 14:2; 18:6; Jdg 20:9; Ne 10:34; Est 3:7; 9:24; Ps 22:18; Pr 16:33 [t] ver 10, 26

[g] 31 Or *my tabernacle* [h] 8 That is, the goat of removal; Hebrew *azazel*; also in verses 10 and 26

16:1–34 THE DAY OF ATONEMENT. This entire chapter describes the Day of Atonement. For comments on this important Jewish day and how the process of atonement points forward to Jesus Christ and the new covenant, see article on THE DAY OF ATONEMENT, p. 174.

sen by lot as the scapegoat shall be presented alive before the LORD to be used for making atonement[u] by sending it into the desert as a scapegoat.

[11]"Aaron shall bring the bull for his own sin offering to make atonement for himself and his household,[v] and he is to slaughter the bull for his own sin offering. [12]He is to take a censer full of burning coals[w] from the altar before the LORD and two handfuls of finely ground fragrant incense[x] and take them behind the curtain. [13]He is to put the incense on the fire before the LORD, and the smoke of the incense will conceal the atonement cover[y] above the Testimony, so that he will not die.[z] [14]He is to take some of the bull's blood[a] and with his finger sprinkle it on the front of the atonement cover; then he shall sprinkle some of it with his finger seven times before the atonement cover.[b]

[15]"He shall then slaughter the goat for the sin offering for the people[c] and take its blood behind the curtain[d] and do with it as he did with the bull's blood: He shall sprinkle[e] it on the atonement cover and in front of it. [16]In this way he will make atonement[f] for the Most Holy Place[g] because of the uncleanness and rebellion of the Israelites, whatever their sins have been. He is to do the same for the Tent of Meeting,[h] which is among them in the midst of their uncleanness. [17]No one is to be in the Tent of Meeting from the time Aaron goes in to make atonement in the Most Holy Place until he comes out, having made atonement for himself, his household and the whole community of Israel.

[18]"Then he shall come out to the altar[i] that is before the LORD and make atonement for it. He shall take some of the bull's blood and some of the goat's blood and put it on all the horns of the altar.[j] [19]He shall sprinkle some of the blood on it with his finger seven times to cleanse it and to consecrate it from the uncleanness of the Israelites.[k]

[20]"When Aaron has finished making atonement for the Most Holy Place, the Tent of Meeting and the altar, he shall bring forward the live goat.[l] [21]He is to lay both hands on the head of the live goat[m] and confess[n] over it all the wickedness and rebellion of the Israelites—all their sins—and put them on the goat's head. He shall send the goat away into the desert in the care of a man appointed for the task. [22]The goat will carry on itself all their sins[o] to a solitary place; and the man shall release it in the desert.

[23]"Then Aaron is to go into the Tent of Meeting and take off the linen garments[p] he put on before he entered the Most Holy Place, and he is to leave them there.[q] [24]He shall bathe himself with water in a holy place[r] and put on his regular garments.[s] Then he shall come out and sacrifice the burnt offering for himself and the burnt offering for the people,[t] to make atonement for himself and for the people.[u] [25]He shall also burn the fat of the sin offering on the altar.

[26]"The man who releases the goat as a scapegoat[v] must wash his clothes[w] and bathe himself with water;[x] afterward he may come into the camp. [27]The bull and the goat for the sin offerings, whose blood was brought into the Most Holy Place to make atonement, must be taken outside the camp;[y] their hides, flesh and offal are to be burned up. [28]The man who burns them must wash his clothes and bathe himself with water; afterward he may come into the camp.[z]

[29]"This is to be a lasting ordinance[a] for you: On the tenth day of the seventh month[b] you must deny yourselves[i][c] and not do any work[d]—whether native-born[e] or an alien living among you— [30]because on this day atonement will be made[f] for you, to cleanse you. Then, before the LORD, you will be clean from all your sins.[g] [31]It is a sabbath of rest, and you must deny yourselves;[h] it is a lasting ordinance.[i] [32]The priest who is anointed and ordained[j] to succeed his father as high priest is to make atonement. He is to put on the sacred linen garments[k] [33]and make atonement for the Most Holy Place, for the Tent of Meeting and the altar, and for the priests and all the people of the community.[l]

[34]"This is to be a lasting ordinance[m] for you: Atonement is to be made once a year[n] for all the sins of the Israelites."

And it was done, as the LORD commanded Moses.

Dt 26:6-9

16:10 [u] Isa 53:4-10; S Ro 3:25
16:11 [v] S ver 6, 24,33
16:12 [w] S Lev 10:1; Rev 8:5 [x] S Ex 25:6; 30:34-38
16:13 [y] S Ex 25:17 [z] S Ex 28:43
16:14 [a] S Lev 4:5; Heb 9:7,13,25 [b] S Lev 4:6
16:15 [c] S Lev 4:13-21; Heb 7:27; 9:7,12; 13:11 [d] Heb 9:3 [e] S Lev 4:17; Nu 19:19; Isa 52:15; Eze 36:25
16:16 [f] S Ex 29:36; S Ro 3:25 [g] S Ex 26:33; Heb 9:25 [h] Ex 29:4; S 40:2
16:18 [i] S Lev 4:7 [j] S Lev 4:25
16:19 [k] Eze 43:20
16:20 [l] S ver 5
16:21 [m] S Ex 29:10 [n] S Lev 5:5
16:22 [o] S Ex 28:38; Isa 53:12
16:23 [p] S Ex 28:42 [q] Eze 42:14
16:24 [r] S Lev 6:16 [s] ver 3-5 [t] Lev 1:3 [u] S ver 11
16:26 [v] S ver 8 [w] S Lev 11:25 [x] Lev 14:8
16:27 [y] S Ex 29:14
16:28 [z] Nu 19:8, 10
16:29 [a] S Ex 12:14 [b] Lev 25:9 [c] ver 31; Lev 23:27,32; Nu 29:7; Isa 58:3 [d] S Ex 31:15; S Lev 23:28 [e] Ex 12:19
16:30 [f] S Ex 30:10 [g] Ps 51:2; Jer 33:8; Eze 36:33; Zec 13:1; Eph 5:26
16:31 [h] Ezr 8:21; Isa 58:3,5; Da 10:12 [i] Ac 27:9
16:32 [j] S Ex 30:30 [k] S ver 4; S Ex 28:2
16:33 [l] S ver 11, 16-18; Eze 45:18
16:34 [m] S Ex 27:21 [n] Heb 9:7,25

i *29* Or *must fast*; also in verse 31

THE DAY OF ATONEMENT

Lev 16:32–33 "He is to . . . make atonement for the Most Holy Place, for the Tent of Meeting and the altar, and for the priests and all the people of the community."

THE NEED FOR ATONEMENT. The word "atonement" (Heb *kippurim*, from *kaphar*, meaning "to cover over") has the idea of covering over sin by making an equivalent payment (i.e., a "ransom"), so that adequate recompense is made for the offense (note the "ransom" principle in Ex 30:12; Nu 35:31; Ps 49:7; Isa 43:3).

(1) The need for atonement arose from the fact that Israel's sins (Lev 16:30), if not atoned for, would subject them to God's wrath (cf. Ro 1:18; Col 3:5; 1Th 2:16). Thus the purpose of the Day of Atonement was to provide a comprehensive sacrifice for all sins that may not have been atoned for in the sacrifices offered throughout the preceding year. Thereby the people would be cleansed from their sins of the past year, avert God's wrath toward them, and maintain God's fellowship with them (Lev 16:30–34; Heb 9:7).

(2) Because God desired to save the Israelites, forgive their sins and reconcile them to himself, he furnished a way of salvation by accepting in their place the death of an innocent life (i.e., the animal that was sacrificed); this animal bore their guilt and penalty (Lev 17:11; cf. Isa 53:4,6,11) and covered over their sins by its shed blood.

THE RITUAL OF THE DAY OF ATONEMENT. Lev 16 describes the Day of Atonement, the most important holy day of the Jewish year. On this day the high priest, clad in sacred garments, first prepared himself by bathing himself with water. Then, before making atonement for the sins of the people, he had to offer a bull for his own sins. Next he took two goats and cast lots: one became the sacrifice, the other became the scapegoat (Lev 16:8). He killed the first goat, took its blood, entered the Most Holy Place behind the curtain, and sprinkled the blood on the atonement cover, placing the blood between God and the tablets of the Law that were inside the ark (laws they had broken but that were now covered by the blood), thus making atonement for the sins of the entire nation (Lev 16:15–16). As a final step he took the live goat, laid his hands on its head, confessed over it all the unforgiven sins of the Israelites, and sent it away into the desert, symbolizing that their sins were being carried out of the camp to disappear in the desert (Lev 16:21–22).

(1) The Day of Atonement was to be a solemn assembly, a day in which the people fasted and humbled themselves before the Lord (Lev 16:31); this response emphasized sin's seriousness and the fact that God's atoning work was effective only for those who had a repentant heart and a persevering faith (cf. Lev 23:27; Nu 15:30; 29:7).

(2) The Day of Atonement accomplished atonement for all sins and transgressions not atoned for during the previous year (Lev 16:16,21). It had to be repeated every year in the same manner.

CHRIST AND THE DAY OF ATONEMENT. The Day of Atonement is replete with symbolism pointing to the work of our Lord and Savior Jesus Christ. In the NT, the author of Hebrews emphasizes the new covenant fulfillment of the typology of the Day of Atonement ritual (see Heb 9:6—10:18; see article on CHRIST IN THE OLD TESTAMENT, p. 518).

(1) The fact that the OT sacrificial rituals had to be repeated annually indicates that there was something temporary about them. They pointed ahead to the time when Christ would come to take away permanently all confessed sin (cf. Heb 9:28; 10:10–18).

(2) The two goats represent the atonement, forgiveness, reconciliation and cleansing accomplished by Christ. The slain goat represents his substitutionary and sacrificial death for sinners as payment for sins (Ro 3:24–26; Heb 9:11–12,24–26). The scapegoat, sent away bearing the sins of the nation, typifies Christ's sacrifice, which removes sin and guilt from all who repent (Ps 103:12; Isa 53:6,11–12; Jn 1:29; Heb 9:26).

(3) The sacrifices on the Day of Atonement provided a "covering over" of sin, *not* a taking away of sin. Christ's blood shed on the cross, however, is God's ultimate atonement for humankind, which takes away sin permanently (cf. Heb 10:4,10–11). Christ as the perfect sacrifice (Heb 9:26; 10:5–10) paid the full penalty for our sins (Ro 3:25–26; 6:23; Gal 3:13; 2Co 5:21) and effected the atoning sacrifice that turns aside God's wrath, reconciles us to him and renews our fellowship with him (Ro 5:6–11; 2Co 5:18–19; 1Pe 1:18–19; 1Jn 2:2).

(4) The Most Holy Place where the high priest entered with the blood to make atonement represents God's throne in heaven; Christ entered this heavenly "Most Holy Place" after his death, bearing his own blood to make atonement for the believer before God's throne (Ex 30:10; Heb 9:7–8,11–12,24–28).

(5) Since animal sacrifices were a type of Christ's perfect sacrifice for sin and found their fulfillment in Christ's sacrifice of himself, there is no more need for animal sacrifices after his death on the cross (Heb 9:12–18).

Eating Blood Forbidden

17 The LORD said to Moses,
2 "Speak to Aaron and his
sons[o] and to all the Israelites and say
to them: 'This is what the LORD has
commanded: 3 Any Israelite who sacrifices an ox,[j] a lamb[p] or a goat[q] in
the camp or outside of it 4 instead of
bringing it to the entrance to the Tent
of Meeting[r] to present it as an offering to the LORD in front of the tabernacle of the LORD[s]—that man shall be
considered guilty of bloodshed; he has
shed blood and must be cut off from his
people.[t] 5 This is so the Israelites will
bring to the LORD the sacrifices they are
now making in the open fields. They
must bring them to the priest, that is,
to the LORD, at the entrance to the Tent
of Meeting and sacrifice them as fellowship offerings.[k u] 6 The priest is to
sprinkle the blood against the altar[v]
of the LORD[w] at the entrance to the
Tent of Meeting and burn the fat as an
aroma pleasing to the LORD.[x] 7 They
must no longer offer any of their sacrifices to the goat idols[l y] to whom they
prostitute themselves.[z] This is to be
a lasting ordinance[a] for them and for
the generations to come.'[b]

8 "Say to them: 'Any Israelite or any
alien living among them who offers a
burnt offering or sacrifice 9 and does
not bring it to the entrance to the
Tent[c] of Meeting[d] to sacrifice it to
the LORD[e]—that man must be cut off
from his people.

10 " 'Any Israelite or any alien living
among them who eats any blood—I
will set my face against that person
who eats blood[f] and will cut him off
from his people. 11 For the life of a creature is in the blood,[g] and I have given
it to you to make atonement for yourselves on the altar; it is the blood that
makes atonement for one's life.[h]
12 Therefore I say to the Israelites,
"None of you may eat blood, nor may an
alien living among you eat blood."

13 " 'Any Israelite or any alien living
among you who hunts any animal or
bird that may be eaten must drain out
the blood and cover it with earth,[i]
14 because the life of every creature is
its blood. That is why I have said to the
Israelites, "You must not eat the blood
of any creature, because the life of every creature is its blood; anyone who
eats it must be cut off."[j]

15 " 'Anyone, whether native-born or
alien, who eats anything[k] found dead
or torn by wild animals[l] must wash
his clothes and bathe with water,[m]
and he will be ceremonially unclean till
evening;[n] then he will be clean. 16 But
if he does not wash his clothes and
bathe himself, he will be held responsible.[o]' "

Unlawful Sexual Relations

18 The LORD said to Moses,
2 "Speak to the Israelites and
say to them: 'I am the LORD your God.[p]
3 You must not do as they do in Egypt,
where you used to live, and you must
not do as they do in the land of Canaan,
where I am bringing you. Do not follow
their practices.[q] 4 You must obey my
laws[r] and be careful to follow my decrees.[s] I am the LORD your God.[t]
5 Keep my decrees and laws,[u] for the

17:2 [o] Lev 10:6, 12
17:3 [p] S Lev 3:7 [q] S Lev 7:23
17:4 [r] ver 9; 1Ki 8:4; 2Ch 1:3 [s] Dt 12:5-21 [t] S Ge 17:14
17:5 [u] S Lev 3:1; Eze 43:27
17:6 [v] S Lev 4:18 [w] S Lev 3:2 [x] S Lev 1:9
17:7 [y] S Ex 22:20 [z] S Ex 34:15; Jer 3:6,9; Eze 23:3; 1Co 10:20 [a] S Ex 12:14 [b] S Ge 9:12
17:9 [c] S Lev 1:3 [d] S ver 4 [e] S Lev 3:7
17:10 [f] S Ge 9:4
17:11 [g] ver 14 [h] Heb 9:22
17:13 [i] Lev 7:26; Eze 24:7; 33:25; Ac 15:20
17:14 [j] S Ge 9:4
17:15 [k] S Lev 7:24 [l] S Ex 22:31 [m] S Lev 14:8 [n] S Lev 11:40
17:16 [o] S Lev 5:1
18:2 [p] S Ge 17:7
18:3 [q] ver 24-30; S Ex 23:24; Dt 18:9; 2Ki 16:3; 17:8; 1Ch 5:25
18:4 [r] S Ge 26:5 [s] Dt 4:1; 1Ki 11:11; Jer 44:10,23; Eze 11:12 [t] ver 2
18:5 [u] S Ge 26:5

j3 The Hebrew word can include both male and female. k5 Traditionally *peace offerings* l7 Or *demons*

17:7 THE GOAT IDOLS. "Goat idols" literally means "hairy ones." Evidently during the time of Moses, Israel offered sacrifices to desert demons in order to gain their help or their favor. This kind of action represented spiritual unfaithfulness to the Lord God and was strictly forbidden.

17:11 LIFE OF A CREATURE IS IN THE BLOOD. This passage gives the reason for shedding the blood of a sacrificial animal, and its meaning for atonement. The blood of the animal was identified with its life (v. 14); thus the blood atoned for human sin at the price of life. In other words, human beings did not have to give their lives, because the animal's life was payment in their place (see article on THE DAY OF ATONEMENT, p. 174). This principle of substitutionary atonement by the blood of another helps us understand the importance of Christ's blood in receiving salvation under the new covenant. As Jesus Christ shed his blood on the cross, he substituted his life for the sinner's life (Ro 5:1). Because his life was without sin and perfect before God, his blood is of infinite worth and results in perfect salvation for all who accept and follow him (cf. Col 1:14; Heb 9:13–14; 1Jn 1:7; Rev 7:14).

18:3 MUST NOT DO AS THEY DO. God's people have always been tempted to accept the practices and standards of morality of the society to which they belong. Therefore, God commands his people to make his laws the only standard by which to judge right and wrong. We must never conform to the surrounding society and accept its way of life. God must be the sole source and standard for all human moral or spiritual conduct (see article on SPIRITUAL SEPARATION FOR BELIEVERS, p. 1794).

man who obeys them will live by
them.[v] I am the LORD.
6"'No one is to approach any close
relative to have sexual relations. I am
the LORD.
7"'Do not dishonor your father[w] by
having sexual relations with your
mother.[x] She is your mother; do not
have relations with her.
8"'Do not have sexual relations with
your father's wife;[y] that would dishonor your father.[z]
9"'Do not have sexual relations with
your sister,[a] either your father's
daughter or your mother's daughter,
whether she was born in the same
home or elsewhere.[b]
10"'Do not have sexual relations
with your son's daughter or your
daughter's daughter; that would dishonor you.
11"'Do not have sexual relations
with the daughter of your father's wife,
born to your father; she is your sister.
12"'Do not have sexual relations
with your father's sister;[c] she is your
father's close relative.
13"'Do not have sexual relations
with your mother's sister,[d] because
she is your mother's close relative.
14"'Do not dishonor your father's
brother by approaching his wife to
have sexual relations; she is your
aunt.[e]
15"'Do not have sexual relations
with your daughter-in-law.[f] She is
your son's wife; do not have relations
with her.[g]
16"'Do not have sexual relations
with your brother's wife;[h] that would
dishonor your brother.
17"'Do not have sexual relations
with both a woman and her daughter.[i]
Do not have sexual relations with either her son's daughter or her daughter's daughter; they are her close relatives. That is wickedness.

18:5 [v] Dt 4:1; Ne 9:29; Isa 55:3; Eze 18:9; 20:11; Am 5:4-6; Mt 19:17; S Ro 10:5*; Gal 3:12* **18:7** [w] ver 8; Lev 20:11; Dt 27:20 [x] Eze 22:10 **18:8** [y] 1Co 5:1 [z] Ge 35:22; Lev 20:11; Dt 22:30; 27:20 **18:9** [a] ver 11; Lev 20:17; Dt 27:22 [b] Lev 20:17; Dt 27:22; 2Sa 13:13; Eze 22:11 **18:12** [c] ver 13; Lev 20:19 **18:13** [d] S ver 12, 14; Lev 20:20 **18:14** [e] S ver 13 **18:15** [f] S Ge 11:31; S 38:16 [g] Eze 22:11 **18:16** [h] Lev 20:21; Mt 14:4; Mk 6:18 **18:17** [i] Lev 20:14; Dt 27:23

18:18 [j] S Ge 30:1 **18:19** [k] S Lev 15:25-30 [l] S Lev 15:24 **18:20** [m] S Ex 20:14; Mt 5:27,28; 1Co 6:9; Heb 13:4 **18:21** [n] Dt 12:31; 18:10; 2Ki 16:3; 17:17; 21:6; 23:10; 2Ch 28:1-4; 33:6; Ps 106:37, 38; Isa 57:5; Jer 7:30,31; 19:5; 32:35; Eze 16:20; Mic 6:7 [o] Lev 20:2-5; Dt 9:4; 1Ki 11:5,7, 33; Isa 57:9; Jer 32:35; 49:1; Zep 1:5 [p] Lev 19:12; 21:6; Isa 48:11; Eze 22:26; 36:20; Am 2:7; Mal 1:12 [q] S Ex 6:2 **18:22** [r] Lev 20:13; Dt 23:18; Ro 1:27; 1Co 6:9 [s] S Ge 19:5 **18:23** [t] Ex 22:19; Lev 20:15; Dt 27:21

18"'Do not take your wife's sister[j]
as a rival wife and have sexual
relations with her while your wife is
living.
19"'Do not approach a woman to
have sexual relations during the uncleanness[k] of her monthly period.[l]
20"'Do not have sexual relations
with your neighbor's wife[m] and defile
yourself with her.
21"'Do not give any of your children[n] to be sacrificed[m] to Molech,[o]
for you must not profane the name of
your God.[p] I am the LORD.[q]
22"'Do not lie with a man as one lies
with a woman;[r] that is detestable.[s]
23"'Do not have sexual relations
with an animal and defile yourself with
it. A woman must not present herself
to an animal to have sexual relations
with it; that is a perversion.[t]
24"'Do not defile yourselves in any
of these ways, because this is how the
nations that I am going to drive out before you[u] became defiled.[v] **25**Even
the land was defiled;[w] so I punished it
for its sin,[x] and the land vomited out
its inhabitants.[y] **26**But you must keep
my decrees and my laws.[z] The native-
born and the aliens living among you
must not do any of these detestable
things, **27**for all these things were done
by the people who lived in the land before you, and the land became defiled.
28And if you defile the land,[a] it will
vomit you out[b] as it vomited out the
nations that were before you.
29"'Everyone who does any of these
detestable things—such persons must
be cut off from their people. **30**Keep my
requirements[c] and do not follow any

18:24 [u] ver 3,27,30; Lev 20:23 [v] Dt 9:4; 18:12 **18:25** [w] Nu 35:34; Dt 21:23 [x] Lev 20:23; Dt 9:5; 12:31; 18:12 [y] ver 28; Lev 20:22; Job 20:15; Jer 51:34 **18:26** [z] S Ge 26:5 **18:28** [a] Lev 20:22; Ezr 9:11; La 1:17 [b] S ver 25 **18:30** [c] S Lev 8:35

[m] 21 Or *to be passed through* ⌊*the fire*⌋

18:6 HAVE SEXUAL RELATIONS. The translation "have sexual relations with" is from a Hebrew phrase that literally means "uncover the nakedness of"; it involves the entire realm of impure sexual activity and play, including acts that fall short of sexual intercourse. Thus, any kind of sexual activity involving the uncovering of the nakedness of another person who is not a lawful wife or husband oversteps God's boundaries of purity and is serious sin against him and his law (see article on STANDARDS OF SEXUAL MORALITY, p. 1936).

18:21 SACRIFICED TO MOLECH. The Canaanites sacrificed infants to their gods as part of their religious rites. This detestable practice was strictly forbidden by God (cf. 20:2–5; Jer 32:35). Today the practice of killing unborn children for the sake of convenience or as a form of birth control is an equally detestable sin and an abomination to God.

18:22 THAT IS DETESTABLE. Sexual activity with a person of the same sex (i.e., sodomy; see Ge 19:5, note) is said to be an abomination to the Lord; this act is especially repugnant to him (see Ro 1:27, note).

of the detestable customs that were
practiced before you came and do not
defile yourselves with them. I am the
LORD your God.[d]' "

Various Laws

19 The LORD said to Moses,
2"Speak to the entire assembly
of Israel[e] and say to them: 'Be holy
because I, the LORD your God,[f] am
holy.[g]
3" 'Each of you must respect his
mother and father,[h] and you must observe my Sabbaths.[i] I am the LORD
your God.[j]
4" 'Do not turn to idols or make gods
of cast metal for yourselves.[k] I am the
LORD your God.[l]
5" 'When you sacrifice a fellowship
offering[n] to the LORD, sacrifice it in
such a way that it will be accepted on
your behalf. 6It shall be eaten on the
day you sacrifice it or on the next day;
anything left over until the third day
must be burned up.[m] 7If any of it is
eaten on the third day, it is impure and
will not be accepted.[n] 8Whoever eats
it will be held responsible[o] because he
has desecrated what is holy[p] to the
LORD; that person must be cut off from
his people.[q]
9" 'When you reap the harvest of
your land, do not reap to the very
edges[r] of your field or gather the
gleanings of your harvest.[s] 10Do not
go over your vineyard a second time[t]
or pick up the grapes that have fall-
en.[u] Leave them for the poor and the
alien.[v] I am the LORD your God.
11" 'Do not steal.[w]
" 'Do not lie.[x]
" 'Do not deceive one another.[y]
12" 'Do not swear falsely[z] by my
name[a] and so profane[b] the name of
your God. I am the LORD.
13" 'Do not defraud your neighbor[c]
or rob[d] him.[e]
" 'Do not hold back the wages of a
hired man[f] overnight.[g]
14" 'Do not curse the deaf or put a
stumbling block in front of the blind,[h]
but fear your God.[i] I am the LORD.
15" 'Do not pervert justice;[j] do not
show partiality[k] to the poor or favoritism to the great,[l] but judge your
neighbor fairly.[m]
16" 'Do not go about spreading slander[n] among your people.
" 'Do not do anything that endan-
gers your neighbor's life.[o] I am the
LORD.
17" 'Do not hate your brother in your
heart.[p] Rebuke your neighbor frankly[q] so you will not share in his guilt.
18" 'Do not seek revenge[r] or bear a
grudge[s] against one of your people,[t]
but love your neighbor[u] as yourself.[v]
I am the LORD.
19" 'Keep my decrees.[w]
" 'Do not mate different kinds of animals.
" 'Do not plant your field with two
kinds of seed.[x]
" 'Do not wear clothing woven of two
kinds of material.[y]
20" 'If a man sleeps with a woman
who is a slave girl promised to another
man[z] but who has not been ransomed

18:30 [d]ver 2 **19:2** [e]Nu 14:5; Ps 68:26 [f]S Ex 20:2 [g]S Ex 15:11; 1Pe 1:16*; S Lev 11:44; S 20:26 **19:3** [h]Ex 20:12 [i]S Ex 20:8 [j]Lev 11:44 **19:4** [k]S Ex 20:4; Jdg 17:3; Ps 96:5; 115:4-7; 135:15 [l]Lev 11:44 **19:6** [m]Lev 7:16-17 **19:7** [n]Lev 7:18 **19:8** [o]S Lev 5:1 [p]Lev 22:2,15,16; Nu 18:32 [q]S Ge 17:14 **19:9** [r]Ru 2:2,3,7, 16,17 [s]Lev 23:10, 22; Dt 24:19-22; Job 24:10 **19:10** [t]Dt 24:20 [u]ver 9 [v]Dt 24:19, 21 **19:11** [w]Ex 20:15; S 23:4; Lk 3:14 [x]S Ex 20:16; S Eph 4:25 [y]S Lev 6:2 **19:12** [z]Jer 5:2; 7:9; Mal 3:5 [a]Ex 3:13; 20:7; Dt 18:19; Pr 18:10; Isa 42:8; Jer 44:16,26; S Mt 5:33 [b]Jer 34:16 **19:13** [c]Lev 25:14,17 [d]S Ex 20:15 [e]S Ex 22:15,25-27 [f]Job 7:2; 24:12; 31:39; Isa 16:14; Mal 3:5 [g]Dt 24:15; Jer 22:13; Mt 20:8; 1Ti 5:18; Jas 5:4 **19:14** [h]S Ex 4:11; Lev 21:18; Dt 27:18 [i]ver 32; Lev 25:17,36 **19:15** [j]S Ex 23:2; Ex 23:2,6 [k]Dt 24:17; Job 13:8,10; 32:21; Pr 28:21 [l]Job 34:19 [m]S Ex 23:8; Pr 24:23; Mal 2:9; Jas 2:1-4 **19:16** [n]Ps 15:3; 31:13; 41:6; 101:5; Jer 6:28; 9:4; Eze 22:9 [o]Ex 23:7; Dt 10:17; 27:25; Ps 15:5; Eze 22:12 **19:17** [p]S 1Jn 2:9 [q]S Mt 18:15 **19:18** [r]S Ge 4:23; Ro 12:19; Heb 10:30 [s]Ps 103:9 [t]S Ex 12:48 [u]S Ex 20:16 [v]ver 34; S Mt 5:43*; 19:16*; 22:39*; Mk 12:31*; Lk 10:27*; Jn 13:34; Ro 13:9*; Gal 5:14*; Jas 2:8* **19:19** [w]S Ge 26:5 [x]Dt 22:9 [y]Dt 22:11 **19:20** [z]Dt 22:23-27

[n]5 Traditionally *peace offering*

19:2 BE HOLY. Because God's people must be like him, he calls them to express his divine nature by being separate from the ungodly customs and sins of the surrounding nations and by serving him in love and righteousness (see 11:44, note). This call to holiness was first given to Adam and Eve, who were created in God's image in order to reflect God's character (Ge 1:26). Every generation of believers should "be imitators of God" (Eph 5:1) and "be holy because I, the LORD your God, am holy" (cf. Mt 5:48; Ro 12:1–2; see articles on SANCTIFICATION, p. 1956, and SPIRITUAL SEPARATION FOR BELIEVERS, p. 1794).

19:18 LOVE YOUR NEIGHBOR. "Neighbor" refers to anyone we come into contact with, not just someone who lives near us. This commandment regulating Israel's treatment of others was cited by Christ (Mt 22:39), Paul (Ro 13:9) and James (Jas 2:8). Vv. 9–18 describe practical ways for us to show love and care for our neighbors.

19:19 TWO KINDS OF MATERIAL. Some of the laws in Leviticus applied only to Israel under the old covenant (e.g., vv. 19–25), while others are still applicable for those under the new covenant (e.g., vv. 11–18,26,31; see Mt 5:17, note). Regarding the former, some were given in order to keep the Israelites from participating in the pagan practices of their surrounding cultures. For example, the prohibition regarding the mixing of two kinds of material may have been based on the fact that pagan priests attempted to practice sorcery by mixing different types of fabrics into their garments. The verse as a whole addresses the principle of purity without mixture.

or given her freedom, there must be
due punishment. Yet they are not to be
put to death, because she had not been
freed. 21 The man, however, must bring
a ram to the entrance to the Tent of
Meeting for a guilt offering to the
LORD.[a] 22 With the ram of the guilt offering the priest is to make atonement
for him before the LORD for the sin he
has committed, and his sin will be forgiven.[b]
23 " 'When you enter the land and
plant any kind of fruit tree, regard its
fruit as forbidden.[o] For three years
you are to consider it forbidden[o]; it
must not be eaten. 24 In the fourth year
all its fruit will be holy,[c] an offering of
praise to the LORD. 25 But in the fifth
year you may eat its fruit. In this way
your harvest will be increased. I am the
LORD your God.
26 " 'Do not eat any meat with the
blood still in it.[d]
" 'Do not practice divination[e] or
sorcery.[f]
27 " 'Do not cut the hair at the sides
of your head or clip off the edges of
your beard.[g]
28 " 'Do not cut[h] your bodies for the
dead or put tattoo marks on yourselves. I am the LORD.
29 " 'Do not degrade your daughter
by making her a prostitute,[i] or the
land will turn to prostitution and be
filled with wickedness.[j]
30 " 'Observe my Sabbaths[k] and
have reverence for my sanctuary. I am
the LORD.[l]
31 " 'Do not turn to mediums[m] or
seek out spiritists,[n] for you will be defiled by them. I am the LORD your God.
32 " 'Rise in the presence of the aged,
show respect[o] for the elderly[p] and
revere your God.[q] I am the LORD.[r]
33 " 'When an alien lives with you in
your land, do not mistreat him. 34 The
alien living with you must be treated as
one of your native-born.[s] Love him as
yourself,[t] for you were aliens[u] in
Egypt.[v] I am the LORD your God.
35 " 'Do not use dishonest standards
when measuring length, weight or
quantity.[w] 36 Use honest scales[x] and
honest weights, an honest ephah[p][y]
and an honest hin.[q][z] I am the LORD
your God, who brought you out of
Egypt.[a]
37 " 'Keep all my decrees[b] and all
my laws[c] and follow them. I am the
LORD.' "

Punishments for Sin

20 The LORD said to Moses, 2 "Say
to the Israelites: 'Any Israelite
or any alien living in Israel who gives[r]
any of his children to Molech must be
put to death.[d] The people of the community are to stone him.[e] 3 I will set
my face against that man and I will cut
him off from his people;[f] for by giving
his children to Molech, he has defiled[g]
my sanctuary[h] and profaned my holy
name.[i] 4 If the people of the community close their eyes when that man gives
one of his children to Molech and they
fail to put him to death,[j] 5 I will set my
face against that man and his family
and will cut off from their people both
him and all who follow him in prostitut-
ing themselves to Molech.
6 " 'I will set my face against the person who turns to mediums and spiritists to prostitute himself by following
them, and I will cut him off from his
people.[k]
7 " 'Consecrate yourselves[l] and be
holy,[m] because I am the LORD your
God.[n] 8 Keep my decrees[o] and follow
them. I am the LORD, who makes you
holy.[s][p]
9 " 'If anyone curses his father[q] or
mother,[r] he must be put to death.[s]
He has cursed his father or his mother,

19:21 [a]S Lev 5:15 **19:22** [b]S Lev 5:15 **19:24** [c]S Ex 22:29 **19:26** [d]S Ge 9:4 [e]S Ge 30:27; S Isa 44:25 [f]S Ex 22:18; 2Ki 17:17 **19:27** [g]Lev 21:5; Dt 14:1; 2Sa 10:4-5; Jer 41:5; 48:37; Eze 5:1-5 **19:28** [h]Lev 21:5; Dt 14:1; 1Ki 18:28; Jer 16:6; 41:5; 47:5 **19:29** [i]Lev 21:9; Dt 23:18 [j]Ge 34:7; Lev 21:9 **19:30** [k]S Ex 20:8 [l]Lev 26:2 **19:31** [m]S Ex 22:18; 1Sa 28:7-20; 1Ch 10:13 [n]Lev 20:6; 2Ki 21:6; 23:24; Isa 8:19; 19:3; 29:4; 47:12; 65:4 **19:32** [o]1Ki 12:8 [p]Job 32:4; Pr 23:22; La 5:12; 1Ti 5:1 [q]S ver 14; Job 29:8 [r]Lev 11:44; 25:17 **19:34** [s]S Ex 12:48 [t]S ver 18 [u]S Ex 22:21 [v]Ex 23:9; Dt 10:19; 23:7; Ps 146:9 **19:35** [w]Dt 25:13-16 **19:36** [x]Job 31:6; Pr 11:1; Hos 12:7; Mic 6:11 [y]Jdg 6:19; Ru 2:17; 1Sa 1:24; 17:17; Eze 45:10 [z]Dt 25:13-15; Pr 20:10; Eze 45:11 [a]S Ex 12:17 **19:37** [b]2Ki 17:37; 2Ch 7:17; Ps 119:5; Eze 18:9 [c]S Ge 26:5 **20:2** [d]ver 10; Ge 26:11; Ex 19:12 [e]ver 27; Lev 24:14; Nu 15:35,36; Dt 21:21; Jos 7:25 **20:3** [f]ver 5,6; Lev 23:30 [g]Ps 74:7; 79:1; Jer 7:30; Eze 5:11 [h]S Lev 15:31 [i]S Lev 18:21 **20:4** [j]Dt 17:2-5 **20:6** [k]S ver 3; S Lev 19:31 **20:7** [l]S Lev 11:44 [m]S Ex 29:1; 31:13; Lev 11:45; Eph 1:4; 1Pe 1:16* [n]S Ex 6:2; S 20:2 **20:8** [o]S Ge 26:5 [p]S Ex 31:13; Eze 20:12 **20:9** [q]Ex 20:12; Jer 35:16; Mal 1:6; 2:10 [r]S Ex 20:12; Dt 27:16; Eze 22:7 [s]Ex 21:17; Dt 21:20-21; Mt 15:4*; Mk 7:10*

[o] *23* Hebrew *uncircumcised* [p] *36* An ephah was a dry measure. [q] *36* A hin was a liquid measure. [r] *2* Or *sacrifices*; also in verses 3 and 4 [s] *8* Or *who sanctifies you*; or *who sets you apart as holy*

19:31 MEDIUMS OR . . . SPIRITISTS. Mediums and spiritists were those who sought to contact the dead for the purpose of obtaining prophetic knowledge. Anyone who transgresses God's commands by turning to spiritists is in reality dealing with Satan and demons (20:6; Dt 18:10–11).

19:34 LOVE HIM AS YOURSELF. Loving one's neighbor includes loving foreigners and resident aliens who come to live in one's community. Jesus emphasizes the same thing in the parable of the Good Samaritan (Lk 10:25–37). God himself loved his people while they were aliens, and he expects us to do the same. He is the kind of God who wants to bless all the nations of the world (Ge 12:3; Jn 3:16).

and his blood will be on his own
head.[t]
10" 'If a man commits adultery with
another man's wife[u]—with the wife
of his neighbor—both the adulterer
and the adulteress must be put to
death.[v]
11" 'If a man sleeps with his father's
wife, he has dishonored his father.[w]
Both the man and the woman must be
put to death; their blood will be on their
own heads.[x]
12" 'If a man sleeps with his daughter-in-law,[y] both of them must be put
to death. What they have done is a perversion; their blood will be on their
own heads.
13" 'If a man lies with a man as one
lies with a woman, both of them have
done what is detestable.[z] They must
be put to death; their blood will be on
their own heads.
14" 'If a man marries both a woman
and her mother,[a] it is wicked. Both he
and they must be burned in the fire,[b]
so that no wickedness will be among
you.[c]
15" 'If a man has sexual relations
with an animal,[d] he must be put to
death,[e] and you must kill the animal.
16" 'If a woman approaches an animal to have sexual relations with it,
kill both the woman and the animal.
They must be put to death; their blood
will be on their own heads.
17" 'If a man marries his sister[f],
the daughter of either his father or his
mother, and they have sexual relations, it is a disgrace. They must be cut
off before the eyes[g] of their people. He
has dishonored his sister and will be
held responsible.[h]
18" 'If a man lies with a woman during her monthly period[i] and has sexual relations with her, he has exposed
the source of her flow, and she has also
uncovered it. Both of them must be cut
off from their people.[j]
19" 'Do not have sexual relations
with the sister of either your mother or
your father,[k] for that would dishonor
a close relative; both of you would be
held responsible.
20" 'If a man sleeps with his aunt,[l]
he has dishonored his uncle. They will

20:9 [t]ver 11; Dt 22:30; Jos 2:19; 2Sa 1:16; 3:29; 1Ki 2:37; Eze 18:13; 33:4,5
20:10 [u]Ex 20:14; Dt 5:18; 22:22; Jn 8:5 [v]S Ge 38:24; S Ex 21:12
20:11 [w]S Lev 18:7 [x]S ver 9; S Lev 18:8
20:12 [y]S Ge 11:31; S 38:16
20:13 [z]Lev 18:22
20:14 [a]S Lev 18:17 [b]Lev 21:9; Nu 16:39; Jdg 14:15; 15:6 [c]S Lev 18:8; Dt 27:23
20:15 [d]S Ex 22:19 [e]ver 10
20:17 [f]S Lev 18:9 [g]S Ge 17:14 [h]S Lev 5:1
20:18 [i]S Lev 15:24 [j]Eze 18:6
20:19 [k]S Lev 18:12
20:20 [l]S Lev 18:13
[m]ver 21; Ge 15:2
20:21 [n]S Lev 18:16; Mt 14:4; Mk 6:18 [o]S ver 20
20:22 [p]S Ge 26:5 [q]S Lev 18:25-28
20:23 [r]S Lev 18:3 [s]S Lev 18:24 [t]S Lev 18:25
20:24 [u]S Ex 3:8; Nu 14:8; 16:14 [v]S Ex 33:16
20:25 [w]Lev 10:10; Dt 14:3-21; Ac 10:14
20:26 [x]Dt 14:2 [y]ver 8; Lev 19:2; Jos 24:19; 2Ki 19:22; Ps 99:3 [z]S Ex 33:16
20:27 [a]S Ex 22:18 [b]S Lev 19:31 [c]S ver 2; S Lev 24:14
21:1 [d]S Ex 28:1; S Lev 1:5 [e]S Lev 5:3; S 13:3 [f]ver 11; Nu 5:2; 6:6; 19:11; 31:19
21:2 [g]ver 11
21:3 [h]Nu 6:6
21:5 [i]S Lev 13:40; Jer 7:29; 16:6

be held responsible; they will die childless.[m]
21" 'If a man marries his brother's
wife,[n] it is an act of impurity; he has
dishonored his brother. They will be
childless.[o]
22" 'Keep all my decrees and laws[p]
and follow them, so that the land[q]
where I am bringing you to live may not
vomit you out. **23**You must not live according to the customs of the nations[r]
I am going to drive out before you.[s]
Because they did all these things, I abhorred them.[t] **24**But I said to you,
"You will possess their land; I will give
it to you as an inheritance, a land flowing with milk and honey."[u] I am the
LORD your God, who has set you apart
from the nations.[v]
25" 'You must therefore make a distinction between clean and unclean animals and between unclean and clean
birds.[w] Do not defile yourselves by
any animal or bird or anything that
moves along the ground—those which
I have set apart as unclean for you.
26You are to be holy to me[t][x] because
I, the LORD, am holy,[y] and I have set
you apart from the nations[z] to be my
own.
27" 'A man or woman who is a medium[a] or spiritist among you must be
put to death.[b] You are to stone
them;[c] their blood will be on their own
heads.' "

Rules for Priests

21 The LORD said to Moses, "Speak
to the priests, the sons of Aaron,[d] and say to them: 'A priest must
not make himself ceremonially unclean[e] for any of his people who die,[f]
2except for a close relative, such as his
mother or father,[g] his son or daughter, his brother, **3**or an unmarried sister who is dependent on him since she
has no husband—for her he may make
himself unclean.[h] **4**He must not make
himself unclean for people related to
him by marriage,[u] and so defile himself.
5" 'Priests must not shave[i] their
heads or shave off the edges of their

[t]26 Or *be my holy ones* [u]4 Or *unclean as a leader among his people*

21:1 PRIESTS. Ch. 21 deals with the qualifications and high standards for those who were to serve as ministers of God's people. They were to be examples of godliness both in their ceremonial duties and in their personal character and deeds; consequently God placed on them a higher standard than was required for membership among God's covenant people.

beards[j] or cut their bodies.[k] 6They
must be holy to their God[l] and must
not profane the name of their God.[m]
Because they present the offerings
made to the LORD by fire,[n] the food of
their God,[o] they are to be holy.[p]
7" 'They must not marry women defiled by prostitution or divorced from
their husbands,[q] because priests are
holy to their God.[r] 8Regard them as
holy,[s] because they offer up the food
of your God.[t] Consider them holy, because I the LORD am holy—I who make
you holy.[v][u]
9" 'If a priest's daughter defiles herself by becoming a prostitute, she disgraces her father; she must be burned
in the fire.[v]
10" 'The high priest, the one among
his brothers who has had the anointing
oil poured on his head[w] and who has
been ordained to wear the priestly garments,[x] must not let his hair become
unkempt[w] or tear his clothes.[y] 11He
must not enter a place where there is
a dead body.[z] He must not make himself unclean,[a] even for his father or
mother,[b] 12nor leave the sanctuary[c]
of his God or desecrate it, because he
has been dedicated by the anointing
oil[d] of his God. I am the LORD.
13" 'The woman he marries must be
a virgin.[e] 14He must not marry a widow, a divorced woman, or a woman defiled by prostitution, but only a virgin
from his own people, 15so he will not
defile his offspring among his people.
I am the LORD, who makes him
holy.[x]' "
16The LORD said to Moses, 17"Say to
Aaron: 'For the generations to come
none of your descendants who has a
defect[f] may come near to offer the
food of his God.[g] 18No man who has
any defect[h] may come near: no man
who is blind[i] or lame,[j] disfigured or
deformed; 19no man with a crippled
foot or hand, 20or who is hunchbacked
or dwarfed, or who has any eye defect,
or who has festering or running sores
or damaged testicles.[k] 21No descendant of Aaron the priest who has any
defect[l] is to come near to present the
offerings made to the LORD by fire.[m] He
has a defect; he must not come near to
offer the food of his God.[n] 22He may
eat the most holy food of his God,[o] as
well as the holy food; 23yet because of
his defect,[p] he must not go near the
curtain or approach the altar, and so
desecrate my sanctuary.[q] I am the
LORD, who makes them holy.[y][r]' "
24So Moses told this to Aaron and
his sons and to all the Israelites.

22 The LORD said to Moses, 2"Tell
Aaron and his sons to treat
with respect the sacred offerings[s] the
Israelites consecrate to me, so they
will not profane my holy name.[t] I am
the LORD.[u]
3"Say to them: 'For the generations
to come, if any of your descendants is
ceremonially unclean and yet comes
near the sacred offerings that the Israelites consecrate to the LORD,[v] that

21:5 [j]Eze 5:1; 44:20 [k]S Lev 19:28
21:6 [l]ver 8; Ezr 8:28 [m]Lev 18:21 [n]S Lev 3:11 [o]ver 17,22; Lev 22:25 [p]S Ex 19:22; S Lev 10:3
21:7 [q]ver 13,14 [r]Eze 44:22
21:8 [s]ver 6 [t]Lev 3:11 [u]S Ex 31:13
21:9 [v]S Ge 38:24; S Lev 19:29
21:10 [w]S Ex 29:7 [x]S Lev 8:7-9,13; S 16:4 [y]S Lev 10:6
21:11 [z]Nu 5:2; 6:6; 9:6; 19:11,13, 14; 31:19 [a]Lev 19:28 [b]ver 2
21:12 [c]S Ex 25:8 [d]S Ex 28:41
21:13 [e]Eze 44:22
21:17 [f]ver 18,21, 23 [g]S ver 6
21:18 [h]Lev 22:19-25 [i]S Lev 19:14 [j]2Sa 4:4; 9:3; 19:26
21:20 [k]Lev 22:24; Dt 23:1; Isa 56:3
21:21 [l]S ver 17 [m]S Lev 3:11 [n]Lev 22:19
21:22 [o]1Co 9:13
21:23 [p]S ver 17 [q]S Ex 25:8 [r]Lev 20:8
22:2 [s]S Lev 19:8 [t]S Ex 20:7; S Mt 5:33 [u]Eze 44:8
22:3 [v]Ezr 8:28

[v]8 Or *who sanctify you*; or *who set you apart as holy* [w]10 Or *not uncover his head* [x]15 Or *who sanctifies him*; or *who sets him apart as holy* [y]23 Or *who sanctifies them*; or *who sets them apart as holy*

21:6 HOLY TO THEIR GOD. Priests were to be separated from all ungodly customs and to live blameless lives that conformed to God's will. Failure to do so would "profane the name of their God" (to "profane" means to desecrate the Lord's name and to deprive it of its holiness). This principle of holiness is continued in the new covenant, for God desires only those who live holy and righteous lives to be his chosen overseers (1Ti 3:1–7; see 4:12, note).

21:7 NOT MARRY WOMEN DEFILED BY PROSTITUTION. Priests were forbidden to marry women who had been immoral or even those who had been divorced. They were to marry only virgins or widows of priests (cf. vv. 13–15; Eze 44:22). Through this law God revealed that his spiritual leaders were expected to serve as examples of God's highest ideals for marriage and the family. In the NT God requires that a man must serve as a model of faithfulness to his wife and family in order to be chosen for the office of an overseer (see article on MORAL QUALIFICATIONS FOR OVERSEERS, p. 1882).

21:17 HAS A DEFECT. Physical defects disqualified Aaron's descendants from serving as priests and presenting offerings on behalf of the people (vv. 17–23). (1) Wholeness of body represented God's purpose that the priests were to serve as examples of the fullness of life as God intended; consequently they would be most effective in God's service when free from physical imperfections. However, those who were disqualified from serving as ministers of God could still eat the most holy food (v. 22), i.e., the full salvation provided by God's covenant. (2) God's requirement for a perfect body in the priesthood prefigures Christ's moral perfection (Heb 9:13–14) and hints at God's spiritual requirements for NT overseers. Any who serve in this capacity must be blameless and above reproach spiritually (see 1Ti 3:2, note; see article on MORAL QUALIFICATIONS FOR OVERSEERS, p. 1882).

person must be cut off from my presence.[w] I am the LORD.
4" 'If a descendant of Aaron has an
infectious skin disease[z] or a bodily
discharge,[x] he may not eat the sacred
offerings until he is cleansed. He will
also be unclean if he touches something defiled by a corpse[y] or by anyone who has an emission of semen, **5**or
if he touches any crawling thing[z] that
makes him unclean, or any person[a]
who makes him unclean, whatever the
uncleanness may be. **6**The one who
touches any such thing will be unclean[b] till evening.[c] He must not eat
any of the sacred offerings unless he
has bathed himself with water.[d]
7When the sun goes down, he will be
clean, and after that he may eat the
sacred offerings, for they are his
food.[e] **8**He must not eat anything
found dead[f] or torn by wild animals,[g]
and so become unclean[h] through it. I
am the LORD.[i]
9" 'The priests are to keep my requirements[j] so that they do not become guilty[k] and die[l] for treating
them with contempt. I am the LORD,
who makes them holy.[a m]
10" 'No one outside a priest's family
may eat the sacred offering, nor may
the guest of a priest or his hired worker
eat it.[n] **11**But if a priest buys a slave
with money, or if a slave is born in his
household, that slave may eat his
food.[o] **12**If a priest's daughter marries
anyone other than a priest, she may
not eat any of the sacred contributions.
13But if a priest's daughter becomes a
widow or is divorced, yet has no children, and she returns to live in her father's house as in her youth, she may
eat of her father's food. No unauthorized person, however, may eat any
of it.
14" 'If anyone eats a sacred offering
by mistake,[p] he must make restitution to the priest for the offering and
add a fifth of the value[q] to it. **15**The
priests must not desecrate the sacred
offerings[r] the Israelites present to
the LORD[s] **16**by allowing them to eat[t]
the sacred offerings and so bring upon
them guilt[u] requiring payment.[v] I am
the LORD, who makes them holy.[w]' "

Unacceptable Sacrifices

17The LORD said to Moses, **18**"Speak
to Aaron and his sons and to all the
Israelites and say to them: 'If any of
you—either an Israelite or an alien living in Israel[x]—presents a gift[y] for a
burnt offering to the LORD, either to fulfill a vow[z] or as a freewill offering,[a]
19you must present a male without defect[b] from the cattle, sheep or goats in
order that it may be accepted on your
behalf.[c] **20**Do not bring anything with
a defect,[d] because it will not be accepted on your behalf.[e] **21**When anyone brings from the herd or flock[f] a
fellowship offering[b g] to the LORD to
fulfill a special vow or as a freewill offering,[h] it must be without defect or
blemish[i] to be acceptable.[j] **22**Do not
offer to the LORD the blind, the injured
or the maimed, or anything with warts
or festering or running sores. Do not
place any of these on the altar as an
offering made to the LORD by fire. **23**You
may, however, present as a freewill offering an ox[c] or a sheep that is deformed or stunted, but it will not be accepted in fulfillment of a vow. **24**You
must not offer to the LORD an animal
whose testicles are bruised, crushed,
torn or cut.[k] You must not do this in
your own land, **25**and you must not accept such animals from the hand of a
foreigner and offer them as the food of
your God.[l] They will not be accepted
on your behalf, because they are deformed and have defects.[m]' "
26The LORD said to Moses, **27**"When
a calf, a lamb or a goat[n] is born, it is
to remain with its mother for seven
days.[o] From the eighth day[p] on, it
will be acceptable[q] as an offering
made to the LORD by fire. **28**Do not
slaughter a cow or a sheep and its
young on the same day.[r]
29"When you sacrifice a thank offering[s] to the LORD, sacrifice it in such a
way that it will be accepted on your behalf. **30**It must be eaten that same day;
leave none of it till morning.[t] I am the
LORD.[u]
31"Keep[v] my commands and follow
them.[w] I am the LORD. **32**Do not profane my holy name.[x] I must be acknowledged as holy by the Israelites.[y]
I am the LORD, who makes[d] you

22:3 [w] Lev 7:20, 21; Nu 19:13
22:4 [x] Lev 15:2-15 [y] Lev 11:24-28,39
22:5 [z] Lev 11:24-28,43 [a] S Lev 15:7
22:6 [b] Hag 2:13 [c] S Lev 11:24 [d] S Lev 14:8
22:7 [e] Nu 18:11
22:8 [f] S Lev 11:39 [g] S Ex 22:31 [h] S Lev 11:40 [i] Lev 11:44
22:9 [j] S Lev 8:35 [k] S Ex 28:38 [l] ver 16; S Ex 28:43 [m] Lev 20:8
22:10 [n] ver 13; Ex 12:45; 29:33
22:11 [o] Ge 17:13; Ex 12:44
22:14 [p] S Lev 4:2 [q] Lev 5:15
22:15 [r] S Lev 19:8 [s] Nu 18:32
22:16 [t] Nu 18:11 [u] S Ex 28:38 [v] S ver 9 [w] Lev 20:8
22:18 [x] Nu 15:16; 19:10; Jos 8:33 [y] S Lev 1:2 [z] ver 21; S Ge 28:20; Nu 15:8; Ps 22:25; 76:11; 116:18 [a] S Lev 7:16
22:19 [b] S Lev 1:3; 21:18-21; Nu 28:11; Dt 15:21 [c] S Lev 1:2
22:20 [d] S Lev 1:3; Dt 15:21; 17:1; Eze 43:23; 45:18; 46:6; Mal 1:8; Heb 9:14; 1Pe 1:19 [e] S Ex 28:38
22:21 [f] S Lev 1:2 [g] S Ex 32:6; S Lev 3:6 [h] S Lev 7:16 [i] S Ex 12:5; Mal 1:14 [j] Am 4:5
22:24 [k] S Lev 21:20
22:25 [l] S Lev 21:6 [m] S Lev 1:3; S 3:1; Nu 19:2
22:27 [n] S Lev 1:3 [o] S Ex 22:30 [p] S Ex 22:30 [q] S Ex 28:38
22:28 [r] Dt 22:6,7
22:29 [s] S Lev 7:12
22:30 [t] Lev 7:15 [u] Lev 11:44
22:31 [v] Dt 4:2,40; Ps 105:45 [w] S Ex 22:31
22:32 [x] Lev 18:21 [y] S Lev 10:3

[z] *4* Traditionally *leprosy*; the Hebrew word was used for various diseases affecting the skin—not necessarily leprosy. [a] *9* Or *who sanctifies them*; or *who sets them apart as holy*; also in verse 16 [b] *21* Traditionally *peace offering* [c] *23* The Hebrew word can include both male and female. [d] *32* Or *made*

holy[e][z] **33**and who brought you out of Egypt[a] to be your God.[b] I am the LORD."

23

The LORD said to Moses, **2**"Speak to the Israelites and say to them: 'These are my appointed feasts,[c] the appointed feasts of the LORD, which you are to proclaim as sacred assemblies.[d]

The Sabbath

3" 'There are six days when you may work,[e] but the seventh day is a Sabbath of rest,[f] a day of sacred assembly. You are not to do any work;[g] wherever you live, it is a Sabbath to the LORD.

The Passover and Unleavened Bread

23:4–8pp — Ex 12:14–20; Nu 28:16–25; Dt 16:1–8

4" 'These are the LORD's appointed feasts, the sacred assemblies you are to proclaim at their appointed times:[h] **5**The LORD's Passover[i] begins at twilight on the fourteenth day of the first month.[j] **6**On the fifteenth day of that month the LORD's Feast of Unleavened Bread[k] begins; for seven days[l] you must eat bread made without yeast. **7**On the first day hold a sacred assembly[m] and do no regular work. **8**For seven days present an offering made to the LORD by fire.[n] And on the seventh day hold a sacred assembly and do no regular work.' "

Firstfruits

9The LORD said to Moses, **10**"Speak to the Israelites and say to them: 'When you enter the land I am going to give you[o] and you reap its harvest,[p] bring to the priest a sheaf[q] of the first grain you harvest.[r] **11**He is to wave the sheaf before the LORD[s] so it will be accepted[t] on your behalf; the priest is to wave it on the day after the Sabbath. **12**On the day you wave the sheaf, you must sacrifice as a burnt offering to the LORD a lamb a year old[u] without defect,[v] **13**together with its grain offering[w] of two-tenths of an ephah[f][x] of fine flour mixed with oil—an offering made to the LORD by fire, a pleasing aroma—and its drink offering[y] of a quarter of a hin[g] of wine.[z] **14**You must not eat any bread, or roasted or new grain,[a] until the very day you bring this offering to your God.[b] This is to be a lasting ordinance for the generations to come,[c] wherever you live.[d]

Feast of Weeks

23:15–22pp — Nu 28:26–31; Dt 16:9–12

15" 'From the day after the Sabbath, the day you brought the sheaf of the wave offering, count off seven full weeks. **16**Count off fifty days up to the day after the seventh Sabbath,[e] and then present an offering of new grain to the LORD. **17**From wherever you live, bring two loaves made of two-tenths of an ephah[f] of fine flour, baked with yeast, as a wave offering of firstfruits[g] to the LORD. **18**Present with this bread seven male lambs, each a year old and without defect, one young bull and two rams. They will be a burnt offering to

22:32 [z] Lev 20:8
22:33 [a] S Ex 6:6 [b] S Ge 17:7
23:2 [c] ver 4,37, 44; Nu 29:39; Eze 44:24; Col 2:16 [d] ver 21, 27
23:3 [e] Ex 20:9 [f] S Ex 20:10; Heb 4:9,10 [g] ver 7, 21,35; Nu 28:26
23:4 [h] Na 1:15
23:5 [i] S Ex 12:11 [j] S Ex 12:6
23:6 [k] Ex 12:17 [l] S Ex 12:19
23:7 [m] ver 3,8
23:8 [n] S Lev 1:9
23:10 [o] Nu 15:2, 18 [p] S Lev 19:9 [q] S Lev 19:9 [r] S Ex 22:29; S 34:22; Ro 11:16
23:11 [s] S Ex 29:24 [t] S Ex 28:38
23:12 [u] S Lev 12:6 [v] S Ex 12:5
23:13 [w] Lev 2:14-16; S 6:20 [x] ver 17; Lev 24:5; Nu 15:6; 28:9 [y] S Ge 35:14 [z] S Lev 10:9
23:14 [a] Jos 5:11; Ru 2:14; 1Sa 17:17; 25:18; 2Sa 17:28 [b] Ex 34:26 [c] Lev 3:17; Nu 10:8; 15:21 [d] Jer 2:3
23:16 [e] Ac 2:1; 20:16
23:17 [f] S ver 13 [g] S Ex 34:22

[e] *32* Or *who sanctifies you*; or *who sets you apart as holy* [f] *13* That is, probably about 4 quarts (about 4.5 liters); also in verse 17 [g] *13* That is, probably about 1 quart (about 1 liter)

23:2 APPOINTED FEASTS OF THE LORD. This chapter presents a list of the "feasts of the LORD," i.e., the sacred days of celebration and worship. These days were symbols of redemption and consecration, demonstrating that Israel and all they possessed belonged to God. There were two cycles of these feasts: a weekly cycle and an annual cycle. All were feasts except for the Day of Atonement, which was the one fast day required by the law. These cycles helped to tie their worship to the events in their daily lives, for they were not to separate worship from life.

23:5 THE LORD'S PASSOVER. See article on THE PASSOVER, p. 104.

23:6 FEAST OF UNLEAVENED BREAD. See Ex 12:17, note.

23:10 FIRST GRAIN YOU HARVEST. The Feast of Firstfruits (vv. 10–14), acknowledging that the fruit of the ground came from the Lord, occurred in connection with the Feast of Unleavened Bread. The firstfruits were to be consecrated to the Lord, which pointed to the NT believer's dedication of all of life to God. Christians are the firstfruits of Christ's saving work (Jas 1:18; Rev 14:4).

23:15 SEVEN FULL WEEKS. The Feast of Weeks (cf. Dt 16:10), also called the Feast of Pentecost, occurred at the end of the wheat harvest, fifty days ("Pentecost" means "fifty") after the Feast of Firstfruits (v. 16). On this day God's people gave thanks for his abundant gifts of food and for all that sustained them. It was on the day of Pentecost that God poured out the Holy Spirit on Christ's disciples (Ac 2:1–4).

OLD TESTAMENT FEASTS

Name	OT References	OT Time	Today	Description	NT References
Sabbath	Ex 20:8-11; 31:12-17; Lev 23:3; Dt 5:12-15	7th day	Same	Day of rest; no work	Mt 12:1-14; Mk 2:23–3:5; Lk 4 4:16-30; 6:1-10; 13:10 -16; 14:1-5; Jn 5:1-15; 9:1-34; Ac 13:14-48; 17:2; 18:4; Heb 4:1-11
Sabbath Year	Ex 23:10-11; Lev 25:1-7	7th year	Same	Year of rest; fallow fields	
Year of Jubilee	Lev 25:8-55; 27:17-24; Nu 36:4	50th year	Same	Cancelled debts; liberation of slaves and endentured servants; land returned to original family owners	
Passover	Ex 12:1-14; Lev 23:5; Nu 9:1-14; 28:16; Dt 16:1-3a, 4b-7	1st month (Abib) 14	Mar-Apr	Slaying and eating a lamb, together with bitter herbs and bread made without yeast, in every household	Mt 26:1-2, 17-29; Mk 14:12-26; Lk 22:7-38; Jn 2:13-25; 11:55-56; Jn 13:1-30; 1Co 5:7
Unleavened Bread	Ex 12:15-20; 13:3-10; 23:15; 34:18; Lev 23:6-8; Nu 28:17-25; Dt 16:3b,4a,8	1st month (Abib) 15-21	Mar-Apr	Eating bread made without yeast; holding several assemblies; making designated offerings	Mt 26:17; Mk 14:1,12; Luke 22:1,7; Ac 12:3; 20:6; 1Co 5:6-8
Firstfruits	Lev 23:9-14	1st month (Abib) 16	Mar-Apr	Presenting a sheaf of the first of the barley harvest as a wave offering; making a burnt offering and a grain offering	Ro 8:23; 1Co 15:20-23
Weeks (Pentecost)(Harvest)	Ex 23:16a; 34:22a; Lev 23:15-21; Nu 28:26-31; Dt 16:9-12	3rd month (Sivan) 6	May-June	A festival of joy; mandatory and voluntary offerings, including the firstfruits of the wheat harvest	Ac 2:1-41; 20:16; 1Co 16:8
Trumpets (Later: Rosh Hashanah–New Year's Day)	Lev 23:23-25; Nu 29:1-6	7th month (Tishri) 1	Sept-Oct	An assembly on a day of rest commemorated with trumpet blasts and sacrifices	
Day of Atonement (Yom Kippur)	Lev 16; 23:26-32; Nu 29:7-11	7th month (Tishri) 10	Sept-Oct	A day of rest, fasting and sacrifices of atonement for priests and people and atonement for the tabernacle and altar	Ac 27:9; Ro 3:24-26; Heb 9:1-14, 23-26; 10:19-22
Tabernacles (Booths)(Ingathering)	Ex 23:16b;34:22b; Lev 23:33-36a, 39-43; Nu 29:12-34; Dt 16:13-15; Zec 14:16-19	7th month (Tishri) 15-21	Sept-Oct	A week of celebration for the harvest; living in booths and offering sacrifices	Jn 7:2-37
Sacred Assembly	Lev 23:36b; Nu 29:35-38	7th month (Tishri) 22	Sept-Oct	A day of convocation, rest and offering sacrifices	Jn 7:37-44
Dedication		9th month	Dec	A commemoration of the purification of the temple in Maccabean era (166-164 B.C.)	Jn 10:22-39
Purim	Est 9:18-32	12th month (Adar) 14,15	Feb-Mar	A day of joy and feasting and giving presents	

the LORD, together with their grain offerings and drink offerings[h]—an offering made by fire, an aroma pleasing
to the LORD. 19Then sacrifice one male
goat for a sin offering and two lambs,
each a year old, for a fellowship offering.[h] 20The priest is to wave the two
lambs before the LORD as a wave offering,[i] together with the bread of the
firstfruits. They are a sacred offering
to the LORD for the priest. 21On that
same day you are to proclaim a sacred
assembly[j] and do no regular work.[k]
This is to be a lasting ordinance for the
generations to come, wherever you
live.
22" 'When you reap the harvest[l] of
your land, do not reap to the very edges
of your field or gather the gleanings of
your harvest.[m] Leave them for the
poor and the alien.[n] I am the LORD
your God.' "

Feast of Trumpets

23:23–25pp — Nu 29:1–6

23The LORD said to Moses, 24"Say to
the Israelites: 'On the first day of the
seventh month you are to have a day of
rest, a sacred assembly[o] commemorated with trumpet blasts.[p] 25Do no
regular work,[q] but present an offering
made to the LORD by fire.[r]' "

Day of Atonement

23:26–32pp — Lev 16:2–34; Nu 29:7–11

26The LORD said to Moses, 27"The
tenth day of this seventh month[s] is
the Day of Atonement.[t] Hold a sacred
assembly[u] and deny yourselves,[i]
and present an offering made to the
LORD by fire. 28Do no work[v] on that
day, because it is the Day of Atonement, when atonement is made for you
before the LORD your God. 29Anyone
who does not deny himself on that day
must be cut off from his people.[w] 30I
will destroy from among his people[x]
anyone who does any work on that day.
31You shall do no work at all. This is
to be a lasting ordinance[y] for the generations to come, wherever you live.
32It is a sabbath of rest[z] for you, and
you must deny yourselves. From the
evening of the ninth day of the month
until the following evening you are to
observe your sabbath."[a]

Feast of Tabernacles

23:33–43pp — Nu 29:12–39; Dt 16:13–17

33The LORD said to Moses, 34"Say to
the Israelites: 'On the fifteenth day of
the seventh[b] month the LORD's Feast
of Tabernacles[c] begins, and it lasts
for seven days. 35The first day is a sacred assembly;[d] do no regular work.[e]
36For seven days present offerings
made to the LORD by fire, and on the
eighth day hold a sacred assembly[f]
and present an offering made to the
LORD by fire.[g] It is the closing assembly; do no regular work.
37(" 'These are the LORD's appointed
feasts, which you are to proclaim as
sacred assemblies for bringing offerings made to the LORD by fire—the
burnt offerings and grain offerings,
sacrifices and drink offerings[h] required for each day. 38These offerings[i] are in addition to those for the
LORD's Sabbaths[j] and[j] in addition to
your gifts and whatever you have
vowed and all the freewill offerings[k]
you give to the LORD.)
39" 'So beginning with the fifteenth
day of the seventh month, after you
have gathered the crops of the land,
celebrate the festival[l] to the LORD for
seven days;[m] the first day is a day of
rest, and the eighth day also is a day
of rest. 40On the first day you are to
take choice fruit from the trees, and
palm fronds, leafy branches[n] and poplars,[o] and rejoice[p] before the LORD
your God for seven days. 41Celebrate

23:18 [h]ver 13; Ex 29:41; 30:9; 37:16; Jer 19:13; 44:18
23:20 [i]S Ex 29:24
23:21 [j]S ver 2; Ex 32:5 [k]S ver 3
23:22 [l]S Lev 19:9 [m]S Lev 19:10; Dt 24:19-21; Ru 2:15 [n]Ru 2:2
23:24 [o]ver 27,36; Ezr 3:1 [p]Lev 25:9; Nu 10:9,10; 29:1; 31:6; 2Ki 11:14; 2Ch 13:12; Ps 98:6
23:25 [q]ver 21 [r]S Lev 1:9
23:27 [s]S Lev 16:29 [t]S Ex 30:10 [u]S ver 2,S 24
23:28 [v]ver 31
23:29 [w]Ge 17:14; Lev 7:20; Nu 5:2
23:30 [x]S Lev 20:3
23:31 [y]Lev 3:17
23:32 [z]S Lev 16:31 [a]Ne 13:19
23:34 [b]1Ki 8:2; Hag 2:1 [c]S Ex 23:16; Jn 7:2
23:35 [d]ver 2 [e]ver 3
23:36 [f]S ver 24; 1Ki 8:2; 2Ch 7:9; Ne 8:18; Jn 7:37 [g]S Lev 1:9
23:37 [h]ver 13
23:38 [i]S Lev 1:2 [j]S Ex 20:10; 2Ch 2:4; Eze 45:17 [k]S Lev 7:16
23:39 [l]Isa 62:9 [m]S Ex 23:16
23:40 [n]Ps 118:27 [o]Ne 8:14-17; Ps 137:2; Isa 44:4 [p]Dt 12:7; 14:26; 28:47; Ne 8:10; Ps 9:2; 66:6; 105:43; Joel 2:26

[h] *19* Traditionally *peace offering* [i] *27* Or *and fast*; also in verses 29 and 32 [j] *38* Or *These feasts are in addition to the LORD's Sabbaths, and these offerings are*

23:24 TRUMPET BLASTS. The Feast of Trumpets occurred on the first day of the seventh month, probably as a reminder of and a preparation for the approaching Day of Atonement (cf. vv. 26–32). God wanted Israel to think about spiritual things, especially about their covenant relationship with him.

23:27 DAY OF ATONEMENT. See article on THE DAY OF ATONEMENT, p. 174.

23:34–43 FEAST OF TABERNACLES. The Feast of Tabernacles was so called because during this feast the people left their houses and lived in temporary booths or tents made from tree branches (vv. 40–42); this act reminded the people of God's goodness to them during their forty years in the desert when they had no permanent dwelling place. The Feast of Tabernacles was also called the Feast of Ingathering, for it celebrated the conclusion of the harvest of summer fruits and nuts.

this as a festival to the LORD for seven
days each year. This is to be a lasting
ordinance for the generations to come;
celebrate it in the seventh month.
42Live in booths[q] for seven days: All
native-born Israelites are to live in
booths 43so your descendants will
know[r] that I had the Israelites live in
booths when I brought them out of
Egypt. I am the LORD your God.' "
44So Moses announced to the Israelites the appointed feasts of the LORD.

Oil and Bread Set Before the LORD

24:1–3pp — Ex 27:20–21

24 The LORD said to Moses, 2"Command the Israelites to bring
you clear oil of pressed olives for the
light so that the lamps may be kept
burning continually. 3Outside the curtain of the Testimony in the Tent of
Meeting, Aaron is to tend the lamps before the LORD from evening till morning, continually. This is to be a lasting
ordinance[s] for the generations to
come. 4The lamps on the pure gold
lampstand[t] before the LORD must be
tended continually.
5"Take fine flour and bake twelve
loaves of bread,[u] using two-tenths of
an ephah[k v] for each loaf. 6Set them
in two rows, six in each row, on the
table of pure gold[w] before the LORD.
7Along each row put some pure incense[x] as a memorial portion[y] to represent the bread and to be an offering
made to the LORD by fire. 8This bread
is to be set out before the LORD regularly,[z] Sabbath after Sabbath,[a] on behalf of the Israelites, as a lasting covenant. 9It belongs to Aaron and his
sons,[b] who are to eat it in a holy
place,[c] because it is a most holy[d]
part of their regular share of the offerings made to the LORD by fire."

A Blasphemer Stoned

10Now the son of an Israelite mother
and an Egyptian father went out
among the Israelites, and a fight broke
out in the camp between him and an
Israelite. 11The son of the Israelite
woman blasphemed the Name[e] with a
curse;[f] so they brought him to Moses.[g] (His mother's name was Shelomith, the daughter of Dibri the Danite.)[h] 12They put him in custody until
the will of the LORD should be made
clear to them.[i]
13Then the LORD said to Moses:
14"Take the blasphemer outside the
camp. All those who heard him are to
lay their hands on his head, and the
entire assembly is to stone him.[j]
15Say to the Israelites: 'If anyone
curses his God,[k] he will be held
responsible;[l] 16anyone who blasphemes[m] the name of the LORD must
be put to death.[n] The entire assembly
must stone him. Whether an alien or
native-born, when he blasphemes the
Name, he must be put to death.
17" 'If anyone takes the life of a human being, he must be put to death.[o]
18Anyone who takes the life of someone's animal must make restitution[p]—life for life. 19If anyone injures
his neighbor, whatever he has done
must be done to him: 20fracture for
fracture, eye for eye, tooth for tooth.[q]
As he has injured the other, so he is to
be injured. 21Whoever kills an animal
must make restitution,[r] but whoever
kills a man must be put to death.[s]
22You are to have the same law for the
alien[t] and the native-born.[u] I am the
LORD your God.' "
23Then Moses spoke to the Israelites, and they took the blasphemer outside the camp and stoned him.[v] The
Israelites did as the LORD commanded
Moses.

The Sabbath Year

25 The LORD said to Moses on
Mount Sinai,[w] 2"Speak to the
Israelites and say to them: 'When you
enter the land I am going to give you,
the land itself must observe a sabbath
to the LORD. 3For six years sow your
fields, and for six years prune your
vineyards and gather their crops.[x]
4But in the seventh year the land is to
have a sabbath of rest,[y] a sabbath to
the LORD. Do not sow your fields or
prune your vineyards.[z] 5Do not reap
what grows of itself[a] or harvest the
grapes[b] of your untended vines.[c] The

[k] 5 That is, probably about 4 quarts (about 4.5 liters)

23:42 [q] S Ex 23:16
23:43 [r] Ps 78:5
24:3 [s] S Ex 12:14
24:4 [t] S Ex 25:31
24:5 [u] S Ex 25:30; Heb 9:2 [v] S Lev 23:13
24:6 [w] Ex 25:23-30; Nu 4:7
24:7 [x] S Lev 2:1 [y] S Lev 2:2
24:8 [z] Ex 25:30; Nu 4:7; 1Ch 9:32; 2Ch 2:4 [a] Mt 12:5
24:9 [b] Mt 12:4; Mk 2:26; Lk 6:4 [c] S Lev 6:16 [d] S Lev 6:17
24:11 [e] S Ex 3:15 [f] S Ex 20:7; S 2Ki 6:33; S Job 1:11 [g] S Ex 18:22 [h] Ex 31:2; Nu 1:4; 7:2; 10:15; 13:2; 17:2; Jos 7:18; 1Ki 7:14
24:12 [i] S Ex 18:16
24:14 [j] ver 23; S Lev 20:2; Dt 13:9; 17:5,7; Ac 7:58
24:15 [k] S Ex 22:28 [l] S Lev 5:1
24:16 [m] S Ex 22:28 [n] S Ex 21:12; 1Ki 21:10,13; Mt 26:66; Mk 14:64; Jn 10:33; 19:7; Ac 7:58
24:17 [o] ver 21; Ge 9:6; S Ex 21:12; Dt 27:24
24:18 [p] ver 21
24:20 [q] S Ex 21:24; Mt 5:38*
24:21 [r] S ver 18 [s] S ver 17
24:22 [t] S Ex 12:49; S 22:21; Eze 47:22 [u] Nu 9:14
24:23 [v] S ver 14
25:1 [w] Ex 19:11
25:3 [x] Ex 23:10
25:4 [y] ver 5,6,20; Lev 26:35; 2Ch 36:21 [z] Isa 36:16; 37:30
25:5 [a] 2Ki 19:29 [b] Ge 40:10; Nu 6:3; 13:20; Dt 23:24; Ne 13:15; Isa 5:2 [c] ver 4,11

24:2 THE LIGHT. See Ex 27:20–21, note.
24:5 TWELVE LOAVES. The twelve loaves (the bread of the Presence) represented the twelve tribes of Israel and the Israelites' realization that they lived in God's presence and were always to be dedicated to him (cf. Ex 25:30, note).

land is to have a year of rest. **6**Whatever the land yields during the sabbath
year[d] will be food for you—for yourself, your manservant and maidservant, and the hired worker and temporary resident who live among you, **7**as
well as for your livestock and the wild
animals[e] in your land. Whatever the
land produces may be eaten.

The Year of Jubilee

25:8–38Ref — Dt 15:1–11
25:39–55Ref — Ex 21:2–11; Dt 15:12–18

8" 'Count off seven sabbaths of
years—seven times seven years—so
that the seven sabbaths of years
amount to a period of forty-nine years.
9Then have the trumpet[f] sounded everywhere on the tenth day of the seventh month;[g] on the Day of Atonement[h] sound the trumpet throughout
your land. **10**Consecrate the fiftieth
year and proclaim liberty[i] throughout
the land to all its inhabitants. It shall
be a jubilee[j] for you; each one of you
is to return to his family property[k] and
each to his own clan. **11**The fiftieth
year shall be a jubilee[l] for you; do not
sow and do not reap what grows of itself or harvest the untended vines.[m]
12For it is a jubilee and is to be holy for
you; eat only what is taken directly
from the fields.

13" 'In this Year of Jubilee[n] everyone is to return to his own property.

14" 'If you sell land to one of your
countrymen or buy any from him, do
not take advantage of each other.[o]
15You are to buy from your countryman
on the basis of the number of years[p]
since the Jubilee. And he is to sell to
you on the basis of the number of years
left for harvesting crops. **16**When the
years are many, you are to increase the
price, and when the years are few, you
are to decrease the price,[q] because
what he is really selling you is the
number of crops. **17**Do not take advantage of each other,[r] but fear your
God.[s] I am the LORD your God.[t]

18" 'Follow my decrees and be careful to obey my laws,[u] and you will live
safely in the land.[v] **19**Then the land
will yield its fruit,[w] and you will eat
your fill and live there in safety.[x]
20You may ask, "What will we eat in
the seventh year[y] if we do not plant or
harvest our crops?" **21**I will send you
such a blessing[z] in the sixth year that
the land will yield enough for three
years.[a] **22**While you plant during the
eighth year, you will eat from the old
crop and will continue to eat from it
until the harvest of the ninth year
comes in.[b]

23" 'The land[c] must not be sold permanently, because the land is mine[d]
and you are but aliens[e] and my tenants. **24**Throughout the country that
you hold as a possession, you must
provide for the redemption[f] of the
land.

25" 'If one of your countrymen becomes poor and sells some of his property, his nearest relative[g] is to come
and redeem[h] what his countryman
has sold. **26**If, however, a man has no
one to redeem it for him but he himself
prospers[i] and acquires sufficient
means to redeem it, **27**he is to determine the value for the years[j] since he
sold it and refund the balance to the
man to whom he sold it; he can then go
back to his own property.[k] **28**But if he
does not acquire the means to repay
him, what he sold will remain in the
possession of the buyer until the Year
of Jubilee. It will be returned[l] in the
Jubilee, and he can then go back to his
property.[m]

29" 'If a man sells a house in a
walled city, he retains the right of redemption a full year after its sale. During that time he may redeem it. **30**If it
is not redeemed before a full year has
passed, the house in the walled city
shall belong permanently to the buyer
and his descendants. It is not to be returned in the Jubilee. **31**But houses in
villages without walls around them are

25:6 [d]S ver 4
25:7 [e]Ex 23:11
25:9 [f]Lev 23:24; Nu 10:8; Jos 6:4; Jdg 3:27; 7:16; 1Sa 13:3; Isa 27:13; Zec 9:14 [g]S Lev 16:29 [h]S Ex 30:10
25:10 [i]Isa 61:1; Jer 34:8,15,17; S Lk 4:19 [j]ver 11, 28,50; Lev 27:17, 21; Nu 36:4; Eze 46:17 [k]ver 27
25:11 [l]S ver 10 [m]S ver 5
25:13 [n]ver 10
25:14 [o]S Lev 19:13; 1Sa 12:3,4; 1Co 6:8
25:15 [p]ver 27; Lev 27:18,23
25:16 [q]ver 27,51, 52
25:17 [r]S Lev 19:13; Job 31:16; Pr 22:22; Jer 7:5, 6; 21:12; 22:3,15; Zec 7:9-10; 1Th 4:6 [s]S Lev 19:14 [t]S Lev 19:32
25:18 [u]S Ge 26:5 [v]ver 19; Lev 26:4, 5; Dt 12:10; 33:28; Job 5:22; Ps 4:8; Jer 23:6; 30:10; 32:37; 33:16; Eze 28:26; 34:25; 38:14
25:19 [w]Lev 26:4; Dt 11:14; 28:12; Isa 55:10 [x]S ver 18
25:20 [y]S ver 4
25:21 [z]Dt 28:8, 12; Ps 133:3; 134:3; 147:13; Eze 44:30; Hag 2:19; Mal 3:10 [a]S Ex 16:5
25:22 [b]Lev 26:10
25:23 [c]Nu 36:7; 1Ki 21:3; Eze 46:18 [d]Ex 19:5 [e]S Ge 23:4; S Heb 11:13
25:24 [f]ver 29,48; Ru 4:7
25:25 [g]ver 48; Ru 2:20; Jer 32:7 [h]Lev 27:13,19,31; Ru 4:4
25:26 [i]ver 49
25:27 [j]S ver 15 [k]ver 10
25:28 [l]Lev 27:24 [m]S ver 10

25:8–34 PERIOD OF FORTY-NINE YEARS. Three features characterized the Year of Jubilee (a year that came every fifty years). (1) All Israelite slaves were to be freed. (2) All ancestral property that had been sold had to be returned to the original family. (3) The land was to be left untilled. God's purpose in instituting this special year was to guarantee justice and to keep the rich from accumulating wealth and land at the expense of the disadvantaged.

25:23 THE LAND. God told the Israelites that they were not the real owners of the land, for it belonged to him; they were simply its stewards. Similarly, the material possessions of NT believers belong to the Lord. We have been appointed as stewards who must manage all our possessions justly for God, for ourselves and for others (cf. Mt 25:14–27; Lk 16:10–12; 1Co 4:1–7).

to be considered as open country. They
can be redeemed, and they are to be
returned in the Jubilee.
32“ ‘The Levites always have the
right to redeem their houses in the Levitical towns,[n] which they possess.
33So the property of the Levites is re-
deemable—that is, a house sold in any
town they hold—and is to be returned
in the Jubilee, because the houses in
the towns of the Levites are their property among the Israelites. 34But the
pastureland belonging to their towns
must not be sold; it is their permanent
possession.[o]
35“ ‘If one of your countrymen becomes poor[p] and is unable to support
himself among you, help him[q] as you
would an alien or a temporary resident,
so he can continue to live among you.
36Do not take interest[r] of any kind[1]
from him, but fear your God,[s] so that
your countryman may continue to live
among you. 37You must not lend him
money at interest[t] or sell him food at
a profit. 38I am the LORD your God, who
brought you out of Egypt to give you
the land of Canaan[u] and to be your
God.[v]
39“ ‘If one of your countrymen becomes poor among you and sells himself to you, do not make him work as
a slave.[w] 40He is to be treated as a
hired worker[x] or a temporary resident
among you; he is to work for you until
the Year of Jubilee. 41Then he and his
children are to be released, and he will
go back to his own clan and to the
property[y] of his forefathers.[z] 42Be-
cause the Israelites are my servants,
whom I brought out of Egypt,[a] they
must not be sold as slaves. 43Do not
rule over them ruthlessly,[b] but fear
your God.[c]
44“ ‘Your male and female slaves are
to come from the nations around you;
from them you may buy slaves. 45You
may also buy some of the temporary
residents living among you and members of their clans born in your country, and they will become your property. 46You can will them to your children
as inherited property and can make
them slaves for life, but you must not
rule over your fellow Israelites ruthlessly.
47“ ‘If an alien or a temporary resident among you becomes rich and one
of your countrymen becomes poor and
sells himself[d] to the alien living
among you or to a member of the
alien's clan, 48he retains the right of
redemption[e] after he has sold himself.
One of his relatives[f] may redeem him:
49An uncle or a cousin or any blood relative in his clan may redeem him. Or if
he prospers,[g] he may redeem himself.
50He and his buyer are to count the
time from the year he sold himself up
to the Year of Jubilee.[h] The price for
his release is to be based on the rate
paid to a hired man[i] for that number
of years. 51If many years remain, he
must pay for his redemption a larger
share of the price paid for him. 52If
only a few years remain until the Year
of Jubilee, he is to compute that and
pay for his redemption accordingly.[j]
53He is to be treated as a man hired
from year to year; you must see to it
that his owner does not rule over him
ruthlessly.[k]
54“ ‘Even if he is not redeemed in
any of these ways, he and his children
are to be released in the Year of Jubilee, 55for the Israelites belong to me as
servants. They are my servants, whom
I brought out of Egypt.[l] I am the LORD
your God.[m]

Reward for Obedience

26 “ ‘Do not make idols[n] or set up
an image[o] or a sacred stone[p]
for yourselves, and do not place a
carved stone[q] in your land to bow
down before it. I am the LORD your God.
2“ ‘Observe my Sabbaths[r] and have
reverence for my sanctuary.[s] I am the
LORD.
3“ ‘If you follow my decrees and are
careful to obey[t] my commands, 4I will
send you rain[u] in its season,[v] and the
ground will yield its crops and the
trees of the field their fruit.[w] 5Your

25:32 [n] Nu 35:1-8; Jos 21:2
25:34 [o] Nu 35:2-5; Eze 48:14
25:35 [p] Dt 24:14,15 [q] Dt 15:8; Ps 37:21,26; Pr 21:26; Lk 6:35
25:36 [r] S Ex 22:25; Jer 15:10 [s] S Lev 19:32
25:37 [t] S Ex 22:25
25:38 [u] S Ge 10:19 [v] S Ge 17:7
25:39 [w] 1Ki 5:13; 9:22; Jer 34:14
25:40 [x] ver 53
25:41 [y] ver 28 [z] Jer 34:8
25:42 [a] ver 38
25:43 [b] S Ex 1:13; Eze 34:4; Col 4:1 [c] S Ge 42:18
25:47 [d] Ne 5:5; Job 24:9
25:48 [e] S ver 24 [f] S ver 25
25:49 [g] ver 26
25:50 [h] S ver 10 [i] Job 7:1; 14:6; Isa 16:14; 21:16
25:52 [j] S ver 16
25:53 [k] Col 4:1
25:55 [l] S Lev 11:45 [m] Lev 11:44
26:1 [n] S Ex 20:4 [o] Ps 97:7; Isa 48:5; Jer 44:19; Hab 2:18 [p] S Ex 23:24 [q] Nu 33:52
26:2 [r] S Ex 20:8 [s] Lev 19:30
26:3 [t] S Ge 26:5; S Ex 24:8; Dt 6:17; 7:12; 11:13,22; 28:1,9
26:4 [u] Dt 11:14; 28:12; Ps 68:9; Jer 5:24; Hos 6:3; Joel 2:23; Zec 10:1 [v] Job 5:10; Ps 65:9; 104:13; 147:8; Jer 5:24 [w] S Ex 23:26; S Lev 25:19; S Job 14:9; Ps 67:6

[1] 36 Or *take excessive interest*; similarly in verse 37

25:36 DO NOT TAKE INTEREST. See Ex 22:25, note.

25:44 SLAVES ... FROM THE NATIONS. Slavery was a fact of life in Biblical days. That God allowed Israel to buy slaves from the pagan nations around them was a blessing for the slaves purchased, for God required his people to treat their slaves with much more dignity than they would have received in their own country (cf. Ex 20:10).

threshing will continue until grape harvest and the grape harvest will continue until planting, and you will eat all
the food you want[x] and live in safety
in your land.[y]
6" 'I will grant peace in the land,[z]
and you will lie down[a] and no one will
make you afraid.[b] I will remove savage beasts[c] from the land, and the
sword will not pass through your country. 7You will pursue your enemies,[d]
and they will fall by the sword before
you. 8Five[e] of you will chase a hundred, and a hundred of you will chase
ten thousand, and your enemies will
fall by the sword before you.[f]
9" 'I will look on you with favor and
make you fruitful and increase your
numbers,[g] and I will keep my covenant[h] with you. 10You will still be
eating last year's harvest when you
will have to move it out to make room
for the new.[i] 11I will put my dwelling
place[m][j] among you, and I will not abhor you.[k] 12I will walk[l] among you
and be your God,[m] and you will be my
people.[n] 13I am the LORD your God,[o]
who brought you out of Egypt[p] so that
you would no longer be slaves to the
Egyptians; I broke the bars of your
yoke[q] and enabled you to walk with
heads held high.

Punishment for Disobedience

14" 'But if you will not listen to me
and carry out all these commands,[r]
15and if you reject my decrees and abhor my laws[s] and fail to carry out all
my commands and so violate my covenant,[t] 16then I will do this to you: I
will bring upon you sudden terror,
wasting diseases and fever[u] that will
destroy your sight and drain away your
life.[v] You will plant seed in vain, because your enemies will eat it.[w] 17I
will set my face[x] against you so that
you will be defeated[y] by your enemies;[z] those who hate you will rule
over you,[a] and you will flee even when
no one is pursuing you.[b]
18" 'If after all this you will not listen to me,[c] I will punish[d] you for
your sins seven times over.[e] 19I will
break down your stubborn pride[f] and
make the sky above you like iron and
the ground beneath you like bronze.[g]
20Your strength will be spent in vain,[h]
because your soil will not yield its
crops, nor will the trees of the land
yield their fruit.[i]
21" 'If you remain hostile[j] toward
me and refuse to listen to me, I will
multiply your afflictions seven times
over,[k] as your sins deserve. 22I will
send wild animals[l] against you, and
they will rob you of your children, destroy your cattle and make you so
few[m] in number that your roads will be
deserted.[n]
23" 'If in spite of these things you do
not accept my correction[o] but continue to be hostile toward me, 24I myself
will be hostile[p] toward you and will
afflict you for your sins seven times
over. 25And I will bring the sword[q]
upon you to avenge[r] the breaking of
the covenant. When you withdraw into
your cities, I will send a plague[s]
among you, and you will be given into
enemy hands. 26When I cut off your
supply of bread,[t] ten women will be
able to bake your bread in one oven,
and they will dole out the bread by

26:5 [x]Dt 6:11; 11:15; Eze 36:29-30; Joel 2:19,26 [y]S Lev 25:18
26:6 [z]Ps 29:11; 37:11; 85:8; 147:14; Isa 26:3; 54:13; 60:18; Hag 2:9 [a]Ps 3:5; 4:8; Pr 3:24 [b]Job 11:18,19; Isa 17:2; Jer 30:10; Mic 4:4; Zep 3:13 [c]S ver 22; S Ge 37:20
26:7 [d]Ps 18:37; 44:5
26:8 [e]Isa 30:17 [f]Dt 28:7; 32:30; Jos 23:10; Jdg 15:15; 1Ch 12:14
26:9 [g]S Ge 1:22; S 17:6; Ne 9:23 [h]S Ge 17:7
26:10 [i]Lev 25:22
26:11 [j]Ex 25:8; Ps 74:7; 76:2; Eze 37:27 [k]ver 15, 43,44; Dt 31:6; 1Sa 12:22; 1Ki 6:13; 2Ki 17:15
26:12 [l]S Ge 3:8 [m]S Ge 17:7 [n]Ex 6:7; Jer 7:23; 11:4; 24:7; 30:22; 31:1; Zec 13:9; 2Co 6:16*
26:13 [o]Lev 11:44 [p]S Ex 6:6; S 13:3 [q]Isa 10:27; Jer 2:20; 27:2; 28:10; 30:8; Eze 30:18; 34:27; Hos 11:4
26:14 [r]Dt 28:15-68; Mal 2:2
26:15 [s]S ver 11 [t]S Ge 17:7
26:16 [u]Dt 28:22, 35; Ps 78:33 [v]ver 39; 1Sa 2:33; Ps 107:17; Eze 4:17; 24:23; 33:10 [w]Jdg 6:3-6; Job 31:8
26:17 [x]Lev 17:10; Eze 15:7 [y]Dt 28:48; Jos 7:12; Jdg 2:15; 1Ki 8:33; 2Ch 6:24 [z]Jos 7:4; Jer 19:7; 21:7 [a]Ps 106:41 [b]ver 36,37; Dt 28:7,25; Ps 53:5; Pr 28:1; Isa 30:17
26:18 [c]ver 14 [d]Ps 99:8; Jer 21:14; Am 3:14 [e]ver 21
26:19 [f]Ps 10:4; 73:6; Isa 16:6; 25:11; 28:1-3; Jer 13:9; 48:29; Eze 24:21; Am 6:8; Zep 3:11 [g]Dt 28:23; Job 38:38
26:20 [h]Dt 28:38; Ps 127:1; Isa 17:11; 49:4; Jer 12:13; Mic 6:15; Hag 1:6 [i]Dt 11:17; 28:24 **26:21** [j]ver 41 [k]ver 18; S Ge 4:15 **26:22** [l]S Ge 37:20 [m]Dt 28:62; Jer 42:2 [n]Jer 5:6; 14:16; 15:3; 16:4; Eze 14:15 **26:23** [o]Jer 2:30; 5:3; 7:28; 17:23; 32:33; Zep 3:2 **26:24** [p]2Sa 22:27 **26:25** [q]Jer 5:17; 15:3; 47:6; Eze 11:8; 14:17; 21:4; 33:2 [r]Jer 50:28; 51:6,11 [s]S Ex 5:3; S 9:3; Nu 16:46; 1Ki 8:37; Hab 3:5 **26:26** [t]1Ki 8:37; 18:2; 2Ki 4:38; 6:25; 8:1; 25:3; Ps 105:16; Isa 3:1; 9:20; Jer 37:21; 52:6; Eze 4:16,17; 5:16; 14:13; Hos 4:10; Mic 6:14

[m] *11* Or *my tabernacle*

26:14 IF YOU WILL NOT LISTEN TO ME. Ch. 26 reveals the pathos, anguish and heartache of God as he lamented the fact that he might be compelled to punish the people he had redeemed. If they, in utter ingratitude, rejected his love and were unwilling to have him as their God, he would have no other choice but to bring upon them sorrow and calamity. The Lord's promises and warnings were spoken from the depths of divine love and with the sincere desire that such discipline and judgment would never be necessary for his chosen people (read also Dt 28—30).

26:17 SET MY FACE AGAINST YOU. The greatest tragedy of sin, rebellion and disobedience is that God may set his face against us, i.e., withdraw his presence and care, his grace and strength, from us. In its place, we will be exposed to his direct judgment and to all the problems and dangers of life without his protection and guidance. The price of rejecting God and his righteous standards is enormous. To be in his will, in his presence and in his care are the greatest blessings of life (vv. 3–13).

weight. You will eat, but you will not be
satisfied.
27“ ‘If in spite of this you still do not
listen to me[u] but continue to be hostile toward me, **28**then in my anger[v] I
will be hostile[w] toward you, and I myself will punish you for your sins seven
times over.[x] **29**You will eat[y] the flesh
of your sons and the flesh of your
daughters.[z] **30**I will destroy your high
places,[a] cut down your incense altars[b] and pile your dead bodies on the
lifeless forms of your idols,[c] and I will
abhor[d] you. **31**I will turn your cities
into ruins[e] and lay waste[f] your sanctuaries,[g] and I will take no delight in
the pleasing aroma of your offerings.[h]
32I will lay waste the land,[i] so that
your enemies who live there will be appalled.[j] **33**I will scatter[k] you among
the nations[l] and will draw out my
sword[m] and pursue you. Your land will
be laid waste,[n] and your cities will lie
in ruins.[o] **34**Then the land will enjoy
its sabbath years all the time that it
lies desolate[p] and you are in the country of your enemies;[q] then the land
will rest and enjoy its sabbaths. **35**All
the time that it lies desolate, the land
will have the rest[r] it did not have during the sabbaths you lived in it.
36“ ‘As for those of you who are left,
I will make their hearts so fearful in
the lands of their enemies that the
sound of a windblown leaf[s] will put
them to flight.[t] They will run as
though fleeing from the sword, and
they will fall, even though no one is
pursuing them.[u] **37**They will stumble
over one another[v] as though fleeing
from the sword, even though no one is
pursuing them. So you will not be able
to stand before your enemies.[w] **38**You
will perish[x] among the nations; the
land of your enemies will devour you.[y]
39Those of you who are left will waste
away in the lands of their enemies because of their sins; also because of
their fathers’[z] sins they will waste
away.[a]
40“ ‘But if they will confess[b] their
sins[c] and the sins of their fathers[d]—
their treachery against me and their
hostility toward me, **41**which made me
hostile[e] toward them so that I sent
them into the land of their enemies—
then when their uncircumcised
hearts[f] are humbled[g] and they pay[h]
for their sin, **42**I will remember my covenant with Jacob[i] and my covenant
with Isaac[j] and my covenant with
Abraham,[k] and I will remember the
land. **43**For the land will be deserted[l]
by them and will enjoy its sabbaths
while it lies desolate without them.
They will pay for their sins because
they rejected[m] my laws and abhorred
my decrees.[n] **44**Yet in spite of this,
when they are in the land of their enemies,[o] I will not reject them or abhor[p] them so as to destroy them completely,[q] breaking my covenant[r]
with them. I am the LORD their God.
45But for their sake I will remember[s]
the covenant with their ancestors
whom I brought out of Egypt[t] in the
sight of the nations to be their God. I
am the LORD.’ ”
46These are the decrees, the laws
and the regulations that the LORD established on Mount Sinai[u] between
himself and the Israelites through Moses.[v]

Redeeming What Is the LORD’s

27 The LORD said to Moses,
2“Speak to the Israelites and
say to them: ‘If anyone makes a special
vow[w] to dedicate persons to the LORD
by giving equivalent values, **3**set the
value of a male between the ages of
twenty and sixty at fifty shekels[n] of
silver, according to the sanctuary
shekel[o];[x] **4**and if it is a female, set
her value at thirty shekels.[p] **5**If it is a
person between the ages of five and

26:27 [u]ver 14 **26:28** [v]Dt 32:19; Jdg 2:14; Ps 78:59; 106:40 [w]Dt 7:10; Job 34:11; Isa 59:18; 65:6-7; 66:6; Jer 17:10; 25:29; Joel 3:4 [x]ver 18 **26:29** [y]2Ki 6:29; Jer 19:9; La 4:10; Eze 5:10 [z]Dt 28:53 **26:30** [a]Dt 12:2; 1Sa 9:12; 10:5; 1Ki 3:2,4; 12:31; 13:2,32; 2Ki 17:29; 23:20; 2Ch 34:3; Ps 78:58; Eze 6:3; 16:16; Am 7:9 [b]2Ch 34:4; Isa 17:8; 27:9; Eze 6:6 [c]Isa 21:9; Jer 50:2; Eze 6:13 [d]Ps 106:40; Am 6:8 **26:31** [e]Ne 1:3; Isa 1:7; 3:8,26; 6:11; 24:12; 61:4; Jer 4:7; 9:11; 25:11; 34:22; 44:2,6,22; Eze 36:33; Mic 2:4; 3:12; Zep 2:5; 3:6 [f]2Ki 22:19 [g]Ps 74:3-7; Isa 63:18; 64:11; La 2:7; Eze 24:21; Am 7:9 [h]Am 5:21, 22; 8:10 **26:32** [i]Isa 5:6; Jer 9:11; 12:11; 25:11; 26:9; 33:10; 34:22; 44:22 [j]1Ki 9:8; 2Ch 29:8; Isa 52:14; Jer 18:16; 19:8; 48:39; Eze 5:14; 26:16; 27:35; 28:19 **26:33** [k]Jer 40:15; 50:17; Eze 34:6; Joel 3:2 [l]Dt 4:27; 28:64; Ne 1:8; Ps 44:11; 106:27; Jer 4:11; 9:16; 13:24; 31:10; Eze 5:10; 12:15; 17:21; 20:23; 22:15; Zec 7:14 [m]Jer 42:16; Am 9:4 [n]Isa 49:19; Jer 7:34 [o]ver 31; 1Sa 15:22; Job 36:11; Jer 40:3 **26:34** [p]Isa 1:7; Jer 7:34; 25:11; 44:6; Eze 33:29 [q]ver 43; 2Ch 36:21 **26:35** [r]S Lev 25:4 **26:36** [s]Job 13:25 [t]2Ki 25:5; Ps 58:7; La 1:3,6; 4:19; Eze 21:7 [u]S ver 17 **26:37** [v]Jer 6:21; 13:16; 46:16; Eze 3:20; Na 3:3 [w]Jos 7:12

26:38 [x]Job 4:9; 36:12; Ps 1:6; Isa 1:28; Jer 16:4; 44:27 [y]Dt 4:26 **26:39** [z]Ex 20:5; Isa 14:21 [a]S ver 16; Isa 24:16 **26:40** [b]S Lev 5:5 [c]Ps 32:5; 38:18 [d]Ne 9:2; Ps 106:6; Jer 3:12-15; 14:20; Hos 5:15; Lk 15:18; 1Jn 1:9 **26:41** [e]S ver 21 [f]Dt 10:16; 30:6; Jer 4:4; 9:25,26; Eze 44:7,9; Ac 7:51 [g]2Ch 7:14; 12:6; Eze 20:43 [h]Isa 6:7; 33:24; 40:2; 53:5,6,11 **26:42** [i]Ge 28:15; 35:11-12 [j]S Ge 26:5 [k]S Ex 2:24 **26:43** [l]Ps 69:25; Isa 6:11; 32:14; 62:4; Jer 2:15; 44:2; La 1:1; Eze 36:4 [m]Nu 11:20; 14:31; 1Sa 8:7; Ps 106:24 [n]S ver 11; Eze 20:13 **26:44** [o]S ver 33; 2Ki 17:20; 25:11; 2Ch 6:36; 36:20 [p]S ver 11; Ro 11:2 [q]Dt 4:31; Jer 4:27; 5:10; 30:11 [r]Jdg 2:1; Jer 31:37; 33:26; 51:5 **26:45** [s]Dt 4:31 [t]Ex 6:8; Lev 25:38 **26:46** [u]S Ex 19:11 [v]S Lev 7:38; 27:34 **27:2** [w]S Ge 28:20 **27:3** [x]S Ex 30:13

[n] *3* That is, about 1 1/4 pounds (about 0.6 kilogram); also in verse 16 [o] *3* That is, about 2/5 ounce (about 11.5 grams); also in verse 25 [p] *4* That is, about 12 ounces (about 0.3 kilogram)

27:2 VOW. Ch. 27 deals with things vowed or promised to the Lord, such as persons, animals, houses and land. A value was placed on them in case the one who made the promise wanted to buy back the gift.

twenty, set the value of a male at twenty shekels[q][y] and of a female at ten
shekels.[r] 6If it is a person between
one month and five years, set the value
of a male at five shekels[s][z] of silver
and that of a female at three shekels[t]
of silver. 7If it is a person sixty years
old or more, set the value of a male at
fifteen shekels[u] and of a female at ten
shekels. 8If anyone making the vow is
too poor to pay[a] the specified amount,
he is to present the person to the
priest, who will set the value[b] for him
according to what the man making the
vow can afford.

9" 'If what he vowed is an animal
that is acceptable as an offering to the
LORD,[c] such an animal given to the
LORD becomes holy.[d] 10He must not
exchange it or substitute a good one
for a bad one, or a bad one for a good
one;[e] if he should substitute one animal for another, both it and the substitute become holy. 11If what he vowed
is a ceremonially unclean animal[f]—
one that is not acceptable as an offering to the LORD—the animal must be
presented to the priest, 12who will
judge its quality as good or bad. Whatever value the priest then sets, that is
what it will be. 13If the owner wishes
to redeem[g] the animal, he must add a
fifth to its value.[h]

14" 'If a man dedicates his house as
something holy to the LORD, the priest
will judge its quality as good or bad.
Whatever value the priest then sets, so
it will remain. 15If the man who dedicates his house redeems it,[i] he must
add a fifth to its value, and the house
will again become his.

16" 'If a man dedicates to the LORD
part of his family land, its value is to
be set according to the amount of seed
required for it—fifty shekels of silver
to a homer[v] of barley seed. 17If he
dedicates his field during the Year of
Jubilee, the value that has been set remains. 18But if he dedicates his field
after the Jubilee,[j] the priest will determine the value according to the
number of years that remain[k] until
the next Year of Jubilee, and its set value will be reduced. 19If the man who
dedicates the field wishes to redeem
it,[l] he must add a fifth to its value,
and the field will again become his.
20If, however, he does not redeem the
field, or if he has sold it to someone
else, it can never be redeemed. 21When
the field is released in the Jubilee,[m] it
will become holy,[n] like a field devoted
to the LORD;[o] it will become the property of the priests.[w]

22" 'If a man dedicates to the LORD a
field he has bought, which is not part
of his family land, 23the priest will determine its value up to the Year of Jubilee,[p] and the man must pay its value
on that day as something holy to the
LORD. 24In the Year of Jubilee the field
will revert to the person from whom he
bought it,[q] the one whose land it was.
25Every value is to be set according to
the sanctuary shekel,[r] twenty gerahs[s] to the shekel.

26" 'No one, however, may dedicate
the firstborn of an animal, since the
firstborn already belongs to the
LORD;[t] whether an ox[x] or a sheep, it
is the LORD's. 27If it is one of the unclean animals,[u] he may buy it back at
its set value, adding a fifth of the value
to it. If he does not redeem it, it is to
be sold at its set value.

28" 'But nothing that a man owns
and devotes[y][v] to the LORD—whether
man or animal or family land—may be
sold or redeemed; everything so devoted is most holy[w] to the LORD.

29" 'No person devoted to destruction[z] may be ransomed; he must be
put to death.[x]

30" 'A tithe[y] of everything from the
land, whether grain from the soil or
fruit from the trees, belongs to the
LORD; it is holy[z] to the LORD. 31If a man

27:5 [y] S Ge 37:28 **27:6** [z] Nu 3:47; 18:16 **27:8** [a] S Lev 5:11 [b] ver 12,14 **27:9** [c] S Ge 28:20; S Lev 1:2 [d] ver 21, 26,28; Ex 40:9; Nu 6:20; 18:17; Dt 15:19 **27:10** [e] ver 33 **27:11** [f] ver 27; S Ex 13:13; Nu 18:15 **27:13** [g] S Lev 25:25 [h] S Lev 5:16 **27:15** [i] ver 13,20 **27:18** [j] Lev 25:10 [k] Lev 25:15

27:19 [l] S Lev 25:25 **27:21** [m] S Lev 25:10 [n] S ver 9 [o] ver 28; Nu 18:14; Eze 44:29 **27:23** [p] S Lev 25:15 **27:24** [q] Lev 25:28 **27:25** [r] S Ex 30:13 [s] Nu 3:47; Eze 45:12 **27:26** [t] S Ex 13:12 **27:27** [u] S ver 11 **27:28** [v] Nu 18:14; Jos 6:17-19 [w] S ver 9 **27:29** [x] Dt 7:26 **27:30** [y] Nu 18:26; Dt 12:6,17; 14:22, 28; 2Ch 31:6; Ne 10:37; 12:44; 13:5; Mal 3:8 [z] Dt 7:6; Ezr 9:2; Isa 6:13

[q] *5* That is, about 8 ounces (about 0.2 kilogram) [r] *5* That is, about 4 ounces (about 110 grams); also in verse 7 [s] *6* That is, about 2 ounces (about 55 grams) [t] *6* That is, about 1 1/4 ounces (about 35 grams) [u] *7* That is, about 6 ounces (about 170 grams) [v] *16* That is, probably about 6 bushels (about 220 liters) [w] *21* Or *priest* [x] *26* The Hebrew word can include both male and female. [y] *28* The Hebrew term refers to the irrevocable giving over of things or persons to the LORD. [z] *29* The Hebrew term refers to the irrevocable giving over of things or persons to the LORD, often by totally destroying them.

27:30 TITHE. A tithe is a tenth of both the produce of the land and the livestock that was given to the Lord. The tithe of Israel was given to support the Levites (Nu 18:21) and priests (Nu 18:28), to assist in sacred meals (Dt 14:22–27), and to aid the poor, the fatherless and the widows (Dt 14:28–29; see article on TITHES AND OFFERINGS, p. 1392).

redeems[a] any of his tithe, he must add
a fifth of the value[b] to it. 32The entire
tithe of the herd and flock—every
tenth animal that passes under the
shepherd's rod[c]—will be holy to the
LORD. 33He must not pick out the good
from the bad or make any substitution.[d] If he does make a substitution,
both the animal and its substitute become holy and cannot be redeemed.[e]' "

34These are the commands the LORD
gave Moses on Mount Sinai[f] for the
Israelites.[g]

27:31 [a]S Lev 25:25 [b]Lev 5:16 **27:32** [c]Ps 89:32; Jer 33:13; Eze 20:37 **27:33** [d]ver 10 [e]Nu 18:21 **27:34** [f]S Ex 19:11 [g]S Lev 7:38; Ac 7:38

NUMBERS

Outline

I. God Prepares the "Exodus Generation" to Inherit the Land (1:1—10:10)
  A. Preparing to March (1:1—4:49)
    1. Numbering Israel's Fighting Men (1:1–54)
    2. Arranging the Camp (2:1–34)
    3. Organizing the Levites (3:1—4:49)
  B. Sanctifying the People (5:1—10:10)

II. The "Exodus Generation" Forfeits Their Inheritance Through Sin and Unbelief (10:11—25:18)
  A. Murmurings on the Way to Kadesh (10:11—12:16)
  B. Rebellion and Unbelief at Kadesh (13:1—14:45)
  C. Sin and Rebellion in the Desert (15:1—19:22)
  D. Disobedience on the Way to Moab (20:1—25:18)

III. God Prepares a New Generation to Possess the Land (26:1—36:13)
  A. Numbering the New Generation (26:1–65)
  B. Instructing the People (27:1—30:16)
  C. Defeating the Midianites (31:1–54)
  D. Settling the Transjordan (32:1–42)
  E. Recounting the Journey from Egypt to Moab (33:1–49)
  F. Promise of Victory over Canaan (33:50–56)
  G. Preparing to Enter and Divide the Land (34:1—36:13)

Author: Moses

Theme: Desert Wanderings

Date of Writing: c. 1405 B.C.

Background

The book's title, "Numbers," first occurs in the Greek and Latin versions and is derived from the two censuses or "numberings" of Israelite men in the book (chs. 1 and 26). Most of the book, however, describes Israel's experiences while wandering "in the desert"; thus this book is known in the Hebrew OT as "In the Desert" (*bemidbar*).

Chronologically, Numbers is a sequel to the history recorded in the book of Exodus. After approximately one year at Mount Sinai—during which time God established his covenant with Israel, gave Moses the law and the pattern for the tabernacle, and instructed him about the contents of Leviticus—the Israelites prepared to continue their journey to the land God had promised them as the descendants of Abraham, Isaac and Jacob. Shortly before departing from Mount Sinai, however, God directed Moses to take a census of all the Israelite men who were eligible to go to war (1:2–3). Nineteen days afterwards, the nation departed from there on a brief journey to Kadesh (10:11). Numbers records Israel's serious rebellion at Kadesh and her subsequent 39 years of judgment in the desert, until God brought an entirely new generation of Israelites to the plains of Moab, which lay across the Jordan River from Jericho and the promised land.

Authorship has historically been ascribed to Moses (1) by the Jewish and Samaritan Pentateuch, (2) by Jewish tradition, (3) by Jesus and NT writers, (4) by ancient Christian writers, (5) by modern conservative scholars and (6) by internal evidence of the book itself (e.g., 33:1–2). Moses undoubtedly kept a diary during the desert wanderings and then put the contents of Numbers in narrative form sometime shortly before his death (c. 1405 B.C.). Moses' practice of referring to himself in the third person was commonplace in ancient writings and does not weaken the credibility of his authorship.

Purpose

Numbers was written to tell why Israel did not enter the promised land immediately after leaving Mount Sinai. It illustrates God's requirement of faith for his people, his chastisements and judgments for rebellion, and how his ongoing purpose was eventually realized.

Survey

The primary message of Numbers is clear: God's people progressed forward only by trusting him and his promises and by obeying his word. Although passing through the desert was necessary for a season, it was not God's original intention that the desert test be prolonged so that a whole generation of Israelites live and die there. The short journey from Mount Sinai to Kadesh, however, became a 39-year affliction and judgment because of their unbelief. Throughout most of Numbers the "exodus generation" of Israelites was faithless, rebellious and ungrateful for God's miracles and provisions. Major murmuring occurred among the people soon after leaving Mount Sinai (ch. 11); Miriam and Aaron talked against Moses (ch. 12); Israel as a whole rebelled in stubborn unbelief at Kadesh and refused to advance into Canaan (ch. 14); Korah and many Levites rebelled against Moses (ch. 16); pushed to the limits by a rebellious people, Moses finally sinned in angry exasperation (ch. 20); and Israel worshiped Baal (ch. 25). All Israelites who were 20 years old and older at Kadesh (except Joshua and Caleb) perished in the desert. A new generation of Israelites was finally brought to the eastern border of the promised land (chs. 26—36).

Special Features

Six major features characterize Numbers. (1) It is the "Book of Desert Wanderings," revealing clearly why Israel did not immediately possess the promised land after leaving Mount Sinai but instead had to wander aimlessly in the desert for 39 more years. (2) It is the "Book of Murmurings," recording again and again the murmuring discontent and bitter complaint of the Israelites against God and his dealings with them. (3) The book illustrates the principle that without faith, it is impossible to please God (cf. Heb 11:6). Throughout the book one sees that God's people move forward only by trusting him with unwavering faith, believing his promises and leaning on him as their source of life and hope. (4) Numbers profoundly reveals the principle that if one generation fails, God will raise up another one to fulfill his promises and carry out his mission. (5) The census prior to Kadesh (chs. 1—4) and the census later at the plains of Moab before entering Canaan (ch. 26) reveal that it was not the insufficient size of Israel's army that kept her out of Canaan at Kadesh but the inadequacy of her faith and obedience. (6) It is the "Book of Divine Discipline," demonstrating that God does discipline and exercise judgment against his own people when they persist in complaint and unbelief (cf. chs. 13—14).

New Testament Fulfillment

Israel's murmurings and unbelief are mentioned as warnings for believers under the new covenant (1Co 10:5–11; Heb 3:16—4:6). The seriousness of Balaam's sin (chs. 22—24) and Korah's rebellion (ch. 16) are also mentioned (2Pe 2:15–16; Jude 11; Rev 2:14). Jesus refers to the bronze snake (21:7–9) to illustrate his being lifted up so that those who believe in him might not perish but have eternal life (Jn 3:14–16); also, Christ Jesus is compared to the rock from which the Israelites drank in the desert (1Co 10:4) and the heavenly manna they ate (Jn 6:31–33).

Reading Numbers

In order to read the entire Old Testament in one year, the book of Numbers should be read in 16 days, according to the following schedule: □ 1–2 □ 3–4 □ 5–6 □ 7–8 □ 9–10 □ 11–13 □ 14–15 □ 16–17 □ 18–19 □ 20–21 □ 22–23 □ 24–26 □ 27–28 □ 29–31 □ 32–33 □ 34–36

NOTES

The Census

1 The LORD spoke to Moses in the
Tent of Meeting[a] in the Desert of
Sinai[b] on the first day of the second
month[c] of the second year after the
Israelites came out of Egypt.[d] He
said: 2 "Take a census[e] of the whole
Israelite community by their clans and
families,[f] listing every man by
name,[g] one by one. 3 You and Aaron[h]
are to number by their divisions all the
men in Israel twenty years old or
more[i] who are able to serve in the
army.[j] 4 One man from each tribe,[k]
each the head of his family,[l] is to help
you.[m] 5 These are the names[n] of the
men who are to assist you:

from Reuben,[o] Elizur son of Shedeur;[p]
6 from Simeon,[q] Shelumiel son of Zurishaddai;[r]
7 from Judah,[s] Nahshon son of Amminadab;[t]
8 from Issachar,[u] Nethanel son of Zuar;[v]
9 from Zebulun,[w] Eliab son of Helon;[x]
10 from the sons of Joseph:
from Ephraim,[y] Elishama son of Ammihud;[z]
from Manasseh,[a] Gamaliel son of Pedahzur;[b]
11 from Benjamin,[c] Abidan son of Gideoni;[d]
12 from Dan,[e] Ahiezer son of Ammishaddai;[f]
13 from Asher,[g] Pagiel son of Ocran;[h]
14 from Gad,[i] Eliasaph son of Deuel;[j]
15 from Naphtali,[k] Ahira son of Enan.[l]"

16 These were the men appointed
from the community, the leaders[m] of
their ancestral tribes.[n] They were the
heads of the clans of Israel.[o]
17 Moses and Aaron took these men
whose names had been given, 18 and
they called the whole community together on the first day of the second
month.[p] The people indicated their
ancestry[q] by their clans and families,[r] and the men twenty years old or
more[s] were listed by name, one by
one, 19 as the LORD commanded Moses.
And so he counted[t] them in the
Desert of Sinai:

20 From the descendants of Reuben[u] the firstborn son[v] of Israel:
All the men twenty years old or more who were able to serve in the army were listed by name, one by one, according to the records of their clans and families.
21 The number from the tribe of Reuben[w] was 46,500.

22 From the descendants of Simeon:[x]
All the men twenty years old or more who were able to serve in the army were counted and listed by name, one by one, according to the records of their clans and families.
23 The number from the tribe of Simeon was 59,300.[y]

24 From the descendants of Gad:[z]
All the men twenty years old or more who were able to serve in the army were listed by name, according to the records of their clans and families.
25 The number from the tribe of Gad[a] was 45,650.

26 From the descendants of Judah:[b]
All the men twenty years old or more who were able to serve in the army were listed by name, according to the records of their clans and families.
27 The number from the tribe of Judah[c] was 74,600.

28 From the descendants of Issachar:[d]

1:1 [a] S Ex 27:21; S 40:2 [b] S Ex 19:1 [c] ver 18 [d] S Ex 6:14 **1:2** [e] Ex 30:11-16 [f] ver 18 [g] Nu 3:40 **1:3** [h] Ex 4:14; Nu 17:3 [i] S Ex 30:14 [j] ver 20; Nu 26:2; Jos 5:4; 1Ch 5:18 **1:4** [k] S Lev 24:11; S Jos 7:1 [l] ver 16; Nu 7:2; 30:1; 31:26 [m] Ex 18:21; Nu 34:18; Dt 1:15; Jos 22:14 **1:5** [n] Nu 17:2 [o] S Ge 29:32; Rev 7:5 [p] Nu 2:10; 7:30; 10:18 **1:6** [q] ver 22; Nu 25:14 [r] Nu 2:12; 7:36,41; 10:19 **1:7** [s] ver 26; S Ge 29:35; Ps 78:68 [t] Ex 6:23; Nu 7:12; Ru 4:20; 1Ch 2:10; Mt 1:4; Lk 3:32 **1:8** [u] S Ge 30:18; Nu 10:15 [v] Nu 2:5; 7:18 **1:9** [w] ver 30; Nu 10:16 [x] Nu 2:7; 7:24 **1:10** [y] ver 32 [z] Nu 2:18; 7:48,53; 10:22 [a] ver 34; Nu 10:23 [b] Nu 2:20; 7:54 **1:11** [c] Nu 10:24 [d] Nu 2:22; 7:60; Ps 68:27 **1:12** [e] ver 38 [f] Nu 2:25; 7:66; 10:25 **1:13** [g] ver 40; Nu 10:26 [h] Nu 2:27; 7:72 **1:14** [i] ver 24; Nu 10:20 [j] Nu 2:14; 7:42 **1:15** [k] ver 42; Nu 10:27 [l] Nu 2:29; 7:78 **1:16** [m] S Ex 18:25 [n] Nu 32:28 [o] S ver 4 **1:18** [p] ver 1 [q] Ezr 2:59; Heb 7:3 [r] ver 2 [s] S Ex 30:14 **1:19** [t] Ex 30:12; Nu 26:63; 31:49 **1:20** [u] S Ge 29:32; S 46:9; Rev 7:5 [v] S Ge 10:15 **1:21** [w] Nu 26:7 **1:22** [x] S Ge 29:33; Rev 7:7 **1:23** [y] Nu 26:14 **1:24** [z] S Ge 30:11; S Jos 13:24-28; Rev 7:5 **1:25** [a] Ge 46:16; Nu 26:18; 1Ch 5:11 **1:26** [b] S ver 7; Mt 1:2; Rev 7:5 **1:27** [c] Nu 26:22 **1:28** [d] S Ge 30:18; Rev 7:7

1:1 THE LORD SPOKE TO MOSES. What Moses wrote was by inspiration from God, a fact repeated over and over. It is emphasized in the first verse, the last verse, and at the beginning of many of the chapters of this book.

1:1 DESERT OF SINAI. God's command to Moses came ten and a half months after the people arrived at Mount Sinai (i.e, thirteen months after the exodus). The events recorded in Numbers occurred over a period of approximately thirty-nine years, the total time of Israel's wandering in the desert.

1:2 CENSUS OF THE WHOLE ISRAELITE COMMUNITY. The purpose of the census was to organize Israel into a nation and an army (v. 3). Taking a census emphasized that each individual was important to God's redemptive purposes and that the nation's activity was to be ordered and fully accountable to him (cf. Php 4:3; 2Ti 2:19).

All the men twenty years old or
more who were able to serve in
the army were listed by name,
according to the records of
their clans and families. 29 The
number from the tribe of Issachar[e] was 54,400.[f]

30 From the descendants of Zebulun:[g]
All the men twenty years old or
more who were able to serve in
the army were listed by name,
according to the records of
their clans and families. 31 The
number from the tribe of Zebulun was 57,400.[h]

32 From the sons of Joseph:[i]
From the descendants of Ephraim:[j]
All the men twenty years old or
more who were able to serve in
the army were listed by name,
according to the records of
their clans and families. 33 The
number from the tribe of Ephraim[k] was 40,500.
34 From the descendants of Manasseh:[l]
All the men twenty years old or
more who were able to serve in
the army were listed by name,
according to the records of
their clans and families. 35 The
number from the tribe of Manasseh was 32,200.

36 From the descendants of Benjamin:[m]
All the men twenty years old or
more who were able to serve in
the army were listed by name,
according to the records of
their clans and families. 37 The
number from the tribe of Benjamin[n] was 35,400.

38 From the descendants of Dan:[o]
All the men twenty years old or
more who were able to serve in
the army were listed by name,
according to the records of
their clans and families. 39 The
number from the tribe of Dan
was 62,700.[p]

40 From the descendants of Asher:[q]
All the men twenty years old or
more who were able to serve in
the army were listed by name,
according to the records of
their clans and families. 41 The
number from the tribe of Asher[r] was 41,500.

42 From the descendants of Naphtali:[s]
All the men twenty years old or
more who were able to serve in
the army were listed by name,
according to the records of
their clans and families. 43 The
number from the tribe of Naphtali[t] was 53,400.[u]

44 These were the men counted by
Moses and Aaron[v] and the twelve
leaders of Israel, each one representing his family. 45 All the Israelites
twenty years old or more[w] who were
able to serve in Israel's army were
counted according to their families.[x]
46 The total number was 603,550.[y]
47 The families of the tribe of Levi,[z]
however, were not counted[a] along
with the others. 48 The LORD had said to
Moses: 49 "You must not count the tribe
of Levi or include them in the census
of the other Israelites. 50 Instead,
appoint the Levites to be in charge of
the tabernacle[b] of the Testimony[c]—
over all its furnishings[d] and everything belonging to it. They are to carry
the tabernacle and all its furnishings;
they are to take care of it and encamp
around it. 51 Whenever the tabernacle[e] is to move,[f] the Levites are to
take it down, and whenever the tabernacle is to be set up, the Levites shall
do it.[g] Anyone else who goes near it
shall be put to death.[h] 52 The Israel-

1:29 e S Ge 30:18 f Nu 26:25
1:30 g S Ge 30:20; Rev 7:8
1:31 h Nu 26:27
1:32 i Ge 49:26 j S Ge 41:52
1:33 k Nu 26:37; 1Ch 7:20
1:34 l S Ge 41:51; Rev 7:6
1:36 m S Ge 35:18; 2Ch 17:17; Jer 32:44; Ob 1:19; Rev 7:8
1:37 n Nu 26:41
1:38 o Ge 30:6; Dt 33:22
1:39 p Nu 26:43
1:40 q S Ge 30:13; Nu 26:44; Rev 7:6
1:41 r Nu 26:47
1:42 s S Ge 30:8; Rev 7:6
1:43 t Nu 26:50 u S Ex 1:1-4
1:44 v Nu 26:64
1:45 w ver 3; Nu 14:29 x Nu 2:32
1:46 y S Ex 12:37; 2Sa 24:9
1:47 z S Nu 3:17-20 a Nu 4:3,49
1:50 b Ex 25:9; S 26:1 c S 16:34; Ac 7:44; Rev 15:5 d Nu 3:31
1:51 e S Ex 26:1 f Nu 4:5 g Nu 3:38; 4:15 h S Ex 21:12

1:46 603,550. This was the total number of males above the age of twenty, not including the Levites (vv. 45–47). The nation of Israel, therefore, totaled perhaps at least two million people. For this many people to have been sustained in the desert would have required a perpetual miracle, a truth that God's Word clearly stresses (cf. Ex 16:4–15,31–33; Nu 20:8; Dt 8:2–4; 29:5; Ps 78:26–28; 1Co 10:4).

1:52 EACH MAN ... UNDER HIS OWN STANDARD. The Israelite camp was organized with an inner circle of Levites around the tabernacle and an outer circle of the twelve tribes, with three tribes on each side of the tabernacle. The line of march was also organized in such a way that when the cloud lifted, they could move quickly, and when the cloud settled, they could find their places in the camp without confusion. The Bible teaches organization, not for organization's sake, but for smooth operation of the work that needs to be done. The tabernacle in the center of the camp symbolized that the life of the nation revolved around the Lord and the worship of him as their Redeemer.

ites are to set up their tents by divisions, each man in his own camp under
his own standard.[i] 53The Levites,
however, are to set up their tents
around the tabernacle[j] of the Testimony so that wrath will not fall[k] on
the Israelite community. The Levites
are to be responsible for the care of the
tabernacle of the Testimony.[l]"
54The Israelites did all this just as
the LORD commanded Moses.

The Arrangement of the Tribal Camps

2 The LORD said to Moses and Aaron:
2"The Israelites are to camp
around the Tent of Meeting some distance from it, each man under his standard[m] with the banners of his family."

3On the east, toward the sunrise, the divisions of the camp of
Judah are to encamp under their
standard. The leader of the people
of Judah is Nahshon son of Amminadab.[n] 4His division numbers
74,600.
5The tribe of Issachar[o] will
camp next to them. The leader of
the people of Issachar is Nethanel
son of Zuar.[p] 6His division numbers 54,400.
7The tribe of Zebulun will be
next. The leader of the people of
Zebulun is Eliab son of Helon.[q]
8His division numbers 57,400.
9All the men assigned to the
camp of Judah, according to their
divisions, number 186,400. They
will set out first.[r]

10On the south[s] will be the divisions of the camp of Reuben under their standard. The leader of
the people of Reuben is Elizur son
of Shedeur.[t] 11His division numbers 46,500.
12The tribe of Simeon[u] will
camp next to them. The leader of
the people of Simeon is Shelumiel
son of Zurishaddai.[v] 13His division numbers 59,300.
14The tribe of Gad[w] will be
next. The leader of the people of
Gad is Eliasaph son of Deuel.[a][x]
15His division numbers 45,650.
16All the men assigned to the
camp of Reuben,[y] according to
their divisions, number 151,450.
They will set out second.

17Then the Tent of Meeting and
the camp of the Levites[z] will set
out in the middle of the camps.
They will set out in the same order as they encamp, each in
his own place under his standard.

18On the west[a] will be the divisions of the camp of Ephraim[b]
under their standard. The leader
of the people of Ephraim is Elishama son of Ammihud.[c] 19His division numbers 40,500.
20The tribe of Manasseh[d] will
be next to them. The leader of the
people of Manasseh is Gamaliel
son of Pedahzur.[e] 21His division
numbers 32,200.
22The tribe of Benjamin[f] will
be next. The leader of the people
of Benjamin is Abidan son of Gideoni.[g] 23His division numbers
35,400.
24All the men assigned to the
camp of Ephraim,[h] according to
their divisions, number 108,100.
They will set out third.[i]

25On the north[j] will be the divisions of the camp of Dan, under
their standard.[k] The leader of
the people of Dan is Ahiezer son
of Ammishaddai.[l] 26His division
numbers 62,700.
27The tribe of Asher will camp
next to them. The leader of the
people of Asher is Pagiel son of
Ocran.[m] 28His division numbers
41,500.
29The tribe of Naphtali[n] will be
next. The leader of the people of
Naphtali is Ahira son of Enan.[o]
30His division numbers 53,400.
31All the men assigned to the
camp of Dan number 157,600.
They will set out last,[p] under
their standards.

32These are the Israelites,
counted according to their families.[q] All those in the camps,
by their divisions, number
603,550.[r] 33The Levites, however, were not counted[s] along with

1:52 [i]Nu 10:14; Ps 20:5; SS 2:4; 6:4
1:53 [j]Nu 2:10; 3:23,29,38 [k]Lev 10:6; Nu 16:46; 18:5; Dt 9:22 [l]S Ex 38:21; Nu 18:2-4
2:2 [m]Ps 74:4; Isa 31:9; Jer 4:21
2:3 [n]S Ex 6:23
2:5 [o]Nu 10:15 [p]S Nu 1:8
2:7 [q]Nu 1:9; 10:16
2:9 [r]Nu 10:14; Jdg 1:1
2:10 [s]S Nu 1:53 [t]Nu 1:5
2:12 [u]Nu 10:19 [v]S Nu 1:6
2:14 [w]Nu 10:20 [x]Nu 1:14; 10:20
2:16 [y]Nu 10:18
2:17 [z]Nu 1:50; 10:21
2:18 [a]S Nu 1:53 [b]S Ge 48:20; Jer 31:18-20 [c]Nu 1:10
2:20 [d]S Ge 48:20 [e]S Nu 1:10
2:22 [f]Nu 10:24 [g]S Nu 1:11
2:24 [h]Nu 10:22 [i]Ps 80:2
2:25 [j]S Nu 1:53 [k]Nu 10:25 [l]S Nu 1:12
2:27 [m]Nu 1:13; 10:26
2:29 [n]Nu 10:27 [o]Nu 1:15; 10:27
2:31 [p]Nu 10:25; Jos 6:9
2:32 [q]Nu 1:45 [r]S Ex 12:37
2:33 [s]Nu 1:47; 26:57-62

[a] *14* Many manuscripts of the Masoretic Text, Samaritan Pentateuch and Vulgate (see also Num. 1:14); most manuscripts of the Masoretic Text *Reuel*

the other Israelites, as the LORD commanded Moses.

34So the Israelites did everything the LORD commanded Moses; that is the way they encamped under their standards, and that is the way they set out, each with his clan and family.

The Levites

3 This is the account of the family of Aaron and Moses[t] at the time the LORD talked with Moses on Mount Sinai.[u]

2The names of the sons of Aaron were Nadab the firstborn[v] and Abihu, Eleazar and Ithamar.[w] **3**Those were the names of Aaron's sons, the anointed priests,[x] who were ordained to serve as priests. **4**Nadab and Abihu, however, fell dead before the LORD[y] when they made an offering with unauthorized fire before him in the Desert of Sinai.[z] They had no sons; so only Eleazar and Ithamar[a] served as priests during the lifetime of their father Aaron.[b]

5The LORD said to Moses, **6**"Bring the tribe of Levi[c] and present them to Aaron the priest to assist him.[d] **7**They are to perform duties for him and for the whole community[e] at the Tent of Meeting by doing the work[f] of the tabernacle. **8**They are to take care of all the furnishings of the Tent of Meeting, fulfilling the obligations of the Israelites by doing the work of the tabernacle. **9**Give the Levites to Aaron and his sons;[g] they are the Israelites who are to be given wholly to him.**b** **10**Appoint Aaron[h] and his sons to serve as priests;[i] anyone else who approaches the sanctuary must be put to death."[j]

11The LORD also said to Moses, **12**"I have taken the Levites[k] from among the Israelites in place of the first male offspring[l] of every Israelite woman. The Levites are mine,[m] **13**for all the firstborn are mine.[n] When I struck down all the firstborn in Egypt, I set apart for myself every firstborn in Israel, whether man or animal. They are to be mine. I am the LORD."[o]

14The LORD said to Moses in the Desert of Sinai,[p] **15**"Count[q] the Levites by their families and clans. Count every male a month old or more."[r] **16**So Moses counted them, as he was commanded by the word of the LORD.

17These were the names of the sons of Levi:[s]

Gershon,[t] Kohath[u] and Merari.[v]

18These were the names of the Gershonite clans:

Libni and Shimei.[w]

19The Kohathite clans:

Amram, Izhar, Hebron and Uzziel.[x]

20The Merarite clans:[y]

Mahli and Mushi.[z]

These were the Levite clans, according to their families.

21To Gershon[a] belonged the clans of the Libnites and Shimeites;[b] these were the Gershonite clans. **22**The number of all the males a month old or more who were counted was 7,500. **23**The Gershonite clans were to camp on the west, behind the tabernacle.[c] **24**The leader of the families of the Gershonites was Eliasaph son of Lael. **25**At the Tent of Meeting the Gershonites were responsible for the care of the tabernacle[d] and tent, its coverings,[e] the curtain at the entrance[f] to the Tent of Meeting,[g] **26**the curtains of the courtyard[h], the curtain at the entrance to the courtyard surrounding the tabernacle and altar,[i] and the ropes[j]—and everything[k] related to their use.

27To Kohath[l] belonged the clans of the Amramites, Izharites, Hebronites and Uzzielites;[m] these were the Kohathite[n] clans. **28**The number of all the males a month old or more[o] was 8,600.**c** The Kohathites were re-

3:1 [t]S Ex 6:27 [u]S Ex 19:11
3:2 [v]Nu 1:20 [w]S Ex 6:23
3:3 [x]S Ex 28:41; S 29:30
3:4 [y]S Lev 10:2 [z]S Lev 10:1 [a]Lev 10:6,12; Nu 4:28 [b]1Ch 24:1
3:6 [c]Dt 10:8; 31:9; 1Ch 15:2 [d]Nu 8:6-22; 18:1-7; 2Ch 29:11
3:7 [e]Nu 1:53; 8:19 [f]S Lev 8:35
3:9 [g]ver 12,45; Nu 8:19; 18:6
3:10 [h]S Ex 30:7 [i]S Ex 29:9 [j]Nu 1:51
3:12 [k]Ne 13:29; Mal 2:4 [l]ver 41; Nu 8:16,18 [m]S ver 9; Ex 13:2; Nu 8:14; 16:9
3:13 [n]S Ex 13:12 [o]Lev 11:44
3:14 [p]S Ex 19:1
3:15 [q]ver 39; S Nu 1:19 [r]ver 22; Nu 18:16; 26:62
3:17 [s]S Ge 29:34; S 46:11; Nu 1:47; 1Ch 15:4; 23:6; 2Ch 29:12 [t]Jos 21:6 [u]Jos 21:4 [v]S Ex 6:16
3:18 [w]Ex 6:17
3:19 [x]S Ex 6:18
3:20 [y]S Ge 46:11 [z]S Ex 6:19
3:21 [a]S Ge 46:11 [b]Ex 6:17
3:23 [c]S Nu 2:18
3:25 [d]Ex 25:9; Nu 7:1 [e]Ex 26:14 [f]Ex 26:36; Nu 4:25 [g]Ex 40:2
3:26 [h]Ex 27:9 [i]ver 31 [j]Ex 35:18 [k]Nu 4:26
3:27 [l]S Ge 46:11; S Ex 6:18 [m]Ex 6:18; 1Ch 26:23 [n]Nu 4:15,37
3:28 [o]ver 15

b9 Most manuscripts of the Masoretic Text; some manuscripts of the Masoretic Text, Samaritan Pentateuch and Septuagint (see also Num. 8:16) *to me* **c**28 Hebrew; some Septuagint manuscripts *8,300*

3:3 ANOINTED PRIESTS. The purpose of anointing the priests was to "ordain" them to God's service. (1) Likewise, in the NT, when believers are anointed by the Holy Spirit, they are set apart and empowered for service and witness in God's kingdom (Ac 1:8; 2:4). (2) The Hebrew name "Messiah" and the Greek name "Christ" both mean "the Anointed One" (see Mt 1:1, note). Everything Christ did, he did under the anointing of the Holy Spirit (see article on JESUS AND THE HOLY SPIRIT, p. 1546).

3:4 OFFERING WITH UNAUTHORIZED FIRE. See Lev 10:1–2, notes.

sponsible[p] for the care of the sanctuary.[q] 29The Kohathite clans were to
camp on the south side[r] of the tabernacle. 30The leader of the families of
the Kohathite clans was Elizaphan[s]
son of Uzziel. 31They were responsible
for the care of the ark,[t] the table,[u]
the lampstand,[v] the altars,[w] the articles[x] of the sanctuary used in ministering, the curtain,[y] and everything
related to their use.[z] 32The chief leader of the Levites was Eleazar[a] son of
Aaron, the priest. He was appointed
over those who were responsible[b] for
the care of the sanctuary.[c]

33To Merari belonged the clans of
the Mahlites and the Mushites;[d] these
were the Merarite clans.[e] 34The number of all the males a month old or
more[f] who were counted was 6,200.
35The leader of the families of the Merarite clans was Zuriel son of Abihail;
they were to camp on the north side of
the tabernacle.[g] 36The Merarites
were appointed[h] to take care of the
frames of the tabernacle,[i] its crossbars,[j] posts,[k] bases, all its equipment, and everything related to their
use,[l] 37as well as the posts of the surrounding courtyard[m] with their bases,
tent pegs[n] and ropes.

38Moses and Aaron and his sons
were to camp to the east[o] of the tabernacle, toward the sunrise, in front of
the Tent of Meeting.[p] They were responsible for the care of the sanctuary[q] on behalf of the Israelites. Anyone else who approached the
sanctuary was to be put to death.[r]

39The total number of Levites counted[s] at the LORD's command by Moses
and Aaron according to their clans, including every male a month old or
more, was 22,000.[t]

40The LORD said to Moses, "Count all
the firstborn Israelite males who are a
month old or more[u] and make a list of
their names.[v] 41Take the Levites for
me in place of all the firstborn of the
Israelites,[w] and the livestock of the
Levites in place of all the firstborn of
the livestock of the Israelites. I am the
LORD."[x]

42So Moses counted all the firstborn
of the Israelites, as the LORD commanded him. 43The total number of firstborn
males a month old or more,[y] listed by
name, was 22,273.[z]

44The LORD also said to Moses,
45"Take the Levites in place of all the
firstborn of Israel, and the livestock of
the Levites in place of their livestock.
The Levites are to be mine.[a] I am the
LORD.[b] 46To redeem[c] the 273 firstborn Israelites who exceed the number
of the Levites, 47collect five shekels[d][d] for each one, according to the
sanctuary shekel,[e] which weighs
twenty gerahs.[f] 48Give the money for
the redemption[g] of the additional Israelites to Aaron and his sons."[h]

49So Moses collected the redemption money[i] from those who exceeded
the number redeemed by the Levites.
50From the firstborn of the Israelites[j]
he collected silver weighing 1,365
shekels,[e][k] according to the sanctuary shekel. 51Moses gave the redemption money to Aaron and his sons, as
he was commanded by the word of the
LORD.

The Kohathites

4 The LORD said to Moses and Aaron:
2"Take a census[l] of the Kohathite branch of the Levites by their clans
and families. 3Count[m] all the men
from thirty to fifty years of age[n] who
come to serve in the work in the Tent
of Meeting.

4"This is the work[o] of the Kohathites[p] in the Tent of Meeting: the care
of the most holy things.[q] 5When the
camp is to move,[r] Aaron and his sons
are to go in and take down the shielding curtain[s] and cover the ark of the
Testimony with it.[t] 6Then they are to
cover this with hides of sea cows,[f][u]
spread a cloth of solid blue over that
and put the poles[v] in place.

7"Over the table of the Presence[w]
they are to spread a blue cloth and put

3:28 [p] Nu 4:4,15 [q] S Ex 25:8; 30:13; 2Ch 30:19; Ps 15:1; 20:2; Eze 44:27 **3:29** [r] S Nu 1:53 **3:30** [s] S Ex 6:22 **3:31** [t] S Ex 25:10-22; Dt 10:1-8; 2Ch 5:2; Jer 3:16 [u] S Ex 25:23 [v] S Ex 25:31; 1Ch 28:15; Jer 52:19 [w] ver 26 [x] Nu 1:50 [y] S Ex 26:33; Nu 4:5 [z] Nu 4:15; 18:3 **3:32** [a] S Ex 6:23 [b] ver 28 [c] Nu 4:19; 18:3 **3:33** [d] S Ex 6:19 [e] S Ge 46:11 **3:34** [f] ver 15 **3:35** [g] S Nu 2:25 **3:36** [h] Nu 4:32 [i] Ex 26:15-25; 35:20-29 [j] Ex 26:26-29 [k] Ex 36:36 [l] Nu 18:3 **3:37** [m] Ex 27:10-17 [n] Ex 27:19 **3:38** [o] Nu 2:3 [p] S Nu 1:53; 1Ch 9:27; 23:32 [q] ver 7; Nu 18:5 [r] ver 10; Nu 1:51 **3:39** [s] S ver 15 [t] Nu 26:62 **3:40** [u] ver 15 [v] Nu 1:2 **3:41** [w] ver 12 [x] Lev 11:44 **3:43** [y] ver 15 [z] ver 39 **3:45** [a] S ver 9 [b] Lev 11:44 **3:46** [c] Ex 13:13; Nu 18:15 **3:47** [d] S Lev 27:6 [e] S Ex 30:13 [f] S Lev 27:25 **3:48** [g] ver 51 [h] ver 50 **3:49** [i] ver 48 **3:50** [j] ver 41,45 [k] S ver 46-48 **4:2** [l] S Ex 30:12 **4:3** [m] S Nu 1:47 [n] ver 23; Nu 8:25; 1Ch 23:3,24,27; Ezr 3:8 **4:4** [o] S Nu 3:28 [p] Nu 7:9 [q] ver 19 **4:5** [r] Nu 1:51 [s] S Ex 26:31,33 [t] 1Ch 23:26 **4:6** [u] S Ex 25:5 [v] S Ex 25:13-15; 1Ki 8:7; 2Ch 5:8 **4:7** [w] S Lev 24:6

[d] *47* That is, about 2 ounces (about 55 grams) [e] *50* That is, about 35 pounds (about 15.5 kilograms) [f] *6* That is, dugongs; also in verses 8, 10, 11, 12, 14 and 25

3:43 FIRSTBORN. The low number of "firstborn males" compared with the approximately 600,000 men of 1:46 has been explained by some to be a reference to only those "firstborn" who were born between the time of the exodus (cf. Ex 13:1–2) and the numbering of the tribes that occurred thirteen months later.

on it the plates, dishes and bowls, and
the jars for drink offerings;[x] the bread
that is continually there[y] is to remain
on it. 8Over these they are to spread a
scarlet cloth, cover that with hides of
sea cows and put its poles[z] in place.
9"They are to take a blue cloth and
cover the lampstand that is for light,
together with its lamps, its wick trimmers and trays,[a] and all its jars for
the oil used to supply it. 10Then they
are to wrap it and all its accessories in
a covering of hides of sea cows and put
it on a carrying frame.[b]
11"Over the gold altar[c] they are to
spread a blue cloth and cover that with
hides of sea cows and put its poles[d] in
place.
12"They are to take all the articles[e]
used for ministering in the sanctuary,
wrap them in a blue cloth, cover that
with hides of sea cows and put them on
a carrying frame.[f]
13"They are to remove the ashes[g]
from the bronze altar[h] and spread a
purple cloth over it. 14Then they are to
place on it all the utensils[i] used for
ministering at the altar, including the
firepans,[j] meat forks,[k] shovels[l]
and sprinkling bowls.[m] Over it they
are to spread a covering of hides of sea
cows and put its poles[n] in place.
15"After Aaron and his sons have
finished covering the holy furnishings
and all the holy articles, and when the
camp is ready to move,[o] the Kohathites[p] are to come to do the carrying.[q]
But they must not touch the holy
things[r] or they will die.[st] The Kohathites are to carry those things that
are in the Tent of Meeting.
16"Eleazar[u] son of Aaron, the
priest, is to have charge of the oil for
the light,[v] the fragrant incense,[w] the
regular grain offering[x] and the anointing oil. He is to be in charge of the entire tabernacle and everything in it, including its holy furnishings and
articles."
17The LORD said to Moses and Aaron, 18"See that the Kohathite tribal
clans are not cut off from the Levites.
19So that they may live and not die
when they come near the most holy
things,[y] do this for them: Aaron and
his sons[z] are to go into the sanctuary
and assign to each man his work and
what he is to carry.[a] 20But the Kohathites must not go in to look[b] at the
holy things, even for a moment, or they
will die."

The Gershonites

21The LORD said to Moses, 22"Take a
census also of the Gershonites by their
families and clans. 23Count all the men
from thirty to fifty years of age[c] who
come to serve in the work at the Tent
of Meeting.
24"This is the service of the Gershonite clans as they work and carry
burdens: 25They are to carry the curtains of the tabernacle,[d] the Tent of
Meeting,[e] its covering[f] and the outer
covering of hides of sea cows, the curtains for the entrance to the Tent of
Meeting, 26the curtains of the courtyard surrounding the tabernacle and
altar,[g] the curtain for the entrance,[h]
the ropes and all the equipment[i] used
in its service. The Gershonites are to
do all that needs to be done with these
things. 27All their service, whether
carrying or doing other work, is to be
done under the direction of Aaron and
his sons.[j] You shall assign to them as
their responsibility[k] all they are to
carry. 28This is the service of the Gershonite clans[l] at the Tent of Meeting.
Their duties are to be under the direction of Ithamar[m] son of Aaron, the
priest.

The Merarites

29"Count[n] the Merarites by their
clans and families.[o] 30Count all the
men from thirty to fifty years of age
who come to serve in the work at the
Tent of Meeting. 31This is their duty as
they perform service at the Tent of
Meeting: to carry the frames of the tabernacle, its crossbars, posts and bases,[p] 32as well as the posts of the surrounding courtyard with their bases,
tent pegs, ropes,[q] all their equipment
and everything related to their use. Assign to each man the specific things he
is to carry. 33This is the service of the
Merarite clans as they work at the
Tent of Meeting under the direction of
Ithamar[r] son of Aaron, the priest."

4:7 x Ex 39:36; Jer 52:19 y S Ex 25:30
4:8 z Ex 26:26-28
4:9 a S Ex 25:38
4:10 b ver 12
4:11 c S Ex 30:1 d Ex 30:4
4:12 e Nu 3:31 f ver 10
4:13 g S Lev 1:16 h Ex 27:1-8; Nu 3:31
4:14 i S Ex 31:9 j S Ex 27:3 k 1Ch 28:17; 2Ch 4:16 l 2Ch 4:11 m Ex 27:3; Nu 7:84; 2Ch 4:8; Jer 52:18 n Ex 27:6
4:15 o ver 5 p S Nu 3:27 q Nu 7:9 r ver 4 s S Ex 28:43 t Nu 1:51; 2Sa 6:6, 7
4:16 u Lev 10:6; Nu 3:32 v S Ex 25:6 w S Ex 25:6 x S Ex 29:41; Lev 6:14-23
4:19 y S ver 15 z ver 27 a S Nu 3:32
4:20 b S Ex 19:21
4:23 c S ver 3
4:25 d Ex 27:10-18 e Nu 3:25 f Ex 26:14
4:26 g Ex 27:9 h Ex 27:16 i Nu 3:26
4:27 j ver 19 k Nu 3:25,26
4:28 l Nu 7:7 m S Ex 6:23
4:29 n S Ex 30:12 o S Ge 46:11
4:31 p Nu 3:36
4:32 q Nu 3:37
4:33 r S Ex 38:21

4:20 OR THEY WILL DIE. God's holiness will either destroy (vv. 15,20; see Lev 10:2, note) or sanctify (Isa 6:1–7; see Lev 19:2, note). God was teaching that his presence brings blessing if he is obeyed and honored, but judgment if he is treated with irreverence and dishonor (cf. 1Co 11:27–29).

The Numbering of the Levite Clans

34Moses, Aaron and the leaders of the community counted the Kohathites[s] by their clans and families. 35All the men from thirty to fifty years of age[t] who came to serve in the work in the Tent of Meeting, 36counted by clans, were 2,750. 37This was the total of all those in the Kohathite clans[u] who served in the Tent of Meeting. Moses and Aaron counted them according to the LORD's command through Moses.

38The Gershonites[v] were counted by their clans and families. 39All the men from thirty to fifty years of age who came to serve in the work at the Tent of Meeting, 40counted by their clans and families, were 2,630. 41This was the total of those in the Gershonite clans who served at the Tent of Meeting. Moses and Aaron counted them according to the LORD's command.

42The Merarites were counted by their clans and families. 43All the men from thirty to fifty years of age[w] who came to serve in the work at the Tent of Meeting, 44counted by their clans, were 3,200. 45This was the total of those in the Merarite clans.[x] Moses and Aaron counted them according to the LORD's command through Moses.

46So Moses, Aaron and the leaders of Israel counted[y] all the Levites by their clans and families. 47All the men from thirty to fifty years of age[z] who came to do the work of serving and carrying the Tent of Meeting 48numbered 8,580.[a] 49At the LORD's command through Moses, each was assigned his work and told what to carry.

Thus they were counted,[b] as the LORD commanded Moses.

The Purity of the Camp

5 The LORD said to Moses, 2"Command the Israelites to send away from the camp anyone who has an infectious skin disease[g][c] or a discharge[d] of any kind, or who is ceremonially unclean[e] because of a dead body.[f] 3Send away male and female alike; send them outside the camp so they will not defile their camp, where I dwell among them.[g]" 4The Israelites did this; they sent them outside the camp. They did just as the LORD had instructed Moses.

Restitution for Wrongs

5The LORD said to Moses, 6"Say to the Israelites: 'When a man or woman wrongs another in any way[h] and so is unfaithful[h] to the LORD, that person is guilty[i] 7and must confess[j] the sin he has committed. He must make full restitution[k] for his wrong, add one fifth to it and give it all to the person he has wronged. 8But if that person has no close relative to whom restitution can be made for the wrong, the restitution belongs to the LORD and must be given to the priest, along with the ram[l] with which atonement is made for him.[m] 9All the sacred contributions the Israelites bring to a priest will belong to him.[n] 10Each man's sacred gifts are his own, but what he gives to the priest will belong to the priest.[o]' "

The Test for an Unfaithful Wife

11Then the LORD said to Moses, 12"Speak to the Israelites and say to them: 'If a man's wife goes astray[p] and is unfaithful to him 13by sleeping with another man,[q] and this is hidden from her husband and her impurity is undetected (since there is no witness against her and she has not been caught in the act), 14and if feelings of jealousy[r] come over her husband and he suspects his wife and she is impure—or if he is jealous and suspects her even though she is not impure—15then he is to take his wife to the priest. He must also take an offering of a tenth of an ephah[i][s] of barley flour[t] on her behalf. He must not pour

4:34 [s] ver 2
4:35 [t] ver 3
4:37 [u] S Nu 3:27
4:38 [v] S Ge 46:11
4:43 [w] ver 3
4:45 [x] ver 29
4:46 [y] Nu 1:19
4:47 [z] ver 3
4:48 [a] Nu 3:39
4:49 [b] S Nu 1:47
5:2 [c] S Lev 13:2 [d] S Lev 15:2; Mt 9:20 [e] Lev 13:3; Nu 9:6-10 [f] S Lev 21:11
5:3 [g] S Ex 29:45; Lev 26:12; 2Co 6:16
5:6 [h] S Lev 6:2 [i] Lev 5:14-6:7
5:7 [j] S Lev 5:5; S Lk 19:8 [k] S Lev 5:16
5:8 [l] S Lev 5:15 [m] Lev 6:6,7
5:9 [n] Lev 6:17
5:10 [o] Lev 7:29-34
5:12 [p] ver 19-21; S Ex 20:14
5:13 [q] S Ex 20:14
5:14 [r] ver 30; Pr 6:34; 27:4; SS 8:6
5:15 [s] S Ex 16:36 [t] S Lev 6:20

g 2 Traditionally *leprosy*; the Hebrew word was used for various diseases affecting the skin—not necessarily leprosy. h 6 Or *woman commits any wrong common to mankind* i 15 That is, probably about 2 quarts (about 2 liters)

5:2 SEND AWAY FROM THE CAMP. People who had infectious skin diseases or discharges, or those who had come into contact with the dead, were ceremonially unclean (see Lev 12:2; 13:3, notes). Such people were sent outside the camp because God would not dwell in the midst of uncleanness (v. 3). The NT applies the moral principle behind this regulation to church members who flagrantly spurn God's truth or righteousness; they must be put out of the congregation if the body of believers expects to receive God's blessing and presence (cf. 1Co 5; 2Co 6:14–18; 2Th 3:14; 2Jn 10–11; see Mt 18:15, note).

oil on it or put incense on it, because
it is a grain offering for jealousy,[u] a
reminder[v] offering to draw attention
to guilt.
16 “ ‘The priest shall bring her and
have her stand before the LORD. 17 Then
he shall take some holy water in a clay
jar and put some dust from the tabernacle floor into the water. 18 After the
priest has had the woman stand before
the LORD, he shall loosen her hair[w] and
place in her hands the reminder offering, the grain offering for jealousy,[x]
while he himself holds the bitter water
that brings a curse.[y] 19 Then the
priest shall put the woman under oath
and say to her, “If no other man has
slept with you and you have not gone
astray[z] and become impure while
married to your husband, may this bitter water that brings a curse[a] not
harm you. 20 But if you have gone
astray[b] while married to your husband and you have defiled yourself by
sleeping with a man other than your
husband”— 21 here the priest is to put
the woman under this curse of the
oath[c]—“may the LORD cause your
people to curse and denounce you
when he causes your thigh to waste
away and your abdomen to swell.[j]
22 May this water[d] that brings a
curse[e] enter your body so that your
abdomen swells and your thigh wastes
away.[k]”
“ ‘Then the woman is to say, “Amen.
So be it.[f]”
23 “ ‘The priest is to write these
curses on a scroll[g] and then wash
them off into the bitter water. 24 He
shall have the woman drink the bitter
water that brings a curse, and this water will enter her and cause bitter suffering. 25 The priest is to take from her
hands the grain offering for jealousy,
wave it before the LORD[h] and bring it
to the altar. 26 The priest is then to take
a handful of the grain offering as a memorial offering[i] and burn it on the altar; after that, he is to have the woman
drink the water. 27 If she has defiled
herself and been unfaithful to her husband, then when she is made to drink
the water that brings a curse, it will go
into her and cause bitter suffering; her
abdomen will swell and her thigh
waste away,[l] and she will become accursed[j] among her people. 28 If, however, the woman has not defiled herself
and is free from impurity, she will be
cleared of guilt and will be able to have
children.
29 “ ‘This, then, is the law of jealousy
when a woman goes astray[k] and defiles herself while married to her husband, 30 or when feelings of jealousy[l]
come over a man because he suspects
his wife. The priest is to have her stand
before the LORD and is to apply this entire law to her. 31 The husband will be
innocent of any wrongdoing, but the
woman will bear the consequences[m] of
her sin.’ ”

The Nazirite

6 The LORD said to Moses, 2 “Speak
to the Israelites and say to them:
‘If a man or woman wants to make a
special vow[n], a vow of separation[o] to
the LORD as a Nazirite,[p] 3 he must abstain from wine[q] and other fermented

j21 Or *causes you to have a miscarrying womb and barrenness* k22 Or *body and cause you to be barren and have a miscarrying womb* l27 Or *suffering; she will have barrenness and a miscarrying womb*

5:15 u ver 18,25 v Eze 21:23; 29:16 **5:18** w S Lev 10:6; 1Co 11:6 x ver 15 y ver 19 **5:19** z ver 12,29 a ver 18 **5:20** b ver 12 **5:21** c Jos 6:26; 1Sa 14:24; Ne 10:29 **5:22** d Ps 109:18 e ver 18 f Dt 27:15 **5:23** g Jer 45:1 **5:25** h Lev 8:27 **5:26** i S Lev 2:2 **5:27** j Isa 43:28; 65:15; Jer 26:6; 29:18; 42:18; 44:12,22; Zec 8:13 **5:29** k S ver 19 **5:30** l S ver 14 **5:31** m S Lev 5:1 **6:2** n ver 5; S Ge 28:20; Ac 21:23 o ver 6 p Jdg 13:5; 16:17 **6:3** q S Lev 10:9; S Lk 1:15

5:18 WOMAN STAND BEFORE THE LORD. If a husband had reason to suspect that his wife had committed adultery but there was no evidence, the husband could have the wife brought before the Lord in order to determine her guilt or innocence. This protected her from false accusation, as well as provided a means for determining guilt if necessary. If she was guilty, she became ill as the result of God's judgment (vv. 21–28).

6:2 A NAZIRITE. The word "Nazirite" (Heb *nazir*, from *nazar*, "to set apart") designated one who was set apart and dedicated wholly to the Lord. The dedication could be for a specific period of time or for life (Jdg 13:5; 1Sa 1:11). (1) The Nazirites were raised up by God himself in order that through their lifestyle they might demonstrate his highest standard of holiness, sanctity and commitment in the people's presence (cf. Am 2:11–12). (2) The Nazirite vow was totally voluntary and was designed to teach Israel that total devotion to God must come first from a person's heart and then come to expression in self-denial (vv. 3–4), visible profession (v. 5) and personal purity (vv. 6–8). The Nazirite's complete devotion serves as an example of what every Christian should seek to be.

6:3 WINE . . . FERMENTED DRINK. For comments on how the Nazirite was to relate to wine and fermented drink, see article on WINE IN THE OLD TESTAMENT, p. 204.

6:3 GRAPE JUICE. The word translated "juice" (Heb *mishrah*) refers to a drink made by steeping the grapes or the remains of pressed grapes in water.

WINE IN THE OLD TESTAMENT

***Nu 6:3** "He must abstain from wine and other fermented drink and must not drink vinegar made from wine or from other fermented drink. He must not drink grape juice or eat grapes or raisins."*

HEBREW WORDS FOR WINE. In general, there are two Hebrew words that are translated as "wine" in the Bible. (1) The first and most common word is *yayin*, a generic term used 141 times in the OT to indicate various kinds of fermented or unfermented wine (see Ne 5:18, which speaks of "wine [*yayin*] of all kinds"). (a) On the one hand, *yayin* is applied to all kinds of fermented grape juice (see Ge 9:20–21; 19:32–33; 1Sa 25:36–37; Pr 23:30–31). The tragic results of using fermented wine are described in various places in the OT, notably Pr 23:29–35 (see next section).

(b) On the other hand, *yayin* is also used for the sweet unfermented juice of the grape. It can refer to fresh juice as it is pressed from grapes. Isaiah prophesies, "No one treads out wine [*yayin*] at the presses" (Isa 16:10); likewise Jeremiah says, "I have stopped the flow of wine [*yayin*] from the presses; no one treads them with shouts of joy" (Jer 48:33). In fact, Jeremiah even refers to the juice still in the grape as *yayin* (see Jer 40:10,12). Further evidence that *yayin* at times refers to unfermented juice of the grape is found in Lamentations, where the author describes nursing infants as crying out to their mothers for their normal food of "bread and wine" (La 2:12). The fact that unfermented grape juice can go by the term "wine" is supported by various scholarly studies. *The Jewish Encyclopedia* (1901) states: "Fresh wine before fermentation was called *yayin-migat* [wine of the vat] (Sanh, 70a)." Also, the *Encyclopaedia Judaica* (1971) attests to the fact that the term *yayin* was used to refer to the juice of the grape in several stages, including "the newly pressed wine prior to fermentation." The Babylonian Talmud ascribes to Rabbi Hiyya a statement concerning "wine [*yayin*] from the press" (*Baba Bathra*, 97a). And in *Halakot Gedalot* it is said, "One may press out a cluster of grapes, since the juice of the grape is considered wine [*yayin*] in connection with the laws of the Nazirite" (cited by Louis Ginzberg in *American Jewish Yearbook*, 1923, pp. 408–409). For a discussion of *oinos*, the NT Greek equivalent of the Hebrew word *yayin*, see articles on WINE IN NEW TESTAMENT TIMES (1) and (2), p. 1534 and p. 1586.

(2) The other Hebrew word translated "wine" is *tirosh*, a word meaning "new wine" or "harvest wine." *Tirosh* occurs 38 times in the OT; it never refers to fermented drink, but always to the unfermented fruit of the vine, such as the juice that is still in the grape cluster (Isa 65:8) or sweet juice from newly harvested grapes (Dt 11:14; Pr 3:10; Joel 2:24). Brown, Driver, Briggs (*A Hebrew and English Lexicon of the Old Testament*) states that *tirosh* means "must, fresh or new wine"; *The Jewish Encyclopedia* (1901) says that "'*tirosh*' includes all kinds of sweet juices and must, and does not include fermented wine." *Tirosh* has "some good in it" (Isa 65:8); fermented wine, however, "is a mocker" (Pr 20:1) and brings drunkenness (see Pr 23:31, note).

(3) In addition to these two words for wine, there is another Hebrew word that occurs 23 times in the OT and often in the same context—*shekar*, usually translated as "beer" (e.g., 1Sa 1:15) or "fermented drink" (e.g., Nu 6:3). Some scholars say *shekar* most often refers to a fermented drink, perhaps made from palm juice, pomegranates, apples, or dates. *The Jewish Encyclopedia* (1901) suggests that when *yayin* was distinguished from *shekar*, the former was a form of fermented drink diluted with water whereas the latter was undiluted. At times, however, it can refer to a sweet satisfying unfermented juice (Robert P. Teachout, "The Use of 'Wine' in the Old Testament," Th.D. dissertation, Dallas Theological Seminary, 1979). *Shekar* is related to *shakar*, a Hebrew verb that can mean "to drink freely," in addition to "to make drunk." In most instances, it is best to

understand that when *yayin* and *shekar* are used together, they form a single figure of speech referring to intoxicating beverages.

OLD TESTAMENT PERSPECTIVE ON FERMENTED WINE. There are various places in the OT where the use of *yayin* and *shekar* as fermented beverages is condemned. (1) The Bible first describes the evil effects of intoxicating wine in the story of Noah (Ge 9:20–27). He planted a vineyard, harvested it, made intoxicating wine from the grapes and drank from it. Doing so led to drunkenness, immodesty, indiscretion and the family tragedy of a curse placed on Canaan. During Abraham's time, intoxicating wine was a factor in the incest that led to the pregnancies of Lot's daughters (Ge 19:31–38).

(2) Because of the corrupting potential of alcoholic drinks, God commanded all priests of Israel to abstain from wine and other fermented drink during their time of ministry. God regarded the violation of this command sufficiently serious to warrant the death penalty for the offending priest (Lev 10:9–11).

(3) God also revealed his will concerning wine and fermented drink by making abstinence a requirement for all who took the Nazirite vow (see next section).

(4) Solomon's God-given wisdom led him to write: "Wine is a mocker and beer a brawler; whoever is led astray by them is not wise" (see Pr 20:1, note). Alcoholic beverages can cause one to mock God's standard of righteousness and to lose self-control with regard to sin and immorality.

(5) Finally, the Bible unequivocally states that in order to avoid woe and sorrow and instead to follow God's will, the righteous must not even gaze at or desire any fermented wine that can intoxicate and cause addiction (see Pr 23:29–35, notes).

THE NAZIRITES AND WINE. Nazirites were expected to declare that any Israelite should live on as high a level of separation and commitment to God as they themselves did (see Nu 6:2, note). God gave them clear instructions concerning the use of wine. (1) Nazirites were to abstain from "wine and other fermented drink" (Nu 6:3; see Dt 14:26, note); in fact, they were not permitted to eat or drink any product made from the grape, either in liquid or solid form. Most likely God gave this command as a safeguard against the temptation to use intoxicating drinks and against the possibility of a Nazirite drinking alcoholic wine by mistake (Nu 6:3–4). God did not want a totally devoted person to be exposed to the possibility of intoxication or addiction (cf. Lev 10:8–11; Pr 31:4–5). Thus, the highest standard put before God's people with respect to alcoholic beverages was total abstinence (Nu 6:3–4).

(2) Drinking alcohol often leads to various other sins (such as sexual immorality or criminal activity). The Nazirites were to eat or drink nothing that came from the vine in order to teach them that they must avoid sin and anything that borders on it, leads to it, or tempts one to commit it.

(3) God's standard for the Nazirites of total abstinence from wine and fermented drink was ridiculed and rejected by many in Israel during Amos's day. This prophet stated that the ungodly "made the Nazirites drink wine" (see Am 2:12, note). The prophet Isaiah also declared, "Priests and prophets stagger from beer and are befuddled with wine; they reel from beer, they stagger when seeing visions, they stumble when rendering decisions. All the tables are covered with vomit and there is not a spot without filth" (Isa 28:7–8). This occurred because these leaders refused God's high standard of total abstinence (see Pr 31:4–5, note).

(4) The essential spirit of Naziritism—i.e., total consecration to God and his highest standards—is a demand placed on the believer in Christ (cf. Ro 12:1; 2Co 6:17; 7:1). Abstinence from anything that might draw one into sin, stimulate a desire for harmful things, open the way to drug or alcohol addiction, or cause a brother or sister to stumble is as necessary for the believer today as it was for the Nazirite in OT times (see 1Th 5:6, note; Tit 2:2, note; see articles on WINE IN NEW TESTAMENT TIMES (1) and (2), p. 1534 and p. 1586).

drink and must not drink vinegar[r]
made from wine or from other fermented drink. He must not drink grape juice
or eat grapes[s] or raisins. **4**As long as
he is a Nazirite, he must not eat anything that comes from the grapevine,
not even the seeds or skins.
5" 'During the entire period of his
vow of separation no razor[t] may be
used on his head.[u] He must be holy
until the period of his separation to the
LORD is over; he must let the hair of his
head grow long. **6**Throughout the period of his separation to the LORD he
must not go near a dead body.[v] **7**Even
if his own father or mother or brother
or sister dies, he must not make himself ceremonially unclean[w] on account
of them, because the symbol of his separation to God is on his head.
8Throughout the period of his separation he is consecrated to the LORD.
9" 'If someone dies suddenly in his
presence, thus defiling the hair he has
dedicated,[x] he must shave his head on
the day of his cleansing[y]—the seventh day. **10**Then on the eighth day[z]
he must bring two doves or two young
pigeons[a] to the priest at the entrance
to the Tent of Meeting.[b] **11**The priest
is to offer one as a sin offering[c] and
the other as a burnt offering[d] to make
atonement[e] for him because he sinned
by being in the presence of the dead
body. That same day he is to consecrate his head. **12**He must dedicate
himself to the LORD for the period of his
separation and must bring a year-old
male lamb[f] as a guilt offering.[g] The
previous days do not count, because he
became defiled during his separation.
13" 'Now this is the law for the Nazirite when the period of his separation
is over.[h] He is to be brought to the
entrance to the Tent of Meeting.[i]
14There he is to present his offerings
to the LORD: a year-old male lamb without defect[j] for a burnt offering, a
year-old ewe lamb without defect for a
sin offering,[k] a ram[l] without defect
for a fellowship offering,[m][m] **15**together with their grain offerings[n] and
drink offerings,[o] and a basket of
bread made without yeast—cakes
made of fine flour mixed with oil, and
wafers spread with oil.[p]
16" 'The priest is to present them[q]
before the LORD[r] and make the sin offering and the burnt offering.[s] **17**He is
to present the basket of unleavened
bread and is to sacrifice the ram as a
fellowship offering[t] to the LORD, together with its grain offering[u] and
drink offering.[v]
18" 'Then at the entrance to the Tent
of Meeting, the Nazirite must shave off
the hair that he dedicated.[w] He is to
take the hair and put it in the fire that
is under the sacrifice of the fellowship
offering.
19" 'After the Nazirite has shaved off
the hair of his dedication, the priest is
to place in his hands a boiled shoulder
of the ram, and a cake and a wafer from
the basket, both made without yeast.[x]
20The priest shall then wave them before the LORD as a wave offering;[y] they
are holy[z] and belong to the priest, together with the breast that was waved
and the thigh that was presented.[a] After that, the Nazirite may drink wine.[b]
21" 'This is the law of the Nazirite[c]
who vows his offering to the LORD in
accordance with his separation, in ad-

[m] *14* Traditionally *peace offering*; also in verses 17 and 18

6:3 [r] Ru 2:14; Ps 69:21; Pr 10:26 [s] S Lev 25:5 **6:5** [t] Ps 52:2; 57:4; 59:7; Isa 7:20; Eze 5:1 [u] 1Sa 1:11 **6:6** [v] S Lev 21:1-3; Nu 19:11-22 **6:7** [w] Nu 9:6 **6:9** [x] ver 18 [y] S Lev 14:9 **6:10** [z] S Lev 14:10 [a] S Lev 5:7 [b] Lev 14:11 **6:11** [c] S Ex 30:10 [d] S Ge 8:20 [e] S Ex 29:36 **6:12** [f] S Lev 12:6 [g] S Lev 5:15 **6:13** [h] Ac 21:26 [i] Lev 14:11 **6:14** [j] S Ex 12:5 [k] ver 11; Lev 4:3; 14:10 [l] S Lev 5:15 [m] Lev 3:1 **6:15** [n] Lev 2:1; S 6:14 [o] S Ge 35:14 [p] S Ex 29:2 **6:16** [q] Lev 1:3 [r] ver 10 [s] ver 11 **6:17** [t] Lev 3:1 [u] S Ex 29:41 [v] Lev 23:13 **6:18** [w] ver 9; Ac 21:24 **6:19** [x] Lev 7:12 **6:20** [y] Lev 7:30 [z] S Lev 27:9 [a] S Lev 7:34 [b] Ecc 9:7 **6:21** [c] ver 13

6:5 HAIR . . . GROW LONG. The Nazirite was to let his hair grow long as a visible symbol of his consecration to the Lord. According to Paul, long hair was normally a disgrace to a man (1Co 11:14); thus, for a Nazirite, to have long hair may have symbolized his willingness to bear reproach and ridicule for the Lord. The command not to go near a dead person (v. 6) stressed that death was never God's will when he created the human race. Death is the antithesis of life and the consequence of sin; thus a corpse was viewed as unclean (see Lev 12:2, note; 13:3, note).

6:14 PRESENT HIS OFFERINGS. After completing his vow of separation, the Nazirite was to offer the same kind of sacrifices that the high priest offered on the day of his ordination (cf. Lev 8–9); all those in Israel, men or women (v. 2), who completely dedicated themselves to God were as important in God's sight as the highest minister in the congregation. Greatness in God's kingdom is not based on position and power, but on consecration and commitment (see Lk 22:24–30, note).

6:20 THE NAZIRITE MAY DRINK WINE. After the Nazirite terminated his vow, he was permitted to drink wine (Heb *yayin*; see article on WINE IN THE OLD TESTAMENT, p. 204). God had not yet specifically forbidden the use of fermented *yayin*. Its prohibition applied at this time only to situations involving total consecration to God (vv. 1–4; Lev 10:9–11). In the process of progressive revelation, God later stated explicitly that *all* his people were to refrain from fermented *yayin* that could intoxicate (see Pr 23:29–35; see 23:31, note).

dition to whatever else he can afford.
He must fulfill the vow[d] he has made,
according to the law of the Nazirite.' "

The Priestly Blessing

22The LORD said to Moses, **23**"Tell
Aaron and his sons, 'This is how you
are to bless[e] the Israelites. Say to
them:

24" ' "The LORD bless you[f]
and keep you;[g]
25the LORD make his face shine upon
you[h]
and be gracious to you;[i]
26the LORD turn his face[j] toward
you
and give you peace.[k]" '

27"So they will put my name[l] on the
Israelites, and I will bless them."

Offerings at the Dedication of the Tabernacle

7 When Moses finished setting up
the tabernacle,[m] he anointed[n] it
and consecrated it and all its furnishings.[o] He also anointed and consecrated the altar and all its utensils.[p]
2Then the leaders of Israel,[q] the
heads of families who were the tribal
leaders in charge of those who were
counted,[r] made offerings. **3**They
brought as their gifts before the LORD
six covered carts[s] and twelve oxen—
an ox from each leader and a cart from
every two. These they presented before
the tabernacle.

4The LORD said to Moses, **5**"Accept
these from them, that they may be used
in the work at the Tent of Meeting.
Give them to the Levites as each man's
work requires."

6So Moses took the carts and oxen

6:21 [d]ver 2
6:23 [e]Dt 21:5; 1Ch 23:13
6:24 [f]S Ge 28:3; Dt 28:3-6; Ps 28:9; 128:5 [g]1Sa 2:9; Ps 17:8
6:25 [h]Job 29:24; Ps 4:6; 31:16; 80:3; 119:135 [i]Ge 43:29; Ps 25:16; 86:16; 119:29
6:26 [j]Ps 4:6; 44:3 [k]Ps 4:8; 29:11; 37:11,37; 127:2; Isa 14:7; Jer 33:6; Jn 14:27
6:27 [l]Dt 28:10; 2Sa 7:23; 2Ch 7:14; Ne 9:10; Jer 25:29; Eze 36:23
7:1 [m]Ex 40:17 [n]S Ex 30:26 [o]S Ex 40:9 [p]ver 84,88; Ex 40:10; 2Ch 7:9
7:2 [q]Nu 1:5-16 [r]Nu 1:19
7:3 [s]Ge 45:19; 1Sa 6:7-14; 1Ch 13:7
7:7 [t]Nu 4:24-26, 28
7:8 [u]Nu 4:31-33
7:9 [v]Nu 4:4 [w]Nu 4:15
7:10 [x]ver 1; S Ex 29:36 [y]2Ch 7:9
7:12 [z]S Nu 1:7
7:13 [a]S Ex 27:3 [b]ver 85 [c]S Ex 30:13; Lev 27:3-7 [d]Lev 2:1; Nu 6:15; 15:4
7:14 [e]ver 20; 1Ki 7:50; 2Ki 25:14; 2Ch 4:22; 24:14 [f]ver 86 [g]S Ex 25:6
7:15 [h]Ex 24:5; 29:3; Nu 28:11 [i]Lev 1:3
7:16 [j]Lev 4:3

and gave them to the Levites. **7**He gave
two carts and four oxen to the Gershonites,[t] as their work required,
8and he gave four carts and eight oxen
to the Merarites,[u] as their work required. They were all under the direction of Ithamar son of Aaron, the
priest. **9**But Moses did not give any to
the Kohathites,[v] because they were to
carry on their shoulders[w] the holy
things, for which they were responsible.

10When the altar was anointed,[x]
the leaders brought their offerings for
its dedication[y] and presented them
before the altar. **11**For the LORD had
said to Moses, "Each day one leader is
to bring his offering for the dedication
of the altar."

12The one who brought his offering on
the first day was Nahshon[z] son of Amminadab of the tribe of Judah.

13His offering was one silver plate
weighing a hundred and thirty
shekels,[n] and one silver sprinkling bowl[a] weighing seventy
shekels,[o][b] both according to the
sanctuary shekel,[c] each filled
with fine flour mixed with oil as a
grain offering;[d] **14**one gold
dish[e] weighing ten shekels,[p][f]
filled with incense;[g] **15**one young
bull,[h] one ram and one male lamb
a year old, for a burnt offering;[i]
16one male goat for a sin offering;[j] **17**and two oxen, five rams,
five male goats and five male

[n] *13* That is, about 3 1/4 pounds (about 1.5 kilograms); also elsewhere in this chapter
[o] *13* That is, about 1 3/4 pounds (about 0.8 kilogram); also elsewhere in this chapter
[p] *14* That is, about 4 ounces (about 110 grams); also elsewhere in this chapter

6:23 BLESS THE ISRAELITES. Vv. 22–27 show God's gracious response to his people if they maintained purity in the congregation and expressed the kind of heart-devotion seen in a Nazirite vow (see v. 2, note). To "bless" (Heb *barak*) carries the idea that God's presence, activity and love are brought into a person's life and environment. (1) This blessing was set before God's faithful servants under the conditions he had established (Dt 11:27).

(2) The priestly blessing consisted of three parts: (a) The imparting of God's blessing and his protection from evil forces and all that was adverse to one's welfare in life (v. 24; cf. Ps 71:1–6). (b) The shining of the Lord's face, i.e., God's favor, goodwill and grace toward the people (v. 25) is the opposite of his anger (cf. Ps 27:1; 31:16; Pr 15:30; 16:14; Isa 57:17). Grace is God's mercy, love and saving power (see article on FAITH AND GRACE, p. 1720). (c) The turning of the Lord's face toward them (v. 26), i.e., caring for and giving to them with heartfelt love (cf. Ps 4:7–8; 33:18; 34:17). What God gives is "peace" (v. 26). Peace (Heb *shalom*) means being complete so that nothing is lacking and receiving all that is necessary to make life truly life (cf. Mal 2:5), including hope for the future (Jer 29:11). The opposite of "peace" is not only lack of harmony, but evil in all its forms (cf. Ro 1:7; 1Co 1:3; 1Th 5:23; see article on THE PEACE OF GOD, p. 1134).

(3) God's blessing on his people would result in salvation going out like a lighted torch to all the nations (Ps 67; 133:3; Eze 34:26; see Mt 28:19, note; Lk 24:50, note).

lambs a year old, to be sacrificed as a fellowship offering.[q][k] This was the offering of Nahshon son of Amminadab.[l]

18 On the second day Nethanel son of Zuar,[m] the leader of Issachar, brought his offering.
19 The offering he brought was one silver plate weighing a hundred and thirty shekels, and one silver sprinkling bowl weighing seventy shekels, both according to the sanctuary shekel, each filled with fine flour mixed with oil as a grain offering; 20 one gold dish[n] weighing ten shekels, filled with incense; 21 one young bull, one ram and one male lamb a year old, for a burnt offering; 22 one male goat for a sin offering; 23 and two oxen, five rams, five male goats and five male lambs a year old, to be sacrificed as a fellowship offering. This was the offering of Nethanel son of Zuar.

24 On the third day, Eliab son of Helon,[o] the leader of the people of Zebulun, brought his offering.
25 His offering was one silver plate weighing a hundred and thirty shekels, and one silver sprinkling bowl weighing seventy shekels, both according to the sanctuary shekel, each filled with fine flour mixed with oil as a grain offering; 26 one gold dish weighing ten shekels, filled with incense; 27 one young bull, one ram and one male lamb a year old, for a burnt offering; 28 one male goat for a sin offering; 29 and two oxen, five rams, five male goats and five male lambs a year old, to be sacrificed as a fellowship offering. This was the offering of Eliab son of Helon.

30 On the fourth day Elizur son of Shedeur,[p] the leader of the people of Reuben, brought his offering.
31 His offering was one silver plate weighing a hundred and thirty shekels, and one silver sprinkling bowl weighing seventy shekels, both according to the sanctuary shekel, each filled with fine flour mixed with oil as a grain offering; 32 one gold dish weighing ten shekels, filled with incense; 33 one young bull, one ram and one male lamb a year old, for a burnt offering; 34 one male goat for a sin offering; 35 and two oxen, five rams, five male goats and five male lambs a year old, to be sacrificed as a fellowship offering. This was the offering of Elizur son of Shedeur.

36 On the fifth day Shelumiel son of Zurishaddai,[q] the leader of the people of Simeon, brought his offering.
37 His offering was one silver plate weighing a hundred and thirty shekels, and one silver sprinkling bowl weighing seventy shekels, both according to the sanctuary shekel, each filled with fine flour mixed with oil as a grain offering; 38 one gold dish weighing ten shekels, filled with incense; 39 one young bull, one ram and one male lamb a year old, for a burnt offering; 40 one male goat for a sin offering; 41 and two oxen, five rams, five male goats and five male lambs a year old, to be sacrificed as a fellowship offering. This was the offering of Shelumiel son of Zurishaddai.

42 On the sixth day Eliasaph son of Deuel,[r] the leader of the people of Gad, brought his offering.
43 His offering was one silver plate weighing a hundred and thirty shekels, and one silver sprinkling bowl weighing seventy shekels, both according to the sanctuary shekel, each filled with fine flour mixed with oil as a grain offering; 44 one gold dish weighing ten shekels, filled with incense; 45 one young bull, one ram and one male lamb a year old, for a burnt offering; 46 one male goat for a sin offering; 47 and two oxen, five rams, five male goats and five male lambs a year old, to be sacrificed as a fellowship offering. This was the offering of Eliasaph son of Deuel.

48 On the seventh day Elishama son of Ammihud,[s] the leader of the people of Ephraim, brought his offering.
49 His offering was one silver plate weighing a hundred and thirty

7:17 [k] Lev 3:1 [l] Nu 1:7
7:18 [m] S Nu 1:8
7:20 [n] S ver 14
7:24 [o] S Nu 1:9
7:30 [p] S Nu 1:5
7:36 [q] S Nu 1:6
7:42 [r] S Nu 1:14
7:48 [s] S Nu 1:10

[q] 17 Traditionally *peace offering*; also elsewhere in this chapter

shekels, and one silver sprinkling
bowl weighing seventy shekels,
both according to the sanctuary
shekel, each filled with fine flour
mixed with oil as a grain offering;
50one gold dish weighing ten
shekels, filled with incense; **51**one
young bull, one ram and one male
lamb a year old, for a burnt offering; **52**one male goat for a sin offering; **53**and two oxen, five rams,
five male goats and five male
lambs a year old, to be sacrificed
as a fellowship offering. This was
the offering of Elishama son of
Ammihud.[t]

54On the eighth day Gamaliel son of
Pedahzur,[u] the leader of the people of
Manasseh, brought his offering.
55His offering was one silver plate
weighing a hundred and thirty
shekels, and one silver sprinkling
bowl weighing seventy shekels,
both according to the sanctuary
shekel, each filled with fine flour
mixed with oil as a grain offering;
56one gold dish weighing ten
shekels, filled with incense; **57**one
young bull, one ram and one male
lamb a year old, for a burnt offering; **58**one male goat for a sin offering; **59**and two oxen, five rams,
five male goats and five male
lambs a year old, to be sacrificed
as a fellowship offering. This was
the offering of Gamaliel son of Pedahzur.

60On the ninth day Abidan son of Gideoni,[v] the leader of the people of Benjamin, brought his offering.
61His offering was one silver plate
weighing a hundred and thirty
shekels, and one silver sprinkling
bowl weighing seventy shekels,
both according to the sanctuary
shekel, each filled with fine flour
mixed with oil as a grain offering;
62one gold dish weighing ten
shekels, filled with incense; **63**one
young bull, one ram and one male
lamb a year old, for a burnt offering; **64**one male goat for a sin offering; **65**and two oxen, five rams,
five male goats and five male
lambs a year old, to be sacrificed
as a fellowship offering. This was
the offering of Abidan son of Gideoni.

7:53 t S Nu 1:10
7:54 u S Nu 1:10
7:60 v S Nu 1:11

66On the tenth day Ahiezer son of Ammishaddai,[w] the leader of the people
of Dan, brought his offering.
67His offering was one silver plate
weighing a hundred and thirty
shekels, and one silver sprinkling
bowl weighing seventy shekels,
both according to the sanctuary
shekel, each filled with fine flour
mixed with oil as a grain offering;
68one gold dish weighing ten
shekels, filled with incense; **69**one
young bull, one ram and one male
lamb a year old, for a burnt offering; **70**one male goat for a sin offering; **71**and two oxen, five rams,
five male goats and five male
lambs a year old, to be sacrificed
as a fellowship offering. This was
the offering of Ahiezer son of Ammishaddai.

72On the eleventh day Pagiel son of Ocran,[x] the leader of the people of Asher, brought his offering.
73His offering was one silver plate
weighing a hundred and thirty
shekels, and one silver sprinkling
bowl weighing seventy shekels,
both according to the sanctuary
shekel, each filled with fine flour
mixed with oil as a grain offering;
74one gold dish weighing ten
shekels, filled with incense; **75**one
young bull, one ram and one male
lamb a year old, for a burnt offering; **76**one male goat for a sin offering; **77**and two oxen, five rams,
five male goats and five male
lambs a year old, to be sacrificed
as a fellowship offering. This was
the offering of Pagiel son of Ocran.

78On the twelfth day Ahira son of
Enan,[y] the leader of the people of
Naphtali, brought his offering.
79His offering was one silver plate
weighing a hundred and thirty
shekels, and one silver sprinkling
bowl weighing seventy shekels,
both according to the sanctuary
shekel, each filled with fine flour
mixed with oil as a grain offering;
80one gold dish weighing ten
shekels, filled with incense; **81**one
young bull, one ram and one male
lamb a year old, for a burnt offering; **82**one male goat for a sin offering; **83**and two oxen, five rams,
five male goats and five male

7:66 w S Nu 1:12
7:72 x S Nu 1:13
7:78 y S Nu 1:15

lambs a year old, to be sacrificed
as a fellowship offering. This was
the offering of Ahira son of Enan.

84These were the offerings of the Israelite leaders for the dedication of the
altar when it was anointed:[z] twelve
silver plates, twelve silver sprinkling
bowls[a] and twelve gold dishes.[b]
85Each silver plate weighed a hundred
and thirty shekels, and each sprinkling
bowl seventy shekels. Altogether, the
silver dishes weighed two thousand
four hundred shekels,[r] according to
the sanctuary shekel.[c] **86**The twelve
gold dishes filled with incense weighed
ten shekels each, according to the
sanctuary shekel.[d] Altogether, the
gold dishes weighed a hundred and
twenty shekels.[s] **87**The total number
of animals for the burnt offering[e]
came to twelve young bulls, twelve
rams and twelve male lambs a year old,
together with their grain offering.[f]
Twelve male goats were used for the
sin offering.[g] **88**The total number of
animals for the sacrifice of the fellowship offering[h] came to twenty-four
oxen, sixty rams, sixty male goats and
sixty male lambs[i] a year old. These
were the offerings for the dedication of
the altar after it was anointed.[j]

89When Moses entered the Tent of
Meeting[k] to speak with the LORD,[l] he
heard the voice speaking to him from
between the two cherubim above the
atonement cover[m] on the ark of the
Testimony.[n] And he spoke with him.

Setting Up the Lamps

8 The LORD said to Moses, **2**"Speak
to Aaron and say to him, 'When
you set up the seven lamps, they are to
light the area in front of the lampstand.[o]' "

3Aaron did so; he set up the lamps
so that they faced forward on the lampstand, just as the LORD commanded
Moses. **4**This is how the lampstand
was made: It was made of hammered
gold[p]—from its base to its blossoms.
The lampstand was made exactly like
the pattern[q] the LORD had shown Moses.

The Setting Apart of the Levites

5The LORD said to Moses: **6**"Take the
Levites from among the other Israelites and make them ceremonially
clean.[r] **7**To purify them, do this:
Sprinkle the water of cleansing[s] on
them; then have them shave their
whole bodies[t] and wash their
clothes,[u] and so purify themselves.[v]
8Have them take a young bull with its
grain offering of fine flour mixed with
oil;[w] then you are to take a second
young bull for a sin offering.[x] **9**Bring
the Levites to the front of the Tent of
Meeting[y] and assemble the whole Israelite community.[z] **10**You are to
bring the Levites before the LORD, and
the Israelites are to lay their hands on
them.[a] **11**Aaron is to present the Levites before the LORD as a wave offering[b] from the Israelites, so that they
may be ready to do the work of the
LORD.

12"After the Levites lay their hands
on the heads of the bulls,[c] use the one
for a sin offering[d] to the LORD and the
other for a burnt offering,[e] to make
atonement[f] for the Levites. **13**Have
the Levites stand in front of Aaron and
his sons and then present them as a
wave offering[g] to the LORD. **14**In this
way you are to set the Levites apart
from the other Israelites, and the Levites will be mine.[h]

15"After you have purified the Levites and presented them as a wave offering,[i] they are to come to do their
work at the Tent of Meeting.[j] **16**They
are the Israelites who are to be given
wholly to me. I have taken them as my
own in place of the firstborn,[k] the first
male offspring[l] from every Israelite
woman. **17**Every firstborn male in Isra-

7:84 [z]ver 1,10 [a]S Nu 4:14 [b]ver 14 **7:85** [c]ver 13 **7:86** [d]ver 13 **7:87** [e]ver 15 [f]ver 13 [g]ver 16 **7:88** [h]ver 17 [i]Ge 32:14 [j]S ver 1,10 **7:89** [k]S Ex 40:2 [l]S Ex 29:42 [m]S Ex 16:34; Ps 80:1; 99:1 [n]Nu 3:31 **8:2** [o]Ex 25:37 **8:4** [p]S Ex 25:18, 36 [q]S Ex 25:9 **8:6** [r]Lev 22:2; Isa 1:16; 52:11 **8:7** [s]Nu 19:9,17; 31:23 [t]S Lev 14:9; Nu 6:9; Dt 21:12 [u]S Ge 35:2; Lev 14:8 [v]S Ge 35:2 **8:8** [w]Lev 2:1; Nu 15:8-10 [x]Lev 4:3 **8:9** [y]Ex 40:12 [z]Lev 8:3 **8:10** [a]S Lev 3:2; Ac 6:6 **8:11** [b]S Ex 29:24 **8:12** [c]S Ex 29:10 [d]Lev 4:3; Nu 6:11 [e]Lev 1:3 [f]S Ex 29:36 **8:13** [g]S Ex 29:24 **8:14** [h]S Nu 3:12 **8:15** [i]S Ex 29:24 [j]Ex 40:2 **8:16** [k]Nu 1:20 [l]S Nu 3:12

[r] *85* That is, about 60 pounds (about 28 kilograms) [s] *86* That is, about 3 pounds (about 1.4 kilograms)

8:6–26 THE LEVITES. These verses describe the purification and consecration of the Levites, who were appointed to help the priests in the ministry of worship (v. 19).

8:11 LEVITES ... AS A WAVE OFFERING. The "wave offering" was the priests' portion of the fellowship offering (Lev 7:28–34). It was waved toward the sanctuary as a sign of dedication to God and then waved toward the offerer or priest, indicating that the Lord was putting the offering at his or her disposal. Here the Levites themselves are a wave offering to the Lord. Seeing that they could not be waved literally, the dedication was carried out symbolically.

8:14 SET THE LEVITES APART. By their example, the Levites symbolized the godly separation that ought to characterize the entire nation.

el, whether man or animal,[m] is mine.
When I struck down all the firstborn in
Egypt, I set them apart for myself.[n][o]
18And I have taken the Levites in place
of all the firstborn sons in Israel.[p]
19Of all the Israelites, I have given the
Levites as gifts to Aaron and his
sons[q] to do the work at the Tent of
Meeting on behalf of the Israelites[r]
and to make atonement for them[s] so
that no plague will strike the Israelites
when they go near the sanctuary."
20Moses, Aaron and the whole Israelite community did with the Levites
just as the LORD commanded Moses.
21The Levites purified themselves and
washed their clothes.[t] Then Aaron
presented them as a wave offering before the LORD and made atonement[u]
for them to purify them.[v] **22**After that,
the Levites came to do their work[w] at
the Tent of Meeting under the supervision of Aaron and his sons. They did
with the Levites just as the LORD commanded Moses.
23The LORD said to Moses, **24**"This
applies to the Levites: Men twenty-five
years old or more[x] shall come to take
part in the work at the Tent of Meeting,[y] **25**but at the age of fifty,[z] they
must retire from their regular service
and work no longer. **26**They may assist
their brothers in performing their duties at the Tent of Meeting, but they
themselves must not do the work.[a]
This, then, is how you are to assign the
responsibilities of the Levites."

The Passover

9 The LORD spoke to Moses in the
Desert of Sinai in the first month[b]
of the second year after they came out
of Egypt.[c] He said, **2**"Have the Israelites celebrate the Passover[d] at the appointed time.[e] **3**Celebrate it at the appointed time, at twilight on the
fourteenth day of this month,[f] in accordance with all its rules and regulations.[g]"

8:17 [m]S Ex 4:23 [n]S Ex 22:29 [o]S Ex 13:2 **8:18** [p]S Nu 3:12 **8:19** [q]S Nu 3:9 [r]S Nu 3:7 [s]Nu 16:46 **8:21** [t]ver 7; S Ge 35:2 [u]Nu 16:47 [v]ver 12 **8:22** [w]ver 11 **8:24** [x]1Ch 23:3 [y]S Ex 38:21 **8:25** [z]S Nu 4:3 **8:26** [a]ver 11 **9:1** [b]S Ex 40:2 [c]Nu 1:1 **9:2** [d]S Ex 12:11 [e]ver 7 **9:3** [f]S Ex 12:6,42 [g]Ex 12:2-11, 43-49; Lev 23:5-8; Dt 16:1-8

9:4 [h]ver 2; S Ex 12:11 **9:5** [i]ver 1 [j]S Ex 12:6 [k]ver 3 **9:6** [l]S Lev 5:3; S 13:3 [m]S Lev 21:11 [n]Ex 18:15; Nu 27:2 **9:7** [o]ver 2 **9:8** [p]Ex 18:15; Lev 24:12; Nu 15:34; 27:5,21; Ps 85:8 **9:10** [q]ver 6 [r]2Ch 30:2 **9:11** [s]S Ex 12:6 [t]Ex 12:8 **9:12** [u]S Ex 12:8 [v]S Ex 12:46; Jn 19:36* [w]ver 3 **9:13** [x]S Ge 17:14 **9:14** [y]S Ex 12:19, 43

4So Moses told the Israelites to celebrate the Passover,[h] **5**and they did so
in the Desert of Sinai[i] at twilight on
the fourteenth day of the first month.[j]
The Israelites did everything just as
the LORD commanded Moses.[k]
6But some of them could not celebrate the Passover on that day because
they were ceremonially unclean[l] on
account of a dead body.[m] So they came
to Moses and Aaron[n] that same day
7and said to Moses, "We have become
unclean because of a dead body, but
why should we be kept from presenting
the LORD's offering with the other Israelites at the appointed time?[o]"
8Moses answered them, "Wait until
I find out what the LORD commands
concerning you."[p]
9Then the LORD said to Moses,
10"Tell the Israelites: 'When any of you
or your descendants are unclean because of a dead body[q] or are away on
a journey, they may still celebrate[r]
the LORD's Passover. **11**They are to celebrate it on the fourteenth day of the
second month[s] at twilight. They are
to eat the lamb, together with unleavened bread and bitter herbs.[t] **12**They
must not leave any of it till morning[u]
or break any of its bones.[v] When they
celebrate the Passover, they must follow all the regulations.[w] **13**But if a
man who is ceremonially clean and not
on a journey fails to celebrate the Passover, that person must be cut off from
his people[x] because he did not
present the LORD's offering at the appointed time. That man will bear the
consequences of his sin.
14" 'An alien[y] living among you
who wants to celebrate the LORD's
Passover must do so in accordance
with its rules and regulations. You
must have the same regulations for the
alien and the native-born.' "

The Cloud Above the Tabernacle

15On the day the tabernacle, the

8:17 EVERY FIRSTBORN . . . IS MINE. All Israelite firstborn belonged to the Lord (Ex 13:11–16); however, God allowed the Levites to become substitutes for all the firstborn (3:9, 11–13,40–41,45–51; 8:14–19).

9:15–23 CLOUD . . . FIRE. The cloud by day that looked like fire at night served as a sign of divine provision, protection and guidance for Israel in the desert. (1) The Bible emphasizes that the people were to set out or remain in camp only as the supernatural sign indicated. However, God's guidance did not eliminate the need for human wisdom and planning, for Moses asked Hobab to advise them about the best places to camp in the desert (10:29–32).

(2) Obeying God and following his will are thus dependent on both God's supernatural guidance and our own wisdom based on the principles of his word. It is important that we remain near him at all times and not separate ourselves from his protection and will.

(3) God's promise of leading for his OT people

Tent of the Testimony,[z] was set up,[a] the cloud[b] covered it. From evening till morning the cloud above the tabernacle looked like fire.[c] **16**That is how it continued to be; the cloud covered it, and at night it looked like fire.[d] **17**Whenever the cloud lifted from above the Tent, the Israelites set out;[e] wherever the cloud settled, the Israelites encamped.[f] **18**At the LORD's command the Israelites set out, and at his command they encamped. As long as the cloud stayed over the tabernacle, they remained[g] in camp. **19**When the cloud remained over the tabernacle a long time, the Israelites obeyed the LORD's order[h] and did not set out.[i] **20**Sometimes the cloud was over the tabernacle only a few days; at the LORD's command they would encamp, and then at his command they would set out. **21**Sometimes the cloud stayed only from evening till morning, and when it lifted in the morning, they set out. Whether by day or by night, whenever the cloud lifted, they set out. **22**Whether the cloud stayed over the tabernacle for two days or a month or a year, the Israelites would remain in camp and not set out; but when it lifted, they would set out. **23**At the LORD's command they encamped, and at the LORD's command they set out. They obeyed the LORD's order, in accordance with his command through Moses.

The Silver Trumpets

10 The LORD said to Moses: **2**"Make two trumpets[j] of hammered silver, and use them for calling the community[k] together and for having the camps set out.[l] **3**When both are sounded, the whole community is to assemble before you at the entrance to the Tent of Meeting. **4**If only one is sounded, the leaders[m]—the heads of the clans of Israel—are to assemble before you. **5**When a trumpet blast is sounded, the tribes camping on the east are to set out.[n] **6**At the sounding of a second blast, the camps on the south are to set out.[o] The blast will be the signal for setting out. **7**To gather the assembly, blow the trumpets,[p] but not with the same signal.[q]

8"The sons of Aaron, the priests, are to blow the trumpets. This is to be a lasting ordinance for you and the generations to come.[r] **9**When you go into battle in your own land against an enemy who is oppressing you,[s] sound a blast on the trumpets.[t] Then you will be remembered[u] by the LORD your God and rescued from your enemies.[v] **10**Also at your times of rejoicing—your appointed feasts and New Moon festivals[w]—you are to sound the trumpets[x] over your burnt offerings[y] and fellowship offerings,[t][z] and they will be a memorial for you before your God. I am the LORD your God.[a]"

The Israelites Leave Sinai

11On the twentieth day of the second month of the second year,[b] the cloud lifted[c] from above the tabernacle of the Testimony.[d] **12**Then the Israelites set out from the Desert of Sinai and traveled from place to place until the cloud came to rest in the Desert of Paran.[e] **13**They set out, this first time, at the LORD's command through Moses.[f]

14The divisions of the camp of Judah went first, under their standard.[g] Nahshon son of Amminadab[h] was in command. **15**Nethanel son of Zuar was over the division of the tribe[i] of Issachar,[j] **16**and Eliab son of Helon[k] was over the division of the tribe of Zebulun.[l] **17**Then the tabernacle was taken down, and the Gershonites and Merarites, who carried it, set out.[m]

18The divisions of the camp of Reuben[n] went next, under their standard.[o] Elizur son of Shedeur[p] was in command. **19**Shelumiel son of Zurishaddai was over the division of the tribe of Simeon,[q] **20**and Eliasaph son of Deuel was over the division of the tribe of Gad.[r] **21**Then the Kohathites[s] set out, carrying the holy things.[t] The tabernacle was to be set up before they arrived.[u]

22The divisions of the camp of Ephraim[v] went next, under their standard.

9:15 [z] S Ex 38:21 [a] S Ex 26:30 [b] S Ex 33:16 [c] Ex 13:21 **9:16** [d] S Ex 40:38 **9:17** [e] ver 21 [f] 1Co 10:1 **9:18** [g] Ex 40:37 **9:19** [h] S Lev 8:35 [i] Ex 40:37 **10:2** [j] ver 8,9; Nu 31:6; Ne 12:35; Ps 47:5; 98:6; 150:3 [k] Ne 4:18; Jer 4:5,19; 6:1; Hos 5:8; 8:1; Joel 2:1,15; Am 3:6 [l] Nu 33:3 **10:4** [m] S Ex 18:21 **10:5** [n] ver 14 **10:6** [o] ver 18 **10:7** [p] Jer 4:5; 6:1; Eze 33:3; Joel 2:1 [q] 1Co 14:8 **10:8** [r] S Ge 9:12; Nu 15:14; 35:29 **10:9** [s] Ex 3:9; Jdg 2:18; 6:9; 1Sa 10:18; 2Ki 13:4; Ps 106:42 [t] S Lev 23:24 [u] S Ge 8:1 [v] 2Ch 13:12; Ps 106:4 **10:10** [w] Nu 28:11; 1Sa 20:5,24; 2Ki 4:23; 2Ch 8:13; Ps 81:3; Isa 1:13; Eze 45:17; 46:6; Am 8:5 [x] S Lev 23:24 [y] Lev 1:3 [z] Lev 3:1; Nu 6:14 [a] Lev 11:44 **10:11** [b] Ex 40:17 [c] Nu 9:17 [d] S Ex 38:21 **10:12** [e] S Ge 14:6; Dt 1:1; 33:2 **10:13** [f] Dt 1:6 **10:14** [g] S Nu 1:52; S 2:3-9 [h] Nu 1:7 **10:15** [i] S Lev 24:11 [j] S Nu 1:8 **10:16** [k] S Nu 2:7 [l] S Nu 1:9 **10:17** [m] ver 21; Nu 4:21-32 **10:18** [n] Nu 2:16 [o] Nu 2:10-16 [p] S Nu 1:5 **10:19** [q] Nu 1:6 **10:20** [r] S Nu 1:14 **10:21** [s] S Nu 2:17 [t] Nu 4:20 [u] S ver 17 **10:22** [v] Nu 2:24

[t] *10* Traditionally *peace offerings*

still applies to believers. He will guide us by his word and by his Spirit (Ro 8:4). He will make straight the paths of all who acknowledge him (Pr 3:6; cf. Ps 37:23; Ac 5:19–20; 8:26; 13:1–4).

10:9 YOU WILL BE REMEMBERED. God would help his people in war only if he was summoned by the sound of the trumpets (cf. Ex 28:12, 29; 39:7). In other words, God placed certain conditions on the Israelites for receiving his help. God may not move on our behalf if we refuse to draw near to him in prayer, crying out for his grace, protection and presence.

dard. Elishama son of Ammihud[w] was
in command. 23Gamaliel son of Pedahzur was over the division of the tribe of
Manasseh,[x] 24and Abidan son of Gideoni was over the division of the tribe
of Benjamin.[y]
25Finally, as the rear guard[z] for all
the units, the divisions of the camp of
Dan set out, under their standard. Ahiezer son of Ammishaddai[a] was in
command. 26Pagiel son of Ocran was
over the division of the tribe of Asher,[b] 27and Ahira son of Enan was over
the division of the tribe of Naphtali.[c]
28This was the order of march for the
Israelite divisions as they set out.
29Now Moses said to Hobab[d] son of
Reuel[e] the Midianite, Moses' father-
in-law,[f] "We are setting out for the
place about which the LORD said, 'I will
give it to you.'[g] Come with us and we
will treat you well, for the LORD has
promised good things to Israel."
30He answered, "No, I will not go;[h]
I am going back to my own land and my
own people.[i]"
31But Moses said, "Please do not
leave us. You know where we should
camp in the desert, and you can be our
eyes.[j] 32If you come with us, we will
share with you[k] whatever good things
the LORD gives us.[l]"
33So they set out[m] from the mountain of the LORD and traveled for three
days. The ark of the covenant of the
LORD[n] went before them during those
three days to find them a place to
rest.[o] 34The cloud of the LORD was
over them by day when they set out
from the camp.[p]
35Whenever the ark set out, Moses
said,

"Rise up,[q] O LORD!
May your enemies be
scattered;[r]
may your foes flee before
you."[s][t]

36Whenever it came to rest, he said,

"Return,[u] O LORD,
to the countless thousands of
Israel."[v]

Fire From the LORD

11 Now the people complained[w]
about their hardships in the
hearing of the LORD,[x] and when he
heard them his anger was aroused.[y]
Then fire from the LORD burned among
them[z] and consumed[a] some of the
outskirts of the camp. 2When the people cried out to Moses, he prayed[b] to
the LORD[c] and the fire died down. 3So
that place was called Taberah,[u][d] because fire from the LORD had burned
among them.[e]

Quail From the LORD

4The rabble with them began to
crave other food,[f] and again the Israelites started wailing[g] and said, "If
only we had meat to eat! 5We remember the fish we ate in Egypt at no
cost—also the cucumbers, melons,
leeks, onions and garlic.[h] 6But now
we have lost our appetite; we never see
anything but this manna![i]"
7The manna was like coriander
seed[j] and looked like resin.[k] 8The
people went around gathering it,[l] and
then ground it in a handmill or crushed
it in a mortar. They cooked it in a pot
or made it into cakes. And it tasted like
something made with olive oil. 9When
the dew[m] settled on the camp at night,
the manna also came down.
10Moses heard the people of every
family wailing,[n] each at the entrance

10:22 [w]S Nu 1:10 **10:23** [x]S Nu 1:10 **10:24** [y]Nu 1:11 **10:25** [z]S Nu 2:31 [a]S Nu 1:12 **10:26** [b]S Nu 1:13 **10:27** [c]S Nu 1:15 **10:29** [d]Jdg 4:11 [e]S Ex 2:18 [f]S Ex 3:1 [g]S Ge 12:7; S 15:14 **10:30** [h]Mt 21:29 [i]S Ex 18:27 **10:31** [j]Job 29:15 **10:32** [k]S Ex 12:48; Dt 10:18 [l]Ps 22:27-31; 67:5-7 **10:33** [m]ver 12; Dt 1:33 [n]Dt 10:8; 31:9; Jos 3:3; Jdg 20:27; 2Sa 15:24 [o]Jer 31:2 **10:34** [p]Nu 9:15-23 **10:35** [q]2Ch 6:41; Ps 17:13; 44:26; 94:2; 132:8 [r]Jdg 5:31; 1Sa 2:1; Ps 68:1; 92:9 [s]Dt 5:9; 7:10; 32:41; Ps 68:2; Isa 17:12-14 [t]Isa 59:18 **10:36** [u]Isa 52:8; 63:17 [v]Ge 15:5; 26:4; Dt 1:10; 10:22; Ne 9:23 **11:1** [w]S Ex 14:11; S 16:7; La 3:39 [x]Nu 12:2; Dt 1:34 [y]S Ex 4:14 [z]S Lev 10:2 [a]Nu 21:28; Ps 78:63; Isa 26:11 **11:2** [b]Dt 9:19; 1Sa 2:25; 12:23; Ps 106:23 [c]S Ge 20:7; Nu 21:7; Dt 9:20; Jnh 2:1 **11:3** [d]Dt 9:22 [e]Nu 16:35; Job 1:16; Isa 10:17 **11:4** [f]S Ex 16:3 [g]ver 18 **11:5** [h]S Ex 16:3; Nu 21:5 **11:6** [i]Ex 16:14 **11:7** [j]S Ex 16:31 [k]Ge 2:12 **11:8** [l]Ex 16:16 **11:9** [m]Ex 16:13 **11:10** [n]ver 4

[u]3 *Taberah* means *burning.*

10:29 COME WITH US. Moses invited his brother-in-law, a non-Israelite, to come with them and share the good things God had promised to Israel. The door was always open for Gentiles to join Israel, to make the God of Israel their God, and to share in God's promises and blessings. Hobab appeared to have rejected the invitation (but see Jdg 1:16; 4:11); later on Rahab, Ruth and many other Gentiles found acceptance and blessing with the Lord and his people.

11:1 THE PEOPLE COMPLAINED. After only three days into their journey (10:33), the people began to grumble and complain because circumstances were not ideal. (1) How quickly they forgot their deliverance from slavery and God's mighty acts on their behalf. They would not trust God and commit their lives and future to him, which brought on them God's anger and judgment. (2) As NT believers we must never stop being grateful for Christ's sacrificial death for us, our deliverance from sin, and God's gracious provision for guidance and blessing in life.

11:4 THE RABBLE . . . BEGAN TO CRAVE. These were the non-Israelites who joined the people in the exodus (Ex 12:38); they influenced Israel to rebel against God and desire the presumed pleasures of Egypt (v. 5).

11:6 MANNA. See Ex 16:4, note.

to his tent. The LORD became exceedingly angry, and Moses was troubled.
11He asked the LORD, "Why have you
brought this trouble[o] on your servant?
What have I done to displease you that
you put the burden of all these people
on me?[p] 12Did I conceive all these
people? Did I give them birth? Why do
you tell me to carry them in my arms,
as a nurse carries an infant,[q] to the
land you promised on oath[r] to their
forefathers?[s] 13Where can I get meat
for all these people?[t] They keep wailing to me, 'Give us meat to eat!' 14I
cannot carry all these people by myself; the burden is too heavy for me.[u]
15If this is how you are going to treat
me, put me to death[v] right now[w]—if
I have found favor in your eyes—and
do not let me face my own ruin."

16The LORD said to Moses: "Bring me
seventy of Israel's elders[x] who are
known to you as leaders and officials
among the people.[y] Have them come
to the Tent of Meeting,[z] that they may
stand there with you. 17I will come
down and speak with you[a] there, and
I will take of the Spirit that is on you
and put the Spirit on them.[b] They will
help you carry the burden of the people
so that you will not have to carry it
alone.[c]

18"Tell the people: 'Consecrate
yourselves[d] in preparation for tomorrow, when you will eat meat. The LORD
heard you when you wailed,[e] "If only
we had meat to eat! We were better off
in Egypt!"[f] Now the LORD will give you
meat,[g] and you will eat it. 19You will
not eat it for just one day, or two days,
or five, ten or twenty days, 20but for a
whole month—until it comes out of
your nostrils and you loathe it[h]—because you have rejected the LORD,[i]
who is among you, and have wailed before him, saying, "Why did we ever
leave Egypt?"'"[j]

21But Moses said, "Here I am among
six hundred thousand men[k] on foot,
and you say, 'I will give them meat to
eat for a whole month!' 22Would they
have enough if flocks and herds were
slaughtered for them? Would they have
enough if all the fish in the sea were
caught for them?"[l]

23The LORD answered Moses, "Is the
LORD's arm too short?[m] You will now
see whether or not what I say will
come true for you.[n]"

24So Moses went out and told the
people what the LORD had said. He
brought together seventy of their elders and had them stand around the
Tent. 25Then the LORD came down in
the cloud[o] and spoke with him,[p] and
he took of the Spirit[q] that was on him
and put the Spirit on the seventy elders.[r] When the Spirit rested on
them, they prophesied,[s] but they did
not do so again.[v]

26However, two men, whose names
were Eldad and Medad, had remained
in the camp. They were listed among
the elders, but did not go out to the
Tent. Yet the Spirit also rested on
them,[t] and they prophesied in the
camp. 27A young man ran and told Moses, "Eldad and Medad are prophesying in the camp."

28Joshua son of Nun,[u] who had
been Moses' aide[v] since youth, spoke
up and said, "Moses, my lord, stop
them!"[w]

11:11 [o]S Ge 34:30 [p]S Ex 5:22; S 18:18 **11:12** [q]Isa 40:11; 49:23; 66:11,12 [r]Nu 14:16 [s]S Ge 12:7; Ex 13:5 **11:13** [t]S Ex 12:37; Jn 6:5-9 **11:14** [u]S Ex 18:18 **11:15** [v]Ex 32:32 [w]1Ki 19:4; Job 6:9; 7:15-16; 9:21; 10:1; Isa 38:12; Jnh 4:3 **11:16** [x]S Ex 3:16 [y]S Ex 18:25 [z]S Ex 40:2 **11:17** [a]Ex 19:20 [b]ver 25,29; 1Sa 10:6; 2Ki 2:9, 15; 3:12; Isa 32:15; 40:5; 63:11; Joel 2:28; Hag 2:5 [c]S Ex 18:18; Jer 19:1 **11:18** [d]S Ex 19:10 [e]S Ex 16:7 [f]ver 5; Ac 7:39 [g]Ps 78:20 **11:20** [h]Ps 78:29; 106:14,15 [i]S Lev 26:43; Jos 24:27; Jdg 8:23; 1Sa 10:19; Job 31:28; Isa 59:13; Hos 13:11 [j]ver 33; Job 20:13,23 **11:21** [k]S Ex 12:37 **11:22** [l]Mt 15:33 **11:23** [m]Isa 50:2; 59:1 [n]Nu 23:19; 1Sa 15:29; Eze 12:25; 24:14 **11:25** [o]S Ex 19:9; Nu 12:5 [p]ver 17 [q]ver 29; 1Sa 10:6; 19:23 [r]S Ac 2:17 [s]ver 26; Nu 24:2; Jdg 3:10; 1Sa 10:10; 19:20; 2Ch 15:1 **11:26** [t]S ver 25; 1Ch 12:18; Rev 1:10 **11:28** [u]Ex 17:9; Nu 13:8; 26:65; Jos 14:10 [v]Ex 33:11; Jos 1:1 [w]Mk 9:38-40

[v]25 Or *prophesied and continued to do so*

11:12 CARRY THEM . . . AS A NURSE. Moses expected to lead a triumphant army into the promised land. Instead, the people were acting like spiritual babies, and Moses felt it was too much for him to carry them. God then took of the Spirit that was on Moses and put it on the seventy elders to help him in spiritual leadership (vv. 16–17). Thus Moses knew that by the Spirit's power he could face the challenges of any task to which God called him, for he did not have to bear the burdens in his own strength.

11:20 YOU HAVE REJECTED THE LORD. The people complained bitterly about God's ways with them; they were like spoiled children who cried to have their own way (vv. 1,4–6). God let them have what they wanted, but "sent a wasting disease upon them" (Ps 106:15; cf. Ps 78:29–33). This episode is a solemn warning about insisting on our way and desires, rather than humbly submitting to God's way and being grateful for his provisions. To reject God's ways of dealing with us is tantamount to unbelief and rebellion, which brings his judgment (cf. Ps 78:17–22).

11:25 SPIRIT RESTED ON THEM, THEY PROPHESIED. Scripture teaches that prophecy often accompanies the moving of God's Spirit upon his people (cf. 1Sa 10:5–6; Joel 2:28). The account in Acts about the outpouring of the Holy Spirit at Pentecost and afterward indicates that Spirit-filled believers prophesied and spoke in other tongues by the impulse of the Spirit (Ac 2:4; 10:44–47; 19:6; see article on SPIRITUAL GIFTS FOR BELIEVERS, p. 1770).

29But Moses replied, "Are you jealous for my sake? I wish that all the
LORD's people were prophets[x] and
that the LORD would put his Spirit[y] on
them!"[z] 30Then Moses and the elders
of Israel returned to the camp.
31Now a wind went out from the
LORD and drove quail[a] in from the sea.
It brought them[w] down all around the
camp to about three feet[x] above the
ground, as far as a day's walk in any
direction. 32All that day and night and
all the next day the people went out
and gathered quail. No one gathered
less than ten homers.[y] Then they
spread them out all around the camp.
33But while the meat was still between
their teeth[b] and before it could be consumed, the anger[c] of the LORD burned
against the people, and he struck them
with a severe plague.[d] 34Therefore
the place was named Kibroth Hattaavah,[z][e] because there they buried the
people who had craved other food.
35From Kibroth Hattaavah the people traveled to Hazeroth[f] and stayed
there.

Miriam and Aaron Oppose Moses

12 Miriam[g] and Aaron began to
talk against Moses because of
his Cushite wife,[h] for he had married
a Cushite. 2"Has the LORD spoken only
through Moses?" they asked. "Hasn't
he also spoken through us?"[i] And the
LORD heard this.[j]

11:29 [x] 1Sa 10:5; 19:20; 2Ch 24:19; Jer 7:25; 44:4; 1Co 14:5 [y] S ver 17 [z] Nu 27:18
11:31 [a] S Ex 16:13; Ps 78:26-28
11:33 [b] Ps 78:30 [c] Nu 14:18; Dt 9:7; Jdg 2:12; 2Ki 22:17; Ps 106:29; Jer 44:3; Eze 8:17 [d] S ver 18-20; Ps 106:15; Isa 10:16
11:34 [e] Nu 33:16; Dt 9:22
11:35 [f] Nu 33:17
12:1 [g] S Ex 15:20 [h] S Ex 2:21
12:2 [i] Nu 16:3 [j] S Nu 11:1
12:3 [k] Mt 11:29
12:5 [l] S Ex 13:21; S Nu 11:25
12:6 [m] 1Sa 3:7,21 [n] S Ge 15:1 [o] S Ge 20:3; S Mt 27:19; Heb 1:1
12:7 [p] Dt 34:5; Jos 1:1-2; Ps 105:26 [q] Heb 3:2,5
12:8 [r] Jdg 14:12; 1Ki 10:1; Ps 49:4; Pr 1:6; Da 5:12 [s] Ex 20:4; Job 19:26; Ps 17:15; 140:13; Isa 6:1 [t] Ex 24:2
12:9 [u] S Ex 4:14 [v] S Ge 17:22
12:10 [w] Ex 40:2

3(Now Moses was a very humble
man,[k] more humble than anyone else
on the face of the earth.)
4At once the LORD said to Moses,
Aaron and Miriam, "Come out to the
Tent of Meeting, all three of you." So
the three of them came out. 5Then the
LORD came down in a pillar of cloud;[l]
he stood at the entrance to the Tent
and summoned Aaron and Miriam.
When both of them stepped forward,
6he said, "Listen to my words:

"When a prophet of the LORD is
among you,
I reveal[m] myself to him in
visions,[n]
I speak to him in dreams.[o]
7But this is not true of my servant
Moses;[p]
he is faithful in all my house.[q] Ru 3:10-11
8With him I speak face to face,
clearly and not in riddles;[r]
he sees the form of the LORD.[s]
Why then were you not afraid
to speak against my servant
Moses?"[t]

9The anger of the LORD burned
against them,[u] and he left them.[v]
10When the cloud lifted from above
the Tent,[w] there stood Miriam—lep-

[w] 31 Or *They flew* [x] 31 Hebrew *two cubits* (about 1 meter) [y] 32 That is, probably about 60 bushels (about 2.2 kiloliters)
[z] 34 *Kibroth Hattaavah* means *graves of craving.*

11:29 THAT ALL ... WERE PROPHETS. When Eldad and Medad kept prophesying in the camp, Joshua wanted Moses to stop them. Moses, however, had learned his lesson. He saw that the normal level of spiritual life desired for all God's people was that they could prophesy when God's Spirit was on them. In OT times the Holy Spirit only came upon or filled a few to empower them for service or for prophecy. Joel prophesied that a time would come when all God's people would be filled with the Spirit (Joel 2:28–29). This prophecy was fulfilled on the day of Pentecost when the Spirit was poured out on "all people" (Ac 2:4, 16–17). Believers who have not been baptized in the Holy Spirit are not experiencing what God has promised them and what Jesus waits to give them (Ac 1:8; 2:39; 1Co 14:1–2,5,39).

12:1 CUSHITE WIFE. Moses' marriage to a Cushite woman was neither morally nor legally wrong. Miriam and Aaron's complaint was a pretense to cover their jealousy of Moses' authority (v. 2).

12:3 MOSES ... HUMBLE. This reference to Moses as the most humble man on earth is probably a parenthetical comment added by Joshua after Moses' death. Moses' humility lay in his trust in God as Lord, so that he was free of selfishness and ungodly ambitions. When challenged or threatened, Moses depended on God and trusted him for aid and defense. Scripture assures us that God delights to come to the aid of the humble (Ps 22:26; 25:9; 147:6; 149:4; Mt 5:5; 1Pe 5:6). Jesus, a prophet like Moses (Ac 7:37), was gentle and humble in heart (Mt 11:29), and he too trusted in God during persecution (1Pe 2:23).

12:10 THERE STOOD MIRIAM—LEPROUS. The sin of Miriam and Aaron in questioning Moses' authority was that they did not fear God or respect God's word through his prophet Moses. Moses was the mediator of the old covenant, just as Jesus is the mediator of the new (cf. Heb 3:2–6). God spoke directly to Moses (v. 8), and thus Moses' word to the people was the authoritative word of God. Though Miriam and Aaron were leaders in Israel, they had no right to challenge Moses' authority. Just as God showed them that they were not on the same level as Moses, so believers today have no right to put themselves on the same level as Scripture.

rous,[a] like snow.[x] Aaron turned toward her and saw that she had leprosy;[y] **11**and he said to Moses, "Please, my lord, do not hold against us the sin we have so foolishly committed.[z] **12**Do not let her be like a stillborn infant coming from its mother's womb with its flesh half eaten away."

13So Moses cried out to the LORD, "O God, please heal her![a]"

14The LORD replied to Moses, "If her father had spit in her face,[b] would she not have been in disgrace for seven days? Confine her outside the camp[c] for seven days; after that she can be brought back." **15**So Miriam was confined outside the camp[d] for seven Nu 21:7-9 days,[e] and the people did not move on till she was brought back.

16After that, the people left Hazeroth[f] and encamped in the Desert of Paran.[g]

Exploring Canaan

13 The LORD said to Moses, **2**"Send some men to explore[h] the land of Canaan,[i] which I am giving to the Israelites.[j] From each ancestral tribe[k] send one of its leaders."

3So at the LORD's command Moses sent them out from the Desert of Paran. All of them were leaders of the Israelites.[l] **4**These are their names:

from the tribe of Reuben, Shammua son of Zaccur;
5from the tribe of Simeon, Shaphat son of Hori;
6from the tribe of Judah, Caleb son of Jephunneh;[m]
7from the tribe of Issachar, Igal son of Joseph;
8from the tribe of Ephraim, Hoshea son of Nun;[n]
9from the tribe of Benjamin, Palti son of Raphu;
10from the tribe of Zebulun, Gaddiel son of Sodi;
11from the tribe of Manasseh (a tribe of Joseph), Gaddi son of Susi;
12from the tribe of Dan, Ammiel son of Gemalli;
13from the tribe of Asher, Sethur son of Michael;
14from the tribe of Naphtali, Nahbi son of Vophsi;
15from the tribe of Gad, Geuel son of Maki.

16These are the names of the men Moses sent to explore[o] the land. (Moses gave Hoshea son of Nun[p] the name Joshua.)[q]

17When Moses sent them to explore Canaan,[r] he said, "Go up through the Negev[s] and on into the hill country.[t] **18**See what the land is like and whether the people who live there are strong or weak, few or many. **19**What kind of land do they live in? Is it good or bad? What kind of towns do they live in? Are they unwalled or fortified? **20**How is the soil? Is it fertile or poor? Are there trees on it or not? Do your best to bring back some of the fruit of the land.[u]" (It was the season for the first ripe grapes.)[v]

21So they went up and explored the land from the Desert of Zin[w] as far as Rehob,[x] toward Lebo[b] Hamath.[y] **22**They went up through the Negev and came to Hebron,[z] where Ahiman, Sheshai and Talmai,[a] the descendants of Anak,[b] lived. (Hebron had been built seven years before Zoan in Egypt.)[c] **23**When they reached the Valley of Eshcol,[c][d] they cut off a branch bearing a single cluster of grapes. Two of them carried it on a pole between them, along with some pomegranates[e] and figs.[f] **24**That place was called the Valley of Eshcol because of the cluster of grapes the Israelites cut off there. **25**At the end of forty days[g] they returned from exploring the land.[h]

Report on the Exploration

26They came back to Moses and Aaron and the whole Israelite community at Kadesh[i] in the Desert of Paran.[j] There they reported to them[k] and to the whole assembly and showed them the fruit of the land.[l] **27**They gave Moses this account: "We went into the land to which you sent us, and it does flow with milk and honey![m] Here is its fruit.[n] **28**But the people who live there are powerful, and the cities are fortified and very large.[o] We even saw descendants of Anak[p] there.[q] **29**The Amalekites[r] live in the Negev; the Hittites,[s] Jebusites[t] and Amorites[u] live in the hill country;[v]

12:10 [x] S Ex 4:6; Dt 24:9 [y] S Lev 13:11; 2Ki 5:1,27; 2Ch 16:12; 21:12-15; 26:19
12:11 [z] 2Sa 19:19; 24:10
12:13 [a] Ex 15:26; Ps 6:2; 147:3; Isa 1:6; 30:26; 53:5; Jer 17:14; Hos 6:1
12:14 [b] Dt 25:9; Job 17:6; 30:9-10; Isa 50:6 [c] S Lev 13:46
12:15 [d] S Lev 14:8 [e] S Lev 13:4
12:16 [f] Nu 11:35 [g] Ge 21:21; Nu 10:12; 15:32
13:2 [h] ver 16; Dt 1:22 [i] S Lev 14:34 [j] Jos 1:3 [k] S Lev 24:11
13:3 [l] Nu 1:16
13:6 [m] ver 30; Nu 14:6,24; 34:19; Dt 1:36; Jdg 1:12-15
13:8 [n] S Nu 11:28
13:16 [o] S ver 2 [p] ver 8 [q] Dt 32:44
13:17 [r] ver 2; Jos 14:7 [s] S Ge 12:9 [t] Dt 1:7; Jos 9:1; Jdg 1:9
13:20 [u] Dt 1:25 [v] S Lev 25:5
13:21 [w] Nu 20:1; 27:14; 33:36; Dt 32:51; Jos 15:1 [x] Jos 19:28; Jdg 1:31; 18:28; 2Sa 10:6; 1Ch 6:75 [y] Nu 34:8; Jos 13:5; Jdg 3:3; 1Ki 8:65; 2Ki 14:25; 1Ch 13:5; 2Ch 7:8; Jer 52:9; Eze 47:16,20; Am 6:14
13:22 [z] S Ge 13:18; S 23:19 [a] Jos 15:14; Jdg 1:10 [b] ver 28; Dt 2:10; 9:2; Jos 11:21; 15:13; Jdg 1:20 [c] Ps 78:12,43; Isa 19:11,13; 30:4; Eze 30:14
13:23 [d] S Ge 14:13 [e] S Ex 28:33 [f] Ge 3:7; Nu 20:5; Dt 8:8; 2Ki 18:31; Ne 13:15
13:25 [g] S Ge 7:4 [h] Nu 14:34
13:26 [i] S Ge 14:7 [j] S Ge 14:6 [k] Nu 32:8 [l] Dt 1:25
13:27 [m] S Ex 3:8 [n] Dt 1:25; Jer 2:7
13:28 [o] Dt 1:28; 9:1,2 [p] S ver 22 [q] Jos 14:12
13:29 [r] S Ge 14:7 [s] S Ge 10:15; Dt 7:1; 20:17; 1Ki 9:20; 10:29; 2Ki 7:6 [t] S Ex 3:8 [u] S Ge 10:16 [v] ver 17

[a] *10* The Hebrew word was used for various diseases affecting the skin—not necessarily leprosy. [b] *21* Or *toward the entrance to* [c] *23* *Eshcol* means *cluster*; also in verse 24.

and the Canaanites[w] live near the sea
and along the Jordan.[x]"
30Then Caleb[y] silenced the people
before Moses and said, "We should go
up and take possession of the land, for
we can certainly do it."
31But the men who had gone up with
him said, "We can't attack those people; they are stronger than we are."[z]
32And they spread among the Israelites a bad report[a] about the land they
had explored. They said, "The land we
explored devours[b] those living in it.
All the people we saw there are of
great size.[c] **33**We saw the Nephilim[d]
there (the descendants of Anak[e] come
from the Nephilim). We seemed like
grasshoppers[f] in our own eyes, and
we looked the same to them."

The People Rebel

14 That night all the people of the
community raised their voices
and wept aloud.[g] **2**All the Israelites
grumbled[h] against Moses and Aaron,
and the whole assembly said to them,
"If only we had died in Egypt![i] Or in
this desert![j] **3**Why is the LORD bringing us to this land only to let us fall by
the sword?[k] Our wives and children[l]
will be taken as plunder.[m] Wouldn't it
be better for us to go back to Egypt?[n]"
4And they said to each other, "We
should choose a leader and go back to
Egypt.[o]"
5Then Moses and Aaron fell facedown[p] in front of the whole Israelite
assembly[q] gathered there. **6**Joshua
son of Nun[r] and Caleb son of Jephunneh, who were among those who had
explored the land, tore their clothes[s]
7and said to the entire Israelite assembly, "The land we passed through and
explored is exceedingly good.[t] **8**If the
LORD is pleased with us,[u] he will lead
us into that land, a land flowing with
milk and honey,[v] and will give it to
us.[w] **9**Only do not rebel[x] against the
LORD. And do not be afraid[y] of the people of the land,[z] because we will swallow them up. Their protection is gone,
but the LORD is with[a] us.[b] Do not be
afraid of them."[c]
10But the whole assembly talked
about stoning[d] them. Then the glory
of the LORD[e] appeared at the Tent of
Meeting to all the Israelites. **11**The
LORD said to Moses, "How long will
these people treat me with contempt?[f] How long will they refuse to
believe in me,[g] in spite of all the miraculous signs[h] I have performed
among them? **12**I will strike them down
with a plague[i] and destroy them, but
I will make you into a nation[j] greater
and stronger than they."[k]
13Moses said to the LORD, "Then the
Egyptians will hear about it! By your
power you brought these people up
from among them.[l] **14**And they will
tell the inhabitants of this land about

13:29 [w]Ge 10:18 [x]S Ge 13:10; Nu 22:1; 32:5; Dt 1:1; Jos 1:2; Jdg 3:28; Ps 42:6 **13:30** [y]S ver 6 **13:31** [z]Dt 9:1; Jos 14:8 **13:32** [a]Nu 14:36, 37 [b]Eze 36:13,14 [c]Dt 1:28; Am 2:9 **13:33** [d]Ge 6:4 [e]ver 28; Dt 1:28; Jos 11:22; 14:12 [f]Ecc 12:5; Isa 40:22 **14:1** [g]S Ge 27:38; Ex 33:4; Nu 25:6; Dt 1:45; Jdg 20:23,26; 2Sa 3:32; Job 31:29 **14:2** [h]S Ex 15:24; Heb 3:16 [i]S Ex 16:3 [j]S Nu 11:1; 16:13; 20:4; 21:5 **14:3** [k]S Ex 5:21 [l]ver 31 [m]S Ge 34:29; Dt 1:39; Ps 109:11; Isa 33:4; Eze 7:21; 25:7; 26:5 [n]Ac 7:39 **14:4** [o]Ne 9:17 **14:5** [p]S Lev 9:24; Nu 16:4,22,45; 20:6; Jos 5:14; 2Sa 14:4; 1Ch 21:16; Eze 1:28 [q]S Lev 19:2 **14:6** [r]Nu 11:28 [s]S Ge 37:29,34; Jdg 11:35; 2Sa 13:31; 2Ki 19:1; Ezr 9:3; Est 4:1; S Mk 14:63 **14:7** [t]Nu 13:27; Dt 1:25 **14:8** [u]Dt 7:8; 10:15; Ps 18:19; 22:8; 37:23; 41:11; 56:9; 147:11; Pr 11:20; Isa 62:4; Mal 2:17 [v]Nu 13:27 [w]Dt 1:21 **14:9** [x]Dt 1:26; 9:7,23,24 [y]Ge 26:24; 2Ch 32:7; Ps 118:6; Jer 41:18; 42:11 [z]Dt 1:21; 7:18; 20:1 [a]Hag 2:4 [b]S Ge 21:22; Dt 1:30; 2Ch 13:12; Jer 15:20; 46:28; Hag 1:13 [c]ver 24 **14:10** [d]S Ex 17:4 [e]S Ex 24:16 **14:11** [f]Ex 23:21; Nu 15:31; 16:30; 1Sa 2:17; Eze 31:14; Mal 1:13 [g]Dt 1:32; Ps 78:22; 106:24; Jn 3:15 [h]S Ex 3:20; S 4:17; S 10:1 **14:12** [i]S Ex 5:3; S 30:12 [j]S Ex 32:10 [k]Dt 9:14; 29:20; 32:26; Ps 109:13 **14:13** [l]Ex 32:11-14; Ps 106:23

13:32 A BAD REPORT. The unbelief of the ten spies had two dimensions: (1) God's past faithfulness to his people did not bring these ten men into a loyal relationship with him, and (2) they did not trust in God and his promises concerning their future (cf. Ge 15:18; 17:8; Ex 33:2); their lack of faith stood in marked contrast to that of Caleb and Joshua (see next note).

14:6 JOSHUA . . . CALEB. Both Joshua and Caleb opposed the majority opinion of the spies (13:25–33). Basing their report on a firm commitment to God and full confidence in his promises to Israel, they refused to accept the overwhelming decision of God's people—even at the risk of their lives (vv. 6–10). This crucial event in Israel's desert journey teaches us that we must not assume that the majority opinion, even of the church, is always right. Faithful believers must be willing to stand on God's word even if the majority are against them (see 2Ti 1:15, note).

14:11 REFUSE TO BELIEVE IN ME. At the heart of Israel's rebellion was *unbelief*, which grew out of their failure to remember God's past faithfulness, to trust him as their Lord and to accept him at his word. To their way of thinking, they could no longer rely on the Lord under all circumstances. (1) To believe in God means to accept all he says as truth and act accordingly, to anchor your life on his promises, to walk in his ways, and to love him with all your heart and with all your soul (Dt 10:12; see article on FAITH AND GRACE, p. 1720). (2) The presence of faith leads us to be accepted by God and counted righteous before him (see Ge 15:6, note); the absence of faith condemns us (Jn 3:36).

14:13 EGYPTIANS WILL HEAR ABOUT IT! Moses is a classic example of a person so dedicated to the Lord that he is more concerned about God's reputation than his own success and honor (see v. 12). When believers gratefully comprehend all that God has done for them through Christ, they too will desire above all to exalt the Lord and his glory (cf. vv. 21–22) and to keep his name from falling into reproach among unbelievers.

it. They have already heard[m] that you,
O LORD, are with these people[n] and
that you, O LORD, have been seen face
to face,[o] that your cloud stays over
them,[p] and that you go before them in
a pillar of cloud by day and a pillar of
fire by night.[q] 15 If you put these people to death all at one time, the nations
who have heard this report about you
will say, 16 'The LORD was not able to
bring these people into the land he
promised them on oath;[r] so he
slaughtered them in the desert.'[s]
17 "Now may the Lord's strength be
displayed, just as you have declared:
18 'The LORD is slow to anger, abounding in love and forgiving sin and rebellion.[t] Yet he does not leave the guilty
unpunished; he punishes the children
for the sin of the fathers to the third
and fourth generation.'[u] 19 In accordance with your great love, forgive[v]
the sin of these people,[w] just as you
have pardoned them from the time they
left Egypt until now."[x]
20 The LORD replied, "I have forgiven
them,[y] as you asked. 21 Nevertheless,
as surely as I live[z] and as surely as
the glory of the LORD[a] fills the whole
earth,[b] 22 not one of the men who saw
my glory and the miraculous signs[c] I
performed in Egypt and in the desert
but who disobeyed me and tested me
ten times[d]— 23 not one of them will
ever see the land I promised on oath[e]
to their forefathers. No one who has
treated me with contempt[f] will ever
see it.[g] 24 But because my servant Caleb[h] has a different spirit and follows
me wholeheartedly,[i] I will bring him
into the land he went to, and his
descendants will inherit it.[j] 25 Since
the Amalekites[k] and Canaanites[l] are
living in the valleys, turn[m] back tomorrow and set out toward the desert
along the route to the Red Sea.[d][n]"
26 The LORD said to Moses and Aaron: 27 "How long will this wicked community grumble against me? I have
heard the complaints of these grumbling Israelites.[o] 28 So tell them, 'As
surely as I live,[p] declares the LORD, I
will do to you[q] the very things I heard
you say: 29 In this desert your bodies
will fall[r]—every one of you twenty
years old or more[s] who was counted
in the census[t] and who has grumbled
against me. 30 Not one of you will enter
the land[u] I swore with uplifted hand[v]
to make your home, except Caleb son
of Jephunneh[w] and Joshua son of
Nun.[x] 31 As for your children that you
said would be taken as plunder, I will
bring them in to enjoy the land you
have rejected.[y] 32 But you—your bodies will fall[z] in this desert. 33 Your
children will be shepherds here for forty years,[a] suffering for your unfaithfulness, until the last of your bodies
lies in the desert. 34 For forty years[b]—
one year for each of the forty days you
explored the land[c]—you will suffer
for your sins and know what it is like
to have me against you.' 35 I, the LORD,
have spoken, and I will surely do these
things[d] to this whole wicked community, which has banded together
against me. They will meet their end in
this desert; here they will die.[e]"
36 So the men Moses had sent[f] to
explore the land, who returned and
made the whole community grumble[g]

14:14 [m] Ex 15:14 [n] Nu 5:3; 16:3; Jos 2:9 [o] Dt 5:4; 34:10 [p] S Ex 33:16 [q] S Ex 13:21 **14:16** [r] Nu 11:12 [s] Ex 32:12; Jos 7:7 **14:18** [t] S Ex 20:6; 34:6; Ps 145:8; Jnh 4:2; Jas 5:11 [u] Ex 20:5 **14:19** [v] S Ex 34:9; 1Ki 8:34; Ps 85:2; 103:3 [w] Ps 106:45 [x] Ps 78:38 **14:20** [y] Ex 34:6; Ps 99:8; 106:23; Mic 7:18-20 **14:21** [z] ver 28; Dt 32:40; Jdg 8:19; Ru 3:13; 1Sa 14:39; 19:6; Isa 49:18; Jer 4:2; Eze 5:11; Zep 2:9 [a] Lev 9:6 [b] Ps 72:19; Isa 6:3; 40:5; Hab 2:14 **14:22** [c] ver 11 [d] S Ex 14:11; 17:7; 32:1; Ps 81:7; 1Co 10:5 **14:23** [e] ver 16; S Ex 33:1; Nu 32:11; Dt 1:34; Ps 95:11; 106:26 [f] ver 11 [g] Heb 3:18 **14:24** [h] Nu 13:6 [i] ver 6-9; Dt 1:36; Jos 14:8,14 [j] Nu 26:65; 32:12; Ps 25:13; 37:9,11 **14:25** [k] S Ge 14:7 [l] S Ge 10:18 [m] Dt 1:40 [n] Ex 23:31; Nu 21:4; 1Ki 9:26 **14:27** [o] Ex 16:12; Dt 1:34,35 **14:28** [p] S ver 21 [q] Nu 33:56 **14:29** [r] ver 23,30, 32; Nu 26:65; 32:13; 1Co 10:5; Heb 3:17; Jude 1:5 [s] S Nu 1:45 [t] S Ex 30:12 **14:30** [u] S ver 29 [v] Ex 6:8; Dt 32:40; Ne 9:15; Ps 106:26; Eze 20:5; 36:7 [w] Nu 13:6 [x] Nu 11:28 **14:31** [y] S Lev 26:43 **14:32** [z] S ver 29,35 **14:33** [a] ver 34; S Ex 16:35; Ac 13:18; Heb 3:9 **14:34** [b] S ver 33 [c] Nu 13:25 **14:35** [d] Nu 23:19 [e] S ver 32 **14:36** [f] Nu 13:4-16 [g] ver 2

[d] 25 Hebrew *Yam Suph*; that is, Sea of Reeds

14:20 I HAVE FORGIVEN. The granting of pardon or forgiveness does not always mean the end of punishment (see vv. 21–23,27–37; cf. 2Sa 7:14).

14:29 YOUR BODIES WILL FALL. The NT explicitly declares that God intended his judgment on Israel for her disobedience and unbelief to serve as a warning for all believers (1Co 10:11). (1) The Israelites had the good news preached to them (Heb 4:6), were redeemed by the blood (Ex 6:6; 12:13), passed through the Red Sea (Ex 14:22), were baptized (compare Ex 14:19,29–30 with 1Co 10:2), ate spiritual food (Ex 16:4; 1Co 10:3), drank spiritual drink, the living water of Christ (1Co 10:4), and were led by the Holy Spirit (Nu 11:17,25).

(2) In spite of this redemption and experience of grace, the people grumbled against God (vv. 2,27), hardened their hearts (Heb 3:8), rebelled against him (v. 2,9), treated him with contempt, refused to believe in him (vv. 11,23), tested him (v. 22), failed to obey his commands (v. 41) and turned away from following him (v. 43).

(3) Their disobedience brought on them God's wrath (1Co 10:5–10; Heb 3:10,17), death and destruction (14:29,35), failure to enter the land of Canaan (14:22–23) and forfeiture of God's rest (Ps 95:7–11; Heb 3:11,18; see article on GOD'S COVENANT WITH THE ISRAELITES, p. 290).

(4) Based on Israel's failure in the desert, believers in Christ are exhorted to "see to it . . . that none of you has a sinful, unbelieving heart that turns away from the living God" (Heb 3:12) and so to fail to "enter that rest," i.e., heaven (Heb 4:11).

against him by spreading a bad report[h] about it— 37these men responsible for spreading the bad report[i]
about the land were struck down and
died of a plague[j] before the LORD. 38Of
the men who went to explore the
land,[k] only Joshua son of Nun and Caleb son of Jephunneh survived.[l]

39When Moses reported this[m] to all
the Israelites, they mourned[n] bitterly.
40Early the next morning they went up
toward the high hill country.[o] "We
have sinned[p]," they said. "We will go
up to the place the LORD promised."

41But Moses said, "Why are you disobeying the LORD's command? This will
not succeed![q] 42Do not go up, because
the LORD is not with you. You will be
defeated by your enemies,[r] 43for the
Amalekites[s] and Canaanites[t] will
face you there. Because you have
turned away from the LORD, he will not
be with you[u] and you will fall by the
sword."

44Nevertheless, in their presumption they went up[v] toward the high
hill country, though neither Moses nor
the ark of the LORD's covenant moved
from the camp.[w] 45Then the Amalekites and Canaanites[x] who lived in that
hill country[y] came down and attacked
them and beat them down all the way
to Hormah.[z]

Supplementary Offerings

15 The LORD said to Moses,
2"Speak to the Israelites and
say to them: 'After you enter the land
I am giving you[a] as a home 3and you
present to the LORD offerings made by
fire, from the herd or the flock,[b] as an
aroma pleasing to the LORD[c]—whether burnt offerings[d] or sacrifices, for
special vows or freewill offerings[e] or
festival offerings[f]— 4then the one
who brings his offering shall present to
the LORD a grain offering[g] of a tenth of
an ephah[e] of fine flour[h] mixed with a
quarter of a hin[f] of oil. 5With each
lamb[i] for the burnt offering or the
sacrifice, prepare a quarter of a hin of
wine[j] as a drink offering.[k]

6" 'With a ram[l] prepare a grain offering[m] of two-tenths of an ephah[g][n]
of fine flour mixed with a third of a
hin[h] of oil,[o] 7and a third of a hin of
wine[p] as a drink offering.[q] Offer it as
an aroma pleasing to the LORD.[r]

8" 'When you prepare a young bull[s]
as a burnt offering or sacrifice, for a
special vow[t] or a fellowship offering[i][u] to the LORD, 9bring with the bull
a grain offering[v] of three-tenths of an
ephah[j][w] of fine flour mixed with half
a hin[k] of oil. 10Also bring half a hin of
wine[x] as a drink offering.[y] It will be
an offering made by fire, an aroma
pleasing to the LORD.[z] 11Each bull or
ram, each lamb or young goat, is to be
prepared in this manner. 12Do this for
each one, for as many as you prepare.[a]

13" 'Everyone who is native-born[b]
must do these things in this way when
he brings an offering made by fire as an
aroma pleasing to the LORD.[c] 14For
the generations to come,[d] whenever
an alien[e] or anyone else living among
you presents an offering[f] made by
fire[g] as an aroma pleasing to the LORD,
he must do exactly as you do. 15The
community is to have the same rules
for you and for the alien living among
you; this is a lasting ordinance for the
generations to come.[h] You and the
alien shall be the same before the LORD:
16The same laws and regulations will
apply both to you and to the alien living
among you.[i]' "

17The LORD said to Moses, 18"Speak
to the Israelites and say to them:
'When you enter the land to which I am
taking you[j] 19and you eat the food of

14:36 [h] S Nu 13:32 **14:37** [i] S Nu 13:32; 1Co 10:10; Heb 3:17 [j] Nu 16:49; 5:9; 26:1; 31:16; Dt 4:3 **14:38** [k] ver 30; Nu 13:4-16 [l] ver 24; Jos 14:6 **14:39** [m] ver 28-35 [n] S Ex 33:4 **14:40** [o] ver 45; Nu 13:17 [p] S Ex 9:27 **14:41** [q] 2Ch 24:20 **14:42** [r] Dt 1:42 **14:43** [s] Jdg 3:13 [t] ver 45; Nu 13:29 [u] S Ge 39:23; Dt 31:8; Jos 6:27; Jdg 1:19; 6:16; 1Sa 3:19; 18:14; 2Ch 1:1 **14:44** [v] Dt 1:43 [w] Nu 31:6 **14:45** [x] S ver 43 [y] S ver 40 [z] Nu 21:3; Dt 1:44; Jos 12:14; 15:30; 19:4; Jdg 1:17; 1Sa 30:30; 1Ch 4:30 **15:2** [a] S Lev 23:10 **15:3** [b] S Lev 1:2 [c] ver 24; S Lev 1:9 [d] Lev 1:3; Nu 28:13 [e] S Lev 7:16; S Ezr 1:4 [f] Lev 23:1-44 **15:4** [g] S Lev 6:14 [h] S Ex 16:36 **15:5** [i] S Lev 3:7 [j] S Lev 10:9 [k] S Ge 35:14 **15:6** [l] S Lev 5:15 [m] Nu 28:12; 29:14 [n] S Lev 23:13 [o] Eze 46:14 **15:7** [p] ver 5 [q] Lev 23:13; Nu 28:14; 29:18 [r] S Lev 1:9 **15:8** [s] S Ex 12:5; S Lev 1:5 [t] S Lev 22:18 [u] S Lev 3:6 **15:9** [v] Lev 2:1 [w] S Lev 14:10 **15:10** [x] Nu 28:14 [y] Lev 23:13 [z] Lev 1:9 **15:12** [a] Ezr 7:17 **15:13** [b] S Lev 16:29 [c] Lev 1:9 **15:14** [d] Lev 3:17; Nu 10:8 [e] S Ex 12:19,43; S 22:21 [f] S Lev 22:18 [g] ver 25 **15:15** [h] ver 14,21 **15:16** [i] Ex 12:49; S Lev 22:18; Nu 9:14 **15:18** [j] S Lev 23:10

[e] *4* That is, probably about 2 quarts (about 2 liters) [f] *4* That is, probably about 1 quart (about 1 liter); also in verse 5 [g] *6* That is, probably about 4 quarts (about 4.5 liters) [h] *6* That is, probably about 1 1/4 quarts (about 1.2 liters); also in verse 7 [i] *8* Traditionally *peace offering* [j] *9* That is, probably about 6 quarts (about 6.5 liters) [k] *9* That is, probably about 2 quarts (about 2 liters); also in verse 10

14:43 THE LORD ... WILL NOT BE WITH YOU. Despite their shallow repentance and momentary expression of trust in God's promises (v. 40), the Israelites ignored God's warning. They made the fatal mistake of believing they could possess the promised land without obedience, faith and devoted fellowship with God (vv. 40–44). In their momentary but misguided trust, they were defeated (v. 45). The crucial lesson for all who are in Christ is that the riches of God's covenant cannot be obtained without the obedience that comes from faith (cf. Ro 1:5). Simply mouthing words of trust by itself is not adequate; this message is emphasized throughout Scripture (e.g., ch. 32; Dt 1:20–40; Ps 95:10; 106:24ff; Am 2:10; 5:25; 1Co 10:1–11; Heb 3:7—4:13).

the land,[k] present a portion as an offering to the LORD.[l] 20Present a cake from the first of your ground meal[m] and present it as an offering from the threshing floor.[n][o] 21Throughout the generations to come[p] you are to give this offering to the LORD from the first of your ground meal.[q]

Offerings for Unintentional Sins

22" 'Now if you unintentionally fail to keep any of these commands the LORD gave Moses[r]— 23any of the LORD's commands to you through him, from the day the LORD gave them and continuing through the generations to come[s]— 24and if this is done unintentionally[t] without the community being aware of it,[u] then the whole community is to offer a young bull for a burnt offering[v] as an aroma pleasing to the LORD,[w] along with its prescribed grain offering[x] and drink offering,[y] and a male goat for a sin offering.[z] 25The priest is to make atonement for the whole Israelite community, and they will be forgiven,[a] for it was not intentional[b] and they have brought to the LORD for their wrong an offering made by fire[c] and a sin offering.[d] 26The whole Israelite community and the aliens living among them will be forgiven, because all the people were involved in the unintentional wrong.[e]

27" 'But if just one person sins unintentionally,[f] he must bring a year-old female goat for a sin offering.[g] 28The priest is to make atonement[h] before the LORD for the one who erred by sinning unintentionally, and when atonement has been made for him, he will be forgiven.[i] 29One and the same law applies to everyone who sins unintentionally, whether he is a native-born Israelite or an alien.[j]

30" 'But anyone who sins defiantly,[k] whether native-born or alien,[l] blasphemes the LORD,[m] and that person must be cut off from his people.[n] 31Because he has despised[o] the LORD's word and broken his commands,[p] that person must surely be cut off; his guilt remains on him.[q]' "

15:19 [k]Jos 5:11, 12 [l]Nu 18:8
15:20 [m]S Lev 23:14 [n]S Lev 2:14; S Nu 18:27 [o]S Ge 50:10
15:21 [p]S Lev 23:14 [q]Eze 44:30; Ro 11:16
15:22 [r]S Lev 4:2
15:23 [s]ver 21
15:24 [t]ver 25,26 [u]S Lev 5:15 [v]Lev 4:14 [w]S ver 3 [x]Lev 2:1 [y]Lev 23:13; Nu 6:15 [z]Lev 4:3
15:25 [a]Lev 4:20; S Ro 3:25 [b]ver 22, S 24 [c]ver 14 [d]Lev 4:3
15:26 [e]S ver 24
15:27 [f]Lev 4:27 [g]Lev 4:3; Nu 6:14
15:28 [h]Nu 8:12; 28:22 [i]Lev 4:20
15:29 [j]S Ex 12:49
15:30 [k]Nu 14:40-44; Dt 1:43; 17:13; Ps 19:13 [l]ver 14 [m]2Ki 19:6,20; Isa 37:6,23; Eze 20:27 [n]S Ge 17:14; S Job 31:22
15:31 [o]S Nu 14:11 [p]1Sa 15:23,26; 2Sa 11:27; 12:9; Ps 119:126; Pr 13:13 [q]S Lev 5:1; Eze 18:20
15:32 [r]S Nu 12:16 [s]Ex 31:14,15; 35:2,3
15:34 [t]Nu 9:8
15:35 [u]Ex 31:14, 15 [v]S Lev 20:2; Lk 4:29; Ac 7:58
15:36 [w]S Lev 20:2 [x]S Ex 31:14 [y]Jer 17:21
15:38 [z]Lev 3:17; Nu 10:8 [a]Dt 22:12; Mt 23:5
15:39 [b]Dt 4:23; 6:12; Ps 73:27 [c]S Lev 17:7; Jdg 2:17; Ps 106:39; Jer 3:2; Hos 4:12 [d]Ps 78:37; Jer 7:24; Eze 20:16
15:40 [e]S Ge 26:5; Dt 11:13; Ps 103:18; 119:56 [f]S Lev 11:44; Ro 12:1; Col 1:22; 1Pe 1:15
15:41 [g]S Ge 17:7 [h]S Ex 20:2

The Sabbath-Breaker Put to Death

32While the Israelites were in the desert,[r] a man was found gathering wood on the Sabbath day.[s] 33Those who found him gathering wood brought him to Moses and Aaron and the whole assembly, 34and they kept him in custody, because it was not clear what should be done to him.[t] 35Then the LORD said to Moses, "The man must die.[u] The whole assembly must stone him outside the camp.[v]" 36So the assembly took him outside the camp and stoned him[w] to death,[x] as the LORD commanded Moses.[y]

Tassels on Garments

37The LORD said to Moses, 38"Speak to the Israelites and say to them: 'Throughout the generations to come[z] you are to make tassels on the corners of your garments,[a] with a blue cord on each tassel. 39You will have these tassels to look at and so you will remember[b] all the commands of the LORD, that you may obey them and not prostitute yourselves[c] by going after the lusts of your own hearts[d] and eyes. 40Then you will remember to obey all my commands[e] and will be consecrated to your God.[f] 41I am the LORD your God, who brought you out of Egypt to be your God.[g] I am the LORD your God.[h]' "

Korah, Dathan and Abiram

16 Korah[i] son of Izhar, the son of Kohath, the son of Levi, and certain Reubenites—Dathan and Abiram[j], sons of Eliab,[k] and On son of Peleth—became insolent[1] 2and rose up against Moses.[l] With them were 250 Israelite men, well-known community leaders who had been appointed members of the council.[m] 3They came as a group to oppose Moses and Aaron[n] and said to them, "You have gone

16:1 [i]S Ex 6:24; Jude 1:11 [j]ver 24; Ps 106:17 [k]Nu 26:8; Dt 11:6 16:2 [l]Nu 27:3 [m]Nu 1:16; 26:9 16:3 [n]ver 7; Ps 106:16

[1] 1 Or *Peleth—took* ⌊*men*⌋

15:31 DESPISED THE LORD'S WORD. God distinguished between unintentional sins (vv. 22–29) and intentional sins, i.e., those committed willfully in defiance of him and his word (vv. 30–31). Unintentional sin required atonement (vv. 24–28), though it did not separate one from God's chosen people. Deliberate and defiant sin, however, separated a person from the people of God and the redemption provided for them (vv. 30–31; see 1Jn 3:15).

16:3 TO OPPOSE MOSES. The story of Korah, Dathan and Abiram concerns three ambitious Le-

too far! The whole community is
holy,[o] every one of them, and the LORD
is with them.[p] Why then do you set
yourselves above the LORD's assembly?"[q]
4When Moses heard this, he fell
facedown.[r] **5**Then he said to Korah
and all his followers: "In the morning
the LORD will show who belongs to him
and who is holy,[s] and he will have that
person come near him.[t] The man he
chooses[u] he will cause to come near
him. **6**You, Korah, and all your followers[v] are to do this: Take censers[w]
7and tomorrow put fire[x] and incense[y] in them before the LORD. The
man the LORD chooses[z] will be the one
who is holy.[a] You Levites have gone
too far!"
8Moses also said to Korah, "Now listen, you Levites! **9**Isn't it enough[b] for
you that the God of Israel has separated you from the rest of the Israelite
community and brought you near himself to do the work at the LORD's tabernacle and to stand before the community and minister to them?[c] **10**He has
brought you and all your fellow Levites
near himself, but now you are trying to
get the priesthood too.[d] **11**It is against
the LORD that you and all your followers
have banded together. Who is Aaron
that you should grumble[e] against
him?[f]"
12Then Moses summoned Dathan
and Abiram,[g] the sons of Eliab. But
they said, "We will not come![h] **13**Isn't
it enough that you have brought us up
out of a land flowing with milk and
honey[i] to kill us in the desert?[j] And
now you also want to lord it over us?[k]
14Moreover, you haven't brought us
into a land flowing with milk and honey[l] or given us an inheritance of fields
and vineyards.[m] Will you gouge out
the eyes of[m] these men?[n] No, we will
not come![o]"

15Then Moses became very angry[p]
and said to the LORD, "Do not accept
their offering. I have not taken so
much as a donkey[q] from them, nor
have I wronged any of them."
16Moses said to Korah, "You and all
your followers are to appear before the
LORD tomorrow—you and they and
Aaron.[r] **17**Each man is to take his
censer and put incense in it—250 censers in all—and present it before the
LORD. You and Aaron are to present
your censers also.[s]" **18**So each man
took his censer,[t] put fire and incense
in it, and stood with Moses and Aaron
at the entrance to the Tent of Meeting.
19When Korah had gathered all his followers in opposition to them[u] at the
entrance to the Tent of Meeting, the
glory of the LORD[v] appeared to the entire assembly. **20**The LORD said to Moses and Aaron, **21**"Separate yourselves[w] from this assembly so I can
put an end to them at once."[x]
22But Moses and Aaron fell facedown[y] and cried out, "O God, God of
the spirits of all mankind,[z] will you be
angry with the entire assembly[a] when
only one man sins?"[b]
23Then the LORD said to Moses,
24"Say to the assembly, 'Move away
from the tents of Korah, Dathan and
Abiram.' "
25Moses got up and went to Dathan
and Abiram, and the elders of Israel[c]
followed him. **26**He warned the assembly, "Move back from the tents of these
wicked men![d] Do not touch anything
belonging to them, or you will be swept
away[e] because of all their sins.[f]"
27So they moved away from the tents
of Korah, Dathan and Abiram.[g] Dathan and Abiram had come out and
were standing with their wives, chil-

16:3 [o]Ex 19:6 [p]S Nu 14:14 [q]Nu 12:2
16:4 [r]Nu 14:5
16:5 [s]S Lev 10:3; 2Ti 2:19* [t]Jer 30:21 [u]Nu 17:5; Ps 65:4; 105:26; Jer 50:44
16:6 [v]ver 7,16 [w]S Lev 10:1; Rev 8:3
16:7 [x]S Lev 10:1 [y]S Ex 30:9 [z]S ver 6 [a]ver 5
16:9 [b]S Ge 30:15 [c]Nu 3:6; Dt 10:8; 17:12; 21:5; 1Sa 2:11; Ps 134:1; Eze 44:11
16:10 [d]Nu 3:10; 18:7; Jdg 17:5,12
16:11 [e]ver 41; 1Co 10:10 [f]S Ex 16:7
16:12 [g]S ver 1, 27 [h]ver 14
16:13 [i]Nu 13:27 [j]Nu 14:2 [k]S Ge 13:8; Ac 7:27,35
16:14 [l]S Lev 20:24 [m]Ex 22:5; 23:11; Nu 20:5; 1Ki 4:25; Ne 13:15; Ps 105:33; Jer 5:17; Hos 2:12; Joel 2:22; Hag 2:19; Zec 3:10 [n]Jdg 16:21; 1Sa 11:2; Jer 39:7 [o]ver 12
16:15 [p]S Ex 4:14 [q]1Sa 12:3
16:16 [r]S ver 6
16:17 [s]Eze 8:11
16:18 [t]Lev 10:1
16:19 [u]ver 42; Nu 20:2 [v]S Ex 16:7; Nu 14:10; 20:6
16:21 [w]ver 24 [x]S Ge 19:14; S Ex 32:10
16:22 [y]S Nu 14:5 [z]Nu 27:16; Job 12:10; 27:8; 33:4; 34:14; Jer 32:27; Eze 18:4; Heb 12:9 [a]S Lev 10:6 [b]S Ge 18:23; S Job 21:20
16:25 [c]S Ex 19:7
16:26 [d]Isa 52:11 [e]S Ge 19:15 [f]Jer 51:6
16:27 [g]S ver 12

[m]14 Or *you make slaves of*; or *you deceive*

vites maneuvering to get more power and a higher position for themselves as priests (v. 10). They challenged Moses' authority and the command that Aaron alone was to be high priest (vv. 3–11). By this action they were rejecting God and his revealed word about who would lead God's people (see 12:10, note); consequently, they received God's just condemnation (vv. 31–35), as will all those in God's kingdom who "love the place of honor at banquets and the most important seats" (Mt 23:6).

16:10 TRYING TO GET THE PRIESTHOOD TOO. Korah and the men thought they could choose for themselves who would lead the people. But God made it plain that he was in charge. Under the new covenant God still decides the type of people who are to serve as overseers of his church. He has set certain holy standards for those who desire to serve (1Ti 3:1–12; 4:12–16; Tit 1:5–9; see article on MORAL QUALIFICATIONS FOR OVERSEERS, p. 1882). When church members set aside God's standards for overseers and seek to choose leadership while disregarding his word, they are reflecting the rebellious attitude of Korah and the others who stood with him. Leadership must be based on God's revealed will for his church.

dren[h] and little ones at the entrances
to their tents.[i]
28Then Moses said, "This is how you
will know[j] that the LORD has sent
me[k] to do all these things and that it
was not my idea: 29If these men die a
natural death and experience only
what usually happens to men, then the
LORD has not sent me.[l] 30But if the
LORD brings about something totally
new, and the earth opens its mouth[m]
and swallows them, with everything
that belongs to them, and they go down
alive into the grave,[n][n] then you will
know that these men have treated the
LORD with contempt.[o]"
31As soon as he finished saying all
this, the ground under them split
apart[p] 32and the earth opened its
mouth and swallowed them,[q] with
their households and all Korah's men
and all their possessions. 33They went
down alive into the grave,[r] with everything they owned; the earth closed
over them, and they perished and were
gone from the community. 34At their
cries, all the Israelites around them
fled, shouting, "The earth is going to
swallow us too!"
35And fire came out from the LORD[s]
and consumed[t] the 250 men who
were offering the incense.
36The LORD said to Moses, 37"Tell
Eleazar[u] son of Aaron, the priest, to
take the censers[v] out of the smoldering remains and scatter the coals some
distance away, for the censers are
holy— 38the censers of the men who
sinned at the cost of their lives.[w] Hammer the censers into sheets to overlay
the altar,[x] for they were presented before the LORD and have become holy.
Let them be a sign[y] to the Israelites."
39So Eleazar the priest[z] collected
the bronze censers brought by those
who had been burned up,[a] and he had
them hammered out to overlay the altar, 40as the LORD directed him through
Moses. This was to remind the Israelites that no one except a descendant of
Aaron should come to burn incense[b]
before the LORD,[c] or he would become
like Korah and his followers.[d]
41The next day the whole Israelite
community grumbled against Moses
and Aaron. "You have killed the LORD's
people," they said.
42But when the assembly gathered
in opposition[e] to Moses and Aaron
and turned toward the Tent of Meeting,
suddenly the cloud covered it and the
glory of the LORD[f] appeared. 43Then
Moses and Aaron went to the front of
the Tent of Meeting, 44and the LORD
said to Moses, 45"Get away from this
assembly so I can put an end[g] to them
at once." And they fell facedown.
46Then Moses said to Aaron, "Take
your censer[h] and put incense in it,
along with fire from the altar, and hurry to the assembly[i] to make atonement[j] for them. Wrath has come out
from the LORD;[k] the plague[l] has
started." 47So Aaron did as Moses
said, and ran into the midst of the assembly. The plague had already started among the people,[m] but Aaron offered the incense and made atonement
for them. 48He stood between the living and the dead, and the plague
stopped.[n] 49But 14,700 people died
from the plague, in addition to those
who had died because of Korah.[o]
50Then Aaron returned to Moses at the
entrance to the Tent of Meeting, for the
plague had stopped.

The Budding of Aaron's Staff

17 The LORD said to Moses,
2"Speak to the Israelites and
get twelve staffs[p] from them, one
from the leader of each of their ancestral tribes.[q] Write the name of each
man on his staff. 3On the staff of Levi

16:27 [h] ver 32; Jos 7:24; Isa 13:16; 14:21 [i] S Ex 33:8
16:28 [j] 1Ki 18:36 [k] Ex 3:12; Jn 5:36; 6:38
16:29 [l] Nu 24:13; Job 31:2; Ecc 3:19
16:30 [m] Ps 141:7; Isa 5:14 [n] ver 33; S Ge 37:35; 1Sa 2:6; Job 5:26; 21:13; Ps 9:17; 16:10; 55:15; Isa 14:11; 38:18 [o] S Nu 14:11; S Eze 26:20
16:31 [p] Isa 64:1-2; Eze 47:1-12; Mic 1:3-4; Zec 14:4
16:32 [q] S Ex 15:12
16:33 [r] S ver 30; S Ecc 9:10
16:35 [s] S Nu 11:1-3; 26:10; Rev 11:5 [t] S Lev 10:2
16:37 [u] S Ex 6:23 [v] ver 6
16:38 [w] Lev 10:1; Pr 20:2 [x] S Ex 20:24; 38:1-7 [y] Nu 26:10; Dt 28:46; Jer 44:29; Eze 14:8; 2Pe 2:6
16:39 [z] 2Ch 26:18 [a] S Lev 20:14
16:40 [b] S Ex 30:1; 2Ki 12:3; Isa 1:13; 66:3; Jer 41:5; 44:3 [c] S Ex 30:9; 2Ch 26:18 [d] S Nu 3:10
16:42 [e] S ver 19 [f] Ex 16:7; Nu 14:10
16:45 [g] S Ex 32:10
16:46 [h] S Lev 10:1 [i] Lev 10:6 [j] S Ex 29:36 [k] S Nu 1:53 [l] S Lev 26:25; Nu 8:19; Ps 106:29
16:47 [m] Nu 25:6-8
16:48 [n] Nu 25:8; Ps 106:30
16:49 [o] ver 32
17:2 [p] S Ge 32:10; S Ex 4:2 [q] Nu 1:4

[n] 30 Hebrew *Sheol*; also in verse 33

16:32 WITH THEIR HOUSEHOLDS. The sons of Korah did not die along with their father, for they evidently did not participate in his rebellion (see 26:11).

16:41–50 YOU HAVE KILLED THE LORD'S PEOPLE. When God's judgment fell on Korah and his allies, the Israelites complained against Moses as if he had brought the judgment. The people had been so deceived that they thought the rebels were the most spiritual men among them. God's people need discernment to make sure that they do not follow leaders who are not from God (see article on FALSE TEACHERS, p. 1506).

17:3 ON THE STAFF OF LEVI WRITE AARON'S NAME. Ch. 17 defends God's choice of the tribe of Levi as ministers and Aaron as high priest. The Lord performed a miracle to demonstrate his choice of leadership (v. 8). Under the new covenant, godly leaders who faithfully proclaim God's word must be recognized and obeyed (Heb 13:17; cf. Ro 13:1–4; 1Ti 2:1–3).

write Aaron's name,[r] for there must
be one staff for the head of each ancestral tribe. 4Place them in the Tent of
Meeting[s] in front of the Testimony,[t]
where I meet with you.[u] 5The staff belonging to the man I choose[v] will
sprout,[w] and I will rid myself of this
constant grumbling[x] against you by
the Israelites."
6So Moses spoke to the Israelites,
and their leaders gave him twelve
staffs, one for the leader of each of
their ancestral tribes, and Aaron's
staff was among them. 7Moses placed
the staffs before the LORD in the Tent
of the Testimony.[y]
8The next day Moses entered the
Tent of the Testimony[z] and saw that
Aaron's staff,[a] which represented the
house of Levi, had not only sprouted
but had budded, blossomed and produced almonds.[b] 9Then Moses
brought out all the staffs[c] from the
LORD's presence to all the Israelites.
They looked at them, and each man
took his own staff.
10The LORD said to Moses, "Put back
Aaron's staff[d] in front of the Testimony, to be kept as a sign to the rebellious.[e] This will put an end to their
grumbling against me, so that they will
not die." 11Moses did just as the LORD
commanded him.
12The Israelites said to Moses, "We
will die! We are lost, we are all lost![f]
13Anyone who even comes near the
tabernacle of the LORD will die.[g] Are
we all going to die?"

Duties of Priests and Levites

18 The LORD said to Aaron, "You,
your sons and your father's
family are to bear the responsibility for
offenses against the sanctuary,[h] and
you and your sons alone are to bear the
responsibility for offenses against the
priesthood. 2Bring your fellow Levites
from your ancestral tribe to join you
and assist you when you and your sons
minister[i] before the Tent of the Testimony. 3They are to be responsible to
you[j] and are to perform all the duties
of the Tent,[k] but they must not go

17:3 [r] S Nu 1:3
17:4 [s] S Ex 40:2 [t] ver 7; Ex 16:34 [u] Ex 25:22
17:5 [v] S Nu 16:5 [w] ver 8 [x] S Ex 16:7
17:7 [y] S Ex 38:21
17:8 [z] ver 7; Nu 1:50 [a] ver 2,10 [b] Eze 17:24; Heb 9:4
17:9 [c] ver 2
17:10 [d] S ver 8 [e] S Ex 23:21; Dt 9:24; Ps 66:7; 68:18; Pr 24:21
17:12 [f] Jdg 13:22; Isa 6:5; 15:1
17:13 [g] Nu 1:51
18:1 [h] S Ex 28:38
18:2 [i] Nu 3:10
18:3 [j] S Nu 3:32 [k] Nu 1:51
[l] ver 7
18:4 [m] S Nu 3:38
18:5 [n] ver 3; Lev 6:12
18:6 [o] S Nu 3:9 [p] Nu 3:8
18:7 [q] Heb 9:3,6 [r] ver 20; Ex 29:9; 40:13; Heb 5:4 [s] ver 3; Nu 3:10
18:8 [t] S Lev 2:2 [u] Lev 6:16; 7:6, 31-34,36; Dt 18:1; 2Ch 31:4
18:9 [v] S Lev 6:17 [w] Lev 2:1 [x] Lev 6:25 [y] S Lev 5:15
18:10 [z] S Lev 6:16 [a] Lev 6:17,18
18:11 [b] Ex 29:26; Lev 7:30; Nu 6:20 [c] Lev 7:31-34 [d] Lev 13:3; 22:1-16
18:12 [e] Dt 7:13; 11:14; 12:17; 28:51; 2Ki 18:32; 2Ch 31:5; Ne 10:37; Jer 31:12; Eze 23:41; Hos 2:8; Joel 1:10; Hag 1:11 [f] S Ge 4:3 [g] Ex 23:19; 34:26; Ne 10:35
18:13 [h] S Ex 29:27 [i] ver 11

near the furnishings of the sanctuary
or the altar, or both they and you will
die.[l] 4They are to join you and be responsible for the care of the Tent of
Meeting—all the work at the Tent—
and no one else may come near where
you are.[m]
5"You are to be responsible for the
care of the sanctuary and the altar,[n]
so that wrath will not fall on the Israelites again. 6I myself have selected your
fellow Levites from among the Israelites as a gift to you,[o] dedicated to the
LORD to do the work at the Tent of
Meeting.[p] 7But only you and your
sons may serve as priests in connection with everything at the altar and
inside the curtain.[q] I am giving you
the service of the priesthood as a
gift.[r] Anyone else who comes near the
sanctuary must be put to death.[s]"

Offerings for Priests and Levites

8Then the LORD said to Aaron, "I myself have put you in charge of the offerings presented to me; all the holy offerings the Israelites give me I give to you
and your sons as your portion[t] and
regular share.[u] 9You are to have the
part of the most holy offerings[v] that is
kept from the fire. From all the gifts
they bring me as most holy offerings,
whether grain[w] or sin[x] or guilt offerings,[y] that part belongs to you and
your sons. 10Eat it as something most
holy; every male shall eat it.[z] You
must regard it as holy.[a]
11"This also is yours: whatever is
set aside from the gifts of all the wave
offerings[b] of the Israelites. I give this
to you and your sons and daughters as
your regular share.[c] Everyone in your
household who is ceremonially clean[d]
may eat it.
12"I give you all the finest olive oil
and all the finest new wine and grain[e]
they give the LORD[f] as the firstfruits of
their harvest.[g] 13All the land's firstfruits that they bring to the LORD will
be yours.[h] Everyone in your household who is ceremonially clean may
eat it.[i]
14"Everything in Israel that is devot-

18:1 BEAR THE RESPONSIBILITY FOR OFFENSES. The priests and Levites were held responsible for any desecration against the Lord's tabernacle. They had to take great care to serve God and do what the Lord required (cf. Lev 10:7).

18:8 IN CHARGE OF THE OFFERINGS. God determined that the priests and Levites be supported through the offerings of the people (vv. 8–24). In the same manner those who minister today must be supported by the offerings of those to whom they minister (1Co 9:13–14).

ed[o] to the LORD[j] is yours. 15The first
offspring of every womb, both man and
animal, that is offered to the LORD is
yours.[k] But you must redeem[l] every
firstborn[m] son and every firstborn
male of unclean animals.[n] 16When
they are a month old,[o] you must redeem them at the redemption price set
at five shekels[p][p] of silver, according
to the sanctuary shekel,[q] which
weighs twenty gerahs.[r]
17"But you must not redeem the
firstborn of an ox, a sheep or a goat;
they are holy.[s] Sprinkle their blood[t]
on the altar and burn their fat[u] as an
offering made by fire, an aroma pleasing to the LORD.[v] 18Their meat is to be
yours, just as the breast of the wave
offering[w] and the right thigh are
yours.[x] 19Whatever is set aside from
the holy[y] offerings the Israelites
present to the LORD I give to you and
your sons and daughters as your regular share. It is an everlasting covenant
of salt[z] before the LORD for both you
and your offspring."
20The LORD said to Aaron, "You will
have no inheritance in their land, nor
will you have any share among them;[a]
I am your share and your inheritance[b]
among the Israelites.
21"I give to the Levites all the
tithes[c] in Israel as their inheritance[d]
in return for the work they do while
serving at the Tent of Meeting.[e]
22From now on the Israelites must not
go near the Tent of Meeting, or they
will bear the consequences of their sin
and will die.[f] 23It is the Levites who
are to do the work at the Tent of Meeting and bear the responsibility for offenses against it. This is a lasting ordinance[g] for the generations to come.[h]
They will receive no inheritance[i]
among the Israelites.[j] 24Instead, I
give to the Levites as their inheritance
the tithes that the Israelites present as
an offering to the LORD.[k] That is why
I said concerning them: 'They will have
no inheritance among the Israelites.' "
25The LORD said to Moses, 26"Speak
to the Levites and say to them: 'When
you receive from the Israelites the
tithe I give you[l] as your inheritance,
you must present a tenth of that tithe
as the LORD's offering.[m] 27Your offering will be reckoned[n] to you as grain
from the threshing floor[o] or juice from
the winepress.[p] 28In this way you also
will present an offering to the LORD
from all the tithes[q] you receive from
the Israelites. From these tithes you
must give the LORD's portion to Aaron
the priest. 29You must present as the
LORD's portion the best and holiest part
of everything given to you.'
30"Say to the Levites: 'When you
present the best part, it will be reckoned to you as the product of the
threshing floor or the winepress.[r]
31You and your households may eat
the rest of it anywhere, for it is your
wages for your work at the Tent of
Meeting.[s] 32By presenting the best
part[t] of it you will not be guilty in this
matter;[u] then you will not defile the
holy offerings[v] of the Israelites, and
you will not die.' "

The Water of Cleansing

19 The LORD said to Moses and
Aaron: 2"This is a requirement
of the law that the LORD has commanded: Tell the Israelites to bring you a red
heifer[w] without defect or blemish[x]
and that has never been under a
yoke.[y] 3Give it to Eleazar[z] the priest;
it is to be taken outside the camp[a] and
slaughtered in his presence. 4Then Eleazar the priest is to take some of its

18:14 [j]S Lev 27:21; Jos 6:17-19
18:15 [k]Ex 13:2 [l]S Nu 3:46 [m]S Ge 10:15 [n]S Ex 13:13
18:16 [o]S Nu 3:15 [p]S Lev 27:6 [q]S Ex 30:13 [r]Nu 3:47
18:17 [s]S Lev 27:9 [t]S Lev 3:2 [u]S Ex 29:13 [v]S Lev 1:9
18:18 [w]Lev 7:30 [x]ver 11
18:19 [y]2Ki 12:4 [z]S Lev 2:13
18:20 [a]Nu 26:62; Dt 12:12 [b]ver 24; Dt 10:9; 14:27; 18:1-2; Jos 13:33; Eze 44:28
18:21 [c]ver 24; S Ge 28:22; Nu 31:28; Dt 14:22; Ne 10:37; 13:5; Mal 3:8 [d]Lev 27:30-33; Heb 7:5 [e]Nu 1:53
18:22 [f]S Ex 28:43
18:23 [g]S Ex 12:14; S 27:21 [h]Nu 10:8 [i]ver 20; Nu 26:62; Dt 10:9 [j]Eze 44:10
18:24 [k]Lev 27:30; Dt 26:12
18:26 [l]ver 21 [m]ver 28; Ne 10:38
18:27 [n]Lev 7:18 [o]Ge 50:10; Dt 15:14; Jdg 6:37; Ru 3:3,6, 14; 1Sa 23:1 [p]ver 12,30
18:28 [q]Mal 3:8
18:30 [r]S ver 27
18:31 [s]ver 23
18:32 [t]Lev 22:15 [u]ver 29 [v]S Lev 19:8
19:2 [w]S Ge 15:9; Heb 9:13 [x]S Lev 22:19-25 [y]Dt 21:3; 1Sa 6:7
19:3 [z]Nu 3:4 [a]S Ex 29:14

[o] *14* The Hebrew term refers to the irrevocable giving over of things or persons to the LORD. [p] *16* That is, about 2 ounces (about 55 grams)

18:19 COVENANT OF SALT. Salt represents preservation and permanence and highlights the irrevocability of the covenant (cf. Lev 2:13).

18:20 I AM ... YOUR INHERITANCE. The priests and Levites were to have no earthly inheritance, for God himself was their share and inheritance. In principle, this promise extends to all believers in Christ. Our inheritance is not on this earth, for we are but aliens and strangers. We must seek heavenly things, for God dwells in heaven (Heb 11:9–16). Our witness is this: "I say to myself, 'The LORD is my portion; therefore I will wait for him' " (La 3:24).

19:2 RED HEIFER. The sacrifice of the red heifer provided for the cleansing of anyone who was ritually unclean or defiled and therefore unable to draw near to God in worship (vv. 11,14,16). A red heifer without defect was killed and burned outside the camp (vv. 3–6). The ashes were kept, mixed with water (vv. 9,17) and applied to those who were defiled (vv. 12,18). This purification rite cleansed that person, allowing him or her to approach God once again. The book of Hebrews contrasts the cleansing effect of Christ's blood to that of the ashes of the red heifer (Heb 9:13–14; see next note).

blood on his finger and sprinkle[b] it
seven times toward the front of the
Tent of Meeting. 5While he watches,
the heifer is to be burned—its hide,
flesh, blood and offal.[c] 6The priest is
to take some cedar wood, hyssop[d] and
scarlet wool[e] and throw them onto the
burning heifer. 7After that, the priest
must wash his clothes and bathe himself with water.[f] He may then come
into the camp, but he will be ceremonially unclean till evening. 8The man
who burns it must also wash his
clothes and bathe with water, and he
too will be unclean till evening.
9"A man who is clean shall gather up
the ashes of the heifer[g] and put them
in a ceremonially clean place[h] outside
the camp. They shall be kept by the
Israelite community for use in the water of cleansing;[i] it is for purification
from sin.[j] 10The man who gathers
up[k] the ashes of the heifer must also
wash his clothes, and he too will be unclean till evening.[l] This will be a lasting ordinance[m] both for the Israelites
and for the aliens living among them.[n]
11"Whoever touches the dead body[o]
of anyone will be unclean for seven
days.[p] 12He must purify himself with
the water on the third day and on the
seventh day;[q] then he will be clean.
But if he does not purify himself on the
third and seventh days, he will not be
clean.[r] 13Whoever touches the dead
body[s] of anyone and fails to purify
himself defiles the LORD's tabernacle.[t]
That person must be cut off from Israel.[u] Because the water of cleansing
has not been sprinkled on him, he is
unclean;[v] his uncleanness remains on
him.
14"This is the law that applies when
a person dies in a tent: Anyone who
enters the tent and anyone who is in it
will be unclean for seven days, 15and
every open container[w] without a lid
fastened on it will be unclean.
16"Anyone out in the open who
touches someone who has been killed
with a sword or someone who has died
a natural death,[x] or anyone who
touches a human bone[y] or a grave,[z]
will be unclean for seven days.[a]
17"For the unclean person, put some
ashes[b] from the burned purification
offering into a jar and pour fresh water[c] over them. 18Then a man who is
ceremonially clean is to take some hyssop,[d] dip it in the water and sprinkle[e] the tent and all the furnishings
and the people who were there. He
must also sprinkle anyone who has
touched a human bone or a grave[f] or
someone who has been killed or someone who has died a natural death.
19The man who is clean is to sprinkle[g]
the unclean person on the third and
seventh days, and on the seventh day
he is to purify him.[h] The person being
cleansed must wash his clothes[i] and
bathe with water, and that evening he
will be clean. 20But if a person who is
unclean does not purify himself, he
must be cut off from the community,
because he has defiled[j] the sanctuary
of the LORD.[k] The water of cleansing
has not been sprinkled on him, and he
is unclean.[l] 21This is a lasting ordinance[m] for them.
"The man who sprinkles the water of
cleansing must also wash his clothes,
and anyone who touches the water of
cleansing will be unclean till evening.
22Anything that an unclean[n] person
touches becomes unclean, and anyone
who touches it becomes unclean till
evening."

Water From the Rock

20 In the first month the whole Israelite community arrived at
the Desert of Zin,[o] and they stayed at
Kadesh.[p] There Miriam[q] died and
was buried.
2Now there was no water[r] for the
community,[s] and the people gathered
in opposition[t] to Moses and Aaron.
3They quarreled[u] with Moses and
said, "If only we had died when our
brothers fell dead[v] before the LORD![w]
4Why did you bring the LORD's commu-

19:4 [b] S Lev 4:17
19:5 [c] S Ex 29:14
19:6 [d] ver 18; Ps 51:7 [e] S Lev 14:4
19:7 [f] S Lev 11:25; S 14:8
19:9 [g] Heb 9:13 [h] S Ex 29:31; S Lev 4:12 [i] ver 13; Nu 8:7 [j] S Ge 35:2
19:10 [k] Lev 15:10 [l] Lev 14:46 [m] Lev 3:17 [n] S Lev 22:18
19:11 [o] S Lev 21:1 [p] S Lev 8:33; Nu 31:19
19:12 [q] ver 19; Nu 31:19 [r] ver 20; 2Ch 26:21
19:13 [s] S Lev 21:11 [t] S Lev 15:31; 2Ch 36:14; Ps 79:1 [u] Lev 7:20; 22:3 [v] ver 22; Hag 2:13
19:15 [w] S Lev 6:28
19:16 [x] Nu 31:19 [y] 1Ki 13:2; 2Ki 23:14; Eze 6:5 [z] 2Ki 23:6; Mt 23:27 [a] S Lev 5:3
19:17 [b] ver 9 [c] S Nu 8:7
19:18 [d] S ver 6; S Ex 12:22 [e] S Lev 4:17 [f] ver 16
19:19 [g] S Lev 16:14-15 [h] Nu 31:19; Eze 36:25; Heb 10:22 [i] S Ge 35:2
19:20 [j] Ps 74:7 [k] S Lev 15:31 [l] S ver 12; S Lev 14:8
19:21 [m] S Ex 27:21
19:22 [n] S Lev 5:2; 15:4-12
20:1 [o] Nu 13:21 [p] ver 14; Nu 13:26; 33:36; Dt 1:46; Jdg 11:17; Ps 29:8 [q] S Ex 15:20
20:2 [r] S Ex 15:22 [s] Ex 17:1 [t] S Nu 16:19
20:3 [u] ver 13; S Ge 13:7; Ex 17:2; 21:18 [v] S Ex 5:21 [w] S Nu 14:2; 16:31-35

19:9 FOR PURIFICATION FROM SIN. Heb 9:13–14 contrasts the blood of Christ with the ashes of the red heifer. As the Israelites had in the ashes a ready means of purification, so believers in Christ have a ready fountain of Christ's blood in which, by faith and repentance, they may find cleansing "from all sin" (1Jn 1:7). By this cleansing they may draw near to God, receive mercy and find grace to help in their time of need (Heb 4:16; 7:25).

20:1 IN THE FIRST MONTH. The events in this chapter begin in the fortieth year after the exodus from Egypt (see vv. 22–29; 33:38). The people had wandered in the desert for thirty-nine years. Most of the first generation had died because of their unbelief without receiving what was promised (see chs. 13—14); soon their children would enter the promised land.

nity into this desert,[x] that we and our
livestock should die here?[y] **5**Why did
you bring us up out of Egypt to this
terrible place? It has no grain or figs,
grapevines or pomegranates.[z] And
there is no water to drink![a]"
6Moses and Aaron went from the assembly to the entrance to the Tent of
Meeting[b] and fell facedown,[c] and the
glory of the LORD[d] appeared to them.
7The LORD said to Moses, **8**"Take the
staff,[e] and you and your brother Aaron gather the assembly together.
Speak to that rock before their eyes
and it will pour out its water.[f] You
will bring water out of the rock for the
community so they and their livestock
can drink."
9So Moses took the staff[g] from the
LORD's presence,[h] just as he commanded him. **10**He and Aaron gathered
the assembly together[i] in front of the
rock and Moses said to them, "Listen,
you rebels, must we bring you water
out of this rock?"[j] **11**Then Moses
raised his arm and struck the rock
twice with his staff. Water[k] gushed
out, and the community and their livestock drank.
12But the LORD said to Moses and
Aaron, "Because you did not trust in
me enough to honor me as holy[l] in the
sight of the Israelites, you will not
bring this community into the land I
give them."[m]
13These were the waters of Meribah,[q][n] where the Israelites quarreled[o] with the LORD and where he
showed himself holy among them.[p]

Edom Denies Israel Passage

14Moses sent messengers from Kadesh[q] to the king of Edom,[r] saying:
"This is what your brother Israel says: You know[s] about all the
hardships[t] that have come upon
us. **15**Our forefathers went down
into Egypt,[u] and we lived there
many years.[v] The Egyptians mistreated[w] us and our fathers,
16but when we cried out to the
LORD, he heard our cry[x] and sent
an angel[y] and brought us out of
Egypt.[z]
"Now we are here at Kadesh, a
town on the edge of your territory.[a] **17**Please let us pass through
your country. We will not go
through any field or vineyard, or
drink water from any well. We will
travel along the king's highway
and not turn to the right or to the
left until we have passed through
your territory.[b]"
18But Edom[c] answered:
"You may not pass through
here; if you try, we will march out
and attack you with the sword.[d]"
19The Israelites replied:
"We will go along the main
road, and if we or our livestock[e]
drink any of your water, we will
pay for it.[f] We only want to pass
through on foot—nothing else."
20Again they answered:
"You may not pass through.[g]"
Then Edom[h] came out against them
with a large and powerful army.

20:4 [x]S Nu 14:2 [y]S Ex 14:11; Nu 14:3; 16:13 **20:5** [z]Nu 13:23; 16:14 [a]S Ex 17:1 **20:6** [b]S Ex 40:2 [c]Nu 14:5 [d]S Nu 16:19 **20:8** [e]S Ex 4:2; S 10:12-13 [f]Ex 17:6; Isa 41:18; 43:20; Jer 31:9 **20:9** [g]Nu 17:2 [h]Nu 17:10 **20:10** [i]ver 8 [j]Ps 106:32,33 **20:11** [k]S Ex 17:6; S Isa 33:21 **20:12** [l]Nu 27:14; Dt 32:51; Isa 5:16; 8:13 [m]ver 24; Dt 1:37; 3:27 **20:13** [n]S Ex 17:7 [o]S ver 3 [p]S Lev 10:3
20:14 [q]S ver 1 [r]S ver 16; S Ge 25:30; S 36:16 [s]Ge 24:3; Dt 4:39; Jos 2:11; 9:9 [t]S Ex 18:8 **20:15** [u]S Ge 46:6 [v]S Ge 15:13 [w]S Ex 1:14 **20:16** [x]S Ge 16:11; S 21:17; S Ex 2:23 [y]Ex 14:19 [z]Ex 12:42; Dt 26:8 [a]ver 14, 23; Nu 33:37 **20:17** [b]ver 20; Nu 21:22; Dt 2:27; Jdg 11:17 **20:18** [c]ver 14 [d]Nu 21:23 **20:19** [e]Ex 12:38 [f]Dt 2:6,28 **20:20** [g]S ver 17, 18 [h]ver 14

[q]*13 Meribah* means *quarreling.*

20:8 SPEAK TO THAT ROCK. Moses and Aaron were commanded by God to speak to the rock, not to strike it as had been done at Horeb (Ex 17:1–7; see next note).

20:12 YOU WILL NOT BRING THIS COMMUNITY INTO THE LAND. Moses was forbidden to lead God's people into Canaan because he had not carefully followed the Lord's command (compare v. 8 with v. 11). Moses was the spiritual leader of God's people, the one through whom God gave the law. His responsibility to obey the Lord's word was greater because of his greater position and influence (cf. Jas 3:1). (1) Moses' sin was twofold. First, he spoke rashly as if God's glory and power resided in himself and Aaron (v. 10; cf. Ps 106:33). Second, he then acted rashly by angrily striking the rock twice rather than speaking to it as God had instructed (v. 11).

(2) In speaking and acting rashly, Moses showed that he did not trust in God (v. 12) and thus "rebelled" against his command (v. 24). At that critical time, Moses lacked faith and obedience, always the correct response to God's revealed word (cf. Dt 9:23; 1Sa 12:15; 1Ki 13:21; 2Ki 17:14; Ps 106:33). In addition, Moses failed to treat God as the holy and worthy God, choosing not to fear him and obey his command.

(3) Through these verses God reminds all ministers of the gospel that their responsibility to obey the word of God is greater because of their position and influence. Just as Moses disqualified himself from leading the people into Canaan, so also ministers today can permanently disqualify themselves from certain areas of leadership by their unfaithfulness to God's commands (1Ti 3:1–7; see article on MORAL QUALIFICATIONS FOR OVERSEERS, p. 1882).

21 Since Edom refused to let them go through their territory,[i] Israel turned away from them.[j]

The Death of Aaron

22 The whole Israelite community set out from Kadesh[k] and came to Mount Hor.[l] 23 At Mount Hor, near the border of Edom,[m] the LORD said to Moses and Aaron, 24 "Aaron will be gathered to his people.[n] He will not enter the land I give the Israelites, because both of you rebelled against my command[o] at the waters of Meribah.[p] 25 Get Aaron and his son Eleazar and take them up Mount Hor.[q] 26 Remove Aaron's garments[r] and put them on his son Eleazar, for Aaron will be gathered to his people;[s] he will die there."

27 Moses did as the LORD commanded: They went up Mount Hor[t] in the sight of the whole community. 28 Moses removed Aaron's garments and put them on his son Eleazar.[u] And Aaron died there[v] on top of the mountain. Then Moses and Eleazar came down from the mountain, 29 and when the whole community learned that Aaron had died,[w] the entire house of Israel mourned for him[x] thirty days.

Arad Destroyed

21 When the Canaanite king of Arad,[y] who lived in the Negev,[z] heard that Israel was coming along the road to Atharim, he attacked the Israelites and captured some of them. 2 Then Israel made this vow[a] to the LORD: "If you will deliver these people into our hands, we will totally destroy[r][b] their cities." 3 The LORD listened to Israel's plea and gave the Canaanites[c] over to them. They completely destroyed them[d] and their towns; so the place was named Hormah.[s][e]

The Bronze Snake

4 They traveled from Mount Hor[f] along the route to the Red Sea,[t][g] to go around Edom.[h] But the people grew impatient on the way;[i] 5 they spoke against God[j] and against Moses, and said, "Why have you brought us up out of Egypt[k] to die in the desert?[l] There is no bread! There is no water![m] And we detest this miserable food!"[n]

6 Then the LORD sent venomous snakes[o] among them; they bit the people and many Israelites died.[p] 7 The people came to Moses[q] and said, "We sinned[r] when we spoke against the LORD and against you. Pray that the LORD[s] will take the snakes away from us." So Moses prayed[t] for the people.

8 The LORD said to Moses, "Make a snake and put it up on a pole;[u] anyone who is bitten can look at it and live." 9 So Moses made a bronze snake[v] and put it up on a pole. Then when anyone was bitten by a snake and looked at the bronze snake, he lived.[w] Dt 7:15

The Journey to Moab

10 The Israelites moved on and camped at Oboth.[x] 11 Then they set out from Oboth and camped in Iye Abarim, in the desert that faces Moab[y] toward the sunrise. 12 From there they moved on and camped in the Zered Valley.[z] 13 They set out from there and camped alongside the Arnon[a], which is in the desert extending into Amorite territory. The Arnon is the border of Moab, between Moab and the Amo-

20:21 *i* Nu 21:23 *j* Nu 21:4; Dt 2:8; Jdg 11:18 **20:22** *k* Dt 1:46 *l* Nu 33:37; 34:7; Dt 32:50 **20:23** *m* S ver 16 **20:24** *n* S Ge 25:8 *o* S ver 10 *p* S Ex 17:7 **20:25** *q* Nu 33:38 **20:26** *r* Ex 28:1-4; 40:13; S Lev 16:4 *s* ver 24; Nu 27:13; 31:2 **20:27** *t* Nu 33:38 **20:28** *u* S Ex 29:29 *v* ver 26; Nu 33:38; Dt 10:6; 32:50 **20:29** *w* Dt 32:50 *x* S Ge 27:41; S Lev 10:6; S Dt 34:8 **21:1** *y* Nu 33:40; Jos 12:14 *z* S Ge 12:9; Nu 13:17; Dt 1:7; Jdg 1:9,16 **21:2** *a* Lev 7:16 *b* ver 3; Ex 22:20; Dt 2:34; Jos 2:10; 8:26; Jer 25:9; 50:21 **21:3** *c* S Ge 10:18 *d* S ver 2 *e* S Nu 14:45

21:4 *f* Nu 20:22 *g* Nu 14:25; Dt 2:1; 11:4 *h* S Nu 20:21 *i* Dt 2:8; Jdg 11:18 **21:5** *j* Ps 78:19 *k* Nu 11:20 *l* S Ex 14:11; Nu 14:2,3 *m* Nu 20:5 *n* S Nu 11:5 **21:6** *o* ver 7; Dt 8:15; 32:33; Job 20:14; Ps 58:4; 140:3; Jer 8:17 *p* 1Co 10:9 **21:7** *q* Ps 78:34; Hos 5:15 *r* Nu 14:40 *s* Ex 8:8; 1Sa 7:8; Jer 27:18; 37:3; Ac 8:24 *t* S Nu 11:2 **21:8** *u* Jn 3:14 **21:9** *v* 2Ki 18:4 *w* Jn 3:14-15 **21:10** *x* Nu 33:43 **21:11** *y* S Ge 36:35; Nu 33:44; Dt 34:8; Jer 40:11 **21:12** *z* Dt 2:13, 14 **21:13** *a* Nu 22:36; Dt 2:24; Jos 12:1; Jdg 11:13,18; 2Ki 10:33; Isa 16:2; Jer 48:20

r 2 The Hebrew term refers to the irrevocable giving over of things or persons to the LORD, often by totally destroying them; also in verse 3. *s* 3 *Hormah* means *destruction*. *t* 4 Hebrew *Yam Suph*; that is, Sea of Reeds

21:3 COMPLETELY DESTROYED THEM. God, through Israel, totally destroyed the Canaanites in the Negev. Total destruction was his just action upon those who were irreparably committed to sin, immorality, violence and unrighteousness. As the Lord of history God has the right to decide when it is best to destroy the wicked to accomplish his redemptive purpose for the human race. In the OT God often used Israel to accomplish his purpose. Under the new covenant he no longer uses believers to destroy the ungodly. At the end of the age, however, God himself will again execute judgment on all who reject Christ and his way of salvation (Rev 6—19).

21:9 BRONZE SNAKE. The life-giving power of the bronze snake anticipates the sacrificial death of Jesus Christ, who was lifted up on the cross in order to bring life to all who look to him. About this event Jesus himself said: "Just as Moses lifted up the snake in the desert, so the Son of Man must be lifted up, that everyone who believes in him may have eternal life" (Jn 3:14–15). Those who desire to be delivered from their sin and receive salvation must turn their hearts in believing obedience to the word of God in Christ.

rites.[b] **14**That is why the Book of the Wars[c] of the LORD says:

"... Waheb in Suphah[u] and the
ravines,
the Arnon **15**and[v] the slopes of
the ravines
that lead to the site of Ar[d]
and lie along the border of
Moab."

16From there they continued on to Beer,[e] the well where the LORD said to Moses, "Gather the people together and I will give them water."

17Then Israel sang this song:[f]

"Spring up, O well!
Sing about it,
18about the well that the princes
dug,
that the nobles of the people
sank—
the nobles with scepters and
staffs."

Then they went from the desert to Mattanah, **19**from Mattanah to Nahaliel, from Nahaliel to Bamoth, **20**and from Bamoth to the valley in Moab where the top of Pisgah[g] overlooks the wasteland.

Defeat of Sihon and Og

21Israel sent messengers[h] to say to Sihon[i] king of the Amorites:[j]

22"Let us pass through your country. We will not turn aside into any field or vineyard, or drink water from any well. We will travel along the king's highway until we have passed through your territory.[k]"

23But Sihon would not let Israel pass through his territory.[l] He mustered his entire army and marched out into the desert against Israel. When he reached Jahaz,[m] he fought with Israel.[n] **24**Israel, however, put him to the sword[o] and took over his land[p] from the Arnon to the Jabbok,[q] but only as far as the Ammonites,[r] because their border was fortified. **25**Israel captured all the cities of the Amorites[s] and occupied them,[t] including Heshbon[u] and all its surrounding settlements. **26**Heshbon was the city of Sihon[v] king of the Amorites,[w] who had fought against the former king of Moab[x] and had taken from him all his land as far as the Arnon.[y]

27That is why the poets say:

"Come to Heshbon and let it be
rebuilt;
let Sihon's city be restored.

28"Fire went out from Heshbon,
a blaze from the city of Sihon.[z]
It consumed[a] Ar[b] of Moab,
the citizens of Arnon's
heights.[c]
29Woe to you, O Moab![d]
You are destroyed, O people of
Chemosh![e]
He has given up his sons as
fugitives[f]
and his daughters as captives[g]
to Sihon king of the Amorites.

30"But we have overthrown them;
Heshbon is destroyed all the
way to Dibon.[h]
We have demolished them as far
as Nophah,
which extends to Medeba.[i]"

31So Israel settled in the land of the Amorites.[j]

32After Moses had sent spies[k] to Jazer,[l] the Israelites captured its surrounding settlements and drove out the Amorites who were there. **33**Then they turned and went up along the road toward Bashan[m],[n] and Og king of Bashan and his whole army marched out to meet them in battle at Edrei.[o]

34The LORD said to Moses, "Do not be afraid of him, for I have handed him over to you, with his whole army and his land. Do to him what you did to Sihon king of the Amorites, who reigned in Heshbon.[p]"

35So they struck him down, together with his sons and his whole army, leaving them no survivors.[q] And they took possession of his land.[r]

Balak Summons Balaam

22 Then the Israelites traveled to the plains of Moab[s] and camped along the Jordan[t] across from Jericho.[w][u]

21:13 [b]S Ge 10:16
21:14 [c]1Sa 17:47; 18:17; 25:28
21:15 [d]ver 28; Dt 2:9,18; Isa 15:1
21:16 [e]Nu 25:1; 33:49; Jdg 9:21; Isa 15:8
21:17 [f]S Ex 15:1
21:20 [g]Nu 23:14; Dt 3:17,27; 34:1; Jos 12:3; 13:20
21:21 [h]S Ge 32:3 [i]Nu 32:33; Dt 1:4; Jos 2:10; 12:2,4; 13:10; Jdg 11:19-21; 1Ki 4:19; Ne 9:22; Ps 135:11; 136:19; Jer 48:45 [j]S Ex 23:23
21:22 [k]S Nu 20:17
21:23 [l]Nu 20:21 [m]Dt 2:32; Jos 13:18; 21:36; Jdg 11:20; Isa 15:4; Jer 48:21,34 [n]Nu 20:18
21:24 [o]Dt 2:33; 3:3; 29:7; Ps 135:10-11; Am 2:9 [p]ver 35; Dt 3:4 [q]S Ge 32:22; Nu 32:33; Jdg 11:13,22 [r]S Ge 19:38; Dt 2:37; Jos 13:10
21:25 [s]Nu 13:29; Jdg 10:11; Am 2:10 [t]Jdg 11:26 [u]ver 30; Nu 32:3; Dt 1:4; 29:7; Jos 9:10; 12:2; Isa 15:4; 16:8; Jer 48:2,34
21:26 [v]ver 21; Dt 29:7; Ps 135:11 [w]Nu 13:29 [x]ver 11 [y]ver 13
21:28 [z]Jer 48:45 [a]S Nu 11:1 [b]S ver 15 [c]Nu 22:41; Dt 12:2; Jos 13:17; Isa 15:2; Jer 19:5
21:29 [d]Nu 24:17; 2Sa 8:2; 1Ch 18:2; Ps 60:8; Isa 25:10; Jer 48:46 [e]Jdg 10:6; 11:24; Ru 1:15; 1Ki 11:7, 33; 2Ki 23:13; Jer 48:7,46 [f]Isa 15:5 [g]Isa 16:2
21:30 [h]Nu 32:3; Jos 13:9,17; Ne 11:25; Isa 15:2; Jer 48:18,22 [i]Jos 13:16; 1Ch 19:7
21:31 [j]Nu 13:29
21:32 [k]Jos 2:1; 6:22; 7:2; Jdg 18:2; 2Sa 10:3; 1Ch 19:3 [l]Nu 32:1,3,35; Jos 13:25; 2Sa 24:5; 1Ch 6:81; Isa 16:8; Jer 48:32
21:33 [m]Nu 32:33; Dt 3:3; 31:4; Jos 2:10; 12:4; 13:30; 1Ki 4:19; Ne 9:22; Ps 135:11; 136:20 [n]Dt 3:4; 32:14; Jos 9:10; 1Ki 4:13 [o]Dt 1:4; 3:1,10; Jos 12:4; 13:12,31; 19:37 **21:34** [p]Dt 3:2 **21:35** [q]Jos 9:10 [r]S ver 24 **22:1** [s]S Nu 21:11 [t]S Nu 13:29; S Jos 2:7 [u]Nu 31:12; 33:48; Dt 32:49; Jos 2:1

[u] *14* The meaning of the Hebrew for this phrase is uncertain. [v] *14,15* Or *"I have been given from Suphah and the ravines / of the Arnon* [15]*to* [w] *1* Hebrew *Jordan of Jericho*; possibly an ancient name for the Jordan River

2Now Balak son of Zippor[v] saw all
that Israel had done to the Amorites,
3and Moab was terrified because there
were so many people. Indeed, Moab
was filled with dread[w] because of the
Israelites.
4The Moabites[x] said to the elders
of Midian,[y] "This horde is going to
lick up everything[z] around us, as an
ox licks up the grass of the field.[a]"
So Balak son of Zippor, who was
king of Moab at that time, 5sent messengers to summon Balaam son of
Beor,[b] who was at Pethor, near the
River,[x][c] in his native land. Balak
said:

"A people has come out of
Egypt;[d] they cover the face of the
land and have settled next to me.
6Now come and put a curse[e] on
these people, because they are too
powerful for me. Perhaps then I
will be able to defeat them and
drive them out of the country.[f]
For I know that those you bless
are blessed, and those you curse
are cursed."

7The elders of Moab and Midian left,
taking with them the fee for divination.[g] When they came to Balaam,
they told him what Balak had said.
8"Spend the night here," Balaam
said to them, "and I will bring you back
the answer the LORD gives me.[h]" So
the Moabite princes stayed with him.
9God came to Balaam[i] and
asked,[j] "Who are these men with
you?"
10Balaam said to God, "Balak son of
Zippor, king of Moab, sent me this
message: 11'A people that has come
out of Egypt covers the face of the
land. Now come and put a curse on
them for me. Perhaps then I will be
able to fight them and drive them
away.' "
12But God said to Balaam, "Do not
go with them. You must not put a curse
on those people, because they are
blessed.[k]"
13The next morning Balaam got up
and said to Balak's princes, "Go back
to your own country, for the LORD has
refused to let me go with you."
14So the Moabite princes returned to
Balak and said, "Balaam refused to
come with us."
15Then Balak sent other princes,
more numerous and more distinguished than the first. 16They came to
Balaam and said:

"This is what Balak son of Zippor says: Do not let anything keep
you from coming to me, 17because
I will reward you handsomely[l]
and do whatever you say. Come
and put a curse[m] on these people
for me."

18But Balaam answered them,
"Even if Balak gave me his palace filled
with silver and gold, I could not do anything great or small to go beyond the
command of the LORD my God.[n] 19Now
stay here tonight as the others did, and
I will find out what else the LORD will
tell me.[o]"
20That night God came to Balaam[p]
and said, "Since these men have come
to summon you, go with them, but do
only what I tell you."[q]

Balaam's Donkey

21Balaam got up in the morning,
saddled his donkey and went with the
princes of Moab. 22But God was very
angry[r] when he went, and the angel of
the LORD[s] stood in the road to oppose
him. Balaam was riding on his donkey,
and his two servants were with him.
23When the donkey saw the angel of

22:2 [v] Nu 23:1-3; Jos 24:9; Jdg 11:25; Mic 6:5; Rev 2:14
22:3 [w] S Ex 15:15
22:4 [x] S Ge 19:37 [y] S Ge 25:2 [z] Nu 32:17,18,29 [a] Job 5:25; Ps 72:16
22:5 [b] ver 7; Nu 24:25; 31:8,16; Dt 23:4; Jos 13:22; Ne 13:2; Mic 6:5; S 2Pe 2:15 [c] S Ge 2:14 [d] S Ex 13:3
22:6 [e] ver 12,17; Nu 23:7,11,13; 24:9,10 [f] ver 11
22:7 [g] S Ge 30:27
22:8 [h] ver 19
22:9 [i] S Ge 20:3 [j] ver 20; Nu 23:5; 24:4,16
22:12 [k] S Ge 12:2
22:17 [l] ver 37; Nu 24:11 [m] S ver 6
22:18 [n] ver 38; Nu 23:12,26; 24:13; 1Ki 22:14; 2Ch 18:13; Jer 42:4
22:19 [o] ver 8
22:20 [p] S Ge 20:3 [q] ver 35,38; Nu 23:5,12,16,26; 24:13; 2Ch 18:13
22:22 [r] S Ex 4:14 [s] S Ge 16:7; Jdg 13:3,6,13

[x] 5 That is, the Euphrates

22:5 BALAAM. Balaam was not an Israelite but an internationally known priest-diviner. Balak thought that this man could put curses on others (v. 6) by influencing the will of the gods and spirits through his secret knowledge of sorcery, incantations and mysterious manipulations (vv. 2–7; cf. 24:1). (1) Balaam may at one time have been a true follower of God (cf. v. 18) who later departed from the faith and became a diviner (v. 7; cf. 31:16; Dt 23:4–5; 2Pe 2:15; Jude 11). (2) Like all false prophets, he had no genuine concern for God's honor or the holiness of God's people. Unable to curse the people, Balaam led them into sin and immorality (25:1–6; 31:16; Rev 2:14). For this he was killed (31:8; see 25:2, note).

22:18 THE LORD MY GOD. Balaam's reference to "the LORD my God" may indicate that his worship of many gods included the worship of the God of Israel. Scripture depicts Balaam as an example of a man motivated by money rather than by righteousness (Dt 23:3–6; 2Pe 2:15–16; Jude 11).

22:22 GOD WAS VERY ANGRY. God permitted Balaam to go, but he was angry with him because he was still considering Balak's offer. Balaam's spiritual blindness was revealed through the incident of the donkey (vv. 22,32–33).

the LORD standing in the road with a
drawn sword[t] in his hand, she turned
off the road into a field. Balaam beat
her[u] to get her back on the road.
24Then the angel of the LORD stood
in a narrow path between two vineyards, with walls on both sides.
25When the donkey saw the angel of
the LORD, she pressed close to the wall,
crushing Balaam's foot against it. So
he beat her again.
26Then the angel of the LORD moved
on ahead and stood in a narrow place
where there was no room to turn, either to the right or to the left. **27**When
the donkey saw the angel of the LORD,
she lay down under Balaam, and he
was angry[v] and beat her with his
staff. **28**Then the LORD opened the donkey's mouth,[w] and she said to Balaam,
"What have I done to you to make you
beat me these three times?[x]"
29Balaam answered the donkey,
"You have made a fool of me! If I had
a sword in my hand, I would kill you
right now.[y]"
30The donkey said to Balaam, "Am I
not your own donkey, which you have
always ridden, to this day? Have I been
in the habit of doing this to you?"
"No," he said.
31Then the LORD opened Balaam's
eyes,[z] and he saw the angel of the
LORD standing in the road with his
sword drawn. So he bowed low and fell
facedown.
32The angel of the LORD asked him,
"Why have you beaten your donkey
these three times? I have come here to
oppose you because your path is a
reckless one before me.[y] **33**The donkey saw me and turned away from me
these three times. If she had not
turned away, I would certainly have
killed you by now,[a] but I would have
spared her."
34Balaam said to the angel of the
LORD, "I have sinned.[b] I did not realize
you were standing in the road to oppose me. Now if you are displeased, I
will go back."
35The angel of the LORD said to Balaam, "Go with the men, but speak only
what I tell you." So Balaam went with
the princes of Balak.
36When Balak[c] heard that Balaam
was coming, he went out to meet him
at the Moabite town on the Arnon[d]
border, at the edge of his territory.
37Balak said to Balaam, "Did I not
send you an urgent summons? Why
didn't you come to me? Am I really not
able to reward you?"
38"Well, I have come to you now,"
Balaam replied. "But can I say just
anything? I must speak only what God
puts in my mouth."[e]
39Then Balaam went with Balak to
Kiriath Huzoth. **40**Balak sacrificed cattle and sheep,[f] and gave some to Balaam and the princes who were with
him. **41**The next morning Balak took
Balaam up to Bamoth Baal,[g] and from
there he saw part of the people.[h]

Balaam's First Oracle

23 Balaam said, "Build me seven
altars here, and prepare seven
bulls and seven rams[i] for me." **2**Balak
did as Balaam said, and the two of
them offered a bull and a ram on each
altar.[j]
3Then Balaam said to Balak, "Stay
here beside your offering while I go
aside. Perhaps the LORD will come to
meet with me.[k] Whatever he reveals
to me I will tell you." Then he went off
to a barren height.
4God met with him,[l] and Balaam
said, "I have prepared seven altars,
and on each altar I have offered a bull
and a ram."
5The LORD put a message in Balaam's mouth[m n] and said, "Go back
to Balak and give him this message."[o]
6So he went back to him and found
him standing beside his offering, with
all the princes of Moab.[p] **7**Then Balaam[q] uttered his oracle:[r]

"Balak brought me from Aram,[s]
the king of Moab from the
eastern mountains.[t]
'Come,' he said, 'curse Jacob for
me;
come, denounce Israel.'[u]
8How can I curse
those whom God has not
cursed?[v]
How can I denounce
those whom the LORD has not
denounced?[w]

22:23 [t]Jos 5:13 [u]ver 25,27
22:27 [v]Nu 11:1; Jas 1:19
22:28 [w]2Pe 2:16 [x]ver 32
22:29 [y]ver 33; Dt 25:4; Pr 12:10; 27:23-27; Mt 15:19
22:31 [z]Ge 21:19
22:33 [a]S ver 29
22:34 [b]Ge 39:9; Nu 14:40; 1Sa 15:24,30; 2Sa 12:13; 24:10; Job 33:27; Ps 51:4
22:36 [c]ver 2
[d]S Nu 21:13
22:38 [e]Nu 23:5, 16,26
22:40 [f]Nu 23:1, 14,29; Eze 45:23
22:41 [g]S Nu 21:28 [h]Nu 23:13
23:1 [i]S Nu 22:40
23:2 [j]ver 14,30
23:3 [k]ver 15
23:4 [l]ver 16
23:5 [m]S Ex 4:12; Isa 59:21 [n]S Ex 4:15 [o]S Nu 22:20
23:6 [p]ver 17
23:7 [q]Nu 22:5; Jos 24:9 [r]ver 18; Nu 24:3,21; 2Sa 23:1 [s]2Ki 5:1 [t]S Ge 24:10 [u]S Nu 22:6; Ne 13:2
23:8 [v]Nu 22:12 [w]ver 20; Isa 43:13

[y]32 The meaning of the Hebrew for this clause is uncertain.

22:28 OPENED THE DONKEY'S MOUTH. The NT states that the donkey "spoke with a man's voice and restrained the prophet's madness" (2Pe 2:16).

[9]From the rocky peaks I see them,
from the heights I view them.[x]
I see a people who live apart
and do not consider themselves
one of the nations.[y]
[10]Who can count the dust of Jacob[z]
or number the fourth part of
Israel?
Let me die the death of the
righteous,[a]
and may my end be like
theirs![b]"

[11]Balak said to Balaam, "What have
you done to me? I brought you to curse
my enemies,[c] but you have done nothing but bless them!"[d]
[12]He answered, "Must I not speak
what the LORD puts in my mouth?"[e]

Balaam's Second Oracle

[13]Then Balak said to him, "Come
with me to another place[f] where you
can see them; you will see only a part
but not all of them.[g] And from there,
curse them for me.[h]" [14]So he took him
to the field of Zophim on the top of Pisgah,[i] and there he built seven altars
and offered a bull and a ram on each
altar.[j]
[15]Balaam said to Balak, "Stay here
beside your offering while I meet with
him over there."
[16]The LORD met with Balaam and put
a message in his mouth[k] and said, "Go
back to Balak and give him this message."
[17]So he went to him and found him
standing beside his offering, with the
princes of Moab.[l] Balak asked him,
"What did the LORD say?"
[18]Then he uttered his oracle:[m]

"Arise, Balak, and listen;
hear me, son of Zippor.[n]
[19]God is not a man,[o] that he should
lie,[p]
nor a son of man, that he should
change his mind.[q]
Does he speak and then not act?
Does he promise[r] and not
fulfill?
[20]I have received a command to
bless;[s]
he has blessed,[t] and I cannot
change it.[u]

[21]"No misfortune is seen in Jacob,[v]
no misery observed in Israel.[z][w]
The LORD their God is with them;[x]
the shout of the King[y] is
among them.
[22]God brought them out of Egypt;[z]
they have the strength of a wild
ox.[a]
[23]There is no sorcery against Jacob,
no divination[b] against Israel.
It will now be said of Jacob
and of Israel, 'See what God has
done!'
[24]The people rise like a lioness;[c]
they rouse themselves like a
lion[d]
that does not rest till he devours
his prey
and drinks the blood[e] of his
victims."

[25]Then Balak said to Balaam, "Neither curse them at all nor bless them
at all!"
[26]Balaam answered, "Did I not tell
you I must do whatever the LORD
says?"[f]

Balaam's Third Oracle

[27]Then Balak said to Balaam,
"Come, let me take you to another
place.[g] Perhaps it will please God to
let you curse them for me[h] from
there." [28]And Balak took Balaam to
the top of Peor,[i] overlooking the
wasteland.
[29]Balaam said, "Build me seven altars here, and prepare seven bulls and
seven rams for me." [30]Balak did as Balaam had said, and offered a bull and
a ram on each altar.[j]

24 Now when Balaam saw that it
pleased the LORD to bless Isra-
el,[k] he did not resort to sorcery[l] as
at other times, but turned his face toward the desert.[m] [2]When Balaam
looked out and saw Israel encamped

23:9 [x]Nu 22:41 [y]S Ex 33:16; S Dt 32:8 **23:10** [z]S Ge 13:16 [a]Ps 16:3; 116:15; Isa 57:1 [b]Ps 37:37 **23:11** [c]S Nu 22:6 [d]Nu 24:10; Jos 24:10; Ne 13:2 **23:12** [e]S Nu 22:18,20 **23:13** [f]ver 27 [g]Nu 22:41 [h]S Nu 22:6 **23:14** [i]S Nu 21:20; 27:12 [j]S ver 2 **23:16** [k]S Ex 4:15; S Nu 22:38 **23:17** [l]ver 6 **23:18** [m]S ver 7 [n]Nu 22:2 **23:19** [o]Job 9:32; Isa 55:9; Hos 11:9 [p]S Nu 11:23 [q]1Sa 15:29; Job 12:13; 36:5; Ps 33:11; 89:34; 102:27; 110:4; Jer 4:28; 7:16; Mal 3:6; Tit 1:2; Heb 6:18; 7:21; Jas 1:17 [r]2Sa 7:25; Ps 119:38 **23:20** [s]ver 5,16; Nu 24:1 [t]Ge 22:17; Nu 22:12 [u]S ver 8; S Job 9:12 **23:21** [v]Ps 32:2,5; 85:2; Ro 4:7-8 [w]Isa 33:24; 40:2; Jer 50:20 [x]S Ge 26:3; Ex 29:45,46; Dt 4:7; Ps 34:17-18; 145:18; Zec 2:10 [y]Dt 32:15; 33:5; Ps 89:15-18; Isa 44:2 **23:22** [z]Nu 24:8; Jos 2:10; 9:9 [a]Dt 33:17; Job 39:9; Ps 22:21; 29:6; 92:10; Isa 34:7 **23:23** [b]ver 3; S Ge 30:27; Nu 24:1 **23:24** [c]Nu 24:9; Eze 19:2; Na 2:11 [d]S Ge 49:9 [e]Isa 49:26 **23:26** [f]S Nu 22:18,20 **23:27** [g]ver 13 [h]Nu 24:10 **23:28** [i]Nu 25:3,18; 31:16; Dt 3:29; 4:3; Jos 22:17; Ps 106:28; Hos 9:10 **23:30** [j]S ver 2

24:1 [k]S Nu 23:20 [l]S Nu 23:23 [m]Nu 23:28

[z]*21* Or *He has not looked on Jacob's offenses / or on the wrongs found in Israel.*

23:19 NOT A MAN, THAT HE SHOULD LIE . . . CHANGE HIS MIND. God is not unreliable, fickle or changeable, but by his very nature he is faithful to his promises and commitments. This attribute of God does not exclude the possibility, however, of God changing his mind or plans under certain circumstances. For example, God does on occasion change his plans in regard to judgment as a response to the intercessory prayers of his faithful people (see Ex 32:11,14, notes) or as a result of the repentance of wicked people (Jnh 3:1–10; 4:2).

tribe by tribe, the Spirit of God came
upon him[n] 3and he uttered his oracle:

"The oracle of Balaam son of Beor,
  the oracle of one whose eye sees
    clearly,[o]
4the oracle of one who hears the
    words of God,[p]
  who sees a vision from the
    Almighty,[a][q]
  who falls prostrate, and whose
    eyes are opened:

5"How beautiful are your tents,[r]
    O Jacob,
  your dwelling places, O Israel!

6"Like valleys they spread out,
  like gardens beside a river,[s]
like aloes[t] planted by the LORD,
  like cedars beside the waters.[u]
7Water will flow from their buckets;
  their seed will have abundant
    water.

"Their king will be greater than
    Agag;[v]
  their kingdom will be exalted.[w]

8"God brought them out of Egypt;
  they have the strength of a wild
    ox.
They devour hostile nations
  and break their bones in
    pieces;[x]
  with their arrows they pierce
    them.[y]
9Like a lion they crouch and lie
    down,
  like a lioness[z]—who dares to
    rouse them?

"May those who bless you be
    blessed[a]
  and those who curse you be
    cursed!"[b]

10Then Balak's anger burned[c]
against Balaam. He struck his hands
together[d] and said to him, "I summoned you to curse my enemies,[e] but
you have blessed them[f] these three
times.[g] 11Now leave at once and go
home![h] I said I would reward you
handsomely,[i] but the LORD has kept
you from being rewarded."

24:2 [n]S Nu 11:25,26 **24:3** [o]ver 15 **24:4** [p]S Nu 22:9 [q]S Ge 15:1 **24:5** [r]Jer 4:20; 30:18; Mal 2:12 **24:6** [s]S Ge 2:10 [t]Ps 45:8; SS 4:14 [u]Job 29:19; Ps 1:3; 104:16; Eze 31:5 **24:7** [v]S Ex 17:8-16 [w]Dt 28:1; 2Sa 5:12; 1Ch 14:2; Ps 89:27; 145:11-13 **24:8** [x]S Ex 15:6; Jer 50: 17 [y]2Sa 18:14; Ps 45:5 **24:9** [z]S Nu 23:24 [a]S Ge 12:2 [b]S Ge 12:3 **24:10** [c]S Ex 4:14 [d]Job 27:23; 34:37; La 2:15; Eze 21:14; 22:13; 25:6 [e]S Nu 22:6 [f]S Nu 23:11; S Dt 23:5 [g]ver 3-9; Nu 23:7-10,18-24 **24:11** [h]ver 14,25 [i]S Nu 22:17

24:12 [j]Nu 22:18 **24:13** [k]S Nu 22:18 [l]S Nu 22:20 **24:14** [m]S Ge 49:1; Nu 31:8,16; Mic 6:5 **24:16** [n]S Nu 22:9 [o]Ge 14:18; Isa 14:14 **24:17** [p]Rev 1:7 [q]Mt 2:2 [r]S Ge 49:10 [s]S Ge 19:37; S Nu 21:29; S Dt 23:6; Isa 15:1-16:14 [t]Jer 48:45 **24:18** [u]2Sa 8:12; 1Ch 18:11; Ps 60:8; Isa 11:14; Am 9:12 [v]S Ge 14:6; Dt 1:44; Jos 12:7; 15:10; Jdg 5:4 [w]Ob 1:2 [x]S Ge 9:25 **24:19** [y]S Ge 49:10; Mic 5:2 **24:20** [z]S Ge 14:7; S Ex 17:14

12Balaam answered Balak, "Did I
not tell the messengers you sent me,[j]
13'Even if Balak gave me his palace
filled with silver and gold, I could not
do anything of my own accord, good or
bad, to go beyond the command of the
LORD[k]—and I must say only what the
LORD says'?[l] 14Now I am going back
to my people, but come, let me warn
you of what this people will do to your
people in days to come."[m]

Balaam's Fourth Oracle

15Then he uttered his oracle:

"The oracle of Balaam son of Beor,
  the oracle of one whose eye sees
    clearly,
16the oracle of one who hears the
    words[n] of God,
  who has knowledge from the
    Most High,[o]
  who sees a vision from the
    Almighty,
  who falls prostrate, and whose
    eyes are opened:

17"I see him, but not now;
  I behold him, but not near.[p]
A star will come out of Jacob;[q]
  a scepter will rise out of
    Israel.[r]
He will crush the foreheads of
    Moab,[s]
  the skulls[b][t] of[c] all the sons
    of Sheth.[d]
18Edom[u] will be conquered;
  Seir,[v] his enemy, will be
    conquered,[w]
  but Israel[x] will grow strong.
19A ruler will come out of Jacob[y]
  and destroy the survivors of the
    city."

Balaam's Final Oracles

20Then Balaam saw Amalek[z] and
uttered his oracle:

[a] *4* Hebrew *Shaddai*; also in verse 16
[b] *17* Samaritan Pentateuch (see also Jer. 48:45); the meaning of the word in the Masoretic Text is uncertain.
[c] *17* Or possibly *Moab, / batter*
[d] *17* Or *all the noisy boasters*

24:2 SPIRIT OF GOD CAME UPON HIM. The Spirit coming upon Balaam is not synonymous with the filling with the Spirit recorded in the NT (Ac 2:1–4). The Spirit came upon him for the purpose of revelation, not for endorsement as a prophet. God does occasionally use individuals who are not in a right relationship with him to accomplish his purpose (cf. Jn 11:49–52).

24:17 A STAR WILL COME. Many commentators see vv. 15–19 as referring to the coming of Christ and his universal reign over all the nations (cf. Ge 49:10; Ps 45:6; Mt 2:2; Rev 2:28; 19:15; 22:16). Others believe it refers only to King David (cf. 2Sa 7:12).

"Amalek was first among the
nations,
but he will come to ruin at
last."[a]

21Then he saw the Kenites[b] and uttered his oracle:

"Your dwelling place is secure,[c]
your nest is set in a rock;
22yet you Kenites will be destroyed
when Asshur[d] takes you
captive."

23Then he uttered his oracle:

"Ah, who can live when God does
this?[e]
24 Ships will come from the shores
of Kittim;[e]
they will subdue Asshur[f] and
Eber,[g]
but they too will come to
ruin.[h]"

25Then Balaam[i] got up and returned home and Balak went his own
way.

Moab Seduces Israel

25 While Israel was staying in
Shittim,[j] the men began to indulge in sexual immorality[k] with Moabite[l] women,[m] **2**who invited them to
the sacrifices[n] to their gods.[o] The
people ate and bowed down before
these gods. **3**So Israel joined in worshiping[p] the Baal of Peor.[q] And the
LORD's anger burned against them.
4The LORD said to Moses, "Take all
the leaders[r] of these people, kill them
and expose[s] them in broad daylight
before the LORD,[t] so that the LORD's
fierce anger[u] may turn away from Israel."
5So Moses said to Israel's judges,
"Each of you must put to death[v] those
of your men who have joined in worshiping the Baal of Peor."[w]
6Then an Israelite man brought to
his family a Midianite[x] woman right
before the eyes of Moses and the whole
assembly of Israel while they were
weeping[y] at the entrance to the Tent
of Meeting. **7**When Phinehas[z] son of
Eleazar, the son of Aaron, the priest,
saw this, he left the assembly, took a
spear[a] in his hand **8**and followed the
Israelite into the tent. He drove the
spear through both of them—through
the Israelite and into the woman's
body. Then the plague against the Israelites was stopped;[b] **9**but those who
died in the plague[c] numbered
24,000.[d]
10The LORD said to Moses, **11**"Phinehas son of Eleazar, the son of Aaron,
the priest, has turned my anger away
from the Israelites;[e] for he was as
zealous as I am for my honor[f] among
them, so that in my zeal I did not put
an end to them. **12**Therefore tell him I
am making my covenant of peace[g]
with him. **13**He and his descendants
will have a covenant of a lasting priesthood,[h] because he was zealous[i] for
the honor[j] of his God and made atonement[k] for the Israelites."[l]
14The name of the Israelite who was
killed with the Midianite woman[m] was
Zimri son of Salu, the leader of a Sime-
onite family.[n] **15**And the name of the
Midianite woman who was put to death
was Cozbi[o] daughter of Zur, a tribal
chief of a Midianite family.[p]
16The LORD said to Moses,[q]
17"Treat the Midianites[r] as enemies[s] and kill them,[t] **18**because they
treated you as enemies when they de-

24:20 [a]Dt 25:19; 1Sa 15:20; 30:17-20; 2Sa 8:12; 1Ch 18:11 **24:21** [b]S Ge 15:19 [c]Ps 37:27; Pr 1:33; Isa 32:18; Eze 34:27 **24:22** [d]S Ge 10:22 **24:24** [e]S Ge 10:4 [f]ver 22 [g]S Ge 10:21 [h]ver 20 **24:25** [i]S Nu 22:5 **25:1** [j]S Nu 21:16; Jos 2:1; Isa 66:11; Joel 3:18; Mic 6:5 [k]Jer 5:7; 7:9; 9:2; 1Co 10:8; Rev 2:14 [l]S Ge 19:37 [m]Nu 31:16 **25:2** [n]S Ex 32:6 [o]Ex 20:5; Dt 32:38; 1Co 10:20 **25:3** [p]Dt 4:19; Jdg 2:19; 1Ki 9:9; Jer 1:16; 44:3 [q]S Nu 23:28 **25:4** [r]Nu 7:2; 13:3 [s]2Sa 21:6 [t]Dt 4:3 [u]Ex 32:12; Dt 13:17; Jos 7:26; 2Ki 23:26; 2Ch 28:11; 29:10; 30:8; Ezr 10:14; Jer 44:3 **25:5** [v]S Ex 32:27 [w]Hos 9:10 **25:6** [x]S Ge 25:2 [y]S Nu 14:1; Jdg 2:4; Ru 1:9; 1Sa 11:4; 2Sa 15:30; Ezr 10:1; Ps 126:6; Jer 41:6 **25:7** [z]S Ex 6:25; Jos 22:13; Jdg 20:28 [a]Jdg 5:8; 1Sa 13:19,22; 1Ki 18:28; Ps 35:3; 46:9; Joel 3:10; Mic 4:3 **25:8** [b]Ps 106:30 **25:9** [c]S Nu 14:37; 1Co 10:8 [d]Nu 31:16 **25:11** [e]Ps 106:30 [f]Ex 20:5; Dt 32:16,21; Ps 78:58 **25:12** [g]Isa 11:9; 54:10; Eze 34:25; 37:26; Mal 2:4,5 **25:13** [h]S Ex 29:9 [i]1Ki 19:10; 2Ki 10:16 [j]ver 11

[k]S Ex 29:36; S Ro 3:25 [l]Ps 106:31; Jer 33:18 **25:14** [m]ver 6 [n]S Nu 1:6 **25:15** [o]ver 18 [p]Nu 31:8; Jos 13:21; Hab 3:7 **25:16** [q]Nu 31:7 **25:17** [r]Nu 31:1-3 [s]Ex 23:22; Jdg 2:16-18; Ne 9:27; Ps 8:2; 21:8; 74:23 [t]Dt 21:1; 1Sa 17:9,35; 2Ki 9:27; 10:25

[e] *23* Masoretic Text; with a different word division of the Hebrew *A people will gather from the north.*

25:2 BOWED DOWN BEFORE THESE GODS. After Balaam had failed in his attempt to separate the Israelites from the Lord, he counseled the Moabites to try turning the Israelites away from God by enticing them into immorality and the sensual worship of false gods (see 31:16; Rev 2:14, note). As punishment, Balaam was killed (31:8; cf. Jos 13:22).

25:4 THE LEADERS OF THESE PEOPLE, KILL THEM. This verse reveals the intensity of God's displeasure with the leaders of his covenant people. They were executed for their outrageous behavior and their failure to be examples of separation from sexual immorality and idolatry.

25:11 AS ZEALOUS AS I AM. Phinehas reacted to the moral degeneration and idolatry among God's people in holy anger (vv. 1–8). (1) His exceptional zeal for God's honor (v. 13) and cause was evident in his love of righteousness and his hatred of sin, as God himself shows. His zeal typifies Christ's zeal for God's holiness (see Heb 1:9, note). (2) The Lord gave Phinehas the promise of "a lasting priesthood" (vv. 12–13; cf. 1Ch 6:4ff). To be sincerely zealous for the Lord's sake is always rewarded with great blessings from God.

ceived you in the affair of Peor[u] and
their sister Cozbi, the daughter of a
Midianite leader, the woman who was
killed when the plague came as a result of Peor."

The Second Census

26 After the plague[v] the LORD
said to Moses and Eleazar son
of Aaron, the priest, **2**"Take a census[w]
of the whole Israelite community by
families—all those twenty years old or
more who are able to serve in the
army[x] of Israel." **3**So on the plains of
Moab[y] by the Jordan across from Jericho,[f][z] Moses and Eleazar the priest
spoke with them and said, **4**"Take a
census of the men twenty years old or
more, as the LORD commanded Moses."

These were the Israelites who came
out of Egypt:[a]

5The descendants of Reuben,[b] the
firstborn son of Israel, were:
through Hanoch,[c] the Hanochite clan;
through Pallu,[d] the Palluite clan;
6through Hezron,[e] the Hezronite clan;
through Carmi,[f] the Carmite clan.
7These were the clans of Reuben;
those numbered were 43,730.

8The son of Pallu was Eliab, **9**and
the sons of Eliab[g] were Nemuel, Dathan and Abiram. The same Dathan
and Abiram were the community[h] officials who rebelled against Moses and
Aaron and were among Korah's followers when they rebelled against the
LORD.[i] **10**The earth opened its mouth
and swallowed them[j] along with Korah, whose followers died when the fire
devoured the 250 men.[k] And they
served as a warning sign.[l] **11**The line
of Korah,[m] however, did not die out.[n]

12The descendants of Simeon by their
clans were:
through Nemuel,[o] the Nemuelite clan;
through Jamin,[p] the Jaminite clan;
through Jakin, the Jakinite clan;
13through Zerah,[q] the Zerahite clan;
through Shaul, the Shaulite clan.
14These were the clans of Simeon;[r]
there were 22,200 men.[s]

15The descendants of Gad by their
clans were:
through Zephon,[t] the Zephonite clan;
through Haggi, the Haggite clan;
through Shuni, the Shunite clan;
16through Ozni, the Oznite clan;
through Eri, the Erite clan;
17through Arodi,[g] the Arodite clan;
through Areli, the Arelite clan.
18These were the clans of Gad;[u] those
numbered were 40,500.

19Er[v] and Onan[w] were sons of Judah,
but they died[x] in Canaan.
20The descendants of Judah by their
clans were:
through Shelah,[y] the Shelanite clan;
through Perez,[z] the Perezite clan;
through Zerah, the Zerahite clan.[a]
21The descendants of Perez[b] were:
through Hezron,[c] the Hezronite clan;
through Hamul, the Hamulite clan.
22These were the clans of Judah;[d]
those numbered were 76,500.

23The descendants of Issachar by their
clans were:
through Tola,[e] the Tolaite clan;
through Puah, the Puite[h] clan;
24through Jashub,[f] the Jashubite clan;
through Shimron, the Shimronite clan.
25These were the clans of Issachar;[g]
those numbered were 64,300.

26The descendants of Zebulun[h] by
their clans were:
through Sered, the Seredite clan;
through Elon, the Elonite clan;

25:18 [u] S Nu 23:28
26:1 [v] S Nu 14:37; 25:8
26:2 [w] Ex 30:11-16 [x] S Nu 1:3
26:3 [y] ver 63; Nu 33:48; Jos 13:32 [z] Nu 22:1
26:4 [a] S Ex 6:14; S 13:3
26:5 [b] Nu 1:20 [c] S Ge 46:9 [d] 1Ch 5:3
26:6 [e] 1Ch 5:3 [f] Ge 46:9
26:9 [g] Nu 16:1 [h] Nu 1:16 [i] S Nu 16:2
26:10 [j] S Ex 15:12 [k] S Nu 16:35 [l] S Ex 3:12; S Nu 16:38
26:11 [m] Ex 6:24 [n] Nu 16:33; Dt 5:9; 24:16; 2Ki 14:6; 2Ch 25:4; Eze 18:20
26:12 [o] S Ge 46:10 [p] 1Ch 4:24
26:13 [q] S Ge 46:10
26:14 [r] S Ge 46:10 [s] Nu 1:23
26:15 [t] Ge 46:16
26:18 [u] S Ge 30:11; S Nu 1:25; S Jos 13:24-28
26:19 [v] S Ge 38:3 [w] S Ge 38:4 [x] Ge 38:7
26:20 [y] S Ge 38:5 [z] S Ge 38:29 [a] Jos 7:17
26:21 [b] S Ge 38:29 [c] Ru 4:19; 1Ch 2:9
26:22 [d] Nu 1:27
26:23 [e] S Ge 46:13
26:24 [f] Ge 46:13
26:25 [g] S Ge 30:18
26:26 [h] Nu 1:30

[f] *3* Hebrew *Jordan of Jericho*; possibly an ancient name for the Jordan River; also in verse 63 [g] *17* Samaritan Pentateuch and Syriac (see also Gen. 46:16); Masoretic Text *Arod* [h] *23* Samaritan Pentateuch, Septuagint, Vulgate and Syriac (see also 1 Chron. 7:1); Masoretic Text *through Puvah, the Punite*

26:2 CENSUS OF THE WHOLE ISRAELITE COMMUNITY. God ordered a second census (see 1:2–3) in order to prepare the nation for their military responsibilities upon entering Canaan (v. 2) to possess their inheritance of land (vv. 53–56).

through Jahleel, the Jahleelite clan.
27These were the clans of Zebulun;[i] those numbered were 60,500.

28The descendants of Joseph[j] by their clans through Manasseh and Ephraim[k] were:

29The descendants of Manasseh:[l]
through Makir,[m] the Makirite clan (Makir was the father of Gilead[n]);
through Gilead, the Gileadite clan.
30These were the descendants of Gilead:[o]
through Iezer,[p] the Iezerite clan;
through Helek, the Helekite clan;
31through Asriel, the Asrielite clan;
through Shechem, the Shechemite clan;
32through Shemida, the Shemidaite clan;
through Hepher, the Hepherite clan.
33(Zelophehad[q] son of Hepher had no sons;[r] he had only daughters, whose names were Mahlah, Noah, Hoglah, Milcah and Tirzah.)[s]
34These were the clans of Manasseh; those numbered were 52,700.[t]

35These were the descendants of Ephraim[u] by their clans:
through Shuthelah, the Shuthelahite clan;
through Beker, the Bekerite clan;
through Tahan, the Tahanite clan.
36These were the descendants of Shuthelah:
through Eran, the Eranite clan.
37These were the clans of Ephraim;[v] those numbered were 32,500.

These were the descendants of Joseph by their clans.

38The descendants of Benjamin[w] by their clans were:
through Bela, the Belaite clan;
through Ashbel, the Ashbelite clan;
through Ahiram, the Ahiramite clan;
39through Shupham,[i] the Shuphamite clan;
through Hupham, the Huphamite clan.
40The descendants of Bela through Ard[x] and Naaman were:
through Ard,[j] the Ardite clan;
through Naaman, the Naamite clan.
41These were the clans of Benjamin;[y] those numbered were 45,600.

42These were the descendants of Dan[z] by their clans:[a]
through Shuham,[b] the Shuhamite clan.
These were the clans of Dan: 43All of them were Shuhamite clans; and those numbered were 64,400.

44The descendants of Asher[c] by their clans were:
through Imnah, the Imnite clan;
through Ishvi, the Ishvite clan;
through Beriah, the Beriite clan;
45and through the descendants of Beriah:
through Heber, the Heberite clan;
through Malkiel, the Malkielite clan.
46(Asher had a daughter named Serah.)
47These were the clans of Asher;[d] those numbered were 53,400.

48The descendants of Naphtali[e] by their clans were:
through Jahzeel, the Jahzeelite clan;
through Guni, the Gunite clan;
49through Jezer, the Jezerite clan;
through Shillem, the Shillemite clan.
50These were the clans of Naphtali;[f] those numbered were 45,400.[g]

51The total number of the men of Israel was 601,730.[h]

52The LORD said to Moses, 53"The land is to be allotted to them as an inheritance based on the number of names.[i] 54To a larger group give a larger inheritance, and to a smaller group a smaller one; each is to receive

26:27 [i]S Ge 30:20
26:28 [j]Nu 1:32; 36:1 [k]S Ge 41:52
26:29 [l]Nu 1:34 [m]S Ge 50:23 [n]Jdg 11:1
26:30 [o]Nu 27:1; 36:1; 1Ch 7:14,17 [p]Jos 17:2; Jdg 6:11; 8:2
26:33 [q]Nu 27:1; 36:2; Jos 17:3; 1Ch 7:15 [r]Nu 27:3 [s]Nu 36:11
26:34 [t]Nu 1:35
26:35 [u]Nu 1:32
26:37 [v]S Nu 1:33
26:38 [w]Ge 46:21; Nu 1:36; 1Ch 8:40
26:40 [x]S Ge 46:21
26:41 [y]Nu 1:37
26:42 [z]Nu 1:38 [a]Jdg 18:19 [b]Ge 46:23
26:44 [c]S Nu 1:40
26:47 [d]Nu 1:41
26:48 [e]S Ge 30:8
26:50 [f]Nu 1:43 [g]Nu 1:42
26:51 [h]S Ex 12:37
26:53 [i]ver 55; Jos 11:23; 14:1; Eze 45:8

i 39 A few manuscripts of the Masoretic Text, Samaritan Pentateuch, Vulgate and Syriac (see also Septuagint); most manuscripts of the Masoretic Text *Shephupham* j 40 Samaritan Pentateuch and Vulgate (see also Septuagint); Masoretic Text does not have *through Ard.*

its inheritance according to the number[j] of those listed.[k] **55**Be sure that
the land is distributed by lot.[l] What
each group inherits will be according
to the names for its ancestral tribe.
56Each inheritance is to be distributed
by lot among the larger and smaller
groups."

57These were the Levites[m] who were
counted by their clans:
through Gershon, the Gershonite clan;
through Kohath, the Kohathite clan;
through Merari, the Merarite clan.
58These also were Levite clans:
the Libnite clan,
the Hebronite clan,
the Mahlite clan,
the Mushite clan,
the Korahite clan.
(Kohath was the forefather of Amram;[n] **59**the name of Amram's
wife was Jochebed,[o] a descendant of Levi, who was born to the
Levites[k] in Egypt. To Amram she
bore Aaron, Moses[p] and their
sister[q] Miriam.[r] **60**Aaron was
the father of Nadab and Abihu, Eleazar and Ithamar.[s] **61**But Nadab
and Abihu[t] died when they made
an offering before the LORD with
unauthorized fire.)[u]

62All the male Levites a month old or
more numbered 23,000.[v] They were
not counted[w] along with the other Israelites because they received no inheritance[x] among them.[y]

63These are the ones counted[z] by
Moses and Eleazar the priest when
they counted the Israelites on the
plains of Moab[a] by the Jordan across
from Jericho.[b] **64**Not one of them was
among those counted[c] by Moses and
Aaron[d] the priest when they counted
the Israelites in the Desert of Sinai.
65For the LORD had told those Israelites
they would surely die in the desert,[e]
and not one of them was left except
Caleb[f] son of Jephunneh and Joshua
son of Nun.[g]

26:54 [j]Nu 33:54 [k]Nu 35:8
26:55 [l]S Lev 16:8
26:57 [m]S Ge 46:11
26:58 [n]Ex 6:20
26:59 [o]S Ex 2:1 [p]S Ex 6:20 [q]S Ex 2:4 [r]S Ex 15:20
26:60 [s]Ex 6:23
26:61 [t]S Lev 10:1-2 [u]Nu 3:4
26:62 [v]Nu 3:39 [w]Nu 1:47 [x]S Nu 18:23 [y]S Nu 2:33
26:63 [z]S Nu 1:19 [a]S ver 3 [b]Nu 22:1
26:64 [c]S Nu 14:29 [d]Nu 1:44
26:65 [e]Nu 14:28; 1Co 10:5 [f]Nu 13:6 [g]S Nu 11:28

27:1 [h]S Nu 26:33 [i]Jos 17:2,3 [j]S Nu 26:30 [k]S Ge 50:23; 1Ch 2:21
27:2 [l]Ex 40:2,17 [m]S Nu 9:6 [n]Nu 1:16; 31:13; 32:2; 36:1
27:3 [o]Nu 26:65 [p]Nu 16:2 [q]Nu 26:33
27:5 [r]S Ge 25:22; S Ex 18:19 [s]S Nu 9:8
27:7 [t]Job 42:15 [u]ver 8; Jos 17:4
27:11 [v]Nu 35:29
27:12 [w]Nu 23:14 [x]Nu 33:47; Jer 22:20 [y]Dt 3:23-27; 32:48-52 [z]S Lev 14:34
27:13 [a]Nu 20:12; 31:2; Dt 4:22; 31:14; 32:50; 1Ki 2:1 [b]Nu 20:28
27:14 [c]S Nu 20:1,2-5

Zelophehad's Daughters

27:1-11pp — Nu 36:1-12

27 The daughters of Zelophehad[h]
son of Hepher,[i] the son of Gilead,[j] the son of Makir,[k] the son of
Manasseh, belonged to the clans of
Manasseh son of Joseph. The names of
the daughters were Mahlah, Noah,
Hoglah, Milcah and Tirzah. They approached **2**the entrance to the Tent of
Meeting[l] and stood before Moses,[m]
Eleazar the priest, the leaders[n] and
the whole assembly, and said, **3**"Our father died in the desert.[o] He was not
among Korah's followers, who banded
together against the LORD,[p] but he
died for his own sin and left no sons.[q]
4Why should our father's name disappear from his clan because he had no
son? Give us property among our father's relatives."

5So Moses brought their case[r] before the LORD[s] **6**and the LORD said to
him, **7**"What Zelophehad's daughters
are saying is right. You must certainly
give them property as an inheritance[t]
among their father's relatives and turn
their father's inheritance over to
them.[u]

8"Say to the Israelites, 'If a man dies
and leaves no son, turn his inheritance
over to his daughter. **9**If he has no
daughter, give his inheritance to his
brothers. **10**If he has no brothers, give
his inheritance to his father's brothers.
11If his father had no brothers, give his
inheritance to the nearest relative in
his clan, that he may possess it. This
is to be a legal requirement[v] for the
Israelites, as the LORD commanded Moses.' "

Joshua to Succeed Moses

12Then the LORD said to Moses, "Go
up this mountain[w] in the Abarim
range[x] and see the land[y] I have given
the Israelites.[z] **13**After you have seen
it, you too will be gathered to your people,[a] as your brother Aaron[b] was,
14for when the community rebelled at
the waters in the Desert of Zin,[c] both
of you disobeyed my command to honor

[k]59 Or *Jochebed, a daughter of Levi, who was born to Levi*

27:4 GIVE US PROPERTY. Hebrew law made no provision for the inheritance of the land if a father left no sons. God therefore established the law that the father's daughter could inherit the family's share of land (vv. 3–11). This law shows the place of dignity and honor that women were given in Israel.

me as holy[d] before their eyes." (These
were the waters of Meribah[e] Kadesh,
in the Desert of Zin.)
15Moses said to the LORD, **16**"May
the LORD, the God of the spirits of all
mankind,[f] appoint a man over this
community **17**to go out and come in before them, one who will lead them out
and bring them in, so the LORD's people
will not be like sheep without a shepherd."[g]
18So the LORD said to Moses, "Take
Joshua son of Nun, a man in whom is
the spirit,[l][h] and lay your hand on
him.[i] **19**Have him stand before Eleazar the priest and the entire assembly
and commission him[j] in their presence.[k] **20**Give him some of your authority so the whole Israelite community will obey him.[l] **21**He is to stand
before Eleazar the priest, who will obtain decisions for him by inquiring[m] of
the Urim[n] before the LORD. At his command he and the entire community of
the Israelites will go out, and at his
command they will come in."
22Moses did as the LORD commanded
him. He took Joshua and had him stand
before Eleazar the priest and the whole
assembly. **23**Then he laid his hands on
him and commissioned him,[o] as the
LORD instructed through Moses.

Daily Offerings

28 The LORD said to Moses, **2**"Give
this command to the Israelites
and say to them: 'See that you present
to me at the appointed time[p] the
food[q] for my offerings made by fire, as
an aroma pleasing to me.'[r] **3**Say to
them: 'This is the offering made by fire
that you are to present to the LORD: two
lambs a year old without defect,[s] as a
regular burnt offering each day.[t]
4Prepare one lamb in the morning and
the other at twilight,[u] **5**together with
a grain offering[v] of a tenth of an
ephah[m] of fine flour[w] mixed with a
quarter of a hin[n] of oil[x] from pressed
olives. **6**This is the regular burnt offering[y] instituted at Mount Sinai[z] as a
pleasing aroma, an offering made to
the LORD by fire.[a] **7**The accompanying
drink offering[b] is to be a quarter of a
hin of fermented drink[c] with each
lamb. Pour out the drink offering to the
LORD at the sanctuary.[d] **8**Prepare the
second lamb at twilight,[e] along with
the same kind of grain offering and
drink offering that you prepare in the
morning.[f] This is an offering made by
fire, an aroma pleasing to the LORD.[g]

Sabbath Offerings

9" 'On the Sabbath[h] day, make an
offering of two lambs a year old without defect,[i] together with its drink offering and a grain offering of two-
tenths of an ephah[o][j] of fine flour
mixed with oil.[k] **10**This is the burnt
offering for every Sabbath,[l] in addition to the regular burnt offering[m] and
its drink offering.

Monthly Offerings

11" 'On the first of every month,[n]
present to the LORD a burnt offering of
two young bulls,[o] one ram[p] and sev-
en male lambs a year old, all without
defect.[q] **12**With each bull there is to be
a grain offering[r] of three-tenths of an
ephah[p][s] of fine flour mixed with oil;
with the ram, a grain offering of two-
tenths[t] of an ephah of fine flour mixed
with oil; **13**and with each lamb, a grain
offering[u] of a tenth[v] of an ephah of

[l] *18* Or *Spirit* [m] *5* That is, probably about 2 quarts (about 2 liters); also in verses 13, 21 and 29 [n] *5* That is, probably about 1 quart (about 1 liter); also in verses 7 and 14 [o] *9* That is, probably about 4 quarts (about 4.5 liters); also in verses 12, 20 and 28 [p] *12* That is, probably about 6 quarts (about 6.5 liters); also in verses 20 and 28

27:14 [d]S Nu 20:12 [e]S Ex 17:7 **27:16** [f]S Nu 16:22; S Job 21:20 **27:17** [g]1Ki 22:17; 2Ch 18:16; Eze 34:5; Zec 10:2; S Mt 9:36 **27:18** [h]S Ge 41:38; Nu 11:25-29 [i]ver 23; Dt 34:9; Ac 6:6 **27:19** [j]ver 23; Dt 3:28; 31:14,23 [k]Dt 31:7 **27:20** [l]Jos 1:16, 17 **27:21** [m]S Ge 25:22; Jos 9:14; Ps 106:13; Isa 8:19; Hag 1:13; Mal 2:7; 3:1 [n]S Ex 28:30 **27:23** [o]S ver 19 **28:2** [p]Lev 23:1-44 [q]S Lev 3:11 [r]Lev 1:9 **28:3** [s]S Ex 12:5 [t]Ex 29:38; Am 4:4 **28:4** [u]S Ex 29:39 **28:5** [v]Nu 29:6 [w]Lev 6:20 [x]S Lev 2:1 **28:6** [y]Lev 1:3 [z]Ex 19:3 [a]S Lev 1:9 **28:7** [b]Nu 6:15 [c]S Lev 10:9; S 23:13 [d]S Lev 3:7; Nu 3:28 **28:8** [e]S Ex 29:39 [f]S Lev 3:7 [g]ver 2; Lev 1:9 **28:9** [h]S Ex 20:10; Mt 12:5 [i]ver 3 [j]S Lev 23:13 [k]ver 5 **28:10** [l]S Lev 23:38 [m]ver 3 **28:11** [n]S Nu 10:10 [o]S Nu 7:15 [p]S Lev 5:15 [q]Lev 1:3 **28:12** [r]S Nu 15:6; S 29:3 [s]Nu 15:9 [t]ver 20 **28:13** [u]S Lev 6:14 [v]ver 21

27:18 IN WHOM IS THE SPIRIT. "Spirit" here refers to the Holy Spirit (cf. NIV text note). Among Joshua's many qualifications for leadership, the greatest was that he was Spirit-led. As a man who was anointed and who had proven himself open to being led by the Spirit of the Lord, he was preeminently qualified to be commissioned (v. 19) and invested with authority (v. 20) for leading the people.

27:21 INQUIRING OF THE URIM. See Ex 28:30, note.

28:3 REGULAR BURNT OFFERING EACH DAY. Chs. 28—29 stress the importance of continual sacrifices and offerings presented to the Lord. They were to be made (1) daily (vv. 3–8), (2) on the weekly Sabbath days (vv. 9–10), (3) at the beginning of each month (vv. 11–15), and (4) on certain days of the sacred year (28:16—29:40). The ongoing need to draw near to God with sacrifice emphasized the truth that regular, unceasing communion with God was necessary for his continued presence and blessing. This spiritual principle has not changed; believers today must draw near to God daily in prayer and worship in order to receive his saving grace and help (Lk 18:1; 1Th 5:17; cf. Heb 4:16; 7:25).

fine flour mixed with oil. This is for a
burnt offering,[w] a pleasing aroma, an
offering made to the LORD[x] by fire.
14With each bull there is to be a drink
offering[y] of half a hin[q] of wine; with
the ram, a third of a hin[r]; and with
each lamb, a quarter of a hin. This is
the monthly burnt offering to be made
at each new moon[z] during the year.
15Besides the regular burnt offering[a]
with its drink offering, one male goat[b]
is to be presented to the LORD as a sin
offering.[c]

The Passover

28:16–25pp — Ex 12:14–20; Lev 23:4–8; Dt 16:1–8

16" 'On the fourteenth day of the
first month the LORD's Passover[d] is to
be held. 17On the fifteenth day of this
month there is to be a festival; for sev-
en days[e] eat bread made without
yeast.[f] 18On the first day hold a sacred assembly and do no regular
work.[g] 19Present to the LORD an offering made by fire,[h] a burnt offering of
two young bulls, one ram and seven
male lambs a year old, all without defect.[i] 20With each bull prepare a grain
offering of three-tenths of an ephah[j]
of fine flour mixed with oil; with the
ram, two-tenths;[k] 21and with each of
the seven lambs, one-tenth.[l] 22In-
clude one male goat as a sin offering[m]
to make atonement for you.[n] 23Pre-
pare these in addition to the regular
morning burnt offering. 24In this way
prepare the food for the offering made
by fire every day for seven days as an
aroma pleasing to the LORD;[o] it is to be
prepared in addition to the regular
burnt offering and its drink offering.
25On the seventh day hold a sacred assembly and do no regular work.

Feast of Weeks

28:26–31pp — Lev 23:15–22; Dt 16:9–12

26" 'On the day of firstfruits,[p] when
you present to the LORD an offering of
new grain during the Feast of Weeks,[q]
hold a sacred assembly and do no regular work.[r] 27Present a burnt offering
of two young bulls, one ram and seven
male lambs a year old as an aroma
pleasing to the LORD.[s] 28With each
bull there is to be a grain offering of
three-tenths of an ephah of fine flour
mixed with oil; with the ram, two-
tenths;[t] 29and with each of the seven
lambs, one-tenth.[u] 30Include one
male goat[v] to make atonement for
you. 31Prepare these together with
their drink offerings, in addition to the
regular burnt offering[w] and its grain
offering. Be sure the animals are without defect.

Feast of Trumpets

29:1–6pp — Lev 23:23–25

29 " 'On the first day of the seventh month hold a sacred assembly and do no regular work.[x] It is
a day for you to sound the trumpets.
2As an aroma pleasing to the LORD,[y]
prepare a burnt offering[z] of one young
bull, one ram and seven male lambs a
year old,[a] all without defect.[b] 3With
the bull prepare a grain offering[c] of
three-tenths of an ephah[s] of fine flour
mixed with oil; with the ram, two-
tenths[t]; 4and with each of the seven
lambs, one-tenth.[u][d] 5Include one
male goat[e] as a sin offering to make
atonement for you. 6These are in addition to the monthly[f] and daily burnt
offerings[g] with their grain offerings[h]
and drink offerings[i] as specified.
They are offerings made to the LORD by
fire—a pleasing aroma.[j]

Day of Atonement

29:7–11pp — Lev 16:2–34; 23:26–32

7" 'On the tenth day of this seventh
month hold a sacred assembly. You
must deny yourselves[v][k] and do no
work.[l] 8Present as an aroma pleasing
to the LORD a burnt offering of one
young bull, one ram and seven male
lambs a year old, all without defect.[m]
9With the bull prepare a grain offering[n] of three-tenths of an ephah of
fine flour mixed with oil; with the ram,
two-tenths;[o] 10and with each of the
seven lambs, one-tenth.[p] 11Include
one male goat[q] as a sin offering, in
addition to the sin offering for atonement and the regular burnt offering[r]
with its grain offering, and their drink
offerings.[s]

28:13 [w] S Nu 15:3 [x] Lev 1:9 **28:14** [y] S Nu 15:7 [z] ver 11; 2Ch 2:4; Ezr 3:5 **28:15** [a] ver 3,23, 24 [b] ver 30 [c] Lev 4:3; Nu 29:16,19 **28:16** [d] S Ex 12:11; 2Ch 30:13; 35:1 **28:17** [e] S Ex 12:19 [f] S Ex 12:15 **28:18** [g] S Ex 12:16 **28:19** [h] S Lev 1:9 [i] ver 11 **28:20** [j] S Lev 14:10 [k] ver 12 **28:21** [l] ver 13 **28:22** [m] Lev 4:3; Ro 8:3 [n] S Nu 15:28 **28:24** [o] Lev 1:9 **28:26** [p] S Ex 34:22 [q] S Ex 23:16 [r] ver 18 **28:27** [s] ver 19 **28:28** [t] ver 12

28:29 [u] ver 13 **28:30** [v] ver 15 **28:31** [w] ver 3,19 **29:1** [x] Nu 28:18 **29:2** [y] Nu 28:2 [z] Lev 1:9; Nu 28:11 [a] ver 36 [b] Lev 1:3; Nu 28:3 **29:3** [c] ver 14; Nu 28:12 **29:4** [d] Nu 28:13 **29:5** [e] Nu 28:15 **29:6** [f] Nu 28:11 [g] Nu 28:3 [h] Nu 28:5 [i] Nu 28:7 [j] Lev 1:9; Nu 28:2 **29:7** [k] Ac 27:9 [l] S Ex 31:15 **29:8** [m] ver 2 **29:9** [n] S ver 3,18 [o] Nu 28:12 **29:10** [p] Nu 28:13 **29:11** [q] ver 5; Nu 28:15 [r] S Lev 16:3 [s] S ver 6

[q] *14* That is, probably about 2 quarts (about 2 liters) [r] *14* That is, probably about 1 1/4 quarts (about 1.2 liters) [s] *3* That is, probably about 6 quarts (about 6.5 liters); also in verses 9 and 14 [t] *3* That is, probably about 4 quarts (about 4.5 liters); also in verses 9 and 14 [u] *4* That is, probably about 2 quarts (about 2 liters); also in verses 10 and 15 [v] *7* Or *must fast*

Feast of Tabernacles

29:12–39pp — Lev 23:33–43; Dt 16:13–17

12“ ‘On the fifteenth day of the seventh[t] month,[u] hold a sacred assembly and do no regular work. Celebrate
a festival to the LORD for seven days.
13Present an offering made by fire as
an aroma pleasing to the LORD,[v] a
burnt offering of thirteen young bulls,
two rams and fourteen male lambs a
year old, all without defect.[w] **14**With
each of the thirteen bulls prepare a
grain offering[x] of three-tenths of an
ephah of fine flour mixed with oil; with
each of the two rams, two-tenths;
15and with each of the fourteen lambs,
one-tenth.[y] **16**Include one male goat
as a sin offering,[z] in addition to the
regular burnt offering with its grain offering and drink offering.[a]
17“ ‘On the second day[b] prepare
twelve young bulls, two rams and fourteen male lambs a year old, all without
defect.[c] **18**With the bulls, rams and
lambs, prepare their grain offerings[d]
and drink offerings[e] according to the
number specified.[f] **19**Include one
male goat as a sin offering,[g] in addition to the regular burnt offering[h]
with its grain offering, and their drink
offerings.[i]
20“ ‘On the third day prepare eleven
bulls, two rams and fourteen male
lambs a year old, all without defect.[j]
21With the bulls, rams and lambs, prepare their grain offerings and drink offerings according to the number specified.[k] **22**Include one male goat as a sin
offering, in addition to the regular
burnt offering with its grain offering
and drink offering.
23“ ‘On the fourth day prepare ten
bulls, two rams and fourteen male
lambs a year old, all without defect.
24With the bulls, rams and lambs, prepare their grain offerings and drink offerings according to the number specified. **25**Include one male goat as a sin
offering, in addition to the regular
burnt offering with its grain offering
and drink offering.
26“ ‘On the fifth day prepare nine
bulls, two rams and fourteen male
lambs a year old, all without defect.
27With the bulls, rams and lambs, prepare their grain offerings and drink offerings according to the number specified. **28**Include one male goat as a sin
offering, in addition to the regular
burnt offering with its grain offering
and drink offering.
29“ ‘On the sixth day prepare eight
bulls, two rams and fourteen male
lambs a year old, all without defect.
30With the bulls, rams and lambs, prepare their grain offerings and drink offerings according to the number specified. **31**Include one male goat as a sin
offering, in addition to the regular
burnt offering with its grain offering
and drink offering.
32“ ‘On the seventh day prepare sev-
en bulls, two rams and fourteen male
lambs a year old, all without defect.
33With the bulls, rams and lambs, prepare their grain offerings and drink offerings according to the number specified. **34**Include one male goat as a sin
offering, in addition to the regular
burnt offering with its grain offering
and drink offering.
35“ ‘On the eighth day hold an assembly[l] and do no regular work.
36Present an offering made by fire as
an aroma pleasing to the LORD,[m] a
burnt offering of one bull, one ram and
seven male lambs a year old,[n] all
without defect. **37**With the bull, the
ram and the lambs, prepare their grain
offerings and drink offerings according
to the number specified. **38**Include one
male goat as a sin offering, in addition
to the regular burnt offering with its
grain offering and drink offering.
39“ ‘In addition to what you vow[o]
and your freewill offerings,[p] prepare
these for the LORD at your appointed
feasts:[q] your burnt offerings,[r] grain
offerings, drink offerings and fellowship offerings.[w][s]’ ”
40Moses told the Israelites all that
the LORD commanded him.

Vows

30 Moses said to the heads of the
tribes of Israel:[t] “This is what
the LORD commands: **2**When a man
makes a vow to the LORD or takes an

29:12 [t] 1Ki 8:2; 12:32 [u] S Lev 23:24
29:13 [v] ver 2; Nu 28:2 [w] Nu 28:3
29:14 [x] S ver 3; S Nu 15:6
29:15 [y] ver 4; Nu 28:13
29:16 [z] ver 5; S Nu 28:15 [a] ver 6
29:17 [b] Lev 23:36 [c] ver 2; Nu 28:3
29:18 [d] S ver 9 [e] Nu 28:7 [f] Nu 15:4-12
29:19 [g] S Nu 28:15 [h] Nu 28:3 [i] ver 6
29:20 [j] S ver 17
29:21 [k] S ver 18
29:35 [l] S Lev 23:36
29:36 [m] Lev 1:9 [n] ver 2
29:39 [o] Nu 6:2 [p] S Lev 7:16 [q] S Lev 23:2 [r] Lev 1:3; 1Ch 23:31; 2Ch 31:3 [s] Lev 3:1
30:1 [t] S Nu 1:4

[w] *39* Traditionally *peace offerings*

30:2 MAKES A VOW. This chapter makes it clear that God required his people to keep their promises to him and to others. Through these laws he impressed on them the serious nature of any vows and pledges made, and he emphasized that insincerity, lying and hypocrisy had no place among God's people. However, special provisions were made for rash vows of youth (v. 3–5) and

oath to obligate himself by a pledge, he
must not break his word but must do
everything he said.[u]
3“When a young woman still living in
her father’s house makes a vow to the
LORD or obligates herself by a pledge
4and her father hears about her vow or
pledge but says nothing to her, then all
her vows and every pledge by which
she obligated herself will stand.[v] **5**But
if her father forbids her[w] when he
hears about it, none of her vows or the
pledges by which she obligated herself
will stand; the LORD will release her because her father has forbidden her.
6“If she marries after she makes a
vow[x] or after her lips utter a rash
promise by which she obligates herself
7and her husband hears about it but
says nothing to her, then her vows or
the pledges by which she obligated herself will stand. **8**But if her husband[y]
forbids her when he hears about it, he
nullifies the vow that obligates her or
the rash promise by which she obligates herself, and the LORD will release
her.[z]
9“Any vow or obligation taken by a
widow or divorced woman will be binding on her.
10“If a woman living with her husband makes a vow or obligates herself
by a pledge under oath **11**and her husband hears about it but says nothing to
her and does not forbid her, then all her
vows or the pledges by which she obligated herself will stand. **12**But if her
husband nullifies them when he hears
about them, then none of the vows or
pledges that came from her lips will
stand.[a] Her husband has nullified
them, and the LORD will release her.
13Her husband may confirm or nullify
any vow she makes or any sworn
pledge to deny herself. **14**But if her
husband says nothing to her about it
from day to day, then he confirms all
her vows or the pledges binding on her.
He confirms them by saying nothing to
her when he hears about them. **15**If,
however, he nullifies them[b] some
time after he hears about them, then he
is responsible for her guilt.”
16These are the regulations the LORD
gave Moses concerning relationships
between a man and his wife, and between a father and his young daughter
still living in his house.

Vengeance on the Midianites

31 The LORD said to Moses, **2**“Take
vengeance on the Midianites[c]
for the Israelites. After that, you will
be gathered to your people.[d]”
3So Moses said to the people, “Arm
some of your men to go to war against
the Midianites and to carry out the
LORD’s vengeance[e] on them. **4**Send
into battle a thousand men from each
of the tribes of Israel.” **5**So twelve
thousand men armed for battle,[f] a
thousand from each tribe, were supplied from the clans of Israel. **6**Moses
sent them into battle,[g] a thousand
from each tribe, along with Phinehas[h]
son of Eleazar, the priest, who took
with him articles from the sanctuary[i]
and the trumpets[j] for signaling.
7They fought against Midian, as the
LORD commanded Moses,[k] and killed
every man.[l] **8**Among their victims
were Evi, Rekem, Zur, Hur and
Reba[m]—the five kings of Midian.[n]
They also killed Balaam son of Beor[o]
with the sword.[p] **9**The Israelites captured the Midianite women[q] and children and took all the Midianite herds,
flocks and goods as plunder.[r] **10**They
burned[s] all the towns where the Midianites had settled, as well as all their
camps.[t] **11**They took all the plunder
and spoils, including the people and
animals,[u] **12**and brought the captives,
spoils[v] and plunder to Moses and Eleazar the priest and the Israelite assembly[w] at their camp on the plains of
Moab, by the Jordan across from Jericho.[x][x]
13Moses, Eleazar the priest and all
the leaders of the community went to
meet them outside the camp. **14**Moses
was angry with the officers of the
army[y]—the commanders of thousands and commanders of hundreds—
who returned from the battle.
15“Have you allowed all the women
to live?” he asked them. **16**“They were
the ones who followed Balaam’s ad-

30:2 [u]Dt 23:21-23; Jdg 11:35; Job 22:27; Ps 22:25; 50:14; 61:5,8; 76:11; 116:14; Pr 20:25; Ecc 5:4,5; Isa 19:21; Jnh 1:16; 2:9
30:4 [v]ver 7
30:5 [w]ver 8,12, 15
30:6 [x]S Lev 5:4
30:8 [y]S Ge 3:16 [z]ver 5
30:12 [a]Eph 5:22; Col 3:18
30:15 [b]S ver 5
31:2 [c]S Ge 25:2 [d]S Nu 20:26
31:3 [e]Jdg 11:36; 1Sa 24:12; 2Sa 4:8; 22:48; Ps 94:1; 149:7; Isa 34:8; Jer 11:20; 46:10; Eze 25:17
31:5 [f]ver 6,21
31:6 [g]S ver 5 [h]S Ex 6:25 [i]Nu 14:44 [j]S Nu 10:2
31:7 [k]Nu 25:16 [l]Dt 20:13; Jdg 21:11; 1Ki 11:15,16
31:8 [m]Jos 13:21 [n]S Nu 25:15 [o]S Nu 22:5; S 24:14 [p]Jos 13:22
31:9 [q]ver 15 [r]S Ge 34:29
31:10 [s]Jos 6:24; 8:28; 11:11; Jdg 18:27 [t]Ge 25:16; 1Ch 6:54; Ps 69:25; Eze 25:4
31:11 [u]ver 26; Dt 20:14; 2Ch 28:8
31:12 [v]ver 32,53; Ge 49:27; Ex 15:9 [w]S Nu 27:2 [x]Nu 22:1
31:14 [y]ver 48; Ex 18:21; Dt 1:15; 2Sa 18:1

[x] 12 Hebrew *Jordan of Jericho*; possibly an ancient name for the Jordan River

---

vows that affected the relationship between husband and wife or father and daughter.
31:3 GO TO WAR AGAINST THE MIDIANITES. Just as many in Israel had died because of their sins (11:1; 14:37; 16:31–34; 25:9; Ex 32:35; Lev 10:2), so would the Midianites die because of their attempt to corrupt God’s people (vv. 7–8; 25:1–9).

vice[z] and were the means of turning the Israelites away from the LORD in what happened at Peor,[a] so that a plague[b] struck the LORD's people. 17Now kill all the boys. And kill every woman who has slept with a man,[c] 18but save for yourselves every girl who has never slept with a man.

19"All of you who have killed anyone or touched anyone who was killed[d] must stay outside the camp seven days.[e] On the third and seventh days you must purify yourselves[f] and your captives. 20Purify every garment[g] as well as everything made of leather, goat hair or wood.[h]"

21Then Eleazar the priest said to the soldiers who had gone into battle,[i] "This is the requirement of the law that the LORD gave Moses: 22Gold, silver, bronze, iron,[j] tin, lead 23and anything else that can withstand fire must be put through the fire,[k] and then it will be clean. But it must also be purified with the water of cleansing.[l] And whatever cannot withstand fire must be put through that water. 24On the seventh day wash your clothes and you will be clean.[m] Then you may come into the camp.[n]"

Dividing the Spoils

25The LORD said to Moses, 26"You and Eleazar the priest and the family heads[o] of the community are to count all the people[p] and animals that were captured.[q] 27Divide[r] the spoils between the soldiers who took part in the battle and the rest of the community. 28From the soldiers who fought in the battle, set apart as tribute for the LORD[s] one out of every five hundred, whether persons, cattle, donkeys, sheep or goats. 29Take this tribute from their half share and give it to Eleazar the priest as the LORD's part. 30From the Israelites' half, select one out of every fifty, whether persons, cattle, donkeys, sheep, goats or other animals. Give them to the Levites, who are responsible for the care of the LORD's tabernacle.[t]" 31So Moses and Eleazar the priest did as the LORD commanded Moses.

32The plunder remaining from the spoils[u] that the soldiers took was 675,000 sheep, 3372,000 cattle, 3461,000 donkeys 35and 32,000 women who had never slept with a man.

36The half share of those who fought in the battle was:

337,500 sheep, 37of which the tribute for the LORD[v] was 675;
3836,000 cattle, of which the tribute for the LORD was 72;
3930,500 donkeys, of which the tribute for the LORD was 61;
4016,000 people, of which the tribute for the LORD was 32.

41Moses gave the tribute to Eleazar the priest as the LORD's part,[w] as the LORD commanded Moses.[x]

42The half belonging to the Israelites, which Moses set apart from that of the fighting men— 43the community's half—was 337,500 sheep, 4436,000 cattle, 4530,500 donkeys 46and 16,000 people. 47From the Israelites' half, Moses selected one out of every fifty persons and animals, as the LORD commanded him, and gave them to the Levites, who were responsible for the care of the LORD's tabernacle.

48Then the officers[y] who were over the units of the army—the commanders of thousands and commanders of hundreds—went to Moses 49and said to him, "Your servants have counted[z] the soldiers under our command, and not one is missing.[a] 50So we have brought as an offering to the LORD the gold articles each of us acquired—armlets, bracelets, signet rings, earrings and necklaces—to make atonement for ourselves[b] before the LORD."

51Moses and Eleazar the priest accepted from them the gold—all the crafted articles. 52All the gold from the commanders of thousands and commanders of hundreds that Moses and Eleazar presented as a gift to the LORD weighed 16,750 shekels.[y] 53Each soldier had taken plunder[c] for himself. 54Moses and Eleazar the priest accepted the gold from the commanders of thousands and commanders of hundreds and brought it into the Tent of Meeting[d] as a memorial[e] for the Israelites before the LORD.

The Transjordan Tribes

32 The Reubenites and Gadites, who had very large herds and flocks,[f] saw that the lands of Jazer[g]

31:16 [z] S Nu 22:5; S 24:14; S 2Pe 2:15 [a] S Nu 23:28; 25:1-9 [b] S Nu 14:37
31:17 [c] Dt 7:2; 20:16-18; Jdg 21:11
31:19 [d] Nu 19:16 [e] S Lev 21:1 [f] Nu 19:12
31:20 [g] Nu 19:19 [h] S Lev 11:32
31:21 [i] S ver 5
31:22 [j] Jos 6:19; 22:8
31:23 [k] S 1Co 3:13 [l] S Nu 8:7
31:24 [m] S Lev 11:25 [n] S Lev 14:8
31:26 [o] S Nu 1:4 [p] S Nu 1:19 [q] S ver 11,12
31:27 [r] Jos 22:8; 1Sa 25:13; 30:24
31:28 [s] ver 37-41; S Nu 18:21
31:30 [t] Nu 3:7; 18:3
31:32 [u] S ver 12
31:37 [v] ver 38-41
31:41 [w] Nu 5:9; 18:8 [x] ver 21,28
31:48 [y] S ver 14
31:49 [z] S Nu 1:19 [a] Jer 23:4
31:50 [b] S Ex 30:16
31:53 [c] S Ge 34:29; Dt 20:14
31:54 [d] S Ex 27:21; 40:2 [e] S Ex 28:12
32:1 [f] ver 24,36; Jdg 5:16 [g] S Nu 21:32

[y] 52 That is, about 420 pounds (about 190 kilograms)

and Gilead[h] were suitable for livestock.[i] **2**So they came to Moses and
Eleazar the priest and to the leaders of
the community,[j] and said, **3**"Ataroth,[k] Dibon,[l] Jazer,[m] Nimrah,[n]
Heshbon,[o] Elealeh,[p] Sebam,[q]
Nebo[r] and Beon[s]— **4**the land the
LORD subdued[t] before the people of Israel—are suitable for livestock,[u] and
your servants have livestock. **5**If we
have found favor in your eyes," they
said, "let this land be given to your servants as our possession. Do not make
us cross the Jordan.[v]"

6Moses said to the Gadites and Reubenites, "Shall your countrymen go to
war while you sit here? **7**Why do you
discourage the Israelites from going
over into the land the LORD has given
them?[w] **8**This is what your fathers did
when I sent them from Kadesh Barnea
to look over the land.[x] **9**After they
went up to the Valley of Eshcol[y] and
viewed the land, they discouraged the
Israelites from entering the land the
LORD had given them. **10**The LORD's anger was aroused[z] that day and he
swore this oath:[a] **11**'Because they
have not followed me wholeheartedly,
not one of the men twenty years old or
more[b] who came up out of Egypt[c]
will see the land I promised on oath[d]
to Abraham, Isaac and Jacob[e]— **12**not
one except Caleb son of Jephunneh the
Kenizzite and Joshua son of Nun, for
they followed the LORD wholeheartedly.'[f] **13**The LORD's anger burned
against Israel[g] and he made them
wander in the desert forty years, until
the whole generation of those who had
done evil in his sight was gone.[h]

14"And here you are, a brood of sinners, standing in the place of your fathers and making the LORD even more
angry with Israel.[i] **15**If you turn away
from following him, he will again leave
all this people in the desert, and you
will be the cause of their destruction.[j]"

16Then they came up to him and
said, "We would like to build pens[k]
here for our livestock[l] and cities for
our women and children. **17**But we are
ready to arm ourselves and go ahead of
the Israelites[m] until we have brought
them to their place.[n] Meanwhile our
women and children will live in fortified cities, for protection from the inhabitants of the land. **18**We will not return to our homes until every Israelite
has received his inheritance.[o] **19**We
will not receive any inheritance with
them on the other side of the Jordan,
because our inheritance[p] has come
to us on the east side of the Jordan."[q]

20Then Moses said to them, "If you
will do this—if you will arm yourselves
before the LORD for battle,[r] **21**and if all
of you will go armed over the Jordan
before the LORD until he has driven his
enemies out before him[s]— **22**then
when the land is subdued before the
LORD, you may return[t] and be free
from your obligation to the LORD and to
Israel. And this land will be your possession[u] before the LORD.[v]

23"But if you fail to do this, you will
be sinning against the LORD; and you
may be sure that your sin will find you
out.[w] **24**Build cities for your women
and children, and pens for your
flocks,[x] but do what you have promised.[y]"

25The Gadites and Reubenites said
to Moses, "We your servants will do as
our lord commands.[z] **26**Our children
and wives, our flocks and herds will remain here in the cities of Gilead.[a]
27But your servants, every man armed
for battle, will cross over to fight[b]
before the LORD, just as our lord
says."

28Then Moses gave orders about
them[c] to Eleazar the priest and Joshua son of Nun[d] and to the family heads
of the Israelite tribes.[e] **29**He said to
them, "If the Gadites and Reubenites,
every man armed for battle, cross over
the Jordan with you before the LORD,
then when the land is subdued before
you,[f] give them the land of Gilead as
their possession.[g] **30**But if they do not
cross over[h] with you armed, they
must accept their possession with you
in Canaan.[i]"

31The Gadites and Reubenites answered, "Your servants will do what
the LORD has said.[j] **32**We will cross
over before the LORD into Canaan

32:1 [h] S Ge 31:21 [i] Ex 12:38
32:2 [j] Lev 4:22; Nu 27:2
32:3 [k] ver 34; Jos 16:2,7; 18:13 [l] ver 34; S Nu 21:30 [m] ver 1 [n] ver 36; Jos 13:27 [o] Nu 21:25 [p] ver 37; Isa 15:4; 16:9; Jer 48:34 [q] Jos 13:19; Isa 16:8,9; Jer 48:32 [r] Nu 33:47; Dt 32:49; 34:1; 1Ch 5:8 [s] ver 38; Jos 13:17; Eze 25:9
32:4 [t] Nu 21:34 [u] Ex 12:38
32:5 [v] S Nu 13:29
32:7 [w] Nu 13:27-14:4
32:8 [x] Nu 13:3, 26; Dt 1:19-25
32:9 [y] Nu 13:23; Dt 1:24
32:10 [z] Nu 11:1 [a] S Nu 14:20-23
32:11 [b] S Ex 30:14 [c] Nu 1:1 [d] S Nu 14:23 [e] Nu 14:28-30
32:12 [f] Nu 14:24, 30
32:13 [g] S Ex 4:14 [h] Nu 14:28-35; 26:64,65
32:14 [i] S ver 10; Dt 1:34; Ps 78:59
32:15 [j] Dt 30:17-18; 2Ch 7:20
32:16 [k] ver 24, 36; 1Sa 24:3; Ps 50:9; 78:70 [l] Ex 12:38; Dt 3:19
32:17 [m] Dt 3:18; Jos 4:12,13 [n] S Nu 22:4; Dt 3:20
32:18 [o] Jos 22:1-4
32:19 [p] ver 22,29 [q] Nu 21:33; Jos 12:1; 22:7
32:20 [r] ver 17
32:21 [s] ver 17
32:22 [t] Jos 22:4 [u] S Lev 14:34 [v] Dt 3:18-20
32:23 [w] S Ge 4:7; S Isa 3:9
32:24 [x] S ver 1, 16 [y] Nu 30:2
32:25 [z] ver 29; Jos 1:16,18; 22:2
32:26 [a] ver 16,24; Jos 1:14; 12:2; 22:9; 2Sa 2:9; 1Ch 5:9
32:27 [b] ver 17,21
32:28 [c] ver 29; Dt 3:18-20; Jos 1:13 [d] Nu 11:28 [e] Nu 1:16
32:29 [f] S Nu 22:4 [g] S ver 19
32:30 [h] ver 23 [i] ver 29,32
32:31 [j] ver 29

32:20 IF YOU WILL ARM YOURSELVES. Moses would allow the tribes of Reuben and Gad to settle on the east side of Jordan only if they promised to help the other tribes in their conquest of Canaan. It would be considered a great sin if they pursued their own selfish interest while others gave of themselves to do battle for the Lord (v. 23).

armed,[k] but the property we inherit
will be on this side of the Jordan.[l]"
33Then Moses gave to the Gadites,[m]
the Reubenites and the half-tribe of
Manasseh[n] son of Joseph the kingdom
of Sihon king of the Amorites[o] and the
kingdom of Og king of Bashan[p]—the
whole land with its cities and the territory around them.[q]
34The Gadites built up Dibon, Ataroth, Aroer,[r] **35**Atroth Shophan, Jazer,[s] Jogbehah,[t] **36**Beth Nimrah[u]
and Beth Haran as fortified cities, and
built pens for their flocks.[v] **37**And the
Reubenites rebuilt Heshbon,[w] Elealeh[x] and Kiriathaim,[y] **38**as well as
Nebo[z] and Baal Meon (these names
were changed) and Sibmah.[a] They
gave names to the cities they rebuilt.
39The descendants of Makir[b] son of
Manasseh went to Gilead,[c] captured
it and drove out the Amorites[d] who
were there. **40**So Moses gave Gilead to
the Makirites,[e] the descendants of
Manasseh, and they settled there.
41Jair,[f] a descendant of Manasseh,
captured their settlements and called
them Havvoth Jair.[z][g] **42**And Nobah
captured Kenath[h] and its surrounding
settlements and called it Nobah[i] after
himself.[j]

Stages in Israel's Journey

33 Here are the stages in the journey[k] of the Israelites when
they came out of Egypt[l] by divisions
under the leadership of Moses and Aaron.[m] **2**At the LORD's command Moses
recorded[n] the stages in their journey[o]. This is their journey by stages:

3The Israelites set out[p] from
Rameses[q] on the fifteenth day of
the first month, the day after the
Passover.[r] They marched out
boldly[s] in full view of all the
Egyptians, **4**who were burying all
their firstborn,[t] whom the LORD
had struck down among them; for
the LORD had brought judgment[u]
on their gods.[v]
5The Israelites left Rameses
and camped at Succoth.[w]
6They left Succoth and camped
at Etham, on the edge of the
desert.[x]
7They left Etham, turned back
to Pi Hahiroth, to the east of Baal
Zephon,[y] and camped near Migdol.[z]
8They left Pi Hahiroth[a][a] and
passed through the sea[b] into the
desert, and when they had traveled for three days in the Desert
of Etham, they camped at Marah.[c]
9They left Marah and went to
Elim, where there were twelve
springs and seventy palm trees,
and they camped[d] there.
10They left Elim[e] and camped
by the Red Sea.[b]
11They left the Red Sea and
camped in the Desert of Sin.[f]
12They left the Desert of Sin
and camped at Dophkah.
13They left Dophkah and
camped at Alush.
14They left Alush and camped
at Rephidim, where there was no
water for the people to drink.[g]
15They left Rephidim[h] and
camped in the Desert of Sinai.[i]
16They left the Desert of Sinai
and camped at Kibroth Hattaavah.[j]
17They left Kibroth Hattaavah
and camped at Hazeroth.[k]
18They left Hazeroth and
camped at Rithmah.
19They left Rithmah and
camped at Rimmon Perez.
20They left Rimmon Perez
and camped at Libnah.[l]
21They left Libnah and camped
at Rissah.
22They left Rissah and camped
at Kehelathah.
23They left Kehelathah and
camped at Mount Shepher.
24They left Mount Shepher
and camped at Haradah.
25They left Haradah and
camped at Makheloth.
26They left Makheloth and
camped at Tahath.
27They left Tahath and camped
at Terah.
28They left Terah and camped
at Mithcah.
29They left Mithcah and
camped at Hashmonah.
30They left Hashmonah and
camped at Moseroth.[m]

32:32 [k]ver 17 [l]S ver 30; Jos 12:6 **32:33** [m]Jos 13:24-28; 1Sa 13:7 [n]Jos 1:12 [o]Nu 21:21; Dt 2:26 [p]S ver 19; S Jos 12:5 [q]S Nu 21:24; 34:14; Dt 2:36; Jos 12:6 **32:34** [r]Dt 2:36; 3:12; 4:48; Jos 12:2; 13:9; Jdg 11:26; 1Sa 30:28; 1Ch 5:8; Jer 48:19 **32:35** [s]ver 3 [t]Jdg 8:11 **32:36** [u]S ver 3 [v]S ver 1 **32:37** [w]Nu 21:25 [x]S ver 3 [y]Jos 13:19; 1Ch 6:76; Jer 48:1, 23; Eze 25:9 **32:38** [z]S ver 3; Isa 15:2; Jer 48:1, 22 [a]S ver 3 **32:39** [b]S Ge 50:23 [c]Nu 26:29; Dt 2:36 [d]S Ge 10:16 **32:40** [e]S Ge 50:23; Dt 3:15 **32:41** [f]1Ki 4:13 [g]Dt 3:14; Jos 13:30; Jdg 10:4; 1Ch 2:23 **32:42** [h]1Ch 2:23 [i]Jdg 8:11 [j]1Sa 15:12; 2Sa 18:18; Ps 49:11; Isa 22:16; 56:5 **33:1** [k]Ex 17:1; 40:36 [l]Nu 1:1 [m]S Ex 4:16; 6:26 **33:2** [n]S Ex 17:14 [o]S ver 1 **33:3** [p]Nu 10:2 [q]S Ge 47:11 [r]Jos 5:10 [s]S Ex 14:8 **33:4** [t]S Ex 4:23 [u]2Ch 24:24; Jer 15:3; Eze 14:21 [v]S Ex 12:12 **33:5** [w]Ex 12:37 **33:6** [x]Ex 13:20 **33:7** [y]Ex 14:9 [z]S Ex 14:2 **33:8** [a]Ex 14:2 [b]S Ex 14:22 [c]S Ex 15:23 **33:9** [d]Ex 15:27 **33:10** [e]Ex 16:1 **33:11** [f]S Ex 16:1 **33:14** [g]S Ex 15:22; S 17:2 **33:15** [h]S Ex 17:1 [i]S Ex 19:1 **33:16** [j]S Nu 11:34 **33:17** [k]Nu 11:35 **33:20** [l]Jos 10:29; 12:15; 15:42; 21:13; 2Ki 8:22; 19:8; 23:31; 1Ch 6:57; 2Ch 21:10; Isa 37:8; Jer 52:1 **33:30** [m]Dt 10:6

[z] *41* Or *them the settlements of Jair* [a] *8* Many manuscripts of the Masoretic Text, Samaritan Pentateuch and Vulgate; most manuscripts of the Masoretic Text *left from before Hahiroth*
[b] *10* Hebrew *Yam Suph*; that is, Sea of Reeds; also in verse 11

31 They left Moseroth and camped at Bene Jaakan.[n]

32 They left Bene Jaakan and camped at Hor Haggidgad.

33 They left Hor Haggidgad and camped at Jotbathah.[o]

34 They left Jotbathah and camped at Abronah.

35 They left Abronah and camped at Ezion Geber.[p]

36 They left Ezion Geber and camped at Kadesh, in the Desert of Zin.[q]

37 They left Kadesh and camped at Mount Hor,[r] on the border of Edom.[s] 38 At the LORD's command Aaron the priest went up Mount Hor, where he died[t] on the first day of the fifth month of the fortieth year[u] after the Israelites came out of Egypt.[v] 39 Aaron was a hundred and twenty-three years old when he died on Mount Hor.

40 The Canaanite king[w] of Arad,[x] who lived in the Negev[y] of Canaan, heard that the Israelites were coming.

41 They left Mount Hor and camped at Zalmonah.

42 They left Zalmonah and camped at Punon.

43 They left Punon and camped at Oboth.[z]

44 They left Oboth and camped at Iye Abarim, on the border of Moab.[a]

45 They left Iyim[c] and camped at Dibon Gad.

46 They left Dibon Gad and camped at Almon Diblathaim.

47 They left Almon Diblathaim and camped in the mountains of Abarim,[b] near Nebo.[c]

48 They left the mountains of Abarim[d] and camped on the plains of Moab[e] by the Jordan[f] across from Jericho.[d][g] 49 There on the plains of Moab they camped along the Jordan from Beth Jeshimoth[h] to Abel Shittim.[i]

50 On the plains of Moab by the Jordan across from Jericho[j] the LORD said to Moses, 51 "Speak to the Israelites and say to them: 'When you cross the Jordan into Canaan,[k] 52 drive out all the inhabitants of the land before you. Destroy all their carved images and their cast idols, and demolish all their high places.[l] 53 Take possession of the land and settle in it, for I have given you the land to possess.[m] 54 Distribute the land by lot,[n] according to your clans.[o] To a larger group give a larger inheritance, and to a smaller group a smaller one.[p] Whatever falls to them by lot will be theirs. Distribute it according to your ancestral tribes.[q]

55 " 'But if you do not drive out the inhabitants of the land, those you allow to remain will become barbs in your eyes and thorns[r] in your sides. They will give you trouble in the land where you will live. 56 And then I will do to you what I plan to do to them.[s]' "

33:31 [n]Dt 10:6
33:33 [o]Dt 10:7
33:35 [p]Dt 2:8; 1Ki 9:26; 22:48
33:36 [q]S Nu 13:21
33:37 [r]S Nu 20:22 [s]S Ge 36:16; S Nu 20:16
33:38 [t]S Nu 27:13 [u]S Ex 16:35 [v]Nu 20:25-28
33:40 [w]S Ge 10:18 [x]S Nu 21:1 [y]S Ge 12:9
33:43 [z]Nu 21:10
33:44 [a]S Nu 21:11
33:47 [b]Nu 27:12 [c]Nu 32:3
33:48 [d]Nu 27:12 [e]S Nu 26:3 [f]S Ge 13:10 [g]Nu 22:1; Jos 12:9
33:49 [h]Jos 12:3; 13:20; Eze 25:9 [i]S Nu 21:16
33:50 [j]ver 48
33:51 [k]Nu 34:2; Jos 3:17
33:52 [l]S Lev 26:1; Ps 106:34-36
33:53 [m]Dt 11:31; 17:14; Jos 1:11; 21:43
33:54 [n]S Lev 16:8; Nu 36:2 [o]Nu 26:54 [p]Nu 35:8 [q]Jos 18:10
33:55 [r]Jos 23:13; Jdg 2:3; Ps 106:36; Isa 55:13; Eze 2:6; 28:24; Mic 7:4; 2Co 12:7
33:56 [s]Nu 14:28
34:2 [t]S Nu 33:51 [u]Ge 17:8; Dt 1:7-8; Jos 23:4; Ps 78:54-55; 105:11 [v]Eze 47:15
34:3 [w]Nu 13:21; Jos 15:1-3 [x]S Ge 14:3
34:4 [y]Jos 15:3; Jdg 1:36 [z]Nu 32:8 [a]Jos 15:4
34:5 [b]Ge 15:18
34:6 [c]Jos 1:4; 9:1; 15:12,47; 23:4; Eze 47:10, 15; 48:28 [d]Eze 47:19-20
34:7 [e]Eze 47:15-17

Boundaries of Canaan

34 The LORD said to Moses, 2 "Command the Israelites and say to them: 'When you enter Canaan,[t] the land that will be allotted to you as an inheritance[u] will have these boundaries:[v]

3 " 'Your southern side will include some of the Desert of Zin[w] along the border of Edom. On the east, your southern boundary will start from the end of the Salt Sea,[e][x] 4 cross south of Scorpion[f] Pass,[y] continue on to Zin and go south of Kadesh Barnea.[z] Then it will go to Hazar Addar and over to Azmon,[a] 5 where it will turn, join the Wadi of Egypt[b] and end at the Sea.[g]

6 " 'Your western boundary will be the coast of the Great Sea.[c] This will be your boundary on the west.[d]

7 " 'For your northern boundary,[e] run a line from the Great Sea to Mount

[c] 45 That is, Iye Abarim [d] 48 Hebrew *Jordan of Jericho*; possibly an ancient name for the Jordan River; also in verse 50 [e] 3 That is, the Dead Sea; also in verse 12 [f] 4 Hebrew *Akrabbim* [g] 5 That is, the Mediterranean; also in verses 6 and 7

33:55 IF YOU DO NOT DRIVE OUT THE INHABITANTS. If the Israelites failed to drive out completely the wicked Canaanites and destroy their idolatrous worship centers, then God would allow those Canaanites to give them trouble, and he himself would judge them. Likewise, if the church of Jesus Christ tolerates sin in its midst, trouble, destruction and death will come on the church and on the souls of her members. God will allow his people to be trampled by the evil world that they have failed to resist (see Mt 5:13, note).

Hor[f] 8and from Mount Hor to Lebo[h]
Hamath.[g] Then the boundary will go
to Zedad, 9continue to Ziphron and end
at Hazar Enan. This will be your
boundary on the north.
10" 'For your eastern boundary,[h]
run a line from Hazar Enan to Shepham. 11The boundary will go down
from Shepham to Riblah[i] on the east
side of Ain[j] and continue along the
slopes east of the Sea of Kinnereth.[i][k] 12Then the boundary will go
down along the Jordan and end at the
Salt Sea.
" 'This will be your land, with its
boundaries on every side.' "
13Moses commanded the Israelites:
"Assign this land by lot[l] as an inheritance.[m] The LORD has ordered that it
be given to the nine and a half tribes,
14because the families of the tribe of
Reuben, the tribe of Gad and the half-
tribe of Manasseh have received their
inheritance.[n] 15These two and a half
tribes have received their inheritance
on the east side of the Jordan of Jericho,[j] toward the sunrise."
16The LORD said to Moses, 17"These
are the names of the men who are to
assign the land for you as an inheritance: Eleazar the priest and Joshua[o]
son of Nun. 18And appoint one leader
from each tribe to help[p] assign the
land.[q] 19These are their names:[r]

Caleb[s] son of Jephunneh,
from the tribe of Judah;[t]
20Shemuel son of Ammihud,
from the tribe of Simeon;[u]
21Elidad son of Kislon,
from the tribe of Benjamin;[v]
22Bukki son of Jogli,
the leader from the tribe of
Dan;
23Hanniel son of Ephod,
the leader from the tribe of Manasseh[w] son of Joseph;
24Kemuel son of Shiphtan,
the leader from the tribe of
Ephraim[x] son of Joseph;
25Elizaphan son of Parnach,
the leader from the tribe of Zebulun;[y]
26Paltiel son of Azzan,
the leader from the tribe of Issachar;
27Ahihud son of Shelomi,
the leader from the tribe of
Asher;[z]
28Pedahel son of Ammihud,
the leader from the tribe of
Naphtali."

29These are the men the LORD commanded to assign the inheritance to
the Israelites in the land of Canaan.[a]

Towns for the Levites

35 On the plains of Moab by the
Jordan across from Jericho,[k][b]
the LORD said to Moses, 2"Command
the Israelites to give the Levites towns
to live in[c] from the inheritance the Israelites will possess. And give them
pasturelands[d] around the towns.
3Then they will have towns to live in
and pasturelands for their cattle,
flocks and all their other livestock.[e]
4"The pasturelands around the
towns that you give the Levites will extend out fifteen hundred feet[l] from
the town wall. 5Outside the town, measure three thousand feet[m][f] on the
east side, three thousand on the south
side, three thousand on the west and
three thousand on the north, with the
town in the center. They will have this
area as pastureland for the towns.[g]

Cities of Refuge

35:6–34Ref — Dt 4:41–43; 19:1–14; Jos 20:1–9

6"Six of the towns you give the Levites will be cities of refuge, to which
a person who has killed someone may
flee.[h] In addition, give them forty-two
other towns. 7In all you must give the
Levites forty-eight towns, together
with their pasturelands. 8The towns
you give the Levites from the land the
Israelites possess are to be given in
proportion to the inheritance of each
tribe: Take many towns from a tribe
that has many, but few from one that
has few."[i]
9Then the LORD said to Moses:
10"Speak to the Israelites and say to
them: 'When you cross the Jordan into
Canaan,[j] 11select some towns to be
your cities of refuge, to which a person
who has killed someone[k] accidentally[l] may flee. 12They will be places of
refuge from the avenger,[m] so that a
person accused of murder[n] may not

34:7 [f]S Nu 20:22
34:8 [g]Nu 13:21; Jos 13:5
34:10 [h]Jos 15:5
34:11 [i]2Ki 23:33; 25:6,21; Jer 39:5; 52:9,27 [j]Jos 15:32; 21:16; 1Ch 4:32 [k]Dt 3:17; Jos 11:2; 13:27
34:13 [l]S Lev 16:8; Jos 18:10; Mic 2:5 [m]Jos 13:6; 14:1-5; Isa 49:8; 65:9; Eze 45:1
34:14 [n]Nu 32:19; Dt 33:21; Jos 14:3
34:17 [o]Nu 11:28; Dt 1:38
34:18 [p]S Nu 1:4 [q]Jos 14:1
34:19 [r]ver 29 [s]S Nu 26:65 [t]Ge 29:35; Dt 33:7; Ps 60:7
34:20 [u]S Ge 29:33
34:21 [v]Ge 49:27; Jdg 5:14; Ps 68:27
34:23 [w]Nu 1:34
34:24 [x]Nu 1:32
34:25 [y]S Ge 30:20
34:27 [z]Nu 1:40
34:29 [a]ver 19
35:1 [b]Nu 22:1
35:2 [c]Lev 25:32-34; Jos 14:3,4 [d]Jos 21:1-42
35:3 [e]Dt 18:6; Jos 14:4; 21:2
35:5 [f]Jos 3:4 [g]Lev 25:34; 2Ch 11:14; 13:9; 23:2; 31:19
35:6 [h]ver 11; Jos 21:13
35:8 [i]Nu 26:54; 33:54
35:10 [j]Nu 33:51; Dt 9:1; Jos 1:2,11
35:11 [k]ver 22-25 [l]S Ex 21:13
35:12 [m]ver 19; Dt 19:6; Jos 20:3; 2Sa 14:11 [n]ver 26,27,28

[h] 8 Or *to the entrance to* [i] 11 That is, Galilee [j] 15 *Jordan of Jericho* was possibly an ancient name for the Jordan River. [k] 1 Hebrew *Jordan of Jericho*; possibly an ancient name for the Jordan River [l] 4 Hebrew *a thousand cubits* (about 450 meters) [m] 5 Hebrew *two thousand cubits* (about 900 meters)

die before he stands trial before the assembly.[o] 13These six towns you give
will be your cities of refuge.[p] 14Give
three on this side of the Jordan and
three in Canaan as cities of refuge.
15These six towns will be a place of
refuge for Israelites, aliens and any
other people living among them, so
that anyone who has killed another accidentally can flee there.
16" 'If a man strikes someone with
an iron object so that he dies, he is a
murderer; the murderer shall be put to
death.[q] 17Or if anyone has a stone in
his hand that could kill, and he strikes
someone so that he dies, he is a murderer; the murderer shall be put to
death. 18Or if anyone has a wooden object in his hand that could kill, and he
hits someone so that he dies, he is a
murderer; the murderer shall be put to
death. 19The avenger of blood[r] shall
put the murderer to death; when he
meets him, he shall put him to death.[s]
20If anyone with malice aforethought
shoves another or throws something at
him intentionally[t] so that he dies 21or
if in hostility he hits him with his fist
so that he dies, that person shall be put
to death;[u] he is a murderer. The
avenger of blood[v] shall put the murderer to death when he meets him.
22" 'But if without hostility someone
suddenly shoves another or throws
something at him unintentionally[w]
23or, without seeing him, drops a stone
on him that could kill him, and he dies,
then since he was not his enemy and he
did not intend to harm him, 24the assembly[x] must judge between him and
the avenger of blood according to these
regulations. 25The assembly must protect the one accused of murder from
the avenger of blood and send him back
to the city of refuge to which he fled.
He must stay there until the death of
the high priest,[y] who was anointed[z]
with the holy oil.[a]
26" 'But if the accused ever goes outside the limits of the city of refuge to
which he has fled 27and the avenger of
blood finds him outside the city, the
avenger of blood may kill the accused
without being guilty of murder. 28The
accused must stay in his city of refuge
until the death of the high priest; only
after the death of the high priest may
he return to his own property.
29" 'These are to be legal requirements[b] for you throughout the generations to come,[c] wherever you live.[d]
30" 'Anyone who kills a person is to
be put to death as a murderer only on
the testimony of witnesses. But no one
is to be put to death on the testimony
of only one witness.[e]
31" 'Do not accept a ransom[f] for
the life of a murderer, who deserves to
die. He must surely be put to death.
32" 'Do not accept a ransom for anyone who has fled to a city of refuge and
so allow him to go back and live on his
own land before the death of the high
priest.
33" 'Do not pollute the land where
you are. Bloodshed pollutes the land,[g]
and atonement cannot be made for the
land on which blood has been shed, except by the blood of the one who shed
it. 34Do not defile the land[h] where you
live and where I dwell,[i] for I, the
LORD, dwell among the Israelites.' "

Inheritance of Zelophehad's Daughters

36:1–12pp — Nu 27:1–11

36 The family heads of the clan of
Gilead[j] son of Makir,[k] the
son of Manasseh, who were from the
clans of the descendants of Joseph,[l]
came and spoke before Moses and the
leaders,[m] the heads of the Israelite
families. 2They said, "When the LORD
commanded my lord to give the land as
an inheritance to the Israelites by
lot,[n] he ordered you to give the inheritance of our brother Zelophehad[o] to
his daughters. 3Now suppose they mar-

35:12 [o] ver 24,25
35:13 [p] ver 6,14
35:16 [q] S Ex 21:12
35:19 [r] S ver 12 [s] ver 21
35:20 [t] S Ex 21:14
35:21 [u] Ex 21:14 [v] ver 19
35:22 [w] S Ex 21:13
35:24 [x] S ver 12
35:25 [y] ver 32 [z] S Ex 28:41 [a] S Ex 29:7
35:29 [b] Nu 27:11 [c] Nu 10:8 [d] S Ex 12:20
35:30 [e] Dt 17:6; 19:15; S Mt 18:16; Jn 7:51
35:31 [f] Ex 21:30; Job 6:22; Ps 49:8; Pr 13:8
35:33 [g] S Ge 4:10
35:34 [h] Lev 18:24,25 [i] S Ex 29:45
36:1 [j] S Nu 26:30 [k] S Ge 50:23 [l] S Nu 26:28 [m] S Nu 27:2
36:2 [n] S Nu 33:54 [o] S Nu 26:33

35:11 CITIES OF REFUGE. Cities of refuge were established to provide protection for someone who killed a person accidentally. Those accused of murder could flee to one of the cities and find refuge until a trial could be arranged (v. 12). If found guilty of willful murder, the individual was put to death immediately (vv. 16–21). If found guilty of involuntary manslaughter, he or she could remain in that city until the death of the high priest; then the offender could safely return to his or her home (vv. 22–28).

35:33 NOT POLLUTE THE LAND. To fail to put a murderer to death polluted and defiled the land. To "pollute" means that the failure to avenge the death of the innocent person would cause God to withdraw his presence, blessing and help from the land (see Dt 21:1–9). God's holiness and justice required that no murderer be allowed to go free. Capital punishment in Israel expressed God's holy desire that righteousness and the sanctity of innocent life be maintained among his people as a holy nation (see Ge 9:6, note).

ry men from other Israelite tribes; then their inheritance will be taken from our ancestral inheritance and added to that of the tribe they marry into. And so part of the inheritance allotted to us will be taken away. **4**When the Year of Jubilee[p] for the Israelites comes, their inheritance will be added to that of the tribe into which they marry, and their property will be taken from the tribal inheritance of our forefathers."

5Then at the LORD's command Moses gave this order to the Israelites: "What the tribe of the descendants of Joseph is saying is right. **6**This is what the LORD commands for Zelophehad's daughters: They may marry anyone they please as long as they marry within the tribal clan of their father. **7**No inheritance[q] in Israel is to pass from tribe to tribe, for every Israelite shall keep the tribal land inherited from his forefathers. **8**Every daughter who inherits land in any Israelite tribe must marry someone in her father's tribal clan,[r] so that every Israelite will possess the inheritance of his fathers. **9**No inheritance may pass from tribe to tribe, for each Israelite tribe is to keep the land it inherits."

10So Zelophehad's daughters did as the LORD commanded Moses. **11**Zelophehad's daughters—Mahlah, Tirzah, Hoglah, Milcah and Noah[s]—married their cousins on their father's side. **12**They married within the clans of the descendants of Manasseh son of Joseph, and their inheritance remained in their father's clan and tribe.[t]

13These are the commands and regulations the LORD gave through Moses[u] to the Israelites on the plains of Moab by the Jordan across from Jericho.[n][v]

36:4 [p] S Lev 25:10
36:7 [q] S Lev 25:23
36:8 [r] 1Ch 23:22
36:11 [s] Nu 26:33
36:12 [t] 1Ch 7:15
36:13 [u] S Lev 7:38; S 27:34 [v] Nu 22:1

[n] *13* Hebrew *Jordan of Jericho*; possibly an ancient name for the Jordan River

DEUTERONOMY

Outline

Introduction (1:1–5)

I. Moses' First Address: Recounting Israel's Recent History (1:6—4:43)
   - A. Leaving Mount Sinai (1:6–18)
   - B. Unbelief at Kadesh Barnea (1:19–46)
   - C. Desert Wanderings (2:1–15)
   - D. Advancing to the Plains of Moab (2:16—3:29)
   - E. Moses' Exhortation to Obedience (4:1–43)

II. Moses' Second Address: Main Obligations of the Covenant (4:44—26:19)
   - A. The Ten Commandments (4:44—5:33)
   - B. The Shema and Imperatives (6:1–25)
   - C. Practical Commands, Promises and Warnings (7:1—11:32)
   - D. Commands Concerning Worship (12:1–32)
   - E. Commands Concerning False Prophets (13:1–18)
   - F. Commands Concerning Food, Tithes and the Sabbatical Year (14:1—15:23)
   - G. Commands Concerning Annual Feasts (16:1–17)
   - H. Commands Concerning Leaders (16:18—18:22)
   - I. Civil and Social Laws (19:1—26:19)

III. Moses' Third Address: Renewing and Ratifying the Covenant (27:1—30:20)
   - A. Moses Solemnly Charges Israel (27:1–26)
   - B. Promised Blessings for Obedience and Curses for Disobedience (28:1–68)
   - C. Restatement of the Covenant and Pertinent Exhortations (29:1–30:20)

IV. Moses' Final Activities and His Death (31:1—34:12)
   - A. Moses Charges Israel and Commissions Joshua (31:1–29)
   - B. Song of Moses (31:30—32:47)
   - C. God's Instruction to Moses (32:48–52)
   - D. Moses Blesses the Tribes (33:1–29)
   - E. Death and Burial of Moses, and Final Summary (34:1–12)

Author: Moses

Theme: Covenant Renewal

Date of Writing: c. 1405 B.C.

Background

The title "Deuteronomy" (derived from the Septuagint) means "Second Law." The book consists of Moses' farewell messages in which he reviewed and renewed God's covenant with Israel for the sake of the new generation of Israelites. They had come to the end of their desert wandering and were now ready to enter the land of Canaan. For the most part this new generation had no personal recollection of the first Passover, the Red Sea crossing or the giving of the Law at Mount Sinai. They needed an inspired recounting of God's covenant, law and faithfulness, as well as a fresh declaration concerning the accompanying blessings for obedience and curses for disobedience. Unlike Numbers, which records the desert wanderings of the rebellious "exodus generation" of Israelites over a span of 39 years, Deuteronomy covers a short span of perhaps one month at one location on the plains of Moab directly east of Jericho and the Jordan River.

Deuteronomy was written by Moses (31:9,24–26; cf. 4:44–46; 29:1) and bequeathed to Israel as a covenant document to be read before all the people in its entirety every seven years (31:10–13). Moses probably completed the book shortly before his death about 1405 B.C. Mosaic authorship of Deuteronomy is attested to (1) by the Jewish and Samaritan Pentateuch, (2) by OT writers (e.g., Jos 1:7; 1Ki 2:3; 2Ki 14:6; Ezr 3:2; Ne 1:8–9; Da 9:11), (3) by Jesus (Mt 19:7–9; Jn 5:45–47) and other NT writers (e.g., Ac 3:22–23; Ro 10:19), (4) by ancient Christian scholars, (5) by modern conservative scholars and (6) by internal evidence (e.g., similarity in literary structure to secular suzerainty covenant treaties written in the 15th century B.C.). The account of Moses' death (ch. 34) was undoubtedly added soon after its occurrence (most likely by Joshua) as a fitting tribute to Moses, the servant of the Lord.

Purpose

Moses' original purpose in addressing Israel's new generation before turning the reins of leadership over to Joshua for the conquest was to exhort and instruct them about (1) God's mighty deeds and promises, (2) their own covenant obligations of faith and obedience, and (3) their need to consecrate themselves to fear the Lord, to walk in his ways, and to love and honor him with all their heart, soul and strength.

Survey

As a covenant renewal document, Deuteronomy is organized like a suzerainty covenant treaty of that time: (1) preamble (1:1–5); (2) historical prologue (1:6—4:43); (3) main stipulations (4:44—26:19); (4) curses and blessings (27:1—30:20); and (5) arrangements for its continuation (31:1—33:39).

With all the earnestness that he possessed, Moses reviewed and renewed God's covenant with Israel primarily by means of three inspired addresses. (1) Moses' first address reviewed Israel's history and failure since Mount Sinai and summoned the new generation to fear God and obey him (1:6—4:43). (2) Moses' second address reviewed and applied many covenant laws dealing with issues such as Sabbath observance, worship, the poor, annual festivals, inheritance and property rights, sexual immorality, treatment of servants and administration of justice (4:44—26:19). (3) Moses' third address prophesied blessings and curses that would fall on the Israelites according to their obedience or disobedience (27:1—30:20). The remaining chapters include Moses' appointment of Joshua as his successor and a testimony about Moses' death (31:1—34:12).

Special Features

Four major features characterize Deuteronomy. (1) It provided the new generation of Israelites (who were soon to enter Canaan) the necessary foundation and motivation for inheriting the promised land by focusing on the nature of God and his covenant with Israel. (2) It is "The Book of the Second Law" in that Moses, Israel's 120-year-old leader, restated and summarized (in sermonic form) the word of the Lord embodied in the four preceding books of the Pentateuch. (3) It is "The Book of Remembrance." A characteristic admonition of Deuteronomy is, "Remember . . . and never forget." Rather than representing a quest for "new truth," Deuteronomy exhorts Israel to retain and obey the previously revealed truth of God as already given in his absolute and unchanging word. (4) An important keynote of the book is the "faith-plus-obedience" formula. Israel was called to trust God with their whole being and to obey his commands unswervingly. Faith-plus-obedience would enable them to inherit the promises with God's full blessing; the absence of faith and obedience, on the other hand, would introduce the cycle of failure and judgment.

New Testament Fulfillment

When Jesus was tempted by the devil, he responded by quoting passages from Deuteronomy (Mt 4:4,7,10, quoting Dt 8:3; 6:16; 6:13). When Jesus was asked what was the greatest commandment, his reply was from Deuteronomy (Mt 22:37; cf. Dt 6:5). The NT books quote or allude to Deuteronomy nearly 100 times. A clear Messianic prophecy (18:15–19) is referred to twice in the book of Acts (3:22–23; 7:37). Deuteronomy's spiritual character is foundational to NT revelation.

Reading Deuteronomy

In order to read the entire Old Testament in one year, the book of Deuteronomy should be read in 14 days, according to the following schedule: ☐ 1–2 ☐ 3–4 ☐ 5–7 ☐ 8–10 ☐ 11–12 ☐ 13–15 ☐ 16–17 ☐ 18–21 ☐ 22–24 ☐ 25–27 ☐ 28 ☐ 29–30 ☐ 31–32 ☐ 33–34

NOTES

The Command to Leave Horeb

1 These are the words Moses spoke to all Israel in the desert east of the Jordan[a]—that is, in the Arabah[b]—opposite Suph, between Paran[c] and Tophel, Laban, Hazeroth and Dizahab. **2**(It takes eleven days to go from Horeb[d] to Kadesh Barnea[e] by the Mount Seir[f] road.)[g]

3In the fortieth year,[h] on the first day of the eleventh month,[i] Moses proclaimed[j] to the Israelites all that the LORD had commanded him concerning them. **4**This was after he had defeated Sihon[k] king of the Amorites,[l] who reigned in Heshbon,[m] and at Edrei had defeated Og[n] king of Bashan, who reigned in Ashtaroth.[o]

5East of the Jordan in the territory of Moab,[p] Moses began to expound this law, saying:

6The LORD our God said to us[q] at Horeb,[r] "You have stayed long enough[s] at this mountain. **7**Break camp and advance into the hill country of the Amorites;[t] go to all the neighboring peoples in the Arabah,[u] in the mountains, in the western foothills, in the Negev[v] and along the coast, to the land of the Canaanites[w] and to Lebanon,[x] as far as the great river, the Euphrates.[y] **8**See, I have given you this land[z].[a] Go in and take possession of the land that the LORD swore[b] he would give to your fathers—to Abraham, Isaac and Jacob—and to their descendants after them."

The Appointment of Leaders

9At that time I said to you, "You are too heavy a burden[c] for me to carry alone.[d] **10**The LORD your God has increased[e] your numbers[f] so that today you are as many[g] as the stars in the sky.[h] **11**May the LORD, the God of your fathers, increase[i] you a thousand times and bless you as he has promised![j] **12**But how can I bear your problems and your burdens and your disputes all by myself?[k] **13**Choose some wise, understanding and respected men[l] from each of your tribes, and I will set them over you."

14You answered me, "What you propose to do is good."

15So I took[m] the leading men of your tribes,[n] wise and respected men,[o] and appointed them to have authority over you—as commanders[p] of thousands, of hundreds, of fifties and of tens and as tribal officials.[q] **16**And I charged your judges at that time: Hear the disputes between your brothers and judge[r] fairly,[s] whether the case is between brother Israelites or between one of them and an alien.[t] **17**Do not show partiality[u] in judging; hear both small and great alike. Do not be afraid of any man,[v] for judgment belongs to God. Bring me any case too hard for you, and I will hear it.[w] **18**And at that time I told you everything you were to do.[x]

Spies Sent Out

19Then, as the LORD our God commanded us, we set out from Horeb and went toward the hill country of the Amorites[y] through all that vast and dreadful desert[z] that you have seen, and so we reached Kadesh Barnea.[a] **20**Then I said to you, "You have reached the hill country of the Amorites, which the LORD our God is giving us. **21**See, the LORD your God has given you the land. Go up and take possession[b] of it as the LORD, the God of your fathers, told you. Do not be afraid;[c] do not be discouraged."[d]

22Then all of you came to me and said, "Let us send men ahead to spy[e] out the land[f] for us and bring back a report about the route we are to take and the towns we will come to."

23The idea seemed good to me; so I selected[g] twelve of you, one man from each tribe. **24**They left and went up into the hill country, and came to the Valley of Eshcol[h] and explored it. **25**Taking with them some of the fruit of the land, they brought it down to us and reported,[i] "It is a good land[j] that the LORD our God is giving us."[k]

1:1 [a]S Nu 13:29; Dt 4:46 [b]ver 7; Dt 2:8; 3:17; Jos 3:16; 8:14; 11:2; Eze 47:8 [c]S Nu 10:12 **1:2** [d]S Ex 3:1 [e]S Ge 14:7; Dt 2:14; 9:23; Jos 15:3 [f]S Nu 24:18 [g]ver 19 **1:3** [h]Nu 14:33; 32:13; Dt 8:2; Heb 3:7-9 [i]Ge 50:3; Dt 34:8; Jos 4:19 [j]Dt 4:1-2 **1:4** [k]Nu 21:21-26 [l]S Ge 10:16; S 14:7 [m]S Nu 21:25 [n]Nu 21:33-35; Dt 3:10 [o]Jos 9:10; 12:4; 1Ch 11:44 **1:5** [p]S Nu 21:11 **1:6** [q]Nu 10:13 [r]S Ex 3:1 [s]Dt 2:3 **1:7** [t]ver 19; Dt 2:24; 7:1; Jos 10:5 [u]S ver 1 [v]S Nu 21:1; Jos 11:16; 12:8; 2Sa 24:7 [w]S Ge 10:18 [x]Dt 11:24 [y]S Ge 2:14 **1:8** [z]S Jos 23:13 [a]S Nu 34:2 [b]S Ex 13:11; S Nu 14:23; Heb 6:13-14 **1:9** [c]S Nu 11:14; Ps 38:4 [d]S Ex 18:18 **1:10** [e]ver 11; Eze 16:7 [f]S Dt 7:13 [g]S Ge 15:5; Isa 51:2; 60:22; Eze 33:24 [h]S Ge 22:17; S Nu 10:36 **1:11** [i]S ver 10 [j]ver 8; Ex 32:13; 2Sa 24:3; 1Ch 21:3 **1:12** [k]S Ex 5:22; S 18:18 **1:13** [l]S Ge 47:6 **1:15** [m]Ex 18:25 [n]Ex 5:14; Nu 11:16; Jos 1:10; 3:2 [o]S Ge 47:6 [p]Nu 31:14; 1Sa 8:12; 22:7; 1Ki 14:27 [q]S Nu 1:4 **1:16** [r]1Ki 3:9; Ps 72:1; Pr 2:9 [s]S Ge 31:37; Jn 7:24 [t]S Ex 12:19,49; S 22:21 **1:17** [u]S Ex 18:16; S Lev 19:15; Ac 10:34; Jas 2:1 [v]Pr 29:25 [w]Ex 18:26 **1:18** [x]S Ge 39:11 **1:19** [y]S ver 7 [z]Dt 2:7; 8:15; 32:10; Ps 136:16; Jer 2:2,6; Hos 13:5 [a]ver 2; Nu 13:26 **1:21** [b]Dt 9:23 [c]S Nu 14:9; Jos 1:6,9,18; 2Sa 10:12; Ps 27:14 [d]Dt 7:18; Jos 8:1; 10:8 **1:22** [e]Nu 13:1-3 [f]S Ge 42:9 **1:23** [g]Nu 13:1-3 **1:24** [h]Nu 13:21-25; S 32:9 **1:25** [i]S Nu 13:27 [j]S Nu 14:7 [k]Jos 1:2

1:1 THE WORDS MOSES SPOKE. The NT often refers to the contents of Deuteronomy. Jesus quoted from the book when he was tempted by Satan (Mt 4:4,7,10; cf. Dt 6:13,16; 8:3) and as he taught about our relationship with God as embodied in "the first and greatest commandment" (Mt 22:37–38; cf. Dt 6:5; 10:12; 30:6; compare Dt 17:6; 19:15 with Mt 18:16; Jn 8:17).

Rebellion Against the Lord

26But you were unwilling to go up;[l]
you rebelled[m] against the command of
the LORD your God. **27**You grumbled[n]
in your tents and said, "The LORD hates
us; so he brought us out of Egypt to
deliver us into the hands of the Amorites to destroy us. **28**Where can we go?
Our brothers have made us lose heart.
They say, 'The people are stronger and
taller[o] than we are; the cities are
large, with walls up to the sky. We
even saw the Anakites[p] there.' "
29Then I said to you, "Do not be terrified; do not be afraid[q] of them.[r]
30The LORD your God, who is going before you, will fight[s] for you, as he did
for you in Egypt, before your very eyes,
31and in the desert. There you saw how
the LORD your God carried[t] you, as a
father carries his son, all the way you
went until you reached this place."[u]
32In spite of this,[v] you did not
trust[w] in the LORD your God, **33**who
went ahead of you on your journey, in
fire by night and in a cloud by day,[x] to
search[y] out places for you to camp
and to show you the way you should go.
34When the LORD heard[z] what you
said, he was angry[a] and solemnly
swore:[b] **35**"Not a man of this evil generation shall see the good land[c] I
swore to give your forefathers, **36**except Caleb[d] son of Jephunneh. He will
see it, and I will give him and his
descendants the land he set his feet on,
because he followed the LORD wholeheartedly.[e]"
37Because of you the LORD became
angry[f] with me also and said, "You
shall not enter[g] it, either. **38**But your
assistant, Joshua[h] son of Nun, will enter it. Encourage[i] him, because he
will lead[j] Israel to inherit[k] it. **39**And
the little ones that you said would be
taken captive,[l] your children who do
not yet know[m] good from bad—they
will enter the land. I will give it to them
and they will take possession of it.
40But as for you, turn around and set
out toward the desert along the route
to the Red Sea.[a][n]"
41Then you replied, "We have sinned
against the LORD. We will go up and
fight, as the LORD our God commanded
us." So every one of you put on his
weapons, thinking it easy to go up into
the hill country.
42But the LORD said to me, "Tell
them, 'Do not go up and fight, because
I will not be with you. You will be defeated by your enemies.' "[o]
43So I told you, but you would not
listen. You rebelled against the LORD's
command and in your arrogance you
marched up into the hill country. **44**The
Amorites who lived in those hills came
out against you; they chased you like
a swarm of bees[p] and beat you down
from Seir[q] all the way to Hormah.[r]
45You came back and wept before the
LORD,[s] but he paid no attention[t] to
your weeping and turned a deaf ear[u]
to you. **46**And so you stayed in Kadesh[v] many days—all the time you
spent there.

Wanderings in the Desert

2 Then we turned back and set out
toward the desert along the route
to the Red Sea,[a][w] as the LORD had directed me. For a long time we made our
way around the hill country of Seir.[x]
2Then the LORD said to me, **3**"You
have made your way around this hill
country long enough;[y] now turn
north. **4**Give the people these orders:[z]
'You are about to pass through the territory of your brothers the descendants
of Esau,[a] who live in Seir.[b] They will
be afraid[c] of you, but be very careful.

[a] *40,1* Hebrew *Yam Suph*; that is, Sea of Reeds

1:26 [l] Nu 14:1-4 [m] S Nu 14:9
1:27 [n] Dt 9:28; Ps 106:25
1:28 [o] S Nu 13:32 [p] S Nu 13:33; Dt 9:1-3
1:29 [q] Dt 3:22; 20:3; Ne 4:14 [r] Dt 7:18; 20:1; 31:6
1:30 [s] S Ex 14:14
1:31 [t] Ex 19:4; Dt 32:10-12; Ps 28:9; Isa 46:3-4; 63:9; Hos 11:3; Ac 13:18 [u] Jer 31:32
1:32 [v] S Nu 14:11 [w] Dt 9:23; Ps 78:22; 106:24; Zep 3:2; Heb 3:19; Jude 1:5
1:33 [x] Ex 13:21; Nu 9:15-23; Ne 9:12; Ps 78:14 [y] S Nu 10:33
1:34 [z] S Nu 11:1 [a] S Nu 32:14 [b] S Nu 14:23, 28-30; Eze 20:15; Heb 3:11
1:35 [c] S Nu 14:29
1:36 [d] S Nu 13:6 [e] S Nu 14:24
1:37 [f] Ps 106:32 [g] S Nu 27:13
1:38 [h] S Nu 11:28 [i] Dt 31:7 [j] Dt 3:28 [k] Jos 11:23; Ps 78:55; 136:21
1:39 [l] S Nu 14:3 [m] Isa 7:15-16
1:40 [n] S Ex 14:27; Jdg 11:16
1:42 [o] S Nu 14:41-43
1:44 [p] Ps 118:12 [q] S Nu 24:18 [r] S Nu 14:45
1:45 [s] S Nu 14:1 [t] Job 27:9; 35:13; Ps 18:41; 66:18; Pr 1:28; Isa 1:15; Jer 14:12; La 3:8; Mic 3:4; S Jn 9:31 [u] Ps 28:1; 39:12; Pr 28:9
1:46 [v] S Nu 20:1
2:1 [w] S Ex 14:27; S Nu 21:4 [x] S Nu 24:18
2:3 [y] Dt 1:6
2:4 [z] Nu 20:14-21 [a] Ge 36:8 [b] ver 1 [c] Ex 15:16

1:26 REBELLED AGAINST THE COMMAND. The people of Israel should have entered the promised land thirty-nine years before (vv. 2–3), but because of their disobedience and their failure to do the will of God, their entrance was delayed (Nu 14:33–34). Failure to live in God's will and by his Spirit (Ro 8:12–15; Gal 5:16) can result in a delay in or even in a total loss of God's plan for our lives. We should have a holy fear of being out of the Lord's will and losing his presence, grace and protection in our lives (see article on THE WILL OF GOD, p. 1056).

1:35 NOT A MAN . . . SHALL SEE THE GOOD LAND. All Israelites who were unwilling to enter the promised land (see previous note) were thereafter denied entrance in that land. Disobedience can often be tragic because it may result in an irreversibly lost opportunity as well as in divine judgment.

1:36 FOLLOWED THE LORD WHOLEHEARTEDLY. Notice God's blessings reserved for those who follow the Lord "wholeheartedly." God "will fight for you" (v. 30), carry you "as a father carries his son" (v. 31), go "ahead of you" and "show you the way you should go" (v. 33).

5Do not provoke them to war, for I will
not give you any of their land, not even
enough to put your foot on. I have giv-
en Esau the hill country of Seir as his
own.[d] **6**You are to pay them in silver
for the food you eat and the water you
drink.' "
7The LORD your God has blessed you
in all the work of your hands. He has
watched[e] over your journey through
this vast desert.[f] These forty years[g]
the LORD your God has been with you,
and you have not lacked anything.[h]
8So we went on past our brothers
the descendants of Esau, who live in
Seir. We turned from[i] the Arabah[j]
road, which comes up from Elath and
Ezion Geber,[k] and traveled along the
desert road of Moab.[l]
9Then the LORD said to me, "Do not
harass the Moabites or provoke them
to war, for I will not give you any part
of their land. I have given Ar[m] to the
descendants of Lot[n] as a possession."
10(The Emites[o] used to live there—
a people strong and numerous, and as
tall as the Anakites.[p] **11**Like the Anakites, they too were considered Rephaites,[q] but the Moabites called them
Emites. **12**Horites[r] used to live in
Seir, but the descendants of Esau
drove them out. They destroyed the
Horites from before them and settled in
their place, just as Israel did[s] in the
land the LORD gave them as their possession.)
13And the LORD said, "Now get up
and cross the Zered Valley.[t]" So we
crossed the valley.
14Thirty-eight years[u] passed from
the time we left Kadesh Barnea[v] until
we crossed the Zered Valley. By then,
that entire generation[w] of fighting
men had perished from the camp, as
the LORD had sworn to them.[x] **15**The
LORD's hand was against them until he
had completely eliminated[y] them
from the camp.
16Now when the last of these fighting men among the people had died,
17the LORD said to me, **18**"Today you
are to pass by the region of Moab at
Ar.[z] **19**When you come to the Ammonites,[a] do not harass them or provoke
them to war,[b] for I will not give you
possession of any land belonging to the
Ammonites. I have given it as a possession to the descendants of Lot.[c]"
20(That too was considered a land of
the Rephaites,[d] who used to live
there; but the Ammonites called them
Zamzummites. **21**They were a people
strong and numerous, and as tall as
the Anakites.[e] The LORD destroyed
them from before the Ammonites, who
drove them out and settled in their
place. **22**The LORD had done the same
for the descendants of Esau, who lived
in Seir,[f] when he destroyed the Horites from before them. They drove
them out and have lived in their place
to this day. **23**And as for the Avvites[g]
who lived in villages as far as Gaza,[h]
the Caphtorites[i] coming out from
Caphtor[b][j] destroyed them and settled in their place.)

Defeat of Sihon King of Heshbon

24"Set out now and cross the Arnon
Gorge.[k] See, I have given into your
hand Sihon the Amorite,[l] king of
Heshbon, and his country. Begin to
take possession of it and engage[m] him
in battle. **25**This very day I will begin
to put the terror[n] and fear[o] of you on
all the nations under heaven. They will
hear reports of you and will tremble[p]
and be in anguish because of you."
26From the desert of Kedemoth[q] I
sent messengers to Sihon[r] king of
Heshbon offering peace[s] and saying,
27"Let us pass through your country.
We will stay on the main road; we will
not turn aside to the right or to the
left.[t] **28**Sell us food to eat[u] and water
to drink for their price in silver. Only
let us pass through on foot[v]— **29**as
the descendants of Esau, who live in
Seir, and the Moabites, who live in Ar,
did for us—until we cross the Jordan
into the land the LORD our God is giving
us." **30**But Sihon king of Heshbon refused to let us pass through. For the

2:5 [d] Jos 24:4 **2:7** [e] Dt 8:2-4 [f] S Ex 13:21; S Dt 1:19 [g] ver 14; S Nu 14:33; 32:13; Jos 5:6 [h] Ne 9:21; Am 2:10 **2:8** [i] S Nu 20:21 [j] S Dt 1:1 [k] Nu 33:35; 1Ki 9:26 [l] S Nu 21:4 **2:9** [m] S Nu 21:15 [n] Ge 19:38; Ps 83:8 **2:10** [o] Ge 14:5 [p] S Nu 13:22,33 **2:11** [q] S Ge 14:5 **2:12** [r] S Ge 14:6 [s] Nu 21:25,35 **2:13** [t] S Nu 21:12 **2:14** [u] S ver 7 [v] S Dt 1:2 [w] Nu 14:29-35 [x] Dt 1:34-35; Jos 5:6 **2:15** [y] Ps 106:26; Jude 1:5 **2:18** [z] S Nu 21:15 **2:19** [a] S Ge 19:38 [b] 2Ch 20:10 [c] S ver 9 **2:20** [d] S Ge 14:5 **2:21** [e] ver 10 **2:22** [f] S Ge 14:6 **2:23** [g] Jos 13:3; 18:23; 2Ki 17:31 [h] S Ge 10:19 [i] S Ge 10:14 [j] Jer 47:4; Am 9:7 **2:24** [k] Nu 21:13-14; Jdg 11:13,18 [l] S Dt 1:7 [m] Dt 3:6 **2:25** [n] S Ge 35:5; Dt 11:25 [o] Jos 2:9, 11; 1Ch 14:17; 2Ch 14:14; 17:10; 20:29; Isa 2:19; 13:13; 19:16 [p] Ex 15:14-16 **2:26** [q] Jos 13:18; 1Ch 6:79 [r] Dt 1:4; Jdg 11:21-22 [s] Dt 20:10; Jdg 21:13; 2Sa 20:19 **2:27** [t] Nu 21:21-22 **2:28** [u] Dt 23:4 [v] S Nu 20:19

[b] *23* That is, Crete

2:7 GOD HAS BEEN WITH YOU. Although the Israelites had to pay for their sins of rebellion and unbelief (v. 15; 1:26–40), God continued, in a measure, to be with them because they confessed their sin (1:45–46). God will continue to bless and guide those who repent, in spite of their failure and their temporary departure from a life of holiness according to God's law.

2:30 THE LORD ... MADE HIS SPIRIT STUBBORN. God does not harden anyone's heart arbitrarily (Heb 3:7–13). He hardened Sihon's heart because Sihon had already set his heart against Israel and against Israel's God (see Ex 7:3, note).

LORD[w] your God had made his spirit
stubborn[x] and his heart obstinate[y] in
order to give him into your hands,[z] as
he has now done.
31The LORD said to me, "See, I have
begun to deliver Sihon and his country
over to you. Now begin to conquer and
possess his land."[a]
32When Sihon and all his army came
out to meet us in battle[b] at Jahaz,
33the LORD our God delivered[c] him
over to us and we struck him down,[d]
together with his sons and his whole
army. 34At that time we took all his
towns and completely destroyed[c][e]
them—men, women and children. We
left no survivors. 35But the livestock[f]
and the plunder[g] from the towns we
had captured we carried off for ourselves. 36From Aroer[h] on the rim of
the Arnon Gorge, and from the town in
the gorge, even as far as Gilead,[i] not
one town was too strong for us. The
LORD our God gave[j] us all of them.
37But in accordance with the command
of the LORD our God,[k] you did not encroach on any of the land of the Ammonites,[l] neither the land along the
course of the Jabbok[m] nor that around
the towns in the hills.

Defeat of Og King of Bashan

3 Next we turned and went up along
the road toward Bashan, and Og
king of Bashan[n] with his whole army
marched out to meet us in battle at Edrei.[o] 2The LORD said to me, "Do not be
afraid[p] of him, for I have handed him
over to you with his whole army and his
land. Do to him what you did to Sihon
king of the Amorites, who reigned in
Heshbon."
3So the LORD our God also gave into
our hands Og king of Bashan and all
his army. We struck them down,[q]
leaving no survivors.[r] 4At that time
we took all his cities.[s] There was not
one of the sixty cities that we did not
take from them—the whole region of
Argob, Og's kingdom[t] in Bashan.[u]
5All these cities were fortified with
high walls and with gates and bars,
and there were also a great many unwalled villages. 6We completely destroyed[c] them, as we had done with
Sihon king of Heshbon, destroying[c][v]
every city—men, women and children.
7But all the livestock[w] and the plunder from their cities we carried off for
ourselves.
8So at that time we took from these
two kings of the Amorites[x] the territory east of the Jordan, from the Arnon
Gorge as far as Mount Hermon.[y]
9(Hermon is called Sirion[z] by the Sidonians; the Amorites call it Senir.)[a]
10We took all the towns on the plateau,
and all Gilead, and all Bashan as far as
Salecah[b] and Edrei, towns of Og's
kingdom in Bashan. 11(Only Og king of
Bashan was left of the remnant of the
Rephaites.[c] His bed[d] was made of
iron and was more than thirteen feet
long and six feet wide.[e] It is still in
Rabbah[d] of the Ammonites.)

Division of the Land

12Of the land that we took over at
that time, I gave the Reubenites and
the Gadites the territory north of Aroer[e] by the Arnon Gorge, including half
the hill country of Gilead, together
with its towns. 13The rest of Gilead and
also all of Bashan, the kingdom of Og,
I gave to the half tribe of Manasseh.[f]
(The whole region of Argob in Bashan
used to be known as a land of the
Rephaites.[g] 14Jair,[h] a descendant of
Manasseh, took the whole region of Argob as far as the border of the Geshurites and the Maacathites;[i] it was
named[j] after him, so that to this day
Bashan is called Havvoth Jair.[f])
15And I gave Gilead to Makir.[k] 16But
to the Reubenites and the Gadites I
gave the territory extending from Gilead down to the Arnon Gorge (the middle of the gorge being the border) and
out to the Jabbok River,[l] which is the
border of the Ammonites. 17Its western border was the Jordan in the Arabah,[m] from Kinnereth[n] to the Sea of
the Arabah[o] (the Salt Sea[g][p]), below
the slopes of Pisgah.
18I commanded you at that time:
"The LORD your God has given[q] you
this land to take possession of it. But
all your able-bodied men, armed for
battle, must cross over ahead of your
brother Israelites.[r] 19However, your
wives,[s] your children and your livestock[t] (I know you have much live-

2:30 [w] Jdg 14:4; 1Ki 12:15 [x] S Ex 4:21; Ro 9:18 [y] S Ex 14:17 [z] La 3:65
2:31 [a] S Ge 12:7
2:32 [b] S Nu 21:23
2:33 [c] Ex 23:31; Dt 7:2; 31:5 [d] S Nu 21:24
2:34 [e] S Nu 21:2; Dt 3:6; 7:2; Ps 106:34
2:35 [f] Dt 3:7 [g] S Ge 34:29; S 49:27
2:36 [h] S Nu 32:34 [i] S Nu 32:39 [j] Ps 44:3
2:37 [k] ver 18-19 [l] S Nu 21:24 [m] S Ge 32:22
3:1 [n] S Nu 32:19 [o] S Nu 21:33
3:2 [p] Jos 10:8; 2Ki 19:6; Isa 7:4
3:3 [q] S Nu 21:24 [r] Nu 21:35
3:4 [s] S Nu 21:24 [t] ver 13 [u] S Nu 21:33
3:6 [v] Dt 2:24
3:7 [w] Dt 2:35
3:8 [x] Nu 32:33; Jos 13:8-12 [y] Dt 4:48; Jos 11:3, 17; 12:1; 13:5; Jdg 3:3; 1Ch 5:23; Ps 42:6; 89:12; 133:3; SS 4:8
3:9 [z] Ps 29:6 [a] 1Ch 5:23; SS 4:8; Eze 27:5
3:10 [b] Jos 12:5; 1Ch 5:11
3:11 [c] Ge 14:5 [d] Jos 13:25; 15:60; 2Sa 11:1; 12:26; 17:27; 1Ch 20:1; Jer 49:2; Eze 21:20; 25:5; Am 1:14
3:12 [e] Dt 2:36
3:13 [f] Dt 29:8 [g] S Ge 14:5
3:14 [h] S Nu 32:41 [i] Jos 12:5; 13:11, 13; 2Sa 10:6; 23:34; 2Ki 25:23; 1Ch 4:19; Jer 40:8 [j] Jos 19:47; Ps 49:11
3:15 [k] S Ge 50:23; Nu 32:39-40
3:16 [l] S Nu 21:24
3:17 [m] 2Sa 2:29; 4:7; Eze 47:8 [n] S Nu 34:11 [o] S Dt 1:1 [p] S Ge 14:3
3:18 [q] Jos 1:13 [r] S Nu 32:17
3:19 [s] Jos 1:14 [t] S Nu 32:16

[c] *34,6* The Hebrew term refers to the irrevocable giving over of things or persons to the LORD, often by totally destroying them. [d] *11* Or *sarcophagus* [e] *11* Hebrew *nine cubits long and four cubits wide* (about 4 meters long and 1.8 meters wide) [f] *14* Or *called the settlements of Jair* [g] *17* That is, the Dead Sea

stock) may stay in the towns I have
given you, 20until the LORD gives rest to
your brothers as he has to you, and
they too have taken over the land that
the LORD your God is giving them,
across the Jordan. After that, each of
you may go back to the possession I
have given you."

Moses Forbidden to Cross the Jordan

21At that time I commanded Joshua:
"You have seen with your own eyes all
that the LORD your God has done to
these two kings. The LORD will do the
same to all the kingdoms over there
where you are going. 22Do not be
afraid[u] of them;[v] the LORD your God
himself will fight[w] for you."
23At that time I pleaded[x] with the
LORD: 24"O Sovereign LORD, you have
begun to show to your servant your
greatness[y] and your strong hand. For
what god[z] is there in heaven or on
earth who can do the deeds and mighty
works[a] you do?[b] 25Let me go over
and see the good land[c] beyond the Jordan—that fine hill country and Lebanon.[d]"
26But because of you the LORD was
angry[e] with me and would not listen
to me. "That is enough," the LORD said.
"Do not speak to me anymore about
this matter. 27Go up to the top of Pisgah[f] and look west and north and
south and east.[g] Look at the land with
your own eyes, since you are not going
to cross[h] this Jordan.[i] 28But commission[j] Joshua, and encourage[k]
and strengthen him, for he will lead
this people across[l] and will cause
them to inherit the land that you will
see." 29So we stayed in the valley near
Beth Peor.[m]

Obedience Commanded

4 Hear now, O Israel, the decrees[n]
and laws I am about to teach[o]
you. Follow them so that you may
live[p] and may go in and take possession of the land that the LORD, the God
of your fathers, is giving you. 2Do not
add[q] to what I command you and do
not subtract[r] from it, but keep[s] the
commands[t] of the LORD your God that
I give you.
3You saw with your own eyes what
the LORD did at Baal Peor.[u] The LORD
your God destroyed from among you
everyone who followed the Baal of
Peor, 4but all of you who held fast to
the LORD your God are still alive today.
5See, I have taught[v] you decrees
and laws[w] as the LORD my God commanded[x] me, so that you may follow
them in the land you are entering[y] to
take possession of it. 6Observe[z] them
carefully, for this will show your wis-

3:22 [u]S Dt 1:29 [v]Dt 7:18; 20:1; 31:6; 2Ch 32:8; Ps 23:4; Isa 41:10 [w]S Ex 14:14 **3:23** [x]Dt 1:37; 31:2; 32:52; 34:4 **3:24** [y]Dt 5:24; 11:2; 32:3 [z]S Ex 8:10 [a]Ps 71:16; 106:2; 145:12; 150:2 [b]2Sa 7:22 **3:25** [c]Dt 4:22 [d]Dt 1:7; Jos 1:4; 9:1; 11:17; 12:7; 13:5; Jdg 3:3; 9:15; 1Ki 4:33 **3:26** [e]ver 27; Dt 1:37; 31:2 **3:27** [f]S Nu 21:20 [g]S Ge 13:14 [h]S ver 26; S Nu 20:12; Dt 32:52 [i]S Nu 27:12 **3:28** [j]Nu 27:18-23 [k]Dt 31:7 [l]Dt 1:38; 31:3,23 **3:29** [m]S Nu 23:28; Dt 4:46; 34:6; Jos 13:20 **4:1** [n]S Lev 18:4 [o]Dt 1:3 [p]S Lev 18:5; Dt 30:15-20; S Ro 10:5 **4:2** [q]Dt 12:32; Jos 1:7; Pr 30:6; Rev 22:18-19 [r]Jer 26:2 [s]S Lev 22:31 [t]Dt 10:12-13; Ecc 12:13 **4:3** [u]Nu 25:1-9; Ps 106:28 **4:5** [v]Ps 71:17; 119:102; Jer 32:33 [w]S Ex 18:20 [x]S Lev 27:34 [y]Ezr 9:11 **4:6** [z]Dt 29:9; 1Ki 2:3

3:22 THE LORD ... WILL FIGHT FOR YOU. The Israelites faced powerful enemies whom they could not defeat in their own strength. Israel's natural tendency was to fear the awful consequences of defeat. Only by looking to God could they gain victory (see vv. 2–3; 1:30; 2:24–25,31,33,36; 20:4). When committed believers face seemingly insurmountable difficulties and overwhelming opposition, God promises to be with them and to give them strength to accomplish his will for them (see Mt 6:30, note; Php 4:6–7, notes).

3:25 LET ME GO OVER. Moses had seriously disobeyed God and was told he would not be allowed to enter Canaan (Nu 20:8–12). Yet he pleaded with God to change his mind and allow him to cross the Jordan River and enter the promised land. God refused (v. 26) in order to teach that sin by a spiritual leader has grave consequences and will incur a stricter judgment (cf. Jas 3:1); spiritual leaders of God's people can disqualify themselves from certain areas of ministry if they seriously fail to be examples of obedience (cf. Nu 20:12; see 20:8,12, notes).

4:1 FOLLOW THEM SO THAT YOU MAY LIVE. Life, blessing and the possession of Canaan were dependent on Israel's relationship to God (vv. 1,6,15–26,40). God's promises are linked, for every succeeding generation, with holding fast to the Lord (v. 4), revering him (v. 10), teaching our children the ways of the Lord (vv. 9–10), and seeking him with all our heart and all our soul (v. 29) in true faith and love (5:29; 6:5; see Jn 14:21, note; Ro 1:5, note; Gal 5:6, note; cf. Hab 2:4; Am 5:4).

4:2 DO NOT ADD ... DO NOT SUBTRACT. Anything that contradicts, modifies or changes Scripture must be rejected by those who follow God. His Word, the Bible itself, is our highest authority and the ultimate guide to truth (12:32; Pr 30:6; Gal 3:15; Rev 22:18–19; see article on THE INSPIRATION AND AUTHORITY OF SCRIPTURE, p. 1898).

4:6 OBSERVE THEM CAREFULLY. See Mt 5:17, note on OT law and the Christian.

4:6 THE NATIONS. One important reason that Israel had for remaining faithful to God's law was to draw other nations to the Lord by demonstrating the wisdom and benefits of following his ways (vv. 5–8). Like Israel, NT believers are a chosen people, a royal priesthood, a holy nation and a people belonging to God—whom God calls to proclaim his praises and lordship (1Pe 2:9; Rev 1:6; 5:10).

dom[a] and understanding to the nations, who will hear about all these decrees and say, "Surely this great nation
is a wise and understanding people."[b]
7What other nation is so great[c] as to
have their gods near[d] them the way
the LORD our God is near us whenever
we pray to him? 8And what other nation is so great as to have such righteous decrees and laws[e] as this body
of laws I am setting before you today?
9Only be careful,[f] and watch yourselves closely so that you do not forget
the things your eyes have seen or let
them slip from your heart as long as
you live. Teach[g] them to your children[h] and to their children after them.
10Remember the day you stood before
the LORD your God at Horeb,[i] when he
said to me, "Assemble the people before me to hear my words so that they
may learn[j] to revere[k] me as long as
they live in the land[l] and may teach[m]
them to their children." 11You came
near and stood at the foot of the mountain[n] while it blazed with fire[o] to the
very heavens, with black clouds and
deep darkness.[p] 12Then the LORD
spoke[q] to you out of the fire. You
heard the sound of words but saw no
form;[r] there was only a voice.[s] 13He
declared to you his covenant,[t] the
Ten Commandments,[u] which he commanded you to follow and then wrote
them on two stone tablets. 14And the
LORD directed me at that time to teach
you the decrees and laws[v] you are to
follow in the land that you are crossing
the Jordan to possess.

Idolatry Forbidden

15You saw no form[w] of any kind the
day the LORD spoke to you at Horeb[x]
out of the fire. Therefore watch your-

4:6 [a]Dt 30:19-20; 32:46-47; Ps 19:7; 119:98; Pr 1:7; 2Ti 3:15 [b]Job 1:1; 28:28; Ps 111:10; Pr 2:5; 3:7; 9:10; Ecc 12:13; Eze 5:5
4:7 [c]ver 32-34; 2Sa 7:23 [d]S Nu 23:21; S Ps 46:1; Ac 17:27
4:8 [e]Ps 89:14; 97:2; 119:7,62, 144,160,172; Ro 3:2
4:9 [f]S Ex 23:13 [g]S Ge 14:14; 18:19; Dt 6:20-25; Eph 6:4 [h]S Ex 10:2
4:10 [i]S Ex 3:1 [j]Dt 14:23; 17:19; 31:12-13; Ps 2:11; 111:10; 147:11; Isa 8:13; Jer 32:40 [k]S Ex 20:20 [l]Dt 12:1 [m]ver 9
4:11 [n]S Ex 3:1; S 19:17 [o]S Ex 19:18 [p]S Ex 19:9; Ps 18:11; 97:2
4:12 [q]Ex 20:22; Dt 5:4,22; S Mt 3:17; Heb 12:19 [r]Jn 5:37 [s]S Ex 19:9
4:13 [t]Dt 9:9; Ro 9:4 [u]S Ex 24:12
4:14 [v]S Ex 21:1
4:15 [w]Isa 40:18; 41:22-24 [x]S Ex 3:1
[y]Jos 23:11; Mal 2:15
4:16 [z]S Ge 6:11-12; Dt 9:12; 31:29; 32:5; Jdg 2:19 [a]Ex 20:4-5; Ro 1:23
4:17 [b]Ro 1:23
4:19 [c]Dt 17:3; 2Ki 23:11; Job 31:26; Jer 8:2; 43:13; Eze 8:16 [d]S Ge 1:16 [e]S Ge 2:1; S 37:9; Ro 1:25 [f]Dt 13:5 [g]S Nu 25:3
4:20 [h]S Ex 1:13 [i]S Ex 3:10 [j]S Ge 17:7; S Ex 8:22; S 34:9;

selves very carefully,[y] 16so that you
do not become corrupt[z] and make for
yourselves an idol,[a] an image of any
shape, whether formed like a man or a
woman, 17or like any animal on earth
or any bird that flies in the air,[b] 18or
like any creature that moves along the
ground or any fish in the waters below.
19And when you look up to the sky and
see the sun,[c] the moon and the
stars[d]—all the heavenly array[e]—do
not be enticed[f] into bowing down to
them and worshiping[g] things the LORD
your God has apportioned to all the nations under heaven. 20But as for you,
the LORD took you and brought you out
of the iron-smelting furnace,[h] out of
Egypt,[i] to be the people of his inheritance,[j] as you now are.
21The LORD was angry with me[k] because of you, and he solemnly swore
that I would not cross the Jordan and
enter the good land the LORD your God
is giving you as your inheritance. 22I
will die in this land;[l] I will not cross
the Jordan; but you are about to cross
over and take possession of that good
land.[m] 23Be careful not to forget the
covenant[n] of the LORD your God that
he made with you; do not make for
yourselves an idol[o] in the form of anything the LORD your God has forbidden.
24For the LORD your God is a consuming fire,[p] a jealous God.[q]
25After you have had children and
grandchildren and have lived in the
land a long time—if you then become
corrupt[r] and make any kind of idol,[s]
doing evil[t] in the eyes of the LORD your
God and provoking him to anger, 26I

Tit 2:14 4:21 [k]Nu 20:12; Dt 1:37 4:22 [l]Nu 27:13-14 [m]Dt 3:25 4:23 [n]ver 9 [o]S Ex 20:4 4:24 [p]S Ex 15:7; S 19:18; Heb 12:29 [q]S Ex 20:5 4:25 [r]ver 16 [s]ver 23 [t]1Ki 11:6; 15:26; 16:25,30; 2Ki 17:2,17; 21:2

4:9 THAT YOU DO NOT FORGET . . . TEACH THEM TO YOUR CHILDREN. We must diligently remember God's past work in our lives and remain in his word so that love for God and spiritual realities does not diminish from our hearts. Negligence in this area can result in tragic spiritual ruin for our children and grandchildren. A diligent and persevering adherence to God and his laws is necessary in order to pass on a spiritual inheritance to our children.

4:9 TO YOUR CHILDREN AND TO THEIR CHILDREN. See 6:7, note.

4:10 LEARN TO REVERE ME. See article on THE FEAR OF THE LORD, p. 260.

4:16 IDOL, AN IMAGE OF ANY SHAPE. See Ex 20:4, note.

4:24 A CONSUMING FIRE. This descriptive phrase refers to God's holy jealousy, anger and judgment against those who depart from his word and righteous ways into some form of idolatry (v. 23; Heb 12:25,29; cf. Eze 1:13–14,27–28; Da 7:9–10; Rev 1:14–15; 19:11–12).

4:24 JEALOUS GOD. God is a "jealous God" in that he will not tolerate unfaithfulness (i.e., the worship of other gods) on the part of his people (v. 23). This type of jealousy is holy and righteous. Likewise, in the marriage union, there should be a holy jealousy that guards the affection and love of one spouse for the other. Marriage partners must expect exclusive love and loyalty, demanding that each remain completely faithful and true in the marriage relationship.

call heaven and earth as witnesses[u]
against you[v] this day that you will
quickly perish[w] from the land that you
are crossing the Jordan to possess. You
will not live there long but will certainly be destroyed. **27**The LORD will scatter[x] you among the peoples, and only
a few of you will survive[y] among the
nations to which the LORD will drive
you. **28**There you will worship man-
made gods[z] of wood and stone,[a]
which cannot see or hear or eat or
smell.[b] **29**But if from there you seek[c]
the LORD your God, you will find him if
you look for him with all your heart[d]
and with all your soul.[e] **30**When you
are in distress[f] and all these things
have happened to you, then in later
days[g] you will return[h] to the LORD
your God and obey him. **31**For the LORD
your God is a merciful[i] God; he will
not abandon[j] or destroy[k] you or forget[l] the covenant with your forefathers, which he confirmed to them by
oath.

The LORD Is God

32Ask[m] now about the former days,
long before your time, from the day
God created man on the earth;[n] ask
from one end of the heavens to the other.[o] Has anything so great[p] as this
ever happened, or has anything like it
ever been heard of? **33**Has any other
people heard the voice of God[h] speaking out of fire, as you have, and
lived?[q] **34**Has any god ever tried to
take for himself one nation out of another nation,[r] by testings,[s] by miraculous signs[t] and wonders,[u] by war,
by a mighty hand and an outstretched
arm,[v] or by great and awesome
deeds,[w] like all the things the LORD
your God did for you in Egypt before
your very eyes?

35You were shown these things so
that you might know that the LORD is
God; besides him there is no other.[x]
36From heaven he made you hear his
voice[y] to discipline[z] you. On earth he
showed you his great fire, and you
heard his words from out of the fire.
37Because he loved[a] your forefathers
and chose their descendants after
them, he brought you out of Egypt by
his Presence and his great strength,[b]
38to drive out before you nations greater and stronger than you and to bring
you into their land to give it to you for
your inheritance,[c] as it is today.

39Acknowledge[d] and take to heart
this day that the LORD is God in heaven
above and on the earth below. There is
no other.[e] **40**Keep[f] his decrees and
commands,[g] which I am giving you today, so that it may go well[h] with you
and your children after you and that
you may live long[i] in the land the
LORD your God gives you for all time.

Cities of Refuge

4:41–43Ref — Nu 35:6–34; Dt 19:1–14; Jos 20:1–9

41Then Moses set aside three cities
east of the Jordan, **42**to which anyone
who had killed a person could flee if he
had unintentionally[j] killed his neighbor without malice aforethought. He
could flee into one of these cities and
save his life. **43**The cities were these:
Bezer in the desert plateau, for the
Reubenites; Ramoth[k] in Gilead, for
the Gadites; and Golan in Bashan, for
the Manassites.

Introduction to the Law

44This is the law Moses set before
the Israelites. **45**These are the stipulations, decrees and laws Moses gave

4:26 [u] Ge 31:50; Pr 14:5 [v] Dt 30:18-19; 31:28; 32:1; Ps 50:4; Isa 1:2; 34:1; Jer 6:19; Mic 6:2 [w] Dt 6:15; 7:4 **4:27** [x] S Lev 26:33; Dt 28:36,64; 29:28; 1Ki 8:46; 2Ki 17:6; Ps 44:11; 106:27; Jer 3:8; Mic 1:16 [y] Isa 17:6; 21:17; Ob 1:5 **4:28** [z] Dt 13:2; 28:36,64; 1Sa 26:19; Jer 5:19; 16:13; Ac 19:26 [a] Dt 29:17 [b] Ps 115:4-8; 135:15-18; Isa 8:19; 26:14; 44:17-20; Rev 9:20 **4:29** [c] 1Sa 13:12; 2Ki 13:4; 2Ch 7:14; 15:4; 33:12; Ps 78:34; 119:58; Isa 45:19, 22; 55:6; Jer 26:19; Da 9:13; Hos 3:5; Am 5:4 [d] 1Sa 7:3; 1Ki 8:48; Jer 29:13 [e] Dt 6:5; 30:1-3,10 **4:30** [f] Lev 26:41; Dt 31:17,21; Ps 4:1; 18:6; 46:1; 59:16; 107:6 [g] Dt 31:29; Jer 23:20; Hos 3:5; Heb 1:2 [h] Dt 30:2; 1Ki 8:48; Ne 1:9; Jer 3:1,12,22; 4:1; 18:11; Joel 2:12 **4:31** [i] Ex 34:6; Ne 9:31; Ps 111:4 [j] Dt 31:6,8; Jos 1:5; 1Ki 8:57; 1Ch 28:9,20; Ps 9:10; 27:9; 71:9; Isa 42:16; Heb 13:5 [k] S Lev 26:44 [l] Lev 26:45 **4:32** [m] Dt 32:7 [n] S Ge 1:27; Isa 45:12 [o] Dt 28:64; 30:1; Jer 9:16; Mt 24:31 [p] ver 7; 2Sa 7:23 **4:33** [q] Ex 20:22; Dt 5:24-26 **4:34** [r] Ex 14:30 [s] Isa 7:12 [t] S Ex 4:17 [u] Dt 7:19; 26:8; 29:3; 1Ch 16:12; Ps 9:1; 40:5; Jer 32:20

[v] S Ex 3:20; Dt 5:15; 6:21; 15:15 [w] Ex 15:11; Dt 34:12; Ps 45:4; 65:5 **4:35** [x] ver 39; Ex 8:10; Dt 7:9; 32:4,12; 1Sa 2:2; 1Ki 8:60; 2Ki 19:19; Isa 43:10; Mk 12:32 **4:36** [y] S Ex 19:19; Heb 12:25 [z] Dt 8:5 **4:37** [a] Dt 7:8; 10:15; 23:5; 33:3; Ps 44:3; Jer 31:3; Hos 11:1; Mal 1:2; 2:11 [b] S Ex 3:20; S 33:14 **4:38** [c] Nu 34:14-15; Dt 7:1; 9:5 **4:39** [d] Ex 8:10 [e] S ver 35; Ex 15:11 **4:40** [f] S Lev 22:31 [g] ver 1; S Ge 26:5; Dt 5:29; 11:1; Ps 105:45; Isa 48:18 [h] Dt 5:16; 12:25; Isa 3:10 [i] S Ex 23:26; Eph 6:2-3 **4:42** [j] S Ex 21:13 **4:43** [k] Jos 21:38; 1Ki 22:3; 2Ki 8:28; 9:14

[h] 33 Or *of a god*

4:26 HEAVEN AND EARTH AS WITNESSES. Moses gives six predictions about Israel's history in the event that they became disobedient and unfaithful (vv. 25–31): (1) dispersion among the nations (vv. 26–27); (2) suffering in exile (vv. 27–28); (3) reconciliation with God for those who seek him with all their heart and soul (vv. 29–31); (4) distress (v. 30); (5) a return to God "in later days" (v. 30); and (6) restoration of the covenant with their forefathers (v. 31; see also Dt 29—30; Mt 23:39, note; Ro 11:1, note).

4:29 ALL YOUR HEART ... SOUL. To find God and know him in his fullness, a person must seek him with wholehearted devotion (cf. 6:5; 10:12; 11:13; 13:3; 26:16; 30:6,10; see Php 3:8–11, note). Knowing God and experiencing the power, blessing and righteousness of his kingdom do not come easily; that will happen only to those who earnestly seek God (Heb 11:6) and desire his nearness, the fullness of his Spirit and his gift of eternal life.

them when they came out of Egypt
46and were in the valley near Beth
Peor east of the Jordan, in the land of
Sihon[l] king of the Amorites, who
reigned in Heshbon and was defeated
by Moses and the Israelites as they
came out of Egypt. 47They took possession of his land and the land of Og
king of Bashan, the two Amorite kings
east of the Jordan. 48This land extended from Aroer[m] on the rim of the Arnon Gorge to Mount Siyon[i][n] (that is,
Hermon[o]), 49and included all the Arabah east of the Jordan, as far as the Sea
of the Arabah,[j] below the slopes of
Pisgah.

The Ten Commandments

5:6–21pp — Ex 20:1–17

5 Moses summoned all Israel and
said:
Hear, O Israel, the decrees and
laws[p] I declare in your hearing today.
Learn them and be sure to follow them.
2The LORD our God made a covenant[q]
with us at Horeb.[r] 3It was not with
our fathers that the LORD made this
covenant, but with us,[s] with all of us
who are alive here today.[t] 4The LORD
spoke[u] to you face to face[v] out of the
fire[w] on the mountain. 5(At that time
I stood between[x] the LORD and you to
declare to you the word of the LORD,
because you were afraid[y] of the fire
and did not go up the mountain.) And
he said:

6"I am the LORD your God, who
brought you out of Egypt,[z]
out of the land of slavery.[a]
7"You shall have no other gods before[k] me.
8"You shall not make for yourself
an idol in the form of anything in heaven above or on
the earth beneath or in the
waters below.[b] 9You shall
not bow down to them or
worship them; for I, the LORD
your God, am a jealous God,
punishing the children for
the sin of the fathers[c] to the
third and fourth generation
of those who hate me,[d]
10but showing love to a thousand[e] ⌞generations⌟ of those
who love me and keep my
commandments.[f]
11"You shall not misuse the name[g]
of the LORD your God, for the
LORD will not hold anyone
guiltless who misuses his
name.[h]
12"Observe the Sabbath day by
keeping it holy,[i] as the LORD
your God has commanded
you. 13Six days you shall labor and do all your work,
14but the seventh day[j] is a
Sabbath to the LORD your
God. On it you shall not do
any work, neither you, nor
your son or daughter, nor
your manservant or maidservant,[k] nor your ox, your
donkey or any of your animals, nor the alien within
your gates, so that your manservant and maidservant
may rest, as you do.[l] 15Re-
member that you were
slaves[m] in Egypt and that
the LORD your God brought
you out of there with a
mighty hand[n] and an outstretched arm.[o] Therefore
the LORD your God has commanded you to observe the
Sabbath day.
16"Honor your father[p] and your
mother,[q] as the LORD your
God has commanded you, so
that you may live long[r] and
that it may go well with you
in the land the LORD your God
is giving you.

4:46 [l]Nu 21:26 **4:48** [m]Dt 2:36 [n]Dt 3:9 [o]S Dt 3:8 **5:1** [p]S Ex 18:20 **5:2** [q]Ex 19:5; Jer 11:2; Heb 9:15; 10:15-17 [r]S Ge 17:9; S Ex 3:1 **5:3** [s]Dt 11:2-7 [t]Nu 26:63-65; Heb 8:9 **5:4** [u]S Dt 4:12 [v]S Nu 14:14 [w]S Ex 19:18 **5:5** [x]Gal 3:19 [y]S Ge 3:10; Heb 12:18-21 **5:6** [z]S Ex 13:3; S 29:46 [a]Lev 26:1; Dt 6:4; Ps 81:10 **5:8** [b]Lev 26:1; Dt 4:15-18; Ps 78:58; 97:7 **5:9** [c]S Nu 26:11 [d]Ex 34:7; S Nu 10:35; 14:18 **5:10** [e]S Ex 34:7 [f]Nu 14:18; Dt 7:9; Ne 1:5; Jer 32:18; Da 9:4 **5:11** [g]Ps 139:20 [h]Lev 19:12; Dt 10:20; Mt 5:33-37 **5:12** [i]Ex 16:23-30; 31:13-17; Mk 2:27-28 **5:14** [j]S Ge 2:2; Mt 12:2; Mk 2:27; Heb 4:4 [k]Job 31:13; Jer 34:9-11 [l]Jer 17:21,24 **5:15** [m]S Ge 15:13 [n]Ex 6:1; Ps 108:6; Jer 32:21 [o]S Dt 4:34 **5:16** [p]Mal 1:6 [q]Ex 21:17; Lev 19:3; Eze 22:7; Mt 15:4*; 19:19*; Mk 7:10*; 10:19*; Lk 18:20*; Eph 6:2-3* [r]S Dt 4:40; 11:9; Pr 3:1-2

i 48 Hebrew; Syriac (see also Deut. 3:9) *Sirion*
j 49 That is, the Dead Sea
k 7 Or *besides*

5:2 A COVENANT. Israel's salvation was a divine gift given according to God's covenant agreement that he would adopt the Israelites as his sons and daughters in order to care for them and bless them, that they might live long in the land God gave them (4:40); in grateful response Israel was to accept God as their Lord to be worshiped, loved, honored and obeyed in living faith. For a discussion of God's covenant with Israel, see articles on GOD'S COVENANT WITH ABRAHAM, ISAAC AND JACOB, p. 46, and GOD'S COVENANT WITH THE ISRAELITES, p. 290; for a discussion of the covenant that believers in Christ have committed themselves to, see Lk 22:20, note; see article on THE OLD COVENANT AND THE NEW COVENANT, p. 1926.

5:7–21 TEN COMMANDMENTS. This section repeats the Ten Commandments as recorded in Ex 20 (see notes on that chapter for comments; see article on THE OLD TESTAMENT LAW, p. 118).

17“You shall not murder.[s]
18“You shall not commit adultery.[t]
19“You shall not steal.[u]
20“You shall not give false testimony against your neighbor.[v]
21“You shall not covet your neighbor’s wife. You shall not set
your desire on your neighbor’s house or land, his manservant or maidservant, his
ox or donkey, or anything
that belongs to your neighbor.”[w]

22These are the commandments the
LORD proclaimed in a loud voice to your
whole assembly there on the mountain
from out of the fire, the cloud and the
deep darkness;[x] and he added nothing
more. Then he wrote them on two
stone tablets[y] and gave them to me.
23When you heard the voice out of
the darkness, while the mountain was
ablaze with fire, all the leading men of
your tribes and your elders[z] came to
me. 24And you said, “The LORD our God
has shown us[a] his glory and his majesty,[b] and we have heard his voice
from the fire. Today we have seen that
a man can live even if God speaks with
him.[c] 25But now, why should we die?
This great fire will consume us, and we
will die if we hear the voice of the LORD
our God any longer.[d] 26For what mortal man has ever heard the voice of the
living God speaking out of fire, as we
have, and survived?[e] 27Go near and
listen to all that the LORD our God
says.[f] Then tell us whatever the LORD
our God tells you. We will listen and
obey.”[g]
28The LORD heard you when you
spoke to me and the LORD said to me,
“I have heard what this people said to
you. Everything they said was good.[h]
29Oh, that their hearts would be inclined to fear me[i] and keep all my
commands[j] always, so that it might
go well with them and their children
forever![k]
30“Go, tell them to return to their
tents. 31But you stay here[l] with me so
that I may give you all the commands,
decrees and laws you are to teach them
to follow in the land I am giving them
to possess.”
32So be careful to do what the LORD
your God has commanded you;[m] do
not turn aside to the right or to the
left.[n] 33Walk in all the way that the
LORD your God has commanded you,[o]
so that you may live and prosper and
prolong your days[p] in the land that
you will possess.

Love the LORD Your God

6 These are the commands, decrees
and laws the LORD your God directed me to teach you to observe in the
land that you are crossing the Jordan
to possess, 2so that you, your children
and their children after them may
fear[q] the LORD your God as long as you
live[r] by keeping all his decrees and
commands[s] that I give you, and so
that you may enjoy long life.[t] 3Hear,
O Israel, and be careful to obey[u] so
that it may go well with you and that
you may increase greatly[v] in a land
flowing with milk and honey,[w] just as
the LORD, the God of your fathers,
promised[x] you.
4Hear, O Israel: The LORD our God,
the LORD is one.[1][y] 5Love[z] the LORD
your God with all your heart[a] and with

5:17 [s] Ge 9:6; Lev 24:17; Ecc 3:3; Jer 40:15; 41:3; Mt 5:21-22*; 19:19*; Mk 10:19*; Lk 18:20*; Ro 13:9*; Jas 2:11* **5:18** [t] Lev 20:10; Mt 5:27-30; 19:18*; Mk 10:19*; Lk 18:20*; Ro 13:9*; Jas 2:11* **5:19** [u] Lev 19:11; Mt 19:19*; Mk 10:19*; Lk 18:20*; Ro 13:9* **5:20** [v] S Ex 23:1; Mt 19:18*; Mk 10:19*; Lk 18:20* **5:21** [w] Ro 7:7*; 13:9* **5:22** [x] S Ex 20:21 [y] S Ex 24:12 **5:23** [z] S Ex 3:16 **5:24** [a] Dt 4:34; 8:5; 11:2; Isa 53:4 [b] S Dt 3:24 [c] Ex 19:19 **5:25** [d] Ex 20:18-19; Dt 18:16; Heb 12:19 **5:26** [e] S Ex 33:20; Dt 4:33; Jdg 6:22-23; 13:22; Isa 6:5 **5:27** [f] S Ex 19:8 [g] S Ex 24:7 **5:28** [h] Dt 18:17 **5:29** [i] Ps 81:8,13 [j] Jos 22:5; Ps 78:7 [k] ver 33; S Dt 4:1, 40; 12:25; 22:7 **5:31** [l] Ex 24:12 **5:32** [m] S Dt 4:29; 10:12 [n] Dt 17:11, 20; 28:14; Jos 1:7; 1Ki 15:5; 2Ki 22:2; Pr 4:27 **5:33** [o] Isa 3:10; Jer 7:23; 38:20; S Lk 1:6 [p] S ver 29 **6:2** [q] S Ex 20:20; S 1Sa 12:24 [r] Dt 4:9 [s] S Ge 26:5 [t] S Ex 20:12 **6:3** [u] S Ex 19:5 [v] Ge 15:5; Dt 5:33 [w] S Ex 3:8; Dt 32:13-14 [x] Ex 13:5 **6:4** [y] Dt 4:35,39; Ne 9:6; Ps 86:10; Isa 44:6; Zec 14:9; Mk 12:29*; Jn 10:30; 1Co 8:4; Eph 4:6; Jas 2:19 **6:5** [z] Dt 11:1,22; Mt 22:37*; Mk 12:30*; Lk 10:27* [a] 1Sa 12:24

[1] 4 Or *The LORD our God is one LORD*; or *The LORD is our God, the LORD is one*; or *The LORD is our God, the LORD alone*

5:29 OH, THAT THEIR HEARTS WOULD BE INCLINED TO FEAR ME. The Biblical history of salvation is nothing other than God’s tireless attempts to draw men and women away from their sin and its destructive consequences, and to himself.

6:4–9 HEAR, O ISRAEL. This passage is commonly referred to as “the Shema” (from Heb *shama‘*, “to hear”). It was familiar to the Jews in Jesus’ time, being recited daily by devout Jews and regularly in synagogue services. The Shema is the classic declaration of God’s monotheistic character (see next note); it is followed by a twofold injunction to the Israelites: (1) to love God with all their heart, soul and strength (vv. 5–6), and (2) to teach their faith diligently to their children (vv. 7–9).

6:4 THE LORD OUR GOD, THE LORD IS ONE. This verse—along with vv. 5–9; 11:13–21; Nu 15:37–41—teaches monotheism; this doctrine affirms that God is the one true God, not a pantheon of different gods, and is all-powerful among all the gods and spirits of the world (Ex 15:11). This God must be the sole object of Israel’s love and obedience (vv. 4–5). This aspect of “oneness” serves as the basis for prohibiting the worship of other gods (Ex 20:3). It does not contradict the NT revelation of God as a triune being who, though one in essence, is manifested as Father, Son and Holy Spirit (see Mt 3:17, note, and Mk 1:11, note, for comments on God’s triune nature).

THE FEAR OF THE LORD

***Dt 6:1–2** "These are the commands, the decrees and laws the LORD your God directed me to teach you to observe in the land that you are crossing the Jordan to possess, so that you, your children and their children after them may fear the LORD your God as long as you live by keeping all his decrees and commands that I give you, and so that you may enjoy long life."*

A frequent command given to God's people in the Old Testament is to "fear God" or "fear the LORD." It is important that we know what this command means for us as believers. Only as we truly fear the Lord will we be delivered from slavery to all abnormal and satanic fears.

THE MEANING OF THE FEAR OF THE LORD. The comprehensive command to "fear the LORD" includes a variety of different aspects of the believer's relationship with God. (1) Essential to fearing God is a recognition of his holiness, justice and righteousness as a counterpart to his love and mercy, i.e., knowing him and understanding fully who he is (cf. Pr 2:5). Such fear is based on the acknowledgment that God is a holy God, whose very nature causes him to judge sin.

(2) To fear the Lord is to regard him with holy awe and reverence and to honor God as God because of his great glory, holiness, majesty and power (see Php 2:12, note). For example, when the Israelites at Mount Sinai saw God manifest himself through "thunder and lightning, with a thick cloud over the mountain, and a very loud trumpet blast," they all "trembled" in fear (Ex 19:16) and begged Moses to speak to them rather than God himself (Ex 20:18–19; Dt 5:22–27). Also, the psalmist, in his reflections on God as Creator, states explicitly: "Let all the earth fear the LORD; let all the people of the world revere him. For he spoke, and it came to be; he commanded, and it stood firm" (Ps 33:8–9).

(3) True fear of the Lord causes believers to place their faith and trust in him alone for salvation. For example, after the Israelites crossed over the Red Sea on dry ground and saw the enormous destruction of the Egyptian army, they "feared the LORD and put their trust in him" (see Ex 14:31, note). Similarly, the psalmist calls on all who fear the Lord to "trust in the LORD—he is their help and shield" (Ps 115:11). In other words, the fear of the Lord produces in God's people a confident hope and trust in him. It is little wonder, then, that such people are saved (Ps 85:9) and receive his forgiving love and mercy (Lk 1:50; cf. Ps 103:11; 130:4).

(4) Finally, to fear God involves recognizing that he is a God who is angry about sin and has the power to punish those who break his righteous laws, both in time and in eternity (cf. Ps 76:7–8). When Adam and Eve sinned in the Garden of Eden, they were afraid and tried to hide from God's presence (Ge 3:8–10). Moses experienced this aspect of the fear of God when he spent forty days and nights in prayer on behalf of the sinful Israelites: "I feared the anger and wrath of the LORD, for he was angry enough with you to destroy you" (Dt 9:19). Similarly in the NT, immediately after acknowledging God's coming vengeance and judgment, the author of Hebrews wrote: "It is a dreadful thing to fall into the hands of the living God" (Heb 10:31).

REASONS FOR THE FEAR OF THE LORD. The reasons for fearing the Lord proceed from the meaning of the fear of the Lord. (1) We should fear him because of his great power as the Creator of all things and all people (Ps 33:6–9; 96:4–5; Jnh 1:9). (2) Furthermore, the awesome power that he continues to exercise over the elements of creation and over us is cause for fearing God (Ex 20:18–20; Ecc 3:14; Jnh 1:11–16; Mk 4:39–41). (3) When we realize the holiness of our God, i.e., his separation from and constant opposition to sin, the normal response of the human spirit is to fear him (Rev

15:4). (4) Anyone who sees the brightness of God's glory cannot help but become afraid (Mt 17:1–8). (5) The continual blessings we receive from God, especially the forgiveness of our sins (Ps 130:4), should lead us to fear and love him (1Sa 12:24; Ps 34:9; 67:7; Jer 5:24; see article on THE PROVIDENCE OF GOD, p. 78). (6) Beyond all doubt, the fact that God is a God of justice who will judge the entire human race generates the fear of him (Dt 17:12–13; Isa 59:18–19; Mal 3:5; Heb 10:26–31). It is a solemn and holy truth that God is constantly watching and evaluating our actions, both good and bad, and that we will be held accountable for those actions, both now and in the day of our personal judgment.

PERSONAL IMPLICATIONS ABOUT THE FEAR OF THE LORD. The fear of the Lord is far more than a mere Biblical doctrine; it directly applies to our daily lives in numerous ways. (1) First, if we truly fear the Lord, we will live a life of obedience to his commandments and speak a resounding "No" to sin. One reason why God inspired fear in the Israelites at Mount Sinai was so that they might learn to turn away from sin and obey his law (Ex 20:20). Repeatedly in Moses' final address to the Israelites, he related the fear of the Lord to serving and obeying him (e.g., Dt 5:29; 6:2,24; 8:6; 10:12; 13:4; 17:19; 31:12). According to the psalmists, fearing the Lord is equivalent to delighting in his commands (Ps 112:1) and following his precepts (Ps 119:63). Solomon taught that "through the fear of the LORD a man avoids evil" (Pr 16:6; cf. 8:13). In Ecclesiastes, the whole duty of the human race is summarized in two brief imperatives: "Fear God and keep his commandments" (Ecc 12:13). Conversely, anyone who is content to live a life of wickedness does so because "there is no fear of God before his eyes" (Ps 36:1–4).

(2) An important corollary to the previous implication is that believers must teach their children to fear the Lord by training them to hate sin and keep God's holy commands (Dt 4:10; 6:1–2,6–9). The Bible often states that "the fear of the LORD is the beginning of wisdom" (Ps 111:10; Pr 9:10; cf. Job 28:28; Pr 1:7). Since a basic goal for our children's education is for them to live according to God's principles of wisdom (Pr 1:1–6), teaching them to fear the Lord is a critical first step (see article on PARENTS AND CHILDREN, p. 1854).

(3) The fear of the Lord has a sanctifying effect on God's people. Just as there is a sanctifying effect in the truth of God's word (Jn 17:17), so there is a sanctifying effect in the fear of God. It moves us to hate sin and turn away from evil (Pr 3:7; 8:13; 16:6). It causes us to to be careful and restrained in our speech (Pr 10:19; Ecc 5:2,6–7). It protects us from the breakdown of our consciences and of our moral resolve. The fear of the Lord is pure and cleansing (Ps 19:9), holy and redeeming in its effect.

(4) The holy fear of the Lord motivates God's people to worship him with their whole being. If we truly fear God, we will worship and glorify him as Lord of all (Ps 22:23). David equates the worshiping congregation with "those who fear" him (Ps 22:25). Likewise, at the end of history when the heavenly angel who proclaims the eternal gospel calls all on earth to fear God, he immediately adds, "and give him glory . . . Worship him who made the heavens, and earth, the sea and the springs of water" (Rev 14:6–7).

(5) God has promised to reward all those who fear him. "Humility and the fear of the LORD bring wealth and honor and life" (Pr 22:4). Other promised rewards include protection from death (Pr 14:26–27), provisions for our daily needs (Ps 34:9; 111:5), and a long life (Pr 10:27). Those who fear the Lord know that "it will go better with God-fearing men," regardless of what happens in the world around them (Ecc 8:12–13).

(6) Finally, the fear of the Lord is accompanied by assurance and unspeakable spiritual comfort for God's people. The NT directly links the fear of the Lord with the encouragement of the Holy Spirit (Ac 9:31). On the one hand, those who live without fearing the Lord have no sense of his presence, grace and protection (see Dt 1:26, note); on the other hand, those who fear God and keep his commandments have a deep experience of spiritual security in their lives and of the anointing of the Holy Spirit. They can be sure that God will "deliver them from death" (Ps 33:18–19; see articles on DEATH, p. 732, and ASSURANCE OF SALVATION, p. 1982).

all your soul and with all your
strength.[b] 6These commandments
that I give you today are to be upon
your hearts.[c] 7Impress them on your
children. Talk about them when you sit
at home and when you walk along the
road, when you lie down and when you
get up.[d] 8Tie them as symbols on your
hands and bind them on your foreheads.[e] 9Write them on the doorframes of your houses and on your
gates.[f]
10When the LORD your God brings
you into the land he swore to your fathers, to Abraham, Isaac and Jacob, to
give you—a land with large, flourishing cities you did not build,[g] 11houses
filled with all kinds of good things you
did not provide, wells you did not dig,[h]
and vineyards and olive groves you did
not plant—then when you eat and are
satisfied,[i] 12be careful that you do not
forget[j] the LORD, who brought you out
of Egypt, out of the land of slavery.
13Fear the LORD[k] your God, serve
him only[l] and take your oaths[m] in his
name.[n] 14Do not follow other gods,
the gods of the peoples around you;
15for the LORD your God[o], who is
among you, is a jealous God and his
anger will burn against you, and he will
destroy you from the face of the land.
16Do not test the LORD your God[p] as
you did at Massah. 17Be sure to keep[q]
the commands of the LORD your God
and the stipulations and decrees he
has given you.[r] 18Do what is right and
good in the LORD's sight,[s] so that it
may go well[t] with you and you may go
in and take over the good land that the
LORD promised on oath to your forefathers, 19thrusting out all your enemies[u] before you, as the LORD said.
20In the future, when your son asks
you,[v] "What is the meaning of the
stipulations, decrees and laws the LORD
our God has commanded you?" 21tell
him: "We were slaves of Pharaoh in
Egypt, but the LORD brought us out of
Egypt with a mighty hand.[w] 22Before
our eyes the LORD sent miraculous
signs and wonders—great and terrible—upon Egypt and Pharaoh and his
whole household. 23But he brought us
out from there to bring us in and give
us the land that he promised on oath to
our forefathers. 24The LORD commanded us to obey all these decrees and to
fear the LORD our God,[x] so that we
might always prosper and be kept
alive, as is the case today.[y] 25And if
we are careful to obey all this law[z]
before the LORD our God, as he has
commanded us, that will be our righteousness.[a]"

Driving Out the Nations

7 When the LORD your God brings
you into the land you are entering
to possess[b] and drives out before you
many nations[c]—the Hittites,[d] Girga-

6:5 [b] Dt 4:29; 10:12; Jos 22:5
6:6 [c] ver 8; Dt 11:18; 30:14; 32:46; Ps 26:2; 37:31; 40:8; 119:11; Pr 3:3; Isa 51:7; Jer 17:1; 31:33; Eze 40:4
6:7 [d] Dt 4:9; 11:19; Pr 22:6; Eph 6:4
6:8 [e] S ver 6; S Ex 13:9; Mt 23:5
6:9 [f] Dt 11:20
6:10 [g] S Ge 11:4; Dt 12:29; 19:1; Jos 24:13; Ps 105:44
6:11 [h] Jer 2:13 [i] S Lev 26:5; Dt 8:10; 14:29; 31:20
6:12 [j] Dt 4:9,23; 2Ki 17:38; Ps 44:17; 78:7; 103:2
6:13 [k] Ps 33:8; 34:9 [l] Dt 13:4; 1Sa 7:3; Jer 44:10; Mt 4:10*; Lk 4:4*; 4:8* [m] 1Sa 20:3 [n] S Ex 20:7; S Mt 5:33
6:15 [o] Dt 4:24; 5:9
6:16 [p] S Ex 17:2; Mt 4:7*; Lk 4:12*
6:17 [q] S Lev 26:3 [r] Dt 11:22; Ps 119:4,56,100, 134,168
6:18 [s] 2Ki 18:6; Isa 36:7; 38:3 [t] Dt 4:40
6:19 [u] Ex 23:27; Jos 21:44; Ps 78:53; 107:2; 136:24
6:20 [v] S Ex 10:2
6:21 [w] S Dt 4:34
6:24 [x] Dt 10:12; 30:6; Ps 86:11; Jer 32:39 [y] Ps 27:12; 41:2; S Ro 10:5
6:25 [z] Ps 103:18; 119:34,55 [a] Dt 24:13; S Ro 9:31; Ro 10:3,5
7:1 [b] S Lev 14:34; S Dt 4:38 [c] Dt 20:16-18; 31:3 [d] Ge 15:20

6:5 LOVE THE LORD YOUR GOD. God seeks fellowship with his people and gives them this one indispensable command that will attach them to himself. (1) By responding to his love with love, gratitude and loyalty (4:37), they will come to know and enjoy him in a covenant relationship. (2) On this, the "first and greatest commandment," along with the second commandment to love one's neighbor (cf. Lev 19:18), hang all the Law and the Prophets (Mt 22:37–40). (3) True obedience to God and his commandments is possible only when it springs from faith in and love for God (cf. 7:9; 10:12; 11:1,13,22; 13:3; 19:9; 30:6,16,20; see Mt 22:39, note; Jn 14:15; 21:16; 1Jn 4:19).

6:6 THESE COMMANDMENTS ... UPON YOUR HEARTS. It is God's firm desire that his word be in the hearts of his people (cf. Ps 119:11; Jer 31:33; see article on THE HEART, p. 906). The apostle Paul states explicitly, "Let the word of Christ dwell in you richly" (Col 3:16; cf. 2Ti 3:15–17). This can be accomplished only by daily and continually searching the Scriptures (Ps 119:97–100; Jn 8:31–32); one approach is to read the NT through twice every year and the OT once (cf. Isa 29:13; see Jas 1:21, note).

6:7 IMPRESS THEM ON YOUR CHILDREN. One key way to express love for God (v. 5) is to be concerned with the spiritual welfare of our children and to strive to bring them into a faithful relationship with God. (1) The godly training of children should be a foremost concern of parents (cf. Ps 103:13; see Lk 1:17, note; 2Ti 3:3, note; see article on PARENTS AND CHILDREN, p. 1854).

(2) Spiritual instruction must be centered in the home, with both the father and mother taking part. Devotion to the Lord in the home is not an option; it is a direct commandment from the Lord (vv. 7–9; cf. 21:18; Ex 20:12; Lev 20:9; Pr 1:8; 6:20; 2Ti 1:5).

(3) The purpose of parental instruction is to teach the children to fear the Lord, to walk in all his ways, to love and appreciate him, and to serve him with all their heart and soul (10:12; Eph 6:4).

(4) The believer must diligently give his/her children a God-centered education where everything is related to God and his ways (cf. 4:9; 11:19; 32:46; Ge 18:19; Ex 10:2; 12:26–27; 13:14–16; Isa 38:19).

shites,[e] Amorites,[f] Canaanites, Perizzites,[g] Hivites[h] and Jebusites,[i]
seven nations larger and stronger than
you— **2**and when the LORD your God
has delivered[j] them over to you and
you have defeated them, then you must
destroy[k] them totally.[m][l] Make no
treaty[m] with them, and show them no
mercy.[n] **3**Do not intermarry with
them.[o] Do not give your daughters to
their sons or take their daughters for
your sons, **4**for they will turn your sons
away from following me to serve other
gods,[p] and the LORD's anger will burn
against you and will quickly destroy[q]
you. **5**This is what you are to do to
them: Break down their altars, smash
their sacred stones, cut down their
Asherah poles[n][r] and burn their idols
in the fire.[s] **6**For you are a people
holy[t] to the LORD your God.[u] The
LORD your God has chosen[v] you out of
all the peoples on the face of the earth
to be his people, his treasured possession.[w]

7The LORD did not set his affection
on you and choose you because you
were more numerous[x] than other peoples, for you were the fewest[y] of all
peoples.[z] **8**But it was because the
LORD loved[a] you and kept the oath he
swore[b] to your forefathers that he
brought you out with a mighty hand[c]
and redeemed[d] you from the land of
slavery,[e] from the power of Pharaoh
king of Egypt. **9**Know therefore that
the LORD your God is God;[f] he is the
faithful God,[g] keeping his covenant of
love[h] to a thousand generations[i] of
those who love him and keep his commands.[j] **10**But

> those who hate him he will repay
> to their face by destruction;
> he will not be slow to repay to
> their face those who hate
> him.[k]

11Therefore, take care to follow the
commands, decrees and laws I give
you today.

12If you pay attention to these laws
and are careful to follow them, then the
LORD your God will keep his covenant
of love with you, as he swore to your
forefathers.[l] **13**He will love you and
bless you[m] and increase your numbers.[n] He will bless the fruit of your
womb,[o] the crops of your land—your
grain, new wine[p] and oil[q]—the
calves of your herds and the lambs of
your flocks in the land that he swore to
your forefathers to give you.[r] **14**You
will be blessed more than any other
people; none of your men or women
will be childless, nor any of your livestock without young.[s] **15**The LORD will
keep you free from every disease.[t] He
will not inflict on you the horrible diseases you knew in Egypt,[u] but he will
inflict them on all who hate you.[v] Dt 32:39
16You must destroy all the peoples the
LORD your God gives over to you.[w] Do
not look on them with pity[x] and do not
serve their gods,[y] for that will be a
snare[z] to you.

17You may say to yourselves, "These
nations are stronger than we are. How
can we drive them out?[a]" **18**But do not
be afraid[b] of them; remember well
what the LORD your God did to Pharaoh
and to all Egypt.[c] **19**You saw with
your own eyes the great trials, the miraculous signs and wonders, the
mighty hand[d] and outstretched arm,
with which the LORD your God brought
you out. The LORD your God will do the
same to all the peoples you now fear.[e]
20Moreover, the LORD your God will
send the hornet[f] among them until
even the survivors who hide from you
have perished. **21**Do not be terrified by

7:1 [e]S Ge 10:16 [f]S Dt 1:7 [g]Ge 13:7 [h]S Ge 10:17 [i]Jos 3:10 **7:2** [j]S Dt 2:33 [k]S Dt 2:34 [l]Nu 31:17; Dt 33:27; Jos 11:11 [m]S Ex 23:32 [n]ver 16; Dt 13:8; 19:13; 25:12 **7:3** [o]Ex 34:15-16; Jos 22:16; Da 9:7 **7:4** [p]Jdg 3:6 [q]S Dt 4:26 **7:5** [r]S Ex 34:13; Dt 16:21 [s]S Ex 23:24 **7:6** [t]Ex 19:6; S Lev 27:30 [u]Dt 26:19; Ps 30:4; 37:28; 50:5; 52:9 [v]Dt 14:2; 1Ki 3:8; Isa 41:9; Eze 20:5 [w]S Ge 17:7; S Ex 8:22; S 34:9; Isa 43:1; Ro 9:4; Tit 2:14 **7:7** [x]S Ge 22:17 [y]Ge 34:30 [z]Dt 4:37; 10:22 **7:8** [a]S Dt 4:37; 1Ki 10:9; 2Ch 2:11; Ps 44:3 [b]Ex 32:13; S Nu 14:8; Ro 11:28 [c]S Ex 3:20 [d]S Ex 6:6 [e]S Ex 13:14 **7:9** [f]S Dt 4:35 [g]Ps 18:25; 33:4; 108:4; 145:13; 146:6; Isa 49:7; Jer 42:5; Hos 11:12; S 1Co 1:9 [h]ver 12; 1Ki 8:23; 2Ch 6:14; Ne 1:5; 9:32 [i]S Ex 20:6 [j]S Dt 5:10 **7:10** [k]S Lev 26:28; S Nu 10:35; Na 1:2 **7:12** [l]Lev 26:3-13; Dt 28:1-14; Ps 105:8-9; Mic 7:20 **7:13** [m]Ps 11:5; 146:8; Pr 15:9; Isa 51:1; Jn 14:21 [n]S Ge 17:6; Ex 1:7; Dt 1:10; 13:17; 30:5; Ps 107:38 [o]S Ge 49:25 [p]S Ge 27:28 [q]S Nu 18:12 [r]Dt 28:4 **7:14** [s]Ex 23:26 **7:15** [t]S Ex 15:26 [u]S Ex 9:9 [v]S Ex 23:25; Dt 30:8-10 **7:16** [w]ver 24; Jos 6:2; 10:26 [x]S ver 2 [y]Jdg 3:6; Ezr 9:1; Ps 106:36 [z]ver 25; S Ex 10:7 **7:17** [a]Nu 33:53 **7:18** [b]S Nu 14:9; S Dt 1:21,29 [c]Ps 105:5; 119:52 **7:19** [d]Ps 136:12 [e]Dt 4:34 **7:20** [f]S Ex 23:28

[m]*2* The Hebrew term refers to the irrevocable giving over of things or persons to the LORD, often by totally destroying them; also in verse 26. [n]*5* That is, symbols of the goddess Asherah; here and elsewhere in Deuteronomy

7:3 DO NOT INTERMARRY WITH THEM. Any intimate association with people of the world will eventually destroy the separateness and holiness of God's people. Such matters as intermarriage of God's people with unbelievers or close friendship with unbelievers may turn believers away from following God (v. 4; see article on SPIRITUAL SEPARATION FOR BELIEVERS, p. 1794).

7:9 COVENANT OF LOVE TO ... THOSE WHO LOVE HIM. God's choice of Israel was motivated by his love for them (vv. 7–8). Moreover, God promised to faithfully keep his covenant and show mercy to generation after generation of "those who love him and keep his commands" (cf. 6:4–9). Not only was God's love contingent on this response of love and obedience, but also their prosperity (vv. 13–14), good health (v. 15) and military success (v. 16).

7:15 NOT INFLICT ... HORRIBLE DISEASES. See Ex 23:25–26, note.

them, for the LORD your God, who is
among you,[g] is a great and awesome
God.[h] 22 The LORD your God will drive
out those nations before you, little by
little.[i] You will not be allowed to eliminate them all at once, or the wild animals will multiply around you. 23 But
the LORD your God will deliver them
over to you, throwing them into great
confusion until they are destroyed.[j]
24 He will give their kings[k] into your
hand,[l] and you will wipe out their
names from under heaven. No one will
be able to stand up against you;[m] you
will destroy them.[n] 25 The images of
their gods you are to burn[o] in the fire.
Do not covet[p] the silver and gold on
them, and do not take it for yourselves,
or you will be ensnared[q] by it, for it is
detestable[r] to the LORD your God.
26 Do not bring a detestable thing into
your house or you, like it, will be set
apart for destruction.[s] Utterly abhor
and detest it, for it is set apart for destruction.

Do Not Forget the LORD

8 Be careful to follow every command I am giving you today, so
that you may live[t] and increase and
may enter and possess the land that
the LORD promised on oath to your forefathers.[u] 2 Remember how the LORD
your God led[v] you all the way in the
desert these forty years, to humble you
and to test[w] you in order to know what
was in your heart, whether or not you
would keep his commands. 3 He humbled[x] you, causing you to hunger and
then feeding you with manna,[y] which
neither you nor your fathers had
known, to teach[z] you that man does
not live on bread[a] alone but on every
word that comes from the mouth[b] of
the LORD.[c] 4 Your clothes did not wear
out and your feet did not swell during
these forty years.[d] 5 Know then in
your heart that as a man disciplines his
son, so the LORD your God disciplines
you.[e]

6 Observe the commands of the LORD
your God, walking in his ways[f] and
revering him.[g] 7 For the LORD your God
is bringing you into a good land[h]—a
land with streams and pools of water,
with springs flowing in the valleys and
hills;[i] 8 a land with wheat and barley,[j] vines[k] and fig trees,[l] pomegranates, olive oil and honey;[m] 9 a land
where bread[n] will not be scarce and
you will lack nothing;[o] a land where
the rocks are iron and you can dig copper out of the hills.[p]

10 When you have eaten and are satisfied,[q] praise the LORD your God for
the good land he has given you. 11 Be
careful that you do not forget[r] the
LORD your God, failing to observe his
commands, his laws and his decrees
that I am giving you this day. 12 Otherwise, when you eat and are satisfied,
when you build fine houses and settle

7:21 [g] S Ge 17:7; Jos 3:10 [h] Dt 10:17; Ne 1:5; 9:32; Ps 47:2; 66:3; 68:35; Isa 9:6; Da 9:4 **7:22** [i] Ex 23:28-30 **7:23** [j] Ex 23:27; Jos 10:10 **7:24** [k] Jos 10:24; Ps 110:5 [l] S ver 16 [m] S Ex 23:31; Dt 11:25; Jos 1:5; 10:8; 23:9 [n] Jos 21:44 **7:25** [o] S Ex 4:14; S 32:20 [p] Ex 20:17; Jos 7:21 [q] S ver 16 [r] Dt 17:1 **7:26** [s] Lev 27:28-29 **8:1** [t] Dt 4:1 [u] S Ex 19:5; Job 36:11; Ps 16:11; Eze 20:19 **8:2** [v] Dt 29:5; Ps 136:16; Am 2:10 [w] S Ge 22:1 **8:3** [x] 2Ch 36:12; Ps 44:9; Pr 18:12; Isa 2:11; Jer 44:10 [y] S Ex 16:4 [z] 1Ki 8:36; Ps 25:5; 94:12; 119:171 [a] ver 9; S Ge 3:19; Job 23:12; Ps 104:15; Pr 28:21; Isa 51:14; Jer 42:14 [b] Job 22:22; Ps 119:13; 138:4 [c] S Ex 16:2-3; Mt 4:4*; Lk 4:4* **8:4** [d] Dt 29:5; Ne 9:21 **8:5** [e] Dt 4:36; 2Sa 7:14; Job 5:17; 33:19; Pr 3:11-12; Heb 12:5-11; Rev 3:19 **8:6** [f] S Ex 33:13; 1Ki 3:14; Ps 81:13; 95:10 [g] Dt 5:33 **8:7** [h] Ps 106:24; Jer 3:19; Eze 20:6 [i] Dt 11:9-12; Jer 2:7 **8:8** [j] S Ex 9:31 [k] S Ge 49:11 [l] S Nu 13:23; S 1Ki 4:25 [m] Dt 32:13; Ps 81:16 **8:9** [n] S ver 3 [o] Jdg 18:10 [p] Job 28:2 **8:10** [q] Dt 6:10-12 **8:11** [r] Dt 4:9

7:26 DETESTABLE THING INTO YOUR HOUSE. The "detestable thing" refers to the silver and gold on the Canaanite idols (v. 25); anything tied to idolatry had to be destroyed. This admonition to the Israelites to remove whatever was detestable from their houses applies today as well. Anything that promotes sin and immorality and is contrary to God's holy nature must not be allowed into our homes (cf. Eze 5:7,9). Therefore, believers must be extremely careful that they do not allow the influence of immoral lifestyles to penetrate their homes through people or through entertainment media (cf. 12:29–31; 18:12–13; Pr 6:16–19). Rather than permitting evil and ungodliness to be brought into our homes, we must instead "utterly abhor and detest it," for to tolerate and enjoy evil within our homes is to fall under God's curse (cf. 23:14; see Ro 1:32, note).

8:3 MAN DOES NOT LIVE ON BREAD ALONE. The Lord brought testings and troubles to his people in the desert in order to teach them that one's life does not consist merely in the physical, but rather that well-being (both physically and spiritually) depends on one's relationship to God and obedience to his word. The Lord Jesus quoted this passage in the hour of his temptation (Mt 4:4; cf. Ge 3:4, note). At times the Lord may permit difficulties in our lives as a form of fatherly discipline in order to train us to depend on him more firmly and receive his word more willingly (vv. 4–5; cf. Heb 12:3–13).

8:7 LAND WITH STREAMS AND POOLS. At the time of Israel's entrance into Canaan it was a land with brooks, streams, springs of water and deep pools. Israel's scarcity of water in Elijah's time was a judgment of God (1Ki 17:1—18:46). Even today God may use drought to humble his people and bring judgment to sinners (vv. 19–20; see 11:17).

8:12–14 EAT AND ARE SATISFIED ... FORGET THE LORD. In times of prosperity and abundance people are inclined to become satisfied with life on earth as it is and to find their enjoyment in material blessings. Prosperity brings the temptation to forget God and his commands, to no longer seek spiritual blessings, and to fail to

down,[s] **13**and when your herds and
flocks grow large and your silver and
gold increase and all you have is multiplied, **14**then your heart will become
proud and you will forget[t] the LORD
your God, who brought you out of
Egypt, out of the land of slavery. **15**He
led you through the vast and dreadful
desert,[u] that thirsty and waterless
land, with its venomous snakes[v] and
scorpions. He brought you water out of
hard rock.[w] **16**He gave you manna[x] to
eat in the desert, something your fathers had never known,[y] to humble
and to test[z] you so that in the end it
might go well with you. **17**You may say
to yourself,[a] "My power and the
strength of my hands[b] have produced
this wealth for me." **18**But remember
the LORD your God, for it is he who
gives you the ability to produce
wealth,[c] and so confirms his covenant, which he swore to your forefathers, as it is today.
19If you ever forget the LORD your
God and follow other gods[d] and worship and bow down to them, I testify
against you today that you will surely
be destroyed.[e] **20**Like the nations[f]
the LORD destroyed before you, so you
will be destroyed for not obeying the
LORD your God.[g]

Not Because of Israel's Righteousness

9 Hear, O Israel. You are now about
to cross the Jordan[h] to go in and
dispossess nations greater and stronger than you,[i] with large cities[j] that
have walls up to the sky.[k] **2**The people
are strong and tall—Anakites! You
know about them and have heard it
said: "Who can stand up against the
Anakites?"[l] **3**But be assured today
that the LORD your God is the one who
goes across ahead of you[m] like a devouring fire.[n] He will destroy them; he
will subdue them before you. And you
will drive them out and annihilate them
quickly,[o] as the LORD has promised
you.
4After the LORD your God has driven
them out before you, do not say to
yourself,[p] "The LORD has brought me
here to take possession of this land because of my righteousness." No, it is on
account of the wickedness[q] of these
nations[r] that the LORD is going to
drive them out before you. **5**It is not
because of your righteousness or your
integrity[s] that you are going in to take
possession of their land; but on account of the wickedness[t] of these nations,[u] the LORD your God will drive
them out[v] before you, to accomplish
what he swore[w] to your fathers, to
Abraham, Isaac and Jacob.[x] **6**Understand, then, that it is not because of
your righteousness that the LORD your
God is giving you this good land to possess, for you are a stiff-necked people.[y]

The Golden Calf

7Remember this and never forget
how you provoked[z] the LORD your God
to anger in the desert. From the day
you left Egypt until you arrived here,
you have been rebellious[a] against the
LORD.[b] **8**At Horeb you aroused the
LORD's wrath[c] so that he was angry

8:12 [s] Pr 30:9; Hos 13:6
8:14 [t] ver 11; Ps 78:7; 106:21
8:15 [u] S Dt 1:19; S 32:10 [v] Nu 21:6; Isa 14:29; 30:6 [w] Ex 17:6; Dt 32:13; Job 28:9; Ps 78:15; 114:8
8:16 [x] S Ex 16:14 [y] Ex 16:15 [z] S Ge 22:1
8:17 [a] Dt 9:4,7, 24; 31:27 [b] Jdg 7:2; Ps 44:3; Isa 10:13
8:18 [c] Ge 26:13; Dt 26:10; 28:4; 1Sa 2:7; Ps 25:13; 112:3; Pr 8:18; 10:22; Ecc 9:11; Hos 2:8
8:19 [d] Dt 6:14; Ps 16:4; Jer 7:6; 13:10; 25:6 [e] Dt 4:26; 30:18
8:20 [f] 2Ki 21:2; Ps 10:16 [g] Eze 5:5-17
9:1 [h] S Nu 35:10 [i] Dt 4:38 [j] S Nu 13:28 [k] S Ge 11:4
9:2 [l] Nu 13:22; Jos 11:22
9:3 [m] Dt 31:3; Jos 3:11 [n] S Ex 15:7; S 19:18; Heb 12:29 [o] S Ex 23:31
9:4 [p] S Dt 8:17 [q] 2Ki 16:3; 17:8; 21:2; Ezr 9:11 [r] S Ex 23:24; S Lev 18:21,24-30; Dt 18:9-14
9:5 [s] S Eph 2:9 [t] Dt 18:9 [u] S Lev 18:25 [v] Dt 4:38; 11:23 [w] S Ge 12:7 [x] Eze 36:32
9:6 [y] S Ex 32:9; Ac 7:51
9:7 [z] S Nu 11:33 [a] S Ex 23:21 [b] S Ex 14:11
9:8 [c] Nu 16:46; 1Sa 28:18; Job 20:28; Ps 2:12; 7:11; 69:24; 110:5; Isa 9:19; Eze 20:13

grieve over the sin and evil in the world (see article on RICHES AND POVERTY, p. 1562).

8:18 ABILITY TO PRODUCE WEALTH. This verse affirms that God at times blessed Israel as a sign or confirmation that he was fulfilling his covenant with Abraham and his descendants. Unfortunately, many times wealth is gained by means that are contrary to godly principles and practices (see article on RICHES AND POVERTY, p. 1562); such wealth is not to be construed as a sign of God's blessing.

9:4 WICKEDNESS OF THESE NATIONS. The Canaanite nations were destroyed by God because of their extreme wickedness; their depravity was so terrible and widespread that God determined that they had to be completely removed like a dreaded cancer. Thus Israel's conquest and extermination of the Canaanites were capital punishment on a national level. Likewise, virtually uncontrolled wickedness had existed in Noah's day (see Ge 6:1–7) and will characterize the world at the end of time (Mt 24:37–39; 2Ti 3:1–5; Rev 9:20–21; 19:11–21).

9:5 NOT BECAUSE OF YOUR RIGHTEOUSNESS. Israel's possession of the land was not a reward for their own past faithfulness. Rather, it was God's gracious gift based on his love and mercy. However, Moses warned the people that continued possession of the land would be contingent on their perseverance in faith and in obedience to God; if the Israelites became wicked like the Canaanites, they too would be dispossessed of the land (30:15–20). In other words, God's love and mercy in his gift of the land were not unconditional; if the people turned away from the Lord and forgot his word, they too would surely perish (8:11,14,19–20; cf. 11:22–28).

enough to destroy you.[d] **9**When I went up on the mountain to receive the tablets of stone, the tablets of the covenant[e] that the LORD had made with you, I stayed on the mountain forty days[f] and forty nights; I ate no bread and drank no water.[g] **10**The LORD gave me two stone tablets inscribed by the finger of God.[h] On them were all the commandments the LORD proclaimed to you on the mountain out of the fire, on the day of the assembly.[i]

11At the end of the forty days and forty nights,[j] the LORD gave me the two stone tablets,[k] the tablets of the covenant. **12**Then the LORD told me, "Go down from here at once, because your people whom you brought out of Egypt have become corrupt.[l] They have turned away quickly[m] from what I commanded them and have made a cast idol for themselves."

13And the LORD said to me, "I have seen this people[n], and they are a stiff-necked people indeed! **14**Let me alone,[o] so that I may destroy them and blot out[p] their name from under heaven.[q] And I will make you into a nation stronger and more numerous than they."

15So I turned and went down from the mountain while it was ablaze with fire. And the two tablets of the covenant were in my hands.[o][r] **16**When I looked, I saw that you had sinned against the LORD your God; you had made for yourselves an idol cast in the shape of a calf.[s] You had turned aside quickly from the way that the LORD had commanded you. **17**So I took the two tablets and threw them out of my hands, breaking them to pieces before your eyes.

18Then once again I fell[t] prostrate before the LORD for forty days and forty nights; I ate no bread and drank no water,[u] because of all the sin you had committed,[v] doing what was evil in the LORD's sight and so provoking him to anger. **19**I feared the anger and wrath of the LORD, for he was angry enough with you to destroy you.[w] But again the LORD listened to me.[x] **20**And the LORD was angry enough with Aaron to destroy him, but at that time I prayed for Aaron too. **21**Also I took that sinful thing of yours, the calf you had made, and burned it in the fire. Then I crushed it and ground it to powder as fine as dust[y] and threw the dust into a stream that flowed down the mountain.[z]

22You also made the LORD angry[a] at Taberah,[b] at Massah[c] and at Kibroth Hattaavah.[d]

23And when the LORD sent you out from Kadesh Barnea,[e] he said, "Go up and take possession[f] of the land I have given you." But you rebelled[g] against the command of the LORD your God. You did not trust[h] him or obey him. **24**You have been rebellious against the LORD ever since I have known you.[i]

25I lay prostrate before the LORD those forty days and forty nights[j] because the LORD had said he would destroy you.[k] **26**I prayed to the LORD and said, "O Sovereign LORD, do not destroy your people,[l] your own inheritance[m] that you redeemed[n] by your great power and brought out of Egypt with a mighty hand.[o] **27**Remember your servants Abraham, Isaac and Jacob. Overlook the stubbornness[p] of this people, their wickedness and their sin. **28**Otherwise, the country[q] from which you brought us will say, 'Because the LORD was not able to take them into the land he had promised them, and because he hated them,[r] he brought them out to put them to death in the desert.'[s] **29**But they are your people,[t] your inheritance[u] that you brought out by your great power and your outstretched arm.[v]"

Tablets Like the First Ones

10 At that time the LORD said to me, "Chisel out two stone tablets[w] like the first ones and come up to me on the mountain. Also make a wooden chest.[p] **2**I will write on the tablets the words that were on the first tablets, which you broke. Then you are to put them in the chest."[x]

3So I made the ark out of acacia wood[y] and chiseled[z] out two stone tablets like the first ones, and I went up on the mountain with the two tablets in my hands. **4**The LORD wrote on these tablets what he had written be-

9:8 [d]Ex 32:7-10; Ezr 9:14; Ps 106:19
9:9 [e]S Dt 4:13 [f]S Ge 7:4 [g]S Ex 24:12
9:10 [h]S Ex 31:18 [i]Dt 10:4; 18:16
9:11 [j]S Ge 7:4 [k]S Ex 24:12
9:12 [l]S Dt 4:16 [m]Jdg 2:17
9:13 [n]ver 6; Dt 10:16
9:14 [o]Ex 32:10 [p]S Nu 14:12 [q]Jer 7:16
9:15 [r]S Ex 32:15
9:16 [s]S Ex 32:4
9:18 [t]S Ex 34:28 [u]ver 9 [v]S Ex 32:31
9:19 [w]S Ex 32:14; Heb 12:21* [x]ver 26; Ex 34:10; S Nu 11:2; 1Sa 7:9; Jer 15:1
9:21 [y]Ps 18:42; Isa 29:5; 40:15 [z]Ex 32:20; Isa 2:18; Mic 1:7
9:22 [a]S Nu 1:53 [b]Nu 11:3 [c]S Ex 17:7 [d]Nu 11:34
9:23 [e]S Dt 1:2 [f]Dt 1:21 [g]S Nu 14:9 [h]S Dt 1:32; Ps 106:24
9:24 [i]S Dt 8:17
9:25 [j]S Ge 7:4 [k]ver 18; S Ex 33:17
9:26 [l]S Ex 33:13 [m]S Ex 34:9 [n]S Ex 6:6; Dt 15:15; 2Sa 7:23; Ps 78:35 [o]S ver 19; S Ex 32:11
9:27 [p]ver 6; S Ex 32:9
9:28 [q]Dt 32:27 [r]S Dt 1:27 [s]S Ex 32:12; Jos 7:9
9:29 [t]S Ex 33:13 [u]S Ex 34:9; Dt 32:9 [v]Dt 4:34; Ne 1:10; Jer 27:5; 32:17
10:1 [w]Ex 34:1-2
10:2 [x]Ex 25:16, 21; 2Ch 5:10; 6:11
10:3 [y]Ex 37:1-9 [z]Ex 34:4

o 15 Or *And I had the two tablets of the covenant with me, one in each hand*
p 1 That is, an ark

fore, the Ten Commandments[a] he had
proclaimed[b] to you on the mountain,
out of the fire, on the day of the assembly.[c] And the LORD gave them to me.
5Then I came back down the mountain[d] and put the tablets in the ark[e]
I had made,[f] as the LORD commanded
me, and they are there now.[g]
6(The Israelites traveled from the
wells of the Jaakanites to Moserah.[h]
There Aaron died[i] and was buried,
and Eleazar[j] his son succeeded him
as priest.[k] 7From there they traveled
to Gudgodah and on to Jotbathah, a
land with streams of water.[l] 8At that
time the LORD set apart the tribe of
Levi[m] to carry the ark of the covenant[n] of the LORD, to stand before the
LORD to minister[o] and to pronounce
blessings[p] in his name, as they still do
today.[q] 9That is why the Levites have
no share or inheritance among their
brothers; the LORD is their inheritance,[r] as the LORD your God told
them.)
10Now I had stayed on the mountain
forty days and nights, as I did the first
time, and the LORD listened to me at
this time also. It was not his will to
destroy you.[s] 11"Go," the LORD said to
me, "and lead the people on their way,
so that they may enter and possess the
land that I swore to their fathers to
give them."

Fear the LORD

12And now, O Israel, what does the
LORD your God ask of you[t] but to
fear[u] the LORD your God, to walk[v] in
all his ways, to love him,[w] to serve the
LORD[x] your God with all your heart[y]
and with all your soul,[z] 13and to observe the LORD's commands[a] and decrees that I am giving you today for
your own good?[b]
14To the LORD your God belong the
heavens,[cde] even the highest heavens,[fg] the earth and everything in
it.[h] 15Yet the LORD set his affection on
your forefathers and loved[i] them, and
he chose you,[j] their descendants,
above all the nations, as it is today.[k]
16Circumcise[l] your hearts,[m] therefore, and do not be stiff-necked[n] any
longer. 17For the LORD your God is God
of gods[o] and Lord of lords,[p] the great
God, mighty and awesome,[q] who
shows no partiality[r] and accepts no
bribes.[s] 18He defends the cause of the
fatherless and the widow,[t] and loves
the alien, giving him food and clothing.[u] 19And you are to love[v] those
who are aliens,[w] for you yourselves
were aliens in Egypt.[x] 20Fear the LORD
your God and serve him.[y] Hold fast[z]
to him and take your oaths in his
name.[a] 21He is your praise;[b] he is
your God, who performed for you those
great[c] and awesome wonders[d] you
saw with your own eyes. 22Your forefathers who went down into Egypt were
seventy in all,[e] and now the LORD your
God has made you as numerous as the
stars in the sky.[f]

Love and Obey the LORD

11 Love[g] the LORD your God and
keep his requirements, his decrees, his laws and his commands always.[h] 2Remember today that your
children[i] were not the ones who saw
and experienced the discipline of the
LORD your God:[j] his majesty,[k] his
mighty hand, his outstretched arm;[l]
3the signs he performed and the things
he did in the heart of Egypt, both to
Pharaoh king of Egypt and to his whole
country;[m] 4what he did to the Egyptian army, to its horses and chariots,[n]
how he overwhelmed them with the

10:4 [a]S Ex 24:12; S 34:28 [b]Ex 20:1 [c]S Dt 9:10 **10:5** [d]S Ex 19:11 [e]S Ex 25:10; S 1Sa 3:3 [f]S Ex 25:21 [g]1Ki 8:9 **10:6** [h]Nu 33:30 [i]S Nu 27:13 [j]S Ex 6:23 [k]S Nu 20:25-28 **10:7** [l]Nu 33:32-34; Ps 42:1; SS 5:12; Isa 32:2 **10:8** [m]S Nu 3:6 [n]S Nu 10:33 [o]S Nu 16:9 [p]S Ge 48:20 [q]1Ch 23:26 **10:9** [r]S Nu 18:20 **10:10** [s]S Ex 33:17 **10:12** [t]Mic 6:8 [u]S Ex 20:20 [v]1Ki 2:3; 3:3; 9:4 [w]Dt 5:33; 6:13; Mt 22:37; 1Ti 1:5 [x]Dt 11:13; 28:47; Ps 100:2 [y]S Dt 6:5; Ps 119:2 [z]S Dt 5:32 **10:13** [a]S Dt 4:2 [b]Dt 5:33; 6:24 **10:14** [c]Ps 148:4; Isa 19:1; Hab 3:8 [d]Ne 9:6; Job 35:5; Ps 8:3; 89:11; 104:3 [e]Dt 33:26 [f]Ps 115:16 [g]1Ki 8:27 [h]Ex 19:5; Ps 24:1; Ac 17:24 **10:15** [i]S Dt 4:37 [j]Ps 105:6; 135:4 [k]S Nu 14:8; Ro 11:28; 1Pe 2:9 **10:16** [l]S Ge 17:11 [m]S Lev 26:41; Dt 30:6; Jer 32:39 [n]S Ex 32:9; S Dt 9:13 **10:17** [o]Jos 22:22; Ps 135:5; 136:2; Da 2:47; 11:36 [p]Ps 136:3; S 1Ti 6:15 [q]S Dt 7:21 [r]Dt 1:17; Mal 2:9 [s]S Ex 23:8; S Lev 19:16 **10:18** [t]Ex 22:21, 22-24; 23:9; Lev 19:33; Dt 27:19; Job 29:13; Ps 94:6; Isa 10:2; Jer 49:11 [u]S Nu 10:32 **10:19** [v]Dt 7:12 [w]S Ex 22:21; S Dt 24:19 [x]S Lev 19:34; Eze 47:22-23 **10:20** [y]Mt 4:10 [z]Dt 11:22; 13:4; 30:20; Jos 23:8; Ru 1:14; 2Ki 18:6; Ps 119:31; Isa 38:3 [a]S Ex 20:7 **10:21** [b]S Ex 15:2 [c]1Sa 12:24; Ps 126:2 [d]2Sa 7:23 **10:22** [e]S Ge 34:30; S 46:26; Ac 7:14 [f]S Ge 12:2; S Nu 10:36 **11:1** [g]S Dt 6:5 [h]S Lev 8:35 **11:2** [i]Dt 31:13; Ps 78:6 [j]S Dt 5:24 [k]S Dt 3:24 [l]Ps 136:12 **11:3** [m]Ex 7:8-21 **11:4** [n]S Ex 15:1

10:12 LOVE HIM ... WITH ALL YOUR HEART. Repeatedly God emphasized the necessity of love that comes from "the heart" (see 4:29, note; 6:5, note; see article on THE HEART, p. 906). (1) God did not want his people to substitute heartfelt love for him with mere outward religious forms, such as keeping commandments, offering sacrifices, and the like. It was necessary that they always obey God from a heart that sincerely loved and honored him. For NT believers, faith and love from the heart are also essential to our relationship with God (see Jn 21:15, note; Col 3:4, note). (2) It is indeed possible to read Scripture, pray, attend church and partake of the Lord's Supper without a heartfelt devotion to God himself; this is what is meant by legalism (see Mk 7:6, note). Outward obedience and correct religious practices have validity and significance only if they are based on knowing Jesus Christ through sincere faith in and love for him, because of who he is and what he has done for us.

waters of the Red Sea[q][o] as they were pursuing you, and how the LORD brought lasting ruin on them. **5**It was not your children who saw what he did for you in the desert until you arrived at this place, **6**and what he did[p] to Dathan and Abiram, sons of Eliab the Reubenite, when the earth opened[q] its mouth right in the middle of all Israel and swallowed them up with their households, their tents and every living thing that belonged to them. **7**But it was your own eyes that saw all these great things the LORD has done.[r]

8Observe therefore all the commands[s] I am giving you today, so that you may have the strength to go in and take over the land that you are crossing the Jordan to possess,[t] **9**and so that you may live long[u] in the land that the LORD swore[v] to your forefathers to give to them and their descendants, a land flowing with milk and honey.[w] **10**The land you are entering to take over is not like the land of Egypt,[x] from which you have come, where you planted your seed and irrigated it by foot as in a vegetable garden. **11**But the land you are crossing the Jordan to take possession of is a land of mountains and valleys[y] that drinks rain from heaven.[z] **12**It is a land the LORD your God cares for; the eyes[a] of the LORD your God are continually on it from the beginning of the year to its end.

13So if you faithfully obey[b] the commands I am giving you today—to love[c] the LORD your God and to serve him with all your heart and with all your soul[d]— **14**then I will send rain[e] on your land in its season, both autumn and spring rains,[f] so that you may gather in your grain, new wine and oil. **15**I will provide grass[g] in the fields for your cattle, and you will eat and be satisfied.[h]

16Be careful, or you will be enticed to turn away and worship other gods and bow down to them.[i] **17**Then the LORD's anger[j] will burn against you, and he will shut[k] the heavens so that it will not rain and the ground will yield no produce,[l] and you will soon perish[m] from the good land the LORD is giving you. **18**Fix these words of mine in your hearts and minds; tie them as symbols on your hands and bind them on your foreheads.[n] **19**Teach them to your children,[o] talking about them when you sit at home and when you walk along the road, when you lie down and when you get up.[p] **20**Write them on the doorframes of your houses and on your gates,[q] **21**so that your days and the days of your children may be many[r] in the land that the LORD swore to give your forefathers, as many as the days that the heavens are above the earth.[s]

22If you carefully observe[t] all these commands I am giving you to follow—to love[u] the LORD your God, to walk in all his ways and to hold fast[v] to him— **23**then the LORD will drive out[w] all these nations[x] before you, and you will dispossess nations larger and stronger than you.[y] **24**Every place where you set your foot will be yours:[z] Your territory will extend from the desert to Lebanon, and from the Euphrates River[a] to the western sea.[r] **25**No man will be able to stand against you. The LORD your God, as he promised you, will put the terror[b] and fear of you on the whole land, wherever you go.[c]

26See, I am setting before you today a blessing[d] and a curse[e]— **27**the blessing[f] if you obey the commands of the LORD your God that I am giving you today; **28**the curse if you disobey[g] the commands of the LORD your God and turn from the way that I command you today by following other gods,[h] which

11:4 [o]S Ex 14:27; S Nu 21:4 **11:6** [p]Nu 16:1-35; Ps 106:16-18 [q]Isa 24:19 **11:7** [r]Dt 5:3 **11:8** [s]Ezr 9:10 [t]Dt 31:6-7,23; Jos 1:7 **11:9** [u]S Dt 5:16 [v]Dt 9:5 [w]S Ex 3:8 **11:10** [x]Isa 11:15; 37:25 **11:11** [y]Eze 36:4 [z]Dt 8:7; Ne 9:25 **11:12** [a]1Ki 8:29; 9:3 **11:13** [b]S Dt 6:17 [c]S Dt 10:12 [d]Dt 4:29; Jer 17:24 **11:14** [e]S Lev 26:4; Ac 14:17 [f]Ps 147:8; Jer 3:3; 5:24; Joel 2:23; Jas 5:7 **11:15** [g]Ps 104:14 [h]S Lev 26:5 **11:16** [i]Dt 4:19; 8:19; 29:18; Job 31:9,27 **11:17** [j]Dt 6:15; 9:19 [k]1Ki 17:1; 2Ch 6:26; 7:13 [l]S Lev 26:20 [m]Dt 4:26; 28:12, 24 **11:18** [n]S Ex 13:9; Dt 6:6-8 **11:19** [o]S Ex 12:26; Dt 6:7; Ps 145:4; Isa 38:19; Jer 32:39 [p]Dt 4:9-10 **11:20** [q]Dt 6:9 **11:21** [r]Job 5:26; Pr 3:2; 4:10; 9:11 [s]Ps 72:5 **11:22** [t]S Dt 6:17 [u]S Dt 6:5 [v]S Dt 10:20 **11:23** [w]S Dt 9:5 [x]S Ex 23:28 [y]Dt 9:1 **11:24** [z]Ge 15:18; Dt 1:36; 12:20; 19:8; Jos 1:3; 14:9 [a]S Ge 2:14 **11:25** [b]S Dt 2:25 [c]Ex 23:27; Dt 7:24 **11:26** [d]Ps 24:5 [e]Lev 26:14-17; Dt 27:13-26; 30:1, 15,19; La 2:17; Da 9:11; Hag 1:11; Mal 2:2; 3:9; 4:6 **11:27** [f]Dt 28:1-14; Ps 24:5 **11:28** [g]2Ch 24:20; Jer 42:13; 44:16 [h]S Dt 4:28; 13:6,13; 29:26; 1Sa 26:19

[q]4 Hebrew *Yam Suph*; that is, Sea of Reeds
[r]24 That is, the Mediterranean

11:19 TEACH THEM TO YOUR CHILDREN. See 6:7, note.

11:26 A BLESSING AND A CURSE. God set before his people the choice of receiving a blessing or a curse. If they obeyed God's word and remained separated from the sin of the surrounding nations, then God's blessing would come upon them and accompany them (see 28:1–14). On the other hand, if they conformed to the ways of the ungodly, God's curse would come upon them and overtake them (see 28:15–68). (1) Unfortunately, for the most part Israel did not take God's warning seriously. All too often they adopted the ways of the unbelievers and thus fell under his curse. (2) God places the same choice (i.e., "a blessing and a curse") before NT believers. If we abhor sin, follow Christ and seek to serve him continually, then his blessing and power will be ours. If we depart from God and his righteous ways, we will lose God's presence, help and covenant protection.

you have not known. 29When the LORD
your God has brought you into the land
you are entering to possess, you are to
proclaim on Mount Gerizim[i] the
blessings, and on Mount Ebal[j] the
curses.[k] 30As you know, these mountains are across the Jordan, west of the
road,[s] toward the setting sun, near
the great trees of Moreh,[l] in the territory of those Canaanites living in the
Arabah in the vicinity of Gilgal.[m]
31You are about to cross the Jordan to
enter and take possession[n] of the land
the LORD your God is giving[o] you.
When you have taken it over and are
living there, 32be sure that you obey all
the decrees and laws I am setting before you today.

The One Place of Worship

12 These are the decrees[p] and
laws you must be careful to follow in the land that the LORD, the God
of your fathers, has given you to possess—as long as you live in the land.[q]
2Destroy completely all the places on
the high mountains[r] and on the hills
and under every spreading tree[s]
where the nations you are dispossessing worship their gods. 3Break down
their altars, smash[t] their sacred
stones and burn[u] their Asherah[v]
poles in the fire; cut down the idols of
their gods and wipe out their names[w]
from those places.
4You must not worship the LORD your
God in their way.[x] 5But you are to
seek the place the LORD your God will
choose from among all your tribes to
put his Name[y] there for his dwelling.[z] To that place you must go;
6there bring your burnt offerings and
sacrifices, your tithes[a] and special
gifts, what you have vowed[b] to give
and your freewill offerings, and the
firstborn of your herds and flocks.[c]
7There, in the presence[d] of the LORD
your God, you and your families shall
eat and shall rejoice[e] in everything
you have put your hand to, because the
LORD your God has blessed you.
8You are not to do as we do here today, everyone as he sees fit,[f] 9since
you have not yet reached the resting
place[g] and the inheritance[h] the LORD
your God is giving you. 10But you will
cross the Jordan and settle in the land
the LORD your God is giving[i] you as an
inheritance, and he will give you rest[j]
from all your enemies around you so
that you will live in safety. 11Then to
the place the LORD your God will choose
as a dwelling for his Name[k]—there
you are to bring everything I command
you: your burnt offerings and sacrifices, your tithes and special gifts, and
all the choice possessions you have
vowed to the LORD.[l] 12And there rejoice[m] before the LORD your God, you,
your sons and daughters, your menservants and maidservants, and the Levites[n] from your towns, who have no
allotment or inheritance[o] of their
own. 13Be careful not to sacrifice your
burnt offerings anywhere you please.[p]
14Offer them only at the place the LORD
will choose[q] in one of your tribes, and
there observe everything I command
you.
15Nevertheless, you may slaughter
your animals in any of your towns and
eat as much of the meat as you want,
as if it were gazelle or deer,[r] according to the blessing the LORD your God
gives you. Both the ceremonially unclean and the clean may eat it. 16But
you must not eat the blood;[s] pour[t] it
out on the ground like water.[u] 17You
must not eat in your own towns the
tithe[v] of your grain and new wine and
oil,[w] or the firstborn of your herds and
flocks, or whatever you have vowed to
give,[x] or your freewill offerings or

11:29 [i]Jdg 9:7 [j]Dt 27:4; Jos 8:30 [k]Dt 27:12-13; Jos 8:33; Jn 4:20 **11:30** [l]S Ge 12:6 [m]Jos 4:19; 5:9; 9:6; 10:6; 14:6; 15:7; Jdg 2:1; 2Ki 2:1; Mic 6:5 **11:31** [n]S Nu 33:53 [o]Dt 12:10; Jos 11:23 **12:1** [p]Ps 119:5 [q]Dt 4:9-10; 6:15; 1Ki 8:40; Eze 20:19 **12:2** [r]S Nu 21:28 [s]1Ki 14:23; 2Ki 17:10; Isa 57:5; Jer 2:20; 3:6,13 **12:3** [t]2Ki 11:18 [u]S Ex 32:20 [v]Ex 34:13; 1Ki 14:15,23 [w]S Ex 23:13 **12:4** [x]ver 30; 2Ki 17:15; Jer 10:2 **12:5** [y]S Ex 20:24; S 2Sa 7:13 [z]ver 11,13; Dt 14:23; 15:20; 16:2,11; 18:6; 26:2; 1Sa 2:29; 1Ki 5:5; 8:16; 9:3; 2Ch 2:4; 6:6; 7:12, 16; Ezr 6:12; 7:15; Ps 26:8; 78:68; Zec 2:12 **12:6** [a]S Lev 27:30 [b]S Ge 28:20 [c]Jos 22:27; Isa 66:20 **12:7** [d]S Ex 18:12 [e]S Lev 23:40; Ecc 3:12-13; 5:18-20; S Isa 62:9 **12:8** [f]Jdg 17:6; 21:25 **12:9** [g]S Ex 33:14; Dt 3:20; Ps 95:11; Mic 2:10 [h]Dt 4:21 **12:10** [i]S Dt 11:31 [j]S Ex 33:14 **12:11** [k]S ver 5 [l]S Lev 1:3; Jos 22:23 **12:12** [m]ver 7 [n]Dt 26:11-13 [o]S Nu 18:20 **12:13** [p]S ver 5 **12:14** [q]ver 11 **12:15** [r]ver 22; Dt 14:5; 15:22 **12:16** [s]S Ge 9:4; Ac 15:20 [t]ver 23-24; S Ge 35:14; 1Ch 11:18; Jer 7:18 [u]S Lev 17:13; S Dt 15:23; Jn 19:34 **12:17** [v]S Lev 27:30 [w]S Nu 18:12 [x]ver 26; Nu 18:19

[s]30 Or *Jordan, westward*

12:2 DESTROY COMPLETELY ALL THE PLACES. The Israelites were ordered to destroy all the worship places of the pagan nations and to worship God only at the divinely appointed place and in the manner he commanded (vv. 2–15). To leave the altars of pagan worship in place would tempt the Israelites into taking up pagan worship practices.

12:5 THE PLACE ... GOD WILL CHOOSE. The Israelites were not only to worship the Lord in their homes, but also at a particular place chosen by God himself (eventually the temple in Jerusalem). Believers still need a common place where they can meet with other believers to worship God and call on him in faith. It must be a place where God has "put his Name" (v. 5), i.e., a place where his word is truly believed, his Spirit is present and holiness is characteristic of his people's lives (cf. 1Co 1:2).

special gifts.[y] **18**Instead, you are to
eat[z] them in the presence of the LORD
your God at the place the LORD your
God will choose[a]—you, your sons and
daughters, your menservants and
maidservants, and the Levites from
your towns—and you are to rejoice[b]
before the LORD your God in everything
you put your hand to. **19**Be careful not
to neglect the Levites[c] as long as you
live in your land.[d]

20When the LORD your God has enlarged your territory[e] as he promised[f] you, and you crave meat[g] and
say, "I would like some meat," then
you may eat as much of it as you want.
21If the place where the LORD your God
chooses to put his Name[h] is too far
away from you, you may slaughter animals from the herds and flocks the
LORD has given you, as I have commanded you, and in your own towns
you may eat as much of them as you
want.[i] **22**Eat them as you would gazelle or deer.[j] Both the ceremonially
unclean and the clean may eat. **23**But
be sure you do not eat the blood,[k] because the blood is the life, and you
must not eat the life with the meat.[l]
24You must not eat the blood; pour it
out on the ground like water.[m] **25**Do
not eat it, so that it may go well[n] with
you and your children after you, because you will be doing what is right[o]
in the eyes of the LORD.

26But take your consecrated things
and whatever you have vowed to
give,[p] and go to the place the LORD will
choose. **27**Present your burnt offerings[q] on the altar of the LORD your
God, both the meat and the blood. The
blood of your sacrifices must be poured
beside the altar of the LORD your God,
but you may eat[r] the meat. **28**Be careful to obey all these regulations I am
giving you, so that it may always go
well[s] with you and your children after
you, because you will be doing what is
good and right in the eyes of the LORD
your God.

29The LORD your God will cut off[t]
before you the nations you are about to
invade and dispossess. But when you
have driven them out and settled in
their land,[u] **30**and after they have
been destroyed before you, be careful
not to be ensnared[v] by inquiring about
their gods, saying, "How do these nations serve their gods? We will do the
same."[w] **31**You must not worship the
LORD your God in their way, because in
worshiping their gods, they do all
kinds of detestable things the LORD
hates.[x] They even burn their sons[y]
and daughters in the fire as sacrifices
to their gods.[z]

32See that you do all I command
you; do not add[a] to it or take away
from it.

Worshiping Other Gods

13 If a prophet,[b] or one who foretells by dreams,[c] appears
among you and announces to you a miraculous sign or wonder, **2**and if the
sign[d] or wonder of which he has spoken takes place, and he says, "Let us
follow other gods"[e] (gods you have
not known) "and let us worship them,"
3you must not listen to the words of
that prophet[f] or dreamer.[g] The LORD
your God is testing[h] you to find out
whether you love[i] him with all your
heart and with all your soul. **4**It is the
LORD your God you must follow,[j] and

12:17 [y]Dt 14:23; 15:20
12:18 [z]Dt 14:23; 15:20 [a]ver 5 [b]ver 7,12; Dt 14:26; Ne 8:10; Ecc 3:12-13; 5:18-20
12:19 [c]ver 12; Dt 14:27; Ne 13:10 [d]Mal 3:8
12:20 [e]S Ex 34:24 [f]S Ge 15:8; S Dt 11:24 [g]S Ex 16:3
12:21 [h]Dt 14:24 [i]Lev 17:4
12:22 [j]S ver 15
12:23 [k]S Lev 7:26 [l]Eze 33:25
12:24 [m]ver 16
12:25 [n]S Dt 4:40 [o]ver 28; Ex 15:26; Dt 13:18; 1Ki 11:38; 2Ki 12:2
12:26 [p]S ver 17; Nu 5:9-10
12:27 [q]S Lev 1:13 [r]Lev 3:1-17
12:28 [s]Dt 4:40; Ecc 8:12
12:29 [t]Jos 23:4 [u]S Dt 6:10
12:30 [v]S Ex 10:7 [w]S ver 4
12:31 [x]S Lev 18:25 [y]S Lev 18:21 [z]S 2Ki 3:27
12:32 [a]S Dt 4:2; Rev 22:18-19
13:1 [b]Mt 24:24; Mk 13:22; 2Th 2:9 [c]S Ge 20:3; Jer 23:25; 27:9; 29:8
13:2 [d]Dt 18:22; 1Sa 2:34; 10:9; 2Ki 19:29; 20:9; Isa 7:11 [e]S Dt 11:28
13:3 [f]2Pe 2:1 [g]1Sa 28:6,15 [h]S Ge 22:1; 1Ki 13:18; 22:22-23; Jer 29:31; 43:2; Eze 13:9; 1Co 11:19 [i]Dt 6:5
13:4 [j]2Ki 23:3; 2Ch 34:31; 2Jn 1:6

13:3 NOT LISTEN TO . . . THAT PROPHET. Fundamental to the believers' relationship to the Lord is their faithfulness to God and his revealed word (8:3). Vv. 1–5 teach that the temptation to compromise our allegiance to God will come at times from those who appear to be spiritual. Several implications follow for our lives as believers. (1) God will at times test the sincerity of our love and our commitment to him and his word (cf. 8:2).

(2) God sometimes tests us by allowing to appear among his people those who claim to speak for God and who provide "a miraculous sign or wonder" (vv. 1–2). Such individuals may speak under great anointing, prophesy the future correctly, and perform miracles, signs and wonders. At the same time, however, they may preach a gospel that is contrary to Biblical revelation, adding to God's Word or subtracting from it (cf. 4:2; 12:32). If we follow these false leaders, we will be led away from absolute loyalty to him and his inspired Word (v. 5).

(3) The NT also warns that false prophets and teachers will greatly distort the gospel of Christ in the last days. Believers must resolve to remain faithful to God's written revelation as found in the Bible. The validity of an individual's ministry and teaching must not be evaluated solely on his gift of preaching, powers of prophecy, performance of miracles or numbers of conversions; such criteria will become increasingly undependable as the end of this age approaches. The standard for truth must always be the infallible Word of God (see articles on FALSE TEACHERS, p. 1506, and THE INSPIRATION AND AUTHORITY OF SCRIPTURE, p. 1898).

him you must revere.[k] Keep his commands and obey him; serve him and
hold fast[l] to him. 5That prophet or
dreamer must be put to death,[m] because he preached rebellion against
the LORD your God, who brought you
out of Egypt and redeemed you from
the land of slavery; he has tried to
turn[n] you from the way the LORD your
God commanded you to follow. You
must purge the evil[o] from among you.
6If your very own brother, or your
son or daughter, or the wife you love,
or your closest friend secretly entices[p] you, saying, "Let us go and worship other gods"[q] (gods that neither
you nor your fathers have known,
7gods of the peoples around you,
whether near or far, from one end of
the land to the other), 8do not yield[r]
to him or listen to him. Show him no
pity.[s] Do not spare him or shield him.
9You must certainly put him to
death.[t] Your hand[u] must be the first
in putting him to death, and then the
hands of all the people. 10Stone him to
death, because he tried to turn you
away[v] from the LORD your God, who
brought you out of Egypt, out of the
land of slavery. 11Then all Israel will
hear and be afraid,[w] and no one among
you will do such an evil thing again.
12If you hear it said about one of the
towns the LORD your God is giving you
to live in 13that wicked men[x] have
arisen among you and have led the people of their town astray, saying, "Let us
go and worship other gods" (gods you
have not known), 14then you must inquire, probe and investigate it thoroughly.[y] And if it is true and it has
been proved that this detestable thing
has been done among you,[z] 15you
must certainly put to the sword all who
live in that town. Destroy it completely,[t][a] both its people and its livestock.[b] 16Gather all the plunder of the
town into the middle of the public
square and completely burn the town[c]
and all its plunder as a whole burnt offering to the LORD your God.[d] It is to
remain a ruin[e] forever, never to be rebuilt. 17None of those condemned
things[t] shall be found in your hands,
so that the LORD will turn from his
fierce anger;[f] he will show you mercy,[g] have compassion[h] on you, and
increase your numbers,[i] as he promised[j] on oath to your forefathers,
18because you obey the LORD your God,
keeping all his commands that I am
giving you today and doing what is
right[k] in his eyes.

Clean and Unclean Food

14:3–20pp — Lev 11:1–23

14 You are the children[l] of the
LORD your God. Do not cut yourselves or shave the front of your heads
for the dead, 2for you are a people
holy[m] to the LORD your God.[n] Out of
all the peoples on the face of the earth,
the LORD has chosen you to be his treasured possession.[o]
3Do not eat any detestable thing.[p]
4These are the animals you may eat:[q]
the ox, the sheep, the goat,[r] 5the
deer,[s] the gazelle, the roe deer, the
wild goat,[t] the ibex, the antelope and
the mountain sheep.[u] 6You may eat
any animal that has a split hoof divided
in two and that chews the cud. 7How-
ever, of those that chew the cud or that
have a split hoof completely divided
you may not eat the camel, the rabbit
or the coney.[v] Although they chew the
cud, they do not have a split hoof; they
are ceremonially unclean for you. 8The
pig is also unclean; although it has a
split hoof, it does not chew the cud.
You are not to eat their meat or touch
their carcasses.[u]
9Of all the creatures living in the water, you may eat any that has fins and
scales. 10But anything that does not
have fins and scales you may not eat;
for you it is unclean.
11You may eat any clean bird. 12But
these you may not eat: the eagle, the
vulture, the black vulture, 13the red
kite, the black kite, any kind[v] of falcon,[w] 14any kind of raven,[x] 15the
horned owl, the screech owl, the gull,
any kind of hawk, 16the little owl, the
great owl, the white owl, 17the desert
owl,[y] the osprey, the cormorant, 18the
stork, any kind of heron, the hoopoe
and the bat.
19All flying insects that swarm are
unclean to you; do not eat them. 20But
any winged creature that is clean you
may eat.[z]
21Do not eat anything you find already dead.[a] You may give it to an

13:4 [k]S Dt 6:13; S Ps 5:7 [l]S Dt 10:20
13:5 [m]S Ex 21:12; S 22:20 [n]ver 10; Dt 4:19 [o]Dt 17:7, 12; 19:19; 24:7; Jdg 20:13; S 1Co 5:13
13:6 [p]Dt 17:2-7; 29:18 [q]S Dt 11:28
13:8 [r]Pr 1:10 [s]S Dt 7:2
13:9 [t]ver 5 [u]S Lev 24:14
13:10 [v]S Ex 20:3
13:11 [w]Dt 17:13; 19:20; 21:21; 1Ti 5:20
13:13 [x]ver 2,6; Jdg 19:22; 20:13; 1Sa 2:12; 10:27; 11:12; 25:17; 1Ki 21:10
13:14 [y]Jdg 20:12 [z]Dt 17:4
13:15 [a]Isa 24:6; 34:5; 43:28; 47:6; La 2:6; Da 9:11; Zec 8:13; Mal 4:6 [b]Ex 22:20
13:16 [c]2Ki 25:9; Jer 39:8; 52:13; Eze 16:41 [d]Dt 7:25,26; Jos 6:24 [e]Jos 8:28; Isa 7:16; 17:1; 24:10; 25:2; 27:10; 32:14,19; 37:26; Jer 49:2; Mic 1:6
13:17 [f]Ex 32:12; Nu 25:4 [g]S Ge 43:14 [h]Dt 30:3 [i]S Dt 7:13 [j]S Ge 12:2; S 13:14; S 26:24
13:18 [k]S Dt 12:25
14:1 [l]S Jn 1:12; S Ro 8:14; 9:8
14:2 [m]S Ge 28:14; Ex 22:31; Isa 6:13; Mal 2:15 [n]S Lev 20:26; Ro 12:1 [o]S Ex 8:22; S Dt 7:6
14:3 [p]Eze 4:14
14:4 [q]Ac 10:14 [r]S Lev 7:23
14:5 [s]S Dt 12:15 [t]Job 39:1; Ps 104:18
14:8 [u]S Lev 5:2
14:13 [v]S Ge 1:11 [w]Isa 34:15
14:14 [x]S Ge 8:7
14:17 [y]Ps 102:6; Isa 13:21; 14:23; 34:11; Zep 2:14
14:20 [z]S Lev 20:25
14:21 [a]S Lev 11:39

[t] *15* The Hebrew term refers to the irrevocable giving over of things or persons to the LORD, often by totally destroying them. [u] *5* The precise identification of some of the birds and animals in this chapter is uncertain.
[v] *7* That is, the hyrax or rock badger

alien living in any of your towns, and
he may eat it, or you may sell it to a
foreigner. But you are a people holy to
the LORD your God.[b]

Do not cook a young goat in its
mother's milk.[c]

Tithes

22Be sure to set aside a tenth[d] of all
that your fields produce each year.
23Eat[e] the tithe of your grain, new
wine[f] and oil, and the firstborn of
your herds and flocks in the presence
of the LORD your God at the place he
will choose as a dwelling for his
Name,[g] so that you may learn[h] to revere[i] the LORD your God always.
24But if that place is too distant and
you have been blessed by the LORD your
God and cannot carry your tithe (because the place where the LORD will
choose to put his Name is so far away),
25then exchange[j] your tithe for silver,
and take the silver with you and go to
the place the LORD your God will
choose. **26**Use the silver to buy whatever you like: cattle, sheep, wine or other
fermented drink,[k] or anything you
wish. Then you and your household
shall eat there in the presence of the
LORD your God and rejoice.[l] **27**And do
not neglect the Levites[m] living in your
towns, for they have no allotment or
inheritance of their own.[n]

28At the end of every three years,
bring all the tithes[o] of that year's produce and store it in your towns,[p] **29**so
that the Levites (who have no allotment[q] or inheritance[r] of their own)
and the aliens,[s] the fatherless and the
widows who live in your towns may
come and eat and be satisfied,[t] and so
that the LORD your God may bless[u] you
in all the work of your hands.

The Year for Canceling Debts

15:1–11Ref — Lev 25:8–38

15 At the end of every seven years
you must cancel debts.[v] **2**This
is how it is to be done: Every creditor
shall cancel the loan he has made to
his fellow Israelite. He shall not require payment from his fellow Israelite
or brother, because the LORD's time for
canceling debts has been proclaimed.
3You may require payment from a foreigner,[w] but you must cancel any debt
your brother owes you. **4**However,
there should be no poor among you, for
in the land the LORD your God is giving
you to possess as your inheritance, he
will richly bless[x] you, **5**if only you fully obey the LORD your God and are careful to follow[y] all these commands I am
giving you today. **6**For the LORD your
God will bless you as he has promised,
and you will lend to many nations but
will borrow from none. You will rule
over many nations but none will rule
over you.[z]

7If there is a poor man[a] among your
brothers in any of the towns of the land

14:21 [b]ver 2 [c]S Ex 23:19
14:22 [d]S Ge 14:20; S Lev 27:30; S Nu 18:21
14:23 [e]S Dt 12:17,18 [f]Ps 4:7 [g]S Dt 12:5; 1Ki 3:2 [h]S Dt 4:10 [i]Ps 22:23; 33:8; Mal 2:5
14:25 [j]Mt 21:12; Jn 2:14
14:26 [k]S Lev 10:9; Ecc 10:16-17 [l]S Lev 23:40; S Dt 12:18
14:27 [m]S Dt 12:19 [n]S Nu 18:20; 26:62; Dt 18:1-2
14:28 [o]S Lev 27:30
[p]Dt 26:12
14:29 [q]Ge 47:22 [r]Nu 26:62 [s]Dt 16:11; 24:19-21; Ps 94:6; Isa 1:17; 58:6 [t]S Dt 6:11 [u]Dt 15:10; Ps 41:1; Pr 22:9; Mal 3:10
15:1 [v]Dt 31:10; Ne 10:31
15:3 [w]S Ge 31:15; Dt 23:20; 28:12; Ru 2:10
15:4 [x]Dt 28:8
15:5 [y]S Ex 15:26; Dt 7:12; 28:1
15:6 [z]Dt 28:12-13,44
15:7 [a]ver 11; Mt 26:11

14:26 WINE OR OTHER FERMENTED DRINK . . . YOU AND YOUR HOUSEHOLD. This verse applies to special occasions for worship and thanksgiving by the entire household, including men, women, youth and little children. The Hebrew word used here for "wine" (*yayin*) can indicate either fermented grape juice or unfermented grape juice. The Hebrew word for "fermented drink" (*shekar*) can be rendered "sweet drink" (see article on WINE IN THE OLD TESTAMENT, p. 204, for the usual meaning of the two Hebrew words used here). This rendering removes the difficulty of suggesting that adults and children are commanded to worship God by consuming addicting and intoxicating beverages. Any attempt to arrive at a correct interpretation of this verse must take into account the following observations.

(1) The purpose of the worship service was "that you may learn to revere the LORD your God always" (v. 23). In order to properly worship God and learn to revere him, we need to be alert and self-controlled (see Eph 5:18, note; 1Th 5:6–8, note; see article on THE FEAR OF THE LORD, p. 260). Note that God requires total abstinence from intoxicating beverages in order to distinguish between the holy and the profane, to rightly teach his commandments (Lev 10:9) and to ensure we do not forget God's law and do wrong (see Pr 31:4–5, note).

(2) The Levite priests were to be present at the worship service (vv. 27–29). God commanded these priests to abstain from intoxicating types of drink (on penalty of death) during the time of their priestly ministry (Lev 10:9). It would be totally contrary to God's holy character to commend the free use of intoxicants by the worshipers while in the company of the priests.

(3) The nature of the festival was a harvest feast, during which time fresh harvest products would be used (v. 23); this suggests that new fresh juice is in view here.

(4) Also the modern discovery of the terrible deformative consequences of alcohol on unborn children must be considered before alleging that an all-knowing God blessed, sanctioned or commanded Israelite fathers, mothers and small children to "rejoice" in his presence while consuming intoxicating beverages (see Pr 23:31, note; see article on WINE IN NEW TESTAMENT TIMES (2), p. 1586).

that the LORD your God is giving you, do not be hardhearted or tightfisted[b] toward your poor brother. 8Rather be openhanded[c] and freely lend him whatever he needs. 9Be careful not to harbor this wicked thought: "The seventh year, the year for canceling debts,[d] is near," so that you do not show ill will[e] toward your needy brother and give him nothing. He may then appeal to the LORD against you, and you will be found guilty of sin.[f] 10Give generously to him and do so without a grudging heart;[g] then because of this the LORD your God will bless[h] you in all your work and in everything you put your hand to. 11There will always be poor people[i] in the land. Therefore I command you to be openhanded toward your brothers and toward the poor and needy in your land.[j]

Freeing Servants

15:12–18pp — Ex 21:2–6
15:12–18Ref — Lev 25:38–55

12If a fellow Hebrew, a man or a woman, sells himself to you and serves you six years, in the seventh year you must let him go free.[k] 13And when you release him, do not send him away empty-handed. 14Supply him liberally from your flock, your threshing floor[l] and your winepress. Give to him as the LORD your God has blessed you. 15Remember that you were slaves[m] in Egypt and the LORD your God redeemed you.[n] That is why I give you this command today.

16But if your servant says to you, "I do not want to leave you," because he loves you and your family and is well off with you, 17then take an awl and push it through his ear lobe into the door, and he will become your servant for life. Do the same for your maidservant.

18Do not consider it a hardship to set your servant free, because his service to you these six years has been worth twice as much as that of a hired hand. And the LORD your God will bless you in everything you do.

The Firstborn Animals

19Set apart for the LORD[o] your God every firstborn male[p] of your herds and flocks.[q] Do not put the firstborn of your oxen to work, and do not shear the firstborn of your sheep.[r] 20Each year you and your family are to eat them in the presence of the LORD your God at the place he will choose.[s] 21If an animal has a defect,[t] is lame or blind, or has any serious flaw, you must not sacrifice it to the LORD your God.[u] 22You are to eat it in your own towns. Both the ceremonially unclean and the clean may eat it, as if it were gazelle or deer.[v] 23But you must not eat the blood; pour it out on the ground like water.[w]

Passover

16:1–8pp — Ex 12:14–20; Lev 23:4–8; Nu 28:16–25

16 Observe the month of Abib[x] and celebrate the Passover[y] of the LORD your God, because in the month of Abib he brought you out of Egypt by night. 2Sacrifice as the Passover to the LORD your God an animal from your flock or herd at the place the LORD will choose as a dwelling for his Name.[z] 3Do not eat it with bread made with yeast, but for seven days eat unleavened bread, the bread of affliction,[a] because you left Egypt in haste[b]—so that all the days of your life you may remember the time of your departure from Egypt.[c] 4Let no yeast be found in your possession in all your land for seven days. Do not let any of the meat you sacrifice on the evening[d]

15:7 [b] 1Jn 3:17
15:8 [c] Mt 5:42; Lk 6:34; S Ac 24:17
15:9 [d] ver 1 [e] Mt 20:15 [f] S Ex 22:23; S Job 5:15; Jas 5:4
15:10 [g] 2Co 9:5 [h] S Dt 14:29
15:11 [i] S ver 7 [j] Mt 26:11; Mk 14:7; Jn 12:8
15:12 [k] Jer 34:14
15:14 [l] S Nu 18:27
15:15 [m] Ex 13:3; Jer 34:13 [n] Ex 20:2; S Dt 4:34; S 9:26; 16:12; 24:18; Jer 16:14; 23:7
15:19 [o] S Lev 27:9 [p] S Ex 13:2 [q] S Ge 4:4 [r] S Ex 22:30
15:20 [s] S Lev 7:15-18; Dt 12:5-7,17,18
15:21 [t] S Ex 12:5 [u] S Lev 22:19-25; Dt 17:1; Mal 1:8, 13
15:22 [v] S Dt 12:15
15:23 [w] S Ge 9:4; Dt 12:16; Eze 33:25
16:1 [x] S Ex 12:2 [y] S Ex 12:11; 2Ki 23:21; Mt 26:17-29
16:2 [z] Dt 12:5,26
16:3 [a] Ex 12:8,39; 34:18; 1Co 5:8 [b] S Ex 12:11 [c] Dt 4:9
16:4 [d] S Ex 12:6

15:7–11 A POOR MAN. Obedience to God's law was expected to grow out of a sincere desire to help those in need (cf. 24:14–15; Pr 14:21,31). (1) God cares about our attitude and our desire to help the poor and unfortunate. We must use our material possessions to help those who have real needs (see article on THE CARE OF THE POOR AND NEEDY, p. 1316). To have a spirit of greed and selfishness that ignores the needs of others deprives us of God's blessing (vv. 9–10). (2) The NT emphasizes the need for compassion, empathy and kindness toward those who have suffered setbacks or experienced unfortunate circumstances bringing poverty or need (Mt 25:31–36; Gal 6:2, 10).

15:13 NOT SEND HIM AWAY EMPTY-HANDED. The Israelites were not allowed to send their slaves away without adequate provision (cf. v. 12). Love for others (cf. Lev 19:18) demanded that sufficient food and supplies be given to them so that they could get by until they began to earn a living. Similarly, the principle of love and justice under the new covenant requires that we treat our employees with compassion, fairness and justice.

16:1 PASSOVER. See article on THE PASSOVER, p. 104.

of the first day remain until morning.[e]
5You must not sacrifice the Passover in any town the LORD your God
gives you 6except in the place he will
choose as a dwelling for his Name.
There you must sacrifice the Passover
in the evening, when the sun goes
down, on the anniversary[wf] of your
departure from Egypt. 7Roast[g] it and
eat it at the place the LORD your God
will choose. Then in the morning return to your tents. 8For six days eat
unleavened bread and on the seventh
day hold an assembly[h] to the LORD
your God and do no work.[i]

Feast of Weeks

16:9–12pp — Lev 23:15–22; Nu 28:26–31

9Count off seven weeks[j] from the
time you begin to put the sickle to the
standing grain.[k] 10Then celebrate the
Feast of Weeks to the LORD your God by
giving a freewill offering in proportion
to the blessings the LORD your God has
given you. 11And rejoice[l] before the
LORD your God at the place he will
choose as a dwelling for his Name[m]—
you, your sons and daughters, your
menservants and maidservants, the
Levites[n] in your towns, and the
aliens,[o] the fatherless and the widows
living among you.[p] 12Remember that
you were slaves in Egypt,[q] and follow
carefully these decrees.

Feast of Tabernacles

16:13–17pp — Lev 23:33–43; Nu 29:12–39

13Celebrate the Feast of Tabernacles for seven days after you have gathered the produce of your threshing
floor[r] and your winepress.[s] 14Be joyful[t] at your Feast—you, your sons
and daughters, your menservants and
maidservants, and the Levites, the
aliens, the fatherless and the widows
who live in your towns. 15For seven
days celebrate the Feast to the LORD
your God at the place the LORD will
choose. For the LORD your God will
bless you in all your harvest and in all
the work of your hands, and your joy[u]
will be complete.
16Three times a year all your men
must appear[v] before the LORD your
God at the place he will choose: at the
Feast of Unleavened Bread,[w] the
Feast of Weeks and the Feast of Tabernacles.[x] No man should appear before
the LORD empty-handed:[y] 17Each of
you must bring a gift in proportion to
the way the LORD your God has blessed
you.

Judges

18Appoint judges[z] and officials for
each of your tribes in every town the
LORD your God is giving you, and they
shall judge the people fairly.[a] 19Do
not pervert justice[b] or show partiality.[c] Do not accept a bribe,[d] for a
bribe blinds the eyes of the wise and
twists the words of the righteous.
20Follow justice and justice alone, so
that you may live and possess the land
the LORD your God is giving you.

Worshiping Other Gods

21Do not set up any wooden Asherah
pole[xe] beside the altar you build to
the LORD your God,[f] 22and do not
erect a sacred stone,[g] for these the
LORD your God hates.

17 Do not sacrifice to the LORD
your God an ox or a sheep that
has any defect[h] or flaw in it, for that
would be detestable[i] to him.[j]
2If a man or woman living among
you in one of the towns the LORD gives
you is found doing evil in the eyes of
the LORD your God in violation of his
covenant,[k] 3and contrary to my command[l] has worshiped other gods,[m]
bowing down to them or to the sun[n] or
the moon or the stars of the sky,[o]
4and this has been brought to your attention, then you must investigate it
thoroughly. If it is true[p] and it has
been proved that this detestable thing
has been done in Israel,[q] 5take the
man or woman who has done this evil
deed to your city gate and stone that
person to death.[r] 6On the testimony
of two or three witnesses a man shall
be put to death, but no one shall be put
to death on the testimony of only one
witness.[s] 7The hands of the witnesses
must be the first in putting him to
death,[t] and then the hands of all the

16:4 [e]S Ex 12:8; Mk 14:12
16:6 [f]S Ex 12:42
16:7 [g]S Ex 12:8
16:8 [h]S Lev 23:8 [i]Mt 26:17; Lk 2:41; 22:7; Jn 2:13
16:9 [j]Ac 2:1 [k]S Ex 23:16
16:11 [l]Dt 12:7 [m]S Ex 20:24; S 2Sa 7:13 [n]Dt 12:12 [o]S Dt 14:29 [p]Ne 8:10
16:12 [q]S Dt 15:15
16:13 [r]S Lev 2:14 [s]S Ge 27:37; S Ex 23:16
16:14 [t]ver 11
16:15 [u]Job 38:7; Ps 4:7; 28:7; 30:11
16:16 [v]Dt 31:11; Ps 84:7 [w]S Ex 12:17 [x]S Ex 23:14,16; Ezr 3:4 [y]S Ex 34:20
16:18 [z]S Ex 18:21,26 [a]S Ge 31:37
16:19 [b]S Ex 23:2 [c]S Lev 19:15 [d]S Ex 18:21; S 1Sa 8:3
16:21 [e]S Dt 7:5 [f]Ex 34:13; 1Ki 14:15; 2Ki 17:16; 21:3; 2Ch 33:3
16:22 [g]S Ex 23:24
17:1 [h]S Ex 12:5; S Lev 22:20 [i]Dt 7:25 [j]S Dt 15:21
17:2 [k]Dt 13:6-11
17:3 [l]Jer 7:31 [m]Ex 22:20 [n]S Ge 1:16 [o]S Ge 2:1; S 37:9
17:4 [p]Dt 22:20 [q]Dt 13:12-14
17:5 [r]S Lev 24:14
17:6 [s]Nu 35:30; Dt 19:15; S Mt 18:16
17:7 [t]Jn 8:7

[w]6 Or *down, at the time of day* [x]21 Or *Do not plant any tree dedicated to Asherah*

16:10 FEAST OF WEEKS. For comments on Israel's holy days and feasts, see Lev 23, notes.
17:7 PURGE THE EVIL. The Israelites were commanded to keep themselves pure by removing from among them those who lived ungodly lives and transgressed the covenant. The NT also requires that congregations discipline sinning members and expel those who continue to live in sin

people.[u] You must purge the evil[v]
from among you.

Law Courts

8If cases come before your courts
that are too difficult for you to
judge[w]—whether bloodshed, lawsuits
or assaults[x]—take them to the place
the LORD your God will choose.[y] 9Go to
the priests, who are Levites,[z] and to
the judge[a] who is in office at that
time. Inquire of them and they will give
you the verdict.[b] 10You must act according to the decisions they give you
at the place the LORD will choose. Be
careful to do everything they direct you
to do. 11Act according to the law they
teach you and the decisions they give
you. Do not turn aside from what they
tell you, to the right or to the left.[c]
12The man who shows contempt[d] for
the judge or for the priest who stands
ministering[e] there to the LORD your
God must be put to death.[f] You must
purge the evil from Israel.[g] 13All the
people will hear and be afraid, and will
not be contemptuous again.[h]

The King

14When you enter the land the LORD
your God is giving you and have taken
possession[i] of it and settled in it,[j]
and you say, "Let us set a king over us
like all the nations around us,"[k] 15be
sure to appoint[l] over you the king the
LORD your God chooses. He must be
from among your own brothers.[m] Do
not place a foreigner over you, one who
is not a brother Israelite. 16The king,
moreover, must not acquire great numbers of horses[n] for himself[o] or make
the people return to Egypt[p] to get
more of them,[q] for the LORD has told
you, "You are not to go back that way
again."[r] 17He must not take many
wives,[s] or his heart will be led
astray.[t] He must not accumulate[u]
large amounts of silver and gold.[v]
18When he takes the throne[w] of his
kingdom, he is to write[x] for himself on
a scroll a copy[y] of this law, taken from
that of the priests, who are Levites.
19It is to be with him, and he is to read
it all the days of his life[z] so that he
may learn to revere the LORD his God
and follow carefully all the words of
this law and these decrees[a] 20and not
consider himself better than his brothers and turn from the law[b] to the right
or to the left.[c] Then he and his
descendants will reign a long time over
his kingdom in Israel.[d]

Offerings for Priests and Levites

18 The priests, who are Levites[e]—indeed the whole
tribe of Levi—are to have no allotment
or inheritance with Israel. They shall
live on the offerings[f] made to the LORD
by fire, for that is their inheritance.[g]
2They shall have no inheritance among
their brothers; the LORD is their inheritance,[h] as he promised them.[i]
3This is the share due the priests[j]
from the people who sacrifice a bull[k]
or a sheep: the shoulder, the jowls and
the inner parts.[l] 4You are to give
them the firstfruits of your grain, new
wine and oil, and the first wool from
the shearing of your sheep,[m] 5for the
LORD your God has chosen them[n] and
their descendants out of all your tribes
to stand and minister[o] in the LORD's
name always.[p]
6If a Levite moves from one of your
towns anywhere in Israel where he is
living, and comes in all earnestness to
the place the LORD will choose,[q] 7he
may minister in the name[r] of the LORD
his God like all his fellow Levites who
serve there in the presence of the LORD.
8He is to share equally in their benefits, even though he has received money from the sale of family possessions.[s]

Detestable Practices

9When you enter the land the LORD
your God is giving you, do not learn to
imitate[t] the detestable ways[u] of the
nations there. 10Let no one be found

17:7 [u] S Lev 24:14; Ac 7:58 [v] S Dt 13:5; 1Co 5:13* **17:8** [w] Ex 21:6 [x] 2Ch 19:10 [y] Dt 12:5; Ps 122:3-5 **17:9** [z] Dt 24:8; 27:9 [a] S Ex 21:6 [b] S Ge 25:22; Dt 19:17; Eze 44:24; Hag 2:11 **17:11** [c] S Lev 10:11; S Dt 5:32 **17:12** [d] Nu 15:30 [e] S Nu 16:9 [f] ver 13; S Ge 17:14; Dt 13:11; 18:20; 19:20; 1Ki 18:40; Jer 14:14; Hos 4:4; Zec 13:3 [g] S Dt 13:5 **17:13** [h] S ver 12 **17:14** [i] S Nu 33:53 [j] Jos 21:43 [k] 1Sa 8:5,19-20; 10:19 **17:15** [l] 1Sa 16:3; 2Sa 5:3 [m] Jer 30:21 **17:16** [n] Isa 2:7; 30:16 [o] 1Sa 8:11; 1Ki 4:26; 9:19; 10:26; 2Ch 1:14; Ps 20:7 [p] 1Ki 10:29; Isa 31:1; Jer 42:14 [q] 1Ki 10:28; Isa 31:1; Eze 17:15 [r] S Ex 13:17 **17:17** [s] S Ex 34:16; 2Sa 5:13; 12:11; 1Ki 11:3; 2Ch 11:21 [t] 1Ki 11:2; Pr 31:3 [u] 1Ki 10:27 [v] 2Ch 1:11; Isa 2:7 **17:18** [w] 1Ki 1:46; 1Ch 29:23 [x] Dt 31:22,24; Jos 24:26; 1Sa 10:25 [y] 2Ch 23:11 **17:19** [z] Dt 4:9-10; Jos 1:8 [a] Dt 11:13; 1Ki 3:3; 11:38; 2Ki 22:2 **17:20** [b] Jos 23:6; Job 23:12; Ps 119:102 [c] S Dt 5:32; S 1Ki 9:4 [d] 1Sa 8:5; 10:25; 1Ki 2:3; 1Ch 28:8 **18:1** [e] Jer 33:18, 21 [f] S Nu 18:8 [g] S Nu 18:20; 1Co 9:13 **18:2** [h] Nu 18:20 [i] Jos 13:14 **18:3** [j] S Ex 29:27 [k] S Lev 1:5 [l] Lev 7:28-34; Nu 18:12 **18:4** [m] Ex 22:29; Nu 18:12 **18:5** [n] S Ex 28:1 [o] Dt 10:8 [p] S Ex 29:9 **18:6** [q] S Nu 35:2-3; S Dt 12:5 **18:7** [r] ver 19; 1Ki 18:32; 22:16; Ps 118:26 **18:8** [s] Nu 18:24; 2Ch 31:4; Ne 12:44,47; 13:12 **18:9** [t] Dt 9:5; 12:29-31 [u] S Lev 18:3; 2Ki 21:2; 2Ch 28:3; 33:2; 34:33; Ezr 6:21; 9:11; Jer 44:4

---

and immorality (cf. Mt 18:15–17; 1Co 5:1–13; 2Co 2:6–7).

18:9–11 DETESTABLE WAYS OF THE NATIONS. These verses contain a list of occult magic practices, common in the religions of Canaan, which were an abomination to God and forbidden by him. Those among God's OT people who practiced such things were to be put to death (Lev 20:27). Likewise, the NT declares that those who practice such things will not enter God's kingdom (Gal 5:20–21; Rev 22:15).

among you who sacrifices his son or
daughter in[y] the fire,[v] who practices
divination[w] or sorcery,[x] interprets
omens, engages in witchcraft,[y] 11or
casts spells,[z] or who is a medium or
spiritist[a] or who consults the dead.
12Anyone who does these things is detestable to the LORD, and because of
these detestable practices the LORD
your God will drive out those nations
before you.[b] 13You must be blameless[c] before the LORD your God.[d]

The Prophet

14The nations you will dispossess
listen to those who practice sorcery or
divination.[e] But as for you, the LORD
your God has not permitted you to do
so. 15The LORD your God will raise up
for you a prophet like me from among
your own brothers.[f] You must listen
to him. 16For this is what you asked of
the LORD your God at Horeb on the day
of the assembly when you said, "Let us
not hear the voice of the LORD our God
nor see this great fire anymore, or we
will die."[g]
17The LORD said to me: "What they
say is good. 18I will raise up for them
a prophet[h] like you from among their
brothers; I will put my words[i] in his
mouth,[j] and he will tell them everything I command him.[k] 19If anyone
does not listen[l] to my words that the
prophet speaks in my name,[m] I myself
will call him to account.[n] 20But a
prophet who presumes to speak in my
name anything I have not commanded
him to say, or a prophet who speaks in
the name of other gods,[o] must be put
to death."[p]
21You may say to yourselves, "How
can we know when a message has not
been spoken by the LORD?" 22If what a
prophet proclaims in the name of the
LORD does not take place or come
true,[q] that is a message the LORD has
not spoken.[r] That prophet has spoken
presumptuously.[s] Do not be afraid of
him.

Cities of Refuge

19:1-14Ref — Nu 35:6-34; Dt 4:41-43; Jos 20:1-9

19 When the LORD your God has
destroyed the nations whose
land he is giving you, and when you
have driven them out and settled in
their towns and houses,[t] 2then set
aside for yourselves three cities cen-
trally located in the land the LORD your
God is giving you to possess. 3Build
roads to them and divide into three
parts the land the LORD your God is giving you as an inheritance, so that anyone who kills a man may flee there.
4This is the rule concerning the man
who kills another and flees there to
save his life—one who kills his neighbor unintentionally, without malice
aforethought. 5For instance, a man
may go into the forest with his neighbor to cut wood, and as he swings his
ax to fell a tree, the head may fly off
and hit his neighbor and kill him. That
man may flee to one of these cities and
save his life. 6Otherwise, the avenger
of blood[u] might pursue him in a rage,
overtake him if the distance is too
great, and kill him even though he is
not deserving of death, since he did it
to his neighbor without malice aforethought. 7This is why I command you
to set aside for yourselves three cities.
8If the LORD your God enlarges your
territory,[v] as he promised[w] on oath
to your forefathers, and gives you the
whole land he promised them, 9be-
cause you carefully follow all these
laws I command you today—to love

18:10 [v] S Lev 18:21 [w] 1Sa 15:23 [x] S Ex 7:11 [y] S Lev 19:31 **18:11** [z] Isa 47:9 [a] S Ex 22:18; S 1Sa 28:13 **18:12** [b] S Lev 18:24 **18:13** [c] S Ge 6:9; Ps 119:1 [d] Mt 5:48 **18:14** [e] 2Ki 21:6 **18:15** [f] S Mt 21:11; Lk 2:25-35; Jn 1:21; Ac 3:22*; 7:37* **18:16** [g] S Ex 20:19; Dt 5:23-27 **18:18** [h] S Ge 20:7 [i] Isa 2:3; 26:8; 51:4; Mic 4:2 [j] S Ex 4:12 [k] Jn 4:25-26; S 14:24; Ac 3:22* **18:19** [l] S Ex 23:21 [m] S ver 7; S Lev 19:12; 2Ki 2:24 [n] Jos 22:23; Ac 3:23*; Heb 12:25 **18:20** [o] S Ex 23:13 [p] Dt 13:1-5; S 17:12 **18:22** [q] S Dt 13:2; 1Sa 3:20 [r] 1Ki 22:28; Jer 28:9 [s] ver 20 **19:1** [t] Dt 6:10-11 **19:6** [u] S Nu 35:12 **19:8** [v] S Ex 34:24 [w] S Ge 15:8; S Dt 11:24

[y] *10* Or *who makes his son or daughter pass through*

18:10 WHO SACRIFICES ... IN THE FIRE. Moses reminds the Israelites not to emulate the Canaanite practice of child sacrifices to pagan gods, performed in order to try to influence the course of future events (cf. Lev 20:2–5).

18:10 DIVINATION ... OMENS. Those who practiced divination sought to predict future events or uncover secrets by the aid of evil spirits or by some human means (see Rev 9:21, note). In contrast, God's way for us to gain truth is to listen to faithful prophets who declare his word (vv. 14–22).

18:11 CASTS SPELLS ... IS A MEDIUM. This list includes mediums, spiritists, or anyone who calls up the dead or consults with the world of spirits (i.e., demons) in order to discover secrets, predict the future or gain power. Communication with the dead is actually a communication with demons (cf. 1Sa 28:8–14; 2Ki 21:6; Isa 8:19).

18:15 A PROPHET LIKE ME. The ultimate prophet like Moses (vv. 15,18) was Jesus Christ, the Messiah (see Ac 3:22, note). Like Moses, this Prophet was to be an Israelite who would speak God's word (vv. 18–19). The Jews of Jesus' time expected the coming of this great Prophet (Jn 1:21, 45; 4:19,29; 6:14; Ac 3:22–26; 7:37).

the LORD your God and to walk always
in his ways[x]—then you are to set
aside three more cities. 10Do this so
that innocent blood[y] will not be shed
in your land, which the LORD your God
is giving you as your inheritance, and
so that you will not be guilty of bloodshed.[z]
11But if a man hates his neighbor
and lies in wait for him, assaults and
kills him,[a] and then flees to one of
these cities, 12the elders of his town
shall send for him, bring him back from
the city, and hand him over to the
avenger of blood to die. 13Show him no
pity.[b] You must purge from Israel the
guilt of shedding innocent blood,[c] so
that it may go well with you.
14Do not move your neighbor's
boundary stone set up by your predecessors in the inheritance you receive
in the land the LORD your God is giving
you to possess.[d]

Witnesses

15One witness is not enough to convict a man accused of any crime or offense he may have committed. A matter must be established by the
testimony of two or three witnesses.[e]
16If a malicious witness[f] takes the
stand to accuse a man of a crime, 17the
two men involved in the dispute must
stand in the presence of the LORD before the priests and the judges[g] who
are in office at the time. 18The judges
must make a thorough investigation,[h]
and if the witness proves to be a liar,
giving false testimony against his
brother, 19then do to him as he intended to do to his brother.[i] You must
purge the evil from among you. 20The
rest of the people will hear of this and
be afraid,[j] and never again will such
an evil thing be done among you.
21Show no pity:[k] life for life, eye for
eye, tooth for tooth, hand for hand, foot
for foot.[l]

Going to War

20 When you go to war against
your enemies and see horses
and chariots and an army greater than
yours,[m] do not be afraid[n] of them,[o]
because the LORD your God, who
brought you up out of Egypt, will be
with[p] you. 2When you are about to go
into battle, the priest shall come forward and address the army. 3He shall
say: "Hear, O Israel, today you are going into battle against your enemies.
Do not be fainthearted[q] or afraid; do
not be terrified or give way to panic before them. 4For the LORD your God is
the one who goes with you[r] to fight[s]
for you against your enemies to give
you victory.[t]"
5The officers shall say to the army:
"Has anyone built a new house and not
dedicated[u] it? Let him go home, or he
may die in battle and someone else
may dedicate it. 6Has anyone planted[v] a vineyard and not begun to enjoy
it?[w] Let him go home, or he may die
in battle and someone else enjoy it.
7Has anyone become pledged to a
woman and not married her? Let him
go home, or he may die in battle and
someone else marry her.[x]" 8Then the
officers shall add, "Is any man afraid or
fainthearted? Let him go home so that
his brothers will not become disheartened too."[y] 9When the officers have
finished speaking to the army, they
shall appoint commanders over it.
10When you march up to attack a
city, make its people an offer of
peace.[z] 11If they accept and open
their gates, all the people in it shall be
subject[a] to forced labor[b] and shall
work for you. 12If they refuse to make
peace and they engage you in battle,
lay siege to that city. 13When the LORD
your God delivers it into your hand, put
to the sword all the men in it.[c] 14As
for the women, the children, the livestock[d] and everything else in the
city,[e] you may take these as plunder[f] for yourselves. And you may use
the plunder the LORD your God gives
you from your enemies. 15This is how
you are to treat all the cities that are
at a distance[g] from you and do not belong to the nations nearby.
16However, in the cities of the nations the LORD your God is giving you
as an inheritance, do not leave alive
anything that breathes.[h] 17Complete-

19:9 [x]Dt 6:5 **19:10** [y]Pr 6:17; Jer 7:6; 26:15 [z]Dt 21:1-9 **19:11** [a]S Ex 21:12; 1Jn 3:15 **19:13** [b]Dt 7:2 [c]Dt 21:9; 1Ki 2:31 **19:14** [d]Dt 27:17; Job 24:2; Ps 16:6; Pr 15:25; 22:28; 23:10; Isa 1:23; Hos 5:10 **19:15** [e]S Dt 17:6; S Mt 18:16*; 26:60; 2Co 13:1* **19:16** [f]Ex 23:1; Pr 6:19 **19:17** [g]S Ex 21:6 **19:18** [h]S Ex 23:7 **19:19** [i]Pr 19:5,9; 1Co 5:13* **19:20** [j]S Dt 13:11 **19:21** [k]ver 13 [l]S Ex 21:24; Mt 5:38* **20:1** [m]Ps 20:7; Isa 31:1 [n]S Nu 14:9 [o]S Dt 3:22; S 1Sa 17:45

[p]Isa 41:10 **20:3** [q]1Sa 17:32; Job 23:16; Ps 22:14; Isa 7:4; 35:4; Jer 51:46 **20:4** [r]2Ch 20:14-22 [s]S Ex 14:14; 1Ch 5:22; Ne 4:20 [t]Jdg 12:3; 15:18; Ps 44:7; 144:10 **20:5** [u]Ne 12:27 **20:6** [v]Jer 31:5; Eze 28:26; Mic 1:6 [w]1Co 9:7 **20:7** [x]Dt 24:5; Pr 5:18 **20:8** [y]Jdg 7:3 **20:10** [z]S Dt 2:26; Lk 14:31-32 **20:11** [a]ver 15; 2Ki 6:22 [b]1Ki 9:21; 1Ch 22:2; Isa 31:8 **20:13** [c]Nu 31:7 **20:14** [d]Jos 8:2; 22:8 [e]S Nu 31:11 [f]S Nu 31:53 **20:15** [g]S ver 11; Jos 9:9 **20:16** [h]Ex 23:31-33; Nu 21:2-3; S Dt 7:2; Jos 6:21; 10:1; 11:14

19:21 SHOW NO PITY. The principle stated here is that punishment of crime should be commensurate with the offense, but not excessive (see Ex 21:23–25; Lev 24:17–20). Leniency toward those who harm the innocent and unprotected encourages evil and violence in the land (v. 19). The NT does not abrogate this principle for the governing of society (cf. Ro 13:1–4), but it does forbid the law of retaliation in personal relationships (cf. Mt 5:38–41).

ly destroy[z] them—the Hittites, Amorites, Canaanites, Perizzites, Hivites and Jebusites—as the LORD your God has commanded you. 18 Otherwise, they will teach you to follow all the detestable things they do in worshiping their gods,[i] and you will sin[j] against the LORD your God.

19 When you lay siege to a city for a long time, fighting against it to capture it, do not destroy its trees by putting an ax to them, because you can eat their fruit. Do not cut them down. Are the trees of the field people, that you should besiege them?[a] 20 However, you may cut down trees that you know are not fruit trees[k] and use them to build siege works until the city at war with you falls.

Atonement for an Unsolved Murder

21 If a man is found slain, lying in a field in the land the LORD your God is giving you to possess, and it is not known who killed him,[l] 2 your elders and judges shall go out and measure the distance from the body to the neighboring towns. 3 Then the elders of the town nearest the body shall take a heifer that has never been worked and has never worn a yoke[m] 4 and lead her down to a valley that has not been plowed or planted and where there is a flowing stream. There in the valley they are to break the heifer's neck. 5 The priests, the sons of Levi, shall step forward, for the LORD your God has chosen them to minister and to pronounce blessings[n] in the name of the LORD and to decide all cases of dispute and assault.[o] 6 Then all the elders of the town nearest the body shall wash their hands[p] over the heifer whose neck was broken in the valley, 7 and they shall declare: "Our hands did not shed this blood, nor did our eyes see it done. 8 Accept this atonement for your people Israel, whom you have redeemed, O LORD, and do not hold your people guilty of the blood of an innocent man." And the bloodshed will be atoned for.[q] 9 So you will purge[r] from yourselves the guilt of shedding innocent blood, since you have done what is right in the eyes of the LORD.

Marrying a Captive Woman

10 When you go to war against your enemies and the LORD your God delivers them into your hands[s] and you take captives,[t] 11 if you notice among the captives a beautiful[u] woman and are attracted to her,[v] you may take her as your wife. 12 Bring her into your home and have her shave her head,[w] trim her nails 13 and put aside the clothes she was wearing when captured. After she has lived in your house and mourned her father and mother for a full month,[x] then you may go to her and be her husband and she shall be your wife. 14 If you are not pleased with her, let her go wherever she wishes. You must not sell her or treat her as a slave, since you have dishonored her.[y]

The Right of the Firstborn

15 If a man has two wives,[z] and he loves one but not the other, and both bear him sons but the firstborn is the son of the wife he does not love,[a] 16 when he wills his property to his sons, he must not give the rights of the firstborn to the son of the wife he loves in preference to his actual firstborn, the son of the wife he does not love.[b] 17 He must acknowledge the son of his unloved wife as the firstborn by giving him a double[c] share of all he has. That son is the first sign of his father's strength.[d] The right of the firstborn belongs to him.[e]

A Rebellious Son

18 If a man has a stubborn and rebellious[f] son[g] who does not obey his fa-

20:18 [i] S Ex 34:16 [j] S Ex 10:7 **20:20** [k] Jer 6:6 **21:1** [l] S Nu 25:17 **21:3** [m] S Nu 19:2 **21:5** [n] S Ge 48:20; S Ex 39:43 [o] Dt 17:8-11 **21:6** [p] Mt 27:24 **21:8** [q] Nu 35:33-34 **21:9** [r] Dt 19:13 **21:10** [s] Jos 21:44 [t] 1Ki 8:46; 1Ch 9:1; Ezr 5:12; Jer 40:1; Eze 1:1; 17:12; Da 2:25; Mic 4:10 **21:11** [u] Ge 6:2 [v] S Ge 34:8 **21:12** [w] S Lev 14:9; S Nu 8:7; 1Co 11:5 **21:13** [x] Ps 45:10 **21:14** [y] S Ge 34:2 **21:15** [z] S Ge 4:19 [a] Ge 29:33 **21:16** [b] 1Ch 26:10 **21:17** [c] 2Ki 2:9; Isa 40:2; 61:7; Zec 9:12 [d] S Ge 49:3 [e] Ge 25:31; Lk 15:12 **21:18** [f] Ps 78:8; Jer 5:23; Zep 3:1 [g] Pr 30:17

[z] *17* The Hebrew term refers to the irrevocable giving over of things or persons to the LORD, often by totally destroying them.
[a] *19* Or *down to use in the siege, for the fruit trees are for the benefit of man.*

21:10 YOUR ENEMIES. The "enemies" referred to here are those *outside* of Canaan (cf. 20:15); God's people had earlier been instructed not to marry Canaanite people (7:1,3–4). The instructions given in vv. 10–14 protected the dignity of women captives by forbidding their mistreatment.

21:15 TWO WIVES. Having more than one wife (polygamy) typically produces strained relationships, for favoritism and preferential treatment inevitably enter such marital arrangements (cf. Ge 29:30). Polygamy existed in the patriarchal age; though God did not approve of multiple wives, he did give guidelines to regulate an already existing practice (see Ge 2:24, note; 4:19, note; 29:28, note).

ther and mother[h] and will not listen to
them when they discipline him, **19**his
father and mother shall take hold of
him and bring him to the elders at the
gate of his town. **20**They shall say to
the elders, "This son of ours is stubborn and rebellious. He will not obey
us. He is a profligate and a drunkard."
21Then all the men of his town shall
stone him to death.[i] You must purge
the evil[j] from among you. All Israel
will hear of it and be afraid.[k]

Various Laws

22If a man guilty of a capital offense[l] is put to death and his body is
hung on a tree, **23**you must not leave
his body on the tree overnight.[m] Be
sure to bury[n] him that same day, because anyone who is hung on a tree is
under God's curse.[o] You must not
desecrate[p] the land the LORD your God
is giving you as an inheritance.

22 If you see your brother's ox or
sheep straying, do not ignore it
but be sure to take it back to him.[q] **2**If
the brother does not live near you or if
you do not know who he is, take it
home with you and keep it until he
comes looking for it. Then give it back
to him. **3**Do the same if you find your
brother's donkey or his cloak or anything he loses. Do not ignore it.

4If you see your brother's donkey[r]
or his ox fallen on the road, do not
ignore it. Help him get it to its
feet.[s]

5A woman must not wear men's
clothing, nor a man wear women's
clothing, for the LORD your God detests
anyone who does this.

6If you come across a bird's nest beside the road, either in a tree or on the
ground, and the mother is sitting on
the young or on the eggs, do not take
the mother with the young.[t] **7**You may
take the young, but be sure to let the
mother go,[u] so that it may go well
with you and you may have a long
life.[v]

8When you build a new house, make
a parapet around your roof so that you
may not bring the guilt of bloodshed on
your house if someone falls from the
roof.[w]

9Do not plant two kinds of seed in
your vineyard;[x] if you do, not only the
crops you plant but also the fruit of the
vineyard will be defiled.[b]

10Do not plow with an ox and a donkey yoked together.[y]

11Do not wear clothes of wool and
linen woven together.[z]

12Make tassels on the four corners
of the cloak you wear.[a]

Marriage Violations

13If a man takes a wife and, after
lying with her[b], dislikes her **14**and
slanders her and gives her a bad name,
saying, "I married this woman, but
when I approached her, I did not find
proof of her virginity," **15**then the girl's
father and mother shall bring proof
that she was a virgin to the town elders
at the gate.[c] **16**The girl's father will
say to the elders, "I gave my daughter
in marriage to this man, but he dislikes
her. **17**Now he has slandered her and
said, 'I did not find your daughter to be
a virgin.' But here is the proof of my
daughter's virginity." Then her parents
shall display the cloth before the elders of the town, **18**and the elders[d]
shall take the man and punish him.
19They shall fine him a hundred shekels of silver[c] and give them to the
girl's father, because this man has giv-
en an Israelite virgin a bad name. She
shall continue to be his wife; he must
not divorce her as long as he lives.

20If, however, the charge is true[e]
and no proof of the girl's virginity can
be found, **21**she shall be brought to the
door of her father's house and there
the men of her town shall stone her to
death. She has done a disgraceful
thing[f] in Israel by being promiscuous
while still in her father's house. You
must purge the evil from among you.

22If a man is found sleeping with another man's wife, both the man who
slept[g] with her and the woman must

21:18 [h] S Ge 31:35; Pr 1:8; Isa 30:1; Eph 6:1-3 **21:21** [i] S Lev 20:9 [j] Dt 19:19; 1Co 5:13* [k] S Dt 13:11 **21:22** [l] Dt 22:26; Mt 26:66; Mk 14:64; Ac 23:29 **21:23** [m] Jos 8:29; 10:27; Jn 19:31 [n] Eze 39:12 [o] Ezr 6:11; Est 2:23; 7:9; 8:7; 9:13,25; Isa 50:11; Gal 3:13* [p] S Lev 18:25 **22:1** [q] Ex 23:4-5; Pr 27:10; Zec 7:9 **22:4** [r] Ex 23:5 [s] 1Co 9:9 **22:6** [t] Lev 22:28 **22:7** [u] S Lev 22:28 [v] S Dt 5:29 **22:8** [w] Jos 2:8; 1Sa 9:25; 2Sa 11:2 **22:9** [x] Lev 19:19 **22:10** [y] 2Co 6:14 **22:11** [z] Lev 19:19 **22:12** [a] Nu 15:37-41; Mt 23:5 **22:13** [b] Dt 24:1 **22:15** [c] S Ge 23:10 **22:18** [d] Ex 18:21; Dt 1:9-18 **22:20** [e] Dt 17:4 **22:21** [f] S Ge 34:7; S 38:24; S Lev 19:29; Dt 23:17-18; 1Co 5:13* **22:22** [g] 2Sa 11:4

[b] 9 Or *be forfeited to the sanctuary* [c] 19 That is, about 2 1/2 pounds (about 1 kilogram)

22:17 DAUGHTER'S VIRGINITY. It was important that an Israelite girl remain pure and be a virgin at marriage. Much of the responsibility for this fell upon the parents (v. 15). Likewise, Christian parents have the same responsibility to make every effort to protect their daughters (and their sons) against premarital sexual activities. They must teach them God's principle of purity and guide them into godly and chaste convictions with regard to sexual matters (see article on STANDARDS OF SEXUAL MORALITY, p. 1936).

MAJOR ETHICAL CONCERNS IN THE COVENANT

1. PERSONHOOD
Everyone's person is to be secure (Ex 20:13; Dt 5:17; Ex 21:16-21, 26-31; Lev 19:14; Dt 24:7; 27:18).

2. FALSE ACCUSATION
Everyone is to be secure against slander and false accusation (Ex 20:16; Dt 5:20; Ex 23:1-3; Lev 19:16; Dt 19:15-21).

3. WOMAN
No woman is to be taken advantage of within her subordinate status in society (Ex 21:7-11, 20, 26-32; 22:16-17; Dt. 21:10-14; 22:13-30; 24:1-5).

4. PUNISHMENT
Punishment for wrongdoing shall not be excessive so that the culprit is dehumanized (Dt 25:1-5).

5. DIGNITY
Every Israelite's dignity and right to be God's freedman and servant are to be honored and safeguarded (Ex 21:2, 5-6; Lev 25; Dt 15:12-18).

6. INHERITANCE
Every Israelite's inheritance in the promised land is to be secure (Lev 25; Nu 27:5-7; 36:1-9; Dt 25:5-10).

7. PROPERTY
Everyone's property is to be secure (Ex 20:15; Dt 5:19; Ex 21:33-36; 22:1-15; 23:4-5; Lev 19:35-36; Dt 22: 1-4; 25:13-15).

8. FRUIT OF LABOR
Everyone is to receive the fruit of his labors (Lev 19:13; Dt 24:14; 25:4).

9. FRUIT OF THE GROUND
Everyone is to share the fruit of the ground (Ex 23:10-11; Lev 19:9-10; 23:22; 25:3-55; Dt. 14:28-29; 24:19-21).

10. REST ON SABBATH
Everyone, down to the humblest servant and the resident alien, is to share in the weekly rest of God's Sabbath (Ex 20:8-11; Dt 5:12-15; Ex 23:12).

11. MARRIAGE
The marriage relationship is to be kept inviolate (Ex 20:14; Dt 5:18; see also Lev 18:6-23; 20:10-21; Dt 22:13-30).

12. EXPLOITATION
No one, however disabled, impoverished or powerless, is to be oppressed or exploited (Ex 22:21-27; Lev 19:14, 33-34; 25:35-36; Dt 23:19; 24:6, 12-15, 17; 27:18).

13. FAIR TRIAL
Everyone is to have free access to the courts and is to be afforded a fair trial (Ex 23:6,8; Lev 19:15; Dt 1:17; 10:17-18; 16:18-20; 17:8-13; 19:15-21).

14. SOCIAL ORDER
Every person's God-given place in the social order is to be honored (Ex 20:12; Dt 5:16; Ex 21:15, 17; 22:28; Lev 19:3, 32; 20:9; Dt 17:8-13; 21:15-21; 27:16).

15. LAW
No one shall be above the law, not even the king (Dt 17:18-20).

16. ANIMALS
Concern for the welfare of other creatures is to be extended to the animal world (Ex 23:5, 11; Lev 25:7, Dt 22:4, 6-7; 25:4).

die.[h] You must purge the evil from Israel.
23 If a man happens to meet in a town
a virgin pledged to be married and he
sleeps with her, 24 you shall take both
of them to the gate of that town and
stone them to death—the girl because
she was in a town and did not scream
for help, and the man because he violated another man's wife. You must
purge the evil from among you.[i]
25 But if out in the country a man
happens to meet a girl pledged to be
married and rapes her, only the man
who has done this shall die. 26 Do nothing to the girl; she has committed no
sin deserving death. This case is like
that of someone who attacks and murders his neighbor, 27 for the man found
the girl out in the country, and though
the betrothed girl screamed,[j] there
was no one to rescue her.
28 If a man happens to meet a virgin
who is not pledged to be married and
rapes her and they are discovered,[k]
29 he shall pay the girl's father fifty
shekels of silver.[d] He must marry the
girl, for he has violated her. He can
never divorce her as long as he lives.
30 A man is not to marry his father's
wife; he must not dishonor his father's
bed.[l]

Exclusion From the Assembly

23 No one who has been emascu-
lated[m] by crushing or cutting
may enter the assembly of the LORD.
2 No one born of a forbidden marriage[e] nor any of his descendants may
enter the assembly of the LORD, even
down to the tenth generation.
3 No Ammonite[n] or Moabite or any
of his descendants may enter the assembly of the LORD, even down to the
tenth generation.[o] 4 For they did not
come to meet you with bread and water[p] on your way when you came out
of Egypt, and they hired Balaam[q] son
of Beor from Pethor in Aram Naharaim[f][r] to pronounce a curse on you.[s]
5 However, the LORD your God would
not listen to Balaam but turned the
curse[t] into a blessing for you, because the LORD your God loves[u] you.
6 Do not seek a treaty[v] of friendship
with them as long as you live.[w]
7 Do not abhor an Edomite,[x] for he
is your brother.[y] Do not abhor an
Egyptian, because you lived as an alien
in his country.[z] 8 The third generation
of children born to them may enter the
assembly of the LORD.

Uncleanness in the Camp

9 When you are encamped against
your enemies, keep away from everything impure.[a] 10 If one of your men is
unclean because of a nocturnal emission, he is to go outside the camp and
stay there.[b] 11 But as evening approaches he is to wash himself, and at
sunset[c] he may return to the camp.[d]
12 Designate a place outside the
camp where you can go to relieve yourself. 13 As part of your equipment have
something to dig with, and when you
relieve yourself, dig a hole and cover
up your excrement. 14 For the LORD
your God moves[e] about in your camp
to protect you and to deliver your enemies to you. Your camp must be holy,[f]
so that he will not see among you anything indecent and turn away from you.

Miscellaneous Laws

15 If a slave has taken refuge[g] with
you, do not hand him over to his master.[h] 16 Let him live among you wherever he likes and in whatever town he
chooses. Do not oppress[i] him.
17 No Israelite man[j] or woman is to
become a shrine prostitute.[k] 18 You
must not bring the earnings of a female
prostitute or of a male prostitute[g] into
the house of the LORD your God to pay
any vow, because the LORD your God
detests them both.[l]
19 Do not charge your brother interest, whether on money or food or anything else that may earn interest.[m]
20 You may charge a foreigner[n] interest, but not a brother Israelite, so that
the LORD your God may bless[o] you in

22:22 [h] S Ge 38:24; S Ex 21:12; Mt 5:27-28; Jn 8:5; 1Co 6:9; Heb 13:4
22:24 [i] 1Co 5:13*
22:27 [j] S Ge 39:14
22:28 [k] Ex 22:16
22:30 [l] S Ge 29:29; S Lev 18:8; S 20:9; 1Co 5:1
23:1 [m] S Lev 21:20
23:3 [n] S Ge 19:38 [o] ver 4; Ne 13:2
23:4 [p] Dt 2:28 [q] S Nu 23:7; S 2Pe 2:15 [r] S Ge 24:10 [s] S ver 3
23:5 [t] Nu 24:10; Jos 24:10; Pr 26:2 [u] S Dt 4:37
23:6 [v] S Nu 24:17; Isa 15:1; 25:10; Jer 25:21; 27:3; 48:1; Eze 25:8; Zep 2:9 [w] Ezr 9:12; Mt 5:43
23:7 [x] S Ge 25:30 [y] S Ge 25:26 [z] S Lev 19:34
23:9 [a] Lev 15:1-33
23:10 [b] Lev 15:16
23:11 [c] S Lev 15:16 [d] 1Sa 21:5
23:14 [e] S Ge 3:8 [f] Ex 3:5
23:15 [g] 2Sa 22:3; Ps 2:12; 71:1 [h] 1Sa 30:15
23:16 [i] Ex 22:21; S 23:6
23:17 [j] 1Ki 14:24; 15:12; 22:46; 2Ki 23:7; Job 36:14 [k] S Ge 38:21
23:18 [l] S Ge 19:5; S Lev 20:13; Rev 22:15
23:19 [m] S Lev 25:35-37; Ne 5:2-7
23:20 [n] S Ge 31:15; S Dt 15:3 [o] Dt 15:10

[d] *29* That is, about 1 1/4 pounds (about 0.6 kilogram)
[e] *2* Or *one of illegitimate birth*
[f] *4* That is, Northwest Mesopotamia
[g] *18* Hebrew *of a dog*

23:1 NO ONE . . . MAY ENTER THE ASSEMBLY. This should be understood to mean that the individual was excluded only from active participation in corporate worship. The individual could still enjoy fellowship with God and participate in the blessings he provided for all those who had faith in him (cf. Isa 56:3–5).

23:4 BALAAM. See Nu 22:4—24:25 and notes.

23:19 INTEREST. See Ex 22:25, note.

everything you put your hand to in the land you are entering to possess.

21 If you make a vow to the LORD your God, do not be slow to pay it,[p] for the LORD your God will certainly demand it of you and you will be guilty of sin.[q] 22 But if you refrain from making a vow, you will not be guilty.[r] 23 Whatever your lips utter you must be sure to do, because you made your vow freely to the LORD your God with your own mouth.

24 If you enter your neighbor's vineyard, you may eat all the grapes you want, but do not put any in your basket. 25 If you enter your neighbor's grainfield, you may pick kernels with your hands, but you must not put a sickle to his standing grain.[s]

24 If a man marries a woman who becomes displeasing to him[t] because he finds something indecent about her, and he writes her a certificate of divorce,[u] gives it to her and sends her from his house, 2 and if after she leaves his house she becomes the wife of another man, 3 and her second husband dislikes her and writes her a certificate of divorce, gives it to her and sends her from his house, or if he dies, 4 then her first husband, who divorced her, is not allowed to marry her again after she has been defiled. That would be detestable in the eyes of the LORD. Do not bring sin upon the land the LORD[v] your God is giving you as an inheritance.

5 If a man has recently married, he must not be sent to war or have any other duty laid on him. For one year he is to be free to stay at home and bring happiness to the wife he has married.[w]

6 Do not take a pair of millstones—not even the upper one—as security for a debt, because that would be taking a man's livelihood as security.[x]

7 If a man is caught kidnapping one of his brother Israelites and treats him as a slave or sells him, the kidnapper must die.[y] You must purge the evil from among you.[z]

8 In cases of leprous[h] diseases be very careful to do exactly as the priests, who are Levites,[a] instruct you. You must follow carefully what I have commanded them.[b] 9 Remember what the LORD your God did to Miriam along the way after you came out of Egypt.[c]

10 When you make a loan of any kind to your neighbor, do not go into his house to get what he is offering as a pledge.[d] 11 Stay outside and let the man to whom you are making the loan bring the pledge out to you. 12 If the man is poor, do not go to sleep with his pledge[e] in your possession. 13 Return his cloak to him by sunset[f] so that he may sleep in it.[g] Then he will thank you, and it will be regarded as a righteous act in the sight of the LORD your God.[h]

14 Do not take advantage of a hired man who is poor and needy, whether he is a brother Israelite or an alien living in one of your towns.[i] 15 Pay him his wages each day before sunset, because he is poor[j] and is counting on it.[k] Otherwise he may cry to the LORD against you, and you will be guilty of sin.[l]

16 Fathers shall not be put to death for their children, nor children put to

23:21 [p] S Nu 6:21; Jdg 11:35; Ps 15:4 [q] Nu 30:1-2; Job 22:27; Ps 61:8; 65:1; 76:11; Isa 19:21; S Mt 5:33; Ac 5:3
23:22 [r] Ac 5:4
23:25 [s] Mt 12:1; Mk 2:23; Lk 6:1
24:1 [t] Dt 22:13 [u] ver 3; 2Ki 17:6; Isa 50:1; Jer 3:8; Mal 2:16; Mt 1:19; 5:31*; 19:7-9; Mk 10:4-5
24:4 [v] Jer 3:1
24:5 [w] S Dt 20:7
24:6 [x] S Ex 22:22
24:7 [y] S Ex 21:16 [z] 1Co 5:13*
24:8 [a] S Dt 17:9 [b] Lev 13:1-46; S 14:2
24:9 [c] S Nu 12:10
24:10 [d] Ex 22:25-27
24:12 [e] S Ex 22:26
24:13 [f] Ex 22:26 [g] S Ex 22:27 [h] Dt 6:25; Ps 106:31; Da 4:27
24:14 [i] Lev 19:13; 25:35-43; Dt 15:12-18; Job 24:4; Pr 14:31; 19:17; Am 4:1; 1Ti 5:18
24:15 [j] S Lev 25:35 [k] S Lev 19:13; Mt 20:8 [l] S Ex 22:23; S Job 12:19; Jas 5:4

[h] *8* The Hebrew word was used for various diseases affecting the skin—not necessarily leprosy.

23:21 VOW. See Nu 30:1, note.

24:1 CERTIFICATE OF DIVORCE. Divorce is the result of human sin (cf. Mt 19:8). The instructions in vv. 1–4 were God-given guidelines to regulate divorce in ancient Israel. Note the following concerning these verses: (1) The word "displeasing" probably refers to disgraceful or immoral conduct less serious than adultery; it cannot refer to adultery because the penalty for adultery was death, not divorce (cf. 22:13–22).

(2) The "certificate of divorce" was a legal document given to the woman in order to break the marriage covenant, protect her and release her from all obligation to her former husband.

(3) After receiving the certificate of divorce, the woman was free to remarry; however, she was never to return to her former husband if her second marriage was terminated (vv. 2–4).

(4) When divorce happens, it is a tragedy (cf. Mal 2:16; see Ge 2:24, note), but it is not a sin if based on Biblical grounds (see Mt 19:9, note; 1Co 7:15, note). God himself divorced Israel because of its unfaithfulness and spiritual adultery (Isa 50:1; Jer 3:1,6–8).

24:14 POOR AND NEEDY. God often warned Israel not to take advantage of the poor but to treat them with compassion and respect. Believers who fail to treat the poor and needy fairly will bring God's condemnation on themselves (v. 15; cf. Jas 5:1–6; see article on THE CARE OF THE POOR AND NEEDY, p. 1316).

death for their fathers; each is to die
for his own sin.[m]
17Do not deprive the alien or the fatherless[n] of justice,[o] or take the
cloak of the widow as a pledge. 18Re-
member that you were slaves in
Egypt[p] and the LORD your God redeemed you from there. That is why I
command you to do this.
19When you are harvesting in your
field and you overlook a sheaf, do not
go back to get it.[q] Leave it for the
alien,[r] the fatherless and the widow,[s] so that the LORD your God may
bless[t] you in all the work of your
hands. 20When you beat the olives
from your trees, do not go over the
branches a second time.[u] Leave what
remains for the alien, the fatherless
and the widow. 21When you harvest
the grapes in your vineyard, do not go
over the vines again. Leave what remains for the alien, the fatherless and
the widow. 22Remember that you were
slaves in Egypt. That is why I command you to do this.[v]

25 When men have a dispute, they
are to take it to court and the
judges[w] will decide the case,[x] acquitting[y] the innocent and condemning
the guilty.[z] 2If the guilty man deserves to be beaten,[a] the judge shall
make him lie down and have him
flogged in his presence with the number of lashes his crime deserves, 3but
he must not give him more than forty
lashes.[b] If he is flogged more than
that, your brother will be degraded in
your eyes.[c]
4Do not muzzle an ox while it is
treading out the grain.[d]
5If brothers are living together and
one of them dies without a son, his widow must not marry outside the family.
Her husband's brother shall take her
and marry her and fulfill the duty of a
brother-in-law to her.[e] 6The first son
she bears shall carry on the name of
the dead brother so that his name will
not be blotted out from Israel.[f]
7However, if a man does not want to
marry his brother's wife,[g] she shall go
to the elders at the town gate[h] and
say, "My husband's brother refuses to
carry on his brother's name in Israel.
He will not fulfill the duty of a brother-
in-law to me."[i] 8Then the elders of his
town shall summon him and talk to
him. If he persists in saying, "I do not
want to marry her," 9his brother's widow shall go up to him in the presence
of the elders, take off one of his sandals,[j] spit in his face[k] and say, "This
is what is done to the man who will not
build up his brother's family line."
10That man's line shall be known in Israel as The Family of the Unsandaled.
11If two men are fighting and the
wife of one of them comes to rescue her
husband from his assailant, and she
reaches out and seizes him by his private parts, 12you shall cut off her hand.
Show her no pity.[l]
13Do not have two differing weights
in your bag—one heavy, one light.[m]
14Do not have two differing measures
in your house—one large, one small.
15You must have accurate and honest
weights and measures, so that you may
live long[n] in the land the LORD your
God is giving you. 16For the LORD your
God detests anyone who does these
things, anyone who deals dishonest-
ly.[o]
17Remember what the Amalekites[p]
did to you along the way when you
came out of Egypt. 18When you were
weary and worn out, they met you on
your journey and cut off all who were
lagging behind; they had no fear of
God.[q] 19When the LORD your God
gives you rest[r] from all the enemies[s]
around you in the land he is giving you
to possess as an inheritance, you shall
blot out the memory of Amalek[t] from
under heaven. Do not forget!

Firstfruits and Tithes

26 When you have entered the
land the LORD your God is giving
you as an inheritance and have taken
possession of it and settled in it, 2take
some of the firstfruits[u] of all that you
produce from the soil of the land the

24:16 [m] S Nu 26:11; Jer 31:29-30 **24:17** [n] Ex 22:22; Job 6:27; 24:9; 29:12; Ps 10:18; 82:3; Pr 23:10; Eze 22:7 [o] S Ex 22:21; S 23:2; S Dt 10:18 **24:18** [p] S Dt 15:15 **24:19** [q] S Lev 19:9 [r] Dt 10:19; 27:19; Eze 47:22; Zec 7:10; Mal 3:5 [s] ver 20; Dt 14:29 [t] S Dt 14:29; Pr 19:17; 28:27; Ecc 11:1 **24:20** [u] Lev 19:10 **24:22** [v] ver 18 **25:1** [w] S Ex 21:6 [x] Dt 17:8-13; 19:17; Ac 23:3 [y] 1Ki 8:32 [z] S Ex 23:7; Dt 1:16-17 **25:2** [a] Pr 10:13; 19:29; Lk 12:47-48 **25:3** [b] Mt 27:26; Jn 19:1; 2Co 11:24 [c] Jer 20:2 **25:4** [d] S Nu 22:29; 1Co 9:9*; 1Ti 5:18* **25:5** [e] Ru 4:10,13; Mt 22:24; Mk 12:19; Lk 20:28 **25:6** [f] Ge 38:9; Ru 4:5,10 **25:7** [g] Ru 1:15 [h] S Ge 23:10 [i] Ru 4:1-2,5-6 **25:9** [j] Jos 24:22; Ru 4:7-8,11 [k] Nu 12:14; Job 17:6; 30:10; Isa 50:6 **25:12** [l] S Dt 7:2 **25:13** [m] Pr 11:1; 20:23; Mic 6:11 **25:15** [n] S Ex 20:12 **25:16** [o] Pr 11:1 **25:17** [p] S Ge 36:12 **25:18** [q] Ps 36:1; Ro 3:18 **25:19** [r] S Ex 33:14; Heb 3:18-19 [s] Est 9:16 [t] S Ge 36:12 **26:2** [u] S Ex 22:29

24:17 ALIEN . . . FATHERLESS . . . WIDOW. God is especially concerned for the refugee, orphan and widow (Ex 22:21–22; 23:9). To help those who are disadvantaged greatly pleases God (see Lk 7:13, note; Heb 13:2; Jas 1:27).

25:4 NOT MUZZLE AN OX. This command provided that working animals be given sufficient feed to maintain strength and health. They were to be treated humanely and rewarded for their labor. Even more, people deserve fair treatment for their labor. The NT applies this principle to ministers of the gospel (see 1Co 9:9–11; 1Ti 5:17–18). Those who labor in the ministry or for Christian institutions should be paid reasonable, fair wages.

LORD your God is giving you and put them in a basket. Then go to the place the LORD your God will choose as a dwelling for his Name[v] **3**and say to the priest in office at the time, "I declare today to the LORD your God that I have come to the land the LORD swore to our forefathers to give us." **4**The priest shall take the basket from your hands and set it down in front of the altar of the LORD your God. **5**Then you shall declare before the LORD your God: "My father was a wandering[w] Aramean,[x] and he went down into Egypt with a few people[y] and lived there and became a great nation,[z] powerful and numerous. **6**But the Egyptians mistreated us and made us suffer,[a] putting us to hard labor.[b] **7**Then we cried out to the LORD, the God of our fathers, and the LORD heard our voice[c] and saw[d] our misery,[e] toil and oppression.[f] **8**So the LORD brought us out of Egypt[g] with a mighty hand and an outstretched arm,[h] with great terror and with miraculous signs and wonders.[i] **9**He brought us to this place and gave us this land, a land flowing with milk
1Sa 2:1-2 and honey;[j] **10**and now I bring the firstfruits of the soil that you, O LORD, have given me.[k]" Place the basket before the LORD your God and bow down before him. **11**And you and the Levites[l] and the aliens among you shall rejoice[m] in all the good things the LORD your God has given to you and your household.

12When you have finished setting aside a tenth[n] of all your produce in the third year, the year of the tithe,[o] you shall give it to the Levite, the alien, the fatherless and the widow, so that they may eat in your towns and be satisfied. **13**Then say to the LORD your God: "I have removed from my house the sacred portion and have given it to the Levite, the alien, the fatherless and the widow, according to all you commanded. I have not turned aside from your commands nor have I forgotten any of them.[p] **14**I have not eaten any of the sacred portion while I was in mourning, nor have I removed any of it while I was unclean,[q] nor have I offered any of it to the dead. I have obeyed the LORD my God; I have done everything you commanded me. **15**Look down from heaven,[r] your holy dwelling place, and bless[s] your people Israel and the land you have given us as you promised on oath to our forefathers, a land flowing with milk and honey."

26:2 [v] S Ex 20:24; S Dt 12:5 **26:5** [w] S Ge 20:13 [x] S Ge 25:20 [y] S Ge 34:30; 43:14 [z] S Ge 12:2 **26:6** [a] S Nu 20:15 [b] S Ex 1:13 **26:7** [c] S Ge 21:17 [d] Ex 3:9; 2Ki 13:4; 14:26 [e] S Ge 16:11 [f] Ps 42:9; 44:24; 72:14 **26:8** [g] S Nu 20:16 [h] S Ex 3:20 [i] S Dt 4:34; 34:11-12 **26:9** [j] S Ex 3:8 **26:10** [k] S Dt 8:18 **26:11** [l] Dt 12:12 [m] S Dt 16:11 **26:12** [n] S Ge 14:20 [o] S Nu 18:24; Dt 14:28-29; Heb 7:5,9 **26:13** [p] Ps 119:141,153, 176 **26:14** [q] Lev 7:20; Hos 9:4 **26:15** [r] Ps 68:5; 80:14; 102:19; Isa 63:15; Zec 2:13 [s] S Ex 39:43 **26:16** [t] Dt 4:29 **26:17** [u] Ex 19:8; Ps 48:14 **26:18** [v] Ex 6:7; Dt 7:6 **26:19** [w] Isa 62:7; Zep 3:20 [x] Dt 4:7-8; 28:1, 13,44; 1Ch 14:2; Ps 148:14; Isa 40:11 [y] S Dt 7:6 **27:1** [z] Ps 78:7 **27:2** [a] Jos 4:1 [b] Ex 24:4; Jos 24:26; 1Sa 7:12 [c] Jos 8:31 **27:3** [d] S Ex 3:8 **27:4** [e] S Dt 11:29 **27:5** [f] S Ex 20:24

Follow the LORD's Commands

16The LORD your God commands you this day to follow these decrees and laws; carefully observe them with all your heart and with all your soul.[t] **17**You have declared this day that the LORD is your God and that you will walk in his ways, that you will keep his decrees, commands and laws, and that you will obey him.[u] **18**And the LORD has declared this day that you are his people, his treasured possession[v] as he promised, and that you are to keep all his commands. **19**He has declared that he will set you in praise,[w] fame and honor high above all the nations[x] he has made and that you will be a people holy[y] to the LORD your God, as he promised.

The Altar on Mount Ebal

27 Moses and the elders of Israel commanded the people: "Keep all these commands[z] that I give you today. **2**When you have crossed the Jordan[a] into the land the LORD your God is giving you, set up some large stones[b] and coat them with plaster.[c] **3**Write on them all the words of this law when you have crossed over to enter the land the LORD your God is giving you, a land flowing with milk and honey,[d] just as the LORD, the God of your fathers, promised you. **4**And when you have crossed the Jordan, set up these stones on Mount Ebal,[e] as I command you today, and coat them with plaster. **5**Build there an altar[f] to the LORD your

26:8 THE LORD BROUGHT US OUT. The Israelites were expected to remember always that their existence and redemption came about because of what God had done for them. (1) They were to confess this truth publicly (vv. 3–9) and respond with offerings, thanksgiving, joy, goodness toward others and obedience to God's commands (vv. 12–15). (2) As believers in Christ, we likewise owe our lives and salvation to God's mercy through Christ. We have been redeemed and purchased by his death and have become his own possession (cf. Eph 1:14; 1Pe 1:18–19; 2:9–10). From now on we must live in gratitude as living sacrifices to our Lord, not being conformed to this world but being transformed by the Holy Spirit, that we may do his will (Ro 12:1–2; see Eph 2:9, note).

God, an altar of stones. Do not use any
iron tool[g] upon them. **6**Build the altar
of the LORD your God with fieldstones
and offer burnt offerings on it to the
LORD your God. **7**Sacrifice fellowship
offerings[i][h] there, eating them and
rejoicing[i] in the presence of the LORD
your God.[j] **8**And you shall write very
clearly all the words of this law on
these stones[k] you have set up."[l]

Curses From Mount Ebal

9Then Moses and the priests, who
are Levites,[m] said to all Israel, "Be silent, O Israel, and listen! You have now
become the people of the LORD your
God.[n] **10**Obey the LORD your God and
follow his commands and decrees that
I give you today."

11On the same day Moses commanded the people:

12When you have crossed the Jor-
dan, these tribes shall stand on Mount
Gerizim[o] to bless the people: Simeon,
Levi, Judah, Issachar,[p] Joseph and
Benjamin.[q] **13**And these tribes shall
stand on Mount Ebal[r] to pronounce
curses: Reuben, Gad, Asher, Zebulun,
Dan and Naphtali.

14The Levites shall recite to all the
people of Israel in a loud voice:

15"Cursed is the man who
carves an image or casts an
idol[s]—a thing detestable[t] to
the LORD, the work of the craftsman's hands—and sets it up in
secret."

Then all the people shall say,
"Amen!"[u]

16"Cursed is the man who dishonors his father or his mother."[v]

Then all the people shall say,
"Amen!"

17"Cursed is the man who
moves his neighbor's boundary
stone."[w]

Then all the people shall say,
"Amen!"

18"Cursed is the man who leads
the blind astray on the road."[x]

Then all the people shall say,
"Amen!"

19"Cursed is the man who withholds justice from the alien,[y] the
fatherless or the widow."[z]

Then all the people shall say,
"Amen!"

20"Cursed is the man who
sleeps with his father's wife, for
he dishonors his father's bed."[a]

Then all the people shall say,
"Amen!"

21"Cursed is the man who has
sexual relations with any animal."[b]

Then all the people shall say,
"Amen!"

22"Cursed is the man who
sleeps with his sister, the daughter of his father or the daughter of
his mother."[c]

Then all the people shall say,
"Amen!"

23"Cursed is the man who
sleeps with his mother-in-law."[d]

Then all the people shall say,
"Amen!"

24"Cursed is the man who
kills[e] his neighbor secretly."[f]

Then all the people shall say,
"Amen!"

25"Cursed is the man who accepts a bribe to kill an innocent
person."[g]

Then all the people shall say,
"Amen!"

26"Cursed is the man who does
not uphold the words of this law
by carrying them out."[h]

Then all the people shall say,
"Amen!"[i]

Blessings for Obedience

28 If you fully obey the LORD your
God and carefully follow[j] all
his commands[k] I give you today, the
LORD your God will set you high above
all the nations on earth.[l] **2**All these
blessings will come upon you[m] and accompany you if you obey the LORD your
God:

3You will be blessed[n] in the
city and blessed in the country.[o]

4The fruit of your womb will be
blessed, and the crops of your
land and the young of your live-

27:5 [g]Ex 20:25
27:7 [h]S Ex 32:6
[i]S Dt 16:11
[j]Jos 8:31
27:8 [k]Isa 8:1; 30:8; Hab 2:2
[l]Jos 8:32
27:9 [m]S Dt 17:9
[n]Dt 26:18
27:12 [o]S Dt 11:29
[p]S Ge 30:18
[q]Jos 8:35
27:13 [r]S Dt 11:29
27:15 [s]S Ex 20:4
[t]1Ki 11:5,7; 2Ki 23:13; Isa 44:19; 66:3
[u]Nu 5:22; S 1Co 14:16
27:16 [v]S Ge 31:35; S Ex 21:12; S Dt 5:16
27:17 [w]S Dt 19:14
27:18 [x]S Lev 19:14
27:19 [y]S Ex 22:21; S Dt 24:19
[z]S Ex 23:2; S Dt 10:18
27:20 [a]S Ge 34:5; S Lev 18:7
27:21 [b]S Ex 22:19
27:22 [c]S Lev 18:9
27:23 [d]S Lev 20:14
27:24 [e]S Ge 4:23
[f]Ex 21:12
27:25 [g]Ex 23:7-8; S Lev 19:16
27:26 [h]S Lev 26:14; Dt 28:15; Ps 119:21; Jer 11:3; Gal 3:10*
[i]Jer 11:5
28:1 [j]S Dt 15:5
[k]S Lev 26:3
[l]S Nu 24:7; S Dt 26:19
28:2 [m]Jer 32:24; Zec 1:6
28:3 [n]Ps 144:15
[o]S Ge 39:5

i 7 Traditionally *peace offerings*

27:15 SETS IT UP IN SECRET. Many of the sins listed here were done in secret (vv. 15,24). Israel thereby acknowledged that a person was accountable to God even when he or she was alone. All our actions and thoughts occur in God's sight and in his presence (see Ps 139).

28:3 YOU WILL BE BLESSED. See Lk 24:50, note.

stock—the calves of your herds
and the lambs of your flocks.[p]
[5]Your basket and your kneading trough will be blessed.
[6]You will be blessed when you
come in and blessed when you go
out.[q]

[7]The LORD will grant that the enemies[r] who rise up against you will be
defeated before you. They will come at
you from one direction but flee from
you in seven.[s]
[8]The LORD will send a blessing on
your barns and on everything you put
your hand to. The LORD your God will
bless[t] you in the land he is giving you.
[9]The LORD will establish you as his
holy people,[u] as he promised you on
oath, if you keep the commands[v] of
the LORD your God and walk in his
ways. [10]Then all the peoples on earth
will see that you are called by the
name[w] of the LORD, and they will fear
you. [11]The LORD will grant you abundant prosperity—in the fruit of your
womb, the young of your livestock[x]
and the crops of your ground—in the
land he swore to your forefathers to
give you.[y]
[12]The LORD will open the heavens,
the storehouse[z] of his bounty,[a] to
send rain[b] on your land in season and
to bless[c] all the work of your hands.
You will lend to many nations but will
borrow from none.[d] [13]The LORD will
make you the head, not the tail. If you
pay attention to the commands of the
LORD your God that I give you this day
and carefully follow[e] them, you will
always be at the top, never at the bottom.[f] [14]Do not turn aside from any of
the commands I give you today, to the
right or to the left,[g] following other
gods and serving them.

Curses for Disobedience

[15]However, if you do not obey[h] the
LORD your God and do not carefully follow all his commands and decrees I am
giving you today,[i] all these curses
will come upon you and overtake
you:[j]

[16]You will be cursed in the city
and cursed in the country.[k]
[17]Your basket and your kneading trough will be cursed.[l]

28:4 [p]S Ge 49:25; S Dt 8:18
28:6 [q]Ps 121:8
28:7 [r]2Ch 6:34 [s]S Lev 26:8,17
28:8 [t]Dt 15:4
28:9 [u]S Ex 19:6 [v]S Lev 26:3
28:10 [w]S Nu 6:27; 1Ki 8:43; Jer 25:29; Da 9:18
28:11 [x]S Ge 30:27 [y]ver 4; Dt 30:9
28:12 [z]Job 38:22; Ps 135:7; Jer 10:13; 51:16 [a]Ps 65:11; 68:10; Jer 31:12 [b]S Lev 26:4; 1Ki 8:35-36; 18:1; Ps 104:13; Isa 5:6; 30:23; 32:20 [c]Isa 61:9; 65:23; Jer 32:38-41; Mal 3:12 [d]ver 44; S Lev 25:19; S Dt 15:3,6; Eze 34:26
28:13 [e]Jer 11:6 [f]S Dt 26:19
28:14 [g]S Dt 5:32; Jos 1:7
28:15 [h]1Ki 9:6; 2Ch 7:19 [i]S Dt 27:26 [j]Dt 29:27; Jos 23:15; 2Ch 12:5; Da 9:11; Mal 2:2
28:16 [k]ver 3
28:17 [l]ver 5
28:18 [m]ver 4
28:19 [n]ver 6
28:20 [o]ver 8,15; Lev 26:16; Jer 42:18; Mal 2:2; 3:9; 4:6 [p]Ps 39:11; 76:6; 80:16; Isa 17:13; 51:20; 54:9; 66:15; Eze 5:15 [q]Dt 4:26 [r]S Ex 32:22
28:21 [s]Lev 26:25; Nu 14:12; Jer 24:10; Am 4:10
28:22 [t]ver 48; Dt 32:24 [u]Lev 26:16; 2Ki 8:1; Job 12:15; Ps 105:16; Jer 14:1; Hag 1:11; Mal 3:9 [v]Hag 2:17 [w]S Lev 26:25 [x]Dt 4:26; Am 4:9
28:23 [y]S Lev 26:19
28:24 [z]Lev 26:19; Dt 11:17; 1Ki 8:35; 17:1; Isa 5:6; Jer 14:1; Hag 1:10
28:25 [a]1Sa 4:10; Ps 78:62 [b]S Lev 26:17 [c]ver 37 [d]2Ch 29:8; 30:7; Jer 15:4; 24:9;

[18]The fruit of your womb will be
cursed, and the crops of your
land, and the calves of your herds
and the lambs of your flocks.[m]
[19]You will be cursed when you
come in and cursed when you go
out.[n]

[20]The LORD will send on you
curses,[o] confusion and rebuke[p] in
everything you put your hand to, until
you are destroyed and come to sudden
ruin[q] because of the evil[r] you have
done in forsaking him.[j] [21]The LORD
will plague you with diseases until he
has destroyed you from the land you
are entering to possess.[s] [22]The LORD
will strike you with wasting disease,[t]
with fever and inflammation, with
scorching heat and drought,[u] with
blight[v] and mildew, which will
plague[w] you until you perish.[x] [23]The
sky over your head will be bronze, the
ground beneath you iron.[y] [24]The LORD
will turn the rain[z] of your country into
dust and powder; it will come down
from the skies until you are destroyed.
[25]The LORD will cause you to be defeated[a] before your enemies. You will
come at them from one direction but
flee from them in seven,[b] and you will
become a thing of horror[c] to all the
kingdoms on earth.[d] [26]Your carcasses will be food for all the birds of
the air[e] and the beasts of the earth,
and there will be no one to frighten
them away.[f] [27]The LORD will afflict
you with the boils of Egypt[g] and with
tumors, festering sores and the itch,
from which you cannot be cured. [28]The
LORD will afflict you with madness,
blindness and confusion of mind. [29]At
midday you will grope[h] about like a
blind man in the dark. You will be unsuccessful in everything you do; day after day you will be oppressed and
robbed, with no one to rescue[i] you.
[30]You will be pledged to be married
to a woman, but another will take her
and ravish her.[j] You will build a
house, but you will not live in it.[k] You

26:6; 29:18; 44:12; Eze 23:46 **28:26** [e]S Ge 40:19 [f]Ps 79:2; Isa 18:6; Jer 7:33; 12:9; 15:2; 16:4; 19:7; 34:20 **28:27** [g]Dt 7:15 **28:29** [h]Ge 19:11; Ex 10:21; Job 5:14; 12:25; 24:13; 38:15; Isa 59:10 [i]Jdg 3:9; 2Ki 13:5; Est 4:14; Isa 19:20; 43:11; Hos 13:4; Ob 1:21 **28:30** [j]Job 31:10 [k]Isa 65:22; Am 5:11

[j]20 Hebrew *me*

28:15 WILL COME UPON YOU. Moses prophesied the consequences of turning away from God: chastisement, destruction, great sorrow, captivity and dispersion among the nations (vv. 15–68).

will plant a vineyard, but you will not
even begin to enjoy its fruit.[l] **31**Your
ox will be slaughtered before your
eyes, but you will eat none of it. Your
donkey will be forcibly taken from you
and will not be returned. Your sheep
will be given to your enemies, and no
one will rescue them. **32**Your sons and
daughters will be given to another nation,[m] and you will wear out your eyes
watching for them day after day, powerless to lift a hand. **33**A people that
you do not know will eat what your
land and labor produce, and you will
have nothing but cruel oppression[n] all
your days.[o] **34**The sights you see will
drive you mad.[p] **35**The LORD will afflict
your knees and legs with painful
boils[q] that cannot be cured, spreading
from the soles of your feet to the top of
your head.[r]

36The LORD will drive you and the
king[s] you set over you to a nation unknown to you or your fathers.[t] There
you will worship other gods, gods of
wood and stone.[u] **37**You will become a
thing of horror[v] and an object of
scorn[w] and ridicule[x] to all the nations where the LORD will drive you.[y]

38You will sow much seed in the
field but you will harvest little,[z] because locusts[a] will devour[b] it. **39**You
will plant vineyards and cultivate them
but you will not drink the wine[c] or
gather the grapes, because worms will
eat[d] them.[e] **40**You will have olive
trees throughout your country but you
will not use the oil, because the olives
will drop off.[f] **41**You will have sons
and daughters but you will not keep
them, because they will go into captivity.[g] **42**Swarms of locusts[h] will take
over all your trees and the crops of
your land.

43The alien who lives among you
will rise above you higher and higher,
but you will sink lower and lower.[i]
44He will lend to you, but you will not
lend to him.[j] He will be the head, but
you will be the tail.[k]

45All these curses will come upon
you. They will pursue you and overtake
you[l] until you are destroyed,[m] because you did not obey the LORD your
God and observe the commands and
decrees he gave you. **46**They will be a
sign and a wonder to you and your
descendants forever.[n] **47**Because you
did not serve[o] the LORD your God joyfully and gladly[p] in the time of prosperity, **48**therefore in hunger and
thirst,[q] in nakedness and dire poverty, you will serve the enemies the LORD
sends against you. He will put an iron
yoke[r] on your neck[s] until he has destroyed you.

49The LORD will bring a nation
against you[t] from far away, from the
ends of the earth,[u] like an eagle[v]
swooping down, a nation whose language you will not understand,[w] **50**a
fierce-looking nation without respect
for the old[x] or pity for the young.
51They will devour the young of your
livestock and the crops of your land until you are destroyed. They will leave
you no grain, new wine[y] or oil,[z] nor
any calves of your herds or lambs of
your flocks until you are ruined.[a]
52They will lay siege[b] to all the cities
throughout your land until the high fortified walls in which you trust fall
down. They will besiege all the cities
throughout the land the LORD your God
is giving you.[c]

53Because of the suffering that your
enemy will inflict on you during the
siege, you will eat the fruit of the
womb, the flesh of the sons and daughters the LORD your God has given you.[d]
54Even the most gentle and sensitive
man among you will have no compassion on his own brother or the wife he
loves or his surviving children, **55**and
he will not give to one of them any of
the flesh of his children that he is eating. It will be all he has left because of
the suffering your enemy will inflict on
you during the siege of all your cities.[e] **56**The most gentle and sensitive[f] woman among you—so sensitive and gentle that she would not
venture to touch the ground with the
sole of her foot—will begrudge the
husband she loves and her own son or
daughter[g] **57**the afterbirth from her

28:30 [l] Jer 12:13
28:32 [m] ver 41
28:33 [n] Jer 6:6; 22:17 [o] Jer 5:15-17; Eze 25:4
28:34 [p] ver 67
28:35 [q] Dt 7:15; Rev 16:2 [r] Job 2:7; 7:5; 13:28; 30:17, 30; Isa 1:6
28:36 [s] 1Sa 12:25 [t] S Dt 4:27; 2Ki 24:14; 25:7, 11; 2Ch 33:11; 36:21; Ezr 5:12; Jer 15:14; 16:13; 27:20; 39:1-9; 52:28; La 1:3 [u] S Dt 4:28
28:37 [v] ver 25; Jer 42:18; Eze 5:15 [w] Ps 22:7; 39:8; 44:13; 64:8; Jer 18:16; 48:27; Mic 6:16 [x] 2Ch 7:20; Ezr 9:7; Jer 44:8 [y] 1Ki 9:7; Ps 44:14; Jer 19:8; 24:9; 25:9,18; 29:18; La 2:15
28:38 [z] Lev 26:20; Ps 129:7; Isa 5:10; Jer 12:13; Hos 8:7; Mic 6:15; Hag 1:6, 9; 2:16 [a] S Ex 10:4 [b] S Ex 10:15
28:39 [c] S Lev 10:9 [d] Joel 1:4; 2:25; Mal 3:11 [e] Isa 5:10; 17:10-11; Zep 1:13
28:40 [f] Jer 11:16; Mic 6:15
28:41 [g] ver 32
28:42 [h] ver 38; Jdg 6:5; 7:12; Jer 46:23
28:43 [i] ver 13
28:44 [j] S ver 12 [k] S Dt 26:19
28:45 [l] S Ex 15:9 [m] ver 15; Dt 4:25-26
28:46 [n] S Nu 16:38; Ps 71:7; Isa 8:18; 20:3; Eze 5:15; Zec 3:8
28:47 [o] S Dt 10:12 [p] S Lev 23:40; Ne 9:35
28:48 [q] Jer 14:3; La 4:4 [r] Jer 28:13-14; La 1:14 [s] Ge 49:8
28:49 [t] S Lev 26:44 [u] Isa 5:26-30,26; 7:18-20; 39:3; Jer 4:16; 5:15; 6:22; 25:32; 31:8; Hab 1:6 [v] 2Sa 1:23; Jer 4:13; 48:40; 49:22; La 4:19; Eze 17:3 [w] S Ge 11:7; 1Co 14:21*
28:50 [x] Isa 47:6
28:51 [y] Ps 4:7; Isa 36:17; Hag 1:11 [z] S Nu 18:12 [a] ver 33; Jdg 6:4
28:52 [b] 2Ki 6:24 [c] Jer 10:18; Eze 6:10; Zep 1:14-16,17
28:53 [d] ver 57; Lev 26:29; 2Ki 6:28-29; La 2:20
28:55 [e] 2Ki 6:29
28:56 [f] Isa 47:1 [g] La 4:10

28:49–57 A NATION AGAINST YOU. These verses describe an invasion of the land of Canaan that could apply to the Assyrian invasion (described in Hos 8:1 as like that of an eagle), the Babylonian invasion (described in Jer 48:40 as like that of an eagle; cf. 2Ki 25:1–21; Jer 39:1–10; 52:28–30) or to the siege by the Romans in A.D. 70 (see Lk 21:20, note).

womb and the children she bears. For
she intends to eat them[h] secretly during the siege and in the distress that
your enemy will inflict on you in your
cities.
58If you do not carefully follow all
the words of this law,[i] which are written in this book, and do not revere[j]
this glorious and awesome name[k]—
the LORD your God— **59**the LORD will
send fearful plagues on you and your
descendants, harsh and prolonged disasters, and severe and lingering illnesses. **60**He will bring upon you all the
diseases of Egypt[l] that you dreaded,
and they will cling to you. **61**The LORD
will also bring on you every kind of
sickness and disaster not recorded in
this Book of the Law,[m] until you are
destroyed.[n] **62**You who were as numerous as the stars in the sky[o] will be
left but few[p] in number, because you
did not obey the LORD your God. **63**Just
as it pleased[q] the LORD to make you
prosper and increase in number, so
it will please[r] him to ruin and destroy you.[s] You will be uprooted[t]
from the land you are entering to possess.
64Then the LORD will scatter[u] you
among all nations,[v] from one end of
the earth to the other.[w] There you will
worship other gods—gods of wood and
stone, which neither you nor your fathers have known.[x] **65**Among those
nations you will find no repose, no resting place[y] for the sole of your foot.
There the LORD will give you an anxious
mind, eyes[z] weary with longing, and
a despairing heart.[a] **66**You will live in
constant suspense, filled with dread
both night and day, never sure of your
life. **67**In the morning you will say, "If
only it were evening!" and in the evening, "If only it were morning!"—because of the terror that will fill your
hearts and the sights that your eyes
will see.[b] **68**The LORD will send you
back in ships to Egypt on a journey I
said you should never make again.[c]
There you will offer yourselves for sale
to your enemies as male and female
slaves, but no one will buy you.

Renewal of the Covenant

29 These are the terms of the covenant the LORD commanded Mo-
ses to make with the Israelites in
Moab,[d] in addition to the covenant he
had made with them at Horeb.[e]
2Moses summoned all the Israelites
and said to them:

Your eyes have seen all that the
LORD did in Egypt to Pharaoh, to all his
officials and to all his land.[f] **3**With
your own eyes you saw those great trials, those miraculous signs and great
wonders.[g] **4**But to this day the LORD
has not given you a mind that understands or eyes that see or ears that
hear.[h] **5**During the forty years that I
led[i] you through the desert, your
clothes did not wear out, nor did the
sandals on your feet.[j] **6**You ate no
bread and drank no wine or other fermented drink.[k] I did this so that you
might know that I am the LORD your
God.[l]
7When you reached this place, Sihon[m] king of Heshbon[n] and Og king
of Bashan came out to fight against us,
but we defeated them.[o] **8**We took their
land and gave it as an inheritance[p] to
the Reubenites, the Gadites and the
half-tribe of Manasseh.[q]
9Carefully follow[r] the terms of this
covenant,[s] so that you may prosper in
everything you do.[t] **10**All of you are
standing today in the presence of the
LORD your God—your leaders and chief
men, your elders and officials, and all
the other men of Israel, **11**together
with your children and your wives, and
the aliens living in your camps who
chop your wood and carry your wa-
ter.[u] **12**You are standing here in order
to enter into a covenant with the LORD
your God, a covenant the LORD is making with you this day and sealing with
an oath, **13**to confirm you this day as
his people,[v] that he may be your
God[w] as he promised you and as he
swore to your fathers, Abraham, Isaac
and Jacob. **14**I am making this covenant,[x] with its oath, not only with

28:57 [h] S ver 53
28:58 [i] Dt 31:24 [j] Ps 96:4; Jer 5:22; Mal 1:14; 2:5; 3:5, 16; 4:2 [k] S Ex 3:15; S Jos 7:9
28:60 [l] Ex 15:26
28:61 [m] Dt 29:21; 30:10; 31:26; Jos 1:8; 8:34; 23:6; 24:26; 2Ki 14:6; 22:8; 2Ch 17:9; 25:4; Ne 8:1,18; Mal 4:4 [n] Dt 4:25-26
28:62 [o] S Ge 22:17; Dt 4:27; 10:22 [p] S Lev 26:22
28:63 [q] Dt 30:9; Isa 62:5; 65:19; Jer 32:41; Zep 3:17 [r] Pr 1:26 [s] S Ge 6:7 [t] Ps 52:5; Jer 12:14; 31:28; 45:4
28:64 [u] S Dt 4:27; Ezr 9:7; Isa 6:12; Jer 32:23; 43:11; 52:27 [v] Ne 1:8; Ps 44:11; Jer 13:24; 18:17; 22:22 [w] S Dt 4:32; S Jer 8:19 [x] Dt 11:28; 32:17
28:65 [y] La 1:3 [z] Job 11:20 [a] Lev 26:16,36; Hos 9:17
28:67 [b] ver 34
28:68 [c] S Ex 13:14

29:1 [d] S Lev 7:38 [e] S Ex 3:1
29:2 [f] Ex 19:4
29:3 [g] S Dt 4:34
29:4 [h] Isa 6:10; 32:3; 48:8; Jer 5:21; Eze 12:2; S Mt 13:15; Eph 4:18
29:5 [i] S Dt 8:2 [j] S Dt 8:4
29:6 [k] S Lev 10:9 [l] Dt 8:3
29:7 [m] S Nu 21:26 [n] S Nu 21:25 [o] Nu 21:21-24, 33-35; Dt 2:26-3:11
29:8 [p] Ps 78:55; 135:12; 136:22 [q] Nu 32:33; Dt 3:12-13
29:9 [r] S Dt 4:6; S Jos 1:7 [s] Ex 19:5; Ps 25:10; 103:18 [t] Jos 1:8; 2Ch 31:21
29:11 [u] Jos 9:21, 23,27; 1Ch 20:3
29:13 [v] S Ge 6:18; S Ex 19:6 [w] S Ge 17:7
29:14 [x] Ex 19:5; Isa 59:21; Jer 31:31; 32:40; 50:5; Eze 16:62; 37:26; Heb 8:7-8

28:64 SCATTER YOU AMONG ALL NATIONS. The scattering of Israel occurred several times throughout their history—when they were taken captive by the Assyrians (722–721 B.C.; see 2Ki 17:6), the Babylonians (586 B.C.; see 2Ki 25:21), the Greeks (to Alexandria in Egypt, 3rd century B.C.), and the Romans (A.D. 70; see Lk 21:20–24; see also Dt 30:3, note on Israel's restoration).

29:1 TERMS OF THE COVENANT. See article on GOD'S COVENANT WITH THE ISRAELITES, p. 290.

you **15**who are standing here with us
today in the presence of the LORD our
God but also with those who are not
here today.[y]
16You yourselves know how we lived
in Egypt and how we passed through
the countries on the way here. **17**You
saw among them their detestable images and idols of wood and stone, of
silver and gold.[z] **18**Make sure there is
no man or woman, clan or tribe among
you today whose heart turns[a] away
from the LORD our God to go and worship the gods of those nations; make
sure there is no root among you that
produces such bitter poison.[b]
19When such a person hears the
words of this oath, he invokes a blessing[c] on himself and therefore thinks,
"I will be safe, even though I persist in
going my own way."[d] This will bring
disaster on the watered land as well as
the dry.[k] **20**The LORD will never be
willing to forgive[e] him; his wrath and
zeal[f] will burn[g] against that man. All
the curses written in this book will fall
upon him, and the LORD will blot[h] out
his name from under heaven. **21**The
LORD will single him out from all the
tribes of Israel for disaster,[i] according to all the curses of the covenant
written in this Book of the Law.[j]
22Your children who follow you in
later generations and foreigners who
come from distant lands will see the
calamities that have fallen on the land
and the diseases with which the LORD
has afflicted it.[k] **23**The whole land will
be a burning waste[l] of salt[m] and sulfur—nothing planted, nothing sprouting, no vegetation growing on it. It will
be like the destruction of Sodom and
Gomorrah,[n] Admah and Zeboiim,
which the LORD overthrew in fierce anger.[o] **24**All the nations will ask: "Why
has the LORD done this to this land?[p]
Why this fierce, burning anger?"
25And the answer will be: "It is because this people abandoned the covenant of the LORD, the God of their fathers, the covenant he made with them
when he brought them out of Egypt.[q]
26They went off and worshiped other
gods and bowed down to them, gods
they did not know, gods he had not giv-
en them. **27**Therefore the LORD's anger
burned against this land, so that he
brought on it all the curses written in
this book.[r] **28**In furious anger and in
great wrath[s] the LORD uprooted[t]
them from their land and thrust them
into another land, as it is now."
29The secret things belong to the
LORD our God,[u] but the things revealed belong to us and to our children
forever, that we may follow all the
words of this law.[v]

Prosperity After Turning to the LORD

30 When all these blessings and
curses[w] I have set before you
come upon you and you take them to
heart wherever the LORD your God disperses you among the nations,[x] **2**and
when you and your children return[y] to
the LORD your God and obey him with
all your heart[z] and with all your soul
according to everything I command
you today, **3**then the LORD your God will
restore your fortunes[1][a] and have
compassion[b] on you and gather[c] you
again from all the nations where he

29:15 [y]S Ge 6:18; Ac 2:39
29:17 [z]Ex 20:23; Dt 4:28
29:18 [a]S Dt 13:6 [b]S Dt 11:16; Heb 12:15
29:19 [c]Ps 72:17; Isa 65:16 [d]Ps 36:2
29:20 [e]S Ex 23:21 [f]Ex 34:14; Eze 23:25; Zep 1:18 [g]Ps 74:1; 79:5; 80:4; Eze 36:5 [h]2Ki 13:23; 14:27; Rev 3:5
29:21 [i]Dt 32:23; Eze 7:26 [j]S Dt 28:61
29:22 [k]Jer 19:8; 49:17; 50:13
29:23 [l]Isa 1:7; 6:11; 9:18; 64:10; Jer 12:11; 44:2,6; Mic 5:11 [m]S Ge 13:10; Eze 47:11 [n]S Ge 19:24,25; Zep 2:9; S Mt 10:15; Ro 9:29 [o]S Ge 14:8
29:24 [p]1Ki 9:8; 2Ch 36:19; Jer 16:10; 22:8-9; 52:13
29:25 [q]2Ki 17:23; 2Ch 36:21
29:27 [r]S Dt 28:15
29:28 [s]Ps 7:11 [t]1Ki 14:15; 2Ch 7:20; Ps 9:6; 52:5; Pr 2:22; Jer 12:14; 31:28; 42:10; Eze 19:12
29:29 [u]Ac 1:7 [v]Jn 5:39; Ac 17:11; 2Ti 3:16
30:1 [w]S Dt 11:26 [x]Lev 26:40-45; S Dt 4:32; 29:28
30:2 [y]S Dt 4:30 [z]Dt 4:29; Ps 119:2
30:3 [a]Ps 14:7; 53:6; 85:1; 126:4; Jer 30:18; 33:11; Eze 16:53; Joel 3:1; Zep 2:7 [b]Dt 13:17 [c]S Ge 48:21

k *19* Or *way, in order to add drunkenness to thirst."* **1** *3* Or *will bring you back from captivity*

29:18–21 HEART TURNS AWAY FROM THE LORD. These verses concern an *individual* among God's elect people who turned away from the Lord. (1) The promises of life and blessing were made to Israel as a whole, i.e., as a corporate body or nation (cf. 28:1; 30:15–20). An individual within God's chosen people participated in the promised blessings only as he or she entered into a faith relationship with God and persevered in that relationship (see article on ELECTION AND PREDESTINATION, p. 1824).

(2) Eternal life and temporal blessing could be forfeited by any individual in Israel who turned his or her heart away from God (v. 18).

(3) For those in Israel who belonged to God, and then turned away from him (v. 18) and persisted in going their own way (v. 19), there remained no longer any opportunity for forgiveness. They could expect only God's wrath and the blotting out of their names from under heaven (v. 20; see article on PERSONAL APOSTASY, p. 1918).

29:19 SAFE, EVEN THOUGH I PERSIST IN GOING MY OWN WAY. Among God's chosen people would be those who went their own sinful way, yet claimed to "be safe." Similarly, the NT speaks of those within the church who profess to have peace, salvation and eternal life, yet make no attempt to follow God's will (see 1Jn 2:4, note; Rev 2:14, note). God says that their profession of salvation is not valid and compares them to a root that spreads defilement and death like a poison throughout the congregation (cf. Heb 12:15). Terrible judgment will come on those individuals (see previous note).

GOD'S COVENANT WITH THE ISRAELITES

***Dt 29:1** "These are the terms of the covenant the* LORD *commanded Moses to make with the Israelites in Moab, in addition to the covenant he had made with them at Horeb."*

THE COVENANT AT MOUNT SINAI (HOREB). God had made a covenant with Abraham and renewed it with Isaac and Jacob (see article on GOD'S COVENANT WITH ABRAHAM, ISAAC AND JACOB, p. 46). His covenant with the Israelites, made at the foot of Mount Sinai (see Ex 19:1, note), encompasses the two basic principles discussed in the above-mentioned article: (1) God alone establishes the promises and obligations of his covenant, and (2) humans are expected to accept them in obedient faith. The main difference between this covenant and the earlier one is that God outlined its promises and responsibilities before ratification (Ex 24:1–8).

(1) God's promises in this covenant were essentially the same as those made to Abraham (see Ex 19:1, note). He promised (a) to give the Israelites the land of Canaan after redeeming them from slavery in Egypt (Ex 6:3–6; 19:4; 23:20,23), and (b) to be their God and to adopt them as his people (Ex 6:7; 19:6; see Dt 5:2, note). God's ultimate goal was to bring the Savior into the world through the covenant people.

(2) Before God would fulfill all these promises, he required the Israelites to commit themselves to keep his laws spoken to them while they were stationed at Mount Sinai. After God revealed the Ten Commandments and many other laws of the covenant (see article on THE OLD TESTAMENT LAW, p. 118), the Israelites vowed with one voice, "Everything the LORD has said we will do" (Ex 24:3). Without this solemn promise to accept the requirements of God's law, the covenant between them and the Lord God would not have been confirmed (cf. Ex 24:8, note).

(3) This agreement to keep God's law remained a condition of the covenant. Only by persevering in obedience to the Lord's commands and by offering the prescribed sacrifices of his covenant would Israel continue as God's treasured possession and keep on receiving his blessings. In other words, Israel's continued election as the people of God was conditioned on obeying him as their Lord (see Ex 19:5, note).

(4) God also stipulated clearly what would happen if his people failed to keep the covenant obligations. The penalty for disobedience was removal from the covenant people, either by banishment or death (see Ex 31:14–15). This penalty repeats God's warning at the time of the exodus that those who did not follow his instructions for the Passover would be cut off from the people (Ex 12:15,19; 12:15, note). These were not idle threats. At Kadesh, for example, when the Israelites rebelled against the Lord in unbelief and refused to enter Canaan because they feared the inhabitants, God became angry with them and caused them to wander in the desert for the next thirty-nine years; there all Israelites over age twenty died (excluding Caleb and Joshua, see Nu 13:26—14:39; 14:29, note). Their disobedience and unbelief caused them to forfeit living in the land of God's promised rest (cf. Ps 95:7–11; Heb 3:9–11,18).

(5) The obedience God expected from his people was not perfection but a sincere and earnest obedience. Inherent in the covenant was a recognition that at times, because of the weakness of human nature, they would fail (see Dt 30:20, note). In order to remove the guilt of sin and to reconcile the people to himself, God provided the sacrificial system in general and the annual Day of Atonement in particular (see article on THE DAY OF ATONEMENT, p. 174). The people could confess their sins, offer various sacrifices, and so become reconciled to their Lord. However, God would judge severely willful disobedience, rebellion and apostasy.

(6) Through his covenant with the Israelites, God intended that people in other nations, by observing Israel's faithfulness to God and the accompanying blessings, would want to draw near to the Lord and become a part of the community of faith (see Dt 4:6,

note). Eventually, through the promised Redeemer, the nations of the world would be invited to accept these promises too. Thus, the covenant had a missionary emphasis.

THE COVENANT RENEWED ON THE PLAINS OF MOAB. After the rebellious and unfaithful generation of Israelites had died during their thirty-nine years of wandering in the desert, God called a whole new generation of Israelites and prepared them to enter the promised land by renewing the covenant with him. To conquer the land of Canaan successfully would require their commitment to this covenant and the assurance that the Lord God would be with them.

(1) This covenant renewal is the main focus of the book of Deuteronomy (see introduction to Deuteronomy). After an opening preamble (Dt 1:1–5), Deuteronomy summarizes the history of God's dealings with his people from the time they left Sinai (Dt 1:6—4:43), recites the main stipulations of the covenant (Dt 4:44—26:19), reminds the Israelites of the curses and blessings of the covenant (Dt 27:1—30:20), and closes with the arrangements for its continuation (Dt 31:1—33:29). Though not specifically mentioned in the book, we may assume that the nation of Israel with one voice agreed with a hearty "Amen" to the covenant stipulations, even as the previous generation had done at Mount Sinai (cf. Ex 24:1–8; Dt 27).

(2) The basic format of this covenant remained the same as the covenant at Mount Sinai. A recurring theme throughout Deuteronomy is that if God's people obeyed all the words of the covenant, God would bless them; if they did not, God would curse and punish them instead (see especially Dt 27—30). The only way in which they and their descendants could remain forever in the land of Canaan was by keeping the covenant through loving the Lord (see Dt 6:5, note) and obeying God's law (Dt 30:15–20).

(3) Moses instructed the people to refresh their memories periodically concerning the covenant. Every seven years, at the Feast of Tabernacles, all the Israelites were to appear in the place God would choose; there they would be reminded of their covenant by listening to the reading of the Law of Moses and by promising to obey what they had heard (Dt 31:9–13).

(4) The OT records several notable examples of this covenant remembrance and renewal. After the land had been conquered and shortly before Joshua died, he called all the people together for this purpose (Jos 24). The people's response was clear and unmistakable: "We will serve the LORD our God and obey him" (Jos 24:24). Thereupon "Joshua made a covenant for the people" (Jos 24:25). Similarly, Jehoiada led a covenant renewal ceremony at the crowning of Joash (2Ki 11:17), as did Josiah (2Ki 23:1–3), Hezekiah (cf. 2Ch 29:10) and Ezra (Ne 8:1—10:39).

(5) The call to covenant remembrance and renewal is relevant today. The NT is God's covenant with us. We remember his covenant with us as we read and study his revelation with its promises and stipulations, as we hear it proclaimed in the preaching of God's word, and most specifically, as we participate in the Lord's Supper (see 1Co 11:17–34). Through the Lord's Supper we also renew our commitment to love the Lord and to serve him with our whole heart (see 1Co 11:20, note).

scattered[d] you.[e] 4Even if you have
been banished to the most distant land
under the heavens,[f] from there the
LORD your God will gather[g] you and
bring you back.[h] 5He will bring[i] you
to the land that belonged to your fathers, and you will take possession of
it. He will make you more prosperous
and numerous[j] than your fathers.
6The LORD your God will circumcise
your hearts and the hearts of your
descendants,[k] so that you may love[l]
him with all your heart and with all
your soul, and live. 7The LORD your God
will put all these curses[m] on your enemies who hate and persecute you.[n]
8You will again obey the LORD and follow all his commands I am giving you
today. 9Then the LORD your God will
make you most prosperous in all the
work of your hands and in the fruit of
your womb, the young of your livestock
and the crops of your land.[o] The LORD
will again delight[p] in you and make
you prosperous, just as he delighted in
your fathers, 10if you obey the LORD
your God and keep his commands and
decrees that are written in this Book of
the Law[q] and turn to the LORD your
God with all your heart and with all
your soul.[r]

The Offer of Life or Death

11Now what I am commanding you
today is not too difficult for you or beyond your reach.[s] 12It is not up in
heaven, so that you have to ask, "Who
will ascend into heaven[t] to get it and
proclaim it to us so we may obey it?"[u]
13Nor is it beyond the sea,[v] so that
you have to ask, "Who will cross the
sea to get it and proclaim it to us so we
may obey it?"[w] 14No, the word is very
near you; it is in your mouth and in
your heart so you may obey it.[x]

15See, I set before you today life[y]
and prosperity,[z] death[a] and destruction.[b] 16For I command you today to
love[c] the LORD your God, to walk in his
ways, and to keep his commands, decrees and laws; then you will live[d] and
increase, and the LORD your God will
bless you in the land you are entering
to possess.

17But if your heart turns away and
you are not obedient, and if you are
drawn away to bow down to other gods
and worship them, 18I declare to you
this day that you will certainly be destroyed.[e] You will not live long in the
land you are crossing the Jordan to enter and possess.

19This day I call heaven and earth as
witnesses against you[f] that I have set
before you life and death, blessings
and curses.[g] Now choose life, so that
you and your children may live 20and
that you may love[h] the LORD your God,
listen to his voice, and hold fast to him.
For the LORD is your life,[i] and he will
give[j] you many years in the land[k] he

30:3 [d]S Ge 11:4; Dt 4:27 [e]Isa 11:11; Jer 12:15; 16:15; 24:6; 29:14; 48:47; 49:6 **30:4** [f]Ps 19:6 [g]Isa 17:6; 24:13; 27:12; 40:11; 49:5; 56:8; Eze 20:34,41; 34:13 [h]Ne 1:8-9; Isa 11:12; 41:5; 42:10; 43:6; 48:20; 62:11; Jer 31:8,10; 50:2 **30:5** [i]Jer 29:14 [j]S Dt 7:13 **30:6** [k]S Dt 6:24; S 10:16 [l]Dt 6:5 **30:7** [m]S Ge 12:3 [n]Dt 7:15 **30:9** [o]Jer 1:10; 24:6; 31:28; 32:41; 42:10; 45:4 [p]S Dt 28:63 **30:10** [q]S Dt 28:61 [r]S Dt 4:29 **30:11** [s]Ps 19:8; Isa 45:19,23; 63:1 **30:12** [t]Pr 30:4 [u]Ro 10:6* **30:13** [v]Job 28:14 [w]Ro 10:7* **30:14** [x]S Dt 6:6; Ro 10:8* **30:15** [y]Pr 10:16; 11:19; 12:28; Jer 21:8 [z]Dt 28:11; Job 36:11; Ps 25:13; 106:5; Pr 3:1-2 [a]S Ge 2:17 [b]S Dt 11:26 **30:16** [c]Dt 6:5 [d]ver 19; Dt 4:1; 32:47; Ne 9:29 **30:18** [e]S Dt 8:19 **30:19** [f]Dt 4:26 [g]S Dt 11:26 **30:20** [h]Dt 6:5 [i]Dt 4:1; S 8:3; 32:47; Ps 27:1; Pr 3:22; S Jn 5:26; Ac 17:28 [j]Ge 12:7 [k]Ps 37:3

30:3 GATHER YOU AGAIN FROM ALL THE NATIONS. Moses prophesied a restoration of Israel that would involve repentance and return to God (v. 2), restored fortunes and release from captivity (vv. 3–4), a regathering to the Lord (v. 5), spiritual renewal (v. 6), and prosperity and blessing (vv. 7–10). Israel's final restoration includes: (1) universal restoration of the "remnant" of Israel (vv. 3–5; Isa 10:21–23; 11:11–12; Jer 30:24; 31:1,8,10; Eze 39:25,28);

(2) repentance and turning to the Messiah (vv. 2,8,10; Isa 11:10,12; Jer 23:5–8; Eze 37:21–25; Hos 5:15; 6:1–3; Ro 11:25–27; see Mt 23:39, note; see article on ISRAEL IN GOD'S PLAN OF SALVATION, p. 1730);

(3) spiritual renewal (vv. 3–6; Jer 32:37–41; Eze 11:17–20);

(4) blessing for Israel (Jer 31:8,10,12–13,28; Eze 28:25–26; Am 9:11–15);

(5) Israel's ministering for God to the nations (Isa 49:5–6; 55:3–5; 60:1–5; 61:5–6);

(6) judgment on Israel (Eze 20:34–38; Mal 3:2–5; 4:1) and of the nations (Jer 25:29–33; Da 2:44–45; Joel 3:1–2,12–14; see Mt 25:32, note; see article on THE GREAT TRIBULATION, p. 1456);

(7) great blessing on all who survive Christ's judgments after the great tribulation (Isa 19:22–24; 49:5; Mic 4:1–4; Zec 2:10–12; Rev 20:1–4; see Mt 25:32, note);

(8) Israel's permanent possession of the land in peace, safety and security (Jer 32:37–41);

(9) restoration in the last days (Hos 3:4–5);

(10) Christ and the church reigning over Israel and the nations (see Rev 20:4, note).

30:20 LOVE THE LORD YOUR GOD. The Israelites were commanded to maintain their relationship with God by loving him and listening to his voice (see 6:5, note). To express that obedience, however, they had to recognize their inability to fulfill the law and thus they had to bring sacrifices of atonement for their shortcomings (see Lev 1:2, note; see article on THE DAY OF ATONEMENT, p. 174). Life and salvation were never promised as a reward for perfect obedience; the law assumed the imperfection of faith and obedience on the part of God's people and thus provided the sacrificial system that atoned for sin. Israel's ultimate hope rested in God's mercy and grace.

swore to give to your fathers, Abraham, Isaac and Jacob.

Joshua to Succeed Moses

31 Then Moses went out and spoke these words to all Israel: **2**"I am now a hundred and twenty years old[l] and I am no longer able to lead you.[m] The LORD has said to me, 'You shall not cross the Jordan.'[n] **3**The LORD your God himself will cross[o] over ahead of you.[p] He will destroy these nations[q] before you, and you will take possession of their land. Joshua also will cross[r] over ahead of you, as the LORD said. **4**And the LORD will do to them what he did to Sihon and Og,[s] the kings of the Amorites, whom he destroyed along with their land. **5**The LORD will deliver[t] them to you, and you must do to them all that I have commanded you. **6**Be strong and courageous.[u] Do not be afraid or terrified[v] because of them, for the LORD your God goes with you;[w] he will never leave you[x] nor forsake[y] you."

7Then Moses summoned Joshua and said[z] to him in the presence of all Israel, "Be strong and courageous, for you must go with this people into the land that the LORD swore to their forefathers to give them,[a] and you must divide it among them as their inheritance. **8**The LORD himself goes before you and will be with you;[b] he will never leave you nor forsake you.[c] Do not be afraid; do not be discouraged."

The Reading of the Law

9So Moses wrote[d] down this law and gave it to the priests, the sons of Levi, who carried[e] the ark of the covenant of the LORD, and to all the elders of Israel. **10**Then Moses commanded them: "At the end of every seven years, in the year for canceling debts,[f] during the Feast of Tabernacles,[g] **11**when all Israel comes to appear[h] before the LORD your God at the place he will choose,[i] you shall read this law[j] before them in their hearing. **12**Assemble the people—men, women and children, and the aliens living in your towns—so they can listen and learn[k] to fear[l] the LORD your God and follow carefully all the words of this law. **13**Their children,[m] who do not know this law, must hear it and learn to fear the LORD your God as long as you live in the land you are crossing the Jordan to possess."

Israel's Rebellion Predicted

14The LORD said to Moses, "Now the day of your death[n] is near. Call Joshua[o] and present yourselves at the Tent of Meeting, where I will commission him.[p]" So Moses and Joshua came and presented themselves at the Tent of Meeting.[q]

15Then the LORD appeared at the Tent in a pillar of cloud, and the cloud stood over the entrance to the Tent.[r] **16**And the LORD said to Moses: "You are going to rest with your fathers,[s] and these people will soon prostitute[t] themselves to the foreign gods of the land they are entering. They will forsake[u] me and break the covenant I made with them. **17**On that day I will become angry[v] with them and forsake[w] them; I will hide[x] my face[y] from them, and they will be destroyed. Many disasters[z] and difficulties will come upon them, and on that day they will ask, 'Have not these disasters come upon us because our God is not

31:2 [l]S Ex 7:7 [m]Nu 27:17; 1Ki 3:7 [n]S Dt 3:23,26 **31:3** [o]Nu 27:18 [p]S Dt 9:3 [q]S Dt 7:1 [r]S Dt 3:28 **31:4** [s]S Nu 21:33 **31:5** [t]S Dt 2:33 **31:6** [u]ver 7,23; Jos 1:6,9,18; 10:25; 1Ch 22:13; 28:20; 2Ch 32:7 [v]Jer 1:8,17; Eze 2:6 [w]S Ge 28:15; S Dt 1:29; 20:4; S Mt 28:20 [x]Ps 56:9; 118:6 [y]S Dt 4:31; 1Sa 12:22; 1Ki 6:13; Ps 94:14; Isa 41:17; Heb 13:5* **31:7** [z]ver 23; Nu 27:23 [a]Jos 1:6 **31:8** [b]S Ex 13:21 [c]S Ge 28:15; S Dt 4:31 **31:9** [d]S Ex 17:14 [e]ver 25; 1Ch 15:2 **31:10** [f]S Dt 15:1 [g]S Ex 23:16; Dt 16:13 **31:11** [h]S Dt 16:16 [i]Dt 12:5 [j]Jos 8:34-35; 2Ki 23:2; Ne 8:2 **31:12** [k]Dt 4:10 [l]Hag 1:12; Mal 1:6; 3:5,16 **31:13** [m]S Dt 11:2 **31:14** [n]S Ge 25:8; S Nu 27:13 [o]Nu 27:23; Dt 34:9; Jos 1:1-9 [p]S Nu 27:19 [q]Ex 33:9-11 **31:15** [r]S Ex 33:9 **31:16** [s]S Ge 15:15 [t]S Ex 34:15; Dt 4:25-28; Jdg 2:12 [u]Jdg 10:6,13; 1Ki 9:9; 18:18; 19:10; Jer 2:13; 5:19; 19:4 **31:17** [v]Dt 32:16; Jdg 2:14,20; 10:7; 2Ki 13:3; 22:13; Ps 106:29,40; Jer 7:18; 21:5; 36:7 [w]Jdg 6:13; 2Ch 15:2; 24:20; Ezr 8:22; Ps 44:9; Isa 2:6 [x]Dt 32:20; Isa 1:15; 45:15; 53:3; 54:8 [y]Job 13:24; Ps 13:1; 27:9; 30:7; 104:29; Isa 50:6; Jer 33:5; Eze 39:29; Mic 3:4 [z]Jer 4:20; Eze 7:26

31:8 NEVER LEAVE YOU NOR FORSAKE YOU. The NT applies this promise to all who sincerely receive Christ as Lord and Savior (Heb 13:5). (1) Believers are assured that if they love God above all else and depend on him rather than on material security, the Lord will never desert nor forsake them, but will be their helper (cf. 1Ki 8:57; Jas 1:5; see Mt 6:30,33, notes). (2) Because of this promise, we must "be strong and courageous" (v. 6), persevering in trials, resisting temptations, trusting in the Lord and fully obeying him.

31:9 MOSES WROTE DOWN THIS LAW. God's commands were delivered to the people by Moses in written form. These commands included not just the words of Deuteronomy but the entire Pentateuch (i.e., the first five books of the Bible). They were the Word of God in written form, the holy Scriptures inspired, preserved and formed in Biblical history (cf. vv. 24–26; Ex 24:4,7; Nu 33:2; Mt 8:4; Jn 5:46; 7:19; see article on THE INSPIRATION AND AUTHORITY OF SCRIPTURE, p. 1898).

31:16 WILL FORSAKE ME. The Lord knew the Israelites' history and their basic disposition toward unfaithfulness (see v. 21). Thus God prophetically revealed to Moses their future apostasy and his corresponding judgments (vv. 16–18). This prophecy was to be preserved in the form of a song as God's warning to later generations (v. 19; ch. 32).

with us?'[a] 18And I will certainly hide
my face on that day because of all their
wickedness in turning to other gods.
19"Now write[b] down for yourselves
this song and teach it to the Israelites
and have them sing it, so that it may be
a witness[c] for me against them.
20When I have brought them into the
land flowing with milk and honey, the
land I promised on oath to their forefathers,[d] and when they eat their fill
and thrive, they will turn to other
gods[e] and worship them,[f] rejecting
me and breaking my covenant.[g]
21And when many disasters and difficulties come upon them,[h] this song
will testify against them, because it
will not be forgotten by their descendants. I know what they are disposed
to do,[i] even before I bring them into
the land I promised them on oath."
22So Moses wrote[j] down this song
that day and taught it to the Israelites.
23The LORD gave this command[k] to
Joshua son of Nun: "Be strong and courageous,[l] for you will bring the Israelites into the land I promised them on
oath, and I myself will be with you."
24After Moses finished writing[m] in
a book the words of this law[n] from beginning to end, 25he gave this command to the Levites who carried[o] the
ark of the covenant of the LORD:
26"Take this Book of the Law and place
it beside the ark of the covenant of the
LORD your God. There it will remain as
a witness against you.[p] 27For I know
how rebellious[q] and stiff-necked[r]
you are. If you have been rebellious
against the LORD while I am still alive
and with you, how much more will you
rebel after I die! 28Assemble before me
all the elders of your tribes and all your
officials, so that I can speak these
words in their hearing and call heaven
and earth to testify against them.[s]
29For I know that after my death you
are sure to become utterly corrupt[t]
and to turn from the way I have commanded you. In days to come, disaster[u] will fall upon you because you
will do evil in the sight of the LORD and
provoke him to anger by what your
hands have made."

The Song of Moses

30And Moses recited the words of
this song from beginning to end in the
hearing of the whole assembly of Israel:

32 Listen,[v] O heavens,[w] and I
will speak;
hear, O earth, the words of my
mouth.[x]
2Let my teaching fall like rain[y]
and my words descend like
dew,[z][a]
like showers[b] on new grass,
like abundant rain on tender
plants.

3I will proclaim[c] the name of the
LORD.[d]
Oh, praise the greatness[e] of
our God!
4He is the Rock,[f] his works are
perfect,[g]
and all his ways are just.
A faithful God[h] who does no
wrong,
upright[i] and just is he.[j]

5They have acted corruptly toward
him;
to their shame they are no
longer his children,
but a warped and crooked
generation.[m][k]
6Is this the way you repay[l] the
LORD,
O foolish[m] and unwise people?[n]
Is he not your Father,[o] your
Creator,[n]
who made you and formed
you?[p]

7Remember the days of old;[q]
consider the generations long
past.[r]
Ask your father and he will tell
you,
your elders, and they will
explain to you.[s]
8When the Most High[t] gave the
nations their inheritance,
when he divided all mankind,[u]

31:17 [a]Nu 14:42; Hos 9:12
31:19 [b]ver 22 [c]S Ge 31:50
31:20 [d]Dt 6:10-12 [e]Ps 4:2; 16:4; 40:4; Jer 13:25; Da 3:28; Am 2:4 [f]Dt 8:19; 11:16-17 [g]ver 16
31:21 [h]S Dt 4:30 [i]1Ch 28:9; Hos 5:3; Jn 2:24-25
31:22 [j]ver 19
31:23 [k]S ver 7 [l]Jos 1:6
31:24 [m]Dt 17:18; 2Ki 22:8 [n]Dt 28:58
31:25 [o]S ver 9
31:26 [p]ver 19
31:27 [q]S Ex 23:21 [r]S Dt 9:27
31:28 [s]Dt 4:26; 30:19; 32:1; Job 20:27; Isa 26:21
31:29 [t]S Dt 4:16; Rev 9:20 [u]1Ki 9:9; 22:23; 2Ki 22:16

32:1 [v]Ps 49:1; Mic 1:2 [w]Jer 2:12 [x]S Dt 4:26
32:2 [y]2Sa 23:4 [z]Ps 107:20; Isa 9:8; 55:11 [a]Mic 5:7 [b]Ps 65:10; 68:9; 72:6; 147:8
32:3 [c]Ps 118:17; 145:6 [d]Ex 33:19; 34:5-6 [e]S Dt 3:24
32:4 [f]S Ge 49:24 [g]2Sa 22:31; Ps 18:30; 19:7 [h]S Dt 4:35 [i]Ps 92:15 [j]S Ge 18:25
32:5 [k]ver 20; Mt 17:17; Lk 9:41; Ac 2:40
32:6 [l]Ps 116:12 [m]Ps 94:8; Jer 5:21 [n]ver 28 [o]S Ex 4:22; 2Sa 7:24 [p]ver 15
32:7 [q]Ps 44:1; 74:2; 77:5; Isa 51:9; 63:9 [r]Dt 4:32; Job 8:8; 20:4; Ps 78:4; Isa 46:9 [s]S Ex 10:2; Job 15:18
32:8 [t]Ps 7:8 [u]S Ge 11:8; Ac 8:1

[m] 5 Or *Corrupt are they and not his children, / a generation warped and twisted to their shame*
[n] 6 Or *Father, who bought you*

31:30 THIS SONG. Moses' song (ch. 32) was designed to impress upon the Israelites that their whole existence was a result of God's faithfulness and mercy. The Lord alone guided them and sustained them (cf. 32:9–13). Israel's response, on the other hand, was in large measure one of wickedness and foolishness (32:5–6). The song concluded by warning Israel that future infidelity, rebellion and apostasy would bring God's severe judgments on the nation (see previous note).

he set up boundaries[v] for the
peoples
according to the number of the
sons of Israel.[o][w]
9For the LORD's portion[x] is his
people,
Jacob his allotted inheritance.[y]

10In a desert[z] land he found him,
in a barren and howling waste.[a]
He shielded[b] him and cared for
him;
he guarded him as the apple of
his eye,[c]
11like an eagle that stirs up its nest
and hovers over its young,[d]
that spreads its wings to catch
them
and carries them on its
pinions.[e]
12The LORD alone led[f] him;[g]
no foreign god was with him.[h]

13He made him ride on the heights[i]
of the land
and fed him with the fruit of the
fields.
He nourished him with honey from
the rock,[j]
and with oil[k] from the flinty
crag,
14with curds and milk from herd and
flock
and with fattened lambs and
goats,
with choice rams of Bashan[l]
and the finest kernels of
wheat.[m]
You drank the foaming blood of
the grape.[n]

15Jeshurun[p][o] grew fat[p] and
kicked;
filled with food, he became
heavy and sleek.
He abandoned[q] the God who
made him
and rejected the Rock[r] his
Savior.
16They made him jealous[s] with
their foreign gods
and angered[t] him with their
detestable idols.
17They sacrificed[u] to demons,[v]
which are not God—
gods they had not known,[w]
gods that recently appeared,[x]
gods your fathers did not
fear.
18You deserted the Rock, who
fathered you;
you forgot[y] the God who gave
you birth.

19The LORD saw this and rejected
them[z]
because he was angered by his
sons and daughters.[a]
20"I will hide my face[b] from them,"
he said,
"and see what their end will be;
for they are a perverse
generation,[c]
children who are unfaithful.[d]
21They made me jealous[e] by what
is no god
and angered me with their
worthless idols.[f]
I will make them envious by those
who are not a people;
I will make them angry by a
nation that has no
understanding.[g]
22For a fire has been kindled by my
wrath,[h]
one that burns to the realm of
death[q] below.[i]
It will devour[j] the earth and its
harvests[k]
and set afire the foundations of
the mountains.[l]

23"I will heap calamities[m] upon
them

32:8 [v] Ps 74:17 [w] Nu 23:9; Dt 33:12,28; Jer 23:6 **32:9** [x] Ps 16:5; 73:26; 119:57; 142:5; Jer 10:16 [y] S Dt 9:29; S 1Sa 26:19 **32:10** [z] S Dt 1:19 [a] Dt 8:15; Job 12:24; Ps 107:40 [b] Ps 32:10; Jer 31:22 [c] Ps 17:8; Pr 7:2; Hos 13:5; Zec 2:8 **32:11** [d] S Ex 19:4 [e] Ps 17:8; 18:10-19; 61:4 **32:12** [f] Ps 106:9; Isa 63:13; Jer 31:32 [g] Dt 4:35 [h] ver 39; Jdg 2:12; Ps 18:31; 81:9; Isa 43:12; 45:5 **32:13** [i] Dt 33:29; 2Sa 22:34; Ps 18:33; Isa 33:16; 58:14; Eze 36:2; Hab 3:19 [j] S Dt 8:8 [k] Dt 33:24; Job 29:6 **32:14** [l] S Nu 21:33 [m] Ps 65:9; 81:16; 147:14 [n] S Ge 49:11 **32:15** [o] Dt 33:5, 26; Isa 44:2 [p] Dt 31:20; Jer 5:28 [q] Dt 31:16; Isa 1:4,28; 58:2; 65:11; Jer 15:6; Eze 14:5 [r] S Ge 49:24 **32:16** [s] S Nu 25:11; S 1Co 10:22 [t] S Dt 31:17; S 1Ki 14:9 **32:17** [u] S Ex 32:8 [v] S Ex 22:20; 1Co 10:20 [w] S Dt 28:64 [x] Jdg 5:8 **32:18** [y] Jdg 3:7; 1Sa 12:9; Ps 44:17,20; 106:21; Jer 2:32; Eze 23:35; Hos 8:14; 13:6 **32:19** [z] Lev 26:30; Ps 78:59 [a] Am 6:8 **32:20** [b] Dt 31:17, 29; Ps 4:6; 44:24 [c] S ver 5 [d] Dt 9:23 **32:21** [e] S Nu 25:11; S 1Co 10:22 [f] ver 17; 1Ki 16:13,26; 2Ki 17:15; Ps 31:6; Jer 2:5; 8:19; 10:8; 16:19; Jnh 2:8 [g] Ro 10:19* **32:22** [h] Ps 7:11 [i] Nu 16:31-35; Ps 18:7-8; Jer 15:14; La 4:11 [j] Am 7:4 [k] Lev 26:20 [l] Ps 83:14 **32:23** [m] S Dt 29:21

[o] *8* Masoretic Text; Dead Sea Scrolls (see also Septuagint) *sons of God* [p] *15 Jeshurun* means *the upright one*, that is, Israel.
[q] *22* Hebrew *to Sheol*

32:15 GREW FAT. Prosperity was a major factor in Israel's forgetting God and embracing idolatry (cf. 8:7–20). History has shown repeatedly that in times of ease and plenty, God's people are most prone to forget God and to stop seeking his face. During adverse circumstances, however, God's people are more likely to approach God earnestly and ask for his help (cf. the book of Judges).

32:17 DEMONS. Behind the false gods and religions of this world are the spiritual powers of demons (Ps 106:37; 1Co 10:20; see article on THE NATURE OF IDOLATRY, p. 394). Demons may act through their followers even to the point of performing miracles (Ex 7:11,22; 2Th 2:9–10; Rev 13:13; 19:20). The NT recognizes the existence of such evil spirits and urges believers to battle against them through Christ's power and authority (Eph 6:12; see article on POWER OVER SATAN AND DEMONS, p. 1484).

and spend my arrows[n] against
them.
24I will send wasting famine[o]
against them,
consuming pestilence[p] and
deadly plague;[q]
I will send against them the fangs
of wild beasts,[r]
the venom of vipers[s] that glide
in the dust.[t]
25In the street the sword will make
them childless;
in their homes terror[u] will
reign.[v]
Young men and young women will
perish,
infants and gray-haired men.[w]
26I said I would scatter[x] them
and blot out their memory from
mankind,[y]
27but I dreaded the taunt of the
enemy,
lest the adversary
misunderstand[z]
and say, 'Our hand has triumphed;
the LORD has not done all
this.' "[a]
28They are a nation without sense,
there is no discernment[b] in
them.
29If only they were wise and would
understand this[c]
and discern what their end will
be![d]
30How could one man chase a
thousand,
or two put ten thousand to
flight,[e]
unless their Rock had sold them,[f]
unless the LORD had given them
up?[g]
31For their rock is not like our
Rock,[h]
as even our enemies concede.[i]
32Their vine comes from the vine of
Sodom[j]
and from the fields of Gomorrah.
Their grapes are filled with
poison,[k]
and their clusters with
bitterness.[l]
33Their wine is the venom of
serpents,
the deadly poison of cobras.[m]
34"Have I not kept this in reserve
and sealed it in my vaults?[n]
35It is mine to avenge;[o] I will
repay.[p]
In due time their foot will slip;[q]

32:23 [n]ver 42; 2Sa 22:15; Job 6:4; Ps 7:13; 18:14; 45:5; 77:17; 120:4; Isa 5:28; 49:2; Eze 5:16; Hab 3:9, 11
32:24 [o]Ge 26:1; S 41:55; 42:5; 2Sa 24:13; 1Ch 21:12 [p]S Dt 28:22 [q]Ps 91:6 [r]S Ge 37:20 [s]ver 33; Job 20:16; Ps 58:4; Jer 8:17; Am 5:18-19; Mic 7:17 [t]Job 20:16
32:25 [u]Isa 24:17 [v]Jer 14:18; La 1:20; Eze 7:15; 2Co 7:5 [w]2Ch 36:17; Isa 13:18; Jer 4:31; La 2:21
32:26 [x]Dt 4:27 [y]S Nu 14:12; Job 18:17; Ps 34:16; 37:28; 109:15; Isa 14:20
32:27 [z]Dt 9:26-28 [a]Ps 140:8; Isa 10:13; Jer 40:2-3
32:28 [b]Isa 1:3; 5:13; 27:11; Jer 8:7
32:29 [c]Dt 5:29; Ps 81:13 [d]Isa 47:7; La 1:9
32:30 [e]S Lev 26:8 [f]Jdg 2:14; 3:8; 4:2; 10:7; 1Sa 12:9 [g]Nu 21:34; 1Sa 23:7; Ps 31:8; 44:12; 106:41; Isa 50:1; 54:6
32:31 [h]S Ge 49:24 [i]S Ex 14:25
32:32 [j]Jer 23:14 [k]Job 6:4; 20:16 [l]Dt 29:18
32:33 [m]S ver 24
32:34 [n]Job 14:17; Jer 2:22; Hos 13:12
32:35 [o]S ver 41; S Ge 4:24; S Jer 51:6 [p]S Ge 30:2; S Ex 32:34; S Ps 54:5; S Ro 12:19*; Heb 10:30* [q]Ps 17:5; 35:6; 37:31; 38:16; 66:9; 73:2,18; 94:18; 121:3; Pr 4:19; Jer 23:12
[r]Eze 7:8-9
32:36 [s]Heb 10:30* [t]Am 7:3 [u]Lev 26:43-45; Dt 30:1-3; Jdg 2:18; Ps 90:13; 102:13; 103:13; 106:45; 135:14; Joel 2:14 [v]1Ki 14:10; 21:21; 2Ki 9:8
32:37 [w]Jdg 10:14; Jer 2:28; 11:12

their day of disaster is near
and their doom rushes upon
them.[r]"
36The LORD will judge his people[s]
and have compassion[t] on his
servants[u]
when he sees their strength is
gone
and no one is left, slave[v] or
free.
37He will say: "Now where are their
gods,
the rock they took refuge in,[w]
38the gods who ate the fat of their
sacrifices
and drank the wine of their
drink offerings?[x]
Let them rise up to help you!
Let them give you shelter!
39"See now that I myself am He![y]
There is no god besides me.[z]
I put to death[a] and I bring to
life,[b]
I have wounded and I will
heal,[c]
and no one can deliver out of my
hand.[d]
40I lift my hand[e] to heaven and
declare:
As surely as I live forever,[f]
41when I sharpen my flashing
sword[g]
and my hand grasps it in
judgment,
I will take vengeance[h] on my
adversaries
and repay those who hate me.[i]
42I will make my arrows drunk with
blood,[j]
while my sword devours flesh:[k]
the blood of the slain and the
captives,
the heads of the enemy leaders."
43Rejoice,[l] O nations, with his
people,[r,s]

32:38 [x]Nu 25:1-2; Jer 11:12; 44:8,25 **32:39** [y]Isa 41:4; 43:10; 44:7; 46:4; 48:12 [z]S ver 12 [a]1Sa 2:6 [b]1Sa 2:6; 2Ki 5:7; Ps 68:20; Jn 11:25-26 [c]Ex 15:26; Job 5:18; 15:11; Ps 147:3; Isa 6:10; 19:22; 30:26; 53:5; 57:18; Jer 33:6; Hos 6:1; Mal 4:2; 1Pe 2:24 [d]Job 9:12; 10:7; Ps 7:2; 50:22; Isa 43:13; Da 4:35; Hos 5:14 **32:40** [e]S Ge 14:22 [f]S Ge 21:33; Rev 1:18 **32:41** [g]Jdg 7:20; Ps 7:12; 45:3; Isa 27:1; 34:6; 66:16; Jer 12:12; Eze 21:9-10 [h]ver 35; Ps 149:7; Jer 46:10; Na 1:2 [i]Ps 137:8; Jer 25:14; 50:29; 51:24,56 **32:42** [j]S ver 23 [k]2Sa 2:26; Jer 12:12; 44:1; 46:10,14 **32:43** [l]Ps 137:6; Isa 25:9; 65:18; 66:10; Ro 15:10*

r *43* Or *Make his people rejoice, O nations*
s *43* Masoretic Text; Dead Sea Scrolls (see also Septuagint) *people, / and let all the angels worship him /*

for he will avenge the blood of
his servants;[m]
he will take vengeance on his
enemies[n]
and make atonement for his land
and people.[o]

44 Moses came with Joshua[t][p] son
of Nun and spoke all the words of this
song in the hearing of the people.
45 When Moses finished reciting all
these words to all Israel, 46 he said to
them, "Take to heart all the words I
have solemnly declared to you this
day,[q] so that you may command[r]
your children to obey carefully all the
words of this law. 47 They are not just
idle words for you—they are your
life.[s] By them you will live long[t] in
the land you are crossing the Jordan to
possess."

Moses to Die on Mount Nebo

48 On that same day the LORD told
Moses,[u] 49 "Go up into the Abarim[v]
Range to Mount Nebo[w] in Moab,
across from Jericho,[x] and view Canaan,[y] the land I am giving the Israelites as their own possession. 50 There
on the mountain that you have climbed
you will die[z] and be gathered to your
people, just as your brother Aaron
died[a] on Mount Hor[b] and was gathered to his people. 51 This is because
both of you broke faith with me in the
presence of the Israelites at the waters
of Meribah Kadesh[c] in the Desert of
Zin[d] and because you did not uphold
my holiness among the Israelites.[e]
52 Therefore, you will see the land only
from a distance;[f] you will not enter[g]
the land I am giving to the people of
Israel."

Moses Blesses the Tribes

33:1–29Ref — Ge 49:1–28

33 This is the blessing[h] that Moses the man of God[i] pronounced on the Israelites before his death. 2 He said:

"The LORD came from Sinai[j]
and dawned over them from
Seir;[k]
he shone forth[l] from Mount
Paran.[m]
He came with[u] myriads of holy
ones[n]
from the south, from his
mountain slopes.[v]
3 Surely it is you who love[o] the
people;
all the holy ones are in your
hand.[p]
At your feet they all bow down,[q]
and from you receive instruction,
4 the law that Moses gave us,[r]
the possession of the assembly
of Jacob.[s]
5 He was king[t] over Jeshurun[w][u]
when the leaders of the people
assembled,
along with the tribes of Israel.

6 "Let Reuben live and not die,
nor[x] his men be few."[v]

7 And this he said about Judah:[w]

"Hear, O LORD, the cry of Judah;
bring him to his people.
With his own hands he defends his
cause.
Oh, be his help against his
foes!"

8 About Levi[x] he said:

"Your Thummim and Urim[y] belong
to the man you favored.[z]
You tested[a] him at Massah;
you contended with him at the
waters of Meribah.[b]
9 He said of his father and mother,[c]
'I have no regard for them.'
He did not recognize his brothers
or acknowledge his own
children,
but he watched over your word
and guarded your covenant.[d]
10 He teaches[e] your precepts to
Jacob
and your law to Israel.[f]
He offers incense before you[g]

32:43 [m] 2Ki 9:7; S Rev 6:10 [n] Isa 1:24; Jer 9:9 [o] Ps 65:3; 79:9 **32:44** [p] Nu 13:8, 16 **32:46** [q] S Dt 6:6; Jn 1:17; 7:19 [r] Dt 6:7 **32:47** [s] S Dt 30:20 [t] S Ex 23:26; Dt 33:25; Isa 65:22 **32:48** [u] Nu 27:12 **32:49** [v] Nu 27:12 [w] S Nu 32:3 [x] S Nu 22:1 [y] S Lev 14:34 **32:50** [z] S Ge 25:8; S Nu 27:13 [a] Nu 20:29 [b] S Nu 20:22 **32:51** [c] Eze 47:19 [d] S Nu 13:21; 20:11-13 [e] Nu 27:14 **32:52** [f] Dt 34:1-3 [g] S Dt 3:27 **33:1** [h] S Ge 27:4 [i] Jos 14:6; 1Sa 2:27; 9:6; 1Ki 12:22; 13:1; 2Ki 1:9-13; 5:8; Jer 35:4 **33:2** [j] Ex 19:18; Ps 68:8 [k] Jos 11:17; Jdg 5:4 [l] Ps 50:2; 80:1; 94:1 [m] S Nu 10:12 [n] Ps 89:7; Da 4:13; 7:10; 8:13; Zec 14:5; Ac 7:53; Gal 3:19; Heb 2:2; Rev 5:11 **33:3** [o] S Dt 4:37 [p] Dt 7:6 [q] Lk 10:39; Rev 4:10 **33:4** [r] Dt 4:2; Jn 1:17; 7:19 [s] Ps 119:111 **33:5** [t] S Ex 16:8; 1Sa 10:19; Ps 10:16; 149:2 [u] S Nu 23:21; S Dt 32:15 **33:6** [v] S Ge 34:5 **33:7** [w] S Ge 49:10 **33:8** [x] S Ge 29:34 [y] Ex 28:30 [z] Ps 106:16 [a] S Nu 14:22 [b] S Ex 17:7 **33:9** [c] Ex 32:26-29 [d] Ps 61:5; Mal 2:5 **33:10** [e] Ezr 7:10; Ne 8:18; Ps 119:151; Jer 23:22; Mal 2:6 [f] S Lev 10:11; Dt 17:8-11; 31:9-13 [g] S Ex 30:7; Lev 16:12-13

[t] *44* Hebrew *Hoshea,* a variant of *Joshua* [u] *2* Or *from* [v] *2* The meaning of the Hebrew for this phrase is uncertain. [w] *5 Jeshurun* means *the upright one,* that is, Israel; also in verse 26. [x] *6* Or *but let*

33:9 DID NOT RECOGNIZE HIS BROTHERS. After Israel's sin with the golden calf (see Ex 32), the Levites stood with God even against their nearest relatives. They held firmly to the covenant and chastened those who participated in the worship of the golden calf. God rewarded them for their zeal for his cause by appointing them as guardians of the law (v. 10) and as those who would offer sacrifices (v. 10). Our love for and dedication to God and his word must always be first in our lives and take priority over friends, family or church (Mt 10:37–38; Lk 14:26).

and whole burnt offerings on
your altar.[h]
11Bless all his skills, O LORD,
and be pleased with the work of
his hands.[i]
Smite the loins of those who rise
up against him;
strike his foes till they rise no
more."

12About Benjamin[j] he said:

"Let the beloved of the LORD rest
secure in him,[k]
for he shields him all day
long,[l]
and the one the LORD loves[m]
rests between his
shoulders.[n]"

13About Joseph[o] he said:

"May the LORD bless his land
with the precious dew from
heaven above
and with the deep waters that
lie below;[p]
14with the best the sun brings forth
and the finest the moon can
yield;
15with the choicest gifts of the
ancient mountains[q]
and the fruitfulness of the
everlasting hills;
16with the best gifts of the earth and
its fullness
and the favor of him who dwelt
in the burning bush.[r]
Let all these rest on the head of
Joseph,
on the brow of the prince
among[y] his brothers.[s]
17In majesty he is like a firstborn
bull;
his horns[t] are the horns of a
wild ox.[u]
With them he will gore[v] the
nations,
even those at the ends of the
earth.
Such are the ten thousands of
Ephraim;[w]
such are the thousands of
Manasseh.[x]"

18About Zebulun[y] he said:

"Rejoice, Zebulun, in your going
out,
and you, Issachar,[z] in your
tents.
19They will summon peoples to the
mountain[a]
and there offer sacrifices of
righteousness;[b]
they will feast on the abundance of
the seas,[c]
on the treasures hidden in the
sand."

20About Gad[d] he said:

"Blessed is he who enlarges Gad's
domain![e]
Gad lives there like a lion,
tearing at arm or head.
21He chose the best land for
himself;[f]
the leader's portion was kept for
him.[g]
When the heads of the people
assembled,
he carried out the LORD's
righteous will,[h]
and his judgments concerning
Israel."

22About Dan[i] he said:

"Dan is a lion's cub,
springing out of Bashan."

23About Naphtali[j] he said:

"Naphtali is abounding with the
favor of the LORD
and is full of his blessing;
he will inherit southward to the
lake."

24About Asher[k] he said:

"Most blessed of sons is Asher;
let him be favored by his
brothers,
and let him bathe his feet in
oil.[l]
25The bolts of your gates will be
iron and bronze,[m]
and your strength will equal
your days.[n]

26"There is no one like the God of
Jeshurun,[o]
who rides[p] on the heavens to
help you[q]
and on the clouds[r] in his
majesty.[s]
27The eternal[t] God is your
refuge,[u]
and underneath are the
everlasting[v] arms.
He will drive out your enemy
before you,[w]
saying, 'Destroy him!'[x]

33:10 [h]Ps 51:19
33:11 [i]2Sa 24:23; Ps 20:3; 51:19
33:12 [j]S Ge 35:18 [k]Dt 4:37-38; 12:10; S 32:8 [l]S Ex 19:4 [m]Ps 60:5; 127:2; Isa 5:1 [n]S Ex 28:12
33:13 [o]S Ge 30:24 [p]Ge 27:28; Ps 148:7
33:15 [q]Hab 3:6
33:16 [r]S Ex 3:2 [s]S Ge 37:8
33:17 [t]1Sa 2:10; 2Sa 22:3; Eze 34:21 [u]S Nu 23:22 [v]1Ki 22:11; Ps 44:5 [w]S Ge 41:52 [x]S Ge 41:51
33:18 [y]S Ge 30:20 [z]S Ge 30:18
33:19 [a]S Ex 15:17; Ps 48:1; Isa 2:3; 65:11; 66:20; Jer 31:6 [b]Ps 4:5; 51:19 [c]Isa 18:7; 23:18; 45:14; 60:5,11; 61:6; Hag 2:7; Zec 14:14
33:20 [d]Ge 30:11 [e]Dt 3:12-17
33:21 [f]Nu 32:1-5, 31-32 [g]S Nu 34:14 [h]Jos 22:1-3
33:22 [i]Ge 49:16; S Nu 1:38
33:23 [j]S Ge 30:8
33:24 [k]S Ge 30:13 [l]S Ge 49:20; S Dt 32:13
33:25 [m]Ne 3:3; 7:3; Ps 147:13 [n]S Dt 32:47
33:26 [o]S Dt 32:15 [p]Ps 18:10; 68:33 [q]S Dt 10:14; S Ps 104:3 [r]2Sa 22:10; Ps 18:9; 68:4; Da 7:13 [s]S Ex 15:7
33:27 [t]Ex 15:18; Isa 40:28; 57:15 [u]Ps 9:9; 84:1; 90:1; 91:9 [v]S Ge 21:33 [w]Ex 34:11; Jos 24:18 [x]S Dt 7:2

[y]16 Or *of the one separated from*

28So Israel will live in safety
alone;[y]
Jacob's spring is secure
in a land of grain and new wine,
where the heavens drop dew.[z]
29Blessed are you, O Israel![a]
Who is like you,[b]
a people saved by the LORD?[c]
He is your shield and helper[d]
and your glorious sword.
Your enemies will cower before
you,
and you will trample down their
high places.[z][e]"

The Death of Moses

34 Then Moses climbed Mount
Nebo[f] from the plains of Moab
to the top of Pisgah,[g] across from Jericho.[h] There the LORD showed[i] him
the whole land—from Gilead to Dan,[j]
2all of Naphtali, the territory of Ephraim and Manasseh, all the land of Judah
as far as the western sea,[a][k] 3the
Negev[l] and the whole region from the
Valley of Jericho, the City of Palms,[m]
as far as Zoar.[n] 4Then the LORD said
to him, "This is the land I promised on
oath[o] to Abraham, Isaac and Jacob[p]
when I said, 'I will give it[q] to your
descendants.' I have let you see it with
your eyes, but you will not cross[r] over
into it."
5And Moses the servant of the
LORD[s] died[t] there in Moab, as the
LORD had said. 6He buried him[b] in
Moab, in the valley opposite Beth
Peor,[u] but to this day no one knows
where his grave is.[v] 7Moses was a
hundred and twenty years old[w] when
he died, yet his eyes were not weak[x]
nor his strength gone.[y] 8The Israelites grieved for Moses in the plains of
Moab[z] thirty days,[a] until the time of
weeping and mourning[b] was over.
9Now Joshua son of Nun was filled
with the spirit[c] of wisdom[c] because
Moses had laid his hands on him.[d] So
the Israelites listened to him and did
what the LORD had commanded Moses.
10Since then, no prophet[e] has risen
in Israel like Moses,[f] whom the LORD
knew face to face,[g] 11who did all
those miraculous signs and wonders[h]
the LORD sent him to do in Egypt—to
Pharaoh and to all his officials[i] and to
his whole land. 12For no one has[j] ever
shown the mighty power or performed
the awesome deeds[k] that Moses did in
the sight of all Israel.

33:28 [y]S Ex 33:16; S Lev 25:18; S Dt 32:8; Ps 16:9; Pr 1:33; Isa 14:30 [z]ver 13; Ge 27:28 **33:29** [a]Ps 1:1; 32:1-2; 144:15 [b]2Sa 22:45; Ps 18:44; 66:3; 81:15 [c]Dt 4:7 [d]Ge 15:1; Ex 18:4; Ps 10:14; 18:1; 27:1,9; 30:10; 54:4; 70:5; 115:9-11; 118:7; Isa 45:24; Hos 13:9; Hab 3:19 [e]S Nu 33:52; S Dt 32:13 **34:1** [f]S Nu 32:3 [g]S Nu 21:20 [h]Dt 32:49 [i]Dt 32:52 [j]S Ge 14:14 **34:2** [k]S Ex 23:31 **34:3** [l]S Ge 12:9 [m]Jdg 1:16; 3:13; 2Ch 28:15 [n]S Ge 13:10 **34:4** [o]Ge 28:13 [p]Jos 21:43 [q]Ge 12:7 [r]S Dt 3:23 **34:5** [s]S Nu 12:7 [t]S Ge 25:8 **34:6** [u]S Dt 3:29 [v]Jude 1:9 **34:7** [w]S Ex 7:7 [x]S Ge 27:1 [y]S Ge 15:15 **34:8** [z]S Nu 21:11 [a]S Ge 37:34; S Dt 1:3 [b]2Sa 11:27 **34:9** [c]S Ge 41:38; S Ex 28:3; Isa 11:2 [d]S Dt 31:14; Ac 6:6 **34:10** [e]S Ge 20:7 [f]Dt 18:15,18 [g]S Ex 33:11 **34:11** [h]Dt 4:34 [i]S Ex 11:3 **34:12** [j]Heb 3:1-6 [k]S Dt 4:34

[z]29 Or *will tread upon their bodies* [a]2 That is, the Mediterranean [b]6 Or *He was buried* [c]9 Or *Spirit*

34:1 MOSES CLIMBED MOUNT NEBO. Those who have lived their lives in fellowship with God do not fear death. Because of their trust in God, they can even anticipate death with peace and joy (cf. Lk 2:29; Php 1:23). Like Moses, they have been given only a glimpse of the promised land (vv. 1–4); only after death do they inherit the "city with foundations, whose architect and builder is God" (Heb 11:10; see Php 1:21, note).

34:5 MOSES THE SERVANT OF THE LORD DIED. This record of Moses' death was probably written by Joshua soon after the great leader's death (v. 9). Moses was not allowed to enter the promised land before his death (v. 4); however, many years later Moses did enter it when he appeared on the Mount of Transfiguration and spoke with Jesus (Mt 17:3).

34:10 NO PROPHET HAS RISEN ... LIKE MOSES. Moses' great distinctions were his intimate fellowship with God and his understanding of God's nature and person. The foremost desire of all believers should be to know God and experience his close fellowship; it is their greatest privilege and right as God's children (Jn 1:12; 17:3; Ro 8:14–15; Gal 4:6). No person in Christ, possessing an inner life of devotion and an outer life of godliness, will be denied God's presence and grace. The fellowship of God—the Father, the Son and the Holy Spirit—is the believer's greatest promise and reward (Jn 14:15–21,23,26; Rev 3:20).

JOSHUA

Outline

I. Preparing for Entry and Entering Canaan (1:1—5:15)
- A. Joshua Is Commissioned by God (1:1–9)
- B. Preparations for Crossing the Jordan (1:10—3:13)
- C. Crossing the Jordan River (3:14—4:25)
- D. Circumcision, Passover and Encounter at Gilgal (5:1–15)

II. Conquering the Promised Land (6:1—13:7)
- A. Conquests in Central Canaan (6:1—8:35)
  1. Victory at Jericho (6:1–27)
  2. Defeat at Ai because of Achan's Sin (7:1–26)
  3. Victory at Ai (8:1–29)
  4. Worship and Covenant Renewal at Shechem (8:30–35)
- B. Conquests in Southern Canaan (9:1—10:43)
  1. Treaty with the Gibeonites (9:1–27)
  2. Destruction of the Amorite Coalition (10:1–43)
- C. Conquests in Northern Canaan (11:1–15)
- D. Summary of the Conquered Territories (11:16—12:24)
- E. Summary of the Unconquered Territories (13:1–7)

III. Dividing the Inheritance (13:8—22:34)
- A. Tribes East of the Jordan (13:8–33)
- B. Tribes West of the Jordan (14:1—19:51)
- C. Special Allotments (20:1—21:45)
  1. Six Cities of Refuge (20:1–9)
  2. Cities of the Levites (21:1–45)
- D. Return of the Eastern Tribes (22:1–34)

IV. Joshua's Farewell Messages (23:1—24:28)
- A. Addresses Israel's Rulers (23:1–16)
- B. Addresses All Israel; Covenant Renewal at Shechem (24:1–28)

Conclusion (24:29–33)
- A. Death and Burial of Joshua (24:29–31)
- B. Burial of Joseph's Bones (24:32)
- C. Death and Burial of Eleazar (24:33)

Author: Joshua

Theme: Conquering Canaan

Date of Writing: 14th century B.C.

Background

The book of Joshua is a continuation of the history of the Pentateuch. It records Israel's crossing the Jordan River into Canaan after Moses' death, as well as the conquest and settlement of Canaan by the twelve tribes under Joshua's leadership. The Biblical date for Israel's invasion of Canaan is about 1405 B.C. The book covers the next 25–30 years of

Israel's history, telling how God "gave Israel all the land he had sworn to give their forefathers" (21:43).

Appropriately, the book is named after its principal character, who predominates as God's leader throughout the book. Joshua's personal history prepared him well as leader for the conquest. Living near the end of Israel's oppression in Egypt, Joshua witnessed God's ten plague judgments, the first Passover, the miraculous Red Sea crossing, and the supernatural signs (and judgments) during Israel's desert journeys. He served Moses as military leader in the battle against the Amalekites soon after leaving Egypt (Ex 17:8–16), and he alone accompanied Moses up Mount Sinai when God gave Israel the Ten Commandments (Ex 24:12–18). As Moses' assistant, Joshua demonstrated an intense devotion and heart for God by often staying for a long time in the Lord's presence (Ex 33:11); he was a man who treasured God's holy presence. He must have learned much from Moses, his trusted counselor and guide, about the ways of God and the difficulties of leading the people. At Kadesh Joshua served Moses as one of the twelve spies that scouted the land of Canaan; along with Caleb, Joshua vigorously resisted the majority report of unbelief (Nu 14). For many years before replacing Moses as Israel's leader Joshua showed himself to be a man of faith, vision, courage, loyalty, resolute obedience, prayer and dedication to God and his word. By the time he was chosen to replace Moses, he was a man "in whom is the spirit" (Nu 27:18; cf. Dt 34:9).

Authorship of the book is credited to Joshua by Jewish tradition (the Talmud). The act of writing is mentioned twice in the book in connection with Joshua (18:9; 24:26). Internal evidence strongly indicates that the author was an eyewitness of the conquest (cf. "us" in 5:6; note that Rahab was still alive when the author wrote, 6:25). The parts of the book added after Joshua's death—e.g., 15:13–17 (cf. Jdg 1:9–13); 24:29–33—were perhaps written by one of the "elders who outlived him" (24:31). Joshua died about 1375 B.C. at the age of 110 (24:29).

Purpose

Joshua was written as a record of God's faithfulness in fulfilling his covenant promises to Israel concerning the land of Canaan (23:14; cf. Ge 12:6–7). The conquest victories are presented as God's acts of redemption for Israel and his acts of judgment on a decadent Canaanite culture (see Dt 9:4). Violence in the book must be viewed from this perspective. Archaeology confirms that gross immorality and cruelty characterized the Canaanite people whom Israel replaced in the land.

Survey

Joshua begins where Deuteronomy ends. Israel was still encamped on the plains of Moab (Dt 34:1), directly east of Jericho and the Jordan River. The book divides into three sections. (1) Section one (1:1—5:15) describes Joshua's commissioning by God as Moses' successor and Israel's preparation for entering Canaan (1:1—3:13), their crossing the Jordan (3:14—4:24), and their first covenant activities in the land (ch. 5). God promised Joshua: "I will give you every place where you set your foot" (1:3).

(2) Section two (6:1—13:7) describes how Israel marched obediently against well-armed city-states with fortified walls. God gave his people decisive victories in central (chs. 6–8), southern (chs. 9–10) and northern (chs. 11–12) Canaan, whereby Israel gained control of the hill country (south to north) and the Negev. The highly unusual manner in which Jericho was conquered clearly demonstrated to Israel who the Captain of their salvation was (ch. 6). Israel's defeat at Ai reveals the book's honesty and the serious obedience that God required of Israel (ch. 7).

(3) Section three (13:8—22:34) records the distribution of the land by Joshua to the twelve tribes, the inheritance of Caleb, the six cities of refuge, and the 48 Levite cities among the tribes. The book concludes with two farewell messages by Joshua (23:1—24:28) and an epitaph to Joshua and Eleazar (24:29–33).

Special Features

Seven major features characterize this book. (1) It is the first of the OT historical books to describe Israel's history as a nation in Palestine. (2) It provides considerable insight into the remarkable life of Joshua as God's choice for completing Moses' work; his task was to establish Israel as the covenant people in the land of promise. (3) The book records numerous divine miracles on Israel's behalf, the two most dramatic being the fall of Jericho (ch. 6) and the prolongation of the daylight hours at the battle at Gibeon (ch. 10). (4) It is the foremost OT book describing the concept of "holy war" as a specific and limited mission prescribed by God within the larger context of salvation history. (5) The book emphasizes three grand truths about God's relationship to his covenant people: (a) his faithfulness, (b) his holiness and (c) his salvation. (6) It highlights the importance of keeping alive the heritage of God's saving acts on behalf of his people and of perpetuating that heritage from one generation to the next. (7) The book's lengthy account of Achan's transgression and subsequent punishment (ch. 7), along with other admonitions, warnings and punishments, emphasizes the importance of the fear of the Lord in the hearts of God's people.

New Testament Fulfillment

Joshua's name (Heb *Yehoshua* or *Yeshua*) is the Hebrew equivalent of the name "Jesus" in the NT (see 1:1, note). In his role of leading Israel into the promised land, Joshua is an OT type or foreshadowing of Jesus, whose role is to bring "many sons to glory" (Heb 2:10; 4:1–13; cf. 2Co 2:14). Also, as the first Joshua wielded the sword of God's terrible judgment in conquest, so the second Joshua will wield it in conquest over the nations at the end of history (Rev 19:11–16).

Reading Joshua

In order to read the entire Old Testament in one year, the book of Joshua should be read in 9 days, according to the following schedule: ☐ 1–2 ☐ 3–4 ☐ 5–6 ☐ 7–9 ☐ 10–12 ☐ 13–15 ☐ 16–19 ☐ 20–22 ☐ 23–24

NOTES

The Lord Commands Joshua

1 After the death of Moses the servant of the Lord,[a] the Lord said to
Joshua[b] son of Nun, Moses' aide:
2"Moses my servant is dead. Now then,
you and all these people, get ready to
cross the Jordan River[cd] into the
land[e] I am about to give to them[f]—
to the Israelites. 3I will give you every
place where you set your foot,[g] as
I promised Moses.[h] 4Your territory
will extend from the desert to Lebanon,[i] and from the great river,
the Euphrates[j]—all the Hittite[k]
country—to the Great Sea[a] on the
west.[l] 5No one will be able to stand
up against you[m] all the days of your
life. As I was with[n] Moses, so I will be
with you; I will never leave you nor
forsake[o] you.
6"Be strong[p] and courageous,[q] because you will lead these people to inherit the land I swore to their forefathers[r] to give them. 7Be strong and
very courageous. Be careful to obey[s]
all the law[t] my servant Moses[u] gave
you; do not turn from it to the right or
to the left,[v] that you may be successful wherever you go.[w] 8Do not let this
Book of the Law[x] depart from your

1:1 [a] Ex 14:31; Dt 34:5; Rev 15:3 [b] S Ex 17:9 1:2 [c] S Nu 13:29 [d] S Nu 35:10 [e] S Ge 15:14 [f] Ge 12:7; Dt 1:25 1:3 [g] S Dt 11:24 [h] Ge 50:24; Nu 13:2; Dt 1:8 1:4 [i] S Dt 3:25 [j] S Ge 2:14 [k] S Ge 10:15; 23:10; Ex 3:8 [l] Nu 34:2-12; Ezr 4:20 1:5 [m] S Dt 7:24 [n] ver 17; S Ge 26:3; S 39:2; Jdg 6:12; 1Sa 10:7; Jer 1:8; 30:11 [o] S Ge 28:15; S Dt 4:31 1:6 [p] 2Sa 2:7; 1Ki 2:2; Isa 41:6; Joel 3:9-10 [q] S Dt 1:21; S 31:6; S Jdg 5:21 [r] Jer 3:18; 7:7 1:7 [s] Dt 29:9; 1Ki 2:3; 3:3 [t] Ezr 7:26; Ps 78:10; 119:136; Isa 42:24; Jer 26:4-6; 32:23; 44:10 [u] ver 2,15; S Nu 12:7; Job 1:8; 42:7 [v] S Dt 5:32; Jos 23:6 [w] ver 9; S Dt 4:2; 5:33; S 11:8; Jos 11:15 1:8 [x] S Dt 28:61; S Ps 147:19

[a] 4 That is, the Mediterranean

1:1 JOSHUA SON OF NUN. Joshua had been an intimate and faithful assistant of Moses during the forty years of desert wandering (Ex 17:8–13; 24:13; 32:17–19; Nu 13:8,16). As one filled with the Holy Spirit, he had been commissioned as Moses' successor (Nu 27:18–23; Dt 34:9). God was now calling him to lead his people into the land of promise (see Ge 12:6–7; 15:18–21). The name Joshua means "the Lord saves" (or "the Lord is salvation"); the Greek form of this name is "Jesus" (see Mt 1:21, note). Joshua is a type (or representative) of Jesus Christ in that he led God's people into the promised land and to victory over their enemies (Heb 4:1,6–8; see article on CHRIST IN THE OLD TESTAMENT, p. 518). The conquest of Canaan (Palestine) began about 1405 B.C.; Joshua's leadership of Israel covered about twenty-five years.

1:2 CROSS THE JORDAN RIVER INTO THE LAND. Like Israel's experiences in the desert, their entrance into and conquest of Canaan can be called an example written down as a warning for us (cf. 1Co 10:11). (1) The promised land and its conquest by God's people typifies not heaven, but believers' present spiritual inheritance and salvation in Christ.

(2) Although believers already possess salvation and in one sense are in the "heavenly realms . . . in Christ" (Eph 1:3), they must yet fight the fight of faith to ensure their possession of final salvation and eternal rest (1Ti 1:18–20; 4:16; 6:12). As with the taking of Canaan, the possession of salvation and eternal life involves spiritual warfare and conquest (Eph 6:10–20).

(3) For Joshua and the Israelites, the possession of the promised land was realized and maintained by faith in God, expressed in obedience to his word and in warfare against God's enemies (vv. 7–9; cf. Dt 28). For the believer under the new covenant, the possession of salvation and God's blessings are likewise maintained by a present living faith in Christ (see article on FAITH AND GRACE, p. 1720) expressed in obedience to his word (see Jn 3:36, note) and in spiritual warfare against sin, the sinful nature and Satan (Gal 5:16–21; see Eph 6:11, note). Thus, possession of the land (i.e., the Lord's inheritance) may be forfeited, as Joshua warns (23:16). The hope of final possession of God's ultimate rest lies in faith in God's promises (v. 6), in his power (3:14–17) and in his personal presence (vv. 5,9).

1:5 I WILL BE WITH YOU. God's foundational promise to Joshua—"I will be with you; I will never leave you nor forsake you"—is likewise God's commitment to all believers in the struggles of their faith (Mt 28:20; Heb 13:5–6; cf. Dt 31:6; see Ex 3:14, note). God's abiding presence with us is now a reality through his Son (Mt 1:23) and the gift of the Holy Spirit (Lk 24:49).

1:7 OBEY ALL THE LAW. In order to possess the promised land, Joshua and the Israelites had to commit themselves to obeying God's written Word (see next note). The Word of God written in the "Book" (i.e., Scripture, v. 8) was to be their central authority as opposed to all human ideas, tradition or religions; this principle is applicable to believers under both the old and new covenants.

1:8 BOOK OF THE LAW. This phrase refers to the first five books of the Bible, which record God's words, commands and revelation to Moses (cf. Dt 31:9–12,24–26). Joshua was to be faithful to God's word by talking about it (cf. Dt 6:7), meditating on it (cf. Ps 1:2; 119:97) and obeying it fully (cf. Ezr 7:10; Jas 1:22–25).

1:8 MEDITATE ON IT DAY AND NIGHT. "Meditate" (Heb *hagah*) means to read quietly or to talk to yourself as you think. It involves reflecting on God's words and ways and applying them to every area of your life (Ps 1:2; 63:6; 77:12; 143:5).

1:8 PROSPEROUS AND SUCCESSFUL. Those who know and obey God's word and law will be prosperous and successful in that they possess the wisdom to live righteously and to achieve God's goal for their lives (Ps 14:2; 119:99; Pr 1:3; 10:5). The requirements for prosperity and success are: (1) be strong, courageous and diligent (vv. 6–7); (2) make God's Word your authoritative guide for all beliefs and actions (v. 7); (3) study and meditate daily on God's Word (v. 8); and (4) determine

mouth;[y] meditate[z] on it day and night, so that you may be careful to do everything written in it. Then you will be prosperous and successful.[a] 9Have I not commanded you? Be strong and courageous. Do not be terrified;[b] do not be discouraged,[c] for the LORD your God will be with you wherever you go."[d]

Jos 22:5

10So Joshua ordered the officers of the people:[e] 11"Go through the camp[f] and tell the people, 'Get your supplies[g] ready. Three days[h] from now you will cross the Jordan[i] here to go in and take possession[j] of the land the LORD your God is giving you for your own.' "

12But to the Reubenites, the Gadites and the half-tribe of Manasseh,[k] Joshua said, 13"Remember the command that Moses the servant of the LORD gave you: 'The LORD your God is giving you rest[l] and has granted you this land.' 14Your wives,[m] your children and your livestock may stay in the land[n] that Moses gave you east of the Jordan, but all your fighting men, fully armed,[o] must cross over ahead of your brothers.[p] You are to help your brothers 15until the LORD gives them rest, as he has done for you, and until they too have taken possession of the land that the LORD your God is giving them. After that, you may go back and occupy your own land, which Moses the servant of the LORD gave you east of the Jordan toward the sunrise."[q]

16Then they answered Joshua, "Whatever you have commanded us we will do, and wherever you send us we will go.[r] 17Just as we fully obeyed Moses, so we will obey you.[s] Only may the LORD your God be with you as he was with Moses. 18Whoever rebels against your word and does not obey[t] your words, whatever you may command them, will be put to death. Only be strong and courageous!"[u]

Rahab and the Spies

2 Then Joshua son of Nun secretly sent two spies[v] from Shittim.[w] "Go, look over[x] the land," he said, "especially Jericho.[y]" So they went and entered the house of a prostitute[b] named Rahab[z] and stayed there.

2The king of Jericho was told, "Look! Some of the Israelites have come here tonight to spy out the land." 3So the king of Jericho sent this message to Rahab:[a] "Bring out the men who came to you and entered your house, because they have come to spy out the whole land."

4But the woman had taken the two men[b] and hidden them.[c] She said, "Yes, the men came to me, but I did not know where they had come from. 5At dusk, when it was time to close the city gate,[d] the men left. I don't know which way they went. Go after them quickly. You may catch up with them."[e] 6(But she had taken them up to the roof and hidden them under the stalks of flax[f] she had laid out on the roof.)[g] 7So the men set out in pursuit of the spies on the road that leads to the fords of the Jordan,[h] and as soon as the pursuers[i] had gone out, the gate was shut.

8Before the spies lay down for the night, she went up on the roof[j] 9and said to them, "I know that the LORD has

1:8 y S Ex 4:15; Isa 59:21 z S Ge 24:63 a Dt 29:9; 1Sa 18:14; Ps 1:1-3; Isa 52:13; 53:10; Jer 23:5
1:9 b S Dt 31:6; Jos 10:8; 2Ki 19:6; Isa 35:4; 37:6 c S Dt 1:21; Job 4:5 d S ver 7; Dt 31:7-8; Jer 1:8
1:10 e S Dt 1:15
1:11 f Jos 3:2 g 1Sa 17:22; Isa 10:28 h S Ge 40:13 i S Nu 35:10 j S Nu 33:53
1:12 k Nu 32:33
1:13 l S Ex 33:14; Ps 55:6; Isa 11:10; 28:12; 30:15; 32:18; 40:31; Jer 6:16; 45:3; La 5:5
1:14 m Dt 3:19 n S Nu 32:26 o S Ex 13:18 p Jos 4:12
1:15 q Nu 32:20-22; Jos 22:1-4
1:16 r S Nu 27:20; S 32:25
1:17 s S Nu 27:20
1:18 t S Nu 32:25 u S Dt 1:21; S 31:6
2:1 v S ver 4; S Ge 42:9 w S Nu 25:1; Jos 3:1; Joel 3:18 x S Nu 21:32; Jdg 18:2 y S Nu 33:48 z Jos 6:17,25; S Heb 11:31
2:3 a Jos 6:23
2:4 b ver 1; Jos 6:22 c Jos 6:17
2:5 d Jdg 5:8; 9:35; 16:2 e S Heb 11:31
2:6 f Jdg 15:14; Pr 31:13; Isa 19:9 g S Ex 1:17,19; Jos 6:25; 2Sa 17:19
2:7 h Nu 22:1; Jdg 3:28; 7:24; 12:5,6; Isa 16:2 i ver 16,22
2:8 j S Dt 22:8; Jdg 16:27; 2Sa 16:22; Ne 8:16; Isa 15:3; 22:1; Jer 32:29

[b] *1* Or possibly *an innkeeper*

---

to seek earnestly God's presence throughout your life (vv. 5,9). This message to Joshua provides us with a set of general principles for successful living; however, we must never conclude that God is bound to furnish material prosperity to everyone who follows these conditions. Such general principles are not absolute guarantees, for they are subject to God's higher choices for each of us; sometimes he permits us to undergo suffering and adversity (see 3Jn 2, note).

2:1 HOUSE OF A PROSTITUTE. Rahab's house (perhaps an inn) would have been a good place for strangers to enter and gain information without undue alarm or suspicion.

2:1 RAHAB. Rahab was a sinful woman from a pagan background who recognized the God of Israel as the true God of heaven and earth (vv. 10–11). She abandoned Canaan's gods, in faith joined with Israel and its God (Heb 11:31; Jas 2:25), and eventually became an ancestor of the Messiah (Mt 1:5–6). Rahab's salvation illustrates that even while God is in the process of judgment, he "accepts men from every nation who fear him and do what is right" (Ac 10:35).

2:5 I DON'T KNOW WHICH WAY THEY WENT. Rahab's lie does not justify lying by NT believers in special circumstances (cf. Ex 20:16; Dt 5:20). At this time, Rahab was not a member of the covenant community and was not bound to the moral laws of the covenant. Her lying never received approval in Scripture, only her faith and actions (Heb 11:31; Jas 2:25). God in no way needed to rely on deception to fulfill his covenant promises or to protect the spies (1:5–6).

given this land to you and that a great
fear[k] of you has fallen on us, so that
all who live in this country are melting
in fear because of you. 10 We have
heard how the LORD dried up[l] the water of the Red Sea[c] for you when you
came out of Egypt,[m] and what you did
to Sihon and Og,[n] the two kings of the
Amorites[o] east of the Jordan,[p] whom
you completely destroyed.[d][q] 11 When
we heard of it, our hearts melted[r] and
everyone's courage failed[s] because of
you,[t] for the LORD your God[u] is God
in heaven above and on the earth[v] below. 12 Now then, please swear to me[w]
by the LORD that you will show kindness[x] to my family, because I have
shown kindness to you. Give me a sure
sign[y] 13 that you will spare the lives of
my father and mother, my brothers and
sisters, and all who belong to them,[z]
and that you will save us from death."
14 "Our lives for your lives!"[a] the
men assured her. "If you don't tell
what we are doing, we will treat you
kindly and faithfully[b] when the LORD
gives us the land."
15 So she let them down by a rope[c]
through the window,[d] for the house
she lived in was part of the city wall.
16 Now she had said to them, "Go to the
hills[e] so the pursuers[f] will not find
you. Hide yourselves there three
days[g] until they return, and then go
on your way."[h]
17 The men said to her, "This oath[i]
you made us swear will not be binding
on us 18 unless, when we enter the
land, you have tied this scarlet cord[j]
in the window[k] through which you let
us down, and unless you have brought
your father and mother, your brothers
and all your family[l] into your house.
19 If anyone goes outside your house
into the street, his blood will be on his
own head;[m] we will not be responsible.
As for anyone who is in the house with
you, his blood will be on our head[n] if
a hand is laid on him. 20 But if you tell
what we are doing, we will be released
from the oath you made us swear.[o]"
21 "Agreed," she replied. "Let it be as
you say." So she sent them away and
they departed. And she tied the scarlet
cord[p] in the window.[q]
22 When they left, they went into the
hills and stayed there three days,[r] until the pursuers[s] had searched all
along the road and returned without
finding them. 23 Then the two men
started back. They went down out of
the hills, forded the river and came to
Joshua son of Nun and told him everything that had happened to them.
24 They said to Joshua, "The LORD has
surely given the whole land into our
hands;[t] all the people are melting in
fear[u] because of us."

Crossing the Jordan

3 Early in the morning Joshua and
all the Israelites set out from
Shittim[v] and went to the Jordan,[w]
where they camped before crossing
over. 2 After three days[x] the officers[y]
went throughout the camp,[z] 3 giving
orders to the people: "When you see
the ark of the covenant[a] of the LORD
your God, and the priests,[b] who are
Levites,[c] carrying it, you are to move
out from your positions and follow it.
4 Then you will know which way to go,
since you have never been this way before. But keep a distance of about a
thousand yards[e][d] between you and
the ark; do not go near it."
5 Joshua told the people, "Consecrate

c 10 Hebrew *Yam Suph*; that is, Sea of Reeds
d 10 The Hebrew term refers to the irrevocable giving over of things or persons to the LORD, often by totally destroying them.
e 4 Hebrew *about two thousand cubits* (about 900 meters)

2:9 [k]S Ge 35:5; S Ex 15:14 **2:10** [l]S Ge 8:1; Ex 14:21; Jos 3:17; Ps 74:15 [m]S Nu 23:22 [n]S Nu 21:21 [o]S Ge 10:16; S 14:7 [p]Jos 9:10 [q]S Nu 21:2 **2:11** [r]S Ge 42:28 [s]S Dt 2:25; Ps 107:26; Jnh 1:5 [t]Ex 15:14; Jos 5:1; 7:5; 2Sa 4:1; Ps 22:14; Isa 13:7; 19:1; Jer 51:30; Na 2:10 [u]2Ki 5:15; 19:15; Da 6:26 [v]S Ge 14:19; S Nu 20:14 **2:12** [w]S Ge 24:8; S 47:31 [x]S Ge 24:12; Ru 3:10 [y]S Ge 24:14; S Ex 3:12; Jos 4:6; 1Sa 2:34; 2Ki 19:29 **2:13** [z]ver 18; Jos 6:23 **2:14** [a]1Ki 20:39, 42; 2Ki 10:24 [b]S Ge 47:29 **2:15** [c]Jer 38:6,11 [d]ver 18,21; Ge 26:8; Jdg 5:28; 1Sa 19:12 **2:16** [e]S Ge 14:10 [f]S ver 7 [g]ver 22 [h]S Heb 11:31 **2:17** [i]S Ge 24:8 **2:18** [j]ver 21 [k]S ver 15 [l]S ver 13 **2:19** [m]S Lev 20:9 [n]Mt 27:25 **2:20** [o]S Ge 24:8; S 47:31 **2:21** [p]ver 18 [q]S ver 15 **2:22** [r]ver 16 [s]S ver 7 **2:24** [t]Jos 10:8; 11:6; Jdg 3:28; 7:9,14; 20:28; 1Sa 14:10 [u]S Ex 15:15 **3:1** [v]S Jos 2:1 [w]S Ge 13:10; Job 40:23 **3:2** [x]S Ge 40:13; Jos 2:16 [y]S Dt 1:15 [z]Jos 1:11 **3:3** [a]S Nu 10:33 [b]ver 8,17; Nu 4:15; Dt 31:9; 1Ki 8:3 [c]1Sa 6:15 **3:4** [d]Nu 35:5

2:21 SCARLET CORD. The scarlet cord parallels the Passover lamb; just as the blood of the lamb was put on the houses of the Israelites in order to protect them from God's judgment (Ex 12:21–23), so the scarlet cord hanging from Rahab's home brought safety and deliverance for her household. For this reason, some see the scarlet cord as a type of Christ's blood, similar to the blood of the Passover lamb (see article on THE PASSOVER, p. 104).

3:3 ARK OF THE COVENANT. God was more than invisibly present among his people, for the "ark of the covenant" stood as a symbol of his presence among them (Ex 25:22; cf. Nu 10:35). As they were now led into the possession of the promised land, the Lord also openly manifested himself in miracles (vv. 5,14–17; 4:18).

3:5 CONSECRATE YOURSELVES. The act of consecration (cf. Ex 19:10,14–15) points to the principle that God will not act powerfully on behalf of his people if they are not inwardly clean and aligned with his will. Before we ask God to perform signs and wonders in our midst, we must first make sure our hearts are pure and our desires guided by his Holy Spirit (see Ac 2:38, note; 3:26, note).

yourselves,[e] for tomorrow the LORD
will do amazing things[f] among you."
6Joshua said to the priests, "Take up
the ark of the covenant and pass on
ahead of the people." So they took it up
and went ahead of them.
7And the LORD said to Joshua, "Today I will begin to exalt you[g] in the
eyes of all Israel, so they may know
that I am with you as I was with Moses.[h] **8**Tell the priests[i] who carry the
ark of the covenant: 'When you reach
the edge of the Jordan's waters, go and
stand in the river.' "
9Joshua said to the Israelites, "Come
here and listen to the words of the LORD
your God. **10**This is how you will know
that the living God[j] is among you[k]
and that he will certainly drive out before you the Canaanites, Hittites,[l] Hivites, Perizzites,[m] Girgashites, Amorites and Jebusites.[n] **11**See, the ark of
the covenant of the Lord of all the
earth[o] will go into the Jordan ahead of
you.[p] **12**Now then, choose twelve
men[q] from the tribes of Israel, one
from each tribe. **13**And as soon as the
priests who carry the ark of the LORD—
the Lord of all the earth[r]—set foot in
the Jordan, its waters flowing downstream[s] will be cut off[t] and stand up
in a heap.[u]"
14So when the people broke camp to
cross the Jordan, the priests carrying
the ark of the covenant[v] went ahead[w]
of them. **15**Now the Jordan[x] is at flood
stage[y] all during harvest.[z] Yet as
soon as the priests who carried the ark
reached the Jordan and their feet
touched the water's edge, **16**the water
from upstream stopped flowing.[a] It
piled up in a heap[b] a great distance
away, at a town called Adam in the vicinity of Zarethan,[c] while the water
flowing down[d] to the Sea of the Arabah[e] (the Salt Sea[f]) was completely cut off.[g] So the people crossed
over opposite Jericho.[h] **17**The
priests[i] who carried the ark of the
covenant of the LORD stood firm on dry
ground in the middle of the Jordan,[j]
while all Israel passed by until the
whole nation had completed the crossing on dry ground.[k]

4 When the whole nation had finished crossing the Jordan,[l] the
LORD said to Joshua, **2**"Choose twelve
men[m] from among the people, one
from each tribe, **3**and tell them to take
up twelve stones[n] from the middle of
the Jordan[o] from right where the
priests stood and to carry them over
with you and put them down at the
place where you stay tonight.[p]"
4So Joshua called together the
twelve men[q] he had appointed from
the Israelites, one from each tribe,
5and said to them, "Go over before the
ark of the LORD your God into the middle of the Jordan.[r] Each of you is to
take up a stone on his shoulder, according to the number of the tribes of
the Israelites, **6**to serve as a sign[s]
among you. In the future, when your
children[t] ask you, 'What do these
stones mean?'[u] **7**tell them that the
flow of the Jordan was cut off[v] before
the ark of the covenant of the LORD.
When it crossed the Jordan, the waters
of the Jordan were cut off. These
stones are to be a memorial[w] to the
people of Israel forever."
8So the Israelites did as Joshua commanded them. They took twelve
stones[x] from the middle of the Jordan,[y] according to the number of the
tribes of the Israelites, as the LORD had
told Joshua;[z] and they carried them
over with them to their camp, where
they put them down. **9**Joshua set up the
twelve stones[a] that had been[g] in the
middle of the Jordan at the spot where
the priests who carried the ark of the

3:5 [e] S Ex 29:1; S Lev 11:44 [f] Jdg 6:13; 1Ch 16:9,24; Ps 26:7; 75:1 **3:7** [g] Jos 4:14; 1Ch 29:25 [h] Jos 1:5 **3:8** [i] S ver 3 **3:10** [j] Dt 5:26; 1Sa 17:26,36; 2Ki 19:4,16; Ps 18:46; 42:2; 84:2; Isa 37:4,17; Jer 10:10; 23:36; Da 6:26; Hos 1:10; S Mt 16:16 [k] S Dt 7:21 [l] S Ge 26:34 [m] Jos 17:15; 24:11; Jdg 1:4; 3:5 [n] S Ex 3:8; S 23:23; S Dt 7:1; Jos 9:1; 11:3; 12:8; Jdg 19:11; 1Ch 11:4 **3:11** [o] ver 13; Ex 19:5; Dt 10:14; Job 9:10; 28:24; 41:11; Ps 50:12; 97:5; Zec 6:5 [p] S Dt 9:3 **3:12** [q] Jos 4:2,4 **3:13** [r] S ver 11 [s] ver 16 [t] Jos 4:7 [u] S Ex 14:22; S Isa 11:15 **3:14** [v] Ps 132:8 [w] Ac 7:44-45 **3:15** [x] 2Ki 2:6 [y] Jos 4:18; 1Ch 12:15; Isa 8:7 [z] S Ge 8:22 **3:16** [a] Ps 66:6; 74:15; 114:3 [b] Job 38:37; Ps 33:7 [c] 1Ki 4:12; 7:46 [d] ver 13 [e] S Dt 1:1 [f] S Ge 14:3 [g] S Ge 8:1; S Ex 14:22 [h] 2Ki 2:4 **3:17** [i] S ver 3 [j] Jos 4:3,5,8,9,10 [k] S Ex 14:22; S Jos 2:10 **4:1** [l] Dt 27:2 **4:2** [m] S Jos 3:12 **4:3** [n] ver 20 [o] S Jos 3:17 [p] ver 19 **4:4** [q] S Jos 3:12 **4:5** [r] S Jos 3:17 **4:6** [s] S Jos 2:12 [t] S Ex 10:2 [u] ver 21; Ex 12:26; S 13:14 **4:7** [v] Jos 3:13 [w] S Ex 28:12 **4:8** [x] Ex 28:21 [y] S Jos 3:17 [z] ver 20 **4:9** [a] S Ge 28:18; Jos 24:26; 1Sa 7:12

[f] *16* That is, the Dead Sea [g] *9* Or *Joshua also set up twelve stones*

3:13 WATERS . . . STAND UP IN A HEAP. God divided the waters at the Jordan just as he had divided the waters at the Red Sea (Ex 14). This miracle provided clear evidence that the living God was among his people. By this experiential demonstration of his power, God strengthened his people's faith so they could face the challenges of possessing the promised land. Without such power, they could not have taken walled cities and advanced forward in spite of the giants of opposition to conquer the new land.

4:6 YOUR CHILDREN. God wanted his people always to be concerned about the faith of their children (see Dt 6:7, note). The stones of remembrance set up on the banks of the Jordan provided an occasion for parents to teach their children about God's power and faithfulness. Through such teaching these children "might always fear the LORD your God" (v. 24; see article on THE FEAR OF THE LORD, p. 260).

covenant had stood. And they are there
to this day.[b]
10Now the priests who carried the
ark remained standing in the middle of
the Jordan until everything the LORD
had commanded Joshua was done by
the people, just as Moses had directed
Joshua. The people hurried over, 11and
as soon as all of them had crossed, the
ark of the LORD and the priests came to
the other side while the people
watched. 12The men of Reuben,[c]
Gad[d] and the half-tribe of Manasseh[e]
crossed over, armed, in front of the Israelites,[f] as Moses had directed
them.[g] 13About forty thousand armed
for battle[h] crossed over[i] before the
LORD to the plains of Jericho for war.
14That day the LORD exalted[j] Joshua in the sight of all Israel; and they
revered him all the days of his life, just
as they had revered Moses.
15Then the LORD said to Joshua,
16"Command the priests carrying the
ark of the Testimony[k] to come up out
of the Jordan."
17So Joshua commanded the priests,
"Come up out of the Jordan."
18And the priests came up out of the
river carrying the ark of the covenant
of the LORD. No sooner had they set
their feet on the dry ground than the
waters of the Jordan returned to their
place[l] and ran at flood stage[m] as before.
19On the tenth day of the first month
the people went up from the Jordan and
camped at Gilgal[n] on the eastern border of Jericho. 20And Joshua set up at
Gilgal the twelve stones[o] they had
taken out of the Jordan. 21He said to
the Israelites, "In the future when your
descendants ask their fathers, 'What
do these stones mean?'[p] 22tell them,
'Israel crossed the Jordan on dry
ground.'[q] 23For the LORD your God
dried up the Jordan before you until
you had crossed over. The LORD your
God did to the Jordan just what he had
done to the Red Sea[h] when he dried it
up before us until we had crossed
over.[r] 24He did this so that all the
peoples of the earth might know[s] that
the hand of the LORD is powerful[t] and
so that you might always fear the LORD
your God.[u]"

4:9 [b] S Ge 35:20
4:12 [c] S Ge 29:32 [d] S Ge 30:11 [e] S Ge 41:51 [f] S Nu 32:27 [g] Nu 32:29
4:13 [h] S Ex 13:18 [i] S Nu 32:17
4:14 [j] S Jos 3:7
4:16 [k] Ex 25:22
4:18 [l] Ex 14:27 [m] S Jos 3:15
4:19 [n] S Dt 11:30
4:20 [o] ver 3,8
4:21 [p] S ver 6
4:22 [q] S Ex 14:22
4:23 [r] Ex 14:19-22
4:24 [s] 1Ki 8:60; 18:36; 2Ki 5:15; Ps 67:2; 83:18; 106:8; Isa 37:20; 52:10 [t] Ex 15:16; 1Ch 29:12; Ps 44:3; 89:13; 98:1; 118:15-16 [u] S Ex 14:31
5:1 [v] S Nu 13:29 [w] S Ge 42:28
5:2 [x] S Ex 4:25 [y] S Ge 17:10,12,14
5:4 [z] S Nu 1:3 [a] Dt 2:14
5:6 [b] Nu 32:13; Jos 14:10; Ps 107:4 [c] S Ex 16:35 [d] Nu 14:23,29-35; Dt 2:14 [e] S Ex 3:8
5:8 [f] Ge 34:25

Circumcision at Gilgal

5 Now when all the Amorite kings
west of the Jordan and all the Canaanite kings along the coast[v] heard
how the LORD had dried up the Jordan
before the Israelites until we had
crossed over, their hearts melted[w]
and they no longer had the courage to
face the Israelites.
2At that time the LORD said to Joshua, "Make flint knives[x] and circumcise[y] the Israelites again." 3So Joshua
made flint knives and circumcised the
Israelites at Gibeath Haaraloth.[i]
4Now this is why he did so: All those
who came out of Egypt—all the men of
military age[z]—died in the desert on
the way after leaving Egypt.[a] 5All the
people that came out had been circumcised, but all the people born in the
desert during the journey from Egypt
had not. 6The Israelites had moved
about in the desert[b] forty years[c] until all the men who were of military age
when they left Egypt had died, since
they had not obeyed the LORD. For the
LORD had sworn to them that they
would not see the land that he had solemnly promised their fathers to give
us,[d] a land flowing with milk and honey.[e] 7So he raised up their sons in
their place, and these were the ones
Joshua circumcised. They were still
uncircumcised because they had not
been circumcised on the way. 8And after the whole nation had been circumcised, they remained where they were
in camp until they were healed.[f]
9Then the LORD said to Joshua,
"Today I have rolled away the reproach

[h] 23 Hebrew *Yam Suph*; that is, Sea of Reeds
[i] 3 *Gibeath Haaraloth* means *hill of foreskins.*

4:21 WHAT DO THESE STONES MEAN? A monument of stones was frequently used to remind future generations about God's salvation and his grace toward his people. Believers today can still choose certain things or places as memorials to commemorate the good things God has done for them; these memorials should help us instruct our children to look to God for guidance and help throughout their lives.

5:2 CIRCUMCISE. Under the old covenant circumcision marked every male as a child of Abraham and a servant of the Lord. Circumcision qualified them to partake of the blessings of the covenant (see Ge 17:11, note). It was, moreover, a sign of their obedience to the covenant. Even though God's people had invaded the promised land, the spiritual preparation of circumcision and the Passover (v. 10) was needed before they could begin the actual conquest.

of Egypt from you." So the place has
been called Gilgal[j][g] to this day.
10On the evening of the fourteenth
day of the month,[h] while camped at
Gilgal on the plains of Jericho, the Israelites celebrated the Passover.[i]
11The day after the Passover, that very
day, they ate some of the produce of
the land:[j] unleavened bread[k] and
roasted grain.[l] **12**The manna stopped
the day after[k] they ate this food from
the land; there was no longer any manna for the Israelites, but that year they
ate of the produce of Canaan.[m]

The Fall of Jericho

13Now when Joshua was near Jericho, he looked up and saw a man[n]
standing in front of him with a drawn
sword[o] in his hand. Joshua went up to
him and asked, "Are you for us or for
our enemies?"
14"Neither," he replied, "but as commander of the army of the LORD I have
now come." Then Joshua fell facedown[p] to the ground[q] in reverence,
and asked him, "What message does
my Lord[l] have for his servant?"
15The commander of the LORD's
army replied, "Take off your sandals,
for the place where you are standing is
holy."[r] And Joshua did so.

6 Now Jericho[s] was tightly shut up
because of the Israelites. No one
went out and no one came in.
2Then the LORD said to Joshua, "See,
I have delivered[t] Jericho into your
hands, along with its king and its fighting men. **3**March around the city once
with all the armed men. Do this for six
days. **4**Have seven priests carry trumpets of rams' horns[u] in front of the
ark. On the seventh day, march around
the city seven times, with the priests
blowing the trumpets.[v] **5**When you
hear them sound a long blast[w] on the
trumpets, have all the people give a
loud shout;[x] then the wall of the city
will collapse and the people will go up,
every man straight in."
6So Joshua son of Nun called the
priests and said to them, "Take up the
ark of the covenant of the LORD and
have seven priests carry trumpets in
front of it."[y] **7**And he ordered the people, "Advance[z]! March around the
city, with the armed guard going ahead
of the ark[a] of the LORD."
8When Joshua had spoken to the
people, the seven priests carrying the
seven trumpets before the LORD went
forward, blowing their trumpets, and
the ark of the LORD's covenant followed
them. **9**The armed guard marched
ahead of the priests who blew the
trumpets, and the rear guard[b] followed the ark. All this time the trumpets were sounding. **10**But Joshua had
commanded the people, "Do not give a
war cry, do not raise your voices, do
not say a word until the day I tell you
to shout. Then shout![c]" **11**So he had
the ark of the LORD carried around the
city, circling it once. Then the people
returned to camp and spent the night
there.
12Joshua got up early the next morning and the priests took up the ark of
the LORD. **13**The seven priests carrying
the seven trumpets went forward,
marching before the ark of the LORD
and blowing the trumpets. The armed
men went ahead of them and the rear
guard followed the ark of the LORD,
while the trumpets kept sounding.
14So on the second day they marched
around the city once and returned to
the camp. They did this for six days.
15On the seventh day, they got up at
daybreak and marched around the city
seven times in the same manner, except that on that day they circled the
city seven times.[d] **16**The seventh time

5:9 [g]S Dt 11:30 **5:10** [h]S Ex 12:6 [i]S Ex 12:11 **5:11** [j]S Nu 15:19 [k]Ex 12:15 [l]S Lev 23:14 **5:12** [m]Ex 16:35 **5:13** [n]S Ge 18:2 [o]Nu 22:23 **5:14** [p]S Ge 17:3 [q]S Ge 19:1 **5:15** [r]S Ge 28:17; Ex 3:5; Ac 7:33 **6:1** [s]Jos 24:11 **6:2** [t]ver 16; Dt 7:24; Jos 8:1 **6:4** [u]S Ex 19:13 [v]S Lev 25:9 **6:5** [w]Ex 19:13 [x]ver 20; 1Sa 4:5; 2Sa 6:15; Ezr 3:11; 10:12; Ps 42:4; 95:1; Isa 8:9; 42:13

6:6 [y]ver 4 **6:7** [z]Ex 14:15 [a]Nu 10:35; 1Sa 4:3; 7:1 **6:9** [b]ver 13; S Nu 2:31; Isa 52:12 **6:10** [c]ver 20; 1Sa 4:5; Ezr 3:11 **6:15** [d]1Ki 18:44; 2Ki 4:35; 5:14

j9 *Gilgal* sounds like the Hebrew for *roll.*
k12 Or *the day* l14 Or *lord*

5:14 COMMANDER OF THE ARMY OF THE LORD. Joshua is made aware of God's unseen presence and his heavenly army, prepared to do battle alongside his faithful people (cf. Ac 12:5–11; 18:9–10; 23:11; 27:23). Joshua's experience teaches us that we are not alone in our struggles on this earth. There are spiritual forces fighting on our behalf as well as against us (see Heb 1:14). We have the Holy Spirit, who remains constantly at our side as our helper and defender (Jn 14:16–23).

6:1 JERICHO. The city of Jericho covered about eight acres. It was a fortress city not just for its residents, but also for the inhabitants of the nearby countryside. The walls may have been as much as thirty feet high and twenty feet thick. Jericho was considered to be invincible, protected by the gods of the Canaanites. The capture of Jericho was the key to Joshua's whole war strategy, for it would demonstrate that Israel's God was superior to the Canaanite gods; thus the defeat of the Canaanites was certain.

around, when the priests sounded the trumpet blast, Joshua commanded the people, "Shout! For the LORD has given you the city![e] **17**The city and all that is in it are to be devoted[m][f] to the LORD. Only Rahab the prostitute[n][g] and all who are with her in her house shall be spared, because she hid[h] the spies we sent. **18**But keep away from the devoted things,[i] so that you will not bring about your own destruction by taking any of them. Otherwise you will make the camp of Israel liable to destruction[j] and bring trouble[k] on it. **19**All the silver and gold and the articles of bronze and iron[l] are sacred to the LORD and must go into his treasury."

20When the trumpets sounded,[m] the people shouted, and at the sound of the trumpet, when the people gave a loud shout,[n] the wall collapsed; so every man charged straight in, and they took the city.[o] **21**They devoted[p] the city to the LORD and destroyed[q] with the sword every living thing in it—men and women, young and old, cattle, sheep and donkeys.

22Joshua said to the two men[r] who had spied out[s] the land, "Go into the prostitute's house and bring her out and all who belong to her, in accordance with your oath to her.[t]" **23**So the young men who had done the spying went in and brought out Rahab, her father and mother and brothers and all who belonged to her.[u] They brought out her entire family and put them in a place outside the camp of Israel.

24Then they burned the whole city[v] and everything in it, but they put the silver and gold and the articles of bronze and iron[w] into the treasury of the LORD's house.[x] **25**But Joshua spared[y] Rahab the prostitute,[z] with her family and all who belonged to her, because she hid the men Joshua had sent as spies to Jericho[a]—and she lives among the Israelites to this day.

26At that time Joshua pronounced this solemn oath:[b] "Cursed[c] before the LORD is the man who undertakes to rebuild this city, Jericho:

"At the cost of his firstborn son
  will he lay its foundations;
at the cost of his youngest
  will he set up its gates."[d]

27So the LORD was with Joshua,[e] and his fame spread[f] throughout the land.

Achan's Sin

7 But the Israelites acted unfaithfully in regard to the devoted

6:16 [e] S ver 2
6:17 [f] ver 21; Lev 27:28; Dt 20:17; Isa 13:5; 24:1; 34:2,5; Mal 4:6 [g] S Jos 2:1 [h] ver 25; Jos 2:4
6:18 [i] Jos 7:1; 1Ch 2:7 [j] Jos 7:12 [k] Jos 7:25,26
6:19 [l] ver 24; Nu 31:22
6:20 [m] Lev 25:9; Jdg 6:34; 7:22; 1Ki 1:41; Isa 18:3; 27:13; Jer 4:21; 42:14; Am 2:2 [n] S ver 5; S 10 [o] Heb 11:30
6:21 [p] S ver 17 [q] S Dt 20:16
6:22 [r] S Ge 42:9; S Jos 2:4 [s] S Nu 21:32 [t] Jos 2:14; Heb 11:31
6:23 [u] S Jos 2:13
6:24 [v] S Nu 31:10 [w] S ver 19 [x] S Dt 13:16
6:25 [y] Jdg 1:25 [z] S Jos 2:1 [a] S ver 17; S Jos 2:6
6:26 [b] 1Sa 14:24 [c] S Nu 5:21 [d] 1Ki 16:34
6:27 [e] S Ge 39:2; S Nu 14:43 [f] Jos 9:1; 1Ch 14:17

[m] *17* The Hebrew term refers to the irrevocable giving over of things or persons to the LORD, often by totally destroying them; also in verses 18 and 21. [n] *17* Or possibly *innkeeper*; also in verses 22 and 25

6:17 THE CITY ... TO BE DEVOTED. To be devoted (Heb *herem*) means that the object or person was devoted to God either for judgment or for his service. All the people of Jericho were sentenced to total destruction (Dt 13:16). The principle of *herem* teaches that our Creator God may justly destroy those who are given over to evil and unrighteousness (cf. Jer 18:6–7; 45:4; Mt 10:28; Lk 13:3; see article on THE DESTRUCTION OF THE CANAANITES, p. 310). Note also that Jericho was the firstfruits of the conquest; other cities were not treated the same way as Jericho.

6:20 WALL COLLAPSED. The wall collapsed by a direct act of God. The city was taken because of Israel's obedience to God's word and their faith in his miraculous power (Heb 11:30; 1Jn 5:4). Because the city was not rebuilt for several hundred years, very little of the remains of this level of the destroyed city have been found; most of what was left weathered away.

6:21 DESTROYED ... EVERY LIVING THING IN IT. For comments on how the mass destruction of the Canaanites is consistent with God's love and righteousness, see article on THE DESTRUCTION OF THE CANAANITES, p. 310.

7:1–26 ACHAN ... LORD'S ANGER. Achan's sin, its consequence within Israel, and the severe penalty on Achan and his family reveal several principles of judgment when God's people flagrantly sin. (1) When there is serious sin or the toleration of serious sin among God's people, his blessing is either diminished, hindered or lost altogether. God will not bless a people who refuse to remove sin from their midst (vv. 1, 11–13, 20–21,25; cf. 1Co 5:1–13).

(2) Open sin within the congregation of God's people exposes its members to the destructive influence of the enemy from outside (e.g., Satan and the world; vv. 4–13).

(3) If such sin is tolerated and not corrected, it will result in eventual judgment (v. 13). If, however, the sin is exposed, confessed and removed, then God's blessing, presence and grace return (vv. 22–26; 8:1,18–19; cf. Ac 4:31—5:11).

(4) Sin among the people of God, therefore, must be regarded with the utmost seriousness. Purity must be guarded and obedience demanded; otherwise, the congregation's spiritual development will either be stunted or cease altogether (cf. Rev 3:1–3,14–18).

THE DESTRUCTION OF THE CANAANITES

Jos 6:21 "They devoted the city to the LORD and destroyed with the sword every living thing in it—men and women, young and old, cattle, sheep and donkeys."

(1) Before the nation of Israel entered the promised land, God had given strict instructions as to what they should do to the people there—they were to be completely destroyed. "In the cities of the nations the LORD your God is giving you as an inheritance, do not leave anything alive that breathes. Completely destroy them—the Hittites, Amorites, Canaanites, Perizzites, Hivites and Jebusites—as the LORD your God has commanded you" (Dt 20:16–17; cf. Nu 33:51–53).

(2) The Lord repeated this command after the Israelites crossed over the Jordan into Canaan. On several occasions the author of Joshua states that Israel's destruction of the cities and the Canaanites was at the Lord's command (Jos 6:2; 8:1–2; 10:8). Believers who live under the new covenant have often wondered how this order of mass destruction of human beings is consistent with the revelation of God's love, righteousness and hatred of evil elsewhere in the Bible.

(3) The destruction of Jericho is an account of God's righteous judgment on a desperately wicked people whose sin had now reached its full measure (Ge 15:16; Dt 9:4–5). In other words, God annihilated the people of that city and other inhabitants of Canaan because they had given themselves over fully to moral depravity. Archaeology reveals that the Canaanites were involved in all kinds of idolatry, cult prostitution, violence, burning of children as sacrifices to their gods, and spiritism (cf. Dt 12:31; 18:9–13; see Jos 23:12, note).

(4) The complete destruction of the Canaanites was necessary to safeguard Israel from the overwhelming influence of Canaanite idolatry and sin. God knew that if the wicked nations had been allowed to continue, they would "teach you to follow all the detestable things they do in worshiping their gods, and you will sin against the LORD your God" (Dt 20:18); this verse expresses the continuing Biblical principle that God's people must keep themselves separate from their surrounding evil society (Dt 7:2–4; 12:1–4; see articles on SPIRITUAL SEPARATION FOR BELIEVERS, p. 1794, and THE CHRISTIAN'S RELATIONSHIP TO THE WORLD, p. 1976).

(5) The destruction of Canaanite cities and people demonstrates a basic principle of God's judgment: when a people's sin reaches its full measure, God's mercy gives way to judgment (cf. Jos 11:20). God had earlier applied this same principle at the time of the flood (Ge 6:5,11–12) and at the destruction of the wicked cities of Sodom and Gomorrah (Ge 18:20–33; 19:24–25).

(6) Israel's subsequent history confirms the importance of this principle and of God's command that all the pagan nations be destroyed. The Israelites in fact disobeyed the Lord's command and did not drive out completely all of the people living in Canaan. As a result, they began to follow their detestable ways and serve their idol gods (see Jdg 1:28, note; 2:2,17, notes). The book of Judges is the story of what the Lord did in response to this apostasy.

(7) Finally, the destruction of that generation of Canaanites is a type and foreshadowing of God's final judgment on the unrighteous at the end of the age. God's second and true Joshua, i.e., Jesus Christ, will return in righteousness with the armies of heaven to judge and to wage war against all the ungodly (Rev 19:11–21). All who have rejected his offer of grace and salvation and have continued in sin will perish as did the Canaanites. God will overthrow every worldly power and establish his righteous kingdom on earth (Rev 18:20–21; 20:4–10; 21:1–4).

things[o];[g] Achan[h] son of Carmi, the
son of Zimri,[p] the son of Zerah,[i] of
the tribe of Judah,[j] took some of
them. So the LORD's anger burned[k]
against Israel.[l]
2Now Joshua sent men from Jericho
to Ai,[m] which is near Beth Aven[n] to
the east of Bethel,[o] and told them,
"Go up and spy out[p] the region." So
the men went up and spied out Ai.
3When they returned to Joshua, they
said, "Not all the people will have to go
up against Ai. Send two or three thousand men to take it and do not weary
all the people, for only a few men are
there." **4**So about three thousand men
went up; but they were routed by the
men of Ai,[q] **5**who killed about thirty-
six[r] of them. They chased the Israelites from the city gate as far as the
stone quarries[q] and struck them
down on the slopes. At this the hearts
of the people melted[s] and became like
water.
6Then Joshua tore his clothes[t] and
fell facedown[u] to the ground before
the ark of the LORD, remaining there till
evening.[v] The elders of Israel[w] did
the same, and sprinkled dust[x] on their
heads. **7**And Joshua said, "Ah, Sovereign LORD, why[y] did you ever bring
this people across the Jordan to deliver
us into the hands of the Amorites to
destroy us?[z] If only we had been content to stay on the other side of the
Jordan! **8**O Lord, what can I say, now
that Israel has been routed by its enemies? **9**The Canaanites and the other
people of the country will hear about
this and they will surround us and wipe
out our name from the earth.[a] What
then will you do for your own great
name?[b]"
10The LORD said to Joshua, "Stand
up! What are you doing down on your
face? **11**Israel has sinned;[c] they have
violated my covenant,[d] which I commanded them to keep. They have taken
some of the devoted things; they have
stolen, they have lied,[e] they have put
them with their own possessions.[f]
12That is why the Israelites cannot
stand against their enemies;[g] they
turn their backs[h] and run[i] because
they have been made liable to destruction.[j] I will not be with you anymore[k]
unless you destroy whatever among
you is devoted to destruction.
13"Go, consecrate the people. Tell
them, 'Consecrate yourselves[l] in
preparation for tomorrow; for this is
what the LORD, the God of Israel, says:
That which is devoted is among you, O
Israel. You cannot stand against your
enemies until you remove it.
14" 'In the morning, present[m] yourselves tribe by tribe. The tribe that the
LORD takes[n] shall come forward clan
by clan; the clan that the LORD takes
shall come forward family by family;
and the family that the LORD takes shall
come forward man by man. **15**He who
is caught with the devoted things[o]
shall be destroyed by fire,[p] along with
all that belongs to him.[q] He has violated the covenant[r] of the LORD and has
done a disgraceful thing in Israel!' "[s]
16Early the next morning Joshua had
Israel come forward by tribes, and Judah was taken. **17**The clans of Judah
came forward, and he took the Zerahites.[t] He had the clan of the Zerahites come forward by families, and
Zimri was taken. **18**Joshua had his family come forward man by man, and
Achan son of Carmi, the son of Zimri,
the son of Zerah, of the tribe of Judah,[u] was taken.[v]
19Then Joshua said to Achan, "My
son, give glory[w] to the LORD,[r] the God
of Israel, and give him the praise.[s]
Tell[x] me what you have done; do not
hide it from me."
20Achan replied, "It is true! I have
sinned against the LORD, the God of Israel. This is what I have done: **21**When
I saw in the plunder[y] a beautiful robe

7:1 [g]S Jos 6:18 [h]ver 26; 1Ch 2:7 [i]Jos 22:20 [j]ver 18; Nu 1:4 [k]S Ex 4:14; S 32:20 [l]S Lev 10:6 **7:2** [m]S Ge 12:8; S Jos 8:1,28 [n]Jos 18:12; 1Sa 13:5; 14:23; Hos 4:15; 5:8; 10:5 [o]Ge 12:8; Jos 12:16; 16:1; Jdg 1:22; 1Sa 30:27; 2Ki 23:15; Jer 48:13; Am 3:14; 4:4; 5:5-6; 7:10,13 [p]S Nu 21:32 **7:4** [q]S Lev 26:17; S Dt 28:25 **7:5** [r]Jos 22:20 [s]S Ge 42:28; Ps 22:14; Isa 13:7; Eze 21:7; Na 2:10 **7:6** [t]S Ge 37:29 [u]S Ge 17:3; 1Ch 21:16; Eze 9:8 [v]Jdg 20:23 [w]Jos 8:10; 9:11; 20:4; 23:2 [x]1Sa 4:12; 2Sa 13:19; 15:32; Ne 9:1; Job 2:12; La 2:10; Eze 27:30; Rev 18:19 **7:7** [y]1Sa 4:3 [z]S Ex 5:22; S Nu 14:16 **7:9** [a]Ex 32:12; S Dt 9:28 [b]Dt 28:58; 1Sa 12:22; Ps 48:10; 106:8; Jer 14:21 **7:11** [c]S Ex 9:27; Dt 29:27; Jos 24:16-27; 2Ki 17:7; Hos 10:9 [d]ver 15; Jos 6:17-19; 23:16; Jdg 2:20; 1Sa 15:24; Ps 78:10 [e]Ac 5:1-2 [f]ver 21 **7:12** [g]Lev 26:37 [h]Ps 18:40; 21:12 [i]S Lev 26:17 [j]Jos 6:18 [k]Ps 44:9; 60:10 **7:13** [l]S Lev 11:44 **7:14** [m]1Sa 10:19 [n]Pr 16:33 **7:15** [o]Jos 6:18 [p]Dt 7:25; 2Ki 25:9; 1Ch 14:12; Isa 37:19; Jer 43:12; Eze 30:16 [q]1Sa 14:39 [r]S ver 11 [s]S Ge 34:7 **7:17** [t]Nu 26:20 **7:18** [u]S ver 1; S Lev 24:11 [v]Jnh 1:7 **7:19** [w]Ex 14:17; 1Sa 6:5; Ps 96:8; Isa 42:12; Jer 13:16; Jn 9:24* [x]S Lev 5:5; 1Sa 14:43 **7:21** [y]S Ge 34:29; S 49:27

[o]*1* The Hebrew term refers to the irrevocable giving over of things or persons to the LORD, often by totally destroying them; also in verses 11, 12, 13 and 15. [p]*1* See Septuagint and 1 Chron. 2:6; Hebrew *Zabdi*; also in verses 17 and 18. [q]*5* Or *as far as Shebarim* [r]*19* A solemn charge to tell the truth [s]*19* Or *and confess to him*

7:12 CANNOT STAND AGAINST THEIR ENEMIES. The truth of this verse applies not only to God's people corporately, but also to individual members. Persistent and unrepentant sin in a person's life will cut him or her off from God's grace. Such individuals no longer live under the help and protection of God and will not be able to stand against the enemies of their souls who attack and seek to destroy them. Slavery to sin and spiritual death will result unless sin is removed (v. 13).

from Babylonia,[t] two hundred shekels[u] of silver and a wedge of gold
weighing fifty shekels,[v] I coveted[z]
them and took them. They are hidden
in the ground inside my tent, with the
silver underneath."
22 So Joshua sent messengers, and
they ran to the tent, and there it was,
hidden in his tent, with the silver underneath. 23 They took the things from
the tent, brought them to Joshua and
all the Israelites and spread them out
before the LORD.
24 Then Joshua, together with all Israel, took Achan son of Zerah, the silver, the robe, the gold wedge, his
sons[a] and daughters, his cattle, donkeys and sheep, his tent and all that he
had, to the Valley of Achor.[b] 25 Joshua
said, "Why have you brought this trouble[c] on us? The LORD will bring trouble
on you today."
Then all Israel stoned him,[d] and after they had stoned the rest, they
burned them.[e] 26 Over Achan they
heaped[f] up a large pile of rocks,
which remains to this day.[g] Then the
LORD turned from his fierce anger.[h]
Therefore that place has been called
the Valley of Achor[w][i] ever since.

Ai Destroyed

8 Then the LORD said to Joshua, "Do
not be afraid;[j] do not be discouraged.[k] Take the whole army[l]
with you, and go up and attack Ai.[m]
For I have delivered[n] into your hands
the king of Ai, his people, his city and
his land. 2 You shall do to Ai and its
king as you did to Jericho and its king,
except that you may carry off their
plunder[o] and livestock for yourselves.[p] Set an ambush[q] behind the
city."
3 So Joshua and the whole army
moved out to attack Ai. He chose thirty
thousand of his best fighting men and
sent them out at night 4 with these orders: "Listen carefully. You are to set
an ambush behind the city. Don't go
very far from it. All of you be on the
alert. 5 I and all those with me will advance on the city, and when the men
come out against us, as they did before, we will flee from them. 6 They will
pursue us until we have lured them
away from the city, for they will say,
'They are running away from us as
they did before.' So when we flee from
them, 7 you are to rise up from ambush
and take the city. The LORD your God
will give it into your hand.[r] 8 When
you have taken the city, set it on fire.[s]
Do what the LORD has commanded.[t]
See to it; you have my orders."
9 Then Joshua sent them off, and
they went to the place of ambush[u] and
lay in wait between Bethel and Ai, to
the west of Ai—but Joshua spent that
night with the people.
10 Early the next morning[v] Joshua
mustered his men, and he and the leaders of Israel[w] marched before them to
Ai. 11 The entire force that was with
him marched up and approached the
city and arrived in front of it. They set
up camp north of Ai, with the valley
between them and the city. 12 Joshua
had taken about five thousand men and
set them in ambush between Bethel
and Ai, to the west of the city. 13 They
had the soldiers take up their positions—all those in the camp to the
north of the city and the ambush to the
west of it. That night Joshua went into
the valley.
14 When the king of Ai saw this, he
and all the men of the city hurried out
early in the morning to meet Israel in
battle at a certain place overlooking
the Arabah.[x] But he did not know[y]
that an ambush had been set against
him behind the city. 15 Joshua and all
Israel let themselves be driven back[z]
before them, and they fled toward the
desert.[a] 16 All the men of Ai were
called to pursue them, and they pursued Joshua and were lured away[b]

7:21 [z] S Dt 7:25; Eph 5:5; 1Ti 6:10
7:24 [a] S Nu 16:27 [b] ver 26; Jos 15:7; Isa 65:10; Hos 2:15
7:25 [c] S Jos 6:18 [d] S Lev 20:2; Dt 17:5; 1Ki 12:18; 2Ch 10:18; 24:21; Ne 9:26 [e] S Ge 38:24
7:26 [f] 2Sa 18:17 [g] S Ge 35:20 [h] S Nu 25:4 [i] S ver 24
8:1 [j] Ge 26:24; Dt 31:6 [k] S Nu 14:9; S Dt 1:21 [l] Jos 10:7 [m] Jos 7:2; 9:3; 10:1; 12:9 [n] S Jos 6:2
8:2 [o] S Ge 49:27 [p] ver 27; Dt 20:14 [q] ver 4,12; Jdg 9:43; 20:29
8:7 [r] Jdg 7:7; 1Sa 23:4
8:8 [s] Jdg 20:29-38 [t] ver 19
8:9 [u] 2Ch 13:13
8:10 [v] Ge 22:3 [w] S Jos 7:6
8:14 [x] S Dt 1:1 [y] Jdg 20:34
8:15 [z] Jdg 20:36 [a] Jos 15:61; 16:1; 18:12
8:16 [b] Jdg 20:31

[t] *21* Hebrew *Shinar* [u] *21* That is, about 5 pounds (about 2.3 kilograms) [v] *21* That is, about 1 1/4 pounds (about 0.6 kilogram) [w] *26* *Achor* means *trouble.*

7:24 TOOK ACHAN . . . HIS SONS. God punished Achan's family because the narrative clearly implies that they knew about his sin and probably condoned it. Note that Dt 24:16 prohibits the punishment of the children for the sins of their fathers. As a close-knit unit, all members of the family had the mutual responsibility to encourage and warn one another so that all would remain committed to God and his word. Having evidently failed in this regard, they suffered the same consequences as Achan.

7:25 STONED HIM. The eternal destiny of Achan and his family cannot be easily determined. The OT emphasizes physical death as punishment for sin, but it is not clear with regard to the eternal and ultimate judgment of individuals.

from the city. **17**Not a man remained in
Ai or Bethel who did not go after Israel.
They left the city open and went in pursuit of Israel.
18Then the LORD said to Joshua,
"Hold out toward Ai the javelin[c] that
is in your hand,[d] for into your hand I
will deliver the city." So Joshua held
out his javelin[e] toward Ai. **19**As soon
as he did this, the men in the ambush
rose quickly[f] from their position and
rushed forward. They entered the city
and captured it and quickly set it on
fire.[g]
20The men of Ai looked back and
saw the smoke of the city rising
against the sky,[h] but they had no
chance to escape in any direction, for
the Israelites who had been fleeing toward the desert had turned back
against their pursuers. **21**For when
Joshua and all Israel saw that the ambush had taken the city and that smoke
was going up from the city, they turned
around[i] and attacked the men of Ai.
22The men of the ambush also came
out of the city against them, so that
they were caught in the middle, with
Israelites on both sides. Israel cut
them down, leaving them neither survivors nor fugitives.[j] **23**But they took
the king of Ai alive[k] and brought him
to Joshua.
24When Israel had finished killing
all the men of Ai in the fields and in the
desert where they had chased them,
and when every one of them had been
put to the sword, all the Israelites returned to Ai and killed those who were
in it. **25**Twelve thousand men and wom-
en fell that day—all the people of Ai.[l]
26For Joshua did not draw back the
hand that held out his javelin[m] until he
had destroyed[x][n] all who lived in Ai.[o]
27But Israel did carry off for themselves the livestock and plunder of this
city, as the LORD had instructed Joshua.[p]
28So Joshua burned[q] Ai[r] and made
it a permanent heap of ruins,[s] a desolate place to this day.[t] **29**He hung the
king of Ai on a tree and left him there
until evening. At sunset,[u] Joshua ordered them to take his body from the
tree and throw it down at the entrance
of the city gate. And they raised a large
pile of rocks[v] over it, which remains
to this day.

The Covenant Renewed at Mount Ebal

30Then Joshua built on Mount
Ebal[w] an altar[x] to the LORD, the God
of Israel, **31**as Moses the servant of the
LORD had commanded the Israelites.
He built it according to what is written
in the Book of the Law of Moses—an
altar of uncut stones, on which no iron
tool[y] had been used. On it they offered
to the LORD burnt offerings and sacrificed fellowship offerings.[y][z] **32**There,
in the presence of the Israelites, Joshua copied on stones the law of Moses,
which he had written.[a] **33**All Israel,
aliens and citizens[b] alike, with their
elders, officials and judges, were
standing on both sides of the ark of the
covenant of the LORD, facing those who
carried it—the priests, who were Levites.[c] Half of the people stood in
front of Mount Gerizim and half of
them in front of Mount Ebal,[d] as Moses the servant of the LORD had formerly commanded when he gave instructions to bless the people of Israel.
34Afterward, Joshua read all the
words of the law—the blessings and
the curses—just as it is written in the
Book of the Law.[e] **35**There was not a
word of all that Moses had commanded
that Joshua did not read to the whole
assembly of Israel, including the wom-
en and children, and the aliens who
lived among them.[f]

8:18 [c]Job 41:26; Ps 35:3 [d]S Ex 4:2; 17:9-12 [e]ver 26
8:19 [f]Jdg 20:33 [g]S ver 8
8:20 [h]Jdg 20:40
8:21 [i]Jdg 20:41
8:22 [j]Dt 7:2; Jos 10:1
8:23 [k]1Sa 15:8
8:25 [l]Dt 20:16-18
8:26 [m]ver 18 [n]S Nu 21:2 [o]Ex 17:12
8:27 [p]S ver 2
8:28 [q]S Nu 31:10 [r]Jos 7:2; Jer 49:3 [s]S Dt 13:16; Jos 10:1 [t]S Ge 35:20
8:29 [u]S Dt 21:23; Jn 19:31 [v]2Sa 18:17
8:30 [w]ver 33; S Dt 11:29 [x]S Ex 20:24
8:31 [y]S Ex 20:25 [z]Dt 27:6-7
8:32 [a]Dt 27:8
8:33 [b]S Lev 16:29 [c]Dt 31:12 [d]Dt 11:29; Jn 4:20
8:34 [e]S Dt 28:61; 31:11
8:35 [f]S Ex 12:38; Dt 31:12

[x] *26* The Hebrew term refers to the irrevocable giving over of things or persons to the LORD, often by totally destroying them.
[y] *31* Traditionally *peace offerings*

8:30 JOSHUA BUILT . . . AN ALTAR. This episode of building an altar and reading the law (v. 34) reveals four principles for understanding the book of Joshua. (1) The right to possess the promised land was dependent on the proclamation of and loyalty to God's covenant (Dt 30:15–18).

(2) Israel's access to God was always by faith through sacrifice and blood atonement (vv. 30–31).

(3) The continuance of God's blessings was dependent on their holding firmly to him with heartfelt faith and love (Dt 28—29; 30:11–20; see Jos 7:1–26, note). Life, blessing, peace and salvation in Canaan were not unconditional. Faith in God's promises as embodied in the altar, blood atonement and the commandments was essential in maintaining a covenant relationship with God (Dt 29:18–21).

(4) The written Word of God was the ultimate authority for his people and the basis upon which they experienced either his blessing or curse (vv. 31–32,34; 1:8; cf. Dt 27—30; Mt 7:24–27).

The Gibeonite Deception

9 Now when all the kings west of the
Jordan heard about these things —
those in the hill country,[g] in the western foothills, and along the entire coast
of the Great Sea[z][h] as far as Lebanon[i] (the kings of the Hittites, Amorites, Canaanites, Perizzites,[j] Hivites[k] and Jebusites)[l] — 2they came
together to make war against Joshua
and Israel.
3However, when the people of Gibeon[m] heard what Joshua had done to
Jericho and Ai,[n] 4they resorted to a
ruse: They went as a delegation whose
donkeys were loaded[a] with worn-out
sacks and old wineskins, cracked and
mended. 5The men put worn and
patched sandals on their feet and wore
old clothes. All the bread of their food
supply was dry and moldy. 6Then
they went to Joshua in the camp at
Gilgal[o] and said to him and the
men of Israel, "We have come from a
distant country;[p] make a treaty[q]
with us."
7The men of Israel said to the Hivites,[r] "But perhaps you live near us.
How then can we make a treaty[s] with
you?"
8"We are your servants,[t]" they said
to Joshua.
But Joshua asked, "Who are you and
where do you come from?"
9They answered: "Your servants
have come from a very distant country[u] because of the fame of the LORD
your God. For we have heard reports[v]
of him: all that he did in Egypt,[w] 10and
all that he did to the two kings of the
Amorites east of the Jordan — Sihon
king of Heshbon,[x] and Og king of Bashan,[y] who reigned in Ashtaroth.[z]
11And our elders and all those living in
our country said to us, 'Take provisions for your journey; go and meet
them and say to them, "We are your
servants; make a treaty with us." '
12This bread of ours was warm when
we packed it at home on the day we left
to come to you. But now see how dry
and moldy it is. 13And these wineskins
that we filled were new, but see how
cracked they are. And our clothes and
sandals are worn out by the very long
journey."
14The men of Israel sampled their
provisions but did not inquire[a] of the
LORD. 15Then Joshua made a treaty of
peace[b] with them to let them live,[c]
and the leaders of the assembly ratified it by oath.
16Three days after they made the
treaty with the Gibeonites, the Israelites heard that they were neighbors,
living near[d] them. 17So the Israelites
set out and on the third day came to
their cities: Gibeon, Kephirah, Beeroth[e] and Kiriath Jearim.[f] 18But the
Israelites did not attack them, because
the leaders of the assembly had sworn
an oath[g] to them by the LORD, the God
of Israel.
The whole assembly grumbled[h]
against the leaders, 19but all the leaders answered, "We have given them
our oath by the LORD, the God of Israel,
and we cannot touch them now. 20This
is what we will do to them: We will let
them live, so that wrath will not fall on
us for breaking the oath[i] we swore to
them." 21They continued, "Let them
live,[j] but let them be woodcutters and
water carriers[k] for the entire community." So the leaders' promise to them
was kept.
22Then Joshua summoned the Gibeonites and said, "Why did you deceive
us by saying, 'We live a long way[l]
from you,' while actually you live
near[m] us? 23You are now under a
curse:[n] You will never cease to serve
as woodcutters and water carriers for
the house of my God."
24They answered Joshua, "Your servants were clearly told[o] how the LORD
your God had commanded his servant
Moses to give you the whole land and
to wipe out all its inhabitants from before you. So we feared for our lives because of you, and that is why we did
this. 25We are now in your hands.[p] Do

9:1 g S Nu 13:17 h S Nu 34:6 i S Dt 3:25 j Ge 13:7; S Jos 3:10 k ver 7; Jos 11:19 l S Jos 3:10 **9:3** m ver 17; Jos 10:10; 11:19; 18:25; 21:17; 2Sa 2:12; 5:25; 20:8; 1Ki 3:4; 9:2; 1Ch 8:29; 14:16; 16:39; 21:29; 2Ch 1:3; Ne 3:7; Isa 28:21; Jer 28:1; 41:12 n Ge 12:8; S Jos 8:1 **9:6** o S Dt 11:30 p ver 22 q S Ge 26:28 **9:7** r S ver 1 s S Ex 23:32; S 1Ki 5:12 **9:8** t 2Ki 10:5 **9:9** u S Dt 20:15 v ver 24 w S Nu 23:22 **9:10** x S Nu 21:25 y S Nu 21:33 z S Nu 21:24,35; Jos 2:10

9:14 a S Ex 16:28; S Nu 27:21 **9:15** b S ver 3,7; Jos 10:1,4; 11:19; 2Sa 21:2; 24:1 c ver 21; Jdg 1:21; Ps 106:34 **9:16** d ver 22 **9:17** e Jos 18:25; 2Sa 4:2; 23:37 f Jos 15:9,60; 18:14,15; Jdg 18:12; 1Sa 6:21; 7:2; Ps 132:6; Jer 26:20 **9:18** g ver 15; Jdg 21:1,7,18; 1Sa 20:17; Ps 15:4 h S Ex 15:24 **9:20** i S Ge 24:8 **9:21** j S ver 15 k S Dt 29:11 **9:22** l ver 6 m ver 16 **9:23** n S Ge 9:25 **9:24** o ver 9 **9:25** p Ge 16:6

z 1 That is, the Mediterranean a 4 Most Hebrew manuscripts; some Hebrew manuscripts, Vulgate and Syriac (see also Septuagint) *They prepared provisions and loaded their donkeys*

9:14 DID NOT INQUIRE OF THE LORD. Joshua and the leaders of Israel failed to pray and seek God's will with regard to the Gibeonites. They presumptuously entered into a covenant they could not break (v. 18). This ill-advised decision brought the ungodly Canaanites within Israel's midst (an action forbidden in Dt 7). In all the decisions of life we should seek God's will and pray for his wisdom and guidance, thereby enabling us to avoid sorrows and tragedies.

to us whatever seems good and right[q]
to you."
26So Joshua saved them from the Israelites, and they did not kill them.
27That day he made the Gibeonites[r]
woodcutters and water carriers[s] for
the community and for the altar of the
LORD at the place the LORD would
choose.[t] And that is what they are to
this day.

The Sun Stands Still

10 Now Adoni-Zedek[u] king of Jerusalem[v] heard that Joshua
had taken Ai[w] and totally destroyed[b][x] it, doing to Ai and its king
as he had done to Jericho and its king,
and that the people of Gibeon[y] had
made a treaty of peace[z] with Israel
and were living near them. 2He and his
people were very much alarmed at this,
because Gibeon was an important city,
like one of the royal cities; it was larger than Ai, and all its men were good
fighters. 3So Adoni-Zedek king of Jerusalem appealed to Hoham king of Hebron,[a] Piram king of Jarmuth,[b] Japhia king of Lachish[c] and Debir[d]
king of Eglon.[e] 4"Come up and help
me attack Gibeon," he said, "because it
has made peace[f] with Joshua and the
Israelites."
5Then the five kings[g] of the Amorites[h]—the kings of Jerusalem, Hebron, Jarmuth, Lachish and Eglon—
joined forces. They moved up with all
their troops and took up positions
against Gibeon and attacked it.
6The Gibeonites then sent word to
Joshua in the camp at Gilgal:[i] "Do not
abandon your servants. Come up to us
quickly and save us! Help us, because
all the Amorite kings from the hill
country have joined forces against us."
7So Joshua marched up from Gilgal
with his entire army,[j] including all
the best fighting men. 8The LORD said
to Joshua, "Do not be afraid[k] of them;
I have given them into your hand.[l]
Not one of them will be able to withstand you."[m]
9After an all-night march from Gilgal, Joshua took them by surprise.
10The LORD threw them into confusion[n] before Israel,[o] who defeated
them in a great victory at Gibeon.[p] Israel pursued them along the road going
up to Beth Horon[q] and cut them down
all the way to Azekah[r] and Makkedah.[s] 11As they fled before Israel on
the road down from Beth Horon to Azekah, the LORD hurled large hailstones[t]
down on them from the sky,[u] and
more of them died from the hailstones
than were killed by the swords of the
Israelites.
12On the day the LORD gave the Amorites[v] over to Israel, Joshua said to
the LORD in the presence of Israel:

"O sun, stand still over Gibeon,
O moon, over the Valley of
Aijalon."[w]
13So the sun stood still,[x]
and the moon stopped,
till the nation avenged itself
on[c] its enemies,

as it is written in the Book of Jashar.[y]
The sun stopped[z] in the middle of
the sky and delayed going down about
a full day. 14There has never been a
day like it before or since, a day when
the LORD listened to a man. Surely the
LORD was fighting[a] for Israel!
15Then Joshua returned with all Israel to the camp at Gilgal.[b]

9:25 [q] Jer 26:14 **9:27** [r] S Ex 1:11 [s] S Dt 29:11 [t] Dt 12:5 **10:1** [u] ver 3 [v] Jos 12:10; 15:8, 63; 18:28; Jdg 1:7 [w] S Jos 8:1 [x] S Dt 20:16; S Jos 8:22 [y] Jos 9:3 [z] S Jos 9:15 **10:3** [a] S Ge 13:18 [b] ver 5; Jos 12:11; 15:35; 21:29; Ne 11:29 [c] ver 5, 31; Jos 12:11; 15:39; 2Ki 14:19; 2Ch 11:9; 25:27; 32:9; Ne 11:30; Isa 36:2; 37:8; Jer 34:7; Mic 1:13 [d] ver 38; Jos 11:21; 12:13; 13:26; 15:7,49; 21:15; Jdg 1:11; 1Ch 6:58 [e] ver 23, 34,36; Jos 12:12; 15:39 **10:4** [f] S Jos 9:15 **10:5** [g] ver 16 [h] Nu 13:29; S Dt 1:7 **10:6** [i] S Dt 11:30 **10:7** [j] Jos 8:1
10:8 [k] S Dt 3:2; S Jos 1:9 [l] S Jos 2:24 [m] S Dt 7:24 **10:10** [n] S Ex 14:24 [o] S Dt 7:23 [p] S Jos 9:3 [q] Jos 16:3,5; 18:13,14; 21:22; 1Sa 13:18; 1Ki 9:17; 1Ch 6:68; 7:24; 2Ch 8:5; 25:13 [r] Jos 15:35; 1Sa 17:1; 2Ch 11:9; Ne 11:30; Jer 34:7 [s] ver 16,17,21; Jos 12:16; 15:41 **10:11** [t] S Ex 9:18; Ps 18:12; Isa 28:2,17; 32:19; Eze 13:11, 13 [u] Jdg 5:20 **10:12** [v] Am 2:9 [w] Jos 19:42; 21:24; Jdg 1:35; 12:12; 1Sa 14:31; 1Ch 6:69; 8:13; 2Ch 11:10; 28:18 **10:13** [x] Hab 3:11 [y] 2Sa 1:18 [z] Isa 38:8 **10:14** [a] ver 42; S Ex 14:14; Ps 106:43; 136:24; Isa 63:10; Jer 21:5 **10:15** [b] ver 43

[b] *1* The Hebrew term refers to the irrevocable giving over of things or persons to the LORD, often by totally destroying them; also in verses 28, 35, 37, 39 and 40. [c] *13* Or *nation triumphed over*

10:8 DO NOT BE AFRAID OF THEM. Even though Israel had made a mistake in entering into a covenant with the Gibeonites (see previous note), God helped his people defend them (cf. 9:18–20). Often failures that cause us to miss God's perfect will are used by him as occasions to demonstrate his faithfulness and love to us.

10:12 JOSHUA SAID TO THE LORD. Joshua prayed for a miracle, and God answered his prayer. Believers should not hesitate to pray that the Lord would work in extraordinary ways on their behalf. God's people live in a hostile and evil world and are faced with such challenges and difficulties that miracles are sometimes needed to fulfill his plan and purpose in their lives.

10:13 SUN STOOD STILL. The precise method God used in prolonging the daylight is not given. God could have slowed the earth's rotation, tilted the earth on its axis as in the north where the sun does not set, or caused a refraction of the sun's rays. Whatever God chose to do, the extending of that day was an extraordinary answer to prayer (vv. 12–14). The God who created the world and the heavenly bodies with their functions can also suspend their natural movements for his own purposes (cf. Isa 38:7–8).

Five Amorite Kings Killed

16Now the five kings had fled[c] and
hidden in the cave at Makkedah.
17When Joshua was told that the five
kings had been found hiding in the
cave at Makkedah, 18he said, "Roll
large rocks up to the mouth of the
cave, and post some men there to
guard it. 19But don't stop! Pursue your
enemies, attack them from the rear
and don't let them reach their cities,
for the LORD your God has given them
into your hand."
20So Joshua and the Israelites destroyed them completely[d]—almost to
a man—but the few who were left
reached their fortified cities.[e] 21The
whole army then returned safely to
Joshua in the camp at Makkedah, and
no one uttered a word against the Israelites.
22Joshua said, "Open the mouth of
the cave and bring those five kings out
to me." 23So they brought the five
kings out of the cave—the kings of Jerusalem, Hebron, Jarmuth, Lachish
and Eglon. 24When they had brought
these kings[f] to Joshua, he summoned
all the men of Israel and said to the
army commanders who had come with
him, "Come here and put your feet[g] on
the necks of these kings." So they
came forward and placed their feet[h]
on their necks.
25Joshua said to them, "Do not be
afraid; do not be discouraged. Be
strong and courageous.[i] This is what
the LORD will do to all the enemies you
are going to fight." 26Then Joshua
struck and killed the kings and hung
them on five trees, and they were left
hanging on the trees until evening.
27At sunset[j] Joshua gave the order
and they took them down from the
trees and threw them into the cave
where they had been hiding. At the
mouth of the cave they placed large
rocks, which are there to this day.[k]
28That day Joshua took Makkedah.
He put the city and its king to the
sword and totally destroyed everyone
in it. He left no survivors.[l] And he did
to the king of Makkedah as he had
done to the king of Jericho.[m]

Southern Cities Conquered

29Then Joshua and all Israel with
him moved on from Makkedah to Libnah[n] and attacked it. 30The LORD also
gave that city and its king into Israel's
hand. The city and everyone in it Joshua put to the sword. He left no survivors there. And he did to its king as he
had done to the king of Jericho.
31Then Joshua and all Israel with
him moved on from Libnah to Lachish;[o] he took up positions against it
and attacked it. 32The LORD handed Lachish over to Israel, and Joshua took it
on the second day. The city and everyone in it he put to the sword, just as he
had done to Libnah. 33Meanwhile, Horam king of Gezer[p] had come up to
help Lachish, but Joshua defeated him
and his army—until no survivors were
left.
34Then Joshua and all Israel with
him moved on from Lachish to Eglon;[q]
they took up positions against it and
attacked it. 35They captured it that
same day and put it to the sword and
totally destroyed everyone in it, just as
they had done to Lachish.
36Then Joshua and all Israel with
him went up from Eglon to Hebron[r]
and attacked it. 37They took the city
and put it to the sword, together with
its king, its villages and everyone[s] in
it. They left no survivors. Just as at Eglon, they totally destroyed it and everyone in it.
38Then Joshua and all Israel with
him turned around and attacked Debir.[t] 39They took the city, its king and
its villages, and put them to the sword.
Everyone in it they totally destroyed.
They left no survivors. They did to Debir and its king as they had done to
Libnah and its king and to Hebron.[u]
40So Joshua subdued the whole region, including the hill country, the
Negev,[v] the western foothills and the
mountain slopes,[w] together with all
their kings.[x] He left no survivors. He
totally destroyed all who breathed, just
as the LORD, the God of Israel, had commanded.[y] 41Joshua subdued them
from Kadesh Barnea[z] to Gaza[a] and
from the whole region of Goshen[b] to
Gibeon. 42All these kings and their
lands Joshua conquered in one campaign, because the LORD, the God of Israel, fought[c] for Israel.
43Then Joshua returned with all Israel to the camp at Gilgal.[d]

Northern Kings Defeated

11 When Jabin[e] king of Hazor[f]
heard of this, he sent word to

10:16 [c]Ps 68:12
10:20 [d]Dt 20:16 [e]2Ch 11:10; Jer 4:5; 5:17; 8:14; 35:11
10:24 [f]S Dt 7:24 [g]Mal 4:3 [h]2Sa 22:40; Ps 110:1; Isa 51:23
10:25 [i]S Dt 31:6
10:27 [j]S Dt 21:23 [k]S Ge 35:20
10:28 [l]Dt 20:16 [m]ver 30,32,35,39; Jos 6:21
10:29 [n]S Nu 33:20
10:31 [o]S ver 3
10:33 [p]Jos 12:12; 16:3,10; 21:21; Jdg 1:29; 2Sa 5:25; 1Ki 9:15; 1Ch 6:67
10:34 [q]S ver 3
10:36 [r]S Ge 13:18; Jos 14:13; 15:13; 20:7; 21:11; Jdg 16:3
10:37 [s]S ver 28
10:38 [t]S ver 3
10:39 [u]S ver 28
10:40 [v]S Ge 12:9; Jos 12:8; 15:19, 21; 18:25; 19:8; 1Sa 30:27 [w]S Dt 1:7 [x]Dt 7:24 [y]Dt 20:16-17
10:41 [z]S Ge 14:7 [a]S Ge 10:19 [b]Jos 11:16; 15:51
10:42 [c]S ver 14
10:43 [d]ver 15; Jos 5:9; 1Sa 7:16; 10:8; 11:14; 13:12
11:1 [e]Jdg 4:2,7, 23; Ps 83:9 [f]ver 10; Jos 12:19; 15:23,25; 19:36; Jdg 4:2,17; 1Sa 12:9; 1Ki 9:15; 2Ki 15:29; Ne 11:33; Jer 49:28,33

Jobab king of Madon, to the kings of
Shimron[g] and Acshaph,[h] **2**and to the
northern kings who were in the mountains, in the Arabah[i] south of Kinnereth,[j] in the western foothills and in
Naphoth Dor[d][k] on the west; **3**to the
Canaanites in the east and west; to the
Amorites, Hittites, Perizzites[l] and
Jebusites in the hill country;[m] and to
the Hivites[n] below Hermon[o] in the
region of Mizpah.[p] **4**They came out
with all their troops and a large number of horses and chariots—a huge
army, as numerous as the sand on the
seashore.[q] **5**All these kings joined
forces[r] and made camp together at
the Waters of Merom,[s] to fight
against Israel.

6The LORD said to Joshua, "Do not be
afraid of them, because by this time tomorrow I will hand all of them over[t]
to Israel, slain. You are to hamstring[u]
their horses and burn their chariots."[v]

7So Joshua and his whole army came
against them suddenly at the Waters of
Merom and attacked them, **8**and the
LORD gave them into the hand of Israel.
They defeated them and pursued them
all the way to Greater Sidon,[w] to Misrephoth Maim,[x] and to the Valley of
Mizpah on the east, until no survivors
were left. **9**Joshua did to them as the
LORD had directed: He hamstrung their
horses and burned their chariots.

10At that time Joshua turned back
and captured Hazor and put its king to
the sword.[y] (Hazor had been the head
of all these kingdoms.) **11**Everyone in
it they put to the sword. They totally
destroyed[e] them,[z] not sparing anything that breathed,[a] and he burned
up[b] Hazor itself.

12Joshua took all these royal cities
and their kings and put them to the
sword. He totally destroyed them, as
Moses the servant of the LORD had commanded.[c] **13**Yet Israel did not burn
any of the cities built on their
mounds—except Hazor, which Joshua
burned. **14**The Israelites carried off for
themselves all the plunder and livestock of these cities, but all the people
they put to the sword until they completely destroyed them, not sparing
anyone that breathed.[d] **15**As the LORD
commanded his servant Moses, so Moses commanded Joshua, and Joshua did
it; he left nothing undone of all that the
LORD commanded Moses.[e]

16So Joshua took this entire land:
the hill country,[f] all the Negev,[g] the
whole region of Goshen, the western
foothills,[h] the Arabah and the mountains of Israel with their foothills,
17from Mount Halak, which rises toward Seir,[i] to Baal Gad[j] in the Valley of Lebanon[k] below Mount Hermon.[l] He captured all their kings and
struck them down, putting them to
death.[m] **18**Joshua waged war against
all these kings for a long time. **19**Except for the Hivites[n] living in Gibeon,[o] not one city made a treaty of
peace[p] with the Israelites, who took
them all in battle. **20**For it was the LORD
himself who hardened their hearts[q] to
wage war against Israel, so that he
might destroy them totally, exterminating them without mercy, as the
LORD had commanded Moses.[r]

21At that time Joshua went and destroyed the Anakites[s] from the hill
country: from Hebron, Debir[t] and
Anab,[u] from all the hill country of Judah, and from all the hill country of Israel. Joshua totally destroyed them
and their towns. **22**No Anakites were
left in Israelite territory; only in
Gaza,[v] Gath[w] and Ashdod[x] did any
survive. **23**So Joshua took the entire
land,[y] just as the LORD had directed

11:1 g Jos 19:15 h Jos 12:20; 19:25
11:2 i ver 16; S Dt 1:1; Jos 12:1; 18:18 j S Nu 34:11; Dt 3:17; Jos 19:35; 1Ki 15:20 k Jos 12:23; 17:11; Jdg 1:27; 1Ki 4:11; 1Ch 7:29
11:3 l S Jos 3:10 m Nu 13:17 n S Ex 3:8; Dt 7:1; Jdg 3:3,5; 1Ki 9:20 o S Dt 3:8 p ver 8; S Ge 31:49; Jos 15:38; 18:26; Jdg 11:11; 20:1; 21:1; 1Sa 7:5,6; 1Ki 15:22; 2Ki 25:23
11:4 q S Ge 12:2; Jdg 7:12; 1Sa 13:5
11:5 r Jdg 5:19 s ver 7
11:6 t S Jos 2:24 u S Ge 49:6 v ver 9
11:8 w S Ge 10:15; S Jdg 18:7 x Jos 13:6
11:10 y Isa 3:25; Jer 41:2; 44:18
11:11 z S Dt 7:2 a Dt 20:16-17 b S Nu 31:10
11:12 c Nu 33:50-52; Dt 7:2
11:14 d S Dt 20:16
11:15 e Ex 34:11; Dt 7:2; S Jos 1:7
11:16 f Nu 13:17 g S Dt 1:7 h S Jos 10:41
11:17 i S Ge 14:6; S Nu 24:18; S Dt 33:2 j Jos 13:5 k S Dt 3:25; Jos 12:7 l Dt 3:9; Jos 12:8 m Dt 7:24
11:19 n S Jos 9:1 o S Jos 9:3 p S Jos 9:15
11:20 q S Ex 4:21; S 14:17; Ro 9:18 r Dt 7:16; Jdg 14:4
11:21 s S Nu 13:22,33 t S Jos 10:3 u Jos 15:50
11:22 v S Ge 10:19 w Jos 12:17; 19:13; 1Sa 5:8; 17:4; 1Ki 2:39; 2Ki 14:25; 1Ch 8:13; Am 6:2 x Jos 15:47; 1Sa 5:1; Isa 20:1
11:23 y Jos 21:43-45; Ne 9:24

d *2* Or *in the heights of Dor* e *11* The Hebrew term refers to the irrevocable giving over of things or persons to the LORD, often by totally destroying them; also in verses 12, 20 and 21.

11:18 JOSHUA WAGED WAR ... FOR A LONG TIME. The conquest of Canaan was an extended series of campaigns lasting about five years; this can be deduced from the age of Caleb, for five years had elapsed from the beginning of the conquest until Caleb was given Hebron (see 14:6–13; Dt 2:14).

11:20 LORD ... HARDENED THEIR HEARTS. Because the wickedness of the Canaanites was so terrible, God decided they must be destroyed (see article on THE DESTRUCTION OF THE CANAANITES, p. 310). To accomplish this he hardened their hearts so that they resolved stubbornly to wage war against Israel. There may come a time when a person or nation becomes so wicked that mercy is withdrawn and judgment is inevitable (cf. Heb 10:26–31).

11:23 JOSHUA TOOK THE ENTIRE LAND. This verse summarizes the book of Joshua; ch. 12 follows with a brief review of the conquests of Moses and Joshua.

Moses, and he gave it as an inheritance[z] to Israel according to their
tribal divisions.[a b]
Then the land had rest[c] from
war.[d]

List of Defeated Kings

12 These are the kings of the land
whom the Israelites had defeated and whose territory they took[e]
over east of the Jordan,[f] from the Arnon[g] Gorge to Mount Hermon,[h] including all the eastern side of the Arabah:[i]

2Sihon king of the Amorites,
who reigned in Heshbon.[j] He
ruled from Aroer[k] on the rim of
the Arnon Gorge—from the middle of the gorge—to the Jabbok
River,[l] which is the border of the
Ammonites.[m] This included half
of Gilead.[n] 3He also ruled over
the eastern Arabah from the Sea
of Kinnereth[f][o] to the Sea of the
Arabah (the Salt Sea[g][p]), to Beth
Jeshimoth,[q] and then southward
below the slopes of Pisgah.[r]

4And the territory of Og king of Bashan,[s]
one of the last of the Rephaites,[t]
who reigned in Ashtaroth[u] and
Edrei. 5He ruled over Mount Hermon, Salecah,[v] all of Bashan[w]
to the border of the people of Geshur[x] and Maacah,[y] and half of
Gilead[z] to the border of Sihon
king of Heshbon.

6Moses, the servant of the LORD, and
the Israelites conquered them.[a] And
Moses the servant of the LORD gave
their land to the Reubenites, the Gadites and the half-tribe of Manasseh to
be their possession.[b]

7These are the kings of the land that
Joshua and the Israelites conquered on
the west side of the Jordan, from Baal
Gad in the Valley of Lebanon[c] to
Mount Halak, which rises toward Seir
(their lands Joshua gave as an inheritance to the tribes of Israel according
to their tribal divisions— 8the hill
country, the western foothills, the Arabah, the mountain slopes, the desert
and the Negev[d]—the lands of the Hittites, Amorites, Canaanites, Perizzites, Hivites and Jebusites):[e]

9the king of Jericho[f] one
the king of Ai[g] (near
Bethel[h]) one
10the king of Jerusalem[i] one
the king of Hebron one
11the king of Jarmuth one
the king of Lachish[j] one
12the king of Eglon[k] one
the king of Gezer[l] one
13the king of Debir[m] one
the king of Geder one
14the king of Hormah[n] one
the king of Arad[o] one
15the king of Libnah[p] one
the king of Adullam[q] one
16the king of Makkedah[r] one
the king of Bethel[s] one
17the king of Tappuah[t] one
the king of Hepher[u] one
18the king of Aphek[v] one
the king of Lasharon one
19the king of Madon one
the king of Hazor[w] one
20the king of Shimron
Meron one
the king of Acshaph[x] one
21the king of Taanach[y] one
the king of Megiddo[z] one
22the king of Kedesh[a] one
the king of Jokneam[b] in
Carmel[c] one
23the king of Dor (in
Naphoth Dor[h][d]) one
the king of Goyim in
Gilgal one
24the king of Tirzah[e] one
thirty-one kings in all.[f]

Land Still to Be Taken

13 When Joshua was old and well
advanced in years,[g] the LORD
said to him, "You are very old, and
there are still very large areas of land
to be taken over.

2"This is the land that remains:
all the regions of the Philistines[h]

11:23 z S Dt 1:38; 12:9-10; S 25:19; S Jos 13:7 a S Nu 26:53 b Ps 105:44 c S Ex 33:14 d Jos 14:15
12:1 e Ps 136:21 f S Nu 32:19 g S Nu 21:13 h S Dt 3:8 i S Jos 11:2
12:2 j ver 5; S Nu 21:21,25; Jos 13:10; Jdg 11:19 k S Nu 32:34; S Jos 13:16 l S Ge 32:22 m S Ge 19:38 n S Ge 31:21; S Nu 32:26; Dt 2:36; S 3:15; Jos 13:11,25; 17:1; 20:8; 21:38; Jdg 5:17; 7:3; 10:8
12:3 o Jos 11:2 p S Ge 14:3 q S Nu 33:49; Jos 13:20 r S Nu 21:20
12:4 s S Nu 21:21, 33; Jos 13:30 t S Ge 14:5 u S Dt 1:4
12:5 v S Dt 3:10 w Nu 32:33; Jos 17:1; 20:8; 21:27; 22:7 x Jos 13:2,13; 1Sa 27:8 y S Dt 3:14 z ver 2
12:6 a S Dt 3:8 b Nu 32:29,33; Jos 13:8
12:7 c S Jos 11:17
12:8 d S Dt 1:7 e S Jos 3:10; S 11:17; Ezr 9:1
12:9 f S Nu 33:48 g S Ge 12:8; S Jos 8:1 h S Jos 7:2; 8:9; 18:13; Jdg 1:23; 4:5; 20:18; 21:2; Ne 11:31
12:10 i S Jos 10:1
12:11 j S Jos 10:3
12:12 k S Jos 10:3 l S Jos 10:33
12:13 m S Jos 10:3
12:14 n S Nu 14:45 o S Nu 21:1
12:15 p S Nu 33:20 q S Ge 38:1; Jos 15:35; Mic 1:15
12:16 r S Jos 10:10 s S Jos 7:2
12:17 t Jos 15:34; 16:8; 17:8 u S Jos 11:22; 1Ki 4:10
12:18 v Jos 13:4; 19:30; Jdg 1:31; 1Sa 4:1; 29:1
12:19 w S Jos 11:1
12:20 x S Jos 11:1
12:21 y Jos 17:11; 21:25 z Jdg 1:27; 5:19; 1Ki 4:12
12:22 a Jos 15:23; 19:37; 20:7; 21:32; Jdg 4:6,9 b Jos 19:11; 21:34 c Jos 15:55; 19:26; 1Sa 15:12; 2Sa 23:35
12:23 d S Jos 11:2
12:24 e 1Ki 14:17; 15:33; 16:8,23; SS 6:4 f Ps 135:11; 136:18
13:1 g Ge 24:1; Jos 14:10; 23:1,2; 1Ki 1:1
13:2 h S Ge 10:14; S Jdg 3:31

f *3* That is, Galilee g *3* That is, the Dead Sea h *23* Or *in the heights of Dor*

13:1 JOSHUA WAS OLD. This chapter begins the second part of the book of Joshua. The land had now been taken over to the extent that organized resistance was destroyed. The land "had rest from war" (11:23), though portions remained to be conquered (vv. 2–6).

CONQUEST OF CANAAN

When the Israelite tribes approached Canaan after four decades of desert existence, they first had to subdue the tribes in Transjordanian region, under Moses' leadership.

The military strategy of Joshua was brilliant in its simplicity. It had four goals: first, to cross the Jordan and gain a foothold in Canaan by seizing Jericho and its strategic plains, fords and roads; second, to capture the high ground around Bethel, Gibeon and Upper Beth Horon in order to dominate the hill country north and south of the ridge; third, to attack and neutralize lowland towns like Lachish; and finally, to break the power of the mighty urban coalition of northern towns led by Hazor. All of this took place about 1400 B.C.

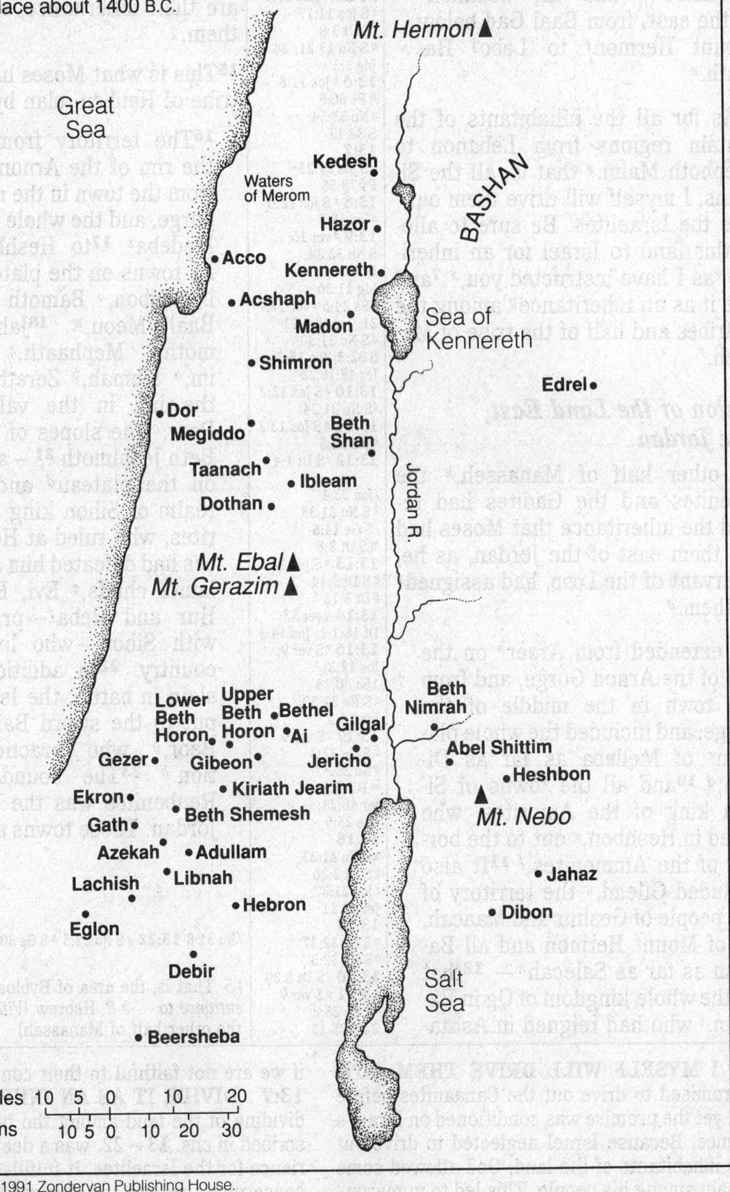

and Geshurites:[i] **3**from the Shihor River[j] on the east of Egypt to
the territory of Ekron[k] on the
north, all of it counted as Canaanite (the territory of the five Philistine rulers[l] in Gaza, Ashdod,[m]
Ashkelon,[n] Gath and Ekron—
that of the Avvites);[o] **4**from the
south, all the land of the Canaanites, from Arah of the Sidonians
as far as Aphek,[p] the region of
the Amorites,[q] **5**the area of the
Gebalites[i];[r] and all Lebanon[s]
to the east, from Baal Gad below
Mount Hermon[t] to Lebo[j] Hamath.[u]

6"As for all the inhabitants of the
mountain regions from Lebanon to
Misrephoth Maim,[v] that is, all the Sidonians, I myself will drive them out[w]
before the Israelites. Be sure to allo-
cate this land to Israel for an inheritance, as I have instructed you,[x] **7**and
divide it as an inheritance[y] among the
nine tribes and half of the tribe of Manasseh."

Division of the Land East of the Jordan

8The other half of Manasseh,[k] the
Reubenites and the Gadites had received the inheritance that Moses had
given them east of the Jordan, as he,
the servant of the LORD, had assigned[z]
it to them.[a]

9It extended from Aroer[b] on the
rim of the Arnon Gorge, and from
the town in the middle of the
gorge, and included the whole plateau[c] of Medeba as far as Dibon,[d] **10**and all the towns of Sihon king of the Amorites, who
ruled in Heshbon,[e] out to the border of the Ammonites.[f] **11**It also
included Gilead,[g] the territory of
the people of Geshur and Maacah,
all of Mount Hermon and all Bashan as far as Salecah[h]— **12**that
is, the whole kingdom of Og in Bashan,[i] who had reigned in Ashtaroth[j] and Edrei[k] and had survived as one of the last of the
Rephaites.[l] Moses had defeated
them and taken over their land.[m]
13But the Israelites did not drive
out the people of Geshur[n] and
Maacah,[o] so they continue to
live among the Israelites to this
day.[p]

14But to the tribe of Levi he gave no
inheritance, since the offerings made
by fire to the LORD, the God of Israel,
are their inheritance, as he promised
them.[q]

15This is what Moses had given to the
tribe of Reuben, clan by clan:

16The territory from Aroer[r] on
the rim of the Arnon Gorge, and
from the town in the middle of the
gorge, and the whole plateau past
Medeba[s] **17**to Heshbon and all
its towns on the plateau,[t] including Dibon,[u] Bamoth Baal,[v] Beth
Baal Meon,[w] **18**Jahaz,[x] Kedemoth,[y] Mephaath,[z] **19**Kiriathaim,[a] Sibmah,[b] Zereth Shahar on
the hill in the valley, **20**Beth
Peor,[c] the slopes of Pisgah, and
Beth Jeshimoth **21**—all the towns
on the plateau[d] and the entire
realm of Sihon king of the Amorites, who ruled at Heshbon. Moses had defeated him and the Midianite chiefs,[e] Evi, Rekem, Zur,
Hur and Reba[f]—princes allied
with Sihon—who lived in that
country. **22**In addition to those
slain in battle, the Israelites had
put to the sword Balaam son of
Beor,[g] who practiced divination.[h] **23**The boundary of the
Reubenites was the bank of the
Jordan. These towns and their vil-

13:2 [i]S Jos 12:5 **13:3** [j]1Ch 13:5; Isa 23:3; Jer 2:18 [k]Jos 15:11,45; 19:43; Jdg 1:18; 1Sa 5:10; 7:14 [l]Jdg 3:3; 16:5,18; 1Sa 6:4,17; Isa 14:29; Jer 25:20; Eze 25:15 [m]S Jos 11:22; Am 3:9 [n]Jdg 1:18; 14:19; 2Sa 1:20 [o]S Dt 2:23 **13:4** [p]S Jos 12:18 [q]S Ge 14:7; S 15:16; Am 2:10 **13:5** [r]1Ki 5:18; Ps 83:7; Eze 27:9 [s]S Jos 11:17 [t]S Dt 3:8 [u]S Nu 13:21; 34:8; Jdg 3:3 **13:6** [v]Jos 11:8 [w]Ps 80:8 [x]Nu 33:54; S 34:13 **13:7** [y]S Jos 11:23; Ps 78:55 **13:8** [z]S Jos 12:6 [a]Jos 18:7 **13:9** [b]ver 16; S Nu 32:34; Dt 2:36; Jdg 11:26; 2Sa 24:5 [c]ver 17, 21; Jer 48:8,21 [d]S Nu 21:30; S 32:3; Isa 15:2; Jer 48:18,22 **13:10** [e]S Jos 12:2 [f]S Nu 21:24 **13:11** [g]S Jos 12:2 [h]Jos 12:5 **13:12** [i]S Dt 1:4 [j]Jos 12:4 [k]S Nu 21:33 [l]S Ge 14:5 [m]S Dt 3:8 **13:13** [n]S Jos 12:5 [o]S Dt 3:14 [p]Dt 3:12 **13:14** [q]ver 33; Dt 18:1-2; Jos 14:3 **13:16** [r]S ver 9; Jos 12:2; 1Sa 30:28 [s]S Nu 21:30; Isa 15:2 **13:17** [t]S ver 9 [u]S Nu 32:3 [v]Nu 22:41 [w]1Ch 5:8; Jer 48:23; Eze 25:9 **13:18** [x]S Nu 21:23 [y]S Dt 2:26 [z]Jos 21:37; Jer 48:21 **13:19** [a]S Nu 32:37 [b]S Nu 32:3 **13:20** [c]S Dt 3:29 **13:21** [d]S ver 9 [e]S Ge 25:2; S Nu 25:15 [f]Nu 31:8 **13:22** [g]S Nu 22:5 [h]S Ge 30:27; S Nu 23:23

[i]5 That is, the area of Byblos [j]5 Or *to the entrance to* [k]8 Hebrew *With it* (that is, with the other half of Manasseh)

13:6 I MYSELF WILL DRIVE THEM OUT. God promised to drive out the Canaanites before Israel, yet the promise was conditioned on Israel's obedience. Because Israel neglected to drive out all the inhabitants of the land, God allowed some to remain among his people. This led to numerous problems for the Israelites, especially that of falling into idolatry. God is not bound to his promises if we are not faithful to their conditions.

13:7 DIVIDE IT AS AN INHERITANCE. The dividing of the land among the twelve tribes, described in chs. 13—22, was a deep spiritual experience for the Israelites. It fulfilled God's promise concerning the land and inspired hope for a greater fulfillment of the peace they now enjoyed (cf. Ps 16:6).

lages were the inheritance of the
Reubenites, clan by clan.[i]

24This is what Moses had given to the
tribe of Gad, clan by clan:

25The territory of Jazer,[j] all the
towns of Gilead[k] and half the
Ammonite country as far as Aroer, near Rabbah;[l] 26and from
Heshbon[m] to Ramath Mizpah and
Betonim, and from Mahanaim[n]
to the territory of Debir;[o] 27and
in the valley, Beth Haram, Beth
Nimrah,[p] Succoth[q] and Zaphon[r] with the rest of the realm
of Sihon king of Heshbon (the east
side of the Jordan, the territory up
to the end of the Sea of Kinnereth[1s]). 28These towns and
their villages were the inheritance
of the Gadites,[t] clan by clan.

29This is what Moses had given to the
half-tribe of Manasseh, that is, to half
the family of the descendants of Manasseh, clan by clan:

30The territory extending from
Mahanaim[u] and including all of
Bashan,[v] the entire realm of Og
king of Bashan[w]—all the settlements of Jair[x] in Bashan, sixty
towns, 31half of Gilead, and Ashtaroth and Edrei (the royal cities
of Og in Bashan).[y] This was for
the descendants of Makir[z] son of
Manasseh—for half of the sons of
Makir, clan by clan.[a]

32This is the inheritance Moses had
given when he was in the plains of
Moab[b] across the Jordan east of Jericho.[c] 33But to the tribe of Levi, Moses
had given no inheritance;[d] the LORD,
the God of Israel, is their inheritance,[e] as he promised them.[f]

Division of the Land West of the Jordan

14 Now these are the areas the Israelites received as an inheritance[g] in the land of Canaan, which
Eleazar[h] the priest, Joshua son of Nun
and the heads of the tribal clans of Israel[i] allotted[j] to them.[k] 2Their inheritances were assigned by lot[l] to
the nine-and-a-half tribes,[m] as the
LORD had commanded through Moses.
3Moses had granted the two-and-a-half
tribes their inheritance east of the Jordan[n] but had not granted the Levites
an inheritance among the rest,[o] 4for
the sons of Joseph had become two
tribes—Manasseh and Ephraim.[p]
The Levites received no share of the
land but only towns to live in, with pasturelands for their flocks and herds.[q]
5So the Israelites divided the land, just
as the LORD had commanded Moses.[r]

Hebron Given to Caleb

6Now the men of Judah approached
Joshua at Gilgal,[s] and Caleb son of Jephunneh[t] the Kenizzite said to him,
"You know what the LORD said to Moses the man of God[u] at Kadesh Barnea[v] about you and me.[w] 7I was forty
years old when Moses the servant of
the LORD sent me from Kadesh Barnea[x] to explore the land.[y] And I
brought him back a report according to
my convictions,[z] 8but my brothers
who went up with me made the hearts
of the people melt with fear.[a] I, however, followed the LORD my God wholeheartedly.[b] 9So on that day Moses
swore to me, 'The land on which your
feet have walked will be your inheritance[c] and that of your children[d] forever, because you have followed the
LORD my God wholeheartedly.'[m]

10"Now then, just as the LORD promised,[e] he has kept me alive for forty-
five years since the time he said this to
Moses, while Israel moved[f] about in
the desert. So here I am today, eighty-
five years old![g] 11I am still as
strong[h] today as the day Moses sent
me out; I'm just as vigorous[i] to go out
to battle now as I was then. 12Now give
me this hill country that the LORD
promised me that day.[j] You yourself
heard then that the Anakites[k] were
there and their cities were large and
fortified,[l] but, the LORD helping me, I
will drive them out just as he said."

13Then Joshua blessed[m] Caleb son
of Jephunneh[n] and gave him Hebron[o]
as his inheritance.[p] 14So Hebron has
belonged to Caleb son of Jephunneh the

13:23 [i]1Ch 5:7
13:25 [j]S Nu 21:32; Jos 21:39 [k]S Jos 12:2 [l]S Dt 3:11
13:26 [m]S Nu 21:25; Jer 49:3 [n]S Ge 32:2 [o]S Jos 10:3
13:27 [p]S Nu 32:3 [q]S Ge 33:17 [r]Jdg 12:1; Ps 48:2 [s]S Nu 34:11
13:28 [t]Ge 46:16; S Nu 32:33; Eze 48:27
13:30 [u]S Ge 32:2 [v]S Nu 21:33 [w]S Jos 12:4 [x]S Nu 32:41
13:31 [y]Nu 21:33 [z]S Ge 50:23 [a]Jos 17:5
13:32 [b]S Nu 26:3 [c]S Nu 22:1
13:33 [d]Nu 26:62 [e]S Nu 18:20 [f]S ver 14; Jos 18:7; Eze 44:28
14:1 [g]S Jos 11:23; Ps 16:6; 136:21 [h]S Ex 6:23 [i]Jos 21:1 [j]S Nu 26:53 [k]Nu 34:17-18; Jos 19:51
14:2 [l]S Lev 16:8 [m]Nu 34:13
14:3 [n]S Nu 32:33; S 34:14 [o]S Nu 35:2; S Jos 13:14
14:4 [p]S Ge 41:52; S Jdg 1:29 [q]S Nu 35:2-3; Jos 21:2
14:5 [r]S Nu 34:13
14:6 [s]S Dt 11:30 [t]Nu 13:6; 14:30 [u]S Dt 33:1 [v]Nu 13:26 [w]S Nu 14:38
14:7 [x]Jos 15:3 [y]S Nu 13:17 [z]Nu 13:30; S 14:6-9
14:8 [a]S Nu 13:31 [b]S Nu 14:24; S 32:12
14:9 [c]S Dt 11:24 [d]S Nu 14:24
14:10 [e]S Nu 11:28; 14:30 [f]S Jos 5:6 [g]S Jos 13:1
14:11 [h]S Dt 34:7 [i]S Ge 15:15
14:12 [j]S Nu 14:24 [k]S Nu 13:33 [l]Nu 13:28
14:13 [m]Jos 22:6, 7 [n]1Sa 25:3; 30:14 [o]S Ge 23:19; S Jos 10:36 [p]Jdg 1:20; 1Ch 6:56

[1]27 That is, Galilee [m]9 Deut. 1:36

14:14 CALEB . . . FOLLOWED THE LORD . . . WHOLEHEARTEDLY. Caleb remained faithful to God and received fully his promised inheritance (vv. 9–14). His life illustrates the believer's faithfulness and acceptance of the Father's promise under the new covenant—i.e., the Holy Spirit (Ac 1:4–5). After repentance and acceptance of God's new covenant terms, believers must go on to re-

Kenizzite ever since, because he followed the LORD, the God of Israel,
wholeheartedly.[q] 15(Hebron used to
be called Kiriath Arba[r] after Arba,[s]
who was the greatest man among the
Anakites.)
Then the land had rest[t] from war.

Allotment for Judah

15:15–19pp — Jdg 1:11–15

15 The allotment for the tribe of
Judah, clan by clan, extended
down to the territory of Edom,[u] to the
Desert of Zin[v] in the extreme south.[w]
2Their southern boundary
started from the bay at the southern end of the Salt Sea,[n][x]
3crossed south of Scorpion[o]
Pass,[y] continued on to Zin and
went over to the south of Kadesh
Barnea.[z] Then it ran past Hezron
up to Addar and curved around to
Karka. 4It then passed along to
Azmon[a] and joined the Wadi of
Egypt,[b] ending at the sea. This is
their[p] southern boundary.
5The eastern boundary[c] is the
Salt Sea[d] as far as the mouth of
the Jordan.
The northern boundary[e] started from the bay of the sea at the
mouth of the Jordan, 6went up to
Beth Hoglah[f] and continued
north of Beth Arabah[g] to the
Stone of Bohan[h] son of Reuben.
7The boundary then went up to
Debir[i] from the Valley of
Achor[j] and turned north to Gilgal,[k] which faces the Pass of
Adummim south of the gorge. It
continued along to the waters of
En Shemesh[l] and came out at En
Rogel.[m] 8Then it ran up the Valley of Ben Hinnom[n] along the
southern slope of the Jebusite[o]
city (that is, Jerusalem[p]). From
there it climbed to the top of the
hill west of the Hinnom Valley[q]
at the northern end of the Valley
of Rephaim.[r] 9From the hilltop
the boundary headed toward the
spring of the waters of Nephtoah,[s] came out at the towns of
Mount Ephron and went down toward Baalah[t] (that is, Kiriath Jearim).[u] 10Then it curved westward from Baalah[v] to Mount
Seir,[w] ran along the northern
slope of Mount Jearim (that is,
Kesalon), continued down to Beth
Shemesh[x] and crossed to Timnah.[y] 11It went to the northern
slope of Ekron,[z] turned toward
Shikkeron, passed along to
Mount Baalah[a] and reached Jabneel.[b] The boundary ended at the
sea.
12The western boundary is the
coastline of the Great Sea.[q][c]
These are the boundaries around the
people of Judah by their clans.

13In accordance with the LORD's
command to him, Joshua gave to Caleb[d] son of Jephunneh a portion in Judah—Kiriath Arba[e], that is, Hebron.[f] (Arba was the forefather of
Anak.)[g] 14From Hebron Caleb drove
out the three Anakites[h]—Sheshai,
Ahiman and Talmai[i]—descendants
of Anak.[j] 15From there he marched
against the people living in Debir (formerly called Kiriath Sepher). 16And
Caleb said, "I will give my daughter Acsah[k] in marriage to the man who attacks and captures Kiriath Sepher."
17Othniel[l] son of Kenaz, Caleb's
brother, took it; so Caleb gave his
daughter Acsah to him in marriage.
18One day when she came to Othniel, she urged him[r] to ask her father
for a field. When she got off her donkey, Caleb asked her, "What can I do
for you?"
19She replied, "Do me a special favor. Since you have given me land in
the Negev,[m] give me also springs of
water." So Caleb gave her the upper
and lower springs.[n]

20This is the inheritance of the tribe
of Judah, clan by clan:

21The southernmost towns of the tribe

14:14 [q] S Nu 14:24 **14:15** [r] S Ge 23:2 [s] Jos 15:13 [t] Jos 11:23; Jdg 3:11; 1Ki 4:24; 5:4; 1Ch 22:9 **15:1** [u] Nu 34:3 [v] S Nu 13:21 [w] Jos 18:5 **15:2** [x] S Ge 14:3 **15:3** [y] S Nu 34:4 [z] S Dt 1:2 **15:4** [a] Nu 34:4 [b] S Ge 15:18 **15:5** [c] Nu 34:10 [d] S Ge 14:3 [e] Jos 18:15-19 **15:6** [f] Jos 18:19, 21 [g] ver 61; Jos 18:18 [h] Jos 18:17 **15:7** [i] S Jos 10:3 [j] S Jos 7:24 [k] S Dt 11:30 [l] Jos 18:17 [m] Jos 18:16; 2Sa 17:17; 1Ki 1:9 **15:8** [n] 2Ch 28:3; Jer 19:6 [o] ver 63; Jos 18:16,28; Jdg 1:21; 19:10; 2Sa 5:6; 1Ch 11:4; Ezr 9:1 [p] S Jos 10:1 [q] 2Ki 23:10; Jer 7:31; 19:2 [r] 2Sa 5:18,22; 1Ch 14:9; Isa 17:5 **15:9** [s] Jos 18:15 [t] ver 10,11,29; 2Sa 6:2; 1Ch 13:6

[u] S Jos 9:17 **15:10** [v] S ver 9 [w] S Nu 24:18 [x] Jos 19:22,38; 21:16; Jdg 1:33; 1Sa 6:9; 1Ki 4:9; 2Ki 14:11 [y] S Ge 38:12 **15:11** [z] S Jos 13:3 [a] S ver 9 [b] Jos 19:33 **15:12** [c] S Nu 34:6 **15:13** [d] 1Sa 25:3; 30:14 [e] S Ge 23:2 [f] S Jos 10:36; 21:12; 1Ch 6:56 [g] S Nu 13:22 **15:14** [h] S Nu 13:33 [i] S Nu 13:22 [j] Jdg 1:10,20 **15:16** [k] 1Ch 2:49 **15:17** [l] Jdg 3:9, 11; 1Ch 4:13; 27:15 **15:19** [m] S Jos 10:40 [n] Ge 36:24

[n] *2* That is, the Dead Sea; also in verse 5
[o] *3* Hebrew *Akrabbim*
[p] *4* Hebrew *your*
[q] *12* That is, the Mediterranean; also in verse 47
[r] *18* Hebrew and some Septuagint manuscripts; other Septuagint manuscripts (see also note at Judges 1:14) *Othniel, he urged her*

ceive whatever spiritual gifts God wishes to bestow (cf. Ro 12:6–8; 1Co 12:4–31), to show the fruit of the Spirit (cf. Gal 5:22–25) and to demonstrate wisdom (cf. Ac 6:3; 1Co 2:6–16; Eph 1:17; Jas 3:13–18). All of these are the proper inheritance of those filled with the Spirit and power (cf. Ac 1:4–8; 2:4).

of Judah in the Negev[o] toward the
boundary of Edom were:
Kabzeel,[p] Eder,[q] Jagur, **22**Ki-
nah, Dimonah, Adadah, **23**Kedesh,[r] Hazor,[s] Ithnan,
24Ziph,[t] Telem, Bealoth, **25**Hazor Hadattah, Kerioth Hezron
(that is, Hazor),[u] **26**Amam, Shema, Moladah,[v] **27**Hazar Gaddah,
Heshmon, Beth Pelet, **28**Hazar
Shual,[w] Beersheba,[x] Biziothiah,
29Baalah,[y] Iim, Ezem,[z] **30**Eltolad,[a] Kesil, Hormah,[b] **31**Ziklag,[c] Madmannah,[d] Sansannah,
32Lebaoth, Shilhim, Ain[e] and
Rimmon[f]—a total of twenty-
nine towns and their villages.

33In the western foothills:
Eshtaol,[g] Zorah,[h] Ashnah,[i]
34Zanoah,[j] En Gannim,[k] Tappuah,[l] Enam, **35**Jarmuth,[m] Adullam,[n] Socoh,[o] Azekah,[p] **36**Shaaraim,[q] Adithaim and Gederah[r]
(or Gederothaim)[s]—fourteen
towns and their villages.
37Zenan, Hadashah, Migdal
Gad, **38**Dilean, Mizpah,[s] Joktheel,[t] **39**Lachish,[u] Bozkath,[v] Eglon,[w] **40**Cabbon, Lahmas, Kitlish,
41Gederoth,[x] Beth Dagon,[y] Naamah and Makkedah[z]—sixteen
towns and their villages.
42Libnah,[a] Ether, Ashan,[b]
43Iphtah, Ashnah,[c] Nezib, **44**Keilah,[d] Aczib[e] and Mareshah[f]—
nine towns and their villages.
45Ekron,[g] with its surrounding settlements and villages;
46west of Ekron, all that were in
the vicinity of Ashdod,[h] together
with their villages; **47**Ashdod,[i]
its surrounding settlements and
villages; and Gaza, its settlements and villages, as far as the
Wadi of Egypt[j] and the coastline
of the Great Sea.[k]

48In the hill country:
Shamir,[l] Jattir,[m] Socoh,[n]
49Dannah, Kiriath Sannah (that
is, Debir[o]), **50**Anab,[p] Eshte-
moh,[q] Anim, **51**Goshen,[r] Holon[s] and Giloh[t]—eleven towns
and their villages.
52Arab, Dumah,[u] Eshan, **53**Ja-
nim, Beth Tappuah, Aphekah,
54Humtah, Kiriath Arba[v] (that
is, Hebron) and Zior—nine towns
and their villages.
55Maon,[w] Carmel,[x] Ziph,[y]
Juttah,[z] **56**Jezreel,[a] Jokdeam,
Zanoah,[b] **57**Kain, Gibeah[c] and
Timnah[d]—ten towns and their
villages.
58Halhul, Beth Zur,[e] Gedor,[f]
59Maarath, Beth Anoth and Elte-
kon—six towns and their villages.
60Kiriath Baal[g] (that is, Kiriath Jearim[h]) and Rabbah[i]—two
towns and their villages.

61In the desert:[j]
Beth Arabah,[k] Middin, Seca-
cah, **62**Nibshan, the City of Salt
and En Gedi[l]—six towns and
their villages.
63Judah could not[m] dislodge the
Jebusites[n], who were living in Jerusalem;[o] to this day the Jebusites live
there with the people of Judah.[p]

Allotment for Ephraim and Manasseh

16 The allotment for Joseph
began at the Jordan of Jericho,[t] east of the waters of Jericho, and went up from there
through the desert[q] into the hill
country of Bethel.[r] **2**It went on
from Bethel (that is, Luz[s]),[u]
crossed over to the territory of the
Arkites[t] in Ataroth,[u] **3**descended westward to the territory of the
Japhletites as far as the region of
Lower Beth Horon[v] and on to Gezer,[w] ending at the sea.

15:21 [o] S Jos 10:40 [p] 2Sa 23:20; 1Ch 11:22 [q] Ge 35:21 **15:23** [r] S Jos 12:22 [s] S Jos 11:1 **15:24** [t] ver 55; 1Sa 23:14; 2Ch 11:8 **15:25** [u] S Jos 11:1 **15:26** [v] Jos 19:2; 1Ch 4:28; Ne 11:26 **15:28** [w] Jos 19:3; 1Ch 4:28 [x] S Ge 21:14 **15:29** [y] S ver 9 [z] Jos 19:3; 1Ch 4:29 **15:30** [a] Jos 19:4 [b] S Nu 14:45 **15:31** [c] Jos 19:5; 1Sa 27:6; 1Ch 4:30; 12:1; Ne 11:28 [d] 1Ch 2:49 **15:32** [e] S Nu 34:11 [f] Jos 19:7; Jdg 20:45; 21:13; Zec 14:10 **15:33** [g] Jos 19:41; Jdg 13:25; 16:31; 18:2 [h] Jdg 13:2; 18:11; 2Ch 11:10; Ne 11:29 [i] ver 43 **15:34** [j] ver 56; 1Ch 4:18; Ne 3:13; 11:30 [k] Jos 19:21; 21:29 [l] S Jos 12:17 **15:35** [m] S Jos 10:3 [n] S Ge 38:1 [o] ver 48; 1Ki 4:10 [p] S Jos 10:10 **15:36** [q] 1Sa 17:52; 1Ch 4:31 [r] 1Ch 12:4 **15:38** [s] S Jos 11:3 [t] 2Ki 14:7 **15:39** [u] S Jos 10:3 [v] 2Ki 22:1 [w] S Jos 10:3 **15:41** [x] 2Ch 28:18 [y] Jos 19:27 [z] S Jos 10:10 **15:42** [a] S Nu 33:20 [b] Jos 19:7; 1Sa 30:30; 1Ch 4:32; 6:59 **15:43** [c] ver 33 **15:44** [d] 1Sa 23:1-2,1; 1Ch 4:19; Ne 3:17, 18 [e] Jos 19:29; Jdg 1:31; Mic 1:14 [f] Mic 1:15 **15:45** [g] S Jos 13:3 **15:46** [h] Jos 11:22 **15:47** [i] S Jos 11:22 [j] S Ge 15:18 [k] S Nu 34:6 **15:48** [l] Jdg 10:1 [m] Jos 21:14; 1Sa 30:27; 1Ch 6:57 [n] S ver 35 **15:49** [o] S Jos 10:3 **15:50** [p] Jos 11:21 [q] Jos 21:14; 1Sa 30:28 **15:51** [r] S Jos 10:41 [s] Jos 21:15; Jer 48:21 [t] 2Sa 15:12 **15:52** [u] S Ge 25:14 **15:54** [v] S Ge 35:27 **15:55** [w] Jdg 10:12; 1Sa 23:24,25; 25:1,2; 1Ch 2:45 [x] S Jos 12:22 [y] S ver 24 [z] Jos 21:16 **15:56** [a] Jos 17:16; 19:18; Jdg 6:33; 1Sa 25:43; 1Ki 18:45; 1Ch 3:1; Hos 1:5 [b] S ver 34 **15:57** [c] Jos 18:28; 24:33; Jdg 19:12; 20:4; 2Sa 23:29; 1Ch 11:31 [d] S Ge 38:12 **15:58** [e] 1Ch 2:45; 2Ch 11:7; Ne 3:16 [f] 1Ch 4:39; 12:7 **15:60** [g] ver 9 [h] S Jos 9:17 [i] S Dt 3:11 **15:61** [j] S Jos 8:15 [k] S ver 6 **15:62** [l] 1Sa 23:29; 24:1; Eze 47:10 **15:63** [m] Jos 16:10; 17:12; Jdg 1:21; 1Ki 9:21 [n] S ver 8 [o] S Jos 10:1 [p] Eze 48:7 **16:1** [q] S Jos 8:15 [r] S Jos 12:9 **16:2** [s] S Ge 28:19 [t] 2Sa 15:32 [u] S ver 5; S Nu 32:3 **16:3** [v] S Jos 10:10 [w] S Jos 10:33

[s] *36* Or *Gederah and Gederothaim* [t] *1* *Jordan of Jericho* was possibly an ancient name for the Jordan River. [u] *2* Septuagint; Hebrew *Bethel to Luz*

16:1 ALLOTMENT FOR JOSEPH. Joseph, the eleventh son of Jacob, did not have a tribe named after him because his inheritance was given to his two sons, Ephraim and Manasseh (Ge 48:14–22). As a result, Joseph received a double portion of the land in that Ephraim and Manasseh constituted two separate, complete tribes.

4 So Manasseh and Ephraim, the
descendants of Joseph, received their
inheritance.[x]

5 This was the territory of Ephraim,
clan by clan:
The boundary of their inheritance went from Ataroth Addar[y]
in the east to Upper Beth Horon[z]
6 and continued to the sea. From
Micmethath[a] on the north it
curved eastward to Taanath Shiloh, passing by it to Janoah[b] on
the east. 7 Then it went down from
Janoah[c] to Ataroth[d] and Naarah, touched Jericho and came out
at the Jordan. 8 From Tappuah[e]
the border went west to the Kanah Ravine[f] and ended at the
sea. This was the inheritance of
the tribe of the Ephraimites, clan
by clan. 9 It also included all the
towns and their villages that were
set aside for the Ephraimites
within the inheritance of the Manassites.[g]
10 They did not dislodge the Canaanites
living in Gezer; to this day the Canaanites live among the people of Ephraim
but are required to do forced labor.[h]

17 This was the allotment for the
tribe of Manasseh[i] as Jo-
seph's firstborn,[j] that is, for Makir,[k]
Manasseh's firstborn. Makir was the
ancestor of the Gileadites, who had received Gilead[l] and Bashan[m] because
the Makirites were great soldiers. 2 So
this allotment was for the rest of the
people of Manasseh[n]—the clans of
Abiezer,[o] Helek, Asriel,[p] Shechem,
Hepher[q] and Shemida.[r] These are
the other male descendants of Manasseh son of Joseph by their clans.

3 Now Zelophehad son of Hepher,[s]
the son of Gilead, the son of Makir, the
son of Manasseh, had no sons but only
daughters,[t] whose names were Mahlah, Noah, Hoglah, Milcah and Tirzah.
4 They went to Eleazar the priest, Joshua son of Nun, and the leaders and
said, "The LORD commanded Moses to
give us an inheritance among our
brothers." So Joshua gave them an inheritance along with the brothers of
their father, according to the LORD's
command.[u] 5 Manasseh's share consisted of ten tracts of land besides Gilead and Bashan east of the Jordan,[v]
6 because the daughters of the tribe of
Manasseh received an inheritance
among the sons. The land of Gilead belonged to the rest of the descendants
of Manasseh.

7 The territory of Manasseh extended from Asher[w] to Micmethath[x] east of Shechem.[y] The
boundary ran southward from
there to include the people living
at En Tappuah. 8 (Manasseh had
the land of Tappuah, but Tappuah[z] itself, on the boundary of Manasseh, belonged to the Ephraimites.) 9 Then the boundary
continued south to the Kanah Ravine.[a] There were towns belonging to Ephraim lying among the
towns of Manasseh, but the
boundary of Manasseh was the
northern side of the ravine and
ended at the sea. 10 On the south
the land belonged to Ephraim, on
the north to Manasseh. The territory of Manasseh reached the sea
and bordered Asher[b] on the
north and Issachar[c] on the
east.[d]

11 Within Issachar[e] and Asher,
Manasseh also had Beth Shan,[f]
Ibleam[g] and the people of Dor,[h]
Endor,[i] Taanach[j] and Megiddo,[k] together with their surrounding settlements (the third in
the list is Naphoth[v]).[l]
12 Yet the Manassites were not able[m]
to occupy these towns, for the Canaanites were determined to live in that region. 13 However, when the Israelites
grew stronger, they subjected the Ca-

16:4 [x] Jos 18:5 **16:5** [y] ver 2; Jos 18:13 [z] S Jos 10:10 **16:6** [a] Jos 17:7 [b] ver 7; 2Ki 15:29 **16:7** [c] S ver 6 [d] S Nu 32:3 **16:8** [e] S Jos 12:17 [f] Jos 17:9; 19:28 **16:9** [g] Eze 48:5 **16:10** [h] S Jos 15:63; 17:13; Jdg 1:28-29; 1Ki 9:16 **17:1** [i] S Nu 1:34; 1Ch 7:14 [j] S Ge 41:51 [k] S Ge 50:23 [l] S Jos 12:2 [m] S Jos 12:5 **17:2** [n] Jos 22:7 [o] S Nu 26:30; Jdg 6:11,34; 8:2; 1Ch 7:18 [p] 1Ch 7:14 [q] S Nu 27:1 [r] 1Ch 7:19 **17:3** [s] S Nu 27:1 [t] S Nu 26:33 **17:4** [u] Nu 27:5-7 **17:5** [v] Jos 13:30-31 **17:7** [w] ver 10; Jos 19:24,31; 21:6,30; Jdg 1:31; 5:17; 6:35; 7:23 [x] Jos 16:6 [y] S Ge 12:6; Jos 21:21; 24:25; Jdg 9:1 **17:8** [z] S Jos 12:17 **17:9** [a] S Jos 16:8 **17:10** [b] S ver 7 [c] S Ge 30:18 [d] Eze 48:5 **17:11** [e] ver 10 [f] ver 16; Jdg 1:27; 1Sa 31:10; 2Sa 21:12; 1Ki 4:12; 1Ch 7:29 [g] 2Ki 9:27 [h] S Jos 11:2 [i] 1Sa 28:7; Ps 83:10 [j] S Jos 12:21 [k] 1Ki 9:15 [l] Eze 48:4 **17:12** [m] S Jos 15:63

[v] *11* That is, Naphoth Dor

17:4 THE LORD COMMANDED MOSES. This verse makes it clear that the people regarded the Pentateuch as the word of God to be obeyed in every detail. The written Word of God, revealed to Moses, constituted the standard of authority for all God's people, including Eleazar the priest and Joshua (v. 4).

17:13 DID NOT DRIVE THEM OUT COMPLETELY. Israel failed to possess the land fully and to completely drive out the Canaanites for two reasons. (1) They wanted the profit and affluence gained from the forced labor and tribute of the Canaanites. Compromising God's will for ease and money sowed the seeds for later widespread apostasy (cf. Jdg 1:21,27–29; 2:11–13). (2) Some of the Canaanites, with their "iron chariots" (vv. 16–18; Jdg 1:19), had armaments superior to the Israelites', which they could not overcome in their own strength. They were beginning to lose their confidence in the power of their God to

naanites to forced labor but did not
drive them out completely.[n]
14The people of Joseph said to Joshua, "Why have you given us only one
allotment and one portion for an inheritance? We are a numerous people and
the LORD has blessed us abundantly."[o]
15"If you are so numerous," Joshua
answered, "and if the hill country of
Ephraim is too small for you, go up into
the forest[p] and clear land for yourselves there in the land of the Perizzites[q] and Rephaites.[r]"
16The people of Joseph replied, "The
hill country is not enough for us, and
all the Canaanites who live in the plain
have iron chariots,[s] both those in
Beth Shan[t] and its settlements and
those in the Valley of Jezreel."[u]
17But Joshua said to the house of Joseph—to Ephraim and Manasseh—
"You are numerous and very powerful.
You will have not only one allotment[v]
18but the forested hill country[w] as
well. Clear it, and its farthest limits
will be yours; though the Canaanites
have iron chariots[x] and though they
are strong, you can drive them out."

Division of the Rest of the Land

18 The whole assembly of the Israelites gathered at Shiloh[y] and
set up the Tent of Meeting[z] there. The
country was brought under their control, 2but there were still seven Israelite tribes who had not yet received
their inheritance.
3So Joshua said to the Israelites:
"How long will you wait before you begin to take possession of the land that
the LORD, the God of your fathers, has
given you? 4Appoint three men from
each tribe. I will send them out to
make a survey of the land and to write
a description of it,[a] according to the
inheritance of each.[b] Then they will
return to me. 5You are to divide the
land into seven parts. Judah is to remain in its territory on the south[c] and
the house of Joseph in its territory on
the north.[d] 6After you have written
descriptions of the seven parts of the
land, bring them here to me and I will
cast lots[e] for you in the presence of
the LORD our God. 7The Levites, however, do not get a portion among you, because the priestly service of the LORD is
their inheritance.[f] And Gad, Reuben
and the half-tribe of Manasseh have already received their inheritance on the
east side of the Jordan. Moses the servant of the LORD gave it to them.[g]"
8As the men started on their way to
map out the land, Joshua instructed
them, "Go and make a survey of the
land and write a description of it.[h]
Then return to me, and I will cast lots
for you here at Shiloh[i] in the presence
of the LORD." 9So the men left and went
through the land. They wrote its description on a scroll, town by town, in
seven parts, and returned to Joshua in
the camp at Shiloh. 10Joshua then cast
lots[j] for them in Shiloh in the presence[k] of the LORD, and there he distributed the land to the Israelites according to their tribal divisions.[l]

Allotment for Benjamin

11The lot came up for the tribe of Benjamin, clan by clan. Their allotted territory lay between the tribes of Judah
and Joseph:
12On the north side their
boundary began at the Jordan,
passed the northern slope of Jericho and headed west into the hill
country, coming out at the
desert[m] of Beth Aven.[n] 13From
there it crossed to the south slope
of Luz[o] (that is, Bethel[p]) and
went down to Ataroth Addar[q] on
the hill south of Lower Beth Horon.
14From the hill facing Beth Horon[r] on the south the boundary
turned south along the western
side and came out at Kiriath Baal
(that is, Kiriath Jearim),[s] a town
of the people of Judah. This was
the western side.
15The southern side began at
the outskirts of Kiriath Jearim on
the west, and the boundary came
out at the spring of the waters
of Nephtoah.[t] 16The boundary

17:13 [n]Jdg 1:27-28 **17:14** [o]Nu 26:28-37 **17:15** [p]2Sa 18:6 [q]S Jos 3:10 [r]S Ge 14:5; Jos 15:8; 18:16; 2Sa 5:18; 23:13; Isa 17:5 **17:16** [s]ver 18; Jdg 1:19; 4:3,13 [t]S ver 11 [u]S Jos 15:56; S 1Sa 29:1 **17:17** [v]Eze 48:5 **17:18** [w]1Sa 1:1 [x]S ver 16 **18:1** [y]ver 8; Jos 19:51; 21:2; Jdg 18:31; 21:12, 19; 1Sa 1:3; 3:21; 4:3; 1Ki 14:2; Ps 78:60; Jer 7:12; 26:6; 41:5 [z]S ver 10; S Ex 27:21; S 40:2; Ac 7:45 **18:4** [a]ver 8 [b]Mic 2:5 **18:5** [c]Jos 15:1 [d]Jos 16:1-4 **18:6** [e]S Lev 16:8 **18:7** [f]S Jos 13:33 [g]Jos 13:8 **18:8** [h]ver 4 [i]S ver 1 **18:10** [j]S Nu 34:13 [k]S ver 1; Jer 7:12 [l]Nu 33:54; Jos 19:51 **18:12** [m]S Jos 8:15 [n]S Jos 7:2 **18:13** [o]S Ge 28:19 [p]S Jos 12:9 [q]S Nu 32:3; S Jos 16:5 **18:14** [r]Jos 10:10 [s]S Jos 9:17 **18:15** [t]Jos 15:9

overcome their enemies (cf. Ps 20:6–8).

18:1 SET UP THE TENT OF MEETING. Israel moved its center of worship from Gilgal to Shiloh. There they set up the Tent of Meeting (tabernacle), the place in which the ark of the covenant was kept and where God manifested his presence among the people in a special way (cf. Ex 25:8; 27:21; 34:26). The tabernacle remained at Shiloh throughout the time of the judges (i.e., about 300 years), until such time as it was captured by the Philistines during the time of Samuel (1Sa 4:3—5:1).

went down to the foot of the hill
facing the Valley of Ben Hinnom,
north of the Valley of Rephaim.[u]
It continued down the Hinnom
Valley[v] along the southern slope
of the Jebusite city and so to En
Rogel.[w] **17**It then curved north,
went to En Shemesh, continued to
Geliloth,[x] which faces the Pass
of Adummim,[y] and ran down to
the Stone of Bohan[z] son of Reuben. **18**It continued to the northern slope of Beth Arabah[w][a] and
on down into the Arabah.[b] **19**It
then went to the northern slope of
Beth Hoglah[c] and came out at
the northern bay of the Salt
Sea,[x][d] at the mouth of the Jordan in the south. This was the
southern boundary.

20The Jordan formed the
boundary on the eastern side.
These were the boundaries that
marked out the inheritance of the clans
of Benjamin on all sides.[e]

21The tribe of Benjamin, clan by clan,
had the following cities:

Jericho, Beth Hoglah,[f] Emek
Keziz, **22**Beth Arabah,[g] Zemara-
im,[h] Bethel,[i] **23**Avvim,[j] Parah,
Ophrah,[k] **24**Kephar Ammoni,
Ophni and Geba[l]—twelve towns
and their villages.

25Gibeon,[m] Ramah,[n] Beeroth,[o] **26**Mizpah,[p] Kephirah,[q]
Mozah, **27**Rekem, Irpeel, Taralah,
28Zelah,[r] Haeleph, the Jebusite
city[s] (that is, Jerusalem[t]), Gibeah[u] and Kiriath—fourteen towns
and their villages.[v]

This was the inheritance of Benjamin
for its clans.[w]

Allotment for Simeon

19:2–10pp — 1Ch 4:28–33

19 The second lot came out for the
tribe of Simeon, clan by clan.
Their inheritance lay within the territory of Judah.[x] **2**It included:

Beersheba[y] (or Sheba),[y] Moladah,[z] **3**Hazar Shual,[a] Balah,
Ezem,[b] **4**Eltolad,[c] Bethul, Hormah,[d] **5**Ziklag,[e] Beth Marcaboth, Hazar Susah, **6**Beth Lebaoth
and Sharuhen—thirteen towns
and their villages;

7Ain, Rimmon,[f] Ether and
Ashan[g]—four towns and their
villages— **8**and all the villages
around these towns as far as Baalath Beer (Ramah in the Negev).[h]

This was the inheritance of the tribe of
the Simeonites, clan by clan. **9**The inheritance of the Simeonites was taken
from the share of Judah,[i] because Judah's portion was more than they
needed. So the Simeonites received
their inheritance within the territory of
Judah.[j]

Allotment for Zebulun

10The third lot came up for Zebulun,[k]
clan by clan:

The boundary of their inheritance went as far as Sarid.[l]
11Going west it ran to Maralah,
touched Dabbesheth, and extended to the ravine near Jokneam.[m]
12It turned east from Sarid[n] toward the sunrise to the territory
of Kisloth Tabor and went on to
Daberath[o] and up to Japhia.
13Then it continued eastward to
Gath Hepher[p] and Eth Kazin; it
came out at Rimmon[q] and turned
toward Neah. **14**There the boundary went around on the north to
Hannathon and ended at the Valley of Iphtah El.[r] **15**Included
were Kattath, Nahalal,[s] Shimron,[t] Idalah and Bethlehem.[u]
There were twelve towns and
their villages.

16These towns and their villages were
the inheritance of Zebulun,[v] clan by
clan.[w]

Allotment for Issachar

17The fourth lot came out for Issachar,[x] clan by clan. **18**Their territory
included:

Jezreel,[y] Kesulloth, Shunem,[z] **19**Hapharaim, Shion, Ana-
harath, **20**Rabbith, Kishion,[a]
Ebez, **21**Remeth, En Gannim,[b]
En Haddah and Beth Pazzez.
22The boundary touched Tabor,[c]
Shahazumah and Beth She-
mesh,[d] and ended at the Jordan.
There were sixteen towns and
their villages.

23These towns and their villages were

18:16 [u]S Jos 17:15 [v]Jos 15:8 [w]S Jos 15:7
18:17 [x]Jos 22:10 [y]Jos 15:7 [z]Jos 15:6
18:18 [a]S Jos 15:6 [b]S Jos 11:2
18:19 [c]S Jos 15:6 [d]S Ge 14:3
18:20 [e]1Sa 9:1
18:21 [f]S Jos 15:6
18:22 [g]Jos 15:6 [h]2Ch 13:4 [i]Jos 16:1
18:23 [j]S Dt 2:23 [k]Jdg 6:11,24; 8:27,32; 9:5; 1Sa 13:17
18:24 [l]Jos 21:17; 1Sa 13:3,16; 14:5; 1Ki 15:22; 2Ki 23:8; Isa 10:29
18:25 [m]Jos 9:3 [n]S Jos 10:40; Jdg 4:5; 19:13; Isa 10:29; Jer 31:15; 40:1 [o]S Jos 9:17; Ezr 2:25; Ne 7:29
18:26 [p]S Jos 11:3 [q]Jos 9:17; Ezr 2:25; Ne 7:29
18:28 [r]2Sa 21:14 [s]S Jos 15:8 [t]S Jos 10:1 [u]S Jos 15:57 [v]S Jos 9:17 [w]Eze 48:23
19:1 [x]S Ge 49:7
19:2 [y]S Ge 21:14; 1Ki 19:3 [z]S Jos 15:26
19:3 [a]S Jos 15:28 [b]S Jos 15:29
19:4 [c]Jos 15:30 [d]S Nu 14:45
19:5 [e]S Jos 15:31
19:7 [f]S Jos 15:32 [g]S Jos 15:42
19:8 [h]S Jos 10:40
19:9 [i]S Ge 49:7 [j]Eze 48:24
19:10 [k]ver 16,27,34; Jos 21:7,34 [l]ver 12
19:11 [m]S Jos 12:22
19:12 [n]ver 10 [o]Jos 21:28; 1Ch 6:72
19:13 [p]S Jos 11:22 [q]Jos 15:32
19:14 [r]ver 27
19:15 [s]Jos 21:35 [t]Jos 11:1 [u]S Ge 35:19
19:16 [v]S ver 10 [w]Eze 48:26
19:17 [x]S Ge 30:18
19:18 [y]S Jos 15:56 [z]1Sa 28:4; 1Ki 1:3; 2Ki 4:8
19:20 [a]Jos 21:28
19:21 [b]S Jos 15:34
19:22 [c]Jdg 4:6,12; 8:18; Ps 89:12; Jer 46:18 [d]S Jos 15:10

[w]18 Septuagint; Hebrew *slope facing the Arabah* [x]19 That is, the Dead Sea
[y]2 Or *Beersheba, Sheba*; 1 Chron. 4:28 does not have *Sheba.*

the inheritance of the tribe of Issachar,[e] clan by clan.[f]

Allotment for Asher

24The fifth lot came out for the tribe of Asher,[g] clan by clan. 25Their territory included:

Helkath, Hali, Beten, Acshaph,[h] 26Allammelech, Amad and Mishal.[i] On the west the boundary touched Carmel[j] and Shihor Libnath. 27It then turned east toward Beth Dagon,[k] touched Zebulun[l] and the Valley of Iphtah El,[m] and went north to Beth Emek and Neiel, passing Cabul[n] on the left. 28It went to Abdon,[z][o] Rehob,[p] Hammon[q] and Kanah,[r] as far as Greater Sidon.[s] 29The boundary then turned back toward Ramah[t] and went to the fortified city of Tyre,[u] turned toward Hosah and came out at the sea[v] in the region of Aczib,[w] 30Ummah, Aphek[x] and Rehob.[y] There were twenty-two towns and their villages.

31These towns and their villages were the inheritance of the tribe of Asher,[z] clan by clan.

Allotment for Naphtali

32The sixth lot came out for Naphtali, clan by clan:

33Their boundary went from Heleph and the large tree in Zaanannim,[a] passing Adami Nekeb and Jabneel[b] to Lakkum and ending at the Jordan. 34The boundary ran west through Aznoth Tabor and came out at Hukkok.[c] It touched Zebulun[d] on the south, Asher on the west and the Jordan[a] on the east. 35The fortified cities were Ziddim, Zer, Hammath,[e] Rakkath, Kinnereth,[f] 36Adamah, Ramah,[g] Hazor,[h] 37Kedesh,[i] Edrei,[j] En Hazor, 38Iron, Migdal El, Horem, Beth Anath[k] and Beth Shemesh.[l] There were nineteen towns and their villages.

39These towns and their villages were the inheritance of the tribe of Naphtali, clan by clan.[m]

Allotment for Dan

40The seventh lot came out for the tribe of Dan, clan by clan. 41The territory of their inheritance included:

Zorah, Eshtaol,[n] Ir Shemesh, 42Shaalabbin, Aijalon,[o] Ithlah, 43Elon, Timnah,[p] Ekron,[q] 44Eltekeh, Gibbethon,[r] Baalath,[s] 45Jehud, Bene Berak, Gath Rimmon,[t] 46Me Jarkon and Rakkon, with the area facing Joppa.[u]

47(But the Danites had difficulty taking possession of their territory,[v] so they went up and attacked Leshem[w], took it, put it to the sword and occupied it. They settled in Leshem and named[x] it Dan after their forefather.)[y]

48These towns and their villages were the inheritance of the tribe of Dan,[z] clan by clan.

Allotment for Joshua

49When they had finished dividing the land into its allotted portions, the Israelites gave Joshua son of Nun an inheritance among them, 50as the LORD had commanded. They gave him the town he asked for—Timnath Serah[b][a] in the hill country of Ephraim. And he built up the town and settled there.

51These are the territories that Eleazar the priest, Joshua son of Nun and the heads of the tribal clans of Israel assigned by lot at Shiloh in the presence of the LORD at the entrance to the Tent of Meeting. And so they finished dividing[b] the land.[c]

Cities of Refuge

20:1-9Ref — Nu 35:9-34; Dt 4:41-43; 19:1-14

20 Then the LORD said to Joshua: 2"Tell the Israelites to designate the cities of refuge, as I instructed you through Moses, 3so that anyone who kills a person accidentally and unintentionally[d] may flee there and find protection from the avenger of blood.[e]

4"When he flees to one of these cities, he is to stand in the entrance of the city gate[f] and state his case before the elders[g] of that city. Then they are to admit him into their city and give

19:23 e Jos 17:10 f Ge 49:15; Eze 48:25
19:24 g S Jos 17:7
19:25 h S Jos 11:1
19:26 i Jos 21:30 j S Jos 12:22; 1Ki 18:19; 2Ki 2:25
19:27 k Jos 15:41 l S ver 10 m ver 14 n 1Ki 9:13
19:28 o Jos 21:30; 1Ch 6:74 p ver 30; Nu 13:21; Jos 21:31; Jdg 1:31 q 1Ch 6:76 r S Jos 16:8 s S Ge 10:19
19:29 t Jos 18:25 u 2Sa 5:11; 24:7; Ezr 3:7; Ps 45:12; Isa 23:1; Jer 25:22; Eze 26:2 v Jdg 5:17 w S Jos 15:44
19:30 x S Jos 12:18 y S ver 28
19:31 z S Ge 30:13; S Jos 17:7; Eze 48:2
19:33 a Jdg 4:11 b Jos 15:11
19:34 c 1Ch 6:75 d S ver 10
19:35 e 1Ch 2:55 f S Jos 11:2
19:36 g Jos 18:25 h S Jos 11:1
19:37 i S Jos 12:22 j S Nu 21:33
19:38 k Jdg 1:33 l S Jos 15:10
19:39 m Eze 48:3
19:41 n S Jos 15:33
19:42 o S Jos 10:12
19:43 p S Ge 38:12 q S Jos 13:3
19:44 r Jos 21:23; 1Ki 15:27; 16:15 s 1Ki 9:18; 2Ch 8:6
19:45 t Jos 21:24; 1Ch 6:69
19:46 u 2Ch 2:16; Ezr 3:7; Jnh 1:3; Ac 9:36
19:47 v Jdg 18:1 w Jdg 18:7,14 x S Dt 3:14 y Jdg 18:27,29
19:48 z S Ge 30:6
19:50 a Jos 24:30; Jdg 2:9
19:51 b Jos 23:4 c S Jos 14:1; S 18:10; Ac 13:19
20:3 d S Lev 4:2 e S Nu 35:12
20:4 f S Ge 23:10; Jer 38:7 g S Jos 7:6

[z] 28 Some Hebrew manuscripts (see also Joshua 21:30); most Hebrew manuscripts *Ebron* [a] 34 Septuagint; Hebrew *west, and Judah, the Jordan,* [b] 50 Also known as *Timnath Heres* (see Judges 2:9)

him a place to live with them. 5If the
avenger of blood pursues him, they
must not surrender the one accused,
because he killed his neighbor unintentionally and without malice aforethought. 6He is to stay in that city until
he has stood trial before the assembly[h] and until the death of the high
priest who is serving at that time. Then
he may go back to his own home in the
town from which he fled."
7So they set apart Kedesh[i] in Galilee in the hill country of Naphtali, Shechem[j] in the hill country of Ephraim,
and Kiriath Arba[k] (that is, Hebron[l])
in the hill country of Judah.[m] 8On the
east side of the Jordan of Jericho[c] they
designated Bezer[n] in the desert on the
plateau in the tribe of Reuben, Ramoth
in Gilead[o][p] in the tribe of Gad, and
Golan in Bashan[q] in the tribe of Manasseh. 9Any of the Israelites or any
alien living among them who killed
someone accidentally[r] could flee to
these designated cities and not be
killed by the avenger of blood prior to
standing trial before the assembly.[s]

Towns for the Levites

21:4–39pp — 1Ch 6:54–80

21 Now the family heads of the Levites approached Eleazar the
priest, Joshua son of Nun, and the
heads of the other tribal families of Israel[t] 2at Shiloh[u] in Canaan and said
to them, "The LORD commanded
through Moses that you give us
towns[v] to live in, with pasturelands
for our livestock."[w] 3So, as the LORD
had commanded, the Israelites gave
the Levites the following towns and
pasturelands out of their own inheritance:
4The first lot came out for the Kohathites,[x] clan by clan. The Levites
who were descendants of Aaron the
priest were allotted thirteen towns
from the tribes of Judah, Simeon and
Benjamin.[y] 5The rest of Kohath's
descendants were allotted ten towns
from the clans of the tribes of Ephraim,
Dan and half of Manasseh.[z]
6The descendants of Gershon[a]
were allotted thirteen towns from the
clans of the tribes of Issachar,[b] Asher,[c] Naphtali and the half-tribe of Manasseh in Bashan.
7The descendants of Merari,[d] clan
by clan, received twelve[e] towns from
the tribes of Reuben, Gad and Zebulun.[f]
8So the Israelites allotted to the Levites these towns and their pasturelands, as the LORD had commanded
through Moses.
9From the tribes of Judah and Simeon
they allotted the following towns by
name 10(these towns were assigned to
the descendants of Aaron who were
from the Kohathite clans of the Levites, because the first lot fell to them):
11They gave them Kiriath
Arba[g] (that is, Hebron[h]), with
its surrounding pastureland, in
the hill country of Judah. (Arba
was the forefather of Anak.)
12But the fields and villages
around the city they had given to
Caleb son of Jephunneh as his
possession.[i]
13So to the descendants of Aaron the priest they gave Hebron (a
city of refuge[j] for one accused of
murder), Libnah,[k] 14Jattir,[l]
Eshtemoa,[m] 15Holon,[n] Debir,[o]
16Ain,[p] Juttah[q] and Beth Shemesh,[r] together with their pasturelands—nine towns from
these two tribes.
17And from the tribe of Benjamin they gave them Gibeon,[s]
Geba,[t] 18Anathoth[u] and Almon,
together with their pasturelands—four towns.
19All the towns[v] for the priests, the
descendants of Aaron, were thirteen,
together with their pasturelands.[w]
20The rest of the Kohathite clans of the
Levites were allotted towns from the
tribe of Ephraim:
21In the hill country of Ephraim
they were given Shechem[x] (a city
of refuge for one accused of murder) and Gezer,[y] 22Kibzaim and
Beth Horon,[z] together with their
pasturelands—four towns.[a]
23Also from the tribe of Dan
they received Eltekeh, Gibbethon,[b] 24Aijalon[c] and Gath Rimmon,[d] together with their pasturelands—four towns.
25From half the tribe of Manasseh they received Taanach[e] and
Gath Rimmon, together with their
pasturelands—two towns.

20:6 [h] S Nu 35:12
20:7 [i] S Jos 12:22
[j] S Ge 12:6
[k] S Ge 35:27
[l] S Jos 10:36
[m] Lk 1:39
20:8 [n] Jos 21:36; 1Ch 6:78
[o] 1Ch 6:80
[p] S Jos 12:2
[q] S Jos 12:5; 1Ch 6:71
20:9 [r] S Lev 4:2
[s] S Ex 21:13
21:1 [t] Jos 14:1
21:2 [u] S Jos 18:1
[v] S Lev 25:32
[w] S Nu 35:2-3; S Jos 14:4
21:4 [x] Nu 3:17
[y] ver 19
21:5 [z] ver 26
21:6 [a] Nu 3:17
[b] S Ge 30:18
[c] S Jos 17:7
21:7 [d] S Ex 6:16
[e] ver 40
[f] S Jos 19:10
21:11 [g] S Ge 23:2
[h] S Jos 10:36
21:12
[i] S Jos 15:13
21:13 [j] Nu 35:6
[k] S Nu 33:20
21:14
[l] S Jos 15:48
[m] S Jos 15:50
21:15
[n] S Jos 15:51
[o] S Jos 10:3
21:16
[p] S Nu 34:11
[q] Jos 15:55
[r] S Jos 15:10
21:17 [s] S Jos 9:3
[t] S Jos 18:24; S Ne 11:31
21:18
[u] 2Sa 23:27; 1Ki 2:26; Ezr 2:23; Ne 7:27; 11:32; Isa 10:30; Jer 1:1; 11:21; 32:7
21:19
[v] 2Ch 31:15 [w] ver 4
21:21 [x] S Jos 17:7
[y] S Jos 10:33
21:22
[z] S Jos 10:10
[a] 1Sa 1:1
21:23
[b] S Jos 19:44
21:24
[c] S Jos 10:12
[d] S Jos 19:45
21:25
[e] S Jos 12:21

[c] 8 *Jordan of Jericho* was possibly an ancient name for the Jordan River.

26All these ten towns and their pasturelands were given to the rest of the
Kohathite clans.[f]

27The Levite clans of the Gershonites
were given:
from the half-tribe of Manasseh,
Golan in Bashan[g] (a city of refuge for one accused of murder[h])
and Be Eshtarah, together with
their pasturelands—two towns;
28from the tribe of Issachar,[i]
Kishion,[j] Daberath,[k] **29**Jarmuth[l] and En Gannim,[m] together with their pasturelands—four
towns;
30from the tribe of Asher,[n]
Mishal,[o] Abdon,[p] **31**Helkath
and Rehob,[q] together with their
pasturelands—four towns;
32from the tribe of Naphtali,
Kedesh[r] in Galilee (a city of refuge for one accused of murder[s]),
Hammoth Dor and Kartan, together with their pasturelands—three
towns.
33All the towns of the Gershonite[t]
clans were thirteen, together with
their pasturelands.

34The Merarite clans (the rest of the
Levites) were given:
from the tribe of Zebulun,[u]
Jokneam,[v] Kartah, **35**Dimnah
and Nahalal,[w] together with their
pasturelands—four towns;
36from the tribe of Reuben,
Bezer,[x] Jahaz,[y] **37**Kedemoth
and Mephaath,[z] together with
their pasturelands—four towns;
38from the tribe of Gad,
Ramoth[a] in Gilead[b] (a city of
refuge for one accused of murder), Mahanaim,[c] **39**Heshbon
and Jazer,[d] together with their
pasturelands—four towns in all.
40All the towns allotted to the Merarite
clans, who were the rest of the Levites,
were twelve.[e]
41The towns of the Levites in the
territory held by the Israelites were
forty-eight in all, together with their
pasturelands.[f] **42**Each of these towns
had pasturelands surrounding it; this
was true for all these towns.

43So the LORD gave Israel all the
land he had sworn to give their forefathers,[g] and they took possession[h] of
it and settled there.[i] **44**The LORD gave
them rest[j] on every side, just as he
had sworn to their forefathers. Not one
of their enemies[k] withstood them; the
LORD handed all their enemies[l] over to
them.[m] **45**Not one of all the LORD's
good promises[n] to the house of Israel
failed; every one was fulfilled.

Eastern Tribes Return Home

22 Then Joshua summoned the
Reubenites, the Gadites and
the half-tribe of Manasseh **2**and said to
them, "You have done all that Moses
the servant of the LORD commanded,[o]
and you have obeyed me in everything
I commanded. **3**For a long time now—
to this very day—you have not deserted your brothers but have carried out
the mission the LORD your God gave
you. **4**Now that the LORD your God has
given your brothers rest[p] as he promised, return to your homes[q] in the
land that Moses the servant of the LORD
gave you on the other side of the Jordan.[r] **5**But be very careful to keep the
commandment[s] and the law that Moses the servant of the LORD gave you:
to love the LORD[t] your God, to walk in
all his ways, to obey his commands,[u]
to hold fast to him and to serve him 1Sa 12:14-15
with all your heart and all your soul.[v]"
6Then Joshua blessed[w] them and
sent them away, and they went to their
homes. **7**(To the half-tribe of Manasseh
Moses had given land in Bashan,[x] and
to the other half of the tribe Joshua
gave land on the west side[y] of the Jordan with their brothers.) When Joshua
sent them home, he blessed them,[z]

21:26 [f]ver 5 **21:27** [g]S Jos 12:5 [h]Nu 35:6 **21:28** [i]S Ge 30:18 [j]Jos 19:20 [k]S Jos 19:12 **21:29** [l]S Jos 10:3 [m]S Jos 15:34 **21:30** [n]S Jos 17:7 [o]Jos 19:26 [p]S Jos 19:28 **21:31** [q]S Jos 19:28 **21:32** [r]S Jos 12:22 [s]Nu 35:6 **21:33** [t]ver 6 **21:34** [u]S Jos 19:10 [v]S Jos 12:22 **21:35** [w]Jos 19:15 **21:36** [x]S Jos 20:8 [y]S Nu 21:23; Dt 2:32; Jdg 11:20 **21:37** [z]S Jos 13:18 **21:38** [a]S Dt 4:43 [b]S Jos 12:2 [c]S Ge 32:2 **21:39** [d]S Jos 13:25 **21:40** [e]ver 7

21:41 [f]Nu 35:7 **21:43** [g]Dt 34:4 [h]Dt 11:31 [i]S Dt 17:14 **21:44** [j]S Ex 33:14 [k]S Dt 6:19 [l]S Ex 23:31 [m]Dt 21:10 **21:45** [n]Jos 23:14; Ne 9:8 **22:2** [o]S Nu 32:25 **22:4** [p]S Ex 33:14 [q]Nu 32:22; Dt 3:20 [r]Nu 32:18; S Jos 1:13-15 **22:5** [s]Isa 43:22; Mal 3:14 [t]Jos 23:11 [u]S Dt 5:29 [v]S Dt 6:5 **22:6** [w]S Ge 24:60; S Ex 39:43 **22:7** [x]S Nu 32:19; S Jos 12:5 [y]Jos 17:2 [z]S Jos 14:13; Lk 24:50

21:45 NOT ONE OF ALL THE LORD'S GOOD PROMISES . . . FAILED. Vv. 43–45 emphasize God's faithfulness in keeping his word to the forefathers (Ge 24:7; 26:3; 50:24), for he had given the promised land to Abraham's descendants. (1) Note that the book of Joshua presents the conquest of Canaan as both complete (10:40–42; 11:23; 12:7–24) and incomplete (13:2–6; 14:12; 17:12–18; 23:5). God was faithful in fulfilling his promise to the Israelites; yet they had to do their part in faithfully obeying the covenant, or they would fail to possess the land completely (1:6–9; 23:6–14).

(2) Likewise, under the new covenant God will faithfully fulfill all his promises to us as believers; yet we have to do our part in faithful obedience if we are to possess fully God's promises and kingdom (Lk 12:31). If receiving God's promises falls short, the failure lies with us, not with our Lord. It is God's desire to give his people the kingdom (cf. Lk 12:32).

8saying, "Return to your homes with
your great wealth—with large herds of
livestock,[a] with silver, gold, bronze
and iron,[b] and a great quantity of
clothing—and divide[c] with your
brothers the plunder[d] from your enemies."
9So the Reubenites, the Gadites and
the half-tribe of Manasseh left the Israelites at Shiloh[e] in Canaan to return
to Gilead,[f] their own land, which they
had acquired in accordance with the
command of the LORD through Moses.
10When they came to Geliloth[g] near
the Jordan in the land of Canaan, the
Reubenites, the Gadites and the half-
tribe of Manasseh built an imposing altar[h] there by the Jordan. 11And when
the Israelites heard that they had built
the altar on the border of Canaan at
Geliloth near the Jordan on the Israelite side, 12the whole assembly of Israel
gathered at Shiloh[i] to go to war
against them.
13So the Israelites sent Phinehas[j]
son of Eleazar,[k] the priest, to the land
of Gilead—to Reuben, Gad and the
half-tribe of Manasseh. 14With him
they sent ten of the chief men, one for
each of the tribes of Israel, each the
head of a family division among the Israelite clans.[l]
15When they went to Gilead—to
Reuben, Gad and the half-tribe of Manasseh—they said to them: 16"The
whole assembly of the LORD says: 'How
could you break faith[m] with the God of
Israel like this? How could you turn
away from the LORD and build yourselves an altar in rebellion[n] against
him now? 17Was not the sin of Peor[o]
enough for us? Up to this very day we
have not cleansed ourselves from that
sin, even though a plague fell on the
community of the LORD! 18And are you
now turning away from the LORD?
" 'If you rebel against the LORD today, tomorrow he will be angry with
the whole community[p] of Israel. 19If
the land you possess is defiled, come
over to the LORD's land, where the
LORD's tabernacle[q] stands, and share
the land with us. But do not rebel
against the LORD or against us by building an altar[r] for yourselves, other
than the altar of the LORD our God.
20When Achan son of Zerah acted unfaithfully regarding the devoted
things,[d][s] did not wrath[t] come upon
the whole community[u] of Israel? He
was not the only one who died for his
sin.' "[v]
21Then Reuben, Gad and the half-
tribe of Manasseh replied to the heads
of the clans of Israel: 22"The Mighty
One, God, the LORD! The Mighty One,
God,[w] the LORD![x] He knows![y] And
let Israel know! If this has been in rebellion or disobedience to the LORD, do
not spare us this day. 23If we have built
our own altar to turn away from the
LORD and to offer burnt offerings and
grain offerings,[z] or to sacrifice fellowship offerings[e] on it, may the LORD
himself call us to account.[a]
24"No! We did it for fear that some
day your descendants might say to
ours, 'What do you have to do with the
LORD, the God of Israel? 25The LORD has
made the Jordan a boundary between
us and you—you Reubenites and Gadites! You have no share in the LORD.' So
your descendants might cause ours to
stop fearing the LORD.
26"That is why we said, 'Let us get
ready and build an altar—but not for
burnt offerings or sacrifices.' 27On the
contrary, it is to be a witness[b] between us and you and the generations
that follow, that we will worship the
LORD at his sanctuary with our burnt

22:8 [a] S Dt 20:14 [b] S Nu 31:22 [c] S Nu 31:27 [d] S Ge 49:27; 1Sa 30:16; 2Sa 1:1; Isa 9:3 **22:9** [e] Jos 18:1 [f] S Nu 32:26 **22:10** [g] Jos 18:17 [h] ver 19,26-27; Isa 19:19; 56:7 **22:12** [i] Jos 18:1 **22:13** [j] S Nu 25:7 [k] Nu 3:32; Jos 24:33 **22:14** [l] ver 32; S Nu 1:4 **22:16** [m] S Dt 7:3; 1Sa 13:13; 15:11 [n] Dt 12:13-14 **22:17** [o] S Nu 23:28; 25:1-9 **22:18** [p] S Lev 10:6 **22:19** [q] S Ex 26:1 [r] S ver 10 **22:20** [s] Jos 7:1 [t] Ps 7:11 [u] Lev 10:6 [v] Jos 7:5 **22:22** [w] S Dt 10:17 [x] Ps 50:1 [y] 1Sa 2:3; 16:7; 1Ki 8:39; 1Ch 28:9; Ps 11:4; 40:9; 44:21; 139:4; Jer 17:10 **22:23** [z] Jer 41:5 [a] S Dt 12:11; S 18:19; 1Sa 20:16 **22:27** [b] S Ge 21:30; Jos 24:27; Isa 19:20

[d] *20* The Hebrew term refers to the irrevocable giving over of things or persons to the LORD, often by totally destroying them.
[e] *23* Traditionally *peace offerings*; also in verse 27

22:12 GO TO WAR AGAINST THEM. The children of Israel were ready to go to war against some of their brothers because they believed they had built an altar in rebellion against the Lord (vv. 10–11). Note the following elements: (1) Joshua and the Israelites felt that God's holiness and truth were being abandoned (vv. 12,16,18; cf. Lev 17:8–9; Dt 13:12–15); they were willing to fight their own people in order to defend God's truth and purity (cf. Eph 4:15).

(2) To demonstrate their love for their fellow Israelites, Joshua and the children of Israel first sent a delegation to try to resolve the problem and achieve reconciliation (vv. 13–20).

(3) Understanding and reconciliation were accomplished without war (vv. 21–34), and both faithfulness to God and love for others were upheld.

(4) Truth and love continue under the new covenant. Believers must stand for God's truth and holiness without compromise, while at the same time acting in love toward those they must oppose (see Eph 4:15, note).

offerings, sacrifices and fellowship offerings.[c] Then in the future your descendants will not be able to say to ours, 'You have no share in the LORD.'

28"And we said, 'If they ever say this to us, or to our descendants, we will answer: Look at the replica of the LORD's altar, which our fathers built, not for burnt offerings and sacrifices, but as a witness[d] between us and you.'

29"Far be it from us to rebel[e] against the LORD and turn away from him today by building an altar for burnt offerings, grain offerings and sacrifices, other than the altar of the LORD our God that stands before his tabernacle.[f]"

30When Phinehas the priest and the leaders of the community—the heads of the clans of the Israelites—heard what Reuben, Gad and Manasseh had to say, they were pleased. **31**And Phinehas son of Eleazar, the priest, said to Reuben, Gad and Manasseh, "Today we know that the LORD is with us,[g] because you have not acted unfaithfully toward the LORD in this matter. Now you have rescued the Israelites from the LORD's hand."

32Then Phinehas son of Eleazar, the priest, and the leaders returned to Canaan from their meeting with the Reubenites and Gadites in Gilead and reported to the Israelites.[h] **33**They were glad to hear the report and praised God.[i] And they talked no more about going to war against them to devastate the country where the Reubenites and the Gadites lived.

34And the Reubenites and the Gadites gave the altar this name: A Witness[j] Between Us that the LORD is God.

22:27 [c]S Dt 12:6 **22:28** [d]S Ge 21:30 **22:29** [e]Jos 24:16 [f]S Ex 26:1 **22:31** [g]2Ch 15:2 **22:32** [h]S ver 14 **22:33** [i]1Ch 29:20; Da 2:19; Lk 2:28 **22:34** [j]S Ge 21:30

23:1 [k]S Dt 12:9; Jos 21:44 [l]S Jos 13:1 **23:2** [m]S Jos 7:6 [n]Jos 24:1 [o]S Jos 13:1 **23:3** [p]S Ex 14:14; S Dt 20:4 **23:4** [q]Jos 19:51 [r]S Nu 34:2; Ps 78:55 [s]S Nu 34:6 **23:5** [t]ver 13; Jdg 2:21 [u]Ps 44:5; Jer 46:15 [v]Ex 23:30 **23:6** [w]S Dt 28:61 [x]S Dt 17:20 [y]Jos 1:7 **23:7** [z]Ex 23:13; Jer 5:7; 12:16 [a]S Ex 20:5 **23:8** [b]S Dt 10:20 **23:9** [c]Dt 11:23 [d]Dt 7:24 **23:10** [e]Lev 26:8; Jdg 3:31 [f]S Ex 14:14 **23:11** [g]S Dt 4:15 [h]Jos 22:5

Joshua's Farewell to the Leaders

23 After a long time had passed and the LORD had given Israel rest[k] from all their enemies around them, Joshua, by then old and well advanced in years,[l] **2**summoned all Israel—their elders,[m] leaders, judges and officials[n]—and said to them: "I am old and well advanced in years.[o] **3**You yourselves have seen everything the LORD your God has done to all these nations for your sake; it was the LORD your God who fought for you.[p] **4**Remember how I have allotted[q] as an inheritance[r] for your tribes all the land of the nations that remain—the nations I conquered—between the Jordan and the Great Sea[f][s] in the west. **5**The LORD your God himself will drive them out[t] of your way. He will push them out[u] before you, and you will take possession of their land, as the LORD your God promised you.[v]

6"Be very strong; be careful to obey all that is written in the Book of the Law[w] of Moses, without turning aside[x] to the right or to the left.[y] **7**Do not associate with these nations that remain among you; do not invoke the names of their gods or swear[z] by them. You must not serve them or bow down[a] to them. **8**But you are to hold fast to the LORD[b] your God, as you have until now.

9"The LORD has driven out before you great and powerful nations;[c] to this day no one has been able to withstand you.[d] **10**One of you routs a thousand,[e] because the LORD your God fights for you,[f] just as he promised. **11**So be very careful[g] to love the LORD[h] your God. 

12"But if you turn away and ally

[f]4 That is, the Mediterranean

22:34 A WITNESS . . . THAT THE LORD IS GOD. The altar erected on the east side of the Jordan was to function as a witness and memorial to future generations that those tribes were bound to remain faithful to the Lord and to serve only him. Visible ties of faith passed on between generations, such as a special Bible, a gift, a photo, a memorial or a family tradition, can similarly remind Christians and their children of their commitment to God.

23:11 LOVE THE LORD. Joshua exhorted Israel to cling to the Lord and love him diligently, just as he had loved them (cf. Dt 7:7,13; 11:1; 19:9). Love for and gratitude to God provided the inner motivation for them to obey his word (v. 6) and to remain separate from the ungodly ways of the nations (vv. 7,12). NT believers are called to the same kind of love and commitment (cf. Mt 22:37; Mk 12:30; Jn 14:15; Gal 5:6; 1Jn 4:19).

23:12 ALLY YOURSELVES WITH . . . THESE NATIONS. With Baal as one of the principal male deities, the religion of the Canaanites was most degrading. (1) Their religion promoted both female and male cult prostitution, and their worship consisted in immoral orgies and sexual acts. Their prophets and priests were the official murderers of little children, sacrificing newborn babies in their temples (see article on THE DESTRUCTION OF THE CANAANITES, p. 310). (2) God knew that if his people associated with the Canaanites, they

yourselves with the survivors of these nations that remain among you and if you intermarry with them[i] and associate with them,[j] **13**then you may be sure that the LORD your God will no longer drive out[k] these nations before you. Instead, they will become snares[l] and traps for you, whips on your backs and thorns in your eyes,[m] until you perish from this good land,[n]
1Ki 19:18 which the LORD your God has given you.

14"Now I am about to go the way of all the earth.[o] You know with all your heart and soul that not one of all the good promises the LORD your God gave you has failed. Every promise[p] has been fulfilled; not one has failed.[q] **15**But just as every good promise[r] of the LORD your God has come true, so the LORD will bring on you all the evil[s] he has threatened, until he has destroyed you[t] from this good land he has given you.[u] **16**If you violate the covenant of the LORD your God, which he commanded you, and go and serve other gods and bow down to them, the LORD's anger will burn against you, and you will quickly perish from the good land he has given you.[v]"

The Covenant Renewed at Shechem

24 Then Joshua assembled[w] all the tribes of Israel at Shechem.[x] He summoned[y] the elders,[z] leaders, judges and officials of Israel,[a] and they presented themselves before God.

2Joshua said to all the people, "This is what the LORD, the God of Israel, says: 'Long ago your forefathers, including Terah the father of Abraham and Nahor,[b] lived beyond the River[g] and worshiped other gods.[c] **3**But I took your father Abraham from the land beyond the River and led him throughout Canaan[d] and gave him many descendants.[e] I gave him Isaac,[f] **4**and to Isaac I gave Jacob and Esau.[g] I assigned the hill country of Seir[h] to Esau, but Jacob and his sons went down to Egypt.[i]

5" 'Then I sent Moses and Aaron,[j] and I afflicted the Egyptians by what I did there, and I brought you out.[k] **6**When I brought your fathers out of Egypt, you came to the sea,[l] and the Egyptians pursued them with chariots and horsemen[h][m] as far as the Red Sea.[i][n] **7**But they cried[o] to the LORD for help, and he put darkness[p] between you and the Egyptians; he brought the sea over them and covered them.[q] You saw with your own eyes what I did to the Egyptians.[r] Then you lived in the desert for a long time.[s]

8" 'I brought you to the land of the Amorites[t] who lived east of the Jordan. They fought against you, but I gave them into your hands. I destroyed them from before you, and you took possession of their land.[u] **9**When Balak son of Zippor,[v] the king of Moab, prepared to fight against Israel, he sent for Balaam son of Beor[w] to put a curse on you.[x] **10**But I would not listen to Balaam, so he blessed you[y] again and again, and I delivered you out of his hand.

11" 'Then you crossed the Jordan[z] and came to Jericho.[a] The citizens of Jericho fought against you, as did also the Amorites, Perizzites,[b] Canaanites, Hittites, Girgashites, Hivites and Jebusites,[c] but I gave them into your hands.[d] **12**I sent the hornet[e] ahead of you, which drove them out[f] before

23:12 [i] S Ge 34:9 [j] S Ex 34:16; Ps 106:34-35
23:13 [k] S ver 5 [l] S Ex 10:7 [m] S Nu 33:55 [n] Dt 1:8; 1Ki 9:7; 2Ki 25:21
23:14 [o] 1Ki 2:2 [p] Ps 119:140; 145:13 [q] S Jos 21:45
23:15 [r] 1Ki 8:56; Jer 33:14 [s] 1Ki 14:10; 2Ki 22:16; Isa 24:6; 34:5; 43:28; Jer 6:19; 11:8; 35:17; 39:16; Mal 4:6 [t] Jos 24:20 [u] Lev 26:17; Dt 28:15; Jer 40:2
23:16 [v] Dt 4:25-26
24:1 [w] Ge 49:2 [x] S Ge 12:6 [y] 1Sa 12:7; 1Ki 8:14 [z] Jos 7:6 [a] Jos 23:2
24:2 [b] Ge 11:26 [c] Ge 11:32
24:3 [d] S Ge 12:1 [e] S Ge 1:28; S 12:2 [f] S Ge 21:3
24:4 [g] S Ge 25:26 [h] S Ge 14:6; S Nu 24:18 [i] Ge 46:5-6
24:5 [j] S Ex 3:10 [k] Ex 12:51
24:6 [l] S Ex 14:22 [m] S Ex 14:9 [n] Ex 14:23
24:7 [o] S Ex 14:10 [p] Ex 14:20 [q] S Ex 14:28 [r] S Ex 19:4 [s] Dt 1:46
24:8 [t] S Ex 23:23 [u] S Nu 21:31
24:9 [v] Nu 22:2 [w] S Nu 23:7 [x] S Nu 22:6
24:10 [y] S Nu 23:11; S Dt 23:5
24:11 [z] S Ex 14:29 [a] Jos 6:1 [b] S Jos 3:10 [c] S Ge 15:18-21 [d] Ex 23:23; Dt 7:1
24:12 [e] S Ex 23:28; Ps 44:3,6-7 [f] S Ex 23:31

[g] *2* That is, the Euphrates; also in verses 3, 14 and 15 [h] *6* Or *charioteers* [i] *6* Hebrew *Yam Suph*; that is, Sea of Reeds

too would adopt those shameful ways. God's call for the separation of his people from the ungodly world remains the same in the NT (see article on THE CHRISTIAN'S RELATIONSHIP TO THE WORLD, p. 1976).

23:13 YOU MAY BE SURE. God's promises were not unconditional for the Israelites. Love for God expressed in obedience to his commandments, faith in his provision and separation from the ungodly were the conditions for his blessings, fellowship and strength (vv. 3–13). God himself provided the grace necessary for maintaining the covenant fellowship between God and the people.

24:1 ASSEMBLED ALL THE TRIBES. At the end of his life, Joshua called all the people together one final time to lead them in a ceremony of covenant renewal in which they committed themselves to serve the Lord in faithfulness and loyal devotion. He did not focus on himself as their leader; rather, he drew attention to God's past goodness to and care of Israel (vv. 2–13) and repeatedly urged them to remain loyal to the Lord (vv. 14–28). Genuine leaders of God's people must share Joshua's concern for God's honor. They must exhort the people to love the Lord, serve him only and remain separated from the world.

you—also the two Amorite kings. You
did not do it with your own sword and
bow.[g] 13So I gave you a land[h] on
which you did not toil and cities you did
not build; and you live in them and eat
from vineyards and olive groves that
you did not plant.'[i]
14"Now fear the LORD[j] and serve
him with all faithfulness.[k] Throw
away the gods[l] your forefathers worshiped beyond the River and in
Egypt,[m] and serve the LORD. 15But if
serving the LORD seems undesirable to
you, then choose for yourselves this
day whom you will serve, whether the
gods your forefathers served beyond
the River, or the gods of the Amorites,[n] in whose land you are living.
But as for me and my household,[o] we
will serve the LORD."[p]
16Then the people answered, "Far be
it from us to forsake[q] the LORD to
serve other gods! 17It was the LORD our
God himself who brought us and our
fathers up out of Egypt, from that land
of slavery,[r] and performed those
great signs[s] before our eyes. He protected us on our entire journey and
among all the nations through which
we traveled. 18And the LORD drove
out[t] before us all the nations,[u] including the Amorites, who lived in the
land.[v] We too will serve the LORD, because he is our God.[w]"
19Joshua said to the people, "You are
not able to serve the LORD. He is a holy
God;[x] he is a jealous God.[y] He will
not forgive[z] your rebellion[a] and your
sins. 20If you forsake the LORD[b] and
serve foreign gods, he will turn[c] and
bring disaster[d] on you and make an
end of you,[e] after he has been good to
you."
21But the people said to Joshua, "No!
We will serve the LORD."
22Then Joshua said, "You are witnesses[f] against yourselves that you
have chosen[g] to serve the LORD."
"Yes, we are witnesses,[h]" they replied.
23"Now then," said Joshua, "throw
away the foreign gods[i] that are
among you and yield your hearts[j] to
the LORD, the God of Israel."
24And the people said to Joshua,
"We will serve the LORD our God and
obey him."[k]
25On that day Joshua made a covenant[l] for the people, and there at
Shechem[m] he drew up for them decrees and laws.[n] 26And Joshua recorded[o] these things in the Book of
the Law of God.[p] Then he took a large
stone[q] and set it up there under the
oak[r] near the holy place of the LORD.
27"See!" he said to all the people.
"This stone[s] will be a witness[t]
against us. It has heard all the words
the LORD has said to us. It will be a
witness against you if you are untrue[u]
to your God."[v]

Buried in the Promised Land

24:29–31pp — Jdg 2:6–9

28Then Joshua sent the people away,
each to his own inheritance.[w]
29After these things, Joshua son of
Nun, the servant of the LORD, died[x] at

24:12 [g]Ps 135:11 **24:13** [h]Ex 6:8 [i]Dt 6:10-11 **24:14** [j]1Sa 12:14; Job 23:15; Ps 19:9; 119:120 [k]Dt 10:12; 18:13; 1Sa 12:24; 2Co 1:12 [l]ver 23; S Ge 31:19; Ex 12:12; 18:11; 20:3; Nu 25:2; Dt 11:28; Jdg 10:16; Ru 1:15; Isa 55:7 [m]Eze 23:3 **24:15** [n]Jdg 6:10; Ru 1:15 [o]S Ge 35:2 [p]Ru 1:16; 2:12; 1Ki 18:21; Da 3:18 **24:16** [q]Jos 22:29 **24:17** [r]Jdg 6:8 [s]S Ex 10:1 **24:18** [t]S Ex 23:31 [u]S Dt 33:27 [v]Ac 7:45 [w]S Ge 28:21 **24:19** [x]S Lev 11:44; S 20:26 [y]S Ex 20:5 [z]S Ex 34:7 [a]S Ex 23:21 **24:20** [b]1Ch 28:9, 20; 2Ch 24:18 [c]Ac 7:42 [d]1Sa 12:25; Hos 13:11 [e]Jos 23:15 **24:22** [f]ver 27; Ru 4:10; Isa 8:2; 43:10; 44:8; Jer 42:5; Mal 2:14 [g]Ps 119:30,173 [h]S Dt 25:9 **24:23** [i]S ver 14 [j]1Ki 8:58; Ps 119:36; 141:4; Jer 31:33 **24:24** [k]Ex 19:8; Jer 42:6 **24:25** [l]S Ex 24:8 [m]S Jos 17:7 [n]Ex 15:25 **24:26** [o]S Dt 17:18 [p]S Dt 28:61; S 31:24 [q]S Ge 28:18; S Dt 27:2 [r]S Ge 12:6; S Jdg 4:11 **24:27** [s]S Ge 28:18; Hab 2:11 [t]S ver 22; S Ge 21:30; S Jos 22:27 [u]S Jos 7:11 [v]S Nu 11:20; S Pr 30:9 **24:28** [w]Jdg 21:23,24 **24:29** [x]Jdg 1:1

24:15 AS FOR ME AND MY HOUSEHOLD, WE WILL SERVE THE LORD. Inherent in the salvation provided by God is the issue of personal choice. Each believer must continually choose whom he or she will serve. As with Joshua and the Israelites, serving the Lord is not merely a one-time choice (cf. 1:16–18; Dt 30:19–20); we must choose time after time to persevere in the faith and to obey the Lord. The renewal of right choices by the believer involves the fear of the Lord, loyalty to the truth, obedience from a sincere heart and the renunciation of sin with its associated pleasures (vv. 14–16). Failure to choose to serve and love the Lord will eventually result in judgment and destruction (v. 20; 23:11–13).

24:16 FAR BE IT FROM US TO FORSAKE THE LORD. The people's promise to serve only the Lord was kept, but only as long as Joshua and the elders lived. Not long after Joshua's death the people forsook the Lord and began serving other gods (Jdg 2:11–19).

24:25 JOSHUA MADE A COVENANT FOR THE PEOPLE. The renewal of the covenant between the Lord and Israel involved a twofold commitment: (1) God committed himself to care for his people, and (2) the Israelites committed themselves to serve the Lord God alone. It was a permanent and binding contract between Israel and God. Under the new covenant established by Christ's death, believers have also made a commitment to follow Christ in repentance, faith and obedience. He in return has committed himself to be our Lord and Savior and to lead us to a heavenly home with the Father. As with Israel, God first came to us in mercy and grace and established the terms of the new covenant; we, like Israel of old, must live under the terms of the covenant (see article on THE OLD COVENANT AND THE NEW COVENANT, p. 1926).

the age of a hundred and ten.[y] 30And
they buried him in the land of his inheritance, at Timnath Serah[j][z] in the hill
country of Ephraim, north of Mount
Gaash.[a]
31Israel served the LORD throughout
the lifetime of Joshua and of the elders[b] who outlived him and who had
experienced everything the LORD had
done for Israel.
32And Joseph's bones,[c] which the
Israelites had brought up from
Egypt,[d] were buried at Shechem in
the tract of land[e] that Jacob bought
for a hundred pieces of silver[k] from
the sons of Hamor, the father of Shechem. This became the inheritance of
Joseph's descendants.
33And Eleazar son of Aaron[f] died
and was buried at Gibeah,[g] which had
been allotted to his son Phinehas[h] in
the hill country[i] of Ephraim.

24:29 [y] S Ge 50:22 **24:30** [z] S Jos 19:50 [a] 2Sa 23:30 **24:31** [b] Jos 7:6 **24:32** [c] Heb 11:22 [d] S Ge 47:29-30 [e] Ge 33:19; Jn 4:5; Ac 7:16 **24:33** [f] S Jos 22:13 [g] S Jos 15:57 [h] S Ex 6:25 [i] 1Sa 9:4; 1Ki 4:8

[j] *30* Also known as *Timnath Heres* (see Judges 2:9) [k] *32* Hebrew *hundred kesitahs*; a kesitah was a unit of money of unknown weight and value.

JUDGES

Outline

I. Israel's Disobedience and Apostasy Introduced (1:1—3:6)
   A. Israel Fails to Purge the Land (1:1—2:5)
   B. Israel Experiences a Downward Spiral (2:6—3:6)
II. History of Israel's Foreign Oppression and Delivering Judges (3:7—16:31)
   A. Mesopotamian Oppression / Othniel's Deliverance (3:7–11)
   B. Moabite Oppression / Ehud's Deliverance (3:12–30)
   C. Philistine Oppression / Shamgar's Deliverance (3:31)
   D. Canaanite Oppression / Deborah-Barak's Deliverance (4:1—5:31)
   E. Midianite Oppression / Gideon's Deliverance (6:1—8:35)
   F. Hard Times Under Abimelech, Tola and Jair (9:1—10:5)
   G. Ammonite Oppression / Jephthah's Deliverance (10:6—12:7)
   H. Minor Judges—Ibzan, Elon and Abdon (12:8–15)
   I. Philistine Oppression / Samson's Life (13:1—16:31)
      1. Samson's Birth and Calling (13:1–25)
      2. Samson's Marriage to an Unbeliever (14:1–20)
      3. Samson's Exploits (15:1–20)
      4. Samson's Downfall and Restoration (16:1–31)
III. Illustrations of Israel's Spiritual, Moral and Social Chaos (17:1—21:25)
   A. Idolatry (17:1—18:31)
      1. An Example of Personal Idolatry (17:1–13)
      2. An Example of Tribal Idolatry (18:1–31)
   B. Immorality (19:1–30)
      1. An Example of Personal Immorality (19:1–9)
      2. An Example of Tribal Immorality (19:10–30)
   C. Tribal Strife (20:1—21:25)

Author: Anonymous

Theme: Apostasy and Deliverance

Date of Writing: c. 1050–1000 B.C.

Background

The book of Judges is the main historical link between Joshua and the time of Israel's kings. The period of the judges dates from about 1375 to 1050 B.C., during which time Israel was a confederacy of tribes. The book derives its name from the individuals whom God raised up periodically to lead and deliver the Israelites after they had backslidden and fallen under the oppression of foreign neighbors. The judges (13 are mentioned in this book) came from different tribes and functioned as military leaders and civil magistrates; many remained tribal in their sphere of influence, while some served the whole territory of Israel. Samuel, generally regarded as the last of the judges and the first of the prophets, is not included in this book.

The authorship of Judges is uncertain. The book itself indicates the following time frame for its composition: (1) its writing occurred after the removal of the ark from Shiloh at the time of Eli and Samuel (18:31; 20:27; cf. 1Sa 4:3–11); (2) the author's frequent reference to the time of the judges by stating that "in those days Israel had no king" (17:6; 18:1; 19:1; 21:25) suggests that Israel's monarchy already existed when the book was written; (3) Jerusalem had not yet been taken from the Jebusites (1:21; cf. 2Sa 5:7). These three clues indicate the book was completed sometime after the beginning of King Saul's reign (c. 1050 B.C.) but before King David captured Jerusalem (c. 1000 B.C.). The Jewish Talmud associates the origin of the book with Samuel, which is a real possibility.

This much is certain: the book records and evaluates the period of the judges from the perspective of the covenant (e.g., 2:1–5). Moses had prophesied that oppression from foreign nations would come on the Israelites as one of God's curses if they departed from the covenant (Dt 28:25,33,48). The book of Judges underscores the historical reality of that prophecy.

Purpose

Historically, Judges provides the main record of Israel's history in the promised land from Joshua's death to the time of Samuel. Theologically, it reveals the spiritual and moral decline of the tribes after settling in the promised land, showing clearly the adverse consequences that always occurred when Israel forgot its covenant with the Lord and went instead in the direction of idolatry and immorality.

Survey

Judges divides into three basic sections. (1) Section one (1:1—3:6) records Israel's failure to thoroughly complete the conquest and describes its downward direction after Joshua's death. (2) Section two (3:7—16:31) comprises the main body of the book. It records six examples of Israel's recurring experience during the time of the judges involving cycles of apostasy, foreign oppression, servitude, crying out to God in distress, and God delivering the Israelites through leaders anointed by his Spirit. Among the 13 judges (all are included in this section of the book), the best known are Deborah and Barak (as a team), Gideon, Jephthah and Samson (cf. Heb 11:32). (3) Section three (17:1—21:25) closes with vivid stories from the time of the judges that illustrate the depth of moral and social corruption resulting from Israel's spiritual apostasy. The book reminds us that the only lesson we as humans learn consistently from history is that we do not learn from history.

Special Features

Six major features characterize the book of Judges. (1) It records events in Israel's turbulent history between the conquest of Palestine and the beginning of the monarchy. (2) It underscores three simple but profound truths: (a) to be God's people means that God must be King and Lord of his people; (b) sin is always destructive to God's people; and (c) when God's people humble themselves, pray and turn from their wicked ways, he will hear from heaven and heal their land (cf. 2Ch 7:14). (3) It emphasizes that whenever Israel lost sight of her identity as the covenant people under God's kingship, the nation plunged into repeated cycles of spiritual, moral and social chaos with the result that "everyone did as he saw fit" (21:25; cf. 17:6). (4) It reveals several oft-repeated patterns that occur in the history of God's people under both covenants: (a) unless God's people give him their whole hearts in loving obedience and diligent spiritual vigilance, their hearts become hardened and unresponsive to God, leading to backsliding and eventual apostasy; (b) God is long-suffering, and whenever his people cry out in repentance, he is merciful to restore them by raising up Spirit-endowed and empowered individuals to deliver them from sin's oppressive judgment; and (c) the very anointed leaders whom God uses to deliver his people often become corrupt themselves because of a fundamental deficiency in humility, character or righteousness. (5) The six major cycles in the book involving apostasy, oppression, distress and deliverance all begin in the same way: "the Israelites did evil in the eyes of the LORD" (e.g., 2:11; 3:7). (6) The book reveals that God used foreign nations that were more evil than his own people in order to judge the latter for their sins and to bring about their repentance and revival. Only this intervention of God kept the Israelites from completely being absorbed by the paganism all around them.

New Testament Fulfillment

The book of Judges reveals an enduring divine principle: when God uses a person greatly in his service, the Spirit of the Lord comes upon him or her (3:10; cf. 6:34; 11:29; 14:6,19; 15:14). At the outset of Jesus' ministry, the Spirit descended on him at his baptism (Mt 3:16; Lk 3:21–22a). Before ascending to his Father, Jesus instructed his disciples to wait for the gift promised by the Father—i.e., the Spirit (Ac 1:4–5); the reason given was that they would receive power when the Holy Spirit came on them (Ac 1:8; cf. 4:33). Under both covenants, God's way of overthrowing the enemy and advancing his kingdom is by the energy, strength and power of the Holy Spirit working through yielded and obedient human vessels.

Reading Judges

In order to read the entire Old Testament in one year, the book of Judges should be read in 10 days, according to the following schedule: ☐ 1–2 ☐ 3–4 ☐ 5–6 ☐ 7–8 ☐ 9 ☐ 10–11 ☐ 12–13 ☐ 14–16 ☐ 17–18 ☐ 19–21

NOTES

Israel Fights the Remaining Canaanites

1:11–15pp — Jos 15:15–19

1 After the death[a] of Joshua, the Israelites asked the LORD, "Who will
be the first[b] to go up and fight for us
against the Canaanites?[c]"
2 The LORD answered, "Judah[d] is to
go; I have given the land into their
hands.[e]"
3 Then the men of Judah said to the
Simeonites their brothers, "Come up
with us into the territory allotted to us,
to fight against the Canaanites. We in
turn will go with you into yours." So
the Simeonites[f] went with them.
4 When Judah attacked, the LORD
gave the Canaanites and Perizzites[g]
into their hands and they struck down
ten thousand men at Bezek.[h] 5 It was
there that they found Adoni-Bezek[i]
and fought against him, putting to rout
the Canaanites and Perizzites. 6 Adoni-
Bezek fled, but they chased him and
caught him, and cut off his thumbs and
big toes.
7 Then Adoni-Bezek said, "Seventy
kings with their thumbs and big toes
cut off have picked up scraps under my table. Now God has paid me
back[j] for what I did to them." They
brought him to Jerusalem,[k] and he
died there.
8 The men of Judah attacked Jerusalem[l] also and took it. They put the
city to the sword and set it on fire.
9 After that, the men of Judah went
down to fight against the Canaanites
living in the hill country,[m] the Negev[n]
and the western foothills. 10 They advanced against the Canaanites living in
Hebron[o] (formerly called Kiriath
Arba[p]) and defeated Sheshai, Ahiman
and Talmai.[q]
11 From there they advanced against
the people living in Debir[r] (formerly
called Kiriath Sepher). 12 And Caleb
said, "I will give my daughter Acsah in
marriage to the man who attacks and
captures Kiriath Sepher." 13 Othniel
son of Kenaz, Caleb's younger brother,
took it; so Caleb gave his daughter Acsah to him in marriage.
14 One day when she came to Othniel, she urged him[a] to ask her father
for a field. When she got off her donkey, Caleb asked her, "What can I do
for you?"
15 She replied, "Do me a special favor. Since you have given me land in
the Negev, give me also springs of water." Then Caleb gave her the upper
and lower springs.[s]
16 The descendants of Moses' father-
in-law,[t] the Kenite,[u] went up from
the City of Palms[b][v] with the men of
Judah to live among the people of the
Desert of Judah in the Negev near
Arad.[w]
17 Then the men of Judah went with
the Simeonites[x] their brothers and attacked the Canaanites living in Ze-
phath, and they totally destroyed[c] the
city. Therefore it was called Hormah.[d][y] 18 The men of Judah also
took[e] Gaza,[z] Ashkelon[a] and Ekron—each city with its territory.
19 The LORD was with[b] the men of
Judah. They took possession of the hill
country,[c] but they were unable to
drive the people from the plains, because they had iron chariots.[d] 20 As
Moses had promised, Hebron[e] was
given to Caleb, who drove from it the
three sons of Anak.[f] 21 The Benjamites, however, failed[g] to dislodge
the Jebusites, who were living in Jerusalem;[h] to this day the Jebusites live
there with the Benjamites.
22 Now the house of Joseph[i] attacked Bethel,[j] and the LORD was with
them. 23 When they sent men to spy out
Bethel (formerly called Luz),[k] 24 the
spies saw a man coming out of the city
and they said to him, "Show us how to
get into the city and we will see that

1:1 [a]Jos 24:29 [b]S Nu 2:3-9; Jdg 20:18; 1Ki 20:14 [c]ver 27; S Ge 10:18; Jdg 3:1-6
1:2 [d]S Ge 49:10 [e]ver 4; Jdg 3:28; 4:7,14; 7:9
1:3 [f]ver 17
1:4 [g]S Ge 13:7; S Jos 3:10 [h]1Sa 11:8
1:5 [i]ver 6,7
1:7 [j]Lev 24:19; Jer 25:12 [k]S Jos 10:1
1:8 [l]ver 21; Jos 15:63; 2Sa 5:6
1:9 [m]S Nu 13:17 [n]S Ge 12:9; S Nu 21:1; Isa 30:6
1:10 [o]S Ge 13:18 [p]S Ge 35:27 [q]ver 20; S Nu 13:22; Jos 15:14
1:11 [r]Jos 10:38
1:15 [s]S Nu 13:6
1:16 [t]Nu 10:29 [u]S Ge 15:19 [v]Dt 34:3; Jdg 3:13; 2Ch 28:15 [w]Nu 21:1; Jos 12:14
1:17 [x]ver 3 [y]S Nu 14:45
1:18 [z]Jos 11:22 [a]S Jos 13:3
1:19 [b]S Nu 14:43 [c]Nu 13:17 [d]S Jos 17:16
1:20 [e]Jos 10:36 [f]S ver 10; S Jos 14:13
1:21 [g]S Jos 9:15; S 15:63 [h]S ver 8
1:22 [i]Jdg 10:9 [j]S Jos 7:2
1:23 [k]S Ge 28:19

[a] *14* Hebrew; Septuagint and Vulgate *Othniel, he urged her* [b] *16* That is, Jericho
[c] *17* The Hebrew term refers to the irrevocable giving over of things or persons to the LORD, often by totally destroying them.
[d] *17* *Hormah* means *destruction.*
[e] *18* Hebrew; Septuagint *Judah did not take*

1:1 AFTER THE DEATH OF JOSHUA. The events recorded in the book of Judges extend from about 1375 B.C. to 1050 B.C., when Saul was anointed king. Thirteen judges are generally associated with the book. They are Othniel (3:7–11), Ehud (3:12–30), Shamgar (3:31), Deborah and Barak (4:1—5:31), Gideon (6:1—8:35), Tola (10:1–2), Jair (10:3–5), Jephthah (10:6—12:7), Ibzan (12:8–10), Elon (12:11–12), Abdon (12:13–15) and Samson (13:1—16:31). Their leadership was primarily regional rather than over all the tribes. The ministry of some of the judges overlap (cf. Jdg 3:30—4:1).

1:6 CUT OFF HIS THUMBS. This was done in order to disable the king and thus prevent him from ever again entering into military battle.

you are treated well.[l]" **25**So he
showed them, and they put the city to
the sword but spared[m] the man and
his whole family. **26**He then went to the
land of the Hittites,[n] where he built a
city and called it Luz,[o] which is its
name to this day.
27But Manasseh did not[p] drive out
the people of Beth Shan or Taanach or
Dor[q] or Ibleam[r] or Megiddo[s] and
their surrounding settlements, for the
Canaanites[t] were determined to live
in that land. **28**When Israel became
strong, they pressed the Canaanites
into forced labor but never drove them
out completely.[u] **29**Nor did Ephraim[v]
drive out the Canaanites living in Gezer,[w] but the Canaanites continued to
live there among them.[x] **30**Neither did
Zebulun drive out the Canaanites living
in Kitron or Nahalol, who remained
among them; but they did subject them
to forced labor. **31**Nor did Asher[y] drive
out those living in Acco or Sidon[z] or
Ahlab or Aczib[a] or Helbah or Aphek[b]
or Rehob,[c] **32**and because of this the
people of Asher lived among the Canaanite inhabitants of the land. **33**Neither did Naphtali drive out those living
in Beth Shemesh[d] or Beth Anath[e];
but the Naphtalites too lived among
the Canaanite inhabitants of the land,
and those living in Beth Shemesh and
Beth Anath became forced laborers for
them. **34**The Amorites[f] confined the
Danites[g] to the hill country, not allowing them to come down into the
plain.[h] **35**And the Amorites were determined also to hold out in Mount Heres,[i] Aijalon[j] and Shaalbim,[k] but
when the power of the house of Joseph
increased, they too were pressed into
forced labor. **36**The boundary of the
Amorites was from Scorpion[f] Pass[l]
to Sela[m] and beyond.[n]

1:24 [l] S Ge 47:29
1:25 [m] Jos 6:25
1:26 [n] S Dt 7:1; Eze 16:3
[o] S Ge 28:19
1:27 [p] 1Ki 9:21
[q] S Jos 11:2
[r] S Jos 17:11
[s] S Jos 12:21
[t] S ver 1
1:28 [u] Jos 17:12-13
1:29 [v] Jos 14:4; Jdg 5:14
[w] S Jos 10:33
[x] Jos 16:10
1:31 [y] S Jos 17:7
[z] S Ge 49:13
[a] S Jos 15:44
[b] S Jos 12:18
[c] S Nu 13:21
1:33 [d] S Jos 15:10
[e] Jos 19:38
1:34 [f] Nu 13:29; Jdg 10:11; 1Sa 7:14
[g] S Ge 30:6
[h] Jdg 18:1
1:35 [i] Jdg 8:13
[j] Jos 19:42
[k] 1Ki 4:9
1:36 [l] Jos 15:3
[m] 2Ki 14:7; Isa 16:1; 42:11
[n] Ps 106:34

2:1 [o] S Ge 16:7
[p] S Dt 11:30
[q] ver 5 [r] Ex 20:2; Jdg 6:8 [s] Ge 17:8
[t] S Lev 26:42-44; Dt 7:9
2:2 [u] S Ex 23:32; S 34:12; Dt 7:2
[v] S Ex 23:24; 34:13; Dt 7:5; 2Ch 14:3
[w] Jer 7:28
2:3 [x] Jos 23:13
[y] S Nu 33:55
[z] S Ex 10:7
2:4 [a] S Ge 27:38; S Nu 25:6; 2Ki 17:13
2:5 [b] ver 1
2:7 [c] ver 17
2:8 [d] Jos 1:1
2:9 [e] S Jos 19:50

The Angel of the LORD *at Bokim*

2 The angel of the LORD[o] went up
from Gilgal[p] to Bokim[q] and said,
"I brought you up out of Egypt[r] and
led you into the land that I swore to
give to your forefathers.[s] I said, 'I will
never break my covenant with you,[t]
2and you shall not make a covenant
with the people of this land,[u] but you
shall break down their altars.[v]' Yet
you have disobeyed[w] me. Why have
you done this? **3**Now therefore I tell
you that I will not drive them out before you;[x] they will be ⌊thorns⌋[y] in
your sides and their gods will be a
snare[z] to you."
4When the angel of the LORD had spoken these things to all the Israelites,
the people wept aloud,[a] **5**and they
called that place Bokim.[g][b] There
they offered sacrifices to the LORD.

Disobedience and Defeat

2:6–9pp — Jos 24:29–31

6After Joshua had dismissed the Israelites, they went to take possession
of the land, each to his own inheritance. **7**The people served the LORD
throughout the lifetime of Joshua and
of the elders who outlived him and who
had seen all the great things the LORD
had done for Israel.[c]
8Joshua son of Nun,[d] the servant of
the LORD, died at the age of a hundred
and ten. **9**And they buried him in the
land of his inheritance, at Timnath Heres[h][e] in the hill country of Ephraim,
north of Mount Gaash.
10After that whole generation had
been gathered to their fathers, another
generation grew up, who knew neither

[f] *36* Hebrew *Akrabbim* [g] *5* *Bokim* means *weepers.* [h] *9* Also known as *Timnath Serah* (see Joshua 19:50 and 24:30)

1:28 NEVER DROVE THEM OUT COMPLETELY. Joshua had destroyed many of the Canaanites; yet after his death a considerable number remained within the land (vv. 1,28–30,32–33,35). God had commanded Israel to drive out the Canaanites completely because of their corrupt and sensual form of religion (Dt 7:2–4; see article on THE DESTRUCTION OF THE CANAANITES, p. 310). Israel's ultimate failure to do this led to compromise with the Canaanites and brought ruin and defeat to God's people.

2:1 ANGEL OF THE LORD. The angel of the Lord rebuked Israel for her failure to drive out the Canaanites (see Ex 3:2, note; see article on ANGELS AND THE ANGEL OF THE LORD, p. 340).

2:2 NOT MAKE A COVENANT WITH THE PEOPLE. God's refusal to help the Israelites drive out the enemy completely was largely due to their failure to be a separated and holy people who abhorred the evil ways of the pagan people around them (cf. Dt 7:2,5,16; 12:3; 30:16).

2:3 THEREFORE ... I WILL NOT DRIVE THEM OUT. Our failure to seek God earnestly and to follow his righteous ways will cause him to withdraw his help, power, and protection from our lives.

2:10 ANOTHER GENERATION GREW UP. The cyclical pattern of spiritual decline and renewal began with the passing of the generation that had taken the promised land and the emergence of

ANGELS AND THE ANGEL OF THE LORD

Jdg 2:1 "The angel of the LORD went up from Gilgal to Bokim and said, 'I brought you up out of Egypt and led you into the land that I swore to give to your forefathers. I said, "I will never break my covenant with you." '"

The Bible mentions angels frequently; this article provides an overview of the Biblical teaching about angels.

ANGELS. The word "angel" (Heb *malak*; Gk *angelos*) means "messenger." Angels are God's heavenly messengers or servants (Heb 1:13–14), created by God before the earth began (Job 38:4–7; Ps 148:2,5; Col 1:16). (1) The Bible speaks of good and evil angels, though it stresses that all angels were originally created good and holy (Ge 1:31). Having the freedom of choice, numerous angels joined in Satan's rebellion (Eze 28:12–17; 2Pe 2:4; Jude 6; Rev 12:9; see Mt 4:10, note) and turned from their original state of grace as God's servants, thereby forfeiting their heavenly role. Undoubtedly, the demons of the NT must be identified with these fallen angels (Mt 25:41; see Jude 6, note; see article on POWER OVER SATAN AND DEMONS, p. 1484).

(2) The Bible speaks of a vast host of good angels (1Ki 22:19; Ps 68:17; 148:2; Da 7:9–10; Rev 5:11), though the names of only two are recorded in Scripture: Michael (Da 12:1; Jude 9; Rev 12:7) and Gabriel (Da 9:21; Lk 1:19,26). Apparently they are divided into different ranks: Michael is called an archangel (literally, "leading angel," Jude 9; cf. 1Th 4:16); there are seraphs (Isa 6:2), cherubim (Eze 10:1–3), angels with authority and dominion (Eph 3:10; Col 1:16), and the myriads of angelic ministering spirits (Heb 1:13–14; Rev 5:11).

(3) As spiritual beings, good angels praise God (Heb 1:6; Rev 5:11; 7:11), do his will (Nu 22:22; Ps 103:20), see his face (Mt 18:10), are in submission to Christ (1Pe 3:22), are superior to humans (Heb 2:6–7), and inhabit heaven (Mk 13:32; Gal 1:8). They do not marry (Mt 22:30), will never die (Lk 20:34–36), and must not be worshiped (Col 2:18; Rev 19:9–10). They can appear in human form (usually as young men without wings, cf. Ge 18:2,16; 19:1; Heb 13:2).

(4) Angels carry out numerous activities on earth at God's command. They had a distinct role in revealing God's law to Moses (Ac 7:38; cf. Gal 3:19; Heb 2:2). Their duties are primarily related to their part in Christ's redemptive mission (see Mt 1:20–24; 2:13; 28:2; Lk 1—2; Ac 1:10; Rev 14:6–7). They rejoice over one sinner who repents (Lk 15:10), serve on behalf of God's people (Da 3:25; 6:22; Mt 18:10; Heb 1:14), observe the life of the Christian congregation (1Co 11:10; Eph 3:10; 1Ti 5:21), bring messages from God (Zec 1:14–17; Ac 10:1–8; 27:23–24), bring answers to prayer (Da 9:21–23; Ac 10:4), sometimes help interpret prophetic dreams and visions (Da 7:15–16), strengthen God's people in trials (Mt 4:11; Lk 22:43), protect saints who fear God and hate evil (Ps 34:7; 91:11; Da 6:22; Ac 12:7–10), punish those who are God's enemies (2Ki 19:35; Ac 12:23; Rev 14:17—16:21), fight against the demonic (Rev 12:7–9), and carry the saved to heaven (Lk 16:22).

(5) During the events of the end times, the war between Michael with the good angels and Satan with his demonic host will intensify (Rev 12:7–9). Angels will come with Christ when he returns (Mt 24:30–31) and will be present at the judgment of the entire human race (Lk 12:8–9).

THE ANGEL OF THE LORD. Special mention must be made of "the angel of the LORD" (sometimes, "the angel of God"), a unique angel who appears in both OT and NT. (1) The first appearance was to Hagar in the desert (Ge 16:7); other appearances involved such people as Abraham (Ge 22:11,15), Jacob (Ge 31:11–13), Moses (Ex 3:2), all the Israelites during the exodus (Ex 14:19) and later at Bokim (Jdg 2:1,4), Balaam (Nu 22:22–36), Joshua (Jos 5:13–15, where the "commander of the army of the LORD" is most likely the angel of the Lord), Gideon (Jdg 6:11), David (1Ch 21:16), Elijah (2Ki 1:3–4), Daniel (Da 6:22) and Joseph (Mt 1:20; 2:13).

(2) The angel of the Lord carried out several tasks similar to those of angels in general. Sometimes he simply brought messages from the Lord to his people (Ge 22:15–18; 31:11–13; Mt 1:20). At other times, God sent his angel to provide for the needs of his people (1Ki 19:5–7), to protect them from danger (Ex 14:19; 23:20; Da 6:22), and on occasion to destroy their enemies (Ex 23:23; 2Ki 19:34–35; cf. Isa 63:9). When God's people themselves rebelled and sinned greatly, his angel could be used to destroy them (2Sa 24:16–17).

(3) The identity of the angel of the Lord has been debated, particularly because of the way he often addressed people. Note the following: (a) In Jdg 2:1, the angel of the Lord says, "*I* brought you up out of Egypt and led you into the land that *I* swore to give to your forefathers. *I* said, '*I* will never break my covenant with you' " (italics added). When compared with other Scripture passages describing the same event, these actions were the actions of the Lord, the covenant God of the Israelites. He was the one who swore to Abraham, Isaac and Jacob to give their descendants the land of Canaan (Ge 13:14–17; 17:8; 26:2–4; 28:13); he swore that this covenant would be everlasting (Ge 17:7); he brought the Israelites up out of Egypt (Ex 20:1–2); and he brought them into the promised land (Jos 1:1–2). (b) When the angel of the Lord appeared before Joshua, Joshua fell down and worshiped him (Jos 5:14). Such a response has led many to believe that this angel was a visible manifestation of the Lord God himself; otherwise, the angel would have instructed Joshua not to worship him (cf. Rev 19:10; 22:8–9). (c) Even more explicitly, the angel of the Lord who appeared to Moses in the burning bush said in no uncertain terms: "I am the God of your father, the God of Abraham, the God of Isaac and the God of Jacob" (Ex 3:6; see Ge 16:7, note; Ex 3:2, note).

(4) Because the angel of the Lord is so closely identified with the Lord himself, and because he appeared in human form, some consider him to be an appearance of the eternal Christ, the second person of the Trinity, prior to his incarnation and virgin birth.

the LORD nor what he had done for Israel.[f] **11**Then the Israelites did evil[g] in
the eyes of the LORD[h] and served the
Baals.[i] **12**They forsook the LORD, the
God of their fathers, who had brought
them out of Egypt. They followed and
worshiped various gods[j] of the peoples around them.[k] They provoked[l]
the LORD to anger[m] **13**because they forsook[n] him and served Baal and the
Ashtoreths.[o] **14**In his anger[p] against
Israel the LORD handed them over[q] to
raiders who plundered[r] them. He sold
them[s] to their enemies all around,
whom they were no longer able to resist.[t] **15**Whenever Israel went out to
fight, the hand of the LORD was against
them[u] to defeat them, just as he had
sworn to them. They were in great distress.[v]

16Then the LORD raised up
judges,[i][w] who saved[x] them out of
the hands of these raiders. **17**Yet they
would not listen to their judges but
prostituted[y] themselves to other
gods[z] and worshiped them.[a] Unlike
their fathers, they quickly turned[b]
from the way in which their fathers had
walked, the way of obedience to the
LORD's commands.[c] **18**Whenever the
LORD raised up a judge for them, he was
with the judge and saved[d] them out of
the hands of their enemies as long as
the judge lived; for the LORD had compassion[e] on them as they groaned[f]
under those who oppressed and afflicted[g] them. **19**But when the judge died,
the people returned to ways even more

2:10 [f]S Ex 5:2; Gal 4:8 **2:11** [g]1Ki 15:26 [h]Jdg 3:12; 4:1; 6:1; 10:6 [i]Jdg 3:7; 8:33; 1Ki 16:31; 22:53; 2Ki 10:18; 17:16 **2:12** [j]S Dt 32:12; Ps 106:36 [k]S Dt 31:16; Jdg 10:6 [l]S Nu 11:33 [m]Dt 4:25; Ps 78:58; 106:40 **2:13** [n]1Sa 7:3; 1Ki 11:5,33; 2Ki 23:13 [o]Jdg 3:7; 5:8; 6:25; 8:33; 10:6; 1Sa 31:10; Ne 9:26; Ps 78:56; Jer 11:10 **2:14** [p]S Dt 31:17 [q]Ne 9:27; Ps 106:41 [r]Ps 44:10; 89:41; Eze 34:8 [s]S Dt 32:30; S Jdg 3:8 [t]S Dt 28:25 **2:15** [u]Ru 1:13; Job 19:21; Ps 32:4 [v]Ge 35:3; 2Sa 22:7; 2Ch 15:4; Job 5:5; 20:22; Ps 4:1; 18:6 **2:16** [w]Ru 1:1; 1Sa 4:18; 7:6,15; 2Sa 7:11; 1Ch 17:10; Ac 13:20 [x]1Sa 11:3; Ps 106:43 **2:17** [y]S Ex 34:15; S Nu 15:39 [z]S Ps 4:2 [a]Ne 9:28; Ps 106:36 [b]Dt 9:12 [c]ver 7 **2:18** [d]1Sa 7:3; 2Ki 13:5; Isa 19:20; 43:3,11; 45:15,21; 49:26; 60:16; 63:8 [e]S Dt 32:36 [f]S Ex 2:23 [g]S Nu 10:9

[i] *16* Or *leaders*; similarly in verses 17-19

a new generation of Israelites. The pattern reflected in Judges revolves around the following process: (1) the new generation drifts away from the righteous commitment of their fathers and departs from a personal relationship with the Lord (v. 10); (2) this leads to conformity to the lifestyles and values of the surrounding culture and results in general apostasy (vv. 11–13); (3) God's judgment comes to Israel in the form of oppression and bondage from one of their enemies (vv. 14–15); (4) the Israelites subsequently cry out to God in their distress and repent of their backsliding (vv. 15,18); (5) God raises up a Spirit-empowered leader who serves as a deliverer to free the Israelites from their bondage and to restore them to God (vv. 16, 18).

2:13 BAAL AND THE ASHTORETHS. Baal, the chief god worshiped by the Canaanites, was the god of fertility, rain and vegetation. Baal worship included cult prostitution and child sacrifice. Israel's compromise with Baalism was repeatedly condemned by the prophets (1Ki 17—18; 22:17–27; 2Ki 1; 13; 17; Jer 10:12–16; 14:22; Hos 2:8,16–17). Ashtoreth, the goddess of war and fertility and the female consort of Baal, was depicted by figurines or statues.

2:16 THE LORD RAISED UP JUDGES. The judges served as military and tribal leaders in a time when Israel was undergoing spiritual, social and moral decline. God raised them up to deliver his people from their enemies after they repented and returned to God. The judges possessed outstanding qualities of leadership and accomplished great feats through God's help and power (v. 18; 6:11–16; 13:24–25; 14:6).

2:17 TURNED FROM THE WAY IN WHICH THEIR FATHERS HAD WALKED. The key to understanding the fundamental nature of Israel's spiritual decline is found in vv. 10–17. (1) During the time of the judges the new generation of Israelites departed from the ways and teachings of their fathers. They forsook their covenant relationship with God (v. 10) and turned to evil (v. 11–13). They began to question the standards and laws of the founding generation (v. 17).

(2) They turned away from obeying God's word (vv. 2,17) and lived instead according to their own desires (cf. 17:6; 21:25).

(3) The Israelites failed to separate themselves completely from the evil culture of the Canaanites (vv. 11–13; 1:28); instead, they preferred the materialistic benefits and immoral pleasures of the Canaanites (vv. 12–13; 1:27–28,30,33; see article on THE NATURE OF IDOLATRY, p. 394). They intermarried with the Canaanites (3:5–6) and began to worship Baal and the Ashtoreths (v. 13). Thus, the inevitable syncretism of the two cultures and lifestyles took place.

(4) This history illustrates that the natural direction of human nature since the fall is downward; the spiritual vitality of an individual or group of believers will diminish unless spiritual renewal periodically occurs by God's grace through repentance, prayer and recommitment (cf. 2Ch 7:14; Isa 57:15; Mt 5:6; Jude 20).

2:19 MORE CORRUPT THAN THOSE OF THEIR FATHERS. This verse unveils a progressive deterioration in Israel. Each successive generation is characterized by greater apostasy and spiritual corruption. Similarly, second- and third-generation believers under the new covenant should ask themselves if they are as committed to God as was the generation that preceded them. Or are they conforming more and more to the ways of their society, while rejecting their fathers' original standards?

2:19 REFUSED TO GIVE UP THEIR EVIL PRACTICES. The failure of many of God's chosen people to remain faithful to him and his word is a recurring theme throughout Biblical history. (1)

corrupt[h] than those of their fathers,[i]
following other gods and serving and
worshiping them.[j] They refused to
give up their evil practices and stubborn[k] ways.
20Therefore the LORD was very angry[l] with Israel and said, "Because
this nation has violated the covenant[m]
that I laid down for their forefathers
and has not listened to me, **21**I will no
longer drive out[n] before them any of
the nations Joshua left when he died.
22I will use them to test[o] Israel and
see whether they will keep the way of
the LORD and walk in it as their forefathers did." **23**The LORD had allowed
those nations to remain; he did not
drive them out at once by giving them
into the hands of Joshua.[p]

3 These are the nations the LORD left
to test[q] all those Israelites who
had not experienced any of the wars in
Canaan **2**(he did this only to teach warfare to the descendants of the Israelites who had not had previous battle
experience): **3**the five[r] rulers of the
Philistines,[s] all the Canaanites, the
Sidonians, and the Hivites[t] living in
the Lebanon mountains from Mount
Baal Hermon[u] to Lebo[j] Hamath.[v]
4They were left to test[w] the Israelites
to see whether they would obey the
LORD's commands, which he had given
their forefathers through Moses.
5The Israelites lived[x] among the
Canaanites, Hittites, Amorites, Perizzites,[y] Hivites and Jebusites.[z] **6**They
took their daughters[a] in marriage and
gave their own daughters to their sons,
and served their gods.[b c]

Othniel

7The Israelites did evil in the eyes of
the LORD; they forgot the LORD[d] their
God and served the Baals and the
Asherahs.[e] **8**The anger of the LORD
burned against Israel so that he sold[f]
them into the hands of Cushan-Rishathaim[g] king of Aram Naharaim,[k h] to
whom the Israelites were subject for
eight years. **9**But when they cried out[i]
to the LORD, he raised up for them a
deliverer,[j] Othniel[k] son of Kenaz,

2:19 [h] S Ge 6:11; S Dt 4:16 [i] Dt 32:17; Ne 9:2; Ps 78:57; Jer 44:3, 9 [j] Jdg 4:1; 8:33 [k] S Ex 32:9 **2:20** [l] S Dt 31:17; Jos 23:16 [m] S Jos 7:11; S 2Ki 17:15 **2:21** [n] S Jos 23:5 **2:22** [o] S Ge 22:1; S Ex 15:25 **2:23** [p] Jdg 1:1 **3:1** [q] S Ex 15:25 **3:3** [r] S Jos 13:3 [s] S Ge 10:14 [t] S Ge 10:17; S Ex 3:8 [u] S Dt 3:8 [v] S Nu 13:21 **3:4** [w] S Ex 15:25 **3:5** [x] Ps 106:35 [y] S Jos 3:10 [z] S Jos 11:3; Ezr 9:1 **3:6** [a] Ezr 10:18; Ne 13:23; Mal 2:11 [b] S Ex 34:16; Dt 7:3-4 [c] S Dt 7:16 **3:7** [d] Dt 4:9; S 32:18; Jdg 8:34; Ps 78:11,42; 106:7; Jer 23:27 [e] S Ex 34:13; S Jdg 2:11,13; 1Ki 16:33; 2Ch 34:7; Isa 17:8 **3:8** [f] Jdg 2:14; Ps 44:12; Isa 50:1; 52:3 [g] ver 10 [h] S Ge 24:10 **3:9** [i] ver 15; Jdg 6:6,7; 10:10; 1Sa 12:10; Ps 106:44; 107:13 [j] S Dt 28:29; Ne 9:27 [k] S Jos 15:17

[j] *3* Or *to the entrance to* [k] *8* That is, Northwest Mesopotamia

The OT reveals God's people repeatedly turning from his love, righteousness, forgiveness and revelation. Some noteworthy examples are the rejection of God's will by Adam (Ge 3:1–7), Adam's descendants (Ge 6:1–7), Noah's descendants (Ge 11:1–9) and the children of Israel (Ex 32; Jdg 1—21; 1Ki; 2Ki; Ac 7:34–53).

(2) Likewise, in the NT, Christ and the apostles reveal that toward the end of the age many within the church will turn from true faith in Christ and his revelation in the Bible (Mt 24:10–12,24; 2Ti 1:15; 4:1–4; Rev 2—3).

(3) However, Scripture emphasizes that a righteous remnant will remain faithful to God and his revelation during times of spiritual decline. Among the many Biblical examples of faithful men and women are Enoch (Ge 5:21–24); Noah (Ge 6:9–12); Abraham (Ge 12–24; 18:19); Joseph (Ge 37–50); Moses (Ex 33:11–14; Dt 34); Joshua and Caleb (Nu 14:1–10); Ruth (Ru 2:12); Samuel (1Sa 2:26; 3:19); Elijah (1Ki 18:20–22; 19:9–18; Ro 11:2–5); the prophets (Ac 7:52); John the Baptist (Lk 1:15–17); Simeon and Anna (Lk 2:25–38); the disciples (Ac 5:27–42); Paul (2Ti 4:6–8); the overcomers of Rev 2—3; and the blameless of Rev 14:1–5,12, who constitute a great multitude of people from every nation who have washed their robes and made them white in the blood of the Lamb (cf. Rev 7:9–17).

3:6 TOOK THEIR DAUGHTERS. Israel's syncretism of Canaanite culture through intermarriage nearly destroyed their identity as a distinct people of God. Such intermarriage had been forbidden by Israel's covenant with the Lord (Ex 34:15–16; Dt 7:3–4; Jos 23:12–13). The book of Judges demonstrates the disastrous effects of Israel's compromise.

3:7 ISRAELITES DID EVIL. The book of Judges records that Israel went through six major cycles of apostasy, bondage, crying out to God, God's deliverance, and then falling away again (see 2:10, note). There are several basic truths revealed in these historical events: (1) The natural direction of God's people, even after revival and restoration, is spiritual decline again. Only a fervent faith, a sincere gratitude, a persistent attempt to seek God's face, and a constant rejection of the ungodly ways of pagan society will enable God's people to maintain their first love, vision and purity.

(2) The history of salvation reveals a people reluctant to learn and profit from the spiritual decline and tragic consequences of previous generations of believers.

(3) Rebellion and unbelief are not insignificant; they are an affront to a righteous God and as such will be visited by his judgment. When God's people lower or compromise their God-given standards, they will lose God's promised blessings and fatherly presence.

(4) God is a merciful God ready to respond to the cries of repentance from his people. He always makes possible a new beginning by grace through faith in him (see article on CHRIST'S MESSAGE TO THE SEVEN CHURCHES, p. 2008).

Caleb's younger brother, who saved them. 10 The Spirit of the LORD came upon him,[l] so that he became Israel's judge[1] and went to war. The LORD gave Cushan-Rishathaim[m] king of Aram[n] into the hands of Othniel, who overpowered him. 11 So the land had peace[o] for forty years,[p] until Othniel son of Kenaz[q] died.

Jdg 6:34

Ehud

12 Once again the Israelites did evil in the eyes of the LORD,[r] and because they did this evil the LORD gave Eglon king of Moab[s] power over Israel. 13 Getting the Ammonites[t] and Amalekites[u] to join him, Eglon came and attacked Israel, and they took possession of the City of Palms.[m][v] 14 The Israelites were subject to Eglon king of Moab[w] for eighteen years.

15 Again the Israelites cried out to the LORD, and he gave them a deliverer[x]—Ehud[y], a left-handed[z] man, the son of Gera the Benjamite. The Israelites sent him with tribute[a] to Eglon king of Moab. 16 Now Ehud[b] had made a double-edged sword about a foot and a half[n] long, which he strapped to his right thigh under his clothing. 17 He presented the tribute[c] to Eglon king of Moab, who was a very fat man.[d] 18 After Ehud had presented the tribute, he sent on their way the men who had carried it. 19 At the idols[o] near Gilgal he himself turned back and said, "I have a secret message for you, O king."

The king said, "Quiet!" And all his attendants left him.

20 Ehud then approached him while he was sitting alone in the upper room of his summer palace[p][e] and said, "I have a message from God for you." As the king rose[f] from his seat, 21 Ehud reached with his left hand, drew the sword[g] from his right thigh and plunged it into the king's belly. 22 Even the handle sank in after the blade, which came out his back. Ehud did not pull the sword out, and the fat closed in over it. 23 Then Ehud went out to the porch[q]; he shut the doors of the upper room behind him and locked them.

24 After he had gone, the servants came and found the doors of the upper room locked. They said, "He must be relieving himself[h] in the inner room of the house." 25 They waited to the point of embarrassment,[i] but when he did not open the doors of the room, they took a key and unlocked them. There they saw their lord fallen to the floor, dead.

26 While they waited, Ehud got away. He passed by the idols and escaped to Seirah. 27 When he arrived there, he blew a trumpet[j] in the hill country of Ephraim, and the Israelites went down with him from the hills, with him leading them.

28 "Follow me," he ordered, "for the LORD has given Moab,[k] your enemy, into your hands.[l]" So they followed him down and, taking possession of the fords of the Jordan[m] that led to Moab, they allowed no one to cross over. 29 At that time they struck down about ten thousand Moabites, all vigorous and strong; not a man escaped. 30 That day Moab[n] was made subject to Israel, and the land had peace[o] for eighty years.

Shamgar

31 After Ehud came Shamgar son of Anath,[p] who struck down six hundred[q] Philistines[r] with an oxgoad. He too saved Israel.

Deborah

4 After Ehud[s] died, the Israelites once again did evil[t] in the eyes of the LORD.[u] 2 So the LORD sold them[v] into the hands of Jabin, a king of Canaan, who reigned in Hazor.[w] The commander of his army was Sisera,[x]

3:10 [l] S Nu 11:25, 29; Jdg 6:34; 11:29; 13:25; 14:6,19; 15:14; 1Sa 11:6; 16:13; 1Ki 18:46; 1Ch 12:18; 2Ch 24:20; Isa 11:2 [m] ver 8 [n] S Ge 10:22
3:11 [o] ver 30; S Jos 14:15; Jdg 5:31; 8:28 [p] S Ex 16:35 [q] S Jos 15:17
3:12 [r] S Jdg 2:11, 14 [s] 1Sa 12:9
3:13 [t] S Ge 19:38; Jdg 10:11 [u] S Ge 14:7 [v] S Jdg 1:16
3:14 [w] Jer 48:1
3:15 [x] S ver 9 [y] ver 16; Jdg 4:1 [z] Jdg 20:16; 1Ch 12:2 [a] ver 17, 18; 2Sa 8:2,6; 1Ki 4:21; 2Ki 17:3; Est 10:1; Ps 68:29; 72:10; 89:22; Ecc 2:8; Isa 60:5; Hos 10:6
3:16 [b] S ver 15
3:17 [c] S ver 15 [d] Job 15:27; Ps 73:4
3:20 [e] Am 3:15 [f] Ne 8:5
3:21 [g] 2Sa 2:16; 3:27; 20:10
3:24 [h] 1Sa 24:3
3:25 [i] 2Ki 2:17; 8:11
3:27 [j] S Lev 25:9; Jdg 6:34; 7:18; 2Sa 2:28; Isa 18:3; Jer 42:14
3:28 [k] S Ge 19:37 [l] S Jos 2:24; S Jdg 1:2 [m] S Nu 13:29; S Jos 2:7
3:30 [n] S Ge 36:35 [o] S ver 11
3:31 [p] Jdg 5:6 [q] S Jos 23:10 [r] Jos 13:2; Jdg 10:11; 13:1; 1Sa 5:1; 31:1; 2Sa 8:1; Jer 25:20; 47:1
4:1 [s] S Jdg 3:15 [t] S Jdg 2:19 [u] S Jdg 2:11
4:2 [v] S Dt 32:30 [w] S Jos 11:1 [x] 1Sa 12:9; Ps 83:9

[1] *10* Or *leader* [m] *13* That is, Jericho
[n] *16* Hebrew *a cubit* (about 0.5 meter)
[o] *19* Or *the stone quarries*; also in verse 26
[p] *20* The meaning of the Hebrew for this phrase is uncertain. [q] *23* The meaning of the Hebrew for this word is uncertain.

3:10 SPIRIT OF THE LORD CAME UPON HIM. The judges of Israel were supernaturally empowered by God's Spirit (cf. Gideon, 6:34; Jephthah, 11:29; Samson, 13:25; 14:6,19; 15:14); i.e., they were charismatic leaders. Through this spiritual enabling, they received the power and wisdom needed to perform extraordinary works for God and Israel (see 10:7, note).

3:21 EHUD . . . DREW THE SWORD. Ehud's action was not murder, but an act of war under the direct command of God (v. 15). Under the new covenant, the holy war of Israel as a theocracy has been replaced by spiritual warfare against Satan and his demonic forces (see Ro 8:13, note; Eph 6:11, note).

who lived in Harosheth Haggoyim. **3**Because he had nine hundred iron chariots[y] and had cruelly oppressed[z] the Israelites for twenty years, they cried to the LORD for help.

4Deborah,[a] a prophetess,[b] the wife of Lappidoth, was leading[r] Israel at that time. **5**She held court[c] under the Palm of Deborah between Ramah[d] and Bethel[e] in the hill country of Ephraim, and the Israelites came to her to have their disputes decided. **6**She sent for Barak son of Abinoam[f] from Kedesh[g] in Naphtali and said to him, "The LORD, the God of Israel, commands you: 'Go, take with you ten thousand men of Naphtali[h] and Zebulun[i] and lead the way to Mount Tabor.[j] **7**I will lure Sisera, the commander of Jabin's[k] army, with his chariots and his troops to the Kishon River[l] and give him into your hands.[m]' "

8Barak said to her, "If you go with me, I will go; but if you don't go with me, I won't go."

9"Very well," Deborah said, "I will go with you. But because of the way you are going about this,[s] the honor will not be yours, for the LORD will hand Sisera over to a woman." So Deborah went with Barak to Kedesh,[n] **10**where he summoned[o] Zebulun and Naphtali. Ten thousand men followed him, and Deborah also went with him.

11Now Heber the Kenite had left the other Kenites,[p] the descendants of Hobab,[q] Moses' brother-in-law,[t] and pitched his tent by the great tree[r] in Zaanannim[s] near Kedesh.

12When they told Sisera that Barak son of Abinoam had gone up to Mount Tabor,[t] **13**Sisera gathered together his nine hundred iron chariots[u] and all the men with him, from Harosheth Haggoyim to the Kishon River.[v]

14Then Deborah said to Barak, "Go! This is the day the LORD has given Sisera into your hands.[w] Has not the LORD gone ahead[x] of you?" So Barak went down Mount Tabor, followed by ten thousand men. **15**At Barak's advance, the LORD routed[y] Sisera and all his chariots and army by the sword, and Sisera abandoned his chariot and fled on foot. **16**But Barak pursued the chariots and army as far as Harosheth Haggoyim. All the troops of Sisera fell by the sword; not a man was left.[z]

17Sisera, however, fled on foot to the tent of Jael,[a] the wife of Heber the Kenite,[b] because there were friendly relations between Jabin king of Hazor[c] and the clan of Heber the Kenite.

18Jael[d] went out to meet Sisera and said to him, "Come, my lord, come right in. Don't be afraid." So he entered her tent, and she put a covering over him.

19"I'm thirsty," he said. "Please give me some water." She opened a skin of milk,[e] gave him a drink, and covered him up.

20"Stand in the doorway of the tent," he told her. "If someone comes by and asks you, 'Is anyone here?' say 'No.' "

21But Jael,[f] Heber's wife, picked up a tent peg and a hammer and went quietly to him while he lay fast asleep,[g] exhausted. She drove the peg through his temple into the ground, and he died.[h]

22Barak came by in pursuit of Sisera, and Jael[i] went out to meet him. "Come," she said, "I will show you the man you're looking for." So he went in with her, and there lay Sisera with the tent peg through his temple—dead.[j]

23On that day God subdued[k] Jabin,[l] the Canaanite king, before the Israelites. **24**And the hand of the Israelites grew stronger and stronger against Jabin, the Canaanite king, until they destroyed him.[m]

The Song of Deborah

5 On that day Deborah[n] and Barak son of Abinoam[o] sang this song:[p]

[r] 4 Traditionally *judging* [s] 9 Or *But on the expedition you are undertaking* [t] 11 Or *father-in-law*

4:3 y S Jos 17:16 z Jdg 10:12; Ps 106:42
4:4 a Jdg 5:1,7,12,15 b S Ex 15:20
4:5 c 1Sa 14:2; 22:6 d S Jos 18:25 e S Jos 12:9
4:6 f Jdg 5:1,12,15; 1Sa 12:11; Heb 11:32 g S Jos 12:22 h S Ge 30:8 i Jdg 5:18; 6:35 j S Jos 19:22
4:7 k S Jos 11:1 l ver 13; Jdg 5:21; 1Ki 18:40; Ps 83:9 m S Jdg 1:2
4:9 n S Jos 12:22
4:10 o 2Ch 36:23; Ezr 1:2; Isa 41:2; 42:6; 45:3; 46:11; 48:15
4:11 p S Ge 15:19 q Nu 10:29 r Jos 24:26; Jdg 9:6 s Jos 19:33
4:12 t S Jos 19:22
4:13 u S Jos 17:16 v S ver 7; Jdg 5:19
4:14 w S Jdg 1:2 x Dt 9:3; 1Sa 8:20; 2Sa 5:24; Ps 68:7
4:15 y S
4:16 z S Ex 14:28; Ps 83:9
4:17 a ver 18,21,22; Jdg 5:6,24 b S Ge 15:19 c S Jos 11:1
4:18 d S ver 17
4:19 e S Ge 18:8
4:21 f S ver 17 g Ge 2:21; 15:12; 1Sa 26:12; Isa 29:10; Jnh 1:5 h Jdg 5:26
4:22 i S ver 17 j Jdg 5:27
4:23 k Ne 9:24; Ps 18:47; 44:2; 47:3; 144:2 l S Jos 11:1
4:24 m Ps 83:9; 106:43
5:1 n S Jdg 4:4 o S Jdg 4:6 p S Ex 15:1; Ps 32:7

4:4 DEBORAH. Deborah was a prophetess; she had prophetic gifts, which enabled her to hear messages from God and to communicate his will to the people (vv. 6–7; see article on THE PROPHET IN THE OLD TESTAMENT, p. 986). Deborah's close relationship with God gave her great influence among her people (v. 8).

4:14 HAS NOT THE LORD GONE AHEAD OF YOU? It is essential that God goes before us to prepare the way; unless he guides us along the way, our endeavors will fail. Consequently, we must earnestly seek to be open to God's continual leading in our lives (cf. Ex 33:15).

5:1 DEBORAH AND BARAK . . . SANG. The song of Deborah and Barak is a song of praise to God (v. 3) for his mercy and righteous acts on behalf of Israel (v. 11). Throughout the OT heartfelt singing to the Lord by the saints was an important

2Sa 22:47-50

[2]"When the princes in Israel take
the lead,
when the people willingly offer[q]
themselves—
praise the LORD![r]

[3]"Hear this, you kings! Listen, you
rulers!
I will sing to[u] the LORD, I will
sing;[s]
I will make music to[v] the LORD,
the God of Israel.[t]

[4]"O LORD, when you went out[u]
from Seir,[v]
when you marched from the land
of Edom,
the earth shook,[w] the heavens
poured,
the clouds poured down water.[x]
[5]The mountains quaked[y] before
the LORD, the One of Sinai,
before the LORD, the God of
Israel.

[6]"In the days of Shamgar son of
Anath,[z]
in the days of Jael,[a] the roads[b]
were abandoned;
travelers took to winding
paths.[c]
[7]Village life[w] in Israel ceased,
ceased until I,[x] Deborah,[d]
arose,
arose a mother in Israel.
[8]When they chose new gods,[e]
war came to the city gates,[f]
and not a shield or spear[g] was
seen
among forty thousand in Israel.
[9]My heart is with Israel's princes,
with the willing volunteers[h]
among the people.
Praise the LORD!

[10]"You who ride on white donkeys,[i]
sitting on your saddle blankets,
and you who walk along the
road,
consider [11]the voice of the
singers[y] at the watering
places.
They recite the righteous acts[j]
of the LORD,
the righteous acts of his
warriors[z] in Israel.

"Then the people of the LORD
went down to the city gates.[k]
[12]'Wake up,[l] wake up, Deborah![m]
Wake up, wake up, break out in
song!
Arise, O Barak![n]
Take captive your captives,[o]
O son of Abinoam.'

[13]"Then the men who were left
came down to the nobles;
the people of the LORD
came to me with the mighty.
[14]Some came from Ephraim,[p] whose
roots were in Amalek;[q]
Benjamin[r] was with the people
who followed you.
From Makir[s] captains came down,
from Zebulun those who bear a
commander's staff.
[15]The princes of Issachar[t] were
with Deborah;[u]
yes, Issachar was with Barak,[v]
rushing after him into the valley.
In the districts of Reuben
there was much searching of
heart.
[16]Why did you stay among the
campfires[a][w]
to hear the whistling for the
flocks?[x]
In the districts of Reuben
there was much searching of
heart.
[17]Gilead[y] stayed beyond the Jordan.
And Dan, why did he linger by
the ships?
Asher[z] remained on the coast[a]
and stayed in his coves.
[18]The people of Zebulun[b] risked
their very lives;
so did Naphtali[c] on the heights
of the field.[d]

[19]"Kings came[e], they fought;
the kings of Canaan fought

5:2 [q]2Ch 17:16; Ps 110:3 [r]ver 9 **5:3** [s]S Ex 15:1 [t]Ps 27:6 **5:4** [u]S Ex 13:21 [v]S Nu 24:18; S Dt 33:2 [w]2Sa 22:8; Ps 18:7; 77:18; 82:5; Isa 2:19,21; 13:13; 24:18; 64:3; Jer 10:10; 50:46; 51:29; Joel 3:16; Na 1:5; Hab 3:6 [x]Ps 68:8; 77:17 **5:5** [y]S Ex 19:18; Ps 29:6; 46:3; 77:18; 114:4; Isa 64:3 **5:6** [z]Jdg 3:31 [a]S Jdg 4:17 [b]Lev 26:22; Isa 33:8 [c]Ps 125:5; Isa 59:8 **5:7** [d]S Jdg 4:4 **5:8** [e]Dt 32:17; S Jdg 2:13 [f]ver 11; S Jos 2:5 [g]S Nu 25:7 **5:9** [h]S ver 2 **5:10** [i]S Ge 49:11; Jdg 12:14 **5:11** [j]1Sa 12:7; Da 9:16; Mic 6:5 [k]S ver 8 **5:12** [l]Ps 44:23; 57:8; Isa 51:9,17 [m]S Jdg 4:4 [n]S Jdg 4:6 [o]Ps 68:18; Eph 4:8 **5:14** [p]S Ge 41:52; S Jdg 1:29 [q]Jdg 3:13 [r]S Nu 34:21 [s]S Ge 50:23 **5:15** [t]S Ge 30:18 [u]S Jdg 4:4 [v]S Jdg 4:6 **5:16** [w]S Ge 49:14 [x]S Nu 32:1 **5:17** [y]S Jos 12:2 [z]S Jos 17:7 [a]Jos 19:29 **5:18** [b]S Ge 30:20 [c]S Ge 30:8; Ps 68:27 [d]S Jdg 4:6,10 **5:19** [e]Jos 11:5; S Jdg 4:13; Rev 16:16

[u]3 Or *of* [v]3 Or / *with song I will praise* [w]7 Or *Warriors* [x]7 Or *you* [y]11 Or *archers*; the meaning of the Hebrew for this word is uncertain. [z]11 Or *villagers* [a]16 Or *saddlebags*

part of expressing gratitude to God for his redeeming power (cf. Ex 15; 1Ch 15—16; 2Ch 20:22; Ps 1—150; see article on PRAISE, p. 770). NT believers are also told to give God praise for his love toward them. Praise, considered by God as a holy sacrifice to him (Heb 13:15), often takes the form of song (Heb 2:12; Jas 5:13; Rev 15:3). Spiritual songs of praise (cf. Eph 5:19; Col 3:16) can be sung with the mind (i.e., using understood language) or with the spirit (i.e., using the language of the Spirit; see 1Co 14:15).

at Taanach by the waters of
Megiddo,[f]
but they carried off no silver, no
plunder.[g]
20 From the heavens[h] the stars
fought,
from their courses they fought
against Sisera.
21 The river Kishon[i] swept them
away,
the age-old river, the river
Kishon.
March on, my soul; be strong![j]
22 Then thundered the horses'
hoofs—
galloping, galloping go his
mighty steeds.[k]
23 'Curse Meroz,' said the angel of
the LORD.
'Curse its people bitterly,
because they did not come to help
the LORD,
to help the LORD against the
mighty.'

24 "Most blessed of women[l] be
Jael,[m]
the wife of Heber the Kenite,[n]
most blessed of tent-dwelling
women.
25 He asked for water, and she gave
him milk;[o]
in a bowl fit for nobles she
brought him curdled milk.
26 Her hand reached for the tent peg,
her right hand for the
workman's hammer.
She struck Sisera, she crushed his
head,
she shattered and pierced his
temple.[p]
27 At her feet he sank,
he fell; there he lay.
At her feet he sank, he fell;
where he sank, there he
fell—dead.[q]

28 "Through the window[r] peered
Sisera's mother;
behind the lattice she cried
out,[s]
'Why is his chariot so long in
coming?
Why is the clatter of his chariots
delayed?'
29 The wisest of her ladies answer
her;
indeed, she keeps saying to
herself,
30 'Are they not finding and dividing
the spoils:[t]
a girl or two for each man,
colorful garments as plunder for
Sisera,
colorful garments embroidered,
highly embroidered garments[u]
for my neck—
all this as plunder?[v]'

31 "So may all your enemies perish,[w]
O LORD!
But may they who love you be
like the sun[x]
when it rises in its strength."[y]

Then the land had peace[z] forty
years.

Gideon

6 Again the Israelites did evil in the
eyes of the LORD,[a] and for seven
years he gave them into the hands of
the Midianites.[b] 2 Because the power
of Midian was so oppressive,[c] the Israelites prepared shelters for themselves in mountain clefts, caves[d] and
strongholds.[e] 3 Whenever the Israelites planted their crops, the Midianites, Amalekites[f] and other eastern
peoples[g] invaded the country. 4 They
camped on the land and ruined the
crops[h] all the way to Gaza[i] and did
not spare a living thing for Israel, neither sheep nor cattle nor donkeys.
5 They came up with their livestock and
their tents like swarms of locusts.[j] It
was impossible to count the men and
their camels;[k] they invaded the land
to ravage it. 6 Midian so impoverished
the Israelites that they cried out[l] to
the LORD for help.

5:19 [f] S Jos 12:21 [g] ver 30
5:20 [h] S Jos 10:11
5:21 [i] S Jdg 4:7 [j] Jos 1:6
5:22 [k] Jer 8:16
5:24 [l] Lk 1:42 [m] S Jdg 4:17 [n] S Ge 15:19
5:25 [o] S Ge 18:8
5:26 [p] Jdg 4:21
5:27 [q] Jdg 4:22
5:28 [r] S Jos 2:15 [s] Pr 7:6
5:30 [t] Ex 15:9; 1Sa 30:24; Ps 68:12 [u] Ps 45:14; Eze 16:10 [v] ver 19; 2Sa 1:24
5:31 [w] S Nu 10:35 [x] 2Sa 23:4; Job 37:21; Ps 19:4; 89:36; Isa 18:4 [y] 2Sa 18:32 [z] S Jdg 3:11
6:1 [a] S Jdg 2:11 [b] S Ge 25:2
6:2 [c] 1Sa 13:6; Isa 5:30; 8:21; 26:16; 37:3 [d] Isa 2:19; Jer 48:28; 49:8,30 [e] Job 24:8; Jer 41:9; Heb 11:38
6:3 [f] Nu 13:29 [g] S Ge 25:6; Isa 11:14; Jer 49:28
6:4 [h] Lev 26:16; Dt 28:30,51; Isa 10:6; 39:6; 42:22 [i] S Ge 10:19
6:5 [j] S Dt 28:42 [k] Jdg 8:10; Isa 21:7; 60:6; Jer 49:32
6:6 [l] S Jdg 3:9

6:1 ISRAELITES DID EVIL. Once more God's people reverted to a syncretistic religion that conformed to the ways of the Canaanites. As a result, for seven years God permitted the Midianites, assisted by the Amalekites and tribes from the east, to invade and oppress Israel (6:3). They were forced to hide in caves and conceal their produce (vv. 2–5); they called on God only when the situation became unbearable (v. 6).

6:6 CRIED OUT TO THE LORD. Israel turned to God as a last resort, and only because of their oppression. (1) The fundamental problem with the Israelites was that their faith in God was founded not on love for and gratitude to the Lord, but on self-centered desires and ambitions; they sought God only in times of crisis when they felt they needed him. (2) NT believers also need to examine their type of faith. As believers, do we follow the

7When the Israelites cried[m] to the
LORD because of Midian, **8**he sent them
a prophet,[n] who said, "This is what
the LORD, the God of Israel, says: I
brought you up out of Egypt,[o] out of
the land of slavery.[p] **9**I snatched you
from the power of Egypt and from the
hand of all your oppressors.[q] I drove
them from before you and gave you
their land.[r] **10**I said to you, 'I am the
LORD your God; do not worship[s] the
gods of the Amorites,[t] in whose land
you live.' But you have not listened to
me."

11The angel of the LORD[u] came and
sat down under the oak in Ophrah[v]
that belonged to Joash[w] the Abiez-
rite,[x] where his son Gideon[y] was
threshing[z] wheat in a winepress[a] to
keep it from the Midianites. **12**When
the angel of the LORD appeared to Gideon, he said, "The LORD is with you,[b]
mighty warrior.[c]"

13"But sir," Gideon replied, "if the
LORD is with us, why has all this happened to us? Where are all his wonders[d] that our fathers told[e] us about
when they said, 'Did not the LORD bring
us up out of Egypt?' But now the LORD
has abandoned[f] us and put us into the
hand of Midian."

14The LORD turned to him and said,
"Go in the strength you have[g] and
save[h] Israel out of Midian's hand.
Am I not sending you?"

15"But Lord,[b]" Gideon asked, "how
can I save Israel? My clan[i] is the
weakest in Manasseh, and I am the
least in my family.[j]"

16The LORD answered, "I will be with
you[k], and you will strike down all the
Midianites together."

17Gideon replied, "If now I have
found favor in your eyes, give me a
sign[l] that it is really you talking to
me. **18**Please do not go away until I
come back and bring my offering and
set it before you."

And the LORD said, "I will wait until
you return."

19Gideon went in, prepared a young
goat,[m] and from an ephah[c][n] of flour
he made bread without yeast. Putting
the meat in a basket and its broth in a
pot, he brought them out and offered
them to him under the oak.[o]

20The angel of God said to him,
"Take the meat and the unleavened
bread, place them on this rock,[p] and
pour out the broth." And Gideon did so.
21With the tip of the staff[q] that was in
his hand, the angel of the LORD touched
the meat and the unleavened bread.[r]
Fire flared from the rock, consuming
the meat and the bread. And the angel
of the LORD disappeared. **22**When Gideon realized[s] that it was the angel of
the LORD, he exclaimed, "Ah, Sovereign
LORD! I have seen the angel of the LORD
face to face!"[t]

23But the LORD said to him, "Peace!
Do not be afraid.[u] You are not going
to die."[v]

24So Gideon built an altar to the
LORD there and called[w] it The LORD is
Peace. To this day it stands in Oph-
rah[x] of the Abiezrites.

25That same night the LORD said to
him, "Take the second bull from your
father's herd, the one seven years
old.[d] Tear down your father's altar to
Baal and cut down the Asherah
pole[e][y] beside it. **26**Then build a proper kind of[f] altar to the LORD your God
on the top of this height. Using the

6:7 [m] S Jdg 3:9
6:8 [n] Dt 18:15; 1Ki 20:13,22; 2Ki 17:13,23; Ne 9:29; Job 36:10; Jer 25:5; Eze 18:30-31 [o] S Jdg 2:1 [p] Jos 24:17
6:9 [q] S Nu 10:9; Ps 136:24 [r] Ps 44:2
6:10 [s] S Ex 20:5 [t] S Jos 24:15
6:11 [u] S Ge 16:7 [v] S Jos 18:23 [w] ver 29; Jdg 7:14; 8:13,29 [x] S Nu 26:30 [y] Jdg 7:1; 8:1; Heb 11:32 [z] Ru 2:17; 3:2; 1Sa 23:1; 1Ch 21:20 [a] Ne 13:15; Isa 16:10; 63:3; La 1:15; Joel 3:13
6:12 [b] S Jos 1:5; Ru 2:4; 1Sa 10:7; Ps 129:8 [c] Jdg 11:1
6:13 [d] S Jos 3:5 [e] 2Sa 7:22; Ps 44:1; 78:3 [f] S Dt 31:17
6:14 [g] Heb 11:34 [h] ver 36; Jdg 10:1; 2Ki 14:27
6:15 [i] Isa 60:22 [j] 1Sa 9:21
6:16 [k] Ex 3:12; S Nu 14:43; Jos 1:5
6:17 [l] ver 36-37; S Ge 24:14; S Ex 3:12; S 4:8
6:19 [m] Jdg 13:15 [n] S Lev 19:36 [o] Ge 18:7-8
6:20 [p] Jdg 13:19
6:21 [q] S Ex 4:2 [r] S Lev 9:24
6:22 [s] Jdg 13:16, 21 [t] Ge 32:30; Jdg 13:22
6:23 [u] Da 10:19 [v] S Ge 16:13; S Dt 5:26
6:24 [w] S Ge 22:14 [x] S Jos 18:23
6:25 [y] ver 26,28, 30; Ex 34:13; S Jdg 2:13

[b] 15 Or *sir* [c] 19 That is, probably about 3/5 bushel (about 22 liters) [d] 25 Or *Take a full-grown, mature bull from your father's herd* [e] 25 That is, a symbol of the goddess Asherah; here and elsewhere in Judges [f] 26 Or *build with layers of stone an*

Lord because we truly love and appreciate him for who he is and what he has done? Or do we serve him primarily for what we can receive from him? If our faith and our devotion to God are genuine, we will follow the Lord even if it means trouble, suffering, persecution and loss (see article on FAITH AND GRACE, p. 1720).

6:13 WHERE ARE ALL HIS WONDERS? Gideon's question should also be asked by NT believers. If God's miraculous power is lacking among us, we need to seek his kingdom and righteousness until his mighty acts are again manifested in our midst (see articles on SIGNS OF BELIEVERS, p. 1513, THE KINGDOM OF GOD, p. 1430 and DIVINE HEALING, p. 1420).

6:14 THE LORD TURNED TO HIM. Evidently the "LORD" here and "the angel of the LORD" (v. 12) are identical. Theologians refer to this appearance as a theophany, i.e., a manifestation of God in physical form (cf. v. 22; see Ge 12:7, note; see article on ANGELS AND THE ANGEL OF THE LORD, p. 340).

6:16 I WILL BE WITH YOU. All those who, like Gideon, earnestly seek to serve God can depend on God's active presence with them. This promise is made to NT believers by Jesus Christ himself (Mt 28:19–20).

wood of the Asherah pole that you cut
down, offer the second[g] bull as a
burnt offering.[z]"
27So Gideon took ten of his servants
and did as the LORD told him. But because he was afraid of his family and
the men of the town, he did it at night
rather than in the daytime.
28In the morning when the men of
the town got up, there was Baal's altar,[a] demolished, with the Asherah
pole beside it cut down and the second
bull sacrificed on the newly built altar!
29They asked each other, "Who did
this?"
When they carefully investigated,
they were told, "Gideon son of Joash[b]
did it."
30The men of the town demanded of
Joash, "Bring out your son. He must
die, because he has broken down
Baal's altar[c] and cut down the Asherah pole beside it."
31But Joash replied to the hostile
crowd around him, "Are you going to
plead Baal's cause?[d] Are you trying to
save him? Whoever fights for him shall
be put to death by morning! If Baal
really is a god, he can defend himself
when someone breaks down his altar."
32So that day they called Gideon "Jerub-Baal,[h][e]" saying, "Let Baal contend with him," because he broke down
Baal's altar.
33Now all the Midianites, Amalekites[f] and other eastern peoples[g]
joined forces and crossed over the Jordan and camped in the Valley of Jezreel.[h] 34Then the Spirit of the LORD
came upon[i] Gideon, and he blew a
trumpet,[j] summoning the Abiez-
rites[k] to follow him. 35He sent mes- Jdg 11:29
sengers throughout Manasseh, calling
them to arms, and also into Asher,[l]
Zebulun and Naphtali,[m] so that they
too went up to meet them.[n]
36Gideon said to God, "If you will
save[o] Israel by my hand as you have
promised— 37look, I will place a wool
fleece[p] on the threshing floor.[q] If
there is dew only on the fleece and all
the ground is dry, then I will know[r]
that you will save Israel by my hand, as
you said." 38And that is what happened. Gideon rose early the next day;
he squeezed the fleece and wrung out
the dew—a bowlful of water.
39Then Gideon said to God, "Do not
be angry with me. Let me make just
one more request.[s] Allow me one
more test with the fleece. This time
make the fleece dry and the ground
covered with dew." 40That night God
did so. Only the fleece was dry; all the
ground was covered with dew.[t]

Gideon Defeats the Midianites

7 Early in the morning, Jerub-Baal[u]
(that is, Gideon[v]) and all his men
camped at the spring of Harod.[w] The
camp of Midian[x] was north of them in
the valley near the hill of Moreh.[y]
2The LORD said to Gideon, "You have
too many men for me to deliver Midian
into their hands. In order that Israel
may not boast against me that her own
strength[z] has saved her, 3announce
now to the people, 'Anyone who trem-

6:26 [z] S Ge 8:20
6:28 [a] ver 30; 1Ki 16:32; 2Ki 21:3
6:29 [b] S ver 11
6:30 [c] S ver 28
6:31 [d] 1Sa 24:15; Ps 43:1; Jer 30:13
6:32 [e] Jdg 7:1; 8:29,35; 9:1; 1Sa 12:11
6:33 [f] Nu 13:29 [g] S Ge 25:6 [h] S Jos 15:56; Eze 25:4; Hos 1:5
6:34 [i] S Jdg 3:10 [j] S Jos 6:20; S Jdg 3:27 [k] S Jos 17:2
6:35 [l] S Jos 17:7 [m] S Jdg 4:6 [n] Jdg 7:23
6:36 [o] S ver 14
6:37 [p] Job 31:20 [q] S Nu 18:27; 2Sa 6:6; 24:16 [r] S Ge 24:14
6:39 [s] S Ge 18:32
6:40 [t] Ex 4:3-7; Isa 38:7
7:1 [u] S Jdg 6:32 [v] S Jdg 6:11 [w] 2Sa 23:25 [x] S Ge 25:2 [y] S Ge 12:6
7:2 [z] S Dt 8:17; 2Co 4:7

g 26 Or *full-grown*; also in verse 28
h 32 *Jerub-Baal* means *let Baal contend.*

6:34 SPIRIT OF THE LORD CAME UPON GIDEON. The verb "came upon" literally means "to put on, clothe." God's Spirit clothed himself with Gideon in order to equip him to serve God's people, and Gideon went out in the power of the Spirit (cf. 1Ch 12:18; 2Ch 24:20; Lk 24:49). The experience of having the Spirit come upon and live in a person is promised to all who believe in Jesus Christ (see Ac 2:4,38–39; see article on BAPTISM IN THE HOLY SPIRIT, p. 1642).

6:37 A WOOL FLEECE. Gideon put out a fleece in order to strengthen his faith and bolster his confidence that God had indeed called him to deliver Israel (v. 36). Gideon's request for reassurance was accompanied by an attitude of faith, humility and obedience. (1) The God who understands human nature (cf. Ps 103:14) responded with love and grace. All God's faithful children have the right to ask God to strengthen their faith (cf. Ge 17:17–20; Ex 3:2; 4:1–9; Mk 9:24). (2) Even those who are filled with the Spirit may sometimes experience fear or uncertainty in difficult circumstances. In such times, God desires to encourage us and strengthen our faith (vv. 38–40).

7:2 YOU HAVE TOO MANY MEN. The command to reduce the army from 32,000 to 300 (vv. 2–7) illustrates four Biblical truths. (1) Only God's presence and activity can ensure victory for his people. God is able to work mightily through a small number of dedicated people. It is "not by might nor by power, but by my Spirit, says the LORD" (Zec 4:6). (2) Spiritual alertness and dedication, not great numbers, are of primary importance to God (cf. Rev 3:4–5). (3) Our ultimate resource and strength to meet all of life's challenges can be found in God and in him alone (Php 4:13). (4) Pride in "our" accomplishment inevitably becomes a hindrance to receiving fully God's power and help (Pr 8:13).

bles with fear may turn back and leave Mount Gilead.[a]' " So twenty-two thousand men left, while ten thousand remained.

4But the LORD said to Gideon, "There are still too many[b] men. Take them down to the water, and I will sift them for you there. If I say, 'This one shall go with you,' he shall go; but if I say, 'This one shall not go with you,' he shall not go."

5So Gideon took the men down to the water. There the LORD told him, "Separate those who lap the water with their tongues like a dog from those who kneel down to drink." 6Three hundred men[c] lapped with their hands to their mouths. All the rest got down on their knees to drink.

7The LORD said to Gideon, "With the three hundred men that lapped I will save you and give the Midianites into your hands.[d] Let all the other men go, each to his own place."[e] 8So Gideon sent the rest of the Israelites to their tents but kept the three hundred, who took over the provisions and trumpets of the others.

Now the camp of Midian lay below him in the valley. 9During that night the LORD said to Gideon, "Get up, go down against the camp, because I am going to give it into your hands.[f] 10If you are afraid to attack, go down to the camp with your servant Purah 11and listen to what they are saying. Afterward, you will be encouraged to attack the camp." So he and Purah his servant went down to the outposts of the camp. 12The Midianites, the Amalekites[g] and all the other eastern peoples had settled in the valley, thick as locusts.[h] Their camels[i] could no more be counted than the sand on the seashore.[j]

13Gideon arrived just as a man was telling a friend his dream. "I had a dream," he was saying. "A round loaf of barley bread came tumbling into the Midianite camp. It struck the tent with such force that the tent overturned and collapsed."

14His friend responded, "This can be nothing other than the sword of Gideon son of Joash,[k] the Israelite. God has given the Midianites and the whole camp into his hands."

15When Gideon heard the dream and its interpretation, he worshiped God.[l] He returned to the camp of Israel and called out, "Get up! The LORD has given the Midianite camp into your hands."[m] 16Dividing the three hundred men[n] into three companies,[o] he placed trumpets[p] and empty jars[q] in the hands of all of them, with torches[r] inside.

17"Watch me," he told them. "Follow my lead. When I get to the edge of the camp, do exactly as I do. 18When I and all who are with me blow our trumpets,[s] then from all around the camp blow yours and shout, 'For the LORD and for Gideon.' "

19Gideon and the hundred men with him reached the edge of the camp at the beginning of the middle watch, just after they had changed the guard. They blew their trumpets and broke the jars[t] that were in their hands. 20The three companies blew the trumpets and smashed the jars. Grasping the torches[u] in their left hands and holding in their right hands the trumpets they were to blow, they shouted, "A sword[v] for the LORD and for Gideon!" 21While each man held his position around the camp, all the Midianites ran, crying out as they fled.[w]

22When the three hundred trumpets sounded,[x] the LORD caused the men throughout the camp to turn on each other[y] with their swords.[z] The army fled to Beth Shittah toward Zererah as far as the border of Abel Meholah[a] near Tabbath. 23Israelites from Naphtali, Asher[b] and all Manasseh were called out,[c] and they pursued the Midianites.[d] 24Gideon sent messengers throughout the hill country of Ephraim, saying, "Come down against the Midianites and seize the waters of the Jordan[e] ahead of them as far as Beth Barah."

So all the men of Ephraim were called out and they took the waters of the Jordan as far as Beth Barah. 25They also captured two of the Midianite leaders, Oreb and Zeeb[f]. They killed Oreb at the rock of Oreb,[g] and

7:3 [a] Dt 20:8; S Jos 12:2
7:4 [b] 1Sa 14:6
7:6 [c] Ge 14:14
7:7 [d] S Jos 8:7 [e] 1Sa 14:6
7:9 [f] ver 13-15; S Jos 2:24; S Jdg 1:2
7:12 [g] Nu 13:29 [h] S Dt 28:42; Jer 46:23 [i] Jer 49:29 [j] S Jos 11:4
7:14 [k] S Jdg 6:11
7:15 [l] 1Sa 15:31 [m] S ver 9
7:16 [n] Ge 14:15 [o] Jdg 9:43; 1Sa 11:11; 2Sa 18:2 [p] S Lev 25:9 [q] ver 19; Ge 24:14 [r] S Ge 15:17
7:18 [s] S Jdg 3:27
7:19 [t] S ver 16
7:20 [u] S Ge 15:17 [v] S Dt 32:41
7:21 [w] 2Ki 7:7
7:22 [x] S Jos 6:20 [y] 1Sa 14:20; 2Ch 20:23; Isa 9:21; 19:2; Eze 38:21; Hag 2:22; Zec 14:13 [z] Hab 3:14 [a] 1Sa 18:19; 1Ki 4:12; 19:16
7:23 [b] S Jos 17:7 [c] Jdg 6:35 [d] Ps 83:9
7:24 [e] S Jos 2:7
7:25 [f] Jdg 8:3; Ps 83:11 [g] Isa 10:26

7:11 YOU WILL BE ENCOURAGED. God encouraged Gideon in order to alleviate his fear and strengthen his faith (cf. v. 10). Believers, committed to God's will and faithfully serving him, will at times need God's encouragement. When those times come, we should pray that God will inspire us through his Spirit with faith, hope and courage (see 2Co 1:4–11; Php 4:6–7).

Zeeb at the winepress of Zeeb. They pursued the Midianites[h] and brought the heads of Oreb and Zeeb to Gideon, who was by the Jordan.[i]

Zebah and Zalmunna

8 Now the Ephraimites asked Gideon,[j] "Why have you treated us like this? Why didn't you call us when you went to fight Midian?[k]"[l] And they criticized him sharply.[m]

2 But he answered them, "What have I accomplished compared to you? Aren't the gleanings of Ephraim's grapes better than the full grape harvest of Abiezer?[n] 3 God gave Oreb and Zeeb,[o] the Midianite leaders, into your hands. What was I able to do compared to you?" At this, their resentment against him subsided.

4 Gideon and his three hundred men, exhausted yet keeping up the pursuit, came to the Jordan[p] and crossed it. 5 He said to the men of Succoth,[q] "Give my troops some bread; they are worn out,[r] and I am still pursuing Zebah and Zalmunna,[s] the kings of Midian."

6 But the officials of Succoth[t] said, "Do you already have the hands of Zebah and Zalmunna in your possession? Why should we give bread[u] to your troops?"[v]

7 Then Gideon replied, "Just for that, when the LORD has given Zebah and Zalmunna[w] into my hand, I will tear your flesh with desert thorns and briers."

8 From there he went up to Peniel[i][x] and made the same request of them, but they answered as the men of Succoth had. 9 So he said to the men of Peniel, "When I return in triumph, I will tear down this tower."[y]

10 Now Zebah and Zalmunna were in Karkor with a force of about fifteen thousand men, all that were left of the armies of the eastern peoples; a hundred and twenty thousand swordsmen had fallen.[z] 11 Gideon went up by the route of the nomads east of Nobah[a] and Jogbehah[b] and fell upon the unsuspecting army. 12 Zebah and Zalmunna, the two kings of Midian, fled, but he pursued them and captured them, routing their entire army.

13 Gideon son of Joash[c] then returned from the battle by the Pass of Heres.[d] 14 He caught a young man of Succoth and questioned him, and the young man wrote down for him the names of the seventy-seven officials of Succoth,[e] the elders[f] of the town. 15 Then Gideon came and said to the men of Succoth, "Here are Zebah and Zalmunna, about whom you taunted me by saying, 'Do you already have the hands of Zebah and Zalmunna in your possession? Why should we give bread to your exhausted men?[g]' " 16 He took the elders of the town and taught the men of Succoth a lesson[h] by punishing them with desert thorns and briers. 17 He also pulled down the tower of Peniel[i] and killed the men of the town.[j]

18 Then he asked Zebah and Zalmunna, "What kind of men did you kill at Tabor?[k]"

"Men like you," they answered, "each one with the bearing of a prince."

19 Gideon replied, "Those were my brothers, the sons of my own mother. As surely as the LORD lives,[l] if you had spared their lives, I would not kill you." 20 Turning to Jether, his oldest son, he said, "Kill them!" But Jether did not draw his sword, because he was only a boy and was afraid.

21 Zebah and Zalmunna said, "Come, do it yourself. 'As is the man, so is his strength.' " So Gideon stepped forward and killed them, and took the ornaments[m] off their camels' necks.

Gideon's Ephod

22 The Israelites said to Gideon, "Rule over us — you, your son and your grandson — because you have saved us out of the hand of Midian."

23 But Gideon told them, "I will not rule over you, nor will my son rule over

7:25 [h] Isa 9:4 [i] Jdg 8:4; Ps 106:43
8:1 [j] S Jdg 6:11 [k] S Ge 25:2 [l] Jdg 12:1 [m] 2Sa 19:41
8:2 [n] S Nu 26:30
8:3 [o] S Jdg 7:25
8:4 [p] Jdg 7:25
8:5 [q] S Ge 33:17 [r] Job 16:7; Ps 6:6; Jer 45:3 [s] ver 7,12; Ps 83:11
8:6 [t] ver 14 [u] 1Sa 25:11 [v] ver 15
8:7 [w] S ver 5
8:8 [x] ver 9,17; Ge 32:30; 1Ki 12:25
8:9 [y] ver 17
8:10 [z] S Jdg 6:5; Isa 9:4
8:11 [a] Nu 32:42 [b] S Nu 32:35
8:13 [c] S Jdg 6:11 [d] Jdg 1:35
8:14 [e] ver 6 [f] S Ex 3:16
8:15 [g] ver 6
8:16 [h] 1Sa 14:12
8:17 [i] S ver 8 [j] ver 9
8:18 [k] S Jos 19:22
8:19 [l] S Nu 14:21
8:21 [m] ver 26; Isa 3:18

[i] 8 Hebrew *Penuel*, a variant of *Peniel*; also in verses 9 and 17

8:6 GIVE BREAD TO YOUR TROOPS? By refusing to help Gideon's army, the Israelites of Succoth and Peniel (v. 8) were allying themselves with Israel's enemy, a decision for which they were punished (vv. 15–17). Likewise, NT believers are required to take a definite stand for Christ and righteousness; otherwise, they are viewed in reality as being against him (Mt 12:30).

8:16–17 TOOK THE ELDERS ... KILLED THE MEN. The punishment inflicted by Gideon on the Israelites of Succoth and Peniel was severe but justifiable. To be a member of God's people while refusing to stand by those fighting God's battle is a terrible offense in the Lord's eyes (see previous note).

you. The LORD will rule[n] over you."
24And he said, "I do have one request,
that each of you give me an earring[o]
from your share of the plunder.[p]" (It
was the custom of the Ishmaelites[q] to
wear gold earrings.)
25They answered, "We'll be glad to
give them." So they spread out a garment, and each man threw a ring from
his plunder onto it. 26The weight of the
gold rings he asked for came to seventeen hundred shekels,[j] not counting
the ornaments, the pendants and the
purple garments worn by the kings of
Midian or the chains[r] that were on
their camels' necks. 27Gideon made
the gold into an ephod,[s] which he
placed in Ophrah,[t] his town. All Israel
prostituted themselves by worshiping
it there, and it became a snare[u] to Gideon and his family.[v]

Gideon's Death

28Thus Midian was subdued before
the Israelites and did not raise its
head[w] again. During Gideon's lifetime, the land enjoyed peace[x] forty
years.
29Jerub-Baal[y] son of Joash[z] went
back home to live. 30He had seventy
sons[a] of his own, for he had many
wives. 31His concubine,[b] who lived in
Shechem, also bore him a son, whom
he named Abimelech.[c] 32Gideon son
of Joash died at a good old age[d] and
was buried in the tomb of his father
Joash in Ophrah of the Abiezrites.
33No sooner had Gideon died than
the Israelites again prostituted themselves to the Baals.[e] They set up
Baal-Berith[f] as their god[g] and 34did
not remember[h] the LORD their God,
who had rescued them from the hands
of all their enemies on every side.
35They also failed to show kindness to
the family of Jerub-Baal[i] (that is, Gideon) for all the good things he had done
for them.[j]

Abimelech

9 Abimelech[k] son of Jerub-Baal[l]
went to his mother's brothers in
Shechem and said to them and to all
his mother's clan, 2"Ask all the citizens of Shechem, 'Which is better for
you: to have all seventy of Jerub-Baal's
sons rule over you, or just one man?'
Remember, I am your flesh and
blood.[m]"
3When the brothers repeated all this
to the citizens of Shechem, they were
inclined to follow Abimelech, for they
said, "He is our brother." 4They gave
him seventy shekels[k] of silver from
the temple of Baal-Berith,[n] and Abimelech used it to hire reckless adventurers,[o] who became his followers. 5He
went to his father's home in Ophrah
and on one stone murdered his seventy
brothers,[p] the sons of Jerub-Baal. But
Jotham,[q] the youngest son of Jerub-
Baal, escaped by hiding.[r] 6Then all
the citizens of Shechem and Beth Millo[s] gathered beside the great tree[t] at
the pillar in Shechem to crown Abimelech king.
7When Jotham[u] was told about this,
he climbed up on the top of Mount Gerizim[v] and shouted to them, "Listen to
me, citizens of Shechem, so that God
may listen to you. 8One day the trees
went out to anoint a king for themselves. They said to the olive tree, 'Be
our king.'
9"But the olive tree answered,
'Should I give up my oil, by which both
gods and men are honored, to hold
sway over the trees?'

8:23 [n]S Ex 16:8; S Nu 11:20; 1Sa 12:12
8:24 [o]S Ge 35:4 [p]S Ge 49:27 [q]S Ge 16:11
8:26 [r]S ver 21
8:27 [s]S Ex 25:7; Jdg 17:5; 18:14 [t]S Jos 18:23 [u]S Ex 10:7 [v]S Ex 32:2
8:28 [w]Ps 83:2 [x]S Jdg 3:11
8:29 [y]S Jdg 6:32 [z]S Jdg 6:11
8:30 [a]Jdg 9:2,5, 18,24; 12:14; 2Ki 10:1
8:31 [b]S Ge 22:24 [c]Jdg 9:1; 10:1; 2Sa 11:21
8:32 [d]S Ge 15:15
8:33 [e]S Jdg 2:11, 13,19 [f]Jdg 9:4 [g]Jdg 9:27,46
8:34 [h]S Jdg 3:7; S Ne 9:17
8:35 [i]S Jdg 6:32 [j]Jdg 9:16
9:1 [k]S Jdg 8:31 [l]S Jdg 6:32
9:2 [m]S Ge 29:14
9:4 [n]S Jdg 8:33 [o]Jdg 11:3; 1Sa 25:25; 2Ch 13:7; Job 30:8
9:5 [p]S Jdg 8:30 [q]ver 7,21,57 [r]2Ki 11:2; 2Ch 22:9
9:6 [s]ver 20; 2Ki 12:20 [t]S Ge 12:6; S Jdg 4:11
9:7 [u]S ver 5 [v]S Dt 11:29; Jn 4:20

[j]26 That is, about 43 pounds (about 19.5 kilograms) [k]4 That is, about 1 3/4 pounds (about 0.8 kilogram)

8:27 AN EPHOD. This ephod was probably a copy of the outer garment used by the high priest when serving God (Ex 28:6, note). Gideon probably made it with good intentions, as a memorial to Israel's success in the work of God. However, the ephod was unauthorized by God and became an object of veneration, glorifying Gideon and Israel's achievement; this idolatrous act brought spiritual disaster to the nation and to Gideon's household. We can learn from Gideon's tragic mistake that: (1) To exalt and glorify churches, institutions or human leaders who possess special charisma will result in spiritual corruption and death. (2) When planning to do something for God, we must pray for wisdom to foresee potential consequences that may eventually do great damage to God's kingdom.

9:4–5 ABIMELECH ... MURDERED HIS SEVENTY BROTHERS. This great tragedy in Gideon's family was the result of Gideon's polygamy (8:30–31). His concubine in Shechem gave birth to Abimelech, who later killed seventy of his brothers. Gideon had leadership ability on the battlefield, but not in the home. God, on the other hand, places a great importance on the family. Under the new covenant he commands that no one be appointed as an overseer of God's people who cannot manage himself or his family well (1Ti 3:1–5).

10"Next, the trees said to the fig
tree, 'Come and be our king.'
11"But the fig tree replied, 'Should I
give up my fruit, so good and sweet, to
hold sway over the trees?'
12"Then the trees said to the vine,
'Come and be our king.'
13"But the vine answered, 'Should I
give up my wine,[w] which cheers both
gods and men, to hold sway over the
trees?'
14"Finally all the trees said to the
thornbush, 'Come and be our king.'
15"The thornbush said to the trees,
'If you really want to anoint me king
over you, come and take refuge in my
shade;[x] but if not, then let fire come
out[y] of the thornbush and consume
the cedars of Lebanon!'[z]
16"Now if you have acted honorably
and in good faith when you made Abimelech king, and if you have been fair to
Jerub-Baal and his family, and if you
have treated him as he deserves—
17and to think that my father fought for
you, risked[a] his life to rescue you
from the hand of Midian **18**(but today
you have revolted against my father's
family, murdered his seventy sons[b] on
a single stone, and made Abimelech,
the son of his slave girl, king over the
citizens of Shechem because he is your
brother)— **19**if then you have acted
honorably and in good faith toward Jerub-Baal and his family today,[c] may
Abimelech be your joy, and may you be
his, too! **20**But if you have not, let fire
come out[d] from Abimelech and consume you, citizens of Shechem[e] and
Beth Millo,[f] and let fire come out
from you, citizens of Shechem and
Beth Millo, and consume Abimelech!"
21Then Jotham[g] fled, escaping to
Beer,[h] and he lived there because he
was afraid of his brother Abimelech.
22After Abimelech had governed Israel three years, **23**God sent an evil
spirit[i] between Abimelech and the citizens of Shechem, who acted treacherously against Abimelech. **24**God did
this in order that the crime against Jerub-Baal's seventy sons,[j] the shedding[k] of their blood, might be
avenged[l] on their brother Abimelech
and on the citizens of Shechem, who
had helped him[m] murder his brothers.
25In opposition to him these citizens of
Shechem set men on the hilltops to ambush and rob everyone who passed by,
and this was reported to Abimelech.
26Now Gaal son of Ebed[n] moved
with his brothers into Shechem, and its
citizens put their confidence in him.
27After they had gone out into the
fields and gathered the grapes and
trodden[o] them, they held a festival in
the temple of their god.[p] While they
were eating and drinking, they cursed
Abimelech. **28**Then Gaal son of Ebed[q]
said, "Who[r] is Abimelech, and who is
Shechem, that we should be subject to
him? Isn't he Jerub-Baal's son, and
isn't Zebul his deputy? Serve the men
of Hamor,[s] Shechem's father! Why
should we serve Abimelech? **29**If only
this people were under my command![t] Then I would get rid of him. I
would say to Abimelech, 'Call out your
whole army!' "[1u]
30When Zebul the governor of the
city heard what Gaal son of Ebed said,
he was very angry. **31**Under cover he
sent messengers to Abimelech, saying,
"Gaal son of Ebed and his brothers
have come to Shechem and are stirring
up the city against you. **32**Now then,
during the night you and your men
should come and lie in wait[v] in the
fields. **33**In the morning at sunrise, advance against the city. When Gaal and
his men come out against you, do whatever your hand finds to do.[w]"
34So Abimelech and all his troops
set out by night and took up concealed
positions near Shechem in four companies. **35**Now Gaal son of Ebed had gone
out and was standing at the entrance
to the city gate[x] just as Abimelech
and his soldiers came out from their
hiding place.[y]
36When Gaal saw them, he said to
Zebul, "Look, people are coming down
from the tops of the mountains!"
Zebul replied, "You mistake the
shadows of the mountains for men."
37But Gaal spoke up again: "Look,

9:13 [w]S Ge 14:18; Ecc 2:3; SS 4:10 **9:15** [x]Isa 30:2 [y]ver 20 [z]S Dt 3:25; 1Ki 5:6; Ps 29:5; 92:12; Isa 2:13 **9:17** [a]Jdg 12:3; 1Sa 19:5; 28:21; Job 13:14; Ps 119:109 **9:18** [b]S Jdg 8:30 **9:19** [c]ver 16 **9:20** [d]ver 15 [e]ver 45 [f]S ver 6 **9:21** [g]S ver 5 [h]Nu 21:16 **9:23** [i]1Sa 16:14, 23; 18:10; 19:9; 1Ki 22:22 **9:24** [j]S Jdg 8:30 [k]S Ge 9:6; Nu 35:33; 1Ki 2:32 [l]ver 56-57 [m]Dt 27:25 **9:26** [n]ver 28,31, 41 **9:27** [o]Isa 16:10; Am 5:11; 9:13 [p]S Jdg 8:33 **9:28** [q]S ver 26 [r]1Sa 25:10 [s]S Ge 33:19 **9:29** [t]2Sa 15:4 [u]ver 38 **9:32** [v]Jos 8:2 **9:33** [w]1Sa 10:7 **9:35** [x]S Jos 2:5 [y]Ps 32:7; Isa 28:15,17; Jer 49:10

[1]29 Septuagint; Hebrew *him." Then he said to Abimelech, "Call out your whole army!"*

9:13 WINE. The Hebrew word used here for wine is *tirosh*, meaning "new wine." *Tirosh* typically refers to fresh, pure juice of the grape, the produce of the vine (see Isa 65:8, note; see article on WINE IN THE OLD TESTAMENT, p. 204).

9:23 GOD SENT AN EVIL SPIRIT. God used demonic spirits to punish Abimelech and the citizens of Shechem for the murder of Gideon's sons. The evil spirit caused strife and distrust (see 1Sa 16:14,23, notes).

people are coming down from the center of the land, and a company is coming from the direction of the soothsay-
ers' tree."
38Then Zebul said to him, "Where is
your big talk now, you who said, 'Who
is Abimelech that we should be subject
to him?' Aren't these the men you ridiculed?[z] Go out and fight them!"
39So Gaal led out[m] the citizens of
Shechem and fought Abimelech.
40Abimelech chased him, and many fell
wounded in the flight—all the way to
the entrance to the gate. **41**Abimelech
stayed in Arumah, and Zebul drove
Gaal and his brothers out of Shechem.
42The next day the people of Shechem went out to the fields, and this
was reported to Abimelech. **43**So he
took his men, divided them into three
companies[a] and set an ambush[b] in
the fields. When he saw the people
coming out of the city, he rose to attack them. **44**Abimelech and the companies with him rushed forward to a
position at the entrance to the city
gate. Then two companies rushed upon
those in the fields and struck them
down. **45**All that day Abimelech
pressed his attack against the city until he had captured it and killed its people. Then he destroyed the city[c] and
scattered salt[d] over it.
46On hearing this, the citizens in the
tower of Shechem went into the stronghold of the temple[e] of El-Berith.
47When Abimelech heard that they had
assembled there, **48**he and all his men
went up Mount Zalmon.[f] He took an
ax and cut off some branches, which he
lifted to his shoulders. He ordered the
men with him, "Quick! Do what you
have seen me do!" **49**So all the men cut
branches and followed Abimelech.
They piled them against the stronghold and set it on fire over the people
inside. So all the people in the tower of
Shechem, about a thousand men and
women, also died.
50Next Abimelech went to Thebez[g]
and besieged it and captured it. **51**Inside the city, however, was a strong
tower, to which all the men and wom-
en—all the people of the city—fled.
They locked themselves in and climbed
up on the tower roof. **52**Abimelech
went to the tower and stormed it. But
as he approached the entrance to the
tower to set it on fire, **53**a woman
dropped an upper millstone on his head
and cracked his skull.[h]
54Hurriedly he called to his armor-
bearer, "Draw your sword and kill
me,[i] so that they can't say, 'A woman
killed him.'" So his servant ran him
through, and he died. **55**When the Israelites saw that Abimelech was dead,
they went home.
56Thus God repaid the wickedness
that Abimelech had done to his father
by murdering his seventy brothers.
57God also made the men of Shechem
pay for all their wickedness.[j] The
curse of Jotham[k] son of Jerub-Baal
came on them.

Tola

10 After the time of Abimelech[l] a
man of Issachar,[m] Tola son of
Puah,[n] the son of Dodo, rose to save[o]
Israel. He lived in Shamir,[p] in the hill
country of Ephraim. **2**He led[n] Israel
twenty-three years; then he died, and
was buried in Shamir.

Jair

3He was followed by Jair[q] of Gilead,
who led Israel twenty-two years. **4**He
had thirty sons, who rode thirty donkeys.[r] They controlled thirty towns in
Gilead, which to this day are called
Havvoth Jair.[o][s] **5**When Jair[t] died, he
was buried in Kamon.

Jephthah

6Again the Israelites did evil in the

9:38 [z] ver 28-29
9:43 [a] S Jdg 7:16 [b] Jos 8:2
9:45 [c] ver 20 [d] Jer 48:9
9:46 [e] S Jdg 8:33
9:48 [f] Ps 68:14
9:50 [g] 2Sa 11:21
9:53 [h] 2Sa 11:21
9:54 [i] 1Sa 31:4; 2Sa 1:9
9:57 [j] ver 24; Ps 94:23 [k] S ver 5
10:1 [l] S Jdg 8:31 [m] S Ge 30:18 [n] S Ge 46:13 [o] S Jdg 6:14 [p] Jos 15:48
10:3 [q] S Nu 32:41
10:4 [r] S Ge 49:11; S 1Ki 1:33 [s] S Nu 32:41
10:5 [t] S Nu 32:41

[m] 39 Or *Gaal went out in the sight of*
[n] 2 Traditionally *judged*; also in verse 3
[o] 4 Or *called the settlements of Jair*

10:6 AGAIN THE ISRAELITES DID EVIL. Once again the Israelites forsook the Lord and served other gods (see article on THE NATURE OF IDOLATRY, p. 394). (1) In the Canaanite religion a person could be devoted to religion and at the same time indulge in cult prostitution. In seeking fertility from the gods, the adherents of those religions found that religion and sinful sexual pleasures were compatible.

(2) In a similar vein, some who profess to be Christians teach that salvation is compatible with sexual looseness. They allege that because salvation is by grace, grace automatically blots out any and all sins; thus sexual immorality, drunkenness, theft, homosexuality, cruelty, and the like need not be forsaken in order to have salvation in Christ.

(3) Such a doctrine is a perversion of God's redemption for his people and must be rejected by all who are loyal to God and his word (see Mt 7:21,

eyes of the LORD.[u] They served the Baals and the Ashtoreths,[v] and the gods
of Aram,[w] the gods of Sidon,[x] the
gods of Moab, the gods of the Ammonites[y][z] and the gods of the Philistines.[a] And because the Israelites forsook the LORD[b] and no longer served
him, **7**he became angry[c] with them.
He sold them[d] into the hands of the
Philistines and the Ammonites, **8**who
that year shattered and crushed them.
For eighteen years they oppressed all
the Israelites on the east side of the
Jordan in Gilead,[e] the land of the Amorites. **9**The Ammonites also crossed
the Jordan to fight against Judah,[f]
Benjamin and the house of Ephraim;[g]
and Israel was in great distress.
10Then the Israelites cried[h] out to the
LORD, "We have sinned[i] against you,
forsaking our God and serving the Baals."[j]
11The LORD replied, "When the Egyptians,[k] the Amorites,[l] the Ammonites,[m] the Philistines,[n] **12**the Sidonians, the Amalekites[o] and the
Maonites[p][p] oppressed you[q] and you
cried to me for help, did I not save you
from their hands? **13**But you have forsaken[r] me and served other gods,[s]
so I will no longer save you. **14**Go and
cry out to the gods you have chosen.
Let them save[t] you when you are in
trouble![u]"
15But the Israelites said to the LORD,
"We have sinned. Do with us whatever
you think best,[v] but please rescue us
now." **16**Then they got rid of the foreign
gods among them and served the
LORD.[w] And he could bear Israel's misery[x] no longer.[y]
17When the Ammonites were called
to arms and camped in Gilead, the Israelites assembled and camped at Mizpah.[z] **18**The leaders of the people of
Gilead said to each other, "Whoever
will launch the attack against the Ammonites will be the head[a] of all those
living in Gilead."
11 Jephthah[b] the Gileadite was a
mighty warrior.[c] His father
was Gilead;[d] his mother was a prostitute.[e] **2**Gilead's wife also bore him
sons, and when they were grown up,
they drove Jephthah away. "You are
not going to get any inheritance in our
family," they said, "because you are
the son of another woman." **3**So Jephthah fled from his brothers and settled
in the land of Tob,[f] where a group of
adventurers[g] gathered around him
and followed him.
4Some time later, when the Ammonites[h] made war on Israel, **5**the elders
of Gilead went to get Jephthah from the
land of Tob. **6**"Come," they said, "be
our commander, so we can fight the
Ammonites."
7Jephthah said to them, "Didn't you
hate me and drive me from my father's
house?[i] Why do you come to me now,
when you're in trouble?"
8The elders of Gilead said to him,
"Nevertheless, we are turning to you
now; come with us to fight the Ammonites, and you will be our head[j] over all
who live in Gilead."
9Jephthah answered, "Suppose you
take me back to fight the Ammonites
and the LORD gives them to me—will I
really be your head?"
10The elders of Gilead replied, "The
LORD is our witness;[k] we will certainly
do as you say." **11**So Jephthah went
with the elders[l] of Gilead, and the

10:6 [u]S Jdg 2:11 [v]S Jdg 2:13 [w]Eze 27:16 [x]S Ge 10:15 [y]S Ge 19:38 [z]S Nu 21:29 [a]S Ge 26:1; S Jdg 2:12 [b]S Dt 32:15 **10:7** [c]S Dt 31:17 [d]S Dt 32:30 **10:8** [e]S Jos 12:2 **10:9** [f]ver 17; Jdg 11:4 [g]Jdg 1:22 **10:10** [h]S Jdg 3:9 [i]S Ex 9:27; Ps 32:5; Jer 3:25; 8:14; 14:20 [j]Jer 2:27 **10:11** [k]Ex 14:30 [l]S Ge 14:7 [m]S Jdg 3:13 [n]S Jdg 3:31 **10:12** [o]S Ge 14:7 [p]S Jos 15:55 [q]S Jdg 4:3 **10:13** [r]S Dt 32:15 [s]Jer 11:10; 13:10 **10:14** [t]Isa 44:17; 57:13 [u]Dt 32:37; Jer 2:28; 11:12; Hab 2:18 **10:15** [v]1Sa 3:18; 2Sa 10:12; 15:26; Job 1:21; Isa 39:8 **10:16** [w]Jos 24:23; Jer 18:8 [x]Isa 63:9 [y]S Dt 32:36 **10:17** [z]S Ge 31:49; Jdg 11:29 **10:18** [a]Jdg 11:8, 9 **11:1** [b]Jdg 12:1; 1Sa 12:11; Heb 11:32 [c]Jdg 6:12 [d]Nu 26:29 [e]S Ge 38:15 **11:3** [f]ver 5; 2Sa 10:6,8 [g]S Jdg 9:4 **11:4** [h]S Jdg 10:9 **11:7** [i]S Ge 26:16 **11:8** [j]S Jdg 10:18 **11:10** [k]S Ge 31:50; S Isa 1:2 **11:11** [l]1Sa 8:4; 2Sa 3:17

[p]*12* Hebrew; some Septuagint manuscripts *Midianites*

note; 1Jn 2:4, note; Rev 21:8, note; see article on STANDARDS OF SEXUAL MORALITY, p. 1936).

10:7 HE BECAME ANGRY. Anger at sin and wickedness is an inherent attribute of God (see article on THE ATTRIBUTES OF GOD, p. 882). It is an expression of his goodness and his love for righteousness. When believers express anger against sin, cruelty, evil or injustice, it is not wrong, for such individuals share in the divine nature and participate in God's love of righteousness and hatred of evil (see Mk 3:5; Ro 1:18, note; Heb 1:9, note).

10:16 COULD BEAR ISRAEL'S MISERY NO LONGER. Although the Israelites justly deserved the suffering they were undergoing, God was still deeply moved by their misery. (1) Their suffering and plight grieved his heart, just as the miseries of a child grieve and hurt a loving father. In a sense, God was heartbroken by their trouble (cf. Eze 6:9) and was moved by compassion to be merciful toward them (cf. Hos 11:7–9).

(2) God's tender mercies are available to all who have sinned, who are suffering grievous consequences, and who repent and seek forgiveness. In such situations we can depend on God to be touched by our misery and suffering, to have pity on us, and to restore us to a place of fellowship and blessing.

(3) God's compassion for a lost world moved him to send his Son to reconcile sinners to himself (Jn 3:16).

people made him head and commander
over them. And he repeated[m] all his
words before the LORD in Mizpah.[n]
12Then Jephthah sent messengers to
the Ammonite king with the question:
"What do you have against us that you
have attacked our country?"
13The king of the Ammonites answered Jephthah's messengers, "When
Israel came up out of Egypt, they took
away my land from the Arnon[o] to the
Jabbok,[p] all the way to the Jordan.
Now give it back peaceably."
14Jephthah sent back messengers to
the Ammonite king, **15**saying:

"This is what Jephthah says: Israel did not take the land of Moab[q]
or the land of the Ammonites.[r]
16But when they came up out of
Egypt, Israel went through the
desert to the Red Sea[q][s] and on
to Kadesh.[t] **17**Then Israel sent
messengers[u] to the king of
Edom, saying, 'Give us permission to go through your country,'[v] but the king of Edom would
not listen. They sent also to the
king of Moab,[w] and he refused.[x]
So Israel stayed at Kadesh.
18"Next they traveled through
the desert, skirted the lands of
Edom[y] and Moab, passed along
the eastern side[z] of the country
of Moab, and camped on the other
side of the Arnon.[a] They did not
enter the territory of Moab, for the
Arnon was its border.
19"Then Israel sent messengers[b] to Sihon king of the Amorites, who ruled in Heshbon,[c]
and said to him, 'Let us pass
through your country to our own
place.'[d] **20**Sihon, however, did
not trust Israel[r] to pass through
his territory. He mustered all his
men and encamped at Jahaz and
fought with Israel.[e]
21"Then the LORD, the God of Israel, gave Sihon and all his men
into Israel's hands, and they defeated them. Israel took over all
the land of the Amorites who lived
in that country, **22**capturing all of
it from the Arnon to the Jabbok
and from the desert to the Jordan.[f]
23"Now since the LORD, the God
of Israel, has driven the Amorites
out before his people Israel, what
right have you to take it over?
24Will you not take what your god
Chemosh[g] gives you? Likewise,
whatever the LORD our God has
given us,[h] we will possess. **25**Are
you better than Balak son of Zippor,[i] king of Moab? Did he ever
quarrel with Israel or fight with
them?[j] **26**For three hundred
years Israel occupied[k] Heshbon,
Aroer,[l] the surrounding settlements and all the towns along the
Arnon. Why didn't you retake
them during that time? **27**I have
not wronged you, but you are doing me wrong by waging war
against me. Let the LORD, the
Judge,[s][m] decide[n] the dispute
this day between the Israelites
and the Ammonites.[o]"

28The king of Ammon, however, paid
no attention to the message Jephthah
sent him.
29Then the Spirit[p] of the LORD came
upon Jephthah. He crossed Gilead and
Manasseh, passed through Mizpah[q]
of Gilead, and from there he advanced
against the Ammonites.[r] **30**And Jephthah made a vow[s] to the LORD: "If you
give the Ammonites into my hands,
31whatever comes out of the door of my
house to meet me when I return in triumph[t] from the Ammonites will be
the LORD's, and I will sacrifice it as a
burnt offering.[u]"
32Then Jephthah went over to fight
the Ammonites, and the LORD gave
them into his hands. **33**He devastated
twenty towns from Aroer to the vicinity
of Minnith,[v] as far as Abel Keramim.
Thus Israel subdued Ammon.
34When Jephthah returned to his
home in Mizpah, who should come out
to meet him but his daughter, dancing[w] to the sound of tambourines![x]
She was an only child.[y] Except for her
he had neither son nor daughter.
35When he saw her, he tore his
clothes[z] and cried, "Oh! My daughter!
You have made me miserable and
wretched, because I have made a vow
to the LORD that I cannot break.[a]"

11:11 [m] Ex 19:9; 1Sa 8:21 [n] S Jos 11:3
11:13 [o] S Nu 21:13 [p] S Nu 21:24
11:15 [q] Dt 2:9 [r] Dt 2:19
11:16 [s] Nu 14:25; S Dt 1:40 [t] S Ge 14:7
11:17 [u] ver 19; S Ge 32:3; Nu 20:14 [v] S Nu 20:17 [w] Jer 48:1 [x] S Jos 24:9
11:18 [y] S Nu 20:21 [z] Dt 2:8 [a] S Nu 21:13
11:19 [b] S ver 17 [c] S Jos 12:2 [d] Nu 21:21-22
11:20 [e] Nu 21:23
11:22 [f] Nu 21:21-26; S Dt 2:26
11:24 [g] S Nu 21:29; S Jos 3:10 [h] Dt 2:36
11:25 [i] Nu 22:2 [j] S Jos 24:9
11:26 [k] Nu 21:25 [l] S Nu 32:34; S Jos 13:9
11:27 [m] S Ge 18:25 [n] S Ge 16:5 [o] 2Ch 20:12
11:29 [p] S Jdg 3:10 [q] S Ge 31:49 [r] S Jdg 10:17
11:30 [s] S Ge 28:20; Nu 30:10; 1Sa 1:11; Pr 31:2
11:31 [t] Ge 28:21 [u] S Ge 8:20; Lev 1:3; Jdg 13:16
11:33 [v] Eze 27:17
11:34 [w] S Ex 15:20 [x] S Ge 31:27; S Ex 15:20 [y] Zec 12:10
11:35 [z] S Nu 14:6 [a] Nu 30:2; S Dt 23:21; Ecc 5:2,4,5

[q] *16* Hebrew *Yam Suph*; that is, Sea of Reeds
[r] *20* Or *however, would not make an agreement for Israel*
[s] *27* Or *Ruler*

11:29 SPIRIT OF THE LORD. See 3:10, note.

36"My father," she replied, "you
have given your word to the LORD. Do
to me just as you promised,[b] now that
the LORD has avenged you[c] of your enemies,[d] the Ammonites. 37But grant
me this one request," she said. "Give
me two months to roam the hills and
weep with my friends, because I will
never marry."
38"You may go," he said. And he let
her go for two months. She and the
girls went into the hills and wept because she would never marry. 39After
the two months, she returned to her
father and he did to her as he had
vowed. And she was a virgin.
From this comes the Israelite custom 40that each year the young women
of Israel go out for four days to commemorate the daughter of Jephthah
the Gileadite.

Jephthah and Ephraim

12 The men of Ephraim called out
their forces, crossed over to Zaphon[e] and said to Jephthah,[f] "Why
did you go to fight the Ammonites without calling us to go with you?[g] We're
going to burn down your house over
your head."
2Jephthah answered, "I and my people were engaged in a great struggle
with the Ammonites, and although I
called, you didn't save me out of their
hands. 3When I saw that you wouldn't
help, I took my life in my hands[h] and
crossed over to fight the Ammonites,
and the LORD gave me the victory[i]
over them. Now why have you come up
today to fight me?"
4Jephthah then called together the
men of Gilead[j] and fought against
Ephraim. The Gileadites struck them
down because the Ephraimites had
said, "You Gileadites are renegades
from Ephraim and Manasseh.[k]" 5The
Gileadites captured the fords of the
Jordan[l] leading to Ephraim, and
whenever a survivor of Ephraim said,
"Let me cross over," the men of Gilead
asked him, "Are you an Ephraimite?" If
he replied, "No," 6they said, "All right,
say 'Shibboleth.'" If he said, "Sibbo-
leth," because he could not pronounce
the word correctly, they seized him and
killed him at the fords of the Jordan.
Forty-two thousand Ephraimites were
killed at that time.
7Jephthah led[t] Israel six years.
Then Jephthah the Gileadite died, and
was buried in a town in Gilead.

Ibzan, Elon and Abdon

8After him, Ibzan of Bethlehem[m]
led Israel. 9He had thirty sons and thirty daughters. He gave his daughters
away in marriage to those outside his
clan, and for his sons he brought in
thirty young women as wives from outside his clan. Ibzan led Israel seven
years. 10Then Ibzan died, and was buried in Bethlehem.
11After him, Elon the Zebulunite led
Israel ten years. 12Then Elon died, and
was buried in Aijalon[n] in the land of
Zebulun.
13After him, Abdon son of Hillel,
from Pirathon,[o] led Israel. 14He had
forty sons and thirty grandsons,[p] who
rode on seventy donkeys.[q] He led Israel eight years. 15Then Abdon son of
Hillel died, and was buried at Pirathon
in Ephraim, in the hill country of the
Amalekites.[r]

The Birth of Samson

13 Again the Israelites did evil in
the eyes of the LORD, so the
LORD delivered them into the hands of
the Philistines[s] for forty years.[t]
2A certain man of Zorah,[u] named
Manoah,[v] from the clan of the Danites,[w] had a wife who was sterile and
remained childless.[x] 3The angel of
the LORD[y] appeared to her[z] and said,
"You are sterile and childless, but you

11:36 [b] Lk 1:38 [c] S Nu 31:3 [d] 2Sa 18:19
12:1 [e] S Jos 13:27 [f] S Jdg 11:1 [g] Jdg 8:1
12:3 [h] S Jdg 9:17 [i] S Dt 20:4
12:4 [j] 1Ki 17:1 [k] S Ge 46:20; Isa 9:21; 19:2
12:5 [l] S Jos 2:7
12:8 [m] S Ge 35:19
12:12 [n] S Jos 10:12
12:13 [o] ver 15; 2Sa 23:30; 1Ch 11:31; 27:14
12:14 [p] S Jdg 8:30 [q] S Jdg 5:10
12:15 [r] Jdg 5:14
13:1 [s] S Jdg 3:31 [t] Jdg 14:4
13:2 [u] S Jos 15:33 [v] ver 8; Jdg 16:31 [w] S Ge 30:6 [x] S Ge 11:30
13:3 [y] S Ge 16:7 [z] ver 10

[t] 7 Traditionally *judged*; also in verses 8-14

11:39 SHE WAS A VIRGIN. It seems apparent that Jephthah did not physically sacrifice his daughter's life (vv. 30–31) for at least two reasons. (1) He would have been acquainted with God's law sternly forbidding human sacrifice and would know that God considered such action an intolerable abomination (Lev 18:21; 20:2–5; Dt 12:31; 18:10–12). (2) The emphasis that "she was a virgin" (i.e., did not marry) implies that she was presented to God as a living sacrifice, to devote her entire life to chastity and to service at the national sanctuary (cf. Ex 38:8; 1Sa 2:22).

13:1 THE PHILISTINES. A great movement of Philistines migrated to the south coast of Canaan about 1200 B.C., possibly from Crete (Jer 47:4; Am 9:7, where Caphtor means Crete). They became the principal enemy of the Hebrews during the years 1200–1000 B.C. (i.e., until the time of David). Because of their ability to make iron weapons, they possessed a military advantage over Israel (1Sa 13:19–22). The word "Palestine" is derived from the term "Philistine."

are going to conceive and have a son.[a]
4Now see to it that you drink no wine
or other fermented drink[b] and that
you do not eat anything unclean,[c] 5be-
cause you will conceive and give birth
to a son.[d] No razor[e] may be used on
his head, because the boy is to be a
Nazirite,[f] set apart to God from birth,
and he will begin[g] the deliverance of
Israel from the hands of the Philistines."
6Then the woman went to her husband and told him, "A man of God[h]
came to me. He looked like an angel of
God,[i] very awesome.[j] I didn't ask
him where he came from, and he didn't
tell me his name. 7But he said to me,
'You will conceive and give birth to a
son. Now then, drink no wine[k] or other fermented drink[l] and do not eat
anything unclean, because the boy will
be a Nazirite of God from birth until the
day of his death.[m]' "
8Then Manoah[n] prayed to the LORD:
"O Lord, I beg you, let the man of
God[o] you sent to us come again to
teach us how to bring up the boy who
is to be born."
9God heard Manoah, and the angel
of God came again to the woman while
she was out in the field; but her husband Manoah was not with her. 10The
woman hurried to tell her husband,
"He's here! The man who appeared to
me[p] the other day!"
11Manoah got up and followed his
wife. When he came to the man, he
said, "Are you the one who talked to
my wife?"
"I am," he said.
12So Manoah asked him, "When
your words are fulfilled, what is to be
the rule for the boy's life and work?"
13The angel of the LORD answered,
"Your wife must do all that I have told
her. 14She must not eat anything that
comes from the grapevine, nor drink
any wine or other fermented drink[q]
nor eat anything unclean.[r] She must
do everything I have commanded her."
15Manoah said to the angel of the
LORD, "We would like you to stay until
we prepare a young goat[s] for you."
16The angel of the LORD replied,
"Even though you detain me, I will not
eat any of your food. But if you prepare
a burnt offering,[t] offer it to the LORD."
(Manoah did not realize[u] that it was
the angel of the LORD.)
17Then Manoah inquired of the angel of the LORD, "What is your name,[v]
so that we may honor you when your
word comes true?"
18He replied, "Why do you ask my
name?[w] It is beyond understanding.[u]" 19Then Manoah took a young
goat, together with the grain offering,
and sacrificed it on a rock[x] to the
LORD. And the LORD did an amazing
thing while Manoah and his wife
watched: 20As the flame[y] blazed up
from the altar toward heaven, the angel of the LORD ascended in the flame.
Seeing this, Manoah and his wife fell
with their faces to the ground.[z]
21When the angel of the LORD did not
show himself again to Manoah and his
wife, Manoah realized[a] that it was the
angel of the LORD.
22"We are doomed[b] to die!" he said
to his wife. "We have seen[c] God!"
23But his wife answered, "If the LORD
had meant to kill us, he would not have
accepted a burnt offering and grain offering from our hands, nor shown us all
these things or now told us this."[d]
24The woman gave birth to a boy and
named him Samson.[e] He grew[f] and
the LORD blessed him,[g] 25and the Spirit of the LORD began to stir[h] him while
he was in Mahaneh Dan,[i] between Zorah and Eshtaol.

Samson's Marriage

14 Samson[j] went down to Timnah[k] and saw there a young

13:3 [a]Isa 7:14; Lk 1:13
13:4 [b]S Lev 10:9 [c]ver 14; Nu 6:2-4; S Lk 1:15
13:5 [d]S Ge 3:15 [e]1Sa 1:11 [f]S Nu 6:2,13; Am 2:11,12 [g]1Sa 7:13
13:6 [h]ver 8; 1Sa 2:27; 9:6; 1Ki 13:1; 17:18 [i]S Nu 22:22 [j]Ps 66:5
13:7 [k]Jer 35:6 [l]Lev 10:9 [m]1Sa 1:11,28
13:8 [n]S ver 2 [o]S ver 6
13:10 [p]ver 3
13:14 [q]Lev 10:9 [r]S ver 4
13:15 [s]Jdg 6:19
13:16 [t]S Jdg 11:31 [u]S Jdg 6:22
13:17 [v]S Ge 32:29
13:18 [w]S Ge 32:29
13:19 [x]Jdg 6:20
13:20 [y]S Lev 9:24 [z]S Ge 17:3
13:21 [a]S Jdg 6:22
13:22 [b]S Nu 17:12; S Dt 5:26 [c]S Ge 16:13; S Ex 3:6; S 24:10; S Jdg 6:22
13:23 [d]Ps 25:14
13:24 [e]Jdg 14:1; 15:1; 16:1; Heb 11:32 [f]1Sa 2:21,26; 3:19 [g]Lk 1:80
13:25 [h]S Jdg 3:10 [i]Jdg 18:12
14:1 [j]S Jdg 13:24 [k]S Ge 38:12

[u]*18* Or *is wonderful*

13:4 DRINK NO WINE OR OTHER FERMENTED DRINK. Whereas Samson's mother was instructed to be careful not to drink wine or any fermented drink during the time of her conception and pregnancy for spiritual reasons (vv. 4–5), modern medical science advises the same for physical reasons. Leading authorities on human birth defects warn that women who drink even moderate amounts of alcohol during conception or pregnancy stand a greater chance of having miscarriages or causing incurable birth defects in their babies (see article on WINE IN NEW TESTAMENT TIMES (2), p. 1586).

13:5 BOY IS TO BE A NAZIRITE. God intended Samson to be a Nazirite and live according to God's highest standards for his people (for an explanation of the Nazirite vow, see Nu 6:2, note; see article on WINE IN THE OLD TESTAMENT, p. 204).

13:7 WINE OR OTHER FERMENTED DRINK. See article on WINE IN THE OLD TESTAMENT, p. 204.

Philistine woman. 2When he returned,
he said to his father and mother, "I
have seen a Philistine woman in Timnah; now get her for me as my wife."[l]
3His father and mother replied,
"Isn't there an acceptable woman
among your relatives or among all our
people?[m] Must you go to the uncircumcised[n] Philistines to get a
wife?[o]"

But Samson said to his father, "Get
her for me. She's the right one for me."
4(His parents did not know that this
was from the LORD,[p] who was seeking
an occasion to confront the Philistines;[q] for at that time they were ruling over Israel.)[r] 5Samson went down
to Timnah together with his father and
mother. As they approached the vineyards of Timnah, suddenly a young lion
came roaring toward him. 6The Spirit
of the LORD came upon him in power[s]
so that he tore the lion apart[t] with his
bare hands as he might have torn a
young goat. But he told neither his father nor his mother what he had done.
7Then he went down and talked with
the woman, and he liked her.

8Some time later, when he went
back to marry her, he turned aside to
look at the lion's carcass. In it was a
swarm of bees and some honey, 9which
he scooped out with his hands and ate
as he went along. When he rejoined his
parents, he gave them some, and they
too ate it. But he did not tell them that
he had taken the honey from the lion's
carcass.

10Now his father went down to see
the woman. And Samson made a
feast[u] there, as was customary for
bridegrooms. 11When he appeared, he
was given thirty companions.

12"Let me tell you a riddle,[v]" Samson said to them. "If you can give me
the answer within the seven days of
the feast,[w] I will give you thirty linen
garments and thirty sets of clothes.[x]
13If you can't tell me the answer, you
must give me thirty linen garments and
thirty sets of clothes."

"Tell us your riddle," they said.
"Let's hear it."

14He replied,

> "Out of the eater, something to
> eat;
> out of the strong, something
> sweet."[y]

For three days they could not give the
answer.

15On the fourth[v] day, they said to
Samson's wife, "Coax[z] your husband
into explaining the riddle for us, or we
will burn you and your father's household to death.[a] Did you invite us here
to rob us?"

16Then Samson's wife threw herself
on him, sobbing, "You hate me! You
don't really love me.[b] You've given my
people a riddle, but you haven't told me
the answer."

"I haven't even explained it to my
father or mother," he replied, "so why
should I explain it to you?" 17She cried
the whole seven days[c] of the feast. So
on the seventh day he finally told her,
because she continued to press him.

14:2 [l]S Ge 21:21
14:3 [m]S Ge 24:4 [n]S Ge 34:14; S 1Sa 14:6 [o]S Ex 34:16
14:4 [p]S Dt 2:30 [q]S Jos 11:20 [r]Jdg 13:1; 15:11
14:6 [s]S Jdg 3:10 [t]1Sa 17:35
14:10 [u]S Ge 29:22
14:12 [v]S Nu 12:8; Eze 17:2; 20:49; 24:3; Hos 12:10 [w]Ge 29:27 [x]S Ge 45:22; S 2Ki 5:5
14:14 [y]ver 18
14:15 [z]Jdg 16:5; Ecc 7:26 [a]S Lev 20:14; Jdg 15:6
14:16 [b]Jdg 16:15
14:17 [c]Est 1:5

[v] *15* Some Septuagint manuscripts and Syriac; Hebrew *seventh*

14:3 MUST YOU GO TO THE UNCIRCUMCISED? Although the Lord had blessed Samson and empowered him with the Spirit (13:24–25; 14:6,19; 15:14), Samson made fatal errors that led to spiritual failure and physical death. Among these are the following: (1) He did not anchor his life in the word of God. He showed a lack of concern and respect for God's commandments, specifically ignoring God's law concerning mixed marriages (Ex 34:16; Dt 7:3; cf. Ge 24:3–4; 26:34–35).

(2) He disregarded his parents' God-given instruction and rejected his godly heritage in order to fulfill his own desires (13:5,8,14,24–25).

(3) Unlike Moses, who chose to be mistreated along with God's people rather than enjoy the pleasures of sin for a short time (Heb 11:25), Samson chose to express his human emotions and desires in ways that did not please God (14:3; 16:1,4; see 15:7, note).

(4) He misused God's gifts and empowerment for personal gain and advantage.

14:4 THIS WAS FROM THE LORD. This statement does not mean that God initiated Samson's intention to marry an unbeliever. Samson was motivated by his own desire to seek marital companionship with those outside of God's people (cf. Jas 1:13–14). However, God did use Samson's sin as an occasion to accomplish his purpose against the Philistines (v. 4; cf. Ge 50:20).

14:6 SPIRIT OF THE LORD. Samson's great physical strength was not his own, but was the result of the Spirit coming upon him (v. 19; 15:14; 16:28–30). Under the new covenant, the Holy Spirit also comes upon believers, though not to make us physically strong; rather, the Holy Spirit empowers us to live and witness for Christ (see article on BAPTISM IN THE HOLY SPIRIT, p. 1642).

She in turn explained the riddle to her people.

18Before sunset on the seventh day the men of the town said to him,

"What is sweeter than honey?
What is stronger than a lion?"[d]

Samson said to them,

"If you had not plowed with my heifer,
you would not have solved my riddle."

19Then the Spirit of the LORD came upon him in power.[e] He went down to Ashkelon,[f] struck down thirty of their men, stripped them of their belongings and gave their clothes to those who had explained the riddle. Burning with anger,[g] he went up to his father's house. **20**And Samson's wife was given to the friend[h] who had attended him at his wedding.

Samson's Vengeance on the Philistines

15 Later on, at the time of wheat harvest,[i] Samson[j] took a young goat[k] and went to visit his wife. He said, "I'm going to my wife's room."[l] But her father would not let him go in.

2"I was so sure you thoroughly hated her," he said, "that I gave her to your friend.[m] Isn't her younger sister more attractive? Take her instead."

3Samson said to them, "This time I have a right to get even with the Philistines; I will really harm them." **4**So he went out and caught three hundred foxes[n] and tied them tail to tail in pairs. He then fastened a torch[o] to every pair of tails, **5**lit the torches[p] and let the foxes loose in the standing grain of the Philistines. He burned up the shocks[q] and standing grain, together with the vineyards and olive groves.

6When the Philistines asked, "Who did this?" they were told, "Samson, the Timnite's son-in-law, because his wife was given to his friend."[r]

So the Philistines went up and burned her[s] and her father to death.[t] **7**Samson said to them, "Since you've acted like this, I won't stop until I get my revenge on you." **8**He attacked them viciously and slaughtered many of them. Then he went down and stayed in a cave in the rock[u] of Etam.[v]

9The Philistines went up and camped in Judah, spreading out near Lehi.[w] **10**The men of Judah asked, "Why have you come to fight us?"

"We have come to take Samson prisoner," they answered, "to do to him as he did to us."

11Then three thousand men from Judah went down to the cave in the rock of Etam and said to Samson, "Don't you realize that the Philistines are rulers over us?[x] What have you done to us?"

He answered, "I merely did to them what they did to me."

12They said to him, "We've come to tie you up and hand you over to the Philistines."

Samson said, "Swear to me[y] that you won't kill me yourselves."

13"Agreed," they answered. "We will only tie you up and hand you over to them. We will not kill you." So they bound him with two new ropes[z] and led him up from the rock. **14**As he approached Lehi,[a] the Philistines came toward him shouting. The Spirit of the LORD came upon him in power.[b] The ropes on his arms became like charred flax,[c] and the bindings dropped from his hands. **15**Finding a fresh jawbone of a donkey, he grabbed it and struck down a thousand men.[d]

16Then Samson said,

"With a donkey's jawbone
I have made donkeys of them.[w][e]
With a donkey's jawbone
I have killed a thousand men."

17When he finished speaking, he threw

[w]16 Or *made a heap or two*; the Hebrew for *donkey* sounds like the Hebrew for *heap*.

14:18 [d]ver 14
14:19 [e]S Jdg 3:10 [f]S Jos 13:3 [g]1Sa 11:6
14:20 [h]Jdg 15:2, 6; Jn 3:29
15:1 [i]S Ge 30:14 [j]S Jdg 13:24 [k]S Ge 38:17 [l]Ge 29:21
15:2 [m]S Jdg 14:20
15:4 [n]SS 2:15 [o]S Ge 15:17
15:5 [p]S Ge 15:17 [q]Ex 22:6; 2Sa 14:30-31
15:6 [r]S Jdg 14:20 [s]S Ge 38:24 [t]S Jdg 14:15
15:8 [u]Isa 2:21 [v]ver 11
15:9 [w]ver 14,17, 19
15:11 [x]S Jdg 14:4; Ps 106:40-42
15:12 [y]S Ge 47:31
15:13 [z]Jdg 16:11, 12
15:14 [a]S ver 9 [b]S Jdg 3:10 [c]S Jos 2:6
15:15 [d]S Lev 26:8
15:16 [e]Jer 22:19

15:7 MY REVENGE ON YOU. Samson's fight with the Philistines was primarily motivated by personal anger and revenge rather than by concern for God's deliverance of the Hebrew people. This selfishness and lack of commitment to God eventually led to his ruin (16:1,20–21).

15:14 SPIRIT OF THE LORD CAME UPON HIM IN POWER. An empowerment from the Spirit in the OT does not mean that God endorsed that person's way of life (cf. Nu 24:2). Indeed, there were many objectionable aspects to Samson's lifestyle.

away the jawbone; and the place was
called Ramath Lehi.[x][f]
18Because he was very thirsty, he
cried out to the LORD,[g] "You have giv-
en your servant this great victory.[h]
Must I now die of thirst and fall into
the hands of the uncircumcised?"
19Then God opened up the hollow
place in Lehi, and water came out of it.
When Samson drank, his strength returned and he revived.[i] So the
spring[j] was called En Hakkore,[y] and
it is still there in Lehi.
20Samson led[z] Israel for twenty
years[k] in the days of the Philistines.

Samson and Delilah

16 One day Samson[l] went to
Gaza,[m] where he saw a prostitute.[n] He went in to spend the night
with her. 2The people of Gaza were
told, "Samson is here!" So they surrounded the place and lay in wait for
him all night at the city gate.[o] They
made no move during the night, saying,
"At dawn[p] we'll kill him."
3But Samson lay there only until the
middle of the night. Then he got up and
took hold of the doors of the city gate,
together with the two posts, and tore
them loose, bar and all. He lifted them
to his shoulders and carried them to
the top of the hill that faces Hebron.[q]
4Some time later, he fell in love[r]
with a woman in the Valley of Sorek
whose name was Delilah.[s] 5The rulers of the Philistines[t] went to her and
said, "See if you can lure[u] him into
showing you the secret of his great
strength[v] and how we can overpower
him so we may tie him up and subdue
him. Each one of us will give you elev-
en hundred shekels[a] of silver."[w]
6So Delilah[x] said to Samson, "Tell
me the secret of your great strength
and how you can be tied up and subdued."
7Samson answered her, "If anyone
ties me with seven fresh thongs[b] that
have not been dried, I'll become as
weak as any other man."
8Then the rulers of the Philistines
brought her seven fresh thongs that
had not been dried, and she tied him
with them. 9With men hidden in the
room,[y] she called to him, "Samson,
the Philistines are upon you!"[z] But he
snapped the thongs as easily as a piece
of string snaps when it comes close to
a flame. So the secret of his strength
was not discovered.
10Then Delilah said to Samson, "You
have made a fool of me;[a] you lied to
me. Come now, tell me how you can be
tied."
11He said, "If anyone ties me securely with new ropes[b] that have never
been used, I'll become as weak as any
other man."
12So Delilah took new ropes and tied
him with them. Then, with men hidden
in the room, she called to him, "Samson, the Philistines are upon you!"[c]
But he snapped the ropes off his arms
as if they were threads.
13Delilah then said to Samson, "Until now, you have been making a fool of
me and lying to me. Tell me how you
can be tied."
He replied, "If you weave the seven
braids of my head into the fabric ⌞on the
loom⌟ and tighten it with the pin, I'll
become as weak as any other man." So
while he was sleeping, Delilah took the
seven braids of his head, wove them
into the fabric 14and[c] tightened it with
the pin.
Again she called to him, "Samson,
the Philistines are upon you!"[d] He
awoke from his sleep and pulled up the
pin and the loom, with the fabric.
15Then she said to him, "How can
you say, 'I love you,'[e] when you won't
confide in me? This is the third time[f]
you have made a fool of me and haven't
told me the secret of your great
strength.[g] 16With such nagging she

15:17 [f]S ver 9
15:18 [g]Jdg 16:28 [h]S Dt 20:4
15:19 [i]Ge 45:27; 1Sa 30:12; Isa 40:29 [j]S Ex 17:6
15:20 [k]Jdg 16:31
16:1 [l]S Jdg 13:24 [m]S Ge 10:19 [n]S Ge 38:15
16:2 [o]S Jos 2:5 [p]1Sa 19:11
16:3 [q]S Jos 10:36
16:4 [r]S Ge 24:67; S 34:3 [s]ver 6
16:5 [t]S Jos 13:3 [u]S Ex 10:7; S Jdg 14:15 [v]ver 6,15 [w]ver 18
16:6 [x]ver 4
16:9 [y]ver 12 [z]ver 14
16:10 [a]ver 13
16:11 [b]S Jdg 15:13
16:12 [c]ver 14
16:14 [d]ver 9,20
16:15 [e]Jdg 14:16 [f]Nu 24:10 [g]S ver 5

[x] 17 *Ramath Lehi* means *jawbone hill.*
[y] 19 *En Hakkore* means *caller's spring.*
[z] 20 Traditionally *judged*
[a] 5 That is, about 28 pounds (about 13 kilograms)
[b] 7 Or *bowstrings*; also in verses 8 and 9
[c] 13,14 Some Septuagint manuscripts; Hebrew *"⌞I can⌟ if you weave the seven braids of my head into the fabric ⌞on the loom⌟." 14So she*

15:20 LED ISRAEL FOR TWENTY YEARS. During the twenty years Samson was judge of Israel, he never succeeded in delivering the people from the oppression of the Philistines. His record consisted only of sporadic exploits against that pagan nation. What might God have accomplished through Samson if he had been faithful to his calling and genuinely dedicated to God's purpose for his life as the chosen deliverer of Israel?

16:1 A PROSTITUTE. Samson's problem of insatiable lust eventually led to his downfall (cf. vv. 4,19–21). He was more concerned with satisfying his sexual passion than with pleasing his holy God (vv. 1–3).

prodded him day after day until he was
tired to death.
17So he told her everything.[h] "No
razor has ever been used on my head,"
he said, "because I have been a Nazirite[i] set apart to God since birth. If
my head were shaved, my strength
would leave me, and I would become as
weak as any other man."
18When Delilah saw that he had told
her everything, she sent word to the
rulers of the Philistines[j], "Come back
once more; he has told me everything."
So the rulers of the Philistines returned with the silver in their hands.[k]
19Having put him to sleep on her lap,
she called a man to shave off the seven
braids of his hair, and so began to subdue him.[d] And his strength left him.[l]
20Then she called, "Samson, the
Philistines are upon you!"[m]

He awoke from his sleep and
thought, "I'll go out as before and
shake myself free." But he did not
know that the LORD had left him.[n]
21Then the Philistines[o] seized him,
gouged out his eyes[p] and took him
down to Gaza.[q] Binding him with
bronze shackles, they set him to grinding[r] in the prison. **22**But the hair on
his head began to grow again after it
had been shaved.

The Death of Samson

23Now the rulers of the Philistines
assembled to offer a great sacrifice to
Dagon[s] their god and to celebrate,
saying, "Our god has delivered Samson, our enemy, into our hands."
24When the people saw him, they
praised their god,[t] saying,

"Our god has delivered our enemy
into our hands,[u]
the one who laid waste our land
and multiplied our slain."

25While they were in high spirits,[v]
they shouted, "Bring out Samson to entertain us." So they called Samson out
of the prison, and he performed for
them.

When they stood him among the pillars, **26**Samson said to the servant who
held his hand, "Put me where I can feel
the pillars that support the temple, so
that I may lean against them." **27**Now
the temple was crowded with men and
women; all the rulers of the Philistines
were there, and on the roof[w] were
about three thousand men and women
watching Samson perform. **28**Then
Samson prayed to the LORD,[x] "O Sovereign LORD, remember me. O God,
please strengthen me just once more,
and let me with one blow get revenge[y]
on the Philistines for my two eyes."
29Then Samson reached toward the
two central pillars on which the temple
stood. Bracing himself against them,
his right hand on the one and his left
hand on the other, **30**Samson said, "Let
me die with the Philistines!" Then he
pushed with all his might, and down
came the temple on the rulers and
all the people in it. Thus he killed
many more when he died than while he
lived.
31Then his brothers and his father's
whole family went down to get him.
They brought him back and buried him
between Zorah and Eshtaol in the tomb
of Manoah[z] his father. He had led[e][a]
Israel twenty years.[b]

Micah's Idols

17 Now a man named Micah[c]
from the hill country of Ephra-

16:17 [h] ver 18; Mic 7:5 [i] S Nu 6:2
16:18 [j] S Jos 13:3; 1Sa 5:8 [k] ver 5
16:19 [l] Pr 7:26-27
16:20 [m] S ver 14 [n] Nu 14:42; Jos 7:12; 1Sa 16:14; 18:12; 28:15
16:21 [o] Jer 47:1 [p] S Nu 16:14 [q] S Ge 10:19 [r] Job 31:10; Isa 47:2
16:23 [s] 1Sa 5:2; 1Ch 10:10
16:24 [t] Da 5:4 [u] 1Sa 31:9; 1Ch 10:9
16:25 [v] Jdg 9:27; 19:6,9,22; Ru 3:7; Est 1:10
16:27 [w] S Jos 2:8
16:28 [x] Jdg 15:18 [y] Jer 15:15
16:31 [z] S Jdg 13:2 [a] Ru 1:1; 1Sa 4:18; 7:6 [b] Jdg 15:20
17:1 [c] Jdg 18:2,13

d *19* Hebrew; some Septuagint manuscripts *and he began to weaken* **e** *31* Traditionally *judged*

16:19 HIS STRENGTH LEFT HIM. Samson entered into compromise with Delilah by continuing to disregard God's instruction to remain separate from the wicked nations in Canaan (Dt 7:1–4). He failed to realize that compromise with idol worshipers and immoral people opens up one's life to Satan's power, to delusion and to total defeat (vv. 19–21).

16:20 THE LORD HAD LEFT HIM. Samson is an example of those believers who think that God will remain with them even as they continue in sinful and immoral conduct. The Lord left this judge because of his continued disobedience (cf. 1Co 9:27; Heb 3:6–19). This passage strongly warns us that it is possible for the Lord to depart from a persistently sinful person without him or her realizing it.

16:28 SAMSON PRAYED TO THE LORD. Samson, now with a repentant spirit and a renewed faith in God, called on the Lord, and his prayer was answered. This demonstration of Samson's faith resulted in his inclusion among the heroes of faith (see Heb 11:32).

17:1 MICAH. The chronological history of the book of Judges ends with ch. 16. Beginning with the episode of Micah, the book's final section (17:1—21:25) illustrates the low moral standards, the perverted religious practices and the chaotic social order of Israel during the period of the judges. These illustrations demonstrate that if

im 2said to his mother, "The eleven
hundred shekels[f] of silver that were
taken from you and about which I
heard you utter a curse—I have that
silver with me; I took it."
Then his mother said, "The LORD
bless you,[d] my son!"
3When he returned the eleven hundred shekels of silver to his mother,
she said, "I solemnly consecrate my
silver to the LORD for my son to make
a carved image and a cast idol.[e] I will
give it back to you."
4So he returned the silver to his
mother, and she took two hundred
shekels[g] of silver and gave them to a
silversmith, who made them into the
image and the idol.[f] And they were
put in Micah's house.
5Now this man Micah had a
shrine,[g] and he made an ephod[h] and
some idols[i] and installed[j] one of his
sons as his priest.[k] 6In those days Israel had no king;[l] everyone did as he
saw fit.[m]
7A young Levite[n] from Bethlehem
in Judah,[o] who had been living within
the clan of Judah, 8left that town in
search of some other place to stay. On
his way[h] he came to Micah's house in
the hill country of Ephraim.
9Micah asked him, "Where are you
from?"
"I'm a Levite from Bethlehem in Judah,[p]" he said, "and I'm looking for a
place to stay."
10Then Micah said to him, "Live
with me and be my father[q] and
priest,[r] and I'll give you ten shekels[i]
of silver a year, your clothes and your
food." 11So the Levite agreed to live
with him, and the young man was to
him like one of his sons. 12Then Micah
installed[s] the Levite, and the young
man became his priest[t] and lived in
his house. 13And Micah said, "Now I
know that the LORD will be good to me,
since this Levite has become my
priest."[u]

Danites Settle in Laish

18 In those days Israel had no
king.[v]
And in those days the tribe of the
Danites was seeking a place of their
own where they might settle, because
they had not yet come into an inheritance among the tribes of Israel.[w] 2So
the Danites[x] sent five warriors[y] from
Zorah and Eshtaol to spy out[z] the
land and explore it. These men represented all their clans. They told them,
"Go, explore the land."[a]
The men entered the hill country of
Ephraim and came to the house of Micah,[b] where they spent the night.
3When they were near Micah's house,
they recognized the voice of the young
Levite;[c] so they turned in there and
asked him, "Who brought you here?
What are you doing in this place? Why
are you here?"
4He told them what Micah had done
for him, and said, "He has hired me and
I am his priest.[d]"
5Then they said to him, "Please inquire of God[e] to learn whether our
journey will be successful."
6The priest answered them, "Go in
peace[f]. Your journey has the LORD's
approval."
7So the five men[g] left and came to

17:2 [d] Ru 2:20; 3:10; 1Sa 15:13; 23:21; 2Sa 2:5
17:3 [e] S Ex 20:4
17:4 [f] S Ex 32:4; S Isa 17:8
17:5 [g] Isa 44:13; Eze 8:10 [h] S Jdg 8:27 [i] S Ge 31:19 [j] S Nu 16:10 [k] S Ex 29:9
17:6 [l] Jdg 18:1; 19:1; 21:25 [m] S Dt 12:8
17:7 [n] Jdg 18:3 [o] S Ge 35:19; Mt 2:1
17:9 [p] Ru 1:1
17:10 [q] S Ge 45:8 [r] Jdg 18:19
17:12 [s] S Nu 16:10 [t] Jdg 18:4
17:13 [u] Nu 18:7
18:1 [v] S Jdg 17:6 [w] Jos 19:47; Jdg 1:34
18:2 [x] S Ge 30:6 [y] ver 17 [z] S Nu 21:32 [a] S Jos 2:1 [b] S Jdg 17:1
18:3 [c] Jdg 17:7
18:4 [d] Jdg 17:12
18:5 [e] S Ge 25:22; Jdg 20:18,23,27; 1Sa 14:18; 2Sa 5:19; 2Ki 1:2; 8:8
18:6 [f] 1Ki 22:6
18:7 [g] ver 17

[f] 2 That is, about 28 pounds (about 13 kilograms) [g] 4 That is, about 5 pounds (about 2.3 kilograms) [h] 8 Or *To carry on his profession* [i] 10 That is, about 4 ounces (about 110 grams)

God's word and sound moral principles are disregarded, both individuals and society as a whole will be destroyed (cf. Pr 14:34; 21:7). Twice the writer observes that "everyone did as he saw fit" (17:6; 21:25; cf. Pr 14:12). God's way was rejected, resulting in despair, disorder and death.

17:5 A SHRINE. Because Micah did not submit to the authority of God's inspired, written revelation through Moses, he deceived himself and did what was right in his own eyes (v. 6; cf. Dt 11:18–25; Jos 1:5–8). He deceived himself into believing that he could receive God's blessing (v. 13) and at the same time break the clear commands of Scripture. His sin involved stealing (v. 2), worshiping idols (vv. 3–5), disobeying God's commands (v. 6) and appointing his own son as priest (vv. 5–13; Nu 16:17; Dt 21:5; cf. 2Ti 4:3). Proper discernment and sound moral judgment were lost in Israel when the nation departed from God's covenant.

17:6 EVERYONE DID AS HE SAW FIT. People who do what is right in their own eyes inevitably do what is evil in God's eyes (cf. 2:11; 4:1; 6:1; 10:6). This lawless attitude is as prevalent in our day as it was in Micah's day. People want to do their own thing and resent being told what they can or cannot do—even by God and his Word. Those who disregard God's absolute standards in favor of human subjective wishes will end in chaos spiritually, morally and socially. True believers, on the other hand, will gladly submit to God's standards and values as revealed in his written Word.

Laish,[h] where they saw that the people were living in safety, like the Sidonians, unsuspecting and secure.[i] And
since their land lacked nothing, they
were prosperous.[j] Also, they lived a
long way from the Sidonians[j] and had
no relationship with anyone else.[k]
8When they returned to Zorah and
Eshtaol, their brothers asked them,
"How did you find things?"
9They answered, "Come on, let's attack them! We have seen that the land
is very good. Aren't you going to do
something? Don't hesitate to go there
and take it over.[k] 10When you get
there, you will find an unsuspecting
people and a spacious land that God
has put into your hands, a land that
lacks nothing[l] whatever.[m]"
11Then six hundred men[n] from the
clan of the Danites,[o] armed for battle,
set out from Zorah and Eshtaol. 12On
their way they set up camp near Kiriath Jearim[p] in Judah. This is why the
place west of Kiriath Jearim is called
Mahaneh Dan[l][q] to this day. 13From
there they went on to the hill country
of Ephraim and came to Micah's
house.[r]
14Then the five men who had spied
out the land of Laish[s] said to their
brothers, "Do you know that one of
these houses has an ephod,[t] other
household gods, a carved image and a
cast idol?[u] Now you know what to do."
15So they turned in there and went to
the house of the young Levite at Micah's place and greeted him. 16The six
hundred Danites,[v] armed for battle,
stood at the entrance to the gate.
17The five men who had spied out the
land went inside and took the carved
image, the ephod, the other household
gods[w] and the cast idol while the
priest and the six hundred armed
men[x] stood at the entrance to the
gate.
18When these men went into Micah's house and took[y] the carved image, the ephod, the other household
gods[z] and the cast idol, the priest said
to them, "What are you doing?"
19They answered him, "Be quiet![a]
Don't say a word. Come with us, and be
our father and priest.[b] Isn't it better
that you serve a tribe and clan[c] in Israel as priest rather than just one
man's household?" 20Then the priest
was glad. He took the ephod, the other
household gods and the carved image
and went along with the people. 21Put-
ting their little children, their livestock
and their possessions in front of them,
they turned away and left.
22When they had gone some distance from Micah's house, the men
who lived near Micah were called together and overtook the Danites. 23As
they shouted after them, the Danites
turned and said to Micah, "What's the
matter with you that you called out
your men to fight?"
24He replied, "You took[d] the gods I
made, and my priest, and went away.
What else do I have? How can you ask,
'What's the matter with you?' "
25The Danites answered, "Don't argue with us, or some hot-tempered
men will attack you, and you and your
family will lose your lives." 26So the
Danites went their way, and Micah,
seeing that they were too strong for
him,[e] turned around and went back
home.
27Then they took what Micah had
made, and his priest, and went on to
Laish, against a peaceful and unsuspecting people.[f] They attacked them
with the sword and burned[g] down
their city.[h] 28There was no one to rescue them because they lived a long way
from Sidon[i] and had no relationship
with anyone else. The city was in a valley near Beth Rehob.[j]
The Danites rebuilt the city and settled there. 29They named it Dan[k] after
their forefather Dan, who was born to
Israel—though the city used to be
called Laish.[l] 30There the Danites set
up for themselves the idols, and Jonathan son of Gershom,[m] the son of Moses,[m] and his sons were priests for the
tribe of Dan until the time of the captivity of the land. 31They continued to use
the idols Micah had made,[n] all the

18:7 [h]S Jos 19:47 [i]S Ge 34:25 [j]ver 28; Jos 11:8 **18:9** [k]Nu 13:30; 1Ki 22:3 **18:10** [l]Dt 8:9 [m]1Ch 4:40 **18:11** [n]ver 16,17 [o]Jdg 13:2 **18:12** [p]S Jos 9:17 [q]Jdg 13:25 **18:13** [r]S Jdg 17:1 **18:14** [s]S Jos 19:47 [t]S Jdg 8:27 [u]S Ge 31:19 **18:16** [v]S ver 11 **18:17** [w]S Ge 31:19; Mic 5:13 [x]ver 11 **18:18** [y]ver 24; Isa 46:2; Jer 43:11; 48:7; 49:3; Hos 10:5 [z]S Ge 31:19 **18:19** [a]Job 13:5; 21:5; 29:9; 40:4; Isa 52:15; Mic 7:16 [b]Jdg 17:10 [c]Nu 26:42 **18:24** [d]S ver 17-18 **18:26** [e]2Sa 3:39; Ps 18:17; 35:10 **18:27** [f]S Ge 34:25 [g]S Nu 31:10 [h]Ge 49:17; S Jos 19:47 **18:28** [i]S ver 7; S Ge 10:19 [j]S Nu 13:21 **18:29** [k]S Ge 14:14 [l]S Jos 19:47; 1Ki 15:20 **18:30** [m]Ex 2:22 **18:31** [n]ver 17

[j] *7* The meaning of the Hebrew for this clause is uncertain. [k] *7* Hebrew; some Septuagint manuscripts *with the Arameans*
[l] *12 Mahaneh Dan* means *Dan's camp.*
[m] *30* An ancient Hebrew scribal tradition, some Septuagint manuscripts and Vulgate; Masoretic Text *Manasseh*

18:20 THE PRIEST WAS GLAD. The prominence given to the priest in chs. 17—18 emphasizes that not only the people but also the sacred ministry had become corrupt. This priest was willing to serve as priest of other gods solely for money and position (17:12).

time the house of God[o] was in Shiloh.[p]

A Levite and His Concubine

19 In those days Israel had no
king.
Now a Levite who lived in a remote
area in the hill country of Ephraim[q]
took a concubine from Bethlehem in
Judah.[r] 2 But she was unfaithful to
him. She left him and went back to her
father's house in Bethlehem, Judah.
After she had been there four months,
3 her husband went to her to persuade
her to return. He had with him his servant and two donkeys. She took him
into her father's house, and when her
father saw him, he gladly welcomed
him. 4 His father-in-law, the girl's father, prevailed upon him to stay; so he
remained with him three days, eating
and drinking,[s] and sleeping there.
5 On the fourth day they got up early
and he prepared to leave, but the girl's
father said to his son-in-law, "Refresh
yourself[t] with something to eat; then
you can go." 6 So the two of them sat
down to eat and drink together. Afterward the girl's father said, "Please
stay tonight and enjoy yourself.[u]"
7 And when the man got up to go, his
father-in-law persuaded him, so he
stayed there that night. 8 On the morning of the fifth day, when he rose to go,
the girl's father said, "Refresh yourself. Wait till afternoon!" So the two of
them ate together.
9 Then when the man, with his concubine and his servant, got up to leave,
his father-in-law, the girl's father, said,
"Now look, it's almost evening. Spend
the night here; the day is nearly over.
Stay and enjoy yourself. Early tomorrow morning you can get up and be on
your way home." 10 But, unwilling to
stay another night, the man left and
went toward Jebus[v] (that is, Jerusalem), with his two saddled donkeys
and his concubine.
11 When they were near Jebus and
the day was almost gone, the servant
said to his master, "Come, let's stop at
this city of the Jebusites[w] and spend
the night."
12 His master replied, "No. We won't
go into an alien city, whose people are
not Israelites. We will go on to Gibeah." 13 He added, "Come, let's try to
reach Gibeah or Ramah[x] and spend
the night in one of those places." 14 So
they went on, and the sun set as they
neared Gibeah in Benjamin.[y] 15 There
they stopped to spend the night.[z]
They went and sat in the city square,[a]
but no one took them into his home for
the night.
16 That evening[b] an old man from
the hill country of Ephraim,[c] who was
living in Gibeah (the men of the place
were Benjamites), came in from his
work in the fields. 17 When he looked
and saw the traveler in the city square,
the old man asked, "Where are you going? Where did you come from?"[d]
18 He answered, "We are on our way
from Bethlehem in Judah to a remote
area in the hill country of Ephraim
where I live. I have been to Bethlehem
in Judah and now I am going to the
house of the LORD.[e] No one has taken
me into his house. 19 We have both
straw and fodder[f] for our donkeys[g]
and bread and wine[h] for ourselves
your servants—me, your maidservant,
and the young man with us. We don't
need anything."
20 "You are welcome at my house,"
the old man said. "Let me supply whatever you need. Only don't spend the
night in the square." 21 So he took him
into his house and fed his donkeys. After they had washed their feet, they
had something to eat and drink.[i]
22 While they were enjoying them-

18:31 [o] Jdg 19:18; 20:18 [p] S Jos 18:1; Jer 7:14
19:1 [q] ver 16,18 [r] Ru 1:1
19:4 [s] ver 6,8; S Ex 32:6
19:5 [t] ver 8; Ge 18:5
19:6 [u] S Jdg 16:25
19:10 [v] S Ge 10:16; S Jos 15:8
19:11 [w] S Ge 10:16; S Jos 3:10
19:13 [x] S Jos 18:25
19:14 [y] Jos 15:57; 1Sa 10:26; 11:4; 13:2; 15:34; Isa 10:29
19:15 [z] S Ge 24:23 [a] S Ge 19:2
19:16 [b] Ps 104:23 [c] S ver 1
19:17 [d] S Ge 29:4
19:18 [e] S Jdg 18:31
19:19 [f] Ge 24:25 [g] S Ge 42:27 [h] S Ge 14:18
19:21 [i] Ge 24:32-33; Lk 7:44

19:1 IN THOSE DAYS. The events recorded in ch. 19 reveal how depraved and immoral some in Israel had become after they turned from God. (1) Some Israelites (i.e., Benjamites) became homosexuals, rapists and murderers (vv. 22–30). (2) A Levite (i.e., minister of God's word) gave his wife over to rape and death in order to save himself (vv. 1,22,25–30). Thus, both laity and ministers alike fall into the depths of depravity when God and his word are forsaken (cf. Hos 9:9; 10:9).

19:1 CONCUBINE. In the Bible a concubine was a woman lawfully united in marriage to a man, but in a position inferior to that of a regular wife. Nowhere does the OT sanction this polygamous practice (Ex 21:7–11; Dt 21:10–14; see Ge 29:28, note).

19:22 BRING OUT THE MAN. One of the greatest examples of corruption and depravity occurred at Gibeah, when those who were once God's people gave themselves over to the lust of homosexuality and rape (cf. Hos 9:9; 10:9); they had become like the Sodomites (Ge 19:1–11). Scripture views homosexuality and lesbianism as one of the end results of God's rejection of a perverse person or people (see Ro 1:27, note). If not repented of, homosexuality will lead to "a depraved

selves,[j] some of the wicked men[k] of the city surrounded the house. Pounding on the door, they shouted to the old man who owned the house, "Bring out the man who came to your house so we can have sex with him.[l]"

23 The owner of the house went outside[m] and said to them, "No, my friends, don't be so vile. Since this man is my guest, don't do this disgraceful thing.[n] 24 Look, here is my virgin daughter,[o] and his concubine. I will bring them out to you now, and you can use them and do to them whatever you wish. But to this man, don't do such a disgraceful thing."

25 But the men would not listen to him. So the man took his concubine and sent her outside to them, and they raped her[p] and abused her[q] throughout the night, and at dawn they let her go. 26 At daybreak the woman went back to the house where her master was staying, fell down at the door and lay there until daylight.

27 When her master got up in the morning and opened the door of the house and stepped out to continue on his way, there lay his concubine, fallen in the doorway of the house, with her hands on the threshold. 28 He said to her, "Get up; let's go." But there was no answer. Then the man put her on his donkey and set out for home.

29 When he reached home, he took a knife[r] and cut up his concubine, limb by limb, into twelve parts and sent them into all the areas of Israel.[s] 30 Everyone who saw it said, "Such a thing has never been seen or done, not since the day the Israelites came up out of Egypt.[t] Think about it! Consider it! Tell us what to do![u]"

Israelites Fight the Benjamites

20 Then all the Israelites[v] from Dan to Beersheba[w] and from the land of Gilead came out as one man[x] and assembled[y] before the LORD in Mizpah.[z] 2 The leaders of all the people of the tribes of Israel took their places in the assembly of the people of God, four hundred thousand soldiers[a] armed with swords. 3 (The Benjamites heard that the Israelites had gone up to Mizpah.) Then the Israelites said, "Tell us how this awful thing happened."

4 So the Levite, the husband of the murdered woman, said, "I and my concubine came to Gibeah[b] in Benjamin to spend the night.[c] 5 During the night the men of Gibeah came after me and surrounded the house, intending to kill me.[d] They raped my concubine, and she died.[e] 6 I took my concubine, cut her into pieces and sent one piece to each region of Israel's inheritance,[f] because they committed this lewd and disgraceful act[g] in Israel. 7 Now, all you Israelites, speak up and give your verdict.[h]"

8 All the people rose as one man, saying, "None of us will go home. No, not one of us will return to his house. 9 But now this is what we'll do to Gibeah: We'll go up against it as the lot directs.[i] 10 We'll take ten men out of every hundred from all the tribes of Israel, and a hundred from a thousand, and a thousand from ten thousand, to get provisions for the army. Then, when the army arrives at Gibeah[n] in Benjamin, it can give them what they deserve for all this vileness done in Israel." 11 So all the men of Israel got together and united as one man[j] against the city.

12 The tribes of Israel sent men throughout the tribe of Benjamin, saying, "What about this awful crime that was committed among you?[k] 13 Now surrender those wicked men[l] of Gibe-

19:22 [j]S Jdg 16:25 [k]S Dt 13:13 [l]Ge 19:4-5; Jdg 20:5; Ro 1:26-27 **19:23** [m]Ge 19:6 [n]S Ge 34:7; S Lev 19:29; S Jos 7:15; S Jdg 20:6; Ro 1:27 **19:24** [o]Ge 19:8 **19:25** [p]Jdg 20:5 [q]1Sa 31:4 **19:29** [r]S Ge 22:6 [s]Jdg 20:6; 1Sa 11:7 **19:30** [t]Hos 9:9 [u]Jdg 20:7; Pr 13:10 **20:1** [v]Jdg 21:5 [w]S Ge 21:14; 1Sa 3:20; 2Sa 3:10; 17:11; 24:15; 1Ki 4:25; 2Ch 30:5 [x]ver 11; 1Sa 11:7 [y]1Sa 7:5 [z]S Jos 11:3 **20:2** [a]1Sa 11:8 **20:4** [b]S Jos 15:57 [c]S Ge 24:23 **20:5** [d]S Jdg 19:22 [e]Jdg 19:25-26 **20:6** [f]S Jdg 19:29 [g]S Jdg 19:23; 2Sa 13:12 **20:7** [h]S Jdg 19:30 **20:9** [i]S Lev 16:8 **20:11** [j]S ver 1 **20:12** [k]Dt 13:14 **20:13** [l]S Dt 13:13

[n] *10* One Hebrew manuscript; most Hebrew manuscripts *Geba,* a variant of *Gibeah*

mind" (Ro 1:28) and may produce the kind of brutality described in ch. 19.

20:1 THE ISRAELITES . . . CAME OUT. Because the tribes of Israel had failed to enforce God's law or promote righteousness, the result was the horrible sin described in ch. 19 and the refusal of the Benjamites to punish the evildoers (vv. 12–14). Israel as a whole departed from sincere obedience to God's word, and the Benjamites entered into complete apostasy. Civil war broke out, many thousands were killed and the tribe of Benjamin was almost annihilated.

20:13 THE BENJAMITES WOULD NOT LISTEN. The Benjamites sympathized more with the evil individuals among them than with the innocent victim who had undergone such cruelty (19:25). (1) By refusing to punish these evil members of their group, the Benjamites demonstrated (a) that they did not value justice, and (b) that they had lost all moral sensitivity and loyalty to God's law. Because of this, God punished the whole tribe of Benjamin (cf. vv. 18,35,48).

(2) A parallel exists today under the new covenant when churches refuse to discipline or expel

ah so that we may put them to death
and purge the evil from Israel.[m]"
But the Benjamites would not listen
to their fellow Israelites. 14From their
towns they came together at Gibeah to
fight against the Israelites. 15At once
the Benjamites mobilized twenty-six
thousand swordsmen from their towns,
in addition to seven hundred chosen
men from those living in Gibeah.
16Among all these soldiers there were
seven hundred chosen men who were
left-handed,[n] each of whom could
sling a stone at a hair and not miss.
17Israel, apart from Benjamin, mustered four hundred thousand swordsmen, all of them fighting men.
18The Israelites went up to Bethel[o][o] and inquired of God.[p] They
said, "Who of us shall go first[q] to
fight[r] against the Benjamites?"
The LORD replied, "Judah[s] shall go
first."
19The next morning the Israelites
got up and pitched camp near Gibeah.
20The men of Israel went out to fight
the Benjamites and took up battle positions against them at Gibeah. 21The
Benjamites came out of Gibeah and cut
down twenty-two thousand Israelites[t] on the battlefield that day. 22But
the men of Israel encouraged one another and again took up their positions
where they had stationed themselves
the first day. 23The Israelites went up
and wept before the LORD[u] until evening,[v] and they inquired of the LORD.[w]
They said, "Shall we go up again to battle[x] against the Benjamites, our
brothers?"
The LORD answered, "Go up against
them."
24Then the Israelites drew near to
Benjamin the second day. 25This time,
when the Benjamites came out from
Gibeah to oppose them, they cut down
another eighteen thousand Israelites,[y] all of them armed with swords.
26Then the Israelites, all the people,
went up to Bethel, and there they sat
weeping before the LORD.[z] They fasted[a] that day until evening and presented burnt offerings[b] and fellowship offerings[p][c] to the LORD.[d] 27And
the Israelites inquired of the LORD.[e]
(In those days the ark of the covenant
of God[f] was there, 28with Phinehas
son of Eleazar,[g] the son of Aaron,
ministering before it.)[h] They asked,
"Shall we go up again to battle with
Benjamin our brother, or not?"
The LORD responded, "Go, for tomorrow I will give them into your
hands.[i]"
29Then Israel set an ambush[j]
around Gibeah. 30They went up
against the Benjamites on the third
day and took up positions against Gibeah as they had done before. 31The Benjamites came out to meet them and
were drawn away[k] from the city. They
began to inflict casualties on the Israelites as before, so that about thirty
men fell in the open field and on the
roads—the one leading to Bethel[l]
and the other to Gibeah.
32While the Benjamites were saying,
"We are defeating them as before,"[m]
the Israelites were saying, "Let's retreat and draw them away from the city
to the roads."
33All the men of Israel moved from
their places and took up positions at
Baal Tamar, and the Israelite ambush
charged out of its place[n] on the west[q]
of Gibeah.[r] 34Then ten thousand of Israel's finest men made a frontal attack
on Gibeah. The fighting was so heavy
that the Benjamites did not realize[o]
how near disaster was.[p] 35The LORD
defeated Benjamin[q] before Israel, and
on that day the Israelites struck down
25,100 Benjamites, all armed with
swords. 36Then the Benjamites saw
that they were beaten.
Now the men of Israel had given
way[r] before Benjamin, because they
relied on the ambush[s] they had set
near Gibeah. 37The men who had been
in ambush made a sudden dash into
Gibeah, spread out and put the whole
city to the sword.[t] 38The men of Israel had arranged with the ambush that

20:13 [m] S Dt 13:5; S 1Co 5:13 **20:16** [n] S Jdg 3:15 **20:18** [o] S Jos 12:9; S Jdg 18:31 [p] S Jdg 18:5 [q] S Jdg 1:1 [r] ver 23, 28 [s] S Ge 49:10 **20:21** [t] ver 25 **20:23** [u] S Nu 14:1 [v] Jos 7:6 [w] S Jdg 18:5 [x] S ver 18 **20:25** [y] ver 21 **20:26** [z] S Nu 14:1 [a] 2Sa 12:21 [b] Lev 1:3 [c] S Ex 32:6 [d] Jdg 21:4 **20:27** [e] S Jdg 18:5 [f] S Nu 10:33 **20:28** [g] Nu 25:7 [h] Dt 18:5 [i] S Jos 2:24 **20:29** [j] S Jos 8:2, 4 **20:31** [k] Jos 8:16 [l] Jos 16:1 **20:32** [m] ver 39 **20:33** [n] Jos 8:19 **20:34** [o] Jos 8:14 [p] ver 41 **20:35** [q] 1Sa 9:21 **20:36** [r] Jos 8:15 [s] Jos 8:2 **20:37** [t] Jos 8:19

[o] *18* Or *to the house of God*; also in verse 26 [p] *26* Traditionally *peace offerings* [q] *33* Some Septuagint manuscripts and Vulgate; the meaning of the Hebrew for this word is uncertain. [r] *33* Hebrew *Geba*, a variant of *Gibeah*

sinning members. The toleration of sin and immorality (i.e., an attitude that does not want to apply Biblical discipline) indicates the loss of moral sensitivity and loyalty to God and his Word by the congregation itself. God's judgment on such a congregation is certain (see Mt 13:30, note; 18:15, note; 1Co 5:1, notes).

they should send up a great cloud of
smoke[u] from the city,[v] 39 and then
the men of Israel would turn in the battle.
The Benjamites had begun to inflict
casualties on the men of Israel (about
thirty), and they said, "We are defeating them as in the first battle."[w] 40 But
when the column of smoke began to
rise from the city, the Benjamites
turned and saw the smoke of the whole
city going up into the sky.[x] 41 Then the
men of Israel turned on them,[y] and
the men of Benjamin were terrified, because they realized that disaster had
come[z] upon them. 42 So they fled before the Israelites in the direction of
the desert, but they could not escape
the battle. And the men of Israel who
came out of the towns cut them down
there. 43 They surrounded the Benjamites, chased them and easily[s] over-
ran them in the vicinity of Gibeah on
the east. 44 Eighteen thousand Benjamites fell, all of them valiant fighters.[a] 45 As they turned and fled toward the desert to the rock of
Rimmon,[b] the Israelites cut down five
thousand men along the roads. They
kept pressing after the Benjamites as
far as Gidom and struck down two
thousand more.
46 On that day twenty-five thousand
Benjamite[c] swordsmen fell, all of
them valiant fighters. 47 But six hundred men turned and fled into the
desert to the rock of Rimmon, where
they stayed four months. 48 The men of
Israel went back to Benjamin and put
all the towns to the sword, including
the animals and everything else they
found. All the towns they came across
they set on fire.[d]

Wives for the Benjamites

21 The men of Israel had taken an
oath[e] at Mizpah:[f] "Not one of
us will give[g] his daughter in marriage
to a Benjamite."
2 The people went to Bethel,[t] where
they sat before God until evening, raising their voices and weeping bitterly.
3 "O LORD, the God of Israel," they
cried, "why has this happened to Israel? Why should one tribe be missing[h]
from Israel today?"
4 Early the next day the people built
an altar and presented burnt offerings
and fellowship offerings.[u][i]
5 Then the Israelites asked, "Who
from all the tribes of Israel[j] has failed
to assemble before the LORD?" For they
had taken a solemn oath that anyone
who failed to assemble before the LORD
at Mizpah should certainly be put to
death.
6 Now the Israelites grieved for their
brothers, the Benjamites. "Today one
tribe is cut off from Israel," they said.
7 "How can we provide wives for those
who are left, since we have taken an
oath[k] by the LORD not to give them any
of our daughters in marriage?" 8 Then
they asked, "Which one of the tribes of
Israel failed to assemble before the
LORD at Mizpah?" They discovered that
no one from Jabesh Gilead[l] had come
to the camp for the assembly. 9 For
when they counted the people, they
found that none of the people of Jabesh
Gilead were there.
10 So the assembly sent twelve thousand fighting men with instructions to
go to Jabesh Gilead and put to the
sword those living there, including the
women and children. 11 "This is what
you are to do," they said. "Kill every
male[m] and every woman who is not a
virgin.[n]" 12 They found among the people living in Jabesh Gilead four hundred young women who had never
slept with a man, and they took them
to the camp at Shiloh[o] in Canaan.
13 Then the whole assembly sent an
offer of peace[p] to the Benjamites at
the rock of Rimmon.[q] 14 So the Benjamites returned at that time and were
given the women of Jabesh Gilead who
had been spared. But there were not
enough for all of them.
15 The people grieved for Benjamin,[r] because the LORD had made a
gap in the tribes of Israel. 16 And the
elders of the assembly said, "With the
women of Benjamin destroyed, how

20:38 [u] Jos 8:20 [v] Jos 8:4-8 **20:39** [w] ver 32; Ps 78:9 **20:40** [x] Jos 8:20 **20:41** [y] Jos 8:21 [z] ver 34 **20:44** [a] 1Sa 10:26; Ps 76:5 **20:45** [b] S Jos 15:32 **20:46** [c] 1Sa 9:21 **20:48** [d] Jdg 21:23 **21:1** [e] S Jos 9:18 [f] S Jos 11:3 [g] ver 18,22

21:3 [h] ver 6,17 **21:4** [i] Jdg 20:26 **21:5** [j] Jdg 20:1 **21:7** [k] S Jos 9:18 **21:8** [l] 1Sa 11:1; 31:11; 2Sa 2:4; 21:12; 1Ch 10:11 **21:11** [m] S Nu 31:7 [n] Nu 31:17-18 **21:12** [o] S Jos 18:1 **21:13** [p] S Dt 2:26 [q] S Jos 15:32 **21:15** [r] ver 6

[s] *43* The meaning of the Hebrew for this word is uncertain. [t] *2* Or *to the house of God*
[u] *4* Traditionally *peace offerings*

21:7 FOR THOSE WHO ARE LEFT. Only 600 Benjamites survived the war (see 20:47).

21:10 PUT TO THE SWORD THOSE LIVING THERE. Most of the Israelites in Jabesh Gilead were killed because they refused to join with Israel in the war against the Benjamites. Their sin was seen in not standing with God and his people against the heinous sin committed by some of their brothers (19:22–25).

shall we provide wives for the men who
are left? **17**The Benjamite survivors
must have heirs," they said, "so that a
tribe of Israel will not be wiped out.[s]
18We can't give them our daughters as
wives, since we Israelites have taken
this oath:[t] 'Cursed be anyone who
gives[u] a wife to a Benjamite.' **19**But
look, there is the annual festival of the
LORD in Shiloh,[v] to the north of Bethel[w], and east of the road that goes
from Bethel to Shechem,[x] and to the
south of Lebonah."
20So they instructed the Benjamites,
saying, "Go and hide in the vineyards
21and watch. When the girls of Shiloh
come out to join in the dancing,[y] then
rush from the vineyards and each of
you seize a wife from the girls of Shiloh
and go to the land of Benjamin. **22**When
their fathers or brothers complain to
us, we will say to them, 'Do us a kindness by helping them, because we did
not get wives for them during the war,
and you are innocent, since you did not
give[z] your daughters to them.' "
23So that is what the Benjamites
did. While the girls were dancing,[a]
each man caught one and carried her
off to be his wife. Then they returned
to their inheritance[b] and rebuilt the
towns and settled in them.[c]
24At that time the Israelites left that
place and went home to their tribes
and clans, each to his own inheritance.
25In those days Israel had no king;
everyone did as he saw fit.[d]

21:17 [s] S ver 3
21:18 [t] S Jos 9:18
[u] S ver 1
21:19 [v] S Jos 18:1
[w] Jos 16:1
[x] S Jos 17:7
21:21
[y] S Ex 15:20
21:22 [z] S ver 1; ver 1,18
21:23 [a] ver 21
[b] S Jos 24:28
[c] Jdg 20:48
21:25 [d] S Dt 12:8

21:25 EVERYONE DID AS HE SAW FIT. The book of Judges ends by emphasizing that during the time of the judges, the Israelites ignored God's standards for them and did what was right in their own judgment. But as Proverbs points out, human thoughts and opinions are a poor judgment of what is right (Pr 14:12; 16:25). To make our opinions rather than God's Word the guide for our lives is nothing less than rebellion against him. About God's people Nehemiah wrote, "They were disobedient and rebelled against you; they put your law behind their backs. . . . In your great mercy you did not put an end to them or abandon them, for you are a gracious and merciful God" (Ne 9:26,31).

RUTH

Outline

I. Naomi's Adversity (1:1–5)
II. Naomi and Ruth (1:6–22)
  A. Naomi's Decision to Leave Moab (1:6–13)
  B. Ruth's Steadfast Love (1:14–18)
  C. Naomi and Ruth Go to Bethlehem (1:19–22)
III. Ruth Meets Boaz in the Harvest Field (2:1–23)
  A. God's Providence in Ruth's Decision (2:1–3)
  B. God's Provision through Ruth's Decision (2:4–16)
  C. Ruth Shares with Naomi (2:17–23)
IV. Ruth and Boaz at the Threshing Floor (3:1–18)
  A. Naomi's Instruction about Boaz (3:1–5)
  B. Ruth's Kinsman-Redeemer Request to Boaz (3:6–9)
  C. Boaz's Response to Ruth (3:10–18)
V. Boaz Marries Ruth (4:1–13)
  A. The Kinsman-Redeemer Agreement (4:1–12)
  B. Marriage and a Son (4:13)
VI. Naomi's Fulfillment (4:14–17)
VII. Genealogy: Perez to David (4:18–22)

Author: Anonymous

Theme: Redeeming Love

Date of Writing: 10th century B.C.

Background

Historically, the book of Ruth describes events in the life of an Israelite family during the time of the judges (1:1; c. 1375–1050 B.C.). Geographically, the setting for the first 18 verses is the land of Moab (east of the Dead Sea). The remainder of the book is located in or near Bethlehem of Judah. Liturgically, the book of Ruth became one of the five scrolls of the third part of the Hebrew Bible, the *Hagiographa* ("Holy Writings"), each of which was read publicly at one of the annual Jewish feasts. Since the central drama of Ruth occurred at harvest time, the book was customarily read at the Harvest Feast (Pentecost).

Inasmuch as the book traces Ruth's descendants no further than King David (4:21–22), it was most likely written during David's reign. The book's author is nowhere identified in Scripture, though Jewish tradition (e.g., the Talmud) attributes authorship to Samuel.

Purpose

Ruth was written to describe how through self-giving love and the righteous fulfillment of God's law a virtuous and devout young Moabite woman became the great-grandmother of Israel's King David. The book was also written to preserve an admirable story from the time of the judges about a godly family whose faithfulness in hardship stood in sharp contrast to the general spiritual and moral decline in Israel at that time (see the introduction to Judges).

Survey

This story of redeeming love opens with Elimelech leaving Judah and relocating his family in Moab because of famine (1:1–2). Adversity continued to follow Elimelech as he and his two sons died in Moab (1:3–5), leaving their wives widows. Four main episodes then follow. (1) Naomi (Elimelech's widow) and her devout Moabite daughter-in-law, Ruth, returned to Bethlehem in Judah (1:6–22). (2) In God's providence Ruth met Boaz, a wealthy kinsman of Elimelech (ch. 2). (3) Prompted by Naomi, Ruth conveyed to Boaz her interest in the possibility of marriage according to the kinsman-redeemer law (ch. 3). (4) As a kinsman-redeemer, Boaz bought Naomi's property and married Ruth, and they bore a son named Obed—the grandfather of David (ch. 4). Whereas the book opens with bleak adversity, it concludes with glorious fulfillment—for Naomi, Ruth, Boaz and Israel.

Special Features

Six major features characterize the book of Ruth. (1) It is one of two Bible books named after a woman (the other one being Esther). (2) Written against the dark backdrop of Israel's unfaithfulness and apostasy during the period of the judges, this book describes the joys and sorrows of a godly family at Bethlehem during those chaotic times. (3) It illustrates that God's plan of redemption included Gentiles who, during OT times, were grafted into the commonwealth of Israel upon repentance and faith in the Lord. (4) Redemption is a central theme throughout the book, with the kinsman-redeemer role of Boaz being one of the clearest OT illustrations or types of the mediatorial ministry of Jesus Christ. (5) The most recognized verse in the book is Ruth's words to Naomi while still in Moab: "Where you go I will go, and where you stay I will stay. Your people will be my people and your God my God" (1:16). (6) It gives a realistic portrait of life with its struggles and tragedies, yet describes how the faith and faithfulness of godly people enabled God to turn tragedy into triumph and defeat into redemption.

New Testament Fulfillment

Four NT truths are illustrated in the book. (1) Human adversity becomes God's opportunity for advancing his great redemptive purposes (cf. Php 1:12). (2) Ruth's inclusion in redemption demonstrates that participation in God's kingdom is not by physical descent, but by conforming one's life to God's will through the "obedience that comes from faith" (Ro 1:5; cf. 16:26). (3) Ruth's place in the ancestry of David and Jesus (see Mt 1:5) signifies that people of all nations will be represented in the kingdom of the great "Son of David" (Rev 5:9; 7:9). (4) Boaz as the kinsman-redeemer is a type of the great Redeemer, Jesus Christ (Mt 20:28; see Ru 4:10, note).

Reading Ruth

In order to read the entire Old Testament in one year, the book of Ruth should be read in 1 day: ☐ Ruth

NOTES

Naomi and Ruth

1 In the days when the judges
ruled,[a][a] there was a famine in
the land,[b] and a man from Bethlehem
in Judah,[c] together with his wife and
two sons, went to live for a while[d] in
the country of Moab.[e] 2The man's
name was Elimelech,[f] his wife's name
Naomi, and the names of his two sons
were Mahlon and Kilion.[g] They were
Ephrathites[h] from Bethlehem,[i] Judah. And they went to Moab and lived
there.
3Now Elimelech, Naomi's husband,
died, and she was left with her two
sons. 4They married Moabite wom-
en,[j] one named Orpah and the other
Ruth.[k] After they had lived there
about ten years, 5both Mahlon and Kilion[l] also died,[m] and Naomi was left
without her two sons and her husband.
6When she heard in Moab[n] that the
LORD had come to the aid of his people[o] by providing food[p] for them, Naomi and her daughters-in-law[q] prepared to return home from there. 7With
her two daughters-in-law she left the
place where she had been living and
set out on the road that would take
them back to the land of Judah.
8Then Naomi said to her two daughters-in-law, "Go back, each of you, to
your mother's home.[r] May the LORD
show kindness[s] to you, as you have
shown to your dead[t] and to me. 9May
the LORD grant that each of you will find
rest[u] in the home of another husband."
Then she kissed[v] them and they
wept aloud[w] 10and said to her, "We
will go back with you to your people."
11But Naomi said, "Return home, my
daughters. Why would you come with
me? Am I going to have any more sons,
who could become your husbands?[x]
12Return home, my daughters; I am
too old to have another husband. Even
if I thought there was still hope for
me—even if I had a husband tonight
and then gave birth to sons— 13would
you wait until they grew up?[y] Would
you remain unmarried for them? No,
my daughters. It is more bitter[z] for
me than for you, because the LORD's
hand has gone out against me![a]"
14At this they wept[b] again. Then
Orpah kissed her mother-in-law[c]
good-by,[d] but Ruth clung to her.[e]
15"Look," said Naomi, "your sister-
in-law[f] is going back to her people
and her gods.[g] Go back with her."
16But Ruth replied, "Don't urge me
to leave you[h] or to turn back from you.
Where you go I will go,[i] and where

1:1 [a]Jdg 2:16-18 [b]S Ge 12:10; 2Ki 6:25; Ps 105:16; Hag 1:11 [c]S Ge 35:19 [d]Ge 47:4 [e]S Ge 36:35 **1:2** [f]ver 3; Ru 2:1; 4:3 [g]ver 5; Ru 4:9 [h]S Ge 35:16 [i]Ge 35:19; 1Sa 16:18 **1:4** [j]1Ki 11:1; 2Ch 24:26; Ezr 9:2; Ne 13:23 [k]ver 14; Ru 4:13; Mt 1:5 **1:5** [l]S ver 2 [m]ver 8; Ru 2:11 **1:6** [n]S Ge 36:35 [o]S Ge 50:24; Ex 4:31; Jer 29:10; Zep 2:7 [p]Ps 132:15; Mt 6:11 [q]S Ge 11:31; S 38:16 **1:8** [r]Ge 38:11 [s]S Ge 19:19; 2Ti 1:16 [t]S ver 5 **1:9** [u]Ru 3:1 [v]S Ge 27:27; S 29:11 [w]S Ge 27:38; S Nu 25:6 **1:11** [x]Ge 38:11; Dt 25:5 **1:13** [y]Ge 38:11 [z]ver 20; Ex 1:14; 15:23; 1Sa 30:6 [a]S Jdg 2:15; S Job 4:5 **1:14** [b]ver 9 [c]Ru 2:11; 3:1; Mic 7:6 [d]S Ge 31:28 [e]S Dt 10:20 **1:15** [f]Dt 25:7 [g]S Jos 24:14 **1:16** [h]2Ki 2:2 [i]Ge 24:58

a *1* Traditionally *judged*

1:1 WHEN THE JUDGES RULED. The story of Ruth takes place during the time of the judges; it reveals that during the pathetic moral and spiritual apostasy of that time (cf. Jdg 17:6, note; 21:25, note), there was a godly remnant that continued to love and honor God. The book emphasizes that God is active in the lives of those who remain faithful to him and his word (see 2:12, note).

1:3 ELIMELECH, NAOMI'S HUSBAND, DIED. Although Naomi was a faithful follower of the Lord, she experienced great adversity. (1) She and her family suffered the effects of famine and were displaced from their home (v. 1). Furthermore, she lost her husband (v. 3) and her two sons. It appeared that the Lord had forsaken her and even turned against her (cf. vv. 13,21). (2) However, the story shows that God continued to be concerned for her, working through others to help her in her time of need. Like Naomi, believers may be faithful to Christ, yet experience great adversity in their lives; this does not mean that God has forsaken them or is punishing them. Scripture repeatedly emphasizes that God lovingly continues in all things to work for our good in times of trouble (see Ro 8:28,36, notes).

1:12 RETURN HOME, MY DAUGHTERS. Although it would likely mean loneliness for Naomi, she urged her two daughters-in-law to stay in their own homeland. She believed that they would have no opportunity for remarriage and happiness with her. The book emphasizes the selfless devotion and love that existed between Naomi and Ruth and teaches us that true piety always includes loving care and personal sacrifice for members of our own families (see Eph 5:21—6:4, notes).

1:13 THE LORD'S HAND HAS GONE OUT AGAINST ME. Naomi believed that her adversity demonstrated that she no longer had God's favor, but that he was against her (vv. 13,20–21). This personal viewpoint turned out to be erroneous (2:20; 4:14–15). We must not consider all adversity and hardship to be the result of God's actions or displeasure with us, for Satan and ordinary human experiences will at times inflict difficulties and trouble on us irrespective of our dedication to the Lord (see Lk 13:11, note).

1:16 YOUR GOD MY GOD. Naomi had evidently imparted to Ruth her faith in the Lord God by example and teaching (cf. Dt 11:18–19). Ruth's faith in God caused her to remain faithful in her love for Naomi. Ruth illustrates the divine principle that "whoever loses his life for my sake will find it" (Mt 10:39; cf. Ru 4:13–17).

you stay I will stay. Your people will be
my people[j] and your God my God.[k]
17Where you die I will die, and there I
will be buried. May the LORD deal with
me, be it ever so severely,[l] if anything
but death separates you and me."[m]
18When Naomi realized that Ruth was
determined to go with her, she stopped
urging her.[n]
19So the two women went on until
they came to Bethlehem.[o] When they
arrived in Bethlehem, the whole town
was stirred[p] because of them, and the
women exclaimed, "Can this be Naomi?"
20"Don't call me Naomi,[b]" she told
them. "Call me Mara,[c] because the Almighty[d][q] has made my life very bitter.[r] 21I went away full, but the LORD
has brought me back empty.[s] Why
call me Naomi? The LORD has afflicted[e] me;[t] the Almighty has brought
misfortune upon me."
22So Naomi returned from Moab accompanied by Ruth the Moabitess,[u]
her daughter-in-law,[v] arriving in
Bethlehem as the barley harvest[w] was
beginning.[x]

Ruth Meets Boaz

2 Now Naomi had a relative[y] on her
husband's side, from the clan of
Elimelech,[z] a man of standing,[a]
whose name was Boaz.[b]
2And Ruth the Moabitess[c] said to
Naomi, "Let me go to the fields and
pick up the leftover grain[d] behind anyone in whose eyes I find favor.[e]"
Naomi said to her, "Go ahead, my
daughter." 3So she went out and began
to glean in the fields behind the harvesters.[f] As it turned out, she found
herself working in a field belonging to
Boaz, who was from the clan of Elimelech.[g]
4Just then Boaz arrived from Bethlehem and greeted the harvesters, "The
LORD be with you![h]"
"The LORD bless you![i]" they called
back.
5Boaz asked the foreman of his harvesters, "Whose young woman is
that?"
6The foreman replied, "She is the
Moabitess[j] who came back from
Moab with Naomi. 7She said, 'Please
let me glean and gather among the
sheaves[k] behind the harvesters.' She
went into the field and has worked
steadily from morning till now, except
for a short rest[l] in the shelter."
8So Boaz said to Ruth, "My daughter, listen to me. Don't go and glean in
another field and don't go away from
here. Stay here with my servant girls.
9Watch the field where the men are
harvesting, and follow along after the
girls. I have told the men not to touch
you. And whenever you are thirsty, go
and get a drink from the water jars the
men have filled."
10At this, she bowed down with her
face to the ground.[m] She exclaimed,
"Why have I found such favor in your
eyes that you notice me[n]—a foreigner?[o]"
11Boaz replied, "I've been told all
about what you have done for your
mother-in-law[p] since the death of
your husband[q]—how you left your father and mother and your homeland
and came to live with a people you did
not know[r] before.[s] 12May the LORD
repay you for what you have done. May
you be richly rewarded by the LORD,[t]
the God of Israel,[u] under whose
wings[v] you have come to take refuge.[w]"
13"May I continue to find favor in
your eyes,[x] my lord," she said. "You
have given me comfort and have spoken kindly to your servant—though I

1:16 [j]Ps 45:10 [k]S Jos 24:15 **1:17** [l]1Sa 3:17; 14:44; 20:13; 25:22; 2Sa 3:9,35; 2Sa 19:13; 1Ki 2:23; 19:2; 20:10; 2Ki 6:31 [m]2Sa 15:21 **1:18** [n]Ac 21:14 **1:19** [o]S Jdg 17:7 [p]Mt 21:10 **1:20** [q]S Ge 15:1; S 17:1; Ps 91:1 [r]S ver 13 **1:21** [s]Job 1:21 [t]Job 30:11; Ps 88:7; Isa 53:4 **1:22** [u]Ru 2:2,6, 21; 4:5,10 [v]S Ge 11:31 [w]S Ex 9:31; S Lev 19:9 [x]2Sa 21:9 **2:1** [y]Ru 3:2; Pr 7:4 [z]S Ru 1:2 [a]1Sa 9:1; 1Ki 11:28 [b]Ru 4:21; 1Ch 2:12; Mt 1:5; Lk 3:32 **2:2** [c]S Ru 1:22 [d]S Lev 19:9; S 23:22 [e]S Ge 6:8; S 18:3 **2:3** [f]ver 14; 2Ki 4:18; Jer 9:22; Am 9:13 [g]ver 1 **2:4** [h]S Jdg 6:12; Lk 1:28; 2Th 3:16 [i]S Ge 28:3; S Nu 6:24 **2:6** [j]S Ru 1:22 **2:7** [k]S Ge 37:7; S Lev 19:9 [l]2Sa 4:5 **2:10** [m]S Ge 19:1; S 1Sa 20:41 [n]ver 19; Ps 41:1 [o]S Ge 31:15; S Dt 15:3 **2:11** [p]S Ru 1:14 [q]S Ru 1:5 [r]Isa 55:5 [s]Ru 1:16-17 **2:12** [t]1Sa 24:19; 26:23,25; Ps 18:20; Pr 25:22; Jer 31:16 [u]S Jos 24:15 [v]Ps 17:8; 36:7; 57:1; 61:4; 63:7; 91:4 [w]Ps 71:1 **2:13** [x]S Ge 18:3

[b]20 Naomi means *pleasant*; also in verse 21. [c]20 *Mara* means *bitter*. [d]20 Hebrew *Shaddai*; also in verse 21 [e]21 Or *has testified against*

2:2 PICK UP THE LEFTOVER GRAIN. In the law of Moses, God had commanded Israel to permit the poor and needy to gather the grain left in the fields after harvest (Lev 19:9; 23:22; Dt 24:19). God wants those who have enough to share with those in need (cf. 2Co 8:13–15; see article on THE CARE OF THE POOR AND NEEDY, p. 1316).

2:4 BOAZ. Boaz's prayerful greetings and his care for Ruth and Naomi (vv. 8–12) show him to be a righteous believer in the Lord.

2:12 UNDER WHOSE WINGS YOU HAVE COME TO TAKE REFUGE. This is the key verse in the book of Ruth. Even in the midst of great apostasy during the period of the judges, God watched over those who sought him in sincere trust and committed faith (cf. Ps 17:8; 36:7; 63:7). Ruth's story is the story of God's providence and provision in the lives of all who trust in him and follow his ways. As Abraham responded to the Lord's call in faith, so Ruth's trust in the Lord caused her to leave her country and relatives in order to follow his redemptive purpose (cf. Ge 12:1–4).

do not have the standing of one of your
servant girls."
14At mealtime Boaz said to her,
"Come over here. Have some bread[y]
and dip it in the wine vinegar."
When she sat down with the harvesters,[z] he offered her some roasted
grain.[a] She ate all she wanted and had
some left over.[b] 15As she got up to
glean, Boaz gave orders to his men,
"Even if she gathers among the
sheaves,[c] don't embarrass her.
16Rather, pull out some stalks for her
from the bundles and leave them for
her to pick up, and don't rebuke[d]
her."
17So Ruth gleaned in the field until
evening. Then she threshed[e] the barley she had gathered, and it amounted
to about an ephah.[f][f] 18She carried it
back to town, and her mother-in-law
saw how much she had gathered. Ruth
also brought out and gave her what she
had left over[g] after she had eaten
enough.
19Her mother-in-law asked her,
"Where did you glean today? Where did
you work? Blessed be the man who
took notice of you![h]"
Then Ruth told her mother-in-law
about the one at whose place she had
been working. "The name of the man I
worked with today is Boaz," she said.
20"The LORD bless him![i]" Naomi
said to her daughter-in-law.[j] "He has
not stopped showing his kindness[k] to
the living and the dead." She added,
"That man is our close relative;[l] he is
one of our kinsman-redeemers.[m]"
21Then Ruth the Moabitess[n] said,
"He even said to me, 'Stay with my
workers until they finish harvesting all
my grain.' "
22Naomi said to Ruth her daughter-
in-law, "It will be good for you, my
daughter, to go with his girls, because
in someone else's field you might be
harmed."
23So Ruth stayed close to the servant girls of Boaz to glean until the
barley[o] and wheat harvests[p] were
finished. And she lived with her mother-in-law.

Ruth and Boaz at the Threshing Floor

3 One day Naomi her mother-in-
law[q] said to her, "My daughter,
should I not try to find a home[g][r] for
you, where you will be well provided
for? 2Is not Boaz, with whose servant
girls you have been, a kinsman[s] of
ours? Tonight he will be winnowing
barley on the threshing floor.[t]
3Wash[u] and perfume yourself,[v] and
put on your best clothes.[w] Then go
down to the threshing floor, but don't
let him know you are there until he has
finished eating and drinking.[x] 4When
he lies down, note the place where he
is lying. Then go and uncover his feet
and lie down. He will tell you what to
do."
5"I will do whatever you say,"[y]
Ruth answered. 6So she went down to
the threshing floor[z] and did everything her mother-in-law told her to do.
7When Boaz had finished eating and
drinking and was in good spirits,[a] he
went over to lie down at the far end of
the grain pile.[b] Ruth approached quietly, uncovered his feet and lay down.
8In the middle of the night something
startled the man, and he turned and
discovered a woman lying at his feet.
9"Who are you?" he asked.
"I am your servant Ruth," she said.
"Spread the corner of your garment[c]

2:14 [y]S Ge 3:19 [z]S ver 3 [a]S Lev 23:14 [b]ver 18
2:15 [c]S Ge 37:7; S Lev 19:9
2:16 [d]S Ge 37:10
2:17 [e]S Jdg 6:11 [f]S Lev 19:36
2:18 [g]ver 14
2:19 [h]S ver 10
2:20 [i]S Jdg 17:2; S 1Sa 23:21 [j]S Ge 11:31 [k]S Ge 19:19 [l]S Lev 25:25 [m]Ru 3:9,12; 4:1, 14
2:21 [n]S Ru 1:22
2:23 [o]S Ex 9:31 [p]S Ge 30:14; S 1Sa 6:13
3:1 [q]Ru 1:14 [r]Ru 1:9
3:2 [s]S Ru 2:1 [t]S Lev 2:14; S Nu 18:27; S Jdg 6:11
3:3 [u]2Sa 12:20; 2Ki 5:10; Ps 26:6; 51:2; Isa 1:16; Jer 4:14; Eze 16:9 [v]2Sa 14:2; Isa 61:3 [w]S Ge 41:14 [x]S Ex 32:6; S Ecc 2:3; S Jer 15:17
3:5 [y]Eph 6:1; Col 3:20
3:6 [z]S Nu 18:27
3:7 [a]Jdg 19:6,9, 22; 1Sa 25:36; 2Sa 13:28; 1Ki 21:7; Est 1:10 [b]2Ch 31:6; SS 7:2; Jer 50:26; Hag 2:16
3:9 [c]Eze 16:8

[f] *17* That is, probably about 3/5 bushel (about 22 liters) [g] *1* Hebrew *find rest* (see Ruth 1:9)

2:20 NOT STOPPED SHOWING HIS KINDNESS. Naomi began to understand that God had not forsaken her and that his love and kindness toward her were indeed continuing. Her attitude changed from her earlier perception that God had turned against her (see 1:13, note).

2:20 ONE OF OUR KINSMAN-REDEEMERS. Boaz, as a close relative of Naomi and Ruth, was required by the law of Moses to provide for the needs of his relatives (cf. Lev 25:25–28,47–49; Dt 25:5–10). Boaz fulfilled this obligation by marrying Ruth and purchasing the land of her former husband's father (cf. 2:20—4:14).

3:4 UNCOVER HIS FEET AND LIE DOWN. Ruth's lying down at Boaz's feet must be viewed in the light of the customs of that day. It was done discreetly and without sexual connotations. As Boaz remained at the threshing floor during the night to protect his crop, Ruth went there and by her action conveyed to Boaz her desire for him to marry her as her deceased husband's next of kin (i.e., as the kinsman-redeemer, see vv. 6–9).

3:9 SPREAD THE CORNER OF YOUR GARMENT OVER ME. By this gesture, Ruth was asking Boaz to take her for his wife (see also Eze 16:8). The covering symbolizes protection, care and support.

over me, since you are a kinsman-redeemer.[d]"
10"The LORD bless you,[e] my daughter," he replied. "This kindness is
greater than that which you showed
earlier:[f] You have not run after the
younger men, whether rich or poor.
11And now, my daughter, don't be
afraid. I will do for you all you ask. All
my fellow townsmen know that you are
a woman of noble character.[g] **12**Although it is true that I am near of kin,
there is a kinsman-redeemer[h] nearer
than[i] I. **13**Stay here for the night, and
in the morning if he wants to redeem,[j]
good; let him redeem. But if he is not
willing, as surely as the LORD lives[k] I
will do it.[l] Lie here until morning."
14So she lay at his feet until morning, but got up before anyone could be
recognized; and he said, "Don't let it be
known that a woman came to the
threshing floor."[m][n]
15He also said, "Bring me the
shawl[o] you are wearing and hold it
out." When she did so, he poured into
it six measures of barley and put it on
her. Then he[h] went back to town.
16When Ruth came to her mother-in-
law, Naomi asked, "How did it go, my
daughter?"
Then she told her everything Boaz
had done for her **17**and added, "He gave
me these six measures of barley, saying, 'Don't go back to your mother-in-
law empty-handed.' "
18Then Naomi said, "Wait, my
daughter, until you find out what happens. For the man will not rest until
the matter is settled today."[p]

Boaz Marries Ruth

4 Meanwhile Boaz went up to the
town gate[q] and sat there. When
the kinsman-redeemer[r] he had mentioned[s] came along, Boaz said, "Come
over here, my friend, and sit down." So
he went over and sat down.
2Boaz took ten of the elders[t] of the
town and said, "Sit here," and they did
so.[u] **3**Then he said to the kinsman-redeemer, "Naomi, who has come back
from Moab, is selling the piece of land
that belonged to our brother Elimelech.[v] **4**I thought I should bring the
matter to your attention and suggest
that you buy it in the presence of these
seated here and in the presence of the
elders of my people. If you will redeem
it, do so. But if you[i] will not, tell me,
so I will know. For no one has the right
to do it except you,[w] and I am next in
line."
"I will redeem it," he said.
5Then Boaz said, "On the day you
buy the land from Naomi and from
Ruth the Moabitess,[x] you acquire[j]
the dead man's widow, in order to
maintain the name of the dead with his
property."[y]
6At this, the kinsman-redeemer
said, "Then I cannot redeem[z] it because I might endanger my own estate.
You redeem it yourself. I cannot do
it."[a]
7(Now in earlier times in Israel, for
the redemption[b] and transfer of property to become final, one party took off
his sandal[c] and gave it to the other.
This was the method of legalizing
transactions[d] in Israel.)[e]
8So the kinsman-redeemer said to
Boaz, "Buy it yourself." And he removed his sandal.[f]
9Then Boaz announced to the elders
and all the people, "Today you are witnesses[g] that I have bought from Naomi all the property of Elimelech, Kilion
and Mahlon. **10**I have also acquired
Ruth the Moabitess,[h] Mahlon's widow, as my wife,[i] in order to maintain
the name of the dead with his property,
so that his name will not disappear
from among his family or from the

3:9 [d]S Ru 2:20 **3:10** [e]S Jdg 17:2 [f]S Jos 2:12 **3:11** [g]Pr 12:4; 14:1; 31:10 **3:12** [h]S Ru 2:20 [i]Ru 4:1 **3:13** [j]Dt 25:5; Ru 4:5; Mt 22:24 [k]S Nu 14:21; Hos 4:15 [l]Ru 4:6 **3:14** [m]S Nu 18:27 [n]Ro 14:16; 2Co 8:21 **3:15** [o]Isa 3:22 **3:18** [p]Ps 37:3-5 **4:1** [q]S Ge 18:1; S 23:10 [r]S Ru 2:20 [s]Ru 3:12 **4:2** [t]S Ex 3:16

[u]S Dt 25:7 **4:3** [v]S Lev 25:25; S Ru 1:2 **4:4** [w]S Lev 25:25; Jer 32:7-8 **4:5** [x]S Ru 1:22 [y]S Ge 38:8; S Ru 3:13 **4:6** [z]Lev 25:25; Ru 3:13 [a]S Dt 25:7 **4:7** [b]S Lev 25:24 [c]ver 8 [d]Isa 8:1-2, 16,20 [e]Dt 25:7-9 **4:8** [f]Dt 25:9 **4:9** [g]Isa 8:2; Jer 32:10,44 **4:10** [h]S Ru 1:22 [i]S Dt 25:5

[h] *15* Most Hebrew manuscripts; many Hebrew manuscripts, Vulgate and Syriac *she*
[i] *4* Many Hebrew manuscripts, Septuagint, Vulgate and Syriac; most Hebrew manuscripts *he*
[j] *5* Hebrew; Vulgate and Syriac *Naomi, you acquire Ruth the Moabitess,*

3:12 KINSMAN-REDEEMER. The nearest relative had the first right to marry Ruth and also inherit the family land. Only if he refused was Boaz free to marry Ruth (see 4:1–6).

4:10 ACQUIRED RUTH ... AS MY WIFE. Boaz became a redeemer in two ways. (1) He married Ruth and preserved the name of Elimelech, Naomi's deceased husband. The firstborn son of Boaz and Ruth was considered a son of Elimelech's line (vv. 5,10). (2) Boaz redeemed (i.e., bought) the family land that Naomi had sold and restored it to Elimelech's line (vv. 3,7–10).

Boaz is an OT type of Jesus Christ, who likewise redeems the believer in two ways. (1) Christ has purchased us by his own blood and thereby keeps our lives and names from perishing in sin (Jn 3:16; 1Pe 1:18–19). (2) He includes us as the redeemed in his eternal inheritance in the new heaven and earth (Mt 5:5; Rev 21:1–7).

town records.[j] Today you are witnesses![k]"
11Then the elders and all those at
the gate[l] said, "We are witnesses.[m]
May the LORD make the woman who is
coming into your home like Rachel and
Leah,[n] who together built up the
house of Israel. May you have standing
in Ephrathah[o] and be famous in Bethlehem.[p] **12**Through the offspring the
LORD gives you by this young woman,
may your family be like that of Perez,[q]
whom Tamar[r] bore to Judah."

The Genealogy of David

4:18–22pp — 1Ch 2:5–15; Mt 1:3–6; Lk 3:31–33

13So Boaz took Ruth and she became his wife. Then he went to her,
and the LORD enabled her to conceive,[s] and she gave birth to a son.[t]
14The women[u] said to Naomi: "Praise
be to the LORD,[v] who this day has not
left you without a kinsman-redeemer.[w] May he become famous throughout Israel! **15**He will renew your life
and sustain you in your old age. For
your daughter-in-law,[x] who loves you
and who is better to you than seven
sons,[y] has given him birth."
16Then Naomi took the child, laid
him in her lap and cared for him. **17**The
women living there said, "Naomi has a
son." And they named him Obed. He
was the father of Jesse,[z] the father of
David.[a]
18This, then, is the family line of Perez[b]:

Perez was the father of Hezron,[c]
19Hezron the father of Ram,
Ram the father of Amminadab,[d]
20Amminadab the father of Nahshon,[e]
Nahshon the father of Salmon,[k]
21Salmon the father of Boaz,[f]
Boaz the father of Obed,
22Obed the father of Jesse,
and Jesse the father of David.

4:10 [j] S Dt 25:6 [k] S Jos 24:22 **4:11** [l] S Ge 23:10 [m] S Dt 25:9 [n] S Ge 4:19; S 29:16 [o] S Ge 35:16 [p] Ru 1:19 **4:12** [q] S Ge 38:29 [r] Ge 38:6,24 **4:13** [s] S Ge 8:1; S 29:31 [t] S Ge 29:32; S 30:6; Lk 1:57 **4:14** [u] Lk 1:58 [v] S Ge 24:27 [w] S Ru 2:20
4:15 [x] S Ge 11:31 [y] 1Sa 1:8; 2:5; Job 1:2 **4:17** [z] ver 22; 1Sa 16:1,18; 17:12,17,58; 1Ch 2:12,13; Ps 72:20 [a] 1Sa 16:13; 1Ch 2:15 **4:18** [b] S Ge 38:29 [c] Nu 26:21 **4:19** [d] S Ex 6:23 **4:20** [e] S Nu 7:12 **4:21** [f] S Ru 2:1

[k] *20* A few Hebrew manuscripts, some Septuagint manuscripts and Vulgate (see also verse 21 and Septuagint of 1 Chron. 2:11); most Hebrew manuscripts *Salma*

4:14 HAS NOT LEFT YOU. Although Naomi had experienced great sorrow and adversity in her life, she had maintained her faith in God. Because of her persevering faith, God so ordered events that her life ended in goodness and blessing. She could testify at the end of her life that "the Lord is full of compassion and mercy" (Jas 5:11).

4:17 A SON . . . THE FATHER OF DAVID. God honored the decision of a virtuous young woman who forsook her pagan homeland in order to remain loyal to her mother-in-law and to the God of Israel (1:16), by allowing her to become a part of the earthly family through whom Jesus Christ came into the world (cf. Mt 1:5).

1 SAMUEL

Outline

I. Samuel: Prophetic Leader of Israel (1:1—8:22)
   A. Birth of a Prophetic Leader (1:1—2:11)
      1. Hannah's Sorrow and Supplication (1:1–18)
      2. Hannah's Prophetic Son (1:19–28)
      3. Hannah's Prophetic Song (2:1–11)
   B. Corruption of the Old Leadership (2:12–36)
   C. Transition from Eli to Samuel (3:1—6:21)
      1. Samuel's Prophetic Calling (3:1–21)
      2. Judgment of Eli's House and Ministry (4:1–22)
      3. The Ark Taken and Restored (5:1—6:21)
   D. Revival Under the Leadership of Samuel (7:1–17)
   E. Israel Demands a King (8:1–22)
      1. Israel Rejects Samuel's Sons as Leaders (8:1–5)
      2. Israel Rejects God as King (8:6–22)

II. Saul: First King of Israel (9:1—15:35)
   A. Transition from Samuel to Saul (9:1—12:25)
      1. Selection of Saul (9:1–27)
      2. Samuel Anoints Saul (10:1–27)
      3. Saul's Victory over the Ammonites (11:1–11)
      4. Samuel Renews the Kingdom at Gilgal (11:12–15)
      5. Samuel's Farewell Address (12:1–25)
   B. The Early Kingship of Saul (13:1—15:35)
      1. Saul's Wars and Foolishness (13:1—14:52)
      2. Saul's Disobedience and Rejection (15:1–35)

III. David: An Anointed Man in Waiting (16:1—31:13)
   A. Samuel Anoints David (16:1–13)
   B. God Takes His Spirit from Saul (16:14–23)
   C. David in Contest with Goliath (17:1–58)
   D. David in the Court of Saul (18:1—19:17)
      1. David and Jonathan (18:1–4)
      2. David Serves Saul (18:5–16)
      3. David Marries Michal (18:17–28)
      4. Saul Fears David and Seeks His Life (18:29—19:17)
   E. David in Exile (19:18—31:13)
      1. David with Samuel (19:18–24)
      2. David Protected by Jonathan (20:1–42)
      3. David Aided by Ahimelech the Priest (21:1–9)
      4. David at Gath (21:10–15)
      5. A Band of Outlaws Rally Around David (22:1—26:25)
      6. David's Refuge in Philistia (27:1—30:31)
      7. The Death of Saul (31:1–13)

Author: Anonymous

Theme: Theocratic Kingship

Date of Writing: Late 10th century B.C.

Background

1 and 2 Samuel are one book in the Hebrew OT. They are named after the prophet Samuel, who was held in high esteem as a strong spiritual leader of Israel and the one whom God used to set in order the theocratic monarchy. 1 Samuel covers nearly one century of Israel's history—from Samuel's birth to Saul's death (c. 1105–1010 B.C.)—and forms the main historical link between the time of the judges and the first of Israel's kings. Whereas 2 Samuel deals solely with King David, 1 Samuel covers three major transitions in national leadership: from Eli to Samuel, from Samuel to Saul, and from Saul to David.

The issue of authorship involves 1 and 2 Samuel as a single literary unit. Since part of 1 Samuel and all of 2 Samuel were written after Samuel's death, Samuel served only as one contributing author (cf. 1Sa 10:25). The final composition was written by an inspired prophetic historian who used several sources, including the records of Samuel (cf. 2Sa 1:18; 1Ch 27:24; 29:29); the identity of this inspired historian is unknown to us. The book was completed probably soon after 930 B.C., for 1 Samuel seems to assume the division of the kingdom (1Sa 27:6) and 2 Samuel ends with the last days of David.

Purpose

1 Samuel describes the crucial turning point in Israel's history from rule by the judges to rule by a king. The book sets forth the tension between the people's expectation of a king (a despotic ruler "such as all the other nations have," 8:5) and God's pattern of a theocracy, in which he was their King. The book shows clearly that Saul's disobedience and his violation of the theocratic requirements of his office led God to reject and replace him as king.

Survey

The content of 1 Samuel focuses on three key national leaders: Samuel, Saul and David. (1) Samuel was the last of the judges and the first to occupy the prophetic office (though he was not the first prophet, cf. Dt 34:10; Jdg 4:4). As a man of great piety and prophetic gifts, Samuel (a) wisely directed Israel in a revival of true worship (ch. 7), (b) laid the foundation that gave the prophets their due place in Israel (19:20; cf. Ac 3:24; 13:20; Heb 11:32), and (c) clearly established the monarchy as a theocratic kingship (15:1,12,28; 16:1). Samuel's importance as spiritual leader of God's people during a period of great change in Israel's history is second only to that of Moses at the time of the exodus.

(2) Saul became Israel's first king because of the people's demand for a human king "such as all the other nations have" (8:5,20). Saul quickly demonstrated that he was spiritually unfit to fill the theocratic office; thus he was later rejected by God (chs. 13; 15).

(3) David, God's next choice to be his representative as king, was anointed by Samuel (ch. 16). David refused to usurp Saul's throne by force or subversion and left his own promotion in God's hands. Chs. 19—30 largely describe David's flight from an insanely jealous Saul, and the patience with which David waited for God to act in his own time. The book concludes with Saul's tragic death (ch. 31).

Special Features

Six major features characterize 1 Samuel. (1) It sets forth clearly God's holy standards for Israel's kingship. Israel's kings were to be leaders who submitted to God as the true King of Israel, obeyed his laws, and allowed themselves to be guided and corrected by his revelation through the prophets. (2) It records the foundational beginning of prominence for the prophetic office in Israel as a spiritual equal to the priesthood. The book contains the first OT references to a group of prophets (10:5; 19:18–24). (3) It stresses the importance and power of prayer (1:10–28; 2:1–10; 7:5–10; 8:5–6; 9:15; 12:19–23), God's word (1:23; 9:27; 15:1,10,23) and the Spirit of prophecy (2:27–36; 3:20; 10:6,10; 19:20–24: 28:6). (4) It contains rich biographical information about and insights into the lives of three key leaders of Israel—Samuel (chs. 1—7), Saul (chs. 8—31) and David (chs. 16—31). (5) It is replete with well-known Bible stories, such as God speaking to young Samuel (ch. 3), David and Goliath (ch. 17), David and Jonathan (chs. 18—20), Saul's jealousy and fear of David (chs. 18—30), and Saul and the witch of Endor (ch. 28). (6) It is the source of some oft-quoted words: "Ichabod"—meaning "no glory," for "the glory has departed from Israel" (4:21); "Ebenezer"—meaning "stone of help," for "thus far has the LORD helped us"(7:12); and "Long live the king!" (10:24). Also, it is the first OT book to use the phrase "the LORD Almighty" (e.g., 1:3).

New Testament Fulfillment

1 Samuel records two prophetic types of Jesus' ministry as prophet, priest and king. (1) Samuel—God's main prophetic and priestly representative to Israel, foreshadowed Jesus' ministry as God's foremost prophetic and priestly representative to Israel. (2) David—born in Bethlehem, a shepherd and God's anointed king who served God's purposes for his own generation (Ac 13:36)—became the primary OT type and forerunner of Israel's Messianic king. The NT speaks of Jesus Christ as "the son of David" (e.g., Mt 1:1; 9:27; 21:9), "a descendant of David" (Ro 1:3), and "the Root and the Offspring of David" (Rev 22:16).

Reading 1 Samuel

In order to read the entire Old Testament in one year, the book of 1 Samuel should be read in 11 days, according to the following schedule: ☐ 1–2 ☐ 3–7 ☐ 8–10 ☐ 11–13 ☐ 14–15 ☐ 16–17 ☐ 18–19 ☐ 20–22 ☐ 23–25 ☐ 26–28 ☐ 29–31

NOTES

The Birth of Samuel

1 There was a certain man from Ramathaim,[a] a Zuphite[ab] from the
hill country[c] of Ephraim,[d] whose
name was Elkanah[e] son of Jeroham,
the son of Elihu, the son of Tohu, the
son of Zuph, an Ephraimite. **2**He had
two wives;[f] one was called Hannah
and the other Peninnah. Peninnah had
children, but Hannah had none.

3Year after year[g] this man went up
from his town to worship[h] and sacrifice to the LORD Almighty at Shiloh,[i]
where Hophni and Phinehas, the two
sons of Eli,[j] were priests of the LORD.
4Whenever the day came for Elkanah
to sacrifice,[k] he would give portions of
the meat to his wife Peninnah and to
all her sons and daughters.[l] **5**But to
Hannah he gave a double portion[m] because he loved her, and the LORD had
closed her womb.[n] **6**And because the
LORD had closed her womb, her rival
kept provoking her in order to irritate
her.[o] **7**This went on year after year.
Whenever Hannah went up to the
house of the LORD, her rival provoked
her till she wept and would not eat.[p]
8Elkanah her husband would say to
her, "Hannah, why are you weeping?
Why don't you eat? Why are you down-
hearted? Don't I mean more to you
than ten sons?[q]"

9Once when they had finished eating
and drinking in Shiloh, Hannah stood
up. Now Eli the priest was sitting on a
chair by the doorpost of the LORD's temple.[br] **10**In bitterness of soul[s] Hannah wept much and prayed to the LORD.
11And she made a vow,[t] saying,
"O LORD Almighty[u], if you will only
look upon your servant's misery and
remember[v] me, and not forget your
servant but give her a son, then I will
give him to the LORD for all the days of
his life,[w] and no razor[x] will ever be
used on his head."

12As she kept on praying to the
LORD, Eli observed her mouth. **13**Hannah was praying in her heart, and her
lips were moving but her voice was not
heard. Eli thought she was drunk
14and said to her, "How long will you
keep on getting drunk? Get rid of your
wine."

15"Not so, my lord," Hannah replied,
"I am a woman who is deeply troubled.[y] I have not been drinking wine
or beer; I was pouring[z] out my soul to
the LORD. **16**Do not take your servant
for a wicked woman; I have been praying here out of my great anguish and
grief."[a]

17Eli answered, "Go in peace,[b] and
may the God of Israel grant you what
you have asked of him.[c]"

18She said, "May your servant find
favor in your eyes.[d]" Then she went
her way and ate something, and her
face was no longer downcast.[e]

19Early the next morning they arose
and worshiped before the LORD and
then went back to their home at Ramah.[f] Elkanah lay with Hannah his
wife, and the LORD remembered[g] her.
20So in the course of time Hannah conceived and gave birth to a son.[h] She
named[i] him Samuel,[cj] saying, "Because I asked the LORD for him."

1:1 [a] S Jos 18:25 [b] 1Sa 9:5 [c] Jos 17:17-18 [d] Jos 21:20-22 [e] 1Ch 6:27,34 **1:2** [f] S Ge 4:19 **1:3** [g] ver 21; Ex 23:14; 1Sa 2:19; 20:6,29; Lk 2:41 [h] Dt 12:5-7 [i] S Jos 18:1 [j] 1Sa 2:31; 14:3 **1:4** [k] Lev 7:15-18; Dt 12:17-18 [l] S Ge 29:34 **1:5** [m] S Ge 37:3 [n] S Ge 11:30; S 29:31 **1:6** [o] S Ge 16:4 **1:7** [p] 2Sa 12:17; Ps 102:4 **1:8** [q] S Ru 4:15 **1:9** [r] 1Sa 3:3 **1:10** [s] Job 3:20; 7:11; 10:1; 21:25; 23:2; 27:2; Isa 38:15; Jer 20:18 **1:11** [t] S Jdg 11:30 [u] S Ge 17:1; Ps 24:10; 46:7; Isa 1:9 [v] S Ge 8:1 [w] S Jdg 13:7 [x] Nu 6:1-21; Jdg 13:5; Lk 1:15 **1:15** [y] 2Ki 4:27 [z] Ps 42:4; 62:8; La 2:19 **1:16** [a] Ps 55:2 **1:17** [b] Nu 6:26; 1Sa 20:42; 2Ki 5:19; S Ac 15:33 [c] S Ge 25:21; Ps 20:3-5 **1:18** [d] S Ge 18:3; Ru 2:13 [e] Ro 15:13 **1:19** [f] S Jos 18:25 [g] S Ge 8:1; S 29:31 **1:20** [h] S Ge 17:19; S 29:32; S 30:6 [i] Ex 2:10; Mt 1:21 [j] 1Sa 7:5; 12:23; 1Ch 6:27; Jer 15:1; Heb 11:32

[a] *1* Or *from Ramathaim Zuphim* [b] *9* That is, tabernacle [c] *20* *Samuel* sounds like the Hebrew for *heard of God.*

1:5 THE LORD HAD CLOSED HER WOMB. Hannah's barrenness is ascribed directly to the activity of God. He had withheld children to prepare her for the birth of her son Samuel. In the same way, at times God may cause us to experience disappointments or lead us into situations in which we feel inadequate or inferior in order to work out his will in our lives. We should do as Hannah did—take our situations and hurts directly to the Lord and wait for him (cf. vv. 10–19; see Ro 8:28, note).

1:11 I WILL GIVE HIM TO THE LORD. Hannah showed her devotion to the Lord by her willingness to dedicate her son to the Lord's work. In the same way, Christian parents today may express their commitment to God and his kingdom by giving their sons and daughters to the ministry or to the work of missions in other lands. Those parents who support, encourage and pray for their children will find great favor with God.

1:11 NO RAZOR ... HEAD. Uncut hair was a sign of the Nazirite vow (see Nu 6:5,14, notes).

1:20 GAVE BIRTH TO A SON ... SAMUEL. Although this book deals largely with the transition in Israel's history from the period of the judges to the establishment of the kingship, the first eight chapters concentrate on the birth, early life and prophetic leadership of Samuel, the last judge. This prophet of God preceded the institution of the king in Israel who stood under the word and Spirit of God as represented by Samuel (11:14—12:25). Throughout the Bible, the prophet as God's representative to Israel took precedence over the kingship and all other offices (cf. Mal 4:5–6; Lk 7:24–28).

Hannah Dedicates Samuel

21When the man Elkanah went up
with all his family to offer the annual[k]
sacrifice to the LORD and to fulfill his
vow,[l] 22Hannah did not go. She said
to her husband, "After the boy is
weaned, I will take him and present[m]
him before the LORD, and he will live
there always."
23"Do what seems best to you," Elkanah her husband told her. "Stay here
until you have weaned him; only may
the LORD make good[n] his[d] word." So
the woman stayed at home and nursed
her son until she had weaned[o] him.
24After he was weaned, she took the
boy with her, young as he was, along
with a three-year-old bull,[e][p] an
ephah[f] of flour and a skin of wine, and
brought him to the house of the LORD at
Shiloh. 25When they had slaughtered
the bull, they brought the boy to Eli,
26and she said to him, "As surely as
you live, my lord, I am the woman who
stood here beside you praying to the
LORD. 27I prayed[q] for this child, and
the LORD has granted me what I asked
of him. 28So now I give him to the LORD.
For his whole life[r] he will be given
over to the LORD." And he worshiped
the LORD there.

Hannah's Prayer

2 Then Hannah prayed and said:[s]
"My heart rejoices[t] in the LORD;
in the LORD my horn[g][u] is lifted
high.
My mouth boasts[v] over my
enemies,[w]
for I delight in your deliverance.

2"There is no one holy[h][x] like[y]
the LORD;
there is no one besides you;
there is no Rock[z] like our God.

3"Do not keep talking so proudly
or let your mouth speak such
arrogance,[a]
for the LORD is a God who
knows,[b]
and by him deeds[c] are
weighed.[d]

4"The bows of the warriors are
broken,[e]
but those who stumbled are
armed with strength.[f]
5Those who were full hire
themselves out for food,
but those who were hungry[g]
hunger no more.
She who was barren[h] has borne
seven children,
but she who has had many sons
pines away.

6"The LORD brings death and makes
alive;[i]
he brings down to the grave[i]
and raises up.[j]
7The LORD sends poverty and
wealth;[k]
he humbles and he exalts.[l]
8He raises[m] the poor[n] from the
dust[o]
and lifts the needy[p] from the
ash heap;
he seats them with princes
and has them inherit a throne of
honor.[q]
"For the foundations[r] of the earth
are the LORD's;
upon them he has set the world.
9He will guard the feet[s] of his
saints,[t]
but the wicked will be silenced
in darkness.[u]

1:21 [k]S ver 3 [l]S Ge 28:20; Nu 30:2; Dt 12:11 1:22 [m]Ex 13:2; Lk 2:22 1:23 [n]S Ge 25:21 [o]Ge 21:8 1:24 [p]Nu 15:8-10 1:27 [q]1Sa 2:20; Ps 66:19-20 1:28 [r]S Jdg 13:7 2:1 [s]Lk 1:46-55 [t]Ps 13:5; 33:21; Zec 10:7 [u]Ps 18:2; 89:17,24; 148:14 [v]Ps 6:8 [w]S Nu 10:35; Ps 6:10 2:2 [x]S Ex 15:11; S Lev 11:44 [y]S Ex 8:10; Isa 40:25; 46:5 [z]S Ge 49:24; S Ex 33:22; Dt 32:37; 2Sa 22:2,32; 23:3; Ps 31:3; 71:3 2:3 [a]Ps 17:10; 31:18; 73:8; 75:4; 94:4

[b]S Jos 22:22 [c]1Sa 16:7; 1Ki 8:39; 1Ch 28:9; 2Ch 6:30; Pr 15:11; Jer 11:20; 17:10 [d]Pr 16:2; 24:11-12 2:4 [e]2Sa 1:27; Ps 37:15; 46:9; 76:3 [f]Job 17:9; Isa 40:31; 41:1; 52:1; 57:10 2:5 [g]Lk 1:53 [h]Ps 113:9; Isa 54:1; Jer 15:9 2:6 [i]Dt 32:39 [j]Isa 26:19; Eze 37:3,12 2:7 [k]S Dt 8:18 [l]Job 5:11; 40:12; Ps 75:7; Isa 2:12; 13:11; 22:19; Da 4:37 2:8 [m]Ps 113:7-8 [n]Jas 2:5 [o]1Ki 16:2 [p]Ps 72:12; 107:41; 145:14; 146:8; S Mt 23:12 [q]2Sa 7:8; Job 36:7; Isa 22:23; Eze 21:26 [r]Job 15:7; 38:4; Ps 104:5; Pr 8:29; Isa 40:12; Jer 10:12 2:9 [s]Ps 91:12; 121:3; Pr 3:26 [t]Pr 2:8 [u]Job 10:22; Isa 5:30; 8:22; 59:9; 60:2; Jer 13:16; Am 5:18,20; Zep 1:14-15; Mt 8:12

[d]*23* Masoretic Text; Dead Sea Scrolls, Septuagint and Syriac *your* [e]*24* Dead Sea Scrolls, Septuagint and Syriac; Masoretic Text *with three bulls* [f]*24* That is, probably about 3/5 bushel (about 22 liters) [g]*1* *Horn* here symbolizes strength; also in verse 10. [h]*2* Or *no Holy One* [i]*6* Hebrew *Sheol*

1:28 GIVEN OVER TO THE LORD. Hannah should be lifted up as an example of godly motherhood. From the time she first desired to have a child, she prayerfully and purposefully presented her child before the Lord (vv. 10–28). She regarded her son as a gracious gift from God and expressed her intention to fulfill her vow by dedicating him to the Lord (vv. 11,24–28; see article on PARENTS AND CHILDREN, p. 1854).

2:1 HANNAH PRAYED. Hannah's prophetic song celebrates God's providential care of those who remain faithful to him (v. 9; cf. Mary's song in Lk 1:46–55). She rejoiced also in his salvation, for he is holy, and he alone is God (v. 2). All followers of the Lord Jesus should trust in the Lord's ways with them. Anything that he allows to come into our lives should be brought to him in prayer, with full confidence that not only can nothing separate us from his love, but also he will ultimately bring good out of whatever happens to us (Ro 8:31–39).

"It is not by strength[v] that one
prevails;
10 those who oppose the LORD will
be shattered.[w]
He will thunder[x] against them
from heaven;
the LORD will judge[y] the ends of
the earth.

"He will give strength[z] to his
king
and exalt the horn[a] of his
anointed."

11 Then Elkanah went home to Ramah,[b] but the boy ministered[c] before
the LORD under Eli the priest.

Eli's Wicked Sons

12 Eli's sons were wicked men; they
had no regard[d] for the LORD. **13** Now it
was the practice[e] of the priests with
the people that whenever anyone offered a sacrifice and while the meat[f]
was being boiled, the servant of the
priest would come with a three-
pronged fork in his hand. **14** He would
plunge it into the pan or kettle or caldron or pot, and the priest would take
for himself whatever the fork brought
up. This is how they treated all the Israelites who came to Shiloh. **15** But
even before the fat was burned, the servant of the priest would come and say
to the man who was sacrificing, "Give
the priest some meat to roast; he won't
accept boiled meat from you, but only
raw."

16 If the man said to him, "Let the
fat[g] be burned up first, and then take
whatever you want," the servant would
then answer, "No, hand it over now; if
you don't, I'll take it by force."

17 This sin of the young men was
very great in the LORD's sight, for
they[j] were treating the LORD's offering with contempt.[h]

18 But Samuel was ministering[i] before the LORD—a boy wearing a linen
ephod.[j] **19** Each year his mother made
him a little robe and took it to him
when she went up with her husband to
offer the annual[k] sacrifice. **20** Eli
would bless Elkanah and his wife, saying, "May the LORD give you children by
this woman to take the place of the one
she prayed[l] for and gave to the LORD."
Then they would go home. **21** And the
LORD was gracious to Hannah;[m] she
conceived and gave birth to three sons
and two daughters. Meanwhile, the
boy Samuel grew[n] up in the presence
of the LORD.

22 Now Eli, who was very old, heard
about everything[o] his sons were doing
to all Israel and how they slept with
the women[p] who served at the entrance to the Tent of Meeting. **23** So he
said to them, "Why do you do such
things? I hear from all the people about
these wicked deeds of yours. **24** No, my
sons; it is not a good report that I hear
spreading among the LORD's people.
25 If a man sins against another man,
God[k] may mediate for him; but if a
man sins against the LORD, who will[q]
intercede[r] for him?" His sons, however, did not listen to their father's rebuke, for it was the LORD's will to put
them to death.

26 And the boy Samuel continued to
grow[s] in stature and in favor with the
LORD and with men.[t]

Prophecy Against the House of Eli

27 Now a man of God[u] came to Eli
and said to him, "This is what the LORD
says: 'Did I not clearly reveal myself to
your father's house when they were in
Egypt under Pharaoh? **28** I chose[v]

2:9 [v] 1Sa 17:47; Ps 33:16-17; Zec 4:6
2:10 [w] S Ex 15:6 [x] S Ex 19:16; 1Sa 7:10; 12:17; 2Sa 22:14; Job 37:4,5; 38:1; Ps 18:13; 29:3; Isa 66:6 [y] Ps 96:13; 98:9; Mt 25:31-32 [z] Ps 18:1; 21:1; 59:16 [a] S Dt 33:17; Ps 89:24; S Lk 1:69
2:11 [b] S Jos 18:25 [c] ver 18; S Nu 16:9; 1Sa 3:1
2:12 [d] Jer 2:8; 9:6
2:13 [e] Dt 18:3 [f] Lev 7:35-36
2:16 [g] Lev 3:3, 14-16; 7:29-34
2:17 [h] ver 22,29; S Nu 14:11; Jer 7:21; Eze 22:26; Mal 2:7-9
2:18 [i] S ver 11 [j] ver 28; 1Sa 22:18; 23:9; 2Sa 6:14; 1Ch 15:27
2:19 [k] S 1Sa 1:3
2:20 [l] S 1Sa 1:27
2:21 [m] Ge 21:1 [n] S Jdg 13:24; Lk 1:80; 2:40
2:22 [o] S ver 17 [p] S Ex 38:8
2:25 [q] Ex 4:21; Jos 11:20 [r] S Ex 32:10; S Nu 11:2; 1Sa 3:14; 1Ki 13:6; Job 9:33; Ps 106:30; Isa 1:18; 22:14; Jer 15:1; Heb 10:26
2:26 [s] S Jdg 13:24; Lk 2:52 [t] Pr 3:4
2:27 [u] S Dt 33:1; S Jdg 13:6
2:28 [v] S Ex 28:1

[j] 17 Or *men* [k] 25 Or *the judges*

2:12 WICKED MEN. The sons of Eli were corrupt ministers in God's house who used their position as an opportunity for greedy gain and for sexual immorality (vv. 13–17,22; cf. Php 3:17–18). Their father Eli, the high priest, refused to discipline them or to disqualify them from the priesthood (see v. 29, note).

2:23 I HEAR . . . ABOUT THESE WICKED DEEDS. Eli protested the evil actions of his sons, yet he failed to remove them from their ministerial office (cf. Nu 15:30–31). Eli's failure was regarded as equivalent to despising God (i.e., God's holy nature and his standard for the priesthood, v. 30). God's Word declares that no immoral minister may serve as a leader of God's people; such persons must be removed from their positions of leadership (see article on MORAL QUALIFICATIONS FOR OVERSEERS, p. 1882).

2:25 THE LORD'S WILL TO PUT THEM TO DEATH. Eli's sons had hardened their hearts and were sinning openly and without shame (cf. Nu 15:30–31). Therefore Eli's instruction had no moral effect on them. For them the day of salvation had passed, and they were already appointed by God to condemnation and death (cf. Ro 1:21–32; Heb 3; 10:26–31). They would die as a result of their own willful disobedience and failure to repent.

your father out of all the tribes of Israel to be my priest, to go up to my altar, to burn incense,[w] and to wear an ephod[x] in my presence. I also gave your father's house all the offerings[y] made with fire by the Israelites. **29**Why do you[l] scorn my sacrifice and offering[z] that I prescribed for my dwelling?[a] Why do you honor your sons more than me by fattening yourselves on the choice parts of every offering made by my people Israel?'

30"Therefore the LORD, the God of Israel, declares: 'I promised that your house and your father's house would minister before me forever.[b]' But now the LORD declares: 'Far be it from me! Those who honor me I will honor,[c] but those who despise[d] me will be disdained.[e] **31**The time is coming when I will cut short your strength and the strength of your father's house, so that there will not be an old man in your family line[f] **32**and you will see distress[g] in my dwelling. Although good will be done to Israel, in your family line there will never be an old man.[h] **33**Every one of you that I do not cut off from my altar will be spared only to blind your eyes with tears and to grieve your heart, and all your descendants[i] will die in the prime of life.

34" 'And what happens to your two sons, Hophni and Phinehas, will be a sign[j] to you—they will both die[k] on the same day.[l] **35**I will raise up for myself a faithful priest,[m] who will do according to what is in my heart and mind. I will firmly establish his house, and he will minister before my anointed[n] one always. **36**Then everyone left in your family line will come and bow down before him for a piece of silver and a crust of bread and plead,[o] "Appoint me to some priestly office so I can have food to eat.[p]" ' "

The LORD Calls Samuel

3 The boy Samuel ministered[q] before the LORD under Eli. In those days the word of the LORD was rare;[r] there were not many visions.[s]

2One night Eli, whose eyes[t] were becoming so weak that he could barely see,[u] was lying down in his usual place. **3**The lamp[v] of God had not yet gone out, and Samuel was lying down in the temple[m][w] of the LORD, where the ark[x] of God was. **4**Then the LORD called Samuel.

Samuel answered, "Here I am.[y]" **5**And he ran to Eli and said, "Here I am; you called me."

But Eli said, "I did not call; go back and lie down." So he went and lay down.

6Again the LORD called, "Samuel!" And Samuel got up and went to Eli and said, "Here I am; you called me."

"My son," Eli said, "I did not call; go back and lie down."

7Now Samuel did not yet know[z] the LORD: The word[a] of the LORD had not yet been revealed[b] to him.

2:28 [w] S Ex 30:7 [x] 1Sa 22:18; 23:6, 9; 30:7 [y] Lev 7:35-36 **2:29** [z] ver 12-17 [a] S Dt 12:5 **2:30** [b] S Ex 29:9 [c] Ps 50:23; 91:15; Pr 8:17 [d] Isa 53:3; Na 3:6; Mal 2:9 [e] Jer 18:10 **2:31** [f] 1Sa 4:11-18; 22:16 **2:32** [g] 1Sa 4:3; 22:17-20; Jer 7:12, 14 [h] 1Ki 2:26-27 **2:33** [i] Jer 29:32; Mal 2:12 **2:34** [j] S Dt 13:2 [k] 1Sa 4:11 [l] 1Ki 13:3 **2:35** [m] 2Sa 8:17; 20:25; 1Ki 1:8,32; 2:35; 4:4; 1Ch 16:39; 29:22; Eze 44:15-16 [n] 1Sa 9:16; 10:1; 16:13; 2Sa 2:4; 12:7; 23:1; 1Ki 1:34; Ps 89:20 **2:36** [o] Eze 44:10-14 [p] 1Sa 3:12; 1Ki 2:27 **3:1** [q] S 1Sa 2:11 [r] Ps 74:9; La 2:9; Eze 7:26 [s] Am 8:11 **3:2** [t] 1Sa 4:15 [u] S Ge 27:1 **3:3** [v] Ex 25:31-38; Lev 24:1-4 [w] 1Sa 1:9 [x] Dt 10:1-5; 1Ki 6:19; 8:1 **3:4** [y] S Ge 22:1; S Ex 3:4 **3:7** [z] 1Sa 2:12 [a] Jer 1:2 [b] S Nu 12:6; Am 3:7

[l] *29* The Hebrew is plural. [m] *3* That is, tabernacle

2:29 HONOR YOUR SONS MORE THAN ME. Eli failed completely to provide spiritual leadership for his family and thus for Israel. (1) As a father he was unable to train his sons in the way of righteousness. When they seduced the women serving at the door of the Tent of Meeting (v. 22), Eli demonstrated neither the will nor the spiritual authority necessary to remove them from the ministry (3:13; cf. Dt 21:18–21).

(2) Eli's failure as a father and a minister of the Lord resulted in: (a) God's judgment on Eli, his sons and his family (vv. 30–36; 4:17–18); (b) a decline in respect for the office of the priesthood (v. 17); (c) the general spiritual decline of God's people (v. 22–24; 4:1–11); and (d) the departure of the glory of the Lord from Israel (4:21).

(3) The entire Bible emphasizes the necessity of godliness and the true fear of God as his standard for those who would lead God's people (cf. 1Ti 3:1–10).

2:31 I WILL CUT SHORT YOUR STRENGTH. Eli and his descendants were removed from their priestly service forever. Their unfaithfulness and immorality had permanently disqualified them from being spiritual leaders and godly examples for Israel (cf. vv. 30–34; 3:13–14).

2:35 FAITHFUL PRIEST. This refers initially to Samuel, who served as priest, judge (7:6,15–17) and prophet (3:20–21). From an early age he was trained by the high priest Eli for his sacred duties (vv. 1–11; 1:24–28), and he eventually succeeded Eli as high priest. He was consistently faithful to God throughout his life. In this way he points forward to the perfect priest, Jesus the Messiah (the Anointed One—Ps 110; Heb 5:6). (1) Above all a priest was called to be faithful, i.e., to adhere firmly to what is in God's heart and Word; that implies steadfast allegiance, devotion, fidelity, and an unwillingness to be turned aside from God and his ways. (2) The NT teaches that only those who have clearly demonstrated faithfulness to God are to be spiritual leaders of God's people (cf. Mt 24:45; 25:21; 1Ti 3:1–13; 4:16; 2Ti 2:2).

8The LORD called Samuel a third
time, and Samuel got up and went to
Eli and said, "Here I am; you called
me."
Then Eli realized that the LORD was
calling the boy. **9**So Eli told Samuel,
"Go and lie down, and if he calls you,
say, 'Speak, LORD, for your servant is
listening.'" So Samuel went and lay
down in his place.
10The LORD came and stood there,
calling as at the other times, "Samuel!
Samuel![c]"
Then Samuel said, "Speak, for your
servant is listening."
11And the LORD said to Samuel: "See,
I am about to do something in Israel
that will make the ears of everyone
who hears of it tingle.[d] **12**At that time
I will carry out against Eli everything[e]
I spoke against his family—from beginning to end. **13**For I told him that I
would judge his family forever because
of the sin he knew about; his sons
made themselves contemptible,[n] and
he failed to restrain[f] them. **14**Therefore, I swore to the house of Eli, 'The
guilt of Eli's house will never be
atoned[g] for by sacrifice or offering.'"
15Samuel lay down until morning
and then opened the doors of the house
of the LORD. He was afraid to tell Eli the
vision, **16**but Eli called him and said,
"Samuel, my son."
Samuel answered, "Here I am."
17"What was it he said to you?" Eli
asked. "Do not hide[h] it from me. May
God deal with you, be it ever so severely,[i] if you hide from me anything he
told you." **18**So Samuel told him everything, hiding nothing from him. Then
Eli said, "He is the LORD; let him do
what is good in his eyes."[j]
19The LORD was with[k] Samuel as he
grew[l] up, and he let none[m] of his
words fall to the ground. **20**And all Israel from Dan to Beersheba[n] recognized that Samuel was attested as a
prophet of the LORD.[o] **21**The LORD continued to appear at Shiloh, and there
he revealed[p] himself to Samuel
through his word.

4 And Samuel's word came to all
Israel.

The Philistines Capture the Ark

Now the Israelites went out to fight
against the Philistines. The Israelites
camped at Ebenezer,[q] and the Philistines at Aphek.[r] **2**The Philistines deployed their forces to meet Israel, and
as the battle spread, Israel was defeated by the Philistines, who killed about
four thousand of them on the battlefield. **3**When the soldiers returned to
camp, the elders of Israel asked,
"Why[s] did the LORD bring defeat upon
us today before the Philistines? Let us

3:10 [c]Ex 3:4
3:11 [d]2Ki 21:12; Job 15:21; Jer 19:3
3:12 [e]S 1Sa 2:27-36
3:13 [f]1Ki 1:6
3:14 [g]S 1Sa 2:25
3:17 [h]1Ki 22:14; Jer 23:28; 38:14; 42:4 [i]S Ru 1:17
3:18 [j]S Jdg 10:15
3:19 [k]S Ge 21:22; S Nu 14:43 [l]S Jdg 13:24 [m]1Sa 9:6
3:20 [n]S Jdg 20:1 [o]S Dt 18:22; Eze 33:33
3:21 [p]S Nu 12:6
4:1 [q]1Sa 5:1; 7:12 [r]Jos 12:18; 1Sa 29:1; 1Ki 20:26
4:3 [s]Jos 7:7

[n] *13* Masoretic Text; an ancient Hebrew scribal tradition and Septuagint *sons blasphemed God*

3:13 JUDGE HIS FAMILY FOREVER. Although Eli personally could be forgiven for his failure in the ministry, God would not restore him or his descendants to their position as priests. No calling to be a minister or overseer can be considered irrevocable (see Ro 11:29, note).

3:20 PROPHET OF THE LORD. Samuel is one of the first persons to occupy the prophetic office, though he was not the first person with a prophetic gift (cf. Abraham, Ge 20:7; Moses, Dt 18:15,18; Deborah, Jdg 4:4). (1) Because of the corruption of the priesthood and the spiritual decline among God's people, God called Samuel to proclaim his word (vv. 19–21), to provide an example of faithfulness to his will (2:35), to call for repentance and renewal (7:3), and to act as a mediator between God and the people (7:8–9).

(2) Around Samuel gathered other prophets, called a "group of prophets" or "company of the prophets" (19:20; 2Ki 2:3,5; 4:38); the group of prophets at Ramah was under Samuel's leadership (cf. 19:20–22). Through him these prophets were edified, nurtured and instructed concerning God's will for Israel. The aim of such a community of prophets was to bring about spiritual renewal and the recovery of God's covenant purpose for Israel. Anyone could come and learn God's ways from them.

4:2 ISRAEL WAS DEFEATED. Israel suffered defeat because the priesthood had become corrupt and the people were living in disobedience to God's commands. They took the ark of the covenant into battle, thinking that it would assure them victory (see next note); instead, they should have repented of and corrected their sinful ways if they wanted God's blessing.

4:3 ARK OF THE LORD'S COVENANT. The ark represented God's presence in Israel (cf. Ex 25:10–22; Nu 10:33–36). The people thought that the ark would unconditionally guarantee God's favor and power. They failed to understand that a symbol of spiritual things does not itself assure one of the reality to which it points. God remained with his people only as long as they sought to maintain their covenant relationship with him. So too, under the new covenant, submitting to water baptism or partaking of the Lord's Supper will be of no spiritual benefit unless one truly submits to the Lord and his righteous ways (cf. 1Co 11:27–30).

bring the ark[t] of the LORD's covenant
from Shiloh,[u] so that it[o] may go with
us[v] and save us from the hand of our
enemies."
4So the people sent men to Shiloh,
and they brought back the ark of the
covenant of the LORD Almighty, who is
enthroned between the cherubim.[w]
And Eli's two sons, Hophni and Phinehas, were there with the ark of the covenant of God.
5When the ark of the LORD's covenant came into the camp, all Israel
raised such a great shout[x] that the
ground shook. 6Hearing the uproar,
the Philistines asked, "What's all this
shouting in the Hebrew[y] camp?"
When they learned that the ark of
the LORD had come into the camp, 7the
Philistines were afraid.[z] "A god has
come into the camp," they said. "We're
in trouble! Nothing like this has happened before. 8Woe to us! Who will deliver us from the hand of these mighty
gods? They are the gods who struck[a]
the Egyptians with all kinds of
plagues[b] in the desert. 9Be strong,
Philistines! Be men, or you will be subject to the Hebrews, as they[c] have
been to you. Be men, and fight!"
10So the Philistines fought, and the
Israelites were defeated[d] and every
man fled to his tent. The slaughter was
very great; Israel lost thirty thousand
foot soldiers. 11The ark of God was
captured, and Eli's two sons, Hophni
and Phinehas, died.[e]

Death of Eli

12That same day a Benjamite[f] ran
from the battle line and went to Shiloh,
his clothes torn and dust[g] on his head.
13When he arrived, there was Eli[h] sitting on his chair by the side of the road,
watching, because his heart feared for
the ark of God. When the man entered
the town and told what had happened,
the whole town sent up a cry.
14Eli heard the outcry and asked,
"What is the meaning of this uproar?"
The man hurried over to Eli, 15who
was ninety-eight years old and whose
eyes[i] were set so that he could not
see. 16He told Eli, "I have just come
from the battle line; I fled from it this
very day."
Eli asked, "What happened, my
son?"
17The man who brought the news replied, "Israel fled before the Philistines, and the army has suffered heavy
losses. Also your two sons, Hophni and
Phinehas, are dead,[j] and the ark of
God has been captured."[k]
18When he mentioned the ark of
God, Eli fell backward off his chair by
the side of the gate. His neck was broken and he died, for he was an old man
and heavy. He had led[p][l] Israel forty
years.[m]
19His daughter-in-law, the wife of
Phinehas, was pregnant and near the
time of delivery. When she heard the
news that the ark of God had been captured and that her father-in-law and
her husband were dead, she went into
labor and gave birth, but was overcome
by her labor pains. 20As she was dying,
the women attending her said, "Don't
despair; you have given birth to a son."
But she did not respond or pay any attention.
21She named the boy Ichabod,[q][n]
saying, "The glory[o] has departed from
Israel"—because of the capture of the
ark of God and the deaths of her father-
in-law and her husband. 22She said,
"The glory[p] has departed from Israel,
for the ark of God has been captured."[q]

The Ark in Ashdod and Ekron

5 After the Philistines had captured
the ark of God, they took it from
Ebenezer[r] to Ashdod.[s] 2Then they
carried the ark into Dagon's temple
and set it beside Dagon.[t] 3When the
people of Ashdod rose early the next
day, there was Dagon, fallen[u] on his
face on the ground before the ark of the
LORD! They took Dagon and put him
back in his place. 4But the following

4:3 [t] S Jos 6:7 [u] S Jos 18:1; S 1Sa 2:32 [v] 2Ch 13:8 **4:4** [w] S Ge 3:24; S Ex 25:22 **4:5** [x] S Jos 6:5,10 **4:6** [y] S Ge 14:13 **4:7** [z] S Ex 15:14 **4:8** [a] Ex 12:30; 1Sa 5:12 [b] Rev 11:6 **4:9** [c] S Jdg 13:1 **4:10** [d] S Dt 28:25 **4:11** [e] Ps 78:64; Jer 7:12 **4:12** [f] Eze 24:26; 33:21 [g] S Jos 7:6; S 2Sa 1:2 **4:13** [h] ver 18
4:15 [i] S 1Sa 3:2 **4:17** [j] 1Sa 22:18; Ps 78:64 [k] Ps 78:61 **4:18** [l] S Jdg 2:16; S 16:31 [m] 1Sa 2:31 **4:21** [n] S Ge 35:18 [o] S Ex 24:16; Ps 106:20; Jer 2:11; Eze 1:28; 9:3; 10:18 **4:22** [p] S Ex 24:16; Ps 78:61 [q] Jer 7:12 **5:1** [r] S 1Sa 4:1 [s] S Jos 11:22; S 13:3 **5:2** [t] S Jdg 16:23; Isa 2:18; 19:1; 46:1 **5:3** [u] Isa 40:20; 41:7; 46:7; Jer 10:4

[o] 3 Or *he* [p] 18 Traditionally *judged*
[q] 21 *Ichabod* means *no glory.*

4:17 HOPHNI AND PHINEHAS, ARE DEAD. The deaths of Hophni and Phinehas and the ark's capture emphasize that God will judge, i.e., bring personal disaster to and remove his glory from those who accept immoral spiritual leaders.

4:21 ICHABOD. Ichabod means "no glory." The glory of Israel was God and his manifested presence on earth among his people (see Ex 24:16, note). Phinehas's widow was rightly concerned about the departure of God's glory (vv. 19–22), just as new covenant believers must be concerned if the Spirit's presence, power, holiness and gifts are absent from them.

morning when they rose, there was Dagon, fallen on his face on the ground
before the ark of the LORD! His head
and hands had been broken[v] off and
were lying on the threshold; only his
body remained. **5**That is why to this
day neither the priests of Dagon nor
any others who enter Dagon's temple
at Ashdod step on the threshold.[w]
6The LORD's hand[x] was heavy upon
the people of Ashdod and its vicinity;
he brought devastation[y] upon them
and afflicted them with tumors.[r z]
7When the men of Ashdod saw what
was happening, they said, "The ark of
the god of Israel must not stay here
with us, because his hand is heavy
upon us and upon Dagon our god." **8**So
they called together all the rulers[a] of
the Philistines and asked them, "What
shall we do with the ark of the god of
Israel?"
They answered, "Have the ark of the
god of Israel moved to Gath.[b]" So they
moved the ark of the God of Israel.
9But after they had moved it, the
LORD's hand was against that city,
throwing it into a great panic.[c] He afflicted the people of the city, both
young and old, with an outbreak of tumors.[s] **10**So they sent the ark of God
to Ekron.[d]
As the ark of God was entering Ekron, the people of Ekron cried out,
"They have brought the ark of the god
of Israel around to us to kill us and our
people." **11**So they called together all
the rulers[e] of the Philistines and said,
"Send the ark of the god of Israel away;
let it go back to its own place, or it[t]
will kill us and our people." For death
had filled the city with panic; God's
hand was very heavy upon it. **12**Those
who did not die[f] were afflicted with
tumors, and the outcry of the city went
up to heaven.

The Ark Returned to Israel

6 When the ark of the LORD had been
in Philistine territory seven
months, **2**the Philistines called for the
priests and the diviners[g] and said,
"What shall we do with the ark of the
LORD? Tell us how we should send it
back to its place."
3They answered, "If you return the
ark of the god of Israel, do not send it
away empty,[h] but by all means send a
guilt offering[i] to him. Then you will
be healed, and you will know why his
hand[j] has not been lifted from you."
4The Philistines asked, "What guilt
offering should we send to him?"
They replied, "Five gold tumors and
five gold rats, according to the number[k] of the Philistine rulers, because
the same plague[l] has struck both you
and your rulers. **5**Make models of the
tumors[m] and of the rats that are destroying the country, and pay honor[n]
to Israel's god. Perhaps he will lift his
hand from you and your gods and your
land. **6**Why do you harden[o] your
hearts as the Egyptians and Pharaoh
did? When he[u] treated them harshly,[p] did they[q] not send the Israelites
out so they could go on their way?
7"Now then, get a new cart[r] ready,
with two cows that have calved and
have never been yoked.[s] Hitch the
cows to the cart, but take their calves
away and pen them up. **8**Take the ark
of the LORD and put it on the cart, and
in a chest beside it put the gold objects
you are sending back to him as a guilt
offering. Send it on its way, **9**but keep
watching it. If it goes up to its own territory, toward Beth Shemesh,[t] then
the LORD has brought this great disaster on us. But if it does not, then we
will know that it was not his hand that
struck us and that it happened to us by
chance."
10So they did this. They took two
such cows and hitched them to the cart
and penned up their calves. **11**They
placed the ark of the LORD on the cart
and along with it the chest containing
the gold rats and the models of the tumors. **12**Then the cows went straight
up toward Beth Shemesh, keeping on
the road and lowing all the way; they
did not turn to the right or to the left.
The rulers of the Philistines followed
them as far as the border of Beth Shemesh.
13Now the people of Beth Shemesh
were harvesting their wheat[u] in the
valley, and when they looked up and

5:4 [v]Eze 6:6; Mic 1:7
5:5 [w]Zep 1:9
5:6 [x]S Ex 9:3; Ac 13:11 [y]2Sa 6:7; Ps 78:66 [z]S Ex 15:26; 1Sa 6:5
5:8 [a]S Jdg 16:18 [b]S Jos 11:22
5:9 [c]S Ex 14:24
5:10 [d]S Jos 13:3
5:11 [e]ver 8
5:12 [f]S 1Sa 4:8
6:2 [g]S Ex 7:11; S Isa 44:25
6:3 [h]S Ex 22:29; S 34:20 [i]S Lev 5:15 [j]ver 9
6:4 [k]S Jos 13:3 [l]2Sa 24:25
6:5 [m]S 1Sa 5:6-11 [n]S Jos 7:19; Rev 14:7
6:6 [o]S Ex 4:21 [p]Ex 10:2 [q]S Ex 12:33
6:7 [r]2Sa 6:3; 1Ch 13:7 [s]S Nu 19:2
6:9 [t]S Jos 15:10; 21:16
6:13 [u]S Ge 30:14; Ru 2:23; 1Sa 12:17

[r] *6* Hebrew; Septuagint and Vulgate *tumors. And rats appeared in their land, and death and destruction were throughout the city* [s] *9* Or *with tumors in the groin* (see Septuagint) [t] *11* Or *he* [u] *6* That is, God

6:12 STRAIGHT UP TOWARD BETH SHEMESH. God caused the cows to take the ark back to Israel. Beth Shemesh was a town across the border within the territory of Judah (cf. Jos 21:16).

saw the ark, they rejoiced at the sight.
14The cart came to the field of Joshua
of Beth Shemesh, and there it stopped
beside a large rock. The people
chopped up the wood of the cart and
sacrificed the cows as a burnt offering[v] to the LORD. 15The Levites[w] took
down the ark of the LORD, together with
the chest containing the gold objects,
and placed them on the large rock.[x]
On that day the people of Beth Shemesh[y] offered burnt offerings and
made sacrifices to the LORD. 16The five
rulers of the Philistines saw all this
and then returned that same day to Ekron.
17These are the gold tumors the Philistines sent as a guilt offering to the
LORD—one each[z] for Ashdod, Gaza,
Ashkelon, Gath and Ekron. 18And the
number of the gold rats was according
to the number of Philistine towns belonging to the five rulers—the fortified
towns with their country villages. The
large rock, on which[v] they set the ark
of the LORD, is a witness to this day in
the field of Joshua of Beth Shemesh.
19But God struck down[a] some of
the men of Beth Shemesh, putting seventy[w] of them to death because they
had looked[b] into the ark of the LORD.
The people mourned because of the
heavy blow the LORD had dealt them,
20and the men of Beth Shemesh asked,
"Who can stand[c] in the presence of
the LORD, this holy[d] God? To whom
will the ark go up from here?"
21Then they sent messengers to the
people of Kiriath Jearim,[e] saying,
"The Philistines have returned the ark
of the LORD. Come down and take it up
7 to your place." 1So the men of Kiriath Jearim came and took up the
ark[f] of the LORD. They took it to Abinadab's[g] house on the hill and consecrated Eleazar his son to guard the ark
of the LORD.

Samuel Subdues the Philistines at Mizpah

2It was a long time, twenty years in
all, that the ark remained at Kiriath Jearim,[h] and all the people of Israel
mourned and sought after the LORD.[i]
3And Samuel said to the whole house
of Israel, "If you are returning[j] to the
LORD with all your hearts, then rid[k]
yourselves of the foreign gods and the
Ashtoreths[l] and commit[m] yourselves
to the LORD and serve him only,[n] and
he will deliver[o] you out of the hand of
the Philistines." 4So the Israelites put
away their Baals and Ashtoreths, and
served the LORD only.
5Then Samuel[p] said, "Assemble all
Israel at Mizpah[q] and I will intercede[r] with the LORD for you." 6When
they had assembled at Mizpah,[s] they
drew water and poured[t] it out before
the LORD. On that day they fasted and
there they confessed, "We have sinned
against the LORD." And Samuel was
leader[x][u] of Israel at Mizpah.
7When the Philistines heard that Israel had assembled at Mizpah, the rulers of the Philistines came up to attack
them. And when the Israelites heard of
it, they were afraid[v] because of the
Philistines. 8They said to Samuel, "Do
not stop crying[w] out to the LORD our
God for us, that he may rescue us from
the hand of the Philistines." 9Then
Samuel[x] took a suckling lamb and of-

6:14 [v] 1Sa 11:7; 2Sa 24:22; 1Ki 19:21
6:15 [w] Jos 3:3 [x] ver 18 [y] Jos 21:16
6:17 [z] S Jos 13:3
6:19 [a] 2Sa 6:7 [b] S Ex 19:21
6:20 [c] 2Sa 6:9; Ps 130:3; Mal 3:2; Rev 6:17 [d] S Lev 11:45
6:21 [e] S Jos 9:17
7:1 [f] S Jos 6:7 [g] 2Sa 6:3; 1Ch 13:7
7:2 [h] 1Ch 13:5; Ps 132:6 [i] 1Ch 13:3
7:3 [j] Dt 30:10; 2Ki 18:5; 23:25; Jer 24:7 [k] S Ge 31:19; S Jos 24:14 [l] S Jdg 2:12-13; 1Sa 12:10; 31:10 [m] Joel 2:12 [n] S Dt 6:13; Mt 4:10; Lk 4:8 [o] S Jdg 2:18
7:5 [p] S 1Sa 1:20; Ps 99:6; Jer 15:1 [q] S Jos 11:3; Jdg 21:5; 1Sa 10:17 [r] S ver 8; S Ge 20:7; S Dt 9:19
7:6 [s] S Jos 11:3 [t] La 2:19 [u] S Jdg 2:16; S 16:31
7:7 [v] 1Sa 17:11
7:8 [w] ver 5; S Ex 32:30; S Nu 21:7; 1Sa 12:19,23; 1Ki 18:24; Isa 37:4; Jer 15:1; 27:18
7:9 [x] Ps 99:6

[v] *18* A few Hebrew manuscripts (see also Septuagint); most Hebrew manuscripts *villages as far as Greater Abel, where*
[w] *19* A few Hebrew manuscripts; most Hebrew manuscripts and Septuagint *50,070*
[x] *6* Traditionally *judge*

6:19 STRUCK DOWN SOME OF THE MEN. Many of the people of Beth Shemesh disregarded the command of the Lord not to look at or touch the holy objects of the sanctuary (Nu 4:15,20). By examining the ark, they demonstrated a total absence of the fear of the Lord and of reverence for what is holy. Honor, respect and a reverent fear should characterize God's people in their relationship to their holy God.

7:3 IF YOU ARE RETURNING TO THE LORD . . . HE WILL DELIVER YOU. Samuel emphasized the Biblical principle that if God's people hope to receive his protection and deliverance, they must first turn to him with all their hearts and put away all forms of idolatry and compromise (cf. Ro 12:1–2). All those who sincerely desire to please God may expect his care, blessing and deliverance (cf. Ex 23:22; Dt 20:1–4; Jos 1:5–9).

7:8 DO NOT STOP CRYING OUT TO THE LORD. Throughout our lives, victory over spiritual adversaries is dependent on unceasing prayer to God. Prayer brings God into every aspect of our lives: our work, plans, family, problems and successes (see Lk 18:1,7, notes). To fail to pray opens us up to Satan's attack and our defeat. Samuel's response to the people's request (v. 9) was to offer a lamb as a burnt offering, signifying renewed dedication to the Lord, and to offer prayers on the people's behalf.

fered it up as a whole burnt offering to
the LORD. He cried out to the LORD on
Israel's behalf, and the LORD answered
him.[y]
10While Samuel was sacrificing the
burnt offering, the Philistines drew
near to engage Israel in battle. But
that day the LORD thundered[z] with
loud thunder against the Philistines
and threw them into such a panic[a]
that they were routed before the Israelites. **11**The men of Israel rushed out of
Mizpah and pursued the Philistines,
slaughtering them along the way to a
point below Beth Car.
12Then Samuel took a stone[b] and
set it up between Mizpah and Shen. He
named it Ebenezer,[y][c] saying, "Thus
far has the LORD helped us." **13**So the
Philistines were subdued[d] and did not
invade Israelite territory again.
Throughout Samuel's lifetime, the
hand of the LORD was against the Philistines. **14**The towns from Ekron[e] to
Gath that the Philistines had captured
from Israel were restored to her, and
Israel delivered the neighboring territory from the power of the Philistines.
And there was peace between Israel
and the Amorites.[f]
15Samuel[g] continued as judge[h]
over Israel all[i] the days of his life.
16From year to year he went on a circuit from Bethel[j] to Gilgal[k] to Mizpah, judging[l] Israel in all those
places. **17**But he always went back to
Ramah,[m] where his home was, and
there he also judged[n] Israel. And he
built an altar[o] there to the LORD.

Israel Asks for a King

8 When Samuel grew old, he appointed[p] his sons as judges for Israel. **2**The name of his firstborn was
Joel and the name of his second was
Abijah,[q] and they served at Beersheba.[r] **3**But his sons[s] did not walk in
his ways. They turned aside[t] after
dishonest gain and accepted bribes[u]
and perverted[v] justice.
4So all the elders[w] of Israel gathered together and came to Samuel at
Ramah.[x] **5**They said to him, "You are
old, and your sons do not walk in your
ways; now appoint a king[y] to lead[zz]
us, such as all the other nations[a]
have."
6But when they said, "Give us a
king[b] to lead us," this displeased[c]
Samuel; so he prayed to the LORD. **7**And
the LORD told him: "Listen[d] to all that
the people are saying to you; it is not
you they have rejected,[e] but they have
rejected me as their king.[f] **8**As they
have done from the day I brought them
up out of Egypt until this day, forsaking[g] me and serving other gods, so
they are doing to you. **9**Now listen to
them; but warn them solemnly and let

7:9 [y]S Ex 32:11; S Dt 9:19 **7:10** [z]S Ex 9:23; S 1Sa 2:10 [a]S Ge 35:5; S Ex 14:24 **7:12** [b]S Ge 28:22; S Dt 27:2; Jos 4:9 [c]S 1Sa 4:1 **7:13** [d]Jdg 13:1,5 **7:14** [e]S Jos 13:3 [f]S Jdg 1:34 **7:15** [g]ver 6; 1Sa 12:11 [h]S Jdg 2:16 [i]Jdg 2:18 **7:16** [j]S Ge 12:8 [k]S Jos 10:43; S 1Sa 10:8; Am 5:5 [l]ver 6; Ac 13:20 **7:17** [m]S Jos 18:25; 1Sa 8:4; 15:34; 19:18; 25:1; 28:3 [n]ver 6 [o]1Sa 9:12; 14:35; 20:6; 2Sa 24:25 **8:1** [p]Dt 16:18-19 **8:2** [q]1Ch 6:28 [r]Ge 22:19; 1Ki 19:3; Am 5:4-5 **8:3** [s]1Sa 2:12 [t]Ne 9:29; Job 34:27; Ps 14:3; 58:3; Isa 53:6 [u]Ex 23:8; 1Sa 12:3; Job 8:22; Pr 17:23 [v]S Ex 23:2 **8:4** [w]S Jdg 11:11; 1Sa 11:3 [x]S 1Sa 7:17 **8:5** [y]ver 19; S Dt 17:14-20; 1Sa 10:19; 12:12, 13; Hos 13:11 [z]1Sa 3:20; 12:2 [a]ver 20 **8:6** [b]Hos 13:10 [c]1Sa 12:17; 15:11; 16:1 **8:7** [d]ver 22; 1Sa 12:1 [e]S Nu 11:20 [f]S Ex 16:8 **8:8** [g]1Sa 12:10; 2Ki 21:22; Jer 2:17

[y] *12 Ebenezer* means *stone of help.*
[z] *5* Traditionally *judge;* also in verses 6 and 20

8:1–3 HIS SONS. Samuel made his sons judges in the southern part of Israel, but they did not follow their father's good example (v. 3). This was their choice, however, and the Bible does not blame Samuel the way it does Eli (2:29). Evidently Samuel had not allowed them to function as priests; their behavior shows that children of godly parents must still make their own choices.

8:5 APPOINT A KING. Kingship was part of God's promise in his covenant with Abraham (Ge 17:6); in Jacob's blessing of his sons, he assigned the kingship to the tribe of Judah (Ge 49:10). Moses foretold of the day when Israel would no longer be content with God's direct rule (Dt 17:14–15; 28:36); that prophecy came to pass here through Israel's demand for a human king. God saw their request as a rejection of himself as King of Israel (v. 7) and as a demonstration of their eagerness to compromise their role as God's special people. (1) The people asked for a human king so that they would "be like all the other nations, with a king to lead us and to go out before us and fight our battles" (v. 20). They mistakenly believed the reason for their troubles and defeats was inadequate government, when in reality it was their sin. Consequently, they conformed to the ways of the pagan societies around them instead of trusting in God.

(2) Although this was not the time God had chosen for them to have a king, and although their motivation was wrong, the Lord gave them what they asked for. Afterward, he purposed to guide his people in spite of the flawed government of Israel's monarchy (12:14–15,19–25), pointing to God's love and patience with human weakness.

8:7 THEY HAVE REJECTED ME. Up to this time Israel's government had been a theocracy, i.e., God himself ruled Israel as their King. He ruled through direct guidance, through special revelation and the written Word, and through chosen and anointed leaders. When Israel requested a monarchial government, her kings took office by virtue of hereditary succession rather than by God's direct choice; this resulted in the reign of evil and immoral kings and thereby impaired God's lordship over his people. At the end of history, God will again resume direct reign over his people through Jesus Christ, and "his kingdom will never end" (Lk 1:33; cf. 1Ti 1:17; Rev 20:4–6; 21:1–8).

them know[h] what the king who will
reign over them will do."
10Samuel told[i] all the words of the
LORD to the people who were asking
him for a king. **11**He said, "This is what
the king who will reign over you will
do: He will take[j] your sons and make
them serve[k] with his chariots and
horses, and they will run in front of his
chariots.[l] **12**Some he will assign to be
commanders[m] of thousands and commanders of fifties, and others to plow
his ground and reap his harvest, and
still others to make weapons of war
and equipment for his chariots. **13**He
will take your daughters to be perfum-
ers and cooks and bakers. **14**He will
take the best of your[n] fields and vineyards[o] and olive groves and give them
to his attendants.[p] **15**He will take a
tenth[q] of your grain and of your vin-
tage and give it to his officials and attendants. **16**Your menservants and
maidservants and the best of your cattle[a] and donkeys he will take for his
own use. **17**He will take a tenth of your
flocks, and you yourselves will become
his slaves. **18**When that day comes, you
will cry out for relief from the king you
have chosen, and the LORD will not answer[r] you in that day.[s]"
19But the people refused[t] to listen
to Samuel. "No!" they said. "We want[u]
a king[v] over us. **20**Then we will be like
all the other nations,[w] with a king to
lead us and to go out before us and
fight our battles."
21When Samuel heard all that the
people said, he repeated[x] it before the
LORD. **22**The LORD answered, "Listen[y]
to them and give them a king."
Then Samuel said to the men of Israel, "Everyone go back to his town."

Samuel Anoints Saul

9 There was a Benjamite,[z] a man of
standing,[a] whose name was
Kish[b] son of Abiel, the son of Zeror,
the son of Becorath, the son of Aphiah
of Benjamin. **2**He had a son named
Saul, an impressive[c] young man without equal[d] among the Israelites—a
head taller[e] than any of the others.
3Now the donkeys[f] belonging to
Saul's father Kish were lost, and Kish
said to his son Saul, "Take one of the
servants with you and go and look for
the donkeys." **4**So he passed through
the hill[g] country of Ephraim and
through the area around Shalisha,[h]
but they did not find them. They went
on into the district of Shaalim, but the
donkeys[i] were not there. Then he
passed through the territory of Benjamin, but they did not find them.
5When they reached the district of
Zuph,[j] Saul said to the servant who
was with him, "Come, let's go back, or
my father will stop thinking about the
donkeys and start worrying[k] about
us."
6But the servant replied, "Look, in
this town there is a man of God;[l] he
is highly respected, and everything[m]
he says comes true. Let's go there
now. Perhaps he will tell us what way
to take."
7Saul said to his servant, "If we go,
what can we give the man? The food in
our sacks is gone. We have no gift[n] to
take to the man of God. What do we
have?"
8The servant answered him again.
"Look," he said, "I have a quarter of a
shekel[b] of silver. I will give it to the
man of God so that he will tell us what
way to take." **9**(Formerly in Israel, if a
man went to inquire[o] of God, he would
say, "Come, let us go to the seer," because the prophet of today used to be
called a seer.)[p]

8:9 [h] ver 11-18; S Dt 17:14-20; 1Sa 10:25
8:10 [i] S Ex 19:7
8:11 [j] 1Sa 14:52 [k] S Ge 41:46 [l] S Dt 17:16; 2Sa 15:1; 1Ki 1:5; 2Ch 1:14; 9:25; SS 3:7
8:12 [m] S Dt 1:15
8:14 [n] Eze 46:18 [o] 1Ki 21:7,15; Mic 2:2 [p] 2Ki 22:12
8:15 [q] S Ge 41:34; 1Sa 17:25
8:18 [r] 1Sa 28:6; Job 27:9; 35:12, 13; Ps 18:41; 66:18; Pr 1:28; Isa 1:15; 58:4; 59:2; Jer 14:12; Eze 8:18; Mic 3:4 [s] 1Sa 10:25; 1Ki 12:4
8:19 [t] Pr 1:24; Isa 50:2; 66:4; Jer 7:13; 8:12; 13:10; 44:16 [u] Ac 13:21 [v] S ver 5
8:20 [w] S ver 5
8:21 [x] S Jdg 11:11
8:22 [y] S ver 7
9:1 [z] Jos 18:11-20 [a] S Ru 2:1 [b] 1Sa 14:51; 1Ch 8:33; 9:39; Est 2:5; Ac 13:21
9:2 [c] S Ge 39:6 [d] 1Sa 10:24 [e] 1Sa 10:23
9:3 [f] ver 20; 1Sa 10:14,16
9:4 [g] S Jos 24:33 [h] 2Ki 4:42 [i] 1Sa 10:2
9:5 [j] 1Sa 1:1 [k] 1Sa 10:2
9:6 [l] S Dt 33:1; S Jdg 13:6 [m] 1Sa 3:19
9:7 [n] S Ge 32:20; 1Ki 13:7; 14:3; 2Ki 4:42; 5:5,15; Jer 40:5
9:9 [o] S Ge 25:22 [p] 2Sa 15:27; 24:11; 2Ki 17:13; 1Ch 9:22; 21:9; 26:28; 29:29; 2Ch 19:2; Isa 29:10; 30:10; Am 7:12

[a] *16* Septuagint; Hebrew *young men*
[b] *8* That is, about 1/10 ounce (about 3 grams)

8:22 GIVE THEM A KING. Although it was not God's will to give Israel a king at this time, he nevertheless did so. This is an example of history proceeding according to God's permissive will rather than his perfect will (see 1Ti 2:4, note; see article on THE WILL OF GOD, p. 1056). God permitted the appointment of a king and monarchial government in spite of its eventual trouble and disaster (vv. 10–18): (1) to show the need for God's perfect kingdom and thus to foreshadow Jesus Christ as King of kings (Mt 2:2; 21:5; 1Ti 1:17; 6:15; Rev 19:16); (2) to teach his people that no type of government on earth will resolve their problems or guarantee peace and safety as long as sinful people exist. Only in the new heaven and new earth will righteousness reign and complete peace and happiness be the lot of all people (Rev 21—22).

9:9 SEER. A seer (Heb *ro'eh*, "one who sees") was a person with a special God-given ability to see in the spiritual realm or foresee future events (cf. v. 19; 2Sa 24:11; 2Ch 29:25; 35:15). Often God revealed present or future events to the prophet through dreams and visions (cf. Nu 12:6); thus when the gift of prophecy was rare, it was reported that "there were not many visions" (3:1). Later in

10"Good," Saul said to his servant.
"Come, let's go." So they set out for the
town where the man of God was.
11As they were going up the hill to
the town, they met some girls coming
out to draw[q] water, and they asked
them, "Is the seer here?"
12"He is," they answered. "He's
ahead of you. Hurry now; he has just
come to our town today, for the people
have a sacrifice[r] at the high place.[s]
13As soon as you enter the town, you
will find him before he goes up to the
high place to eat. The people will not
begin eating until he comes, because
he must bless[t] the sacrifice; afterward, those who are invited will eat.
Go up now; you should find him about
this time."
14They went up to the town, and as
they were entering it, there was Samuel, coming toward them on his way up
to the high place.
15Now the day before Saul came, the
LORD had revealed this to Samuel:
16"About this time tomorrow I will
send you a man from the land of Benjamin. Anoint[u] him leader[v] over my
people Israel; he will deliver[w] my people from the hand of the Philistines.[x]
I have looked upon my people, for their
cry[y] has reached me."
17When Samuel caught sight of
Saul, the LORD said to him, "This[z] is
the man I spoke to you about; he will
govern my people."
18Saul approached Samuel in the
gateway and asked, "Would you please
tell me where the seer's house is?"
19"I am the seer," Samuel replied.
"Go up ahead of me to the high place,
for today you are to eat with me, and
in the morning I will let you go and will
tell you all that is in your heart. 20As
for the donkeys[a] you lost three days
ago, do not worry about them; they
have been found. And to whom is all
the desire[b] of Israel turned, if not to
you and all your father's family?"
21Saul answered, "But am I not a
Benjamite, from the smallest tribe[c] of
Israel, and is not my clan the least[d] of
all the clans of the tribe of Benjamin?[e]
Why do you say such a thing to me?"
22Then Samuel brought Saul and his
servant into the hall and seated them
at the head of those who were invited—about thirty in number. 23Samuel
said to the cook, "Bring the piece of
meat I gave you, the one I told you to
lay aside."
24So the cook took up the leg[f] with
what was on it and set it in front of
Saul. Samuel said, "Here is what has
been kept for you. Eat, because it was
set aside for you for this occasion, from
the time I said, 'I have invited
guests.' " And Saul dined with Samuel
that day.
25After they came down from the
high place to the town, Samuel talked
with Saul on the roof[g] of his house.
26They rose about daybreak and Samuel called to Saul on the roof, "Get
ready, and I will send you on your
way." When Saul got ready, he and
Samuel went outside together. 27As
they were going down to the edge of
the town, Samuel said to Saul, "Tell
the servant to go on ahead of us"—and
the servant did so—"but you stay here
awhile, so that I may give you a message from God."

10 Then Samuel took a flask[h] of
oil and poured it on Saul's head
and kissed him, saying, "Has not the
LORD anointed[i] you leader over his inheritance?[c][j] 2When you leave me today, you will meet two men near Rachel's tomb,[k] at Zelzah on the border
of Benjamin. They will say to you, 'The
donkeys[l] you set out to look for have
been found. And now your father has
stopped thinking about them and is

9:11 [q] S Ge 24:11, 13 **9:12** [r] Nu 28:11-15; S 1Sa 7:17 [s] S Lev 26:30 **9:13** [t] S Mt 14:19; 1Co 10:16; 1Ti 4:3-5 **9:16** [u] Ex 30:25; S 1Sa 2:35; 12:3; 15:1; 26:9; 2Ki 11:12; Ps 2:2 [v] 2Sa 7:8; 1Ki 8:16; 1Ch 5:2 [w] Ex 3:7-9 [x] 1Sa 23:4; 2Sa 3:18 [y] S Ge 16:11; Ps 102:1 **9:17** [z] 1Sa 16:12 **9:20** [a] S ver 3 [b] 1Sa 12:13; Ezr 6:8; Isa 60:4-9; Da 2:44; Hag 2:7; Mal 3:1

9:21 [c] Ps 68:27 [d] S Ex 3:11; Mt 2:6; 1Co 15:9 [e] Jdg 6:15; 20:35, 46; 1Sa 18:18 **9:24** [f] S Lev 7:32-34 **9:25** [g] S Dt 22:8; S Jos 2:8; S Mt 24:17; Lk 5:19 **10:1** [h] 1Sa 16:1; 2Ki 9:1,3,6 [i] S Ex 29:7; S 1Sa 9:16; S 1Ki 1:39 [j] S Ex 34:9; 2Sa 20:19; Ps 78:62,71 **10:2** [k] Ge 35:20 [l] 1Sa 9:4

c *1* Hebrew; Septuagint and Vulgate *over his people Israel? You will reign over the LORD's people and save them from the power of their enemies round about. And this will be a sign to you that the LORD has anointed you leader over his inheritance:*

Israel's history the seer came to be less prominent than the prophet, whose primary task was to speak to God's covenant people about what he saw or heard from God concerning their loyalty to God (see article on THE PROPHET IN THE OLD TESTAMENT, p. 986).

10:1 THE LORD ANOINTED YOU. The purpose of Saul's anointing was (1) to dedicate him to God for the special task to which he was called, and (2) to impart to him enabling grace and gifts for his God-appointed task. "The LORD's anointed" became a common term for Israel's king (26:9; cf. 12:3; La 4:20). God's ultimate anointed king is Jesus, the Messiah (Heb *mashiah*, "the Anointed One"), whom God anointed with the Holy Spirit (Jn 1:32–33). Subsequently, all Jesus' followers must be anointed with the same Holy Spirit (2Co 1:21; 1Jn 2:20) as new covenant priests and kings (cf. 1Pe 2:5,9).

worried[m] about you. He is asking,
"What shall I do about my son?" '
3 "Then you will go on from there until you reach the great tree of Tabor.
Three men going up to God at Bethel[n]
will meet you there. One will be carrying three young goats, another three
loaves of bread, and another a skin of
wine. 4 They will greet you and offer
you two loaves of bread,[o] which you
will accept from them.
5 "After that you will go to Gibeah[p]
of God, where there is a Philistine outpost.[q] As you approach the town, you
will meet a procession of prophets[r]
coming down from the high place[s]
with lyres, tambourines,[t] flutes[u] and
harps[v] being played before them, and
they will be prophesying.[w] 6 The Spirit[x] of the LORD will come upon you in
power, and you will prophesy with
them; and you will be changed[y] into a
different person. 7 Once these signs are
fulfilled, do whatever[z] your hand[a]
finds to do, for God is with[b] you.
8 "Go down ahead of me to Gilgal.[c]
I will surely come down to you to sacrifice burnt offerings and fellowship offerings,[d] but you must wait seven[d]
days until I come to you and tell you
what you are to do."

Saul Made King

9 As Saul turned to leave Samuel,
God changed[e] Saul's heart, and all
these signs[f] were fulfilled[g] that day.
10 When they arrived at Gibeah, a procession of prophets met him; the Spirit[h] of God came upon him in power,
and he joined in their prophesying.[i]
11 When all those who had formerly
known him saw him prophesying with
the prophets, they asked each other,
"What is this[j] that has happened to
the son of Kish? Is Saul also among the
prophets?"[k]
12 A man who lived there answered,
"And who is their father?" So it became
a saying: "Is Saul also among the
prophets?"[l] 13 After Saul stopped
prophesying,[m] he went to the high
place.
14 Now Saul's uncle[n] asked him and
his servant, "Where have you been?"
"Looking for the donkeys,[o]" he
said. "But when we saw they were not
to be found, we went to Samuel."
15 Saul's uncle said, "Tell me what
Samuel said to you."
16 Saul replied, "He assured us that
the donkeys[p] had been found." But he
did not tell his uncle what Samuel had
said about the kingship.
17 Samuel summoned the people of
Israel to the LORD at Mizpah[q] 18 and
said to them, "This is what the LORD,
the God of Israel, says: 'I brought Israel up out of Egypt, and I delivered you
from the power of Egypt and all the
kingdoms that oppressed[r] you.' 19 But
you have now rejected[s] your God, who
saves[t] you out of all your calamities
and distresses. And you have said, 'No,
set a king[u] over us.'[v] So now
present[w] yourselves before the LORD
by your tribes and clans."
20 When Samuel brought all the
tribes of Israel near, the tribe of Benjamin was chosen. 21 Then he brought
forward the tribe of Benjamin, clan by
clan, and Matri's clan was chosen.[x]
Finally Saul son of Kish was chosen.
But when they looked for him, he was
not to be found. 22 So they inquired[y]
further of the LORD, "Has the man come
here yet?"
And the LORD said, "Yes, he has hidden himself among the baggage."
23 They ran and brought him out, and
as he stood among the people he was
a head taller[z] than any of the others.
24 Samuel said to all the people, "Do
you see the man the LORD has cho-

10:2 [m] 1Sa 9:5
10:3 [n] S Ge 35:7-8
10:4 [o] ver 27; 1Sa 16:20; Pr 18:16
10:5 [p] ver 26; 1Sa 11:4; 15:34 [q] 1Sa 13:3 [r] S Nu 11:29; 1Ki 20:35; 2Ki 2:3,15; 4:1; 6:1; 9:1; Am 7:14 [s] S Lev 26:30 [t] S Ge 31:27; Jer 31:4 [u] 1Ki 1:40; Isa 30:29 [v] 1Sa 16:16; 18:10; 19:9; 2Ki 3:15; Ps 92:3 [w] ver 10; 1Sa 19:20; 1Ch 25:1; 1Co 14:1
10:6 [x] S Nu 11:25 [y] ver 9
10:7 [z] 2Sa 7:3; 1Ki 8:17; 1Ch 22:7; 28:2; 2Ch 6:7; Ecc 9:10 [a] Jdg 9:33 [b] S Jos 1:5; Lk 1:28; Heb 13:5
10:8 [c] Jos 4:20; S 10:43; 1Sa 7:16; 11:14-15 [d] 1Sa 13:8
10:9 [e] ver 6 [f] S Dt 13:2 [g] ver 7
10:10 [h] S Nu 11:25; 1Sa 11:6 [i] S ver 5-6
10:11 [j] Mt 13:54; Jn 7:15 [k] ver 12; 1Sa 19:24; 2Ki 9:11; Jer 29:26; Hos 9:7
10:12 [l] S ver 11
10:13 [m] 1Sa 19:23
10:14 [n] 1Sa 14:50 [o] S 1Sa 9:3
10:16 [p] S 1Sa 9:3
10:17 [q] S 1Sa 7:5
10:18 [r] S Ex 1:14; S Nu 10:9
10:19 [s] S Nu 11:20; S Dt 33:5 [t] Ps 7:10; 18:48; 68:20; 145:19 [u] S 1Sa 8:5-7 [v] S Dt 17:14 [w] Jos 7:14
10:21 [x] Est 3:7; Pr 16:33
10:22 [y] S Ge 25:22; S Jdg 18:5
10:23 [z] 1Sa 9:2

[d] 8 Traditionally *peace offerings*

10:5 THEY WILL BE PROPHESYING. This prophesying (vv. 6,10–11,13) most likely involved praise to God through both prophetic utterance and songs inspired by the Holy Spirit (cf. Nu 11:25).

10:6 A DIFFERENT PERSON. God changed Saul's inner disposition through his anointing by the Holy Spirit (cf. v. 9). This change was not unconditional or permanent, but something that could be maintained only by obedience to God. He later refused to obey God, after which the Spirit left him (13:13–14; 15:11; 16:14).

10:9 GOD CHANGED SAUL'S HEART. Saul possessed many God-given endowments to help him serve God and Israel in a righteous manner. He had a changed heart, an empowering by the Holy Spirit (v. 6), a strong body (v. 23), a humble attitude (9:21), and Samuel's guidance and prayers (12:23–25). Note especially the gift of prophecy (vv. 10–13), which was a sign that he had been anointed to kingship. Nevertheless, by his foolishness Saul soon failed to remain faithful to God and his word (13:13–14).

sen?[a] There is no one like[b] him
among all the people."
Then the people shouted, "Long
live[c] the king!"
25Samuel explained[d] to the people
the regulations[e] of the kingship.[f] He
wrote them down on a scroll and deposited it before the LORD. Then Samuel dismissed the people, each to his
own home.
26Saul also went to his home in Gibeah,[g] accompanied by valiant men[h]
whose hearts God had touched. 27But
some troublemakers[i] said, "How can
this fellow save us?" They despised
him and brought him no gifts.[j] But
Saul kept silent.

Saul Rescues the City of Jabesh

11 Nahash[k] the Ammonite went
up and besieged Jabesh Gile-
ad.[l] And all the men of Jabesh said to
him, "Make a treaty[m] with us, and we
will be subject to you."
2But Nahash the Ammonite replied,
"I will make a treaty with you only on
the condition[n] that I gouge[o] out the
right eye of every one of you and so
bring disgrace[p] on all Israel."
3The elders[q] of Jabesh said to him,
"Give us seven days so we can send
messengers throughout Israel; if no
one comes to rescue[r] us, we will surrender[s] to you."
4When the messengers came to Gibeah[t] of Saul and reported these terms
to the people, they all wept[u] aloud.
5Just then Saul was returning from the
fields, behind his oxen, and he asked,
"What is wrong with the people? Why
are they weeping?" Then they repeated
to him what the men of Jabesh had
said.
6When Saul heard their words, the
Spirit[v] of God came upon him in power, and he burned with anger. 7He took
a pair of oxen,[w] cut them into pieces,
and sent the pieces by messengers
throughout Israel,[x] proclaiming,
"This is what will be done to the oxen
of anyone[y] who does not follow Saul
and Samuel." Then the terror of the
LORD fell on the people, and they turned
out as one man.[z] 8When Saul mustered[a] them at Bezek,[b] the men of
Israel numbered three hundred thousand and the men of Judah thirty thousand.
9They told the messengers who had
come, "Say to the men of Jabesh Gilead, 'By the time the sun is hot tomorrow, you will be delivered.' " When the
messengers went and reported this to
the men of Jabesh, they were elated.
10They said to the Ammonites, "Tomorrow we will surrender[c] to you,
and you can do to us whatever seems
good to you."
11The next day Saul separated his
men into three divisions;[d] during the
last watch of the night they broke into
the camp of the Ammonites[e] and
slaughtered them until the heat of the
day. Those who survived were scattered, so that no two of them were left
together.

Saul Confirmed as King

12The people then said to Samuel,
"Who[f] was it that asked, 'Shall Saul
reign over us?' Bring these men to us
and we will put them to death."
13But Saul said, "No one shall be put
to death today,[g] for this day the LORD
has rescued[h] Israel."
14Then Samuel said to the people,
"Come, let us go to Gilgal[i] and there
reaffirm the kingship.[j]" 15So all the
people went to Gilgal[k] and confirmed
Saul as king[l] in the presence of the
LORD. There they sacrificed fellowship
offerings[e] before the LORD, and Saul
and all the Israelites held a great celebration.

Samuel's Farewell Speech

12 Samuel said to all Israel, "I
have listened[m] to everything

e 15 Traditionally *peace offerings*

10:24 a Dt 17:15; 2Sa 21:6 b 1Sa 9:2 c 1Ki 1:25,34,39; 2Ki 11:12 **10:25** d S 1Sa 8:9 e S Dt 17:14-20; S 1Sa 8:11-18; 2Ki 11:12 f 1Sa 11:14 **10:26** g S ver 5; S Jdg 19:14 h S Jdg 20:44 **10:27** i S Dt 13:13; S 1Sa 20:7 j S ver 4; 1Ki 10:25; 2Ch 17:5; 32:23; Ps 68:29 **11:1** k S Ge 19:38; 1Sa 12:12; 2Sa 10:2; 17:27; 1Ch 19:1 l Jdg 21:8; 1Sa 31:11; 2Sa 2:4,5; 21:12 m S Ex 23:32; S Jer 37:1 **11:2** n Ge 34:15 o S Nu 16:14 p 1Sa 17:26 **11:3** q S 1Sa 8:4 r S Jdg 2:16 s ver 10 **11:4** t S 1Sa 10:5, 26 u S Ge 27:38; S Nu 25:6 **11:6** v S Jdg 3:10 **11:7** w S 1Sa 6:14 x S Jdg 19:29 y Jdg 21:5 z S Jdg 20:1 **11:8** a Jdg 20:2 b Jdg 1:4 **11:10** c ver 3 **11:11** d S Jdg 7:16 e S Ge 19:38 **11:12** f S Dt 13:13; Lk 19:27 **11:13** g 2Sa 19:22 h 1Sa 19:5; 1Ch 11:14 **11:14** i S Jos 10:43; S 1Sa 10:8 j 1Sa 10:25 **11:15** k S Jos 5:9; 2Sa 19:15 l 1Sa 12:1 **12:1** m S 1Sa 8:7

10:25 REGULATIONS OF THE KINGSHIP. Israel's king was to be distinctly different from the kings of other nations. Rather than being an absolute monarch, he was to be a theocratic king, subject to God as the ultimate Ruler of the people. (See Dt 17:14–20 for duties and regulations for kings.)

11:6 SPIRIT OF GOD CAME UPON HIM, AND HE BURNED WITH ANGER. The promise of the empowering of the Spirit spoken by Samuel at Saul's anointing as king (10:6) is here fulfilled. Note that Saul, as king, gave the same kind of military leadership against Israel's enemies as the judges did (cf. Jdg 14:6, where this phrase is used of Samson). One dimension of the Holy Spirit's work in the believer is genuine anger at sin and at the mistreatment of others. Jesus himself expressed such anger at sin and evil on several occasions (see Lk 19:45, note; Jn 11:33, note).

you said to me and have set a king[n]
over you. **2**Now you have a king as your
leader.[o] As for me, I am old and gray,
and my sons[p] are here with you. I
have been your leader from my youth
until this day. **3**Here I stand. Testify
against me in the presence of the LORD
and his anointed.[q] Whose ox have I
taken? Whose donkey[r] have I taken?
Whom have I cheated? Whom have I
oppressed? From whose hand have I
accepted a bribe[s] to make me shut my
eyes? If I have done[t] any of these, I
will make it right."[u]
4"You have not cheated or oppressed
us," they replied. "You have not taken
anything from anyone's hand."
5Samuel said to them, "The LORD is
witness[v] against you, and also his
anointed is witness this day, that you
have not found anything[w] in my
hand.[x]"
"He is witness," they said.
6Then Samuel said to the people, "It
is the LORD who appointed Moses and
Aaron and brought[y] your forefathers
up out of Egypt. **7**Now then, stand[z]
here, because I am going to confront[a]
you with evidence before the LORD as to
all the righteous acts[b] performed by
the LORD for you and your fathers.
8"After Jacob[c] entered Egypt, they
cried[d] to the LORD for help, and the
LORD sent[e] Moses and Aaron, who
brought your forefathers out of Egypt
and settled them in this place.
9"But they forgot[f] the LORD their
God; so he sold them[g] into the hand
of Sisera,[h] the commander of the
army of Hazor,[i] and into the hands of
the Philistines[j] and the king of
Moab,[k] who fought against them.
10They cried[l] out to the LORD and
said, 'We have sinned; we have forsak-
en[m] the LORD and served the Baals and
the Ashtoreths.[n] But now deliver us
from the hands of our enemies, and we
will serve you.' **11**Then the LORD sent
Jerub-Baal,[f][o] Barak,[g][p] Jephthah[q]
and Samuel,[h][r] and he delivered you
from the hands of your enemies on every side, so that you lived securely.
12"But when you saw that Nahash[s]
king[t] of the Ammonites was moving
against you, you said to me, 'No, we
want a king to rule[u] over us'—even
though the LORD your God was your
king. **13**Now here is the king[v] you
have chosen, the one you asked[w] for;
see, the LORD has set a king over you.
14If you fear[x] the LORD and serve and
obey him and do not rebel[y] against his
commands, and if both you and the
king who reigns over you follow the
LORD your God—good! **15**But if you do
not obey the LORD, and if you rebel
against[z] his commands, his hand will
be against you, as it was against your 1Sa 15:22-23
fathers.
16"Now then, stand still[a] and see[b]
this great thing the LORD is about to do
before your eyes! **17**Is it not wheat harvest[c] now? I will call[d] upon the LORD
to send thunder[e] and rain.[f] And you
will realize what an evil[g] thing you did
in the eyes of the LORD when you asked
for a king."
18Then Samuel called upon the
LORD,[h] and that same day the LORD
sent thunder and rain. So all the people
stood in awe[i] of the LORD and of Samuel.
19The people all said to Samuel,
"Pray[j] to the LORD your God for your
servants so that we will not die,[k] for
we have added to all our other sins the
evil of asking for a king."
20"Do not be afraid," Samuel replied.
"You have done all this evil;[l] yet do
not turn away from the LORD, but serve
the LORD with all your heart. **21**Do not
turn away after useless[m] idols.[n] They
can do you no good, nor can they res-

12:1 [n] 1Sa 11:15 **12:2** [o] S 1Sa 8:5 [p] 1Sa 8:3 **12:3** [q] S 1Sa 9:16; 24:6; 26:9,11; 2Sa 1:14; 19:21; Ps 105:15 [r] Nu 16:15 [s] S Ex 18:21; S 1Sa 8:3 [t] Ex 20:17; Ac 20:33 [u] S Lev 25:14 **12:5** [v] S Ge 31:50 [w] Ac 23:9; 24:20 [x] Ex 22:4 **12:6** [y] S Ex 3:10; Mic 6:4 **12:7** [z] S Jos 24:1 [a] Isa 1:18; 3:14; Jer 2:9; 25:31; Eze 17:20; 20:35; Mic 6:1-5 [b] S Jdg 5:11 **12:8** [c] S Ge 46:6 [d] S Ex 2:23 [e] S Ex 3:10; 4:16 **12:9** [f] S Dt 32:18; S Jdg 3:7 [g] S Dt 32:30 [h] Jdg 4:2 [i] S Jos 11:1 [j] Jdg 10:7 [k] Jdg 3:12 **12:10** [l] S Jdg 3:9 [m] S 1Sa 8:8 [n] S 1Sa 7:3 **12:11** [o] Jdg 6:32 [p] S Jdg 4:6 [q] S Jdg 11:1 [r] S 1Sa 7:15 **12:12** [s] S 1Sa 11:1 [t] S 1Sa 8:5 [u] 1Sa 25:30; 2Sa 5:2; 1Ch 5:2 **12:13** [v] S 1Sa 8:5 [w] S 1Sa 9:20 **12:14** [x] S Jos 24:14 [y] Jer 4:17; La 1:18 **12:15** [z] Lev 26:16; Jos 24:20; Isa 1:20; Jer 4:17; 26:4 **12:16** [a] S Ex 14:14 [b] S Ex 14:13 **12:17** [c] S Ge 30:14; S 1Sa 6:13 [d] 1Ki 18:42; Jas 5:18 [e] S Ex 9:23; S 1Sa 2:10 [f] Ge 7:12; Ex 9:18; Job 37:13; Pr 26:1 [g] S 1Sa 8:6-7 **12:18** [h] Ps 99:6 [i] S Ge 3:10; S Ex 14:31 **12:19** [j] S Ex 8:8; S 1Sa 7:8; S Jer 37:3; Jas 5:18; 1Jn 5:16 [k] S Dt 9:19 **12:20** [l] S Ex 32:30 **12:21** [m] Isa 40:20; 41:24, 29; 44:9; Jer 2:5,11; 14:22; 16:19; Jnh 2:8; Hab 2:18; Ac 14:15 [n] Dt 11:16

[f] *11* Also called *Gideon* [g] *11* Some Septuagint manuscripts and Syriac; Hebrew *Bedan* [h] *11* Hebrew; some Septuagint manuscripts and Syriac *Samson*

12:7–18 I AM GOING TO CONFRONT YOU. Samuel manifested the true prophet's heart by pleading with the people to remain faithful to God and his commands. Samuel himself remained faithful to God and his purpose throughout his life, and never deviated from his original personal integrity, mission or message (vv. 3–5; 2:35).

12:14 FEAR THE LORD . . . OBEY HIM. Samuel made it clear that God's blessing and the nation's welfare are conditioned not on having a king, but on their response of reverence for and service to God with a full obedience to his covenant word (vv. 24–25).

12:21 DO NOT TURN AWAY AFTER USELESS IDOLS. Samuel warned the Israelites not to worship powerless idol gods; only the Lord God could give them the help they needed in any time of crisis. For more about idolatry, see article on THE NATURE OF IDOLATRY, p. 394.

THE NATURE OF IDOLATRY

***1Sa 12:20–21** "Do not be afraid . . . You have done all this evil; yet do not turn away from the LORD, but serve the LORD with all your heart. Do not turn away after useless idols. They can do you no good, nor can they rescue you, because they are useless."*

Idolatry is a sin that recurs throughout the history of God's people. The first recorded instance was in the family of Jacob (Israel); note that just before he arrived in Bethel, Jacob commanded that their foreign gods be put away (Ge 35:1–4). The first story recorded in the Bible in which Israel as a whole engaged in idolatry was the worship of the golden calf while Moses was on Mount Sinai (Ex 32:1–6). During the time of the judges God's people frequently turned to idols. Though there is no evidence of idolatry during the time of Saul or David, the latter years of King Solomon set in motion a consistent pattern of idolatry in Israel (1Ki 11:1–8). In the history of the divided kingdom, all of the kings of the northern kingdom of Israel were idolatrous, as were many of the kings of the southern kingdom of Judah. Only after the exile did the idolatrous worship of other gods cease among the Jews.

ATTRACTIVENESS OF IDOLATRY. Why was idolatry so attractive to the Israelites? Several factors were involved. (1) The Israelites were surrounded by pagan nations who believed that the worship of several gods was superior to the worship of a single God. In other words, more was better. God's people were influenced by these nations, and they constantly imitated them instead of obeying God's command to keep themselves holy and separate from them.

(2) The gods of the other nations did not require the kind of obedience that the God of Israel demanded. For example, many of the pagan religions included sexual immorality with temple prostitutes as part of their religious rituals. This practice undoubtedly seemed appealing to many within Israel. God, on the other hand, required his people to obey the high moral standards as defined in his law in order to maintain a saving relationship with him. They had to resist consistently the tendency toward immorality and other sinful practices condoned or blessed by the pagan religions.

(3) Because of the demonic character of idols (see next section), idolatry at times produced genuine and demonstrable results for those who worshiped idols. The demonic powers behind the idols were able, though on a limited basis, to impart temporary material and physical benefits. Fertility gods promised the birth of children; weather gods (sun, moon, rain, etc.) promised the appropriate conditions for abundant crops; and warrior gods promised protection from enemies and victory in battle. Such promised benefits were attractive to the Israelites, and for this reason many were willing to serve these idols.

ESSENTIAL CHARACTER OF IDOLATRY. We cannot understand idolatry's attractiveness unless we understand its true nature. (1) The Bible makes it plain that an idol in and of itself is nothing (Jer 2:11; 16:20). An idol is a mere piece of wood or stone, carved by human hands, that has no power of its own. Samuel calls idols useless things (1Sa 12:21), and Paul states explicitly: "we know that an idol is nothing at all in the world" (1Co 8:4; cf. 10:19–20). For this reason the psalmists (e.g., Ps 115:4–8; 135:15–18) and prophets (e.g., 1Ki 18:27; Isa 44:9–20; 46:1–7; Jer 10:3–5) frequently mocked idols.

(2) However, behind all idols are demons, spiritual beings controlled by the devil. Both Moses (see Dt 32:17, note) and the psalmist (Ps 106:36–37) equate false gods with demons. Note too what Paul says in his letter to the Corinthians about eating meat

sacrificed to idols: "the sacrifices of pagans are offered to demons, not to God" (1Co 10:20). In other words, the power behind idolatry is the power and activity of demons, and demons do indeed have great power in this world. Christians know, of course, that the power of Jesus Christ is greater than that of demons (see article on POWER OVER SATAN AND DEMONS, p. 1484). Nevertheless, Satan as "the god of this age" (2Co 4:4) exercises tremendous power in this present evil age (see 1Jn 5:19, note; cf. Lk 13:16; Gal 1:4; Eph 6:12; Heb 2:14). He has the power to produce counterfeit miracles, signs and wonders (2Th 2:9; Rev 13:2–8,13; 16:13–14; 19:20) and to bestow physical and material benefits on people. Undoubtedly, this power sometimes contributes to the prosperity of the wicked (cf. Ps 10:2–6; 37:16,35; 49:6; 73:3–12).

(3) The relationship between idolatry and demons is seen more clearly when we realize how intricately pagan religious practices are linked with spiritism, sorcery, divination, enchantment, witchcraft, necromancy, and the like (cf. 2Ki 21:3–6; Isa 8:19; see Dt 18:9–11, notes; Rev 9:21, note). According to Scripture, all of these occult practices involve paying homage to demons. For example, when the witch at Endor was asked by Saul to bring up Samuel from the dead, she saw a spirit "coming up out of the ground," which proved to represent Samuel (1Sa 28:8–14); she had expected a demon to come out of the underworld (see 1Sa 28:12, note).

(4) The NT calls greed a form of idolatry (Col 3:5). The connection is obvious; because demons are able to give material benefits, people who are not satisfied with what they have but are always greedy for more will not hesitate to give their allegiance to the principles and desires of those spiritual beings who can get them what they want. Though such people may not worship gods made out of wood and stone, they do in reality worship the demons that stand behind greed and evil desires; thus, they are idolaters. Thus Jesus' statement that we "cannot serve both God and Money" (Mt 6:24) is essentially the same as Paul's admonition that believers may "not drink the cup of the Lord and the cup of demons" (1Co 10:21).

GOD'S RESPONSE TO IDOLATRY. God will not tolerate any form of idolatry. (1) He frequently warned against it in the OT (a) In the Ten Commandments, the first two take a direct stand against the worship of any other god than the Lord God of Israel (see Ex 20:3–4, notes). (b) This type of instruction was repeated elsewhere by God (e.g., Ex 23:13,24; 34:14–17; Dt 4:23–24; 6:14; Jos 23:7; Jdg 6:10; 2Ki 17:35,37–38). (c) Linked with the command not to serve other gods was a command to destroy all the idols and to break down the images of the pagan nations in the land of Canaan (Ex 23:24; 34:13; Dt 7:4–5; 12:2–3).

(2) The history of the Israelites was all too often the history of idol worship. God became very angry with his people for failing to destroy all of the idols in the promised land and for adopting the worship of false gods instead; he punished them by allowing their enemies to gain control over them. (a) The book of Judges presents an ever-recurring cycle: the Israelites began to serve the idol gods of the nations that they failed to drive out; God allowed their enemies to gain power over them; God's people cried out to the Lord; the Lord heard and sent a judge to deliver them. (b) The idolatry of the northern kingdom went on unhindered for nearly two centuries. Finally, God's patience ran out, and he allowed the Assyrians to destroy Israel's capital and to scatter the ten tribes (2Ki 17:6–18). (c) The southern kingdom of Judah did have a number of God-fearing kings such as Hezekiah and Josiah, but because of wicked kings like Manasseh, idolatry became entrenched in the nation of Judah (2Ki 21:1–9). As a result, through the prophets God said that he would allow Jerusalem to be destroyed (2Ki 21:10–16). In spite of these warnings, idolatry continued (see, e.g., Isa 48:4–5; Jer 2:4–30; 16:18–21; Eze 8), until God finally fulfilled his prophecy through King Nebuchadnezzar of Babylon, who captured Jerusalem, burned the temple and sacked the city (2Ki 25).

(3) The NT also warns all believers against idolatry. (a) Idolatry manifests itself in various forms today. It explicitly appears in the false world religions, as well as in sorcery, satanism and other forms of the occult. It is found wherever men and women

give themselves over to greed and materialism rather than trusting in God alone. Finally, it occurs within the church when people believe that at one and the same time they can serve God and experience his salvation and blessings, and still participate in the immoral and wicked practices of the world. (b) Consequently, the NT admonishes us not to be covetous, greedy or immoral (Col 3:5; cf. Mt 6:19–24; Ro 7:7; Heb 13:5–6; see article on RICHES AND POVERTY, p. 1562), but rather to flee from all forms of idolatry (1Co 10:14; 1Jn 5:21). God backs up his warnings with the statement that those who engage in any form of idolatry will not inherit his kingdom (1Co 6:9–10; Gal 5:20–21; Rev 22:15).

cue you, because they are useless.
22For the sake[o] of his great name[p]
the LORD will not reject[q] his people,
because the LORD was pleased to
make[r] you his own. 23As for me, far
be it from me that I should sin against
the LORD by failing to pray[s] for you.
And I will teach[t] you the way that is
good and right. 24But be sure to fear[u]
the LORD and serve him faithfully with
all your heart;[v] consider[w] what
great[x] things he has done for you.
25Yet if you persist[y] in doing evil, both
you and your king[z] will be swept[a]
away."

Samuel Rebukes Saul

13 Saul was ⌊thirty,⌋[i] years old
when he became king, and he
reigned over Israel ⌊forty-⌋[j] two years.
2Saul[k] chose three thousand men
from Israel; two thousand[b] were with
him at Micmash[c] and in the hill country of Bethel, and a thousand were with
Jonathan at Gibeah[d] in Benjamin. The
rest of the men he sent back to their
homes.
3Jonathan attacked the Philistine
outpost[e] at Geba,[f] and the Philistines heard about it. Then Saul had the
trumpet[g] blown throughout the land
and said, "Let the Hebrews hear!" 4So
all Israel heard the news: "Saul has attacked the Philistine outpost, and now
Israel has become a stench[h] to the
Philistines." And the people were summoned to join Saul at Gilgal.
5The Philistines assembled[i] to
fight Israel, with three thousand[l]
chariots, six thousand charioteers, and
soldiers as numerous as the sand[j] on
the seashore. They went up and
camped at Micmash,[k] east of Beth
Aven.[l] 6When the men of Israel saw
that their situation was critical and
that their army was hard pressed, they
hid[m] in caves and thickets, among the
rocks, and in pits and cisterns.[n]
7Some Hebrews even crossed the Jordan to the land of Gad[o] and Gilead.
Saul remained at Gilgal, and all the
troops with him were quaking[p] with
fear. 8He waited seven[q] days, the time
set by Samuel; but Samuel did not
come to Gilgal, and Saul's men began
to scatter. 9So he said, "Bring me the
burnt offering and the fellowship offerings.[m]" And Saul offered[r] up the
burnt offering. 10Just as he finished
making the offering, Samuel[s] arrived,
and Saul went out to greet[t] him.
11"What have you done?" asked
Samuel.
Saul replied, "When I saw that the
men were scattering, and that you did
not come at the set time, and that the
Philistines were assembling at Micmash,[u] 12I thought, 'Now the Philistines will come down against me at Gilgal,[v] and I have not sought the LORD's
favor.[w]' So I felt compelled to offer the
burnt offering."
13"You acted foolishly,[x]" Samuel

12:22 [o]Ps 25:11; 106:8; Isa 48:9, 11; Jer 14:7; Da 9:19 [p]S Jos 7:9; 2Sa 7:23; Jn 17:12 [q]S Lev 26:11; S Dt 31:6 [r]Dt 7:7; 1Pe 2:9
12:23 [s]S Nu 11:2; S 1Sa 1:20; S 7:8; Ro 1:9-10 [t]1Ki 8:36; Ps 25:4; 34:11; 86:11; 94:12; Pr 4:11
12:24 [u]Dt 6:2; Ecc 12:13 [v]Dt 6:5; S Jos 24:14 [w]Job 34:27; Isa 5:12; 22:11; 26:10 [x]S Dt 10:21
12:25 [y]1Sa 31:1-5 [z]Dt 28:36 [a]S Jos 24:20; S 1Ki 14:10
13:2 [b]ver 15 [c]ver 5,11,23; Ne 11:31; Isa 10:28 [d]S Jdg 19:14
13:3 [e]S 1Sa 10:5 [f]S Jos 18:24 [g]S Lev 25:9; S Jdg 3:27
13:4 [h]S Ge 34:30
13:5 [i]1Sa 17:1 [j]S Jos 11:4; Rev 20:8 [k]S ver 2 [l]S Jos 7:2
13:6 [m]1Sa 14:11, 22 [n]S Jdg 6:2; Eze 33:27
13:7 [o]S Nu 32:33 [p]S Ge 35:5; S Ex 19:16
13:8 [q]1Sa 10:8
13:9 [r]Dt 12:5-14; 2Sa 24:25; 1Ki 3:4
13:10 [s]1Sa 15:13 [t]1Sa 25:14
13:11 [u]S ver 2
13:12 [v]S Jos 10:43 [w]S Dt 4:29; Ps 119:58; Jer 26:19
13:13 [x]2Ch 16:9

[i]*1* A few late manuscripts of the Septuagint; Hebrew does not have *thirty.* [j]*1* See the round number in Acts 13:21; Hebrew does not have *forty-.* [k]*1,2* Or *and when he had reigned over Israel two years, 2he* [l]*5* Some Septuagint manuscripts and Syriac; Hebrew *thirty thousand* [m]*9* Traditionally *peace offerings*

12:22 THE LORD WILL NOT REJECT HIS PEOPLE. God continued to work with the Israelites even though they had made a wrong choice and departed from his perfect will for them. In his mercy and patience, God will often keep on helping us even when we make wrong choices and enter a path that is not wholly his will for our lives. When we stray, we must seek forgiveness and resume obeying and serving God with all our heart (v. 24). If we do so, God will bless us in our present situation. But if we persist in going our own way, we will bring destruction upon ourselves (v. 25).

12:23 FAR BE IT FROM ME THAT I SHOULD SIN . . . BY FAILING TO PRAY. Samuel was a man of prayer. (1) He was born in answer to his mother's prayer (1:10–20); he prayed for God's people and through prayer saw Israel delivered from their enemy (7:5–14); he prayed when Israel rejected God (8:6); he prayed continually for God's people to fear the Lord and serve him faithfully (12:23–24). (2) Ps 99:6 states that he was "among those who called on his [God's] name." Jer 15:1 indicates that as an intercessor, Samuel had the same stature before God as Moses. (3) Samuel so understood the nature, significance and power of intercessory prayer that he considered it a sin to stop interceding (see article on INTERCESSION, p. 1268).

12:24 BE SURE TO FEAR THE LORD AND SERVE HIM. Although King Saul now was ruler of Israel, Samuel as a prophet of God continued to call both the king and the people to walk in God's way (v. 23). Representing God and his word, the prophet stood apart from Saul and all future kings of Israel as God's voice (3:20; 15:1; Ex 7:1–2). Israel's kings were to remain subject to God's authority, teaching and rebuke through his prophets (cf. 13:13–14; 15:17–23; 2Sa 12:1–15).

13:13 NOT KEPT THE COMMAND THE LORD . . . GAVE YOU. The Lord had specifically

said. "You have not kept[y] the command the LORD your God gave you; if
you had, he would have established
your kingdom over Israel for all time.[z]
14But now your kingdom[a] will not endure; the LORD has sought out a man
after his own heart[b] and appointed[c]
him leader[d] of his people, because you
have not kept[e] the LORD's command."
15Then Samuel left Gilgal[n] and
went up to Gibeah[f] in Benjamin, and
Saul counted the men who were with
him. They numbered about six hundred.[g]

Israel Without Weapons

16Saul and his son Jonathan and the
men with them were staying in Gibeah[o][h] in Benjamin, while the Philistines camped at Micmash. **17**Raiding[i]
parties went out from the Philistine
camp in three detachments. One
turned toward Ophrah[j] in the vicinity
of Shual, **18**another toward Beth Horon,[k] and the third toward the border-
land overlooking the Valley of Zeboim[l] facing the desert.
19Not a blacksmith[m] could be found
in the whole land of Israel, because the
Philistines had said, "Otherwise the
Hebrews will make swords or
spears![n]" **20**So all Israel went down to
the Philistines to have their plowshares, mattocks, axes and sickles[p]
sharpened. **21**The price was two thirds
of a shekel[q] for sharpening plowshares and mattocks, and a third of a
shekel[r] for sharpening forks and axes
and for repointing goads.

13:13 [y]ver 14; S Jos 22:16; 1Sa 15:23,24; 2Sa 7:15; 1Ch 10:13 [z]Ps 72:5
13:14 [a]1Sa 15:28; 18:8; 24:20; 1Ch 10:14 [b]Ac 7:46; 13:22 [c]2Sa 6:21 [d]1Sa 25:30; 2Sa 5:2; Ps 18:43; Isa 16:5; 55:4; Jer 30:9; Eze 34:23-24; 37:24; Da 9:25; Hos 3:5; Mic 5:2 [e]1Sa 15:26; 16:1; 2Sa 12:9; 1Ki 13:21; Hos 13:11
13:15 [f]1Sa 14:2 [g]ver 2
13:16 [h]S Jos 18:24
13:17 [i]1Sa 14:15 [j]S Jos 18:23
13:18 [k]S Jos 10:10 [l]Ne 11:34
13:19 [m]S Ge 4:22 [n]S Nu 25:7
13:22 [o]1Ch 9:39 [p]S Nu 25:7; 1Sa 14:6; 17:47; Zec 4:6
13:23 [q]1Sa 14:4 [r]S ver 2
14:2 [s]S Jdg 4:5 [t]1Sa 13:15 [u]S Ex 28:33 [v]Isa 10:28
14:3 [w]S Ge 35:18 [x]1Sa 22:11,20 [y]S 1Sa 1:3 [z]Ps 78:60
14:4 [a]1Sa 13:23
14:5 [b]S Jos 18:24

22So on the day of the battle not a
soldier with Saul and Jonathan[o] had a
sword or spear[p] in his hand; only Saul
and his son Jonathan had them.

Jonathan Attacks the Philistines

23Now a detachment of Philistines
had gone out to the pass[q] at Micmash.[r]

14

1One day Jonathan son
of Saul said to the young man
bearing his armor, "Come, let's go over
to the Philistine outpost on the other
side." But he did not tell his father.
2Saul was staying[s] on the outskirts
of Gibeah[t] under a pomegranate
tree[u] in Migron.[v] With him were
about six hundred men, **3**among whom
was Ahijah, who was wearing an
ephod. He was a son of Ichabod's[w]
brother Ahitub[x] son of Phinehas, the
son of Eli,[y] the LORD's priest in Shiloh.[z] No one was aware that Jonathan
had left.
4On each side of the pass[a] that Jonathan intended to cross to reach the
Philistine outpost was a cliff; one was
called Bozez, and the other Seneh.
5One cliff stood to the north toward
Micmash, the other to the south toward Geba.[b]
6Jonathan said to his young armor-

n *15* Hebrew; Septuagint *Gilgal and went his way; the rest of the people went after Saul to meet the army, and they went out of Gilgal*
o *16* Two Hebrew manuscripts; most Hebrew manuscripts *Geba,* a variant of *Gibeah*
p *20* Septuagint; Hebrew *plowshares*
q *21* Hebrew *pim;* that is, about 1/4 ounce (about 8 grams) **r** *21* That is, about 1/8 ounce (about 4 grams)

---

commanded Saul to wait in Gilgal for the arrival of Samuel, who would offer sacrifices and give instruction (10:8). God tested Saul's obedience by the providential delay of Samuel beyond the agreed-upon seven days. In desperation (v. 8) and presumption (v. 9), Saul himself proceeded to offer a sacrifice contrary to God's word. Because Saul failed to keep the Lord's command, Samuel told him that God would take the kingdom away from him (vv. 13–14). Though Saul retained the kingship for the rest of his life, his son Jonathan would not succeed him to the throne.

13:14 A MAN AFTER HIS OWN HEART. (1)David is this man—a man after God's heart in the following ways: (a) he believed in God from his youth (17:34,37); (b) he diligently and continually sought God's face and counsel in childlike dependence (23:2,4; 30:8; 2Sa 2:1; 5:19,23); (c) he worshiped God with his whole being and directed all of Israel to do the same (1Ch 15—16); (d) he humbly recognized that God was the real King of Israel and that he was only God's representative (2Sa 5:12); and (e) in his public conduct he largely obeyed the Lord and carried out his will (cf. Ac 13:22).

(2) In later life, however, on several occasions David caused God deep grief and ceased to be a man after God's own heart. He despised God and his word by committing the sins of adultery and murder (2Sa 12:7–14) and by numbering Israel against God's will (1Ch 21:1–17).

14:1 PHILISTINE OUTPOST. This chapter emphasizes that the Israelites defeated the Philistines only because God acted on their behalf. They were discouraged, outnumbered and inadequately armed (13:19–22), with no reasonable hope for victory, yet they won the battle because "the LORD rescued Israel that day" (v. 23). When circumstances seem to be against us and our resources seem inadequate, as God's children we have the right to call on him to help us in our time of need (see Heb 4:16, note). He has promised to be "an ever-present help in trouble" (Ps 46:1) and to supply grace for all our needs (2Co 12:9).

bearer, “Come, let’s go over to the outpost of those uncircumcised[c] fellows.
Perhaps the LORD will act in our behalf.
Nothing[d] can hinder the LORD from
saving, whether by many[e] or by
few.[f]”
7“Do all that you have in mind,” his
armor-bearer said. “Go ahead; I am
with you heart and soul.”
8Jonathan said, “Come, then; we will
cross over toward the men and let
them see us. 9If they say to us, ‘Wait
there until we come to you,’ we will
stay where we are and not go up to
them. 10But if they say, ‘Come up to
us,’ we will climb up, because that will
be our sign[g] that the LORD has given
them into our hands.[h]”
11So both of them showed themselves to the Philistine outpost.
“Look!” said the Philistines. “The Hebrews[i] are crawling out of the holes
they were hiding[j] in.” 12The men of
the outpost shouted to Jonathan and
his armor-bearer, “Come up to us and
we’ll teach you a lesson.[k]”
So Jonathan said to his armor-bearer, “Climb up after me; the LORD has
given them into the hand[l] of Israel.”
13Jonathan climbed up, using his
hands and feet, with his armor-bearer
right behind him. The Philistines fell
before Jonathan, and his armor-bearer
followed and killed behind him. 14In
that first attack Jonathan and his armor-bearer killed some twenty men in
an area of about half an acre.[s]

Israel Routs the Philistines

15Then panic[m] struck the whole
army—those in the camp and field,
and those in the outposts and raiding[n]
parties—and the ground shook. It was
a panic sent by God.[t]
16Saul’s lookouts[o] at Gibeah in
Benjamin saw the army melting away
in all directions. 17Then Saul said to
the men who were with him, “Muster
the forces and see who has left us.”
When they did, it was Jonathan and his
armor-bearer who were not there.
18Saul said to Ahijah, “Bring[p] the
ark[q] of God.” (At that time it was with
the Israelites.)[u] 19While Saul was
talking to the priest, the tumult in the
Philistine camp increased more and
more. So Saul said to the priest,[r]
“Withdraw your hand.”
20Then Saul and all his men assembled and went to the battle. They found
the Philistines in total confusion, striking[s] each other with their swords.
21Those Hebrews who had previously
been with the Philistines and had gone
up with them to their camp went[t] over
to the Israelites who were with Saul
and Jonathan. 22When all the Israelites
who had hidden[u] in the hill country of
Ephraim heard that the Philistines
were on the run, they joined the battle
in hot pursuit. 23So the LORD rescued[v]
Israel that day, and the battle moved
on beyond Beth Aven.[w]

Jonathan Eats Honey

24Now the men of Israel were in distress that day, because Saul had bound
the people under an oath,[x] saying,
“Cursed be any man who eats food before evening comes, before I have
avenged myself on my enemies!” So
none of the troops tasted food.
25The entire army[v] entered the
woods, and there was honey on the
ground. 26When they went into the
woods, they saw the honey oozing out,
yet no one put his hand to his mouth,
because they feared the oath. 27But
Jonathan had not heard that his father
had bound the people with the oath, so
he reached out the end of the staff that
was in his hand and dipped it into the
honeycomb.[y] He raised his hand to his
mouth, and his eyes brightened.[w]
28Then one of the soldiers told him,
“Your father bound the army under a
strict oath, saying, ‘Cursed be any man
who eats food today!’ That is why the
men are faint.”
29Jonathan said, “My father has
made trouble[z] for the country. See
how my eyes brightened[x] when I tasted a little of this honey. 30How much
better it would have been if the men
had eaten today some of the plunder
they took from their enemies. Would
not the slaughter of the Philistines
have been even greater?”
31That day, after the Israelites had
struck down the Philistines from Micmash[a] to Aijalon,[b] they were ex-

14:6 [c]Jdg 14:3; 1Sa 17:26,36; 31:4; Jer 9:26; Eze 28:10 [d]S 1Sa 13:22; S 1Ki 19:12; S Mt 19:26; Heb 11:34 [e]Jdg 7:4 [f]Ps 33:16
14:10 [g]S Ge 24:14 [h]S Jos 2:24
14:11 [i]S Ge 14:13 [j]S 1Sa 13:6
14:12 [k]Jdg 8:16 [l]1Sa 17:46; 2Sa 5:24
14:15 [m]S Ge 35:5; S Ex 14:24; S 19:16; 2Ki 7:5-7 [n]1Sa 13:17
14:16 [o]2Sa 18:24; 2Ki 9:17; Isa 52:8; Eze 33:2
14:18 [p]1Sa 30:7 [q]S Jdg 18:5
14:19 [r]Nu 27:21
14:20 [s]S Jdg 7:22; Eze 38:21; Zec 14:13
14:21 [t]1Sa 29:4
14:22 [u]S 1Sa 13:6
14:23 [v]S Ex 14:30 [w]S Jos 7:2
14:24 [x]Jos 6:26
14:27 [y]ver 43; Ps 19:10; Pr 16:24; 24:13
14:29 [z]Jos 7:25; 1Ki 18:18
14:31 [a]ver 5 [b]S Jos 10:12

[s]*14* Hebrew *half a yoke*; a “yoke” was the land plowed by a yoke of oxen in one day. [t]*15* Or *a terrible panic* [u]*18* Hebrew; Septuagint *“Bring the ephod.” (At that time he wore the ephod before the Israelites.)* [v]*25* Or *Now all the people of the land* [w]*27* Or *his strength was renewed* [x]*29* Or *my strength was renewed*

hausted. **32**They pounced on the plunder[c] and, taking sheep, cattle and
calves, they butchered them on the
ground and ate them, together with the
blood.[d] **33**Then someone said to Saul,
"Look, the men are sinning against the
LORD by eating meat that has blood[e] in
it."
"You have broken faith," he said.
"Roll a large stone over here at once."
34Then he said, "Go out among the
men and tell them, 'Each of you bring
me your cattle and sheep, and slaughter them here and eat them. Do not sin
against the LORD by eating meat with
blood still[f] in it.' "
So everyone brought his ox that
night and slaughtered it there. **35**Then
Saul built an altar[g] to the LORD; it was
the first time he had done this.
36Saul said, "Let us go down after
the Philistines by night and plunder
them till dawn, and let us not leave one
of them alive."
"Do whatever seems best to you,"
they replied.
But the priest said, "Let us inquire[h]
of God here."
37So Saul asked God, "Shall I go
down after the Philistines? Will you
give them into Israel's hand?" But God
did not answer[i] him that day.
38Saul therefore said, "Come here,
all you who are leaders of the army,
and let us find out what sin has been
committed[j] today. **39**As surely as the
LORD who rescues Israel lives,[k] even if
it lies with my son Jonathan,[l] he must
die."[m] But not one of the men said a
word.
40Saul then said to all the Israelites,
"You stand over there; I and Jonathan
my son will stand over here."
"Do what seems best to you," the
men replied.
41Then Saul prayed to the LORD, the
God of Israel, "Give[n] me the right[o]
answer."[y] And Jonathan and Saul
were taken by lot, and the men were
cleared. **42**Saul said, "Cast the lot[p] between me and Jonathan my son." And
Jonathan was taken.
43Then Saul said to Jonathan, "Tell
me what you have done."[q]
So Jonathan told him, "I merely tasted a little honey[r] with the end of my
staff. And now must I die?"
44Saul said, "May God deal with me,
be it ever so severely,[s] if you do not
die, Jonathan.[t]"
45But the men said to Saul, "Should
Jonathan die—he who has brought
about this great deliverance in Israel?
Never! As surely as the LORD lives, not
a hair[u] of his head will fall to the
ground, for he did this today with God's
help." So the men rescued[v] Jonathan,
and he was not put to death.
46Then Saul stopped pursuing the
Philistines, and they withdrew to their
own land.
47After Saul had assumed rule over
Israel, he fought against their enemies
on every side: Moab,[w] the Ammonites,[x] Edom,[y] the kings[z] of Zobah,[z]
and the Philistines. Wherever he
turned, he inflicted punishment on
them.[a] **48**He fought valiantly and defeated the Amalekites,[a] delivering Israel from the hands of those who had
plundered them.

Saul's Family

49Saul's sons were Jonathan, Ishvi
and Malki-Shua.[b] The name of his older daughter was Merab, and that of the
younger was Michal.[c] **50**His wife's
name was Ahinoam daughter of Ahimaaz. The name of the commander of
Saul's army was Abner[d] son of Ner,
and Ner was Saul's uncle.[e] **51**Saul's
father Kish[f] and Abner's father Ner
were sons of Abiel.
52All the days of Saul there was bitter war with the Philistines, and whenever Saul saw a mighty or brave man,
he took[g] him into his service.

The LORD Rejects Saul as King

15 Samuel said to Saul, "I am the
one the LORD sent to anoint[h]
you king over his people Israel; so listen now to the message from the LORD.
2This is what the LORD Almighty says:

14:32 c 1Sa 15:19; Est 9:10 d S Ge 9:4
14:33 e S Ge 9:4
14:34 f Lev 19:26
14:35 g S 1Sa 7:17
14:36 h S Ge 25:22; S Jdg 18:5
14:37 i 1Sa 28:6, 15; 2Sa 22:42; Ps 18:41
14:38 j Jos 7:11
14:39 k S Nu 14:21; 2Sa 12:5; Job 19:25; Ps 18:46; 42:2 l ver 44 m Jos 7:15
14:41 n Ac 1:24 o Pr 16:33
14:42 p Jnh 1:7
14:43 q S Jos 7:19
r S ver 27
14:44 s S Ru 1:17 t ver 39
14:45 u 1Ki 1:52; S Mt 10:30 v 2Sa 14:11
14:47 w S Ge 19:37 x S Ge 19:38; 2Sa 12:31 y 1Sa 21:7 z 2Sa 8:3; 10:6; 23:36
14:48 a S Ge 36:12; Nu 13:29; Jdg 3:13; 1Sa 15:2,7; 27:8; 28:18; 30:13; 2Sa 1:13; 1Ch 4:43
14:49 b 1Sa 31:2; 1Ch 8:33 c S Ge 29:26
14:50 d 2Sa 2:8; 3:6; 1Ki 2:5 e 1Sa 10:14
14:51 f S 1Sa 9:1
14:52 g 1Sa 8:11
15:1 h S 1Sa 9:16

y *41* Hebrew; Septuagint *"Why have you not answered your servant today? If the fault is in me or my son Jonathan, respond with Urim, but if the men of Israel are at fault, respond with Thummim."* z *47* Masoretic Text; Dead Sea Scrolls and Septuagint *king* a *47* Hebrew; Septuagint *he was victorious*

15:2 PUNISH THE AMALEKITES FOR WHAT THEY DID. The Amalekites (i.e., descendants of Amalek) had been the first to oppose God and the nation of Israel in the desert (Ex 17:8–13). They represented evil power and opposition to God, his people and his truth. It was Saul's responsibility to totally destroy the Amalekites and their evil ways (v. 3). Under the cloak of religious zeal,

'I will punish the Amalekites[i] for
what they did to Israel when they way-
laid them as they came up from Egypt.
3Now go, attack the Amalekites and totally[j] destroy[b] everything that belongs to them. Do not spare them; put
to death men and women, children and
infants, cattle and sheep, camels and
donkeys.' "
4So Saul summoned the men and
mustered them at Telaim—two hundred thousand foot soldiers and ten
thousand men from Judah. **5**Saul went
to the city of Amalek and set an ambush in the ravine. **6**Then he said to the
Kenites,[k] "Go away, leave the Amalekites so that I do not destroy you
along with them; for you showed kindness to all the Israelites when they
came up out of Egypt." So the Kenites
moved away from the Amalekites.
7Then Saul attacked the Amalekites[l] all the way from Havilah to
Shur,[m] to the east of Egypt. **8**He took
Agag[n] king of the Amalekites alive,[o]
and all his people he totally destroyed
with the sword. **9**But Saul and the army
spared[p] Agag and the best of the
sheep and cattle, the fat calves[c] and
lambs—everything that was good.
These they were unwilling to destroy
completely, but everything that was
despised and weak they totally destroyed.
10Then the word of the LORD came to
Samuel: **11**"I am grieved[q] that I have
made Saul king, because he has
turned[r] away from me and has not
carried out my instructions."[s] Samuel
was troubled,[t] and he cried out to the
LORD all that night.
12Early in the morning Samuel got
up and went to meet Saul, but he was
told, "Saul has gone to Carmel.[u]
There he has set up a monument[v] in
his own honor and has turned and gone
on down to Gilgal."
13When Samuel reached him, Saul
said, "The LORD bless you! I have carried out the LORD's instructions."
14But Samuel said, "What then is
this bleating of sheep in my ears? What
is this lowing of cattle that I hear?"
15Saul answered, "The soldiers
brought them from the Amalekites;
they spared the best of the sheep and
cattle to sacrifice to the LORD your God,
but we totally destroyed the rest."
16"Stop!" Samuel said to Saul. "Let
me tell you what the LORD said to me
last night."
"Tell me," Saul replied.
17Samuel said, "Although you were
once small[w] in your own eyes, did you
not become the head of the tribes of
Israel? The LORD anointed you king
over Israel. **18**And he sent you on a
mission, saying, 'Go and completely
destroy those wicked people, the Amalekites; make war on them until you
have wiped them out.' **19**Why did you
not obey the LORD? Why did you pounce
on the plunder[x] and do evil in the eyes
of the LORD?"
20"But I did obey[y] the LORD," Saul
said. "I went on the mission the LORD
assigned me. I completely destroyed
the Amalekites and brought back Agag
their king. **21**The soldiers took sheep
and cattle from the plunder, the best of
what was devoted to God, in order to
sacrifice them to the LORD your God at
Gilgal."
22But Samuel replied:

15:2 [i]S Ge 14:7; S 1Sa 14:48; S 2Sa 1:8
15:3 [j]ver 9,19; S Ge 14:23; Jos 6:17; 1Sa 22:19; 27:9; 28:18; Est 3:13; 9:5
15:6 [k]S Ge 15:19; Nu 24:22; Jdg 1:16; 1Sa 30:29
15:7 [l]S 1Sa 14:48 [m]S Ge 16:7
15:8 [n]Ex 17:8-16; S Nu 24:7 [o]S Jos 8:23
15:9 [p]S ver 3
15:11 [q]S Ge 6:6; S Ex 32:14 [r]S Jos 22:16 [s]Job 21:14; 34:27; Ps 28:5; Isa 5:12; 53:6; Jer 48:10; Eze 18:24 [t]S ver 35; S 1Sa 8:6
15:12 [u]Jos 15:55 [v]S Nu 32:42
15:17 [w]S Ex 3:11
15:19 [x]S Ge 14:23; S 1Sa 14:32
15:20 [y]1Sa 28:18

[b]*3* The Hebrew term refers to the irrevocable giving over of things or persons to the LORD, often by totally destroying them; also in verses 8, 9, 15, 18, 20 and 21. [c]*9* Or *the grown bulls*; the meaning of the Hebrew for this phrase is uncertain.

he refused to obey fully God's command regarding the Amalekites and was subsequently rejected by God as king (vv. 18–23).

15:3 PUT TO DEATH ... CHILDREN AND INFANTS. The extent of the Amalekites' wickedness, cruelty and continued rebellion was so great that the removal of innocent children from earth was an act of mercy. Note that because of the extreme wickedness of humankind in Noah's day, God in sorrow and grief had decided to destroy everyone, including children and infants (Ge 6:5–7). Here also God decided that the Amalekites had to be utterly blotted out. It was better that the children of the Amalekites die in infancy than live under their parents' corrupt and wicked influence.

15:9 SAUL AND THE ARMY ... WERE UNWILLING TO DESTROY COMPLETELY. Saul rebelled against and disobeyed God and his clear instructions (vv. 2–3,18–19) because he was not committed to God's will with all his heart. He felt God's word was good but not so sacred that it must be followed in every detail. His rejection of the Lord's word (vv. 22–23) is all the more significant because he had already been confronted for his disobedience (13:13).

15:22 TO OBEY IS BETTER THAN SACRIFICE. Obeying God's word from the heart is better than any outward form of worship, service or personal sacrifice. Saul's sin was placing his own conception of what was right above Biblical revela-

"Does the LORD delight in burnt
offerings and sacrifices
as much as in obeying the voice
of the LORD?
To obey is better than sacrifice,[z]
and to heed is better than the
fat of rams.
23For rebellion is like the sin of
divination,[a]
and arrogance like the evil of
idolatry.
Because you have rejected[b] the
word of the LORD,
1Ki 2:2-4 he has rejected you as king."

24Then Saul said to Samuel, "I have
sinned.[c] I violated[d] the LORD's command and your instructions. I was
afraid[e] of the people and so I gave in
to them. 25Now I beg you, forgive[f] my
sin and come back with me, so that I
may worship the LORD."
26But Samuel said to him, "I will
not go back with you. You have rejected[g] the word of the LORD, and the
LORD has rejected you as king over
Israel!"
27As Samuel turned to leave, Saul
caught hold of the hem of his robe,[h]
and it tore.[i] 28Samuel said to him,
"The LORD has torn[j] the kingdom[k] of
Israel from you today and has given it
to one of your neighbors—to one better than you.[l] 29He who is the Glory
of Israel does not lie[m] or change[n] his
mind; for he is not a man, that he
should change his mind."
30Saul replied, "I have sinned.[o] But
please honor[p] me before the elders of
my people and before Israel; come
back with me, so that I may worship
the LORD your God." 31So Samuel went

15:22 [z]Ps 40:6-8; 51:16; Pr 21:3; Isa 1:11-15; Jer 7:22; Hos 6:6; Am 5:25; Mic 6:6-8; S Mk 12:33
15:23 [a]Dt 18:10 [b]S 1Sa 13:13
15:24 [c]S Ex 9:27; S Nu 22:34; Ps 51:4 [d]S 1Sa 13:13 [e]Pr 29:25; Isa 51:12-13; Jer 42:11
15:25 [f]Ex 10:17
15:26 [g]S Nu 15:31; S 1Sa 13:14; S 1Ki 14:10
15:27 [h]1Sa 28:14 [i]1Ki 11:11,31; 14:8; 2Ki 17:21
15:28 [j]1Sa 28:17 [k]S 1Sa 13:14 [l]2Sa 6:21; 7:15
15:29 [m]Tit 1:2 [n]S Nu 23:19; Heb 7:21
15:30 [o]S Nu 22:34 [p]Isa 29:13; Jn 12:43
15:33 [q]Est 9:7-10; Jer 18:21
15:34 [r]S 1Sa 7:17 [s]S Jdg 19:14; S 1Sa 10:5
15:35 [t]1Sa 19:24 [u]ver 11; 1Sa 16:1 [v]S Ge 6:6
16:1 [w]S 1Sa 8:6; S 15:35 [x]S 1Sa 13:14 [y]S 1Sa 10:1 [z]S Ru 4:17 [a]2Sa 5:2; 7:8; 1Ki 8:16; 1Ch 12:23; Ps 78:70; Ac 13:22
16:3 [b]Ex 4:15 [c]S Dt 17:15

back with Saul, and Saul worshiped
the LORD.
32Then Samuel said, "Bring me
Agag king of the Amalekites."
Agag came to him confidently,[d]
thinking, "Surely the bitterness of
death is past."
33But Samuel said,

"As your sword has made women
childless,
so will your mother be childless
among women."[q]
And Samuel put Agag to death before
the LORD at Gilgal.
34Then Samuel left for Ramah,[r] but
Saul went up to his home in Gibeah[s]
of Saul. 35Until the day Samuel[t] died,
he did not go to see Saul again, though
Samuel mourned[u] for him. And the
LORD was grieved[v] that he had made
Saul king over Israel.

Samuel Anoints David

16 The LORD said to Samuel, "How
long will you mourn[w] for Saul,
since I have rejected[x] him as king
over Israel? Fill your horn with oil[y]
and be on your way; I am sending you
to Jesse[z] of Bethlehem. I have chosen[a] one of his sons to be king."
2But Samuel said, "How can I go?
Saul will hear about it and kill me."
The LORD said, "Take a heifer with
you and say, 'I have come to sacrifice
to the LORD.' 3Invite Jesse to the sacrifice, and I will show[b] you what to do.
You are to anoint[c] for me the one I
indicate."
4Samuel did what the LORD said.

[d]32 Or *him trembling, yet*

tion; this sin will be the focal point of the final apostasy predicted for the period just before Jesus returns to the earth (Mt 24:11,24; 2Th 2:9–12; 2Ti 4:3–4; cf. 2Pe 2). Worship, prayer, praise, spiritual gifts and service to God are worthless in his sight if not accompanied by explicit obedience to him and his righteous standards (cf. Isa 58:2; 59:2; 1Co 13).

15:23 REBELLION . . . DIVINATION. The sin of "divination" is seeking to manipulate events, people or the future by the spirits of the departed dead (cf. Lev 19:26; Dt 18:9–12). Rebellion against God's word is like this sin in that both involve a rejection of God's lordship and an attempt to determine the outcome of things in a manner other than God's way. Furthermore, both sins take transgressors out from under God's protection and put them under the destructive power of Satan and evil spirits (cf. 16:14; 18:10; 19:9).

15:23 HE HAS REJECTED YOU AS KING. (1) Saul's disqualification from being king and the consequent rejection of his dynasty did not mean that God had forever rejected Saul personally. Although Saul's position as king would never again be restored, he could still be forgiven and enjoy a saving relationship with God by sincerely repenting and serving the Lord (vv. 24–25,31).

(2) This same principle operates under the new covenant. A spiritual leader may fail morally, and thus be rejected permanently by God from his spiritual office, yet be open to full forgiveness, salvation and fellowship with God (see article on MORAL QUALIFICATIONS FOR OVERSEERS, p. 1882).

15:35 THE LORD WAS GRIEVED. "Grieved" (Heb *naham*) expresses God's deep emotion and sorrow at Saul's rebellion; God's grief included regret that he had made Saul king over Israel.

When he arrived at Bethlehem,[d] the elders of the town trembled[e] when they met him. They asked, "Do you come in peace?[f]"

[5]Samuel replied, "Yes, in peace; I have come to sacrifice to the LORD. Consecrate[g] yourselves and come to the sacrifice with me." Then he consecrated Jesse and his sons and invited them to the sacrifice.

[6]When they arrived, Samuel saw Eliab[h] and thought, "Surely the LORD's anointed stands here before the LORD."

[7]But the LORD said to Samuel, "Do not consider his appearance or his height, for I have rejected him. The LORD does not look at the things man looks at. Man looks at the outward appearance,[i] but the LORD looks at the heart."[j]

[8]Then Jesse called Abinadab[k] and had him pass in front of Samuel. But Samuel said, "The LORD has not chosen this one either." [9]Jesse then had Shammah[l] pass by, but Samuel said, "Nor has the LORD chosen this one." [10]Jesse had seven of his sons pass before Samuel, but Samuel said to him, "The LORD has not chosen these." [11]So he asked Jesse, "Are these all[m] the sons you have?"

"There is still the youngest," Jesse answered, "but he is tending the sheep."[n]

Samuel said, "Send for him; we will not sit down[e] until he arrives."

[12]So he[o] sent and had him brought in. He was ruddy, with a fine appearance and handsome[p] features.

Then the LORD said, "Rise and anoint him; he is the one."

[13]So Samuel took the horn of oil and anointed[q] him in the presence of his brothers, and from that day on the Spirit of the LORD[r] came upon David in power.[s] Samuel then went to Ramah.

David in Saul's Service

[14]Now the Spirit of the LORD had departed[t] from Saul, and an evil[f] spirit[u] from the LORD tormented him.[v]

[15]Saul's attendants said to him, "See, an evil spirit from God is tormenting you. [16]Let our lord command his servants here to search for someone who can play the harp.[w] He will play when the evil spirit from God comes upon you, and you will feel better."

[17]So Saul said to his attendants, "Find someone who plays well and bring him to me."

[18]One of the servants answered, "I have seen a son of Jesse[x] of Bethlehem who knows how to play the harp. He is a brave man and a warrior.[y] He speaks well and is a fine-looking man. And the LORD is with[z] him."

[19]Then Saul sent messengers to Jesse and said, "Send me your son David, who is with the sheep.[a]" [20]So Jesse took a donkey loaded with bread,[b] a skin of wine and a young goat and sent them with his son David to Saul.

[21]David came to Saul and entered his service.[c] Saul liked him very much, and David became one of his armor-bearers. [22]Then Saul sent word to Jesse, saying, "Allow David to remain in my service, for I am pleased with him."

[23]Whenever the spirit from God came upon Saul, David would take his harp and play. Then relief would come to Saul; he would feel better, and the evil spirit[d] would leave him. 1Ki 18:21-39

David and Goliath

17 Now the Philistines gathered their forces for war and assembled[e] at Socoh in Judah. They pitched camp at Ephes Dammim, between Socoh[f] and Azekah.[g] [2]Saul and the Israelites assembled and camped in the Valley of Elah[h] and drew up their bat-

16:4 [d]S Ge 48:7; Lk 2:4 [e]1Sa 21:1 [f]1Ki 2:13; 2Ki 9:17 **16:5** [g]S Ex 19:10, 22 **16:6** [h]1Sa 17:13; 1Ch 2:13 **16:7** [i]Ps 147:10 [j]S 1Sa 2:3; 2Sa 7:20; S Ps 44:21; S 139:23; S Rev 2:23 **16:8** [k]1Sa 17:13 **16:9** [l]1Sa 17:13; 2Sa 13:3; 21:21 **16:11** [m]1Sa 17:12 [n]S Ge 37:2; 2Sa 7:8 **16:12** [o]1Sa 9:17 [p]S Ge 39:6 **16:13** [q]S 1Sa 2:35; S 2Sa 22:51 [r]1Sa 18:12 [s]S 1Sa 11:6 **16:14** [t]S Jdg 16:20 [u]ver 23; S Jdg 9:23; 1Sa 18:10 [v]2Sa 7:15 **16:16** [w]ver 23; S 1Sa 10:5,6; 2Ch 29:26-27; Ps 49:4 **16:18** [x]S Ru 4:17 [y]2Sa 17:8 [z]S Ge 39:2; 1Sa 17:32-37; 20:13; 1Ch 22:11; Mt 1:23 **16:19** [a]1Sa 17:15 **16:20** [b]S Ge 32:13; S 1Sa 10:4 **16:21** [c]S Ge 41:46 **16:23** [d]S ver 14; S Jdg 9:23 **17:1** [e]1Sa 13:5 [f]Jos 15:35; 2Ch 28:18 [g]S Jos 10:10,11 **17:2** [h]1Sa 21:9

[e] *11* Some Septuagint manuscripts; Hebrew *not gather around* [f] *14* Or *injurious*; also in verses 15, 16 and 23

16:12 RISE AND ANOINT HIM. Already at an early age David developed a heart and desire for God as his spiritual Shepherd (see Ps 23). David's earnest heart for God (v. 7) was the primary reason God chose him as Israel's next king.

16:14 THE SPIRIT OF THE LORD HAD DEPARTED FROM SAUL. Because Saul had rebelled against God's will, he was given over to demonic influence (see 15:23). Evil spirits operate under the permissive will of our sovereign God and at times under his direct will (Jdg 9:23; 1Ki 22:19–23; see also Lk 11:26, note; 22:3; Ro 1:21–32; 2Th 2:8–12; see article on THE WILL OF GOD, p. 1056).

16:23 THE EVIL SPIRIT WOULD LEAVE. Apparently the Holy Spirit was active in David's music so that Saul received temporary relief from the demonic oppression that had come as God's judgment.

tle line to meet the Philistines. **3**The Philistines occupied one hill and the Israelites another, with the valley between them.

4A champion named Goliath,[i] who was from Gath, came out of the Philistine camp. He was over nine feet[g] tall. **5**He had a bronze helmet on his head and wore a coat of scale armor of bronze weighing five thousand shekels[h]; **6**on his legs he wore bronze greaves, and a bronze javelin[j] was slung on his back. **7**His spear shaft was like a weaver's rod,[k] and its iron point weighed six hundred shekels.[i] His shield bearer[l] went ahead of him.

8Goliath stood and shouted to the ranks of Israel, "Why do you come out and line up for battle? Am I not a Philistine, and are you not the servants of Saul? Choose[m] a man and have him come down to me. **9**If he is able to fight and kill me, we will become your subjects; but if I overcome him and kill him, you will become our subjects and serve us." **10**Then the Philistine said, "This day I defy[n] the ranks of Israel! Give me a man and let us fight each other.[o]" **11**On hearing the Philistine's words, Saul and all the Israelites were dismayed and terrified.

12Now David was the son of an Ephrathite[p] named Jesse,[q] who was from Bethlehem[r] in Judah. Jesse had eight[s] sons, and in Saul's time he was old and well advanced in years. **13**Jesse's three oldest sons had followed Saul to the war: The firstborn was Eliab;[t] the second, Abinadab;[u] and the third, Shammah.[v] **14**David was the youngest. The three oldest followed Saul, **15**but David went back and forth from Saul to tend[w] his father's sheep[x] at Bethlehem.

16For forty days the Philistine came forward every morning and evening and took his stand.

17Now Jesse said to his son David, "Take this ephah[j][y] of roasted grain[z] and these ten loaves of bread for your brothers and hurry to their camp. **18**Take along these ten cheeses to the commander of their unit.[k] See how your brothers[a] are and bring back some assurance[l] from them. **19**They are with Saul and all the men of Israel in the Valley of Elah, fighting against the Philistines."

20Early in the morning David left the flock with a shepherd, loaded up and set out, as Jesse had directed. He reached the camp as the army was going out to its battle positions, shouting the war cry. **21**Israel and the Philistines were drawing up their lines facing each other. **22**David left his things with the keeper of supplies,[b] ran to the battle lines and greeted his brothers. **23**As he was talking with them, Goliath, the Philistine champion from Gath, stepped out from his lines and shouted his usual[c] defiance, and David heard it. **24**When the Israelites saw the man, they all ran from him in great fear.

25Now the Israelites had been saying, "Do you see how this man keeps coming out? He comes out to defy Israel. The king will give great wealth to the man who kills him. He will also give him his daughter[d] in marriage and will exempt his father's family from taxes[e] in Israel."

26David asked the men standing near him, "What will be done for the man who kills this Philistine and removes this disgrace[f] from Israel? Who is this uncircumcised[g] Philistine that he should defy[h] the armies of the living[i] God?"

27They repeated to him what they had been saying and told him, "This is what will be done for the man who kills him."

28When Eliab, David's oldest brother, heard him speaking with the men, he burned with anger[j] at him and asked, "Why have you come down here? And with whom did you leave those few sheep in the desert? I know how conceited you are and how wicked your heart is; you came down only to watch the battle."

29"Now what have I done?" said David. "Can't I even speak?" **30**He then turned away to someone else and brought up the same matter, and the men answered him as before. **31**What David said was overheard and reported to Saul, and Saul sent for him.

32David said to Saul, "Let no one lose heart[k] on account of this Philis-

17:4 [i] 1Sa 21:9; 2Sa 21:19
17:6 [j] ver 45; 1Sa 18:10
17:7 [k] 2Sa 21:19; 1Ch 11:23; 20:5 [l] ver 41
17:8 [m] 2Sa 2:12-17
17:10 [n] ver 26, 45; 2Sa 21:21 [o] ver 23
17:12 [p] S Ge 35:16; S 48:7; Ps 132:6 [q] S Ru 4:17 [r] S Ge 35:19 [s] 1Sa 16:11
17:13 [t] S 1Sa 16:6 [u] 1Sa 16:8 [v] S 1Sa 16:9
17:15 [w] S Ge 37:2 [x] 1Sa 16:19
17:17 [y] S Lev 19:36 [z] S Lev 23:14; 1Sa 25:18
17:18 [a] Ge 37:14
17:22 [b] S Jos 1:11
17:23 [c] ver 8-10
17:25 [d] 1Sa 18:17 [e] S 1Sa 8:15
17:26 [f] 1Sa 11:2 [g] S 1Sa 14:6 [h] S ver 10 [i] Dt 5:26; S Jos 3:10; 2Ki 18:35
17:28 [j] S Ge 27:41; Pr 18:19
17:32 [k] S Dt 20:3; Ps 18:45; Isa 7:4; Jer 4:9; 38:4; Da 11:30

[g] *4* Hebrew *was six cubits and a span* (about 3 meters) [h] *5* That is, about 125 pounds (about 57 kilograms) [i] *7* That is, about 15 pounds (about 7 kilograms) [j] *17* That is, probably about 3/5 bushel (about 22 liters) [k] *18* Hebrew *thousand* [l] *18* Or *some token*; or *some pledge of spoils*

tine; your servant will go and fight
him."
33Saul replied,[l] "You are not able
to go out against this Philistine and
fight him; you are only a boy, and he
has been a fighting man from his
youth."
34But David said to Saul, "Your servant has been keeping his father's
sheep. When a lion[m] or a bear came
and carried off a sheep from the flock,
35I went after it, struck it and rescued
the sheep from its mouth. When it
turned on me, I seized[n] it by its hair,
struck it and killed it. 36Your servant
has killed both the lion[o] and the bear;
this uncircumcised Philistine will be
like one of them, because he has defied
the armies of the living God. 37The
LORD who delivered[p] me from the paw
of the lion[q] and the paw of the bear
will deliver me from the hand of this
Philistine."
Saul said to David, "Go, and the LORD
be with[r] you."
38Then Saul dressed David in his
own[s] tunic. He put a coat of armor on
him and a bronze helmet on his head.
39David fastened on his sword over the
tunic and tried walking around, because he was not used to them.
"I cannot go in these," he said to
Saul, "because I am not used to them."
So he took them off. 40Then he took his
staff in his hand, chose five smooth
stones from the stream, put them in
the pouch of his shepherd's bag and,
with his sling in his hand, approached
the Philistine.
41Meanwhile, the Philistine, with
his shield bearer[t] in front of him, kept
coming closer to David. 42He looked
David over and saw that he was only a
boy, ruddy and handsome,[u] and he despised[v] him. 43He said to David,
"Am I a dog,[w] that you come at me
with sticks?" And the Philistine cursed
David by his gods. 44"Come here," he
said, "and I'll give your flesh to the
birds of the air[x] and the beasts of the
field![y]"
45David said to the Philistine, "You
come against me with sword and spear
and javelin,[z] but I come against you in
the name[a] of the LORD Almighty, the
God of the armies of Israel, whom you
have defied.[b] 46This day the LORD will
hand[c] you over to me, and I'll strike
you down and cut off your head. Today
I will give the carcasses[d] of the Philistine army to the birds of the air and the
beasts of the earth, and the whole
world[e] will know that there is a God
in Israel.[f] 47All those gathered here
will know that it is not by sword[g] or
spear that the LORD saves;[h] for the
battle[i] is the LORD's, and he will give
all of you into our hands."
48As the Philistine moved closer to
attack him, David ran quickly toward
the battle line to meet him. 49Reaching
into his bag and taking out a stone, he
slung it and struck the Philistine on
the forehead. The stone sank into his
forehead, and he fell facedown on the
ground.
50So David triumphed over the Philistine with a sling[j] and a stone; without a sword in his hand he struck down
the Philistine and killed him.
51David ran and stood over him. He
took hold of the Philistine's sword and
drew it from the scabbard. After he
killed him, he cut[k] off his head with 1Ki
the sword.[l] 18:41-46
When the Philistines saw that their
hero was dead, they turned and ran.
52Then the men of Israel and Judah
surged forward with a shout and pursued the Philistines to the entrance of
Gath[m] and to the gates of Ekron.[m]

17:33 [l] Nu 13:31 **17:34** [m] Job 10:16; Isa 31:4; Jer 49:19; Hos 13:8; Am 3:12 **17:35** [n] Jdg 14:6 **17:36** [o] 1Ch 11:22 **17:37** [p] 2Co 1:10 [q] 2Ti 4:17 [r] S 1Sa 16:18; S 18:12 **17:38** [s] S Ge 41:42 **17:41** [t] ver 7 **17:42** [u] 1Sa 16:12 [v] Ps 123:3-4; Pr 16:18 **17:43** [w] 1Sa 24:14; 2Sa 3:8; 9:8; 2Ki 8:13

17:44 [x] S Ge 40:19; Rev 19:17 [y] 2Sa 21:10; Jer 34:20 **17:45** [z] S ver 6 [a] Dt 20:1; 2Ch 13:12; 14:11; 32:8; Ps 20:7-8; 124:8; Heb 11:32-34 [b] S ver 10 **17:46** [c] S 1Sa 14:12 [d] S Dt 28:26 [e] S Jos 4:24; S Isa 11:9 [f] 1Ki 18:36; 2Ki 5:8; 19:19; Isa 37:20 **17:47** [g] Hos 1:7 [h] 1Sa 14:6; 2Ch 14:11; Jer 39:18 [i] S Ex 14:14; S Nu 21:14; S 1Sa 2:9; 2Ch 20:15; Ps 44:6-7 **17:50** [j] 1Sa 25:29 **17:51** [k] Heb 11:34 [l] 1Sa 21:9; 22:10 **17:52** [m] Jos 15:11

m *52* Some Septuagint manuscripts; Hebrew *a valley*

17:50 DAVID TRIUMPHED OVER THE PHILISTINE. David's victory over Goliath came as a result of his faith in God that had already been tested and proven in his life. We can identify five specific factors that led to his triumph: (1) David had a heart for God (16:7) that caused him to seek the Lord and his face always (cf. 1Ch 16:10–11).

(2) David had a zealous and deep concern for the honor and reputation of the Lord God of Israel (vv. 26,36,46). He recognized that Goliath was defying not just the armies of Israel, but the Lord Almighty.

(3) David's confidence in the Lord's power had been strengthened by his memory of previous times when he had prayed for and experienced God's deliverance (vv. 34–37; cf. Ps 29:3–4).

(4) David trusted not in himself but in God to win the victory over Goliath and the Philistines (vv. 37,45–47; cf. Ps 33:16–17; 44:6–7; Hos 1:7).

(5) The Spirit of the Lord came upon him in power (16:13; cf. Zec 4:6).

Whenever God's children face seemingly insurmountable problems and situations, those giants can be overcome if we exercise faith like David and depend on the power of the Holy Spirit (see Eph 3:20–21; Php 4:13).

Their dead were strewn along the Shaaraim[n] road to Gath and Ekron. **53**When the Israelites returned from chasing the Philistines, they plundered their camp. **54**David took the Philistine's head and brought it to Jerusalem, and he put the Philistine's weapons in his own tent.

55As Saul watched David[o] going out to meet the Philistine, he said to Abner, commander of the army, "Abner,[p] whose son is that young man?"

Abner replied, "As surely as you live, O king, I don't know."

56The king said, "Find out whose son this young man is."

57As soon as David returned from killing the Philistine, Abner took him and brought him before Saul, with David still holding the Philistine's head.

58"Whose son are you, young man?" Saul asked him.

David said, "I am the son of your servant Jesse[q] of Bethlehem."

Saul's Jealousy of David

18 After David had finished talking with Saul, Jonathan[r] became one in spirit with David, and he loved[s] him as himself.[t] **2**From that day Saul kept David with him and did not let him return to his father's house. **3**And Jonathan made a covenant[u] with David because he loved him as himself. **4**Jonathan took off the robe[v] he was wearing and gave it to David, along with his tunic, and even his sword, his bow and his belt.[w]

5Whatever Saul sent him to do, David did it so successfully[n][x] that Saul gave him a high rank in the army.[y] This pleased all the people, and Saul's officers as well.

6When the men were returning home after David had killed the Philistine, the women came out from all the towns of Israel to meet King Saul with singing and dancing,[z] with joyful songs and with tambourines[a] and lutes. **7**As they danced, they sang:[b]

"Saul has slain his thousands,
and David his tens[c] of
thousands."

8Saul was very angry; this refrain galled him. "They have credited David with tens of thousands," he thought, "but me with only thousands. What more can he get but the kingdom?[d]" **9**And from that time on Saul kept a jealous[e] eye on David.

10The next day an evil[o] spirit[f] from God came forcefully upon Saul. He was prophesying in his house, while David was playing the harp,[g] as he usually[h] did. Saul had a spear[i] in his hand **11**and he hurled it, saying to himself,[j] "I'll pin David to the wall." But David eluded[k] him twice.[l]

12Saul was afraid[m] of David, because the LORD[n] was with[o] David but had left[p] Saul. **13**So he sent David away from him and gave him command over a thousand men, and David led[q] the troops in their campaigns.[r] **14**In everything he did he had great success,[p][s] because the LORD was with[t] him. **15**When Saul saw how successful[q] he was, he was afraid of him. **16**But all Israel and Judah loved David, because he led them in their campaigns.[u]

17Saul said to David, "Here is my older daughter[v] Merab. I will give her to you in marriage;[w] only serve me bravely and fight the battles[x] of the LORD." For Saul said to himself,[y] "I will not raise a hand against him. Let the Philistines do that!"

18But David said to Saul, "Who am I,[z] and what is my family or my father's clan in Israel, that I should become the king's son-in-law?[a]" **19**So[r] when the time came for Merab,[b] Saul's daughter, to be given to David, she was given in marriage to Adriel of Meholah.[c]

20Now Saul's daughter Michal[d] was in love with David, and when they told Saul about it, he was pleased.[e] **21**"I will give her to him," he thought, "so that she may be a snare[f] to him and so that the hand of the Philistines may be against him." So Saul said to

17:52 [n] S Jos 15:36
17:55 [o] 1Sa 16:21 [p] 1Sa 26:5
17:58 [q] S Ru 4:17
18:1 [r] 1Sa 19:1; 20:16; 31:2; 2Sa 4:4 [s] 2Sa 1:26 [t] S Ge 44:30
18:3 [u] 1Sa 20:8, 16,17,42; 22:8; 23:18; 24:21; 2Sa 21:7
18:4 [v] S Ge 41:42 [w] 2Sa 18:11
18:5 [x] ver 30 [y] 2Sa 5:2
18:6 [z] S Ex 15:20; 2Sa 1:20 [a] Ps 68:25
18:7 [b] Ex 15:21 [c] 1Sa 21:11; 29:5; 2Sa 18:3
18:8 [d] S 1Sa 13:14; 1Sa 15:8
18:9 [e] 1Sa 19:1
18:10 [f] S Jdg 9:23; S 1Sa 16:14 [g] S 1Sa 10:5 [h] 1Sa 16:21; 19:7 [i] S 1Sa 17:6
18:11 [j] ver 25; 1Sa 20:7,33 [k] 1Sa 19:10 [l] Ps 132:1
18:12 [m] ver 29 [n] 1Sa 16:13 [o] Jos 1:5; 1Sa 17:37; 20:13; 1Ch 22:11 [p] S Jdg 16:20
18:13 [q] Nu 27:17 [r] 2Sa 5:2
18:14 [s] S Ge 39:3 [t] S Ge 39:2; S Nu 14:43; 2Sa 7:9
18:16 [u] 2Sa 5:2
18:17 [v] 1Sa 17:25 [w] S Ge 29:26 [x] S Nu 21:14 [y] ver 25; 1Sa 20:33
18:18 [z] S Ex 3:11; S 1Sa 9:21 [a] ver 23
18:19 [b] 2Sa 21:8 [c] S Jdg 7:22
18:20 [d] ver 28; S Ge 29:26 [e] ver 29
18:21 [f] S Ex 10:7; S Dt 7:16

[n] 5 Or *wisely* [o] 10 Or *injurious* [p] 14 Or *he was very wise* [q] 15 Or *wise* [r] 19 Or *However,*

18:10 EVIL SPIRIT FROM GOD CAME FORCEFULLY UPON SAUL. HE WAS PROPHESYING. We must not understand this to mean that God directly sent a demonic spirit into Saul, but rather that God permitted an evil spirit to enter him (see 16:14, note; see article on THE WILL OF GOD, p. 1056). The Hebrew word for prophesy can refer to either true or false prophecy. Saul was not prophesying here by God's Spirit; rather, his prophecy was probably demonic utterances and ravings.

David, "Now you have a second opportunity to become my son-in-law."
22Then Saul ordered his attendants:
"Speak to David privately and say,
'Look, the king is pleased with you,
and his attendants all like you; now become his son-in-law.' "
23They repeated these words to David. But David said, "Do you think it is
a small matter to become the king's
son-in-law?[g] I'm only a poor man and
little known."
24When Saul's servants told him
what David had said, **25**Saul replied,
"Say to David, 'The king wants no other price[h] for the bride than a hundred
Philistine foreskins, to take revenge[i]
on his enemies.' " Saul's plan[j] was to
have David fall by the hands of the Philistines.
26When the attendants told David
these things, he was pleased to become the king's son-in-law. So before
the allotted time elapsed, **27**David and
his men went out and killed two hundred Philistines. He brought their foreskins and presented the full number to
the king so that he might become the
king's son-in-law. Then Saul gave him
his daughter Michal[k] in marriage.
28When Saul realized that the LORD
was with David and that his daughter
Michal[l] loved David, **29**Saul became
still more afraid[m] of him, and he remained his enemy the rest of his days.
30The Philistine commanders continued to go out to battle, and as often
as they did, David met with more success[s][n] than the rest of Saul's officers, and his name became well
known.

Saul Tries to Kill David

19 Saul told his son Jonathan[o]
and all the attendants to kill[p]
David. But Jonathan was very fond of
David **2**and warned him, "My father
Saul is looking for a chance to kill you.
Be on your guard tomorrow morning;
go into hiding[q] and stay there. **3**I will
go out and stand with my father in the
field where you are. I'll speak[r] to him
about you and will tell you what I find
out."
4Jonathan spoke[s] well of David to
Saul his father and said to him, "Let
not the king do wrong[t] to his servant
David; he has not wronged you, and
what he has done has benefited you
greatly. **5**He took his life[u] in his hands
when he killed the Philistine. The LORD
won a great victory[v] for all Israel, and
you saw it and were glad. Why then
would you do wrong to an innocent[w]
man like David by killing him for no
reason?"
6Saul listened to Jonathan and took
this oath: "As surely as the LORD lives,
David will not be put to death."
7So Jonathan called David and told
him the whole conversation. He
brought him to Saul, and David was
with Saul as before.[x]
8Once more war broke out, and David went out and fought the Philistines.
He struck them with such force that
they fled before him.
9But an evil[t] spirit[y] from the LORD
came upon Saul as he was sitting in his
house with his spear in his hand. While
David was playing the harp,[z] **10**Saul
tried to pin him to the wall with his
spear, but David eluded[a] him as Saul
drove the spear into the wall. That
night David made good his escape.
11Saul sent men to David's house to
watch[b] it and to kill him in the morning.[c] But Michal, David's wife,
warned him, "If you don't run for your
life tonight, tomorrow you'll be killed."
12So Michal let David down through a
window,[d] and he fled and escaped.
13Then Michal took an idol[u][e] and
laid it on the bed, covering it with a
garment and putting some goats' hair
at the head.
14When Saul sent the men to capture David, Michal said,[f] "He is ill."
15Then Saul sent the men back to
see David and told them, "Bring him up
to me in his bed so that I may kill him."
16But when the men entered, there
was the idol in the bed, and at the head
was some goats' hair.
17Saul said to Michal, "Why did you
deceive me like this and send my enemy away so that he escaped?"
Michal told him, "He said to me, 'Let
me get away. Why should I kill you?' "
18When David had fled and made his
escape, he went to Samuel at Ramah[g]
and told him all that Saul had done to
him. Then he and Samuel went to Naioth and stayed there. **19**Word came to
Saul: "David is in Naioth at Ramah";
20so he sent men to capture him. But

[s] *30* Or *David acted more wisely* [t] *9* Or *injurious* [u] *13* Hebrew *teraphim;* also in verse 16

18:23 [g] ver 18
18:25 [h] S Ge 34:12 [i] Ps 8:2; 44:16; Jer 20:10 [j] S ver 11,S 17; ver 17
18:27 [k] 2Sa 3:14; 6:16
18:28 [l] S ver 20
18:29 [m] ver 12
18:30 [n] ver 5
19:1 [o] S 1Sa 18:1 [p] 1Sa 18:9
19:2 [q] 1Sa 20:5, 19
19:3 [r] 1Sa 20:12
19:4 [s] 1Sa 20:32; 22:14; Pr 31:8,9; Jer 18:20 [t] 1Sa 25:21; Pr 17:13
19:5 [u] S Jdg 9:17; S 12:3 [v] S 1Sa 11:13 [w] S Ge 31:36; Dt 19:10-13
19:7 [x] S 1Sa 18:2, 13
19:9 [y] S Jdg 9:23 [z] S 1Sa 10:5
19:10 [a] 1Sa 18:11
19:11 [b] Ps 59 Title [c] Jdg 16:2
19:12 [d] S Jos 2:15; Ac 9:25; 2Co 11:33
19:13 [e] S Ge 31:19
19:14 [f] S Ex 1:19; Jos 2:4
19:18 [g] S 1Sa 7:17

when they saw a group of prophets[h] prophesying, with Samuel standing there as their leader, the Spirit of God came upon[i] Saul's men and they also prophesied.[j] 21Saul was told about it, and he sent more men, and they prophesied too. Saul sent men a third time, and they also prophesied. 22Finally, he himself left for Ramah and went to the great cistern at Secu. And he asked, "Where are Samuel and David?"

"Over in Naioth at Ramah," they said.

23So Saul went to Naioth at Ramah. But the Spirit of God came even upon him, and he walked along prophesying[k] until he came to Naioth. 24He stripped[l] off his robes and also prophesied in Samuel's[m] presence. He lay that way all that day and night. This is why people say, "Is Saul also among the prophets?"[n]

David and Jonathan

20 Then David fled from Naioth at Ramah and went to Jonathan and asked, "What have I done? What is my crime? How have I wronged[o] your father, that he is trying to take my life?"[p]

2"Never!" Jonathan replied. "You are not going to die! Look, my father doesn't do anything, great or small, without confiding in me. Why would he hide this from me? It's not so!"

3But David took an oath[q] and said, "Your father knows very well that I have found favor in your eyes, and he has said to himself, 'Jonathan must not know this or he will be grieved.' Yet as surely as the LORD lives and as you live, there is only a step between me and death."

4Jonathan said to David, "Whatever you want me to do, I'll do for you."

5So David said, "Look, tomorrow is the New Moon festival,[r] and I am supposed to dine with the king; but let me go and hide[s] in the field until the evening of the day after tomorrow. 6If your father misses me at all, tell him, 'David earnestly asked my permission[t] to hurry to Bethlehem,[u] his hometown, because an annual[v] sacrifice is being made there for his whole clan.' 7If he says, 'Very well,' then your servant is safe. But if he loses his temper,[w] you can be sure that he is determined[x] to harm me. 8As for you, show kindness to your servant, for you have brought him into a covenant[y] with you before the LORD. If I am guilty, then kill[z] me yourself! Why hand me over to your father?"

9"Never!" Jonathan said. "If I had the least inkling that my father was determined to harm you, wouldn't I tell you?"

10David asked, "Who will tell me if your father answers you harshly?"

11"Come," Jonathan said, "let's go out into the field." So they went there together.

12Then Jonathan said to David: "By the LORD, the God of Israel, I will surely sound[a] out my father by this time the day after tomorrow! If he is favorably disposed toward you, will I not send you word and let you know? 13But if my father is inclined to harm you, may the LORD deal with me, be it ever so severely,[b] if I do not let you know and send you away safely. May the LORD be with[c] you as he has been with my father. 14But show me unfailing kindness[d] like that of the LORD as long as I live, so that I may not be killed, 15and do not ever cut off your kindness from my family[e]—not even when the LORD has cut off every one of David's enemies from the face of the earth."

16So Jonathan[f] made a covenant[g] with the house of David, saying, "May the LORD call David's enemies to ac-

19:20 [h] S Nu 11:29 [i] S Nu 11:25 [j] S 1Sa 10:5 **19:23** [k] 1Sa 10:13 **19:24** [l] 2Sa 6:20; Isa 20:2 [m] 1Sa 15:35 [n] S 1Sa 10:11 **20:1** [o] 1Sa 24:9 [p] 1Sa 22:23; 23:15; 24:11; 25:29; Ps 40:14; 54:3; 63:9; 70:2 **20:3** [q] Dt 6:13 **20:5** [r] S Nu 10:10 [s] S 1Sa 19:2 **20:6** [t] ver 28 [u] 1Sa 17:58 [v] S 1Sa 1:3 **20:7** [w] 1Sa 10:27; 25:17 [x] S 1Sa 18:11 **20:8** [y] S 1Sa 18:3 [z] 2Sa 14:32 **20:12** [a] 1Sa 19:3 **20:13** [b] S Ru 1:17 [c] S 1Sa 16:18; S 18:12 **20:14** [d] S Ge 40:14 **20:15** [e] 1Sa 24:21; 2Sa 9:7 **20:16** [f] S 1Sa 18:1 [g] S 1Sa 18:3

19:20 A GROUP OF PROPHETS. Samuel had founded a school of the prophets. An association of prophets is also referred to in the time of Elijah and Elisha (cf. 1Ki 20:35; 2Ki 6:1–7). Such schools were organized in order to encourage those who were prophetically gifted to develop righteous and devout lives through spiritual training, so that their ministry might help check apostasy and encourage righteous obedience to God's word. Of special note is the great prominence these companies of prophets gave to the Holy Spirit (cf. 10:5–6).

19:21 THEY ALSO PROPHESIED. Vv. 18–24 reveal that the Spirit of God may come upon individuals for judgment or for blessing. (1) Saul had sent men to arrest David. To hinder their mission the Spirit of God overpowered them with his presence and influence. Saul himself was later overcome by the Spirit and humiliated by being laid out in a trance all day and all night. (2) This passage makes clear that the Holy Spirit's coming upon an individual for prophecy or any other charismatic manifestation does not always mean that the person has a right relationship with God. Saul was in rebellion against God, yet slain by the Spirit (cf. Mt 7:22–23).

count.[h]" 17And Jonathan had David
reaffirm his oath[i] out of love for him,
because he loved him as he loved himself.
18Then Jonathan said to David: "Tomorrow is the New Moon festival. You
will be missed, because your seat will
be empty.[j] 19The day after tomorrow,
toward evening, go to the place where
you hid[k] when this trouble began, and
wait by the stone Ezel. 20I will shoot
three arrows[l] to the side of it, as
though I were shooting at a target.
21Then I will send a boy and say, 'Go,
find the arrows.' If I say to him, 'Look,
the arrows are on this side of you;
bring them here,' then come, because,
as surely as the LORD lives, you are
safe; there is no danger. 22But if I say
to the boy, 'Look, the arrows are beyond[m] you,' then you must go, because
the LORD has sent you away. 23And
about the matter you and I discussed—remember, the LORD is witness[n] between you and me forever."
24So David hid in the field, and when
the New Moon festival[o] came, the
king sat down to eat. 25He sat in his
customary place by the wall, opposite
Jonathan,[v] and Abner sat next to
Saul, but David's place was empty.[p]
26Saul said nothing that day, for he
thought, "Something must have happened to David to make him ceremonially unclean—surely he is unclean.[q]"
27But the next day, the second day of
the month, David's place was empty
again. Then Saul said to his son Jonathan, "Why hasn't the son of Jesse
come to the meal, either yesterday or
today?"
28Jonathan answered, "David earnestly asked me for permission[r] to go
to Bethlehem. 29He said, 'Let me go,
because our family is observing a sacrifice[s] in the town and my brother has
ordered me to be there. If I have found
favor in your eyes, let me get away to
see my brothers.' That is why he has
not come to the king's table."
30Saul's anger flared up at Jonathan
and he said to him, "You son of a perverse and rebellious woman! Don't I
know that you have sided with the son
of Jesse to your own shame and to the
shame of the mother who bore you?
31As long as the son of Jesse lives on
this earth, neither you nor your kingdom[t] will be established. Now send
and bring him to me, for he must die!"
32"Why[u] should he be put to death?
What[v] has he done?" Jonathan asked
his father. 33But Saul hurled his spear
at him to kill him. Then Jonathan knew
that his father intended[w] to kill David.
34Jonathan got up from the table in
fierce anger; on that second day of the
month he did not eat, because he was
grieved at his father's shameful treatment of David.
35In the morning Jonathan went out
to the field for his meeting with David.
He had a small boy with him, 36and he
said to the boy, "Run and find the arrows I shoot." As the boy ran, he shot
an arrow beyond him. 37When the boy
came to the place where Jonathan's arrow had fallen, Jonathan called out after him, "Isn't the arrow beyond[x]
you?" 38Then he shouted, "Hurry! Go
quickly! Don't stop!" The boy picked
up the arrow and returned to his master. 39(The boy knew nothing of all
this; only Jonathan and David knew.)
40Then Jonathan gave his weapons to
the boy and said, "Go, carry them back
to town."
41After the boy had gone, David got
up from the south side ⌞of the stone⌟
and bowed down before Jonathan three
times, with his face to the ground.[y]
Then they kissed each other and wept
together—but David wept the most.
42Jonathan said to David, "Go in
peace,[z] for we have sworn friendship[a] with each other in the name of
the LORD,[b] saying, 'The LORD is witness[c] between you and me, and between your descendants and my
descendants forever.[d]'" Then David
left, and Jonathan went back to the
town.

David at Nob

21 David went to Nob,[e] to Ahimelech the priest. Ahimelech

20:16 [h]S Jos 22:23
20:17 [i]S Jos 9:18; S 1Sa 18:3
20:18 [j]ver 25
20:19 [k]S 1Sa 19:2
20:20 [l]2Ki 13:15
20:22 [m]ver 37
20:23 [n]S Ge 31:50
20:24 [o]S Nu 10:10
20:25 [p]ver 18
20:26 [q]Lev 7:20-21
20:28 [r]ver 6
20:29 [s]S Ge 8:20
20:31 [t]1Sa 23:17; 24:20
20:32 [u]S 1Sa 19:4; Mt 27:23 [v]S Ge 31:36
20:33 [w]S 1Sa 18:11,17
20:37 [x]ver 22
20:41 [y]S Ge 33:3; Ru 2:10; 1Sa 24:8; 25:23; 2Sa 1:2
20:42 [z]S 1Sa 1:17; S Ac 15:33 [a]S Ge 40:14; 2Sa 1:26; Pr 18:24 [b]Isa 48:1 [c]S Ge 31:50; S 1Sa 18:3 [d]2Sa 9:1
21:1 [e]1Sa 22:9, 19; Ne 11:32; Isa 10:32

[v]*25* Septuagint; Hebrew *wall. Jonathan arose*

21:1 DAVID WENT TO NOB. Chs. 21—22 record David's flight from Saul and his failure to trust God completely. In an attempt to save his life, David lied (v. 2), sought refuge among the ungodly Philistines (vv. 10–15), and indirectly caused the death of the priests and many others (22:11–23; cf. Ps 52). By resorting to deception, David failed to commit his life unconditionally to the Lord and his protection.

trembled[f] when he met him, and asked, "Why are you alone? Why is no one with you?"

2David answered Ahimelech the priest, "The king charged me with a certain matter and said to me, 'No one is to know anything about your mission and your instructions.' As for my men, I have told them to meet me at a certain place. 3Now then, what do you have on hand? Give me five loaves of bread, or whatever you can find."

4But the priest answered David, "I don't have any ordinary bread[g] on hand; however, there is some consecrated[h] bread here—provided the men have kept[i] themselves from women."

5David replied, "Indeed women have been kept from us, as usual[j] whenever[w] I set out. The men's things[x] are holy[k] even on missions that are not holy. How much more so today!" 6So the priest gave him the consecrated bread,[l] since there was no bread there except the bread of the Presence that had been removed from before the LORD and replaced by hot bread on the day it was taken away.

7Now one of Saul's servants was there that day, detained before the LORD; he was Doeg[m] the Edomite,[n] Saul's head shepherd.

8David asked Ahimelech, "Don't you have a spear or a sword here? I haven't brought my sword or any other weapon, because the king's business was urgent."

9The priest replied, "The sword[o] of Goliath[p] the Philistine, whom you killed in the Valley of Elah,[q] is here; it is wrapped in a cloth behind the ephod. If you want it, take it; there is no sword here but that one."

David said, "There is none like it; give it to me."

David at Gath

10That day David fled from Saul and went[r] to Achish king of Gath. 11But the servants of Achish said to him, "Isn't this David, the king of the land? Isn't he the one they sing about in their dances:

" 'Saul has slain his thousands,
and David his tens of
thousands'?"[s]

12David took these words to heart and was very much afraid of Achish king of Gath. 13So he pretended to be insane[t] in their presence; and while he was in their hands he acted like a madman, making marks on the doors of the gate and letting saliva run down his beard.

14Achish said to his servants, "Look at the man! He is insane! Why bring him to me? 15Am I so short of madmen that you have to bring this fellow here to carry on like this in front of me? Must this man come into my house?"

David at Adullam and Mizpah

22 David left Gath and escaped to the cave[u] of Adullam.[v] When his brothers and his father's household heard about it, they went down to him there. 2All those who were in distress or in debt or discontented gathered[w] around him, and he became their leader. About four hundred men were with him.

3From there David went to Mizpah in Moab and said to the king of Moab, "Would you let my father and mother come and stay with you until I learn what God will do for me?" 4So he left them with the king of Moab,[x] and they stayed with him as long as David was in the stronghold.

5But the prophet Gad[y] said to David, "Do not stay in the stronghold. Go into the land of Judah." So David left and went to the forest of Hereth.[z]

Saul Kills the Priests of Nob

6Now Saul heard that David and his men had been discovered. And Saul, spear in hand, was seated[a] under the tamarisk[b] tree on the hill at Gibeah, with all his officials standing around him. 7Saul said to them, "Listen, men of Benjamin! Will the son of Jesse give all of you fields and vineyards? Will he make all of you commanders[c] of thousands and commanders of hundreds? 8Is that why you have all conspired[d] against me? No one tells me when my son makes a covenant[e] with the son of Jesse.[f] None of you is concerned[g] about me or tells me that my son has incited my servant to lie in wait for me, as he does today."

9But Doeg[h] the Edomite, who was standing with Saul's officials, said, "I saw the son of Jesse come to Ahime-

w5 Or *from us in the past few days since*
x5 Or *bodies*

21:1 [f] 1Sa 16:4
21:4 [g] Lev 24:8-9 [h] Mt 12:4 [i] S Ex 19:15; S Lev 15:18
21:5 [j] Dt 23:9-11; Jos 3:5; 2Sa 11:11 [k] 1Th 4:4
21:6 [l] S Ex 25:30; 1Sa 22:10; Mt 12:3-4; Mk 2:25-28; Lk 6:1-5
21:7 [m] 1Sa 22:9, 22 [n] 1Sa 14:47; Ps 52 Title
21:9 [o] S 1Sa 17:51 [p] S 1Sa 17:4 [q] 1Sa 17:2
21:10 [r] 1Sa 25:13; 27:2
21:11 [s] S 1Sa 18:7
21:13 [t] Ps 34 Title
22:1 [u] Ps 57 Title; 142 Title [v] S Ge 38:1
22:2 [w] 1Sa 23:13; 25:13; 2Sa 15:20
22:4 [x] S Ge 19:37
22:5 [y] 2Sa 24:11; 1Ch 21:9; 29:29; 2Ch 29:25 [z] 2Sa 23:14
22:6 [a] S Jdg 4:5 [b] S Ge 21:33
22:7 [c] S Dt 1:15
22:8 [d] ver 13 [e] S 1Sa 18:3 [f] 2Sa 20:1 [g] 1Sa 23:21
22:9 [h] S 1Sa 21:7

lech son of Ahitub[i] at Nob.[j] 10Ahim-
elech inquired[k] of the LORD for him; he
also gave him provisions[l] and the
sword[m] of Goliath the Philistine."
11Then the king sent for the priest
Ahimelech son of Ahitub and his father's whole family, who were the
priests at Nob, and they all came to the
king. 12Saul said, "Listen now, son of
Ahitub."
"Yes, my lord," he answered.
13Saul said to him, "Why have you
conspired[n] against me, you and the
son of Jesse, giving him bread and a
sword and inquiring of God for him, so
that he has rebelled against me and
lies in wait for me, as he does today?"
14Ahimelech answered the king,
"Who[o] of all your servants is as loyal
as David, the king's son-in-law, captain of your bodyguard and highly respected in your household? 15Was that
day the first time I inquired of God for
him? Of course not! Let not the king
accuse your servant or any of his father's family, for your servant knows
nothing at all about this whole affair."
16But the king said, "You will surely
die, Ahimelech, you and your father's
whole family.[p]"
17Then the king ordered the guards
at his side: "Turn and kill the priests
of the LORD, because they too have sided with David. They knew he was fleeing, yet they did not tell me."
But the king's officials were not willing[q] to raise a hand to strike the
priests of the LORD.
18The king then ordered Doeg, "You
turn and strike down the priests."[r] So
Doeg the Edomite turned and struck
them down. That day he killed eighty-
five men who wore the linen ephod.[s]
19He also put to the sword[t] Nob,[u] the
town of the priests, with its men and
women, its children and infants, and
its cattle, donkeys and sheep.
20But Abiathar,[v] a son of Ahimelech son of Ahitub,[w] escaped and fled
to join David.[x] 21He told David that
Saul had killed the priests of the LORD.
22Then David said to Abiathar: "That
day, when Doeg[y] the Edomite was
there, I knew he would be sure to tell
Saul. I am responsible for the death of
your father's whole family. 23Stay with
me; don't be afraid; the man who is
seeking your life[z] is seeking mine
also. You will be safe with me."

David Saves Keilah

23 When David was told, "Look,
the Philistines are fighting
against Keilah[a] and are looting the
threshing floors,"[b] 2he inquired[c] of
the LORD, saying, "Shall I go and attack
these Philistines?"
The LORD answered him, "Go, attack
the Philistines and save Keilah."
3But David's men said to him, "Here
in Judah we are afraid. How much
more, then, if we go to Keilah against
the Philistine forces!"
4Once again David inquired[d] of the
LORD, and the LORD answered him, "Go
down to Keilah, for I am going to give
the Philistines[e] into your hand.[f]"
5So David and his men went to Keilah,
fought the Philistines and carried off
their livestock. He inflicted heavy
losses on the Philistines and saved the
people of Keilah. 6(Now Abiathar[g] son
of Ahimelech had brought the ephod[h]
down with him when he fled to David
at Keilah.)

Saul Pursues David

7Saul was told that David had gone
to Keilah, and he said, "God has handed him over[i] to me, for David has imprisoned himself by entering a town
with gates and bars."[j] 8And Saul
called up all his forces for battle, to go
down to Keilah to besiege David and
his men.
9When David learned that Saul was
plotting against him, he said to Abiathar[k] the priest, "Bring the ephod.[l]"
10David said, "O LORD, God of Israel,
your servant has heard definitely that
Saul plans to come to Keilah and destroy the town on account of me. 11Will
the citizens of Keilah surrender me to
him? Will Saul come down, as your servant has heard? O LORD, God of Israel,
tell your servant."
And the LORD said, "He will."
12Again David asked, "Will the citi-

22:9 [i] 1Sa 14:3 [j] S 1Sa 21:1
22:10 [k] S Ge 25:22; S 1Sa 23:2 [l] S 1Sa 21:6 [m] S 1Sa 17:51
22:13 [n] ver 8
22:14 [o] S 1Sa 19:4
22:16 [p] S 1Sa 2:31
22:17 [q] S Ex 1:17
22:18 [r] S 1Sa 4:17 [s] S 1Sa 2:18,31
22:19 [t] S 1Sa 15:3 [u] S 1Sa 21:1
22:20 [v] 1Sa 23:6, 9; 30:7; 2Sa 15:24; 20:25; 1Ki 1:7; 2:22,26, 27; 4:4; 1Ch 15:11; 27:34 [w] S 1Sa 14:3 [x] S 1Sa 2:32
22:22 [y] S 1Sa 21:7
22:23 [z] S 1Sa 20:1
23:1 [a] S Jos 15:44 [b] S Nu 18:27; S Jdg 6:11
23:2 [c] ver 4,12; 1Sa 22:10; 30:8; 2Sa 2:1; 5:19,23; Ps 50:15
23:4 [d] S ver 2 [e] S 1Sa 9:16 [f] S Jos 8:7
23:6 [g] S 1Sa 22:20 [h] S 1Sa 2:28
23:7 [i] S Dt 32:30 [j] Ps 31:21
23:9 [k] S 1Sa 22:20 [l] S 1Sa 2:18

22:18 HE KILLED EIGHTY-FIVE MEN. God allowed Doeg to kill God's ministers and other innocent men, women and children. In a fallen world, the innocent sometimes suffer unjustly. God's people should not be alarmed when they suffer at the hands of evil people. In this life we will experience hardships (Ac 14:22) but in the life to come abundant blessing that far exceeds our present suffering and agonies (Ro 8:18–39).

zens of Keilah surrender[m] me and my
men to Saul?"
And the LORD said, "They will."
13So David and his men,[n] about six
hundred in number, left Keilah and
kept moving from place to place. When
Saul was told that David had escaped
from Keilah, he did not go there.
14David stayed in the desert[o]
strongholds and in the hills of the
Desert of Ziph.[p] Day after day Saul
searched[q] for him, but God did not[r]
give David into his hands.
15While David was at Horesh in the
Desert of Ziph, he learned that Saul
had come out to take his life.[s] 16And
Saul's son Jonathan went to David at
Horesh and helped him find strength[t]
in God. 17"Don't be afraid," he said.
"My father Saul will not lay a hand on
you. You will be king[u] over Israel, and
I will be second to you. Even my father
Saul knows this." 18The two of them
made a covenant[v] before the LORD.
Then Jonathan went home, but David
remained at Horesh.
19The Ziphites[w] went up to Saul at
Gibeah and said, "Is not David hiding
among us[x] in the strongholds at Horesh, on the hill of Hakilah,[y] south of
Jeshimon? 20Now, O king, come down
whenever it pleases you to do so, and
we will be responsible for handing[z]
him over to the king."
21Saul replied, "The LORD bless[a]
you for your concern[b] for me. 22Go
and make further preparation. Find out
where David usually goes and who has
seen him there. They tell me he is very
crafty. 23Find out about all the hiding
places he uses and come back to me
with definite information.[y] Then I will
go with you; if he is in the area, I will
track[c] him down among all the clans
of Judah."
24So they set out and went to Ziph
ahead of Saul. Now David and his men
were in the Desert of Maon,[d] in the
Arabah south of Jeshimon.[e] 25Saul
and his men began the search, and
when David was told about it, he went
down to the rock and stayed in the
Desert of Maon. When Saul heard this,
he went into the Desert of Maon in pursuit of David.
26Saul[f] was going along one side of
the mountain, and David and his men
were on the other side, hurrying to get
away from Saul. As Saul and his forces
were closing in on David and his men
to capture them, 27a messenger came
to Saul, saying, "Come quickly! The
Philistines are raiding the land."
28Then Saul broke off his pursuit of
David and went to meet the Philistines.
That is why they call this place Sela
Hammahlekoth.[z] 29And David went
up from there and lived in the strongholds[g] of En Gedi.[h]

David Spares Saul's Life

24 After Saul returned from pursuing the Philistines, he was told,
"David is in the Desert of En Gedi.[i]"
2So Saul took three thousand chosen
men from all Israel and set out to
look[j] for David and his men near the
Crags of the Wild Goats.
3He came to the sheep pens along
the way; a cave[k] was there, and Saul
went in to relieve[l] himself. David and
his men were far back in the cave. 4The
men said, "This is the day the LORD
spoke[m] of when he said[a] to you, 'I
will give your enemy into your hands
for you to deal with as you wish.'"[n]
Then David crept up unnoticed and
cut[o] off a corner of Saul's robe.
5Afterward, David was conscience-
stricken[p] for having cut off a corner of
his robe. 6He said to his men, "The
LORD forbid that I should do such a
thing to my master, the LORD's anointed,[q] or lift my hand against him; for he
is the anointed of the LORD." 7With
these words David rebuked his men
and did not allow them to attack Saul.
And Saul left the cave and went his
way.
8Then David went out of the cave
and called out to Saul, "My lord the

23:12 [m] ver 20 **23:13** [n] S 1Sa 22:2 **23:14** [o] Ps 55:7 [p] S Jos 15:24,55 [q] Ps 54:3-4 [r] Ps 32:7 **23:15** [s] S 1Sa 20:1 **23:16** [t] 1Sa 30:6; Ps 18:2; 27:14 **23:17** [u] S 1Sa 20:31 **23:18** [v] S 1Sa 18:3; 2Sa 9:1 **23:19** [w] 1Sa 26:1 [x] Ps 54 Title [y] 1Sa 26:3 **23:20** [z] ver 12 **23:21** [a] Ru 2:20; 2Sa 2:5 [b] 1Sa 22:8 **23:23** [c] S Ge 31:36 **23:24** [d] S Jos 15:55 [e] 1Sa 26:1

23:26 [f] Ps 17:9 **23:29** [g] 1Sa 24:22 [h] S Jos 15:62; 2Ch 20:2; SS 1:14 **24:1** [i] S Jos 15:62 **24:2** [j] 1Sa 26:2 **24:3** [k] Ps 57 Title; 142 Title [l] Jdg 3:24 **24:4** [m] 1Sa 25:28-30 [n] 2Sa 4:8 [o] ver 10, 11 **24:5** [p] 1Sa 26:9; 2Sa 24:10 **24:6** [q] S Ge 26:11; S 1Sa 12:3

[y] 23 Or *me at Nacon* [z] 28 *Sela Hammahlekoth* means *rock of parting.* [a] 4 Or *"Today the LORD is saying*

24:6 THE ANOINTED OF THE LORD. This phrase refers only to Saul in his appointed role as king of Israel; it does not mean that he was presently anointed by the Holy Spirit. David had received no direction from God to remove Saul from the throne through assassination. (1) Vv. 6–10 provide no basis for the failure to discipline or to oppose church leaders who fail morally or who depart from the teachings of God's Word (see 1Ti 3:1–13; 5:19–20; Tit 1:5–9). Such leaders must be removed from their positions. (2) Furthermore, church leaders may not use these verses to claim they are not accountable for their conduct to other leaders and to the body of Christ.

king!" When Saul looked behind him,
David bowed down and prostrated himself with his face to the ground.[r] **9**He
said to Saul, "Why do you listen[s]
when men say, 'David is bent on harming[t] you'? **10**This day you have seen
with your own eyes how the LORD delivered you into my hands in the cave.
Some urged me to kill you, but I
spared[u] you; I said, 'I will not lift my
hand against my master, because he is
the LORD's anointed.' **11**See, my father,
look at this piece of your robe in my
hand! I cut[v] off the corner of your robe
but did not kill you. Now understand
and recognize that I am not guilty[w] of
wrongdoing[x] or rebellion. I have not
wronged[y] you, but you are hunting[z]
me down to take my life.[a] **12**May the
LORD judge[b] between you and me. And
may the LORD avenge[c] the wrongs you
have done to me, but my hand will not
touch you. **13**As the old saying goes,
'From evildoers come evil deeds,[d]' so
my hand will not touch you.

14"Against whom has the king of Israel come out? Whom are you pursuing? A dead dog?[e] A flea?[f] **15**May the
LORD be our judge[g] and decide[h] between us. May he consider my cause
and uphold[i] it; may he vindicate[j] me
by delivering[k] me from your hand."

16When David finished saying this,
Saul asked, "Is that your voice,[l] David my son?" And he wept aloud.
17"You are more righteous than I,"[m]
he said. "You have treated me well,[n]
but I have treated you badly.[o] **18**You
have just now told me of the good you
did to me; the LORD delivered[p] me into
your hands, but you did not kill me.
19When a man finds his enemy, does he
let him get away unharmed? May the
LORD reward[q] you well for the way you
treated me today. **20**I know that you
will surely be king[r] and that the kingdom[s] of Israel will be established in
your hands. **21**Now swear[t] to me by
the LORD that you will not cut off my
descendants or wipe out my name from
my father's family.[u]"

22So David gave his oath to Saul.
Then Saul returned home, but David
and his men went up to the stronghold.[v]

24:8 [r] S 1Sa 20:41
24:9 [s] 1Sa 26:19
[t] 1Sa 20:1
24:10 [u] S ver 4
24:11 [v] S ver 4
[w] Ps 7:3
[x] 1Sa 25:28
[y] Ps 35:7
[z] S Ge 31:36; 1Sa 26:20
[a] S 1Sa 20:1
24:12
[b] S Ge 16:5; S 1Sa 25:38; S Job 9:15
[c] S Nu 31:3
24:13 [d] Mt 7:20
24:14
[e] S 1Sa 17:43
[f] 1Sa 26:20
24:15 [g] ver 12
[h] S Ge 16:5
[i] Ps 35:1,23; Isa 49:25
[j] Ps 26:1; 35:24; 43:1; 50:4; 54:1; 135:14
[k] Ps 119:134,154
24:16 [l] 1Sa 26:17
24:17 [m] Ge 38:26
[n] Mt 5:44
[o] S Ex 9:27
24:18
[p] 1Sa 26:23
24:19
[q] S Ru 2:12; S 2Ch 15:7
24:20
[r] S 1Sa 20:31
[s] S 1Sa 13:14
24:21 [t] Ge 21:23; S 47:31; S 1Sa 18:3; 2Sa 21:1-9
[u] S 1Sa 20:14-15

24:22 [v] 1Sa 23:29
25:1 [w] 1Sa 28:3
[x] S Lev 10:6; Dt 34:8
[y] S 1Sa 7:17
25:2 [z] S Jos 15:55
[a] 2Sa 19:32
[b] S Ge 31:19
25:3 [c] Pr 31:10
[d] S Jos 14:13; S 15:13
25:6 [e] Ps 122:7; Mt 10:12
[f] 1Ch 12:18
25:7 [g] ver 15
25:8 [h] Ne 8:10
25:10 [i] Jdg 9:28
25:11 [j] Jdg 8:6

David, Nabal and Abigail

25 Now Samuel died,[w] and all Israel assembled and mourned[x]
for him; and they buried him at his
home in Ramah.[y]

Then David moved down into the
Desert of Maon.[b] **2**A certain man in
Maon,[z] who had property there at
Carmel, was very wealthy.[a] He had a
thousand goats and three thousand
sheep, which he was shearing[b] in Carmel. **3**His name was Nabal and his
wife's name was Abigail.[c] She was an
intelligent and beautiful woman, but
her husband, a Calebite,[d] was surly
and mean in his dealings.

4While David was in the desert, he
heard that Nabal was shearing sheep.
5So he sent ten young men and said to
them, "Go up to Nabal at Carmel and
greet him in my name. **6**Say to him:
'Long life to you! Good health[e] to you
and your household! And good health
to all that is yours![f]

7" 'Now I hear that it is sheep-shear-
ing time. When your shepherds were
with us, we did not mistreat[g] them,
and the whole time they were at Carmel nothing of theirs was missing.
8Ask your own servants and they will
tell you. Therefore be favorable toward
my young men, since we come at a festive time. Please give your servants
and your son David whatever[h] you can
find for them.' "

9When David's men arrived, they
gave Nabal this message in David's
name. Then they waited.

10Nabal answered David's servants,
"Who[i] is this David? Who is this son
of Jesse? Many servants are breaking
away from their masters these days.
11Why should I take my bread[j] and
water, and the meat I have slaughtered
for my shearers, and give it to men
coming from who knows where?"

[b] *1* Some Septuagint manuscripts; Hebrew *Paran*

25:1 SAMUEL DIED. Samuel's death brought to an end the life of one of God's most faithful servants. (1) He was zealous for God and did more than any other person of his day to follow what was in God's heart (2:35; 12:7–25; 15:10–11,35). He provides a high example of integrity, honesty, faithfulness and moral blamelessness (12:1–5). (2) He left behind him a reputation that ranks him among the greatest of God's OT people. God himself spoke of him in the same breath as Moses (Jer 15:1). Samuel and other righteous prophets, not the kings, represent the highest moral and spiritual leadership under the old covenant.

12David's men turned around and
went back. When they arrived, they reported every word. **13**David said to his
men[k], "Put on your swords!" So they
put on their swords, and David put on
his. About four hundred men went[l] up
with David, while two hundred stayed
with the supplies.[m]
14One of the servants told Nabal's
wife Abigail: "David sent messengers
from the desert to give our master his
greetings,[n] but he hurled insults at
them. **15**Yet these men were very good
to us. They did not mistreat[o] us, and
the whole time we were out in the
fields near them nothing was missing.[p] **16**Night and day they were a
wall[q] around us all the time we were
herding our sheep near them. **17**Now
think it over and see what you can do,
because disaster is hanging over our
master and his whole household. He is
such a wicked[r] man that no one can
talk to him."
18Abigail lost no time. She took two
hundred loaves of bread, two skins of
wine, five dressed sheep, five seahs[c]
of roasted grain,[s] a hundred cakes of
raisins[t] and two hundred cakes of
pressed figs, and loaded them on donkeys.[u] **19**Then she told her servants,
"Go on ahead;[v] I'll follow you." But
she did not tell[w] her husband Nabal.
20As she came riding her donkey
into a mountain ravine, there were David and his men descending toward
her, and she met them. **21**David had
just said, "It's been useless—all my
watching over this fellow's property in
the desert so that nothing of his was
missing.[x] He has paid[y] me back
evil[z] for good. **22**May God deal with
David,[d] be it ever so severely,[a] if by
morning I leave alive one male[b] of all
who belong to him!"
23When Abigail saw David, she
quickly got off her donkey and bowed
down before David with her face to the
ground.[c] **24**She fell at his feet and
said: "My lord, let the blame[d] be on
me alone. Please let your servant
speak to you; hear what your servant
has to say. **25**May my lord pay no attention to that wicked man Nabal. He is
just like his name—his name is
Fool[e],[f] and folly goes with him. But
as for me, your servant, I did not see
the men my master sent.
26"Now since the LORD has kept you,
my master, from bloodshed[g] and from
avenging[h] yourself with your own
hands, as surely as the LORD lives and
as you live, may your enemies and all
who intend to harm my master be like
Nabal.[i] **27**And let this gift,[j] which
your servant has brought to my master, be given to the men who follow
you. **28**Please forgive[k] your servant's
offense, for the LORD will certainly
make a lasting[l] dynasty for my master, because he fights the LORD's battles.[m] Let no wrongdoing[n] be found
in you as long as you live. **29**Even
though someone is pursuing you to
take your life,[o] the life of my master
will be bound securely in the bundle of
the living by the LORD your God. But the
lives of your enemies he will hurl[p]
away as from the pocket of a sling.[q]
30When the LORD has done for my master every good thing he promised concerning him and has appointed him
leader[r] over Israel, **31**my master will
not have on his conscience the staggering burden of needless bloodshed or of
having avenged himself. And when the
LORD has brought my master success,
remember[s] your servant."[t]
32David said to Abigail, "Praise[u] be
to the LORD, the God of Israel, who has
sent you today to meet me. **33**May you
be blessed for your good judgment and
for keeping me from bloodshed[v] this
day and from avenging myself with my
own hands. **34**Otherwise, as surely as
the LORD, the God of Israel, lives, who
has kept me from harming you, if you
had not come quickly to meet me, not
one male belonging to Nabal[w] would
have been left alive by daybreak."
35Then David accepted from her
hand what she had brought him and
said, "Go home in peace. I have heard
your words and granted[x] your request."

[c] *18* That is, probably about a bushel (about 37 liters) [d] *22* Some Septuagint manuscripts; Hebrew *with David's enemies*

25:13 [k]S 1Sa 22:2 [l]S 1Sa 21:10 [m]S Nu 31:27 **25:14** [n]1Sa 13:10 **25:15** [o]ver 7 [p]ver 21 **25:16** [q]Ex 14:22; Job 1:10; Ps 139:5 **25:17** [r]S Dt 13:13; S 1Sa 20:7 **25:18** [s]S Lev 23:14; S 1Sa 17:17 [t]1Ch 12:40 [u]S Ge 42:26; 2Sa 16:1; Isa 30:6 **25:19** [v]Ge 32:20 [w]ver 36 **25:21** [x]ver 15 [y]Ps 109:5 [z]S 1Sa 19:4 **25:22** [a]S Ru 1:17 [b]1Ki 14:10; 21:21; 2Ki 9:8 **25:23** [c]S Ge 19:1; S 1Sa 20:41 **25:24** [d]2Sa 14:9 **25:25** [e]Pr 17:12 [f]Pr 12:16; 14:16; 20:3; Isa 32:5 **25:26** [g]ver 33 [h]Heb 10:30 [i]ver 34; 2Sa 18:32 **25:27** [j]S Ge 33:11 **25:28** [k]ver 24; 2Sa 14:9 [l]2Sa 7:11,26 [m]1Sa 18:17 [n]1Sa 24:11 **25:29** [o]S 1Sa 20:1 [p]Jer 10:18; 22:26 [q]1Sa 17:50; 2Sa 4:8 **25:30** [r]S 1Sa 12:12; S 13:14 **25:31** [s]S Ge 40:14 [t]2Sa 3:10 **25:32** [u]S Ge 24:27 **25:33** [v]ver 26 **25:34** [w]S ver 26 **25:35** [x]S Ge 19:21

25:32 GOD . . . SENT YOU. God sent Abigail to prevent David from doing a great injustice to all of Nabal's men (v. 34). David recognized how wrong he had been in planning to take such extreme revenge against them. At times God sends others to us with godly advice that opens our eyes and protects us from doing wrong. When others counsel us, we must judge our plans by God's Word and the Spirit's leading in our hearts (see Ro 8:14, note).

36When Abigail went to Nabal, he
was in the house holding a banquet
like that of a king. He was in high[y]
spirits and very drunk.[z] So she told[a]
him nothing until daybreak. 37Then in
the morning, when Nabal was sober,
his wife told him all these things, and
his heart failed him and he became like
a stone.[b] 38About ten days later, the
LORD struck[c] Nabal and he died.

39When David heard that Nabal was
dead, he said, "Praise be to the LORD,
who has upheld my cause against Nabal for treating me with contempt. He
has kept his servant from doing wrong
and has brought Nabal's wrongdoing
down on his own head."

Then David sent word to Abigail,
asking her to become his wife. 40His
servants went to Carmel and said to
Abigail, "David has sent us to you to
take you to become his wife."

41She bowed down with her face to
the ground and said, "Here is your
maidservant, ready to serve you and
wash the feet of my master's servants." 42Abigail[d] quickly got on a
donkey and, attended by her five
maids, went with David's messengers
and became his wife. 43David had also
married Ahinoam[e] of Jezreel, and they
both were his wives.[f] 44But Saul had
given his daughter Michal, David's
wife, to Paltiel[e][g] son of Laish, who
was from Gallim.[h]

David Again Spares Saul's Life

26 The Ziphites[i] went to Saul at
Gibeah and said, "Is not David
hiding[j] on the hill of Hakilah, which
faces Jeshimon?[k]"

2So Saul went down to the Desert of
Ziph, with his three thousand chosen
men of Israel, to search[l] there for David. 3Saul made his camp beside the
road on the hill of Hakilah[m] facing Jeshimon, but David stayed in the desert.
When he saw that Saul had followed
him there, 4he sent out scouts and
learned that Saul had definitely arrived.[f]

5Then David set out and went to the
place where Saul had camped. He saw
where Saul and Abner[n] son of Ner, the
commander of the army, had lain
down. Saul was lying inside the camp,
with the army encamped around him.

6David then asked Ahimelech the
Hittite[o] and Abishai[p] son of Zeruiah,[q] Joab's brother, "Who will go
down into the camp with me to Saul?"

"I'll go with you," said Abishai.

7So David and Abishai went to the
army by night, and there was Saul, lying asleep inside the camp with his
spear stuck in the ground near his
head. Abner and the soldiers were lying around him.

8Abishai said to David, "Today God
has delivered your enemy into your
hands. Now let me pin him to the
ground with one thrust of my spear; I
won't strike him twice."

9But David said to Abishai, "Don't
destroy him! Who can lay a hand on the
LORD's anointed[r] and be guiltless?[s]
10As surely as the LORD lives," he said,
"the LORD himself will strike[t] him; either his time[u] will come and he will
die,[v] or he will go into battle and perish. 11But the LORD forbid that I should
lay a hand on the LORD's anointed. Now
get the spear and water jug that are
near his head, and let's go."

12So David took the spear and water
jug near Saul's head, and they left. No
one saw or knew about it, nor did anyone wake up. They were all sleeping,
because the LORD had put them into a
deep sleep.[w]

13Then David crossed over to the
other side and stood on top of the hill
some distance away; there was a wide
space between them. 14He called out to
the army and to Abner son of Ner,
"Aren't you going to answer me, Abner?"

Abner replied, "Who are you who
calls to the king?"

15David said, "You're a man, aren't
you? And who is like you in Israel?
Why didn't you guard your lord the
king? Someone came to destroy your
lord the king. 16What you have done is
not good. As surely as the LORD lives,
you and your men deserve to die, because you did not guard your master,
the LORD's anointed. Look around you.

25:36 [y] S Ru 3:7 [z] Pr 20:1; Ecc 10:17; Isa 5:11,22; 22:13; 28:7; 56:12; Hos 4:11 [a] ver 19
25:37 [b] Ex 15:16
25:38 [c] Dt 32:35; 1Sa 24:12; 26:10; 2Sa 6:7; 12:15
25:42 [d] 2Sa 2:2; 3:3; 1Ch 3:1
25:43 [e] 2Sa 3:2; 1Ch 3:1 [f] 1Sa 27:3; 30:5; 2Sa 2:2
25:44 [g] 2Sa 3:15 [h] Isa 10:30
26:1 [i] 1Sa 23:19 [j] Ps 54 Title [k] 1Sa 23:24
26:2 [l] 1Sa 24:2
26:3 [m] 1Sa 23:19
26:5 [n] 1Sa 17:55
26:6 [o] S Ge 10:15 [p] 2Sa 2:18; 10:10; 16:9; 18:2; 19:21; 23:18; 1Ch 11:20; 19:11 [q] 1Ch 2:16
26:9 [r] ver 16; S Ge 26:11; S 1Sa 9:16; 2Sa 1:14; 19:21; La 4:20 [s] S 1Sa 24:5
26:10 [t] S Ge 16:5; S 1Sa 25:38; S Ro 12:19 [u] Dt 31:14; Ps 37:13 [v] 1Sa 31:6; 2Sa 1:1
26:12 [w] S Jdg 4:21

e 44 Hebrew *Palti*, a variant of *Paltiel*
f 4 Or *had come to Nacon*

26:9 THE LORD'S ANOINTED. David refused to kill Saul because he had been assured that God himself would remove Saul and that David would become king at God's appointed time (see v. 10; 13:13–14; 15:23; 16:12–13). David and Saul's unique situation must not be deemed grounds for permitting spiritual leaders in the church to continue in sin or evil (see 24:6, note).

Where are the king's spear and water
jug that were near his head?"
17Saul recognized David's voice and
said, "Is that your voice,[x] David my
son?"
David replied, "Yes it is, my lord the
king." **18**And he added, "Why is my lord
pursuing his servant? What have I
done, and what wrong[y] am I guilty of?
19Now let my lord the king listen[z] to
his servant's words. If the LORD has incited you against me, then may he accept an offering.[a] If, however, men
have done it, may they be cursed before
the LORD! They have now driven me
from my share in the LORD's inheritance[b] and have said, 'Go, serve other
gods.'[c] **20**Now do not let my blood[d]
fall to the ground far from the presence
of the LORD. The king of Israel has
come out to look for a flea[e]—as one
hunts a partridge in the mountains.[f]"
21Then Saul said, "I have sinned.[g]
Come back, David my son. Because
you considered my life precious[h] today, I will not try to harm you again.
Surely I have acted like a fool and have
erred greatly."
22"Here is the king's spear," David
answered. "Let one of your young men
come over and get it. **23**The LORD rewards[i] every man for his righteousness[j] and faithfulness. The LORD delivered[k] you into my hands today, but
I would not lay a hand on the LORD's
anointed. **24**As surely as I valued your
life today, so may the LORD value my
life and deliver[l] me from all trouble."
25Then Saul said to David, "May you
be blessed,[m] my son David; you will do
great things and surely triumph."
So David went on his way, and Saul
returned home.

David Among the Philistines

27 But David thought to himself,
"One of these days I will be destroyed by the hand of Saul. The best
thing I can do is to escape to the land
of the Philistines. Then Saul will give
up searching for me anywhere in Israel, and I will slip out of his hand."
2So David and the six hundred
men[n] with him left and went[o] over to
Achish[p] son of Maoch king of Gath.
3David and his men settled in Gath
with Achish. Each man had his family
with him, and David had his two
wives:[q] Ahinoam of Jezreel and Abigail of Carmel, the widow of Nabal.
4When Saul was told that David had
fled to Gath, he no longer searched for
him.
5Then David said to Achish, "If I
have found favor in your eyes, let a
place be assigned to me in one of the
country towns, that I may live there.
Why should your servant live in the
royal city with you?"
6So on that day Achish gave him Ziklag,[r] and it has belonged to the kings
of Judah ever since. **7**David lived[s] in
Philistine territory a year and four
months.
8Now David and his men went up
and raided the Geshurites,[t] the Gir-
zites and the Amalekites.[u] (From ancient times these peoples had lived in
the land extending to Shur[v] and
Egypt.) **9**Whenever David attacked an
area, he did not leave a man or woman
alive,[w] but took sheep and cattle, donkeys and camels, and clothes. Then he
returned to Achish.
10When Achish asked, "Where did
you go raiding today?" David would
say, "Against the Negev of Judah" or
"Against the Negev of Jerahmeel[x]" or
"Against the Negev of the Kenites.[y]"
11He did not leave a man or woman
alive to be brought to Gath, for he
thought, "They might inform on us and
say, 'This is what David did.' " And
such was his practice as long as he
lived in Philistine territory. **12**Achish
trusted David and said to himself, "He
has become so odious[z] to his people,
the Israelites, that he will be my servant forever.[a]"

Saul and the Witch of Endor

28 In those days the Philistines
gathered[b] their forces to fight
against Israel. Achish said to David,
"You must understand that you and

26:17 [x] 1Sa 24:16
26:18 [y] Job 13:23; Jer 37:18
26:19 [z] 1Sa 24:9 [a] 2Sa 16:11 [b] Dt 20:16; 32:9; 2Sa 14:16; 20:19; 21:3 [c] S Dt 4:28; S 11:28
26:20 [d] S 1Sa 24:11 [e] 1Sa 24:14 [f] Jer 4:29; 16:16; Am 9:3
26:21 [g] S Ex 9:27 [h] Ps 72:14
26:23 [i] S Ge 16:5; S Ru 2:12; Ps 62:12 [j] 2Sa 22:21,25; Ps 7:8; 18:20,24 [k] 1Sa 24:18
26:24 [l] Ps 54:7
26:25 [m] S Ru 2:12
27:2 [n] 1Sa 30:9; 2Sa 2:3 [o] S 1Sa 21:10 [p] 1Ki 2:39
27:3 [q] S 1Sa 25:43
27:6 [r] Jos 15:31; 19:5; 1Sa 30:1; 1Ch 12:20; Ne 11:28
27:7 [s] 1Sa 29:3
27:8 [t] S Jos 12:5 [u] S Ex 17:14; S 1Sa 14:48; 30:1; 2Sa 1:8; 8:12 [v] S Ge 16:7
27:9 [w] S 1Sa 15:3
27:10 [x] 1Sa 30:29 [y] Jdg 1:16
27:12 [z] S Ge 34:30 [a] 1Sa 29:6
28:1 [b] 1Sa 29:1

27:1 LAND OF THE PHILISTINES. Fearing Saul's instability, David here failed to trust in God; this chapter records his consequent unethical behavior. He took refuge among God's enemies (v. 1), acted in an inhuman manner without God's approval (vv. 8–11) and resorted to deception (vv. 10–12). The inspired writer of this account tells us about David's actions without approving of them. Events recorded in Scripture do not necessarily mean they are sanctioned by God. Read 1Ch 22:8 for God's evaluation of David's career as a warrior.

your men will accompany me in the
army."
2David said, "Then you will see for
yourself what your servant can do."
Achish replied, "Very well, I will
make you my bodyguard[c] for life."
3Now Samuel was dead,[d] and all Israel had mourned for him and buried
him in his own town of Ramah.[e] Saul
had expelled[f] the mediums and spiritists[g] from the land.
4The Philistines assembled and
came and set up camp at Shunem,[h]
while Saul gathered all the Israelites
and set up camp at Gilboa.[i] 5When
Saul saw the Philistine army, he was
afraid; terror[j] filled his heart. 6He inquired[k] of the LORD, but the LORD did
not answer him by dreams[l] or Urim[m]
or prophets.[n] 7Saul then said to his
attendants, "Find me a woman who is
a medium,[o] so I may go and inquire of
her."
"There is one in Endor,[p]" they said.
8So Saul disguised[q] himself, putting on other clothes, and at night he
and two men went to the woman. "Consult[r] a spirit for me," he said, "and
bring up for me the one I name."
9But the woman said to him, "Surely
you know what Saul has done. He has
cut off[s] the mediums and spiritists
from the land. Why have you set a
trap[t] for my life to bring about my
death?"
10Saul swore to her by the LORD, "As
surely as the LORD lives, you will not be
punished for this."
11Then the woman asked, "Whom
shall I bring up for you?"
"Bring up Samuel," he said.
12When the woman saw Samuel, she
cried out at the top of her voice and
said to Saul, "Why have you deceived
me?[u] You are Saul!"
13The king said to her, "Don't be
afraid. What do you see?"

28:2 [c]1Sa 29:2
28:3 [d]1Sa 25:1
[e]S 1Sa 7:17 [f]ver 9
[g]S Ex 22:18
28:4 [h]S Jos 19:18
[i]1Sa 31:1,3;
2Sa 1:6,21; 21:12
28:5 [j]S Ex 19:16
28:6 [k]S 1Sa 8:18;
14:37 [l]S Dt 13:3
[m]S Ex 28:30;
S Lev 8:8
[n]Eze 20:3;
Am 8:11; Mic 3:7
28:7 [o]1Ch 10:13;
Ac 16:16
[p]Jos 17:11;
Ps 83:10
28:8 [q]1Ki 22:30;
2Ch 18:29; 35:22
[r]2Ki 1:3; Isa 8:19
28:9 [s]ver 3
[t]Job 18:10;
Ps 31:4; 69:22;
Isa 8:14
28:12
[u]S Ge 27:36;
1Ki 14:6
28:13 [v]ver 15;
S Lev 19:31;
2Ch 33:6
28:14
[w]1Sa 15:27
28:15
[x]S Jdg 16:20
[y]S 1Sa 14:37
[z]S Dt 13:3
28:17 [a]1Sa 15:28
28:18 [b]1Sa 15:20
[c]S Dt 9:8;
S 1Sa 15:3
[d]S Ge 14:7;
S 1Sa 14:48
28:19 [e]1Sa 31:2;
1Ch 8:33
28:21
[f]S Jdg 9:17; S 12:3

The woman said, "I see a spirit[g]
coming up out of the ground."[v]
14"What does he look like?" he
asked.
"An old man wearing a robe[w] is
coming up," she said.
Then Saul knew it was Samuel, and
he bowed down and prostrated himself
with his face to the ground.
15Samuel said to Saul, "Why have
you disturbed me by bringing me up?"
"I am in great distress," Saul said.
"The Philistines are fighting against
me, and God has turned[x] away from
me. He no longer answers[y] me, either
by prophets or by dreams.[z] So I have
called on you to tell me what to do."
16Samuel said, "Why do you consult
me, now that the LORD has turned away
from you and become your enemy?
17The LORD has done what he predicted
through me. The LORD has torn[a] the
kingdom out of your hands and given it
to one of your neighbors—to David.
18Because you did not obey[b] the LORD
or carry out his fierce wrath[c] against
the Amalekites,[d] the LORD has done
this to you today. 19The LORD will hand
over both Israel and you to the Philistines, and tomorrow you and your
sons[e] will be with me. The LORD will
also hand over the army of Israel to the
Philistines."
20Immediately Saul fell full length
on the ground, filled with fear because
of Samuel's words. His strength was
gone, for he had eaten nothing all that
day and night.
21When the woman came to Saul
and saw that he was greatly shaken,
she said, "Look, your maidservant has
obeyed you. I took my life[f] in my
hands and did what you told me to do.
22Now please listen to your servant
and let me give you some food so you

[g]13 Or *see spirits*; or *see gods*

28:6 THE LORD DID NOT ANSWER HIM. Saul sought a prophetic word from God in the midst of his trouble, but received none. In despair he then turned to a medium (vv. 7–25). Persisting in ungodly ways instead of following the Spirit's leading cuts us off from God's help. Calling on him will be useless unless we turn from our ungodly ways (see Mt 3:2, note).

28:12 THE WOMAN SAW SAMUEL. God sent the spirit of Samuel to appear to Saul. Note the following facts: (1) Spiritism is sternly condemned in Scripture (Dt 18:9–12; cf. Lev 19:31; 20:6). Mediums do not really contact the dead, but usually communicate with deceiving spirits. This story gives no justification for attempting to make contact with the dead.

(2) The woman was amazed and terrified when Samuel actually appeared; this implies that she was expecting not Samuel but a demonic spirit. Clearly Samuel's appearance was not the result of her witchcraft.

(3) The appearance of the prophet was brought about by an extraordinary act of God himself in order to deliver God's final message of judgment to the king.

may eat and have the strength to go on
your way."
23 He refused[g] and said, "I will not
eat."
But his men joined the woman in
urging him, and he listened to them.
He got up from the ground and sat on
the couch.
24 The woman had a fattened calf[h]
at the house, which she butchered at
once. She took some flour, kneaded it
and baked bread without yeast. 25 Then
she set it before Saul and his men, and
they ate. That same night they got up
and left.

Achish Sends David Back to Ziklag

29 The Philistines gathered[i] all
their forces at Aphek,[j] and Israel camped by the spring in Jezreel.[k]
2 As the Philistine rulers marched with
their units of hundreds and thousands,
David and his men were marching at
the rear[l] with Achish. 3 The commanders of the Philistines asked,
"What about these Hebrews?"
Achish replied, "Is this not David,[m]
who was an officer of Saul king of Israel? He has already been with me for
over a year,[n] and from the day he left
Saul until now, I have found no fault in
him."
4 But the Philistine commanders
were angry with him and said, "Send[o]
the man back, that he may return to
the place you assigned him. He must
not go with us into battle, or he will
turn[p] against us during the fighting.
How better could he regain his master's favor than by taking the heads of
our own men? 5 Isn't this the David
they sang about in their dances:

" 'Saul has slain his thousands,
and David his tens of
thousands'?"[q]

6 So Achish called David and said to
him, "As surely as the LORD lives, you
have been reliable, and I would be
pleased to have you serve with me in
the army. From the day[r] you came to
me until now, I have found no fault in
you, but the rulers[s] don't approve of
you. 7 Turn back and go in peace; do

28:23 [g] 1Ki 21:4
28:24 [h] S Ge 18:7
29:1 [i] 1Sa 28:1
[j] S 1Sa 4:1
[k] Jos 17:16; 1Ki 18:45; 21:1, 23; 2Ki 9:30; Jer 50:5; Hos 1:4, 5,11; 2:22
29:2 [l] 1Sa 28:2
29:3 [m] 1Ch 12:19
[n] 1Sa 27:7
29:4 [o] 1Ch 12:19
[p] 1Sa 14:21
29:5 [q] S 1Sa 18:7
29:6
[r] 1Sa 27:8-12
[s] ver 3
29:9 [t] 2Sa 14:17, 20; 19:27 [u] ver 4
29:10
[v] 1Ch 12:19
30:1 [w] S 1Sa 27:6
[x] S 1Sa 27:8
[y] ver 14
30:3 [z] S Ge 31:26
30:4 [a] S Ge 27:38
30:5
[b] S 1Sa 25:43
30:6 [c] S Ex 17:4; Jn 8:59
[d] S Ru 1:13
[e] S 1Sa 23:16; Ro 4:20
30:7
[f] S 1Sa 22:20
[g] S 1Sa 2:28
30:8 [h] S 1Sa 23:2
[i] S Ge 14:16
[j] S Ex 2:17
30:9 [k] S 1Sa 27:2

nothing to displease the Philistine rulers."
8 "But what have I done?" asked David. "What have you found against your
servant from the day I came to you until now? Why can't I go and fight
against the enemies of my lord the
king?"
9 Achish answered, "I know that you
have been as pleasing in my eyes as an
angel[t] of God; nevertheless, the Philistine commanders[u] have said, 'He
must not go up with us into battle.'
10 Now get up early, along with your
master's servants who have come with
you, and leave[v] in the morning as
soon as it is light."
11 So David and his men got up early
in the morning to go back to the land
of the Philistines, and the Philistines
went up to Jezreel.

David Destroys the Amalekites

30 David and his men reached Ziklag[w] on the third day. Now the
Amalekites[x] had raided the Negev
and Ziklag. They had attacked Ziklag
and burned[y] it, 2 and had taken captive the women and all who were in it,
both young and old. They killed none of
them, but carried them off as they went
on their way.
3 When David and his men came to
Ziklag, they found it destroyed by fire
and their wives and sons and daughters taken captive.[z] 4 So David and his
men wept[a] aloud until they had no
strength left to weep. 5 David's two
wives[b] had been captured—Ahinoam
of Jezreel and Abigail, the widow of Nabal of Carmel. 6 David was greatly distressed because the men were talking
of stoning[c] him; each one was bitter[d]
in spirit because of his sons and daughters. But David found strength[e] in the
LORD his God.
7 Then David said to Abiathar[f] the
priest, the son of Ahimelech, "Bring me
the ephod.[g]" Abiathar brought it to
him, 8 and David inquired[h] of the LORD,
"Shall I pursue this raiding party? Will
I overtake them?"
"Pursue them," he answered. "You
will certainly overtake them and succeed[i] in the rescue.[j]"
9 David and the six hundred men[k]

30:7 EPHOD. The ephod was a sacred garment worn by the high priest. It was adorned with precious stones that enabled a person to learn God's will in certain situations, similar to how the Urim and Thummim were used (see Ex 28:30, note).

with him came to the Besor Ravine,
where some stayed behind, **10**for two
hundred men were too exhausted[l] to
cross the ravine. But David and four
hundred men continued the pursuit.
11They found an Egyptian in a field
and brought him to David. They gave
him water to drink and food to eat—
12part of a cake of pressed figs and two
cakes of raisins. He ate and was revived,[m] for he had not eaten any food
or drunk any water for three days and
three nights.
13David asked him, "To whom do
you belong, and where do you come
from?"
He said, "I am an Egyptian, the slave
of an Amalekite.[n] My master abandoned me when I became ill three days
ago. **14**We raided the Negev of the Kerethites[o] and the territory belonging to
Judah and the Negev of Caleb.[p] And
we burned[q] Ziklag."
15David asked him, "Can you lead
me down to this raiding party?"
He answered, "Swear to me before
God that you will not kill me or hand
me over to my master,[r] and I will take
you down to them."
16He led David down, and there they
were, scattered over the countryside,
eating, drinking and reveling[s] because of the great amount of plunder[t]
they had taken from the land of the
Philistines and from Judah. **17**David
fought[u] them from dusk until the evening of the next day, and none of them
got away, except four hundred young
men who rode off on camels and fled.[v]
18David recovered[w] everything the
Amalekites had taken, including his
two wives. **19**Nothing was missing:
young or old, boy or girl, plunder or
anything else they had taken. David
brought everything back. **20**He took all
the flocks and herds, and his men
drove them ahead of the other livestock, saying, "This is David's plunder."
21Then David came to the two hundred men who had been too exhausted[x] to follow him and who were left
behind at the Besor Ravine. They came
out to meet David and the people with
him. As David and his men approached, he greeted them. **22**But all
the evil men and troublemakers among
David's followers said, "Because they
did not go out with us, we will not
share with them the plunder we recovered. However, each man may take his
wife and children and go."
23David replied, "No, my brothers,
you must not do that with what the
LORD has given us. He has protected us
and handed over to us the forces that
came against us. **24**Who will listen to
what you say? The share of the man
who stayed with the supplies is to be
the same as that of him who went down
to the battle. All will share alike.[y]"
25David made this a statute and ordinance for Israel from that day to this.
26When David arrived in Ziklag, he
sent some of the plunder to the elders
of Judah, who were his friends, saying,
"Here is a present[z] for you from the
plunder of the LORD's enemies."
27He sent it to those who were in
Bethel,[a] Ramoth[b] Negev and Jattir;[c] **28**to those in Aroer,[d] Siph-
moth,[e] Eshtemoa[f] **29**and Racal; to
those in the towns of the Jerahmeel-
ites[g] and the Kenites;[h] **30**to those in
Hormah,[i] Bor Ashan,[j] Athach **31**and
Hebron;[k] and to those in all the other
places where David and his men had
roamed.

Saul Takes His Life

31:1–13pp — 2Sa 1:4–12; 1Ch 10:1–12

31 Now the Philistines fought
against Israel; the Israelites
fled before them, and many fell slain on
Mount Gilboa.[l] **2**The Philistines
pressed hard after Saul and his sons,[m]
and they killed his sons Jonathan,[n]
Abinadab and Malki-Shua.[o] **3**The
fighting grew fierce around Saul, and
when the archers overtook him, they
wounded[p] him critically.
4Saul said to his armor-bearer,
"Draw your sword and run me
through,[q] or these uncircumcised[r]
fellows will come and run me through
and abuse me."

30:10 [l] ver 21 **30:12** [m] S Jdg 15:19 **30:13** [n] S 1Sa 14:48 **30:14** [o] 2Sa 8:18; 15:18; 20:7,23; 1Ki 1:38,44; 1Ch 18:17; Eze 25:16; Zep 2:5 [p] S Jos 14:13; S 15:13 [q] ver 1 **30:15** [r] Dt 23:15 **30:16** [s] Lk 12:19 [t] S ver 17; S Jos 22:8 **30:17** [u] ver 16; 1Sa 11:11; 2Sa 1:1 [v] 2Sa 1:8 **30:18** [w] S Ge 14:16 **30:21** [x] ver 10
30:24 [y] S Nu 31:27; S Jdg 5:30 **30:26** [z] S Ge 33:11 **30:27** [a] S Jos 7:2 [b] S Jos 10:40 [c] S Jos 15:48 **30:28** [d] S Nu 32:34; S Jos 13:16 [e] 1Ch 27:27 [f] S Jos 15:50 **30:29** [g] 1Sa 27:10 [h] S 1Sa 15:6 **30:30** [i] S Nu 14:45; S 21:3 [j] S Jos 15:42 **30:31** [k] Nu 13:22; S Jos 10:36; 2Sa 2:1,4 **31:1** [l] S 1Sa 28:4 **31:2** [m] S 1Sa 28:19 [n] S 1Sa 18:1 [o] S 1Sa 14:49 **31:3** [p] S 1Sa 28:4 **31:4** [q] S Jdg 9:54 [r] S Ge 34:14; S 1Sa 14:6

30:24 SHARE OF THE MAN WHO STAYED ... IS TO BE THE SAME. David determined that those who remained at home to care faithfully for the supplies of those who went to war were to have an equal share in the spoils of battle. This principle may be applied to the sending of foreign missionaries into other lands to preach the gospel. Those who stay home, faithfully supporting and praying for those who go, will share equally in the heavenly rewards and in God's approval (see Mt 10:41, note).

But his armor-bearer was terrified
and would not do it; so Saul took his
own sword and fell on it. 5When the
armor-bearer saw that Saul was dead,
he too fell on his sword and died with
him. 6So Saul and his three sons and
his armor-bearer and all his men died[s]
together that same day.

7When the Israelites along the valley and those across the Jordan saw
that the Israelite army had fled and
that Saul and his sons had died, they
abandoned their towns and fled. And
the Philistines came and occupied
them.

8The next day, when the Philistines[t] came to strip the dead, they
found Saul and his three sons fallen on
Mount Gilboa. 9They cut off his head
and stripped off his armor, and they
sent messengers throughout the land
of the Philistines to proclaim the
news[u] in the temple of their idols and
among their people.[v] 10They put his
armor in the temple of the Ashtoreths[w] and fastened his body to the
wall of Beth Shan.[x]

11When the people of Jabesh Gilead[y] heard of what the Philistines had
done to Saul, 12all their valiant men[z]
journeyed through the night to Beth
Shan. They took down the bodies of
Saul and his sons from the wall of Beth
Shan and went to Jabesh, where they
burned[a] them. 13Then they took their
bones[b] and buried them under a tamarisk[c] tree at Jabesh, and they fasted[d]
seven days.[e]

31:6 [s]S 1Sa 26:10
31:8 [t]2Sa 1:20
31:9 [u]2Sa 1:20; 4:4 [v]S Jdg 16:24
31:10 [w]S Jdg 2:12-13; S 1Sa 7:3 [x]S Jos 17:11
31:11 [y]S Jdg 21:8; S 1Sa 11:1
31:12 [z]Ps 76:5 [a]S Ge 38:24; Am 6:10
31:13 [b]2Sa 21:12-14 [c]S Ge 21:33 [d]2Sa 3:35; 12:19-23 [e]S Ge 50:10

2 SAMUEL

Outline

I. David's Remarkable Success as King (1:1—10:19)
  A. David's Political Success (1:1—5:25)
    1. David Laments the Death of Saul and Jonathan (1:1–27)
    2. David's Years as King Over Judah (2:1—4:12)
    3. David Enthroned King Over all Israel (5:1–5)
    4. David Conquers Jerusalem and Establishes It as the Political Center (5:6–10)
    5. David Extends the Kingdom (5:11–25)
  B. David's Spiritual Success (6:1—7:29)
    1. David Establishes Jerusalem as the Religious Center (6:1–23)
    2. David Wishes to Build God a House (7:1–3)
    3. God's Covenant with David (7:4–17)
    4. David's Response (7:18–29)
  C. David's Military Success (8:1—10:19)
    1. David's Victories Over Philistia, Moab, Zobah, Aram, Edom (8:1–12)
    2. David's Righteous Rule in Jerusalem (8:13—9:13)
    3. David's Victory Over Ammon (10:1–19)

II. David's Shameful Transgression as King (11:1—12:14)
  A. David's Adultery with Bathsheba (11:1–5)
  B. David's Murder of Uriah and Cover-up (11:6–27)
  C. David's Guilt and Judgment Pronounced by the Prophet Nathan (12:1–14)

III. David's Years of Reaping Sin's Consequences (12:15—20:26)
  A. Judgment on David's Household: Immorality and Death (12:15—15:6)
    1. Death of His Son of Adultery (12:15–25)
    2. Joab's Loyalty (12:26–31)
    3. Amnon Rapes Tamar, a Half Sister (13:1–20)
    4. Absalom Kills Amnon in Revenge (13:21–36)
    5. Absalom's Flight, Return and Deceit (13:37—15:6)
  B. Judgment on David's Kingdom: Insurrection and Murder (15:7—20:26)
    1. Absalom's Insurrection (15:7–12)
    2. David Flees Jerusalem in Disgrace (15:13—16:14)
    3. Absalom Rules in Jerusalem (16:15—17:29)
    4. Absalom Overthrown and Murdered (18:1–32)
    5. David's Lament and Joab's Rebuke (18:33—19:8)
    6. David Restored as King (19:9–43)
    7. Sheba's Insurrection and Murder (20:1–26)

IV. The Last Years of David as King (21:1—24:25)
  A. A Three-Year Famine (21:1–14)
  B. War with the Philistines (21:15–22)
  C. David's Psalm of Praise (22:1–51)
  D. David's Last Words (23:1–7)
  E. David's Mighty Men (23:8–39)
  F. David's Census and God's Plague (24:1–17)
  G. David's Intercession and God's Mercy (24:18–25)

Author: Anonymous

Theme: David's Reign

Date of Writing: Late 10th century B.C.

Background

Since 1 and 2 Samuel were originally a single book in the Hebrew OT, the background of 2 Samuel is discussed more fully at the beginning of 1 Samuel (see the introduction to 1 Samuel). It may be noted here that whereas the events in 1 Samuel (extending from Samuel's birth to Saul's death) cover almost a century of time (c. 1105–1010 B.C.), 2 Samuel records only the reign of David, a period of forty years (c. 1010–970 B.C.).

Purpose

2 Samuel continues the prophetic history of the theocratic character of Israel's monarchy. It profoundly illustrates from David's kingship and personal life the terms of the covenant for Israel as set forth by Moses in Deuteronomy: covenant obedience results in God's blessings; disregard for God's law results in curses and judgment (see Dt 27—30).

Survey

The full record of David's life extends from 1Sa 16:1 to 1Ki 2:11. 2 Samuel begins with Saul's death and David's anointing at Hebron as king over Judah for seven and one-half years (chs. 1—4). The rest of the book focuses on David's next 33 years as king over all Israel at Jerusalem (chs. 5—24). The watershed of the book and of David's life is his adultery with Bathsheba and murder of Uriah (ch. 11). Before this dark chapter, David represented many of the ideals of a theocratic king. Under the favor, wisdom and anointing of God, David (1) captured Jerusalem from the Jebusites and made it his capital (ch. 5), (2) brought back the ark of the covenant to Jerusalem amidst great rejoicing and celebration (ch. 6), and (3) subdued Israel's enemies, beginning with the Philistines (ch. 8—10); he became "more and more powerful, because the LORD God Almighty was with him" (5:10). His strong leadership attracted "mighty men" and inspired intense loyalty. David understood that God had established him as king over Israel, and he openly acknowledged God's rule over himself and the nation. God prophetically promised that a descendant of David would sit on his throne, one who would perfectly fulfill the role of theocratic king (7:12–17; cf. Isa. 9:6–7; 11:1–5; Jer 23:5–6; 33:14–16).

However, after David's tragic sins of adultery and murder, moral disintegration and rebellion plagued his family (chs. 12—17) and the entire nation (chs. 18—20); great national blessing was changed to national judgment. Although David sincerely repented and experienced the mercy of God's forgiveness (12:13; cf. Ps 51), the consequences of his transgression continued to the end of his life and even afterwards (cf. 12:7–12). Nevertheless, God did not reject David as king as he had rejected Saul (cf. 1Sa 15:23). Indeed David's heart for God (see his psalms) and his abhorrence of all idolatry made him the example by which all subsequent kings of Israel were measured (cf. 2Ki 18:3; 22:2). 2 Samuel ends with David purchasing the threshing floor of Araunah, which became the future site of the temple (24:18–25).

Special Features

Five major features characterize 2 Samuel. (1) It records key events in King David's 40-year reign, including his capture of Jerusalem from the Jebusites and his formation of it into Israel's political and religious center. His life falls exactly midway between Abraham and Jesus Christ. (2) The book's pivotal center (ch. 11) records David's tragic sins involving Bathsheba and her husband Uriah. The prophetic historian of this book emphasizes that though David's adultery and murder were done secretly, the sin was judged openly by God at every level of David's life—personal, family and national. (3) It reveals an important and enduring principle of leadership in God's kingdom: the greater God's favor and anointing on a leader's life, the greater will be God's judgment if that leader violates God's trust by committing moral or ethical transgression. Though David is commended in Scripture as a man after God's own heart, God's favor changed to judgment and his blessings to curses after David sinned, just as Moses had warned Israel (cf. Dt 28). (4) The chapters describing the ongoing rippling effects of David's sin on his family and the entire nation (chs. 12—21) reveal how intricately the well-being of an entire people is tied to the spiritual and moral condition of their leader. (5) It highlights the enduring moral lesson that success and prosperity often lead to moral flabbiness, which in turn leads to moral failure. David's exemplary life and reign were tragically marred by adultery and murder at the pinnacle of his success and power as king.

New Testament Fulfillment

David's rule as king in chs. 1—10 is a type of the Messianic King. His establishment of Jerusalem as the holy city, God's gift to him of the Davidic covenant, and his reception of the prophetic promise of an everlasting kingdom all point ahead to the final "Son of David," Jesus Christ, and to his present and future kingdom as revealed in the NT (cf. Isa 9:7; Mt 21:9; 22:45; Lk 1:32–33). For further insight into the NT application related to David, see the introduction to 1 Samuel.

Reading 2 Samuel

In order to read the entire Old Testament in one year, the book of 2 Samuel should be read in 10 days, according to the following schedule: □ 1–3 □ 4–6 □ 7–8 □ 9–11 □ 12–14 □ 15–17 □ 18–19 □ 20–21 □ 22 □ 23–24

NOTES

David Hears of Saul's Death

1:4–12pp — 1Sa 31:1–13; 1Ch 10:1–12

1 After the death[a] of Saul, David returned from defeating[b] the Amalekites[c] and stayed in Ziklag two
days. **2**On the third day a man[d] arrived
from Saul's camp, with his clothes torn
and with dust on his head.[e] When he
came to David, he fell[f] to the ground
to pay him honor.[g]
3"Where have you come from?" David asked him.
He answered, "I have escaped from
the Israelite camp."
4"What happened?" David asked.
"Tell me."
He said, "The men fled from the battle. Many of them fell and died. And
Saul and his son Jonathan are dead."
5Then David said to the young man
who brought him the report, "How do
you know that Saul and his son Jonathan are dead?"
6"I happened to be on Mount Gilboa,[h]" the young man said, "and there
was Saul, leaning on his spear, with
the chariots and riders almost upon
him. **7**When he turned around and saw
me, he called out to me, and I said,
'What can I do?'
8"He asked me, 'Who are you?'
" 'An Amalekite,[i]' I answered.
9"Then he said to me, 'Stand over
me and kill me![j] I am in the throes of
death, but I'm still alive.'
10"So I stood over him and killed
him, because I knew that after he had
fallen he could not survive. And I took
the crown[k] that was on his head and
the band on his arm and have brought
them here to my lord."
11Then David and all the men with
him took hold of their clothes and
tore[l] them. **12**They mourned and
wept and fasted till evening for Saul
and his son Jonathan, and for the
army of the LORD and the house of Israel, because they had fallen by the
sword.
13David said to the young man who
brought him the report, "Where are you
from?"
"I am the son of an alien, an Amalekite,[m]" he answered.
14David asked him, "Why were you
not afraid to lift your hand to destroy
the LORD's anointed?[n]"
15Then David called one of his men
and said, "Go, strike him down!"[o] So
he struck him down, and he died.[p]
16For David had said to him, "Your
blood be on your own head.[q] Your own
mouth testified against you when you
said, 'I killed the LORD's anointed.' "

David's Lament for Saul and Jonathan

17David took up this lament[r] concerning Saul and his son Jonathan,[s]
18and ordered that the men of Judah be
taught this lament of the bow (it is
written in the Book of Jashar):[t]

19"Your glory, O Israel, lies slain on
your heights.
How the mighty[u] have fallen![v]

20"Tell it not in Gath,[w]
proclaim it not in the streets of
Ashkelon,[x]
lest the daughters of the
Philistines[y] be glad,
lest the daughters of the
uncircumcised rejoice.[z]

21"O mountains of Gilboa,[a]
may you have neither dew[b] nor
rain,[c]
nor fields that yield offerings[d]
⌞of grain⌟.
For there the shield of the mighty
was defiled,
the shield of Saul—no longer
rubbed with oil.[e]
22From the blood[f] of the slain,
from the flesh of the mighty,
the bow[g] of Jonathan did not turn
back,
the sword of Saul did not return
unsatisfied.

23"Saul and Jonathan—
in life they were loved and
gracious,
and in death they were not
parted.
They were swifter than eagles,[h]
they were stronger than lions.[i]

24"O daughters of Israel,
weep for Saul,
who clothed you in scarlet and
finery,

1:1 [a] S 1Sa 26:10; 1Ch 10:13 [b] S Jos 22:8; S 1Sa 30:17 [c] S Ge 14:7; Nu 13:29 **1:2** [d] 2Sa 4:10 [e] S 1Sa 4:12; Job 2:12; Eze 27:30 [f] S 1Sa 20:41 [g] S Ge 37:7 **1:6** [h] ver 21; S 1Sa 28:4 **1:8** [i] ver 13; S 1Sa 15:2; S 27:8; 30:13,17 **1:9** [j] S Jdg 9:54 **1:10** [k] 2Ki 11:12 **1:11** [l] S Ge 37:29; S Nu 14:6 **1:13** [m] S ver 8; S 1Sa 14:48 **1:14** [n] S 1Sa 12:3; S 26:9 **1:15** [o] 2Sa 4:12 [p] 2Sa 4:10 **1:16** [q] S Lev 20:9; Mt 27:24-25; Ac 18:6 **1:17** [r] S Ge 50:10; S Eze 32:2 [s] ver 26 **1:18** [t] Jos 10:13 **1:19** [u] 2Sa 23:8; Ps 29:1; 45:3 [v] 2Sa 3:38 **1:20** [w] Mic 1:10 [x] S Jos 13:3 [y] 1Sa 31:8 [z] S 1Sa 18:6 **1:21** [a] S ver 6 [b] S Ge 27:28; S Isa 18:4 [c] Dt 11:17; 1Ki 8:35; 17:1; 18:1; 2Ch 6:26; Job 36:27; 38:28; Ps 65:10; 147:8; Isa 5:6; Jer 5:24; 14:4; Am 1:2 [d] Jer 12:4; Eze 31:15 [e] Isa 21:5 **1:22** [f] Isa 34:3,7; 49:26 [g] Dt 32:42 **1:23** [h] S Dt 28:49 [i] Jdg 14:18

1:10 I . . . KILLED HIM. The Amalekite lied about the manner of Saul's death (see the true account in 1Sa 31:3–6). He was seeking honor and favor from David, but instead his fabricated story resulted in his death (v. 15).

who adorned your garments with
ornaments of gold.[j]

25 “How the mighty have fallen in
battle!
Jonathan lies slain on your
heights.
26 I grieve[k] for you, Jonathan[l] my
brother;[m]
you were very dear to me.
Your love for me was wonderful,[n]
more wonderful than that of
women.

27 “How the mighty have fallen!
The weapons of war have
perished!”[o]

David Anointed King Over Judah

2 In the course of time, David inquired[p] of the LORD. “Shall I go up
to one of the towns of Judah?” he
asked.
The LORD said, “Go up.”
David asked, “Where shall I go?”
“To Hebron,”[q] the LORD answered.
2 So David went up there with his
two wives,[r] Ahinoam of Jezreel and
Abigail,[s] the widow of Nabal of Carmel. 3 David also took the men who
were with him,[t] each with his family,
and they settled in Hebron[u] and its
towns. 4 Then the men of Judah came to
Hebron[v] and there they anointed[w]
David king over the house of
Judah.
When David was told that it was the
men of Jabesh Gilead[x] who had buried
Saul, 5 he sent messengers to the men
of Jabesh Gilead to say to them, “The
LORD bless[y] you for showing this kindness to Saul your master by burying
him. 6 May the LORD now show you
kindness and faithfulness,[z] and I too
will show you the same favor because
you have done this. 7 Now then, be
strong[a] and brave, for Saul your master is dead, and the house of Judah has
anointed me king over them.”

1:24 [j] S Jdg 5:30
1:26 [k] Jer 22:18; 34:5 [l] ver 17 [m] S 1Sa 20:42 [n] S 1Sa 18:1
1:27 [o] S 1Sa 2:4
2:1 [p] S 1Sa 23:2, 11-12 [q] S Ge 13:18; S 23:19
2:2 [r] S 1Sa 25:43 [s] S 1Sa 25:42
2:3 [t] S 1Sa 27:2; 1Ch 12:22 [u] S Ge 13:18; 23:2; 37:14
2:4 [v] S 1Sa 30:31 [w] S 1Sa 2:35; 2Sa 5:3-5; 1Ch 12:23-40 [x] S Jdg 21:8; S 1Sa 11:1
2:5 [y] S Jdg 17:2; S 1Sa 23:21; 2Ti 1:16
2:6 [z] Ex 34:6
2:7 [a] S Jos 1:6; S Jdg 5:21
2:8 [b] S 1Sa 14:50; S 2Sa 3:27 [c] 2Sa 4:5; 1Ch 8:33; 9:39 [d] S Ge 32:2
2:9 [e] S Nu 32:26 [f] S Jos 19:24-31 [g] 1Ch 12:29
2:11 [h] 2Sa 5:5
2:12 [i] S Jos 9:3
2:13 [j] 2Sa 8:16; 19:13; 1Ki 1:7; 1Ch 2:16; 11:6; 27:34
2:16 [k] S Jdg 3:21
2:17 [l] 2Sa 3:1 [m] S 1Sa 17:8
2:18 [n] 2Sa 3:39; 16:10; 19:22 [o] 2Sa 3:30; 10:7; 11:1; 14:1; 18:14; 20:8; 24:3; 1Ki 1:7; 2:5,34 [p] S 1Sa 26:6 [q] 2Sa 23:24; 1Ch 2:16; 11:26; 27:7 [r] 1Ch 12:8; Pr 6:5; SS 2:9

War Between the Houses of David and Saul

3:2–5pp — 1Ch 3:1–4

8 Meanwhile, Abner[b] son of Ner, the
commander of Saul’s army, had taken
Ish-Bosheth[c] son of Saul and brought
him over to Mahanaim.[d] 9 He made
him king over Gilead,[e] Ashuri[a][f] and
Jezreel, and also over Ephraim, Benjamin and all Israel.[g]
10 Ish-Bosheth son of Saul was forty
years old when he became king over
Israel, and he reigned two years. The
house of Judah, however, followed David. 11 The length of time David was
king in Hebron over the house of Judah
was seven years and six months.[h]
12 Abner son of Ner, together with
the men of Ish-Bosheth son of Saul,
left Mahanaim and went to Gibeon.[i]
13 Joab[j] son of Zeruiah and David’s
men went out and met them at the pool
of Gibeon. One group sat down on one
side of the pool and one group on the
other side.
14 Then Abner said to Joab, “Let’s
have some of the young men get up and
fight hand to hand in front of us.”
“All right, let them do it,” Joab said.
15 So they stood up and were counted
off—twelve men for Benjamin and Ish-
Bosheth son of Saul, and twelve for David. 16 Then each man grabbed his opponent by the head and thrust his
dagger[k] into his opponent’s side, and
they fell down together. So that place
in Gibeon was called Helkath Hazzurim.[b]
17 The battle that day was very
fierce, and Abner and the men of Israel
were defeated[l] by David’s men.[m]
18 The three sons of Zeruiah[n] were
there: Joab,[o] Abishai[p] and Asahel.[q]
Now Asahel was as fleet-footed as a
wild gazelle.[r] 19 He chased Abner,
turning neither to the right nor to the

[a] *9* Or *Asher* [b] *16 Helkath Hazzurim* means *field of daggers* or *field of hostilities.*

1:26 YOUR LOVE FOR ME. David spoke of Jonathan’s extraordinary friendship in terms of their devotion, commitment and oneness of purpose. Jonathan had accepted the Lord’s choice of David as the next king without jealousy or bitterness (1Sa 20:13–16).

2:4 ANOINTED DAVID KING OVER . . . JUDAH. Chs. 2—4 describe the placing of David as king over Judah and his civil war with Ish-Bosheth, Saul’s son and successor as the king of the remaining tribes of Israel (vv. 8–11). Seven and a half years later David became king over the entire nation (5:1–5). Possibly Ps 18 represents David’s celebration of his complete deliverance from his enemies at this time (cf. 1Sa 30:1–31, which describes another victory immediately preceding Saul’s death and David’s ascension to the throne). David did not rush to take control of the entire nation. He inquired of the Lord (v. 1) and was willing to be king over one tribe until the Lord opened the door for him to be king over all Israel.

left as he pursued him. 20Abner looked
behind him and asked, "Is that you, Asahel?"
"It is," he answered.
21Then Abner said to him, "Turn
aside to the right or to the left; take on
one of the young men and strip him of
his weapons." But Asahel would not
stop chasing him.
22Again Abner warned Asahel,
"Stop chasing me! Why should I strike
you down? How could I look your
brother Joab in the face?"[s]
23But Asahel refused to give up the
pursuit; so Abner thrust the butt of his
spear into Asahel's stomach,[t] and the
spear came out through his back. He
fell there and died on the spot. And every man stopped when he came to the
place where Asahel had fallen and
died.[u]
24But Joab and Abishai pursued Abner, and as the sun was setting, they
came to the hill of Ammah, near Giah
on the way to the wasteland of Gibeon.
25Then the men of Benjamin rallied behind Abner. They formed themselves
into a group and took their stand on
top of a hill.
26Abner called out to Joab, "Must
the sword devour[v] forever? Don't you
realize that this will end in bitterness?
How long before you order your men to
stop pursuing their brothers?"
27Joab answered, "As surely as God
lives, if you had not spoken, the men
would have continued the pursuit of
their brothers until morning.[c]"
28So Joab[w] blew the trumpet,[x] and
all the men came to a halt; they no
longer pursued Israel, nor did they
fight anymore.
29All that night Abner and his men
marched through the Arabah.[y] They
crossed the Jordan, continued through
the whole Bithron[d] and came to Mahanaim.[z]
30Then Joab returned from pursuing
Abner and assembled all his men. Besides Asahel, nineteen of David's men
were found missing. 31But David's
men had killed three hundred and sixty
Benjamites who were with Abner.
32They took Asahel and buried him in
his father's tomb[a] at Bethlehem.
Then Joab and his men marched all
night and arrived at Hebron by daybreak.

3 The war between the house of Saul
and the house of David lasted a
long time.[b] David grew stronger and
stronger,[c] while the house of Saul
grew weaker and weaker.[d]
2Sons were born to David in Hebron:
His firstborn was Amnon[e] the
son of Ahinoam[f] of Jezreel;
3his second, Kileab the son of
Abigail[g] the widow of Nabal of
Carmel;
the third, Absalom[h] the son of
Maacah daughter of Talmai
king of Geshur;[i]
4the fourth, Adonijah[j] the son
of Haggith;
the fifth, Shephatiah the son of
Abital;
5and the sixth, Ithream the son
of David's wife Eglah.
These were born to David in
Hebron.

Abner Goes Over to David

6During the war between the house
of Saul and the house of David, Abner[k] had been strengthening his own
position in the house of Saul. 7Now
Saul had had a concubine[l] named Rizpah[m] daughter of Aiah. And Ish-Bosheth said to Abner, "Why did you
sleep with my father's concubine?"
8Abner was very angry because of
what Ish-Bosheth said and he answered, "Am I a dog's head[n]—on Judah's side? This very day I am loyal to
the house of your father Saul and to his
family and friends. I haven't handed
you over to David. Yet now you accuse
me of an offense involving this woman!
9May God deal with Abner, be it ever
so severely, if I do not do for David
what the LORD promised[o] him on oath
10and transfer the kingdom from the
house of Saul and establish David's
throne over Israel and Judah from Dan
to Beersheba."[p] 11Ish-Bosheth did not
dare to say another word to Abner, because he was afraid of him.
12Then Abner sent messengers on
his behalf to say to David, "Whose land
is it? Make an agreement with me, and
I will help you bring all Israel over to
you."
13"Good," said David. "I will make

2:22 [s] 2Sa 3:27
2:23 [t] 2Sa 3:27; 4:6 [u] 2Sa 20:12
2:26 [v] S Dt 32:42; Jer 46:10,14; Na 2:13; 3:15
2:28 [w] 2Sa 18:16; 20:23 [x] S Jdg 3:27
2:29 [y] S Dt 3:17 [z] S Ge 32:2
2:32 [a] S Ge 49:29
3:1 [b] 1Ki 14:30 [c] 2Sa 5:10 [d] 2Sa 2:17; 22:44; Est 9:4
3:2 [e] 2Sa 13:1 [f] S 1Sa 25:43
3:3 [g] S 1Sa 25:42 [h] 2Sa 13:1,28 [i] 2Sa 13:37; 14:32; 15:8
3:4 [j] 1Ki 1:5,11; 2:13,22
3:6 [k] S 1Sa 14:50
3:7 [l] S Ge 22:24; 2Sa 16:21-22; S 1Ki 1:3 [m] 2Sa 21:8-11
3:8 [n] S 1Sa 17:43; 2Sa 9:8; 16:9; 2Ki 8:13
3:9 [o] S 1Sa 15:28
3:10 [p] S Jdg 20:1; 1Sa 25:28-31; 2Sa 24:2

[c] *27* Or *spoken this morning, the men would not have taken up the pursuit of their brothers*; or *spoken, the men would have given up the pursuit of their brothers by morning* [d] *29* Or *morning*; or *ravine*; the meaning of the Hebrew for this word is uncertain.

an agreement with you. But I demand
one thing of you: Do not come into my
presence unless you bring Michal
daughter of Saul when you come to see
me."[q] **14**Then David sent messengers
to Ish-Bosheth son of Saul, demanding, "Give me my wife Michal,[r] whom
I betrothed to myself for the price of a
hundred Philistine foreskins."
15So Ish-Bosheth gave orders and
had her taken away from her husband[s] Paltiel[t] son of Laish. **16**Her
husband, however, went with her,
weeping behind her all the way to Bahurim.[u] Then Abner said to him, "Go
back home!" So he went back.
17Abner conferred with the elders[v]
of Israel and said, "For some time you
have wanted to make David your king.
18Now do it! For the LORD promised David, 'By my servant David I will rescue
my people Israel from the hand of the
Philistines[w] and from the hand of all
their enemies.[x]' "
19Abner also spoke to the Benjamites in person. Then he went to Hebron to tell David everything that Israel and the whole house of Benjamin[y]
wanted to do. **20**When Abner, who had
twenty men with him, came to David at
Hebron, David prepared a feast[z] for
him and his men. **21**Then Abner said to
David, "Let me go at once and assemble all Israel for my lord the king, so
that they may make a compact[a] with
you, and that you may rule over all that
your heart desires."[b] So David sent
Abner away, and he went in peace.

Joab Murders Abner

22Just then David's men and Joab returned from a raid and brought with
them a great deal of plunder. But Abner was no longer with David in Hebron, because David had sent him
away, and he had gone in peace.
23When Joab and all the soldiers with
him arrived, he was told that Abner son
of Ner had come to the king and that
the king had sent him away and that he
had gone in peace.
24So Joab went to the king and said,
"What have you done? Look, Abner
came to you. Why did you let him go?
Now he is gone! **25**You know Abner son
of Ner; he came to deceive you and observe your movements and find out everything you are doing."
26Joab then left David and sent messengers after Abner, and they brought
him back from the well of Sirah. But
David did not know it. **27**Now when Abner[c] returned to Hebron, Joab took
him aside into the gateway, as though
to speak with him privately. And there,
to avenge the blood of his brother Asahel, Joab stabbed him[d] in the stomach,
and he died.[e]
28Later, when David heard about
this, he said, "I and my kingdom are
forever innocent[f] before the LORD concerning the blood of Abner son of Ner.
29May his blood[g] fall upon the head of
Joab and upon all his father's house![h]
May Joab's house never be without
someone who has a running sore[i] or
leprosy[e] or who leans on a crutch or
who falls by the sword or who lacks
food."
30(Joab and his brother Abishai murdered Abner because he had killed
their brother Asahel in the battle at
Gibeon.)
31Then David said to Joab and all the
people with him, "Tear your clothes
and put on sackcloth[j] and walk in
mourning[k] in front of Abner." King
David himself walked behind the bier.
32They buried Abner in Hebron, and
the king wept[l] aloud at Abner's tomb.
All the people wept also.
33The king sang this lament[m] for
Abner:

"Should Abner have died as the
　lawless die?
34 Your hands were not bound,
　your feet were not fettered.[n]
You fell as one falls before wicked
　men."

And all the people wept over him
again.
35Then they all came and urged David to eat something while it was still
day; but David took an oath, saying,
"May God deal with me, be it ever so
severely,[o] if I taste bread[p] or anything else before the sun sets!"
36All the people took note and were
pleased; indeed, everything the king
did pleased them. **37**So on that day all
the people and all Israel knew that the
king had no part[q] in the murder of Abner son of Ner.
38Then the king said to his men, "Do
you not realize that a prince and a

[e] 29 The Hebrew word was used for various diseases affecting the skin—not necessarily leprosy.

3:13 [q] S Ge 43:5
3:14 [r] S 1Sa 18:27
3:15 [s] Dt 24:1-4 [t] 1Sa 25:44
3:16 [u] 2Sa 16:5; 17:18
3:17 [v] S Jdg 11:11
3:18 [w] S 1Sa 9:16 [x] 2Sa 8:6
3:19 [y] 1Ch 12:2, 16,29
3:20 [z] 1Ch 12:39
3:21 [a] 2Sa 5:3 [b] 1Ki 11:37
3:27 [c] 2Sa 2:8; 4:1; 1Ki 2:5,32 [d] S Ex 21:14; S Jdg 3:21; S 2Sa 2:23 [e] 2Sa 2:22
3:28 [f] ver 37; Dt 21:9
3:29 [g] S Lev 20:9 [h] 1Ki 2:31-33 [i] S Lev 15:2
3:31 [j] Ps 30:11; 35:13; 69:11; Isa 20:2 [k] S Ge 37:34
3:32 [l] S Nu 14:1; Pr 24:17
3:33 [m] S Ge 50:10
3:34 [n] Job 36:8; Ps 2:3; 149:8; Isa 45:14; Na 3:10
3:35 [o] S Ru 1:17 [p] S 1Sa 31:13; 2Sa 12:17; Jer 16:7
3:37 [q] S ver 28

great man has fallen[r] in Israel this
day? 39And today, though I am the
anointed king, I am weak, and these
sons of Zeruiah[s] are too strong[t] for
me.[u] May the LORD repay[v] the evildoer according to his evil deeds!"

Ish-Bosheth Murdered

4 When Ish-Bosheth son of Saul
heard that Abner[w] had died in Hebron, he lost courage, and all Israel became alarmed. 2Now Saul's son had
two men who were leaders of raiding
bands. One was named Baanah and the
other Recab; they were sons of Rimmon the Beerothite from the tribe of
Benjamin—Beeroth[x] is considered
part of Benjamin, 3because the people
of Beeroth fled to Gittaim[y] and have
lived there as aliens to this day.

4(Jonathan[z] son of Saul had a son
who was lame in both feet. He was five
years old when the news[a] about Saul
and Jonathan came from Jezreel. His
nurse picked him up and fled, but as
she hurried to leave, he fell and became crippled.[b] His name was Mephibosheth.)[c]

5Now Recab and Baanah, the sons of
Rimmon the Beerothite, set out for the
house of Ish-Bosheth,[d] and they arrived there in the heat of the day while
he was taking his noonday rest.[e]
6They went into the inner part of the
house as if to get some wheat, and they
stabbed[f] him in the stomach. Then
Recab and his brother Baanah slipped
away.

7They had gone into the house while
he was lying on the bed in his bedroom.
After they stabbed and killed him, they
cut off his head. Taking it with them,
they traveled all night by way of the
Arabah.[g] 8They brought the head[h] of
Ish-Bosheth to David at Hebron and
said to the king, "Here is the head of
Ish-Bosheth son of Saul,[i] your enemy, who tried to take your life. This
day the LORD has avenged[j] my lord the
king against Saul and his offspring."

9David answered Recab and his
brother Baanah, the sons of Rimmon

3:38 [r] 2Sa 1:19
3:39 [s] S 2Sa 2:18 [t] 2Sa 16:9; 18:11 [u] S Jdg 18:26 [v] 1Ki 2:32; Ps 41:10; 101:8
4:1 [w] S 2Sa 3:27
4:2 [x] S Jos 9:17
4:3 [y] Ne 11:33
4:4 [z] S 1Sa 18:1 [a] S 1Sa 31:9 [b] S Lev 21:18 [c] 2Sa 9:8,12; 16:1-4; 19:24; 21:7-8; 1Ch 8:34; 9:40
4:5 [d] S 2Sa 2:8 [e] Ru 2:7
4:6 [f] S 2Sa 2:23
4:7 [g] S Dt 3:17
4:8 [h] 2Sa 20:21; 2Ki 10:7 [i] 1Sa 24:4; 25:29 [j] S Nu 31:3
4:9 [k] S Ge 48:16; 1Ki 1:29
4:10 [l] 2Sa 1:2-16
4:11 [m] S Ge 4:10; 9:5; Ps 9:12; 72:14
4:12 [n] 2Sa 1:15
5:1 [o] 2Sa 19:43 [p] S Ge 29:14; 35:26
5:2 [q] 1Sa 18:5,13, 16 [r] S 1Sa 11:6 [s] S Ge 48:15; S 1Sa 16:1; 2Sa 7:7; Mt 2:6; Jn 21:16 [t] S 1Sa 12:12; S 13:14; S 2Sa 6:21
5:3 [u] 2Sa 3:21 [v] S Dt 17:15; 2Sa 2:4
5:4 [w] S Ge 37:2; Lk 3:23 [x] 1Ki 2:11; 1Ch 3:4 [y] 1Ch 26:31
5:5 [z] 2Sa 2:11; 1Ki 2:11; 1Ch 3:4
5:6 [a] S Jdg 1:8 [b] S Jos 15:8

the Beerothite, "As surely as the LORD
lives, who has delivered[k] me out of all
trouble, 10when a man told me, 'Saul is
dead,' and thought he was bringing
good news, I seized him and put him to
death in Ziklag.[l] That was the reward
I gave him for his news! 11How much
more—when wicked men have killed
an innocent man in his own house and
on his own bed—should I not now demand his blood[m] from your hand and
rid the earth of you!"

12So David gave an order to his men,
and they killed them.[n] They cut off
their hands and feet and hung the bodies by the pool in Hebron. But they took
the head of Ish-Bosheth and buried it
in Abner's tomb at Hebron.

David Becomes King Over Israel

5:1–3pp — 1Ch 11:1–3

5 All the tribes of Israel[o] came to
David at Hebron and said, "We are
your own flesh and blood.[p] 2In the
past, while Saul was king over us, you
were the one who led Israel on their
military campaigns.[q] And the LORD
said[r] to you, 'You will shepherd[s] my
people Israel, and you will become
their ruler.[t]' "

3When all the elders of Israel had
come to King David at Hebron, the king
made a compact[u] with them at Hebron
before the LORD, and they anointed[v]
David king over Israel.

4David was thirty years old[w] when
he became king, and he reigned[x] forty[y] years. 5In Hebron he reigned over
Judah seven years and six months,[z]
and in Jerusalem he reigned over all
Israel and Judah thirty-three years.

David Conquers Jerusalem

5:6–10pp — 1Ch 11:4–9
5:11–16pp — 1Ch 3:5–9; 14:1–7

6The king and his men marched to
Jerusalem[a] to attack the Jebusites,[b]
who lived there. The Jebusites said to
David, "You will not get in here; even
the blind and the lame can ward you
off." They thought, "David cannot get

4:12 THEY KILLED THEM. David's ascent to the throne was a bloody one, involving civil war between the tribes and much political maneuvering—all of which illustrates why God's perfect will for Israel was not a human king (1Sa 8:5–7,19–22).

5:6 JERUSALEM. David captured Jerusalem and made it the capital of Israel. Spiritually, it eventually became the most important city on earth, the center of God's redemptive action for the human race. It was in Jerusalem that Christ was crucified and rose from the dead, and the Holy Spirit was poured out upon the assembled followers of Jesus. The Bible calls it the city of God (Ps 46:4; 48:1; 87:3; Heb 12:22; Rev 3:12; see article on THE CITY OF JERUSALEM, p. 576).

in here." 7Nevertheless, David captured the fortress of Zion,[c] the City of
David.[d e]
8On that day, David said, "Anyone
who conquers the Jebusites will have
to use the water shaft[f f] to reach
those 'lame and blind'[g] who are David's enemies.[g]" That is why they say,
"The 'blind and lame' will not enter the
palace."
9David then took up residence in the
fortress and called it the City of David.
He built up the area around it, from the
supporting terraces[h h] inward. 10And
he became more and more powerful,[i]
because the LORD God Almighty[j] was
with him.[k]
11Now Hiram[l] king of Tyre sent
messengers to David, along with cedar
logs and carpenters and stonemasons,
and they built a palace for David.
12And David knew that the LORD had
established him as king over Israel and
had exalted his kingdom[m] for the sake
of his people Israel.
13After he left Hebron, David took
more concubines and wives[n] in Jerusalem, and more sons and daughters
were born to him. 14These are the
names of the children born to him
there:[o] Shammua, Shobab, Nathan,[p]
Solomon, 15Ibhar, Elishua, Nepheg,
Japhia, 16Elishama, Eliada and
Eliphelet.

David Defeats the Philistines

5:17–25pp — 1Ch 14:8–17

17When the Philistines heard that
David had been anointed king over Israel, they went up in full force to
search for him, but David heard about
it and went down to the stronghold.[q]
18Now the Philistines had come and
spread out in the Valley of Rephaim;[r]
19so David inquired[s] of the LORD,
"Shall I go and attack the Philistines?
Will you hand them over to me?"
The LORD answered him, "Go, for I
will surely hand the Philistines over to
you."
20So David went to Baal Perazim,
and there he defeated them. He said,
"As waters break out, the LORD has broken out against my enemies before
me." So that place was called Baal Perazim.[i t] 21The Philistines abandoned
their idols there, and David and his
men carried them off.[u]
22Once more the Philistines came up
and spread out in the Valley of Rephaim; 23so David inquired of the LORD,
and he answered, "Do not go straight
up, but circle around behind them and
attack them in front of the balsam
trees. 24As soon as you hear the
sound[v] of marching in the tops of the
balsam trees, move quickly, because
that will mean the LORD has gone out
in front[w] of you to strike the Philistine
army." 25So David did as the LORD commanded him, and he struck down the
Philistines[x] all the way from Gibeon[j y] to Gezer.[z]

The Ark Brought to Jerusalem

6:1–11pp — 1Ch 13:1–14
6:12–19pp — 1Ch 15:25–16:3

6 David again brought together out
of Israel chosen men, thirty thousand in all. 2He and all his men set out
from Baalah[a] of Judah[k] to bring up
from there the ark[b] of God, which is
called by the Name,[l c] the name of
the LORD Almighty, who is enthroned[d]
between the cherubim[e] that are on the
ark. 3They set the ark of God on a new
cart[f] and brought it from the house of
Abinadab, which was on the hill.[g] Uz-

5:7 [c]Ps 76:2 [d]Jer 21:13 [e]2Sa 6:12,16; 1Ki 2:10; 8:1; Isa 29:1; Jer 25:29
5:8 [f]2Ki 20:20; 2Ch 32:30 [g]Mt 21:14
5:9 [h]1Ki 9:15,24
5:10 [i]2Sa 3:1 [j]Ps 24:10 [k]2Sa 7:9
5:11 [l]1Ki 5:1,18; 2Ch 2:3
5:12 [m]S Nu 24:7
5:13 [n]S Dt 17:17
5:14 [o]1Ch 3:5 [p]Lk 3:31
5:17 [q]2Sa 23:14; 1Ch 11:16
5:18 [r]S Jos 15:8; S 17:15
5:19 [s]S Jdg 18:5; S 1Sa 23:2
5:20 [t]S Ge 38:29
5:21 [u]Dt 7:5; Isa 46:2
5:24 [v]S Ex 14:24 [w]Jdg 4:14
5:25 [x]2Sa 8:12; 21:15 [y]Isa 28:21 [z]S Jos 10:33
6:2 [a]S Jos 15:9 [b]1Sa 4:4; 7:1 [c]Lev 24:16; Dt 28:10; Isa 63:14 [d]Ps 99:1; 132:14 [e]S Ge 3:24; S Ex 25:22
6:3 [f]ver 7; Nu 7:4-9; S 1Sa 6:7 [g]2Sa 7:1

[f]8 Or *use scaling hooks* [g]8 Or *are hated by David* [h]9 Or *the Millo* [i]20 *Baal Perazim* means *the lord who breaks out.* [j]25 Septuagint (see also 1 Chron. 14:16); Hebrew *Geba* [k]2 That is, Kiriath Jearim; Hebrew *Baale Judah*, a variant of *Baalah of Judah* [l]2 Hebrew; Septuagint and Vulgate do not have *the Name.*

5:13 DAVID TOOK MORE CONCUBINES AND WIVES. This verse reveals David's most serious character weakness—his strong desire for women (cf. 3:1–5; 5:13). (1) David's failure to resist and subdue his sensual desires led him to violate God's command in Dt 17:15–17 (which forbade Israel's kings to take many wives), to act cruelly toward Michal and her husband (3:14–16), to commit adultery with Bathsheba (11:1–5) and to have her husband Uriah murdered (11:6–27). (2) David's lust for women was the source of great sin, sorrow and suffering for his family (12:9–14; chs. 13—18). After David's sin with Bathsheba, God sent judgment and calamity upon David for the rest of his life (12:10).

5:19 DAVID INQUIRED OF THE LORD. One of David's greatest strengths was his conviction that God's help and direction were absolutely essential for success in battle; thus he made it a regular practice to inquire of the Lord. So too, fulfilling God's purpose for our lives will depend on our seeking God's guidance through prayer and on our being led by the Holy Spirit who lives within us (cf. Ro 8:1–17).

zah and Ahio, sons of Abinadab, were
guiding the new cart **4**with the ark of
God on it,[m] and Ahio was walking in
front of it. **5**David and the whole house
of Israel were celebrating[h] with all
their might before the LORD, with
songs[n] and with harps, lyres, tambourines, sistrums and cymbals.[i]
6When they came to the threshing
floor of Nacon, Uzzah reached out and
took hold of[j] the ark of God, because
the oxen stumbled. **7**The LORD's anger
burned against Uzzah because of his irreverent act;[k] therefore God struck
him down[l] and he died there beside
the ark of God.
8Then David was angry because the
LORD's wrath[m] had broken out against
Uzzah, and to this day that place is
called Perez Uzzah.[o][n]
9David was afraid of the LORD that
day and said, "How[o] can the ark of the
LORD ever come to me?" **10**He was not
willing to take the ark of the LORD to be
with him in the City of David. Instead,
he took it aside to the house of Obed-
Edom[p] the Gittite. **11**The ark of the
LORD remained in the house of Obed-
Edom the Gittite for three months, and
the LORD blessed him and his entire
household.[q]
12Now King David[r] was told, "The
LORD has blessed the household of
Obed-Edom and everything he has, because of the ark of God." So David went
down and brought up the ark of God
from the house of Obed-Edom to the
City of David with rejoicing. **13**When
those who were carrying the ark of the
LORD had taken six steps, he sacrificed[s] a bull and a fattened calf. **14**David, wearing a linen ephod,[t] danced[u]
before the LORD with all his might,
15while he and the entire house of Israel brought up the ark of the LORD with
shouts[v] and the sound of trumpets.[w]
16As the ark of the LORD was entering the City of David,[x] Michal[y]
daughter of Saul watched from a window. And when she saw King David
leaping and dancing before the LORD,
she despised him in her heart.
17They brought the ark of the LORD
and set it in its place inside the tent
that David had pitched for it,[z] and David sacrificed burnt offerings[a] and fellowship offerings[p] before the LORD.
18After he had finished sacrificing[b]
the burnt offerings and fellowship offerings, he blessed[c] the people in the
name of the LORD Almighty. **19**Then he
gave a loaf of bread, a cake of dates
and a cake of raisins[d] to each person
in the whole crowd of Israelites, both
men and women.[e] And all the people
went to their homes.
20When David returned home to
bless his household, Michal daughter
of Saul came out to meet him and said,
"How the king of Israel has distinguished himself today, disrobing[f] in
the sight of the slave girls of his servants as any vulgar fellow would!"
21David said to Michal, "It was before the LORD, who chose me rather

6:5 [h] S Ex 15:20 [i] Ezr 3:10; Ne 12:27; Ps 150:5 **6:6** [j] S Nu 4:15, 19-20 **6:7** [k] 1Ch 15:13-15 [l] S Ex 19:22; S 1Sa 5:6; 6:19; S 25:38 **6:8** [m] Ps 7:11 [n] S Ge 38:29 **6:9** [o] S 1Sa 6:20 **6:10** [p] 1Ch 15:18; 26:4-5 **6:11** [q] S Ge 30:27; 39:5 **6:12** [r] 1Ki 8:1 **6:13** [s] 1Ki 8:5,62; Ezr 6:17 **6:14** [t] Ex 19:6; S 1Sa 2:18 [u] S Ex 15:20

6:15 [v] S Jos 6:5 [w] Ps 47:5; 98:6 **6:16** [x] S 2Sa 5:7 [y] S 1Sa 18:27 **6:17** [z] 1Ki 8:6; 1Ch 15:1; 2Ch 1:4 [a] Lev 1:1-17; 1Ki 8:62-64 **6:18** [b] 1Ki 8:22 [c] S Ex 39:43 **6:19** [d] Hos 3:1 [e] Dt 26:13; Ne 8:10 **6:20** [f] S 1Sa 19:24

[m] *3,4* Dead Sea Scrolls and some Septuagint manuscripts; Masoretic Text *cart* [4]*and they brought it with the ark of God from the house of Abinadab, which was on the hill* [n] *5* See Dead Sea Scrolls, Septuagint and 1 Chronicles 13:8; Masoretic Text *celebrating before the LORD with all kinds of instruments made of pine.* [o] *8* *Perez Uzzah* means *outbreak against Uzzah.* [p] *17* Traditionally *peace offerings*; also in verse 18

6:7 THE LORD'S ANGER. God struck down Uzzah because David and the high priest had not assigned the Levites to handle the ark in accordance with God's command (Nu 1:47–52). (1) God had ordered that no one was to touch the ark, the symbol of his presence and majesty (Nu 4:15; cf. 1Ch 15:13–15). Uzzah's action grew out of his ignorance of God's word or his lack of the fear of the Lord (cf. 1Ch 15:2).

(2) Uzzah is an example of the inherent dangers in having a zeal for God without knowledge of God's word and ways. David's plan to bring back the ark to Jerusalem, and Uzzah's desire to steady it when it teetered on the cart, demonstrated a zeal for God's kingdom, yet at the same time led to a careless attitude toward the standards of God's sacred word. Ignorance is no excuse. God's inspired revelation expresses his will regarding all of life and must be followed by those who claim him as their Lord (cf. Lev 10:1–3; Jos 7; Ac 5:1–11).

6:12 ARK . . . TO THE CITY OF DAVID. David brought the ark to Jerusalem (cf. 5:6–7) and transformed that city into the worship center and capital of Israel. This time he followed the Lord's instructions and had Levites carry the ark (1Ch 15:12). Two of David's greatest achievements as king centered around "the City of David": (1) his formation of Israel into a strong unified nation with its capital being the well-fortified city of Jerusalem, and (2) the establishment in that central location of the worship of the Lord as Israel's greatest priority (cf. 7:1–29; 1Ch 15:1 – 17:27).

6:20 DISROBING. Michal felt that David had behaved in a manner unbecoming to the king of Israel (cf. v. 16). "Disrobing" means that David had laid aside his royal clothing and appeared in a simple tunic such as slaves wore.

than your father or anyone from his house when he appointed[g] me ruler[h] over the LORD's people Israel—I will
celebrate before the LORD. 22I will be-
come even more undignified than this, and I will be humiliated in my own eyes. But by these slave girls you spoke of, I will be held in honor."
23And Michal daughter of Saul had no children to the day of her death.

God's Promise to David

7:1–17pp — 1Ch 17:1–15

7 After the king was settled in his palace[i] and the LORD had given him rest from all his enemies[j] around
him,[k] 2he said to Nathan[l] the proph-
et, "Here I am, living in a palace[m] of cedar, while the ark of God remains in a tent."[n]
3Nathan replied to the king, "What-
ever you have in mind,[o] go ahead and do it, for the LORD is with you."
4That night the word of the LORD came to Nathan, saying:

5"Go and tell my servant David, 'This is what the LORD says: Are you[p] the one to build me a house
to dwell in?[q] 6I have not dwelt in a house from the day I brought the Israelites up out of Egypt to this day.[r] I have been moving from place to place with a tent[s] as my
dwelling.[t] 7Wherever I have moved with all the Israelites,[u] did I ever say to any of their rulers whom I commanded to shep-herd[v] my people Israel, "Why have you not built me a house[w] of cedar?[x]" '
8"Now then, tell my servant Da-vid, 'This is what the LORD Al-mighty says: I took you from the pasture and from following the flock[y] to be ruler[z] over my peo-
ple Israel.[a] 9I have been with you wherever you have gone,[b] and I have cut off all your enemies from before you.[c] Now I will make your name great, like the names of the greatest men of the earth.[d]
10And I will provide a place for my people Israel and will plant[e] them so that they can have a home of their own and no longer be disturbed.[f] Wicked[g] people will not oppress them anymore,[h]
as they did at the beginning 11and have done ever since the time I appointed leaders[q][i] over my people Israel. I will also give you rest from all your enemies.[j]
" 'The LORD declares[k] to you that the LORD himself will establish[l] a house[m] for you: 12When
your days are over and you rest[n] with your fathers, I will raise up your offspring to succeed you, who will come from your own body,[o] and I will establish his
kingdom.[p] 13He is the one who will build a house[q] for my Name,[r] and I will establish the throne of his kingdom forever.[s]
14I will be his father, and he will be my son.[t] When he does wrong, I will punish him[u] with the rod[v] of men, with floggings
inflicted by men. 15But my love will never be taken away from him,[w] as I took it away from Saul,[x] whom I removed from before you. 16Your house and your kingdom will endure forever be-fore me[r]; your throne[y] will be established[z] forever.[a]' "
17Nathan reported to David all the words of this entire revelation.

David's Prayer

7:18–29pp — 1Ch 17:16–27

18Then King David went in and sat before the LORD, and he said:

6:21 [g] 1Sa 13:14; S 15:28 [h] 2Sa 5:2; 7:8; 1Ch 5:2; 17:7; Mic 5:2 **7:1** [i] 2Sa 6:3 [j] ver 11 [k] 1Ch 22:18 **7:2** [l] 2Sa 12:1; 1Ki 1:8,22; 1Ch 29:29; 2Ch 9:29 [m] 2Sa 5:11; 1Ki 3:1; 7:1,2,7; 9:1; 2Ch 8:1; Jer 22:14; Hag 1:4 [n] S Ex 26:1; Ps 132:3; Ac 7:45-46 **7:3** [o] S 1Sa 10:7; Ps 132:1-5 **7:5** [p] 1Ki 8:19; 1Ch 22:8 [q] 1Ki 5:3-5; 1Ch 28:3 **7:6** [r] Ac 7:45 [s] Ex 40:18,34; Jos 18:1 [t] 1Ki 8:16 **7:7** [u] Dt 23:14 [v] S 2Sa 5:2 [w] 1Ki 8:27; Isa 66:1 [x] Lev 26:11-12 **7:8** [y] S 1Sa 16:11; 1Ch 21:17; Ps 74:1; Am 7:15 [z] S 1Sa 2:7-8; S 9:16; S 16:1; S 2Sa 6:21 [a] Ps 78:70-72; 2Co 6:18* **7:9** [b] S 1Sa 18:14; 2Sa 5:10 [c] Ps 18:37-42 [d] S Ex 11:3 **7:10** [e] S Ex 15:17; Isa 5:1-7 [f] 2Ki 21:8; 2Ch 33:8 [g] Ps 89:22-23 [h] Ps 147:14; Isa 54:14; 60:18 **7:11** [i] S Jdg 2:16; 1Sa 12:9-11 [j] ver 1 [k] 1Ki 2:24 [l] 1Sa 25:28; Ps 89:35-37; S Mt 1:1; Lk 1:32-33; Ac 13:22-23; 2Ti 2:8 [m] S Ex 1:21; Isa 7:2 **7:12** [n] S Ge 15:15; 1Ki 2:1; Ac 13:36 [o] 1Ki 8:20; Ps 132:11-12; Jer 30:21; 33:15 [p] 2Ch 23:3 **7:13** [q] S Dt 12:5; 1Ki 6:12 [r] Dt 16:11; 1Ki 5:5; 8:19,29; 2Ki 21:4,7 [s] ver 16; S Ge 9:16; 2Sa 22:51; 1Ki 2:4,45; 1Ch 22:10; 28:6; 2Ch 6:16; 7:18; 13:5; 21:7; Ps 89:3-4,29,35-37; Pr 25:5; Isa 9:7; 16:5; Jer 17:25; 33:17,21; Da 7:27 **7:14** [t] Ps 2:7; 89:26; Jer 3:19; S Mt 3:17; Jn 1:49; 2Co 6:18*; Heb 1:5*; Rev 21:7 [u] S Dt 8:5; 1Ki 11:34; 1Ch 22:10; Heb 12:7 [v] Ps 89:30-33; Pr 13:24 **7:15** [w] ver 25; 1Ki 2:4; 6:12; 8:25; 9:5; 11:13,32; 2Ki 19:34; 2Ch 6:16; 7:18; 21:7; Ps 89:24,33; Jer 33:17 [x] S 1Sa 13:13; S 15:28; 16:14 **7:16** [y] Ps 89:36-37; S Lk 1:33 [z] Ps 9:7; 93:2; 103:19 [a] S ver 13

[q] *11* Traditionally *judges* [r] *16* Some Hebrew manuscripts and Septuagint; most Hebrew manuscripts *you*

7:12 I WILL ESTABLISH HIS KINGDOM. Using the voice of the prophet Nathan, God established his covenant with David (see article on GOD'S COVENANT WITH DAVID, p. 432).

7:16 YOUR KINGDOM WILL ENDURE FOREVER. God's covenant with David was fulfilled ultimately in Jesus Christ (see article on GOD'S COVENANT WITH DAVID, p. 432).

7:18 WHO AM I . . . THAT YOU HAVE BROUGHT ME THIS FAR? The Lord did not give David his covenant promise because of David's merit, righteousness or good deeds; rather, it was established out of his mercy and grace—for the sake of his word (v. 21), the glory of his name (v.

GOD'S COVENANT WITH DAVID

2Sa 7:16 "Your house and your kingdom will endure forever before me; your throne will be established forever."

THE NATURE OF THE COVENANT WITH DAVID. (1) Though the word "covenant" does not actually occur in 2Sa 7, it is clear that God was establishing a covenant with David. In Ps 89:3–4, for example, God says: "I have made a covenant with my chosen one, I have sworn to David my servant, 'I will establish your line forever and make your throne firm through all generations' " (see also Ps 89:34–36). This promise that the throne of God's people would be established forever by David's seed is precisely the promise that God made with David in 2Sa 7 (note especially v. 16). Furthermore, later in 2 Samuel, David himself makes a reference to the "everlasting covenant" that God made with him (2Sa 23:5), undoubtedly referring back to 2Sa 7.

(2) The same two principles at work in other covenants in the OT are also evident here: God alone established the promises and obligation of his covenant, and human beings were expected to accept them in obedient faith (see articles on GOD'S COVENANT WITH ABRAHAM, ISAAC AND JACOB, p. 46, and GOD'S COVENANT WITH THE ISRAELITES, p. 290). (a) In this covenant arrangement with David, God made an immediate promise to establish the kingdom of David's son, Solomon, who would build a house for the Lord, i.e., the temple (2Sa 7:11–13). (b) At the same time, God's promise that David's house or dynasty would endure forever over the Israelites was conditioned on the faithful obedience of David and his descendants. In other words, this covenant was everlasting only in the sense that God intended to keep always a son of David on the throne in Jerusalem, provided the rulers of Judah remained faithful and obedient to him.

(3) For the next four centuries, the line of David remained unbroken on Judah's throne. But when the kings of Judah, particularly Manasseh and those who reigned after King Josiah, continually rebelled against God by worshiping idols and disobeying his law, God finally did remove them from occupying the throne. He allowed King Nebuchadnezzar of Babylon to invade the land of Judah, lay siege to the city of Jerusalem and eventually destroy the city along with its temple (see 2Ki 25; 2Ch 36). God's people were now, for the first time since their slavery in Egypt, under the control of foreign rulers.

JESUS CHRIST AND THIS COVENANT. There was one aspect to God's covenant with David, however, that was unconditional—that the kingdom of David would *ultimately* be established forever. (1) The apex of God's promise was that from the Davidic family line would come a descendant who would be the Messianic and eternal King. This King would be ruler over the faithful of Israel and of all the nations (cf. Isa 9:6–7; 11:1,10; Mic 5:2,4). He would come out of the city of Bethlehem (Mic 5:2,4), and his rule would extend to the ends of the earth (Zec 9:10). He would be called "The LORD Our Righteousness" (Jer 23:5–6) and would bring salvation from sin (Zec 13:1). The fulfillment of the Davidic promise began with the birth of Jesus Christ, announced by the angel Gabriel to Mary, a devout daughter from David's family (Lk 1:30–33; cf. Ac 2:29–35).

(2) This promise was an extension of the covenant given in Ge 3:15, which predicted Satan's defeat through Eve's offspring (see Ge 3:15, note); it was a continuation of the covenant given to Abraham and his descendants (see article on GOD'S COVENANT WITH ABRAHAM, ISAAC AND JACOB, p. 46).

(3) The fulfillment of this promise involved Christ's resurrection from the dead and his exaltation to the right hand of God in heaven (Ac 2:29–33), from where he now rules as King of kings and Lord of lords. Christ's first task as exalted Lord was the outpouring of the Holy Spirit upon his people (Ac 1:8; 2:4,33).

(4) Christ's kingly rule is characterized by a call to all people to turn from sin and the perverse world, to accept Christ as Lord and Savior, and to receive the Holy Spirit (Ac 2:32–40).

(5) Christ's eternal kingship includes (a) his present rulership over God's kingdom and his headship over the church, (b) his future millennial rule over the nations (Rev 2:26–27; 20:4), and (c) his everlasting kingdom in the new heaven and the new earth (Rev 21—22).

"Who am I,[b] O Sovereign LORD, and what is my family, that you have brought me this far? 19And as if this were not enough in your sight, O Sovereign LORD, you have also spoken about the future of the house of your servant. Is this your usual way of dealing with man,[c] O Sovereign LORD?

20"What more can David say[d] to you? For you know[e] your servant,[f] O Sovereign LORD. 21For the sake of your word and according to your will, you have done this great thing and made it known to your servant.

22"How great[g] you are,[h] O Sovereign LORD! There is no one like[i] you, and there is no God[j] but you, as we have heard with our own ears.[k] 23And who is like your people Israel[l]—the one nation on earth that God went out to redeem as a people for himself, and to make a name[m] for himself, and to perform great and awesome wonders[n] by driving out nations and their gods from before your people, whom you redeemed[o] from Egypt?[s] 24You have established your people Israel as your very own[p] forever, and you, O LORD, have become their God.[q]

25"And now, LORD God, keep forever the promise[r] you have made concerning your servant and his house. Do as you promised, 26so that your name[s] will be great forever. Then men will say, 'The LORD Almighty is God over Israel!' And the house of your servant David will be established[t] before you.

27"O LORD Almighty, God of Israel, you have revealed this to your servant, saying, 'I will build a house for you.' So your servant has found courage to offer you this prayer. 28O Sovereign LORD, you are God! Your words are trustworthy,[u] and you have promised these good things to your servant. 29Now be pleased to bless the house of your servant, that it may continue forever in your sight; for you, O Sovereign LORD, have spoken, and with your blessing[v] the house of your servant will be blessed forever."

David's Victories

8:1-14pp — 1Ch 18:1-13

8 In the course of time, David defeated the Philistines[w] and subdued[x] them, and he took Metheg Ammah from the control of the Philistines.

2David also defeated the Moabites.[y] He made them lie down on the ground and measured them off with a length of cord. Every two lengths of them were put to death, and the third length was allowed to live. So the Moabites became subject to David and brought tribute.[z]

3Moreover, David fought Hadadezer[a] son of Rehob, king of Zobah,[b] when he went to restore his control along the Euphrates[c] River. 4David captured a thousand of his chariots, seven thousand charioteers[t] and twenty thousand foot soldiers. He hamstrung[d] all but a hundred of the chariot horses.

5When the Arameans of Damascus[e] came to help Hadadezer king of Zobah, David struck down twenty-two thousand of them. 6He put garrisons[f] in the Aramean kingdom of Damascus, and the Arameans became subject[g] to him and brought tribute. The LORD gave David victory wherever he went.[h]

7David took the gold shields[i] that belonged to the officers of Hadadezer and brought them to Jerusalem. 8From Tebah[u] and Berothai,[j] towns that belonged to Hadadezer, King David took a great quantity of bronze.

9When Tou[v] king of Hamath[k] heard that David had defeated the entire army of Hadadezer,[l] 10he sent his son Joram[w] to King David to greet him and congratulate him on his victory in battle over Hadadezer, who had been at war with Tou. Joram brought with

7:18 [b]S Ex 3:11
7:19 [c]Isa 55:8-9
7:20 [d]Isa 38:15 [e]Jn 21:17 [f]S 1Sa 16:7
7:22 [g]Ps 48:1; 77:13; 86:10; Jer 10:6 [h]Dt 3:24 [i]S Ex 9:14 [j]S Ex 8:10; S 20:4 [k]Ex 10:2; S Jdg 6:13; Ps 44:1
7:23 [l]Dt 4:32-38; S 33:29; S 1Sa 12:22 [m]S Nu 6:27 [n]Dt 10:21 [o]Dt 7:7-8; S 9:26
7:24 [p]Dt 26:18 [q]Ex 6:6-7; Ps 48:14
7:25 [r]S ver 15; S Nu 23:19; 2Ch 1:9
7:26 [s]S Ex 6:3; Ne 9:5; Ps 72:19; 96:8; Mt 6:9 [t]S 1Sa 25:28
7:28 [u]Ex 34:6; Jn 17:17
7:29 [v]Nu 6:23-27
8:1 [w]Ps 60:8; 87:4; 108:9 [x]Heb 11:32-33
8:2 [y]S Ge 19:37; S Nu 21:29 [z]S Jdg 3:15; S Isa 45:14
8:3 [a]2Sa 10:16, 19; 1Ki 11:23 [b]S 1Sa 14:47 [c]S Ge 2:14
8:4 [d]S Ge 49:6; Jos 11:9
8:5 [e]S Ge 14:15; 2Sa 10:6; 1Ki 11:24; 2Ki 8:7; 14:28
8:6 [f]1Ki 20:34 [g]2Sa 10:19 [h]2Sa 3:18
8:7 [i]1Ki 10:16; 14:26; 2Ki 11:10
8:8 [j]Eze 47:16
8:9 [k]1Ki 8:65; 2Ki 14:28; 2Ch 8:4 [l]Lk 14:31-32

[s] *23* See Septuagint and 1 Chron. 17:21; Hebrew *wonders for your land and before your people, whom you redeemed from Egypt, from the nations and their gods.* [t] *4* Septuagint (see also Dead Sea Scrolls and 1 Chron. 18:4); Masoretic Text *captured seventeen hundred of his charioteers* [u] *8* See some Septuagint manuscripts (see also 1 Chron. 18:8); Hebrew *Betah.* [v] *9* Hebrew *Toi,* a variant of *Tou;* also in verse 10 [w] *10* A variant of *Hadoram*

26), the destiny of his people Israel (5:12) and ultimately the salvation of all nations (Isa 11:1,10). David accepted God's promise in humility and faith.

him articles of silver and gold and
bronze.
11King David dedicated[m] these articles to the LORD, as he had done with
the silver and gold from all the nations
he had subdued: **12**Edom[x][n] and
Moab,[o] the Ammonites[p] and the Philistines,[q] and Amalek.[r] He also dedicated the plunder taken from Hadadezer son of Rehob, king of Zobah.
13And David became famous[s] after
he returned from striking down eighteen thousand Edomites[y] in the Valley of Salt.[t]
14He put garrisons throughout
Edom, and all the Edomites[u] became
subject to David.[v] The LORD gave David victory[w] wherever he went.[x]

David's Officials

8:15–18pp — 1Ch 18:14–17

15David reigned over all Israel, doing what was just and right[y] for all his
people. **16**Joab[z] son of Zeruiah was
over the army; Jehoshaphat[a] son of
Ahilud was recorder;[b] **17**Zadok[c] son
of Ahitub and Ahimelech son of Abiathar[d] were priests; Seraiah was secretary;[e] **18**Benaiah[f] son of Jehoiada
was over the Kerethites[g] and Pelethites; and David's sons were royal advisers.[z]

David and Mephibosheth

9 David asked, "Is there anyone still
left of the house of Saul to whom
I can show kindness for Jonathan's
sake?"[h]
2Now there was a servant of Saul's
household named Ziba.[i] They called
him to appear before David, and the
king said to him, "Are you Ziba?"
"Your servant," he replied.
3The king asked, "Is there no one
still left of the house of Saul to whom
I can show God's kindness?"
Ziba answered the king, "There is
still a son of Jonathan;[j] he is crippled[k] in both feet."
4"Where is he?" the king asked.
Ziba answered, "He is at the house
of Makir[l] son of Ammiel in Lo Debar."
5So King David had him brought
from Lo Debar, from the house of Makir son of Ammiel.
6When Mephibosheth son of Jonathan, the son of Saul, came to David,
he bowed down to pay him honor.[m]
David said, "Mephibosheth!"
"Your servant," he replied.
7"Don't be afraid," David said to
him, "for I will surely show you kindness for the sake of your father Jonathan.[n] I will restore to you all the land
that belonged to your grandfather
Saul, and you will always eat at my table.[o]" Ps 1:3
8Mephibosheth[p] bowed down and
said, "What is your servant, that you
should notice a dead dog[q] like me?"
9Then the king summoned Ziba,
Saul's servant, and said to him, "I have
given your master's grandson everything that belonged to Saul and his
family. **10**You and your sons and your
servants are to farm the land for him
and bring in the crops, so that your
master's grandson[r] may be provided
for. And Mephibosheth, grandson of
your master, will always eat at my table." (Now Ziba had fifteen sons and
twenty servants.)
11Then Ziba said to the king, "Your
servant will do whatever my lord the
king commands his servant to do." So
Mephibosheth ate at David's[a] table
like one of the king's sons.[s]
12Mephibosheth had a young son
named Mica, and all the members of
Ziba's household were servants of Mephibosheth.[t] **13**And Mephibosheth
lived in Jerusalem, because he always
ate at the king's table, and he was crippled in both feet.

8:11 [m]ver 12; 1Ki 7:51; 15:15; 1Ch 26:26; 2Ch 5:1
8:12 [n]S Nu 24:18 [o]ver 2 [p]2Sa 10:14 [q]S 2Sa 5:25 [r]S Nu 24:20; S 1Sa 27:8
8:13 [s]2Sa 7:9 [t]2Ki 14:7; 1Ch 18:12; Ps 60 Title
8:14 [u]Nu 24:17-18; Ps 108:9; Isa 34:5; 63:1; Jer 49:7; Eze 25:12 [v]S Ge 27:29,37-40 [w]Ps 144:10 [x]2Sa 22:44; Ps 18:43
8:15 [y]S Ge 18:19; 1Ki 11:38; 14:8; 15:11; 22:43; 2Ki 12:2; Job 29:14; Ps 5:12; 119:121; Heb 11:33
8:16 [z]S 2Sa 2:13 [a]2Sa 20:24; 1Ki 4:3 [b]Isa 36:3, 22
8:17 [c]S 1Sa 2:35; 2Sa 15:24,29; 20:25; 1Ki 1:8; 4:4; 1Ch 6:8,53; 16:39; 24:3; 27:17; 2Ch 31:10; Eze 40:46; 43:19; 44:15; 48:11 [d]Mk 2:26 [e]1Ki 4:3; 2Ki 12:10; 19:2; 22:3; Isa 36:3; Jer 36:12
8:18 [f]2Sa 20:23; 23:20; 1Ki 1:8,38; 2:25,35,46; 4:4 [g]S 1Sa 30:14
9:1 [h]S 1Sa 20:14-17, 42; S 23:18
9:2 [i]2Sa 16:1-4; 19:17,26,29
9:3 [j]1Ch 8:34; 1Sa 20:14 [k]S Lev 21:18
9:4 [l]2Sa 17:27-29
9:6 [m]S Ge 37:7
9:7 [n]S 1Sa 20:14-15 [o]ver 13; 2Sa 19:28; 21:7; 1Ki 2:7; 2Ki 25:29; Jer 52:33
9:8 [p]S 2Sa 4:4 [q]S 2Sa 3:8
9:10 [r]2Sa 16:3
9:11 [s]Job 36:7; Ps 113:8
9:12 [t]S 2Sa 4:4

[x]*12* Some Hebrew manuscripts, Septuagint and Syriac (see also 1 Chron. 18:11); most Hebrew manuscripts *Aram* [y]*13* A few Hebrew manuscripts, Septuagint and Syriac (see also 1 Chron. 18:12); most Hebrew manuscripts *Aram* (that is, Arameans) [z]*18* Or *were priests* [a]*11* Septuagint; Hebrew *my*

9:1 SHOW KINDNESS FOR JONATHAN'S SAKE. Ch. 9 records how David kept his promise to his close friend Jonathan. David had made a covenant with Jonathan years before to show kindness to his family always (1Sa 20:11–23). Mephibosheth was a son of Jonathan (vv. 3,6; cf. 4:4). This is the first of two acts of kindness reported of David (cf. 10:1–5). David's remarkable kindness stands in sharp contrast to the two acts of wickedness (adultery and murder) that immediately follow (11:1–27).

David Defeats the Ammonites

10:1–19pp — 1Ch 19:1–19

10 In the course of time, the king of the Ammonites died, and his son Hanun succeeded him as king. 2David thought, "I will show kindness to Hanun son of Nahash,[u] just as his father showed kindness to me." So David sent a delegation to express his sympathy to Hanun concerning his father.

When David's men came to the land of the Ammonites, 3the Ammonite nobles said to Hanun their lord, "Do you think David is honoring your father by sending men to you to express sympathy? Hasn't David sent them to you to explore the city and spy it out[v] and overthrow it?" 4So Hanun seized David's men, shaved off half of each man's beard,[w] cut off their garments in the middle at the buttocks,[x] and sent them away.

5When David was told about this, he sent messengers to meet the men, for they were greatly humiliated. The king said, "Stay at Jericho till your beards have grown, and then come back."

6When the Ammonites realized that they had become a stench[y] in David's nostrils, they hired twenty thousand Aramean[z] foot soldiers from Beth Rehob[a] and Zobah,[b] as well as the king of Maacah[c] with a thousand men, and also twelve thousand men from Tob.[d]

7On hearing this, David sent Joab[e] out with the entire army of fighting men. 8The Ammonites came out and drew up in battle formation at the entrance to their city gate, while the Arameans of Zobah and Rehob and the men of Tob and Maacah were by themselves in the open country.

9Joab saw that there were battle lines in front of him and behind him; so he selected some of the best troops in Israel and deployed them against the Arameans. 10He put the rest of the men under the command of Abishai[f] his brother and deployed them against the Ammonites. 11Joab said, "If the Arameans are too strong for me, then you are to come to my rescue; but if the Ammonites are too strong for you, then I will come to rescue you. 12Be strong[g] and let us fight bravely for our people and the cities of our God. The LORD will do what is good in his sight."[h]

13Then Joab and the troops with him advanced to fight the Arameans, and they fled before him. 14When the Ammonites[i] saw that the Arameans were fleeing, they fled before Abishai and went inside the city. So Joab returned from fighting the Ammonites and came to Jerusalem.

15After the Arameans saw that they had been routed by Israel, they regrouped. 16Hadadezer had Arameans brought from beyond the River[b]; they went to Helam, with Shobach the commander of Hadadezer's army leading them.

17When David was told of this, he gathered all Israel, crossed the Jordan and went to Helam. The Arameans formed their battle lines to meet David and fought against him. 18But they fled before Israel, and David killed seven hundred of their charioteers and forty thousand of their foot soldiers.[c] He also struck down Shobach the commander of their army, and he died there. 19When all the kings who were vassals of Hadadezer saw that they had been defeated by Israel, they made peace with the Israelites and became subject[j] to them.

So the Arameans[k] were afraid to help the Ammonites anymore.

David and Bathsheba

11 In the spring,[l] at the time when kings go off to war, David sent Joab[m] out with the king's men and the whole Israelite army.[n] They destroyed the Ammonites and besieged Rabbah.[o] But David remained in Jerusalem.

2One evening David got up from his

[b] *16* That is, the Euphrates [c] *18* Some Septuagint manuscripts (see also 1 Chron. 19:18); Hebrew *horsemen*

10:2 [u]S 1Sa 11:1 **10:3** [v]S Nu 21:32 **10:4** [w]S Lev 19:27; Isa 7:20; 15:2; 50:6; 52:14; Jer 48:37; Eze 5:1 [x]Isa 20:4 **10:6** [y]S Ge 34:30 [z]S 2Sa 8:5 [a]S Nu 13:21 [b]S 1Sa 14:47 [c]S Dt 3:14 [d]Jdg 11:3-5 **10:7** [e]S 2Sa 2:18 **10:10** [f]S 1Sa 26:6 **10:12** [g]S Dt 1:21; 31:6; S Eph 6:10 [h]S Jdg 10:15; Ne 4:14 **10:14** [i]2Sa 8:12 **10:19** [j]2Sa 8:6 [k]1Ki 11:25; 22:31; 2Ki 5:1 **11:1** [l]1Ki 20:22, 26 [m]S 2Sa 2:18 [n]1Ch 20:1 [o]S Dt 3:11

11:1 DAVID REMAINED IN JERUSALEM. Ch. 11 records David's tragic sin and fall. Instead of leading his army into battle as he had done before, David stayed behind in Jerusalem. He had developed a softness that soon led to his spiritual and moral collapse. His life of ease and luxury as king bred self-confidence and self-indulgence. At about this time he ceased to be a man after God's own heart (see 1Sa 13:14). David's fall from grace (cf. Gal 5:4) stands as a warning to all believers: "So, if you think you are standing firm, be careful that you don't fall!" (1Co 10:12).

11:2 HE SAW A WOMAN. Chs. 11–24 record David's serious spiritual failures and God's subse-

bed and walked around on the roof[p] of
the palace. From the roof he saw[q] a
woman bathing. The woman was very
beautiful, **3**and David sent someone to
find out about her. The man said, "Isn't
this Bathsheba,[r] the daughter of Eliam[s] and the wife of Uriah[t] the Hittite?" **4**Then David sent messengers to
get her.[u] She came to him, and he
slept[v] with her. (She had purified herself from her uncleanness.)[w] Then[d]
she went back home. **5**The woman conceived and sent word to David, saying,
"I am pregnant."
6So David sent this word to Joab:
"Send me Uriah[x] the Hittite." And
Joab sent him to David. **7**When Uriah
came to him, David asked him how
Joab was, how the soldiers were and
how the war was going. **8**Then David
said to Uriah, "Go down to your house
and wash your feet."[y] So Uriah left the
palace, and a gift from the king was
sent after him. **9**But Uriah slept at the
entrance to the palace with all his master's servants and did not go down to
his house.
10When David was told, "Uriah did
not go home," he asked him, "Haven't
you just come from a distance? Why
didn't you go home?"
11Uriah said to David, "The ark[z]
and Israel and Judah are staying in
tents, and my master Joab and my
lord's men are camped in the open
fields. How could I go to my house to
eat and drink and lie[a] with my wife?
As surely as you live, I will not do such
a thing!"
12Then David said to him, "Stay here
one more day, and tomorrow I will send
you back." So Uriah remained in Jerusalem that day and the next. **13**At David's invitation, he ate and drank with
him, and David made him drunk. But in
the evening Uriah went out to sleep on
his mat among his master's servants;
he did not go home.
14In the morning David wrote a letter[b] to Joab and sent it with Uriah.
15In it he wrote, "Put Uriah in the front
line where the fighting is fiercest. Then
withdraw from him so he will be struck
down[c] and die.[d]"
16So while Joab had the city under

11:2 [p] S Dt 22:8; S Jos 2:8 [q] Mt 5:28
11:3 [r] 1Ch 3:5 [s] 2Sa 23:34 [t] 2Sa 23:39
11:4 [u] S Lev 20:10; Ps 51 Title; Jas 1:14-15 [v] Dt 22:22 [w] S Lev 15:25-30
11:6 [x] 1Ch 11:41
11:8 [y] S Ge 18:4
11:11 [z] 2Sa 7:2 [a] S 1Sa 21:5
11:14 [b] 1Ki 21:8
11:15 [c] ver 14-17; 2Sa 12:9 [d] 2Sa 12:12

[d] 4 Or *with her. When she purified herself from her uncleanness,*

quent judgment on him for the rest of his life. (1) This account of David's sins and the consequent tragedies in his personal and family life serves as a serious example and warning for the NT believer, not just for Israel. Concerning similar events at the time of the exodus, the Holy Spirit through the apostle Paul emphasized, "These things happened to them as examples and were written down as warnings for us, on whom the fulfillment of the ages has come" (1Co 10:11); thus we should take every precaution not to desire evil things, act immorally or test the Lord (cf. 1Co 10:6–9).

(2) David's experience demonstrates how far a person may fall when he or she turns away from God and the guidance of the Holy Spirit. When God first called him to be king, David was a man after God's own heart (1Sa 13:14; Ac 13:22); in striking down Uriah and taking his wife, however, David was despising God and his word (12:9–10; cf. 1Co 10:12).

(3) Although David repented of his sins and received God's forgiveness, God did not eliminate the consequences. Likewise, a believer may commit terrible sins and then through godly sorrow and sincere repentance receive God's grace and forgiveness. Nevertheless, the restoration of one's relationship with God does not necessarily mean he or she will escape temporal punishment or be delivered from the consequences of specific sins (vv. 10–11,14).

(4) God did not condone or excuse David's sins under the pretense that David was only human, that his sins were merely weaknesses or human failures, or that he as king could understandably resort to evil and cruelty. The recorded events reveal that David did not have to do what he did. Even in the imperfect redemption of the old covenant, people such as the prophet Samuel manifested a persevering loyalty to and faith in God through the grace available to them (cf. 1Sa 12:1–5,23; see 1Sa 25:1 note). The writer of this book clearly condemns rather than excuses David's great transgressions.

(5) The correct response to sin is to repent in all sincerity, to come to God in order to receive forgiveness, grace and mercy (Ps 51; Heb 4:16; 7:25), and to be willing to accept God's punishment without bitterness or rebellion. David recognized and admitted his terrible sins, turned his heart back to God and accepted God's rebuke in humility (12:9–13,20; 16:5–12; 24:10–25; Ps 51).

11:11 THE ARK AND ISRAEL. Uriah proved to be a better man than David. His actions were based on his commitment to God and his comradeship with those fighting the Lord's battle. He paid for his dedication with his life.

11:15 SO HE WILL BE STRUCK DOWN AND DIE. Instead of confessing his sin, David decided to have Uriah murdered and then to take his wife. The words that the apostle John applied to Cain and all other murderers (1Jn 3:12–15) apply also to David at this time: "Anyone who hates his brother is a murderer, and you know that no murderer has eternal life in him" (1Jn 3:15). He could be restored only through sincere and heartfelt repentance before God (see ch. 12; Ps 51).

siege, he put Uriah at a place where he
knew the strongest defenders were.
17When the men of the city came out
and fought against Joab, some of the
men in David's army fell; moreover,
Uriah the Hittite died.
18Joab sent David a full account of
the battle. 19He instructed the messenger: "When you have finished giving
the king this account of the battle,
20the king's anger may flare up, and he
may ask you, 'Why did you get so close
to the city to fight? Didn't you know
they would shoot arrows from the
wall? 21Who killed Abimelech[e] son of
Jerub-Besheth[e]? Didn't a woman
throw an upper millstone on him from
the wall,[f] so that he died in Thebez?
Why did you get so close to the wall?'
If he asks you this, then say to him,
'Also, your servant Uriah the Hittite is
dead.'"
22The messenger set out, and when
he arrived he told David everything
Joab had sent him to say. 23The messenger said to David, "The men overpowered us and came out against us in
the open, but we drove them back to
the entrance to the city gate. 24Then
the archers shot arrows at your servants from the wall, and some of the
king's men died. Moreover, your servant Uriah the Hittite is dead."
25David told the messenger, "Say
this to Joab: 'Don't let this upset you;
the sword devours one as well as another. Press the attack against the city
and destroy it.' Say this to encourage
Joab."
26When Uriah's wife heard that her
husband was dead, she mourned for
him. 27After the time of mourning[g]
was over, David had her brought to his
house, and she became his wife and
bore him a son. But the thing David
had done displeased[h] the LORD.

11:21 [e] S Jdg 8:31 [f] Jdg 9:50-54 **11:27** [g] Dt 34:8 [h] 2Sa 12:9; Ps 51:4-5

Nathan Rebukes David

11:1; 12:29–31pp — 1Ch 20:1–3

12 The LORD sent Nathan[i] to David.[j] When he came to him,[k]
he said, "There were two men in a certain town, one rich and the other poor.
2The rich man had a very large number
of sheep and cattle, 3but the poor man
had nothing except one little ewe lamb
he had bought. He raised it, and it grew
up with him and his children. It shared
his food, drank from his cup and even
slept in his arms. It was like a daughter to him.
4"Now a traveler came to the rich
man, but the rich man refrained from
taking one of his own sheep or cattle
to prepare a meal for the traveler who
had come to him. Instead, he took the
ewe lamb that belonged to the poor
man and prepared it for the one who
had come to him."
5David[l] burned with anger[m]
against the man[n] and said to Nathan,
"As surely as the LORD lives,[o] the man
who did this deserves to die! 6He must
pay for that lamb four times over,[p] because he did such a thing and had no
pity."
7Then Nathan said to David, "You
are the man![q] This is what the LORD,
the God of Israel, says: 'I anointed[r]
you[s] king over Israel, and I delivered
you from the hand of Saul. 8I gave your
master's house to you,[t] and your master's wives into your arms. I gave you
the house of Israel and Judah. And if all
this had been too little, I would have
given you even more. 9Why did you despise[u] the word of the LORD by doing
what is evil in his eyes? You struck
down[v] Uriah[w] the Hittite with the
sword and took his wife to be your own.

12:1 [i] S 2Sa 7:2 [j] Ps 51 Title [k] 2Sa 14:4 **12:5** [l] 1Ki 20:40 [m] S Ge 34:7 [n] Ro 2:1 [o] S 1Sa 14:39 **12:6** [p] Ex 22:1 **12:7** [q] 2Sa 14:13; Da 4:22 [r] S 1Sa 2:35 [s] 1Ki 20:42 **12:8** [t] S 2Sa 9:7 **12:9** [u] S Nu 15:31; S 1Sa 13:14 [v] S 2Sa 11:15 [w] 1Ki 15:5

e *21* Also known as *Jerub-Baal* (that is, Gideon)

11:27 THE THING ... DISPLEASED THE LORD. David's sins of adultery, cold-blooded murder, and subsequent cover-up were an exceptional evil in God's sight. He became guilty of breaking the sixth, seventh, eighth, ninth and tenth commandments (Ex 20:13–17). His sins were made greater because he was a shepherd over God's people (5:2) and the one who was responsible to administer justice and righteousness in Israel (8:15).

12:9 WHY DID YOU DESPISE THE WORD OF THE LORD? The prophet Nathan declared that David, in committing adultery, murder and deceit, was guilty of despising "the word of the LORD" and despising God himself (v. 10). "Despise" (Heb *bazah*) means to treat contemptuously, to scorn, to make of little account; thus by his actions, David was declaring God to be of little account, unworthy of love and devotion.

(1) In the church today, ministers of God who commit adultery reflect their estimate of God and his holy Word. They treat the gospel and the blood of Christ contemptuously, as if they are petty and unworthy of fidelity.

(2) The Bible states that any professed believer who enters into an adulterous relationship disqualifies himself from the office of overseer (1Ti 3:2; see article on MORAL QUALIFICATIONS FOR OVERSEERS, p. 1882).

You killed[x] him with the sword of the
Ammonites. **10**Now, therefore, the
sword[y] will never depart from your
house, because you despised me and
took the wife of Uriah the Hittite to be
your own.'
11"This is what the LORD says: 'Out
of your own household[z] I am going to
bring calamity upon you.[a] Before your
very eyes I will take your wives and
give them to one who is close to you,
and he will lie with your wives in broad
daylight.[b] **12**You did it in secret,[c] but
I will do this thing in broad daylight[d]
before all Israel.' "
13Then David said to Nathan, "I
have sinned[e] against the LORD."
Nathan replied, "The LORD has taken
away[f] your sin.[g] You are not going to
die.[h] **14**But because by doing this you
have made the enemies of the LORD
show utter contempt,[f][i] the son born
to you will die."
15After Nathan had gone home, the
LORD struck[j] the child that Uriah's
wife had borne to David, and he became ill. **16**David pleaded with God for
the child. He fasted and went into his
house and spent the nights lying[k] on
the ground. **17**The elders of his household stood beside him to get him up
from the ground, but he refused,[l] and
he would not eat any food with them.[m]
18On the seventh day the child died.
David's servants were afraid to tell him
that the child was dead, for they
thought, "While the child was still living, we spoke to David but he would
not listen to us. How can we tell him
the child is dead? He may do something desperate."
19David noticed that his servants
were whispering among themselves
and he realized the child was dead. "Is
the child dead?" he asked.
"Yes," they replied, "he is dead."
20Then David got up from the
ground. After he had washed,[n] put on
lotions and changed his clothes,[o] he
went into the house of the LORD and
worshiped. Then he went to his own
house, and at his request they served
him food, and he ate.
21His servants asked him, "Why are
you acting this way? While the child
was alive, you fasted and wept,[p] but
now that the child is dead, you get up
and eat!"
22He answered, "While the child was
still alive, I fasted and wept. I thought,
'Who knows?[q] The LORD may be gracious to me and let the child live.'[r]
23But now that he is dead, why should
I fast? Can I bring him back again? I
will go to him,[s] but he will not return
to me."[t]

12:9 [x]Ps 26:9; 51:14
12:10 [y]2Sa 13:28; 18:14-15; 1Ki 2:25
12:11 [z]2Sa 16:11 [a]Dt 28:30; 2Sa 16:21-22 [b]S Dt 17:17
12:12 [c]2Sa 11:4-15 [d]2Sa 16:22
12:13 [e]S Ge 13:13; S 20:6; S Nu 22:34 [f]Ps 32:1-5; 51:1,9; 103:12; Isa 43:25; 44:22; Zec 3:4,9 [g]Pr 28:13; Jer 2:35; Mic 7:18-19 [h]Lev 20:10; 24:17
12:14 [i]Isa 52:5; Ro 2:24
12:15 [j]S 1Sa 25:38
12:16 [k]Ps 5:7; 95:6
12:17 [l]S Ge 37:35; S 1Sa 1:7 [m]S 2Sa 3:35; Da 6:18
12:20 [n]Mt 6:17 [o]S Ge 41:14
12:21 [p]Jdg 20:26
12:22 [q]Jnh 3:9 [r]Isa 38:1-5
12:23 [s]Ge 37:35 [t]S 1Sa 31:13; 2Sa 13:39; Job 7:10; 10:21

f *14* Masoretic Text; an ancient Hebrew scribal tradition *this you have shown utter contempt for the LORD*

12:10 SWORD WILL NEVER DEPART FROM YOUR HOUSE. Because David had despised God and killed Uriah in order to take Uriah's wife for himself, God pronounced judgment on David and his family that would be fulfilled in violence, strife and murder (i.e., the sword) for the rest of his life (approximately twenty-five years). The Scriptures record at least four events as a result of this curse: the death of the child (v. 14), the murder of Amnon by Absalom (13:29), the killing of Absalom when he turned against his father (18:9–17) and the execution of Adonijah (1Ki 2:24–25).

12:11–12 THIS IS WHAT THE LORD SAYS. David's dreadful punishment, prophesied by Nathan, was not merely the natural consequences of his sin, nor was God passively permitting things to happen to David; rather, his punishment was the result of God's direct actions. Three times God used a phrase of intention: "*I am going* to bring calamity upon you"; "Before your very eyes *I will* take your wives"; "*I will* do this thing . . . before all Israel." David would experience atrocities at the hands of his own children, such as the raping of his daughter Tamar by Amnon (13:7–14; see 13:1, note) and the violation of his wives by Absalom (16:22).

12:12 BEFORE ALL ISRAEL. The prescribed punishment in Israel for adultery and murder was death (Lev 20:10; 24:17). However, God laid aside the punishment in this instance, not so much because of David's repentance, but because God had to vindicate himself and his righteousness publicly before all Israel and the nations. For the rest of David's life he was an example of God's righteous judgment on a spiritual leader who had sinned greatly.

12:13 THE LORD HAS TAKEN AWAY YOUR SIN. David's sin was forgiven by God in that the death penalty and eternal punishment were laid aside (cf. 1Jn 3:15); thus, David was restored to salvation and fellowship with God (cf. Ps 51). In spite of this, his reputation was forever blemished and the effects of his sin continued throughout the rest of his life and family history. David's experience after he was forgiven and restored is a sober lesson for those who casually treat sin as something that God simply forgives and forgets.

12:15 NATHAN HAD GONE HOME. David admitted his sin to Nathan (v. 13). Shortly thereafter, David repented before God and accepted his judgment (see Ps 51 for David's prayer of confession and repentance).

24 Then David comforted his wife
Bathsheba,[u] and he went to her and
lay with her. She gave birth to a son,
and they named him Solomon.[v] The
LORD loved him; 25 and because the
LORD loved him, he sent word through
Nathan the prophet to name him Jedidiah.[g][w]
26 Meanwhile Joab fought against
Rabbah[x] of the Ammonites and captured the royal citadel. 27 Joab then
sent messengers to David, saying, "I
have fought against Rabbah and taken
its water supply. 28 Now muster the
rest of the troops and besiege the city
and capture it. Otherwise I will take
the city, and it will be named after me."
29 So David mustered the entire
army and went to Rabbah, and attacked and captured it. 30 He took the
crown[y] from the head of their
king[h]—its weight was a talent[i] of
gold, and it was set with precious
stones—and it was placed on David's
head. He took a great quantity of plunder from the city 31 and brought out the
people who were there, consigning
them to labor with saws and with iron
picks and axes, and he made them
work at brickmaking.[j] He did this to
all the Ammonite[z] towns. Then David
and his entire army returned to Jerusalem.

Amnon and Tamar

13 In the course of time, Amnon[a]
son of David fell in love with
Tamar,[b] the beautiful sister of Absalom[c] son of David.
2 Amnon became frustrated to the
point of illness on account of his sister
Tamar, for she was a virgin, and it
seemed impossible for him to do anything to her.
3 Now Amnon had a friend named
Jonadab son of Shimeah,[d] David's
brother. Jonadab was a very shrewd
man. 4 He asked Amnon, "Why do you,
the king's son, look so haggard morning after morning? Won't you tell me?"
Amnon said to him, "I'm in love with
Tamar, my brother Absalom's sister."
5 "Go to bed and pretend to be ill,"
Jonadab said. "When your father comes
to see you, say to him, 'I would like my
sister Tamar to come and give me
something to eat. Let her prepare the
food in my sight so I may watch her and
then eat it from her hand.' "
6 So Amnon lay down and pretended
to be ill. When the king came to see
him, Amnon said to him, "I would like
my sister Tamar to come and make
some special bread in my sight, so I
may eat from her hand."
7 David sent word to Tamar at the
palace: "Go to the house of your brother Amnon and prepare some food for
him." 8 So Tamar went to the house of
her brother Amnon, who was lying
down. She took some dough, kneaded
it, made the bread in his sight and
baked it. 9 Then she took the pan and
served him the bread, but he refused to
eat.
"Send everyone out of here,"[e] Amnon said. So everyone left him. 10 Then
Amnon said to Tamar, "Bring the food
here into my bedroom so I may eat
from your hand." And Tamar took the
bread she had prepared and brought it
to her brother Amnon in his bedroom.
11 But when she took it to him to eat,
he grabbed[f] her and said, "Come to
bed with me, my sister."[g]
12 "Don't, my brother!" she said to

12:24 [u] 1Ki 1:11 [v] 1Ki 1:10; 1Ch 22:9; 28:5; Mt 1:6
12:25 [w] Ne 13:26
12:26 [x] S Dt 3:11
12:30 [y] Est 8:15; Ps 21:3; 132:18
12:31 [z] S 1Sa 14:47
13:1 [a] 2Sa 3:2 [b] 2Sa 14:27; 1Ch 3:9 [c] S 2Sa 3:3
13:3 [d] S 1Sa 16:9
13:9 [e] Ge 45:1
13:11 [f] S Ge 39:12 [g] S Ge 38:16

[g] *25 Jedidiah* means *loved by the LORD.*
[h] *30* Or *of Milcom* (that is, Molech)
[i] *30* That is, about 75 pounds (about 34 kilograms)
[j] *31* The meaning of the Hebrew for this clause is uncertain.

12:24 HIS WIFE BATHSHEBA. Did David benefit from his sins of lust and murder? He engineered the death of Bathsheba's husband and then possessed the woman he desired. Perhaps the severity of God's punishment of David for the next twenty-five years was due partly to the fact that David had not faced the reality that he had no legal or moral right to take and keep Uriah's wife: (1) God had commanded that kings were not to take many wives (Dt 17:17); and (2) he had disobeyed several of the Ten Commandments in this episode (see 11:27, note). For this God declared, "the sword will never depart from your house, because you . . . took the wife of Uriah the Hittite to be your own" (v. 10).

13:1 AMNON . . . TAMAR. The series of narratives in chs. 13—22 are mainly accounts of the fulfillment of God's purpose to bring calamity upon David. (1) Ch. 13 records the first result of David's sins of lust, adultery and murder (cf. Gal 6:7). Incest and murder broke out within his own home as David's lust was first reproduced in his son Amnon. (2) Because David destroyed the happiness of Uriah's house, God destroyed the happiness of David's house. Many times, God lays upon the transgressor great suffering and sorrow so that he or she, as well as others, might fear God and turn away from sin (cf. Nu 14:20–36).

him. "Don't force me. Such a thing
should not be done in Israel![h] Don't
do this wicked thing.[i] **13**What about
me?[j] Where could I get rid of my disgrace? And what about you? You would
be like one of the wicked fools in Israel. Please speak to the king; he will not
keep me from being married to you."
14But he refused to listen to her, and
since he was stronger than she, he
raped her.[k]

15Then Amnon hated her with intense hatred. In fact, he hated her
more than he had loved her. Amnon
said to her, "Get up and get out!"

16"No!" she said to him. "Sending me
away would be a greater wrong than
what you have already done to me."

But he refused to listen to her. **17**He
called his personal servant and said,
"Get this woman out of here and bolt
the door after her." **18**So his servant
put her out and bolted the door after
her. She was wearing a richly ornamented[k] robe,[l] for this was the kind
of garment the virgin daughters of the
king wore. **19**Tamar put ashes[m] on her
head and tore the ornamented[1] robe
she was wearing. She put her hand on
her head and went away, weeping
aloud as she went.

20Her brother Absalom said to her,
"Has that Amnon, your brother, been
with you? Be quiet now, my sister; he
is your brother. Don't take this thing to
heart." And Tamar lived in her brother
Absalom's house, a desolate woman.

21When King David heard all this, he
was furious.[n] **22**Absalom never said a
word to Amnon, either good or bad;[o]
he hated[p] Amnon because he had disgraced his sister Tamar.

Absalom Kills Amnon

23Two years later, when Absalom's
sheepshearers[q] were at Baal Hazor
near the border of Ephraim, he invited
all the king's sons to come there. **24**Absalom went to the king and said, "Your
servant has had shearers come. Will
the king and his officials please join
me?"

25"No, my son," the king replied.
"All of us should not go; we would only
be a burden to you." Although Absalom
urged him, he still refused to go, but
gave him his blessing.

26Then Absalom said, "If not, please
let my brother Amnon come with us."

The king asked him, "Why should he
go with you?" **27**But Absalom urged
him, so he sent with him Amnon and
the rest of the king's sons.

28Absalom[r] ordered his men, "Listen! When Amnon is in high[s] spirits
from drinking wine and I say to you,
'Strike Amnon down,' then kill him.
Don't be afraid. Have not I given you
this order? Be strong and brave.[t]"
29So Absalom's men did to Amnon
what Absalom had ordered. Then all
the king's sons got up, mounted their
mules and fled.

30While they were on their way, the
report came to David: "Absalom has
struck down all the king's sons; not
one of them is left." **31**The king stood
up, tore[u] his clothes and lay down on
the ground; and all his servants stood
by with their clothes torn.

32But Jonadab son of Shimeah, David's brother, said, "My lord should not
think that they killed all the princes;
only Amnon is dead. This has been Absalom's expressed intention ever since
the day Amnon raped his sister Tamar.
33My lord the king should not be concerned about the report that all the
king's sons are dead. Only Amnon is
dead."

34Meanwhile, Absalom had fled.

Now the man standing watch looked
up and saw many people on the road
west of him, coming down the side of

13:12 [h] Lev 20:17 [i] S Ge 34:7
13:13 [j] S Lev 18:9; S Dt 22:21,23-24
13:14 [k] S Ge 34:2; Eze 22:11
13:18 [l] S Ge 37:23
13:19 [m] S Jos 7:6; Est 4:1; Da 9:3
13:21 [n] S Ge 34:7
13:22 [o] Ge 31:24 [p] Lev 19:17-18; 1Jn 2:9-11
13:23 [q] 1Sa 25:7
13:28 [r] S 2Sa 3:3 [s] S Ru 3:7 [t] S 2Sa 12:10
13:31 [u] S Nu 14:6

[k] *18* The meaning of the Hebrew for this phrase is uncertain. [1] *19* The meaning of the Hebrew for this word is uncertain.

13:21 DAVID . . . WAS FURIOUS. David was very angry at the rape of his daughter by his firstborn son (1Ch 3:1). Yet, he could not bring himself to rebuke and punish Amnon as he should have (see Lev 20:17). (1) David's own sexual immorality with Bathsheba weakened and undermined his ability to discipline his sons and manage his own household. Since David was not above reproach himself (see Pr 6:32–33), he lacked the authority and moral courage to rebuke his son. His own poor example destroyed his moral influence with those under his care. (2) Under the new covenant, leaders in the church must be examples of holiness so that when they rebuke sin, they need not fear any examination of their life that would reveal a compromise of God's standards as revealed in his Word (1Ti 3:1–13).

13:28 STRIKE AMNON DOWN, THEN KILL HIM. God permitted Absalom's vengeance to punish Amnon's crime against Tamar. At times God uses human sin to achieve his purposes, punishing one wrongdoer through the sin of another.

the hill. The watchman went and told
the king, "I see men in the direction of
Horonaim, on the side of the hill."[m]
35Jonadab said to the king, "See, the
king's sons are here; it has happened
just as your servant said."
36As he finished speaking, the
king's sons came in, wailing loudly.
The king, too, and all his servants wept
very bitterly.
37Absalom fled and went to Talmai[v] son of Ammihud, the king of Geshur. But King David mourned for his
son every day.
38After Absalom fled and went to
Geshur, he stayed there three years.
39And the spirit of the king[n] longed to
go to Absalom,[w] for he was consoled[x]
concerning Amnon's death.

Absalom Returns to Jerusalem

14 Joab[y] son of Zeruiah knew
that the king's heart longed for
Absalom. 2So Joab sent someone to Tekoa[z] and had a wise woman[a] brought
from there. He said to her, "Pretend
you are in mourning. Dress in mourning clothes, and don't use any cosmetic
lotions.[b] Act like a woman who has
spent many days grieving for the dead.
3Then go to the king and speak these
words to him." And Joab[c] put the
words in her mouth.
4When the woman from Tekoa
went[o] to the king, she fell with her
face to the ground to pay him honor,
and she said, "Help me, O king!"
5The king asked her, "What is troubling you?"
She said, "I am indeed a widow; my
husband is dead. 6I your servant had
two sons. They got into a fight with
each other in the field, and no one was
there to separate them. One struck the
other and killed him. 7Now the whole
clan has risen up against your servant;
they say, 'Hand over the one who
struck his brother down, so that we
may put him to death[d] for the life of
his brother whom he killed; then we
will get rid of the heir[e] as well.' They
would put out the only burning coal I
have left,[f] leaving my husband neither name nor descendant on the face
of the earth."
8The king said to the woman, "Go
home,[g] and I will issue an order in
your behalf."
9But the woman from Tekoa said to
him, "My lord the king, let the blame[h]
rest on me and on my father's family,[i]
and let the king and his throne be without guilt.[j]"
10The king replied, "If anyone says
anything to you, bring him to me, and
he will not bother you again."
11She said, "Then let the king invoke the LORD his God to prevent the
avenger[k] of blood from adding to the
destruction, so that my son will not be
destroyed."
"As surely as the LORD lives," he
said, "not one hair[l] of your son's head
will fall to the ground.[m]"
12Then the woman said, "Let your
servant speak a word to my lord the
king."
"Speak," he replied.
13The woman said, "Why then have
you devised a thing like this against
the people of God? When the king says
this, does he not convict himself,[n] for
the king has not brought back his banished son?[o] 14Like water[p] spilled on
the ground, which cannot be recovered, so we must die.[q] But God does
not take away life; instead, he devises
ways so that a banished person[r] may
not remain estranged from him.
15"And now I have come to say this
to my lord the king because the people
have made me afraid. Your servant
thought, 'I will speak to the king; perhaps he will do what his servant asks.
16Perhaps the king will agree to deliver his servant from the hand of the man
who is trying to cut off both me and my

13:37 [v] S 2Sa 3:3 **13:39** [w] 2Sa 14:13 [x] S 2Sa 12:19-23 **14:1** [y] S 2Sa 2:18 **14:2** [z] Ne 3:5; Jer 6:1; Am 1:1 [a] 2Sa 20:16 [b] S Ru 3:3; S Isa 1:6 **14:3** [c] ver 19 **14:7** [d] Nu 35:19 [e] Mt 21:38 [f] Dt 19:10-13 **14:8** [g] 1Sa 25:35 **14:9** [h] 1Sa 25:24 [i] Mt 27:25 [j] 1Sa 25:28 **14:11** [k] S Nu 35:12,21 [l] S Mt 10:30 [m] S 1Sa 14:45 **14:13** [n] S 2Sa 12:7; 1Ki 20:40 [o] 2Sa 13:38-39 **14:14** [p] Job 14:11; Ps 58:7; Isa 19:5 [q] Job 10:8; 17:13; 30:23; Ps 22:15; Heb 9:27 [r] Nu 35:15,25-28

[m] *34* Septuagint; Hebrew does not have this sentence. [n] *39* Dead Sea Scrolls and some Septuagint manuscripts; Masoretic Text *But the spirit of* David the king [o] *4* Many Hebrew manuscripts, Septuagint, Vulgate and Syriac; most Hebrew manuscripts *spoke*

13:36 THE KING . . . WEPT VERY BITTERLY. After Absalom killed Amnon, David was grief-stricken. David's agony as a result of God's chastisement has no parallel in Biblical history. God permitted sin and Satan to inflict great suffering on him. Though David was forgiven by God and did not suffer eternal punishment for his sin (see 12:13, note), nevertheless the temporal consequences, both natural and divine, continued unabated until his death. The actions of Absalom and Amnon were only the beginning of the calamity that God brought upon David (12:11) because he had despised God and his Word by cruelly killing Uriah in order to conceal his sin with Bathsheba (12:9–10).

son from the inheritance[s] God gave us.'

[17]"And now your servant says, 'May the word of my lord the king bring me rest, for my lord the king is like an angel[t] of God in discerning[u] good and evil. May the LORD your God be with you.' "

[18]Then the king said to the woman, "Do not keep from me the answer to what I am going to ask you."

"Let my lord the king speak," the woman said.

[19]The king asked, "Isn't the hand of Joab[v] with you in all this?"

The woman answered, "As surely as you live, my lord the king, no one can turn to the right or to the left from anything my lord the king says. Yes, it was your servant Joab who instructed me to do this and who put all these words into the mouth of your servant. [20]Your servant Joab did this to change the present situation. My lord has wisdom[w] like that of an angel of God—he knows everything that happens in the land.[x]"

[21]The king said to Joab, "Very well, I will do it. Go, bring back the young man Absalom."

[22]Joab fell with his face to the ground to pay him honor, and he blessed the king.[y] Joab said, "Today your servant knows that he has found favor in your eyes, my lord the king, because the king has granted his servant's request."

[23]Then Joab went to Geshur and brought Absalom back to Jerusalem. [24]But the king said, "He must go to his own house; he must not see my face." So Absalom went to his own house and did not see the face of the king.

[25]In all Israel there was not a man so highly praised for his handsome appearance as Absalom. From the top of his head to the sole of his foot there was no blemish in him. [26]Whenever he cut the hair of his head[z]—he used to cut his hair from time to time when it became too heavy for him—he would weigh it, and its weight was two hundred shekels[p] by the royal standard.

[27]Three sons[a] and a daughter were born to Absalom. The daughter's name was Tamar,[b] and she became a beautiful woman.

[28]Absalom lived two years in Jerusalem without seeing the king's face. [29]Then Absalom sent for Joab in order to send him to the king, but Joab refused to come to him. So he sent a second time, but he refused to come. [30]Then he said to his servants, "Look, Joab's field is next to mine, and he has barley[c] there. Go and set it on fire." So Absalom's servants set the field on fire.

[31]Then Joab did go to Absalom's house and he said to him, "Why have your servants set my field on fire?[d]"

[32]Absalom said to Joab, "Look, I sent word to you and said, 'Come here so I can send you to the king to ask, "Why have I come from Geshur?[e] It would be better for me if I were still there!" ' Now then, I want to see the king's face, and if I am guilty of anything, let him put me to death."[f]

[33]So Joab went to the king and told him this. Then the king summoned Absalom, and he came in and bowed down with his face to the ground before the king. And the king kissed[g] Absalom.

Absalom's Conspiracy

15 In the course of time,[h] Absalom provided himself with a chariot[i] and horses and with fifty men to run ahead of him. [2]He would get up early and stand by the side of the road leading to the city gate.[j] Whenever anyone came with a complaint to be placed before the king for a decision, Absalom would call out to him, "What town are you from?" He would answer, "Your servant is from one of the tribes of Israel." [3]Then Absalom would say to him, "Look, your claims are valid and proper, but there is no representative of the king to hear you."[k] [4]And Absalom would add, "If only I were appointed judge in the land![l] Then everyone who has a complaint or case could come to me and I would see that he gets justice."

[5]Also, whenever anyone approached him to bow down before him, Absalom would reach out his hand, take hold of him and kiss him. [6]Absalom behaved in this way toward all the Israelites who

14:16 [s] S Ex 34:9; S 1Sa 26:19
14:17 [t] S 1Sa 29:9 [u] 1Ki 3:9; Da 2:21
14:19 [v] ver 3
14:20 [w] 1Ki 3:12, 28; 10:23-24; Isa 28:6 [x] 2Sa 18:13
14:22 [y] S Ge 47:7
14:26 [z] 2Sa 18:9
14:27 [a] 2Sa 18:18 [b] S 2Sa 13:1
14:30 [c] S Ex 9:31
14:31 [d] S Jdg 15:5
14:32 [e] S 2Sa 3:3 [f] 1Sa 20:8
14:33 [g] Lk 15:20
15:1 [h] S 2Sa 12:11 [i] S 1Sa 8:11
15:2 [j] S Ge 23:10; 2Sa 19:8
15:3 [k] Pr 12:2
15:4 [l] Jdg 9:29

[p] 26 That is, about 5 pounds (about 2.3 kilograms)

15:6 ABSALOM . . . STOLE THE HEARTS OF THE MEN. Absalom conspired for four years to steal the throne from his father, and the people increasingly turned against David (vv. 1–15).

came to the king asking for justice, and
so he stole the hearts[m] of the men of
Israel.
7At the end of four[q] years, Absalom
said to the king, "Let me go to Hebron
and fulfill a vow I made to the LORD.
8While your servant was living at Geshur[n] in Aram, I made this vow:[o] 'If
the LORD takes me back to Jerusalem,
I will worship the LORD in Hebron.[r]' "
9The king said to him, "Go in peace."
So he went to Hebron.
10Then Absalom sent secret messengers throughout the tribes of Israel
to say, "As soon as you hear the sound
of the trumpets,[p] then say, 'Absalom
is king in Hebron.' " 11Two hundred
men from Jerusalem had accompanied
Absalom. They had been invited as
guests and went quite innocently,
knowing nothing about the matter.
12While Absalom was offering sacrifices, he also sent for Ahithophel[q] the
Gilonite, David's counselor,[r] to come
from Giloh,[s] his hometown. And so
the conspiracy gained strength, and
Absalom's following kept on increasing.[t]

David Flees

13A messenger came and told David,
"The hearts of the men of Israel are
with Absalom."
14Then David said to all his officials
who were with him in Jerusalem,
"Come! We must flee,[u] or none of us
will escape from Absalom.[v] We must
leave immediately, or he will move
quickly to overtake us and bring ruin
upon us and put the city to the sword."
15The king's officials answered him,
"Your servants are ready to do whatever our lord the king chooses."
16The king set out, with his entire
household following him; but he left
ten concubines[w] to take care of the
palace. 17So the king set out, with all
the people following him, and they
halted at a place some distance away.
18All his men marched past him, along
with all the Kerethites[x] and Pelethites; and all the six hundred Gittites
who had accompanied him from Gath
marched before the king.
19The king said to Ittai[y] the Gittite,
"Why should you come along with us?
Go back and stay with King Absalom.
You are a foreigner,[z] an exile from
your homeland. 20You came only yesterday. And today shall I make you
wander[a] about with us, when I do not
know where I am going? Go back, and
take your countrymen. May kindness
and faithfulness[b] be with you."
21But Ittai replied to the king, "As
surely as the LORD lives, and as my lord
the king lives, wherever my lord the
king may be, whether it means life or
death, there will your servant be."[c]
22David said to Ittai, "Go ahead,
march on." So Ittai the Gittite marched
on with all his men and the families
that were with him.
23The whole countryside wept
aloud[d] as all the people passed by.
The king also crossed the Kidron Valley,[e][f] and all the people moved on
toward the desert.
24Zadok[g] was there, too, and all the
Levites who were with him were carrying the ark[h] of the covenant of God.
They set down the ark of God, and Abiathar[i] offered sacrifices[s] until all
the people had finished leaving the
city.
25Then the king said to Zadok,
"Take the ark of God back into the city.
If I find favor in the LORD's eyes, he will
bring me back and let me see it and his
dwelling place[j] again. 26But if he
says, 'I am not pleased with you,' then
I am ready; let him do to me whatever
seems good to him.[k]"
27The king also said to Zadok the
priest, "Aren't you a seer?[l] Go back to
the city in peace, with your son Ahimaaz and Jonathan[m] son of Abiathar. You
and Abiathar take your two sons with
you. 28I will wait at the fords[n] in the

15:6 [m]Ro 16:18
15:8 [n]S 2Sa 3:3 [o]S Ge 28:20
15:10 [p]1Ki 1:34, 39; 2Ki 9:13
15:12 [q]ver 31,34; 2Sa 16:15,23; 17:14; 23:34; 1Ch 27:33 [r]Job 19:14; Ps 41:9; 55:13; Jer 9:4 [s]Jos 15:51 [t]Ps 3:1
15:14 [u]1Ki 2:26; Ps 132:1; Ps 3 Title [v]2Sa 19:9
15:16 [w]2Sa 16:21-22; 20:3
15:18 [x]S 1Sa 30:14; 2Sa 20:7,23; 1Ki 1:38,44; 1Ch 18:17
15:19 [y]2Sa 18:2 [z]S Ge 31:15
15:20 [a]S 1Sa 22:2 [b]2Sa 2:6
15:21 [c]Ru 1:16-17; Pr 17:17
15:23 [d]1Sa 11:4; Job 2:12 [e]1Ki 2:37; 2Ki 23:12; 2Ch 15:16; 29:16; 30:14; Jer 31:40 [f]Jn 18:1
15:24 [g]S 2Sa 8:17; 19:11 [h]Nu 4:15; S 10:33; 1Ki 2:26 [i]S 1Sa 22:20
15:25 [j]Ex 15:13; S Lev 15:31; Ps 43:3; 46:4; 84:1; 132:7
15:26 [k]S Jdg 10:15; 2Sa 22:20
15:27 [l]S 1Sa 9:9 [m]ver 36; 2Sa 17:17; 1Ki 1:42
15:28 [n]2Sa 17:16

[q]7 Some Septuagint manuscripts, Syriac and Josephus; Hebrew *forty* [r]8 Some Septuagint manuscripts; Hebrew does not have *in Hebron.* [s]24 Or *Abiathar went up*

Absalom's success reveals that David, because of his sin and consequent failure to manage his own house, had lost much of the people's respect. His ability to lead, once based on a persevering faithfulness to his God, was now eroded because of his sin and severely marred reputation.

15:14 COME! WE MUST FLEE. David was forced to flee from his own son, who now sought to kill him and gain the throne. David left Jerusalem, "weeping as he went" (v. 30). David likely remembered his sin and recognized that this was part of God's retribution (cf. 12:9–12; 16:10–11). David, now a humiliated fugitive, humbly accepted God's dealing with him (vv. 25–26; cf. 16:9–13).

desert until word comes from you to
inform me." 29So Zadok and Abiathar
took the ark of God back to Jerusalem
and stayed there.

30But David continued up the Mount
of Olives, weeping[o] as he went; his
head[p] was covered and he was barefoot. All the people with him covered
their heads too and were weeping as
they went up. 31Now David had been
told, "Ahithophel[q] is among the conspirators with Absalom." So David
prayed, "O LORD, turn Ahithophel's
counsel into foolishness."

32When David arrived at the summit, where people used to worship
God, Hushai[r] the Arkite[s] was there
to meet him, his robe torn and dust[t]
on his head. 33David said to him, "If
you go with me, you will be a burden[u]
to me. 34But if you return to the city
and say to Absalom, 'I will be your servant, O king; I was your father's servant in the past, but now I will be your
servant,'[v] then you can help me by
frustrating[w] Ahithophel's advice.
35Won't the priests Zadok and Abiathar be there with you? Tell them anything you hear in the king's palace.[x]
36Their two sons, Ahimaaz[y] son of Zadok and Jonathan[z] son of Abiathar,
are there with them. Send them to me
with anything you hear."

37So David's friend Hushai[a] arrived
at Jerusalem as Absalom[b] was entering the city.

David and Ziba

16 When David had gone a short
distance beyond the summit,
there was Ziba,[c] the steward of Mephibosheth, waiting to meet him. He
had a string of donkeys saddled and
loaded with two hundred loaves of
bread, a hundred cakes of raisins, a
hundred cakes of figs and a skin of
wine.[d]

2The king asked Ziba, "Why have
you brought these?"

Ziba answered, "The donkeys are for
the king's household to ride on, the
bread and fruit are for the men to eat,
and the wine is to refresh[e] those who
become exhausted in the desert."

3The king then asked, "Where is
your master's grandson?"[f]

Ziba[g] said to him, "He is staying in
Jerusalem, because he thinks, 'Today
the house of Israel will give me back
my grandfather's kingdom.' "

4Then the king said to Ziba, "All that
belonged to Mephibosheth[h] is now
yours."

"I humbly bow," Ziba said. "May I
find favor in your eyes, my lord the
king."

Shimei Curses David

5As King David approached Bahurim,[i] a man from the same clan as
Saul's family came out from there. His
name was Shimei[j] son of Gera, and he
cursed[k] as he came out. 6He pelted
David and all the king's officials with
stones, though all the troops and the
special guard were on David's right
and left. 7As he cursed, Shimei said,
"Get out, get out, you man of blood, you
scoundrel! 8The LORD has repaid you
for all the blood you shed in the household of Saul, in whose place you have
reigned.[l] The LORD has handed the
kingdom over to your son Absalom.
You have come to ruin because you are
a man of blood!"[m]

9Then Abishai[n] son of Zeruiah said
to the king, "Why should this dead
dog[o] curse my lord the king? Let me
go over and cut off his head."[p]

10But the king said, "What do you
and I have in common, you sons of Zeruiah?[q] If he is cursing because the
LORD said to him, 'Curse David,' who
can ask, 'Why do you do this?' "[r]

11David then said to Abishai and all
his officials, "My son,[s] who is of my
own flesh, is trying to take my life.
How much more, then, this Benjamite!
Leave him alone; let him curse, for the
LORD has told him to.[t] 12It may be that
the LORD will see my distress[u] and repay me with good[v] for the cursing I
am receiving today.[w]"

13So David and his men continued
along the road while Shimei was going
along the hillside opposite him, cursing as he went and throwing stones at
him and showering him with dirt.
14The king and all the people with
him arrived at their destination exhausted.[x] And there he refreshed
himself.

15:30 [o] S Nu 25:6; S Ps 30:5 [p] Est 6:12
15:31 [q] S ver 12
15:32 [r] ver 37; 2Sa 16:16; 17:5; 1Ki 4:16 [s] Jos 16:2 [t] S Jos 7:6
15:33 [u] 2Sa 19:35
15:34 [v] 2Sa 16:19 [w] 2Sa 17:14; Pr 11:14
15:35 [x] 2Sa 17:15-16
15:36 [y] 2Sa 18:19 [z] S ver 27; 2Sa 17:17; 1Ki 1:42
15:37 [a] 1Ch 27:33 [b] 2Sa 16:15
16:1 [c] 2Sa 9:1-13 [d] S 1Sa 25:18; 1Ch 12:40
16:2 [e] 2Sa 17:27-29
16:3 [f] 2Sa 9:9-10 [g] S 2Sa 9:2
16:4 [h] S 2Sa 4:4
16:5 [i] S 2Sa 3:16 [j] 2Sa 19:16-23; 1Ki 2:8-9,36,44 [k] S Ex 22:28
16:8 [l] 2Sa 19:28; 21:9 [m] 2Sa 19:19; Ps 55:3
16:9 [n] S 1Sa 26:6 [o] S 2Sa 3:8 [p] S 2Sa 3:39; Lk 9:54
16:10 [q] S 2Sa 2:18; 19:22 [r] Ro 9:20
16:11 [s] 2Sa 12:11 [t] S Ge 45:5; 1Sa 26:19
16:12 [u] Ps 4:1; 25:18 [v] Dt 23:5; Ro 8:28 [w] Ps 109:28
16:14 [x] 2Sa 17:2

16:3 HE IS STAYING IN JERUSALEM. For more on this allegation about Mephibosheth, see 19:24–30. For more on the relationship between Ziba and Mephibosheth, see 9:1-13.

The Advice of Hushai and Ahithophel

15 Meanwhile, Absalom[y] and all the men of Israel came to Jerusalem, and Ahithophel[z] was with him. 16 Then Hushai[a] the Arkite, David's friend, went to Absalom and said to him, "Long live the king! Long live the king!"

17 Absalom asked Hushai, "Is this the love you show your friend? Why didn't you go with your friend?"[b]

18 Hushai said to Absalom, "No, the one chosen by the LORD, by these people, and by all the men of Israel—his I will be, and I will remain with him. 19 Furthermore, whom should I serve? Should I not serve the son? Just as I served your father, so I will serve you."[c]

20 Absalom said to Ahithophel, "Give us your advice. What should we do?"

21 Ahithophel answered, "Lie with your father's concubines whom he left to take care of the palace. Then all Israel will hear that you have made yourself a stench in your father's nostrils, and the hands of everyone with you will be strengthened." 22 So they pitched a tent for Absalom on the roof, and he lay with his father's concubines in the sight of all Israel.[d]

23 Now in those days the advice[e] Ahithophel gave was like that of one who inquires of God. That was how both David[f] and Absalom regarded all of Ahithophel's advice.

17 Ahithophel said to Absalom, "I would[t] choose twelve thousand men and set out tonight in pursuit of David. 2 I would[u] attack him while he is weary and weak.[g] I would[u] strike him with terror, and then all the people with him will flee. I would[u] strike down only the king[h] 3 and bring all the people back to you. The death of the man you seek will mean the return of all; all the people will be unharmed." 4 This plan seemed good to Absalom and to all the elders of Israel.

5 But Absalom said, "Summon also Hushai[i] the Arkite, so we can hear what he has to say." 6 When Hushai came to him, Absalom said, "Ahithophel has given this advice. Should we do what he says? If not, give us your opinion."

7 Hushai replied to Absalom, "The advice Ahithophel has given is not good this time. 8 You know your father and his men; they are fighters, and as fierce as a wild bear robbed of her cubs.[j] Besides, your father is an experienced fighter;[k] he will not spend the night with the troops. 9 Even now, he is hidden in a cave or some other place.[l] If he should attack your troops first,[v] whoever hears about it will say, 'There has been a slaughter among the troops who follow Absalom.' 10 Then even the bravest soldier, whose heart is like the heart of a lion,[m] will melt[n] with fear, for all Israel knows that your father is a fighter and that those with him are brave.[o]

11 "So I advise you: Let all Israel, from Dan to Beersheba[p]—as numerous as the sand[q] on the seashore—be gathered to you, with you yourself leading them into battle. 12 Then we will attack him wherever he may be found, and we will fall on him as dew settles on the ground. Neither he nor any of his men will be left alive. 13 If he withdraws into a city, then all Israel will bring ropes to that city, and we will drag it down to the valley[r] until not even a piece of it can be found."

14 Absalom and all the men of Israel said, "The advice[s] of Hushai the Arkite is better than that of Ahithophel."[t] For the LORD had determined to frustrate[u] the good advice of Ahithophel in order to bring disaster[v] on Absalom.[w]

15 Hushai told Zadok and Abiathar, the priests, "Ahithophel has advised Absalom and the elders of Israel to do such and such, but I have advised them to do so and so. 16 Now send a message immediately and tell David, 'Do not spend the night at the fords in the

16:15 [y] S 2Sa 15:37 [z] S 2Sa 15:12 **16:16** [a] S 2Sa 15:32 **16:17** [b] 2Sa 19:25 **16:19** [c] 2Sa 15:34 **16:22** [d] S 2Sa 3:7; 12:11-12; S 15:16 **16:23** [e] 2Sa 17:14,23 [f] S 2Sa 15:12 **17:2** [g] 2Sa 16:14 [h] 1Ki 22:31; Zec 13:7 **17:5** [i] S 2Sa 15:32 **17:8** [j] Hos 13:8 [k] 1Sa 16:18 **17:9** [l] Jer 41:9 **17:10** [m] 1Ch 12:8 [n] Jos 2:9,11; Eze 21:15 [o] 2Sa 23:8; 1Ch 11:11 **17:11** [p] S Jdg 20:1 [q] S Ge 12:2; S Jos 11:4 **17:13** [r] Mic 1:6 **17:14** [s] S 2Sa 16:23 [t] S 2Sa 15:12 [u] S 2Sa 15:34; Ne 4:15 [v] Ps 9:16 [w] 2Ch 10:8

[t] 1 Or *Let me* [u] 2 Or *will* [v] 9 Or *When some of the men fall at the first attack*

16:22 HIS FATHER'S CONCUBINES. In open defiance toward his father, Absalom committed adultery with David's own wives. Scripture states that the evil deed of Absalom took place "on the roof" and "in the sight of all Israel." This was in fulfillment of God's judgment: "Out of your own household I am going to bring calamity upon you. Before your very eyes I will take your wives and give them to one who is close to you, and he will lie with your wives in broad daylight. . . . I will do this thing in broad daylight before all Israel" (12:11–12). For a son to violate his father's wives was the greatest insult to a father. David had sinned grievously and suffered for it here.

desert;[x] cross over without fail, or the
king and all the people with him will be
swallowed up.[y]' "
17Jonathan[z] and Ahimaaz were
staying at En Rogel.[a] A servant girl
was to go and inform them, and they
were to go and tell King David, for they
could not risk being seen entering the
city. **18**But a young man saw them and
told Absalom. So the two of them left
quickly and went to the house of a man
in Bahurim.[b] He had a well in his
courtyard, and they climbed down into
it. **19**His wife took a covering and
spread it out over the opening of the
well and scattered grain over it. No one
knew anything about it.[c]
20When Absalom's men came to the
woman[d] at the house, they asked,
"Where are Ahimaaz and Jonathan?"
The woman answered them, "They
crossed over the brook."[w] The men
searched but found no one, so they returned to Jerusalem.
21After the men had gone, the two
climbed out of the well and went to inform King David. They said to him,
"Set out and cross the river at once;
Ahithophel has advised such and such
against you." **22**So David and all the
people with him set out and crossed
the Jordan. By daybreak, no one was
left who had not crossed the Jordan.
23When Ahithophel saw that his advice[e] had not been followed, he saddled his donkey and set out for his
house in his hometown. He put his
house in order[f] and then hanged himself. So he died and was buried in his
father's tomb.
24David went to Mahanaim,[g] and
Absalom crossed the Jordan with all
the men of Israel. **25**Absalom had appointed Amasa[h] over the army in
place of Joab. Amasa was the son of a
man named Jether,[x][i] an Israelite[y]
who had married Abigail,[z] the daughter of Nahash and sister of Zeruiah the
mother of Joab. **26**The Israelites and
Absalom camped in the land of Gilead.
27When David came to Mahanaim,
Shobi son of Nahash[j] from Rabbah[k]
of the Ammonites, and Makir[l] son
of Ammiel from Lo Debar, and Barzillai[m] the Gileadite[n] from Rogelim
28brought bedding and bowls and articles of pottery. They also brought
wheat and barley, flour and roasted
grain, beans and lentils,[a] **29**honey and
curds, sheep, and cheese from cows'
milk for David and his people to eat.[o]
For they said, "The people have become hungry and tired and thirsty in
the desert.[p]"

Absalom's Death

18 David mustered the men who
were with him and appointed
over them commanders of thousands
and commanders of hundreds. **2**David
sent the troops out[q]—a third under
the command of Joab, a third under
Joab's brother Abishai[r] son of Zeruiah, and a third under Ittai[s] the Gittite.
The king told the troops, "I myself will
surely march out with you."
3But the men said, "You must not go
out; if we are forced to flee, they won't
care about us. Even if half of us die,
they won't care; but you are worth
ten[t] thousand of us.[b] It would be better now for you to give us support from
the city."[u]
4The king answered, "I will do whatever seems best to you."
So the king stood beside the gate
while all the men marched out in units
of hundreds and of thousands. **5**The
king commanded Joab, Abishai and Ittai, "Be gentle with the young man Absalom for my sake." And all the troops
heard the king giving orders concerning Absalom to each of the commanders.
6The army marched into the field to
fight Israel, and the battle took place
in the forest[v] of Ephraim. **7**There the
army of Israel was defeated by David's
men, and the casualties that day were
great—twenty thousand men. **8**The
battle spread out over the whole countryside, and the forest claimed more
lives that day than the sword.
9Now Absalom happened to meet
David's men. He was riding his mule,
and as the mule went under the thick
branches of a large oak, Absalom's
head[w] got caught in the tree. He was

17:16 [x]2Sa 15:28 [y]2Sa 15:35
17:17 [z]S 2Sa 15:27,36 [a]Jos 15:7; 18:16; 1Ki 1:9
17:18 [b]S 2Sa 3:16
17:19 [c]S Jos 2:6
17:20 [d]S Ex 1:19
17:23 [e]2Sa S 2Sa 16:23 [f]2Ki 20:1
17:24 [g]S Ge 32:2
17:25 [h]2Sa 19:13; 20:4, 9-12; 1Ki 2:5,32; 1Ch 12:18 [i]1Ch 2:13-17
17:27 [j]S 1Sa 11:1 [k]S Dt 3:11 [l]2Sa 9:4 [m]2Sa 19:31-39; 1Ki 2:7 [n]2Sa 19:31; Ezr 2:61
17:29 [o]1Ch 12:40 [p]2Sa 16:2; S Ro 12:13
18:2 [q]S Jdg 7:16; 1Sa 11:11 [r]S 1Sa 26:6 [s]2Sa 15:19
18:3 [t]S 1Sa 18:7 [u]2Sa 21:17
18:6 [v]S Jos 17:15
18:9 [w]2Sa 14:26

[w]*20* Or *"They passed by the sheep pen toward the water."* [x]*25* Hebrew *Ithra,* a variant of *Jether* [y]*25* Hebrew and some Septuagint manuscripts; other Septuagint manuscripts (see also 1 Chron. 2:17) *Ishmaelite* or *Jezreelite* [z]*25* Hebrew *Abigal,* a variant of *Abigail* [a]*28* Most Septuagint manuscripts and Syriac; Hebrew *lentils, and roasted grain* [b]*3* Two Hebrew manuscripts, some Septuagint manuscripts and Vulgate; most Hebrew manuscripts *care; for now there are ten thousand like us*

left hanging in midair, while the mule
he was riding kept on going.
10When one of the men saw this, he
told Joab, "I just saw Absalom hanging
in an oak tree."
11Joab said to the man who had told
him this, "What! You saw him? Why
didn't you strike[x] him to the ground
right there? Then I would have had to
give you ten shekels[c] of silver and a
warrior's belt.[y]"
12But the man replied, "Even if a
thousand shekels[d] were weighed out
into my hands, I would not lift my hand
against the king's son. In our hearing
the king commanded you and Abishai
and Ittai, 'Protect the young man Absalom for my sake.[e]' 13And if I had
put my life in jeopardy[f]—and nothing
is hidden from the king[z]—you would
have kept your distance from me."
14Joab[a] said, "I'm not going to wait
like this for you." So he took three jave-
lins in his hand and plunged them into
Absalom's heart while Absalom was
still alive in the oak tree. 15And ten of
Joab's armor-bearers surrounded Absalom, struck him and killed him.[b]
16Then Joab[c] sounded the trumpet,
and the troops stopped pursuing Israel, for Joab halted them. 17They took
Absalom, threw him into a big pit in the
forest and piled up[d] a large heap of
rocks[e] over him. Meanwhile, all the
Israelites fled to their homes.
18During his lifetime Absalom had
taken a pillar and erected it in the
King's Valley[f] as a monument[g] to
himself, for he thought, "I have no
son[h] to carry on the memory of my
name." He named the pillar after himself, and it is called Absalom's Monument to this day.

David Mourns

19Now Ahimaaz[i] son of Zadok said,
"Let me run and take the news to the
king that the LORD has delivered him
from the hand of his enemies.[j]"
20"You are not the one to take the
news today," Joab told him. "You may
take the news another time, but you
must not do so today, because the
king's son is dead."
21Then Joab said to a Cushite, "Go,
tell the king what you have seen." The
Cushite bowed down before Joab and
ran off.
22Ahimaaz son of Zadok again said
to Joab, "Come what may, please let me
run behind the Cushite."
But Joab replied, "My son, why do
you want to go? You don't have any
news that will bring you a reward."
23He said, "Come what may, I want
to run."
So Joab said, "Run!" Then Ahimaaz
ran by way of the plain[g] and outran
the Cushite.
24While David was sitting between
the inner and outer gates, the watchman[k] went up to the roof of the gateway by the wall. As he looked out, he
saw a man running alone. 25The
watchman called out to the king and
reported it.
The king said, "If he is alone, he
must have good news." And the man
came closer and closer.
26Then the watchman saw another
man running, and he called down to the
gatekeeper, "Look, another man running alone!"
The king said, "He must be bringing
good news,[l] too."
27The watchman said, "It seems to
me that the first one runs like[m] Ahimaaz son of Zadok."
"He's a good man," the king said.
"He comes with good news."
28Then Ahimaaz called out to the
king, "All is well!" He bowed down before the king with his face to the
ground and said, "Praise be to the LORD
your God! He has delivered up the men
who lifted their hands against my lord
the king."
29The king asked, "Is the young man
Absalom safe?"
Ahimaaz answered, "I saw great
confusion just as Joab was about to
send the king's servant and me, your
servant, but I don't know what it was."
30The king said, "Stand aside and
wait here." So he stepped aside and
stood there.
31Then the Cushite arrived and said,
"My lord the king, hear the good news!
The LORD has delivered you today from
all who rose up against you."

18:11 [x]S 2Sa 3:39 [y]1Sa 18:4
18:13 [z]2Sa 14:19-20
18:14 [a]S 2Sa 2:18
18:15 [b]S 2Sa 12:10
18:16 [c]S 2Sa 2:28
18:17 [d]Jos 7:26 [e]Jos 8:29
18:18 [f]Ge 14:17 [g]S Ge 50:5; S Nu 32:42 [h]2Sa 14:27
18:19 [i]S 2Sa 15:36 [j]Jdg 11:36
18:24 [k]S 1Sa 14:16; S Jer 51:12
18:26 [l]1Ki 1:42; Isa 52:7; 61:1
18:27 [m]2Ki 9:20

[c] *11* That is, about 4 ounces (about 115 grams) [d] *12* That is, about 25 pounds (about 11 kilograms) [e] *12* A few Hebrew manuscripts, Septuagint, Vulgate and Syriac; most Hebrew manuscripts may be translated *Absalom, whoever you may be.* [f] *13* Or *Otherwise, if I had acted treacherously toward him* [g] *23* That is, the plain of the Jordan

32The king asked the Cushite, "Is
the young man Absalom safe?"
The Cushite replied, "May the enemies of my lord the king and all who
rise up to harm you be like that young
man."[n]
33The king was shaken. He went up
to the room over the gateway and wept.
As he went, he said: "O my son Absalom! My son, my son Absalom! If only
I had died[o] instead of you—O Absalom, my son, my son!"[p]

19 Joab was told, "The king is
weeping and mourning for Absalom." 2And for the whole army the
victory that day was turned into
mourning, because on that day the
troops heard it said, "The king is grieving for his son." 3The men stole into
the city that day as men steal in who
are ashamed when they flee from battle. 4The king covered his face and
cried aloud, "O my son Absalom! O Absalom, my son, my son!"
5Then Joab went into the house to
the king and said, "Today you have humiliated all your men, who have just
saved your life and the lives of your
sons and daughters and the lives of
your wives and concubines. 6You love
those who hate you and hate those who
love you. You have made it clear today
that the commanders and their men
mean nothing to you. I see that you
would be pleased if Absalom were alive
today and all of us were dead. 7Now go
out and encourage your men. I swear
by the LORD that if you don't go out, not
a man will be left with you by nightfall.
This will be worse for you than all the
calamities that have come upon you
from your youth till now."[q]
8So the king got up and took his seat
in the gateway. When the men were
told, "The king is sitting in the gateway,[r]" they all came before him.

David Returns to Jerusalem

Meanwhile, the Israelites had fled to
their homes. 9Throughout the tribes of
Israel, the people were all arguing with
each other, saying, "The king delivered
us from the hand of our enemies; he is
the one who rescued us from the hand
of the Philistines.[s] But now he has
fled the country because of Absalom;[t]
10and Absalom, whom we anointed to
rule over us, has died in battle. So why
do you say nothing about bringing the
king back?"
11King David sent this message to
Zadok[u] and Abiathar, the priests:
"Ask the elders of Judah, 'Why should
you be the last to bring the king back
to his palace, since what is being said
throughout Israel has reached the king
at his quarters? 12You are my brothers,
my own flesh and blood. So why should
you be the last to bring back the king?'
13And say to Amasa,[v] 'Are you not my
own flesh and blood?[w] May God deal
with me, be it ever so severely,[x] if
from now on you are not the commander of my army in place of Joab.[y]' "
14He won over the hearts of all the
men of Judah as though they were one
man. They sent word to the king, "Return, you and all your men." 15Then the
king returned and went as far as the
Jordan.
Now the men of Judah had come to
Gilgal[z] to go out and meet the king
and bring him across the Jordan.
16Shimei[a] son of Gera, the Benjamite
from Bahurim, hurried down with the
men of Judah to meet King David.
17With him were a thousand Benjamites, along with Ziba,[b] the steward
of Saul's household,[c] and his fifteen
sons and twenty servants. They rushed
to the Jordan, where the king was.
18They crossed at the ford to take the
king's household over and to do whatever he wished.
When Shimei son of Gera crossed
the Jordan, he fell prostrate before the
king 19and said to him, "May my lord
not hold me guilty. Do not remember
how your servant did wrong on the day
my lord the king left Jerusalem.[d] May
the king put it out of his mind. 20For I
your servant know that I have sinned,
but today I have come here as the first
of the whole house of Joseph to come
down and meet my lord the king."
21Then Abishai[e] son of Zeruiah
said, "Shouldn't Shimei be put to death
for this? He cursed[f] the LORD's anointed."[g]
22David replied, "What do you and I
have in common, you sons of Zeruiah?[h] This day you have become my adversaries! Should anyone be put to
death in Israel today?[i] Do I not know

18:32 [n] Jdg 5:31; S 1Sa 25:26
18:33 [o] Ex 32:32 [p] S Ge 43:14; 2Sa 19:4
19:7 [q] Pr 14:28
19:8 [r] S 2Sa 15:2
19:9 [s] 2Sa 8:1-14 [t] 2Sa 15:14
19:11 [u] S 2Sa 15:24
19:13 [v] S 2Sa 17:25 [w] S Ge 29:14 [x] S Ru 1:17 [y] S 2Sa 2:13
19:15 [z] S 1Sa 11:15
19:16 [a] 2Sa 16:5-13
19:17 [b] S 2Sa 9:2 [c] S Ge 43:16
19:19 [d] S 2Sa 16:6-8
19:21 [e] S 1Sa 26:6 [f] S Ex 22:28 [g] S 1Sa 12:3; S 26:9
19:22 [h] S 2Sa 2:18; S 16:10 [i] 1Sa 11:13

18:33 ABSALOM! IF ONLY I HAD DIED INSTEAD OF YOU. David's unremitting grief was more than that of a father for his son; it was grief for a son killed in the very act of rebellion and sin.

that today I am king over Israel?" 23So the king said to Shimei, "You shall not die." And the king promised him on oath.[j]

24Mephibosheth,[k] Saul's grandson, also went down to meet the king. He had not taken care of his feet or trimmed his mustache or washed his clothes from the day the king left until the day he returned safely. 25When he came from Jerusalem to meet the king, the king asked him, "Why didn't you go with me,[l] Mephibosheth?"

26He said, "My lord the king, since I your servant am lame,[m] I said, 'I will have my donkey saddled and will ride on it, so I can go with the king.' But Ziba[n] my servant betrayed me. 27And he has slandered your servant to my lord the king. My lord the king is like an angel[o] of God; so do whatever pleases you. 28All my grandfather's descendants deserved nothing but death[p] from my lord the king, but you gave your servant a place among those who eat at your table.[q] So what right do I have to make any more appeals to the king?"

29The king said to him, "Why say more? I order you and Ziba to divide the fields."

30Mephibosheth said to the king, "Let him take everything, now that my lord the king has arrived home safely."

31Barzillai[r] the Gileadite also came down from Rogelim to cross the Jordan with the king and to send him on his way from there. 32Now Barzillai was a very old man, eighty years of age. He had provided for the king during his stay in Mahanaim, for he was a very wealthy[s] man. 33The king said to Barzillai, "Cross over with me and stay with me in Jerusalem, and I will provide for you."

34But Barzillai answered the king, "How many more years will I live, that I should go up to Jerusalem with the king? 35I am now eighty[t] years old. Can I tell the difference between what is good and what is not? Can your servant taste what he eats and drinks? Can I still hear the voices of men and women singers?[u] Why should your servant be an added[v] burden to my lord the king? 36Your servant will cross over the Jordan with the king for a short distance, but why should the king reward me in this way? 37Let your servant return, that I may die in my own town near the tomb of my father[w] and mother. But here is your servant Kimham.[x] Let him cross over with my lord the king. Do for him whatever pleases you."

38The king said, "Kimham shall cross over with me, and I will do for him whatever pleases you. And anything you desire from me I will do for you."

39So all the people crossed the Jordan, and then the king crossed over. The king kissed Barzillai and gave him his blessing,[y] and Barzillai returned to his home.

40When the king crossed over to Gilgal, Kimham crossed with him. All the troops of Judah and half the troops of Israel had taken the king over.

41Soon all the men of Israel were coming to the king and saying to him, "Why did our brothers, the men of Judah, steal the king away and bring him and his household across the Jordan, together with all his men?"[z]

42All the men of Judah answered the men of Israel, "We did this because the king is closely related to us. Why are you angry about it? Have we eaten any of the king's provisions? Have we taken anything for ourselves?"

43Then the men of Israel[a] answered the men of Judah, "We have ten shares in the king; and besides, we have a greater claim on David than you have. So why do you treat us with contempt? Were we not the first to speak of bringing back our king?"

But the men of Judah responded even more harshly than the men of Israel.

Sheba Rebels Against David

20 Now a troublemaker named Sheba son of Bicri, a Benjamite, happened to be there. He sounded the trumpet and shouted,

"We have no share[b] in David,[c]
no part in Jesse's son![d]
Every man to his tent, O Israel!"

2So all the men of Israel deserted David to follow Sheba son of Bicri. But the men of Judah stayed by their king all the way from the Jordan to Jerusalem.

3When David returned to his palace in Jerusalem, he took the ten concubines[e] he had left to take care of the palace and put them in a house under

19:23 [j] 1Ki 2:8,42 **19:24** [k] S 2Sa 4:4 **19:25** [l] 2Sa 16:17 **19:26** [m] S Lev 21:18 [n] S 2Sa 9:2 **19:27** [o] S 1Sa 29:9 **19:28** [p] S 2Sa 16:8 [q] S 2Sa 9:7,13 **19:31** [r] S 2Sa 17:27-29, 27; 1Ki 2:7 **19:32** [s] 1Sa 25:2 **19:35** [t] Ps 90:10 [u] 2Ch 35:25; Ezr 2:65; Ecc 2:8; 12:1 [v] 2Sa 15:33 **19:37** [w] S Ge 49:29 [x] Jer 41:17 **19:39** [y] S Ge 47:7 **19:41** [z] Jdg 8:1; 12:1 **19:43** [a] S 2Sa 5:1 **20:1** [b] S Ge 31:14 [c] S Ge 29:14; 1Ki 12:16 [d] 1Sa 22:7-8 **20:3** [e] S 2Sa 15:16

guard. He provided for them, but did
not lie with them. They were kept in
confinement till the day of their death,
living as widows.
4Then the king said to Amasa,[f]
"Summon the men of Judah to come to
me within three days, and be here yourself." **5**But when Amasa went to summon Judah, he took longer than the
time the king had set for him.
6David said to Abishai,[g] "Now Sheba son of Bicri will do us more harm
than Absalom did. Take your master's
men and pursue him, or he will find fortified cities and escape from us." **7**So
Joab's men and the Kerethites[h] and
Pelethites and all the mighty warriors
went out under the command of Abishai. They marched out from Jerusalem
to pursue Sheba son of Bicri.
8While they were at the great rock in
Gibeon,[i] Amasa came to meet them.
Joab[j] was wearing his military tunic,
and strapped over it at his waist was a
belt with a dagger in its sheath. As he
stepped forward, it dropped out of its
sheath.
9Joab said to Amasa, "How are you,
my brother?" Then Joab took Amasa by
the beard with his right hand to kiss
him. **10**Amasa was not on his guard
against the dagger[k] in Joab[l]'s hand,
and Joab plunged it into his belly, and
his intestines spilled out on the
ground. Without being stabbed again,
Amasa died. Then Joab and his brother
Abishai pursued Sheba son of Bicri.
11One of Joab's men stood beside
Amasa and said, "Whoever favors Joab,
and whoever is for David, let him follow Joab!" **12**Amasa lay wallowing in
his blood in the middle of the road, and
the man saw that all the troops came
to a halt[m] there. When he realized that
everyone who came up to Amasa
stopped, he dragged him from the road
into a field and threw a garment over
him. **13**After Amasa had been removed
from the road, all the men went on with
Joab to pursue Sheba son of Bicri.
14Sheba passed through all the
tribes of Israel to Abel Beth Maacah[h]
and through the entire region of the
Berites,[n] who gathered together and
followed him. **15**All the troops with

20:4 [f] S 2Sa 17:25
20:6 [g] 2Sa 21:17
20:7 [h] S 1Sa 30:14; S 2Sa 15:18
20:8 [i] S Jos 9:3 [j] S 2Sa 2:18
20:10 [k] S Jdg 3:21 [l] 1Ki 2:5
20:12 [m] S 2Sa 2:23
20:14 [n] Nu 21:16
20:15 [o] 1Ki 15:20; 2Ki 15:29 [p] Isa 37:33; Jer 6:6; 32:24
20:16 [q] 2Sa 14:2
20:19 [r] S Dt 2:26 [s] S 1Sa 26:19
20:21 [t] S 2Sa 4:8
20:22 [u] Ecc 9:13
20:23 [v] S 2Sa 2:28; 8:16-18; 24:2
20:24 [w] 1Ki 4:6; 5:14; 12:18; 2Ch 10:18 [x] S 2Sa 8:16
20:25 [y] S 1Sa 2:35; S 2Sa 8:17
21:1 [z] S Ge 12:10; S Dt 32:24

Joab came and besieged Sheba in Abel
Beth Maacah.[o] They built a siege
ramp[p] up to the city, and it stood
against the outer fortifications. While
they were battering the wall to bring it
down, **16**a wise woman[q] called from
the city, "Listen! Listen! Tell Joab to
come here so I can speak to him." **17**He
went toward her, and she asked, "Are
you Joab?"
"I am," he answered.
She said, "Listen to what your servant has to say."
"I'm listening," he said.
18She continued, "Long ago they
used to say, 'Get your answer at Abel,'
and that settled it. **19**We are the peaceful[r] and faithful in Israel. You are trying to destroy a city that is a mother in
Israel. Why do you want to swallow up
the LORD's inheritance?"[s]
20"Far be it from me!" Joab replied,
"Far be it from me to swallow up or
destroy! **21**That is not the case. A man
named Sheba son of Bicri, from the hill
country of Ephraim, has lifted up his
hand against the king, against David.
Hand over this one man, and I'll withdraw from the city."
The woman said to Joab, "His head[t]
will be thrown to you from the wall."
22Then the woman went to all the
people with her wise advice,[u] and they
cut off the head of Sheba son of Bicri
and threw it to Joab. So he sounded the
trumpet, and his men dispersed from
the city, each returning to his home.
And Joab went back to the king in Jerusalem.
23Joab[v] was over Israel's entire
army; Benaiah son of Jehoiada was
over the Kerethites and Pelethites;
24Adoniram[i][w] was in charge of
forced labor; Jehoshaphat[x] son of Ahilud was recorder; **25**Sheva was secretary; Zadok[y] and Abiathar were
priests; **26**and Ira the Jairite was David's priest.

The Gibeonites Avenged

21 During the reign of David, there
was a famine[z] for three suc-

[h] *14* Or *Abel, even Beth Maacah;* also in verse 15 [i] *24* Some Septuagint manuscripts (see also 1 Kings 4:6 and 5:14); Hebrew *Adoram*

21:1 THERE WAS A FAMINE. Chs. 21—24 contain supplementary accounts of events related to David's reign. They are not presented in chronological order; rather, they comprise an appendix to 1 and 2 Samuel. Several of the events occurred early in David's reign.

21:1 BECAUSE HE PUT THE GIBEONITES TO DEATH. Joshua and Israel had made a treaty

cessive years; so David sought[a] the
face of the LORD. The LORD said, "It is
on account of Saul and his blood-
stained house; it is because he put the
Gibeonites to death."
2The king summoned the Gibeonites[b] and spoke to them. (Now the
Gibeonites were not a part of Israel but
were survivors of the Amorites; the Israelites had sworn to ⌞spare⌟ them, but
Saul in his zeal for Israel and Judah
had tried to annihilate them.) 3David
asked the Gibeonites, "What shall I do
for you? How shall I make amends so
that you will bless the LORD's inheritance?"[c]
4The Gibeonites answered him, "We
have no right to demand silver or gold
from Saul or his family, nor do we have
the right to put anyone in Israel to
death."[d]
"What do you want me to do for
you?" David asked.
5They answered the king, "As for
the man who destroyed us and plotted
against us so that we have been deci-
mated and have no place anywhere in
Israel, 6let seven of his male descendants be given to us to be killed and
exposed[e] before the LORD at Gibeah of
Saul—the LORD's chosen[f] one."
So the king said, "I will give them to
you."
7The king spared Mephibosheth[g]
son of Jonathan, the son of Saul, because of the oath[h] before the LORD between David and Jonathan son of Saul.
8But the king took Armoni and Mephibosheth, the two sons of Aiah's
daughter Rizpah,[i] whom she had
borne to Saul, together with the five
sons of Saul's daughter Merab,[j]
whom she had borne to Adriel son of
Barzillai the Meholathite.[j] 9He handed them over to the Gibeonites, who
killed and exposed them on a hill before the LORD. All seven of them fell together; they were put to death[k] during
the first days of the harvest, just as the
barley harvest was beginning.[l]
10Rizpah daughter of Aiah took
sackcloth and spread it out for herself
on a rock. From the beginning of the
harvest till the rain poured down from
the heavens on the bodies, she did not
let the birds of the air touch them by
day or the wild animals by night.[m]
11When David was told what Aiah's
daughter Rizpah, Saul's concubine,
had done, 12he went and took the
bones of Saul[n] and his son Jonathan
from the citizens of Jabesh Gilead.[o]
(They had taken them secretly from
the public square at Beth Shan,[p]
where the Philistines had hung[q] them
after they struck Saul down on Gilboa.)[r] 13David brought the bones of
Saul and his son Jonathan from there,
and the bones of those who had been
killed and exposed were gathered up.
14They buried the bones of Saul and
his son Jonathan in the tomb of Saul's
father Kish, at Zela[s] in Benjamin, and
did everything the king commanded.
After that,[t] God answered prayer[u] in
behalf of the land.[v]

Wars Against the Philistines

21:15–22pp — 1Ch 20:4–8

15Once again there was a battle between the Philistines[w] and Israel. David went down with his men to fight
against the Philistines, and he became
exhausted. 16And Ishbi-Benob, one of
the descendants of Rapha, whose
bronze spearhead weighed three hundred shekels[k] and who was armed
with a new ⌞sword⌟, said he would kill
David. 17But Abishai[x] son of Zeruiah
came to David's rescue; he struck the
Philistine down and killed him. Then
David's men swore to him, saying,
"Never again will you go out with us to
battle, so that the lamp[y] of Israel will
not be extinguished.[z]"
18In the course of time, there was
another battle with the Philistines, at
Gob. At that time Sibbecai[a] the Hu-

21:1 [a]S Ex 32:11 **21:2** [b]S Jos 9:15 **21:3** [c]S 1Sa 26:19 **21:4** [d]Nu 35:33-34 **21:6** [e]Nu 25:4 [f]S 1Sa 10:24 **21:7** [g]2Sa 4:4 [h]S 1Sa 18:3; S 2Sa 9:7 **21:8** [i]2Sa 3:7 [j]1Sa 18:19 **21:9** [k]S 2Sa 16:8 [l]S Ru 1:22 **21:10** [m]S Ge 40:19; S 1Sa 17:44 **21:12** [n]1Sa 31:11-13 [o]S Jdg 21:8; S 1Sa 11:1 [p]S Jos 17:11 [q]1Sa 31:10 [r]S 1Sa 28:4 **21:14** [s]Jos 18:28 [t]Jos 7:26 [u]2Sa 24:25 [v]1Ch 8:34 **21:15** [w]S 2Sa 5:25 **21:17** [x]2Sa 20:6 [y]1Ki 11:36; 15:4; 2Ki 8:19; 2Ch 21:7; Ps 132:17 [z]2Sa 18:3 **21:18** [a]1Ch 11:29; 27:11

[j] *8* Two Hebrew manuscripts, some Septuagint manuscripts and Syriac (see also 1 Samuel 18:19); most Hebrew and Septuagint manuscripts *Michal* [k] *16* That is, about 7 1/2 pounds (about 3.5 kilograms)

with the Gibeonites that they would not be killed along with the other Canaanites (Jos 9:15–21). Evidently Saul had broken this vow (v. 2). To break a vow was a serious transgression against God's law (Nu 30:1–2). The term "his blood-stained house" implies that Saul's sons had participated in killing the Gibeonites (v. 8; see next note).

21:14 AFTER THAT, GOD ANSWERED PRAYER. After the deaths of the seven descendants of Saul (vv. 8–9), God once again answered the prayers of his people (cf. Jos 7—8). This text also indicates that these seven men had been implicated in the killing of the Gibeonites; in cases where the children were not involved in the sins of their father, they were not to be punished (see Dt 24:16; 2Ki 14:6; Eze 18:1–4,14–17).

shathite killed Saph, one of the descendants of Rapha.
19In another battle with the Philistines at Gob, Elhanan son of Jaare-Ore-
gim[l] the Bethlehemite killed Goliath[m] the Gittite,[b] who had a spear
with a shaft like a weaver's rod.[c]
20In still another battle, which took
place at Gath, there was a huge man
with six fingers on each hand and six
toes on each foot—twenty-four in all.
He also was descended from Rapha.
21When he taunted[d] Israel, Jonathan
son of Shimeah,[e] David's brother,
killed him.
22These four were descendants of
Rapha in Gath, and they fell at the
hands of David and his men.

David's Song of Praise

22:1–51pp — Ps 18:1–50

22 David sang[f] to the LORD the
words of this song when the
LORD delivered him from the hand of all
his enemies and from the hand of Saul.
2He said:

"The LORD is my rock,[g] my
fortress[h] and my
deliverer;[i]
3 my God is my rock, in whom I
take refuge,[j]
my shield[k] and the horn[n][l] of
my salvation.
He is my stronghold,[m] my refuge
and my savior—
from violent men you save me.
4I call to the LORD, who is worthy[n]
of praise,
and I am saved from my
enemies.

5"The waves[o] of death swirled
about me;
the torrents of destruction
overwhelmed me.
6The cords of the grave[o][p] coiled
around me;
the snares of death confronted
me.
7In my distress[q] I called[r] to the
LORD;
I called out to my God.
From his temple he heard my
voice;
my cry came to his ears.

8"The earth[s] trembled and
quaked,[t]
the foundations[u] of the
heavens[p] shook;

21:19
[b]S 1Sa 17:4
[c]S 1Sa 17:7
21:21
[d]S 1Sa 17:10
[e]S 1Sa 16:9
22:1 [f]S Ex 15:1
22:2 [g]S 1Sa 2:2
[h]Ps 31:3; 91:2
[i]Ps 144:2
22:3 [j]S Dt 23:15;
S 32:37; Ps 14:6;
31:2; 59:16; 71:7;
91:2; 94:22;
Pr 10:29; Isa 25:4;
Jer 16:19;
Joel 3:16
[k]S Ge 15:1
[l]S Dt 33:17;
S Lk 1:69
[m]Ps 9:9; 52:7
22:4 [n]Ps 48:1;
96:4; 145:3
22:5
[o]Ps 69:14-15;
Jnh 2:3
22:6 [p]Ps 116:3;
Ac 2:24
22:7 [q]Ge 35:3;
S Jdg 2:15;
2Ch 15:4; Ps 4:1;
77:2; 120:1;
Isa 26:16
[r]Ps 34:6,15; 116:4
22:8 [s]Jdg 5:4;
Ps 97:4
[t]S Ex 19:18;
S Jdg 5:4; Ps 68:8;
77:18; Jer 10:10
[u]Job 9:6; 26:11;
Ps 75:3
22:9 [v]Ps 50:3;
97:3; Heb 12:29;
S Rev 11:5
[w]Isa 6:6;
Eze 1:13; 10:2
22:10
[x]S Ex 19:9;
Lev 16:2;
S Dt 33:26;
1Ki 8:12; Job 26:9;
Ps 104:3;
Isa 19:1; Jer 4:13;
Na 1:3
22:11
[y]S Ge 3:24;
S Ex 25:22
[z]Ps 104:3
22:12 [a]S Ex 19:9
22:13 [b]Job 37:3;
Ps 77:18
22:14
[c]S 1Sa 2:10
22:15
[d]S Dt 32:23
22:16 [e]Ps 6:1;
50:8,21; 106:9;
Na 1:4
[f]S Ex 14:21;
Isa 30:33; 40:24
22:17 [g]Ps 144:7
[h]Ex 2:10
22:18 [i]Lk 1:71
22:19 [j]Ps 23:4
22:20
[k]Job 36:16;
Ps 31:8

they trembled because he was
angry.
9Smoke rose from his nostrils;
consuming fire[v] came from his
mouth,
burning coals[w] blazed out of it.
10He parted the heavens and came
down;
dark clouds[x] were under his
feet.
11He mounted the cherubim[y] and
flew;
he soared[q] on the wings of the
wind.[z]
12He made darkness[a] his canopy
around him—
the dark[r] rain clouds of the
sky.
13Out of the brightness of his
presence
bolts of lightning[b] blazed forth.
14The LORD thundered[c] from
heaven;
the voice of the Most High
resounded.
15He shot arrows[d] and scattered
⌊the enemies⌋,
bolts of lightning and routed
them.
16The valleys of the sea were
exposed
and the foundations of the earth
laid bare
at the rebuke[e] of the LORD,
at the blast[f] of breath from his
nostrils.

17"He reached down from on high[g]
and took hold of me;
he drew[h] me out of deep
waters.
18He rescued[i] me from my powerful
enemy,
from my foes, who were too
strong for me.
19They confronted me in the day of
my disaster,
but the LORD was my support.[j]
20He brought me out into a
spacious[k] place;

[l]19 Or *son of Jair the weaver* [m]19 Hebrew and Septuagint; 1 Chron. 20:5 *son of Jair killed Lahmi the brother of Goliath* [n]3 *Horn* here symbolizes strength. [o]6 Hebrew *Sheol* [p]8 Hebrew; Vulgate and Syriac (see also Psalm 18:7) *mountains* [q]11 Many Hebrew manuscripts (see also Psalm 18:10); most Hebrew manuscripts *appeared* [r]12 Septuagint and Vulgate (see also Psalm 18:11); Hebrew *massed*

he rescued[l] me because he
delighted[m] in me.[n]

21"The LORD has dealt with me
according to my
righteousness;[o]
according to the cleanness[p] of
my hands[q] he has
rewarded me.
22For I have kept[r] the ways of the
LORD;
I have not done evil by turning
from my God.
23All his laws are before me;[s]
I have not turned[t] away from
his decrees.
24I have been blameless[u] before
him
and have kept myself from sin.
25The LORD has rewarded me
according to my
righteousness,[v]
according to my cleanness[s] in
his sight.

26"To the faithful you show yourself
faithful,
to the blameless you show
yourself blameless,
27to the pure[w] you show yourself
pure,
but to the crooked you show
yourself shrewd.[x]
28You save the humble,[y]
but your eyes are on the
haughty[z] to bring them
low.[a]
29You are my lamp,[b] O LORD;
the LORD turns my darkness into
light.
30With your help I can advance
against a troop[t];
with my God I can scale a wall.

31"As for God, his way is perfect;[c]
the word of the LORD is
flawless.[d]
He is a shield[e]
for all who take refuge in him.
32For who is God besides the LORD?
And who is the Rock[f] except
our God?[g]
33It is God who arms me with
strength[u]
and makes my way perfect.
34He makes my feet like the feet of
a deer;[h]
he enables me to stand on the
heights.[i]
35He trains my hands[j] for battle;
my arms can bend a bow[k] of
bronze.
36You give me your shield[l] of
victory;
you stoop down to make me
great.
37You broaden the path[m] beneath
me,
so that my ankles do not turn.

38"I pursued my enemies and
crushed them;
I did not turn back till they were
destroyed.
39I crushed[n] them completely, and
they could not rise;
they fell beneath my feet.
40You armed me with strength for
battle;
you made my adversaries bow at
my feet.[o]
41You made my enemies turn their
backs[p] in flight,
and I destroyed my foes.
42They cried for help,[q] but there
was no one to save
them—[r]
to the LORD, but he did not
answer.[s]
43I beat them as fine as the dust[t]
of the earth;
I pounded and trampled[u] them
like mud[v] in the streets.

44"You have delivered[w] me from the
attacks of my people;
you have preserved[x] me as the
head of nations.
People[y] I did not know are
subject to me,
45 and foreigners come cringing[z]
to me;
as soon as they hear me, they
obey me.[a]

22:20 [l]Ps 118:5 [m]Ps 22:8; Isa 42:1; Mt 12:18 [n]S 2Sa 15:26 **22:21** [o]S 1Sa 26:23 [p]Ps 26:6 [q]Job 17:9; 22:30; 42:7-8; Ps 24:4 **22:22** [r]Ge 18:19; Ps 128:1; Pr 8:32 **22:23** [s]Dt 6:4-9; Ps 119:30-32 [t]Ps 119:102 **22:24** [u]S Ge 6:9; Eph 1:4 **22:25** [v]S 1Sa 26:23 **22:27** [w]Mt 5:8 [x]Lev 26:23-24 **22:28** [y]S Ex 3:8; 1Sa 2:8-9; Ps 72:12-13 [z]Ps 131:1; Pr 30:13; Da 4:31; Zep 3:11 [a]Isa 2:12,17; 5:15; S Lk 1:51 **22:29** [b]Ps 27:1; Isa 2:5; Mic 7:8; Rev 21:23; 22:5 **22:31** [c]S Dt 32:4; Mt 5:48 [d]Ps 12:6; 119:140; Pr 30:5-6 [e]S Ge 15:1 **22:32** [f]S 1Sa 2:2 [g]S 2Sa 7:22
22:34 [h]Isa 35:6; Hab 3:19 [i]S Dt 32:13 **22:35** [j]Ps 144:1 [k]Ps 7:12; 11:2; Zec 9:13 **22:36** [l]Eph 6:16 **22:37** [m]Pr 4:11 **22:39** [n]Ps 44:5; 110:6; Mal 4:3 **22:40** [o]S Jos 10:24; S 1Ki 5:3 **22:41** [p]S Ex 23:27 **22:42** [q]Isa 1:15 [r]Ps 50:22 [s]S 1Sa 14:37 **22:43** [t]1Ki 20:10; 2Ki 13:7; Isa 41:2; Am 1:3 [u]Ps 7:5; Isa 41:25; Mic 7:10; Zec 10:5 [v]Isa 5:25; 10:6; 22:5; Mic 7:10 **22:44** [w]S Ex 11:3; S 2Sa 3:1 [x]Dt 28:13 [y]S 2Sa 8:1-14; Isa 55:3-5 **22:45** [z]Ps 66:3; 81:15 [a]S Dt 33:29

[s]*25* Hebrew; Septuagint and Vulgate (see also Psalm 18:24) *to the cleanness of my hands*
[t]*30* Or *can run through a barricade*
[u]*33* Dead Sea Scrolls, some Septuagint manuscripts, Vulgate and Syriac (see also Psalm 18:32); Masoretic Text *who is my strong refuge*

22:22 I HAVE KEPT THE WAYS OF THE LORD. David was not maintaining that he had never sinned or that he was perfect. He was expressing his desire to please the Lord with a heart that had been, up to this point, habitually turned toward him in faith. The psalm was probably composed shortly after God delivered him from Saul (2:4; 1Sa 31:6) and before he fell into his sins of murder and adultery (11:1—12:15).

46They all lose heart;
they come trembling[v][b] from
their strongholds.

47"The LORD lives! Praise be to my
Rock!
Exalted[c] be God, the Rock, my
Savior![d]
48He is the God who avenges[e]
me,[f]
who puts the nations under me,
49 who sets me free from my
enemies.[g]
You exalted me[h] above my foes;
from violent men you rescued
me.
50Therefore I will praise you,
O LORD, among the nations;
I will sing praises[i] to your
name.[j]
51He gives his king great victories;[k]
he shows unfailing kindness to
his anointed,[l]
to David[m] and his descendants
forever."[n]

The Last Words of David

23 These are the last words of
David:

"The oracle of David son of Jesse,
the oracle of the man exalted[o]
by the Most High,
the man anointed[p] by the God of
Jacob,
Israel's singer of songs[w]:

2"The Spirit[q] of the LORD spoke
through me;
his word was on my tongue.
3The God of Israel spoke,
the Rock[r] of Israel said to me:
'When one rules over men in
righteousness,[s]
when he rules in the fear[t] of
God,[u]
4he is like the light[v] of morning[w]
at sunrise[x]
on a cloudless morning,
like the brightness after rain[y]
that brings the grass from the
earth.'

5"Is not my house right with God?
Has he not made with me an
everlasting covenant,[z]
arranged and secured in every
part?
Will he not bring to fruition my
salvation
and grant me my every desire?

22:46 [b]Mic 7:17
22:47 [c]S Ex 15:2
[d]Dt 32:15;
Ps 18:31; 89:26;
95:1
22:48 [e]S Nu 31:3
[f]Ps 144:2
22:49 [g]Ps 140:1,
4 [h]Ps 27:6
22:50 [i]Ps 9:11;
47:6; 68:4
[j]Ro 15:9*
22:51 [k]Ps 21:1;
144:9-10
[l]1Sa 16:13;
Ps 89:20;
Ac 13:23
[m]S 2Sa 7:13
[n]Ps 89:24,29
23:1 [o]S Ex 11:3;
Ps 78:70-71;
89:27 [p]1Sa 2:10,
35; Ps 18:50;
20:6; 84:9;
Isa 45:1; Hab 3:13
23:2 [q]Mt 22:43;
Mk 12:36;
2Pe 1:21
23:3 [r]Dt 32:4;
S 1Sa 2:2;
Ps 18:31 [s]Ps 72:2
[t]S Ge 42:18
[u]Isa 11:1-5
23:4 [v]Jn 1:5
[w]Ps 119:147;
130:6; Pr 4:18
[x]S Jdg 5:31;
Mt 13:43
[y]S Dt 32:2
23:5 [z]S Ge 9:16;
Ps 89:29

23:6 [a]Isa 5:6;
9:18; 10:17; 27:4;
33:12; Mic 7:4;
Na 1:10;
Mt 13:40-41
23:8
[b]S 2Sa 17:10
[c]1Ch 27:2
23:9 [d]1Ch 27:4
[e]1Ch 8:4
23:13 [f]S Ge 38:1;
S Jos 12:15
[g]S Jos 17:15
23:14
[h]1Sa 22:4-5;
S 2Sa 5:17
[i]Ru 1:19

6But evil men are all to be cast
aside like thorns,[a]
which are not gathered with the
hand.
7Whoever touches thorns
uses a tool of iron or the shaft
of a spear;
they are burned up where they
lie."

David's Mighty Men

23:8–39pp — 1Ch 11:10–41

8These are the names of David's
mighty men:[b]
Josheb-Basshebeth,[x][c] a Tahkemonite,[y] was chief of the Three; he
raised his spear against eight hundred
men, whom he killed[z] in one encounter.
9Next to him was Eleazar son of Dodai[d] the Ahohite.[e] As one of the
three mighty men, he was with David
when they taunted the Philistines
gathered ⌊at Pas Dammim⌋[a] for battle.
Then the men of Israel retreated, 10but
he stood his ground and struck down
the Philistines till his hand grew tired
and froze to the sword. The LORD
brought about a great victory that day.
The troops returned to Eleazar, but
only to strip the dead.
11Next to him was Shammah son of
Agee the Hararite. When the Philistines banded together at a place where
there was a field full of lentils, Israel's
troops fled from them. 12But Shammah
took his stand in the middle of the
field. He defended it and struck the
Philistines down, and the LORD brought
about a great victory.
13During harvest time, three of the
thirty chief men came down to David at
the cave of Adullam,[f] while a band of
Philistines was encamped in the Valley
of Rephaim.[g] 14At that time David
was in the stronghold,[h] and the Philistine garrison was at Bethlehem.[i]
15David longed for water and said, "Oh,
that someone would get me a drink of

[v] *46* Some Septuagint manuscripts and Vulgate (see also Psalm 18:45); Masoretic Text *they arm themselves.* [w] *1* Or *Israel's beloved singer* [x] *8* Hebrew; some Septuagint manuscripts suggest *Ish-Bosheth,* that is, *Esh-Baal* (see also 1 Chron. 11:11 *Jashobeam*). [y] *8* Probably a variant of *Hacmonite* (see 1 Chron. 11:11) [z] *8* Some Septuagint manuscripts (see also 1 Chron. 11:11); Hebrew and other Septuagint manuscripts *Three; it was Adino the Eznite who killed eight hundred men* [a] *9* See 1 Chron. 11:13; Hebrew *gathered there.*

water from the well near the gate of
Bethlehem!" 16So the three mighty
men broke through the Philistine lines,
drew water from the well near the gate
of Bethlehem and carried it back to David. But he refused to drink it; instead,
he poured[j] it out before the LORD.
17"Far be it from me, O LORD, to do
this!" he said. "Is it not the blood[k] of
men who went at the risk of their
lives?" And David would not drink it.

Such were the exploits of the three
mighty men.

18Abishai[l] the brother of Joab son
of Zeruiah was chief of the Three.[b] He
raised his spear against three hundred
men, whom he killed, and so he became as famous as the Three. 19Was
he not held in greater honor than the
Three? He became their commander,
even though he was not included
among them.

20Benaiah[m] son of Jehoiada was a
valiant fighter from Kabzeel,[n] who
performed great exploits. He struck
down two of Moab's best men. He also
went down into a pit on a snowy day
and killed a lion. 21And he struck down
a huge Egyptian. Although the Egyptian had a spear in his hand, Benaiah
went against him with a club. He
snatched the spear from the Egyptian's hand and killed him with his own
spear. 22Such were the exploits of Benaiah son of Jehoiada; he too was as
famous as the three mighty men. 23He
was held in greater honor than any of
the Thirty, but he was not included
among the Three. And David put him in
charge of his bodyguard.

24Among the Thirty were:
Asahel[o] the brother of Joab,
Elhanan son of Dodo from Bethlehem,
25Shammah the Harodite,[p]
Elika the Harodite,
26Helez[q] the Paltite,
Ira[r] son of Ikkesh from Tekoa,
27Abiezer[s] from Anathoth,[t]
Mebunnai[c] the Hushathite,
28Zalmon the Ahohite,
Maharai[u] the Netophathite,[v]
29Heled[d][w] son of Baanah the Netophathite,
Ithai son of Ribai from Gibeah[x] in Benjamin,
30Benaiah the Pirathonite,[y]
Hiddai[e] from the ravines of Gaash,[z]
31Abi-Albon the Arbathite,
Azmaveth the Barhumite,[a]
32Eliahba the Shaalbonite,
the sons of Jashen,
Jonathan 33son of[f] Shammah the Hararite,
Ahiam son of Sharar[g] the Hararite,
34Eliphelet son of Ahasbai the Maacathite,[b]
Eliam[c] son of Ahithophel[d] the Gilonite,
35Hezro the Carmelite,[e]
Paarai the Arbite,
36Igal son of Nathan from Zobah,[f]
the son of Hagri,[h]
37Zelek the Ammonite,
Naharai the Beerothite,[g] the armor-bearer of Joab son of Zeruiah,
38Ira the Ithrite,[h]
Gareb the Ithrite
39and Uriah[i] the Hittite.
There were thirty-seven in all.

23:16 [j]S Ge 35:14 **23:17** [k]Lev 17:10-12 **23:18** [l]S 1Sa 26:6 **23:20** [m]S 2Sa 8:18; 1Ch 27:5 [n]Jos 15:21 **23:24** [o]S 2Sa 2:18 **23:25** [p]Jdg 7:1 **23:26** [q]1Ch 27:10 [r]1Ch 27:9 **23:27** [s]1Ch 27:12 [t]S Jos 21:18 **23:28** [u]1Ch 27:13 [v]2Ki 25:23; Ezr 2:22; Ne 7:26; Jer 40:8 **23:29** [w]1Ch 27:15 [x]S Jos 15:57 **23:30** [y]S Jdg 12:13 [z]Jos 24:30 **23:31** [a]2Sa 3:16 **23:34** [b]S Dt 3:14 [c]S 2Sa 11:3 [d]S 2Sa 15:12 **23:35** [e]S Jos 12:22 **23:36** [f]S 1Sa 14:47 **23:37** [g]S Jos 9:17 **23:38** [h]1Ch 2:53 **23:39** [i]2Sa 11:3 **24:1** [j]S Jos 9:15 [k]Job 1:6; Zec 3:1

David Counts the Fighting Men

24:1–17pp — 1Ch 21:1–17

24 Again[j] the anger of the LORD burned against Israel,[k] and he

[b] *18* Most Hebrew manuscripts (see also 1 Chron. 11:20); two Hebrew manuscripts and Syriac *Thirty* [c] *27* Hebrew; some Septuagint manuscripts (see also 1 Chron. 11:29) *Sibbecai* [d] *29* Some Hebrew manuscripts and Vulgate (see also 1 Chron. 11:30); most Hebrew manuscripts *Heleb* [e] *30* Hebrew; some Septuagint manuscripts (see also 1 Chron. 11:32) *Hurai* [f] *33* Some Septuagint manuscripts (see also 1 Chron. 11:34); Hebrew does not have *son of.* [g] *33* Hebrew; some Septuagint manuscripts (see also 1 Chron. 11:35) *Sacar* [h] *36* Some Septuagint manuscripts (see also 1 Chron. 11:38); Hebrew *Haggadi*

24:1 TAKE A CENSUS OF ISRAEL AND JUDAH. Note the following concerning David's sin in taking a census of the people: (1) Here it is stated that God incited David, whereas 1Ch 21:1 says that Satan "incited David to take a census of Israel." God at times will use Satan to achieve his divine purposes by permitting him to test God's people (cf. Job 1:12; 2:6; Mt 4:1–11; 1Pe 4:19; 5:8). God evidently allowed Satan to tempt David because of David's pride and lack of trust in God. David's will was involved in the sin (vv. 3–4; 1Ch 21:3–4), for he could have resisted Satan.

(2) The mention of "the anger of the LORD ... against Israel" presupposes that Israel had committed a grave offense against God. God's anger is stirred only when people sin, and the people evi-

incited David against them, saying,
"Go and take a census of[l] Israel and
Judah."
2So the king said to Joab[m] and the
army commanders[i] with him, "Go
throughout the tribes of Israel from
Dan to Beersheba[n] and enroll[o] the
fighting men, so that I may know how
many there are."
3But Joab[p] replied to the king,
"May the LORD your God multiply the
troops a hundred times over,[q] and
may the eyes of my lord the king see
it. But why does my lord the king want
to do such a thing?"
4The king's word, however, over-
ruled Joab and the army commanders;
so they left the presence of the king to
enroll the fighting men of Israel.
5After crossing the Jordan, they
camped near Aroer,[r] south of the
town in the gorge, and then went
through Gad and on to Jazer.[s] 6They
went to Gilead and the region of Tah-
tim Hodshi, and on to Dan Jaan and
around toward Sidon.[t] 7Then they
went toward the fortress of Tyre[u] and
all the towns of the Hivites[v] and Canaanites. Finally, they went on to Beersheba[w] in the Negev[x] of Judah.
8After they had gone through the entire land, they came back to Jerusalem
at the end of nine months and twenty
days.
9Joab reported the number of the
fighting men to the king: In Israel
there were eight hundred thousand
able-bodied men who could handle a
sword, and in Judah five hundred thousand.[y]
10David was conscience-stricken[z]
after he had counted the fighting men,
and he said to the LORD, "I have
sinned[a] greatly in what I have done.
Now, O LORD, I beg you, take away the
guilt of your servant. I have done a
very foolish thing.[b]"
11Before David got up the next
morning, the word of the LORD had
come to Gad[c] the prophet, David's
seer:[d] 12"Go and tell David, 'This is
what the LORD says: I am giving you
three options. Choose one of them for
me to carry out against you.' "
13So Gad went to David and said to
him, "Shall there come upon you
three[j] years of famine[e] in your land?
Or three months of fleeing from your
enemies while they pursue you? Or
three days of plague[f] in your land?
Now then, think it over and decide how
I should answer the one who sent me."
14David said to Gad, "I am in deep
distress. Let us fall into the hands of
the LORD, for his mercy[g] is great; but
do not let me fall into the hands of
men."
15So the LORD sent a plague on Israel
from that morning until the end of the
time designated, and seventy thousand
of the people from Dan to Beersheba
died.[h] 16When the angel stretched out
his hand to destroy Jerusalem, the
LORD was grieved[i] because of the calamity and said to the angel who was
afflicting the people, "Enough! Withdraw your hand." The angel of the
LORD[j] was then at the threshing floor
of Araunah the Jebusite.
17When David saw the angel who
was striking down the people, he said
to the LORD, "I am the one who has
sinned and done wrong. These are but
sheep.[k] What have they done?[l] Let
your hand fall upon me and my family."[m]

David Builds an Altar

24:18–25pp — 1Ch 21:18–26

18On that day Gad went to David and
said to him, "Go up and build an altar
to the LORD on the threshing floor of
Araunah[n] the Jebusite." 19So David
went up, as the LORD had commanded
through Gad. 20When Araunah looked
and saw the king and his men coming
toward him, he went out and bowed

24:1 [l] S Ex 30:12; 1Ch 27:23
24:2 [m] S 2Sa 20:23 [n] S 2Sa 3:10 [o] 2Ch 2:17; 17:14; 25:5
24:3 [p] S 2Sa 2:18 [q] S Dt 1:11
24:5 [r] S Jos 13:9 [s] S Nu 21:32
24:6 [t] S Ge 10:19; Jdg 1:31
24:7 [u] S Jos 19:29 [v] S Ex 3:8 [w] Ge 21:31 [x] S Dt 1:7
24:9 [y] S Nu 1:44-46
24:10 [z] S 1Sa 24:5 [a] S Nu 22:34 [b] S Nu 12:11
24:11 [c] S 1Sa 22:5 [d] 1Sa 9:9
24:13 [e] Dt 28:38-42,48; S 32:24; Eze 14:21 [f] S Ex 5:3; S 30:12; S Lev 26:25; Dt 28:21-22,27-28, 35
24:14 [g] Ne 9:28; Ps 4:1; 51:1; 86:5; 103:8,13; 119:132; 130:4; Isa 54:7; 55:7; Jer 33:8; 42:12; Da 9:9
24:15 [h] 1Ch 27:24
24:16 [i] S Ge 6:6 [j] S Ge 16:7; S 19:13; S Ex 12:23; Ac 12:23
24:17 [k] Ps 74:1; 100:3; Jer 49:20 [l] S Ge 18:23 [m] Jnh 1:12
24:18 [n] Ge 22:2; 2Ch 3:1

[i] *2* Septuagint (see also verse 4 and 1 Chron. 21:2); Hebrew *Joab the army commander*
[j] *13* Septuagint (see also 1 Chron. 21:12); Hebrew *seven*

---

dently had done something to merit this punishment (although the nature of their sin is not mentioned).

(3) The nature of David's sin was probably pride, expressed (a) in his leadership of a powerful and numerous people, and (b) in his self-exaltation and boasting of his great accomplishments and strength. David was glorying in human ability and great numbers rather than in God's power and righteousness.

24:17 LET YOUR HAND FALL UPON ME. David knew that because he was the leader of Israel, his sin was greater than the sin of the people. In concern for them, he was ready to accept all the punishment. One of David's greatest character traits was his willingness to accept humbly God's punishment for his misdeeds (cf. 15:26; 16:10–12).

down before the king with his face to
the ground.
21Araunah said, "Why has my lord
the king come to his servant?"
"To buy your threshing floor," David
answered, "so I can build an altar to
the LORD, that the plague on the people
may be stopped."[o]
22Araunah said to David, "Let my
lord the king take whatever pleases
him and offer it up. Here are oxen[p] for
the burnt offering, and here are threshing
sledges and ox yokes for the wood.
23O king, Araunah gives[q] all this to
the king." Araunah also said to him,
"May the LORD your God accept you."

24But the king replied to Araunah,
"No, I insist on paying you for it. I will
not sacrifice to the LORD my God burnt
offerings that cost me nothing."[r]
So David bought the threshing floor
and the oxen and paid fifty shekels[k][s]
of silver for them. 25David built an altar[t]
to the LORD there and sacrificed
burnt offerings and fellowship offerings.[l]
Then the LORD answered
prayer[u] in behalf of the land, and the
plague on Israel was stopped.

24:21 [o] Nu 16:44-50
24:22 [p] S 1Sa 6:14
24:23 [q] Ge 23:11
24:24 [r] Mal 1:13-14 [s] S Ge 23:16
24:25 [t] S 1Sa 7:17 [u] 2Sa 21:14

[k] 24 That is, about 1 1/4 pounds (about 0.6 kilogram) [l] 25 Traditionally *peace offerings*

24:24 OFFERINGS THAT COST ME NOTHING. David's words express the truth that the true value to God of our gifts, service and life is measured primarily by the sacrifice and cost involved. Self-denial and the willingness to suffer because of righteousness are principles of Christ's kingdom (Mt 5:10–12; Mk 8:34; 10:21–27). Christianity that costs nothing is worth nothing (cf. Isa 1:11).

1 KINGS

Outline

I. The Reign of Solomon (1:1—11:43)
  A. Solomon Succeeds David as King (1:1—2:11)
  B. Solomon Solidifies His Position as King (2:12–46)
  C. Solomon's Wisdom and Administration (3:1—4:34)
  D. Solomon's Success and Fame (5:1—10:29)
    1. Preparations for the Temple (5:1–18)
    2. Construction of the Temple (6:1–38)
    3. Construction of Solomon's Palace (7:1–12)
    4. Furnishings of the Temple (7:13–51)
    5. Dedication of the Temple (8:1–66)
    6. Ratification of the Davidic Covenant (9:1–9)
    7. Solomon's Activities and Fame (9:10—10:29)
  E. Solomon's Downfall and Death (11:1–43)
    1. Solomon's Flagrant Polygamy and Idolatry (11:1–8)
    2. The Judgment of Division Foretold by God (11:9–13)
    3. God Raises Adversaries Against Solomon (11:14–28)
    4. The Prophecy of Ahijah (11:29–40)
    5. The Death of Solomon (11:41–43)

II. The Division of the Kingdom: Israel and Judah (12:1—22:53)
  A. The Judgment of Division Occurs (12:1–24)
  B. Reign of Jeroboam (Israel) (12:25—14:20)
  C. Reign of Rehoboam (Judah) (14:21–31)
  D. Reign of Abijah (Judah) (15:1–8)
  E. Reign of Asa (Judah) (15:9–24)
  F. Reign of Nadab (Israel) (15:25–31)
  G. Reign of Baasha (Israel) (15:32—16:7)
  H. Reign of Elah (Israel) (16:8–14)
  I. Reign of Zimri (Israel) (16:15–20)
  J. Reign of Omri (Israel) (16:21–28)
  K. Reign of Ahab (Israel) (16:29—22:40)
    1. The Beginning of Ahab's Reign (16:29–34)
    2. Ahab and the Prophet Elijah (17:1—19:21)
    3. Ahab's Battles with Aram (20:1–43)
    4. Ahab and Naboth's Vineyard (21:1–29)
    5. Ahab's Fatal Battle with Aram (22:1–40)
  L. Reign of Jehoshaphat (Judah) (22:41–50)
  M. Reign of Ahaziah (Israel) (22:51–53)

Author: Anonymous

Theme: Kings of Israel and Judah

Date of Writing: c. 560–550 B.C.

Background

1 and 2 Kings follow immediately upon the history recorded in 1 and 2 Samuel. Together these four books selectively cover the entire history of the kings of Israel and Judah (c. 1050–586 B.C.). 1 and 2 Kings chronologically cover four centuries of that history—from the time of King Solomon (970 B.C.) to the time of the Babylonian exile (586 B.C.); 1 Kings alone covers about 120 years—Solomon's reign of 40 years (970–930 B.C.) and approximately the first 80 years after the kingdom was divided (c. 930–852 B.C.).

1 and 2 Kings were originally a single volume in the Hebrew OT; therefore, the issue of authorship relates to them as one book. The last recorded event (2Ki 25:27) is the release of King Jehoiachin from prison in Babylon (c. 560 B.C.) Thus 1 and 2 Kings in their completed form likely date from the decade 560–550 B.C. Although the author is undesignated, it is clear that he was an inspired prophetic historian who interpreted the reigns of all the kings of Israel and Judah in the light of God's covenant with the Hebrew people. It is also clear that he used various written sources by name: (1) "the book of the annals of Solomon" (11:41), (2) "the book of the annals of the kings of Israel" (e.g., 14:19), (3) "the book of the annals of the kings of Judah" (e.g., 14:29). These sources were probably written records kept by prophets rather than the official court annals; it is also probable that the author consulted other prophetic sources such as those mentioned in 1Ch 29:29. For an overview of the kings of Israel and Judah, see the chart on KINGS OF ISRAEL AND JUDAH, p. 553.

Purpose

1 and 2 Kings were written to provide the Hebrew people in the Babylonian exile with a prophetic interpretation of their history so that they would understand why the nation split in 930 B.C., why the northern kingdom of Israel fell in 722 B.C., and why the Davidic kingdom and Jerusalem fell in 586 B.C. The author emphasizes that the division and collapse of Israel and Judah were the direct and inevitable consequence of idolatry and unrighteousness on the part of the kings and the nation as a whole; in that light, the author evaluates the success or failure of each king according to his faithfulness or unfaithfulness to God and the covenant. No matter what success a king had politically or economically, he was judged a failure if he did not uphold the covenant. This prophetic understanding was presented so that the captives might forever turn away from idolatry, turn to God and obey his commands in future generations.

Survey

1 Kings divides into two major parts. (1) Part One describes the reign of King Solomon (chs. 1—11). The opening chapters describe the circumstances under which he became king (chs. 1—2) and his request for wisdom by which to rule the nation (ch. 3). The next seven chapters describe Solomon's rise to world prominence and Israel's zenith in prosperity, peace, power and glory—all during the first 20 years of Solomon's reign. During this time Solomon built and dedicated the temple in Jerusalem (chs. 6; 8). Ch. 11 describes Solomon's second 20 years—years of indulgence, flagrant polygamy, idolatry and erosion of the nation's foundations. By the time of Solomon's death, the seeds had been sown for the kingdom's division and decline.

(2) Part Two describes the split of the kingdom under Solomon's son, Rehoboam, and the next 80 years of the political and spiritual decline of both kingdoms under their separate succession of kings (chs. 12—22). The major personalities in this half of the book are kings Rehoboam in the southern kingdom and Jeroboam in the northern kingdom, King Ahab and his wicked wife Jezebel (north), and the prophet Elijah (north).

Special Features

Four major features characterize 1 Kings. (1) It presents the prophets as God's representatives and spokesmen to the kings of Israel and Judah—e.g., Ahijah (11:29–40; 14:5–18),

Shemaiah (12:22–24), Micaiah (22:8–28), and especially Elijah (chs. 17—19). (2) It emphasizes prophecy and its fulfillment in the history of the kings. Numerous times a recorded prophecy is stated as having been fulfilled (e.g., 2Sa 7:13 and 1 Ki 8:20; 11:29–39 and 12:15; ch. 13 and 2Ki 23:16–18). (3) It contains many well-known Bible stories—e.g., the wisdom of Solomon (chs. 3—4), the dedication of the temple (ch. 8), the visit of the queen of Sheba to Jerusalem (ch. 10), and the ministry of Elijah, especially his showdown with Baalism on Mount Carmel (ch. 18). (4) It includes vast amounts of chronological data about the kings of Israel and Judah that is sometimes difficult to synchronize. However, most problems are satisfactorily resolved by recognizing the probability of overlapping reigns, co-regencies of sons with their fathers, and different ways to calculate the beginning of a king's reign.

New Testament Fulfillment

The NT records that Jesus declared to his generation that the significance of his life and kingdom surpassed the wisdom, authority, glory and splendor of Solomon and his reign: "now one greater than Solomon is here" (Mt 12:42). Moreover, the glory of God that filled Solomon's temple at its dedication came to tabernacle among the human race in Jesus, the One and Only Son of the Father (Jn 1:14).

Reading 1 Kings

In order to read the entire Old Testament in one year, the book of 1 Kings should be read in 11 days, according to the following schedule: ☐ 1 ☐ 2–3 ☐ 4–6 ☐ 7–8 ☐ 9 ☐ 10–11 ☐ 12–14 ☐ 15–17 ☐ 18–19 ☐ 20–21 ☐ 22

NOTES

Adonijah Sets Himself Up as King

1 When King David was old and well advanced in years, he could not keep warm even when they put covers over him. 2So his servants said to him, "Let us look for a young virgin to attend the king and take care of him. She can lie beside him so that our lord the king may keep warm."

3Then they searched throughout Israel for a beautiful girl and found Abishag,[a] a Shunammite,[b] and brought her to the king. 4The girl was very beautiful; she took care of the king and waited on him, but the king had no intimate relations with her.

5Now Adonijah,[c] whose mother was Haggith, put himself forward and said, "I will be king." So he got chariots[d] and horses[a] ready, with fifty men to run ahead of him. 6(His father had never interfered[e] with him by asking, "Why do you behave as you do?" He was also very handsome and was born next after Absalom.)

7Adonijah conferred with Joab[f] son of Zeruiah and with Abiathar[g] the priest, and they gave him their support. 8But Zadok[h] the priest, Benaiah[i] son of Jehoiada, Nathan[j] the prophet, Shimei[k] and Rei[b] and David's special guard[l] did not join Adonijah.

9Adonijah then sacrificed sheep, cattle and fattened calves at the Stone of Zoheleth near En Rogel.[m] He invited all his brothers, the king's sons,[n] and all the men of Judah who were royal officials, 10but he did not invite[o] Nathan the prophet or Benaiah or the special guard or his brother Solomon.[p]

11Then Nathan asked Bathsheba,[q] Solomon's mother, "Have you not heard that Adonijah,[r] the son of Haggith, has become king without our lord David's knowing it? 12Now then, let me advise[s] you how you can save your own life and the life of your son Solomon. 13Go in to King David and say to him, 'My lord the king, did you not swear[t] to me your servant: "Surely Solomon your son shall be king after me, and he will sit on my throne"? Why then has Adonijah become king?' 14While you are still there talking to the king, I will come in and confirm what you have said."

15So Bathsheba went to see the aged king in his room, where Abishag[u] the Shunammite was attending him. 16Bathsheba bowed low and knelt before the king.

"What is it you want?" the king asked.

17She said to him, "My lord, you yourself swore[v] to me your servant by the LORD your God: 'Solomon your son shall be king after me, and he will sit on my throne.' 18But now Adonijah has become king, and you, my lord the king, do not know about it. 19He has sacrificed[w] great numbers of cattle, fattened calves, and sheep, and has invited all the king's sons, Abiathar the priest and Joab the commander of the army, but he has not invited Solomon your servant. 20My lord the king, the eyes of all Israel are on you, to learn from you who will sit on the throne of my lord the king after him. 21Otherwise, as soon as my lord the king is laid to rest[x] with his fathers, I and my son Solomon will be treated as criminals."

22While she was still speaking with the king, Nathan the prophet arrived. 23And they told the king, "Nathan the prophet is here." So he went before the king and bowed with his face to the ground.

1:3 [a]ver 15; S 2Sa 3:7; 1Ki 2:17,22 [b]S Jos 19:18
1:5 [c]S 2Sa 3:4 [d]S 1Sa 8:11
1:6 [e]1Sa 3:13
1:7 [f]S 2Sa 2:13, 18 [g]S 1Sa 22:20
1:8 [h]S 1Sa 2:35; S 2Sa 8:17 [i]S 2Sa 8:18 [j]S 2Sa 7:2 [k]1Ki 4:18 [l]2Sa 23:8
1:9 [m]S 2Sa 17:17 [n]1Ch 29:24
1:10 [o]ver 26 [p]S 2Sa 12:24
1:11 [q]2Sa 12:24 [r]S 2Sa 3:4
1:12 [s]Pr 15:22
1:13 [t]ver 17,30
1:15 [u]S ver 3
1:17 [v]S ver 13
1:19 [w]ver 9
1:21 [x]S Ge 15:15; 1Ki 2:10

[a]5 Or *charioteers* [b]8 Or *and his friends*

1:6 HIS FATHER HAD NEVER INTERFERED. Adonijah, David's fourth son, rebelled against his father by proclaiming himself king of Israel, even though God and David had designated Solomon as the next king (vv. 5,17,30; 2:15). (1) Until his death David had trouble with his sons. In spite of his record as a good ruler, he failed greatly as a father, neglecting or refusing to teach, guide and "interfere with" (i.e., discipline) his sons properly as described in Dt 6:1–9. As a result, David's life was full of grief and sorrow. His first son, Amnon, raped his half sister Tamar and was subsequently killed by his half brother Absalom (2Sa 13:1–33). David's third son, Absalom, rebelled against and attempted to kill his father (2Sa 15–18). Now his fourth son was rebelling and was later executed by Solomon (2:23–25).

(2) Because David failed to follow God's will regarding his family, he experienced one sorrow after another throughout his life. There is no fruit of discipleship more important in our lives than striving with all our hearts to remain faithful to our spouse and children and to lead them into lives of godliness through teaching and example (see article on PARENTS AND CHILDREN, p. 1854).

24Nathan said, "Have you, my lord the king, declared that Adonijah shall be king after you, and that he will sit on your throne? **25**Today he has gone down and sacrificed great numbers of cattle, fattened calves, and sheep. He has invited all the king's sons, the commanders of the army and Abiathar the priest. Right now they are eating and drinking with him and saying, 'Long live King Adonijah!' **26**But me your servant, and Zadok the priest, and Benaiah son of Jehoiada, and your servant Solomon he did not invite.[y] **27**Is this something my lord the king has done without letting his servants know who should sit on the throne of my lord the king after him?"

David Makes Solomon King

1:28–53pp — 1Ch 29:21–25

28Then King David said, "Call in Bathsheba." So she came into the king's presence and stood before him.

29The king then took an oath: "As surely as the LORD lives, who has delivered me out of every trouble,[z] **30**I will surely carry out today what I swore[a] to you by the LORD, the God of Israel: Solomon your son shall be king after me, and he will sit on my throne in my place."

31Then Bathsheba bowed low with her face to the ground and, kneeling before the king, said, "May my lord King David live forever!"

32King David said, "Call in Zadok[b] the priest, Nathan the prophet and Benaiah son of Jehoiada." When they came before the king, **33**he said to them: "Take your lord's servants with you and set Solomon my son on my own mule[c] and take him down to Gihon.[d] **34**There have Zadok the priest and Nathan the prophet anoint[e] him king over Israel. Blow the trumpet[f] and shout, 'Long live King Solomon!' **35**Then you are to go up with him, and he is to come and sit on my throne and reign in my place. I have appointed him ruler over Israel and Judah."

36Benaiah son of Jehoiada answered the king, "Amen! May the LORD, the God of my lord the king, so declare it. **37**As the LORD was with my lord the king, so may he be with[g] Solomon to make his throne even greater[h] than the throne of my lord King David!"

38So Zadok[i] the priest, Nathan the prophet, Benaiah son of Jehoiada, the Kerethites[j] and the Pelethites went down and put Solomon on King David's mule and escorted him to Gihon.[k] **39**Zadok the priest took the horn of oil[l] from the sacred tent[m] and anointed Solomon. Then they sounded the trumpet[n] and all the people shouted,[o] "Long live King Solomon!" **40**And all the people went up after him, playing flutes[p] and rejoicing greatly, so that the ground shook with the sound.

41Adonijah and all the guests who were with him heard it as they were finishing their feast. On hearing the sound of the trumpet, Joab asked, "What's the meaning of all the noise in the city?"[q]

42Even as he was speaking, Jonathan[r] son of Abiathar the priest arrived. Adonijah said, "Come in. A worthy man like you must be bringing good news."[s]

43"Not at all!" Jonathan answered. "Our lord King David has made Solomon king. **44**The king has sent with him Zadok the priest, Nathan the prophet, Benaiah son of Jehoiada, the Kerethites and the Pelethites, and they have put him on the king's mule, **45**and Zadok the priest and Nathan the prophet have anointed him king at Gihon. From there they have gone up cheering, and the city resounds[t] with it. That's the noise you hear. **46**Moreover, Solomon has taken his seat[u] on the royal throne. **47**Also, the royal officials have come to congratulate our lord King David, saying, 'May your God make Solomon's name more famous than yours and his throne greater[v] than yours!' And the king bowed in worship on his bed **48**and said, 'Praise be to the LORD, the God of Israel, who has allowed my eyes to see a successor[w] on my throne today.' "

49At this, all Adonijah's guests rose in alarm and dispersed. **50**But Adonijah, in fear of Solomon, went and took hold of the horns[x] of the altar. **51**Then Solomon was told, "Adonijah is afraid of King Solomon and is clinging to the horns of the altar. He says, 'Let King

1:26 [y] ver 10
1:29 [z] S 2Sa 4:9
1:30 [a] S ver 13; 1Ch 23:1
1:32 [b] S 1Sa 2:35
1:33 [c] Jdg 10:4; Zec 9:9 [d] ver 38; 2Ch 32:30; 33:14
1:34 [e] S 1Sa 2:35; 10:1 [f] S 2Sa 15:10
1:37 [g] Jos 1:5,17 [h] ver 47
1:38 [i] ver 8 [j] S 1Sa 30:14; S 2Sa 15:18 [k] S ver 33
1:39 [l] S Ex 29:7; S 1Sa 10:1; 2Ki 11:12; Ps 89:20 [m] S Ex 26:1; S 27:21 [n] S 2Sa 15:10; 2Ki 11:14 [o] ver 34; Nu 23:21; Ps 47:5; Zec 9:9
1:40 [p] S 1Sa 10:5
1:41 [q] 2Ch 23:12-13
1:42 [r] S 2Sa 15:27,36 [s] S 2Sa 18:26
1:45 [t] ver 40
1:46 [u] S Dt 17:18
1:47 [v] ver 37
1:48 [w] 1Ki 3:6
1:50 [x] S Ex 27:2

1:50 THE HORNS OF THE ALTAR. The horns of the altar were symbolic of God's mercy, forgiveness and protection. Adonijah fled to the altar, believing that Solomon would not kill him in such a sacred place (cf. Ex 21:13–14).

Solomon swear to me today that he will not put his servant to death with the sword.'"

52Solomon replied, "If he shows himself to be a worthy man, not a hair[y] of his head will fall to the ground; but if evil is found in him, he will die." 53Then King Solomon sent men, and they brought him down from the altar. And Adonijah came and bowed down to King Solomon, and Solomon said, "Go to your home."

David's Charge to Solomon

2:10–12pp — 1Ch 29:26–28

2 When the time drew near for David to die,[z] he gave a charge to Solomon his son.

2"I am about to go the way of all the earth,"[a] he said. "So be strong,[b] show yourself a man, 3and observe[c] what the LORD your God requires: Walk in his ways, and keep his decrees and commands, his laws and requirements, as written in the Law of Moses, so that you may prosper[d] in all you do and wherever you go, 4and that the LORD may keep his promise[e] to me: 'If your descendants watch how they live, and if they walk faithfully[f] before me with all their heart and soul, you will never fail to have a man on the throne of Israel.'

1Ki 9:3-8

5"Now you yourself know what Joab[g] son of Zeruiah did to me—what he did to the two commanders of Israel's armies, Abner[h] son of Ner and Amasa[i] son of Jether. He killed them, shedding their blood in peacetime as if in battle, and with that blood stained the belt around his waist and the sandals on his feet. 6Deal with him according to your wisdom,[j] but do not let his gray head go down to the grave[c] in peace.

7"But show kindness[k] to the sons of Barzillai[l] of Gilead and let them be among those who eat at your table.[m] They stood by me when I fled from your brother Absalom.

8"And remember, you have with you Shimei[n] son of Gera, the Benjamite from Bahurim, who called down bitter curses on me the day I went to Mahanaim.[o] When he came down to meet me at the Jordan, I swore[p] to him by the LORD: 'I will not put you to death by the sword.' 9But now, do not consider him innocent. You are a man of wisdom;[q] you will know what to do to him. Bring his gray head down to the grave in blood."

10Then David rested with his fathers and was buried[r] in the City of David.[s] 11He had reigned[t] forty years over Israel—seven years in Hebron and thirty-three in Jerusalem. 12So Solomon sat on the throne[u] of his father David, and his rule was firmly established.[v]

Solomon's Throne Established

13Now Adonijah,[w] the son of Haggith, went to Bathsheba, Solomon's mother. Bathsheba asked him, "Do you come peacefully?"[x]

He answered, "Yes, peacefully." 14Then he added, "I have something to say to you."

"You may say it," she replied.

15"As you know," he said, "the kingdom was mine. All Israel looked to me as their king. But things changed, and the kingdom has gone to my brother; for it has come to him from the LORD. 16Now I have one request to make of you. Do not refuse me."

"You may make it," she said.

1:52 y S 1Sa 14:45
2:1 z S Ge 27:2; S Nu 27:13
2:2 a Jos 23:14 b S Jos 1:6
2:3 c S Dt 4:6; S 10:12; S 17:14-20; S Jos 1:7 d 1Ch 22:13
2:4 e S 2Sa 7:13, 25; 2Ch 23:3 f 2Ki 18:3-6; 20:3; Ps 26:1-3; 132:12
2:5 g S 2Sa 2:18 h S 1Sa 14:50; S 2Sa 3:27 i S 2Sa 17:25
2:6 j ver 9
2:7 k S Ge 40:14 l S 2Sa 17:27; 19:31-39 m S 2Sa 9:7
2:8 n ver 36-46; 2Sa 16:5-13 o S Ge 32:2 p 2Sa 19:18-23
2:9 q ver 6
2:10 r Ac 2:29 s S 2Sa 5:7
2:11 t S 2Sa 5:4,5
2:12 u 1Ch 17:14; 29:23; 2Ch 9:8 v ver 46; 2Ch 1:1; 12:13; 17:1; 21:4
2:13 w S 2Sa 3:4 x S 1Sa 16:4

c6 Hebrew *Sheol*; also in verse 9

2:4 IF YOUR DESCENDANTS WATCH HOW THEY LIVE. David had learned through painful experience and discipline that success and God's blessing depended on remaining in God's ways and truth. Thus, David was deeply concerned that Solomon live a life of obedience and faithfulness to God. Yet Solomon and his sons ultimately failed to listen to David's pleas and turned from God and his covenant (cf. 2Ch 7:17–22); the result was God's judgment on Solomon (11:1–13), the division of the kingdom (12:1–33) and the eventual destruction of both the northern and southern kingdoms. The ultimate fulfillment of God's promises to David was realized only in Jesus Christ (Ac 15:16–18).

2:5 JOAB . . . DID TO THE TWO COMMANDERS. David instructed Solomon to begin his reign by exercising justice on Joab, who was worthy of death for murdering Abner and Amasa (2Sa 3:27; 20:9–10; cf. Mt 26:52).

2:9 BRING . . . DOWN TO THE GRAVE IN BLOOD. How sad that David's final recorded instruction to Solomon was to do an evil that he himself had sworn he would not do (cf. v. 8); David was thus breaking his word to Shimei (see 2Sa 19:23). This unforgiving severity must not be justified as pleasing to and blameless before God, but neither should it be judged entirely by NT standards (cf. Ac 17:30).

17So he continued, "Please ask King Solomon—he will not refuse you—to give me Abishag[y] the Shunammite as my wife."

18"Very well," Bathsheba replied, "I will speak to the king for you."

19When Bathsheba went to King Solomon to speak to him for Adonijah, the king stood up to meet her, bowed down to her and sat down on his throne. He had a throne brought for the king's mother,[z] and she sat down at his right hand.[a]

20"I have one small request to make of you," she said. "Do not refuse me."

The king replied, "Make it, my mother; I will not refuse you."

21So she said, "Let Abishag[b] the Shunammite be given in marriage to your brother Adonijah."

22King Solomon answered his mother, "Why do you request Abishag[c] the Shunammite for Adonijah? You might as well request the kingdom for him—after all, he is my older brother[d]—yes, for him and for Abiathar[e] the priest and Joab son of Zeruiah!"

23Then King Solomon swore by the LORD: "May God deal with me, be it ever so severely,[f] if Adonijah does not pay with his life for this request! **24**And now, as surely as the LORD lives—he who has established me securely on the throne of my father David and has founded a dynasty for me as he promised[g]—Adonijah shall be put to death today!" **25**So King Solomon gave orders to Benaiah[h] son of Jehoiada, and he struck down Adonijah and he died.[i]

26To Abiathar[j] the priest the king said, "Go back to your fields in Anathoth.[k] You deserve to die, but I will not put you to death now, because you carried the ark[l] of the Sovereign LORD before my father David and shared all my father's hardships."[m] **27**So Solomon removed Abiathar from the priesthood of the LORD, fulfilling[n] the word the LORD had spoken at Shiloh about the house of Eli.

28When the news reached Joab, who had conspired with Adonijah though not with Absalom, he fled to the tent of the LORD and took hold of the horns[o] of the altar. **29**King Solomon was told that Joab had fled to the tent of the LORD and was beside the altar.[p] Then Solomon ordered Benaiah[q] son of Jehoiada, "Go, strike him down!"

30So Benaiah entered the tent[r] of the LORD and said to Joab, "The king says, 'Come out![s]' "

But he answered, "No, I will die here."

Benaiah reported to the king, "This is how Joab answered me."

31Then the king commanded Benaiah, "Do as he says. Strike him down and bury him, and so clear me and my father's house of the guilt of the innocent blood[t] that Joab shed. **32**The LORD will repay[u] him for the blood he shed,[v] because without the knowledge of my father David he attacked two men and killed them with the sword. Both of them—Abner son of Ner, commander of Israel's army, and Amasa[w] son of Jether, commander of Judah's army—were better[x] men and more upright than he. **33**May the guilt of their blood rest on the head of Joab and his descendants forever. But on David and his descendants, his house and his throne, may there be the LORD's peace forever."

34So Benaiah[y] son of Jehoiada went up and struck down Joab[z] and killed him, and he was buried on his own land[d] in the desert. **35**The king put Benaiah[a] son of Jehoiada over the army in Joab's position and replaced Abiathar with Zadok[b] the priest.

36Then the king sent for Shimei[c] and said to him, "Build yourself a house in Jerusalem and live there, but do not go anywhere else. **37**The day you leave and cross the Kidron Valley,[d] you can be sure you will die; your blood will be on your own head."[e]

38Shimei answered the king, "What you say is good. Your servant will do as my lord the king has said." And Shimei stayed in Jerusalem for a long time.

2:17 y S 1Ki 1:3
2:19 z 1Ki 15:13; 2Ki 10:13; 24:15; 2Ch 15:16; Jer 13:18; 22:26; 29:2 a Ps 45:9
2:21 b 1Ki 1:3
2:22 c S Ge 22:24; S 1Ki 1:3 d 1Ch 3:2 e S 1Sa 22:20
2:23 f S Ru 1:17
2:24 g 2Sa 7:11
2:25 h S 2Sa 8:18 i S 2Sa 12:10
2:26 j S 1Sa 22:20 k S Jos 21:18 l S 2Sa 15:24 m S 2Sa 15:14
2:27 n S 1Sa 2:27-36
2:28 o S Ex 27:2
2:29 p Ex 21:14 q ver 25
2:30 r 2Ki 11:15 s Ex 21:14
2:31 t S Dt 19:13
2:32 u Jdg 9:57 v S Ge 4:14; S Jdg 9:24 w S 2Sa 17:25 x 2Ch 21:13
2:34 y ver 25 z S 2Sa 2:18
2:35 a S 2Sa 8:18 b S 1Sa 2:35
2:36 c S 2Sa 16:5
2:37 d S 2Sa 15:23; Jn 18:1 e S Lev 20:9

[d] *34* Or *buried in his tomb*

2:27 FULFILLING THE WORD THE LORD HAD SPOKEN. Nearly 120 years before this, a man of God had given a prophetic word to Eli the high priest about God's judgment on his house (cf. 1Sa 2:27–36). Part of his prophecy was fulfilled quickly (1Sa 4:10–22); part of it covered a long period of time. Abiathar's removal from the priesthood was part of the fulfillment of God's word to Eli. God never forgets; he always watches to see that his word is fulfilled (Jer 1:12), though it sometimes encompasses a long span of time, even decades and generations. God's word will be fully realized.

[39]But three years later, two of Shimei's slaves ran off to Achish[f] son of
Maacah, king of Gath, and Shimei was
told, "Your slaves are in Gath." [40]At
this, he saddled his donkey and went to
Achish at Gath in search of his slaves.
So Shimei went away and brought the
slaves back from Gath.
[41]When Solomon was told that
Shimei had gone from Jerusalem to
Gath and had returned, [42]the king
summoned Shimei and said to him,
"Did I not make you swear by the LORD
and warn[g] you, 'On the day you leave
to go anywhere else, you can be sure
you will die'? At that time you said to
me, 'What you say is good. I will obey.'
[43]Why then did you not keep your oath
to the LORD and obey the command I
gave you?"
[44]The king also said to Shimei, "You
know in your heart all the wrong[h] you
did to my father David. Now the LORD
will repay you for your wrongdoing.
[45]But King Solomon will be blessed,
and David's throne will remain secure[i] before the LORD forever."
[46]Then the king gave the order to
Benaiah[j] son of Jehoiada, and he went
out and struck Shimei[k] down and
killed him.
The kingdom was now firmly established[l] in Solomon's hands.

Solomon Asks for Wisdom

3:4–15pp — 2Ch 1:2–13

3 Solomon made an alliance with
Pharaoh king of Egypt and married[m] his daughter.[n] He brought her
to the City of David[o] until he finished
building his palace[p] and the temple of
the LORD, and the wall around Jerusalem. [2]The people, however, were still
sacrificing at the high places,[q] because a temple had not yet been built
for the Name[r] of the LORD. [3]Solomon
showed his love[s] for the LORD by walking[t] according to the statutes[u] of his

2:39 [f]1Sa 27:2
2:42 [g]S 2Sa 19:23
2:44 [h]2Sa 16:5-13
2:45 [i]S 2Sa 7:13
2:46 [j]S 2Sa 8:18 [k]S ver 8 [l]S ver 12
3:1 [m]1Ki 7:8; 11:1-13 [n]1Ki 9:24; 2Ch 8:11 [o]2Sa 5:7; 1Ki 2:10 [p]S 2Sa 7:2; 1Ki 9:10
3:2 [q]Lev 17:3-5; S 26:30; Dt 12:14; 1Ki 15:14; 22:43 [r]S Dt 14:23
3:3 [s]Dt 6:5; Ps 31:23; 145:20 [t]S Dt 10:12; S Jos 1:7 [u]S Dt 17:19; S 1Ki 14:8

3:2 SACRIFICING AT THE HIGH PLACES. Before the temple was built in Jerusalem as the central place of sacrifice, Israel offered sacrifices to God on hilltops or other elevated places, sometimes at the former sites of Canaanite pagan worship. Offering sacrifices at these places was forbidden by OT law, for all the Canaanite high places were to be destroyed (Lev 17:3–5; Dt 7:5; 12:3). Altars for worship and sacrifice were to be built only at divinely designated places (Ex 20:24; Dt 12:5,8,13–14).

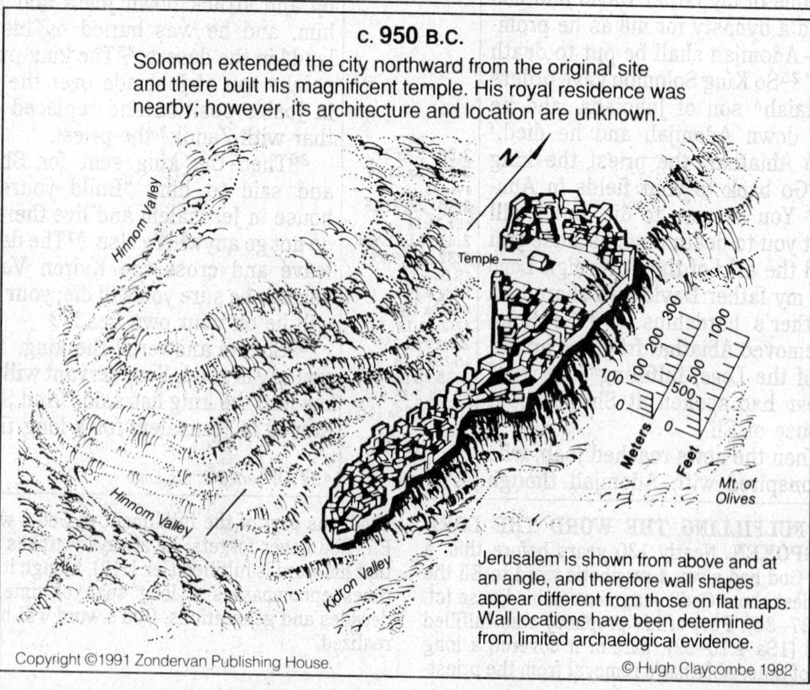
SOLOMON'S JERUSALEM
c. 950 B.C.
Solomon extended the city northward from the original site and there built his magnificent temple. His royal residence was nearby; however, its architecture and location are unknown.
N
Hinnom Valley
Temple
Hinnom Valley
Kidron Valley
Mt. of Olives
Meters
Feet
0
100
200
300
0
100
500
1000
Jerusalem is shown from above and at an angle, and therefore wall shapes appear different from those on flat maps. Wall locations have been determined from limited archaelogical evidence.

father David, except that he offered sacrifices and burned incense on the high places.[v]

4The king went to Gibeon[w] to offer sacrifices, for that was the most important high place, and Solomon offered a thousand burnt offerings on that altar. 5At Gibeon the LORD appeared[x] to Solomon during the night in a dream,[y] and God said, "Ask[z] for whatever you want me to give you."

6Solomon answered, "You have shown great kindness to your servant, my father David, because he was faithful[a] to you and righteous and upright in heart. You have continued this great kindness to him and have given him a son[b] to sit on his throne this very day.

7"Now, O LORD my God, you have made your servant king in place of my father David. But I am only a little child[c] and do not know how to carry out my duties. 8Your servant is here among the people you have chosen,[d] a great people, too numerous to count or number.[e] 9So give your servant a discerning[f] heart to govern your people and to distinguish[g] between right and wrong. For who is able[h] to govern this great people of yours?"

10The Lord was pleased that Solomon had asked for this. 11So God said to him, "Since you have asked[i] for this and not for long life or wealth for yourself, nor have asked for the death of your enemies but for discernment[j] in administering justice, 12I will do what you have asked.[k] I will give you a wise[l] and discerning heart, so that there will never have been anyone like you, nor will there ever be. 13Moreover, I will give you what you have not[m] asked for—both riches and honor[n]—so that in your lifetime you will have no equal[o] among kings. 14And if you walk[p] in my ways and obey my statutes and commands as David your father did, I will give you a long life."[q] 15Then Solomon awoke[r]—and he realized it had been a dream.[s]

He returned to Jerusalem, stood before the ark of the Lord's covenant and sacrificed burnt offerings[t] and fellowship offerings.[e][u] Then he gave a feast[v] for all his court.

A Wise Ruling

16Now two prostitutes came to the king and stood before him. 17One of them said, "My lord, this woman and I live in the same house. I had a baby while she was there with me. 18The third day after my child was born, this woman also had a baby. We were alone; there was no one in the house but the two of us.

19"During the night this woman's son died because she lay on him. 20So she got up in the middle of the night and took my son from my side while I your servant was asleep. She put him by her breast and put her dead son by my breast. 21The next morning, I got up to nurse my son—and he was dead! But when I looked at him closely in the morning light, I saw that it wasn't the son I had borne."

22The other woman said, "No! The living one is my son; the dead one is yours."

But the first one insisted, "No! The dead one is yours; the living one is mine." And so they argued before the king.

23The king said, "This one says, 'My son is alive and your son is dead,' while that one says, 'No! Your son is dead and mine is alive.' "

24Then the king said, "Bring me a sword." So they brought a sword for the king. 25He then gave an order: "Cut the living child in two and give half to one and half to the other."

26The woman whose son was alive was filled with compassion[w] for her son and said to the king, "Please, my lord, give her the living baby! Don't kill him!"

3:3 [v]S ver 2; Lev 17:3-5; 2Ki 12:3; 15:4,35; 16:4; 21:3
3:4 [w]S Jos 9:3
3:5 [x]1Ki 9:2; 11:9 [y]S Mt 27:19 [z]S Mt 7:7
3:6 [a]S Ge 17:1 [b]1Ki 1:48
3:7 [c]Nu 27:17; 1Ch 22:5; 29:1; Jer 1:6
3:8 [d]S Dt 7:6 [e]S Ge 12:2; 15:5; S 1Ch 27:23
3:9 [f]S 2Sa 14:17; Jas 1:5 [g]S Dt 1:16 [h]2Co 2:16
3:11 [i]Jas 4:3 [j]1Ch 22:12
3:12 [k]1Jn 5:14-15 [l]S 2Sa 14:20; 1Ki 4:29,30,31; 5:12; 10:23; Ecc 1:16
3:13 [m]Mt 6:33; Eph 3:20 [n]Pr 3:1-2,16; 8:18 [o]1Ki 10:23; 2Ch 9:22; Ne 13:26
3:14 [p]1Ki 9:4; Ps 25:13; 101:2; 128:1; Pr 3:1-2,16 [q]Ps 61:6
3:15 [r]S Ge 28:16 [s]ver 5 [t]Lev 6:8-13 [u]Lev 7:11-21 [v]Est 1:3,9; 2:18; 5:8; 6:14; 9:17; Da 5:1
3:26 [w]Ps 102:13; Isa 49:15; 63:15; Jer 3:12; 31:20; Hos 11:8

[e] *15* Traditionally *peace offerings*

3:9 GIVE YOUR SERVANT A DISCERNING HEART. Solomon began his reign in faith in and love for the Lord (v. 3). He prayed for wisdom and a discerning heart (vv. 5–9); God was pleased with his request (v. 10) and answered his prayer (vv. 11–14). However, God's gift of wisdom did not guarantee that Solomon would always persist in godliness; for this reason God emphasized that long life would be his "if you walk in my ways" (v. 14). Solomon's unfaithfulness later in life prevented the full realization of God's will for his life (11:1–8).

3:10 THE LORD WAS PLEASED. God is pleased when believers sincerely seek and pray for godly wisdom and a discerning heart. "If any of you lacks wisdom, he should ask God, who gives generously to all without finding fault, and it will be given to him" (Jas 1:5; cf. Pr 2:2–6; 3:15; Lk 12:31; Eph 5:17; Jas 3:17).

But the other said, "Neither I nor
you shall have him. Cut him in two!"
27 Then the king gave his ruling:
"Give the living baby to the first
woman. Do not kill him; she is his
mother."
28 When all Israel heard the verdict
the king had given, they held the king
in awe, because they saw that he had
wisdom[x] from God to administer justice.

Solomon's Officials and Governors

4 So King Solomon ruled over all Israel. 2 And these were his chief officials:[y]

Azariah[z] son of Zadok—the priest;
3 Elihoreph and Ahijah, sons of Shisha—secretaries;[a]
Jehoshaphat[b] son of Ahilud—recorder;
4 Benaiah[c] son of Jehoiada—commander in chief;
Zadok[d] and Abiathar—priests;
5 Azariah son of Nathan—in charge of the district officers;
Zabud son of Nathan—a priest and personal adviser to the king;
6 Ahishar—in charge of the palace;[e]
Adoniram[f] son of Abda—in charge of forced labor.[g]

7 Solomon also had twelve district
governors[h] over all Israel, who supplied provisions for the king and the
royal household. Each one had to provide supplies for one month in the year.
8 These are their names:

Ben-Hur—in the hill country[i] of Ephraim;
9 Ben-Deker—in Makaz, Shaalbim,[j] Beth Shemesh[k] and Elon Bethhanan;
10 Ben-Hesed—in Arubboth (Socoh[l] and all the land of Hepher[m] were his);
11 Ben-Abinadab—in Naphoth Dor[f][n] (he was married to Taphath daughter of Solomon);
12 Baana son of Ahilud—in Taanach and Megiddo, and in all of Beth Shan[o] next to Zarethan[p] below Jezreel, from Beth Shan to Abel Meholah[q] across to Jokmeam;[r]
13 Ben-Geber—in Ramoth Gilead (the settlements of Jair[s] son of Manasseh in Gilead[t] were his, as well as the district of Argob in Bashan and its sixty large walled cities[u] with bronze gate bars);
14 Ahinadab son of Iddo—in Mahanaim;[v]
15 Ahimaaz[w]—in Naphtali (he had married Basemath daughter of Solomon);
16 Baana son of Hushai[x]—in Asher and in Aloth;
17 Jehoshaphat son of Paruah—in Issachar;
18 Shimei[y] son of Ela—in Benjamin;
19 Geber son of Uri—in Gilead (the country of Sihon[z] king of the Amorites and the country of Og[a] king of Bashan). He was the only governor over the district.

Solomon's Daily Provisions

20 The people of Judah and Israel
were as numerous as the sand[b] on the
seashore; they ate, they drank and
they were happy.[c] 21 And Solomon
ruled[d] over all the kingdoms from the
River[g][e] to the land of the Philistines,
as far as the border of Egypt.[f] These
countries brought tribute[g] and were
Solomon's subjects all his life.
22 Solomon's daily provisions[h] were
thirty cors[h] of fine flour and sixty
cors[i] of meal, 23 ten head of stall-fed
cattle, twenty of pasture-fed cattle and
a hundred sheep and goats, as well as
deer, gazelles, roebucks and choice
fowl.[i] 24 For he ruled over all the king-

3:28 [x] S 2Sa 14:20; Col 2:3 **4:2** [y] 1Ki 12:6; Job 12:12 [z] 1Ch 6:10; 2Ch 26:17 **4:3** [a] S 2Sa 8:17 [b] S 2Sa 8:16 **4:4** [c] S 2Sa 8:18 [d] S 2Sa 8:17 **4:6** [e] S Ge 41:40 [f] S 2Sa 20:24 [g] S Ge 49:15 **4:7** [h] ver 27 **4:8** [i] S Jos 24:33 **4:9** [j] Jdg 1:35 [k] S Jos 15:10 **4:10** [l] S Jos 15:35 [m] S Jos 12:17 **4:11** [n] S Jos 11:2 **4:12** [o] S Jos 17:11 [p] S Jos 3:16 [q] S Jdg 7:22 [r] 1Ch 6:68 **4:13** [s] S Nu 32:41 [t] Nu 32:40 [u] Dt 3:4 **4:14** [v] Jos 13:26 **4:15** [w] 2Sa 15:27 **4:16** [x] S 2Sa 15:32 **4:18** [y] 1Ki 1:8 **4:19** [z] S Jos 12:2 [a] Dt 3:8-10; S Jos 12:4 **4:20** [b] S Ge 12:2; S 32:12 [c] 1Ch 22:9 **4:21** [d] 2Ch 9:26; Ezr 4:20; Ps 72:11; La 1:1 [e] S Ge 2:14; Ps 72:8 [f] S Ex 23:31 [g] S Jdg 3:15; Eze 16:13 **4:22** [h] 1Ki 10:5 **4:23** [i] Ne 5:18

[f] *11* Or *in the heights of Dor* [g] *21* That is, the Euphrates; also in verse 24 [h] *22* That is, probably about 185 bushels (about 6.6 kiloliters) [i] *22* That is, probably about 375 bushels (about 13.2 kiloliters)

4:24 PEACE ON ALL SIDES. During Solomon's rule, Israel as a nation reached its pinnacle of power, peace and prosperity (vv. 20–28). Politically and materially Solomon's reign was a success; spiritually, however, Solomon's slide into idolatry would leave his reign judged to be a failure (11:1–8).

doms west of the River, from Tiphsah[j] to Gaza, and had peace[k] on all
sides. **25**During Solomon's lifetime Judah and Israel, from Dan to Beersheba,[l] lived in safety,[m] each man under
his own vine and fig tree.[n]

26Solomon had four[j] thousand
stalls for chariot horses,[o] and twelve
thousand horses.[k]

27The district officers,[p] each in his
month, supplied provisions for King
Solomon and all who came to the
king's table. They saw to it that nothing was lacking. **28**They also brought
to the proper place their quotas of barley and straw for the chariot horses
and the other horses.

Solomon's Wisdom

29God gave Solomon wisdom[q] and
very great insight, and a breadth of understanding as measureless as the
sand[r] on the seashore. **30**Solomon's
wisdom was greater than the wisdom
of all the men of the East,[s] and greater than all the wisdom of Egypt.[t] **31**He
was wiser[u] than any other man, including Ethan the Ezrahite—wiser
than Heman, Calcol and Darda, the
sons of Mahol. And his fame spread to
all the surrounding nations. **32**He
spoke three thousand proverbs[v] and
his songs[w] numbered a thousand
and five. **33**He described plant life,
from the cedar of Lebanon to the
hyssop[x] that grows out of walls. He
also taught about animals and birds,
reptiles and fish. **34**Men of all nations came to listen to Solomon's
wisdom, sent by all the kings[y] of
the world, who had heard of his
wisdom.

4:24 [j] 2Ki 15:16 [k] S Jos 14:15 **4:25** [l] S Jdg 20:1 [m] 1Ch 22:9; Jer 23:6; Eze 28:26; 39:26 [n] Dt 8:8; 2Ki 18:31; Ps 105:33; Isa 36:16; Jer 5:17; Joel 2:22; Mic 4:4; Zec 3:10 **4:26** [o] S Dt 17:16 **4:27** [p] ver 7 **4:29** [q] S 1Ki 3:12 [r] S Ge 32:12 **4:30** [s] S Ge 25:6; S Jdg 6:3; Da 1:20; Mt 2:1 [t] Isa 19:11; Ac 7:22 **4:31** [u] S 1Ki 3:12 **4:32** [v] Pr 1:1; 10:1; 25:1; Ecc 12:9 [w] Ps 78:63; SS 1:1; Eze 33:32 **4:33** [x] S Lev 14:49 **4:34** [y] 2Ch 9:23

5:1 [z] S 2Sa 5:11 **5:3** [a] 1Ch 22:8; 28:3 [b] S 2Sa 7:5 [c] 2Sa 22:40; Ps 8:6; 110:1; S Mt 22:44; 1Co 15:25 **5:4** [d] S Jos 14:15; 1Ch 22:9; Lk 2:14 [e] 1Ki 11:14,23 **5:5** [f] S Dt 12:5; 1Ch 17:12; 1Co 3:16; Rev 21:22 [g] Dt 12:5; 2Sa 7:13 **5:6** [h] 1Ch 14:1; 22:4 **5:7** [i] 1Ki 10:9; Isa 60:6

Preparations for Building the Temple

5:1–16pp — 2Ch 2:1–18

5 When Hiram[z] king of Tyre heard
that Solomon had been anointed
king to succeed his father David, he
sent his envoys to Solomon, because
he had always been on friendly terms
with David. **2**Solomon sent back this
message to Hiram:

3"You know that because of the
wars[a] waged against my father
David from all sides, he could not
build[b] a temple for the Name of
the LORD his God until the LORD
put his enemies under his feet.[c]
4But now the LORD my God has
given me rest[d] on every side, and
there is no adversary[e] or disaster. **5**I intend, therefore, to build a
temple[f] for the Name of the LORD
my God, as the LORD told my father David, when he said, 'Your
son whom I will put on the throne
in your place will build the temple
for my Name.'[g]

6"So give orders that cedars[h]
of Lebanon be cut for me. My men
will work with yours, and I will
pay you for your men whatever
wages you set. You know that we
have no one so skilled in felling
timber as the Sidonians."

7When Hiram heard Solomon's message, he was greatly pleased and said,
"Praise be to the LORD[i] today, for he

[j] *26* Some Septuagint manuscripts (see also 2 Chron. 9:25); Hebrew *forty* [k] *26* Or *charioteers*

4:29–34 GOD GAVE SOLOMON WISDOM. Solomon's wisdom involved a breadth of understanding and discernment about life and his responsibilities as king (cf. 3:9). He wrote 3,000 proverbs (v. 32), many of which have been preserved in the book of Proverbs. (1) How could Solomon, who was given such godly wisdom, eventually turn from the Lord to serve other gods? Clearly, to have wisdom and to follow wisdom are two different issues. Solomon's greatest failure was that he did not apply his own spiritual wisdom to every area of his life. Though he was the wisest man of his time, he did not live as wisely as some of God's faithful people did.

(2) Solomon was brought to spiritual ruin primarily because he married so many foreign women (11:1–8). Two factors were involved: (a) He did this to form political and military alliances, and in so doing failed to trust that the Lord would keep his kingdom secure from foreign threats. (b) He undoubtedly found it difficult to resist the lusts of the flesh in his desire for women—also a character flaw of his father David.

5:5 TO BUILD A TEMPLE FOR THE NAME OF THE LORD. Chs. 5–8 record the steps taken by Solomon to build the temple where God would continuously reveal his presence and glory. The temple was a dwelling place for God and a place for the people to gather to worship him (cf. 8:15–21; 2Sa 7:12–13). It was built in Jerusalem on Mount Moriah (2Ch 3:1; cf. Ge 22:2) and took seven years to complete (6:38; see 6:2, note). God gave David the plans for the temple by revelation of the Holy Spirit (1Ch 28:12), and David provided many of the resources before he died.

has given David a wise son to rule over this great nation."

8So Hiram sent word to Solomon:

> "I have received the message you sent me and will do all you want in providing the cedar and pine logs. **9**My men will haul them down from Lebanon to the sea[j], and I will float them in rafts by sea to the place you specify. There I will separate them and you can take them away. And you are to grant my wish by providing food[k] for my royal household."

10In this way Hiram kept Solomon supplied with all the cedar and pine logs he wanted, **11**and Solomon gave Hiram twenty thousand cors[l] of wheat as food[l] for his household, in addition to twenty thousand baths[m,n] of pressed olive oil. Solomon continued to do this for Hiram year after year. **12**The LORD gave Solomon wisdom,[m] just as he had promised him. There were peaceful relations between Hiram and Solomon, and the two of them made a treaty.[n]

13King Solomon conscripted laborers[o] from all Israel—thirty thousand men. **14**He sent them off to Lebanon in shifts of ten thousand a month, so that they spent one month in Lebanon and two months at home. Adoniram[p] was in charge of the forced labor. **15**Solomon had seventy thousand carriers and eighty thousand stonecutters in the hills, **16**as well as thirty-three hundred[o] foremen[q] who supervised the project and directed the workmen. **17**At the king's command they removed from the quarry[r] large blocks of quality stone[s] to provide a foundation of dressed stone for the temple. **18**The craftsmen of Solomon and Hiram[t] and the men of Gebal[p][u] cut and prepared the timber and stone for the building of the temple.

5:9 [j] Ezr 3:7 [k] ver 11; Eze 27:17; Ac 12:20
5:11 [l] S ver 9
5:12 [m] S 1Ki 3:12 [n] Jos 9:7; 1Ki 15:19; Am 1:9
5:13 [o] S Ge 49:15; S Lev 25:39; 1Ki 9:15
5:14 [p] S 2Sa 20:24; 1Ki 4:6; 2Ch 10:18
5:16 [q] 1Ki 9:23
5:17 [r] 1Ki 6:7 [s] 1Ch 22:2
5:18 [t] S 2Sa 5:11 [u] S Jos 13:5

Solomon Builds the Temple

6:1–29pp — 2Ch 3:1–14

6 In the four hundred and eightieth[q] year after the Israelites had come out of Egypt, in the fourth year of Solomon's reign over Israel, in the month of Ziv, the second month,[v] he began to build the temple of the LORD.[w]

2The temple[x] that King Solomon built for the LORD was sixty cubits long, twenty wide and thirty high.[r] **3**The portico[y] at the front of the main hall of the temple extended the width of the temple, that is twenty cubits,[s] and projected ten cubits[t] from the front of the temple. **4**He made narrow clerestory windows[z] in the temple. **5**Against the walls of the main hall and inner sanctuary he built a structure around the building, in which there were side rooms.[a] **6**The lowest floor was five cubits[u] wide, the middle floor six cubits[v] and the third floor seven.[w] He made offset ledges around the outside of the temple so that nothing would be inserted into the temple walls.

7In building the temple, only blocks dressed[b] at the quarry were used, and no hammer, chisel or any other iron tool[c] was heard at the temple site while it was being built.

8The entrance to the lowest[x] floor

6:1 [v] Ezr 3:8 [w] Ezr 5:11
6:2 [x] Ex 26:1
6:3 [y] Eze 40:49
6:4 [z] Eze 41:16
6:5 [a] Jer 35:2; Eze 41:5-6
6:7 [b] S Ex 20:25 [c] S Dt 27:5

[l] *11* That is, probably about 125,000 bushels (about 4,400 kiloliters) [m] *11* Septuagint (see also 2 Chron. 2:10); Hebrew *twenty cors* [n] *11* That is, about 115,000 gallons (about 440 kiloliters) [o] *16* Hebrew; some Septuagint manuscripts (see also 2 Chron. 2:2, 18) *thirty-six hundred* [p] *18* That is, Byblos [q] *1* Hebrew; Septuagint *four hundred and fortieth* [r] *2* That is, about 90 feet (about 27 meters) long and 30 feet (about 9 meters) wide and 45 feet (about 13.5 meters) high [s] *3* That is, about 30 feet (about 9 meters) [t] *3* That is, about 15 feet (about 4.5 meters) [u] *6* That is, about 7 1/2 feet (about 2.3 meters); also in verses 10 and 24 [v] *6* That is, about 9 feet (about 2.7 meters) [w] *6* That is, about 10 1/2 feet (about 3.1 meters) [x] *8* Septuagint; Hebrew *middle*

6:1 FOUR HUNDRED AND EIGHTIETH YEAR AFTER. This verse is crucial in establishing the date for Israel's exodus out of Egypt. Solomon began to build the temple of the Lord about 966 B.C.; this date has been determined by integrating Biblical data with Assyrian chronological records. The exodus occurred 480 years before that date, placing the exodus at about 1446 B.C. (cf. Ac 13:19–20).

6:2 THE TEMPLE . . . FOR THE LORD. The temple, housing the ark of the covenant (see Ex 25:16), symbolized God's presence and character among his people. The temple communicated the truth that God desired to live among his people (Lev 26:12; cf. Jn 14:21–23). It was a visible sign and pledge of his covenant relationship with the people (Ex 29:45–46), and it was built that God's Name might dwell there (5:5; 8:16; 9:3). The name of God is "holy" (Lev 20:3; 1Ch 16:10,35; Eze 39:7). Thus, God wanted to be known and worshiped by Israel as the Holy One and the Sanctifier of his people (Ex 29:43–46; Eze 37:26–28). For more detail, see article on THE TEMPLE, p. 608.

was on the south side of the temple; a
stairway led up to the middle level and
from there to the third. 9So he built the
temple and completed it, roofing it with
beams and cedar[d] planks. 10And he
built the side rooms all along the temple. The height of each was five cubits,
and they were attached to the temple
by beams of cedar.
11The word of the LORD came[e] to
Solomon: 12"As for this temple you are
building, if you follow my decrees, carry out my regulations and keep all my
commands[f] and obey them, I will fulfill through you the promise[g] I gave to
David your father. 13And I will live
among the Israelites and will not abandon[h] my people Israel."
14So Solomon[i] built the temple and
completed[j] it. 15He lined its interior
walls with cedar boards, paneling them
from the floor of the temple to the ceiling,[k] and covered the floor of the temple with planks of pine.[l] 16He parti-
tioned off twenty cubits[y] at the rear of
the temple with cedar boards from
floor to ceiling to form within the temple an inner sanctuary, the Most Holy
Place.[m] 17The main hall in front of this
room was forty cubits[z] long. 18The inside of the temple was cedar,[n] carved
with gourds and open flowers. Everything was cedar; no stone was to be
seen.
19He prepared the inner sanctuary[o]
within the temple to set the ark of the
covenant[p] of the LORD there. 20The inner sanctuary[q] was twenty cubits
long, twenty wide and twenty high.[a]
He overlaid the inside with pure gold,
and he also overlaid the altar of cedar.[r] 21Solomon covered the inside of
the temple with pure gold, and he extended gold chains across the front of
the inner sanctuary, which was overlaid with gold. 22So he overlaid the
whole interior with gold. He also overlaid with gold the altar that belonged
to the inner sanctuary.
23In the inner sanctuary he made a
pair of cherubim[s] of olive wood, each
ten cubits[b] high. 24One wing of the
first cherub was five cubits long, and
the other wing five cubits—ten cubits
from wing tip to wing tip. 25The second
cherub also measured ten cubits, for
the two cherubim were identical in size

6:9 [d]SS 1:17
6:11 [e]1Ki 12:22; 13:20; 16:1,7; 17:2; 21:17; Jer 40:1
6:12 [f]1Ki 11:10 [g]2Sa 7:12-16; 1Ki 9:5
6:13 [h]S Lev 26:11; S Dt 31:6; Jn 14:18; Heb 13:5
6:14 [i]Ac 7:47 [j]1Ch 28:20; 2Ch 5:1
6:15 [k]1Ki 7:7 [l]Eze 41:15-16
6:16 [m]S Ex 26:33
6:18 [n]ver 29; Ps 74:6; Eze 41:18
6:19 [o]1Ki 8:6 [p]S Ex 25:10; S 1Sa 3:3
6:20 [q]Eze 41:3-4 [r]S Ex 30:1
6:23 [s]S Ex 37:1-9
6:27 [t]S Ge 3:24; S Ex 25:18
6:29 [u]S ver 18 [v]ver 32,35; Eze 41:18,25
6:32 [w]Eze 41:23
6:36 [x]2Ch 4:9 [y]1Ki 7:12; Ezr 6:4
6:38 [z]1Ch 28:19 [a]Ex 25:9; Heb 8:5
7:1 [b]S 2Sa 7:2
7:2 [c]S 2Sa 7:2 [d]1Ki 10:17; 2Ch 9:16; Isa 22:8; 37:24; Jer 22:6,23

and shape. 26The height of each cherub
was ten cubits. 27He placed the cherubim[t] inside the innermost room of the
temple, with their wings spread out.
The wing of one cherub touched one
wall, while the wing of the other
touched the other wall, and their wings
touched each other in the middle of the
room. 28He overlaid the cherubim with
gold.
29On the walls[u] all around the temple, in both the inner and outer rooms,
he carved cherubim,[v] palm trees and
open flowers. 30He also covered the
floors of both the inner and outer
rooms of the temple with gold.
31For the entrance of the inner sanctuary he made doors of olive wood with
five-sided jambs. 32And on the two olive wood doors[w] he carved cherubim,
palm trees and open flowers, and overlaid the cherubim and palm trees with
beaten gold. 33In the same way he
made four-sided jambs of olive wood
for the entrance to the main hall. 34He
also made two pine doors, each having
two leaves that turned in sockets. 35He
carved cherubim, palm trees and open
flowers on them and overlaid them
with gold hammered evenly over the
carvings.
36And he built the inner courtyard[x]
of three courses[y] of dressed stone and
one course of trimmed cedar beams.
37The foundation of the temple of
the LORD was laid in the fourth year, in
the month of Ziv. 38In the eleventh
year in the month of Bul, the eighth
month, the temple was finished in all
its details[z] according to its specifications.[a] He had spent seven years
building it.

Solomon Builds His Palace

7 It took Solomon thirteen years,
however, to complete the construction of his palace.[b] 2He built the
Palace[c] of the Forest of Lebanon[d] a
hundred cubits long, fifty wide and
thirty high,[c] with four rows of cedar

[y] 16 That is, about 30 feet (about 9 meters)
[z] 17 That is, about 60 feet (about 18 meters)
[a] 20 That is, about 30 feet (about 9 meters) long, wide and high
[b] 23 That is, about 15 feet (about 4.5 meters)
[c] 2 That is, about 150 feet (about 46 meters) long, 75 feet (about 23 meters) wide and 45 feet (about 13.5 meters) high

6:12 IF YOU FOLLOW MY DECREES. The books of 1 and 2 Kings record the tragic history of the persistent failure of God's people to meet this condition (cf. 2:3–4; 3:14).

SOLOMON'S TEMPLE

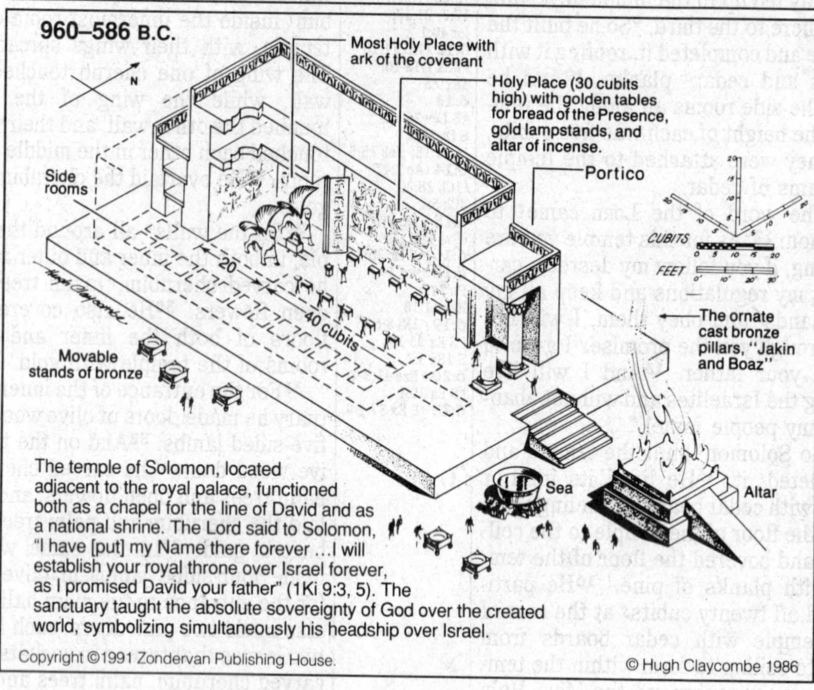

The temple of Solomon, located adjacent to the royal palace, functioned both as a chapel for the line of David and as a national shrine. The Lord said to Solomon, "I have [put] my Name there forever ... I will establish your royal throne over Israel forever, as I promised David your father" (1Ki 9:3, 5). The sanctuary taught the absolute sovereignty of God over the created world, symbolizing simultaneously his headship over Israel.

TEMPLE FURNISHINGS

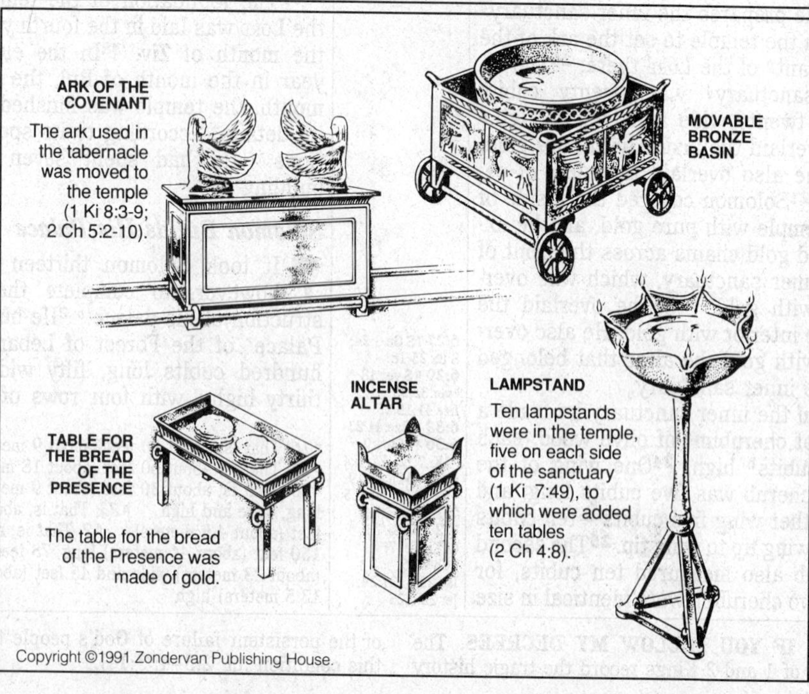

ARK OF THE COVENANT

The ark used in the tabernacle was moved to the temple (1 Ki 8:3-9; 2 Ch 5:2-10).

MOVABLE BRONZE BASIN

TABLE FOR THE BREAD OF THE PRESENCE

The table for the bread of the Presence was made of gold.

INCENSE ALTAR

LAMPSTAND

Ten lampstands were in the temple, five on each side of the sanctuary (1 Ki 7:49), to which were added ten tables (2 Ch 4:8).

columns supporting trimmed cedar
beams. 3It was roofed with cedar above
the beams that rested on the columns—forty-five beams, fifteen to a
row. 4Its windows were placed high in
sets of three, facing each other. 5All
the doorways had rectangular frames;
they were in the front part in sets of
three, facing each other.[d]

6He made a colonnade fifty cubits
long and thirty wide.[e] In front of it
was a portico, and in front of that were
pillars and an overhanging roof.

7He built the throne hall, the Hall of
Justice, where he was to judge,[e] and
he covered it with cedar from floor to
ceiling.[f][f] 8And the palace in which
he was to live, set farther back, was
similar in design. Solomon also made a
palace like this hall for Pharaoh's
daughter, whom he had married.[g]

9All these structures, from the outside to the great courtyard and from
foundation to eaves, were made of
blocks of high-grade stone cut to size
and trimmed with a saw on their inner
and outer faces. 10The foundations
were laid with large stones of good
quality, some measuring ten cubits[g]
and some eight.[h] 11Above were high-
grade stones, cut to size, and cedar
beams. 12The great courtyard was surrounded by a wall of three courses[h] of
dressed stone and one course of
trimmed cedar beams, as was the inner
courtyard of the temple of the LORD
with its portico.

The Temple's Furnishings

7:23–26pp — 2Ch 4:2–5
7:38–51pp — 2Ch 4:6,10–5:1

13King Solomon sent to Tyre and
brought Huram,[i][i] 14whose mother
was a widow from the tribe of Naphtali
and whose father was a man of Tyre
and a craftsman in bronze. Huram was
highly skilled[j] and experienced in all
kinds of bronze work. He came to King
Solomon and did all[k] the work assigned to him.

15He cast two bronze pillars,[l] each
eighteen cubits high and twelve cubits
around,[j] by line. 16He also made two
capitals[m] of cast bronze to set on the
tops of the pillars; each capital was
five cubits[k] high. 17A network of interwoven chains festooned the capitals
on top of the pillars, seven for each
capital. 18He made pomegranates in
two rows[l] encircling each network to
decorate the capitals on top of the pillars.[m] He did the same for each capital. 19The capitals on top of the pillars
in the portico were in the shape of lilies, four cubits[n] high. 20On the capitals of both pillars, above the bowl-
shaped part next to the network, were
the two hundred pomegranates[n] in
rows all around. 21He erected the pillars at the portico of the temple. The
pillar to the south he named Jakin[o]
and the one to the north Boaz.[p][o]
22The capitals on top were in the shape
of lilies. And so the work on the pillars[p] was completed.

23He made the Sea[q] of cast metal,
circular in shape, measuring ten cubits[g] from rim to rim and five cubits
high. It took a line[r] of thirty cubits[q]
to measure around it. 24Below the rim,
gourds encircled it—ten to a cubit.
The gourds were cast in two rows in
one piece with the Sea.

25The Sea stood on twelve bulls,[s]
three facing north, three facing west,
three facing south and three facing
east. The Sea rested on top of them,
and their hindquarters were toward
the center. 26It was a handbreadth[r] in
thickness, and its rim was like the rim
of a cup, like a lily blossom. It held two
thousand baths.[s]

27He also made ten movable
stands[t] of bronze; each was four cubits long, four wide and three high.[t]
28This is how the stands were made:

7:7 [e] 1Sa 7:15; Ps 122:5; Pr 20:8 [f] 1Ki 6:15
7:8 [g] S 1Ki 3:1
7:12 [h] S 1Ki 6:36
7:13 [i] ver 45; 2Ch 2:13; 4:16
7:14 [j] Ex 31:2-5; S 35:31 [k] 2Ch 4:11,16
7:15 [l] 2Ki 11:14; 23:3; 25:17; 2Ch 3:15; 23:13; 34:31; Jer 27:19; 52:17,21; Eze 40:49
7:16 [m] ver 20,42; 2Ki 25:17; Jer 52:22
7:20 [n] ver 18; 2Ch 3:16; 4:13
7:21 [o] 2Ch 3:17
7:22 [p] 2Ki 25:17
7:23 [q] ver 47; 2Ki 25:13; 1Ch 18:8; 2Ch 4:18; Jer 52:17; Rev 4:6 [r] Jer 31:39; Zec 2:1
7:25 [s] Jer 52:20
7:27 [t] 2Ki 16:17

[d] *5* The meaning of the Hebrew for this verse is uncertain. [e] *6* That is, about 75 feet (about 23 meters) long and 45 feet (about 13.5 meters) wide [f] *7* Vulgate and Syriac; Hebrew *floor* [g] *10* That is, about 15 feet (about 4.5 meters) [h] *10* That is, about 12 feet (about 3.6 meters) [i] *13* Hebrew *Hiram,* a variant of *Huram*; also in verses 40 and 45 [j] *15* That is, about 27 feet (about 8.1 meters) high and 18 feet (about 5.4 meters) around [k] *16* That is, about 7 1/2 feet (about 2.3 meters); also in verse 23 [l] *18* Two Hebrew manuscripts and Septuagint; most Hebrew manuscripts *made the pillars, and there were two rows* [m] *18* Many Hebrew manuscripts and Syriac; most Hebrew manuscripts *pomegranates* [n] *19* That is, about 6 feet (about 1.8 meters); also in verse 38 [o] *21 Jakin* probably means *he establishes.* [p] *21 Boaz* probably means *in him is strength.* [q] *23* That is, about 45 feet (about 13.5 meters) [r] *26* That is, about 3 inches (about 8 centimeters) [s] *26* That is, probably about 11,500 gallons (about 44 kiloliters); the Septuagint does not have this sentence. [t] *27* That is, about 6 feet (about 1.8 meters) long and wide and about 4 1/2 feet (about 1.3 meters) high

They had side panels attached to uprights. 29On the panels between the
uprights were lions, bulls and cherubim—and on the uprights as well.
Above and below the lions and bulls
were wreaths of hammered work.
30Each stand[u] had four bronze wheels
with bronze axles, and each had a basin resting on four supports, cast with
wreaths on each side. 31On the inside
of the stand there was an opening that
had a circular frame one cubit[u] deep.
This opening was round, and with its
basework it measured a cubit and a
half.[v] Around its opening there was
engraving. The panels of the stands
were square, not round. 32The four
wheels were under the panels, and the
axles of the wheels were attached to
the stand. The diameter of each wheel
was a cubit and a half. 33The wheels
were made like chariot wheels; the axles, rims, spokes and hubs were all of
cast metal.

34Each stand had four handles, one
on each corner, projecting from the
stand. 35At the top of the stand there
was a circular band half a cubit[w] deep.
The supports and panels were attached to the top of the stand. 36He engraved cherubim, lions and palm trees
on the surfaces of the supports and on
the panels, in every available space,
with wreaths all around. 37This is the
way he made the ten stands. They were
all cast in the same molds and were
identical in size and shape.

38He then made ten bronze basins,[v]
each holding forty baths[x] and measuring four cubits across, one basin to go
on each of the ten stands. 39He placed
five of the stands on the south side of
the temple and five on the north. He
placed the Sea on the south side, at the
southeast corner of the temple. 40He
also made the basins and shovels and
sprinkling bowls.[w]

So Huram finished all the work he
had undertaken for King Solomon in
the temple of the LORD:

41the two pillars;
the two bowl-shaped capitals on top of the pillars;
the two sets of network decorating the two bowl-shaped capitals on top of the pillars;
42the four hundred pomegranates for the two sets of network (two rows of pomegranates for each network, decorating the bowl-shaped capitals[x] on top of the pillars);
43the ten stands with their ten basins;
44the Sea and the twelve bulls under it;
45the pots, shovels and sprinkling bowls.[y]

7:30 [u] 2Ki 16:17
7:38 [v] S Ex 30:18
7:40 [w] S Ex 27:3; Jer 52:18
7:42 [x] S ver 16
7:45 [y] S Ex 27:3; Jer 52:18
[z] S ver 13
7:46 [a] S Ge 13:10
[b] S Ge 33:17
[c] Jos 3:16
7:47 [d] 1Ch 22:3; Jer 52:20
[e] Ex 36:5-7
[f] S ver 23
7:48 [g] Ex 39:32-43
[h] S Ex 25:23
[i] S Ex 25:30
7:49 [j] S Ex 25:31-38
7:50 [k] S Nu 7:14
[l] 2Ki 25:13; Jer 52:19
7:51 [m] S 2Sa 8:11
[n] 2Ki 12:13; 24:13; Jer 27:19
8:1 [o] Nu 7:2
[p] S 1Sa 3:3; Rev 11:19

All these objects that Huram[z] made
for King Solomon for the temple of the
LORD were of burnished bronze. 46The
king had them cast in clay molds in the
plain[a] of the Jordan between Succoth[b] and Zarethan.[c] 47Solomon left
all these things unweighed,[d] because
there were so many;[e] the weight of
the bronze[f] was not determined.

48Solomon also made all[g] the furnishings that were in the LORD's temple:

the golden altar;
the golden table[h] on which was the bread of the Presence;[i]
49the lampstands[j] of pure gold (five on the right and five on the left, in front of the inner sanctuary);
the gold floral work and lamps and tongs;
50the pure gold basins, wick trimmers, sprinkling bowls, dishes[k] and censers;[l]
and the gold sockets for the doors of the innermost room, the Most Holy Place, and also for the doors of the main hall of the temple.

51When all the work King Solomon
had done for the temple of the LORD
was finished, he brought in the things
his father David had dedicated[m]—the
silver and gold and the furnishings[n]—and he placed them in the
treasuries of the LORD's temple.

The Ark Brought to the Temple

8:1-21pp — 2Ch 5:2-6:11

8 Then King Solomon summoned
into his presence at Jerusalem the
elders of Israel, all the heads of the
tribes and the chiefs[o] of the Israelite
families, to bring up the ark[p] of the

[u] *31* That is, about 1 1/2 feet (about 0.5 meter) [v] *31* That is, about 2 1/4 feet (about 0.7 meter); also in verse 32 [w] *35* That is, about 3/4 foot (about 0.2 meter) [x] *38* That is, about 230 gallons (about 880 liters)

LORD's covenant from Zion, the City of
David.[q] **2**All the men of Israel came
together to King Solomon at the time
of the festival[r] in the month of Etha-
nim, the seventh month.[s]
3When all the elders of Israel had
arrived, the priests[t] took up the ark,
4and they brought up the ark of the
LORD and the Tent of Meeting[u] and all
the sacred furnishings in it. The
priests and Levites[v] carried them up,
5and King Solomon and the entire assembly of Israel that had gathered
about him were before the ark, sacrificing[w] so many sheep and cattle that
they could not be recorded or counted.
6The priests then brought the ark of
the LORD's covenant[x] to its place in
the inner sanctuary of the temple, the
Most Holy Place,[y] and put it beneath
the wings of the cherubim.[z] **7**The
cherubim spread their wings over the
place of the ark and overshadowed[a]
the ark and its carrying poles. **8**These
poles were so long that their ends
could be seen from the Holy Place in
front of the inner sanctuary, but not
from outside the Holy Place; and they
are still there today.[b] **9**There was
nothing in the ark except the two stone
tablets[c] that Moses had placed in it at
Horeb, where the LORD made a covenant with the Israelites after they
came out of Egypt.
10When the priests withdrew from
the Holy Place, the cloud[d] filled the
temple of the LORD. **11**And the priests
could not perform their service[e] because of the cloud, for the glory[f] of
the LORD filled his temple.
12Then Solomon said, "The LORD has
said that he would dwell in a dark
cloud;[g] **13**I have indeed built a magnificent temple for you, a place for you to
dwell[h] forever."
14While the whole assembly of Israel was standing there, the king turned
around and blessed[i] them. **15**Then he
said:

"Praise be to the LORD,[j] the
God of Israel, who with his own
hand has fulfilled what he promised with his own mouth to my father David. For he said, **16**'Since
the day I brought my people Israel
out of Egypt,[k] I have not chosen
a city in any tribe of Israel to have
a temple built for my Name[l] to be
there, but I have chosen[m] David[n] to rule my people Israel.'
17"My father David had it in his
heart[o] to build a temple[p] for the
Name of the LORD, the God of Israel. **18**But the LORD said to my father David, 'Because it was in
your heart to build a temple for
my Name, you did well to have
this in your heart. **19**Nevertheless,
you[q] are not the one to build the
temple, but your son, who is your
own flesh and blood—he is the
one who will build the temple for
my Name.'[r]
20"The LORD has kept the prom-

8:1 [q] S 2Sa 5:7
8:2 [r] ver 65; S Lev 23:36; Ne 8:17 [s] S Lev 23:34; S Nu 29:12
8:3 [t] S Jos 3:3
8:4 [u] S Lev 17:4 [v] 1Ch 15:13
8:5 [w] S 2Sa 6:13; S 2Ch 30:24
8:6 [x] S Ex 26:33; S 2Sa 6:17; Rev 11:19 [y] S Ex 26:33 [z] S Ge 3:24; S Ex 25:18
8:7 [a] S Ex 25:20
8:8 [b] Ex 25:13-15
8:9 [c] S Ex 16:34; S 25:16; Heb 9:4
8:10 [d] S Ex 16:10; S Lev 16:2; Rev 15:8
8:11 [e] 2Ch 7:2; Rev 15:8 [f] S Ex 16:7; S 29:43
8:12 [g] S Ex 40:34; S 2Sa 22:10
8:13 [h] Ex 15:17; Ps 132:13; 135:21; Mt 23:21
8:14 [i] S Ex 39:43
8:15 [j] 1Ch 16:36; Lk 1:68
8:16 [k] S Ex 3:10 [l] S Dt 12:5 [m] S 1Sa 9:16; S 16:1 [n] Ps 89:3-4
8:17 [o] S 1Sa 10:7; Ac 7:46 [p] 2Sa 7:27; 1Ch 22:7; Ps 26:8; 132:5
8:19 [q] S 2Sa 7:5 [r] S 2Sa 7:13

8:1 ARK OF THE LORD'S COVENANT. The ark of the covenant was the only article of furniture in the Most Holy Place. It was a rectangular chest 3 and 3/4 feet long by 2 and 1/4 feet wide by 2 and 1/4 feet high, made of acacia wood and overlaid inside and out with pure gold. The ark originally contained three reminders of God's kingship over Israel: (1) the stone tablets on which the Ten Commandments were engraved (cf. Ex 25:16,21; 40:20; see Ex 25:10, note); (2) a gold jar full of manna, which God had provided daily for Israel during her years in the desert; and (3) Aaron's almond staff that supernaturally budded. However, by Solomon's time the ark contained only the two tablets of stone (2Ch 5:10). Fitting over the top of the ark was the "atonement cover," on which the blood of sacrifices was sprinkled once a year by the high priest on the Day of Atonement. Two gold cherubim carved as one piece, facing each other with their wings spread forward, hovered over the atonement cover in an arch. At the center of the atonement cover, God's presence was symbolized by a brilliant supernatural light called the *shekinah* (see article on THE GLORY OF GOD, p. 1192).

8:4 TENT OF MEETING. The Tent of Meeting was the tentlike structure that had provided a portable place of worship for the Israelites as they had moved about in the desert. After the Israelites had settled in their homeland, David expressed a desire to build a permanent house of worship for the Lord (see 2Sa 7:1–13; see article on THE TEMPLE, p. 608).

8:11 THE GLORY OF THE LORD. The glory of the Lord filled the temple after the ark of the covenant was brought into it (vv. 5–11). Where God's word is living and is obeyed, there his glory abides (see Ex 40:34, note; cf. Jn 15:7–11; 17:17–22; see article on THE GLORY OF GOD, p. 1192).

8:13 A PLACE FOR YOU TO DWELL. The fact that God lived in the temple did not mean that he lived in no other place, for God is everywhere (cf. v. 27). What it did mean was that God's presence and power would be manifested in a special way in the temple; in the same manner, Christ's presence with his people is manifested in a special way when they gather together in his name (Mt 18:20).

ise he made: I have succeeded[s]
David my father and now I sit on
the throne of Israel, just as the
LORD promised, and I have built[t]
the temple for the Name of the
LORD, the God of Israel. **21**I have
provided a place there for the ark,
in which is the covenant of the
LORD that he made with our fathers when he brought them out
of Egypt."

Solomon's Prayer of Dedication

8:22–53pp — 2Ch 6:12–40

22Then Solomon stood before the altar of the LORD in front of the whole
assembly of Israel, spread out his
hands[u] toward heaven **23**and said:

"O LORD, God of Israel, there is
no God like[v] you in heaven above
or on earth below—you who keep
your covenant of love[w] with your
servants who continue wholeheartedly in your way. **24**You have
kept your promise to your servant
David my father; with your mouth
you have promised and with your
hand you have fulfilled it—as it is
today.

25"Now LORD, God of Israel,
keep for your servant David my father the promises[x] you made to
him when you said, 'You shall
never fail to have a man to sit before me on the throne of Israel, if
only your sons are careful in all
they do to walk before me as you
have done.' **26**And now, O God of
Israel, let your word that you
promised[y] your servant David
my father come true.

27"But will God really dwell[z]
on earth? The heavens, even the
highest heaven,[a] cannot contain[b] you. How much less this
temple I have built! **28**Yet give attention to your servant's prayer
and his plea for mercy, O LORD my
God. Hear the cry and the prayer
that your servant is praying in
your presence this day. **29**May
your eyes be open[c] toward[d] this
temple night and day, this place of
which you said, 'My Name[e] shall
be there,' so that you will hear the
prayer your servant prays toward
this place. **30**Hear the supplication of your servant and of your
people Israel when they pray[f] toward this place. Hear[g] from
heaven, your dwelling place, and
when you hear, forgive.[h]

31"When a man wrongs his
neighbor and is required to take
an oath and he comes and swears
the oath[i] before your altar in this
temple, **32**then hear from heaven
and act. Judge between your servants, condemning the guilty and
bringing down on his own head
what he has done. Declare the innocent not guilty, and so establish
his innocence.[j]

33"When your people Israel
have been defeated[k] by an enemy
because they have sinned[l]
against you, and when they turn
back to you and confess your
name, praying and making supplication to you in this temple,[m]
34then hear from heaven and forgive the sin of your people Israel
and bring them back to the land
you gave to their fathers.

35"When the heavens are shut
up and there is no rain[n] because
your people have sinned[o] against
you, and when they pray toward
this place and confess your name
and turn from their sin because
you have afflicted them, **36**then
hear from heaven and forgive the
sin of your servants, your people
Israel. Teach[p] them the right
way[q] to live, and send rain[r] on
the land you gave your people for
an inheritance.

37"When famine[s] or plague[t]
comes to the land, or blight[u] or
mildew, locusts or grasshoppers,[v] or when an enemy be-
sieges them in any of their cities,
whatever disaster or disease may
come, **38**and when a prayer or plea
is made by any of your people Israel—each one aware of the afflictions of his own heart, and
spreading out his hands[w] toward
this temple— **39**then hear[x] from
heaven, your dwelling place. Forgive[y] and act; deal with each

8:20 [s] S 2Sa 7:12 [t] 1Ch 28:6
8:22 [u] S Ex 9:29
8:23 [v] S Ex 9:14 [w] S Dt 7:9,12; Ne 1:5; 9:32; Da 9:4
8:25 [x] S 2Sa 7:15; 1Ch 17:23; 2Ch 1:9
8:26 [y] S 2Sa 7:25
8:27 [z] Ac 7:48; 17:24 [a] S Dt 10:14 [b] 2Ch 2:6; Ps 139:7-16; Isa 66:1; Jer 23:24
8:29 [c] ver 52; 2Ki 19:16; 2Ch 7:15; Ne 1:6; Ps 5:1; 31:2; 102:17; 130:2; Isa 37:17 [d] Ps 28:2; 138:2; Da 6:10 [e] S Dt 11:12; 12:11; S 2Sa 7:13
8:30 [f] ver 47; Lev 26:40; Ne 1:6; Jer 29:12; Da 9:4 [g] ver 39; Ps 34:6 [h] S Ex 34:7,9; Lev 26:40-42; Ps 85:2
8:31 [i] S Ex 22:11
8:32 [j] Dt 25:1; Eze 18:20
8:33 [k] S Lev 26:17 [l] Lev 26:39 [m] Isa 37:1,14,38
8:35 [n] S Dt 28:24; S 2Sa 1:21 [o] Jer 5:25
8:36 [p] S Dt 8:3; S 1Sa 12:23 [q] Ps 5:8; 27:11; 107:7; Pr 11:5; Isa 45:13; Jer 6:16; 7:23; 31:21 [r] ver 35; 1Ki 17:1; 18:1,45; Jer 5:24; 10:3; 14:22; Zec 10:1
8:37 [s] S Lev 26:26 [t] S Ex 30:12; S Lev 26:25 [u] S Dt 28:22 [v] S Ex 10:13; Ps 105:34
8:38 [w] S Ex 9:29
8:39 [x] S ver 30 [y] Ps 130:4

8:29 MY NAME. The Name of God represents his presence, character and glory.

8:39 FORGIVE AND ACT; DEAL WITH EACH MAN ACCORDING TO ALL HE DOES. Solomon understood that God would forgive his people if they turned from their sin and sincerely repented

man according to all he does,
since you know[z] his heart (for
you alone know the hearts of all
men), **40**so that they will fear[a]
you all the time they live in the
land[b] you gave our fathers.
41"As for the foreigner[c] who
does not belong to your people Israel but has come from a distant
land because of your name—
42for men will hear[d] of your great
name and your mighty hand[e] and
your outstretched arm—when he
comes and prays toward this temple, **43**then hear from heaven,
your dwelling place, and do whatever the foreigner asks of you, so
that all the peoples of the earth
may know[f] your name and fear[g]
you, as do your own people Israel,
and may know that this house I
have built bears your Name.[h]
44"When your people go to war
against their enemies, wherever
you send them, and when they
pray[i] to the LORD toward the city
you have chosen and the temple I
have built for your Name, **45**then
hear from heaven their prayer and
their plea, and uphold their
cause.[j]
46"When they sin against
you—for there is no one who does
not sin[k]—and you become angry
with them and give them over to
the enemy, who takes them captive[l] to his own land, far away or
near; **47**and if they have a change
of heart in the land where they are
held captive, and repent and
plead[m] with you in the land of
their conquerors and say, 'We
have sinned, we have done wrong,
we have acted wickedly';[n] **48**and
if they turn back[o] to you with all
their heart[p] and soul in the land
of their enemies who took them
captive, and pray[q] to you toward
the land you gave their fathers, toward the city you have chosen and
the temple[r] I have built for your
Name;[s] **49**then from heaven, your
dwelling place, hear their prayer
and their plea, and uphold their
cause. **50**And forgive your people,
who have sinned against you; forgive all the offenses they have
committed against you, and cause
their conquerors to show them
mercy;[t] **51**for they are your people and your inheritance,[u] whom
you brought out of Egypt, out of
that iron-smelting furnace.[v]
52"May your eyes be open[w] to
your servant's plea and to the
plea of your people Israel, and
may you listen to them whenever
they cry out to you.[x] **53**For you
singled them out from all the nations of the world to be your own
inheritance,[y] just as you declared through your servant Moses when you, O Sovereign LORD,
brought our fathers out of Egypt."

54When Solomon had finished all
these prayers and supplications to the
LORD, he rose from before the altar of
the LORD, where he had been kneeling
with his hands spread out toward heav-
en. **55**He stood and blessed[z] the whole
assembly of Israel in a loud voice, saying:

56"Praise be to the LORD, who
has given rest[a] to his people Israel just as he promised. Not one
word has failed of all the good
promises[b] he gave through his
servant Moses. **57**May the LORD
our God be with us as he was with
our fathers; may he never leave us
nor forsake[c] us. **58**May he turn
our hearts[d] to him, to walk in all
his ways and to keep the com-

8:39 [z] S Jos 22:22; S Ps 44:21; Jn 2:24; S Rev 2:23
8:40 [a] ver 39-40; Dt 6:13; Ps 103:11; 130:4 [b] S Dt 12:1
8:41 [c] S Ge 31:15; Isa 56:3,6; 61:5
8:42 [d] 1Ki 10:1; Isa 60:3; Ac 8:27 [e] Dt 3:24
8:43 [f] S Jos 4:24; S 1Sa 17:46 [g] Ps 102:15 [h] S Dt 28:10
8:44 [i] 1Ch 5:20; 2Ch 14:11
8:45 [j] Ps 9:4; 140:12
8:46 [k] Ps 130:3; 143:2; Pr 20:9; S Ro 3:9 [l] Lev 26:33-39; S Dt 4:27; S 21:10; S 28:64; 2Ki 25:21
8:47 [m] S ver 30; S Lev 5:5; Ezr 9:15; Ne 1:6; Jer 14:20 [n] Ezr 9:7; Ps 106:6; Jer 3:25
8:48 [o] S Dt 4:30 [p] S Dt 4:29 [q] 1Jn 1:8-10 [r] Ps 5:7; 11:4; Jnh 2:4 [s] S Dt 12:11-14; Ne 1:9; Jer 23:3; 31:8
8:50 [t] 2Ki 25:28; 2Ch 30:9; Ps 106:46; Da 1:9
8:51 [u] S Ex 34:9; S Dt 9:29 [v] S Ex 1:13; Isa 48:10; Jer 11:4
8:52 [w] S ver 29 [x] Job 30:20; Ps 3:4; 22:2; 77:1; 142:1
8:53 [y] Ex 19:5; S 34:9
8:55 [z] S Ex 39:43; Nu 6:23
8:56 [a] S Ex 33:14; Dt 12:10; Heb 4:8 [b] S Jos 23:15; S Jer 29:10
8:57 [c] S Dt 4:31; S 31:6; S Mt 28:20; Heb 13:5
8:58 [d] S Jos 24:23

in regret and sorrow (vv. 35–36); he also acknowledged that God might have to discipline them, in order that "they will fear you all the time they live in the land" (v. 40).

8:46 THERE IS NO ONE WHO DOES NOT SIN. Solomon's words are not an attempt to justify his or Israel's sins; rather, he was expressing the truth that because sin is universally present, turning away from God is always a possibility for his people (vv. 46–50; cf. Ro 3:23; 1Jn 1:10). If apostasy does occur, deliverance is also possible if they repent and return to God (vv. 46–51).

8:57 MAY THE LORD OUR GOD BE WITH US. Solomon's prayer is an ideal model for what we should desire in our walk with the Lord. He asked: (1) for the Lord's protecting presence and help (v. 57), (2) for God to confirm his word by fulfilling his good promises (vv. 26,56), (3) for a work of divine grace in their hearts to keep God's commands and to love his righteous ways (v. 58), (4) for God to answer daily prayers and to supply daily needs (v. 59), (5) for increased understanding of God's great and awesome nature (v. 60), and (6) for a heart fully committed to God and his will (v. 61).

mands, decrees and regulations
he gave our fathers. **59**And may
these words of mine, which I have
prayed before the LORD, be near to
the LORD our God day and night,
that he may uphold the cause of
his servant and the cause of his
people Israel according to each
day's need, **60**so that all the peoples[e] of the earth may know that
the LORD is God and that there is
no other.[f] **61**But your hearts[g]
must be fully committed[h] to the
LORD our God, to live by his decrees and obey his commands, as
at this time."

The Dedication of the Temple

8:62–66pp — 2Ch 7:1–10

62Then the king and all Israel with
him offered sacrifices[i] before the
LORD. **63**Solomon offered a sacrifice of
fellowship offerings[y] to the LORD:
twenty-two thousand cattle and a hundred and twenty thousand sheep and
goats. So the king and all the Israelites
dedicated[j] the temple of the LORD.
64On that same day the king consecrated the middle part of the courtyard
in front of the temple of the LORD, and
there he offered burnt offerings, grain
offerings and the fat[k] of the fellowship offerings, because the bronze altar[l] before the LORD was too small to
hold the burnt offerings, the grain offerings and the fat of the fellowship offerings.[m]
65So Solomon observed the festival[n] at that time, and all Israel with
him—a vast assembly, people from
Lebo[z] Hamath[o] to the Wadi of
Egypt.[p] They celebrated it before the
LORD our God for seven days and seven
days more, fourteen days in all. **66**On
the following day he sent the people
away. They blessed the king and then
went home, joyful and glad in heart for
all the good[q] things the LORD had done
for his servant David and his people Israel.

8:60 [e]S Jos 4:24 [f]S Dt 4:35
8:61 [g]Dt 6:5 [h]1Ki 9:4; 11:4; 15:3,14; 22:43; 2Ki 20:3; 1Ch 28:9; 29:19; 2Ch 16:9; 17:6; 25:2; Ps 119:80; Isa 38:3
8:62 [i]S 2Sa 6:13; 1Ch 29:21; Eze 45:17
8:63 [j]Ezr 6:16
8:64 [k]S Ex 29:13 [l]S Ex 27:1; 2Ki 16:14; 2Ch 4:1; 8:12; 15:8; Eze 43:13-17 [m]S 2Sa 6:17
8:65 [n]S ver 2 [o]S Nu 13:21 [p]S Ge 15:18
8:66 [q]S Ex 18:9
9:1 [r]S 2Sa 7:2
9:2 [s]S 1Ki 3:5
9:3 [t]S 1Sa 9:16; 2Ki 19:20; 20:5; Ps 10:17; 34:17 [u]S Ex 20:24; S Dt 12:5 [v]S Dt 11:12
9:4 [w]S Ge 17:1 [x]Dt 17:20; 1Ki 14:8; 15:5 [y]S 1Ki 3:14; 1Ch 28:9; Pr 4:4
9:5 [z]1Ch 22:10 [a]S 2Sa 7:15
9:6 [b]Dt 28:15; 2Sa 7:14; 2Ki 18:12; Jer 17:27; 26:4; 32:23; 44:23 [c]1Ki 11:10
9:7 [d]Lev 18:24-28; Dt 4:26; S Jos 23:13; 2Ki 17:23; Jer 24:10 [e]Dt 12:5; Jer 7:14 [f]Job 17:6; Ps 44:14; Jer 24:9; Joel 2:17 [g]S Dt 28:37; Eze 5:15
9:8 [h]S Lev 26:32 [i]S Dt 29:24; Jer 7:4-15; Mt 23:38
9:9 [j]Dt 29:25; 2Ki 22:17; Jer 5:19; 13:22; 16:11,13; 22:9 [k]S Nu 25:3; Jer 40:3; 44:23; La 4:12

The LORD Appears to Solomon

9:1–9pp — 2Ch 7:11–22

9 When Solomon had finished[r]
building the temple of the LORD and
the royal palace, and had achieved all
he had desired to do, **2**the LORD appeared[s] to him a second time, as he
had appeared to him at Gibeon. **3**The
LORD said to him:

"I have heard[t] the prayer and
plea you have made before me; I
have consecrated this temple,
which you have built, by putting
my Name[u] there forever. My
eyes[v] and my heart will always
be there.
4"As for you, if you walk before
me in integrity of heart[w] and uprightness, as David[x] your father
did, and do all I command and observe my decrees and laws,[y] **5**I
will establish[z] your royal throne
over Israel forever, as I promised
David your father when I said,
'You shall never fail[a] to have a
man on the throne of Israel.'
6"But if you[a] or your sons turn
away[b] from me and do not observe the commands and decrees
I have given you[a] and go off to
serve other gods[c] and worship
them, **7**then I will cut off Israel
from the land[d] I have given them
and will reject this temple I have
consecrated for my Name.[e] Israel will then become a byword[f]
and an object of ridicule[g] among
all peoples. **8**And though this temple is now imposing, all who pass
by will be appalled[h] and will scoff
and say, 'Why has the LORD done
such a thing to this land and to
this temple?'[i] **9**People will answer,[j] 'Because they have forsaken[k] the LORD their God, who

[y] *63* Traditionally *peace offerings*; also in verse 64 [z] *65* Or *from the entrance to* [a] *6* The Hebrew is plural.

9:3 THE LORD SAID TO HIM. God's response to Solomon's prayer affirmed that he had heard and answered; however, God added that he would establish Solomon's throne and the kingdom of Israel only if he and the people would remain faithful and not turn away from his commands (vv. 4–9). All of Scripture expresses this principle: God's promises are fulfilled only when we seek to follow him and his ways (see Jn 14:13–21; 15:7).

9:7 WILL REJECT THIS TEMPLE. God said he would no longer manifest his presence, power and glory in the temple if the people failed to follow his ways sincerely (vv. 6–9); this warning applies under the new covenant as well. If a church fails to obey Christ's words and the teachings of the NT apostles, turning instead to false doctrine and the ungodly ways of the world, then God's Spirit and power will be withdrawn from it, and God will remove it from his kingdom (see Rev 2:5, note).

brought their fathers out of
Egypt, and have embraced other
gods, worshiping and serving
them—that is why the LORD
brought all this disaster[l] on
them.' "

Solomon's Other Activities

9:10–28pp — 2Ch 8:1–18

10At the end of twenty years, during
which Solomon built these two buildings—the temple of the LORD and the
royal palace— 11King Solomon gave
twenty towns in Galilee to Hiram king
of Tyre, because Hiram had supplied
him with all the cedar and pine and
gold[m] he wanted. 12But when Hiram
went from Tyre to see the towns that
Solomon had given him, he was not
pleased with them. 13"What kind of
towns are these you have given me, my
brother?" he asked. And he called them
the Land of Cabul,[b][n] a name they
have to this day. 14Now Hiram had sent
to the king 120 talents[c] of gold.[o]
15Here is the account of the forced
labor King Solomon conscripted[p] to
build the LORD's temple, his own palace, the supporting terraces,[d][q] the
wall of Jerusalem, and Hazor,[r] Megiddo and Gezer.[s] 16(Pharaoh king of
Egypt had attacked and captured Gezer. He had set it on fire. He killed its
Canaanite inhabitants and then gave it
as a wedding gift to his daughter,[t]
Solomon's wife. 17And Solomon rebuilt
Gezer.) He built up Lower Beth Horon,[u] 18Baalath,[v] and Tadmor[e] in
the desert, within his land, 19as well as
all his store cities[w] and the towns for
his chariots[x] and for his horses[f]—
whatever he desired to build in Jerusalem, in Lebanon and throughout all the
territory he ruled.
20All the people left from the Amorites, Hittites,[y] Perizzites, Hivites
and Jebusites[z] (these peoples were
not Israelites), 21that is, their descendants[a] remaining in the land, whom
the Israelites could not exterminate[g][b]—these Solomon conscripted
for his slave labor force,[c] as it is to
this day. 22But Solomon did not make
slaves[d] of any of the Israelites; they
were his fighting men, his government
officials, his officers, his captains, and
the commanders of his chariots and
charioteers. 23They were also the chief
officials[e] in charge of Solomon's

9:9 [l] S Dt 31:29
9:11 [m] ver 14
9:13 [n] Jos 19:27
9:14 [o] ver 11
9:15 [p] 1Ki 5:13
[q] S 2Sa 5:9
[r] Jos 11:10-11
[s] S Jos 10:33
9:16 [t] 1Ki 3:1; Ps 45:12; 68:29; 72:10
9:17 [u] S Jos 10:10
9:18 [v] S Jos 19:44
9:19 [w] S Ex 1:11
[x] S Dt 17:16; 1Ki 4:26; 2Ch 1:14; 9:25
9:20 [y] S Nu 13:29
[z] S Jos 11:3
9:21
[a] S Ge 9:25-26
[b] S Jos 15:63
[c] S Ge 49:15; S Ex 1:11; S Dt 20:11
9:22
[d] S Lev 25:39
9:23 [e] 1Ki 5:16
9:24 [f] S 1Ki 3:1
[g] 2Sa 5:9; 1Ki 11:27
9:25 [h] S Ex 23:14
9:26 [i] 1Ki 10:22; 22:48; 2Ch 20:37; Isa 2:16
[j] S Nu 33:35
[k] 2Ki 14:22; 16:6
9:27 [l] Eze 27:8
9:28 [m] S Ge 10:29
[n] ver 14; 1Ki 10:10,11,14, 21; 2Ch 1:15; Ecc 2:8
10:1 [o] S Ge 10:7, 28; S 25:3; Mt 12:42; Lk 11:31
[p] Eze 16:14
[q] S Nu 12:8; S Jdg 14:12
10:2 [r] S Ge 24:10
10:5 [s] 1Ki 4:22

projects—550 officials supervising the
men who did the work.
24After Pharaoh's daughter[f] had
come up from the City of David to the
palace Solomon had built for her, he
constructed the supporting terraces.[g]
25Three[h] times a year Solomon sacrificed burnt offerings and fellowship
offerings[h] on the altar he had built for
the LORD, burning incense before the
LORD along with them, and so fulfilled
the temple obligations.
26King Solomon also built ships[i] at
Ezion Geber,[j] which is near Elath[k] in
Edom, on the shore of the Red Sea.[i]
27And Hiram sent his men—sailors[l]
who knew the sea—to serve in the
fleet with Solomon's men. 28They
sailed to Ophir[m] and brought back 420
talents[j] of gold,[n] which they delivered to King Solomon.

The Queen of Sheba Visits Solomon

10:1–13pp — 2Ch 9:1–12

10 When the queen of Sheba[o]
heard about the fame[p] of Solomon and his relation to the name of the
LORD, she came to test him with hard
questions.[q] 2Arriving at Jerusalem
with a very great caravan[r]—with
camels carrying spices, large quantities of gold, and precious stones—she
came to Solomon and talked with him
about all that she had on her mind.
3Solomon answered all her questions;
nothing was too hard for the king to
explain to her. 4When the queen of
Sheba saw all the wisdom of Solomon
and the palace he had built, 5the food
on his table,[s] the seating of his officials, the attending servants in their
robes, his cupbearers, and the burnt offerings he made at[k] the temple of the
LORD, she was overwhelmed.
6She said to the king, "The report I
heard in my own country about your
achievements and your wisdom is true.

[b] *13* *Cabul* sounds like the Hebrew for *good-for-nothing.* [c] *14* That is, about 4 1/2 tons (about 4 metric tons) [d] *15* Or *the Millo*; also in verse 24 [e] *18* The Hebrew may also be read *Tamar.* [f] *19* Or *charioteers* [g] *21* The Hebrew term refers to the irrevocable giving over of things or persons to the LORD, often by totally destroying them. [h] *25* Traditionally *peace offerings* [i] *26* Hebrew *Yam Suph*; that is, Sea of Reeds [j] *28* That is, about 16 tons (about 14.5 metric tons) [k] *5* Or *the ascent by which he went up to*

7But I did not believe[t] these things
until I came and saw with my own
eyes. Indeed, not even half was told
me; in wisdom and wealth[u] you have
far exceeded the report I heard. **8**How
happy your men must be! How happy
your officials, who continually stand
before you and hear[v] your wisdom!
9Praise[w] be to the LORD your God, who
has delighted in you and placed you on
the throne of Israel. Because of the
LORD's eternal love[x] for Israel, he has
made you king, to maintain justice[y]
and righteousness."

10And she gave the king 120 talents[l] of gold,[z] large quantities of
spices, and precious stones. Never
again were so many spices brought in
as those the queen of Sheba gave to
King Solomon.

11(Hiram's ships brought gold from
Ophir;[a] and from there they brought
great cargoes of almugwood[m] and precious stones. **12**The king used the almugwood to make supports for the
temple of the LORD and for the royal
palace, and to make harps and lyres for
the musicians. So much almugwood
has never been imported or seen since
that day.)

13King Solomon gave the queen of
Sheba all she desired and asked for,
besides what he had given her out of
his royal bounty. Then she left and returned with her retinue to her own
country.

Solomon's Splendor

10:14–29pp — 2Ch 1:14–17; 9:13–28

14The weight of the gold[b] that Solomon received yearly was 666 talents,[n]
15not including the revenues from merchants and traders and from all the
Arabian kings and the governors of the
land.

16King Solomon made two hundred
large shields[c] of hammered gold; six
hundred bekas[o] of gold went into each
shield. **17**He also made three hundred
small shields of hammered gold, with
three minas[p] of gold in each shield.
The king put them in the Palace of the
Forest of Lebanon.[d]

18Then the king made a great throne
inlaid with ivory and overlaid with fine
gold. **19**The throne had six steps, and
its back had a rounded top. On both
sides of the seat were armrests, with a
lion standing beside each of them.
20Twelve lions stood on the six steps,
one at either end of each step. Nothing
like it had ever been made for any other
kingdom. **21**All King Solomon's goblets
were gold, and all the household articles in the Palace of the Forest of Lebanon were pure gold.[e] Nothing was
made of silver, because silver was considered of little value in Solomon's
days. **22**The king had a fleet of trading
ships[q][f] at sea along with the ships[g]
of Hiram. Once every three years it returned, carrying gold, silver and ivory,
and apes and baboons.

23King Solomon was greater in
riches[h] and wisdom[i] than all the other kings of the earth. **24**The whole
world sought audience with Solomon
to hear the wisdom[j] God had put in
his heart. **25**Year after year, everyone
who came brought a gift[k]—articles of
silver and gold, robes, weapons and
spices, and horses and mules.

26Solomon accumulated chariots
and horses;[l] he had fourteen hundred
chariots and twelve thousand
horses,[r] which he kept in the chariot
cities and also with him in Jerusalem.
27The king made silver as common[m]
in Jerusalem as stones,[n] and cedar as
plentiful as sycamore-fig[o] trees in the
foothills. **28**Solomon's horses were imported from Egypt[s] and from Kue[t]—
the royal merchants purchased them
from Kue. **29**They imported a chariot
from Egypt for six hundred shekels[u]
of silver, and a horse for a hundred and
fifty.[v] They also exported them to all
the kings of the Hittites[p] and of the
Arameans.

Solomon's Wives

11 King Solomon, however, loved
many foreign women[q] besides

10:7 [t]S Ge 45:26 [u]1Ch 29:25
10:8 [v]Pr 8:34
10:9 [w]S 1Ki 5:7; S Isa 42:10 [x]S Dt 7:8 [y]Ps 11:7; 33:5; 72:2; 99:4; 103:6
10:10 [z]S 1Ki 9:28; Isa 60:6
10:11 [a]S Ge 10:29
10:14 [b]S 1Ki 9:28
10:16 [c]S 2Sa 8:7
10:17 [d]S 1Ki 7:2
10:21 [e]Isa 60:17
10:22 [f]S 1Ki 9:26 [g]1Ki 9:27; Ps 48:7; Isa 2:16; 23:1,14; 60:6,9
10:23 [h]1Ki 3:13; Mt 6:29 [i]S 1Ki 3:12; Mt 12:42
10:24 [j]S 2Sa 14:20
10:25 [k]S 1Sa 10:27
10:26 [l]S Dt 17:16
10:27 [m]Dt 17:17 [n]Job 27:16; Isa 60:17 [o]1Ch 27:28; Am 7:14
10:29 [p]S Nu 13:29
11:1 [q]S ver 3; S Ex 34:16

[l]*10* That is, about 4 1/2 tons (about 4 metric tons) [m]*11* Probably a variant of *algumwood*; also in verse 12 [n]*14* That is, about 25 tons (about 23 metric tons) [o]*16* That is, about 7 1/2 pounds (about 3.5 kilograms) [p]*17* That is, about 3 3/4 pounds (about 1.7 kilograms) [q]*22* Hebrew *of ships of Tarshish* [r]*26* Or *charioteers* [s]*28* Or possibly *Muzur*, a region in Cilicia; also in verse 29 [t]*28* Probably *Cilicia* [u]*29* That is, about 15 pounds (about 7 kilograms) [v]*29* That is, about 3 3/4 pounds (about 1.7 kilograms)

11:1 SOLOMON . . . LOVED MANY FOREIGN WOMEN. Ch. 11 describes Solomon's spiritual decline and its results. (1) Solomon began as a man who loved the Lord, walked according to his stat-

Pharaoh's daughter—Moabites, Ammonites,[r] Edomites, Sidonians and
Hittites. 2They were from nations
about which the LORD had told the Israelites, "You must not intermarry[s]
with them, because they will surely
turn your hearts after their gods." Nevertheless, Solomon held fast to them in
love. 3He had seven hundred wives of
royal birth and three hundred concubines,[t] and his wives led him
astray.[u] 4As Solomon grew old, his
wives turned his heart after other
gods,[v] and his heart was not fully devoted[w] to the LORD his God, as the
heart of David his father had been. 5He
followed Ashtoreth[x] the goddess of
the Sidonians, and Molech[w][y] the detestable god of the Ammonites. 6So
Solomon did evil[z] in the eyes of the
LORD; he did not follow the LORD completely, as David his father had done.
7On a hill east[a] of Jerusalem, Solomon built a high place for Chemosh[b]
the detestable god of Moab, and for

11:1 r 1Ki 14:21, 31
11:2 s S Ex 34:16; 1Ki 16:31
11:3 t S Ge 22:24; S Est 2:14 u ver 1; Dt 17:17; Ne 13:26; Pr 31:3
11:4 v S Ex 34:16 w S 1Ki 8:61; S 1Ch 29:19
11:5 x S Jdg 2:13 y ver 7; S Lev 18:21; Isa 57:9; Zep 1:5
11:6 z S Dt 4:25
11:7 a 2Ki 23:13 b S Nu 21:29 c S Lev 18:21; 20:2-5; Ac 7:43
11:9 d S 1Ki 3:5
11:10 e S 1Ki 9:6 f 1Ki 6:12
11:11 g S Lev 18:4 h ver 31; S 1Sa 15:27; 2Ki 17:21; Mt 21:43
11:12 i Ps 89:33
11:13 j 1Ki 12:20 k S 2Sa 7:15

Molech[c] the detestable god of the Ammonites. 8He did the same for all his
foreign wives, who burned incense and
offered sacrifices to their gods.
9The LORD became angry with Solomon because his heart had turned
away from the LORD, the God of Israel,
who had appeared[d] to him twice. 10Al-
though he had forbidden Solomon to
follow other gods,[e] Solomon did not
keep the LORD's command.[f] 11So the
LORD said to Solomon, "Since this is
your attitude and you have not kept my
covenant and my decrees,[g] which I
commanded you, I will most certainly
tear[h] the kingdom away from you and
give it to one of your subordinates.
12Nevertheless, for the sake of David[i]
your father, I will not do it during your
lifetime. I will tear it out of the hand of
your son. 13Yet I will not tear the
whole kingdom from him, but will give
him one tribe[j] for the sake[k] of David

w5 Hebrew *Milcom;* also in verse 33

utes and built his temple (3:3; 6:1). He experienced God's love, grace and salvation; he was given special spiritual understanding (3:10–14; 2Sa 12:24), and he wrote holy Scripture under the inspiration of the Holy Spirit (see 4:29–34, note).

(2) Nevertheless, Solomon became hardened by sin's deceitfulness and turned away from the Lord to serve other gods; he provoked the Lord to anger, and was consequently punished by God (vv. 1–13; cf. Dt 29:14–21; 30:15–20; Heb 3:12–14).

(3) Solomon's fatal error was to seek power, success, wealth and sensual pleasure through compromise with and tolerance of idolatry and sin. Solomon sought (a) unholy alliances with foreign nations (Tyre, 9:10–14; Egypt, 3:1; 10:28–29; other nations, 9:25—10:13), (b) many foreign wives and concubines to seal these alliances (vv. 1–8; see next note; Ge 29:28, note), and (c) more and more wealth and glory (10:14–19; cf. 1Ti 6:9).

(4) Read Dt 17:14–20 for God's commands for kings about allying with foreigners, acquiring horses from Egypt, taking many wives, and accumulating more silver or gold. The Bible nowhere states that Solomon ever repented of his sins (see v. 43, note).

11:2 YOU MUST NOT INTERMARRY WITH THEM. Solomon's possession of many wives not only ignored God's command for kings not to take many wives (cf. Dt 17:17), but also transgressed God's prohibition against marrying pagan wives from the Canaanites (Ex 34:12–16; Jos 23:12–13). Solomon clearly failed to meditate carefully on God's law "so that he may learn to revere the LORD his God and follow carefully all the words of this law" (Dt 17:19).

11:4 FULLY DEVOTED . . . HEART OF DAVID HIS FATHER. David's heart was "fully devoted" not in the sense that he never failed God miserably, but that he never turned to idolatry and the worship of other gods. In his adultery with Bathsheba and his attempted coverup, David grievously sinned to the point of despising God and his word (2Sa 12:9–10); yet, he never worshiped or depended on other gods, as did many of Israel's kings (cf. 15:5).

11:5–7 HE FOLLOWED ASHTORETH . . . MOLECH. Solomon first tolerated the false gods of his wives, then turned his own heart after them (vv. 2–9). (1) In addition to his worship of the Lord, Solomon added the worship of the Sidonian goddess Ashtoreth (involving immoral rituals and the worship of the stars), the Moabite god Molech (involving child sacrifice, cf. Lev 18:21; 20:1–5), and the Ammonite god Chemosh (a sun-god). No longer could Solomon say that the covenant Lord was the only true God (cf. Dt 6:4).

(2) Solomon's apostasy shows that mere knowledge of God and his word is not an adequate defense against sin and apostasy. Sin comes from the heart and can be resisted only so long as one's heart is turned in faith and love toward God (Dt 6:4–9; cf. 1Ki 3:9, note). Solomon, a preacher who warned others, fell into such blatant sin that he directly sanctioned spiritism, encouraged immorality and cruelty, defiled Israel and dishonored the one true God.

11:11 TEAR THE KINGDOM AWAY FROM YOU. God's judgment on Solomon resulted in the division of Israel into two kingdoms, only one of which was ruled by Solomon's successors (vv. 9–13,31)—the tribe of Judah (but including Simeon, cf. Jos 19:1), given to his son Rehoboam in order to preserve the Messianic line (vv. 13,32). The ten tribes were soon to be given to Jeroboam (vv. 31–36).

my servant and for the sake of Jerusalem, which I have chosen."[l]

Solomon's Adversaries

14 Then the LORD raised up against
Solomon an adversary,[m] Hadad the
Edomite, from the royal line of Edom.
15 Earlier when David was fighting with
Edom, Joab the commander of the
army, who had gone up to bury the
dead, had struck down all the men in
Edom.[n] 16 Joab and all the Israelites
stayed there for six months, until they
had destroyed all the men in Edom.
17 But Hadad, still only a boy, fled to
Egypt with some Edomite officials who
had served his father. 18 They set out
from Midian and went to Paran.[o]
Then taking men from Paran with
them, they went to Egypt, to Pharaoh
king of Egypt, who gave Hadad a house
and land and provided him with food.
19 Pharaoh was so pleased with Hadad that he gave him a sister of his own
wife, Queen Tahpenes, in marriage.
20 The sister of Tahpenes bore him a
son named Genubath, whom Tahpenes
brought up in the royal palace. There
Genubath lived with Pharaoh's own
children.
21 While he was in Egypt, Hadad
heard that David rested with his fathers and that Joab the commander of
the army was also dead. Then Hadad
said to Pharaoh, "Let me go, that I may
return to my own country."
22 "What have you lacked here that
you want to go back to your own country?" Pharaoh asked.
"Nothing," Hadad replied, "but do let
me go!"
23 And God raised up against Solomon another adversary,[p] Rezon son of
Eliada, who had fled from his master,
Hadadezer[q] king of Zobah. 24 He gathered men around him and became the
leader of a band of rebels when David
destroyed the forces[x] ⌊of Zobah⌋; the
rebels went to Damascus,[r] where
they settled and took control. 25 Rezon
was Israel's adversary as long as Solomon lived, adding to the trouble caused
by Hadad. So Rezon ruled in Aram[s]
and was hostile toward Israel.

Jeroboam Rebels Against Solomon

26 Also, Jeroboam son of Nebat rebelled[t] against the king. He was one

11:13 [l]Dt 12:11
11:14 [m]S 1Ki 5:4
11:15 [n]1Ch 18:12
11:18 [o]Nu 10:12
11:23 [p]S 1Ki 5:4 [q]S 2Sa 8:3
11:24 [r]S 2Sa 8:5
11:25 [s]S Ge 10:22; S 2Sa 10:19
11:26 [t]2Ch 13:6
11:27 [u]S 1Ki 9:24
11:28 [v]S Ru 2:1 [w]S Ge 39:4; Pr 22:29
11:29 [x]1Ki 12:15; 14:2; 2Ch 9:29; 10:15
11:30 [y]1Sa 15:27
11:31 [z]S ver 11; S 1Sa 15:27
11:32 [a]S 2Sa 7:15
11:33 [b]S Jdg 2:13 [c]2Ki 21:22 [d]1Ki 3:3
11:36 [e]1Ki 12:17 [f]S 2Sa 21:17
11:37 [g]1Ki 14:7 [h]2Sa 3:21
11:38 [i]S Dt 12:25; S 2Sa 8:15 [j]S Dt 17:19

of Solomon's officials, an Ephraimite
from Zeredah, and his mother was a
widow named Zeruah.
27 Here is the account of how he rebelled against the king: Solomon had
built the supporting terraces[y][u] and
had filled in the gap in the wall of the
city of David his father. 28 Now Jeroboam was a man of standing,[v] and when
Solomon saw how well[w] the young
man did his work, he put him in charge
of the whole labor force of the house of
Joseph.
29 About that time Jeroboam was going out of Jerusalem, and Ahijah[x] the
prophet of Shiloh met him on the way,
wearing a new cloak. The two of them
were alone out in the country, 30 and
Ahijah took hold of the new cloak he
was wearing and tore[y] it into twelve
pieces. 31 Then he said to Jeroboam,
"Take ten pieces for yourself, for this
is what the LORD, the God of Israel,
says: 'See, I am going to tear[z] the
kingdom out of Solomon's hand and
give you ten tribes. 32 But for the
sake[a] of my servant David and the
city of Jerusalem, which I have chosen
out of all the tribes of Israel, he will
have one tribe. 33 I will do this because
they have[z] forsaken me and worshiped[b] Ashtoreth the goddess of the
Sidonians, Chemosh the god of the Moabites, and Molech the god of the Ammonites, and have not walked[c] in my
ways, nor done what is right in my
eyes, nor kept my statutes[d] and laws
as David, Solomon's father, did.
34 " 'But I will not take the whole
kingdom out of Solomon's hand; I have
made him ruler all the days of his life
for the sake of David my servant,
whom I chose and who observed my
commands and statutes. 35 I will take
the kingdom from his son's hands and
give you ten tribes. 36 I will give one
tribe[e] to his son so that David my servant may always have a lamp[f] before
me in Jerusalem, the city where I chose
to put my Name. 37 However, as for you,
I will take you, and you will rule[g] over
all that your heart desires;[h] you will
be king over Israel. 38 If you do whatever I command you and walk in my ways
and do what is right[i] in my eyes by
keeping my statutes[j] and commands,

[x]24 Hebrew *destroyed them* [y]27 Or *the Millo* [z]33 Hebrew; Septuagint, Vulgate and Syriac *because he has*

as David my servant did, I will be with
you. I will build you a dynasty[k] as enduring as the one I built for David and
will give Israel to you. 39I will humble
David's descendants because of this,
but not forever.' "
40Solomon tried to kill Jeroboam,
but Jeroboam fled[l] to Egypt, to Shishak[m] the king, and stayed there until
Solomon's death.

Solomon's Death

11:41–43pp — 2Ch 9:29–31

41As for the other events of Solomon's reign—all he did and the wisdom he displayed—are they not written in the book of the annals of
Solomon? 42Solomon reigned in Jerusalem over all Israel forty years.
43Then he rested with his fathers and
was buried in the city of David his father. And Rehoboam[n] his son succeeded him as king.

Israel Rebels Against Rehoboam

12:1–24pp — 2Ch 10:1–11:4

12 Rehoboam went to Shechem,[o]
for all the Israelites had gone
there to make him king. 2When Jeroboam son of Nebat heard this (he was still
in Egypt, where he had fled[p] from
King Solomon), he returned from[a]
Egypt. 3So they sent for Jeroboam, and
he and the whole assembly of Israel
went to Rehoboam and said to him:
4"Your father put a heavy yoke[q] on us,
but now lighten the harsh labor and the
heavy yoke he put on us, and we will
serve you."
5Rehoboam answered, "Go away for
three days and then come back to me."
So the people went away.
6Then King Rehoboam consulted
the elders[r] who had served his father
Solomon during his lifetime. "How
would you advise me to answer these
people?" he asked.
7They replied, "If today you will be
a servant to these people and serve
them and give them a favorable answer,[s] they will always be your servants."
8But Rehoboam rejected[t] the advice the elders gave him and consulted
the young men who had grown up with
him and were serving him. 9He asked
them, "What is your advice? How
should we answer these people who
say to me, 'Lighten the yoke your father put on us'?"
10The young men who had grown up
with him replied, "Tell these people
who have said to you, 'Your father put
a heavy yoke on us, but make our yoke
lighter'—tell them, 'My little finger is
thicker than my father's waist. 11My
father laid on you a heavy yoke; I will
make it even heavier. My father
scourged you with whips; I will
scourge you with scorpions.' "
12Three days later Jeroboam and all
the people returned to Rehoboam, as
the king had said, "Come back to me in
three days." 13The king answered the
people harshly. Rejecting the advice
given him by the elders, 14he followed
the advice of the young men and said,
"My father made your yoke heavy; I
will make it even heavier. My father
scourged[u] you with whips; I will
scourge you with scorpions." 15So the
king did not listen to the people, for
this turn of events was from the
LORD,[v] to fulfill the word the LORD had
spoken to Jeroboam son of Nebat
through Ahijah[w] the Shilonite.
16When all Israel saw that the king
refused to listen to them, they answered the king:

"What share[x] do we have in
David,
what part in Jesse's son?
To your tents, O Israel![y]
Look after your own house,
O David!"

So the Israelites went home.[z] 17But
as for the Israelites who were living in
the towns of Judah,[a] Rehoboam still
ruled over them.
18King Rehoboam sent out Adoniram,[b b] who was in charge of forced
labor, but all Israel stoned him to

11:38 [k] S Ex 1:21 **11:40** [l] 1Ki 12:2; 2Ch 10:2 [m] 2Ch 12:2 **11:43** [n] Mt 1:7 **12:1** [o] ver 25; S Ge 12:6; Jos 24:32 **12:2** [p] S 1Ki 11:40 **12:4** [q] S 1Sa 8:11-18; 1Ki 4:20-28 **12:6** [r] S 1Ki 4:2 **12:7** [s] Pr 15:1 **12:8** [t] Lev 19:32 **12:14** [u] Ex 1:14 **12:15** [v] S Dt 2:30; 2Ch 25:20 [w] S 1Ki 11:29 **12:16** [x] S Ge 31:14 [y] S 2Sa 20:1 [z] Isa 7:17 **12:17** [a] 1Ki 11:13,36 **12:18** [b] S 2Sa 20:24

[a] 2 Or *he remained in* [b] 18 Some Septuagint manuscripts and Syriac (see also 1 Kings 4:6 and 5:14); Hebrew *Adoram*

11:43 THEN HE RESTED. The same chapter that mentions Solomon's apostasy speaks of his death, without any indication that he repented and returned to God. The Chronicler records David's warning to Solomon: "if you forsake [God], he will reject you forever" (1Ch 28:9). The Biblical truth revealed here is that Solomon, who was once in grace, did not remain in that grace. God's Word warns us here: if a king who had experienced such great gifts, ministry and graces could fall, then let all who stand be careful that they do not fall (1Co 10:12).

death.[c] King Rehoboam, however,
managed to get into his chariot and escape to Jerusalem. 19So Israel has
been in rebellion against the house of
David[d] to this day.
20When all the Israelites heard that
Jeroboam had returned, they sent and
called him to the assembly and made
him king over all Israel. Only the tribe
of Judah remained loyal to the house of
David.[e]
21When Rehoboam arrived in Jerusalem, he mustered the whole house of
Judah and the tribe of Benjamin—a
hundred and eighty thousand fighting
men—to make war[f] against the
house of Israel and to regain the kingdom for Rehoboam son of Solomon.
22But this word of God came to Shemaiah[g] the man of God:[h] 23"Say to
Rehoboam son of Solomon king of Judah, to the whole house of Judah and
Benjamin, and to the rest of the people,
24'This is what the LORD says: Do not
go up to fight against your brothers,
the Israelites. Go home, every one of
you, for this is my doing.' " So they
obeyed the word of the LORD and went
home again, as the LORD had ordered.

Golden Calves at Bethel and Dan

25Then Jeroboam fortified Shechem[i] in the hill country of Ephraim
and lived there. From there he went
out and built up Peniel.[c][j]
26Jeroboam thought to himself, "The
kingdom will now likely revert to the
house of David. 27If these people go up
to offer sacrifices at the temple of the
LORD in Jerusalem,[k] they will again
give their allegiance to their lord, Rehoboam king of Judah. They will kill
me and return to King Rehoboam."
28After seeking advice, the king
made two golden calves.[l] He said to
the people, "It is too much for you to
go up to Jerusalem. Here are your
gods, O Israel, who brought you up out
of Egypt."[m] 29One he set up in Bethel,[n] and the other in Dan.[o] 30And this
thing became a sin;[p] the people went
even as far as Dan to worship the one
there.
31Jeroboam built shrines[q] on high
places and appointed priests[r] from all
sorts of people, even though they were
not Levites. 32He instituted a festival

12:18 [c]S Jos 7:25
12:19 [d]2Ki 17:21
12:20 [e]1Ki 11:13,32; Eze 37:16
12:21 [f]1Ki 14:30; 15:6,16; 2Ch 11:1
12:22 [g]2Ch 12:5-7 [h]S Dt 33:1; 2Ki 4:7
12:25 [i]S ver 1 [j]S Jdg 8:8,17
12:27 [k]Dt 12:5-6
12:28 [l]S Ex 32:4; S 2Ch 11:15 [m]S Ex 32:8
12:29 [n]S Ge 12:8; S Jos 7:2 [o]Jdg 18:27-31; Am 8:14
12:30 [p]1Ki 13:34; 14:16; 15:26,30; 16:2; 2Ki 3:3; 10:29; 13:2; 17:21
12:31 [q]S Lev 26:30; 1Ki 13:32; 2Ki 17:29 [r]S Ex 29:9; 1Ki 13:33; 2Ki 17:32; 2Ch 11:14-15; 13:9

[c]25 Hebrew *Penuel,* a variant of *Peniel*

12:20 JEROBOAM . . . KING OVER ALL ISRAEL. At Solomon's death (11:43), the Hebrew nation split into two kingdoms. (1) The northern kingdom, called Israel, was first ruled by Jeroboam. The southern kingdom, called Judah, was first ruled by Rehoboam, Solomon's son (v. 17). The division continued until the ten northern tribes were taken into captivity by Assyria in 722 B.C. The southern kingdom was carried into captivity in 586 B.C. by the Babylonians. The history of the two kingdoms is recorded in 1Ki 12—22; 2Ki 1—25; and 2Ch 10—36.

(2) The story of Israel and Judah reveals their persistence in breaking God's covenant. The Bible indicates that all the kings of the northern kingdom did evil in the eyes of the Lord (e.g., 16:25,30; 22:52; 2Ki 3:3; 10:29); the majority of the kings of Judah departed from the covenant. Only a few of the kings of Judah, notably Hezekiah (2Ki 18:1—20:21) and Josiah (2Ki 22:1—23:29), "did what was right in the eyes of the LORD" (2Ki 18:3; 22:2).

12:24 FOR THIS IS MY DOING. It was the Lord who brought about the division of his people. The existence of two nations was designed by him (1) as a punishment for their idolatry, and (2) as a means for preserving a faithful remnant through Judah (11:13). Though Israel as a whole departed from God, a remnant in Judah remained faithful to the covenant, and through them God was able to fulfill his promises and redemptive purpose.

12:28 TWO GOLDEN CALVES. . . HERE ARE YOUR GODS. Jeroboam of the northern kingdom established a counterfeit religious system by offering the people worship of their gods through idols (vv. 27–30; cf. Ex 20:3–4), after the pattern of the golden calf made by Aaron (Ex 32:8). He appointed priests, "even though they were not Levites" (v. 31), thus ordaining men to the ministry who were not qualified according to God's law (see next note).

Jeroboam's establishment of a false religious system produced two results: (1) Most people who remained in the northern kingdom accepted Baal worship along with its immoral practice of cult prostitution. (2) The majority of the godly remnant that desired to remain loyal to God and his law suffered greatly as they "abandoned their . . . property" and moved to the southern kingdom in order to worship the Lord according to his original revelation and commands (2Ch 11:13–14). "Those from every tribe of Israel who set their hearts on seeking the LORD, the God of Israel, followed the Levites to Jerusalem to offer sacrifices to the LORD, the God of their fathers" (2Ch 11:16; cf. 15:9).

12:31 APPOINTED PRIESTS . . . THOUGH THEY WERE NOT LEVITES. Jeroboam appointed priests who were not qualified according to God's standards in Nu 3:6–9; 8:5–20. Under the new covenant the Levitical priesthood no longer exists, but God has still established certain essential qualifications for those who would be ordained for pastoral or church leadership; these spiritual and moral qualifications are listed in 1Ti 3:1–7 and Tit 1:5–9 (see article on MORAL QUALIFICATIONS FOR OVERSEERS, p. 1882).

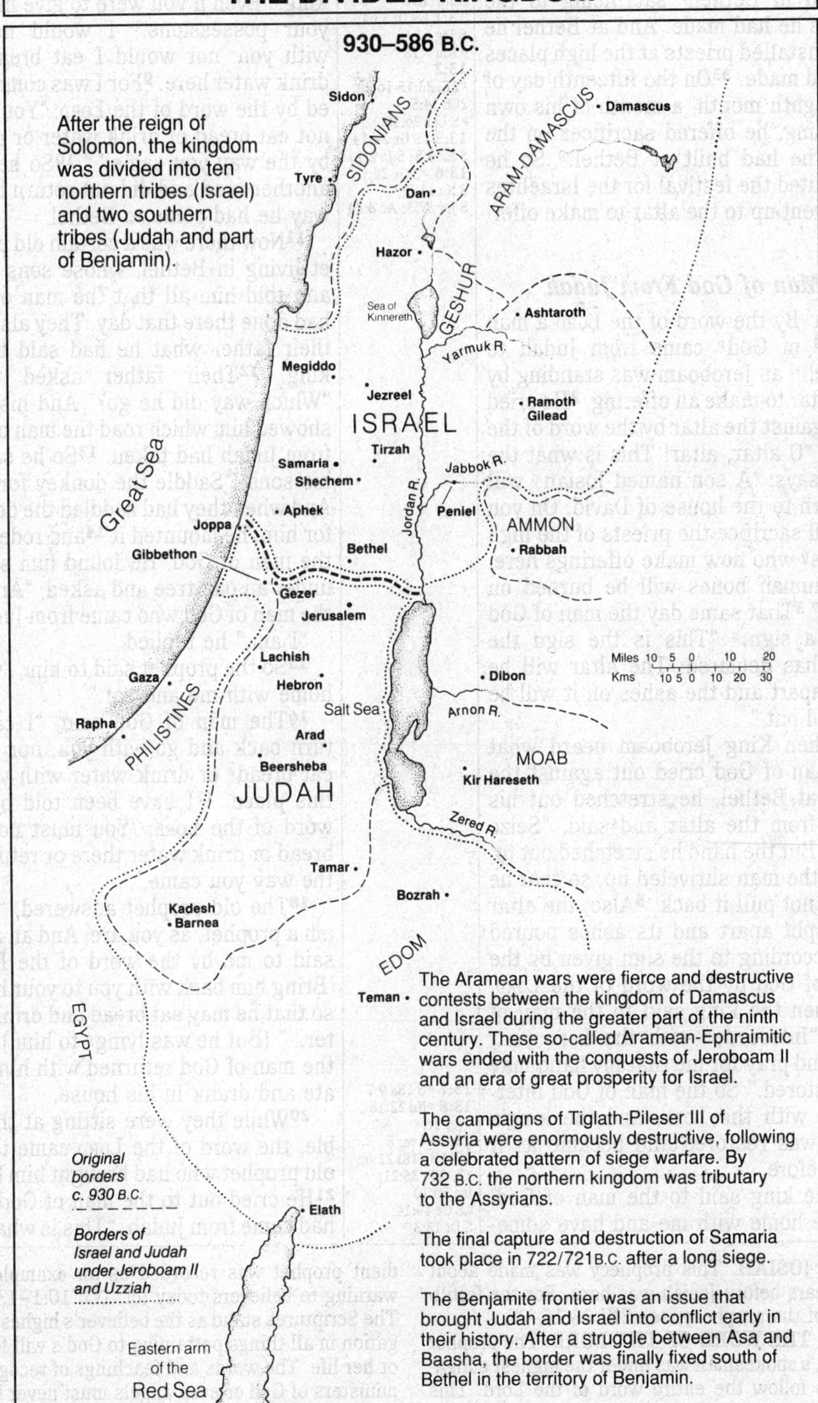
THE DIVIDED KINGDOM
930–586 B.C.
After the reign of Solomon, the kingdom was divided into ten northern tribes (Israel) and two southern tribes (Judah and part of Benjamin).
Sidon
Damascus
SIDONIANS
ARAM-DAMASCUS
Tyre
Dan
Hazor
GESHUR
Sea of Kinnereth
Ashtaroth
Yarmuk R.
Megiddo
Jezreel
Ramoth Gilead
ISRAEL
Great Sea
Tirzah
Samaria
Shechem
Jabbok R.
Jordan R.
Aphek
Peniel
AMMON
Joppa
Gibbethon
Bethel
Rabbah
Gezer
Jerusalem
Lachish
Miles 10 5 0 10 20
Kms 10 5 0 10 20 30
Gaza
Hebron
Dibon
Salt Sea
Arnon R.
Rapha
PHILISTINES
Arad
Beersheba
MOAB
JUDAH
Kir Hareseth
Zered R.
Tamar
Bozrah
Kadesh Barnea
EDOM
Teman
EGYPT
The Aramean wars were fierce and destructive contests between the kingdom of Damascus and Israel during the greater part of the ninth century. These so-called Aramean-Ephraimitic wars ended with the conquests of Jeroboam II and an era of great prosperity for Israel.
The campaigns of Tiglath-Pileser III of Assyria were enormously destructive, following a celebrated pattern of siege warfare. By 732 B.C. the northern kingdom was tributary to the Assyrians.
The final capture and destruction of Samaria took place in 722/721 B.C. after a long siege.
The Benjamite frontier was an issue that brought Judah and Israel into conflict early in their history. After a struggle between Asa and Baasha, the border was finally fixed south of Bethel in the territory of Benjamin.
Original borders c. 930 B.C.
Elath
Borders of Israel and Judah under Jeroboam II and Uzziah
Eastern arm of the Red Sea

on the fifteenth day of the eighth[s]
month, like the festival held in Judah,
and offered sacrifices on the altar. This
he did in Bethel,[t] sacrificing to the
calves he had made. And at Bethel he
also installed priests at the high places
he had made. **33**On the fifteenth day of
the eighth month, a month of his own
choosing, he offered sacrifices on the
altar he had built at Bethel.[u] So he
instituted the festival for the Israelites
and went up to the altar to make offerings.

The Man of God From Judah

13 By the word of the LORD a man
of God[v] came from Judah to
Bethel,[w] as Jeroboam was standing by
the altar to make an offering. **2**He cried
out against the altar by the word of the
LORD: "O altar, altar! This is what the
LORD says: 'A son named Josiah[x] will
be born to the house of David. On you
he will sacrifice the priests of the high
places[y] who now make offerings here,
and human bones will be burned on
you.' " **3**That same day the man of God
gave a sign:[z] "This is the sign the
LORD has declared: The altar will be
split apart and the ashes on it will be
poured out."

4When King Jeroboam heard what
the man of God cried out against the
altar at Bethel, he stretched out his
hand from the altar and said, "Seize
him!" But the hand he stretched out toward the man shriveled up, so that he
could not pull it back. **5**Also, the altar
was split apart and its ashes poured
out according to the sign given by the
man of God by the word of the LORD.

6Then the king said to the man of
God, "Intercede[a] with the LORD your
God and pray for me that my hand may
be restored." So the man of God interceded with the LORD, and the king's
1Ki 17:17-24 hand was restored and became as it
was before.

7The king said to the man of God,
"Come home with me and have something to eat, and I will give you a
gift."[b]

8But the man of God answered the
king, "Even if you were to give me half
your possessions,[c] I would not go
with you, nor would I eat bread[d] or
drink water here. **9**For I was commanded by the word of the LORD: 'You must
not eat bread or drink water or return
by the way you came.' " **10**So he took
another road and did not return by the
way he had come to Bethel.

11Now there was a certain old prophet living in Bethel, whose sons came
and told him all that the man of God
had done there that day. They also told
their father what he had said to the
king. **12**Their father asked them,
"Which way did he go?" And his sons
showed him which road the man of God
from Judah had taken. **13**So he said to
his sons, "Saddle the donkey for me."
And when they had saddled the donkey
for him, he mounted it **14**and rode after
the man of God. He found him sitting
under an oak tree and asked, "Are you
the man of God who came from Judah?"

"I am," he replied.

15So the prophet said to him, "Come
home with me and eat."

16The man of God said, "I cannot
turn back and go with you, nor can I
eat bread[e] or drink water with you in
this place. **17**I have been told by the
word of the LORD: 'You must not eat
bread or drink water there or return by
the way you came.' "

18The old prophet answered, "I too
am a prophet, as you are. And an angel
said to me by the word of the LORD:[f]
'Bring him back with you to your house
so that he may eat bread and drink water.' " (But he was lying[g] to him.) **19**So
the man of God returned with him and
ate and drank in his house.

20While they were sitting at the table, the word of the LORD came to the
old prophet who had brought him back.
21He cried out to the man of God who
had come from Judah, "This is what the

12:32 [s] S Nu 29:12 [t] 2Ki 10:29 **12:33** [u] 2Ki 23:15; Am 7:13 **13:1** [v] S Dt 33:1; S Jdg 13:6 [w] Am 7:13 **13:2** [x] 2Ki 23:15-16,20; 2Ch 34:5 [y] S Lev 26:30 **13:3** [z] S Ge 24:14; S Ex 4:8; S Jn 2:11 **13:6** [a] S Ge 20:7; S Nu 11:2; S Jer 37:3; Ac 8:24 **13:7** [b] S 1Sa 9:7 **13:8** [c] Nu 22:18 [d] ver 16 **13:16** [e] ver 8 **13:18** [f] 1Ki 22:6, 12; 2Ch 35:21; Isa 36:10 [g] S Ge 19:14; S Dt 13:3

13:2 JOSIAH. This prophecy was made about 300 years before Josiah was born. For the fulfillment of the prophecy, see 2Ki 23:15–20.

13:9 THE WORD OF THE LORD. The prophet as God's spokesman was under the highest obligation to follow the entire word of the Lord. This particular prophet later failed to obey God's instruction and paid with his life (vv. 11–24).

13:21–22 YOU HAVE DEFIED THE WORD OF THE LORD. The story of the unnamed disobedient prophet was recorded as an example and warning to believers today (cf. 1Co 10:1–13). (1) The Scriptures stand as the believer's highest obligation in all things pertaining to God's will for his or her life. The words and teachings of recognized ministers of God or even angels must never be accepted if they contradict the instructions and standards of written revelation found in the original and fundamental testimony of Christ and the apostles (1Co 14:29; Gal 1:8–9; see 1Jn 4:1, note).

LORD says: 'You have defied[h] the word
of the LORD and have not kept the command the LORD your God gave you.
22 You came back and ate bread and
drank water in the place where he told
you not to eat or drink. Therefore your
body will not be buried in the tomb of
your fathers.' "
23 When the man of God had finished
eating and drinking, the prophet who
had brought him back saddled his donkey for him. 24 As he went on his way,
a lion[i] met him on the road and killed
him, and his body was thrown down on
the road, with both the donkey and the
lion standing beside it. 25 Some people
who passed by saw the body thrown
down there, with the lion standing beside the body, and they went and reported it in the city where the old
prophet lived.
26 When the prophet who had
brought him back from his journey
heard of it, he said, "It is the man of
God who defied[j] the word of the LORD.
The LORD has given him over to the
lion, which has mauled him and killed
him, as the word of the LORD had
warned him."
27 The prophet said to his sons, "Saddle the donkey for me," and they did so.
28 Then he went out and found the body
thrown down on the road, with the donkey and the lion standing beside it. The
lion had neither eaten the body nor
mauled the donkey. 29 So the prophet
picked up the body of the man of God,
laid it on the donkey, and brought it
back to his own city to mourn for him
and bury him. 30 Then he laid the body
in his own tomb,[k] and they mourned
over him and said, "Oh, my brother!"[l]
31 After burying him, he said to his
sons, "When I die, bury me in the grave
where the man of God is buried; lay my
bones[m] beside his bones. 32 For the
message he declared by the word of the
LORD against the altar in Bethel and
against all the shrines on the high
places[n] in the towns of Samaria[o] will
certainly come true."[p]
33 Even after this, Jeroboam did not
change his evil ways,[q] but once more
appointed priests for the high places
from all sorts[r] of people. Anyone who
wanted to become a priest he consecrated for the high places. 34 This was
the sin[s] of the house of Jeroboam that
led to its downfall and to its destruction[t] from the face of the earth.

Ahijah's Prophecy Against Jeroboam

14 At that time Abijah son of Jeroboam became ill, 2 and Jerobo-
am said to his wife, "Go, disguise yourself, so you won't be recognized as the
wife of Jeroboam. Then go to Shiloh.
Ahijah[u] the prophet is there—the one
who told me I would be king over this
people. 3 Take ten loaves of bread[v]
with you, some cakes and a jar of honey, and go to him. He will tell you what
will happen to the boy." 4 So Jeroboam's wife did what he said and went to
Ahijah's house in Shiloh.
Now Ahijah could not see; his sight
was gone because of his age. 5 But the
LORD had told Ahijah, "Jeroboam's wife
is coming to ask you about her son, for
he is ill, and you are to give her such
and such an answer. When she arrives,
she will pretend to be someone else."
6 So when Ahijah heard the sound of
her footsteps at the door, he said,
"Come in, wife of Jeroboam. Why this
pretense?[w] I have been sent to you
with bad news. 7 Go, tell Jeroboam that
this is what the LORD, the God of Israel,
says:[x] 'I raised you up from among
the people and made you a leader[y]
over my people Israel. 8 I tore[z] the
kingdom away from the house of David
and gave it to you, but you have not
been like my servant David, who kept
my commands and followed me with all
his heart, doing only what was right[a]
in my eyes. 9 You have done more evil[b]
than all who lived before you.[c] You
have made for yourself other gods,
idols[d] made of metal; you have provoked[e] me to anger and thrust me behind your back.[f]

13:21 [h] ver 26; S 1Sa 13:14; 1Ki 20:35 **13:24** [i] 1Ki 20:36 **13:26** [j] S ver 21 **13:30** [k] 2Ki 23:17 [l] Jer 22:18 **13:31** [m] 2Ki 23:18 **13:32** [n] S Lev 26:30; S 1Ki 12:31 [o] 1Ki 16:24,28; 20:1; 2Ki 10:1; 15:13 [p] 2Ki 23:16

13:33 [q] 1Ki 15:26 [r] S 1Ki 12:31 **13:34** [s] S 1Ki 12:30 [t] 1Ki 14:10; 15:29; 2Ki 9:9; Jer 35:17; Am 7:9 **14:2** [u] S 1Ki 11:29 **14:3** [v] S 1Sa 9:7 **14:6** [w] S 1Sa 28:12 **14:7** [x] 1Ki 15:29 [y] 1Ki 11:37 **14:8** [z] S 1Sa 15:27 [a] S 2Sa 8:15; 1Ki 3:3; 15:5; 2Ki 14:3; 15:3,34; 16:2; 18:3; 20:3; 22:2 **14:9** [b] 1Ki 16:30, 33; 21:25; 2Ki 21:9,11; 24:3 [c] 1Ki 16:2 [d] S Ex 20:4; S 32:4; 2Ch 11:15 [e] Dt 32:16; 1Ki 16:2; Ps 78:58; Jer 7:18; 8:19; 32:32; 44:3; Eze 8:17; 16:26 [f] Ne 9:26; Ps 50:17; Jer 2:27; 32:33; Eze 23:35

(2) Disobedience to what God has commanded brings punishment, regardless of past faithfulness and service (vv. 20–25).

(3) The most perilous position of any believer is to maintain a careless attitude toward the Word of God. The greatest cause of failure among God's people is not taking God's Word as a matter of life and death (see Ge 3:4, note).

(4) God demands the greatest measure of faithfulness to his commands from those who are called to proclaim his word (cf. 1Ti 3:1–11; Tit 1:5–9; Jas 3:1); they must set an example for God's people.

13:24 A LION . . . KILLED HIM. It must not be assumed that the prophet received eternal punishment after he died. His disobedience is in the same category as that of Moses (see Nu 20:12, note).

10“ ‘Because of this, I am going to
bring disaster[g] on the house of Jeroboam. I will cut off from Jeroboam every
last male in Israel—slave or free.[h] I
will burn up the house of Jeroboam as
one burns dung, until it is all gone.[i]
11Dogs[j] will eat those belonging to
Jeroboam who die in the city, and the
birds of the air[k] will feed on those who
die in the country. The LORD has spoken!’

12“As for you, go back home. When
you set foot in your city, the boy will
die. 13All Israel will mourn for him and
bury him. He is the only one belonging
to Jeroboam who will be buried, because he is the only one in the house
of Jeroboam in whom the LORD, the God
of Israel, has found anything good.[l]

14“The LORD will raise up for himself
a king over Israel who will cut off the
family of Jeroboam. This is the day!
What? Yes, even now.[d] 15And the
LORD will strike Israel, so that it will be
like a reed swaying in the water. He
will uproot[m] Israel from this good land
that he gave to their forefathers and
scatter them beyond the River,[e] because they provoked[n] the LORD to anger by making Asherah[o] poles.[f]
16And he will give Israel up because of
the sins[p] Jeroboam has committed
and has caused Israel to commit.”

17Then Jeroboam’s wife got up and
left and went to Tirzah.[q] As soon as
she stepped over the threshold of the
house, the boy died. 18They buried him,
and all Israel mourned for him, as the
LORD had said through his servant the
prophet Ahijah.

19The other events of Jeroboam’s
reign, his wars and how he ruled, are
written in the book of the annals of the
kings of Israel. 20He reigned for twenty-two years and then rested with his
fathers. And Nadab his son succeeded
him as king.

14:10 [g]S Jos 23:15; S 1Ki 13:34 [h]S Dt 32:36; 2Ki 9:8-9 [i]1Sa 12:25; 15:26; 1Ki 15:29; Hos 13:11
14:11 [j]1Ki 16:4; 21:24 [k]S Ge 40:19; S Dt 28:26
14:13 [l]2Ch 12:12; 19:3
14:15 [m]S Dt 29:28; S 2Ch 7:20 [n]Jer 44:3 [o]S Dt 12:3
14:16 [p]S 1Ki 12:30; S 15:26
14:17 [q]S Jos 12:24; S 1Ki 15:33
14:21 [r]S 1Ki 11:1
14:22 [s]2Ki 17:19; 2Ch 12:1 [t]Dt 32:21; Ps 78:58; Jer 44:3; S 1Co 10:22
14:23 [u]S Ex 23:24; Dt 16:22; Hos 10:1 [v]S Dt 12:3 [w]S Dt 12:2; Eze 6:13
14:24 [x]S Dt 23:17 [y]1Ki 11:5-7; 2Ki 21:2; Ezr 9:11; Pr 21:27; Isa 1:13; Jer 16:18; 32:35; 44:4
14:25 [z]2Ch 12:2
14:26 [a]1Ki 15:15,18 [b]S 2Sa 8:7
14:27 [c]2Ki 11:5

Rehoboam King of Judah

14:21,25–31pp — 2Ch 12:9–16

21Rehoboam son of Solomon was
king in Judah. He was forty-one years
old when he became king, and he
reigned seventeen years in Jerusalem,
the city the LORD had chosen out of all
the tribes of Israel in which to put his
Name. His mother’s name was Naamah; she was an Ammonite.[r]

22Judah[s] did evil in the eyes of the
LORD. By the sins they committed they
stirred up his jealous anger[t] more
than their fathers had done. 23They
also set up for themselves high places,
sacred stones[u] and Asherah poles[v]
on every high hill and under every
spreading tree.[w] 24There were even
male shrine prostitutes[x] in the land;
the people engaged in all the detestable[y] practices of the nations the LORD
had driven out before the Israelites.

25In the fifth year of King Rehoboam, Shishak king of Egypt attacked[z]
Jerusalem. 26He carried off the treasures of the temple[a] of the LORD and
the treasures of the royal palace. He
took everything, including all the gold
shields[b] Solomon had made. 27So
King Rehoboam made bronze shields
to replace them and assigned these to
the commanders of the guard on duty
at the entrance to the royal palace.[c]
28Whenever the king went to the
LORD’s temple, the guards bore the
shields, and afterward they returned
them to the guardroom.

29As for the other events of Rehoboam’s reign, and all he did, are they not
written in the book of the annals of the
kings of Judah? 30There was continual

[d] *14* The meaning of the Hebrew for this sentence is uncertain. [e] *15* That is, the Euphrates [f] *15* That is, symbols of the goddess Asherah; here and elsewhere in 1 Kings

14:15 SCATTER THEM BEYOND THE RIVER. Ahijah prophesied the captivity of Israel; in 722 B.C. Israel was defeated and thousands were carried away across the river Euphrates by the Assyrians (cf. 2Ki 15:29; 17:6,18).

14:22 JUDAH DID EVIL. The tribe of Judah, ruled by Rehoboam (v. 21), did little better than the ten tribes of Israel; they also forsook the Lord and gave themselves over to terrible sin (see next note; cf. 2Ch 11—12).

14:24 MALE SHRINE PROSTITUTES. Judah’s apostasy led to the depraved sin of homosexuality and male prostitution (cf. Ro 1:25–28). God’s people accepted “all the detestable practices of the nations” and were thus conquered by the ungodly nations (vv. 25–26). Christ reemphasized this principle of judgment for believers who conform to the world (see Mt 5:13, note).

14:26 CARRIED OFF THE TREASURES OF THE TEMPLE. God permitted Shishak, the king of Egypt, to invade the temple and to carry away its treasures. The temple, where God had manifested his glory during Solomon’s early rule (8:11), became a scene of disgrace just five years after Solomon’s death, as God’s own people had cast aside his righteous ways.

warfare[d] between Rehoboam and Jeroboam. 31 And Rehoboam rested with
his fathers and was buried with them
in the City of David. His mother's name
was Naamah; she was an Ammonite.[e]
And Abijah[g] his son succeeded him as
king.

Abijah King of Judah

15:1-2,6-8pp — 2Ch 13:1-2,22-14:1

15 In the eighteenth year of the
reign of Jeroboam son of Nebat,
Abijah[h] became king of Judah, 2 and he
reigned in Jerusalem three years. His
mother's name was Maacah[f] daughter of Abishalom.[i]

3 He committed all the sins his father
had done before him; his heart was not
fully devoted[g] to the LORD his God, as
the heart of David his forefather had
been. 4 Nevertheless, for David's sake
the LORD his God gave him a lamp[h] in
Jerusalem by raising up a son to succeed him and by making Jerusalem
strong. 5 For David had done what was
right in the eyes of the LORD and had
not failed to keep[i] any of the LORD's
commands all the days of his life—except in the case of Uriah[j] the Hittite.
6 There was war[k] between Rehoboam[j] and Jeroboam throughout ⌊Abi-
jah's⌋ lifetime. 7 As for the other events
of Abijah's reign, and all he did, are
they not written in the book of the annals of the kings of Judah? There was
war between Abijah and Jeroboam.
8 And Abijah rested with his fathers
and was buried in the City of David.
And Asa his son succeeded him as
king.

Asa King of Judah

15:9-22pp — 2Ch 14:2-3; 15:16-16:6
15:23-24pp — 2Ch 16:11-17:1

9 In the twentieth year of Jeroboam
king of Israel, Asa became king of Judah, 10 and he reigned in Jerusalem forty-one years. His grandmother's name
was Maacah[l] daughter of Abishalom.
11 Asa did what was right in the eyes
of the LORD, as his father David[m] had
done. 12 He expelled the male shrine
prostitutes[n] from the land and got rid
of all the idols[o] his fathers had made.
13 He even deposed his grandmother
Maacah[p] from her position as queen
mother,[q] because she had made a repulsive Asherah pole. Asa cut the pole
down[r] and burned it in the Kidron Valley. 14 Although he did not remove[s]
the high places, Asa's heart was fully
committed[t] to the LORD all his life.
15 He brought into the temple of the
LORD the silver and gold and the articles that he and his father had dedicated.[u]

16 There was war[v] between Asa and
Baasha king of Israel throughout their
reigns. 17 Baasha king of Israel went
up against Judah and fortified Ramah[w] to prevent anyone from leaving
or entering the territory of Asa king of
Judah.

18 Asa then took all the silver and
gold that was left in the treasuries of
the LORD's temple[x] and of his own palace. He entrusted it to his officials and
sent[y] them to Ben-Hadad[z] son of
Tabrimmon, the son of Hezion, the
king of Aram, who was ruling in Damascus. 19 "Let there be a treaty[a] between me and you," he said, "as there
was between my father and your father. See, I am sending you a gift of
silver and gold. Now break your treaty
with Baasha king of Israel so he will
withdraw from me."

20 Ben-Hadad agreed with King Asa

14:30 [d] 2Sa 3:1; S 1Ki 12:21
14:31 [e] S 1Ki 11:1
15:2 [f] ver 10,13; 2Ch 11:20
15:3 [g] S 1Ki 8:61
15:4 [h] S 2Sa 21:17
15:5 [i] S Dt 5:32; S 1Ki 9:4 [j] 2Sa 11:2-27; 12:9
15:6 [k] ver 16,32; S 1Ki 12:21; 2Ch 16:9
15:10 [l] S ver 2
15:11 [m] 1Ki 9:4
15:12 [n] 1Ki 14:24 [o] 2Ch 15:8
15:13 [p] S ver 2 [q] S 1Ki 2:19 [r] S Ex 34:13
15:14 [s] 2Ch 14:5; 17:6 [t] S 1Ki 8:61
15:15 [u] S 2Sa 8:11
15:16 [v] S ver 6; S 1Ki 12:21
15:17 [w] S Jos 18:25
15:18 [x] S 1Ki 14:26 [y] 2Ki 12:18; 16:8; 18:14-16,15; Joel 3:5 [z] ver 18-20; 1Ki 20:1; 2Ki 6:24; 13:3; Jer 49:27
15:19 [a] S Ex 23:32; S 1Ki 5:12

[g] *31* Some Hebrew manuscripts and Septuagint (see also 2 Chron. 12:16); most Hebrew manuscripts *Abijam* [h] *1* Some Hebrew manuscripts and Septuagint (see also 2 Chron. 12:16); most Hebrew manuscripts *Abijam*; also in verses 7 and 8 [i] *2* A variant of *Absalom*; also in verse 10 [j] *6* Most Hebrew manuscripts; some Hebrew manuscripts and Syriac *Abijam* (that is, Abijah)

15:3 HEART WAS NOT FULLY DEVOTED. The undevoted heart typically refers to one who was an idolater. David's heart is said to be fully devoted to the Lord because he never turned after other gods; to have a fully devoted heart does not imply moral perfection (cf. v. 5; see 11:4, note).

15:4 A LAMP. "Lamp" as used here means that God had determined never to extinguish the Davidic line and covenant. The lamp eventually became "the light of the world" in the person of Jesus Christ (Jn 8:12; cf. Lk 2:4).

15:9 ASA. Asa was a good king whose reign was characterized by faithfulness to God. However, he failed to trust God fully in his later years (see 2Ch 16). His reign was significant because he led the people to renounce their ungodly ways and turn away from the wicked practices of the Canaanites. True revival always includes turning away from practices that offend God and violate his word (see 2Ch 14—16 for more about Asa's reign).

and sent the commanders of his forces
against the towns of Israel. He conquered[b] Ijon, Dan, Abel Beth Maacah
and all Kinnereth in addition to Naphtali. 21When Baasha heard this, he
stopped building Ramah[c] and withdrew to Tirzah.[d] 22Then King Asa issued an order to all Judah—no one was
exempt—and they carried away from
Ramah[e] the stones and timber Baasha had been using there. With them
King Asa[f] built up Geba[g] in Benjamin, and also Mizpah.[h]
23As for all the other events of Asa's
reign, all his achievements, all he did
and the cities he built, are they not
written in the book of the annals of the
kings of Judah? In his old age, however, his feet became diseased. 24Then
Asa rested with his fathers and was
buried with them in the city of his father David. And Jehoshaphat[i] his son
succeeded him as king.

Nadab King of Israel

25Nadab son of Jeroboam became
king of Israel in the second year of Asa
king of Judah, and he reigned over Israel two years. 26He did evil[j] in the eyes
of the LORD, walking in the ways of his
father[k] and in his sin, which he had
caused Israel to commit.
27Baasha son of Ahijah of the house
of Issachar plotted against him, and he
struck him down[l] at Gibbethon,[m] a
Philistine town, while Nadab and all Israel were besieging it. 28Baasha killed
Nadab in the third year of Asa king of
Judah and succeeded him as king.
29As soon as he began to reign, he
killed Jeroboam's whole family.[n] He
did not leave Jeroboam anyone that
breathed, but destroyed them all, according to the word of the LORD given
through his servant Ahijah the Shilonite— 30because of the sins[o] Jeroboam had committed and had caused[p]
Israel to commit, and because he provoked the LORD, the God of Israel, to
anger.
31As for the other events of Nadab's
reign, and all he did, are they not written in the book of the annals[q] of the
kings of Israel? 32There was war[r] between Asa and Baasha king of Israel
throughout their reigns.

Baasha King of Israel

33In the third year of Asa king of Judah, Baasha son of Ahijah became king
of all Israel in Tirzah,[s] and he reigned
twenty-four years. 34He did evil[t] in
the eyes of the LORD, walking in the
ways of Jeroboam and in his sin, which
he had caused Israel to commit.

16 Then the word of the LORD came
to Jehu[u] son of Hanani[v]
against Baasha: 2"I lifted you up from
the dust[w] and made you leader[x] of
my people Israel, but you walked in the
ways of Jeroboam and caused[y] my
people Israel to sin and to provoke me
to anger by their sins. 3So I am about
to consume Baasha[z] and his house,[a]
and I will make your house like that of
Jeroboam son of Nebat. 4Dogs[b] will
eat those belonging to Baasha who die
in the city, and the birds of the air[c]
will feed on those who die in the country."
5As for the other events of Baasha's
reign, what he did and his achievements, are they not written in the book
of the annals[d] of the kings of Israel?
6Baasha rested with his fathers and
was buried in Tirzah.[e] And Elah his
son succeeded him as king.
7Moreover, the word of the LORD
came[f] through the prophet Jehu[g] son
of Hanani to Baasha and his house, because of all the evil he had done in the
eyes of the LORD, provoking him to anger by the things he did, and becoming
like the house of Jeroboam—and also
because he destroyed it.

Elah King of Israel

8In the twenty-sixth year of Asa king
of Judah, Elah son of Baasha became
king of Israel, and he reigned in Tirzah
two years.
9Zimri, one of his officials, who had
command of half his chariots, plotted
against him. Elah was in Tirzah at the

15:20 [b] 1Ki 20:34
15:21 [c] S Jos 18:25 [d] 1Ki 16:15-17
15:22 [e] ver 17 [f] ver 9-24; Jer 41:9 [g] S Jos 18:24; 2Ki 23:8 [h] S Jos 11:3
15:24 [i] Mt 1:8
15:26 [j] S Dt 4:25 [k] S 1Ki 12:30
15:27 [l] 1Ki 14:14 [m] S Jos 19:44
15:29 [n] S 1Ki 13:34
15:30 [o] S 1Ki 12:30 [p] 1Ki 16:26; 2Ki 3:3; 14:24; 15:28; 21:16
15:31 [q] 1Ki 11:41
15:32 [r] S ver 6
15:33 [s] 1Ki 14:17; 16:6, 23; 2Ki 15:14; SS 6:4
15:34 [t] ver 26
16:1 [u] ver 7; 2Ch 19:2; 20:34 [v] 2Ch 16:7
16:2 [w] 1Sa 2:8 [x] S 1Ki 14:7-9 [y] S 1Ki 12:30
16:3 [z] 2Ki 9:9 [a] ver 11; 1Ki 21:22
16:4 [b] S 1Ki 14:11 [c] S Ge 40:19
16:5 [d] 1Ki 15:31
16:6 [e] S 1Ki 15:33
16:7 [f] S 1Ki 6:11 [g] S ver 1

15:24 JEHOSHAPHAT. Jehoshaphat was a good king who tried to teach the people God's word and who sought to remain faithful to the Lord (for details about his reign, see 22:41–50; 2Ch 17:1–21:1).

16:7 THE PROPHET JEHU. When God's leaders and people rejected his law and adopted the ungodly ways of the Canaanites, God sent prophets to proclaim his truth and righteousness. Such prophets are needed today as well (see articles on THE PROPHET IN THE OLD TESTAMENT, p. 986, and THE MINISTRY GIFTS OF THE CHURCH, p. 1830).

time, getting drunk[h] in the home of
Arza, the man in charge[i] of the palace
at Tirzah. 10Zimri came in, struck him
down and killed him in the twenty-seventh year of Asa king of Judah. Then he
succeeded him as king.[j]
11As soon as he began to reign and
was seated on the throne, he killed off
Baasha's whole family.[k] He did not
spare a single male, whether relative
or friend. 12So Zimri destroyed the
whole family of Baasha, in accordance
with the word of the LORD spoken
against Baasha through the prophet
Jehu— 13because of all the sins Baasha and his son Elah had committed
and had caused Israel to commit, so
that they provoked the LORD, the God of
Israel, to anger by their worthless
idols.[l]
14As for the other events of Elah's
reign, and all he did, are they not written in the book of the annals of the
kings of Israel?

Zimri King of Israel

15In the twenty-seventh year of Asa
king of Judah, Zimri reigned in Tirzah
seven days. The army was encamped
near Gibbethon,[m] a Philistine town.
16When the Israelites in the camp
heard that Zimri had plotted against
the king and murdered him, they proclaimed Omri, the commander of the
army, king over Israel that very day
there in the camp. 17Then Omri and all
the Israelites with him withdrew from
Gibbethon and laid siege to Tirzah.
18When Zimri saw that the city was
taken, he went into the citadel of the
royal palace and set the palace on fire
around him. So he died, 19because of
the sins he had committed, doing evil
in the eyes of the LORD and walking in
the ways of Jeroboam and in the sin he
had committed and had caused Israel
to commit.
20As for the other events of Zimri's
reign, and the rebellion he carried out,
are they not written in the book of the
annals of the kings of Israel?

Omri King of Israel

21Then the people of Israel were
split into two factions; half supported
Tibni son of Ginath for king, and the
other half supported Omri. 22But
Omri's followers proved stronger than
those of Tibni son of Ginath. So Tibni
died and Omri became king.
23In the thirty-first year of Asa king
of Judah, Omri became king of Israel,
and he reigned twelve years, six of
them in Tirzah.[n] 24He bought the hill
of Samaria from Shemer for two talents[k] of silver and built a city on the
hill, calling it Samaria,[o] after Shemer,
the name of the former owner of the
hill.
25But Omri did evil[p] in the eyes of
the LORD and sinned more than all
those before him. 26He walked in all
the ways of Jeroboam son of Nebat and
in his sin, which he had caused[q] Israel
to commit, so that they provoked the
LORD, the God of Israel, to anger by
their worthless idols.[r]
27As for the other events of Omri's
reign, what he did and the things he
achieved, are they not written in the
book of the annals of the kings of Israel? 28Omri rested with his fathers and
was buried in Samaria.[s] And Ahab his
son succeeded him as king.

Ahab Becomes King of Israel

29In the thirty-eighth year of Asa
king of Judah, Ahab son of Omri became king of Israel, and he reigned in
Samaria over Israel twenty-two years.
30Ahab son of Omri did more[t] evil in
the eyes of the LORD than any of those
before him. 31He not only considered it
trivial to commit the sins of Jeroboam
son of Nebat, but he also married[u] Jezebel daughter[v] of Ethbaal king of the
Sidonians, and began to serve Baal[w]
and worship him. 32He set up an altar[x] for Baal in the temple[y] of Baal
that he built in Samaria. 33Ahab also
made an Asherah pole[z] and did
more[a] to provoke the LORD, the God of
Israel, to anger than did all the kings
of Israel before him.
34In Ahab's time, Hiel of Bethel rebuilt Jericho. He laid its foundations at

16:9 [h] 1Ki 20:12, 16; Pr 31:4-5 [i] 1Ki 18:3 **16:10** [j] 2Ki 9:31 **16:11** [k] S ver 3 **16:13** [l] S Dt 32:21 **16:15** [m] S Jos 19:44

16:23 [n] S Jos 12:24; S 1Ki 15:33 **16:24** [o] S 1Ki 13:32; S Mt 10:5 **16:25** [p] ver 25-26; S Dt 4:25; Mic 6:16 **16:26** [q] S 1Ki 15:30 [r] S Dt 32:21 **16:28** [s] S 1Ki 13:32 **16:30** [t] S 1Ki 14:9 **16:31** [u] S 1Ki 11:2 [v] S Jdg 3:6; 2Ki 9:34 [w] S Jdg 2:11 **16:32** [x] S Jdg 6:28 [y] 2Ki 10:21,27; 11:18; Jer 43:12 **16:33** [z] S Jdg 3:7; 2Ki 13:6 [a] S 1Ki 14:9; 21:25

[k] *24* That is, about 150 pounds (about 70 kilograms)

16:30 AHAB. Sin and evil became progressively worse in Israel during King Ahab's reign. Outright rebellion and hardness of heart against God's commands prevailed; the worship of Baal increased. In the face of such apostasy, God sent the mighty prophet Elijah to oppose the corrupt religious system and to proclaim God's purpose for his kingdom (17:1).

16:31 BAAL. See Jos 23:12, note; Jdg 2:13, note.

the cost of his firstborn son Abiram, and he set up its gates at the cost of his youngest son Segub, in accordance with the word of the LORD spoken by Joshua son of Nun.[b]

Elijah Fed by Ravens

17 Now Elijah[c] the Tishbite, from Tishbe[1] in Gilead,[d] said to Ahab, "As the LORD, the God of Israel, lives, whom I serve, there will be neither dew nor rain[e] in the next few years except at my word."
2Then the word of the LORD came to Elijah: 3"Leave here, turn eastward and hide[f] in the Kerith Ravine, east of the Jordan. 4You will drink from the brook, and I have ordered the ravens[g] to feed you there."
5So he did what the LORD had told him. He went to the Kerith Ravine, east of the Jordan, and stayed there. 6The ravens brought him bread and meat in the morning[h] and bread and meat in the evening, and he drank from the brook.

The Widow at Zarephath

7Some time later the brook dried up because there had been no rain in the land. 8Then the word of the LORD came to him: 9"Go at once to Zarephath[i] of Sidon and stay there. I have commanded a widow[j] in that place to supply you with food." 10So he went to Zarephath. When he came to the town gate, a widow was there gathering sticks. He called to her and asked, "Would you bring me a little water in a jar so I may have a drink?"[k] 11As she was going to get it, he called, "And bring me, please, a piece of bread."
12"As surely as the LORD your God lives," she replied, "I don't have any bread—only a handful of flour in a jar and a little oil[l] in a jug. I am gathering a few sticks to take home and make a meal for myself and my son, that we may eat it—and die."
13Elijah said to her, "Don't be afraid. Go home and do as you have said. But first make a small cake of bread for me from what you have and bring it to me, and then make something for yourself and your son. 14For this is what the LORD, the God of Israel, says: 'The jar of flour will not be used up and the jug of oil will not run dry until the day the LORD gives rain[m] on the land.' "
15She went away and did as Elijah

16:34 [b]Jos 6:26
17:1 [c]Mal 4:5; Mt 11:14; 17:3 [d]Jdg 12:4 [e]S Dt 11:17; S 28:24; S 2Sa 1:21; S 1Ki 8:36; Job 12:15; S Lk 4:25
17:3 [f]1Ki 18:4, 10; Jer 36:19,26
17:4 [g]S Ge 8:7
17:6 [h]Ex 16:8
17:9 [i]Ob 1:20 [j]Lk 4:26
17:10 [k]S Ge 24:17; Jn 4:7
17:12 [l]2Ki 4:2
17:14 [m]ver 1

[1]*1* Or *Tishbite, of the settlers*

17:1 ELIJAH. Elijah was a prophet in the northern kingdom during the reigns of Ahab and his son Ahaziah. The name Elijah, meaning "The LORD is my God," represents the unshakable conviction of Elijah's life (18:21,39). The principal narratives about his life are found in 1Ki 17—19; 21:17–29; 2Ki 1—2.

(1) Elijah's life centered around the conflict between the worship of the Lord and the worship of Baal. His mission was to awaken the Israelites to their apostasy and to call them back to loyalty to the God of Israel (18:21,36–37). Thus, Elijah was a restorer and a reformer who sought to reestablish the covenant.

(2) The OT ends with the prophecy that Elijah would appear again before "that great and dreadful day of the LORD comes" (Mal 4:5); this prophecy was partially fulfilled in the appearance of John the Baptist (Mt 11:7–14; Lk 1:17) and may have a future fulfillment before Christ's return (cf. Mt 17:11; Rev 11:3–6; see Rev 11:3, note).

(3) Elijah's unwavering devotion to God and his covenant makes him forever both an example of faith, courage and loyalty to God in the face of intense opposition and persecution and an example of faithful persistence in opposing false religion and false prophets.

17:1 NEITHER DEW NOR RAIN. As God's messenger, Elijah spoke a word of judgment from the Lord against disobedient Israel. God would withhold rain for three and a half years (cf. Dt 11:13–17). This word of judgment also mocked Baal, for Baal worshipers believed he controlled rain and was responsible for abundant crops. The NT states that this drought in Israel came as the result of Elijah's earnest prayers (Jas 5:17).

17:4 ORDERED THE RAVENS TO FEED YOU THERE. God sustained Elijah at the Kerith Ravine because he had stood with God against the people's apostasy (vv. 3–7; cf. Ps 25:10). As Elijah had borne God's burden, the Lord would now bear his burden (cf. Ps 68:19–20).

17:7 THE BROOK DRIED UP. When the brook dried up, God directed Elijah to go to a pagan territory inhabited by Baal worshipers, and there God provided for Elijah through a poor widow (v. 9). The experience further strengthened Elijah's confidence in God's providence. Sometimes adversity occurs even though we are in God's will; through such experiences he may help us in a different and greater way than we had expected.

17:15 THERE WAS FOOD EVERY DAY. The needs and misery of a poor widow were not insignificant to God; he sent Elijah to strengthen her faith and give material blessings at a time when she felt all was lost (v. 12). The widow's faith in God and his word through the prophet Elijah led her to exchange the certain for the uncertain, the seen for the unseen (vv. 10–16; cf. Heb 11:27). The believing widow not only received from God's prophet a material blessing, but also a spiritual blessing.

had told her. So there was food every
day for Elijah and for the woman and
her family. 16For the jar of flour was
not used up and the jug of oil did not
run dry, in keeping with the word of the
LORD spoken by Elijah.
17Some time later the son of the
woman who owned the house became
ill. He grew worse and worse, and finally stopped breathing. 18She said to
Elijah, "What do you have against me,
man of God? Did you come to remind
me of my sin[n] and kill my son?"
19"Give me your son," Elijah replied.
He took him from her arms, carried
him to the upper room where he was
staying, and laid him on his bed.
20Then he cried[o] out to the LORD,
"O LORD my God, have you brought
tragedy also upon this widow I am
staying with, by causing her son to
die?" 21Then he stretched[p] himself
out on the boy three times and cried to
the LORD, "O LORD my God, let this
boy's life return to him!"
22The LORD heard Elijah's cry, and
the boy's life returned to him, and he
lived. 23Elijah picked up the child and
carried him down from the room into
the house. He gave him to his mother[q]
and said, "Look, your son is alive!"
24Then the woman said to Elijah,
"Now I know[r] that you are a man of
God[s] and that the word of the LORD
from your mouth is the truth."[t]

Elijah and Obadiah

18 After a long time, in the third[u]
year, the word of the LORD came
to Elijah: "Go and present[v] yourself to
Ahab, and I will send rain[w] on the
land." 2So Elijah went to present himself to Ahab.
Now the famine was severe[x] in Samaria, 3and Ahab had summoned Obadiah, who was in charge[y] of his palace. (Obadiah was a devout believer[z]
in the LORD. 4While Jezebel[a] was killing off the LORD's prophets, Obadiah
had taken a hundred prophets and hidden[b] them in two caves, fifty in each,
and had supplied[c] them with food and
water.) 5Ahab had said to Obadiah, "Go
through the land to all the springs[d]
and valleys. Maybe we can find some
grass to keep the horses and mules
alive so we will not have to kill any of
our animals."[e] 6So they divided the
land they were to cover, Ahab going in
one direction and Obadiah in another.
7As Obadiah was walking along, Elijah met him. Obadiah recognized[f]
him, bowed down to the ground, and
said, "Is it really you, my lord Elijah?"
8"Yes," he replied. "Go tell your master, 'Elijah is here.' "
9"What have I done wrong," asked
Obadiah, "that you are handing your
servant over to Ahab to be put to
death? 10As surely as the LORD your
God lives, there is not a nation or kingdom where my master has not sent
someone to look[g] for you. And whenever a nation or kingdom claimed you
were not there, he made them swear
they could not find you. 11But now you
tell me to go to my master and say,
'Elijah is here.' 12I don't know where
the Spirit[h] of the LORD may carry you
when I leave you. If I go and tell Ahab
and he doesn't find you, he will kill me.
Yet I your servant have worshiped the
LORD since my youth. 13Haven't you
heard, my lord, what I did while Jezebel
was killing the prophets of the LORD? I
hid a hundred of the LORD's prophets in
two caves, fifty in each, and supplied
them with food and water. 14And now
you tell me to go to my master and say,
'Elijah is here.' He will kill me!"
15Elijah said, "As the LORD Almighty
lives, whom I serve, I will surely
present[i] myself to Ahab today."

Elijah on Mount Carmel

16So Obadiah went to meet Ahab
and told him, and Ahab went to meet
Elijah. 17When he saw Elijah, he said
to him, "Is that you, you troubler[j] of
Israel?"
18"I have not made trouble for Israel," Elijah replied. "But you[k] and your

17:18 [n] Lk 5:8 **17:20** [o] 2Ki 4:33 **17:21** [p] 2Ki 4:34; Ac 20:10 **17:23** [q] Heb 11:35 **17:24** [r] Jn 16:30 [s] ver 18 [t] 1Ki 22:16; Ps 119:43; Jn 17:17 **18:1** [u] 1Ki 17:1; Lk 4:25 [v] ver 15 [w] S Dt 28:12 **18:2** [x] S Lev 26:26 **18:3** [y] 1Ki 16:9 [z] Ne 7:2 **18:4** [a] 1Ki 21:23; 2Ki 9:7 [b] S 1Ki 17:3; Isa 16:3; 25:4; 32:2; Ob 1:14 [c] Jer 26:24 **18:5** [d] Jer 14:3 [e] S Ge 47:4 **18:7** [f] 2Ki 1:8; Zec 13:4 **18:10** [g] S 1Ki 17:3 **18:12** [h] 2Ki 2:16; Eze 3:14; Ac 8:39 **18:15** [i] ver 1 **18:17** [j] Jos 7:25; 1Sa 14:29; 1Ki 21:20; Jer 38:4 **18:18** [k] 1Ki 16:31,33; 21:25

17:17 THE SON . . . STOPPED BREATHING. We confront here one of life's perplexing mysteries. At the very time God was miraculously providing flour and oil, trouble and sorrow occurred. Sometimes sickness or even greater tragedy may come to those who are doing God's will and who are actively involved in the work of his kingdom.

17:22 THE LORD HEARD ELIJAH'S CRY. God restored the boy to life in answer to Elijah's prayer. This is the first instance recorded in the Bible of someone being raised from the dead (cf. 2Ki 4:34; Ac 20:10). The three miracles listed in ch. 17 strikingly manifested God's glory and love; they demonstrated to Elijah and the woman that in the midst of tragic circumstances, God's power and love are active on behalf of those who love him and are called according to his purpose (see Ro 8:28, note).

father's family have. You have abandoned[l] the LORD's commands and
have followed the Baals. **19**Now summon[m] the people from all over Israel
to meet me on Mount Carmel.[n] And
bring the four hundred and fifty prophets of Baal and the four hundred prophets of Asherah, who eat at Jezebel's table."[o]
20So Ahab sent word throughout all
Israel and assembled the prophets on
Mount Carmel.[p] **21**Elijah went before
the people and said, "How long will you
waver[q] between two opinions? If the
LORD[r] is God, follow him; but if Baal
is God, follow him."
But the people said nothing.
22Then Elijah said to them, "I am the
only one of the LORD's prophets left,[s]
but Baal has four hundred and fifty
prophets.[t] **23**Get two bulls for us. Let
them choose one for themselves, and
let them cut it into pieces and put it on
the wood but not set fire to it. I will
prepare the other bull and put it on the
wood but not set fire to it. **24**Then you
call[u] on the name of your god, and I
will call on the name of the LORD.[v] The
god who answers by fire[w]—he is
God."
Then all the people said, "What you
say is good."
25Elijah said to the prophets of Baal,
"Choose one of the bulls and prepare it
first, since there are so many of you.
Call on the name of your god, but do
not light the fire." **26**So they took the
bull given them and prepared it.
Then they called[x] on the name of
Baal from morning till noon. "O Baal,
answer us!" they shouted. But there
was no response;[y] no one answered.

18:18 [l]S Dt 31:16 **18:19** [m]2Ki 10:19 [n]S Jos 19:26 [o]2Ki 9:22 **18:20** [p]2Ki 2:25; 4:25 **18:21** [q]Jos 24:15; 2Ki 17:41; Ps 119:113; Mt 6:24 [r]ver 39; Ps 100:3; 118:27 **18:22** [s]1Ki 19:10 [t]Jer 2:8; 23:13 **18:24** [u]S 1Sa 7:8 [v]S Ge 4:26 [w]S ver 38; S Ex 19:18; S Lev 9:24 **18:26** [x]Isa 44:17; 45:20 [y]Ps 115:4-5; 135:16; Isa 41:26, 28; 46:7; Jer 10:5; 1Co 8:4; 12:2

18:27 [z]Hab 2:19 **18:28** [a]S Lev 19:28 **18:29** [b]S Ex 29:41 [c]2Ki 19:12; Isa 16:12; Jer 10:5 **18:30** [d]1Ki 19:10 **18:31** [e]S Ge 17:5; 2Ki 17:34 **18:32** [f]S Dt 18:7; Col 3:17 **18:33** [g]S Ge 22:9 **18:36** [h]S Ex 29:39,41

And they danced around the altar they
had made.
27At noon Elijah began to taunt
them. "Shout louder!" he said. "Surely
he is a god! Perhaps he is deep in
thought, or busy, or traveling. Maybe
he is sleeping and must be awakened."[z] **28**So they shouted louder and
slashed[a] themselves with swords and
spears, as was their custom, until their
blood flowed. **29**Midday passed, and
they continued their frantic prophesying until the time for the evening sacrifice.[b] But there was no response, no
one answered, no one paid attention.[c]
30Then Elijah said to all the people,
"Come here to me." They came to him,
and he repaired the altar[d] of the LORD,
which was in ruins. **31**Elijah took
twelve stones, one for each of the
tribes descended from Jacob, to whom
the word of the LORD had come, saying,
"Your name shall be Israel."[e] **32**With
the stones he built an altar in the
name[f] of the LORD, and he dug a
trench around it large enough to hold
two seahs[m] of seed. **33**He arranged[g]
the wood, cut the bull into pieces and
laid it on the wood. Then he said to
them, "Fill four large jars with water
and pour it on the offering and on the
wood."
34"Do it again," he said, and they did
it again.
"Do it a third time," he ordered, and
they did it the third time. **35**The water
ran down around the altar and even
filled the trench.
36At the time[h] of sacrifice, the

[m]*32* That is, probably about 13 quarts (about 15 liters)

18:18 ABANDONED THE LORD'S COMMANDS. Elijah's courageous confrontation with Ahab and with unrighteousness in Israel made him a model prophet to Israel and the most qualified person to be a prototype of the forerunner of the Lord Jesus Christ (cf. Mal 4:5–6; Lk 1:17). (1) He was a true "man of God" (17:24), one who spoke not as a people-pleaser but as a faithful servant of God (cf. Gal 1:10; 1Th 2:4; see Lk 1:17, note).

(2) As Elijah was called to defend the true God of Israel, all ministers of the new covenant are called to defend the gospel of Christ against distortion, compromise and corruption (see Php 1:17, note; Jude 3, note).

18:21 IF THE LORD IS GOD, FOLLOW HIM. Elijah challenged the people to make a definitive choice between following God or following Baal (cf. Eze 20:31,39). Israel believed they could worship both deities at the same time. They were guilty of a divided heart (cf. Dt 6:4–5) that tried to serve two masters; Christ himself warned against this fatal attitude (Mt 6:24; cf. Dt 30:19; Jos 24:14–15; see article on SPIRITUAL SEPARATION FOR BELIEVERS, p. 1794).

18:27 ELIJAH BEGAN TO TAUNT THEM. Elijah's mockery of the prophets of Baal shows his fierce indignation at the immoral and cruel idolatry that Israel had embraced; his sarcasm and his uncompromising attitude expressed unwavering loyalty to the God whom he loved and served. Compare Elijah's reaction with Jesus' anger and intolerance at the defiling of the temple in Jerusalem (see Lk 19:45, note).

18:36 ELIJAH ... PRAYED: O LORD, GOD OF ABRAHAM. Elijah's courage and faith have virtually no parallel in the entire history of redemption. His challenge to the king (vv. 16–19), rebuke of all Israel (vv. 21–24) and confrontation

prophet Elijah stepped forward and
prayed: "O LORD, God of Abraham,[i]
Isaac and Israel, let it be known[j] today that you are God in Israel and that
I am your servant and have done all
these things at your command.[k] 37An-
swer me, O LORD, answer me, so these
people will know[l] that you, O LORD,
are God, and that you are turning their
hearts back again."

38Then the fire[m] of the LORD fell and
burned up the sacrifice, the wood, the
stones and the soil, and also licked up
the water in the trench.

39When all the people saw this, they
fell prostrate[n] and cried, "The LORD—
he is God! The LORD—he is God!"[o]

40Then Elijah commanded them,
"Seize the prophets of Baal. Don't let
anyone get away!" They seized them,
and Elijah had them brought down to
the Kishon Valley[p] and slaughtered[q]
there.

41And Elijah said to Ahab, "Go, eat
and drink, for there is the sound of a
heavy rain." 42So Ahab went off to eat
and drink, but Elijah climbed to the top
of Carmel, bent down to the ground and
put his face between his knees.[r]

43"Go and look toward the sea," he
told his servant. And he went up and
looked.

"There is nothing there," he said.

Seven times Elijah said, "Go back."

44The seventh time[s] the servant reported, "A cloud[t] as small as a man's
hand is rising from the sea."

So Elijah said, "Go and tell Ahab,

18:36 [i]S Ge 24:12; S Ex 4:5; Mt 22:32 [j]S Jos 4:24; S 1Sa 17:46; S Ps 46:10 [k]Nu 16:28 **18:37** [l]S Jos 4:24 **18:38** [m]ver 24; S Ex 19:18; S Lev 9:24; 2Ki 1:10; 1Ch 21:26; 2Ch 7:1; Job 1:16 **18:39** [n]S Lev 9:24 [o]S ver 24; S Ps 46:10 **18:40** [p]S Jdg 4:7 [q]S Ex 22:20; S Dt 17:12; S 2Ki 11:18 **18:42** [r]S 1Sa 12:17; Jas 5:18 **18:44** [s]S Jos 6:15 [t]Lk 12:54

with the 450 prophets of Baal (vv. 22,27) were undertaken with only the weapons of prayer and faith in God. His confidence in God is indicated by the brevity (41 words in Hebrew) and simplicity of his prayer (vv. 36–37; see article on EFFECTIVE PRAYING, p. 496).

18:37 TURNING THEIR HEARTS BACK AGAIN. The purpose of Elijah's confrontation with the prophets of Baal and then his prayer was to reveal God's grace to his people. He wanted to turn their hearts back to God (v. 37). Similarly, John the Baptist, the "Elijah" of the NT (see 17:1, note), had as his goal to turn the hearts of many back to God in preparation for Christ's coming.

18:38 FIRE OF THE LORD FELL. The Lord miraculously provided fire to consume the sacrifice (cf. 1Ch 21:26; 2Ch 7:1). The miracle vindicated Elijah as God's prophet and proved that Israel's Lord alone was the living God whom they were to serve. In a similar way, believers should pray for and expect the manifestation of God in their midst through the Holy Spirit (see 1Co 12:4–11; 14:1–40).

18:40 SLAUGHTERED THERE. Note the following about the slaughter of the prophets of Baal: (1) Their death sentence was just, for it was done in obedience to the law of Moses (Dt 13:6–9; 17:2–5). The NT has no such command; violent action against false teachers is prohibited (Mt 5:44), though God does command rejection of and separation from them (Mt 24:23–24; 2Co 6:14–18; Gal 1:6–9; 2Jn 7–11; Jude 3–4; see article on FALSE TEACHERS, p. 1506).

(2) Elijah's action against the false prophets represented God's wrath against those who were trying to destroy his chosen people's faith and spiritual heritage, and expressed Elijah's own love for and loyalty to his Lord. Thus, his spirit and heart were in harmony with God; his moral and spiritual sensitivity was outraged at Israel's tragic defection from their covenant God, the One who had loved and redeemed them.

(3) Elijah's slaughter of the false prophets also showed a deep concern for the Israelites themselves who were being spiritually destroyed by false religion. Jesus had this same attitude (Mt 23; see also Lk 19:27), as did Paul (Gal 1:6–9; see Gal 1:9, note). Furthermore, note that God's wrath will be poured out on all stubborn and unrepentant people at "the day of God's wrath, when his righteous judgment will be revealed" (Ro 2:5; cf. 11:22; Rev 19:11–21; 20:7–10).

18:42 ELIJAH . . . PUT HIS FACE BETWEEN HIS KNEES. The NT cites Elijah's faith and persistent prayer as an example and encouragement to all God's faithful people with regard to the power of prayer (Jas 5:18; see article on EFFECTIVE PRAYING, p. 496). Elijah's prayer was (1) the prayer of a righteous man (Jas 5:16; cf. Ps 66:18), (2) the prayer of a man with a human nature like ours (Jas 5:17), (3) an earnest and persistent prayer of faith (vv. 18:42–44; Jas 5:17; cf. Mt 21:21–22; Mk 9:23; Lk 18:1; Eph 6:18; Heb 11:6), and (4) a prayer that accomplished much (v. 45; Jas 5:16–17).

18:43 SEVEN TIMES ELIJAH SAID. The number seven in Scripture symbolizes something that is full and complete. In this chapter Elijah engaged in a complete intercession with three aspects: (1) he interceded to restore the altar and the honor of God in the land (vv. 21,24,30–39); (2) he interceded by engaging in spiritual warfare against the false religion and cult of Baalism and Asherah (vv. 19,27,40); and (3) he interceded with God by intense and persistent prayer for the outpouring of rain (vv. 41–46).

Insofar as the OT compares the outpouring of the Spirit with the outpouring of rain (e.g., Hos 6:1–3; Joel 2:23–29), Elijah's confrontation with Baalism illustrates the three main kinds of intercession that must characterize the prayers of God's people: (1) intercession for the restoration of God's honor and glory and for a revival among God's people; (2) intercession involving spiritual warfare against demonic strongholds; and (3) intercession for spiritual drought to be broken by the outpouring of God's Spirit and by a spiritual awakening (see article on INTERCESSION, p. 1268).

EFFECTIVE PRAYING

***1Ki 18:42b-45** "Elijah climbed to the top of Carmel, bent down to the earth and put his face between his knees. 'Go and look toward the sea,' he told his servant. And he went up and looked. 'There is nothing there,' he said. Seven times Elijah said, 'Go back.' The seventh time the servant reported, 'A cloud as small as a man's hand is rising from the sea.' So Elijah said, 'Go and tell Ahab, "Hitch up your chariot and go down before the rain stops you."' Meanwhile, the sky grew black with clouds, the wind rose, a heavy rain came on and Ahab rode off to Jezreel."*

Prayer refers to the multifaceted communication of believers with the Lord. In addition to such words as "prayer" and "praying," this activity is described as calling on God (Ps 17:6), calling on the name of the Lord (Ge 4:26), crying aloud to the Lord (Ps 3:4), lifting up one's soul to the Lord (Ps 25:1), seeking the Lord (Isa 55:6), approaching the throne of grace with confidence (Heb 4:16), and drawing near to God (Heb 10:22).

REASONS FOR PRAYER. The Bible provides clear reasons why God's people ought to pray. (1) First and foremost, believers are commanded by God to pray. The command to pray comes from the lips of psalmists (1Ch 16:11; Ps 105:4), prophets (Isa 55:6; Am 5:4,6), apostles (Eph 6:17–18; Col 4:2; 1Th 5:17), and the Lord Jesus himself (Mt 26:41; Lk 18:1; Jn 16:24). God desires our fellowship; by prayer we maintain our relationship with him.

(2) Prayer is the necessary link to receiving God's blessings and power, and the fulfillment of his promises. Numerous Bible passages illustrate this principle. Jesus, for example, promised that his followers would receive the Holy Spirit if they persisted in asking, seeking and knocking at the door of their heavenly Father (Lk 11:5–13). Thus, after Jesus' ascension, his followers joined together constantly in prayer in the upper room (Ac 1:14) until with power (cf. Ac 1:8) the Holy Spirit was poured out on the day of Pentecost (Ac 2:1–4). When the apostles gathered together after their arrest and release by the Jewish authorities, they prayed earnestly for the Holy Spirit to give them boldness and influence when speaking his word. "After they prayed, the place where they were meeting was shaken. And they were all filled with the Holy Spirit and spoke the word of God boldly" (Ac 4:31). The apostle Paul frequently requested prayers on his behalf, knowing that his work would not be successful unless Christians were praying for him (e.g., Ro 15:30–32; 2Co 1:11; Eph 6:18–20; Php 1:19; Col 4:3–4; see article on INTERCESSION, p. 1268). James states explicitly that physical healing can come to the believer in response to "the prayer offered in faith" (Jas 5:14–15).

(3) In his plan of salvation for humankind God has ordained that believers be co-workers with him in the redemptive process. In some respect God has limited himself to the holy, believing, persevering prayers of his people. There are many things that will not be accomplished in God's kingdom without the intercessory prayers of believers (see Ex 33:11, note). For example, God desires to send out workers into the gospel harvest; Christ teaches that this will only be accomplished to God's full purpose through his people's prayers: "Ask the Lord of the harvest, therefore, to send out workers into his harvest field" (Mt 9:38). In other words, God's power to accomplish many of his purposes is released only through his people's earnest prayers on behalf of the progress of his kingdom. If we fail to pray, we may actually be hindering the accomplishment of God's redemptive purpose, both for ourselves as individuals and for the church as a body.

REQUIREMENTS OF EFFECTIVE PRAYING. Several conditions must be met for our prayers to be effective. (1) Our prayers will not be answered unless we have a sincere, true faith. Jesus states explicitly: "Whatever you ask for in prayer, believe that you have received it, and it will be yours" (Mk 11:24). To the father of a demon-possessed boy, he spoke these words: "Everything is possible for him who believes" (Mk 9:23). The author of Hebrews urges us to "draw near to God with a sincere heart in full assurance of faith" (Heb 10:22), and James encourages us, when asking, to "believe and not doubt" (Jas 1:6; cf. 5:15).

(2) Prayer must also be made in Jesus' name. Jesus himself expressed this principle when he said: "And I will do whatever you ask in my name, so that the Son may bring glory to the Father. You may ask me for anything in my name, and I will do it" (Jn 14:13–14). Our prayers should be made in harmony with the person, character and will of our Lord (see Jn 14:13, note).

(3) Prayer can only be effective if it is made according to God's perfect will. "This is the confidence we have in approaching God: that if we ask anything according to his will, he hears us" (1Jn 5:14; see article on THE WILL OF GOD, p. 1056). One of the petitions in Jesus' model prayer, the Lord's Prayer, confirms this: "Your will be done on earth as it is in heaven" (Mt 6:10; cf. Lk 11:2; note Jesus' own prayer in Gethsemane, Mt 26:42). In many instances we know God's will because he has revealed it to us in the Bible. We can be sure that any prayer truly based on God's promises in his Word will indeed be effective. Elijah was certain that the God of Israel would answer his prayer with fire and later with rain because the Lord's prophetic word had come to him (1Ki 18:1), and he was fully confident that none of the pagan gods was greater than or even as powerful as the Lord God of Israel (1Ki 18:21–24). At other times God's will becomes clear only as we earnestly seek to determine what it is; then once we know his will about any given issue, we can pray with confidence and faith that God will answer (see 1Jn 5:14, note).

(4) Not only must we pray according to God's will, but we must be *in* God's will if we expect him to hear and answer us. God will give us the things we ask for only if we seek first his kingdom and his righteousness (see Mt 6:33, note). The apostle John unequivocally states that we "receive from him anything we ask, because we obey his commands and do what pleases him" (1Jn 3:22, see note). Obeying God's commands, loving him and pleasing him are indispensable conditions for receiving answers to prayer. When James wrote that the prayers of the righteous are effective, he meant both a person who has been made righteous through faith in Christ and one who is living a righteous, God-fearing and obedient life—such as the prophet Elijah (Jas 5:16–18; cf. Ps 34:13–14). Already in the OT this same point is stressed. God made clear that Moses' prayers on behalf of the Israelites were effective because of his obedient relationship with the Lord and his loyalty to him (see Ex 33:17, note). Conversely, the psalmist claims that if we cherish sin in our lives, the Lord will not listen to our prayers (Ps 66:18; see Jas 4:3, note); this sort of attitude was the main reason the Lord did not listen to the prayers of the idolatrous and wicked Israelites (Isa 1:15). But if God's people repent and turn from their wicked ways, the Lord promises to again hear them, forgive their sin and heal their land (2Ch 7:14; cf. 6:36–39; Lk 18:14). Note that the high priest's prayer for the forgiveness of the Israelites' sins on the Day of Atonement would not be heard until his own sinful condition had been cleansed (see Ex 26:33, note; see article on THE DAY OF ATONEMENT, p. 174).

(5) Finally, for prayer to be effective we must be persistent. This is the main point of the parable of the persistent widow (see Lk 18:1–7; see 18:1, note). Jesus' instruction to "ask . . . seek . . . knock" (Mt 7:7–8) teaches perseverance in prayer (see Mt 7:7–8, note). The apostle Paul also urges us to devote ourselves to prayer (Col 4:2, note; 1Th 5:17, note). Likewise, OT saints recognized this principle. For example, only as long as Moses persevered in prayer with his hands lifted toward God were the Israelites successful in their battle against the Amalekites (see Ex 17:11, note). After Elijah received the prophetic word that rain was coming, he still persisted in prayer until the rain came (1Ki 18:41–45). On a previous occasion, this great prophet had persistently and earnestly prayed that God would give life back to the dead son of the widow of Zarephath until the Lord answered his prayer (1Ki 17:17–23).

SCRIPTURAL ELEMENTS AND METHODS OF EFFECTIVE PRAYING. (1) What elements constitute effective praying? (a) To pray effectively, we must genuinely praise and adore God (Ps 150; Ac 2:47; Ro 15:11; see article on PRAISE, p. 770). (b) Closely related and equally important is thanksgiving to God (see Ps 100:4; Mt 11:25–26; Php 4:6). (c) Sincere confession of known sins is essential to the prayer offered in faith (Jas 5:15–16; cf. Ps 51; Lk 18:13; 1Jn 1:9). (d) God also instructs us to ask according to our needs; as James writes, we do not receive the things we want because we do not ask, or we ask with wrong motives (Jas 4:2–3; cf. Ps 27:7–12; Mt 7:7–11; Php 4:6). (e) And we must pray fervently for others (Nu 14:13–19; Ps 122:6–9; Lk 22:31–32; 23:34; see article on INTERCESSION, p. 1268).

(2) How ought we to pray? Jesus emphasizes the sincerity of our hearts, for we are not heard simply for all our empty words (Mt 6:7). We can pray silently (1Sa 1:13), or we can pray aloud (Ne 9:4; Eze 11:13). We can pray in our own words or using the words of Scripture. We can pray with the mind, or we can pray with the Spirit (i.e., in tongues, 1Co 14:14–18). We can even pray by groaning, i.e., not using any human words (Ro 8:26), knowing that the Spirit will bring those inaudible requests to the Lord. Yet another method of praying is singing to the Lord (Ps 92:1–2; Eph 5:19–20; Col 3:16). Earnest prayer to the Lord will at times be accompanied with fasting (Ezr 8:21; Ne 1:4; Da 9:3–4; Lk 2:37; Ac 14:23; see Mt 6:16, note).

(3) What posture is appropriate for prayer? The Bible records praying while standing (1Ki 8:22; Ne 9:4–5), sitting (1Ch 17:16; Lk 10:13), kneeling (Ezr 9:5; Da 6:10; Ac 20:36), lying on a bed (Ps 63:6), bowing down to the ground (Ex 34:8; Ps 95:6), lying on the ground (2Sa 12:16; Mt 26:39), and lifting up hands to heaven (Ps 28:2; Isa 1:15; 1Ti 2:8).

EXAMPLES OF EFFECTIVE PRAYING. The Bible is filled with examples of prayers that were powerful and effective. (1) Moses had numerous intercessory prayers that God answered, even when he had told Moses that he would follow a different course of action (see article on INTERCESSION, p. 1268). (2) A repentant Samson prayed for one more opportunity to fulfill his life's task of defeating the Philistines; God answered this prayer by giving him strength to pull down the pillars of the building in which they were celebrating the power of their gods (Jdg 16:21–30). (3) The prophet Elijah had at least four powerful prayers answered, all of which brought glory to the God of Israel (see 1Ki 17—18; cf. Jas 5:17–18). (4) King Hezekiah became sick and was told by Isaiah that he would die (2Ki 20:1; Isa 38:1). Feeling that his life and work were incomplete, Hezekiah turned his face to the wall and prayed intensely for God to give him more time; God sent Isaiah back to Hezekiah, assuring him of healing and fifteen more years of life (2Ki 20:2–6; Isa 38:2–6). (5) Daniel undoubtedly prayed to the Lord in the lions' den, asking for deliverance from their mouths, and the Lord granted his request (Da 6:10,16–22). (6) The early Christians prayed earnestly for Peter's release from prison, and God sent an angel to free him (Ac 12:3–11; cf. 12:5, note). Such examples should fill us with holy desire and faith to pray effectively according to the principles outlined in the Bible.

'Hitch up your chariot and go down before the rain stops you.' "
45Meanwhile, the sky grew black
with clouds, the wind rose, a heavy
rain[u] came on and Ahab rode off to
Jezreel.[v] 46The power[w] of the LORD
came upon Elijah and, tucking his
cloak into his belt,[x] he ran ahead of
Ahab all the way to Jezreel.

Elijah Flees to Horeb

19 Now Ahab told Jezebel[y] everything Elijah had done and how
he had killed[z] all the prophets with
the sword. 2So Jezebel sent a messenger to Elijah to say, "May the gods
deal with me, be it ever so severely,[a]
if by this time tomorrow I do not
make your life like that of one of
them."[b]
3Elijah was afraid[n] and ran[c] for
his life.[d] When he came to Beersheba[e] in Judah, he left his servant there,
4while he himself went a day's journey
into the desert. He came to a broom
tree,[f] sat down under it and prayed
that he might die. "I have had enough,
LORD," he said. "Take my life;[g] I am no
better than my ancestors." 5Then he
lay down under the tree and fell
asleep.[h]
All at once an angel[i] touched him
and said, "Get up and eat." 6He looked
around, and there by his head was a
cake of bread baked over hot coals, and
a jar of water. He ate and drank and
then lay down again.
7The angel of the LORD came back a
second time and touched him and said,
"Get up and eat, for the journey is too
much for you." 8So he got up and ate
and drank. Strengthened by that food,
he traveled forty[j] days and forty
nights until he reached Horeb,[k] the
mountain of God. 9There he went into
a cave[l] and spent the night.

The LORD Appears to Elijah

And the word of the LORD came to
him: "What are you doing here, Elijah?"[m]
10He replied, "I have been very zealous[n] for the LORD God Almighty. The
Israelites have rejected your covenant,[o] broken down your altars,[p]
and put your prophets to death with

18:45 [u] S 1Ki 8:36; Job 37:13 [v] S 1Sa 29:1; S Hos 1:4 **18:46** [w] S Jdg 3:10; S 1Sa 11:6; Lk 1:35; 4:14 [x] 2Ki 4:29; 9:1 **19:1** [y] 1Ki 16:31 [z] S Ex 22:20 **19:2** [a] S Ru 1:17 [b] Ps 13:4; Jer 20:10; 26:21; 36:26 **19:3** [c] S Ge 31:21 [d] S Ge 19:17 [e] S Jos 19:2 **19:4** [f] Job 30:4 [g] S Nu 11:15; Job 6:9; 7:16; 10:1; Ps 69:19; Jer 20:18; Jnh 4:8 **19:5** [h] Ge 28:11 [i] S Ge 16:7 **19:8** [j] Ex 24:18; Mt 4:2 [k] S Ex 3:1 **19:9** [l] S Ex 33:22 [m] S Ge 3:9 **19:10** [n] S Nu 25:13; Ac 22:3; Gal 4:18 [o] S Dt 31:16 [p] 1Ki 18:30

[n] *3* Or *Elijah saw*

19:3 ELIJAH WAS AFRAID AND RAN FOR HIS LIFE. Elijah's expression of faith and the supernatural victories in ch. 18 were followed by fear, flight for his life and discouragement—all results of Jezebel's intention to destroy his life (v. 2). (1) Since Elijah had received no word from the Lord to remain in Jezreel, to have stayed would have been to risk his life unnecessarily (cf. 18:1); his destiny was Mount Horeb (i.e., Mount Sinai).

(2) Elijah's forced departure from Israel for Judah and the desert is an example of those who "because of righteousness" (see Mt 5:10, note) have been ill-treated and forced to wander in deserts, mountains, caves and holes in the ground (Heb 11:37–38). Like Elijah there are prophets who have had to leave their churches, preachers their pulpits, professors their classrooms and laypeople their work because they stood against sin, spoke according to God's Word and followed the path of righteousness for his name's sake. Great is their reward in heaven (Mt 5:10–12).

19:4 TAKE MY LIFE. Elijah—overcome by exhaustion, discouragement and grief—prayed that God would deliver him from the heavy prophetic burden and let him depart to his heavenly rest. (1) Elijah's feelings were not unlike that of (a) the apostle Paul, when he spoke of having a desire "to depart and be with Christ" (Php 1:23), or (b) the heroes of faith, who "were longing for a better country—a heavenly one" (Heb 11:16; cf. also Moses in Nu 11:15).

(2) The following are some reasons why Elijah was profoundly discouraged. (a) Apparent failure: he had expected the conversion of all Israel and possibly even Jezebel, yet he now had to flee for his life instead. The hope, labor and struggle of his whole life appeared to be ending in failure (vv. 1–4). (b) Loneliness: he felt that he stood alone in the battle for God's truth and righteousness (v. 10; cf. Paul, 2Ti 4:16). (c) Physical exhaustion after a long and strenuous journey (vv. 3–4; 18:46).

19:5 AN ANGEL TOUCHED HIM. God dealt with the discouraged Elijah in an understanding and caring manner (cf. Heb 4:14–15). (1) He allowed Elijah to sleep (vv. 5–6). (2) He nourished him with food (vv. 5–7). (3) He visited him with an awe-inspiring revelation of his power and presence (vv. 11–13). (4) He provided additional revelation and direction (vv. 15–18). (5) He gave him a faithful companion with a kindred spirit (vv. 16, 19–21). In other words, when God's children are discouraged in the place God has put them, they can through Christ ask God to give strength, grace and encouragement, and to make them adequate for their situation (see Heb 2:18; 3:6; 7:25).

19:8 FORTY DAYS AND FORTY NIGHTS. Some take this fast, along with the experiences of Moses (Ex 34:28) and Christ (Mt 4:2), to be examples of long fasts. However, these individuals did not fast in the ordinary sense. Moses, in the presence of God in the cloud, was supernaturally sustained. Elijah was given two supernatural meals that kept giving him strength for forty days (vv. 6–8). Jesus was led by the Spirit into the desert and did not become hungry until after the forty days (see Mt 4:2, note; 6:16, note).

the sword. I am the only one left,[q] and
now they are trying to kill me too."
11The LORD said, "Go out and stand
on the mountain[r] in the presence of
the LORD, for the LORD is about to pass
by."[s]

Then a great and powerful wind[t]
tore the mountains apart and shattered[u] the rocks before the LORD, but
the LORD was not in the wind. After the
wind there was an earthquake, but the
LORD was not in the earthquake. 12Af-
ter the earthquake came a fire,[v] but
the LORD was not in the fire. And after
the fire came a gentle whisper.[w]
13When Elijah heard it, he pulled his
cloak over his face[x] and went out and
stood at the mouth of the cave.

Then a voice said to him, "What are
you doing here, Elijah?"
14He replied, "I have been very zealous for the LORD God Almighty. The Israelites have rejected your covenant,
broken down your altars, and put your
prophets to death with the sword. I am
the only one left,[y] and now they are
trying to kill me too."
15The LORD said to him, "Go back the
way you came, and go to the Desert of
Damascus. When you get there, anoint
Hazael[z] king over Aram. 16Also,
anoint[a] Jehu son of Nimshi king over
Israel, and anoint Elisha[b] son of Shaphat from Abel Meholah[c] to succeed
you as prophet. 17Jehu will put to death
any who escape the sword of Hazael,[d]
and Elisha will put to death any who
escape the sword of Jehu.[e] 18Yet I reserve[f] seven thousand in Israel—all
whose knees have not bowed down to
Baal and all whose mouths have not
kissed[g] him."

The Call of Elisha

19So Elijah went from there and
found Elisha son of Shaphat. He was
plowing with twelve yoke of oxen, and
he himself was driving the twelfth pair.
Elijah went up to him and threw his
cloak[h] around him. 20Elisha then left
his oxen and ran after Elijah. "Let me
kiss my father and mother good-by,"[i]
he said, "and then I will come with
you."

"Go back," Elijah replied. "What
have I done to you?"
21So Elisha left him and went back.
He took his yoke of oxen[j] and slaughtered them. He burned the plowing
equipment to cook the meat and gave
it to the people, and they ate. Then he
set out to follow Elijah and became his
attendant.[k]

Ben-Hadad Attacks Samaria

20 Now Ben-Hadad[l] king of Aram
mustered his entire army. Accompanied by thirty-two kings with
their horses and chariots, he went up
and besieged Samaria[m] and attacked
it. 2He sent messengers into the city to
Ahab king of Israel, saying, "This is
what Ben-Hadad says: 3'Your silver

19:10 [q] 1Ki 18:4, 22; Jer 5:11; 9:2; Ro 11:3* **19:11** [r] Ex 34:2; Mt 17:1-3 [s] Ex 33:19 [t] S Ex 14:21; S 2Ki 2:1 [u] Na 1:6 **19:12** [v] S Ex 3:2 [w] ver 11; S 1Sa 14:6; Job 4:16; Zec 4:6; 2Co 12:9 **19:13** [x] Ex 3:6 **19:14** [y] 1Ki 18:22; Ro 11:3* **19:15** [z] 2Ki 8:7-15 **19:16** [a] 2Ki 9:1-3, 6 [b] ver 21; 2Ki 2:1; 3:11 [c] S Jdg 7:22 **19:17** [d] 2Ki 8:12, 29; 10:32; 12:17; 13:3,7,22; Am 1:4 [e] Jer 48:44 **19:18** [f] Ro 11:4* [g] Hos 13:2 **19:19** [h] S Ge 41:42; 2Ki 2:8,14 **19:20** [i] Lk 9:61 **19:21** [j] S 1Sa 6:14 [k] S ver 16 **20:1** [l] S 1Ki 15:18 [m] S 1Ki 13:32

19:11–12 THE LORD IS ABOUT TO PASS BY. To encourage and strengthen Elijah's faith, God visited him on Mount Horeb (i.e., Mount Sinai, the mountain of revelation). This visitation was accompanied by a great wind, earthquake and fire, but the Lord was in none of those events. Instead, God's revelation came in the form of "a gentle whisper." Elijah learned that God's work proceeds and advances " 'Not by might nor by power, but by my Spirit,' says the LORD Almighty" (cf. Zec 4:6). God had in fact not deserted his prophet or his faithful people. By his Spirit and eternal word, he would bring redemption, righteousness and eternal salvation.

19:16 ANOINT ELISHA ... TO SUCCEED YOU. God directed Elijah to anoint Elisha to be his successor. Note that not only were priests and kings anointed to their respective offices, but prophets as well. Elisha was to (1) minister to Elijah, (2) help Hazael (king of Aram) and Jehu (king of Israel) defeat the enemies of God (vv. 16–17), and (3) proclaim the word of God to the faithful remnant (v. 18). Elijah and Elisha's ministries covered a span of 75 years (875–800 B.C., during the reigns of Ahab, Ahaziah, Joram, Jehu, Jehoahaz and Jehoash). Elisha was a faithful servant to the older prophet and was known as the one who "used to pour water on the hands of Elijah" (2Ki 3:11).

19:18 SEVEN THOUSAND IN ISRAEL. The 7, 000 in Israel who did not bow their knees to Baal are joined by the suffering faithful of all generations who overcome apostasy, compromise and worldliness among God's people, and who persevere in love, faith and obedience to God and his Word. They are those who refuse to be caught up in the evil ways of the world, who have washed their robes and made them white in the blood of the Lamb (Rev 7:14), who are persecuted because of righteousness (Mt 5:10), and who steadfastly remain on the narrow road (Mt 7:14; see articles on SPIRITUAL SEPARATION FOR BELIEVERS, p. 1794, and THE CHRISTIAN'S RELATIONSHIP TO THE WORLD, p. 1976). Throughout Scripture it is the faithful and overcoming remnant that is known by the Lord (2Ti 2:19). God promises to shield them by his power through faith (1Pe 1:5), and the Lamb will lead them home (Rev 7:17).

and gold are mine, and the best of your
wives and children are mine.' "
[4]The king of Israel answered, "Just
as you say, my lord the king. I and all
I have are yours."
[5]The messengers came again and
said, "This is what Ben-Hadad says: 'I
sent to demand your silver and gold,
your wives and your children. [6]But
about this time tomorrow I am going to
send my officials to search your palace
and the houses of your officials. They
will seize everything you value and carry it away.' "
[7]The king of Israel summoned all
the elders[n] of the land and said to
them, "See how this man is looking for
trouble![o] When he sent for my wives
and my children, my silver and my
gold, I did not refuse him."

20:7 [n] 1Sa 11:3 [o] 2Ki 5:7

[8]The elders and the people all answered, "Don't listen to him or agree to
his demands."
[9]So he replied to Ben-Hadad's messengers, "Tell my lord the king, 'Your
servant will do all you demanded the
first time, but this demand I cannot
meet.' " They left and took the answer
back to Ben-Hadad.
[10]Then Ben-Hadad sent another
message to Ahab: "May the gods deal
with me, be it ever so severely, if
enough dust[p] remains in Samaria to
give each of my men a handful."
[11]The king of Israel answered, "Tell
him: 'One who puts on his armor
should not boast[q] like one who takes
it off.' "
[12]Ben-Hadad heard this message
while he and the kings were drinking[r]

20:10 [p] S 2Sa 22:43
20:11 [q] Pr 27:1; Jer 9:23; Am 2:14
20:12 [r] S 1Ki 16:9

THE LIVES OF ELIJAH AND ELISHA

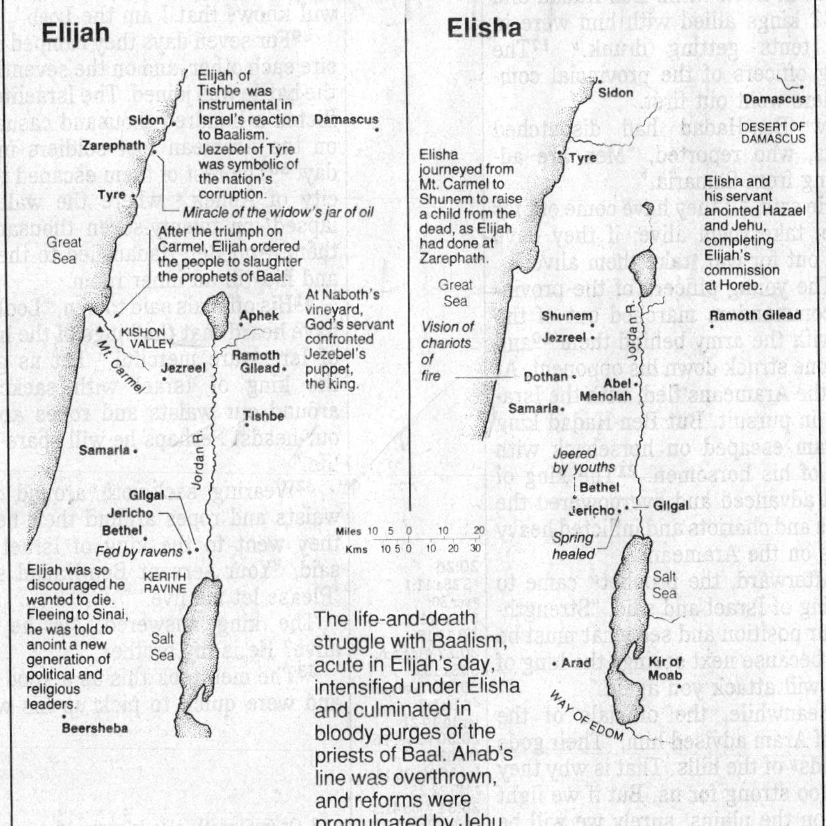
Elijah
Elijah of Tishbe was instrumental in Israel's reaction to Baalism. Jezebel of Tyre was symbolic of the nation's corruption.
Sidon
Zarephath
Damascus
Tyre
Miracle of the widow's jar of oil
After the triumph on Carmel, Elijah ordered the people to slaughter the prophets of Baal.
Great Sea
Aphek
At Naboth's vineyard, God's servant confronted Jezebel's puppet, the king.
KISHON VALLEY
Mt. Carmel
Jezreel
Ramoth Gilead
Tishbe
Samaria
Jordan R.
Gilgal
Jericho
Bethel
Fed by ravens
KERITH RAVINE
Elijah was so discouraged he wanted to die. Fleeing to Sinai, he was told to anoint a new generation of political and religious leaders.
Salt Sea
Beersheba
Elisha
Sidon
Damascus
DESERT OF DAMASCUS
Elisha journeyed from Mt. Carmel to Shunem to raise a child from the dead, as Elijah had done at Zarephath.
Tyre
Elisha and his servant anointed Hazael and Jehu, completing Elijah's commission at Horeb.
Great Sea
Shunem
Jezreel
Jordan R.
Ramoth Gilead
Vision of chariots of fire
Dothan
Abel-Meholah
Samaria
Jeered by youths
Bethel
Jericho
Gilgal
Spring healed
Miles 10 5 0 10 20
Kms 10 5 0 10 20 30
Salt Sea
Arad
Kir of Moab
WAY OF EDOM
The life-and-death struggle with Baalism, acute in Elijah's day, intensified under Elisha and culminated in bloody purges of the priests of Baal. Ahab's line was overthrown, and reforms were promulgated by Jehu.
Copyright ©1991 Zondervan Publishing House.

in their tents,[o] and he ordered his men: "Prepare to attack." So they prepared to attack the city.

Ahab Defeats Ben-Hadad

13Meanwhile a prophet[s] came to Ahab king of Israel and announced, "This is what the LORD says: 'Do you see this vast army? I will give it into your hand today, and then you will know[t] that I am the LORD.' "

14"But who will do this?" asked Ahab.

The prophet replied, "This is what the LORD says: 'The young officers of the provincial commanders will do it.' "

"And who will start[u] the battle?" he asked.

The prophet answered, "You will."

15So Ahab summoned the young officers of the provincial commanders, 232 men. Then he assembled the rest of the Israelites, 7,000 in all. **16**They set out at noon while Ben-Hadad and the 32 kings allied with him were in their tents getting drunk.[v] **17**The young officers of the provincial commanders went out first.

Now Ben-Hadad had dispatched scouts, who reported, "Men are advancing from Samaria."

18He said, "If they have come out for peace, take them alive; if they have come out for war, take them alive."

19The young officers of the provincial commanders marched out of the city with the army behind them **20**and each one struck down his opponent. At that, the Arameans fled, with the Israelites in pursuit. But Ben-Hadad king of Aram escaped on horseback with some of his horsemen. **21**The king of Israel advanced and overpowered the horses and chariots and inflicted heavy losses on the Arameans.

22Afterward, the prophet[w] came to the king of Israel and said, "Strengthen your position and see what must be done, because next spring[x] the king of Aram will attack you again."

23Meanwhile, the officials of the king of Aram advised him, "Their gods are gods[y] of the hills. That is why they were too strong for us. But if we fight them on the plains, surely we will be stronger than they. **24**Do this: Remove all the kings from their commands and replace them with other officers. **25**You must also raise an army like the one you lost—horse for horse and chariot for chariot—so we can fight Israel on the plains. Then surely we will be stronger than they." He agreed with them and acted accordingly.

26The next spring[z] Ben-Hadad mustered the Arameans and went up to Aphek[a] to fight against Israel. **27**When the Israelites were also mustered and given provisions, they marched out to meet them. The Israelites camped opposite them like two small flocks of goats, while the Arameans covered the countryside.[b]

28The man of God came up and told the king of Israel, "This is what the LORD says: 'Because the Arameans think the LORD is a god of the hills and not a god[c] of the valleys, I will deliver this vast army into your hands, and you will know[d] that I am the LORD.' "

29For seven days they camped opposite each other, and on the seventh day the battle was joined. The Israelites inflicted a hundred thousand casualties on the Aramean foot soldiers in one day. **30**The rest of them escaped to the city of Aphek,[e] where the wall collapsed[f] on twenty-seven thousand of them. And Ben-Hadad fled to the city and hid[g] in an inner room.

31His officials said to him, "Look, we have heard that the kings of the house of Israel are merciful.[h] Let us go to the king of Israel with sackcloth[i] around our waists and ropes around our heads. Perhaps he will spare your life."

32Wearing sackcloth around their waists and ropes around their heads, they went to the king of Israel and said, "Your servant Ben-Hadad says: 'Please let me live.' "

The king answered, "Is he still alive? He is my brother."

33The men took this as a good sign and were quick to pick up his word.

20:13 [s] S Jdg 6:8 [t] S Ex 6:7 **20:14** [u] S Jdg 1:1 **20:16** [v] S 1Ki 16:9 **20:22** [w] S Jdg 6:8 [x] S 2Sa 11:1 **20:23** [y] ver 28; Isa 36:20; Ro 1:21-23

20:26 [z] S 2Sa 11:1 [a] ver 30; S 1Sa 4:1; 2Ki 13:17 **20:27** [b] Jdg 6:6; S 1Sa 13:6 **20:28** [c] S ver 23 [d] S Ex 6:7; Jer 16:19-21 **20:30** [e] S ver 26 [f] Ps 62:4; Isa 26:21; 30:13 [g] 1Ki 22:25 **20:31** [h] Job 41:3 [i] S Ge 37:34

[o] *12* Or *in Succoth*; also in verse 16

20:13 I WILL GIVE IT INTO YOUR HAND. In spite of the unfaithfulness of Ahab and the people of Israel, God showed them mercy and delivered Samaria from the Aramean army (v. 20). A year later God gave Israel a great victory over Aram east of the Jordan River near the city of Aphek (vv. 22–29). Ahab, however, refused to submit to and worship the true God of Israel.

"Yes, your brother Ben-Hadad!" they
said.
"Go and get him," the king said.
When Ben-Hadad came out, Ahab had
him come up into his chariot.
34"I will return the cities[j] my father took from your father," Ben-Hadad[k] offered. "You may set up your
own market areas[l] in Damascus,[m] as
my father did in Samaria."
⌊Ahab said,⌋ "On the basis of a treaty[n] I will set you free." So he made a
treaty with him, and let him go.

A Prophet Condemns Ahab

35By the word of the LORD one of the
sons of the prophets[o] said to his companion, "Strike me with your weapon,"
but the man refused.[p]
36So the prophet said, "Because you
have not obeyed the LORD, as soon as
you leave me a lion[q] will kill you."
And after the man went away, a lion
found him and killed him.
37The prophet found another man
and said, "Strike me, please." So the
man struck him and wounded him.
38Then the prophet went and stood by
the road waiting for the king. He disguised himself with his headband down
over his eyes. 39As the king passed by,
the prophet called out to him, "Your
servant went into the thick of the battle, and someone came to me with a
captive and said, 'Guard this man. If
he is missing, it will be your life for
his life,[r] or you must pay a talent[p]
of silver.' 40While your servant was
busy here and there, the man disappeared."
"That is your sentence,"[s] the king
of Israel said. "You have pronounced it
yourself."
41Then the prophet quickly removed
the headband from his eyes, and the
king of Israel recognized him as one of
the prophets. 42He said to the king,
"This is what the LORD says: 'You[t]
have set free a man I had determined
should die.[q][u] Therefore it is your
life for his life,[v] your people for his
people.'" 43Sullen and angry,[w] the
king of Israel went to his palace in
Samaria.

Naboth's Vineyard

21 Some time later there was an
incident involving a vineyard
belonging to Naboth[x] the Jezreelite.
The vineyard was in Jezreel,[y] close to
the palace of Ahab king of Samaria.
2Ahab said to Naboth, "Let me have
your vineyard to use for a vegetable
garden, since it is close to my palace.
In exchange I will give you a better
vineyard or, if you prefer, I will pay you
whatever it is worth."
3But Naboth replied, "The LORD forbid that I should give you the inheritance[z] of my fathers."
4So Ahab went home, sullen and angry[a] because Naboth the Jezreelite
had said, "I will not give you the inheritance of my fathers." He lay on his bed
sulking and refused[b] to eat.
5His wife Jezebel came in and asked
him, "Why are you so sullen? Why
won't you eat?"
6He answered her, "Because I said
to Naboth the Jezreelite, 'Sell me your
vineyard; or if you prefer, I will give
you another vineyard in its place.' But
he said, 'I will not give you my vineyard.'"
7Jezebel his wife said, "Is this how
you act as king over Israel? Get up and
eat! Cheer up. I'll get you the vineyard[c] of Naboth the Jezreelite."
8So she wrote letters[d] in Ahab's
name, placed his seal[e] on them, and
sent them to the elders and nobles who
lived in Naboth's city with him. 9In
those letters she wrote:

> "Proclaim a day of fasting and
> seat Naboth in a prominent place
> among the people. 10But seat two
> scoundrels[f] opposite him and
> have them testify that he has
> cursed[g] both God and the king.
> Then take him out and stone him
> to death."

11So the elders and nobles who lived
in Naboth's city did as Jezebel directed

20:34 [j] 1Ki 15:20 [k] S Ge 10:22 [l] 2Sa 8:6 [m] S Ge 14:15; Jer 49:23-27 [n] S Ex 23:32 **20:35** [o] S 1Sa 10:5; Am 7:14 [p] S 1Ki 13:21 **20:36** [q] 1Ki 13:24 **20:39** [r] S Jos 2:14 **20:40** [s] 2Sa 12:5; S 14:13 **20:42** [t] S 2Sa 12:7 [u] Jer 48:10 [v] S Jos 2:14 **20:43** [w] 1Ki 21:4

21:1 [x] 2Ki 9:21 [y] S 1Sa 29:1; 2Ki 10:1 **21:3** [z] S Lev 25:23 **21:4** [a] 1Ki 20:43 [b] 1Sa 28:23 **21:7** [c] S 1Sa 8:14 **21:8** [d] 2Sa 11:14 [e] S Ge 38:18 **21:10** [f] S Dt 13:13; Ac 6:11 [g] S Ex 22:28; Lev 24:15-16

[p] *39* That is, about 75 pounds (about 34 kilograms) [q] *42* The Hebrew term refers to the irrevocable giving over of things or persons to the LORD, often by totally destroying them.

20:35 SONS OF THE PROPHETS. These were students of the prophets who in some sense were discipled by older and more renowned prophets like Elisha (cf. 2Ki 2:3,5,7,15; 4:1,38; 5:22; 6:1; 9:1). They stood in close association with the master prophet, opposed Baal worship, and promoted obedience and faithfulness to the Lord God. They were known for prophesying by the power of the Spirit.

in the letters she had written to them.
12 They proclaimed a fast[h] and seated
Naboth in a prominent place among the
people. 13 Then two scoundrels came
and sat opposite him and brought
charges against Naboth before the people, saying, "Naboth has cursed both
God and the king." So they took him
outside the city and stoned him to
death.[i] 14 Then they sent word to Jezebel: "Naboth has been stoned and is
dead."

15 As soon as Jezebel heard that Naboth had been stoned to death, she said
to Ahab, "Get up and take possession
of the vineyard[j] of Naboth the Jezreelite that he refused to sell you. He is no
longer alive, but dead." 16 When Ahab
heard that Naboth was dead, he got up
and went down to take possession of
Naboth's vineyard.

17 Then the word of the LORD came to
Elijah the Tishbite: 18 "Go down to
meet Ahab king of Israel, who rules in
Samaria. He is now in Naboth's vineyard, where he has gone to take possession of it. 19 Say to him, 'This is
what the LORD says: Have you not murdered a man and seized his property?'[k] Then say to him, 'This is what
the LORD says: In the place where dogs
licked up Naboth's blood,[l] dogs[m] will
lick up your blood—yes, yours!' "

20 Ahab said to Elijah, "So you have
found me, my enemy!"[n]

"I have found you," he answered,
"because you have sold[o] yourself to
do evil in the eyes of the LORD. 21 'I am
going to bring disaster on you. I will
consume your descendants and cut off
from Ahab every last male[p] in Israel—slave or free.[q] 22 I will make your
house[r] like that of Jeroboam son of
Nebat and that of Baasha son of Ahijah, because you have provoked me to
anger and have caused Israel to sin.'[s]

23 "And also concerning Jezebel the
LORD says: 'Dogs[t] will devour Jezebel
by the wall of[r] Jezreel.'

24 "Dogs[u] will eat those belonging
to Ahab who die in the city, and the
birds of the air[v] will feed on those who
die in the country."

25 (There was never[w] a man like
Ahab, who sold himself to do evil in the
eyes of the LORD, urged on by Jezebel
his wife. 26 He behaved in the vilest
manner by going after idols, like the
Amorites[x] the LORD drove out before
Israel.)

27 When Ahab heard these words, he
tore his clothes, put on sackcloth[y]
and fasted. He lay in sackcloth and
went around meekly.[z]

28 Then the word of the LORD came to
Elijah the Tishbite: 29 "Have you noticed how Ahab has humbled himself
before me? Because he has humbled[a]
himself, I will not bring this disaster in
his day,[b] but I will bring it on his
house in the days of his son."[c]

Micaiah Prophesies Against Ahab

22:1–28pp — 2Ch 18:1–27

22 For three years there was no
war between Aram and Israel.
2 But in the third year Jehoshaphat king
of Judah went down to see the king of
Israel. 3 The king of Israel had said to
his officials, "Don't you know that Ramoth Gilead[d] belongs to us and yet we
are doing nothing to retake it from the
king of Aram?"

4 So he asked Jehoshaphat, "Will you

21:12 [h] Isa 58:4 **21:13** [i] S Lev 24:16 **21:15** [j] S 1Sa 8:14 **21:19** [k] Job 24:6; 31:39 [l] 2Ki 9:26; Ps 9:12; Isa 14:20 [m] 1Ki 22:38; Ps 68:23; Jer 15:3 **21:20** [n] S 1Ki 18:17 [o] 2Ki 17:17; Ro 7:14 **21:21** [p] Jdg 9:5; 2Ki 10:7 [q] S Dt 32:36 **21:22** [r] 1Ki 16:3 [s] S 1Ki 12:30 **21:23** [t] 2Ki 9:10, 34-36 **21:24** [u] 1Ki 14:11 [v] S Ge 40:19; S Dt 28:26 **21:25** [w] S 1Ki 14:9; S 16:33 **21:26** [x] S Ge 15:16 **21:27** [y] S Ge 37:34; S Jer 4:8 [z] Isa 38:15 **21:29** [a] S Ex 10:3 [b] S Ex 32:14; 2Ki 22:20 [c] Ex 20:5; 2Ki 9:26; 10:6-10 **22:3** [d] S Dt 4:43

[r] *23* Most Hebrew manuscripts; a few Hebrew manuscripts, Vulgate and Syriac (see also 2 Kings 9:26) *the plot of ground at*

21:17 THE WORD OF THE LORD CAME TO ELIJAH. God hates injustice within the community of his people. Because of the death of the innocent Naboth, Elijah prophesied that Ahab and Jezebel would suffer (vv. 17–29). God's principle of retribution and justice continues under the new covenant. For example, Paul states that "anyone who does wrong [to another person] will be repaid for his wrong, and there is no favoritism" (see Col 3:25, note). God's people must treat one another justly, fairly and mercifully (Mic 6:8; Col 4:1; cf. Gal 6:7).

21:19 DOGS WILL LICK UP YOUR BLOOD. This prophecy was fulfilled when Ahab was killed in battle, and the dogs licked up the blood washed from his chariot (22:35,38). Ahab's sons also died violent deaths: Ahaziah was injured in, and later died from, a fall (2Ki 1:2,17); Joram was killed by Jehu and his body thrown into Naboth's plot of ground (2Ki 9:22–26). Ahab's wife, Jezebel, also died a violent death (see 2Ki 9:30–37).

21:25 JEZEBEL. The goal of Ahab's wicked wife was to uproot the worship of the Lord and to substitute the Baal of Tyre as the chief god of Israel; she failed to do so. Instead, her name has become synonymous with wickedness, witchcraft, treachery and spiritual seduction. John uses the name Jezebel for a false prophetess within the church in Thyatira who was leading God's people into immorality and worldliness (see Rev 2:20, note).

go with me to fight[e] against Ramoth
Gilead?"
Jehoshaphat replied to the king of
Israel, "I am as you are, my people as
your people, my horses as your
horses." 5But Jehoshaphat also said to
the king of Israel, "First seek the counsel[f] of the LORD."
6So the king of Israel brought together the prophets—about four hundred men—and asked them, "Shall I
go to war against Ramoth Gilead, or
shall I refrain?"
"Go,"[g] they answered, "for the Lord
will give it into the king's hand."[h]
7But Jehoshaphat asked, "Is there
not a prophet[i] of the LORD here whom
we can inquire[j] of?"
8The king of Israel answered Jehoshaphat, "There is still one man
through whom we can inquire of the
LORD, but I hate[k] him because he never prophesies anything good[l] about
me, but always bad. He is Micaiah son
of Imlah."
"The king should not say that," Jehoshaphat replied.
9So the king of Israel called one of
his officials and said, "Bring Micaiah
son of Imlah at once."
10Dressed in their royal robes, the
king of Israel and Jehoshaphat king of
Judah were sitting on their thrones at
the threshing floor[m] by the entrance of
the gate of Samaria, with all the prophets prophesying before them. 11Now
Zedekiah[n] son of Kenaanah had made
iron horns[o] and he declared, "This is
what the LORD says: 'With these you
will gore the Arameans until they are
destroyed.'"
12All the other prophets were prophesying the same thing. "Attack Ramoth Gilead and be victorious," they
said, "for the LORD will give it into the
king's hand."
13The messenger who had gone to
summon Micaiah said to him, "Look,
as one man the other prophets are predicting success for the king. Let your
word agree with theirs, and speak favorably."[p]
14But Micaiah said, "As surely as
the LORD lives, I can tell him only what
the LORD tells me."[q]
15When he arrived, the king asked
him, "Micaiah, shall we go to war
against Ramoth Gilead, or shall I refrain?"
"Attack and be victorious," he answered, "for the LORD will give it into
the king's hand."
16The king said to him, "How many
times must I make you swear to tell me
nothing but the truth in the name of the
LORD?"
17Then Micaiah answered, "I saw all
Israel scattered[r] on the hills like
sheep without a shepherd,[s] and the
LORD said, 'These people have no master. Let each one go home in peace.'"
18The king of Israel said to Jehoshaphat, "Didn't I tell you that he never
prophesies anything good about me,
but only bad?"
19Micaiah continued, "Therefore
hear the word of the LORD: I saw the
LORD sitting on his throne[t] with all the
host[u] of heaven standing around him
on his right and on his left. 20And the
LORD said, 'Who will entice Ahab into
attacking Ramoth Gilead and going to
his death there?'
"One suggested this, and another
that. 21Finally, a spirit came forward,
stood before the LORD and said, 'I will
entice him.'
22"'By what means?' the LORD
asked.
"'I will go out and be a lying[v] spirit
in the mouths of all his prophets,' he
said.
"'You will succeed in enticing him,'
said the LORD. 'Go and do it.'
23"So now the LORD has put a lying[w]
spirit in the mouths of all these proph-

22:4 [e] 2Ki 3:7 **22:5** [f] Ex 33:7; 2Ki 3:11; Job 38:2; Ps 32:8; 73:24; 107:11 **22:6** [g] S Jdg 18:6 [h] S 1Ki 13:18 **22:7** [i] Dt 18:15; 2Ki 3:11; 5:8 [j] S Nu 27:21; 2Ki 3:11 **22:8** [k] Am 5:10 [l] ver 13; Isa 5:20; 30:10; Jer 23:17 **22:10** [m] S Jdg 6:37 **22:11** [n] ver 24 [o] Dt 33:17; Jer 27:2; 28:10; Zec 1:18-21 **22:13** [p] S ver 8 **22:14** [q] S Nu 22:18; S 1Sa 3:17 **22:17** [r] S Ge 11:4; Na 3:18 [s] Nu 27:17; Isa 13:14; S Mt 9:36 **22:19** [t] Ps 47:8; Isa 6:1; 63:15; Eze 1:26; Da 7:9 [u] Job 1:6; 15:8; 38:7; Ps 103:20-21; 148:2; Jer 23:18, 22; Lk 2:13 **22:22** [v] S Jdg 9:23; 2Th 2:11 **22:23** [w] S Dt 13:3

22:6 FOUR HUNDRED MEN. These four hundred prophets of Ahab (see vv. 22–23) were not true prophets of the Lord, but religionists who prophesied what the king wanted to hear (cf. v. 8; see article on THE PROPHET IN THE OLD TESTAMENT, p. 986).

22:15 ATTACK AND BE VICTORIOUS. Micaiah mimicked the prediction of the false prophets in such a way that Ahab knew he was not serious (cf. v. 16). Micaiah then proceeded to make known the true prophetic vision he had received (v. 17). The meaning was clear: Ahab would die and Israel would retreat home.

22:23 A LYING SPIRIT. The lying spirit can be understood as one of Satan's agents, i.e., an evil spirit sent by God to condemn Ahab and the false prophets in their sin. Their hearts were hardened against the truth to such an extent that God finally gave them over to a lie as the due penalty for their sin (cf. Ro 1:21–27). The same kind of judging will take place in the last days of this age, when God will send "a powerful delusion" (2Th 2:11) to all who "refused to love the truth . . . but have delighted in wickedness" (2Th 2:10,12). The deception

ets[x] of yours. The LORD has decreed
disaster[y] for you."
24 Then Zedekiah[z] son of Kenaanah
went up and slapped[a] Micaiah in the
face. "Which way did the spirit from[s]
the LORD go when he went from me to
speak[b] to you?" he asked.
25 Micaiah replied, "You will find out
on the day you go to hide[c] in an inner
room."
26 The king of Israel then ordered,
"Take Micaiah and send him back to
Amon the ruler of the city and to Joash
the king's son 27 and say, 'This is what
the king says: Put this fellow in prison[d] and give him nothing but bread
and water until I return safely.'"
28 Micaiah declared, "If you ever return safely, the LORD has not spoken[e]
through me." Then he added, "Mark
my words, all you people!"

Ahab Killed at Ramoth Gilead

22:29–36pp — 2Ch 18:28–34

29 So the king of Israel and Jehoshaphat king of Judah went up to Ramoth
Gilead. 30 The king of Israel said to Jehoshaphat, "I will enter the battle in
disguise,[f] but you wear your royal
robes." So the king of Israel disguised
himself and went into battle.
31 Now the king of Aram[g] had ordered his thirty-two chariot commanders, "Do not fight with anyone, small or
great, except the king[h] of Israel."
32 When the chariot commanders saw
Jehoshaphat, they thought, "Surely
this is the king of Israel." So they
turned to attack him, but when Jehoshaphat cried out, 33 the chariot commanders saw that he was not the king
of Israel and stopped pursuing him.
34 But someone drew his bow[i] at
random and hit the king of Israel between the sections of his armor. The
king told his chariot driver, "Wheel
around and get me out of the fighting.
I've been wounded." 35 All day long the
battle raged, and the king was propped
up in his chariot facing the Arameans.
The blood from his wound ran onto the
floor of the chariot, and that evening he
died. 36 As the sun was setting, a cry
spread through the army: "Every man
to his town; everyone to his land!"[j]
37 So the king died and was brought
to Samaria, and they buried him there.
38 They washed the chariot at a pool in
Samaria (where the prostitutes
bathed),[t] and the dogs[k] licked up his
blood, as the word of the LORD had declared.
39 As for the other events of Ahab's
reign, including all he did, the palace
he built and inlaid with ivory,[l] and the
cities he fortified, are they not written
in the book of the annals of the kings
of Israel? 40 Ahab rested with his fathers. And Ahaziah his son succeeded
him as king.

Jehoshaphat King of Judah

22:41–50pp — 2Ch 20:31–21:1

41 Jehoshaphat son of Asa became
king of Judah in the fourth year of Ahab
king of Israel. 42 Jehoshaphat was thirty-five years old when he became king,
and he reigned in Jerusalem twenty-
five years. His mother's name was
Azubah daughter of Shilhi. 43 In everything he walked in the ways of his father Asa[m] and did not stray from
them; he did what was right in the eyes
of the LORD. The high places,[n] however, were not removed, and the people
continued to offer sacrifices and burn
incense there. 44 Jehoshaphat was also
at peace with the king of Israel.
45 As for the other events of Jehoshaphat's reign, the things he achieved
and his military exploits, are they not
written in the book of the annals of the
kings of Judah? 46 He rid the land of the
rest of the male shrine prostitutes[o]
who remained there even after the
reign of his father Asa. 47 There was
then no king[p] in Edom; a deputy
ruled.
48 Now Jehoshaphat built a fleet of
trading ships[u][q] to go to Ophir for
gold, but they never set sail—they
were wrecked at Ezion Geber.[r] 49 At
that time Ahaziah son of Ahab said to
Jehoshaphat, "Let my men sail with
your men," but Jehoshaphat refused.
50 Then Jehoshaphat rested with his
fathers and was buried with them in

22:23 [x] Eze 14:9 [y] S Dt 31:29
22:24 [z] ver 11 [a] Ac 23:2 [b] Job 26:4
22:25 [c] 1Ki 20:30
22:27 [d] 2Ch 16:10; Jer 20:2; 26:21; 37:15; Heb 11:36
22:28 [e] S Dt 18:22
22:30 [f] S 1Sa 28:8
22:31 [g] S Ge 10:22; S 2Sa 10:19 [h] S 2Sa 17:2
22:34 [i] 2Ki 9:24; 2Ch 35:23
22:36 [j] 2Ki 14:12
22:38 [k] S 1Ki 21:19
22:39 [l] 2Ch 9:17; Ps 45:8; Am 3:15
22:43 [m] S 1Ki 8:61; 2Ch 17:3 [n] S 1Ki 3:2
22:46 [o] S Dt 23:17
22:47 [p] 1Ki 11:14-18; 2Ki 3:9; 8:20
22:48 [q] S 1Ki 9:26 [r] S Nu 33:35

[s] *24* Or *Spirit of* [t] *38* Or *Samaria and cleaned the weapons* [u] *48* Hebrew *of ships of Tarshish*

will come from the "work of Satan . . . so that all will be condemned who have not believed the truth" (2Th 2:9,12; see 2Th 2:10–12, notes).

22:41 JEHOSHAPHAT SON OF ASA BECAME KING. For more on Jehoshaphat's reign, see 15:24, note.

the city of David his father. And Jehoram his son succeeded him.

Ahaziah King of Israel

51 Ahaziah son of Ahab became king
of Israel in Samaria in the seventeenth
year of Jehoshaphat king of Judah, and
he reigned over Israel two years. 52 He
did evil[s] in the eyes of the LORD, because he walked in the ways of his father and mother and in the ways of Jeroboam son of Nebat, who caused Israel
to sin. 53 He served and worshiped
Baal[t] and provoked the LORD, the God
of Israel, to anger, just as his father[u]
had done.

22:52 [s] 1Ki 15:26
22:53 [t] S Jdg 2:11 [u] 1Ki 21:25

2 KINGS

Outline

- I. The Divided Kingdom: Israel and Judah (1:1—17:41)
  - A. Reign of Ahaziah Continued (Israel) (1:1–18; cf. 1Ki 22:51–53)
  - B. Reign of Joram (Israel) (2:1—8:15)
    - 1. Prophetic Transition from Elijah to Elisha (2:1–25)
    - 2. Evaluation of Joram (3:1–3)
    - 3. Joram Defeats Moab (3:4–27)
    - 4. Elisha's Miraculous Ministry (4:1—8:15)
  - C. Reign of Jehoram (Judah) (8:16–24)
  - D. Reign of Ahaziah (Judah) (8:25–29)
  - E. Reign of Jehu (Israel) (9:1—10:36)
    - 1. Jehu Anointed by Elisha (9:1–10)
    - 2. Jehu's Bloody Purge of Israel (9:11—10:36)
  - F. Reign of Athaliah (Judah) (11:1–16)
  - G. Reign of Joash (Judah) (11:17—12:21)
  - H. Reign of Jehoahaz (Israel) (13:1–9)
  - I. Reign of Jehoash (Israel) (13:10–25)
  - J. Reign of Amaziah (Judah) (14:1–22)
  - K. Reign of Jeroboam II (Israel) (14:23–29)
  - L. Reign of Azariah (Judah) (15:1–7)
  - M. Reign of Zechariah (Israel) (15:8–12)
  - N. Reign of Shallum (Israel) (15:13–15)
  - O. Reign of Menahem (Israel) (15:16–22)
  - P. Reign of Pekahiah (Israel) 15:23–26)
  - Q. Reign of Pekah (Israel) (15:27–31)
  - R. Reign of Jotham (Judah) (15:32–38)
  - S. Reign of Ahaz (Judah) (16:1–20)
  - T. Reign of Hoshea (Israel) (17:1–41)
    - 1. Evaluation and Imprisonment of Hoshea (17:1–4)
    - 2. Final Collapse of Israel (17:5–23)
    - 3. Israel's Captivity and Resettlement of the Land (17:24–41)
- II. The Single Kingdom: Judah After Israel's Collapse (18:1—25:21)
  - A. Reign of Hezekiah (18:1—20:21)
    - 1. Revival and Reform (18:1–8)
    - 2. Review of Israel's Fall and God's Deliverance of Judah from Two Assyrian Invasions (18:9—19:37)
    - 3. Hezekiah's Illness and Healing (20:1–11)
    - 4. Hezekiah's Foolishness and Death (20:12–21)
  - B. Reign of Manasseh (21:1–18)
  - C. Reign of Amon (21:19–26)
  - D. Reign of Josiah (22:1—23:30)
    - 1. Revival and Reform (22:1—23:25)
    - 2. God's Wrath Delayed but not Averted and Josiah's Death (23:26–30)
  - E. Reign of Jehoahaz (23:31–33)
  - F. Reign of Jehoiakim (23:34—24:7)

G. Reign of Jehoiachin (24:8–16)
H. Reign of Zedekiah (24:17—25:21)
1. Fall of Jerusalem (25:1–7)
2. Destruction of the Temple and City Walls (25:8–10,13–17)
3. Final Deportation of the People to Babylon (25:11–21)
III. Postlude (25:22–30)

Author: Anonymous

Theme: Kings of Israel and Judah

Date of Writing: c. 560–550 B.C.

Background

Because 1 and 2 Kings are one continuous history, important background information for 2 Kings is contained in the introduction to 1 Kings. 2 Kings resumes tracing the decline of Israel and Judah, beginning at about 852 B.C. It records the two great national calamities that brought about the dissolution of the kingdoms of Israel and Judah: (1) the destruction of Israel's capital, Samaria, and that nation's deportation to Assyria in 722 B.C. and (2) the destruction of Jerusalem and Judah's deportation to Babylon in 586 B.C. 2 Kings covers the last 130 years of Judah's 345-year history. The greater instability of Israel (i.e., the northern ten tribes) is evidenced by its constant change of kings (19) and dynasties (nine) in 210 years, compared with Judah's 20 kings and one dynasty (briefly interrupted) over 345 years.

Many OT writing prophets ministered during the time recorded in 2 Kings. They reminded, warned and exhorted the kings concerning their responsibilities to God as his theocratic representatives. Amos and Hosea prophesied in Israel, while Joel, Isaiah, Micah, Nahum, Habakkuk, Zephaniah and Jeremiah prophesied in Judah. These prophets' books provide important historical and theological revelation not contained in 2 Kings concerning the spiritual and moral decline of both nations.

Purpose

2 Kings has the same purpose as 1 Kings (see the introduction to 1 Kings). In brief the original purpose was to provide the Hebrew people, especially the exiles in Babylon, with a prophetic interpretation and understanding of their history during the divided monarchy, so that they might not repeat the sins of their forefathers.

Survey

The history of 2 Kings divides into two major eras: (1) the history of both kingdoms before the fall of Israel (the ten tribes) in 722 B.C. (chs. 1—17) and (2) the history of Judah after Israel's collapse until her own fall in 586 B.C. (chs. 18—25). On the one hand, Israel had an unbroken succession of kings who "did evil in the eyes of the LORD" (e.g., 3:2). 2 Kings records that in the midst of Israel's terrible apostasy, God raised up mighty prophets such as Elijah and Elisha to call the nation and its leaders back to God and his covenant (chs. 1—9).

Judah, on the other hand, did at times have a reprieve from evil kings in godly rulers like Hezekiah (chs. 18—21) and Josiah (chs. 22—23), who sought to turn the heart of the nation back to God. Nevertheless, such kings were unable to alter permanently the prevailing tide of idolatry, immorality and violence. After Josiah's death (ch. 23), Judah's slide to destruction was rapid, culminating in Nebuchadnezzar's sack of Jerusalem in 586 B.C. (ch. 25).

Special Features

Five major features characterize 2 Kings. (1) It emphasizes (as did 1 Kings) the importance of the prophets and their revelation as God's primary means for getting his message through to the kings and people of Israel and Judah—e.g., Elijah and Elisha (chs. 1—13),

Jonah (14:25), Isaiah (19:1–7,20–34) and Huldah (22:14–20). (2) Elisha's miraculous ministry is highlighted throughout much of the first half of the book (chs. 2—13). (3) It gives only two kings in all of Israel and Judah unqualified approval as being faithful to God and the people: Hezekiah (18:1—20:21) and Josiah (22:1—23:29). (4) It reveals that unrighteous leaders will eventually lead a people to ruin and illustrates the enduring principle that "righteousness exalts a nation, but sin is a disgrace to any people" (Pr 14:34). (5) It contains many well-known Bible stories, such as Elijah going to heaven in a whirlwind (ch. 2), Elisha raising the Shunammite's son from the dead (ch. 4), the healing of Naaman (ch. 5), the floating of an axhead in water (ch. 6), Jezebel's violent death as prophesied by Elijah (ch. 9), the great revivals under Hezekiah (ch. 18) and Josiah (ch. 23), and Hezekiah's serious sickness and his healing (ch. 20).

New Testament Fulfillment

2 Kings makes clear that the sin and unfaithfulness of Judah's kings (i.e., David's descendants) resulted in the destruction of Jerusalem and the Davidic kingdom. The NT makes it equally clear, however, that God in his faithfulness fulfilled his covenant promise to David through Jesus Christ, "the son of David" (Mt 1:1; 9:27–31; 21:9), whose reign and kingdom will never end (Lk 1:32–33; cf. Isa 9:7).

Reading 2 Kings

In order to read the entire Old Testament in one year, the book of 2 Kings should be read in 10 days, according to the following schedule: ☐ 1–3 ☐ 4–5 ☐ 6–7 ☐ 8–9 ☐ 10–12 ☐ 13–15 ☐ 16–17 ☐ 18–19 ☐ 20–22 ☐ 23–25

NOTES

The LORD's Judgment on Ahaziah

1 After Ahab's death, Moab[a] rebelled against Israel. 2Now Ahaziah had fallen through the lattice of his
upper room in Samaria and injured
himself. So he sent messengers,[b] saying to them, "Go and consult Baal-Zebub,[c] the god of Ekron,[d] to see if I
will recover[e] from this injury."
3But the angel[f] of the LORD said to
Elijah[g] the Tishbite, "Go up and meet
the messengers of the king of Samaria
and ask them, 'Is it because there is no
God in Israel[h] that you are going off
to consult Baal-Zebub, the god of Ekron?' 4Therefore this is what the LORD
says: 'You will not leave[i] the bed you
are lying on. You will certainly die!' "
So Elijah went.
5When the messengers returned to
the king, he asked them, "Why have
you come back?"
6"A man came to meet us," they replied. "And he said to us, 'Go back to
the king who sent you and tell him,
"This is what the LORD says: Is it because there is no God in Israel that you
are sending men to consult Baal-Zebub, the god of Ekron? Therefore you
will not leave[j] the bed you are lying
on. You will certainly die!" ' "
7The king asked them, "What kind
of man was it who came to meet you
and told you this?"
8They replied, "He was a man with
a garment of hair[k] and with a leather
belt around his waist."
The king said, "That was Elijah the
Tishbite."
9Then he sent[l] to Elijah a captain[m]
with his company of fifty men. The captain went up to Elijah, who was sitting
on the top of a hill, and said to him,
"Man of God, the king says, 'Come
down!' "
10Elijah answered the captain, "If I
am a man of God, may fire come down
from heaven and consume you and
your fifty men!" Then fire[n] fell from
heaven and consumed the captain and
his men.
11At this the king sent to Elijah another captain with his fifty men. The
captain said to him, "Man of God, this
is what the king says, 'Come down at
once!' "
12"If I am a man of God," Elijah replied, "may fire come down from heav-
en and consume you and your fifty
men!" Then the fire of God fell from
heaven and consumed him and his fifty
men.
13So the king sent a third captain
with his fifty men. This third captain
went up and fell on his knees before
Elijah. "Man of God," he begged,
"please have respect for my life[o] and
the lives of these fifty men, your servants! 14See, fire has fallen from heav-
en and consumed the first two captains
and all their men. But now have respect for my life!"
15The angel[p] of the LORD said to Elijah, "Go down with him; do not be
afraid[q] of him." So Elijah got up and
went down with him to the king.
16He told the king, "This is what the
LORD says: Is it because there is no God
in Israel for you to consult that you
have sent messengers[r] to consult
Baal-Zebub, the god of Ekron? Because
you have done this, you will never
leave[s] the bed you are lying on. You
will certainly die!" 17So he died,[t] according to the word of the LORD that
Elijah had spoken.
Because Ahaziah had no son, Joram[a][u] succeeded him as king in the
second year of Jehoram son of Jehoshaphat king of Judah. 18As for all the other events of Ahaziah's reign, and what
he did, are they not written in the book
of the annals of the kings of Israel?

Elijah Taken Up to Heaven

2 When the LORD was about to take[v]
Elijah up to heaven in a whirl-
wind,[w] Elijah and Elisha[x] were on
their way from Gilgal.[y] 2Elijah said to
Elisha, "Stay here;[z] the LORD has sent
me to Bethel."
But Elisha said, "As surely as the
LORD lives and as you live, I will not

1:1 [a]S Ge 19:37; 2Ki 3:5
1:2 [b]ver 16 [c]S Mk 3:22 [d]1Sa 6:2; Isa 2:6; 14:29 [e]S Jdg 18:5
1:3 [f]ver 15 [g]1Ki 17:1 [h]S 1Sa 28:8
1:4 [i]ver 6,16; Ps 41:8
1:6 [j]S ver 4
1:8 [k]S 1Ki 18:7; Mt 3:4; Mk 1:6
1:9 [l]2Ki 6:14 [m]Ex 18:25; Isa 3:3
1:10 [n]S 1Ki 18:38; S Rev 11:5; S 13:13
1:13 [o]Ps 72:14
1:15 [p]ver 3 [q]Isa 51:12; 57:11; Jer 1:17; Eze 2:6
1:16 [r]S ver 2 [s]ver 4
1:17 [t]2Ki 8:15; Jer 20:6; 28:17 [u]2Ki 3:1; 8:16
2:1 [v]S Ge 5:24 [w]ver 11; 1Ki 19:11; Isa 5:28; 66:15; Jer 4:13; Na 1:3 [x]S 1Ki 19:16,21 [y]S Dt 11:30; 2Ki 4:38
2:2 [z]ver 6

[a] 17 Hebrew *Jehoram,* a variant of *Joram*

1:8 A GARMENT OF HAIR. A shaggy mantle of sheepskin, goatskin or camel's hair was a mark of the prophetic office from Elijah on, including John the Baptist (cf. Zec 13:4; Mt 3:4; Heb 11:37). Elijah's leather belt was what the poor normally wore. The prophet's dress was a sign of contempt for the materialistic display of the wealthy upper class (cf. Isa 20:2; Mt 11:7–8).

1:10 FIRE FELL FROM HEAVEN. The king and his soldiers, in rebellion against God and his word, tried to arrest Elijah. The fire came directly by God's hand (v. 12) as a judgment against Ahaziah, who had stubbornly persisted in opposing God and the prophet.

leave you."[a] So they went down to Bethel.

3The company[b] of the prophets at Bethel came out to Elisha and asked, "Do you know that the LORD is going to take your master from you today?"

"Yes, I know," Elisha replied, "but do not speak of it."

4Then Elijah said to him, "Stay here, Elisha; the LORD has sent me to Jericho.[c]"

And he replied, "As surely as the LORD lives and as you live, I will not leave you." So they went to Jericho.

5The company[d] of the prophets at Jericho went up to Elisha and asked him, "Do you know that the LORD is going to take your master from you today?"

"Yes, I know," he replied, "but do not speak of it."

6Then Elijah said to him, "Stay here;[e] the LORD has sent me to the Jordan."[f]

And he replied, "As surely as the LORD lives and as you live, I will not leave you."[g] So the two of them walked on.

7Fifty men of the company of the prophets went and stood at a distance, facing the place where Elijah and Elisha had stopped at the Jordan. 8Elijah took his cloak,[h] rolled it up and struck[i] the water with it. The water divided[j] to the right and to the left, and the two of them crossed over on dry[k] ground.

9When they had crossed, Elijah said to Elisha, "Tell me, what can I do for you before I am taken from you?"

"Let me inherit a double[l] portion of your spirit,"[m] Elisha replied.

10"You have asked a difficult thing," Elijah said, "yet if you see me when I am taken from you, it will be yours—otherwise not."

11As they were walking along and talking together, suddenly a chariot of fire[n] and horses of fire appeared and separated the two of them, and Elijah went up to heaven[o] in a whirlwind.[p] 12Elisha saw this and cried out, "My father! My father! The chariots[q] and horsemen of Israel!" And Elisha saw him no more. Then he took hold of his own clothes and tore[r] them apart.

13He picked up the cloak that had fallen from Elijah and went back and stood on the bank of the Jordan. 14Then he took the cloak[s] that had fallen from him and struck[t] the water with it. "Where now is the LORD, the God of Elijah?" he asked. When he struck the water, it divided to the right and to the left, and he crossed over.

15The company[u] of the prophets from Jericho, who were watching, said, "The spirit[v] of Elijah is resting on Elisha." And they went to meet him and bowed to the ground before him. 16"Look," they said, "we your servants have fifty able men. Let them go and look for your master. Perhaps the Spirit[w] of the LORD has picked him up[x] and set him down on some mountain or in some valley."

"No," Elisha replied, "do not send them."

17But they persisted until he was too ashamed[y] to refuse. So he said, "Send them." And they sent fifty men, who searched for three days but did not find him. 18When they returned to Elisha, who was staying in Jericho, he said to them, "Didn't I tell you not to go?"

2:2 [a]Ru 1:16
2:3 [b]S 1Sa 10:5
2:4 [c]Jos 3:16
2:5 [d]ver 3
2:6 [e]ver 2 [f]Jos 3:15 [g]Ru 1:16
2:8 [h]S 1Ki 19:19 [i]ver 14 [j]S Ex 14:21 [k]Ex 14:22,29
2:9 [l]S Dt 21:17 [m]S Nu 11:17
2:11 [n]2Ki 6:17; Ps 68:17; 104:3,4; Isa 66:15; Hab 3:8; Zec 6:1 [o]S Ge 5:24 [p]S ver 1
2:12 [q]2Ki 6:17; 13:14 [r]S Ge 37:29
2:14 [s]S 1Ki 19:19 [t]ver 8
2:15 [u]S 1Sa 10:5 [v]S Nu 11:17
2:16 [w]S 1Ki 18:12 [x]Ac 8:39
2:17 [y]S Jdg 3:25

2:3 COMPANY OF THE PROPHETS. The companies of the prophets (see 1Ki 20:35, note) appear to have been located primarily in three areas—Gilgal, Bethel and Jericho (see 2:3,5,15; 4:38). God evidently sent Elijah to these communities in order to encourage them one last time and to announce that Elisha would be their new leader (cf. vv. 1,15).

2:9 DOUBLE PORTION OF YOUR SPIRIT. The term "double portion" does not necessarily mean twice the spiritual power of Elijah; rather, it refers to a father-son relationship, where the firstborn son received twice the inheritance the other sons received (Dt 21:17). Elisha was asking his spiritual father to give him an abundant measure of his prophetic spirit in order that he might carry on Elijah's mission. God granted Elisha's request, knowing that the young prophet was willing to remain faithful to him in the face of the spiritual, moral and doctrinal apostasy all around him.

2:11–12 CHARIOT OF FIRE AND HORSES OF FIRE. Elijah was taken to heaven, as was Enoch (Ge 5:24), without experiencing death. (1) The miraculous transporting of Elijah to heaven was God's emphatic seal of approval on the prophet's work, spirit and ministry. Elijah had been totally united to the word of God throughout his ministry. To the very last he had lived for God's honor, stood against the sin and idolatry of an apostate people, and encouraged the faithful remnant in Israel. He was given a dramatic escort to heaven in triumph. (2) The translation of Elijah and Enoch is like the future catching up of God's faithful people at Christ's return (1Th 4:16–17).

Healing of the Water

19 The men of the city said to Elisha,
"Look, our lord, this town is well situated, as you can see, but the water is
bad and the land is unproductive."
20 "Bring me a new bowl," he said,
"and put salt in it." So they brought it
to him.
21 Then he went out to the spring and
threw[z] the salt into it, saying, "This is
what the LORD says: 'I have healed this
water. Never again will it cause death
or make the land unproductive.' "
22 And the water has remained wholesome[a] to this day, according to the
word Elisha had spoken.

Elisha Is Jeered

23 From there Elisha went up to
Bethel. As he was walking along the
road, some youths came out of the
town and jeered[b] at him. "Go on up,
you baldhead!" they said. "Go on up,
you baldhead!" 24 He turned around,
looked at them and called down a
curse[c] on them in the name[d] of the
LORD. Then two bears came out of the
woods and mauled forty-two of the
youths. 25 And he went on to Mount
Carmel[e] and from there returned to
Samaria.

Moab Revolts

3 Joram[b][f] son of Ahab became
king of Israel in Samaria in the
eighteenth year of Jehoshaphat king of
Judah, and he reigned twelve years.
2 He did evil[g] in the eyes of the LORD,
but not as his father[h] and mother had
done. He got rid of the sacred stone[i]
of Baal that his father had made. 3 Nevertheless he clung to the sins[j] of Jeroboam son of Nebat, which he had
caused Israel to commit; he did not
turn away from them.
4 Now Mesha king of Moab[k] raised
sheep, and he had to supply the king of
Israel with a hundred thousand
lambs[l] and with the wool of a hundred
thousand rams. 5 But after Ahab died,
the king of Moab rebelled[m] against the
king of Israel. 6 So at that time King
Joram set out from Samaria and mobilized all Israel. 7 He also sent this message to Jehoshaphat king of Judah:
"The king of Moab has rebelled against
me. Will you go with me to fight[n]
against Moab?"
"I will go with you," he replied. "I am
as you are, my people as your people,
my horses as your horses."
8 "By what route shall we attack?" he
asked.
"Through the Desert of Edom," he
answered.
9 So the king of Israel set out with
the king of Judah and the king of
Edom.[o] After a roundabout march of
seven days, the army had no more water for themselves or for the animals
with them.
10 "What!" exclaimed the king of Israel. "Has the LORD called us three
kings together only to hand us over to
Moab?"
11 But Jehoshaphat asked, "Is there
no prophet of the LORD here, that we
may inquire[p] of the LORD through
him?"
An officer of the king of Israel answered, "Elisha[q] son of Shaphat is
here. He used to pour water on the
hands of Elijah."[c][r]
12 Jehoshaphat said, "The word[s] of
the LORD is with him." So the king of
Israel and Jehoshaphat and the king of
Edom went down to him.
13 Elisha said to the king of Israel,
"What do we have to do with each oth-

2:21 [z] S Ex 15:25; 2Ki 4:41; 6:6
2:22 [a] Ex 15:25
2:23 [b] S Ex 22:28; 2Ch 30:10; 36:16; Job 19:18; Ps 31:18
2:24 [c] S Ge 4:11 [d] S Dt 18:19
2:25 [e] S 1Ki 18:20
3:1 [f] S 2Ki 1:17
3:2 [g] 1Ki 15:26 [h] 1Ki 16:30-32 [i] S Ex 23:24
3:3 [j] S 1Ki 12:28-32
3:4 [k] S Ge 19:37; 2Ki 1:1 [l] Ezr 7:17; Isa 16:1
3:5 [m] S 2Ki 1:1
3:7 [n] 1Ki 22:4
3:9 [o] S 1Ki 22:47
3:11 [p] S Ge 25:22; S 1Ki 22:5 [q] S Ge 20:7 [r] S 1Ki 19:16
3:12 [s] S Nu 11:17

b *1* Hebrew *Jehoram,* a variant of *Joram;* also in verse 6 c *11* That is, he was Elijah's personal servant.

2:23 JEERED AT HIM. Some believe that the youths who mocked Elisha were a gang organized to oppose his ministry. Though the Hebrew word *na'ar* is used as a general word for "boy" and is often applied to older youths when used alone (cf. Ge 22:5; 41:12), the Hebrew here is *na'arim qatanim* ("little boys"). Older youths would undoubtedly have been out in the fields. But as happens even today, this outsider coming into a village attracted a group of small boys. These children may have heard their parents mock the news that Elijah had gone up to heaven, possibly saying, "If Elisha says that, then let him show us how it is done. Let him go on up, the old baldhead." The mockery against the prophet demonstrated disdain for the Lord himself (cf. Eze 16:8; Ac 5:4).

2:24 A CURSE ON THEM IN THE NAME OF THE LORD. To avenge the Lord's honor, Elisha pronounced on them the divine judgment expressed in the covenant law of blessings and curses (Lev 26:21–22; Dt 30:19). God himself judged the depraved children by sending the two bears (cf. Gal 6:7). The judgment at Bethel was a warning to Israel that God's covenant curses awaited them if they persisted in rebellion against God (cf. Dt 30:15–20). Note that the bears injured the youths, but apparently did not kill them.

er? Go to the prophets of your father
and the prophets of your mother."
"No," the king of Israel answered,
"because it was the LORD who called us
three kings together to hand us over to
Moab."
14Elisha said, "As surely as the LORD
Almighty lives, whom I serve, if I did
not have respect for the presence of Jehoshaphat king of Judah, I would not
look at you or even notice you. 15But
now bring me a harpist."[t]
While the harpist was playing, the
hand[u] of the LORD came upon Elisha
16and he said, "This is what the LORD
says: Make this valley full of ditches.
17For this is what the LORD says: You
will see neither wind nor rain, yet this
valley will be filled with water,[v] and
you, your cattle and your other animals
will drink. 18This is an easy[w] thing in
the eyes of the LORD; he will also hand
Moab over to you. 19You will overthrow
every fortified city and every major
town. You will cut down every good
tree, stop up all the springs, and ruin
every good field with stones."
20The next morning, about the
time[x] for offering the sacrifice, there
it was—water flowing from the direction of Edom! And the land was filled
with water.[y]
21Now all the Moabites had heard
that the kings had come to fight
against them; so every man, young and
old, who could bear arms was called up
and stationed on the border. 22When
they got up early in the morning, the
sun was shining on the water. To the
Moabites across the way, the water
looked red—like blood. 23"That's
blood!" they said. "Those kings must
have fought and slaughtered each other. Now to the plunder, Moab!"
24But when the Moabites came to
the camp of Israel, the Israelites rose
up and fought them until they fled. And
the Israelites invaded the land and
slaughtered the Moabites. 25They destroyed the towns, and each man threw
a stone on every good field until it was
covered. They stopped up all the
springs and cut down every good tree.
Only Kir Hareseth[z] was left with its
stones in place, but men armed with
slings surrounded it and attacked it as
well.
26When the king of Moab saw that
the battle had gone against him, he
took with him seven hundred swordsmen to break through to the king of
Edom, but they failed. 27Then he took
his firstborn[a] son, who was to succeed him as king, and offered him as a
sacrifice on the city wall. The fury
against Israel was great; they withdrew and returned to their own land.

The Widow's Oil

4 The wife of a man from the company[b] of the prophets cried out to
Elisha, "Your servant my husband is
dead, and you know that he revered the
LORD. But now his creditor[c] is coming
to take my two boys as his slaves."
2Elisha replied to her, "How can I
help you? Tell me, what do you have in
your house?"
"Your servant has nothing there at
all," she said, "except a little oil."[d]

3:15 [t] S 1Sa 10:5 [u] Jer 15:17; Eze 1:3
3:17 [v] Ps 107:35; Isa 12:3; 32:2; 35:6; 41:18; 65:13
3:18 [w] S Ge 18:14; 2Ki 20:10; Isa 49:6; Jer 32:17,27; Mk 10:27
3:20 [x] S Ex 29:41 [y] S Ex 17:6
3:25 [z] Isa 15:1; 16:7; Jer 48:31,36
3:27 [a] S Dt 12:31; 2Ki 16:3; 21:6; 2Ch 28:3; Ps 106:38; Jer 19:4-5; Mic 6:7
4:1 [b] S 1Sa 10:5 [c] S Ex 22:26; Lev 25:39-43; Ne 5:3-5; Job 22:6; 24:9
4:2 [d] S 1Ki 17:12

3:15 THE HARPIST WAS PLAYING. The music of the harp helped seal off all outside distraction and the unbelief around him, bringing Elisha into a frame of mind and spirit to receive the Lord's revelation.

3:27 FIRSTBORN SON .... OFFERED HIM AS A SACRIFICE. The king of Moab put his oldest son to death as an offering to the god Chemosh (see 1Ki 11:7), in an effort to persuade the supposed deity to help his army in battle. This human sacrifice was in reality a sacrifice to Satan and demons (see article on THE NATURE OF IDOLATRY, p. 394); "the sacrifices of pagans are offered to demons" (1Co 10:20). Archaeologists have discovered a Moabite stone confirming that Moab's king really did carry out this wicked deed.

3:27 THE FURY AGAINST ISRAEL WAS GREAT. Israel's armies withdrew in a hasty retreat. The wrath of the Moabite army that came against them was presumably the result of the human sacrifice offered to the demonic power behind Chemosh (see previous note). It appears that power is unleashed in the spiritual realm by blood sacrifices—both for incomparably great good, as through Christ's blood, and for abominable evil, as in the sacrifice here; it could well be that blood sacrifices offered to demonic powers release them to do battle more effectively against the spiritual forces of the Lord (cf. Eph 6:12).

4:1 WIFE OF A MAN FROM THE COMPANY OF THE PROPHETS. Elisha's miraculous acts recorded in ch. 4 present spiritual truths in dramatic action. The narrative of the widow and her two children reveals that God cares for his faithful who are in need and trouble. The widow and her children represent God's forsaken and oppressed people. In both the OT and NT, compassion for and care of the needy are signs of genuine faith in God and true piety (Ex 22:22–24; Dt 10:18; 14:29; Job 29:12; Jas 1:27; see article on THE CARE OF THE POOR AND NEEDY, p. 1316).

3Elisha said, "Go around and ask all
your neighbors for empty jars. Don't
ask for just a few. **4**Then go inside and
shut the door behind you and your
sons. Pour oil into all the jars, and as
each is filled, put it to one side."
5She left him and afterward shut the
door behind her and her sons. They
brought the jars to her and she kept
pouring. **6**When all the jars were full,
she said to her son, "Bring me another
one."
But he replied, "There is not a jar
left." Then the oil stopped flowing.
7She went and told the man of
God,[e] and he said, "Go, sell the oil and
pay your debts. You and your sons can
live on what is left."

The Shunammite's Son Restored to Life

8One day Elisha went to Shunem.[f]
And a well-to-do woman was there.
who urged him to stay for a meal. So
whenever he came by, he stopped there
to eat. **9**She said to her husband, "I
know that this man who often comes
our way is a holy man of God. **10**Let's
make a small room on the roof and put
in it a bed and a table, a chair and a
lamp for him. Then he can stay[g] there
whenever he comes to us."
11One day when Elisha came, he
went up to his room and lay down
there. **12**He said to his servant Gehazi,
"Call the Shunammite."[h] So he called
her, and she stood before him. **13**Elisha
said to him, "Tell her, 'You have gone
to all this trouble for us. Now what can
be done for you? Can we speak on your
behalf to the king or the commander of
the army?' "
She replied, "I have a home among
my own people."
14"What can be done for her?" Elisha
asked.
Gehazi said, "Well, she has no son
and her husband is old."
15Then Elisha said, "Call her." So he
called her, and she stood in the doorway. **16**"About this time[i] next year,"
Elisha said, "you will hold a son in your
arms."
"No, my lord," she objected. "Don't
mislead your servant, O man of God!"
17But the woman became pregnant,
and the next year about that same time
she gave birth to a son, just as Elisha
had told her.
18The child grew, and one day he
went out to his father, who was with
the reapers.[j] **19**"My head! My head!"
he said to his father.
His father told a servant, "Carry him
to his mother." **20**After the servant had
lifted him up and carried him to his
mother, the boy sat on her lap until
noon, and then he died. **21**She went up
and laid him on the bed[k] of the man
of God, then shut the door and went
out.
22She called her husband and said,
"Please send me one of the servants
and a donkey so I can go to the man of
God quickly and return."
23"Why go to him today?" he asked.
"It's not the New Moon[l] or the Sabbath."
"It's all right," she said.
24She saddled the donkey and said
to her servant, "Lead on; don't slow
down for me unless I tell you." **25**So
she set out and came to the man of God
at Mount Carmel.[m]
When he saw her in the distance, the
man of God said to his servant Gehazi,
"Look! There's the Shunammite!
26Run to meet her and ask her, 'Are

4:7 [e] S 1Ki 12:22
4:8 [f] S Jos 19:18
4:10 [g] Mt 10:41; S Ro 12:13
4:12 [h] 2Ki 8:1
4:16 [i] S Ge 18:10
4:18 [j] S Ru 2:3
4:21 [k] ver 32
4:23 [l] S Nu 10:10; 1Ch 23:31; Ps 81:3
4:25 [m] S 1Ki 18:20

4:8 SHUNEM . . . WELL-TO-DO WOMAN. The narrative of this wealthy Shunammite woman contains three key episodes. (1) God blessed the faithful woman by giving her a son (vv. 8–17). (2) God caused her to be severely tested by permitting the son to be taken from her (vv. 18–21). (3) God restored her son's life as she held firmly to God's word of promise (vv. 22–37). Many times God allows his faithful ones to pass through inexplicable trials and afflictions (cf. Heb 11:17–40; Job 1—2), but then later they experience his love, grace and compassion as they hold firmly to him in faith (cf. Ps 25:10; Ro 8:28; Heb 11:6).

4:21 MAN OF GOD. Elisha was especially known by people from all walks of life as "the man of God" (e.g., 4:9,16,22,25,27,40; 5:8; 6:6,9–10; 7:18; 8:4,8,11). The highest tribute that can be paid to any minister is that he is a "man of God." The following are five characteristics of this man of God. (1) He maintained intimate and persevering communion with God. He knew God and was known by him. (2) He was a holy man, fully set apart from the religious and moral compromise of his day and dedicated to the Lord God of Israel. (3) He empathized with God over the sins of the covenant people and opposed the tide of idolatry and apostasy in Israel. (4) The Spirit of the Lord was upon him, enabling him to speak with spiritual authority as God's representative and to proclaim the word of the Lord faithfully. (5) As a prophet of enormous stature and gifts, his ministry was affirmed by God with mighty miracles and signs.

you all right? Is your husband all right?
Is your child all right?' "
"Everything is all right," she said.
27When she reached the man of God
at the mountain, she took hold of his
feet. Gehazi came over to push her
away, but the man of God said, "Leave
her alone! She is in bitter distress,[n]
but the LORD has hidden it from me and
has not told me why."
28"Did I ask you for a son, my lord?"
she said. "Didn't I tell you, 'Don't raise
my hopes'?"
29Elisha said to Gehazi, "Tuck your
cloak into your belt,[o] take my staff[p]
in your hand and run. If you meet anyone, do not greet him, and if anyone
greets you, do not answer. Lay my staff
on the boy's face."
30But the child's mother said, "As
surely as the LORD lives and as you live,
I will not leave you." So he got up and
followed her.
31Gehazi went on ahead and laid the
staff on the boy's face, but there was
no sound or response. So Gehazi went
back to meet Elisha and told him, "The
boy has not awakened."
32When Elisha reached the house,
there was the boy lying dead on his
couch.[q] 33He went in, shut the door
on the two of them and prayed[r] to the
LORD. 34Then he got on the bed and lay
upon the boy, mouth to mouth, eyes to
eyes, hands to hands. As he
stretched[s] himself out upon him, the
boy's body grew warm. 35Elisha turned
away and walked back and forth in the
room and then got on the bed and
stretched out upon him once more. The
boy sneezed seven times[t] and opened
his eyes.[u]
36Elisha summoned Gehazi and
said, "Call the Shunammite." And he
did. When she came, he said, "Take
your son."[v] 37She came in, fell at his
feet and bowed to the ground. Then she
took her son and went out.

Death in the Pot

38Elisha returned to Gilgal[w] and
there was a famine[x] in that region.
While the company of the prophets was
meeting with him, he said to his servant, "Put on the large pot and cook
some stew for these men."
39One of them went out into the
fields to gather herbs and found a wild
vine. He gathered some of its gourds
and filled the fold of his cloak. When he
returned, he cut them up into the pot
of stew, though no one knew what they
were. 40The stew was poured out for
the men, but as they began to eat it,
they cried out, "O man of God, there is
death in the pot!" And they could not
eat it.
41Elisha said, "Get some flour." He
put it into the pot and said, "Serve it to
the people to eat." And there was nothing harmful in the pot.[y]

Feeding of a Hundred

42A man came from Baal Shalishah,[z] bringing the man of God twenty loaves[a] of barley bread[b] baked
from the first ripe grain, along with
some heads of new grain. "Give it to
the people to eat," Elisha said.
43"How can I set this before a hundred men?" his servant asked.
But Elisha answered, "Give it to the
people to eat.[c] For this is what the
LORD says: 'They will eat and have
some left over.[d]' " 44Then he set it before them, and they ate and had some
left over, according to the word of the
LORD.

Naaman Healed of Leprosy

5 Now Naaman was commander of
the army of the king of Aram.[e] He

4:27 [n] 1Sa 1:15
4:29 [o] S 1Ki 18:46 [p] S Ex 4:2
4:32 [q] ver 21
4:33 [r] 1Ki 17:20; Mt 6:6
4:34 [s] 1Ki 17:21; Ac 20:10
4:35 [t] S Jos 6:15 [u] 2Ki 8:5
4:36 [v] Heb 11:35
4:38 [w] S 2Ki 2:1 [x] S Lev 26:26; 2Ki 8:1
4:41 [y] S Ex 15:25; S 2Ki 2:21
4:42 [z] 1Sa 9:4 [a] Mt 14:17; 15:36 [b] S 1Sa 9:7
4:43 [c] Lk 9:13 [d] Mt 14:20; Jn 6:12
5:1 [e] S Ge 10:22; S 2Sa 10:19

4:38–44 FAMINE IN THAT REGION. These two narratives about the needs of the "company of the prophets" illustrate the truth that "the eyes of the LORD are on those who fear him, on those whose hope is in his unfailing love, to deliver them from death and keep them alive in famine" (Ps 33:18–19). The remnant who remain faithful to God's Word are under the Lord's special care (cf. Mk 16:18).

4:39 TO GATHER HERBS. Unlike the affluent lifestyle of the wealthy, the lifestyle of the company of the prophets (see 1Ki 20:35, note) was simple, involving faithful service and self-denial (cf. 2Co 4:7–12; 6:4–10).

4:42 BRINGING THE MAN OF GOD . . . NEW GRAIN. Evidently the man from Baal Shalishah refused to give his offering to the corrupt priests and Levites (1Ki 12:28–31); instead, being a godly man, he brought his offering to true prophets of the Lord, those who were faithful to his word and covenant obligations.

5:1 NAAMAN. The story of Naaman demonstrates God's providence (vv. 1–14), his saving power and grace (vv. 15–19), and his judgment on sin (vv. 20–27). Prominent in the narrative is the truth that God's grace and salvation were not confined to Israel, but that he desired to have compassion on non-Israelites and lead them to know the

was a great man in the sight of his
master and highly regarded, because
through him the LORD had given victory
to Aram. He was a valiant soldier, but
he had leprosy.[d][f]
2Now bands[g] from Aram had gone
out and had taken captive a young girl
from Israel, and she served Naaman's
wife. **3**She said to her mistress, "If only
my master would see the prophet[h]
who is in Samaria! He would cure him
of his leprosy."
4Naaman went to his master and
told him what the girl from Israel had
said. **5**"By all means, go," the king of
Aram replied. "I will send a letter to
the king of Israel." So Naaman left,
taking with him ten talents[e] of silver,
six thousand shekels[f] of gold and ten
sets of clothing.[i] **6**The letter that he
took to the king of Israel read: "With
this letter I am sending my servant Naaman to you so that you may cure him
of his leprosy."
7As soon as the king of Israel read
the letter,[j] he tore his robes and said,
"Am I God?[k] Can I kill and bring back
to life?[l] Why does this fellow send
someone to me to be cured of his leprosy? See how he is trying to pick a quarrel[m] with me!"
8When Elisha the man of God heard
that the king of Israel had torn his
robes, he sent him this message: "Why
have you torn your robes? Have the
man come to me and he will know that
there is a prophet[n] in Israel." **9**So Naaman went with his horses and chariots
and stopped at the door of Elisha's
house. **10**Elisha sent a messenger to
say to him, "Go, wash[o] yourself seven
times[p] in the Jordan, and your flesh
will be restored and you will be
cleansed."
11But Naaman went away angry and
said, "I thought that he would surely
come out to me and stand and call on
the name of the LORD his God, wave his
hand[q] over the spot and cure me of my
leprosy. **12**Are not Abana and Pharpar,
the rivers of Damascus, better than
any of the waters[r] of Israel? Couldn't
I wash in them and be cleansed?" So he
turned and went off in a rage.[s]
13Naaman's servants went to him
and said, "My father,[t] if the prophet
had told you to do some great thing,
would you not have done it? How much
more, then, when he tells you, 'Wash
and be cleansed'!" **14**So he went down
and dipped himself in the Jordan seven
times,[u] as the man of God had told
him, and his flesh was restored[v] and
became clean like that of a young
boy.[w] 2Ki 20:1-7
15Then Naaman and all his attendants went back to the man of God[x].
He stood before him and said, "Now I
know[y] that there is no God in all the
world except in Israel. Please accept
now a gift[z] from your servant."
16The prophet answered, "As surely
as the LORD lives, whom I serve, I will
not accept a thing." And even though
Naaman urged him, he refused.[a]
17"If you will not," said Naaman,
"please let me, your servant, be given
as much earth[b] as a pair of mules can
carry, for your servant will never again

5:1 [f]S Ex 4:6; S Nu 12:10; Lk 4:27 **5:2** [g]2Ki 6:23; 13:20; 24:2 **5:3** [h]S Ge 20:7 **5:5** [i]ver 22; S Ge 24:53; Jdg 14:12; S 1Sa 9:7 **5:7** [j]2Ki 19:14 [k]S Ge 30:2 [l]S Dt 32:39 [m]1Ki 20:7 **5:8** [n]S 1Ki 22:7 **5:10** [o]Jn 9:7 [p]S Ge 33:3; S Lev 14:7 **5:11** [q]S Ex 7:19 **5:12** [r]Isa 8:6 [s]Pr 14:17,29; 19:11; 29:11 **5:13** [t]2Ki 6:21; 13:14 **5:14** [u]S Ge 33:3; S Lev 14:7; S Jos 6:15 [v]S Ex 4:7 [w]Job 33:25 **5:15** [x]S Jos 2:11 [y]S Jos 4:24; S 1Sa 17:46 [z]S 1Sa 9:7 **5:16** [a]ver 20,26; Ge 14:23; Da 5:17 **5:17** [b]Ex 20:24

[d] *1* The Hebrew word was used for various diseases affecting the skin—not necessarily leprosy; also in verses 3, 6, 7, 11 and 27.
[e] *5* That is, about 750 pounds (about 340 kilograms) [f] *5* That is, about 150 pounds (about 70 kilograms)

one true God (see Lk 4:18–19,25–27).

5:10 WASH YOURSELF . . . IN THE JORDAN. Elisha instructed Naaman to wash himself in the muddy waters of the Jordan River as a simple demonstration of humility and obedience. Furthermore, by doing so, Naaman would find it impossible to ascribe the cure to humans or to natural means; both the Israelites and Arameans knew that the Jordan could not heal leprosy. Naaman needed to know that his healing came miraculously by God's grace and power through the word of his prophet.

5:13–14 WASH AND BE CLEANSED! This passage, along with many others in the OT, is prophetic of Jesus Christ, God's promised Messiah. For an analysis of this subject, see article on CHRIST IN THE OLD TESTAMENT, p. 518.

5:15 NO GOD IN ALL THE WORLD EXCEPT IN ISRAEL. It is amazing that Naaman, a foreigner, was miraculously delivered from leprosy and converted to the true God, while many lepers in Israel remained unclean. Jesus himself mentioned Naaman (Lk 4:27) in order to emphasize that when God's people disobey him and his word, he will take his kingdom from them and raise up others to experience his salvation, righteousness and kingdom power (cf. Mt 8:10–13; 23:37–39).

5:16 I WILL NOT ACCEPT A THING. God does not offer his services for a price only to those who can afford it; thus Elisha felt it would be inappropriate for him to profit from what God had done through him (cf. Mt 10:8; 2Co 2:17). Naaman's healing was a merciful act of God, which no amount of money could repay; he was now under an obligation of lifetime devotion to God (v. 17).

CHRIST IN THE OLD TESTAMENT

***2Ki 5:14** "So he went down and dipped himself in the Jordan seven times, as the man of God had told him, and his flesh was restored and became clean like that of a young boy."*

One of the fundamental NT teachings is that Jesus Christ (the Messiah) is the fulfillment of the OT. The writer to the Hebrews suggests that Christ is the heir of all that God had spoken through the prophets (Heb 1:1–2). Jesus himself asserted that he had come to fulfill the Law and the Prophets (Mt 5:17). After his glorious resurrection, he demonstrated to his followers from the Law of Moses, the Prophets and the Psalms (i.e., from the three main divisions of the Hebrew OT) that God had long ago predicted everything that had happened to him (Lk 24:25–27,44–46). To better understand the OT's prophecies about Jesus Christ, we must say something about *typology*.

PRINCIPLES OF TYPOLOGY. A careful study of the OT reveals elements (called *types*, from Gk *tupos*) that are fulfilled in the coming of the Messiah (who is the *antitype*); in other words, there is a correspondence between persons, events or things in the OT and Jesus Christ in the NT. Note two basic principles with respect to this pattern of prophecy and fulfillment: (1) In seeing how an OT passage points forward to Christ, we must always begin by looking at the passage as revealing an event within God's history of redemption, i.e., we must first examine an OT passage as a historical event and then see how it points forward to the coming of Jesus Christ as the promised Messiah.

(2) We must recognize that the Messianic fulfillment of an OT passage is often on a higher spiritual plane than the OT event. In fact, the OT people involved in the story may not themselves have seen that what they were experiencing was prophetic of the coming Son of God. For example, David probably did not realize when he wrote Ps 22 that his suffering was prophetic of Christ's suffering on the cross. Nor did the weeping exiles going past Rachel's tomb in Ramah (Jer 31:15) know that some day their tears would be fulfilled in the deaths of all boys two years old and under in Bethlehem (Mt 2:18). Often we are able to see an OT passage as prophetic of our Lord only in the light of NT revelation.

CATEGORIES OF PROPHETIC TYPES. We can identify at least four different patterns in which the OT points forward to and is prophetic of the coming of Christ in the NT. (1) *Specific OT texts quoted in the NT.* Certain passages of the OT are obviously prophetic of Christ because they are quoted as such in the NT; for example, Matthew cites Isa 7:14 to prove that the OT prophesied Christ's virgin birth (Mt 1:23), and Mic 5:2 to prove that Jesus was to be born in Bethlehem (Mt 2:6). Mark reminds his readers (Mk 1:2–3) that the coming of John the Baptist as the forerunner of Christ was prophesied both by Isaiah (Isa 40:3) and Malachi (Mal 3:1). Zechariah foretold Jesus' triumphal entry into Jerusalem on Palm Sunday (Zec. 9:9; cf. Mt 21:1–5; Jn 12:14–15). David's experience expressed in Ps 22:18 anticipates the soldiers at the cross dividing up Jesus' clothing (Jn 19:23–24), and his statement in Ps 16:8–11 is interpreted as a clear prediction of Jesus' resurrection (Ac 2:25–32; 13:35–37). The writer of the letter to the Hebrews asserts that Melchizedek (cf. Ge 14:18–20; Ps 110:4) is a type of Christ, our eternal high priest. There are many other examples that could be cited.

(2) *Allusions by NT writers to OT passages.* Another pattern whereby Christ can be found in the OT are those NT passages that, without actually quoting a specific text, refer to OT persons, events or things as prophetic of Christ. For example, in the Bible's very first prophetic text (Ge 3:15), God promises to send the offspring of the woman to destroy the serpent's offspring. Surely Paul had this passage in mind when he says that Christ was born of a woman to redeem those under law (Gal 4:4–5; cf. Ro 16:20), as did the apostle John when he maintains that the Son of God came to "destroy the devil's work" (1Jn 3:8). John the Baptist's reference to Jesus as the Lamb of God who takes

away the sin of the world (Jn 1:29,36) points back to Lev 16 and Isa 53:7, and Paul's reference to Jesus as "our Passover lamb" (1Co 5:7) shows that the killing of the Passover lamb prophesied of Christ's death for us (Ex 12:1–14). Jesus himself said that Moses lifting up the snake in the desert (Nu 21:4–9) was prophetic of him hanging on a cross. And when John says that Jesus, the Word of God, was involved in the creation of all things (Jn 1:1–3), we cannot help but think of Ps 33:6: "By the word of the LORD were the heavens made" (cf. Heb 1:3,10–12). These are only a few of the many NT allusions to OT passages that relate to Christ.

(3) *OT persons, events or things that focus on the theme of redemption.* Israel's exodus from Egypt, which is viewed throughout the OT as the greatest redemptive event under the old covenant, foreshadows Christ and the redemption he brings under the new covenant. Some types in the book of Exodus that foreshadow Christ and his redemption are Moses, the Passover, the Red Sea crossing, manna, the water from the rock, the tabernacle and its furnishings, and the high priest.

(4) *Patterns in OT events that foreshadow the way God deals with us in Christ.* Many of the stories in the OT reveal a pattern of God's dealings with his people that is brought to fulfillment in Jesus Christ. Note the following examples: (a) Abraham had to wait patiently nearly twenty-five years for God to open Sarah's womb and give them Isaac. Nothing he did could hurry along the birth of that son of God's promise. This pattern is fulfilled in the NT, as God sent his own Son as Savior of the world, when the time had fully come (Gal 4:4); nothing humans did could hurry it along. Our salvation comes only by God's initiative (cf. Jn 3:16), not by human effort. (b) Before the Israelites were redeemed out of Egypt by God's gracious power, they had to cry out in desperation to their God to be freed from their enemies (Ex 2:23–24; 3:7). This is prophetic of God's redemptive plan in Christ for us. Before we can expect deliverance by God's grace from our sins and spiritual enemies, we must cry out in repentance and ask for his saving grace (cf. Ac 2:37–38; 16:29–33; 17:30–31). All those who call on the name of the Lord will be saved. (c) When Naaman the Aramean sought healing from the God of Israel for his leprosy, he was told to wash himself seven times in the Jordan River. Though this made him angry initially, he had to humble himself and submit to the Jordan washing in order to be healed (2Ki 5:1–14). This passage foreshadows Jesus and the new covenant—both that God's saving grace reaches beyond the limits of the nation of Israel (cf. Lk 4:27; Ac 22:21; Ro 15:8–12), and that in order to receive salvation, we must forsake our pride, humble ourselves before God (cf. Jas 4:10; 1Pe 5:6), and seek to be washed in the blood of Jesus, God's provision for our cleansing (cf. Ac 22:16; 1Co 6:11; Tit 3:5; 1Jn 1:7,9; Rev 1:5).

In summary, though the OT tells the stories of godly people in the past who serve as our models and examples (cf. 1Co 10:1–13; Heb 11; Jas 5:16–18), it does much more than that; it "was put in charge to lead us to Christ that we might be justified by faith" (Gal 3:24).

make burnt offerings and sacrifices to
any other god but the LORD. 18But may
the LORD forgive your servant for this
one thing: When my master enters the
temple of Rimmon to bow down and he
is leaning[c] on my arm and I bow there
also—when I bow down in the temple
of Rimmon, may the LORD forgive your
servant for this."
19"Go in peace,"[d] Elisha said.
After Naaman had traveled some
distance, 20Gehazi, the servant of Elisha the man of God, said to himself,
"My master was too easy on Naaman,
this Aramean, by not accepting from
him what he brought. As surely as the
LORD[e] lives, I will run after him and
get something from him."
21So Gehazi hurried after Naaman.
When Naaman saw him running toward him, he got down from the chariot
to meet him. "Is everything all right?"
he asked.
22"Everything is all right," Gehazi
answered. "My master sent me to say,
'Two young men from the company of
the prophets have just come to me
from the hill country of Ephraim.
Please give them a talent[g] of silver
and two sets of clothing.' "[f]
23"By all means, take two talents,"
said Naaman. He urged Gehazi to accept them, and then tied up the two talents of silver in two bags, with two sets
of clothing. He gave them to two of his
servants, and they carried them ahead
of Gehazi. 24When Gehazi came to the
hill, he took the things from the servants and put them away in the house.
He sent the men away and they left.
25Then he went in and stood before his
master Elisha.
"Where have you been, Gehazi?" Elisha asked.
"Your servant didn't go anywhere,"
Gehazi answered.

5:18 [c]2Ki 7:2
5:19 [d]1Sa 1:17; S Ac 15:33
5:20 [e]Ex 20:7
5:22 [f]S ver 5; S Ge 45:22
5:26 [g]S ver 16 [h]Jer 45:5
5:27 [i]S Nu 12:10 [j]Col 3:5 [k]S Ex 4:6
6:1 [l]S 1Sa 10:5
6:6 [m]S Ex 15:25; S 2Ki 2:21
6:9 [n]ver 12

26But Elisha said to him, "Was not
my spirit with you when the man got
down from his chariot to meet you? Is
this the time[g] to take money, or to accept clothes, olive groves, vineyards,
flocks, herds, or menservants and
maidservants?[h] 27Naaman's leprosy[i] will cling to you and to your
descendants forever." Then Gehazi[j]
went from Elisha's presence and he
was leprous, as white as snow.[k]

An Axhead Floats

6 The company[l] of the prophets
said to Elisha, "Look, the place
where we meet with you is too small
for us. 2Let us go to the Jordan, where
each of us can get a pole; and let us
build a place there for us to live."
And he said, "Go."
3Then one of them said, "Won't you
please come with your servants?"
"I will," Elisha replied. 4And he went
with them.
They went to the Jordan and began
to cut down trees. 5As one of them was
cutting down a tree, the iron axhead
fell into the water. "Oh, my lord," he
cried out, "it was borrowed!"
6The man of God asked, "Where did
it fall?" When he showed him the place,
Elisha cut a stick and threw[m] it there,
and made the iron float. 7"Lift it out,"
he said. Then the man reached out his
hand and took it.

Elisha Traps Blinded Arameans

8Now the king of Aram was at war
with Israel. After conferring with his
officers, he said, "I will set up my camp
in such and such a place."
9The man of God sent word to the
king[n] of Israel: "Beware of passing
that place, because the Arameans are

[g] *22* That is, about 75 pounds (about 34 kilograms)

5:20 I WILL ... GET SOMETHING FROM HIM. Elisha's servant Gehazi had a covetous heart and therefore tried to corrupt God's gracious act for the sake of material prosperity. His transgressions included betraying Elisha, lying to Naaman and Elisha, and dishonoring God's name. Likewise, the NT refers to people who peddle the word of God for profit (2Co 2:17). Unfortunately, there are ministers who seek to enrich themselves and accumulate great material abundance by proclaiming Christ's shed blood, offering salvation to the lost, healing the sick or counseling those in distress. They are using the word of God and making merchandise of God's mercy; they turn the "riches of Christ" (Eph 3:8) into "the treasures of Egypt" (Heb 11:26).

6:5 IRON AXHEAD. The story of the lost axhead illustrates God's interest and care in what might appear to be an insignificant matter. An iron axhead at that time was a very expensive tool, and this poor man felt keenly his responsibility for the borrowed tool. The miracle served (1) to communicate God's heart of compassion for the man in his predicament, (2) to demonstrate God's power at work through the prophet and thus to further confirm Elisha's authority and ministry, and (3) to increase the faith of the younger prophets with Elisha (cf. vv. 1–7).

going down there." **10**So the king of Israel checked on the place indicated by
the man of God. Time and again Elisha
warned[o] the king, so that he was on
his guard in such places.
11This enraged the king of Aram. He
summoned his officers and demanded
of them, "Will you not tell me which
of us is on the side of the king of
Israel?"
12"None of us, my lord the king[p],"
said one of his officers, "but Elisha, the
prophet who is in Israel, tells the king
of Israel the very words you speak in
your bedroom."
13"Go, find out where he is," the king
ordered, "so I can send men and capture him." The report came back: "He
is in Dothan."[q] **14**Then he sent[r]
horses and chariots and a strong force
there. They went by night and surrounded the city.
15When the servant of the man of
God got up and went out early the next
morning, an army with horses and
chariots had surrounded the city. "Oh,
my lord, what shall we do?" the servant
asked.
16"Don't be afraid,"[s] the prophet
answered. "Those who are with us are
more[t] than those who are with them."
17And Elisha prayed, "O LORD, open
his eyes so he may see." Then the LORD
opened the servant's eyes, and he
looked and saw the hills full of horses
and chariots[u] of fire all around Elisha.
18As the enemy came down toward
him, Elisha prayed to the LORD, "Strike
these people with blindness."[v] So he
struck them with blindness, as Elisha
had asked.
19Elisha told them, "This is not the
road and this is not the city. Follow me,
and I will lead you to the man you are
looking for." And he led them to Samaria.
20After they entered the city, Elisha
said, "LORD, open the eyes of these men
so they can see." Then the LORD opened
their eyes and they looked, and there
they were, inside Samaria.
21When the king of Israel saw them,
he asked Elisha, "Shall I kill them, my
father?[w] Shall I kill them?"
22"Do not kill them," he answered.
"Would you kill men you have captured[x] with your own sword or bow?
Set food and water before them so that
they may eat and drink and then go
back to their master." **23**So he prepared a great feast for them, and after
they had finished eating and drinking,
he sent them away, and they returned
to their master. So the bands[y] from
Aram stopped raiding Israel's territory.

Famine in Besieged Samaria

24Some time later, Ben-Hadad[z]
king of Aram mobilized his entire army
and marched up and laid siege[a] to Samaria. **25**There was a great famine[b] in
the city; the siege lasted so long that
a donkey's head sold for eighty shekels[h] of silver, and a quarter of a cab[i]
of seed pods[j][c] for five shekels.[k]
26As the king of Israel was passing
by on the wall, a woman cried to him,
"Help me, my lord the king!"
27The king replied, "If the LORD does
not help you, where can I get help for
you? From the threshing floor? From
the winepress?" **28**Then he asked her,
"What's the matter?"

[h] 25 That is, about 2 pounds (about 1 kilogram) [i] 25 That is, probably about 1/2 pint (about 0.3 liter) [j] 25 Or *of dove's dung* [k] 25 That is, about 2 ounces (about 55 grams)

6:10 [o] Jer 11:18
6:12 [p] ver 9
6:13 [q] Ge 37:17
6:14 [r] 2Ki 1:9
6:16 [s] S Ge 15:1 [t] 2Ch 32:7; Ps 55:18; Ro 8:31; 1Jn 4:4
6:17 [u] S 2Ki 2:11, 12
6:18 [v] Ge 19:11; Ac 13:11
6:21 [w] S 2Ki 5:13
6:22 [x] S Dt 20:11; 2Ch 28:8-15
6:23 [y] S 2Ki 5:2
6:24 [z] S 1Ki 15:18; 2Ki 8:7 [a] Dt 28:52
6:25 [b] S Lev 26:26; S Ru 1:1 [c] Isa 36:12

6:16–17 MORE THAN THOSE WHO ARE WITH THEM. An unseen spiritual realm exists, consisting of a host of ministering angels who are active in the lives of God's people (Ge 32:2; Isa 63:9). Several principles may be derived from this event. (1) Not only is God for his people (Ro 8:31), but also armies of his angels stand by, ready to defend the believer and God's kingdom (v. 17; Ps 34:7; see article on ANGELS AND THE ANGEL OF THE LORD, p. 340).

(2) All Bible-believing Christians should continually pray that God would deliver them from spiritual blindness and open the eyes of their hearts to see more clearly the spiritual reality of God's kingdom (cf. Lk 24:31; Eph 1:18–21) and its heavenly hosts (cf. Heb 1:14).

(3) God's ministering spirits are not far away, but are very close (Ge 32:1–2), observing the actions and faith of God's children and working on their behalf (Ac 7:55–60; 1Co 4:9; Eph 3:10; 1Ti 5:21).

(4) The real battle in God's kingdom is not against flesh and blood; it is a spiritual battle "against the powers of this dark world and against the spiritual forces of evil in the heavenly realms" (Eph 6:12; cf. Rev 12:7–9; see Eph 6:11, note).

(5) There is a cause and effect relationship in spiritual battles; the outcome of spiritual battles is determined in part by the faith and prayers of the saints (vv. 16–20; Eph 6:18–19; see Mt 9:38, note).

6:28 SO WE MAY EAT HIM. Because Israel

She answered, "This woman said to
me, 'Give up your son so we may eat
him today, and tomorrow we'll eat my
son.' 29 So we cooked my son and ate[d]
him. The next day I said to her, 'Give
up your son so we may eat him,' but
she had hidden him."
30 When the king heard the woman's
words, he tore[e] his robes. As he went
along the wall, the people looked, and
there, underneath, he had sackcloth[f]
on his body. 31 He said, "May God deal
with me, be it ever so severely, if the
head of Elisha son of Shaphat remains
on his shoulders today!"
32 Now Elisha was sitting in his
house, and the elders[g] were sitting
with him. The king sent a messenger
ahead, but before he arrived, Elisha
said to the elders, "Don't you see how
this murderer[h] is sending someone to
cut off my head?[i] Look, when the
messenger comes, shut the door and
hold it shut against him. Is not the
sound of his master's footsteps behind
him?"
33 While he was still talking to them,
the messenger came down to him. And
⌞the king⌟ said, "This disaster is from
the LORD. Why should I wait[j] for the
LORD any longer?"

7 Elisha said, "Hear the word of the
LORD. This is what the LORD says:
About this time tomorrow, a seah[l] of
flour will sell for a shekel[m] and two
seahs[n] of barley for a shekel[k] at the
gate of Samaria."
2 The officer on whose arm the king
was leaning[l] said to the man of God,
"Look, even if the LORD should open the
floodgates[m] of the heavens, could this
happen?"
"You will see it with your own eyes,"
answered Elisha, "but you will not
eat[n] any of it!"

The Siege Lifted

3 Now there were four men with leprosy[o][o] at the entrance of the city
gate. They said to each other, "Why
stay here until we die? 4 If we say,
'We'll go into the city'—the famine is
there, and we will die. And if we stay
here, we will die. So let's go over to the
camp of the Arameans and surrender.
If they spare us, we live; if they kill us,
then we die."
5 At dusk they got up and went to the
camp of the Arameans. When they
reached the edge of the camp, not a
man was there, 6 for the Lord had
caused the Arameans to hear the
sound[p] of chariots and horses and a
great army, so that they said to one
another, "Look, the king of Israel has
hired[q] the Hittite[r] and Egyptian
kings to attack us!" 7 So they got up
and fled[s] in the dusk and abandoned
their tents and their horses and donkeys. They left the camp as it was and
ran for their lives.
8 The men who had leprosy[t]
reached the edge of the camp and entered one of the tents. They ate and
drank, and carried away silver, gold
and clothes, and went off and hid them.
They returned and entered another
tent and took some things from it and
hid them also.
9 Then they said to each other,
"We're not doing right. This is a day of
good news and we are keeping it to
ourselves. If we wait until daylight,
punishment will overtake us. Let's go
at once and report this to the royal palace."
10 So they went and called out to the
city gatekeepers and told them, "We
went into the Aramean camp and not a
man was there—not a sound of anyone—only tethered horses and donkeys, and the tents left just as they
were." 11 The gatekeepers shouted the
news, and it was reported within the
palace.
12 The king got up in the night and
said to his officers, "I will tell you what
the Arameans have done to us. They

6:29 [d] S Lev 26:29; Dt 28:53-55 **6:30** [e] 2Ki 18:37; Isa 22:15 [f] S Ge 37:34 **6:32** [g] Eze 8:1; 14:1; 20:1 [h] 1Ki 18:4 [i] ver 31 **6:33** [j] Lev 24:11; Job 2:9; 14:14; Isa 40:31 **7:1** [k] ver 16 **7:2** [l] 2Ki 5:18 [m] ver 19; Ge 7:11; Ps 78:23; Mal 3:10 [n] ver 17 **7:3** [o] Lev 13:45-46; Nu 5:1-4

7:6 [p] S Ex 14:24; Eze 1:24 [q] 2Sa 10:6; Jer 46:21 [r] S Nu 13:29 **7:7** [s] Jdg 7:21; Ps 48:4-6; Pr 28:1; Isa 30:17 **7:8** [t] Isa 33:23; 35:6

[l] *1* That is, probably about 7 quarts (about 7.3 liters); also in verses 16 and 18 [m] *1* That is, about 2/5 ounce (about 11 grams); also in verses 16 and 18 [n] *1* That is, probably about 13 quarts (about 15 liters); also in verses 16 and 18 [o] *3* The Hebrew word is used for various diseases affecting the skin—not necessarily leprosy; also in verse 8.

had departed from a covenant trust in God, his people committed horrible deeds against their own children during a time of severe famine. A major result of throwing aside God and his word is the loss of family love and affection (cf. Dt 28:15, 53–57).

7:1 A SEAH OF FLOUR WILL SELL FOR A SHEKEL. Elisha prophesied that the shortage of food would soon end and that food prices would drop to a normal level (cf. v. 16).

know we are starving; so they have left
the camp to hide[u] in the countryside,
thinking, 'They will surely come out,
and then we will take them alive and
get into the city.' "
13One of his officers answered,
"Have some men take five of the horses
that are left in the city. Their plight will
be like that of all the Israelites left
here—yes, they will only be like all
these Israelites who are doomed. So let
us send them to find out what happened."
14So they selected two chariots with
their horses, and the king sent them
after the Aramean army. He commanded the drivers, "Go and find out what
has happened." 15They followed them
as far as the Jordan, and they found the
whole road strewn with the clothing
and equipment the Arameans had
thrown away in their headlong flight.[v]
So the messengers returned and reported to the king. 16Then the people
went out and plundered[w] the camp of
the Arameans. So a seah of flour sold
for a shekel, and two seahs of barley
sold for a shekel,[x] as the LORD had
said.
17Now the king had put the officer
on whose arm he leaned in charge of
the gate, and the people trampled him
in the gateway, and he died,[y] just as
the man of God had foretold when the
king came down to his house. 18It happened as the man of God had said to
the king: "About this time tomorrow, a
seah of flour will sell for a shekel and
two seahs of barley for a shekel at the
gate of Samaria."
19The officer had said to the man of
God, "Look, even if the LORD should
open the floodgates[z] of the heavens,
could this happen?" The man of God
had replied, "You will see it with your
own eyes, but you will not eat any of
it!" 20And that is exactly what happened to him, for the people trampled
him in the gateway, and he died.

7:12 [u]Jos 8:4
7:15 [v]Job 27:22
7:16 [w]Isa 33:4, 23 [x]ver 1
7:17 [y]S ver 2
7:19 [z]S ver 2

The Shunammite's Land Restored

8 Now Elisha had said to the woman[a] whose son he had restored to
life, "Go away with your family and
stay for a while wherever you can, because the LORD has decreed a famine[b]
in the land that will last seven
years."[c] 2The woman proceeded to do
as the man of God said. She and her
family went away and stayed in the
land of the Philistines seven years.
3At the end of the seven years she
came back from the land of the Philistines and went to the king to beg for
her house and land. 4The king was
talking to Gehazi, the servant of the
man of God, and had said, "Tell me
about all the great things Elisha has
done." 5Just as Gehazi was telling the
king how Elisha had restored[d] the
dead to life, the woman whose son Elisha had brought back to life came to
beg the king for her house and land.

Gehazi said, "This is the woman, my
lord the king, and this is her son whom
Elisha restored to life." 6The king
asked the woman about it, and she told
him.

Then he assigned an official to her
case and said to him, "Give back everything that belonged to her, including
all the income from her land from the
day she left the country until now."

Hazael Murders Ben-Hadad

7Elisha went to Damascus,[e] and
Ben-Hadad[f] king of Aram was ill.
When the king was told, "The man of
God has come all the way up here," 8he
said to Hazael,[g] "Take a gift[h] with
you and go to meet the man of God.
Consult[i] the LORD through him; ask
him, 'Will I recover from this illness?' "
9Hazael went to meet Elisha, taking
with him as a gift forty camel-loads of
all the finest wares of Damascus. He
went in and stood before him, and said,

8:1 [a]2Ki 4:8-37 [b]S Lev 26:26; S Dt 28:22; S Ru 1:1 [c]S Ge 12:10
8:5 [d]2Ki 4:35
8:7 [e]S 2Sa 8:5 [f]S 2Ki 6:24
8:8 [g]1Ki 19:15 [h]S Ge 32:20; S 1Sa 9:7 [i]S Jdg 18:5

7:16 AS THE LORD HAD SAID. Through the event recorded in this chapter, the Israelites understood that the word of the Lord was indeed true, that in mercy God had saved the apostate nation from calamity in order that they might repent and return to him, and that unbelief and failure to follow God's word would result in further judgment (vv. 2,17–20).

8:1 DECREED A FAMINE. God sent a famine to Israel as a punishment for their apostasy (cf. Dt 11:16–17; 28:38–40). The author does not say when it occurred, though it was evidently before the judgment on Gehazi (v. 5; 5:27) and after the raising of the Shunammite's son (v. 1; 4:32–37); it is probably the same famine as the one mentioned in 4:38.

8:2 THE WOMAN PROCEEDED TO DO. Because the woman demonstrated a sincere faith and remained faithful to God's prophet in a time of general apostasy (4:8–37), the Lord helped her in her time of need (cf. Mt 10:41; Rev 3:10).

“Your son Ben-Hadad king of Aram has
sent me to ask, ‘Will I recover from this
illness?’ ”
10Elisha answered, “Go and say to
him, ‘You will certainly recover’;[j]
but[p] the LORD has revealed to me that
he will in fact die.” 11He stared at him
with a fixed gaze until Hazael felt
ashamed.[k] Then the man of God began to weep.[l]
12“Why is my lord weeping?” asked
Hazael.
“Because I know the harm[m] you will
do to the Israelites,” he answered.
“You will set fire to their fortified
places, kill their young men with the
sword, dash[n] their little children[o] to
the ground, and rip open[p] their pregnant women.”
13Hazael said, “How could your servant, a mere dog,[q] accomplish such a
feat?”
“The LORD has shown me that you
will become king[r] of Aram,” answered
Elisha.
14Then Hazael left Elisha and returned to his master. When Ben-Hadad
asked, “What did Elisha say to you?”
Hazael replied, “He told me that you
would certainly recover.” 15But the
next day he took a thick cloth, soaked
it in water and spread it over the king’s
face, so that he died.[s] Then Hazael
succeeded him as king.

Jehoram King of Judah

8:16–24pp — 2Ch 21:5–10,20

16In the fifth year of Joram[t] son of
Ahab king of Israel, when Jehoshaphat
was king of Judah, Jehoram[u] son of
Jehoshaphat began his reign as king of
Judah. 17He was thirty-two years old
when he became king, and he reigned
in Jerusalem eight years. 18He walked
in the ways of the kings of Israel, as
the house of Ahab had done, for he
married a daughter[v] of Ahab. He did
evil in the eyes of the LORD. 19Neverthe-
less, for the sake of his servant David,
the LORD was not willing to destroy[w]
Judah. He had promised to maintain a
lamp[x] for David and his descendants
forever.
20In the time of Jehoram, Edom rebelled against Judah and set up its own
king.[y] 21So Jehoram[q] went to Zair
with all his chariots. The Edomites
surrounded him and his chariot commanders, but he rose up and broke
through by night; his army, however,
fled back home. 22To this day Edom
has been in rebellion[z] against Judah.
Libnah[a] revolted at the same time.
23As for the other events of Jehoram’s reign, and all he did, are they not
written in the book of the annals of the
kings of Judah? 24Jehoram rested with
his fathers and was buried with them
in the City of David. And Ahaziah his
son succeeded him as king.

Ahaziah King of Judah

8:25–29pp — 2Ch 22:1–6

25In the twelfth[b] year of Joram son
of Ahab king of Israel, Ahaziah son of
Jehoram king of Judah began to reign.
26Ahaziah was twenty-two years old
when he became king, and he reigned
in Jerusalem one year. His mother’s
name was Athaliah,[c] a granddaughter
of Omri[d] king of Israel. 27He walked
in the ways of the house of Ahab[e] and
did evil[f] in the eyes of the LORD, as the
house of Ahab had done, for he was related by marriage to Ahab’s family.
28Ahaziah went with Joram son of
Ahab to war against Hazael king of
Aram at Ramoth Gilead.[g] The Arameans wounded Joram; 29so King Joram
returned to Jezreel[h] to recover from
the wounds the Arameans had inflicted
on him at Ramoth[r] in his battle with
Hazael[i] king of Aram.
Then Ahaziah[j] son of Jehoram king
of Judah went down to Jezreel to see

8:10 [j] Isa 38:1
8:11 [k] S Jdg 3:25 [l] Lk 19:41
8:12 [m] S 1Ki 19:17 [n] Ps 137:9; Isa 13:16; Hos 13:16; Na 3:10; Lk 19:44 [o] S Ge 34:29 [p] 2Ki 15:16; Am 1:13
8:13 [q] S 1Sa 17:43; S 2Sa 3:8 [r] 1Ki 19:15
8:15 [s] S 2Ki 1:17
8:16 [t] S 2Ki 1:17 [u] 2Ch 21:1-4
8:18 [v] ver 26; 2Ki 11:1
8:19 [w] S Ge 6:13 [x] S 2Sa 21:17; Rev 21:23
8:20 [y] S 1Ki 22:47
8:22 [z] Ge 27:40 [a] S Nu 33:20; Jos 21:13; 2Ki 19:8
8:25 [b] 2Ki 9:29
8:26 [c] S ver 18 [d] 1Ki 16:23
8:27 [e] 1Ki 16:30 [f] 1Ki 15:26
8:28 [g] S Dt 4:43; 2Ki 9:1,14
8:29 [h] 1Ki 21:29; 2Ki 9:21 [i] 1Ki 19:15,17 [j] 2Ki 10:13

[p] *10* The Hebrew may also be read *Go and say, ‘You will certainly not recover,’ for.*
[q] *21* Hebrew *Joram,* a variant of *Jehoram;* also in verses 23 and 24
[r] *29* Hebrew *Ramah,* a variant of *Ramoth*

8:11–12 THE MAN OF GOD BEGAN TO WEEP. In a vision from the Spirit of revelation, Elisha saw that Hazael would become king of Aram and perpetrate terrible evil against Israel (vv. 12–13). Elisha wept because of what was coming upon Israel as a result of their apostasy. As a true man of God, he felt a deep sorrow both for God, who had been abandoned by his own people, and for those people who now had to suffer severe judgment for their sins. In like manner Jesus wept over Jerusalem (Lk 19:41) and Paul over the church (Ac 20:28–31). The words of Elisha do not endorse the future cruelty of Hazael, but only describe the terrible practices of depraved humans in times of war (cf. Isa 13:15; Hos 10:14).

Joram son of Ahab, because he had
been wounded.

Jehu Anointed King of Israel

9 The prophet Elisha summoned a
man from the company[k] of the
prophets and said to him, "Tuck your
cloak into your belt,[l] take this flask
of oil[m] with you and go to Ramoth Gilead.[n] 2When you get there, look for
Jehu son of Jehoshaphat, the son of
Nimshi. Go to him, get him away from
his companions and take him into an
inner room. 3Then take the flask and
pour the oil[o] on his head and declare,
'This is what the LORD says: I anoint
you king over Israel.' Then open the
door and run; don't delay!"

4So the young man, the prophet,
went to Ramoth Gilead. 5When he arrived, he found the army officers sitting together. "I have a message for
you, commander," he said.

"For which of us?" asked Jehu.

"For you, commander," he replied.

6Jehu got up and went into the
house. Then the prophet poured the
oil[p] on Jehu's head and declared,
"This is what the LORD, the God of Israel, says: 'I anoint you king over the
LORD's people Israel. 7You are to destroy the house of Ahab your master,
and I will avenge[q] the blood of my servants[r] the prophets and the blood of
all the LORD's servants shed by Jezebel.[s] 8The whole house[t] of Ahab will
perish. I will cut off from Ahab every
last male[u] in Israel—slave or free. 9I
will make the house of Ahab like the
house of Jeroboam[v] son of Nebat and
like the house of Baasha[w] son of Ahijah. 10As for Jezebel, dogs[x] will devour her on the plot of ground at Jezreel, and no one will bury her.' " Then he
opened the door and ran.

11When Jehu went out to his fellow
officers, one of them asked him, "Is everything all right? Why did this madman[y] come to you?"

"You know the man and the sort of
things he says," Jehu replied.

12"That's not true!" they said. "Tell
us."

Jehu said, "Here is what he told me:
'This is what the LORD says: I anoint
you king over Israel.' "

13They hurried and took their cloaks
and spread[z] them under him on the
bare steps. Then they blew the trumpet[a] and shouted, "Jehu is king!"

Jehu Kills Joram and Ahaziah

9:21–29pp — 2Ch 22:7–9

14So Jehu son of Jehoshaphat, the
son of Nimshi, conspired against Joram. (Now Joram and all Israel had
been defending Ramoth Gilead[b]
against Hazael king of Aram, 15but
King Joram[s] had returned to Jezreel to
recover[c] from the wounds the Arameans had inflicted on him in the battle
with Hazael king of Aram.) Jehu said,
"If this is the way you feel, don't let
anyone slip out of the city to go and tell
the news in Jezreel." 16Then he got into
his chariot and rode to Jezreel, because
Joram was resting there and Ahaziah[d]
king of Judah had gone down to see
him.

17When the lookout[e] standing on
the tower in Jezreel saw Jehu's troops
approaching, he called out, "I see some
troops coming."

"Get a horseman," Joram ordered.
"Send him to meet them and ask, 'Do
you come in peace?[f]' "

18The horseman rode off to meet
Jehu and said, "This is what the king
says: 'Do you come in peace?' "

"What do you have to do with
peace?" Jehu replied. "Fall in behind
me."

The lookout reported, "The messenger has reached them, but he isn't coming back."

19So the king sent out a second
horseman. When he came to them he
said, "This is what the king says: 'Do
you come in peace?' "

[s] *15* Hebrew *Jehoram,* a variant of *Joram;* also in verses 17 and 21-24

9:1 [k] S 1Sa 10:5 [l] S 1Ki 18:46 [m] S 1Sa 10:1 [n] S 2Ki 8:28
9:3 [o] 1Ki 19:16
9:6 [p] 1Ki 19:16
9:7 [q] S Ge 4:24; S Rev 6:10 [r] S Dt 32:43 [s] S 1Ki 18:4
9:8 [t] 2Ki 10:17 [u] S 1Sa 25:22
9:9 [v] S 1Ki 13:34; S 14:10 [w] 1Ki 16:3
9:10 [x] S 1Ki 21:23
9:11 [y] S 1Sa 10:11; S Jn 10:20
9:13 [z] Mt 21:8; Lk 19:36 [a] S 2Sa 15:10
9:14 [b] S Dt 4:43; S 2Ki 8:28
9:15 [c] S 2Ki 8:29
9:16 [d] 2Ch 22:7
9:17 [e] S 1Sa 14:16; Isa 21:6 [f] S 1Sa 16:4

9:7 DESTROY THE HOUSE OF AHAB. Years earlier Elijah had foretold the complete destruction of Ahab's descendants (1Ki 21:19–24).

9:8 WHOLE HOUSE OF AHAB WILL PERISH. God caused the fall of the house of Ahab because it had remained stubborn and unrepentant in its idolatry and apostasy, corrupting the entire nation of Israel (cf. Ro 2:5–6). God's righteous judgment on Ahab's house (ch. 10), Ahab's son Joram (vv. 22–26; see 1Ki 21:19) and Ahab's wife Jezebel (vv. 30–37) shows that God will surely judge all who lead his people into unrighteousness. Scripture teaches plainly that God will reward every person according to his or her deeds (Ro 2:6; cf. 2Ti 4:14), and that there will be "trouble and distress for every human being who does evil" (Ro 2:9).

Jehu replied, "What do you have to
do with peace? Fall in behind me."
20The lookout reported, "He has
reached them, but he isn't coming back
either. The driving is like[g] that of Jehu
son of Nimshi—he drives like a madman."
21"Hitch up my chariot," Joram ordered. And when it was hitched up, Joram king of Israel and Ahaziah king of
Judah rode out, each in his own chariot, to meet Jehu. They met him at the
plot of ground that had belonged to Naboth[h] the Jezreelite. **22**When Joram
saw Jehu he asked, "Have you come in
peace, Jehu?"
"How can there be peace," Jehu replied, "as long as all the idolatry and
witchcraft of your mother Jezebel[i]
abound?"
23Joram turned about and fled, calling out to Ahaziah, "Treachery,[j] Ahaziah!"
24Then Jehu drew his bow[k] and
shot Joram between the shoulders. The
arrow pierced his heart and he
slumped down in his chariot. **25**Jehu
said to Bidkar, his chariot officer,
"Pick him up and throw him on the
field that belonged to Naboth the Jezreelite. Remember how you and I were
riding together in chariots behind Ahab
his father when the LORD made this
prophecy[l] about him: **26**'Yesterday I
saw the blood of Naboth[m] and the
blood of his sons, declares the LORD,
and I will surely make you pay for it on
this plot of ground, declares the
LORD.'[t] Now then, pick him up and
throw him on that plot, in accordance
with the word of the LORD."[n]
27When Ahaziah king of Judah saw
what had happened, he fled up the road
to Beth Haggan.[u] Jehu chased him,
shouting, "Kill him too!" They wounded him in his chariot on the way up to
Gur near Ibleam,[o] but he escaped to
Megiddo[p] and died there. **28**His servants took him by chariot[q] to Jerusalem and buried him with his fathers in
his tomb in the City of David. **29**(In the
eleventh[r] year of Joram son of Ahab,
Ahaziah had become king of Judah.)

Jezebel Killed

30Then Jehu went to Jezreel. When
Jezebel heard about it, she painted[s]
her eyes, arranged her hair and looked
out of a window. **31**As Jehu entered the
gate, she asked, "Have you come in
peace, Zimri,[t] you murderer of your
master?"[v]
32He looked up at the window and
called out, "Who is on my side? Who?"
Two or three eunuchs looked down at
him. **33**"Throw her down!" Jehu said.
So they threw her down, and some of
her blood spattered the wall and the
horses as they trampled her underfoot.[u]
34Jehu went in and ate and drank.
"Take care of that cursed woman," he
said, "and bury her, for she was a
king's daughter."[v] **35**But when they
went out to bury her, they found nothing except her skull, her feet and her
hands. **36**They went back and told
Jehu, who said, "This is the word of the
LORD that he spoke through his servant
Elijah the Tishbite: On the plot of
ground at Jezreel dogs[w] will devour
Jezebel's flesh.[wx] **37**Jezebel's body
will be like refuse[y] on the ground in
the plot at Jezreel, so that no one will
be able to say, 'This is Jezebel.' "

Ahab's Family Killed

10 Now there were in Samaria[z]
seventy sons[a] of the house of
Ahab. So Jehu wrote letters and sent
them to Samaria: to the officials of Jezreel,[xb] to the elders and to the guardians[c] of Ahab's children. He said,
2"As soon as this letter reaches you,
since your master's sons are with you
and you have chariots and horses, a
fortified city and weapons, **3**choose the
best and most worthy of your master's

9:20 [g] 2Sa 18:27
9:21 [h] 1Ki 21:1-7, 15-19
9:22 [i] 1Ki 18:19; Rev 2:20
9:23 [j] 2Ki 11:14
9:24 [k] S 1Ki 22:34
9:25 [l] 1Ki 21:19-22, 24-29
9:26 [m] S 1Ki 21:19 [n] S 1Ki 21:29
9:27 [o] S Jdg 1:27 [p] 2Ki 23:29
9:28 [q] 2Ki 14:20; 23:30
9:29 [r] 2Ki 8:25
9:30 [s] Jer 4:30; Eze 23:40
9:31 [t] 1Ki 16:9-10
9:33 [u] Ps 7:5
9:34 [v] S 1Ki 16:31
9:36 [w] Ps 68:23; Jer 15:3 [x] S 1Ki 21:23
9:37 [y] Ps 83:10; Isa 5:25; Jer 8:2; 9:22; 16:4; 25:33; Zep 1:17
10:1 [z] S 1Ki 13:32 [a] S Jdg 8:30 [b] S 1Ki 21:1 [c] ver 5

[t] *26* See 1 Kings 21:19. [u] *27* Or *fled by way of the garden house* [v] *31* Or *"Did Zimri have peace, who murdered his master?"* [w] *36* See 1 Kings 21:23. [x] *1* Hebrew; some Septuagint manuscripts and Vulgate *of the city*

9:25 ON THE FIELD THAT BELONGED TO NABOTH. Ahab and Jezebel, the parents of King Joram, had ruthlessly defrauded Naboth in order to steal his field (1Ki 21:1–24). Now the dead body of their son was thrown into that very field. The sins of parents may bear fruit in their children years after the parents' death.

10:1 JEHU WROTE LETTERS. Jehu challenged the officials of Samaria to choose a king from the sons of Ahab and then face the consequences of conflict with Jehu himself (vv. 1–4). The rulers, however, became terrified by this psychological warfare and swore allegiance to Jehu; they then obeyed Jehu's order to kill Ahab's descendants (vv. 5–8).

sons and set him on his father's
throne. Then fight for your master's
house."
4But they were terrified and said, "If
two kings could not resist him, how
can we?"
5So the palace administrator, the
city governor, the elders and the
guardians sent this message to Jehu:
"We are your servants[d] and we will do
anything you say. We will not appoint
anyone as king; you do whatever you
think best."
6Then Jehu wrote them a second letter, saying, "If you are on my side and
will obey me, take the heads of your
master's sons and come to me in Jezreel by this time tomorrow."
Now the royal princes, seventy of
them, were with the leading men of the
city, who were rearing them. 7When
the letter arrived, these men took the
princes and slaughtered all seventy[e]
of them. They put their heads[f] in baskets and sent them to Jehu in Jezreel.
8When the messenger arrived, he told
Jehu, "They have brought the heads of
the princes."
Then Jehu ordered, "Put them in two
piles at the entrance of the city gate
until morning."
9The next morning Jehu went out.
He stood before all the people and said,
"You are innocent. It was I who conspired against my master and killed
him, but who killed all these? 10Know
then, that not a word the LORD has spoken against the house of Ahab will fail.
The LORD has done what he promised[g]
through his servant Elijah."[h] 11So
Jehu[i] killed everyone in Jezreel who
remained of the house of Ahab, as well
as all his chief men, his close friends
and his priests, leaving him no survivor.[j]
12Jehu then set out and went toward
Samaria. At Beth Eked of the Shepherds, 13he met some relatives of Ahaziah king of Judah and asked, "Who are
you?"
They said, "We are relatives of Ahaziah,[k] and we have come down to
greet the families of the king and of the
queen mother."[l]
14"Take them alive!" he ordered. So
they took them alive and slaughtered
them by the well of Beth Eked—forty-
two men. He left no survivor.[m]
15After he left there, he came upon
Jehonadab[n] son of Recab,[o] who was
on his way to meet him. Jehu greeted
him and said, "Are you in accord with
me, as I am with you?"
"I am," Jehonadab answered.
"If so," said Jehu, "give me your
hand."[p] So he did, and Jehu helped
him up into the chariot. 16Jehu said,
"Come with me and see my zeal[q] for
the LORD." Then he had him ride along
in his chariot.
17When Jehu came to Samaria, he
killed all who were left there of Ahab's
family;[r] he destroyed them, according
to the word of the LORD spoken to Elijah.

Ministers of Baal Killed

18Then Jehu brought all the people
together and said to them, "Ahab
served[s] Baal a little; Jehu will serve
him much. 19Now summon[t] all the
prophets of Baal, all his ministers and
all his priests. See that no one is missing, because I am going to hold a great
sacrifice for Baal. Anyone who fails to
come will no longer live." But Jehu was
acting deceptively in order to destroy
the ministers of Baal.
20Jehu said, "Call an assembly[u] in
honor of Baal." So they proclaimed it.
21Then he sent word throughout Israel, and all the ministers of Baal came;
not one stayed away. They crowded
into the temple of Baal until it was full
from one end to the other. 22And Jehu
said to the keeper of the wardrobe,
"Bring robes for all the ministers of
Baal." So he brought out robes for
them.
23Then Jehu and Jehonadab son of
Recab went into the temple of Baal.
Jehu said to the ministers of Baal,
"Look around and see that no servants
of the LORD are here with you—only
ministers of Baal." 24So they went in to
make sacrifices and burnt offerings.
Now Jehu had posted eighty men outside with this warning: "If one of you
lets any of the men I am placing in your
hands escape, it will be your life for his
life."[v]
25As soon as Jehu had finished making the burnt offering, he ordered the
guards and officers: "Go in and kill[w]
them; let no one escape."[x] So they cut
them down with the sword. The guards
and officers threw the bodies out and
then entered the inner shrine of the
temple of Baal. 26They brought the sacred stone[y] out of the temple of Baal

10:5 [d] Jos 9:8
10:7 [e] S 1Ki 21:21 [f] S 2Sa 4:8
10:10 [g] 2Ki 9:7-10 [h] S 1Ki 21:29
10:11 [i] Hos 1:4 [j] ver 14; Job 18:19; Mal 4:1
10:13 [k] 2Ki 8:24, 29; 2Ch 22:8 [l] S 1Ki 2:19
10:14 [m] S ver 11
10:15 [n] Jer 35:6, 14-19 [o] 1Ch 2:55; Jer 35:2
[p] Ezr 10:19; Eze 17:18
10:16 [q] S Nu 25:13
10:17 [r] 2Ki 9:8
10:18 [s] S Jdg 2:11
10:19 [t] 1Ki 18:19
10:20 [u] S Ex 32:5
10:24 [v] S Jos 2:14
10:25 [w] S Ex 22:20; S 2Ki 11:18 [x] S 1Ki 18:40
10:26 [y] S Ex 23:24

and burned it. **27**They demolished the
sacred stone of Baal and tore down the
temple[z] of Baal, and people have used
it for a latrine to this day.
28So Jehu[a] destroyed Baal worship
in Israel. **29**However, he did not turn
away from the sins[b] of Jeroboam son
of Nebat, which he had caused Israel to
commit—the worship of the golden
calves[c] at Bethel[d] and Dan.
30The LORD said to Jehu, "Because
you have done well in accomplishing
what is right in my eyes and have done
to the house of Ahab all I had in mind
to do, your descendants will sit on the
throne of Israel to the fourth generation."[e] **31**Yet Jehu was not careful[f] to
keep the law of the LORD, the God of
Israel, with all his heart. He did not
turn away from the sins[g] of Jeroboam,
which he had caused Israel to commit.
32In those days the LORD began to
reduce[h] the size of Israel. Hazael[i]
overpowered the Israelites throughout
their territory **33**east of the Jordan in
all the land of Gilead (the region of
Gad, Reuben and Manasseh), from
Aroer[j] by the Arnon[k] Gorge through
Gilead to Bashan.
34As for the other events of Jehu's
reign, all he did, and all his achievements, are they not written in the book
of the annals[l] of the kings of Israel?
35Jehu rested with his fathers and
was buried in Samaria. And Jehoahaz
his son succeeded him as king. **36**The
time that Jehu reigned over Israel in
Samaria was twenty-eight years.

Athaliah and Joash

11:1–21pp — 2Ch 22:10–23:21

11 When Athaliah[m] the mother of
Ahaziah saw that her son was
dead, she proceeded to destroy the
whole royal family. **2**But Jehosheba,
the daughter of King Jehoram[y] and
sister of Ahaziah, took Joash[n] son of
Ahaziah and stole him away from
among the royal princes, who were
about to be murdered. She put him and
his nurse in a bedroom to hide him
from Athaliah; so he was not killed.[o]
3He remained hidden with his nurse at
the temple of the LORD for six years
while Athaliah ruled the land.
4In the seventh year Jehoiada sent
for the commanders of units of a hundred, the Carites[p] and the guards and
had them brought to him at the temple
of the LORD. He made a covenant with
them and put them under oath at the
temple of the LORD. Then he showed
them the king's son. **5**He commanded
them, saying, "This is what you are to
do: You who are in the three companies
that are going on duty on the Sab-

10:27 [z] S 1Ki 16:32
10:28 [a] 1Ki 19:17
10:29 [b] S 1Ki 12:30 [c] S Ex 32:4 [d] 1Ki 12:32
10:30 [e] 2Ki 15:12
10:31 [f] Dt 4:9; Pr 4:23 [g] 1Ki 12:30
10:32 [h] 2Ki 13:25; Ps 107:39 [i] S 1Ki 19:17
10:33 [j] S Nu 32:34; Dt 2:36; Jdg 11:26; Isa 17:2 [k] S Nu 21:13
10:34 [l] 1Ki 15:31
11:1 [m] S 2Ki 8:18
11:2 [n] 2Ki 12:1 [o] S Jdg 9:5
11:4 [p] ver 19

[y] 2 Hebrew *Joram,* a variant of *Jehoram*

10:28 JEHU DESTROYED BAAL WORSHIP. Jehu had been chosen by God to destroy the idolatrous dynasty of Ahab (cf. v. 30; 9:6–10). Inherent in that call was the commission to eradicate Baalism, an unspeakably vile and cruel religion associated with immorality, drunkenness and human sacrifice (vv. 18–28; see Jdg 2:13, note). The complete destruction of the house of Ahab and the religion of Baal was an act of mercy for the Israelites. Had both continued, Israel would have quickly become spiritually and morally ripe for judgment and destruction.

10:31 NOT CAREFUL TO KEEP THE LAW. Jehu, though zealous for God, did not serve him with all his heart. He permitted the worship of the golden calves for political reasons (v. 29) and took little interest in God's law. Thus, the spiritual reformation God had intended for Israel was hindered because of a leadership failure involving personal ambition and love of power. Great revivals and reformations die when self-seeking interest takes priority over God's purpose. Because Jehu served God out of motives tainted by worldly self-interest rather than out of a sincere concern for truth and righteousness, God later punished his house (cf. Hos 1:4).

11:1 ATHALIAH . . . DESTROY THE WHOLE ROYAL FAMILY. Athaliah, the only non-Davidic ruler in Judah's history, was queen during a six-year reign of terror. This daughter of wicked Ahab and Jezebel had married Jehoram, the son of Judah's King Jehoshaphat. When King Ahaziah (see 9:27), the only son of Jehoram and Athaliah, was killed in Jehu's purge of Ahab's house during a visit to the north, the treacherous Athaliah mounted Judah's throne and attempted to purge it of David's descendants, including all her own grandsons. However Jehosheba, the wife of the high priest Jehoiada, hid the infant son of Ahaziah named Joash and thereby preserved the Davidic line from which the Messiah would be born (vv. 2–3; 2Sa 7:11,16; 1Ki 8:25; cf. Mt 1:8–9).

11:4 JEHOIADA. Jehoiada, the husband of Jehosheba, was the high priest of the Lord during Athaliah's reign in the southern kingdom (v. 2; cf. 2Ch 22:11). He instigated Athaliah's overthrow (cf. 2Ch 23), set Joash on the throne and guided him in devotion to the Lord (v. 12; 2Ch 23:11). What Jehoiada did preserved the Messianic line. He effectively directed the young king Joash in renewing the covenant between the Lord and his people and in destroying the religion of Baal (vv. 17–18).

bath[q]—a third of you guarding the royal palace,[r] **6**a third at the Sur Gate, and a third at the gate behind the guard, who take turns guarding the temple— **7**and you who are in the other two companies that normally go off Sabbath duty are all to guard the temple for the king. **8**Station yourselves around the king, each man with his weapon in his hand. Anyone who approaches your ranks[z] must be put to death. Stay close to the king wherever he goes."

9The commanders of units of a hundred did just as Jehoiada the priest ordered. Each one took his men—those who were going on duty on the Sabbath and those who were going off duty—and came to Jehoiada the priest. **10**Then he gave the commanders the spears and shields[s] that had belonged to King David and that were in the temple of the LORD. **11**The guards, each with his weapon in his hand, stationed themselves around the king—near the altar and the temple, from the south side to the north side of the temple.

12Jehoiada brought out the king's son and put the crown on him; he presented him with a copy of the covenant[t] and proclaimed him king. They anointed[u] him, and the people clapped their hands[v] and shouted, "Long live the king!"[w]

13When Athaliah heard the noise made by the guards and the people, she went to the people at the temple of the LORD. **14**She looked and there was the king, standing by the pillar,[x] as the custom was. The officers and the trumpeters were beside the king, and all the people of the land were rejoicing and blowing trumpets.[y] Then Athaliah tore[z] her robes and called out, "Treason! Treason!"[a]

15Jehoiada the priest ordered the commanders of units of a hundred, who were in charge of the troops: "Bring her out between the ranks[a] and put to the sword anyone who follows her." For the priest had said, "She must not be put to death in the temple[b] of the LORD." **16**So they seized her as she reached the place where the horses enter[c] the palace grounds, and there she was put to death.[d]

17Jehoiada then made a covenant[e] between the LORD and the king and people that they would be the LORD's people. He also made a covenant between the king and the people.[f] **18**All the people of the land went to the temple[g] of Baal and tore it down. They smashed[h] the altars and idols to pieces and killed Mattan the priest[i] of Baal in front of the altars.

Then Jehoiada the priest posted guards at the temple of the LORD. **19**He took with him the commanders of hundreds, the Carites,[j] the guards and all the people of the land, and together they brought the king down from the temple of the LORD and went into the palace, entering by way of the gate of the guards. The king then took his place on the royal throne, **20**and all the people of the land rejoiced.[k] And the city was quiet, because Athaliah had been slain with the sword at the palace.

21Joash[b] was seven years old when he began to reign.

Joash Repairs the Temple

12:1–21pp — 2Ch 24:1–14; 24:23–27

12 In the seventh year of Jehu, Joash[c][l] became king, and he reigned in Jerusalem forty years. His mother's name was Zibiah; she was from Beersheba. **2**Joash did what was right[m] in the eyes of the LORD all the years Jehoiada the priest instructed him. **3**The high places,[n] however, were not removed; the people continued to offer sacrifices and burn incense there.

4Joash said to the priests, "Collect[o] all the money that is brought as sacred offerings[p] to the temple of the LORD—the money collected in the census,[q] the money received from personal

11:5 [q]1Ch 9:25 [r]1Ki 14:27 **11:10** [s]S 2Sa 8:7 **11:12** [t]Ex 25:16; 2Ki 23:3 [u]S 1Sa 9:16; S 1Ki 1:39 [v]Ps 47:1; 98:8; Isa 55:12 [w]S 1Sa 10:24 **11:14** [x]S 1Ki 7:15 [y]S 1Ki 1:39 [z]S Ge 37:29 [a]2Ki 9:23 **11:15** [b]1Ki 2:30 **11:16** [c]Ne 3:28; Jer 31:40 [d]S Ge 4:14 **11:17** [e]S Ex 24:8; 2Sa 5:3; 2Ch 15:12; 23:3; 29:10; 34:31; Ezr 10:3 [f]2Ki 23:3; Jer 34:8 **11:18** [g]S 1Ki 16:32 [h]S Dt 12:3 [i]1Ki 18:40; 2Ki 10:25; 23:20 **11:19** [j]ver 4 **11:20** [k]Pr 11:10; 28:12; 29:2 **12:1** [l]2Ki 11:2 **12:2** [m]S Dt 12:25; S 2Sa 8:15 **12:3** [n]S 1Ki 3:3; S 2Ki 18:4 **12:4** [o]2Ki 22:4 [p]Nu 18:19 [q]S Ex 30:12

[z]*8* Or *approaches the precincts* [a]*15* Or *out from the precincts* [b]*21* Hebrew *Jehoash,* a variant of *Joash* [c]*1* Hebrew *Jehoash,* a variant of *Joash*; also in verses 2, 4, 6, 7 and 18

12:2 JOASH. As long as Jehoiada the high priest was his counselor, Joash served the Lord. However, after Jehoiada's death, Joash forsook the Lord and began to serve idols (2Ch 24:17–18). He multiplied his sin by murdering Jehoiada's son Zechariah, who had condemned him for forsaking the Lord (2Ch 24:20–22). In just recompense, Joash was killed by his own officials for this murder (v. 20; 2Ch 24:25; see next note). Joash began well as king but ended in spiritual ruin (cf. Mt 24:13; Gal 3:3; Rev 2:10).

vows and the money brought voluntarily[r] to the temple. 5Let every priest receive the money from one of the treasurers, and let it be used to repair[s] whatever damage is found in the temple."

6But by the twenty-third year of King Joash the priests still had not repaired the temple. 7Therefore King Joash summoned Jehoiada the priest and the other priests and asked them, "Why aren't you repairing the damage done to the temple? Take no more money from your treasurers, but hand it over for repairing the temple." 8The priests agreed that they would not collect any more money from the people and that they would not repair the temple themselves.

9Jehoiada the priest took a chest and bored a hole in its lid. He placed it beside the altar, on the right side as one enters the temple of the LORD. The priests who guarded the entrance[t] put into the chest all the money[u] that was brought to the temple of the LORD. 10Whenever they saw that there was a large amount of money in the chest, the royal secretary[v] and the high priest came, counted the money that had been brought into the temple of the LORD and put it into bags. 11When the amount had been determined, they gave the money to the men appointed to supervise the work on the temple. With it they paid those who worked on the temple of the LORD—the carpenters and builders, 12the masons and stonecutters.[w] They purchased timber and dressed stone for the repair of the temple of the LORD, and met all the other expenses of restoring the temple.

13The money brought into the temple was not spent for making silver basins, wick trimmers, sprinkling bowls, trumpets or any other articles of gold[x] or silver for the temple of the LORD; 14it was paid to the workmen, who used it to repair the temple. 15They did not require an accounting from those to whom they gave the money to pay the workers, because they acted with complete honesty.[y] 16The money from the guilt offerings[z] and sin offerings[a] was not brought into the temple of the LORD; it belonged[b] to the priests.

17About this time Hazael[c] king of Aram went up and attacked Gath and captured it. Then he turned to attack Jerusalem. 18But Joash king of Judah took all the sacred objects dedicated by his fathers—Jehoshaphat, Jehoram and Ahaziah, the kings of Judah—and the gifts he himself had dedicated and all the gold found in the treasuries of the temple of the LORD and of the royal palace, and he sent[d] them to Hazael king of Aram, who then withdrew[e] from Jerusalem.

19As for the other events of the reign of Joash, and all he did, are they not written in the book of the annals of the kings of Judah? 20His officials[f] conspired against him and assassinated[g] him at Beth Millo,[h] on the road down to Silla. 21The officials who murdered him were Jozabad son of Shimeath and Jehozabad son of Shomer. He died and was buried with his fathers in the City of David. And Amaziah his son succeeded him as king.

Jehoahaz King of Israel

13 In the twenty-third year of Joash son of Ahaziah king of Judah, Jehoahaz son of Jehu became king of Israel in Samaria, and he reigned seventeen years. 2He did evil[i] in the eyes of the LORD by following the sins of Jeroboam son of Nebat, which he had caused Israel to commit, and he did not turn away from them. 3So the LORD's anger[j] burned against Israel, and for a long time he kept them under the power[k] of Hazael king of Aram and Ben-Hadad[l] his son.

4Then Jehoahaz sought[m] the LORD's favor, and the LORD listened to him, for he saw[n] how severely the king of Aram was oppressing[o] Israel. 5The LORD provided a deliverer[p] for Israel, and they escaped from the power of Aram. So the Israelites lived in their own homes as they had before. 6But they did not turn away from the sins[q] of the house of Jeroboam, which he had caused Israel to commit; they continued in them. Also, the Asherah pole[d][r] remained standing in Samaria.

7Nothing had been left[s] of the army

12:4 [r] S Ex 25:2; S 35:29
12:5 [s] 2Ki 22:5
12:9 [t] 2Ki 25:18; Jer 35:4; 52:24 [u] Mk 12:41; Lk 21:1
12:10 [v] S 2Sa 8:17
12:12 [w] 2Ki 22:5-6
12:13 [x] S 1Ki 7:48-51
12:15 [y] 2Ki 22:7; 1Co 4:2
12:16 [z] Lev 5:14-19 [a] Lev 4:1-35 [b] S Lev 7:7
12:17 [c] 2Ki 8:12
12:18 [d] S 1Ki 15:18; S 2Ch 21:16-17 [e] 1Ki 15:21; 2Ki 15:20; 19:36
12:20 [f] 2Ki 14:5 [g] 2Ki 14:19; 15:10, 14,25,30; 21:23; 25:25 [h] Jdg 9:6
13:2 [i] 1Ki 12:26-33
13:3 [j] S Dt 31:17 [k] S 1Ki 19:17 [l] ver 24
13:4 [m] S Dt 4:29 [n] S Dt 26:7 [o] S Nu 10:9; 2Sa 7:10
13:5 [p] S Ge 45:7; S Dt 28:29; S Jdg 2:18
13:6 [q] 1Ki 12:30 [r] S 1Ki 16:33
13:7 [s] 2Ki 10:32-33

[d] 6 That is, a symbol of the goddess Asherah; here and elsewhere in 2 Kings

12:20 ASSASSINATED HIM. The conspiracy against Joash occurred because he had rejected the Lord, begun to worship other gods and killed Zechariah (2Ch 24:17–22,25).

of Jehoahaz except fifty horsemen, ten
chariots and ten thousand foot soldiers, for the king of Aram had destroyed the rest and made them like
the dust[t] at threshing time.
8As for the other events of the reign
of Jehoahaz, all he did and his achievements, are they not written in the book
of the annals of the kings of Israel? 9Je-
hoahaz rested with his fathers and was
buried in Samaria. And Jehoash[e] his
son succeeded him as king.

Jehoash King of Israel

10In the thirty-seventh year of Joash
king of Judah, Jehoash son of Jehoahaz
became king of Israel in Samaria, and
he reigned sixteen years. 11He did evil
in the eyes of the LORD and did not turn
away from any of the sins of Jeroboam
son of Nebat, which he had caused Israel to commit; he continued in them.
12As for the other events of the reign
of Jehoash, all he did and his achievements, including his war against Amaziah[u] king of Judah, are they not written in the book of the annals[v] of the
kings of Israel? 13Jehoash rested with
his fathers, and Jeroboam[w] succeeded
him on the throne. Jehoash was buried
in Samaria with the kings of Israel.
14Now Elisha was suffering from the
illness from which he died. Jehoash
king of Israel went down to see him
and wept over him. "My father! My father!" he cried. "The chariots[x] and
horsemen of Israel!"
15Elisha said, "Get a bow and some
arrows,"[y] and he did so. 16"Take the
bow in your hands," he said to the king
of Israel. When he had taken it, Elisha
put his hands on the king's hands.
17"Open the east window," he said,
and he opened it. "Shoot!"[z] Elisha
said, and he shot. "The LORD's arrow of
victory, the arrow of victory over
Aram!" Elisha declared. "You will completely destroy the Arameans at
Aphek."[a]
18Then he said, "Take the arrows,"
and the king took them. Elisha told
him, "Strike the ground." He struck it
three times and stopped. 19The man of
God was angry with him and said, "You
should have struck the ground five or
six times; then you would have defeated Aram and completely destroyed it.
But now you will defeat it only three
times."[b]
20Elisha died and was buried.
Now Moabite raiders[c] used to enter
the country every spring. 21Once while
some Israelites were burying a man,
suddenly they saw a band of raiders; so
they threw the man's body into Elisha's tomb. When the body touched
Elisha's bones, the man came to life[d]
and stood up on his feet.
22Hazael king of Aram oppressed[e]
Israel throughout the reign of Jehoahaz. 23But the LORD was gracious to
them and had compassion and showed
concern for them because of his covenant[f] with Abraham, Isaac and Jacob. To this day he has been unwilling
to destroy[g] them or banish them from
his presence.[h]
24Hazael king of Aram died, and

13:7 [t] S 2Sa 22:43 **13:12** [u] 2Ki 14:15 [v] 1Ki 15:31 **13:13** [w] 2Ki 14:23; Hos 1:1 **13:14** [x] S 2Ki 2:12 **13:15** [y] 1Sa 20:20

13:17 [z] Jos 8:18 [a] S 1Ki 20:26 **13:19** [b] ver 25 **13:20** [c] S 2Ki 5:2 **13:21** [d] Mt 27:52 **13:22** [e] S 1Ki 19:17 **13:23** [f] S Ex 2:24 [g] S Dt 29:20 [h] S Ex 33:15; 2Ki 17:18; 24:3,20

[e] 9 Hebrew *Joash,* a variant of *Jehoash;* also in verses 12-14 and 25

13:14 ELISHA WAS SUFFERING FROM THE ILLNESS. Elisha, through whom God had performed many wonderful miracles, eventually succumbed to a fatal illness. Reality dictates that great people of faith die, and ironically death sometimes comes through sickness even to those who have themselves had a healing ministry. Among the consequences of the fall of Adam and Eve are sickness and death; no one is exempt from them.

13:14 THE CHARIOTS AND HORSEMEN OF ISRAEL. King Jehoash recognized Elisha's God as the real defender of Israel (cf. 2:12); he knew beyond a doubt that with the death of Elisha, Israel's strength and protection would be gone. In any age when there is no prophetic word to God's people, spiritual death and apostasy are sure to occur (cf. Jer 21—22; see article on THE MINISTRY GIFTS OF THE CHURCH, p. 1830).

13:17–18 EAST WINDOW . . . THE ARROW. The shooting of the arrow toward the east (i.e., the area held by Aram, 10:32–33) was a symbolic action predicting that Israel was going to overthrow Aram's oppression; it was a pledge that God would keep Israel safe. By striking the ground with arrows only three times, King Jehoash demonstrated that he lacked the zeal, commitment and faith necessary for the Lord to fulfill his promise; consequently, he would not completely defeat the Arameans (v. 19).

13:21 TOUCHED ELISHA'S BONES . . . CAME TO LIFE. Elisha died and was buried, but even in the grave God revealed his power as a testimony to Elisha's character as a life-giving prophet (cf. 4:32–37; 1Ki 17:17–24). This miracle suggests that a godly person's influence does not necessarily end at death but can yet be a source of spiritual life for others (cf. Jn 12:24; 2Co 4:11–12).

Ben-Hadad[i] his son succeeded him as
king. **25**Then Jehoash son of Jehoahaz
recaptured from Ben-Hadad son of
Hazael the towns he had taken in battle from his father Jehoahaz. Three
times[j] Jehoash defeated him, and so
he recovered[k] the Israelite towns.

Amaziah King of Judah

14:1–7pp — 2Ch 25:1–4,11–12
14:8–22pp — 2Ch 25:17–26:2

14 In the second year of Jehoash[f]
son of Jehoahaz king of Israel,
Amaziah son of Joash king of Judah began to reign. **2**He was twenty-five years
old when he became king, and he
reigned in Jerusalem twenty-nine
years. His mother's name was Jehoaddin; she was from Jerusalem. **3**He did
what was right in the eyes of the LORD,
but not as his father David had done.
In everything he followed the example
of his father Joash. **4**The high places,[l]
however, were not removed; the people
continued to offer sacrifices and burn
incense there.

5After the kingdom was firmly in his
grasp, he executed[m] the officials[n]
who had murdered his father the king.
6Yet he did not put the sons of the as-
sassins to death, in accordance with
what is written in the Book of the
Law[o] of Moses where the LORD commanded: "Fathers shall not be put to
death for their children, nor children
put to death for their fathers; each is
to die for his own sins."[g][p]

7He was the one who defeated ten
thousand Edomites in the Valley of
Salt[q] and captured Sela[r] in battle,
calling it Joktheel, the name it has to
this day.

8Then Amaziah sent messengers to
Jehoash son of Jehoahaz, the son of
Jehu, king of Israel, with the challenge:
"Come, meet me face to face."

9But Jehoash king of Israel replied
to Amaziah king of Judah: "A thistle[s]
in Lebanon sent a message to a cedar
in Lebanon, 'Give your daughter to my
son in marriage.' Then a wild beast in
Lebanon came along and trampled the
thistle underfoot. **10**You have indeed
defeated Edom and now you are arrogant.[t] Glory in your victory, but stay
at home! Why ask for trouble and
cause your own downfall and that of
Judah also?"

11Amaziah, however, would not listen, so Jehoash king of Israel attacked.
He and Amaziah king of Judah faced
each other at Beth Shemesh[u] in Judah. **12**Judah was routed by Israel, and
every man fled to his home.[v] **13**Jehoash king of Israel captured Amaziah
king of Judah, the son of Joash, the son
of Ahaziah, at Beth Shemesh. Then Jehoash went to Jerusalem and broke
down the wall[w] of Jerusalem from
the Ephraim Gate[x] to the Corner
Gate[y]—a section about six hundred
feet long.[h] **14**He took all the gold and
silver and all the articles found in the
temple of the LORD and in the treasuries of the royal palace. He also took
hostages and returned to Samaria.

15As for the other events of the reign
of Jehoash, what he did and his
achievements, including his war[z]
against Amaziah king of Judah, are
they not written in the book of the annals of the kings of Israel? **16**Jehoash
rested with his fathers and was buried
in Samaria with the kings of Israel.
And Jeroboam his son succeeded him
as king.

17Amaziah son of Joash king of Judah lived for fifteen years after the
death of Jehoash son of Jehoahaz king
of Israel. **18**As for the other events of
Amaziah's reign, are they not written
in the book of the annals of the kings
of Judah?

19They conspired[a] against him in
Jerusalem, and he fled to Lachish,[b]
but they sent men after him to Lachish
and killed him there. **20**He was brought
back by horse[c] and was buried in Jerusalem with his fathers, in the City of
David.

21Then all the people of Judah took
Azariah,[i][d] who was sixteen years
old, and made him king in place of his
father Amaziah. **22**He was the one who

13:24 [i] ver 3
13:25 [j] ver 18,19 [k] S 2Ki 10:32
14:4 [l] 2Ki 12:3
14:5 [m] 2Ki 21:24 [n] 2Ki 12:20
14:6 [o] S Dt 28:61 [p] S Nu 26:11; Job 21:20; Jer 31:30; 44:3; Eze 18:4,20
14:7 [q] S 2Sa 8:13 [r] S Jdg 1:36
14:9 [s] Jdg 9:8-15
14:10 [t] 2Ch 26:16; 32:25
14:11 [u] S Jos 15:10
14:12 [v] 1Ki 22:36
14:13 [w] 1Ki 3:1; 2Ch 33:14; 36:19; Jer 39:2 [x] Ne 8:16; 12:39 [y] 2Ch 26:9; Jer 31:38; Zec 14:10
14:15 [z] 2Ki 13:12
14:19 [a] S 2Ki 12:20 [b] S Jos 10:3
14:20 [c] S 2Ki 9:28
14:21 [d] 2Ki 15:1; 2Ch 26:23; Isa 1:1; Hos 1:1; Am 1:1

[f] *1* Hebrew *Joash,* a variant of *Jehoash*; also in verses 13, 23 and 27 [g] *6* Deut. 24:16
[h] *13* Hebrew *four hundred cubits* (about 180 meters) [i] *21* Also called *Uzziah*

14:1 AMAZIAH. This king began well, but later fell into idolatry (2Ch 25:14), for he did not act "wholeheartedly" (2Ch 25:2); i.e., he had not firmly resolved to do God's will at any cost. Essential to perseverance in the faith is a unwavering intention to remain faithful to God and his commands until the end of our time on this earth, regardless of what may happen to us (Php 3:8–16).

rebuilt Elath[e] and restored it to Judah
after Amaziah rested with his fathers.

Jeroboam II King of Israel

23In the fifteenth year of Amaziah
son of Joash king of Judah, Jeroboam[f]
son of Jehoash king of Israel became
king in Samaria, and he reigned forty-
one years. **24**He did evil in the eyes of
the LORD and did not turn away from
any of the sins of Jeroboam son of Nebat, which he had caused Israel to commit.[g] **25**He was the one who restored
the boundaries of Israel from Lebo[j]
Hamath[h] to the Sea of the Arabah,[k][i] in accordance with the word
of the LORD, the God of Israel, spoken
through his servant Jonah[j] son of Amittai, the prophet from Gath Hepher.
26The LORD had seen how bitterly everyone in Israel, whether slave or
free,[k] was suffering;[l] there was no
one to help them.[m] **27**And since the
LORD had not said he would blot out[n]
the name of Israel from under heaven,
he saved[o] them by the hand of Jeroboam son of Jehoash.
28As for the other events of Jeroboam's reign, all he did, and his military
achievements, including how he recovered for Israel both Damascus[p] and
Hamath,[q] which had belonged to Yau-
di,[1] are they not written in the book of
the annals[r] of the kings of Israel?
29Jeroboam rested with his fathers, the
kings of Israel. And Zechariah his son
succeeded him as king.

Azariah King of Judah

15:1–7pp — 2Ch 26:3–4,21–23

15 In the twenty-seventh year of
Jeroboam king of Israel, Azariah[s] son of Amaziah king of Judah began to reign. **2**He was sixteen years old
when he became king, and he reigned
in Jerusalem fifty-two years. His mother's name was Jecoliah; she was from
Jerusalem. **3**He did what was right[t] in
the eyes of the LORD, just as his father
Amaziah had done. **4**The high places,
however, were not removed; the people
continued to offer sacrifices and burn
incense there.
5The LORD afflicted[u] the king with
leprosy[m] until the day he died, and he
lived in a separate house.[n][v] Jotham[w]
the king's son had charge of the palace[x] and governed the people of the
land.
6As for the other events of Azariah's
reign, and all he did, are they not written in the book of the annals of the
kings of Judah? **7**Azariah rested[y] with
his fathers and was buried near them

14:22 [e] S 1Ki 9:26
14:23 [f] S 2Ki 13:13; 1Ch 5:17; Am 1:1; 7:10
14:24 [g] S 1Ki 15:30
14:25 [h] S Nu 13:21 [i] Dt 3:17 [j] Jnh 1:1; Mt 12:39
14:26 [k] Dt 32:36 [l] 2Ki 13:4 [m] Ps 18:41; 22:11; 72:12; 107:12; Isa 63:5; La 1:7
14:27 [n] S Dt 29:20 [o] S Jdg 6:14
14:28 [p] S 2Sa 8:5 [q] S 2Sa 8:9 [r] 1Ki 15:31
15:1 [s] S ver 32; S 2Ki 14:21
15:3 [t] S 1Ki 14:8
15:5 [u] S Ge 12:17 [v] Lev 13:46 [w] ver 7,32; 2Ch 27:1; Mic 1:1 [x] S Ge 41:40
15:7 [y] Isa 6:1; 14:28

[j] *25* Or *from the entrance to* [k] *25* That is, the Dead Sea [l] *28* Or *Judah* [m] *5* The Hebrew word was used for various diseases affecting the skin—not necessarily leprosy. [n] *5* Or *in a house where he was relieved of responsibility*

14:25 RESTORED THE BOUNDARIES. Israel regained land and the people attained great material prosperity during the reign of Jeroboam II (cf. Am 6:4–6; Hos 12:8). However, the prophets Amos and Hosea, who ministered to Israel during his reign, saw clearly the rotten foundations on which Israel's prosperity was built and foretold Israel's approaching doom in no uncertain terms. In reality, the prosperity that occurred during Jeroboam's reign contributed to the spiritual complacency, moral degeneracy, social injustice and religious apostasy that brought Israel's downfall about twenty-eight years later (see v. 26, note).

14:25 JONAH. Jonah son of Amittai is the well-known prophet who was swallowed by a great fish and who brought God's message of repentance to the Assyrians (Jnh 1:1,17; 3:1–10). He lived and prophesied during the reign of Jeroboam II and was a contemporary of Hosea and Amos.

14:26 HOW BITTERLY EVERYONE IN ISRAEL . . . WAS SUFFERING. In compassion for the people, God used Jeroboam to help Israel (vv. 26–27). (1) However, God's goodness did not lead to repentance. The time of Israel's prosperity was also a time of corruption spiritually, morally and socially. Both Amos and Hosea (see v. 25, note) spoke of a people deeply depraved. Luxury, debauchery, immorality, injustice, violence and deceit of all kinds were the normal way of life (Am 2:6–8; 3:9; 5:11–13; 6:4–7). About this period in Israel's history Hosea wrote: "There is no faithfulness, no love, no acknowledgment of God in the land. There is only cursing, lying and murder, stealing and adultery; they break all bounds, and bloodshed follows bloodshed" (Hos 4:1–2).

(2) This was an agonizing time for both God and his prophets (Hos 1:1–2; 3:1–5; 11:1–12). The prophets spoke, but Israel would not hear. Therefore, the Lord caused the people of Israel to be "taken from their homeland into exile in Assyria" (17:23).

15:1 AZARIAH. Azariah, also called Uzziah (2Ch 26), was king of Judah for 52 years (v. 2). The very year that he died God commissioned the prophet Isaiah as a messenger to Judah and Israel (Isa 6; see 2Ch 26 for more details about Azariah's life).

15:5 AFFLICTED THE KING. Azariah was afflicted with leprosy because (1) he disobeyed God by assuming the function of the priesthood, and (2) in pride he refused to repent of his presumptuous sin (see 2Ch 26:16–21).

in the City of David. And Jotham[z] his
son succeeded him as king.

Zechariah King of Israel

8In the thirty-eighth year of Azariah
king of Judah, Zechariah son of Jeroboam became king of Israel in Samaria,
and he reigned six months. 9He did
evil[a] in the eyes of the LORD, as his
fathers had done. He did not turn away
from the sins of Jeroboam son of Nebat,
which he had caused Israel to commit.
10Shallum son of Jabesh conspired
against Zechariah. He attacked him in
front of the people,[o] assassinated[b]
him and succeeded him as king. 11The
other events of Zechariah's reign are
written in the book of the annals[c] of
the kings of Israel. 12So the word of
the LORD spoken to Jehu was fulfilled:[d] "Your descendants will sit on
the throne of Israel to the fourth generation."[p]

Shallum King of Israel

13Shallum son of Jabesh became
king in the thirty-ninth year of Uzziah
king of Judah, and he reigned in Samaria[e] one month. 14Then Menahem son
of Gadi went from Tirzah[f] up to Samaria. He attacked Shallum son of Jabesh in Samaria, assassinated[g] him
and succeeded him as king.
15The other events of Shallum's
reign, and the conspiracy he led, are
written in the book of the annals[h] of
the kings of Israel.
16At that time Menahem, starting
out from Tirzah, attacked Tiphsah[i]
and everyone in the city and its vicinity, because they refused to open[j]
their gates. He sacked Tiphsah and
ripped open all the pregnant women.

Menahem King of Israel

17In the thirty-ninth year of Azariah
king of Judah, Menahem son of Gadi
became king of Israel, and he reigned
in Samaria ten years. 18He did evil[k] in
the eyes of the LORD. During his entire
reign he did not turn away from the
sins of Jeroboam son of Nebat, which
he had caused Israel to commit.
19Then Pul[q][l] king of Assyria invaded the land, and Menahem gave
him a thousand talents[r] of silver to
gain his support and strengthen his
own hold on the kingdom. 20Menahem
exacted this money from Israel. Every
wealthy man had to contribute fifty
shekels[s] of silver to be given to the
king of Assyria. So the king of Assyria
withdrew[m] and stayed in the land no
longer.
21As for the other events of Menahem's reign, and all he did, are they not
written in the book of the annals of the
kings of Israel? 22Menahem rested
with his fathers. And Pekahiah his son
succeeded him as king.

Pekahiah King of Israel

23In the fiftieth year of Azariah king
of Judah, Pekahiah son of Menahem
became king of Israel in Samaria, and
he reigned two years. 24Pekahiah did
evil[n] in the eyes of the LORD. He did
not turn away from the sins of Jeroboam son of Nebat, which he had caused
Israel to commit. 25One of his chief officers, Pekah[o] son of Remaliah, conspired against him. Taking fifty men of
Gilead with him, he assassinated[p]
Pekahiah, along with Argob and Arieh,
in the citadel of the royal palace at Samaria. So Pekah killed Pekahiah and
succeeded him as king.
26The other events of Pekahiah's
reign, and all he did, are written in
the book of the annals of the kings of
Israel.

Pekah King of Israel

27In the fifty-second year of Azariah
king of Judah, Pekah[q] son of Remaliah[r] became king of Israel in Samaria,
and he reigned twenty years. 28He did
evil in the eyes of the LORD. He did not
turn away from the sins of Jeroboam
son of Nebat, which he had caused Israel to commit.
29In the time of Pekah king of Israel,
Tiglath-Pileser[s] king of Assyria came

15:7 [z] S ver 5
15:9 [a] 1Ki 15:26
15:10 [b] S 2Ki 12:20
15:11 [c] 1Ki 15:31
15:12 [d] 2Ki 10:30
15:13 [e] S 1Ki 13:32
15:14 [f] S 1Ki 15:33 [g] S 2Ki 12:20
15:15 [h] 1Ki 15:31
15:16 [i] 1Ki 4:24 [j] S 2Ki 8:12; S Hos 13:16
15:18 [k] 1Ki 15:26
15:19 [l] 1Ch 5:6, 26
15:20 [m] S 2Ki 12:18
15:24 [n] 1Ki 15:26
15:25 [o] 2Ch 28:6; Isa 7:1 [p] S 2Ki 12:20
15:27 [q] 2Ch 28:6; Isa 7:1 [r] Isa 7:4
15:29 [s] 2Ki 16:7; 17:6; 1Ch 5:26; 2Ch 28:20; Jer 50:17

[o] *10* Hebrew; some Septuagint manuscripts *in Ibleam* [p] *12* 2 Kings 10:30 [q] *19* Also called *Tiglath-Pileser* [r] *19* That is, about 37 tons (about 34 metric tons) [s] *20* That is, about 1 1/4 pounds (about 0.6 kilogram)

15:16 RIPPED OPEN ALL THE PREGNANT WOMEN. Some of Israel's kings committed the most barbarous atrocities (see Isa 13:18; Hos 10:14; 13:16; Am 1:13); furthermore, God had predicted that its kings would lead God's people into apostasy (see 1Sa 8:7; 10:19). By now, Israel had become so evil that her doom and destruction were imminent (see next note).

15:29 DEPORTED THE PEOPLE TO ASSYRIA. This invasion by Tiglath-Pileser III of Assyria

and took Ijon,[t] Abel Beth Maacah, Janoah, Kedesh and Hazor. He took Gilead and Galilee, including all the land of
Naphtali,[u] and deported[v] the people
to Assyria. 30Then Hoshea[w] son of
Elah conspired against Pekah son of
Remaliah. He attacked and assassinated[x] him, and then succeeded him as
king in the twentieth year of Jotham
son of Uzziah.
31As for the other events of Pekah's
reign, and all he did, are they not written in the book of the annals[y] of the
kings of Israel?

Jotham King of Judah

15:33–38pp — 2Ch 27:1–4,7–9

32In the second year of Pekah son of
Remaliah king of Israel, Jotham[z] son
of Uzziah king of Judah began to reign.
33He was twenty-five years old when
he became king, and he reigned in Jerusalem sixteen years. His mother's
name was Jerusha daughter of Zadok.
34He did what was right[a] in the eyes
of the LORD, just as his father Uzziah
had done. 35The high places,[b] however, were not removed; the people continued to offer sacrifices and burn incense there. Jotham rebuilt the Upper
Gate[c] of the temple of the LORD.
36As for the other events of Jotham's
reign, and what he did, are they not
written in the book of the annals of the
kings of Judah? 37(In those days the
LORD began to send Rezin[d] king of
Aram and Pekah son of Remaliah
against Judah.) 38Jotham rested with
his fathers and was buried with them
in the City of David, the city of his father. And Ahaz his son succeeded him
as king.

Ahaz King of Judah

16:1–20pp — 2Ch 28:1–27

16 In the seventeenth year of Pekah son of Remaliah, Ahaz[e]
son of Jotham king of Judah began to
reign. 2Ahaz was twenty years old
when he became king, and he reigned
in Jerusalem sixteen years. Unlike David his father, he did not do what was
right[f] in the eyes of the LORD his God.
3He walked in the ways of the kings of
Israel[g] and even sacrificed his son[h]
in[t] the fire, following the detestable[i]
ways of the nations the LORD had driven
out before the Israelites. 4He offered
sacrifices and burned incense[j] at the
high places, on the hilltops and under
every spreading tree.[k]
5Then Rezin[l] king of Aram and Pekah son of Remaliah king of Israel
marched up to fight against Jerusalem
and besieged Ahaz, but they could not
overpower him. 6At that time, Rezin[m]
king of Aram recovered Elath[n] for
Aram by driving out the men of Judah.
Edomites then moved into Elath and
have lived there to this day.
7Ahaz sent messengers to say to
Tiglath-Pileser[o] king of Assyria, "I
am your servant and vassal. Come up
and save[p] me out of the hand of the
king of Aram and of the king of Israel,
who are attacking me." 8And Ahaz
took the silver and gold found in the
temple of the LORD and in the treasuries of the royal palace and sent it as a
gift[q] to the king of Assyria. 9The king
of Assyria complied by attacking Damascus[r] and capturing it. He deported its inhabitants to Kir[s] and put Rezin to death.
10Then King Ahaz went to Damascus to meet Tiglath-Pileser king of Assyria. He saw an altar in Damascus
and sent to Uriah[t] the priest a sketch
of the altar, with detailed plans for its
construction. 11So Uriah the priest
built an altar in accordance with all the
plans that King Ahaz had sent from Damascus and finished it before King
Ahaz returned. 12When the king came
back from Damascus and saw the al-

15:29 [t]1Ki 15:20 [u]2Ki 16:9; 17:24; 2Ch 16:4; Isa 7:9; 9:1; 10:9,10; 28:1; 36:19; 37:18 [v]2Ki 24:14-16; 1Ch 5:22; Isa 14:6,17; 36:17; 45:13
15:30 [w]2Ki 17:1 [x]S 2Ki 12:20
15:31 [y]1Ki 15:31
15:32 [z]ver 1,S 5; 1Ch 5:17; Isa 1:1; Hos 1:1
15:34 [a]S 1Ki 14:8
15:35 [b]2Ki 12:3 [c]S Ge 23:10; 2Ch 23:20
15:37 [d]2Ki 16:5; Isa 7:1; 8:6; 9:11
16:1 [e]Isa 1:1; 7:1; 14:28; Hos 1:1; Mic 1:1
16:2 [f]S 1Ki 14:8
16:3 [g]2Ki 17:19 [h]S Lev 18:21; S 2Ki 3:27 [i]S Lev 18:3; S Dt 9:4
16:4 [j]2Ki 22:17; 23:5 [k]Dt 12:2; Eze 6:13
16:5 [l]S 2Ki 15:37
16:6 [m]Isa 9:12 [n]S 1Ki 9:26
16:7 [o]S 2Ki 15:29 [p]Isa 2:6; 10:20; Jer 2:18; 3:1; Eze 16:28; 23:5; Hos 10:6
16:8 [q]S 1Ki 15:18; 2Ki 12:18
16:9 [r]S Ge 14:15; S 2Ki 15:29 [s]Isa 22:6; Am 1:5; 9:7
16:10 [t]ver 11,15, 16; Isa 8:2

[t]3 Or *even made his son pass through*

(733 B.C.) represented the first stage of Israel's captivity in exile. Those living in the northern and eastern sections of Israel were carried away from their homeland into Mesopotamia (cf. 16:5–9; 2Ch 28:16–21; Isa 7:1–17). This beginning of the end for the northern kingdom came as a result of God's judgment for their continued sin. Samaria, the capital of the northern kingdom, was captured eleven years later (17:6).

16:3 SACRIFICED HIS SON IN THE FIRE. Under the reign of Ahaz, Judah entered into a dark time of spiritual chaos and corruption. Apostasy reached such depths that the king himself performed the pagan religious practice of sacrificing children by fire to pagan gods (cf. Lev 18:21; 2Ch 28:3; Jer 19:5).

16:9 ASSYRIA COMPLIED BY ATTACKING DAMASCUS. See Amos's prophecy about the Assyrian capture of Damascus (Am 1:3–5; cf. Isa 8:4; 17:1).

tar, he approached it and presented offerings[u][u] on it. **13**He offered up his
burnt offering[v] and grain offering,[w]
poured out his drink offering,[x] and
sprinkled the blood of his fellowship offerings[v][y] on the altar. **14**The bronze
altar[z] that stood before the LORD he
brought from the front of the temple—
from between the new altar and the
temple of the LORD—and put it on the
north side of the new altar.
15King Ahaz then gave these orders
to Uriah the priest: "On the large new
altar, offer the morning[a] burnt offering and the evening grain offering, the
king's burnt offering and his grain offering, and the burnt offering of all the
people of the land, and their grain offering and their drink offering. Sprinkle on the altar all the blood of the
burnt offerings and sacrifices. But I
will use the bronze altar for seeking
guidance."[b] **16**And Uriah the priest
did just as King Ahaz had ordered.
17King Ahaz took away the side panels and removed the basins from the
movable stands. He removed the Sea
from the bronze bulls that supported it
and set it on a stone base.[c] **18**He took
away the Sabbath canopy[w] that had
been built at the temple and removed
the royal entryway outside the temple
of the LORD, in deference to the king of
Assyria.[d]
19As for the other events of the reign
of Ahaz, and what he did, are they not
written in the book of the annals of the
kings of Judah? **20**Ahaz rested[e] with
his fathers and was buried with them
in the City of David. And Hezekiah his
son succeeded him as king.

16:12 [u]2Ch 26:16 **16:13** [v]Lev 6:8-13 [w]Lev 6:14-23 [x]S Ex 29:40 [y]Lev 7:11-21 **16:14** [z]S Ex 20:24; S 40:6; S 1Ki 8:64 **16:15** [a]Ex 29:38-41 [b]1Sa 9:9 **16:17** [c]1Ki 7:27 **16:18** [d]Eze 16:28 **16:20** [e]Isa 14:28

17:1 [f]2Ki 15:30 **17:2** [g]S Dt 4:25 **17:3** [h]Hos 10:14 [i]S Jdg 3:15 **17:4** [j]Ps 146:3; Isa 30:1,7; 36:6; Jer 2:36; Hos 12:1 [k]Hos 13:10 **17:5** [l]Hos 13:16 **17:6** [m]ver 20; S 2Ki 15:29; Isa 42:24 [n]Isa 10:9 [o]S Dt 4:27; S 24:1; S 2Ki 15:29; Am 7:17 [p]1Ch 5:26 **17:7** [q]S Jos 7:11 [r]Ex 14:15-31 **17:8** [s]S Ex 34:15; S Lev 18:3; S Dt 9:4

Hoshea Last King of Israel

17:3-7pp — 2Ki 18:9-12

17 In the twelfth year of Ahaz king
of Judah, Hoshea[f] son of Elah
became king of Israel in Samaria, and
he reigned nine years. **2**He did evil[g] in
the eyes of the LORD, but not like the
kings of Israel who preceded him.
3Shalmaneser[h] king of Assyria
came up to attack Hoshea, who had
been Shalmaneser's vassal and had
paid him tribute.[i] **4**But the king of Assyria discovered that Hoshea was a
traitor, for he had sent envoys to So[x]
king of Egypt,[j] and he no longer paid
tribute to the king of Assyria, as he had
done year by year. Therefore Shalmaneser seized him and put him in prison.[k] **5**The king of Assyria invaded the
entire land, marched against Samaria
and laid siege[l] to it for three years.
6In the ninth year of Hoshea, the king
of Assyria[m] captured Samaria[n] and
deported[o] the Israelites to Assyria.
He settled them in Halah, in Gozan[p]
on the Habor River and in the towns of
the Medes.

Israel Exiled Because of Sin

7All this took place because the Israelites had sinned[q] against the LORD
their God, who had brought them up
out of Egypt[r] from under the power of
Pharaoh king of Egypt. They worshiped other gods **8**and followed the
practices of the nations[s] the LORD had

[u] *12* Or *and went up* [v] *13* Traditionally *peace offerings* [w] *18* Or *the dais of his throne* (see Septuagint) [x] *4* Or *to Sais, to the*; *So* is possibly an abbreviation for *Osorkon*.

17:6 DEPORTED THE ISRAELITES TO ASSYRIA. In 722 B.C., after 210 years of idolatry, spiritual rebellion and moral corruption, God decreed the ultimate fall and exile of the nation of Israel (i.e., the ten tribes of the northern kingdom). The relentless progress of evil among God's people had reached a point of no return; their sin had reached its full measure. God's only recourse was a judgment that dissolved the nation; only a believing and faithful remnant was left to experience the fulfillment of God's promises (cf. Ro 9:27).

17:7 SINNED AGAINST THE LORD. In vv. 7–41 the Holy Spirit gives the theological and moral reasons why God brought about the downfall of his redeemed covenant people and removed them from his presence (v. 18). (1) They forgot God's love and grace manifested in their redemption from Egypt (v. 7). (2) They served the gods of the pagan societies around them, thinking that they would find success, well-being and guidance (vv. 7,12,17; see Col 3:5, note). (3) They adopted the customs and lifestyles of the ungodly world (vv. 8–11,15–17). (4) They rejected God's prophets and their message of righteousness (vv. 13–15; cf. Ac 7:51). (5) They openly rebelled against God's written revelation and covenant (vv. 13–16). (6) They gave themselves over to divination and sorcery and all kinds of immorality (vv. 9,15–17).

This message warns all God's people under the new covenant (see 1Co 10:1–12). God will remove from his kingdom all those (both individuals and churches) who fail to remain faithfully in his Word and love. The results of abandoning God are judgment, ruin, suffering and ultimate rejection (cf. Rev 2:5; 3:15–16).

17:8 FOLLOWED THE PRACTICES OF THE NATIONS. Israel all too eagerly accepted the lifestyles and standards of those who were not God's

driven out before them, as well as the
practices that the kings of Israel had
introduced. 9The Israelites secretly
did things against the LORD their God
that were not right. From watchtower
to fortified city[t] they built themselves
high places in all their towns. 10They
set up sacred stones[u] and Asherah
poles[v] on every high hill and under every spreading tree.[w] 11At every high
place they burned incense, as the nations whom the LORD had driven out before them had done. They did wicked
things that provoked the LORD to anger.
12They worshiped idols,[x] though the
LORD had said, "You shall not do
this."[y] 13The LORD warned[y] Israel
and Judah through all his prophets and
seers:[z] "Turn from your evil ways.[a]
Observe my commands and decrees, in
accordance with the entire Law that I
commanded your fathers to obey and
that I delivered to you through my servants the prophets."[b]

14But they would not listen and were
as stiff-necked[c] as their fathers, who
did not trust in the LORD their God.
15They rejected his decrees and the
covenant[d] he had made with their fathers and the warnings he had given
them. They followed worthless idols[e]
and themselves became worthless.[f]
They imitated the nations[g] around
them although the LORD had ordered
them, "Do not do as they do," and they
did the things the LORD had forbidden
them to do.

16They forsook all the commands of
the LORD their God and made for themselves two idols cast in the shape of
calves,[h] and an Asherah[i] pole. They
bowed down to all the starry hosts,[j]
and they worshiped Baal.[k] 17They
sacrificed[l] their sons and daughters
in[z] the fire. They practiced divination
and sorcery[m] and sold[n] themselves
to do evil in the eyes of the LORD, provoking him to anger.

18So the LORD was very angry with
Israel and removed them from his presence.[o] Only the tribe of Judah was left,
19and even Judah did not keep the commands of the LORD their God. They followed the practices Israel had introduced.[p] 20Therefore the LORD rejected
all the people of Israel; he afflicted
them and gave them into the hands of
plunderers,[q] until he thrust them
from his presence.[r]

21When he tore[s] Israel away from
the house of David, they made Jeroboam son of Nebat their king.[t] Jeroboam
enticed Israel away from following the
LORD and caused them to commit a
great sin.[u] 22The Israelites persisted
in all the sins of Jeroboam and did not
turn away from them 23until the LORD
removed them from his presence,[v] as
he had warned[w] through all his servants the prophets. So the people of
Israel were taken from their homeland[x] into exile in Assyria, and they
are still there.

17:9 [t] 2Ki 18:8 **17:10** [u] S Ex 23:24 [v] Ex 34:13; Isa 17:8; Mic 5:14 [w] S Dt 12:2 **17:12** [x] S Ex 20:4 **17:13** [y] S Jdg 6:8; S 2Ch 7:14; S Job 34:33; Eze 3:17-19 [z] S 1Sa 9:9 [a] Jer 4:1; 18:11; 23:22; 25:5; 35:15; 36:3; Zec 1:4 [b] Mt 23:34 **17:14** [c] S Ex 32:9; Ac 7:51 **17:15** [d] S Lev 26:11; Dt 29:25; Jdg 2:20; 1Ki 11:11; 2Ki 18:12; Ps 78:10; Eze 5:6; Mal 2:10 [e] S Dt 32:21; Hos 11:2; Ro 1:21-23 [f] Jer 2:5 [g] S Dt 12:4 **17:16** [h] S Ex 32:4 [i] S Dt 16:21 [j] S Ge 2:1; Isa 40:26; Jer 19:13 [k] S Jdg 2:11 **17:17** [l] S Dt 12:31; 18:10-12; 2Ki 16:3; Eze 16:21 [m] S Lev 19:26 [n] S 1Ki 21:20; Ro 7:14 **17:18** [o] S Ge 4:14; S Ex 33:15; S 2Ki 13:23; 2Th 1:9 **17:19** [p] 2Ki 16:3; Jer 3:6-10; Eze 23:13 **17:20** [q] S ver 6 [r] Jer 7:15; 15:1 **17:21** [s] S 1Sa 15:27; S 1Ki 11:11 [t] 1Ki 12:20 [u] S 1Ki 12:30 **17:23** [v] Eze 39:23-24 [w] S Jdg 6:8 [x] S 1Ki 9:7

[y] 12 Exodus 20:4, 5 [z] 17 Or *They made their sons and daughters pass through*

---

people. Although separation from the nations was one of God's fundamental requirements for Israel (Lev 18:3,30; Dt 12:29–31; 18:9–14), the people adopted pagan customs from surrounding nations (see article on SPIRITUAL SEPARATION FOR BELIEVERS, p. 1794). Conforming to the world's way of living is one of the great dangers that God's people face in every generation and culture (see Ro 12:2).

17:13 HIS PROPHETS. Israel rejected God's prophets, those who spoke against sin and called for repentance and obedience to the Lord's word and commands (e.g. Jdg 6:8–10; 1Ki 13:1–3; 14:6–16; cf. Ac 7:51–53). They rejected the ministries of Elijah, Elisha, Amos, Hosea and other prophets. The refusal to hear and obey God's word, along with the spurning of the prophetic message against sin and evil, are unmistakable signs of apostasy (see 2Ti 4:3–4, note).

17:16 BOWED DOWN TO ALL THE STARRY HOSTS. The Israelites worshiped astral deities and other gods because they believed such gods would provide a better life, i.e., greater prosperity, fertility, health, pleasure, well-being and security (see Jdg 2:13, note). For this reason Paul calls greed "idolatry" (see Col 3:5, note); Jesus himself states that the pursuit of prosperity and wealth as one's major goal in life is incompatible with serving God (Mt 6:24; cf. Eph 5:5).

17:18 TRIBE OF JUDAH. The southern kingdom consisted of the tribe of Judah, elements of the tribes of Benjamin and Simeon, and some from the ten tribes in Israel who had migrated to the southern kingdom to worship God at Jerusalem (see 2Ch 19:4; 30:1,10–11,25–26; 34:5–7; 35:17–18). Thus, the nation of Judah became the people through whom God's covenant with the Hebrew people was maintained. Note that descendants from the tribes of Israel were present in Palestine in NT times (Ac 26:7; cf. Lk 2:36; Php 3:5).

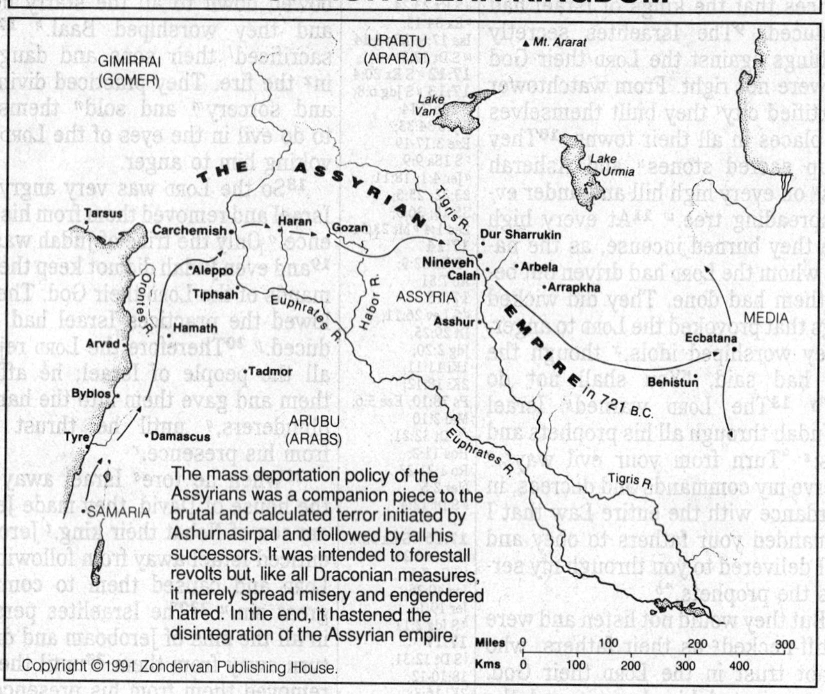
EXILE OF NORTHERN KINGDOM
URARTU
(ARARAT)
Mt. Ararat
GIMIRRAI
(GOMER)
Lake Van
Lake Urmia
THE ASSYRIAN EMPIRE in 721 B.C.
Tigris R.
Tarsus
Carchemish
Haran
Gozan
Dur Sharrukin
Nineveh
Calah
Arbela
Arrapkha
Aleppo
Orontes R.
Tiphsah
Euphrates R.
Habor R.
ASSYRIA
Asshur
MEDIA
Hamath
Arvad
Ecbatana
Tadmor
Behistun
Byblos
ARUBU
(ARABS)
Tyre
Damascus
Euphrates R.
Tigris R.
SAMARIA
The mass deportation policy of the Assyrians was a companion piece to the brutal and calculated terror initiated by Ashurnasirpal and followed by all his successors. It was intended to forestall revolts but, like all Draconian measures, it merely spread misery and engendered hatred. In the end, it hastened the disintegration of the Assyrian empire.
Miles 0 100 200 300
Kms 0 100 200 300 400
Copyright ©1991 Zondervan Publishing House.

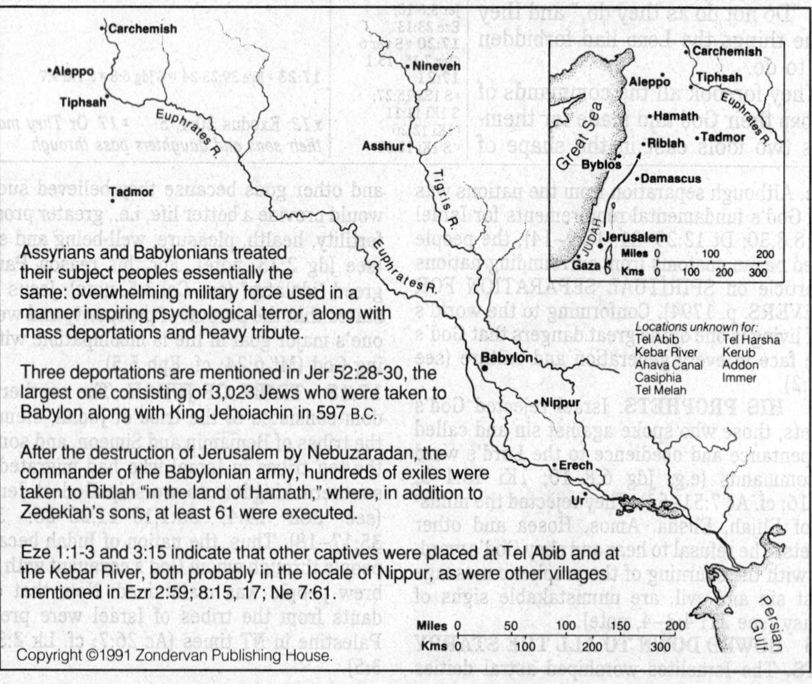
EXILE OF THE SOUTHERN KINGDOM
Carchemish
Aleppo
Tiphsah
Euphrates R.
Nineveh
Asshur
Tadmor
Tigris R.
Euphrates R.
Carchemish
Aleppo
Tiphsah
Euphrates R.
Great Sea
Hamath
Riblah
Tadmor
Byblos
Damascus
JUDAH
Jerusalem
Gaza
Miles 0 100 200
Kms 0 100 200 300
Assyrians and Babylonians treated their subject peoples essentially the same: overwhelming military force used in a manner inspiring psychological terror, along with mass deportations and heavy tribute.
Locations unknown for:
Tel Abib
Kebar River
Ahava Canal
Casiphia
Tel Melah
Tel Harsha
Kerub
Addon
Immer
Babylon
Three deportations are mentioned in Jer 52:28-30, the largest one consisting of 3,023 Jews who were taken to Babylon along with King Jehoiachin in 597 B.C.
Nippur
After the destruction of Jerusalem by Nebuzaradan, the commander of the Babylonian army, hundreds of exiles were taken to Riblah "in the land of Hamath," where, in addition to Zedekiah's sons, at least 61 were executed.
Erech
Ur
Eze 1:1-3 and 3:15 indicate that other captives were placed at Tel Abib and at the Kebar River, both probably in the locale of Nippur, as were other villages mentioned in Ezr 2:59; 8:15, 17; Ne 7:61.
Persian Gulf
Miles 0 50 100 150 200
Kms 0 100 200 300
Copyright ©1991 Zondervan Publishing House.

Samaria Resettled

24The king of Assyria[y] brought
people from Babylon, Cuthah, Avva,
Hamath and Sepharvaim[z] and settled
them in the towns of Samaria to replace the Israelites. They took over Samaria and lived in its towns. 25When
they first lived there, they did not worship the LORD; so he sent lions[a] among
them and they killed some of the people. 26It was reported to the king of
Assyria: "The people you deported and
resettled in the towns of Samaria do
not know what the god of that country
requires. He has sent lions among
them, which are killing them off, because the people do not know what he
requires."
27Then the king of Assyria gave this
order: "Have one of the priests you
took captive from Samaria go back to
live there and teach the people what
the god of the land requires." 28So one
of the priests who had been exiled from
Samaria came to live in Bethel and
taught them how to worship the LORD.
29Nevertheless, each national group
made its own gods in the several
towns[b] where they settled, and set
them up in the shrines[c] the people of
Samaria had made at the high
places.[d] 30The men from Babylon
made Succoth Benoth, the men from
Cuthah made Nergal, and the men from
Hamath made Ashima; 31the Avvites
made Nibhaz and Tartak, and the Se-
pharvites burned their children in the
fire as sacrifices to Adrammelech[e]
and Anammelech, the gods of Sepharvaim.[f] 32They worshiped the LORD,
but they also appointed all sorts[g] of
their own people to officiate for them
as priests in the shrines at the high
places. 33They worshiped the LORD, but
they also served their own gods in accordance with the customs of the nations from which they had been
brought.
34To this day they persist in their
former practices. They neither worship
the LORD nor adhere to the decrees and
ordinances, the laws and commands
that the LORD gave the descendants of
Jacob, whom he named Israel.[h]
35When the LORD made a covenant with
the Israelites, he commanded them:
"Do not worship[i] any other gods or
bow down to them, serve them or sacrifice to them.[j] 36But the LORD, who
brought you up out of Egypt with
mighty power and outstretched arm,[k]
is the one you must worship. To him
you shall bow down and to him offer
sacrifices. 37You must always be careful[l] to keep the decrees[m] and ordinances, the laws and commands he
wrote for you. Do not worship other
gods. 38Do not forget[n] the covenant I
have made with you, and do not worship other gods. 39Rather, worship the
LORD your God; it is he who will deliver
you from the hand of all your enemies."
40They would not listen, however,
but persisted in their former practices.
41Even while these people were worshiping the LORD,[o] they were serving
their idols. To this day their children
and grandchildren continue to do as
their fathers did.

Hezekiah King of Judah

18:2-4pp — 2Ch 29:1-2; 31:1
18:5-7pp — 2Ch 31:20-21
18:9-12pp — 2Ki 17:3-7

18 In the third year of Hoshea son
of Elah king of Israel, Hezekiah[p] son of Ahaz king of Judah began
to reign. 2He was twenty-five years old
when he became king, and he reigned
in Jerusalem twenty-nine years.[q] His
mother's name was Abijah[a] daughter
of Zechariah. 3He did what was right[r]
in the eyes of the LORD, just as his father David[s] had done. 4He removed[t]
the high places,[u] smashed the sacred
stones[v] and cut down the Asherah
poles. He broke into pieces the bronze
snake[w] Moses had made, for up to
that time the Israelites had been burn-

[a] 2 Hebrew *Abi,* a variant of *Abijah*

17:24 [y] 2Ki 19:37; Ezr 4:2,10; Isa 37:38 [z] ver 31; S 2Ki 15:29; 18:34; Isa 36:19; 37:13; Am 6:2
17:25 [a] S Ge 37:20; Isa 5:29; 15:9; Jer 50:17
17:29 [b] Jer 2:28; 11:13 [c] S Lev 26:30; S 1Ki 12:31 [d] Mic 4:5
17:31 [e] 2Ki 19:37 [f] S ver 24
17:32 [g] S 1Ki 12:31
17:34 [h] S Ge 17:5; S 1Ki 18:31
17:35 [i] S Ex 20:5 [j] S Ex 20:3
17:36 [k] S Ex 3:20; Ps 136:12
17:37 [l] Dt 5:32 [m] S Lev 19:37
17:38 [n] S Dt 6:12
17:41 [o] S 1Ki 18:21; Ezr 4:2; Mt 6:24
18:1 [p] Isa 1:1; Hos 1:1; Mic 1:1
18:2 [q] ver 13; Isa 38:5
18:3 [r] S 1Ki 14:8 [s] Isa 38:5
18:4 [t] 2Ch 31:1; Isa 36:7 [u] 2Ki 12:3; 21:3 [v] S Ex 23:24 [w] Nu 21:9

17:24 SETTLED THEM IN THE TOWNS OF SAMARIA. The king of Assyria imported foreign captives to inhabit the "towns of Samaria" (i.e., the entire northern kingdom) in order to destroy any remaining nationalism. Intermarriage between Israelites not taken to Assyria and foreigners brought to the land of Israel produced the people called the "Samaritans." The result was a mixture of foreign religious and cultural traditions with Hebrew customs and faith (vv. 29–33). By NT times, however, many Samaritans had left their pagan ways and developed a faith based exclusively on the Pentateuch (first five books of the Bible). Jesus witnessed to a Samaritan woman, speaking of the incompleteness of Samaritan traditions (Jn 4:4–26). Later many Samaritans became believers in Christ through Philip's ministry (Ac 8:5–25).

ing incense to it. (It was called[b] Nehushtan.[c])
5Hezekiah trusted[x] in the LORD, the
God of Israel. There was no one like
him among all the kings of Judah, either before him or after him. **6**He held
fast[y] to the LORD and did not cease to
follow him; he kept the commands the
LORD had given Moses. **7**And the LORD
was with him; he was successful[z] in
whatever he undertook. He rebelled[a]
against the king of Assyria and did not
serve him. **8**From watchtower to fortified city,[b] he defeated the Philistines,
as far as Gaza and its territory.
9In King Hezekiah's fourth year,[c]
which was the seventh year of Hoshea
son of Elah king of Israel, Shalmaneser king of Assyria marched against
Samaria and laid siege to it. **10**At the
end of three years the Assyrians took
it. So Samaria was captured in Hezekiah's sixth year, which was the ninth
year of Hoshea king of Israel. **11**The
king[d] of Assyria deported Israel to
Assyria and settled them in Halah, in
Gozan on the Habor River and in towns
of the Medes.[e] **12**This happened because they had not obeyed the LORD
their God, but had violated his covenant[f]—all that Moses the servant of
the LORD commanded.[g] They neither
listened to the commands[h] nor carried them out.
13In the fourteenth year[i] of King
Hezekiah's reign, Sennacherib king of
Assyria attacked all the fortified cities
of Judah[j] and captured them. **14**So
Hezekiah king of Judah sent this message to the king of Assyria at Lachish:[k] "I have done wrong.[l] Withdraw from me, and I will pay whatever
you demand of me." The king of Assyria exacted from Hezekiah king of Judah
three hundred talents[d] of silver and
thirty talents[e] of gold. **15**So Hezekiah
gave[m] him all the silver that was
found in the temple of the LORD and in
the treasuries of the royal palace.
16At this time Hezekiah king of Judah stripped off the gold with which he
had covered the doors[n] and doorposts
of the temple of the LORD, and gave it
to the king of Assyria.

Sennacherib Threatens Jerusalem

18:13, 17–37pp — Isa 36:1–22
18:17–35pp — 2Ch 32:9–19

17The king of Assyria sent his supreme commander,[o] his chief officer
and his field commander with a large
army, from Lachish to King Hezekiah
at Jerusalem. They came up to Jerusalem and stopped at the aqueduct of the
Upper Pool,[p] on the road to the Washerman's Field. **18**They called for the
king; and Eliakim[q] son of Hilkiah the
palace administrator, Shebna[r] the
secretary, and Joah son of Asaph the
recorder went out to them.
19The field commander said to them,
"Tell Hezekiah:

" 'This is what the great king,
the king of Assyria, says: On what
are you basing this confidence[s]
of yours? **20**You say you have
strategy and military strength—
but you speak only empty words.
On whom are you depending, that
you rebel against me? **21**Look

18:5 [x] ver 19; S 1Sa 7:3; 2Ki 19:10; Ps 21:7; 125:1; Pr 3:26 **18:6** [y] Dt 10:20; S Dt 6:18 **18:7** [z] S Ge 39:3; S Job 22:25 [a] 2Ki 24:1; Ezr 4:19; Isa 36:5 **18:8** [b] 2Ki 17:9 **18:9** [c] Isa 1:1; 36:1 **18:11** [d] Isa 37:12 [e] Eze 16:39; 23:9 **18:12** [f] S 2Ki 17:15 [g] 2Ki 21:8; Da 9:6, 10 [h] S 1Ki 9:6 **18:13** [i] S ver 2 [j] Isa 1:7; Mic 1:9 **18:14** [k] 2Ki 19:8 [l] Isa 24:5; 33:8 **18:15** [m] S 1Ki 15:18; Isa 39:2 **18:16** [n] 2Ch 29:3 **18:17** [o] Isa 20:1 [p] 2Ki 20:20; 2Ch 32:4,30; Ne 2:14; Isa 22:9 **18:18** [q] 2Ki 19:2; Isa 22:20; 36:3, 11,22; 37:2 [r] ver 26,37; Isa 22:15 **18:19** [s] S ver 5; S Job 4:6

[b] *4* Or *He called it* [c] *4* Nehushtan sounds like the Hebrew for *bronze* and *snake* and *unclean thing.* [d] *14* That is, about 11 tons (about 10 metric tons) [e] *14* That is, about 1 ton (about 1 metric ton)

18:5 TRUSTED IN THE LORD. After telling of the fall of Samaria and the northern kingdom, the author resumes the history of Judah (the southern kingdom), beginning with the reign of the good king Hezekiah. He was considered to be one of the greatest kings Judah ever had because of his trust in and reliance on God. Hezekiah trusted deeply in the Lord, kept his commands (vv. 3–6), and urged the people to turn from sin and return to God (2Ch 30:6–9). At the beginning of his reign he repaired and purified the house of the Lord, restored the priests and Levites to their ministry and reinstated the celebration of the Passover feast (2Ch 29:3; 30:5). He vigorously sought to destroy all idolatrous altars and high places in Judah (v. 4). See chs. 19—20; 2Ch 29—32 and Isa 36—39 for more information on Hezekiah's reign.

18:7 REBELLED AGAINST THE KING OF ASSYRIA. At this time in Judah's history, the southern kingdom also fell under Assyrian dominance, being required to pay an annual tribute. Hezekiah identified with an international conspiracy against Assyria and refused to pay any more money; the result of this attempt at independence is recorded in 18:13—19:37.

18:13 CITIES OF JUDAH AND CAPTURED THEM. In 701 B.C. the Assyrian king Sennacherib responded to Judah's rebellion by capturing many of its important cities; his personal records indicate that he took 46 fortified cities. Hezekiah, seeing no hope in further resistance, apologetically submitted to Sennacherib and depleted Judah's treasury in order to pay Assyria's assessment (vv. 14–16).

now, you are depending on
Egypt,[t] that splintered reed of a
staff,[u] which pierces a man's
hand and wounds him if he leans
on it! Such is Pharaoh king of
Egypt to all who depend on him.
22And if you say to me, "We are
depending on the LORD our God"—
isn't he the one whose high places
and altars Hezekiah removed,
saying to Judah and Jerusalem,
"You must worship before this altar in Jerusalem"?
23" 'Come now, make a bargain
with my master, the king of Assyria: I will give you two thousand
horses—if you can put riders on
them! 24How can you repulse one
officer[v] of the least of my master's officials, even though you
are depending on Egypt for chariots and horsemen[f]? 25Further-
more, have I come to attack and
destroy this place without word
from the LORD?[w] The LORD himself
told me to march against this
country and destroy it.' "

26Then Eliakim son of Hilkiah, and
Shebna and Joah said to the field commander, "Please speak to your servants in Aramaic,[x] since we understand it. Don't speak to us in Hebrew
in the hearing of the people on the
wall."
27But the commander replied, "Was
it only to your master and you that my
master sent me to say these things,
and not to the men sitting on the
wall—who, like you, will have to eat
their own filth and drink their own
urine?"
28Then the commander stood and
called out in Hebrew: "Hear the word
of the great king, the king of Assyria!
29This is what the king says: Do not let
Hezekiah deceive[y] you. He cannot deliver you from my hand. 30Do not let
Hezekiah persuade you to trust in the
LORD when he says, 'The LORD will surely deliver us; this city will not be given
into the hand of the king of Assyria.'
31"Do not listen to Hezekiah. This is
what the king of Assyria says: Make
peace with me and come out to me.
Then every one of you will eat from his
own vine and fig tree[z] and drink water
from his own cistern,[a] 32until I come
and take you to a land like your own,
a land of grain and new wine, a land of
bread and vineyards, a land of olive
trees and honey. Choose life[b] and not
death!
"Do not listen to Hezekiah, for he is
misleading you when he says, 'The
LORD will deliver us.' 33Has the god[c]
of any nation ever delivered his land
from the hand of the king of Assyria?
34Where are the gods of Hamath[d] and
Arpad?[e] Where are the gods of Sepharvaim, Hena and Ivvah? Have they
rescued Samaria from my hand? 35Who
of all the gods of these countries has
been able to save his land from me?
How then can the LORD deliver Jerusalem from my hand?"[f]
36But the people remained silent
and said nothing in reply, because the
king had commanded, "Do not answer
him."
37Then Eliakim[g] son of Hilkiah the
palace administrator, Shebna the secretary and Joah son of Asaph the recorder went to Hezekiah, with their
clothes torn,[h] and told him what the
field commander had said.

Jerusalem's Deliverance Foretold

19:1–13pp — Isa 37:1–13

19 When King Hezekiah heard
this, he tore[i] his clothes and
put on sackcloth and went into the
temple of the LORD. 2He sent Eliakim[j]
the palace administrator, Shebna the
secretary and the leading priests,[k] all
wearing sackcloth,[l] to the prophet
Isaiah[m] son of Amoz. 3They told him,

18:21 [t] Isa 20:5; 31:1; Eze 29:6 [u] 2Ki 24:7; Isa 20:6; 30:5,7; Jer 25:19; 37:7; 46:2
18:24 [v] Isa 10:8
18:25 [w] 2Ki 19:6, 22; 24:3; 2Ch 35:21
18:26 [x] Ezr 4:7
18:29 [y] 2Ki 19:10
18:31 [z] S Nu 13:23; S 1Ki 4:25 [a] Jer 14:3; La 4:4
18:32 [b] Dt 30:19
18:33 [c] 2Ki 19:12
18:34 [d] S 2Ki 17:24; S Jer 49:23 [e] Isa 10:9
18:35 [f] Ps 2:1-2
18:37 [g] S ver 18; Isa 33:7; 36:3,22 [h] S 2Ki 6:30
19:1 [i] S Ge 37:34; S Nu 14:6
19:2 [j] S 2Ki 18:18 [k] Jer 19:1 [l] S Ge 37:34 [m] Isa 1:1

[f]24 Or *charioteers*

18:30 DO NOT LET HEZEKIAH PERSUADE YOU TO TRUST. For some unspecified reason, King Sennacherib of Assyria again invaded Judah with a large army and besieged Jerusalem (v. 17). The Assyrian generals sought to intimidate Hezekiah and all of Jerusalem by defiantly belittling the Lord and mocking the people's trust in him. This blasphemy against God resulted in an angelic intervention by God, whereby 185,000 men of Sennacherib's army were killed and Judah was delivered (19:6–37; 2Ch 32:21–22; Isa 37:14–20,33–38).

19:1 HEZEKIAH . . . WENT INTO THE TEMPLE. Hezekiah had great confidence in God (18:5). Faced with the threat of the Assyrians (18:17–37) and horrified at the mockery of the Lord (18:30–35), he turned to God and urged Isaiah to pray for Jerusalem and God's remnant people (vv. 2–4).

"This is what Hezekiah says: This day
is a day of distress and rebuke and disgrace, as when children come to the
point[n] of birth and there is no
strength to deliver them. 4It may be
that the LORD your God will hear all the
words of the field commander, whom
his master, the king of Assyria, has
sent to ridicule[o] the living God, and
that he will rebuke[p] him for the words
the LORD your God has heard. Therefore pray for the remnant[q] that still
survives."

5When King Hezekiah's officials
came to Isaiah, 6Isaiah said to them,
"Tell your master, 'This is what the
LORD says: Do not be afraid[r] of what
you have heard—those words with
which the underlings of the king of Assyria have blasphemed[s] me. 7Listen!
I am going to put such a spirit in him
that when he hears a certain report,[t]
he will return to his own country, and
there I will have him cut down with the
sword.[u]' "

8When the field commander heard
that the king of Assyria had left Lachish,[v] he withdrew and found the
king fighting against Libnah.[w]

9Now Sennacherib received a report
that Tirhakah, the Cushite[g] king ⌞of
Egypt⌟, was marching out to fight
against him. So he again sent messengers to Hezekiah with this word:
10"Say to Hezekiah king of Judah: Do
not let the god you depend[x] on deceive[y] you when he says, 'Jerusalem
will not be handed over to the king of
Assyria.' 11Surely you have heard what
the kings of Assyria have done to all
the countries, destroying them completely. And will you be delivered?
12Did the gods of the nations that were
destroyed by my forefathers deliver[z]
them: the gods of Gozan,[a] Haran,[b]
Rezeph and the people of Eden who
were in Tel Assar? 13Where is the king
of Hamath, the king of Arpad, the king
of the city of Sepharvaim, or of Hena or
Ivvah?"[c]

Hezekiah's Prayer

19:14–19pp — Isa 37:14–20

14Hezekiah received the letter[d]
from the messengers and read it. Then
he went up to the temple of the LORD
and spread it out before the LORD.
15And Hezekiah prayed to the LORD:
"O LORD, God of Israel, enthroned between the cherubim,[e] you alone[f] are
God over all the kingdoms of the earth.
You have made heaven and earth.
16Give ear,[g] O LORD, and hear;[h] open
your eyes,[i] O LORD, and see; listen to
the words Sennacherib has sent to insult the living God.

17"It is true, O LORD, that the Assyrian kings have laid waste these nations
and their lands. 18They have thrown
their gods into the fire and destroyed
them, for they were not gods[j] but only
wood and stone, fashioned by men's
hands.[k] 19Now, O LORD our God, deliver[l] us from his hand, so that all kingdoms[m] on earth may know[n] that you
alone, O LORD, are God."

Isaiah Prophesies Sennacherib's Fall

19:20–37pp — Isa 37:21–38
19:35–37pp — 2Ch 32:20–21

20Then Isaiah son of Amoz sent a
message to Hezekiah: "This is what
the LORD, the God of Israel, says: I have
heard[o] your prayer concerning Sennacherib king of Assyria. 21This is the
word that the LORD has spoken
against[p] him:

" 'The Virgin Daughter[q] of Zion
despises[r] you and mocks[s] you.
The Daughter of Jerusalem
tosses her head[t] as you flee.

19:3 [n]Hos 13:13 **19:4** [o]S 1Sa 17:26 [p]2Sa 16:12 [q]S Ge 45:7; S Jer 37:3 **19:6** [r]S Dt 3:2; S Jos 1:9 [s]S 2Ki 18:25 **19:7** [t]S Ex 14:24; Jer 51:46 [u]ver 37; 2Ch 32:21; Isa 10:12 **19:8** [v]2Ki 18:14 [w]S Nu 33:20; S 2Ki 8:22 **19:10** [x]S 2Ki 18:5 [y]2Ki 18:29 **19:12** [z]2Ki 18:33; 2Ch 32:17 [a]2Ki 17:6 [b]S Ge 11:31 **19:13** [c]Isa 10:9-11; Jer 49:23 **19:14** [d]2Ki 5:7 **19:15** [e]S Ge 3:24; S Ex 25:22 [f]S Ge 1:1; S Jos 2:11 **19:16** [g]Ps 31:2; 71:2; 88:2; 102:2 [h]S 1Ki 8:29 [i]S Ex 3:16 **19:18** [j]Isa 44:9-11; Jer 10:3-10 [k]Dt 4:28; Ps 115:4; Ac 17:29 **19:19** [l]1Sa 12:10; Job 6:23; Ps 3:7; 71:4 [m]S 1Ki 8:43; 1Ch 16:8 [n]S Jos 4:24; S 1Sa 17:46 **19:20** [o]S 1Ki 9:3 **19:21** [p]Isa 10:5; 33:1 [q]Isa 47:1; Jer 14:17; 18:13; 31:4; 46:11; La 2:13; Am 5:2 [r]Ps 53:5 [s]Pr 1:26; 3:34 [t]Job 16:4; Ps 44:14; 64:8; 109:25; Jer 18:16

[g]9 That is, from the upper Nile region

19:15 HEZEKIAH PRAYED. Hezekiah took the defiant letter that demanded Jerusalem's surrender, spread it out before the Lord and prayed earnestly. When troubles come into our lives and circumstances seem out of control, we must do just as Hezekiah did—draw near to God in fervent and trusting prayer. God has promised to deliver his people from the hands of their enemies and permit nothing to happen that is out of his will (Mt 6:25–34); by clinging to God in trust and faith, we will have his peace to guard our hearts and minds (Php 4:6–7).

19:19 KNOW THAT YOU ALONE, O LORD, ARE GOD. Hezekiah's prayer for God's glory and the vindication of his ways and purposes in history manifests the highest desire of all who love the Lord. Moses (Ex 32:12; Nu 14:13–16; Dt 9:26–29) and David (Ps 59:13; 83:18) exhibited this desire in their prayers. We as believers must be so identified with God that our main concern is to uphold his reputation and honor (cf. Jn 17:4–6); our chief prayer should be, "Hallowed be your name" (Mt 6:9).

22Who is it you have insulted and blasphemed?[u]
Against whom have you raised your voice
and lifted your eyes in pride?
Against the Holy One[v] of Israel!
23By your messengers
you have heaped insults on the Lord.
And you have said,[w]
"With my many chariots[x]
I have ascended the heights of the mountains,
the utmost heights of Lebanon.
I have cut down[y] its tallest cedars,
the choicest of its pines.
I have reached its remotest parts,
the finest of its forests.
24I have dug wells in foreign lands
and drunk the water there.
With the soles of my feet
I have dried up all the streams of Egypt."

25" 'Have you not heard?[z]
Long ago I ordained it.
In days of old I planned[a] it;
now I have brought it to pass,
that you have turned fortified cities
into piles of stone.[b]
26Their people, drained of power,[c]
are dismayed[d] and put to shame.
They are like plants in the field,
like tender green shoots,[e]
like grass sprouting on the roof,
scorched[f] before it grows up.

27" 'But I know[g] where you stay
and when you come and go
and how you rage against me.
28Because you rage against me
and your insolence has reached my ears,
I will put my hook[h] in your nose
and my bit[i] in your mouth,
and I will make you return[j]
by the way you came.'

29"This will be the sign[k] for you,
O Hezekiah:

"This year you will eat what grows by itself,[l]
and the second year what springs from that.
But in the third year sow and reap,
plant vineyards[m] and eat their fruit.
30Once more a remnant[n] of the house of Judah
will take root[o] below and bear fruit above.
31For out of Jerusalem will come a remnant,[p]
and out of Mount Zion a band of survivors.[q]

The zeal[r] of the LORD Almighty will
accomplish this.

32"Therefore this is what the LORD
says concerning the king of Assyria:

"He will not enter this city
or shoot an arrow here.
He will not come before it with shield
or build a siege ramp against it.
33By the way that he came he will return;[s]
he will not enter this city,
declares the LORD.
34I will defend[t] this city and save it,
for my sake and for the sake of David[u] my servant."

35That night the angel of the LORD[v]
went out and put to death a hundred
and eighty-five thousand men in the
Assyrian camp. When the people got
up the next morning—there were all
the dead bodies![w] 36So Sennacherib
king of Assyria broke camp and with-
drew.[x] He returned to Nineveh[y] and 2Ch 20:20-24
stayed there.
37One day, while he was worshiping
in the temple of his god Nisroch, his
sons Adrammelech[z] and Sharezer cut
him down with the sword,[a] and they
escaped to the land of Ararat.[b] And
Esarhaddon[c] his son succeeded him
as king.

19:22 [u]S 2Ki 18:25 [v]Lev 19:2; 1Sa 2:2; Job 6:10; Ps 16:10; 22:3; 71:22; 78:41; 89:18; Isa 1:4; 6:3; 57:15; Hos 11:9
19:23 [w]Isa 10:18; Jer 21:14; Eze 20:47 [x]Ps 20:7; Jer 50:37 [y]Isa 10:34; 14:8; 33:9; Eze 31:3
19:25 [z]Isa 40:21, 28 [a]Isa 22:11 [b]Mic 1:6
19:26 [c]Isa 13:7; Eze 7:17; Zep 3:16 [d]Ps 6:10; 71:24; 83:17; Isa 41:23; Jer 8:9 [e]Isa 4:2; 11:1; 53:2; Jer 23:5 [f]Job 8:12; Ps 37:2; 129:6
19:27 [g]Ps 139:1-4
19:28 [h]2Ch 33:11; Eze 19:9; 29:4; 38:4; Am 4:2 [i]Isa 30:28 [j]ver 33
19:29 [k]S Ex 7:9; S Dt 13:2; Lk 2:12 [l]Lev 25:5 [m]Ps 107:37; Isa 65:21; Am 9:14
19:30 [n]S Ge 45:7 [o]Isa 5:24; 11:1; 27:6; Eze 17:22; Am 2:9
19:31 [p]S Ge 45:7 [q]Isa 66:19; Zep 2:9; Zec 14:16 [r]Isa 9:7
19:33 [s]ver 28
19:34 [t]2Ki 20:6 [u]S 2Sa 7:15
19:35 [v]S Ge 19:13; S Ex 12:23 [w]Job 24:24; Isa 17:14; 41:12; Na 3:3
19:36 [x]S 2Ki 12:18 [y]S Ge 10:11
19:37 [z]2Ki 17:31 [a]S ver 7 [b]S Ge 8:4 [c]S 2Ki 17:24

19:35 ANGEL OF THE LORD. Judah's miraculous deliverance from the Assyrians is one of the great redemptive moments in OT history, recorded no less than three times in Scripture (vv. 35–36; 2Ch 32:21–22: Isa 37:36). The most powerful political kingdom on earth stood against the little nation of Judah. When defeat seemed inevitable, God intervened and delivered his people. In mercy God showed his willingness to renew the covenant and to be Judah's God and Protector if the people would place their trust in him.

Hezekiah's Illness

20:1–11pp — 2Ch 32:24–26; Isa 38:1–8

20 In those days Hezekiah became ill and was at the point of death. The prophet Isaiah son of Amoz went to him and said, "This is what the LORD says: Put your house in order, because you are going to die; you will not recover."

2Hezekiah turned his face to the wall and prayed to the LORD, **3**"Remember,[d] O LORD, how I have walked[e] before you faithfully[f] and with wholehearted devotion and have done what is good in your eyes." And Hezekiah wept bitterly.

4Before Isaiah had left the middle court, the word of the LORD came to him: **5**"Go back and tell Hezekiah, the leader of my people, 'This is what the LORD, the God of your father David, says: I have heard[g] your prayer and seen your tears;[h] I will heal you. On the third day from now you will go up to the temple of the LORD. **6**I will add fifteen years to your life. And I will deliver you and this city from the hand of the king of Assyria. I will defend[i] this city for my sake and for the sake of my servant David.' "

7Then Isaiah said, "Prepare a poul-
2Ch 7:14 tice of figs." They did so and applied it to the boil,[j] and he recovered.

8Hezekiah had asked Isaiah, "What will be the sign that the LORD will heal me and that I will go up to the temple of the LORD on the third day from now?"

9Isaiah answered, "This is the LORD's sign[k] to you that the LORD will do what he has promised: Shall the shadow go forward ten steps, or shall it go back ten steps?"

10"It is a simple[l] matter for the shadow to go forward ten steps," said Hezekiah. "Rather, have it go back ten steps."

11Then the prophet Isaiah called upon the LORD, and the LORD made the shadow go back[m] the ten steps it had gone down on the stairway of Ahaz.

20:3 [d]S Ge 8:1; Ne 1:8; 5:19; 13:14 [e]S Ge 5:22 [f]S 1Ki 2:4; 2Ch 31:20
20:5 [g]S 1Ki 9:3 [h]Ps 6:6,8; 39:12; 56:8
20:6 [i]S 2Ki 19:34; S 1Ch 17:19
20:7 [j]S Ex 9:9
20:9 [k]S Dt 13:2; Jer 44:29
20:10 [l]S 2Ki 3:18
20:11 [m]Jos 10:13; 2Ch 32:31
20:17 [n]2Ki 24:13; 2Ch 36:10; Jer 20:5; 27:22; 52:17-23
20:18 [o]2Ki 24:15; Da 1:3 [p]Mic 4:10
20:20 [q]S 2Ki 18:17 [r]S 2Sa 5:8

Envoys From Babylon

20:12–19pp — Isa 39:1–8
20:20–21pp — 2Ch 32:32–33

12At that time Merodach-Baladan son of Baladan king of Babylon sent Hezekiah letters and a gift, because he had heard of Hezekiah's illness. **13**Hezekiah received the messengers and showed them all that was in his storehouses—the silver, the gold, the spices and the fine oil—his armory and everything found among his treasures. There was nothing in his palace or in all his kingdom that Hezekiah did not show them.

14Then Isaiah the prophet went to King Hezekiah and asked, "What did those men say, and where did they come from?"

"From a distant land," Hezekiah replied. "They came from Babylon."

15The prophet asked, "What did they see in your palace?"

"They saw everything in my palace," Hezekiah said. "There is nothing among my treasures that I did not show them."

16Then Isaiah said to Hezekiah, "Hear the word of the LORD: **17**The time will surely come when everything in your palace, and all that your fathers have stored up until this day, will be carried off to Babylon.[n] Nothing will be left, says the LORD. **18**And some of your descendants,[o] your own flesh and blood, that will be born to you, will be taken away, and they will become eunuchs in the palace of the king of Babylon."[p]

19"The word of the LORD you have spoken is good," Hezekiah replied. For he thought, "Will there not be peace and security in my lifetime?"

20As for the other events of Hezekiah's reign, all his achievements and how he made the pool[q] and the tunnel[r] by which he brought water into the city, are they not written in the book of the annals of the kings of Judah? **21**Hezekiah rested with his fathers. And Manasseh his son succeeded him as king.

20:1 YOU ARE GOING TO DIE. See Isa 38:1, note.
20:5 HEARD YOUR PRAYER . . . I WILL HEAL YOU. See Isa 38:5, note.
20:11 MADE THE SHADOW GO BACK THE TEN STEPS. See Isa 38:8, note.
20:17 CARRIED OFF TO BABYLON. Isaiah's prediction of Judah's exile to Babylon was fulfilled about 115 years later when Nebuchadnezzar, king of Babylon, destroyed Jerusalem, stripped the land and temple of all their riches and took the people of Judah away as captives to his nation (cf. 24:10–13; 2Ch 33:11; Da 1:1–3).

Manasseh King of Judah

21:1–10pp — 2Ch 33:1–10
21:17–18pp — 2Ch 33:18–20

21 Manasseh was twelve years old
when he became king, and he
reigned in Jerusalem fifty-five years.
His mother's name was Hephzibah.[s]
2He did evil[t] in the eyes of the LORD,
following the detestable practices[u] of
the nations the LORD had driven out before the Israelites. 3He rebuilt the high
places[v] his father Hezekiah had destroyed; he also erected altars to
Baal[w] and made an Asherah pole,[x] as
Ahab king of Israel had done. He
bowed down to all the starry hosts[y]
and worshiped them. 4He built altars[z]
in the temple of the LORD, of which the
LORD had said, "In Jerusalem I will put
my Name."[a] 5In both courts[b] of the
temple of the LORD, he built altars to all
the starry hosts. 6He sacrificed his
own son[c] in[h] the fire, practiced sorcery and divination,[d] and consulted
mediums and spiritists.[e] He did much
evil in the eyes of the LORD, provoking[f] him to anger.
7He took the carved Asherah pole[g]
he had made and put it in the temple,[h]
of which the LORD had said to David and
to his son Solomon, "In this temple and
in Jerusalem, which I have chosen out
of all the tribes of Israel, I will put my
Name[i] forever. 8I will not again[j]
make the feet of the Israelites wander
from the land I gave their forefathers,
if only they will be careful to do everything I commanded them and will keep
the whole Law that my servant Moses[k] gave them." 9But the people did
not listen. Manasseh led them astray,
so that they did more evil[l] than the
nations[m] the LORD had destroyed before the Israelites.
10The LORD said through his servants the prophets: 11"Manasseh king
of Judah has committed these detestable sins. He has done more evil[n] than
the Amorites[o] who preceded him and
has led Judah into sin with his idols.[p]
12Therefore this is what the LORD, the
God of Israel, says: I am going to bring
such disaster[q] on Jerusalem and Judah that the ears of everyone who
hears of it will tingle.[r] 13I will stretch
out over Jerusalem the measuring line
used against Samaria and the plumb
line[s] used against the house of Ahab.
I will wipe[t] out Jerusalem as one
wipes a dish, wiping it and turning it
upside down. 14I will forsake[u] the
remnant[v] of my inheritance and hand
them over to their enemies. They will
be looted and plundered by all their
foes, 15because they have done evil[w]
in my eyes and have provoked[x] me to
anger from the day their forefathers
came out of Egypt until this day."
16Moreover, Manasseh also shed so
much innocent blood[y] that he filled Jerusalem from end to end—besides the
sin that he had caused Judah[z] to commit, so that they did evil in the eyes of
the LORD.
17As for the other events of Manasseh's reign, and all he did, including
the sin he committed, are they not written in the book of the annals of the
kings of Judah? 18Manasseh rested
with his fathers and was buried in his

21:1 [s] Isa 62:4
21:2 [t] ver 16; S Dt 4:25; Jer 15:4 [u] Dt 9:4; S 18:9; S 1Ki 14:24; 2Ki 16:3
21:3 [v] S 1Ki 3:3; S 2Ki 18:4 [w] S Jdg 6:28 [x] S Dt 16:21 [y] S Ge 2:1; Dt 17:3; Jer 19:13
21:4 [z] Isa 66:4; Jer 4:1; 7:30; 23:11; 32:34; Eze 23:39 [a] S Ex 20:24; S 2Sa 7:13
21:5 [b] 1Ki 7:12; 2Ki 23:12
21:6 [c] S Lev 18:21; S Dt 18:10; S 2Ki 3:27 [d] Dt 18:14 [e] S Lev 19:31 [f] 2Ki 23:26
21:7 [g] Dt 16:21; 2Ki 23:4 [h] S Lev 15:31 [i] S Ex 20:24; S 2Sa 7:13
21:8 [j] S 2Sa 7:10 [k] S 2Ki 18:12
21:9 [l] S 1Ki 14:9; Eze 5:7 [m] Dt 9:4
21:11 [n] S 1Ki 14:9 [o] S Ge 15:16 [p] Eze 18:12
21:12 [q] 2Ki 23:26; 24:3; Jer 15:4; Eze 7:5 [r] S 1Sa 3:11
21:13 [s] Isa 28:17; 34:11; La 2:8; Am 7:7-9 [t] 2Ki 23:27
21:14 [u] Ps 78:58-60; Jer 12:7; 23:33 [v] 2Ki 19:4; Ezr 9:8; Ne 1:2; Isa 1:9; 10:21; Jer 6:9; 40:15; 42:2; 44:7,28; 50:20; Mic 2:12
21:15 [w] S Ex 32:22 [x] Jer 25:7
21:16 [y] 2Ki 24:4; Job 22:14; Ps 10:11; 94:7; 106:38; Isa 29:15; 47:10; 59:3,7; Jer 2:34; 7:6; 19:4; 22:17; La 4:13; Eze 7:23; 8:12; 9:9; 22:3-4; Hos 4:2; Zep 1:12 [z] S ver 2,11

[h] 6 Or *He made his own son pass through*

21:9 MANASSEH LED THEM ASTRAY. During his long reign of 55 years, Manasseh plunged Judah into her darkest era of idolatry. This wicked king had nothing but contempt for the God of his father Hezekiah. He led God's people into greater evil than the pagan nations that Joshua had destroyed. Why did God allow Manasseh to influence Judah to do such great wickedness? The answer: God does not always remove ungodly leaders from their positions of influence. He holds his people responsible for requiring their leaders to align themselves with his Word; he expects them to reject as false any leader who is not faithful to the teachings of his Word. In this way, God tests his people's loyalty to him, to his revelation and to his godly standards (see Dt 13:3, note).

21:10 THE PROPHETS. Isaiah was probably still prophesying during Manasseh's time. Among other things, a prophet was to be a voice for righteousness when God's people were conforming to the ways of the world (see article on THE PROPHET IN THE OLD TESTAMENT, p. 986).

21:14 FORSAKE THE REMNANT OF MY INHERITANCE. Judah was the focus of redemptive history at this time, forming what was left of God's elect people. Like the northern kingdom, however, a large number of them, by worshiping false gods, threw aside the salvation God had prepared for them. Only those who persevere in genuine faith are assured of remaining a part of God's elect people (see article on ELECTION AND PREDESTINATION, p. 1824).

21:17 OTHER EVENTS OF MANASSEH'S REIGN. See 2Ch 33:1–19 for a record of other events, including Manasseh's repentance at the end of his life.

palace garden,[a] the garden of Uzza.
And Amon his son succeeded him as
king.

Amon King of Judah

21:19–24pp — 2Ch 33:21–25

19Amon was twenty-two years old
when he became king, and he reigned
in Jerusalem two years. His mother's
name was Meshullemeth daughter of
Haruz; she was from Jotbah. 20He did
evil[b] in the eyes of the LORD, as his
father Manasseh had done. 21He
walked in all the ways of his father; he
worshiped the idols his father had worshiped, and bowed down to them. 22He
forsook[c] the LORD, the God of his fathers, and did not walk[d] in the way of
the LORD.
23Amon's officials conspired against
him and assassinated[e] the king in his
palace. 24Then the people of the land
killed[f] all who had plotted against
King Amon, and they made Josiah[g] his
son king in his place.
25As for the other events of Amon's
reign, and what he did, are they not
written in the book of the annals of the
kings of Judah? 26He was buried in his
grave in the garden[h] of Uzza. And Josiah his son succeeded him as king.

The Book of the Law Found

22:1–20pp — 2Ch 34:1–2,8–28

22 Josiah[i] was eight years old
when he became king, and he
reigned in Jerusalem thirty-one years.
His mother's name was Jedidah daughter of Adaiah; she was from Bozkath.[j]
2He did what was right[k] in the eyes of
the LORD and walked in all the ways of
his father David, not turning aside to
the right[l] or to the left.
3In the eighteenth year of his reign,
King Josiah sent the secretary, Shaphan[m] son of Azaliah, the son of Meshullam, to the temple of the LORD. He
said: 4"Go up to Hilkiah[n] the high
priest and have him get ready the money that has been brought into the temple of the LORD, which the doorkeepers
have collected[o] from the people.
5Have them entrust it to the men appointed to supervise the work on the
temple. And have these men pay the
workers who repair[p] the temple of the
LORD— 6the carpenters, the builders
and the masons. Also have them purchase timber and dressed stone to repair the temple.[q] 7But they need not
account for the money entrusted to
them, because they are acting faithfully."[r]
8Hilkiah the high priest said to Shaphan the secretary, "I have found the
Book of the Law[s] in the temple of the
LORD." He gave it to Shaphan, who read
it. 9Then Shaphan the secretary went
to the king and reported to him: "Your
officials have paid out the money that
was in the temple of the LORD and have
entrusted it to the workers and supervisors at the temple." 10Then Shaphan
the secretary informed the king, "Hilkiah the priest has given me a book."
And Shaphan read from it in the presence of the king.[t]
11When the king heard the words of
the Book of the Law,[u] he tore his
robes. 12He gave these orders to Hilkiah the priest, Ahikam[v] son of Shaphan, Acbor son of Micaiah, Shaphan
the secretary and Asaiah the king's attendant:[w] 13"Go and inquire[x] of the
LORD for me and for the people and for
all Judah about what is written in this

21:18 [a] ver 26; Est 1:5; 7:7
21:20 [b] 1Ki 15:26
21:22 [c] S 1Sa 8:8 [d] 1Ki 11:33
21:23 [e] S 2Ki 12:20
21:24 [f] 2Ki 14:5 [g] 2Ch 33:21; Zep 1:1
21:26 [h] S ver 18
22:1 [i] Jer 1:2; 25:3 [j] Jos 15:39
22:2 [k] S Dt 17:19; S 1Ki 14:8 [l] S Dt 5:32
22:3 [m] 2Ch 34:20; Jer 39:14
22:4 [n] Ezr 7:1 [o] 2Ki 12:4-5
22:5 [p] 2Ki 12:5, 11-14
22:6 [q] 2Ki 12:11-12
22:7 [r] S 2Ki 12:15
22:8 [s] S Dt 28:61; S 31:24; Gal 3:10
22:10 [t] Jer 36:21
22:11 [u] ver 8
22:12 [v] 2Ki 25:22; Jer 26:24; 39:14 [w] 1Sa 8:14
22:13 [x] S Ge 25:22; S 1Sa 9:9

22:1 JOSIAH. Josiah was the last of the righteous kings of Judah. At an early age (sixteen years old) he began earnestly to seek the Lord (2Ch 34:3), and four years later he began to purge Judah of false worship (2Ch 34:3–4). As the temple was being repaired, Hilkiah found the Book of the Law written by Moses (2Ch 34:15); this discovery brought a renewed commitment to God's Word, and a measure of spiritual reform was accomplished throughout the land (23:1–30). The prophets Jeremiah and Habakkuk aided Josiah in his attempt to bring the people back to God; for the spiritual condition of the people of Josiah's time, see Jer 1—12; Hab 1:2–4.

22:3 EIGHTEENTH YEAR OF HIS REIGN. Josiah's dedication to God reveals that a young person (Josiah was 26 years old at this time) can have a zeal for the Lord and his cause equal to or greater than that of many older adults.

22:8 THE BOOK OF THE LAW. The Book of the Law found by Hilkiah had been "given through Moses" (2Ch 34:14); it was most likely a copy of the entire Pentateuch, the first five books of the Bible (cf. 23:25; Dt 31:24–26). This discovery bears witness to God's guiding and controlling hand, which had watched over his inspired Word and protected it from destruction by idolators and apostates; indeed, the inspired written Word of God is indestructible (Isa 40:8).

22:13 GO AND INQUIRE OF THE LORD. Josiah wanted to know whether the sins of Judah had reached such a point that divine judgment was inevitable. (1) Through the prophetess Huldah, God said that his people would someday surely be de-

book that has been found. Great is the LORD's anger[y] that burns against us because our fathers have not obeyed the words of this book; they have not acted in accordance with all that is written there concerning us."

14Hilkiah the priest, Ahikam, Acbor, Shaphan and Asaiah went to speak to the prophetess[z] Huldah, who was the wife of Shallum son of Tikvah, the son of Harhas, keeper of the wardrobe. She lived in Jerusalem, in the Second District.

15She said to them, "This is what the LORD, the God of Israel, says: Tell the man who sent you to me, **16**'This is what the LORD says: I am going to bring disaster[a] on this place and its people, according to everything written in the book[b] the king of Judah has read. **17**Because they have forsaken[c] me and burned incense to other gods and provoked me to anger by all the idols their hands have made,[i] my anger will burn against this place and will not be quenched.' **18**Tell the king of Judah, who sent you to inquire[d] of the LORD, 'This is what the LORD, the God of Israel, says concerning the words you heard: **19**Because your heart was responsive and you humbled[e] yourself before the LORD when you heard what I have spoken against this place and its people, that they would become accursed[f] and laid waste,[g] and because you tore your robes and wept in my presence, I have heard you, declares the LORD. **20**Therefore I will gather you to your fathers, and you will be buried in peace.[h] Your eyes[i] will not see all the disaster I am going to bring on this place.' "

22:13 [y] Dt 29:24-28; S 31:17; Isa 5:25; 42:25; Am 2:4
22:14 [z] S Ex 15:20
22:16 [a] S Dt 31:29; S Jos 23:15; Jer 6:19; 11:11; 18:11; 35:17 [b] Da 9:11
22:17 [c] S 1Ki 9:9
22:18 [d] Jer 21:2; 37:3,7
22:19 [e] S Ex 10:3; Isa 57:15; 61:1; Mic 6:8 [f] Jer 24:9; 25:18; 26:6 [g] Lev 26:31
22:20 [h] Isa 47:11; 57:1; Jer 18:11 [i] S 1Ki 21:29
23:2 [j] S Dt 31:11 [k] S Ex 24:7
23:3 [l] S 1Ki 7:15 [m] S 2Ki 11:12 [n] S Dt 13:4
23:4 [o] 2Ki 25:18; Jer 35:4 [p] S 2Ki 21:7
23:5 [q] S 2Ki 16:4 [r] Jer 8:2 [s] Jer 43:13

So they took her answer back to the king.

Josiah Renews the Covenant

23:1–3pp — 2Ch 34:29–32
23:4–20Ref — 2Ch 34:3–7,33
23:21–23pp — 2Ch 35:1,18–19
23:28–30pp — 2Ch 35:20–36:1

23 Then the king called together all the elders of Judah and Jerusalem. **2**He went up to the temple of the LORD with the men of Judah, the people of Jerusalem, the priests and the prophets—all the people from the least to the greatest. He read[j] in their hearing all the words of the Book of the Covenant,[k] which had been found in the temple of the LORD. **3**The king stood by the pillar[l] and renewed the covenant[m] in the presence of the LORD—to follow[n] the LORD and keep his commands, regulations and decrees with all his heart and all his soul, thus confirming the words of the covenant written in this book. Then all the people pledged themselves to the covenant.

4The king ordered Hilkiah the high priest, the priests next in rank and the doorkeepers[o] to remove[p] from the temple of the LORD all the articles made for Baal and Asherah and all the starry hosts. He burned them outside Jerusalem in the fields of the Kidron Valley and took the ashes to Bethel. **5**He did away with the pagan priests appointed by the kings of Judah to burn incense on the high places of the towns of Judah and on those around Jerusalem—those who burned incense[q] to Baal, to the sun and moon, to the constellations and to all the starry hosts.[r][s]

[i] 17 Or *by everything they have done*

livered into the hands of their enemies (vv. 14–17). In other words, when God's people persist in sin, there comes a time when his judgment can no longer be averted. (2) For far too many years, God's people had "mocked God's messengers, despised his words and scoffed at his prophets until the wrath of the LORD was aroused against his people and there was no remedy" (2Ch 36:16). Josiah's revival merely delayed the approaching destruction of Judah, but could not avert it (vv. 18–20; 23:24–27).

22:19 YOU HUMBLED YOURSELF. Josiah pleased God because he humbled himself before the Lord. Humbling oneself before God is a primary condition for becoming renewed and receiving God's grace. It involves: (1) believing that God's judgments toward us are right and just, in accordance with what we deserve (v. 13); (2) knowing that we, without his grace, are captives to sin and evil, and that we are dependent on him for all good (cf. Pr 3:7; Ro 12:3; 1Co 1:4); (3) having a contrite heart before God because of our spiritually poor condition (Ps 51:17; cf. Lev 26:40–41; Nu 12:3; 2Ch 12:5–6; Pr 22:4); (4) fearing God's Word with deep sincerity (v. 11; 2Ch 34:18–19).

23:4 HE BURNED THEM. Josiah's reforms follow the Scriptural principle that repentance for specific sins is essential to true revival. Whenever genuine repentance occurs, specific sins will be identified, false brothers and sisters expelled, worldly practices forsaken and godly standards restored. Any talk of the need for revival and repentance in the churches without specifying what must be changed indicates that the commitment to real change in people's hearts and lifestyles is lacking.

6He took the Asherah pole from the
temple of the LORD to the Kidron Valley[t] outside Jerusalem and burned it
there. He ground it to powder[u] and
scattered the dust over the graves[v] of
the common people.[w] 7He also tore
down the quarters of the male shrine
prostitutes,[x] which were in the temple of the LORD and where women did
weaving for Asherah.
8Josiah brought all the priests from
the towns of Judah and desecrated the
high places, from Geba[y] to Beersheba, where the priests had burned incense. He broke down the shrines[j] at
the gates—at the entrance to the Gate
of Joshua, the city governor, which is
on the left of the city gate. 9Although
the priests of the high places did not
serve[z] at the altar of the LORD in Jerusalem, they ate unleavened bread with
their fellow priests.
10He desecrated Topheth,[a] which
was in the Valley of Ben Hinnom,[b] so
no one could use it to sacrifice his
son[c] or daughter in[k] the fire to Molech. 11He removed from the entrance
to the temple of the LORD the horses
that the kings of Judah[d] had dedicated
to the sun. They were in the court near
the room of an official named Nathan-
Melech. Josiah then burned the chariots dedicated to the sun.[e]
12He pulled down[f] the altars the
kings of Judah had erected on the
roof[g] near the upper room of Ahaz,
and the altars Manasseh had built in
the two courts[h] of the temple of the
LORD. He removed them from there,
smashed them to pieces and threw the
rubble into the Kidron Valley.[i] 13The
king also desecrated the high places
that were east of Jerusalem on the
south of the Hill of Corruption—the
ones Solomon[j] king of Israel had built
for Ashtoreth the vile goddess of the
Sidonians, for Chemosh the vile god of
Moab, and for Molech[l] the detestable[k] god of the people of Ammon.[l]
14Josiah smashed[m] the sacred stones
and cut down the Asherah poles and
covered the sites with human bones.[n]
15Even the altar[o] at Bethel, the
high place made by Jeroboam[p] son of
Nebat, who had caused Israel to sin—
even that altar and high place he demolished. He burned the high place
and ground it to powder, and burned
the Asherah pole also. 16Then Josiah[q]
looked around, and when he saw the
tombs that were there on the hillside,
he had the bones removed from them
and burned on the altar to defile it, in
accordance[r] with the word of the LORD
proclaimed by the man of God who
foretold these things.
17The king asked, "What is that
tombstone I see?"

The men of the city said, "It marks
the tomb of the man of God who came
from Judah and pronounced against
the altar of Bethel the very things you
have done to it."
18"Leave it alone," he said. "Don't
let anyone disturb his bones[s]." So
they spared his bones and those of the
prophet[t] who had come from Samaria.
19Just as he had done at Bethel, Josiah removed and defiled all the shrines
at the high places that the kings of Israel had built in the towns of Samaria
that had provoked the LORD to anger.
20Josiah slaughtered[u] all the priests
of those high places on the altars and
burned human bones[v] on them. Then
he went back to Jerusalem.
21The king gave this order to all the
people: "Celebrate the Passover[w] to
the LORD your God, as it is written in
this Book of the Covenant."[x] 22Not
since the days of the judges who led
Israel, nor throughout the days of the
kings of Israel and the kings of Judah,
had any such Passover been observed.
23But in the eighteenth year of King
Josiah, this Passover was celebrated to
the LORD in Jerusalem.[y]
24Furthermore, Josiah got rid of the
mediums and spiritists,[z] the household gods,[a] the idols and all the other
detestable[b] things seen in Judah and
Jerusalem. This he did to fulfill the requirements of the law written in the
book that Hilkiah the priest had discovered in the temple of the LORD.
25Neither before nor after Josiah was
there a king like him who turned[c] to

23:6 [t] Jer 31:40 [u] S Ex 32:20 [v] S Nu 19:16 [w] Jer 26:23 **23:7** [x] S Ge 38:21; 1Ki 14:24; Eze 16:16 **23:8** [y] S Jos 18:24; S 1Ki 15:22 **23:9** [z] Eze 44:10-14 **23:10** [a] Isa 30:33; Jer 7:31,32; 19:6 [b] S Jos 15:8 [c] S Lev 18:21; S Dt 18:10 **23:11** [d] ver 5,19; Ne 9:34; Jer 44:9 [e] S Dt 4:19 **23:12** [f] 2Ch 33:15 [g] Jer 19:13; Zep 1:5 [h] S 2Ki 21:5 [i] S 2Sa 15:23 **23:13** [j] 1Ki 11:7 [k] S Dt 27:15 [l] Jer 11:13 **23:14** [m] S Ex 23:24 [n] S Nu 19:16; S Ps 53:5 **23:15** [o] S Jos 7:2; 1Ki 13:1-3 [p] S 1Ki 12:33 **23:16** [q] S 1Ki 13:2 [r] 1Ki 13:32 **23:18** [s] 1Ki 13:31 [t] 1Ki 13:29 **23:20** [u] S Ex 22:20; S 2Ki 11:18 [v] S 1Ki 13:2 **23:21** [w] S Ex 12:11; Dt 16:1-8 [x] S Ex 24:7 **23:23** [y] S Ex 12:11; S Nu 28:16 **23:24** [z] S Lev 19:31; S Dt 18:11 [a] S Ge 31:19 [b] Dt 7:26; 2Ki 16:3 **23:25** [c] S 1Sa 7:3

[j] *8* Or *high places* [k] *10* Or *to make his son or daughter pass through* [l] *13* Hebrew *Milcom*

23:25 NEITHER BEFORE NOR AFTER JOSIAH. Josiah is described here as the most faithful and dedicated of all the kings who had reigned over God's people, including David himself (see 2Sa 12:7–15). In terms of personal commitment and faithfulness to God's word, Josiah was the greatest (cf. 18:5; Dt 6:5; Jer 22:15–16).

the LORD as he did—with all his heart
and with all his soul and with all his
strength, in accordance with all the
Law of Moses.[d]
26Nevertheless, the LORD did not
turn away from the heat of his fierce
anger,[e] which burned against Judah
because of all that Manasseh[f] had
done to provoke him to anger. 27So the
LORD said, "I will remove[g] Judah also
from my presence[h] as I removed Israel, and I will reject[i] Jerusalem, the
city I chose, and this temple, about
which I said, 'There shall my Name
be.'[m]"
28As for the other events of Josiah's
reign, and all he did, are they not written in the book of the annals of the
kings of Judah?
29While Josiah was king, Pharaoh
Neco[j] king of Egypt went up to the
Euphrates River to help the king of Assyria. King Josiah marched out to meet
him in battle, but Neco faced him and
killed him at Megiddo.[k] 30Josiah's
servants brought his body in a chariot[l] from Megiddo to Jerusalem and
buried him in his own tomb. And the
people of the land took Jehoahaz son of
Josiah and anointed him and made him
king in place of his father.

Jehoahaz King of Judah

23:31–34pp — 2Ch 36:2–4

31Jehoahaz[m] was twenty-three
years old when he became king, and he
reigned in Jerusalem three months. His
mother's name was Hamutal[n] daughter of Jeremiah; she was from Libnah.
32He did evil[o] in the eyes of the LORD,
just as his fathers had done. 33Pharaoh
Neco put him in chains at Riblah[p] in
the land of Hamath[n][q] so that he
might not reign in Jerusalem, and he
imposed on Judah a levy of a hundred
talents[o] of silver and a talent[p] of
gold. 34Pharaoh Neco made Eliakim[r]
son of Josiah king in place of his father
Josiah and changed Eliakim's name to
Jehoiakim. But he took Jehoahaz and
carried him off to Egypt, and there he
died.[s] 35Jehoiakim paid Pharaoh Neco
the silver and gold he demanded. In order to do so, he taxed the land and exacted the silver and gold from the people of the land according to their
assessments.[t]

Jehoiakim King of Judah

23:36–24:6pp — 2Ch 36:5–8

36Jehoiakim[u] was twenty-five years
old when he became king, and he
reigned in Jerusalem eleven years. His
mother's name was Zebidah daughter
of Pedaiah; she was from Rumah.
37And he did evil[v] in the eyes of the
LORD, just as his fathers had done.

24 During Jehoiakim's reign, Nebuchadnezzar[w] king of Babylon
invaded[x] the land, and Jehoiakim
became his vassal for three years.
But then he changed his mind and

23:25 [d]Jer 22:15 **23:26** [e]2Ki 21:6; Jer 23:20; 30:24 [f]S 2Ki 21:12 **23:27** [g]2Ki 21:13 [h]S Ex 33:15; 2Ki 24:3 [i]Jer 27:10; 32:31 **23:29** [j]ver 33-35; Jer 46:2 [k]2Ki 9:27 **23:30** [l]S 2Ki 9:28 **23:31** [m]1Ch 3:15; Jer 22:11 [n]2Ki 24:18

23:32 [o]1Ki 15:26 **23:33** [p]S Nu 34:11 [q]1Ki 8:65 **23:34** [r]2Ki 24:6; 1Ch 3:15; 2Ch 36:5-8; Jer 1:3 [s]Jer 22:12 **23:35** [t]Jer 2:16 **23:36** [u]Jer 26:1 **23:37** [v]1Ki 15:26 **24:1** [w]ver 10; 2Ki 25:11; Ezr 5:12; Jer 4:7; 25:1,9; 39:1; 40:1; 50:17; 52:15; Eze 32:2; Da 1:1; 7:4 [x]Jer 35:11

[m]*27* 1 Kings 8:29 [n]*33* Hebrew; Septuagint (see also 2 Chron. 36:3) *Neco at Riblah in Hamath removed him* [o]*33* That is, about 3 3/4 tons (about 3.4 metric tons) [p]*33* That is, about 75 pounds (about 34 kilograms)

23:26 NOT TURN AWAY . . . HIS FIERCE ANGER. In spite of Josiah's moral leadership and his spiritual revival and reforms, Judah had declined so far as a nation that deep and lasting national change was no longer possible. Judgment against Judah was only postponed (see Jer 11; 13:27), for both the people and the priests were evil at heart. Thus, after Josiah's death, spiritual and moral degeneration occurred rapidly, and God was obliged to destroy the kingdom only 22 years later.

24:1 NEBUCHADNEZZAR KING OF BABYLON. Nebuchadnezzar, the powerful king of the Neo-Babylonian empire, reigned from 605–562 B.C. In 605 he invaded Palestine and took back to Babylon certain hostages from Jerusalem. This began the 70-year captivity of Judah predicted by Jeremiah (Jer 25:11–12). Jeremiah, Ezekiel and Daniel prophesied during Nebuchadnezzar's time. The destruction and captivity of Judah by Nebuchadnezzar occurred in three phases.

(1) In 605 B.C. King Jehoiakim was conquered; along with temple treasures and royal personnel (including Daniel and his three Hebrew friends, Da 1:1–7), the king was bound in chains to be taken to Babylon (vv. 1–7; 2Ch 36:6–7).

(2) In 597 B.C., Jerusalem was again invaded, and King Jehoiachin, the rest of the temple treasures, and 10,000 men were carried away to Babylon (vv. 14–16), among whom was the prophet Ezekiel.

(3) In 586 B.C., the Babylonians invaded Jerusalem for the final time; this time they destroyed the city and its temple. King Zedekiah and all but some of the poorest people were deported to Babylon (25:1–12; Jer 52:29).

24:1 BABYLON. Babylon, also called the Neo-Babylonian empire, broke the supremacy of Assyria and dominated the world from 605–539 B.C. The Babylonian empire lasted about 70 years, the same 70 years of Judah's captivity. Babylon was in turn conquered by King Cyrus of Persia (539 B.C.), who allowed the Jews to return to their homeland (2Ch 36:22–23; Ezr 1:1–4).

rebelled[y] against Nebuchadnezzar.
2The LORD sent Babylonian,[q][z] Aramean,[a] Moabite and Ammonite raiders[b] against him. He sent them to destroy[c] Judah, in accordance with the
word of the LORD proclaimed by his servants the prophets.[d] 3Surely these
things happened to Judah according to
the LORD's command,[e] in order to remove them from his presence[f] because of the sins of Manasseh[g] and all
he had done, 4including the shedding
of innocent blood.[h] For he had filled
Jerusalem with innocent blood, and the
LORD was not willing to forgive.[i]
5As for the other events of Jehoiakim's reign,[j] and all he did, are they
not written in the book of the annals
of the kings of Judah? 6Jehoiakim
rested[k] with his fathers. And Jehoiachin[l] his son succeeded him as
king.
7The king of Egypt[m] did not march
out from his own country again, because the king of Babylon[n] had taken
all his territory, from the Wadi of Egypt
to the Euphrates River.

Jehoiachin King of Judah

24:8–17pp — 2Ch 36:9–10

8Jehoiachin[o] was eighteen years
old when he became king, and he
reigned in Jerusalem three months. His
mother's name was Nehushta[p] daughter of Elnathan; she was from Jerusalem. 9He did evil[q] in the eyes of the
LORD, just as his father had done.
10At that time the officers of Nebuchadnezzar[r] king of Babylon advanced on Jerusalem and laid siege to
it, 11and Nebuchadnezzar himself
came up to the city while his officers
were besieging it. 12Jehoiachin king of
Judah, his mother, his attendants, his
nobles and his officials all surrendered[s] to him.
In the eighth year of the reign of the
king of Babylon, he took Jehoiachin
prisoner. 13As the LORD had declared,[t] Nebuchadnezzar removed all
the treasures[u] from the temple of the
LORD and from the royal palace, and
took away all the gold articles[v] that
Solomon[w] king of Israel had made for
the temple of the LORD. 14He carried
into exile[x] all Jerusalem: all the officers and fighting men,[y] and all the
craftsmen and artisans—a total of ten
thousand. Only the poorest[z] people of
the land were left.
15Nebuchadnezzar took Jehoiachin[a] captive to Babylon. He also took
from Jerusalem to Babylon the king's
mother,[b] his wives, his officials and
the leading men[c] of the land. 16The
king of Babylon also deported to Babylon the entire force of seven thousand
fighting men, strong and fit for war,
and a thousand craftsmen and artisans.[d] 17He made Mattaniah, Jehoiachin's uncle, king in his place and
changed his name to Zedekiah.[e]

Zedekiah King of Judah

24:18–20pp — 2Ch 36:11–16; Jer 52:1–3

18Zedekiah[f] was twenty-one years
old when he became king, and he
reigned in Jerusalem eleven years. His
mother's name was Hamutal[g] daughter of Jeremiah; she was from Libnah.
19He did evil[h] in the eyes of the LORD,
just as Jehoiakim had done. 20It was
because of the LORD's anger that all

24:1 [y]S 2Ki 18:7 **24:2** [z]Jer 5:15; Hab 1:6 [a]Jer 35:11 [b]S 2Ki 5:2 [c]Isa 28:18-19 [d]Jer 12:7-9; 25:1; 26:1; 36:1; Eze 23:23; Da 1:2 **24:3** [e]S 2Ki 18:25 [f]2Ki 13:23 [g]S 1Ki 14:9; S 2Ki 21:12; Jer 15:4 **24:4** [h]S 2Ki 21:16; Jer 22:3 [i]S Ex 23:21; La 3:42 **24:5** [j]Jer 22:18-19 **24:6** [k]Jer 22:19; 36:30 [l]1Ch 3:16; Jer 22:24,28; Eze 19:1 **24:7** [m]S Ge 15:18; S 2Ki 18:21; S Jer 46:25 [n]Jer 1:14; 25:9; 46:24 **24:8** [o]1Ch 3:16; Jer 22:24; 37:1 [p]ver 15; Jer 13:18; 22:26; 29:2 **24:9** [q]1Ki 15:26 **24:10** [r]S ver 1 **24:12** [s]2Ki 25:27; Jer 13:18; 22:24-30; 24:1; 29:2 **24:13** [t]2Ki 20:17 [u]2Ki 25:15; Isa 39:6; 42:22 [v]2Ki 25:14; Ezr 1:7; Isa 39:6; Jer 15:13; 17:3; 20:5; 27:16; 28:3; Eze 7:21; Da 1:2; 5:2,23; Zep 1:13 [w]S 1Ki 7:51 **24:14** [x]S Dt 28:36; S 2Ch 36:20; S Mt 1:11 [y]Isa 3:1-3 [z]Dt 15:11; 2Ki 25:12; Job 5:16; Ps 9:18; Jer 40:7; 52:16 **24:15** [a]S 2Ki 20:18; Eze 19:9 [b]S ver 8; S 1Ki 2:19 [c]Est 2:6; Isa 39:7; La 2:9; Eze 1:2; 17:12-14; Da 1:3 **24:16** [d]Ezr 2:1; Jer 24:1 **24:17** [e]1Ch 3:15; 2Ch 36:11; Jer 1:3; 37:1; 52:1; Eze 17:13 **24:18** [f]1Ch 3:16; Jer 39:1 [g]2Ki 23:31 **24:19** [h]1Ki 15:26; Jer 37:2

[q]2 Or *Chaldean*

24:2 IN ACCORDANCE WITH THE WORD OF THE LORD. The captivity of the southern kingdom by Babylon had been predicted 150 years before it occurred (Isa 6:11–12; 39:6); Jeremiah foretold that it would last seventy years (Jer 25:11–12).

24:3 REMOVE THEM FROM HIS PRESENCE. Judah's fall was God's judgment on an obstinate and unrepentant people who followed the terrible sins of Manasseh. (1) Apostasy had reached its limit. The priests and prophets uttered lies (Jer 5:31; 6:13). Greediness and deceit (Jer 6:13), immorality and prostitution (Jer 5:8–9), injustice and violence (Jer 6:7), rejection of God's word (Jer 8:9–10) and unfaithfulness (Jer 9:2–3) characterized the lifestyles of the people. (2) God's severe judgment on his OT people serves as a warning to believers today. If God did not spare the natural branches, neither will he spare those who have been grafted in if they conform to the world and a sinful lifestyle (see Ro 11:18–25).

24:20 ZEDEKIAH REBELLED AGAINST THE KING. Zedekiah rebelled partly because false prophets had declared a positive message that God would destroy Babylon and not Judah. Jeremiah's message, though unpopular, proclaimed the opposite—that God would bring his rebellious people under Babylon's rule. It was Jeremiah's message that came to pass, demonstrating that he was a true prophet of the Lord (cf. Dt 18:21–22; see article on THE PROPHET IN THE OLD TESTAMENT, p. 986).

this happened to Jerusalem and Judah,
and in the end he thrust[i] them from
his presence.[j]

The Fall of Jerusalem

25:1–12pp — Jer 39:1–10
25:1–21pp — 2Ch 36:17–20; Jer 52:4–27
25:22–26pp — Jer 40:7–9; 41:1–3, 16–18

Now Zedekiah rebelled against the
king of Babylon.

25 So in the ninth[k] year of Zedekiah's reign, on the tenth day of
the tenth month, Nebuchadnezzar[l]
king of Babylon marched against Jerusalem with his whole army. He encamped outside the city and built siege
works[m] all around it. 2The city was
kept under siege until the eleventh
year of King Zedekiah. 3By the ninth
day of the ⌊fourth⌋[r] month the famine[n] in the city had become so severe
that there was no food for the people
to eat. 4Then the city wall was broken
through,[o] and the whole army fled at
night through the gate between the
two walls near the king's garden,
though the Babylonians[s] were surrounding[p] the city. They fled toward
the Arabah,[t] 5but the Babylonian[u]
army pursued the king and overtook
him in the plains of Jericho. All his soldiers were separated from him and
scattered,[q] 6and he was captured.[r]
He was taken to the king of Babylon at
Riblah,[s] where sentence was pronounced on him. 7They killed the sons
of Zedekiah before his eyes. Then they
put out his eyes, bound him with
bronze shackles and took him to Babylon.[t]

8On the seventh day of the fifth
month, in the nineteenth year of Nebuchadnezzar king of Babylon, Nebuzaradan commander of the imperial guard,
an official of the king of Babylon, came
to Jerusalem. 9He set fire[u] to the temple of the LORD, the royal palace and all
the houses of Jerusalem. Every important building he burned down.[v] 10The
whole Babylonian army, under the
commander of the imperial guard,
broke down the walls[w] around Jerusalem. 11Nebuzaradan the commander of
the guard carried into exile[x] the people who remained in the city, along
with the rest of the populace and those
who had gone over to the king of Babylon.[y] 12But the commander left behind some of the poorest people[z] of
the land to work the vineyards and
fields.

13The Babylonians broke[a] up the
bronze pillars, the movable stands and
the bronze Sea that were at the temple
of the LORD and they carried the bronze
to Babylon. 14They also took away the
pots, shovels, wick trimmers, dishes[b]
and all the bronze articles[c] used in
the temple service. 15The commander
of the imperial guard took away the
censers and sprinkling bowls—all that
were made of pure gold or silver.[d]

16The bronze from the two pillars,
the Sea and the movable stands, which
Solomon had made for the temple of
the LORD, was more than could be
weighed. 17Each pillar[e] was twenty-
seven feet[v] high. The bronze capital
on top of one pillar was four and a half
feet[w] high and was decorated with a
network and pomegranates of bronze
all around. The other pillar, with its
network, was similar.

18The commander of the guard took
as prisoners Seraiah[f] the chief priest,
Zephaniah[g] the priest next in rank
and the three doorkeepers.[h] 19Of
those still in the city, he took the officer in charge of the fighting men and
five royal advisers. He also took the
secretary who was chief officer in
charge of conscripting the people of
the land and sixty of his men who were
found in the city. 20Nebuzaradan the
commander took them all and brought

24:20 [i]Dt 4:26; 29:27 [j]S Ex 33:15; S 2Ki 13:23
25:1 [k]Jer 32:1 [l]Jer 21:2; 34:1-7 [m]Isa 23:13; 29:3; Jer 4:16-17; 32:2; 33:4; Eze 21:22; 24:2
25:3 [n]S Lev 26:26; Isa 22:2; Jer 14:18; 37:21; La 2:20; 4:9
25:4 [o]Job 30:14; Ps 144:14; Jer 50:15; 51:44, 58; Eze 33:21 [p]Jer 4:17; 6:3
25:5 [q]S Lev 26:36; Eze 12:14; 17:21
25:6 [r]Isa 22:3; Jer 38:23 [s]S Nu 34:11
25:7 [t]S Dt 28:36; Jer 21:7; 32:4-5; 34:3,21; Eze 12:11; 19:9; 40:1
25:9 [u]Isa 60:7; 63:15,18; 64:11 [v]S Dt 13:16; Ne 1:3; Ps 74:3-8; 79:1; Jer 2:15; 17:27; 21:10; 26:6,18; La 4:11; Am 2:5; Mic 3:12
25:10 [w]Ne 1:3; Jer 50:15
25:11 [x]S Lev 26:44; 2Ki 24:14 [y]S Dt 28:36; S 2Ki 24:1
25:12 [z]S 2Ki 24:14
25:13 [a]S 1Ki 7:50
25:14 [b]S Nu 7:14 [c]S 2Ki 24:13; Ezr 1:7
25:15 [d]S 2Ki 24:13; Jer 15:13; 20:5; 27:16-22
25:17 [e]1Ki 7:15-22
25:18 [f]ver 18-21; 1Ch 6:14; Ezr 7:1; Ne 11:11 [g]Jer 21:1; 29:25; 37:3 [h]S 2Ki 12:9; S 23:4

[r]3 See Jer. 52:6. [s]4 Or *Chaldeans*; also in verses 13, 25 and 26 [t]4 Or *the Jordan Valley* [u]5 Or *Chaldean*; also in verses 10 and 24 [v]17 Hebrew *eighteen cubits* (about 8.1 meters) [w]17 Hebrew *three cubits* (about 1.3 meters)

25:1 BUILT SIEGE WORKS ALL AROUND IT. The siege against Jerusalem began in 588 B.C. and lasted 18 months (vv. 1–3); its calamities are described in La 2:20–21; 4:3–20; 5:2–15; Eze 5:10. One-third of the people died of hunger and plague, while another one-third died by the sword (Eze 5:12; see also Jer 38:17–19; 39:1; 52:4; Eze 24:1–2).

25:7 KILLED THE SONS OF ZEDEKIAH. Zedekiah, the youngest son of Josiah, reigned for eleven years. He departed from the faith of his righteous father and often persecuted the prophet Jeremiah. Zedekiah could have avoided the tragedies that overtook him if he had listened to Jeremiah (see Jer 38:14–28). Likewise, if a church and its people do not listen to a godly pastor, the church runs the risk of finding itself destroyed and its children captivated by the evil of the world.

them to the king of Babylon at Riblah.
21There at Riblah,[i] in the land of Hamath, the king had them executed.[j]
So Judah went into captivity,[k] away
from her land.[l]
22Nebuchadnezzar king of Babylon
appointed Gedaliah[m] son of Ahikam,[n]
the son of Shaphan, to be over the people he had left behind in Judah. 23When
all the army officers and their men
heard that the king of Babylon had appointed Gedaliah as governor, they
came to Gedaliah at Mizpah—Ishmael
son of Nethaniah, Johanan son of Kareah, Seraiah son of Tanhumeth the Netophathite, Jaazaniah the son of the
Maacathite, and their men. 24Gedaliah
took an oath to reassure them and
their men. "Do not be afraid of the Babylonian officials," he said. "Settle down
in the land and serve the king of Babylon, and it will go well with you."
25In the seventh month, however,
Ishmael son of Nethaniah, the son of
Elishama, who was of royal blood,
came with ten men and assassinated[o]
Gedaliah and also the men of Judah
and the Babylonians who were with
him at Mizpah.[p] 26At this, all the people from the least to the greatest, together with the army officers, fled to
Egypt[q] for fear of the Babylonians.

Jehoiachin Released

25:27–30pp — Jer 52:31–34

27In the thirty-seventh year of the
exile of Jehoiachin king of Judah, in the
year Evil-Merodach[x] became king of
Babylon, he released Jehoiachin[r]
from prison on the twenty-seventh day
of the twelfth month. 28He spoke kindly[s] to him and gave him a seat of hon-
or[t] higher than those of the other
kings who were with him in Babylon.
29So Jehoiachin put aside his prison
clothes and for the rest of his life ate
regularly at the king's table.[u] 30Day
by day the king gave Jehoiachin a regular allowance as long as he lived.[v]

25:21 [i] S Nu 34:11 [j] Jer 34:21 [k] S 1Ki 8:46 [l] S Ge 12:7; S Jos 23:13 **25:22** [m] Jer 39:14; 40:5, 7; 41:18 [n] S 2Ki 22:12 **25:25** [o] S 2Ki 12:20 [p] Zec 7:5 **25:26** [q] Isa 30:2; Jer 43:7 **25:27** [r] S 2Ki 24:12 **25:28** [s] S 1Ki 8:50 [t] Ezr 5:5; 7:6,28; 9:9; Ne 2:1; Da 2:48 **25:29** [u] S 2Sa 9:7 **25:30** [v] Ge 43:34; Est 2:9; 9:22; Jer 28:4

[x] *27* Also called *Amel-Marduk*

25:21 JUDAH WENT INTO CAPTIVITY, AWAY FROM HER LAND. When Judah was led away into captivity, the earthly political kingdom of David ended. But in spite of the destruction of the nation, the promise concerning David's descendants remained (see 2Sa 7:14–16; see article on GOD'S COVENANT WITH DAVID, p. 432). God continued preparing for the coming of David's Son, the Christ, whose kingdom would never end (Lk 1:33). Through David's Messianic descendant, God would eventually form "a chosen people, a royal priesthood, a holy nation, a people belonging to God" (1Pe 2:9).

KINGS OF ISRAEL AND JUDAH

This chart depicts the reigns of the kings of Israel and Judah from Jeroboam of Israel and Rehoboam of Judah until the fall of Jerusalem. As best can be determined, the dates reflect the official reign of each king and not any years of his co-regency with another king. The center column is divided into increments of twenty years; the outside columns give the passages in 1 and 2 Kings and 2 Chronicles where the reign of each king is described. By using this chart, you can see at a glance both the length of each reign and the kings in Israel and Judah who were contemporaries. The final column depicts when the major prophets lived and ministered.

PASSAGES	KINGS OF ISRAEL	DATE B.C	KINGS OF JUDAH	PASSAGES		PROPHETS
I Kings				**I Kings**	**2 Chron.**	
12:25–14:20	JEROBOAM I	930	REHOBOAM	12:1-24; 14:21-31	10:1–12:16	
			ABIJAH	15:1-8	13:1-14:1	
15:25-31	NADAB	910	ASA	15:9-24	14:2–16:14	
15:32–16:7	BAASHA					
		890				
16:8-14	ELAH					
16:15-22	ZIMRI, TIBNI/OMRI					
16:23-28	OMRI					
16:29–22:40	AHAB					Elijah
		870	JEHOSHAPHAT	22:41-50	17:1–21:3	
2 Kings						
1:1-18	AHAZIAH					
3:1–8:15	JORAM					Elisha
		850				

KINGS OF ISRAEL AND JUDAH

PASSAGES	KINGS OF ISRAEL	DATE B.C	KINGS OF JUDAH	PASSAGES		PROPHETS
2 Kings				2 Kings	2 Chron.	
		850				Elisha (cont.)
			JEHORAM	8:16-24	21:4-20	
9:30 –10:36	JEHU		AHAZIAH	8:25-29	22:1-9	
			ATHALIAH	11:1-21	22:10 –23:21	
			JOASH	12:1-21	24:1-27	
		830				
13:1-9	JEHOAHAZ					
		810				
13:10-25	JEHOASH					
			AMAZIAH	14:1-22	25:1-28	
		790				
14:23-29	JEROBOAM II					Jonah
			AZARIAH (UZZIAH)	15:1-7	26:1-23	
		770				Amos
						Hosea
15:8-15	ZECHARIAH, SHALLUM					
15:16-22	MENAHEM	750				

KINGS OF ISRAEL AND JUDAH

PASSAGES	KINGS OF ISRAEL	DATE B.C	KINGS OF JUDAH	PASSAGES		PROPHETS
2 Kings		750		2 Kings	2 Chron.	Hosea (cont.)
15:23-26	PEKAHIAH					Isaiah
15:27-31	PEKAH		JOTHAM	15:32-38	27:1-8	Micah
17:1-6	HOSHEA	730	AHAZ	16:1-20	28:1-27	
	FALL OF SAMARIA	722				
			HEZEKIAH	18:1 –20:21	29:1 –32:33	
		710				
		690				
			MANASSEH	21:1-18	33:1-20	
		670				
		650				

KINGS OF ISRAEL AND JUDAH

PASSAGES	KINGS OF ISRAEL	DATE B.C	KINGS OF JUDAH	PASSAGES 2 Kings	PASSAGES 2 Chron.	PROPHETS
		650				
			AMON	21:19-26	33:21-25	
			JOSIAH	22:1 –23:30	34:1 –35:27	Zephaniah, Nahum
		630				Jeremiah
		610	JEHOAHAZ	23:31-33	36:1-4	Habakkuk
			JEHOIAKIM	23:36 –24:7	36:5-8	Daniel
			JEHOIACHIN	24:8-17	36:9-10	
			ZEDEKIAH	24:18 –25:21	36:11-21	Ezekiel
		590				
		586	FALL OF JERUSALEM	25:8-17	36:15-19	
		570				
		550				

1 CHRONICLES

Outline

I. Genealogies: Adam to Post-exilic Restoration (1:1—9:44)
   A. Adam to Abraham (1:1–27)
   B. Abraham to Jacob (1:28–54)
   C. Jacob to David (2:1–55)
   D. David to the Babylonian Exile (3:1–24)
   E. Genealogies of the Twelve Tribes (4:1—8:40)
   F. Genealogies of the Remnant (9:1–34)
      1. The Tribes That Returned (9:1–9)
      2. The Priests Who Returned (9:10–13)
      3. The Levites Who Returned (9:14–34)
   G. Genealogy of Saul (9:35–44)

II. David: The Enduring Significance of His Reign (10:1—29:30)
   A. The Death of Saul and His Sons (10:1–14)
   B. The Capture of Jerusalem, and David's Mighty Men (11:1—12:40)
   C. Returning the Ark, Restoring Worship and Establishing the Kingdom (13:1—16:43)
   D. The Davidic Covenant (17:1–27)
   E. David's Military Victories (18:1—20:8)
   F. David's Sinful Census (21:1–30)
   G. David Thoroughly Prepares for Building the Temple (22:1–19)
   H. David Organizes the Levites for Temple Ministry (23:1—26:32)
   I. David's Administrative Organization (27:1–34)
   J. David's Final Preparation for Succession and the Temple (28:1—29:20)
   K. Solomon Made King and David's Death (29:21–30)

Author: Ezra (?)

Theme: Israel's "Redemptive" History

Date of Writing: 450–420 B.C.

Background

The history recorded in 1 and 2 Chronicles is pre-exilic; the origin and perspective of the books, however, are post-exilic—written in the second half of the 5th century B.C., sometime after Ezra and a second large company of Jewish exiles from Babylon and Persia had returned to Palestine (457 B.C.). The invasions and destruction of Jerusalem by King Nebuchadnezzar (605–586 B.C.), along with the subsequent 70+ years of Babylonian captivity, had crushed many of the Jews' hopes and ideals as the covenant people; therefore, the exiles who returned to rebuild Jerusalem and the temple needed a spiritual foundation laid, i.e., a sense of identity with their past redemptive history and an understanding concerning the character of their present faith and future hope as the covenant people. 1 and 2 Chronicles were written to address this need among the returned exiles.

The books of Chronicles, Ezra and Nehemiah were all written for the Jews who had returned to Palestine from exile, and they closely resemble one another in style, language, perspective and purpose. Scholars commonly believe that these were all the work of one author or compiler, who, according to the Talmud and most ancient Jewish and Christian scholars, was Ezra, the priest and scribe. Because 1 and 2 Chronicles were written from a priestly perspective and probably in Ezra's lifetime, and because the closing verses of 2 Chronicles (36:22–23) are repeated in Ezr 1:1–3, the talmudic tradition that Ezra was "the Chronicler" is substantiated.

The author consulted numerous written sources when writing Chronicles, including certain OT books and noncanonical records of kings and prophets (see 1Ch 29:29; 2Ch 9:29; 12:15; 20:34; 32:32). According to the apocryphal book 2 Maccabees (2:13–15), Nehemiah during his governorship established a library in Jerusalem in which he placed numerous records of the kings and the prophets. As a spiritual leader, Ezra was given access to all available documents to use in compiling Chronicles. This tradition is ancient and may accurately reflect the means by which the Holy Spirit guided and inspired the composition of these two books.

Purpose

Chronicles was written to reconnect the returned Jewish exiles with their ancestry and redemptive history. In doing so, it underscored three issues: (1) the importance for the Jews to preserve their racial and spiritual heritage; (2) the importance of the law, the temple and the priesthood in their ongoing relationship with God, far more important than allegiance to an earthly king; and (3) Israel's ultimate hope in God's promise of a Messianic descendant of David to sit on the throne forever (1Ch 17:14).

Survey

Although the origin and perspective of 1 and 2 Chronicles is post-exilic, they contain an overview of OT history from Adam to the decree of Cyrus (c. 538 B.C.), when the Jews were permitted to return to their homeland from exile in Babylon and Persia. 1 Chronicles is organized around two major topics: Israel's genealogical history (chs. 1—9) and King David's reign (chs. 10—29).

(1) Chs. 1—9 trace Israel's unique redemptive history from Adam to Abraham to David to the Babylonian exile. The tribe of Judah is placed first among Jacob's twelve sons because the house of David, the temple and the Messiah all came from Judah. The genealogies reveal how God chose and preserved a remnant for himself from the beginning of human history to the post-exilic present. The priestly perspective of this book is evident in the special attention given to the families of the priests and Levites.

(2) Chs. 10—29 are devoted to the reign of David. David's mighty men (chs. 11—12) and his great victories (chs. 14; 18—20) are commended. Also, the Levites, priests and musicians in his administration are highlighted (chs. 23—26). The author placed emphasis on David's recovery of the ark of the covenant and his establishment of Jerusalem as Israel's center of worship (chs. 13—16; 22; 28—29). 1 Chronicles differs from 2 Samuel in its omission of the prophetic revelation of David's dark sins of adultery and murder and the subsequent trail of tragic consequences. In its place, 1 Chronicles inserts what 2 Samuel omits: David's diligent and detailed provisions for building the temple and establishing the worship of the Lord God. Under the Holy Spirit's leading, its omissions and additions were designed to meet the needs of God's people in the post-exilic community.

Special Features

Five major features characterize 1 Chronicles. (1) It covers roughly the same scope of history as does 1 and 2 Samuel. (2) Its genealogies (chs. 1—9) are the longest and most comprehensive genealogical records in the Bible. Since 1 and 2 Chronicles were located last in the original Hebrew arrangement of OT books, these genealogies were conveniently located so as to provide inspiration and content for the genealogies of the Messiah at the beginning of the NT. (3) It vividly describes the unprecedented revival and restoration of all forms of worship when David brought the ark of the covenant to Jerusalem (chs. 15—16). (4) It emphasizes God's covenant with David (ch. 17) as central to Israel's hope for the promised Messiah. (5) Its selective history reflects the priestly perspective of the inspired author concerning the reestablishment of the temple, the law and the priesthood in the post-exilic Jerusalem community.

New Testament Fulfillment

The genealogical record from Adam to the Babylonian exile, including the Davidic kings and their descendants (chs. 3–4), provides the necessary data for the NT genealogies of Jesus the Messiah in Matthew (1:1–17) and of Jesus the Son of God in Luke (3:23–28). The portrait of David in 1 Chronicles, seated on the throne of the Lord and ruling over his kingdom (17:14), foreshadows the coming of the Messianic "Son of David," Jesus Christ.

Historical Reliability of Chronicles

Careless critics have viewed Chronicles as invented or distorted history, generally less reliable than what is recorded in Samuel and Kings. It is true that Chronicles is a highly selective history; it is not true, however, that it is invented or unreliable. It is true that Chronicles stresses the bright side of Jewish history; it is not true that it denies her failures (e.g., 1Ch 21). When omitting history recorded in Samuel and Kings, the Chronicler presupposes a knowledge of these books by his readers. Both the prophetic judgments of Samuel and Kings and the priestly hopes of Chronicles are true and necessary. Many of the historical statements found only in 1 Chronicles have been authenticated as reliable by archaeological discoveries; none has been proven untenable. Also, careful scholarship has provided legitimate explanations concerning the superficial problem of large figures in Chronicles. Chronicles stands as an important and reliable part of the whole of God's inspired record of the old covenant.

Reading 1 Chronicles

In order to read the entire Old Testament in one year, the book of 1 Chronicles should be read in 11 days, according to the following schedule: ☐ 1–2 ☐ 3–4 ☐ 5–6 ☐ 7–8 ☐ 9–10 ☐ 11–13 ☐ 14–16 ☐ 17–19 ☐ 20–22 ☐ 23–25 ☐ 26–29

NOTES

Historical Records From Adam to Abraham

To Noah's Sons

1 Adam,[a] Seth, Enosh, 2Kenan,[b]
Mahalalel,[c] Jared,[d] 3Enoch,[e]
Methuselah,[f] Lamech,[g] Noah.[h]
4The sons of Noah:[a][i]
Shem, Ham and Japheth.[j]

The Japhethites

1:5–7pp — Ge 10:2–5

5The sons[b] of Japheth:
Gomer, Magog, Madai, Javan, Tubal, Meshech and Tiras.
6The sons of Gomer:
Ashkenaz, Riphath[c] and Togarmah.
7The sons of Javan:
Elishah, Tarshish, the Kittim and the Rodanim.

The Hamites

1:8–16pp — Ge 10:6–20

8The sons of Ham:
Cush, Mizraim,[d] Put and Canaan.
9The sons of Cush:
Seba, Havilah, Sabta, Raamah and Sabteca.
The sons of Raamah:
Sheba and Dedan.
10Cush was the father[e] of
Nimrod, who grew to be a mighty warrior on earth.
11Mizraim was the father of
the Ludites, Anamites, Lehabites, Naphtuhites, 12Pathrusites, Casluhites (from whom the Philistines came) and Caphtorites.
13Canaan was the father of
Sidon his firstborn,[f] and of the Hittites, 14Jebusites, Amorites, Girgashites, 15Hivites, Arkites, Sinites, 16Arvadites, Zemarites and Hamathites.

The Semites

1:17–23pp — Ge 10:21–31; 11:10–27

17The sons of Shem:
Elam, Asshur, Arphaxad, Lud and Aram.
The sons of Aram[g]:
Uz, Hul, Gether and Meshech.
18Arphaxad was the father of Shelah,
and Shelah the father of Eber.
19Two sons were born to Eber:
One was named Peleg,[h] because in his time the earth was divided; his brother was named Joktan.
20Joktan was the father of
Almodad, Sheleph, Hazarmaveth, Jerah, 21Hadoram, Uzal, Diklah, 22Obal,[i] Abimael, Sheba, 23Ophir, Havilah and Jobab. All these were sons of Joktan.

1:1 [a] Ge 5:1-32; Lk 3:36-38
1:2 [b] S Ge 5:9 [c] S Ge 5:12 [d] S Ge 5:15
1:3 [e] S Ge 5:18; Jude 1:14 [f] S Ge 5:21 [g] S Ge 5:25 [h] S Ge 5:29
1:4 [i] Ge 6:10; 10:1 [j] S Ge 5:32

[a] *4* Septuagint; Hebrew does not have *The sons of Noah:* [b] *5 Sons* may mean *descendants* or *successors* or *nations*; also in verses 6-10, 17 and 20. [c] *6* Many Hebrew manuscripts and Vulgate (see also Septuagint and Gen. 10:3); most Hebrew manuscripts *Diphath* [d] *8* That is, Egypt; also in verse 11 [e] *10 Father* may mean *ancestor* or *predecessor* or *founder*; also in verses 11, 13, 18 and 20. [f] *13* Or *of the Sidonians, the foremost* [g] *17* One Hebrew manuscript and some Septuagint manuscripts (see also Gen. 10:23); most Hebrew manuscripts do not have this line. [h] *19 Peleg* means *division.* [i] *22* Some Hebrew manuscripts and Syriac (see also Gen. 10:28); most Hebrew manuscripts *Ebal*

1:1 THE GENEALOGIES. The inclusion of genealogies in this book serves several purposes: (1) Like all of 1 Chronicles, the genealogies served to reconnect the returned exiles with their ancestry and their redemptive past, thus enabling them to recover a sense of their roots and heritage.

(2) The genealogies revealed how God chose and preserved a remnant for himself from the beginning of human history to the post-exilic present.

(3) The genealogies' immediate objective was to help Israelite families resettle the land according to previous family ownership (cf. Lev 25) and to mark clearly the tribe of Levi from which the priests were to come.

(4) Their ultimate objective was to trace the descendants of the family line through which God would bring salvation to the world. God had chosen Abraham (v. 27), and from Abraham another family, Israel (v. 34), and from Israel's family (2:1), the tribe of Judah, from which came the Davidic line (3:1). From the family of David, God promised that the Messianic Son would come, who would bring redemption from Satan and sin (see Ge 3:15, note; see articles on GOD'S COVENANT WITH ABRAHAM, ISAAC AND JACOB, p. 46, and GOD'S COVENANT WITH DAVID, p. 432).

1:1–4 ADAM, SETH, ENOSH. These names are taken from Ge 5:1–32 and show that the Chronicler believed Genesis's first chapters to be reliable history and not legend.

24Shem,[k] Arphaxad,[j] Shelah,
25Eber, Peleg, Reu,
26Serug, Nahor, Terah
27and Abram (that is, Abraham).

The Family of Abraham

28The sons of Abraham:
Isaac and Ishmael.

Descendants of Hagar

1:29–31pp — Ge 25:12–16

29These were their descendants:
Nebaioth the firstborn of Ishmael, Kedar, Adbeel, Mibsam,
30Mishma, Dumah, Massa, Hadad, Tema,
31Jetur, Naphish and Kedemah. These were the sons of Ishmael.

Descendants of Keturah

1:32–33pp — Ge 25:1–4

32The sons born to Keturah, Abraham's concubine:[l]
Zimran, Jokshan, Medan, Midian, Ishbak and Shuah.
The sons of Jokshan:
Sheba and Dedan.[m]
33The sons of Midian:
Ephah, Epher, Hanoch, Abida and Eldaah.
All these were descendants of Keturah.

Descendants of Sarah

1:35–37pp — Ge 36:10–14

34Abraham[n] was the father of Isaac.[o]
The sons of Isaac:
Esau and Israel.[p]

Esau's Sons

35The sons of Esau:[q]
Eliphaz, Reuel,[r] Jeush, Jalam and Korah.
36The sons of Eliphaz:
Teman, Omar, Zepho,[k] Gatam and Kenaz;
by Timna: Amalek.[l][s]
37The sons of Reuel:[t]
Nahath, Zerah, Shammah and Mizzah.

The People of Seir in Edom

1:38–42pp — Ge 36:20–28

38The sons of Seir:
Lotan, Shobal, Zibeon, Anah, Dishon, Ezer and Dishan.
39The sons of Lotan:
Hori and Homam. Timna was Lotan's sister.
40The sons of Shobal:
Alvan,[m] Manahath, Ebal, Shepho and Onam.
The sons of Zibeon:
Aiah and Anah.[u]
41The son of Anah:
Dishon.
The sons of Dishon:
Hemdan,[n] Eshban, Ithran and Keran.
42The sons of Ezer:
Bilhan, Zaavan and Akan.[o]
The sons of Dishan[p]:
Uz and Aran.

The Rulers of Edom

1:43–54pp — Ge 36:31–43

43These were the kings who reigned in Edom before any Israelite king reigned[q]:
Bela son of Beor, whose city was named Dinhabah.
44When Bela died, Jobab son of Zerah from Bozrah succeeded him as king.
45When Jobab died, Husham from the land of the Temanites[v] succeeded him as king.
46When Husham died, Hadad son of Bedad, who defeated Midian in the country of Moab, succeeded him as king. His city was named Avith.
47When Hadad died, Samlah from Masrekah succeeded him as king.
48When Samlah died, Shaul from Rehoboth on the river[r] succeeded him as king.
49When Shaul died, Baal-Hanan son

1:24 [k]S Ge 10:21-25; Lk 3:34-36
1:32 [l]S Ge 22:24 [m]S Ge 10:7
1:34 [n]Lk 3:34 [o]Mt 1:2; Ac 7:8 [p]S Ge 17:5
1:35 [q]Ge 36:19 [r]S Ge 36:4
1:36 [s]S Ex 17:14
1:37 [t]Ge 36:17
1:40 [u]S Ge 36:2
1:45 [v]S Ge 36:11

[j] *24* Hebrew; some Septuagint manuscripts *Arphaxad, Cainan* (see also note at Gen. 11:10)
[k] *36* Many Hebrew manuscripts, some Septuagint manuscripts and Syriac (see also Gen. 36:11); most Hebrew manuscripts *Zephi*
[l] *36* Some Septuagint manuscripts (see also Gen. 36:12); Hebrew *Gatam, Kenaz, Timna and Amalek*
[m] *40* Many Hebrew manuscripts and some Septuagint manuscripts (see also Gen. 36:23); most Hebrew manuscripts *Alian*
[n] *41* Many Hebrew manuscripts and some Septuagint manuscripts (see also Gen. 36:26); most Hebrew manuscripts *Hamran*
[o] *42* Many Hebrew and Septuagint manuscripts (see also Gen. 36:27); most Hebrew manuscripts *Zaavan, Jaakan*
[p] *42* Hebrew *Dishon,* a variant of *Dishan*
[q] *43* Or *before an Israelite king reigned over them*
[r] *48* Possibly the Euphrates

of Acbor succeeded him as
king.
50When Baal-Hanan died, Hadad
succeeded him as king. His city
was named Pau,[s] and his
wife's name was Mehetabel
daughter of Matred, the daughter
of Me-Zahab.
51Hadad also
died.

The chiefs of Edom were:
Timna, Alvah, Jetheth,
52Oholibamah, Elah, Pinon,
53Kenaz,
Teman, Mibzar,
54Magdiel and
Iram. These were the chiefs of
Edom.

Israel's Sons

2:1–2pp — Ge 35:23–26

2 These were the sons of Israel:
Reuben, Simeon, Levi, Judah,
Issachar, Zebulun,
2Dan, Joseph, Benjamin, Naphtali, Gad
and Asher.

Judah

2:5–15pp — Ru 4:18–22; Mt 1:3–6

To Hezron's Sons

3The sons of Judah:[w]
Er, Onan and Shelah.[x] These
three were born to him by a Canaanite woman, the daughter
of Shua.[y] Er, Judah's firstborn, was wicked in the LORD's
sight; so the LORD put him to
death.[z]
4Tamar,[a] Judah's
daughter-in-law,[b] bore him
Perez[c] and Zerah. Judah had
five sons in all.

5The sons of Perez:[d]
Hezron[e] and Hamul.
6The sons of Zerah:
Zimri, Ethan, Heman, Calcol
and Darda[t]—five in all.
7The son of Carmi:
Achar,[u][f] who brought trouble on Israel by violating
the ban on taking devoted
things.[v][g]
8The son of Ethan:
Azariah.
9The sons born to Hezron[h] were:
Jerahmeel, Ram and Caleb.[w]

From Ram Son of Hezron

10Ram[i] was the father of
Amminadab[j], and Amminadab the father of Nahshon,[k]
the leader of the people of Judah.
11Nahshon was the father
of Salmon,[x] Salmon the father
of Boaz,
12Boaz[l] the father of
Obed and Obed the father of
Jesse.[m]
13Jesse[n] was the father of
Eliab[o] his firstborn; the second son was Abinadab, the
third Shimea,
14the fourth Nethanel, the fifth Raddai,
15the
sixth Ozem and the seventh David.
16Their sisters were Zeruiah[p] and Abigail. Zeruiah's[q]
three sons were Abishai, Joab[r]
and Asahel.
17Abigail was the
mother of Amasa,[s] whose father was Jether the Ishmaelite.

Caleb Son of Hezron

18Caleb son of Hezron had children
by his wife Azubah (and by Jerioth). These were her sons: Jesher, Shobab and Ardon.
19When Azubah died, Caleb[t]
married Ephrath, who bore him
Hur.
20Hur was the father of
Uri, and Uri the father of Bezalel.[u]

2:3 [w] S Ge 29:35; 38:2-10 [x] S Ge 38:5 [y] S Ge 38:2 [z] S Nu 26:19 2:4 [a] Ge 38:11-30 [b] S Ge 11:31 [c] S Ge 38:29 2:5 [d] S Ge 46:12 [e] Nu 26:21 2:7 [f] S Jos 7:1 [g] S Jos 6:18
2:9 [h] S Nu 26:21 2:10 [i] Lk 3:32-33 [j] S Ex 6:23 [k] S Nu 1:7 2:12 [l] S Ru 2:1 [m] S Ru 4:17 2:13 [n] S Ru 4:17 [o] S 1Sa 16:6 2:16 [p] 1Sa 26:6 [q] 2Sa 2:18 [r] S 2Sa 2:13 2:17 [s] 2Sa 17:25 2:19 [t] ver 42,50 2:20 [u] S Ex 31:2

[s] *50* Many Hebrew manuscripts, some Septuagint manuscripts, Vulgate and Syriac (see also Gen. 36:39); most Hebrew manuscripts *Pai* [t] *6* Many Hebrew manuscripts, some Septuagint manuscripts and Syriac (see also 1 Kings 4:31); most Hebrew manuscripts *Dara* [u] *7* *Achar* means *trouble*; *Achar* is called *Achan* in Joshua. [v] *7* The Hebrew term refers to the irrevocable giving over of things or persons to the LORD, often by totally destroying them. [w] *9* Hebrew *Kelubai*, a variant of *Caleb* [x] *11* Septuagint (see also Ruth 4:21); Hebrew *Salma*

2:1 SONS OF ISRAEL. In ch. 1 the author of Chronicles lists descendants from Adam (v. 1) to Abraham (v. 27) to Israel (v. 34). Through the sons of Israel (i.e., Jacob) came the chosen people, through whom God had determined to bless "all peoples on earth" (Ge 12:3). In chs. 2—8 the author traces the genealogy of Israel's twelve sons. Judah's genealogy is placed first among the tribes (v. 3) because the main stream of redemptive history flowed through it, and particularly through David and his descendants (cf. 3:1; 2Sa 23:5), to the Messiah.

2:5 THE SONS OF. The genealogies are selective, choosing only certain descendants. The phrase "the son of" can also mean "the descendant of"; thus some sons or generations may be omitted.

21Later, Hezron lay with the daughter of Makir the father of Gilead[v] (he had married her when
he was sixty years old), and she
bore him Segub. 22Segub was
the father of Jair, who controlled twenty-three towns in
Gilead. 23(But Geshur and
Aram captured Havvoth
Jair,[y][w] as well as Kenath[x]
with its surrounding settlements — sixty towns.) All these
were descendants of Makir the
father of Gilead.

24After Hezron died in Caleb Ephrathah, Abijah the wife of Hezron
bore him Ashhur[y] the father[z]
of Tekoa.

Jerahmeel Son of Hezron

25The sons of Jerahmeel the firstborn of Hezron:
Ram his firstborn, Bunah,
Oren, Ozem and[a] Ahijah. 26Je-
rahmeel had another wife,
whose name was Atarah; she
was the mother of Onam.
27The sons of Ram the firstborn of
Jerahmeel:
Maaz, Jamin and Eker.
28The sons of Onam:
Shammai and Jada.
The sons of Shammai:
Nadab and Abishur.
29Abishur's wife was named Abihail, who bore him Ahban and
Molid.
30The sons of Nadab:
Seled and Appaim. Seled died
without children.
31The son of Appaim:
Ishi, who was the father of Sheshan.
Sheshan was the father of Ahlai.
32The sons of Jada, Shammai's
brother:
Jether and Jonathan. Jether
died without children.
33The sons of Jonathan:
Peleth and Zaza.
These were the descendants of Jerahmeel.
34Sheshan had no sons — only
daughters.
He had an Egyptian servant
named Jarha. 35Sheshan gave
his daughter in marriage to his
servant Jarha, and she bore him
Attai.
36Attai was the father of Nathan,
Nathan the father of Zabad,[z]
37Zabad the father of Ephlal,
Ephlal the father of Obed,
38Obed the father of Jehu,
Jehu the father of Azariah,
39Azariah the father of Helez,
Helez the father of Eleasah,
40Eleasah the father of Sismai,
Sismai the father of Shallum,
41Shallum the father of Jekamiah,
and Jekamiah the father of
Elishama.

The Clans of Caleb

42The sons of Caleb[a] the brother of
Jerahmeel:
Mesha his firstborn, who was
the father of Ziph, and his son
Mareshah,[b] who was the father of Hebron.
43The sons of Hebron:
Korah, Tappuah, Rekem and
Shema. 44Shema was the father of Raham, and Raham the
father of Jorkeam. Rekem was
the father of Shammai. 45The
son of Shammai was Maon[b],
and Maon was the father of
Beth Zur.[c]
46Caleb's concubine Ephah was the
mother of Haran, Moza and Gazez. Haran was the father of
Gazez.
47The sons of Jahdai:
Regem, Jotham, Geshan, Pelet,
Ephah and Shaaph.
48Caleb's concubine Maacah was
the mother of Sheber and Tir-
hanah. 49She also gave birth to
Shaaph the father of Madmannah[d] and to Sheva the father
of Macbenah and Gibea. Caleb's daughter was Acsah.[e]
50These were the descendants
of Caleb.

The sons of Hur[f] the firstborn of
Ephrathah:
Shobal the father of Kiriath Jea-
rim,[g] 51Salma the father of

2:21 [v]S Nu 27:1
2:23 [w]S Nu 32:41; Dt 3:14 [x]Nu 32:42
2:24 [y]1Ch 4:5
2:36 [z]1Ch 11:41
2:42 [a]S ver 19
2:45 [b]S Jos 15:55 [c]S Jos 15:58
2:49 [d]Jos 15:31 [e]Jos 15:16
2:50 [f]1Ch 4:4 [g]S ver 19

[y] 23 Or *captured the settlements of Jair*
[z] 24 *Father* may mean *civic leader* or *military leader*; also in verses 42, 45, 49-52 and possibly elsewhere.
[a] 25 Or *Oren and Ozem, by*
[b] 42 The meaning of the Hebrew for this phrase is uncertain.

Bethlehem, and Hareph the father of Beth Gader.

52 The descendants of Shobal the father of Kiriath Jearim were:
Haroeh, half the Manahathites,
53 and the clans of Kiriath Jearim: the Ithrites,[h] Puthites, Shumathites and Mishraites. From these descended the Zorathites and Eshtaolites.

54 The descendants of Salma:
Bethlehem, the Netophathites,[i] Atroth Beth Joab, half the Manahathites, the Zorites,
55 and the clans of scribes[c] who lived at Jabez: the Tirathites, Shimeathites and Sucathites. These are the Kenites[j] who came from Hammath,[k] the father of the house of Recab.[d][l]

The Sons of David

3:1–4pp — 2Sa 3:2–5
3:5–8pp — 2Sa 5:14–16; 1Ch 14:4–7

3 These were the sons of David[m] born to him in Hebron:
The firstborn was Amnon the son of Ahinoam[n] of Jezreel;[o]
the second, Daniel the son of Abigail[p] of Carmel;
2 the third, Absalom the son of Maacah daughter of Talmai king of Geshur;
the fourth, Adonijah[q] the son of Haggith;
3 the fifth, Shephatiah the son of Abital;
and the sixth, Ithream, by his wife Eglah.
4 These six were born to David in Hebron,[r] where he reigned seven years and six months.[s]
David reigned in Jerusalem thirty-three years,
5 and these were the children born to him there:
Shammua,[e] Shobab, Nathan and Solomon. These four were by Bathsheba[f][t] daughter of Ammiel.
6 There were also Ibhar, Elishua,[g] Eliphelet,
7 Nogah, Nepheg, Japhia,
8 Elishama, Eliada and Eliphelet—nine in all.
9 All these were the sons of David, besides his sons by his concubines. And Tamar[u] was their sister.[v]

The Kings of Judah

10 Solomon's son was Rehoboam,[w]
Abijah[x] his son,
Asa[y] his son,
Jehoshaphat[z] his son,
11 Jehoram[h][a] his son,
Ahaziah[b] his son,
Joash[c] his son,
12 Amaziah[d] his son,
Azariah[e] his son,
Jotham[f] his son,
13 Ahaz[g] his son,
Hezekiah[h] his son,
Manasseh[i] his son,
14 Amon[j] his son,
Josiah[k] his son.

15 The sons of Josiah:
Johanan the firstborn,
Jehoiakim[l] the second son,
Zedekiah[m] the third,
Shallum[n] the fourth.

16 The successors of Jehoiakim:
Jehoiachin[i][o] his son,
and Zedekiah.[p]

The Royal Line After the Exile

17 The descendants of Jehoiachin the captive:
Shealtiel[q] his son,
18 Malkiram, Pedaiah, Shenazzar,[r] Jekamiah, Hoshama and Nedabiah.[s]

19 The sons of Pedaiah:
Zerubbabel[t] and Shimei.
The sons of Zerubbabel:
Meshullam and Hananiah.
Shelomith was their sister.
20 There were also five others:
Hashubah, Ohel, Berekiah, Hasadiah and Jushab-Hesed.

21 The descendants of Hananiah:

2:53 [h] 2Sa 23:38
2:54 [i] Ezr 2:22; Ne 7:26; 12:28
2:55 [j] S Ge 15:19; S Jdg 4:11 [k] Jos 19:35 [l] 2Ki 10:15,23; Jer 35:2-19
3:1 [m] 1Ch 14:3; 28:5 [n] S 1Sa 25:43 [o] S Jos 15:56 [p] S 1Sa 25:42
3:2 [q] 1Ki 2:22
3:4 [r] S 2Sa 5:4; 1Ch 29:27 [s] S 2Sa 5:5
3:5 [t] 2Sa 11:3
3:9 [u] S 2Sa 13:1 [v] 1Ch 14:4
3:10 [w] 1Ki 14:21-31; 2Ch 12:16 [x] 1Ki 15:1-8; 2Ch 13:1 [y] 1Ki 15:9-24 [z] 2Ch 17:1-21:3
3:11 [a] 2Ki 8:16-24; 2Ch 21:1 [b] 2Ki 8:25-10:14; 2Ch 22:1-10 [c] 2Ki 11:1-12:21; 2Ch 22:11-24:27
3:12 [d] 2Ki 14:1-22; 2Ch 25:1-28 [e] 2Ki 15:1-7; 2Ch 26:1-23 [f] 2Ki 15:32-38; 2Ch 27:1; Isa 1:1; Hos 1:1; Mic 1:1
3:13 [g] 2Ki 16:1-20; 2Ch 28:1; Isa 7:1 [h] 2Ki 18:1-20:21; 2Ch 29:1; Isa 1:1; Jer 26:19; Hos 1:1; Mic 1:1 [i] 2Ki 21:1-18; 2Ch 33:1
3:14 [j] 2Ki 21:19-26; 2Ch 33:21; Zep 1:1 [k] 2Ki 22:1; 2Ch 34:1; Jer 1:2; 3:6; 25:3
3:15 [l] S 2Ki 23:34 [m] Jer 37:1 [n] S 2Ki 23:31
3:16 [o] S 2Ki 24:6, 8 [p] S 2Ki 24:18
3:17 [q] Ezr 3:2
3:18 [r] Ezr 1:8; 5:14 [s] Jer 22:30
3:19 [t] Ezr 2:2; 3:2; 5:2; Ne 7:7; 12:1; Hag 1:1; 2:2; Zec 4:6

[c] *55* Or *of the Sopherites* [d] *55* Or *father of Beth Recab* [e] *5* Hebrew *Shimea,* a variant of *Shammua* [f] *5* One Hebrew manuscript and Vulgate (see also Septuagint and 2 Samuel 11:3); most Hebrew manuscripts *Bathshua* [g] *6* Two Hebrew manuscripts (see also 2 Samuel 5:15 and 1 Chron. 14:5); most Hebrew manuscripts *Elishama* [h] *11* Hebrew *Joram,* a variant of *Jehoram* [i] *16* Hebrew *Jeconiah,* a variant of *Jehoiachin*; also in verse 17

3:1 SONS OF DAVID. The author gives special attention to David's descendants. It was from the family of David that God had promised to bring the Messianic king to rule God's people (see 2Sa 7:12–17). The author wants to show that although David's kingdom had been destroyed, his descendants lived on. Thus God could and would fulfill his promises.

Pelatiah and Jeshaiah, and the
sons of Rephaiah, of Arnan, of
Obadiah and of Shecaniah.
22 The descendants of Shecaniah:
Shemaiah and his sons:
Hattush,[u] Igal, Bariah, Neari-
ah and Shaphat—six in all.
23 The sons of Neariah:
Elioenai, Hizkiah and Azri-
kam—three in all.
24 The sons of Elioenai:
Hodaviah, Eliashib, Pelaiah,
Akkub, Johanan, Delaiah and
Anani—seven in all.

Other Clans of Judah

4 The descendants of Judah:[v]
Perez, Hezron,[w] Carmi, Hur
and Shobal.
2 Reaiah son of Shobal was the father of Jahath, and Jahath the
father of Ahumai and Lahad.
These were the clans of the Zorathites.
3 These were the sons[j] of Etam:
Jezreel, Ishma and Idbash.
Their sister was named Hazze-
lelponi. 4 Penuel was the father
of Gedor, and Ezer the father of
Hushah.
These were the descendants of
Hur,[x] the firstborn of Ephrathah and father[k] of Bethlehem.[y]
5 Ashhur[z] the father of Tekoa had
two wives, Helah and Naarah.
6 Naarah bore him Ahuzzam, Hepher, Temeni and Haahashtari.
These were the descendants of
Naarah.
7 The sons of Helah:
Zereth, Zohar, Ethnan, 8 and
Koz, who was the father of
Anub and Hazzobebah and of
the clans of Aharhel son of Ha-
rum.

9 Jabez was more honorable than his
brothers. His mother had named him
Jabez,[l] saying, "I gave birth to him in
pain." 10 Jabez cried out to the God of
Israel, "Oh, that you would bless me
and enlarge my territory! Let your
hand be with me, and keep me from
harm so that I will be free from pain."
And God granted his request.

11 Kelub, Shuhah's brother, was the
father of Mehir, who was the father of Eshton. 12 Eshton was
the father of Beth Rapha, Paseah and Tehinnah the father of
Ir Nahash.[m] These were the
men of Recah.

13 The sons of Kenaz:
Othniel[a] and Seraiah.
The sons of Othniel:
Hathath and Meonothai.[n]
14 Meonothai was the father of
Ophrah.
Seraiah was the father of Joab,
the father of Ge Harashim.[o] It
was called this because its people were craftsmen.
15 The sons of Caleb son of Jephunneh:
Iru, Elah and Naam.
The son of Elah:
Kenaz.
16 The sons of Jehallelel:
Ziph, Ziphah, Tiria and Asarel.
17 The sons of Ezrah:
Jether, Mered, Epher and Jalon.
One of Mered's wives gave
birth to Miriam,[b] Shammai
and Ishbah the father of Eshtemoa. 18 (His Judean wife gave
birth to Jered the father of Gedor, Heber the father of Soco,
and Jekuthiel the father of Zanoah.[c]) These were the children of Pharaoh's daughter Bi-
thiah, whom Mered had
married.

3:22 [u] Ezr 8:2-3
4:1 [v] S Ge 29:35; S 1Ch 2:3 [w] Nu 26:21
4:4 [x] 1Ch 2:50 [y] Ru 1:19
4:5 [z] 1Ch 2:24
4:13 [a] S Jos 15:17
4:17 [b] S Ex 15:20
4:18 [c] S Jos 15:34

[j] *3* Some Septuagint manuscripts (see also Vulgate); Hebrew *father* [k] *4* *Father* may mean *civic leader* or *military leader*; also in verses 12, 14, 17, 18 and possibly elsewhere. [l] *9* *Jabez* sounds like the Hebrew for *pain.* [m] *12* Or *of the city of Nahash* [n] *13* Some Septuagint manuscripts and Vulgate; Hebrew does not have *and Meonothai.* [o] *14* *Ge Harashim* means *valley of craftsmen.*

4:10 JABEZ CRIED OUT TO THE GOD OF ISRAEL. The righteous example of Jabez stresses the truth that God blesses those who faithfully call on him. Note that Jabez was "more honorable than his brothers" (v. 9). Jabez demonstrates that God's divine blessing and protection do not come automatically, but occur as the result of our commitment to him and his cause on earth and as a result of our prayers (see Mt 6:13; see article on EFFECTIVE PRAYING, p. 496). The Chronicler's point of view is well expressed in 2Ch 20:20, "Have faith in the LORD your God and you will be upheld." Jabez's prayer is a model for all believers.

4:10 KEEP ME FROM HARM. See Mt 6:13, note.

19The sons of Hodiah's wife, the sister of Naham:
the father of Keilah[d] the Garmite, and Eshtemoa the Maacathite.[e]
20The sons of Shimon:
Amnon, Rinnah, Ben-Hanan and Tilon.
The descendants of Ishi:
Zoheth and Ben-Zoheth.
21The sons of Shelah[f] son of Judah:
Er the father of Lecah, Laadah the father of Mareshah and the clans of the linen workers at Beth Ashbea,
22Jokim, the men of Cozeba, and Joash and Saraph, who ruled in Moab and Jashubi Lehem. (These records are from ancient times.)
23They were the potters who lived at Netaim and Gederah; they stayed there and worked for the king.

Simeon

4:28–33pp — Jos 19:2–10

24The descendants of Simeon:[g]
Nemuel, Jamin, Jarib,[h] Zerah and Shaul;
25Shallum was Shaul's son, Mibsam his son and Mishma his son.
26The descendants of Mishma:
Hammuel his son, Zaccur his son and Shimei his son.

27Shimei had sixteen sons and six daughters, but his brothers did not have many children; so their entire clan did not become as numerous as the people of Judah.
28They lived in Beersheba,[i] Moladah,[j] Hazar Shual,
29Bilhah, Ezem,[k] Tolad,
30Bethuel, Hormah,[l] Ziklag,[m]
31Beth Marcaboth, Hazar Susim, Beth Biri and Shaaraim.[n] These were their towns until the reign of David.
32Their surrounding villages were Etam, Ain,[o] Rimmon, Token and Ashan[p]—five towns—
33and all the villages around these towns as far as Baalath.[p] These were their settlements. And they kept a genealogical record.

34Meshobab, Jamlech, Joshah son of Amaziah,
35Joel, Jehu son of Joshibiah, the son of Seraiah, the son of Asiel,
36also Elioenai, Jaakobah, Jeshohaiah, Asaiah, Adiel, Jesimiel, Benaiah,
37and Ziza son of Shiphi, the son of Allon, the son of Jedaiah, the son of Shimri, the son of Shemaiah.

38The men listed above by name were leaders of their clans. Their families increased greatly,
39and they went to the outskirts of Gedor[q] to the east of the valley in search of pasture for their flocks.
40They found rich, good pasture, and the land was spacious, peaceful and quiet.[r] Some Hamites had lived there formerly.

41The men whose names were listed came in the days of Hezekiah king of Judah. They attacked the Hamites in their dwellings and also the Meunites[s] who were there and completely destroyed[q] them, as is evident to this day. Then they settled in their place, because there was pasture for their flocks.
42And five hundred of these Simeonites, led by Pelatiah, Neariah, Rephaiah and Uzziel, the sons of Ishi, invaded the hill country of Seir.[t]
43They killed the remaining Amalekites[u] who had escaped, and they have lived there to this day.

Reuben

5 The sons of Reuben[v] the firstborn of Israel (he was the firstborn, but when he defiled his father's marriage bed,[w] his rights as firstborn were given to the sons of Joseph[x] son of Israel;[y] so he could not be listed in the genealogical record in accordance with his birthright,[z]
2and though Judah[a] was the strongest of his brothers and a ruler[b] came from him, the rights of the firstborn[c] belonged to Joseph)—
3the sons of Reuben[d] the firstborn of Israel:
Hanoch, Pallu,[e] Hezron[f] and Carmi.
4The descendants of Joel:
Shemaiah his son, Gog his son, Shimei his son,
5Micah his son, Reaiah his son, Baal his son,
6and Beerah his son, whom Tiglath-Pileser[r][g] king of Assyria took into exile. Beerah was a leader of the Reubenites.

4:19 [d] S Jos 15:44 [e] S Dt 3:14 **4:21** [f] S Ge 38:5 **4:24** [g] S Ge 29:33 [h] Nu 26:12 **4:28** [i] S Ge 21:14 [j] S Jos 15:26 **4:29** [k] S Jos 15:29 **4:30** [l] S Nu 14:45 [m] S Jos 15:31 **4:31** [n] S Jos 15:36 **4:32** [o] S Nu 34:11 [p] S Jos 15:42

4:39 [q] S Jos 15:58 **4:40** [r] Jdg 18:7-10 **4:41** [s] 2Ch 20:1; 26:7 **4:42** [t] S Ge 14:6 **4:43** [u] S Ge 14:7; Est 3:1; 9:16 **5:1** [v] S Ge 29:32 [w] Ge 35:22; 49:4 [x] S Ge 48:16,22; S 49:26 [y] Ge 48:5 [z] 1Ch 26:10 **5:2** [a] S Ge 49:10, 12 [b] S 1Sa 9:16; S 12:12; S 2Sa 6:21; 1Ch 11:2; S 2Ch 7:18; Mt 2:6 [c] S Ge 25:31 **5:3** [d] S Ge 29:32; 46:9; Ex 6:14; Nu 26:5-11 [e] S Nu 26:5 [f] S Nu 26:6 **5:6** [g] ver 26; S 2Ki 15:19; 16:10; 2Ch 28:20

[p] *33* Some Septuagint manuscripts (see also Joshua 19:8); Hebrew *Baal* [q] *41* The Hebrew term refers to the irrevocable giving over of things or persons to the LORD, often by totally destroying them. [r] *6* Hebrew *Tilgath-Pilneser*, a variant of *Tiglath-Pileser*; also in verse 26

7Their relatives by clans,[h] listed
according to their genealogical
records:
Jeiel the chief, Zechariah, 8and
Bela son of Azaz, the son of
Shema, the son of Joel. They
settled in the area from Aroer[i]
to Nebo[j] and Baal Meon.[k]
9To the east they occupied the
land up to the edge of the
desert that extends to the Euphrates[l] River, because their
livestock had increased in Gilead.[m]
10During Saul's reign they
waged war against the Hagrites[n], who were defeated at
their hands; they occupied the
dwellings of the Hagrites throughout the entire region east of
Gilead.

Gad

11The Gadites[o] lived next to them
in Bashan, as far as Salecah:[p]
12Joel was the chief, Shapham
the second, then Janai and Shaphat, in Bashan.
13Their relatives, by families, were:
Michael, Meshullam, Sheba,
Jorai, Jacan, Zia and Eber—
seven in all.
14These were the sons of Abihail
son of Huri, the son of Jaroah,
the son of Gilead, the son of Michael, the son of Jeshishai, the
son of Jahdo, the son of Buz.
15Ahi son of Abdiel, the son of
Guni, was head of their family.
16The Gadites lived in Gilead, in Bashan and its outlying villages,
and on all the pasturelands of
Sharon as far as they extended.
17All these were entered in the genealogical records during the reigns of
Jotham[q] king of Judah and Jeroboam[r] king of Israel.

18The Reubenites, the Gadites and
the half-tribe of Manasseh had 44,760
men ready for military service[s]—
able-bodied men who could handle
shield and sword, who could use a bow,
and who were trained for battle.
19They waged war against the Hagrites, Jetur,[t] Naphish and Nodab.
20They were helped[u] in fighting them,
and God handed the Hagrites and all
their allies over to them, because they
cried[v] out to him during the battle. He
answered their prayers, because they
trusted[w] in him. 21They seized the
livestock of the Hagrites—fifty thousand camels, two hundred fifty thousand sheep and two thousand donkeys.
They also took one hundred thousand
people captive, 22and many others fell
slain, because the battle[x] was God's.
And they occupied the land until the
exile.[y]

The Half-Tribe of Manasseh

23The people of the half-tribe of Manasseh[z] were numerous; they settled
in the land from Bashan to Baal Hermon, that is, to Senir (Mount Hermon).[a]
24These were the heads of their families: Epher, Ishi, Eliel, Azriel, Jeremiah, Hodaviah and Jahdiel. They were
brave warriors, famous men, and
heads of their families. 25But they
were unfaithful[b] to the God of their
fathers and prostituted[c] themselves
to the gods of the peoples of the land,
whom God had destroyed before them.
26So the God of Israel stirred up the
spirit[d] of Pul[e] king of Assyria (that
is, Tiglath-Pileser[f] king of Assyria),
who took the Reubenites, the Gadites
and the half-tribe of Manasseh into exile. He took them to Halah,[g] Habor,
Hara and the river of Gozan, where
they are to this day.

Levi

6 The sons of Levi:[h]
Gershon, Kohath and Merari.
2The sons of Kohath:
Amram, Izhar, Hebron and Uzziel.[i]
3The children of Amram:

5:7 [h]Jos 13:15-23 **5:8** [i]S Nu 32:34; Jdg 11:26 [j]S Nu 32:3 [k]S **5:9** [l]S Ge 2:14 [m]S Nu 32:26 **5:10** [n]ver 22; 1Ch 27:31 **5:11** [o]S Ge 30:11; S Nu 1:25; S Jos 13:24-28 [p]S Dt 3:10 **5:17** [q]S 2Ki 15:32 [r]S 2Ki 14:23 **5:18** [s]S Nu 1:3 **5:19** [t]Ge 25:15 **5:20** [u]Ps 37:40; 46:5; 54:4 [v]1Ki 8:44; 2Ch 6:34; 13:14; 14:11; Ps 20:7-9; 22:5; 107:6 [w]Ps 26:1; Isa 26:3; Da 6:23 **5:22** [x]S Dt 20:4; 2Ch 32:8 [y]S ver 10; S 2Ki 15:29 **5:23** [z]1Ch 7:14 [a]S Dt 3:8,9; SS 4:8 **5:25** [b]Dt 32:15-18; 1Ch 9:1; 10:13; 2Ch 12:2; 26:16; 28:19; 29:6; 30:7; 36:14 [c]S Ex 34:15; S Lev 18:3 **5:26** [d]Isa 37:7 [e]S 2Ki 15:19 [f]S ver 6; S 2Ki 15:29 [g]2Ki 17:6 **6:1** [h]S Ge 29:34; S Nu 3:17 **6:2** [i]S Ex 6:18

5:25–26 UNFAITHFUL TO THE GOD OF THEIR FATHERS. Throughout Chronicles, the writer underscores the truth that disobedience and sin bring judgment and calamity, whereas obedience and faithfulness bring peace and blessing (see 2Ch 7:14; 15:2–7; 19:2; 21:12–15; 24:20; 28:9; 34:24–25). This spiritual principle, which holds true in the NT, should motivate us to fear the Lord and to obey the leadership of the Holy Spirit (see Ro 2:6–10; 8:5–17; 1Co 10:1–13).

6:1 THE SONS OF LEVI. Ch. 6 gives the descendants of Levi, the line of the high priests, down to the captivity, and lists the Levitical cities. The sons of Levi had been chosen by God for spiritual service in the tabernacle (Nu 3—4) and in the temple (1Ch 23—26). In effect, this chapter points to the importance of true worship according to God's instruction.

Aaron, Moses and Miriam.[j]
The sons of Aaron:
Nadab, Abihu,[k] Eleazar[l] and Ithamar.[m]
4Eleazar was the father of Phinehas,[n]
Phinehas the father of Abishua,
5Abishua the father of Bukki,
Bukki the father of Uzzi,
6Uzzi the father of Zerahiah,
Zerahiah the father of Meraioth,
7Meraioth the father of Amariah,
Amariah the father of Ahitub,
8Ahitub the father of Zadok,[o]
Zadok the father of Ahimaaz,
9Ahimaaz the father of Azariah,
Azariah the father of Johanan,
10Johanan the father of Azariah[p]
(it was he who served as priest
in the temple Solomon built in
Jerusalem),
11Azariah the father of Amariah,
Amariah the father of Ahitub,
12Ahitub the father of Zadok,
Zadok the father of Shallum,
13Shallum the father of Hilkiah,[q]
Hilkiah the father of Azariah,
14Azariah the father of Seraiah,[r]
and Seraiah the father of Jehozadak.
15Jehozadak[s] was deported when the LORD sent Judah and Jerusalem into exile by the hand of Nebuchadnezzar.
16The sons of Levi:[t]
Gershon,[s] Kohath and Merari.[u]
17These are the names of the sons of Gershon:
Libni and Shimei.[v]
18The sons of Kohath:
Amram, Izhar, Hebron and Uzziel.[w]
19The sons of Merari:[x]
Mahli and Mushi.[y]
These are the clans of the Levites listed according to their fathers:
20Of Gershon:
Libni his son, Jehath his son,
Zimmah his son, 21Joah his son,
Iddo his son, Zerah his son
and Jeatherai his son.
22The descendants of Kohath:
Amminadab his son, Korah[z] his son,
Assir his son, 23Elkanah his son,
Ebiasaph his son, Assir his son,
24Tahath his son, Uriel[a] his son,
Uzziah his son and Shaul his son.
25The descendants of Elkanah:
Amasai, Ahimoth,
26Elkanah his son,[t] Zophai his son,
Nahath his son, 27Eliab his son,
Jeroham his son, Elkanah[b] his son
and Samuel[c] his son.[u]
28The sons of Samuel:
Joel[v][d] the firstborn
and Abijah the second son.
29The descendants of Merari:
Mahli, Libni his son,
Shimei his son, Uzzah his son,
30Shimea his son, Haggiah his son
and Asaiah his son.

The Temple Musicians

6:54–80pp — Jos 21:4–39

31These are the men[e] David put in
charge of the music[f] in the house of
the LORD after the ark came to rest
there. 32They ministered with music
before the tabernacle, the Tent of
Meeting, until Solomon built the temple of the LORD in Jerusalem. They performed their duties according to the regulations laid down for them.
33Here are the men who served, together with their sons:
From the Kohathites:
Heman,[g] the musician,
the son of Joel,[h] the son of Samuel,

6:3 [j] S Ex 15:20 [k] S Lev 10:1; S 10:1-20:2 [l] Lev 10:6 [m] S Ex 6:23 **6:4** [n] Ezr 7:5 **6:8** [o] S 2Sa 8:17; S 1Ch 12:28; S Ezr 7:2 **6:10** [p] S 1Ki 4:2 **6:13** [q] 2Ki 22:1-20; 2Ch 34:9; 35:8 **6:14** [r] S 2Ki 25:18; S Ezr 2:2 **6:15** [s] Ne 12:1; Hag 1:1,14; 2:2,4; Zec 6:11 **6:16** [t] S Ge 29:34; S Nu 3:17-20 [u] S Nu 26:57 **6:17** [v] S Ex 6:17 **6:18** [w] S Ex 6:18 **6:19** [x] S Ge 46:11; 1Ch 23:21; 24:26 [y] S Ex 6:19
6:22 [z] S Ex 6:24 **6:24** [a] 1Ch 15:5 **6:27** [b] S 1Sa 1:1 [c] S 1Sa 1:20 **6:28** [d] ver 33; 1Sa 8:2 **6:31** [e] 1Ch 25:1; 2Ch 29:25-26; Ne 12:45 [f] 1Ch 9:33; 15:19; Ezr 3:10; Ps 68:25 **6:33** [g] 1Ki 4:31; 1Ch 15:17; 25:1 [h] S ver 28

[s] *16* Hebrew *Gershom,* a variant of *Gershon;* also in verses 17, 20, 43, 62 and 71
[t] *26* Some Hebrew manuscripts, Septuagint and Syriac; most Hebrew manuscripts *Ahimoth 26and Elkanah. The sons of Elkanah:*
[u] *27* Some Septuagint manuscripts (see also 1 Samuel 1:19,20 and 1 Chron. 6:33,34); Hebrew does not have *and Samuel his son.*
[v] *28* Some Septuagint manuscripts and Syriac (see also 1 Samuel 8:2 and 1 Chron. 6:33); Hebrew does not have *Joel.*

6:32 MINISTERED WITH MUSIC. Worshiping God in song is a form of ministry to him (cf. Eph 5:18–20) and something with which he is well pleased. Through singing we may present ourselves to him in faith and love (see Eph 5:19, note).

[34]the son of Elkanah,[i] the son of Jeroham,
the son of Eliel, the son of Toah,
[35]the son of Zuph, the son of Elkanah,
the son of Mahath, the son of Amasai,
[36]the son of Elkanah, the son of Joel,
the son of Azariah, the son of Zephaniah,
[37]the son of Tahath, the son of Assir,
the son of Ebiasaph, the son of Korah,[j]
[38]the son of Izhar,[k] the son of Kohath,
the son of Levi, the son of Israel;
[39]and Heman's associate Asaph,[l] who served at his right hand:
Asaph son of Berekiah, the son of Shimea,[m]
[40]the son of Michael, the son of Baaseiah,[w]
the son of Malkijah, [41]the son of Ethni,
the son of Zerah, the son of Adaiah,
[42]the son of Ethan, the son of Zimmah,
the son of Shimei, [43]the son of Jahath,
the son of Gershon, the son of Levi;
[44]and from their associates, the Merarites,[n] at his left hand:
Ethan son of Kishi, the son of Abdi,
the son of Malluch, [45]the son of Hashabiah,
the son of Amaziah, the son of Hilkiah,
[46]the son of Amzi, the son of Bani,
the son of Shemer, [47]the son of Mahli,
the son of Mushi, the son of Merari,
the son of Levi.

[48]Their fellow Levites[o] were assigned to all the other duties of the tabernacle, the house of God. [49]But Aaron and his descendants were the ones who presented offerings on the altar[p] of burnt offering and on the altar of incense[q] in connection with all that was done in the Most Holy Place, making atonement for Israel, in accordance with all that Moses the servant of God had commanded.

[50]These were the descendants of Aaron:
Eleazar his son, Phinehas his son,
Abishua his son, [51]Bukki his son,
Uzzi his son, Zerahiah his son,
[52]Meraioth his son, Amariah his son,
Ahitub his son, [53]Zadok[r] his son
and Ahimaaz his son.

[54]These were the locations of their settlements[s] allotted as their territory (they were assigned to the descendants of Aaron who were from the Kohathite clan, because the first lot was for them):
[55]They were given Hebron in Judah with its surrounding pasturelands.
[56]But the fields and villages around the city were given to Caleb son of Jephunneh.[t]
[57]So the descendants of Aaron were given Hebron (a city of refuge), and Libnah,[x][u] Jattir,[v] Eshtemoa,
[58]Hilen, Debir,[w]
[59]Ashan,[x] Juttah[y] and Beth Shemesh, together with their pasturelands.
[60]And from the tribe of Benjamin they were given Gibeon,[z] Geba, Alemeth and Anathoth,[y] together with their pasturelands.
These towns, which were distributed among the Kohathite clans, were thirteen in all.
[61]The rest of Kohath's descendants were allotted ten towns from the clans of half the tribe of Manasseh.
[62]The descendants of Gershon, clan by clan, were allotted thirteen towns from the tribes of Issachar, Asher and Naphtali, and from the part of the tribe of Manasseh that is in Bashan.
[63]The descendants of Merari, clan by clan, were allotted twelve towns

6:34 [i]S 1Sa 1:1
6:37 [j]S Ex 6:24
6:38 [k]Ex 6:21
6:39 [l]1Ch 25:1,9; 2Ch 29:13; Ne 11:17 [m]1Ch 15:17
6:44 [n]1Ch 15:17
6:48 [o]1Ch 23:32
6:49 [p]Ex 27:1-8 [q]S Ex 30:1-7,10; 2Ch 26:18
6:53 [r]S 2Sa 8:17
6:54 [s]S Nu 31:10
6:56 [t]S Jos 14:13; S 15:13
6:57 [u]S Nu 33:20 [v]S Jos 15:48
6:58 [w]S Jos 10:3
6:59 [x]S Jos 15:42
6:60 [y]Jer 1:1

[w]40 Most Hebrew manuscripts; some Hebrew manuscripts, one Septuagint manuscript and Syriac *Maaseiah* [x]57 See Joshua 21:13; Hebrew *given the cities of refuge: Hebron, Libnah.* [y]59 Syriac (see also Septuagint and Joshua 21:16); Hebrew does not have *Juttah.* [z]60 See Joshua 21:17; Hebrew does not have *Gibeon.*

from the tribes of Reuben, Gad and
Zebulun.

64So the Israelites gave the Levites
these towns[z] and their pasturelands.
65From the tribes of Judah, Simeon and
Benjamin they allotted the previously
named towns.

66Some of the Kohathite clans were
given as their territory towns from the
tribe of Ephraim.

67In the hill country of Ephraim
they were given Shechem (a city
of refuge), and Gezer,[a][a] 68Jok-
meam,[b] Beth Horon,[c] 69Aija-
lon[d] and Gath Rimmon,[e] together with their pasturelands.

70And from half the tribe of Manasseh the Israelites gave Aner
and Bileam, together with their
pasturelands, to the rest of the
Kohathite clans.

71The Gershonites[f] received the
following:
From the clan of the half-tribe of
Manasseh
they received Golan in Bashan[g] and also Ashtaroth, together with their pasturelands;
72from the tribe of Issachar
they received Kedesh, Daberath,[h] 73Ramoth and Anem,
together with their pasturelands;
74from the tribe of Asher
they received Mashal, Ab-
don,[i] 75Hukok[j] and Rehob,[k] together with their pasturelands;
76and from the tribe of Naphtali
they received Kedesh in Galilee, Hammon[l] and Kiriathaim,[m] together with their pasturelands.

77The Merarites (the rest of the Levites) received the following:
From the tribe of Zebulun
they received Jokneam, Kartah,[b] Rimmono and Tabor, together with their pasturelands;
78from the tribe of Reuben across
the Jordan east of Jericho
they received Bezer[n] in the
desert, Jahzah, 79Kedemoth[o]
and Mephaath, together with
their pasturelands;
80and from the tribe of Gad
they received Ramoth in Gilead,[p] Mahanaim,[q] 81Heshbon
and Jazer,[r] together with their
pasturelands.[s]

Issachar

7 The sons of Issachar:[t]
Tola, Puah,[u] Jashub and Shimron—four in all.

2The sons of Tola:
Uzzi, Rephaiah, Jeriel, Jahmai,
Ibsam and Samuel—heads of
their families. During the reign
of David, the descendants of
Tola listed as fighting men in
their genealogy numbered
22,600.

3The son of Uzzi:
Izrahiah.
The sons of Izrahiah:
Michael, Obadiah, Joel and Isshiah. All five of them were
chiefs. 4According to their family genealogy, they had 36,000
men ready for battle, for they
had many wives and children.

5The relatives who were fighting
men belonging to all the clans
of Issachar, as listed in their
genealogy, were 87,000 in all.

Benjamin

6Three sons of Benjamin:[v]
Bela, Beker and Jediael.
7The sons of Bela:
Ezbon, Uzzi, Uzziel, Jerimoth
and Iri, heads of families—five
in all. Their genealogical
record listed 22,034 fighting
men.
8The sons of Beker:
Zemirah, Joash, Eliezer, Elioenai, Omri, Jeremoth, Abijah,
Anathoth and Alemeth. All
these were the sons of Beker.
9Their genealogical record listed the heads of families and
20,200 fighting men.
10The son of Jediael:
Bilhan.
The sons of Bilhan:
Jeush, Benjamin, Ehud, Kenaanah, Zethan, Tarshish and
Ahishahar. 11All these sons of
Jediael were heads of families.
There were 17,200 fighting
men ready to go out to war.

6:64 z Nu 35:1-8
6:67 a S Jos 10:33
6:68 b 1Ki 4:12
c S Jos 10:10
6:69 d S Jos 10:12
e S Jos 19:45
6:71 f 1Ch 23:7
g S Jos 20:8
6:72 h S Jos 19:12
6:74 i S Jos 19:28
6:75 j Jos 19:34
k S Nu 13:21
6:76 l Jos 19:28
m S Nu 32:37
6:78 n S Jos 20:8
6:79 o S Dt 2:26
6:80 p Jos 20:8
q S Ge 32:2
6:81 r S Nu 21:32
s 2Ch 11:14
7:1 t S Ge 30:18
u S Ge 46:13
7:6 v S Nu 26:38

[a] 67 See Joshua 21:21; Hebrew *given the cities of refuge: Shechem, Gezer.* [b] 77 See Septuagint and Joshua 21:34; Hebrew does not have *Jokneam, Kartah.*

12The Shuppites and Huppites were
the descendants of Ir, and the
Hushites the descendants of
Aher.

Naphtali

13The sons of Naphtali:[w]
Jahziel, Guni, Jezer and Shillem[c]—the descendants of Bilhah.

Manasseh

14The descendants of Manasseh:[x]
Asriel was his descendant
through his Aramean concubine. She gave birth to Makir
the father of Gilead.[y] 15Makir
took a wife from among the
Huppites and Shuppites. His
sister's name was Maacah.
Another descendant was
named Zelophehad,[z] who had
only daughters.
16Makir's wife Maacah gave
birth to a son and named him
Peresh. His brother was named
Sheresh, and his sons were
Ulam and Rakem.
17The son of Ulam:
Bedan.
These were the sons of Gilead[a]
son of Makir, the son of Manasseh. 18His sister Hammoleketh
gave birth to Ishhod, Abiezer[b]
and Mahlah.
19The sons of Shemida[c] were:
Ahian, Shechem, Likhi and
Aniam.

Ephraim

20The descendants of Ephraim:[d]
Shuthelah, Bered his son,
Tahath his son, Eleadah his
son,
Tahath his son, 21Zabad his
son
and Shuthelah his son.
Ezer and Elead were killed by
the native-born men of Gath,
when they went down to seize
their livestock. 22Their father
Ephraim mourned for them
many days, and his relatives
came to comfort him. 23Then he
lay with his wife again, and she
became pregnant and gave birth
to a son. He named him Beriah,[d] because there had been
misfortune in his family. 24His
daughter was Sheerah, who
built Lower and Upper Beth Horon[e] as well as Uzzen Sheerah.
25Rephah was his son, Resheph his
son,[e]
Telah his son, Tahan his son,
26Ladan his son, Ammihud his
son,
Elishama his son, 27Nun his
son
and Joshua his son.
28Their lands and settlements included Bethel and its surrounding villages, Naaran to the east, Gezer[f] and
its villages to the west, and Shechem
and its villages all the way to Ayyah
and its villages. 29Along the borders of
Manasseh were Beth Shan,[g] Taanach,
Megiddo and Dor,[h] together with their
villages. The descendants of Joseph
son of Israel lived in these towns.

Asher

30The sons of Asher:[i]
Imnah, Ishvah, Ishvi and Beri-
ah. Their sister was Serah.
31The sons of Beriah:
Heber and Malkiel, who was
the father of Birzaith.
32Heber was the father of Japhlet,
Shomer and Hotham and of
their sister Shua.
33The sons of Japhlet:
Pasach, Bimhal and Ashvath.
These were Japhlet's sons.
34The sons of Shomer:
Ahi, Rohgah,[f] Hubbah and
Aram.
35The sons of his brother Helem:
Zophah, Imna, Shelesh and
Amal.
36The sons of Zophah:
Suah, Harnepher, Shual, Beri,
Imrah, 37Bezer, Hod, Shamma,
Shilshah, Ithran[g] and Beera.
38The sons of Jether:
Jephunneh, Pispah and Ara.
39The sons of Ulla:
Arah, Hanniel and Rizia.
40All these were descendants of
Asher—heads of families, choice men,
brave warriors and outstanding lead-
ers. The number of men ready for bat-

7:13 [w]S Ge 30:8
7:14 [x]S Ge 41:51; S Jos 17:1; 1Ch 5:23 [y]S Nu 26:30
7:15 [z]S Nu 26:33; 36:1-12
7:17 [a]S Nu 26:30
7:18 [b]S Jos 17:2
7:19 [c]Jos 17:2
7:20 [d]S Ge 41:52; S Nu 1:33
7:24 [e]S Jos 10:10
7:28 [f]Jos 10:33
7:29 [g]S Jos 17:11 [h]S Jos 11:2
7:30 [i]S Nu 1:40

[c] *13* Some Hebrew and Septuagint manuscripts (see also Gen. 46:24 and Num. 26:49); most Hebrew manuscripts *Shallum*
[d] *23 Beriah* sounds like the Hebrew for *misfortune.*
[e] *25* Some Septuagint manuscripts; Hebrew does not have *his son.*
[f] *34* Or *of his brother Shomer: Rohgah*
[g] *37* Possibly a variant of *Jether*

tle, as listed in their genealogy, was
26,000.

The Genealogy of Saul the Benjamite

8:28–38pp — 1Ch 9:34–44

8 Benjamin[j] was the father of Bela
his firstborn,
Ashbel the second son, Aharah
the third,
2 Nohah the fourth and Rapha
the fifth.
3 The sons of Bela were:
Addar,[k] Gera, Abihud,[h]
4 Abishua, Naaman, Ahoah,[l]
5 Gera, Shephuphan and Huram.
6 These were the descendants of
Ehud,[m] who were heads of
families of those living in Geba
and were deported to Manahath:
7 Naaman, Ahijah, and Gera, who
deported them and who was the
father of Uzza and Ahihud.
8 Sons were born to Shaharaim in
Moab after he had divorced his
wives Hushim and Baara. 9 By
his wife Hodesh he had Jobab,
Zibia, Mesha, Malcam, 10 Jeuz,
Sakia and Mirmah. These were
his sons, heads of families.
11 By Hushim he had Abitub
and Elpaal.
12 The sons of Elpaal:
Eber, Misham, Shemed (who
built Ono[n] and Lod with its
surrounding villages), 13 and
Beriah and Shema, who were
heads of families of those living
in Aijalon[o] and who drove out
the inhabitants of Gath.[p]
14 Ahio, Shashak, Jeremoth, 15 Zebadiah, Arad, Eder, 16 Michael,
Ishpah and Joha were the sons
of Beriah.
17 Zebadiah, Meshullam, Hizki, Heber, 18 Ishmerai, Izliah and Jobab were the sons of Elpaal.
19 Jakim, Zicri, Zabdi, 20 Elienai, Zillethai, Eliel, 21 Adaiah, Beraiah
and Shimrath were the sons of
Shimei.
22 Ishpan, Eber, Eliel, 23 Abdon, Zicri, Hanan, 24 Hananiah, Elam,
Anthothijah, 25 Iphdeiah and
Penuel were the sons of Shashak.
26 Shamsherai, Shehariah, Athaliah,
27 Jaareshiah, Elijah and Zicri
were the sons of Jeroham.
28 All these were heads of families,
chiefs as listed in their genealogy, and
they lived in Jerusalem.

29 Jeiel[i] the father[j] of Gibeon lived
in Gibeon.[q]
His wife's name was Maacah,
30 and his firstborn son was Abdon, followed by Zur, Kish,
Baal, Ner,[k] Nadab, 31 Gedor,
Ahio, Zeker 32 and Mikloth,
who was the father of Shimeah.
They too lived near their relatives in Jerusalem.
33 Ner[r] was the father of Kish,[s]
Kish the father of Saul[t], and
Saul the father of Jonathan,
Malki-Shua, Abinadab and
Esh-Baal.[l][u]
34 The son of Jonathan:[v]
Merib-Baal,[m][w] who was the
father of Micah.
35 The sons of Micah:
Pithon, Melech, Tarea and
Ahaz.
36 Ahaz was the father of Jehoaddah, Jehoaddah was the father
of Alemeth, Azmaveth and Zimri, and Zimri was the father of
Moza. 37 Moza was the father of
Binea; Raphah was his son, Eleasah his son and Azel his son.
38 Azel had six sons, and these were
their names:
Azrikam, Bokeru, Ishmael,
Sheariah, Obadiah and Hanan.
All these were the sons of Azel.
39 The sons of his brother Eshek:
Ulam his firstborn, Jeush the
second son and Eliphelet the
third. 40 The sons of Ulam were
brave warriors who could handle the bow. They had many
sons and grandsons—150 in
all.
All these were the descendants of
Benjamin.[x]

9 All Israel[y] was listed in the genealogies recorded in the book of the
kings of Israel.

8:1 [j]S Ge 46:21 **8:3** [k]S Ge 46:21 **8:4** [l]2Sa 23:9 **8:6** [m]Jdg 3:12-30 **8:12** [n]Ezr 2:33; Ne 6:2; 7:37; 11:35 **8:13** [o]S Jos 10:12 [p]S Jos 11:22 **8:29** [q]S Jos 9:3 **8:33** [r]S 1Sa 28:19 [s]S 1Sa 9:1 [t]1Sa 14:49 [u]S 2Sa 2:8 **8:34** [v]S 2Sa 9:12 [w]S 2Sa 4:4; S 21:7-14 **8:40** [x]S Nu 26:38 **9:1** [y]1Ch 11:1,10; 12:38; 14:8; 15:3, 28; 18:14; 19:17; 21:5; 28:4,8; 29:21,23; 2Ch 1:2; 5:3; 7:8; 10:3,16; 12:1; 13:4,15; 18:16; 24:5; 28:23; 29:24; 30:1

h *3* Or *Gera the father of Ehud* **i** *29* Some Septuagint manuscripts (see also 1 Chron. 9:35); Hebrew does not have *Jeiel.* **j** *29* *Father* may mean *civic leader* or *military leader.* **k** *30* Some Septuagint manuscripts (see also 1 Chron. 9:36); Hebrew does not have *Ner.* **l** *33* Also known as *Ish-Bosheth* **m** *34* Also known as *Mephibosheth*

The People in Jerusalem

9:1–17pp — Ne 11:3–19

The people of Judah were taken captive to Babylon[z] because of their unfaithfulness.[a] 2Now the first to resettle on their own property in their own
towns[b] were some Israelites, priests,
Levites and temple servants.[c]
3Those from Judah, from Benjamin,
and from Ephraim and Manasseh who
lived in Jerusalem were:
4Uthai son of Ammihud, the son of
Omri, the son of Imri, the son of
Bani, a descendant of Perez
son of Judah.[d]
5Of the Shilonites:
Asaiah the firstborn and his
sons.
6Of the Zerahites:
Jeuel.
The people from Judah numbered 690.
7Of the Benjamites:
Sallu son of Meshullam, the
son of Hodaviah, the son of
Hassenuah;
8Ibneiah son of Jeroham; Elah
son of Uzzi, the son of Micri;
and Meshullam son of Shephatiah, the son of Reuel, the son
of Ibnijah.
9The people from Benjamin, as
listed in their genealogy, numbered 956. All these men were
heads of their families.
10Of the priests:
Jedaiah; Jehoiarib; Jakin;
11Azariah son of Hilkiah, the son
of Meshullam, the son of Zadok, the son of Meraioth, the
son of Ahitub, the official in
charge of the house of God;
12Adaiah son of Jeroham, the son
of Pashhur,[e] the son of Malkijah; and Maasai son of Adiel,
the son of Jahzerah, the son of
Meshullam, the son of Meshil-
lemith, the son of Immer.
13The priests, who were heads of
families, numbered 1,760.
They were able men, responsible for ministering in the house
of God.
14Of the Levites:
Shemaiah son of Hasshub, the
son of Azrikam, the son of
Hashabiah, a Merarite; 15Bak-
bakkar, Heresh, Galal and Mattaniah[f] son of Mica, the son of
Zicri, the son of Asaph; 16Oba-
diah son of Shemaiah, the son
of Galal, the son of Jeduthun;
and Berekiah son of Asa, the
son of Elkanah, who lived in
the villages of the Netophathites.[g]
17The gatekeepers:[h]
Shallum, Akkub, Talmon, Ahiman and their brothers, Shallum their chief 18being stationed at the King's Gate[i] on
the east, up to the present time.
These were the gatekeepers
belonging to the camp of the
Levites. 19Shallum[j] son of
Kore, the son of Ebiasaph, the
son of Korah, and his fellow
gatekeepers from his family
(the Korahites) were responsible for guarding the thresholds
of the Tent[n] just as their fathers had been responsible for
guarding the entrance to the
dwelling of the LORD. 20In earlier times Phinehas[k] son of Eleazar was in charge of the gatekeepers, and the LORD was with
him. 21Zechariah[l] son of Meshelemiah was the gatekeeper
at the entrance to the Tent of
Meeting.
22Altogether, those chosen to be
gatekeepers[m] at the thresholds numbered 212. They were registered by genealogy in their villages. The gatekeepers had been assigned to their
positions of trust by David and Samuel
the seer.[n] 23They and their descendants were in charge of guarding the
gates of the house of the LORD—the
house called the Tent. 24The gatekeepers were on the four sides: east, west,
north and south. 25Their brothers in
their villages had to come from time to
time and share their duties for seven-
day[o] periods. 26But the four principal

n *19* That is, the temple; also in verses 21 and 23

9:1 z S Dt 21:10 a S 1Ch 5:25 **9:2** b Jos 9:27; Ezr 2:70 c Ezr 2:43,58; 8:20; Ne 7:60 **9:4** d S Ge 38:29; 46:12 **9:12** e Ezr 2:38; 10:22; Ne 10:3; Jer 21:1; 38:1 **9:15** f 2Ch 20:14; Ne 11:22 **9:16** g Ne 12:28 **9:17** h ver 22; 1Ch 26:1; 2Ch 8:14; 31:14; Ezr 2:42; Ne 7:45 **9:18** i 1Ch 26:14; Eze 43:1; 46:1 **9:19** j Jer 35:4 **9:20** k Nu 25:7-13 **9:21** l 1Ch 26:2, 14 **9:22** m S ver 17 n S 1Sa 9:9 **9:25** o 2Ki 11:5

9:1 ALL ISRAEL. Ch. 9 is concerned with the community of God's people (i.e., "all Israel") after their return from exile in Babylon, emphasizing their continuity with Israel before the exile (cf. Ne 9). This first verse gives the reason for their captivity, while the rest of the chapter deals with the "priests, Levites and temple servants" (v. 2) whom God appointed to restore the true order of worship that had been lost during the captivity.

gatekeepers, who were Levites, were
entrusted with the responsibility for
the rooms and treasures[p] in the
house of God. 27 They would spend the
night stationed around the house of
God,[q] because they had to guard it;
and they had charge of the key[r] for
opening it each morning.
28 Some of them were in charge of
the articles used in the temple service;
they counted them when they were
brought in and when they were taken
out. 29 Others were assigned to take
care of the furnishings and all the other articles of the sanctuary,[s] as well
as the flour and wine, and the oil, incense and spices. 30 But some[t] of the
priests took care of mixing the spices.
31 A Levite named Mattithiah, the firstborn son of Shallum the Korahite, was
entrusted with the responsibility for
baking the offering bread. 32 Some of
their Kohathite brothers were in
charge of preparing for every Sabbath
the bread set out on the table.[u]
33 Those who were musicians,[v]
heads of Levite families, stayed in the
rooms of the temple and were exempt
from other duties because they were
responsible for the work day and
night.[w]
34 All these were heads of Levite
families, chiefs as listed in their genealogy, and they lived in Jerusalem.

The Genealogy of Saul

9:34–44pp — 1Ch 8:28–38

35 Jeiel[x] the father[o] of Gibeon
lived in Gibeon.
His wife's name was Maacah,
36 and his firstborn son was Ab-
don, followed by Zur, Kish,
Baal, Ner, Nadab, 37 Gedor,
Ahio, Zechariah and Mikloth.
38 Mikloth was the father of
Shimeam. They too lived near
their relatives in Jerusalem.
39 Ner[y] was the father of Kish,[z]
Kish the father of Saul, and
Saul the father of Jonathan,[a]
Malki-Shua, Abinadab and
Esh-Baal.[p][b]
40 The son of Jonathan:
Merib-Baal,[q][c] who was the
father of Micah.

9:26 *p* 1Ch 26:22
9:27 *q* S Nu 3:38
r Isa 22:22
9:29 *s* S Nu 3:28; 1Ch 23:29
9:30 *t* S Ex 30:23-25
9:32 *u* Lev 24:5-8; 1Ch 23:29; 2Ch 13:11
9:33 *v* S 1Ch 6:31; 25:1-31; S 2Ch 5:12
w Ps 134:1
9:35 *x* 1Ch 8:29
9:39 *y* S 1Ch 8:33
z S 1Sa 9:1
a 1Sa 13:22
b S 2Sa 2:8
9:40 *c* S 2Sa 4:4

41 The sons of Micah:
Pithon, Melech, Tahrea and
Ahaz.[r]
42 Ahaz was the father of Jadah,
Jadah[s] was the father of Alemeth, Azmaveth and Zimri, and
Zimri was the father of Moza.
43 Moza was the father of Binea; Rephaiah was his son, Eleasah his son and Azel his son.
44 Azel had six sons, and these were
their names:
Azrikam, Bokeru, Ishmael,
Sheariah, Obadiah and Hanan.
These were the sons of Azel.

Saul Takes His Life

10:1–12pp — 1Sa 31:1–13; 2Sa 1:4–12

10 Now the Philistines fought
against Israel; the Israelites
fled before them, and many fell slain
on Mount Gilboa. 2 The Philistines
pressed hard after Saul and his sons,
and they killed his sons Jonathan,
Abinadab and Malki-Shua. 3 The fighting grew fierce around Saul, and when
the archers overtook him, they wounded him.
4 Saul said to his armor-bearer,
"Draw your sword and run me through,
or these uncircumcised fellows will
come and abuse me."
But his armor-bearer was terrified
and would not do it; so Saul took his
own sword and fell on it. 5 When the
armor-bearer saw that Saul was dead,
he too fell on his sword and died. 6 So
Saul and his three sons died, and all
his house died together.
7 When all the Israelites in the valley
saw that the army had fled and that
Saul and his sons had died, they abandoned their towns and fled. And the
Philistines came and occupied them.
8 The next day, when the Philistines
came to strip the dead, they found Saul

[o] *35* *Father* may mean *civic leader* or *military leader.* [p] *39* Also known as *Ish-Bosheth* [q] *40* Also known as *Mephibosheth* [r] *41* Vulgate and Syriac (see also Septuagint and 1 Chron. 8:35); Hebrew does not have *and Ahaz.* [s] *42* Some Hebrew manuscripts and Septuagint (see also 1 Chron. 8:36); most Hebrew manuscripts *Jarah, Jarah*

10:1 THE PHILISTINES FOUGHT AGAINST ISRAEL. With ch. 10 the writer begins a historical summary of Israel's past, starting with the monarchical era. In this chapter he states the reason for the rejection of Saul and the transfer of the kingdom to David (vv. 13–14). The remaining events in this book deal with the history of David and the enduring significance of his reign.

and his sons fallen on Mount Gilboa.
9They stripped him and took his head
and his armor, and sent messengers
throughout the land of the Philistines
to proclaim the news among their
idols and their people. 10They put his
armor in the temple of their gods and
hung up his head in the temple of
Dagon.[d]
11When all the inhabitants of Jabesh
Gilead[e] heard of everything the Philistines had done to Saul, 12all their
valiant men went and took the bodies
of Saul and his sons and brought them
to Jabesh. Then they buried their bones
under the great tree in Jabesh, and
they fasted seven days.
13Saul died[f] because he was unfaithful[g] to the LORD; he did not
keep[h] the word of the LORD and even
consulted a medium[i] for guidance,
14and did not inquire of the LORD. So
the LORD put him to death and turned[j]
the kingdom[k] over to David son of
Jesse.

David Becomes King Over Israel

11:1–3pp — 2Sa 5:1–3

11 All Israel[l] came together to
David at Hebron[m] and said,
"We are your own flesh and blood. 2In
the past, even while Saul was king, you
were the one who led Israel on their
military campaigns.[n] And the LORD
your God said to you, 'You will shepherd[o] my people Israel, and you will
become their ruler.[p]' "
3When all the elders of Israel had
come to King David at Hebron, he
made a compact with them at Hebron
before the LORD, and they anointed[q]
David king over Israel, as the LORD had
promised through Samuel.

10:10 [d]S Jdg 16:23
10:11 [e]S Jdg 21:8
10:13 [f]S 2Sa 1:1 [g]S 1Ch 5:25 [h]S 1Sa 13:13 [i]S Lev 19:31; S 20:6; Dt 18:9-14
10:14 [j]1Ch 12:23 [k]S 1Sa 13:14
11:1 [l]S 1Ch 9:1 [m]S Ge 13:18; S 23:19
11:2 [n]S 1Sa 18:5, 16 [o]Ps 78:71; Mt 2:6 [p]S 1Ch 5:2
11:3 [q]1Sa 16:1-13
11:4 [r]S Ge 10:16; S 15:18-21; S Jos 3:10; S 15:8
11:6 [s]S 2Sa 2:13
11:8 [t]S 2Sa 5:9; 2Ch 32:5
11:9 [u]Est 9:4
11:10 [v]ver 1 [w]
11:11 [x]S 2Sa 17:10

David Conquers Jerusalem

11:4–9pp — 2Sa 5:6–10

4David and all the Israelites
marched to Jerusalem (that is, Jebus).
The Jebusites[r] who lived there 5said
to David, "You will not get in here."
Nevertheless, David captured the fortress of Zion, the City of David.
6David had said, "Whoever leads the
attack on the Jebusites will become
commander-in-chief." Joab[s] son of
Zeruiah went up first, and so he received the command.
7David then took up residence in the
fortress, and so it was called the City
of David. 8He built up the city around
it, from the supporting terraces[t][t] to
the surrounding wall, while Joab restored the rest of the city. 9And David
became more and more powerful,[u] because the LORD Almighty was with him.

David's Mighty Men

11:10–41pp — 2Sa 23:8–39

10These were the chiefs of David's
mighty men—they, together with all
Israel,[v] gave his kingship strong support to extend it over the whole land,
as the LORD had promised[w]— 11this is
the list of David's mighty men:[x]
Jashobeam,[u] a Hacmonite, was
chief of the officers[v]; he raised his
spear against three hundred men,
whom he killed in one encounter.
12Next to him was Eleazar son of Dodai the Ahohite, one of the three
mighty men. 13He was with David at
Pas Dammim when the Philistines

[t] 8 Or *the Millo* [u] 11 Possibly a variant of *Jashob-Baal* [v] 11 Or *Thirty*; some Septuagint manuscripts *Three* (see also 2 Samuel 23:8)

10:13 SAUL DIED BECAUSE HE WAS UNFAITHFUL. See 1Sa 15:23, note on Saul's rejection by God; 1Sa 28:12, note on Saul's encounter with the medium of Endor.

11:1 DAVID. Ch. 11 begins David's story; 2Sa 2—5 tells more fully just how David became king over Judah and then over all Israel. (1) A comparison with the parallel accounts in 2 Samuel makes it apparent that the writer of Chronicles omits most of the difficulties David experienced, along with his personal moral failures and shame (2Sa 1—4; 11—21). These omissions coincide with the writer's twofold purpose: (a) to emphasize those historical events that were important to God's purpose in salvation history, and (b) to encourage the disheartened post-exilic community that was resettling in its homeland. (2) This same purpose is reflected in the author's focus on Solomon's building of the temple and his omission of Solomon's apostasy and idolatry as described in 1Ki 11.

11:1 ALL ISRAEL CAME TOGETHER. The first seven years of David's reign as king at Hebron over two tribes are assumed but not described. The narrative begins with David becoming king over all Israel.

11:5 FORTRESS OF ZION. Zion was one of the hills on which Jerusalem stood; it was formerly the site of a Jebusite fortress that David had captured (2Sa 5:6–9; see article on THE CITY OF JERUSALEM, p. 576). The hill became sacred when David brought the ark of the covenant to Zion. Later the name Zion was applied to the city of Jerusalem (2Ki 19:21; Ps 48; Isa 1:8), the nation of Judah (Isa 33:14; 34:8), and heaven itself (Heb 12:22; cf. Rev 14:1).

THE CITY OF JERUSALEM

1Ch 11:7–8 "David then took up residence in the fortress, and so it was called the City of David. He built up the city around it, from the supporting terraces to the surrounding wall, while Joab restored the rest of the city."

HISTORY OF THE CITY OF JERUSALEM. The first reference to the city of Jerusalem is probably Ge 14:18, where Melchizedek is listed as the king of Salem (i.e., Jerusalem; see Ge 14:18, note). When the Israelites were ready to cross over the Jordan to enter the promised land, the city then was called "the Jebusite city" (Jos 15:8) or "Jebus" (1Ch 11:4). It was never captured during Joshua's conquest of the land of Canaan, and remained in the hands of the Canaanites until David became king. David's army stormed Jebus and took possession of it, and David made it his capital city (2Sa 5:5–7; 1Ch 11:4–7). Jerusalem served as the political capital of Israel during the united kingdom and later of the southern kingdom of Judah. Solomon, David's successor, built the temple of the Lord in Jerusalem (1Ki 5—8; 2Ch 2—5; see article on THE TEMPLE, p. 608), so that the city also became the religious center for the worship of the covenant God.

Because of Israel's sin, in 586 B.C. Nebuchadnezzar of Babylon besieged the city and eventually destroyed it along with its temple (2Ki 25:1–11; 2Ch 36:17–19); Jerusalem remained a pile of rubble until the Jews returned in 536 B.C. from Persia to rebuild both the temple and the city (Ezr 3:8–13; 5:1—6:15; Ne 3—4). By NT times, Jerusalem had once again become the center of Jewish political and religious life. In A.D. 70, however, after frequent rebellion by the Jews against the Roman authorities, the city and its temple were once again destroyed.

When David made Jerusalem his capital city, it began to take on various other names in keeping with its character—names such as: "Zion" (2Sa 5:7), "the City of David" (1Ki 2:10), "the holy city" (Ne 11:1), "the city of God" (Ps 46:4), "the city of the Great King" (Ps 48:2), "the City of righteousness, the Faithful City" (Isa 1:26), "the City of the LORD" (Isa 60:14), "THE LORD IS THERE" (Eze 48:35), and "the City of Truth" (Zec 8:3). Some of these names are prophetic names for the future city of Jerusalem.

THE MEANING OF JERUSALEM FOR THE ISRAELITES. The city of Jerusalem had special meaning for God's people in the OT. (1) When God reviewed his law with the Israelites on the border of Canaan, he prophesied through Moses that at some point in the future he would choose a place in which "to put his Name" (Dt 12:5,11,21; 14:23–24). This place was to be the city of Jerusalem (1Ki 11:13; 14:21) where the temple of the living God was erected; thus it received the names of "the holy city," "the City of God," and "the City of the LORD." Three times a year all the Israelite males were expected to travel to Jerusalem, to "appear before the LORD your God at the place he will choose: at the Feast of Unleavened Bread, the Feast of Weeks and the Feast of Tabernacles" (Dt 16:16; cf. 16:2,6,11,15).

(2) Jerusalem was the city where God revealed his word to his people (Isa 2:3); that is, it was "the Valley of Vision" (Isa 22:1). Furthermore, it was the place where God ruled over his people Israel (Ps 99:1–2; cf. 48:1–3,12–14). Thus, when the Israelites prayed, they were instructed to pray "toward the city" (1Ki 8:44; cf. Da 6:10). The mountains surrounding Jerusalem symbolized the Lord surrounding his people in eternal steadfastness (Ps 125:1–2). In essence, therefore, Jerusalem was a symbol of all that God wanted for his people. Whenever God's people were in Jerusalem, they were to remember God's ruling power, his holiness, his faithfulness to his people, and his eternal commitment to be their God.

(3) When God's people destroyed their relationship with him by their constant idolatry and refusal to obey his commands (see article on THE NATURE OF IDOLATRY, p. 394), the Lord allowed the Babylonians to destroy Jerusalem, along with the temple. By al-

lowing this long-standing symbol of his constant presence among them to be destroyed, God was signifying that he himself was withdrawing from his people. Note that God's promise of an "everlasting covenant" with his people was always conditioned on their obedience to his revealed will (see article on GOD'S COVENANT WITH THE ISRAELITES, p. 290). Thus, God was warning his people then and now that they must remain faithful to him and obey his law if they want to continue to receive his blessings and promises.

THE MEANING OF JERUSALEM FOR THE CHRISTIAN CHURCH. The city of Jerusalem was also important for the Christian church. (1) Jerusalem was the birthplace of Christianity. It was there that Jesus Christ was crucified and rose from the dead. It was also in Jerusalem that the exalted Christ poured out the Holy Spirit on his disciples at Pentecost (Ac 2). From that city the gospel message of Jesus Christ spread "to the ends of the earth" (Ac 1:8: cf. Lk 24:47). The church in Jerusalem was the mother church of all churches and the home church of the apostles (Ac 1:12–26; 8:1). When controversy broke out over whether Gentiles who believed in Jesus had to be circumcised, Jerusalem was the city where the first major church council convened to decide this issue (Ac 15:1–31; Gal 2:1–10).

(2) NT writers accepted much of the OT significance of Jerusalem, but changed its application from the earthly city to a heavenly city. In other words, to them Jerusalem as the holy city was no longer here on earth but in heaven where God dwells and Christ rules at his right hand; from there he sends his blessings, and from there Jesus will return. Paul speaks about the Jerusalem "that is above," who is our mother (Gal 4:26). The author to the Hebrews indicates that in coming to Jesus Christ for salvation, believers have come not to an earthly mountain, but "to Mount Zion, to the heavenly Jerusalem, the city of the living God" (Heb 12:22). And instead of preparing a city on earth for believers, God is busy preparing the new Jerusalem, which will some day come "down out of heaven from God, prepared as a bride beautifully dressed for her husband" (Rev 21:2; cf. 3:12). On that great day, God's covenant promises will be fully realized: "Now the dwelling of God is with men, and he will live with them. They will be his people, and God himself will be with them and be their God" (Rev 21:3). God and the Lamb will reign for ever and ever on their throne in this holy city (Rev 22:3).

(3) Does the earthly city of Jerusalem still have a future role in God's millennial kingdom? Isaiah points to "new heavens and a new earth" (Isa 65:17), and then notes with emphasis, "*but* . . . " (italics added) the present Jerusalem will have its fulfillment; the remainder of Isa 65 deals with millennial conditions. Many believe that when Christ returns to establish his millennial rule (Rev 20:1–6), he will set up his throne in the city of Jerusalem. After the great white throne judgment (Rev 20:11–15), the heavenly Jerusalem will descend to the new earth and become the headquarters of God's eternal kingdom (see Rev 21:2, note).

gathered there for battle. At a place
where there was a field full of barley,
the troops fled from the Philistines.
14 But they took their stand in the middle of the field. They defended it and
struck the Philistines down, and the
LORD brought about a great victory.[y]
15 Three of the thirty chiefs came
down to David to the rock at the cave
of Adullam, while a band of Philistines
was encamped in the Valley[z] of Rephaim. 16 At that time David was in the
stronghold,[a] and the Philistine garrison was at Bethlehem. 17 David longed
for water and said, "Oh, that someone
would get me a drink of water from the
well near the gate of Bethlehem!" 18 So
the Three broke through the Philistine
lines, drew water from the well near
the gate of Bethlehem and carried it
back to David. But he refused to drink
it; instead, he poured[b] it out before
the LORD. 19 "God forbid that I should do
this!" he said. "Should I drink the blood
of these men who went at the risk of
their lives?" Because they risked their
lives to bring it back, David would not
drink it.

Such were the exploits of the three
mighty men.

20 Abishai[c] the brother of Joab was
chief of the Three. He raised his spear
against three hundred men, whom he
killed, and so he became as famous as
the Three. 21 He was doubly honored
above the Three and became their commander, even though he was not included among them.

22 Benaiah son of Jehoiada was a valiant fighter from Kabzeel,[d] who performed great exploits. He struck down
two of Moab's best men. He also went
down into a pit on a snowy day and
killed a lion.[e] 23 And he struck down
an Egyptian who was seven and a half
feet[w] tall. Although the Egyptian had
a spear like a weaver's rod[f] in his
hand, Benaiah went against him with a
club. He snatched the spear from the
Egyptian's hand and killed him with
his own spear. 24 Such were the exploits of Benaiah son of Jehoiada; he
too was as famous as the three mighty
men. 25 He was held in greater honor
than any of the Thirty, but he was not
included among the Three. And David
put him in charge of his bodyguard.

26 The mighty men were:
Asahel[g] the brother of Joab,
Elhanan son of Dodo from Bethlehem,
27 Shammoth[h] the Harorite,
Helez the Pelonite,
28 Ira son of Ikkesh from Tekoa,
Abiezer[i] from Anathoth,
29 Sibbecai[j] the Hushathite,
Ilai the Ahohite,
30 Maharai the Netophathite,
Heled son of Baanah the Netophathite,
31 Ithai son of Ribai from Gibeah in Benjamin,
Benaiah[k] the Pirathonite,[l]
32 Hurai from the ravines of Gaash,
Abiel the Arbathite,
33 Azmaveth the Baharumite,
Eliahba the Shaalbonite,
34 the sons of Hashem the Gizonite,
Jonathan son of Shagee the Hararite,
35 Ahiam son of Sacar the Hararite,
Eliphal son of Ur,
36 Hepher the Mekerathite,
Ahijah the Pelonite,
37 Hezro the Carmelite,
Naarai son of Ezbai,
38 Joel the brother of Nathan,
Mibhar son of Hagri,
39 Zelek the Ammonite,
Naharai the Berothite, the armor-bearer of Joab son of Zeruiah,
40 Ira the Ithrite,
Gareb the Ithrite,
41 Uriah[m] the Hittite,
Zabad[n] son of Ahlai,
42 Adina son of Shiza the Reubenite, who was chief of the Reubenites, and the thirty with him,
43 Hanan son of Maacah,
Joshaphat the Mithnite,
44 Uzzia the Ashterathite,[o]

11:14 [y] S Ex 14:30; S 1Sa 11:13
11:15 [z] 1Ch 14:9; Isa 17:5
11:16 [a] S 2Sa 5:17
11:18 [b] S Dt 12:16
11:20 [c] S 1Sa 26:6
11:22 [d] S Jos 15:21 [e] 1Sa 17:36
11:23 [f] S 1Sa 17:7
11:26 [g] S 2Sa 2:18
11:27 [h] 1Ch 27:8
11:28 [i] 1Ch 27:12
11:29 [j] S 2Sa 21:18
11:31 [k] 1Ch 27:14 [l] S Jdg 12:13
11:41 [m] 2Sa 11:6 [n] 1Ch 2:36
11:44 [o] S Dt 1:4

[w] *23* Hebrew *five cubits* (about 2.3 meters)

11:41 URIAH THE HITTITE. Uriah is listed as one of the mighty men who faithfully gave David's kingship strong support (v. 10). Yet David took this warrior's wife for himself and had Uriah murdered (see 2Sa 11). David's sin was considered so terrible that he lived under God's punishment for the rest of his life. This sin is alluded to in the first chapter of the NT (Mt 1:6; see 2Sa 12, notes on David's sin).

Shama and Jeiel the sons of Hotham the Aroerite,
45Jediael son of Shimri,
his brother Joha the Tizite,
46Eliel the Mahavite,
Jeribai and Joshaviah the sons of Elnaam,
Ithmah the Moabite,
47Eliel, Obed and Jaasiel the Mezobaite.

Warriors Join David

12 These were the men who came to David at Ziklag,[p] while he was banished from the presence of Saul son of Kish (they were among the warriors who helped him in battle;
2they were armed with bows and were able to shoot arrows or to sling stones right-handed or left-handed;[q] they were kinsmen of Saul[r] from the tribe of Benjamin):

3Ahiezer their chief and Joash the sons of Shemaah the Gibeathite;
Jeziel and Pelet the sons of Azmaveth; Beracah, Jehu the Anathothite,
4and Ishmaiah the Gibeonite, a mighty man among the Thirty, who was a leader of the Thirty; Jeremiah, Jahaziel, Johanan, Jozabad the Gederathite,[s]
5Eluzai, Jerimoth, Bealiah, Shemariah and Shephatiah the Haruphite;
6Elkanah, Isshiah, Azarel, Joezer and Jashobeam the Korahites;
7and Joelah and Zebadiah the sons of Jeroham from Gedor.[t]

8Some Gadites[u] defected to David at his stronghold in the desert. They were brave warriors, ready for battle and able to handle the shield and spear. Their faces were the faces of lions,[v] and they were as swift as gazelles[w] in the mountains.

9Ezer was the chief,
Obadiah the second in command,
Eliab the third,
10Mishmannah the fourth, Jeremiah the fifth,
11Attai the sixth, Eliel the seventh,
12Johanan the eighth, Elzabad the ninth,
13Jeremiah the tenth and Macbannai the eleventh.

14These Gadites were army commanders; the least was a match for a hundred,[x] and the greatest for a thousand.[y]
15It was they who crossed the Jordan in the first month when it was overflowing all its banks,[z] and they put to flight everyone living in the valleys, to the east and to the west.
16Other Benjamites[a] and some men from Judah also came to David in his stronghold.
17David went out to meet them and said to them, "If you have come to me in peace, to help me, I am ready to have you unite with me. But if you have come to betray me to my enemies when my hands are free from violence, may the God of our fathers see it and judge you."
18Then the Spirit[b] came upon Amasai,[c] chief of the Thirty, and he said:

"We are yours, O David!
We are with you, O son of Jesse!
Success,[d] success to you,
and success to those who help you,
for your God will help you."

So David received them and made them leaders of his raiding bands. 2Ch 24:20-21

19Some of the men of Manasseh defected to David when he went with the Philistines to fight against Saul. (He and his men did not help the Philistines because, after consultation, their rulers sent him away. They said, "It will cost us our heads if he deserts to his master Saul.")[e]
20When David went to Ziklag,[f] these were the men of Manasseh who defected to him: Adnah, Jozabad, Jediael, Michael, Jozabad, Elihu and Zillethai, leaders of units of a thousand in Manasseh.
21They helped David against raiding bands, for all of them were brave warriors, and they were commanders in his army.
22Day after day men came to help David, until he had a great army, like the army of God.[x]

x 22 Or *a great and mighty army*

12:1 p S Jos 15:31 12:2 q S Jdg 3:15 r S 2Sa 3:19 12:4 s Jos 15:36 12:7 t S Jos 15:58 12:8 u S Ge 30:11 v 2Sa 17:10 w S 2Sa 2:18 12:14 x S Lev 26:8 y S Dt 32:30 12:15 z S Jos 3:15 12:16 a S 2Sa 3:19 12:18 b S Jdg 3:10; 1Ch 28:12; 2Ch 15:1; 20:14; 24:20 c S 2Sa 17:25 d 1Sa 25:5-6 12:19 e 1Sa 29:2-11 12:20 f S 1Sa 27:6

12:18 THE SPIRIT CAME UPON AMASAI. Under the old covenant the Holy Spirit equipped certain persons with power and ability to do tasks to which God had called them (e.g., see Ex 31:1–5; Jdg 3:10; 6:34; 11:29; 13:25; 1Sa 10:10; 11:6; 16:13). In Amasai's case it was the gift of prophetic inspiration. Under the new covenant, Jesus promised that *all* his followers would "receive power when the Holy Spirit comes on [them]" (Ac 1:8; cf. 2:4; see article on BAPTISM IN THE HOLY SPIRIT, p. 1642).

Others Join David at Hebron

23 These are the numbers of the men armed for battle who came to David at Hebron[g] to turn[h] Saul's kingdom over to him, as the LORD had said:[i]
24 men of Judah, carrying shield and spear—6,800 armed for battle;
25 men of Simeon, warriors ready for battle—7,100;
26 men of Levi—4,600, 27 including Jehoiada, leader of the family of Aaron, with 3,700 men, 28 and Zadok,[j] a brave young warrior, with 22 officers from his family;
29 men of Benjamin,[k] Saul's kinsmen—3,000, most[l] of whom had remained loyal to Saul's house until then;
30 men of Ephraim, brave warriors, famous in their own clans—20,800;
31 men of half the tribe of Manasseh, designated by name to come and make David king—18,000;
32 men of Issachar, who understood the times and knew what Israel should do[m]—200 chiefs, with all their relatives under their command;
33 men of Zebulun, experienced soldiers prepared for battle with every type of weapon, to help David with undivided loyalty—50,000;
34 men of Naphtali—1,000 officers, together with 37,000 men carrying shields and spears;
35 men of Dan, ready for battle—28,600;
36 men of Asher, experienced soldiers prepared for battle—40,000;
37 and from east of the Jordan, men of Reuben, Gad and the half-tribe of Manasseh, armed with every type of weapon—120,000.

38 All these were fighting men who
volunteered to serve in the ranks. They
came to Hebron fully determined to
make David king over all Israel.[n] All
the rest of the Israelites were also of
one mind to make David king. 39 The
men spent three days there with David,
eating and drinking,[o] for their families had supplied provisions for them.
40 Also, their neighbors from as far
away as Issachar, Zebulun and Naphtali came bringing food on donkeys,
camels, mules and oxen. There were
plentiful supplies[p] of flour, fig cakes,
raisin[q] cakes, wine, oil, cattle and
sheep, for there was joy[r] in Israel.

Bringing Back the Ark

13:1–14pp — 2Sa 6:1–11

13 David conferred with each of his officers, the commanders of thousands and commanders of hundreds.
2 He then said to the whole assembly of Israel, "If it seems good to
you and if it is the will of the LORD our
God, let us send word far and wide to
the rest of our brothers throughout the
territories of Israel, and also to the
priests and Levites who are with them
in their towns and pasturelands, to
come and join us. 3 Let us bring the ark
of our God back to us,[s] for we did not
inquire[t] of[y] it[z] during the reign of
Saul." 4 The whole assembly agreed to
do this, because it seemed right to all
the people.
5 So David assembled all the Israel-

12:23 [g] 2Sa 2:3-4 [h] 1Ch 10:14 [i] S 1Sa 16:1; 1Ch 11:10 **12:28** [j] 1Ch 6:8; 15:11; 16:39; 27:17 **12:29** [k] S 2Sa 3:19 [l] 2Sa 2:8-9 **12:32** [m] Est 1:13 **12:38** [n] S 1Ch 9:1 **12:39** [o] 2Sa 3:20; Isa 25:6-8 **12:40** [p] S 2Sa 16:1; 17:29 [q] 1Sa 25:18 [r] 1Ch 29:22 **13:3** [s] 1Sa 7:1-2 [t] 2Ch 1:5

[y] 3 Or *we neglected* [z] 3 Or *him*

12:32 UNDERSTOOD THE TIMES. According to God's sovereign wisdom, he has a season and a time for all his purposes and for the fulfillment of his promises (cf. Ecc 3:1). We see this in the realm of nature, and also in his kingdom, where there are appointed times (Ps 102:13) and seasons of change (Isa 43:18–19) that are crucially important in his ongoing redemptive purpose.

(1) Scripture reveals again and again how God's people are often blind to what he is doing or about to do. Israel as a whole was blind and ignorant when God in the fullness of time sent his Son to be their Messiah. Likewise, too often the church doesn't know or discern when God is fulfilling some aspect of his purpose.

(2) The men of Issachar are given special mention in Scripture because they, from among Israel's twelve tribes, understood the times and discerned what God was doing in bringing David to the throne as his anointed. Discernment of God's times and seasons is necessary in order to cooperate with God in purposeful action and to embrace or sustain a God-given vision during times of change.

13:3 BRING THE ARK OF OUR GOD BACK. The ark had been captured and held by the Philistines for seven months (1Sa 4:11; 6:1; see 1Sa 4:3,21, notes); it was then returned to Israel and kept at Kiriath Jearim, ten miles from Jerusalem (1Sa 7:2). Throughout Saul's reign it had been neglected and had remained in obscurity.

ites,[u] from the Shihor River[v] in
Egypt to Lebo[a] Hamath,[w] to bring the
ark of God from Kiriath Jearim.[x] 6Da-
vid and all the Israelites with him went
to Baalah[y] of Judah (Kiriath Jearim) to
bring up from there the ark of God the
LORD, who is enthroned between the
cherubim[z]—the ark that is called by
the Name.

7They moved the ark of God from
Abinadab's[a] house on a new cart, with
Uzzah and Ahio guiding it. 8David and
all the Israelites were celebrating with
all their might before God, with songs
and with harps, lyres, tambourines,
cymbals and trumpets.[b]

9When they came to the threshing
floor of Kidon, Uzzah reached out his
hand to steady the ark, because the
oxen stumbled. 10The LORD's anger[c]
burned against Uzzah, and he struck
him down[d] because he had put his
hand on the ark. So he died there before God.

11Then David was angry because the
LORD's wrath had broken out against
Uzzah, and to this day that place is
called Perez Uzzah.[b][e]

12David was afraid of God that day
and asked, "How can I ever bring the
ark of God to me?" 13He did not take
the ark to be with him in the City of
David. Instead, he took it aside to the
house of Obed-Edom[f] the Gittite.
14The ark of God remained with the
family of Obed-Edom in his house for
three months, and the LORD blessed his
household[g] and everything he had.

David's House and Family

14:1–7pp — 2Sa 5:11–16; 1Ch 3:5–8

14 Now Hiram king of Tyre sent
messengers to David, along
with cedar logs,[h] stonemasons and
carpenters to build a palace for him.
2And David knew that the LORD had established him as king over Israel and
that his kingdom had been highly exalted[i] for the sake of his people Israel.

3In Jerusalem David took more
wives and became the father of more
sons[j] and daughters. 4These are the
names of the children born to him
there:[k] Shammua, Shobab, Nathan,
Solomon, 5Ibhar, Elishua, Elpelet,
6Nogah, Nepheg, Japhia, 7Elishama,
Beeliada[c] and Eliphelet.

David Defeats the Philistines

14:8–17pp — 2Sa 5:17–25

8When the Philistines heard that David had been anointed king over all Israel,[l] they went up in full force to
search for him, but David heard about
it and went out to meet them. 9Now the
Philistines had come and raided the
Valley[m] of Rephaim; 10so David inquired of God: "Shall I go and attack
the Philistines? Will you hand them
over to me?"

The LORD answered him, "Go, I will
hand them over to you."

11So David and his men went up to
Baal Perazim,[n] and there he defeated
them. He said, "As waters break out,
God has broken out against my enemies by my hand." So that place was
called Baal Perazim.[d] 12The Philistines had abandoned their gods there,
and David gave orders to burn[o] them
in the fire.[p]

13Once more the Philistines raided
the valley;[q] 14so David inquired of
God again, and God answered him, "Do

13:5 [u]1Ch 11:1; 15:3 [v]S Jos 13:3 [w]S Nu 13:21 [x]S 1Sa 7:2 **13:6** [y]S Jos 15:9 [z]S Ex 25:22; 2Ki 19:15 **13:7** [a]S 1Sa 7:1 **13:8** [b]1Ch 15:16, 19,24; 2Ch 5:12; Ps 92:3 **13:10** [c]1Ch 15:13,15 [d]S Lev 10:2 **13:11** [e]1Ch 15:13; Ps 7:11 **13:13** [f]1Ch 15:18,24; 16:38; 26:4-5,15 **13:14** [g]S 2Sa 6:11 **14:1** [h]S 1Ki 5:6; 1Ch 17:6; 22:4; 2Ch 2:3; Ezr 3:7; Hag 1:8 **14:2** [i]S Nu 24:7; S Dt 26:19 **14:3** [j]S 1Ch 3:1 **14:4** [k]S 1Ch 3:9 **14:8** [l]1Ch 11:1 **14:9** [m]ver 13; S Jos 15:8; S 1Ch 11:15 **14:11** [n]Ps 94:16; Isa 28:21 **14:12** [o]S Ex 32:20 [p]S Jos 7:15 **14:13** [q]S ver 9

[a]*5* Or *to the entrance to* [b]*11* *Perez Uzzah* means *outbreak against Uzzah.* [c]*7* A variant of *Eliada* [d]*11* *Baal Perazim* means *the lord who breaks out.*

13:10 THE LORD'S ANGER BURNED AGAINST UZZAH. Uzzah was destroyed because of his action contrary to God's command (see also 2Sa 6:1–8; cf. 1Ch 15:2,13,15; see Ex 25:12–15; Nu 4:15, where God had given specific instructions for handling the ark). This story teaches that worship of and service to God must be according to his revelation and word (see 2Sa 6:7, note).

13:14 BLESSED HIS HOUSEHOLD. The Lord blessed Obed-Edom's family because he undoubtedly received the ark with reverence and in obedience to God. What brought death to one man brought blessing to another.

14:2 FOR THE SAKE OF HIS PEOPLE ISRAEL. David's kingdom was highly exalted, not for his own sake, but for the sake of all God's people. David was to establish Israel's position in the world in order that they might serve God in righteousness and truth (see 2Sa 7:18, note). Under the new covenant, God may exalt a person, not for that person's own sake, but in order that God's people might be built up morally and spiritually.

14:3 DAVID TOOK MORE WIVES. For commentary on David taking many wives, see 2Sa 5:13, note. This glaring personal fault in David brought terrible tragedy on himself and his family (see 2Sa 12:13, note; 13:1, note).

14:14 DAVID INQUIRED OF GOD AGAIN. David did not assume that because it had been God's will to attack the Philistines before (v. 10), it was

not go straight up, but circle around
them and attack them in front of the
balsam trees. 15As soon as you hear
the sound of marching in the tops of
the balsam trees, move out to battle,
because that will mean God has gone
out in front of you to strike the Philistine army." 16So David did as God commanded him, and they struck down the
Philistine army, all the way from Gibeon[r] to Gezer.[s]
17So David's fame[t] spread
throughout every land, and the LORD
made all the nations fear[u] him.

The Ark Brought to Jerusalem

15:25–16:3pp — 2Sa 6:12–19

15 After David had constructed
buildings for himself in the City
of David, he prepared[v] a place for the
ark of God and pitched[w] a tent for it.
2Then David said, "No one but the Levites[x] may carry[y] the ark of God, because the LORD chose them to carry the
ark of the LORD and to minister[z] before
him forever."

3David assembled all Israel[a] in Jerusalem to bring up the ark of the LORD
to the place he had prepared for it. 4He
called together the descendants of
Aaron and the Levites:[b]

5From the descendants of Kohath,
Uriel[c] the leader and 120 relatives;
6from the descendants of Merari,
Asaiah the leader and 220 relatives;
7from the descendants of Gershon,[e]
Joel the leader and 130 relatives;
8from the descendants of Elizaphan,[d]
Shemaiah the leader and 200
relatives;

14:16 [r] S Jos 9:3 [s] Jos 10:33 **14:17** [t] S Jos 6:27 [u] Ex 15:14-16; S Dt 2:25; Ps 2:1-12 **15:1** [v] Ps 132:1-18 [w] S 2Sa 6:17; 1Ch 16:1; 17:1 **15:2** [x] S Nu 3:6; 4:15; Dt 10:8; 31:25; 2Ch 5:5 [y] S Dt 31:9 [z] 1Ch 16:4; 23:13; 2Ch 29:11; 31:2; Ps 134:1; 135:2 **15:3** [a] S 1Ch 13:5 **15:4** [b] S Nu 3:17-20 **15:5** [c] 1Ch 6:24 **15:8** [d] S Ex 6:22

15:9 [e] Ex 6:18 **15:11** [f] S 1Ch 12:28 [g] S 1Sa 22:20 **15:12** [h] S Ex 29:1; 30:19-21,30; 40:31-32; S Lev 11:44 **15:13** [i] 1Ki 8:4 [j] S 1Ch 13:7-10 [k] S Lev 5:10 **15:15** [l] S Ex 25:14 [m] 2Sa 6:7 **15:16** [n] 1Ch 6:31 [o] 2Ch 7:6 [p] Ezr 2:41; Ne 11:23; Ps 68:25 [q] S 1Ch 13:8; 23:5; 2Ch 29:26; Ne 12:27,36; Job 21:12; Ps 150:5; Am 6:5 **15:17** [r] S 1Ch 6:33 [s] 1Ch 6:39 [t] 1Ch 6:44

9from the descendants of Hebron,[e]
Eliel the leader and 80 relatives;
10from the descendants of Uzziel,
Amminadab the leader and 112
relatives.
11Then David summoned Zadok[f]
and Abiathar[g] the priests, and Uriel,
Asaiah, Joel, Shemaiah, Eliel and Amminadab the Levites. 12He said to
them, "You are the heads of the Levitical families; you and your fellow Levites are to consecrate[h] yourselves
and bring up the ark of the LORD, the
God of Israel, to the place I have prepared for it. 13It was because you, the
Levites,[i] did not bring it up the first
time that the LORD our God broke out
in anger against us.[j] We did not inquire of him about how to do it in the
prescribed way.[k]" 14So the priests
and Levites consecrated themselves in
order to bring up the ark of the LORD,
the God of Israel. 15And the Levites
carried the ark of God with the poles on
their shoulders, as Moses had commanded[l] in accordance with the word
of the LORD.[m]
16David[n] told the leaders of the Levites[o] to appoint their brothers as
singers[p] to sing joyful songs, accompanied by musical instruments: lyres,
harps and cymbals.[q]
17So the Levites appointed Heman[r]
son of Joel; from his brothers, Asaph[s]
son of Berekiah; and from their brothers the Merarites,[t] Ethan son of Ku-
shaiah; 18and with them their brothers
next in rank: Zechariah,[f] Jaaziel, She-

[e] 7 Hebrew *Gershom,* a variant of *Gershon*
[f] 18 Three Hebrew manuscripts and most Septuagint manuscripts (see also verse 20 and 1 Chron. 16:5); most Hebrew manuscripts *Zechariah son and* or *Zechariah, Ben and*

also true on this occasion. David's example teaches believers that we will not succeed in life if we do not consistently seek the Lord's will, guidance and help. Calling on God for his special grace and presence is an ongoing need for our lives. If we fail to turn continually to God for his help, we will find ourselves facing life's troubles and demands alone, without the presence of the Holy Spirit (see 2Sa 5:19, note).

15:1 HE PREPARED A PLACE FOR THE ARK. The ark of God contained the two tablets of the law, a jar of manna and Aaron's staff (see Ex 25:10–22; Dt 10:2–5). It represented the instruction, provision, power and mercy of God found in faithful obedience to him and his covenant (see Ps 132:8; Heb 9). David's placing the ark in Jerusalem was representative of his desire to return the nation to its original and fundamental purpose for existence, i.e., to keep God and his Word central (see Ex 25:10, note).

15:12 CONSECRATE YOURSELVES. To do the Lord's work, believers must separate themselves from all that offends God and present themselves to him as instruments of righteousness (cf. Ro 6:17–22; 12:1–2; see article on SPIRITUAL SEPARATION FOR BELIEVERS, p. 1794). As a holy God, he requires that his servants be holy and consecrated.

15:13 WE DID NOT INQUIRE OF HIM. See 13:10, note.

miramoth, Jehiel, Unni, Eliab, Benaiah,
Maaseiah, Mattithiah, Eliphelehu,
Mikneiah, Obed-Edom[u] and Jeiel,[g]
the gatekeepers.
19The musicians Heman,[v] Asaph
and Ethan were to sound the bronze
cymbals; 20Zechariah, Aziel, Shemiramoth, Jehiel, Unni, Eliab, Maaseiah
and Benaiah were to play the lyres according to *alamoth*,[h] 21and Mattithiah,
Eliphelehu, Mikneiah, Obed-Edom, Jeiel and Azaziah were to play the harps,
directing according to *sheminith*.[h]
22Kenaniah the head Levite was in
charge of the singing; that was his responsibility because he was skillful at
it.
23Berekiah and Elkanah were to be
doorkeepers for the ark. 24Shebaniah,
Joshaphat, Nethanel, Amasai, Zechariah, Benaiah and Eliezer the priests
were to blow trumpets[w] before the ark
of God. Obed-Edom and Jehiah were
also to be doorkeepers for the ark.
25So David and the elders of Israel
and the commanders of units of a thousand went to bring up the ark[x] of the
covenant of the LORD from the house of
Obed-Edom, with rejoicing. 26Because
God had helped the Levites who were
carrying the ark of the covenant of the
LORD, seven bulls and seven rams[y]
were sacrificed. 27Now David was
clothed in a robe of fine linen, as were
all the Levites who were carrying the
ark, and as were the singers, and Kenaniah, who was in charge of the singing
of the choirs. David also wore a linen
ephod.[z] 28So all Israel[a] brought up
the ark of the covenant of the LORD with
shouts,[b] with the sounding of rams'
horns[c] and trumpets, and of cymbals,
and the playing of lyres and harps.
29As the ark of the covenant of the
LORD was entering the City of David,
Michal daughter of Saul watched from
a window. And when she saw King David dancing and celebrating, she despised him in her heart.

16 They brought the ark of God
and set it inside the tent that
David had pitched[d] for it, and they
presented burnt offerings and fellowship offerings[i] before God. 2After David had finished sacrificing the burnt
offerings and fellowship offerings, he
blessed[e] the people in the name of the
LORD. 3Then he gave a loaf of bread, a
cake of dates and a cake of raisins[f] to
each Israelite man and woman.
4He appointed some of the Levites to
minister[g] before the ark of the LORD,
to make petition, to give thanks, and to
praise the LORD, the God of Israel:
5Asaph was the chief, Zechariah second, then Jeiel, Shemiramoth, Jehiel,
Mattithiah, Eliab, Benaiah, Obed-
Edom and Jeiel. They were to play the
lyres and harps, Asaph was to sound
the cymbals, 6and Benaiah and Jahaziel the priests were to blow the trumpets regularly before the ark of the covenant of God.

David's Psalm of Thanks

16:8–22pp — Ps 105:1–15
16:23–33pp — Ps 96:1–13
16:34–36pp — Ps 106:1,47–48

7That day David first committed to
Asaph and his associates this psalm[h]
of thanks to the LORD:

8Give thanks[i] to the LORD, call on
his name;
make known among the
nations[j] what he has done.
9Sing to him, sing praise[k] to him;
tell of all his wonderful acts.
10Glory in his holy name;[l]
let the hearts of those who seek
the LORD rejoice.

15:18 [u]S 2Sa 6:10; 1Ch 26:4-5 **15:19** [v]1Ch 16:41; 25:6 **15:24** [w]2Ch 5:12; 7:6; 29:26 **15:25** [x]2Ch 1:4; 5:2; Jer 3:16 **15:26** [y]Nu 23:1-4,29 **15:27** [z]S 1Sa 2:18 **15:28** [a]S 1Ch 9:1 [b]S 1Ki 1:39; Zec 4:7 [c]S Ex 19:13

16:1 [d]S 1Ch 15:1 **16:2** [e]S Ex 39:43; Nu 6:23-27 **16:3** [f]Isa 16:7 **16:4** [g]S 1Ch 15:2 **16:7** [h]Ps 47:7 **16:8** [i]ver 34; Ps 107:1; 118:1; 136:1 [j]S 2Ki 19:19 **16:9** [k]S Ex 15:1; Ps 7:17 **16:10** [l]Ps 8:1; 29:2; 66:2

[g]*18* Hebrew; Septuagint (see also verse 21) *Jeiel and Azaziah* [h]*20* Probably a musical term [i]*1* Traditionally *peace offerings*; also in verse 2

16:7 THIS PSALM OF THANKS. This psalm is a composite of Ps 105:1–15; 96:1–13; 106:1, 47–48. The manner in which David celebrated God's mercy and wonderful acts for Israel consisted largely of praise and thanksgiving. Under the new covenant all believers are priests of God (1Pe 2:5,9; Rev 20:6) and as such should offer the spiritual ministry of praise and thanksgiving to God. "Through Jesus, therefore, let us continually offer to God a sacrifice of praise—the fruit of lips that confess his name" (Heb 13:15). The believer's praise and worship must be both in word and in deed (see v. 29, note) and are pleasing to God only as long as he or she is committed to his Word and not conformed to the pattern of this world (Ro 12:1–2).

16:10 LET THE HEARTS OF THOSE WHO SEEK THE LORD REJOICE. Our happiness and security and our freedom from anxiety are dependent on our gratitude to God and our perseverance in seeking his face daily (vv. 8–11). Those who continually call out to the Lord with thanksgiving can have confidence that he will walk by their side and be an ever-present help throughout all of life (Ps 46:1; see Php 4:6–7, notes).

11Look to the LORD and his strength;
seek[m] his face always.
12Remember[n] the wonders[o] he has
done,
his miracles,[p] and the
judgments he pronounced,
13O descendants of Israel his
servant,
O sons of Jacob, his chosen
ones.

14He is the LORD our God;
his judgments[q] are in all the
earth.
15He remembers[j r] his covenant
forever,
the word he commanded, for a
thousand generations,
16the covenant[s] he made with
Abraham,
the oath he swore to Isaac.
17He confirmed it to Jacob[t] as a
decree,
to Israel as an everlasting
covenant:
18"To you I will give the land of
Canaan[u]
as the portion you will inherit."

19When they were but few in
number,[v]
few indeed, and strangers in it,
20they[k] wandered[w] from nation to
nation,
from one kingdom to another.
21He allowed no man to oppress
them;
for their sake he rebuked
kings:[x]
22"Do not touch my anointed ones;
do my prophets[y] no harm."

23Sing to the LORD, all the earth;
proclaim his salvation day after
day.
24Declare his glory[z] among the
nations,
his marvelous deeds among all
peoples.
25For great is the LORD and most
worthy of praise;[a]
he is to be feared[b] above all
gods.[c]
26For all the gods of the nations are
idols,
but the LORD made the
heavens.[d]
27Splendor and majesty are before
him;
strength and joy in his dwelling
place.

28Ascribe to the LORD, O families of
nations,
ascribe to the LORD glory and
strength,[e]
29 ascribe to the LORD the glory
due his name.[f]
Bring an offering and come before
him;
worship the LORD in the splendor
of his[l] holiness.[g]
30Tremble[h] before him, all the
earth!
The world is firmly established;
it cannot be moved.[i]

31Let the heavens rejoice, let the
earth be glad;[j]
let them say among the nations,
"The LORD reigns![k]"
32Let the sea resound, and all that
is in it;[l]
let the fields be jubilant, and
everything in them!
33Then the trees[m] of the forest will
sing,
they will sing for joy before the
LORD,
for he comes to judge[n] the
earth.

34Give thanks[o] to the LORD, for he
is good;[p]
his love endures forever.[q]
35Cry out, "Save us, O God our
Savior;[r]
gather us and deliver us from
the nations,
that we may give thanks to your
holy name,
that we may glory in your
praise."
36Praise be to the LORD, the God of
Israel,[s]
from everlasting to everlasting.

16:11 [m] ver 10; 1Ch 28:9; 2Ch 7:14; 14:4; 15:2,12; 16:12; 18:4; 20:4; 34:3; Ps 24:6; 27:8; 105:4; 119:2,58; Pr 8:17
16:12 [n] Ps 77:11 [o] S Dt 4:34 [p] Ps 78:43
16:14 [q] Isa 4:4; 26:9
16:15 [r] S Ge 8:1; Ps 98:3; 111:5; 115:12; 136:23
16:16 [s] S Ge 12:7; S 15:18; 22:16-18
16:17 [t] Ge 35:9-12
16:18 [u] Ge 13:14-17
16:19 [v] Dt 7:7
16:20 [w] S Ge 20:13
16:21 [x] Ge 12:17; S 20:3; Ex 7:15-18; Ps 9:5
16:22 [y] S Ge 20:7
16:24 [z] Isa 42:12; 66:19
16:25 [a] Ps 18:3; 48:1 [b] Ps 76:7; 89:7 [c] Ex 18:11; Dt 32:39; 2Ch 2:5; Ps 135:5; Isa 40:25
16:26 [d] Ps 8:3; 102:25
16:28 [e] Ps 29:1-2
16:29 [f] Ps 8:1 [g] 2Ch 20:21; Ps 29:1-2
16:30 [h] Ps 2:11; 33:8; 76:8; 99:1; 114:7 [i] Ps 93:1
16:31 [j] Isa 44:23; 49:13 [k] Ps 9:7; 47:8; 93:1; 97:1; 99:1; 146:10; Isa 52:7; La 5:19
16:32 [l] Ex 20:11; Isa 42:10
16:33 [m] Isa 14:8; 55:12 [n] 1Sa 2:10; Ps 7:8; 96:10; 98:9; 110:6; Isa 2:4
16:34 [o] S ver 8; Ps 105:1; Isa 12:4 [p] Ps 25:7; 34:8; 100:5; 135:3; 145:9; Na 1:7 [q] 2Ch 5:13; 7:3; Ezr 3:11; Ps 136:1-26; Jer 33:11
16:35 [r] Dt 32:15; Ps 18:46; 38:22; Mic 7:7
16:36 [s] S 1Ki 8:15; Ps 72:18-19

j *15* Some Septuagint manuscripts (see also Psalm 105:8); Hebrew *Remember*
k *18-20* One Hebrew manuscript, Septuagint and Vulgate (see also Psalm 105:12); most Hebrew manuscripts *inherit, / 19though you are but few in number, / few indeed, and strangers in it." / 20They*
l *29* Or *LORD with the splendor of*

16:29 IN THE SPLENDOR OF HIS HOLINESS. Genuine worship must be done in "holiness" (cf. 2Ch 20:21). God accepts spiritual and jubilant worship (15:28) only as long as it is accompanied by an inward disposition of reverence and purity, an earnest desire to be near him, and the fervent commitment to resist all that offends his holy nature (see v. 7, note).

Then all the people said "Amen" and "Praise the LORD."

37David left Asaph and his associates before the ark of the covenant of the LORD to minister there regularly, according to each day's requirements.[t] 38He also left Obed-Edom[u] and his sixty-eight associates to minister with them. Obed-Edom son of Jeduthun, and also Hosah,[v] were gatekeepers.

39David left Zadok[w] the priest and his fellow priests before the tabernacle of the LORD at the high place in Gibeon[x] 40to present burnt offerings to the LORD on the altar of burnt offering regularly, morning and evening, in accordance with everything written in the Law[y] of the LORD, which he had given Israel. 41With them were Heman[z] and Jeduthun and the rest of those chosen and designated by name to give thanks to the LORD, "for his love endures forever." 42Heman and Jeduthun were responsible for the sounding of the trumpets and cymbals and for the playing of the other instruments for sacred song.[a] The sons of Jeduthun[b] were stationed at the gate.

43Then all the people left, each for his own home, and David returned home to bless his family.

God's Promise to David

17:1–15pp — 2Sa 7:1–17

17 After David was settled in his palace, he said to Nathan the prophet, "Here I am, living in a palace of cedar, while the ark of the covenant of the LORD is under a tent.[c]"

2Nathan replied to David, "Whatever you have in mind,[d] do it, for God is with you."

3That night the word of God came to Nathan, saying:

4"Go and tell my servant David, 'This is what the LORD says: You[e] are not the one to build me a house to dwell in. 5I have not dwelt in a house from the day I brought Israel up out of Egypt to this day. I have moved from one tent site to another, from one dwelling place to another. 6Wherever I have moved with all the Israelites, did I ever say to any of their leaders[m] whom I commanded to shepherd my people, "Why have you not built me a house of cedar?[f]" '

7"Now then, tell my servant David, 'This is what the LORD Almighty says: I took you from the pasture and from following the flock, to be ruler[g] over my people Israel. 8I have been with you wherever you have gone, and I have cut off all your enemies from before you. Now I will make your name like the names of the greatest men of the earth. 9And I will provide a place for my people Israel and will plant them so that they can have a home of their own and no longer be disturbed. Wicked people will not oppress them anymore, as they did at the beginning 10and have done ever since the time I appointed leaders[h] over my people Israel. I will also subdue all your enemies.

" 'I declare to you that the LORD will build a house for you: 11When your days are over and you go to be with your fathers, I will raise up your offspring to succeed you, one of your own sons, and I will establish his kingdom. 12He is the one who will build[i] a house for me, and I will establish his throne forever.[j] 13I will be his father,[k] and he will be my son.[l] I will never take my love away from him, as I took it away from your predecessor. 14I will set him over my house and my kingdom forever; his throne[m] will be established forever.[n]' "

15Nathan reported to David all the words of this entire revelation.

David's Prayer

17:16–27pp — 2Sa 7:18–29

16Then King David went in and sat before the LORD, and he said:

"Who am I, O LORD God, and what is my family, that you have brought me this far? 17And as if this were not enough in your sight, O God, you have spoken

16:37 [t]2Ch 8:14
16:38 [u]S 1Ch 13:13; 26:4-5 [v]1Ch 26:10
16:39 [w]S 1Sa 2:35; S 2Sa 8:17; S 1Ch 12:28 [x]S Jos 9:3; 2Ch 1:3
16:40 [y]S Ex 29:38; Nu 28:1-8
16:41 [z]S 1Ch 15:19
16:42 [a]2Ch 7:6 [b]1Ch 25:3
17:1 [c]S 1Ch 15:1
17:2 [d]1Ch 22:7; 28:2; 2Ch 6:7
17:4 [e]1Ch 22:10; 28:3
17:6 [f]S 1Ch 14:1
17:7 [g]S 2Sa 6:21
17:10 [h]S Jdg 2:16
17:12 [i]S 1Ki 5:5 [j]1Ch 22:10; 2Ch 7:18; 13:5
17:13 [k]2Co 6:18 [l]1Ch 28:6; Lk 1:32; Heb 1:5*
17:14 [m]S 1Ki 2:12; 1Ch 28:5; 29:23; 2Ch 9:8 [n]Ps 132:11; Jer 33:17

m6 Traditionally *judges*; also in verse 10

17:1–27 GOD'S COVENANT WITH DAVID. Ch. 17 is almost identical with 2Sa 7:1–29; see article on GOD'S COVENANT WITH DAVID, p. 432, for the various aspects of this covenant.

about the future of the house of
your servant. You have looked on
me as though I were the most exalted of men, O LORD God.
18"What more can David say to
you for honoring your servant?
For you know your servant,
19O LORD. For the sake[o] of your
servant and according to your
will, you have done this great
thing and made known all these
great promises.[p]
20"There is no one like you,
O LORD, and there is no God but
you,[q] as we have heard with our
own ears. 21And who is like your
people Israel—the one nation on
earth whose God went out to redeem[r] a people for himself, and
to make a name for yourself, and
to perform great and awesome
wonders by driving out nations
from before your people, whom
you redeemed from Egypt? 22You
made your people Israel your very
own forever,[s] and you, O LORD,
have become their God.
23"And now, LORD, let the promise[t] you have made concerning
your servant and his house be established forever. Do as you promised, 24so that it will be established and that your name will be
great forever. Then men will say,
'The LORD Almighty, the God over
Israel, is Israel's God!' And the
house of your servant David will
be established before you.
25"You, my God, have revealed
to your servant that you will build
a house for him. So your servant
has found courage to pray to you.
26O LORD, you are God! You have
promised these good things to
your servant. 27Now you have
been pleased to bless the house of
your servant, that it may continue
forever in your sight;[u] for you,
O LORD, have blessed it, and it will
be blessed forever."

David's Victories

18:1–13pp — 2Sa 8:1–14

18 In the course of time, David defeated the Philistines and subdued them, and he took Gath and its
surrounding villages from the control
of the Philistines.
2David also defeated the Moabites,[v] and they became subject to him
and brought tribute.
3Moreover, David fought Hadadezer
king of Zobah,[w] as far as Hamath,
when he went to establish his control
along the Euphrates River.[x] 4David
captured a thousand of his chariots,
seven thousand charioteers and twenty thousand foot soldiers. He hamstrung[y] all but a hundred of the chariot horses.
5When the Arameans of Damascus[z] came to help Hadadezer king of
Zobah, David struck down twenty-two
thousand of them. 6He put garrisons in
the Aramean kingdom of Damascus,
and the Arameans became subject to
him and brought tribute. The LORD gave
David victory everywhere he went.
7David took the gold shields carried
by the officers of Hadadezer and
brought them to Jerusalem. 8From Tebah[n] and Cun, towns that belonged to
Hadadezer, David took a great quantity of bronze, which Solomon used to
make the bronze Sea,[a] the pillars and
various bronze articles.
9When Tou king of Hamath heard
that David had defeated the entire
army of Hadadezer king of Zobah, 10he
sent his son Hadoram to King David to
greet him and congratulate him on his
victory in battle over Hadadezer, who
had been at war with Tou. Hadoram
brought all kinds of articles of gold and
silver and bronze.
11King David dedicated these articles to the LORD, as he had done with
the silver and gold he had taken from
all these nations: Edom[b] and Moab,
the Ammonites and the Philistines,
and Amalek.[c]
12Abishai son of Zeruiah struck
down eighteen thousand Edomites[d] in
the Valley of Salt. 13He put garrisons
in Edom, and all the Edomites became
subject to David. The LORD gave David
victory everywhere he went.

17:19 [o] 2Sa 7:16-17; 2Ki 20:6; Isa 9:7; 37:35; 55:3 [p] S 2Sa 7:25
17:20 [q] S Ex 8:10; S 9:14; S 15:11; Isa 44:6; 46:9
17:21 [r] S Ex 6:6
17:22 [s] Ex 19:5-6
17:23 [t] S 1Ki 8:25
17:27 [u] Ps 16:11; 21:6

18:2 [v] S Nu 21:29
18:3 [w] 1Ch 19:6 [x] S Ge 2:14
18:4 [y] S Ge 49:6
18:5 [z] 2Ki 16:9
18:8 [a] S 1Ki 7:23; 2Ch 4:2-5
18:11 [b] S Nu 24:18 [c] Nu 24:20
18:12 [d] 1Ki 11:15

[n] 8 Hebrew *Tibhath,* a variant of *Tebah*

18:6 VICTORY EVERYWHERE HE WENT. God desires to help, protect and give victory to his faithful people. As we look to the Lord and his strength and seek his face always (16:11), a channel of blessing is opened to our lives whereby God helps us in trouble, gives us freedom from Satan's power and leads us by his Spirit.

David's Officials

18:14–17pp — 2Sa 8:15–18

14David reigned[e] over all Israel,[f]
doing what was just and right for all
his people. **15**Joab[g] son of Zeruiah was
over the army; Jehoshaphat son of Ahilud was recorder; **16**Zadok[h] son of
Ahitub and Ahimelech[o][i] son of Abiathar were priests; Shavsha was secretary; **17**Benaiah son of Jehoiada was
over the Kerethites and Pelethites;[j]
and David's sons were chief officials at
the king's side.

The Battle Against the Ammonites

19:1–19pp — 2Sa 10:1–19

19 In the course of time, Nahash
king of the Ammonites[k] died,
and his son succeeded him as king.
2David thought, "I will show kindness
to Hanun son of Nahash, because his
father showed kindness to me." So David sent a delegation to express his
sympathy to Hanun concerning his father.

When David's men came to Hanun in
the land of the Ammonites to express
sympathy to him, **3**the Ammonite nobles said to Hanun, "Do you think David is honoring your father by sending
men to you to express sympathy?
Haven't his men come to you to explore
and spy out[l] the country and overthrow it?" **4**So Hanun seized David's
men, shaved them, cut off their garments in the middle at the buttocks,
and sent them away.

5When someone came and told David about the men, he sent messengers
to meet them, for they were greatly humiliated. The king said, "Stay at Jericho till your beards have grown, and
then come back."

6When the Ammonites realized that
they had become a stench[m] in David's
nostrils, Hanun and the Ammonites
sent a thousand talents[p] of silver to
hire chariots and charioteers from
Aram Naharaim,[q] Aram Maacah and
Zobah.[n] **7**They hired thirty-two thousand chariots and charioteers, as well
as the king of Maacah with his troops,
who came and camped near Medeba,[o]
while the Ammonites were mustered
from their towns and moved out for
battle.

8On hearing this, David sent Joab
out with the entire army of fighting
men. **9**The Ammonites came out and
drew up in battle formation at the entrance to their city, while the kings
who had come were by themselves in
the open country.

10Joab saw that there were battle
lines in front of him and behind him; so
he selected some of the best troops in
Israel and deployed them against the
Arameans. **11**He put the rest of the
men under the command of Abishai[p]
his brother, and they were deployed
against the Ammonites. **12**Joab said, "If
the Arameans are too strong for me,
then you are to rescue me; but if the
Ammonites are too strong for you, then
I will rescue you. **13**Be strong and let
us fight bravely for our people and the
cities of our God. The LORD will do what
is good in his sight."

14Then Joab and the troops with him
advanced to fight the Arameans, and
they fled before him. **15**When the Ammonites saw that the Arameans were
fleeing, they too fled before his brother
Abishai and went inside the city. So
Joab went back to Jerusalem.

16After the Arameans saw that they
had been routed by Israel, they sent
messengers and had Arameans
brought from beyond the River,[r] with
Shophach the commander of Hadadezer's army leading them.

17When David was told of this, he
gathered all Israel[q] and crossed the
Jordan; he advanced against them and
formed his battle lines opposite them.
David formed his lines to meet the Arameans in battle, and they fought
against him. **18**But they fled before Israel, and David killed seven thousand
of their charioteers and forty thousand
of their foot soldiers. He also killed
Shophach the commander of their
army.

19When the vassals of Hadadezer
saw that they had been defeated by Israel, they made peace with David and
became subject to him.

So the Arameans were not willing to
help the Ammonites anymore.

18:14 [e]1Ch 29:26 [f]1Ch 11:1
18:15 [g]2Sa 5:6-8
18:16 [h]1Ch 6:8 [i]1Ch 24:6
18:17 [j]S 1Sa 30:14; S 2Sa 15:18
19:1 [k]S Ge 19:38; Jdg 10:17-11:33; 2Ch 20:1-2; Zep 2:8-11
19:3 [l]S Nu 21:32
19:6 [m]S Ge 34:30 [n]S 1Ch 18:3
19:7 [o]S Nu 21:30
19:11 [p]S 1Sa 26:6
19:17 [q]S 1Ch 9:1

[o] *16* Some Hebrew manuscripts, Vulgate and Syriac (see also 2 Samuel 8:17); most Hebrew manuscripts *Abimelech* [p] *6* That is, about 37 tons (about 34 metric tons) [q] *6* That is, Northwest Mesopotamia [r] *16* That is, the Euphrates

The Capture of Rabbah

20:1–3pp — 2Sa 11:1; 12:29–31

20 In the spring, at the time when
kings go off to war, Joab led out
the armed forces. He laid waste the
land of the Ammonites and went to
Rabbah[r] and besieged it, but David
remained in Jerusalem. Joab attacked
Rabbah and left it in ruins.[s] 2David
took the crown from the head of their
king[s]—its weight was found to be a
talent[t] of gold, and it was set with
precious stones—and it was placed on
David's head. He took a great quantity
of plunder from the city 3and brought
out the people who were there, consigning them to labor with saws and
with iron picks and axes.[t] David did
this to all the Ammonite towns. Then
David and his entire army returned to
Jerusalem.

War With the Philistines

2:4–8pp — 2Sa 21:15–22

4In the course of time, war broke out
with the Philistines, at Gezer.[u] At
that time Sibbecai the Hushathite
killed Sippai, one of the descendants of
the Rephaites,[v] and the Philistines
were subjugated.

5In another battle with the Philistines, Elhanan son of Jair killed Lahmi
the brother of Goliath the Gittite, who
had a spear with a shaft like a weaver's
rod.[w]

6In still another battle, which took
place at Gath, there was a huge man
with six fingers on each hand and six
toes on each foot—twenty-four in all.
He also was descended from Rapha.
7When he taunted Israel, Jonathan son
of Shimea, David's brother, killed him.

8These were descendants of Rapha
in Gath, and they fell at the hands of
David and his men.

David Numbers the Fighting Men

21:1–26pp — 2Sa 24:1–25

21 Satan[x] rose up against Israel
and incited David to take a census[y] of Israel. 2So David said to Joab
and the commanders of the troops, "Go
and count[z] the Israelites from Beersheba to Dan. Then report back to me
so that I may know how many there
are."

3But Joab replied, "May the LORD
multiply his troops a hundred times
over.[a] My lord the king, are they not
all my lord's subjects? Why does my
lord want to do this? Why should he
bring guilt on Israel?"

4The king's word, however, over-
ruled Joab; so Joab left and went
throughout Israel and then came back
to Jerusalem. 5Joab reported the number of the fighting men to David: In all
Israel[b] there were one million one
hundred thousand men who could handle a sword, including four hundred
and seventy thousand in Judah.

6But Joab did not include Levi and
Benjamin in the numbering, because
the king's command was repulsive to
him. 7This command was also evil in
the sight of God; so he punished Israel.

8Then David said to God, "I have
sinned greatly by doing this. Now, I beg

20:1 [r] S Dt 3:11 [s] Am 1:13-15
20:3 [t] S Dt 29:11
20:4 [u] Jos 10:33 [v] S Ge 14:5
20:5 [w] S 1Sa 17:7
21:1 [x] S 2Ch 18:21; S Ps 109:6 [y] 2Ch 14:8; 25:5
21:2 [z] 1Ch 27:23-24
21:3 [a] S Dt 1:11
21:5 [b] S 1Ch 9:1

[s] *2* Or *of Milcom,* that is, Molech [t] *2* That is, about 75 pounds (about 34 kilograms)

21:1 SATAN . . . INCITED DAVID TO TAKE A CENSUS. God allowed Satan to tempt David after David had accomplished much and gained great victories (see 2Sa 24:1, note). We learn the following truths from Satan's temptation of David: (1) "Satan" means "accuser" (cf. Job 1:6); he actively opposes the believer's efforts to conform to God's will and righteous standards (see Eph 6:11–12; 1Pe 5:8; Rev 12:17).

(2) Satan often directs his activity toward the human mind, mostly by way of deception (see Ge 3:1–7,13; 2Co 4:4; Eph 2:2; 1Ti 4:1); he deceived David into thinking that God would endorse this census of the nation.

(3) Satan loves to lead believers into the sins of pride and self-exaltation (see Ge 3:5; see 1Ch 21:8, note); note that it was after David's great victories and accomplishments (chs. 14—21) that Satan was able to gain this foothold in the king's life (vv. 7–8; see 1Ti 3:6).

21:7 HE PUNISHED ISRAEL. It is likely that the people of Israel were in sympathy with David's sinful desire to number the people. Joab himself knew that taking a census was a great sin that would bring guilt on all Israel (v. 3). Presumably, therefore, a majority of the people were guilty of favoring the census. Through their spirit of national pride, they participated in David's sin and became subject to judgment (see next note).

21:8 I HAVE SINNED GREATLY. David sinned by taking personal pride in God's using him for great purposes within the kingdom of Israel. By counting the people, he was trying to exalt himself and Israel and to rely on their national strength. Such boasting inevitably leads to a spirit of self-trust and superiority and to a life no longer lived in faith and humility. David should have remembered that all Israel's victories had been accomplished by God's help. Similarly, believers should never boast in their own "greatness" within God's

you, take away the guilt of your servant. I have done a very foolish thing."
9 The LORD said to Gad,[c] David's
seer,[d] 10 "Go and tell David, 'This is
what the LORD says: I am giving you
three options. Choose one of them for
me to carry out against you.' "
11 So Gad went to David and said to
him, "This is what the LORD says: 'Take
your choice: 12 three years of famine,[e]
three months of being swept away[u]
before your enemies, with their swords
overtaking you, or three days of the
sword[f] of the LORD[g]—days of plague
in the land, with the angel of the LORD
ravaging every part of Israel.' Now
then, decide how I should answer the
one who sent me."
13 David said to Gad, "I am in deep
distress. Let me fall into the hands of
the LORD, for his mercy[h] is very great;
but do not let me fall into the hands of
men."
14 So the LORD sent a plague on Israel, and seventy thousand men of Israel
fell dead.[i] 15 And God sent an angel[j]
to destroy Jerusalem.[k] But as the angel was doing so, the LORD saw it and
was grieved[l] because of the calamity
and said to the angel who was destroying[m] the people, "Enough! Withdraw
your hand." The angel of the LORD was
then standing at the threshing floor of
Araunah[v] the Jebusite.
16 David looked up and saw the angel
of the LORD standing between heaven
and earth, with a drawn sword in his
hand extended over Jerusalem. Then
David and the elders, clothed in sackcloth, fell facedown.[n]
17 David said to God, "Was it not I
who ordered the fighting men to be
counted? I am the one who has sinned
and done wrong. These are but
sheep.[o] What have they done? O LORD
my God, let your hand fall upon me and
my family,[p] but do not let this plague
remain on your people."
18 Then the angel of the LORD ordered
Gad to tell David to go up and build an
altar to the LORD on the threshing
floor[q] of Araunah the Jebusite. 19 So
David went up in obedience to the word
that Gad had spoken in the name of the
LORD.
20 While Araunah was threshing
wheat,[r] he turned and saw the angel;
his four sons who were with him hid
themselves. 21 Then David approached,
and when Araunah looked and saw
him, he left the threshing floor and
bowed down before David with his face
to the ground.
22 David said to him, "Let me have
the site of your threshing floor so I can
build an altar to the LORD, that the
plague on the people may be stopped.
Sell it to me at the full price."
23 Araunah said to David, "Take it!
Let my lord the king do whatever
pleases him. Look, I will give the oxen
for the burnt offerings, the threshing
sledges for the wood, and the wheat for
the grain offering. I will give all this."
24 But King David replied to Araunah, "No, I insist on paying the full
price. I will not take for the LORD what
is yours, or sacrifice a burnt offering
that costs me nothing."
25 So David paid Araunah six hundred shekels[w] of gold for the site.
26 David built an altar to the LORD there
and sacrificed burnt offerings and fellowship offerings.[x] He called on the
LORD, and the LORD answered him with
fire[s] from heaven on the altar of burnt
offering.
27 Then the LORD spoke to the angel,
and he put his sword back into its
sheath. 28 At that time, when David
saw that the LORD had answered him on
the threshing floor of Araunah the Jeb-

21:9 [c] S 1Sa 22:5 [d] S 1Sa 9:9 **21:12** [e] S Dt 32:24 [f] Eze 30:25 [g] S Ge 19:13 **21:13** [h] Ps 6:4; 86:15; 130:4,7 **21:14** [i] 1Ch 27:24 **21:15** [j] S Ge 32:1 [k] Ps 125:2 [l] S Ge 6:6; S Ex 32:14 [m] S Ge 19:13 **21:16** [n] S Nu 14:5; S Jos 7:6 **21:17** [o] S 2Sa 7:8 [p] Jnh 1:12 **21:18** [q] 2Ch 3:1 **21:20** [r] S Jdg 6:11 **21:26** [s] S Ex 19:18; S Jdg 6:21

[u] *12* Hebrew; Septuagint and Vulgate (see also 2 Samuel 24:13) *of fleeing* [v] *15* Hebrew *Ornan*, a variant of *Araunah*; also in verses 18-28 [w] *25* That is, about 15 pounds (about 7 kilograms) [x] *26* Traditionally *peace offerings*

kingdom but in their weaknesses, "so that Christ's power may rest on [them]" (2Co 12:9).

21:14 THE LORD SENT A PLAGUE. David confessed his sin, sincerely repented, and was forgiven (v. 8). Yet God carried out the temporal punishment on him and the people. The fact that sin often receives divine punishment even after confession and forgiveness is a recurring Biblical principle (see 2Sa 11:2, note; 12:13, note). By causing his disobedient children to endure the temporal consequences of sin, God honors his own law, upholds his own authority, purifies his people and shows himself to be a righteous Ruler.

21:15 ENOUGH! WITHDRAW YOUR HAND. The Lord is a God who can have feelings of compassion even for those who deserve punishment; because of his love, mercy and compassion, God may shorten or even cancel a punishment he has intended to carry out (cf. Jnh 3).

21:24 BURNT OFFERING THAT COSTS ME NOTHING. See 2Sa 24:24, note.

usite, he offered sacrifices there. 29The
tabernacle of the LORD, which Moses
had made in the desert, and the altar
of burnt offering were at that time on
the high place at Gibeon.[t] 30But David could not go before it to inquire of
God, because he was afraid of the
sword of the angel of the LORD.

22 Then David said, "The house of
the LORD God[u] is to be here,
and also the altar of burnt offering for
Israel."

Preparations for the Temple

2So David gave orders to assemble
the aliens[v] living in Israel, and from
among them he appointed stonecutters[w] to prepare dressed stone for
building the house of God. 3He provided a large amount of iron to make nails
for the doors of the gateways and for
the fittings, and more bronze than
could be weighed.[x] 4He also provided
more cedar logs[y] than could be counted, for the Sidonians and Tyrians had
brought large numbers of them to David.
5David said, "My son Solomon is
young[z] and inexperienced, and the
house to be built for the LORD should be
of great magnificence and fame and
splendor[a] in the sight of all the nations. Therefore I will make preparations for it." So David made extensive
preparations before his death.
6Then he called for his son Solomon
and charged him to build[b] a house for
the LORD, the God of Israel. 7David said
to Solomon: "My son, I had it in my
heart[c] to build[d] a house for the
Name[e] of the LORD my God. 8But this
word of the LORD came to me: 'You have
shed much blood and have fought
many wars.[f] You are not to build a
house for my Name,[g] because you
have shed much blood on the earth in
my sight. 9But you will have a son who
will be a man of peace[h] and rest,[i]
and I will give him rest from all his enemies on every side. His name will be
Solomon,[y][j] and I will grant Israel
peace and quiet[k] during his reign.
10He is the one who will build a house
for my Name.[l] He will be my son,[m]
and I will be his father. And I will establish[n] the throne of his kingdom
over Israel forever.'[o]
11"Now, my son, the LORD be with[p]
you, and may you have success and
build the house of the LORD your God,
as he said you would. 12May the LORD
give you discretion and understanding[q] when he puts you in command
over Israel, so that you may keep the
law of the LORD your God. 13Then you
will have success[r] if you are careful to
observe the decrees and laws[s] that
the LORD gave Moses for Israel. Be
strong and courageous.[t] Do not be
afraid or discouraged.
14"I have taken great pains to provide for the temple of the LORD a hundred thousand talents[z] of gold, a million talents[a] of silver, quantities of
bronze and iron too great to be
weighed, and wood and stone. And you
may add to them.[u] 15You have many
workmen: stonecutters, masons and
carpenters,[v] as well as men skilled in
every kind of work 16in gold and silver,
bronze and iron—craftsmen[w] beyond
number. Now begin the work, and the
LORD be with you."
17Then David ordered[x] all the leaders of Israel to help his son Solomon.
18He said to them, "Is not the LORD
your God with you? And has he not
granted you rest[y] on every side?[z] For
he has handed the inhabitants of the
land over to me, and the land is subject
to the LORD and to his people. 19Now
devote your heart and soul to seeking
the LORD your God.[a] Begin to build the
sanctuary of the LORD God, so that you
may bring the ark of the covenant of
the LORD and the sacred articles belonging to God into the temple that will
be built for the Name of the LORD."

The Levites

23 When David was old and full of
years, he made his son Solomon[b] king over Israel.[c]

21:29 [t] S Jos 9:3
22:1 [u] S Ge 28:17
22:2 [v] S Ex 1:11; S Dt 20:11; 2Ch 8:10; S Isa 56:6 [w] 1Ki 5:17-18; Ezr 3:7
22:3 [x] S 1Ki 7:47; 1Ch 29:2-5
22:4 [y] S 1Ki 5:6
22:5 [z] S 1Ki 3:7; 1Ch 29:1 [a] 2Ch 2:5
22:6 [b] Ac 7:47
22:7 [c] S 1Ch 17:2 [d] S 1Ki 8:17 [e] Dt 12:5,11
22:8 [f] S 1Ki 5:3 [g] 1Ch 28:3
22:9 [h] S Jos 14:15; S 1Ki 5:4 [i] ver 18; 1Ch 23:25; 2Ch 14:6,7; 15:15; 20:30; 36:21 [j] S 2Sa 12:24; S 1Ch 23:1 [k] 1Ki 4:20
22:10 [l] S 1Ch 17:12 [m] S 2Sa 7:13 [n] 1Ki 9:5 [o] S 2Sa 7:14; S 1Ch 17:4; 2Ch 6:15
22:11 [p] S 1Sa 16:18; S 18:12
22:12 [q] 1Ki 3:9-12
22:13 [r] 1Ki 2:3 [s] 1Ch 28:7 [t] S Dt 31:6
22:14 [u] 1Ch 29:2-5,19
22:15 [v] Ezr 3:7
22:16 [w] 2Ch 2:7
22:17 [x] 1Ch 28:1-6
22:18 [y] S ver 9 [z] 2Sa 7:1
22:19 [a] 2Ch 7:14
23:1 [b] 1Ch 22:9; 28:5; 2Ch 1:8 [c] S 1Ki 1:30; 1Ch 29:28

[y] 9 *Solomon* sounds like and may be derived from the Hebrew for *peace*. [z] 14 That is, about 3,750 tons (about 3,450 metric tons) [a] 14 That is, about 37,500 tons (about 34,500 metric tons)

22:11 NOW, MY SON. Although David was not allowed to build the temple (vv. 7–8), he faithfully dedicated himself to preparing for its construction. His concern was not only for the temple but for his son Solomon, who would oversee the project. Above all, he instructed his son to be careful to observe God's laws and seek the Lord with all his heart and soul (vv. 11–13,19; see Jn 17:1, note on the way parents ought to pray for their children).

2He also gathered together all the
leaders of Israel, as well as the priests
and Levites. 3The Levites thirty years
old or more[d] were counted,[e] and the
total number of men was thirty-eight
thousand.[f] 4David said, "Of these,
twenty-four thousand are to supervise[g] the work[h] of the temple of the
LORD and six thousand are to be officials and judges.[i] 5Four thousand are
to be gatekeepers and four thousand
are to praise the LORD with the musical
instruments[j] I have provided for that
purpose."[k]
6David divided[l] the Levites into
groups corresponding to the sons of
Levi:[m] Gershon, Kohath and Merari.

Gershonites

7Belonging to the Gershonites:[n]
Ladan and Shimei.
8The sons of Ladan:
Jehiel the first, Zetham and
Joel—three in all.
9The sons of Shimei:
Shelomoth, Haziel and Haran—three in all.
These were the heads of the
families of Ladan.
10And the sons of Shimei:
Jahath, Ziza,[b] Jeush and Beriah.
These were the sons of Shimei—four in all.
11Jahath was the first and Ziza
the second, but Jeush and Beriah did not have many sons; so
they were counted as one family with one assignment.

Kohathites

12The sons of Kohath:[o]
Amram, Izhar, Hebron and Uzziel—four in all.
13The sons of Amram:[p]
Aaron and Moses.
Aaron was set apart,[q] he and
his descendants forever, to
consecrate the most holy
things, to offer sacrifices before the LORD, to minister[r] before him and to pronounce
blessings[s] in his name forever. 14The sons of Moses the
man[t] of God were counted as
part of the tribe of Levi.
15The sons of Moses:
Gershom and Eliezer.[u]
16The descendants of Gershom:[v]
Shubael was the first.
17The descendants of Eliezer:
Rehabiah[w] was the first.
Eliezer had no other sons, but
the sons of Rehabiah were very
numerous.
18The sons of Izhar:
Shelomith[x] was the first.
19The sons of Hebron:[y]
Jeriah the first, Amariah the
second, Jahaziel the third and
Jekameam the fourth.
20The sons of Uzziel:
Micah the first and Isshiah the
second.

Merarites

21The sons of Merari:[z]
Mahli and Mushi.[a]
The sons of Mahli:
Eleazar and Kish.
22Eleazar died without having
sons: he had only daughters.
Their cousins, the sons of Kish,
married them.[b]
23The sons of Mushi:
Mahli, Eder and Jerimoth—
three in all.

24These were the descendants of
Levi by their families—the heads of
families as they were registered under
their names and counted individually,
that is, the workers twenty years old or
more[c] who served in the temple of the
LORD. 25For David had said, "Since the
LORD, the God of Israel, has granted
rest[d] to his people and has come to
dwell in Jerusalem forever, 26the Levites no longer need to carry the tabernacle or any of the articles used in its
service."[e] 27According to the last instructions of David, the Levites were
counted from those twenty years old or
more.
28The duty of the Levites was to
help Aaron's descendants in the ser-

23:3 [d]Nu 8:24 [e]1Ch 21:7 [f]Nu 4:3-49 23:4 [g]Ezr 3:8 [h]2Ch 34:13; Ne 4:10 [i]1Ch 26:29; 2Ch 19:8; Eze 44:24 23:5 [j]S 1Ch 15:16; Ps 92:3 [k]Ne 12:45 23:6 [l]2Ch 8:14; 23:18; 29:25 [m]S Nu 3:17; 1Ch 24:20 23:7 [n]1Ch 6:71 23:12 [o]S Ge 46:11; S Ex 6:18 23:13 [p]Ex 6:20 [q]Ex 30:7-10 [r]S 1Ch 15:2 [s]S Nu 6:23 23:14 [t]Dt 33:1 23:15 [u]Ex 18:4 23:16 [v]1Ch 26:24-28 23:17 [w]1Ch 24:21 23:18 [x]1Ch 26:25 23:19 [y]1Ch 24:23; 26:31 23:21 [z]S 1Ch 6:19 [a]S Ex 6:19 23:22 [b]Nu 36:8 23:24 [c]S Nu 4:3 23:25 [d]S 1Ch 22:9 23:26 [e]Nu 4:5, 15; 7:9; Dt 10:8

[b] *10* One Hebrew manuscript, Septuagint and Vulgate (see also verse 11); most Hebrew manuscripts *Zina*

23:2 GATHERED TOGETHER ALL THE LEADERS. David demonstrated kingly leadership at its best when he arranged for the proper conducting of divine worship. Among other things, he specified the work of the Levites (vv. 4–5); in so doing, he established a foundation for his leadership and strengthened the religious and political structure of the nation.

vice of the temple of the LORD: to be in
charge of the courtyards, the side
rooms, the purification[f] of all sacred
things and the performance of other
duties at the house of God. 29They
were in charge of the bread set out on
the table,[g] the flour for the grain offerings,[h] the unleavened wafers, the
baking and the mixing, and all measurements of quantity and size.[i]
30They were also to stand every morning to thank and praise the LORD. They
were to do the same in the evening[j]
31and whenever burnt offerings were
presented to the LORD on Sabbaths and
at New Moon[k] festivals and at appointed feasts.[l] They were to serve
before the LORD regularly in the proper
number and in the way prescribed for
them.
32And so the Levites[m] carried out
their responsibilities for the Tent of
Meeting,[n] for the Holy Place and, under their brothers the descendants of
Aaron, for the service of the temple of
the LORD.[o]

The Divisions of Priests

24 These were the divisions[p] of
the sons of Aaron:[q]
The sons of Aaron were Nadab, Abihu, Eleazar and Ithamar.[r] 2But Nadab
and Abihu died before their father
did,[s] and they had no sons; so Eleazar
and Ithamar served as the priests.
3With the help of Zadok[t] a descendant of Eleazar and Ahimelech a
descendant of Ithamar, David separated them into divisions for their appointed order of ministering. 4A larger
number of leaders were found among
Eleazar's descendants than among Ithamar's, and they were divided accordingly: sixteen heads of families from
Eleazar's descendants and eight heads
of families from Ithamar's descendants. 5They divided them impartially
by drawing lots,[u] for there were officials of the sanctuary and officials of
God among the descendants of both Eleazar and Ithamar.
6The scribe Shemaiah son of Nethanel, a Levite, recorded their names
in the presence of the king and of the
officials: Zadok the priest, Ahimelech[v] son of Abiathar and the heads of
families of the priests and of the Levites—one family being taken from Eleazar and then one from Ithamar.

7The first lot fell to Jehoiarib,
the second to Jedaiah,[w]
8the third to Harim,[x]
the fourth to Seorim,
9the fifth to Malkijah,
the sixth to Mijamin,
10the seventh to Hakkoz,
the eighth to Abijah,[y]
11the ninth to Jeshua,
the tenth to Shecaniah,
12the eleventh to Eliashib,
the twelfth to Jakim,
13the thirteenth to Huppah,
the fourteenth to Jeshebeab,
14the fifteenth to Bilgah,
the sixteenth to Immer,[z]
15the seventeenth to Hezir,[a]
the eighteenth to Happizzez,
16the nineteenth to Pethahiah,
the twentieth to Jehezkel,
17the twenty-first to Jakin,
the twenty-second to Gamul,
18the twenty-third to Delaiah
and the twenty-fourth to Maaziah.

19This was their appointed order of
ministering when they entered the
temple of the LORD, according to the
regulations prescribed for them by
their forefather Aaron, as the LORD, the
God of Israel, had commanded him.

The Rest of the Levites

20As for the rest of the descendants of
Levi:[b]
from the sons of Amram: Shubael;
from the sons of Shubael: Jehdeiah.
21As for Rehabiah,[c] from his
sons:
Isshiah was the first.
22From the Izharites: Shelomoth;
from the sons of Shelomoth: Jahath.
23The sons of Hebron:[d] Jeriah the

23:28 [f] 2Ch 29:15; Ne 13:9; Mal 3:3
23:29 [g] S Ex 25:30 [h] Lev 2:4-7; 6:20-23 [i] Lev 19:35-36; S 1Ch 9:29,32
23:30 [j] S 1Ch 9:33; Ps 134:1
23:31 [k] S 2Ki 4:23 [l] Nu 28:9-29:39; Isa 1:13-14; Col 2:16
23:32 [m] 1Ch 6:48 [n] Nu 3:6-8,38 [o] 2Ch 23:18; 31:2; Eze 44:14
24:1 [p] 1Ch 23:6; 28:13; 2Ch 5:11; 8:14; 23:8; 31:2; 35:4,5; Ezr 6:18 [q] Nu 3:2-4 [r] S Ex 6:23
24:2 [s] Lev 10:1-2
24:3 [t] S 2Sa 8:17
24:5 [u] ver 31; 1Ch 25:8; 26:13
24:6 [v] 1Ch 18:16
24:7 [w] Ezr 2:36; Ne 12:6
24:8 [x] Ezr 2:39; 10:21; Ne 10:5
24:10 [y] Ne 12:4, 17; Lk 1:5
24:14 [z] Ezr 2:37; 10:20; Jer 20:1
24:15 [a] Ne 10:20
24:20 [b] S 1Ch 23:6
24:21 [c] 1Ch 23:17
24:23 [d] S 1Ch 23:19

24:1 THE DIVISIONS OF THE SONS OF AARON. Ch. 24 deals with the organization of the priests. Their duty consisted in offering sacrifices by which the people might approach God to receive forgiveness and offer obedience to his will; that task ceased with the coming of Jesus and the establishment of the new covenant through his blood (see Heb 3:1; 4:14–16; 7:23–25; 8:1–13; see article on THE OLD COVENANT AND THE NEW COVENANT, p. 1926). Ironically, in NT times the priests had so departed from the truth of God's word that they were the ones who instigated Jesus' crucifixion (Mt 27:1,6,20). Today all believers are to be a holy priesthood (see 1Pe 2:5, note).

first,[c] Amariah the second, Jahaziel the third and Jekameam the fourth.
24The son of Uzziel: Micah;
from the sons of Micah: Shamir.
25The brother of Micah: Isshiah;
from the sons of Isshiah: Zechariah.
26The sons of Merari:[e] Mahli and Mushi.
The son of Jaaziah: Beno.
27The sons of Merari:
from Jaaziah: Beno, Shoham, Zaccur and Ibri.
28From Mahli: Eleazar, who had no sons.
29From Kish: the son of Kish: Jerahmeel.
30And the sons of Mushi: Mahli, Eder and Jerimoth.

These were the Levites, according to
their families. 31They also cast lots,[f]
just as their brothers the descendants
of Aaron did, in the presence of King
David and of Zadok, Ahimelech, and
the heads of families of the priests and
of the Levites. The families of the oldest brother were treated the same as those of the youngest.

The Singers

25 David, together with the commanders of the army, set apart some of the sons of Asaph,[g] Heman[h] and Jeduthun[i] for the ministry of prophesying,[j] accompanied by harps, lyres and cymbals.[k] Here is the list of the men[l] who performed this service:[m]

2From the sons of Asaph:
Zaccur, Joseph, Nethaniah and Asarelah. The sons of Asaph were under the supervision of Asaph, who prophesied under the king's supervision.
3As for Jeduthun, from his sons:[n]
Gedaliah, Zeri, Jeshaiah, Shimei,[d] Hashabiah and Mattithiah, six in all, under the supervision of their father Jeduthun, who prophesied, using the harp[o] in thanking and praising the LORD.
4As for Heman, from his sons:
Bukkiah, Mattaniah, Uzziel, Shubael and Jerimoth; Hananiah, Hanani, Eliathah, Giddalti and Romamti-Ezer; Joshbekashah, Mallothi, Hothir and Mahazioth.
5All these were sons of Heman the king's seer. They were given him through the promises of God to exalt him.[e] God gave Heman fourteen sons and three daughters.

6All these men were under the supervision of their fathers[p] for the music of the temple of the LORD, with cymbals, lyres and harps, for the ministry at the house of God. Asaph, Jeduthun
and Heman[q] were under the supervi-
sion of the king.[r] 7Along with their
relatives—all of them trained and skilled in music for the LORD—they
numbered 288. 8Young and old alike,
teacher as well as student, cast lots[s] for their duties.

9The first lot, which was for Asaph,[t] fell to Joseph,
his sons and relatives,[f] 12[g]
the second to Gedaliah,
he and his relatives and sons, 12
10the third to Zaccur,
his sons and relatives, 12
11the fourth to Izri,[h]
his sons and relatives, 12
12the fifth to Nethaniah,
his sons and relatives, 12
13the sixth to Bukkiah,
his sons and relatives, 12

24:26 [e]S 1Ch 6:19
24:31 [f]S ver 5
25:1 [g]S 1Ch 6:39 [h]S 1Ch 6:33 [i]1Ch 16:41,42; Ne 11:17 [j]S 1Sa 10:5; 2Ki 3:15 [k]S 1Ch 15:16 [l]S 1Ch 6:31 [m]2Ch 5:12; 8:14; 34:12; 35:15; Ezr 3:10
25:3 [n]1Ch 16:41-42 [o]S Ge 4:21; Ps 33:2
25:6 [p]S 1Ch 15:16 [q]S 1Ch 15:19 [r]2Ch 23:18; 29:25
25:8 [s]1Ch 26:13
25:9 [t]S 1Ch 6:39

[c]23 Two Hebrew manuscripts and some Septuagint manuscripts (see also 1 Chron. 23:19); most Hebrew manuscripts *The sons of Jeriah:* [d]3 One Hebrew manuscript and some Septuagint manuscripts (see also verse 17); most Hebrew manuscripts do not have *Shimei.* [e]5 Hebrew *exalt the horn* [f]9 See Septuagint; Hebrew does not have *his sons and relatives.* [g]9 See the total in verse 7; Hebrew does not have *twelve.* [h]11 A variant of *Zeri*

25:1 PROPHESYING, ACCOMPANIED BY HARPS. The usual meaning of "to prophesy" is to use one's voice for God's service and to his glory under divine impulse. Here it is used to signify singing and playing music to the praise of God, most likely under the direct influence of the Holy Spirit. Under the new covenant, prophesying came to be a predominant manifestation of the Holy Spirit among those who believe in Christ and who are filled with the Spirit (see Ac 2:17, note; see article on SPIRITUAL GIFTS FOR BELIEVERS, p. 1770).

25:7 MUSIC FOR THE LORD. Singing was primarily a medium to praise God and to glorify his name (see Eph 5:19, note).

14 the seventh to Jesarelah,[i]
his sons and relatives, 12
15 the eighth to Jeshaiah,
his sons and relatives, 12
16 the ninth to Mattaniah,
his sons and relatives, 12
17 the tenth to Shimei,
his sons and relatives, 12
18 the eleventh to Azarel,[j]
his sons and relatives, 12
19 the twelfth to Hashabiah,
his sons and relatives, 12
20 the thirteenth to Shubael,
his sons and relatives, 12
21 the fourteenth to
Mattithiah,
his sons and relatives, 12
22 the fifteenth to Jerimoth,
his sons and relatives, 12
23 the sixteenth to Hananiah,
his sons and relatives, 12
24 the seventeenth to
Joshbekashah,
his sons and relatives, 12
25 the eighteenth to Hanani,
his sons and relatives, 12
26 the nineteenth to Mallothi,
his sons and relatives, 12
27 the twentieth to Eliathah,
his sons and relatives, 12
28 the twenty-first to Hothir,
his sons and relatives, 12
29 the twenty-second to
Giddalti,
his sons and relatives, 12
30 the twenty-third to
Mahazioth,
his sons and relatives, 12
31 the twenty-fourth to
Romamti-Ezer,
his sons and relatives, 12[u]

The Gatekeepers

26 The divisions of the gatekeepers:[v]

From the Korahites: Meshelemiah son of Kore, one of the sons of Asaph.
2 Meshelemiah had sons:
Zechariah[w] the firstborn,
Jediael the second,
Zebadiah the third,
Jathniel the fourth,
3 Elam the fifth,
Jehohanan the sixth
and Eliehoenai the seventh.
4 Obed-Edom also had sons:
Shemaiah the firstborn,
Jehozabad the second,
Joah the third,
Sacar the fourth,
Nethanel the fifth,
5 Ammiel the sixth,
Issachar the seventh
and Peullethai the eighth.
(For God had blessed Obed-Edom.[x])

6 His son Shemaiah also had sons,
who were leaders in their father's family because they were
very capable men. 7 The sons of
Shemaiah: Othni, Rephael,
Obed and Elzabad; his relatives
Elihu and Semakiah were also
able men. 8 All these were
descendants of Obed-Edom;
they and their sons and their
relatives were capable men
with the strength to do the
work—descendants of Obed-Edom, 62 in all.
9 Meshelemiah had sons and relatives, who were able men—18
in all.
10 Hosah the Merarite had sons:
Shimri the first (although he
was not the firstborn, his father
had appointed him the first),[y]
11 Hilkiah the second, Tabaliah
the third and Zechariah the
fourth. The sons and relatives
of Hosah were 13 in all.
12 These divisions of the gatekeepers, through their chief men, had duties for ministering[z] in the temple of
the LORD, just as their relatives had.
13 Lots[a] were cast for each gate, according to their families, young and old
alike.
14 The lot for the East Gate[b] fell to
Shelemiah.[k] Then lots were cast for
his son Zechariah,[c] a wise counselor,
and the lot for the North Gate fell to
him. 15 The lot for the South Gate fell
to Obed-Edom,[d] and the lot for the
storehouse fell to his sons. 16 The lots
for the West Gate and the Shalleketh
Gate on the upper road fell to Shuppim
and Hosah.
Guard was alongside of guard:
17 There were six Levites a day on the
east, four a day on the north, four a day
on the south and two at a time at the
storehouse. 18 As for the court to the

25:31 [u]S 1Ch 9:33
26:1 [v]S 1Ch 9:17
26:2 [w]S 1Ch 9:21
26:5 [x]S 2Sa 6:10; S 1Ch 13:13; S 16:38
26:10 [y]Dt 21:16; 1Ch 5:1
26:12 [z]1Ch 9:22
26:13 [a]S 1Ch 24:5,31; 25:8
26:14 [b]S 1Ch 9:18 [c]S 1Ch 9:21
26:15 [d]S 1Ch 13:13; 2Ch 25:24

[i] *14* A variant of *Asarelah* [j] *18* A variant of *Uzziel* [k] *14* A variant of *Meshelemiah*

west, there were four at the road and
two at the court itself.
19These were the divisions of the
gatekeepers who were descendants of
Korah and Merari.[e]

The Treasurers and Other Officials

20Their fellow Levites[f] were[1] in
charge of the treasuries of the house of
God and the treasuries for the dedicated things.[g]
21The descendants of Ladan, who
were Gershonites through Ladan and
who were heads of families belonging
to Ladan the Gershonite,[h] were Jehieli, 22the sons of Jehieli, Zetham and his
brother Joel. They were in charge of
the treasuries[i] of the temple of the
LORD.
23From the Amramites, the Izharites, the Hebronites and the Uzzielites:[j]
24Shubael,[k] a descendant of Gershom son of Moses, was the officer in charge of the treasuries. 25His relatives through
Eliezer: Rehabiah his son, Jeshaiah his son, Joram his son,
Zicri his son and Shelomith[l]
his son. 26Shelomith and his
relatives were in charge of all
the treasuries for the things
dedicated[m] by King David, by
the heads of families who were
the commanders of thousands
and commanders of hundreds,
and by the other army commanders. 27Some of the plunder taken in battle they dedicated for the repair of the
temple of the LORD. 28And everything dedicated by Samuel
the seer[n] and by Saul son of
Kish, Abner son of Ner and Joab
son of Zeruiah, and all the other dedicated things were in the
care of Shelomith and his relatives.
29From the Izharites: Kenaniah and
his sons were assigned duties
away from the temple, as officials and judges[o] over Israel.
30From the Hebronites: Hashabiah[p] and his relatives—seventeen hundred able men—were
responsible in Israel west of
the Jordan for all the work of
the LORD and for the king's service. 31As for the Hebronites,[q]
Jeriah was their chief according
to the genealogical records of
their families. In the fortieth[r]
year of David's reign a search
was made in the records, and
capable men among the He-
bronites were found at Jazer in
Gilead. 32Jeriah had twenty-
seven hundred relatives, who
were able men and heads of
families, and King David put
them in charge of the Reubenites, the Gadites and the half-
tribe of Manasseh for every
matter pertaining to God and
for the affairs of the king.

Army Divisions

27 This is the list of the Israelites—heads of families, commanders of thousands and commanders of hundreds, and their officers, who
served the king in all that concerned
the army divisions that were on duty
month by month throughout the year.
Each division consisted of 24,000 men.
2In charge of the first division, for the
first month, was Jashobeam[s]
son of Zabdiel. There were
24,000 men in his division. 3He
was a descendant of Perez and
chief of all the army officers for
the first month.
4In charge of the division for the second month was Dodai[t] the
Ahohite; Mikloth was the leader
of his division. There were
24,000 men in his division.
5The third army commander, for the
third month, was Benaiah[u] son
of Jehoiada the priest. He was
chief and there were 24,000
men in his division. 6This was
the Benaiah who was a mighty
man among the Thirty and was
over the Thirty. His son Ammiz-
abad was in charge of his division.
7The fourth, for the fourth month, was
Asahel[v] the brother of Joab;
his son Zebadiah was his successor. There were 24,000 men
in his division.
8The fifth, for the fifth month, was the
commander Shamhuth[w] the Iz-

26:19 [e] 2Ch 35:15; Ne 7:1; Eze 44:11
26:20 [f] 2Ch 24:5 [g] 1Ch 28:12
26:21 [h] 1Ch 23:7; 29:8
26:22 [i] 1Ch 9:26
26:23 [j] S Nu 3:27
26:24 [k] 1Ch 23:16
26:25 [l] 1Ch 23:18
26:26 [m] S 2Sa 8:11
26:28 [n] S 1Sa 9:9
26:29 [o] Dt 17:8-13; S 1Ch 23:4
26:30 [p] 1Ch 27:17
26:31 [q] S 1Ch 23:19 [r] S 2Sa 5:4
27:2 [s] 2Sa 23:8
27:4 [t] S 2Sa 23:9
27:5 [u] S 2Sa 23:20
27:7 [v] S 2Sa 2:18
27:8 [w] 1Ch 11:27

[1] 20 Septuagint; Hebrew *As for the Levites, Ahijah was*

rahite. There were 24,000 men
in his division.
9The sixth, for the sixth month, was
Ira[x] the son of Ikkesh the Tekoite. There were 24,000 men
in his division.
10The seventh, for the seventh month,
was Helez[y] the Pelonite, an
Ephraimite. There were 24,000
men in his division.
11The eighth, for the eighth month,
was Sibbecai[z] the Hushathite,
a Zerahite. There were 24,000
men in his division.
12The ninth, for the ninth month, was
Abiezer[a] the Anathothite, a
Benjamite. There were 24,000
men in his division.
13The tenth, for the tenth month, was
Maharai[b] the Netophathite, a
Zerahite. There were 24,000
men in his division.
14The eleventh, for the eleventh
month, was Benaiah[c] the Pirathonite, an Ephraimite. There
were 24,000 men in his division.
15The twelfth, for the twelfth month,
was Heldai[d] the Netophathite,
from the family of Othniel.[e]
There were 24,000 men in his
division.

Officers of the Tribes

16The officers over the tribes of Israel:

over the Reubenites: Eliezer son of Zicri;
over the Simeonites: Shephatiah son of Maacah;
17over Levi: Hashabiah[f] son of Kemuel;
over Aaron: Zadok;[g]
18over Judah: Elihu, a brother of David;
over Issachar: Omri son of Michael;
19over Zebulun: Ishmaiah son of Obadiah;
over Naphtali: Jerimoth son of Azriel;
20over the Ephraimites: Hoshea son of Azaziah;
over half the tribe of Manasseh: Joel son of Pedaiah;
21over the half-tribe of Manasseh in Gilead: Iddo son of Zechariah;
over Benjamin: Jaasiel son of Abner;
22over Dan: Azarel son of Jeroham.

These were the officers over the
tribes of Israel.
23David did not take the number of
the men twenty years old or less,[h] because the LORD had promised to make
Israel as numerous as the stars[i] in
the sky. 24Joab son of Zeruiah began to
count the men but did not finish. Wrath
came on Israel on account of this numbering,[j] and the number was not entered in the book[m] of the annals of
King David.

The King's Overseers

25Azmaveth son of Adiel was in
charge of the royal storehouses.

Jonathan son of Uzziah was in charge of the storehouses in the outlying districts, in the towns, the villages and the watchtowers.

26Ezri son of Kelub was in charge of
the field workers who farmed the land.
27Shimei the Ramathite was in
charge of the vineyards.

Zabdi the Shiphmite was in charge of the produce of the vineyards for the wine vats.

28Baal-Hanan the Gederite was in
charge of the olive and sycamore-fig[k]
trees in the western foothills.

Joash was in charge of the supplies of olive oil.

29Shitrai the Sharonite was in
charge of the herds grazing in Sharon.[l]

Shaphat son of Adlai was in charge of the herds in the valleys.

30Obil the Ishmaelite was in charge
of the camels.

Jehdeiah the Meronothite was in charge of the donkeys.

31Jaziz the Hagrite[m] was in charge
of the flocks.

All these were the officials in charge of King David's property.

32Jonathan, David's uncle, was a
counselor, a man of insight and a
scribe. Jehiel son of Hacmoni took care
of the king's sons.
33Ahithophel[n] was the king's counselor.

Hushai[o] the Arkite was the king's
friend. 34Ahithophel was succeeded by
Jehoiada son of Benaiah and by Abiathar.[p]

Joab[q] was the commander of the royal army.

27:9 [x] 2Sa 23:26 **27:10** [y] 2Sa 23:26 **27:11** [z] S 2Sa 21:18 **27:12** [a] 2Sa 23:27 **27:13** [b] 2Sa 23:28 **27:14** [c] S 1Ch 11:31 **27:15** [d] 2Sa 23:29 [e] S Jos 15:17 **27:17** [f] 1Ch 26:30 [g] S 2Sa 8:17; S 1Ch 12:28 **27:23** [h] S 2Sa 24:1; 1Ch 21:2-5 [i] S Ge 12:2 **27:24** [j] S 2Sa 24:15; 1Ch 21:14 **27:28** [k] S 1Ki 10:27 **27:29** [l] SS 2:1; Isa 33:9; 35:2; 65:10 **27:31** [m] S 1Ch 5:10 **27:33** [n] S 2Sa 15:12 [o] S 2Sa 15:37 **27:34** [p] S 1Sa 22:20 [q] S 2Sa 2:13

m 24 Septuagint; Hebrew *number*

David's Plans for the Temple

28 David summoned[r] all the officials[s] of Israel to assemble at Jerusalem: the officers over the tribes, the commanders of the divisions in the service of the king, the commanders of thousands and commanders of hundreds, and the officials in charge of all the property and livestock belonging to the king and his sons, together with the palace officials, the mighty men and all the brave warriors.

2King David rose to his feet and said: "Listen to me, my brothers and my people. I had it in my heart[t] to build a house as a place of rest[u] for the ark of the covenant of the LORD, for the footstool[v] of our God, and I made plans to build it.[w] **3**But God said to me,[x] 'You are not to build a house for my Name,[y] because you are a warrior and have shed blood.'[z]

4"Yet the LORD, the God of Israel, chose me[a] from my whole family[b] to be king over Israel forever. He chose Judah[c] as leader, and from the house of Judah he chose my family, and from my father's sons he was pleased to make me king over all Israel.[d] **5**Of all my sons—and the LORD has given me many[e]—he has chosen my son Solomon[f] to sit on the throne[g] of the kingdom of the LORD over Israel. **6**He said to me: 'Solomon your son is the one who will build[h] my house and my courts, for I have chosen him to be my son,[i] and I will be his father. **7**I will establish his kingdom forever if he is unswerving in carrying out my commands and laws,[j] as is being done at this time.'

8"So now I charge you in the sight of all Israel[k] and of the assembly of the LORD, and in the hearing of our God: Be careful to follow all the commands[l] of the LORD your God, that you may possess this good land and pass it on as an inheritance to your descendants forever.[m]

28:1 [r]1Ch 22:17 [s]1Ch 27:1-31; 29:6
28:2 [t]S 1Sa 10:7; S 1Ch 17:2 [u]2Ch 6:41 [v]Ps 99:5; 132:7; Isa 60:13 [w]Ps 132:1-5
28:3 [x]S 2Sa 7:5 [y]1Ch 22:8 [z]S 1Ki 5:3; S 1Ch 17:4
28:4 [a]2Ch 6:6 [b]1Sa 16:1-13 [c]S Ge 49:10; Nu 24:17-19 [d]1Ch 11:1
28:5 [e]S 1Ch 3:1 [f]S 2Sa 12:24; S 1Ch 23:1 [g]S 1Ch 17:14
28:6 [h]1Ki 8:20 [i]S 2Sa 7:13; S 1Ch 17:13
28:7 [j]1Ch 22:13
28:8 [k]S 1Ch 9:1 [l]Dt 6:1 [m]Dt 4:1; S 17:14-20
28:9 [n]S 1Ch 29:19 [o]S 1Sa 2:3; 2Ch 6:30; Ps 7:9 [p]S 1Ch 16:11; S Ps 40:16 [q]S Dt 4:31; S Jos 24:20; S 2Ch 7:19; 15:2 [r]1Ki 9:7; Ps 44:23; 74:1; 77:7
28:11 [s]S Ex 25:9; Ac 7:44; Heb 8:5
28:12 [t]S 1Ch 12:18 [u]1Ch 26:20
28:13 [v]S 1Ch 24:1
28:15 [w]Ex 25:31
28:16 [x]S Ex 25:23
28:17 [y]S Ex 27:3
28:18 [z]Ex 30:1-10 [a]S Ex 25:22

9"And you, my son Solomon, acknowledge the God of your father, and serve him with wholehearted devotion[n] and with a willing mind, for the LORD searches every heart[o] and understands every motive behind the thoughts. If you seek him,[p] he will be found by you; but if you forsake[q] him, he will reject[r] you forever. **10**Consider now, for the LORD has chosen you to build a temple as a sanctuary. Be strong and do the work." 2Ch 13:4-12

11Then David gave his son Solomon the plans[s] for the portico of the temple, its buildings, its storerooms, its upper parts, its inner rooms and the place of atonement. **12**He gave him the plans of all that the Spirit[t] had put in his mind for the courts of the temple of the LORD and all the surrounding rooms, for the treasuries of the temple of God and for the treasuries for the dedicated things.[u] **13**He gave him instructions for the divisions[v] of the priests and Levites, and for all the work of serving in the temple of the LORD, as well as for all the articles to be used in its service. **14**He designated the weight of gold for all the gold articles to be used in various kinds of service, and the weight of silver for all the silver articles to be used in various kinds of service: **15**the weight of gold for the gold lampstands[w] and their lamps, with the weight for each lampstand and its lamps; and the weight of silver for each silver lampstand and its lamps, according to the use of each lampstand; **16**the weight of gold for each table[x] for consecrated bread; the weight of silver for the silver tables; **17**the weight of pure gold for the forks, sprinkling bowls[y] and pitchers; the weight of gold for each gold dish; the weight of silver for each silver dish; **18**and the weight of the refined gold for the altar of incense.[z] He also gave him the plan for the chariot,[a] that is, the cherubim of gold that spread their

---

28:8 BE CAREFUL TO FOLLOW ALL THE COMMANDS. The condition for establishing Solomon's kingdom was a life of obedience and faithfulness to God. Solomon heeded his father's advice in the beginning, but later departed from God (see 1Ki 2:4; 11:1, notes).

28:9 ACKNOWLEDGE THE GOD OF YOUR FATHER. David's charge to Solomon was that he should acknowledge God, serve him and seek him "with wholehearted devotion and with a willing mind." (1) To acknowledge God means to have practical knowledge of his person and ways and to live in close fellowship with him and his word (see Jn 17:3, note; cf. 15:4, note). (2) To serve God means to desire his grace, kingdom power and righteousness to such an extent that we continually pray for his active presence in our lives and earnestly seek to obey his will (see Mt 5:6, note on hungering and thirsting for righteousness).

wings and shelter[b] the ark of the covenant of the LORD.

19"All this," David said, "I have in writing from the hand of the LORD upon me, and he gave me understanding in all the details[c] of the plan.[d]"

20David also said to Solomon his son, "Be strong and courageous,[e] and do the work. Do not be afraid or discouraged, for the LORD God, my God, is with you. He will not fail you or forsake[f] you until all the work for the service of the temple of the LORD is finished.[g] 21The divisions of the priests and Levites are ready for all the work on the temple of God, and every willing man skilled[h] in any craft will help you in all the work. The officials and all the people will obey your every command."

Gifts for Building the Temple

29 Then King David said to the whole assembly: "My son Solomon, the one whom God has chosen, is young and inexperienced.[i] The task is great, because this palatial structure is not for man but for the LORD God. 2With all my resources I have provided for the temple of my God—gold[j] for the gold work, silver for the silver, bronze for the bronze, iron for the iron and wood for the wood, as well as onyx for the settings, turquoise,[n][k] stones of various colors, and all kinds of fine stone and marble—all of these in large quantities.[l] 3Besides, in my devotion to the temple of my God I now give my personal treasures of gold and silver for the temple of my God, over and above everything I have provided[m] for this holy temple: 4three thousand talents[o] of gold (gold of Ophir)[n] and seven thousand talents[p] of refined silver,[o] for the overlaying of the walls of the buildings, 5for the gold work and the silver work, and for all the work to be done by the craftsmen. Now, who is willing to consecrate himself today to the LORD?"

6Then the leaders of families, the officers of the tribes of Israel, the commanders of thousands and commanders of hundreds, and the officials[p] in charge of the king's work gave willingly.[q] 7They[r] gave toward the work on the temple of God five thousand talents[q] and ten thousand darics[r] of gold, ten thousand talents[s] of silver, eighteen thousand talents[t] of bronze and a hundred thousand talents[u] of iron. 8Any who had precious stones[s] gave them to the treasury of the temple of the LORD in the custody of Jehiel the Gershonite.[t] 9The people rejoiced at the willing response of their leaders, for they had given freely and wholeheartedly[u] to the LORD. David the king also rejoiced greatly.

David's Prayer

10David praised the LORD in the presence of the whole assembly, saying,

"Praise be to you, O LORD,
God of our father Israel,
from everlasting to everlasting.
11Yours, O LORD, is the greatness
and the power[v]
and the glory and the majesty
and the splendor,
for everything in heaven and
earth is yours.[w]
Yours, O LORD, is the kingdom;
you are exalted as head over
all.[x]
12Wealth and honor[y] come from
you;
you are the ruler[z] of all things.
In your hands are strength and
power
to exalt and give strength to all.
13Now, our God, we give you thanks,
and praise your glorious name.

14"But who am I, and who are my

28:18 [b]S Ex 25:20
28:19 [c]1Ki 6:38 [d]S Ex 25:9
28:20 [e]S Dt 31:6; 1Ch 22:13; 2Ch 19:11; Hag 2:4 [f]S Dt 4:31; S Jos 24:20 [g]S 1Ki 6:14; 2Ch 7:11
28:21 [h]Ex 35:25-36:5
29:1 [i]1Ki 3:7; 1Ch 22:5; 2Ch 13:7
29:2 [j]ver 7,14,16; Ezr 1:4; 6:5; Hag 2:8 [k]Isa 54:11 [l]1Ch 22:2-5
29:3 [m]2Ch 24:10; 31:3; 35:8
29:4 [n]S Ge 10:29 [o]1Ch 22:14
29:6 [p]1Ch 27:1; S 28:1 [q]ver 9; Ex 25:1-8; 35:20-29; 36:2; 2Ch 24:10; Ezr 7:15
29:7 [r]S Ex 25:2; Ne 7:70-71
29:8 [s]Ex 35:27 [t]S 1Ch 26:21
29:9 [u]1Ki 8:61
29:11 [v]Ps 24:8; 59:17; 62:11 [w]Ps 89:11 [x]Rev 5:12-13
29:12 [y]2Ch 1:12; 32:27; Ezr 7:27; Ecc 5:19 [z]2Ch 20:6

[n]2 The meaning of the Hebrew for this word is uncertain. [o]4 That is, about 110 tons (about 100 metric tons) [p]4 That is, about 260 tons (about 240 metric tons) [q]7 That is, about 190 tons (about 170 metric tons) [r]7 That is, about 185 pounds (about 84 kilograms) [s]7 That is, about 375 tons (about 345 metric tons) [t]7 That is, about 675 tons (about 610 metric tons) [u]7 That is, about 3,750 tons (about 3,450 metric tons)

29:5 CONSECRATE HIMSELF TODAY. Ch. 29 illustrates the right attitude in giving to God's kingdom work. We must have: (1) a delight and commitment to God's kingdom (vv. 3,17); (2) a willingness to consecrate ourselves as well as our possessions to God (vv. 5–6); (3) joy arising out of wholehearted giving (v. 9); (4) an acknowledgment that what we have justly gained has come from God (v. 12); (5) humility and thanksgiving for the privilege of having a part in God's eternal purposes (vv. 13–15); (6) motives for giving that come out of a sincere heart and a righteous life (v. 17); (7) prayer that God might continue to direct our hearts to a steadfast faithfulness to him and his cause on earth (v. 18; see also 2Co 9).

people, that we should be able to give
as generously as this?[a] Everything
comes from you, and we have given you
only what comes from your hand.[b]
15We are aliens and strangers[c] in
your sight, as were all our forefathers.
Our days on earth are like a shadow,[d]
without hope. 16O LORD our God, as for
all this abundance that we have provided for building you a temple for your
Holy Name, it comes from your hand,
and all of it belongs to you. 17I know,
my God, that you test the heart[e] and
are pleased with integrity. All these
things have I given willingly and with
honest intent. And now I have seen
with joy how willingly your people who
are here have given to you.[f] 18O LORD,
God of our fathers Abraham, Isaac and
Israel, keep this desire in the hearts of
your people forever, and keep their
hearts loyal to you. 19And give my son
Solomon the wholehearted devotion[g]
to keep your commands, requirements
and decrees[h] and to do everything to
build the palatial structure for which I
have provided."[i]
20Then David said to the whole assembly, "Praise the LORD your God." So
they all praised the LORD, the God of
their fathers; they bowed low and fell
prostrate before the LORD and the king.

Solomon Acknowledged as King

29:21–25pp — 1Ki 1:28–53

21The next day they made sacrifices
to the LORD and presented burnt offerings to him:[j] a thousand bulls, a thousand rams and a thousand male lambs,
together with their drink offerings, and
other sacrifices in abundance for all Israel.[k] 22They ate and drank with
great joy[l] in the presence of the LORD
that day.
Then they acknowledged Solomon
son of David as king a second time,
anointing him before the LORD to be ruler and Zadok[m] to be priest. 23So Solomon sat[n] on the throne[o] of the LORD
as king in place of his father David. He
prospered and all Israel obeyed him.
24All the officers and mighty men, as
well as all of King David's sons,[p]
pledged their submission to King Solomon.
25The LORD highly exalted[q] Solomon in the sight of all Israel and bestowed on him royal splendor[r] such
as no king over Israel ever had before.[s]

The Death of David

29:26–28pp — 1Ki 2:10–12

26David son of Jesse was king[t] over
all Israel.[u] 27He ruled over Israel forty years—seven in Hebron[v] and thirty-three in Jerusalem.[w] 28He died[x] at
a good old age, having enjoyed long
life, wealth and honor. His son Solomon succeeded him as king.[y]
29As for the events of King David's
reign, from beginning to end, they are
written in the records of Samuel the
seer,[z] the records of Nathan[a] the
prophet and the records of Gad[b] the
seer, 30together with the details of his
reign and power, and the circumstances that surrounded him and Israel and the kingdoms of all the other
lands.

29:14 [a] Ps 8:4; 144:3 [b] S ver 2
29:15 [c] S Ge 17:8; S 23:4; Ps 39:12; S Heb 11:13 [d] Job 7:6; 8:9; 14:2; 32:7; Ps 102:11; 144:4; Ecc 6:12
29:17 [e] Ps 139:23; Pr 15:11; 17:3; Jer 11:20; 17:10 [f] 1Ch 28:9; Ps 15:1-5; Pr 11:20
29:19 [g] S 1Ki 8:61; 11:4; 1Ch 28:9; Isa 38:3 [h] Ps 72:1 [i] S 1Ch 22:14
29:21 [j] S 1Ki 8:62 [k] 1Ch 11:1
29:22 [l] 1Ch 12:40 [m] S 1Sa 2:35
29:23 [n] S Dt 17:18 [o] S 1Ki 2:12; S 1Ch 17:14
29:24 [p] 1Ki 1:9
29:25 [q] S Jos 3:7 [r] 1Ki 10:7; 2Ch 1:1,12 [s] Ecc 2:9
29:26 [t] 1Ch 18:14 [u] 1Ch 11:1
29:27 [v] S Ge 23:19 [w] 2Sa 5:4-5; S 1Ch 3:4
29:28 [x] S Ge 15:15; Ac 13:36 [y] S 1Ch 23:1
29:29 [z] S 1Sa 9:9 [a] S 2Sa 7:2 [b] S 1Sa 22:5

29:20 PRAISE THE LORD YOUR GOD. To "praise the LORD" is to adore and worship him (Ps 103:1–2). When believers praise God, they begin by recalling God's goodness, righteousness and glory, and then respond in praise and adoration.

2 CHRONICLES

Outline

I. Solomon: Significant Contributions of His Reign (1:1—9:31)
   A. The Establishment of Solomon's Leadership (1:1–17)
   B. The Building of the Temple (2:1—5:1)
   C. The Dedication of the Temple (5:2—7:22)
      1. Installing the Ark (5:2–14)
      2. Solomon's Dedicatory Address (6:1–11)
      3. Solomon's Dedicatory Prayer and God's Glory (6:12—7:3)
      4. Dedicatory Sacrifices and Feasts (7:4–11)
      5. God's Promise and Warning (7:12–22)
   D. The Fame of Solomon (8:1—9:28)
      1. The Accomplishments, Possessions and Policies (8:1–18)
      2. Queen of Sheba's Praise (9:1–12)
      3. Solomon's Wealth (9:13–28)
   E. The Death of Solomon (9:29–31)

II. Judah's Kings From Rehoboam to the Exile (10:1—36:23)
   A. Schism and the Reign of Rehoboam (10:1—12:16)
   B. The Reigns of Abijah and Asa (13:1—16:14)
   C. Jehoshaphat's Reign (17:1—20:37)
   D. The Reigns of Jehoram, Ahaziah and Athaliah (21:1—23:15)
   E. Joash's Reign (23:16—24:27)
   F. The Reigns of Amaziah, Uzziah and Jotham (25:1—27:9)
   G. Ahaz's Reign (28:1–27)
   H. Hezekiah's Reign and Reforms (29:1—32:33)
   I. The Reigns of Manasseh and Amon (33:1–25)
   J. Josiah's Reign and Reforms (34:1—35:27)
   K. Josiah's Successors and the Exile (36:1–21)
   L. Cyrus's Decree (36:22–23)

Author: Ezra (?)

Theme: True Worship, Revival and Reform

Date of Writing: 450–420 B.C.

Background

Since 1 and 2 Chronicles were originally a single book in the Hebrew OT, the background to 2 Chronicles is discussed more fully in the introduction to 1 Chronicles. 2 Chronicles covers the same period of history as 1 and 2 Kings—namely, the reign of Solomon (971–931 B.C.) and the divided kingdom (930–586 B.C.). Unlike 1 and 2 Kings, which traces the history of both halves of the divided kingdom, 2 Chronicles focuses only on Judah's destiny. The Chronicler views the southern kingdom of Judah as the main stream of Israel's "redemptive history," because (1) the temple in Jerusalem remained the center for the true worship of God, (2) Judah's kings were the descendants of David, and (3) Judah was the dominant tribe among the returning Jews who rebuilt Jerusalem and the temple. 2 Chronicles was written from the priestly perspective of the latter half of the 5th century B.C. when the temple, the priesthood and the Davidic covenant were again central in importance.

Purpose

Like 1 Chronicles, 2 Chronicles was written to the returned remnant of Jews who faced the urgent need of recovering their spiritual heritage. Rather than emphasizing the dark side of Israel's past, it stresses revival, reform and the recovery of faith for the beaten-down exiles, who sought a future and a redemptive hope in the promised land.

Survey

The history of 2 Chronicles divides into two major sections. (1) Chs. 1—9 are devoted to Solomon's reign, which became Israel's golden age of peace, power, prosperity and prestige. Nevertheless, in keeping with the overall purpose of Chronicles, a full two-thirds of these nine chapters focus on the building and dedication of the temple as the center of true Israelite worship of God (chs. 2—7).

(2) Chs. 10—36 are a highly selective account of the kings of Judah after Solomon's death and the division of the kingdom. In the midst of Judah's spiritual decline and apostasy, 2 Chronicles features certain praiseworthy kings: Asa (chs. 14—15), Jehoshaphat (ch. 17; 19—20), Joash (ch. 24), Hezekiah (chs. 29—32) and Josiah (chs. 34—35), each of whom initiated and led times of spiritual revival and reform. A full 70 percent of chs. 10—36 focuses on those kings responsible for revival and reform, while only 30 percent focuses on the evil kings responsible for the corruption and collapse of the kingdom. The book ends with King Cyrus of Persia permitting the Jewish exiles to return and rebuild their temple in Jerusalem (36:22–23).

Special Features

Four major features characterize 2 Chronicles. (1) Its scope of history corresponds essentially to the time frame covered in 1 and 2 Kings. (2) Its focus on the temple in Jerusalem most likely accounts for Chronicles being placed in the nonprophetic division of the Hebrew OT, thus separating it from Samuel and Kings, which are located in the prophetic division. (3) It features five national revivals, including: (a) the most extended OT account of a spiritual revival under Hezekiah (chs. 29—32) and (b) the dramatic revival under Josiah, when "the Book of the Law" was found and was read publicly, resulting in a renewal of the covenant and the Passover celebration (chs. 34—35). (4) The book's key exhortation is to seek the Lord; the author stresses again and again the importance of seeking the Lord diligently with all one's heart (e.g., 1:6–13; 6:14; 7:14; 12:14; 15:1–2,12–15; 16:9,12; 17:4; 19:3; 20:3–4,20; 31:21; 32:20–22; 34:26–28).

New Testament Fulfillment

Though the Davidic kingdom was destroyed, the Davidic line remained and found its fulfillment in Jesus Christ (see the genealogies of Mt 1:1–17 and Lk 3:23–38). The Jerusalem temple also has prophetic significance related to Jesus, who declared: "I tell you that one greater than the temple is here" (Mt 12:6). Jesus also compared his body to the temple: "Destroy this temple, and I will raise it again in three days" (Jn 2:19). Finally, in the new Jerusalem, God and the Lamb replace the temple: "I did not see a temple in the city, because the Lord God Almighty and the Lamb are its temple" (Rev 21:22).

Reading 2 Chronicles

In order to read the entire Old Testament in one year, the book of 2 Chronicles should be read in 12 days, according to the following schedule: ☐ 1–4 ☐ 5–7 ☐ 8–11 ☐ 12–15 ☐ 16–19 ☐ 20–22 ☐ 23–25 ☐ 26–28 ☐ 29–30 ☐ 31–32 ☐ 33–34 ☐ 35–36

NOTES

Solomon Asks for Wisdom

1:2–13pp — 1Ki 3:4–15
1:14–17pp — 1Ki 10:26–29; 2Ch 9:25–28

1 Solomon son of David established[a] himself firmly over his
kingdom, for the LORD his God was
with[b] him and made him exceedingly
great.[c]
2Then Solomon spoke to all Israel[d]—to the commanders of thousands
and commanders of hundreds, to the
judges and to all the leaders in Israel,
the heads of families— 3and Solomon
and the whole assembly went to the
high place at Gibeon,[e] for God's Tent
of Meeting[f] was there, which Moses[g] the LORD's servant had made in
the desert. 4Now David had brought up
the ark[h] of God from Kiriath Jearim
to the place he had prepared for it,
because he had pitched a tent[i] for
it in Jerusalem. 5But the bronze altar[j] that Bezalel[k] son of Uri, the
son of Hur, had made was in Gibeon in front of the tabernacle of the
LORD; so Solomon and the assembly
inquired[l] of him there. 6Solomon
went up to the bronze altar before
the LORD in the Tent of Meeting and
offered a thousand burnt offerings
on it.
7That night God appeared[m] to Solomon and said to him, "Ask for whatever you want me to give you."
8Solomon answered God, "You have
shown great kindness to David my father and have made me[n] king in his
place. 9Now, LORD God, let your promise[o] to my father David be confirmed,
for you have made me king over a people who are as numerous as the dust of
the earth.[p] 10Give me wisdom and
knowledge, that I may lead[q] this people, for who is able to govern this great
people of yours?"
11God said to Solomon, "Since this is
your heart's desire and you have not
asked for wealth,[r] riches or honor,
nor for the death of your enemies, and
since you have not asked for a long life
but for wisdom and knowledge to govern my people over whom I have made
you king, 12therefore wisdom and
knowledge will be given you. And I will
also give you wealth, riches and hon-
or,[s] such as no king who was before
you ever had and none after you will
have.[t]"
13Then Solomon went to Jerusalem
from the high place at Gibeon, from before the Tent of Meeting. And he
reigned over Israel.
14Solomon accumulated chariots[u]
and horses; he had fourteen hundred
chariots and twelve thousand
horses,[a] which he kept in the chariot
cities and also with him in Jerusalem.
15The king made silver and gold[v] as
common in Jerusalem as stones, and
cedar as plentiful as sycamore-fig
trees in the foothills. 16Solomon's
horses were imported from Egypt[b]
and from Kue[c]—the royal merchants
purchased them from Kue. 17They
imported a chariot[w] from Egypt for
six hundred shekels[d] of silver, and
a horse for a hundred and fifty.[e]
They also exported them to all the
kings of the Hittites and of the Arameans.

1:1 [a] S 1Ki 2:12, 26; S 2Ch 12:1 [b] S Ge 21:22; S 39:2; S Nu 14:43 [c] S 1Ch 29:25 **1:2** [d] S 1Ch 9:1 **1:3** [e] S Jos 9:3 [f] S Lev 17:4 [g] Ex 40:18 **1:4** [h] S 1Ch 15:25 [i] 2Sa 6:17 **1:5** [j] Ex 38:2 [k] S Ex 31:2 [l] 1Ch 13:3 **1:7** [m] 2Ch 7:12 **1:8** [n] S 1Ch 23:1 **1:9** [o] S 2Sa 7:25; S 1Ki 8:25 [p] S Ge 12:2 **1:10** [q] Nu 27:17; 2Sa 5:2; Pr 8:15-16 **1:11** [r] S Dt 17:17 **1:12** [s] S 1Ch 29:12 [t] S 1Ch 29:25; 2Ch 9:22; Ne 13:26 **1:14** [u] S 1Sa 8:11; S 1Ki 9:19 **1:15** [v] S 1Ki 9:28; Isa 60:5 **1:17** [w] SS 1:9

[a] *14* Or *charioteers* [b] *16* Or possibly *Muzur,* a region in Cilicia; also in verse 17
[c] *16* Probably Cilicia [d] *17* That is, about 15 pounds (about 7 kilograms) [e] *17* That is, about 3 3/4 pounds (about 1.7 kilograms)

1:7 WHATEVER YOU WANT ME TO GIVE YOU. God, who gives good gifts to his children (cf. Mt 7:7–11), offered to give Solomon whatever he asked for. We too may ask for good things from the Lord, for he desires to give us the necessary provisions for life (Mt 6:25–34), the presence of the Holy Spirit (Lk 11:9–13), and grace, mercy and full salvation to help us in all matters of life (Heb 4:16; 7:25).

1:10 GIVE ME WISDOM. Wisdom, i.e., a wise and discerning heart that sees and evaluates everything from the point of view of God and his Word, is one of the greatest treasures in life (Pr 3:15). God desires to give every believer this wisdom. It comes to us through prayer (v. 7; Jas 1:5), the Holy Spirit's enlightenment (Ro 8:5–15; Gal 5:16–25; Eph 5:17–18) and a diligent search of Scripture to learn God's ways (Ps 25:4; 119:2–3; Ac 17:11).

1:12 WISDOM AND KNOWLEDGE WILL BE GIVEN YOU. Solomon was granted wisdom and knowledge, yet this did not guarantee that he would persevere in faithfulness to God. For this reason God told him to be careful to walk in his ways and to obey his commands (see 1Ki 3:14). Possessing wisdom or an exceptional knowledge of God's Word does not guarantee that a person will live for God according to that wisdom and follow his ways. Later in life Solomon departed from God and failed to do what he knew was right; he was consequently rejected by God (see 1Ki 3:9–10; 4:29–34; 11:1; and notes).

Preparations for Building the Temple

2:1–18pp — 1Ki 5:1–16

2 Solomon gave orders to build a
temple[x] for the Name of the LORD
and a royal palace for himself.[y] **2**He
conscripted seventy thousand men as
carriers and eighty thousand as stonecutters in the hills and thirty-six hundred as foremen over them.[z]
3Solomon sent this message to Hiram[f][a] king of Tyre:

"Send me cedar logs[b] as you
did for my father David when you
sent him cedar to build a palace to
live in. **4**Now I am about to build
a temple[c] for the Name of the
LORD my God and to dedicate it to
him for burning fragrant incense[d] before him, for setting out
the consecrated bread[e] regularly, and for making burnt offerings[f] every morning and evening
and on Sabbaths[g] and New
Moons[h] and at the appointed
feasts of the LORD our God. This is
a lasting ordinance for Israel.
5"The temple I am going to
build will be great,[i] because our
God is greater than all other
gods.[j] **6**But who is able to build
a temple for him, since the heavens, even the highest heavens,
cannot contain him?[k] Who then
am I[l] to build a temple for him,
except as a place to burn sacrifices before him?
7"Send me, therefore, a man
skilled to work in gold and silver,
bronze and iron, and in purple,
crimson and blue yarn, and experienced in the art of engraving, to
work in Judah and Jerusalem with
my skilled craftsmen,[m] whom my
father David provided.
8"Send me also cedar, pine and
algum[g] logs from Lebanon, for I
know that your men are skilled in
cutting timber there. My men will
work with yours **9**to provide me
with plenty of lumber, because
the temple I build must be large
and magnificent. **10**I will give your
servants, the woodsmen who cut
the timber, twenty thousand
cors[h] of ground wheat, twenty
thousand cors of barley, twenty
thousand baths[i] of wine and
twenty thousand baths of olive
oil.[n]"

11Hiram king of Tyre replied by letter to Solomon:

"Because the LORD loves[o] his
people, he has made you their
king."

12And Hiram added:

"Praise be to the LORD, the God
of Israel, who made heaven and
earth![p] He has given King David
a wise son, endowed with intelligence and discernment, who will
build a temple for the LORD and a
palace for himself.
13"I am sending you Huram-
Abi,[q] a man of great skill,
14whose mother was from Dan[r]
and whose father was from Tyre.
He is trained[s] to work in gold
and silver, bronze and iron, stone
and wood, and with purple and
blue[t] and crimson yarn and fine
linen. He is experienced in all
kinds of engraving and can execute any design given to him. He
will work with your craftsmen and
with those of my lord, David your
father.
15"Now let my lord send his servants the wheat and barley and
the olive oil[u] and wine he promised, **16**and we will cut all the logs
from Lebanon that you need and
will float them in rafts by sea
down to Joppa.[v] You can then
take them up to Jerusalem."

17Solomon took a census of all the
aliens[w] who were in Israel, after the
census[x] his father David had taken;
and they were found to be 153,600.
18He assigned[y] 70,000 of them to be
carriers and 80,000 to be stonecutters

2:1 [x] S Dt 12:5 [y] Ecc 2:4 **2:2** [z] 2Ch 10:4 **2:3** [a] S 2Sa 5:11 [b] S 1Ch 14:1 **2:4** [c] S Dt 12:5 [d] S Ex 30:7 [e] Ex 25:30 [f] Ex 29:42; 2Ch 13:11; 29:28 [g] S Lev 23:38 [h] S Nu 28:14 **2:5** [i] 1Ch 22:5 [j] S Ex 12:12; S 1Ch 16:25 **2:6** [k] S 1Ki 8:27; Jer 23:24 [l] S Ex 3:11 **2:7** [m] S Ex 35:31; 1Ch 22:16 **2:10** [n] Ezr 3:7 **2:11** [o] 1Ki 10:9; 2Ch 9:8 **2:12** [p] Ne 9:6; Ps 8:3; 33:6; 96:5; 102:25; 146:6 **2:13** [q] S 1Ki 7:13 **2:14** [r] S Ex 31:6 [s] S Ex 35:31 [t] Ex 35:35 **2:15** [u] Ezr 3:7 **2:16** [v] S Jos 19:46; Jnh 1:3 **2:17** [w] 1Ch 22:2 [x] S 2Sa 24:2 **2:18** [y] 1Ch 22:2; 2Ch 8:8

[f] *3* Hebrew *Huram,* a variant of *Hiram;* also in verses 11 and 12 [g] *8* Probably a variant of *almug;* possibly juniper [h] *10* That is, probably about 125,000 bushels (about 4,400 kiloliters) [i] *10* That is, probably about 115,000 gallons (about 440 kiloliters)

2:1 TEMPLE FOR THE NAME OF THE LORD. Solomon inherited from his father David the desire "to build a temple for the Name of the LORD." Solomon was the one to carry out his father's intentions. The foremost inheritance that any father can bequeath his son is the holy desire to see God's house and kingdom established in purity, truth and righteousness.

in the hills, with 3,600 foremen over
them to keep the people working.

Solomon Builds the Temple

3:1–14pp — 1Ki 6:1–29

3 Then Solomon began to build[z] the
temple of the LORD[a] in Jerusalem
on Mount Moriah, where the LORD had
appeared to his father David. It was on
the threshing floor of Araunah[j][b] the
Jebusite, the place provided by David.
2He began building on the second day
of the second month in the fourth year
of his reign.[c]

3The foundation Solomon laid for
building the temple of God was sixty
cubits long and twenty cubits wide[k][d]
(using the cubit of the old standard).
4The portico at the front of the temple
was twenty cubits[l] long across the
width of the building and twenty cubits[m] high.

He overlaid the inside with pure
gold. **5**He paneled the main hall with
pine and covered it with fine gold and
decorated it with palm tree[e] and chain
designs. **6**He adorned the temple with
precious stones. And the gold he used
was gold of Parvaim. **7**He overlaid the
ceiling beams, doorframes, walls and
doors of the temple with gold, and he
carved cherubim[f] on the walls.

8He built the Most Holy Place,[g] its
length corresponding to the width of
the temple—twenty cubits long and
twenty cubits wide. He overlaid the inside with six hundred talents[n] of fine
gold. **9**The gold nails[h] weighed fifty
shekels.[o] He also overlaid the upper
parts with gold.

10In the Most Holy Place he made a
pair[i] of sculptured cherubim and
overlaid them with gold. **11**The total
wingspan of the cherubim was twenty
cubits. One wing of the first cherub
was five cubits[p] long and touched the
temple wall, while its other wing, also
five cubits long, touched the wing of
the other cherub. **12**Similarly one wing
of the second cherub was five cubits
long and touched the other temple
wall, and its other wing, also five cubits long, touched the wing of the first
cherub. **13**The wings of these cherubim[j] extended twenty cubits. They
stood on their feet, facing the main
hall.[q]

14He made the curtain[k] of blue,
purple and crimson yarn and fine linen,
with cherubim[l] worked into it.

15In the front of the temple he made
two pillars,[m] which ⌊together⌋ were
thirty-five cubits[r] long, each with a
capital[n] on top measuring five cubits.
16He made interwoven chains[s][o] and
put them on top of the pillars. He also
made a hundred pomegranates[p] and
attached them to the chains. **17**He

3:1 [z] Ac 7:47 [a] S Ge 28:17 [b] S 2Sa 24:18
3:2 [c] Ezr 5:11
3:3 [d] Eze 41:2
3:5 [e] Eze 40:16
3:7 [f] Ge 3:24; Eze 41:18
3:8 [g] S Ex 26:33
3:9 [h] Ex 26:32
3:10 [i] Ex 25:18
3:13 [j] S Ex 25:18
3:14 [k] S Ex 26:31, 33 [l] Ge 3:24
3:15 [m] S 1Ki 7:15; Rev 3:12 [n] 1Ki 7:22
3:16 [o] 1Ki 7:17 [p] S 1Ki 7:20

[j] *1* Hebrew *Ornan,* a variant of *Araunah*
[k] *3* That is, about 90 feet (about 27 meters) long and 30 feet (about 9 meters) wide
[l] *4* That is, about 30 feet (about 9 meters); also in verses 8, 11 and 13
[m] *4* Some Septuagint and Syriac manuscripts; Hebrew *and a hundred and twenty*
[n] *8* That is, about 23 tons (about 21 metric tons)
[o] *9* That is, about 1 1/4 pounds (about 0.6 kilogram)
[p] *11* That is, about 7 1/2 feet (about 2.3 meters); also in verse 15
[q] *13* Or *facing inward*
[r] *15* That is, about 52 feet (about 16 meters)
[s] *16* Or possibly *made chains in the inner sanctuary*; the meaning of the Hebrew for this phrase is uncertain.

3:1 SOLOMON BEGAN TO BUILD. A comparison of Solomon's temple and the temple of Christ (i.e., the church) reveals the following: (1) Solomon's temple was built by David's son (2:1); the church by David's descendant, the Lord Jesus Christ (Heb 3:3–6).

(2) Solomon's temple was built from gold, silver and precious stone (1Ch 29:3–8); the church is built with the redeemed lives of those purchased at the cost of Christ's precious blood (1Pe 1:18–19; 2:5).

(3) Solomon's temple stood on Mount Moriah (3:1); the church stands on the rock of Jesus' divine person and sacrificial death (Mt 16:18; Eph 2:20).

(4) Solomon's temple had earthly mediating priests (1Ch 24); the church has a heavenly high priest to whom all believers may draw near for eternal salvation (Heb 2:17; 7:25).

(5) Solomon's temple was made beautiful by gold and decorations (1Ch 22:5); the church becomes beautiful by the purity and power of the Holy Spirit within the believer's life (Ac 1:8; 2:4; Gal 5:22; cf. 1Pe 3:3–4).

(6) Solomon's temple provided a place for God's special dwelling among his people; the church is the special dwelling of the Holy Spirit on earth (1Co 3:16; 6:19).

(7) Solomon's temple was earthly and temporal (2Ki 25:8–9); the temple of Christ is heavenly and everlasting (Rev 21—22).

(8) The church, therefore, is the heir and successor of the tabernacle/temple as God's visible dwelling place on earth (see article on THE TEMPLE, p. 608).

3:1 THRESHING FLOOR OF ARAUNAH. For more details about this site for the temple and the circumstances under which it was obtained, see 1Ch 21:16–30.

erected the pillars in the front of the
temple, one to the south and one to the
north. The one to the south he named
Jakin[t] and the one to the north
Boaz.[u]

The Temple's Furnishings

4:2–6,10–5:1pp — 1Ki 7:23–26,38–51

4 He made a bronze altar[q] twenty
cubits long, twenty cubits wide
and ten cubits high.[v] 2He made the
Sea[r] of cast metal, circular in shape,
measuring ten cubits from rim to rim
and five cubits[w] high. It took a line of
thirty cubits[x] to measure around it.
3Below the rim, figures of bulls encircled it—ten to a cubit.[y] The bulls
were cast in two rows in one piece with
the Sea.
4The Sea stood on twelve bulls,
three facing north, three facing west,
three facing south and three facing
east.[s] The Sea rested on top of them,
and their hindquarters were toward
the center. 5It was a handbreadth[z] in
thickness, and its rim was like the rim
of a cup, like a lily blossom. It held
three thousand baths.[a]
6He then made ten basins[t] for
washing and placed five on the south
side and five on the north. In them the
things to be used for the burnt offerings[u] were rinsed, but the Sea was to
be used by the priests for washing.
7He made ten gold lampstands[v] according to the specifications[w] for
them and placed them in the temple,
five on the south side and five on the
north.
8He made ten tables[x] and placed
them in the temple, five on the south
side and five on the north. He also
made a hundred gold sprinkling
bowls.[y]
9He made the courtyard[z] of the
priests, and the large court and the
doors for the court, and overlaid
the doors with bronze. 10He placed the
Sea on the south side, at the southeast
corner.
11He also made the pots and shovels
and sprinkling bowls.

So Huram finished[a] the work he
had undertaken for King Solomon in
the temple of God:

12the two pillars;
the two bowl-shaped capitals on
top of the pillars;
the two sets of network decorating the two bowl-shaped capitals on top of the pillars;
13the four hundred pomegranates
for the two sets of network
(two rows of pomegranates for
each network, decorating the
bowl-shaped capitals on top of
the pillars);
14the stands[b] with their basins;
15the Sea and the twelve bulls under it;
16the pots, shovels, meat forks and
all related articles.

All the objects that Huram-Abi[c]
made for King Solomon for the temple
of the LORD were of polished bronze.
17The king had them cast in clay molds
in the plain of the Jordan between Succoth[d] and Zarethan.[b] 18All these
things that Solomon made amounted
to so much that the weight of the
bronze[e] was not determined.
19Solomon also made all the furnishings that were in God's temple:

the golden altar;
the tables[f] on which was the
bread of the Presence;
20the lampstands[g] of pure gold
with their lamps, to burn in
front of the inner sanctuary as
prescribed;
21the gold floral work and lamps
and tongs (they were solid
gold);
22the pure gold wick trimmers,
sprinkling bowls, dishes[h] and
censers;[i] and the gold doors
of the temple: the inner doors
to the Most Holy Place and the
doors of the main hall.

5 When all the work Solomon had
done for the temple of the LORD

4:1 [q] S Ex 20:24; S 40:6; S 1Ki 8:64 **4:2** [r] Rev 4:6; 15:2 **4:4** [s] Nu 2:3-25; Eze 48:30-34; Rev 21:13 **4:6** [t] S Ex 30:18 [u] Ne 13:5,9; Eze 40:38 **4:7** [v] S Ex 25:31 [w] Ex 25:40 **4:8** [x] S Ex 25:23 [y] S Nu 4:14 **4:9** [z] 1Ki 6:36; 2Ch 33:5 **4:11** [a] 1Ki 7:14 **4:14** [b] 1Ki 7:27-30 **4:16** [c] S 1Ki 7:13 **4:17** [d] S Ge 33:17 **4:18** [e] S 1Ki 7:23 **4:19** [f] S Ex 25:23, 30 **4:20** [g] Ex 25:31 **4:22** [h] S Nu 7:14 [i] S Lev 10:1

[t] *17 Jakin* probably means *he establishes.*
[u] *17 Boaz* probably means *in him is strength.*
[v] *1* That is, about 30 feet (about 9 meters) long and wide, and about 15 feet (about 4.5 meters) high [w] *2* That is, about 7 1/2 feet (about 2.3 meters) [x] *2* That is, about 45 feet (about 13.5 meters) [y] *3* That is, about 1 1/2 feet (about 0.5 meter) [z] *5* That is, about 3 inches (about 8 centimeters)
[a] *5* That is, about 17,500 gallons (about 66 kiloliters) [b] *17* Hebrew *Zeredatha,* a variant of *Zarethan*

5:1 THE TEMPLE. The OT dedicates much attention to the temple because of its crucial importance in maintaining Israel's true faith and their communion with God. See Ex 25:9, note on the

was finished,[j] he brought in the
things his father David had dedicated[k]—the silver and gold and all the
furnishings—and he placed them in
the treasuries of God's temple.

The Ark Brought to the Temple

5:2–6:11pp — 1Ki 8:1–21

2 Then Solomon summoned to Jerusalem the elders of Israel, all the heads
of the tribes and the chiefs of the Israelite families, to bring up the ark[l] of
the LORD's covenant from Zion, the City
of David. 3 And all the men of Israel[m]
came together to the king at the time
of the festival in the seventh month.
4 When all the elders of Israel had
arrived, the Levites took up the ark,
5 and they brought up the ark and the
Tent of Meeting and all the sacred furnishings in it. The priests, who were
Levites,[n] carried them up; 6 and King
Solomon and the entire assembly of Israel that had gathered about him were
before the ark, sacrificing so many
sheep and cattle that they could not be
recorded or counted.
7 The priests then brought the ark[o]
of the LORD's covenant to its place in
the inner sanctuary of the temple, the
Most Holy Place, and put it beneath
the wings of the cherubim. 8 The cherubim[p] spread their wings over the
place of the ark and covered the ark
and its carrying poles. 9 These poles
were so long that their ends, extending
from the ark, could be seen from in
front of the inner sanctuary, but not
from outside the Holy Place; and they
are still there today. 10 There was nothing in the ark except[q] the two tablets[r] that Moses had placed in it at
Horeb, where the LORD made a covenant with the Israelites after they
came out of Egypt.
11 The priests then withdrew from
the Holy Place. All the priests who
were there had consecrated themselves, regardless of their divisions.[s]
12 All the Levites who were musicians[t]—Asaph, Heman, Jeduthun
and their sons and relatives—stood on
the east side of the altar, dressed in
fine linen and playing cymbals, harps
and lyres. They were accompanied by
120 priests sounding trumpets.[u]
13 The trumpeters and singers joined in
unison, as with one voice, to give
praise and thanks to the LORD. Accompanied by trumpets, cymbals and other
instruments, they raised their voices in
praise to the LORD and sang:

"He is good;
his love endures forever."[v]

Then the temple of the LORD was
filled with a cloud,[w] 14 and the priests
could not perform[x] their service because of the cloud,[y] for the glory[z] of
the LORD filled the temple of God.

6 Then Solomon said, "The LORD has
said that he would dwell in a dark
cloud;[a] 2 I have built a magnificent
temple for you, a place for you to dwell
forever.[b]"
3 While the whole assembly of Israel
was standing there, the king turned
around and blessed them. 4 Then he
said:

"Praise be to the LORD, the God
of Israel, who with his hands has
fulfilled what he promised with
his mouth to my father David. For
he said, 5 'Since the day I brought
my people out of Egypt, I have not
chosen a city in any tribe of Israel
to have a temple built for my
Name to be there, nor have I chosen anyone to be the leader over
my people Israel. 6 But now I have
chosen Jerusalem[c] for my
Name[d] to be there, and I have
chosen David[e] to rule my people
Israel.'
7 "My father David had it in his
heart[f] to build a temple for the
Name of the LORD, the God of Israel. 8 But the LORD said to my father
David, 'Because it was in your
heart to build a temple for my
Name, you did well to have this in
your heart. 9 Nevertheless, you
are not the one to build the temple, but your son, who is your own
flesh and blood—he is the one
who will build the temple for my
Name.'
10 "The LORD has kept the prom-

5:1 [j] S 1Ki 6:14 [k] S 2Sa 8:11
5:2 [l] S Nu 3:31; S 1Ch 15:25
5:3 [m] S 1Ch 9:1
5:5 [n] S Nu 3:31; S 1Ch 15:2
5:7 [o] Rev 11:19
5:8 [p] S Ge 3:24
5:10 [q] Heb 9:4 [r] S Ex 16:34; S Dt 10:2
5:11 [s] S 1Ch 24:1
5:12 [t] 1Ki 10:12; 1Ch 9:33; S 25:1; Ps 68:25 [u] S 1Ch 13:8
5:13 [v] S 1Ch 16:34,41; 2Ch 7:3; 20:21; Ezr 3:11; Ps 100:5; 106:1; 107:1; 118:1; 136:1; Jer 33:11 [w] S Ex 40:34
5:14 [x] Ex 40:35; Rev 15:8 [y] Ex 19:16 [z] S Ex 29:43; S 40:35
6:1 [a] S Ex 19:9
6:2 [b] Ezr 6:12; 7:15; Ps 135:21
6:6 [c] S Dt 12:5; S Isa 14:1 [d] S Ex 20:24 [e] S 1Ch 28:4
6:7 [f] S 1Sa 10:7; S 1Ch 17:2; Ac 7:46

significance of the tabernacle and its typological interpretations for the new covenant; also see article on THE TEMPLE, p. 608.

5:14 THE GLORY OF THE LORD. See Ex 40:34, note; 1Ki 8:11, note; see article on THE GLORY OF GOD, p. 1192.

6:10 THE TEMPLE FOR THE NAME OF THE LORD. The Bible often refers to temples in relation to salvation history; the dwelling places of God mentioned are: the tabernacle, Solomon's

THE TEMPLE

***2Ch 5:1** "When all the work Solomon had done for the temple of the Lord was finished, he brought in the things his father David had dedicated—the silver and gold and all the furnishings—and he placed them in the treasuries of God's temple."*

HISTORY OF THE TEMPLE. (1) The forerunner to the temple was the tabernacle, the tent that God instructed the Israelites to build while they were stationed in the desert at Mount Sinai (Ex 25—27; 30; 36—38; 39:32—40:33). After entering the promised land of Canaan, they retained this mobile sanctuary until the time of King Solomon. During the early years of his reign, he commissioned thousands of people to take part in the construction of the temple of the Lord (see 1Ki 5:13–18). In the fourth year of his reign the foundations were laid; seven years later the temple was completed (1Ki 6:37–38). The worship of the Lord, especially the sacrifices offered to him, now had an established place in the city of Jerusalem (see article on THE CITY OF JERUSALEM, p. 576).

(2) During the time of the monarchy, the temple underwent several cycles of defilement and restoration. It was ransacked by Shishak of Egypt during the reign of King Rehoboam (2Ch 12:9), and was refurbished by King Asa (2Ch 15:8,18). After another period of idolatry and spiritual decline, King Joash repaired the house of the Lord (2Ch 24:4–14). Later King Ahaz took some of the temple furnishings, sent them to the king of Assyria as a means of political appeasement, and shut the doors of the temple (2Ch 28:21,24). His son Hezekiah once again opened, repaired and cleansed the temple (2Ch 29:1–19), only to have it defiled again by his son Manasseh (2Ch 33:1–7). Manasseh's grandson Josiah was the last king of Judah to repair the temple (2Ch 34:1,8–13). Idolatry continued among his successors, and God finally allowed King Nebuchadnezzar of Babylon in 586 B.C. to completely destroy the temple (2Ki 25:13–17; 2Ch 36:18–19).

(3) Fifty years later, King Cyrus allowed the Jews to return from Babylon to Palestine and to rebuild the temple (Ezr 1:1–4). Zerubbabel led the reconstruction effort (Ezr 3:8), though not without opposition from the other people living in that land (Ezr 4:1–4). After a delay of a decade or so, the people were permitted to resume the project (Ezr 4:24—5:2), and it was completed and dedicated in 516 B.C. (Ezr 6:14–18). At the outset of the NT era, King Herod spent much time and money repairing and beautifying the second temple (Jn 2:20); this was the temple Jesus cleared on two occasions (see Mt 21:12–13; Jn 2:13–21). In A.D. 70, however, after frequent rebellion by the Jews against the Roman authorities, the temple, along with the entire city of Jerusalem, was once again destroyed and made uninhabitable.

THE MEANING OF THE TEMPLE FOR THE ISRAELITES. In many ways the temple had the same significance among the Israelites as did the city of Jerusalem (see article on THE CITY OF JERUSALEM, p. 576). (1) It symbolized the presence and protection of the Lord God among his people (cf. Ex 25:8; 29:43–46). When the temple was dedicated, God came down from heaven, filled it with his glory (2Ch 7:1–2; cf. Ex 40:34–38) and promised to put his Name there (2Ch 6:20,33). Thus when God's people wanted to pray to the Lord, they could do so facing the temple (2Ch 6:24,26,29,32), and God would hear them "from his temple" (Ps 18:6).

(2) The temple also represented God's redemption of his people. There were two important functions that took place there: the daily sacrifices for sin on the bronze altar and the Day of Atonement, when the high priest went into the Most Holy Place to sprinkle blood on the atonement cover of the ark to atone for the sins of the people (cf. Lev 16; 1Ki 8:6–9). Through these temple rituals, the Israelites were reminded of the costly nature of their redemption and reconciliation.

(3) At no time in the history of God's people did God have more than one physical dwelling place or temple; this demonstrated the fact that there is only one God—the Lord, the covenant God of the Israelites.

(4) However, the temple gave no absolute guarantees of God's presence; it symbolized God's presence only insofar as the people rejected all other gods and obeyed God's holy law. Micah, for example, criticized the leaders of God's people, who were violent and materialistic and at the same time convinced that no disaster would come on them as long as they had the symbol of the Lord's presence among them (Mic 3:9–11); he prophesied that God would teach them a lesson by destroying Jerusalem and its temple. Later Jeremiah took the idolatrous people of Judah to task for taking comfort in their constant repetition of the words, "The temple of the LORD, the temple of the LORD, the temple of the LORD!" (Jer 7:2–4,8–12). Because of their godless lifestyle, God would destroy the symbol of his presence—the temple (Jer 7:14–15); God even told Jeremiah that it was useless for him to pray for Judah, for he would not listen (Jer 7:16). Their only hope was to amend their ways (Jer 7:5–7).

THE MEANING OF THE TEMPLE FOR THE CHRISTIAN CHURCH. The role of the temple in the NT must be understood against the background of what the temple symbolized in the OT. (1) Jesus himself, like the OT prophets, criticized the misuse of the temple. His first (Jn 2:13–17) and last great public acts (Mt 21:12–13) were to clear the temple of those who were destroying its true spiritual purpose (see Lk 19:45, note). He went on to predict the day when the temple would be completely destroyed (Mt 24:1–2; Mk 13:1–2; Lk 21:5–6).

(2) The early church in Jerusalem frequently entered the temple at the time of prayer (Ac 2:46; 3:1; 5:21,42). They did this out of custom, however, knowing full well that it was not the only place where believers could pray (see Ac 4:23–31). Stephen, and later Paul, witnessed that the living God could not be confined to a temple made by human hands (Ac 7:48–50; 17:24).

(3) The focus of worship for Christians shifted from the temple to Jesus Christ himself. He, not the temple, now represents God's presence among his people. He is the Word of God made flesh (Jn 1:14), and in him all the fullness of God lives (Col 2:9). In fact, Jesus goes so far as to call himself the temple (Jn 2:19–22); by his sacrifice on the cross he fulfilled all of the sacrifices that took place in the temple (cf. Heb 9:1—10:18). Note also that in his conversation with the Samaritan woman, Jesus stated that worship would soon take place not in a specific building but "in spirit and truth," i.e., wherever people genuinely believed the truth of God's Word and received God's Spirit through Christ (see Jn 4:23, note).

(4) Since Jesus Christ embodied the meaning of the temple, and since the church is his body (Ro 12:5; 1Co 12:12–27; Eph 1:22–23; Col 1:18), the church was designated as "God's temple," being indwelt by Christ and his Spirit (1Co 3:16; 2Co 6:16; cf. Eph 2:21–22). Through his Spirit, Christ lives in his church and requires his body to be holy. Just as in the OT where God would not tolerate any defilement of his temple, so he promises to destroy anyone who destroys his church (1Co 3:16-17; see 3:17, note, for examples of ways in which people corrupt and destroy the church).

(5) Not only is the Holy Spirit living in the church, but also in the individual believer as his temple (1Co 6:19). For that reason Paul warns strongly against any defilement of the human body by immorality or impurity (see 1Co 6:18–19, notes).

(6) Finally, note that there is no need for a temple in the new Jerusalem (Rev 21:22). The reason for this is clear: because the temple was only a symbol of God's presence among his people and not the full reality, no temple is necessary when God and the Lamb are living among them: "the Lord God Almighty and the Lamb are its temple" (Rev 21:22).

ise he made. I have succeeded David my father and now I sit on the
throne of Israel, just as the LORD
promised, and I have built the
temple for the Name of the LORD,
the God of Israel. **11**There I have
placed the ark, in which is the
covenant[g] of the LORD that he
made with the people of Israel."

Solomon's Prayer of Dedication

6:12–40pp — 1Ki 8:22–53
6:41–42pp — Ps 132:8–10

12Then Solomon stood before the altar of the LORD in front of the whole
assembly of Israel and spread out his
hands. **13**Now he had made a bronze
platform,[h] five cubits[c] long, five cubits wide and three cubits[d] high, and
had placed it in the center of the outer
court. He stood on the platform and
then knelt down[i] before the whole assembly of Israel and spread out his
hands toward heaven. **14**He said:

"O LORD, God of Israel, there is
no God like you[j] in heaven or on
earth—you who keep your covenant of love[k] with your servants
who continue wholeheartedly in
your way. **15**You have kept your
promise to your servant David my
father; with your mouth you have
promised[l] and with your hand
you have fulfilled it—as it is today.

16"Now LORD, God of Israel,
keep for your servant David my father the promises you made to
him when you said, 'You shall
never fail[m] to have a man to sit
before me on the throne of Israel,
if only your sons are careful in all
they do to walk before me according to my law,[n] as you have
done.' **17**And now, O LORD, God of
Israel, let your word that you
promised your servant David
come true.

18"But will God really dwell[o]
on earth with men? The heavens,[p] even the highest heavens,
cannot contain you. How much
less this temple I have built! **19**Yet
give attention to your servant's
prayer and his plea for mercy,
O LORD my God. Hear the cry and
the prayer that your servant is
praying in your presence. **20**May
your eyes[q] be open toward this
temple day and night, this place of
which you said you would put
your Name[r] there. May you
hear[s] the prayer your servant
prays toward this place. **21**Hear
the supplications of your servant
and of your people Israel when
they pray toward this place. Hear
from heaven, your dwelling place;
and when you hear, forgive.[t]

22"When a man wrongs his
neighbor and is required to take
an oath[u] and he comes and
swears the oath before your altar
in this temple, **23**then hear from
heaven and act. Judge between
your servants, repaying[v] the
guilty by bringing down on his
own head what he has done. Declare the innocent not guilty and
so establish his innocence.

24"When your people Israel
have been defeated[w] by an enemy
because they have sinned against
you and when they turn back and
confess your name, praying and
making supplication before you in
this temple, **25**then hear from
heaven and forgive the sin of your
people Israel and bring them back
to the land you gave to them and
their fathers.

26"When the heavens are shut
up and there is no rain[x] because
your people have sinned against
you, and when they pray toward
this place and confess your name
and turn from their sin because
you have afflicted them, **27**then
hear from heaven and forgive[y]
the sin of your servants, your people Israel. Teach them the right
way to live, and send rain on the
land you gave your people for an
inheritance.

28"When famine[z] or plague

6:11 [g] S Dt 10:2; Ps 25:10; 50:5
6:13 [h] Ne 8:4 [i] Ps 95:6
6:14 [j] S Ex 8:10; 15:11 [k] S Dt 7:9
6:15 [l] S 1Ch 22:10
6:16 [m] S 2Sa 7:13,15; 2Ch 23:3 [n] Ps 132:12
6:18 [o] S Rev 21:3 [p] Ps 11:4; Isa 40:22; 66:1
6:20 [q] S Ex 3:16; Ps 34:15 [r] Dt 12:11 [s] 2Ch 7:14; 30:20
6:21 [t] Ps 51:1; Isa 33:24; 40:2; 43:25; 44:22; 55:7; Mic 7:18
6:22 [u] S Ex 22:11
6:23 [v] Isa 3:11; 65:6; S Mt 16:27
6:24 [w] S Lev 26:17
6:26 [x] Lev 26:19; S Dt 11:17; 28:24; S 2Sa 1:21
6:27 [y] ver 30,39; 2Ch 7:14
6:28 [z] 2Ch 20:9

[c] *13* That is, about 7 1/2 feet (about 2.3 meters) [d] *13* That is, about 4 1/2 feet (about 1.3 meters)

temple, Ezekiel's temple, Zerubbabel's temple, Herod's temple, Christ's body, the church, the individual believer's physical body, and the new Jerusalem (Rev 21:22). For more detail, see article on THE TEMPLE, p. 608.

6:11 THE ARK. See 1Ki 8:1, note.

6:18 HEAVENS . . . CANNOT CONTAIN YOU. See 1Ki 8:13, note.

6:21 FORGIVE. See 1Ki 8:39, note.

comes to the land, or blight or mildew, locusts or grasshoppers, or
when enemies besiege them in
any of their cities, whatever disaster or disease may come, **29**and
when a prayer or plea is made by
any of your people Israel—each
one aware of his afflictions and
pains, and spreading out his
hands toward this temple—
30then hear from heaven, your
dwelling place. Forgive,[a] and
deal with each man according to
all he does, since you know his
heart (for you alone know the
hearts of men),[b] **31**so that they
will fear you[c] and walk in your
ways all the time they live in the
land you gave our fathers.
32"As for the foreigner who
does not belong to your people Israel but has come[d] from a distant
land because of your great name
and your mighty hand[e] and your
outstretched arm—when he
comes and prays toward this temple, **33**then hear from heaven,
your dwelling place, and do whatever the foreigner[f] asks of you,
so that all the peoples of the earth
may know your name and fear
you, as do your own people Israel,
and may know that this house I
have built bears your Name.
34"When your people go to war
against their enemies,[g] wherever
you send them, and when they
pray[h] to you toward this city you
have chosen and the temple I
have built for your Name, **35**then
hear from heaven their prayer
and their plea, and uphold their
cause.
36"When they sin against
you—for there is no one who does
not sin[i]—and you become angry
with them and give them over to
the enemy, who takes them captive[j] to a land far away or near;
37and if they have a change of
heart[k] in the land where they are
held captive, and repent and plead
with you in the land of their captivity and say, 'We have sinned,
we have done wrong and acted
wickedly'; **38**and if they turn back

6:30 [a]S ver 27 [b]S 1Sa 2:3; Ps 7:9; 44:21; Pr 16:2; 17:3 **6:31** [c]S Dt 6:13; Ps 34:7,9; 103:11, 13; Pr 8:13 **6:32** [d]2Ch 9:6 [e]S Ex 3:19,20 **6:33** [f]S Ex 12:43 **6:34** [g]Dt 28:7 [h]S 1Ch 5:20 **6:36** [i]S 1Ki 8:46; Job 11:12; 15:14; Ps 143:2; Ecc 7:20; Jer 9:5; 13:23; 17:9; S Ro 3:9; Eph 2:3 [j]S Lev 26:44 **6:37** [k]1Ki 8:48; 2Ch 7:14; 12:6,12; 30:11; 33:12,19, 23; 34:27; 36:12; Isa 58:3; Jer 24:7; 29:13

6:39 [l]S ver 27; 2Ch 30:9 **6:40** [m]S 1Ki 8:29, 52; 2Ch 7:15; Ne 1:6,11; Ps 17:1,6; 116:1; 130:2; Isa 37:17 **6:41** [n]Ps 3:7; 7:6; 59:4; Isa 33:10 [o]1Ch 28:2 [p]Ps 132:16 [q]Ps 13:6; 27:13; 116:12; 142:7 **6:42** [r]Ps 2:2 [s]Ps 89:24,28 **7:1** [t]S Ex 19:18; S Lev 9:24; S 1Ki 18:38 [u]S Ex 16:10 [v]Ps 26:8 **7:2** [w]S 1Ki 8:11 [x]S Ex 29:43; S 40:35 **7:3** [y]S 1Ch 16:34; 2Ch 5:13; Ezr 3:11

to you with all their heart and soul
in the land of their captivity where
they were taken, and pray toward
the land you gave their fathers, toward the city you have chosen and
toward the temple I have built for
your Name; **39**then from heaven,
your dwelling place, hear their
prayer and their pleas, and uphold
their cause. And forgive[l] your
people, who have sinned against
you.
40"Now, my God, may your eyes
be open and your ears attentive[m]
to the prayers offered in this
place.

41"Now arise,[n] O LORD God,
and come to your
resting place,[o]
you and the ark of your
might.
May your priests,[p] O LORD
God, be clothed with
salvation,
may your saints rejoice in
your goodness.[q]
42O LORD God, do not reject
your anointed one.[r]
Remember the great love[s]
promised to David your
servant."

The Dedication of the Temple

7:1–10pp — 1Ki 8:62–66

7 When Solomon finished praying,
fire[t] came down from heaven and
consumed the burnt offering and the
sacrifices, and the glory of the LORD
filled[u] the temple.[v] **2**The priests
could not enter[w] the temple of the
LORD because the glory[x] of the LORD
filled it. **3**When all the Israelites saw
the fire coming down and the glory of
the LORD above the temple, they knelt
on the pavement with their faces to the
ground, and they worshiped and gave
thanks to the LORD, saying,

"He is good;
his love endures forever."[y]

4Then the king and all the people offered sacrifices before the LORD. **5**And
King Solomon offered a sacrifice of
twenty-two thousand head of cattle
and a hundred and twenty thousand

7:1 THE GLORY OF THE LORD. The "glory of the LORD" refers to a visible manifestation of God's presence and splendor (see article on THE GLORY OF GOD, p. 1192).

sheep and goats. So the king and all
the people dedicated the temple of
God. **6**The priests took their positions,
as did the Levites[z] with the LORD's
musical instruments,[a] which King David had made for praising the LORD and
which were used when he gave thanks,
saying, "His love endures forever." Opposite the Levites, the priests blew
their trumpets, and all the Israelites
were standing.
7Solomon consecrated the middle
part of the courtyard in front of the
temple of the LORD, and there he offered burnt offerings and the fat[b] of
the fellowship offerings,[e] because the
bronze altar he had made could not
hold the burnt offerings, the grain offerings and the fat portions.
8So Solomon observed the festival[c]
at that time for seven days, and all Israel[d] with him—a vast assembly, people from Lebo[f] Hamath[e] to the Wadi
of Egypt.[f] **9**On the eighth day they
held an assembly, for they had celebrated[g] the dedication of the altar for
seven days and the festival[h] for seven
days more. **10**On the twenty-third day
of the seventh month he sent the people to their homes, joyful and glad in
heart for the good things the LORD had
done for David and Solomon and for his
people Israel.

7:6 [z] 1Ch 15:16 [a] S 1Ch 15:24
7:7 [b] S Ex 29:13
7:8 [c] 2Ch 30:26; Ne 8:17 [d] S 1Ch 9:1 [e] S Nu 13:21 [f] S Ge 15:18
7:9 [g] 2Ch 30:23 [h] S Lev 23:36
7:11 [i] S 1Ch 28:20
7:12 [j] 2Ch 1:7 [k] Dt 12:11 [l] S Dt 12:5
7:13 [m] S Dt 11:17; Am 4:7
7:14 [n] S Nu 6:27 [o] S Ex 10:3; S Lev 26:41; S 2Ch 6:37 [p] S 1Ch 16:11 [q] S 2Ki 17:13; Isa 55:7; Eze 18:32; Zec 1:4 [r] S 2Ch 6:20 [s] S 2Ch 6:27 [t] S Ex 15:26; 2Ch 30:20; Ps 60:2; Isa 30:26; 53:5; 57:18; Jer 33:6; Mal 4:2
7:15 [u] S 1Ki 8:29; S 2Ch 6:40; Ne 1:6
7:16 [v] S Dt 12:5; 2Ch 33:7

The LORD Appears to Solomon

7:11–22pp — 1Ki 9:1–9

11When Solomon had finished[i] the
temple of the LORD and the royal palace, and had succeeded in carrying out
all he had in mind to do in the temple
of the LORD and in his own palace, **12**the
LORD appeared[j] to him at night and
said:

"I have heard your prayer and
have chosen[k] this place for myself[l] as a temple for sacrifices.
13"When I shut up the heavens
so that there is no rain,[m] or command locusts to devour the land
or send a plague among my people, **14**if my people, who are called
by my name,[n] will humble[o]
themselves and pray and seek my
face[p] and turn[q] from their wicked ways, then will I hear[r] from
heaven and will forgive[s] their sin
and will heal[t] their land. **15**Now
my eyes will be open and my ears
attentive to the prayers offered in
this place.[u] **16**I have chosen[v]
and consecrated this temple so
that my Name may be there forev-

[e] 7 Traditionally *peace offerings* [f] 8 Or *from the entrance to*

7:12 THE LORD APPEARED TO HIM. See 1Ki 9:3, note.

7:14 IF MY PEOPLE . . . HUMBLE . . . PRAY . . . SEEK . . . TURN. God's judgment of his people during times of moral decline, spiritual apathy and worldly compromise is drought, barrenness and plague (v. 13). God's promise (see next note), although originally given to Israel, applies equally to his people of any generation who, after experiencing his judgment, meet the following four conditions for the revival of spiritual life and the restoration of God's holy purpose and blessing for his people (cf. Ac 3:19):

(1) "Humble themselves." God's people must recognize their failures, show sorrow for their sin and renew their commitment to do God's will. Humbling oneself before God and his Word means recognizing one's spiritual poverty (11:16; 15:12–13,15; 34:15–19; Ps 51:17; Mt 5:3).

(2) "Pray." God's people must cry out desperately to him for mercy, and must completely depend on him and trust him for his intervention. The prayer must be earnest and sustained until God answers from heaven (cf. Lk 11:1–13; 18:1–8; Jas 5:17–18).

(3) "Seek my face." God's people must diligently turn to God with the whole heart and long for his presence—and not just try to escape from adversity (11:16; 19:3; 1Ch 16:11; 22:19; Isa 55:6–7).

(4) "Turn from their wicked ways." God's people must genuinely repent by turning from specific sins and all forms of idolatry, renounce conformity to the world, and draw near to God for mercy, forgiveness and cleansing (29:6–11; 2Ki 17:13; Jer 25:5; Zec 1:4; Heb 4:16).

7:14 THEN WILL I HEAR . . . FORGIVE . . . HEAL. When God's four conditions for revival and restoration are met (see previous note), then God's threefold promise of revival will be fulfilled. (1) God will turn away his anger from his people, listen to their desperate cry and be attentive to their prayers (v. 15). In other words, the first evidence of revival is that God begins to hear and answer prayer from heaven (vv. 14–15) and show compassion for his people (cf. Ps 85:4–7; 102:1–2,13; Jer 33:3; Joel 2:12–13,18–19; see article on FAITH AND GRACE, p. 1720).

(2) God will forgive his people, cleanse them from their sins, and restore his favor, presence, peace, truth, righteousness and power among them (cf. Ps 85:9–13; Jer 33:7–8; Hos 10:12; Joel 2:25; 2Co 6:14–18).

(3) God will heal his people and their land by again pouring out rain (i.e., physical favor and blessing) and the Holy Spirit (i.e., spiritual awakening among the covenant people and among the spiritually lost, cf. Ps 51:12–13; Hos 5:14—6:3,11; Joel 2:28–32).

er. My eyes and my heart will always be there.
17"As for you, if you walk before me[w] as David your father
did, and do all I command, and observe my decrees[x] and laws, 18I
will establish your royal throne,
as I covenanted[y] with David your
father when I said, 'You shall never fail to have a man[z] to rule over
Israel.'[a]
19"But if you[g] turn away[b] and
forsake[c] the decrees and commands I have given you[g] and go
off to serve other gods and worship them, 20then I will uproot[d]
Israel from my land,[e] which I
have given them, and will reject
this temple I have consecrated for
my Name. I will make it a byword
and an object of ridicule[f] among
all peoples. 21And though this
temple is now so imposing, all
who pass by will be appalled[g]
and say,[h] 'Why has the LORD done
such a thing to this land and to
this temple?' 22People will answer, 'Because they have forsak-
en the LORD, the God of their fathers, who brought them out of
Egypt, and have embraced other
gods, worshiping and serving
them[i]—that is why he brought
all this disaster on them.'"

Solomon's Other Activities

8:1–18pp — 1Ki 9:10–28

8 At the end of twenty years, during
which Solomon built the temple of
the LORD and his own palace,[j] 2Solo-
mon rebuilt the villages that Hiram[h]
had given him, and settled Israelites in
them. 3Solomon then went to Hamath
Zobah and captured it. 4He also built
up Tadmor in the desert and all the
store cities he had built in Hamath.[k]
5He rebuilt Upper Beth Horon[l] and
Lower Beth Horon as fortified cities,
with walls and with gates and bars, 6as
well as Baalath[m] and all his store cities, and all the cities for his chariots
and for his horses[i]—whatever he desired to build in Jerusalem, in Lebanon
and throughout all the territory he
ruled.
7All the people left from the Hittites,
Amorites, Perizzites, Hivites and Jebusites[n] (these peoples were not Israelites), 8that is, their descendants remaining in the land, whom the
Israelites had not destroyed—these
Solomon conscripted[o] for his slave labor force, as it is to this day. 9But Solomon did not make slaves of the Israelites for his work; they were his fighting
men, commanders of his captains, and
commanders of his chariots and charioteers. 10They were also King Solomon's chief officials—two hundred
and fifty officials supervising the men.
11Solomon brought Pharaoh's
daughter[p] up from the City of David to
the palace he had built for her, for he
said, "My wife must not live in the palace of David king of Israel, because the
places the ark of the LORD has entered
are holy."
12On the altar[q] of the LORD that he
had built in front of the portico, Solomon sacrificed burnt offerings to the
LORD, 13according to the daily requirement[r] for offerings commanded by
Moses for Sabbaths,[s] New Moons[t]
and the three[u] annual feasts—the
Feast of Unleavened Bread,[v] the
Feast of Weeks[w] and the Feast of Tabernacles.[x] 14In keeping with the ordinance of his father David, he appointed
the divisions[y] of the priests for their
duties, and the Levites[z] to lead the
praise and to assist the priests according to each day's requirement. He also
appointed the gatekeepers[a] by divisions for the various gates, because
this was what David the man of God[b]
had ordered.[c] 15They did not deviate
from the king's commands to the
priests or to the Levites in any matter,
including that of the treasuries.

7:17 [w]S 1Ki 9:4 [x]S Lev 19:37
7:18 [y]Isa 9:7; Jer 33:17,21 [z]S 1Ch 5:2; Isa 55:4; Mic 5:2 [a]S 2Sa 7:13; S 1Ch 17:12; 2Ch 13:5; 23:3
7:19 [b]S Dt 28:15 [c]S 1Ch 28:9; 2Ch 12:1; 24:18; Jer 9:13; 11:8
7:20 [d]S Dt 29:28 [e]1Ki 14:15; Jer 12:14; 16:13; 50:11 [f]S Dt 28:37
7:21 [g]Jer 19:8 [h]Dt 29:24
7:22 [i]Jer 16:11
8:1 [j]S 2Sa 7:2
8:4 [k]S 2Sa 8:9
8:5 [l]S Jos 10:10
8:6 [m]S Jos 19:44
8:7 [n]S Ge 10:16; S 15:18-21; Ezr 9:1
8:8 [o]S 2Ch 2:18
8:11 [p]S 1Ki 3:1
8:12 [q]S 1Ki 8:64; 2Ch 15:8
8:13 [r]S Ex 29:38 [s]Nu 28:9 [t]S Nu 10:10 [u]S Ex 23:14 [v]S Ex 12:17; Nu 28:16-25 [w]S Ex 23:16 [x]Nu 29:12-38; Ne 8:17
8:14 [y]S 1Ch 24:1 [z]S 1Ch 25:1 [a]S 1Ch 9:17 [b]Ne 12:24,36 [c]S 1Ch 23:6; Ne 12:45

[g] *19* The Hebrew is plural. [h] *2* Hebrew *Huram,* a variant of *Hiram*; also in verse 18 [i] *6* Or *charioteers*

7:20 REJECT THIS TEMPLE. See 1Ki 9:7, note.

8:11 PHARAOH'S DAUGHTER. Solomon's marriage to Pharaoh's daughter was contrary to God's law (see Dt 17:17; Ex 34:16). Though Solomon was dedicated to building the temple and obeying many of God's commands, this marriage shows that he failed to submit every area of his life to God's rule. Failure to resist his strongest temptation eventually resulted in his ruin; thus he left a vital area of his life open to Satan (see 1Ki 4:29–34, note; 11:1, note). Satan needs only one uncommitted or unresolved area of the believer's life to gain a foothold and lead him or her away from God.

[16]All Solomon's work was carried out, from the day the foundation of the temple of the LORD was laid until its completion. So the temple of the LORD was finished.

[17]Then Solomon went to Ezion Geber and Elath on the coast of Edom. [18]And Hiram sent him ships commanded by his own officers, men who knew the sea. These, with Solomon's men, sailed to Ophir and brought back four hundred and fifty talents[j] of gold,[d] which they delivered to King Solomon.

The Queen of Sheba Visits Solomon

9:1–12pp — 1Ki 10:1–13

9 When the queen of Sheba[e] heard of Solomon's fame, she came to Jerusalem to test him with hard questions. Arriving with a very great caravan—with camels carrying spices, large quantities of gold, and precious stones—she came to Solomon and talked with him about all she had on her mind. [2]Solomon answered all her questions; nothing was too hard for him to explain to her. [3]When the queen of Sheba saw the wisdom of Solomon,[f] as well as the palace he had built, [4]the food on his table, the seating of his officials, the attending servants in their robes, the cupbearers in their robes and the burnt offerings he made at[k] the temple of the LORD, she was overwhelmed.

[5]She said to the king, "The report I heard in my own country about your achievements and your wisdom is true. [6]But I did not believe what they said until I came[g] and saw with my own eyes. Indeed, not even half the greatness of your wisdom was told me; you have far exceeded the report I heard. [7]How happy your men must be! How happy your officials, who continually stand before you and hear your wisdom! [8]Praise be to the LORD your God, who has delighted in you and placed you on his throne[h] as king to rule for the LORD your God. Because of the love of your God for Israel and his desire to uphold them forever, he has made you king[i] over them, to maintain justice and righteousness."

[9]Then she gave the king 120 talents[l] of gold,[j] large quantities of spices, and precious stones. There had never been such spices as those the queen of Sheba gave to King Solomon.

[10](The men of Hiram and the men of Solomon brought gold from Ophir;[k] they also brought algumwood[m] and precious stones. [11]The king used the algumwood to make steps for the temple of the LORD and for the royal palace, and to make harps and lyres for the musicians. Nothing like them had ever been seen in Judah.)

[12]King Solomon gave the queen of Sheba all she desired and asked for; he gave her more than she had brought to him. Then she left and returned with her retinue to her own country.

Solomon's Splendor

9:13–28pp — 1Ki 10:14–29; 2Ch 1:14–17

[13]The weight of the gold that Solomon received yearly was 666 talents,[n] [14]not including the revenues brought in by merchants and traders. Also all the kings of Arabia[l] and the governors of the land brought gold and silver to Solomon.

[15]King Solomon made two hundred large shields of hammered gold; six hundred bekas[o] of hammered gold went into each shield. [16]He also made three hundred small shields[m] of hammered gold, with three hundred bekas[p] of gold in each shield. The king put them in the Palace of the Forest of Lebanon.[n]

[17]Then the king made a great throne inlaid with ivory[o] and overlaid with pure gold. [18]The throne had six steps, and a footstool of gold was attached to it. On both sides of the seat were armrests, with a lion standing beside each of them. [19]Twelve lions stood on the six steps, one at either end of each step. Nothing like it had ever been made for any other kingdom. [20]All King Solomon's goblets were gold, and all the household articles in the Palace of the Forest of Lebanon were pure gold. Nothing was made of silver, because silver was considered of little value in Solomon's day. [21]The king had

8:18 [d]2Ch 9:9
9:1 [e]S Ge 10:7; Eze 23:42; Mt 12:42; Lk 11:31
9:3 [f]1Ki 5:12
9:6 [g]2Ch 6:32
9:8 [h]S 1Ki 2:12; S 1Ch 17:14; 2Ch 13:8 [i]2Ch 2:11
9:9 [j]2Ch 8:18
9:10 [k]2Ch 8:18
9:14 [l]2Ch 17:11; Isa 21:13; Jer 25:24; Eze 27:21; 30:5
9:16 [m]2Ch 12:9 [n]S 1Ki 7:2
9:17 [o]S 1Ki 22:39

[j]*18* That is, about 17 tons (about 16 metric tons) [k]*4* Or *the ascent by which he went up to* [l]*9* That is, about 4 1/2 tons (about 4 metric tons) [m]*10* Probably a variant of *almugwood* [n]*13* That is, about 25 tons (about 23 metric tons) [o]*15* That is, about 7 1/2 pounds (about 3.5 kilograms) [p]*16* That is, about 3 3/4 pounds (about 1.7 kilograms)

a fleet of trading ships[q] manned by Hiram's[r] men. Once every three years it
returned, carrying gold, silver and ivory, and apes and baboons.
22King Solomon was greater in
riches and wisdom than all the other
kings of the earth.[p] **23**All the kings[q]
of the earth sought audience with Solomon to hear the wisdom God had put
in his heart. **24**Year after year, everyone who came brought a gift[r]—articles of silver and gold, and robes,
weapons and spices, and horses and
mules.
25Solomon had four thousand stalls
for horses and chariots,[s] and twelve
thousand horses,[s] which he kept in
the chariot cities and also with him in
Jerusalem. **26**He ruled[t] over all the
kings from the River[t][u] to the land of
the Philistines, as far as the border of
Egypt.[v] **27**The king made silver as
common in Jerusalem as stones, and
cedar as plentiful as sycamore-fig
trees in the foothills. **28**Solomon's
horses were imported from Egypt[u]
and from all other countries.

Solomon's Death

9:29–31pp — 1Ki 11:41–43

29As for the other events of Solomon's reign, from beginning to end, are
they not written in the records of Nathan[w] the prophet, in the prophecy of
Ahijah[x] the Shilonite and in the visions of Iddo the seer concerning Jeroboam[y] son of Nebat? **30**Solomon
reigned in Jerusalem over all Israel forty years. **31**Then he rested with his fathers and was buried in the city of David[z] his father. And Rehoboam his son
succeeded him as king.

Israel Rebels Against Rehoboam

10:1–11:4pp — 1Ki 12:1–24

10 Rehoboam went to Shechem,
for all the Israelites had gone
there to make him king. **2**When Jeroboam[a] son of Nebat heard this (he was
in Egypt, where he had fled[b] from
King Solomon), he returned from
Egypt. **3**So they sent for Jeroboam, and
he and all Israel[c] went to Rehoboam
and said to him: **4**"Your father put a
heavy yoke on us,[d] but now lighten
the harsh labor and the heavy yoke he
put on us, and we will serve you."
5Rehoboam answered, "Come back
to me in three days." So the people
went away.
6Then King Rehoboam consulted
the elders[e] who had served his father
Solomon during his lifetime. "How
would you advise me to answer these
people?" he asked.
7They replied, "If you will be kind to
these people and please them and give
them a favorable answer,[f] they will
always be your servants."
8But Rehoboam rejected[g] the advice the elders[h] gave him and consulted the young men who had grown up
with him and were serving him. **9**He
asked them, "What is your advice?
How should we answer these people
who say to me, 'Lighten the yoke your
father put on us'?"
10The young men who had grown up
with him replied, "Tell the people who
have said to you, 'Your father put a
heavy yoke on us, but make our yoke
lighter'—tell them, 'My little finger is
thicker than my father's waist. **11**My
father laid on you a heavy yoke; I will
make it even heavier. My father
scourged you with whips; I will
scourge you with scorpions.' "
12Three days later Jeroboam and all

9:22 [p] S 1Ki 3:13; S 2Ch 1:12 **9:23** [q] 1Ki 4:34 **9:24** [r] 2Ch 32:23; Ps 45:12; 68:29; 72:10; Isa 18:7 **9:25** [s] S 1Sa 8:11 **9:26** [t] S 1Ki 4:21 [u] Ps 72:8-9 [v] Ge 15:18-21 **9:29** [w] S 2Sa 7:2 [x] S 1Ki 11:29 [y] 2Ch 10:2 **9:31** [z] 1Ki 2:10

10:2 [a] S 2Ch 9:29 [b] S 1Ki 11:40 **10:3** [c] S 1Ch 9:1 **10:4** [d] 2Ch 2:2 **10:6** [e] Job 8:8-9; 12:12; 15:10; 32:7 **10:7** [f] Pr 15:1 **10:8** [g] S 2Sa 17:14 [h] Pr 13:20

[q] *21* Hebrew *of ships that could go to Tarshish* [r] *21* Hebrew *Huram,* a variant of *Hiram* [s] *25* Or *charioteers* [t] *26* That is, the Euphrates [u] *28* Or possibly *Muzur,* a region in Cilicia

9:29 OTHER EVENTS OF SOLOMON'S REIGN. The author of Chronicles refers to the rest of the acts of Solomon that are more fully recorded in 1Ki 11. In Solomon's later years he declined spiritually and departed from God. In the end Solomon was not only a backslider, but he also set the stage for Israel's division and decline, which happened almost immediately after his death. For his tragic spiritual state at the end, see 1Ki 11, notes.

10:1 THE DIVIDING OF THE KINGDOM. This chapter marks the point when the nation of Israel was torn apart into two kingdoms (vv. 15–19; see 1Ki 12:20,24, notes). The northern kingdom was called Israel, the southern kingdom Judah. The main stream of Hebrew history is viewed at all times in this book as being the southern kingdom of Judah. The writer says little of the history of the northern kingdom, focusing attention on the southern kingdom for three reasons: (1) The people of Judah constituted the majority of the post-exilic remnant who returned to Palestine and for whom Chronicles was originally written; (2) Judah remained the center of the worship of the Lord God; and (3) Judah's kings were David's descendants and thus part of the covenant promise.

the people returned to Rehoboam, as
the king had said, "Come back to me in
three days." 13The king answered
them harshly. Rejecting the advice of
the elders, 14he followed the advice of
the young men and said, "My father
made your yoke heavy; I will make it
even heavier. My father scourged you
with whips; I will scourge you with
scorpions." 15So the king did not listen
to the people, for this turn of events
was from God,[i] to fulfill the word the
LORD had spoken to Jeroboam son of
Nebat through Ahijah the Shilonite.[j]
16When all Israel[k] saw that the
king refused to listen to them, they answered the king:

"What share do we have in
David,[l]
what part in Jesse's son?
To your tents, O Israel!
Look after your own house,
O David!"

So all the Israelites went home. 17But
as for the Israelites who were living in
the towns of Judah, Rehoboam still
ruled over them.
18King Rehoboam sent out Adoniram,[v][m] who was in charge of forced
labor, but the Israelites stoned him to
death. King Rehoboam, however, managed to get into his chariot and escape
to Jerusalem. 19So Israel has been in
rebellion against the house of David to
this day.

11 When Rehoboam arrived in Jerusalem,[n] he mustered the
house of Judah and Benjamin—a hundred and eighty thousand fighting
men—to make war against Israel and
to regain the kingdom for Rehoboam.
2But this word of the LORD came to
Shemaiah[o] the man of God: 3"Say to
Rehoboam son of Solomon king of Judah and to all the Israelites in Judah
and Benjamin, 4'This is what the LORD
says: Do not go up to fight against your
brothers.[p] Go home, every one of you,
for this is my doing.' " So they obeyed
the words of the LORD and turned back
from marching against Jeroboam.

Rehoboam Fortifies Judah

5Rehoboam lived in Jerusalem and
built up towns for defense in Judah:
6Bethlehem, Etam, Tekoa, 7Beth Zur,
Soco, Adullam, 8Gath, Mareshah, Ziph,
9Adoraim, Lachish, Azekah, 10Zorah,
Aijalon and Hebron. These were fortified cities[q] in Judah and Benjamin.
11He strengthened their defenses and
put commanders in them, with supplies of food, olive oil and wine. 12He
put shields and spears in all the cities,
and made them very strong. So Judah
and Benjamin were his.
13The priests and Levites from all
their districts throughout Israel sided
with him. 14The Levites[r] even abandoned their pasturelands and property,[s] and came to Judah and Jerusalem
because Jeroboam and his sons had rejected them as priests of the LORD.
15And he appointed[t] his own
priests[u] for the high places and for the
goat[v] and calf[w] idols he had made.
16Those from every tribe of Israel[x]
who set their hearts on seeking the
LORD, the God of Israel, followed the
Levites to Jerusalem to offer sacrifices
to the LORD, the God of their fathers.
17They strengthened[y] the kingdom of
Judah and supported Rehoboam son of
Solomon three years, walking in the
ways of David and Solomon during this
time.

10:15 [i] 2Ch 11:4; 25:16-20 [j] S 1Ki 11:29
10:16 [k] S 1Ch 9:1 [l] S 2Sa 20:1
10:18 [m] S 2Sa 20:24; S 1Ki 5:14
11:1 [n] S 1Ki 12:21
11:2 [o] S 1Ki 12:22; 2Ch 12:5-7,15
11:4 [p] 2Ch 28:8-11
11:10 [q] S Jos 10:20; 2Ch 12:4; 17:2,19; 21:3
11:14 [r] S Nu 35:2-5 [s] 1Ch 6:81
11:15 [t] S 1Ki 13:33 [u] S 1Ki 12:31 [v] Lev 17:7 [w] 1Ki 12:28; 2Ch 13:8
11:16 [x] 2Ch 15:9
11:17 [y] 2Ch 12:1

[v] 18 Hebrew *Hadoram*, a variant of *Adoniram*

11:4 THIS IS MY DOING. It was God who divided Israel in an effort to keep Judah loyal to him and to separate Judah from the growing spiritual corruption in the other tribes. Sometimes God causes division in order to preserve and protect his revealed truth, his righteous standards and those godly people who want to remain faithful to him (see 1Ki 12:24, note; Mt 10:34, note; Eph 4:3,5, 13,15, notes).

11:14–15 JEROBOAM ... APPOINTED HIS OWN PRIESTS. See 1Ki 12:28, note.

11:16 SET THEIR HEARTS ON SEEKING THE LORD. Jeroboam and the northern kingdom abandoned the worship of the Lord as revealed in his Word and covenant and replaced it with idolatry (see 1Ki 12:28, note). (1) For this reason all those who wanted to remain true to God left their homes, separated themselves from the northern kingdom and joined the kingdom of Judah (vv. 14, 17). The challenge to remain true to God in the midst of apostasy or moral decline has frequently faced God's people throughout the history of redemption (see Rev 2:7, note).

(2) Loyalty and commitment to God and his Word may sometimes require separating oneself from one's church and joining or forming another one that is devoted to God's original and fundamental revelation in Christ (see Mt 21:43, note on Jesus' teaching that the kingdom will be taken from the faithless and given to those who respond to the gospel; Eph 4:13, note; see article on SPIRITUAL SEPARATION FOR BELIEVERS, p. 1794).

Rehoboam's Family

18 Rehoboam married Mahalath, who
was the daughter of David's son Jerimoth and of Abihail, the daughter of
Jesse's son Eliab. 19 She bore him sons:
Jeush, Shemariah and Zaham. 20 Then
he married Maacah[z] daughter of Absalom, who bore him Abijah,[a] Attai,
Ziza and Shelomith. 21 Rehoboam loved
Maacah daughter of Absalom more
than any of his other wives and concubines. In all, he had eighteen wives[b]
and sixty concubines, twenty-eight
sons and sixty daughters.

22 Rehoboam appointed Abijah[c] son
of Maacah to be the chief prince among
his brothers, in order to make him
king. 23 He acted wisely, dispersing
some of his sons throughout the districts of Judah and Benjamin, and to all
the fortified cities. He gave them abundant provisions[d] and took many wives
for them.

Shishak Attacks Jerusalem

12:9–16pp — 1Ki 14:21, 25–31

12 After Rehoboam's position as
king was established[e] and he
had become strong,[f] he and all Israel[w][g] with him abandoned[h] the law of
the LORD. 2 Because they had been unfaithful[i] to the LORD, Shishak[j] king
of Egypt attacked Jerusalem in the fifth
year of King Rehoboam. 3 With twelve
hundred chariots and sixty thousand
horsemen and the innumerable troops
of Libyans,[k] Sukkites and Cushites[x][l] that came with him from
Egypt, 4 he captured the fortified cities[m] of Judah and came as far as Jerusalem.

5 Then the prophet Shemaiah[n] came
to Rehoboam and to the leaders of Judah who had assembled in Jerusalem
for fear of Shishak, and he said to
them, "This is what the LORD says, 'You
have abandoned me; therefore, I now
abandon[o] you to Shishak.' "

6 The leaders of Israel and the king
humbled[p] themselves and said, "The
LORD is just."[q]

7 When the LORD saw that they humbled themselves, this word of the LORD
came to Shemaiah: "Since they have
humbled themselves, I will not destroy
them but will soon give them deliverance.[r] My wrath[s] will not be poured
out on Jerusalem through Shishak.
8 They will, however, become subject[t]
to him, so that they may learn the difference between serving me and serving the kings of other lands."

9 When Shishak king of Egypt attacked Jerusalem, he carried off the
treasures of the temple of the LORD and
the treasures of the royal palace. He
took everything, including the gold
shields[u] Solomon had made. 10 So
King Rehoboam made bronze shields
to replace them and assigned these to
the commanders of the guard on duty
at the entrance to the royal palace.
11 Whenever the king went to the
LORD's temple, the guards went with
him, bearing the shields, and afterward
they returned them to the guardroom.

12 Because Rehoboam humbled[v]
himself, the LORD's anger turned from
him, and he was not totally destroyed.
Indeed, there was some good[w] in Judah.

13 King Rehoboam established[x]
himself firmly in Jerusalem and continued as king. He was forty-one years old
when he became king, and he reigned
seventeen years in Jerusalem, the city
the LORD had chosen out of all the
tribes of Israel in which to put his
Name.[y] His mother's name was Naamah; she was an Ammonite. 14 He did

11:20 [z] S 1Ki 15:2 [a] 2Ch 12:16; 13:2 **11:21** [b] S Dt 17:17 **11:22** [c] Dt 21:15-17 **11:23** [d] 2Ch 21:3 **12:1** [e] ver 13; 2Ch 1:1 [f] 2Ch 11:17 [g] S 1Ch 9:1 [h] S 2Ch 7:19 **12:2** [i] 1Ki 14:22-24; S 1Ch 5:25 [j] 1Ki 11:40 **12:3** [k] Da 11:43 [l] S Ge 10:6; 2Ch 14:9; 16:8; Isa 18:2; Am 9:7; Na 3:9 **12:4** [m] S 2Ch 11:10 **12:5** [n] 2Ch 11:2 [o] S Dt 28:15 **12:6** [p] S Lev 26:41; S 2Ch 6:37 [q] Ex 9:27; Ezr 9:15; Ps 11:7; 116:5; Da 9:14 **12:7** [r] Ps 78:38 [s] Dt 9:19; Ps 69:24; Jer 7:20; 42:18; Eze 5:13 **12:8** [t] Dt 28:48 **12:9** [u] 2Ch 9:16 **12:12** [v] S 2Ch 6:37 [w] S 1Ki 14:13; 2Ch 19:3 **12:13** [x] S ver 1; S 1Ki 2:12 [y] S Ex 20:24; Dt 12:5

[w] *1* That is, Judah, as frequently in 2 Chronicles [x] *3* That is, people from the upper Nile region

12:1 ALL ISRAEL. Here the Chronicler uses the term "all Israel" for the southern kingdom (i.e., Judah) alone (cf. v. 4). At other times "all Israel" refers to the northern kingdom (10:16) or to both kingdoms (9:30). Consequently, its meaning must be determined from the context.

12:5 YOU HAVE ABANDONED ME; THEREFORE. The writer of Chronicles often emphasizes that God's blessings follow obedience (11:17) while punishment follows disobedience (12:1–6). When King Rehoboam became unfaithful, God stopped protecting him from his enemies (v. 5). We cannot expect God to protect us from the dangers of life or Satan's attacks if we are unfaithful to him and his will. God's protecting power comes to us only through a living faith in Christ (see Ro 8:28; note; 1Pe 1:5, note). "The LORD is with you when you are with him" (15:2).

12:7 THEY HAVE HUMBLED THEMSELVES. If we have sinned and are being punished for it, we should humble ourselves before God and confess that his judgments are just (v. 6; cf. 7:14, note). The Lord will forgive our sins and restore us to his grace and favor, and he may even reduce the punishment we must bear.

evil because he had not set his heart on
seeking the LORD.
15As for the events of Rehoboam's
reign, from beginning to end, are they
not written in the records of Shemaiah[z] the prophet and of Iddo the seer
that deal with genealogies? There was
continual warfare between Rehoboam
and Jeroboam. 16Rehoboam[a] rested
with his fathers and was buried in the
City of David. And Abijah[b] his son
succeeded him as king.

Abijah King of Judah

13:1–2,22–14:1pp — 1Ki 15:1–2,6–8

13 In the eighteenth year of the
reign of Jeroboam, Abijah became king of Judah, 2and he reigned in
Jerusalem three years. His mother's
name was Maacah,[y][c] a daughter[z] of
Uriel of Gibeah.
There was war between Abijah[d]
and Jeroboam.[e] 3Abijah went into battle with a force of four hundred thousand able fighting men, and Jeroboam
drew up a battle line against him with
eight hundred thousand able troops.
4Abijah stood on Mount Zemara-
im,[f] in the hill country of Ephraim,
and said, "Jeroboam and all Israel,[g]
listen to me! 5Don't you know that the
LORD, the God of Israel, has given the
kingship of Israel to David and his
descendants forever[h] by a covenant of
salt?[i] 6Yet Jeroboam son of Nebat, an
official of Solomon son of David, rebelled[j] against his master. 7Some
worthless scoundrels[k] gathered
around him and opposed Rehoboam
son of Solomon when he was young
and indecisive[l] and not strong
enough to resist them.
8"And now you plan to resist the
kingdom of the LORD, which is in the
hands of David's descendants.[m] You
are indeed a vast army and have with
you[n] the golden calves[o] that Jeroboam made to be your gods. 9But didn't
you drive out the priests[p] of the
LORD,[q] the sons of Aaron, and the Levites, and make priests of your own as
the peoples of other lands do? Whoever
comes to consecrate himself with a
young bull[r] and seven rams[s] may become a priest of what are not gods.[t]
10"As for us, the LORD is our God,
and we have not forsaken him. The
priests who serve the LORD are sons of
Aaron, and the Levites assist them.
11Every morning and evening[u] they
present burnt offerings and fragrant incense[v] to the LORD. They set out the
bread on the ceremonially clean table[w] and light the lamps[x] on the gold
lampstand every evening. We are observing the requirements of the LORD
our God. But you have forsaken him.
12God is with us; he is our leader. His
priests with their trumpets will sound
the battle cry against you.[y] Men of Israel, do not fight against the LORD,[z]
the God of your fathers, for you will not
succeed."[a]
13Now Jeroboam had sent troops
around to the rear, so that while he
was in front of Judah the ambush[b] was
behind them. 14Judah turned and saw
that they were being attacked at both
front and rear. Then they cried out[c] to
the LORD. The priests blew their trumpets 15and the men of Judah raised the
battle cry. At the sound of their battle
cry, God routed Jeroboam and all Israel[d] before Abijah and Judah. 16The Israelites fled before Judah, and God delivered[e] them into their hands.
17Abijah and his men inflicted heavy
losses on them, so that there were five
hundred thousand casualties among
Israel's able men. 18The men of Israel
were subdued on that occasion, and

12:15 [z]S 2Ch 11:2
12:16 [a]S 1Ch 3:10 [b]S 2Ch 11:20
13:2 [c]2Ch 15:16 [d]S 2Ch 11:20 [e]1Ki 15:6
13:4 [f]Jos 18:22 [g]1Ch 11:1
13:5 [h]S 2Sa 7:13; S 1Ch 17:12 [i]S Lev 2:13
13:6 [j]1Ki 11:26
13:7 [k]S Jdg 9:4 [l]S 1Ch 29:1
13:8 [m]S 2Ch 9:8 [n]1Sa 4:3 [o]S Ex 32:4; S 2Ch 11:15
13:9 [p]S 1Ki 12:31 [q]2Ch 11:14-15 [r]Ex 29:35-36 [s]S Ex 29:31 [t]Jer 2:11; Gal 4:8
13:11 [u]S Ex 29:39; S 2Ch 2:4 [v]S Ex 25:6 [w]S 1Ch 9:32 [x]S Ex 25:37
13:12 [y]S Nu 10:8-9 [z]S Jdg 2:15; Ac 5:39 [a]Job 9:4; Pr 21:30; 29:1
13:13 [b]Jos 8:9; 2Ch 20:22
13:14 [c]S 1Ch 5:20; 2Ch 14:11; 18:31
13:15 [d]S 1Ch 9:1
13:16 [e]2Ch 16:8

[y]2 Most Septuagint manuscripts and Syriac (see also 2 Chron. 11:20 and 1 Kings 15:2); Hebrew *Micaiah* [z]2 Or *granddaughter*

12:14 HE DID EVIL . . . NOT SET HIS HEART ON SEEKING THE LORD. There is a direct connection between diligently seeking God and his strength and resisting evil. In order to persevere in the faith, we must firmly resolve to seek God's face in earnest prayer; by doing so, we will be able to resist sin, despise the world, obey God's Word and follow the Holy Spirit's leading until the day we go to be with God. On the other hand, without this determined purpose in our hearts, we will soon forsake God and his salvation, and conform to the ungodly ways of society.

13:1 ABIJAH BECAME KING OF JUDAH. Chronicles records Abijah's victory as coming because he and the men of Judah relied on God (v. 18). The author of Kings does not record the incident, however, and states that Abijah "committed all the sins his father had done" (1Ki 15:3). The difference in emphasis between Chronicles and Kings is due to each author's purpose in writing. The writer of Kings was interested in evaluating the overall picture of each king's reign; the Chronicler wanted to emphasize the exceptional moments of faith and obedience in order to show Israel that God would help and deliver them if they trusted and obeyed God.

the men of Judah were victorious because they relied[f] on the LORD, the
God of their fathers.
19 Abijah pursued Jeroboam and took
from him the towns of Bethel, Jeshanah and Ephron, with their surrounding villages. 20 Jeroboam did not regain
power during the time of Abijah. And
the LORD struck him down and he died.
21 But Abijah grew in strength. He
married fourteen wives and had twenty-two sons and sixteen daughters.
22 The other events of Abijah's reign,
what he did and what he said, are written in the annotations of the prophet
Iddo.

14 And Abijah rested with his fathers and was buried in the City
of David. Asa his son succeeded him as
king, and in his days the country was
at peace for ten years.

Asa King of Judah

14:2–3pp — 1Ki 15:11–12

2 Asa did what was good and right in
the eyes of the LORD his God.[g] 3 He removed the foreign altars[h] and the
high places, smashed the sacred
stones[i] and cut down the Asherah
poles.[a][j] 4 He commanded Judah to
seek the LORD,[k] the God of their fathers, and to obey his laws and commands. 5 He removed the high places[l]
and incense altars[m] in every town in
Judah, and the kingdom was at peace
under him. 6 He built up the fortified
cities of Judah, since the land was at
peace. No one was at war with him during those years, for the LORD gave him
rest.[n]
7 "Let us build up these towns," he
said to Judah, "and put walls around
them, with towers, gates and bars. The
land is still ours, because we have
sought the LORD our God; we sought
him and he has given us rest[o] on every
side." So they built and prospered.
8 Asa had an army of three hundred
thousand[p] men from Judah, equipped
with large shields and with spears, and
two hundred and eighty thousand from
Benjamin, armed with small shields
and with bows. All these were brave
fighting men.
9 Zerah the Cushite[q] marched out
against them with a vast army[b] and
three hundred chariots, and came as
far as Mareshah.[r] 10 Asa went out to
meet him, and they took up battle positions in the Valley of Zephathah near
Mareshah.
11 Then Asa called[s] to the LORD his
God and said, "LORD, there is no one
like you to help the powerless against
the mighty. Help us,[t] O LORD our God,
for we rely[u] on you, and in your
name[v] we have come against this vast
army. O LORD, you are our God; do not
let man prevail[w] against you."
12 The LORD struck down[x] the Cushites before Asa and Judah. The Cushites fled, 13 and Asa and his army pursued them as far as Gerar.[y] Such a
great number of Cushites fell that they
could not recover; they were crushed[z]
before the LORD and his forces. The
men of Judah carried off a large
amount of plunder.[a] 14 They destroyed
all the villages around Gerar, for the
terror[b] of the LORD had fallen upon
them. They plundered all these villages, since there was much booty
there. 15 They also attacked the camps
of the herdsmen and carried off droves

13:18 [f] 2Ch 14:11; 16:7; Ps 22:5
14:2 [g] 2Ch 21:12
14:3 [h] S Jdg 2:2 [i] S Ex 23:24 [j] S Ex 34:13
14:4 [k] S 1Ch 16:11
14:5 [l] S 1Ki 15:14 [m] Isa 27:9; Eze 6:4
14:6 [n] S 1Ch 22:9
14:7 [o] S 1Ch 22:9
14:8 [p] S 1Ch 21:1
14:9 [q] S 2Ch 12:3 [r] S Ge 10:8-9; 2Ch 11:8; 24:24
14:11 [s] S 1Ki 8:44; S 2Ch 13:14; 25:8 [t] Ps 60:11-12; 79:9 [u] S 2Ch 13:18 [v] S 1Sa 17:45 [w] Ps 9:19
14:12 [x] 1Ki 8:45
14:13 [y] Ge 10:19 [z] 2Sa 22:38; Ne 9:24; Ps 44:2, 19; 135:10 [a] 2Ch 15:11,18
14:14 [b] S Ge 35:5; S Dt 2:25; 11:25

[a] *3* That is, symbols of the goddess Asherah; here and elsewhere in 2 Chronicles
[b] *9* Hebrew *with an army of a thousand thousands* or *with an army of thousands upon thousands*

14:2 ASA DID WHAT WAS GOOD. During the reigns of Rehoboam (ch. 12) and Abijah (ch. 13; 1Ki 15:1–8), the true worship of God in Judah declined while idolatry increased; various places for idolatrous worship were erected (1Ki 14:21–24; 15:3). When Asa became king, he set out to purge idolatry and to urge Judah to seek God and obey his commands (vv. 3–5).

14:4 SEEK THE LORD. Essential to any reformation or revival among God's people is seeking the Lord (see 7:14, note). The writer of Chronicles uses the verb "to seek [the LORD]" eight times in chs. 14—16 (14:4,7; 15:2,4,12–13,15; 16:12) and 30 times altogether; it means to desire and pursue earnestly the Lord's presence, fellowship, kingdom and holiness (1Ch 16:11). Seeking the Lord involves: (1) turning to the Lord with the whole heart and in fervent prayer (Isa 55:6; Jer 29:12–13); (2) hungering and thirsting for righteousness and God's presence (15:2; Ps 24:3–6; Isa 51:1; cf. Mt 5:8; Jn 4:14; see Mt 5:6, note); (3) committing yourself firmly to do God's will and abandoning all actions that offend God (vv. 2–7; 7:14); (4) believing in and relying on God as your ultimate helper (Heb 13:6), confident that he "rewards those who earnestly seek him" (Heb 11:6; 2Ch 14:11; see next note).

of sheep and goats and camels. Then
they returned to Jerusalem.

Asa's Reform

15:16–19pp — 1Ki 15:13–16

15 The Spirit of God came upon[c]
Azariah son of Oded. 2He went
out to meet Asa and said to him, "Listen to me, Asa and all Judah and Benjamin. The LORD is with you[d] when you
are with him.[e] If you seek[f] him, he
will be found by you, but if you forsake
him, he will forsake you.[g] 3For a long
time Israel was without the true God,
without a priest to teach[h] and without
the law.[i] 4But in their distress they
turned to the LORD, the God of Israel,
and sought him,[j] and he was found by
them. 5In those days it was not safe to
travel about,[k] for all the inhabitants
of the lands were in great turmoil.
6One nation was being crushed by another and one city by another,[l] because God was troubling them with every kind of distress. 7But as for you, be
strong[m] and do not give up, for your
work will be rewarded."[n]
8When Asa heard these words and
the prophecy of Azariah son of[c] Oded
the prophet, he took courage. He removed the detestable idols[o] from the
whole land of Judah and Benjamin and
from the towns he had captured[p] in
the hills of Ephraim. He repaired the
altar[q] of the LORD that was in front of
the portico of the LORD's temple.
9Then he assembled all Judah and
Benjamin and the people from Ephraim, Manasseh and Simeon who had
settled among them, for large numbers[r] had come over to him from Israel when they saw that the LORD his God
was with him.
10They assembled at Jerusalem in
the third month[s] of the fifteenth year
of Asa's reign. 11At that time they sacrificed to the LORD seven hundred head
of cattle and seven thousand sheep and
goats from the plunder[t] they had
brought back. 12They entered into a
covenant[u] to seek the LORD,[v] the God
of their fathers, with all their heart and
soul. 13All who would not seek the
LORD, the God of Israel, were to be put
to death,[w] whether small or great,
man or woman. 14They took an oath to
the LORD with loud acclamation, with
shouting and with trumpets and horns.
15All Judah rejoiced about the oath because they had sworn it wholeheartedly. They sought God[x] eagerly, and he
was found by them. So the LORD gave
them rest[y] on every side.
16King Asa also deposed his grandmother Maacah[z] from her position as
queen mother,[a] because she had
made a repulsive Asherah pole.[b] Asa
cut the pole down, broke it up and
burned it in the Kidron Valley.[c] 17Al-
though he did not remove the high
places from Israel, Asa's heart was fully committed ⌞to the LORD⌟ all his life.
18He brought into the temple of God
the silver and gold and the articles that
he and his father had dedicated.[d]
19There was no more war until the
thirty-fifth year of Asa's reign.

Asa's Last Years

16:1–6pp — 1Ki 15:17–22
16:11–17:1pp — 1Ki 15:23–24

16 In the thirty-sixth year of Asa's
reign Baasha[e] king of Israel
went up against Judah and fortified Ramah to prevent anyone from leaving or
entering the territory of Asa king of Judah.

15:1 c S Nu 11:25, 26
15:2 d 2Ch 20:17 e Jas 4:8 f 2Ch 7:14; Ps 78:34; Isa 45:19; 55:6; Jer 29:13; Hos 3:5 g S Dt 31:17; S 1Ch 28:9
15:3 h S Lev 10:11 i La 2:9; Am 8:11
15:4 j S Dt 4:29
15:5 k S Jdg 5:6; 19:20; Zec 8:10
15:6 l Isa 19:2; Mt 24:7; Mk 13:8; Lk 21:10
15:7 m Jos 1:7,9 n 1Sa 24:19; Ps 18:20; 58:11; Pr 14:14; Jer 31:16
15:8 o 1Ki 15:12 p 2Ch 17:2 q S 1Ki 8:64; S 2Ch 8:12
15:9 r 2Ch 11:16-17
15:10 s S Lev 23:15-21
15:11 t S 2Ch 14:13
15:12 u S 2Ki 11:17 v S 1Ch 16:11
15:13 w S Ex 22:20; Dt 13:9-16
15:15 x Dt 4:29 y S 1Ch 22:9
15:16 z 2Ch 13:2 a S 1Ki 2:19 b S Ex 34:13 c S 2Sa 15:23
15:18 d S 2Ch 14:13
16:1 e 2Ki 9:9; Jer 41:9

c 8 Vulgate and Syriac (see also Septuagint and verse 1); Hebrew does not have *Azariah son of.*

15:2 IF YOU SEEK HIM. Seeking the Lord faithfully (see previous note) has wonderful results: (1) Those who seek the Lord will experience the peace of God (14:6–7); this means not merely the absence of conflict, but the experience of forgiveness, a clear conscience (Ac 24:16; 1Ti 3:9), and a sense of well-being arising from a right relationship with God (cf. Isa 26:3; Ac 10:36; Ro 5:1; Gal 5:22; see Ro 8:1, note; see article on THE PEACE OF GOD, p. 1134).

(2) Those who seek the Lord will receive mercy, grace and help in time of need (see Heb 4:16, note; cf. 2Ch 14:11–15).

(3) Those who seek the Lord will experience God's presence (vv. 1–4). God promises that those who earnestly seek him will find him. Under the new covenant the presence of God through the Holy Spirit brings strength and comfort to believers, leading them into truth, righteousness and power (see Jn 14:16–26; 15:26–27; Ac 2:4; Ro 8:5–16; Gal 4:6).

(4) Those who seek the Lord will be able to stand firm against their enemies (14:9–15; 16:7–8). Believers will have great strength to wage effective warfare against Satan and his spiritual forces (cf. Eph 6:10–18; see Mt 4:10, note).

15:17 ASA'S HEART WAS FULLY COMMITTED . . . ALL HIS LIFE. Asa's full commitment is seen in his rejection of idolatry, not necessarily in his conduct in all matters (see next note).

2Asa then took the silver and gold
out of the treasuries of the LORD's temple and of his own palace and sent it to
Ben-Hadad king of Aram, who was ruling in Damascus.[f] **3**"Let there be a
treaty[g] between me and you," he said,
"as there was between my father and
your father. See, I am sending you silver and gold. Now break your treaty
with Baasha king of Israel so he will
withdraw from me."
4Ben-Hadad agreed with King Asa
and sent the commanders of his forces
against the towns of Israel. They conquered Ijon, Dan, Abel Maim[d] and all
the store cities of Naphtali.[h] **5**When
Baasha heard this, he stopped building
Ramah and abandoned his work.
6Then King Asa brought all the men of
Judah, and they carried away from Ramah the stones and timber Baasha had
been using. With them he built up Geba
and Mizpah.[i]
7At that time Hanani[j] the seer
came to Asa king of Judah and said to
him: "Because you relied[k] on the king
of Aram and not on the LORD your God,
the army of the king of Aram has escaped from your hand. **8**Were not the
Cushites[e][l] and Libyans a mighty
army with great numbers[m] of chariots
and horsemen[f]? Yet when you relied
on the LORD, he delivered[n] them into
your hand. **9**For the eyes[o] of the LORD
range throughout the earth to
strengthen those whose hearts are fully committed to him. You have done a
foolish[p] thing, and from now on you
will be at war.[q]"
10Asa was angry with the seer because of this; he was so enraged that
he put him in prison.[r] At the same
time Asa brutally oppressed some of
the people.
11The events of Asa's reign, from beginning to end, are written in the book
of the kings of Judah and Israel. **12**In
the thirty-ninth year of his reign Asa
was afflicted[s] with a disease in his
feet. Though his disease was severe,
even in his illness he did not seek[t]
help from the LORD,[u] but only from the
physicians. **13**Then in the forty-first
year of his reign Asa died and rested
with his fathers. **14**They buried him in
the tomb that he had cut out for himself[v] in the City of David. They laid
him on a bier covered with spices and
various blended perfumes,[w] and they
made a huge fire[x] in his honor.

Jehoshaphat King of Judah

17 Jehoshaphat his son succeeded
him as king and strength-
ened[y] himself against Israel. **2**He stationed troops in all the fortified cities[z]
of Judah and put garrisons in Judah and
in the towns of Ephraim that his father
Asa had captured.[a]
3The LORD was with Jehoshaphat because in his early years he walked in
the ways his father David[b] had followed. He did not consult the Baals
4but sought[c] the God of his father and
followed his commands rather than the
practices of Israel. **5**The LORD established the kingdom under his control;
and all Judah brought gifts[d] to Jehoshaphat, so that he had great wealth and

16:2 [f] 2Ch 19:1-20:37; 22:1-9
16:3 [g] 2Ch 20:35; 25:7
16:4 [h] S 2Ki 15:29
16:6 [i] Jer 41:9
16:7 [j] 1Ki 16:1 [k] S 2Ch 13:18
16:8 [l] S Ge 10:6, 8-9; S 2Ch 12:3 [m] 2Ch 24:24 [n] 2Ch 13:16
16:9 [o] Job 24:23; Ps 33:13-15; Pr 15:3; Jer 16:17; Zec 3:9; 4:10 [p] 1Sa 13:13 [q] S 1Ki 15:6; 2Ch 19:2; 25:7; 28:16-21
16:10 [r] S 1Ki 22:27
16:12 [s] 2Ch 21:18; 26:19; Ps 103:3 [t] 2Ch 7:14 [u] Jer 17:5-6
16:14 [v] S Ge 50:5 [w] S Ge 50:2 [x] 2Ch 21:19; Jer 34:5
17:1 [y] S 1Ki 2:12
17:2 [z] S 2Ch 11:10 [a] 2Ch 15:8
17:3 [b] S 1Ki 22:43
17:4 [c] 2Ch 22:9
17:5 [d] S 1Sa 10:27

[d] *4* Also known as *Abel Beth Maacah*
[e] *8* That is, people from the upper Nile region
[f] *8* Or *charioteers*

16:7 BECAUSE YOU RELIED ... NOT ON THE LORD. Asa failed to persevere in seeking God during his later years. He is an example to all believers that it is indeed possible to fall away from faithfulness to God even after participating in a great spiritual reformation. Three evidences of his spiritual decline are given in this chapter. (1) He stopped relying on the Lord and trusted instead in human resources (vv. 7–9). (2) He rejected and persecuted the prophet of God (v. 10). An unmistakable sign of spiritual decline is the spurning of God's prophets who bring God's word of rebuke and correction (vv. 7–10; see Lk 6:23, note). (3) When physically afflicted, rather than first seeking God for discernment and deliverance, he exclusively sought the help of his physicians, who perhaps used incantations and the medical remedies of the occult (v. 12).

16:9 THE EYES OF THE LORD RANGE THROUGHOUT THE EARTH. God so values those who are devoted to him that he searches throughout the earth to mark all who love him faithfully and identify themselves with his cause (Eze 9:3–6). God does this to support and help such people in whatever dangers (see Ex 14:15–20; 2Ki 19:35), affliction (Ge 37:34; Ex 2:23–25) or trials (Ge 22:1–14) they face.

16:9 HEARTS ARE FULLY COMMITTED TO HIM. God distinguishes between those among his people whose hearts are completely his and those whose hearts are divided between him and the world. This truth is also seen in Christ's evaluation of the seven churches in Rev 2—3, where he contrasts the faithful overcomers with the lukewarm members of his churches (Rev 3:15,21; see article on CHRIST'S MESSAGE TO THE SEVEN CHURCHES, p. 2008).

honor.[e] 6His heart was devoted[f] to
the ways of the LORD; furthermore, he
removed the high places[g] and the
Asherah poles[h] from Judah.[i]
7In the third year of his reign he sent
his officials Ben-Hail, Obadiah, Zechariah, Nethanel and Micaiah to teach[j]
in the towns of Judah. 8With them were
certain Levites[k]—Shemaiah, Nethaniah, Zebadiah, Asahel, Shemiramoth,
Jehonathan, Adonijah, Tobijah and
Tob-Adonijah—and the priests Elishama and Jehoram. 9They taught
throughout Judah, taking with them
the Book of the Law[l] of the LORD; they
went around to all the towns of Judah
and taught the people.
10The fear[m] of the LORD fell on all
the kingdoms of the lands surrounding
Judah, so that they did not make war
with Jehoshaphat. 11Some Philistines
brought Jehoshaphat gifts and silver as
tribute, and the Arabs[n] brought him
flocks:[o] seven thousand seven hundred rams and seven thousand seven
hundred goats.
12Jehoshaphat became more and
more powerful; he built forts and store
cities in Judah 13and had large supplies
in the towns of Judah. He also kept experienced fighting men in Jerusalem.
14Their enrollment[p] by families was
as follows:

From Judah, commanders of units of 1,000:
Adnah the commander, with 300,000 fighting men;
15next, Jehohanan the command-
er, with 280,000;
16next, Amasiah son of Zicri, who
volunteered[q] himself for the
service of the LORD, with
200,000.
17From Benjamin:[r]
Eliada, a valiant soldier, with 200,000 men armed with bows and shields;
18next, Jehozabad, with 180,000
men armed for battle.

19These were the men who served
the king, besides those he stationed
in the fortified cities[s] throughout
Judah.[t]

17:5 [e]2Ch 18:1
17:6 [f]S 1Ki 8:61
[g]S 1Ki 15:14; 2Ch 19:3; 20:33
[h]S Ex 34:13
[i]2Ch 21:12
17:7 [j]S Lev 10:11; Dt 6:4-9; 2Ch 19:4-11; 35:3; Ne 8:7; Mal 2:7
17:8 [k]2Ch 19:8; Ne 8:7-8; Hos 4:6
17:9 [l]S Dt 28:61
17:10 [m]S Ge 35:5; S Dt 2:25
17:11 [n]S 2Ch 9:14
[o]2Ch 21:16
17:14 [p]S 2Sa 24:2
17:16 [q]S Jdg 5:9
17:17 [r]S Nu 1:36
17:19 [s]S 2Ch 11:10
[t]2Ch 25:5
18:1 [u]2Ch 17:5
[v]2Ch 19:1-3; 22:3
[w]2Ch 21:6
18:11 [x]2Ch 22:5

Micaiah Prophesies Against Ahab

18:1–27pp — 1Ki 22:1–28

18 Now Jehoshaphat had great
wealth and honor,[u] and he allied[v] himself with Ahab[w] by marriage. 2Some years later he went down
to visit Ahab in Samaria. Ahab slaughtered many sheep and cattle for him
and the people with him and urged him
to attack Ramoth Gilead. 3Ahab king
of Israel asked Jehoshaphat king of Judah, "Will you go with me against Ramoth Gilead?"
Jehoshaphat replied, "I am as you
are, and my people as your people; we
will join you in the war." 4But Jehoshaphat also said to the king of Israel,
"First seek the counsel of the LORD."
5So the king of Israel brought together the prophets—four hundred
men—and asked them, "Shall we go to
war against Ramoth Gilead, or shall I
refrain?"
"Go," they answered, "for God will
give it into the king's hand."
6But Jehoshaphat asked, "Is there
not a prophet of the LORD here whom
we can inquire of?"
7The king of Israel answered Jehoshaphat, "There is still one man
through whom we can inquire of the
LORD, but I hate him because he never
prophesies anything good about me,
but always bad. He is Micaiah son of
Imlah."
"The king should not say that," Jehoshaphat replied.
8So the king of Israel called one of
his officials and said, "Bring Micaiah
son of Imlah at once."
9Dressed in their royal robes, the
king of Israel and Jehoshaphat king of
Judah were sitting on their thrones at
the threshing floor by the entrance to
the gate of Samaria, with all the prophets prophesying before them. 10Now
Zedekiah son of Kenaanah had made
iron horns, and he declared, "This is
what the LORD says: 'With these you
will gore the Arameans until they are
destroyed.' "
11All the other prophets were prophesying the same thing. "Attack Ramoth Gilead[x] and be victorious," they

17:9 THEY TAUGHT . . . THE BOOK OF THE LAW. A spiritual revival will soon die if it is not based solidly on the Word of God and an earnest commitment to follow its teachings. This is as true under the new covenant as it was under the old. Any spiritual movement not firmly based on the original and fundamental revelation of Christ and the apostles is doomed to failure, or prone to emotionalism or humanism (see 34:30, note; Eph 2:20, note).

said, "for the LORD will give it into the
king's hand."
12The messenger who had gone to
summon Micaiah said to him, "Look,
as one man the other prophets are predicting success for the king. Let your
word agree with theirs, and speak favorably."
13But Micaiah said, "As surely as
the LORD lives, I can tell him only what
my God says."[y]
14When he arrived, the king asked
him, "Micaiah, shall we go to war
against Ramoth Gilead, or shall I refrain?"
"Attack and be victorious," he answered, "for they will be given into
your hand."
15The king said to him, "How many
times must I make you swear to tell me
nothing but the truth in the name of the
LORD?"
16Then Micaiah answered, "I saw all
Israel[z] scattered on the hills like
sheep without a shepherd,[a] and the
LORD said, 'These people have no master. Let each one go home in peace.' "
17The king of Israel said to Jehoshaphat, "Didn't I tell you that he never
prophesies anything good about me,
but only bad?"
18Micaiah continued, "Therefore
hear the word of the LORD: I saw the
LORD sitting on his throne[b] with all the
host of heaven standing on his right
and on his left. 19And the LORD said,
'Who will entice Ahab king of Israel
into attacking Ramoth Gilead and going to his death there?'
"One suggested this, and another
that. 20Finally, a spirit came forward,
stood before the LORD and said, 'I will
entice him.'
" 'By what means?' the LORD asked.
21" 'I will go and be a lying spirit[c]
in the mouths of all his prophets,' he
said.
" 'You will succeed in enticing him,'
said the LORD. 'Go and do it.'
22"So now the LORD has put a lying
spirit in the mouths of these prophets
of yours.[d] The LORD has decreed disaster for you."
23Then Zedekiah son of Kenaanah
went up and slapped[e] Micaiah in the
face. "Which way did the spirit from[g]
the LORD go when he went from me to
speak to you?" he asked.
24Micaiah replied, "You will find out
on the day you go to hide in an inner
room."
25The king of Israel then ordered,
"Take Micaiah and send him back to
Amon the ruler of the city and to Joash
the king's son, 26and say, 'This is what
the king says: Put this fellow in prison[f] and give him nothing but bread
and water until I return safely.' "
27Micaiah declared, "If you ever return safely, the LORD has not spoken
through me." Then he added, "Mark
my words, all you people!"

Ahab Killed at Ramoth Gilead

18:28–34pp — 1Ki 22:29–36

28So the king of Israel and Jehoshaphat king of Judah went up to Ramoth
Gilead. 29The king of Israel said to Jehoshaphat, "I will enter the battle in
disguise, but you wear your royal
robes." So the king of Israel disguised[g] himself and went into battle.
30Now the king of Aram had ordered
his chariot commanders, "Do not fight
with anyone, small or great, except the
king of Israel." 31When the chariot
commanders saw Jehoshaphat, they
thought, "This is the king of Israel." So
they turned to attack him, but Jehoshaphat cried out,[h] and the LORD helped
him. God drew them away from him,
32for when the chariot commanders
saw that he was not the king of Israel,
they stopped pursuing him.
33But someone drew his bow at random and hit the king of Israel between
the sections of his armor. The king told
the chariot driver, "Wheel around and
get me out of the fighting. I've been
wounded." 34All day long the battle
raged, and the king of Israel propped
himself up in his chariot facing the Arameans until evening. Then at sunset
he died.[i]

19 When Jehoshaphat king of Judah returned safely to his palace in Jerusalem, 2Jehu[j] the seer, the
son of Hanani, went out to meet him

18:13 [y] Nu 22:18, 20,35
18:16 [z] S 1Ch 9:1 [a] S Nu 27:17
18:18 [b] Da 7:9
18:21 [c] 1Ch 21:1; Job 1:6; Zec 3:1; Jn 8:44
18:22 [d] Job 12:16; Eze 14:9
18:23 [e] Ac 23:2
18:26 [f] Heb 11:36
18:29 [g] S 1Sa 28:8
18:31 [h] S 2Ch 13:14
18:34 [i] 2Ch 22:5
19:2 [j] S 1Ki 16:1

[g] 23 Or *Spirit of*

18:14 GO TO WAR. See 1Ki 22:15, note.
18:22 A LYING SPIRIT. See 1Ki 22:23, note.
19:2 SHOULD YOU HELP THE WICKED. Jehoshaphat is rebuked for associating with Ahab and helping this enemy of God (cf. ch. 18). Believers should not associate with the ungodly if in that relationship the cause of unrighteousness is advanced, our commitment to God is jeopardized or

and said to the king, "Should you help
the wicked[k] and love[h] those who
hate the LORD?[l] Because of this, the
wrath[m] of the LORD is upon you. **3**There
is, however, some good[n] in you, for
you have rid the land of the Asherah
poles[o] and have set your heart on
seeking God.[p]"

Jehoshaphat Appoints Judges

4Jehoshaphat lived in Jerusalem,
and he went out again among the people from Beersheba to the hill country
of Ephraim and turned them back to
the LORD, the God of their fathers. **5**He
appointed judges[q] in the land, in each
of the fortified cities of Judah. **6**He told
them, "Consider carefully what you
do,[r] because you are not judging for
man[s] but for the LORD, who is with you
whenever you give a verdict. **7**Now let
the fear of the LORD be upon you. Judge
carefully, for with the LORD our God
there is no injustice[t] or partiality[u] or
bribery."
8In Jerusalem also, Jehoshaphat
appointed some of the Levites,[v]
priests[w] and heads of Israelite families to administer[x] the law of the LORD
and to settle disputes. And they lived
in Jerusalem. **9**He gave them these orders: "You must serve faithfully and
wholeheartedly in the fear of the LORD.
10In every case that comes before you
from your fellow countrymen who live
in the cities—whether bloodshed or
other concerns of the law, commands,
decrees or ordinances—you are to
warn them not to sin against the
LORD;[y] otherwise his wrath will come
on you and your brothers. Do this, and
you will not sin.
11"Amariah the chief priest will be
over you in any matter concerning the
LORD, and Zebadiah son of Ishmael, the
leader of the tribe of Judah, will be over

19:2 [k]S 2Ch 16:2-9 [l]Ps 139:21-22 [m]2Ch 24:18; 32:25; Ps 7:11
19:3 [n]S 1Ki 14:13 [o]S 2Ch 17:6 [p]S 2Ch 18:1; 20:35; 25:7
19:5 [q]S Ge 47:6; S Ex 18:26
19:6 [r]S Lev 19:15 [s]Dt 16:18-20; 17:8-13
19:7 [t]S Ge 18:25; S Job 8:3 [u]S Ex 18:16; Dt 10:17; Job 13:10; 32:21; 34:19
19:8 [v]S 1Ch 23:4 [w]Eze 44:24 [x]2Ch 17:8-9
19:10 [y]Dt 17:8-13
19:11 [z]S 1Ch 28:20
20:1 [a]Ps 83:6 [b]S 1Ch 4:41
20:2 [c]2Ch 24:24 [d]S Ge 14:7 [e]S 1Sa 23:29; SS 1:14
20:3 [f]1Sa 7:6; Ezr 8:23; Ne 1:4; Est 4:16; Isa 58:6; Jer 36:9; Da 9:3; Joel 1:14; 2:15; Jnh 3:5,7
20:4 [g]Jer 36:6
20:6 [h]Mt 6:9 [i]Dt 4:39 [j]1Ch 29:11-12 [k]2Ch 25:8; Job 25:2; 41:10; 42:2; Isa 14:27; Jer 32:27; 49:19
20:7 [l]S Ge 12:7 [m]Isa 41:8; Jas 2:23
20:8 [n]2Ch 6:20

you in any matter concerning the king,
and the Levites will serve as officials
before you. Act with courage,[z] and
may the LORD be with those who do
well."

Jehoshaphat Defeats Moab and Ammon

20 After this, the Moabites[a] and
Ammonites with some of the
Meunites[i b] came to make war on Jehoshaphat.
2Some men came and told Jehoshaphat, "A vast army[c] is coming against
you from Edom,[j] from the other
side of the Sea.[k] It is already in
Hazazon Tamar[d]" (that is, En Gedi).[e]
3Alarmed, Jehoshaphat resolved to inquire of the LORD, and he proclaimed a
fast[f] for all Judah. **4**The people of Judah[g] came together to seek help from
the LORD; indeed, they came from every
town in Judah to seek him.
5Then Jehoshaphat stood up in the
assembly of Judah and Jerusalem at
the temple of the LORD in the front of
the new courtyard **6**and said:

"O LORD, God of our fathers,[h]
are you not the God who is in
heaven?[i] You rule over all the
kingdoms[j] of the nations. Power
and might are in your hand, and
no one can withstand you.[k]
7O our God, did you not drive out
the inhabitants of this land[l] before your people Israel and give it
forever to the descendants of
Abraham your friend?[m] **8**They
have lived in it and have built in
it a sanctuary[n] for your Name,
saying, **9**'If calamity comes upon

[h] *2* Or *and make alliances with* [i] *1* Some Septuagint manuscripts; Hebrew *Ammonites*
[j] *2* One Hebrew manuscript; most Hebrew manuscripts, Septuagint and Vulgate *Aram*
[k] *2* That is, the Dead Sea

the truth of God's Word is compromised.

20:3 ALARMED, JEHOSHAPHAT RESOLVED. Faced with the greatest crisis of his life (vv. 1–2), Jehoshaphat met a seemingly impossible circumstance in an exemplary manner. He began to seek the Lord through fasting (v. 3), gathered together others to pray and fast (v. 4), confessed his helplessness (v. 12), obeyed the Holy Spirit (vv. 14–18), put his trust in the Lord and his word (v. 20), and gave thanks to the Lord (vv. 21–22).

20:3 PROCLAIMED A FAST. Seeking the Lord (see 15:2, note) can be intensified through fasting. Fasting should regularly accompany prayer and the believer's desire that God's will be done (see Ezr 8:23; Ne 9:1–2; Da 9:3; see Mt 4:2; 6:16, notes).

20:6 O LORD, GOD OF OUR FATHERS. Jehoshaphat based his prayer and his confidence in God on five principal truths. (1) God has power over all people and situations (vv. 6–7); (2) God has been faithful to his people in the past and present (vv. 7–9); (3) God's people are helpless without him (v. 12); (4) God's promises are a sure foundation for faith (vv. 14–17,20); and (5) God's active presence among his people means deliverance and victory (v. 17).

us, whether the sword of judgment, or plague or famine,[o] we
will stand in your presence before
this temple that bears your Name
and will cry out to you in our distress, and you will hear us and
save us.'
10"But now here are men from
Ammon, Moab and Mount Seir,
whose territory you would not allow Israel to invade when they
came from Egypt;[p] so they
turned away from them and did
not destroy them. 11See how they
are repaying us by coming to drive
us out of the possession[q] you
gave us as an inheritance.
12O our God, will you not judge
them?[r] For we have no power to
face this vast army that is attacking us. We do not know what to
do, but our eyes are upon you.[s]"

13All the men of Judah, with their
wives and children and little ones,
stood there before the LORD.
14Then the Spirit[t] of the LORD came
upon Jahaziel son of Zechariah, the son
of Benaiah, the son of Jeiel, the son of
Mattaniah,[u] a Levite and descendant
of Asaph, as he stood in the assembly.
15He said: "Listen, King Jehoshaphat and all who live in Judah and Jerusalem! This is what the LORD says to
you: 'Do not be afraid or discouraged[v]
because of this vast army. For the battle[w] is not yours, but God's. 16Tomor-
row march down against them. They
will be climbing up by the Pass of Ziz,
and you will find them at the end of the
gorge in the Desert of Jeruel. 17You
will not have to fight this battle. Take
up your positions; stand firm and see[x]
the deliverance the LORD will give you,
O Judah and Jerusalem. Do not be
afraid; do not be discouraged. Go out to
face them tomorrow, and the LORD will
be with you.' "
18Jehoshaphat bowed[y] with his
face to the ground, and all the people
of Judah and Jerusalem fell down in
worship before the LORD. 19Then some
Levites from the Kohathites and Korahites stood up and praised the LORD,
the God of Israel, with very loud voice.
20Early in the morning they left for

20:9 [o] S 2Ch 6:28
20:10 [p] Nu 20:14-21; Dt 2:4-6,9,18-19
20:11 [q] Ps 83:1-12
20:12 [r] Jdg 11:27 [s] Ps 25:15; Isa 30:15; 45:22; Mic 7:7
20:14 [t] S 1Ch 12:18 [u] S 1Ch 9:15
20:15 [v] 2Ch 32:7 [w] S 1Sa 17:47; Ps 91:8
20:17 [x] S Ex 14:13
20:18 [y] S Ge 24:26; 2Ch 29:29
20:20 [z] Isa 7:9 [a] S Ge 39:3; Pr 16:3
20:21 [b] S 1Ch 16:29 [c] S 2Ch 5:13; Ps 136:1
20:22 [d] S 2Ch 13:13
20:23 [e] S Ge 19:38 [f] 2Ch 21:8 [g] S Jdg 7:22; 1Sa 14:20; Eze 38:21
20:29 [h] S Ge 35:5; S Dt 2:25 [i] S Ex 14:14

the Desert of Tekoa. As they set out,
Jehoshaphat stood and said, "Listen to
me, Judah and people of Jerusalem!
Have faith[z] in the LORD your God and
you will be upheld; have faith in his
prophets and you will be successful.[a]"
21After consulting the people, Jehoshaphat appointed men to sing to the LORD
and to praise him for the splendor of
his[1] holiness[b] as they went out at the
head of the army, saying:

"Give thanks to the LORD,
for his love endures forever."[c]

22As they began to sing and praise,
the LORD set ambushes[d] against the
men of Ammon and Moab and Mount
Seir who were invading Judah, and
they were defeated. 23The men of Ammon[e] and Moab rose up against the
men from Mount Seir[f] to destroy and
annihilate them. After they finished
slaughtering the men from Seir, they
helped to destroy one another.[g]
24When the men of Judah came to
the place that overlooks the desert and
looked toward the vast army, they saw
only dead bodies lying on the ground; 2Ch 32:20-23
no one had escaped. 25So Jehoshaphat
and his men went to carry off their
plunder, and they found among them a
great amount of equipment and clothing[m] and also articles of value—more
than they could take away. There was
so much plunder that it took three days
to collect it. 26On the fourth day they
assembled in the Valley of Beracah,
where they praised the LORD. This is
why it is called the Valley of Beracah[n]
to this day.
27Then, led by Jehoshaphat, all the
men of Judah and Jerusalem returned
joyfully to Jerusalem, for the LORD had
given them cause to rejoice over their
enemies. 28They entered Jerusalem
and went to the temple of the LORD with
harps and lutes and trumpets.
29The fear[h] of God came upon all
the kingdoms of the countries when
they heard how the LORD had fought[i]
against the enemies of Israel. 30And

[1] 21 Or *him with the splendor of* [m] 25 Some Hebrew manuscripts and Vulgate; most Hebrew manuscripts *corpses* [n] 26 *Beracah* means *praise.*

20:15 THE BATTLE IS NOT YOURS, BUT GOD'S. Here the strength and power of faith are demonstrated by praising God in song in the face of battle (vv. 18–19). Similarly, Paul exhorts believers to "be strong in the Lord and in his mighty power" as they fight against the powers and spiritual forces of Satan (Eph 6:10).

the kingdom of Jehoshaphat was at
peace, for his God had given him rest[j]
on every side.

The End of Jehoshaphat's Reign

20:31–21:1pp — 1Ki 22:41–50

31 So Jehoshaphat reigned over Judah. He was thirty-five years old when
he became king of Judah, and he
reigned in Jerusalem twenty-five years.
His mother's name was Azubah daughter of Shilhi. 32 He walked in the ways
of his father Asa and did not stray from
them; he did what was right in the eyes
of the LORD. 33 The high places,[k] however, were not removed, and the people
still had not set their hearts on the God
of their fathers.

34 The other events of Jehoshaphat's
reign, from beginning to end, are written in the annals of Jehu[l] son of Hanani, which are recorded in the book of
the kings of Israel.

35 Later, Jehoshaphat king of Judah
made an alliance[m] with Ahaziah king
of Israel, who was guilty of wickedness.[n] 36 He agreed with him to construct a fleet of trading ships.[o] After
these were built at Ezion Geber, 37 Eliezer son of Dodavahu of Mareshah
prophesied against Jehoshaphat, saying, "Because you have made an alliance with Ahaziah, the LORD will destroy what you have made." The
ships[o] were wrecked and were not
able to set sail to trade.[p]

21 Then Jehoshaphat rested with
his fathers and was buried with
them in the City of David. And Jehoram[p] his son succeeded him as king.
2 Jehoram's brothers, the sons of Jehoshaphat, were Azariah, Jehiel, Zechariah, Azariahu, Michael and Shephatiah. All these were sons of Jehoshaphat
king of Israel.[q] 3 Their father had giv-
en them many gifts[q] of silver and gold
and articles of value, as well as fortified cities[r] in Judah, but he had given
the kingdom to Jehoram because he
was his firstborn son.

Jehoram King of Judah

21:5–10,20pp — 2Ki 8:16–24

4 When Jehoram established[s] himself firmly over his father's kingdom,
he put all his brothers[t] to the sword
along with some of the princes of Israel. 5 Jehoram was thirty-two years old
when he became king, and he reigned
in Jerusalem eight years. 6 He walked
in the ways of the kings of Israel,[u] as
the house of Ahab had done, for he
married a daughter of Ahab.[v] He did
evil in the eyes of the LORD. 7 Nevertheless, because of the covenant the LORD
had made with David,[w] the LORD was
not willing to destroy the house of David.[x] He had promised to maintain a
lamp[y] for him and his descendants
forever.

8 In the time of Jehoram, Edom[z] rebelled against Judah and set up its own
king. 9 So Jehoram went there with his
officers and all his chariots. The Edomites surrounded him and his chariot
commanders, but he rose up and broke
through by night. 10 To this day Edom
has been in rebellion against Judah.

Libnah[a] revolted at the same time,
because Jehoram had forsaken the
LORD, the God of his fathers. 11 He had
also built high places on the hills of
Judah and had caused the people of Jerusalem to prostitute themselves and
had led Judah astray.

12 Jehoram received a letter from Elijah[b] the prophet, which said:

"This is what the LORD, the God of
your father[c] David, says: 'You
have not walked in the ways of
your father Jehoshaphat or of
Asa[d] king of Judah. 13 But you
have walked in the ways of the
kings of Israel, and you have led
Judah and the people of Jerusalem
to prostitute themselves, just as
the house of Ahab did.[e] You have
also murdered your own brothers,
members of your father's house,
men who were better[f] than you.
14 So now the LORD is about to
strike your people, your sons,
your wives and everything that is
yours, with a heavy blow. 15 You
yourself will be very ill with a lingering disease[g] of the bowels,

20:30 [j] S 1Ch 22:9 **20:33** [k] S 2Ch 17:6 **20:34** [l] S 1Ki 16:1 **20:35** [m] S 2Ch 16:3 [n] S 2Ch 19:1-3 **20:37** [o] S 1Ki 9:26 **21:1** [p] S 1Ch 3:11 **21:3** [q] 2Ch 11:23 [r] S 2Ch 11:10 **21:4** [s] S 1Ki 2:12 [t] Jdg 9:5 **21:6** [u] 1Ki 12:28-30 [v] 2Ch 18:1; 22:3 **21:7** [w] S 2Sa 7:13 [x] S 2Sa 7:15; 2Ch 23:3 [y] S 2Sa 21:17 **21:8** [z] 2Ch 20:22-23 **21:10** [a] S Nu 33:20 **21:12** [b] 2Ki 1:16-17 [c] 2Ch 17:3-6 [d] 2Ch 14:2 **21:13** [e] 1Ki 16:29-33 [f] 1Ki 2:32 **21:15** [g] S Nu 12:10

o 36 Hebrew *of ships that could go to Tarshish*
p 37 Hebrew *sail for Tarshish* q 2 That is, Judah, as frequently in 2 Chronicles

20:33 HIGH PLACES. These were elevated areas where idolatrous worship took place. God wanted his people to destroy these places completely, lest they be led into such worship (Nu 33:52). The attraction that God's people had for these places indicated that they lacked a firm and total commitment to the Lord God.

until the disease causes your bowels to come out.' "

16The LORD aroused against Jehoram
the hostility of the Philistines and of
the Arabs[h] who lived near the Cushites. 17They attacked Judah, invaded it
and carried off all the goods found in
the king's palace, together with his
sons and wives. Not a son was left to
him except Ahaziah,[r] the youngest.[i]
18After all this, the LORD afflicted Jehoram with an incurable disease of the
bowels. 19In the course of time, at the
end of the second year, his bowels
came out because of the disease, and
he died in great pain. His people made
no fire in his honor,[j] as they had for
his fathers.
20Jehoram was thirty-two years old
when he became king, and he reigned
in Jerusalem eight years. He passed
away, to no one's regret, and was buried[k] in the City of David, but not in the
tombs of the kings.

Ahaziah King of Judah

22:1–6pp — 2Ki 8:25–29
22:7–9pp — 2Ki 9:21–29

22 The people[l] of Jerusalem[m]
made Ahaziah, Jehoram's youngest son, king in his place, since the
raiders,[n] who came with the Arabs
into the camp, had killed all the older
sons. So Ahaziah son of Jehoram king
of Judah began to reign.
2Ahaziah was twenty-two[s] years
old when he became king, and he
reigned in Jerusalem one year. His
mother's name was Athaliah, a granddaughter of Omri.
3He too walked[o] in the ways of the
house of Ahab,[p] for his mother encouraged him in doing wrong. 4He did
evil in the eyes of the LORD, as the
house of Ahab had done, for after his
father's death they became his advisers, to his undoing. 5He also followed
their counsel when he went with Joram[t] son of Ahab king of Israel to war
against Hazael king of Aram at Ramoth Gilead.[q] The Arameans wounded Joram; 6so he returned to Jezreel to
recover from the wounds they had inflicted on him at Ramoth[u] in his battle
with Hazael[r] king of Aram.
Then Ahaziah[v] son of Jehoram king
of Judah went down to Jezreel to see
Joram son of Ahab because he had been
wounded.
7Through Ahaziah's[s] visit to Joram, God brought about Ahaziah's
downfall. When Ahaziah arrived, he
went out with Joram to meet Jehu son
of Nimshi, whom the LORD had anointed
to destroy the house of Ahab. 8While
Jehu was executing judgment on the
house of Ahab,[t] he found the princes
of Judah and the sons of Ahaziah's relatives, who had been attending Ahaziah, and he killed them. 9He then went
in search of Ahaziah, and his men captured him while he was hiding[u] in Samaria. He was brought to Jehu and put
to death. They buried him, for they
said, "He was a son of Jehoshaphat,
who sought[v] the LORD with all his
heart." So there was no one in the
house of Ahaziah powerful enough to
retain the kingdom.

Athaliah and Joash

22:10–23:21pp — 2Ki 11:1–21

10When Athaliah the mother of Ahaziah saw that her son was dead, she
proceeded to destroy the whole royal
family of the house of Judah. 11But Jehosheba,[w] the daughter of King Jehoram, took Joash son of Ahaziah and
stole him away from among the royal
princes who were about to be murdered
and put him and his nurse in a bedroom. Because Jehosheba,[w] the
daughter of King Jehoram and wife of
the priest Jehoiada, was Ahaziah's sister, she hid the child from Athaliah so
she could not kill him. 12He remained
hidden with them at the temple of God
for six years while Athaliah ruled the
land.

23 In the seventh year Jehoiada
showed his strength. He made
a covenant with the commanders of
units of a hundred: Azariah son of Jero-

21:16 [h]2Ch 17:10-11; 22:1; 26:7
21:17 [i]2Ki 12:18; 2Ch 22:1; Joel 3:5
21:19 [j]S 2Ch 16:14
21:20 [k]2Ch 24:25; 28:27; 33:20
22:1 [l]2Ch 33:25; 36:1 [m]2Ch 23:20-21; 26:1 [n]S 2Ch 21:16-17
22:3 [o]S 2Ch 18:1 [p]S 2Ch 21:6
22:5 [q]2Ch 18:11, 34
22:6 [r]1Ki 19:15; 2Ki 8:13-15
22:7 [s]2Ki 9:16
22:8 [t]S 2Ki 10:13
22:9 [u]S Jdg 9:5 [v]2Ch 17:4

[r]17 Hebrew *Jehoahaz,* a variant of *Ahaziah*
[s]2 Some Septuagint manuscripts and Syriac (see also 2 Kings 8:26); Hebrew *forty-two*
[t]5 Hebrew *Jehoram,* a variant of *Joram*; also in verses 6 and 7
[u]6 Hebrew *Ramah,* a variant of *Ramoth*
[v]6 Some Hebrew manuscripts, Septuagint, Vulgate and Syriac (see also 2 Kings 8:29); most Hebrew manuscripts *Azariah*
[w]11 Hebrew *Jehoshabeath,* a variant of *Jehosheba*

22:7 JEHU . . . WHOM THE LORD HAD ANOINTED. See 2Ki 9:8; 10:28, notes.
22:10 ATHALIAH. See 2Ki 11:1, note.
23:1 JEHOIADA. See 2Ki 11:4, note on Jehoiada's overthrow of Athaliah (23:10–15) and the placing of Joash on the throne.

ham, Ishmael son of Jehohanan, Azariah son of Obed, Maaseiah son of Adaiah, and Elishaphat son of Zicri. 2They
went throughout Judah and gathered
the Levites[w] and the heads of Israelite
families from all the towns. When they
came to Jerusalem, 3the whole assembly made a covenant[x] with the king at
the temple of God.

Jehoiada said to them, "The king's
son shall reign, as the LORD promised
concerning the descendants of David.[y] 4Now this is what you are to do:
A third of you priests and Levites who
are going on duty on the Sabbath are
to keep watch at the doors, 5a third of
you at the royal palace and a third at
the Foundation Gate, and all the other
men are to be in the courtyards of the
temple of the LORD. 6No one is to enter
the temple of the LORD except the
priests and Levites on duty; they may
enter because they are consecrated,
but all the other men are to guard[z]
what the LORD has assigned to them.[x]
7The Levites are to station themselves
around the king, each man with his
weapons in his hand. Anyone who enters the temple must be put to death.
Stay close to the king wherever he
goes."

8The Levites and all the men of Judah did just as Jehoiada the priest ordered.[a] Each one took his men—
those who were going on duty on the
Sabbath and those who were going off
duty—for Jehoiada the priest had not
released any of the divisions.[b] 9Then
he gave the commanders of units of a
hundred the spears and the large and
small shields that had belonged to
King David and that were in the temple
of God. 10He stationed all the men,
each with his weapon in his hand,
around the king—near the altar and
the temple, from the south side to the
north side of the temple.

11Jehoiada and his sons brought out
the king's son and put the crown on
him; they presented him with a copy[c]
of the covenant and proclaimed him
king. They anointed him and shouted,
"Long live the king!"

12When Athaliah heard the noise of
the people running and cheering the
king, she went to them at the temple of
the LORD. 13She looked, and there was
the king,[d] standing by his pillar[e] at
the entrance. The officers and the
trumpeters were beside the king, and
all the people of the land were rejoicing
and blowing trumpets, and singers
with musical instruments were leading
the praises. Then Athaliah tore her
robes and shouted, "Treason! Treason!"

14Jehoiada the priest sent out the
commanders of units of a hundred, who
were in charge of the troops, and said
to them: "Bring her out between the
ranks[y] and put to the sword anyone
who follows her." For the priest had
said, "Do not put her to death at the
temple of the LORD." 15So they seized
her as she reached the entrance of the
Horse Gate[f] on the palace grounds,
and there they put her to death.

16Jehoiada then made a covenant[g]
that he and the people and the king[z]
would be the LORD's people. 17All the
people went to the temple of Baal and
tore it down. They smashed the altars
and idols and killed[h] Mattan the
priest of Baal in front of the altars.

18Then Jehoiada placed the oversight of the temple of the LORD in the
hands of the priests, who were Levites,[i] to whom David had made as-
signments in the temple,[j] to present
the burnt offerings of the LORD as written in the Law of Moses, with rejoicing
and singing, as David had ordered.
19He also stationed doorkeepers[k] at
the gates of the LORD's temple so that
no one who was in any way unclean
might enter.

20He took with him the commanders
of hundreds, the nobles, the rulers of
the people and all the people of the
land and brought the king down from
the temple of the LORD. They went into
the palace through the Upper Gate[l]
and seated the king on the royal
throne, 21and all the people of the land
rejoiced. And the city was quiet, because Athaliah had been slain with the
sword.[m]

Joash Repairs the Temple

24:1–14pp — 2Ki 12:1–16
24:23–27pp — 2Ki 12:17–21

24 Joash was seven years old
when he became king, and he
reigned in Jerusalem forty years. His
mother's name was Zibiah; she was

23:2 [w]S Nu 35:2-5
23:3 [x]S 2Ki 11:17 [y]S 2Sa 7:12; S 1Ki 2:4; S 2Ch 6:16; S 7:18; S 21:7
23:6 [z]Zec 3:7
23:8 [a]2Ki 11:9 [b]S 1Ch 24:1
23:11 [c]Dt 17:18
23:13 [d]1Ki 1:41 [e]S 1Ki 7:15
23:15 [f]Jer 31:40
23:16 [g]2Ch 29:10; 34:31; Ne 9:38
23:17 [h]Dt 13:6-9
23:18 [i]S 1Ch 23:28-32 [j]S 1Ch 23:6; S 25:6
23:19 [k]1Ch 9:22
23:20 [l]S 2Ki 15:35
23:21 [m]S 2Ch 22:1

[x]6 Or *to observe the LORD's command* ⌊*not to enter*⌋ [y]14 Or *out from the precincts*
[z]16 Or *covenant between* ⌊*the LORD*⌋ *and the people and the king that they* (see 2 Kings 11:17)

from Beersheba. 2Joash did what was right in the eyes of the LORD[n] all the years of Jehoiada the priest. 3Jehoiada chose two wives for him, and he had sons and daughters.

4Some time later Joash decided to restore the temple of the LORD. 5He called together the priests and Levites and said to them, "Go to the towns of Judah and collect the money[o] due annually from all Israel,[p] to repair the temple of your God. Do it now." But the Levites[q] did not act at once.

6Therefore the king summoned Jehoiada the chief priest and said to him, "Why haven't you required the Levites to bring in from Judah and Jerusalem the tax imposed by Moses the servant of the LORD and by the assembly of Israel for the Tent of the Testimony?"[r]

7Now the sons of that wicked woman Athaliah had broken into the temple of God and had used even its sacred objects for the Baals.

8At the king's command, a chest was made and placed outside, at the gate of the temple of the LORD. 9A proclamation was then issued in Judah and Jerusalem that they should bring to the LORD the tax that Moses the servant of God had required of Israel in the desert. 10All the officials and all the people brought their contributions gladly,[s] dropping them into the chest until it was full. 11Whenever the chest was brought in by the Levites to the king's officials and they saw that there was a large amount of money, the royal secretary and the officer of the chief priest would come and empty the chest and carry it back to its place. They did this regularly and collected a great amount of money. 12The king and Jehoiada gave it to the men who carried out the work required for the temple of the LORD. They hired[t] masons and carpenters to restore the LORD's temple, and also workers in iron and bronze to repair the temple.

13The men in charge of the work were diligent, and the repairs progressed under them. They rebuilt the temple of God according to its original design and reinforced it. 14When they had finished, they brought the rest of the money to the king and Jehoiada, and with it were made articles for the LORD's temple: articles for the service and for the burnt offerings, and also dishes and other objects of gold and silver. As long as Jehoiada lived, burnt offerings were presented continually in the temple of the LORD.

15Now Jehoiada was old and full of years, and he died at the age of a hundred and thirty. 16He was buried with the kings in the City of David, because of the good he had done in Israel for God and his temple.

The Wickedness of Joash

17After the death of Jehoiada, the officials of Judah came and paid homage to the king, and he listened to them. 18They abandoned[u] the temple of the LORD, the God of their fathers, and worshiped Asherah poles and idols.[v] Because of their guilt, God's anger[w] came upon Judah and Jerusalem. 19Although the LORD sent prophets to the people to bring them back to him, and though they testified against them, they would not listen.[x]

20Then the Spirit[y] of God came

24:2 [n] 2Ch 25:2; 26:5
24:5 [o] S Ex 30:16; Ne 10:32-33; Mt 17:24 [p] 1Ch 11:1 [q] S 1Ch 26:20
24:6 [r] S Ex 38:21
24:10 [s] S Ex 25:2; S 1Ch 29:3,6,9
24:12 [t] 2Ch 34:11
24:18 [u] S Jos 24:20; S 2Ch 7:19 [v] S Ex 34:13; 2Ch 33:3; Jer 17:2 [w] S 2Ch 19:2
24:19 [x] S Nu 11:29; Jer 7:25; Zec 1:4
24:20 [y] S Jdg 3:10; S 1Ch 12:18

24:14 BURNT OFFERINGS WERE PRESENTED. Offerings to God were first made after the sin of Adam and Eve (Ge 4:3–4). Thereafter various types of offerings were established so that God's people might understand the seriousness of sin and the significance of worshiping God (see Lev 1:2, note). In addition to the burnt offerings mentioned here (cf. Lev 1:3–17), God required sin offerings (Lev 4:3–21), guilt offerings (Lev 5:14—6:7) and fellowship offerings (Lev 3:1–17). The important element in making an offering to God was a sincere heart that brought before him the best that one possessed (see Lev 22:21). In the book of Malachi God rebuked the people because they were offering crippled or diseased animals (Mal 1:6–14).

24:17 AFTER THE DEATH OF JEHOIADA. See 2Ki 12:2, note.

24:19 SENT PROPHETS ... THEY WOULD NOT LISTEN. Under the old covenant, God sent prophets to urge his people to be faithful to their God and to live according to the covenant stipulations. Under the new covenant, prophets and their messages remain essential to the life of the church. To ignore or reject God's true prophets will result in spiritual death for the church (see article on THE MINISTRY GIFTS OF THE CHURCH, p. 1830).

24:20 THE SPIRIT OF GOD CAME UPON ZECHARIAH. The Holy Spirit came upon (lit. "clothed") Zechariah, and he exposed and rebuked the sin of Joash and the officials of Judah. The work of conviction in regard to sin is a primary function of the Holy Spirit (Jn 16:8). Often through using a godly spokesman such as Zechariah, the Spirit uncovers guilt in order to lead people to repentance.

upon Zechariah[z] son of Jehoiada the
priest. He stood before the people and
said, "This is what God says: 'Why do
you disobey the LORD's commands? You
will not prosper.[a] Because you have
forsaken the LORD, he has forsaken[b]
you.' "
21But they plotted against him, and
by order of the king they stoned[c] him
Ps 51:10-12 to death[d] in the courtyard of the
LORD's temple.[e] 22King Joash did not
remember the kindness Zechariah's father Jehoiada had shown him but killed
his son, who said as he lay dying, "May
the LORD see this and call you to account."[f]
23At the turn of the year,[a] the army
of Aram marched against Joash; it invaded Judah and Jerusalem and killed
all the leaders of the people.[g] They
sent all the plunder to their king in Damascus. 24Although the Aramean
army had come with only a few men,[h]
the LORD delivered into their hands a
much larger army.[i] Because Judah
had forsaken the LORD, the God of their
fathers, judgment was executed on Joash. 25When the Arameans withdrew,
they left Joash severely wounded. His
officials conspired against him for murdering the son of Jehoiada the priest,
and they killed him in his bed. So he
died and was buried[j] in the City of
David, but not in the tombs of the
kings.
26Those who conspired against
him were Zabad,[b] son of Shimeath
an Ammonite woman, and Jehozabad, son of Shimrith[c][k] a Moabite
woman.[l] 27The account of his sons,
the many prophecies about him,
and the record of the restoration of
the temple of God are written in the
annotations on the book of the kings.
And Amaziah his son succeeded him
as king.

24:20 [z] Mt 23:35; Lk 11:51 [a] Nu 14:41 [b] S Dt 31:17 **24:21** [c] S Jos 7:25 [d] Jer 26:21 [e] Jer 20:2 **24:22** [f] S Ge 9:5 **24:23** [g] 2Ki 12:17-18 **24:24** [h] S 2Ch 14:9; 16:8; 20:2,12 [i] Lev 26:23-25; Dt 28:25 **24:25** [j] S 2Ch 21:20 **24:26** [k] 2Ki 12:21 [l] S Ru 1:4

25:2 [m] S 1Ki 8:61; S 2Ch 24:2 **25:4** [n] S Dt 28:61 [o] S Nu 26:11 **25:5** [p] S 2Sa 24:2 [q] S Ex 30:14 [r] S 1Ch 21:1; 2Ch 17:14-19 **25:7** [s] S 2Ch 16:2-9; S 19:1-3

Amaziah King of Judah

25:1–4pp — 2Ki 14:1–6
25:11–12pp — 2Ki 14:7
25:17–28pp — 2Ki 14:8–20

25 Amaziah was twenty-five years
old when he became king, and
he reigned in Jerusalem twenty-nine
years. His mother's name was Jehoaddin[d]; she was from Jerusalem. 2He did
what was right in the eyes of the LORD,
but not wholeheartedly.[m] 3After the
kingdom was firmly in his control, he
executed the officials who had murdered his father the king. 4Yet he did
not put their sons to death, but acted
in accordance with what is written in
the Law, in the Book of Moses,[n]
where the LORD commanded: "Fathers
shall not be put to death for their children, nor children put to death for their
fathers; each is to die for his own
sins."[e][o]
5Amaziah called the people of Judah
together and assigned them according
to their families to commanders of
thousands and commanders of hundreds for all Judah and Benjamin. He
then mustered[p] those twenty years
old[q] or more and found that there
were three hundred thousand men
ready for military service,[r] able to
handle the spear and shield. 6He also
hired a hundred thousand fighting men
from Israel for a hundred talents[f] of
silver.
7But a man of God came to him and
said, "O king, these troops from Israel[s] must not march with you, for the
LORD is not with Israel—not with any
of the people of Ephraim. 8Even if you
go and fight courageously in battle,

[a] *23* Probably in the spring [b] *26* A variant of *Jozabad* [c] *26* A variant of *Shomer*
[d] *1* Hebrew *Jehoaddan,* a variant of *Jehoaddin*
[e] *4* Deut. 24:16 [f] *6* That is, about 3 3/4 tons (about 3.4 metric tons); also in verse 9

24:21 THEY STONED HIM TO DEATH. Zechariah was the first recorded prophet in Judah to suffer martyrdom. He died because he remained loyal to God's truth and righteous ways and testified against the apostasy of the king and the people. Jesus referred to this martyrdom and God's planned vengeance on the generation of that time (Mt 23:35; Lk 11:51). He called Zechariah's blood "righteous" because the prophet stood with God when the majority had forsaken God's ways. The prophet was killed "between the altar and the sanctuary" (Lk 11:51), i.e., the most sacred part of the court of the priests. Israel's rejection of the words of God's prophets ultimately resulted in their own destruction and rejection by God (see 36:16).

25:2 NOT WHOLEHEARTEDLY. See 2Ki 14:1, note.

25:7 TROOPS FROM ISRAEL MUST NOT MARCH WITH YOU. The writer of Chronicles emphasizes God's condemnation of alliances that demonstrated Judah's failure to trust in God (cf. 16:2–9; 22:5; Ezr 4:3). An alliance with those whom God opposes (i.e., God's enemies) could result in God causing defeat for his people (vv. 7–8); this truth was often reiterated by God's prophets (see Isa 57:13; Jer 17:5–8; 39:18).

God will overthrow you before the enemy, for God has the power to help or to
overthrow."[t]
9 Amaziah asked the man of God,
"But what about the hundred talents I
paid for these Israelite troops?"
The man of God replied, "The LORD
can give you much more than that."[u]
10 So Amaziah dismissed the troops
who had come to him from Ephraim
and sent them home. They were furious with Judah and left for home in a
great rage.[v]
11 Amaziah then marshaled his
strength and led his army to the Valley
of Salt, where he killed ten thousand
men of Seir. 12 The army of Judah also
captured ten thousand men alive, took
them to the top of a cliff and threw
them down so that all were dashed to
pieces.[w]
13 Meanwhile the troops that Amaziah had sent back and had not allowed
to take part in the war raided Judean
towns from Samaria to Beth Horon.
They killed three thousand people and
carried off great quantities of plunder.
14 When Amaziah returned from
slaughtering the Edomites, he brought
back the gods of the people of Seir. He
set them up as his own gods,[x] bowed
down to them and burned sacrifices to
them. 15 The anger of the LORD burned
against Amaziah, and he sent a prophet to him, who said, "Why do you consult this people's gods, which could
not save[y] their own people from your
hand?"
16 While he was still speaking, the
king said to him, "Have we appointed
you an adviser to the king? Stop! Why
be struck down?"
So the prophet stopped but said, "I
know that God has determined to destroy you, because you have done this
and have not listened to my counsel."
17 After Amaziah king of Judah consulted his advisers, he sent this challenge to Jehoash[g] son of Jehoahaz, the
son of Jehu, king of Israel: "Come,
meet me face to face."
18 But Jehoash king of Israel replied
to Amaziah king of Judah: "A thistle[z]
in Lebanon sent a message to a cedar
in Lebanon, 'Give your daughter to my
son in marriage.' Then a wild beast in
Lebanon came along and trampled the
thistle underfoot. 19 You say to yourself
that you have defeated Edom, and now
you are arrogant and proud. But stay at
home! Why ask for trouble and cause
your own downfall and that of Judah
also?"
20 Amaziah, however, would not listen, for God so worked that he might
hand them over to ⌊Jehoash⌋, because
they sought the gods of Edom.[a] 21 So
Jehoash king of Israel attacked. He
and Amaziah king of Judah faced each
other at Beth Shemesh in Judah. 22 Judah was routed by Israel, and every
man fled to his home. 23 Jehoash king
of Israel captured Amaziah king of Judah, the son of Joash, the son of Ahaziah,[h] at Beth Shemesh. Then Jehoash
brought him to Jerusalem and broke
down the wall of Jerusalem from
the Ephraim Gate[b] to the Corner
Gate[c]—a section about six hundred
feet[i] long. 24 He took all the gold and
silver and all the articles found in the
temple of God that had been in the care
of Obed-Edom,[d] together with the palace treasures and the hostages, and returned to Samaria.
25 Amaziah son of Joash king of Judah lived for fifteen years after the
death of Jehoash son of Jehoahaz king
of Israel. 26 As for the other events of
Amaziah's reign, from beginning to
end, are they not written in the book of
the kings of Judah and Israel? 27 From
the time that Amaziah turned away
from following the LORD, they conspired against him in Jerusalem and he
fled to Lachish[e], but they sent men
after him to Lachish and killed him
there. 28 He was brought back by horse
and was buried with his fathers in the
City of Judah.

Uzziah King of Judah

26:1–4pp — 2Ki 14:21–22; 15:1–3
26:21–23pp — 2Ki 15:5–7

26 Then all the people of Judah[f]
took Uzziah,[j] who was sixteen
years old, and made him king in place

25:8 [t] S 2Ch 14:11; S 20:6
25:9 [u] Dt 8:18; Pr 10:22
25:10 [v] ver 13
25:12 [w] Ps 141:6; Ob 1:3
25:14 [x] Ex 20:3; 2Ch 28:23; Isa 44:15
25:15 [y] Isa 36:20
25:18 [z] Jdg 9:8-15
25:20 [a] S 2Ch 10:15
25:23 [b] 2Ki 14:13; Ne 8:16; 12:39 [c] 2Ch 26:9; Jer 31:38
25:24 [d] S 1Ch 26:15
25:27 [e] S Jos 10:3
26:1 [f] S 2Ch 22:1

[g] 17 Hebrew *Joash*, a variant of *Jehoash*; also in verses 18, 21, 23 and 25
[h] 23 Hebrew *Jehoahaz*, a variant of *Ahaziah*
[i] 23 Hebrew *four hundred cubits* (about 180 meters)
[j] 1 Also called *Azariah*

26:1 UZZIAH. Uzziah's reign is divided into two parts: the years he sought the Lord and the years he was unfaithful to the Lord. The Bible emphasizes that seeking God results in blessing and help, whereas failure to seek God results in spiritual decline and judgment (see vv. 5–7 and

of his father Amaziah. 2He was the one
who rebuilt Elath and restored it to Judah after Amaziah rested with his fathers.
3Uzziah was sixteen years old when
he became king, and he reigned in Jerusalem fifty-two years. His mother's
name was Jecoliah; she was from Jerusalem. 4He did what was right in the
eyes of the LORD, just as his father Amaziah had done. 5He sought God during
the days of Zechariah, who instructed
him in the fear[k] of God.[g] As long as
he sought the LORD, God gave him success.[h]
6He went to war against the Philistines[i] and broke down the walls of
Gath, Jabneh and Ashdod.[j] He then
rebuilt towns near Ashdod and elsewhere among the Philistines. 7God
helped him against the Philistines and
against the Arabs[k] who lived in Gur
Baal and against the Meunites.[l] 8The
Ammonites[m] brought tribute to Uzziah, and his fame spread as far as the
border of Egypt, because he had become very powerful.
9Uzziah built towers in Jerusalem at
the Corner Gate,[n] at the Valley Gate[o]
and at the angle of the wall, and he
fortified them. 10He also built towers
in the desert and dug many cisterns,
because he had much livestock in the
foothills and in the plain. He had people working his fields and vineyards in
the hills and in the fertile lands, for he
loved the soil.
11Uzziah had a well-trained army,
ready to go out by divisions according
to their numbers as mustered by Jeiel
the secretary and Maaseiah the officer
under the direction of Hananiah, one of
the royal officials. 12The total number
of family leaders over the fighting men
was 2,600. 13Under their command
was an army of 307,500 men trained
for war, a powerful force to support the
king against his enemies. 14Uzziah
provided shields, spears, helmets,
coats of armor, bows and slingstones
for the entire army.[p] 15In Jerusalem
he made machines designed by skillful
men for use on the towers and on the
corner defenses to shoot arrows and
hurl large stones. His fame spread far
and wide, for he was greatly helped until he became powerful.
16But after Uzziah became powerful,
his pride[q] led to his downfall.[r] He
was unfaithful[s] to the LORD his God,
and entered the temple of the LORD to
burn incense[t] on the altar of incense.
17Azariah[u] the priest with eighty other courageous priests of the LORD followed him in. 18They confronted him
and said, "It is not right for you, Uzziah, to burn incense to the LORD. That is
for the priests,[v] the descendants[w] of
Aaron,[x] who have been consecrated
to burn incense.[y] Leave the sanctuary, for you have been unfaithful; and
you will not be honored by the LORD
God."
19Uzziah, who had a censer in his
hand ready to burn incense, became
angry. While he was raging at the
priests in their presence before the incense altar in the LORD's temple, leprosy[l][z] broke out on his forehead.
20When Azariah the chief priest and all
the other priests looked at him, they
saw that he had leprosy on his forehead, so they hurried him out. Indeed,
he himself was eager to leave, because
the LORD had afflicted him.
21King Uzziah had leprosy until
the day he died. He lived in a separate house[m][a]—leprous, and excluded
from the temple of the LORD. Jotham his
son had charge of the palace and governed the people of the land.
22The other events of Uzziah's reign,
from beginning to end, are recorded by
the prophet Isaiah[b] son of Amoz.
23Uzziah[c] rested with his fathers and
was buried near them in a field for burial that belonged to the kings, for people said, "He had leprosy." And Jotham
his son succeeded him as king.[d]

26:5 [g] S 2Ch 24:2 [h] 2Ch 27:6
26:6 [i] Isa 2:6; 11:14; 14:29; Jer 25:20 [j] Am 1:8; 3:9
26:7 [k] S 2Ch 21:16 [l] 2Ch 20:1
26:8 [m] S Ge 19:38
26:9 [n] S 2Ki 14:13; S 2Ch 25:23 [o] Ne 2:13; 3:13
26:14 [p] Jer 46:4
26:16 [q] S 2Ki 14:10 [r] Dt 32:15 [s] S 1Ch 5:25 [t] 2Ki 16:12
26:17 [u] S 1Ki 4:2
26:18 [v] Nu 16:39 [w] Nu 18:1-7 [x] S Ex 30:7 [y] S 1Ch 6:49
26:19 [z] S Nu 12:10
26:21 [a] S Ex 4:6; Lev 13:46; S 14:8; Nu 5:2; S 19:12
26:22 [b] 2Ki 15:1; Isa 1:1; 6:1
26:23 [c] Isa 1:1; 6:1 [d] S 2Ki 14:21; Am 1:1

[k] *5* Many Hebrew manuscripts, Septuagint and Syriac; other Hebrew manuscripts *vision*
[l] *19* The Hebrew word was used for various diseases affecting the skin—not necessarily leprosy; also in verses 20, 21 and 23.
[m] *21* Or *in a house where he was relieved of responsibilities*

16–20; see 15:2, note).

26:5 AS LONG AS HE SOUGHT THE LORD. As long as Uzziah continued to seek the Lord and follow his righteous ways, he was given grace, strength and help to rule as king of Judah (see 14:4, note).

26:16 HIS PRIDE LED TO HIS DOWNFALL. Uzziah failed to realize that all he had accomplished had been with the help of God (vv. 5,7) and others (vv. 8,11–13); the result was pride, and it led him into the sins of presumption and unfaithfulness (see Php 2:3, note).

Jotham King of Judah

27:1–4,7–9pp — 2Ki 15:33–38

27 Jotham[e] was twenty-five years
old when he became king, and
he reigned in Jerusalem sixteen years.
His mother's name was Jerusha daughter of Zadok. **2**He did what was right in
the eyes of the LORD, just as his father
Uzziah had done, but unlike him he did
not enter the temple of the LORD. The
people, however, continued their corrupt practices. **3**Jotham rebuilt the Upper Gate of the temple of the LORD and
did extensive work on the wall at the
hill of Ophel.[f] **4**He built towns in the
Judean hills and forts and towers in the
wooded areas.

5Jotham made war on the king of the
Ammonites[g] and conquered them.
That year the Ammonites paid him a
hundred talents[n] of silver, ten thousand cors[o] of wheat and ten thousand
cors of barley. The Ammonites brought
him the same amount also in the second and third years.

6Jotham grew powerful[h] because
he walked steadfastly before the LORD
his God.

7The other events in Jotham's reign,
including all his wars and the other
things he did, are written in the book
of the kings of Israel and Judah. **8**He
was twenty-five years old when he became king, and he reigned in Jerusalem
sixteen years. **9**Jotham rested with his
fathers and was buried in the City of
David. And Ahaz his son succeeded
him as king.

Ahaz King of Judah

28:1–27pp — 2Ki 16:1–20

28 Ahaz[i] was twenty years old
when he became king, and he
reigned in Jerusalem sixteen years. Unlike David his father, he did not do
what was right in the eyes of the LORD.
2He walked in the ways of the kings of
Israel and also made cast idols[j] for
worshiping the Baals. **3**He burned sacrifices in the Valley of Ben Hinnom[k]
and sacrificed his sons[l] in the fire, following the detestable[m] ways of the nations the LORD had driven out before
the Israelites. **4**He offered sacrifices
and burned incense at the high places,
on the hilltops and under every spreading tree.

5Therefore the LORD his God handed
him over to the king of Aram.[n] The
Arameans defeated him and took many
of his people as prisoners and brought
them to Damascus.

He was also given into the hands of
the king of Israel, who inflicted heavy
casualties on him. **6**In one day Pekah[o]
son of Remaliah killed a hundred and
twenty thousand soldiers in Judah[p]—
because Judah had forsaken the LORD,
the God of their fathers. **7**Zicri, an
Ephraimite warrior, killed Maaseiah
the king's son, Azrikam the officer in
charge of the palace, and Elkanah, second to the king. **8**The Israelites took
captive from their kinsmen[q] two hundred thousand wives, sons and daughters. They also took a great deal of
plunder, which they carried back to Samaria.[r]

9But a prophet of the LORD named
Oded was there, and he went out to
meet the army when it returned to Samaria. He said to them, "Because the
LORD, the God of your fathers, was angry[s] with Judah, he gave them into
your hand. But you have slaughtered
them in a rage that reaches to heav-
en.[t] **10**And now you intend to make
the men and women of Judah and Jerusalem your slaves.[u] But aren't you
also guilty of sins against the LORD
your God? **11**Now listen to me! Send
back your fellow countrymen you have
taken as prisoners, for the LORD's
fierce anger rests on you.[v]"

12Then some of the leaders in
Ephraim—Azariah son of Jehohanan,
Berekiah son of Meshillemoth, Jehizki-
ah son of Shallum, and Amasa son of
Hadlai—confronted those who were
arriving from the war. **13**"You must not
bring those prisoners here," they said,
"or we will be guilty before the LORD.

27:1 [e]S 2Ki 15:5, 32; S 1Ch 3:12
27:3 [f]2Ch 33:14; Ne 3:26
27:5 [g]S Ge 19:38
27:6 [h]2Ch 26:5
28:1 [i]S 1Ch 3:13; Isa 1:1
28:2 [j]Ex 34:17
28:3 [k]S Jos 15:8 [l]S Lev 18:21; S 2Ki 3:27; Eze 20:26 [m]S Dt 18:9; 2Ch 33:2
28:5 [n]Isa 7:1
28:6 [o]S 2Ki 15:25,27 [p]ver 8; Isa 9:21; 11:13
28:8 [q]Dt 28:25-41 [r]2Ch 29:9
28:9 [s]Isa 10:6; 47:6; Zec 1:15 [t]Ezr 9:6; Rev 18:5
28:10 [u]Lev 25:39-46
28:11 [v]2Ch 11:4

[n]*5* That is, about 3 3/4 tons (about 3.4 metric tons) [o]*5* That is, probably about 62,000 bushels (about 2,200 kiloliters)

28:3 SACRIFICED HIS SONS IN THE FIRE. King Ahaz was so given over to idolatry and occult practices that he destroyed his own sons in fire as a sacrifice to pagan gods (see Lev 20:1–5; Jer 7:31–32; see 2Ki 16:3, note). Children today can also be ruthlessly destroyed—physically through the sins of abortion and child abuse, and spiritually by parents who fail to teach them godly ways based on Scripture (see Dt 6:7, note) or to separate and protect them from the ungodliness of the world (see article on THE CHRISTIAN'S RELATIONSHIP TO THE WORLD, p. 1976).

Do you intend to add to our sin and
guilt? For our guilt is already great,
and his fierce anger rests on Israel."
14 So the soldiers gave up the prisoners and plunder in the presence of the
officials and all the assembly. 15 The
men designated by name took the prisoners, and from the plunder they
clothed all who were naked. They provided them with clothes and sandals,
food and drink,[w] and healing balm.
All those who were weak they put on
donkeys. So they took them back to
their fellow countrymen at Jericho,
the City of Palms,[x] and returned to
Samaria.[y]
16 At that time King Ahaz sent to the
king[p] of Assyria[z] for help. 17 The
Edomites[a] had again come and attacked Judah and carried away prisoners,[b] 18 while the Philistines[c] had
raided towns in the foothills and in the
Negev of Judah. They captured and occupied Beth Shemesh, Aijalon[d] and
Gederoth,[e] as well as Soco,[f] Timnah[g] and Gimzo, with their surrounding villages. 19 The LORD had humbled
Judah because of Ahaz king of Israel,[q]
for he had promoted wickedness in Judah and had been most unfaithful[h] to
the LORD. 20 Tiglath-Pileser[r][i] king of
Assyria[j] came to him, but he gave him
trouble[k] instead of help.[l] 21 Ahaz[m]
took some of the things from the temple of the LORD and from the royal palace and from the princes and presented
them to the king of Assyria, but that
did not help him.[n]
22 In his time of trouble King Ahaz
became even more unfaithful[o] to the
LORD. 23 He offered sacrifices to the
gods[p] of Damascus, who had defeated
him; for he thought, "Since the gods of
the kings of Aram have helped them, I
will sacrifice to them so they will help
me."[q] But they were his downfall and
the downfall of all Israel.[r]
24 Ahaz gathered together the furnishings[s] from the temple of God[t]
and took them away.[s] He shut the
doors[u] of the LORD's temple and set up
altars[v] at every street corner in Jerusalem. 25 In every town in Judah he
built high places to burn sacrifices to
other gods and provoked the LORD, the
God of his fathers, to anger.
26 The other events of his reign and
all his ways, from beginning to end, are
written in the book of the kings of Judah and Israel. 27 Ahaz rested[w] with
his fathers and was buried[x] in the city
of Jerusalem, but he was not placed in
the tombs of the kings of Israel. And
Hezekiah his son succeeded him as
king.

Hezekiah Purifies the Temple

29:1–2pp — 2Ki 18:2–3

29 Hezekiah[y] was twenty-five
years old when he became king,
and he reigned in Jerusalem twenty-
nine years. His mother's name was
Abijah daughter of Zechariah. 2 He did
what was right in the eyes of the LORD,
just as his father David[z] had done.
3 In the first month of the first year
of his reign, he opened the doors of the
temple of the LORD and repaired[a]
them. 4 He brought in the priests and
the Levites, assembled them in the
square on the east side 5 and said: "Listen to me, Levites! Consecrate[b] yourselves now and consecrate the temple
of the LORD, the God of your fathers.

28:15 [w] 2Ki 6:22; Pr 25:21-22 [x] S Dt 34:3; S Jdg 1:16 [y] Lk 10:25-37 **28:16** [z] S 2Ki 16:7; Eze 23:12 **28:17** [a] Ps 137:7; Isa 34:5; 63:1; Jer 25:21; Eze 16:57; 25:12; Am 1:11 [b] 2Ch 29:9 **28:18** [c] Isa 9:12; 11:14; Jer 25:20; Eze 16:27,57; 25:15 [d] S Jos 10:12 [e] Jos 15:41 [f] S 1Sa 17:1 [g] S Ge 38:12 **28:19** [h] S 1Ch 5:25 **28:20** [i] S 2Ki 15:29; S 1Ch 5:6 [j] Isa 7:17; 8:7; 10:5-6; 36:1 [k] Isa 10:20 [l] S 2Ki 16:7 **28:21** [m] S 2Ch 16:2-9 [n] Jer 2:36 **28:22** [o] Jer 5:3; 15:7; 17:23 **28:23** [p] S 2Ch 25:14 [q] Isa 10:20; Jer 44:17-18 [r] 1Ch 11:1; Jer 18:15 **28:24** [s] 2Ch 29:19 [t] S 2Ki 16:18 [u] Mal 1:10 [v] 2Ch 30:14 **28:27** [w] Isa 14:28-32 [x] S 2Ch 21:20 **29:1** [y] S 1Ch 3:13 **29:2** [z] 2Ch 34:2 **29:3** [a] 2Ki 18:16 **29:5** [b] S Lev 11:44; Ne 13:9

[p] *16* One Hebrew manuscript, Septuagint and Vulgate (see also 2 Kings 16:7); most Hebrew manuscripts *kings* [q] *19* That is, Judah, as frequently in 2 Chronicles [r] *20* Hebrew *Tilgath-Pilneser,* a variant of *Tiglath-Pileser* [s] *24* Or *and cut them up*

29:1 HEZEKIAH. See 2Ki 18:5, note.

29:5 CONSECRATE YOURSELVES ... REMOVE ALL DEFILEMENT. In order for God's people to experience revival and renewal, four things are indispensable. (1) Confession of specific sins. We must recognize those areas of our lives where we have departed from God's will and word and must confess those specific sins (vv. 6–7; see Ps 51:3; cf. Mt 5:24).

(2) Purifying the house of the Lord (vv. 5,18). The church is God's house under the new covenant (2Co 6:16; Eph 2:21–22; 1Ti 3:15). Whatever in the church's doctrine, worship and lifestyle that clearly offends God's will as revealed in Scripture must be removed. Likewise, the individual believer, as the temple of the Holy Spirit (1Co 6:19), must be purified from all unrighteousness (see 1Jn 1:9, note; see articles on THE TEMPLE, p. 608, and SANCTIFICATION, p. 1956).

(3) Renewal of the covenant (vv. 10–11). We must renew our dedication to God, his kingdom and his righteous cause on earth, and we must express a sincere desire to turn from the evil of the world and to resist sin.

(4) Proclaim a blood sacrifice for atonement (vv. 20–24). We must appropriate by faith the blood atonement of Jesus Christ, who suffered on the cross to save and sanctify his people (see Heb 9:11–14; see 1Co 10:16, note).

Remove all defilement from the sanctuary. **6**Our fathers[c] were unfaithful;[d] they did evil in the eyes of the
LORD our God and forsook him. They
turned their faces away from the
LORD's dwelling place and turned their
backs on him. **7**They also shut the
doors of the portico and put out the
lamps. They did not burn incense[e] or
present any burnt offerings at the
sanctuary to the God of Israel. **8**Therefore, the anger of the LORD has fallen on
Judah and Jerusalem; he has made
them an object of dread and horror[f]
and scorn,[g] as you can see with your
own eyes. **9**This is why our fathers
have fallen by the sword and why our
sons and daughters and our wives are
in captivity.[h] **10**Now I intend to make
a covenant[i] with the LORD, the God of
Israel, so that his fierce anger[j] will
turn away from us. **11**My sons, do not
be negligent now, for the LORD has chosen you to stand before him and serve
him,[k] to minister[l] before him and to
burn incense."

12Then these Levites[m] set to work:
from the Kohathites,
Mahath son of Amasai and Joel son of Azariah;
from the Merarites,
Kish son of Abdi and Azariah son of Jehallelel;
from the Gershonites,
Joah son of Zimmah and Eden[n] son of Joah;
13from the descendants of Elizaphan,[o]
Shimri and Jeiel;
from the descendants of Asaph,[p]
Zechariah and Mattaniah;
14from the descendants of Heman,
Jehiel and Shimei;
from the descendants of Jeduthun,
Shemaiah and Uzziel.

15When they had assembled their
brothers and consecrated themselves,
they went in to purify[q] the temple of
the LORD, as the king had ordered, following the word of the LORD. **16**The
priests went into the sanctuary of the
LORD to purify it. They brought out to
the courtyard of the LORD's temple everything unclean that they found in the
temple of the LORD. The Levites took it
and carried it out to the Kidron Valley.[r] **17**They began the consecration
on the first day of the first month, and
by the eighth day of the month they
reached the portico of the LORD.
For eight more days they consecrated
the temple of the LORD itself, finishing on the sixteenth day of the first
month.

18Then they went in to King Hezekiah and reported: "We have purified the
entire temple of the LORD, the altar of
burnt offering with all its utensils, and
the table for setting out the consecrated bread, with all its articles. **19**We
have prepared and consecrated all the
articles[s] that King Ahaz removed in
his unfaithfulness while he was king.
They are now in front of the LORD's altar."

20Early the next morning King Hezekiah gathered the city officials together and went up to the temple of the
LORD. **21**They brought seven bulls, sev-
en rams, seven male lambs and seven
male goats[t] as a sin offering[u] for the
kingdom, for the sanctuary and for Judah. The king commanded the priests,
the descendants of Aaron, to offer
these on the altar of the LORD. **22**So
they slaughtered the bulls, and the
priests took the blood and sprinkled it
on the altar; next they slaughtered the
rams and sprinkled their blood on the
altar; then they slaughtered the lambs
and sprinkled their blood[v] on the altar. **23**The goats[w] for the sin offering
were brought before the king and the
assembly, and they laid their hands[x]
on them. **24**The priests then slaughtered the goats and presented their
blood on the altar for a sin offering to
atone[y] for all Israel, because the king
had ordered the burnt offering and the
sin offering for all Israel.[z]

25He stationed the Levites in the
temple of the LORD with cymbals, harps
and lyres in the way prescribed by David[a] and Gad[b] the king's seer and
Nathan the prophet; this was commanded by the LORD through his prophets. **26**So the Levites stood ready with
David's instruments,[c] and the priests
with their trumpets.[d]

27Hezekiah gave the order to sacrifice the burnt offering on the altar. As
the offering began, singing to the LORD
began also, accompanied by trumpets
and the instruments[e] of David king of
Israel. **28**The whole assembly bowed in
worship, while the singers sang and
the trumpeters played. All this contin-

29:6 [c] Ezr 9:7; Ps 106:6-47; Jer 2:27; 18:17; Eze 23:35; Da 9:5-6 [d] S 1Ch 5:25
29:7 [e] S Ex 30:7
29:8 [f] S Dt 28:25 [g] S Lev 26:32; Jer 18:16; 19:8; 25:9,18
29:9 [h] 2Ch 28:5-8, 17
29:10 [i] S 2Ki 11:17; S 2Ch 23:16 [j] S Nu 25:4; 2Ch 30:8; Ezr 10:14
29:11 [k] S Nu 3:6; 8:6,14 [l] S 1Ch 15:2
29:12 [m] S Nu 3:17-20 [n] 2Ch 31:15
29:13 [o] S Ex 6:22 [p] S 1Ch 6:39
29:15 [q] S 1Ch 23:28; S Isa 1:25
29:16 [r] S 2Sa 15:23
29:19 [s] 2Ch 28:24
29:21 [t] Ezr 6:17; 8:35 [u] S Lev 4:13-14
29:22 [v] S Lev 4:18; Nu 18:17
29:23 [w] S Lev 16:5 [x] Lev 4:15
29:24 [y] S Ex 29:36; Lev 4:26 [z] 1Ch 11:1; Ezr 8:35
29:25 [a] S 1Ch 25:6; 28:19 [b] S 1Sa 22:5
29:26 [c] S 1Ch 15:16 [d] S 1Ch 15:24
29:27 [e] S 1Sa 16:16

ued until the sacrifice of the burnt offering[f] was completed.
29When the offerings were finished,
the king and everyone present with
him knelt down and worshiped.[g]
30King Hezekiah and his officials ordered the Levites to praise the LORD
with the words of David and of Asaph
the seer. So they sang praises with
gladness and bowed their heads and
worshiped.
31Then Hezekiah said, "You have
now dedicated yourselves to the LORD.
Come and bring sacrifices[h] and thank
offerings to the temple of the LORD."
So the assembly brought sacrifices
and thank offerings, and all whose
hearts were willing[i] brought burnt offerings.
32The number of burnt offerings[j]
the assembly brought was seventy
bulls, a hundred rams and two hundred
male lambs—all of them for burnt offerings to the LORD. 33The animals consecrated as sacrifices amounted to six
hundred bulls and three thousand
sheep and goats. 34The priests, however, were too few to skin all the burnt
offerings;[k] so their kinsmen the Levites helped them until the task was
finished and until other priests had
been consecrated,[l] for the Levites
had been more conscientious in consecrating themselves than the priests
had been. 35There were burnt offerings
in abundance, together with the fat[m]
of the fellowship offerings[t][n] and the
drink offerings[o] that accompanied the
burnt offerings.
So the service of the temple of the
LORD was reestablished. 36Hezekiah
and all the people rejoiced at what God
had brought about for his people, because it was done so quickly.[p]

29:28 [f]S 2Ch 2:4
29:29 [g]S 2Ch 20:18
29:31 [h]Heb 13:15-16 [i]S Ex 25:2; 35:22
29:32 [j]Lev 1:1-17
29:34 [k]Eze 44:11 [l]2Ch 30:3,15
29:35 [m]S Ge 4:4; S Ex 29:13 [n]Lev 7:11-21 [o]S Ge 35:14
29:36 [p]2Ch 35:8

Hezekiah Celebrates the Passover

30 Hezekiah sent word to all Israel[q] and Judah and also wrote
letters to Ephraim and Manasseh,[r] inviting them to come to the temple of
the LORD in Jerusalem and celebrate
the Passover[s] to the LORD, the God of
Israel. 2The king and his officials and
the whole assembly in Jerusalem decided to celebrate[t] the Passover in
the second month. 3They had not been
able to celebrate it at the regular time
because not enough priests had consecrated[u] themselves and the people
had not assembled in Jerusalem. 4The
plan seemed right both to the king and
to the whole assembly. 5They decided
to send a proclamation throughout Israel, from Beersheba to Dan,[v] calling
the people to come to Jerusalem and
celebrate the Passover to the LORD, the
God of Israel. It had not been celebrated in large numbers according to what
was written.
6At the king's command, couriers
went throughout Israel and Judah with
letters from the king and from his officials, which read:

"People of Israel, return to the
LORD, the God of Abraham, Isaac
and Israel, that he may return to
you who are left, who have escaped from the hand of the kings
of Assyria. 7Do not be like your
fathers[w] and brothers, who were
unfaithful[x] to the LORD, the God
of their fathers, so that he made
them an object of horror,[y] as you
see. 8Do not be stiff-necked,[z] as
your fathers were; submit to the
LORD. Come to the sanctuary,

30:1 [q]S 1Ch 9:1 [r]S Ge 41:52 [s]S Ex 12:11; S Nu 28:16
30:2 [t]Nu 9:10
30:3 [u]Nu 9:6-13; S 2Ch 29:34
30:5 [v]S Jdg 20:1
30:7 [w]Ps 78:8, 57; 106:6; Jer 11:10; Eze 20:18 [x]S 1Ch 5:25 [y]S Dt 28:25
30:8 [z]S Ex 32:9

[t]35 Traditionally *peace offerings*

30:6 RETURN TO THE LORD. Turning from sinful ways to return to God is an essential prerequisite of revival (cf. Zec 1:4). The verb "return" occurs four times in vv. 6–9, implying that God's people were in a backslidden state, attached more to the ways of the world than to God's ways. The message of repentance found here is applicable to all churches that have forsaken their first love, accepted unbiblical doctrine and compromised with the world (see article on CHRIST'S MESSAGE TO THE SEVEN CHURCHES, p. 2008).

30:8 SUBMIT TO THE LORD. Hezekiah emphasizes four truths concerning genuine repentance. (1) God's people must return to him with the desire to forsake sin and confess him as Lord if they want to experience his favor (vv. 6–8). God will not return and bless his people while they take pleasure in sin (Hos 5:4,15).

(2) God's people must return to him with the sincere intention of obeying his commands. Unless God's people forsake the world's sinful ways and pursue purity of heart and obedience to his word, God will bring calamity and destruction upon them and their families (see v. 7; Mt 5:13, note).

(3) God's people must return to him in submission, worship and service if they hope to escape his burning anger toward sin. The words "submit to the LORD" are literally "to give the hand to the LORD." The hand is given as a pledge of absolute loyalty and fidelity to God and his righteous ways (cf. 2Ki 10:15; Ezr 10:19; Eze 17:18).

(4) God's people must return to him in persevering prayer if they are to experience again his grace and compassion (vv. 9,19–20,27; see 14:4, note).

which he has consecrated forever.
Serve the LORD your God, so that
his fierce anger[a] will turn away
from you. **9**If you return[b] to the
LORD, then your brothers and your
children will be shown compassion[c] by their captors and will
come back to this land, for the
LORD your God is gracious and
compassionate.[d] He will not turn
his face from you if you return to
him."

10The couriers went from town to
town in Ephraim and Manasseh, as far
as Zebulun, but the people scorned
and ridiculed[e] them. **11**Nevertheless,
some men of Asher, Manasseh and
Zebulun humbled[f] themselves and
went to Jerusalem.[g] **12**Also in Judah
the hand of God was on the people to
give them unity[h] of mind to carry out
what the king and his officials had ordered, following the word of the LORD.

13A very large crowd of people assembled in Jerusalem to celebrate the
Feast of Unleavened Bread[i] in the
second month. **14**They removed the altars[j] in Jerusalem and cleared away
the incense altars and threw them into
the Kidron Valley.[k]

15They slaughtered the Passover
lamb on the fourteenth day of the second month. The priests and the Levites
were ashamed and consecrated[l]
themselves and brought burnt offerings to the temple of the LORD. **16**Then
they took up their regular positions[m]
as prescribed in the Law of Moses the
man of God. The priests sprinkled the
blood handed to them by the Levites.
17Since many in the crowd had not consecrated themselves, the Levites had
to kill[n] the Passover lambs for all
those who were not ceremonially clean
and could not consecrate ⌞their lambs⌟
to the LORD. **18**Although most of the
many people who came from Ephraim,
Manasseh, Issachar and Zebulun had
not purified themselves,[o] yet they ate
the Passover, contrary to what was
written. But Hezekiah prayed for them,
saying, "May the LORD, who is good,
pardon everyone **19**who sets his heart
on seeking God—the LORD, the God of
his fathers—even if he is not clean according to the rules of the sanctuary."
20And the LORD heard[p] Hezekiah and
healed[q] the people.[r]
21The Israelites who were present in
Jerusalem celebrated the Feast of Unleavened Bread[s] for seven days with
great rejoicing, while the Levites and
priests sang to the LORD every day, accompanied by the LORD's instruments
of praise.[u]
22Hezekiah spoke encouragingly to
all the Levites, who showed good understanding of the service of the LORD.
For the seven days they ate their assigned portion and offered fellowship
offerings[v] and praised the LORD, the
God of their fathers.
23The whole assembly then agreed
to celebrate[t] the festival seven more
days; so for another seven days they
celebrated joyfully. **24**Hezekiah king of
Judah provided[u] a thousand bulls and
seven thousand sheep and goats for
the assembly, and the officials provided them with a thousand bulls and ten
thousand sheep and goats. A great
number of priests consecrated themselves. **25**The entire assembly of Judah
rejoiced, along with the priests and Levites and all who had assembled from
Israel[v], including the aliens who had
come from Israel and those who lived
in Judah. **26**There was great joy in Jerusalem, for since the days of Solomon[w]
son of David king of Israel there had
been nothing like this in Jerusalem.
27The priests and the Levites stood to
bless[x] the people, and God heard
them, for their prayer reached heaven,
his holy dwelling place.

31 When all this had ended, the Israelites who were there went
out to the towns of Judah, smashed the
sacred stones and cut down[y] the
Asherah poles. They destroyed the
high places and the altars throughout
Judah and Benjamin and in Ephraim
and Manasseh. After they had destroyed all of them, the Israelites returned to their own towns and to their
own property.

Contributions for Worship

31:20–21pp — 2Ki 18:5–7

2Hezekiah[z] assigned the priests
and Levites to divisions[a]—each of
them according to their duties as
priests or Levites—to offer burnt offerings and fellowship offerings,[v] to min-

30:8 [a] S Nu 25:4; S 2Ch 29:10 **30:9** [b] Dt 30:2-5; Isa 1:16; 55:7; Jer 25:5; Eze 33:11 [c] S Ex 3:21; S 1Ki 8:50 [d] S Ex 22:27; S Dt 4:31; S 2Ch 6:39; Mic 7:18 **30:10** [e] 2Ch 36:16 **30:11** [f] S 2Ch 6:37 [g] ver 25 **30:12** [h] Jer 32:39; Eze 11:19 **30:13** [i] S Nu 28:16 **30:14** [j] 2Ch 28:24 [k] S 2Sa 15:23 **30:15** [l] S 2Ch 29:34 **30:16** [m] 2Ch 35:10 **30:17** [n] 2Ch 35:11; Ezr 6:20 **30:18** [o] Ex 12:43-49; Nu 9:6-10 **30:20** [p] S 2Ch 6:20 [q] S 2Ch 7:14; Mal 4:2 [r] Jas 5:16

30:21 [s] Ex 12:15, 17; 13:6 **30:23** [t] 2Ch 7:9 **30:24** [u] 1Ki 8:5; 2Ch 35:7; Ezr 6:17; 8:35 **30:25** [v] ver 11 **30:26** [w] S 2Ch 7:8 **30:27** [x] S Ex 39:43 **31:1** [y] S 2Ki 18:4; 2Ch 32:12; Isa 36:7 **31:2** [z] S 2Ch 29:9 [a] S 1Ch 24:1

[u] 21 Or *priests praised the* LORD *every day with resounding instruments belonging to the* LORD
[v] 22,2 Traditionally *peace offerings*

ister,[b] to give thanks and to sing
praises[c] at the gates of the LORD's
dwelling.[d] 3The king contributed[e]
from his own possessions for the morning and evening burnt offerings and for
the burnt offerings on the Sabbaths,
New Moons and appointed feasts as
written in the Law of the LORD.[f] 4He
ordered the people living in Jerusalem
to give the portion[g] due the priests
and Levites so they could devote themselves to the Law of the LORD. 5As soon
as the order went out, the Israelites
generously gave the firstfruits[h] of
their grain, new wine,[i] oil and honey
and all that the fields produced. They
brought a great amount, a tithe of everything. 6The men of Israel and Judah
who lived in the towns of Judah also
brought a tithe[j] of their herds and
flocks and a tithe of the holy things
dedicated to the LORD their God, and
they piled them in heaps.[k] 7They began doing this in the third month and
finished in the seventh month.[l]
8When Hezekiah and his officials came
and saw the heaps, they praised the
LORD and blessed[m] his people Israel.
9Hezekiah asked the priests and Levites about the heaps; 10and Azariah
the chief priest, from the family of Zadok,[n] answered, "Since the people began to bring their contributions to the
temple of the LORD, we have had
enough to eat and plenty to spare,
because the LORD has blessed his people, and this great amount is left
over."[o]
11Hezekiah gave orders to prepare
storerooms in the temple of the LORD,
and this was done. 12Then they faithfully brought in the contributions,
tithes and dedicated gifts. Conaniah,[p]
a Levite, was in charge of these things,
and his brother Shimei was next in
rank. 13Jehiel, Azaziah, Nahath, Asahel, Jerimoth, Jozabad,[q] Eliel, Ismaki-
ah, Mahath and Benaiah were supervisors under Conaniah and Shimei his
brother, by appointment of King Hezekiah and Azariah the official in charge
of the temple of God.
14Kore son of Imnah the Levite,
keeper of the East Gate, was in charge
of the freewill offerings given to God,
distributing the contributions made to
the LORD and also the consecrated
gifts. 15Eden,[r] Miniamin, Jeshua,
Shemaiah, Amariah and Shecaniah assisted him faithfully in the towns[s] of
the priests, distributing to their fellow
priests according to their divisions, old
and young alike.
16In addition, they distributed to the
males three years old or more whose
names were in the genealogical
records[t]—all who would enter the
temple of the LORD to perform the daily
duties of their various tasks, according
to their responsibilities and their divisions. 17And they distributed to the
priests enrolled by their families in the
genealogical records and likewise to
the Levites twenty years old or more,
according to their responsibilities and
their divisions. 18They included all the
little ones, the wives, and the sons and
daughters of the whole community listed in these genealogical records. For
they were faithful in consecrating
themselves.
19As for the priests, the descendants of Aaron, who lived on the farm
lands around their towns or in any other towns,[u] men were designated by
name to distribute portions to every
male among them and to all who were
recorded in the genealogies of the Levites.
20This is what Hezekiah did
throughout Judah, doing what was
good and right and faithful[v] before the
LORD his God. 21In everything that he
undertook in the service of God's temple and in obedience to the law and the
commands, he sought his God and
worked wholeheartedly. And so he
prospered.[w]

31:2 [b] S 1Ch 15:2 [c] Ps 7:17; 9:2; 47:6; 71:22 [d] S 1Ch 23:28-32 **31:3** [e] S 1Ch 29:3; 2Ch 35:7; Eze 45:17 [f] Nu 28:1-29:40 **31:4** [g] S Nu 18:8; S Dt 18:8; Ne 13:10 **31:5** [h] S Nu 18:12,24; Ne 13:12; Eze 44:30 [i] Dt 12:17 **31:6** [j] S Lev 27:30; Ne 13:10-12 [k] S Ru 3:7 **31:7** [l] Ex 23:16 **31:8** [m] Ps 144:13-15 **31:10** [n] S 2Sa 8:17 [o] S Ex 36:5; Eze 44:30; Mal 3:10-12 **31:12** [p] 2Ch 35:9 **31:13** [q] 2Ch 35:9 **31:15** [r] 2Ch 29:12 [s] Jos 21:9-19 **31:16** [t] 1Ch 23:3 **31:19** [u] S Nu 35:2-5 **31:20** [v] S 2Ki 20:3 **31:21** [w] S Dt 29:9

31:4 DEVOTE THEMSELVES TO THE LAW. Hezekiah commanded the people to give the firstfruits and a tithe of all their produce to the priests and Levites (see Ex 23:19; Lev 27:30–33; Nu 18:12,20–24; Dt 26), thus enabling the priests to devote themselves more fully to God and the ministry of his Word (see article on TITHES AND OFFERINGS, p. 1392). Likewise, under the new covenant, spiritual leaders called by God must be paid from the tithes and offerings of God's people in order that they might "give [their] attention to prayer and the ministry of the word" (Ac 6:4; see Gal 6:6–10, note).

31:10 THE LORD HAS BLESSED HIS PEOPLE. As a condition for experiencing God's blessings, we must be both willing and committed to give of our means for God's work and ministry, locally and abroad (cf. 1Co 9:14; Php 4:15–18). Unwillingness to do so is a sign that our love for God and his cause is less than complete. God wants us to serve him, not money (cf. Mt 6:24; see 2Co 8—9, notes).

Sennacherib Threatens Jerusalem

32:9–19pp — 2Ki 18:17–35; Isa 36:2–20
32:20–21pp — 2Ki 19:35–37; Isa 37:36–38

32 After all that Hezekiah had so
faithfully done, Sennacherib[x]
king of Assyria came and invaded Judah. He laid siege to the fortified cities,
thinking to conquer them for himself.
2When Hezekiah saw that Sennacherib
had come and that he intended to make
war on Jerusalem,[y] 3he consulted
with his officials and military staff
about blocking off the water from the
springs outside the city, and they
helped him. 4A large force of men assembled, and they blocked all the
springs[z] and the stream that flowed
through the land. "Why should the
kings[w] of Assyria come and find plenty of water?" they said. 5Then he
worked hard repairing all the broken
sections of the wall[a] and building towers on it. He built another wall outside
that one and reinforced the supporting
terraces[x][b] of the City of David. He
also made large numbers of weapons[c]
and shields.
6He appointed military officers over
the people and assembled them before
him in the square at the city gate and
encouraged them with these words:
7"Be strong and courageous.[d] Do not
be afraid or discouraged[e] because of
the king of Assyria and the vast army
with him, for there is a greater power
with us than with him.[f] 8With him is
only the arm of flesh,[g] but with us[h]
is the LORD our God to help us and to
fight our battles."[i] And the people
gained confidence from what Hezekiah
the king of Judah said.
9Later, when Sennacherib king of
Assyria and all his forces were laying
siege to Lachish,[j] he sent his officers
to Jerusalem with this message for
Hezekiah king of Judah and for all the
people of Judah who were there:
10"This is what Sennacherib
king of Assyria says: On what are
you basing your confidence,[k]
that you remain in Jerusalem under siege? 11When Hezekiah says,
'The LORD our God will save us
from the hand of the king of Assyria,' he is misleading[l] you, to
let you die of hunger and thirst.
12Did not Hezekiah himself remove this god's high places and
altars, saying to Judah and Jerusalem, 'You must worship before
one altar[m] and burn sacrifices on
it'?
13"Do you not know what I and
my fathers have done to all the
peoples of the other lands? Were
the gods of those nations ever
able to deliver their land from my
hand?[n] 14Who of all the gods of
these nations that my fathers destroyed has been able to save his
people from me? How then can
your god deliver you from my
hand? 15Now do not let Hezekiah
deceive[o] you and mislead you
like this. Do not believe him, for
no god of any nation or kingdom
has been able to deliver[p] his people from my hand or the hand of
my fathers.[q] How much less will
your god deliver you from my
hand!"
16Sennacherib's officers spoke further against the LORD God and against
his servant Hezekiah. 17The king also
wrote letters[r] insulting[s] the LORD,
the God of Israel, and saying this
against him: "Just as the gods[t] of the
peoples of the other lands did not rescue their people from my hand, so the
god of Hezekiah will not rescue his
people from my hand." 18Then they
called out in Hebrew to the people of
Jerusalem who were on the wall, to terrify them and make them afraid in order to capture the city. 19They spoke

32:1 [x]Isa 36:1; 37:9,17,37
32:2 [y]Isa 22:7; Jer 1:15
32:4 [z]S 2Ki 18:17; Isa 22:9,11; Na 3:14
32:5 [a]Isa 22:10 [b]S 1Ch 11:8 [c]Isa 22:8
32:7 [d]S Dt 31:6 [e]2Ch 20:15 [f]S Nu 14:9; 2Ki 6:16
32:8 [g]Job 40:9; Isa 52:10; Jer 17:5; 32:21 [h]S Dt 3:22; S 1Sa 17:45 [i]S 1Ch 5:22; Ps 20:7; Isa 28:6
32:9 [j]S Jos 10:3, 31
32:10 [k]Eze 29:16
32:11 [l]Isa 37:10
32:12 [m]S 2Ch 31:1
32:13 [n]ver 15
32:15 [o]Isa 37:10 [p]Da 3:15 [q]Ex 5:2
32:17 [r]Isa 37:14 [s]Ps 74:22; Isa 37:4,17 [t]S 2Ki 19:12

[w]4 Hebrew; Septuagint and Syriac *king*
[x]5 Or *the Millo*

32:1 AFTER ALL THAT. The Chronicler notes that it was after Hezekiah's acts of faithfulness that Sennacherib invaded Judah (see also 2Ki 18—19; Isa 36—37). Trouble and testing sometimes come to a believer who has been completely faithful and obedient to God. However, the assurance of faith is this: the one who is with us is so great that he can overcome all that the enemy throws against us (v. 7; cf. 1Jn 4:4).

32:7 DO NOT BE AFRAID. Hezekiah's words of faith may have been inspired by the experience and words of the prophet Elisha (2Ki 6:16). Hezekiah's exhortation not to be afraid, together with his promise that "with us is the LORD our God to help us and to fight our battles" (v. 8), is applicable to all who follow the Lord with love, a sincere faith and a pure heart. According to Isaiah, "sinners in Zion are terrified" (Isa 33:14), but "he who walks righteously . . . will dwell on the heights" (Isa 33:15–16).

about the God of Jerusalem as they did
about the gods of the other peoples of
the world—the work of men's
hands.[u]
[20]King Hezekiah and the prophet
Isaiah son of Amoz cried out in
prayer[v] to heaven about this. [21]And
the LORD sent an angel,[w] who annihilated all the fighting men and the leaders and officers in the camp of the Assyrian king. So he withdrew to his own
land in disgrace. And when he went
into the temple of his god, some of his
sons cut him down with the sword.[x]
[22]So the LORD saved Hezekiah and
the people of Jerusalem from the hand
of Sennacherib king of Assyria and
from the hand of all others. He took
care of them[y] on every side. [23]Many
brought offerings to Jerusalem for the
LORD and valuable gifts[y] for Hez-
Ne 6:15-16 ekiah king of Judah. From then on
he was highly regarded by all the
nations.

Hezekiah's Pride, Success and Death

32:24–33pp — 2Ki 20:1–21; Isa 37:21–38; 38:1–8

[24]In those days Hezekiah became ill
and was at the point of death. He
prayed to the LORD, who answered him
and gave him a miraculous sign.[z]
[25]But Hezekiah's heart was proud[a]
and he did not respond to the kindness
shown him; therefore the LORD's
wrath[b] was on him and on Judah and
Jerusalem. [26]Then Hezekiah repented[c] of the pride of his heart, as did the
people of Jerusalem; therefore the
LORD's wrath did not come upon them
during the days of Hezekiah.[d]
[27]Hezekiah had very great riches
and honor,[e] and he made treasuries
for his silver and gold and for his precious stones, spices, shields and all
kinds of valuables. [28]He also made
buildings to store the harvest of grain,
new wine and oil; and he made stalls
for various kinds of cattle, and pens for
the flocks. [29]He built villages and acquired great numbers of flocks and
herds, for God had given him very great
riches.[f]
[30]It was Hezekiah who blocked[g]
the upper outlet of the Gihon[h] spring
and channeled[i] the water down to the
west side of the City of David. He succeeded in everything he undertook.
[31]But when envoys were sent by the
rulers of Babylon[j] to ask him about
the miraculous sign[k] that had occurred in the land, God left him to
test[l] him and to know everything that
was in his heart.
[32]The other events of Hezekiah's
reign and his acts of devotion are written in the vision of the prophet Isaiah
son of Amoz in the book of the kings of
Judah and Israel. [33]Hezekiah rested
with his fathers and was buried on the
hill where the tombs of David's descendants are. All Judah and the people of
Jerusalem honored him when he died.
And Manasseh his son succeeded him
as king.

32:19 [u]Ps 115:4-8; Isa 2:8; 17:8; 37:19; Jer 1:16 **32:20** [v]Isa 1:15; 37:15 **32:21** [w]S Ge 19:13 [x]S 2Ki 19:7; Isa 37:7,38; Jer 41:2 **32:23** [y]S 1Sa 10:27; S 2Ch 9:24; Ps 68:18,29; 76:11; Isa 16:1; 18:7; 45:14; Zep 3:10; Zec 14:16-17 **32:24** [z]ver 31 **32:25** [a]S 2Ki 14:10 [b]S 2Ch 19:2 **32:26** [c]Jer 26:18-19 [d]2Ch 34:27,28; Isa 39:8 **32:27** [e]S 1Ch 29:12; S 2Ch 9:24 **32:29** [f]Isa 39:2 **32:30** [g]S 2Ki 18:17 [h]S 1Ki 1:33 [i]S 2Sa 5:8 **32:31** [j]Isa 13:1; 39:1 [k]S ver 24; Isa 38:7 [l]S Ge 22:1; Dt 8:16

[y]22 Hebrew; Septuagint and Vulgate *He gave them rest*

32:19 THEY SPOKE ABOUT THE GOD OF JERUSALEM. See 2Ki 18:30, note.

32:20 CRIED OUT IN PRAYER. See 2Ki 19:1–34 and Isa 37:1–35 for Hezekiah's prayer (see 2Ki 19:15,19, notes).

32:21 THE LORD SENT AN ANGEL. See 2Ki 19:35, note.

32:24 HEZEKIAH BECAME ILL. For a more complete narrative of Hezekiah's sickness and healing and the miraculous sign that accompanied his healing, see 2Ki 20:1–11 (cf. Isa 38:1–8; see 38:1,5 notes).

32:31 TO TEST HIM. The story of Hezekiah's dealings with the envoys from Babylon is told in 2Ki 20:12–19 and Isa 39. God sometimes withdraws evidences of his nearness and favor in order to test the hearts and steadfast trust of his choicest servants. God may also test the genuineness of believers' devotion in order to train them in humility and prepare them for larger tasks or greater responsibilities. (1) Some of the ways that God tests his people are by (a) prolonged adverse circumstances, as with Joseph in Egypt (Ge 39—40), (b) physical and emotional affliction, as with Job (Job 1—2), (c) delayed fulfillment of God's promises, as with Abraham and Sarah (Ge 15—21) and Joseph's dreams (Ge 37; 42:6; cf. Ps 105:17–19), (d) a difficult obedience test, as with Abraham and Isaac (Ge 22) or King Saul (1Sa 15), and (e) seasons of spiritual dryness or darkness that come to most of God's people at some point in life.

(2) Learning to trust God and remaining faithful in the midst of trying experiences produce the full-grown fruit of steadfast faith, proven character, mature obedience and God's approval (cf. 2Co 12:7–10). In the midst of his fiery trial, Job declared: "[God] knows the way that I take; when he has tested me, I will come forth as gold" (Job 23:10; cf. Zec 13:9). To be tested by God is not necessarily a sign of his disfavor or judgment, but may in fact be a sign of his greater purpose for the one whose heart he tests.

Manasseh King of Judah

33:1–10pp — 2Ki 21:1–10
33:18–20pp — 2Ki 21:17–18

33 Manasseh[m] was twelve years
old when he became king, and
he reigned in Jerusalem fifty-five years.
2He did evil in the eyes of the LORD,[n]
following the detestable[o] practices of
the nations the LORD had driven out before the Israelites. 3He rebuilt the high
places his father Hezekiah had demolished; he also erected altars to the Baals and made Asherah poles.[p] He
bowed down[q] to all the starry hosts
and worshiped them. 4He built altars in
the temple of the LORD, of which the
LORD had said, "My Name[r] will remain
in Jerusalem forever." 5In both courts
of the temple of the LORD,[s] he built
altars to all the starry hosts. 6He sacrificed his sons[t] in[z] the fire in the Valley of Ben Hinnom, practiced sorcery,
divination and witchcraft, and consulted mediums[u] and spiritists.[v] He did
much evil in the eyes of the LORD, provoking him to anger.

7He took the carved image he had
made and put it in God's temple,[w] of
which God had said to David and to his
son Solomon, "In this temple and in Jerusalem, which I have chosen out of all
the tribes of Israel, I will put my Name
forever. 8I will not again make the feet
of the Israelites leave the land[x] I assigned to your forefathers, if only they
will be careful to do everything I commanded them concerning all the laws,
decrees and ordinances given through
Moses." 9But Manasseh led Judah and
the people of Jerusalem astray, so that
they did more evil than the nations the
LORD had destroyed before the Israelites.[y]

10The LORD spoke to Manasseh and
his people, but they paid no attention.
11So the LORD brought against them
the army commanders of the king of
Assyria, who took Manasseh prisoner,[z] put a hook[a] in his nose, bound
him with bronze shackles[b] and took
him to Babylon. 12In his distress he
sought the favor of the LORD his God
and humbled[c] himself greatly before
the God of his fathers. 13And when he
prayed to him, the LORD was moved by
his entreaty and listened to his plea; so
he brought him back to Jerusalem and
to his kingdom. Then Manasseh knew
that the LORD is God.

14Afterward he rebuilt the outer
wall of the City of David, west of the
Gihon[d] spring in the valley, as far as
the entrance of the Fish Gate[e] and encircling the hill of Ophel;[f] he also
made it much higher. He stationed military commanders in all the fortified
cities in Judah.

15He got rid of the foreign gods and
removed[g] the image from the temple
of the LORD, as well as all the altars he
had built on the temple hill and in Jerusalem; and he threw them out of the
city. 16Then he restored the altar of the
LORD and sacrificed fellowship offerings[a] and thank offerings[h] on it, and
told Judah to serve the LORD, the God
of Israel. 17The people, however, continued to sacrifice at the high places,
but only to the LORD their God.

18The other events of Manasseh's
reign, including his prayer to his God
and the words the seers spoke to him
in the name of the LORD, the God of
Israel, are written in the annals of
the kings of Israel.[b] 19His prayer and
how God was moved by his entreaty,
as well as all his sins and unfaithfulness, and the sites where he built
high places and set up Asherah poles
and idols before he humbled[i] himself—all are written in the records
of the seers.[c][j] 20Manasseh rested
with his fathers and was buried[k]
in his palace. And Amon his son succeeded him as king.

33:1 [m]S 1Ch 3:13 **33:2** [n]Jer 15:4 [o]S Dt 18:9 **33:3** [p]Dt 16:21-22; S 2Ch 24:18 [q]Dt 17:3 **33:4** [r]2Ch 7:16 **33:5** [s]S 2Ch 4:9 **33:6** [t]S Lev 18:21; S Dt 18:10 [u]S Ex 22:18; S Lev 19:31 [v]S 1Sa 28:13 **33:7** [w]S 2Ch 7:16 **33:8** [x]S 2Sa 7:10 **33:9** [y]Jer 15:4; Eze 5:7 **33:11** [z]S Dt 28:36 [a]S 2Ki 19:28; Isa 37:29; Eze 29:4; 38:4; Am 4:2 [b]Ps 149:8 **33:12** [c]S 2Ch 6:37 **33:14** [d]S 1Ki 1:33 [e]Ne 3:3; 12:39; Zep 1:10 [f]2Ch 27:3; Ne 3:26 **33:15** [g]2Ki 23:12 **33:16** [h]Lev 7:11-18 **33:19** [i]S 2Ch 6:37 [j]2Ki 21:17 **33:20** [k]2Ki 21:18; S 2Ch 21:20

[z] *6* Or *He made his sons pass through*
[a] *16* Traditionally *peace offerings* [b] *18* That is, Judah, as frequently in 2 Chronicles
[c] *19* One Hebrew manuscript and Septuagint; most Hebrew manuscripts *of Hozai*

33:13 PRAYED TO HIM. Manasseh forsook the God of his father, Hezekiah, and became more evil than any other king in Judah's history. However, in a time of crisis and great distress (vv. 11–12), this king genuinely repented and cried out to God (vv. 12–13). God's forgiveness of Manasseh after his deep repentance and humility dramatically illustrates the truth that even the most wicked sinners can find grace whenever they sincerely humble themselves and call out to God. Unfortunately, as the writer of 2 Kings emphasizes, Manasseh's long and ungodly rule had led many into sin and ruin (2Ki 21:9–15); his repentance and restoration did not stop the ongoing rippling consequences of his previous influence for evil (cf. 2Ki 24:3–4; see 23:26, note).

Amon King of Judah

33:21–25pp — 2Ki 21:19–24

21 Amon[l] was twenty-two years old
when he became king, and he reigned
in Jerusalem two years. 22 He did evil in
the eyes of the LORD, as his father Manasseh had done. Amon worshiped and
offered sacrifices to all the idols Manasseh had made. 23 But unlike his father Manasseh, he did not humble[m]
himself before the LORD; Amon increased his guilt.

24 Amon's officials conspired against
him and assassinated him in his palace. 25 Then the people[n] of the land
killed all who had plotted against King
Amon, and they made Josiah his son
king in his place.

Josiah's Reforms

34:1–2pp — 2Ki 22:1–2
34:3–7Ref — 2Ki 23:4–20
34:8–13pp — 2Ki 22:3–7

34 Josiah[o] was eight years old
when he became king,[p] and he
reigned in Jerusalem thirty-one years.
2 He did what was right in the eyes of
the LORD and walked in the ways of his
father David,[q] not turning aside to the
right or to the left.

3 In the eighth year of his reign,
while he was still young, he began to
seek the God[r] of his father David. In
his twelfth year he began to purge Judah and Jerusalem of high places,
Asherah poles, carved idols and cast
images. 4 Under his direction the altars
of the Baals were torn down; he cut to
pieces the incense altars that were
above them, and smashed the Asherah
poles,[s] the idols and the images.
These he broke to pieces and scattered
over the graves of those who had sacrificed to them.[t] 5 He burned[u] the
bones of the priests on their altars, and
so he purged Judah and Jerusalem. 6 In
the towns of Manasseh, Ephraim and
Simeon, as far as Naphtali, and in the
ruins around them, 7 he tore down the
altars and the Asherah poles and
crushed the idols to powder[v] and cut
to pieces all the incense altars
throughout Israel. Then he went back
to Jerusalem.

8 In the eighteenth year of Josiah's
reign, to purify the land and the temple, he sent Shaphan son of Azaliah
and Maaseiah the ruler of the city, with
Joah son of Joahaz, the recorder, to repair the temple of the LORD his God.

9 They went to Hilkiah[w] the high
priest and gave him the money that had
been brought into the temple of God,
which the Levites who were the doorkeepers had collected from the people
of Manasseh, Ephraim and the entire
remnant of Israel and from all the people of Judah and Benjamin and the inhabitants of Jerusalem. 10 Then they
entrusted it to the men appointed to
supervise the work on the LORD's temple. These men paid the workers who
repaired and restored the temple.
11 They also gave money[x] to the carpenters and builders to purchase
dressed stone, and timber for joists
and beams for the buildings that the
kings of Judah had allowed to fall into
ruin.[y]

12 The men did the work faithfully.[z]
Over them to direct them were Jahath
and Obadiah, Levites descended from
Merari, and Zechariah and Meshullam,
descended from Kohath. The Levites—all who were skilled in playing
musical instruments—[a] 13 had charge
of the laborers[b] and supervised all the
workers from job to job. Some of the
Levites were secretaries, scribes and
doorkeepers.

The Book of the Law Found

34:14–28pp — 2Ki 22:8–20
34:29–32pp — 2Ki 23:1–3

14 While they were bringing out the
money that had been taken into the
temple of the LORD, Hilkiah the priest
found the Book of the Law of the LORD
that had been given through Moses.
15 Hilkiah said to Shaphan the secretary, "I have found the Book of the
Law[c] in the temple of the LORD." He
gave it to Shaphan.

16 Then Shaphan took the book to
the king and reported to him: "Your officials are doing everything that has
been committed to them. 17 They have
paid out the money that was in the temple of the LORD and have entrusted it to
the supervisors and workers." 18 Then
Shaphan the secretary informed the
king, "Hilkiah the priest has given me
a book." And Shaphan read from it in
the presence of the king.

33:21 [l] S 1Ch 3:14
33:23 [m] S Ex 10:3; 2Ch 7:14; Ps 18:27; 147:6; Pr 3:34
33:25 [n] S 2Ch 22:1
34:1 [o] S 1Ch 3:14 [p] Zep 1:1
34:2 [q] 2Ch 29:2
34:3 [r] S 1Ch 16:11
34:4 [s] S Ex 34:13 [t] Ex 32:20; S Lev 26:30; 2Ki 23:11; Mic 1:5
34:5 [u] S 1Ki 13:2
34:7 [v] S Ex 32:20
34:9 [w] S 1Ch 6:13
34:11 [x] 2Ch 24:12 [y] 2Ch 33:4-7
34:12 [z] 2Ki 12:15 [a] S 1Ch 25:1
34:13 [b] S 1Ch 23:4
34:15 [c] S 2Ki 22:8; Ezr 7:6; Ne 8:1

34:1 JOSIAH. See 2Ki 22:1, note.
34:14 FOUND THE BOOK OF THE LAW IN THE TEMPLE OF THE LORD. See 2Ki 22:8, note.

19When the king heard the words of
the Law,[d] he tore[e] his robes. **20**He
gave these orders to Hilkiah, Ahikam
son of Shaphan[f], Abdon son of Micah,[d] Shaphan the secretary and Asaiah the king's attendant: **21**"Go and inquire of the LORD for me and for the
remnant in Israel and Judah about
what is written in this book that has
been found. Great is the LORD's anger
that is poured out[g] on us because our
fathers have not kept the word of the
LORD; they have not acted in accordance with all that is written in this
book."

22Hilkiah and those the king had
sent with him[e] went to speak to the
prophetess[h] Huldah, who was the
wife of Shallum son of Tokhath,[f] the
son of Hasrah,[g] keeper of the wardrobe. She lived in Jerusalem, in the
Second District.

23She said to them, "This is what the
LORD, the God of Israel, says: Tell the
man who sent you to me, **24**'This is
what the LORD says: I am going to bring
disaster[i] on this place and its people[j]—all the curses[k] written in the
book that has been read in the presence of the king of Judah. **25**Because
they have forsaken me[l] and burned
incense to other gods and provoked me
to anger by all that their hands have
made,[h] my anger will be poured out on
this place and will not be quenched.'
26Tell the king of Judah, who sent you
to inquire of the LORD, 'This is what the
LORD, the God of Israel, says concerning the words you heard: **27**Because
your heart was responsive[m] and you
humbled[n] yourself before God when
you heard what he spoke against this
place and its people, and because you
humbled yourself before me and tore
your robes and wept in my presence, I
have heard you, declares the LORD.
28Now I will gather you to your fathers,[o] and you will be buried in
peace. Your eyes will not see all the
disaster I am going to bring on this
place and on those who live here.' "[p]

So they took her answer back to the
king.

29Then the king called together all
the elders of Judah and Jerusalem.
30He went up to the temple of the
LORD[q] with the men of Judah, the people of Jerusalem, the priests and the
Levites—all the people from the least
to the greatest. He read in their hearing all the words of the Book of the
Covenant, which had been found in the
temple of the LORD. **31**The king stood by
his pillar[r] and renewed the covenant[s] in the presence of the LORD—
to follow[t] the LORD and keep his commands, regulations and decrees with
all his heart and all his soul, and to
obey the words of the covenant written
in this book.

32Then he had everyone in Jerusalem and Benjamin pledge themselves
to it; the people of Jerusalem did this
in accordance with the covenant of
God, the God of their fathers.

33Josiah removed all the detestable[u] idols from all the territory belonging to the Israelites, and he had all
who were present in Israel serve the
LORD their God. As long as he lived,
they did not fail to follow the LORD, the
God of their fathers.

Josiah Celebrates the Passover

35:1,18–19pp — 2Ki 23:21–23

35 Josiah celebrated the Passover[v] to the LORD in Jerusalem,
and the Passover lamb was slaugh-

34:19 [d]Dt 28:3-68 [e]Isa 36:22; 37:1 **34:20** [f]S 2Ki 22:3 **34:21** [g]La 2:4; 4:11; Eze 36:18 **34:22** [h]S Ex 15:20; Ne 6:14 **34:24** [i]Pr 16:4; Isa 3:9; Jer 40:2; 42:10; 44:2,11 [j]2Ch 36:14-20 [k]Dt 28:15-68 **34:25** [l]2Ch 33:3-6; Jer 22:9 **34:27** [m]S 2Ch 32:26 [n]S Ex 10:3; S 2Ch 6:37 **34:28** [o]2Ch 35:20-25 [p]S 2Ch 32:26 **34:30** [q]S 2Ki 23:2 **34:31** [r]S 1Ki 7:15 [s]S 2Ki 11:17; S 2Ch 23:16 [t]S Dt 13:4 **34:33** [u]S Dt 18:9 **35:1** [v]Ex 12:1-30; S Nu 28:16

[d]20 Also called *Acbor son of Micaiah*
[e]22 One Hebrew manuscript, Vulgate and Syriac; most Hebrew manuscripts do not have *had sent with him.* [f]22 Also called *Tikvah*
[g]22 Also called *Harhas* [h]25 Or *by everything they have done*

34:24 BRING DISASTER ON THIS PLACE. The sins of the people had reached such a point that God's destructive judgment on them was inevitable (see 2Ki 22:13, note).

34:27 YOU HUMBLED YOURSELF BEFORE GOD. See 7:14, note; 2Ki 22:19, note.

34:30 HE READ ... ALL THE WORDS OF THE BOOK. Every spiritual revival recorded in the OT came from a renewed proclamation of and commitment to the word of God. (1) Josiah read the "words of the Book of the Covenant" in the people's presence, and they returned to the Lord (vv. 30–33). (2) Earlier, Jehoshaphat and the Levites "taught throughout Judah, taking with them the Book of the Law of the LORD" (17:9). (3) Later, Ezra read from God's law for six hours a day for seven days (Ne 8:3,18) and explained it in such a way that the people "could understand what was being read" (Ne 8:8). All genuine lasting revivals are accompanied by restoring the Word of God to its appointed place of authority and honor. One sure evidence that revival is beginning among God's people is a great desire to hear, search out and obey the Word of the Lord (see Ac 2:42).

35:1 JOSIAH CELEBRATED THE PASSOVER. See article on THE PASSOVER, p. 104.

tered on the fourteenth day of the first
month. 2He appointed the priests to
their duties and encouraged them in
the service of the LORD's temple. 3He
said to the Levites, who instructed[w]
all Israel and who had been consecrated to the LORD: "Put the sacred ark in
the temple that Solomon son of David
king of Israel built. It is not to be carried about on your shoulders. Now
serve the LORD your God and his people
Israel. 4Prepare yourselves by families
in your divisions,[x] according to the directions written by David king of Israel
and by his son Solomon.
5"Stand in the holy place with a
group of Levites for each subdivision of
the families of your fellow countrymen,
the lay people. 6Slaughter the Passover lambs, consecrate yourselves[y]
and prepare ⌊the lambs⌋ for your fellow
countrymen, doing what the LORD commanded through Moses."
7Josiah provided for all the lay people who were there a total of thirty
thousand sheep and goats for the Passover offerings,[z] and also three thousand cattle—all from the king's own
possessions.[a]
8His officials also contributed[b] voluntarily to the people and the priests
and Levites. Hilkiah,[c] Zechariah and
Jehiel, the administrators of God's
temple, gave the priests twenty-six
hundred Passover offerings and three
hundred cattle. 9Also Conaniah[d]
along with Shemaiah and Nethanel, his
brothers, and Hashabiah, Jeiel and Jozabad,[e] the leaders of the Levites, provided five thousand Passover offerings
and five hundred head of cattle for the
Levites.
10The service was arranged and the
priests stood in their places with the
Levites in their divisions[f] as the king
had ordered.[g] 11The Passover lambs
were slaughtered,[h] and the priests
sprinkled the blood handed to them,
while the Levites skinned the animals.
12They set aside the burnt offerings to
give them to the subdivisions of the
families of the people to offer to the
LORD, as is written in the Book of Moses. They did the same with the cattle.
13They roasted the Passover animals
over the fire as prescribed,[i] and
boiled the holy offerings in pots, cal-
drons and pans and served them quickly to all the people. 14After this, they
made preparations for themselves and
for the priests, because the priests, the
descendants of Aaron, were sacrificing
the burnt offerings and the fat portions[j] until nightfall. So the Levites
made preparations for themselves and
for the Aaronic priests.
15The musicians,[k] the descendants
of Asaph, were in the places prescribed
by David, Asaph, Heman and Jeduthun
the king's seer. The gatekeepers at
each gate did not need to leave their
posts, because their fellow Levites
made the preparations for them.
16So at that time the entire service
of the LORD was carried out for the celebration of the Passover and the offering of burnt offerings on the altar of the
LORD, as King Josiah had ordered.
17The Israelites who were present celebrated the Passover at that time and
observed the Feast of Unleavened
Bread for seven days. 18The Passover
had not been observed like this in Israel since the days of the prophet Samuel; and none of the kings of Israel had
ever celebrated such a Passover as did
Josiah, with the priests, the Levites
and all Judah and Israel who were
there with the people of Jerusalem.
19This Passover was celebrated in the
eighteenth year of Josiah's reign.

The Death of Josiah

35:20–36:1pp — 2Ki 23:28–30

20After all this, when Josiah had set
the temple in order, Neco king of Egypt
went up to fight at Carchemish[l] on
the Euphrates,[m] and Josiah marched
out to meet him in battle. 21But Neco
sent messengers to him, saying, "What
quarrel is there between you and me,
O king of Judah? It is not you I am attacking at this time, but the house with
which I am at war. God has told[n] me
to hurry; so stop opposing God, who is
with me, or he will destroy you."
22Josiah, however, would not turn
away from him, but disguised[o] himself to engage him in battle. He would
not listen to what Neco had said at

35:3 [w]S 2Ch 17:7 **35:4** [x]ver 10; S 1Ch 24:1; Ezr 6:18 **35:6** [y]S Lev 11:44 **35:7** [z]S 2Ch 30:24 [a]S 2Ch 31:3 **35:8** [b]S 1Ch 29:3; 2Ch 29:31-36 [c]S 1Ch 6:13 **35:9** [d]2Ch 31:12 [e]2Ch 31:13 **35:10** [f]S ver 4 [g]2Ch 30:16 **35:11** [h]S 2Ch 30:17

35:13 [i]Ex 12:2-11 **35:14** [j]S Ex 29:13 **35:15** [k]S 1Ch 25:1; S 26:12-19; 2Ch 29:30; Ne 12:46; Ps 68:25 **35:20** [l]Isa 10:9; Jer 46:2 [m]S Ge 2:14 **35:21** [n]S 1Ki 13:18; S 2Ki 18:25 **35:22** [o]S 1Sa 28:8

35:22 WOULD NOT LISTEN TO WHAT NECO HAD SAID AT GOD'S COMMAND. Neco's military campaign against the emerging Babylonian world power was from the Lord. Josiah, although a righteous man, failed to understand God's will in this matter and attempted to hinder Neco's army. Josiah's failure to seek out God's will and purpose cost him his life.

God's command but went to fight him
on the plain of Megiddo.
23Archers[p] shot King Josiah, and
he told his officers, "Take me away; I
am badly wounded." 24So they took
him out of his chariot, put him in the
other chariot he had and brought him
to Jerusalem, where he died. He was
buried in the tombs of his fathers, and
all Judah and Jerusalem mourned for
him.
25Jeremiah composed laments for
Josiah, and to this day all the men and
women singers commemorate Josiah in
the laments.[q] These became a tradition in Israel and are written in the Laments.[r]
26The other events of Josiah's reign
and his acts of devotion, according to
what is written in the Law of the
LORD— 27all the events, from beginning to end, are written in the book of
the kings of Israel and Judah.

36
1And the people[s] of the land
took Jehoahaz son of Josiah and made
him king in Jerusalem in place of his
father.

Jehoahaz King of Judah

36:2–4pp — 2Ki 23:31–34

2Jehoahaz[i] was twenty-three years
old when he became king, and he
reigned in Jerusalem three months.
3The king of Egypt dethroned him in
Jerusalem and imposed on Judah a levy
of a hundred talents[j] of silver and a
talent[k] of gold. 4The king of Egypt
made Eliakim, a brother of Jehoahaz,
king over Judah and Jerusalem and
changed Eliakim's name to Jehoiakim.
But Neco[t] took Eliakim's brother Jehoahaz and carried him off to Egypt.[u]

Jehoiakim King of Judah

36:5–8pp — 2Ki 23:36–24:6

5Jehoiakim[v] was twenty-five years
old when he became king, and he
reigned in Jerusalem eleven years. He
did evil in the eyes of the LORD his God.
6Nebuchadnezzar[w] king of Babylon attacked him and bound him with bronze
shackles to take him to Babylon.[x]
7Nebuchadnezzar also took to Babylon
articles from the temple of the LORD
and put them in his temple[l] there.[y]
8The other events of Jehoiakim's
reign, the detestable things he did and
all that was found against him, are
written in the book of the kings of Israel and Judah. And Jehoiachin his son
succeeded him as king.

Jehoiachin King of Judah

36:9–10pp — 2Ki 24:8–17

9Jehoiachin[z] was eighteen[m] years
old when he became king, and he
reigned in Jerusalem three months and
ten days. He did evil in the eyes of the
LORD. 10In the spring, King Nebuchadnezzar sent for him and brought him to
Babylon,[a] together with articles of
value from the temple of the LORD, and
he made Jehoiachin's uncle,[n] Zedekiah, king over Judah and Jerusalem.

Zedekiah King of Judah

36:11–16pp — 2Ki 24:18–20; Jer 52:1–3

11Zedekiah[b] was twenty-one years
old when he became king, and he
reigned in Jerusalem eleven years.
12He did evil in the eyes of the LORD[c]
his God and did not humble[d] himself
before Jeremiah the prophet, who
spoke the word of the LORD. 13He also
rebelled against King Nebuchadnezzar,
who had made him take an oath[e] in
God's name. He became stiff-necked[f]
and hardened his heart and would not
turn to the LORD, the God of Israel.
14Furthermore, all the leaders of the

35:23 [p] S 1Ki 22:34 **35:25** [q] S Ge 50:10; Jer 22:10,15-16 [r] 2Ch 34:28 **36:1** [s] S 2Ch 22:1 **36:4** [t] Jer 22:10-12 [u] Eze 19:4 **36:5** [v] Jer 22:18; 25:1; 26:1; 35:1; 36:1; 45:1; 46:2 **36:6** [w] Jer 25:9; 27:6; Eze 29:18 [x] Eze 19:9; Da 1:1 **36:7** [y] ver 18; Ezr 1:7; Jer 27:16; Da 1:2 **36:9** [z] Jer 22:24-28; 24:1; 27:20; 29:21; 52:31 **36:10** [a] ver 18; S 2Ki 20:17; Ezr 1:7; Isa 52:11; Jer 14:18; 21:7; 22:25; 24:1; 27:16,20,22; 29:1; 34:21; 40:1; Eze 17:12; Da 5:2 **36:11** [b] S 2Ki 24:17; Jer 27:1; 28:1; 34:2; 37:1; 39:1 **36:12** [c] Jer 37:1-39:18 [d] S Dt 8:3; 2Ch 7:14; Jer 44:10 **36:13** [e] Eze 17:13 [f] S Ex 32:9; S Dt 9:27

[i] *2* Hebrew *Joahaz,* a variant of *Jehoahaz;* also in verse 4 [j] *3* That is, about 3 3/4 tons (about 3.4 metric tons) [k] *3* That is, about 75 pounds (about 34 kilograms) [l] *7* Or *palace* [m] *9* One Hebrew manuscript, some Septuagint manuscripts and Syriac (see also 2 Kings 24:8); most Hebrew manuscripts *eight* [n] *10* Hebrew *brother,* that is, relative (see 2 Kings 24:17)

36:6 NEBUCHADNEZZAR ... ATTACKED HIM. See 2Ki 24:1, note on the three phases of the destruction and captivity of Judah by Nebuchadnezzar.

36:14 UNFAITHFUL, FOLLOWING ALL THE DETESTABLE PRACTICES. The most prevailing sin of God's people throughout redemptive history has been their failure to remain separate from the unrighteous people and society around them. Instead of despising the immoral customs and lifestyles of the ungodly, all too often God's people are attracted to and conform to the culture in which they live. By doing so they show themselves unfaithful to God and thereby defile the house of the Lord (see 2Ki 24:3, note); the sad consequence is the destruction of God's people and their families because of their conformity to the ungodly ways of the world (vv. 5–21; see Ro 12:2, note; see also article on THE CHRISTIAN'S RELATIONSHIP TO THE WORLD, p. 1976).

priests and the people became more
and more unfaithful,[g] following all the
detestable practices of the nations and
defiling the temple of the LORD, which
he had consecrated in Jerusalem.

The Fall of Jerusalem

36:17–20pp — 2Ki 25:1–21; Jer 52:4–27
36:22–23pp — Ezr 1:1–3

15The LORD, the God of their fathers,
sent word to them through his messengers[h] again and again,[i] because he
had pity on his people and on his dwelling place. **16**But they mocked God's
messengers, despised his words and
scoffed[j] at his prophets until the
wrath[k] of the LORD was aroused
against his people and there was no
remedy.[l] **17**He brought up against
them the king of the Babylonians,[o][m]
who killed their young men with the
sword in the sanctuary, and spared neither young man[n] nor young woman,
old man or aged.[o] God handed all of
them over to Nebuchadnezzar.[p] **18**He
carried to Babylon all the articles[q]
from the temple of God, both large and
small, and the treasures of the LORD's
temple and the treasures of the king
and his officials. **19**They set fire[r] to
God's temple[s] and broke down the
wall[t] of Jerusalem; they burned all
the palaces and destroyed[u] everything of value there.[v]

36:14 [g]S 1Ch 5:25
36:15 [h]Isa 5:4; 44:26; Jer 7:25; Hag 1:13; Zec 1:4; Mal 2:7; 3:1; S Mt 5:12 [i]Jer 7:13,25; 11:7; 25:3-4; 35:14,15; 44:4-6
36:16 [j]S 2Ki 2:23; Job 8:2; Isa 28:14, 22; 29:20; 57:4; Jer 5:13; 43:2; Mic 2:11 [k]Ezr 5:12; Pr 1:30-31; Jer 44:3 [l]Ne 9:30; Pr 29:1; Jer 7:26; 20:8; 25:4; 30:12; Da 9:6; Zec 1:2
36:17 [m]S Ge 10:10 [n]Jer 6:11; 9:21; 18:21; 44:7 [o]S Dt 32:25; Jer 51:22 [p]Ezr 5:12; Jer 32:28; La 2:21; Eze 9:6; 23:47
36:18 [q]S ver 7; S ver 10; Jer 27:20
36:19 [r]Jer 11:16; 17:27; 21:10,14; 22:7; 32:29; 39:8; La 4:11; Eze 20:47; Am 2:5; Zec 11:1 [s]1Ki 9:8-9 [t]S 2Ki 14:13 [u]La 2:6 [v]Ps 79:1-3
36:20 [w]S Lev 26:44; S 2Ki 24:14; Ezr 2:1; Ne 7:6 [x]Jer 27:7
36:21 [y]S Lev 25:4 [z]S 1Ch 22:9

20He carried into exile[w] to Babylon
the remnant, who escaped from the
sword, and they became servants[x] to
him and his sons until the kingdom of
Persia came to power. **21**The land enjoyed its sabbath rests;[y] all the time
of its desolation it rested,[z] until the
seventy years[a] were completed in fulfillment of the word of the LORD spoken
by Jeremiah.
22In the first year of Cyrus[b] king of
Persia, in order to fulfill the word of
the LORD spoken by Jeremiah, the LORD
moved the heart of Cyrus king of Persia to make a proclamation throughout
his realm and to put it in writing:

23"This is what Cyrus king of Persia
says:

> " 'The LORD, the God of heaven,
> has given me all the kingdoms of
> the earth and he has appointed[c]
> me to build a temple for him at
> Jerusalem in Judah. Anyone of his
> people among you—may the LORD
> his God be with him, and let him
> go up.' "

[a]Jer 1:1; 25:11; 27:22; 29:10; 40:1; Da 9:2; Zec 1:12; 7:5 **36:22** [b]Isa 44:28; 45:1,13; Da 1:21; 6:28; 10:1 **36:23** [c]S Jdg 4:10

[o]*17* Or *Chaldeans*

36:15 BECAUSE HE HAD PITY. God's messengers who expose and condemn his people when they conform to the world (see previous note) are motivated by the compassion of God. They preach their messages with the intense hope that none might perish. The superficial compassion of those messengers who bring a word that allows God's people to keep compromising with the surrounding society is, like the messengers themselves, not from God (see 2Ti 4:3–4).

36:16 THEY MOCKED GOD'S MESSENGERS. The messengers sent to call God's people to repentance included Isaiah, Jeremiah and Ezekiel (cf. Jer 25:3–7; 35:12–15). Scoffing at God's prophets is the same as despising God's words (v. 16). Anyone who scorns the prophets who expose sin, guilt and apostasy is rejecting God himself (see Ac 9:4). Continual rejection of God's prophets resulted in the Israelites hardening their hearts until there was no longer any remedy (see article on THE PROPHET IN THE OLD TESTAMENT, p. 986).

36:21 THE LAND ENJOYED ITS SABBATH RESTS. According to God's commandment given at Mount Sinai, every seventh year the land was to lie fallow (Lev 25:1–7). Israel and Judah had failed to observe these sabbath years; therefore, through the exile of seventy years, God would enforce the sabbath rests (see Jer 25:11–12; 29:10).

36:22–23 THE LORD MOVED THE HEART OF CYRUS. The writer ends this book by emphasizing that, in spite of Judah's sin and apostasy, God was still at work in fulfilling his promises to the faithful remnant of his people. God would move even the mightiest rulers of the world in order to accomplish his purpose and fulfill his word (cf. Ezr 1:1–3; Jer 25:11–14; 27:22; 29:10; 33:7–10).

EZRA

Outline

I. The First Return of Exiles to Jerusalem (1:1—6:22)
  A. The Decree and Provision of Cyrus (1:1–11)
  B. List of the Returning Exiles (2:1–70)
  C. Restoration of the Temple Begins (3:1–13)
    1. Sacrifices Reinstituted (3:1–6)
    2. Construction of the Temple Started (3:7–13)
  D. Construction of the Temple Ceases Because of Opposition (4:1–24)
  E. Construction of the Temple Resumes and Is Completed (5:1—6:18)
    1. Encouragement from the Prophets (5:1–2)
    2. Protest from the Governor Tattenai (5:3–17)
    3. Darius Affirms the Temple's Construction (6:1–12)
    4. Temple Completed and Dedicated (6:13–18)
  F. Celebration of the Passover (6:19–22)
II. The Second Return of Exiles to Jerusalem Led by Ezra (7:1—10:44)
  A. The Mission of Ezra Authorized by Artaxerxes (7:1–28)
  B. The Journey of Ezra and Those Who Accompanied Him (8:1–36)
  C. The Reforms of Ezra in Jerusalem (9:1—10:44)
    1. Condemnation of Intermarriage with Pagans (9:1–4)
    2. Ezra's Confession and Intercessory Prayer for the People (9:5–15)
    3. Public Repentance and Reform (10:1–44)

Author: Ezra

Theme: Restoration of a Remnant

Date of Writing: 450–420 B.C.

Background

The book of Ezra is part of a continuous history of the Jews written after their exile, consisting of 1 and 2 Chronicles, Ezra and Nehemiah. In the Hebrew OT, Ezra and Nehemiah were originally a single book, as were 1 and 2 Chronicles. Bible scholars commonly believe that the history presented in all these books was primarily the inspired work of one post-exilic author. Although the author is nowhere designated in the Bible, almost all ancient Jewish and Christian sources, as well as many modern scholars, believe that this author was Ezra, the priest and scribe. For more details about Ezra's role as author, see the introduction to 1 Chronicles.

According to tradition, Ezra was the one who collected all the OT books together as a unit, originated the form of worship used in the synagogue, and founded the Great Synagogue in Jerusalem where the canon of OT Scriptures was eventually settled. Ezra was a godly leader with an uncompromising loyalty to and passionate love for God's Word. His written history in the Chronicles and in Ezra and Nehemiah emphasizes the themes of hope, revival, reform and restoration for God's people. The entire history was written during the second half of the 5th century B.C.

The book of Ezra records how God fulfilled his prophetic promise made through Jeremiah (Jer 29:10–14) to restore the Jewish people after 70 years of exile by bringing them back to their own land (1:1). Judah's collapse as a nation and their deportation to Babylon had occurred in three distinct stages. In stage one (605 B.C.), Judah's young nobility, including Daniel, were taken into exile; in stage two (597 B.C.), there were 11,000 more exiles taken, including Ezekiel; and in stage three (586 B.C.), the rest of Judah, except for Jeremiah and the poorest of the people, were carried off. Likewise, the restoration of the exilic remnant, in fulfillment of Jeremiah's prophecy, took place in three stages. In stage one (538 B.C.), 50,000 exiles returned, led by Zerubbabel and Jeshua (cf. Ezr 2); in stage two (457 B.C.), over 1,700 men (plus women and children, totaling 5,000–10,000 Jews) were led back by Ezra (cf. 8:1–14, 18–21); and in stage three (444 B.C.), Nehemiah led another group back (cf. Ne 2:1–10). Note that the first company of Jewish exiles in 538 B.C. returned to Jerusalem approximately 70 years after the first deportation of Jews to exile.

About two years after the Babylonian empire was defeated and replaced by the Persian empire (539 B.C.), the Jewish restoration to their homeland began. The book of Ezra records the first and second stages of the restoration, involving three Persian kings (Cyrus, Darius and Artaxerxes) and five prominent spiritual leaders: (1) Zerubbabel, who led the first exiles in reestablishing Jerusalem and rebuilding the temple; (2) Jeshua, a godly high priest who assisted Zerubbabel; (3) Haggai and (4) Zechariah, two prophets of God who exhorted the people to finish rebuilding the temple; and (5) Ezra, who led the second company of exiles back to Jerusalem and whom God used to restore the people spiritually and morally. If Ezra is the author of this book, as seems likely, he compiled his history under the inspiration of the Holy Spirit by consulting a variety of official letters and documents (e.g., 1:2–4; 4:11–22; 5:7–17; 6:1–12), genealogies (e.g., 2:1–70) and personal memoirs (e.g., 7:27—9:15). The book was written in Hebrew except for 4:8—6:18 and 7:12–26, which were written in Aramaic, the official language of the exiles.

Purpose

This book was written to show God's providence and faithfulness in restoring a Jewish remnant from exile in Babylon (1) by moving the hearts of three different Persian kings to assist God's people in returning to their homeland, resettling Jerusalem and rebuilding the temple; and (2) by providing godly and capable leaders to lead the returning remnant in a revival of worship, commitment to God's word and repentance for unfaithfulness to God.

Survey

Ezra's 10 chapters divide naturally into two main sections: (1) Section one (chs. 1—6) records the first return of Jewish exiles to Jerusalem and the rebuilding of the temple; (2) Section two (chs.7—10) describes the second return under Ezra and the spiritual reformation that followed.

(1) Section one begins where 2 Chronicles ends—with the Jewish captivity and the decree of King Cyrus of Persia (538 B.C.) that permitted the Jews to return to their homeland (1:1–11); ch. 2 lists those who participated in this first return. Significantly, only about 50,000 Jewish exiles from among one million or more were in the first group to return (1:5; 2:64–65). In ch. 3, Zerubbabel (a descendant of David) and Jeshua (the high priest) rallied the people to start rebuilding the destroyed temple. Shrewd enemies of Judah used political means to stop that project for some time (ch. 4), but eventually the work was resumed and the temple was completed in 516 B.C. (chs. 5—6).

(2) A gap of about 60 years occurs between chs. 6 and 7, during which time Esther reigned as queen in Persia with King Xerxes I. Esther became queen about 478 B.C. (see the introduction to Esther). Chs. 7—8 record events about 20 years later when a smaller number of exiles returned from Persia to Jerusalem under Ezra's leadership. Whereas the first returning exiles accomplished the task of rebuilding God's house, Ezra set about to restore God's Law in the hearts of the people (cf. Ne 8:1–8). Ezra found widespread spiritual and moral backsliding among the men in Judah, evident in their intermarriages with pagan women. In deep grief, Ezra confessed their sin to God and interceded on their

behalf (ch. 9) The book ends with Ezra leading the men in public repentance and severing the marriage ties with the pagan wives (ch. 10).

Special Features

Four major features characterize the book of Ezra. (1) Ezra-Nehemiah is the only historical record in the Bible of the post-exilic restoration of the Jews in Palestine. (2) A remarkable feature of this book is that its two main divisions (chs. 1—6; chs. 7—10) have a historical gap between them of about 60 years. The whole book covers about 80 years. (3) Ezra demonstrates clearly how God watches over his word to see that it is fulfilled (cf. Jer 1:12; 29:10); God directed the hearts of Persian kings like a watercourse in order to restore his people to their homeland (1:1; 7:11–28; cf. Pr 21:1). (4) Ezra's treatment of unbelieving pagan women whom the Jewish men (including priests) had married in violation of God's commands profoundly illustrates how God (a) requires his people to be separated from the pagan world, and (b) sometimes uses radical surgery in order to deal with dangerous and cancerous compromise among his people. Ezra's action strongly reminded the covenant people of their primary calling to be a "kingdom of priests and a holy nation" (Ex 19:6), not just another mixed national entity.

New Testament Fulfillment

The return of a Jewish remnant to their homeland and the rebuilding of the temple reveal that God always longs to restore his wayward people. His ways include not only judgment for apostasy, but also restoration and hope for the believing remnant, through whom God directs the stream of redemption on its ultimate course. This principle is seen in the NT, where a believing remnant of Jews accepted Jesus as their Messianic Lord, while the main stream of redemption was rechanneled from unbelieving Jews to Gentiles in the early church.

Reading Ezra

In order to read the entire Old Testament in one year, the book of Ezra should be read in 4 days, according to the following schedule: □ 1–3 □ 4–6 □ 7–8 □ 9–10

NOTES

Cyrus Helps the Exiles to Return

1:1–3pp — 2Ch 36:22–23

1 In the first year of Cyrus king of
Persia, in order to fulfill the word
of the LORD spoken by Jeremiah,[a] the
LORD moved the heart[b] of Cyrus king
of Persia to make a proclamation
throughout his realm and to put it in
writing:

2 "This is what Cyrus king of Persia says:
" 'The LORD, the God of heaven,
has given me all the kingdoms of
the earth and he has appointed[c]
me to build[d] a temple for him at
Jerusalem in Judah. 3 Anyone of
his people among you—may his
God be with him, and let him go up
to Jerusalem in Judah and build
the temple of the LORD, the God of
Israel, the God who is in Jerusalem. 4 And the people of any place
where survivors[e] may now be living are to provide him with silver
and gold,[f] with goods and livestock, and with freewill offerings[g] for the temple of God[h] in
Jerusalem.' "[i]

5 Then the family heads of Judah and
Benjamin,[j] and the priests and Levites—everyone whose heart God had
moved[k]—prepared to go up and build
the house[l] of the LORD in Jerusalem.
6 All their neighbors assisted them with
articles of silver and gold,[m] with
goods and livestock, and with valuable
gifts, in addition to all the freewill offerings. 7 Moreover, King Cyrus
brought out the articles belonging to
the temple of the LORD, which Nebuchadnezzar had carried away from Jerusalem and had placed in the temple
of his god.[a][n] 8 Cyrus king of Persia
had them brought by Mithredath the
treasurer, who counted them out to
Sheshbazzar[o] the prince of Judah.
9 This was the inventory:

gold dishes	30
silver dishes	1,000
silver pans[b]	29
10 gold bowls	30
matching silver bowls	410
other articles	1,000

11 In all, there were 5,400 articles of
gold and of silver. Sheshbazzar
brought all these along when the exiles
came up from Babylon to Jerusalem.

The List of the Exiles Who Returned

2:1–70pp — Ne 7:6–73

2 Now these are the people of the
province who came up from the
captivity of the exiles,[p] whom Nebu-

1:1 [a] Jer 25:11-12; 29:10-14; Zec 1:12-16 [b] Ezr 6:22; 7:27
1:2 [c] S Jdg 4:10; Ps 72:11; Isa 41:2,25; 44:28; 45:13; 46:11; 49:7,23; 60:3,10 [d] Hag 1:2
1:4 [e] Isa 10:20-22 [f] S Ex 3:22 [g] Nu 15:3; Ps 50:14; 54:6; 116:17 [h] Ps 72:8-11; Rev 21:24 [i] Ezr 3:7; 4:3; 5:13; 6:3,14
1:5 [j] 2Ch 11:1,3, 10,12,23; 15:2, 8-9; 25:5; 31:1; 34:9; Ezr 4:1; 10:9; Ne 11:4; 12:34 [k] ver 1; Ex 35:20-22; 2Ch 36:22; Hag 1:14; S Php 2:13 [l] Ps 127:1
1:6 [m] S Ex 3:22
1:7 [n] S 2Ki 24:13; S 2Ch 36:7,10; Ezr 5:14; 6:5; Jer 52:17-19
1:8 [o] S 1Ch 3:18
2:1 [p] S 2Ch 36:20

[a] 7 Or *gods* [b] 9 The meaning of the Hebrew for this word is uncertain.

1:1 FULFILL THE WORD OF THE LORD SPOKEN BY JEREMIAH. Jeremiah had predicted that the Jews would remain in captivity in the land of Babylon for seventy years before returning to Judah (Jer 25:11–12; 29:10). The seventy-year captivity can be calculated from the first captivity in 605 B.C., the third year of Jehoiakim (2Ki 24:1; Da 1:1), to 538 B.C. (approximately seventy years later), when the people began to return to their homeland (see 2:1, note).

1:1 THE LORD MOVED THE HEART OF CYRUS. The Lord God directs the stream of redemption throughout history to its appointed end. In doing so he sometimes chooses to humble mighty rulers (e.g., Nebuchadnezzar, Da 4), send destructive judgment on rulers (e.g., Pharaoh during the exodus, Ex 14; Belshazzar in Babylon, Da 5), or exalt an international leader (e.g., King Cyrus of Persia, v. 2) in order to fulfill his word and accomplish his purposes. By stirring Cyrus's heart to be benevolent toward conquered and exiled peoples, God enabled his word of promise through Jeremiah to be fulfilled on time. Proverbs declares that a king's heart is like a watercourse in the hand of God, which God directs wherever he wishes in order to assure the ongoing course of redemption and the ultimate conclusion of history (Pr 21:1).

1:2 CYRUS KING OF PERSIA. About 160 years before the appearance of Cyrus, Isaiah had foretold of a ruler named Cyrus who would permit the return of the Jews to their homeland in order to rebuild Jerusalem and the temple (Isa 44:26–28; 45:1,13; see also Isa 41:2; 45:4–5).

1:5 WHOSE HEART GOD HAD MOVED. Through the Holy Spirit, God moved the hearts of some of his faithful people to return to their land (cf. Php 2:13, note). About 50,000 responded to the Lord's call to participate in this first pilgrimage to Palestine. Note that others remained behind in exile (vv. 4,6); their purpose was to encourage and support those who were returning to the land of Judah.

1:8 SHESHBAZZAR. Sheshbazzar, the first governor to be appointed over the returning exiles (cf. 5:14,16), may have been another name for Zerubbabel (cf. 2:2; 3:2,8; 4:3).

2:1 CAME UP FROM THE CAPTIVITY. The book of Ezra describes two of the three waves of exiled Israelites who returned to Judah. (1) The first return occurred in 538 B.C. under Zerubbabel's leadership (v. 2; 3:8; cf. Hag 1:1,14; Zec 4:9). Approximately 50,000 people returned (vv. 64–65) and rebuilt the temple, completing it in 516 B.C. (see 6:15, note). The prophets Haggai and Zechari-

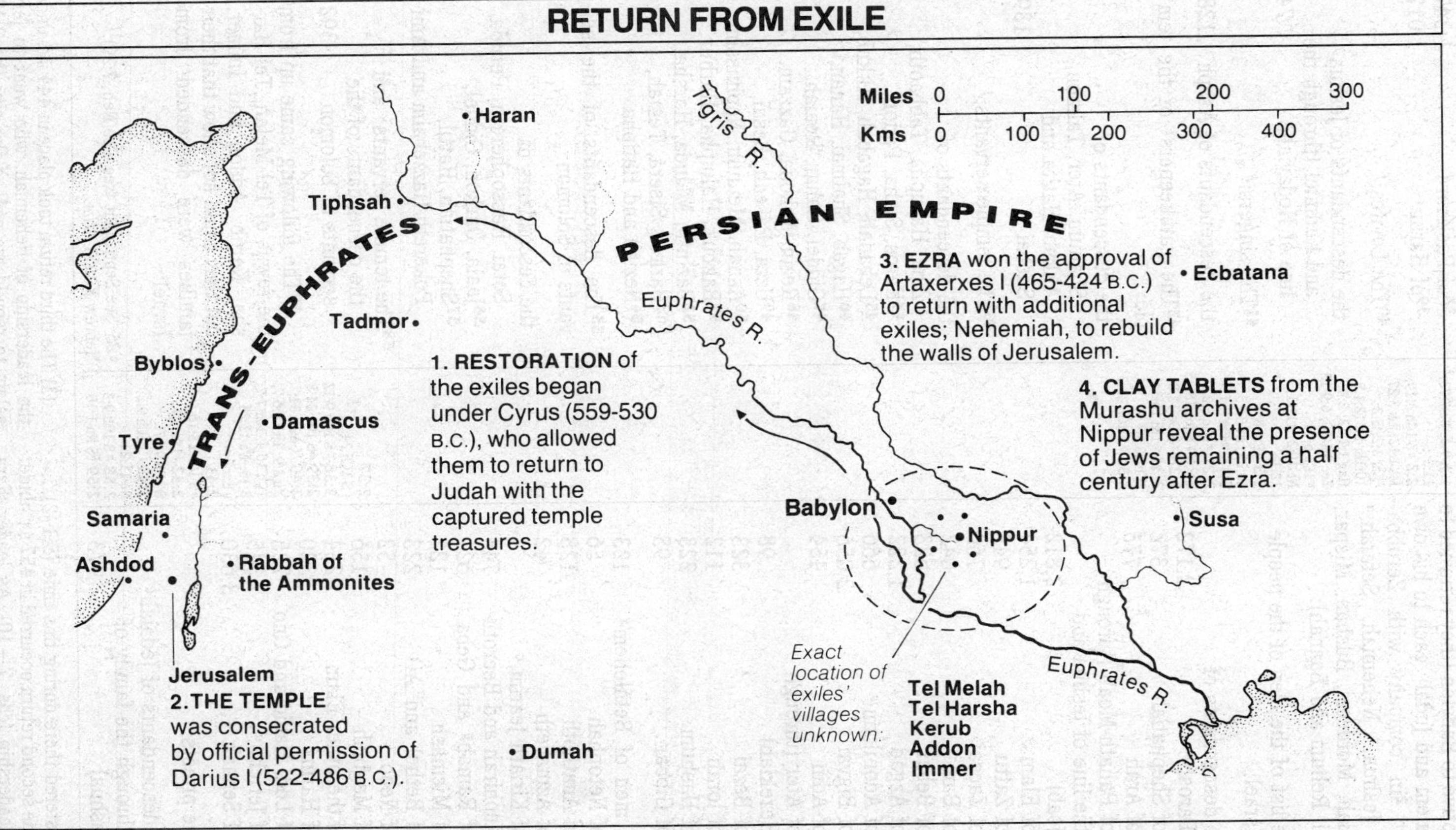

RETURN FROM EXILE
Miles 0 100 200 300
Kms 0 100 200 300 400
PERSIAN EMPIRE
TRANS-EUPHRATES
Tigris R.
Euphrates R.
Euphrates R.
Haran
Tiphsah
Tadmor
Byblos
Damascus
Tyre
Samaria
Ashdod
Rabbah of the Ammonites
Jerusalem
Dumah
Babylon
Nippur
Susa
Ecbatana
Exact location of exiles' villages unknown:
Tel Melah
Tel Harsha
Kerub
Addon
Immer
1. RESTORATION of the exiles began under Cyrus (559-530 B.C.), who allowed them to return to Judah with the captured temple treasures.
2. THE TEMPLE was consecrated by official permission of Darius I (522-486 B.C.).
3. EZRA won the approval of Artaxerxes I (465-424 B.C.) to return with additional exiles; Nehemiah, to rebuild the walls of Jerusalem.
4. CLAY TABLETS from the Murashu archives at Nippur reveal the presence of Jews remaining a half century after Ezra.

chadnezzar king of Babylon[q] had tak-
en captive to Babylon (they returned to
Jerusalem and Judah, each to his own
town,[r] 2 in company with Zerubbabel,[s] Jeshua,[t] Nehemiah, Seraiah,[u]
Reelaiah, Mordecai, Bilshan, Mispar,
Bigvai, Rehum and Baanah):

The list of the men of the people of Israel:

3 the descendants of Parosh[v] 2,172
4 of Shephatiah 372
5 of Arah 775
6 of Pahath-Moab (through the line of Jeshua and Joab) 2,812
7 of Elam 1,254
8 of Zattu 945
9 of Zaccai 760
10 of Bani 642
11 of Bebai 623
12 of Azgad 1,222
13 of Adonikam[w] 666
14 of Bigvai 2,056
15 of Adin 454
16 of Ater (through Hezekiah) 98
17 of Bezai 323
18 of Jorah 112
19 of Hashum 223
20 of Gibbar 95

21 the men of Bethlehem[x] 123
22 of Netophah 56
23 of Anathoth 128
24 of Azmaveth 42
25 of Kiriath Jearim,[c] Kephirah and Beeroth 743
26 of Ramah[y] and Geba 621
27 of Micmash 122
28 of Bethel and Ai[z] 223
29 of Nebo 52
30 of Magbish 156
31 of the other Elam 1,254
32 of Harim 320
33 of Lod, Hadid and Ono 725
34 of Jericho[a] 345
35 of Senaah 3,630

36 The priests:

the descendants of Jedaiah[b] (through the family of Jeshua) 973
37 of Immer[c] 1,052
38 of Pashhur[d] 1,247
39 of Harim[e] 1,017

40 The Levites:[f]

the descendants of Jeshua[g] and Kadmiel (through the line of Hodaviah) 74

41 The singers:[h]

the descendants of Asaph 128

42 The gatekeepers[i] of the temple:

the descendants of Shallum, Ater, Talmon, Akkub, Hatita and Shobai 139

43 The temple servants:[j]

the descendants of
Ziha, Hasupha, Tabbaoth,
44 Keros, Siaha, Padon,
45 Lebanah, Hagabah, Akkub,
46 Hagab, Shalmai, Hanan,
47 Giddel, Gahar, Reaiah,
48 Rezin, Nekoda, Gazzam,
49 Uzza, Paseah, Besai,
50 Asnah, Meunim, Nephussim,
51 Bakbuk, Hakupha, Harhur,
52 Bazluth, Mehida, Harsha,
53 Barkos, Sisera, Temah,
54 Neziah and Hatipha

55 The descendants of the servants of Solomon:

the descendants of
Sotai, Hassophereth, Peruda,
56 Jaala, Darkon, Giddel,
57 Shephatiah, Hattil,
Pokereth-Hazzebaim and Ami

58 The temple servants[k] and the descendants of the servants of Solomon 392

59 The following came up from
the towns of Tel Melah, Tel Harsha, Kerub, Addon and Immer,
but they could not show that their
families were descended[l] from
Israel:

[c] *25* See Septuagint (see also Neh. 7:29); Hebrew *Kiriath Arim.*

2:1 [q] S 2Ki 24:16; 25:12 [r] ver 70; 1Ch 9:2; Ne 7:73; 11:3 **2:2** [s] S 1Ch 3:19; Mt 1:12; Lk 3:27 [t] Ezr 3:2; 5:2; 10:18; Ne 12:1,8; Hag 1:1,12; 2:4; Zec 3:1-10; 6:9-15 [u] 1Ch 6:14; Ne 10:2; 11:11; 12:1 **2:3** [v] Ezr 8:3; 10:25; Ne 3:25 **2:13** [w] Ezr 8:13 **2:21** [x] Mic 5:2 **2:26** [y] S Jos 18:25 **2:28** [z] S Ge 12:8 **2:34** [a] 1Ki 16:34; 2Ch 28:15 **2:36** [b] S 1Ch 24:7 **2:37** [c] S 1Ch 24:14 **2:38** [d] S 1Ch 9:12 **2:39** [e] S 1Ch 24:8 **2:40** [f] Ge 29:34; Nu 3:9; Dt 18:6-7; 1Ch 16:4; Ezr 7:7; 8:15; Ne 12:24 [g] Ezr 3:9 **2:41** [h] S 1Ch 15:16 **2:42** [i] 1Sa 3:15; S 1Ch 9:17 **2:43** [j] S 1Ch 9:2; Ne 11:21 **2:58** [k] S 1Ch 9:2 **2:59** [l] S Nu 1:18

ah ministered there during this time (5:1–2).

(2) The second return occurred in 457 B.C. under Ezra's leadership (chs. 7—10). As leader, Ezra focused on furthering the spiritual life of the people and encouraging their obedience to God's law (7:10; 10:1–6).

(3) The third return took place in 444 B.C. under the leadership of Nehemiah, who went to Jerusalem to rebuild the wall of the city (Ne 2:17). The prophet Malachi probably ministered in Judah during the latter days of Ezra and Nehemiah.

60 The descendants of
Delaiah, Tobiah and
Nekoda 652

61 And from among the priests:

The descendants of
Hobaiah, Hakkoz and
Barzillai (a man who had
married a daughter of
Barzillai the Gileadite[m] and
was called by that name).
62 These searched for their family records, but they could not find
them and so were excluded from
the priesthood[n] as unclean.
63 The governor ordered them not
to eat any of the most sacred
food[o] until there was a priest
ministering with the Urim and
Thummim.[p]

64 The whole company num-
bered 42,360, 65 besides their
7,337 menservants and maidservants; and they also had 200 men
and women singers.[q] 66 They had
736 horses,[r] 245 mules, 67 435
camels and 6,720 donkeys.

68 When they arrived at the house of
the LORD in Jerusalem, some of the
heads of the families[s] gave freewill offerings toward the rebuilding of the
house of God on its site. 69 According to
their ability they gave to the treasury
for this work 61,000 drachmas[d] of
gold, 5,000 minas[e] of silver and 100
priestly garments.
70 The priests, the Levites, the singers, the gatekeepers and the temple
servants settled in their own towns,
along with some of the other people,
and the rest of the Israelites settled in
their towns.[t]

Rebuilding the Altar

3 When the seventh month came and
the Israelites had settled in their
towns,[u] the people assembled[v] as
one man in Jerusalem. 2 Then Jeshua[w]
son of Jozadak[x] and his fellow priests
and Zerubbabel son of Shealtiel[y] and
his associates began to build the altar
of the God of Israel to sacrifice burnt
offerings on it, in accordance with
what is written in the Law of Moses[z]
the man of God. 3 Despite their fear[a]
of the peoples around them, they built
the altar on its foundation and sacrificed burnt offerings on it to the LORD,
both the morning and evening sacrifices.[b] 4 Then in accordance with what
is written, they celebrated the Feast of
Tabernacles[c] with the required number of burnt offerings prescribed for
each day. 5 After that, they presented
the regular burnt offerings, the New
Moon[d] sacrifices and the sacrifices
for all the appointed sacred feasts of
the LORD,[e] as well as those brought as
freewill offerings to the LORD. 6 On the
first day of the seventh month they began to offer burnt offerings to the LORD,
though the foundation of the LORD's
temple had not yet been laid.

Rebuilding the Temple

7 Then they gave money to the ma-

2:61 [m] S 2Sa 17:27
2:62 [n] Nu 3:10; 16:39-40
2:63 [o] Lev 2:3,10 [p] S Ex 28:30
2:65 [q] S 2Sa 19:35
2:66 [r] Isa 66:20
2:68 [s] S Ex 25:2
2:70 [t] S ver 1; S 1Ch 9:2; Ne 11:3-4
3:1 [u] Ne 7:73 [v] S Lev 23:24
3:2 [w] S Ezr 2:2 [x] Hag 1:1; Zec 6:11 [y] 1Ch 3:17 [z] S Ex 20:24; Dt 12:5-6
3:3 [a] Ezr 4:4; Da 9:25 [b] S Ex 29:39; Nu 28:1-8
3:4 [c] S Ex 23:16; Nu 29:12-38; Ne 8:14-18; Zec 14:16-19
3:5 [d] S Nu 28:3,11,14; Col 2:16 [e] Lev 23:1-44; S Nu 29:39

[d] *69* That is, about 1,100 pounds (about 500 kilograms) [e] *69* That is, about 3 tons (about 2.9 metric tons)

2:64 NUMBERED 42,360. The total sum of the numbers given in vv. 3–63 falls about 11,000 short of the 42,360 mentioned here; the additional 11,000 may refer to exiles from tribes other than Judah (cf. v. 70; 6:17; 8:35), women and children, and the unregistered priests (vv. 61–62). Certain numerical differences in Nehemiah's list (7:6–73) may be due to scribal errors in the transmission of numbers.

2:70 THE REST OF THE ISRAELITES. This phrase suggests that people from all twelve tribes were represented in the remnant that returned (see 6:17; 8:35).

3:2 BUILD THE ALTAR OF THE GOD OF ISRAEL. The first priority of the returned exiles was to build an altar to the Lord. The altar was the center of Jewish worship, for on it sacrifices and blood atonement for sin were offered to God (see Ex 27:1, note). (1) The people were motivated to build the altar, at least in part, because of the danger from "the peoples around them" (v. 3). They knew that God would protect them from harm only as they approached him in faith and obedience (see Ex 19:5; 29:43; cf. Heb 4:16). (2) They also understood the basic purpose of their existence. They were to offer sacrifices to God as "a kingdom of priests and a holy nation" (Ex 19:6). Only by fulfilling this spiritual calling could they become what God intended them to be. Likewise, believers in Christ are to be "a royal priesthood, a holy nation, a people belonging to God, that you may declare the praises of him who called you out of darkness into his wonderful light" (1Pe 2:9), and to offer "spiritual sacrifices acceptable to God through Jesus Christ" (1Pe 2:5; see Heb 13:10). In other words, the church as the people of God in NT times is the heir of and successor to Israel.

3:4 FEAST OF TABERNACLES. See Lev 23:34–43, note.

sons and carpenters,[f] and gave food and drink and oil to the people of Sidon and Tyre, so that they would bring cedar logs[g] by sea from Lebanon[h] to Joppa, as authorized by Cyrus[i] king of Persia.

8In the second month[j] of the second year after their arrival at the house of God in Jerusalem, Zerubbabel[k] son of Shealtiel, Jeshua son of Jozadak and the rest of their brothers (the priests and the Levites and all who had returned from the captivity to Jerusalem) began the work, appointing Levites twenty[l] years of age and older to supervise the building of the house of the LORD. 9Jeshua[m] and his sons and brothers and Kadmiel and his sons (descendants of Hodaviah[f]) and the sons of Henadad and their sons and brothers—all Levites—joined together in supervising those working on the house of God.

10When the builders laid[n] the foundation of the temple of the LORD, the priests in their vestments and with trumpets,[o] and the Levites (the sons of Asaph) with cymbals, took their places to praise[p] the LORD, as prescribed by David[q] king of Israel.[r] 11With praise and thanksgiving they sang to the LORD:

"He is good;
his love to Israel endures
forever."[s]

And all the people gave a great shout[t] of praise to the LORD, because the foundation[u] of the house of the LORD was laid. 12But many of the older priests and Levites and family heads, who had seen the former temple,[v] wept[w] aloud when they saw the foundation of this temple being laid, while many others shouted for joy. 13No one could distinguish the sound of the shouts of joy[x] from the sound of weeping, because the people made so much noise. And the sound was heard far away.

Opposition to the Rebuilding

4 When the enemies of Judah and Benjamin heard that the exiles were building[y] a temple for the LORD, the God of Israel, 2they came to Zerubbabel and to the heads of the families and said, "Let us help you build because, like you, we seek your God and have been sacrificing to him since the time of Esarhaddon[z] king of Assyria, who brought us here."[a]

3But Zerubbabel, Jeshua and the

3:7 [f] 1Ch 22:15 [g] S 1Ch 14:1 [h] Isa 35:2; 60:13 [i] S Ezr 1:2-4
3:8 [j] 1Ki 6:1 [k] Zec 4:9 [l] S Nu 4:3
3:9 [m] Ezr 2:40
3:10 [n] Ezr 5:16; 6:3; Hag 2:15 [o] S Nu 10:2; S 2Sa 6:5; 1Ch 16:6; 2Ch 5:13; Ne 12:35 [p] S 1Ch 25:1 [q] S 1Ch 6:31 [r] Zec 6:12
3:11 [s] 1Ch 16:34, 41; S 2Ch 7:3; Ps 30:5; 107:1; 118:1; 138:8 [t] S Jos 6:5,10 [u] Hag 2:18; Zec 4:9; 8:9
3:12 [v] Hag 2:3,9 [w] Jer 31:9; 50:4
3:13 [x] Job 8:21; 33:26; Ps 27:6; 42:4; Isa 16:9; Jer 48:33
4:1 [y] Ne 2:20
4:2 [z] S 2Ki 17:24 [a] S 2Ki 17:41

[f] 9 Hebrew *Yehudah,* probably a variant of *Hodaviah*

3:8 THE HOUSE OF THE LORD. The people's highest priority after returning to Jerusalem was to rebuild the temple and so to reinstate the faithful worship of the Lord. Their years in captivity had taught them that God would not be their protector and helper unless they put him first in their lives. Likewise, we cannot expect the Lord's help or blessing if our lives and desires are not in accord with his kingdom and righteous cause (Mt 6:33, note).

3:11 WITH PRAISE AND THANKSGIVING THEY SANG. The people sang songs of praise to the Lord when they saw the foundation of the temple laid because it represented God's answer to their prayers and his goodness to them. Biblical praise exalts God and his work and is an element of worship in which all the people are to participate (see article on PRAISE, p. 770).

3:12 MANY ... WEPT ALOUD ... MANY OTHERS SHOUTED FOR JOY. Although God's law encouraged worship in an orderly manner, it did not limit worship to a set form or pattern. Some of those who had seen the glory of Solomon's temple burst into tears, undoubtedly relieved that the shame of its destruction was now gone; others broke into shouts of joy. Our worship of the Lord should always be flexible enough to allow for a variety of spontaneous expressions. God made us all different; we should expect variety when his people yield to the Holy Spirit.

4:1 THE ENEMIES OF JUDAH. Believers will always undergo a measure of opposition from the ungodly (2Co 11:13–15; Eph 6:12; 2Ti 3:12). The righteous, who proclaim the truth and rely on God alone, must respond to these threats by constant prayer and sincere faith (see Eph 6:11, note).

4:2 LET US HELP YOU BUILD. God's enemies (probably Samaritans, see 2Ki 17:24–34) attempted to infiltrate the Jews and disrupt the building of the temple by a pretense of unity and by an offer to join together to advance God's work. (1) The enemies of Judah (v. 1) claimed to worship and sacrifice to the Lord God as did the Jews. However, they retained their own gods as well and did not accept the written Word of God as the fundamental authority for his people (see 2Ki 17:24, note). This deceptive offer of help was a sinister plot to undermine the faith and commitment of the restored remnant.

(2) Scripture warns that Satan will seek to distort God's message and bring spiritual ruin to God's holy remnant through offers of cooperation from false believers who are not loyal to the inspired revelation of God's Word (see Mt 24:24; Ac 20:27–31; 2Co 11:13–15; Rev 2—3).

(3) Unity among those who worship the Lord is an important Biblical teaching, but such unity must be based on sincere faith, obedient righteousness and loyalty to God's revealed truth (see Eph 4:3–13, notes).

rest of the heads of the families of Israel answered, "You have no part with us
in building a temple to our God. We
alone will build it for the LORD, the God
of Israel, as King Cyrus, the king of
Persia, commanded us."[b]
4Then the peoples around them set
out to discourage the people of Judah
and make them afraid to go on building.[g][c] 5They hired counselors to
work against them and frustrate their
plans during the entire reign of Cyrus
king of Persia and down to the reign of
Darius king of Persia.

Later Opposition Under Xerxes and Artaxerxes

6At the beginning of the reign of Xerxes,[h][d] they lodged an accusation
against the people of Judah and Jerusalem.[e]
7And in the days of Artaxerxes[f]
king of Persia, Bishlam, Mithredath,
Tabeel and the rest of his associates
wrote a letter to Artaxerxes. The letter
was written in Aramaic script and in
the Aramaic[g] language.[i,j]
8Rehum the commanding officer and
Shimshai the secretary wrote a letter
against Jerusalem to Artaxerxes the
king as follows:

9Rehum the commanding officer
and Shimshai the secretary, together with the rest of their associates[h]—the judges and officials
over the men from Tripolis, Persia,[k] Erech[i] and Babylon, the
Elamites of Susa,[j] 10and the other people whom the great and
honorable Ashurbanipal[l][k] deported and settled in the city of
Samaria and elsewhere in Trans-
Euphrates.[l]

11(This is a copy of the letter they
sent him.)

To King Artaxerxes,

From your servants, the men of
Trans-Euphrates:

12The king should know that
the Jews who came up to us from
you have gone to Jerusalem and
are rebuilding that rebellious and
wicked city. They are restoring
the walls and repairing the foundations.[m]
13Furthermore, the king should
know that if this city is built and
its walls are restored, no more
taxes, tribute or duty[n] will be
paid, and the royal revenues will
suffer. 14Now since we are under
obligation to the palace and it is
not proper for us to see the king
dishonored, we are sending this
message to inform the king, 15so
that a search may be made in the
archives[o] of your predecessors.
In these records you will find that
this city is a rebellious city, troublesome to kings and provinces, a
place of rebellion from ancient
times. That is why this city was
destroyed.[p] 16We inform the
king that if this city is built and its

4:3 [b]Ezr 1:1-4
4:4 [c]S Ezr 3:3
4:6 [d]Est 1:1; Da 9:1 [e]Est 3:13; 9:5
4:7 [f]Ezr 7:1; Ne 2:1 [g]2Ki 18:26; Isa 36:11; Da 1:4; 2:4
4:9 [h]ver 23; Ezr 5:6; 6:6,13 [i]Ge 10:10 [j]Ne 1:1; Est 1:2; Da 8:2
4:10 [k]S 2Ki 17:24 [l]ver 17; Ne 4:2
4:12 [m]Ezr 5:3,9
4:13 [n]Ezr 7:24; Ne 5:4
4:15 [o]Ezr 5:17; 6:1 [p]Est 3:8

[g]4 Or *and troubled them as they built*
[h]6 Hebrew *Ahasuerus,* a variant of Xerxes' Persian name
[i]7 Or *written in Aramaic and translated*
[j]7 The text of Ezra 4:8—6:18 is in Aramaic.
[k]9 Or *officials, magistrates and governors over the men from*
[l]10 Aramaic *Osnappar,* a variant of *Ashurbanipal*

4:3 NO PART WITH US. Zerubbabel and Jeshua refused to enter into fellowship with "the peoples around them" (v. 4), for they lived by the Biblical principle of separation from idolatry and from compromise with the world (see article on SPIRITUAL SEPARATION FOR BELIEVERS, p. 1794). This refusal to accept a pluralistic religion led to opposition and persecution for God's faithful people (vv. 4–24; see 2Ti 3:12, note). The adversaries discouraged the people through intimidation, threats and misrepresention of their intentions (vv. 4–6).

4:5 TO THE REIGN OF DARIUS KING OF PERSIA. This reference to Darius's reign is repeated in v. 24, a way used in the OT to show that v. 24 continues where v. 5 left off. The material between these two verses is a parenthesis that completes the account of Samaritan persecution down to Ezra's own day; then the author comes back to the account of the rebuilding of the temple. Note that vv. 7–23 talk about the city being rebuilt, not the temple. Evidently Ezra had received a decree to rebuild the city, and the Samaritans wanted it revoked.

4:6 REIGN OF XERXES, THEY LODGED AN ACCUSATION. Xerxes (Heb *'ahashwerosh;* also known as Ahasuerus) reigned over the Persian empire from 485 to 465 B.C. The events of the book of Esther took place during this period.

4:11 A COPY OF THE LETTER THEY SENT. Ezra does not give any details of the accusation made by Judah's enemies to King Xerxes (v. 6), but a copy of the letter was sent in Ezra's own day to the next king, Artaxerxes (who reigned from 465 to 424 B.C.). Unfortunately, the letter contained some truth—Jerusalem had rebelled against the Babylonians more than once.

walls are restored, you will be left
with nothing in Trans-Euphrates.

17The king sent this reply:

To Rehum the commanding officer, Shimshai the secretary and
the rest of their associates living
in Samaria and elsewhere in
Trans-Euphrates:[q]

Greetings.

18The letter you sent us has
been read and translated in my
presence. 19I issued an order and
a search was made, and it was
found that this city has a long history of revolt[r] against kings and
has been a place of rebellion and
sedition. 20Jerusalem has had
powerful kings ruling over the
whole of Trans-Euphrates,[s] and
taxes, tribute and duty were paid
to them. 21Now issue an order to
these men to stop work, so that
this city will not be rebuilt until I
so order. 22Be careful not to neglect this matter. Why let this
threat grow, to the detriment of
the royal interests?[t]

23As soon as the copy of the letter of
King Artaxerxes was read to Rehum
and Shimshai the secretary and their
associates,[u] they went immediately to
the Jews in Jerusalem and compelled
them by force to stop.

24Thus the work on the house of God
in Jerusalem came to a standstill until
the second year of the reign of Darius[v] king of Persia.

Tattenai's Letter to Darius

5 Now Haggai[w] the prophet and
Zechariah[x] the prophet, a descendant of Iddo, prophesied[y] to the Jews
in Judah and Jerusalem in the name of
the God of Israel, who was over them.
2Then Zerubbabel[z] son of Shealtiel
and Jeshua[a] son of Jozadak set to
work[b] to rebuild the house of God in
Jerusalem. And the prophets of God
were with them, helping them.

3At that time Tattenai,[c] governor
of Trans-Euphrates, and Shethar-Bozenai[d] and their associates went to
them and asked, "Who authorized you
to rebuild this temple and restore this
structure?"[e] 4They also asked, "What
are the names of the men constructing
this building?"[m] 5But the eye of their
God[f] was watching over the elders of
the Jews, and they were not stopped

4:17 [q]S ver 10 **4:19** [r]S 2Ki 18:7 **4:20** [s]Ge 15:18-21; S Ex 23:31; S Jos 1:4; S 1Ki 4:21; 1Ch 18:3; Ps 72:8-11 **4:22** [t]Da 6:2 **4:23** [u]S ver 9 **4:24** [v]Ne 2:1-8; Da 9:25; Hag 1:1, 15; Zec 1:1 **5:1** [w]Ezr 6:14; Hag 1:1,3,12; 2:1, 10,20 [x]Zec 1:1; 7:1 [y]Hag 1:14-2:9; Zec 4:9-10; 8:9 **5:2** [z]S 1Ch 3:19; Hag 1:14; 2:21; Zec 4:6-10 [a]S Ezr 2:2 [b]ver 8; Hag 2:2-5 **5:3** [c]Ezr 6:6 [d]Ezr 6:6 [e]S Ezr 4:12 **5:5** [f]S 2Ki 25:28; Ezr 7:6,9,28; 8:18, 22,31; Ne 2:8,18; Ps 33:18; Isa 66:14

[m]4 See Septuagint; Aramaic *4We told them the names of the men constructing this building.*

4:23 COMPELLED THEM BY FORCE TO STOP. Ne 1:3 gives more details of what the Jews' opponents did to impede any progress on the city walls. This verse concludes the account of Samaritan persecution (cf. v. 5, note).

4:24 THE WORK ... CAME TO A STANDSTILL. Work on the temple ceased soon after it began in 538 B.C. and did not resume until eighteen years later, in 520 B.C.

5:1 PROPHESIED TO THE JEWS. Work on the temple was renewed and accomplished because of the prophetic ministries of Haggai and Zechariah (see Hag 1:9–11). Their prophecies included (1) direct command (Hag 1:8), (2) warning and rebuke (Hag 1:9–11), (3) exhortation (Hag 2:4), and (4) encouragement through the promise of future blessings (Hag 2:6–9, note; Zec 8:3, note). The word of God through Jeremiah had set in motion the beginning of the rebuilding of the temple (1:1); likewise, the word of the Lord through Haggai and Zechariah was now inspiring its completion (6:14).

5:2 THE PROPHETS ... HELPING THEM. The rebuilding of the temple was undertaken through the godly leadership of Zerubbabel and Jeshua. However, Ezra notes two additional contributing factors in the successful restoration of God's house. (1) The ministry and revelation of the prophets Haggai and Zechariah were influential in seeing the project through to completion in spite of many obstacles and setbacks (see previous note). God's work always requires the participation of God's prophets to realize his holy purpose for any given generation.

(2) The dedication of the elders and the people was another key element (vv. 5,8; cf. 7:23). Instead of being apathctic or taking the challenge casually, they pursued the task with great diligence, and God prospered the work of their hands. God's kingdom always advances through the words and actions of committed leaders and people who, by working together, give themselves fully to God's purpose for their generation.

5:3 WHO AUTHORIZED YOU TO REBUILD. The people had obeyed the word of the Lord that came through his prophets (v. 1). They committed themselves to work for the glory of God (v. 2), and God was with them in a special way (v. 5). Yet the enemy came and opposed the work (v. 3). In every spiritual advance we can expect our efforts to be opposed and tested by Satan and the enemies of Christ. God's people must respond to such opposition by continually praying to God, trusting him and pressing on until the work is done (see Eph 6:11, note).

5:5 EYE OF THEIR GOD WAS WATCHING OVER THE ELDERS. Those who commit their lives to God's cause and work are special objects of his watchful care. If you are striving to exalt our

until a report could go to Darius and his written reply be received.

6This is a copy of the letter that Tattenai, governor of Trans-Euphrates, and Shethar-Bozenai and their associates, the officials of Trans-Euphrates, sent to King Darius. 7The report they sent him read as follows:

To King Darius:

Cordial greetings.

8The king should know that we went to the district of Judah, to the temple of the great God. The people are building it with large stones and placing the timbers in the walls. The work[g] is being carried on with diligence and is making rapid progress under their direction.

9We questioned the elders and asked them, "Who authorized you to rebuild this temple and restore this structure?"[h] 10We also asked them their names, so that we could write down the names of their leaders for your information.

11This is the answer they gave us:

"We are the servants of the God of heaven and earth, and we are rebuilding the temple[i] that was built many years ago, one that a great king of Israel built and finished. 12But because our fathers angered[j] the God of heaven, he handed them over to Nebuchadnezzar the Chaldean, king of Babylon, who destroyed this temple and deported the people to Babylon.[k]

13"However, in the first year of Cyrus king of Babylon, King Cyrus issued a decree[l] to rebuild this house of God. 14He even removed from the temple[n] of Babylon the gold and silver articles of the house of God, which Nebuchadnezzar had taken from the temple in Jerusalem and brought to the temple[n] in Babylon.[m]

"Then King Cyrus gave them to a man named Sheshbazzar,[n] whom he had appointed governor, 15and he told him, 'Take these articles and go and deposit them in the temple in Jerusalem. And rebuild the house of God on its site.' 16So this Sheshbazzar came and laid the foundations of the house of God[o] in Jerusalem. From that day to the present it has been under construction but is not yet finished."

17Now if it pleases the king, let a search be made in the royal archives[p] of Babylon to see if King Cyrus did in fact issue a decree to rebuild this house of God in Jerusalem. Then let the king send us his decision in this matter.

The Decree of Darius

6 King Darius then issued an order, and they searched in the archives[q] stored in the treasury at Babylon. 2A scroll was found in the citadel of Ecbatana in the province of Media, and this was written on it:

Memorandum:

3In the first year of King Cyrus, the king issued a decree concerning the temple of God in Jerusalem:

Let the temple be rebuilt as a place to present sacrifices, and let its foundations be laid.[r] It is to be ninety feet[o] high and ninety feet wide, 4with three courses[s] of large stones and one of timbers. The costs are to be paid by the royal treasury.[t] 5Also, the gold[u] and silver articles of the house of God, which Nebuchadnezzar took from the temple in Jerusalem and brought to Babylon, are to be returned to their places in the temple in Jerusalem; they are to be deposited in the house of God.[v]

6Now then, Tattenai,[w] governor of Trans-Euphrates, and Shethar-Bozenai[x] and you, their fellow officials of that province, stay away from there. 7Do not inter-

5:8 [g] S ver 2
5:9 [h] S Ezr 4:12
5:11 [i] 1Ki 6:1; 2Ch 3:1-2
5:12 [j] S 2Ch 36:16 [k] S Dt 21:10; S 28:36; S 2Ki 24:1; S Jer 1:3
5:13 [l] S Ezr 1:2-4
5:14 [m] Ezr 1:7 [n] S 1Ch 3:18
5:16 [o] S Ezr 3:10
5:17 [p] S Ezr 4:15
6:1 [q] S Ezr 4:15
6:3 [r] S Ezr 3:10; Hag 2:3
6:4 [s] S 1Ki 6:36 [t] ver 8; Ezr 7:20
6:5 [u] S 1Ch 29:2 [v] S Ezr 1:7
6:6 [w] Ezr 5:3 [x] Ezr 5:3

[n] 14 Or *palace* [o] 3 Aramaic *sixty cubits* (about 27 meters)

Lord's kingdom and his righteousness, he will never take his eyes off you (Job 36:7; cf. Mt 6:33). This promise belongs to you: "The eyes of the LORD are on the righteous" (Ps 34:15).

5:16 **SHESHBAZZAR.** See 1:8, note.

fere with the work on this temple
of God. Let the governor of the
Jews and the Jewish elders rebuild
this house of God on its site.
8 Moreover, I hereby decree
what you are to do for these elders
of the Jews in the construction of
this house of God:
The expenses of these men are
to be fully paid out of the royal
treasury,[y] from the revenues[z]
of Trans-Euphrates, so that the
work will not stop.
9 Whatever is
needed—young bulls, rams, male
lambs for burnt offerings[a] to the
God of heaven, and wheat, salt,
wine and oil, as requested by the
priests in Jerusalem—must be
given them daily without fail,
10 so
that they may offer sacrifices
pleasing to the God of heaven and
pray for the well-being of the king
and his sons.[b]
11 Furthermore, I decree that if
anyone changes this edict, a beam
is to be pulled from his house and
he is to be lifted up and impaled[c]
on it. And for this crime his house
is to be made a pile of rubble.[d]
12 May God, who has caused his
Name to dwell there,[e] overthrow
any king or people who lifts a
hand to change this decree or to
destroy this temple in Jerusalem.
I Darius[f] have decreed it. Let
it be carried out with diligence.

Completion and Dedication of the Temple

13 Then, because of the decree King
Darius had sent, Tattenai, governor of
Trans-Euphrates, and Shethar-Bozenai and their associates[g] carried it out
with diligence.
14 So the elders of the
Jews continued to build and prosper
under the preaching[h] of Haggai the
prophet and Zechariah, a descendant
of Iddo. They finished building the
temple according to the command of
the God of Israel and the decrees
of Cyrus,[i] Darius[j] and Artaxerxes,[k]
kings of Persia.
15 The temple was
completed on the third day of the
month Adar, in the sixth year of the
reign of King Darius.[l]
16 Then the people of Israel—the
priests, the Levites and the rest of the
exiles—celebrated the dedication[m] of
the house of God with joy.
17 For the
dedication of this house of God they offered[n] a hundred bulls, two hundred
rams, four hundred male lambs and, as
a sin offering for all Israel, twelve male
goats, one for each of the tribes of Israel.
18 And they installed the priests in
their divisions[o] and the Levites in
their groups[p] for the service of God at
Jerusalem, according to what is written in the Book of Moses.[q]

The Passover

19 On the fourteenth day of the first
month, the exiles celebrated the Passover.[r]
20 The priests and Levites had
purified themselves and were all ceremonially clean. The Levites slaughtered[s] the Passover lamb for all the
exiles, for their brothers the priests
and for themselves.
21 So the Israelites
who had returned from the exile ate it,
together with all who had separated
themselves[t] from the unclean practices[u] of their Gentile neighbors in order to seek the LORD,[v] the God of Israel.
22 For seven days they celebrated
with joy the Feast of Unleavened
Bread,[w] because the LORD had filled
them with joy by changing the attitude[x] of the king of Assyria, so that he
assisted them in the work on the house
of God, the God of Israel.

Ezra Comes to Jerusalem

7 After these things, during the
reign of Artaxerxes[y] king of Persia, Ezra son of Seraiah,[z] the son of
Azariah, the son of Hilkiah,[a]
2 the son
of Shallum, the son of Zadok,[b] the son
of Ahitub,[c]
3 the son of Amariah, the
son of Azariah, the son of Meraioth,
4 the son of Zerahiah, the son of Uzzi,
the son of Bukki,
5 the son of Abishua,
the son of Phinehas,[d] the son of Elea-

6:8 [y] S ver 4 [z] S 1Sa 9:20 **6:9** [a] Lev 1:3,10 **6:10** [b] Ezr 7:23; 1Ti 2:1-2 **6:11** [c] S Dt 21:22-23; Est 2:23; 5:14; 9:14 [d] Ezr 7:26; Da 2:5; 3:29 **6:12** [e] S Ex 20:24; S Dt 12:5; S 2Ch 6:2 [f] ver 14 **6:13** [g] S Ezr 4:9 **6:14** [h] S Ezr 5:1 [i] S Ezr 1:1-4 [j] ver 12 [k] Ezr 7:1; Ne 2:1 **6:15** [l] Zec 1:1; 4:9 **6:16** [m] S 1Ki 8:63 **6:17** [n] S 2Sa 6:13; S 2Ch 29:21; S 30:24 **6:18** [o] S 2Ch 35:4; Lk 1:5 [p] S 1Ch 24:1 [q] Nu 3:6-9; 8:9-11; 18:1-32 **6:19** [r] S Ex 12:11; S Nu 28:16 **6:20** [s] S 2Ch 30:15,17; 35:11 **6:21** [t] Ezr 9:1; Ne 9:2 [u] S Dt 18:9; Eze 36:25 [v] 1Ch 22:19; Ps 14:2 **6:22** [w] S Ex 12:17 [x] S Ezr 1:1 **7:1** [y] S Ezr 4:7; S 6:14 [z] S 2Ki 25:18 [a] 2Ki 22:4 **7:2** [b] 1Ki 1:8; 2:35; 1Ch 6:8; Eze 40:46; 43:19; 44:15 [c] Ne 11:11 **7:5** [d] 1Ch 6:4

6:15 THE TEMPLE WAS COMPLETED. The construction was finished in 516 B.C., twenty-one years after the laying of the foundation (3:10). The ark of the covenant, containing the two tablets of the law, was not in the new temple, having apparently been destroyed at some unknown time earlier in Judah's history.

7:1 EZRA. A gap of about sixty years occurs between chs. 6 and 7, during which time the events recorded in the book of Esther transpired in Persia. Chs. 7—8 record the second return of exiles from Persia to Jerusalem under Ezra's leadership (about 457 B.C.); chs. 9—10 describe the spiritual reforms that Ezra instituted after arriving in Jerusalem.

zar, the son of Aaron the chief priest—
6this Ezra[e] came up from Babylon. He
was a teacher well versed in the Law
of Moses, which the LORD, the God of
Israel, had given. The king had granted[f] him everything he asked, for the
hand of the LORD his God was on him.[g]
7Some of the Israelites, including
priests, Levites, singers, gatekeepers
and temple servants, also came up to
Jerusalem in the seventh year of King
Artaxerxes.[h]

8Ezra arrived in Jerusalem in the
fifth month of the seventh year of the
king. **9**He had begun his journey from
Babylon on the first day of the first
month, and he arrived in Jerusalem on
the first day of the fifth month, for the
gracious hand of his God was on him.[i]
10For Ezra had devoted himself to the
study and observance of the Law of the
LORD, and to teaching[j] its decrees and
laws in Israel.

King Artaxerxes' Letter to Ezra

11This is a copy of the letter King
Artaxerxes had given to Ezra the priest
and teacher, a man learned in matters
concerning the commands and decrees
of the LORD for Israel:

12[p]Artaxerxes, king of kings,[k]

To Ezra the priest, a teacher of
the Law of the God of heaven:

Greetings.

13Now I decree that any of the
Israelites in my kingdom, including priests and Levites, who wish
to go to Jerusalem with you, may
go. **14**You are sent by the king and
his seven advisers[l] to inquire
about Judah and Jerusalem with
regard to the Law of your God,
which is in your hand. **15**Moreover, you are to take with you the
silver and gold that the king and
his advisers have freely given[m] to
the God of Israel, whose dwelling[n] is in Jerusalem, **16**together
with all the silver and gold[o] you
may obtain from the province of
Babylon, as well as the freewill offerings of the people and priests
for the temple of their God in Jerusalem.[p] **17**With this money be
sure to buy bulls, rams and male
lambs,[q] together with their grain
offerings and drink offerings,[r]
and sacrifice[s] them on the altar
of the temple of your God in Jerusalem.

18You and your brother Jews
may then do whatever seems best
with the rest of the silver and
gold, in accordance with the will
of your God. **19**Deliver[t] to the
God of Jerusalem all the articles
entrusted to you for worship in
the temple of your God. **20**And
anything else needed for the temple of your God that you may have
occasion to supply, you may provide from the royal treasury.[u]

21Now I, King Artaxerxes, order all the treasurers of Trans-Euphrates to provide with diligence
whatever Ezra the priest, a teacher of the Law of the God of heav-
en, may ask of you— **22**up to a

7:6 [e]Ne 12:36 [f]S 2Ki 25:28 [g]S Ezr 5:5; S Isa 41:20 **7:7** [h]Ezr 8:1 **7:9** [i]ver 6 **7:10** [j]S Dt 33:10 **7:12** [k]Eze 26:7; Da 2:37 **7:14** [l]Est 1:14 **7:15** [m]S 1Ch 29:6 [n]S Dt 12:5; S 2Ch 6:2 **7:16** [o]S Ex 3:22 [p]Zec 6:10 **7:17** [q]S 2Ki 3:4 [r]Nu 15:5-12 [s]Dt 12:5-11 **7:19** [t]Ezr 5:14; Jer 27:22 **7:20** [u]S Ezr 6:4

[p]*12* The text of Ezra 7:12-26 is in Aramaic.

7:6 THE HAND OF THE LORD HIS GOD WAS ON HIM. Three times this chapter says that the hand of the Lord was on Ezra (vv. 6,9,28; cf. 8:18, 22,31). Three reasons are given in v. 10: Ezra had devoted himself (1) to study God's Word, (2) to practice it and (3) to teach it to others (see next note). Loyalty to God and his Word will always be accompanied by the Lord's blessing and help. This principle is affirmed in such NT passages as Mt 5:6; Jn 14:21; 15:7–10; Ac 10:1–4; 2Co 6:16–18; Heb 11:6; Jas 1:21–25; Rev 3:7–10. In 8:22 Ezra adds another occasion in which the Lord's hand is on his people, namely, that God's favor comes to those who look to him with their whole heart. Any who earnestly seek God and who genuinely demonstrate loyalty to him and his Word will experience the favorable hand of the Lord on them.

7:10 STUDY AND OBSERVANCE OF THE LAW . . . AND TO TEACHING. Ezra is a model for all who would dedicate themselves as people anointed by God to studying, obeying and teaching God's Word (cf. vv. 6,9). (1) Ezra believed that the Law was given through Moses by God himself and that it was therefore the ultimate authority for all God's people (v. 6; cf. Ne 8:14).

(2) Ezra devoted himself to study (literally "seek") God's Word. He sought to know God's ways and thoughts in all things pertaining to life, the world and God's purposes among his people. Thus the wisdom of God was in him (v. 25).

(3) Ezra devoted himself to obey God's decrees and righteous standards. What he taught, he lived (cf. Ac 1:1; 1Co 9:27; 1Ti 4:12,16).

(4) Ezra devoted himself to teach God's Word in order to preserve truth, righteousness and purity among God's people (see 10:10–11; Ne 8:2–18; see 1Ti 1:5, note; see article on BIBLE TRAINING FOR CHRISTIANS, p. 1894).

hundred talents[q] of silver, a hundred cors[r] of wheat, a hundred baths[s] of wine, a hundred baths[s] of olive oil, and salt without limit. 23Whatever the God of heaven has prescribed, let it be done with diligence for the temple of the God of heaven. Why should there be wrath against the realm of the king and of his sons?[v] 24You are also to know that you have no authority to impose taxes, tribute or duty[w] on any of the priests, Levites, singers, gatekeepers, temple servants or other workers at this house of God.[x]

25And you, Ezra, in accordance with the wisdom of your God, which you possess, appoint[y] magistrates and judges to administer justice to all the people of Trans-Euphrates—all who know the laws of your God. And you are to teach[z] any who do not know them. 26Whoever does not obey the law of your God and the law of the king must surely be punished by death, banishment, confiscation of property, or imprisonment.[a]

27Praise be to the LORD, the God of our fathers, who has put it into the king's heart[b] to bring honor[c] to the house of the LORD in Jerusalem in this way 28and who has extended his good favor[d] to me before the king and his advisers and all the king's powerful officials. Because the hand of the LORD my God was on me,[e] I took courage and gathered leading men from Israel to go up with me.

List of the Family Heads Returning With Ezra

8 These are the family heads and those registered with them who came up with me from Babylon during the reign of King Artaxerxes:[f]

2of the descendants of Phinehas, Gershom;
of the descendants of Ithamar, Daniel;
of the descendants of David, Hattush 3of the descendants of Shecaniah;[g]

of the descendants of Parosh,[h] Zechariah, and with him were registered 150 men;
4of the descendants of Pahath-Moab,[i] Eliehoenai son of Zerahiah, and with him 200 men;
5of the descendants of Zattu,[t] Shecaniah son of Jahaziel, and with him 300 men;
6of the descendants of Adin,[j] Ebed son of Jonathan, and with him 50 men;
7of the descendants of Elam, Jeshaiah son of Athaliah, and with him 70 men;
8of the descendants of Shephatiah, Zebadiah son of Michael, and with him 80 men;
9of the descendants of Joab, Obadiah son of Jehiel, and with him 218 men;
10of the descendants of Bani,[u] Shelomith son of Josiphiah, and with him 160 men;
11of the descendants of Bebai, Zechariah son of Bebai, and with him 28 men;
12of the descendants of Azgad, Johanan son of Hakkatan, and with him 110 men;
13of the descendants of Adonikam,[k] the last ones, whose names were Eliphelet, Jeuel and Shemaiah, and with them 60 men;
14of the descendants of Bigvai, Uthai and Zaccur, and with them 70 men.

The Return to Jerusalem

15I assembled them at the canal that flows toward Ahava,[l] and we camped there three days. When I checked among the people and the priests, I found no Levites[m] there. 16So I summoned Eliezer, Ariel, Shemaiah, Elnathan, Jarib, Elnathan, Nathan, Zechariah and Meshullam, who were leaders, and Joiarib and Elnathan, who were men of learning, 17and I sent them to Iddo, the leader in Casiphia. I told them what to say to Iddo and his kinsmen, the temple servants[n] in Casiphia, so that they might bring attendants

7:23 [v]S Ezr 6:10 **7:24** [w]S Ezr 4:13 [x]Ezr 8:36 **7:25** [y]S Ex 18:21, 26 [z]S Lev 10:11 **7:26** [a]S Ezr 6:11 **7:27** [b]S Ezr 1:1 [c]S 1Ch 29:12 **7:28** [d]S 2Ki 25:28 [e]S Ezr 5:5 **8:1** [f]Ezr 7:7 **8:3** [g]1Ch 3:22 [h]S Ezr 2:3 **8:4** [i]Ezr 2:6 **8:6** [j]Ezr 2:15; Ne 7:20; 10:16 **8:13** [k]Ezr 2:13 **8:15** [l]ver 21,31 [m]S Ezr 2:40 **8:17** [n]Ezr 2:43

[q]*22* That is, about 3 3/4 tons (about 3.4 metric tons) [r]*22* That is, probably about 600 bushels (about 22 kiloliters) [s]*22* That is, probably about 600 gallons (about 2.2 kiloliters) [t]*5* Some Septuagint manuscripts (also 1 Esdras 8:32); Hebrew does not have *Zattu.* [u]*10* Some Septuagint manuscripts (also 1 Esdras 8:36); Hebrew does not have *Bani.*

to us for the house of our God. **18**Because the gracious hand of our God was on us,[o] they brought us Sherebiah,[p] a capable man, from the descendants of Mahli son of Levi, the son of Israel, and Sherebiah's sons and brothers, 18 men; **19**and Hashabiah, together with Jeshaiah from the descendants of Merari, and his brothers and nephews, 20 men. **20**They also brought 220 of the temple servants[q]—a body that David and the officials had established to assist the Levites. All were registered by name.

21There, by the Ahava Canal,[r] I proclaimed a fast, so that we might humble ourselves before our God and ask him for a safe journey[s] for us and our children, with all our possessions. **22**I was ashamed to ask the king for soldiers[t] and horsemen to protect us from enemies on the road, because we had told the king, "The gracious hand of our God is on everyone[u] who looks to him, but his great anger is against all who forsake him.[v]" **23**So we fasted[w] and petitioned our God about this, and he answered our prayer.

24Then I set apart twelve of the leading priests, together with Sherebiah,[x] Hashabiah and ten of their brothers, **25**and I weighed out[y] to them the offering of silver and gold and the articles that the king, his advisers, his officials and all Israel present there had donated for the house of our God. **26**I weighed out to them 650 talents[v] of silver, silver articles weighing 100 talents,[w] 100 talents[w] of gold, **27**20 bowls of gold valued at 1,000 darics,[x] and two fine articles of polished bronze, as precious as gold.

28I said to them, "You as well as these articles are consecrated to the LORD.[z] The silver and gold are a freewill offering to the LORD, the God of your fathers. **29**Guard them carefully until you weigh them out in the chambers of the house of the LORD in Jerusalem before the leading priests and the Levites and the family heads of Israel." **30**Then the priests and Levites received the silver and gold and sacred articles that had been weighed out to be taken to the house of our God in Jerusalem.

31On the twelfth day of the first month we set out from the Ahava Canal[a] to go to Jerusalem. The hand of our God was on us,[b] and he protected us from enemies and bandits along the way. **32**So we arrived in Jerusalem, where we rested three days.[c]

33On the fourth day, in the house of our God, we weighed out[d] the silver and gold and the sacred articles into the hands of Meremoth[e] son of Uriah, the priest. Eleazar son of Phinehas was with him, and so were the Levites Jozabad[f] son of Jeshua and Noadiah son of Binnui.[g] **34**Everything was accounted for by number and weight, and the entire weight was recorded at that time.

35Then the exiles who had returned from captivity sacrificed burnt offerings to the God of Israel: twelve bulls[h] for all Israel,[i] ninety-six rams, seventy-seven male lambs and, as a sin offering, twelve male goats.[j] All this was a burnt offering to the LORD. **36**They also delivered the king's orders[k] to the royal satraps and to the governors of Trans-Euphrates,[l] who then gave

8:18 [o] S Ezr 5:5 [p] ver 24
8:20 [q] S 1Ch 9:2
8:21 [r] S ver 15 [s] Ps 5:8; 27:11; 107:7
8:22 [t] Ne 2:9; Jer 41:16 [u] S Ezr 5:5 [v] S Dt 31:17
8:23 [w] S 2Ch 20:3; Ac 14:23
8:24 [x] ver 18
8:25 [y] ver 33
8:28 [z] S Lev 21:6; 22:2-3
8:31 [a] S ver 15 [b] S Ezr 5:5
8:32 [c] S Ge 40:13
8:33 [d] ver 25 [e] Ne 3:4,21 [f] Ne 11:16 [g] Ne 3:24
8:35 [h] S Lev 1:3 [i] S 2Ch 29:24 [j] S 2Ch 29:21; S 30:24
8:36 [k] Ezr 7:21-24 [l] Ne 2:7

[v] *26* That is, about 25 tons (about 22 metric tons) [w] *26* That is, about 3 3/4 tons (about 3.4 metric tons) [x] *27* That is, about 19 pounds (about 8.5 kilograms)

8:21 I PROCLAIMED A FAST. Fasting entails abstaining from food for a limited period of time (see Mt 6:16, note). God's OT people fasted in order to express humility, self-denial and submission to God, and to seek his grace, help, protection and favor (vv. 21,31). Fasting occurred when they (1) were oppressed by great cares (2Sa 12:16–23; 1Ki 21:20–27; Ps 35:13; 69:10); (2) were worshiping God on the Day of Atonement (cf. Lev 16:29–31; 23:26–32); (3) wanted to show repentance and remorse (1Ki 21:27–29; Ne 9:1–2; Joel 2:12–13; Jnh 3:4–10); (4) were faced with danger (2Ch 20:3; Ezr 8:21–23), sickness (2Sa 12:15–16) and death (1Sa 31:13); (5) were preparing for ministry (Ex 34:28; Dt 9:9–18), and (6) were seeking God for revival and restoration (Da 9:3–19).

8:21 ASK HIM FOR A SAFE JOURNEY. It is always appropriate to pray to God for his care and protection when setting out on a journey. God's help should not be taken for granted, for his guidance and protection are mediated to us through our prayers; and when we arrive safely at our destination (v. 32), we should never forget to give him thanks.

8:23 WE FASTED AND PETITIONED OUR GOD. God looks favorably on a people who humbly and earnestly fast and petition him about a matter (cf. Ne 1:4). Just as God responded favorably to Ezra's request, so he will honor all who with sincere hearts seek him in prayer and fasting (see v. 21, note).

assistance to the people and to the
house of God.[m]

Ezra's Prayer About Intermarriage

9 After these things had been done,
the leaders came to me and said,
"The people of Israel, including the
priests and the Levites, have not kept
themselves separate[n] from the neighboring peoples with their detestable
practices, like those of the Canaanites,
Hittites, Perizzites, Jebusites,[o] Ammonites,[p] Moabites,[q] Egyptians and
Amorites.[r] **2**They have taken some of
their daughters[s] as wives for themselves and their sons, and have mingled[t] the holy race[u] with the peoples
around them. And the leaders and officials have led the way in this unfaithfulness."[v]
3When I heard this, I tore[w] my tunic
and cloak, pulled hair from my head
and beard and sat down appalled.[x]
4Then everyone who trembled[y] at the
words of the God of Israel gathered
around me because of this unfaithfulness of the exiles. And I sat there appalled[z] until the evening sacrifice.
5Then, at the evening sacrifice,[a] I
rose from my self-abasement, with my
tunic and cloak torn, and fell on my
knees with my hands[b] spread out to
the LORD my God **6**and prayed:

"O my God, I am too ashamed[c]
and disgraced to lift up my face to
you, my God, because our sins are
higher than our heads and our
guilt has reached to the heavens.[d] **7**From the days of our forefathers[e] until now, our guilt has
been great. Because of our sins,
we and our kings and our priests
have been subjected to the
sword[f] and captivity,[g] to pillage
and humiliation[h] at the hand of
foreign kings, as it is today.
8"But now, for a brief moment,
the LORD our God has been gracious[i] in leaving us a remnant[j]

8:36 [m] Est 9:3 **9:1** [n] S Ezr 6:21 [o] S Ge 10:16; S Jos 15:8 [p] Ge 19:38 [q] S Ge 19:37 [r] Ex 13:5; 23:28; Dt 20:17; S Jos 3:10; S Jdg 3:5; 1Ki 9:20; S 2Ch 8:7; Ne 9:8 **9:2** [s] S Ex 34:16; S Ru 1:4 [t] Ps 106:35 [u] S Ex 22:31; S Lev 27:30; S Dt 14:2 [v] Ezr 10:2 **9:3** [w] S Nu 14:6 [x] S Ex 32:19; S 33:4 **9:4** [y] Ezr 10:3; Ps 119:120; Isa 66:2,5 [z] Ne 1:4; Ps 119:136; Da 10:2 **9:5** [a] S Ex 29:41 [b] Ne 8:6; Ps 28:2; 134:2 **9:6** [c] Jer 31:19 [d] S 2Ch 28:9; Job 42:6; Ps 38:4; Isa 59:12; Jer 3:25; 14:20; Rev 18:5 **9:7** [e] S 2Ch 29:6 [f] Eze 21:1-32 [g] S Dt 28:64 [h] S Dt 28:37 **9:8** [i] Ps 25:16; 67:1; 119:58; Isa 33:2 [j] S Ge 45:7

9:1 THE PEOPLE ... HAVE NOT KEPT THEMSELVES SEPARATE. The Jews' past failure to separate themselves from the sinful societies around them had led them into idolatry and immorality, and it eventually caused their captivity and exile (2Ch 36:14–21). Now, after God had brought a small remnant back to the land (vv. 8–9), the Jews were once again transgressing God's fundamental precept of separation from the lifestyle of the ungodly.

9:2 SOME OF THEIR DAUGHTERS AS WIVES. When Ezra arrived in Jerusalem, he discovered that many of the people, including priests, Levites and officials, had married women who worshiped other gods and followed detestable and impure pagan practices (vv. 1–2,11). Intermarriage with the ungodly was expressly forbidden in the Law of Moses (Ex 34:11–16; Dt 7:1–4; cf. Ps 106:35); the NT likewise forbids God's new covenant people to marry unbelievers (1Co 7:39; cf. 2Co 6:14).

9:2 THE HOLY RACE. Israel's high calling was to be a "holy race" (cf. Ex 19:6; Isa 6:13; Mal 2:15). (1) They were to be God's treasured possession, reflecting his person and holiness while separating themselves from the immoral ways of those who did not belong to him (Dt 7:1–11). (2) NT believers are also called to be separate from the world (2Co 6:14–18). Those who confess Jesus as their Lord must be "a holy nation" (1Pe 2:9–12), consecrated to doing the will and work of the Father. This implies that a Spirit-led believer will live a righteous and separated life in fellowship with God (1Co 6:11), living in a way that differs from this corrupt generation (Ac 2:40; see article on SPIRITUAL SEPARATION FOR BELIEVERS, p. 1794); he or she will always look to fulfill God's will as a true son or daughter of God (Ro 8:13–16).

9:3 WHEN I HEARD THIS. Ezra's response of grief and his prayer are a classic example of the concern and distress that all true ministers of God should have when they see God's people conforming to ungodly customs. (1) Ezra was appalled, ashamed and deeply saddened because of the guilt of the people (vv. 3–6; see 1Sa 15:35; Jer 9; 2Co 11:29).

(2) Ezra possessed a deep sense of the Lord's glory, righteousness and love, which the people had spurned (vv. 4,8–10). He could not accept what the people were doing (vv. 3,5; 10:1; see also the prayers of Nehemiah in Ne 9, and Daniel in Da 9).

(3) Ezra prayed to God in humility and with tears (vv. 3,5; 10:1).

(4) Ezra linked himself with those for whom he prayed by referring to "our sins" and "our evil deeds" (vv. 6–15); he felt the national shame and guilt more deeply than any of them (cf. Isa 53:12).

(5) Ezra comprehended that God's grace and loving-kindness, shown toward the returned remnant in reviving their hope and vision for the future, raising up God's house from the ruins and giving them a wall of protection, were now being jeopardized by the people's disobedience to God's word (vv. 8–15).

(6) Ezra was acutely conscious of God's grace and kindness and thus hoped to see forgiveness and restoration for the people (vv. 8–9,12–14).

(7) Finally, Ezra's remorse attracted others who trembled at "the words of the God of Israel" (v. 4) and understood the disastrous consequences of sin for the people and their families (vv. 7,13–15).

and giving us a firm place[k] in his
sanctuary, and so our God gives
light to our eyes[l] and a little relief in our bondage. 9Though we
are slaves,[m] our God has not deserted us in our bondage. He has
shown us kindness[n] in the sight
of the kings of Persia: He has
granted us new life to rebuild the
house of our God and repair its ruins,[o] and he has given us a wall
of protection in Judah and Jerusalem.
10"But now, O our God, what
can we say after this? For we have
disregarded the commands[p]
11you gave through your servants
the prophets when you said: 'The
land you are entering[q] to possess
is a land polluted[r] by the corruption of its peoples. By their detestable practices[s] they have filled it
with their impurity from one end
to the other. 12Therefore, do not
give your daughters in marriage
to their sons or take their daughters for your sons. Do not seek a
treaty of friendship with them[t]
at any time, that you may be
strong[u] and eat the good
things[v] of the land and leave it to
your children as an everlasting inheritance.'[w]
13"What has happened to us is
a result of our evil[x] deeds and
our great guilt, and yet, our God,
you have punished us less than
our sins have deserved[y] and
have given us a remnant like this.
14Shall we again break your commands and intermarry[z] with the
peoples who commit such detestable practices? Would you not be
angry enough with us to destroy
us,[a] leaving us no remnant[b] or
survivor? 15O LORD, God of Israel,
you are righteous![c] We are left

9:8 [k]Ecc 12:11; Isa 22:23 [l]Ps 13:3; 19:8 **9:9** [m]S Ex 1:14; Ne 9:36 [n]S 2Ki 25:28; Ps 106:46 [o]Ps 69:35; Isa 43:1; 44:26; 48:20; 52:9; 63:9; Jer 32:44; Zec 1:16-17 **9:10** [p]Dt 11:8; Isa 1:19-20 **9:11** [q]Dt 4:5 [r]S Lev 18:25-28 [s]S Dt 9:4; S 18:9; S 1Ki 14:24 **9:12** [t]S Ex 34:15 [u]Dt 11:8 [v]S Ge 45:18 [w]Ps 103:17; Eze 37:25; Joel 3:20 **9:13** [x]S Ex 32:22 [y]Job 11:6; 15:5; 22:5; 33:27; Ps 103:10 **9:14** [z]Ne 13:27 [a]S Dt 9:8 [b]Dt 9:14 **9:15** [c]S Ge 18:25; S 2Ch 12:6; Ne 9:8; Ps 51:4; 129:4; 145:17; Isa 24:16; Jer 12:1; 23:6; 33:16; La 1:18; Da 9:7; Zep 3:5

[d]Ps 76:7; 130:3; Mal 3:2 [e]S 1Ki 8:47 **10:1** [f]2Ch 20:9; Da 9:20 [g]S Nu 25:6 **10:2** [h]ver 26 [i]S Ezr 9:2 [j]Dt 30:8-10 **10:3** [k]S 2Ki 11:17 [l]S Ex 34:16 **10:5** [m]Ne 5:12; 13:25 **10:6** [n]S Ex 34:28; Dt 9:18; Ps 102:4; Jnh 3:7

this day as a remnant. Here we
are before you in our guilt, though
because of it not one of us can
stand[d] in your presence.[e]"

The People's Confession of Sin

10 While Ezra was praying and
confessing,[f] weeping[g] and
throwing himself down before the
house of God, a large crowd of Israelites—men, women and children—
gathered around him. They too wept
bitterly. 2Then Shecaniah son of Jehiel,
one of the descendants of Elam,[h] said
to Ezra, "We have been unfaithful[i] to
our God by marrying foreign women
from the peoples around us. But in
spite of this, there is still hope for Israel.[j] 3Now let us make a covenant[k]
before our God to send away[l] all
these women and their children, in accordance with the counsel of my lord
and of those who fear the commands of
our God. Let it be done according to the
Law. 4Rise up; this matter is in your
hands. We will support you, so take
courage and do it."
5So Ezra rose up and put the leading
priests and Levites and all Israel under
oath[m] to do what had been suggested.
And they took the oath. 6Then Ezra
withdrew from before the house of God
and went to the room of Jehohanan son
of Eliashib. While he was there, he ate
no food and drank no water,[n] because
he continued to mourn over the unfaithfulness of the exiles.
7A proclamation was then issued
throughout Judah and Jerusalem for all
the exiles to assemble in Jerusalem.
8Anyone who failed to appear within
three days would forfeit all his property, in accordance with the decision of
the officials and elders, and would himself be expelled from the assembly of
the exiles.
9Within the three days, all the men

10:3 SEND AWAY ALL THESE WOMEN. Ezra required divorce for the following reasons: (1) Marrying foreign women had constituted an act of unfaithfulness to God and his word (v. 10; 10:2; see 9:2, note). True repentance required separation to rectify the evil. (2) Divorcing foreign wives was necessary to maintain Israel's purpose as a holy nation set apart for God (see 9:2, note). (3) Divorce was necessary to prevent the people from adopting the idolatry and immoral ways of the nations. Moses stated, "Do not intermarry with them . . . for they will turn your sons away from following me" (Dt 7:3–4). Divorce in this instance was radical surgery required in order to stop the rippling consequences of compromise that would inevitably lead another generation into apostasy and subject them to God's severe judgment.

10:4 TAKE COURAGE AND DO IT. Courage and decisive action in a spiritual leader are necessary in order to oppose worldly trends among God's people, to issue an earnest call to sinners to turn away from sin and back to God, and to encourage obedience to his word. Ezra demonstrated these qualities when he required the Jews to separate themselves "from the peoples around you and from your foreign wives" (v. 11).

of Judah and Benjamin[o] had gathered
in Jerusalem. And on the twentieth day
of the ninth month, all the people were
sitting in the square before the house
of God, greatly distressed by the occasion and because of the rain. **10**Then
Ezra[p] the priest stood up and said to
them, "You have been unfaithful; you
have married foreign women, adding to
Israel's guilt.[q] **11**Now make confession to the LORD, the God of your fathers, and do his will. Separate yourselves from the peoples around you
and from your foreign wives."[r]

12The whole assembly responded
with a loud voice:[s] "You are right! We
must do as you say. **13**But there are
many people here and it is the rainy
season; so we cannot stand outside.
Besides, this matter cannot be taken
care of in a day or two, because we
have sinned greatly in this thing. **14**Let
our officials act for the whole assembly. Then let everyone in our towns
who has married a foreign woman
come at a set time, along with the elders and judges[t] of each town, until
the fierce anger[u] of our God in this
matter is turned away from us." **15**Only
Jonathan son of Asahel and Jahzeiah
son of Tikvah, supported by Meshullam and Shabbethai[v] the Levite, opposed this.

16So the exiles did as was proposed.
Ezra the priest selected men who were
family heads, one from each family division, and all of them designated by
name. On the first day of the tenth
month they sat down to investigate the
cases, **17**and by the first day of the first
month they finished dealing with all
the men who had married foreign wom-
en.

Those Guilty of Intermarriage

18Among the descendants of the priests, the following had married foreign women:[w]

From the descendants of Jeshua[x] son of Jozadak, and his brothers: Maaseiah, Eliezer, Jarib and Gedaliah. **19**(They all gave their hands[y] in pledge to put away their wives, and for their guilt they each presented a ram from the flock as a guilt offering.)[z]

20From the descendants of Immer:[a]
Hanani and Zebadiah.

21From the descendants of Harim:[b]
Maaseiah, Elijah, Shemaiah, Jehiel and Uzziah.

22From the descendants of Pashhur:[c]
Elioenai, Maaseiah, Ishmael, Nethanel, Jozabad and Elasah.

23Among the Levites:[d]

Jozabad, Shimei, Kelaiah (that is, Kelita), Pethahiah, Judah and Eliezer.

24From the singers:
Eliashib.[e]

From the gatekeepers:
Shallum, Telem and Uri.

25And among the other Israelites:

From the descendants of Parosh:[f]
Ramiah, Izziah, Malkijah, Mijamin, Eleazar, Malkijah and Benaiah.

26From the descendants of Elam:[g]
Mattaniah, Zechariah, Jehiel, Abdi, Jeremoth and Elijah.

27From the descendants of Zattu:
Elioenai, Eliashib, Mattaniah, Jeremoth, Zabad and Aziza.

28From the descendants of Bebai:
Jehohanan, Hananiah, Zabbai and Athlai.

29From the descendants of Bani:
Meshullam, Malluch, Adaiah, Jashub, Sheal and Jeremoth.

30From the descendants of Pahath-Moab:
Adna, Kelal, Benaiah, Maaseiah, Mattaniah, Bezalel, Binnui and Manasseh.

31From the descendants of Harim:
Eliezer, Ishijah, Malkijah, She-

10:9 [o] S Ezr 1:5
10:10 [p] Ezr 7:21 [q] 2Ch 28:13
10:11 [r] S Dt 24:1; Mal 2:10-16
10:12 [s] S Jos 6:5
10:14 [t] Dt 16:18 [u] S Nu 25:4; S 2Ch 29:10
10:15 [v] Ne 11:16
10:18 [w] S Jdg 3:6 [x] S Ezr 2:2
10:19 [y] S 2Ki 10:15 [z] S Lev 5:15; 6:6
10:20 [a] S 1Ch 24:14
10:21 [b] S 1Ch 24:8
10:22 [c] S 1Ch 9:12
10:23 [d] Ne 8:7; 9:4
10:24 [e] Ne 3:1; 12:10; 13:7,28
10:25 [f] S Ezr 2:3
10:26 [g] S ver 2

10:11 SEPARATE YOURSELVES. The actions of Ezra and the Israelite community at this stage of history should not be considered a standard for those under the new covenant. Concerning marriage and divorce for NT believers, the Bible teaches the following: (1) The believer must not enter into marriage with an unbeliever (1Co 7:39; cf. 2Co 6:14).

(2) If a person becomes a believer after marriage and the spouse remains an unbeliever, the believing spouse must not seek divorce if the unbelieving partner wants the marriage relationship to continue (1Co 7:12; see 7:14, note).

(3) Divorce is allowed in situations of immorality or abandonment (see Mt 19:9, note; 1Co 7:11, 15, notes).

maiah, Shimeon, 32Benjamin,
Malluch and Shemariah.
33From the descendants of Hashum:
Mattenai, Mattattah, Zabad,
Eliphelet, Jeremai, Manasseh
and Shimei.
34From the descendants of Bani:
Maadai, Amram, Uel, 35Bena-
iah, Bedeiah, Keluhi, 36Vaniah,
Meremoth, Eliashib, 37Matta-
niah, Mattenai and Jaasu.
38From the descendants of Binnui:[y]
Shimei, 39Shelemiah, Nathan,
Adaiah, 40Macnadebai, Sha-
shai, Sharai, 41Azarel, Shelemiah, Shemariah, 42Shallum,
Amariah and Joseph.
43From the descendants of Nebo:
Jeiel, Mattithiah, Zabad, Zebina, Jaddai, Joel and Benaiah.

44All these had married foreign women, and some of them had children by these wives.[z]

[y] *37,38* See Septuagint (also 1 Esdras 9:34); Hebrew *Jaasu 38and Bani and Binnui,*
[z] *44* Or *and they sent them away with their children*

10:44 WOMEN ... CHILDREN. The foreign wives and their children were most likely sent back to their own families among their people (see NIV text note).

NEHEMIAH

Outline

I. Rebuilding the Wall of Jerusalem: Led by Nehemiah (1:1—7:73)
  A. Nehemiah's Intercession for Jerusalem (1:1—2:8)
    1. The Burden of His Intercession (1:1–4)
    2. The Content of His Intercession with God (1:5–11)
    3. The Outcome of His Intercession with King Artaxerxes (2:1–8)
  B. Nehemiah Goes to Jerusalem as Governor (2:9–20)
  C. Nehemiah Leads in Reconstructing the Walls (3:1—7:4)
    1. The Builders (3:1–32)
    2. The Opposition (4:1—6:14)
      a. Ridicule (4:1–6)
      b. Conspiracy (4:7–23)
      c. Extortion (5:1–19)
      d. Compromise (6:1–4)
      e. Slander (6:5–9)
      f. Treachery (6:10–14)
    3. The Accomplishment (6:15—7:4)
  D. Nehemiah Registers the Remnant (7:5–73)
II. Reviving the People of Jerusalem: Led by Ezra (8:1—10:39)
  A. Public Declaration of God's Word and Commemoration of the Feast of Tabernacles (8:1–18)
  B. Fasting, Recollection of Past Sins and Public Confession of Those Sins (9:1–37)
  C. Making a Covenant of Obedience (9:38—10:39)
III. Reforming the Nation: Led by Nehemiah (11:1—13:31)
  A. Redistribution of the Remnant (11:1—12:26)
  B. Dedication of the Walls (12:27–47)
  C. Reforms During Nehemiah's Second Administration (13:1–31)

Author: Ezra and Nehemiah (?)

Theme: Rebuilding the Wall of Jerusalem

Date of Writing: c. 430–420 B.C.

Background

The book of Nehemiah concludes OT history, when the Jewish exiles were permitted to return to their homeland from captivity in Babylon and Persia. Together with Ezra (with which it forms a single book in the Hebrew OT; see the introduction to Ezra), it records the history of the three returns of exiles to Jerusalem. Ezra covers events associated with the first two returns (538 B.C.; 457 B.C.), and Nehemiah records events during the third return (444 B.C.). Whereas the focus in Ezra is on rebuilding the temple, in Nehemiah it is on rebuilding the wall of Jerusalem. Both books emphasize the importance of spiritual recovery and of commitment to God and his Word.

Nehemiah, a contemporary of Ezra, was serving as a cupbearer to Artaxerxes I (king of Persia) when he received news that the exiles who returned to Judah from Babylon and Persia were in trouble and the wall of Jerusalem was still in shambles. After praying about Jerusalem's plight, Nehemiah was providentially authorized by King Artaxerxes to go to Jerusalem to serve as governor and to rebuild the city walls. As an inspired leader, he rallied his countrymen to rebuild the wall completely in only 52 days in spite of determined opposition. He served as governor for twelve years; after a brief return to Persia, he served a second term as governor of Judah (cf. 2:1; 13:6–7a).

Ezra the priest assisted Nehemiah in promoting spiritual revival and reform among the returned remnant; possibly Nehemiah helped Ezra in writing this book. The historicity of the book of Nehemiah is confirmed by ancient documents discovered in 1903 called the Elephantine Papyri, which mention Sanballat (2:19), Johanan (12:23) and the replacement of Nehemiah as governor about 410 B.C.

Purpose

This book was written (1) to complete the recording of the post-exilic history begun in the book of Ezra, and (2) to show what God did on behalf of the remnant through the godly leadership of Nehemiah and Ezra during the third stage of the post-exilic restoration.

Survey

Chs. 1—7 record Nehemiah's role as governor and as leader in rebuilding the wall of Jerusalem. Ch. 1 reveals the spiritual depth of Nehemiah as a man of prayer. While serving the king of Persia, he received news about the sorry plight of Jerusalem and began to intercede earnestly with God to intervene on behalf of the city and its inhabitants. Ch. 2 describes how God used Artaxerxes to commission Nehemiah to be governor of Jerusalem and Nehemiah's arrival at Jerusalem. Chs. 3:1—7:1 reveal Nehemiah's bold, wise and decisive leadership in rallying Jerusalem to rebuild its broken-down walls in only 52 days, in spite of serious opposition from inside and outside the city.

The second half of the book describes (1) the spiritual restoration among the people of Jerusalem, led by Ezra the priest (chs. 8—10), and (2) certain national issues addressed by Nehemiah (chs. 11—13). Central to the spiritual restoration was the public reading of God's Law, repentance for sin, and a new resolve by the remnant to remember and keep their covenant with God. The last chapter records certain reforms that Nehemiah initiated during his second term as governor (ch. 13).

Special Features

Five major features characterize the book of Nehemiah. (1) It records the last events of Jewish OT history before the intertestamental period. (2) It provides historical background for Malachi, the last book of the OT, since Nehemiah and Malachi were contemporaries. (3) Nehemiah is a superb Biblical model of a godly leader in government: a man of wisdom, principle, courage, impeccable integrity, unwavering faith, compassion for the oppressed, and great gifts in leadership and organization. Throughout his years as governor, Nehemiah remained righteous, humble, free from greed, self-sacrificing, and uncorrupted by his prominence or power. (4) Nehemiah is one of the foremost OT examples of a praying leader (cf. also Daniel). No less than 11 times he is described as addressing God in prayer or intercession (e.g. 1:4–11; 2:4; 4:4,9; 5:19; 6:9,14; 13:14,22,29,31). He was a man who accomplished seemingly impossible tasks because of his complete dependence on God. (5)The book graphically illustrates that prayer, sacrifice, hard work and tenacity go together in realizing a God-given vision.

New Testament Fulfillment

This book records the completion of all the basic steps in restoration in post-exilic Judaism necessary for the coming of Christ at the outset of the NT era: Jerusalem and the temple were rebuilt, the law was restored, the covenant was renewed and the Davidic lineage was intact. Externally, everything was in place for the Messiah's coming (cf. Da 9:25). The era depicted in Nehemiah concludes with the prophetic hope that the Lord would soon come to his temple (cf. Mal 3:1). The NT opens with the fulfillment of this post-exilic expectation and hope.

Reading Nehemiah

In order to read the entire Old Testament in one year, the book of Nehemiah should be read in 5 days, according to the following schedule: ☐ 1–3 ☐ 4–6 ☐ 7–8 ☐ 9–10 ☐ 11–13

NOTES

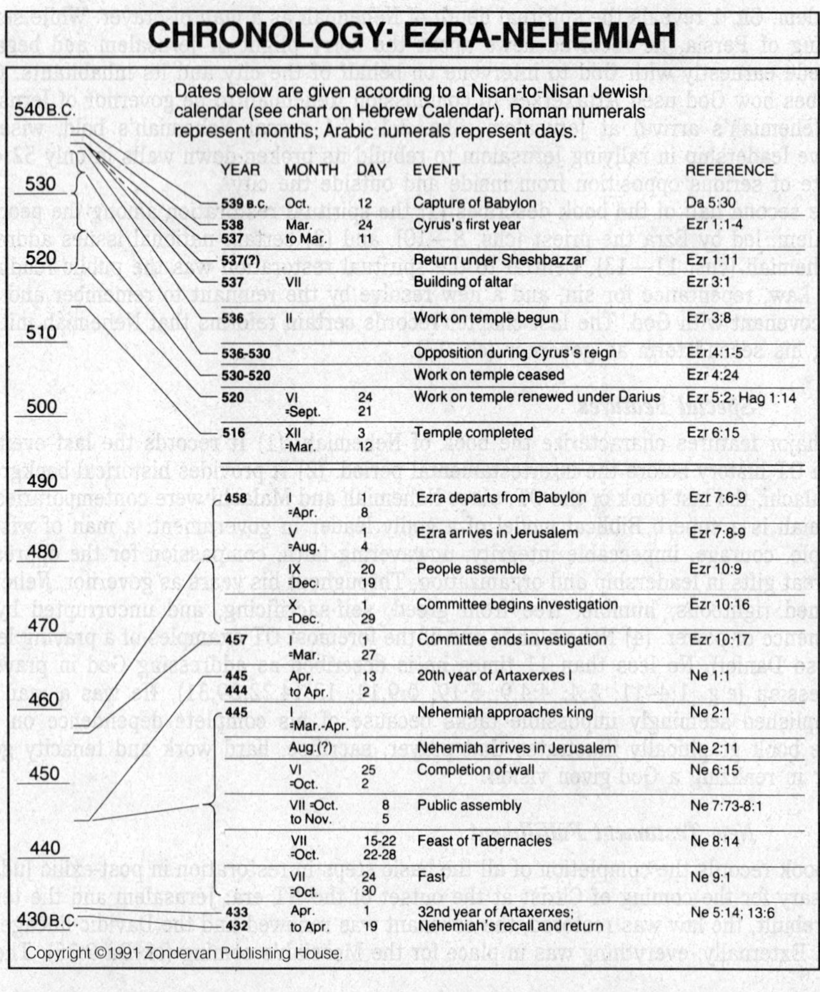

CHRONOLOGY: EZRA-NEHEMIAH

Dates below are given according to a Nisan-to-Nisan Jewish calendar (see chart on Hebrew Calendar). Roman numerals represent months; Arabic numerals represent days.

YEAR	MONTH	DAY	EVENT	REFERENCE
539 B.C.	Oct.	12	Capture of Babylon	Da 5:30
538 537	Mar. to Mar.	24 11	Cyrus's first year	Ezr 1:1-4
537(?)			Return under Sheshbazzar	Ezr 1:11
537	VII		Building of altar	Ezr 3:1
536	II		Work on temple begun	Ezr 3:8
536-530			Opposition during Cyrus's reign	Ezr 4:1-5
530-520			Work on temple ceased	Ezr 4:24
520	VI =Sept.	24 21	Work on temple renewed under Darius	Ezr 5:2; Hag 1:14
516	XII =Mar.	3 12	Temple completed	Ezr 6:15
458	I =Apr.	1 8	Ezra departs from Babylon	Ezr 7:6-9
	V =Aug.	1 4	Ezra arrives in Jerusalem	Ezr 7:8-9
	IX =Dec.	20 19	People assemble	Ezr 10:9
	X =Dec.	1 29	Committee begins investigation	Ezr 10:16
457	I =Mar.	1 27	Committee ends investigation	Ezr 10:17
445 444	Apr. to Apr.	13 2	20th year of Artaxerxes I	Ne 1:1
445	I =Mar.-Apr.		Nehemiah approaches king	Ne 2:1
	Aug.(?)		Nehemiah arrives in Jerusalem	Ne 2:11
	VI =Oct.	25 2	Completion of wall	Ne 6:15
	VII =Oct. to Nov.	8 5	Public assembly	Ne 7:73-8:1
	VII =Oct.	15-22 22-28	Feast of Tabernacles	Ne 8:14
	VII =Oct.	24 30	Fast	Ne 9:1
433 432	Apr. to Apr.	1 19	32nd year of Artaxerxes; Nehemiah's recall and return	Ne 5:14; 13:6

Nehemiah's Prayer

1 The words of Nehemiah son of
Hacaliah:

In the month of Kislev[a] in the twentieth year, while I was in the citadel of
Susa,[b] **2**Hanani,[c] one of my brothers,
came from Judah with some other men,
and I questioned them about the Jewish remnant[d] that survived the exile,
and also about Jerusalem.
3They said to me, "Those who survived the exile and are back in the
province are in great trouble and disgrace. The wall of Jerusalem is broken
down, and its gates have been burned
with fire.[e]"
4When I heard these things, I sat
down and wept.[f] For some days I
mourned and fasted[g] and prayed before the God of heaven. **5**Then I said:

"O LORD, God of heaven, the
great and awesome God,[h] who
keeps his covenant of love[i] with
those who love him and obey his
commands, **6**let your ear be attentive and your eyes open to hear[j]
the prayer[k] your servant is praying before you day and night for
your servants, the people of Israel. I confess[l] the sins we Israelites, including myself and my father's house, have committed
against you. **7**We have acted very
wickedly[m] toward you. We have
not obeyed the commands, decrees and laws you gave your servant Moses.
8"Remember[n] the instruction
you gave your servant Moses, saying, 'If you are unfaithful, I will
scatter[o] you among the nations,
9but if you return to me and obey
my commands, then even if your
exiled people are at the farthest
horizon, I will gather[p] them from
there and bring them to the place
I have chosen as a dwelling for my
Name.'[q]
10"They are your servants and
your people, whom you redeemed
by your great strength and your
mighty hand.[r] **11**O Lord, let your
ear be attentive[s] to the prayer of
this your servant and to the
prayer of your servants who delight in revering your name. Give
your servant success today by
granting him favor[t] in the presence of this man."

I was cupbearer[u] to the king.

Artaxerxes Sends Nehemiah to Jerusalem

2 In the month of Nisan in the twentieth year of King Artaxerxes,[v]
when wine was brought for him, I took
the wine and gave it to the king. I had
not been sad in his presence before;
2so the king asked me, "Why does your
face look so sad when you are not ill?
This can be nothing but sadness of
heart."
I was very much afraid, **3**but I said
to the king, "May the king live forever![w] Why should my face not look sad
when the city[x] where my fathers are
buried lies in ruins, and its gates have
been destroyed by fire?[y]"
4The king said to me, "What is it you
want?"
Then I prayed to the God of heaven,

1:1 [a]Zec 7:1 [b]S Ezr 4:9; S Est 2:8
1:2 [c]Ne 7:2 [d]S 2Ki 21:14; Ne 7:6; Jer 52:28
1:3 [e]S Lev 26:31; 2Ki 25:10; Ne 2:3, 13,17; Isa 22:9; Jer 39:8; 52:14; La 2:9
1:4 [f]Ps 137:1 [g]S 2Ch 20:3; S Ezr 9:4; Da 9:3
1:5 [h]S Dt 7:21; Ne 4:14 [i]S Dt 7:9; S 1Ki 8:23; Da 9:4
1:6 [j]S 1Ki 8:29; S 2Ch 7:15 [k]S 1Ki 8:30 [l]S 1Ki 8:47
1:7 [m]Ps 106:6
1:8 [n]S Ge 8:1; S 2Ki 20:3; Ne 4:14; 5:19; 6:14; 13:22,29,31 [o]S Lev 26:33
1:9 [p]S Dt 30:4; Ps 106:47; 107:3; Isa 11:12; 56:8; Jer 42:12; Eze 11:17 [q]S 1Ki 8:48; Jer 29:14; Eze 11:17; 20:34-38; 36:24-38; Mic 2:12
1:10 [r]S Ex 32:11; Isa 51:9-11
1:11 [s]S 2Ch 6:40 [t]S Ex 3:21 [u]S Ge 40:1
2:1 [v]S Ezr 4:7; S 6:14
2:3 [w]1Ki 1:31; Da 2:4; 3:9; 5:10; 6:6,21 [x]Ps 137:6 [y]S Ne 1:3

1:1 NEHEMIAH. Nehemiah left Persia for Jerusalem in 444 B.C. to be governor of Judah. This was thirteen years after Ezra had arrived there. Nehemiah came with a commission from the king of Persia to rebuild the wall of Jerusalem and fortify the city (2:7–8). In spite of much opposition, Nehemiah completed the wall in 52 days (6:15). He was a man of ability, courage, perseverance and prayer (see 2:4, note), who cooperated with Ezra in bringing spiritual renewal to the people (ch. 8).

1:4 MOURNED AND FASTED AND PRAYED. Nehemiah was deeply burdened for his people and for God's work in Judah. For four months (cf. v. 1 with 2:1) he poured out his heart to God in fasting and prayer with many tears because of the trouble afflicting God's people in Jerusalem and Judah (cf. Ac 20:31). His prayer included confession of sin (vv. 6–7), reminders to God of his own word (v. 8; cf. Lev 26:40–45; Dt 30:1–6), concern for God's glory and purposes (vv. 5–8), and continual intercession for the people of Israel (v. 6).

1:11 FAVOR IN THE PRESENCE OF THIS MAN. "This man" was Artaxerxes, king of Persia (2:1). Nehemiah prayed that God would grant him favor with the king on behalf of the Jews. When we desire to obtain anything from other people, we should first present our concerns to God. He can then move the hearts and minds of influential leaders to do his will (see Est 4:16; Pr 21:1).

2:4 THEN I PRAYED. Nehemiah's first impulse always was to pray. Before answering the king's question, he breathed a prayer to God for help and wisdom—just one of the many times in the book where Nehemiah spontaneously called on God (cf. 4:4–5,9; 5:19; 6:9,14; 13:14,22,29,31). (1) In this case, Nehemiah stood before the king and had time only to cry out to God from his heart. In emergencies we do not have time for long prayers. Nehemi-

5and I answered the king, “If it pleases
the king and if your servant has found
favor in his sight, let him send me to
the city in Judah where my fathers are
buried so that I can rebuild it.”
6Then the king[z], with the queen sitting beside him, asked me, “How long
will your journey take, and when will
you get back?” It pleased the king to
send me; so I set a time.
7I also said to him, “If it pleases the
king, may I have letters to the governors of Trans-Euphrates,[a] so that
they will provide me safe-conduct until
I arrive in Judah? 8And may I have a
letter to Asaph, keeper of the king’s
forest, so he will give me timber to
make beams for the gates of the citadel[b] by the temple and for the city
wall and for the residence I will occupy?” And because the gracious hand of
my God was upon me,[c] the king granted my requests.[d] 9So I went to the
governors of Trans-Euphrates and
gave them the king’s letters. The king
had also sent army officers and cavalry[e] with me.
10When Sanballat[f] the Horonite
and Tobiah[g] the Ammonite official
heard about this, they were very much
disturbed that someone had come to
promote the welfare of the Israelites.[h]

Nehemiah Inspects Jerusalem’s Walls

11I went to Jerusalem, and after
staying there three days[i] 12I set out
during the night with a few men. I had
not told anyone what my God had put
in my heart to do for Jerusalem. There
were no mounts with me except the
one I was riding on.
13By night I went out through the
Valley Gate[j] toward the Jackal[a] Well
and the Dung Gate,[k] examining the
walls[l] of Jerusalem, which had been
broken down, and its gates, which had
been destroyed by fire. 14Then I moved
on toward the Fountain Gate[m] and the
King’s Pool,[n] but there was not
enough room for my mount to get
through; 15so I went up the valley by
night, examining the wall. Finally, I
turned back and reentered through the
Valley Gate. 16The officials did not
know where I had gone or what I was
doing, because as yet I had said nothing to the Jews or the priests or nobles
or officials or any others who would be
doing the work.
17Then I said to them, “You see the
trouble we are in: Jerusalem lies in ruins, and its gates have been burned
with fire.[o] Come, let us rebuild the
wall[p] of Jerusalem, and we will no
longer be in disgrace.[q]” 18I also told
them about the gracious hand of my
God upon me[r] and what the king had
said to me.
They replied, “Let us start rebuilding.” So they began this good work.
19But when Sanballat[s] the Horonite, Tobiah the Ammonite official and
Geshem[t] the Arab heard about it,

2:6 [z] Ne 5:14; 13:6
2:7 [a] S Ezr 8:36
2:8 [b] Ne 7:2 [c] S Ezr 5:5 [d] S Ezr 4:24
2:9 [e] S Ezr 8:22
2:10 [f] ver 19; Ne 4:1,7; 6:1-2,5, 12,14; 13:28 [g] Ne 4:3; 13:4-7 [h] Est 10:3
2:11 [i] S Ge 40:13
2:13 [j] S 2Ch 26:9 [k] Ne 3:13; 12:31 [l] S Ne 1:3
2:14 [m] Ne 3:15; 12:37 [n] S 2Ki 18:17
2:17 [o] S Ne 1:3 [p] Ps 102:16; Isa 30:13; 58:12 [q] Eze 5:14
2:18 [r] S Ezr 5:5
2:19 [s] S ver 10 [t] Ne 6:1,2,6

[a] 13 Or *Serpent* or *Fig*

ah’s brief prayer touched God because it had been preceded by four months of praying and fasting. It pays to be “on praying ground.”

(2) The habit of praying frequently throughout the day will make way for a greater flow of God’s grace, help and wisdom into our lives. To forget our dependence on God and the need for his presence with us throughout the day will limit the working of the Holy Spirit in our lives (see Eph 6:18; 1Th 5:17).

2:8 GRACIOUS HAND OF MY GOD WAS UPON ME. The hand of the Lord upon Nehemiah meant at least five things to him. (1) He was sharing in God’s purposes (ch. 1). (2) God was actively guiding him (v. 12). (3) God was granting him his favor and help (v. 18; cf. Heb 4:16). (4) God was with him, enabling him to prosper and succeed in God’s work (v. 20; cf. Lk 24:50, note). (5) He felt renewed courage and faith in God (4:14,20).

2:12 NOT TOLD ANYONE. Though Nehemiah arrived as governor with the full authority of the Persian empire behind him, he did nothing for three days and told no one his God-given plans. We can be sure he was waiting on God, not rushing ahead by trusting in his own strength (see Isa 40:29–31). Then he made a cautious, careful survey of the damage done to the walls by the Samaritans (see Ezr 4:23–24, notes), while at the same time undoubtedly counting the cost (cf. Lk 14:28–30). Most important, instead of criticizing the people for their problems and sorrows, he wanted to see these problems from their own viewpoint; thus he said nothing until he could understand the situation from their perspective and feel what they felt.

2:19 MOCKED AND RIDICULED US. Ridicule and scorn often become the lot of God’s faithful children who day in and day out sincerely try to live a righteous life among those who do not know God. The world frequently despises the moral standards of Christians and mocks their devotion to Christ. Our confidence and reply should be the same as Nehemiah’s—the God of heaven will help us and in the end vindicate the righteous (v. 20; see Rev 2:7, note; 21:1–7, notes).

they mocked and ridiculed us.[u] "What is this you are doing?" they asked. "Are you rebelling against the king?"

20I answered them by saying, "The God of heaven will give us success. We his servants will start rebuilding,[v] but as for you, you have no share[w] in Jerusalem or any claim or historic right to it."

Builders of the Wall

3 Eliashib[x] the high priest and his fellow priests went to work and rebuilt[y] the Sheep Gate.[z] They dedicated it and set its doors in place, building as far as the Tower of the Hundred, which they dedicated, and as far as the Tower of Hananel.[a] 2The men of Jericho[b] built the adjoining section, and Zaccur son of Imri built next to them.

3The Fish Gate[c] was rebuilt by the sons of Hassenaah. They laid its beams and put its doors and bolts and bars in place. 4Meremoth[d] son of Uriah, the son of Hakkoz, repaired the next section. Next to him Meshullam son of Berekiah, the son of Meshezabel, made repairs, and next to him Zadok son of Baana also made repairs. 5The next section was repaired by the men of Tekoa,[e] but their nobles would not put their shoulders to the work under their supervisors.[b]

6The Jeshanah[c] Gate[f] was repaired by Joiada son of Paseah and Meshullam son of Besodeiah. They laid its beams and put its doors and bolts and bars in place. 7Next to them, repairs were made by men from Gibeon[g] and Mizpah—Melatiah of Gibeon and Jadon of Meronoth—places under the authority of the governor of Trans-Euphrates. 8Uzziel son of Harhaiah, one of the goldsmiths, repaired the next section; and Hananiah, one of the perfume-makers, made repairs next to that. They restored[d] Jerusalem as far as the Broad Wall.[h] 9Rephaiah son of Hur, ruler of a half-district of Jerusalem, repaired the next section. 10Adjoining this, Jedaiah son of Harumaph made repairs opposite his house, and Hattush son of Hashabneiah made repairs next to him. 11Malkijah son of Harim and Hasshub son of Pahath-Moab repaired another section and the Tower of the Ovens.[i] 12Shallum son of Hallohesh, ruler of a half-district of Jerusalem, repaired the next section with the help of his daughters.

13The Valley Gate[j] was repaired by Hanun and the residents of Zanoah.[k] They rebuilt it and put its doors and bolts and bars in place. They also repaired five hundred yards[e] of the wall as far as the Dung Gate.[l]

14The Dung Gate was repaired by Malkijah son of Recab, ruler of the district of Beth Hakkerem.[m] He rebuilt it and put its doors and bolts and bars in place.

15The Fountain Gate was repaired by Shallun son of Col-Hozeh, ruler of the district of Mizpah. He rebuilt it, roofing it over and putting its doors and bolts and bars in place. He also repaired the wall of the Pool of Siloam,[f][n] by the King's Garden, as far as the steps going down from the City of David. 16Beyond him, Nehemiah son of Azbuk, ruler of a half-district of Beth Zur,[o] made repairs up to a point opposite the tombs[g][p] of David, as far as the artificial pool and the House of the Heroes.

17Next to him, the repairs were made by the Levites under Rehum son of Bani. Beside him, Hashabiah, ruler of half the district of Keilah,[q] carried out repairs for his district. 18Next to him, the repairs were made by their

2:19 [u]Ps 44:13-16
2:20 [v]Ezr 4:1 [w]Ezr 4:3; Ac 8:21
3:1 [x]S Ezr 10:24 [y]Isa 58:12 [z]ver 32; Ne 12:39; Jn 5:2 [a]Ne 12:39; Ps 48:12; Jer 31:38; Zec 14:10
3:2 [b]Ne 7:36
3:3 [c]S 2Ch 33:14
3:4 [d]S Ezr 8:33
3:5 [e]ver 27; S 2Sa 14:2
3:6 [f]Ne 12:39
3:7 [g]S Jos 9:3
3:8 [h]Ne 12:38
3:11 [i]Ne 12:38
3:13 [j]S 2Ch 26:9 [k]S Jos 15:34 [l]S Ne 2:13
3:14 [m]Jer 6:1
3:15 [n]Isa 8:6; Jn 9:7
3:16 [o]S Jos 15:58 [p]Ac 2:29
3:17 [q]S Jos 15:44

[b] *5* Or *their Lord* or *the governor* [c] *6* Or *Old*
[d] *8* Or *They left out part of* [e] *13* Hebrew *a thousand cubits* (about 450 meters)
[f] *15* Hebrew *Shelah*, a variant of *Shiloah*, that is, Siloam [g] *16* Hebrew; Septuagint, some Vulgate manuscripts and Syriac *tomb*

2:20 WILL GIVE US SUCCESS. In all matters related to his kingdom, success begins with God. Nehemiah began rebuilding the wall of the city because he knew it was God's will; therefore he was fully confident that God would give him success in doing so. In all God's work, our Lord desires his people to be co-laborers with him (cf. Php 2:12–13). Ch. 4 adds three factors of success that involve effort on our part: (1) the people put their whole heart into the work (4:6); (2) the people were prayerful and watchful as they did the work (4:9); and (3) the people demonstrated courage, determination and faith when confronting opposition from the enemy (4:14). When Jerusalem's wall was finished in 52 days, even the Jews' enemies had to acknowledge that this work was accomplished with the help of God (6:15–16). God always does his part when his people do their part in persevering faith.

countrymen under Binnui[h] son of Henadad, ruler of the other half-district of Keilah. **19**Next to him, Ezer son of Jeshua, ruler of Mizpah, repaired another section, from a point facing the ascent to the armory as far as the angle. **20**Next to him, Baruch son of Zabbai zealously repaired another section, from the angle to the entrance of the house of Eliashib the high priest. **21**Next to him, Meremoth[r] son of Uriah, the son of Hakkoz, repaired another section, from the entrance of Eliashib's house to the end of it.

22The repairs next to him were made by the priests from the surrounding region. **23**Beyond them, Benjamin and Hasshub made repairs in front of their house; and next to them, Azariah son of Maaseiah, the son of Ananiah, made repairs beside his house. **24**Next to him, Binnui[s] son of Henadad repaired another section, from Azariah's house to the angle and the corner, **25**and Palal son of Uzai worked opposite the angle and the tower projecting from the upper palace near the court of the guard.[t] Next to him, Pedaiah son of Parosh[u] **26**and the temple servants[v] living on the hill of Ophel[w] made repairs up to a point opposite the Water Gate[x] toward the east and the projecting tower. **27**Next to them, the men of Tekoa[y] repaired another section, from the great projecting tower[z] to the wall of Ophel.

28Above the Horse Gate,[a] the priests made repairs, each in front of his own house. **29**Next to them, Zadok son of Immer made repairs opposite his house. Next to him, Shemaiah son of Shecaniah, the guard at the East Gate, made repairs. **30**Next to him, Hananiah son of Shelemiah, and Hanun, the sixth son of Zalaph, repaired another section. Next to them, Meshullam son of Berekiah made repairs opposite his living quarters. **31**Next to him, Malkijah, one of the goldsmiths, made repairs as far as the house of the temple servants and the merchants, opposite the Inspection Gate, and as far as the room above the corner; **32**and between the room above the corner and the Sheep Gate[b] the goldsmiths and merchants made repairs.

Opposition to the Rebuilding

4 When Sanballat[c] heard that we were rebuilding the wall, he became angry and was greatly incensed. He ridiculed the Jews, **2**and in the presence of his associates[d] and the army of Samaria, he said, "What are those feeble Jews doing? Will they restore their wall? Will they offer sacrifices? Will they finish in a day? Can they bring the stones back to life from those heaps of rubble[e]—burned as they are?"

3Tobiah[f] the Ammonite, who was at his side, said, "What they are building—if even a fox climbed up on it, he would break down their wall of stones!"[g]

4Hear us, O our God, for we are despised.[h] Turn their insults back on their own heads. Give them over as plunder in a land of captivity. **5**Do not cover up their guilt[i] or blot out their sins from your sight,[j] for they have thrown insults in the face of[i] the builders.

6So we rebuilt the wall till all of it reached half its height, for the people worked with all their heart.

7But when Sanballat, Tobiah,[k] the Arabs, the Ammonites and the men of Ashdod heard that the repairs to Jerusalem's walls had gone ahead and that the gaps were being closed, they were very angry. **8**They all plotted togeth-

3:21 [r]S Ezr 8:33
3:24 [s]S Ezr 8:33
3:25 [t]Jer 32:2; 37:21; 39:14 [u]S Ezr 2:3
3:26 [v]Ne 7:46; 11:21 [w]S 2Ch 33:14 [x]Ne 8:1,3,16; 12:37
3:27 [y]S ver 5 [z]Ps 48:12
3:28 [a]S 2Ki 11:16
3:32 [b]S ver 1; Jn 5:2
4:1 [c]S Ne 2:10
4:2 [d]S Ezr 4:9-10 [e]Ps 79:1; Jer 26:18
4:3 [f]S Ne 2:10 [g]Job 13:12; 15:3
4:4 [h]Ps 44:13; 123:3-4; Jer 33:24
4:5 [i]Isa 2:9; La 1:22 [j]2Ki 14:27; Ps 51:1; 69:27-28; 109:14; Jer 18:23
4:7 [k]S Ne 2:10

h *18* Two Hebrew manuscripts and Syriac (see also Septuagint and verse 24); most Hebrew manuscripts *Bavvai*
i *5* Or *have provoked you to anger before*

4:1 SANBALLAT . . . RIDICULED THE JEWS. The enemies of the small remnant of Jews opposed the rebuilding of Jerusalem's wall. Nehemiah and the people encountered ridicule (vv. 1–6), the threat of force (vv. 7–9), discouragement (v. 10) and fear (vv. 11–13). This chapter shows how opposition to the work of God can be overcome. (1) Ridicule was overcome by prayer and determination (vv. 4–6). (2) The threat of force was overcome by prayer and prudent security (vv. 7–9; see Mk 14:38; Eph 6:18). (3) Discouragement and fear were overcome by the faith of godly leaders, their encouragement and their preparation to resist the enemy (vv. 12–18; see Eph 6:11, note).

4:4 BACK ON THEIR OWN HEADS. Nehemiah's prayer against the enemy was motivated by his faith in God and his love for God's work and people (cf. Jer 18:23; Rev 6:10). It is always right to pray that God will oppose his enemies or turn back the hearts of those who are trying to destroy his work or harm his children.

er[l] to come and fight against Jerusalem and stir up trouble against it. 9But
we prayed to our God and posted a
guard day and night to meet this
threat.
10Meanwhile, the people in Judah
said, "The strength of the laborers[m] is
giving out, and there is so much rubble
that we cannot rebuild the wall."
11Also our enemies said, "Before
they know it or see us, we will be right
there among them and will kill them
and put an end to the work."
12Then the Jews who lived near
them came and told us ten times over,
"Wherever you turn, they will attack
us."
13Therefore I stationed some of the
people behind the lowest points of the
wall at the exposed places, posting
them by families, with their swords,
spears and bows. 14After I looked
things over, I stood up and said to the
nobles, the officials and the rest of the
people, "Don't be afraid[n] of them. Remember[o] the Lord, who is great and
awesome,[p] and fight[q] for your brothers, your sons and your daughters,
your wives and your homes."
15When our enemies heard that we
were aware of their plot and that God
had frustrated it,[r] we all returned to
the wall, each to his own work.
16From that day on, half of my men
did the work, while the other half were
equipped with spears, shields, bows
and armor. The officers posted themselves behind all the people of Judah
17who were building the wall. Those
who carried materials did their work
with one hand and held a weapon[s] in
the other, 18and each of the builders
wore his sword at his side as he
worked. But the man who sounded the
trumpet[t] stayed with me.
19Then I said to the nobles, the officials and the rest of the people, "The
work is extensive and spread out, and
we are widely separated from each other along the wall. 20Wherever you hear
the sound of the trumpet,[u] join us
there. Our God will fight[v] for us!"
21So we continued the work with
half the men holding spears, from the
first light of dawn till the stars came
out. 22At that time I also said to the
people, "Have every man and his helper stay inside Jerusalem at night, so
they can serve us as guards by night
and workmen by day." 23Neither I nor
my brothers nor my men nor the
guards with me took off our clothes;
each had his weapon, even when he
went for water.[j]

Nehemiah Helps the Poor

5 Now the men and their wives
raised a great outcry against their
Jewish brothers. 2Some were saying,
"We and our sons and daughters are
numerous; in order for us to eat and
stay alive, we must get grain."
3Others were saying, "We are mort-
gaging our fields,[w] our vineyards and
our homes to get grain during the famine."[x]
4Still others were saying, "We have
had to borrow money to pay the king's
tax[y] on our fields and vineyards. 5Al-
though we are of the same flesh and
blood[z] as our countrymen and though
our sons are as good as theirs, yet we
have to subject our sons and daughters
to slavery.[a] Some of our daughters
have already been enslaved, but we are
powerless, because our fields and our
vineyards belong to others."[b]
6When I heard their outcry and
these charges, I was very angry. 7I
pondered them in my mind and then

4:8 [l]Ps 2:2; 83:1-18
4:10 [m]S 1Ch 23:4
4:14 [n]S Ge 28:15; S Dt 1:29 [o]S Ne 1:8 [p]S Ne 1:5 [q]S 2Sa 10:12
4:15 [r]S 2Sa 17:14; Job 5:12
4:17 [s]Ps 149:6
4:18 [t]S Nu 10:2
4:20 [u]Eze 33:3 [v]S Ex 14:14; S Dt 20:4; Jos 10:14
5:3 [w]Ps 109:11 [x]Ge 47:23
5:4 [y]S Ezr 4:13
5:5 [z]S Ge 29:14 [a]Lev 25:39-43,47; S 2Ki 4:1; Isa 50:1 [b]Dt 15:7-11; S 2Ki 4:1

[j]*23* The meaning of the Hebrew for this clause is uncertain.

4:20 OUR GOD WILL FIGHT FOR US! When our work for God is genuinely undertaken in faith and humility in order to bring God glory and to advance his kingdom, using the weapons of the Spirit (see 2Co 10:4, note), we can be assured that no matter how great the difficulties, God will fight for us.

5:1 A GREAT OUTCRY. Ch. 5 concerns unjust economic inequities among the Jewish people. (1) The rich, i.e., the nobles and officials (v. 7), were oppressing the poor by making them mortgage their property and borrow money in order to buy food. In some instances the poor were being forced to give their children as slaves to keep from starving (vv. 1–5). In anger, Nehemiah fought against this injustice (v. 6) and brought the offenders to repentance and correction (vv. 12–13). (2) The sin of covetousness, which leads people to take advantage of others in times of trouble, reveals the deep depravity of human nature. God will judge such injustices perpetrated among people (cf. Pr 28:27; see Col 3:25, note; see article on THE CARE OF THE POOR AND NEEDY, p. 1316).

5:6 VERY ANGRY. Nehemiah's anger at injustice and evil was a godly anger. The absence of such anger indicates an indifference to the suffering of the innocent and needy (see Lk 19:45, note).

accused the nobles and officials. I told
them, "You are exacting usury[c] from
your own countrymen!" So I called together a large meeting to deal with
them 8and said: "As far as possible, we
have bought[d] back our Jewish brothers who were sold to the Gentiles. Now
you are selling your brothers, only for
them to be sold back to us!" They kept
quiet, because they could find nothing
to say.[e]

9So I continued, "What you are doing
is not right. Shouldn't you walk in the
fear of our God to avoid the reproach[f]
of our Gentile enemies? 10I and my
brothers and my men are also lending
the people money and grain. But let the
exacting of usury stop![g] 11Give back
to them immediately their fields, vineyards, olive groves and houses, and
also the usury[h] you are charging
them—the hundredth part of the money, grain, new wine and oil."

12"We will give it back," they said.
"And we will not demand anything
more from them. We will do as you
say."

Then I summoned the priests and
made the nobles and officials take an
oath[i] to do what they had promised.
13I also shook[j] out the folds of my
robe and said, "In this way may God
shake out of his house and possessions
every man who does not keep this
promise. So may such a man be shaken
out and emptied!"

At this the whole assembly said,
"Amen,"[k] and praised the LORD. And
the people did as they had promised.

14Moreover, from the twentieth year
of King Artaxerxes,[l] when I was appointed to be their governor[m] in the
land of Judah, until his thirty-second
year—twelve years—neither I nor my
brothers ate the food allotted to the
governor. 15But the earlier governors—those preceding me—placed a
heavy burden on the people and took
forty shekels[k] of silver from them in
addition to food and wine. Their assistants also lorded it over the people.
But out of reverence for God[n] I did not
act like that. 16Instead,[o] I devoted
myself to the work on this wall. All my
men were assembled there for the
work; we[l] did not acquire any land.

17Furthermore, a hundred and fifty
Jews and officials ate at my table, as
well as those who came to us from the
surrounding nations. 18Each day one
ox, six choice sheep and some poul-
try[p] were prepared for me, and every
ten days an abundant supply of wine of
all kinds. In spite of all this, I never
demanded the food allotted to the governor, because the demands were
heavy on these people.

19Remember[q] me with favor, O my
God, for all I have done for these people.

Further Opposition to the Rebuilding

6 When word came to Sanballat, Tobiah,[r] Geshem[s] the Arab and the
rest of our enemies that I had rebuilt
the wall and not a gap was left in it—
though up to that time I had not set the
doors in the gates— 2Sanballat and
Geshem sent me this message: "Come,
let us meet together in one of the villages[m] on the plain of Ono.[t]"

But they were scheming to harm me;
3so I sent messengers to them with
this reply: "I am carrying on a great
project and cannot go down. Why

5:7 [c] Ex 22:25-27; S Lev 25:35-37; Dt 23:19-20; 24:10-13
5:8 [d] Lev 25:47 [e] Jer 34:8
5:9 [f] Isa 52:5
5:10 [g] S Ex 22:25
5:11 [h] Isa 58:6
5:12 [i] S Ezr 10:5
5:13 [j] S Mt 10:14 [k] Dt 27:15-26
5:14 [l] S Ne 2:6 [m] Ge 42:6; Ezr 6:7; Jer 40:7; Hag 1:1
5:15 [n] S Ge 20:11
5:16 [o] 2Th 3:7-10
5:18 [p] 1Ki 4:23
5:19 [q] S Ge 8:1; S 2Ki 20:3; S Ne 1:8
6:1 [r] Ne 2:10 [s] S Ne 2:19
6:2 [t] S 1Ch 8:12

[k] *15* That is, about 1 pound (about 0.5 kilogram) [l] *16* Most Hebrew manuscripts; some Hebrew manuscripts, Septuagint, Vulgate and Syriac *I* [m] *2* Or *in Kephirim*

5:15 REVERENCE FOR GOD. Because Nehemiah revered God, he did not use his authority to take advantage of the people, as some other leaders before him had done. Reverence for God makes us aware of our accountability to him and motivates us to turn away from even subtle practices, such as manipulating or defrauding his people.

5:18 WINE OF ALL KINDS. In OT times there were all kinds of wine—new, old, pure and mixed wines—some fresh from the grape, some boiled and condensed, some sweet and thick like honey, some mixed with water and some mixed with drugs. Of these wines, some were fermented, others were not (see Pr 23:30, note; see also articles on WINE IN THE OLD TESTAMENT, p. 204, and WINE IN NEW TESTAMENT TIMES (1) and (2), p. 1534 and p. 1586).

6:3 CARRYING ON A GREAT PROJECT. God's people must have a vision of the greatness of the work to which he calls them. Even though our task or contribution as individuals may seem small and inconsequential, corporately as God's people we are "carrying on a great project." Nehemiah was resolute in his objective of rebuilding the wall; he would not be distracted by friend or foe until the work was completed. Great vision coupled with unwavering faith achieves the realization of God's purpose for our lives and our generation.

should the work stop while I leave it
and go down to you?" **4**Four times they
sent me the same message, and each
time I gave them the same answer.
5Then, the fifth time, Sanballat[u]
sent his aide to me with the same message, and in his hand was an unsealed
letter **6**in which was written:

"It is reported among the nations—and Geshem[n][v] says it is
true—that you and the Jews are
plotting to revolt, and therefore
you are building the wall. Moreover, according to these reports
you are about to become their
king **7**and have even appointed
prophets to make this proclamation about you in Jerusalem:
'There is a king in Judah!' Now
this report will get back to the
king; so come, let us confer together."

8I sent him this reply: "Nothing like
what you are saying is happening; you
are just making it up out of your head."
9They were all trying to frighten us,
thinking, "Their hands will get too
weak for the work, and it will not be
completed."

⌞But I prayed,⌟ "Now strengthen my
hands."

10One day I went to the house of
Shemaiah son of Delaiah, the son of
Mehetabel, who was shut in at his
home. He said, "Let us meet in the
house of God, inside the temple[w], and
let us close the temple doors, because
men are coming to kill you—by night
they are coming to kill you."
11But I said, "Should a man like me
run away? Or should one like me go
into the temple to save his life? I will
not go!" **12**I realized that God had not
sent him, but that he had prophesied
against me[x] because Tobiah and Sanballat[y] had hired him. **13**He had been
hired to intimidate me so that I would
commit a sin by doing this, and then
they would give me a bad name to discredit me.[z]

14Remember[a] Tobiah and Sanballat,[b] O my God, because of what they
have done; remember also the prophetess[c] Noadiah and the rest of the
prophets[d] who have been trying to intimidate me.

The Completion of the Wall

15So the wall was completed on the
twenty-fifth of Elul, in fifty-two days.
16When all our enemies heard about
this, all the surrounding nations were
afraid and lost their self-confidence,
because they realized that this work Est 4:14–5:2
had been done with the help of our God.
17Also, in those days the nobles of
Judah were sending many letters to Tobiah, and replies from Tobiah kept
coming to them. **18**For many in Judah
were under oath to him, since he was
son-in-law to Shecaniah son of Arah,
and his son Jehohanan had married the
daughter of Meshullam son of Berekiah. **19**Moreover, they kept reporting to
me his good deeds and then telling him
what I said. And Tobiah sent letters to
intimidate me.

7 After the wall had been rebuilt and
I had set the doors in place, the
gatekeepers[e] and the singers[f] and
the Levites[g] were appointed. **2**I put in
charge of Jerusalem my brother Hana-

6:5 [u]S Ne 2:10
6:6 [v]S Ne 2:19
6:10 [w]Nu 18:7
6:12 [x]Eze 13:22-23 [y]S Ne 2:10
6:13 [z]Jer 20:10
6:14 [a]S Ne 1:8 [b]S Ne 2:10 [c]S Ex 15:20; Eze 13:17-23; S Ac 21:9; Rev 2:20 [d]Jer 23:9-40; Zec 13:2-3
7:1 [e]1Ch 9:27; S 26:12-19 [f]Ps 68:25 [g]Ne 8:9

[n]6 Hebrew *Gashmu,* a variant of *Geshem*

6:12 I REALIZED THAT GOD HAD NOT SENT HIM. All who claim to be God's messengers must be tested as to whether they are really from God. Some will claim to be believers and proclaim that they are undertaking a ministry ordained by God, yet in reality they are only seeking glory and prosperity for themselves. God's people need discernment to judge the personal character and loyalty to God and his standards of all who present themselves as spokespersons for God (see article on FALSE TEACHERS, p. 1506).

6:14 PROPHETS . . . TRYING TO INTIMIDATE ME. Nehemiah suffered from false brothers who, although claiming to labor for God's honor, were in reality in league with God's enemies. This betrayal of God and his kingdom by false brothers and sisters is one of the heaviest griefs that true servants of God sometimes have to bear (see Ac 20:28–31; 2Co 11:26).

6:15 THE WALL WAS COMPLETED. The wall was completed (1) because God was with his people (2:20; 4:15,20); (2) because they had a courageous, dedicated and persevering leader, Nehemiah, who depended fully on God as his protection and source of strength (vv. 3,9; 5:14–19); and (3) because the people worked with all their heart (4:6), following their leader in giving themselves courageously to the task until it was completed.

7:2 MAN OF INTEGRITY AND FEARED GOD. The Scriptural principle in selecting leaders for God's work is to appoint those who have persevered in faithfulness to God and his word and have demonstrated a godly fear of sin and its consequences (see articles on MORAL QUALIFICATIONS FOR OVERSEERS, p. 1882, and BIBLE TRAINING FOR CHRISTIANS, p. 1894).

ni,[h] along with[o] Hananiah[i] the commander of the citadel,[j] because he was a man of integrity and feared[k] God more than most men do. 3I said to them, "The gates of Jerusalem are not to be opened until the sun is hot. While the gatekeepers are still on duty, have them shut the doors and bar them. Also appoint residents of Jerusalem as guards, some at their posts and some near their own houses."

The List of the Exiles Who Returned

7:6–73pp — Ezr 2:1–70

4Now the city was large and spacious, but there were few people in it,[l] and the houses had not yet been rebuilt. 5So my God put it into my heart to assemble the nobles, the officials and the common people for registration by families. I found the genealogical record of those who had been the first to return. This is what I found written there:

6These are the people of the province who came up from the captivity of the exiles[m] whom Nebuchadnezzar king of Babylon had taken captive (they returned to Jerusalem and Judah, each to his own town, 7in company with Zerubbabel,[n] Jeshua, Nehemiah, Azariah, Raamiah, Nahamani, Mordecai, Bilshan, Mispereth, Bigvai, Nehum and Baanah):

The list of the men of Israel:

8the descendants of Parosh 2,172
9of Shephatiah 372
10of Arah 652
11of Pahath-Moab (through the line of Jeshua and Joab) 2,818
12of Elam 1,254
13of Zattu 845
14of Zaccai 760
15of Binnui 648
16of Bebai 628
17of Azgad 2,322
18of Adonikam 667
19of Bigvai 2,067
20of Adin[o] 655
21of Ater (through Hezekiah) 98
22of Hashum 328
23of Bezai 324
24of Hariph 112
25of Gibeon 95

26the men of Bethlehem and Netophah[p] 188
27of Anathoth[q] 128
28of Beth Azmaveth 42
29of Kiriath Jearim, Kephirah[r] and Beeroth[s] 743
30of Ramah and Geba 621
31of Micmash 122
32of Bethel and Ai[t] 123
33of the other Nebo 52
34of the other Elam 1,254
35of Harim 320
36of Jericho[u] 345
37of Lod, Hadid and Ono[v] 721
38of Senaah 3,930

39The priests:

the descendants of Jedaiah (through the family of Jeshua) 973
40of Immer 1,052
41of Pashhur 1,247
42of Harim 1,017

43The Levites:

the descendants of Jeshua (through Kadmiel through the line of Hodaviah) 74

44The singers:[w]

the descendants of Asaph 148

45The gatekeepers:[x]

the descendants of Shallum, Ater, Talmon, Akkub, Hatita and Shobai 138

46The temple servants:[y]

the descendants of Ziha, Hasupha, Tabbaoth,
47Keros, Sia, Padon,
48Lebana, Hagaba, Shalmai,
49Hanan, Giddel, Gahar,
50Reaiah, Rezin, Nekoda,
51Gazzam, Uzza, Paseah,
52Besai, Meunim, Nephussim,
53Bakbuk, Hakupha, Harhur,
54Bazluth, Mehida, Harsha,
55Barkos, Sisera, Temah,
56Neziah and Hatipha

7:2 [h]Ne 1:2 [i]Ne 10:23 [j]Ne 2:8 [k]1Ki 18:3 **7:4** [l]Ne 11:1 **7:6** [m]S 2Ch 36:20; S Ne 1:2 **7:7** [n]S 1Ch 3:19 **7:20** [o]S Ezr 8:6 **7:26** [p]S 2Sa 23:28; S 1Ch 2:54 **7:27** [q]S Jos 21:18 **7:29** [r]S Jos 18:26 [s]S Jos 18:25 **7:32** [t]S Ge 12:8 **7:36** [u]Ne 3:2 **7:37** [v]S 1Ch 8:12 **7:44** [w]Ne 11:23 **7:45** [x]S 1Ch 9:17 **7:46** [y]S Ne 3:26

[o]2 Or *Hanani, that is,*

57 The descendants of the servants
of Solomon:

the descendants of
Sotai, Sophereth, Perida,
58 Jaala, Darkon, Giddel,
59 Shephatiah, Hattil,
Pokereth-Hazzebaim and
Amon

60 The temple servants and
the descendants of the
servants of Solomon[z] 392

61 The following came up from
the towns of Tel Melah, Tel Harsha, Kerub, Addon and Immer,
but they could not show that their
families were descended from Israel:

62 the descendants of
Delaiah, Tobiah and
Nekoda 642

63 And from among the priests:

the descendants of
Hobaiah, Hakkoz and
Barzillai (a man who had
married a daughter of
Barzillai the Gileadite and
was called by that name).

64 These searched for their family records, but they could not find
them and so were excluded from
the priesthood as unclean. 65 The
governor, therefore, ordered them
not to eat any of the most sacred
food until there should be a priest
ministering with the Urim and
Thummim.[a]

66 The whole company numbered 42,360, 67 besides their
7,337 menservants and maidservants; and they also had 245 men
and women singers. 68 There were
736 horses, 245 mules,[p] 69 435
camels and 6,720 donkeys.

70 Some of the heads of the families contributed to the work. The
governor gave to the treasury 1,000 drachmas[q] of gold,
50 bowls and 530 garments for
priests. 71 Some of the heads of
the families[b] gave to the treasury for the work 20,000 drachmas[r] of gold and 2,200 minas[s]
of silver. 72 The total given by the
rest of the people was 20,000
drachmas of gold, 2,000 minas[t]
of silver and 67 garments for
priests.[c]

73 The priests, the Levites, the
gatekeepers, the singers and the
temple servants,[d] along with certain of the people and the rest of
the Israelites, settled in their own
towns.[e]

Ezra Reads the Law

When the seventh month came and
the Israelites had settled in their
8 towns,[f] 1 all the people assembled as one man in the square before the Water Gate.[g] They told Ezra
the scribe to bring out the Book of the
Law of Moses,[h] which the LORD had
commanded for Israel.

2 So on the first day of the seventh
month[i] Ezra the priest brought the
Law[j] before the assembly, which was
made up of men and women and all
who were able to understand. 3 He read
it aloud from daybreak till noon as he
faced the square before the Water
Gate[k] in the presence of the men,
women and others who could understand. And all the people listened attentively to the Book of the Law.

4 Ezra the scribe stood on a high
wooden platform[l] built for the occasion. Beside him on his right stood
Mattithiah, Shema, Anaiah, Uriah, Hilkiah and Maaseiah; and on his left
were Pedaiah, Mishael, Malkijah, Ha-

7:60 [z] S 1Ch 9:2
7:65 [a] S Ex 28:30
7:71 [b] S 1Ch 29:7
7:72 [c] S Ex 25:2
7:73 [d] Ne 1:10; Ps 34:22; 103:21; 113:1; 135:1 [e] S Ezr 3:1; Ne 11:1 [f] Ezr 3:1
8:1 [g] S Ne 3:26 [h] S Dt 28:61; S 2Ch 34:15
8:2 [i] Lev 23:23-25; Nu 29:1-6 [j] S Dt 31:11
8:3 [k] S Ne 3:26
8:4 [l] 2Ch 6:13

[p] *68* Some Hebrew manuscripts (see also Ezra 2:66); most Hebrew manuscripts do not have this verse. [q] *70* That is, about 19 pounds (about 8.5 kilograms) [r] *71* That is, about 375 pounds (about 170 kilograms); also in verse 72 [s] *71* That is, about 1 1/3 tons (about 1.2 metric tons) [t] *72* That is, about 1 1/4 tons (about 1.1 metric tons)

8:1 ALL THE PEOPLE ASSEMBLED. Chs. 8—10 describe one of the greatest revivals in OT times and illustrate several fundamental principles for spiritual renewal and revival. Renewal and revival come only from God; they are mediated through God's Word (vv. 1–8), prayer (v. 6), confession (ch. 9), a broken and contrite heart (v. 9), a turning from the sinful ways and behavior of contemporary society (9:2), and a renewed commitment to walk in God's will and to make God's Word the rule for grateful living (10:29).

8:3 LISTENED ATTENTIVELY. The revival was initiated by a sincere return to God's Word and a diligent effort to understand its meaning (v. 8). For seven days, six hours each day, Ezra read from the Book of the Law (vv. 3,18). One of the greatest evidences of true revival among God's people is a deep hunger to hear and to read God's Word.

shum, Hashbaddanah, Zechariah and
Meshullam.
5Ezra opened the book. All the people could see him because he was
standing[m] above them; and as he
opened it, the people all stood up.
6Ezra praised the LORD, the great
God; and all the people lifted their
hands[n] and responded, "Amen!
Amen!" Then they bowed down and
worshiped the LORD with their faces
to the ground.
7The Levites[o]—Jeshua, Bani,
Sherebiah, Jamin, Akkub, Shabbethai,
Hodiah, Maaseiah, Kelita, Azariah,
Jozabad, Hanan and Pelaiah—instructed[p] the people in the Law while
the people were standing there. 8They
read from the Book of the Law of God,
making it clear[u] and giving the meaning so that the people could understand what was being read.
9Then Nehemiah the governor, Ezra
the priest and scribe, and the Levites[q]
who were instructing the people said to
them all, "This day is sacred to the
LORD your God. Do not mourn or
weep."[r] For all the people had been
weeping as they listened to the words
of the Law.
10Nehemiah said, "Go and enjoy
choice food and sweet drinks, and send
some to those who have nothing[s] prepared. This day is sacred to our Lord.
Do not grieve, for the joy[t] of the LORD
is your strength."
11The Levites calmed all the people,
saying, "Be still, for this is a sacred
day. Do not grieve."
12Then all the people went away to
eat and drink, to send portions of food
and to celebrate with great joy,[u] because they now understood the words
that had been made known to them.
13On the second day of the month,
the heads of all the families, along with
the priests and the Levites, gathered
around Ezra the scribe to give attention to the words of the Law. 14They
found written in the Law, which the
LORD had commanded through Moses,
that the Israelites were to live in
booths[v] during the feast of the seventh month 15and that they should proclaim this word and spread it throughout their towns and in Jerusalem: "Go
out into the hill country and bring back
branches from olive and wild olive
trees, and from myrtles, palms and
shade trees, to make booths"—as it is
written.[v]
16So the people went out and
brought back branches and built themselves booths on their own roofs, in

8:5 [m]Jdg 3:20
8:6 [n]S Ezr 9:5; 1Ti 2:8
8:7 [o]S Ezr 10:23 [p]S Lev 10:11; S 2Ch 17:7
8:9 [q]Ne 7:1,65,70 [r]Dt 12:7,12; 16:14-15
8:10 [s]1Sa 25:8; S 2Sa 6:19; Est 9:22; Lk 14:12-14 [t]S Lev 23:40; S Dt 12:18; 16:11, 14-15
8:12 [u]Est 9:22
8:14 [v]S Ex 23:16

[u]8 Or *God, translating it* [v]15 See Lev. 23:37-40.

8:6 BOWED DOWN AND WORSHIPED. This chapter describes one of the greatest worship services of all time. God desires the adoration of his people and calls them to worship him regularly (cf. Ps 29:2; 96:9; see article on WORSHIP, p. 680).

8:7 INSTRUCTED THE PEOPLE IN THE LAW. Ezra and the Levites demonstrate what should happen whenever God's Word is proclaimed to his people. Many of the returned exiles no longer understood Hebrew, for their language was now Aramaic. Thus when the Hebrew Scriptures were read, a group of dedicated men translated it into Aramaic and explained its meaning in a manner that the people could understand and apply to their lives; as a result, the people rejoiced "because they now understood the words that had been made known to them" (v. 12). Revelation, repentance, revival and rejoicing are all potentially present and waiting to be released by the Holy Spirit through anointed messengers who proclaim God's Word with clarity, power and conviction.

8:9 WEEPING AS THEY LISTENED. When the people heard and understood the Word of God, they felt a deep conviction of sin and guilt. (1) The passages of the Law that brought a clear revelation of their spiritual condition may have been Lev 26 and Dt 28; these passages speak of God's blessing or judgment, depending on the people's obedience or disobedience to his Word. (2) In revivals, weeping, when accompanied with profound repentance (cf. ch. 9), is a sign of the work of the Holy Spirit (see Jn 16:8, note). Turning from sin in sorrow brings God's forgiveness and the joy of salvation (see v. 10, note; Mt 5:4).

8:10 ENJOY CHOICE FOOD AND SWEET DRINKS. The Jews highly prized foods prepared with much fat and drinks that were sweet. Much of the ancient wines were boiled and condensed until they were very sweet and thick like honey or jellies. They had to be greatly diluted before they could be drunk (see 5:18, note).

8:10 THE JOY OF THE LORD IS YOUR STRENGTH. The declaration of God's Word, accompanied by a sincere desire to follow its instruction, will result in a true, heartfelt joy. This "joy of the LORD" is based on reconciliation with God and the presence of the Spirit in our lives. It is maintained by the assurance that we have been forgiven in Christ and restored to fellowship with God, and that we now live in harmony with his will (vv. 10–13; cf. Lk 7:50). Such joy acts (1) as a fortress to guard us from the troubles and temptations of each day (cf. Ps 119:165; Gal 5:22; Php 4:4), and (2) as the power and motivation to persevere in faith until the end.

their courtyards, in the courts of the house of God and in the square by the Water Gate[w] and the one by the Gate of Ephraim.[x] **17**The whole company that had returned from exile built booths and lived in them.[y] From the days of Joshua son of Nun until that day, the Israelites had not celebrated[z] it like this. And their joy was very great.

18Day after day, from the first day to the last, Ezra read[a] from the Book of the Law[b] of God. They celebrated the feast for seven days, and on the eighth day, in accordance with the regulation,[c] there was an assembly.[d]

The Israelites Confess Their Sins

9 On the twenty-fourth day of the same month, the Israelites gathered together, fasting and wearing sackcloth and having dust on their heads.[e] **2**Those of Israelite descent had separated themselves from all foreigners.[f] They stood in their places and confessed their sins and the wickedness of their fathers.[g] **3**They stood where they were and read from the Book of the Law of the LORD their God for a quarter of the day, and spent another quarter in confession and in worshiping the LORD their God. **4**Standing on the stairs were the Levites[h]—Jeshua, Bani, Kadmiel, Shebaniah, Bunni, Sherebiah, Bani and Kenani—who called with loud voices to the LORD their God. **5**And the Levites—Jeshua, Kadmiel, Bani, Hashabneiah, Sherebiah, Hodiah, Shebaniah and Pethahiah—said: "Stand up and praise the LORD your God,[i] who is from everlasting to everlasting.[w]"

"Blessed be your glorious name,[j] and may it be exalted above all blessing and praise.
6You alone are the LORD.[k] You made the heavens,[l] even the highest heavens, and all their starry host,[m] the earth[n] and all that is on it, the seas[o] and all that is in them.[p] You give life to everything, and the multitudes of heaven[q] worship you.

7"You are the LORD God, who chose Abram[r] and brought him out of Ur of the Chaldeans[s] and named him Abraham.[t] **8**You found his heart faithful to you, and you made a covenant with him to give to his descendants the land of the Canaanites, Hittites, Amorites, Perizzites, Jebusites and Girgashites.[u] You have kept your promise[v] because you are righteous.[w]

9"You saw the suffering of our forefathers in Egypt;[x] you heard their cry at the Red Sea.[x][y] **10**You sent miraculous signs[z] and wonders[a] against Pharaoh, against all his officials and all the people of his land, for you knew how arrogantly the Egyptians treated them. You made a name[b] for yourself,[c] which remains to this day. **11**You divided the sea before them,[d] so that they passed through it on dry ground, but you hurled their pursuers into the depths,[e] like a stone into mighty waters.[f] **12**By day[g] you led[h] them with a pillar of cloud,[i] and by night with a pillar of fire to give them light on the way they were to take.

13"You came down on Mount Sinai;[j] you spoke[k] to them from heaven.[l] You gave them regulations and laws that are just[m] and right, and decrees and commands that are good.[n] **14**You made known to them your holy Sabbath[o] and gave them commands, decrees and laws through your servant Moses. **15**In their hunger you gave them bread from heaven[p] and in their thirst you brought them water from the rock;[q] you told them to go in and

8:16 [w]S Ne 3:26 [x]S 2Ch 25:23 **8:17** [y]Hos 12:9 [z]S 1Ki 8:2; S 2Ch 7:8; S 8:13 **8:18** [a]Dt 31:11; S 33:10 [b]S Dt 28:61 [c]S Lev 23:36,40; S Ezr 3:4 [d]S Lev 23:36 **9:1** [e]Lev 26:40-45; S Jos 7:6; 2Ch 7:14-16 **9:2** [f]S Ezr 6:21; Ne 10:28; 13:3,30 [g]S Lev 26:40; S Ezr 10:11; Ps 106:6 **9:4** [h]S Ezr 10:23 **9:5** [i]Ps 78:4 [j]S 2Sa 7:26 **9:6** [k]S Dt 6:4 [l]S Ex 8:19 [m]Isa 40:26; 45:12 [n]S Ge 1:1; Isa 37:16 [o]Ps 95:5; 146:6; Jnh 1:9 [p]Dt 10:14; Ac 4:24; Rev 10:6 [q]Ps 103:20; 148:2 **9:7** [r]S Ge 16:11 [s]S Ge 11:28 [t]S Ge 17:5 **9:8** [u]S Ge 15:18-21; S Ezr 9:1 [v]S Jos 21:45 [w]Ge 15:6; S Ezr 9:15 **9:9** [x]Ex 2:23-25; 3:7 [y]Ex 14:10-30 **9:10** [z]S Ex 10:1; Ps 74:9 [a]S Ex 3:20; S 6:6 [b]Jer 32:20; Da 9:15 [c]S Nu 6:27 **9:11** [d]Ps 78:13 [e]S Ex 14:28 [f]Ex 15:4-5,10; Heb 11:29 **9:12** [g]S Dt 1:33 [h]S Ex 15:13 [i]S Ex 13:21 **9:13** [j]S Ex 19:11 [k]S Ex 19:19 [l]S Ex 20:22 [m]Ps 119:137 [n]S Ex 20:1; Dt 4:7-8 **9:14** [o]S Ge 2:3; Ex 20:8-11 **9:15** [p]S Ex 16:4; Ps 78:24-25; Jn 6:31 [q]Ex 17:6; Nu 20:7-13

[w]5 Or *God for ever and ever* [x]9 Hebrew *Yam Suph*; that is, Sea of Reeds

9:2 SEPARATED THEMSELVES ... CONFESSED THEIR SINS. The actions recorded in this chapter show that the people's repentance was deep and sustained. They continued to seek God by fasting, humbling themselves before him, confessing their spiritual poverty and separating themselves from that which offended him (vv. 1–3).

9:6–37 YOU ALONE ARE THE LORD. The primary themes of this outstanding prayer are God's gracious endeavor to provide redemption and salvation for Israel and Israel's ungrateful response to that divine love throughout its history; these are recurring themes in the OT (see Da 9:3–19; Am 2:9–12; Mic 6:1–8; cf. Lk 13:34).

WORSHIP

Ne 8:5–6 "Ezra opened the book. All the people could see him because he was standing above them; and as he opened it, the people all stood up: And Ezra praised the LORD, the great God; and all the people lifted their hands and responded, 'Amen! Amen!' Then they bowed down and worshiped the LORD with their faces to the ground."

The English word "worship" is derived from an Old English word "worthship," and constitutes those actions and attitudes that revere and honor the worthiness of the great God of heaven and earth. Thus, worship is God-centered, not man-centered. In Christian worship we draw near to God in gratitude for what he has done for us in Christ and through the Holy Spirit. It requires a faith commitment and an acknowledgment that he is our God and Lord.

BRIEF HISTORY OF THE WORSHIP OF THE TRUE GOD. Human beings have worshiped God from the beginning of history. Adam and Eve had fellowship regularly with God in the Garden of Eden (cf. Ge 3:8). Cain and Abel both brought offerings (Heb *minhah*, also translated as "tribute," or "gift") of plant life and animal life to the Lord (Ge 4:3–4); Seth's descendants called "on the name of the LORD" (Ge 4:26). Noah built an altar to the Lord for a burnt offering after the flood (Ge 8:20). Abraham dotted the landscape of the promised land with altars for burnt offerings to the Lord (Ge 12:7–8; 13:4,18; 22:9) and talked intimately with him (Ge 18:23–33; 22:11–18).

Not until after the exodus, when the tabernacle was built, however, did *public* worship become formalized. Thereafter, regular sacrifices were offered daily and especially on the Sabbath, and God established several annual religious feasts as occasions for Israelite public worship (Ex 23:14–17; Lev 1—7; 16; 23:4–44; Dt 12; 16). This worship later became centralized around the temple in Jerusalem (cf. David's plans as recorded in 1Ch 22—26). When the temple was destroyed in 586 B.C., the Jews built synagogues as places of instruction and worship while they were in exile and wherever they settled. These buildings continued to be used for worship even after the building of the second temple under Zerubbabel's leadership (Ezr 3—6). There were synagogues in Palestine and all over the Roman world during NT times (e.g., Lk 4:16; Jn 6:59; Ac 6:9; 13:14; 14:1; 17:1,10; 18:4; 19:8; 22:19).

Worship in the early church took place both in the Jerusalem temple and in private homes (Ac 2:46–47). Outside of Jerusalem, Christians worshiped, as long as they were permitted, in the synagogues; when that was no longer allowed, they met elsewhere for worship—usually in private homes (cf. Ac 18:7; Ro 16:5; Col 4:15; Phm 2), though sometimes in public halls (Ac 19:9–10).

EXPRESSIONS OF CHRISTIAN WORSHIP. (1) Two key principles govern Christian worship. (a) True worship takes place in spirit and truth (see Jn 4:23, note), i.e., worship must take place according to God's revelation of himself in the Son (cf. Jn 14:6). Likewise, it involves the human spirit and not just the mind, as well as the manifestations of the Holy Spirit (1Co 12:7–12). (b) The practice of Christian worship must correspond to the NT pattern for the church (see Ac 7:44, note). Believers today ought to desire, seek and expect as the norm for the church all elements found in the worship experience of the NT (cf. the hermeneutical principle discussed in the introduction to Acts).

(2) The key feature of OT worship was the sacrificial system (see Nu 28—29). Since Christ's sacrifice on the cross fulfilled this system, there is no longer any need for the shedding of blood as part of Christian worship (see Heb 9:1—10:18). Through the sacrament of the Lord's Supper, the NT church continually commemorated Christ's once-

for-all sacrifice (1Co 11:23–26). Also, the church is exhorted to "continually offer to God a sacrifice of praise—the fruit of lips that confess his name" (Heb 13:15), and to offer our bodies as "living sacrifices, holy and pleasing to God" (Ro 12:1, note).

(3) Praising God is essential to Christian worship. Praise was a key element in Israel's worship of God (e.g., Ps 100:4; 106:1; 111:1; 113:1; 117), as well as in early Christian worship (Ac 2:46–47; 16:25; Ro 15:10–11; Heb 2:12; see article on PRAISE, p. 770).

(4) One crucial way to praise God is by singing psalms, hymns and spiritual songs. The OT abounds with exhortations to sing to the Lord (e.g., 1Ch 16:23; Ps 95:1; 96:1–2; 98:1,5–6; 100:1–2). At the time of Jesus' birth, the entire heavenly host burst into a song of praise (Lk 2:13–14), and the NT church was a singing community (1Co 14:15; Eph 5:19; Col 3:16; Jas 5:13). The songs of NT Christians were sung either with the mind (i.e., with a known human language) or with the spirit (i.e., in tongues; see 1Co 14:15, note). Under no circumstances did they view singing as a form of entertainment.

(5) Another important element in worship is seeking God's face in prayer. The OT saints constantly communicated with God through prayer (e.g., Ge 20:17; Nu 11:2; 1Sa 8:6; 2Sa 7:27; Da 9:3–19; cf. Jas 5:17–18). The apostles prayed continually after Jesus ascended into heaven (Ac 1:14), and prayer became a regular part of corporate Christian worship (Ac 2:42; 20:36; 1Th 5:17; see article on EFFECTIVE PRAYING, p. 496). These prayers could be on their own behalf (e.g., Ac 4:24–30), or they could be intercessory prayers on behalf of others (e.g., Ro 15:30–32; Eph 6:18). At all times Christian prayer must be accompanied by thanksgiving to God (Eph 5:20; Php 4:6; Col 3:15,17; 1Th 5:18). As with singing, praying could be done with known human languages or in tongues (1Co 14:13–15).

(6) Confession of sin was clearly an important part of OT worship. God had established the Day of Atonement for the Israelites as a time for national confession of sin (Lev 16; see article on THE DAY OF ATONEMENT, p. 174). In his prayer at the temple dedication Solomon acknowledged the importance of confession (1Ki 8:30–39). When Ezra and Nehemiah realized how far God's people had departed from his law, they led the entire nation of Judah in an intense public prayer of confession (Ne 9). So too, in the Lord's Prayer, Jesus teaches believers to ask for forgiveness of sins (Mt 6:12). James instructs believers to confess their sins to each other (Jas 5:16); through such confession we receive assurance of God's gracious pardon (1Jn 1:9).

(7) Worship must also include public reading of Scripture and its true proclamation. In OT times God arranged that every seven years, at the Feast of Tabernacles, all Israelites were to assemble for a public reading of the Law of Moses (Dt 31:9–13); the clearest example of this element of OT worship came during the time of Ezra and Nehemiah (see Ne 8:1–12). The reading of Scripture became a regular part of the synagogue worship on the Sabbath (see Lk 4:16–19; Ac 13:15); similarly, when NT believers gathered for worship, they also heard the Word of God (1Ti 4:13; cf. Col 4:16; 1Th 5:27) along with teaching, preaching and exhortation based on it (1Ti 4:13; 2Ti 4:2; cf. Ac 19:8–10; 20:7).

(8) Whenever God's OT people assembled in the courts of the Lord, they were instructed to bring tithes and offerings (Ps 96:8; Mal 3:10). Similarly, Paul wrote to the Corinthian Christians concerning the collection for the Jerusalem church: "On the first day of every week, each one of you should set aside a sum of money in keeping with his income" (1 Cor 16:2). True worship of God must therefore provide the opportunity to present our tithes and offerings to the Lord.

(9) One unique element in the NT worshiping community was the role of the Holy Spirit and his manifestations. Among his manifestations in the body of Christ were the message of wisdom, the message of knowledge, special expressions of faith, gifts of healing, miraculous powers, prophecy, distinguishing between spirits, speaking in tongues and the interpretation of tongues (1Co 12:7–10). The charismatic nature of early Christian worship is further described in Paul's instructions: "When you come together, everyone has a hymn, or a word of instruction, a revelation, a tongue or an interpretation" (1Co 14:26). In his Corinthian correspondence, Paul provided principles by which

to regulate that aspect of their worship (see 1Co 14:1–33, notes); the overriding principle was that any exercise of the gifts of the Holy Spirit during worship had to strengthen and help the whole congregation (1Co 12:7; 14:26; see article on SPIRITUAL GIFTS FOR BELIEVERS, p. 1770).

(10) The other unique element in NT worship was the celebration of the sacraments—baptism and the Lord's Supper. The Lord's Supper (or the "breaking of bread," see Ac 2:42) appears to have been observed daily among believers right after Pentecost (Ac 2:46–47), and later at least weekly (Ac 20:7,11). Baptism, as commanded by Christ (Mt 28:19–20), occurred as often as there were conversions and people being added to the church (Ac 2:41; 8:12; 9:18; 10:48; 16:30–33; 19:1–5).

GOD'S BLESSINGS FOR TRUE WORSHIPERS. When true worship takes place, God has many blessings in store for his people. He promises: (1) to be with them (Mt 18:20) and to come in intimate communion (Rev 3:20); (2) to overshadow his people with his glory (cf. Ex 40:35; 2Ch 7:1; 1Pe 4:14); (3) to bless his people with showers of blessings (Eze 34:26), especially with peace (Ps 29:11; see article on THE PEACE OF GOD, p. 1134); (4) to impart an abundance of joy (Ps 122:1; Jn 15:11); (5) to answer the prayers of those who pray in sincere faith (Mk 11:24; Jas 5:15; see article on EFFECTIVE PRAYING, p. 496); (6) to freshly fill his people with his Holy Spirit and with boldness (Ac 4:31); (7) to send manifestations of the Holy Spirit among his people (1Co 12:7–13); (8) to guide his people into all truth through the Holy Spirit (Jn 15:26; 16:13); (9) to sanctify his people by his Word and Spirit (Jn 17:17–19); (10) to comfort, encourage and strengthen his people (Isa 40:1; 1Co 14:26; 2Co 1:3–4; 1Th 5:11); (11) to convict his people of sin, righteousness and judgment by the Holy Spirit (see Jn 16:8, note); and (12) to save sinners who become convicted of sin at a worship service (1Co 14:22–25).

HINDRANCES TO TRUE WORSHIP. Just because those who claim to be God's people have assembled for worship is no guarantee that true worship is taking place or that God is accepting their praise and listening to their prayers. (1) If the worship of God is mere form and lip service and the hearts of God's people are far from him, then God does not accept their worship. Christ severely castigated the Pharisees for their hypocrisy—legalistically following God's law while their hearts were far from him (Mt 15:7–9; 23:23–28; Mk 7:5–7). Note the similar criticism that he leveled against the church in Ephesus, which continued to worship the Lord but no longer really loved him supremely (Rev 2:1–5). Paul warns believers that those who participate in the Lord's Supper without departing from sin and without properly recognizing the body of Christian brothers and sisters bring judgment on themselves (1Co 11:28–30; see 11:27, note). Thus, we can expect God to draw near to us and accept our worship only if our hearts are in a right relationship with him (Jas 4:8; cf. Ps 24:3–4).

(2) Another hindrance to true worship is a lifestyle of compromise, sin and immorality. God refused to accept King Saul's sacrifices because he disobeyed his command (1Sa 15:1–23). Isaiah castigates God's people as a "sinful nation, a people loaded with guilt, a brood of evildoers" (Isa 1:4); at the same time, however, they were offering sacrifices and celebrating their holy days. Thus the Lord declared through Isaiah: "Your New Moon festivals and your appointed feasts my soul hates. They have become a burden to me; I am weary of bearing them. When you spread out your hands in prayer, I will hide my eyes from you; even if you offer many prayers, I will not listen. Your hands are full of blood" (Isa 1:14–15). Likewise in the NT church, Jesus urged the worshipers in Sardis to wake up, because "I have not found your deeds complete in the sight of my God" (Rev 3:2). Similarly, James indicates that God will not hear the selfish prayers of those who have not separated themselves from the world (Jas 4:1–5; see article on EFFECTIVE PRAYING, p. 496). God's people can expect him to draw near and accept their worship only if they have clean hands and a pure heart (Ps 24:3–4; Jas 4:8).

take possession of the land you
had sworn with uplifted hand[r] to
give them.[s]
16"But they, our forefathers,
became arrogant and stiff-
necked,[t] and did not obey your
commands.[u] **17**They refused to
listen and failed to remember[v]
the miracles[w] you performed
among them. They became stiff-
necked[x] and in their rebellion appointed a leader in order to return
to their slavery.[y] But you are a
forgiving God,[z] gracious and
compassionate,[a] slow to anger[b]
and abounding in love.[c] Therefore you did not desert them,[d]
18even when they cast for themselves an image of a calf[e] and
said, 'This is your god, who
brought you up out of Egypt,' or
when they committed awful blasphemies.[f]
19"Because of your great compassion you did not abandon[g]
them in the desert. By day the pillar of cloud[h] did not cease to
guide them on their path, nor the
pillar of fire by night to shine on
the way they were to take. **20**You
gave your good Spirit[i] to instruct[j] them. You did not withhold your manna[k] from their
mouths, and you gave them wa-
ter[l] for their thirst. **21**For forty
years[m] you sustained them in the
desert; they lacked nothing,[n]
their clothes did not wear out nor
did their feet become swollen.[o]
22"You gave them kingdoms
and nations, allotting to them
even the remotest frontiers. They
took over the country of Sihon[y][p]
king of Heshbon and the country
of Og king of Bashan.[q] **23**You
made their sons as numerous as
the stars in the sky,[r] and you
brought them into the land that
you told their fathers to enter and
possess. **24**Their sons went in and
took possession of the land.[s] You
subdued[t] before them the Canaanites, who lived in the land;
you handed the Canaanites over
to them, along with their kings
and the peoples of the land, to
deal with them as they pleased.
25They captured fortified cities
and fertile land;[u] they took possession of houses filled with all
kinds of good things,[v] wells already dug, vineyards, olive groves
and fruit trees in abundance. They
ate to the full and were well-nour-
ished;[w] they reveled in your great
goodness.[x]
26"But they were disobedient
and rebelled against you; they put
your law behind their backs.[y]
They killed[z] your prophets,[a]
who had admonished them in order to turn them back to you; they
committed awful blasphemies.[b]
27So you handed them over to
their enemies,[c] who oppressed
them. But when they were oppressed they cried out to you.
From heaven you heard them, and
in your great compassion[d] you
gave them deliverers,[e] who rescued them from the hand of their
enemies.
28"But as soon as they were at
rest, they again did what was evil
in your sight.[f] Then you abandoned them to the hand of their
enemies so that they ruled over
them. And when they cried out to
you again, you heard from heaven,
and in your compassion[g] you delivered them[h] time after time.
29"You warned[i] them to return to your law, but they became
arrogant[j] and disobeyed your
commands. They sinned against
your ordinances, by which a man
will live if he obeys them.[k] Stubbornly they turned their backs[l]
on you, became stiff-necked[m] and
refused to listen.[n] **30**For many
years you were patient with them.

9:15 [r]S Ge 14:22 [s]Dt 1:8,21
9:16 [t]S Ex 32:9; Jer 7:26; 17:23; 19:15 [u]Dt 1:26-33; 31:29
9:17 [v]Jdg 8:34; Ps 78:42 [w]Ps 77:11; 78:12; 105:5; 106:7 [x]Jer 7:26; 19:15 [y]Nu 14:1-4 [z]Ps 130:4; Da 9:9 [a]S Dt 4:31 [b]S Ex 34:6; Ps 103:8; Na 1:3 [c]S Ex 22:27; Nu 14:17-19; Ps 86:15 [d]Ps 78:11; Eze 5:6
9:18 [e]S Ex 32:4 [f]S Ex 20:23
9:19 [g]Ex 13:22 [h]S Ex 13:21
9:20 [i]Nu 9:17; 11:17; Isa 63:11, 14; Hag 2:5; Zec 4:6 [j]Ps 23:3; 143:10 [k]S Ex 16:15 [l]Ex 17:6
9:21 [m]S Ex 16:35 [n]S Dt 2:7 [o]S Dt 8:4
9:22 [p]S Nu 21:21 [q]S Nu 21:33; Dt 2:26-3:11
9:23 [r]S Ge 12:2; S Lev 26:9; S Nu 10:36
9:24 [s]S Jos 11:23 [t]S Jdg 4:23; S 2Ch 14:13
9:25 [u]S Dt 11:11 [v]S Ex 18:9 [w]Dt 6:10-12 [x]8:8-11; 32:12-15; Ps 23:6; 25:7; 69:16
9:26 [y]S 1Ki 14:9; Jer 44:10 [z]S Jos 7:25 [a]Jer 2:30; 26:8; Mt 21:35-36; 23:29-36; Ac 7:52 [b]S Jdg 2:12-13
9:27 [c]S Nu 25:17; S Jdg 2:14 [d]Ps 51:1; 103:8; 106:45; 119:156 [e]S Jdg 3:9
9:28 [f]S Ex 32:22; S Jdg 2:17 [g]S 2Sa 24:14 [h]Ps 22:4; 106:43; 136:24
9:29 [i]S Jdg 6:8 [j]ver 16-17; Ps 5:5; Isa 2:11; Jer 43:2 [k]S Dt 30:16 [l]S 1Sa 8:3 [m]Jer 19:15 [n]Zec 7:11-12

[y]*22* One Hebrew manuscript and Septuagint; most Hebrew manuscripts *Sihon, that is, the country of the*

9:17 GRACIOUS AND COMPASSIONATE. The merciful Lord is ready to accept again those who have forsaken him and sinned against his laws whenever they repent. Moreover, he is patient and long-suffering with the faults and shortcomings of his children, as long as their expressed desire is to follow him fully and to gain complete victory over sin, Satan and the world (see article on SANCTIFICATION, p. 1956).

9:20 YOUR GOOD SPIRIT TO INSTRUCT THEM. The Holy Spirit is our leader to guide us into God's truth and righteous ways (see Jn 14:17, note; 16:13, note; Ro 8:5–14, note).

9:30 BY YOUR SPIRIT YOU ADMONISHED

By your Spirit you admonished
them through your prophets.[o]
Yet they paid no attention, so you
handed them over to the neighbor-
Isa 61:1-3 ing peoples.[p] **31**But in your great
mercy you did not put an end[q]
to them or abandon them, for
you are a gracious and merciful[r]
God.

32"Now therefore, O our God,
the great, mighty[s] and awesome
God,[t] who keeps his covenant of
love,[u] do not let all this hardship
seem trifling in your eyes—the
hardship[v] that has come upon
us, upon our kings and leaders,
upon our priests and prophets,
upon our fathers and all your people, from the days of the kings of
Assyria until today. **33**In all that
has happened to us, you have
been just;[w] you have acted faithfully, while we did wrong.[x] **34**Our
kings,[y] our leaders, our priests
and our fathers[z] did not follow
your law; they did not pay attention to your commands or the
warnings you gave them. **35**Even
while they were in their kingdom,
enjoying your great goodness[a] to
them in the spacious and fertile
land you gave them, they did not
serve you[b] or turn from their evil
ways.

36"But see, we are slaves[c] today, slaves in the land you gave
our forefathers so they could eat
its fruit and the other good things
it produces. **37**Because of our
sins, its abundant harvest goes to
the kings you have placed over us.
They rule over our bodies and our
cattle as they please. We are in
great distress.[d]

The Agreement of the People

38"In view of all this, we are making
a binding agreement,[e] putting it in
writing,[f] and our leaders, our Levites
and our priests are affixing their seals
to it."

9:30 [o] 2Ki 17:13-18; S 2Ch 36:16 [p] Jer 16:11; Zec 7:12 **9:31** [q] Isa 48:9; 65:9 [r] S Dt 4:31 **9:32** [s] Job 9:19; Ps 24:8; 89:8; 93:4 [t] S Dt 7:21 [u] S Dt 7:9; S 1Ki 8:23; Da 9:4 [v] S Ex 18:8 **9:33** [w] S Ge 18:25 [x] Jer 44:3; Da 9:7-8,14 **9:34** [y] S 2Ki 23:11 [z] Jer 44:17 **9:35** [a] Isa 63:7 [b] Dt 28:45-48 **9:36** [c] S Ezr 9:9 **9:37** [d] Dt 28:33; La 5:5 **9:38** [e] S 2Ch 23:16 [f] Isa 44:5

10:2 [g] S Ezr 2:2 **10:3** [h] S 1Ch 9:12 **10:5** [i] S 1Ch 24:8 **10:8** [j] Ne 12:1 **10:9** [k] Ne 12:1 **10:16** [l] S Ezr 8:6 **10:20** [m] 1Ch 24:15 **10:23** [n] S Ne 7:2 **10:28** [o] Ps 135:1 [p] 2Ch 6:26; S Ne 9:2

10 Those who sealed it were:

Nehemiah the governor, the son of Hacaliah.

Zedekiah, **2**Seraiah,[g] Azariah, Jeremiah,
3Pashhur,[h] Amariah, Malkijah,
4Hattush, Shebaniah, Malluch,
5Harim,[i] Meremoth, Obadiah,
6Daniel, Ginnethon, Baruch,
7Meshullam, Abijah, Mijamin,
8Maaziah, Bilgai and Shemaiah.
These were the priests.[j]

9The Levites:[k]

Jeshua son of Azaniah, Binnui of the sons of Henadad, Kadmiel,
10and their associates: Shebaniah,
Hodiah, Kelita, Pelaiah, Hanan,
11Mica, Rehob, Hashabiah,
12Zaccur, Sherebiah, Shebaniah,
13Hodiah, Bani and Beninu.

14The leaders of the people:

Parosh, Pahath-Moab, Elam, Zattu, Bani,
15Bunni, Azgad, Bebai,
16Adonijah, Bigvai, Adin,[l]
17Ater, Hezekiah, Azzur,
18Hodiah, Hashum, Bezai,
19Hariph, Anathoth, Nebai,
20Magpiash, Meshullam, Hezir,[m]
21Meshezabel, Zadok, Jaddua,
22Pelatiah, Hanan, Anaiah,
23Hoshea, Hananiah,[n] Hasshub,
24Hallohesh, Pilha, Shobek,
25Rehum, Hashabnah, Maaseiah,
26Ahiah, Hanan, Anan,
27Malluch, Harim and Baanah.

28"The rest of the people—
priests, Levites, gatekeepers,
singers, temple servants[o] and all
who separated themselves from
the neighboring peoples[p] for the
sake of the Law of God, together
with their wives and all their sons
and daughters who are able to understand— **29**all these now join
their brothers the nobles, and
bind themselves with a curse and

THEM. A principal work of the Holy Spirit in the OT was to rebuke God's people and expose their sin through his faithful prophets. Under the new covenant, the Spirit continues to convict people of sin (see Jn 16:8,13, notes; see article on THE MINISTRY GIFTS OF THE CHURCH, p. 1830).

10:29 BIND THEMSELVES WITH . . . AN OATH. The revival led by Ezra (chs. 8—10) resulted in a firm commitment to obey God's will. This was manifested in the people dedicating themselves: (1) to serve the Lord in faithfulness to his commands (v. 29); (2) to keep themselves unpolluted by and separate from the world (vv. 30–31; cf. Jas 1:27); and (3) to support God's work with their time, money and possessions (vv. 32–39).

an oath[q] to follow the Law of God
given through Moses the servant
of God and to obey carefully all
the commands, regulations and
decrees of the LORD our Lord.
30"We promise not to give our
daughters in marriage to the peoples around us or take their
daughters for our sons.[r]
31"When the neighboring peoples bring merchandise or grain to
sell on the Sabbath,[s] we will not
buy from them on the Sabbath or
on any holy day. Every seventh
year we will forgo working the
land[t] and will cancel all debts.[u]
32"We assume the responsibility for carrying out the commands
to give a third of a shekel[z] each
year for the service of the house of
our God: **33**for the bread set out on
the table;[v] for the regular grain
offerings and burnt offerings; for
the offerings on the Sabbaths,
New Moon[w] festivals and appointed feasts; for the holy offerings; for sin offerings to make
atonement for Israel; and for all
the duties of the house of our
God.[x]
34"We—the priests, the Levites and the people—have cast
lots[y] to determine when each of
our families is to bring to the
house of our God at set times each
year a contribution of wood[z] to
burn on the altar of the LORD our
God, as it is written in the Law.
35"We also assume responsibility for bringing to the house of the
LORD each year the firstfruits[a] of
our crops and of every fruit tree.[b]
36"As it is also written in the
Law, we will bring the firstborn[c]
of our sons and of our cattle, of
our herds and of our flocks to the
house of our God, to the priests
ministering there.[d]
37"Moreover, we will bring to
the storerooms of the house of our
God, to the priests, the first of our
ground meal, of our ⌊grain⌋ offerings, of the fruit of all our trees
and of our new wine and oil.[e]
And we will bring a tithe[f] of our
crops to the Levites,[g] for it is the
Levites who collect the tithes in
all the towns where we work.[h]
38A priest descended from Aaron
is to accompany the Levites when

10:29 [q]S Nu 5:21; Ps 119:106
10:30 [r]S Ex 34:16; Ne 13:23
10:31 [s]Ne 13:16, 18; Jer 17:27; Eze 23:38; Am 8:5 [t]S Ex 23:11; Lev 25:1-7 [u]S Dt 15:1
10:33 [v]Lev 24:6 [w]Nu 10:10; Ps 81:3; Isa 1:14 [x]S 2Ch 24:5
10:34 [y]S Lev 16:8 [z]Ne 13:31
10:35 [a]S Ex 22:29; S Nu 18:12 [b]Dt 26:1-11
10:36 [c]S Ex 13:2; S Nu 18:14-16 [d]Ne 13:31
10:37 [e]S Nu 18:12 [f]S Lev 27:30; S Nu 18:21 [g]Dt 14:22-29 [h]Eze 44:30
10:38 [i]Nu 18:26
10:39 [j]Ne 13:11, 12
11:1 [k]Ne 7:4 [l]Isa 48:2; 52:1; 64:10; Zec 14:20-21 [m]S Ne 7:73
11:3 [n]S Ezr 2:1
11:4 [o]S Ezr 1:5 [p]S Ezr 2:70

they receive the tithes, and the
Levites are to bring a tenth of the
tithes[i] up to the house of our
God, to the storerooms of the treasury. **39**The people of Israel, including the Levites, are to bring
their contributions of grain, new
wine and oil to the storerooms
where the articles for the sanctuary are kept and where the ministering priests, the gatekeepers
and the singers stay.
"We will not neglect the house
of our God."[j] Job 1:1-5

The New Residents of Jerusalem

11:3–19pp — 1Ch 9:1–17

11 Now the leaders of the people
settled in Jerusalem, and the
rest of the people cast lots to bring one
out of every ten to live in Jerusalem,[k]
the holy city,[l] while the remaining
nine were to stay in their own towns.[m]
2The people commended all the men
who volunteered to live in Jerusalem.
3These are the provincial leaders
who settled in Jerusalem (now some Israelites, priests, Levites, temple servants and descendants of Solomon's
servants lived in the towns of Judah,
each on his own property in the various
towns,[n] **4**while other people from both
Judah and Benjamin[o] lived in Jerusalem):[p]

From the descendants of Judah:

Athaiah son of Uzziah, the son of
Zechariah, the son of Amariah,
the son of Shephatiah, the son of
Mahalalel, a descendant of Perez;
5and Maaseiah son of Baruch, the
son of Col-Hozeh, the son of Haza-
iah, the son of Adaiah, the son of
Joiarib, the son of Zechariah, a
descendant of Shelah. **6**The
descendants of Perez who lived in
Jerusalem totaled 468 able men.

7From the descendants of Benjamin:

Sallu son of Meshullam, the son
of Joed, the son of Pedaiah, the
son of Kolaiah, the son of Maaseiah, the son of Ithiel, the son of
Jeshaiah, **8**and his followers, Gab-
bai and Sallai—928 men. **9**Joel
son of Zicri was their chief officer,
and Judah son of Hassenuah was

[z] *32* That is, about 1/8 ounce (about 4 grams)

over the Second District of the
city.

10 From the priests:

Jedaiah; the son of Joiarib; Jakin;
11 Seraiah[q] son of Hilkiah, the
son of Meshullam, the son of Zadok, the son of Meraioth, the son
of Ahitub,[r] supervisor in the
house of God, 12 and their associates, who carried on work for the
temple—822 men; Adaiah son of
Jeroham, the son of Pelaliah, the
son of Amzi, the son of Zechariah,
the son of Pashhur, the son of
Malkijah, 13 and his associates,
who were heads of families—242
men; Amashsai son of Azarel, the
son of Ahzai, the son of Meshillemoth, the son of Immer, 14 and
his[a] associates, who were able
men—128. Their chief officer was
Zabdiel son of Haggedolim.

15 From the Levites:

Shemaiah son of Hasshub, the son
of Azrikam, the son of Hashabiah,
the son of Bunni; 16 Shabbethai[s]
and Jozabad,[t] two of the heads of
the Levites, who had charge of the
outside work of the house of God;
17 Mattaniah[u] son of Mica, the
son of Zabdi, the son of Asaph,[v]
the director who led in thanksgiving and prayer; Bakbukiah, second among his associates; and
Abda son of Shammua, the son of
Galal, the son of Jeduthun.[w]
18 The Levites in the holy city[x]
totaled 284.

19 The gatekeepers:

Akkub, Talmon and their associates, who kept watch at the
gates—172 men.

20 The rest of the Israelites, with the
priests and Levites, were in all the
towns of Judah, each on his ancestral
property.
21 The temple servants[y] lived on the
hill of Ophel, and Ziha and Gishpa were
in charge of them.
22 The chief officer of the Levites in
Jerusalem was Uzzi son of Bani, the
son of Hashabiah, the son of Mattaniah,[z] the son of Mica. Uzzi was one of
Asaph's descendants, who were the
singers responsible for the service of
the house of God. 23 The singers[a] were

11:11 [q] S 2Ki 25:18; S Ezr 2:2 [r] S Ezr 7:2
11:16 [s] Ezr 10:15 [t] S Ezr 8:33
11:17 [u] S 1Ch 9:15; Ne 12:8 [v] 2Ch 5:12 [w] S 1Ch 25:1
11:18 [x] S Rev 21:2
11:21 [y] S Ezr 2:43; S Ne 3:26
11:22 [z] S 1Ch 9:15
11:23 [a] S 1Ch 15:16; Ne 7:44
11:24 [b] S Ge 38:30
11:25 [c] S Ge 35:27 [d] S Nu 21:30
11:26 [e] Jos 15:26 [f] Jos 15:27
11:27 [g] Jos 15:28 [h] S Ge 21:14
11:28 [i] S 1Sa 27:6
11:29 [j] Jos 15:33 [k] S Jos 10:3; S 15:35
11:30 [l] Jos 15:34 [m] Jos 15:35 [n] S Jos 10:3; 15:39 [o] S Jos 10:10 [p] Jos 15:28
11:31 [q] Jos 21:17; Isa 10:29 [r] S 1Sa 13:2 [s] S Jos 12:9
11:32 [t] Jos 21:18; Isa 10:30; Jer 1:1 [u] S 1Sa 21:1
11:33 [v] S Jos 11:1 [w] S Jos 18:25 [x] 2Sa 4:3
11:34 [y] 1Sa 13:18
11:35 [z] S 1Ch 8:12
12:1 [a] Ne 10:1-8 [b] Ne 10:9 [c] S 1Ch 3:19; Ezr 3:2; Zec 4:6-10 [d] Ezr 3:2 [e] S Ezr 2:2 [f] S Ezr 2:2
12:4 [g] ver 16; Zec 1:1 [h] S 1Ch 24:10; Lk 1:5
12:6 [i] S 1Ch 24:7
12:8 [j] S Ezr 2:2 [k] S Ne 11:17

under the king's orders, which regulated their daily activity.
24 Pethahiah son of Meshezabel, one
of the descendants of Zerah[b] son of
Judah, was the king's agent in all affairs relating to the people.
25 As for the villages with their
fields, some of the people of Judah
lived in Kiriath Arba[c] and its surrounding settlements, in Dibon[d] and
its settlements, in Jekabzeel and its
villages, 26 in Jeshua, in Moladah,[e]
in Beth Pelet,[f] 27 in Hazar Shual,[g] in
Beersheba[h] and its settlements, 28 in
Ziklag,[i] in Meconah and its settlements, 29 in En Rimmon, in Zorah,[j] in
Jarmuth,[k] 30 Zanoah,[l] Adullam[m] and
their villages, in Lachish[n] and its
fields, and in Azekah[o] and its settlements. So they were living all the way
from Beersheba[p] to the Valley of Hinnom.
31 The descendants of the Benjamites from Geba[q] lived in Micmash,[r]
Aija, Bethel[s] and its settlements,
32 in Anathoth,[t] Nob[u] and Ananiah,
33 in Hazor,[v] Ramah[w] and Gittaim,[x]
34 in Hadid, Zeboim[y] and Neballat, 35 in
Lod and Ono,[z] and in the Valley of the
Craftsmen.
36 Some of the divisions of the Levites of Judah settled in Benjamin.

Priests and Levites

12 These were the priests[a] and
Levites[b] who returned with
Zerubbabel[c] son of Shealtiel[d] and
with Jeshua:[e]

Seraiah,[f] Jeremiah, Ezra,
2 Amariah, Malluch, Hattush,
3 Shecaniah, Rehum, Meremoth,
4 Iddo,[g] Ginnethon,[b] Abijah,[h]
5 Mijamin,[c] Moadiah, Bilgah,
6 Shemaiah, Joiarib, Jedaiah,[i]
7 Sallu, Amok, Hilkiah and Jedaiah.

These were the leaders of the priests
and their associates in the days of
Jeshua.
8 The Levites were Jeshua,[j] Binnui,
Kadmiel, Sherebiah, Judah, and also
Mattaniah,[k] who, together with his
associates, was in charge of the songs
of thanksgiving. 9 Bakbukiah and Unni,
their associates, stood opposite them
in the services.

[a] *14* Most Septuagint manuscripts; Hebrew *their* [b] *4* Many Hebrew manuscripts and Vulgate (see also Neh. 12:16); most Hebrew manuscripts *Ginnethoi* [c] *5* A variant of *Miniamin*

10Jeshua was the father of Joiakim,
Joiakim the father of Eliashib,[l] Eliashib the father of Joiada, **11**Joiada the
father of Jonathan, and Jonathan the
father of Jaddua.

12In the days of Joiakim, these were
the heads of the priestly families:
of Seraiah's family, Meraiah;
of Jeremiah's, Hananiah;
13of Ezra's, Meshullam;
of Amariah's, Jehohanan;
14of Malluch's, Jonathan;
of Shecaniah's,[d] Joseph;
15of Harim's, Adna;
of Meremoth's,[e] Helkai;
16of Iddo's,[m] Zechariah;
of Ginnethon's, Meshullam;
17of Abijah's,[n] Zicri;
of Miniamin's and of Moadiah's,
Piltai;
18of Bilgah's, Shammua;
of Shemaiah's, Jehonathan;
19of Joiarib's, Mattenai;
of Jedaiah's, Uzzi;
20of Sallu's, Kallai;
of Amok's, Eber;
21of Hilkiah's, Hashabiah;
of Jedaiah's, Nethanel.

22The family heads of the Levites in
the days of Eliashib, Joiada, Johanan
and Jaddua, as well as those of the
priests, were recorded in the reign of
Darius the Persian. **23**The family heads
among the descendants of Levi up to
the time of Johanan son of Eliashib
were recorded in the book of the annals. **24**And the leaders of the Levites[o] were Hashabiah, Sherebiah,
Jeshua son of Kadmiel, and their associates, who stood opposite them to give
praise and thanksgiving, one section
responding to the other, as prescribed
by David the man of God.[p]

25Mattaniah, Bakbukiah, Obadiah,
Meshullam, Talmon and Akkub were
gatekeepers who guarded the storerooms at the gates. **26**They served in
the days of Joiakim son of Jeshua, the
son of Jozadak, and in the days of Nehemiah the governor and of Ezra the
priest and scribe.

Dedication of the Wall of Jerusalem

27At the dedication[q] of the wall of
Jerusalem, the Levites were sought out
from where they lived and were
brought to Jerusalem to celebrate joyfully the dedication with songs of
thanksgiving and with the music of
cymbals,[r] harps and lyres.[s] **28**The
singers also were brought together
from the region around Jerusalem—
from the villages of the Netophathites,[t] **29**from Beth Gilgal, and from
the area of Geba and Azmaveth, for the
singers had built villages for themselves around Jerusalem. **30**When the
priests and Levites had purified themselves ceremonially, they purified the
people,[u] the gates and the wall.

31I had the leaders of Judah go up on
top[f] of the wall. I also assigned two
large choirs to give thanks. One was to
proceed on top[g] of the wall to the
right, toward the Dung Gate.[v] **32**Hoshaiah and half the leaders of Judah
followed them, **33**along with Azariah,
Ezra, Meshullam, **34**Judah, Benjamin,[w] Shemaiah, Jeremiah, **35**as well
as some priests with trumpets,[x] and
also Zechariah son of Jonathan, the son
of Shemaiah, the son of Mattaniah, the
son of Micaiah, the son of Zaccur, the
son of Asaph, **36**and his associates—
Shemaiah, Azarel, Milalai, Gilalai,
Maai, Nethanel, Judah and Hanani—
with musical instruments[y] ⌞pre-
scribed by⌟ David the man of God.[z]
Ezra[a] the scribe led the procession.
37At the Fountain Gate[b] they continued directly up the steps of the City of
David on the ascent to the wall and
passed above the house of David to the
Water Gate[c] on the east.

38The second choir proceeded in the
opposite direction. I followed them on
top[h] of the wall, together with half the
people—past the Tower of the Ov-
ens[d] to the Broad Wall,[e] **39**over the
Gate of Ephraim,[f] the Jeshanah[i]
Gate,[g] the Fish Gate,[h] the Tower of
Hananel[i] and the Tower of the Hundred,[j] as far as the Sheep Gate.[k] At
the Gate of the Guard they stopped.

40The two choirs that gave thanks
then took their places in the house of
God; so did I, together with half the
officials, **41**as well as the priests—Eliakim, Maaseiah, Miniamin, Micaiah,
Elioenai, Zechariah and Hananiah with

12:10 [l]S Ezr 10:24; Ne 3:20
12:16 [m]S ver 4
12:17 [n]S 1Ch 24:10
12:24 [o]S Ezr 2:40 [p]S 2Ch 8:14
12:27 [q]Dt 20:5 [r]S 2Sa 6:5 [s]S 1Ch 15:16,28; 25:6; Ps 92:3
12:28 [t]S 1Ch 2:54; 9:16
12:30 [u]Ex 19:10; Job 1:5
12:31 [v]Ne 2:13
12:34 [w]S Ezr 1:5
12:35 [x]S Ezr 3:10
12:36 [y]S 1Ch 15:16 [z]S 2Ch 8:14 [a]Ezr 7:6
12:37 [b]S Ne 2:14 [c]S Ne 3:26
12:38 [d]Ne 3:11 [e]Ne 3:8
12:39 [f]S 2Ki 14:13 [g]Ne 3:6 [h]S 2Ch 33:14 [i]S Ne 3:1 [j]Ne 3:1 [k]S Ne 3:1

[d] *14* Very many Hebrew manuscripts, some Septuagint manuscripts and Syriac (see also Neh. 12:3); most Hebrew manuscripts *Shebaniah's* [e] *15* Some Septuagint manuscripts (see also Neh. 12:3); Hebrew *Meraioth's* [f] *31* Or *go alongside* [g] *31* Or *proceed alongside* [h] *38* Or *them alongside* [i] *39* Or *Old*

their trumpets — **42**and also Maaseiah,
Shemaiah, Eleazar, Uzzi, Jehohanan,
Malkijah, Elam and Ezer. The choirs
sang under the direction of Jezrahiah.
43And on that day they offered great
sacrifices, rejoicing because God had
given them great joy. The women and
children also rejoiced. The sound of rejoicing in Jerusalem could be heard far
away.
44At that time men were appointed
to be in charge of the storerooms[l] for
the contributions, firstfruits and
tithes.[m] From the fields around the
towns they were to bring into the storerooms the portions required by the
Law for the priests and the Levites, for
Judah was pleased with the ministering priests and Levites.[n] **45**They performed the service of their God and the
service of purification, as did also the
singers and gatekeepers, according to
the commands of David[o] and his son
Solomon.[p] **46**For long ago, in the days
of David and Asaph,[q] there had been
directors for the singers and for the
songs of praise[r] and thanksgiving to
God. **47**So in the days of Zerubbabel
and of Nehemiah, all Israel contributed
the daily portions for the singers and
gatekeepers. They also set aside the
portion for the other Levites, and the
Levites set aside the portion for the
descendants of Aaron.[s]

Nehemiah's Final Reforms

13 On that day the Book of Moses
was read aloud in the hearing
of the people and there it was found
written that no Ammonite or Moabite
should ever be admitted into the assembly of God,[t] **2**because they had
not met the Israelites with food and
water but had hired Balaam[u] to call a
curse down on them.[v] (Our God, however, turned the curse into a blessing.)[w] **3**When the people heard this
law, they excluded from Israel all who
were of foreign descent.[x]
4Before this, Eliashib the priest had
been put in charge of the storerooms[y]
of the house of our God. He was closely
associated with Tobiah,[z] **5**and he had
provided him with a large room formerly used to store the grain offerings and
incense and temple articles, and also
the tithes[a] of grain, new wine and oil
prescribed for the Levites, singers and
gatekeepers, as well as the contributions for the priests.
6But while all this was going on, I
was not in Jerusalem, for in the thirty-
second year of Artaxerxes[b] king of
Babylon I had returned to the king.
Some time later I asked his permission
7and came back to Jerusalem. Here I
learned about the evil thing Eliashib[c]
had done in providing Tobiah[d] a room
in the courts of the house of God. **8**I
was greatly displeased and threw all
Tobiah's household goods out of the
room.[e] **9**I gave orders to purify the
rooms,[f] and then I put back into them
the equipment of the house of God,
with the grain offerings and the incense.[g]
10I also learned that the portions assigned to the Levites had not been giv-
en to them,[h] and that all the Levites
and singers responsible for the service

12:44 [l] Ne 13:4, 13 [m] S Lev 27:30 [n] S Dt 18:8 **12:45** [o] S 2Ch 8:14 [p] S 1Ch 6:31; 23:5 **12:46** [q] S 2Ch 35:15 [r] 2Ch 29:27; Ps 137:4 **12:47** [s] S Dt 18:8
13:1 [t] ver 23; Dt 23:3 **13:2** [u] Nu 22:3-11 [v] S Nu 23:7; S Dt 23:3 [w] S Nu 23:11; Dt 23:4-5 **13:3** [x] ver 23; S Ne 9:2 **13:4** [y] S Ne 12:44 [z] Ne 2:10 **13:5** [a] S Lev 27:30; S Nu 18:21 **13:6** [b] S Ne 2:6 **13:7** [c] S Ezr 10:24 [d] S Ne 2:10 **13:8** [e] Mt 21:12-13; Mk 11:15-17; Lk 19:45-46; Jn 2:13-16 **13:9** [f] S 1Ch 23:28; S 2Ch 29:5 [g] S Lev 2:1 **13:10** [h] S Dt 12:19

13:3 EXCLUDED . . . ALL WHO WERE OF FOREIGN DESCENT. Pagan foreigners were excluded from Israel in order to erect a barrier between God's people and the wicked practices of unbelievers. (1) The key to understanding why God desired this is found in his people's inherent tendency to conform to the ways, pleasures and lifestyles of the world. (2) An essential requirement for God's people who would be holy, therefore, is to remain separate from the ways, values and ungodly customs of our society and to stand against the prevailing and popular expressions of the spirit of this world. Failure to do so will result in the loss of God's presence and all the good he has determined for us (see Ro 12:2, note; see article on SPIRITUAL SEPARATION FOR BELIEVERS, p. 1794).

13:7 CAME BACK TO JERUSALEM. Nehemiah had returned to Persia and was away from Jerusalem for some time (vv. 6–7). When he returned, he discovered that the Jews in Jerusalem had become lax in their moral and spiritual commitment to God. Ch. 13 records a number of these spiritual failures.

13:7 THE EVIL THING ELIASHIB HAD DONE. Tobiah the Ammonite, along with Sanballat, the governor of Samaria, had earlier mocked the Jews' efforts at rebuilding the wall of Jerusalem (2:10,19). Now, however, he had married into a priestly family closely related to Eliashib the high priest. In response, Eliashib himself remodeled and decorated a large room in the temple area as an apartment for Tobiah. When Nehemiah saw this desecration, he burned with righteous indignation and tossed out Tobiah's belongings and the luxurious furnishings Eliashib had put there for him. Nehemiah was hurt because this desecration of God's house was an affront to God's holiness. Modern churches that give space to activities that do not promote God's kingdom might well take note.

had gone back to their own fields.[i]
11So I rebuked the officials and asked
them, "Why is the house of God
neglected?"[j] Then I called them together and stationed them at their
posts.
12All Judah brought the tithes[k] of
grain, new wine and oil into the storerooms.[l] **13**I put Shelemiah the priest,
Zadok the scribe, and a Levite named
Pedaiah in charge of the storerooms
and made Hanan son of Zaccur, the son
of Mattaniah, their assistant, because
these men were considered trustworthy. They were made responsible for
distributing the supplies to their brothers.[m]

14Remember[n] me for this, O my
God, and do not blot out what I have so
faithfully done for the house of my God
and its services.

15In those days I saw men in Judah
treading winepresses on the Sabbath
and bringing in grain and loading it on
donkeys, together with wine, grapes,
figs and all other kinds of loads. And
they were bringing all this into Jerusalem on the Sabbath.[o] Therefore I
warned them against selling food on
that day. **16**Men from Tyre who lived in
Jerusalem were bringing in fish and all
kinds of merchandise and selling them
in Jerusalem on the Sabbath[p] to the
people of Judah. **17**I rebuked the nobles
of Judah and said to them, "What is this
wicked thing you are doing—desecrating the Sabbath day? **18**Didn't your
forefathers do the same things, so that
our God brought all this calamity upon
us and upon this city?[q] Now you are
stirring up more wrath against Israel
by desecrating the Sabbath."[r]
19When evening shadows fell on the
gates of Jerusalem before the Sabbath,[s] I ordered the doors to be shut
and not opened until the Sabbath was
over. I stationed some of my own men
at the gates so that no load could be
brought in on the Sabbath day. **20**Once
or twice the merchants and sellers of
all kinds of goods spent the night outside Jerusalem. **21**But I warned them
and said, "Why do you spend the night
by the wall? If you do this again, I will
lay hands on you." From that time on
they no longer came on the Sabbath.
22Then I commanded the Levites to purify themselves and go and guard the
gates in order to keep the Sabbath day
holy.

Remember[t] me for this also, O my
God, and show mercy to me according
to your great love.

23Moreover, in those days I saw men
of Judah who had married[u] women
from Ashdod, Ammon and Moab.[v]
24Half of their children spoke the language of Ashdod or the language of one
of the other peoples, and did not know
how to speak the language[w] of Judah.
25I rebuked them and called curses
down on them. I beat some of the men
and pulled out their hair. I made them
take an oath[x] in God's name and said:
"You are not to give your daughters in
marriage to their sons, nor are you to
take their daughters in marriage for
your sons or for yourselves.[y] **26**Was it
not because of marriages like these
that Solomon king of Israel sinned?

13:10 [i]S 2Ch 31:4 **13:11** [j]S Ne 10:37-39; Hag 1:1-9; Mal 3:8-9 **13:12** [k]S 2Ch 31:6 [l]S Dt 18:8; 1Ki 7:51; S 2Ch 31:5; S Ne 10:37-39; Mal 3:10 **13:13** [m]S Ne 12:44; Ac 6:1-5 **13:14** [n]S Ge 8:1; S 2Ki 20:3 **13:15** [o]Ex 20:8-11; S 34:21; Dt 5:12-15 **13:16** [p]S Ne 10:31 **13:18** [q]Jer 44:23
[r]S Ne 10:31 **13:19** [s]Lev 23:32 **13:22** [t]S Ge 8:1; S Ne 1:8 **13:23** [u]Ezr 9:1-2; Mal 2:11 [v]ver 1; S ver 1,S 3; Ex 34:16; S Ru 1:4; S Ne 10:30 **13:24** [w]Est 1:22; 3:12; 8:9 **13:25** [x]S Ezr 10:5 [y]S Ex 34:16

13:12 ALL JUDAH BROUGHT THE TITHES. Nehemiah restored full worship in the temple, along with the ministries of the Levites and singers; as a result the people were able to bring their tithes to the very room that Eliashib had given to Tobiah. People are much more willing to tithe when they see the worship of God bringing blessing. God also raised up Malachi about this time; his exhortation emphasized God's blessing for faithful tithers (Mal 3:10). Tithing has always been primarily a matter of blessing rather than law (see article on TITHES AND OFFERINGS, p. 1392). Even before God gave his law at Mount Sinai, Abraham was so blessed by Melchizedek that he gave a tithe of all he had (Ge 14:19–20). The Spirit-filled believer loves to give and to share, just as the early believers did (Ac 2:44–45; 4:34–37; 11:28–30).

13:17 DESECRATING THE SABBATH DAY. God's people were allowing their business interests and their desire for the things of the world to destroy obedience to God's command to make the Sabbath a day of rest. NT believers must constantly beware of the temptation to allow the pursuit of riches and success to usurp their desire to honor and worship God as he commands. We must "seek first his kingdom and his righteousness" (Mt 6:33; see 12:1, note).

13:25 I REBUKED THEM. There are times when leaders, if they are genuinely people of God, must have a holy anger toward unrighteousness and take drastic steps to correct an evil situation. Gentleness and meekness in the face of open and blatant disregard of God's will within the church are in reality weakness and compromise. Nehemiah's correction shows a zeal for God similar to Christ's when with a whip he drove the money changers from the temple in Jerusalem (Mt 21:12–13; Jn 2:13–16; see Lk 19:45, note).

Among the many nations there was no
king like him.[z] He was loved by his
God,[a] and God made him king over all
Israel, but even he was led into sin by
foreign women.[b] 27Must we hear now
that you too are doing all this terrible
wickedness and are being unfaithful to
our God by marrying[c] foreign wom-
en?"
28One of the sons of Joiada son of
Eliashib[d] the high priest was son-in-
law to Sanballat[e] the Horonite. And I
drove him away from me.

13:26 [z]S 1Ki 3:13; S 2Ch 1:12 [a]2Sa 12:25 [b]S Ex 34:16; S 1Ki 11:3
13:27 [c]Ezr 9:14
13:28 [d]S Ezr 10:24 [e]S Ne 2:10
13:29 [f]S Ne 1:8 [g]S Nu 3:12
13:30 [h]S Ne 9:2
13:31 [i]Ne 10:34 [j]Ne 10:35-36 [k]S Ge 8:1; S Ne 1:8

29Remember[f] them, O my God, because they defiled the priestly office
and the covenant of the priesthood and
of the Levites.[g]

30So I purified the priests and the
Levites of everything foreign,[h] and assigned them duties, each to his own
task. 31I also made provision for contributions of wood[i] at designated
times, and for the firstfruits.[j]

Remember[k] me with favor, O my
God.

ESTHER

Outline

I. God's Providence in the Placement of a Queen (1:1—2:18)
  A. Vashti Deposed as Queen of Persia (1:1–22)
    1. The Feast of Xerxes (1:1–9)
    2. The Refusal of Vashti (1:10–12)
    3. The Removal of the Old Queen (1:13–22)
  B. Esther Selected as Queen of Persia (2:1–18)
    1. The Search of Xerxes (2:1–4)
    2. The Agreement of Esther (2:5–11)
    3. The Selection of the New Queen (2:12–18)
II. God's Providence Amidst a Plot Against Mordecai and the Jews (2:19—4:17)
  A. Mordecai Saves the King's Life (2:19–23)
  B. Haman's Pride and Treacherous Plot (3:1–15)
  C. Mordecai Persuades Esther to Intercede with the King (4:1–17)
III. God's Providence in Delivering His People (5:1—9:32)
  A. Esther's First Banquet: An Initial Request (5:1–8)
  B. Haman's Plot Develops (5:9–14)
  C. Providence in the King's Sleepless Night (6:1–14)
  D. Esther's Second Banquet: Haman's Plot Exposed (7:1–10)
  E. The King's Decree and the Jews' Victory (8:1—9:16)
  F. The Feast of Purim Instituted (9:17–32)
IV. God's Providence in Mordecai's Promotion (10:1–3)

Author: Anonymous

Theme: God's Providential Care

Date of Writing: 460–400 B.C.

Background

After the Babylonian empire was captured, defeated and replaced by the Persians in 539 B.C., the center of government for the Jewish exiles transferred to Persia. The capital city of Susa is the setting for the story of Esther, during the reign of King Xerxes I (his Greek name) or Ahasuerus (his Hebrew name) or Khshayarshan (his Persian name)—who ruled from 486–465 B.C. The book covers the years 483–473 B.C. of his reign (1:3; 3:7), with most events occuring in 473 B.C. Esther became queen of Persia in 478 B.C. (2:16).

Chronologically, the Esther episode in Persia falls between Ezra 6 and 7, i.e., between the first return of Jewish exiles from Babylon and Persia to Jerusalem in 538 B.C. under Zerubbabel (Ezr 1—6) and the second return led by Ezra in 457 B.C. (Ezr 7—10; see the introduction to Ezra). Though Esther is placed after Nehemiah in our OT, its events actually occurred 30 years before Nehemiah's return to Jerusalem (444 B.C.) to rebuild the wall (see the introduction to Nehemiah). Whereas the post-exilic books of Ezra and Nehemiah address issues involving the Jewish remnant that returned to Jerusalem, Esther records a development of crucial importance among the Jews who remained in Persia.

The significance of Queen Esther is seen not only in her saving her people from destruction, but also in securing their safety and respect in a foreign land (cf. 8:17; 10:3); this providential action made possible Nehemiah's service in the king's court several decades later and his being selected to rebuild the wall of Jerusalem. If Esther and the Jews (including Nehemiah) had perished in Persia, the distressed remnant in Jerusalem may never have rebuilt their city; the outcome of post-exilic Jewish history would surely have been drastically different.

Though the author of Esther is unknown, it is evident from the book itself that he was personally acquainted with Persian customs, the palace of Susa, and details about King Xerxes, indicating that the author likely lived in Persia during the period described in the book. Furthermore, the author's Jewish sympathies and his knowledge of Jewish customs suggest he was a Jew. Most likely the author was a younger contemporary of Mordecai, with the latter providing much of the book's firsthand information. The book was put in its present form after the lifetime of Mordecai himself (cf. 10:1–3). Its historical and linguistic details do not support a date later than 400 B.C. The apocryphal "Additions to the Book of Esther" originated a considerable time later than canonical Esther.

Purpose

The book has a twofold purpose. (1) It was written to show how the Jewish people were protected and delivered from impending annihilation by God's intervention through Queen Esther. Though God's name is not specifically mentioned, there is evidence of his providence throughout the book. (2) It was written also to provide a record of and historical background for the Jewish Feast of Purim (3:6–7; 9:26–28) and thereby to keep alive for generations to come the memory of this great deliverance of the Jewish people in Persia (cf. the Passover feast and the Israelites' great deliverance from Egypt). The book also outlines the obligation for the annual commemoration of Purim (9:24,28–32).

Survey

Esther provides a character study of five main persons involved in the story: (1) the Persian king, Xerxes; (2) his prime minister, Haman; (3) Vashti, the queen who preceded Esther; (4) Esther, the beautiful Jewish maiden who became queen; and (5) Mordecai, the righteous cousin of Esther who adopted her as his daughter and brought her up. Esther, of course, is the heroine of the story, Haman is the villain, and Mordecai is the hero who, as the primary object of Haman's contempt, is vindicated and exalted in the end. The key figure behind the book's events is Mordecai, for he influenced and gave righteous counsel to Queen Esther.

God's providence is everywhere present in the book. It is first seen in the selection of a Jewish virgin named Hadassah (Heb)—Ester (Persian) or Esther (Gk)—to be queen of Persia at a crucial hour in Jewish history (chs. 1—2; 4:4). God's providence is again evident when Mordecai, the cousin of Esther who had brought her up as his daughter (2:7), overheard an assassination plot against the king, exposed it, saved the king's life and had his deed recorded in the king's chronicles (2:19–34), a fact the king providentially discovered in a timely fashion during a sleepless night (6:1–14).

Haman's hatred for Mordecai was extended to all Jews. He conceived a hideous plot and deceptively persuaded Xerxes to issue a decree to annihilate all Jews on the 13th day of the month Adar (3:13). Mordecai prevailed upon Esther to intercede with the king on behalf of the Jews. After a three-day fast by all the Jews, Esther risked her life in approaching the king's throne uninvited (ch. 4), received the king's favor (5:1–4) and exposed Haman's plot. Subsequently, the king hung Haman on the gallows that Haman had prepared for Mordecai (7:1–10). A second decree by the king enabled the Jews to triumph over their enemies (8:1—9:16); this triumph became an occasion of great celebration and the beginning of the annual Feast of Purim (9:17–32). The book concludes with a note about the fame of Mordecai (10:1–3).

Special Features

Five special features characterize the book of Esther. (1) It is one of two books in the Bible named after a woman, the other being Ruth. (2) The book begins and ends with a feast, and it records a total of ten feasts or banquets around which much of the book's drama unfolds. (3) Esther is the last of the five scrolls in the third part of the Hebrew Bible, the *Hagiographa* ("Holy Writings"), each of which is read publicly at one of the great Jewish festivals; this one is read at the Feast of Purim on Adar 14–15, celebrating the great deliverance of the Jewish people in Persia under Queen Esther. (4) Though the book mentions a three-day fast, there are no explicit references to God, worship or prayer (a feature that has led some critics unwisely to question its spiritual value). (5) Though God's name appears nowhere in Esther, his providence is everywhere evident (e.g., 2:7,17,22; 4:14; 4:16—5:2; 6:1,3–10; 9:1). No other Bible book illustrates as powerfully God's providence in preserving the Jewish people in spite of the demonic hatred of their enemies.

New Testament Fulfillment

There is no reference or allusion to this book anywhere in the NT. However, Haman's hatred for the Jews and his plot to kill and annihilate all Jews in the Persian empire (ch. 3; 7:4) is an OT type of the NT antichrist, who will seek to destroy all Jews and Christians alike at the end of history (see the book of Revelation).

Reading Esther

In order to read the entire Old Testament in one year, the book of Esther should be read in 3 days, according to the following schedule: ☐ 1–4 ☐ 5–7 ☐ 8–10

NOTES

Queen Vashti Deposed

1 This is what happened during the time of Xerxes,[a][a] the Xerxes who ruled over 127 provinces[b] stretching from India to Cush[b]:[c] **2**At that time King Xerxes reigned from his royal throne in the citadel of Susa,[d] **3**and in the third year of his reign he gave a banquet[e] for all his nobles and officials. The military leaders of Persia and Media, the princes, and the nobles of the provinces were present.

4For a full 180 days he displayed the vast wealth of his kingdom and the splendor and glory of his majesty. **5**When these days were over, the king gave a banquet, lasting seven days,[f] in the enclosed garden[g] of the king's palace, for all the people from the least to the greatest, who were in the citadel of Susa. **6**The garden had hangings of white and blue linen, fastened with cords of white linen and purple material to silver rings on marble pillars. There were couches[h] of gold and silver on a mosaic pavement of porphyry, marble, mother-of-pearl and other costly stones. **7**Wine was served in goblets of gold, each one different from the other, and the royal wine was abundant, in keeping with the king's liberality.[i] **8**By the king's command each guest was allowed to drink in his own way, for the king instructed all the wine stewards to serve each man what he wished.

9Queen Vashti also gave a banquet[j] for the women in the royal palace of King Xerxes.

10On the seventh day, when King Xerxes was in high spirits[k] from wine,[l] he commanded the seven eunuchs who served him—Mehuman, Biztha, Harbona,[m] Bigtha, Abagtha, Zethar and Carcas— **11**to bring[n] before him Queen Vashti, wearing her royal crown, in order to display her beauty[o] to the people and nobles, for she was lovely to look at. **12**But when the attendants delivered the king's command, Queen Vashti refused to come. Then the king became furious and burned with anger.[p]

13Since it was customary for the king to consult experts in matters of law and justice, he spoke with the wise men who understood the times[q] **14**and were closest to the king—Carshena, Shethar, Admatha, Tarshish, Meres, Marsena and Memucan, the seven nobles[r] of Persia and Media who had special access to the king and were highest in the kingdom.

15"According to law, what must be done to Queen Vashti?" he asked. "She has not obeyed the command of King Xerxes that the eunuchs have taken to her."

16Then Memucan replied in the presence of the king and the nobles, "Queen Vashti has done wrong, not only against the king but also against all the nobles and the peoples of all the provinces of King Xerxes. **17**For the queen's conduct will become known to all the women, and so they will despise their husbands and say, 'King Xerxes commanded Queen Vashti to be brought before him, but she would not come.' **18**This very day the Persian and Median women of the nobility who have heard about the queen's conduct will respond to all the king's nobles in the same way. There will be no end of disrespect and discord.[s]

19"Therefore, if it pleases the king,[t] let him issue a royal decree and let it be written in the laws of Persia and Media, which cannot be repealed,[u] that Vashti is never again to enter the presence of King Xerxes. Also let the king give her royal position to someone else who is better than she. **20**Then when the king's edict is proclaimed throughout all his vast realm, all the women will respect their husbands, from the least to the greatest."

21The king and his nobles were pleased with this advice, so the king

1:1 [a]S Ezr 4:6 [b]Est 9:30; Da 3:2; 6:1 [c]Est 8:9
1:2 [d]S Ezr 4:9; S Est 2:8
1:3 [e]S 1Ki 3:15
1:5 [f]Jdg 14:17 [g]S 2Ki 21:18
1:6 [h]Est 7:8; Eze 23:41; Am 3:12; 6:4
1:7 [i]Est 2:18; Da 5:2
1:9 [j]S 1Ki 3:15
1:10 [k]S Jdg 16:25; S Ru 3:7 [l]S Ge 14:18; Est 3:15; 5:6; 7:2; Pr 31:4-7; Da 5:1-4 [m]Est 7:9
1:11 [n]SS 2:4 [o]Ps 45:11; Eze 16:14
1:12 [p]Ge 39:19; Est 2:21; 7:7; Pr 19:12
1:13 [q]1Ch 12:32
1:14 [r]Ezr 7:14
1:18 [s]Pr 19:13; 27:15
1:19 [t]Ecc 8:4 [u]Est 8:8; Da 6:8, 12

[a] *1* Hebrew *Ahasuerus,* a variant of Xerxes' Persian name; here and throughout Esther
[b] *1* That is, the upper Nile region

1:1 DURING THE TIME OF XERXES. Xerxes ruled as king over Persia from 486 to 465 B.C. Important dates for the book of Esther are: (1) the Jews' captivity by Nebuchadnezzar in 586 B.C. (2Ki 25); (2) the Jews' authorized return from captivity in 538 B.C. (Ezr 1); (3) Esther's reign as queen of Persia beginning in 479 B.C. (2:16–17); (4) Ezra's authorized trip from Babylon to Jerusalem in 458 B.C. (Ezr 7). Thus the events of Esther happened approximately twenty-one years before Ezra led a second group of exiles to Jerusalem.

1:13 UNDERSTOOD THE TIMES. Sometimes the worldly wise are more in touch with the times than are the supposedly wise leaders among believers. For a discussion on understanding the times, see 1Ch 12:32, note.

did as Memucan proposed. 22He sent
dispatches to all parts of the kingdom,
to each province in its own script and
to each people in its own language,[v]
proclaiming in each people's tongue
that every man should be ruler over his
own household.

Esther Made Queen

2 Later when the anger of King Xerxes had subsided,[w] he remembered Vashti and what she had done
and what he had decreed about her.
2Then the king's personal attendants
proposed, "Let a search be made for
beautiful young virgins for the king.
3Let the king appoint commissioners
in every province of his realm to bring
all these beautiful girls into the harem
at the citadel of Susa. Let them be
placed under the care of Hegai, the
king's eunuch, who is in charge of the
women; and let beauty treatments be
given to them. 4Then let the girl who
pleases the king be queen instead of
Vashti." This advice appealed to the
king, and he followed it.
5Now there was in the citadel of
Susa a Jew of the tribe of Benjamin,
named Mordecai son of Jair, the son of
Shimei, the son of Kish,[x] 6who had
been carried into exile from Jerusalem
by Nebuchadnezzar king of Babylon,
among those taken captive with Jehoiachin[c][y] king of Judah.[z] 7Mordecai
had a cousin named Hadassah, whom
he had brought up because she had neither father nor mother. This girl, who
was also known as Esther,[a] was lovely[b] in form and features, and Mordecai had taken her as his own daughter
when her father and mother died.
8When the king's order and edict
had been proclaimed, many girls were
brought to the citadel of Susa[c] and
put under the care of Hegai. Esther
also was taken to the king's palace and
entrusted to Hegai, who had charge of
the harem. 9The girl pleased him and
won his favor.[d] Immediately he provided her with her beauty treatments
and special food.[e] He assigned to her
seven maids selected from the king's
palace and moved her and her maids
into the best place in the harem.
10Esther had not revealed her nationality and family background, because Mordecai had forbidden her to
do so.[f] 11Every day he walked back
and forth near the courtyard of the harem to find out how Esther was and
what was happening to her.
12Before a girl's turn came to go in
to King Xerxes, she had to complete
twelve months of beauty treatments
prescribed for the women, six months
with oil of myrrh and six with perfumes[g] and cosmetics. 13And this is
how she would go to the king: Anything she wanted was given her to take
with her from the harem to the king's
palace. 14In the evening she would go
there and in the morning return to another part of the harem to the care of
Shaashgaz, the king's eunuch who was
in charge of the concubines.[h] She
would not return to the king unless he
was pleased with her and summoned
her by name.[i]
15When the turn came for Esther
(the girl Mordecai had adopted, the
daughter of his uncle Abihail[j]) to go
to the king,[k] she asked for nothing
other than what Hegai, the king's eunuch who was in charge of the harem,
suggested. And Esther won the favor[l]
of everyone who saw her. 16She was
taken to King Xerxes in the royal residence in the tenth month, the month of
Tebeth, in the seventh year of his
reign.
17Now the king was attracted to Es-

1:22 [v]S Ne 13:24
2:1 [w]Est 7:10
2:5 [x]S 1Sa 9:1
2:6 [y]S 2Ki 24:6, 15 [z]Da 1:1-5; 5:13
2:7 [a]Ge 41:45 [b]S Ge 39:6
2:8 [c]Ne 1:1; Est 1:2; Da 8:2
2:9 [d]S Ge 39:21 [e]S Ge 37:3; 1Sa 9:22-24; S 2Ki 25:30; Est 9:19; Eze 16:9-13; Da 1:5
2:10 [f]ver 20
2:12 [g]Pr 27:9; SS 1:3; Isa 3:24
2:14 [h]1Ki 11:3; SS 6:8; Da 5:2 [i]Est 4:11
2:15 [j]Est 9:29 [k]Ps 45:14 [l]S Ge 18:3; S 30:27; Est 5:8; 7:3; 8:5

[c]6 Hebrew *Jeconiah*, a variant of *Jehoiachin*

2:4 BE QUEEN INSTEAD OF VASHTI. The book of Esther, although it contains no explicit mention of God, shows his continuing providence over the Jewish people. He directs, overrules and uses the actions of men and women to accomplish his purposes and to preserve his chosen people (see article on THE PROVIDENCE OF GOD, p. 78). The book displays God's foresight and providence in the following ways: (1) Because "Vashti refused to come" to the king's party (1:12), Esther, a Jewish maiden, was chosen queen (vv. 15–18); (2) Mordecai, also a Jew and a close relative of Esther, uncovered a plot to kill the king (vv. 21–23); (3) the king regarded Esther with special favor (5:2, 8); (4) the king discovered that Mordecai had saved his life (6:1–2; cf. 2:21–23); (5) the king desired to honor Mordecai at the exact moment that Haman entered (6:1–11); (6) the king helped Esther and the Jewish people who were about to be destroyed (chs. 7—8); (7) Mordecai became very influential with the king (9:4; 10:2–3).

2:6 CARRIED INTO EXILE. It was Kish (v. 5), Mordecai's great-grandfather, not Mordecai himself, who was taken from Jerusalem and exiled along with King Jehoiachin in 597 B.C.

2:17 MADE HER QUEEN. That the Persian

ther more than to any of the other
women, and she won his favor and approval more than any of the other virgins. So he set a royal crown on her
head and made her queen[m] instead of
Vashti. 18And the king gave a great
banquet,[n] Esther's banquet, for all his
nobles and officials.[o] He proclaimed a
holiday throughout the provinces and
distributed gifts with royal liberality.[p]

Mordecai Uncovers a Conspiracy

19When the virgins were assembled
a second time, Mordecai was sitting at
the king's gate.[q] 20But Esther had
kept secret her family background and
nationality just as Mordecai had told
her to do, for she continued to follow
Mordecai's instructions as she had
done when he was bringing her up.[r]
21During the time Mordecai was sitting at the king's gate, Bigthana[d] and
Teresh, two of the king's officers[s]
who guarded the doorway, became angry[t] and conspired to assassinate
King Xerxes. 22But Mordecai found out
about the plot and told Queen Esther,
who in turn reported it to the king, giving credit to Mordecai. 23And when the
report was investigated and found to
be true, the two officials were
hanged[u] on a gallows.[e] All this was
recorded in the book of the annals[v] in
the presence of the king.[w]

Haman's Plot to Destroy the Jews

3 After these events, King Xerxes
honored Haman son of Hammedatha, the Agagite,[x] elevating him and
giving him a seat of honor higher than
that of all the other nobles. 2All the
royal officials at the king's gate knelt
down and paid honor to Haman, for the
king had commanded this concerning
him. But Mordecai would not kneel
down or pay him honor.
3Then the royal officials at the
king's gate asked Mordecai, "Why do
you disobey the king's command?"[y]
4Day after day they spoke to him but he
refused to comply.[z] Therefore they
told Haman about it to see whether
Mordecai's behavior would be tolerated, for he had told them he was a Jew.
5When Haman saw that Mordecai
would not kneel down or pay him hon-
or, he was enraged.[a] 6Yet having
learned who Mordecai's people were,
he scorned the idea of killing only Mordecai. Instead Haman looked for a
way[b] to destroy[c] all Mordecai's people, the Jews,[d] throughout the whole
kingdom of Xerxes.
7In the twelfth year of King Xerxes,
in the first month, the month of Nisan,

2:17 [m]Eze 16:9-13
2:18 [n]S 1Ki 3:15 [o]S Ge 40:20 [p]S Est 1:7
2:19 [q]Est 4:2; 5:13
2:20 [r]ver 10
2:21 [s]S Ge 40:2 [t]S Est 1:12; 3:5; 5:9; 7:7
2:23 [u]S Ge 40:19; S Dt 21:22-23; Ps 7:14-16; Pr 26:27; Ecc 10:8 [v]Est 6:1; 10:2 [w]Est 6:2
3:1 [x]S Ex 17:8-16; S Nu 24:7; Dt 25:17-19; 1Sa 14:48
3:3 [y]Est 5:9; Da 3:12
3:4 [z]Ge 39:10
3:5 [a]S Est 2:21
3:6 [b]Pr 16:25 [c]Ps 74:8; 83:4 [d]Est 9:24

[d] *21* Hebrew *Bigthan,* a variant of *Bigthana*
[e] *23* Or *were hung* (or *impaled*) *on poles;* similarly elsewhere in Esther

---

king appointed Esther as queen illustrates how God can turn the hearts of sinful people in order to serve his purposes (cf. Pr 21:1; see Ezr 1:1, note). Esther was now in a position to help her people when the need arose about five years later. God used the free decisions of those involved to protect his people (4:14).

2:20 JUST AS MORDECAI HAD TOLD HER. Although Esther had been chosen and crowned queen of the great Persian empire (2:17), she was not puffed up with pride and self-importance because of her newly attained status and power. She did not despise her lowly cousin's advice, nor did she disdain her racial or spiritual heritage; rather, she manifested a true spirit of meekness, humility and submissiveness after becoming queen, even as she had done before.

3:2 MORDECAI WOULD NOT KNEEL DOWN. Mordecai refused to bow before Haman because of his loyalty to God (v. 4). Evidently the honor paid to Haman by the king's servants and others was either undeserved or it bordered on conduct reserved by the Jews only for the worship of God. Thus Mordecai would not consent to kneel down before Haman. Daniel's three companions demonstrated the same conviction (Da 3:1–12).

3:4 HE WAS A JEW. Those around Mordecai wanted to know why he did not kneel down. He gave them only one answer: he was a Jew. (1) God sent the Jews into captivity to purge them of their idolatry. We see from Ezra and Nehemiah that the Jews who went back to Jerusalem had learned their lesson and wanted a worship free from idolatry; the book of Esther shows that the Jews who did not go back had also learned their lesson. By this time it meant something to be a Jew, and Jews refused to kneel down to any human or idol. (2) It should mean something to us to be a Christian. Like Mordecai, we must also take a firm and open stand for Christ and the righteous standards of his Word in the midst of the pressures of a worldly society.

3:6 A WAY TO DESTROY . . . THE JEWS. Haman, the prime minister of Persia, is the first political figure in the Bible to devise a sinister plan for exterminating all the Jews within his political sphere. This plot of genocide against the Jewish race has its parallel in Antiochus Epiphanes's plot in the second century B.C. (see Da 11:28, note), in Adolf Hitler's schemes in twentieth-century Europe, and in the antichrist at the end of history who will seek to destroy all Jews and Christians (Rev 13:15–18).

3:7 THEY CAST THE *PUR*. The "*pur*" is something similar to dice. Haman used it to determine the "lucky day" on which to destroy the Jews. Near-

they cast the *pur*[e] (that is, the lot[f]) in the presence of Haman to select a day and month. And the lot fell on[f] the twelfth month, the month of Adar.[g]

8Then Haman said to King Xerxes, "There is a certain people dispersed and scattered among the peoples in all the provinces of your kingdom whose customs[h] are different from those of all other people and who do not obey[i] the king's laws; it is not in the king's best interest to tolerate them.[j] **9**If it pleases the king, let a decree be issued to destroy them, and I will put ten thousand talents[g] of silver into the royal treasury for the men who carry out this business."[k]

10So the king took his signet ring[l] from his finger and gave it to Haman son of Hammedatha, the Agagite, the enemy of the Jews. **11**"Keep the money," the king said to Haman, "and do with the people as you please."

12Then on the thirteenth day of the first month the royal secretaries were summoned. They wrote out in the script of each province and in the language[m] of each people all Haman's orders to the king's satraps, the governors of the various provinces and the nobles of the various peoples. These were written in the name of King Xerxes himself and sealed[n] with his own ring. **13**Dispatches were sent by couriers to all the king's provinces with the order to destroy, kill and annihilate all the Jews[o]—young and old, women and little children—on a single day, the thirteenth day of the twelfth month, the month of Adar,[p] and to plunder[q] their goods. **14**A copy of the text of the edict was to be issued as law in every province and made known to the people of every nationality so they would be ready for that day.[r]

15Spurred on by the king's command, the couriers went out, and the edict was issued in the citadel of Susa.[s] The king and Haman sat down to drink,[t] but the city of Susa was bewildered.[u]

3:7 [e]Est 9:24,26 [f]S Lev 16:8; S 1Sa 10:21 [g]ver 13; Est 9:19
3:8 [h]Ac 16:20-21 [i]Jer 29:7; Da 6:13 [j]Ezr 4:15
3:9 [k]Est 7:4
3:10 [l]S Ge 41:42
3:12 [m]S Ne 13:24 [n]S Ge 38:18
3:13 [o]S 1Sa 15:3; S Ezr 4:6 [p]S ver 7 [q]Est 8:11; 9:10
3:14 [r]Est 8:8; 9:1
3:15 [s]Est 8:14 [t]S Est 1:10 [u]Est 8:15

Mordecai Persuades Esther to Help

4 When Mordecai learned of all that had been done, he tore his clothes,[v] put on sackcloth and ashes,[w] and went out into the city, wailing[x] loudly and bitterly. **2**But he went only as far as the king's gate,[y] because no one clothed in sackcloth was allowed to enter it. **3**In every province to which the edict and order of the king came, there was great mourning among the Jews, with fasting, weeping and wailing. Many lay in sackcloth and ashes.

4When Esther's maids and eunuchs came and told her about Mordecai, she was in great distress. She sent clothes for him to put on instead of his sackcloth, but he would not accept them. **5**Then Esther summoned Hathach, one of the king's eunuchs assigned to attend her, and ordered him to find out what was troubling Mordecai and why.

6So Hathach went out to Mordecai in the open square of the city in front of the king's gate. **7**Mordecai told him everything that had happened to him, including the exact amount of money Haman had promised to pay into the royal treasury for the destruction of the Jews.[z] **8**He also gave him a copy of the text of the edict for their annihilation, which had been published in Susa, to show to Esther and explain it to her, and he told him to urge her to go into the king's presence to beg for mercy and plead with him for her people.

9Hathach went back and reported to Esther what Mordecai had said. **10**Then she instructed him to say to Mordecai, **11**"All the king's officials and the people of the royal provinces know that for any man or woman who approaches the king in the inner court without being summoned[a] the king has but one law:[b] that he be put to death. The only exception to this is for

4:1 [v]S Nu 14:6 [w]S 2Sa 13:19; Eze 27:30-31 [x]S Ex 11:6; Ps 30:11
4:2 [y]S Est 2:19
4:7 [z]Est 7:4
4:11 [a]Est 2:14 [b]Da 2:9

[f] 7 Septuagint; Hebrew does not have *And the lot fell on.* [g] 9 That is, about 375 tons (about 345 metric tons)

ly one year intervened between the casting of the lot and the execution of the plan; this gave Mordecai and Esther, under God's providence, time to counter Haman's evil plot.

3:8 WHOSE CUSTOMS ARE DIFFERENT. One of God's purposes in giving the law to Israel was to make them different from all other people. Haman recognized something different in the Jews and hated them for it. Under the new covenant, God still wants his people to be separate and different from the world, a holy people belonging to him (cf. 1Pe 2:9). Likewise today, the world will hate God's people because they are different, holy and righteous (cf. Jn 15:18–25).

the king to extend the gold scepter[c] to
him and spare his life. But thirty days
have passed since I was called to go to
the king."
12When Esther's words were reported to Mordecai, **13**he sent back this answer: "Do not think that because you
are in the king's house you alone of all
the Jews will escape. **14**For if you remain silent[d] at this time, relief[e] and
deliverance[f] for the Jews will arise
from another place, but you and your
father's family will perish. And who
knows but that you have come to royal
position for such a time as this?"[g]
15Then Esther sent this reply to
Mordecai: **16**"Go, gather together all
the Jews who are in Susa, and fast[h]
for me. Do not eat or drink for three
days, night or day. I and my maids will
fast as you do. When this is done, I will
go to the king, even though it is against
the law. And if I perish, I perish."[i]
17So Mordecai went away and carried out all of Esther's instructions.

Esther's Request to the King

5 On the third day Esther put on her
royal robes[j] and stood in the inner court of the palace, in front of the
king's[k] hall. The king was sitting on
his royal throne in the hall, facing the
entrance. **2**When he saw Queen Esther
standing in the court, he was pleased
with her and held out to her the gold
scepter that was in his hand. So Esther
approached and touched the tip of the
Job 13:15 scepter.[l]
3Then the king asked, "What is it,
Queen Esther? What is your request?
Even up to half the kingdom,[m] it will
be given you."
4"If it pleases the king," replied Esther, "let the king, together with Haman, come today to a banquet I have
prepared for him."
5"Bring Haman at once," the king
said, "so that we may do what Esther
asks."
So the king and Haman went to the
banquet Esther had prepared. **6**As they
were drinking wine,[n] the king again
asked Esther, "Now what is your petition? It will be given you. And what is
your request? Even up to half the kingdom,[o] it will be granted."[p]
7Esther replied, "My petition and my
request is this: **8**If the king regards me
with favor[q] and if it pleases the king
to grant my petition and fulfill my request, let the king and Haman come
tomorrow to the banquet[r] I will prepare for them. Then I will answer the
king's question."

Haman's Rage Against Mordecai

9Haman went out that day happy
and in high spirits. But when he saw
Mordecai at the king's gate and observed that he neither rose nor showed
fear in his presence, he was filled with
rage[s] against Mordecai.[t] **10**Nevertheless, Haman restrained himself and
went home.
Calling together his friends and Zeresh,[u] his wife, **11**Haman boasted[v] to
them about his vast wealth, his many
sons,[w] and all the ways the king had
honored him and how he had elevated
him above the other nobles and officials. **12**"And that's not all," Haman
added. "I'm the only person[x] Queen
Esther invited to accompany the king
to the banquet she gave. And she has
invited me along with the king tomorrow. **13**But all this gives me no satisfaction as long as I see that Jew Mordecai sitting at the king's gate.[y]"

4:11 [c]Est 5:1,2; 8:4; Ps 125:3 **4:14** [d]Job 34:29; Ps 28:1; 35:22; Ecc 3:7; Isa 42:14; 57:11; 62:1; 64:12; Am 5:13 [e]Est 9:16,22 [f]S Ge 45:7; S Dt 28:29 [g]S Ge 50:20 **4:16** [h]S 2Ch 20:3; Est 9:31 [i]S Ge 43:14 **5:1** [j]Eze 16:13 [k]Pr 21:1 **5:2** [l]S Est 4:11 **5:3** [m]Est 7:2; Da 5:16; Mk 6:23

5:6 [n]S Est 1:10 [o]Da 5:16; Mk 6:23 [p]Est 9:12 **5:8** [q]S Est 2:15 [r]S 1Ki 3:15 **5:9** [s]S Est 2:21; Pr 14:17 [t]S Est 3:3,5 **5:10** [u]Est 6:13 **5:11** [v]Pr 13:16 [w]Est 9:7-10,13 **5:12** [x]Job 22:29; Pr 16:18; 29:23 **5:13** [y]S Est 2:19

4:14 IF YOU REMAIN SILENT AT THIS TIME. Mordecai believed that it was God's purpose to use Esther to deliver Israel and that she had become queen for this very reason. However, Mordecai knew that Esther could fall short of that purpose if she did not do her part in God's redemptive plan. If she refused to help the Jews, she too would perish (v. 14). God's sovereign purposes usually include human responsibility (cf. Mt 26:24; see Ex 33:3, note; Php 2:12, note).

4:14 TO ROYAL POSITION FOR SUCH A TIME AS THIS? This passage reveals the book's basic meaning: God is involved in the events of the world in order to save his people from its evil and to accomplish his redemptive purposes on their behalf. All believers must remember that God is working in what happens around us in order to rescue us from this present evil age and to bring us to be with him forever (Ro 8:29–39; Gal 1:4; Jude 24).

4:16 IF I PERISH, I PERISH. Esther was willing to give her life in an attempt to save her people. She would do what was right and leave the consequences with God. God will not honor those who remain silent in order to protect their place or position, but he will honor those who, for the sake of God and his word, speak the truth in the face of great loss (see Jn 16:1–4). Mordecai and Esther were willing to die, if need be, in this battle against the powers of evil. They are examples of loyal obedience to godly convictions (see Lk 1:17, note on the character and convictions of John the Baptist).

14His wife Zeresh and all his friends
said to him, "Have a gallows built, seventy-five feet[h] high,[z] and ask the
king in the morning to have Mordecai
hanged[a] on it. Then go with the king
to the dinner and be happy." This suggestion delighted Haman, and he had
the gallows built.

Mordecai Honored

6 That night the king could not
sleep;[b] so he ordered the book of
the chronicles,[c] the record of his
reign, to be brought in and read to him.
2It was found recorded there that Mordecai had exposed Bigthana and Teresh, two of the king's officers who
guarded the doorway, who had conspired to assassinate King Xerxes.[d]
3"What honor and recognition has
Mordecai received for this?" the king
asked.

"Nothing has been done for him,"[e]
his attendants answered.
4The king said, "Who is in the
court?" Now Haman had just entered
the outer court of the palace to speak
to the king about hanging Mordecai on
the gallows he had erected for him.
5His attendants answered, "Haman
is standing in the court."

"Bring him in," the king ordered.
6When Haman entered, the king
asked him, "What should be done for
the man the king delights to honor?"

Now Haman thought to himself,
"Who is there that the king would rather honor than me?" **7**So he answered
the king, "For the man the king delights to honor, **8**have them bring a royal robe[f] the king has worn and a
horse[g] the king has ridden, one with
a royal crest placed on its head. **9**Then
let the robe and horse be entrusted to
one of the king's most noble princes.
Let them robe the man the king delights to honor, and lead him on the
horse through the city streets, proclaiming before him, 'This is what is
done for the man the king delights to
honor!'[h]"
10"Go at once," the king commanded
Haman. "Get the robe and the horse
and do just as you have suggested for
Mordecai the Jew, who sits at the
king's gate. Do not neglect anything
you have recommended."
11So Haman got[i] the robe and the
horse. He robed Mordecai, and led him
on horseback through the city streets,
proclaiming before him, "This is what
is done for the man the king delights to
honor!"
12Afterward Mordecai returned to
the king's gate. But Haman rushed
home, with his head covered[j] in grief,
13and told Zeresh[k] his wife and all his
friends everything that had happened
to him.

His advisers and his wife Zeresh
said to him, "Since Mordecai, before
whom your downfall[l] has started, is
of Jewish origin, you cannot stand
against him—you will surely come to
ruin!"[m] **14**While they were still talking
with him, the king's eunuchs arrived
and hurried Haman away to the banquet[n] Esther had prepared.

Haman Hanged

7 So the king and Haman went to
dine[o] with Queen Esther, **2**and as
they were drinking wine[p] on that second day, the king again asked, "Queen
Esther, what is your petition? It will be
given you. What is your request? Even
up to half the kingdom,[q] it will be
granted.[r]"
3Then Queen Esther answered, "If I
have found favor[s] with you, O king,
and if it pleases your majesty, grant me
my life—this is my petition. And spare
my people—this is my request. **4**For I
and my people have been sold for destruction and slaughter and annihilation.[t] If we had merely been sold as
male and female slaves, I would have

5:14 [z] Est 7:9 [a] S Ezr 6:11
6:1 [b] Da 2:1; 6:18 [c] S Est 2:23
6:2 [d] Est 2:21-23
6:3 [e] Ecc 9:13-16
6:8 [f] S Ge 41:42; S Isa 52:1 [g] 1Ki 1:33
6:9 [h] Ge 41:43
6:11 [i] S Ge 41:42
6:12 [j] 2Sa 15:30; Est 7:8; Jer 14:3, 4; Mic 3:7
6:13 [k] Est 5:10 [l] Ps 57:6; Pr 26:27; 28:18 [m] Est 7:7
6:14 [n] S 1Ki 3:15
7:1 [o] Ge 40:20-22; Mt 22:1-14
7:2 [p] S Est 1:10 [q] S Est 5:3 [r] Est 9:12
7:3 [s] S Est 2:15
7:4 [t] Est 3:9; S 4:7

[h] 14 Hebrew *fifty cubits* (about 23 meters)

5:13 GIVES ME NO SATISFACTION. Although Haman had riches, glory, power and status, he was a discontented man. Mordecai, on the other hand, had strength of character, godly convictions and assurance in his God. Haman knew in his heart that Mordecai was the better man and thus hated him for it. In God's sight greatness is never found in riches, power or position, but in faithfulness, commitment to him and pursuit of his righteous goals on earth (see Lk 22:24–30, note).

6:1 ORDERED THE BOOK ... TO BE BROUGHT IN. God's providential workings are clearly evident in ch. 6. He used the king's sleeplessness to bring about the exaltation of Mordecai by his enemy (vv. 2–11). Day and night God watches over those who are faithful (see 1Sa 2:8; Ps 121; Ac 5:17–19; 18:9–10; Rev 3:8–9).

kept quiet, because no such distress
would justify disturbing the king.[i]"
5King Xerxes asked Queen Esther,
"Who is he? Where is the man who has
dared to do such a thing?"
6Esther said, "The adversary and enemy is this vile Haman."
Then Haman was terrified before the
king and queen. 7The king got up in a
rage,[u] left his wine and went out into
the palace garden.[v] But Haman, realizing that the king had already decided
his fate,[w] stayed behind to beg Queen
Esther for his life.
8Just as the king returned from the
palace garden to the banquet hall, Haman was falling on the couch[x] where
Esther was reclining.[y]
The king exclaimed, "Will he even
molest the queen while she is with me
in the house?"[z]
As soon as the word left the king's
mouth, they covered Haman's face.[a]
9Then Harbona,[b] one of the eunuchs
attending the king, said, "A gallows
seventy-five feet[j] high[c] stands by
Haman's house. He had it made for
Mordecai, who spoke up to help the
king."
The king said, "Hang him on it!"[d]
10So they hanged[e] Haman[f] on the
gallows[g] he had prepared for Mordecai.[h] Then the king's fury subsided.[i]

The King's Edict in Behalf of the Jews

8 That same day King Xerxes gave
Queen Esther the estate of Haman,[j] the enemy of the Jews. And
Mordecai came into the presence of the
king, for Esther had told how he was
related to her. 2The king took off his
signet ring,[k] which he had reclaimed
from Haman, and presented it to Mordecai. And Esther appointed him over
Haman's estate.[l]
3Esther again pleaded with the king,
falling at his feet and weeping. She
begged him to put an end to the evil
plan of Haman the Agagite,[m] which he
had devised against the Jews. 4Then
the king extended the gold scepter[n] to
Esther and she arose and stood before
him.
5"If it pleases the king," she said,
"and if he regards me with favor[o] and
thinks it the right thing to do, and if he
is pleased with me, let an order be written overruling the dispatches that Haman son of Hammedatha, the Agagite,
devised and wrote to destroy the Jews
in all the king's provinces. 6For how
can I bear to see disaster fall on my
people? How can I bear to see the destruction of my family?"[p]
7King Xerxes replied to Queen Esther and to Mordecai the Jew, "Because Haman attacked the Jews, I have
given his estate to Esther, and they
have hanged[q] him on the gallows.
8Now write another decree[r] in the
king's name in behalf of the Jews as
seems best to you, and seal[s] it with
the king's signet ring[t]—for no document written in the king's name and
sealed with his ring can be revoked."[u]
9At once the royal secretaries were
summoned—on the twenty-third day
of the third month, the month of Sivan.
They wrote out all Mordecai's orders
to the Jews, and to the satraps, governors and nobles of the 127 provinces
stretching from India to Cush.[k][v]
These orders were written in the script
of each province and the language of
each people and also to the Jews in
their own script and language.[w]
10Mordecai wrote in the name of King
Xerxes, sealed the dispatches with the
king's signet ring, and sent them by
mounted couriers, who rode fast
horses especially bred for the king.
11The king's edict granted the Jews
in every city the right to assemble and
protect themselves; to destroy, kill and
annihilate any armed force of any nationality or province that might attack

7:7 [u]S Ge 34:7; S Est 1:12; Pr 19:12; 20:1-2 [v]S 2Ki 21:18 [w]Est 6:13 **7:8** [x]S Est 1:6 [y]Ge 39:14; Jn 13:23 [z]S Ge 34:7 [a]S Est 6:12 **7:9** [b]Est 1:10 [c]Est 5:14 [d]S Dt 21:22-23; Ps 7:14-16; 9:16; Pr 11:5-6; S 26:27; S Mt 7:2 **7:10** [e]Ge 40:22 [f]Pr 10:28 [g]Est 9:25 [h]Da 6:24 [i]Est 2:1 **8:1** [j]Pr 22:22-23 **8:2** [k]S Ge 24:22; S 41:42 [l]S Ge 41:41; Pr 13:22; 14:35; Da 2:48 **8:3** [m]S Ex 17:8-16 **8:4** [n]S Est 4:11 **8:5** [o]S Est 2:15 **8:6** [p]Ge 44:34 **8:7** [q]S Dt 21:22-23 **8:8** [r]S Est 3:12-14 [s]S Ge 38:18 [t]S Ge 41:42 [u]S Est 1:19; Da 6:15 **8:9** [v]Est 1:1 [w]S Ne 13:24

[i]4 Or *quiet, but the compensation our adversary offers cannot be compared with the loss the king would suffer* [j]9 Hebrew *fifty cubits* (about 23 meters) [k]9 That is, the upper Nile region

8:3 PUT AN END TO THE EVIL PLAN. Although Haman was hanged as a result of God's just intervention (7:10), the king's edict to destroy the Jews was still in effect. Even the king himself could not reverse the official decree (v. 8). However, in response to Esther's request, a second decree was written that gave the Jews the right to fight back and defend themselves on the day formerly decreed for their destruction (vv. 9–17). God typically does not save his people apart from their faithful participation, yet he is constantly with them working out their deliverance; i.e., Israel's deliverance was the result of the combined activity of both God and faithful believers (see Php 2:12–13).

them and their women and children;
and to plunder[x] the property of their
enemies. 12The day appointed for the
Jews to do this in all the provinces of
King Xerxes was the thirteenth day of
the twelfth month, the month of
Adar.[y] 13A copy of the text of the edict
was to be issued as law in every province and made known to the people of
every nationality so that the Jews
would be ready on that day[z] to avenge
themselves on their enemies.
14The couriers, riding the royal
horses, raced out, spurred on by the
king's command. And the edict was
also issued in the citadel of Susa.[a]
15Mordecai[b] left the king's presence wearing royal garments of blue
and white, a large crown of gold[c] and
a purple robe of fine linen.[d] And the
city of Susa held a joyous celebration.[e] 16For the Jews it was a time of
happiness and joy,[f] gladness and hon-
or.[g] 17In every province and in every
city, wherever the edict of the king
went, there was joy[h] and gladness
among the Jews, with feasting and celebrating. And many people of other na-
tionalities became Jews because fear[i]
of the Jews had seized them.[j]

Triumph of the Jews

9 On the thirteenth day of the
twelfth month, the month of
Adar,[k] the edict commanded by the
king was to be carried out. On this day
the enemies of the Jews had hoped to
overpower them, but now the tables
were turned and the Jews got the upper
hand[l] over those who hated them.[m]
2The Jews assembled in their cities[n]
in all the provinces of King Xerxes to
attack those seeking their destruction.
No one could stand against them,[o] because the people of all the other na-
tionalities were afraid of them. 3And
all the nobles of the provinces, the satraps, the governors and the king's administrators helped the Jews,[p] because fear of Mordecai had seized
them.[q] 4Mordecai[r] was prominent[s]
in the palace; his reputation spread
throughout the provinces, and he became more and more powerful.[t]
5The Jews struck down all their enemies with the sword, killing and destroying them,[u] and they did what
they pleased to those who hated them.
6In the citadel of Susa, the Jews killed
and destroyed five hundred men. 7They
also killed Parshandatha, Dalphon,
Aspatha, 8Poratha, Adalia, Aridatha,
9Parmashta, Arisai, Aridai and Vaiza-
tha, 10the ten sons[v] of Haman son of
Hammedatha, the enemy of the Jews.[w]
But they did not lay their hands on the
plunder.[x]
11The number of those slain in the
citadel of Susa was reported to the
king that same day. 12The king said to
Queen Esther, "The Jews have killed
and destroyed five hundred men and
the ten sons of Haman in the citadel of
Susa. What have they done in the rest
of the king's provinces? Now what is
your petition? It will be given you.
What is your request? It will also be
granted."[y]
13"If it pleases the king," Esther answered, "give the Jews in Susa permission to carry out this day's edict tomorrow also, and let Haman's ten sons[z]
be hanged[a] on gallows."
14So the king commanded that this
be done. An edict was issued in Susa,
and they hanged[b] the ten sons of Haman. 15The Jews in Susa came together on the fourteenth day of the month
of Adar, and they put to death in Susa
three hundred men, but they did not lay
their hands on the plunder.[c]
16Meanwhile, the remainder of the
Jews who were in the king's provinces
also assembled to protect themselves
and get relief[d] from their enemies.[e]
They killed seventy-five thousand of
them[f] but did not lay their hands on
the plunder.[g] 17This happened on the
thirteenth day of the month of Adar,
and on the fourteenth they rested and
made it a day of feasting[h] and joy.

Purim Celebrated

18The Jews in Susa, however, had

8:11 [x]S Ge 14:23; S Est 3:13; 9:10, 15,16
8:12 [y]Est 3:13; 9:1
8:13 [z]Est 3:14
8:14 [a]Est 3:15
8:15 [b]Est 9:4; 10:2 [c]S 2Sa 12:30 [d]S Ge 41:42 [e]Est 3:15
8:16 [f]Ps 97:10-12 [g]Est 4:1-3; Ps 112:4; Jer 29:4-7
8:17 [h]Ps 35:27; 45:15; 51:8; Pr 11:10 [i]S Ex 15:14,16; Dt 11:25; Da 6:26 [j]Est 9:3
9:1 [k]S Est 8:12 [l]Jer 29:4-7 [m]S Est 3:12-14; Pr 22:22-23
9:2 [n]S Ge 22:17 [o]Ps 35:26; 40:14; 70:2; 71:13,24
9:3 [p]S Ezr 8:36 [q]Est 8:17
9:4 [r]S Est 8:15 [s]S Ex 11:3 [t]S 2Sa 3:1; 1Ch 11:9
9:5 [u]Dt 25:17-19; S 1Sa 15:3; S Ezr 4:6
9:10 [v]S Est 5:11; Ps 127:3-5 [w]S 1Sa 15:33 [x]S Ge 14:23; S 1Sa 14:32; S Est 3:13
9:12 [y]Est 5:6; 7:2
9:13 [z]S Est 5:11 [a]S Dt 21:22-23
9:14 [b]S Ezr 6:11
9:15 [c]S Ge 14:23; S Est 8:11
9:16 [d]S Est 4:14 [e]Dt 25:19 [f]S 1Ch 4:43 [g]S Est 8:11
9:17 [h]S 1Ki 3:15

8:17 FEAR OF THE JEWS HAD SEIZED THEM. Not only did God enable the Jews to defend themselves (see previous note), but God also caused the people of the land to fear the Jews (cf. 9:2; Ne 6:16). In other words, God's people actually gained in stature through Haman's wicked plot.

9:5 STRUCK DOWN ALL THEIR ENEMIES. The destruction of the Jews' enemies on the thirteenth day of Adar was an act of self-defense; the Jews had been placed in a circumstance of having to fight for their very lives. They resisted those who wanted to exterminate them, yet they showed restraint by not plundering their enemies (vv. 10, 15–16).

assembled on the thirteenth and fourteenth, and then on the fifteenth they
rested and made it a day of feasting
and joy.
19That is why rural Jews—those living in villages—observe the fourteenth of the month of Adar[i] as a day
of joy and feasting, a day for giving
presents to each other.[j]
20Mordecai recorded these events,
and he sent letters to all the Jews
throughout the provinces of King Xerxes, near and far, 21to have them celebrate annually the fourteenth and fifteenth days of the month of Adar 22as
the time when the Jews got relief[k]
from their enemies, and as the month
when their sorrow was turned into joy
and their mourning into a day of celebration.[l] He wrote them to observe
the days as days of feasting and joy and
giving presents of food[m] to one another and gifts to the poor.[n]
23So the Jews agreed to continue the
celebration they had begun, doing
what Mordecai had written to them.
24For Haman son of Hammedatha, the
Agagite,[o] the enemy of all the Jews,
had plotted against the Jews to destroy
them and had cast the *pur*[p] (that is,
the lot[q]) for their ruin and destruction.[r] 25But when the plot came to the
king's attention,[1] he issued written
orders that the evil scheme Haman had
devised against the Jews should come
back onto his own head,[s] and that he
and his sons should be hanged[t] on the
gallows.[u] 26(Therefore these days
were called Purim, from the word
pur.[v]) Because of everything written
in this letter and because of what they
had seen and what had happened to
them, 27the Jews took it upon themselves to establish the custom that
they and their descendants and all who
join them should without fail observe
these two days every year, in the way
prescribed and at the time appointed.
28These days should be remembered
and observed in every generation by
every family, and in every province and
in every city. And these days of Purim
should never cease to be celebrated by
the Jews, nor should the memory of
them die out among their descendants.
29So Queen Esther, daughter of Abihail,[w] along with Mordecai the Jew,
wrote with full authority to confirm
this second letter concerning Purim.
30And Mordecai sent letters to all the
Jews in the 127 provinces[x] of the
kingdom of Xerxes—words of goodwill
and assurance— 31to establish these
days of Purim at their designated
times, as Mordecai the Jew and Queen
Esther had decreed for them, and as
they had established for themselves
and their descendants in regard to
their times of fasting[y] and lamentation.[z] 32Esther's decree confirmed
these regulations about Purim, and it
was written down in the records.

The Greatness of Mordecai

10 King Xerxes imposed tribute
throughout the empire, to its
distant shores.[a] 2And all his acts of
power and might, together with a full
account of the greatness of Mordecai[b]
to which the king had raised him,[c] are
they not written in the book of the annals[d] of the kings of Media and Persia? 3Mordecai the Jew was second[e]
in rank[f] to King Xerxes,[g] preeminent among the Jews, and held in high
esteem by his many fellow Jews, because he worked for the good of his
people and spoke up for the welfare of
all the Jews.[h]

9:19 [i]S Est 3:7 [j]S Est 2:9; Rev 11:10
9:22 [k]S Est 4:14 [l]Ne 8:12; Ps 30:11-12 [m]S 2Ki 25:30 [n]S Ne 8:10
9:24 [o]S Ex 17:8-16 [p]S Est 3:7 [q]S Lev 16:8 [r]Est 3:6
9:25 [s]Ps 7:16 [t]S Dt 21:22-23 [u]Est 7:10
9:26 [v]S Est 3:7
9:29 [w]Est 2:15
9:30 [x]S Est 1:1
9:31 [y]S Est 4:16 [z]Est 4:1-3
10:1 [a]Ps 72:10; 97:1
10:2 [b]S Est 8:15 [c]S Ge 41:44 [d]S Est 2:23
10:3 [e]Da 5:7 [f]Ge 41:43 [g]Ge 41:40 [h]Ne 2:10; Jer 29:4-7; Da 6:3

[1]25 Or *when Esther came before the king*

9:26 PURIM. Mordecai established the Feast of Purim (cf. vv. 20–23), a two-day festival celebrating God's deliverance of his people from Haman's sinister plot of Jewish genocide. (1) The feast was called "Purim," recalling that Haman used the "*pur*" or lot to determine the day the Jews were to be destroyed (see 3:7, note). (2) Purim reminds us that God can overrule the laws of chance. God's people should never see themselves as victims of fate or chance. God has a wonderful plan for each of our lives, a plan that fits in with his great plan of redemption. But we must take our stand, as did Mordecai and Esther.

JOB

Outline

I. Prose Prologue: The Crisis (1:1—2:13)
   A. Job an Upright, God-fearing Man (1:1–5)
   B. Conversation Between the Lord and Satan, and Job's Subsequent Calamities (1:6—2:10)
   C. The Visit of Job's Three Friends (2:11–13)

II. The Dialogues Between Job and His Friends: A Search for Intellectual Answers (3:1—31:40)
   A. First Cycle of Dialogue: The Righteousness of God (3:1—14:22)
      1. Job Laments the Day of His Birth (3:1–26)
      2. Eliphaz's Reply (4:1—5:27)
      3. Job's Rejoinder (6:1—7:21)
      4. Bildad's Reply (8:1–22)
      5. Job's Rejoinder (9:1—10:22)
      6. Zophar's Reply (11:1–20)
      7. Job's Rejoinder (12:1—14:22)
   B. Second Cycle of Dialogue: The Fate of Wicked Man (15:1—21:34)
      1. Eliphaz's Response (15:1–35)
      2. Job's Rejoinder (16:1—17:16)
      3. Bildad's Response (18:1–21)
      4. Job's Rejoinder (19:1–29)
      5. Zophar's Response (20:1–29)
      6. Job's Rejoinder (21:1–34)
   C. Third Cycle of Dialogue: The Sinfulness of Job (22:1—31:40)
      1. Eliphaz's Answer (22:1–30)
      2. Job's Rejoinder (23:1—24:25)
      3. Bildad's Answer (25:1–6)
      4. Job's Rejoinder (26:1–14)
      5. Job's Final Summary of His Basic Position (27:1—31:40)

III. The Speeches of Elihu: The Beginning of Insight (32:1—37:24)
   A. Introduction of Elihu (32:1–6a)
   B. First Speech: God's Instruction to Humans through Affliction (32:6b—33:33)
   C. Second Speech: God's Justice and Job's Presumption (34:1–37)
   D. Third Speech: Uprightness Is Not Without Profit (35:1–16)
   E. Fourth Speech: God's Majestic Greatness and Job's Ignorance (36:1—37:24)

IV. The Lord Answers Job: Firsthand Revelation (38:1—42:6)
   A. God Speaks to Job's Ignorance (38:1—40:2)
   B. Job's Humility (40:3–5)
   C. God Challenges Job's Criticism about His Righteous Rule in the World (40:6—41:34)
   D. Job Confesses His Inadequate Knowledge of God's Ways (42:1–6)

V. Prose Epilogue: The Crisis Ends (42:7–17)
   A. Job Prays for His Three Friends (42:7–9)
   B. Job's Double Portion (42:10–17)

Author: Anonymous

Theme: Why Do the Righteous Suffer?

Date of Writing: Uncertain

Background

Job is classified as one of the wisdom and poetic books of the OT: "wisdom" because it deals profoundly with important universal questions of humankind; "poetic" because almost the entire book is in poetic form. Its poetry, however, is based on a real, historical person (see Eze 14:14,20) and a real, historical event (see Jas 5:11). The book's setting is "the land of Uz" (1:1), which later became the territory of Edom located southeast of the Dead Sea or in northern Arabia (cf. La 4:21); thus the historical background of Job is Arabic rather than Hebrew.

There are two important dates to consider in relation to Job: (1) the date for Job himself and the events described in the book, and (2) the date for the inspired writing of the book. Certain facts indicate that Job himself lived about the time of Abraham (2000 B.C.) or before. The most significant facts are: (1) his having lived 140 years after the events in the book (42:16), suggesting a life span close to 200 years (Abraham lived 175 years); (2) his wealth being measured in terms of livestock (1:3; 42:12); (3) his service as priest for his family, like Abraham, Isaac and Jacob (1:5); (4) the patriarchal family-clan being the basic social unit, as in Abraham's day (1:4–5,13); (5) the raids by the Sabeans (1:15) and Chaldeans (1:17), which fit the Abrahamic era; (6) the frequent use (31 times) of the common patriarchal name for God, *Shaddai* ("the Almighty"); and (7) the absence of any reference to Israelite history or Mosaic law, suggesting a pre-Mosaic era (before 1500 B.C.).

Three main views exist concerning when the book itself was written. It may have been composed (1) during the patriarchal age (c. 2000 B.C.), shortly after the events occurred and perhaps by Job himself; (2) during the days of Solomon or soon after (c. 950–900 B.C.), since the book's literary form and style are similar to the wisdom literature of that period; or (3) during the time of the exile (c. 586–538 B.C.), when God's people were wrestling theologically with the meaning of their calamity. The unknown author, if other than Job himself, must have had detailed oral and/or written sources from the time of Job, which he used under divine prompting and inspiration to write the book as we now have it. Certain parts of the book had to be given by direct revelation from God (e.g. 1:6—2:10).

Purpose

The book of Job wrestles with the age-old question, "If God is just and loving, why does he permit a truly righteous man like Job (1:1,8) to suffer intensely?" In struggling with this issue, the author reveals the following truths. (1) As an opponent of God, Satan received permission to test the genuineness of the faith of a righteous man by afflicting him; but God's grace triumphed over suffering because Job by faith remained steadfast and immovable, even when there appeared to be no physical or temporal benefit in his staying committed to God. (2) God is moved by considerations too vast for the human mind to fully comprehend (37:5); because we do not see with the breadth and vision of the Almighty, we need God's gracious self-disclosure. (3) The real foundation of faith lies not in God's blessings, in personal circumstances or in intellectual answers, but in a revelation of God himself. (4) God sometimes permits Satan to test the righteous with adversity in order to purify their faith and lives, just as gold is refined by the fire (23:10; cf. 1Pe 1:6–7); such testing results in an increased measure of spiritual integrity and humility in his people (42:1–10). (5) Though God's dealings at times may seem dark and cruel (as Job himself thought), in the end God is seen to be full of compassion and mercy (42:7–17; cf. Jas 5:11).

Survey

There are five distinct divisions in the structure of the book of Job: (1) the prologue (chs. 1—2), which describes Job's calamity and the cause behind it; (2) three cycles of dialogue between Job and his three friends, in which they search for intellectual answers to Job's affliction (chs. 3—31); (3) four monologues by Elihu, a man younger than Job and his three friends, which contain some glimmer of insight into the meaning (though not the cause) of Job's affliction (chs. 32—37); (4) God himself, who speaks to Job's ignorance and complaint and listens to Job's response to his revelation (38:1—42:6); (5) the epilogue (42:7–17), which records Job's restoration. Job is written entirely in poetic form, except for three passages: (a) the prologue, (b) 32:1–6a, and (c) the epilogue.

Job is presented in ch. 1 as a righteous and God-fearing man (1:1,8) and the greatest of all the people of the East (1:3). His circumstances were suddenly reversed by a series of great calamities that destroyed his possessions, children and health (1:13–22; 2:7–10). Job was completely baffled, not realizing he was deeply involved in a conflict between God and Satan (1:6–12; 2:1–6). Job's three friends—Eliphaz, Bildad and Zophar—came to comfort Job but instead ended up debating with him about why his misfortunes had occurred. They insisted that since God is just, Job's suffering must represent punishment for hidden sins and that his only recourse was repentance. Job rejected their ready-made answers, affirmed his innocence and confessed his inability to understand (chs. 3—31). Elihu offered another perspective, namely, that Job's suffering involved God's redemptive purpose of further purifying Job (chs. 32—37).

In the end everyone was silenced, including Job, as God himself spoke to Job concerning his wisdom and power as the Creator. Job acknowledged his ignorance and insignificance with a repentant and humble heart (chs. 38—41). When Job repented of contending with the Almighty (40:1–4,8; 42:5–6) and prayed for his friends who had cut him deeply (42:8,10), he was delivered from his fiery trial and restored twofold (42:10); also Job was vindicated when God stated that Job had spoken of God "what is right" (42:7). Job's latter days were blessed more than his life before his affliction (42:12–17). Though God never provided Job with a philosophical understanding of why he suffered, the reader receives this important perspective from the prologue.

Special Features

Seven major features characterize the book of Job. (1) Job, a native of northern Arabia, was a righteous and God-fearing non-Israelite, living perhaps before the covenant family of Israel even existed (1:1). (2) This book is the most profound one ever written dealing with the mystery of suffering. As dramatic poetry, the book's drama contains stirring pathos and rousing intellectual dialogue. (3) It discloses an important dynamic that operates in every fiery trial of the saints: while Satan attempts to destroy the faith of the saints, God is at work to prove and deepen it. Job's steadfastness in naked faith enabled God's purpose to prevail over Satan's hope (cf. Jas 5:11). (4) It makes an invaluable contribution to the total Biblical revelation on such key subjects as God, humankind, creation, Satan, sin, righteousness, suffering, justice, repentance and faith. (5) A large portion of the book records the faulty theological evaluation of Job's suffering by his friends. Perhaps their wrong way of thinking is so frequently repeated in this book because it reflects a common error among God's people that needs correction. (6) Satan's role as "accuser" of the righteous is demonstrated in Job more than in any other OT book. Of the 19 OT references to Satan by name, 14 of these occur in Job. (7) Job dramatically demonstrates the Biblical principle that believers are transformed by revelation, not information (42:5–6).

New Testament Fulfillment

The Redeemer whom Job confesses (19:25–27), the mediator for whom he longs (9:32–33), and the answers to his deepest questions and needs all find their fulfillment in Jesus Christ. Jesus identified fully with human suffering (cf. Heb 4:15–16; 5:8) as God's appointed Redeemer, mediator, wisdom, healer, light and life. The Spirit of prophecy concerning the coming of Christ is most clearly expressed in 19:25–27. Explicit mention of Job occurs twice in the NT: (1) as a quotation (5:13 in 1Co 3:19), and (2) as a reference to Job's steadfastness in affliction and the merciful outcome of God's dealings with him (Jas 5:11). Job illustrates vividly the NT truth that when believers experience persecution or some other fiery trial of suffering, they must remain steadfast in faith and keep entrusting themselves to him who judges justly, just as did Jesus himself when he suffered (cf. 1Pe 2:23). Job 1:6—2:10 remains the best illustration of our enemy as described in 1Pe 5:8–9.

Reading Job

In order to read the entire Old Testament in one year, the book of Job should be read in 13 days, according to the following schedule: □ 1–2 □ 3–5 □ 6–8 □ 9–11 □ 12–14 □ 15–18 □ 19–21 □ 22–24 □ 25–28 □ 29–31 □ 32–35 □ 36–39 □ 40–42

NOTES

Prologue

1 In the land of Uz[a] there lived a
man whose name was Job.[b] This
man was blameless[c] and upright;[d]
he feared God[e] and shunned evil.[f]
2He had seven sons[g] and three daughters,[h] **3**and he owned seven thousand
sheep, three thousand camels, five
hundred yoke of oxen and five hundred
donkeys,[i] and had a large number of
servants.[j] He was the greatest man[k]
among all the people of the East.[l]
4His sons used to take turns holding
feasts[m] in their homes, and they
would invite their three sisters to eat
and drink with them. **5**When a period of
feasting had run its course, Job would
send and have them purified.[n] Early in
the morning he would sacrifice a burnt
offering[o] for each of them, thinking,
"Perhaps my children have sinned[p]
and cursed God[q] in their hearts." This
was Job's regular custom.

Job's First Test

6One day the angels[a][r] came to
present themselves before the LORD,
and Satan[b][s] also came with them.[t]
7The LORD said to Satan, "Where have
you come from?"
Satan answered the LORD, "From
roaming through the earth and going
back and forth in it."[u]
8Then the LORD said to Satan, "Have
you considered my servant Job?[v]
There is no one on earth like him; he
is blameless and upright, a man who
fears God[w] and shuns evil."[x]
9"Does Job fear God for nothing?"[y]
Satan replied. **10**"Have you not put a
hedge[z] around him and his household
and everything he has?[a] You have

1:1 [a]S Ge 10:23 [b]Eze 14:14,20; Jas 5:11 [c]S Ge 6:9; S Job 23:10 [d]Job 23:7; Ps 11:7; 107:42; Pr 21:29; Mic 7:2 [e]S Ge 22:12 [f]ver 8; S Dt 4:6; Job 2:3; 1Th 5:22 **1:2** [g]S Ru 4:15 [h]ver 13,18; Job 42:13; Ps 127:3; 144:12 **1:3** [i]S Ge 13:2 [j]S Ge 12:16 [k]ver 8; Job 29:25 [l]S Ge 25:6; Job 42:10; Ps 103:10 **1:4** [m]ver 13,18 **1:5** [n]S Ne 12:30 [o]S Ge 8:20 [p]Job 8:4 [q]1Ki 21:10,13; Ps 10:3; 74:10 **1:6** [r]S 1Ki 22:19; *fn* Ge 6:2 [s]S 2Sa 24:1; S 2Ch 18:21; S Ps 109:6; Lk 22:31 [t]Job 2:1 **1:7** [u]S Ge 3:1; 1Pe 5:8 **1:8** [v]S Jos 1:7 [w]Ps 25:12; 112:1; 128:4 [x]S ver 1; S Ex 20:20 **1:9** [y]1Ti 6:5 **1:10** [z]S 1Sa 25:16 [a]ver 12; Job 2:4; Ps 34:7

[a] *6* Hebrew *the sons of God* [b] *6* *Satan* means *accuser.*

1:1 JOB. It appears that Job lived in the age of the patriarchs (Abraham, Isaac and Jacob, approximately 2100–1800 B.C.). Most scholars believe the land of Uz was located southeast of Palestine and the Dead Sea or in northern Arabia (see the introduction to Job). Others believe that the land of Uz was located northeast of the Sea of Galilee, toward Damascus.

1:1 BLAMELESS AND UPRIGHT ... FEARED GOD AND SHUNNED EVIL. (1) Fearing God and turning away from evil are the foundation for Job's blamelessness and uprightness (cf. Pr 1:7). "Blameless" refers to Job's moral integrity and wholehearted commitment to God; "upright" denotes rightness in word, thought and deed. (2) This declaration about Job's righteousness is restated by God himself in v. 8 and in 2:3, clearly affirming that God through his grace can redeem fallen humans so as to make them genuinely good, righteous and victorious over sin. This statement shames and exposes as error evangelical teachings today that maintain that (a) no believer in Christ, even with the now fully available help of the Holy Spirit, can ever expect to be blameless and upright in this life; and (b) believers must expect to sin every day in word, thought and deed with no hope of overcoming the sinful nature in this life.

1:5 MY CHILDREN. As a godly parent, Job was deeply concerned for his children's spiritual welfare. He watched their conduct and lifestyle, praying that they would be kept from evil and would experience God's blessing and salvation. Job exemplifies a father whose heart is turned to his children by devoting the time and attention necessary to keep them from a life of sin (see Lk 1:17, note; see article on PARENTS AND CHILDREN, p. 1854).

1:6–7 SATAN. Prior to Christ's death and resurrection, Satan had occasional access to God's presence, whereby he could question the sincerity and righteousness of a believer (see 1:6–12; 2:1–6; 38:7; Rev 12:10). However, nowhere in the Bible does it say Satan has direct access to God under the new covenant (see Mt 4:10, note), though he still aims his accusations at believers. We may overcome these accusations by Christ's blood, a good conscience, and the Word of God (cf. Mt 4:3–11; Jas 4:7; Rev 12:11). We can be further encouraged by the fact that we have an advocate with the Father—Jesus Christ (1Jn 2:1), who is at his right hand interceding for us (Heb 7:25).

1:8 HAVE YOU CONSIDERED MY SERVANT JOB? Here the book introduces the struggle between God and his great adversary, Satan. God challenged Satan to observe in Job the triumph of divine grace and redemption. In the life of this faithful servant, God demonstrated that his plan to redeem the human race from sin and evil can be achieved.

1:9 DOES JOB FEAR GOD FOR NOTHING? Satan reacted to God's claim that Job was a godly man by assaulting both Job and God. (1) Satan questioned Job's motives and therefore the reality of Job's righteousness by insisting that Job's love for God was really self-serving, and that he worshiped God only because it profited him. Satan implied that Job's love for God was not genuine.

(2) Satan further implied that God was naive and had deceived himself, having obtained Job's devotion by blessing and bribery (vv. 10–11). Satan concluded that God had thereby failed in his attempt to reconcile the human race to himself. If God were to stop giving Job protection, wealth, health and happiness, Satan maintained that Job would "curse you to your face" (v. 11).

1:10 A HEDGE AROUND HIM. Because Satan comes to steal, kill and destroy (cf. Jn 10:10), God

blessed the work of his hands, so that
his flocks and herds are spread
throughout the land.[b] 11But stretch
out your hand and strike everything he
has,[c] and he will surely curse you to
your face."[d]

12The LORD said to Satan, "Very
well, then, everything he has[e] is in
your hands, but on the man himself do
not lay a finger."[f]

Then Satan went out from the presence of the LORD.

13One day when Job's sons and
daughters[g] were feasting[h] and
drinking wine at the oldest brother's
house, 14a messenger came to Job and
said, "The oxen were plowing and the
donkeys were grazing[i] nearby, 15and
the Sabeans[j] attacked and carried
them off. They put the servants to the
sword, and I am the only one who has
escaped to tell you!"

16While he was still speaking, another messenger came and said, "The
fire of God fell from the sky[k] and
burned up the sheep and the servants,[l] and I am the only one who has
escaped to tell you!"

17While he was still speaking, another messenger came and said, "The
Chaldeans[m] formed three raiding parties and swept down on your camels
and carried them off. They put the servants to the sword, and I am the only
one who has escaped to tell you!"

18While he was still speaking, yet
another messenger came and said,
"Your sons and daughters[n] were
feasting[o] and drinking wine at the
oldest brother's house, 19when suddenly a mighty wind[p] swept in from
the desert and struck the four corners
of the house. It collapsed on them and
they are dead,[q] and I am the only one
who has escaped to tell you!"[r]

20At this, Job got up and tore his
robe[s] and shaved his head.[t] Then he
fell to the ground in worship[u] 21and
said:

"Naked I came from my mother's
womb,
and naked I will depart.[c][v]
The LORD gave and the LORD has
taken away;[w]
may the name of the LORD be
praised."[x]

22In all this, Job did not sin by charging God with wrongdoing.[y]

Job's Second Test

2 On another day the angels[d][z]
came to present themselves before
the LORD, and Satan also came with
them[a] to present himself before him.
2And the LORD said to Satan, "Where
have you come from?"

Satan answered the LORD, "From
roaming through the earth and going
back and forth in it."[b]

1:10 [b] ver 3; Job 8:7; 29:6; 42:12,17 **1:11** [c] Job 19:21; Lk 22:31 [d] Lev 24:11; Job 2:5; Isa 3:8; 65:3; Rev 12:9-10 **1:12** [e] S ver 10 [f] Job 2:6; 1Co 10:13 **1:13** [g] S ver 2 [h] S ver 4 **1:14** [i] Ge 36:24 **1:15** [j] S Ge 10:7; S Job 9:24 **1:16** [k] S 1Ki 18:38; 2Ki 1:12; Job 20:26 [l] S Ge 18:17; S Lev 10:2; S Nu 11:1-3 **1:17** [m] S Ge 11:28,31; S Job 9:24 **1:18** [n] S ver 2 [o] S ver 4 **1:19** [p] Ps 11:6; Isa 5:28; 21:1; Jer 4:11; 13:24; 18:17; Eze 17:10; Hos 13:15; Mt 7:25 [q] Job 16:7; 19:13-15 [r] Eze 24:26 **1:20** [s] S Ge 37:29; S Mk 14:63 [t] Isa 3:24; 15:2; 22:12; Jer 7:29; 16:6; Eze 27:31; 29:18; Mic 1:16 [u] 1Pe 5:6 **1:21** [v] Ecc 5:15; 1Ti 6:7 [w] Ru 1:21; 1Sa 2:7 [x] S Jdg 10:15; Job 2:10; Ecc 7:14; Jer 40:2; S Eph 5:20; 1Th 5:18; Jas 5:11 **1:22** [y] Job 2:10; Ps 39:1; Pr 10:19; 13:3; Isa 53:7; Ro 9:20 **2:1** [z] fn Ge 6:2 [a] S Job 1:6 **2:2** [b] S Ge 3:1

[c] 21 Or *will return there* [d] 1 Hebrew *the sons of God*

places a hedge of protection around his people to shield them from Satan's attacks. (1) The "hedge" is like a spiritual "wall of fire" surrounding God's faithful so that Satan cannot harm them. " 'And I myself will be a wall of fire around it [Jerusalem],' declares the LORD" (Zec 2:5). (2) All believers who are faithfully striving to love God and follow the leading of the Holy Spirit have a right to ask and expect God to place this wall of protection around them and their families.

1:11 AND HE WILL SURELY CURSE YOU. In vv. 6–12 the book's primary questions are proposed. Is it possible for God's people to love and serve him because of who he is and not just for his gifts? Can the righteous maintain their faith in and love for God in the midst of unexplainable tragedy and undeserved suffering?

1:12 DO NOT LAY A FINGER. God gave Satan the authority to destroy Job's property and family; however, he limited Satan as to what he could do, for he was not given the power of death over Job. Satan brought both violent weather and violent people against Job (vv. 13–19).

1:16 THE FIRE OF GOD. The "fire of God" is probably a term for lightning (see Nu 11:1; 1Ki 18:38).

1:20 FELL TO THE GROUND IN WORSHIP. Job reacted to the disasters that happened to him with intense grief, but also with a humility that submitted to God and continued to worship him in the midst of extreme adversity (v. 21; 2:10). (1) Job's later reactions to continued calamity included doubt, anger and a sense of isolation from God (7:11). Yet even in this time of darkness and wavering faith, he did not turn against God but openly expressed his protest and feelings to him. (2) The book of Job shows how faithful believers should face life's calamities. Though we may experience severe sufferings and unexplainable affliction, we should pray for grace to accept what God allows to come upon us and to ask for revelation and understanding concerning its meaning. God will deal with our chaotic feelings and complaints if they are directed to him — not in rebellion, but in sincere trust in him as a loving God. (3) The book reveals that God accepted Job's questionings (chs. 38 — 41) and in the end praised him for speaking "what is right" (42:7).

3 Then the LORD said to Satan, "Have
you considered my servant Job? There
is no one on earth like him; he is blameless and upright, a man who fears God
and shuns evil.[c] And he still maintains his integrity,[d] though you incited me against him to ruin him without
any reason."[e]
4 "Skin for skin!" Satan replied. "A
man will give all he has[f] for his own
life. 5 But stretch out your hand and
strike his flesh and bones,[g] and he
will surely curse you to your face."[h]
6 The LORD said to Satan, "Very well,
then, he is in your hands;[i] but you
must spare his life."[j]
7 So Satan went out from the presence of the LORD and afflicted Job with
painful sores from the soles of his feet
to the top of his head.[k] 8 Then Job took
a piece of broken pottery and scraped
himself with it as he sat among the
ashes.[l]
9 His wife said to him, "Are you still
holding on to your integrity?[m] Curse
God and die!"[n]

2:3 [c] S Ex 20:20; S Job 1:1,8 [d] Job 6:29; 13:18; 27:6; 31:6; 32:1; 40:8 [e] Job 9:17; Ps 44:17 2:4 [f] S Job 1:10 2:5 [g] Job 16:8; 19:20; 33:21; Ps 102:5; La 4:8 [h] S Ex 20:7; S Job 1:11 2:6 [i] 2Co 12:7 [j] S Job 1:12 2:7 [k] S Dt 28:35; S Job 16:16 2:8 [l] Ge 18:27; Est 4:3; Job 16:15; 19:9; 30:19; 42:6; Ps 7:5; Isa 58:5; 61:3; Jer 6:26; La 3:29; Eze 26:16; Jnh 3:5-8,6; Mt 11:21 2:9 [m] Job 6:29; 13:15; 27:5; 33:9; 35:2; 1Th 5:8 [n] S Ex 20:7; S 2Ki 6:33 2:10 [o] S Job 1:21; S Ecc 2:24; La 3:38 [p] S Job 1:22; S 6:24; Jas 1:12; 5:11 2:11 [q] S Ge 36:11 [r] S Ge 25:2 [s] Job 11:1; 20:1 [t] S Ge 37:35;

10 He replied, "You are talking like a
foolish[e] woman. Shall we accept good
from God, and not trouble?"[o]
In all this, Job did not sin in what he
said.[p]

Job's Three Friends

11 When Job's three friends, Eliphaz
the Temanite,[q] Bildad the Shuhite[r]
and Zophar the Naamathite,[s] heard
about all the troubles that had come
upon him, they set out from their
homes and met together by agreement
to go and sympathize with him and
comfort him.[t] 12 When they saw him
from a distance, they could hardly recognize him;[u] they began to weep
aloud,[v] and they tore their robes[w]
and sprinkled dust on their heads.[x]
13 Then they sat on the ground[y] with

S Job 6:10; Jn 11:19 2:12 [u] Job 17:7; Isa 52:14 [v] S 2Sa 15:23 [w] S Ge 37:29; S Mk 14:63 [x] S Jos 7:6; S 2Sa 1:2 2:13 [y] Isa 3:26; 47:1; Jer 48:18; La 2:10; Eze 26:16; Jnh 3:6; Hag 2:22

[e] *10* The Hebrew word rendered *foolish* denotes moral deficiency.

2:3 RUIN HIM WITHOUT ANY REASON. Job, the innocent sufferer, foreshadows both Jesus Christ and all righteous believers under the new covenant. (1) As the OT ideal of the suffering righteous person, Job is a type of Christ—the perfect Righteous Man—who suffered even though he was innocent (see article on CHRIST IN THE OLD TESTAMENT, p. 518). The sinless Christ suffered in his body the consequences of evil and was "stricken by God" (Isa 53:4; cf. 1Pe 2:24; 4:1).

(2) Furthermore, Job exemplifies the patient endurance in adversity that is required of the child of God in Christ (Jas 5:11; cf. also Heb 11, where many of the heroes of faith suffered and died without receiving deliverance). As Job suffered innocently because of his loyalty to God and God's righteousness, all faithful believers will likewise suffer in some measure. The NT states that "everyone who wants to live a godly life in Christ Jesus will be persecuted" (2Ti 3:12)—a suffering seen as entering into the fellowship of sharing in Christ's sufferings (Php 3:10; cf. Col 1:24). Innocent sufferers are thus companions of God (cf. 1Pe 4:1; 5:10; see 2:21, note; 4:13, note; see article on THE SUFFERING OF THE RIGHTEOUS, p. 710).

2:6 HE IS IN YOUR HANDS. God allowed Satan to inflict further pain on Job because neither Job's full commitment to God could be proven nor God's endeavor to redeem him from sin demonstrated effectively without undeserved suffering. (1) The testing of a righteous person's faith through such suffering has great significance, because God's honor is at stake in the greatest spiritual struggle of all times, i.e., the conflict between God and Satan. (2) The apostle Peter, writing from a NT perspective, states: "you may have had to suffer grief in all kinds of trials. These have come so that your faith—of greater worth than gold, which perishes even though refined by fire—may be proved genuine and may result in praise, glory and honor when Jesus Christ is revealed" (1Pe 1:6–7).

2:9 CURSE GOD AND DIE! This advice from Job's wife expresses the heart of Job's test of faith. Throughout the book, his deep anguish caused by the seemingly unjust adversity from God tempted him both to abandon his moral resolve to remain loyal to God and to stop trusting the Lord as a compassionate and merciful God (cf. Jas 5:11).

2:10 AND NOT TROUBLE? True believers must prepare themselves both to be tested by God with adversity and to receive good from his hand. Trusting in God does not mean that he will always exempt us from trouble, nor does faithfulness to God guarantee prosperity and success (see 2:3, note; 3Jn 2, note). When adversity comes, the believer who is not conscious of any sin or rebellion against God must commit his or her soul to God. Faith in God as one's loving Lord in the midst of trials and oppression expresses the ultimate triumph of faith (1Pe 1:3–9).

2:11 JOB'S THREE FRIENDS. After hearing of Job's adversity, three of his friends came to sympathize with him and comfort him. The book of Job records their dialogues with the sufferer. Their perspective represented a popular but incomplete theology, for they believed that only good things happen to the godly, while adversity always indicates sin in one's life. They sincerely tried to help Job by urging him to admit to some grave sin. In the end God rebuked them for their error (42:7).

THE SUFFERING OF THE RIGHTEOUS

Job 2:7–8 "So Satan went out from the presence of the LORD and afflicted Job with painful sores from the soles of his foot to the top of his head. Then Job took a piece of broken pottery and scraped himself with it as he sat among the ashes."

Faithfulness to God does not guarantee believers freedom from trouble, pain and suffering in their lives (see Ac 28:16, note). In fact, Jesus taught that we are to expect it (Jn 16:1–4,33; see 2Ti 3:12, note). The Bible provides numerous examples of godly people who experienced significant amounts of suffering for a variety of reasons—e.g., Joseph, David, Job, Jeremiah and Paul.

REASONS BELIEVERS SUFFER. There are various reasons why believers suffer. (1) Believers experience suffering as an ongoing consequence of the fall of Adam and Eve. When sin entered the world, pain, sorrow, conflict and eventual death invaded the lives of all human beings (Ge 3:16–19). Paul affirms this: "Therefore, just as sin entered the world through one man, and death through sin, and in this way death came to all men, because all sinned" (Ro 5:12; see note). In fact, the whole created universe groans under sin's effects and yearns for the time of a new heaven and a new earth (Ro 8:20–23; 2Pe 3:10–13). Response: we must always cast ourselves on God's grace, strength and comfort (cf. 1Co 10:13).

(2) Some believers suffer for the same reason that unbelievers do, i.e., as a consequence of their own actions (see article on THE PROVIDENCE OF GOD, p. 78). The principle that "A man reaps what he sows" (Gal 6:7) applies in a general sense to everyone. If we drive our cars recklessly, we may get into serious accidents. If we are undisciplined in our eating habits, we are likely to have serious health problems. God may use such suffering as a means of discipline, that we may achieve "a harvest of righteousness and peace" (Heb 12:3–11; see 12:5, note). Response: we must always act in wisdom and in accord with God's Word, and we must avoid whatever will remove us from God's protective care.

(3) Believers also suffer, at least in their inner selves, because they live in a sinful and corrupt world. All around us are the effects of sin; we experience distress and anguish as we see the power that evil holds over so many lives (see Eze 9:4; Ac 17:16; 2Pe 2:8, note). Response: we must pray to God that he will demonstrate his victory over sin's power.

(4) Believers suffer at the hands of the devil. (a) Scripture makes it clear that Satan, as "the god of this age" (2Co 4:4), controls this present evil age (see 1Jn 5:19, note; cf. Gal 1:4; Heb 2:14). He has been given power to afflict us in a variety of ways (cf. 1Pe 5:8–9). The story of Job centers around an upright, God-fearing man whom God permitted to be tormented by Satan with unspeakable sufferings (see especially Job 1—2). Jesus testified that one of the women he healed had been bound by Satan for eighteen years (cf. Lk 13:11,16). Paul recognized that his thorn in the flesh was "a messenger of Satan, to torment me" (2Co 12:7). As we engage in spiritual warfare against "the powers of this dark world" (Eph 6:12), we will inevitably suffer adversity. In order to deal with such assaults, God has given us spiritual armor (Eph 6:10–18; see 6:11, note) and spiritual weapons (2Co 10:3–6). Response: we must put on the full armor of God and pray (Eph 6:10–18), resolving to persevere faithfully in his strength.

(b) Satan and his followers delight to persecute believers. Those who love the Lord Jesus and follow his principles of truth and righteousness will be persecuted for their faith. In fact, such suffering because of righteousness may be an indication of our genuine devotion to Christ (see Mt 5:10, note; 1Pe 4:12, note). Response: since all true believers are called to suffer persecution and reproach because of righteousness, we must stand firm and keep on trusting him who judges justly (Mt 5:10–11; 1Co 15:58; 1Pe 2:23).

(5) More positively, another reason why believers suffer is that "we have the mind of Christ" (see 1Co 2:16, note). To be a Christian means to be in Christ, to be one with him; as a result we share in his sufferings (see 1Pe 2:21, note). For example, just as Christ wept in agony over the wicked city of Jerusalem and their refusal to repent and accept salvation (see Lk 19:41, note), so we are to weep over humanity's sinfulness and lostness. Included in Paul's list of sufferings for Christ's sake (2Co 11:23–32; see 11:23, note) was his daily concern for the churches he had founded: "Who is weak, and I do not feel weak? Who is led into sin, and I do not inwardly burn?" (2Co 11:29). Such mental anguish over those whom we love in Christ should be a natural part of our lives: "mourn with those who mourn" (Ro 12:15). In fact, sharing in Christ's sufferings is a prerequisite for being glorified with Christ (Ro 8:17). Response: we must thank God that just as Christ's sufferings are ours, so also is his comfort (2Co 1:5).

(6) God himself may use suffering in our lives as a catalyst to spiritual growth or change. (a) He often uses suffering to call his straying people to repent of their sins and renew their faith and trust in him (see the book of Judges). Response: we must confess known sin and examine our lives to see if there is anything that displeases the Holy Spirit. (b) God sometimes uses suffering to test our faith, to see whether we will remain faithful to him. To test Job's faith was the reason he allowed Satan to afflict him (see Job 1:6–12; 2:1–6): would Job remain committed to the Lord, or would he curse God to his face? James calls the various trials we face "the testing of your faith" (Jas 1:3; see 1:2, note); through them our faith in Christ becomes more mature (see Dt 8:3, note; 1Pe 1:7, note). Response: we must realize that the genuineness of our faith will result in "praise, glory and honor when Jesus Christ is revealed" (1Pe 1:7). (c) God uses suffering not only to strengthen our faith, but also to help us to grow in Christian character and righteousness. According to both Paul and James, God wants us to learn patience through suffering (Ro 5:3–5; Jas 1:3). In suffering we learn to depend less on ourselves and more on God and his grace (see Ro 5:3, note; 2Co 12:9, note). Response: we must be attuned to what God may want us to learn from our suffering. (d) God may also send us pain and affliction so that we might be better able to comfort and encourage other sufferers (see 2Co 1:4, note); thus the effectiveness of our ministry deepens and increases (2Co 4:7–12; see 4:11–12, note). Response: we must use our experience of pain to encourage and strengthen other believers.

(7) Finally, God can and does use the suffering of the righteous to further the cause of his kingdom and his plan of redemption. For example, all the injustices that Joseph experienced at the hands of his brothers and the Egyptians were part of God's plan "to preserve for you a remnant on earth and to save your lives by a great deliverance" (Ge 45:7; see article on THE PROVIDENCE OF GOD, p. 78). The prime example of this principle is the suffering of Christ, "the Holy and Righteous One" (Ac 3:14), who experienced persecution, agony and death so that God's plan of salvation might be fully realized. This does not excuse the wickedness of those who crucified him (Ac 2:23), but it does indicate how God can use the suffering of the righteous at the hands of sinful people for his own purposes and to his own glory.

GOD'S RELATIONSHIP TO THE SUFFERING OF BELIEVERS. (1) The first thing to remember is this: God is involved in our sufferings. Even though Satan is the god of this age, he is able to afflict our lives only by God's permissive will (cf. Job 1—2; see articles on THE PROVIDENCE OF GOD, p. 78, and THE WILL OF GOD, p. 1056). God has promised in his Word that he will not allow us to be tempted beyond what we can bear (1Co 10:13).

(2) God has also promised to bring good out of all the sufferings and persecution of those who love him and obey his commands (see Ro 8:28, note). Joseph recognized this truth in his own life of suffering (cf. Ge 50:20), and the author of Hebrews shows how God uses the painful parts of our lives for our growth and benefit (see Heb 12:5, note).

(3) In addition, God has promised to stand by us in our pain, to walk with us "through the valley of the shadow of death" (Ps 23:4; cf. Isa 43:2). He does so by his Holy Spirit, who comforts us in all our troubles (see 2Co 1:4, note). To each of his children he sends sufficient grace so that they can bear the trials of life (1Co 10:13; see 2Co 12:9, note).

(4) Finally, do not forget that the Lord Jesus shares your pain. When we pray to him, we have a sympathetic high priest who himself experienced the various dimensions of our trials and sufferings (Heb 4:15). He indeed "took up our infirmities and carried our sorrows" (Isa 53:4); there is healing for our own sufferings through the sufferings that he bore on our behalf (Isa 53:5).

VICTORY OVER PERSONAL SUFFERING. Now we must address an important issue: when experiencing trials and affliction, what steps can we take to cope with such suffering so as to be victorious over it? (1) First, consider the various reasons human beings suffer (see section 1, above) and how those reasons apply to you. If you can identify a specific reason, then follow the appropriate response.

(2) Believe that God cares deeply for you, regardless of how severe your circumstances are (see Ro 8:36, note; 2Co 1:8–10, note; Jas 5:11, note; 1Pe 5:7, note). Suffering should never lead you to deny God's love for you or to reject him as your Lord and Savior.

(3) Turn to God in earnest prayer and seek his face. Wait for him until he delivers you from your affliction (see Ps 27:8–14; 40:1–3; 130).

(4) Expect God to give you the grace necessary to bear your affliction until deliverance comes (1Co 10:13; 2Co 12:7–10). Always remember that "we are more than conquerors through him who loved us" (Ro 8:37; cf. Jn 16:33). The Christian faith lies not in the removal of weakness and suffering, but in the manifestation of divine power through human weakness (see 2Co 4:7, note).

(5) Read the Word of God, especially those psalms that give comfort in times of affliction (e.g., Ps 11; 16; 23; 27; 40; 46; 61; 91; 121; 125; 138).

(6) Seek revelation and discernment from God regarding your particular situation—through prayer, Scripture, the enlightenment of the Holy Spirit or the counsel of a godly, mature believer.

(7) If your suffering is physical in nature, follow the steps as outlined in the article on DIVINE HEALING, p. 1420.

(8) During the time of your suffering, remember Christ's prediction that you will have trouble in your life as a believer (Jn 16:33). Look forward with eager anticipation to that time when God "will wipe every tear from their eyes. There will be no more death or mourning or crying or pain" (Rev 21:4).

him for seven days and seven nights.[z]
No one said a word to him,[a] because
they saw how great his suffering was.

Job Speaks

3 After this, Job opened his mouth
and cursed the day of his birth.[b]
2He said:

3"May the day of my birth perish,
and the night it was said, 'A boy
is born!'[c]
4That day—may it turn to
darkness;
may God above not care about
it;
may no light shine upon it.
5May darkness and deep
shadow[f][d] claim it once
more;
may a cloud settle over it;
may blackness overwhelm its
light.
6That night—may thick darkness[e]
seize it;
may it not be included among
the days of the year
nor be entered in any of the
months.
7May that night be barren;
may no shout of joy[f] be heard
in it.
8May those who curse days[g] curse
that day,[g]
those who are ready to rouse
Leviathan.[h]
9May its morning stars become
dark;
may it wait for daylight in vain
and not see the first rays of
dawn,[i]
10for it did not shut the doors of the
womb on me
to hide trouble from my eyes.

11"Why did I not perish at birth,
and die as I came from the
womb?[j]
12Why were there knees to receive
me[k]
and breasts that I might be
nursed?
13For now I would be lying down[l]
in peace;
I would be asleep and at rest[m]
14with kings and counselors of the
earth,[n]
who built for themselves places
now lying in ruins,[o]
15with rulers[p] who had gold,
who filled their houses with
silver.[q]
16Or why was I not hidden in the
ground like a stillborn
child,[r]
like an infant who never saw the
light of day?[s]
17There the wicked cease from
turmoil,[t]
and there the weary are at
rest.[u]
18Captives[v] also enjoy their ease;
they no longer hear the slave
driver's[w] shout.[x]
19The small and the great are
there,[y]
and the slave is freed from his
master.

20"Why is light given to those in
misery,
and life to the bitter of soul,[z]
21to those who long for death that
does not come,[a]
who search for it more than for
hidden treasure,[b]
22who are filled with gladness
and rejoice when they reach the
grave?[c]
23Why is life given to a man
whose way is hidden,[d]
whom God has hedged in?[e]
24For sighing[f] comes to me instead
of food;[g]

2:13 [z] S Ge 50:10 [a] Pr 17:28; Isa 23:2; 47:5 **3:1** [b] Jer 15:10; 20:14 **3:3** [c] ver 11,16; Job 10:18-19; Ecc 4:2; 6:3; Jer 20:14-18; Mt 26:24 **3:5** [d] Job 10:21, 22; 34:22; 38:17; Ps 23:4; 44:19; 88:12; Jer 2:6; 13:16 **3:6** [e] Job 23:17; 30:26 **3:7** [f] Ps 20:5; 33:3; 65:13; Isa 26:19; Jer 51:48 **3:8** [g] Job 10:18; Jer 20:14 [h] S Ge 1:21; Job 41:1,8,10,25; Ps 74:14; 104:26 **3:9** [i] Job 41:18; Hab 3:4 **3:11** [j] S ver 3 **3:12** [k] S Ge 48:12; Isa 66:12 **3:13** [l] Job 17:13; 30:23 [m] ver 17; Job 7:8-10,21; 10:22; 13:19; 14:10-12; 19:27; 21:13,23; 27:19; Ps 139:11; Isa 8:22 **3:14** [n] Job 9:24; 12:17; Isa 14:9; Eze 32:28-32 [o] Job 15:28; Jer 51:37; Na 3:7 **3:15** [p] Job 12:21; Isa 45:1 [q] Job 15:29; 20:10; 27:17; Ps 49:16-17; Pr 13:22; 28:8; Ecc 2:26; Isa 2:7; Zep 1:11 **3:16** [r] Ps 58:8; Ecc 4:3; 6:3 [s] S ver 3; Ps 71:6 **3:17** [t] ver 26; Job 30:26; Ecc 4:2; Isa 14:3 [u] S ver 13 **3:18** [v] Isa 51:14 [w] S Ge 15:13 [x] Job 39:7 **3:19** [y] Job 9:22; 17:16; 21:33; 24:24; 30:23; Ecc 12:5 **3:20** [z] S 1Sa 1:10; Eze 27:30-31 **3:21** [a] Rev 9:6 [b] Ps 119:127; Pr 2:4 **3:22** [c] Job 7:16; Ecc 4:3; Jer 8:3 **3:23** [d] Pr 4:19; Isa 59:10; Jer 13:16; 23:12 [e] Job 6:4; 16:13; 19:6,8,12; Ps 88:8; La 2:4; 3:7; Hos 2:6 **3:24** [f] Ps 5:1; 38:9; Isa 35:10 [g] Job 6:7; 33:20; Ps 107:18

[f] 5 Or *and the shadow of death* [g] 8 Or *the sea*

3:1 CURSED THE DAY OF HIS BIRTH. Job was bereaved, humiliated and in pain. His greatest hurt was that God seemed to have left him. (1) In his speech (vv. 2–26) Job told God exactly how he felt. He began by cursing the day of his birth and his miserable existence, but note that in all this Job did not curse God. His cry was an expression of pain and despair, not a cry of defiance against God. (2) It is always best for believers to express their doubts and their honest emotions to the Lord in prayer. To go to God with our misery and heartache in order to find him and evoke his compassion is never wrong. Jesus Christ himself asked God the question, "My God, my God, why have you forsaken me?" (Mt 27:46; cf. also Jer 20:14–18; La 3:1–18).

3:13 I WOULD BE ASLEEP AND AT REST. Job conceived of the grave as a place of rest. He did not see it as extinction, but as a place of continuing personal existence (vv. 13–19; see Ps 16:10, note on Sheol).

my groans[h] pour out like
water.[i]
25What I feared has come upon me;
what I dreaded[j] has happened
to me.[k]
26I have no peace,[l] no quietness;
I have no rest,[m] but only
turmoil."[n]

Eliphaz

4 Then Eliphaz the Temanite[o] replied:

2"If someone ventures a word with
you, will you be impatient?
But who can keep from
speaking?[p]
3Think how you have instructed
many,[q]
how you have strengthened
feeble hands.[r]
4Your words have supported those
who stumbled;[s]
you have strengthened faltering
knees.[t]
5But now trouble comes to you, and
you are discouraged;[u]
it strikes[v] you, and you are
dismayed.[w]
6Should not your piety be your
confidence[x]
and your blameless[y] ways your
hope?

7"Consider now: Who, being
innocent, has ever
perished?[z]
Where were the upright ever
destroyed?[a]
8As I have observed,[b] those who
plow evil[c]
and those who sow trouble reap
it.[d]
9At the breath of God[e] they are
destroyed;
at the blast of his anger they
perish.[f]
10The lions may roar[g] and growl,
yet the teeth of the great lions[h]
are broken.[i]
11The lion perishes for lack of
prey,[j]
and the cubs of the lioness are
scattered.[k]

12"A word[l] was secretly brought to
me,
my ears caught a whisper[m] of
it.[n]
13Amid disquieting dreams in the
night,
when deep sleep falls on men,[o]
14fear and trembling[p] seized me
and made all my bones shake.[q]
15A spirit glided past my face,
and the hair on my body stood
on end.[r]
16It stopped,
but I could not tell what it was.
A form stood before my eyes,
and I heard a hushed voice:[s]

3:24 [h]Ps 22:1; 32:3; 38:8 [i]1Sa 1:15; Job 30:16; Ps 6:6; 22:14; 42:3,4; 80:5; Isa 53:12; La 2:12 **3:25** [j]Job 7:9; 9:28; 30:15; Hos 13:3 [k]S Ge 42:36 **3:26** [l]Isa 48:22; Jn 14:27 [m]Job 7:4, 14; Ps 6:6; Da 4:5; Mt 11:28 [n]S ver 17; S Job 10:18; S 19:8 **4:1** [o]S Ge 36:11; Job 15:1; 22:1 **4:2** [p]Job 32:20; Jer 4:19; 20:9 **4:3** [q]Dt 32:2; Job 29:23; Hos 6:3 [r]Job 26:2; Ps 71:9; Isa 13:7; 35:3; Zep 3:16; Heb 12:12 **4:4** [s]Job 16:5; 29:16,25; Isa 1:17 [t]Job 29:11,15; Isa 35:3; Jer 31:8; Heb 12:12 **4:5** [u]S Jos 1:9 [v]Ru 1:13; Job 1:11; 19:21; 30:21; Ps 38:2; Isa 53:4 [w]Job 6:14; Pr 24:10 **4:6** [x]2Ki 18:19; Ps 27:3; 71:5; Pr 3:26 [y]S Ge 6:9 **4:7** [z]Job 5:11; 36:7; Ps 41:12; 2Pe 2:9 [a]Job 8:20; Ps 37:25; 91:9-10; Pr 12:21; 19:23 **4:8** [b]Job 5:3; 15:17 [c]Jdg 14:18; Job 5:6; 15:35; Ps 7:14; Isa 59:4 [d]Ps 7:15; 9:15; Pr 11:18; 22:8; Isa 17:11; Hos 8:7; 10:13; Gal 6:7-8 **4:9** [e]S Ex 15:10; S Job 41:21; 2Th 2:8 [f]S Lev 26:38; Job 40:13; Isa 25:7 **4:10** [g]Ps 22:13 [h]Ps 17:12; 22:21; Pr 28:15 [i]Job 5:15; 29:17; 36:6; 38:15; Ps 35:10; 58:6 **4:11** [j]Dt 28:41; Job 27:14; 29:17; Ps 34:10; 58:6; Pr 30:14 [k]Job 5:4 **4:12** [l]ver 17-21; Job 32:13; Jer 9:23 [m]Job 26:14 [n]Job 33:14 **4:13** [o]Job 33:15 **4:14** [p]Job 21:6; Ps 48:6; 55:5; 119:120,161; Jer 5:22; Hab 3:16; S 2Co 7:15 [q]Jer 23:9; Da 10:8; Hab 3:16 **4:15** [r]Da 5:6; 7:15,28; 10:8; Mt 14:26 **4:16** [s]S 1Ki 19:12

3:25 WHAT I FEARED HAS COME UPON ME. Job's greatest desire had been for the presence and favor of God; now the thing he dreaded most had happened. God seemed to have forsaken him, and he had no idea why. But Job did not curse God; he still prayed to him for mercy and relief (6:8–9).

4:1 ELIPHAZ THE TEMANITE REPLIED. Ch. 4 begins the first of three major cycles of the dialogues of Eliphaz, Bildad and Zophar with Job himself. When reading these dialogues, note the following: (1) Although the words of Job's three friends are recorded in Scripture, everything they said is not necessarily true. The Holy Spirit recorded their words, but did not inspire them. At the end of the book, God himself stated that much of what they had spoken was not right (42:7–8).

(2) Some of their statements are indeed true and are restated in the NT (e.g., part of what Eliphaz says in 5:13 is found in 1Co 3:19).

(3) The basic theology and viewpoint of these counselors were defective. They believed (a) that the truly righteous will always prosper while sinners always suffer, and (b) conversely, that poverty and suffering always imply sinfulness, while prosperity and success imply righteousness. God later revealed that this attitude was in error and the viewpoint it represented was "folly" (42:7–9).

4:7 WHERE WERE THE UPRIGHT EVER DESTROYED? The theology that the righteous will not perish and the wicked will be punished is true from an eternal viewpoint (see Gal 6:7; Heb 10:13); ultimately, justice will be done. However, here on earth, so often just retribution does not occur and the innocent do suffer. Failure to recognize this truth was a fundamental error in Eliphaz's thinking (e.g., Mt 23:35; Lk 13:4–5; Jn 9:1–3; 1Pe 2:19–20).

4:13 DISQUIETING DREAMS. It is not said that Eliphaz's dreams were from God; in fact, they were not from God, for they described him as unconcerned about humankind (vv. 17–21). It is wrong to build theology on dreams and visions that cannot be supported by God's written revelation.

17'Can a mortal be more righteous
than God?[t]
Can a man be more pure than
his Maker?[u]
18If God places no trust in his
servants,[v]
if he charges his angels with
error,[w]
19how much more those who live in
houses of clay,[x]
whose foundations[y] are in the
dust,[z]
who are crushed[a] more readily
than a moth![b]
20Between dawn and dusk they are
broken to pieces;
unnoticed, they perish forever.[c]
21Are not the cords of their tent
pulled up,[d]
so that they die[e] without
wisdom?'[h][f]

5 "Call if you will, but who will
answer you?[g]
To which of the holy ones[h] will
you turn?
2Resentment[i] kills a fool,
and envy slays the simple.[j]
3I myself have seen[k] a fool taking
root,[l]
but suddenly[m] his house was
cursed.[n]
4His children[o] are far from
safety,[p]
crushed in court[q] without a
defender.[r]
5The hungry consume his harvest,[s]
taking it even from among
thorns,
and the thirsty pant after his
wealth.
6For hardship does not spring from
the soil,
nor does trouble sprout from the
ground.[t]
7Yet man is born to trouble[u]
as surely as sparks fly upward.

8"But if it were I, I would appeal to
God;
I would lay my cause before
him.[v]

4:17 [t]Job 9:2; 13:18; Ps 143:2 [u]Job 8:3; 10:3; 14:4; 15:14; 21:14; 25:4; 31:15; 32:22; 35:10; 36:3,13; 37:23; 40:19; Ps 18:26; 51:5; 119:73; Pr 20:9; Ecc 7:20; Isa 51:13; Mal 2:10; Ac 17:24 **4:18** [v]Heb 1:14 [w]Job 15:15; 21:22; 25:5 **4:19** [x]Job 10:9; 33:6; Isa 64:8; Ro 9:21; 2Co 4:7; 5:1 [y]Job 22:16 [z]S Ge 2:7 [a]Job 5:4 [b]Job 7:17; 15:16; 17:14; 25:6; Ps 22:6; Isa 41:14 **4:20** [c]Job 14:2, 20; 15:33; 20:7; 24:24; Ps 89:47; 90:5-6; Jas 4:14 **4:21** [d]Job 8:22; Isa 38:12 [e]Jn 8:24 [f]Job 18:21; 36:12; Pr 5:23; Jer 9:3 **5:1** [g]Hab 1:2 [h]Job 15:15; Ps 89:5,7 **5:2** [i]Job 21:15; 36:13 [j]Pr 12:16; Gal 5:26 **5:3** [k]S Job 4:8 [l]Ps 37:35; Isa 40:24; Jer 12:2; Eze 17:6 [m]Pr 6:15 [n]Job 24:18; Ps 37:22,35-36; 109:9-10; Pr 3:33 **5:4** [o]Job 20:10; 27:14 [p]S Job 4:11 [q]Job 4:19; Am 5:12 [r]Ps 109:12; Isa 9:17; 1Jn 2:1 **5:5** [s]Lev 26:16; S Jdg 2:15; Job 20:18; 31:8; Mic 6:15 **5:6** [t]S Job 4:8 **5:7** [u]S Ge 3:17; Job 10:17; 15:35; Ps 51:5; 58:3; 90:10; Pr 22:8 **5:8** [v]Job 8:5; 11:13; 13:3,15; 23:4; 40:1; Ps 35:23; 50:15; Jer 12:1; 1Co 4:4 **5:9** [w]Ps 78:4; 111:2 [x]Dt 29:29; Job 9:4,10; 11:7; 25:2; 26:14; 33:12; 36:5,22,26; 37:5,14,16,23; 42:3; Ps 40:5; 71:17; 72:18; 86:10; 131:1; 139:6,17; 145:3; Isa 40:28; Ro 11:33 [y]Ps 71:15

9He performs wonders[w] that cannot
be fathomed,[x]
miracles that cannot be
counted.[y]
10He bestows rain on the earth;[z]
he sends water upon the
countryside.[a]
11The lowly he sets on high,[b]
and those who mourn[c] are
lifted[d] to safety.
12He thwarts the plans[e] of the
crafty,
so that their hands achieve no
success.[f]
13He catches the wise[g] in their
craftiness,[h]
and the schemes of the wily are
swept away.[i]
14Darkness[j] comes upon them in
the daytime;
at noon they grope as in the
night.[k]
15He saves the needy[l] from the
sword in their mouth;
he saves them from the clutches
of the powerful.[m]
16So the poor[n] have hope,
and injustice shuts its mouth.[o]

17"Blessed is the man whom God
corrects;[p]
so do not despise the
discipline[q] of the
Almighty.[i][r]
18For he wounds, but he also binds
up;[s]
he injures, but his hands also
heal.[t]

5:10 [z]Mt 5:45 [a]S Lev 26:4; Job 36:28; 37:6,13; 38:28,34; Ps 135:7; Jer 14:22 **5:11** [b]S 1Sa 2:7-8; S Job 4:7; Ps 75:7; 113:7-8 [c]Isa 61:2; Mt 5:4; Ro 12:15 [d]S Mt 23:12; Jas 4:10 **5:12** [e]Ne 4:15; Ps 33:10; Isa 8:10; 19:3; Jer 19:7 [f]Job 12:23; Ps 78:59; 140:8 **5:13** [g]Job 37:24; Isa 29:14; 44:25; Jer 8:8; 18:18; 51:57 [h]Job 15:5; Ps 36:3; Lk 20:23; 1Co 3:19*; 2Co 11:3; Eph 4:14 [i]Job 9:4; 18:7; Pr 21:30; 29:6; Jer 8:9 **5:14** [j]Job 15:22,30; 18:6,18; 20:26; 22:11; 27:20; Isa 8:22; Jn 12:35 [k]S Dt 28:29; S Job 18:5; Am 8:9 **5:15** [l]S Ex 22:23; Job 8:6; 22:27; 33:26; 36:15 [m]S Job 4:10; S 31:22 **5:16** [n]Job 20:19; 31:16; Pr 17:5; 22:22; Isa 11:4; 41:17; 61:1 [o]Ps 63:11; 107:42; Ro 3:19 **5:17** [p]Dt 8:5; Job 33:19; 36:10; Zep 3:7; Jas 1:12 [q]Ps 94:12; Pr 3:11; Jer 31:18 [r]S Ge 17:1; S Job 15:11; Heb 12:5-11 **5:18** [s]Ps 147:3; Isa 57:15; 61:1; Hos 6:1 [t]S Dt 32:39

[h]*21* Some interpreters end the quotation after verse 17. [i]*17* Hebrew *Shaddai*; here and throughout Job

5:17–27 THE MAN WHOM GOD CORRECTS. To Eliphaz, if God corrects a person and he or she responds rightly, then God will deliver that individual from all calamities. (1) This mistaken idea is contradicted by the author of Hebrews, who declares that some of the greatest OT heroes of faith were persecuted, left destitute, mistreated and even put to death; these righteous people never received total deliverance in this life (Heb 11:36–39). (2) The Bible nowhere teaches that God will eliminate from our lives all trouble and suffering. Godly people are not always rescued in this life.

[19]From six calamities he will
rescue[u] you;
in seven no harm will befall
you.[v]
[20]In famine[w] he will ransom you
from death,
and in battle from the stroke of
the sword.[x]
[21]You will be protected from the
lash of the tongue,[y]
and need not fear[z] when
destruction comes.[a]
[22]You will laugh[b] at destruction and
famine,[c]
and need not fear the beasts of
the earth.[d]
[23]For you will have a covenant[e]
with the stones[f] of the
field,
and the wild animals will be at
peace with you.[g]
[24]You will know that your tent is
secure;[h]
you will take stock of your
property and find nothing
missing.[i]
[25]You will know that your children
will be many,[j]
and your descendants like the
grass of the earth.[k]
[26]You will come to the grave in full
vigor,[l]
like sheaves gathered in
season.[m]
[27]"We have examined this, and it is
true.
So hear it[n] and apply it to
yourself."[o]

Job

6 Then Job replied:

[2]"If only my anguish could be
weighed
and all my misery be placed on
the scales![p]
[3]It would surely outweigh the
sand[q] of the seas—
no wonder my words have been
impetuous.[r]
[4]The arrows[s] of the Almighty[t]
are in me,[u]
my spirit drinks[v] in their
poison;[w]
God's terrors[x] are marshaled
against me.[y]
[5]Does a wild donkey[z] bray[a] when
it has grass,
or an ox bellow when it has
fodder?[b]
[6]Is tasteless food eaten without
salt,
or is there flavor in the white of
an egg[j]?[c]
[7]I refuse to touch it;
such food makes me ill.[d]
[8]"Oh, that I might have my request,
that God would grant what I
hope for,[e]
[9]that God would be willing to
crush[f] me,
to let loose his hand and cut me
off![g]
[10]Then I would still have this
consolation[h]—
my joy in unrelenting pain[i]—
that I had not denied the
words[j] of the Holy One.[k]
[11]"What strength do I have, that I
should still hope?
What prospects, that I should be
patient?[l]
[12]Do I have the strength of stone?
Is my flesh bronze?[m]
[13]Do I have any power to help
myself,[n]
now that success has been
driven from me?

5:19 [u]Da 3:17; 6:16 [v]Ps 34:19; 91:10; Pr 3:25-26; 24:15-16 **5:20** [w]ver 22; Ps 33:19; 37:19 [x]Ps 22:20; 91:7; 140:7; 144:10; Jer 39:18 **5:21** [y]Ps 12:2-4; 31:20 [z]Ps 23:4; 27:1; 91:5 [a]ver 15 **5:22** [b]Job 8:21; 39:7,18,22; 41:29 [c]S ver 20 [d]S Lev 25:18; Ps 91:13; Hos 2:18; Mk 1:13 **5:23** [e]Isa 28:15; Hos 2:18 [f]2Ki 3:19,25; Ps 91:12; Mt 13:8 [g]Job 40:20; Isa 11:6-9; 65:25; Eze 34:25 **5:24** [h]Job 12:6; 21:9 [i]Job 8:6; 22:23 **5:25** [j]Dt 28:4; Ps 112:2 [k]Ps 72:16; Isa 44:3-4; 48:19 **5:26** [l]S Ge 15:15; S Dt 11:21; S Ecc 8:13 [m]Pr 3:21-26 **5:27** [n]Job 32:10, 17 [o]Job 8:5; 11:13; 22:27 **6:2** [p]Job 31:6; Pr 11:1; Da 5:27 **6:3** [q]1Ki 4:29; Pr 27:3 [r]ver 11,26; Job 7:11; 16:6; 21:4; 23:2 **6:4** [s]S Dt 32:23; Ps 38:2 [t]S Ge 17:1 [u]Job 7:20; 16:12, 13; 19:12; La 3:12 [v]Job 21:20 [w]S Dt 32:32; Job 30:21; 34:6; Jer 15:18; 30:12 [x]Job 9:34; 13:21; 18:11; 23:6; 27:20; 30:15; 33:16 [y]S Job 3:23; Ps 88:15-18 **6:5** [z]S Ge 16:12 [a]Job 30:7 [b]Job 24:6; Isa 30:24 **6:6** [c]Job 33:20; Ps 107:18 **6:7** [d]S Job 3:24 **6:8** [e]Job 14:13 **6:9** [f]Job 19:2 [g]S Nu 11:15; S Ps 31:22 **6:10** [h]S Job 2:11; 15:11; Ps 94:19 [i]Ps 38:17; Jer 4:19; 45:3 [j]Job 22:22; 23:12; Ps 119:102; Mk 8:38 [k]S Lev 11:44; S 2Ki 19:22; S Isa 31:1 **6:11** [l]S ver 3 **6:12** [m]Job 26:2 **6:13** [n]Job 26:2

j *6* The meaning of the Hebrew for this phrase is uncertain.

6:4 THE ARROWS OF THE ALMIGHTY ARE IN ME. Job recognized that his suffering ultimately came from God, or at least with God's knowledge and permission. His greatest anguish was this: God seemed to be against him and he did not know why. When you experience hardship while sincerely striving to please God, you must not give in to the thought that God has stopped being concerned for you. You may not know why God is allowing such things to happen, but you can know (as did Job) that in the end God himself will make you strong, firm and steadfast, bringing you through victorious (cf. Ro 8:35–39; Jas 5:11; 1Pe 5:10).

6:10 I HAD NOT DENIED THE WORDS OF THE HOLY ONE. In all his suffering, Job's consolation was that he did not turn from his Lord, nor did he deny his words. Unaware of any conscious or inadvertent sins, he affirmed his innocence throughout the book (see 16:17; 27:6), convinced that he had always sought to honor and obey God. Therefore he could rejoice, even in his pain.

14"A despairing man[o] should have
the devotion[p] of his
friends,[q]
even though he forsakes the fear
of the Almighty.[r]
15But my brothers are as
undependable as
intermittent streams,[s]
as the streams that overflow
16when darkened by thawing ice
and swollen with melting
snow,[t]
17but that cease to flow in the dry
season,
and in the heat[u] vanish from
their channels.
18Caravans turn aside from their
routes;
they go up into the wasteland
and perish.
19The caravans of Tema[v] look for
water,
the traveling merchants of
Sheba[w] look in hope.
20They are distressed, because they
had been confident;
they arrive there, only to be
disappointed.[x]
21Now you too have proved to be of
no help;
you see something dreadful and
are afraid.[y]
22Have I ever said, 'Give something
on my behalf,
pay a ransom[z] for me from
your wealth,[a]
23deliver me from the hand of the
enemy,
ransom me from the clutches of
the ruthless'?[b]

24"Teach me, and I will be quiet;[c]
show me where I have been
wrong.[d]
25How painful are honest words![e]
But what do your arguments
prove?
26Do you mean to correct what I
say,
and treat the words of a
despairing man as wind?[f]
27You would even cast lots[g] for the
fatherless[h]
and barter away your friend.

28"But now be so kind as to look at
me.
Would I lie to your face?[i]
29Relent, do not be unjust;[j]
reconsider, for my integrity[k] is
at stake.[k l]
30Is there any wickedness on my
lips?[m]
Can my mouth not discern[n]
malice?

7 "Does not man have hard
service[o] on earth?[p]
Are not his days like those of a
hired man?[q]
2Like a slave longing for the
evening shadows,[r]
or a hired man waiting eagerly
for his wages,[s]
3so I have been allotted months of
futility,
and nights of misery have been
assigned to me.[t]
4When I lie down I think, 'How long
before I get up?'[u]
The night drags on, and I toss
till dawn.[v]
5My body is clothed with worms[w]
and scabs,
my skin is broken and
festering.[x]

6"My days are swifter than a
weaver's shuttle,[y]
and they come to an end without
hope.[z]
7Remember, O God, that my life is
but a breath;[a]
my eyes will never see
happiness again.[b]
8The eye that now sees me will see
me no longer;
you will look for me, but I will
be no more.[c]
9As a cloud vanishes[d] and is gone,
so he who goes down to the
grave[1e] does not return.[f]
10He will never come to his house
again;

6:14 [o]S Job 4:5 [p]1Sa 20:42; Job 15:4 [q]Job 12:4; 17:2,6; 19:19,21; 21:3; 30:1,10; Ps 38:11; 69:20; 1Jn 3:17 [r]S Ge 17:1 **6:15** [s]Job 13:4; 16:2; 21:34; Ps 22:1; 38:11; Jer 15:18 **6:16** [t]Ps 147:18 **6:17** [u]Job 24:19 **6:19** [v]S Ge 25:15 [w]S Ge 10:7,28 **6:20** [x]Jer 14:3; Joel 1:11 **6:21** [y]Ps 38:11 **6:22** [z]S Nu 35:31; Job 33:24; Ps 49:7 [a]Jer 15:10 **6:23** [b]S 2Ki 19:19 **6:24** [c]S Job 2:10; 33:33; Ps 39:1; 141:3; Pr 10:19; 11:12; 17:27; Ecc 5:2 [d]Job 19:4 **6:25** [e]Ecc 12:11; Isa 22:23 **6:26** [f]S ver 3; S Ge 41:6; Job 8:2; 15:3; 16:3; Jer 5:13 **6:27** [g]Eze 24:6; Joel 3:3; Ob 1:11; Na 3:10 [h]S Ex 22:22,24; Job 31:17,21; Isa 10:2 **6:28** [i]Job 9:15; 24:25; 27:4; 32:10; 33:1,3; 34:6; 36:3,4 **6:29** [j]Job 19:6; 27:2; 40:8; Isa 40:27 [k]S Job 2:3 [l]Job 9:21; 10:7; 11:2; 12:4; 23:7, 10; 33:9,32; 34:5, 36; 35:2; 42:6; Ps 66:10; Zec 13:9 **6:30** [m]Job 27:4 [n]Job 12:11 **7:1** [o]Job 14:14; Isa 40:2 [p]S Job 5:7 [q]S Lev 25:50 **7:2** [r]Job 14:1; Ecc 2:23 [s]S Lev 19:13; S Job 14:6 **7:3** [t]Job 16:7; Ps 6:6; 42:3; 56:8; Ecc 4:1; Isa 16:9; Jer 9:1; La 1:2,16 **7:4** [u]Dt 28:67 [v]ver 13-14 **7:5** [w]Job 17:14; 21:26; 24:20; 25:6; Isa 14:11 [x]S Dt 28:35 **7:6** [y]Job 9:25; Ps 39:5; Isa 38:12 [z]Job 13:15; 14:19; 17:11,15; 19:10; Ps 37:4; 52:9 **7:7** [a]ver 16; Ge 27:46; Ps 39:4, 5,11; 62:9; 78:39; 89:47; 144:4; Ecc 7:15; S Jas 4:14 [b]Job 10:20 **7:8** [c]S Job 3:13; 8:18; 15:29; 20:7,9, 21; 27:17; Ps 37:36; 103:16; Isa 41:12; Jn 16:16; Ac 20:25 **7:9** [d]S Job 3:25 [e]S Job 3:13; 11:8; 14:13; 17:16; 26:6; 38:17; Am 9:2 [f]2Sa 12:23

[k]29 Or *my righteousness still stands*
[1]9 Hebrew *Sheol*

7:1 JOB ADDRESSES GOD. Job turned from his friends, who did not seem to understand, and prayed instead to his Lord. Job's greatest concern throughout all his discourses was with God. Even when he spoke about God in the third person, he was always conscious of his presence. Job's heart never turned from the God he loved.

his place[g] will know him no
more.[h]

11"Therefore I will not keep silent;[i]
I will speak out in the anguish[j]
of my spirit,
I will complain[k] in the
bitterness of my soul.[l]
12Am I the sea,[m] or the monster of
the deep,[n]
that you put me under guard?[o]
13When I think my bed will comfort
me
and my couch will ease my
complaint,[p]
14even then you frighten me with
dreams
and terrify[q] me with visions,[r]
15so that I prefer strangling and
death,[s]
rather than this body of mine.[t]
16I despise my life;[u] I would not
live forever.[v]
Let me alone;[w] my days have
no meaning.[x]

17"What is man that you make so
much of him,
that you give him so much
attention,[y]
18that you examine him every
morning[z]
and test him[a] every moment?[b]
19Will you never look away from
me,[c]
or let me alone even for an
instant?[d]
20If I have sinned, what have I done
to you,[e]
O watcher of men?
Why have you made me your
target?[f]
Have I become a burden to
you?[m][g]
21Why do you not pardon my
offenses
and forgive my sins?[h]
For I will soon lie down in the
dust;[i]
you will search for me, but I will
be no more."[j]

Bildad

8 Then Bildad the Shuhite[k] replied:
2"How long will you say such
things?[l]
Your words are a blustering
wind.[m]
3Does God pervert justice?[n]
Does the Almighty pervert what
is right?[o]
4When your children sinned against
him,
he gave them over to the
penalty of their sin.[p]
5But if you will look to God
and plead[q] with the Almighty,[r]
6if you are pure and upright,

7:10 [g]Job 18:21; 21:18; 27:21,23; Ps 58:9; Jer 18:17; 19:8 [h]S ver 8; Ps 37:10; 104:35 **7:11** [i]Job 9:35; 13:13; Ps 22:2; 40:9 [j]Job 10:1; Ps 6:3; Isa 38:15, 17 [k]ver 13; Job 9:27; 21:4; 23:2 [l]S 1Sa 1:10; S Job 6:3 **7:12** [m]Job 38:8-11 [n]S Ge 1:21 [o]ver 20; Isa 1:14 **7:13** [p]S ver 11 **7:14** [q]Job 9:34 [r]S Ge 41:8; S Job 3:26 **7:15** [s]1Ki 19:4; Jnh 4:3 [t]Job 6:9; Rev 9:6 **7:16** [u]S 1Ki 19:4; Job 9:21 [v]S Job 3:22 [w]ver 19; Job 10:20; Ps 39:13 [x]S ver 7 **7:17** [y]S Job 4:19; 22:2; Ps 8:4; 144:3; Heb 2:6 **7:18** [z]Ps 73:14 [a]Job 23:10; Ps 139:23 [b]Job 14:3; Ps 17:3; 26:2; 66:10; 139:1-6; 143:2 **7:19** [c]S ver 16 [d]Job 9:18; 13:26; 14:6; 27:2; Ps 139:7 **7:20** [e]Job 35:6; Jer 7:19 [f]S Job 6:4 [g]S ver 12 **7:21** [h]Job 9:28; 10:14; 16:6; Ps 119:120; Isa 43:25; Jer 31:34; Heb 1:3 [i]S Ge 3:19; Job 10:9; 34:15; Ps 7:5; 22:15; 90:3; 104:29 [j]S ver 8; S Job 3:13 **8:1** [k]S Ge 25:2; Job 18:1; 25:1 **8:2** [l]Job 11:2; 18:2 [m]S 2Ch 36:16; S Job 6:26 **8:3** [n]S Job 4:17; 34:12; Isa 29:15; Ro 3:5 [o]S Ge 18:25; S Jer 12:1 **8:4** [p]Job 1:19 **8:5** [q]Job 9:15 [r]S Job 5:8,27

m *20* A few manuscripts of the Masoretic Text, an ancient Hebrew scribal tradition and Septuagint; most manuscripts of the Masoretic Text *I have become a burden to myself.*

7:11 THE ANGUISH OF MY SPIRIT. Job often spoke of the anguish and bitterness of his spirit and soul (cf. 10:1; 27:2). He had become a man who suffered deeply in every aspect of life. (1) Physically he had lost wealth, children and health (1:13–19; 2:7–8). (2) Socially he was alienated from his friends and family (2:7–8; 19:13–19). He was scorned by the public (16:10; 30:1–10) and betrayed by his closest friends (6:14–23). (3) Spiritually he felt forsaken by God, believing that the Lord had turned against him (vv. 17–19; 6:4). (4) Afflicted in every possible way, Job experienced a wide range of emotions: anxiety (vv. 4,13–14), uncertainty (9:20), rejection and betrayal (10:3; 12:4), fear (6:4; 9:28), loneliness (19:13–19) and despair that led to a desire for death (ch. 3).

7:16 LET ME ALONE. Job spoke honestly to God about his feelings of unfairness, rejection and doubt. He even wished that God would leave him alone (vv. 16–19), though at other times he yearned for God to speak with him (14:15; 23:3,5). The faithful who are undergoing severe trials and suffering should express their feelings openly to God in prayer. Speaking from the heart to God about our anguish and bitterness in an attitude of submission is not wrong. Hannah poured out her soul before the Lord because of great concern and provocation (1Sa 1:13–16). Jesus himself offered up "prayers and petitions with loud cries and tears" (Heb 5:7), and at his death he experienced the indescribable darkness of separation from God (Mt 27:46).

7:20 IF I HAVE SINNED. Job considered the possibility that his counselors were right, that God had directed his anger toward him because of some unknown transgression. What Job did not know was that God was indeed watching, not in displeasure, but in compassion and admiration. Though tempted to the limit, Job consistently refused to curse God (cf. 2:9), and thus God's redemptive power was exalted. In due time, when the test was finished, God revealed his approval publicly (42:8).

8:6 IF YOU ARE PURE AND UPRIGHT. Bildad's argument was essentially the same as Eliphaz's. If Job were really upright, he would be

even now he will rouse himself
on your behalf[s]
and restore you to your rightful
place.[t]
7Your beginnings will seem humble,
so prosperous[u] will your future
be.[v]

8"Ask the former generations[w]
and find out what their fathers
learned,
9for we were born only yesterday
and know nothing,[x]
and our days on earth are but a
shadow.[y]
10Will they not instruct[z] you and
tell you?
Will they not bring forth words
from their understanding?[a]
11Can papyrus grow tall where there
is no marsh?[b]
Can reeds[c] thrive without
water?
12While still growing and uncut,
they wither more quickly than
grass.[d]
13Such is the destiny[e] of all who
forget God;[f]
so perishes the hope of the
godless.[g]
14What he trusts in is fragile[n];
what he relies on is a spider's
web.[h]
15He leans on his web,[i] but it gives
way;
he clings to it, but it does not
hold.[j]
16He is like a well-watered plant in
the sunshine,
spreading its shoots[k] over the
garden;[l]
17it entwines its roots around a pile
of rocks
and looks for a place among the
stones.
18But when it is torn from its spot,
that place disowns[m] it and says,
'I never saw you.'[n]
19Surely its life withers[o] away,
and[o] from the soil other plants
grow.[p]
20"Surely God does not reject a
blameless[q] man
or strengthen the hands of
evildoers.[r]
21He will yet fill your mouth with
laughter[s]
and your lips with shouts of
joy.[t]
22Your enemies will be clothed in
shame,[u]
and the tents[v] of the wicked
will be no more."[w]

Job

9 Then Job replied:

2"Indeed, I know that this is
true.
But how can a mortal be
righteous before God?[x]
3Though one wished to dispute with
him,[y]
he could not answer him one
time out of a thousand.[z]
4His wisdom[a] is profound, his
power is vast.[b]
Who has resisted[c] him and
come out unscathed?[d]
5He moves mountains[e] without
their knowing it
and overturns them in his
anger.[f]
6He shakes the earth[g] from its
place
and makes its pillars tremble.[h]

8:6 [s] S Job 5:15; 22:27; 33:26; 34:28; Isa 58:9; 65:24 [t] S Job 5:24 **8:7** [u] Job 21:13; 22:21; 36:11; Ps 25:13 [v] S Job 1:10; Jer 29:11; 31:17 **8:8** [w] S Dt 32:7; S Ps 71:18 **8:9** [x] S Ge 47:9 [y] S 1Ch 29:15; S 2Ch 10:6; S Ps 39:6 **8:10** [z] Pr 1:8 [a] Pr 2:1-2; 4:1 **8:11** [b] Job 40:21 [c] S Ex 2:3; Isa 19:6; 35:7 **8:12** [d] ver 19; S 2Ki 19:26; Job 18:16; 20:5; Ps 90:5-6; 102:11; Isa 34:4; 40:7,24 **8:13** [e] Ps 37:38; 73:17 [f] Ps 9:17; 50:22; Isa 51:13; Jer 17:6 [g] Job 6:9; 11:20; 13:16; 15:34; 20:5; 27:8; 34:30; Ps 37:1-2; 112:10; Pr 10:28; 11:7; Jer 15:9 **8:14** [h] ver 15; Job 27:18; Isa 59:5 **8:15** [i] S ver 14 [j] Ps 49:11; Mt 7:26-27 **8:16** [k] Ps 80:11; Isa 16:8 [l] Ps 37:35; Jer 11:16 **8:18** [m] Job 20:9; Ps 103:16 [n] S Job 7:8; S 14:20 **8:19** [o] S ver 12; S Job 15:30 [p] Ps 119:90; Ecc 1:4 **8:20** [q] Job 1:1 [r] S Ge 18:25 **8:21** [s] S Job 5:22 [t] S Ezr 3:13; Job 35:10; Ps 47:5; 107:22; 118:15; 126:2; 132:16; Isa 35:6 **8:22** [u] Job 27:7; Ps 6:10; 35:26; 44:7; 53:5; 71:13; 86:17; 109:29; 132:18; Eze 7:27; 26:16 [v] S Job 4:21 [w] S 1Sa 8:3; Job 18:6,14,21; 21:28; 27:8,18; 34:26; 36:6; 38:13; Ps 52:5; Pr 14:11 **9:2** [x] S Job 4:17; Ro 3:20 **9:3** [y] ver 32; Job 40:5 [z] ver 12,14,29,32; Job 10:2; 12:14; 13:9,14; 22:4; 23:7,13; 37:19; 40:2; Ps 44:21; Isa 14:24 **9:4** [a] Job 11:6; 28:12,20,23; 38:36; Ps 51:6; Pr 2:6; Ecc 2:26 [b] ver 19; S Job 5:9; 12:13,16; 23:6; 24:22; 26:12; 30:18; Ps 93:4; 95:3; Pr 8:14; Isa 40:26; 63:1; Da 2:20; 4:35 [c] Jer 50:24 [d] S 2Ch 13:12; S Job 5:13 **9:5** [e] Mt 17:20 [f] Ps 18:7; 46:2-3; Isa 13:13; Mic 1:4 **9:6** [g] S Ex 19:18; Isa 2:21; 13:13; 24:18-20; Am 8:8; Heb 12:26 [h] S 2Sa 22:8; Job 26:14; 36:29; 37:4-5; Ps 75:3; Hab 3:4

[n] *14* The meaning of the Hebrew for this word is uncertain. [o] *19* Or *Surely all the joy it has / is that*

vindicated by God. Job was not vindicated by God; therefore he must be wicked. Bildad based his argument on his belief that because God was just, he would not bring trouble on a righteous individual (vv. 3–4,20). Bildad's error was exposed later by God himself (42:7–8) — and ultimately in Christ's crucifixion, when God delivered his own Son over to suffering and death (Mt 27:31–50).

9:2 BE RIGHTEOUS BEFORE GOD? In ch. 9 Job acknowledged that he could not be perfectly righteous before God. He understood that by nature he was inclined toward self and sin and that he was not faultless in God's sight (cf. 7:21). Yet, with all his heart and soul he had resisted evil and turned from it (1:1,8; 2:3); he was confident he had not sinned greatly and thus did not deserve such suffering (6:24; 7:20). Thus Job complained that God had punished him without cause (vv. 16–20). Yet his faith still held firm, for he persisted in calling on God (see 10:2,8–12; cf. Jas 5:11). He did not curse God as Satan predicted he would (1:11; 2:5), although he did speak words he would later regret (vv. 17,20,22–23,30–31; 42:3–6).

7He speaks to the sun and it does not shine;[i]
he seals off the light of the stars.[j]
8He alone stretches out the heavens[k]
and treads on the waves of the sea.[l]
9He is the Maker[m] of the Bear and Orion,
the Pleiades and the constellations of the south.[n]
10He performs wonders[o] that cannot be fathomed,
miracles that cannot be counted.[p]
11When he passes me, I cannot see him;
when he goes by, I cannot perceive him.[q]
12If he snatches away, who can stop him?[r]
Who can say to him, 'What are you doing?'[s]
13God does not restrain his anger;[t]
even the cohorts of Rahab[u] cowered at his feet.

14"How then can I dispute with him?
How can I find words to argue with him?[v]
15Though I were innocent, I could not answer him;[w]
I could only plead[x] with my Judge[y] for mercy.[z]
16Even if I summoned him and he responded,
I do not believe he would give me a hearing.[a]
17He would crush me[b] with a storm[c]
and multiply[d] my wounds for no reason.[e]
18He would not let me regain my breath
but would overwhelm me with misery.[f]
19If it is a matter of strength, he is mighty![g]
And if it is a matter of justice, who will summon him[p]?[h]
20Even if I were innocent, my mouth would condemn me;
if I were blameless, it would pronounce me guilty.[i]
21"Although I am blameless,[j]
I have no concern for myself;[k]
I despise my own life.[l]
22It is all the same; that is why I say,
'He destroys both the blameless and the wicked.'[m]
23When a scourge[n] brings sudden death,
he mocks the despair of the innocent.[o]
24When a land falls into the hands of the wicked,[p]
he blindfolds its judges.[q]
If it is not he, then who is it?[r]

25"My days are swifter than a runner;[s]
they fly away without a glimpse of joy.[t]
26They skim past[u] like boats of papyrus,[v]
like eagles swooping down on their prey.[w]
27If I say, 'I will forget my complaint,[x]
I will change my expression, and smile,'
28I still dread[y] all my sufferings,
for I know you will not hold me innocent.[z]
29Since I am already found guilty,
why should I struggle in vain?[a]
30Even if I washed myself with soap[q][b]
and my hands[c] with washing soda,[d]
31you would plunge me into a slime pit[e]
so that even my clothes would detest me.[f]

9:7 [i] Isa 34:4; Jer 4:28; Joel 2:2, 10,31; 3:15; Zep 1:15; Zec 14:6 [j] Isa 13:10; Jer 4:23; Eze 32:8 **9:8** [k] S Ge 1:1,8; S Isa 48:13 [l] Job 38:16; Ps 77:19; Pr 8:28; Hab 3:15; Mt 14:25; Mk 6:48; Jn 6:19 **9:9** [m] Job 32:22; 40:15,19 [n] S Ge 1:16 **9:10** [o] Dt 6:22; Ps 72:18; 136:4; Jer 32:20 [p] S Job 5:9 **9:11** [q] Job 23:8-9; 35:14 **9:12** [r] Nu 23:20; Job 11:10; Isa 14:27; 43:13 [s] S ver 3; S Dt 32:39; Isa 29:16; 45:9; Da 2:21; 4:32; Ro 9:20 **9:13** [t] Nu 14:18; Job 10:15; Ps 78:38; Isa 3:11; 6:5; 48:9 [u] Job 26:12; Ps 87:4; 89:10; Isa 30:7; 51:9 **9:14** [v] S ver 3 **9:15** [w] Job 10:15; 13:19; 34:5-6; 40:5; 42:7 [x] Job 8:5 [y] S Ge 18:25; 1Sa 24:12; Ps 50:6; 96:13 [z] ver 20,29; Job 15:6; 23:4; 40:2 **9:16** [a] Job 13:22; Ro 9:20-21 **9:17** [b] Job 16:12; 30:16; Ps 10:10; Isa 38:13 [c] Job 30:22; Ps 83:15; Jnh 1:4 [d] Job 16:14 [e] S Job 2:3 **9:18** [f] S Job 7:19; S 10:1 **9:19** [g] S ver 4; S Ne 9:32 [h] ver 33; Jer 49:19 **9:20** [i] S ver 15 **9:21** [j] S Ge 6:9; Job 34:6,7 [k] ver 14; S Job 6:29; 10:1; 13:13 [l] S Nu 11:15; S Job 7:16 **9:22** [m] S Job 3:19; 10:8; Ecc 9:2,3; Eze 21:3 **9:23** [n] Heb 11:36 [o] Job 24:1,12; Ps 64:4; Hab 1:3; 1Pe 1:7 **9:24** [p] Job 1:15, 17; 10:3; 16:11; 21:16; 22:18; 27:2; 40:8; Ps 73:3 [q] S Job 3:14; 12:6; 19:7; 21:7; 24:23; 31:35; 35:15; Ps 73:12; Ecc 8:11; Jer 12:1; La 3:9 [r] Job 12:9; 13:1; 24:12; Isa 41:20 **9:25** [s] S Job 7:6 [t] Job 7:7; 10:20 **9:26** [u] Job 24:18; Ps 46:3 [v] Isa 18:2 [w] Job 39:29; Hab 1:8 **9:27** [x] S Job 7:11 **9:28** [y] S Job 3:25 [z] S Ex 34:7; S Job 7:21 **9:29** [a] S ver 3,S 15; Ps 37:33 **9:30** [b] Mal 3:2 [c] Job 17:9; 31:7; Isa 1:15 [d] Job 14:4,17; 33:9; Isa 1:18; Jer 2:22; Hos 13:12 **9:31** [e] Ps 35:7; 40:2; 51:9; Jer 2:22; Na 3:6; Mal 2:3 [f] S Job 7:20; 34:9; 35:3; Ps 73:13

p *19* See Septuagint; Hebrew *me.* q *30* Or *snow*

9:17 MULTIPLY MY WOUNDS FOR NO REASON. The most difficult thing for Job to accept was God's continuing silence in the midst of a painful situation that seemed to have no purpose. God will sometimes allow us to pass through a dark time of trial when he himself remains silent and seemingly far away. Yet even in the midst of the darkness of God's silence, he has a plan for our lives, and we must continue to trust him.

32"He is not a man[g] like me that I
might answer him,[h]
that we might confront each
other in court.[i]
33If only there were someone to
arbitrate between us,[j]
to lay his hand upon us both,[k]
34someone to remove God's rod from
me,[l]
so that his terror would frighten
me no more.[m]
35Then I would speak up without
fear of him,[n]
but as it now stands with me, I
cannot.[o]

10 "I loathe my very life;[p]
therefore I will give free rein
to my complaint
and speak out in the bitterness
of my soul.[q]
2I will say to God:[r] Do not
condemn me,
but tell me what charges[s] you
have against me.[t]
3Does it please you to oppress
me,[u]
to spurn the work of your
hands,[v]
while you smile on the schemes
of the wicked?[w]
4Do you have eyes of flesh?
Do you see as a mortal sees?[x]
5Are your days like those of a
mortal
or your years like those of a
man,[y]
6that you must search out my faults
and probe after my sin[z]—
7though you know that I am not
guilty[a]
and that no one can rescue me
from your hand?[b]
8"Your hands shaped[c] me and
made me.
Will you now turn and destroy
me?[d]
9Remember that you molded me
like clay.[e]
Will you now turn me to dust
again?[f]
10Did you not pour me out like milk
and curdle me like cheese,
11clothe me with skin and flesh
and knit me together[g] with
bones and sinews?
12You gave me life[h] and showed me
kindness,[i]
and in your providence[j]
watched over[k] my spirit.

13"But this is what you concealed in
your heart,
and I know that this was in your
mind:[l]
14If I sinned, you would be watching
me[m]
and would not let my offense go
unpunished.[n]
15If I am guilty[o]—woe to me![p]
Even if I am innocent, I cannot
lift my head,[q]
for I am full of shame
and drowned in[r] my affliction.[r]
16If I hold my head high, you stalk
me like a lion[s]

9:32 [g]S Nu 23:19 [h]S ver 3; Ro 9:20 [i]Ps 143:2; Ecc 6:10 9:33 [j]S 1Sa 2:25 [k]S ver 19 9:34 [l]Job 21:9; Ps 39:10; 73:5 [m]S Job 6:4; 7:14; 33:7; Ps 32:4 9:35 [n]S Job 7:11 [o]Job 7:15; 13:21 10:1 [p]S Nu 11:15; S 1Ki 19:4 [q]S 1Sa 1:10; S Job 7:11; 9:18, 21 10:2 [r]Job 13:3; 40:1 [s]Isa 3:13; Hos 4:1; 5:1; 12:2; Mic 6:2; Ro 8:33 [t]S Job 9:3 10:3 [u]S Job 9:22; 16:9,14; 19:6,21; 22:10; 30:13,21; 31:23; 34:6 [v]ver 8; Ge 1:26; S Job 4:17; 14:15; 34:19; Ps 8:6; 95:6; 100:3; 138:8; 149:2; Isa 60:21; 64:8 [w]S Job 9:24 10:4 [x]1Sa 16:7; Job 11:11; 14:16; 24:23; 28:24; 31:4; 34:21; 41:11; Ps 11:4; 33:15; 119:168; 139:12; Pr 5:21; 15:3; Jer 11:20-23; 16:17 10:5 [y]Job 36:26; Ps 39:5; 90:2,4; 102:24; 2Pe 3:8 10:6 [z]Job 14:16 10:7 [a]ver 15; S Job 6:29; 11:4; 16:17; 27:5,6; 31:6; 32:1 [b]S Dt 32:39 10:8 [c]Ge 2:7 [d]S ver 3; S 2Sa 14:14; S Job 30:15 10:9 [e]S Job 4:19; Isa 29:16 [f]S Ge 2:7; S Job 7:21 10:11 [g]Ps 139:13,15 10:12 [h]S Ge 2:7 [i]S Ge 24:12 [j]S Ge 45:5 [k]1Pe 2:25 10:13 [l]Job 23:13; Ps 115:3 10:14 [m]Job 13:27 [n]S Ex 34:7; S Job 7:21 10:15 [o]S ver 7 [p]S Job 9:13 [q]S Job 9:15 [r]Ps 25:16 10:16 [s]S 1Sa 17:34; Ps 7:2; Isa 38:13; Jer 5:6; 25:38; La 3:10; Hos 5:14; 13:7

[r]15 Or *and aware of*

9:33 SOMEONE TO ARBITRATE BETWEEN US. Job saw the need for a mediator who could lay one hand on him and the other hand on God and bring them together. Jesus Christ became such a mediator, for by his death and resurrection he restores us to fellowship with God (1Ti 2:5; Heb 9:15).

10:1 IN THE BITTERNESS OF MY SOUL. In ch. 10 Job continued pouring out to God his bitterness and feelings of being treated unfairly. But even though Job felt that God had withdrawn his love from him, he still maintained a trust in God's justice and continued to wrestle with God for a solution to his dilemma.

10:2 WHAT CHARGES YOU HAVE AGAINST ME. In none of Job's prayers did he pray for healing of his body. Job's greatest concern was the "why" of his suffering and of God's apparent abandonment of his servant; to know this was more important to Job than his actual adversity. Being accepted by God as one of his own, even in adversity, was the most critical thing in his life.

10:16 YOU STALK ME LIKE A LION. Because Job was experiencing severe affliction, he felt that God was against him. The NT gives a more complete revelation about hardship, with the result that the believer can even glory in suffering. (1) Paul wrote to the Corinthians, "We were under great pressure, far beyond our ability to endure, so that we despaired even of life" (2Co 1:8). Yet in his hardships the apostle praised God because his presence and Spirit were with him to comfort him (2Co 1:3–4,22). The foremost glory of Paul's suffering, however, was that in some way he was sharing "the sufferings of Christ" (2Co 1:5; cf. 2Co 4:10; Php 3:10; Col 1:24; 1Pe 4:13).

(2) All the great saints of God have experienced the Scriptural truth that being one with God and his kingdom and being committed to his ways and standards do not necessarily entail deliverance

and again display your awesome
power against me.[t]
17You bring new witnesses against
me[u]
and increase your anger toward
me;[v]
your forces come against me
wave upon wave.[w]

18"Why then did you bring me out of
the womb?[x]
I wish I had died before any eye
saw me.[y]
19If only I had never come into
being,
or had been carried straight
from the womb to the
grave![z]
20Are not my few days[a] almost
over?[b]
Turn away from me[c] so I can
have a moment's joy[d]
21before I go to the place of no
return,[e]
to the land of gloom and deep
shadow,[s][f]
22to the land of deepest night,
of deep shadow[g] and disorder,
where even the light is like
darkness."[h]

Zophar

11

Then Zophar the Naamathite[i]
replied:

2"Are all these words to go
unanswered?[j]
Is this talker to be vindicated?[k]
3Will your idle talk[l] reduce men to
silence?
Will no one rebuke you when
you mock?[m]
4You say to God, 'My beliefs are
flawless[n]
and I am pure[o] in your sight.'
5Oh, how I wish that God would
speak,[p]
that he would open his lips
against you
6and disclose to you the secrets of
wisdom,[q]
for true wisdom has two sides.
Know this: God has even
forgotten some of your
sin.[r]

7"Can you fathom[s] the mysteries of
God?
Can you probe the limits of the
Almighty?
8They are higher[t] than the
heavens[u]—what can you
do?
They are deeper than the depths
of the grave[t][v]—what can
you know?[w]
9Their measure[x] is longer than the
earth
and wider than the sea.[y]

10"If he comes along and confines
you in prison
and convenes a court, who can
oppose him?[z]
11Surely he recognizes deceitful
men;
and when he sees evil, does he
not take note?[a]
12But a witless man can no more
become wise
than a wild donkey's colt[b] can
be born a man.[u][c]

13"Yet if you devote your heart[d] to
him
and stretch out your hands[e] to
him,[f]
14if you put away[g] the sin that is in
your hand
and allow no evil[h] to dwell in
your tent,[i]
15then you will lift up your face[j]
without shame;
you will stand firm[k] and
without fear.[l]
16You will surely forget your
trouble,[m]

10:16 [t]Job 5:9; Isa 28:21; 29:14; 65:7 **10:17** [u]1Ki 21:10; Job 16:8 [v]Ru 1:21 [w]S Job 5:7 **10:18** [x]S Job 3:8; S Ps 22:9 [y]Job 3:26; Ecc 4:2; 7:1 **10:19** [z]S Job 3:3; Jer 15:10 **10:20** [a]Job 14:1; Ecc 6:12 [b]S Job 7:7 [c]S Job 7:16 [d]S Job 9:25 **10:21** [e]S 2Sa 12:23; S Job 3:13; 16:22; Ps 39:13; Ecc 12:5 [f]S Job 3:5 **10:22** [g]S Job 3:5 [h]S 1Sa 2:9; S Job 3:13 **11:1** [i]S Job 2:11 **11:2** [j]S Job 8:2; S 16:3 [k]S Ge 41:6; S Job 6:29 **11:3** [l]Eph 4:29; 5:4 [m]Job 12:4; 16:10; 17:2; 21:3; 30:1; Ps 1:1 **11:4** [n]Job 9:21 [o]S Job 10:7 **11:5** [p]Ex 20:19; Job 23:5; 32:13; 38:1 **11:6** [q]S Job 9:4; 1Co 2:10 [r]S Ezr 9:13; S Job 15:5 **11:7** [s]S Job 5:9; Ecc 3:11 **11:8** [t]Eph 3:18 [u]S Ge 15:5; Job 22:12; 25:2; Ps 57:10; Isa 55:9 [v]S Job 7:9 [w]Job 15:13,25; 33:13; 40:2; Ps 139:8 **11:9** [x]Eph 3:19-20 [y]Job 22:12; 35:5; 36:26; 37:5,23; Isa 40:26 **11:10** [z]S Job 9:12; Rev 3:7 **11:11** [a]S Job 10:4; 31:37; 34:11,25; 36:7; Ps 10:14 **11:12** [b]S Ge 16:12 [c]S 2Ch 6:36 **11:13** [d]1Sa 7:3; Ps 78:8 [e]S Ex 9:29 [f]S Job 5:8,27 **11:14** [g]S Jos 24:14 [h]Ps 101:4 [i]Job 22:23 **11:15** [j]Job 22:26 [k]S 1Sa 2:9; Ps 20:8; 37:23; 40:2; 119:5; Eph 6:14 [l]S Ge 4:7; S Ps 3:6 **11:16** [m]Isa 26:16; 37:3; 65:16

[s]*21* Or *and the shadow of death*; also in verse 22 [t]*8* Hebrew *than Sheol* [u]*12* Or *wild donkey can be born tame*

from earthly suffering, but deliverance *for* earthly suffering with Christ (see Heb 13:12–13; Jas 5:10–11; 1Pe 2:21; 4:1).

11:1 ZOPHAR. Zophar harshly accused Job of self-righteousness (vv. 4–6) and stubbornness (vv. 13–20), telling him that he deserved to suffer even more than he had (v. 6). He maintained that if Job would turn from sin, his sufferings would immediately cease, and security, prosperity and happiness would return (vv. 13–19). Zophar's speech contained serious theological error. The Bible nowhere guarantees a life "brighter than noonday" (v. 17) for the faithful believer. Rather, "we must go through many hardships to enter the kingdom of God" (Ac 14:22).

recalling it only as waters gone
by.[n]
17Life will be brighter than
noonday,[o]
and darkness will become like
morning.[p]
18You will be secure, because there
is hope;
you will look about you and take
your rest[q] in safety.[r]
19You will lie down, with no one to
make you afraid,[s]
and many will court your
favor.[t]
20But the eyes of the wicked will
fail,[u]
and escape will elude them;[v]
their hope will become a dying
gasp."[w]

Job

12 Then Job replied:
2"Doubtless you are the
people,
and wisdom will die with you![x]
3But I have a mind as well as you;
I am not inferior to you.
Who does not know all these
things?[y]

4"I have become a laughingstock[z]
to my friends,[a]
though I called upon God and he
answered[b]—
a mere laughingstock, though
righteous and blameless![c]
5Men at ease have contempt[d] for
misfortune
as the fate of those whose feet
are slipping.[e]
6The tents of marauders are
undisturbed,[f]
and those who provoke God are
secure[g]—
those who carry their god in
their hands.[v]

7"But ask the animals, and they
will teach you,[h]
or the birds of the air,[i] and
they will tell you;[j]
8or speak to the earth, and it will
teach you,
or let the fish of the sea inform
you.
9Which of all these does not know[k]
that the hand of the LORD has
done this?[l]
10In his hand is the life[m] of every
creature
and the breath of all mankind.[n]
11Does not the ear test words
as the tongue tastes food?[o]
12Is not wisdom found among the
aged?[p]
Does not long life bring
understanding?[q]
13"To God belong wisdom[r] and
power;[s]
counsel and understanding are
his.[t]
14What he tears down[u] cannot be
rebuilt;[v]
the man he imprisons cannot be
released.[w]
15If he holds back the waters,[x]
there is drought;[y]

11:16 [n] Jos 7:5; Job 22:11; Ps 58:7; 112:10; Eze 21:7 **11:17** [o] Job 22:28; Ps 37:6; Isa 58:8, 10; 62:1 [p] Job 17:12; 18:6; 29:3; Ps 18:28; 112:4; 119:105; Isa 5:20; Jn 8:12 **11:18** [q] Ps 3:5; 4:8; 127:2; Ecc 5:12 [r] S Lev 26:6; Pr 3:24; Isa 11:10; 14:3; 28:12; 30:15; 32:18; Zec 3:10 **11:19** [s] S Lev 26:6 [t] Isa 45:14 **11:20** [u] Dt 28:65; Job 17:5 [v] Job 12:10; 18:18; 27:22; 34:22; 36:6; Ps 139:11-12; Jer 11:11; 23:24; 25:35; Am 2:14; 9:2-3 [w] S Job 8:13 **12:2** [x] Job 15:8; 17:10 **12:3** [y] Job 13:2; 15:9 **12:4** [z] S Ge 38:23 [a] S Job 6:14; S 11:3; S 16:10; S 19:14 [b] Ps 91:15 [c] S Ge 6:9; S Job 6:29; S 15:16 **12:5** [d] Ps 123:4 [e] Ps 17:5; 37:31; 38:16; 66:9; 73:2; 94:18 **12:6** [f] S Job 5:24 [g] S Job 9:24 **12:7** [h] Job 35:11 *fn* [i] Mt 6:26 [j] Job 18:3; Ro 1:20 **12:9** [k] Isa 1:3 [l] S Job 9:24 **12:10** [m] Da 5:23 [n] S Ge 2:7; S Nu 16:22; S Job 11:20; Ac 17:28 **12:11** [o] Job 34:3 **12:12** [p] S 1Ki 4:2; Job 15:10 [q] ver 20; Job 17:4; 32:7,9; 34:4,10

12:13 [r] Pr 21:30; Isa 45:9 [s] S Job 9:4; S Jer 32:19; 1Co 1:24 [t] S Nu 23:19; 1Ki 3:12; Job 32:8; 38:36; Pr 2:6; Isa 40:13-14; Da 1:17 **12:14** [u] Job 16:9; 19:10 [v] Dt 13:16; Ps 127:1; Isa 24:20; 25:2; Eze 26:14 [w] S Job 9:3; Isa 22:22; Rev 3:7 **12:15** [x] Job 28:25; Isa 40:12 [y] S Dt 28:22; S 1Ki 17:1

[v] 6 Or *secure / in what God's hand brings them*

12:5 MEN AT EASE HAVE CONTEMPT. Job condemned the way prosperous people often think. In contempt they look down on the poor and needy and justify their lack of sympathy by assuming that the unfortunate have brought adversity on themselves. At the same time the prosperous are "at ease" with their own lifestyle because they believe God has rewarded them for their faith and righteousness. Both assumptions are erroneous, for there are numerous exceptions among those who are citizens of God's kingdom.

12:13 TO GOD BELONG WISDOM AND POWER. We must believe that God is wise and powerful and that his ways with us are the best and the surest means of attaining our highest good (cf. 9:4; 36:5; Isa 40:26,28; Da 2:20; Ro 16:25,27; see Ro 8:28, note). (1) Believers must never think that God has promised a trouble-free life (cf. Ps 34:19). God may send both joy and sorrow in order to detach our love from the things of this world and attach it to himself.

(2) God directs events in a committed believer's life for the purpose of personal sanctification and the fulfilling of his or her service in the kingdom of God (cf. Jacob in Ge 28—35; Joseph in Ge 37:28, see note; see article on THE PROVIDENCE OF GOD, p. 78).

(3) In this life believers can never completely discern the ultimate purpose of everything that happens to them, nor will it always be perfectly clear how God is working in all things for good (Ecc 3:11; 7:13; 11:5; Ro 8:28). During those times when we cannot fully understand God's method of dealing with us, we should commit ourselves to our heavenly Father, just as Christ did on the day of his crucifixion (cf. Mt 27:46; Lk 23:46).

if he lets them loose, they
devastate the land.[z]
16 To him belong strength and
victory;[a]
both deceived and deceiver are
his.[b]
17 He leads counselors away
stripped[c]
and makes fools of judges.[d]
18 He takes off the shackles[e] put on
by kings
and ties a loincloth[w] around
their waist.[f]
19 He leads priests away stripped[g]
and overthrows men long
established.[h]
20 He silences the lips of trusted
advisers
and takes away the discernment
of elders.[i]
21 He pours contempt on nobles[j]
and disarms the mighty.[k]
22 He reveals the deep things of
darkness[l]
and brings deep shadows[m] into
the light.[n]
23 He makes nations great, and
destroys them;[o]
he enlarges nations,[p] and
disperses them.[q]
24 He deprives the leaders of the
earth of their reason;[r]
he sends them wandering
through a trackless
waste.[s]
25 They grope in darkness with no
light;[t]
he makes them stagger like
drunkards.[u]

13

"My eyes have seen all this,[v]
my ears have heard and
understood it.
2 What you know, I also know;
I am not inferior to you.[w]
3 But I desire to speak to the
Almighty[x]
and to argue my case with
God.[y]
4 You, however, smear me with
lies;[z]
you are worthless physicians,[a]
all of you![b]
5 If only you would be altogether
silent![c]
For you, that would be
wisdom.[d]
6 Hear now my argument;
listen to the plea of my lips.[e]
7 Will you speak wickedly on God's
behalf?
Will you speak deceitfully for
him?[f]
8 Will you show him partiality?[g]
Will you argue the case for God?
9 Would it turn out well if he
examined you?[h]
Could you deceive him as you
might deceive men?[i]
10 He would surely rebuke you
if you secretly showed
partiality.[j]
11 Would not his splendor[k] terrify
you?
Would not the dread of him fall
on you?[l]
12 Your maxims are proverbs of
ashes;
your defenses are defenses of
clay.[m]
13 "Keep silent[n] and let me speak;[o]
then let come to me what
may.[p]
14 Why do I put myself in jeopardy
and take my life in my hands?[q]
15 Though he slay me, yet will I
hope[r] in him;[s]
I will surely[x] defend my ways
to his face.[t]
16 Indeed, this will turn out for my
deliverance,[u]
for no godless[v] man would dare
come before him![w]
17 Listen carefully to my words;[x]
let your ears take in what I say.
18 Now that I have prepared my
case,[y]

12:15 [z] S Ge 7:24 **12:16** [a] S Job 9:4 [b] 2Ch 18:22; Job 13:7,9; 27:4; Ro 2:11 **12:17** [c] ver 19; Job 19:9; Isa 20:4 [d] S Job 3:14; 1Co 1:20 **12:18** [e] Ps 107:14; 116:16; Na 1:13 [f] ver 21; Job 34:18; Ps 107:40; Isa 5:27; 40:23 **12:19** [g] S ver 17 [h] S Dt 24:15; S Job 9:24; 14:20; 22:8; 24:12,22; 34:20,28; 35:9; Isa 2:22; 31:8; 40:17,23; Jer 25:18; Da 2:21,34; Lk 1:52 **12:20** [i] S ver 12, 24; Da 4:33-34 **12:21** [j] S ver 18; S Isa 34:12 [k] S Job 3:15 **12:22** [l] 1Co 4:5 [m] Job 3:5 [n] Ps 139:12; Da 2:22 **12:23** [o] Ps 2:1; 46:6; Isa 13:4; Jer 25:9 [p] S Ex 34:24; Ps 107:38; Isa 9:3; 26:15; 54:3 [q] S Job 5:12; Ac 17:26 **12:24** [r] S ver 20 [s] Ps 107:40 **12:25** [t] S Dt 28:29; Job 18:6; 21:17; 29:3 [u] Ps 107:27; Isa 24:20 **13:1** [v] S Job 9:24 **13:2** [w] S Job 12:3 **13:3** [x] Job 5:17; 40:2 [y] S Job 5:8; 9:14-20; S 10:2 **13:4** [z] Ps 119:69; Isa 9:15; Jer 23:32 [a] Jer 8:22 [b] S Job 6:15 **13:5** [c] ver 13; S Jdg 18:19 [d] Pr 17:28 **13:6** [e] Job 33:1; 36:4 **13:7** [f] S Job 12:16; S 16:17 **13:8** [g] S Lev 19:15 **13:9** [h] S Job 9:3 [i] S Job 12:16; Gal 6:7 **13:10** [j] S Lev 19:15; S 2Ch 19:7 **13:11** [k] Job 31:23 [l] S Ex 3:6 **13:12** [m] S Ne 4:2-3 **13:13** [n] S ver 5 [o] S Job 7:11 [p] S Job 9:21 **13:14** [q] S Jdg 9:17 **13:15** [r] S Job 7:6 [s] Ps 23:4; 27:1; Pr 14:32; Isa 12:2; Da 3:28 [t] S Job 5:8; 27:5 **13:16** [u] Ps 30:5; Isa 12:1; 54:7-8; Hos 14:4; Php 1:19 [v] S Job 8:13 [w] S Ge 3:8 **13:17** [x] Job 21:2 **13:18** [y] S ver 3; Job 23:4; 37:19

[w] *18* Or *shackles of kings / and ties a belt*
[x] *15* Or *He will surely slay me; I have no hope — / yet I will*

13:15 THOUGH HE SLAY ME, YET WILL I HOPE IN HIM. Here is one of the most astounding declarations of faith in God's goodness ever uttered. Whatever God allowed to happen to Job, whatever burden he laid upon him, even if he should "slay" him, Job believed ultimately that God would not fail him. Paul expressed this same confidence in God's love for his faithful people (Ro 8). Although the Lord may take away comfort after comfort, health may be destroyed and waves of trouble may come upon us, through the grace of Jesus Christ and power of his saving death, we can trust God with unwavering faith, convinced that he is right, just and good (cf. Ro 8:37–39).

I know I will be vindicated.[z]
19 Can anyone bring charges against me?[a]
If so, I will be silent[b] and die.[c]

20 "Only grant me these two things, O God,
and then I will not hide from you:
21 Withdraw your hand[d] far from me,
and stop frightening me with your terrors.[e]
22 Then summon me and I will answer,[f]
or let me speak, and you reply.[g]
23 How many wrongs and sins have I committed?[h]
Show me my offense and my sin.[i]
24 Why do you hide your face[j]
and consider me your enemy?[k]
25 Will you torment[l] a windblown leaf?[m]
Will you chase[n] after dry chaff?[o]
26 For you write down bitter things against me
and make me inherit the sins of my youth.[p]
27 You fasten my feet in shackles;[q]
you keep close watch on all my paths[r]
by putting marks on the soles of my feet.

28 "So man wastes away like something rotten,
like a garment[s] eaten by moths.[t]

14 "Man born of woman[u]
is of few days[v] and full of trouble.[w]
2 He springs up like a flower[x] and withers away;[y]
like a fleeting shadow,[z] he does not endure.[a]
3 Do you fix your eye on such a one?[b]
Will you bring him[y] before you for judgment?[c]
4 Who can bring what is pure[d] from the impure?[e]
No one![f]
5 Man's days are determined;[g]
you have decreed the number of his months[h]
and have set limits he cannot exceed.[i]
6 So look away from him and let him alone,[j]
till he has put in his time like a hired man.[k]

7 "At least there is hope for a tree:[l]
If it is cut down, it will sprout again,
and its new shoots[m] will not fail.[n]
8 Its roots may grow old in the ground
and its stump[o] die in the soil,
9 yet at the scent of water[p] it will bud
and put forth shoots like a plant.[q]
10 But man dies and is laid low;[r]
he breathes his last and is no more.[s]
11 As water disappears from the sea
or a riverbed becomes parched and dry,[t]
12 so man lies down and does not rise;[u]
till the heavens are no more,[v]
men will not awake
or be roused from their sleep.[w]

13 "If only you would hide me in the grave[z][x]
and conceal me till your anger has passed![y]
If only you would set me a time
and then remember[z] me![a]
14 If a man dies, will he live again?

13:18 [z] S Job 2:3; S 9:21 **13:19** [a] Job 40:4; Isa 50:8; Ro 8:33 [b] S Job 9:15 [c] S Job 3:13; 10:8 **13:21** [d] S Ex 9:3; Heb 10:31 [e] S Job 6:4 **13:22** [f] Job 9:35; 14:15 [g] S Job 9:16 **13:23** [h] S 1Sa 26:18 [i] Job 7:21; 9:21; 14:17; 33:9 **13:24** [j] S Dt 32:20 [k] Job 16:9; 19:11; 33:10; Ps 88:14-15; Jer 30:14; La 2:5 **13:25** [l] Job 19:2 [m] Lev 26:36 [n] Job 19:22,28 [o] Job 21:18; Ps 1:4; 35:5; 83:13; Isa 17:13; 42:3; 43:17; Hos 13:3 **13:26** [p] Job 18:7; 20:11; 21:23; Ps 25:7 **13:27** [q] S Ge 40:15; Job 33:11; Jer 20:2; Ac 16:24 [r] Job 10:14 **13:28** [s] Ps 102:26; Mk 2:21 [t] S Dt 28:35; Ps 39:11; Isa 50:9; 51:8; Hos 5:12; Jas 5:2 **14:1** [u] Job 15:14; Mt 11:11 [v] S Job 10:20 [w] S Ge 3:17; S Job 7:2 **14:2** [x] Ps 103:15; S Jas 1:10 [y] Ps 37:2; 90:5-6; Isa 40:6-8 [z] Job 8:9; Ps 39:4; 102:11; 109:23; 144:4; Ecc 6:12 [a] S Job 4:20; Ps 49:12 **14:3** [b] Ps 8:4; 144:3 [c] S Job 7:18 **14:4** [d] Ps 51:10 [e] S Job 4:17; Eph 2:1-3 [f] S Job 9:30; Jn 3:6; Ro 5:12; 7:14 **14:5** [g] Job 24:1; Ps 31:15; 139:16 [h] Job 21:21; Ps 39:4; 90:12 [i] Ac 17:26 **14:6** [j] S Job 7:19 [k] Job 7:1,2; Ps 39:13; Isa 16:14; 21:16 **14:7** [l] Job 19:10; 24:20; Ps 52:5 [m] Isa 11:1; 53:2; 60:21 [n] Isa 6:13 **14:8** [o] Isa 6:13; 11:1; 53:2 **14:9** [p] Job 29:19; Ps 1:3; Jer 17:8; Eze 31:7 [q] Lev 26:4; Eze 34:27; Zec 10:1 **14:10** [r] ver 12 [s] S Job 10:21; 13:19 **14:11** [t] S 2Sa 14:14 **14:12** [u] ver 10 [v] Ps 102:26; Rev 20:11; 21:1 [w] Ac 3:21 **14:13** [x] S Job 7:9 [y] Ps 30:5; Isa 26:20; 54:7 [z] S Ge 8:1 [a] Job 6:8

[y] 3 Septuagint, Vulgate and Syriac; Hebrew *me*
[z] 13 Hebrew *Sheol*

14:1 FULL OF TROUBLE. For the believer, a life that is "full of trouble" may be the result of persecution, injustice, poverty, ill health or Satan's opposition to their fight of faith (see article on THE SUFFERING OF THE RIGHTEOUS, p. 710). God wants all believers who are suffering and oppressed on this earth to know that a day of resurrection (see next note) and victory is coming when they will be with God forever (see Rev 21:1, 4, notes). At that time they will experience first-hand that their "present sufferings are not worth comparing with the glory that will be revealed in us" (see Ro 8:18, note).

14:14 IF A MAN DIES, WILL HE LIVE AGAIN? Job believed that after he died and entered the grave (v. 13), God would call him out

All the days of my hard
service[b]
I will wait for my renewal[a][c] to
come.
15 You will call and I will answer
you;[d]
you will long for the creature
your hands have made.[e]
16 Surely then you will count my
steps[f]
but not keep track of my sin.[g]
17 My offenses will be sealed[h] up in
a bag;[i]
you will cover over my sin.[j]

18 "But as a mountain erodes and
crumbles[k]
and as a rock is moved from its
place,[l]
19 as water wears away stones
and torrents[m] wash away the
soil,[n]
so you destroy man's hope.[o]
20 You overpower him once for all,
and he is gone;[p]
you change his countenance and
send him away.[q]
21 If his sons are honored, he does
not know it;
if they are brought low, he does
not see it.[r]
22 He feels but the pain of his own
body[s]
and mourns only for himself.[t]"

Eliphaz

15 Then Eliphaz the Temanite[u]
replied:

2 "Would a wise man answer with
empty notions
or fill his belly with the hot east
wind?[v]
3 Would he argue with useless
words,
with speeches that have no
value?[w]
4 But you even undermine piety
and hinder devotion to God.[x]
5 Your sin[y] prompts your mouth;[z]
you adopt the tongue of the
crafty.[a]

14:14 [b]S Job 7:1 [c]S 2Ki 6:33 **14:15** [d]S Job 13:22 [e]S Job 10:3 **14:16** [f]S Job 10:4; Ps 139:1-3; Pr 5:21; Jer 16:17; 32:19 [g]Job 10:6; 1Co 13:5 **14:17** [h]Jer 32:10 [i]S Dt 32:34 [j]S Job 9:30; S 13:23 **14:18** [k]Eze 38:20 [l]Job 18:4 **14:19** [m]Eze 13:13 [n]S Ge 7:23 [o]S Job 7:6 **14:20** [p]S Job 4:20 [q]S Job 7:10; 8:18; S 12:19; 27:19; Jas 1:10 **14:21** [r]Job 21:21; Ecc 9:5; Isa 63:16 **14:22** [s]Ps 38:7; Isa 21:3; Jer 4:19 [t]Job 21:21 **15:1** [u]S Job 4:1 **15:2** [v]S Ge 41:6 **15:3** [w]S Ne 4:2-3; S Job 6:26 **15:4** [x]Job 25:6 **15:5** [y]Job 11:6; 22:5 [z]Pr 16:23 [a]S Job 5:13

15:6 [b]S Job 9:15; 18:7; Ps 10:2; S Mt 12:37; Lk 19:22 **15:7** [c]Job 38:21 [d]S 1Sa 2:8; Ps 90:2; Pr 8:25 **15:8** [e]Job 29:4; Isa 9:6; 40:13; 41:28; Jer 23:18; Ro 11:34; 1Co 2:11 [f]S Job 12:2 **15:9** [g]S Job 12:3 **15:10** [h]S Job 12:12 [i]S 2Ch 10:6 **15:11** [j]S Ge 37:35; S Job 6:10; 2Co 1:3-4 [k]Zec 1:13 [l]S Dt 8:3; S 32:39; S Job 5:17; 22:22; 23:12; 36:16; Ps 119:11,72; Jer 15:16 **15:12** [m]Job 11:13; 36:13 **15:13** [n]Pr 29:11; Da 11:30 [o]Ps 94:4 [p]S Job 11:8; 22:5; 32:3 **15:14** [q]S Job 14:1 [r]S 2Ch 6:36; S Job 4:17 **15:15** [s]S Job 5:1 [t]S Job 4:18 **15:16** [u]S Lev 5:2; S Job 4:19; Ps 14:1 [v]Job 20:12 [w]Job 12:4; 34:7; Pr 19:28

6 Your own mouth condemns you,
not mine;
your own lips testify against
you.[b]

7 "Are you the first man ever
born?[c]
Were you brought forth before
the hills?[d]
8 Do you listen in on God's
council?[e]
Do you limit wisdom to
yourself?[f]
9 What do you know that we do not
know?
What insights do you have that
we do not have?[g]
10 The gray-haired and the aged[h] are
on our side,
men even older than your
father.[i]
11 Are God's consolations[j] not
enough for you,
words[k] spoken gently to you?[l]
12 Why has your heart[m] carried you
away,
and why do your eyes flash,
13 so that you vent your rage[n]
against God
and pour out such words[o] from
your mouth?[p]

14 "What is man, that he could be
pure,
or one born of woman,[q] that he
could be righteous?[r]
15 If God places no trust in his holy
ones,[s]
if even the heavens are not pure
in his eyes,[t]
16 how much less man, who is vile
and corrupt,[u]
who drinks up evil[v] like
water![w]

17 "Listen to me and I will explain to
you;

[a] *14* Or *release*

again (v. 15; cf. 1Co 15:20; 1Th 4:16–17); in other words, Job expressed hope in a personal resurrection (see 19:25–26, notes). The basis for this hope-filled expectation was God's fervent love for his people, i.e., "you will long for the creature your hands have made" (v. 15). For a brief moment, Job reached out to God with a towering expression of faith.

15:1 ELIPHAZ THE TEMANITE REPLIED. In chs. 15—21 the four participants continued their dispute, developing what they had said before, only with more tenacity. Job steadfastly clung to God, while at the same time maintaining his innocence and insisting on the unfairness of his calamity (e.g., 16:19–21).

let me tell you what I have
seen,[x]
18what wise men have declared,
hiding nothing received from
their fathers[y]
19(to whom alone the land[z] was
given
when no alien passed among
them):
20All his days the wicked man
suffers torment,[a]
the ruthless through all the
years stored up for him.[b]
21Terrifying sounds fill his ears;[c]
when all seems well, marauders
attack him.[d]
22He despairs of escaping the
darkness;[e]
he is marked for the sword.[f]
23He wanders about[g]—food for
vultures[b];[h]
he knows the day of darkness[i]
is at hand.[j]
24Distress and anguish[k] fill him
with terror;[l]
they overwhelm him, like a
king[m] poised to attack,
25because he shakes his fist[n] at
God
and vaunts himself against the
Almighty,[o]
26defiantly charging against him
with a thick, strong shield.[p]

27"Though his face is covered with
fat
and his waist bulges with
flesh,[q]
28he will inhabit ruined towns
and houses where no one
lives,[r]
houses crumbling to rubble.[s]
29He will no longer be rich and his
wealth will not endure,[t]
nor will his possessions spread
over the land.[u]
30He will not escape the darkness;[v]
a flame[w] will wither his
shoots,[x]
and the breath of God's mouth[y]
will carry him away.[z]
31Let him not deceive[a] himself by
trusting what is
worthless,[b]
for he will get nothing in
return.[c]
32Before his time[d] he will be paid
in full,[e]
and his branches will not
flourish.[f]

15:17 [x]S Job 4:8 **15:18** [y]S Dt 32:7 **15:19** [z]Ge 12:1; Job 22:8 **15:20** [a]ver 24; Isa 8:22; 50:11; 66:24 [b]Job 24:1; 27:13-23; Isa 2:12; Jer 46:10; Ob 1:15; Zep 1:7 **15:21** [c]ver 24; S 1Sa 3:11; Job 18:11; 20:25; Jer 6:25; 20:3 [d]Job 22:10; 27:20; Isa 13:3; Jer 51:25,53,56; 1Th 5:3 **15:22** [e]ver 23; S Job 5:14; 24:17; 38:15; Ps 91:5; SS 3:8 [f]Job 16:13; 18:19; 19:29; 20:24; 27:14; 33:18; 36:12; Pr 7:23; Isa 1:20; Jer 44:27; Hos 9:13; Am 5:19 **15:23** [g]Ps 109:10 [h]Pr 30:17; Eze 39:17; Mt 24:28; Lk 17:37 [i]S ver 22 [j]Job 18:12 **15:24** [k]Isa 8:22; 9:1 [l]S ver 20 [m]Job 18:14 **15:25** [n]Ps 44:16; Isa 10:32; 37:23 [o]S Job 11:8; 35:12; 36:9; 40:8; Ps 2:2-3; 73:9; 75:5; Pr 21:30; Isa 3:16; 45:9 **15:26** [p]Jer 44:16 **15:27** [q]S Jdg 3:17 **15:28** [r]Isa 5:9 [s]S Job 3:14 **15:29** [t]S Job 3:15; S 7:8 [u]Isa 5:8 **15:30** [v]S Job 5:14 [w]ver 34; Job 16:7; 20:26; 22:20; 31:12 [x]ver 32; Job 8:19; 18:16; 29:19; Hos 9:1-16; Mal 4:1 [y]S Ex 15:10 [z]Isa 40:23-24 **15:31** [a]Job 31:5; Pr 1:16; 6:18; Isa 44:20; 59:7; Mic 2:11; S Mk 13:5; Jas 1:16 [b]Isa 30:12; 47:10; 59:4; Jer 7:4,8; S Mt 6:19 [c]Job 20:7; 22:13; 27:9; 35:13; Pr 15:29; Isa 1:15; Jer 11:11; Mic 3:4 **15:32** [d]Ecc 7:17 [e]Job 22:16; 36:14; Ps 55:23; 109:8; Pr 10:27 [f]S ver 30 **15:33** [g]Hab 3:17 [h]S Job 4:20 **15:34** [i]S Job 8:13 [j]S ver 30; Heb 10:27 [k]S Ex 23:8; S 1Sa 8:3 **15:35** [l]S Job 5:7 [m]S Job 4:8; S Isa 29:20; Gal 6:7; Jas 1:15

33He will be like a vine stripped of
its unripe grapes,[g]
like an olive tree shedding its
blossoms.[h]
34For the company of the godless[i]
will be barren,
and fire will consume[j] the
tents of those who love
bribes.[k]
35They conceive trouble[l] and give
birth to evil;[m]
their womb fashions deceit."

Job 16

16 Then Job replied:

2"I have heard many things
like these;
miserable comforters[n] are you
all![o]
3Will your long-winded speeches
never end?[p]
What ails you that you keep on
arguing?[q]
4I also could speak like you,
if you were in my place;
I could make fine speeches against
you
and shake my head[r] at you.
5But my mouth would encourage
you;
comfort[s] from my lips would
bring you relief.[t]

6"Yet if I speak, my pain is not
relieved;
and if I refrain, it does not go
away.[u]
7Surely, O God, you have worn me
out;[v]
you have devastated my entire
household.[w]
8You have bound me—and it has
become a witness;
my gauntness[x] rises up and
testifies against me.[y]
9God assails me and tears[z] me in
his anger[a]
and gnashes his teeth at me;[b]
my opponent fastens on me his
piercing eyes.[c]

16:2 [n]Ps 69:20 [o]S Job 6:15 **16:3** [p]Job 11:2; 18:2 [q]S Job 6:26 **16:4** [r]S 2Ki 19:21; Ps 22:7; Isa 37:22; Jer 48:27; La 2:15; Zep 2:15; S Mt 27:39 **16:5** [s]Job 29:25 [t]S Ge 37:35 **16:6** [u]S Job 6:3; S 7:21 **16:7** [v]S Jdg 8:5; S Job 7:3 [w]S Job 1:19 **16:8** [x]Job 17:7; 19:20; 33:21; Ps 6:7; 22:17; 88:9; 102:5; 109:24; La 5:17 [y]S Job 10:17 **16:9** [z]S Job 12:14; Hos 6:1 [a]S Job 9:5; 18:4; 19:11 [b]Job 30:21; Ps 35:16; 37:12; 112:10; La 2:16; Ac 7:54 [c]S Job 13:24

[b]23 Or *about, looking for food*

10Men open their mouths[d] to jeer at me;[e]
they strike my cheek[f] in scorn
and unite together against me.[g]
11God has turned me over to evil men
and thrown me into the clutches of the wicked.[h]
12All was well with me, but he shattered me;
he seized me by the neck and crushed me.[i]
He has made me his target;[j]
13 his archers surround me.[k]
Without pity, he pierces[l] my kidneys
and spills my gall on the ground.
14Again and again[m] he bursts upon me;
he rushes at me like a warrior.[n]

15"I have sewed sackcloth[o] over my skin
and buried my brow in the dust.[p]
16My face is red with weeping,[q]
deep shadows ring my eyes;[r]
17yet my hands have been free of violence[s]
and my prayer is pure.[t]

18"O earth, do not cover my blood;[u]
may my cry[v] never be laid to rest![w]
19Even now my witness[x] is in heaven;[y]
my advocate is on high.[z]
20My intercessor[a] is my friend[c][b]
as my eyes pour out[c] tears[d] to God;
21on behalf of a man he pleads[e] with God
as a man pleads for his friend.

22"Only a few years will pass
before I go on the journey of no return.[f]

17

1My spirit[g] is broken,
my days are cut short,[h]
the grave awaits me.[i]
2Surely mockers[j] surround me;[k]
my eyes must dwell on their hostility.

3"Give me, O God, the pledge you demand.[l]
Who else will put up security[m] for me?[n]
4You have closed their minds to understanding;[o]
therefore you will not let them triumph.
5If a man denounces his friends for reward,[p]
the eyes of his children will fail.[q]

6"God has made me a byword[r] to everyone,[s]
a man in whose face people spit.[t]
7My eyes have grown dim with grief;[u]
my whole frame is but a shadow.[v]
8Upright men are appalled at this;
the innocent are aroused[w] against the ungodly.
9Nevertheless, the righteous[x] will hold to their ways,
and those with clean hands[y] will grow stronger.[z]

10"But come on, all of you, try again!

16:10 [d]Ps 22:13; 35:21 [e]Job 12:4; 19:18; 21:3; 30:1, 9; Ps 22:13; 69:12; 119:51 [f]Isa 50:6; La 3:30; Mic 5:1; Ac 23:2 [g]ver 7; S Job 11:3; 19:12; 30:12; Ps 27:3; 35:15; Ac 7:57 **16:11** [h]S Job 9:24 **16:12** [i]S Job 9:17 [j]S Job 6:4; La 3:12 **16:13** [k]S Job 3:23 [l]Job 20:24; Pr 7:23; La 3:13 **16:14** [m]Job 9:17 [n]S Job 10:3; Joel 2:7 **16:15** [o]S Ge 37:34 [p]S Job 2:8 **16:16** [q]ver 20; Ps 6:6 [r]Job 2:7; 17:7; 30:17,30; 33:19; Isa 52:14 **16:17** [s]Isa 55:7; 59:6; Jer 18:11; Jnh 3:8 [t]S Job 6:28; S 10:7; 13:7; Isa 53:9; Zep 3:13 **16:18** [u]S Ge 4:10; Isa 26:21 [v]Ps 5:2; 18:6; 102:1; 119:169 [w]Job 19:24; Ps 66:18-19; Heb 11:4 **16:19** [x]S Ge 31:50; S Ro 1:9; 1Th 2:5 [y]Job 22:12; 42:2 [z]Job 19:27; 21:17; 25:2; 27:13; 31:2; Ps 113:5; Isa 33:5; 57:15; 58:4; 66:1; Mk 11:10 **16:20** [a]S Ro 8:34 [b]Jn 15:15 [c]La 2:19 [d]S ver 16 **16:21** [e]1Ki 8:45; Ps 9:4; 140:12 **16:22** [f]S Job 10:21 **17:1** [g]Ps 143:4 [h]Isa 38:12 [i]Ps 88:3-4; Ecc 12:1-7 **17:2** [j]S Job 11:3 [k]S Job 6:14; Ps 22:7; 119:51; Jer 20:7; La 3:14

17:3 [l]Ps 35:27; 119:122 [m]Pr 6:1 [n]Ps 35:2; 40:17; Isa 38:14 **17:4** [o]S Job 12:12 **17:5** [p]S Ex 22:15 [q]S Job 11:20 **17:6** [r]S 1Ki 9:7; Job 30:9; Jer 15:4 [s]S ver 2 [t]S Nu 12:14 **17:7** [u]S Job 16:8 [v]S Job 2:12; S 16:16 **17:8** [w]S Ex 4:14 **17:9** [x]Pr 4:18 [y]S 2Sa 22:21; S Job 9:30 [z]S 1Sa 2:4; Ps 84:7

[c] *20* Or *My friends treat me with scorn*

16:9 TEARS ME IN HIS ANGER. Job's terrible suffering made him feel that God was a cruel tyrant rather than a merciful Lord. His conviction that he had lived justly and purely (v. 17) caused him to question God's justice (cf. 19:6). Yet, Job also held firmly to his belief that God was indeed just; therefore, if only he could enter into direct contact with God (13:13–27; 23:1–7) or find someone to plead his case (see 9:33, note), God as his witness would testify to his innocence (vv. 19–21; see next note).

16:19 MY WITNESS IS IN HEAVEN. In faith Job rose above his doubts about God's goodness, for he declared that God himself would testify as a witness of his innocence. He longed for God to plead his cause in the heavenly court of justice. The desire for a mediator to speak to God in our defense became a reality in Jesus Christ, through whom God "reconciled us to himself" (2Co 5:18); "we have one who speaks to the Father in our defense—Jesus Christ, the Righteous One" (1Jn 2:1).

17:1 MY SPIRIT IS BROKEN. As a broken man, Job firmly believed he would die soon. He saw himself as a man deserted by God and as the object of his companions' scorn. Job could do nothing but persevere in his conviction about the rightness of his cause (v. 9), maintaining confidence in God's justice, all outward appearances to the contrary (16:19–22).

I will not find a wise man
among you.[a]
11My days have passed,[b] my plans
are shattered,
and so are the desires of my
heart.[c]
12These men turn night into day;[d]
in the face of darkness they say,
'Light is near.'[e]
13If the only home I hope for is the
grave,[d][f]
if I spread out my bed[g] in
darkness,[h]
14if I say to corruption,[i] 'You are
my father,'
and to the worm,[j] 'My mother'
or 'My sister,'
15where then is my hope?[k]
Who can see any hope for me?[l]
16Will it go down to the gates of
death[d]?[m]
Will we descend together into
the dust?"[n]

Bildad

18 Then Bildad the Shuhite[o] replied:

2"When will you end these
speeches?[p]
Be sensible, and then we can
talk.
3Why are we regarded as cattle[q]
and considered stupid in your
sight?[r]
4You who tear yourself[s] to pieces
in your anger,[t]
is the earth to be abandoned for
your sake?
Or must the rocks be moved
from their place?[u]

5"The lamp of the wicked is snuffed
out;[v]
the flame of his fire stops
burning.[w]
6The light in his tent[x] becomes
dark;[y]
the lamp beside him goes out.[z]
7The vigor[a] of his step is
weakened;[b]
his own schemes[c] throw him
down.[d]
8His feet thrust him into a net[e]
and he wanders into its mesh.
9A trap seizes him by the heel;
a snare[f] holds him fast.[g]
10A noose[h] is hidden for him on the
ground;
a trap[i] lies in his path.[j]
11Terrors[k] startle him on every
side[l]
and dog[m] his every step.
12Calamity[n] is hungry[o] for him;
disaster[p] is ready for him when
he falls.[q]
13It eats away parts of his skin;[r]
death's firstborn devours his
limbs.[s]
14He is torn from the security of his
tent[t]
and marched off to the king[u] of
terrors.[v]
15Fire resides[e] in his tent;[w]
burning sulfur[x] is scattered
over his dwelling.
16His roots dry up below[y]
and his branches wither above.[z]
17The memory of him perishes from
the earth;[a]
he has no name[b] in the land.[c]
18He is driven from light into
darkness[d]
and is banished[e] from the
world.[f]
19He has no offspring[g] or
descendants[h] among his
people,
no survivor[i] where once he
lived.[j]
20Men of the west are appalled[k] at
his fate;[l]
men of the east are seized with
horror.
21Surely such is the dwelling[m] of an
evil man;[n]
such is the place[o] of one who
knows not God."[p]

Job

19 Then Job replied:

2"How long will you
torment[q] me
and crush[r] me with words?
3Ten times[s] now you have
reproached[t] me;
shamelessly you attack me.
4If it is true that I have gone
astray,

17:10 [a] S Job 12:2 **17:11** [b] ver 15; Isa 38:10 [c] S Job 7:6 **17:12** [d] Isa 50:11 [e] Job 5:17-26; S 11:17 **17:13** [f] S 2Sa 14:14; S Job 3:13 [g] Ps 139:8 [h] Ps 88:18 **17:14** [i] Job 13:28; 30:28,30; Ps 16:10; 49:9 [j] S Job 4:19; S 7:5 **17:15** [k] S Job 7:6 [l] Ps 31:22; La 3:18; Eze 37:11 **17:16** [m] S Job 7:9; 33:28; Ps 9:13; 30:3; 107:18; Isa 38:10,17; Jnh 2:6 [n] S Ge 2:7; S Job 3:19; 20:11; 21:26 **18:1** [o] S Job 8:1 **18:2** [p] S Job 8:2; S 16:3 **18:3** [q] S Job 12:7 [r] Ps 73:22 **18:4** [s] Job 13:14 [t] S Job 16:9 [u] Job 14:18 **18:5** [v] Job 21:17; 35:15; Pr 13:9; 20:20; 24:20; Jer 25:10; Mt 25:8; Jn 8:12 [w] S Job 5:14; 12:25; 24:17; 38:15 **18:6** [x] S Job 8:22 [y] S Job 5:14 [z] S Job 11:17; S 12:25 **18:7** [a] S Job 13:26 [b] Ps 18:36; Pr 4:12 [c] S Job 5:13 [d] S Job 15:6 **18:8** [e] Job 19:6; Ps 9:15; 10:9; 35:7; 57:6; 66:11; 140:5; La 1:13; Mic 7:2; Hab 1:15 **18:9** [f] Job 22:10; 30:12; Isa 24:18; Jer 48:44; Am 5:19 [g] Pr 5:22 **18:10** [h] Pr 7:22; Isa 51:20 [i] S 1Sa 28:9 [j] Ps 140:5 **18:11** [k] ver 14; S Job 6:4; 20:25; 24:17; Ps 55:4; 88:15; Isa 28:19; Jer 15:8; La 2:22 [l] S Job 15:21; Ps 31:13 [m] ver 18; Job 20:8; Isa 22:18 **18:12** [n] Job 21:17 [o] Isa 8:21; 9:20; 65:13 [p] Job 31:3 [q] Job 15:23 **18:13** [r] Nu 12:12 [s] Zec 14:12 **18:14** [t] S Job 8:22 [u] Job 15:24 [v] S ver 11 **18:15** [w] ver 18; Job 20:26 [x] S Ge 19:24 **18:16** [y] Isa 5:24; Hos 5:12; Am 2:9 [z] S Ge 27:28; S Job 8:12; S 15:30 **18:17** [a] S Dt 32:26 [b] Dt 9:14; Ps 9:5; 69:28; Pr 10:7; Isa 14:22 [c] Job 24:20; Ps 34:16; Pr 2:22; 10:7; Isa 49:15 **18:18** [d] S Job 5:14 [e] S ver 11 [f] S Job 11:20; 30:8 **18:19** [g] Ps 37:28; Isa 1:4; 14:20; Jer 22:30 [h] Ps 21:10; 109:13; Isa 14:22 [i] S 2Ki 10:11; S Eze 17:8 [j] Job 27:14-15 **18:20** [k] Ps 22:6-7; Isa 52:14; 53:2-3; Eze 27:35 [l] Ps 37:13; Jer 46:21; 50:27,31; Eze 7:7 **18:21** [m] Job 21:28 [n] Isa 57:20 [o] S Job 7:10 [p] S Job 4:21; 1Th 4:5 **19:2** [q] Job 13:25 [r] Job 6:9 **19:3** [s] S Ge 31:7 [t] Job 20:3

[d] *13* Hebrew *Sheol* [e] *15* Or *Nothing he had remains*

my error[u] remains my concern
alone.
5If indeed you would exalt
yourselves above me[v]
and use my humiliation against
me,
6then know that God has wronged
me[w]
and drawn his net[x] around
me.[y]
7"Though I cry, 'I've been wronged!'
I get no response;[z]
though I call for help,[a] there is
no justice.[b]
8He has blocked my way so I
cannot pass;[c]
he has shrouded my paths in
darkness.[d]
9He has stripped[e] me of my
honor[f]
and removed the crown from my
head.[g]
10He tears me down[h] on every side
till I am gone;
he uproots my hope[i] like a
tree.[j]
11His anger[k] burns against me;
he counts me among his
enemies.[l]
12His troops advance in force;[m]
they build a siege ramp[n]
against me
and encamp around my tent.[o]
13"He has alienated my brothers[p]
from me;
my acquaintances are completely
estranged from me.[q]
14My kinsmen have gone away;
my friends[r] have forgotten me.
15My guests[s] and my
maidservants[t] count me a
stranger;
they look upon me as an alien.
16I summon my servant, but he does
not answer,
though I beg him with my own
mouth.
17My breath is offensive to my wife;
I am loathsome[u] to my own
brothers.
18Even the little boys[v] scorn me;
when I appear, they ridicule
me.[w]
19All my intimate friends[x] detest
me;[y]
those I love have turned against
me.[z]
20I am nothing but skin and bones;[a]
I have escaped with only the
skin of my teeth.[f]
21"Have pity on me, my friends,[b]
have pity,
for the hand of God has struck[c]
me.
22Why do you pursue[d] me as God
does?[e]
Will you never get enough of my
flesh?[f]
23"Oh, that my words were recorded,
that they were written on a
scroll,[g]
24that they were inscribed with an
iron tool[h] on[g] lead,
or engraved in rock forever![i]
25I know that my Redeemer[h][j]
lives,[k]

19:4 [u]Job 6:24 **19:5** [v]Ps 35:26; 38:16; 55:12 **19:6** [w]S Job 6:29 [x]S Job 18:8 [y]S Job 10:3 **19:7** [z]Job 30:20; Ps 22:2 [a]Job 30:24,28; 31:35; Ps 5:2 [b]S Job 9:24; Hab 1:2-4 **19:8** [c]La 3:7; Hos 2:6 [d]Job 3:26; 23:17; 30:26; Ecc 6:4; Isa 59:9; Jer 8:15; 14:19; La 3:2 **19:9** [e]S Job 12:17 [f]Ge 43:28; Ex 12:42; Ps 15:4; 50:23; Pr 14:31 [g]S Job 2:8; 29:14; Ps 89:39,44; La 5:16 **19:10** [h]S Job 12:14 [i]S Job 7:6 [j]S Job 14:7 **19:11** [k]Job 16:9 [l]S Job 13:24 **19:12** [m]S Job 16:13 [n]S Job 16:10 [o]S Job 3:23 **19:13** [p]Ps 69:8 [q]ver 19; Job 16:7; 42:11; Ps 31:11; 38:11; 88:8 **19:14** [r]ver 19; S 2Sa 15:12; Job 12:4; 16:20; Ps 88:18; Jer 20:10; 38:22 **19:15** [s]Ge 14:14 [t]Ecc 2:7 **19:17** [u]Ps 38:5 **19:18** [v]S 2Ki 2:23 [w]S Job 16:10 **19:19** [x]S ver 14; S Job 6:14; Ps 55:12-13 [y]Job 30:10 [z]S ver 13; Jn 13:18 **19:20** [a]S Job 2:5 **19:21** [b]S Job 6:14 [c]S Jdg 2:15; S Job 4:5; S 10:3; La 3:1 **19:22** [d]S Job 13:25 [e]ver 6 [f]S 2Ch 28:9; Ps 14:4; 27:2; 69:26; Pr 30:14; Isa 53:4 **19:23** [g]S Ex 17:14; S Ps 40:7; S Isa 8:1 **19:24** [h]Jer 17:1 [i]S Job 16:18 **19:25** [j]S Ex 6:6; S Lev 25:25; Ps 68:5; 78:35; Pr 23:11; Isa 41:14; 43:14; 44:6,24; 47:4; 48:17; 49:26; 54:5; 59:20; 60:16 [k]S 1Sa 14:39; Job 16:19

[f]20 Or *only my gums* [g]24 Or *and* [h]25 Or *defender*

19:11 COUNTS ME AMONG HIS ENEMIES. Job was now under the serious misconception that God directly caused his suffering (cf. vv. 8–13). (1) He believed that God had become his enemy who delighted in bringing torment and agony on his soul. Job was not aware that Satan was the cause of his unrelenting calamity. Although God was permitting Satan to bring harm to Job, it was nevertheless Satan who inflicted the cruel suffering. (2) Believers should be careful not to blame God for what he only permits. In this world many evil things occur; God takes no pleasure in witnessing them. Tragedies happen among his children, which he permits with regret and pity (see 1Ti 2:4, note; see article on THE WILL OF GOD, p. 1056).

19:25 I KNOW THAT MY REDEEMER LIVES. In the midst of his suffering and despair, Job clung with great faith to God, believing the Lord would vindicate him in the end (cf. 13:15; 14:14–15). Job viewed God as his "redeemer" or helper; in Bible times a "redeemer" was a relative who with great affection came to protect, defend, help in times of trouble (see Lev 25:25; Dt 25:5–10; Ru 1—4; see also Ge 48:16; Ex 6:6; Isa 43:1; Hos 13:14) and vindicate a suffering kinsman.

19:25 IN THE END HE WILL STAND UPON THE EARTH. By the inspiration of the Holy Spirit, Job's testimony pointed toward Jesus Christ the Redeemer, who would come to save his people from sin and condemnation (Ro 3:24; Gal 3:13; 4:5; Eph 1:7; Tit 2:14), free them from the fear of death (Heb 2:14–15; Ro 8:23), give them eternal life (Jn 3:16; Ro 6:23), rescue them from the coming wrath (1Th 1:10) and publicly vindicate them (cf. Rev 19:11–21; 20:1–6). Here Job was predict-

and that in the end he will stand
upon the earth.[i]
26And after my skin has been
destroyed,
yet[j] in[k] my flesh I will see
God;[l]
27I myself will see him
with my own eyes[m]—I, and not
another.
How my heart yearns[n] within
me!

28"If you say, 'How we will hound[o]
him,
since the root of the trouble lies
in him,[1]'
29you should fear the sword
yourselves;
for wrath will bring punishment
by the sword,[p]
and then you will know that
there is judgment.[m]"[q]

Zophar

20

Then Zophar the Naamathite[r]
replied:

2"My troubled thoughts prompt me
to answer
because I am greatly
disturbed.[s]
3I hear a rebuke[t] that dishonors
me,
and my understanding inspires
me to reply.

4"Surely you know how it has been
from of old,[u]
ever since man[n] was placed on
the earth,
5that the mirth of the wicked[v] is
brief,
the joy of the godless[w] lasts but
a moment.[x]
6Though his pride[y] reaches to the
heavens[z]
and his head touches the
clouds,[a]
7he will perish forever,[b] like his
own dung;
those who have seen him will
say, 'Where is he?'[c]
8Like a dream[d] he flies away,[e] no
more to be found,
banished[f] like a vision of the
night.[g]
9The eye that saw him will not see
him again;
his place will look on him no
more.[h]
10His children[i] must make amends
to the poor;
his own hands must give back
his wealth.[j]
11The youthful vigor[k] that fills his
bones[l]
will lie with him in the dust.[m]

12"Though evil[n] is sweet in his
mouth
and he hides it under his
tongue,[o]
13though he cannot bear to let it go
and keeps it in his mouth,[p]
14yet his food will turn sour in his
stomach;[q]
it will become the venom of
serpents[r] within him.
15He will spit out the riches[s] he
swallowed;
God will make his stomach
vomit[t] them up.
16He will suck the poison[u] of
serpents;
the fangs of an adder will kill
him.[v]

19:26 [l] S Nu 12:8; S Mt 5:8; 1Co 13:12; 1Jn 3:2 **19:27** [m] Lk 2:30 [n] Ps 42:1; 63:1; 84:2 **19:28** [o] S Job 13:25 **19:29** [p] Job 15:22 [q] Job 27:13-23; Ps 1:5; 9:7; 58:11; Ecc 3:17; 11:9; 12:14 **20:1** [r] S Job 2:11 **20:2** [s] Ps 42:5; La 1:20 **20:3** [t] Job 19:3 **20:4** [u] Dt 4:32; S 32:7 **20:5** [v] Ps 94:3 [w] S Job 8:13 [x] S Job 8:12; Ps 37:35-36; 73:19 **20:6** [y] Job 33:17; Isa 16:6 [z] S Ge 11:4 [a] Isa 14:13-14; Ob 1:3-4 **20:7** [b] S Job 4:20 [c] S Job 7:8; S 14:20 **20:8** [d] Ps 73:20; Ecc 5:3 [e] Ps 90:10; Ecc 6:12; 12:7 [f] S Job 18:11 [g] Job 27:20; 34:20; Ps 90:5; Isa 17:14; 29:7 **20:9** [h] S Job 7:8 **20:10** [i] S Job 5:4 [j] ver 15,18,20; S Job 3:15; 31:8 **20:11** [k] S Job 13:26 [l] Job 21:24 [m] S Job 17:16 **20:12** [n] S Job 15:16 [o] Ps 10:7; 140:3 **20:13** [p] S Nu 11:18-20 **20:14** [q] Pr 20:17; Jer 2:19; 4:18; Rev 10:9 [r] S Nu 21:6 **20:15** [s] S ver 10 [t] S Lev 18:25 **20:16** [u] S Dt 32:32 [v] Dt 32:24

[i] *25* Or *upon my grave* [j] *26* Or *And after I awake, / though this* ⌊*body*⌋ *has been destroyed, / then* [k] *26* Or */ apart from* [l] *28* Many Hebrew manuscripts, Septuagint and Vulgate; most Hebrew manuscripts *me* [m] *29* Or */ that you may come to know the Almighty* [n] *4* Or *Adam*

ing the visible manifestation of this divine Redeemer.

19:26 IN MY FLESH I WILL SEE GOD. Job prophetically expressed the conviction that after his body had decayed in the grave, he would physically be raised to life and see his Redeemer-God in a resurrected body. This section contains in seed form God's revelation about Christ's future coming at the end of time, the resurrection from the dead and the final vindication of all God's faithful (see previous note; cf. Ps 16:10; 49:15; Isa 26:19; Da 12:2; Hos 13:14; see article on DEATH, p. 732).

19:27 I MYSELF WILL SEE HIM. Job's longing to see his Redeemer-God far outweighed all other desires expressed in this book (see 23:3, note). Job yearned for the day when he could see the Lord's face in full redemption. Likewise, NT believers long for the coming of their Savior (1Co 1:7; 2Ti 4:8) and the day of consummation, when "the dwelling of God is with men, and he will live with them. They will be his people, and God himself will be with them" (Rev 21:3) and "they will see his face" (Rev 22:4).

DEATH

Job 19:25–26 ***"I know that my redeemer lives, and that in the end he will stand upon the earth. And after my skin has been destroyed, yet in my flesh I will see God."***

All humans, believers and unbelievers, are subject to death. The word "death" in the Bible, however, has more than one meaning. It is important to understand the believer's relationship to the various meanings of death.

DEATH AS A RESULT OF SIN. Ge 2—3 teaches that death entered the world because of sin. Our first parents were created with the ability to live forever; when they disobeyed God's command, they came under the penalty of sin, which is death. (1) Adam and Eve became subject to *physical* death. God had set the tree of life in the Garden of Eden in order that by continually eating from it, humans would never die (see Ge 2:9, note). But after Adam and Eve ate fruit from the tree of the knowledge of good and evil, God pronounced these words: "for dust you are and to dust you will return" (Ge 3:19). Though they did not physically die on the day they ate, they did become subject to the law of death as a result of God's curse.

(2) Adam and Eve also died a *moral* death. God warned Adam that *when* he ate of the forbidden fruit, he would surely die (Ge 2:17). This was a serious warning. Even though Adam and his wife did not die physically on that day, they did die morally, i.e., their nature became sinful. Ever since Adam and Eve, every person has been born with a sinful nature (Ro 8:5–8), i.e., an innate desire to go his or her own selfish way without concern for God or others (see Ge 3:6, note; Ro 3:10–18, note; Eph 2:3; Col 2:13).

(3) Adam and Eve also died a *spiritual* death when they disobeyed God, i.e., their former intimate relationship to God was destroyed (see Ge 3:6, note). No longer did they look forward to walking and talking with God in the garden; rather, they hid from his presence (Ge 3:8). Elsewhere, the Bible teaches that apart from Christ, all are alienated from God and from life in him (Eph 4:17–18); they are spiritually dead.

(4) Finally, death as a result of sin involves *eternal* death. Eternal life would have been the consequence of the obedience of Adam and Eve (cf. Ge 3:22); instead, the principle of eternal death has become operative. Eternal death is eternal condemnation and separation from God as a result of disobedience (see Ge 3:4, note), i.e., "punished with everlasting destruction and shut out from the presence of the Lord" (2Th 1:9; see Ro 6:16, note).

(5) The only way to escape death in all its multifaceted aspects is through Jesus Christ, who "destroyed death and has brought life and immortality to light" (2Ti 1:10). By his death he reconciled us with God, thus reversing the spiritual separation and alienation that had come as a result of sin (see Ge 3:24, note; 2Co 5:18, note). By his resurrection, he overcame and broke the power of Satan, sin and physical death (see Ge 3:15, note; Ro 6:10, note; cf. Ro 5:18–19; 1Co 15:12–28; 1Jn 3:8). That believers will not remain forever in the grave was already a part of the testimony of God's OT people (see Job 19:25–26; Ps 16:9–11; see article on THE RESURRECTION OF THE BODY, p. 1779).

THE MEANING OF PHYSICAL DEATH FOR BELIEVERS. Even though believers in Christ have the assurance of resurrection life, they still go through the experience of physical death. But believers approach death differently than do unbelievers. The following are some scripturally revealed truths about the death of a believer.

(1) Death for the Christian is not the end of life, but a new beginning. Rather than something to be feared (1Co 15:55–57), it is the point of transition to a fuller life. Death for believers is a release from the troubles of this world (2Co 4:17) and from an earthly body, in order to be clothed with heavenly life and glory (2Co 5:1–5). Paul speaks of physical death as sleep (1Co 15:6,18,20; 1Th 4:13–15), implying that death is rest from earthly labor and suffering (cf. Rev 14:13). It means going to be with our godly ancestors who have died before us (see Ge 25:8, note) and is a door into the presence of the living God (Php 1:23).

(2) The Bible also speaks of the death of believers in comforting terms. The death of the godly is "precious in the sight of the LORD" (Ps 116:15). It is an entrance "into peace" (Isa 57:1–2) and "into glory" (Ps 73:24); a being carried by the angels "to Abraham's side" (Lk 16:22); a going to "paradise" (Lk 23:43); a going to our Father's house, where there are "many rooms" (Jn 14:2); a blessed departure in order to "be with Christ" (Php 1:23); a being "at home with the Lord" (2Co 5:8); a falling "asleep in Christ" (1Co 15:18; cf. Jn 11:11; 1Th 4:13); a "gain . . . which is better by far" (Php 1:21,23) and a time to receive the "crown of righteousness" (see 2Ti 4:8, note).

(3) Concerning the time between the believer's death and his or her bodily resurrection, Scripture teaches the following: (a) At the time of death believers are brought into Christ's presence (2Co 5:8; Php 1:23). (b) Believers exist in full consciousness (Lk 16:19–31) and experience joy at the kindness and love shown by God (cf. Eph 2:7). (c) Heaven is like a home, i.e., a haven of rest and security (Rev 6:11) and a place of community and fellowship with other believers (Jn 14:2, note). (d) Activities in heaven will include worship and singing (Ps 87; Rev 14:2–3; 15:3), assigned tasks (Lk 19:17), and eating and drinking (Lk 14:15; 22:14–18; Rev 22:2). (e) While awaiting the bodily resurrection, believers are not invisible disembodied spirits, but are clothed with a temporary heavenly form (Lk 9:30–32; 2Co 5:1–4). (f) In heaven believers maintain their personal identity (Mt 8:11; Lk 9:30–32). (g) Believers who have passed on will continue to be concerned about God's purposes on earth (Rev 6:9–11).

(4) Even though much hope and joy awaits the believer at death, believers still grieve when a loved one dies. After Jacob's death, for example, Joseph mourned deeply for his father; his reaction to his father's death is a model for all believers who experience the death of a loved one (see Ge 50:1, note).

17He will not enjoy the streams,
the rivers[w] flowing with
honey[x] and cream.[y]
18What he toiled for he must give
back uneaten;[z]
he will not enjoy the profit from
his trading.[a]
19For he has oppressed the poor[b]
and left them destitute;[c]
he has seized houses[d] he did
not build.

20"Surely he will have no respite
from his craving;[e]
he cannot save himself by his
treasure.[f]
21Nothing is left for him to devour;
his prosperity will not endure.[g]
22In the midst of his plenty, distress
will overtake him;[h]
the full force of misery will
come upon him.[i]
23When he has filled his belly,[j]
God will vent his burning
anger[k] against him
and rain down his blows upon
him.[l]
24Though he flees[m] from an iron
weapon,
a bronze-tipped arrow pierces
him.[n]
25He pulls it out of his back,
the gleaming point out of his
liver.
Terrors[o] will come over him;[p]
26 total darkness[q] lies in wait for
his treasures.
A fire[r] unfanned will consume
him[s]
and devour what is left in his
tent.[t]
27The heavens will expose his guilt;
the earth will rise up against
him.[u]
28A flood will carry off his house,[v]
rushing waters° on the day of
God's wrath.[w]
29Such is the fate God allots the
wicked,
the heritage appointed for them
by God."[x]

Job

21

Then Job replied:

2"Listen carefully to my
words;[y]
let this be the consolation you
give me.[z]
3Bear with me while I speak,
and after I have spoken, mock
on.[a]

4"Is my complaint[b] directed to
man?
Why should I not be
impatient?[c]
5Look at me and be astonished;
clap your hand over your
mouth.[d]
6When I think about this, I am
terrified;[e]
trembling seizes my body.[f]
7Why do the wicked live on,
growing old and increasing in
power?[g]
8They see their children established
around them,
their offspring before their
eyes.[h]
9Their homes are safe and free from
fear;[i]
the rod of God is not upon
them.[j]
10Their bulls never fail to breed;
their cows calve and do not
miscarry.[k]
11They send forth their children as a
flock;[l]
their little ones dance about.
12They sing to the music of
tambourine and harp;[m]
they make merry to the sound of
the flute.[n]
13They spend their years in
prosperity[o]

20:17 [w]Ps 36:8 [x]Dt 32:13 [y]Dt 32:14; Job 29:6 **20:18** [z]S ver 10; S Job 5:5 [a]Ps 109:11 **20:19** [b]S Job 5:16; Ps 10:2; 94:6; 109:16 [c]S Dt 15:11; 24:14; Job 24:4, 14; 35:9; Pr 14:31; 28:28; Am 8:4 [d]Isa 5:8 **20:20** [e]Ecc 5:12-14 [f]S ver 10; Pr 11:4; Zep 1:18; Lk 12:15 **20:21** [g]S Job 7:8 **20:22** [h]S Jdg 2:15; Lk 12:16-20 [i]ver 29; Job 21:17, 30; 31:2-3 **20:23** [j]S Nu 11:18-20 [k]La 4:11; Eze 5:13; 6:12 [l]ver 14; Ps 78:30-31 **20:24** [m]Isa 24:18; Jer 46:21; 48:44 [n]S Job 15:22 **20:25** [o]S Job 18:11 [p]S Job 15:21; Ps 88:15-16 **20:26** [q]S Job 5:14 [r]S Job 1:16 [s]Job 15:34; 26:6; 28:22; 31:12; Ps 21:9 [t]S Job 18:15 **20:27** [u]S Dt 31:28 **20:28** [v]Dt 28:31; Mt 7:26-27 [w]ver 29; Nu 14:28-32; Job 21:17,20,30; 40:11; Ps 60:3; 75:8; Pr 16:4; Isa 24:18; 51:17; Am 5:18; Jn 3:36; Ro 1:18; Eph 5:6 **20:29** [x]S ver 22; S Job 15:20; 22:5; 31:2; 36:17; Jer 13:25; Rev 21:8

21:2 [y]S Job 13:17 [z]ver 34 **21:3** [a]S Job 6:14; S 11:3; S 16:10 **21:4** [b]S Job 7:11 [c]S Job 6:3 **21:5** [d]S Jdg 18:19 **21:6** [e]S Ge 45:3 [f]S Job 4:14 **21:7** [g]ver 13; S Job 9:24; 12:19; Ps 37:1; 73:3; Ecc 7:15; 8:14; Hab 1:13; Mal 3:15 **21:8** [h]Ps 17:14; Mal 3:15 **21:9** [i]S Job 5:24 [j]S Job 9:34 **21:10** [k]Ex 23:26 **21:11** [l]Ps 78:52; 107:41 **21:12** [m]Ps 33:2 [n]S Ge 4:21; S 1Ch 15:16; Ps 71:22; 81:2; 108:2; Isa 5:12; Mt 11:17 **21:13** [o]S ver 7; S Job 8:7; Ps 10:1-12; 94:3

°*28* Or *The possessions in his house will be carried off, / washed away*

21:7 WHY DO THE WICKED LIVE ON. Job questioned the inequities of life, especially the prosperity, success and happiness of many of the wicked. Ps 73 addresses this theological problem. At times the "pure in heart" seem "plagued" (Ps 73:1,14), while the wicked prosper and "have no struggles" (Ps 73:3–5). God responds by revealing the final end of both the godly and the wicked (Ps 73:16–28). Ultimately God will justly rectify all things and give to each one according to his or her deeds and love of the truth (Ro 2:5–11). The wicked will not remain unpunished, nor will the righteous be left unvindicated or unrewarded (Ro 2:5–11; Rev 2:10).

and go down to the grave[p][p] in
peace.[q][q]
14Yet they say to God, 'Leave us
alone![r]
We have no desire to know your
ways.[s]
15Who is the Almighty, that we
should serve him?
What would we gain by praying
to him?'[t]
16But their prosperity is not in their
own hands,
so I stand aloof from the
counsel of the wicked.[u]

17"Yet how often is the lamp of the
wicked snuffed out?[v]
How often does calamity[w] come
upon them,
the fate God allots in his
anger?[x]
18How often are they like straw
before the wind,
like chaff[y] swept away[z][a] by a
gale?[b]
19⌊It is said,⌋ 'God stores up a man's
punishment for his sons.'[c]
Let him repay the man himself,
so that he will know it![d]
20Let his own eyes see his
destruction;[e]
let him drink[f] of the wrath of
the Almighty.[r][g]
21For what does he care about the
family he leaves behind[h]
when his allotted months[i]
come to an end?[j]

22"Can anyone teach knowledge to
God,[k]
since he judges even the
highest?[l]
23One man dies in full vigor,[m]
completely secure and at ease,[n]
24his body[s] well nourished,[o]
his bones[p] rich with marrow.[q]
25Another man dies in bitterness of
soul,[r]
never having enjoyed anything
good.
26Side by side they lie in the dust,[s]
and worms[t] cover them both.[u]

27"I know full well what you are
thinking,
the schemes by which you would
wrong me.
28You say, 'Where now is the great
man's[v] house,
the tents where wicked men
lived?'[w]
29Have you never questioned those
who travel?
Have you paid no regard to their
accounts—
30that the evil man is spared from
the day of calamity,[x]
that he is delivered from[t] the
day of wrath?[y]
31Who denounces his conduct to his
face?
Who repays him for what he has
done?[z]
32He is carried to the grave,
and watch is kept over his
tomb.[a]
33The soil in the valley is sweet to
him;[b]
all men follow after him,
and a countless throng goes[u]
before him.[c]

34"So how can you console me[d]
with your nonsense?
Nothing is left of your answers
but falsehood!"[e]

Eliphaz

22 Then Eliphaz the Temanite[f]
replied:

2"Can a man be of benefit to God?[g]
Can even a wise man benefit
him?[h]
3What pleasure[i] would it give the
Almighty if you were
righteous?[j]
What would he gain if your ways
were blameless?[k]

4"Is it for your piety that he
rebukes you
and brings charges against
you?[l]
5Is not your wickedness great?
Are not your sins[m] endless?[n]
6You demanded security[o] from
your brothers for no
reason;[p]
you stripped men of their
clothing, leaving them
naked.[q]

21:13 [p] Job 24:19; Ps 49:14; Isa 14:15 [q] S Job 3:13
21:14 [r] S Job 4:17; 22:17; Isa 30:11 [s] S Dt 32:15; S 1Sa 15:11; Ps 95:10; Pr 1:29; Jer 2:20,31
21:15 [t] S Job 5:2; 34:9; 35:3; Ps 73:13; 139:20; Isa 48:5; Jer 9:6; 44:17
21:16 [u] Job 22:18; Ps 1:1; 26:5; 36:1
21:17 [v] S Job 18:5 [w] Job 18:12 [x] S Job 20:22,28
21:18 [y] S Job 13:25 [z] S Ge 19:15 [a] S Job 7:10; Pr 10:25 [b] S Ge 7:23
21:19 [c] Ex 20:5; Jer 31:29; Eze 18:2; Jn 9:2 [d] Jer 25:14; 50:29; 51:6,24,56
21:20 [e] S Ex 32:33; Nu 16:22; S 2Ki 14:6; Jer 42:16 [f] Job 6:4 [g] S Job 20:28; Jer 25:15; Rev 14:10
21:21 [h] Job 14:22 [i] S Job 14:5 [j] S Job 14:21; Ecc 9:5-6
21:22 [k] Job 35:11; 36:22; 39:17; Ps 94:12; Isa 40:13-14; Jer 32:33; Ro 11:34 [l] S Job 4:18; Ps 82:1; 86:8; 135:5
21:23 [m] S Ge 15:15; S Job 13:26 [n] S Job 3:13
21:24 [o] Ps 73:4 [p] Job 20:11 [q] Pr 3:8
21:25 [r] S Job 10:1
21:26 [s] S Job 17:16 [t] S Job 7:5 [u] Job 24:20; Ecc 9:2-3; Isa 14:11
21:28 [v] Job 1:3; 12:21; 29:25; 31:37 [w] S Job 8:22
21:30 [x] Job 31:3 [y] S Job 20:22,28; S Isa 5:30; Ro 2:5; 2Pe 2:9
21:31 [z] Job 34:11; Ps 62:12; Pr 24:11-12; Isa 59:18
21:32 [a] Isa 14:18
21:33 [b] Job 3:22 [c] S Job 3:19
21:34 [d] ver 2 [e] S Job 6:15; 8:20
22:1 [f] S Job 4:1
22:2 [g] Lk 17:10 [h] S Job 7:17
22:3 [i] Isa 1:11; Hag 1:8 [j] Ps 143:2 [k] Job 35:7; Pr 9:12
22:4 [l] S Job 9:3; 19:29; Ps 143:2; Isa 3:14; Eze 20:35 **22:5** [m] S Ezr 9:13; S Job 15:5 [n] S Job 15:13; S 20:29; 29:17 **22:6** [o] S Ex 22:26 [p] S 2Ki 4:1 [q] S Ex 22:27; Dt 24:12-13

[p] *13* Hebrew *Sheol* [q] *13* Or *in an instant*
[r] *17-20* Verses 17 and 18 may be taken as exclamations and 19 and 20 as declarations.
[s] *24* The meaning of the Hebrew for this word is uncertain. [t] *30* Or *man is reserved for the day of calamity, / that he is brought forth to*
[u] *33* Or / *as a countless throng went*

7You gave no water[r] to the weary
and you withheld food from the
hungry,[s]
8though you were a powerful man,
owning land[t]—
an honored man,[u] living on it.[v]
9And you sent widows[w] away
empty-handed[x]
and broke the strength of the
fatherless.[y]
10That is why snares[z] are all
around you,[a]
why sudden peril terrifies you,[b]
11why it is so dark[c] you cannot
see,
and why a flood of water covers
you.[d]

12"Is not God in the heights of
heaven?[e]
And see how lofty are the
highest stars!
13Yet you say, 'What does God
know?[f]
Does he judge through such
darkness?[g]
14Thick clouds[h] veil him, so he
does not see us[i]
as he goes about in the vaulted
heavens.'[j]
15Will you keep to the old path
that evil men[k] have trod?[l]
16They were carried off before their
time,[m]
their foundations[n] washed away
by a flood.[o]
17They said to God, 'Leave us alone!
What can the Almighty do to
us?'[p]
18Yet it was he who filled their
houses with good things,[q]
so I stand aloof from the
counsel of the wicked.[r]
19"The righteous see their ruin and
rejoice;[s]
the innocent mock[t] them,
saying,
20'Surely our foes are destroyed,[u]
and fire[v] devours their wealth.'

21"Submit to God and be at peace[w]
with him;[x]
in this way prosperity will come
to you.[y]
22Accept instruction from his
mouth[z]
and lay up his words[a] in your
heart.[b]
23If you return[c] to the Almighty,
you will be restored:[d]
If you remove wickedness far
from your tent[e]
24and assign your nuggets[f] to the
dust,
your gold[g] of Ophir[h] to the
rocks in the ravines,[i]
25then the Almighty will be your
gold,[j]
the choicest silver for you.[k]
26Surely then you will find delight in
the Almighty[l]
and will lift up your face[m] to
God.[n]
27You will pray to him,[o] and he will
hear you,[p]
and you will fulfill your vows.[q]
28What you decide on will be done,[r]

22:7 [r]Mt 10:42 [s]ver 9; Job 29:12; 31:17,21,31; Isa 58:7,10; Eze 18:7; Mt 25:42 **22:8** [t]S Job 15:19 [u]Isa 3:3; 5:13; 9:15 [v]S Job 12:19 **22:9** [w]Job 29:13; 31:16; Ps 146:9 [x]Job 24:3,21; Isa 10:2; Lk 1:53 [y]S ver 7; S Job 6:27; S Isa 1:17 **22:10** [z]S Job 18:9 [a]S Job 10:3 [b]S Job 15:21 **22:11** [c]S Job 5:14 [d]S Ge 7:23; Job 36:28; 38:34, 37; Ps 69:1-2; 124:4-5; Isa 58:10-11; La 3:54 **22:12** [e]S Job 11:8; S 16:19 **22:13** [f]ver 14; Ps 10:11; 59:7; 64:5; 73:11; 94:7; Isa 29:15; Eze 9:9; Zep 1:12 [g]Ps 139:11; Eze 8:12; Eph 6:12 **22:14** [h]Job 26:9; Ps 97:2; 105:39 [i]S ver 13; S 2Ki 21:16 [j]Job 37:18; Ps 18:11; Pr 8:27; Isa 40:22; Jer 23:23-24 **22:15** [k]Job 23:10; 34:36 [l]Job 34:8; Ps 1:1; 50:18 **22:16** [m]S Job 15:32 [n]S Job 4:19 [o]S Ge 7:23; Mt 7:26-27 **22:17** [p]Job 21:15 **22:18** [q]S Job 12:6 [r]S Job 21:16 **22:19** [s]Ps 5:11; 9:2; 32:11; 58:10; 64:10; 97:12; 107:42 [t]Job 21:3; Ps 52:6 **22:20** [u]Ps 18:39 [v]S Job 15:30

22:21 [w]Isa 26:3,12; 27:5; Ro 5:1 [x]S Ge 17:1; Jer 9:24 [y]S Job 8:7; Ps 34:8-10; Pr 3:10; 1Pe 5:6 **22:22** [z]S Dt 8:3 [a]S Job 6:10 [b]S Job 15:11; 28:23; Ps 37:31; 40:8; Pr 2:6; Eze 3:10 **22:23** [c]Isa 31:6; 44:22; 55:7; 59:20; Jer 3:14,22; Eze 18:32; Zec 1:3; Mal 3:7 [d]S Job 5:24; Isa 19:22; Ac 20:32 [e]Job 11:14 **22:24** [f]Job 28:6 [g]Ps 19:10 [h]S Ge 10:29 [i]S Job 1:10; 31:25; Isa 2:20; 30:22; 31:7; 40:19-20; Mt 6:19 **22:25** [j]Job 31:24; Ps 49:6; 52:7; Pr 11:28 [k]2Ki 18:7; Isa 33:6; Mt 6:20-21 **22:26** [l]Job 27:10; Ps 2:8; 16:6; 37:4; Isa 58:14; 61:10 [m]Job 11:15 [n]Job 11:17; 33:26; Ps 27:6; 100:1 **22:27** [o]S Job 5:27 [p]S Job 5:15; S Ps 86:7; S Isa 30:19 [q]S Nu 30:2 **22:28** [r]Ps 103:11; 145:19

22:21–30 PROSPERITY WILL COME TO YOU. Eliphaz appealed to Job with a traditional, yet simplistic, doctrine of repentance: if Job was willing to return to God, to receive instruction from his word, to humble himself and remove sin from his life, and to abandon his trust in earthly things and make the Almighty his delight, then God would surely deliver him from all trouble, his prayers would be answered, and success would follow his every endeavor. However, Eliphaz was mistaken in three respects.

(1) Repentance and salvation do not always result in physical and material prosperity. Sometimes men and women of faith, *because of* their faithfulness, are "destitute, persecuted and mistreated" (Heb 11:37); though they believe God's promises, yet at present they do not receive "what had been promised" (Heb 11:39).

(2) In exhorting Job to repent in order to recover his health and prosperity, Eliphaz was unknowingly siding with Satan and his accusations against Job and God. Satan had earlier accused Job of serving God only for what he could get from God (1:9–11). Note that if Job were to repent of some supposed sin in order to gain God's blessing, then he could indeed be accused of serving God simply for personal gain.

(3) Although Eliphaz's words eloquently express the importance of repentance, they were spoken with the wrong motivation. There was no hint of sympathy in his heart for the suffering Job. Eliphaz's failure demonstrates that the message of repentance spoken to the weak and suffering must be accompanied by words of comfort and compassion.

and light[s] will shine on your
ways.[t]
29When men are brought low[u] and
you say, 'Lift them up!'
then he will save the
downcast.[v]
30He will deliver even one who is
not innocent,[w]
who will be delivered through
the cleanness of your
hands."[x]

Job

23 Then Job replied:
2"Even today my complaint[y]
is bitter;[z]
his hand[v] is heavy in spite of[w]
my groaning.[a]
3If only I knew where to find him;
if only I could go to his
dwelling![b]
4I would state my case[c] before him
and fill my mouth with
arguments.[d]
5I would find out what he would
answer me,[e]
and consider what he would say.
6Would he oppose me with great
power?[f]
No, he would not press charges
against me.[g]
7There an upright man[h] could
present his case before
him,[i]
and I would be delivered forever
from my judge.[j]
8"But if I go to the east, he is not
there;
if I go to the west, I do not find
him.
9When he is at work in the north, I
do not see him;
when he turns to the south, I
catch no glimpse of him.[k]
10But he knows the way that I
take;[l]
when he has tested me,[m] I will
come forth as gold.[n]
11My feet have closely followed his
steps;[o]
I have kept to his way without
turning aside.[p]
12I have not departed from the
commands of his lips;[q]
I have treasured the words of
his mouth more than my
daily bread.[r] Ps 1:1-2
13"But he stands alone, and who can
oppose him?[s]
He does whatever he pleases.[t]
14He carries out his decree against
me,
and many such plans he still has
in store.[u]
15That is why I am terrified before
him;[v]
when I think of all this, I fear
him.[w]
16God has made my heart faint;[x]
the Almighty[y] has terrified
me.[z]
17Yet I am not silenced by the
darkness,[a]
by the thick darkness that
covers my face.

22:28 [s]Job 33:28; Ps 97:11; Pr 4:18 [t]S Job 11:17 **22:29** [u]S Est 5:12 [v]Ps 18:27; S Mt 23:12 **22:30** [w]Isa 1:18; Ro 4:5 [x]S 2Sa 22:21 **23:2** [y]S Job 7:11 [z]S 1Sa 1:10; S Job 6:3 [a]Ps 6:6; 32:4; Jer 45:3; Eze 21:7 **23:3** [b]Dt 4:29 **23:4** [c]S Job 13:18 [d]S Job 9:15 **23:5** [e]S Job 11:5 **23:6** [f]S Job 9:4 [g]S Job 6:4 **23:7** [h]S Job 1:1 [i]S Ge 3:8; S Job 9:3; 13:3 [j]S Job 6:29 **23:9** [k]S Job 9:11 **23:10** [l]Job 1:1; 27:6; 31:6; 36:7; Ps 7:9; 11:5; 34:15; 37:18; 94:11; 119:168; 146:8 [m]S Job 7:18; Ps 139:1-3 [n]S Job 6:29; S 22:15; S Ps 12:6; 1Pe 1:7 **23:11** [o]Ps 17:5 [p]Job 31:7; Ps 40:4; 44:18; 119:51,59,157; 125:5; Jer 11:20 **23:12** [q]S Job 6:10 [r]S Job 15:11; Mt 4:4; Jn 4:32,34 **23:13** [s]S Job 9:3 [t]S Job 10:13; Isa 55:11 **23:14** [u]1Th 3:3; 1Pe 4:12 **23:15** [v]S Ge 45:3 [w]S Jos 24:14; Ps 34:9; 36:1; 111:10; Pr 1:7; Ecc 3:14; 12:13; 2Co 5:11 **23:16** [x]S Dt 20:3 [y]Job 27:2 [z]S Ex 3:6; Rev 6:16 **23:17** [a]S Job 3:6; S 19:8

[v]2 Septuagint and Syriac; Hebrew / *the hand on me* [w]2 Or *heavy on me in*

23:3 IF ONLY I KNEW WHERE TO FIND HIM. Throughout the whole experience of Job's suffering, his greatest longing was for the presence of his Lord. (1) He rarely mentioned the loss of prosperity; he barely alluded to his deep sorrow because of the loss of his children; it was the loss of God's presence that he mourned. In all his misery he desired to find God and to have communion with him again (cf. 13:24; 16:19–21; 29:2–5).

(2) This same yearning for God should characterize all true believers. "As the deer pants for streams of water, so my soul pants for you, O God. My soul thirsts for God, for the living God" (Ps 42:1–2). Again: "O God, you are my God, earnestly I seek you; my soul thirsts for you, my body longs for you, in a dry and weary land where there is no water" (Ps 63:1).

23:10–12 WHEN HE HAS TESTED ME. Job felt confident that God still cared about his life and knew that no adversity would turn Job from faithful adherence to him. (1) Job saw his suffering as a test of his faith in and love for the Lord. His test was similar to that of Abraham when he was told to sacrifice his son Isaac (Ge 22).

(2) Jesus Christ himself was tested by the suffering he underwent (Heb 5:8), and as a result he is now our pattern and example (1Pe 2:21); we as his followers are required to follow in his steps (Heb 13:12–13).

(3) Job's firm conviction that he would pass the test and never abandon his Lord rested on (a) his faithful obedience in the past (vv. 11–12), (b) his love for God's words (v. 12), and (c) his awe and fear of God (vv. 13–15). Likewise, the NT believer must resolve never to be swayed from his or her obedience to God, but rather to fear the consequences of unrighteousness and to love God's words more than daily bread (cf. Ps 40:8; 119:11; see Jas 1:21, note).

24

1 “Why does the Almighty not
set times[b] for judgment?[c]
Why must those who know him
look in vain for such
days?[d]
2 Men move boundary stones;[e]
they pasture flocks they have
stolen.[f]
3 They drive away the orphan’s
donkey
and take the widow’s ox in
pledge.[g]
4 They thrust the needy[h] from the
path
and force all the poor[i] of the
land into hiding.[j]
5 Like wild donkeys[k] in the desert,
the poor go about their labor[l]
of foraging food;
the wasteland[m] provides food
for their children.
6 They gather fodder[n] in the fields
and glean in the vineyards[o] of
the wicked.[p]
7 Lacking clothes, they spend the
night naked;
they have nothing to cover
themselves in the cold.[q]
8 They are drenched[r] by mountain
rains
and hug[s] the rocks for lack of
shelter.[t]
9 The fatherless[u] child is
snatched[v] from the breast;
the infant of the poor is seized[w]
for a debt.[x]
10 Lacking clothes, they go about
naked;[y]
they carry the sheaves,[z] but
still go hungry.
11 They crush olives among the
terraces[x];
they tread the winepresses,[a]
yet suffer thirst.[b]
12 The groans of the dying rise from
the city,
and the souls of the wounded
cry out for help.[c]
But God charges no one with
wrongdoing.[d]

13 “There are those who rebel against
the light,[e]
who do not know its ways
or stay in its paths.[f]
14 When daylight is gone, the
murderer rises up
and kills[g] the poor and
needy;[h]
in the night he steals forth like
a thief.[i]
15 The eye of the adulterer[j] watches
for dusk;[k]
he thinks, ‘No eye will see
me,’[l]
and he keeps his face concealed.
16 In the dark, men break into
houses,[m]
but by day they shut themselves
in;
they want nothing to do with the
light.[n]
17 For all of them, deep darkness is
their morning[y];
they make friends with the
terrors[o] of darkness.[z][p]

18 “Yet they are foam[q] on the
surface of the water;[r]
their portion of the land is
cursed,[s]
so that no one goes to the
vineyards.[t]
19 As heat and drought snatch away
the melted snow,[u]
so the grave[a][v] snatches away
those who have sinned.
20 The womb forgets them,
the worm[w] feasts on them;[x]
evil men are no longer
remembered[y]
but are broken like a tree.[z]
21 They prey on the barren and
childless woman,
and to the widow show no
kindness.[a]
22 But God drags away the mighty by
his power;[b]
though they become
established,[c] they have no
assurance of life.[d]
23 He may let them rest in a feeling
of security,[e]
but his eyes[f] are on their
ways.[g]
24 For a little while they are exalted,
and then they are gone;[h]
they are brought low and
gathered up like all
others;[i]

24:1 [b]S Job 14:5 [c]S Job 9:23; 2Pe 3:7 [d]S Job 15:20; Ac 1:7 **24:2** [e]S Dt 19:14 [f]Ex 20:15; Dt 28:31 **24:3** [g]S Job 6:27; S 22:9 **24:4** [h]Job 29:16; 31:19 [i]Job 29:12; 30:25; Ps 12:5; 41:1; 82:3,4; Isa 11:4 [j]S Job 20:19; S Pr 28:12 **24:5** [k]S Ge 16:12 [l]Ps 104:23 [m]Job 30:3 **24:6** [n]S Job 6:5 [o]ver 18 [p]Ru 2:22; S 1Ki 21:19 **24:7** [q]S Ex 22:27 **24:8** [r]Da 4:25,33 [s]La 4:5 [t]S Jdg 6:2 **24:9** [u]S Dt 24:17 [v]Job 29:17 [w]Ps 14:4; Pr 30:14; Isa 3:14; 10:1-2; Eze 18:12 [x]S Lev 25:47; S 2Ki 4:1 **24:10** [y]Dt 24:12-13 [z]S Lev 19:9 **24:11** [a]Isa 5:2; 16:10; Hag 2:16 [b]Mic 6:15 **24:12** [c]S Job 12:19; 30:28; Ps 5:2; 22:24; 39:12; 119:147; Isa 30:19; Jer 50:46; 51:52, 54; Eze 26:15; Rev 6:10 [d]S Job 9:23 **24:13** [e]ver 16; Job 38:15; Jn 3:19-20; 1Th 5:4-5 [f]Job 17:12; 38:20; Ps 18:28; Isa 5:20; Eph 5:8-14 **24:14** [g]Isa 3:15; Mic 3:3 [h]S Job 20:19; Ps 37:32 [i]Ps 10:9 **24:15** [j]Job 31:9, 27; Pr 1:10 [k]Pr 7:8-9 [l]Ps 10:11 **24:16** [m]S Ex 22:2; Mt 6:19 [n]S ver 13 **24:17** [o]S Job 18:11 [p]S Job 15:22; S 18:5 **24:18** [q]S Job 9:26; Jude 1:13 [r]Job 22:16; Isa 57:20 [s]S Job 5:3 [t]ver 6 **24:19** [u]Job 6:17 [v]S Job 21:13 **24:20** [w]S Job 7:5 [x]S Job 21:26 [y]S Job 18:17 [z]S Job 14:7; Ps 31:12; Da 4:14 **24:21** [a]S Job 22:9 **24:22** [b]S Job 9:4 [c]S Job 12:19 [d]Dt 28:66; Mt 6:27; Jas 4:14 **24:23** [e]S Job 9:24; Am 6:1 [f]S 2Ch 16:9 [g]S Job 10:4 **24:24** [h]S 2Ki 19:35; S Job 4:20; Ps 37:10; 83:13; Isa 5:24; 17:13; 40:24; 41:2,15 [i]S Job 3:19

[x] *11* Or *olives between the millstones*; the meaning of the Hebrew for this word is uncertain. [y] *17* Or *them, their morning is like the shadow of death* [z] *17* Or *of the shadow of death* [a] *19* Hebrew *Sheol*

they are cut off like heads of
grain.[j]
25"If this is not so, who can prove
me false
and reduce my words to
nothing?"[k]

Bildad

25 Then Bildad the Shuhite[l] replied:

2"Dominion and awe belong to
God;[m]
he establishes order in the
heights of heaven.[n]
3Can his forces be numbered?
Upon whom does his light not
rise?[o]
4How then can a man be righteous
before God?
How can one born of woman be
pure?[p]
5If even the moon[q] is not bright
and the stars are not pure in his
eyes,[r]
6how much less man, who is but a
maggot—
a son of man,[s] who is only a
worm!"[t]

Job

26 Then Job replied:

2"How you have helped the
powerless![u]
How you have saved the arm
that is feeble![v]
3What advice you have offered to
one without wisdom!
And what great insight[w] you
have displayed!
4Who has helped you utter these
words?
And whose spirit spoke from
your mouth?[x]

5"The dead are in deep anguish,[y]
those beneath the waters and all
that live in them.

24:24 [j] Isa 17:5
24:25 [k] S Job 6:28; S 16:17
25:1 [l] S Job 8:1
25:2 [m] S Job 9:4; Ps 47:9; 89:18; Zec 9:7; Rev 1:6 [n] S 2Ch 20:6; S Job 11:8; S 16:19
25:3 [o] Mt 5:45; Jas 1:17
25:4 [p] S Job 4:17
25:5 [q] Job 31:26 [r] S Job 4:18
25:6 [s] Ps 80:17; 144:3; Eze 2:1 [t] S Job 4:19; S 7:5
26:2 [u] Job 6:12 [v] S Job 4:3
26:3 [w] Job 34:35
26:4 [x] 1Ki 22:24
26:5 [y] Ps 88:10; Isa 14:9; 26:14
26:6 [z] Ps 139:8 [a] S Job 20:26; S Rev 9:11 [b] Job 10:22; 11:8; 38:17; 41:11; Ps 139:11-12; Pr 15:11; S Heb 4:13
26:7 [c] Job 9:8 [d] Job 38:6; Ps 104:5; Pr 3:19-20; 8:27; Isa 40:22
26:8 [e] Pr 30:4 [f] S Ge 1:2; Job 36:27; 37:11; Ps 147:8
26:9 [g] S 2Sa 22:10; S Job 22:14
26:10 [h] Pr 8:27, 29; Isa 40:22 [i] S Ge 1:4; S Job 28:3; 38:8-11
26:11 [j] S 2Sa 22:8
26:12 [k] S Ex 14:21 [l] Job 12:13 [m] S Job 9:13
26:13 [n] Job 9:8 [o] Isa 27:1
26:14 [p] Job 4:12 [q] Job 42:5; Hab 3:2; 1Co 13:12 [r] S Job 9:6
27:1 [s] Job 29:1
27:2 [t] S Job 6:29; S 9:24; Isa 45:9; 49:4,14 [u] Job 23:16 [v] S 1Sa 1:10; S Job 7:19; S 10:1
27:3 [w] S Ge 2:7; Job 32:8; 33:4; 34:14; S Ps 144:4

6Death[b][z] is naked before God;
Destruction[c][a] lies uncovered.[b]
7He spreads out the northern
⌊skies⌋[c] over empty space;
he suspends the earth over
nothing.[d]
8He wraps up the waters[e] in his
clouds,[f]
yet the clouds do not burst
under their weight.
9He covers the face of the full
moon,
spreading his clouds[g] over it.
10He marks out the horizon on the
face of the waters[h]
for a boundary between light and
darkness.[i]
11The pillars of the heavens
quake,[j]
aghast at his rebuke.
12By his power he churned up the
sea;[k]
by his wisdom[l] he cut Rahab[m]
to pieces.
13By his breath the skies[n] became
fair;
his hand pierced the gliding
serpent.[o]
14And these are but the outer fringe
of his works;
how faint the whisper[p] we hear
of him![q]
Who then can understand the
thunder of his power?"[r]

27 And Job continued his discourse:[s]

2"As surely as God lives, who has
denied me justice,[t]
the Almighty,[u] who has made
me taste bitterness of
soul,[v]
3as long as I have life within me,
the breath of God[w] in my
nostrils,
4my lips will not speak wickedness,

[b]6 Hebrew *Sheol* [c]6 Hebrew *Abaddon*

27:4 MY LIPS WILL NOT SPEAK WICKEDNESS. Job is among the greatest examples of endurance in conviction, adherence to righteousness and perseverance in the faith (see Jas 5:11). His unswerving determination to maintain his integrity and remain faithful to God is unparalleled in the salvation history of the faithful. No temptation, suffering or apparent silence from God could drive him away from allegiance to God and his word (cf. Isa 45:21). He refused to curse God and die (2:9).

(1) Similarly, NT believers must be committed to only one course of action throughout the temptations, sorrows and dark days of life. With the strongest conviction they must confidently continue in their faith, firm to the end (Col 1:23); they must never give up as long as they live, holding fast with integrity to God's word and his love. They must strive always to keep their consciences clear before God and others (Ac 24:16; cf. 23:1; 1Co 4:4; 2Ti 1:3; 1Jn 3:21).

(2) This decision to remain faithful to God and steadfast in faith, hope and love is not optional for the believer (Heb 3:14; 10:35–39; Jude 21). Doing so is their safeguard against experiencing ship-

and my tongue will utter no
deceit.[x]
5I will never admit you are in the
right;
till I die, I will not deny my
integrity.[y]
6I will maintain my righteousness[z]
and never let go of it;
my conscience[a] will not
reproach me as long as I
live.[b]

7"May my enemies be like the
wicked,[c]
my adversaries[d] like the unjust!
8For what hope has the godless[e]
when he is cut off,
when God takes away his life?[f]
9Does God listen to his cry
when distress comes upon
him?[g]
10Will he find delight in the
Almighty?[h]
Will he call upon God at all
times?
11"I will teach you about the power
of God;
the ways[i] of the Almighty I
will not conceal.[j]
12You have all seen this yourselves.
Why then this meaningless talk?

13"Here is the fate God allots to the
wicked,
the heritage a ruthless man
receives from the
Almighty:[k]
14However many his children,[l] their
fate is the sword;[m]
his offspring will never have
enough to eat.[n]
15The plague will bury those who
survive him,
and their widows will not weep
for them.[o]
16Though he heaps up silver like
dust[p]
and clothes like piles of clay,[q]
17what he lays up[r] the righteous
will wear,[s]
and the innocent will divide his
silver.[t]
18The house[u] he builds is like a
moth's cocoon,[v]
like a hut[w] made by a
watchman.

27:4 [x]S Job 6:28; S 12:16; S 16:17
27:5 [y]S Job 2:9; S 10:7; S 32:2
27:6 [z]Job 29:14; Ps 119:121; 132:9; Isa 59:17; 61:10 [a]S Ac 23:1; Ro 2:15 [b]S Job 2:3; S 10:7; S 23:10; S 34:17
27:7 [c]S Job 8:22 [d]Job 31:35
27:8 [e]S Job 8:13 [f]S Nu 16:22; S Job 8:22; S 11:20; Lk 12:20
27:9 [g]S Dt 1:45; S 1Sa 8:18; S Job 15:31
27:10 [h]S Job 22:26
27:11 [i]Job 36:23 [j]ver 13
27:13 [k]S Job 16:19; S 20:29
27:14 [l]S Job 5:4 [m]S Job 15:22; S La 2:22 [n]S Job 4:11
27:15 [o]Ps 78:64
27:16 [p]S 1Ki 10:27 [q]Zec 9:3
27:17 [r]Ps 39:6; 49:10; Ecc 2:26 [s]S Job 7:8; Pr 13:22; 28:8; Ecc 2:26 [t]Ex 3:22; S Job 3:15
27:18 [u]S Job 8:22 [v]S Job 8:14 [w]Isa 1:8; 24:20
27:19 [x]S Job 3:13; S 7:8 [y]S Job 14:20
27:20 [z]S Job 6:4 [a]S Job 15:21 [b]S Job 20:8
27:21 [c]Job 38:24; Jer 13:24; 22:22 [d]Job 30:22 [e]S Job 7:10
27:22 [f]Jer 13:14; Eze 5:11; 24:14 [g]2Ki 7:15 [h]S Job 11:20
27:23 [i]S Nu 24:10; Na 3:19 [j]S Job 7:10
28:1 [k]Ps 12:6; 66:10; Jer 9:7; Da 11:35; Mal 3:3
28:2 [l]Dt 8:9
28:3 [m]Ecc 1:13; 7:25; 8:17 [n]S Job 26:10; 38:19
28:4 [o]ver 10; 2Sa 5:8
28:5 [p]Ge 1:29; Ps 104:14; 145:15
28:6 [q]ver 16; SS 5:14; Isa 54:11 [r]S Job 22:24
28:7 [s]ver 21
28:8 [t]Job 41:34 [u]Isa 35:9
28:9 [v]S Dt 8:15 [w]Jnh 2:6

19He lies down wealthy, but will do
so no more;[x]
when he opens his eyes, all is
gone.[y]
20Terrors[z] overtake him like a
flood;[a]
a tempest snatches him away in
the night.[b]
21The east wind[c] carries him off,
and he is gone;[d]
it sweeps him out of his place.[e]
22It hurls itself against him without
mercy[f]
as he flees headlong[g] from its
power.[h]
23It claps its hands[i] in derision
and hisses him out of his
place.[j]

28 "There is a mine for silver
and a place where gold is
refined.[k]
2Iron is taken from the earth,
and copper is smelted from
ore.[l]
3Man puts an end to the
darkness;[m]
he searches the farthest
recesses
for ore in the blackest
darkness.[n]
4Far from where people dwell he
cuts a shaft,[o]
in places forgotten by the foot of
man;
far from men he dangles and
sways.
5The earth, from which food
comes,[p]
is transformed below as by fire;
6sapphires[d][q] come from its rocks,
and its dust contains nuggets of
gold.[r]
7No bird of prey knows that hidden
path,
no falcon's eye has seen it.[s]
8Proud beasts[t] do not set foot on
it,
and no lion prowls there.[u]
9Man's hand assaults the flinty
rock[v]
and lays bare the roots of the
mountains.[w]

[d] 6 Or *lapis lazuli*; also in verse 16

wreck of their faith when faced with intense persecution, temptations and assaults from Satan (1Ti 1:18–20; cf. 6:11–14; 2Ti 4:5–8; see Php 3:8–16).
(3) On his part, God promises by his power to shield his faithful people and keep them in his grace, so that they may obtain "the salvation that is ready to be revealed in the last time" (see 1Pe 1:5, note).

10He tunnels through the rock;[x]
his eyes see all its treasures.[y]
11He searches[e] the sources of the rivers[z]
and brings hidden things[a] to light.

12"But where can wisdom be found?[b]
Where does understanding dwell?[c]
13Man does not comprehend its worth;[d]
it cannot be found in the land of the living.[e]
14The deep[f] says, 'It is not in me';
the sea[g] says, 'It is not with me.'
15It cannot be bought with the finest gold,
nor can its price be weighed in silver.[h]
16It cannot be bought with the gold of Ophir,[i]
with precious onyx or sapphires.[j]
17Neither gold nor crystal can compare with it,[k]
nor can it be had for jewels of gold.[l]
18Coral[m] and jasper[n] are not worthy of mention;
the price of wisdom is beyond rubies.[o]
19The topaz[p] of Cush[q] cannot compare with it;
it cannot be bought with pure gold.[r]

20"Where then does wisdom come from?
Where does understanding dwell?[s]
21It is hidden from the eyes of every living thing,
concealed even from the birds of the air.[t]
22Destruction[f][u] and Death[v] say,
'Only a rumor of it has reached our ears.'
23God understands the way to it
and he alone[w] knows where it dwells,[x]
24for he views the ends of the earth[y]
and sees everything under the heavens.[z]
25When he established the force of the wind
and measured out the waters,[a]
26when he made a decree for the rain[b]
and a path for the thunderstorm,[c]
27then he looked at wisdom and appraised it;
he confirmed it and tested it.[d]
28And he said to man,
'The fear of the Lord—that is wisdom,
and to shun evil[e] is understanding.[f]'"

29

Job continued his discourse:[g]
2"How I long for the months gone by,[h]
for the days when God watched over me,[i]
3when his lamp shone upon my head
and by his light I walked through darkness![j]
4Oh, for the days when I was in my prime,

28:10 [x]S ver 4 [y]Pr 2:4 **28:11** [z]S Ge 7:11 [a]Isa 48:6; Jer 33:3 **28:12** [b]ver 28; Pr 1:20; 3:13-20; 8:1; 9:1-3; Ecc 7:24 [c]ver 20, 23 **28:13** [d]Pr 3:15; Mt 13:44-46 [e]Dt 29:29; Ps 27:13; 52:5; 116:9; 142:5; Isa 38:11; Jer 11:19; Eze 26:20; 32:24 **28:14** [f]Ps 42:7; Ro 10:7 [g]Dt 30:13 **28:15** [h]ver 17; Pr 3:13-14; 8:10-11; 16:16; Ac 8:20 **28:16** [i]S Ge 10:29 [j]S ver 6; S Ex 24:10 **28:17** [k]Ps 119:72; Pr 8:10 [l]S ver 15 **28:18** [m]Eze 27:16 [n]Rev 21:11 [o]Pr 3:15; 8:11 **28:19** [p]Ex 28:17 [q]Isa 11:11 [r]Pr 3:14-15; 8:10-11,19 **28:20** [s]S Job 9:4 **28:21** [t]ver 7 **28:22** [u]S Job 20:26; S Rev 9:11 [v]Pr 8:32-36 **28:23** [w]Ecc 3:11; 8:17 [x]S Job 9:4; S 22:22; Pr 8:22-31 **28:24** [y]Job 36:32; 37:3; 38:18,24,35; Ps 33:13-14; 66:7; Isa 11:12 [z]S Jos 3:11; S Job 10:4; S Heb 4:13 **28:25** [a]S Job 12:15; 38:8-11 **28:26** [b]Job 36:28; 37:6; Jer 51:16 [c]Job 36:33; 37:3, 8,11; 38:25,27; Ps 65:12; 104:14; 147:8; Isa 35:7 **28:27** [d]Pr 3:19; 8:22-31 **28:28** [e]Ps 11:5; 97:10; Pr 3:7; 8:13 [f]S Ex 20:20; S Dt 4:6; S Job 37:24 **29:1** [g]Job 27:1 **29:2** [h]S Ge 31:30 [i]Jer 1:12; 31:28; 44:27 **29:3** [j]S Job 11:17; S 12:25

[e]*11* Septuagint, Aquila and Vulgate; Hebrew *He dams up* [f]*22* Hebrew *Abaddon*

28:28 THE FEAR OF THE LORD—THAT IS WISDOM. Fear of and reverence for God are fundamental to the believer's relationship with God (Ps 61:5; Pr 1:7). (1) Fearing the Lord makes us concerned and alert that we do not offend our holy God. Without this foundation, no true wisdom exists and no redemptive experience will stand the test of time and temptation.

(2) True fear of God and true Biblical wisdom cause us to shun evil and result in the encouragement of the Holy Spirit (see Ac 9:31, note).

(3) To fear God and yet continue in sin is a moral impossibility. The person that acclaims God's majesty and recognizes his opposition to evil will be characterized by an earnest, decisive and total endeavor to separate from sin (Ps 4:4; Pr 3:7; 8:13; 16:6; Isa 1:16) and follow God's word (Ps 112:1; 119:63; Pr 14:2,16; 2Co 7:1; Eph 5:21; 1Pe 1:17; see article on THE FEAR OF THE LORD, p. 260).

29:2 THE DAYS WHEN GOD WATCHED OVER ME. Job persevered in his desire for the communion with God that he had once known (see 23:3, note). He longed for (1) God's special care and protection (cf. Nu 6:24–26; Ps 91:11; 121:7–8); (2) God's light to show him the way in dark or difficult circumstances (v. 3); (3) God's intimate fellowship and love (vv. 4–5; cf. Pr 3:32); (4) God's grace to help him do good (vv. 12–17); and (5) God's wisdom to share with others (vv. 21–25). What God was to Job, he offers to all those who believe in the Lord Jesus Christ (see Jn 15:15; Ro 8:1,31,33; 2Th 3:3; 1Pe 3:13).

when God's intimate friendship[k] blessed my house,[l]
5when the Almighty was still with me
and my children[m] were around me,[n]
6when my path was drenched with cream[o]
and the rock[p] poured out for me streams of olive oil.[q]

7"When I went to the gate[r] of the city
and took my seat in the public square,
8the young men saw me and stepped aside[s]
and the old men rose to their feet;[t]
9the chief men refrained from speaking[u]
and covered their mouths with their hands;[v]
10the voices of the nobles were hushed,[w]
and their tongues stuck to the roof of their mouths.[x]
11Whoever heard me spoke well of me,
and those who saw me commended me,[y]
12because I rescued the poor[z] who cried for help,
and the fatherless[a] who had none to assist him.[b]
13The man who was dying blessed me;[c]
I made the widow's[d] heart sing.
14I put on righteousness[e] as my clothing;
justice was my robe and my turban.[f]
15I was eyes[g] to the blind
and feet to the lame.[h]
16I was a father to the needy;[i]
I took up the case[j] of the stranger.[k]
17I broke the fangs of the wicked
and snatched the victims[l] from their teeth.[m]

18"I thought, 'I will die in my own house,
my days as numerous as the grains of sand.[n]
19My roots will reach to the water,[o]
and the dew will lie all night on my branches.[p]
20My glory will remain fresh[q] in me,
the bow[r] ever new in my hand.'[s]

21"Men listened to me expectantly,
waiting in silence for my counsel.[t]
22After I had spoken, they spoke no more;[u]
my words fell gently on their ears.[v]
23They waited for me as for showers
and drank in my words as the spring rain.[w]
24When I smiled at them, they scarcely believed it;
the light of my face[x] was precious to them.[g][y]
25I chose the way for them and sat as their chief;[z]
I dwelt as a king[a] among his troops;
I was like one who comforts mourners.[b]

30

"But now they mock me,[c]
men younger than I,
whose fathers I would have disdained
to put with my sheep dogs.[d]
2Of what use was the strength of their hands to me,
since their vigor had gone from them?
3Haggard from want and hunger,
they roamed[h] the parched land[e]
in desolate wastelands[f] at night.[g]
4In the brush they gathered salt herbs,[h]
and their food[i] was the root of the broom tree.[i]
5They were banished from their fellow men,
shouted at as if they were thieves.
6They were forced to live in the dry stream beds,
among the rocks and in holes in the ground.[j]
7They brayed[k] among the bushes[l]
and huddled in the undergrowth.
8A base and nameless brood,[m]
they were driven out of the land.[n]

9"And now their sons mock me[o] in song;[p]

29:4 [k]S Job 15:8 [l]Ps 25:14; Pr 3:32
29:5 [m]Ps 127:3-5; 128:3 [n]Ru 4:1
29:6 [o]S Job 20:17 [p]Ps 81:16 [q]Ge 49:20; S Dt 32:13
29:7 [r]ver 21; Job 5:4; 31:21; Jer 20:2; 38:7
29:8 [s]1Ti 5:1 [t]S Lev 19:32
29:9 [u]ver 21; Job 31:21 [v]S Jdg 18:19; Job 40:4; Pr 30:32
29:10 [w]ver 22 [x]Ps 137:6
29:11 [y]S Job 4:4; Heb 11:4
29:12 [z]S Job 24:4 [a]S Dt 24:17; Job 31:17,21 [b]Ps 72:12; Pr 21:13
29:13 [c]Job 31:20 [d]S Dt 10:18; S Job 22:9
29:14 [e]S 2Sa 8:15; S Job 27:6; Eph 4:24; 6:14 [f]S Job 19:9
29:15 [g]Nu 10:31 [h]S Job 4:4
29:16 [i]S Job 24:4 [j]Ex 18:26 [k]S Job 4:4; Pr 22:22-23
29:17 [l]Job 24:9 [m]S Job 4:10,11; S Ps 3:7
29:18 [n]Ps 1:1-3; 15:5; 16:8; 30:6; 62:2; 139:18; Pr 3:1-2
29:19 [o]S Nu 24:6; S Job 14:9 [p]S Ge 27:8; S Job 15:30; S Ps 133:3
29:20 [q]Ps 92:14 [r]Job 30:11; Ps 18:34; Isa 38:12 [s]Ge 49:24
29:21 [t]S ver 7, S 9
29:22 [u]ver 10 [v]Dt 32:2
29:23 [w]S Job 4:3
29:24 [x]S Nu 6:25 [y]Pr 16:14,15
29:25 [z]S Job 21:28 [a]S Job 1:3 [b]S Job 4:4
30:1 [c]S Job 6:14; S 11:3; S Ps 119:21 [d]Isa 56:10
30:3 [e]Isa 8:21 [f]Job 24:5 [g]Jer 17:6
30:4 [h]Job 39:6 [i]S 1Ki 19:4
30:6 [j]Isa 2:19; Hos 10:8
30:7 [k]Job 6:5 [l]Job 39:5-6
30:8 [m]S Jdg 9:4 [n]S Job 18:18
30:9 [o]S Job 16:10; Ps 69:11 [p]Job 12:4; La 3:14,63

[g]24 The meaning of the Hebrew for this clause is uncertain. [h]3 Or *gnawed* [i]4 Or *fuel*

I have become a byword[q]
among them.
10They detest me[r] and keep their
distance;
they do not hesitate to spit in
my face.[s]
11Now that God has unstrung my
bow[t] and afflicted me,[u]
they throw off restraint[v] in my
presence.
12On my right[w] the tribe[j] attacks;
they lay snares[x] for my feet,[y]
they build their siege ramps
against me.[z]
13They break up my road;[a]
they succeed in destroying
me[b]—
without anyone's helping them.[k]
14They advance as through a gaping
breach;[c]
amid the ruins they come rolling
in.
15Terrors[d] overwhelm me;[e]
my dignity is driven away as by
the wind,
my safety vanishes like a
cloud.[f]

16"And now my life ebbs away;[g]
days of suffering grip me.[h]
17Night pierces my bones;
my gnawing pains never rest.[i]
18In his great power[j] ⌊God⌋ becomes
like clothing to me[l];
he binds me like the neck of my
garment.
19He throws me into the mud,[k]
and I am reduced to dust and
ashes.[l]

20"I cry out to you,[m] O God, but you
do not answer;[n]
I stand up, but you merely look
at me.
21You turn on me ruthlessly;[o]
with the might of your hand[p]
you attack me.[q]
22You snatch me up and drive me
before the wind;[r]
you toss me about in the
storm.[s]
23I know you will bring me down to
death,[t]
to the place appointed for all the
living.[u]

24"Surely no one lays a hand on a
broken man[v]
when he cries for help in his
distress.[w]
25Have I not wept for those in
trouble?[x]
Has not my soul grieved for the
poor?[y]
26Yet when I hoped for good, evil
came;
when I looked for light, then
came darkness.[z]
27The churning inside me never
stops;[a]
days of suffering confront me.[b]
28I go about blackened,[c] but not by
the sun;
I stand up in the assembly and
cry for help.[d]
29I have become a brother of
jackals,[e]
a companion of owls.[f]
30My skin grows black[g] and
peels;[h]
my body burns with fever.[i]
31My harp is tuned to mourning,[j]
and my flute[k] to the sound of
wailing.

31 "I made a covenant with my
eyes[l]
not to look lustfully at a girl.[m]

30:9 [q] S Job 17:6 **30:10** [r] Job 19:19 [s] S Dt 25:9; Mt 26:67 **30:11** [t] S Job 29:20 [u] S Ge 12:17; S Ru 1:21 [v] Job 41:13; Ps 32:9 **30:12** [w] Ps 109:6; Zec 3:1 [x] S Job 18:9 [y] Ps 140:4-5 [z] S Job 16:10 **30:13** [a] Isa 3:12 [b] S Job 10:3 **30:14** [c] S 2Ki 25:4 **30:15** [d] S Job 6:4 [e] S Ex 3:6; Job 10:8; 31:2-3, 23; Ps 55:4-5 [f] S Job 3:25 **30:16** [g] S Job 3:24 [h] ver 27; S Job 9:17 **30:17** [i] S Dt 28:35; S Job 16:16 **30:18** [j] S Job 9:4 **30:19** [k] Ps 40:2; 69:2,14; 130:1; Jer 38:6,22 [l] S Ge 3:19; S Job 2:8 **30:20** [m] S 1Ki 8:52; Ps 34:17; Pr 2:3; Mic 4:9 [n] S Job 19:7; La 3:8 **30:21** [o] Jer 6:23; 30:14; 50:42 [p] Isa 9:12; 14:26; 31:3; Eze 6:14 [q] S Job 4:5; S 6:4; S 10:3 **30:22** [r] Job 27:21; Jude 1:12 [s] S Job 9:17 **30:23** [t] S 2Sa 14:14; S Job 3:13; S 10:3 [u] S Job 3:19 **30:24** [v] Ps 145:14; Isa 42:3; 57:15 [w] S Job 19:7 **30:25** [x] Lk 19:41; Php 3:18 [y] S Job 24:4; Ps 35:13-14; Ro 12:15 **30:26** [z] S Job 3:6, 17; S 19:8; S Ps 82:5; S Jer 4:23 **30:27** [a] Ps 38:8; La 2:11 [b] S ver 16 **30:28** [c] S Job 17:14; La 4:8 [d] S Job 19:7; S 24:12 **30:29** [e] Ps 44:19; Isa 34:13; Jer 9:11 [f] Ps 102:6; Mic 1:8 **30:30** [g] S Job 17:14 [h] La 3:4; 4:8 [i] S Dt 28:35; S Job 16:16; Ps 102:3; La 1:13; 5:10 **30:31** [j] S Ge 8:8; Ps 137:2; Isa 16:11; 24:8; Eze 26:13 [k] S Ge 4:21 **31:1** [l] Pr 4:25; 17:24; 2Pe 2:14 [m] Ex 20:14,17; Dt 5:18; Mt 5:28

[j] *12* The meaning of the Hebrew for this word is uncertain. [k] *13* Or *me. / 'No one can help him,' ⌊they say⌋.* [l] *18* Hebrew; Septuagint *⌊God⌋ grasps my clothing*

30:20 I CRY OUT . . . YOU DO NOT ANSWER. All God's people have this experience at some point in their walk with God, a time in which they cry out to God for help and he does not seem to answer them. Even the Lord Jesus experienced this (Mt 27:46). (1) Through this experiece our faith is tested. At such times we must nevertheless persevere in faith (see Mt 15:21–28; Lk 18:1–7; 1Pe 1:7). (2) We know from God's dealing with Job and with faithful believers throughout history that no true follower of the Lord is ever really abandoned by him (Heb 13:5), and no earnest prayers ever go unheard (cf. Heb 10:32–39).

31:1–34 I MADE A COVENANT WITH MY EYES. In this section Job reviewed his firm spiritual integrity, his adherence to God and his ways, and his goodness to others. (1) Job's declarations about God's redemptive work in him embraced every aspect of life. He spoke of his innocence in the sins of the heart, including sexual lust and impure thoughts (vv. 1–4), lying and cheating for gain (vv. 5–8), and marital infidelity (vv. 9–12). He declared his just treatment of workers (vv. 13–15) and his care for the poor and needy (vv. 16–23).

2For what is man's lot[n] from God
above,
his heritage from the Almighty
on high?[o]
3Is it not ruin[p] for the wicked,
disaster[q] for those who do
wrong?[r]
4Does he not see my ways[s]
and count my every step?[t]

5"If I have walked in falsehood
or my foot has hurried after
deceit[u]—
6let God weigh me[v] in honest
scales[w]
and he will know that I am
blameless[x]—
7if my steps have turned from the
path,[y]
if my heart has been led by my
eyes,
or if my hands[z] have been
defiled,[a]
8then may others eat what I have
sown,[b]
and may my crops be
uprooted.[c]

9"If my heart has been enticed[d] by
a woman,[e]
or if I have lurked at my
neighbor's door,
10then may my wife grind[f] another
man's grain,
and may other men sleep with
her.[g]
11For that would have been
shameful,[h]
a sin to be judged.[i]
12It is a fire[j] that burns to
Destruction[m];[k]
it would have uprooted my
harvest.[l]

13"If I have denied justice to my
menservants and
maidservants[m]
when they had a grievance
against me,[n]
14what will I do when God confronts
me?[o]
What will I answer when called
to account?[p]
15Did not he who made me in the
womb make them?[q]
Did not the same one form us
both within our mothers?[r]

16"If I have denied the desires of the
poor[s]
or let the eyes of the widow[t]
grow weary,[u]
17if I have kept my bread to myself,
not sharing it with the
fatherless[v]—
18but from my youth I reared him as
would a father,
and from my birth I guided the
widow[w]—
19if I have seen anyone perishing for
lack of clothing,[x]
or a needy[y] man without a
garment,
20and his heart did not bless me[z]
for warming him with the
fleece[a] from my sheep,
21if I have raised my hand against
the fatherless,[b]
knowing that I had influence in
court,[c]
22then let my arm fall from the
shoulder,
let it be broken off at the
joint.[d]
23For I dreaded destruction from
God,[e]
and for fear of his splendor[f] I
could not do such things.[g]

31:2 [n]Nu 26:55; Ps 11:6; 16:5; 50:18; Ecc 3:22; 5:19; 9:9 [o]S Job 16:19; S 20:29 **31:3** [p]S Job 21:30 [q]Job 18:12 [r]Job 34:22; Ro 2:9 **31:4** [s]2Ch 16:9; Ps 139:3; Da 4:37; 5:23 [t]S ver 14; S Job 10:4 **31:5** [u]S Job 15:31 **31:6** [v]Ps 139:23 [w]S Lev 19:36; S Job 6:2 [x]S Ge 6:9; S Job 2:3; S 23:10 **31:7** [y]S Job 23:11 [z]S Job 9:30 [a]Ps 7:3 **31:8** [b]S Job 5:5; S 20:10; Jn 4:37 [c]ver 12; Mic 6:15 **31:9** [d]S Dt 11:16; S Job 24:15; Jas 1:14 [e]Pr 5:3; 7:5 **31:10** [f]S Jdg 16:21 [g]Dt 28:30 **31:11** [h]Pr 6:32-33 [i]S Ge 38:24; S Ex 21:12; Jn 8:4-5 **31:12** [j]S Job 15:30 [k]S Job 26:6 [l]S ver 8 **31:13** [m]S Dt 5:14 [n]Ex 21:2-11; Lev 25:39-46; Dt 24:14-15 **31:14** [o]Job 33:5 [p]ver 4,37; Ps 10:13,15; 94:7; Isa 10:3; Jer 5:31; Hos 9:7; Mic 7:4; Col 4:1 **31:15** [q]S Job 4:17; Pr 22:2 [r]S Job 10:3; Eph 6:9 **31:16** [s]S Lev 25:17; S Job 5:16 [t]S Job 22:9; Jas 1:27 [u]Job 22:7 **31:17** [v]S Job 6:27; S 22:7 **31:18** [w]Isa 51:18 **31:19** [x]Job 22:6; Isa 58:7 [y]S Job 24:4 **31:20** [z]Job 29:13 [a]Jdg 6:37 **31:21** [b]S Job 22:7; Jas 1:27 [c]S Job 29:7,9 **31:22** [d]Nu 15:30; Job 5:15; 38:15; Ps 10:15; 37:17; 137:5 **31:23** [e]S Job 10:3; S 30:15 [f]Job 13:11 [g]S Ge 20:11

m *12* Hebrew *Abaddon*

He maintained that he was free from covetousness (vv. 24–25), idolatry (vv. 26–28), revenge (vv. 29–32) and hypocrisy (vv. 33–34).

(2) The moral character and purity of heart and life described here serve as a splendid example for every believer. The godly life that Job lived prior to the new covenant can be abundantly experienced by all who believe in Christ, through the saving power of his death and resurrection (Ro 8:1–17; Gal 2:20).

31:1 NOT TO LOOK LUSTFULLY. Job was committed to the standard of inner holiness that Christ later articulated in the Sermon on the Mount (Mt 5:28). Job had made a covenant with his eyes to avoid stimulating lustful desires that come from gazing at a young woman (cf. Ge 3:6; Nu 15:39). He knew that sensuality would displease his Lord and dissipate the life of God in his soul (vv. 2–4).

31:13 JUSTICE TO MY MANSERVANTS AND MAIDSERVANTS. Job's treatment of his servants exemplifies how employers should care for their employees. He treated his workers with fairness, kindness and equality; he listened to them and responded to any just grievance (cf. Lev 25:42–43,55; Dt 15:12–15; 16:12). Job knew that one day he would have to give account to God for his treatment of others (v. 14; see Col 3:25, note).

24"If I have put my trust in gold[h]
or said to pure gold, 'You are
my security,'[i]
25if I have rejoiced over my great
wealth,[j]
the fortune my hands had
gained,[k]
26if I have regarded the sun[l] in its
radiance
or the moon[m] moving in
splendor,
27so that my heart was secretly
enticed[n]
and my hand offered them a kiss
of homage,[o]
28then these also would be sins to
be judged,[p]
for I would have been unfaithful
to God on high.[q]

29"If I have rejoiced at my enemy's
misfortune[r]
or gloated over the trouble that
came to him[s]—
30I have not allowed my mouth to
sin
by invoking a curse against his
life[t]—
31if the men of my household have
never said,
'Who has not had his fill of Job's
meat?'[u]—
32but no stranger had to spend the
night in the street,
for my door was always open to
the traveler[v]—
33if I have concealed[w] my sin as
men do,[n]
by hiding[x] my guilt in my heart
34because I so feared the crowd[y]
and so dreaded the contempt of
the clans
that I kept silent[z] and would
not go outside
35("Oh, that I had someone to hear
me![a]
I sign now my defense—let the
Almighty answer me;
let my accuser[b] put his
indictment in writing.
36Surely I would wear it on my
shoulder,[c]
I would put it on like a crown.[d]
37I would give him an account of my
every step;[e]
like a prince[f] I would approach
him.)—
38"if my land cries out against me[g]
and all its furrows are wet[h]
with tears,
39if I have devoured its yield without
payment[i]
or broken the spirit of its
tenants,[j]
40then let briers[k] come up instead
of wheat
and weeds[l] instead of barley."

The words of Job are ended.[m]

Elihu

32 So these three men stopped answering Job,[n] because he was
righteous in his own eyes.[o] 2But Elihu
son of Barakel the Buzite,[p] of the family of Ram, became very angry with
Job for justifying himself[q] rather than
God.[r] 3He was also angry with the
three friends,[s] because they had
found no way to refute Job,[t] and yet
had condemned him.[o][u] 4Now Elihu
had waited before speaking to Job because they were older than he.[v] 5But
when he saw that the three men had
nothing more to say, his anger was
aroused.

6So Elihu son of Barakel the Buzite
said:

"I am young in years,
and you are old;[w]
that is why I was fearful,
not daring to tell you what I
know.
7I thought, 'Age should speak;
advanced years should teach
wisdom.'[x]
8But it is the spirit[p][y] in a man,

31:24 [h]S Job 22:25 [i]Mt 6:24; Lk 12:15 **31:25** [j]S Ge 12:16; Ps 49:6; 52:7; 62:10; Isa 10:14 [k]S Job 22:24; Eze 28:5; Lk 12:20-21 **31:26** [l]S Ge 1:16 [m]Job 25:5 **31:27** [n]S Dt 11:16; S Job 24:15; Jas 1:14 [o]Jer 8:2; 16:11 **31:28** [p]S Ge 38:24; Dt 17:2-7 [q]S Nu 11:20; Eze 8:16 **31:29** [r]S Nu 14:1; Ps 35:15; Ob 1:12; Mt 5:44 [s]Pr 17:5; 24:17-18 **31:30** [t]Job 5:3; Ro 12:14 **31:31** [u]S Job 22:7 **31:32** [v]Ge 19:2-3; Jdg 19:20; Mt 25:35; S Ro 12:13 **31:33** [w]Ps 32:5; Pr 28:13 [x]S Ge 3:8 **31:34** [y]Ex 23:2 [z]Ps 32:3; 39:2 **31:35** [a]S Job 9:24; 30:28 [b]Job 27:7 **31:36** [c]S Ex 28:12 [d]Job 29:14 **31:37** [e]S ver 14; S Job 11:11 [f]S Job 21:28 **31:38** [g]S Ge 4:10 [h]Ps 65:10 **31:39** [i]S 1Ki 21:19 [j]S Lev 19:13; Jas 5:4 **31:40** [k]S Ge 3:18; Mt 13:7 [l]Zep 2:9; Mt 13:26 [m]Ps 72:20; Jer 51:64 **32:1** [n]ver 15 [o]S Job 2:3; S 10:7 **32:2** [p]S Ge 22:21 [q]ver 1 [r]S Job 13:19; 27:5; 30:21; 35:2 **32:3** [s]Job 42:7 [t]ver 12-13 [u]S Job 15:13 **32:4** [v]S Lev 19:32 **32:6** [w]Job 15:10 **32:7** [x]S 1Ch 29:15; S 2Ch 10:6 **32:8** [y]ver 18

[n]33 Or *as Adam did* [o]3 Masoretic Text; an ancient Hebrew scribal tradition *Job, and so had condemned God* [p]8 Or *Spirit*; also in verse 18

32:2 ELIHU. A new counselor, Elihu, is introduced here into the narrative. He had refrained from expressing his opinion earlier because he was younger than the others (v. 4). He believed, however, that he had insight into Job's suffering and could instruct him in the correct attitude he should have before God. Elihu's speech differs from the first three in its emphasis that suffering can be God's merciful chastisement in order to enlighten the soul (33:30) and to bring about a more intimate relationship with God (36:7–10). However, like the other counselors, Elihu assumed that Job had sinned and therefore deserved his suffering.

32:8 THE SPIRIT IN A MAN. Despite Elihu's claim to spiritual insight from God (cf. 33:4), his

the breath of the Almighty,[z]
that gives him
understanding.[a]
9 It is not only the old[q] who are
wise,[b]
not only the aged[c] who
understand what is right.[d]

10 "Therefore I say: Listen to me;[e]
I too will tell you what I
know.[f]
11 I waited while you spoke,
I listened to your reasoning;
while you were searching for
words,
12 I gave you my full attention.
But not one of you has proved Job
wrong;
none of you has answered his
arguments.[g]
13 Do not say, 'We have found
wisdom;[h]
let God refute[i] him, not man.'
14 But Job has not marshaled his
words against me,[j]
and I will not answer him with
your arguments.

15 "They are dismayed and have no
more to say;
words have failed them.[k]
16 Must I wait, now that they are
silent,
now that they stand there with
no reply?
17 I too will have my say;
I too will tell what I know.[l]
18 For I am full of words,
and the spirit[m] within me
compels me;[n]
19 inside I am like bottled-up wine,
like new wineskins ready to
burst.[o]
20 I must speak and find relief;
I must open my lips and reply.[p]
21 I will show partiality[q] to no
one,[r]
nor will I flatter any man;[s]
22 for if I were skilled in flattery,
my Maker[t] would soon take me
away.[u]

33

"But now, Job, listen[v] to my
words;
pay attention to everything I
say.[w]
2 I am about to open my mouth;
my words are on the tip of my
tongue.
3 My words come from an upright
heart;[x]
my lips sincerely speak what I
know.[y]
4 The Spirit[z] of God has made
me;[a]
the breath of the Almighty[b]
gives me life.[c]
5 Answer me[d] then, if you can;
prepare[e] yourself and confront
me.[f]
6 I am just like you before God;[g]
I too have been taken from
clay.[h]
7 No fear of me should alarm you,
nor should my hand be heavy
upon you.[i]

8 "But you have said in my
hearing—
I heard the very words—
9 'I am pure[j] and without sin;[k]
I am clean and free from guilt.[l]
10 Yet God has found fault with me;
he considers me his enemy.[m]
11 He fastens my feet in shackles;[n]
he keeps close watch on all my
paths.'[o]

12 "But I tell you, in this you are not
right,
for God is greater than man.[p]
13 Why do you complain to him[q]
that he answers none of man's
words[r]?[r]
14 For God does speak[s]—now one
way, now another[t]—
though man may not perceive
it.[u]
15 In a dream,[v] in a vision[w] of the
night,[x]
when deep sleep[y] falls on men
as they slumber in their beds,
16 he may speak[z] in their ears

32:8 [z] S Job 27:3 [a] S Job 12:13; S Ps 119:34; Jas 1:5 **32:9** [b] 1Co 1:26 [c] Ps 119:100 [d] S Job 12:12,20; Lk 2:47; 1Ti 4:12 **32:10** [e] Job 33:1, 31,33; 34:2,16; 37:2,14; Ps 34:11 [f] S Job 5:27 **32:12** [g] ver 3 **32:13** [h] S Job 4:12; S Ecc 9:11 [i] S Job 11:5 **32:14** [j] Job 23:4 **32:15** [k] ver 1 **32:17** [l] S Job 5:27; 33:3; 36:4 **32:18** [m] ver 8 [n] Ac 4:20; 1Co 9:16; 2Co 5:14 **32:19** [o] Jer 20:9; Am 3:8; Mt 9:17 **32:20** [p] S Job 4:2; S Jer 6:11 **32:21** [q] S Lev 19:15; S 2Ch 19:7; S Job 13:10 [r] Mt 22:16 [s] Pr 29:5; 1Th 2:5 **32:22** [t] S Job 4:17; S 9:9 [u] Ps 12:2-4 **33:1** [v] Job 32:10 [w] S Job 6:28; S 13:6 **33:3** [x] 1Ki 3:6; Ps 7:10; 11:2; 64:10 [y] S Job 6:28 **33:4** [z] S Ge 1:2 [a] Job 10:3 [b] S Job 27:3 [c] S Nu 16:22; S Job 12:10 **33:5** [d] ver 32 [e] Job 13:18 [f] S Job 31:14 **33:6** [g] Ac 14:15; Jas 5:17 [h] S Job 4:19 **33:7** [i] S Job 9:34; 2Co 2:4 **33:9** [j] S Job 10:7 [k] S Job 9:30; S 13:23 [l] S Job 2:9 **33:10** [m] S Job 13:24 **33:11** [n] S Job 13:27 [o] Job 14:16; Pr 3:6; Isa 30:21 **33:12** [p] S Job 5:9; Ps 8:4; 50:21; Ecc 7:20; Isa 55:8-9 **33:13** [q] Job 40:2; Isa 45:9 [r] S Job 11:8 **33:14** [s] Ps 62:11 [t] ver 29 [u] Job 4:12 **33:15** [v] S Ge 20:3; Job 4:13; S Mt 27:19 [w] Ac 16:9 [x] S Ge 15:1; Da 2:19 [y] S Ge 2:21 **33:16** [z] Job 36:10,15

[q] *9* Or *many*; or *great* [r] *13* Or *that he does not answer for any of his actions*

statements and his theology are not thereby infallible. Some are full of insight; others fall short of Biblical revelation.

33:9 I AM PURE AND WITHOUT SIN. Elihu falsely stated that Job was claiming moral perfection, i.e., that he was "without sin" all his life. Job had never insisted that he was sinless (see 13:26), but only that he had followed God's ways with all his heart and could never recall having committed a serious sin that merited such severe punishment (27:5–6; 31:1–40).

and terrify them[a] with
warnings,[b]
17to turn man from wrongdoing
and keep him from pride,[c]
18to preserve his soul from the
pit,[s d]
his life from perishing by the
sword.[t e]
19Or a man may be chastened[f] on a
bed of pain[g]
with constant distress in his
bones,[h]
20so that his very being finds food[i]
repulsive
and his soul loathes the choicest
meal.[j]
21His flesh wastes away to nothing,
and his bones,[k] once hidden,
now stick out.[l]
22His soul draws near to the pit,[u m]
and his life to the messengers of
death.[v n]

23"Yet if there is an angel on his
side
as a mediator,[o] one out of a
thousand,
to tell a man what is right for
him,[p]
24to be gracious to him and say,
'Spare him from going down to
the pit[w];[q]
I have found a ransom for
him'[r]—
25then his flesh is renewed[s] like a
child's;
it is restored as in the days of
his youth.[t]
26He prays to God and finds favor
with him,[u]
he sees God's face and shouts
for joy;[v]
he is restored by God to his
righteous state.[w]
27Then he comes to men and says,
'I sinned,[x] and perverted what
was right,[y]
but I did not get what I
deserved.[z]
28He redeemed[a] my soul from going
down to the pit,[x b]
and I will live to enjoy the
light.'[c]

29"God does all these things to a
man[d]—
twice, even three times[e]—
30to turn back[f] his soul from the
pit,[y g]
that the light of life[h] may shine
on him.[i]

33:16 [a] S Job 6:4 [b] Ps 88:15-16 **33:17** [c] S Job 20:6 **33:18** [d] ver 22,24, 28,30; Ps 28:1; 30:9; 69:15; 88:6; 103:4; Pr 1:12; Isa 14:15; 38:17; Jnh 2:6; Zec 9:11 [e] S Job 15:22; Mt 26:52 **33:19** [f] S Job 5:17 [g] S Ge 17:1; S Dt 8:5; 2Co 12:7-10; Jas 1:3 [h] S Job 16:16; Ps 6:2; 38:3; Isa 38:13 **33:20** [i] Ps 102:4; 107:18 [j] S Job 3:24; S 6:6 **33:21** [k] S Job 2:5 [l] S Job 16:8 **33:22** [m] S ver 18 [n] Job 38:17; Ps 9:13; 88:3; 107:18; 116:3 **33:23** [o] Gal 3:19; Heb 8:6; 9:15 [p] Job 36:9-10; Mic 6:8 **33:24** [q] S ver 18 [r] S Job 6:22 **33:25** [s] Ps 103:5 [t] 2Ki 5:14 **33:26** [u] S Job 5:15; Pr 8:35; 12:2; 18:22; Lk 2:52 [v] S Ezr 3:13; S Job 22:26 [w] Ps 13:5; 50:15; 51:12; 1Jn 1:9 **33:27** [x] S Nu 22:34 [y] Lk 15:21 [z] S Ezr 9:13; Ps 22:27; 51:13; Ro 6:21; Jas 2:13 **33:28** [a] S Ex 15:13; Ps 34:22; 107:20 [b] S ver 18; S Job 17:16 [c] S Job 22:28 **33:29** [d] Ps 139:16; Pr 16:9; 20:24; Jer 10:23; 1Co 12:6; Eph 1:11; Php 2:13 [e] ver 14 **33:30** [f] Jas 5:19 [g] S ver 18 [h] Ps 49:19; 56:13; 116:9; Isa 53:11 [i] Isa 60:1; Eph 5:14 **33:31** [j] Jer 23:18 [k] S Job 32:10 [l] ver 33 **33:32** [m] ver 5 [n] S Job 6:29; 35:2 **33:33** [o] S Job 32:10 [p] ver 31 [q] S Job 6:24; Pr 10:8,10,19 **34:2** [r] S Job 32:10 **34:3** [s] Job 12:11 **34:4** [t] S Job 12:12; Heb 5:14 [u] 1Th 5:21 **34:5** [v] S Job 10:7 [w] S Job 6:29 **34:6** [x] S Job 6:28 [y] S Job 9:21 [z] S Job 6:4; S 10:3; S Jer 10:19

31"Pay attention, Job, and listen[j] to
me;[k]
be silent,[l] and I will speak.
32If you have anything to say,
answer me;[m]
speak up, for I want you to be
cleared.[n]
33But if not, then listen to me;[o]
be silent,[p] and I will teach you
wisdom.[q]"

34

Then Elihu said:

2"Hear my words, you wise
men;
listen to me,[r] you men of
learning.
3For the ear tests words
as the tongue tastes food.[s]
4Let us discern for ourselves what
is right;[t]
let us learn together what is
good.[u]

5"Job says, 'I am innocent,[v]
but God denies me justice.[w]
6Although I am right,
I am considered a liar;[x]
although I am guiltless,[y]
his arrow inflicts an incurable
wound.'[z]
7What man is like Job,
who drinks scorn like water?[a]
8He keeps company with evildoers;
he associates with wicked
men.[b]
9For he says, 'It profits a man
nothing
when he tries to please God.'[c]

10"So listen to me,[d] you men of
understanding.[e]
Far be it from God to do evil,[f]
from the Almighty to do
wrong.[g]
11He repays a man for what he has
done;[h]
he brings upon him what his
conduct deserves.[i]

34:7 [a] S Job 9:21; S 15:16 **34:8** [b] S Job 22:15 **34:9** [c] S Job 9:29-31; S 21:15 **34:10** [d] Job 32:10 [e] ver 16; S Job 12:12 [f] S Ge 18:25 [g] ver 12; Dt 32:4; Job 8:3; 36:23; Ps 92:15; Ro 3:5; 9:14 **34:11** [h] S Job 21:31; S Mt 16:27 [i] Jer 17:10; 32:19; Eze 33:20

[s] *18* Or *preserve him from the grave* [t] *18* Or *from crossing the River* [u] *22* Or *He draws near to the grave* [v] *22* Or *to the dead* [w] *24* Or *grave* [x] *28* Or *redeemed me from going down to the grave* [y] *30* Or *turn him back from the grave*

[12]It is unthinkable that God would
do wrong,[j]
that the Almighty would pervert
justice.[k]
[13]Who appointed[l] him over the
earth?
Who put him in charge of the
whole world?[m]
[14]If it were his intention
and he withdrew his spirit[z][n]
and breath,[o]
[15]all mankind would perish[p]
together
and man would return to the
dust.[q]

[16]"If you have understanding,[r] hear
this;
listen to what I say.[s]
[17]Can he who hates justice
govern?[t]
Will you condemn the just and
mighty One?[u]
[18]Is he not the One who says to
kings, 'You are worthless,'
and to nobles,[v] 'You are
wicked,'[w]
[19]who shows no partiality[x] to
princes
and does not favor the rich over
the poor,[y]
for they are all the work of his
hands?[z]
[20]They die in an instant, in the
middle of the night;[a]
the people are shaken and they
pass away;
the mighty are removed without
human hand.[b]

[21]"His eyes are on the ways of
men;[c]
he sees their every step.[d]
[22]There is no dark place,[e] no deep
shadow,[f]
where evildoers can hide.[g]
[23]God has no need to examine men
further,[h]
that they should come before
him for judgment.[i]
[24]Without inquiry he shatters[j] the
mighty[k]
and sets up others in their
place.[l]
[25]Because he takes note of their
deeds,[m]
he overthrows them in the
night[n] and they are
crushed.[o]
[26]He punishes them for their
wickedness[p]
where everyone can see them,
[27]because they turned from following
him[q]
and had no regard for any of his
ways.[r]
[28]They caused the cry of the poor to
come before him,
so that he heard the cry of the
needy.[s]
[29]But if he remains silent,[t] who can
condemn him?[u]
If he hides his face,[v] who can
see him?
Yet he is over man and nation
alike,[w]
[30] to keep a godless[x] man from
ruling,[y]
from laying snares for the
people.[z]

[31]"Suppose a man says to God,
'I am guilty[a] but will offend no
more.
[32]Teach me what I cannot see;[b]
if I have done wrong, I will not
do so again.'[c]
[33]Should God then reward you on
your terms,
when you refuse to repent?[d]
You must decide, not I;
so tell me what you know.

[34]"Men of understanding declare,
wise men who hear me say to
me,
[35]'Job speaks without knowledge;[e]
his words lack insight.'[f]
[36]Oh, that Job might be tested to the
utmost
for answering like a wicked
man![g]
[37]To his sin he adds rebellion;

34:12 [j]S ver 10; Tit 1:2; Heb 6:18 [k]S Job 8:3; Ps 9:16; Col 3:25; 2Th 1:6 **34:13** [l]Heb 1:2 [m]Job 36:23; 38:4, 6; Isa 40:14 **34:14** [n]S Ge 6:3 [o]S Nu 16:22; S Job 27:3 **34:15** [p]S Ge 6:13; La 3:22; Mal 3:6; Jn 3:16 [q]S Ge 2:7; S Job 7:21; 9:22; Ps 90:10 **34:16** [r]S ver 10 [s]S Job 32:10 **34:17** [t]ver 30; 2Sa 23:3-4; Pr 20:8,26; 24:23-25; 28:28 [u]ver 29; S Job 10:7; 40:8; Ro 3:5-6 **34:18** [v]S Job 12:18 [w]Ex 22:28; Isa 40:24 **34:19** [x]S Job 13:10; S Ac 10:34 [y]S Lev 19:15; Jas 2:5 [z]S Job 10:3 **34:20** [a]ver 25; S Ex 11:4; S Job 20:8 [b]S Job 12:19 **34:21** [c]Jer 32:19 [d]S Job 14:16; Pr 15:3; S Heb 4:13 **34:22** [e]Ps 74:20 [f]S Job 3:5 [g]S Ge 3:8; S Job 11:20 **34:23** [h]Ps 11:4 [i]Job 11:11 **34:24** [j]Isa 8:9; 9:4; Jer 51:20; Da 2:34 [k]Job 12:19 [l]Da 2:21 **34:25** [m]S Job 11:11 [n]S ver 20 [o]Pr 5:21-23 **34:26** [p]S Ge 6:5; S Job 8:22; S 28:24; Ps 9:5; Jer 44:5 **34:27** [q]Ps 14:3 [r]S 1Sa 15:11 **34:28** [s]S Ex 22:23; S Job 5:15; S 12:19 **34:29** [t]Ps 28:1; 83:1; 109:1 [u]S ver 17; Ro 8:34 [v]Ps 13:1 [w]Ps 83:18; 97:9 **34:30** [x]S Job 8:13 [y]S ver 17 [z]Ps 25:15; 31:4; 91:3; 124:7; 140:5; Pr 29:2-12 **34:31** [a]Ps 51:5; Lk 15:21; Ro 7:24; 1Jn 1:8,10 **34:32** [b]Ex 33:13; Job 35:11; 38:36; Ps 15:2; 25:4; 27:11; 51:6; 86:11; 139:23-24; 143:8 [c]Job 33:27; S Lk 19:8 **34:33** [d]S 2Ki 17:13; Job 33:23; 36:10,15,18,21; 41:11; 42:6; Pr 17:23; Jnh 3:8 **34:35** [e]Job 35:16; 38:2; 42:3 [f]Job 26:3 **34:36** [g]S Job 6:29; S 22:15

[z]14 Or *Spirit*

34:37 TO HIS SIN HE ADDS REBELLION. Elihu believed that Job's questioning of and complaints against God (19:6; 27:2) demonstrated outright rebellion against God. Though it may be true that Job seriously erred in his complaints against God, his heart held steadfastly to him as his Lord (19:25–27; 23:8–12; 27:1–6). In his zeal to vindicate God, Elihu failed to understand fully the need Job had to express his innermost feelings to God (cf. Ps 42:9; 43:2).

scornfully he claps his hands[h]
among us
and multiplies his words[i]
against God."[j]

35

Then Elihu said:
2"Do you think this is just?
You say, 'I will be cleared[k] by
God.[a]'[l]
3Yet you ask him, 'What profit is it
to me,[b]
and what do I gain by not
sinning?'[m]

4"I would like to reply to you
and to your friends with you.
5Look up at the heavens[n] and see;
gaze at the clouds so high above
you.[o]
6If you sin, how does that affect
him?
If your sins are many, what does
that do to him?[p]
7If you are righteous, what do you
give to him,[q]
or what does he receive[r] from
your hand?[s]
8Your wickedness affects only a
man like yourself,[t]
and your righteousness only the
sons of men.[u]

9"Men cry out[v] under a load of
oppression;[w]
they plead for relief from the
arm of the powerful.[x]
10But no one says, 'Where is God my
Maker,[y]
who gives songs[z] in the
night,[a]
11who teaches[b] more to[c] us than
to[c] the beasts of the earth
and makes us wiser than[d] the
birds of the air?'
12He does not answer[d] when men
cry out
because of the arrogance[e] of
the wicked.[f]

34:37 [h]S Job 27:23 [i]Job 35:16 [j]Job 23:2
35:2 [k]S Job 33:32 [l]S Job 2:9; S 32:2
35:3 [m]S Job 9:29-31; S 21:15
35:5 [n]S Ge 15:5; S Dt 10:14 [o]S Job 11:7-9; Ps 19:1-4
35:6 [p]S Job 7:20
35:7 [q]Ro 11:35 [r]1Co 4:7 [s]S Job 22:2-3; Lk 17:10
35:8 [t]Eze 18:24 [u]Eze 18:5-9; Zec 7:9-10
35:9 [v]Ex 2:23 [w]S Job 20:19 [x]S Job 5:15; S 12:19
35:10 [y]S Job 4:17 [z]S Job 8:21 [a]Ps 42:8; 77:6; 119:62; 149:5; Ac 16:25
35:11 [b]S Job 21:22; Lk 12:24 [c]Job 12:7
35:12 [d]S 1Sa 8:18 [e]S Job 15:25 [f]Ps 66:18
35:13 [g]S Dt 1:45; S 1Sa 8:18; S Job 15:31; S Pr 15:8
35:14 [h]S Job 9:11 [i]Ps 37:6 [j]Job 31:35
35:15 [k]S Job 9:24 [l]S Job 18:5; Ps 10:11; Hos 7:2; Am 8:7
35:16 [m]Tit 1:10 [n]S Job 34:35,37; 1Co 4:20; Jude 1:10
36:3 [o]S Job 6:28 [p]S Job 4:17
36:4 [q]S Job 6:28; S 13:6 [r]Job 37:5, 16,23 [s]S Job 32:17
36:5 [t]S Job 9:4 [u]Ps 5:2; 22:24; 31:22; 69:33; 102:17; 103:10 [v]S Nu 23:19; Ro 11:29
36:6 [w]S Job 34:26 [x]S Job 4:10

13Indeed, God does not listen to
their empty plea;
the Almighty pays no attention
to it.[g]
14How much less, then, will he
listen
when you say that you do not
see him,[h]
that your case[i] is before him
and you must wait for him,[j]
15and further, that his anger never
punishes[k]
and he does not take the least
notice of wickedness.[e][l]
16So Job opens his mouth with
empty talk;[m]
without knowledge he multiplies
words."[n]

36

Elihu continued:
2"Bear with me a little longer
and I will show you
that there is more to be said in
God's behalf.
3I get my knowledge from afar;[o]
I will ascribe justice to my
Maker.[p]
4Be assured that my words are not
false;[q]
one perfect in knowledge[r] is
with you.[s]

5"God is mighty,[t] but does not
despise men;[u]
he is mighty, and firm in his
purpose.[v]
6He does not keep the wicked
alive[w]
but gives the afflicted their
rights.[x]

[a] 2 Or *My righteousness is more than God's* [b] 3 Or *you* [c] 11 Or *teaches us by* [d] 11 Or *us wise by* [e] 15 Symmachus, Theodotion and Vulgate; the meaning of the Hebrew for this word is uncertain.

35:6 IF YOU SIN, HOW DOES THAT AFFECT HIM? Elihu believed that God is so detached from us (v. 5) that our sins or our righteousness have no affect on him. (1) Elihu's perception is wrong. The Bible reveals that God is not without emotion; he is capable of feeling hurt when men or women reject his love. When they turn against him and sin, he is deeply grieved (Ge 6:6; Ps 78:40; Lk 19:41–44; Eph 4:30).

(2) On the other hand, when God's people sincerely follow him in love, obedience and loyalty, he is greatly pleased (2Co 9:7). God cares for his people with deep feeling, gathering them in his arms like a shepherd (Isa 40:11) and loving them with a tenderness greater than a mother (Isa 49:15). Note the marvelous expression of God's unfailing love recorded by Isaiah: "In all their distress he too was distressed, and the angel of his presence saved them. In his love and mercy he redeemed them; he lifted them up and carried them all the days of old" (Isa 63:9; cf. Isa 53; Heb 4:14–15).

7 He does not take his eyes off the righteous;[y]
he enthrones them with kings[z]
and exalts them forever.[a]
8 But if men are bound in chains,[b]
held fast by cords of affliction,[c]
9 he tells them what they have done—
that they have sinned arrogantly.[d]
10 He makes them listen[e] to correction[f]
and commands them to repent of their evil.[g]
11 If they obey and serve him,[h]
they will spend the rest of their days in prosperity[i]
and their years in contentment.[j]
12 But if they do not listen,
they will perish by the sword[f][k]
and die without knowledge.[l]

13 "The godless in heart[m] harbor resentment;[n]
even when he fetters them, they do not cry for help.[o]
14 They die in their youth,[p]
among male prostitutes of the shrines.[q]
15 But those who suffer[r] he delivers in their suffering;[s]
he speaks[t] to them in their affliction.[u]

16 "He is wooing[v] you from the jaws of distress
to a spacious place[w] free from restriction,[x]
to the comfort of your table[y]
laden with choice food.[z]
17 But now you are laden with the judgment due the wicked;[a]
judgment and justice have taken hold of you.[b]
18 Be careful that no one entices you by riches;
do not let a large bribe[c] turn you aside.[d]
19 Would your wealth[e]
or even all your mighty efforts
sustain you so you would not be in distress?
20 Do not long for the night,[f]
to drag people away from their homes.[g]
21 Beware of turning to evil,[g]
which you seem to prefer to affliction.[h]

22 "God is exalted in his power.[i]
Who is a teacher like him?[j]
23 Who has prescribed his ways[k] for him,[l]
or said to him, 'You have done wrong'?[m]
24 Remember to extol his work,[n]
which men have praised in song.[o]
25 All mankind has seen it;[p]
men gaze on it from afar.
26 How great is God—beyond our understanding![q]
The number of his years is past finding out.[r]

27 "He draws up the drops of water,[s]
which distill as rain to the streams[h];[t]
28 the clouds pour down their moisture
and abundant showers[u] fall on mankind.[v]
29 Who can understand how he spreads out the clouds,
how he thunders[w] from his pavilion?[x]
30 See how he scatters his lightning[y] about him,
bathing the depths of the sea.[z]
31 This is the way he governs[i] the nations[a]
and provides food[b] in abundance.[c]
32 He fills his hands with lightning
and commands it to strike its mark.[d]
33 His thunder announces the coming storm;[e]
even the cattle make known its approach.[j][f]

37 "At this my heart pounds[g]
and leaps from its place.
2 Listen![h] Listen to the roar of his voice,[i]

36:7 [y]S Job 11:11; Ps 11:5; 33:18; 34:15; Mt 6:18 [z]Ps 113:8; Isa 22:23 [a]S 1Sa 2:7-8; S Job 4:7 **36:8** [b]S 2Sa 3:34; 2Ki 23:33; Ps 107:10,14 [c]ver 10,15,21; Ps 119:67,71 **36:9** [d]S Job 15:25 **36:10** [e]S Job 33:16 [f]S Job 5:17 [g]S ver 8; S Jdg 6:8; S Job 34:33; 1Th 5:22 **36:11** [h]S Lev 26:33; Dt 28:1; Isa 1:19; Hag 1:12 [i]S Dt 30:15; S Job 8:7 [j]S Ex 8:22; S Dt 8:1; Jn 14:21; 1Ti 4:8 **36:12** [k]S Lev 26:38; S Job 15:22 [l]S Job 4:21; Eph 4:18 **36:13** [m]S Job 15:12; Ro 2:5 [n]S Job 5:2 [o]S Job 4:17; Am 4:11 **36:14** [p]S Job 15:32 [q]S Dt 23:17 **36:15** [r]S Job 5:15 [s]2Co 12:10 [t]S Job 33:16 [u]S ver 8; S Job 34:33 **36:16** [v]Hos 2:14 [w]S 2Sa 22:20; Ps 18:19 [x]Ps 118:5 [y]Ps 23:5; 78:19 [z]S Ge 17:1; S Job 15:11 **36:17** [a]S Job 20:29 [b]Job 22:11 **36:18** [c]S Ex 23:8; Am 5:12 [d]S Job 34:33 **36:19** [e]Ps 49:6; Jer 9:23 **36:20** [f]Job 34:20, 25 **36:21** [g]S Job 34:33; Ps 66:18 [h]S ver 8; Heb 11:25 **36:22** [i]S Job 5:9; S 9:4 [j]S Job 21:22; S Ro 11:34 **36:23** [k]Job 27:11 [l]S Job 34:13; Ro 11:33 [m]S Ge 18:25; S Job 34:10 **36:24** [n]1Ch 16:24; Ps 35:27; 92:5; 111:2; 138:5; 145:10 [o]S Ex 15:1; Rev 15:3 **36:25** [p]Ro 1:20 **36:26** [q]S Job 5:9; 1Co 13: 12 [r]S Ge 21:33; S Job 10:5; Heb 1:12 **36:27** [s]S Job 26:8 [t]S 2Sa 1:21; Job 28:26; 38:28; Isa 55:10 **36:28** [u]Ps 65:10; 72:6; Joel 2:23 [v]S Job 5:10; S 22:11; S 28:26; Mt 5:45 **36:29** [w]Ps 29:3; Jer 10:13 [x]S Job 9:6; 37:16; Ps 18:7-15; 19:4,5; 104:2; Pr 8:28; Isa 40:22 **36:30** [y]Ex 19:16; Job 37:11,15; Ps 18:12,14; 97:4; Jer 10:13; Hab 3:11 [z]Ps 68:22; Isa 51:10 **36:31** [a]Dt 28:23-24; 1Ki 17:1; Job 37:13; Am 4:7-8 [b]Ps 145:15 [c]Ps 104:14-15,27-28; Isa 30:23; Ac 14:17 **36:32** [d]S Job 28:24; 37:12,15; Ps 18:14; 29:7-9 **36:33** [e]Job 37:5; 40:9 [f]S Job 28:26 **37:1** [g]Ps 38:10; Isa 15:5; Jer 4:19; Hab 3:16 **37:2** [h]S Job 32:10 [i]ver 5

[f] *12* Or *will cross the River* [g] *20* The meaning of the Hebrew for verses 18-20 is uncertain. [h] *27* Or *distill from the mist as rain* [i] *31* Or *nourishes* [j] *33* Or *announces his coming— / the One zealous against evil*

to the rumbling that comes from
his mouth.[j]
3He unleashes his lightning[k]
beneath the whole heaven
and sends it to the ends of the
earth.[l]
4After that comes the sound of his
roar;
he thunders[m] with his majestic
voice.[n]
When his voice resounds,
he holds nothing back.
5God's voice thunders[o] in
marvelous ways;[p]
he does great things beyond our
understanding.[q]
6He says to the snow,[r] 'Fall on the
earth,'
and to the rain shower, 'Be a
mighty downpour.'[s]
7So that all men he has made may
know his work,[t]
he stops every man from his
labor.[k][u]
8The animals take cover;[v]
they remain in their dens.[w]
9The tempest comes out from its
chamber,[x]
the cold from the driving
winds.[y]
10The breath of God produces ice,
and the broad waters become
frozen.[z]
11He loads the clouds with
moisture;[a]
he scatters his lightning[b]
through them.[c]
12At his direction they swirl around
over the face of the whole earth
to do whatever he commands
them.[d]
13He brings the clouds to punish
men,[e]
or to water his earth[1] and show
his love.[f]

14"Listen[g] to this, Job;
stop and consider God's
wonders.[h]
15Do you know how God controls the
clouds
and makes his lightning[i]
flash?[j]
16Do you know how the clouds hang
poised,[k]
those wonders of him who is
perfect in knowledge?[l]
17You who swelter in your clothes
when the land lies hushed under
the south wind,[m]
18can you join him in spreading out
the skies,[n]
hard as a mirror of cast
bronze?[o]

19"Tell us what we should say to
him;[p]
we cannot draw up our case[q]
because of our darkness.[r]
20Should he be told that I want to
speak?
Would any man ask to be
swallowed up?
21Now no one can look at the sun,[s]
bright as it is in the skies
after the wind has swept them
clean.
22Out of the north he comes in
golden splendor;[t]
God comes in awesome
majesty.[u]
23The Almighty is beyond our reach
and exalted in power;[v]
in his justice[w] and great
righteousness, he does not
oppress.[x]
24Therefore, men revere him,[y]
for does he not have regard for
all the wise[z] in heart?[m]"

The LORD *Speaks*

38 Then the LORD answered Job[a]
out of the storm.[b] He said:

37:2 [j] Ps 18:13; 29:3-9 **37:3** [k] S 2Sa 22:13; Ps 18:14 [l] S Job 36:32; Mt 24:27; Lk 17:24 **37:4** [m] S 1Sa 2:10 [n] S Ex 20:19 **37:5** [o] S 1Sa 2:10; Jn 12:29 [p] S Job 36:33 [q] S Job 5:9; S 11:7-9; S 36:4 **37:6** [r] Dt 28:12; Job 38:22 [s] S Ge 7:4; S Job 5:10; S 28:26 **37:7** [t] Ps 109:27 [u] Ps 104:19-23; 111:2 **37:8** [v] S Job 28:26 [w] Job 38:40; Ps 104:22 **37:9** [x] Ps 50:3 [y] Ps 147:17 **37:10** [z] Job 38:29-30; Ps 147:17 **37:11** [a] S Job 26:8 [b] S Job 36:30 [c] S Job 28:26 **37:12** [d] S ver 3; Ps 147:16; 148:8 **37:13** [e] S Ge 7:4; Ex 9:22-23; S 1Sa 12:17 [f] S 1Ki 18:45; S Job 5:10; S 36:31; 38:27 **37:14** [g] S Job 32:10 [h] S Job 5:9 **37:15** [i] S Job 36:30 [j] S Job 36:32 **37:16** [k] S Job 36:29 [l] S Job 5:9; S 36:4 **37:17** [m] Ac 27:13 **37:18** [n] S Ge 1:1, 8; S Job 22:14 [o] Dt 28:23 **37:19** [p] Ro 8:26 [q] S Job 13:18 [r] S Job 9:3 **37:21** [s] S Jdg 5:31; Ac 22:11; 26:13 **37:22** [t] Ps 19:5 [u] Ex 24:17 **37:23** [v] S Job 5:9; S 36:4; Ro 11:33; 1Ti 6:16 [w] S Job 8:3 [x] S Job 4:17; Ps 44:1; Isa 63:9; Jer 25:5; La 3:33; Eze 18:23,32 **37:24** [y] S Ge 22:12; Job 28:28; Ecc 12:13; Mic 6:8; Mt 10:28 [z] S Job 5:13; Eph 5:15 **38:1** [a] S Job 11:5 [b] S Ex 14:21; S 1Sa 2:10; Job 40:6; Isa 21:1; Eze 1:4

[k] 7 Or / *he fills all men with fear by his power*
[1] 13 Or *to favor them* [m] 24 Or *for he does not have regard for any who think they are wise.*

38:1 THEN THE LORD ANSWERED JOB. It was God himself who now addressed Job. He revealed Job's ignorance about the divine role in all that was happening. He humbled Job by revealing how little humans really know and understand about the Almighty. However, through God's response came firsthand revelation to Job of God's presence, mercy and love. (1) Job's constant prayer and deepest yearning to find God was finally answered (see 23:3, note; 29:2, note), confirming that everything was still all right between himself and his Lord.

(2) The Lord's response to his servant Job illustrates that God will ultimately come to all who sincerely and steadfastly call on him; even if our prayers come from hearts of confusion, doubt, frustration or anger, God will eventually respond with his presence, comfort and word.

(3) The most important aspect in our relationship with God is not an intellectual understanding

[2]"Who is this that darkens my
counsel[c]
with words without
knowledge?[d]
[3]Brace yourself like a man;
I will question you,
and you shall answer me.[e]

[4]"Where were you when I laid the
earth's foundation?[f]
Tell me, if you understand.[g]
[5]Who marked off its dimensions?[h]
Surely you know!
Who stretched a measuring
line[i] across it?
[6]On what were its footings set,[j]
or who laid its cornerstone[k]—
[7]while the morning stars[l] sang
together[m]
and all the angels[n][n] shouted
for joy?[o]

[8]"Who shut up the sea behind
doors[p]
when it burst forth from the
womb,[q]
[9]when I made the clouds its
garment
and wrapped it in thick
darkness,[r]
[10]when I fixed limits for it[s]
and set its doors and bars in
place,[t]
[11]when I said, 'This far you may
come and no farther;[u]
here is where your proud waves
halt'?[v]

[12]"Have you ever given orders to the
morning,[w]
or shown the dawn its place,[x]
[13]that it might take the earth by the
edges
and shake the wicked[y] out of
it?[z]
[14]The earth takes shape like clay
under a seal;[a]
its features stand out like those
of a garment.
[15]The wicked are denied their
light,[b]
and their upraised arm is
broken.[c]

[16]"Have you journeyed to the springs
of the sea
or walked in the recesses of the
deep?[d]
[17]Have the gates of death[e] been
shown to you?
Have you seen the gates of the
shadow of death[o]?[f]
[18]Have you comprehended the vast
expanses of the earth?[g]
Tell me, if you know all this.[h]

[19]"What is the way to the abode of
light?
And where does darkness
reside?[i]

38:2 [c]S 1Ki 22:5; Isa 40:13 [d]S Job 34:35; Mk 10:38; 1Ti 1:7 **38:3** [e]Job 40:7; 42:4; Mk 11:29 **38:4** [f]S ver 5; S Ge 1:1; S 1Sa 2:8 [g]ver 18; S Job 34:13; Pr 30:4 **38:5** [h]ver 4; Ps 102:25; Pr 8:29; Isa 40:12; 48:13; Jer 31:37 [i]Jer 31:39; Zec 1:16; 4:9-10 **38:6** [j]Pr 8:25 [k]S Job 26:7 **38:7** [l]S Ge 1:16 [m]Ps 19:1-4; 148:2-3 [n]S 1Ki 22:19 [o]S Dt 16:15 **38:8** [p]ver 11; Ps 33:7; Pr 8:29; Jer 5:22 [q]S Ge 1:9-10 **38:9** [r]S Ge 1:2 **38:10** [s]S Job 28:25; Ps 33:7; 104:9; Isa 40:12 [t]Ne 3:3; Job 7:12; 26:10 **38:11** [u]S ver 8 [v]Ps 65:7; 89:9; 104:6-9 **38:12** [w]Ps 57:8 [x]Ps 74:16; Am 5:8 **38:13** [y]Ps 104:35 [z]S Job 8:22 **38:14** [a]Ex 28:11 **38:15** [b]S Dt 28:29; S Job 15:22; S 18:5 [c]S Ge 17:14; S Job 4:10; S 31:22 **38:16** [d]S Ge 1:7; S Job 9:8 **38:17** [e]S Job 33:22; Mt 16:18; Rev 1:18 [f]S Job 7:9 **38:18** [g]S Job 28:24; Isa 40:12 [h]S ver 4 **38:19** [i]S Ge 1:4; S Job 28:3; Ps 139:11-12

[n]7 Hebrew *the sons of God* [o]17 Or *gates of deep shadows*

of all of God's ways, but the experience and reality of his divine presence and the assurance that all is right between ourselves and God. In fellowship with God we can endure any trial we are called on to undergo.

38:3 BRACE YOURSELF LIKE A MAN. God's words to Job are remarkable both for what they say and do not say. (1) Amazingly, Job was never told why he suffered. He never learned that his suffering involved such grave matters as the integrity and vindication of God's redemptive work among the fallen human race (see 1:8–9, notes). God's silence in this area indicates that the why of Job's suffering was not the most important issue at stake. (2) Also God did not refer to the careless and extreme statements Job uttered in his speeches. God did not severely rebuke him or hold his foolishness against him. He understood and sympathized with Job's suffering and weighed his words and feelings with compassion.

38:4 THE EARTH'S FOUNDATIONS. God's speeches dealt entirely with the natural world of creation and nature. He described the mystery and complexity of the universe and revealed that his method of ruling the world is far beyond our ability to comprehend. God wanted Job to understand that his activity in the world of nature is analogous to his rule in the moral and spiritual order of the universe, and that complete understanding of God's ways will never be found in this life. But the book of Job does reveal that when all truth is finally known, God's ways and actions will be seen as just and righteous.

38:4 TELL ME, IF YOU UNDERSTAND. God rebuked Job for speaking without knowledge (v. 2) and humbled him by making his suffering servant realize that human reasoning is no match for the infinite and eternal God (cf. 40:1–5). Without rejecting Job's claims to moral integrity, God called into question Job's suggestion that he might not be ruling the world justly (e.g., chs. 21; 24). But God went on to assure Job that in his dialogues with the counselors, he had spoken rightly about God (42:7). In other words, God considered Job's error in judgment as stemming from a lack of understanding, not a failure in faith or in sincere love for his Lord.

20Can you take them to their places?
Do you know the paths[j] to their dwellings?
21Surely you know, for you were already born![k]
You have lived so many years!

22"Have you entered the storehouses of the snow[l]
or seen the storehouses[m] of the hail,[n]
23which I reserve for times of trouble,[o]
for days of war and battle?[p]
24What is the way to the place where the lightning is dispersed,[q]
or the place where the east winds[r] are scattered over the earth?[s]
25Who cuts a channel for the torrents of rain,
and a path for the thunderstorm,[t]
26to water[u] a land where no man lives,
a desert with no one in it,[v]
27to satisfy a desolate wasteland
and make it sprout with grass?[w]
28Does the rain have a father?[x]
Who fathers the drops of dew?
29From whose womb comes the ice?
Who gives birth to the frost from the heavens[y]
30when the waters become hard as stone,
when the surface of the deep is frozen?[z]

31"Can you bind the beautiful[p] Pleiades?
Can you loose the cords of Orion?[a]
32Can you bring forth the constellations[b] in their seasons[q]
or lead out the Bear[r] with its cubs?[c]
33Do you know the laws[d] of the heavens?[e]
Can you set up ⌊God's[s]⌋ dominion over the earth?

34"Can you raise your voice to the clouds
and cover yourself with a flood of water?[f]
35Do you send the lightning bolts on their way?[g]
Do they report to you, 'Here we are'?
36Who endowed the heart[t] with wisdom[h]
or gave understanding[i] to the mind[t]?
37Who has the wisdom to count the clouds?
Who can tip over the water jars[j] of the heavens[k]
38when the dust becomes hard[l]
and the clods of earth stick together?[m]

39"Do you hunt the prey for the lioness
and satisfy the hunger of the lions[n]
40when they crouch in their dens[o]
or lie in wait in a thicket?[p]
41Who provides food[q] for the raven[r]
when its young cry out to God
and wander about for lack of food?[s]

39

1"Do you know when the mountain goats[t] give birth?
Do you watch when the doe bears her fawn?[u]
2Do you count the months till they bear?
Do you know the time they give birth?[v]
3They crouch down and bring forth their young;
their labor pains are ended.
4Their young thrive and grow strong in the wilds;
they leave and do not return.

38:20 [j]S Job 24:13
38:21 [k]Job 15:7
38:22 [l]S Job 37:6 [m]S Dt 28:12 [n]Ps 105:32; 147:17
38:23 [o]Ps 27:5; Isa 28:17; 30:30; Eze 13:11 [p]Ex 9:26; Jos 10:11; Eze 13:13; Rev 16:21
38:24 [q]S Job 28:24 [r]S Job 27:21 [s]Jer 10:13; 51:16
38:25 [t]Job 28:26
38:26 [u]Job 36:27 [v]Ps 84:6; 107:35; Isa 41:18
38:27 [w]S Job 28:26; S 37:13; S Ps 104:14
38:28 [x]S 2Sa 1:21; S Job 5:10
38:29 [y]Ps 147:16-17
38:30 [z]Job 37:10
38:31 [a]Job 9:9; Am 5:8
38:32 [b]2Ki 23:5; Isa 13:10; 40:26; 45:12; Jer 19:13 [c]S Ge 1:16
38:33 [d]Ps 148:6; Jer 31:36 [e]S Ge 1:16
38:34 [f]S Job 5:10; S 22:11
38:35 [g]S Job 36:32
38:36 [h]S Job 9:4; S 34:32; Jas 1:5 [i]S Job 12:13
38:37 [j]S Jos 3:16 [k]S Job 22:11
38:38 [l]S Lev 26:19 [m]1Ki 18:45
38:39 [n]S Ge 49:9
38:40 [o]S Job 37:8 [p]S Ge 49:9
38:41 [q]S Ge 1:30 [r]S Ge 8:7; Lk 12:24 [s]Ps 147:9; S Mt 6:26
39:1 [t]S Dt 14:5 [u]Ge 49:21
39:2 [v]S Ge 31:7-9

[p]31 Or *the twinkling*; or *the chains of the*
[q]32 Or *the morning star in its season*
[r]32 Or *out Leo*
[s]33 Or *his*; or *their*
[t]36 The meaning of the Hebrew for this word is uncertain.

39:1 DO YOU KNOW WHEN? God continued to interrogate Job with questions he could not answer. By so doing, God showed Job that his desire to debate God was foolish. Job was humbled and silenced, yet he was reassured of the most important thing—God had not abandoned him. The Lord was there, face to face.

39:2 DO YOU COUNT THE MONTHS? If God could lead Job to perceive his human limitations in understanding God's ways in the world, then he could persuade Job that he is just and merciful, even when Job did not understand the way in which God was working in his life.

5"Who let the wild donkey[w] go
free?
Who untied his ropes?
6I gave him the wasteland[x] as his
home,
the salt flats[y] as his habitat.[z]
7He laughs[a] at the commotion in
the town;
he does not hear a driver's
shout.[b]
8He ranges the hills[c] for his
pasture
and searches for any green
thing.

9"Will the wild ox[d] consent to
serve you?[e]
Will he stay by your manger[f] at
night?
10Can you hold him to the furrow
with a harness?[g]
Will he till the valleys behind
you?
11Will you rely on him for his great
strength?[h]
Will you leave your heavy work
to him?
12Can you trust him to bring in your
grain
and gather it to your threshing
floor?

13"The wings of the ostrich flap
joyfully,
but they cannot compare with
the pinions and feathers of
the stork.[i]
14She lays her eggs on the ground
and lets them warm in the sand,
15unmindful that a foot may crush
them,
that some wild animal may
trample them.[j]
16She treats her young harshly,[k] as
if they were not hers;
she cares not that her labor was
in vain,
17for God did not endow her with
wisdom
or give her a share of good
sense.[l]
18Yet when she spreads her feathers
to run,

39:5 [w]S Ge 16:12
39:6 [x]Job 24:5; Ps 107:34; Jer 2:24 [y]Job 30:4 [z]Job 30:7; Jer 14:6; 17:6
39:7 [a]S Job 5:22 [b]Job 3:18
39:8 [c]Isa 32:20
39:9 [d]S Nu 23:22 [e]S Ex 21:6 [f]S Ge 42:27
39:10 [g]Job 41:13; Ps 32:9
39:11 [h]ver 19; Job 40:16; 41:12, 22; Ps 147:10
39:13 [i]Zec 5:9
39:15 [j]2Ki 14:9
39:16 [k]ver 17; La 4:3
39:17 [l]S ver 16; S Job 21:22
39:18 [m]S Job 5:22
39:19 [n]S ver 11
39:20 [o]Joel 2:4-5; Rev 9:7 [p]Job 41:25 [q]Jer 8:16
39:21 [r]ver 11 [s]Jer 8:6
39:22 [t]S Job 5:22
39:23 [u]Isa 5:28; Jer 5:16 [v]Na 3:3
39:24 [w]Nu 10:9; Jer 4:5,19; Eze 7:14; Am 3:6
39:25 [x]Jos 6:5 [y]Jer 8:6; Am 1:14; 2:2
39:26 [z]Jer 8:7
39:27 [a]Jer 49:16; Ob 1:4; Hab 2:9
39:28 [b]Jer 49:16; Ob 1:3
39:29 [c]S Job 9:26
39:30 [d]Mt 24:28; Lk 17:37
40:1 [e]S Job 5:8; S 10:2
40:2 [f]S Job 13:3 [g]S Job 9:15; S 11:8; S 33:13; Ro 9:20

she laughs[m] at horse and rider.
19"Do you give the horse his
strength[n]
or clothe his neck with a flowing
mane?
20Do you make him leap like a
locust,[o]
striking terror[p] with his proud
snorting?[q]
21He paws fiercely, rejoicing in his
strength,[r]
and charges into the fray.[s]
22He laughs[t] at fear, afraid of
nothing;
he does not shy away from the
sword.
23The quiver[u] rattles against his
side,
along with the flashing spear[v]
and lance.
24In frenzied excitement he eats up
the ground;
he cannot stand still when the
trumpet sounds.[w]
25At the blast of the trumpet[x] he
snorts, 'Aha!'
He catches the scent of battle
from afar,
the shout of commanders and
the battle cry.[y]

26"Does the hawk take flight by your
wisdom
and spread his wings toward the
south?[z]
27Does the eagle soar at your
command
and build his nest on high?[a]
28He dwells on a cliff and stays
there at night;
a rocky crag[b] is his stronghold.
29From there he seeks out his
food;[c]
his eyes detect it from afar.
30His young ones feast on blood,
and where the slain are, there is
he."[d]

40 The LORD said to Job:[e]
2"Will the one who contends
with the Almighty[f] correct
him?[g]

40:2 WILL THE ONE WHO CONTENDS WITH THE ALMIGHTY CORRECT HIM? God once again challenged Job to prove his contention that God was governing the world in an improper manner. (1) If Job could not comprehend the working of God's creation nor understand why things happen as they do, how did he think he could question God about his administration of the affairs of humankind, or even about the suffering God allowed him to experience?

(2) What God was showing his suffering servant was that he had created the world in wisdom and that he was governing it with wisdom and justice. The misfortune that Job had suffered did not mean

Let him who accuses God
answer him!"[h]

3Then Job answered the LORD:

4"I am unworthy[i]—how can I
reply to you?
I put my hand over my mouth.[j]
5I spoke once, but I have no
answer[k]—
twice, but I will say no more."[l]

6Then the LORD spoke to Job out of
the storm:[m]

7"Brace yourself like a man;
I will question you,
and you shall answer me.[n]

8"Would you discredit my justice?[o]
Would you condemn me to
justify yourself?[p]
9Do you have an arm like God's,[q]
and can your voice[r] thunder
like his?[s]
10Then adorn yourself with glory and
splendor,
and clothe yourself in honor and
majesty.[t]
11Unleash the fury of your wrath,[u]
look at every proud man and
bring him low,[v]
12look at every proud[w] man and
humble him,[x]
crush[y] the wicked where they
stand.
13Bury them all in the dust
together;[z]
shroud their faces in the
grave.[a]
14Then I myself will admit to you
that your own right hand can
save you.[b]

15"Look at the behemoth,[u]
which I made[c] along with you
and which feeds on grass like an
ox.[d]
16What strength[e] he has in his
loins,
what power in the muscles of
his belly![f]
17His tail[v] sways like a cedar;
the sinews of his thighs are
close-knit.[g]
18His bones are tubes of bronze,
his limbs[h] like rods of iron.[i]
19He ranks first among the works of
God,[j]

40:2 [h]S Job 9:3 **40:4** [i]Job 42:6 [j]S Jdg 18:19; S Job 29:9 **40:5** [k]S Job 9:3 [l]S Job 9:15 **40:6** [m]S Ex 14:21; S Job 38:1 **40:7** [n]S Job 38:3 **40:8** [o]S Job 15:25; S 27:2; Ro 3:3 [p]S Job 2:3; S 34:17 **40:9** [q]S 2Ch 32:8; S Ps 98:1 [r]Isa 6:8; Eze 10:5 [s]S Ex 20:19; S Job 36:33 **40:10** [t]Ps 29:1-2; 45:3; 93:1; 96:6; 104:1; 145:5 **40:11** [u]S Job 20:28; Ps 7:11; Isa 5:25; 9:12,19; 10:5; 13:3,5; 30:27; 42:25; 51:20; Jer 7:20; Na 1:6; Zep 1:18 [v]Ps 18:27; Isa 2:11,12,17; 23:9; 24:10; 25:12; 26:5; 32:19 **40:12** [w]Ps 10:4; Isa 25:11; Jer 48:29; 49:16; Zep 2:10 [x]S 1Sa 2:7; S Ps 52:5; 1Pe 5:5 [y]Ps 60:12; Isa 22:5; 28:3; 63:2-3,6; Da 5:20; Mic 5:8; 7:10; Zec 10:5; Mal 4:3 **40:13** [z]Nu 16:31-34 [a]S Job 4:9 **40:14** [b]Ex 15:6,12; Ps 18:35; 20:6; 48:10; 60:5; 108:6; Isa 41:10; 63:5 **40:15** [c]S Job 9:9 [d]Isa 11:7; 65:25 **40:16** [e]S Job 39:11 [f]Job 41:9 **40:17** [g]Job 41:15 **40:18** [h]Job 41:12 [i]Isa 11:4; 49:2 **40:19** [j]Job 41:33; Ps 40:5; 139:14; Isa 27:1

[u]*15* Possibly the hippopotamus or the elephant [v]*17* Possibly trunk

that God had abandoned his love for his faithful servant.

(3) The suffering of the righteous does not call into question God's goodness. Their affliction is under the permissive will of God, allowed for his wise, yet often unknown, purpose (see article on THE WILL OF GOD, p. 1056). Adverse circumstances should not destroy our faith in God's love for us; he allows them for our highest good (Ro 8:28, note).

40:3 THEN JOB ANSWERED. Job was now faced with the decision whether to persist in his belief that God had treated him unfairly in view of his years of faithful worship and obedience to his word. Would Job maintain his trust in God in spite of circumstances suggesting that God was unjust and capricious, or would he hold on to the feeling that God had seemingly become his enemy?

40:4 PUT MY HAND OVER MY MOUTH. Job was overwhelmed by this new revelation of God. He understood how insignificant humans are before God's secret wisdom (cf. 1Co 2:7), and he felt he could say no more. Still, he was not quite ready to give up his claim that something had been wrong in God's treatment of him (Job's final response comes in 42:2–6). Yet Job was coming to the realization that his mysterious and perplexing suffering had not been a mystery to God, and that through it all God could be trusted.

40:6 THE LORD SPOKE TO JOB. In order to bring Job to complete submission to his lordship and ways, God continued his argument. He wanted to overcome Job's remaining resistance and to lead him into a full realization of his love. This loving persistence on God's part reveals his patience, mercy and genuine care for his suffering people.

40:8 WOULD YOU CONDEMN ME? Job's contention that he was innocent and that God had been unjustly punishing him (see 19:6) brought him close to condemning God. The Lord now asked Job specifically whether he would continue to assert his limited perspective of God's administration of the world at the cost of rejecting his justice and goodness?

40:15 THE BEHEMOTH. The behemoth is identified by many commentators as the hippopotamus; the leviathan (ch. 41) is often identified as a giant crocodile or a whale. By these illustrations God emphasized that if Job could not subdue the great creatures of the world, then he was in no position to question and counsel the God who had made these creatures (41:10). Job must trustfully submit to God's rule over the universe, the affairs of humankind and the lives of his followers. He must trust God and maintain his faith in God—both during the sufferings and afflictions of life and during the times of blessing.

yet his Maker[k] can approach
him with his sword.[l]
20The hills bring him their
produce,[m]
and all the wild animals play[n]
nearby.[o]
21Under the lotus plants he lies,
hidden among the reeds[p] in the
marsh.[q]
22The lotuses conceal him in their
shadow;
the poplars by the stream[r]
surround him.
23When the river rages,[s] he is not
alarmed;
he is secure, though the
Jordan[t] should surge
against his mouth.
24Can anyone capture him by the
eyes,[w]
or trap him and pierce his
nose?[u]

41 "Can you pull in the
leviathan[x][v] with a
fishhook[w]
or tie down his tongue with a
rope?
2Can you put a cord through his
nose[x]
or pierce his jaw with a hook?[y]
3Will he keep begging you for
mercy?[z]
Will he speak to you with gentle
words?
4Will he make an agreement with
you
for you to take him as your
slave for life?[a]
5Can you make a pet of him like a
bird
or put him on a leash for your
girls?
6Will traders barter for him?
Will they divide him up among
the merchants?
7Can you fill his hide with harpoons
or his head with fishing
spears?[b]
8If you lay a hand on him,
you will remember the struggle
and never do it again![c]
9Any hope of subduing him is
false;
the mere sight of him is
overpowering.[d]
10No one is fierce enough to rouse
him.[e]
Who then is able to stand
against me?[f]
11Who has a claim against me that I
must pay?[g]
Everything under heaven belongs
to me.[h]
12"I will not fail to speak of his
limbs,[i]
his strength[j] and his graceful
form.
13Who can strip off his outer coat?
Who would approach him with a
bridle?[k]
14Who dares open the doors of his
mouth,[l]
ringed about with his fearsome
teeth?
15His back has[y] rows of shields
tightly sealed together;[m]
16each is so close to the next
that no air can pass between.
17They are joined fast to one
another;
they cling together and cannot
be parted.
18His snorting throws out flashes of
light;
his eyes are like the rays of
dawn.[n]
19Firebrands[o] stream from his
mouth;
sparks of fire shoot out.
20Smoke pours from his nostrils[p]
as from a boiling pot over a fire
of reeds.
21His breath[q] sets coals ablaze,
and flames dart from his
mouth.[r]
22Strength[s] resides in his neck;
dismay goes before him.
23The folds of his flesh are tightly
joined;
they are firm and immovable.
24His chest is hard as rock,
hard as a lower millstone.[t]
25When he rises up, the mighty are
terrified;[u]
they retreat before his
thrashing.[v]
26The sword that reaches him has
no effect,
nor does the spear or the dart or
the javelin.[w][x]
27Iron he treats like straw[y]
and bronze like rotten wood.
28Arrows do not make him flee;[z]
slingstones are like chaff to him.

40:19 [k]S Job 4:17; S 9:9 [l]S Ge 3:24
40:20 [m]Ps 104:14 [n]Ps 104:26 [o]S Job 5:23
40:21 [p]S Ge 41:2; Ps 68:30; Isa 35:7 [q]Job 8:11
40:22 [r]Ps 1:3; Isa 44:4
40:23 [s]Isa 8:7; 11:15 [t]S Jos 3:1
40:24 [u]2Ki 19:28; Job 41:2,7,26; Isa 37:29
41:1 [v]S Job 3:8 [w]Am 4:2
41:2 [x]S Job 40:24 [y]Eze 19:4
41:3 [z]1Ki 20:31
41:4 [a]S Ex 21:6
41:7 [b]S Job 40:24
41:8 [c]S Job 3:8
41:9 [d]Job 40:16
41:10 [e]S Job 3:8 [f]S 2Ch 20:6; S Isa 46:5; Jer 50:44; Rev 6:17
41:11 [g]S Job 34:33; Ro 11:35 [h]S Jos 3:11; S Job 10:4; Ac 4:24; 1Co 10:26
41:12 [i]Job 40:18 [j]S Job 39:11
41:13 [k]S Job 30:11; S 39:10
41:14 [l]Ps 22:13
41:15 [m]Job 40:17
41:18 [n]S Job 3:9
41:19 [o]Da 10:6
41:20 [p]Ps 18:8
41:21 [q]S Job 4:9; Isa 11:4; 40:7 [r]Ps 18:8; Isa 10:17; 30:27; 33:14; 66:14-16; Jer 4:4
41:22 [s]S Job 39:11
41:24 [t]Mt 18:6
41:25 [u]Job 39:20 [v]S Job 3:8
41:26 [w]S Jos 8:18 [x]S Job 40:24
41:27 [y]ver 29
41:28 [z]Ps 91:5

[w]24 Or *by a water hole* [x]1 Possibly the crocodile [y]15 Or *His pride is his*

29A club seems to him but a piece of straw;[a]
he laughs[b] at the rattling of the lance.
30His undersides are jagged potsherds,
leaving a trail in the mud like a threshing sledge.[c]
31He makes the depths churn like a boiling caldron[d]
and stirs up the sea like a pot of ointment.[e]
32Behind him he leaves a glistening wake;
one would think the deep had white hair.
33Nothing on earth is his equal[f]—
a creature without fear.
34He looks down on all that are haughty;[g]
he is king over all that are proud.[h]"

Job

42 Then Job replied to the LORD:
2"I know that you can do all things;[i]
no plan of yours can be thwarted.[j]
3⌞You asked,⌟ 'Who is this that obscures my counsel without knowledge?'[k]
Surely I spoke of things I did not understand,
things too wonderful for me to know.[l]
4"You said,⌟ 'Listen now, and I will speak;
I will question you,
and you shall answer me.'[m]
5My ears had heard of you[n]
but now my eyes have seen you.[o]
6Therefore I despise myself[p]
and repent[q] in dust and ashes."[r]

Epilogue

7After the LORD had said these
things to Job[s], he said to Eliphaz the
Temanite, "I am angry with you and
your two friends,[t] because you have

41:29 [a]ver 27 [b]S Job 5:22 41:30 [c]Isa 28:27; 41:15; Am 1:3 41:31 [d]1Sa 2:14 [e]Eze 32:2 41:33 [f]S Job 40:19 41:34 [g]Ps 18:27; 101:5; 131:1; Pr 6:17; 21:4; 30:13 [h]Job 28:8 42:2 [i]S Ge 18:14; S Mt 19:26 [j]S 2Ch 20:6; S Job 16:19; Ac 4:28; Eph 1:11 42:3 [k]S Job 34:35 [l]S Job 5:9 42:4 [m]S Job 38:3 42:5 [n]S Job 26:14; Ro 10:17 [o]Jdg 13:22; Isa 6:5; S Mt 5:8; Lk 2:30; Eph 1:17-18 42:6 [p]Job 40:4; Eze 6:9; Ro 12:3 [q]S Job 34:33 [r]S Ex 10:3; S Ezr 9:6; S Job 2:8; S 6:29 42:7 [s]S Jos 1:7 [t]Job 32:3

42:1 THEN JOB REPLIED. Job's final answer to God was one of absolute humility and submission to his revelation. He confessed that (1) God does all things well; (2) that everything that God permits to occur he does so in wisdom and with purpose; and thus (3) even the suffering of the righteous has meaning and divine purpose.

42:3 SPOKE OF THINGS I DID NOT UNDERSTAND. Job admitted that God's ways are beyond human comprehension and that out of misunderstanding he had declared that they were unjust. (1) Note that Job in his suffering and in his prayers did not sin against God. However, his misunderstanding and his complaints against God had led him close to pride and to the belief that God was in some way not perfectly good. Now with the appearance and revelation of his Lord (cf. v. 5), his perspective completely changes.

(2) Job acknowledged his error and was ready to submit to and serve God no matter what happened to him. He would fear and love God for God's own sake, with or without his health, regardless of any personal gain (v. 4).

(3) By committing himself to God in faith, hope and love while still suffering and not knowing the why of it all, Job proved Satan's accusation wrong (1:9–11) and thereby vindicated God's power to redeem and reconcile the human race to himself (see 1:8–9, notes).

42:5 NOW MY EYES HAVE SEEN YOU. Job had earlier prayed to see his Redeemer (19:27); now that longing was fulfilled. God's word and presence brought Job a greater revelation of God's ways and character. Through this personal experience, Job was transformed by a sense of forgiveness, a renewed confidence in God's goodness and a reassuring experience of his love. (1) God's appearance to Job was a vindication of Job's uprightness, and it is an assurance to all faithful believers that the Lord will accept our sincere questions when we are undergoing unexplained adversity and suffering. (2) God is patient with his own and sympathizes with our weaknesses, our misunderstandings and even our anger (Heb 4:15). As with Job, if we endure, God will manifest his presence and extend his care to us.

42:6 REPENT IN DUST AND ASHES. In response to God's revelation, Job humbled himself in repentance. The word "repent" means that Job considered himself and even his moral rightness as mere "dust and ashes" before a holy God (cf. Isa 6). Job did not retract what he had said about his life of righteousness and moral integrity, but he did admit that his accusations and complaints against God were not appropriate for a finite human to make, and he repented for doing so (cf. Ge 18:27).

42:7 AFTER THE LORD HAD SAID. Although the book of Job never gives a final solution to the problem of undeserved suffering by the righteous, the ultimate answer is found not in theological reasoning, but in a personal encounter between God and the faithful sufferer. (1) Only the personal presence of a comforting and caring God will bring confidence in his grace and purpose for our lives. For those who believe in Christ, God sends the Holy Spirit as a Helper and a Counselor (see Jn 14:16, note). (2) This presence of God through the Holy Spirit teaches us that we may have confidence in God's love, whether in circumstances of

not spoken of me what is right, as my
servant Job has.[u] 8So now take seven
bulls and seven rams[v] and go to my
servant Job[w] and sacrifice a burnt offering[x] for yourselves. My servant
Job will pray for you, and I will accept
his prayer[y] and not deal with you according to your folly.[z] You have not
spoken of me what is right, as my servant Job has."[a] 9So Eliphaz the Temanite, Bildad the Shuhite and Zophar
the Naamathite[b] did what the LORD
told them; and the LORD accepted Job's
prayer.[c]
10After Job had prayed for his
friends, the LORD made him prosperous
again[d] and gave him twice as much as
he had before.[e] 11All his brothers and
sisters and everyone who had known
him before[f] came and ate with him in
his house. They comforted and consoled him over all the trouble the LORD
had brought upon him,[g] and each one
gave him a piece of silver[z] and a gold
ring.
12The LORD blessed the latter part of
Job's life more than the first. He had
fourteen thousand sheep, six thousand
camels, a thousand yoke of oxen and a
thousand donkeys. 13And he also had
seven sons and three daughters. 14The
first daughter he named Jemimah, the
second Keziah and the third Keren-
Happuch. 15Nowhere in all the land
were there found women as beautiful
as Job's daughters, and their father
granted them an inheritance along
with their brothers.
16After this, Job lived a hundred and
forty years; he saw his children and
their children to the fourth generation.
17And so he died, old and full of
years.[h]

42:7 [u] ver 8; S Job 9:15
42:8 [v] Nu 23:1, 29; Eze 45:23 [w] Job 1:8 [x] S Ge 8:20 [y] Jas 5:15-16; 1Jn 5:16 [z] Ge 20:7; Job 22:30 [a] S ver 7
42:9 [b] Job 2:11 [c] S Ge 19:21; S 20:17; Eze 14:14
42:10 [d] Dt 30:3; Ps 14:7 [e] S Job 1:3; Ps 85:1-3; 126:5-6; Php 2:8-9; Jas 5:11
42:11 [f] S Job 19:13 [g] S Ge 37:35
42:17 [h] S Ge 15:15

[z] *11* Hebrew *him a kesitah*; a kesitah was a unit of money of unknown weight and value.

adversity or blessing. The Spirit mediates to us Christ's presence and points us to the cross, by which we have the assurance that God is for us and that he seeks our ultimate good (see Ro 8:28, note).

42:7 YOU HAVE NOT SPOKEN OF ME WHAT IS RIGHT. The Lord condemned Job's three friends for their erroneous theology of prosperity and suffering, evident in their accusations against Job. Their three major errors were: (1) They taught a retributive principle of prosperity and suffering—that the righteous are always blessed and the wicked always experience adversity (see Jn 9:3, note).

(2) They urged Job to admit a sin that he had not committed, so that he might escape his suffering and receive God's blessing. By their counsel they tempted Job to use God for personal gain. If Job had followed their advice, he would have (a) discredited God's faith in him, and (b) confirmed Satan's claim that Job feared God only for blessing and gain.

(3) They had spoken arrogantly in claiming God's sanction for some of their false doctrine and theology.

42:7 RIGHT, AS MY SERVANT JOB HAS. God declared that what Job had said was right. He did not mean that everything Job said was completely accurate, but that Job's response to his three friends was completely honest before God and that his attitude was pleasing to him. God sometimes permits errors in our prayers and allows us to question his ways if our hearts are truly given to him in sincere commitment.

42:8 MY SERVANT JOB. God calls Job "my servant" (vv. 7–8) and states twice that his prayer was accepted (vv. 8–9). Job was fully restored to God's favor and was given spiritual authority with God. God will hear Job's intercessory prayer for his three friends because of Job's righteous standing with God (vv. 8–9).

42:10 GAVE HIM TWICE AS MUCH AS HE HAD BEFORE. The restoration of Job's fortunes reveals God's purpose for all faithful believers. (1) God's redemptive purpose with respect to Job's suffering was accomplished. God had allowed Job to suffer for reasons that Job did not understand. God never allows believers to suffer without a spiritual purpose, even though they may not understand the reasons. We must trust God in such circumstances, knowing that in his perfect justice he will do what is eternally best for us and his kingdom. (2) Job's reconciliation with God and his reception of abundant life emphasize that no matter what hardships or pain the faithful must experience, in God's own time he will reach out to help those who persevere and give them total healing and restoration. "You have heard of Job's perseverance and have seen what the Lord finally brought about. The Lord is full of compassion and mercy" (Jas 5:11). (3) Every person who remains faithful to God in the midst of the trials and afflictions of this life will ultimately come to that joyous and blessed state when he or she enjoys God's presence for all eternity (see 2Ti 4:7–8; 1Pe 5:10; Rev 21; 22:1–5).

PSALMS

Outline

I. Book 1: Psalms 1—41 (41:13)
II. Book 2: Psalms 42—72 (72:19)
III. Book 3: Psalms 73—89 (89:52)
IV. Book 4: Psalms 90—106 (106:48)
V. Book 5: Psalms 107—150 (150:1–6)

Two observations are noteworthy about the above outline. (1) From ancient times, the 150 psalms were organized into these five books, with each book having its own benediction (indicated above in parentheses). Ps 150 is not only the last psalm and a benediction for Book 5, but also a doxology for the entire Psalter. (2) The following chart provides helpful perspective about the five-book division of the Psalms.

	Book I 1–41	Book II 42–72	Book III 73–89	Book IV 90–106	Book V 107–150
Total Psalms	41	31	17	17	44
Authorship	Mainly David	Mainly David and Sons of Korah	Mainly Asaph	Mainly Anonymous	Mainly David or Anonymous
Predominant Divine Name	Yahweh (the "LORD")	El/Elohim ("God")	El/Elohim ("God")	Yahweh (the "LORD")	Yahweh (the "LORD")
Frequent Topics	Humans and Creation	Deliverance and Redemption	Worship and Sanctuary	Desert and God's Ways	God's Word and Praise
Resemblance to Pentateuch	Genesis	Exodus	Leviticus	Numbers	Deuteronomy

Author: David and Others

Theme: Prayers and Praises

Date of Writing: Largely 10th to 5th centuries B.C.

Background

The Hebrew title for the Psalms is *tehillim*, meaning "praises"; the title in the Septuagint (Greek translation of the OT, done about 200 B.C.) is *psalmoi*, meaning "songs to the accompaniment of stringed instruments." The English title, "Psalms," is derived from the Septuagint.

Music played an important role in ancient Israel's worship (cf. Ps 149—150; 1Ch 15:16–22); the psalms were Israel's hymns. Unlike much poetry or songs in the western world that are written with rhyme or meter, OT poetry and songs were based on a parallelism of thought, in which the second (or succeeding) line(s) of poetry essentially restates (synonymous parallelism), contrasts (antithetical parallelism), or progressively completes (synthetic parallelism) the first. All three forms of parallelism characterize the Psalter. The earliest known psalm is from Moses in the 15th century B.C. (Ps 90); the latest ones are from the 6th to 5th centuries B.C. (e.g., Ps 137). The majority of the psalms, however, were written in the 10th century B.C. during Israel's golden age of poetry.

The editorial titles or superscriptions at the beginning of most psalms, though not an original and inspired part of the psalms, are ancient (before the Septuagint) and significant. The content of these superscriptions varies, covering such categories as (1) author's name (e.g., Ps 47, "Of the Sons of Korah"), (2) type of psalm (e.g., Ps 32, a "maskil," meaning a contemplative or didactic poem), (3) musical terms (e.g., Ps 4, "For the director of music. With stringed instruments"), (4) liturgical notations (e.g., Ps 45, "A wedding song"), and (5) brief historical notations (e.g., Ps 3, "A psalm of David. When he fled from his son Absalom").

Concerning authorship of the psalms, the superscriptions ascribe 73 psalms to David, 12 to Asaph (a musically and prophetically gifted Levite, see 1Ch 15:16–19; 2Ch 29:30), 10 to the sons of Korah (a musically gifted family), two to Solomon, one to Heman, one to Ethan and one to Moses. With the exception of Moses, David and Solomon, all other designated authors were priests or Levites with musical gifts and responsibilities in sacred worship during David's reign. Fifty psalms are anonymous. Biblical and historical references suggest that David (cf. 1Ch 15:16–22), Hezekiah (cf. 2Ch 29:25–30; Pr 25:1) and Ezra (cf. Ne 10:39; 11:22; 12:27–36,45–47) were each involved at different stages in collecting the psalms for corporate use in Jerusalem. The final compiling of the Psalter most likely occurred during the time of Ezra and Nehemiah (450–400 B.C.).

Purpose

The psalms, as Spirit-inspired prayers and praises, were written, generally speaking, to express the deep inner emotions of the human heart in relation to God. (1) Many were written as prayers to God, expressing (a) trust, love, adoration, thanksgiving, praise and a longing for close fellowship; (b) discouragement, deep distress, fear, anxiety, humiliation, and a cry for deliverance, healing or vindication. (2) Others were written as songs expressing praise, thanksgiving and adoration for who God is and for the great things he has done. (3) Some psalms contain important Messianic sections.

Survey

As an anthology of 150 psalms, the Psalter covers a great breadth of topics, including revelation about God, creation, humankind, salvation, sin and evil, justice and righteousness, worship and praise, prayer and judgment. It views God in a rich variety of ways: a fortress, rock, shield, shepherd, soldier, creator, ruler, judge, redeemer, sustainer, healer and avenger; he expresses love, anger and compassion, and he is everywhere present, all-knowing and almighty. God's people are also described in various ways: as the apple of his eye, sheep, saints, the upright and the righteous whom he has lifted out of the slimy pit, set their feet on a rock, and put a new song in their mouth. God directs their steps, satisfies their spiritual longings, forgives all their sins, heals all their diseases and provides for them an eternal dwelling.

One helpful method for surveying the book is by general categories used for classifying the psalms (with some overlapping). (1) *Hallelujah or Praise Songs*: These magnify the name, majesty, goodness, greatness and salvation of God (e.g., Ps 8; 21; 33—34; 103—106; 111—113; 115—117; 135; 145—150). (2) *Thanksgiving Songs*: These acknowledge God's saving help and deliverances on behalf of an individual or Israel as a nation (e.g., Ps 18; 30; 34; 41; 66; 92; 100; 106; 116; 118; 124; 126; 136; 138). (3) *Prayer and Supplication Psalms*: These include laments and petitions to God, longings for God, and intercession on behalf of God's people (e.g., Ps 3—6; 13; 43; 54; 67; 69—70; 79—80; 85—86; 88; 90; 102; 141—143). (4) *Penitential Psalms*: These focus on the acknowledgment and confession of sin (e.g., Ps 32; 38; 51; 130). (5) *Sacred History Songs*: These recount God's dealings with Israel as a nation (e.g., Ps 78; 105—106; 108; 114; 126; 137). (6) *Enthronement of the Lord Psalms*: These declare boldly that "the LORD reigns" (e.g., Ps 24; 47; 93; 96—99). (7) *Liturgical Songs*: These were composed for special services or feasts (e.g., Ps 15; 24; 45; 68; 113—118; these last six were used annually at the Passover). (8) *Trust and Devotion*

Psalms: These express (a) the individual's confidence in God's integrity and the help of his presence, and (b) the heart's devotion to God (e.g., Ps 11; 16; 23; 27; 31–32; 40; 46; 56; 62–63; 91; 119; 130–131; 139). (9) *Pilgrimage Songs*: Called also "Songs of Zion" or "Songs of Ascent," these were sung by pilgrims during their journey to Jerusalem for the annual feasts of Passover, Pentecost and Tabernacles (e.g., Ps 43; 46; 48; 76; 84; 87; 120–134). (10) *Creation Songs*: These acknowledge God's handiwork in the heavens and on the earth (e.g. Ps 8; 19; 29; 33; 65; 104). (11) *Wisdom and Didactic Psalms*: These reflect on God's ways and instruct us concerning righteousness (e.g., Ps 1; 34; 37; 73; 112; 119; 133). (12) *Royal or Messianic Psalms*: These describe certain experiences of King David or King Solomon that have prophetic significance and find their ultimate fulfillment in the coming of the Messiah, Jesus Christ (e.g., Ps 2; 8; 16; 22; 40–41; 45; 68–69; 72; 89; 102; 110; 118). (13) *Imprecatory Psalms*: These psalms invoke God's curse or judgment on the wicked (e.g., Ps 7; 35; 55; 58; 59; 69; 109; 137; 139:19–22). Since many Christians are perplexed by these psalms, it must be noted that they were written out of zeal for God's name, his justice and his righteousness, and from a strong abhorrence of evil, not out of a petty vindictiveness. Essentially they call on God to lift up the righteous and bring down the wicked.

Special Features

Nine major features characterize the Psalms. (1) It is the Bible's longest book and contains the Bible's longest chapter (119:1–176), shortest chapter (117:1–2), and middle verse (118:8). (2) As the Hebrew songbook and devotional book, its spiritual depth and breadth make the psalms the most read and most treasured portion of the OT by most believers. (3) "Hallelujah" (translated "Praise the LORD"), a Hebrew term universally recognized among believers, occurs 28 times in the Bible, 24 of which are in the Psalms. In the Psalter it reaches its apex in Ps 150 and conveys complete, rounded and perfect praise to the Lord. (4) No other Bible book so totally expresses the full range of human emotions and needs in relation to God and human life. Its choruses of praise and devotion flow down from the highest mountains, and its cries of desperation arise from the deepest valleys. (5) About half of the psalms involve prayers of faith in times of adversity. (6) It is the OT book most frequently quoted in the NT. (7) It contains many "favorite chapters" of the Bible, such as Ps 1; 23; 24; 34; 37; 84; 91; 103; 119; 121; 139; and 150. (8) Ps 119 is unique in the Bible in (a) its length (176 verses), (b) its majestic love for God's Word, and (c) its literary construction involving 22 stanzas of eight verses each, with every stanza beginning each of its verses with the same letter and each stanza using a successive letter of the Hebrew alphabet as a memory aid (i.e., an alphabetical acrostic). (9) Its foremost literary feature is a poetic style called parallelism, involving rhythm of thought rather than a rhythm of rhyme or meter; this feature has enabled its message to be translated from one language to another without serious difficulty.

New Testament Fulfillment

There are 186 quotations from the Psalms in the NT, far more than from any other OT book. It is clear that Jesus and the NT writers were filled with the psalms and that the Holy Spirit used them often in Jesus' teaching and in other passages where Jesus fulfills Scripture as the prophesied Messiah. For example, the brief Ps 110 (seven verses) is quoted in the NT more times than any other OT chapter; it contains prophecy about Jesus as the Messiah, as the Son of God and as a priest forever in the order of Melchizedek. Other Messianic psalms applied to Jesus in the NT are: 2; 8; 16; 22; 40; 41; 45; 68; 69; 89; 102; 109; and 118. They are applied to (1) Jesus as prophet, priest and king; (2) both his first and second advents; (3) his Sonship and character; (4) his sufferings and atoning death; and (5) his resurrection. In summary, the psalms are among the most meticulous of all OT prophecies about Christ and are everywhere deeply embedded in the message of the NT writers.

Reading Psalms

In order to read the entire Old Testament in one year, the book of Psalms should be read in 44 days, according to the following schedule: ☐ 1–6 ☐ 7–10 ☐ 11–16 ☐ 17–18 ☐ 19–20 ☐ 21–22 ☐ 23–25 ☐ 26–29 ☐ 30–31 ☐ 32–34 ☐ 35–37 ☐ 38–41 ☐ 42–44 ☐ 45–48 ☐ 49–51 ☐ 52–55 ☐ 56–59 ☐ 60–63 ☐ 64–67 ☐ 68–69 ☐ 70–73 ☐ 74–77 ☐ 78 ☐ 79–81 ☐ 82–84 ☐ 85–88 ☐ 89 ☐ 90–93 ☐ 94–98 ☐ 99–101 ☐ 102–103 ☐ 104–106 ☐ 107–108 ☐ 109–112 ☐ 113–116 ☐ 117–118 ☐ 119:1–88 ☐ 119:89–176 ☐ 120–127 ☐ 128–134 ☐ 135–138 ☐ 139–141 ☐ 142–145 ☐ 146–150

NOTES

BOOK I

Psalms 1–41

Psalm 1

1 Blessed is the man[a]
who does not walk[b] in the
counsel of the wicked[c]
or stand in the way[d] of sinners[e]
or sit[f] in the seat of
mockers.[g]
2 But his delight[h] is in the law of
the LORD,[i]
and on his law he meditates[j]
8 day and night.
3 He is like a tree[k] planted by
streams[l] of water,[m]
which yields its fruit[n] in
season
and whose leaf[o] does not wither.
Whatever he does prospers.[p]

4 Not so the wicked!
They are like chaff[q]
that the wind blows away.
5 Therefore the wicked will not
stand[r] in the judgment,[s]
nor sinners in the assembly[t] of
the righteous.

6 For the LORD watches over[u] the
way of the righteous,
but the way of the wicked will
perish.[v]

Psalm 2

1 Why do the nations conspire[a]
and the peoples plot[w] in vain?

1:1 [a] S Dt 33:29; Ps 40:4; 128:4 [b] Ps 89:15 [c] S Job 21:16; Ps 10:2-11 [d] S Ge 49:6 [e] Ps 26:9; 37:38; 51:13; 104:35 [f] Ps 26:4 [g] S Job 11:3; Pr 1:22; Isa 28:14; Hos 7:5 **1:2** [h] Ps 112:1; 119:16,35; Ro 7:22 [i] Ps 19:7; 119:1; Eze 11:20; 18:17 [j] S Ge 24:63 **1:3** [k] Ps 52:8; 92:12; 128:3; Jer 11:16; Zec 4:3 [l] Ps 46:4; 65:9; Isa 33:21; Jer 31:9 [m] S Nu 24:6; S Job 14:9; S Eze 17:5 [n] Ps 92:14; Eze 47:12 [o] Isa 1:30; 64:6 [p] S Ge 39:3 **1:4** [q] S Job 13:25; Isa 40:24; Jer 13:24 **1:5** [r] Ps 5:5 [s] S Job 19:29 [t] Ps 26:12; 35:18; 82:1; 89:5; 107:32; 111:1; 149:1 **1:6** [u] Ps 37:18; 121:5; 145:20; Na 1:7 [v] S Lev 26:38; Ps 9:6 **2:1** [w] Ps 21:11; 83:5; Pr 24:2

[a] *1* Hebrew; Septuagint *rage*

1:1 BLESSED IS THE MAN. Ps 1 serves as an introduction to the book of Psalms. It contrasts the only two kinds of people recognized by God, each with a distinct set of life principles: (1) The godly, who are characterized by righteousness, love, obedience to God's word, and separation from fellowship with the world (vv. 1–2); (2) the ungodly, who represent the ways and counsel of the world, who do not abide in God's word, and who consequently have no part in the assembly of God's people (vv. 4–5). The godly person is known and blessed by God, but the ungodly person has no part in God's kingdom (1Co 6:9) and will perish (v. 6). The separation between these two kinds of people will exist throughout redemptive history and on into eternity.

1:1 DOES NOT WALK IN THE COUNSEL OF THE WICKED. The first verse of the book of Psalms emphasizes the distinction between the righteous and the wicked. True believers can be distinguished by the things they do not do, the places they do not go and the company they do not keep. No person can experience God's blessing without turning from those things that are harmful or destructive.

1:2 HIS DELIGHT IS IN THE LAW. Those who are blessed by God not only turn from evil, but also build their lives around the words of the Lord. They seek to obey God's will out of hearts that genuinely take pleasure in God's ways and commands (see 2Th 2:10, where the wicked perish because "they refused to love the truth"). What motivates their actions are their redeemed spirits and emotions, captivated by God's truth as found in his Word.

1:2 ON HIS LAW HE MEDITATES DAY AND NIGHT. Those seeking to live under God's blessing meditate on God's law (i.e., his Word) in order to shape their thinking, attitudes and actions. They read the words of Scripture, ponder them and compare them with other Scriptures. When meditating on a passage in the Bible, questions such as these cross their minds:

Is God's Spirit applying this verse to my present situation?

Is there a promise here for me to claim?

Is this passage revealing a particular sin I must strive to avoid?

Is God issuing a command I must obey?

Is my spirit in harmony with what the Holy Spirit is saying?

Is the passage expressing a truth about God, salvation, sin, the world or my personal obedience on which I need to be enlightened by the Holy Spirit?

1:3 STREAMS OF WATER. The outcome of those who faithfully seek God and his Word is life in the Spirit. Since water often represents the Spirit of God (e.g., Jn 7:38–39), those who are instructed by God and who abide in his Word will receive an unfailing source of life from the Spirit. The phrase "whatever he does prospers" does not mean that problems or failure will never occur, but rather that a godly person will know God's will and blessing (see 3Jn 2, note).

1:4–6 THE WICKED. Ps 1 describes unrepentant sinners with three awful pictures: (1) they are like "chaff" blown away by forces they cannot see (v. 4; see Eph 2:2, note); (2) they will be condemned before God on the judgment day (v. 5; cf. 76:7; Mal 3:2; Mt 25:31–46; Rev 6:17); (3) they will perish for eternity (v. 6; see Mt 10:28, note).

2:1–12 WHY DO THE NATIONS CONSPIRE. This psalm consists of four distinct scenes. (1) The psalmist begins by speaking of the peoples and the kings of the world taking a stand against God's Anointed One (vv. 1–3; cf. Ac 4:25–27; see next note)—a sad picture of the arrogant rebellion of humankind against God, his law, his redemption, his Messiah and the moral teaching of his revelation. The NT authors likewise see the world in opposition to Christ, the believer and the Biblical faith (Jn 15:19; Eph 6:12).

(2) God responds by mocking the ridiculous ef-

2 The kings[x] of the earth take their
stand
and the rulers gather together
against the LORD
and against his Anointed[y]
One.[b z]
3 "Let us break their chains,[a]" they
say,
"and throw off their fetters."[b]

4 The One enthroned[c] in heaven
laughs;[d]
the Lord scoffs at them.
5 Then he rebukes them in his
anger[e]
and terrifies them in his
wrath,[f] saying,
6 "I have installed my King[c g]
on Zion,[h] my holy hill.[i]"

7 I will proclaim the decree of the
LORD:

He said to me, "You are my
Son[d];[j]
today I have become your
Father.[e k]
8 Ask of me,
and I will make the nations[l]
your inheritance,[m]
the ends of the earth[n] your
possession.
9 You will rule them with an iron
scepter[f];[o]
you will dash them to pieces[p]
like pottery.[q]"

10 Therefore, you kings, be wise;[r]
be warned, you rulers[s] of the
earth.
11 Serve the LORD with fear[t]
and rejoice[u] with trembling.[v]
12 Kiss the Son,[w] lest he be angry
and you be destroyed in your
way,
for his wrath[x] can flare up in a
moment.
Blessed[y] are all who take
refuge[z] in him.

Psalm 3

A psalm of David. When he fled from his son Absalom.[a]

1 O LORD, how many are my foes!
How many rise up against me!
2 Many are saying of me,
"God will not deliver him.[b]"
Selah[g]
3 But you are a shield[c] around me,
O LORD;

2:2 [x] Ps 48:4 [y] S 1Sa 9:16; Jn 1:41 [z] Ac 4:25-26* **2:3** [a] S Job 36:8 [b] S 2Sa 3:34 **2:4** [c] Isa 37:16; 40:22; 66:1 [d] Ps 37:13; Pr 1:26 **2:5** [e] Ps 6:1; 27:9; 38:1 [f] Ps 21:9; 79:6; 90:7; 110:5 **2:6** [g] Ps 10:16; 24:10 [h] 2Ki 19:31; Ps 9:11; 48:2,11; 78:68; 110:2; 133:3 [i] S Ex 15:17 **2:7** [j] S Mt 3:17; S 4:3 [k] S 2Sa 7:14; Ac 13:33*; Heb 1:5*; 5:5* **2:8** [l] Rev 2:26 [m] S Job 22:26; Mt 21:38 [n] Ps 22:27; 67:7 **2:9** [o] S Ge 49:10; Rev 12:5 [p] S Ex 15:6 [q] Isa 30:14; Jer 19:10; Rev 2:27*; 19:15 **2:10** [r] Pr 27:11 [s] Ps 141:6; Pr 8:15; Am 2:3 **2:11** [t] Ps 103:11 [u] Ps 9:2; 35:9; 104:34; Isa 61:10 [v] S 1Ch 16:30 **2:12** [w] ver 7 [x] S Dt 9:8; Rev 6:16 [y] Ps 84:12 [z] Ps 5:11; 34:8; 64:10 **3:1** [a] **Title** 2Sa 15:14 **3:2** [b] Ps 22:8; 71:11; Isa 36:15; 37:20 **3:3** [c] S Ge 15:1

[b] 2 Or *anointed one* [c] 6 Or *king* [d] 7 Or *son*; also in verse 12 [e] 7 Or *have begotten you* [f] 9 Or *will break them with a rod of iron* [g] 2 A word of uncertain meaning, occurring frequently in the Psalms; possibly a musical term

forts of the world to remove him from the scene (vv. 4–6). The time is coming when he will terminate human rebellion and fully establish his kingdom on the earth (see Ro 1:18; 1Th 5:1–11; 2Th 2:8; Rev 19:11–21).

(3) God the Father promises to send his beloved Son (vv. 7–9), the ultimate inheritance of the nations (see Ac 13:33; Heb 1:5; 5:5; cf. Mt 3:17; 17:5; 2Pe 1:17), to defeat all who oppose his rule. This promise will be fulfilled when Christ comes to earth at the end of time and destroys God's enemies (see Rev 12:5; 19:15). Then all faithful believers will share in his rule over the nations (Rev 2:26–27).

(4) Through the psalmist, the Holy Spirit exhorts humankind to be wise before Almighty God and to take refuge in him before that terrible day of God's judgment arrives (vv. 10–12; cf. Heb 3:7–19).

2:2 HIS ANOINTED ONE. Ps 2 is a Messianic psalm, i.e., one that prophesies the coming of God's Messiah, Jesus Christ. "Messiah" means "anointed one" and applies to Jesus, whom God anointed to redeem Israel and rule over God's kingdom (see next note; see Mt 1:1, note).

2:7 MY SON; TODAY I HAVE BECOME YOUR FATHER. "Become your father" literally translates "brought you forth." It was used of a woman bringing forth a child from the womb, but it was also a technical term for a king bringing out his son before the people to proclaim him as king along with his father (cf. 1Ki 1:32–34, where David did this for Solomon). Here it applies to Jesus' public proclamation as God's Son and his anointing as prophet, priest and king (see Mt 3:12; Ac 13:33; Heb 1:5; 5:5; 7:28; 2Pe 1:13).

2:8 THE NATIONS YOUR INHERITANCE. No earthly king was ever given this promise of the nations as an inheritance; it was a promise only to be fulfilled in the Messianic King, Jesus (see Zec 9:10).

3:1–8 HOW MANY ARE MY FOES! This psalm is a lament to God. Nearly a third of the psalms belong to this category. (1) The basic structure of the psalm of lament consists of a fervent calling on God (v. 1), a description of the believer's trouble, suffering or injustice (vv. 1–2), an affirmation of trust in God (vv. 3–6), a plea for help (v. 7), and an expression of praise or thanksgiving (v. 8). (2) The exceptionally large number of psalms of lament in the Bible indicates that God wants his people to call on him in times of need and trouble (see Heb 4:16).

3:2 SELAH. The meaning of this term is uncertain; it may signal a pause, a musical interlude or a musical climax.

you bestow glory on me and
lift[h] up my head.[d]
4To the LORD I cry aloud,[e]
and he answers me from his
holy hill.[f] *Selah*

5I lie down and sleep;[g]
I wake again,[h] because the
LORD sustains me.
6I will not fear[i] the tens of
thousands
drawn up against me on every
side.[j]

7Arise,[k] O LORD!
Deliver me,[l] O my God!
Strike[m] all my enemies on the
jaw;
break the teeth[n] of the wicked.

8From the LORD comes
deliverance.[o]
May your blessing[p] be on your
people. *Selah*

Psalm 4

For the director of music. With stringed instruments. A psalm of David.

1Answer me[q] when I call to you,
O my righteous God.
Give me relief from my distress;[r]
be merciful[s] to me and hear my
prayer.[t]

2How long, O men, will you turn my
glory[u] into shame[i]?[v]
How long will you love delusions
and seek false gods[j]?[w] *Selah*

3Know that the LORD has set apart
the godly[x] for himself;
the LORD will hear[y] when I call
to him.

4In your anger do not sin;[z]
when you are on your beds,[a]
search your hearts and be silent.
Selah

5Offer right sacrifices
and trust in the LORD.[b]

6Many are asking, "Who can show
us any good?"
Let the light of your face shine
upon us,[c] O LORD.
7You have filled my heart[d] with
greater joy[e]
than when their grain and new
wine[f] abound.
8I will lie down and sleep[g] in
peace,[h]
for you alone, O LORD,
make me dwell in safety.[i]

Psalm 5

For the director of music. For flutes. A psalm of David.

1Give ear[j] to my words, O LORD,
consider my sighing.[k]
2Listen to my cry for help,[l]
my King and my God,[m]
for to you I pray.
3In the morning,[n] O LORD, you hear
my voice;

3:3 [d]Ps 27:6 **3:4** [e]S Job 30:20 [f]Ps 2:6 **3:5** [g]S Lev 26:6 [h]Ps 17:15; 139:18 **3:6** [i]Job 11:15; Ps 23:4; 27:3 [j]Ps 118:11 **3:7** [k]S 2Ch 6:41 [l]Ps 6:4; 7:1; 59:1; 109:21; 119:153; Isa 25:9; 33:22; 35:4; 36:15; 37:20; Jer 42:11; Mt 6:13 [m]Job 16:10 [n]Job 29:17; Ps 57:4; Pr 30:14; La 3:16 **3:8** [o]Ps 27:1; 37:39; 62:1; Isa 43:3,11; 44:6, 8; 45:21; Hos 13:4; Jnh 2:9; Rev 7:10 [p]Nu 6:23; Ps 29:11; 129:8 **4:1** [q]Ps 13:3; 27:7; 69:16; 86:7; 102:2 [r]S Ge 32:7; S Jdg 2:15 [s]Ps 30:10 [t]Ps 17:6; 54:2; 84:8; 88:2 **4:2** [u]Ex 16:7; 1Sa 4:21 [v]2Ki 19:26; Job 8:22; Ps 35:26 [w]Jdg 2:17; Ps 31:6; 40:4; Jer 13:25; 16:19; Am 2:4 **4:3** [x]Ps 12:1; 30:4; 31:23; 79:2; Mic 7:2; 1Ti 4:7; 2Pe 3:11 [y]Ps 6:8; Mic 7:7 **4:4** [z]Eph 4:26* [a]Ps 63:6; Da 2:28 **4:5** [b]Ps 31:6; 115:9; Pr 3:5; 28:26; Isa 26:4; Jn 14:1 **4:6** [c]Nu 6:25 **4:7** [d]Ac 14:17 [e]Isa 9:3; 35:10; 65:14,18 [f]S Ge 27:28; S Dt 28:51 **4:8** [g]S Lev 26:6 [h]S Nu 6:26; S Job 11:18 [i]S Dt 33:28; S Jer 32:37 **5:1** [j]S 1Ki 8:29; Ps 17:1; 40:1; 116:2; Da 9:18 [k]Ps 38:9; Isa 35:10; 51:11 **5:2** [l]S Job 19:7; S 24:12; S 36:5 [m]Ps 44:4; 68:24; 84:3 **5:3** [n]Isa 28:19; 50:4; Jer 21:12; Eze 46:13; Zep 3:5

[h] *3* Or *LORD, / my Glorious One, who lifts*
[i] *2* Or *you dishonor my Glorious One* [j] *2* Or *seek lies*

3:3 YOU ARE A SHIELD ... YOU BESTOW GLORY. Believers who live according to God's will but find themselves confronting affliction and opposition (vv. 1–2; see 2Sa 15:12–30) may call on God with a confidence that he will act on their behalf according to his divine purpose. (1) "Shield" refers to God's protection (see Ge 15:1, where God is Abraham's shield; Dt 33:29, where he is Israel's shield). (2) God bestows "glory" on believers in that his presence, fellowship and help are our greatest good. Committing ourselves to God as our provider who bestows glory results in the experience of his grace and presence that enables us to rise above life's troubles.

3:5 I LIE DOWN AND SLEEP. Believers who earnestly call on God and constantly trust in his faithfulness, with the confidence that he hears (v. 4) may lie down in peace and sleep securely (cf. 4:8). God will sustain them and minister his grace even while they sleep (see 127:2; Pr 3:24).

4:1–8 ANSWER ME. This psalm reveals the kind of persons who will be answered by God in times of distress. They must have a personal relationship of trust in God (vv. 5,8), an earnest desire for God's help (vv. 1,3,6) and a godly lifestyle (vv. 3–5; see next note).

4:3 WILL HEAR WHEN I CALL TO HIM. In order to have assurance that God will answer our call for help, we must sincerely strive to live a godly life (cf. Pr 15:29; Jn 9:31; 15:7). Those who faithfully devote themselves to God have been set apart as his own treasured possession. When we belong to God, we can appeal to him as our protector and provider (cf. Heb 10:22; 1Jn 3:21–22).

5:3 YOU HEAR MY VOICE. Firmly determined to seek God with all his heart, David commits himself to three actions. (1) Confident that God will hear his voice, he will persist in prayer and not live

in the morning I lay my requests
before you
and wait in expectation.[o]

4You are not a God who takes
pleasure in evil;
with you the wicked[p] cannot
dwell.
5The arrogant[q] cannot stand[r] in
your presence;
you hate[s] all who do wrong.
6You destroy those who tell lies;[t]
bloodthirsty and deceitful men
the LORD abhors.

7But I, by your great mercy,
will come into your house;
in reverence[u] will I bow down[v]
toward your holy temple.[w]
8Lead me, O LORD, in your
righteousness[x]
because of my enemies—
make straight your way[y] before
me.

9Not a word from their mouth can
be trusted;
their heart is filled with
destruction.
Their throat is an open grave;[z]
with their tongue they speak
deceit.[a]
10Declare them guilty, O God!
Let their intrigues be their
downfall.
Banish them for their many sins,[b]
for they have rebelled[c] against
you.
11But let all who take refuge in you
be glad;
let them ever sing for joy.[d]
Spread your protection over them,
that those who love your name[e]
may rejoice in you.[f]
12For surely, O LORD, you bless the
righteous;[g]
you surround them[h] with your
favor as with a shield.[i]

Psalm 6

For the director of music. With stringed instruments. According to *sheminith.*[k] A psalm of David.

1O LORD, do not rebuke me in your
anger[j]
or discipline me in your wrath.
2Be merciful to me,[k] LORD, for I am
faint;[l]
O LORD, heal me,[m] for my bones
are in agony.[n]
3My soul is in anguish.[o]
How long,[p] O LORD, how long?

4Turn,[q] O LORD, and deliver me;
save me because of your
unfailing love.[r]
5No one remembers you when he is
dead.
Who praises you from the
grave[l]?[s]

6I am worn out[t] from groaning;[u]

5:3 [o]Ps 62:1; 119:81; 130:5; Hab 2:1; Ro 8:19 5:4 [p]Ps 1:5; 11:5; 104:35; Pr 2:22 5:5 [q]2Ki 19:32; Ps 73:3; 75:4; Isa 33:19; 37:33 [r]Ps 1:5 [s]Ps 45:7; 101:3; 119:104; Pr 8:13 5:6 [t]Pr 19:22; S Jn 8:44; Ac 5:3; Rev 21:8 5:7 [u]Dt 13:4; Jer 44:10; Da 6:26 [v]S 2Sa 12:16; Ps 138:2 [w]S 1Ki 8:48 5:8 [x]Ps 23:3; 31:1; 71:2; 85:13; 89:16; Pr 8:20 [y]S 1Ki 8:36; Jn 1:23 5:9 [z]Jer 5:16; Lk 11:44 [a]Ps 12:2; 28:3; 36:3; Pr 15:4; Jer 9:8; Ro 3:13* 5:10 [b]La 1:5 [c]Ps 78:40; 106:7; 107:11; La 3:42 5:11 [d]Ps 33:1; 81:1; 90:14; 92:4; 95:1; 145:7 [e]Ps 69:36; 119:132 [f]S Job 22:19 5:12 [g]Ps 112:2 [h]Ps 32:7 [i]S Ge 15:1 6:1 [j]S Ps 2:5 6:2 [k]Ps 4:1; 26:11; Jer 3:12; 12:15; 31:20 [l]Ps 61:2; 77:3; 142:3; Isa 40:31; Jer 8:18; Eze 21:7 [m]S Nu 12:13 [n]Ps 22:14; 31:10; 32:3; 38:3; 42:10; 102:3 6:3 [o]S Job 7:11; Ps 31:7; 38:8; 55:4; S Jn 12:27; Ro 9:2; 2Co 2:4 [p]1Sa 1:14; 1Ki 18:21; Ps 4:2; 89:46; Isa 6:11; Jer 4:14; Hab 1:2; Zec 1:12 6:4 [q]Ps 25:16; 31:2; 69:16; 71:2; 86:16; 88:2; 102:2; 119:132 [r]Ps 13:5; 31:16; 77:8; 85:7; 119:41; Isa 54:8,10 6:5 [s]Ps 30:9; 88:10-12; 115:17; Ecc 9:10; Isa 38:18 6:6 [t]S Jdg 8:5 [u]S Job 3:24; S 23:2; Ps 12:5; 77:3; 102:5; La 1:8,11,21,22

[k]Title: Probably a musical term [l]5 Hebrew *Sheol*

without it (vv. 1–2; cf. Dt 4:29). (2) He will pray "in the morning." If we orient our lives around God, morning prayers will be the natural thing to do. Each new morning calls for a renewed dedication of ourselves to God (55:16–17; 88:13; 119:147), fellowship with him and a feeding on his Word (cf. 119:9–16). (3) He will "wait in expectation" for answers to his prayer, and throughout the day he will search for signs that God is at work in his life.

5:5–6 YOU HATE ALL WHO DO WRONG. Evil does not exist in the abstract. God not only hates sin, but also in some sense hates those who perpetrate evil. On the other hand, the Bible also reveals God to be One who loves sinners, reaches out to them in compassion and mercy, and seeks to redeem them from sin through the cross of Christ (Jn 3:16).

5:10 BANISH THEM. See Ps 35:1–38, note on the psalmist's prayer for the destruction of God's enemies.

6:1–10 DO NOT REBUKE ME IN YOUR ANGER. This psalm is one of six penitential psalms (i.e., psalms of sorrow for sin; the others are Ps 32; 38; 51; 130; 143). The Holy Spirit inspired this prayer to give encouragement to all who have suffered for a long time under God's discipline and who need pardon and healing.

6:2 HEAL ME. During a time of physical affliction and divine discipline, which he knows he deserves, the psalmist has lost his sense of God's presence (v. 4) and spiritual peace (v. 3). He has suffered for a long time and is in intense grief. His prayer is not so much that God will remove all rebuke from him as it is that God's discipline might be mingled with mercy and not be so severe that he dies (cf. Jer 10:23–24).

6:4 DELIVER ME. Though the penitent one is concerned about the healing of his body (v. 2), his primary concern is for the healing of his soul and the restoration of God's presence and favor. He longs for God to be near him and appeals to his mercy and love (vv. 2,4). Since mercy and love are a part of God's character, believers may appeal to him to be true to his character.

all night long I flood my bed
with weeping[v]
and drench my couch with
tears.[w]
7My eyes grow weak[x] with sorrow;
they fail because of all my
foes.
8Away from me,[y] all you who do
evil,[z]
for the LORD has heard my
weeping.
9The LORD has heard my cry for
mercy;[a]
the LORD accepts my prayer.
10All my enemies will be ashamed
and dismayed;[b]
they will turn back in sudden
disgrace.[c]

Psalm 7

A *shiggaion*[m][d] of David, which he sang to the LORD concerning Cush, a Benjamite.

1O LORD my God, I take refuge[e] in
you;
save and deliver me[f] from all
who pursue me,[g]
2or they will tear me like a lion[h]
and rip me to pieces with no one
to rescue[i] me.
3O LORD my God, if I have done this
and there is guilt on my
hands[j]—
4if I have done evil to him who is at
peace with me
or without cause[k] have robbed
my foe—
5then let my enemy pursue and
overtake[l] me;
let him trample my life to the
ground[m]
and make me sleep in the
dust.[n] *Selah*
6Arise,[o] O LORD, in your anger;
rise up against the rage of my
enemies.[p]
Awake,[q] my God; decree
justice.
7Let the assembled peoples gather
around you.
Rule over them from on high;[r]
8 let the LORD judge[s] the peoples.
Judge me, O LORD, according to my
righteousness,[t]
according to my integrity,[u]
O Most High.[v]
9O righteous God,[w]
who searches minds and
hearts,[x]
bring to an end the violence of the
wicked
and make the righteous
secure.[y]
10My shield[n][z] is God Most High,

6:6 [v] S Job 16:16 [w] S Job 7:3; Lk 7:38; Ac 20:19 **6:7** [x] S Job 16:8; Ps 31:9; 69:3; 119:82; Isa 38:14 **6:8** [y] Ps 119:115; 139:19 [z] Ps 5:5; S Mt 7:23 **6:9** [a] Ps 28:6; 116:1 **6:10** [b] S 2Ki 19:26 [c] Ps 40:14 **7:1** [d] **7 Title** Hab 3:1 [e] Ps 2:12; 11:1; 31:1 [f] S Ps 3:7 [g] Ps 31:15; 119:86,157,161 **7:2** [h] S Ge 49:9; Rev 4:7 [i] Ps 3:2; 71:11 **7:3** [j] Isa 59:3 **7:4** [k] Ps 35:7,19; Pr 24:28 **7:5** [l] S Ex 15:9 [m] S 2Sa 22:43; 2Ki 9:33; Isa 10:6; La 3:16 [n] S Job 7:21 **7:6** [o] S 2Ch 6:41 [p] Ps 138:7 [q] Ps 35:23; 44:23 **7:7** [r] Ps 68:18 **7:8** [s] S 1Ch 16:33 [t] S 1Sa 26:23; Ps 18:20 [u] S Ge 20:5 [v] S Ge 3:5; S Nu 24:16; S Mk 5:7 **7:9** [w] Jer 11:20 [x] S 1Ch 28:9; Ps 26:2; Rev 2:23 [y] Ps 37:23; 40:2 **7:10** [z] Ps 3:3

[m] Title: Probably a literary or musical term
[n] *10* Or *sovereign*

6:6 I AM WORN OUT FROM GROANING. The psalmist's distress and anguish of soul have continued for some time. The statement "How long, O LORD, how long?" (v. 3), along with vv. 6–7, confirms that God has not immediately restored him to spiritual peace and his divine presence and grace. Vv. 8–9 teach that in his own time God will hear our cries for mercy and accept our prayer. We need not despair but must wait on God in faith (cf. 13:1; 74:9); in due time he will answer our prayer.

7:1–17 DELIVER ME FROM ALL WHO PURSUE ME. This psalm serves as a model for all who are unjustly treated, falsely accused or attacked by those who despise them. The prayer may be applied to our greatest enemy who seeks to tear us like a lion (v. 2), i.e., to Satan and his demonic host (Eph 6:11–12; 1Pe 5:8). It is always appropriate to pray for deliverance from the evil one (see Mt 6:13, note).

7:1 I TAKE REFUGE. Those who have sincerely committed themselves to God may with all confidence take refuge in the Lord and commit their life situations to him. In the midst of unjust or troublesome times, we may place ourselves under God's protection and appeal to him on the basis of our faithfulness and righteousness (vv. 3–5,8).

7:10 WHO SAVES THE UPRIGHT IN HEART. The Holy Spirit teaches that the righteous can expect God to deliver and help them in times of affliction. We may appeal to God on the basis of a clear conscience and our sincere endeavor to maintain uprightness of heart.

(1) We may assert our spiritual integrity before God by praying, "Judge me, O LORD, according to my righteousness" (v. 8; cf. Job 29:14). Such a claim is not self-righteous if it is spoken from a sincere heart, purified by love for God through faith (cf. 1Jn 3:21; Jas 5:16).

(2) What a blessed thing it is to pray for God's help with a repentant heart (Ps 6). But it is even better when we can pray to God with a clear conscience and with the knowledge that we have wronged no one and have sought sincerely to love God with all our heart.

(3) Note what the apostle Paul states: "So I strive always to keep my conscience clear before God and man" (Ac 24:16; cf. 2Co 1:12; 1Ti 1:5,19; 2Ti 1:3; 1Pe 3:21). And Jesus affirms, "If you remain in me and my words remain in you, ask whatever you wish, and it will be given you" (Jn 15:7).

who saves the upright in
heart.[a]
11God is a righteous judge,[b]
a God who expresses his
wrath[c] every day.
12If he does not relent,[d]
he[o] will sharpen his sword;[e]
he will bend and string his
bow.[f]
13He has prepared his deadly
weapons;
he makes ready his flaming
arrows.[g]

14He who is pregnant with evil
and conceives trouble gives
birth[h] to disillusionment.
15He who digs a hole and scoops it
out
falls into the pit[i] he has
made.[j]
16The trouble he causes recoils on
himself;
his violence comes down on his
own head.

17I will give thanks to the LORD
because of his
righteousness[k]
and will sing praise[l] to the
name of the LORD Most
High.[m]

Psalm 8

For the director of music. According to *gittith*.[p] A psalm of David.

1O LORD, our Lord,
how majestic is your name[n] in
all the earth!

You have set your glory[o]
above the heavens.[p]
2From the lips of children and
infants
you have ordained praise[q][q]
because of your enemies,
to silence the foe[r] and the
avenger.
3When I consider your heavens,[s]
the work of your fingers,[t]
the moon and the stars,[u]
which you have set in place,
4what is man that you are mindful
of him,
the son of man that you care for
him?[v]
5You made him a little lower than
the heavenly beings[r][w]
and crowned him with glory and
honor.[x]
6You made him ruler[y] over the
works of your hands;[z]
you put everything under his
feet:[a][b]
7all flocks and herds,[c]
and the beasts of the field,[d]
8the birds of the air,
and the fish of the sea,[e]
all that swim the paths of the
seas.

9O LORD, our Lord,
how majestic is your name in all
the earth![f]

Psalm 9[s]

For the director of music. To ⌊the tune of⌋ "The Death of the Son." A psalm of David.

1I will praise you, O LORD, with all
my heart;[g]
I will tell of all your wonders.[h]
2I will be glad and rejoice[i] in you;
I will sing praise[j] to your
name,[k] O Most High.

7:10 [a]S Job 33:3
7:11 [b]S Ge 18:25; Ps 9:8; 67:4; 75:2; 96:13; 98:9; Isa 11:4; Jer 11:20 [c]S Dt 9:8
7:12 [d]Eze 3:19; 33:9 [e]S Dt 32:41 [f]S 2Sa 22:35; Ps 21:12; Isa 5:28; 13:18
7:13 [g]Ps 11:2; 18:14; 64:3
7:14 [h]Isa 59:4; Jas 1:15
7:15 [i]Ps 35:7,8; 40:2; 94:13; Pr 26:27 [j]S Job 4:8
7:17 [k]Ps 5:8 [l]S 2Ch 31:2; Ro 15:11; Heb 2:12 [m]S Ge 14:18
8:1 [n]S 1Ch 16:10 [o]S Ex 15:11; Lk 2:9 [p]Ps 57:5; 108:5; 113:4; 148:13; Hab 3:3
8:2 [q]Mt 21:16* [r]Ps 143:12
8:3 [s]S Ge 15:5; S Dt 10:14 [t]S Ex 8:19; S 1Ch 16:26; S 2Ch 2:12; Ps 102:25 [u]S Ge 1:16; 1Co 15:41
8:4 [v]S 1Ch 29:14
8:5 [w]S Ge 1:26 [x]Ps 21:5; 103:4
8:6 [y]S Ge 1:28 [z]S Job 10:3; Ps 19:1; 102:25; 145:10; Isa 26:12; 29:23; 45:11; Heb 1:10 [a]Heb 2:6-8* [b]S 1Ki 5:3; 1Co 15:25,27*; Eph 1:22
8:7 [c]Ge 13:5; 26:14 [d]S Ge 2:19
8:8 [e]Ge 1:26
8:9 [f]ver 1
9:1 [g]Ps 86:12; 111:1; 119:2,10, 145; 138:1 [h]S Dt 4:34
9:2 [i]S Job 22:19; Ps 14:7; 31:7; 70:4; 97:8; 126:3; Pr 23:15; Isa 25:9; Jer 30:19; Joel 2:21; Zep 3:14; S Mt 5:12; Rev 19:7 [j]S 2Ch 31:2 [k]Ps 92:1

[o] 12 Or *If a man does not repent, / God*
[p] Title: Probably a musical term
[q] 2 Or *strength*
[r] 5 Or *than God*
[s] Psalms 9 and 10 may have been originally a single acrostic poem, the stanzas of which begin with the successive letters of the Hebrew alphabet. In the Septuagint they constitute one psalm.

8:4–6 THE SON OF MAN. The NT quotes these verses from the Septuagint (the Greek translation of the Hebrew OT) and applies them to Jesus (Heb 2:6–8; cf. Eph 1:19–22). It is only in him that these truths are perfectly realized. He is the one who, as a representative of the human race, will be given full dominion over all creation (vv. 6–8; cf. Php 2:10).

8:5 WITH GLORY AND HONOR. This psalm expresses the amazing honor that God has bestowed on humankind. It affirms that we as humans were created by God for a glorious purpose; we are not just animals, the product of natural evolution and chance (v. 5; see article on CREATION, p. 6). So valuable are we to God that we are special objects of his concern and favor (v. 4). He has honored us by choosing us to rule over his creation (vv. 6–8; cf. Ge 1:28; 2:15,19); yet the consciousness of our favored position is no reason for praising ourselves, but a reason for giving thanks and glory to the Creator (v. 9).

9:1–2 I WILL PRAISE YOU, O LORD. At the heart of every believer's relationship with God is the requirement to praise him (see article on PRAISE, p. 770).

3My enemies turn back;
they stumble and perish before
you.
4For you have upheld my right[l]
and my cause;[m]
you have sat on your throne,[n]
judging righteously.[o]
5You have rebuked the nations[p]
and destroyed the wicked;
you have blotted out their
name[q] for ever and ever.
6Endless ruin has overtaken the
enemy,
you have uprooted their cities;[r]
even the memory of them[s] has
perished.

7The LORD reigns forever;[t]
he has established his throne[u]
for judgment.
8He will judge the world in
righteousness;[v]
he will govern the peoples with
justice.[w]
9The LORD is a refuge[x] for the
oppressed,[y]
a stronghold in times of
trouble.[z]
10Those who know your name[a] will
trust in you,
for you, LORD, have never
forsaken[b] those who seek
you.[c]

11Sing praises[d] to the LORD,
enthroned in Zion;[e]
proclaim among the nations[f]
what he has done.[g]
12For he who avenges blood[h]
remembers;
he does not ignore the cry of the
afflicted.[i]

13O LORD, see how my enemies[j]
persecute me!
Have mercy[k] and lift me up
from the gates of death,[l]
14that I may declare your praises[m]
in the gates of the Daughter of
Zion[n]
and there rejoice in your
salvation.[o]

15The nations have fallen into the
pit they have dug;[p]
their feet are caught in the net
they have hidden.[q]
16The LORD is known by his justice;
the wicked are ensnared by the
work of their hands.[r]
Higgaion.[t] *Selah*
17The wicked return to the
grave,[u][s]
all the nations that forget God.[t]
18But the needy will not always be
forgotten,
nor the hope[u] of the afflicted[v]
ever perish.

19Arise,[w] O LORD, let not man
triumph;[x]
let the nations be judged[y] in
your presence.
20Strike them with terror,[z] O LORD;
let the nations know they are
but men.[a] *Selah*

Psalm 10[v]

1Why, O LORD, do you stand far
off?[b]
Why do you hide yourself[c] in
times of trouble?

9:4 [l]S 1Ki 8:45 [m]S Job 16:21 [n]Ps 11:4; 47:8; Isa 6:1 [o]Ps 7:11; 67:4; 98:9; 1Pe 2:23 **9:5** [p]Ge 20:7; S 37:10; S 1Ch 16:21; Ps 59:5; 105:14; Isa 26:14; 66:15 [q]S Job 18:17 **9:6** [r]S Dt 29:28; Jer 2:3; 46:1-51:58; Zep 2:8-10 [s]Ps 34:16; 109:15; Ecc 9:5; Isa 14:22; 26:14 **9:7** [t]S 1Ch 16:31; Rev 19:6 [u]Ps 11:4; 47:8; 93:2; Isa 6:1; 66:1 **9:8** [v]S ver 4; Ps 7:11 [w]Ps 11:7; 45:6; 72:2 **9:9** [x]S Dt 33:27; S 2Sa 22:3 [y]Ps 10:18; 74:21 [z]Ps 32:7; 121:7 **9:10** [a]Ps 91:14 [b]S Ge 28:15; S Dt 4:31; Ps 22:1; 37:25; 71:11; Isa 49:14; Jer 15:18; Heb 13:5 [c]Ps 70:4 **9:11** [d]Ps 7:17 [e]S Ps 2:6 [f]Ps 18:49; 44:11; 57:9; 106:27; Isa 24:13; Eze 20:23; 1Ti 3:16 [g]Ps 105:1 **9:12** [h]S 2Sa 4:11 [i]ver 18; Ps 10:17; 22:24; 72:4; Isa 49:13 **9:13** [j]Nu 10:9; Ps 3:7; 18:3 [k]Ps 6:2; 41:4; 51:1; 86:3,16; 119:132 [l]S Job 17:16; Mt 16:18 **9:14** [m]Ps 51:15; 1Pe 2:9 [n]2Ki 19:21; Isa 1:8; 10:32; 37:22; 62:11; Jer 4:31; 6:2; La 1:6; Mic 1:13; Zep 3:14; Zec 2:10; Mt 21:5; Jn 12:15 [o]Ps 13:5; 35:9; 50:23; 51:12 **9:15** [p]S Job 4:8; Ps 35:7 [q]Ps 35:8; 57:6 **9:16** [r]Pr 5:22 **9:17** [s]S Nu 16:30; Pr 5:5 [t]S Job 8:13 **9:18** [u]Ps 25:3; 39:7; 71:5; Pr 23:18; Jer 14:8 [v]ver 12; Ps 74:19 **9:19** [w]Ps 3:7 [x]2Ch 14:11 [y]Ps 110:6; Isa 2:4; Joel 3:12 **9:20** [z]S Ge 35:5; Ps 31:13; Isa 13:8; Lk 21:26 [a]Ps 62:9; Isa 31:3; Eze 28:2 **10:1** [b]Ps 22:1,11; 35:22; 38:21; 71:12 [c]Ps 13:1

[t]*16* Or *Meditation*; possibly a musical notation [u]*17* Hebrew *Sheol* [v]Psalms 9 and 10 may have been originally a single acrostic poem, the stanzas of which begin with the successive letters of the Hebrew alphabet. In the Septuagint they constitute one psalm.

9:5 DESTROYED THE WICKED. David speaks as if the events recorded here have already happened—a stylistic feature of prophecy in the psalms. He is so certain that the events will occur that he speaks of them as if they have already been fulfilled (see vv. 15–16).

9:8 JUDGE THE WORLD IN RIGHTEOUSNESS. The psalmist thanks and praises the Lord because he will one day fully deliver those who seek him (vv. 8–14) and will bring judgment against his enemies (vv. 3–8,15–20). (1) In order to prevent discouragement and despair at the apparent success of evil in the world, God's people must firmly believe and confess that the Lord will one day vindicate those who, in spite of affliction, persevere against all who would destroy their faith in God (vv. 7–1; see Rev 19—21). (2) NT believers may apply these verses to the enemies of the Lord and his church. Throughout the NT age a conflict rages between the forces of evil and the forces of righteousness. Faithful believers will be opposed by Satan, the world and false believers within the church (see 2Ti 3:12, note).

9:18 THE NEEDY WILL NOT ALWAYS BE FORGOTTEN. The needy and the afflicted among God's people are objects of his special care (vv. 9–10,12). They have the promise that God will not forsake them (v. 10), that he will remember their prayers (v. 12), and that their hopes will eventually be realized (v. 18).

PRAISE

Ps 9:1–2 "I will praise you, O LORD, with all my heart; I will tell of all your wonders. I will be glad and rejoice in you; I will sing praise to your name, O Most High."

IMPORTANCE OF PRAISE. The Bible often exhorts God's people to praise the Lord. (1) The writers of the OT used three basic words to call Israelites to praise God: the word *barak* (which can also be translated "bless"); the word *halal* (from which "hallelujah," meaning "praise the LORD," comes); and the word *yadah* (sometimes translated as "give thanks").

(2) The Bible's first song, sung after the Israelites had crossed the Red Sea, was essentially a song of praise and thanksgiving to God (Ex 15; see v. 2). Moses commanded the Israelites to praise God for his goodness in giving them the promised land (Dt 8:10). Deborah's song specifically called the people to praise the Lord (Jdg 5:9). David's desire to praise God is recorded both in the story of his life (2Sa 22:4,47,50; 1Ch 16:4,9,25,35–36; 29:20) and in the psalms he wrote (Ps 9:1–2; 18:3; 22:23; 52:9; 108:1,3; 145). Other psalmists also call God's people to live their lives praising God (Ps 33:1–2; 47:6–7; 75:9; 96:1–4; 100; 150). Finally, the OT prophets instructed God's people to praise him (Isa 42:10,12; Jer 20:13; cf. Isa 12:1; 25:1; Jer 33:9; Joel 2:26; Hab 3:3).

(3) The call to praise God reverberates throughout the NT. Jesus himself praised his Father in heaven (Mt 11:25; Lk 10:21). Paul expects all the nations to praise God (Ro 15:9–11; Eph 1:3,6,12), and James calls us to praise the Lord (Jas 3:9; 5:13). And in the end the picture given in Revelation is that of a vast throng of both saints and angels praising God continually (Rev 4:9–11; 5:8–14; 7:9–12; 11:16–18).

(4) Praising God is one of the main functions of angels (Ps 103:20; 148:2) and is the privilege of God's people, both children (Mt 21:16; cf. Ps 8:2) and adults (Ps 30:4; 135:1–2,19–21). Furthermore, God calls all nations to praise him (Ps 67:3–5; 117:1; 148:11–13; Isa 42:10–12; Ro 15:11). In other words, everything that has breath is called to shout out the praise of God (Ps 150:6). As if that is not enough, God also commands inanimate nature to praise him—such as the sun, moon and stars (Ps 148:3–4; cf. Ps 19:1–2); lightning, hail, snow and wind (Ps 148:8); mountains, hills, rivers and seas (Ps 98:7–8; 148:9; Isa 44:23); all kinds of trees (Ps 148:9; Isa 55:12); and all kinds of living creatures (Ps 69:34; 148:10).

METHODS OF PRAISE. Praising God can take place in a variety of ways. (1) Praise is a keynote in the corporate worship of God's people (Ps 100:4; see article on WORSHIP, p. 680). (2) Both in the corporate worship setting and in other places, the singing of psalms, hymns and spiritual songs is a way to express praise to God (Ps 96:1–4; 147:1; Eph 5:19–20; Col 3:16–17). Praise can be sung with the mind (i.e., in known human languages) or with the spirit (i.e., in tongues; 1Co 14:14–16, see 14:15, note). (3) Musical praise can be expressed through various instruments—horns such as rams' horns and trumpets (1Ch 15:28; Ps 150:3), wind instruments such as the flute (1Sa 10:5; Ps 150:4), stringed instruments such as the harp and lyre (1Ch 13:8; Ps 149:3; 150:3), and percussion instruments such as the tambourines and cymbals (Ex 15:20; Ps 150:4–5). (4) We can also communicate God's praise by telling others about our God's wonderful deeds. For example, having experienced God's forgiveness, David was eager to tell others about what the Lord had done for him (Ps 51:12–13,15). Other Bible writers urge us to declare God's glory and praise in the congregation of God's people (Ps 22:22–25; 111:1; Heb 2:12) and among the nations (Ps 18:49; 96:3–4; Isa 42:10–12). Peter calls on God's chosen people to "declare the praises of him who called you out of darkness into his wonderful light" (1Pe 2:9). In other words, mission work is a method of praising God.

(5) Finally, a life lived to God's glory is a way to praise the Lord. Jesus reminds us that if we let our light shine, people will see our good deeds and give glory and praise to God (Mt 5:16; cf. Jn 15:8). Similarly, Paul observes that a life filled with the fruit of righteousness praises God (Php 1:11).

REASONS FOR PRAISE. Why do people praise the Lord? (1) One of the obvious reasons is because of the splendor, glory and majesty of our God, the One who created the heavens and the earth (Ps 96:4–6; 145:3; 148:13), the One who is to be exalted in his holiness (Ps 99:3; Isa 6:3). (2) The experience of God's mighty acts, particularly his acts of salvation and redemption, is a key reason to praise his name (Ps 96:1–3; 106:1–2; 148:14; 150:2; Lk 1:68–75; 2:14,20); in doing so, we praise God for his unfailing mercy, grace and love (Ps 57:9–10; 89:1–2; 117; 145:8–10; Eph 1:6). (3) We will also want to praise God for any specific acts of deliverance in our lives, such as being rescued from our enemies or healed of our sicknesses (Ps 9:1–5; 40:1–3; 59:16; 124; Jer 20:13; Lk 13:13; Ac 3:7–9). (4) Finally, God's continual providential care and provision for us day by day, both physically and spiritually, is a powerful reason to praise and bless his name (Ps 68:19; 103; 147; Isa 63:7; see article on THE PROVIDENCE OF GOD, p. 78).

[2]In his arrogance the wicked man
hunts down the weak,[d]
who are caught in the schemes
he devises.
[3]He boasts[e] of the cravings of his
heart;
he blesses the greedy and
reviles the LORD.[f]
[4]In his pride the wicked does not
seek him;
in all his thoughts there is no
room for God.[g]
[5]His ways are always prosperous;
he is haughty[h] and your laws
are far from him;
he sneers at all his enemies.
[6]He says to himself, "Nothing will
shake me;
I'll always be happy[i] and never
have trouble."
[7]His mouth is full of curses[j] and
lies and threats;[k]
trouble and evil are under his
tongue.[l]
[8]He lies in wait[m] near the villages;
from ambush he murders the
innocent,[n]
watching in secret for his
victims.
[9]He lies in wait like a lion in
cover;
he lies in wait to catch the
helpless;[o]
he catches the helpless and
drags them off in his net.[p]
[10]His victims are crushed,[q] they
collapse;
they fall under his strength.

10:2 [d]ver 9; S Job 20:19
10:3 [e]Ps 49:6; 94:4; Jer 48:30 [f]S Job 1:5
10:4 [g]Ps 36:1
10:5 [h]Ps 18:27; 101:5; Pr 6:17; Isa 13:11; Jer 48:29
10:6 [i]Rev 18:7
10:7 [j]Ro 3:14* [k]Ps 73:8; 119:134; Ecc 4:1; Isa 30:12 [l]S Job 20:12
10:8 [m]Ps 37:32; 59:3; 71:10; Pr 1:11; Jer 5:26; Mic 7:2 [n]Hos 6:9
10:9 [o]S ver 2 [p]S Job 18:8
10:10 [q]S Job 9:17
10:11 [r]Job 22:13; Ps 42:9; 77:9 [s]S Job 22:14
10:12 [t]Ps 3:7 [u]Ps 17:7; 20:6; 106:26; Isa 26:11; Mic 5:9 [v]Ps 9:12
10:13 [w]ver 3 [x]S Job 31:14
10:14 [y]ver 7; Ps 22:11 [z]Ps 37:5 [a]S Dt 33:29
10:15 [b]S Job 31:22
10:16 [c]S Ex 15:18 [d]S Dt 8:20
10:17 [e]S Ps 9:12 [f]S Ex 22:23
10:18 [g]S Dt 24:17; Ps 146:9 [h]S Ps 9:9

[11]He says to himself, "God has
forgotten;[r]
he covers his face and never
sees."[s]
[12]Arise,[t] LORD! Lift up your hand,[u]
O God.
Do not forget the helpless.[v]
[13]Why does the wicked man revile
God?[w]
Why does he say to himself,
"He won't call me to account"?[x]
[14]But you, O God, do see trouble[y]
and grief;
you consider it to take it in
hand.
The victim commits himself to
you;[z]
you are the helper[a] of the
fatherless.
[15]Break the arm of the wicked and
evil man;[b]
call him to account for his
wickedness
that would not be found
out.

[16]The LORD is King for ever and
ever;[c]
the nations[d] will perish from
his land.
[17]You hear, O LORD, the desire of the
afflicted;[e]
you encourage them, and you
listen to their cry,[f]
[18]defending the fatherless[g] and the
oppressed,[h]
in order that man, who is of the
earth, may terrify no more.

10:1–18 DO YOU STAND FAR OFF? This prayer wrestles with the question of the seeming delay of the triumph of God's justice (cf. the cry of the martyred saints in Rev 6:9–10). In this present age injustice and evil run rampant, and God sometimes appears to "stand far off" and not interfere. God's people must pray that he will stop evil and suffering. Meanwhile, we may be assured that though the day of justice has not arrived, the Lord has heard our prayers and will give encouragement until the end (vv. 17–18).

10:2 IN HIS ARROGANCE THE WICKED MAN HUNTS. The psalmist grieves over the haughty attitude of cruel and wicked people and their apparent success (vv. 3–11). (1) He prays that God will overthrow the wicked, help the helpless, and reign as king forever in order that sin and terror be abolished from the earth (vv. 12–18). (2) While NT believers must always be vitally concerned about the salvation of the wicked, they must also understand that sin and cruelty will never be completely crushed, nor will righteousness fully reign, until Christ returns to destroy all evil (Rev 19:11 — 20:10). We must therefore pray that God will soon abolish all evil, that Christ will be crowned king forever, and that on the earth sin and sorrow will cease (see Rev 19 — 22).

10:8–10 FROM AMBUSH HE MURDERS THE INNOCENT. These verses can be applied to those who traffic in drugs, alcohol and abortion, where the result is physical, emotional and spiritual ruin for many. (1) Out of greed (cf. v. 3), such people draw the poor, the young and the thoughtless within their nets. Through testimony and advertisement, they craftily emphasize the pleasures of their products while hiding the tragic suffering that comes as a result of their business (v. 9).

(2) These wicked individuals are arrogantly oblivious to their moral accountability before God (vv. 3–4,11,13); their final end will be disastrous (see Ps 73). No believer should participate in the promotion of what will harm another human, but rather in love, compassion and concern seek to help all others avoid such temptations.

Psalm 11

For the director of music. Of David.

1In the LORD I take refuge.[i]
How then can you say to me:
"Flee[j] like a bird to your
mountain.[k]
2For look, the wicked bend their
bows;[l]
they set their arrows[m] against
the strings
to shoot from the shadows[n]
at the upright in heart.[o]
3When the foundations[p] are being
destroyed,
what can the righteous do[w]?"

4The LORD is in his holy
temple;[q]
the LORD is on his heavenly
throne.[r]
He observes the sons of men;[s]
his eyes examine[t] them.
5The LORD examines the
righteous,[u]
but the wicked[x] and those who
love violence
his soul hates.[v]
6On the wicked he will rain
fiery coals and burning sulfur;[w]
a scorching wind[x] will be their
lot.

7For the LORD is righteous,[y]
he loves justice;[z]
upright men[a] will see his
face.[b]

Psalm 12

For the director of music. According
to *sheminith*.[y] A psalm of David.

1Help, LORD, for the godly are no
more;[c]
the faithful have vanished from
among men.
2Everyone lies[d] to his neighbor;
their flattering lips speak with
deception.[e]

3May the LORD cut off all flattering
lips[f]
and every boastful tongue[g]
4that says, "We will triumph with
our tongues;[h]
we own our lips[z]—who is our
master?"

5"Because of the oppression[i] of
the weak
and the groaning[j] of the needy,
I will now arise,[k]" says the LORD.
"I will protect them[l] from those
who malign them."
6And the words of the LORD are
flawless,[m]
like silver refined[n] in a
furnace[o] of clay,
purified seven times.

7O LORD, you will keep us safe[p]
and protect us from such people
forever.[q]
8The wicked freely strut[r] about
when what is vile is honored
among men.

Psalm 13

For the director of music. A psalm
of David.

1How long,[s] O LORD? Will you
forget me[t] forever?

11:1 [i]S Ps 7:1 [j]S Ge 14:10 [k]Ps 50:11 **11:2** [l]S 2Sa 22:35 [m]S Ps 7:13; S 58:7 [n]Ps 10:8 [o]S Job 33:3; Ps 7:10 **11:3** [p]Ps 18:15; 82:5; Isa 24:18 **11:4** [q]S 1Ki 8:48; Ps 18:6; 27:4; Jnh 2:7; Mic 1:2; Hab 2:20 [r]S 2Ch 6:18; S Ps 9:7; Mt 5:34; 23:22; S Rev 4:2 [s]Pr 15:3 [t]Ps 33:18; 66:7 **11:5** [u]S Dt 7:13; S Job 23:10 [v]S Job 28:28; Ps 5:5; 45:7; Isa 1:14 **11:6** [w]S Ge 19:24; S Rev 9:17 [x]S Ge 41:6; S Job 1:19 **11:7** [y]S 2Ch 12:6; S Ezr 9:15; 2Ti 4:8 [z]S Ps 9:8; 33:5; 99:4; Isa 28:17; 30:18; 56:1; 61:8; Jer 9:24 [a]S Job 1:1; Lk 23:50 [b]Ps 17:15; 140:13 **12:1** [c]Isa 57:1; Mic 7:2 **12:2** [d]Ps 5:6; 34:13; 141:3; Pr 6:19; 12:17; 13:3; Isa 32:7 [e]S Ps 5:9; Ro 16:18 **12:3** [f]Pr 26:28; 28:23 [g]Ps 73:9; Da 7:8; Jas 3:5; Rev 13:5 **12:4** [h]Pr 18:21; Jas 3:6 **12:5** [i]Ps 44:24; 62:10; 72:14; 73:8; Ecc 4:1; 5:8; Isa 3:15; 5:7; 30:12; 59:13; Ac 7:34 [j]S Ps 6:6 [k]Ps 3:7 [l]Ps 34:6; 35:10 **12:6** [m]S 2Sa 22:31; Ps 18:30 [n]S Job 23:10; S 28:1; Isa 48:10; Zec 13:9 [o]Ps 119:140 **12:7** [p]Ps 16:1; 27:5 [q]Ps 37:28; Jn 17:12 **12:8** [r]Ps 55:10-11 **13:1** [s]Ps 6:3 [t]Ps 42:9; La 5:20

[w]3 Or *what is the Righteous One doing* [x]5 Or *The LORD, the Righteous One, examines the wicked, /* [y]Title: Probably a musical term [z]4 Or */ our lips are our plowshares*

11:1–7 IN THE LORD I TAKE REFUGE. This psalm rebukes those who counsel flight or compromise when Biblical principles are at stake (vv. 1–3). Faithful believers will take refuge in the Lord (v. 1) and remain committed to righteousness even if the moral and spiritual "foundations are being destroyed" in both society and the church (v. 3); the result will be that "upright men will see his face" (v. 7; cf. 16:8–11; 17:15; 23:6).

11:5 THOSE WHO LOVE VIOLENCE HIS SOUL HATES. Because the Lord "loves justice" (v. 7), he hates those who participate in violence or enjoy being entertained by it. Thus believers must exercise caution concerning the entertainment media and examine themselves to determine whether they take pleasure in and enjoy the portrayal of violence and bloodshed (see Lk 23:35, note; Ro 1:32, note).

12:1–8 HELP, LORD. This psalm describes a time when the ungodly activity of the wicked is keenly felt by those committed to God and his righteousness. In all ages God's people have experienced this, but in the last days of this age these conditions will be especially prevalent (1Ti 4:1). The faithful should know that when they are surrounded by the evils of society and are grieved and oppressed by the wicked and their immorality, they will be especially protected by God's power (v. 5). God will "keep us safe and protect us from such people forever" (v. 7; see 1Pe 1:5, note).

13:1 WILL YOU FORGET ME FOREVER? The psalmist is depressed and discouraged; he is in

How long will you hide your
face[u] from me?
[2]How long must I wrestle with my
thoughts[v]
and every day have sorrow in
my heart?
How long will my enemy
triumph over me?[w]

[3]Look on me[x] and answer,[y]
O LORD my God.
Give light to my eyes,[z] or I will
sleep in death;[a]
[4]my enemy will say, "I have
overcome him,[b]"
and my foes will rejoice when I
fall.[c]

[5]But I trust in your unfailing love;[d]
my heart rejoices in your
salvation.[e]
[6]I will sing[f] to the LORD,
for he has been good to me.

Ps 18:1-3

Psalm 14

14:1–7pp — Ps 53:1–6

For the director of music. Of David.

[1]The fool[a] says in his heart,
"There is no God."[g]
They are corrupt, their deeds are
vile;
there is no one who does good.

[2]The LORD looks down from
heaven[h]
on the sons of men
to see if there are any who
understand,[i]
any who seek God.[j]
[3]All have turned aside,[k]
they have together become
corrupt;[l]
there is no one who does good,[m]
not even one.[n]

[4]Will evildoers never learn—[o]
those who devour my people[p]
as men eat bread
and who do not call on the
LORD?[q]
[5]There they are, overwhelmed with
dread,
for God is present in the
company of the righteous.
[6]You evildoers frustrate the plans of
the poor,
but the LORD is their refuge.[r]

[7]Oh, that salvation for Israel would
come out of Zion![s]
When the LORD restores the
fortunes[t] of his people,
let Jacob rejoice and Israel be
glad!

Psalm 15

A psalm of David.

[1]LORD, who may dwell[u] in your
sanctuary?[v]

13:1 [u]S Dt 31:17; S Ps 22:24; S Isa 8:17; S 54:9 **13:2** [v]Ps 42:4; 55:2; 139:23; Isa 33:18; Da 7:28 [w]Ps 94:3 **13:3** [x]Ps 9:12; 25:18; 31:7; 35:23; 59:4; 80:14; 107:41; 119:50,153 [y]S Ps 4:1 [z]S Ezr 9:8 [a]Ps 76:5; 90:5; Jer 51:39 **13:4** [b]S 1Ki 19:2; Ps 25:2 [c]Ps 38:16; 118:13 **13:5** [d]S Ps 6:4 [e]S Job 33:26; Ps 9:14; Isa 25:9; 33:2 **13:6** [f]S Ex 15:1; Ps 7:17 **14:1** [g]Ps 10:4 **14:2** [h]Job 41:34; Ps 85:11; 102:19; La 3:50 [i]Ps 92:6 [j]S Ezr 6:21 **14:3** [k]S 1Sa 8:3; 1Ti 5:15 [l]2Pe 2:7 [m]1Ki 8:46; Ps 143:2; Ecc 7:20 [n]Ro 3:10-12* **14:4** [o]Ps 82:5; Jer 4:22 [p]Ps 27:2; Mic 3:3 [q]Ps 79:6; Isa 64:7; 65:1; Jer 10:25; Hos 7:7 **14:6** [r]S 2Sa 22:3 **14:7** [s]Ps 2:6 [t]S Dt 30:3; S Jer 48:47 **15:1** [u]Ex 29:46; Ps 23:6; 27:4; 61:4 [v]Ex 25:8; 1Ch 22:19; Ps 20:2; 78:69; 150:1

[a] *1* The Hebrew words rendered *fool* in Psalms denote one who is morally deficient.

---

desperate trouble, yet he feels that God is absent and unwilling to give practical help. Note especially two important lessons: (1) The prayers of the godly may not be answered immediately, for God may appear to pay no attention to our pleas. This feeling of being forsaken by him may occur in times of sickness, financial need or severe problems; it may involve family, work or church. At such times we should pray for the Holy Spirit to give us the assurance that we will yet rejoice in God's salvation (vv. 5–6).

(2) If we are sincerely seeking God's help through genuine faith in Jesus Christ, then God's delay does not mean that we are forsaken by him. He may instead be planning to accomplish some unseen purpose in our lives (cf. 2Co 12:7–10; Heb 12:10–11; Jas 1:2–4; 1Pe 1:6–7).

13:5 MY HEART REJOICES IN YOUR SALVATION. The answer to God's apparent delay is to trust in his unfailing love and to remember that in the past he has delivered us and blessed us. The Lord's unfailing love will appear in his own time and way (see Ro 8:28, note).

14:1–7 THE FOOL. The fool is a person who lives as if there is no God. Fools reveal their rebellion against God in two ways. (1) They reject God's revelation, for they do not believe what the Bible says about God; they scorn the moral principles of God's Word and rely on their own ideas to determine right from wrong (vv. 1–3).

(2) They do not seek God, nor do they call on God in prayer for his presence and help.

(3) This psalm describes the depravity of the wicked and teaches that the human race is by nature separated from God (cf. Eph 2:2–3). Paul quotes the first three verses of this psalm to support the truth that "all have sinned and fall short of the glory of God" (Ro 3:23; see 3:10–12).

15:1 WHO MAY DWELL IN YOUR SANCTUARY? This psalm answers the question: "What sort of person experiences God's intimate presence and fellowship?" It implies that we can cause God to withdraw his presence from our lives through our acts of unrighteousness, deceit, slander or selfishness. Thus we should examine our actions daily, confess our sins, turn from them, constantly seek through Christ to present ourselves to God as those approved (cf. 2Ti 2:15), and realize that to lose communion with God is to lose everything (cf. 1Jn 1:6–7; 2:3–6; 3:21–24).

Who may live on your holy
hill?[w]
²He whose walk is blameless[x]
and who does what is righteous,
who speaks the truth[y] from his
heart
³ and has no slander[z] on his
tongue,
who does his neighbor no wrong
and casts no slur on his
fellowman,
⁴who despises a vile man
but honors[a] those who fear the
LORD,
who keeps his oath[b]
even when it hurts,
⁵who lends his money without
usury[c]
and does not accept a bribe[d]
against the innocent.
He who does these things
will never be shaken.[e]

Psalm 16

A *miktam*[b] of David.

¹Keep me safe,[f] O God,
for in you I take refuge.[g]
²I said to the LORD, "You are my
Lord;[h]
apart from you I have no good
thing."[i]
³As for the saints[j] who are in the
land,[k]
they are the glorious ones in
whom is all my delight.[c]
⁴The sorrows[l] of those will
increase
who run after other gods.[m]
I will not pour out their libations
of blood
or take up their names[n] on my
lips.
⁵LORD, you have assigned me my
portion[o] and my cup;[p]
you have made my lot[q] secure.
⁶The boundary lines[r] have fallen
for me in pleasant places;
surely I have a delightful
inheritance.[s]
⁷I will praise the LORD, who
counsels me;[t]
even at night[u] my heart
instructs me.
⁸I have set the LORD always before
me.
Because he is at my right
hand,[v]
I will not be shaken.[w]
⁹Therefore my heart is glad[x] and
my tongue rejoices;
my body also will rest secure,[y]
¹⁰because you will not abandon me
to the grave,[d][z]

15:1 [w]S Ex 15:17 **15:2** [x]S Ge 6:9; S Ps 18:32; Eph 1:4; S 1Th 3:13; Tit 1:6 [y]Pr 16:13; Isa 45:19; Jer 7:28; 9:5; Zec 8:3,16; Ro 9:1; S Eph 4:25 **15:3** [z]S Lev 19:16 **15:4** [a]S Job 19:9; Ac 28:10 [b]S Dt 23:21; S Jos 9:18; Mt 5:33 **15:5** [c]S Ex 22:25 [d]S Ex 18:21; S 1Sa 8:3; Ac 24:26 [e]S Job 29:18; Ps 21:7; 112:6; Ac 2:25; Heb 12:28; 2Pe 1:10 **16:1** [f]S Ps 12:7 [g]Ps 2:12 **16:2** [h]Ps 31:14; 118:28; 140:6 [i]Ps 73:25 **16:3** [j]Dt 33:3; Ps 30:4; 85:8; Da 7:18; Ac 9:13; Ro 1:7 [k]Ps 101:6 **16:4** [l]Ps 32:10; Pr 23:29 [m]Ex 18:11; 20:3; S Dt 8:19; S 31:20 [n]S Ex 23:13 **16:5** [o]S Lev 2:2 [p]Ps 23:5; 75:8; 116:13; Isa 51:17; La 4:21; Eze 23:32-34; Hab 2:16 [q]S Job 31:2 **16:6** [r]S Dt 19:14; Ps 104:9; Pr 8:29; Jer 5:22 [s]S Job 22:26 **16:7** [t]Ps 73:24; Pr 15:22; Isa 11:2 [u]Job 35:10; Ps 42:8; 77:6 **16:8** [v]1Ki 2:19; 1Ch 6:39; Ps 73:23 [w]Ps 15:5 **16:9** [x]Ps 4:7; 13:5; 28:7; 30:11 [y]S Dt 33:28 **16:10** [z]S Nu 16:30; Ps 30:3; 31:17; 86:13; Hos 13:14

[b] Title: Probably a literary or musical term
[c] *3* Or *As for the pagan priests who are in the land / and the nobles in whom all delight, I said:*
[d] *10* Hebrew *Sheol*

16:2 APART FROM YOU I HAVE NO GOOD THING. Apart from God, the psalmist sees no meaning in life and no personal happiness. Nothing in his life is good if the Lord's presence and blessing are absent. Paul expressed this same truth when he said: "For to me, to live is Christ" (Php 1:21; cf. Gal 2:20).

16:5 ASSIGNED ME MY PORTION AND MY CUP. The "portion" and "cup" are the Lord himself (cf. 73:26; Nu 18:20; Dt 18:2). An important aspect of our inheritance as NT believers is the following: "If anyone loves me, he will obey my teaching. My Father will love him, and we will come to him and make our home with him" (Jn 14:23). Communion with God is the sure source of blessings and happiness.

16:8 SET THE LORD ALWAYS BEFORE ME. Believers should seek and cherish above all else intimate fellowship with God. The Lord's continual presence at our right hand brings his guidance (vv. 7,11), protection (v. 8), joy (v. 9), resurrection (v. 10) and eternal pleasures (v. 11).

16:10 NOT ABANDON ME TO THE GRAVE. A personal relationship with God will give believers confidence in a future life with God and the certainty that he will not abandon them to the grave (Heb *Sheol*; cf. 73:26). The apostles Peter and Paul both applied this verse to Christ and his resurrection (Ac 2:25–31; 13:34–37).

(1) *Sheol*, found 66 times in the OT, is translated 55 times as "the grave" and 6 times as "death." Some scholars believe *Sheol* always means "the grave," while others think it never has that meaning alone.

(2) In general, the OT views *Sheol* as a place associated with some sort of punishment. (a) When Jacob indicated that he would go down to the grave (*Sheol*) because of the loss of his son Joseph (Ge 37:35), he felt he must be under God's judgment; thus he refused to be comforted; there is no evidence that he sought God further until after he heard Joseph was still alive. (b) David clearly indicated that the grave (*Sheol*) was the place where "the wicked" would go (9:17), and Isaiah said that the pagan king Tiglath-Pileser of Assyria, when he died, would meet in the grave the kings he con-

nor will you let your Holy
One[e][a] see decay.[b]
11You have made[f] known to me the
path of life;[c]
you will fill me with joy in your
presence,[d]
with eternal pleasures[e] at your
right hand.[f]

Psalm 17

A prayer of David.

1Hear,[g] O LORD, my righteous plea;
listen to my cry.[h]
Give ear[i] to my prayer—
it does not rise from deceitful
lips.[j]
2May my vindication[k] come from
you;
may your eyes see what is
right.[l]
3Though you probe my heart[m] and
examine me at night,
though you test me,[n] you will
find nothing;[o]
I have resolved that my mouth
will not sin.[p]
4As for the deeds of men—
by the word of your lips
I have kept myself
from the ways of the violent.
5My steps have held to your
paths;[q]
my feet have not slipped.[r]
6I call on you, O God, for you will
answer me;[s]
give ear to me[t] and hear my
prayer.[u]
7Show the wonder of your great
love,[v]
you who save by your right
hand[w]
those who take refuge[x] in you
from their foes.
8Keep me[y] as the apple of your
eye;[z]
hide me[a] in the shadow of your
wings[b]
9from the wicked who assail me,
from my mortal enemies who
surround me.[c]
10They close up their callous
hearts,[d]
and their mouths speak with
arrogance.[e]
11They have tracked me down, they
now surround me,[f]
with eyes alert, to throw me to
the ground.
12They are like a lion[g] hungry for
prey,[h]
like a great lion crouching in
cover.
13Rise up,[i] O LORD, confront them,
bring them down;[j]
rescue me from the wicked by
your sword.
14O LORD, by your hand save me
from such men,
from men of this world[k] whose
reward is in this life.[l]

16:10 [a] S 2Ki 19:22 [b] S Job 17:14; Ac 2:31; 13:35* **16:11** [c] Ps 139:24; Mt 7:14 [d] Ac 2:25-28* [e] Ps 21:6 [f] Ps 80:17 **17:1** [g] Ps 30:10; 64:1; 80:1; 140:6 [h] Ps 5:2; 39:12; 142:6; 143:1 [i] S Ps 5:1 [j] Isa 29:13 **17:2** [k] Ps 24:5; 26:1; Isa 46:13; 50:8-9; 54:17 [l] Ps 99:4 **17:3** [m] Ps 139:1; Jer 12:3 [n] S Job 7:18 [o] Job 23:10; Jer 50:20 [p] Ps 39:1 **17:5** [q] Job 23:11; Ps 44:18; 119:133 [r] Dt 32:35; Ps 73:2; 121:3 **17:6** [s] Ps 86:7 [t] Ps 116:2 [u] S Ps 4:1 **17:7** [v] Ps 31:21; 69:13; 106:45; 107:43; 117:2 [w] S Ps 10:12 [x] Ps 2:12 **17:8** [y] S Nu 6:24 [z] S Dt 32:10; Pr 7:2 [a] Ps 27:5; 31:20; 32:7 [b] Ru 2:12; Ps 36:7; 63:7; Isa 34:15 **17:9** [c] Ps 109:3 **17:10** [d] Ps 73:7; 119:70; Isa 6:10 [e] S 1Sa 2:3 **17:11** [f] Ps 88:17 **17:12** [g] Ps 7:2; Jer 5:6; 12:8; La 3:10 [h] S Ge 49:9 **17:13** [i] S Nu 10:35 [j] Ps 35:8; 55:23; 73:18 **17:14** [k] Lk 16:8 [l] Ps 49:17; Lk 16:25

[e] *10* Or *your faithful one* [f] *11* Or *You will make*

quered (Isa 14:9–10). (c) There are several passages that indicate the Israelites did not expect to go to *Sheol* at all at death, but would instead go where they could enjoy the blessings of God's presence. When David died, he anticipated dwelling in the house of the Lord forever (23:6). Another psalmist believed that God would redeem his life from the grave (*Sheol*) and take him to himself in heaven (49:15; cf. 73:14–15). And Solomon testified that the wise, God-fearing person's paths lead upward "to keep him from going down to the grave" (Pr 15:24).

17:1 HEAR, O LORD. The psalmist's cry to the Lord to hear his prayer is founded not only on God's mercy and grace, but also on his own faithful obedience to God's will and ways (vv. 1–5). God has searched his heart and found that his endeavor to please him is no pretense (cf. 1Jn 3:18–21). That David appeals to God on the basis of his own personal faithfulness expresses the fundamental truth that God has promised to hear the prayers of those who love and honor him (see Jn 15:7, note). The first indispensable condition of true prayer is a clear conscience and a pure life (see 1Jn 3:22, note; see article on EFFECTIVE PRAYING, p. 496).

17:8 THE APPLE OF YOUR EYE. The psalmist uses two figures that recall God's love and care for his faithful people. (1) The "apple" of the eye is the pupil and is a Hebrew metaphor expressing something greatly valued and dear. (2) "The shadow of your wings" is a metaphor drawn from the imagery of a hen protecting her young with her wings; thus it expresses tender protection (cf. 36:7; 57:1; 61:4; 63:7). Christ used this metaphor to express his love for Israel (Mt 23:37). All believers should pray that God will reach out to protect us in times of danger just like someone who instinctively reacts to guard the pupil of the eye from harm (cf. Dt 32:10; Pr 7:2; Zec 2:8), and that the heavenly Father will always be ready to hide and shield us as a mother hen covers her chicks (91:4; Mt 23:37).

You still the hunger of those you
cherish;
their sons have plenty,
and they store up wealth[m] for
their children.
15And I — in righteousness I will see
your face;
when I awake,[n] I will be
satisfied with seeing your
likeness.[o]

Psalm 18

18:Title–50pp — 2Sa 22:1–51

For the director of music. Of David the servant of the LORD. He sang to the LORD the words of this song when the LORD delivered him from the hand of all his enemies and from the hand of Saul. He said:

1I love you, O LORD, my strength.[p]
2The LORD is my rock,[q] my
fortress[r] and my
deliverer;[s]
my God is my rock, in whom I
take refuge.[t]
He is my shield[u] and the
horn[g] of my salvation,[v]
my stronghold.
3I call to the LORD, who is worthy of
praise,[w]
and I am saved from my
enemies.[x]
4The cords of death[y] entangled
me;
the torrents[z] of destruction
overwhelmed me.
5The cords of the grave[h] coiled
around me;
the snares of death[a] confronted
me.
6In my distress[b] I called to the
LORD;[c]
I cried to my God for help.
From his temple he heard my
voice;[d]
my cry came[e] before him, into
his ears.
7The earth trembled[f] and
quaked,[g]
and the foundations of the
mountains shook;[h]
they trembled because he was
angry.[i]
8Smoke rose from his nostrils;[j]
consuming fire[k] came from his
mouth,
burning coals[l] blazed out of it.
9He parted the heavens and came
down;[m]
dark clouds[n] were under his
feet.
10He mounted the cherubim[o] and
flew;
he soared[p] on the wings of the
wind.[q]
11He made darkness his covering,[r]
his canopy[s] around him —
the dark rain clouds of the sky.
12Out of the brightness of his
presence[t] clouds advanced,
with hailstones[u] and bolts of
lightning.[v]
13The LORD thundered[w] from
heaven;
the voice of the Most High
resounded.[i]
14He shot his arrows[x] and scattered
⌊the enemies⌋,
great bolts of lightning[y] and
routed them.[z]
15The valleys of the sea were
exposed
and the foundations[a] of the
earth laid bare

17:14 [m]Isa 2:7; 57:17 **17:15** [n]S Ps 3:5 [o]S Nu 12:8; S Mt 5:8; 1Jn 3:2 **18:1** [p]S Ex 15:2; S Dt 33:29; S 1Sa 2:10; Ps 22:19; 28:7; 59:9; 81:1; Isa 12:2; 49:5; Jer 16:19 **18:2** [q]S Ex 33:22 [r]Ps 28:8; 31:2,3; Isa 17:10; Jer 16:19 [s]Ps 40:17 [t]Ps 2:12; 9:9; 94:22 [u]S Ge 15:1; Ps 28:7; 84:9; 119:114; 144:2 [v]S 1Sa 2:1; S Lk 1:69 **18:3** [w]S 1Ch 16:25 [x]S Ps 9:13 **18:4** [y]Ps 116:3 [z]Ps 93:4; 124:4; Isa 5:30; 17:12; Jer 6:23; 51:42,55; Eze 43:2 **18:5** [a]Pr 13:14 **18:6** [b]S Dt 4:30 [c]Ps 30:2; 99:6; 102:2; 120:1 [d]Ps 66:19; 116:1 [e]S Job 16:18 **18:7** [f]Ps 97:4; Isa 5:25; 64:3 [g]S Jdg 5:4 [h]S Jdg 5:5 [i]S Job 9:5; Jer 10:10 **18:8** [j]S Job 41:20 [k]S Ex 15:7; S 19:18; S Job 41:21; Ps 50:3; 97:3; Da 7:10 [l]Pr 25:22; Ro 12:20 **18:9** [m]S Ge 11:5; S Ps 57:3 [n]S Ex 20:21; S Dt 33:26; S Ps 104:3 **18:10** [o]S Ge 3:24; Eze 10:18 [p]S Dt 33:26 [q]Ps 104:3 **18:11** [r]S Ex 19:9; S Dt 4:11 [s]S Job 22:14; Isa 4:5; Jer 43:10 **18:12** [t]Ps 104:2 [u]S Jos 10:11 [v]S Job 36:30 **18:13** [w]S Ex 9:23; S 1Sa 2:10 **18:14** [x]S Dt 32:23 [y]S Job 36:30; Rev 4:5 [z]S Jdg 4:15 **18:15** [a]S Ps 11:3

[g]*2 Horn* here symbolizes strength.
[h]*5* Hebrew *Sheol*
[i]*13* Some Hebrew manuscripts and Septuagint (see also 2 Samuel 22:14); most Hebrew manuscripts *resounded, / amid hailstones and bolts of lightning*

18:1–50 I LOVE YOU, O LORD. This psalm also occurs in 2Sa 22 with a few changes; it was probably written early in David's reign (cf. 2Sa 8:14), before he committed his terrible sin and suffered greatly under a lifelong chastisement from God (see 2Sa 12:1–14). The psalm may speak prophetically of Christ, for Paul quotes v. 49 as prophesying a time when, through the Messiah, all nations will praise the name of God (cf. Ro 15:9).

18:2 MY ROCK, MY FORTRESS AND MY DELIVERER. The metaphors of this verse can be applied to the believer's perpetual struggles against the physical and spiritual forces of this age. God's care for us is described by six symbols: (1) "my rock" — safety and security in God's immovable strength (cf. 31:2–3; 42:9; 62:7); (2) "my fortress" — a place of refuge and safety where the enemy cannot penetrate; (3) "my deliverer" — a living protector; (4) "my shield" — God stepping between us and harm (cf. Ge 15:1); (5) "horn of my salvation" — strength and victorious power to deliver and save us; (6) "my stronghold" — a safe place to lift us above the dangers of life.

at your rebuke,[b] O LORD,
at the blast of breath from your nostrils.[c]

16He reached down from on high and took hold of me;
he drew me out of deep waters.[d]
17He rescued me from my powerful enemy,[e]
from my foes, who were too strong for me.[f]
18They confronted me in the day of my disaster,[g]
but the LORD was my support.[h]
19He brought me out into a spacious place;[i]
he rescued me because he delighted in me.[j]

20The LORD has dealt with me according to my righteousness;[k]
according to the cleanness of my hands[l] he has rewarded me.[m]
21For I have kept the ways of the LORD;[n]
I have not done evil by turning[o] from my God.
22All his laws are before me;[p]
I have not turned away from his decrees.
23I have been blameless[q] before him
and have kept myself from sin.
24The LORD has rewarded me according to my righteousness,[r]
according to the cleanness of my hands in his sight.

25To the faithful[s] you show yourself faithful,[t]
to the blameless you show yourself blameless,
26to the pure[u] you show yourself pure,
but to the crooked you show yourself shrewd.[v]
27You save the humble[w]
but bring low those whose eyes are haughty.[x]
28You, O LORD, keep my lamp[y] burning;
my God turns my darkness into light.[z]
29With your help[a] I can advance against a troop[j];
with my God I can scale a wall.

30As for God, his way is perfect;[b]
the word of the LORD is flawless.[c]
He is a shield[d]
for all who take refuge[e] in him.
31For who is God besides the LORD?[f]
And who is the Rock[g] except our God?
32It is God who arms me with strength[h]
and makes my way perfect.[i]
33He makes my feet like the feet of a deer;[j]
he enables me to stand on the heights.[k]
34He trains my hands for battle;[l]
my arms can bend a bow of bronze.
35You give me your shield of victory,
and your right hand sustains[m] me;
you stoop down to make me great.
36You broaden the path[n] beneath me,
so that my ankles do not turn.[o]

37I pursued my enemies[p] and overtook them;
I did not turn back till they were destroyed.
38I crushed them[q] so that they could not rise;[r]
they fell beneath my feet.[s]
39You armed me with strength[t] for battle;
you made my adversaries bow[u] at my feet.
40You made my enemies turn their backs[v] in flight,
and I destroyed[w] my foes.
41They cried for help, but there was no one to save them[x]—
to the LORD, but he did not answer.[y]
42I beat them as fine as dust[z] borne on the wind;
I poured them out like mud in the streets.

43You have delivered me from the attacks of the people;
you have made me the head of nations;[a]

18:15 [b]Ps 76:6; 104:7; 106:9; Isa 50:2 [c]S Ex 15:8 **18:16** [d]Ex 15:5; Ps 69:2; Pr 18:4; 20:5 **18:17** [e]ver 48; Ps 38:19; 59:1; 143:9 [f]S Jdg 18:26 **18:18** [g]Pr 1:27; 16:4; Jer 17:17; 40:2; Ob 1:13 [h]Ps 20:2; Isa 3:1 **18:19** [i]Ps 31:8 [j]S Nu 14:8 **18:20** [k]S 1Sa 26:23 [l]Job 22:30; Ps 24:4 [m]S Ru 2:12; S 2Ch 15:7; 1Co 3:8 **18:21** [n]2Ch 34:33; Ps 37:34; 119:2; Pr 8:32; 23:26 [o]Ps 119:102 **18:22** [p]Ps 119:30 **18:23** [q]S Ge 6:9 **18:24** [r]S 1Sa 26:23 **18:25** [s]Ps 31:23; 37:28; 50:5; Pr 2:8 [t]Ps 25:10; 40:11; 89:24; 146:6 **18:26** [u]Pr 15:26; Mt 5:8; Php 1:10; 1Ti 5:22; Tit 1:15; 1Jn 3:3 [v]Pr 3:34; Mt 10:16; Lk 16:8 **18:27** [w]S 2Ch 33:23; S Mt 23:12 [x]S Job 41:34; S Ps 10:5; Pr 3:33-34 **18:28** [y]1Ki 11:36; Ps 132:17 [z]Job 29:3; Ps 97:11; 112:4; Jn 1:5; S Ac 26:18; 2Co 4:6; 2Pe 1:19 **18:29** [a]ver 32,39; Isa 45:5; Heb 11:34 **18:30** [b]S Dt 32:4 [c]S Ps 12:6; Pr 30:5 [d]Ps 3:3 [e]Ps 2:12 **18:31** [f]S Dt 4:35; 32:39; Ps 35:10; 86:8; 89:6; Isa 44:6,8; 45:5,6,14,18,21; 46:9 [g]S Ge 49:24 **18:32** [h]S ver 29; 1Pe 5:10 [i]S Ps 15:2; 19:13; Heb 10:14; Jas 3:2 **18:33** [j]Ps 42:1; Pr 5:19; Isa 35:6; Hab 3:19 [k]S Dt 32:13 **18:34** [l]Ps 144:1 **18:35** [m]Ps 3:5; 37:5,17; 41:3; 51:12; 54:4; 55:22; 119:116; Isa 41:4,10,13; 43:2; 46:4 **18:36** [n]Ps 31:8 [o]S Job 18:7; Ps 66:9 **18:37** [p]S Lev 26:7 **18:38** [q]Ps 68:21; 110:6 [r]Ps 36:12; 140:10; Isa 26:14 [s]Ps 47:3 **18:39** [t]ver 32; Isa 45:5,24 [u]ver 47; Ps 47:3; 144:2 **18:40** [v]S Jos 7:12 [w]ver 37 **18:41** [x]S 2Ki 14:26; Ps 50:22 [y]S 1Sa 8:18; S 14:37; Jer 11:11 **18:42** [z]S Dt 9:21; S Isa 2:22 **18:43** [a]2Sa 8:1-14

[j]29 Or *can run through a barricade*

people I did not know[b] are
subject to me.
44As soon as they hear me, they
obey me;
foreigners[c] cringe before me.
45They all lose heart;[d]
they come trembling[e] from their
strongholds.[f]

46The LORD lives![g] Praise be to my
Rock![h]
Exalted be God[i] my Savior![j]
47He is the God who avenges[k] me,
who subdues nations[l] under
me,
48 who saves[m] me from my
enemies.[n]
You exalted me above my foes;
from violent men[o] you rescued
me.
49Therefore I will praise you among
the nations,[p] O LORD;
I will sing[q] praises to your
name.[r]
50He gives his king great victories;
he shows unfailing kindness to
his anointed,[s]
to David[t] and his descendants
forever.[u]

Psalm 19

For the director of music. A psalm
of David.

1The heavens[v] declare[w] the glory
of God;[x]
the skies[y] proclaim the work of
his hands.[z]
2Day after day they pour forth
speech;
night after night they display
knowledge.[a]
3There is no speech or language
where their voice is not
heard.[k]

18:43 [b]Isa 55:5
18:44 [c]Ps 54:3; 144:7,11; Isa 25:5
18:45 [d]S 1Sa 17:32; 2Co 4:1; Heb 12:3 [e]Isa 66:2; Hos 3:5; 11:10 [f]Ps 9:9; Mic 7:17
18:46 [g]S Jos 3:10; S 1Sa 14:39; 2Co 13:4 [h]ver 31; Ex 33:22 [i]Ps 21:13; 35:27; 40:16; 108:5 [j]S 1Ch 16:35; S Lk 1:47
18:47 [k]S Ge 4:24 [l]S ver 39; S Jdg 4:23
18:48 [m]Ps 7:10; 37:40; Da 3:17 [n]S ver 17 [o]Ps 140:1
18:49 [p]S Ps 9:11 [q]Ps 7:17; 9:2; 101:1; 108:1; 146:2 [r]Ro 15:9*
18:50 [s]S 2Sa 23:1 [t]Ps 144:10 [u]Ps 89:4
19:1 [v]Ps 89:5; Isa 40:22 [w]Ps 50:6; 148:3; Ro 1:19 [x]Ps 4:2; 8:1; 97:6; Isa 6:3 [y]S Ge 1:8 [z]S Ps 8:6; S 103:22
19:2 [a]Ps 74:16
19:4 [b]Ro 10:18* [c]S Job 36:29; Ps 104:2 [d]S Jdg 5:31
19:5 [e]Joel 2:16 [f]S Job 36:29 [g]1Sa 17:4
19:6 [h]Dt 30:4 [i]Ps 113:3; Ecc 1:5
19:7 [j]S Ps 1:2 [k]Ps 119:142; Jas 1:25 [l]Ps 23:3 [m]Ps 93:5; 111:7; 119:138,144 [n]S Dt 4:6; Ps 119:130
19:8 [o]Ps 33:4; 119:128 [p]Ps 119:14 [q]S Ezr 9:8; Ps 38:10
19:9 [r]Ps 34:11; 111:10; Pr 1:7; Ecc 12:13; Isa 33:6 [s]Ps 119:138,142
19:10

4Their voice[l] goes out into all the
earth,
their words to the ends of the
world.[b]
In the heavens he has pitched a
tent[c] for the sun,[d]
5 which is like a bridegroom[e]
coming forth from his
pavilion,[f]
like a champion[g] rejoicing to
run his course.
6It rises at one end of the
heavens[h]
and makes its circuit to the
other;[i]
nothing is hidden from its heat.

7The law of the LORD[j] is perfect,[k]
reviving the soul.[l]
The statutes of the LORD are
trustworthy,[m]
making wise the simple.[n]
8The precepts of the LORD are
right,[o]
giving joy[p] to the heart.
The commands of the LORD are
radiant,
giving light to the eyes.[q]
9The fear of the LORD[r] is pure,
enduring forever.
The ordinances of the LORD are
sure
and altogether righteous.[s]
10They are more precious than
gold,[t]
than much pure gold;
they are sweeter than honey,[u]
than honey from the comb.[v]
11By them is your servant warned;

[t]S Job 22:24; Ps 119:72; Pr 8:10 [u]Ps 119:103; SS 4:11; Eze 3:3 [v]S 1Sa 14:27

[k]3 Or *They have no speech, there are no words; / no sound is heard from them* [l]4 Septuagint, Jerome and Syriac; Hebrew *line*

19:1 THE HEAVENS DECLARE THE GLORY OF GOD. The Judeo-Christian view is that the physical world declares God's glory and creative power (cf. 148:3–5; cf. Ro 1:18–20). The view of many unbelievers, in contrast, is that the creation itself is a divine entity (see Dt 4:19; 2Ki 23:5), with a force that controls human destiny (see Isa 47:13); others believe it came about by chance. The true believer rejects these views, accepts the Scriptural revelation about the universe, and is thus moved to praise the Maker (89:5–8, see article on CREATION, p. 6).

19:7–11 THE LAW OF THE LORD IS PERFECT. These verses speak of the nature, benefits and value of God's law and word. The five facets are: (1) "The law"—a general term for God's revealed will that directs a person in a right relation to him (v. 7).

(2) "The statutes"—God's true word that testifies to his character and will (cf. 1Jn 5:9), the study of which makes us wise (v. 7).

(3) "The precepts"—definite rules concerning righteous living that are a joy to the godly (v. 8).

(4) "The commands"—the authoritative source of guiding light for the faithful who seek his way (v. 8; cf. Ac 26:18); the proper response to God's commands is the "fear of the LORD," which brings freedom from a life of sin (v. 9).

(5) "The ordinances"—laws governing social life that lead to justice and righteousness (v. 9).

in keeping them there is great
reward.

12Who can discern his errors?
Forgive my hidden faults.[w]
13Keep your servant also from willful
sins;[x]
may they not rule over me.[y]
Then will I be blameless,[z]
innocent of great transgression.

14May the words of my mouth and
the meditation of my heart
be pleasing[a] in your sight,
O LORD, my Rock[b] and my
Redeemer.[c]

Psalm 20

For the director of music. A psalm
of David.

1May the LORD answer you when
you are in distress;[d]
may the name of the God of
Jacob[e] protect you.[f]
2May he send you help[g] from the
sanctuary[h]
and grant you support[i] from
Zion.[j]
3May he remember[k] all your
sacrifices
and accept your burnt
offerings.[l] *Selah*
4May he give you the desire of your
heart[m]
and make all your plans
succeed.[n]
5We will shout for joy[o] when you
are victorious
and will lift up our banners[p] in
the name of our God.
May the LORD grant all your
requests.[q]

6Now I know that the LORD saves
his anointed;[r]
he answers him from his holy
heaven
with the saving power of his
right hand.[s]
7Some trust in chariots[t] and some
in horses,[u]
but we trust in the name of the
LORD our God.[v]
8They are brought to their knees
and fall,[w]
but we rise up[x] and stand
firm.[y]
9O LORD, save the king!
Answer[m] us[z] when we call!

Psalm 21

For the director of music. A psalm
of David.

1O LORD, the king rejoices in your
strength.[a]
How great is his joy in the
victories you give![b]
2You have granted him the desire of
his heart[c]
and have not withheld the
request of his lips. *Selah*
3You welcomed him with rich
blessings
and placed a crown of pure
gold[d] on his head.[e]
4He asked you for life, and you
gave it to him—
length of days, for ever and
ever.[f]
5Through the victories[g] you gave,
his glory is great;
you have bestowed on him
splendor and majesty.[h]
6Surely you have granted him
eternal blessings

19:12 [w]Ps 51:2; 90:8; Ecc 12:14 **19:13** [x]S Nu 15:30 [y]Ps 119:133 [z]S Ge 6:9; S Ps 18:32 **19:14** [a]Ps 104:34 [b]Ps 18:31 [c]S Ex 6:6; S Job 19:25 **20:1** [d]Ps 4:1 [e]Ex 3:6; Ps 46:7, 11 [f]Ps 59:1; 69:29; 91:14 **20:2** [g]Ps 30:10; 33:20; 37:40; 40:17; 54:4; 118:7 [h]S Nu 3:28 [i]S Ps 18:18 [j]Ps 2:6; 128:5; 134:3; 135:21 **20:3** [k]Ac 10:4 [l]S Dt 33:11 **20:4** [m]Ps 21:2; 37:4; 145:16,19; Isa 26:8; Eze 24:25; Ro 10:1 [n]Ps 140:8; Pr 16:3; Da 11:17 **20:5** [o]S Job 3:7 [p]S Nu 1:52; Ps 60:4; Isa 5:26; 11:10,12; 13:2; 30:17; 49:22; 62:10; Jer 50:2; 51:12,27 [q]1Sa 1:17 **20:6** [r]S 2Sa 23:1; Ps 28:8 [s]S Job 40:14; Hab 3:13 **20:7** [t]S 2Ki 19:23 [u]S Dt 17:16; Ps 33:17; 147:10; Pr 21:31; Isa 31:1; 36:8,9 [v]S 2Ch 32:8 **20:8** [w]Ps 27:2; Isa 40:30; Jer 46:6; 50:32 [x]Mic 7:8 [y]S Job 11:15; Ps 37:23; Pr 10:25; Isa 7:9 **20:9** [z]Ps 17:6 **21:1** [a]S 1Sa 2:10 [b]S 2Sa 22:51 **21:2** [c]S Ps 20:4 **21:3** [d]S 2Sa 12:30; Rev 14:14 [e]Zec 6:11 **21:4** [f]Ps 10:16; 45:17; 48:14; 133:3 **21:5** [g]ver 1; Ps 18:50; 44:4 [h]S Ps 8:5; 45:3; 93:1; 96:6; 104:1

[m]9 Or *save! / O King, answer*

19:12 FORGIVE MY HIDDEN FAULTS. Sincere believers strive to love and serve God with all their heart (Dt 6:5). Because they are still imperfect in this life, however, they may fall short of God's will without knowing it and thus need to seek God's forgiveness for their errors and hidden faults (cf. Lev 5:2–4). On the other hand, presumptuous or willful sins are a "great transgression" (v. 13) that involves despising God and his word and the loss of a place in his kingdom (cf. Nu 15:30–31; Gal 5:19–21).

19:14 MOUTH . . . HEART BE PLEASING IN YOUR SIGHT. The proper response to the work of salvation in our lives is a constant prayer that God will keep our hearts, words and lives free from sin and pleasing to him. Both the meditation of our hearts and the reflection of our minds should be pleasing to God.

20:1—21:13 ANSWER YOU WHEN YOU ARE IN DISTRESS. Ps 20 and 21 are companion psalms. They are prayers to God about the warfare of his people against their enemies. Ps 20 is a prayer before the battle; Ps 21 is a praise after the battle. For us who believe in Christ, Ps 20 can be applied to our spiritual warfare. We now struggle against unseen, yet very real, forces of evil, and we yearn for victory over and deliverance from Satan and demonic powers (see Eph 6:12, note; see article on POWER OVER SATAN AND DEMONS, p. 1484).

and made him glad with the
joy[i] of your presence.[j]
7For the king trusts in the LORD;[k]
through the unfailing love[l] of
the Most High[m]
he will not be shaken.[n]

8Your hand will lay hold[o] on all
your enemies;
your right hand will seize your
foes.
9At the time of your appearing
you will make them like a fiery
furnace.
In his wrath the LORD will swallow
them up,
and his fire will consume
them.[p]
10You will destroy their descendants
from the earth,
their posterity from mankind.[q]
11Though they plot evil[r] against
you
and devise wicked schemes,[s]
they cannot succeed;
12for you will make them turn their
backs[t]
when you aim at them with
drawn bow.

13Be exalted,[u] O LORD, in your
strength;[v]
we will sing and praise your
might.

Psalm 22

For the director of music. To the tune of "The Doe of the Morning." A psalm of David.

1My God, my God, why have you
forsaken me?[w]
Why are you so far[x] from
saving me,
so far from the words of my
groaning?[y]
2O my God, I cry out by day, but
you do not answer,[z]
by night,[a] and am not silent.

3Yet you are enthroned as the Holy
One;[b]
you are the praise[c] of Israel.[n]
4In you our fathers put their trust;
they trusted and you delivered
them.[d]
5They cried to you[e] and were
saved;
in you they trusted[f] and were
not disappointed.[g]

6But I am a worm[h] and not a man,
scorned by men[i] and
despised[j] by the people.
7All who see me mock me;[k]
they hurl insults,[l] shaking their
heads:[m]
8"He trusts in the LORD;
let the LORD rescue him.[n]
Let him deliver him,[o]
since he delights[p] in him."

9Yet you brought me out of the
womb;[q]
you made me trust[r] in you
even at my mother's breast.
10From birth[s] I was cast upon you;
from my mother's womb you
have been my God.
11Do not be far from me,[t]

21:6 [i] Ps 43:4; 126:3 [j] S 1Ch 17:27 21:7 [k] S 2Ki 18:5 [l] Ps 6:4 [m] Ge 14:18 [n] S Ps 15:5; S 55:22 21:8 [o] Isa 10:10 21:9 [p] S Dt 32:22; Ps 50:3; Jer 15:14 21:10 [q] Dt 28:18 21:11 [r] Ps 2:1 [s] Job 10:3; Ps 10:2; 26:10; 37:7 21:12 [t] S Ex 23:27 21:13 [u] S Ps 18:46 [v] Ps 18:1 22:1 [w] S Job 6:15; S Ps 9:10; Mt 27:46*; Mk 15:34* [x] Ps 10:1 [y] S Job 3:24 22:2 [z] S Job 19:7 [a] Ps 42:3; 88:1 22:3 [b] S 2Ki 19:22; Ps 71:22; S Mk 1:24 [c] S Ex 15:2; Ps 148:14 22:4 [d] Ps 78:53; 107:6 22:5 [e] S 1Ch 5:20 [f] Isa 8:17; 25:9; 26:3; 30:18 [g] S 2Ch 13:18; Ps 25:3; 31:17; 71:1; Isa 49:23; Ro 9:33 22:6 [h] S Job 4:19 [i] S 2Sa 12:14; Ps 31:11; 64:8; 69:19; 109:25 [j] Ps 119:141; Isa 49:7; 53:3; 60:14; Mal 2:9; Mt 16:21 22:7 [k] S Job 17:2; Ps 35:16; 69:12; 74:18; Mt 27:41; Mk 15:31; Lk 23:36 [l] Mt 27:39,44; Mk 15:32; Lk 23:39 [m] Mk 15:29 22:8 [n] Ps 91:14 [o] S Ps 3:2 [p] S 2Sa 22:20; S Mt 3:17; 27:43 22:9 [q] Job 10:18; Ps 71:6 [r] Ps 78:7; Na 1:7 22:10 [s] Ps 71:6; Isa 46:3; 49:1 22:11 [t] ver 19; S Ps 10:1

[n] 3 Or *Yet you are holy, / enthroned on the praises of Israel*

22:1–31 MY GOD. This psalm, one of the most quoted in the NT, is called "the psalm of the cross" because it so precisely portrays Christ's anguished suffering on the cross. Note at least two facts about this psalm: (1) It is a cry of anguish and grief from a godly sufferer who has not yet been delivered from trials and suffering. In this sense all suffering believers can identify with the words of this prayer. (2) The words of the psalm express an experience far beyond that of any ordinary human experience. Inspired by the Holy Spirit, the psalmist both predicts the suffering of Jesus Christ in his crucifixion and points to his subsequent vindication three days later.

22:1 MY GOD, MY GOD, WHY HAVE YOU FORSAKEN ME? Jesus uttered this dreadful cry on the cross when his heavenly Father's caring and protective presence was withdrawn (Isa 53:10–12; 2Co 5:21; see Mt 27:46, note). Jesus was forsaken by God because he suffered in the sinner's place, having become a curse for us (Gal 3:13). By quoting this verse, Jesus was also claiming the entire psalm as a description of himself.

22:2 I CRY OUT . . . YOU DO NOT ANSWER. The believer, like Jesus himself, may at times feel forsaken by God. When this occurs, hold firmly to your belief in God and in his goodness, and continue to pray and trust (vv. 2–5).

22:7 SHAKING THEIR HEADS. See Mt 27:39, which states, "Those who passed by hurled insults at him [Jesus], shaking their heads." The very gestures used by Jesus' enemies were predicted in the OT.

22:8 HE TRUSTS IN THE LORD. This verse recounts the exact words that the Lord's enemies would say to him as they witnessed the crucifixion (Mt 27:43).

22:11–17 THERE IS NO ONE TO HELP.

for trouble is near[u]
and there is no one to help.[v]
12Many bulls[w] surround me;[x]
strong bulls of Bashan[y] encircle me.
13Roaring lions[z] tearing their prey[a]
open their mouths wide[b] against me.
14I am poured out like water,
and all my bones are out of joint.[c]
My heart has turned to wax;[d]
it has melted away[e] within me.
15My strength is dried up like a potsherd,[f]
and my tongue sticks to the roof of my mouth;[g]
you lay me[o] in the dust[h] of death.
16Dogs[i] have surrounded me;
a band of evil men has encircled me,
they have pierced[p][j] my hands and my feet.
17I can count all my bones;
people stare[k] and gloat over me.[l]
18They divide my garments among them
and cast lots[m] for my clothing.[n]
19But you, O LORD, be not far off;[o]
O my Strength,[p] come quickly[q] to help me.[r]
20Deliver my life from the sword,[s]
my precious life[t] from the power of the dogs.[u]
21Rescue me from the mouth of the lions;[v]
save[q] me from the horns of the wild oxen.[w]
22I will declare your name to my brothers;
in the congregation[x] I will praise you.[y]

23You who fear the LORD, praise him![z]
All you descendants of Jacob, honor him![a]
Revere him,[b] all you descendants of Israel!
24For he has not despised[c] or disdained
the suffering of the afflicted one;[d]
he has not hidden his face[e] from him
but has listened to his cry for help.[f]
25From you comes the theme of my praise in the great assembly;[g]
before those who fear you[r] will I fulfill my vows.[h]
26The poor will eat[i] and be satisfied;
they who seek the LORD will praise him—[j]
may your hearts live forever!
27All the ends of the earth[k] will remember and turn to the LORD,
and all the families of the nations will bow down before him,[l]
28for dominion belongs to the LORD[m]
and he rules over the nations.
29All the rich[n] of the earth will feast and worship;[o]
all who go down to the dust[p] will kneel before him—
those who cannot keep themselves alive.[q]
30Posterity[r] will serve him;

22:11 [u]S Ps 10:14 [v]S 2Ki 14:26; S Isa 41:28
22:12 [w]Ps 68:30 [x]Ps 17:9; 27:6; 49:5; 109:3; 140:9 [y]Dt 32:14; Isa 2:13; Eze 27:6; 39:18; Am 4:1
22:13 [z]ver 21; Eze 22:25; Zep 3:3 [a]S Ge 49:9 [b]La 3:46
22:14 [c]S Ps 6:2 [d]Job 23:16; Ps 68:2; 97:5; Mic 1:4 [e]Jos 7:5; Ps 107:26; Da 5:6
22:15 [f]Isa 45:9 [g]Ps 137:6; La 4:4; Eze 3:26; Jn 19:28 [h]S Job 7:21; Ps 104:29
22:16 [i]Php 3:2 [j]Isa 51:9; 53:5; Zec 12:10; Jn 20:25
22:17 [k]Lk 23:35 [l]Ps 25:2; 30:1; 35:19; 38:16; La 2:17; Mic 7:8
22:18 [m]S Lev 16:8; Mt 27:35*; Mk 15:24; Lk 23:34; Jn 19:24* [n]Mk 9:12
22:19 [o]S ver 11 [p]S Ps 18:1 [q]Ps 38:22; 70:5; 141:1 [r]Ps 40:13
22:20 [s]S Job 5:20; Ps 37:14 [t]Ps 35:17 [u]Php 3:2
22:21 [v]S ver 13; S Job 4:10 [w]ver 12; S Nu 23:22
22:22 [x]Ps 26:12; 40:9,10; 68:26 [y]Ps 35:18; Heb 2:12*
22:23 [z]Ps 33:2; 66:8; 86:12; 103:1; 106:1; 113:1; 117:1; 135:19 [a]Ps 50:15; Isa 24:15; 25:3; 49:23; 60:9; Jer 3:17 [b]S Dt 14:23; Ps 33:8
22:24 [c]Ps 102:17 [d]S Ps 9:12 [e]Ps 13:1; 27:9; 69:17; 102:2; 143:7 [f]S Job 24:12; S 36:5; Heb 5:7
22:25 [g]Ps 26:12; 35:18; 40:9; 82:1 [h]S Nu 30:2 22:26 [i]Ps 107:9 [j]Ps 40:16
22:27 [k]S Ps 2:8 [l]Ps 86:9; 102:22; Da 7:27; Mic 4:1
22:28 [m]Ps 47:7-8; Zec 14:9 22:29 [n]Ps 45:12 [o]Ps 95:6; 96:9; 99:5; Isa 27:13; 49:7; 66:23; Zec 14:16 [p]Isa 26:19 [q]Ps 89:48 22:30 [r]Isa 53:10; 54:3; 61:9; 66:22

[o] *15* Or */ I am laid* [p] *16* Some Hebrew manuscripts, Septuagint and Syriac; most Hebrew manuscripts */ like the lion,* [q] *21* Or */ you have heard* [r] *25* Hebrew *him*

These verses describe the Lord's feelings of helplessness while undergoing the brutality of the flogging and crucifixion.

22:16 PIERCED MY HANDS AND MY FEET. Here is another prophetic reference to the crucifixion (cf. Jn 20:25; see Mt 27:35, note).

22:18 DIVIDE MY GARMENTS AMONG THEM. The Roman soldiers did exactly as this verse foretold—an amazing fulfillment of prophecy (see Mt 27:35; Mk 15:24; Lk 23:34; Jn 19:23–24).

22:22 TO MY BROTHERS. Heb 2:11–12 relates this verse to Jesus Christ; it marks the triumph of the cross. Jesus is now the exalted Redeemer who gathers around him his "brothers" (i.e., the redeemed who believe in him and accept his death for them, see Jn 20:17) and stands among them to praise the Lord. His death results in help for the afflicted (v. 24), eternal life (v. 26), the preaching of the gospel (v. 27), his rule over all the nations (vv. 27–29), and ultimate exaltation and glory (vv. 30–31).

future generations[s] will be told
about the Lord.
31They will proclaim his
righteousness[t]
to a people yet unborn[u]—
for he has done it.[v]

Psalm 23

A psalm of David.

1The LORD is my shepherd,[w] I shall
not be in want.[x]
2 He makes me lie down in green
pastures,
he leads me beside quiet waters,[y]
3 he restores my soul.[z]
He guides me[a] in paths of
righteousness[b]
for his name's sake.[c]
4Even though I walk
through the valley of the shadow
of death,[s][d]
I will fear no evil,[e]
for you are with me;[f]
your rod and your staff,
they comfort me.

5You prepare a table[g] before me
in the presence of my enemies.
You anoint my head with oil;[h]
my cup[i] overflows.
6Surely goodness and love[j] will
follow me

22:30 [s]Ps 102:18 22:31 [t]S Ps 5:8; 40:9 [u]Ps 71:18; 78:6; 102:18 [v]Lk 18:31; 24:44 23:1 [w]S Ge 48:15; S Ps 28:9; S Jn 10:11 [x]Ps 34:9,10; 84:11; 107:9; Php 4:19 23:2 [y]Ps 36:8; 46:4; Rev 7:17 23:3 [z]S Ps 19:7 [a]Ps 25:9; 73:24; Isa 42:16 [b]S Ps 5:8 [c]Ps 25:11; 31:3; 79:9; 106:8; 109:21; 143:11 23:4 [d]S Job 3:5; Ps 107:14 [e]Ps 3:6; 27:1 [f]Ps 16:8; Isa 43:2 23:5 [g]S Job 36:16 [h]Ps 45:7; 92:10; Lk 7:46 [i]S Ps 16:5 23:6 [j]S Ne 9:25

[s] 4 Or *through the darkest valley*

23:1–6 THE LORD. This psalm, conceived in the mind of the Lord and inspired by the Holy Spirit, expresses his concern and diligent care for those who follow him. They are the cherished objects of his divine love. He cares for each of them as a father cares for his children and as a shepherd for his sheep.

23:1 MY SHEPHERD. Using a metaphor frequently found in the OT (see 28:9; 79:13; 80:1; 95:7; Isa 40:11; Jer 31:10; Eze 34:6–19), God compares himself to a shepherd in order to illustrate his great love for his people. The Lord Jesus himself adopted the same metaphor to express his relationship to his people (Jn 10:11–16; cf. Heb 13:20; 1Pe 5:4; Rev 7:17). Two truths are emphasized here: (1) God, through Christ and by the Holy Spirit, is so concerned about each of his children that he desires to love, care for, protect, guide and be near that child, just as a good shepherd does for his own sheep (see Jn 10:11,14 notes).

(2) Believers are the Lord's sheep. We belong to him and are the special objects of his affection and attention. Though "we all, like sheep, have gone astray" (Isa 53:6), the Lord has redeemed us with his shed blood (1Pe 1:18–19), and we now belong to him. As his sheep we can claim the promises of this psalm when we respond to his voice and follow him (see Jn 10:3–5; see 10:28, note).

23:1 I SHALL NOT BE IN WANT. To "not be in want" means both (1) that I will not lack anything necessary for God's will to be accomplished in my life (see 3Jn 2, note), and (2) that I will be content in the Good Shepherd's provision and care of my life, even in times of personal hardship, because I trust in his love and his commitment to me (cf. Jn 10:11; Php 4:11–13).

23:2 HE MAKES ME LIE DOWN. Because of the presence and nearness of the shepherd I can "lie down" in peace, free from all fear. The Holy Spirit as my Comforter, Counselor and Helper communicates Christ's shepherdly care and presence to me (Jn 14:16–18; cf. 2Ti 1:7). (1) My confident rest in his presence will be experienced "in green pastures," i.e., in Jesus and the Word of God, which are necessary for an abundant life (Jn 6:32–35,63; 8:31; 10:9; 15:7). (2) "He leads me beside quiet waters" of his Holy Spirit (see 1:3, note; cf. Jer 2:13; Jn 7:37–39).

23:3 HE RESTORES MY SOUL. When I become discouraged (42:11), the Good Shepherd revives and re-energizes my soul through his power and grace (Pr 25:13). "He guides me" by the Spirit of God (Ro 8:14) in his chosen paths, ones that conform to his way of holiness (cf. Ro 8:5–14). My response is obedience: I follow the Shepherd and listen to his voice (Jn 10:3–4); I will not follow "a stranger's voice" (Jn 10:5).

23:4 YOU ARE WITH ME. In times of danger, difficulty and even death, I fear no evil. Why? "For you are with me" in every situation of life (cf. Mt 28:20). The "rod" (a short club) is a weapon of defense or discipline, symbolizing God's strength, power and authority (cf. Ex 21:20; Job 9:34). The "staff" (a long slender stick with a hook on one end) is used to draw a sheep close to the shepherd, guide it in the right way or rescue it from trouble. God's rod and staff reassure us of God's love and guidance in our lives (cf. 71:21; 86:17).

23:5 PREPARE A TABLE. God is pictured as caring for my needs in the midst of the evil forces that attempt to destroy my life and soul (see Ro 8:31–39). (1) Confronted daily by Satan and surrounded by an ungodly society, I am provided with sufficient grace to live and rejoice in God's presence (see 2Co 12:9–10). I may eat at the Lord's table in faith, thanksgiving and hope, fully at peace and protected by the shed blood and broken body of this Good Shepherd (see 1Co 11:23). (2) "Anoint my head with oil" refers to God's special favor and blessing through the anointing of his Holy Spirit on my body, mind and spirit (see Eph 5:18, note). (3) "My cup overflows" literally translates, "My cup is an abundant drink." It refers to a shepherd's cup, which was a large, hollowed-out stone that could hold forty or fifty gallons and from which the sheep drank.

23:6 GOODNESS AND LOVE. With the Shepherd accompanying me through life's pilgrimage, I will receive constant help, kindness and support. No matter what happens I can trust the Good

all the days of my life,
and I will dwell in the house of the LORD
forever.

Psalm 24

Of David. A psalm.

1The earth is the LORD's,[k] and everything in it,
the world, and all who live in it;[l]
2for he founded it upon the seas
and established it upon the waters.[m]

3Who may ascend the hill[n] of the LORD?
Who may stand in his holy place?[o]
4He who has clean hands[p] and a pure heart,[q]
who does not lift up his soul to an idol[r]
or swear by what is false.[t]
5He will receive blessing[s] from the LORD
and vindication[t] from God his Savior.
6Such is the generation of those who seek him,
who seek your face,[u] O God of Jacob.[u] *Selah*
7Lift up your heads, O you gates;[v]
be lifted up, you ancient doors,
that the King[w] of glory[x] may come in.[y]
8Who is this King of glory?
The LORD strong and mighty,[z]
the LORD mighty in battle.[a]
9Lift up your heads, O you gates;
lift them up, you ancient doors,
that the King of glory may come in.
10Who is he, this King of glory?
The LORD Almighty[b]—
he is the King of glory. *Selah*

Psalm 25[v]

Of David.

1To you, O LORD, I lift up my soul;[c]
2 in you I trust,[d] O my God.
Do not let me be put to shame,
nor let my enemies triumph over me.
3No one whose hope is in you
will ever be put to shame,[e]
but they will be put to shame
who are treacherous[f] without excuse.

4Show me your ways, O LORD,
teach me your paths;[g]

24:1 [k]S Ex 9:29; Job 41:11 [l]1Co 10:26* **24:2** [m]S Ge 1:6; Ps 104:3; 2Pe 3:5 **24:3** [n]Ps 2:6 [o]Ps 15:1; 65:4 **24:4** [p]S 2Sa 22:21 [q]Ps 51:10; 73:1; Mt 5:8 [r]Eze 18:15 **24:5** [s]Dt 11:26 [t]Ps 17:2 **24:6** [u]Ps 27:8; 105:4; 119:58; Hos 5:15 **24:7** [v]Ps 118:19, 20; Isa 26:2; 60:11,18; 62:10 [w]Ps 44:4; 74:12 [x]Ps 29:3; Ac 7:2; 1Co 2:8 [y]Zec 9:9; Mt 21:5 **24:8** [z]S 1Ch 29:11; Ps 89:13; Jer 50:34; Eph 6:10 [a]Ex 15:3,6; Dt 4:34 **24:10** [b]S 1Sa 1:11 **25:1** [c]Ps 86:4; 143:8 **25:2** [d]Ps 31:6; 143:8 **25:3** [e]S Ps 22:5; S Isa 29:22 [f]Isa 24:16; Hab 1:13; Zep 3:4; 2Ti 3:4 **25:4** [g]S Job 34:32

[t]*4* Or *swear falsely* [u]*6* Two Hebrew manuscripts and Syriac (see also Septuagint); most Hebrew manuscripts *face, Jacob* [v]This psalm is an acrostic poem, the verses of which begin with the successive letters of the Hebrew alphabet.

Shepherd to work in all things for my good (Ro 8:28; Jas 5:11). The goal of my following the Shepherd and experiencing his goodness and love is that one day I may be with the Lord forever (1Th 4:17), see his face (Rev 22:4), and serve him forever in his house (see Rev 22:3; cf. Jn 14:2–3).

24:4 CLEAN HANDS AND A PURE HEART. David emphasizes that those who want to worship and serve God and receive his blessing must be pursuing a pure heart and a righteous life. "Clean hands" are hands free from external acts of sin (see Isa 1:15; 33:15; 1Ti 2:8). A "pure heart" refers to inward holiness, right motives and goals. Only the pure in heart will see God (Mt 5:8).

24:5 HE WILL RECEIVE BLESSING. Those who receive "blessing from the LORD" are those who "seek him" (v. 6) with "clean hands and a pure heart" (v. 4). We should remind ourselves of this every time we call on God in prayer, worship him in his house or seek his grace in the Lord's Supper (see 1Co 11:23–27; 2Co 6:14–18; Heb 12:14).

24:7–10 KING OF GLORY. These verses are Messianic, for the King of glory is the Lord Jesus (cf. Jn 1:14). The "generation of those who seek him" (i.e., faithful believers) must pray that the "King of glory" will come. This prayer for God's kingdom to come anticipates Christ's eternal reign and the final destruction of evil (see Zec 9:9; Mt 6:10; Rev 19—22).

25:4 SHOW ME YOUR WAYS. Like Moses (Ex 33:13), the psalmist longed intensely to know God's ways. It is possible for believers to know something about God's acts (e.g., salvation, miracles; cf. Ps 103:7), but never really to know God or to understand his ways (i.e., the principles of wisdom by which he works in us and guides us). The basic principles for knowing God's ways in this psalm are the following: (1) We must have a sincere desire to be led into God's righteous ways and the truth of his Word (v. 4).

(2) We must be eager to put our hope in God "all day long" (v. 5).

(3) We must humbly submit to God (v. 9), commit ourselves to godly living (v. 10) and fear the Lord (vv. 12–14).

(4) Since sin is a barrier to knowing God and his ways, we must forsake sin and be cleansed and forgiven (vv. 4–8). "If I had cherished sin in my heart, the Lord would not have listened" (66:18; cf. 1Jn 2:1–6).

(5) Adversity in our lives is not necessarily a sign of God's disfavor (cf. 34:19). Knowing God

5guide me in your truth[h] and teach
me,
for you are God my Savior,[i]
and my hope is in you[j] all day
long.
6Remember, O LORD, your great
mercy and love,[k]
for they are from of old.
7Remember not the sins of my
youth[l]
and my rebellious ways;[m]
according to your love[n] remember
me,
for you are good,[o] O LORD.

8Good and upright[p] is the LORD;
therefore he instructs[q] sinners
in his ways.
9He guides[r] the humble in what is
right
and teaches them[s] his way.
10All the ways of the LORD are loving
and faithful[t]
for those who keep the demands
of his covenant.[u]
11For the sake of your name,[v]
O LORD,
forgive[w] my iniquity,[x] though it
is great.
12Who, then, is the man that fears
the LORD?[y]
He will instruct him in the
way[z] chosen for him.
13He will spend his days in
prosperity,[a]
and his descendants will inherit
the land.[b]
14The LORD confides[c] in those who
fear him;
he makes his covenant known[d]
to them.
15My eyes are ever on the LORD,[e]
for only he will release my feet
from the snare.[f]

16Turn to me[g] and be gracious to
me,[h]
for I am lonely[i] and afflicted.
17The troubles[j] of my heart have
multiplied;
free me from my anguish.[k]
18Look upon my affliction[l] and my
distress[m]
and take away all my sins.[n]
19See how my enemies[o] have
increased
and how fiercely they hate me![p]
20Guard my life[q] and rescue me;[r]
let me not be put to shame,[s]
for I take refuge[t] in you.
21May integrity[u] and uprightness[v]
protect me,
because my hope is in you.[w]

22Redeem Israel,[x] O God,
from all their troubles!

Psalm 26

Of David.

1Vindicate me,[y] O LORD,
for I have led a blameless life;[z]
I have trusted[a] in the LORD
without wavering.[b]
2Test me,[c] O LORD, and try me,

25:5 [h]Ps 31:3; 43:3; Jn 16:13 [i]Ps 24:5 [j]ver 3; Ps 33:20; 39:7; 42:5; 71:5; 130:7; 131:3 **25:6** [k]Ps 5:7; 98:3; Isa 63:7,15; Jer 31:20; Hos 11:8 **25:7** [l]Job 13:26; Isa 54:4; Jer 3:25; 31:19; 32:30; Eze 16:22,60; 23:3; 2Ti 2:22 [m]S Ex 23:21; Ps 107:17 [n]Ps 6:4; 51:1; 69:16; 109:26; 119:124 [o]S 1Ch 16:34; Ps 34:8; 73:1 **25:8** [p]Ps 92:15; Isa 26:7 [q]Ps 32:8; Isa 28:26 **25:9** [r]S Ps 23:3 [s]ver 4; Ps 27:11 **25:10** [t]S Ps 18:25 [u]Ps 103:18; 132:12 **25:11** [v]S Ex 9:16; Ps 31:3; 79:9; Jer 14:7 [w]S Ex 34:9 [x]S Ex 32:30; S Ps 78:38 **25:12** [y]S Job 1:8 [z]ver 8 **25:13** [a]S Dt 30:15; S 1Ki 3:14; S Job 8:7 [b]S Nu 14:24; Mt 5:5 **25:14** [c]Pr 3:32 [d]Ge 17:2; Jn 7:17 **25:15** [e]S 2Ch 20:12; Ps 123:2; Heb 12:2 [f]S Job 34:30; S Ps 119:110 **25:16** [g]S Ps 6:4 [h]S Nu 6:25 [i]Ps 68:6 **25:17** [j]1Ki 1:29; Ps 34:6,17; 40:12; 54:7; 116:3 [k]Ps 6:3; 39:2 **25:18** [l]S Ps 13:3; Ro 12:12 [m]S 2Sa 16:12 [n]Ps 103:3 **25:19** [o]Ps 3:1; 9:13 [p]Ps 35:19; 38:19; 69:4 **25:20** [q]Ps 86:2 [r]Ps 17:13; 22:21; 43:1; 71:2; 116:4; 140:1; 142:6; 144:11 [s]ver 3 [t]Ps 2:12 **25:21** [u]S Ge 20:5; Pr 10:9 [v]1Ki 9:4; Ps 85:10; 111:8; Isa 60:17; Mal 2:6 [w]ver 3 **25:22** [x]Ps 130:8; Lk 24:21 **26:1** [y]S 1Sa 24:15 [z]Ps 15:2; Pr 20:7 [a]Ps 22:4; 40:4; Isa 12:2; 25:9; Jer 17:7; Da 3:28 [b]2Ki 20:3; Heb 10:23 **26:2** [c]Ps 66:10

---

and his ways may lead us into suffering and loss that we would not have otherwise encountered (e.g., Ac 14:22; 20:22–23). The ultimate example of this truth is Jesus himself, who followed God's will perfectly, yet suffered sorrow, betrayal and the cross. The believer, abiding in God's will, must expect the same (Mt 10:24).

25:12 HE WILL INSTRUCT HIM. The main theme of this psalm is how God in his wisdom guides the faithful believer. Note the following truths: (1) God has a plan for every believer. He had a plan for Adam (Ge 1:28; 2:18–25), Abraham (Ge 12:1–3), Joseph (Ge 45:4–9), and his people, Israel (Ge 50:24; Ex 6:6–8); he had a plan for Jesus (Lk 18:31) and Paul (Ac 21:10–14; 22:14–15; 26:16–19; see 21:14, note). God has a definite plan for each of his children (1Co 12; Eph 1:10; 2:10; 3:11; 4:11–13).

(2) God's plans can be communicated to us by extraordinary means, such as dreams, visions and prophecy (Ac 2:17; 9:12; 10:3; 13:2; 1Co 14:1; see Ac 21:10, note). However, the usual way he guides us and imparts wisdom to us is through the holy Scriptures (2Ti 3:16) and through the Holy Spirit living in our hearts (Ac 8:29; 10:19; 13:2; 15:28; 16:6; 1Jn 2:20,27).

(3) God's plan for believers may be missed if we by ignoring God's Word or misreading it make decisions contrary to his will. If the basic convictions, attitudes and teachings found in the Bible are not deeply embedded in our lives, we will go astray.

(4) Righteousness lies at the root of God's guidance (cf. v. 21; Ro 8:11–14), for God guides us "in paths of righteousness" (23:3).

25:14 FEAR HIM. Personal knowledge of God and intimate fellowship with him are reserved for those who fear him and shun evil (cf. Pr 3:5–7; see article on THE FEAR OF THE LORD, p. 260).

examine my heart and my
mind;[d]
3for your love[e] is ever before me,
and I walk continually[f] in your
truth.[g]
4I do not sit[h] with deceitful men,
nor do I consort with
hypocrites;[i]
5I abhor[j] the assembly of evildoers
and refuse to sit with the
wicked.
6I wash my hands in innocence,[k]
and go about your altar, O LORD,
7proclaiming aloud your praise[l]
and telling of all your wonderful
deeds.[m]
8I love[n] the house where you live,
O LORD,
the place where your glory
dwells.[o]

9Do not take away my soul along
with sinners,
my life with bloodthirsty men,[p]
10in whose hands are wicked
schemes,[q]
whose right hands are full of
bribes.[r]
11But I lead a blameless life;
redeem me[s] and be merciful to
me.
12My feet stand on level ground;[t]
in the great assembly[u] I will
praise the LORD.

Psalm 27

Of David.

✝ Ps 37:39-40

1The LORD is my light[v] and my
salvation[w]—
whom shall I fear?
The LORD is the stronghold[x] of my
life—
of whom shall I be afraid?[y]
2When evil men advance against me
to devour my flesh,[w]
when my enemies and my foes
attack me,
they will stumble and fall.[z]

3Though an army besiege me,
my heart will not fear;[a]
though war break out against me,
even then will I be confident.[b]

4One thing[c] I ask of the LORD,
this is what I seek:
that I may dwell in the house of
the LORD
all the days of my life,[d]
to gaze upon the beauty of the
LORD
and to seek him in his temple.
5For in the day of trouble[e]
he will keep me safe[f] in his
dwelling;
he will hide me[g] in the shelter of
his tabernacle
and set me high upon a rock.[h]
6Then my head will be exalted[i]
above the enemies who surround
me;[j]
at his tabernacle will I sacrifice[k]
with shouts of joy;[l]
I will sing[m] and make music[n]
to the LORD.

7Hear my voice[o] when I call,
O LORD;
be merciful to me and answer
me.[p]
8My heart says of you, "Seek his[x]
face![q]"
Your face, LORD, I will seek.
9Do not hide your face[r] from me,
do not turn your servant away in
anger;[s]
you have been my helper.[t]
Do not reject me or forsake[u] me,
O God my Savior.[v]
10Though my father and mother
forsake me,
the LORD will receive me.
11Teach me your way,[w] O LORD;
lead me in a straight path[x]

26:2 [d] S Dt 6:6; S Ps 7:9; Jer 11:20; 20:12; Eze 11:5 **26:3** [e] Ps 6:4 [f] S 1Ki 2:4 [g] Ps 40:11; 43:3; 86:11; 119:30 **26:4** [h] Ps 1:1 [i] Ps 28:3; Mt 6:2 **26:5** [j] Ps 139:21 **26:6** [k] Ps 73:13; Mt 27:24 **26:7** [l] Isa 42:12; 60:6 [m] S Jos 3:5; Ps 9:1 **26:8** [n] Ps 122:6; Isa 66:10 [o] S Ex 29:43; 2Ch 7:1; Ps 96:6 **26:9** [p] Ps 5:6; 28:3; 55:23; 139:19; Pr 29:10 **26:10** [q] S Ps 21:11 [r] S Job 36:18; S Isa 1:23; S Eze 22:12 **26:11** [s] Ps 31:5; 69:18; 119:134; Tit 2:14 **26:12** [t] Ps 27:11; 40:2; 143:10; Isa 26:7; 40:3-4; 45:13; Zec 4:7; Lk 6:17 [u] S Ps 22:25 **27:1** [v] S 2Sa 22:29 [w] S Ex 15:2; S Ps 3:8 [x] Ps 9:9 [y] S Job 13:15; Ps 56:4,11; 118:6 **27:2** [z] Ps 9:3; S 20:8; 37:24; Da 11:19; Ro 11:11

27:3 [a] S Ge 4:7; S Ps 3:6 [b] S Job 4:6 **27:4** [c] Lk 10:42 [d] Ps 23:6; 61:4 **27:5** [e] S Job 38:23 [f] S Ps 12:7 [g] S Ps 17:8 [h] Ps 40:2 **27:6** [i] 2Sa 22:49; Ps 3:3; 18:48 [j] S Ps 22:12 [k] Ps 50:14; 54:6; 107:22; 116:17 [l] S Ezr 3:13; S Job 22:26 [m] S Ex 15:1 [n] Ps 33:2; 92:1; 147:7; S Eph 5:19 **27:7** [o] Ps 5:3; 18:6; 55:17; 119:149; 130:2; Isa 28:23 [p] S Ps 4:1 **27:8** [q] S 1Ch 16:11 **27:9** [r] S Dt 31:17; S Ps 22:24 [s] S Ps 2:5 [t] S Ge 49:25; S Dt 33:29 [u] S Dt 4:31; Ps 37:28; 119:8; Isa 41:17; 62:12; Jer 14:9 [v] Ps 18:46 **27:11** [w] S Ex 33:13 [x] S Ezr 8:21; Ps 5:8

[w]2 Or *to slander me* [x]8 Or *To you, O my heart, he has said, "Seek my*

26:8 I LOVE THE HOUSE WHERE YOU LIVE. The psalmist's happiness does not come from associating with the world (vv. 4–5,9–10), but from being in the "house" and "assembly" of the Lord (v. 12), i.e., where God's divine presence is manifested among his people and where his glory dwells (see article on THE GLORY OF GOD, p. 1192), and from being with fellow believers who walk in God's truth.

27:4 ONE THING I ASK. As in Ps 26, the psalmist seeks God's presence; it is the one thing most treasured in his life, and he prays for it with singleness of purpose. God himself calls all of us to this same purpose: "seek his face" (v. 8). Those who do so, striving to dwell in God's holy presence, are given the firm assurance that no matter what trials come to them, the Lord will never forsake them (vv. 9–10). They have no reason for despair; God's goodness is reserved for them (vv. 13–14).

because of my oppressors.[y]
12Do not turn me over to the desire
of my foes,
for false witnesses[z] rise up
against me,
breathing out violence.

13I am still confident of this:
I will see the goodness of the
LORD[a]
in the land of the living.[b]
14Wait[c] for the LORD;
be strong[d] and take heart
and wait for the LORD.

Psalm 28

Of David.

1To you I call, O LORD my Rock;
do not turn a deaf ear[e] to me.
For if you remain silent,[f]
I will be like those who have
gone down to the pit.[g]
2Hear my cry for mercy[h]
as I call to you for help,
as I lift up my hands[i]
toward your Most Holy Place.[j]

3Do not drag me away with the
wicked,
with those who do evil,
who speak cordially with their
neighbors
but harbor malice in their
hearts.[k]
4Repay them for their deeds
and for their evil work;
repay them for what their hands
have done[l]
and bring back upon them what
they deserve.[m]
5Since they show no regard for the
works of the LORD
and what his hands have done,[n]
he will tear them down
and never build them up again.

6Praise be to the LORD,[o]
for he has heard my cry for
mercy.[p]

27:11 [y]Ps 72:4; 78:42; 106:10; Jer 21:12
27:12 [z]S Dt 19:16; S Mt 26:60; Ac 6:13; 1Co 15:15
27:13 [a]Ex 33:19; S 2Ch 6:41; Ps 23:6; 31:19; 145:7 [b]S Job 28:13
27:14 [c]Ps 33:20; 130:5,6; Isa 8:17; 30:18; Hab 2:3; Zep 3:8; Ac 1:4 [d]S Dt 1:21; S Jdg 5:21; S Eph 6:10
28:1 [e]S Dt 1:45 [f]S Est 4:14 [g]S Job 33:18
28:2 [h]Ps 17:1; 61:1; 116:1; 130:2; 142:1; 143:1 [i]S Ezr 9:5; Ps 63:4; 141:2; La 2:19; 1Ti 2:8 [j]Ps 5:7; 11:4
28:3 [k]Ps 12:2; S 26:4; 55:21; Jer 9:8
28:4 [l]Ps 62:12; 2Ti 4:14; Rev 22:12 [m]La 3:64; Rev 18:6
28:5 [n]Isa 5:12
28:6 [o]S Ge 24:27; 2Co 1:3; Eph 1:3; 1Pe 1:3 [p]ver 2

28:7 [q]S Ps 18:1 [r]Ps 13:5; 112:7; Isa 26:3 [s]S Dt 16:15; S Ps 16:9 [t]Ps 33:3; 40:3; 69:30; 144:9; 149:1
28:8 [u]Ps 18:1 [v]S Ex 15:2; Ps 27:1; Hab 3:13 [w]S Ps 20:6
28:9 [x]1Ch 16:35; Ps 106:47; 118:25 [y]S Ex 34:9 [z]1Ch 11:2; S Ps 23:1; 78:52, 71; 80:1; Isa 40:11; Jer 31:10; Eze 34:12-16,23, 31; Mic 7:14 [a]S Dt 1:31; 32:11; Isa 46:3; 63:9
29:1 [b]ver 2; 1Ch 16:28 [c]S 2Sa 1:19; Ps 103:20; Isa 10:13 [d]Ps 8:1
29:2 [e]S 1Ch 16:29; Ps 96:7-9
29:3 [f]Job 37:5

7The LORD is my strength[q] and my
shield;
my heart trusts[r] in him, and I
am helped.
My heart leaps for joy[s]
and I will give thanks to him in
song.[t]

8The LORD is the strength[u] of his
people,
a fortress of salvation[v] for his
anointed one.[w]
9Save your people[x] and bless your
inheritance;[y]
be their shepherd[z] and carry
them[a] forever.

Psalm 29

A psalm of David.

1Ascribe to the LORD,[b] O mighty
ones,[c]
ascribe to the LORD glory[d] and
strength.
2Ascribe to the LORD the glory due
his name;
worship the LORD in the splendor
of his[y] holiness.[e]

3The voice[f] of the LORD is over the
waters;
the God of glory[g] thunders,[h]
the LORD thunders over the
mighty waters.[i]
4The voice of the LORD is
powerful;[j]
the voice of the LORD is majestic.
5The voice of the LORD breaks the
cedars;
the LORD breaks in pieces the
cedars of Lebanon.[k]
6He makes Lebanon skip[l] like a
calf,

[g]S Ps 24:7; Ac 7:2 [h]S 1Sa 2:10; Ps 18:13; 46:6; 68:33; 77:17; Jer 10:13; 25:30; Joel 2:11; Am 1:2 [i]S Ex 15:10
29:4 [j]Ps 68:33 29:5 [k]S Jdg 9:15 29:6 [l]Ps 114:4

[y]2 Or *LORD with the splendor of*

27:13 I AM STILL CONFIDENT. Trusting in God and experiencing his personal goodness are indispensable for our perseverance in the faith. As believers we may be severely tried, yet nothing can bring us to despair and defeat as long as we keep our eyes on God in faith and hope. In the midst of our darkness we must "wait for the LORD" (v. 14; see 42:5,11; 43:5; 62:5; Isa 40:27–31; Mic 7:8), draw near to him and remain steadfast through his Spirit (see Eph 6:10; 2Ti 2:1; Jas 5:11). We can rest assured that, in his own time, God will manifest his goodness to us.

28:1–9 IF YOU REMAIN SILENT. A faithful believer may at times feel that God is not listening to his or her prayers (vv. 1–3); this experience, however, will not be the norm as long as we continue to draw near to God through Christ (see Heb 4:16; 7:25). After a period of trial, the Lord will respond and help us as a shepherd cares for his sheep (cf. Isa 40:11).

Sirion[z][m] like a young wild
ox.[n]
7The voice of the LORD strikes
with flashes of lightning.[o]
8The voice of the LORD shakes the
desert;
the LORD shakes the Desert of
Kadesh.[p]
9The voice of the LORD twists the
oaks[a][q]
and strips the forests bare.
And in his temple all cry,
"Glory!"[r]

10The LORD sits[b] enthroned over the
flood;[s]
the LORD is enthroned as King
forever.[t]
11The LORD gives strength to his
people;[u]
the LORD blesses his people with
peace.[v]

Psalm 30

A psalm. A song. For the dedication of the temple.[c] Of David.

1I will exalt[w] you, O LORD,
for you lifted me out of the
depths[x]
and did not let my enemies gloat
over me.[y]
2O LORD my God, I called to you for
help[z]
and you healed me.[a]
3O LORD, you brought me up from
the grave[d];[b]
you spared me from going down
into the pit.[c]

4Sing[d] to the LORD, you saints[e] of
his;
praise his holy name.[f]
5For his anger[g] lasts only a
moment,[h]
but his favor lasts a lifetime;[i]
weeping[j] may remain for a
night,
but rejoicing comes in the
morning.[k]

6When I felt secure, I said,
"I will never be shaken."[l]
7O LORD, when you favored me,
you made my mountain[e] stand
firm;
but when you hid your face,[m]
I was dismayed.

8To you, O LORD, I called;
to the Lord I cried for mercy:
9"What gain is there in my
destruction,[f]
in my going down into the pit?[n]
Will the dust praise you?
Will it proclaim your
faithfulness?[o]
10Hear,[p] O LORD, and be merciful to
me;[q]
O LORD, be my help."[r]

11You turned my wailing[s] into
dancing;[t]
you removed my sackcloth[u] and
clothed me with joy,[v]
12that my heart may sing to you and
not be silent.
O LORD my God, I will give you
thanks[w] forever.[x]

Psalm 31

31:1-4pp — Ps 71:1-3

For the director of music. A psalm of David.

1In you, O LORD, I have taken
refuge;[y]
let me never be put to shame;
deliver me in your
righteousness.[z]
2Turn your ear to me,[a]
come quickly to my rescue;[b]

29:6 [m]Dt 3:9 [n]S Nu 23:22; Job 39:9; Ps 92:10 **29:7** [o]Eze 1:14; Rev 8:5 **29:8** [p]Nu 13:26; S 20:1 **29:9** [q]Isa 2:13; Eze 27:6; Am 2:9 [r]Ps 26:8 **29:10** [s]Ge 6:17 [t]S Ex 15:18 **29:11** [u]S Ps 18:1; 28:8; 68:35 [v]S Lev 26:6; S Nu 6:26 **30:1** [w]S Ex 15:2 [x]Job 11:8; Ps 63:9; 107:26; Pr 9:18; Isa 14:15 [y]S Ps 22:17 **30:2** [z]Ps 5:2; 88:13 [a]S Nu 12:13 **30:3** [b]S Ps 16:10; S 56:13 [c]Ps 28:1; 55:23; 69:15; 86:13; 143:7; Pr 1:12; Isa 38:17; Jnh 2:6 **30:4** [d]Ps 33:1; 47:7; 68:4 [e]S Ps 16:3 [f]Ex 3:15; Ps 33:21; 103:1; 145:21 **30:5** [g]Ps 103:9 [h]S Job 14:13 [i]S Ezr 3:11 [j]2Sa 15:30; Ps 6:6; 126:6; Jer 31:16 [k]2Co 4:17 **30:6** [l]S Job 29:18 **30:7** [m]S Dt 31:17 **30:9** [n]S Job 33:18; Isa 38:18 [o]S Ps 6:5; 88:11 **30:10** [p]S Ps 17:1 [q]Ps 4:1 [r]S Ps 20:2 **30:11** [s]S Est 4:1 [t]S Ex 15:20 [u]S 2Sa 3:31; S Ps 35:13 [v]S Dt 16:15; S Ps 16:9 **30:12** [w]Ps 35:18; 75:1; 118:21; Rev 11:17 [x]Ps 44:8; 52:9 **31:1** [y]S Ps 7:1 [z]Ps 5:8 **31:2** [a]S Ps 6:4 [b]S Ex 2:17

[z]6 That is, Mount Hermon [a]9 Or *LORD makes the deer give birth* [b]10 Or *sat* [c]Title: Or *palace* [d]3 Hebrew *Sheol* [e]7 Or *hill country* [f]9 Or *there if I am silenced*

30:6 FELT SECURE. Secure in his prosperity, the psalmist assumed that his wealth and success made him so strong that nothing could destroy his happiness. God then withdrew his protective hand and brought serious trouble and helplessness into his life, causing him to experience the need for God's continual care and presence (vv. 8–10). All believers who feel secure in themselves, who rely on temporal things, and who give God and his kingdom anything but first place in their lives are warned by the words of this psalm.

31:1–24 DELIVER ME. This psalm is a deeply personal prayer expressing distress and lament because of enemies (vv. 4,8), illness (vv. 9–10) and desertion by friends (vv. 11–13). Jeremiah used a phrase from this psalm (v. 13) to express his sorrow and fear (cf. Jer 6:25; 20:10); Jesus also quoted from it (the opening words of v. 5) while on the cross (Lk 23:46). This prayer expresses the heartfelt cry of all believers who suffer affliction because of illness, trouble, or oppression from the world or the enemies of righteousness; it reveals that in times of deep trouble, we can hide "in the shelter of your presence" (v. 20).

be my rock of refuge,[c]
a strong fortress to save me.
3Since you are my rock and my
fortress,[d]
for the sake of your name[e] lead
and guide me.
4Free me from the trap[f] that is set
for me,
for you are my refuge.[g]
5Into your hands I commit my
spirit;[h]
redeem me, O LORD, the God of
truth.[i]

6I hate those who cling to
worthless idols;[j]
I trust in the LORD.[k]
7I will be glad and rejoice in your
love,
for you saw my affliction[l]
and knew the anguish[m] of my
soul.
8You have not handed me over[n] to
the enemy
but have set my feet in a
spacious place.[o]

9Be merciful to me, O LORD, for I
am in distress;[p]
my eyes grow weak with
sorrow,[q]
my soul and my body[r] with
grief.
10My life is consumed by anguish[s]
and my years by groaning;[t]
my strength fails[u] because of my
affliction,[g][v]
and my bones grow weak.[w]
11Because of all my enemies,[x]
I am the utter contempt[y] of my
neighbors;[z]
I am a dread to my friends—
those who see me on the street
flee from me.
12I am forgotten by them as though
I were dead;[a]
I have become like broken
pottery.
13For I hear the slander[b] of many;
there is terror on every side;[c]
they conspire against me[d]
and plot to take my life.[e]
14But I trust[f] in you, O LORD;
I say, "You are my God."
15My times[g] are in your hands;
deliver me from my enemies
and from those who pursue me.
16Let your face shine[h] on your
servant;
save me in your unfailing love.[i]
17Let me not be put to shame,[j]
O LORD,
for I have cried out to you;
but let the wicked be put to shame
and lie silent[k] in the grave.[h]
18Let their lying lips[l] be silenced,
for with pride and contempt
they speak arrogantly[m] against
the righteous.

19How great is your goodness,[n]
which you have stored up for
those who fear you,
which you bestow in the sight of
men[o]
on those who take refuge[p] in
you.
20In the shelter[q] of your presence
you hide[r] them
from the intrigues of men;[s]
in your dwelling you keep them
safe
from accusing tongues.

21Praise be to the LORD,[t]
for he showed his wonderful
love[u] to me
when I was in a besieged city.[v]
22In my alarm[w] I said,
"I am cut off[x] from your sight!"
Yet you heard my cry[y] for mercy
when I called to you for help.

23Love the LORD, all his saints![z]
The LORD preserves the
faithful,[a]
but the proud he pays back[b] in
full.
24Be strong and take heart,[c]
all you who hope in the LORD.

31:2 [c]S 2Sa 22:3; S Ps 18:2
31:3 [d]S Ps 18:2 [e]S Ps 23:3
31:4 [f]S 1Sa 28:9; S Job 18:10 [g]Ps 9:9
31:5 [h]Lk 23:46; Ac 7:59 [i]Isa 45:19; 65:16
31:6 [j]S Dt 32:21 [k]S Ps 4:5
31:7 [l]S Ps 13:3 [m]S Ps 25:17; Lk 22:44
31:8 [n]S Dt 32:30 [o]S 2Sa 22:20
31:9 [p]Ps 4:1 [q]Ps 6:7 [r]Ps 63:1
31:10 [s]ver 7 [t]Ps 6:6 [u]Ps 22:15; 32:4; 38:10; 73:26 [v]Ps 25:18 [w]S Ps 6:2
31:11 [x]Dt 30:7; Ps 3:7; 25:19; 102:8 [y]S Ps 22:6 [z]Ps 38:11
31:12 [a]Ps 28:1; 88:4
31:13 [b]S Lev 19:16; Ps 50:20 [c]S Job 18:11; Isa 13:8; Jer 6:25; 20:3,10; 46:5; 49:5; La 2:22 [d]Ps 41:7; 56:6; 71:10; 83:3 [e]S Ge 37:18; S Mt 12:14
31:14 [f]Ps 4:5
31:15 [g]S Job 14:5
31:16 [h]S Nu 6:25 [i]S Ps 6:4
31:17 [j]S Ps 22:5 [k]1Sa 2:9; Ps 94:17; 115:17
31:18 [l]Ps 120:2; Pr 10:18; 26:24 [m]S 1Sa 2:3; Jude 1:15
31:19 [n]S Ps 27:13; Ro 11:22 [o]Ps 23:5 [p]Ps 2:12
31:20 [q]Ps 55:8 [r]S Ps 17:8 [s]S Ge 37:18
31:21 [t]Ps 28:6 [u]S Ps 17:7 [v]1Sa 23:7
31:22 [w]Ps 116:11 [x]Job 6:9; 17:1; Ps 37:9; 88:5; Isa 38:12 [y]Ps 6:9; 66:19; 116:1; 145:19
31:23 [z]S Ps 4:3 [a]S Ps 18:25; Rev 2:10 [b]Dt 32:41; Ps 94:2
31:24 [c]Ps 27:14

Psalm 32

Of David. A *maskil*.[i]

1Blessed is he
whose transgressions are
forgiven,

[g]10 Or *guilt* [h]17 Hebrew *Sheol* [i]Title: Probably a literary or musical term

31:5 INTO YOUR HANDS I COMMIT MY SPIRIT. These were Jesus' last words before his death (Lk 23:46); these words have often been used by faithful believers in their dying hours (see Ac 7:59). They express dependence on God and faith in his goodness to his people (see 2Sa 24:14; Ro 8:28). To commit ourselves into God's care is equally appropriate during times of danger and difficulty.

32:title MASKIL. This Hebrew word may de-

whose sins are covered.[d]
2 Blessed is the man
whose sin the LORD does not
count against him[e]
and in whose spirit is no
deceit.[f]

3 When I kept silent,[g]
my bones wasted away[h]
through my groaning[i] all day
long.
4 For day and night
your hand was heavy[j] upon me;
my strength was sapped[k]
as in the heat of summer. *Selah*
5 Then I acknowledged my sin to
you
and did not cover up my
iniquity.[l]
I said, "I will confess[m]
my transgressions[n] to the
LORD"—
and you forgave
the guilt of my sin.[o] *Selah*

6 Therefore let everyone who is
godly pray to you
while you may be found;[p]
surely when the mighty waters[q]
rise,[r]
they will not reach him.[s]
7 You are my hiding place;[t]
you will protect me from
trouble[u]
and surround me with songs of
deliverance.[v] *Selah*

8 I will instruct[w] you and teach
you[x] in the way you should
go;
I will counsel you and watch
over[y] you.
9 Do not be like the horse or the
mule,
which have no understanding
but must be controlled by bit and
bridle[z]
or they will not come to you.
10 Many are the woes of the
wicked,[a]
but the LORD's unfailing love
surrounds the man who trusts[b]
in him.

11 Rejoice in the LORD[c] and be glad,
you righteous;
sing, all you who are upright in
heart!

Psalm 33

1 Sing joyfully[d] to the LORD, you
righteous;
it is fitting[e] for the upright[f] to
praise him.
2 Praise the LORD with the harp;[g]
make music to him on the
ten-stringed lyre.[h]
3 Sing to him a new song;[i]
play skillfully, and shout for
joy.[j]

4 For the word of the LORD is right[k]
and true;[l]
he is faithful[m] in all he does.
5 The LORD loves righteousness and
justice;[n]
the earth is full of his unfailing
love.[o]

32:1 [d]Ps 85:2; 103:3 **32:2** [e]S Ro 4:7-8* [f]Jn 1:47; Rev 14:5 **32:3** [g]S Job 31:34 [h]Ps 31:10 [i]S Job 3:24; Ps 6:6 **32:4** [j]1Sa 5:6; S Job 9:34; Ps 38:2; 39:10 [k]Ps 22:15 **32:5** [l]Job 31:33 [m]Pr 28:13 [n]Ps 103:12 [o]S Lev 26:40; 1Jn 1:9 **32:6** [p]Ps 69:13; Isa 55:6 [q]S Ex 15:10 [r]Ps 69:1 [s]Isa 43:2 **32:7** [t]S Jdg 9:35 [u]S Ps 9:9 [v]S Jdg 5:1 **32:8** [w]S Ps 25:8 [x]Ps 34:11 [y]Ps 33:18 **32:9** [z]S Job 30:11; S 39:10; Jas 3:3 **32:10** [a]Ro 2:9 [b]Ps 4:5; Pr 16:20 **32:11** [c]Ps 64:10 **33:1** [d]S Ps 5:11; S 101:1 [e]Ps 147:1 [f]Ps 11:7 **33:2** [g]S Ge 4:21; 1Co 14:7; Rev 5:8 [h]Ps 92:3; 144:9 **33:3** [i]Ps 40:3; Isa 42:10; S Rev 5:9 [j]S Job 3:7; Ps 35:27; 47:1 **33:4** [k]S Ps 19:8 [l]Ps 119:142; Rev 19:9; 22:6 [m]Ps 18:25; 25:10 **33:5** [n]Ps 11:7 [o]Ps 6:4

rive from *sakal*, a Hebrew word meaning "to be wise or skillful." Since *maskil* occurs in the psalm's title, it may indicate that this is a teaching psalm. This particular psalm sets forth the nature of sin and what happens when it is concealed, acknowledged, forsaken and forgiven. Other *maskil* psalms are Ps 42; 44; 45; 52—55; 74; 78; 88; 89; 142.

32:1 BLESSED IS HE WHOSE TRANSGRESSIONS ARE FORGIVEN. The only truly happy people are those who have received forgiveness of their sins from God, so that the guilt of their transgressions does not weigh upon their hearts and minds and their consciences are no longer troubled. Such blessedness is open to all sinners who come to the Lord (Mt 11:28–29). The psalmist describes God's forgiveness in three ways. (1) He forgives the sin, i.e., pardons it. (2) He covers the sin, i.e., puts it out of sight. (3) The sin is not counted against him (v. 2), i.e., the guilt is canceled from the record.

32:2 DOES NOT COUNT AGAINST HIM. Ro 4:6–8 quotes vv. 1–2 to show that God treats sincerely repentant sinners as righteous, not because righteousness is something they earn through works, but rather receive as a gift when they confess their sins and believe in the Lord (cf. v. 5).

32:3–4 WHEN I KEPT SILENT, MY BONES WASTED AWAY. These verses describe the agony and penalty that concealed sin brings. When David hid his sin and did not acknowledge it to God, he lost what was most worthwhile in life—his health, peace of mind, happiness and favor with God. In its place, he experienced guilt and inner torment as God's punishment.

32:5 I ACKNOWLEDGED MY SIN. Acknowledging and confessing sin with an honest, sincere and repentant heart will always result in God's gracious pardon, the removal of guilt and the gift of his abiding presence.

32:8 I WILL INSTRUCT YOU. The Lord promises to instruct and guide a forgiven believer who has a teachable spirit, treasures God's presence and counsel (cf. v. 7), trusts in him (v. 10), rejoices in him (v. 11), and continues upright in heart (v. 11).

6By the word[p] of the LORD were
the heavens made,[q]
their starry host[r] by the breath
of his mouth.
7He gathers the waters[s] of the sea
into jars[j];[t]
he puts the deep into
storehouses.
8Let all the earth fear the LORD;[u]
let all the people of the world[v]
revere him.[w]
9For he spoke, and it came to be;
he commanded,[x] and it stood
firm.
10The LORD foils[y] the plans[z] of the
nations;[a]
he thwarts the purposes of the
peoples.
11But the plans of the LORD stand
firm[b] forever,
the purposes[c] of his heart
through all generations.
12Blessed is the nation whose God is
the LORD,[d]
the people he chose[e] for his
inheritance.[f]
13From heaven the LORD looks
down[g]
and sees all mankind;[h]
14from his dwelling place[i] he
watches
all who live on earth—
15he who forms[j] the hearts of all,
who considers everything they
do.[k]
16No king is saved by the size of his
army;[l]
no warrior escapes by his great
strength.
17A horse[m] is a vain hope for
deliverance;
despite all its great strength it
cannot save.
18But the eyes[n] of the LORD are on
those who fear him,
on those whose hope is in his
unfailing love,[o]
19to deliver them from death[p]
and keep them alive in famine.[q]
20We wait[r] in hope for the LORD;
he is our help and our shield.
21In him our hearts rejoice,[s]
for we trust in his holy name.[t]
22May your unfailing love[u] rest
upon us, O LORD,
even as we put our hope in you.

Psalm 34[k]

Of David. When he pretended to be insane[v] before Abimelech, who drove him away, and he left.

1I will extol the LORD at all times;[w]
his praise will always be on my
lips.
2My soul will boast[x] in the LORD;
let the afflicted hear and
rejoice.[y]
3Glorify the LORD[z] with me;
let us exalt[a] his name together. Ps 92:1-4
4I sought the LORD,[b] and he
answered me;
he delivered[c] me from all my
fears.
5Those who look to him are
radiant;[d]
their faces are never covered
with shame.[e]
6This poor man called, and the LORD
heard him;
he saved him out of all his
troubles.[f]
7The angel of the LORD[g] encamps
around those who fear him,

33:6 [p]S Ge 1:3; Heb 11:3 [q]S Ex 8:19; S 2Ch 2:12 [r]S Ge 1:16 **33:7** [s]S Ge 1:10 [t]S Jos 3:16 **33:8** [u]S Dt 6:13; Ps 2:11 [v]Ps 49:1; Isa 18:3; Mic 1:2 [w]S Dt 14:23 **33:9** [x]Ps 148:5 **33:10** [y]Isa 44:25 [z]S Job 5:12 [a]Ps 2:1 **33:11** [b]S Nu 23:19 [c]Jer 51:12,29 **33:12** [d]Ps 144:15 [e]S Ex 8:22; Dt 7:6; Ps 4:3; 65:4; 84:4 [f]S Ex 34:9 **33:13** [g]Ps 53:2; 102:19 [h]Job 28:24; Ps 11:4; 14:2; S Heb 4:13 **33:14** [i]S Lev 15:31; 1Ki 8:39 **33:15** [j]Job 10:8; Ps 119:73 [k]S Job 10:4; Jer 32:19 **33:16** [l]1Sa 14:6 **33:17** [m]S Ps 20:7 **33:18** [n]S Ex 3:16; S Ps 11:4; 1Pe 3:12 [o]S Ps 6:4 **33:19** [p]Ps 56:13; Ac 12:11 [q]S Job 5:20 **33:20** [r]S Ps 27:14 **33:21** [s]S 1Sa 2:1; S Joel 2:23 [t]S Ps 30:4; S 99:3 **33:22** [u]Ps 6:4 **34:1** [v]34 Title 1Sa 21:13 [w]Ps 71:6; S Eph 5:20; 1Th 5:18 **34:2** [x]Ps 44:8; Jer 9:24; 1Co 1:31 [y]Ps 69:32; 107:42; 119:74 **34:3** [z]Ps 63:3; 86:12; Da 4:37; Jn 17:1; Ro 15:6 [a]S Ex 15:2 **34:4** [b]S Ex 32:11; Ps 77:2 [c]ver 17; Ps 18:43; 22:4; 56:13; 86:13 **34:5** [d]S Ex 34:29 [e]Ps 25:3; 44:15; 69:7; 83:16 **34:6** [f]S Ps 25:17 **34:7** [g]S Ge 32:1; S Da 3:28; S Mt 18:10

j 7 Or *sea as into a heap* k This psalm is an acrostic poem, the verses of which begin with the successive letters of the Hebrew alphabet.

33:6 THE WORD . . . THE BREATH. *Ruach* (here translated "breath") can also mean "spirit"; the breath of God is thus equivalent to the activity of God's Spirit. This verse contains an important Biblical truth: the union of the power of God's word with the power of God's Spirit (through the operation of faith) always releases the creative power of God on behalf of his people.

33:18–19 ON THOSE WHO FEAR HIM. While the "eyes of the LORD" are on all people (vv. 13–14), they rest in a special way on those who "fear him" (see 34:15). God's "eyes" refers to God's caring love and providential oversight of our lives. "To deliver them from death and . . . famine" means that as long as we fear the Lord, put our hope in him, wait for him and remain in his will, God will watch over and protect us so that we will not die unless it be according to his plan. For more on the Biblical meaning of hope in God, see article on BIBLICAL HOPE, p. 792.

34:1–22 I WILL EXTOL THE LORD. The writer of this psalm praises the Lord for a miraculous deliverance from great trouble. His testimony encourages all afflicted believers to believe that they may also experience the goodness of the Lord.

34:7 ANGEL OF THE LORD ENCAMPS. The angel of the Lord probably refers to the angelic host of heaven; they are "ministering spirits sent

BIBLICAL HOPE

***Ps 33:18–19** "But the eyes of the LORD are on those who fear him, on those whose hope is in his unfailing love, to deliver them from death and keep them alive in famine."*

DEFINITION OF BIBLICAL HOPE. By its very nature hope concerns the future (cf. Ro 8:24–25). However, it involves much more than a mere desire or wish for something in the future; Biblical hope consists of assurance in the heart, even a firm confidence, about future things, because these things are based on God's promises and revelation. In other words, Biblical hope is linked inseparably with a firm faith (Ro 15:13; Heb 11:1) and a confident trust in God (Ps 33:21–22). The psalmist puts it most clearly when he parallels "trust" with "hope": "Do not put your trust in princes, in mortal men, who cannot save . . . . Blessed is he whose help is the God of Jacob, whose hope is in the LORD his God" (Ps 146:3–5; cf. Jer 17:7). Consequently, the sure hope of the believer is a hope that "does not disappoint" (Ro 5:5; cf. Ps 22:4–5; Isa 49:23); hope, then, is an anchor for the believer in the midst of life (Heb 6:19–20).

THE BASIS OF THE BELIEVER'S HOPE. The foundation for the believer's confident hope derives from the nature of God, of Jesus Christ, and of God's word. (1) Scripture reveals how God has proved himself faithful in the past on behalf of his people. Ps 22, for example, reveals David's struggle with a personal situation that threatens his life; when he reflects on God's actions in the past, however, he feels confident that God will deliver him: "In you our fathers put their trust; they trusted, and you delivered them" (Ps 22:4). The miraculous power that the Creator God has demonstrated for his faithful people's benefit is evident in the exodus, the conquest of Canaan, the miracles of Jesus and the apostles, and the like—all of which should build confidence in the Lord as our helper (cf. Ps 105; 124:8; Heb 13:6; see Ex 6:7, note). On the other hand, those without God have no reason for hope (Eph 2:12; 1Th 4:13).

(2) The full revelation of the new covenant in Jesus Christ provides even more reason for a confident hope in God. For believers, the Son of God came to destroy the work of the devil (1Jn 3:8), the "god of this age" (2Co 4:4; cf. Gal 1:4; Heb 2:14; see 1Jn 5:19, note; see article on THE SUFFERING OF THE RIGHTEOUS, p. 710). By driving out demons during his earthly ministry, Jesus demonstrated his power over Satan (see article on POWER OVER SATAN AND DEMONS, p. 1484). Moreover, by his death and resurrection he shattered the power of Satan's realm (cf. Jn 12:31) and exhibited the power of God's kingdom (see article on THE KINGDOM OF GOD, p. 1430). Thus Peter exclaims regarding our hope: "Praise be to the God and Father of our Lord Jesus Christ! In his great mercy he has given us new birth into a living hope through the resurrection of Jesus Christ from the dead" (1Pe 1:3). Jesus is therefore called our hope (Col 1:27; 1Ti 1:1); we must set our hope on him through the power of the Holy Spirit (Ro 15:12–13; cf. 1Pe 1:13; see Ex 17:11, note).

(3) God's word is the third basis of hope. God revealed his word through prophets and apostles of old, whom he inspired by the Holy Spirit to write without error (2Ti 3:16; 2Pe 1:19–21; see article on THE INSPIRATION AND AUTHORITY OF SCRIPTURE, p. 1898). Since his eternal word stands firm in the heavens (Ps 119:89), we must place our hope in that word (Ps 119:49,74,81,114,147; 130:5; cf. Ac 26:6; Ro 15:4). In fact, everything we know about God and Jesus Christ is revealed in the infallible Scriptures.

CONTENT OF THE BELIEVER'S HOPE. The believer's ultimate hope and trust must not be in other human beings (Ps 33:16–17; 147:10–11) or in material possessions or money (Ps 20:7; Mt 6:19–21; Lk 12:13–21; 1Ti 6:17; see Nu 18:20, note; see article on RICHES AND POVERTY, p. 1562); rather, it must be in God, in his Son Jesus and in his word. And what does this hope involve? (1) We have hope in God's grace and deliverance in the sufferings we undergo in our present lives (Ps 33:18–19; 42:1–5; 71:1–5,13–14; Jer 17:17–18). (2) We have hope that the time will come when our sufferings on earth will be finally done away with, when the subjection of the earth to corruption will end, and when the redemption (resurrection) of our bodies will occur (Ro 8:18–25; cf. Ps 16:9–10; 2Pe 3:12; see Ac 24:15, note; see article on THE RESURRECTION OF THE BODY, p. 1779). (3) We have the hope of the consummation of our salvation (1Th 5:8; see article on BIBLICAL WORDS FOR SALVATION, p. 1710). (4) We have the hope of an eternal house in the new heaven (2Co 5:1–5; 2Pe 3:13; see Jn 14:2, note), in that city whose architect and builder is God (Heb 11:10). (5) We have the blessed hope of the glorious appearing of our great God and Savior, Jesus Christ (Tit 2:13), when believers will be caught up from the earth to meet him in the air (1Th 4:13–18; see article on THE RAPTURE, p. 1864), and when we shall see him as he is and become like him (Php 3:20–21; 1Jn 3:2–3). (6) We have the hope of receiving a crown—of righteousness (2Ti 4:8), of glory (1Pe 5:4) and of life (Rev 2:10). (7) Finally, we have the hope of eternal life (Tit 1:2; 3:7), the life guaranteed to all who trust and obey the Lord Jesus Christ (Jn 3:16,36; 6:47; 1Jn 5:11–13).

With such great promises in store for those who hope in God and in his Son Jesus, Peter urges us: "Always be prepared to give an answer to everyone who asks you to give a reason for the hope that you have" (1Pe 3:15).

and he delivers[h] them.
8Taste and see that the LORD is
good;[i]
blessed is the man who takes
refuge[j] in him.
9Fear the LORD,[k] you his saints,
for those who fear him lack
nothing.[l]
10The lions may grow weak and
hungry,
but those who seek the LORD
lack no good thing.[m]

11Come, my children, listen[n] to me;
I will teach you[o] the fear of the
LORD.[p]
12Whoever of you loves life[q]
and desires to see many good
days,
13keep your tongue[r] from evil
and your lips from speaking
lies.[s]
14Turn from evil and do good;[t]
seek peace[u] and pursue it.

15The eyes of the LORD[v] are on the
righteous[w]
and his ears are attentive[x] to
their cry;
16the face of the LORD is against[y]
those who do evil,[z]
to cut off the memory[a] of them
from the earth.

17The righteous cry out, and the
LORD hears[b] them;
he delivers them from all their
troubles.
18The LORD is close[c] to the
brokenhearted[d]
and saves those who are
crushed in spirit.

19A righteous man may have many
troubles,[e]
but the LORD delivers him from
them all;[f]
20he protects all his bones,
not one of them will be
broken.[g]

21Evil will slay the wicked;[h]
the foes of the righteous will be
condemned.
22The LORD redeems[i] his servants;
no one will be condemned who
takes refuge[j] in him.

Psalm 35

Of David.

1Contend,[k] O LORD, with those who
contend with me;
fight[l] against those who fight
against me.

34:7 [h] Ps 22:4; 37:40; 41:1; 97:10; Isa 31:5; Ac 12:11 **34:8** [i] Heb 6:5; 1Pe 2:3 [j] S Ps 2:12 **34:9** [k] S Dt 6:13; Rev 14:7 [l] S Ps 23:1 **34:10** [m] S Ps 23:1 **34:11** [n] Ps 66:16 [o] S Ps 32:8 [p] S Ps 19:9 **34:12** [q] Ecc 3:13 **34:13** [r] Ps 39:1; 141:3; Pr 13:3; 21:23; Jas 1:26 [s] S Ps 12:2; 1Pe 2:22 **34:14** [t] Ps 37:27; Isa 1:17; 3Jn 1:11 [u] S Ro 14:19 **34:15** [v] Ps 33:18 [w] S Job 23:10; S 36:7 [x] Mal 3:16; S Jn 9:31 **34:16** [y] Lev 17:10; Jer 23:30 [z] 1Pe 3:10-12* [a] S Ex 17:14; Ps 9:6 **34:17** [b] Ps 145:19 **34:18** [c] Dt 4:7; Ps 119:151; 145:18; Isa 50:8 [d] Ps 51:17; 109:16; 147:3; Isa 61:1 **34:19** [e] ver 17; Ps 25:17 [f] S Job 5:19; 2Ti 3:11 **34:20** [g] Jn 19:36* **34:21** [h] Ps 7:9; 9:16; 11:5; 37:20; 73:27; 94:23; 106:43; 112:10; 140:11; Pr 14:32; 24:16 **34:22** [i] S Ex 6:6; S 15:13; Lk 1:68; Rev 14:3 [j] Ps 2:12 **35:1** [k] S 1Sa 24:15 [l] S Ex 14:14

---

to serve those who will inherit salvation" (Heb 1:14; cf. Ge 32:1–2; 2Ki 6:17; see article on ANGELS AND THE ANGEL OF THE LORD, p. 340). God has appointed his angels to protect and rescue his saints from physical and spiritual harm. This promise of divine intervention is reserved only for those who truly fear God (see next note).

34:9 THOSE WHO FEAR HIM LACK NOTHING. Note that the promises in this psalm are conditional, reserved only for those who genuinely fear the Lord. God promises to deliver us from fear (v. 4), save us from trouble (v. 6,17), send angels to encamp around us (v. 7), supply our needs (v. 9), give us abundant life (v. 12), hear our prayers (v. 15), comfort us with his presence (v. 18) and redeem us (v. 22)—but only if we seek the Lord (vv. 4,10), cry out to him (v. 6), draw close to him, fear him (vv. 7,9), keep our tongues from the evil of lying (v. 13), remain separate from the evil world (v. 14), do good and pursue peace (v. 14), have contrite hearts (v. 18), and become his servants (v. 22).

34:19 HAVE MANY TROUBLES. In the OT God promised blessing and prosperity for those who obeyed his law; yet alongside this promise is the reality that the righteous "may have many troubles" (see Heb 11:33–38; 12:5–10; see article on THE SUFFERING OF THE RIGHTEOUS, p. 710). (1) Believing in God and living righteously will not keep us from trouble and suffering in this life. On the contrary, commitment to God often brings testing and persecution (see Mt 5:10, note). God has ordained that we must go through many hardships to enter his kingdom (Ac 14:22; cf. 1Co 15:19; 2Ti 3:12). (2) The suffering of the righteous must be counterbalanced by the revelation that the Lord wishes to deliver us out of all our troubles. When his purpose in permitting affliction is accomplished, he then delivers us from them either by direct supernatural intervention in this life (cf. Heb 11:33–35) or by victorious death and transference to the life hereafter (cf. Heb 11:35–37).

35:1–38 FIGHT AGAINST THOSE WHO FIGHT AGAINST ME. This psalm is called an imprecatory psalm, meaning that the psalmist prays that God will bring judgment on the enemies of his people and overthrow the wicked (see Ps 35; 69; 109; 137; Ne 6:14; 13:29; Jer 15:15; 17:18; Gal 5:12; 2Ti 4:14; Rev 6:10). Although believers are instructed to forgive their enemies (Lk 23:34) and to pray for their salvation (Mt 5:39,44), a time comes when we must pray for evil to cease and for justice to be done for the innocent. We should be vitally concerned for the victims of cruelty, oppression and evil.

More must be said about imprecatory psalms: (1) They are prayers for deliverance from injustice, crime and oppression. Believers have a right to

[2]Take up shield[m] and buckler;
arise[n] and come to my aid.[o]
[3]Brandish spear[p] and javelin[1q]
against those who pursue me.
Say to my soul,
"I am your salvation.[r]"

[4]May those who seek my life[s]
be disgraced[t] and put to
shame;[u]
may those who plot my ruin
be turned back[v] in dismay.
[5]May they be like chaff[w] before the
wind,
with the angel of the LORD[x]
driving them away;
[6]may their path be dark and
slippery,
with the angel of the LORD
pursuing them.
[7]Since they hid their net[y] for me
without cause[z]
and without cause dug a pit[a]
for me,
[8]may ruin overtake them by
surprise—[b]
may the net they hid entangle
them,
may they fall into the pit,[c] to
their ruin.
[9]Then my soul will rejoice[d] in the
LORD
and delight in his salvation.[e]
[10]My whole being will exclaim,
"Who is like you,[f] O LORD?
You rescue the poor from those too
strong[g] for them,
the poor and needy[h] from those
who rob them."
[11]Ruthless witnesses[i] come
forward;
they question me on things I
know nothing about.
[12]They repay me evil for good[j]
and leave my soul forlorn.
[13]Yet when they were ill, I put on
sackcloth[k]
and humbled myself with
fasting.[l]
When my prayers returned to me
unanswered,
[14] I went about mourning[m]
as though for my friend or
brother.
I bowed my head in grief
as though weeping for my
mother.
[15]But when I stumbled, they
gathered in glee;[n]
attackers gathered against me
when I was unaware.
They slandered[o] me without
ceasing.
[16]Like the ungodly they maliciously
mocked[m,p]
they gnashed their teeth[q] at
me.

35:2 [m]Ps 3:3 [n]Ps 3:7 [o]S Ge 50:24; S Job 17:3
35:3 [p]S Nu 25:7 [q]S Jos 8:18 [r]Ps 27:1
35:4 [s]Ps 38:12; 40:14; Jer 4:30 [t]Ps 69:6,19; 70:2; 83:17; Isa 45:16; Mal 2:9 [u]Ps 25:3 [v]Ps 129:5
35:5 [w]S Job 13:25; Ps 1:4 [x]Ps 34:7
35:7 [y]S Job 18:8 [z]S Ps 7:4 [a]S Job 9:31; S Ps 7:15; S 55:23
35:8 [b]Isa 47:11; 1Th 5:3 [c]S Ps 7:15
35:9 [d]S Ps 2:11; S Lk 1:47 [e]Ps 9:14; 13:5; 27:1
35:10 [f]S Ex 9:14; S Ps 18:31; 113:5 [g]Ps 18:17 [h]Ps 12:5; 37:14; 74:21; 86:1; 109:16; 140:12; Isa 41:17
35:11 [i]S Ex 23:1; S Mt 26:60
35:12 [j]Ps 38:20; 109:5; Pr 17:13; Jer 18:20
35:13 [k]S 2Sa 3:31; 1Ki 20:31; Ps 30:11; 69:11 [l]Job 30:25; Ps 69:10; 109:24
35:14 [m]Ps 38:6; 42:9; 43:2
35:15 [n]S Job 31:29 [o]S Job 16:10
35:16 [p]S Ps 22:7; Mk 10:34 [q]S Job 16:9; Mk 9:18; Ac 7:54

[1]3 Or *and block the way* [m]16 Septuagint; Hebrew may mean *ungodly circle of mockers.*

pray for God's protection from evil people.

(2) They are appeals to God to administer justice and to send penalties on the wicked that are commensurate with their crime (see 28:4). If just retribution is not undertaken by God or by human government, violence and chaos will reign in society (see Dt 25:1–3; Ro 13:3–4; 1Pe 2:13–14).

(3) As you read these prayers, note that the psalmist does not take vengeance into his own hands but commits it to God (cf. Dt 32:35; Pr 20:22; Ro 12:19).

(4) The imprecatory psalms point to the truth that when the sin of the wicked reaches its full measure, the Lord in his righteousness does judge and destroy (see Ge 15:16; Lev 18:24; Rev 6:10, 17).

(5) Remember that these prayers are inspired words of the Holy Spirit (cf. 2Ti 3:16–17; 2Pe 1:19–21), and not just an expression of the psalmist's human desire.

(6) The ultimate goal of an imprecatory prayer is to see injustice and cruelty come to an end, evil destroyed, Satan defeated, godliness exalted, righteousness established and God's kingdom realized. This goal is a dominant concern in the NT. Christ himself states that true believers may pray for the vindication of the righteous. The widow's prayer to "grant me justice against my adversary" (Lk 18:3) is answered by Jesus' assurance that God will "bring about justice for his chosen ones, who cry out to him day and night" (Lk 18:7; cf. Rev 6:9–10).

(7) Believers must keep two Biblical principles in balance: (a) the desire to see all people come to a saving knowledge of Jesus Christ (cf. 2Pe 3:9), and (b) the desire to see evil destroyed and God's kingdom victorious. We must earnestly pray for the salvation of the lost and weep for those who reject the gospel; yet we must know also that righteousness, goodness and love will never be established according to God's purpose until evil is conquered and Satan and his followers are forever put down (see Rev 6:10,17; 19—21). The faithful must pray, "Come, Lord Jesus" (Rev 22:20) as God's ultimate and final solution for evil in the world.

35:4 DISGRACED AND PUT TO SHAME. The NT believer may use this prayer as a call to God to contend with our greatest enemy, Satan, and as a testimony of our hatred of sin and evil.

17O Lord, how long[r] will you look
on?
Rescue my life from their
ravages,
my precious life[s] from these
lions.[t]
18I will give you thanks in the great
assembly;[u]
among throngs[v] of people I will
praise you.[w]

19Let not those gloat over me
who are my enemies[x] without
cause;
let not those who hate me without
reason[y]
maliciously wink the eye.[z]
20They do not speak peaceably,
but devise false accusations[a]
against those who live quietly in
the land.
21They gape[b] at me and say, "Aha!
Aha![c]
With our own eyes we have seen
it."

22O LORD, you have seen[d] this; be
not silent.
Do not be far[e] from me,
O Lord.
23Awake,[f] and rise[g] to my
defense!
Contend[h] for me, my God and
Lord.
24Vindicate me in your
righteousness, O LORD my
God;
do not let them gloat[i] over me.
25Do not let them think, "Aha,[j] just
what we wanted!"
or say, "We have swallowed him
up."[k]

26May all who gloat[l] over my
distress[m]
be put to shame[n] and
confusion;
may all who exalt themselves over
me[o]
be clothed with shame and
disgrace.
27May those who delight in my
vindication[p]
shout for joy[q] and gladness;
may they always say, "The LORD be
exalted,
who delights[r] in the well-being
of his servant."[s]
28My tongue will speak of your
righteousness[t]
and of your praises all day
long.[u]

Psalm 36

For the director of music. Of David
the servant of the LORD.

1An oracle is within my heart
concerning the sinfulness of the
wicked:[n] [v]
There is no fear[w] of God
before his eyes.[x]
2For in his own eyes he flatters
himself
too much to detect or hate his
sin.[y]
3The words of his mouth[z] are
wicked and deceitful;[a]
he has ceased to be wise[b] and
to do good.[c]
4Even on his bed he plots evil;[d]
he commits himself to a sinful
course[e]
and does not reject what is
wrong.[f]

5Your love, O LORD, reaches to the
heavens,
your faithfulness[g] to the
skies.[h]
6Your righteousness[i] is like the
mighty mountains,[j]
your justice like the great
deep.[k]
O LORD, you preserve both man and
beast.[l]
7 How priceless is your unfailing
love![m]
Both high and low among men
find[o] refuge in the shadow of
your wings.[n]
8They feast on the abundance of
your house;[o]

35:17 [r] Ps 6:3 [s] Ps 22:20 [t] Ps 22:21; 57:4; 58:6
35:18 [u] S Ps 22:25 [v] Ps 42:4; 109:30 [w] S Ps 22:22
35:19 [x] Ps 9:13 [y] ver 7; Ps 38:19; 69:4; Jn 15:25* [z] Pr 6:13; 10:10
35:20 [a] Ps 38:12; 55:21; Jer 9:8; Mic 6:12
35:21 [b] S Job 16:10 [c] Ps 40:15; 70:3; Eze 25:3
35:22 [d] Ex 3:7; Ps 10:14 [e] S Ps 10:1
35:23 [f] S Ps 7:6; 80:2 [g] Ps 17:13 [h] S 1Sa 24:15
35:24 [i] Ps 22:17
35:25 [j] ver 21 [k] Ps 124:3; Pr 1:12; La 2:16
35:26 [l] Ps 22:17 [m] Ps 4:1 [n] S Job 8:22; Ps 109:29; Mic 7:10 [o] Job 19:5; Ps 38:16
35:27 [p] Ps 9:4 [q] Ps 20:5; S 33:3 [r] Ps 147:11; 149:4 [s] S Job 17:3
35:28 [t] Ps 5:8; 51:14 [u] Ps 71:15, 24; 72:15
36:1 [v] S Job 21:16 [w] Jer 2:19; 36:16, 24 [x] S Job 23:15; Ro 3:18*
36:2 [y] Dt 29:19
36:3 [z] Ps 10:7 [a] S Job 5:13; Ps 5:6,9; 43:1; 144:8,11; Isa 44:20 [b] Ps 94:8 [c] Jer 4:22; 13:23; Am 3:10
36:4 [d] Pr 4:16 [e] Isa 65:2 [f] Ps 52:3; Ro 12:9
36:5 [g] Ps 89:1; 119:90 [h] Ps 57:10; 71:19; 89:2; 103:11; 108:4
36:6 [i] Ps 5:8 [j] Ps 68:15 [k] S Ge 1:2; S 7:11 [l] Ne 9:6; Ps 104:14; 145:16
36:7 [m] Ps 6:4 [n] S Ru 2:12; S Ps 17:8; 57:1; 91:4
36:8 [o] Ps 65:4; Isa 25:6; Jer 31:12,14

[n] *1* Or *heart: / Sin proceeds from the wicked.*
[o] 7 Or *love, O God! / Men find*; or *love! / Both heavenly beings and men / find*

36:4 DOES NOT REJECT WHAT IS WRONG. The ungodly do not hate evil. (1) Hatred of sin is an essential feature of God's character (Pr 6:16; Jer 44:4; Hab 1:13); it is a fundamental aspect of Christ's ministry and kingship (45:7; see Heb 1:9, note). (2) People may be loving and kind, and do good to the poor, yet if they have no indignation against wrong, contempt for the world's immoral ways, zeal for justice or hatred of evil, they have failed to stand with God or follow the Holy Spirit (cf. Gal 5:16–24). "Let those who love the LORD hate evil" (97:10).

you give them drink from your
river[p] of delights.[q]
9For with you is the fountain of
life;[r]
in your light[s] we see light.
10Continue your love[t] to those who
know you,[u]
your righteousness to the
upright in heart.[v]
11May the foot of the proud not
come against me,
nor the hand of the wicked[w]
drive me away.
12See how the evildoers lie fallen—
thrown down, not able to rise![x]

Psalm 37[p]

Of David.

1Do not fret because of evil men
or be envious[y] of those who do
wrong;[z]
2for like the grass they will soon
wither,[a]
like green plants they will soon
die away.[b]

3Trust in the LORD and do good;
dwell in the land[c] and enjoy
safe pasture.[d]
4Delight[e] yourself in the LORD
and he will give you the desires
of your heart.[f]

5Commit your way to the LORD;
trust in him[g] and he will do
this:
6He will make your righteousness[h]
shine like the dawn,[i]
the justice of your cause like the
noonday sun.

Ps 49:13-15

7Be still[j] before the LORD and wait
patiently[k] for him;
do not fret[l] when men succeed
in their ways,[m]
when they carry out their
wicked schemes.[n]

8Refrain from anger[o] and turn
from wrath;
do not fret[p]—it leads only to
evil.
9For evil men will be cut off,[q]
but those who hope[r] in the
LORD will inherit the land.[s]

10A little while, and the wicked will
be no more;[t]
though you look for them, they
will not be found.
11But the meek will inherit the
land[u]
and enjoy great peace.[v]

12The wicked plot[w] against the
righteous
and gnash their teeth[x] at them;
13but the Lord laughs at the wicked,
for he knows their day is
coming.[y]

36:8 [p]Job 20:17; Rev 22:1 [q]S Ps 23:2; 63:5 **36:9** [r]Ps 87:7; Pr 10:11; 16:22; Jer 2:13 [s]Ps 4:6; 27:1; 76:4; 104:2; Isa 2:5; 9:2; 60:1, 19; Jn 1:4; 1Pe 2:9 **36:10** [t]Jer 31:3 [u]Jer 9:24; 22:16 [v]Ps 7:10; 11:2; 94:15; 125:4 **36:11** [w]Ps 71:4; 140:4 **36:12** [x]S Ps 18:38 **37:1** [y]Pr 3:31; 23:17-18 [z]Ps 73:3; Pr 24:19 **37:2** [a]S 2Ki 19:26; Job 14:2; Ps 102:4; Isa 40:7 [b]ver 38; Ps 90:6; 92:7; Jas 1:10 **37:3** [c]Dt 30:20 [d]Eze 34:14; Jn 10:9 **37:4** [e]S Job 27:10 [f]S Job 7:6; Ps 21:2; 145:19; Mt 6:33 **37:5** [g]Ps 4:5 **37:6** [h]Ps 18:24; 103:17; 112:3 [i]S Job 11:17 **37:7** [j]S Ex 14:14; S Isa 41:1 [k]S Ps 27:14; 40:1; 130:5; Isa 38:13; Hab 3:16; Ro 8:25 [l]ver 1 [m]Jer 12:1 [n]Ps 21:11; 26:10; 119:150 **37:8** [o]Eph 4:31; Col 3:8 [p]ver 1 **37:9** [q]S Ps 31:22; 101:8; 118:10; Pr 2:22 [r]Isa 25:9; 26:8; 40:31; 49:23; 51:5 [s]ver 22; Ps 25:13; Isa 49:8; 57:13; Mt 5:5 **37:10** [t]S Job 7:10; Eze 27:36 **37:11** [u]S Nu 14:24; Mt 5:5 [v]S Lev 26:6; S Nu 6:26 **37:12** [w]Ps 2:1; 31:13 [x]S Job 16:9; Ps 35:16; 112:10 **37:13** [y]1Sa 26:10; Eze 12:23

[p] This psalm is an acrostic poem, the stanzas of which begin with the successive letters of the Hebrew alphabet.

37:1–40 DO NOT FRET. This psalm is not a prayer, but a series of proverbial expressions or instructions about godly wisdom. Its theme concerns the believer's attitude toward the apparent success of the wicked and the hardship of the righteous (see also Ps 49; 73); it teaches that the ungodly will eventually be thrown down and lose all they acquired on earth, whereas the righteous who remain loyal to God will have his presence, help and guidance on earth and will inherit salvation and the promised land. According to the NT, the believer's inheritance is "a new heaven and a new earth" (see Rev 21:1).

37:4 DELIGHT YOURSELF IN THE LORD. To delight yourself in the Lord is to desire and enjoy the nearness of his presence and the truth and righteousness of his word (cf. Job 22:26; 27:10; Isa 58:14). To those who delight themselves in the Lord, God gives the desires of their hearts. (1) God will answer the cry of our hearts if our desires are in accordance with his will (see Jn 15:7, note). (2) When we delight ourselves in God and his will, God himself places desires within our hearts that he then sets out to fulfill (see Php 2:13).

37:6 MAKE YOUR RIGHTEOUSNESS SHINE LIKE THE DAWN. The righteous who are oppressed by sin in the world are promised: (1) answers to their prayers (vv. 4–5); (2) vindication of their righteous standards (v. 6); (3) a heavenly inheritance (vv. 9,11,34); (4) the Lord's sustaining help (vv. 17–19,39); (5) the Lord's guidance, protection and presence (vv. 23–25,28); and (6) salvation (v. 39).

37:7 WAIT PATIENTLY FOR HIM. This psalm reveals how the righteous must react when the wicked prosper in spite of their evil and immoral ways. We must steadfastly persevere in the faith while waiting for God to bring about justice and to vindicate us (cf. v. 1; 73; Pr 3:31; 23:17; 24:1; Jer 12). Patience while undergoing trouble or suffering is possible through the Holy Spirit's help (Gal 5:22; Ro 8:3–4; cf. Eph 4:1–2; Col 1:11; 3:12), who assures us that before long, God will reward us and punish the wicked (cf. Ro 8:28; Heb 12:1–2,5–13).

14 The wicked draw the sword[z]
and bend the bow[a]
to bring down the poor and needy,[b]
to slay those whose ways are upright.
15 But their swords will pierce their own hearts,[c]
and their bows will be broken.[d]

16 Better the little that the righteous have
than the wealth[e] of many wicked;
17 for the power of the wicked will be broken,[f]
but the LORD upholds[g] the righteous.

18 The days of the blameless are known to the LORD,[h]
and their inheritance will endure forever.[i]
19 In times of disaster they will not wither;
in days of famine they will enjoy plenty.

20 But the wicked will perish:[j]
The LORD's enemies will be like the beauty of the fields,
they will vanish—vanish like smoke.[k]

21 The wicked borrow and do not repay,
but the righteous give generously;[l]
22 those the LORD blesses will inherit the land,
but those he curses[m] will be cut off.[n]

23 If the LORD delights[o] in a man's way,
he makes his steps firm;[p]
24 though he stumble, he will not fall,[q]
for the LORD upholds[r] him with his hand.

25 I was young and now I am old,
yet I have never seen the righteous forsaken[s]
or their children begging[t] bread.
26 They are always generous and lend freely;[u]
their children will be blessed.[v]

27 Turn from evil and do good;[w]
then you will dwell in the land forever.[x]
28 For the LORD loves the just
and will not forsake his faithful ones.[y]

They will be protected forever,
but the offspring of the wicked will be cut off;[z]
29 the righteous will inherit the land[a]
and dwell in it forever.[b]

30 The mouth of the righteous man utters wisdom,[c]
and his tongue speaks what is just.
31 The law of his God is in his heart;[d]
his feet do not slip.[e]

32 The wicked lie in wait[f] for the righteous,[g]
seeking their very lives;
33 but the LORD will not leave them in their power
or let them be condemned[h] when brought to trial.[i]

34 Wait for the LORD[j]
and keep his way.[k]
He will exalt you to inherit the land;
when the wicked are cut off,[l] you will see[m] it.

35 I have seen a wicked and ruthless man
flourishing[n] like a green tree in its native soil,
36 but he soon passed away and was no more;
though I looked for him, he could not be found.[o]

37 Consider the blameless,[p] observe the upright;[q]
there is a future[q] for the man of peace.[r]
38 But all sinners[s] will be destroyed;[t]
the future[r] of the wicked will be cut off.[u]

39 The salvation[v] of the righteous comes from the LORD;
he is their stronghold in time of trouble.[w]
40 The LORD helps[x] them and delivers[y] them;
he delivers them from the wicked and saves[z] them,

37:14 [z] S Ps 22:20 [a] Ps 11:2 [b] S Ps 35:10
37:15 [c] S Ps 9:16 [d] S 1Sa 2:4; Ps 46:9; Jer 49:35
37:16 [e] Pr 15:16; 16:8
37:17 [f] Job 38:15; Ps 10:15 [g] Ps 41:12; 140:12; 145:14; 146:7
37:18 [h] S Job 23:10; Ps 44:21 [i] ver 27, 29
37:20 [j] S Ps 34:21 [k] Ps 68:2; 102:3; Isa 51:6
37:21 [l] S Lev 25:35; Ps 112:5
37:22 [m] S Job 5:3 [n] ver 9
37:23 [o] S Nu 14:8; Ps 147:11 [p] S Job 11:15; S Ps 7:9; 66:9
37:24 [q] S Ps 13:4; 27:2; 38:17; 55:22; 119:165; Pr 3:23; 10:9 [r] 2Ch 9:8; Ps 41:12; 145:14
37:25 [s] ver 28; S Ge 15:1; Heb 13:5 [t] Ps 111:5; 145:15; Mk 10:46
37:26 [u] S Lev 25:35 [v] Dt 28:4; Ps 112:2
37:27 [w] Ps 34:14; 3Jn 1:11 [x] S Nu 24:21
37:28 [y] S Dt 7:6; S Ps 18:25; S 97:10 [z] S Ge 17:14; S Dt 32:26; Pr 2:22
37:29 [a] ver 9; Pr 2:21 [b] Isa 34:17
37:30 [c] Ps 49:3; Pr 10:13
37:31 [d] S Dt 6:6; S Job 22:22 [e] S Dt 32:35
37:32 [f] S Ps 10:8 [g] Ps 11:5
37:33 [h] Job 32:3; Ps 34:22; 79:11 [i] 2Pe 2:9
37:34 [j] Ps 27:14 [k] S Ps 18:21 [l] ver 9 [m] Ps 52:6
37:35 [n] S Job 5:3
37:36 [o] ver 10; Pr 12:7; Isa 41:12; Da 11:19
37:37 [p] ver 18; S Ge 6:9; Ps 18:25 [q] Ps 11:7 [r] Isa 57:1-2
37:38 [s] S Ps 1:1 [t] S ver 2; Ps 73:19 [u] ver 9
37:39 [v] S Ps 3:8 [w] S Ps 9:9
37:40 [x] S 1Ch 5:20; S Ps 20:2 [y] S Ps 34:7 [z] S Ps 18:48

[q] 37 Or *there will be posterity* [r] 38 Or *posterity*

because they take refuge[a] in
8 him.

Psalm 38

A psalm of David. A petition.

[1]O LORD, do not rebuke me in your
anger
or discipline me in your wrath.[b]
[2]For your arrows[c] have pierced
me,
and your hand has come down
upon me.
[3]Because of your wrath there is no
health[d] in my body;
my bones[e] have no soundness
because of my sin.
[4]My guilt has overwhelmed[f] me
like a burden too heavy to
bear.[g]

[5]My wounds[h] fester and are
loathsome[i]
because of my sinful folly.[j]
[6]I am bowed down[k] and brought
very low;
all day long I go about
mourning.[l]
[7]My back is filled with searing
pain;[m]
there is no health[n] in my body.
[8]I am feeble and utterly crushed;[o]
I groan[p] in anguish of heart.[q]

[9]All my longings[r] lie open before
you, O Lord;
my sighing[s] is not hidden from
you.
[10]My heart pounds,[t] my strength
fails[u] me;
even the light has gone from my
eyes.[v]
[11]My friends and companions avoid
me because of my
wounds;[w]
my neighbors stay far away.
[12]Those who seek my life set their
traps,[x]
those who would harm me talk
of my ruin;[y]
all day long they plot
deception.[z]

[13]I am like a deaf man, who cannot
hear,[a]
like a mute, who cannot open
his mouth;
[14]I have become like a man who
does not hear,
whose mouth can offer no reply.
[15]I wait[b] for you, O LORD;
you will answer,[c] O Lord my
God.
[16]For I said, "Do not let them
gloat[d]
or exalt themselves over me
when my foot slips."[e]

[17]For I am about to fall,[f]
and my pain[g] is ever with
me.
[18]I confess my iniquity;[h]
I am troubled by my sin.
[19]Many are those who are my
vigorous enemies;[i]
those who hate me[j] without
reason[k] are numerous.
[20]Those who repay my good with
evil[l]
slander[m] me when I pursue
what is good.

[21]O LORD, do not forsake me;[n]
be not far[o] from me, O my God.
[22]Come quickly[p] to help me,[q]
O Lord my Savior.[r]

37:40 [a]Ps 2:12 **38:1** [b]Ps 6:1 **38:2** [c]S Job 6:4 **38:3** [d]Pr 3:8; 4:22 [e]S Job 33:19 **38:4** [f]Ps 40:12; 65:3 [g]S Nu 11:14; S Ezr 9:6; Lk 11:46 **38:5** [h]ver 11; Ps 147:3 [i]Job 19:17 [j]Ps 69:5; Pr 5:23; 12:23; 13:16; Ecc 10:3 **38:6** [k]Ps 57:6; 145:14; 146:8 [l]S Ps 35:14 **38:7** [m]S Job 14:22 [n]ver 3 **38:8** [o]Ps 34:18; Pr 17:22 [p]S Ps 6:6; 22:1; Pr 5:11 [q]S Ps 6:3 **38:9** [r]Ps 119:20; 143:7 [s]S Job 3:24 **38:10** [t]S Job 37:1 [u]S Ps 31:10 [v]S Ps 6:7; S 19:8; 88:9 **38:11** [w]S ver 5 **38:12** [x]Ps 31:4; 140:5; 141:9 [y]Ps 35:4; 41:5 [z]S Ps 35:20 **38:13** [a]Ps 115:6; 135:17; Isa 43:8; Mk 7:37 **38:15** [b]Ps 27:14 [c]Ps 17:6 **38:16** [d]S Ps 22:17 [e]S Dt 32:35 **38:17** [f]S Ps 37:24 [g]ver 7; S Job 6:10 **38:18** [h]S Lev 26:40 **38:19** [i]S Ps 18:17 [j]S Ps 25:19 [k]S Ps 35:19 **38:20** [l]S Ge 44:4; 1Jn 3:12 [m]Ps 54:5; 59:10; 119:23 **38:21** [n]Ps 27:9; 71:18; 119:8 [o]S Ps 10:1; S 22:11; 35:22; 71:12 **38:22** [p]S Ps 22:19 [q]Ps 40:13 [r]S 1Ch 16:35

38:1–22 DO NOT REBUKE ME. This psalm is an anguished prayer for God to withdraw chastisement for sin. David is overcome by a sense of God's wrath (vv. 1–2). His body is racked by disease and failing strength (vv. 3–10), and he knows that his suffering is the result of his own foolish sin (vv. 3–5,18). He accepts his punishment, confesses his sin, and looks to God for help and salvation (vv. 18,21–22). This prayer may be used by all who have sinned and are suffering from guilt, remorse and God's judgment.

38:3 NO HEALTH IN MY BODY. The psalmist emphasizes two consequences of committing serious sin after knowing the Lord and having received his mercy. (1) Divine anger and judgment. The teaching that God always forgives and forgets sin without ever disciplining the repentant believer is not a Biblical teaching. Time may pass before a repentant sinner once again experiences God's favor; even after forgiveness, there may be temporal consequences that continue for months or even years (see 2Sa 12:9–13, notes).

(2) Bodily pain and mental anguish. Sin brings a heavy burden and suffering to the sinner. God may allow severe sickness or even death as the result of our iniquity (vv. 3–10; cf. Ac 12:21–23; 1Co 11:29–30).

38:21 BE NOT FAR FROM ME. One terrible consequence of willful sin is the loss of God's fellowship and the sense of his presence (cf. 22:19; 35:22; 71:12). It is a grievous and bitter experience to commit willful sin after knowing God's mercy and the Holy Spirit's indwelling.

Psalm 39

For the director of music. For Jeduthun. A psalm of David.

1I said, "I will watch my ways[s]
and keep my tongue from sin;[t]
I will put a muzzle on my mouth[u]
as long as the wicked are in my
presence."
2But when I was silent[v] and still,
not even saying anything good,
my anguish[w] increased.
3My heart grew hot[x] within me,
and as I meditated,[y] the fire[z]
burned;
then I spoke with my tongue:

4"Show me, O LORD, my life's end
and the number of my days;[a]
let me know how fleeting[b] is
my life.[c]
5You have made my days[d] a mere
handbreadth;
the span of my years is as
nothing before you.
Each man's life is but a
breath.[e] *Selah*
6Man is a mere phantom[f] as he
goes to and fro:[g]
He bustles about, but only in
vain;[h]
he heaps up wealth,[i] not
knowing who will get it.[j]

7"But now, Lord, what do I look
for?
My hope is in you.[k]
8Save me[l] from all my
transgressions;[m]
do not make me the scorn[n] of
fools.
9I was silent;[o] I would not open
my mouth,[p]
for you are the one who has
done this.[q]
10Remove your scourge from me;
I am overcome by the blow[r] of
your hand.[s]
11You rebuke[t] and discipline[u] men
for their sin;
you consume[v] their wealth like
a moth[w]—
each man is but a breath.[x]
Selah

12"Hear my prayer, O LORD,
listen to my cry for help;[y]
be not deaf[z] to my weeping.[a]
For I dwell with you as an alien,[b]
a stranger,[c] as all my fathers
were.[d]
13Look away from me, that I may
rejoice again
before I depart and am no
more."[e]

Psalm 40

40:13–17pp — Ps 70:1–5

For the director of music. Of David.
A psalm.

1I waited patiently[f] for the LORD;
he turned to me and heard my
cry.[g]
2He lifted me out of the slimy pit,[h]
out of the mud[i] and mire;[j]
he set my feet[k] on a rock[l]
and gave me a firm place to
stand.
3He put a new song[m] in my mouth,
a hymn of praise to our God.
Many will see and fear[n]
and put their trust[o] in the LORD.

4Blessed is the man[p]
who makes the LORD his trust,[q]
who does not look to the proud,[r]

39:1 [s]1Ki 2:4; Ps 119:9,59; Pr 20:11 [t]S Job 1:22; Ps 34:13; Jas 3:2 [u]S Job 6:24; Jas 1:26 **39:2** [v]ver 9; S Job 31:34; Ps 77:4 [w]Ps 6:3; S 25:17; 31:10 **39:3** [x]Lk 24:32 [y]Ps 1:2; 48:9; 77:12; 119:15 [z]Jer 5:14; 20:9; 23:29 **39:4** [a]S Job 14:5 [b]S Job 14:2 [c]S Ge 47:9; S Job 7:7 **39:5** [d]S Job 10:20; Ps 89:45; 102:23 [e]S Job 7:7; Ps 62:9 **39:6** [f]Job 8:9; Ps 102:11; Ecc 6:12; S Jas 4:14 [g]Jas 1:11 [h]Ps 127:2 [i]S Job 27:17 [j]Lk 12:20 **39:7** [k]S Ps 9:18; S 25:5 **39:8** [l]Ps 6:4; 51:14 [m]Ps 32:1; 51:1; Isa 53:5,8, 10 [n]S Dt 28:37; Ps 69:7; 79:4; Isa 43:28; Da 9:16 **39:9** [o]S ver 2 [p]Ps 38:13 [q]Isa 38:15 **39:10** [r]2Ch 21:14; Eze 7:9; 24:16 [s]S Ex 9:3 **39:11** [t]S Dt 28:20; Isa 66:15; Eze 5:15; 2Pe 2:16 [u]Ps 94:10; Isa 26:16 [v]Ps 90:7 [w]S Job 13:28; S Isa 51:8; Lk 12:33; S Jas 5:2 [x]S Job 7:7 **39:12** [y]S Ps 17:1 [z]S Dt 1:45 [a]S 2Ki 20:5 [b]Lev 25:23 [c]S Ge 23:4; S Heb 11:13 [d]S Ge 47:9; S 1Ch 29:15 **39:13** [e]S Job 10:21 **40:1** [f]S Ps 37:7 [g]Ps 6:9; S 31:22; 34:15; 116:1; 145:19 **40:2** [h]S Job 9:31; S Ps 7:15 [i]S Job 30:19 [j]Ps 69:14 [k]Ps 31:8 [l]Ps 27:5 **40:3** [m]S Ps 28:7; S 96:1; Rev 5:9 [n]Ps 52:6; 64:9 [o]S Ex 14:31 **40:4** [p]Ps 34:8 [q]Ps 84:12 [r]Ps 101:5; 138:6; Pr 3:34; 16:5; Isa 65:5; 1Pe 5:5

39:1–13 I WILL WATCH MY WAYS. This psalm continues the theme of Ps 38, for the psalmist is still under God's severe chastisement. He realizes that it is the Lord who is causing his suffering: "I am overcome by the blow of your hand" (v. 10). He wants to know how long he will live and how long he must continue to suffer such direct punishment from God. He prays that he may not die separated from God and his mercy (vv. 12–13).

39:4–6 MY LIFE'S END. David prays that the Lord will help him realize the brief span of his life on earth (cf. v. 11; 62:9; 144:4; Job 7:7). This should be the prayerful concern of every believer. God has given each one of us only a short time on earth as a period of testing to determine our faithfulness to God while living in the midst of a corrupt generation opposed to God and his word. We may spend our days living for the things of this world, with little thought that our real home is in heaven with God; or we may walk in this world as a pilgrim, rejecting the ways of the ungodly, living by God's standards, dedicating ourselves to his ways, and witnessing to the gospel of Christ so that others may be saved. May all of us learn to number our days aright (90:12) and know that only what is done for God and others will endure eternally (see Lk 12:20; Jas 4:14).

to those who turn aside to false
gods.[s s]
5Many, O LORD my God,
are the wonders[t] you have
done.
The things you planned for us
no one can recount[u] to you;
were I to speak and tell of them,
they would be too many[v] to
declare.

6Sacrifice and offering you did not
desire,[w]
but my ears you have
pierced[t,u];[x]
burnt offerings[y] and sin offerings
you did not require.
7Then I said, "Here I am, I have
come—
it is written about me in the
scroll.[v z]
8I desire to do your will,[a] O my
God;[b]
your law is within my heart."[c]

9I proclaim righteousness[d] in the
great assembly;[e]
I do not seal my lips,
as you know,[f] O LORD.
10I do not hide your righteousness in
my heart;
I speak of your faithfulness[g]
and salvation.
I do not conceal your love and
your truth
from the great assembly.[h]

11Do not withhold your mercy[i] from
me, O LORD;
may your love[j] and your
truth[k] always protect[l]
me.

40:4 [s] S Dt 31:20; S Ps 4:2; S 26:1 **40:5** [t] S Dt 4:34; Ps 75:1; 105:5; 136:4 [u] Ps 139:18 [v] Ps 71:15; 139:17 **40:6** [w] S 1Sa 15:22; Jer 6:20; Am 5:22 [x] Ex 21:6 [y] Ps 50:8; 51:16; Isa 1:11; Hos 6:6 **40:7** [z] Job 19:23; Jer 36:2; 45:1; Eze 2:9; Zec 5:1 **40:8** [a] S Mt 26:39 [b] Heb 10:5-7* [c] S Dt 6:6; S Job 22:22; Ro 7:22 **40:9** [d] S Ps 22:31 [e] S Ps 22:25 [f] S Jos 22:22 **40:10** [g] Ps 89:1 [h] S Ps 22:22 **40:11** [i] Zec 1:12 [j] Pr 20:28 [k] S Ps 26:3 [l] Ps 61:7

40:12 [m] S Ps 25:17 [n] Ps 38:4; 65:3 [o] Ps 69:4 [p] Ps 73:26 **40:13** [q] Ps 22:19; 38:22 **40:14** [r] S 1Sa 20:1 [s] S Est 9:2; Ps 35:26 [t] S Ps 35:4 **40:15** [u] S Ps 35:21 **40:16** [v] Dt 4:29; 1Ch 28:9; Ps 9:10; 119:2 [w] Ps 9:2 [x] Ps 35:27 **40:17** [y] Ps 86:1; 109:22 [z] Ps 144:3 [a] S Ps 20:2 [b] S Ps 18:2 [c] Ps 119:60 **41:1** [d] S Dt 14:29 [e] S Job 24:4

12For troubles[m] without number
surround me;
my sins have overtaken me, and
I cannot see.[n]
They are more than the hairs of
my head,[o]
and my heart fails[p] within me.
13Be pleased, O LORD, to save me;
O LORD, come quickly to help
me.[q]
14May all who seek to take my life[r]
be put to shame and
confusion;[s]
may all who desire my ruin[t]
be turned back in disgrace.
15May those who say to me, "Aha!
Aha!"[u]
be appalled at their own shame.
16But may all who seek you[v]
rejoice and be glad[w] in you;
may those who love your salvation
always say,
"The LORD be exalted!"[x]

17Yet I am poor and needy;[y]
may the Lord think[z] of me.
You are my help[a] and my
deliverer;[b]
O my God, do not delay.[c]

Psalm 41

For the director of music. A psalm
of David.

1Blessed[d] is he who has regard for
the weak;[e]

[s] 4 Or *to falsehood* [t] 6 Hebrew; Septuagint *but a body you have prepared for me* (see also Symmachus and Theodotion) [u] 6 Or *opened* [v] 7 Or *come / with the scroll written for me*

40:6 SACRIFICE AND OFFERING YOU DID NOT DESIRE. The psalmist understood that the sacrifices and the symbolic rituals required by God in his law were inadequate by themselves and were no substitute for genuine commitment and heartfelt obedience to him (see 1Sa 15:22; Isa 1:11–17; Jer 7:22–23; Mic 6:6–8). Likewise, the NT believer may participate in water baptism, the Lord's Supper, acts of worship or songs of praise without a heart truly devoted to God and the commands of his word. No religious ritual can compensate for the absence of the obedience that comes from faith (cf. Ro 1:5).

40:8 I DESIRE TO DO YOUR WILL. Heb 10:5–10 quotes vv. 6–8 of this psalm from the Septuagint and applies them to Jesus Christ. V. 6 speaks of the inadequacy of the old covenant; v. 7 refers to the coming of Christ into the world to bring redemption (cf. Lk 24:27; Jn 5:46). His obedience to the heavenly Father and his proclamation of righteousness are emphasized in vv. 8–10 (cf. Php 2:5–8). The motto of Jesus' whole life was, "Here I am, I have come to do your will" (Heb 10:9). It is by Christ's obedience unto death that we have been made holy (Heb 10:10) in order that God's laws may be put in our hearts (Heb 10:16). Thus every believer must also affirm these words of Christ in his or her own life, "Here I am, I come to do your will."

40:8 YOUR LAW IS WITHIN MY HEART. The obedient faith that God desires is a faith that sincerely delights in following God's will and demonstrates that joy by striving to hide God's word in the heart (cf. 119:11; Jn 15:7).

41:1 BLESSED IS HE WHO HAS REGARD FOR THE WEAK. God has a special concern for the weak and helpless, and he blesses those who show loving-kindness to the needy. Vv. 1–3 expand on the principle, "Blessed are the merciful, for they will be shown mercy" (Mt 5:7). If we have

the LORD delivers him in times of
trouble.[f]
2The LORD will protect[g] him and
preserve his life;[h]
he will bless him in the land[i]
and not surrender him to the
desire of his foes.[j]
3The LORD will sustain him on his
sickbed[k]
Ps 103:1-5 and restore him from his bed of
illness.[l]

4I said, "O LORD, have mercy[m] on
me;
heal[n] me, for I have sinned[o]
against you."
5My enemies say of me in malice,
"When will he die and his name
perish?[p]"
6Whenever one comes to see me,
he speaks falsely,[q] while his
heart gathers slander;[r]
then he goes out and spreads[s]
it abroad.

7All my enemies whisper together[t]
against me;
they imagine the worst for me,
saying,
8"A vile disease has beset him;
he will never get up[u] from the
place where he lies."
9Even my close friend,[v] whom I
trusted,
he who shared my bread,
has lifted up his heel against
me.[w]

10But you, O LORD, have mercy[x] on
me;
raise me up,[y] that I may
repay[z] them.
11I know that you are pleased with
me,[a]
for my enemy does not triumph
over me.[b]
12In my integrity[c] you uphold me[d]
and set me in your presence
forever.[e]

13Praise[f] be to the LORD, the God of
Israel,[g]
from everlasting to everlasting.
Amen and Amen.[h]

BOOK II

Psalms 42–72

Psalm 42[w]

For the director of music. A *maskil*[x] of the Sons of Korah.

1As the deer[i] pants for streams of
water,[j]
so my soul pants[k] for you,
O God.
2My soul thirsts[l] for God, for the
living God.[m]
When can I go[n] and meet with
God?
3My tears[o] have been my food
day and night,
while men say to me all day long,
"Where is your God?"[p]
4These things I remember
as I pour out my soul:[q]
how I used to go with the
multitude,
leading the procession to the
house of God,[r]

41:1 [f]Ps 25:17 **41:2** [g]Ps 12:5; 32:7 [h]Ezr 9:9; Ps 71:20; 119:88, 159; 138:7; 143:11 [i]Ps 37:22 [j]S Dt 6:24 **41:3** [k]Ps 6:6 [l]2Sa 13:5; 2Ki 1:4 **41:4** [m]Ps 6:2; S 9:13 [n]S Dt 32:39 [o]Ps 51:4 **41:5** [p]S Ps 38:12 **41:6** [q]Ps 12:2; 101:7; Mt 5:11 [r]Pr 26:24 [s]S Lev 19:16 **41:7** [t]Ps 71:10 **41:8** [u]S 2Ki 1:4 **41:9** [v]S 2Sa 15:12; S Job 19:14 [w]Nu 30:2; Job 19:19; Ps 55:20; 89:34; Mt 26:23; Lk 22:21; Jn 13:18* **41:10** [x]ver 4 [y]Ps 3:3; 9:13 [z]S 2Sa 3:39 **41:11** [a]S Nu 14:8 [b]Ps 25:2 **41:12** [c]S Ps 25:21 [d]Ps 18:35; S 37:17; 63:8 [e]S Job 4:7; Ps 21:6; 61:7 **41:13** [f]S Ge 24:27 [g]Ps 72:18 [h]Ps 72:19; 89:52; 106:48 **42:1** [i]S Ps 18:33 [j]S Dt 10:7 [k]S Job 19:27; Ps 119:131; Joel 1:20 **42:2** [l]Ps 63:1; 143:6 [m]S Jos 3:10; S 1Sa 14:39; S Mt 16:16; Ro 9:26 [n]Ps 43:4; 84:7 **42:3** [o]S Job 3:24 [p]ver 10; Ps 79:10; 115:2; Joel 2:17; Mic 7:10 **42:4** [q]S 1Sa 1:15 [r]Ps 55:14; 122:1; Isa 2:2; 30:29

[w] In many Hebrew manuscripts Psalms 42 and 43 constitute one psalm. [x] Title: Probably a literary or musical term

shared God's compassion for those in need, we can pray with confidence that God will deliver us when we are in trouble (v. 1), protect us from harm (v. 2), bless our lives (v. 2), destroy the power of Satan and our enemies (v. 2), and give us his presence and healing when we are sick (v. 3; cf. 72:2,4, 12; Dt 15:7–11; Pr 29:14; Isa 11:4; Jer 22:16; see Mt 6:30, note).

41:9 LIFTED UP HIS HEEL AGAINST ME. Jesus quoted this verse and applied it to his betrayal by Judas Iscariot, who was a trusted friend (Mt 26:14–16,20–25; Jn 13:18; see Lk 22:3, note).

42:title THE SONS OF KORAH. These were a Levitical family of singers (cf. 2Ch 20:19). For *maskil*, see 32:title, note.

42:2 MY SOUL THIRSTS FOR GOD. As water is essential for physical life, so God and his presence are essential for satisfaction and wholeness of life. True believers will hunger and thirst for God and his grace, blessing and supernatural activity in their lives. (1) To stop thirsting for God is to die spiritually; thus we must not allow anything to diminish our intense desire for the things of God. Beware of the worries of this life, the pursuit of earthly things, and the pleasures that choke out hunger and thirst for God and the desire to seek his face in prayer (Mk 4:19).

(2) We should pray that our longing for God's presence might be strengthened, our love for the full manifestation of the Holy Spirit might be greater, and our passion to see the fullness of Christ's kingdom and righteousness might be deepened until we cry out to him day and night in a heartfelt thirst, even as the deer "pants for streams of water" in times of drought (v. 1; see Mt 5:6; 6:33, notes).

with shouts of joy[s] and
thanksgiving[t]
among the festive throng.[u]

5Why are you downcast,[v] O my
soul?
Why so disturbed[w] within me?
Put your hope in God,[x]
for I will yet praise[y] him,
my Savior[z] and 6my God.[a]

My[y] soul is downcast within me;
therefore I will remember[b] you
from the land of the Jordan,[c]
the heights of Hermon[d]—from
Mount Mizar.
7Deep calls to deep[e]
in the roar of your waterfalls;
all your waves and breakers
have swept over me.[f]

8By day the LORD directs his love,[g]
at night[h] his song[i] is with
me—
a prayer to the God of my life.[j]

9I say to God my Rock,[k]
"Why have you forgotten[l] me?
Why must I go about mourning,[m]
oppressed[n] by the enemy?"[o]
10My bones suffer mortal agony[p]
as my foes taunt[q] me,
saying to me all day long,
"Where is your God?"[r]

11Why are you downcast, O my soul?
Why so disturbed within me?
Put your hope in God,
for I will yet praise him,
my Savior and my God.[s]

Psalm 43[z]

1Vindicate me, O God,
and plead my cause[t] against an
ungodly nation;
rescue me[u] from deceitful and
wicked men.[v]
2You are God my stronghold.
Why have you rejected[w] me?
Why must I go about mourning,[x]
oppressed by the enemy?[y]
3Send forth your light[z] and your
truth,[a]
let them guide me;[b]

42:4 [s]S Ezr 3:13 [t]S Jos 6:5; Ps 95:2; 100:4; 147:7; Jnh 2:9 [u]Ps 35:18; 109:30 **42:5** [v]Ps 38:6; 77:3; La 3:20; Mt 26:38 [w]S Job 20:2 [x]S Ps 25:5; S 71:14 [y]Ps 9:1 [z]Ps 18:46 **42:6** [a]ver 11; Ps 43:5 [b]Ps 63:6; 77:11 [c]Ge 13:10; S Nu 13:29 [d]S Dt 3:8; S 4:48 **42:7** [e]S Ge 1:2; S 7:11 [f]Ps 69:2; Jnh 2:3 **42:8** [g]Ps 57:3 [h]S Ps 16:7 [i]Ps 77:6 [j]Ps 133:3; Ecc 5:18; 8:15 **42:9** [k]Ps 18:31 [l]S Ps 10:11 [m]S Ps 35:14 [n]Job 20:19; Ps 43:2; 106:42 [o]Ps 9:13; 43:2 **42:10** [p]S Ps 6:2 [q]Dt 32:27; Ps 44:16; 89:51; 102:8; 119:42 [r]S ver 3 **42:11** [s]ver 5; Ps 43:5 **43:1** [t]S Jdg 6:31 [u]S Ps 25:20 [v]S Ps 36:3; 109:2 **43:2** [w]Ps 44:9; 74:1; 88:14; 89:38 [x]S Ps 35:14 [y]S Ps 42:9 **43:3** [z]Ps 27:1 [a]S Ps 26:3 [b]S Ps 25:5 [c]Ps 2:6 [d]S 2Sa 15:25 **43:4** [e]S Ps 42:2 [f]Ps 26:6; 84:3 [g]S Ps 21:6 [h]Ps 16:3 [i]S Ge 4:21 **43:5** [j]S Ps 42:6 **44:1** [k]2Sa 7:22; 1Ch 17:20; Jer 26:11 [l]S Jdg 6:13 [m]S Dt 32:7; S Job 37:23 **44:2** [n]S Jos 3:10; Ac 7:45 [o]S Ex 15:17; S Isa 60:21 [p]S Jdg 4:23; S 2Ch 14:13 [q]Ps 80:9; Jer 32:23 **44:3** [r]Jos 24:12 [s]Ps 78:54 [t]Ex 15:16; Ps 77:15; 79:11; 89:10; 98:1; Isa 40:10; 52:10; 63:5 [u]Ps 89:15 [v]S Dt 4:37

let them bring me to your holy
mountain,[c]
to the place where you dwell.[d]
4Then will I go[e] to the altar[f] of
God,
to God, my joy[g] and my
delight.[h]
I will praise you with the harp,[i]
O God, my God.

5Why are you downcast, O my soul?
Why so disturbed within me?
Put your hope in God,
for I will yet praise him,
my Savior and my God.[j]

Psalm 44

For the director of music. Of the Sons of Korah. A *maskil.* [a]

1We have heard with our ears,[k]
O God;
our fathers have told us[l]
what you did in their days,
in days long ago.[m]
2With your hand you drove out[n]
the nations
and planted[o] our fathers;
you crushed[p] the peoples
and made our fathers flourish.[q]
3It was not by their sword[r] that
they won the land,
nor did their arm bring them
victory;
it was your right hand,[s] your
arm,[t]
and the light[u] of your face, for
you loved[v] them.

4You are my King[w] and my God,[x]
who decrees[b] victories[y] for
Jacob.

44:4 [w]S Ps 24:7 [x]Ps 5:2 [y]S Ps 21:5

[y] *5,6* A few Hebrew manuscripts, Septuagint and Syriac; most Hebrew manuscripts *praise him for his saving help. / 6O my God, my* [z] In many Hebrew manuscripts Psalms 42 and 43 constitute one psalm. [a] Title: Probably a literary or musical term [b] *4* Septuagint, Aquila and Syriac; Hebrew *King, O God; / command*

42:6 MY SOUL IS DOWNCAST. Those who thirst for God and yearn for a greater manifestation of his presence may experience delay. Yet the faithful believer will continue thirsting for and seeking God. The Lord promises to bless those who hunger and thirst for righteousness rather than settle for less than his full blessing (Mt 5:6). In the midst of God's silence, we must continue to press on to know God and to experience a greater measure of the Holy Spirit (cf. Hos 6:1–3; Ac 2:38–39; Eph 4:11–13). We must not despair, but put our hope in God and trust in his unfailing love (vv. 8–11).

[5]Through you we push back[z] our enemies;
through your name we trample[a] our foes.
[6]I do not trust in my bow,[b]
my sword does not bring me victory;
[7]but you give us victory[c] over our enemies,
you put our adversaries to shame.[d]
[8]In God we make our boast[e] all day long,[f]
and we will praise your name forever.[g] *Selah*

[9]But now you have rejected[h] and humbled us;[i]
you no longer go out with our armies.[j]
[10]You made us retreat[k] before the enemy,
and our adversaries have plundered[l] us.
[11]You gave us up to be devoured like sheep[m]
and have scattered us among the nations.[n]
[12]You sold your people for a pittance,[o]
gaining nothing from their sale.

[13]You have made us a reproach[p] to our neighbors,[q]
the scorn[r] and derision[s] of those around us.
[14]You have made us a byword[t] among the nations;
the peoples shake their heads[u] at us.
[15]My disgrace[v] is before me all day long,
and my face is covered with shame[w]
[16]at the taunts[x] of those who reproach and revile[y] me,
because of the enemy, who is bent on revenge.[z]

[17]All this happened to us,
though we had not forgotten[a] you
or been false to your covenant.
[18]Our hearts had not turned[b] back;
our feet had not strayed from your path.
[19]But you crushed[c] us and made us a haunt for jackals[d]
and covered us over with deep darkness.[e]

[20]If we had forgotten[f] the name of our God
or spread out our hands to a foreign god,[g]
[21]would not God have discovered it,
since he knows the secrets of the heart?[h]
[22]Yet for your sake we face death all day long;
we are considered as sheep[i] to be slaughtered.[j]

[23]Awake,[k] O Lord! Why do you sleep?[l]
Rouse yourself![m] Do not reject us forever.[n]
[24]Why do you hide your face[o]
and forget[p] our misery and oppression?[q]

[25]We are brought down to the dust;[r]
our bodies cling to the ground.
[26]Rise up[s] and help us;
redeem[t] us because of your unfailing love.[u]

44:5 [z]S Jos 23:5 [a]Ps 60:12; 108:13 **44:6** [b]Ge 48:22; Hos 1:7 **44:7** [c]S Dt 20:4 [d]S Job 8:22 **44:8** [e]S Ps 34:2; 1Co 1:31; 2Co 10:17 [f]Ps 52:1 [g]S Ps 30:12 **44:9** [h]S Ps 43:2 [i]S Dt 8:3; S 31:17; Ps 107:39; Isa 5:15 [j]S Jos 7:12; Ps 108:11 **44:10** [k]S Lev 26:17 [l]S Jdg 2:14 **44:11** [m]ver 22; Jer 12:3 [n]S Lev 26:33; S Ps 9:11; Eze 6:8; Zec 2:6 **44:12** [o]S Dt 32:30; Isa 52:3; Jer 15:13; 50:1; 52:3; Jer 15:13 **44:13** [p]S 2Ch 29:8; Isa 30:3; Jer 25:9; 42:18; 44:8 [q]Ps 79:4; 80:6; 89:41 [r]S Dt 28:37; S Mic 2:6 [s]Eze 23:32 **44:14** [t]S 1Ki 9:7 [u]S 2Ki 19:21 **44:15** [v]Ge 30:23; 2Ch 32:21; Ps 35:26 [w]S Ps 34:5 **44:16** [x]S Ps 42:10 [y]Ps 10:13; 55:3; 74:10 [z]S 1Sa 18:25; S Jer 11:19; Ro 12:19

44:17 [a]S Dt 6:12; S 32:18; Ps 119:16,61,153, 176; Pr 3:1 **44:18** [b]Ps 119:51,157 **44:19** [c]S 2Ch 14:13; Ps 51:8 [d]S Job 30:29; S Isa 34:13 [e]S Job 3:5 **44:20** [f]S Dt 32:18; S Jdg 3:7 [g]S Ex 20:3; Isa 43:12; Jer 5:19 **44:21** [h]S 1Sa 16:7; 1Ki 8:39; Pr 15:11; Jer 12:3; 17:10 **44:22** [i]S ver 11 [j]Isa 53:7; Jer 11:19; 12:3; Ro 8:36* **44:23** [k]S Ps 7:6 [l]Ps 78:65 [m]Ps 59:5 [n]Ps 74:1; 77:7 **44:24** [o]S Dt 32:20; Ps 13:1 [p]La 5:20 [q]S Dt 26:7 **44:25** [r]Ps 119:25 **44:26** [s]S Nu 10:35; S Ps 12:5; 102:13 [t]Ps 26:11 [u]Ps 6:4

44:9 YOU HAVE REJECTED. The psalmist believes that God's people are suffering and being defeated because God has forsaken them (vv. 9–16). Yet he is perplexed because he can find no evidence of sin that would account for such rejection, for they have remained faithful to God and his covenant (vv. 17–19). The psalmist reflects the experience of God's children who, though they are upright and blameless like Job, still undergo great adversity, dark periods of testing, and times when God's presence seems to be withdrawn; the answer to that experience is given in v. 22 (see next note).

44:22 FOR YOUR SAKE WE FACE DEATH ALL DAY LONG. The Holy Spirit reveals that some suffering comes to God's faithful people *because* they maintain loyalty to him in a hostile world. The apostle Paul quotes this verse in Ro 8:36 to teach that all those who identify with Christ and refuse to conform to the evil world will undergo grief, persecution and suffering. At the same time, God's people are assured of victory through Jesus Christ, knowing that no adversity can separate them from God's love (see Ro 8:17, 36, notes).

Psalm 45

For the director of music. To ⌊the tune of⌋ "Lilies." Of the Sons of Korah. A *maskil*.[c] A wedding song.[v]

1 My heart is stirred by a noble
theme
as I recite my verses for the
king;
my tongue is the pen of a
skillful writer.

2 You are the most excellent of men
and your lips have been anointed
with grace,[w]
since God has blessed you
forever.[x]
3 Gird your sword[y] upon your side,
O mighty one;[z]
clothe yourself with splendor
and majesty.[a]
4 In your majesty ride forth
victoriously[b]
in behalf of truth, humility and
righteousness;[c]
let your right hand[d] display
awesome deeds.[e]
5 Let your sharp arrows[f] pierce the
hearts[g] of the king's
enemies;[h]
let the nations fall beneath your
feet.
6 Your throne, O God, will last for
ever and ever;[i]
a scepter of justice will be the
scepter of your kingdom.
7 You love righteousness[j] and hate
wickedness;[k]
therefore God, your God, has set
you above your companions
by anointing[l] you with the oil
of joy.[m]
8 All your robes are fragrant[n] with
myrrh[o] and aloes[p] and
cassia;[q]
from palaces adorned with
ivory[r]
the music of the strings[s] makes
you glad.
9 Daughters of kings[t] are among
your honored women;
at your right hand[u] is the royal
bride[v] in gold of Ophir.[w]

10 Listen, O daughter,[x] consider[y]
and give ear:
Forget your people[z] and your
father's house.
11 The king is enthralled by your
beauty;[a]
honor[b] him, for he is your
lord.[c]
12 The Daughter of Tyre[d] will come
with a gift,[d e]
men of wealth will seek your
favor.
13 All glorious[f] is the princess
within ⌊her chamber⌋;
her gown is interwoven with
gold.[g]
14 In embroidered garments[h] she is
led to the king;[i]
her virgin companions[j] follow
her
and are brought to you.

45:1 [v] 45 Title SS 1:1
45:2 [w] Lk 4:22 [x] Ps 21:6
45:3 [y] S Dt 32:41; Ps 149:6; Rev 1:16 [z] S 2Sa 1:19 [a] S Job 40:10; S Ps 21:5
45:4 [b] Rev 6:2 [c] Zep 2:3 [d] Ps 21:8 [e] S Dt 4:34; Ps 65:5; 66:3
45:5 [f] S Dt 32:23 [g] S Nu 24:8 [h] Ps 9:13; 92:9
45:6 [i] S Ge 21:33; La 5:19
45:7 [j] Ps 33:5 [k] S Ps 11:5 [l] Ps 2:2; Isa 45:1; 61:1; Zec 4:14 [m] S Ps 23:5; Heb 1:8-9*
45:8 [n] Pr 27:9; SS 1:3; 4:10 [o] S Ge 37:25 [p] S Nu 24:6; Jn 19:39 [q] S Ex 30:24 [r] S 1Ki 22:39 [s] Ps 144:9; 150:4; Isa 38:20
45:9 [t] SS 6:8 [u] 1Ki 2:19 [v] Isa 62:5 [w] S Ge 10:29
45:10 [x] Ru 1:11 [y] Jer 5:1 [z] Ru 1:16
45:11 [a] S Est 1:11; S La 2:15 [b] Eph 5:33 [c] 1Pe 3:6
45:12 [d] S Jos 19:29 [e] S 1Ki 9:16; S 2Ch 9:24
45:13 [f] Isa 61:10 [g] Ex 39:3
45:14 [h] S Jdg 5:30 [i] Est 2:15 [j] SS 1:3

[c] Title: Probably a literary or musical term
[d] *12* Or *A Tyrian robe is among the gifts*

45:6–7 YOUR THRONE, O GOD, WILL LAST FOR EVER AND EVER. These two verses find their ultimate fulfillment in Jesus Christ. The author of Hebrews applies these verses to the exaltation, prominence, authority and character of Christ (Heb 1:8). (1) Christ's dominion will be "for ever and ever" (Rev 1:6). The Messianic King is called "God" in v. 6 and is distinguished from "your God" (i.e., the Father) in v. 7. This distinction is consistent with the NT teaching that both Christ and the Father are fully God.

(2) In this psalm, Christ's most significant characteristic is described in terms of loving and hating. (a) He loves righteousness, for it characterizes his kingdom. Since his joy is found in doing his Father's will (Heb 10:7), he intensely loves righteousness in all its manifestations (cf. Eph 5:26; Heb 13:12). (b) As much as he loves righteousness, he hates wickedness. He made this known by dying on the cross to crush evil and to save his people from their sins (Mt 1:21). While on earth, he confronted all forms of sin: a wicked generation (Mt 12:39), the satanic strongholds of unrighteousness (Mk 1:34–39), and hypocrisy among God's people (Mt 23). At the end of this age he will return to establish righteousness upon the earth (Rev 19—22).

(3) Because Jesus Christ loved righteousness and hated wickedness, God set him above all others by anointing him. This anointing refers to the glory, blessedness and authority given him by God. The "oil of joy" is directly related to his anointing with the Holy Spirit (see Mt 3:16–17; Gal 5:22–23; see Heb 1:9, note).

(4) Likewise, the abundant outpouring of the Holy Spirit upon God's people will come only as they share Christ's heartfelt love for righteousness. Furthermore, the right to serve as spiritual leaders of God's people will be based on a Christlike love for righteousness and a persistent resistance to evil (1Ti 3:1–7).

15They are led in with joy and
gladness;[k]
they enter the palace of the
king.
16Your sons will take the place of
your fathers;
you will make them princes[l]
throughout the land.
17I will perpetuate your memory
through all generations;[m]
therefore the nations will praise
you[n] for ever and ever.[o]

Psalm 46

For the director of music. Of the Sons of Korah. According to *alamoth.*[e] A song.

1God is our refuge[p] and strength,[q]
an ever-present[r] help[s] in
trouble.[t]
2Therefore we will not fear,[u]
though the earth give way[v]
and the mountains fall[w] into the
heart of the sea,[x]
3though its waters roar[y] and
foam[z]
and the mountains quake[a] with
their surging. *Selah*
4There is a river[b] whose streams[c]
make glad the city of
God,[d]
the holy place where the Most
High[e] dwells.[f]
5God is within her,[g] she will not
fall;[h]
God will help[i] her at break of
day.
6Nations[j] are in uproar,[k] kingdoms[l]
fall;
he lifts his voice,[m] the earth
melts.[n]
7The LORD Almighty[o] is with us;[p]
the God of Jacob[q] is our
fortress.[r] *Selah*
8Come and see the works of the
LORD,[s]
the desolations[t] he has brought
on the earth.
9He makes wars[u] cease to the
ends of the earth;
he breaks the bow[v] and
shatters the spear,
he burns the shields[f] with
fire.[w]
10"Be still, and know that I am
God;[x]
I will be exalted[y] among the
nations,
I will be exalted in the earth."
11The LORD Almighty is with us;
the God of Jacob[z] is our
fortress.[a] *Selah*

Psalm 47

For the director of music. Of the Sons of Korah. A psalm.

1Clap your hands,[b] all you nations;
shout to God with cries of joy.[c]
2How awesome[d] is the LORD Most
High,[e]

45:15 [k]S Est 8:17 **45:16** [l]1Sa 2:8; Ps 68:27; 113:8 **45:17** [m]S Ex 3:15; Ps 33:11; 119:90; 135:13 [n]Ps 138:4 [o]S Ps 21:4; Rev 22:5 **46:1** [p]Ps 9:9; 37:39; 61:3; 73:26; 91:2,9; 142:5; Isa 33:16; Jer 16:19; 17:17; Joel 3:16; Na 1:7 [q]Ps 18:1 [r]Ps 34:18; La 3:57 [s]Ps 18:6; Lk 1:54 [t]S Dt 4:30; Ps 25:17 **46:2** [u]S Ge 4:7; Ps 3:6 [v]Ps 82:5; Isa 13:13; 24:1, 19,20; Jer 4:23; Da 11:19; Am 8:14; S Rev 6:14 [w]ver 6; Ps 18:7; 97:5; Isa 54:10; Am 9:5; Mic 1:4; Na 1:5; Hab 3:6 [x]Ex 15:8 **46:3** [y]Ps 93:3; Isa 17:13; Jer 5:22; Eze 1:24; Rev 19:6 [z]S Job 9:26 [a]S Jdg 5:5 **46:4** [b]S Ge 2:10; Rev 22:1 [c]S Ps 1:3 [d]Ps 48:1,8; 87:3; 101:8; Rev 3:12 [e]Ge 14:18 [f]S 2Sa 15:25 **46:5** [g]Dt 23:14; S Ps 26:8; Isa 12:6; Zec 2:5 [h]Ps 125:1 [i]S 1Ch 5:20 **46:6** [j]S Job 12:23 [k]Ps 74:23; Isa 5:30; 17:12 [l]Ps 68:32; 102:22; Isa 13:4,13; 23:11; Eze 26:18; Mt 4:8 [m]S Ps 29:3; Isa 33:3 [n]S ver 2 **46:7** [o]S 1Sa 1:11 [p]S Ge 21:22 [q]S Ps 20:1 [r]ver 11; Ps 18:2 **46:8** [s]Ps 66:5 [t]Isa 17:9; 64:10; Da 9:26; Lk 21:20 **46:9** [u]Isa 2:4 [v]S Ps 37:15; S Isa 22:6 [w]Isa 9:5; Eze 39:9; Hos 2:18 **46:10** [x]Dt 4:35; 1Ki 18:36, 39; Ps 100:3; Isa 37:16,20; 43:11; 45:21; Eze 36:23 [y]Ps 18:46; Isa 2:11 **46:11** [z]S Ps 20:1 [a]S ver 7 **47:1** [b]S 2Ki 11:12 [c]S Ps 33:3 **47:2** [d]S Dt 7:21 [e]Ge 14:18

e Title: Probably a musical term f 9 Or *chariots*

46:1–2 OUR REFUGE AND STRENGTH. Although we all experience spiritual barrenness at times (cf. Ps 44), this is not the norm, for God desires to be near his people with help and comfort. This psalm expresses trust and confidence in God during a time of instability and insecurity. (1) The power and ability to face the uncertainties and adversities of life are found in God. "Refuge" pictures a shelter from danger, indicating that God is our true security in the storms of life (see Isa 4:5–6). "Strength" refers to his might when battling our foes (21:8; Ex 15:13) and includes his energy that works powerfully in us (Col 1:29) and enables us to overcome obstacles in life.

(2) The end result is that he is "an ever-present help in trouble." God is available to his people and wants us to call on him for help in any time of need. (Heb 4:16). He is sufficient for any situation and never leaves our side; thus, we need not fear.

46:4 THERE IS A RIVER. God's "river" is the continual flow of his grace, glory and power in the midst of his faithful people (cf. v. 11; Isa 8:6; Eze 47:1; Rev 3:12; 22:1). This pure life-giving river flows from God the Father (Jer 2:13), God the Son (Zec 13:1; Jn 4:14) and God the Holy Spirit (Jn 7:38–39); it flows from the throne of God and constantly refreshes believers, both those on earth (Jn 4:13–14; 7:38) and those in heaven (Rev 22:1). The most significant blessing of this river is that it brings God into the midst of his people (v. 5): "The LORD Almighty is with us" (vv. 7,11).

46:10 BE STILL. The Hebrew here can also be translated, "let go," i.e., quit holding on to things that keep you from exalting God and giving him his proper place in your life.

the great King[f] over all the
earth!
3He subdued[g] nations under us,
peoples under our feet.
4He chose our inheritance[h] for us,
the pride of Jacob,[i] whom he
loved. *Selah*
5God has ascended[j] amid shouts
of joy,[k]
the LORD amid the sounding of
trumpets.[l]
6Sing praises[m] to God, sing
praises;
sing praises to our King, sing
praises.
7For God is the King of all the
earth;[n]
sing to him a psalm[g][o] of
praise.
8God reigns[p] over the nations;
God is seated on his holy
throne.[q]
9The nobles of the nations assemble
as the people of the God of
Abraham,
for the kings[h] of the earth belong
to God;[r]
he is greatly exalted.[s]

Psalm 48

A song. A psalm of the Sons of Korah.

1Great is the LORD,[t] and most
worthy of praise,[u]
in the city of our God,[v] his holy
mountain.[w]
2It is beautiful[x] in its loftiness,
the joy of the whole earth.
Like the utmost heights of
Zaphon[i][y] is Mount
Zion,[z]
the[j] city of the Great King.[a]
3God is in her citadels;[b]
he has shown himself to be her
fortress.[c]

4When the kings joined forces,
when they advanced together,[d]
5they saw ⌊her⌋ and were astounded;
they fled in terror.[e]
6Trembling seized[f] them there,
pain like that of a woman in
labor.[g]
7You destroyed them like ships of
Tarshish[h]
shattered by an east wind.[i]

8As we have heard,
so have we seen
in the city of the LORD Almighty,
in the city of our God:
God makes her secure forever.[j]
Selah

9Within your temple, O God,
we meditate[k] on your unfailing
love.[l]
10Like your name,[m] O God,
your praise reaches to the ends
of the earth;[n]
your right hand is filled with
righteousness.
11Mount Zion rejoices,
the villages of Judah are glad
because of your judgments.[o]

12Walk about Zion, go around her,
count her towers,[p]
13consider well her ramparts,[q]
view her citadels,[r]
that you may tell of them to the
next generation.[s]
14For this God is our God for ever
and ever;
he will be our guide[t] even to
the end.

Psalm 49

For the director of music. Of the Sons of Korah. A psalm.

1Hear[u] this, all you peoples;[v]
listen, all who live in this
world,[w]
2both low and high,[x]
rich and poor alike:

47:2 [f]Ps 2:6; 48:2; 95:3; Mt 5:35 **47:3** [g]Ps 18:39, 47; Isa 14:6 **47:4** [h]Ps 2:8; 16:6; 78:55; 1Pe 1:4 [i]Am 6:8; 8:7 **47:5** [j]Ps 68:18; Eph 4:8 [k]S Job 8:21; S Ps 106:5 [l]S Nu 10:2; S 2Sa 6:15 **47:6** [m]S 2Sa 22:50 **47:7** [n]Zec 14:9 [o]1Ch 16:7; Col 3:16 **47:8** [p]S 1Ch 16:31 [q]S 1Ki 22:19; S Ps 9:4; Rev 4:9 **47:9** [r]S Job 25:2 [s]Ps 46:10; 97:9 **48:1** [t]Ps 86:10; 96:4; 99:2; 135:5; 147:5; Jer 10:6 [u]S 2Sa 22:4; S 1Ch 16:25; Ps 18:3 [v]S Ps 46:4 [w]S Dt 33:19; Ps 2:6; 87:1; Isa 11:9; 32:16; Jer 31:23; Da 9:16; Mic 4:1; Zec 8:3 **48:2** [x]Ps 50:2; La 2:15; Eze 16:14 [y]S Jos 13:27 [z]S Ps 2:6 [a]Mt 5:35 **48:3** [b]ver 13; Ps 122:7 [c]Ps 18:2 **48:4** [d]2Sa 10:1-19 **48:5** [e]Ex 15:16; Isa 13:8; Jer 46:5; Da 5:9 **48:6** [f]S Job 4:14 [g]S Ge 3:16 **48:7** [h]S Ge 10:4; S 1Ki 10:22; 22:48 [i]S Ge 41:6 **48:8** [j]Jer 23:6; Zec 8:13; 14:11 **48:9** [k]S Ps 39:3 [l]Ps 6:4 **48:10** [m]S Ex 6:3; S Jos 7:9 [n]1Sa 2:10; Ps 22:27; 65:5; 98:3; 100:1; Isa 11:12; 24:16; 42:10; 49:6 **48:11** [o]Ps 97:8 **48:12** [p]S Ne 3:1 **48:13** [q]2Sa 20:15; Isa 26:1; La 2:8; Hab 2:1 [r]S ver 3 [s]Ps 71:18; 78:6; 109:13 **48:14** [t]Ps 25:5; 73:24; Pr 6:22; Isa 49:10; 57:18; 58:11 **49:1** [u]Isa 1:2 [v]Ps 78:1 [w]S Ps 33:8 **49:2** [x]Ps 62:9

[g]7 Or *a maskil* (probably a literary or musical term) [h]9 Or *shields* [i]2 *Zaphon* can refer to a sacred mountain or the direction north. [j]2 Or *earth, / Mount Zion, on the northern side / of the*

48:1 THE CITY OF OUR GOD. The city of our God and the Great King (v. 2) is Jerusalem (Mt 5:35). It will be established "forever" (v. 8). What God began in the OT he will complete in the new Jerusalem at the end of the ages (Rev 21:10—22:5; see article on THE CITY OF JERUSALEM, p. 576).

48:14 OUR GUIDE EVEN TO THE END. The Lord has committed himself to be the believer's faithful and constant guide throughout life, in the experience of death and beyond death to the eternal home where we will be with him forever (Jn 14:1–3; 1Th 4:17; Rev 21:3; see Php 1:21, note; see article on DEATH, p. 732).

49:1–20 HEAR THIS. This psalm stresses both the futility of trusting in riches and the transi-

3My mouth will speak words of
wisdom;[y]
the utterance from my heart will
give understanding.[z]
4I will turn my ear to a proverb;[a]
with the harp[b] I will expound
my riddle:[c]

5Why should I fear[d] when evil days
come,
when wicked deceivers surround
me—
6those who trust in their wealth[e]
and boast[f] of their great
riches?[g]
7No man can redeem the life of
another
or give to God a ransom for
him—
8the ransom[h] for a life is costly,
no payment is ever enough—[i]
9that he should live on[j] forever
and not see decay.[k]

10For all can see that wise men
die;[l]
the foolish and the senseless[m]
alike perish
and leave their wealth[n] to
others.[o]
11Their tombs[p] will remain their
houses[k] forever,
their dwellings for endless
generations,[q]
though they had[1] named[r]
lands after themselves.

12But man, despite his riches, does
not endure;[s]
he is[m] like the beasts that
perish.[t]

13This is the fate of those who trust
in themselves,[u]
and of their followers, who
approve their sayings. *Selah*
14Like sheep they are destined[v] for
the grave,[n][w]
and death will feed on them.
The upright will rule[x] over them
in the morning;
their forms will decay in the
grave,[n]
far from their princely mansions.
15But God will redeem my life[o]
from the grave;[y]
he will surely take me to
himself.[z] *Selah*
16Do not be overawed when a man
grows rich,
when the splendor of his house
increases;
17for he will take nothing[a] with him
when he dies,
his splendor will not descend
with him.[b]
18Though while he lived he counted
himself blessed—[c]
and men praise you when you
prosper—
19he will join the generation of his
fathers,[d]
who will never see the light[e] ⌞of
life⌟.
20A man who has riches without
understanding[f]
is like the beasts that perish.[g]

Psalm 50

A psalm of Asaph.

1The Mighty One, God, the LORD,[h]
speaks and summons the earth
from the rising of the sun to the
place where it sets.[i]
2From Zion,[j] perfect in beauty,[k]
God shines forth.[l]
3Our God comes[m] and will not be
silent;[n]
a fire devours[o] before him,[p]
and around him a tempest[q]
rages.
4He summons the heavens above,
and the earth,[r] that he may
judge his people:[s]
5"Gather to me my consecrated
ones,[t]
who made a covenant[u] with me
by sacrifice."
6And the heavens proclaim[v] his
righteousness,
for God himself is judge.[w] *Selah*

49:3 [y]S Ps 37:30 [z]Ps 119:130 **49:4** [a]Ps 78:2; Pr 1:6; Eze 12:22; 16:44; 18:2-3; Lk 4:23 [b]S 1Sa 16:16; Ps 33:2 [c]S Nu 12:8 **49:5** [d]Ps 23:4; 27:1 **49:6** [e]S Job 22:25; Ps 73:12; Jer 48:7 [f]S Ps 10:3 [g]S Job 36:19 **49:8** [h]S Nu 35:31 [i]Mt 16:26 **49:9** [j]Ps 22:29; 89:48 [k]Ps 16:10 **49:10** [l]Ecc 2:16 [m]Ps 92:6; 94:8 [n]S Job 27:17 [o]Ecc 2:18,21; Lk 12:20 **49:11** [p]Mk 5:3; Lk 8:27 [q]Ps 106:31 [r]S Dt 3:14 **49:12** [s]S Job 14:2 [t]ver 20; 2Pe 2:12 **49:13** [u]Lk 12:20 **49:14** [v]Jer 43:11; Eze 31:14 [w]Nu 16:30; S Job 21:13; Ps 9:17; 55:15 [x]Isa 14:2; Da 7:18; 1Co 6:2 **49:15** [y]Ps 56:13; Hos 13:14 [z]S Ge 5:24 **49:17** [a]1Ti 6:7 [b]S Ps 17:14 **49:18** [c]Ps 10:6; Lk 12:19 **49:19** [d]S Ge 15:15 [e]S Job 33:30 **49:20** [f]Pr 16:16 [g]S ver 12 **50:1** [h]Jos 22:22 [i]Ps 113:3 **50:2** [j]Ps 2:6 [k]S Ps 48:2; S La 2:15 [l]S Dt 33:2 **50:3** [m]Ps 96:13 [n]ver 21; Isa 42:14; 64:12; 65:6 [o]S Lev 10:2 [p]S Ps 18:8 [q]Job 37:9; Ps 83:15; 107:25; 147:18; Isa 29:6; 30:28; Jnh 1:4; Na 1:3 **50:4** [r]Dt 4:26; 31:28; Isa 1:2 [s]Heb 10:30 **50:5** [t]S Dt 7:6; S Ps 18:25 [u]Ex 24:7; S 2Ch 6:11 **50:6** [v]S Ps 19:1 [w]S Ge 16:5; S Job 9:15

k *11* Septuagint and Syriac; Hebrew *In their thoughts their houses will remain* l *11* Or / *for they have* m *12* Hebrew; Septuagint and Syriac read verse 12 the same as verse 20. n *14* Hebrew *Sheol*; also in verse 15 o *15* Or *soul*

tory nature of all that this earth has to offer. The psalmist declares that the person whose life consists in an abundance of possessions or in worldly pleasures or fame (Mt 6:19–21; Lk 12:15), rather than in seeking God and his kingdom, will perish (vv. 12–14,16–17); on the other hand, those who live for God will be redeemed from the grave (v. 15; see article on RICHES AND POVERTY, p. 1562).

7"Hear, O my people, and I will
speak,
O Israel, and I will testify[x]
against you:
I am God, your God.[y]
8I do not rebuke[z] you for your
sacrifices
or your burnt offerings,[a] which
are ever before me.
9I have no need of a bull[b] from
your stall
or of goats[c] from your pens,[d]
10for every animal of the forest[e] is
mine,
and the cattle on a thousand
hills.[f]
11I know every bird[g] in the
mountains,
and the creatures of the field[h]
are mine.
12If I were hungry I would not tell
you,
for the world[i] is mine, and all
that is in it.[j]
13Do I eat the flesh of bulls
or drink the blood of goats?
14Sacrifice thank offerings[k] to God,
fulfill your vows[l] to the Most
High,[m]
15and call[n] upon me in the day of
trouble;[o]
I will deliver[p] you, and you will
honor[q] me."

16But to the wicked, God says:

"What right have you to recite my
laws
or take my covenant[r] on your
lips?[s]
17You hate[t] my instruction
and cast my words behind[u] you.
18When you see a thief, you join[v]
with him;
you throw in your lot with
adulterers.[w]
19You use your mouth for evil
and harness your tongue to
deceit.[x]
20You speak continually against your
brother[y]
and slander your own mother's
son.
21These things you have done and I
kept silent;[z]
you thought I was altogether[p]
like you.
But I will rebuke[a] you
and accuse[b] you to your face.

22"Consider this, you who forget
God,[c]
or I will tear you to pieces, with
none to rescue:[d]
23He who sacrifices thank offerings
honors me,
and he prepares the way[e]
so that I may show him[q] the
salvation of God.[f]"

50:7 [x]Heb 2:4 [y]Ex 20:2; Ps 48:14 **50:8** [z]S 2Sa 22:16 [a]S Ps 40:6 **50:9** [b]S Lev 1:5 [c]S Lev 16:5 [d]S Nu 32:16 **50:10** [e]Ps 104:20; Isa 56:9; Mic 5:8 [f]Ps 104:24 **50:11** [g]Mt 6:26 [h]Ps 8:7; 80:13 **50:12** [i]Ex 19:5 [j]Dt 10:14; S Jos 3:11; Ps 24:1; 1Co 10:26 **50:14** [k]S Ezr 1:4; S Ps 27:6 [l]S Nu 30:2; S Ps 66:13; 76:11 [m]Ps 7:8 **50:15** [n]Ps 4:1; 81:7; Isa 55:6; 58:9; Zec 13:9 [o]Ps 69:17; 86:7; 107:6; 142:2; Jas 5:13 [p]Ps 3:7 [q]S Ps 22:23 **50:16** [r]Ps 25:10 [s]Isa 29:13 **50:17** [t]Pr 1:22 [u]S 1Ki 14:9 **50:18** [v]Ro 1:32; 1Ti 5:22 [w]S Job 22:15 **50:19** [x]Ps 10:7; 36:3; 52:2; 101:7 **50:20** [y]Mt 10:21 **50:21** [z]Isa 42:14; 57:11; 62:1; 64:12 [a]Ps 6:1; S 18:15; 76:6; 104:7; Isa 50:2 [b]Ps 85:5; Isa 57:16 **50:22** [c]S Job 8:13; S Isa 17:10 [d]S Dt 32:39; Mic 5:8 **50:23** [e]Ps 85:13 [f]S Ps 9:14; 91:16; 98:3; Isa 52:10 **51:1** [g]**51 Title** 2Sa 11:4; 12:1 [h]S 2Sa 24:14; S Ps 9:13 [i]S Ps 25:7; S 119:88

Psalm 51

For the director of music. A psalm of David. When the prophet Nathan came to him after David had committed adultery with Bathsheba.[g]

1Have mercy[h] on me, O God,
according to your unfailing
love;[i]

[p]*21* Or *thought the 'I AM' was* [q]*23* Or *and to him who considers his way / I will show*

50:15 CALL UPON ME IN THE DAY OF TROUBLE. The Lord invites all faithful believers to call continually on him in times of need and trouble. God desires to hear our prayers, to help us and to have his name exalted as a God who delivers his people.

50:16–23 WHAT RIGHT HAVE YOU TO RECITE MY LAWS? The Lord delivers a stern warning to the wicked hypocrites among his people, threatening to tear to pieces (v. 22) those who pretend to be devoted to him, who claim the covenant salvation and the blessings of his word, and who at the same time ignore his righteous commands and conform to the ungodliness of a wicked society. They will find no deliverance in the end (v. 22); in fact, such people will receive the greater damnation (Mt 23:14; see 1Co 11:27, note).

51:Title A PSALM OF DAVID. The title ascribes this psalm of confession to David, when Nathan the prophet disclosed his sins of adultery and murder (cf. 2Sa 12:1–13). (1) Note that this psalm was written by a believer who had deliberately sinned against God in such a serious way that he was cut off from God's life and presence (cf. v. 11). (2) David probably wrote this psalm after he had repented and Nathan had declared God's forgiveness to him (2Sa 12:13). He pleads earnestly for a full restoration of salvation, purity, God's presence, spiritual vitality and joy (vv. 7–13).

51:1–19 HAVE MERCY ON ME. All who have sinned greatly and are overwhelmed by feelings of guilt can find forgiveness, cleansing from sin, and restoration to God if they approach him in the spirit and words of this psalm. David's appeals for forgiveness and restoration are based on God's grace, mercy, unfailing love and compassion (v. 1), on a truly broken and repentant heart (v. 17), and ultimately on Christ's atoning death for our sins (1Jn 2:1–2).

according to your great
compassion[j]
blot out[k] my transgressions.[l]
2Wash away[m] all my iniquity
and cleanse[n] me from my sin.

3For I know my transgressions,
and my sin is always before
me.[o]
4Against you, you only, have I
sinned[p]
and done what is evil in your
sight,[q]
so that you are proved right when
you speak
and justified when you judge.[r]
5Surely I was sinful[s] at birth,[t]
sinful from the time my mother
conceived me.
6Surely you desire truth in the
inner parts[r];
you teach[s] me wisdom[u] in the
inmost place.[v]

7Cleanse[w] me with hyssop,[x] and I
will be clean;
wash me, and I will be whiter
than snow.[y]
8Let me hear joy and gladness;[z]
let the bones[a] you have
crushed rejoice.
9Hide your face from my sins[b]
and blot out[c] all my iniquity.

10Create in me a pure heart,[d]
O God,
and renew a steadfast spirit
within me.[e]
11Do not cast me[f] from your
presence[g]
or take your Holy Spirit[h] from
me.
12Restore to me the joy of your
salvation[i]
and grant me a willing spirit,[j]
to sustain me.[k]

13Then I will teach transgressors
your ways,[l]
and sinners[m] will turn back to
you.[n]
14Save me[o] from bloodguilt,[p]
O God,
the God who saves me,[q]
and my tongue will sing of your
righteousness.[r]
15O Lord, open my lips,[s]
and my mouth will declare your
praise.
16You do not delight in sacrifice,[t]
or I would bring it;
you do not take pleasure in
burnt offerings.

51:1 [j]S Ne 9:27; Ps 86:15; Isa 63:7 [k]S 2Sa 12:13; S 2Ch 6:21; S Ne 4:5; Ac 3:19 [l]S Ps 39:8 **51:2** [m]S Ru 3:3; Jer 2:22; 13:27; Ac 22:16; 1Jn 1:9 [n]Pr 20:30; Isa 4:4; Eze 36:25; Zec 13:1; Mt 23:25-26; Heb 9:14 **51:3** [o]Isa 59:12 **51:4** [p]S 1Sa 15:24 [q]S Ge 20:6; Lk 15:21 [r]Ro 3:4* **51:5** [s]S Lev 5:2 [t]S Job 5:7 **51:6** [u]Ps 119:66; 143:10 [v]S Job 9:4; S 34:32 **51:7** [w]Isa 4:4; Eze 36:25; Zec 13:1 [x]S Ex 12:22; S Nu 19:6; Heb 9:19 [y]Isa 1:18; 43:25; 44:22 **51:8** [z]Isa 35:10; Jer 33:11; Joel 1:16 [a]S Ex 12:46 **51:9** [b]Jer 16:17; Zec 4:10 [c]S 2Sa 12:13 **51:10** [d]S Ps 24:4; 78:37; Mt 5:8; Ac 15:9 [e]Eze 18:31; 36:26 **51:11** [f]Ps 27:9; 71:9; 138:8 [g]S Ge 4:14; S Ex 33:15 [h]Ps 106:33; Isa 63:10; Eph 4:30 **51:12** [i]S Job 33:26 [j]Ps 110:3 [k]S Ps 18:35 **51:13** [l]S Ex 33:13; Ac 9:21-22 [m]S Ps 1:1 [n]S Job 33:27 **51:14** [o]S Ps 39:8 [p]S 2Sa 12:9 [q]Ps 25:5; 68:20; 88:1 [r]S Ps 5:8; 35:28; 71:15 **51:15** [s]Ex 4:15 **51:16** [t]S 1Sa 15:22

[r]*6* The meaning of the Hebrew for this phrase is uncertain. [s]*6* Or *you desired . . . ; / you taught*

51:3 MY SIN IS ALWAYS BEFORE ME. At times the assurance of forgiveness and the renewed blessing of God do not come easily. A person who has experienced the joy of salvation and then falls into the depths of immorality may experience a prolonged time of repentance and spiritual struggle before receiving the assurance of pardon and a full restoration to God's favor. David's experience reveals how fearful it is to offend a holy God after having been so richly blessed by him.

51:4 AGAINST YOU . . . HAVE I SINNED. David is not saying that his sin was not against others, but that it was preeminently against God and his word (see 2Sa 12:9–10).

51:5 I WAS SINFUL AT BIRTH. David acknowledges that from his infancy he possessed a natural propensity to sin; in other words, he takes responsibility for his own sinful nature. Every person is marred from birth by a selfish inclination to pursue his or her own desires and pleasures, even if it causes pain and suffering for others (see Ro 5:12, note). This inclination can be purged from our lives only through redemption in Christ and the indwelling Holy Spirit (see article on REGENERATION, p. 1589).

51:10 CREATE IN ME A PURE HEART. All believers need God's Spirit to create in them a pure heart that hates sin and a renewed spirit that desires to do God's will. Only God can make us a new creation and restore us to true godliness (Jn 3:3; 2Co 5:17; see article on REGENERATION, p. 1589).

51:11 OR TAKE YOUR HOLY SPIRIT FROM ME. David knows that if God removes the Holy Spirit's convicting and reproving work from his life, then all hope of redemption is gone (see Jn 16:8, note).

51:12 RESTORE TO ME THE JOY OF YOUR SALVATION. The Lord restored to David the joy of salvation, but note the following about David's life: (1) Scripture clearly teaches that we will reap what we sow: if we sow to please the Spirit, we will reap life from the Spirit; if we sow to please the sinful nature, we will reap destruction from the sinful nature (Gal 6:7–8). As a result of David's sin, he suffered lifelong consequences in his own life, in his family life and in his kingdom (2Sa 12:1–14). (2) The dreadful consequences of sin that David experienced, even after his sincere confession and repentance, should instill in all God's children a holy fear about choosing to sin in spiteful rebellion against the redemption provided us in Jesus Christ (see 2Sa 12, notes).

17The sacrifices[u] of God are[t] a
broken spirit;
a broken and contrite heart,[v]
O God, you will not despise.

18In your good pleasure make Zion[w]
prosper;
build up the walls of
Jerusalem.[x]

19Then there will be righteous
sacrifices,[y]
whole burnt offerings[z] to
delight you;
then bulls[a] will be offered on
your altar.

Psalm 52

For the director of music. A *maskil*[u] of David. When Doeg the Edomite[b] had gone to Saul and told him: "David has gone to the house of Ahimelech."

1Why do you boast of evil, you
mighty man?
Why do you boast[c] all day
long,[d]
you who are a disgrace in the
eyes of God?
2Your tongue plots destruction;[e]
it is like a sharpened razor,[f]
you who practice deceit.[g]
3You love evil[h] rather than good,
falsehood[i] rather than speaking
the truth. *Selah*
4You love every harmful word,
O you deceitful tongue![j]

5Surely God will bring you down to
everlasting ruin:
He will snatch you up and tear[k]
you from your tent;
he will uproot[l] you from the
land of the living.[m] *Selah*
6The righteous will see and fear;
they will laugh[n] at him, saying,
7"Here now is the man
who did not make God his
stronghold[o]
but trusted in his great wealth[p]
and grew strong by destroying
others!"

8But I am like an olive tree[q]
flourishing in the house of God;
I trust[r] in God's unfailing love
for ever and ever.
9I will praise you forever[s] for what
you have done;
in your name I will hope,[t] for
your name is good.[u]
I will praise you in the presence
of your saints.[v]

Psalm 53

53:1–6pp — Ps 14:1–7

For the director of music. According to *mahalath.*[v] A *maskil*[u] of David.

1The fool[w] says in his heart,
"There is no God."[x]
They are corrupt, and their ways
are vile;
there is no one who does good.

2God looks down from heaven[y]
on the sons of men
to see if there are any who
understand,[z]
any who seek God.[a]
3Everyone has turned away,
they have together become
corrupt;
there is no one who does good,
not even one.[b]

4Will the evildoers never learn—
those who devour my people as
men eat bread
and who do not call on God?
5There they were, overwhelmed
with dread,
where there was nothing to
dread.[c]
God scattered the bones[d] of those
who attacked you;[e]
you put them to shame,[f] for
God despised them.[g]

6Oh, that salvation for Israel would
come out of Zion!
When God restores the fortunes
of his people,
let Jacob rejoice and Israel be
glad!

51:17 [u]Pr 15:8; Hag 2:14 [v]Mt 11:29 **51:18** [w]Ps 102:16; 147:2; Isa 14:32; 51:3; Zec 1:16-17 [x]Ps 69:35; Isa 44:26 **51:19** [y]Dt 33:19 [z]Ps 66:13; 96:8; Jer 17:26 [a]Ps 66:15 **52:1** [b]**52:1 Title** 1Sa 21:7; 22:9 [c]Ps 10:3; 94:4 [d]Ps 44:8 **52:2** [e]Ps 5:9 [f]S Nu 6:5 [g]S Ps 50:19 **52:3** [h]Ex 10:10; 1Sa 12:25; Am 5:14-15; Jn 3:20 [i]Ps 58:3; Jer 9:5; Rev 21:8 **52:4** [j]Ps 5:9; 10:7; 109:2; 120:2,3; Pr 10:31; 12:19 **52:5** [k]S Dt 29:28; S Job 40:12; Isa 22:19; Eze 17:24 [l]S Dt 28:63 [m]S Job 28:13 **52:6** [n]S Job 22:19 **52:7** [o]S 2Sa 22:3 [p]S Ps 49:6; S Pr 11:28; Mk 10:23 **52:8** [q]S Ps 1:3; S Rev 11:4 [r]Ps 6:4; 13:5 **52:9** [s]S Ps 30:12 [t]S Job 7:6; Ps 25:3 [u]Ps 54:6 [v]S Dt 7:6; Ps 16:3 **53:1** [w]Ps 74:22; 107:17; Pr 10:23 [x]Ps 10:4 **53:2** [y]S Ps 33:13 [z]Ps 82:5; Jer 4:22; 8:8 [a]2Ch 15:2 **53:3** [b]Ro 3:10-12* **53:5** [c]S Lev 26:17 [d]2Ki 23:14; Ps 141:7; Jer 8:1; Eze 6:5 [e]2Ki 17:20 [f]S Job 8:22 [g]Jer 6:30; 14:19; La 5:22

[t]17 Or *My sacrifice, O God, is* [u]Title: Probably a literary or musical term [v]Title: Probably a musical term

51:17 A BROKEN AND CONTRITE HEART. God will not turn away a broken and contrite heart that is full of remorse for sin and heavy with grief because of its wickedness. When our self-seeking, proud attitude is brought low and we cry to God for his forgiving grace, we can be sure that we will be accepted by him (cf. Isa 57:15; Lk 18:10–14).

53:1–6 THE FOOL. This psalm is almost identical with Ps 14 (see 14:1–7, note).

Psalm 54

For the director of music. With stringed instruments. A *maskil*[w] of David. When the Ziphites[h] had gone to Saul and said, "Is not David hiding among us?"

[1]Save me[i], O God, by your
name;[j]
vindicate me by your might.[k]
[2]Hear my prayer, O God;[l]
listen to the words of my mouth.
[3]Strangers are attacking me;[m]
ruthless men[n] seek my life[o]—
men without regard for God.[p]
Selah

[4]Surely God is my help;[q]
the Lord is the one who sustains
me.[r]
[5]Let evil recoil[s] on those who
slander me;
in your faithfulness[t] destroy
them.

[6]I will sacrifice a freewill offering[u]
to you;
I will praise[v] your name,
O LORD,
for it is good.[w]
[7]For he has delivered me[x] from all
my troubles,
and my eyes have looked in
triumph on my foes.[y]

Psalm 55

For the director of music. With stringed instruments. A *maskil*[w] of David.

[1]Listen to my prayer, O God,
do not ignore my plea;[z]
[2] hear me and answer me.[a]
My thoughts trouble me and I am
distraught[b]
[3] at the voice of the enemy,
at the stares of the wicked;
for they bring down suffering upon
me[c]
and revile[d] me in their anger.[e]

[4]My heart is in anguish[f] within
me;
the terrors[g] of death assail me.
[5]Fear and trembling[h] have beset
me;
horror[i] has overwhelmed me.
[6]I said, "Oh, that I had the wings of
a dove!
I would fly away and be at
rest—
[7]I would flee far away
and stay in the desert;[j]
Selah
[8]I would hurry to my place of
shelter,[k]
far from the tempest and
storm.[l]"

[9]Confuse the wicked, O Lord,
confound their speech,[m]
for I see violence and strife[n] in
the city.[o]
[10]Day and night they prowl[p] about
on its walls;
malice and abuse are within it.
[11]Destructive forces[q] are at work in
the city;
threats and lies[r] never leave its
streets.

[12]If an enemy were insulting me,
I could endure it;
if a foe were raising himself
against me,
I could hide from him.
[13]But it is you, a man like myself,
my companion, my close
friend,[s]
[14]with whom I once enjoyed sweet
fellowship[t]
as we walked with the throng at
the house of God.[u]

54:1 [h]54 Title 1Sa 23:19; 26:1 [i]S 1Sa 24:15 [j]Ps 20:1 [k]2Ch 20:6 **54:2** [l]S Ps 4:1; 5:1; 55:1 **54:3** [m]Ps 86:14 [n]Ps 18:48; 140:1, 4,11 [o]S 1Sa 20:1 [p]Ps 36:1 **54:4** [q]S 1Ch 5:20; S Ps 20:2 [r]S Ps 18:35 **54:5** [s]S Dt 32:35; Ps 94:23; Pr 24:12 [t]Ps 89:49; Isa 42:3 **54:6** [u]S Lev 7:12, 16; S Ezr 1:4; S Ps 27:6 [v]Ps 44:8; 69:30; 138:2; 142:7; 145:1 [w]Ps 52:9 **54:7** [x]Ps 34:6 [y]Ps 59:10; 92:11; 112:8; 118:7 **55:1** [z]Ps 27:9; La 3:56 **55:2** [a]Ps 4:1 [b]1Sa 1:15-16; Ps 77:3; 86:6-7; 142:2 **55:3** [c]S 2Sa 16:6-8; Ps 17:9; 143:3 [d]S Ps 44:16 [e]Ps 71:11 **55:4** [f]S Ps 6:3 [g]S Job 18:11 **55:5** [h]S Job 4:14; S 2Co 7:15 [i]Dt 28:67; Isa 21:4; Jer 46:5; 49:5; Eze 7:18 **55:7** [j]1Sa 23:14 **55:8** [k]Ps 31:20 [l]Ps 77:18; Isa 4:6; 25:4; 28:2; 29:6; 32:2 **55:9** [m]Ge 11:9; Ac 2:4 [n]Ps 11:5; Isa 59:6; Jer 6:7; Eze 7:11; Hab 1:3 [o]Ge 4:17 **55:10** [p]1Pe 5:8 **55:11** [q]Ps 5:9 [r]Ps 10:7 **55:13** [s]S 2Sa 15:12 **55:14** [t]Ac 1:16-17 [u]Ps 42:4

[w] Title: Probably a literary or musical term

54:4 GOD IS MY HELP. This psalm is an appropriate prayer for the believer facing dangers or imminent disaster. The psalmist calls for help, expecting that God will respond in his saving, delivering and healing power. Today the Lord sends the Holy Spirit to be our helper on earth and the sustainer of our souls (see Jn 14:16, note).

55:4 MY HEART IS IN ANGUISH WITHIN ME. This psalm may have been written by David after his own son Absalom betrayed him by attempting to usurp the throne; Absalom's rebellion was one of the many dreadful consequences that David suffered because of his sin with Bathsheba (see 2Sa 12:11–12, note).

55:6 WINGS OF A DOVE . . . I WOULD FLY AWAY. When we are oppressed by evil people or spiritual enemies, or when the troubles of the world bring fear, anguish and overwhelming anxiety (vv. 2–5), we too often wish to find rest and relief by escaping from our present distress (cf. Jer 9:2). However, in most cases escape from such situations is not possible. The real solution is found only in seeking refuge in God. We can do as the psalmist did—call on God evening, morning and noon (vv. 16–18) and cast our cares on the Lord by looking to him to sustain us (v. 22; see next note).

[15]Let death take my enemies by
surprise;[v]
let them go down alive to the
grave,[x w]
for evil finds lodging among
them.

[16]But I call to God,
and the LORD saves me.
[17]Evening,[x] morning[y] and noon[z]
I cry out in distress,
and he hears my voice.
[18]He ransoms me unharmed
from the battle waged against
me,
even though many oppose me.
[19]God, who is enthroned forever,[a]
will hear[b] them and afflict
them— *Selah*
men who never change their ways
and have no fear of God.[c]

[20]My companion attacks his
friends;[d]
he violates his covenant.[e]
[21]His speech is smooth as butter,[f]
yet war is in his heart;
his words are more soothing than
oil,[g]
yet they are drawn swords.[h]

[22]Cast your cares on the LORD
and he will sustain you;[i]
he will never let the righteous
fall.[j]
[23]But you, O God, will bring down
the wicked
into the pit[k] of corruption;
bloodthirsty and deceitful men[l]
will not live out half their
days.[m]

But as for me, I trust in you.[n]

55:15 [v]Ps 64:7; Pr 6:15; Isa 29:5; 47:9,11; 1Th 5:3 [w]S Ps 49:14 **55:17** [x]Ps 141:2; Ac 3:1; 10:3,30 [y]Ps 5:3; 88:13; 92:2 [z]Ac 10:9 **55:19** [a]S Ex 15:18; Dt 33:27; Ps 29:10 [b]Ps 78:59 [c]Ps 36:1; 64:4 **55:20** [d]Ps 7:4 [e]S Ps 41:9 **55:21** [f]Ps 12:2 [g]Pr 5:3; 6:24 [h]Ps 57:4; 59:7; 64:3; Pr 12:18; Rev 1:16 **55:22** [i]S Ps 18:35; Mt 6:25-34; 1Pe 5:7 [j]Ps 15:5; 21:7; 37:24; 112:6 **55:23** [k]Ps 9:15; S 30:3; 73:18; 94:13; Isa 14:15; Eze 28:8; S Lk 8:31 [l]Ps 5:6 [m]S Job 15:32 [n]Ps 11:1; 25:2; 56:3

56:1 [o]Ps 6:2 [p]Ps 57:1-3 [q]Ps 17:9 **56:2** [r]Ps 35:25; 124:3 [s]Ps 35:1 **56:3** [t]Ps 55:4-5 [u]S Ps 55:23 **56:4** [v]ver 10 [w]S Ps 27:1 [x]Ps 118:6; Mt 10:28; Heb 13:6 **56:5** [y]Ps 41:7; 2Pe 3:16 **56:6** [z]Ps 59:3; 94:21; Mk 3:6 [a]Ps 17:11 [b]Ps 71:10 **56:7** [c]Pr 19:5; Eze 17:15; Ro 2:3; Heb 12:25 [d]Ps 36:12; 55:23 **56:8** [e]S 2Ki 20:5 [f]Isa 4:3; Da 7:10; 12:1; Mal 3:16 **56:9** [g]Ps 9:3

Psalm 56

For the director of music. To the tune of "A Dove on Distant Oaks." Of David. A *miktam.*[y] When the Philistines had seized him in Gath.

[1]Be merciful to me,[o] O God, for
men hotly pursue me;[p]
all day long they press their
attack.[q]
[2]My slanderers pursue me all day
long;[r]
many are attacking me in their
pride.[s]

[3]When I am afraid,[t]
I will trust in you.[u]
[4]In God, whose word I praise,[v]
in God I trust; I will not be
afraid.[w]
What can mortal man do to
me?[x]

[5]All day long they twist my
words;[y]
they are always plotting to harm
me.
[6]They conspire,[z] they lurk,
they watch my steps,[a]
eager to take my life.[b]
[7]On no account let them escape;[c]
in your anger, O God, bring
down the nations.[d]
[8]Record my lament;
list my tears on your
scroll[z e]—
are they not in your record?[f]

[9]Then my enemies will turn back[g]

[x]15 Hebrew *Sheol* [y]Title: Probably a literary or musical term [z]8 Or / *put my tears in your wineskin*

55:22 CAST YOUR CARES ON THE LORD. When facing trials too great to bear, God invites us to cast our burdens and cares on him. He then bears the weight of them with us and sustains us in every situation. The Holy Spirit has repeated this invitation throughout redemptive history. Jesus gave this invitation in Mt 11:28–30. The apostle Peter stated that believers should humble themselves before God and "cast all your anxiety on him because he cares for you" (1Pe 5:7). And the apostle Paul exhorted us to bring all our anxieties to God in prayer, promising that the peace of God will guard our hearts and minds (see Php 4:7, note).

56:4 WHOSE WORD I PRAISE. In times of fear and trouble, we should praise God for his righteous commands, his promises and every sentence he pronounces in all of Scripture (see Ps 119). As we place our trust in God and his written Word, trust replaces fear (vv. 4,11) and God becomes our helper and deliverer (v. 13). Remember the truth, "God is for me" (v. 9; see next note; cf. Ro 8:31).

56:8 LIST MY TEARS IN YOUR SCROLL. God sees, knows and records in writing all our troubles, distresses and sufferings (cf. 139:16; Mt 6:25–32). (1) Every tear shed by a faithful believer is treasured by God and carefully preserved in his memory; he keeps a record so that he can comfort and reward us according to our suffering on earth. For every trial in which we remain faithful to God, we will reap an abundance of joy and glory when we are with him in heaven (see Ro 8:17, note; 1Pe 4:14, note). (2) Thus when troubles, anxieties, or grievous trials come our way, we must never forget that God looks at us lovingly through all our disappointing experiences, illnesses, sleepless nights, financial trials or hardships in the workplace.

when I call for help.[h]
By this I will know that God is
for me.[i]
10 In God, whose word I praise,
in the LORD, whose word I
praise—
11 in God I trust; I will not be afraid.
What can man do to me?

12 I am under vows[j] to you, O God;
I will present my thank offerings
to you.
13 For you have delivered me[a] from
death[k]
and my feet from stumbling,
that I may walk before God
in the light of life.[b][l]

Psalm 57

57:7–11pp — Ps 108:1–5

For the director of music. ⌊To the tune of⌋ "Do Not Destroy." Of David. A *miktam.*[c] When he had fled from Saul into the cave.[m]

1 Have mercy on me, O God, have
mercy on me,
for in you my soul takes
refuge.[n]
I will take refuge in the shadow of
your wings[o]
until the disaster has passed.[p]

2 I cry out to God Most High,
to God, who fulfills ⌊his purpose⌋
for me.[q]
3 He sends from heaven and saves
me,[r]
rebuking those who hotly pursue
me;[s] *Selah*
God sends his love and his
faithfulness.[t]

4 I am in the midst of lions;[u]
I lie among ravenous beasts—
men whose teeth are spears and
arrows,
whose tongues are sharp
swords.[v]

5 Be exalted, O God, above the
heavens;
let your glory be over all the
earth.[w]

6 They spread a net for my feet[x]—
I was bowed down[y] in distress.
They dug a pit[z] in my path—
but they have fallen into it
themselves.[a] *Selah*

7 My heart is steadfast, O God,
my heart is steadfast;[b]
I will sing and make music.
8 Awake, my soul!
Awake, harp and lyre![c]
I will awaken the dawn.

9 I will praise you, O Lord, among
the nations;
I will sing of you among the
peoples.
10 For great is your love, reaching to
the heavens;
your faithfulness reaches to the
skies.[d]

11 Be exalted, O God, above the
heavens;[e]
let your glory be over all the
earth.[f]

Psalm 58

For the director of music. ⌊To the tune of⌋ "Do Not Destroy." Of David. A *miktam.*[c]

1 Do you rulers indeed speak
justly?[g]
Do you judge uprightly among
men?
2 No, in your heart you devise
injustice,[h]
and your hands mete out
violence on the earth.[i]

3 Even from birth the wicked go
astray;
from the womb they are
wayward and speak lies.
4 Their venom is like the venom of a
snake,[j]
like that of a cobra that has
stopped its ears,
5 that will not heed[k] the tune of the
charmer,[l]
however skillful the enchanter
may be.

56:9 [h] Ps 102:2 [i] S Nu 14:8; S Dt 31:6; Ro 8:31 **56:12** [j] Ps 50:14 **56:13** [k] Ps 30:3; 33:19; 49:15; 86:13; 107:20; 116:8 [l] S Job 33:30 **57:1** [m] 57 Title 1Sa 22:1; 24:3; Ps 142 Title [n] Ps 2:12; 9:9; 34:22 [o] S Ru 2:12; S Mt 23:37 [p] Isa 26:20 **57:2** [q] Ps 138:8 **57:3** [r] Ps 18:9,16; 69:14; 142:6; 144:5,7 [s] Ps 56:1 [t] Ps 25:10; 40:11; 115:1 **57:4** [u] S Ps 35:17 [v] S Ps 55:21; Pr 30:14 **57:5** [w] ver 11; Ps 108:5 **57:6** [x] Ps 10:9; 31:4; 140:5 [y] S Ps 38:6; 145:14 [z] S Ps 9:15 [a] S Est 6:13; Ps 7:15; Pr 28:10; Ecc 10:8 **57:7** [b] Ps 112:7 **57:8** [c] Ps 33:2; 149:3; 150:3 **57:10** [d] S Ps 36:5 **57:11** [e] S Ps 8:1; 113:4 [f] S ver 5 **58:1** [g] Ps 82:2 **58:2** [h] Mt 15:19 [i] Ps 94:20; Isa 10:1; Lk 6:38 **58:4** [j] S Nu 21:6 **58:5** [k] Ps 81:11 [l] Ecc 10:11; Jer 8:17

[a] 13 Or *my soul* [b] 13 Or *the land of the living* [c] Title: Probably a literary or musical term

57:1 IN THE SHADOW OF YOUR WINGS. The shadow of God's wings represents his love, protection, strength and gracious presence. We take refuge under those wings when we come to him in prayer and rely on him in faith (see 17:8; 36:7; 91:4). In the shadow of his wings we are protected from everything that would work contrary to his purpose for our lives (v. 2; see 17:8, note).

6Break the teeth in their mouths,
O God;[m]
tear out, O LORD, the fangs of
the lions![n]
7Let them vanish like water that
flows away;[o]
when they draw the bow, let
their arrows be blunted.[p]
8Like a slug melting away as it
moves along,[q]
like a stillborn child,[r] may they
not see the sun.

9Before your pots can feel ⌊the heat
of⌋ the thorns[s]—
whether they be green or
dry—the wicked will be
swept away.[d][t]
10The righteous will be glad[u] when
they are avenged,[v]
when they bathe their feet in the
blood of the wicked.[w]
11Then men will say,
"Surely the righteous still are
rewarded;[x]
surely there is a God who judges
the earth."[y]

Psalm 59

For the director of music. ⌊To the tune of⌋ "Do Not Destroy." Of David. A *miktam*.[e] When Saul had sent men to watch David's house[z] in order to kill him.

1Deliver me from my enemies,
O God;[a]
protect me from those who rise
up against me.[b]
2Deliver me from evildoers[c]
and save me from bloodthirsty
men.[d]

3See how they lie in wait for me!
Fierce men conspire[e] against
me
for no offense or sin of mine,
O LORD.
4I have done no wrong,[f] yet they
are ready to attack me.[g]
Arise to help me; look on my
plight![h]
5O LORD God Almighty, the God of
Israel,[i]
rouse yourself[j] to punish all
the nations;[k]
show no mercy to wicked
traitors.[l] *Selah*

6They return at evening,
snarling like dogs,[m]
and prowl about the city.
7See what they spew from their
mouths[n]—
they spew out swords[o] from
their lips,
and they say, "Who can hear
us?"[p]
8But you, O LORD, laugh at them;[q]
you scoff at all those nations.[r]
9O my Strength,[s] I watch for you;
you, O God, are my fortress,[t]
10my loving God.

God will go before me
and will let me gloat over those
who slander me.
11But do not kill them, O Lord our
shield,[f][u]
or my people will forget.[v]
In your might make them wander
about,
and bring them down.[w]
12For the sins of their mouths,[x]
for the words of their lips,[y]
let them be caught in their
pride.[z]
For the curses and lies they utter,
13 consume them in wrath,
consume them till they are no
more.[a]
Then it will be known to the ends
of the earth
that God rules over Jacob.[b]
Selah

14They return at evening,
snarling like dogs,
and prowl about the city.
15They wander about for food[c]
and howl if not satisfied.
16But I will sing[d] of your
strength,[e]
in the morning[f] I will sing of
your love;[g]

58:6 [m]Ps 3:7 [n]S Job 4:10 58:7 [o]S Lev 26:36; S Job 11:16 [p]Ps 11:2; 57:4; 64:3 58:8 [q]Isa 13:7 [r]S Job 3:16 58:9 [s]Ps 118:12; Ecc 7:6 [t]S Job 7:10; S 21:18 58:10 [u]S Job 22:19 [v]Dt 32:35; Ps 7:9; 91:8; Jer 11:20; Ro 12:17-21 [w]Ps 68:23 58:11 [x]S Ge 15:1; S Ps 128:2; Lk 6:23 [y]S Ge 18:25 59:1 [z]59 Title 1Sa 19:11 [a]Ps 143:9 [b]S Ps 20:1 59:2 [c]Ps 14:4; 36:12; 53:4; 92:7; 94:16 [d]S Ps 26:9; 139:19; Pr 29:10 59:3 [e]S Ps 56:6 59:4 [f]Ps 119:3 [g]Mt 5:11 [h]S Ps 13:3 59:5 [i]Ps 69:6; 80:4; 84:8 [j]S Ps 44:23 [k]S Ps 9:5; S Isa 10:3 [l]Jer 18:23 59:6 [m]ver 14; Ps 22:16 59:7 [n]Ps 94:4; Pr 10:32; 12:23; 15:2,28 [o]S Ps 55:21 [p]S Job 22:13 59:8 [q]Ps 37:13; Pr 1:26 [r]Ps 2:4 59:9 [s]S Ps 18:1 [t]Ps 9:9; 18:2; 62:2; 71:3 59:11 [u]Ps 3:3; 84:9 [v]Dt 4:9; 6:12 [w]Ps 89:10; 106:27; 144:6; Isa 33:3 59:12 [x]Ps 10:7 [y]Ps 64:8; Pr 10:14; 12:13 [z]Isa 2:12; 5:15; Zep 3:11 59:13 [a]Ps 104:35 [b]Ps 83:18 59:15 [c]Job 15:23 59:16 [d]Ps 108:1 [e]S 1Sa 2:10 [f]Ps 5:3; 88:13 [g]Ps 101:1

[d]9 The meaning of the Hebrew for this verse is uncertain. [e]Title: Probably a literary or musical term [f]11 Or *sovereign*

58:10 RIGHTEOUS WILL BE GLAD WHEN THEY ARE AVENGED. This verse expresses the joy and satisfaction that God's people experience when evil is defeated and overthrown. Likewise, NT believers must desire and pray for the ultimate removal of all evil and for the establishment of God's kingdom in the new heaven and earth (see Rev 6:9–10; 11:15–17; 18:20; 19:1–4,13–18; 21:1–7).

59:13 CONSUME THEM IN WRATH. See 35:1–28, note on prayers to God to bring judgment on the enemies of his people.

for you are my fortress,[h]
my refuge in times of trouble.[i]

17O my Strength, I sing praise to you;
you, O God, are my fortress, my loving God.[j]

Psalm 60

60:5–12pp — Ps 108:6–13

For the director of music. To ⌊the tune of⌋ "The Lily of the Covenant." A *miktam*[g] of David. For teaching. When he fought Aram Naharaim[h] and Aram Zobah,[i] and when Joab returned and struck down twelve thousand Edomites in the Valley of Salt.[k]

1You have rejected us,[l] O God, and burst forth upon us;
you have been angry[m]—now restore us![n]
2You have shaken the land[o] and torn it open;
mend its fractures,[p] for it is quaking.
3You have shown your people desperate times;[q]
you have given us wine that makes us stagger.[r]

4But for those who fear you, you have raised a banner[s]
to be unfurled against the bow. *Selah*

5Save us and help us with your right hand,[t]
that those you love[u] may be delivered.
6God has spoken from his sanctuary:
"In triumph I will parcel out Shechem[v]
and measure off the Valley of Succoth.[w]
7Gilead[x] is mine, and Manasseh is mine;
Ephraim[y] is my helmet,
Judah[z] my scepter.[a]
8Moab is my washbasin,
upon Edom I toss my sandal;
over Philistia I shout in triumph.[b]"

9Who will bring me to the fortified city?
Who will lead me to Edom?
10Is it not you, O God, you who have rejected us
and no longer go out with our armies?[c]
11Give us aid against the enemy,
for the help of man is worthless.[d]
12With God we will gain the victory,
and he will trample down our enemies.[e]

Psalm 61

For the director of music. With stringed instruments. Of David.

1Hear my cry, O God;[f]
listen to my prayer.[g]
2From the ends of the earth I call to you,
I call as my heart grows faint;[h]
lead me to the rock[i] that is higher than I.
3For you have been my refuge,[j]
a strong tower against the foe.[k]
4I long to dwell[l] in your tent forever
and take refuge in the shelter of your wings.[m] *Selah*
5For you have heard my vows,[n] O God;
you have given me the heritage of those who fear your name.[o]

6Increase the days of the king's life,[p]
his years for many generations.[q]

59:16 [h]S 2Sa 22:3 [i]S Dt 4:30
59:17 [j]ver 10
60:1 [k]60 Title 2Sa 8:13 [l]2Sa 5:20; Ps 44:9 [m]Ps 79:5 [n]Ps 80:3
60:2 [o]Ps 18:7 [p]S 2Ch 7:14
60:3 [q]Ps 71:20 [r]Ps 75:8; Isa 29:9; 51:17; 63:6; Jer 25:16; Zec 12:2; Rev 14:10
60:4 [s]Isa 5:26; 11:10,12; 18:3
60:5 [t]S Job 40:14 [u]S Dt 33:12
60:6 [v]S Ge 12:6 [w]S Ge 33:17
60:7 [x]Jos 13:31 [y]S Ge 41:52 [z]S Nu 34:19 [a]S Ge 49:10
60:8 [b]S 2Sa 8:1
60:10 [c]S Jos 7:12
60:11 [d]Ps 146:3; Pr 3:5
60:12 [e]S Job 40:12; Ps 44:5
61:1 [f]Ps 64:1 [g]Ps 4:1; 86:6
61:2 [h]S Ps 6:2 [i]Ps 18:2; 31:2; 94:22
61:3 [j]Ps 9:9; S 46:1; 62:7 [k]Ps 59:9; Pr 18:10
61:4 [l]S Ps 15:1 [m]S Dt 32:11; S Mt 23:37
61:5 [n]S Nu 30:2; Ps 56:12 [o]S Ex 6:3; S Dt 33:9; Ne 1:11; Ps 102:15; Isa 59:19; Mt 6:9
61:6 [p]1Ki 3:14 [q]S Ps 21:4

[g] Title: Probably a literary or musical term
[h] Title: That is, Arameans of Northwest Mesopotamia
[i] Title: That is, Arameans of central Syria

60:1–12 YOU HAVE REJECTED US . . . YOU HAVE BEEN ANGRY. David confesses that God's people suffered a defeat in battle because God withdrew his divine help and protection when they ceased to please him and do his will. The remedy for Israel in this tragic situation is to seek God earnestly in prayer and renew their fear of him (v. 4). In the same manner, we who belong to the new covenant may experience spiritual defeat in our churches, families and personal lives because God's Spirit has been offended by our sin, our conformity to surrounding society, our pride or our forsaking the Biblical principles of truth and righteousness (see article on CHRIST'S MESSAGE TO THE SEVEN CHURCHES, p. 2008).

61:4 IN THE SHELTER OF YOUR WINGS. See 35:1–28, note; 57:1, note.

[7]May he be enthroned in God's
presence forever;[r]
appoint your love and
faithfulness to protect
him.[s]
[8]Then will I ever sing praise to
your name[t]
and fulfill my vows day after
day.[u]

61:7 [r]S Ps 41:12; Lk 22:69; Eph 1:20; Col 3:1 [s]Ps 40:11
61:8 [t]S Ex 15:1; Ps 7:17; 30:4 [u]S Nu 30:2; S Dt 23:21

Psalm 62

For the director of music. For Jeduthun. A psalm of David.

[1]My soul finds rest[v] in God
alone;[w]
my salvation comes from him.
[2]He alone is my rock[x] and my
salvation;[y]
he is my fortress,[z] I will never
be shaken.[a]

[3]How long will you assault a man?
Would all of you throw him
down—
this leaning wall,[b] this tottering
fence?
[4]They fully intend to topple him
from his lofty place;
they take delight in lies.
With their mouths they bless,
but in their hearts they curse.[c]
Selah

[5]Find rest, O my soul, in God
alone;[d]
my hope comes from him.
[6]He alone is my rock and my
salvation;
he is my fortress, I will not be
shaken.
[7]My salvation and my honor depend
on God[j];
he is my mighty rock, my
refuge.[e]
[8]Trust in him at all times,
O people;[f]
pour out your hearts to him,[g]
for God is our refuge. *Selah*

Ps 85:4-7

[9]Lowborn men[h] are but a breath,[i]
the highborn are but a lie;
if weighed on a balance,[j] they are
nothing;
together they are only a breath.
[10]Do not trust in extortion[k]
or take pride in stolen goods;[l]
though your riches increase,
do not set your heart on them.[m]

[11]One thing God has spoken,
two things have I heard:
that you, O God, are strong,[n]
[12] and that you, O Lord, are
loving.[o]
Surely you will reward each person
according to what he has
done.[p]

62:1 [v]S Ps 5:3 [w]ver 5
62:2 [x]Ps 18:31; 89:26 [y]S Ex 15:2 [z]S Ps 59:9 [a]S Job 29:18
62:3 [b]Isa 30:13
62:4 [c]Ps 28:3; 55:21
62:5 [d]ver 1
62:7 [e]S Ps 61:3
62:8 [f]Ps 37:5; Isa 26:4 [g]1Sa 1:15; Ps 42:4; Mt 26:36-46
62:9 [h]Ps 49:2 [i]S Job 7:7 [j]Isa 40:15
62:10 [k]S Ps 12:5; 1Ti 6:17 [l]Isa 61:8; Eze 22:29; Na 3:1 [m]S Job 31:25; Mt 19:23-24; 1Ti 6:6-10
62:11 [n]S 1Ch 29:11; Rev 19:1
62:12 [o]Ps 86:5; 103:8; 130:7 [p]S Job 21:31; Ps 28:4; S Mt 16:27; Ro 2:6*; 1Co 3:8; Col 3:25

Psalm 63

A psalm of David. When he was in the Desert of Judah.

[1]O God, you are my God,
earnestly I seek you;
my soul thirsts for you,[q]
my body longs for you,
in a dry and weary land
where there is no water.[r]

[2]I have seen you in the sanctuary[s]

63:1 [q]Ps 42:2; 84:2 [r]Ps 143:6
63:2 [s]S Ps 15:1; 27:4; 68:24

j 7 Or / *God Most High is my salvation and my honor*

62:1 MY SALVATION COMES FROM HIM. This psalm expresses a fundamental truth by which every believer should live. In times of trouble, affliction or opposition from enemies, we should turn to God as our ultimate refuge and deliverer. Every believer who trusts in God should be able to say: (1) I will allow no trouble, crisis or suffering to shake my confidence in God (vv. 2,6). Not only does my salvation come from him (v. 1), but he himself is my rock, my salvation and my refuge (vv. 6–7).

(2) In times of anxiety or threat I will commit myself to him and by earnest prayer tell him all that is in my heart (see Php 4:6, note).

(3) I will wait for the Lord to act on my behalf, knowing he will respond in love and in compassion for my plight (vv. 11–12).

63:1–11 EARNESTLY I SEEK YOU. Every believer should pray as David did in this psalm. (1) It describes a man's deep longing in his heart for God, one that can only be satisfied by an intimate relationship with him (see Ps 42, notes). (2) Those who profess to know God need to examine themselves by asking the following: Do I really possess a strong desire for God and his presence in my life? Or do I go through life largely consumed with secular pursuits and worldly entertainment, while prayer, Bible reading, and a deep hunger and thirst for God and his righteousness have little place or vitality in my life (see Mt 5:6, note; 6:33, note)?

63:2 BEHELD YOUR POWER AND YOUR GLORY. Not only should we earnestly seek God's presence in our personal lives, but we should also long for his Spirit, power and glory to be manifested in his house. We should pray for God to assert himself in power against satanic dominion, demonic oppression (Mt 12:28; Mk 1:34,39), sin (Ro 6), and sickness and infirmities (Mt 4:23;

and beheld your power and your
glory.[t]
3Because your love is better than
life,[u]
my lips will glorify you.
4I will praise you as long as I
live,[v]
and in your name I will lift up
my hands.[w]
5My soul will be satisfied as with
the richest of foods;[x]
with singing lips my mouth will
praise you.
6On my bed I remember you;
I think of you through the
watches of the night.[y]
7Because you are my help,[z]
I sing in the shadow of your
wings.[a]
8My soul clings to you;[b]
your right hand upholds me.[c]
9They who seek my life will be
destroyed;[d]
they will go down to the depths
of the earth.[e]
10They will be given over to the
sword[f]
and become food for jackals.[g]
11But the king will rejoice in God;
all who swear by God's name
will praise him,[h]
while the mouths of liars will be
silenced.[i]

Psalm 64

For the director of music. A psalm of David.

1Hear me, O God, as I voice my
complaint;[j]
protect my life from the threat
of the enemy.[k]
2Hide me from the conspiracy[l] of
the wicked,[m]
from that noisy crowd of
evildoers.
3They sharpen their tongues like
swords[n]
and aim their words like deadly
arrows.[o]
4They shoot from ambush at the
innocent man;[p]
they shoot at him suddenly,
without fear.[q]

5They encourage each other in evil
plans,
they talk about hiding their
snares;[r]
they say, "Who will see
them[k]?"[s]
6They plot injustice and say,
"We have devised a perfect
plan!"
Surely the mind and heart of
man are cunning.

7But God will shoot them with
arrows;
suddenly they will be struck
down.
8He will turn their own tongues
against them[t]
and bring them to ruin;
all who see them will shake
their heads[u] in scorn.[v]
9All mankind will fear;[w]
they will proclaim the works of
God
and ponder what he has done.[x]
10Let the righteous rejoice in the
LORD[y]
and take refuge in him;[z]
let all the upright in heart praise
him![a]

63:2 [t]S Ex 16:7 **63:3** [u]Ps 36:7; 69:16; 106:45; 109:21 **63:4** [v]Ps 104:33; 146:2; Isa 38:20 [w]S Ps 28:2; 1Ti 2:8 **63:5** [x]S Ps 36:8; Mt 5:6 **63:6** [y]Dt 6:4-9; Ps 16:7; 119:148; Mt 14:25 **63:7** [z]Ps 27:9; 118:7 [a]S Ru 2:12 **63:8** [b]S Nu 32:12; Hos 6:3 [c]S Ps 41:12 **63:9** [d]Ps 40:14 [e]Ps 55:15; 71:20; 95:4; 139:15 **63:10** [f]Jer 18:21; Eze 35:5; Am 1:11 [g]La 5:18 **63:11** [h]Isa 19:18; 45:23; 65:16 [i]S Job 5:16; Ro 3:19 **64:1** [j]Ps 142:2 [k]Ps 140:1 **64:2** [l]S Ex 1:10 [m]Ps 56:6; 59:2

64:3 [n]S Ps 55:21; Isa 49:2 [o]S Ps 7:13; S 58:7 **64:4** [p]S Job 9:23; Ps 10:8; 11:2 [q]S Ps 55:19 **64:5** [r]Ps 91:3; 119:110; 140:5; 141:9 [s]S Job 22:13 **64:8** [t]S Ps 59:12; Pr 18:7 [u]S 2Ki 19:21; Ps 109:25 [v]S Dt 28:37 **64:9** [w]S Ps 40:3 [x]Jer 51:10 **64:10** [y]S Job 22:19 [z]Ps 11:1; 25:20; 31:2 [a]Ps 32:11

[k]5 Or *us*

9:35; Ac 4:30; 8:7). We should fervently desire that the gospel might convict and save sinners (Jn 16:8–11; Ac 4:33), sanctify them (Jn 17:17) and bring them into the Spirit's fullness (Ac 1:8; 2:4; see article on THE KINGDOM OF GOD, p. 1430).

63:6 I REMEMBER YOU; I THINK OF YOU. Along with prayer and reading God's Word, we should strive to center our thoughts on God day and night. Remembering God must not be an occasional occurrence, but a repeated experience of looking to heaven in praise, acknowledging his presence and lordship, and communing with him. Nothing would be better than that our first thought in the morning and our last thought at night be on his grace, character, love and plan for us. And when we find it impossible to sleep during the night, we can again turn our minds and hearts to God.

64:1–10 PROTECT MY LIFE. The psalmist prays to God for protection from the plots and deception of his enemies. We can apply this prayer to our spiritual battles with Satan. We must pray to be protected from the evil one and those whom he uses against us (see Mt 6:13, note). In these struggles, we can be confident of God's saving actions on our behalf (vv. 9–10; see article on POWER OVER SATAN AND DEMONS, p. 1484).

Psalm 65

For the director of music. A psalm of David. A song.

1Praise awaits[l] you, O God, in
Zion;[b]
to you our vows will be
fulfilled.[c]
2O you who hear prayer,
to you all men will come.[d]
3When we were overwhelmed by
sins,[e]
you forgave[m] our
transgressions.[f]
4Blessed are those you choose[g]
and bring near[h] to live in your
courts!
We are filled with the good things
of your house,[i]
of your holy temple.
5You answer us with awesome
deeds of righteousness,[j]
O God our Savior,[k]
the hope of all the ends of the
earth[l]
and of the farthest seas,[m]
6who formed the mountains[n] by
your power,
having armed yourself with
strength,[o]
7who stilled the roaring of the
seas,[p]
the roaring of their waves,
and the turmoil of the nations.[q]
8Those living far away fear your
wonders;
where morning dawns and
evening fades
you call forth songs of joy.[r]
9You care for the land and water
it;[s]
you enrich it abundantly.[t]
The streams of God are filled with
water
to provide the people with
grain,[u]
for so you have ordained it.[n]
10You drench its furrows
and level its ridges;
you soften it with showers[v]
and bless its crops.
11You crown the year with your
bounty,[w]
and your carts overflow with
abundance.[x]
12The grasslands of the desert
overflow;[y]
the hills are clothed with
gladness.[z]
13The meadows are covered with
flocks[a]
and the valleys are mantled with
grain;[b]
they shout for joy and sing.[c]

Psalm 66

For the director of music. A song. A psalm.

1Shout with joy to God, all the
earth![d]
2 Sing the glory of his name;[e]
make his praise glorious![f]
3Say to God, "How awesome are
your deeds![g]
So great is your power
that your enemies cringe[h]
before you.
4All the earth bows down[i] to you;
they sing praise[j] to you,
they sing praise to your name."
Selah

5Come and see what God has done,
how awesome his works[k] in
man's behalf!
6He turned the sea into dry land,[l]

65:1 [b]Ps 2:6 [c]S Dt 23:21; Ps 116:18 **65:2** [d]Ps 86:9; Isa 66:23 **65:3** [e]S Ps 40:12 [f]Ps 79:9; Ro 3:25; Heb 9:14 **65:4** [g]S Ps 33:12 [h]S Nu 16:5 [i]S Ps 36:8 **65:5** [j]S Dt 4:34; S Ps 45:4; 106:22; Isa 64:3 [k]Ps 18:46; 68:19; 85:4 [l]S Ps 48:10 [m]Ps 107:23 **65:6** [n]Am 4:13 [o]S Ps 18:1; 93:1; Isa 51:9 **65:7** [p]Ps 89:9; 93:3-4; 107:29; S Mt 8:26 [q]Dt 32:41; Ps 2:1; 74:23; 139:20; Isa 17:12-13 **65:8** [r]Ps 100:2; 107:22; 126:2; Isa 24:16; 52:9 **65:9** [s]S Lev 26:4 [t]Ps 104:24 [u]S Ge 27:28; S Dt 32:14; Ps 104:14 **65:10** [v]S Dt 32:2; S 2Sa 1:21; S Job 36:28; Ac 14:17 **65:11** [w]S Dt 28:12; Ps 104:28; Jn 10:10 [x]Job 36:28; Ps 147:14; Lk 6:38 **65:12** [y]S Job 28:26; Joel 2:22 [z]Ps 98:8 **65:13** [a]Ps 144:13; Isa 30:23; Zec 8:12 [b]Ps 72:16 [c]Ps 98:8; Isa 14:8; 44:23; 49:13; 55:12 **66:1** [d]Ps 81:1; 84:8; 95:1; 98:4; 100:1 **66:2** [e]Ps 79:9; 86:9 [f]Isa 42:8,12; 43:21 **66:3** [g]S Dt 7:21; S 10:21; Ps 65:5; 106:22; 111:6; 145:6 [h]S 2Sa 22:45 **66:4** [i]Ps 22:27 [j]Ps 7:17; 67:3 **66:5** [k]ver 3; Ps 106:22 **66:6** [l]S Ge 8:1; S Ex 14:22

[l]*1* Or *befits*; the meaning of the Hebrew for this word is uncertain. [m]*3* Or *made atonement for* [n]*9* Or *for that is how you prepare the land*

65:4 BLESSED ARE THOSE YOU . . . BRING NEAR. Our greatest joy is to be near God and to enjoy communion with him; this is now possible for all believers through the sacrifice of Jesus Christ (Heb 10:10–22) and through the indwelling Holy Spirit (Eph 5:18). The Bible exhorts us to draw near to God continually, that we might receive his mercy and strength to help us in our times of need (Heb 4:16; 7:25). Our greatest shame would be to treat lightly this privilege of nearness with God, considering it to be unworthy of our constant endeavor (cf. Heb 10:36–39).

66:5 COME AND SEE WHAT GOD HAS DONE. A community of believers must have the works of the Holy Spirit so manifested in their midst that they can glorify God and say to others, "Come and see what God has done" (see article on SPIRITUAL GIFTS FOR BELIEVERS, p. 1770). Nothing short of the full demonstration of God's power among his people will convince the lost of the truth of the gospel of Christ (see article on SIGNS OF BELIEVERS, p. 1513). We must also witness to others on a personal level, giving testimony to God's continual care in our lives (v. 16).

they passed through[m] the
waters on foot—
come, let us rejoice[n] in him.
7He rules forever[o] by his power,
his eyes watch[p] the nations—
let not the rebellious[q] rise up
against him. *Selah*
8Praise[r] our God, O peoples,
let the sound of his praise be
heard;
9he has preserved our lives[s]
and kept our feet from
slipping.[t]
10For you, O God, tested[u] us;
you refined us like silver.[v]
11You brought us into prison[w]
and laid burdens[x] on our backs.
12You let men ride over our heads;[y]
we went through fire and water,
but you brought us to a place of
abundance.[z]

13I will come to your temple with
burnt offerings[a]
and fulfill my vows[b] to you—
14vows my lips promised and my
mouth spoke
when I was in trouble.
15I will sacrifice fat animals to you
and an offering of rams;
I will offer bulls and goats.[c]
Selah
16Come and listen,[d] all you who
fear God;
let me tell[e] you what he has
done for me.
17I cried out to him with my mouth;
his praise was on my tongue.
18If I had cherished sin in my heart,
the Lord would not have
listened;[f]
19but God has surely listened
and heard my voice[g] in prayer.
20Praise be to God,

66:6 [m] 1Co 10:1 [n] S Lev 23:40 **66:7** [o] S Ex 15:18; Ps 145:13 [p] S Ex 3:16; S Ps 11:4 [q] S Nu 17:10; Ps 112:10; 140:8 **66:8** [r] S Ps 22:23 **66:9** [s] Ps 30:3 [t] S Dt 32:35; S Job 12:5 **66:10** [u] S Ex 15:25 [v] S Job 6:29; S 28:1; S Ps 12:6 **66:11** [w] Ps 142:7; 146:7; Isa 42:7, 22; 61:1 [x] S Ge 3:17; S Ex 1:14; Ps 38:4; Isa 10:27 **66:12** [y] Isa 51:23 [z] Ps 18:19 **66:13** [a] S Ps 51:19 [b] Ps 22:25; 50:14; 116:14; Ecc 5:4; Jnh 2:9 **66:15** [c] S Lev 16:5; Ps 51:19 **66:16** [d] Ps 34:11 [e] Ps 71:15,24 **66:18** [f] S Dt 1:45; S 1Sa 8:18; Jas 4:3 **66:19** [g] S Ps 18:6

66:20 [h] Ps 22:24 **67:1** [i] Nu 6:24-26 **67:2** [j] Isa 40:5; 52:10; 62:1 [k] Ps 98:2; Isa 62:2; Ac 10:35; Tit 2:11 **67:3** [l] ver 5 **67:4** [m] Ps 100:1-2 [n] S Ps 9:4; 96:10-13 [o] Ps 68:32 **67:6** [p] S Ge 8:22; S Lev 26:4; Ps 85:12; Isa 55:10; Eze 34:27; Zec 8:12 [q] S Ge 12:2 **67:7** [r] S Ps 2:8 [s] Ps 33:8 **68:1** [t] Ps 12:5; 132:8 [u] Ps 18:14; 89:10; 92:9; 144:6

who has not rejected[h] my
prayer
or withheld his love from me!

Psalm 67

For the director of music. With
stringed instruments. A psalm.
A song.

1May God be gracious to us and
bless us
and make his face shine upon
us,[i] *Selah*
2that your ways may be known on
earth,
your salvation[j] among all
nations.[k]

3May the peoples praise you,
O God;
may all the peoples praise
you.[l]
4May the nations be glad and sing
for joy,[m]
for you rule the peoples justly[n]
and guide the nations of the
earth.[o] *Selah*
5May the peoples praise you,
O God;
may all the peoples praise you.

6Then the land will yield its
harvest,[p]
and God, our God, will bless
us.[q]
7God will bless us,
and all the ends of the earth[r]
will fear him.[s]

Psalm 68

For the director of music. Of David.
A psalm. A song.

1May God arise,[t] may his enemies
be scattered;[u]

66:18 IF I HAD CHERISHED SIN. Those who take pleasure in unrighteousness have no hope of answered prayer when they call on God. God wants us separated from sin; only then will he respond to us as a Father to a son (2Co 6:14–18; see Jas 4:3, note; 1Jn 3:22, note; see article on EFFECTIVE PRAYING, p. 496).

67:1–2 MAY GOD . . . BLESS US . . . THAT YOUR WAYS MAY BE KNOWN. This psalm speaks of God's plan for his people when he first called Abraham (see Ge 12:1–3; cf. Nu 6:24). (1) God chose this man so that through his descendants, God might become known to the nations of the world. He intended that Israel's reception and enjoyment of his grace and blessings would cause the pagan nations to take notice, so that they might praise him and accept his ways of truth and righteousness.

(2) NT believers should pray that God will bless them and their families with his presence, love, grace, guidance, salvation, healing power and fullness of the Spirit, in order that the lost might seek Christ's truth and salvation (Mt 5:14–16).

(3) The key to effective evangelism and mission work is the blessing of God richly poured out on his people (vv. 2,7). This blessing is described in the NT as the promised Holy Spirit (Gal 3:14), sent by the Father into our hearts (Gal 4:6). Through this Spirit living within us, the proclamation to the nations will achieve its desired results (cf. Ac 1:8).

may his foes flee[v] before him.
2As smoke[w] is blown away by the
wind,
may you blow them away;
as wax melts[x] before the fire,
may the wicked perish[y] before
God.
3But may the righteous be glad
and rejoice[z] before God;
may they be happy and joyful.

4Sing to God, sing praise to his
name,[a]
extol him who rides on the
clouds[o][b]—
his name is the LORD[c]—
and rejoice before him.
5A father to the fatherless,[d] a
defender of widows,[e]
is God in his holy dwelling.[f]
6God sets the lonely[g] in
families,[p][h]
he leads forth the prisoners[i]
with singing;
but the rebellious live in a
sun-scorched land.[j]

7When you went out[k] before your
people, O God,
when you marched through the
wasteland,[l] *Selah*
8the earth shook,[m]
the heavens poured down rain,[n]
before God, the One of Sinai,[o]
before God, the God of Israel.[p]
9You gave abundant showers,[q]
O God;
you refreshed your weary
inheritance.
10Your people settled in it,
and from your bounty,[r] O God,
you provided[s] for the poor.

11The Lord announced the word,
and great was the company[t] of
those who proclaimed it:
12"Kings and armies flee[u] in haste;
in the camps men divide the
plunder.[v]
13Even while you sleep among the
campfires,[q][w]
the wings of ⌊my⌋ dove are
sheathed with silver,
its feathers with shining gold."
14When the Almighty[r] scattered[x]
the kings in the land,
it was like snow fallen on
Zalmon.[y]

15The mountains of Bashan[z] are
majestic mountains;[a]
rugged are the mountains of
Bashan.
16Why gaze in envy, O rugged
mountains,
at the mountain where God
chooses[b] to reign,
where the LORD himself will
dwell forever?[c]
17The chariots[d] of God are tens of
thousands
and thousands of thousands;[e]
the Lord ⌊has come⌋ from Sinai
into his sanctuary.
18When you ascended[f] on high,[g]
you led captives[h] in your train;
you received gifts from men,[i]
even from[s] the rebellious[j]—
that you,[t] O LORD God, might
dwell there.

19Praise be to the Lord, to God our
Savior,[k]
who daily bears our burdens.[l]
Selah
20Our God is a God who saves;[m]
from the Sovereign LORD comes
escape from death.[n]

21Surely God will crush the heads[o]
of his enemies,

68:1 [v]Nu 10:35; Isa 17:13; 21:15; 33:3 **68:2** [w]S Ps 37:20 [x]S Ps 22:14 [y]S Nu 10:35; Ps 9:3; 80:16 **68:3** [z]Ps 64:10; 97:12 **68:4** [a]S 2Sa 22:50; Ps 7:17; S 30:4; 66:2; 96:2; 100:4; 135:3 [b]ver 33; S Ex 20:21; S Dt 33:26 [c]S Ex 6:3; Ps 83:18 **68:5** [d]Ps 10:14 [e]S Ex 22:22; S Dt 10:18 [f]S Dt 26:15; Jer 25:30 **68:6** [g]Ps 25:16 [h]Ps 113:9 [i]Ps 79:11; 102:20; 146:7; Isa 61:1; Lk 4:18 [j]Isa 35:7; 49:10; 58:11 **68:7** [k]S Ex 13:21 [l]Ps 78:40; 106:14 **68:8** [m]S 2Sa 22:8 [n]S Jdg 5:4; 2Sa 21:10; Ecc 11:3 [o]S Dt 33:2 [p]S Jdg 5:5 **68:9** [q]S Dt 32:2; S Job 36:28; S Eze 34:26 **68:10** [r]S Dt 28:12 [s]Ps 65:9 **68:11** [t]Lk 2:13 **68:12** [u]Jos 10:16 [v]S Jdg 5:30 **68:13** [w]S Ge 49:14 **68:14** [x]2Sa 22:15 [y]Jdg 9:48 **68:15** [z]ver 22; Nu 21:33; Jer 22:20 [a]S Ps 36:6 **68:16** [b]Dt 12:5; S Ps 2:6; 132:13 [c]Ps 132:14 **68:17** [d]S 2Ki 2:11; Isa 66:15; Hab 3:8 [e]Da 7:10 **68:18** [f]S Ps 47:5 [g]Ps 7:7 [h]Jdg 5:12 [i]Eph 4:8* [j]S Nu 17:10 **68:19** [k]S Ps 65:5 [l]Ps 81:6 **68:20** [m]S 1Sa 10:19 [n]Ps 56:13; Jer 45:5; Eze 6:8 **68:21** [o]Ps 74:14; 110:5; Hab 3:13

[o]4 Or / *prepare the way for him who rides through the deserts* [p]6 Or *the desolate in a homeland* [q]13 Or *saddlebags* [r]14 Hebrew *Shaddai* [s]18 Or *gifts for men, / even* [t]18 Or *they*

68:1–35 MAY GOD ARISE. This psalm, celebrating God's rule over and care of his people Israel and his victory over his enemies, may foreshadow (1) Christ's destruction of evil and the evil one at the end of the age, and (2) the triumph of all believers in Christ, as they rejoice eternally in God's presence (Rev 19—21).

68:5 A FATHER TO THE FATHERLESS. The fatherhood of God for the believer is emphasized in both the OT and NT. God delights in protecting the weak, disadvantaged, wronged and lonely among his people. If you feel alone in this world, you should ask God to put you under his special care and protection (see Lk 7:13, note).

68:18 WHEN YOU ASCENDED ON HIGH. This verse describes God's triumphal march in Israel's history, culminating with the establishment of his rule in Jerusalem. It also foreshadows Christ's ascension into heaven to rule as head of the church and to bring many into God's kingdom (see Eph 4:8).

68:19 WHO DAILY BEARS OUR BURDENS. See 55:22, note.

the hairy crowns of those who
go on in their sins.
22The Lord says, "I will bring them
from Bashan;
I will bring them from the
depths of the sea,[p]
23that you may plunge your feet in
the blood of your foes,[q]
while the tongues of your dogs[r]
have their share."

24Your procession has come into
view, O God,
the procession of my God and
King into the sanctuary.[s]
25In front are the singers,[t] after
them the musicians;[u]
with them are the maidens
playing tambourines.[v]
26Praise God in the great
congregation;[w]
praise the LORD in the assembly
of Israel.[x]
27There is the little tribe[y] of
Benjamin,[z] leading them,
there the great throng of Judah's
princes,
and there the princes of Zebulun
and of Naphtali.[a]

28Summon your power,[b] O God[u];
show us your strength,[c] O God,
as you have done[d] before.
29Because of your temple at
Jerusalem
kings will bring you gifts.[e]
30Rebuke the beast[f] among the
reeds,[g]
the herd of bulls[h] among the
calves of the nations.
Humbled, may it bring bars of
silver.
Scatter the nations[i] who
delight in war.[j]
31Envoys will come from Egypt;[k]
Cush[v][l] will submit herself to
God.

32Sing to God, O kingdoms of the
earth,[m]
sing praise[n] to the Lord, *Selah*
33to him who rides[o] the ancient
skies above,
who thunders[p] with mighty
voice.[q]
34Proclaim the power[r] of God,
whose majesty[s] is over Israel,
whose power is in the skies.
35You are awesome,[t] O God, in
your sanctuary;[u]
the God of Israel gives power
and strength[v] to his
people.[w]

Praise be to God![x]

Psalm 69

For the director of music. To ⌊the tune of⌋ "Lilies." Of David.

1Save me, O God,
for the waters[y] have come up
to my neck.[z]
2I sink in the miry depths,[a]
where there is no foothold.
I have come into the deep waters;
the floods engulf me.
3I am worn out calling for help;[b]
my throat is parched.
My eyes fail,[c]
looking for my God.
4Those who hate me[d] without
reason[e]
outnumber the hairs of my head;
many are my enemies without
cause,[f]
those who seek to destroy me.[g]
I am forced to restore
what I did not steal.

68:22 [p] S Job 36:30; Mt 18:6 **68:23** [q] Ps 58:10 [r] S 1Ki 21:19; S 2Ki 9:36 **68:24** [s] S Ps 63:2 **68:25** [t] S 1Ch 15:16 [u] S 1Ch 6:31; S 2Ch 5:12; Rev 18:22 [v] S Ge 31:27; S Isa 5:12 **68:26** [w] S Ps 22:22; Heb 2:12 [x] S Lev 19:2 **68:27** [y] S 1Sa 9:21 [z] S Nu 34:21 [a] S Jdg 5:18 **68:28** [b] S Ex 9:16 [c] Ps 29:11 [d] Isa 26:12; 29:23; 45:11; 60:21; 64:8 **68:29** [e] S 2Ch 9:24; S 32:23 **68:30** [f] Isa 27:1; 51:9; Eze 29:3 [g] S Job 40:21 [h] Ps 22:12; Isa 34:7; Jer 50:27 [i] Ps 18:14; 89:10 [j] Ps 120:7; 140:2 **68:31** [k] Isa 19:19; 43:3; 45:14 [l] Isa 11:11; 18:1; Zep 3:10 **68:32** [m] S Ps 46:6; 67:4 [n] Ps 7:17 **68:33** [o] S Dt 33:26 [p] S Ex 9:23; S Ps 29:3 [q] Ps 29:4; Isa 30:30; 33:3; 66:6 **68:34** [r] ver 28 [s] Ps 45:3 **68:35** [t] S Dt 7:21 [u] S Ge 28:17 [v] Ps 18:1; Isa 40:29; 41:10; 50:2 [w] S Ps 29:11 [x] Ps 28:6; 66:20; 2Co 1:3 **69:1** [y] S Ps 42:7 [z] Ps 32:6; Jnh 2:5 **69:2** [a] S Job 30:19 **69:3** [b] Ps 6:6 [c] Ps 119:82 **69:4** [d] S Ps 25:19 [e] Jn 15:25* [f] S Ps 35:19; 38:19 [g] Ps 40:14; 119:95; Isa 32:7

[u] *28* Many Hebrew manuscripts, Septuagint and Syriac; most Hebrew manuscripts *Your God has summoned power for you* [v] *31* That is, the upper Nile region

69:1–36 SAVE ME. This psalm, along with Ps 22, is one of the most frequently quoted psalms in the NT. Ps 69 is quoted as follows: v. 4 - Jn 15:25; v. 9 - Jn 2:17; Ro 15:3; vv. 22–23 - Ro 11:9–10; v. 25 - Ac 1:20. (1) The author describes a person in the depths of despair, suffering greatly in every possible way because of his faithfulness to God and his righteous ways (vv. 7–12). He wants to worship God in the way God has commanded (vv. 9–12). Tradition assigns this psalm to David (see the psalm title), but it may have been written by Hezekiah (cf. 2Ki 18—20; 2Ch 29—32), Jeremiah (cf. Jer 11:19; 12:1) or an unknown Jew desiring to rebuild the temple after the exile (cf. v. 9). (2) Some portions of this psalm prefigure the sufferings of Jesus; however, the confession of v. 5, as well as the curses of vv. 22–28, cannot be applied to Christ.

69:1–4 SAVE ME, O GOD. This expression of the oppressive sufferings of a righteous person also captures the feelings of the Savior as he underwent persecution from the ungodly and experienced the agony of the cross. Similarly, any righteous believer who undergoes great trouble and sees no way out may cry to God, confident that as God eventually delivered Christ from all his suffering, he will likewise deliver all his children at his own appointed time.

5You know my folly,[h] O God;
my guilt is not hidden from
you.[i]
6May those who hope in you
not be disgraced because of me,
O Lord, the LORD Almighty;
may those who seek you
not be put to shame because of
me,
O God of Israel.
7For I endure scorn[j] for your
sake,[k]
and shame covers my face.[l]
8I am a stranger to my brothers,
an alien to my own mother's
sons;[m]
9for zeal for your house consumes
me,[n]
and the insults of those who
insult you fall on me.[o]
10When I weep and fast,[p]
I must endure scorn;
11when I put on sackcloth,[q]
people make sport of me.
12Those who sit at the gate[r] mock
me,
and I am the song of the
drunkards.[s]

13But I pray to you, O LORD,
in the time of your favor;[t]
in your great love,[u] O God,
answer me with your sure
salvation.
14Rescue me from the mire,
do not let me sink;
deliver me from those who hate
me,
from the deep waters.[v]
15Do not let the floodwaters[w] engulf
me
or the depths swallow me up[x]
or the pit close its mouth over
me.[y]
16Answer me, O LORD, out of the
goodness of your love;[z]
in your great mercy turn to me.
17Do not hide your face[a] from your
servant;
answer me quickly,[b] for I am in
trouble.[c]
18Come near and rescue me;
redeem[d] me because of my
foes.
19You know how I am scorned,[e]
disgraced and shamed;
all my enemies are before you.
20Scorn has broken my heart
and has left me helpless;
I looked for sympathy, but there
was none,
for comforters,[f] but I found
none.[g]
21They put gall in my food
and gave me vinegar[h] for my
thirst.[i]
22May the table set before them
become a snare;
may it become retribution and[w]
a trap.[j]
23May their eyes be darkened so
they cannot see,
and their backs be bent
forever.[k]
24Pour out your wrath[l] on them;
let your fierce anger overtake
them.
25May their place be deserted;[m]
let there be no one to dwell in
their tents.[n]
26For they persecute those you
wound
and talk about the pain of those
you hurt.[o]
27Charge them with crime upon
crime;[p]
do not let them share in your
salvation.[q]
28May they be blotted out of the
book of life[r]
and not be listed with the
righteous.[s]

29I am in pain and distress;
may your salvation, O God,
protect me.[t]

30I will praise God's name in song[u]
and glorify him[v] with
thanksgiving.
31This will please the LORD more
than an ox,

69:5 [h]Ps 38:5 [i]S Ps 44:21
69:7 [j]S Ps 39:8 [k]Jer 15:15 [l]Ps 44:15
69:8 [m]Job 19:13-15; Ps 31:11; 38:11; Isa 53:3; Jn 7:5
69:9 [n]Jn 2:17* [o]Ps 89:50-51; Ro 15:3*
69:10 [p]S Ps 35:13
69:11 [q]S 2Sa 3:31; S Ps 35:13
69:12 [r]S Ge 18:1; S 23:10 [s]Job 30:9
69:13 [t]Isa 49:8; 2Co 6:2 [u]S Ps 17:7; 51:1
69:14 [v]ver 2; Ps 144:7
69:15 [w]Ps 124:4-5 [x]Nu 16:33 [y]Ps 28:1
69:16 [z]S Ps 63:3
69:17 [a]S Ps 22:24 [b]Ps 143:7 [c]S Ps 50:15; 66:14
69:18 [d]Ps 49:15
69:19 [e]S Ps 22:6
69:20 [f]Job 16:2 [g]Ps 142:4; Isa 63:5
69:21 [h]S Nu 6:3; Mt 27:48; Mk 15:36; Lk 23:36 [i]Mt 27:34; Mk 15:23; Jn 19:28-30
69:22 [j]S 1Sa 28:9; S Job 18:10
69:23 [k]Ro 11:9-10*
69:24 [l]Ps 79:6; Jer 10:25
69:25 [m]S Lev 26:43; Mt 23:38 [n]Ac 1:20*
69:26 [o]S Job 19:22; Zec 1:15
69:27 [p]Ne 4:5 [q]Ps 109:14
69:28 [r]Ex 32:32-33; S Lk 10:20 [s]Eze 13:9
69:29 [t]S Ps 20:1
69:30 [u]Ps 28:7 [v]Ps 34:3

[w]22 Or *snare / and their fellowship become*

69:9 ZEAL FOR YOUR HOUSE CONSUMES ME. The psalmist bears rejection, shame and alienation because of his righteous zeal for God's house and kingdom (vv. 6–9). He has spoken against sin and has pleaded for revival, cleansing and reformation among God's people; for this he has suffered at the hands of those who were comfortable with the spiritual status quo (vv. 9–11).

69:22–28 MAY THE TABLE . . . BECOME A SNARE. The psalmist prays for judgment to come on those who oppose God and inflict suffering on the righteous. Paul applied these verses to those Jews who continued to reject Christ and his salvation (Ro 11:9–10).

more than a bull with its horns
and hoofs.[w]
32The poor will see and be glad[x]—
you who seek God, may your
hearts live![y]
33The LORD hears the needy[z]
and does not despise his captive
people.
34Let heaven and earth praise
him,
the seas and all that move in
them,[a]
35for God will save Zion[b]
and rebuild the cities of Judah.[c]
Then people will settle there and
possess it;
36 the children of his servants will
inherit it,[d]
and those who love his name
will dwell there.[e]

Psalm 70

70:1–5pp — Ps 40:13–17

For the director of music. Of David.
A petition.

1Hasten, O God, to save me;
O LORD, come quickly to help
me.[f]
2May those who seek my life[g]
be put to shame and confusion;
may all who desire my ruin
be turned back in disgrace.[h]
3May those who say to me, "Aha!
Aha!"[i]
turn back because of their
shame.
4But may all who seek you[j]
rejoice and be glad[k] in you;
may those who love your salvation
always say,
"Let God be exalted!"[l]

5Yet I am poor and needy;[m]
come quickly to me,[n] O God.
You are my help[o] and my
deliverer;[p]
O LORD, do not delay.[q]

69:31 [w]Ps 50:9-13; 51:16 **69:32** [x]S Ps 34:2 [y]Ps 22:26 **69:33** [z]Ps 12:5 **69:34** [a]Ps 96:11; 98:7; Isa 44:23 **69:35** [b]Ob 1:17 [c]S Ezr 9:9; S Ps 51:18 **69:36** [d]Ps 25:13 [e]S Ps 37:29 **70:1** [f]Ps 22:19; 71:12 **70:2** [g]Ps 35:4 [h]Ps 6:10; 35:26; 71:13; 109:29; 129:5 **70:3** [i]S Ps 35:21 **70:4** [j]Ps 9:10 [k]Ps 31:6-7; 32:11; 118:24 [l]Ps 35:27 **70:5** [m]Ps 86:1; 109:22 [n]Ps 141:1 [o]Ps 30:10; 33:20 [p]Ps 18:2 [q]Ps 119:60

71:1 [r]S Dt 23:15; Ru 2:12 [s]S Ps 22:5 **71:2** [t]S 2Ki 19:16 **71:3** [u]Ps 18:2 **71:4** [v]S 2Ki 19:19 [w]Ps 140:4 [x]S Ge 48:16 **71:5** [y]S Ps 9:18; S 25:5 [z]S Job 4:6; Jer 17:7 **71:6** [a]S Ps 22:10 [b]S Job 3:16; S Ps 22:9 [c]Ps 9:1; 34:1; 52:9; 119:164; 145:2 **71:7** [d]S Dt 28:46; Isa 8:18; 1Co 4:9 [e]S 2Sa 22:3; Ps 61:3 **71:8** [f]ver 15; Ps 51:15; 63:5 [g]Ps 96:6; 104:1 **71:9** [h]S Ps 51:11 [i]Ps 92:14; Isa 46:4 [j]S Dt 4:31; S 31:6 **71:10** [k]Ps 3:7 [l]S Ps 10:8; 59:3; Pr 1:18 [m]S Ex 1:10; S Ps 31:13; S Mt 12:14 **71:11** [n]S Ps 9:10; Isa 40:27; 54:7; La 5:20; Mt 27:46 [o]S Ps 7:2 **71:12** [p]S Ps 38:21 [q]Ps 22:19; 38:22

Psalm 71

71:1–3pp — Ps 31:1–4

1In you, O LORD, I have taken
refuge;[r]
let me never be put to shame.[s]
2Rescue me and deliver me in your
righteousness;
turn your ear[t] to me and save
me.
3Be my rock of refuge,
to which I can always go;
give the command to save me,
for you are my rock and my
fortress.[u]
4Deliver[v] me, O my God, from the
hand of the wicked,[w]
from the grasp of evil and cruel
men.[x]
5For you have been my hope,[y]
O Sovereign LORD,
my confidence[z] since my youth.
6From birth[a] I have relied on you;
you brought me forth from my
mother's womb.[b]
I will ever praise[c] you.
7I have become like a portent[d] to
many,
but you are my strong refuge.[e]
8My mouth[f] is filled with your
praise,
declaring your splendor[g] all day
long.
9Do not cast[h] me away when I am
old;[i]
do not forsake[j] me when my
strength is gone.
10For my enemies[k] speak against
me;
those who wait to kill[l] me
conspire[m] together.
11They say, "God has forsaken[n]
him;
pursue him and seize him,
for no one will rescue[o] him."
12Be not far[p] from me, O God;
come quickly, O my God, to
help[q] me.

71:1–24 I HAVE TAKEN REFUGE. This psalm contains a prayer by an older person (v. 9) who faces troubles and needs God's help to rescue him from his enemies and afflictions (vv. 1–2,18). He has walked in God's ways since childhood (vv. 5–6,17) and experienced exceptional troubles in life (v. 20), yet he has maintained his faith and confidence in God. He is determined to live the rest of his life with the confidence that God will demonstrate his power and goodness in his life.

71:9 WHEN I AM OLD. When strength is failing and the troubles of aging are more evident, we should recall God's guidance in days gone by and look to him as our protector, helper and sustainer for the last days of life. And at the hour of death when physical strength fails, we should know that he will not forsake us but will be near (vv. 12,18) as he brings us by the holy angels into his heavenly presence (Lk 16:22).

13May my accusers[r] perish in
shame;[s]
may those who want to harm me
be covered with scorn and
disgrace.[t]

14But as for me, I will always have
hope;[u]
I will praise you more and more.
15My mouth will tell[v] of your
righteousness,[w]
of your salvation all day long,
though I know not its measure.
16I will come and proclaim your
mighty acts,[x] O Sovereign
LORD;
I will proclaim your
righteousness, yours alone.
17Since my youth, O God, you have
taught[y] me,
and to this day I declare your
marvelous deeds.[z]
18Even when I am old and gray,[a]
do not forsake me, O God,
till I declare your power[b] to the
next generation,
your might to all who are to
come.[c]

19Your righteousness reaches to the
skies,[d] O God,
you who have done great
things.[e]
Who, O God, is like you?[f]
20Though you have made me see
troubles,[g] many and bitter,
you will restore[h] my life again;
from the depths of the earth[i]
you will again bring me up.
21You will increase my honor[j]
and comfort[k] me once again.

22I will praise you with the harp[l]
for your faithfulness, O my God;
I will sing praise to you with the
lyre,[m]
O Holy One of Israel.[n]
23My lips will shout for joy[o]
when I sing praise to you—
I, whom you have redeemed.[p]

71:13 [r]Jer 18:19 [s]S Job 8:22; Ps 25:3 [t]S Ps 70:2 **71:14** [u]Ps 25:3; 42:5; 130:7; 131:3 **71:15** [v]S ver 8; S Ps 66:16 [w]S Ps 51:14 **71:16** [x]Ps 9:1; 77:12; 106:2; 118:15; 145:4 **71:17** [y]S Dt 4:5; S Jer 7:13 [z]S Job 5:9; Ps 26:7; 86:10; 96:3 **71:18** [a]Isa 46:4 [b]S Ex 9:16 [c]Job 8:8; Ps 22:30,31; 78:4; 145:4; Joel 1:3 **71:19** [d]S Ps 36:5 [e]Ps 126:2; Lk 1:49 [f]Ps 35:10; 77:13; 89:8 **71:20** [g]Ps 25:17 [h]Ps 80:3,19; 85:4; Hos 6:2 [i]S Ps 63:9 **71:21** [j]Ps 18:35 [k]Ps 23:4; 86:17; Isa 12:1; 40:1-2; 49:13; 54:10 **71:22** [l]Ps 33:2 [m]S Job 21:12; Ps 92:3; 144:9 [n]S 2Ki 19:22 **71:23** [o]Ps 20:5 [p]S Ex 15:13

71:24 [q]S Ps 35:28 [r]ver 13 [s]S Est 9:2 **72:1** [t]S Dt 1:16; S Ps 9:8 **72:2** [u]Isa 9:7; 11:4-5; 16:5; 32:1; 59:17; 63:1; Jer 23:5; 33:15 **72:4** [v]S Ps 9:12; 76:9; Isa 49:13 [w]ver 13; Isa 11:4; 29:19; 32:7 [x]S Ps 27:11 **72:5** [y]1Sa 13:13 [z]Ps 33:11 **72:6** [a]S Dt 32:2 **72:7** [b]Ps 92:12; Pr 14:11 **72:8** [c]S Ex 23:31; S 1Ki 4:21 [d]Zec 9:10

24My tongue will tell of your
righteous acts
all day long,[q]
for those who wanted to harm
me[r]
have been put to shame and
confusion.[s]

Psalm 72

Of Solomon.

1Endow the king with your
justice,[t] O God,
the royal son with your
righteousness.
2He will[x] judge your people in
righteousness,[u]
your afflicted ones with justice.
3The mountains will bring
prosperity to the people,
the hills the fruit of
righteousness.
4He will defend the afflicted[v]
among the people
and save the children of the
needy;[w]
he will crush the oppressor.[x]

5He will endure[y][y] as long as the
sun,
as long as the moon, through all
generations.[z]
6He will be like rain[a] falling on a
mown field,
like showers watering the earth.
7In his days the righteous will
flourish;[b]
prosperity will abound till the
moon is no more.

8He will rule from sea to sea
and from the River[z][c] to the
ends of the earth.[a][d]
9The desert tribes will bow before
him

[x]*2* Or *May he*; similarly in verses 3-11 and 17
[y]*5* Septuagint; Hebrew *You will be feared*
[z]*8* That is, the Euphrates [a]*8* Or *the end of the land*

71:18 DECLARE YOUR POWER TO THE NEXT GENERATION. Our hope and purpose in life should be to abide in God and in the fullness of his Spirit, so that his power and goodness might be clearly manifested in our lives; thus the next generation will be inspired to seek earnestly God's kingdom and his righteousness (Mt 6:33; cf. Ac 1:8; 4:30–33; 11:24).

72:1–19 THE KING. According to the title, this psalm is Solomon's prayer as Israel's king that his reign will be characterized by justice, righteousness, peace, the destruction of evil, and deliverance for the oppressed and needy. It also points to the reign of Jesus Christ over the world (see Rev 20—22), since several of its verses apply fully only to him (vv. 8,11,17; cf. Isa 11:1–5; 60—62). This prayer is similar to the NT prayer: "Your kingdom come, your will be done on earth as it is in heaven" (Mt 6:10). This type of prayer should arise from the hearts of all who desire to see Christ reign as king and his righteousness established on the earth (see Rev 21:1, note).

and his enemies will lick the dust.
10The kings of Tarshish[e] and of distant shores[f]
will bring tribute to him;
the kings of Sheba[g] and Seba
will present him gifts.[h]
11All kings will bow down[i] to him
and all nations will serve[j] him.

12For he will deliver the needy who cry out,
the afflicted who have no one to help.
13He will take pity[k] on the weak and the needy
and save the needy from death.
14He will rescue[l] them from oppression and violence,
for precious[m] is their blood in his sight.

15Long may he live!
May gold from Sheba[n] be given him.
May people ever pray for him
and bless him all day long.[o]
16Let grain[p] abound throughout the land;
on the tops of the hills may it sway.
Let its fruit[q] flourish like Lebanon;[r]
let it thrive like the grass of the field.[s]
17May his name endure forever;[t]
may it continue as long as the sun.[u]
All nations will be blessed through him,
and they will call him blessed.[v]

18Praise be to the LORD God, the God of Israel,[w]
who alone does marvelous deeds.[x]
19Praise be to his glorious name[y] forever;
may the whole earth be filled with his glory.[z]
Amen and Amen.[a]

20This concludes the prayers of David son of Jesse.[b]

72:10 [e]S Ge 10:4 [f]S Est 10:1 [g]S Ge 10:7 [h]S 1Ki 9:16; S 2Ch 9:24 **72:11** [i]S Ge 27:29 [j]S Ezr 1:2 **72:13** [k]Isa 60:10; Joel 2:18; Lk 10:33 **72:14** [l]Ps 69:18; Eze 13:23; 34:10 [m]1Sa 26:21 **72:15** [n]S Ge 10:7 [o]S Ps 35:28 **72:16** [p]S Ge 27:28; Ps 4:7 [q]Isa 4:2; 27:6; Eze 34:27 [r]Ps 92:12; 104:16 [s]S Nu 22:4; Isa 44:4; 58:11; 66:14 **72:17** [t]S Ex 3:15 [u]Ps 89:36 [v]S Ge 12:3; Lk 1:48 **72:18** [w]1Ch 29:10; Ps 41:13; 106:48; Lk 1:68 [x]S Job 5:9 **72:19** [y]S 2Sa 7:26 [z]Nu 14:21 [a]S Ps 41:13 **72:20** [b]S Ru 4:17

73:1 [c]S Ps 24:4; Mt 5:8 **73:2** [d]S Dt 32:35 [e]Ps 69:2; Eph 4:27 **73:3** [f]Pr 3:31; 23:17; 24:1-2 [g]S Job 9:24; S 21:7; Jer 12:1; Mal 3:15 **73:5** [h]ver 12; Eze 23:42 **73:6** [i]S Lev 26:19 [j]S Ge 41:42; SS 4:9; Eze 16:11 [k]S Ge 6:11; S Pr 4:17 **73:7** [l]S Ps 17:10 **73:8** [m]Ps 41:5; Eze 25:15; Col 3:8 [n]Ps 17:10 [o]S Ps 10:7; S 12:5

BOOK III

Psalms 73–89

Psalm 73

A psalm of Asaph.

1Surely God is good to Israel,
to those who are pure in heart.[c]

2But as for me, my feet had almost slipped;[d]
I had nearly lost my foothold.[e]
3For I envied[f] the arrogant
when I saw the prosperity of the wicked.[g]

4They have no struggles;
their bodies are healthy and strong.[b]
5They are free[h] from the burdens common to man;
they are not plagued by human ills.
6Therefore pride[i] is their necklace;[j]
they clothe themselves with violence.[k]
7From their callous hearts[l] comes iniquity[c];
the evil conceits of their minds know no limits.
8They scoff, and speak with malice;[m]
in their arrogance[n] they threaten oppression.[o]
9Their mouths lay claim to heaven,
and their tongues take possession of the earth.
10Therefore their people turn to them
and drink up waters in abundance.[d]
11They say, "How can God know?
Does the Most High have knowledge?"

12This is what the wicked are like—

[b]*4* With a different word division of the Hebrew; Masoretic Text *struggles at their death; / their bodies are healthy* [c]*7* Syriac (see also Septuagint); Hebrew *Their eyes bulge with fat* [d]*10* The meaning of the Hebrew for this verse is uncertain.

73:1–28 GOD IS GOOD TO ISRAEL. This psalm deals with a disturbing problem: though God is sovereign and just, the wicked often prosper (vv. 3–12) while those who serve God seem to suffer more (vv. 13–14). The psalmist, who serves God faithfully (vv. 1,13), has become discouraged when he compares his afflictions with the apparent ease and happiness of many of the wicked (vv. 2–3). However, his confidence in God and in his ways is restored when God reveals the tragic end of the wicked and the true blessing of the righteous (vv. 16–28).

always carefree,[p] they increase
in wealth.[q]

13Surely in vain[r] have I kept my
heart pure;
in vain have I washed my hands
in innocence.[s]

14All day long I have been
plagued;[t]
I have been punished every
morning.

15If I had said, "I will speak thus,"
I would have betrayed your
children.

16When I tried to understand[u] all
this,
it was oppressive to me
17till I entered the sanctuary[v] of
God;
then I understood their final
destiny.[w]

18Surely you place them on slippery
ground;[x]
you cast them down to ruin.[y]

19How suddenly[z] are they
destroyed,
completely swept away[a] by
terrors!

20As a dream[b] when one awakes,[c]
so when you arise, O Lord,
you will despise them as
fantasies.[d]

21When my heart was grieved
and my spirit embittered,
22I was senseless[e] and ignorant;
I was a brute beast[f] before
you.

23Yet I am always with you;
you hold me by my right hand.[g]
24You guide[h] me with your
counsel,[i]
and afterward you will take me
into glory.

73:12 [p] S ver 5 [q] S Ps 49:6
73:13 [r] S Job 9:29-31; S 21:15 [s] S Ge 44:16
73:14 [t] ver 5
73:16 [u] Ecc 8:17
73:17 [v] Ex 15:17; Ps 15:1 [w] S Job 8:13; Php 3:19
73:18 [x] S Dt 32:35; Ps 35:6 [y] S Ps 17:13
73:19 [z] Dt 28:20; Pr 24:22; Isa 47:11 [a] S Ge 19:15
73:20 [b] S Job 20:8 [c] Ps 78:65; Isa 29:8 [d] Pr 12:11; 28:19
73:22 [e] Ps 49:10; 92:6; 94:8 [f] Ps 49:12,20; Ecc 3:18; 9:12
73:23 [g] S Ge 48:13
73:24 [h] S Ps 48:14 [i] S 1Ki 22:5
73:25 [j] Ps 16:2 [k] Php 3:8
73:26 [l] Ps 84:2 [m] S Ps 31:10; 40:12 [n] Ps 18:1 [o] S Dt 32:9
73:27 [p] S Ps 34:21 [q] S Lev 6:2; Jer 5:11; Hos 4:12; 9:1
73:28 [r] Zep 3:2; Heb 10:22; Jas 4:8 [s] Ps 9:9 [t] Ps 26:7; 40:5
74:1 [u] S Ps 43:2 [v] S Ps 44:23 [w] Ps 79:13; 95:7; 100:3
74:2 [x] S Ex 15:16; S 1Co 6:20 [y] S Dt 32:7 [z] S Ex 34:9 [a] S Ex 15:13; S Isa 48:20 [b] Ps 2:6 [c] Ps 43:3; 68:16; Isa 46:13; Joel 3:17,21; Ob 1:17
74:3 [d] Isa 44:26; 52:9
74:4 [e] La 2:7

25Whom have I in heaven but you?[j]
And earth has nothing I desire
besides you.[k]

26My flesh and my heart[l] may
fail,[m]
but God is the strength[n] of my
heart
and my portion[o] forever.

27Those who are far from you will
perish;[p]
you destroy all who are
unfaithful[q] to you.

28But as for me, it is good to be
near God.[r]
I have made the Sovereign LORD
my refuge;[s]
I will tell of all your deeds.[t]

Psalm 74

A *maskil*[e] of Asaph.

1Why have you rejected[u] us
forever,[v] O God?
Why does your anger smolder
against the sheep of your
pasture?[w]

2Remember the people you
purchased[x] of old,[y]
the tribe of your inheritance,[z]
whom you redeemed[a]—
Mount Zion,[b] where you
dwelt.[c]

3Turn your steps toward these
everlasting ruins,[d]
all this destruction the enemy
has brought on the
sanctuary.

4Your foes roared[e] in the place
where you met with us;

[e] Title: Probably a literary or musical term

73:17 I UNDERSTOOD THEIR FINAL DESTINY. God shows the psalmist the destiny of the wicked. (1) This revelation puts his problem in the perspective both of eternity (vv. 17–20) and of the believer's highest blessing (vv. 25–28). In the end all the righteous will succeed and triumph with God, while the wicked will perish. (2) Given the brief span of our lives, if we evaluate things simply from our limited, earth-bound, human perspective, we will almost certainly become discouraged and filled with despair. We must have God's revealed Word and his Holy Spirit in order to complete our life's journey in faith and confidence in God's goodness and justice.

73:23–28 YET I AM ALWAYS WITH YOU. The psalmist discovers the attitude that leads to the triumph of faith. In this life with all of its problems, our greatest good is intimate communion with God (v. 28). Let the wicked prosper; our hope, treasure and life is God himself—always with us, guiding us by his word and Spirit, upholding us by his power (vv. 23–24), and afterward receiving us into the glories of heaven (v. 24). Like the apostle Paul, our motto as we face life's anxieties should be: "For to me, to live is Christ and to die is gain" (Php 1:21)

74:1–23 WHY HAVE YOU REJECTED? The psalmist prays that God's chastisement may not be forever. This prayer warns us that God's patience will not tolerate sin indefinitely; eventually sorrow and calamity will come.

they set up their standards[f] as
signs.
5They behaved like men wielding
axes
to cut through a thicket of
trees.[g]
6They smashed all the carved[h]
paneling
with their axes and hatchets.
7They burned your sanctuary to the
ground;
they defiled[i] the dwelling
place[j] of your Name.[k]
8They said in their hearts, "We will
crush[l] them completely!"
They burned[m] every place
where God was worshiped
in the land.
9We are given no miraculous
signs;[n]
no prophets[o] are left,
and none of us knows how long
this will be.

10How long[p] will the enemy mock[q]
you, O God?
Will the foe revile[r] your name
forever?
11Why do you hold back your hand,
your right hand?[s]
Take it from the folds of your
garment[t] and destroy
them!

12But you, O God, are my king[u]
from of old;
you bring salvation[v] upon the
earth.
13It was you who split open the
sea[w] by your power;
you broke the heads of the
monster[x] in the waters.
14It was you who crushed the heads
of Leviathan[y]
and gave him as food to the
creatures of the desert.[z]
15It was you who opened up
springs[a] and streams;
you dried up[b] the ever flowing
rivers.
16The day is yours, and yours also
the night;
you established the sun and
moon.[c]
17It was you who set all the
boundaries[d] of the earth;
you made both summer and
winter.[e]

18Remember how the enemy has
mocked you, O LORD,

74:4 [f]S Nu 2:2; S Jer 4:6
74:5 [g]Jer 46:22
74:6 [h]S 1Ki 6:18
74:7 [i]S Lev 20:3; Ac 21:28 [j]S Lev 15:31 [k]Ps 75:1
74:8 [l]Ps 94:5 [m]2Ki 25:9; 2Ch 36:19; Jer 21:10; 34:22; 52:13
74:9 [n]S Ex 4:17; S 10:1 [o]S 1Sa 3:1
74:10 [p]Ps 6:3; 79:5; 80:4 [q]ver 22 [r]S Ps 44:16
74:11 [s]S Ex 15:6 [t]Ne 5:13; Eze 5:3
74:12 [u]Ps 2:6; S 24:7; 68:24 [v]Ps 27:1
74:13 [w]S Ex 14:21 [x]Isa 27:1; 51:9; Eze 29:3; 32:2
74:14 [y]S Job 3:8 [z]Isa 13:21; 23:13; 34:14; Jer 50:39
74:15 [a]S Ex 17:6; S Nu 20:11 [b]S Ex 14:29; S Jos 2:10
74:16 [c]S Ge 1:16; Ps 136:7-9
74:17 [d]Dt 32:8; Ac 17:26 [e]S Ge 8:22
74:18 [f]Dt 32:6
74:19 [g]S Ge 8:8; S Isa 59:11 [h]S Ps 9:18
74:20 [i]S Ge 6:18 [j]Job 34:22
74:21 [k]Ps 9:9; 10:18; 103:6; Isa 58:10 [l]S Ps 35:10
74:22 [m]Ps 17:13 [n]S Ps 53:1
74:23 [o]Isa 31:4 [p]S Ps 65:7 [q]S Ps 46:6 [r]S Nu 25:17
75:1 [s]Ps 145:18 [t]S Jos 3:5; Ps 44:1; S 71:16; 77:12; 105:2; 107:8,15; 145:5,12
75:2 [u]S Ex 13:10 [v]S Ps 7:11
75:3 [w]Isa 24:19 [x]1Sa 2:8; S 2Sa 22:8
75:4 [y]S Ps 5:5 [z]S 1Sa 2:3 [a]Zec 1:21
75:5 [b]S Job 15:25
75:7 [c]S Ge 16:5; Ps 50:6; 58:11; Rev 18:8 [d]1Sa 2:7; S Job 5:11; Ps 147:6; Eze 21:26; Da 2:21
75:8 [e]Pr 23:30

how foolish people[f] have
reviled your name.
19Do not hand over the life of your
dove[g] to wild beasts;
do not forget the lives of your
afflicted[h] people forever.
20Have regard for your covenant,[i]
because haunts of violence fill
the dark places[j] of the
land.
21Do not let the oppressed[k] retreat
in disgrace;
may the poor and needy[l] praise
your name.

22Rise up,[m] O God, and defend your
cause;
remember how fools[n] mock you
all day long.
23Do not ignore the clamor[o] of your
adversaries,[p]
the uproar[q] of your enemies,[r]
which rises continually.

Psalm 75

For the director of music. ⌊To the tune of,⌋ "Do Not Destroy." A psalm of Asaph. A song.

1We give thanks to you, O God,
we give thanks, for your Name
is near;[s]
men tell of your wonderful
deeds.[t]

2You say, "I choose the appointed
time;[u]
it is I who judge uprightly.[v]
3When the earth and all its people
quake,[w]
it is I who hold its pillars[x]
firm. *Selah*
4To the arrogant[y] I say, 'Boast no
more,'[z]
and to the wicked, 'Do not lift
up your horns.[a]
5Do not lift your horns against
heaven;
do not speak with outstretched
neck.[b]' "
6No one from the east or the west
or from the desert can exalt a
man.
7But it is God who judges:[c]
He brings one down, he exalts
another.[d]
8In the hand of the LORD is a cup
full of foaming wine mixed[e]
with spices;

he pours it out, and all the wicked
of the earth
drink it down to its very
dregs.[f]
9As for me, I will declare[g] this
forever;
I will sing[h] praise to the God of
Jacob.[i]
10I will cut off the horns of all the
wicked,
but the horns of the righteous
will be lifted up.[j]

Psalm 76

For the director of music. With stringed instruments. A psalm of Asaph. A song.

1In Judah God is known;
his name is great[k] in Israel.
2His tent is in Salem,[l]
his dwelling place in Zion.[m]
3There he broke the flashing
arrows,[n]
the shields and the swords, the
weapons of war.[o] *Selah*
4You are resplendent with light,[p]
more majestic than mountains
rich with game.
5Valiant men[q] lie plundered,
they sleep their last sleep;[r]
not one of the warriors
can lift his hands.
6At your rebuke,[s] O God of Jacob,
both horse and chariot[t] lie still.
7You alone are to be feared.[u]
Who can stand[v] before you
when you are angry?[w]
8From heaven you pronounced
judgment,
and the land feared[x] and was
quiet—
9when you, O God, rise up to
judge,[y]
to save all the afflicted[z] of the
land. *Selah*
10Surely your wrath against men
brings you praise,[a]
and the survivors of your wrath
are restrained.[f]
11Make vows to the LORD your God
and fulfill them;[b]
let all the neighboring lands
bring gifts[c] to the One to be
feared.
12He breaks the spirit of rulers;
he is feared by the kings of the
earth.

Psalm 77

For the director of music. For Jeduthun. Of Asaph. A psalm.

1I cried out to God[d] for help;
I cried out to God to hear me.
2When I was in distress,[e] I sought
the Lord;
at night[f] I stretched out
untiring hands[g]
and my soul refused to be
comforted.[h]
3I remembered[i] you, O God, and I
groaned;[j]
I mused, and my spirit grew
faint.[k] *Selah*
4You kept my eyes from closing;
I was too troubled to speak.[l]
5I thought about the former days,[m]
the years of long ago;
6I remembered my songs in the
night.
My heart mused and my spirit
inquired:
7"Will the Lord reject forever?[n]

75:8 [f]Isa 51:17; Jer 25:15; Zec 12:2
75:9 [g]Ps 40:10 [h]Ps 108:1 [i]S Ge 24:12; Ps 76:6
75:10 [j]Ps 89:17; 92:10; 112:9; 148:14
76:1 [k]Ps 99:3
76:2 [l]S Ge 14:18; Heb 7:1 [m]S 2Sa 5:7; Ps 2:6
76:3 [n]Eze 39:9 [o]Ps 46:9
76:4 [p]S Ps 36:9
76:5 [q]S Jdg 20:44 [r]S Ps 13:3; S Mt 9:24
76:6 [s]S Ps 50:21 [t]S Ex 15:1
76:7 [u]S 1Ch 16:25 [v]S Ezr 9:15; Rev 6:17 [w]Ps 2:5; Na 1:6
76:8 [x]S 1Ch 16:30; Eze 38:20
76:9 [y]S Ps 9:8; 58:11; 74:22; 82:8; 96:13
[z]S Ps 72:4
76:10 [a]Ex 9:16; Ro 9:17
76:11 [b]S Lev 22:18; S Ps 50:14; Ecc 5:4-5 [c]S 2Ch 32:23
77:1 [d]S 1Ki 8:52
77:2 [e]S Ge 32:7; S 2Sa 22:7; S Ps 118:5 [f]Ps 6:6; 22:2; 88:1 [g]S Ex 9:29; S Job 11:13 [h]S Ge 37:35; Mt 2:18
77:3 [i]Ps 78:35 [j]Ex 2:23; S Ps 6:6; Jer 45:3 [k]S Ps 6:2
77:4 [l]S Ps 39:2
77:5 [m]Dt 32:7; Ps 44:1; 143:5; Ecc 7:10
77:7 [n]S 1Ch 28:9

[f]10 Or *Surely the wrath of men brings you praise, / and with the remainder of wrath you arm yourself*

75:8 IN THE HAND OF THE LORD IS A CUP. The picture of God giving the wicked an intoxicating drink is used in Scripture as a symbol of his wrath and punishment. David states: "You have given us wine that makes us stagger" (60:3; cf. Isa 51:17,22; Jer 51:7; Rev 14:10).

76:10 BRINGS YOU PRAISE. (1) God's wrath expressed in judgment against oppressors of his people brings him praise from those who have been delivered. (2) Note also the NIV text note. The wrath of the wicked can provide the occasion for God to rescue his own and to accomplish great things on their behalf; e.g., Pharaoh's wrath against Israel became God's opportunity to demonstrate his miraculous power in delivering them from Egypt (Ex 5—12).

77:1–20 I CRIED OUT TO GOD. This psalm portrays a person in great trouble who cried out to God but could find no evidence that he was responding (vv. 7–9). Faithful believers sometimes find themselves in a similar situation. If so, they should do as this psalmist did: continue to call on God day and night (vv. 1–2) while remembering God's past deeds of love. In the fullness of God's revelation in his Son, we are reassured that "he who did not spare his own Son, but gave him up for us all—how will he not also, along with him, graciously give us all things?" (Ro 8:32).

Will he never show his favor[o]
again?
8Has his unfailing love[p] vanished
forever?
Has his promise[q] failed for all
time?
9Has God forgotten to be
merciful?[r]
Has he in anger withheld his
compassion?[s]" *Selah*
10Then I thought, "To this I will
appeal:
the years of the right hand[t] of
the Most High."
11I will remember the deeds of the
LORD;
yes, I will remember your
miracles[u] of long ago.
12I will meditate[v] on all your works
and consider all your mighty
deeds.[w]

13Your ways, O God, are holy.
What god is so great as our
God?[x]
14You are the God who performs
miracles;[y]
you display your power among
the peoples.
15With your mighty arm you
redeemed your people,[z]
the descendants of Jacob and
Joseph. *Selah*

16The waters[a] saw you, O God,
the waters saw you and
writhed;[b]
the very depths were convulsed.
17The clouds poured down water,[c]
the skies resounded with
thunder;[d]
your arrows[e] flashed back and
forth.
18Your thunder was heard in the
whirlwind,[f]
your lightning[g] lit up the world;
the earth trembled and
quaked.[h]
19Your path[i] led through the sea,[j]
your way through the mighty
waters,
though your footprints were not
seen.

20You led your people[k] like a
flock[l]
by the hand of Moses and
Aaron.[m]

Psalm 78

A *maskil*[g] of Asaph.

1O my people, hear my teaching;[n]
listen to the words of my mouth.
2I will open my mouth in
parables,[o]
I will utter hidden things, things
from of old—
3what we have heard and known,
what our fathers have told us.[p]
4We will not hide them from their
children;[q]
we will tell the next
generation[r]
the praiseworthy deeds[s] of the
LORD,
his power, and the wonders[t] he
has done.
5He decreed statutes[u] for Jacob[v]
and established the law in
Israel,
which he commanded our
forefathers
to teach their children,
6so the next generation would know
them,
even the children yet to be
born,[w]
and they in turn would tell their
children.
7Then they would put their trust in
God
and would not forget[x] his deeds
but would keep his commands.[y]
8They would not be like their
forefathers[z]—

77:7 [o]Ps 85:1; 102:13; 106:4 **77:8** [p]S Ps 6:4; 90:14 [q]2Pe 3:9 **77:9** [r]Ps 25:6; 40:11; 51:1 [s]Isa 49:15 **77:10** [t]S Ex 15:6 **77:11** [u]S Ne 9:17 **77:12** [v]S Ge 24:63 [w]Ps 143:5 **77:13** [x]S Ex 15:11; S Ps 71:19; 86:8 **77:14** [y]S Ex 3:20; S 34:10 **77:15** [z]S Ex 6:6 **77:16** [a]Ex 14:21, 28; Isa 50:2; Hab 3:8 [b]Ps 114:4; Hab 3:10 **77:17** [c]S Jdg 5:4 [d]S Ex 9:23; S Ps 29:3 [e]S Dt 32:23 **77:18** [f]S Ps 55:8 [g]S 2Sa 22:13 [h]S Jdg 5:4 **77:19** [i]S Ex 14:22 [j]S Job 9:8 **77:20** [k]S Ex 13:21 [l]Ps 78:52; Isa 63:11 [m]S Ex 4:16; S Nu 33:1 **78:1** [n]Isa 51:4; 55:3 **78:2** [o]S Ps 49:4; S Mt 13:35* **78:3** [p]S Jdg 6:13 **78:4** [q]S Dt 11:19 [r]S Dt 32:7; S Ps 71:18 [s]Ps 26:7; 71:17 [t]S Job 5:9 **78:5** [u]Ps 19:7; 81:5 [v]Ps 147:19 **78:6** [w]S Ps 22:31 **78:7** [x]S Dt 6:12 [y]S Dt 5:29 **78:8** [z]S 2Ch 30:7

[g] Title: Probably a literary or musical term

78:1 O MY PEOPLE, HEAR MY TEACHING. This psalm was written to remind Israel why so many devastating judgments of God came upon them throughout their history. (1) The song warns them to learn from the spiritual failures of their forefathers and to strive diligently to avoid the same unbelief and unfaithfulness. (2) God's people today should pay close attention to this psalm, for many churches and denominations have lost God's presence and power through unbelief and through disobedience to his word. By failing to make Biblical standards and experience the basis for truth and practice, they have gradually gone astray and turned to their own ways (cf. Isa 53:6).

78:5 TO TEACH THEIR CHILDREN. Teaching our children the godly principles and precepts of God's Word is not optional; it is a commandment he has given to his people. What God commands, he gives grace to fulfill (see Dt 6:7, note; see article on PARENTS AND CHILDREN, p. 1854).

78:8 NOT BE LIKE THEIR FOREFATHERS. God's people are exhorted not to follow in the un-

a stubborn[a] and rebellious[b]
generation,
whose hearts were not loyal to
God,
whose spirits were not faithful
to him.

9The men of Ephraim, though
armed with bows,[c]
turned back on the day of
battle;[d]
10they did not keep God's
covenant[e]
and refused to live by his law.[f]
11They forgot what he had done,[g]
the wonders he had shown them.
12He did miracles[h] in the sight of
their fathers
in the land of Egypt,[i] in the
region of Zoan.[j]
13He divided the sea[k] and led them
through;
he made the water stand firm
like a wall.[l]
14He guided them with the cloud by
day
and with light from the fire all
night.[m]
15He split the rocks[n] in the desert
and gave them water as
abundant as the seas;
16he brought streams out of a rocky
crag
and made water flow down like
rivers.

78:8 [a]S Ex 32:9 [b]S Ex 23:21; S Dt 21:18; Isa 30:9; 65:2 78:9 [c]ver 57; 1Ch 12:2; Hos 7:16 [d]S Jdg 20:39 78:10 [e]S Jos 7:11; S 2Ki 17:15 [f]S Ex 16:28; S Jer 11:8 78:11 [g]Ps 106:13 78:12 [h]S Ne 9:17; Ps 106:22 [i]Ex 11:9 [j]S Nu 13:22 78:13 [k]S Ex 14:21; Ps 66:6; 136:13 [l]S Ex 14:22; S 15:8 78:14 [m]Ex 13:21; Ps 105:39 78:15 [n]S Nu 20:11; 1Co 10:4

78:17 [o]ver 32,40; Dt 9:22; Isa 30:1; 63:10; Heb 3:16 78:18 [p]S Ex 17:2; 1Co 10:9 [q]S Ex 15:24; Nu 11:4 78:19 [r]Nu 21:5 78:20 [s]S Nu 20:11; S Isa 35:6 [t]Nu 11:18 78:21 [u]S Nu 11:1 78:22 [v]S Dt 1:32; Heb 3:19 78:23 [w]Ge 7:11; S 2Ki 7:2 78:24 [x]Ex 16:4; Jn 6:31*

17But they continued to sin[o] against
him,
rebelling in the desert against
the Most High.
18They willfully put God to the
test[p]
by demanding the food they
craved.[q]
19They spoke against God,[r] saying,
"Can God spread a table in the
desert?
20When he struck the rock, water
gushed out,[s]
and streams flowed abundantly.
But can he also give us food?
Can he supply meat[t] for his
people?"
21When the LORD heard them, he was
very angry;
his fire broke out[u] against
Jacob,
and his wrath rose against
Israel,
22for they did not believe in God
or trust[v] in his deliverance.
23Yet he gave a command to the
skies above
and opened the doors of the
heavens;[w]
24he rained down manna[x] for the
people to eat,
he gave them the grain of
heaven.
25Men ate the bread of angels;

---

faithful footsteps of their spiritual ancestors. Applied to the NT age, churches today should be careful not to pattern themselves after those churches, denominations or fellowships that have grown cold and have departed from Biblical Christianity.

Some errors that have brought spiritual ruin to a church are: (1) failure on the part of leaders to discern, and then warn the people, that they are beginning to follow the unbiblical ways of former God-fearing churches; (2) failure to make the NT revelation of Christ and the apostles the only source of life, truth and direction for the church (see Eph 2:20, note); (3) failure to foster church purity in truth, doctrine and moral matters (see article on OVERSEERS AND THEIR DUTIES, p. 1690); (4) failure to be greatly concerned as the church slides farther and farther from the NT norm; (5) failure to keep an intimate devotion to Christ and a fervent life of intercession central in the church's life (Rev 2:4); (6) toleration of sin in church leaders, teachers or laypersons that would have been severely dealt with in the past (Rev 2:14–15,20); (7) substitution of an emphasis on outward success, numbers and affluence for real spirituality, i.e., purity, righteouness, spiritual wisdom, love and the Spirit's power manifested among the people (see article on CHRIST'S MESSAGE TO THE SEVEN CHURCHES, p. 2008).

78:8 HEARTS WERE NOT LOYAL . . . SPIRITS WERE NOT FAITHFUL. No generation of believers will inherit God's kingdom in all its saving purpose and power if they fail to prepare their hearts to seek God and to discern his word and righteous ways. On the other hand, people whose hearts are set steadfastly toward God and who separate themselves from the corrupt world and all unholy compromise will know the praiseworthy deeds, power and wonder of their God (v. 4; see article on SPIRITUAL SEPARATION FOR BELIEVERS, p. 1794).

78:11 THEY FORGOT WHAT HE HAD DONE. Israel failed spiritually, at least in part, because they forgot the deeds and miracles God had performed among their founding fathers. Likewise, we must not forget God's deeds and miracles done in and through the faithful believers of the NT church. The Holy Spirit wants to act today with the same signs, wonders and miracles that he performed in former days, so that the message of redemption might go out through our lives and churches with the same power and effectiveness (see Ac 1:8, note; see article on BAPTISM IN THE HOLY SPIRIT, p. 1642).

he sent them all the food they
could eat.
26He let loose the east wind[y] from
the heavens
and led forth the south wind by
his power.
27He rained meat down on them like
dust,
flying birds[z] like sand on the
seashore.
28He made them come down inside
their camp,
all around their tents.
29They ate till they had more than
enough,[a]
for he had given them what they
craved.
30But before they turned from the
food they craved,
even while it was still in their
mouths,[b]
31God's anger rose against them;
he put to death the sturdiest[c]
among them,
cutting down the young men of
Israel.

32In spite of all this, they kept on
sinning;[d]
in spite of his wonders,[e] they
did not believe.[f]
33So he ended their days in futility[g]
and their years in terror.
34Whenever God slew them, they
would seek[h] him;
they eagerly turned to him
again.
35They remembered that God was
their Rock,[i]
that God Most High was their
Redeemer.[j]
36But then they would flatter him
with their mouths,[k]
lying to him with their tongues;
37their hearts were not loyal[l] to
him,
they were not faithful to his
covenant.
38Yet he was merciful;[m]
he forgave[n] their iniquities[o]
and did not destroy them.
Time after time he restrained his
anger[p]
and did not stir up his full
wrath.
39He remembered that they were but
flesh,[q]
a passing breeze[r] that does not
return.

40How often they rebelled[s] against
him in the desert[t]
and grieved him[u] in the
wasteland!
41Again and again they put God to
the test;[v]
they vexed the Holy One of
Israel.[w]
42They did not remember[x] his
power—
the day he redeemed them from
the oppressor,[y]
43the day he displayed his
miraculous signs[z] in
Egypt,
his wonders[a] in the region of
Zoan.
44He turned their rivers to blood;[b]
they could not drink from their
streams.
45He sent swarms of flies[c] that
devoured them,
and frogs[d] that devastated
them.
46He gave their crops to the
grasshopper,[e]
their produce to the locust.[f]
47He destroyed their vines with
hail[g]
and their sycamore-figs with
sleet.
48He gave over their cattle to the
hail,
their livestock[h] to bolts of
lightning.
49He unleashed against them his hot
anger,[i]
his wrath, indignation and
hostility—
a band of destroying angels.[j]
50He prepared a path for his
anger;

78:26 [y] S Nu 11:31 **78:27** [z] S Ex 16:13; Nu 11:31 **78:29** [a] S Nu 11:20 **78:30** [b] S Nu 11:33 **78:31** [c] Isa 10:16 **78:32** [d] S ver 17 [e] ver 11 [f] ver 22 **78:33** [g] Nu 14:29, 35 **78:34** [h] S Dt 4:29; Hos 5:15 **78:35** [i] S Ge 49:24 [j] S Dt 9:26 **78:36** [k] Eze 33:31 **78:37** [l] ver 8; Ac 8:21 **78:38** [m] S Ex 34:6 [n] Isa 1:25; 27:9; 48:10; Da 11:35 [o] Ps 25:11; 85:2 [p] S Job 9:13; S Isa 30:18 **78:39** [q] S Ge 6:3; S Isa 29:5 [r] S Job 7:7; Jas 4:14 **78:40** [s] S Ex 23:21 [t] Ps 95:8; 106:14 [u] Eph 4:30 **78:41** [v] S Ex 17:2 [w] S 2Ki 19:22; Ps 71:22; 89:18 **78:42** [x] S Jdg 3:7; S Ne 9:17 [y] S Ps 27:11 **78:43** [z] Ex 10:1 [a] S Ex 3:20 **78:44** [b] Ex 7:20-21; Ps 105:29 **78:45** [c] Ex 8:24; Ps 105:31 [d] S Ex 8:2,6 **78:46** [e] Na 3:15 [f] S Ex 10:13 **78:47** [g] Ex 9:23; Ps 105:32; 147:17 **78:48** [h] Ex 9:25 **78:49** [i] Ex 15:7 [j] S Ge 19:13; 1Co 10:10

78:37 HEARTS WERE NOT LOYAL . . . NOT FAITHFUL TO HIS COVENANT. The Israelites failed to set their hearts to follow God faithfully and completely throughout their lives. Essential to maintaining a right relationship with God is the fundamental resolve to remain faithful to God and his covenant until our day of final redemption.

78:38 HE WAS MERCIFUL; HE FORGAVE. God's patience and mercy are clearly revealed in this psalm. Over and over his people rebelled in unfaithfulness, yet God restrained his anger. God will never abandon his children simply because they fail to please him perfectly. However, God's patience and forgiveness must not be presumed upon in willful disobedience and rebellion. If we persistently grieve him by our sin, he will eventually judge us in wrath, just as he did Israel (cf. Heb 3:7–19).

he did not spare them from
death
but gave them over to the
plague.
51 He struck down all the firstborn of
Egypt,[k]
the firstfruits of manhood in the
tents of Ham.[l]
52 But he brought his people out like
a flock;[m]
he led them like sheep through
the desert.
53 He guided them safely, so they
were unafraid;
but the sea engulfed[n] their
enemies.[o]
54 Thus he brought them to the
border of his holy land,
to the hill country his right
hand[p] had taken.
55 He drove out nations[q] before
them
and allotted their lands to them
as an inheritance;[r]
he settled the tribes of Israel in
their homes.

56 But they put God to the test
and rebelled against the Most
High;
they did not keep his statutes.
57 Like their fathers[s] they were
disloyal and faithless,
as unreliable as a faulty bow.[t]
58 They angered him[u] with their
high places;[v]
they aroused his jealousy with
their idols.[w]
59 When God heard[x] them, he was
very angry;[y]
he rejected Israel[z] completely.
60 He abandoned the tabernacle of
Shiloh,[a]
the tent he had set up among
men.[b]
61 He sent ⌊the ark of⌋ his might[c]
into captivity,[d]
his splendor into the hands of
the enemy.
62 He gave his people over to the
sword;[e]
he was very angry with his
inheritance.[f]

78:51 [k]S Ex 12:12; Ps 135:8 [l]Ps 105:23; 106:22 **78:52** [m]S Job 21:11; S Ps 28:9; 77:20 **78:53** [n]S Ex 14:28 [o]Ex 15:7; Ps 106:10 **78:54** [p]Ps 44:3 **78:55** [q]Ps 44:2 [r]S Dt 1:38; S Jos 13:7; Ac 13:19 **78:57** [s]S 2Ch 30:7; Eze 20:27 [t]S ver 9 **78:58** [u]S Jdg 2:12 [v]S Lev 26:30 [w]Ex 20:4; S Dt 5:8; 32:21 **78:59** [x]Ps 55:19 [y]S Lev 26:28; S Nu 32:14 [z]S Dt 32:19 **78:60** [a]S Jos 18:1 [b]Eze 8:6 **78:61** [c]Ps 132:8 [d]S 1Sa 4:17 **78:62** [e]S Dt 28:25 [f]S 1Sa 10:1

78:63 [g]S Nu 11:1 [h]S 1Ki 4:32; Jer 7:34; 16:9; 25:10 **78:64** [i]1Sa 4:17 **78:65** [j]Ps 44:23 **78:66** [k]1Sa 5:6 **78:67** [l]Jer 7:15; Hos 9:13; 12:1 **78:68** [m]S Nu 1:7; Ps 108:8 [n]S Ex 15:17; S Ps 68:16 **78:69** [o]S Ps 15:1 **78:70** [p]S 1Sa 16:1 **78:71** [q]S Ge 37:2 [r]S Ps 28:9 **78:72** [s]S Ge 17:1 **79:1** [t]S Ex 34:9 [u]S Lev 20:3 [v]S 2Ki 25:9; S Ne 4:2; S Isa 6:11 **79:2** [w]Rev 19:17-18 [x]S Dt 28:26; Jer 7:33

63 Fire consumed[g] their young
men,
and their maidens had no
wedding songs;[h]
64 their priests were put to the
sword,[i]
and their widows could not
weep.

65 Then the Lord awoke as from
sleep,[j]
as a man wakes from the stupor
of wine.
66 He beat back his enemies;
he put them to everlasting
shame.[k]
67 Then he rejected the tents of
Joseph,
he did not choose the tribe of
Ephraim;[l]
68 but he chose the tribe of Judah,[m]
Mount Zion,[n] which he loved.
69 He built his sanctuary[o] like the
heights,
like the earth that he
established forever.
70 He chose David[p] his servant
and took him from the sheep
pens;
71 from tending the sheep[q] he
brought him
to be the shepherd[r] of his
people Jacob,
of Israel his inheritance.
72 And David shepherded them with
integrity of heart;[s]
with skillful hands he led them.

Psalm 79

A psalm of Asaph.

1 O God, the nations have invaded
your inheritance;[t]
they have defiled[u] your holy
temple,
they have reduced Jerusalem to
rubble.[v]
2 They have given the dead bodies of
your servants
as food to the birds of the air,[w]
the flesh of your saints to the
beasts of the earth.[x]

79:1–13 THE NATIONS HAVE INVADED. The psalmist here intercedes with God to forgive the Israelites for their apostasy (vv. 8–9) and to punish the nations that have destroyed Jerusalem and God's temple (vv. 6–7; Jerusalem was destroyed by the Babylonians in 586 B.C.). He acknowledges that the pagan nations were instruments of God's anger (v. 5), yet what they had done against Israel was executed out of hatred for God and his chosen people (vv. 1–7; cf. Isa 10:5–11; 47:6–7). The psalmist is motivated by concern for God's glory and the promotion of his name among the unbelieving nations (vv. 9–13).

[3]They have poured out blood like
water
all around Jerusalem,
and there is no one to bury[y]
the dead.[z]
[4]We are objects of reproach to our
neighbors,
of scorn[a] and derision to those
around us.[b]

[5]How long,[c] O LORD? Will you be
angry[d] forever?
How long will your jealousy burn
like fire?[e]
[6]Pour out your wrath[f] on the
nations
that do not acknowledge[g] you,
on the kingdoms
that do not call on your name;[h]
[7]for they have devoured[i] Jacob
and destroyed his homeland.
[8]Do not hold against us the sins of
the fathers;[j]
may your mercy come quickly to
meet us,
for we are in desperate need.[k]

[9]Help us,[l] O God our Savior,
for the glory of your name;
deliver us and forgive our sins
for your name's sake.[m]
[10]Why should the nations say,
"Where is their God?"[n]
Before our eyes, make known
among the nations
that you avenge[o] the outpoured
blood[p] of your servants.
[11]May the groans of the prisoners
come before you;
by the strength of your arm
preserve those condemned to die.
[12]Pay back into the laps[q] of our
neighbors seven times[r]
the reproach they have hurled at
you, O Lord.
[13]Then we your people, the sheep of
your pasture,[s]
will praise you forever;[t]
from generation to generation
we will recount your praise.

79:3 [y]Jer 25:33; Rev 11:9 [z]Jer 16:4
79:4 [a]S Ps 39:8; S Eze 5:14 [b]Ps 44:13; 80:6
79:5 [c]S Ps 74:10 [d]Ps 74:1; 85:5 [e]S Dt 29:20; Ps 89:46; Zep 3:8
79:6 [f]S Ps 2:5; 69:24; 110:5; Rev 16:1 [g]Ps 147:20; Jer 10:25 [h]S Ps 14:4
79:7 [i]Isa 9:12; Jer 10:25
79:8 [j]S Ge 9:25; Jer 44:21 [k]Ps 116:6; 142:6
79:9 [l]S 2Ch 14:11 [m]Ps 25:11; 31:3; Jer 14:7
79:10 [n]S Ps 42:3 [o]Ps 94:1; S Rev 6:10 [p]ver 3
79:12 [q]Isa 65:6; Jer 32:18 [r]S Ge 4:15
79:13 [s]S Ps 74:1 [t]Ps 44:8

80:1 [u]Ps 77:20 [v]S Ex 25:22
80:2 [w]Nu 2:18-24 [x]S Ps 35:23 [y]Ps 54:1; 69:1; 71:2; 109:26; 116:4; 119:94
80:3 [z]S Ps 71:20; 85:4; Jer 31:18; La 5:21 [a]S Nu 6:25 [b]ver 7, 19
80:4 [c]S Ps 74:10 [d]S Dt 29:20
80:5 [e]S Job 3:24 [f]Isa 30:20
80:6 [g]S Ps 79:4
80:7 [h]ver 3
80:8 [i]Isa 5:1-2; Jer 2:21; Mt 21:33-41 [j]Ex 23:28-30; S Jos 13:6; Ac 7:45 [k]S Ex 15:17

Psalm 80

For the director of music. To ⌊the tune of⌋ "The Lilies of the Covenant." Of Asaph. A psalm.

[1]Hear us, O Shepherd of Israel,
you who lead Joseph like a
flock;[u]
you who sit enthroned between the
cherubim,[v] shine forth
[2] before Ephraim, Benjamin and
Manasseh.[w]
Awaken[x] your might;
come and save us.[y]

[3]Restore[z] us,[a] O God;
make your face shine upon us,
that we may be saved.[b]

[4]O LORD God Almighty,
how long[c] will your anger
smolder[d]
against the prayers of your
people?
[5]You have fed them with the bread
of tears;[e]
you have made them drink tears
by the bowlful.[f]
[6]You have made us a source of
contention to our neighbors,
and our enemies mock us.[g]

[7]Restore us, O God Almighty;
make your face shine upon us,
that we may be saved.[h]

[8]You brought a vine[i] out of Egypt;
you drove out[j] the nations and
planted[k] it.
[9]You cleared the ground for it,
and it took root and filled the
land.
[10]The mountains were covered with
its shade,
the mighty cedars with its
branches.
[11]It sent out its boughs to the Sea,[h]

[h] *11* Probably the Mediterranean

80:1–19 HEAR US, O SHEPHERD OF ISRAEL. In this psalm of intercession, the psalmist pleads for the revival and restoration of God's people to their place of full blessing and favor with God. (1) The psalm depicts a people whose divine protection has collapsed, laying them open to assaults from the outside (vv. 12–13). They have eaten the bread of tears and are objects of derision (vv. 5–6). In great humility, the psalmist repeatedly intercedes for God to show his favor once again and to make his face shine upon the remnant who call on his name (vv. 1,3,7,14–15,19).

(2) This psalm's sentiments are characteristic of the plight and prayer of God's people immediately preceding a time of great revival.

(3) This psalm speaks to all believers, individually and corporately, who are not experiencing the full life, power and righteousness of God as promised in his Word. We must pray that God will revive and renew us by his power and mercy.

its shoots as far as the
River.[i][l]
12Why have you broken down its
walls[m]
so that all who pass by pick its
grapes?
13Boars from the forest ravage[n] it
and the creatures of the field
feed on it.
14Return to us, O God Almighty!
Look down from heaven and
see![o]
Watch over this vine,
15 the root your right hand has
planted,
the son[j] you have raised up for
yourself.

16Your vine is cut down, it is burned
with fire;[p]
at your rebuke[q] your people
perish.
17Let your hand rest on the man at
your right hand,
the son of man[r] you have
raised up for yourself.
18Then we will not turn away from
you;
revive[s] us, and we will call on
your name.

19Restore us, O LORD God Almighty;
make your face shine upon us,
that we may be saved.

Psalm 81

For the director of music. According to *gittith*.[k] Of Asaph.

1Sing for joy to God our strength;
shout aloud to the God of
Jacob![t]
2Begin the music, strike the
tambourine,[u]
play the melodious harp[v] and
lyre.[w]

3Sound the ram's horn[x] at the New
Moon,[y]
and when the moon is full, on
the day of our Feast;
4this is a decree for Israel,
an ordinance of the God of
Jacob.[z]
5He established it as a statute for
Joseph
when he went out against
Egypt,[a]
where we heard a language we
did not understand.[l][b]

80:11 [l]Ps 72:8
80:12 [m]Ps 89:40; Isa 5:5; 30:13; Jer 39:8
80:13 [n]Jer 5:6
80:14 [o]S Dt 26:15
80:16 [p]Ps 79:1 [q]S Dt 28:20
80:17 [r]S Job 25:6
80:18 [s]Ps 85:6; Isa 57:15; Hos 6:2
81:1 [t]S Ps 66:1
81:2 [u]S Ex 15:20 [v]Ps 92:3 [w]S Job 21:12
81:3 [x]S Ex 19:13 [y]S Ne 10:33
81:4 [z]ver 1
81:5 [a]S Ex 11:4 [b]Ps 114:1
81:6 [c]S Ex 1:14 [d]Isa 9:4; 52:2
81:7 [e]S Ex 2:23 [f]Ex 19:19 [g]S Ex 17:7; S Dt 33:8
81:8 [h]Ps 50:7; 78:1
81:9 [i]S Ex 20:3
81:10 [j]S Ex 6:6; S 13:3; S 29:46 [k]Eze 2:8 [l]Ps 107:9
81:11 [m]Ex 32:1-6
81:12 [n]Eze 20:25; Ac 7:42; Ro 1:24
81:13 [o]S Dt 5:29
81:14 [p]Ps 47:3 [q]Am 1:8
81:15 [r]S 2Sa 22:45
81:16 [s]S Dt 32:14
82:1 [t]Ps 7:8; 58:11; Isa 3:13; 66:16; Joel 3:12 [u]S Job 21:22

6He says, "I removed the burden[c]
from their shoulders;[d]
their hands were set free from
the basket.
7In your distress you called[e] and I
rescued you,
I answered[f] you out of a
thundercloud;
I tested you at the waters of
Meribah.[g] *Selah*

8"Hear, O my people,[h] and I will
warn you—
if you would but listen to me,
O Israel!
9You shall have no foreign god[i]
among you;
you shall not bow down to an
alien god.
10I am the LORD your God,
who brought you up out of
Egypt.[j]
Open[k] wide your mouth and I
will fill[l] it.

11"But my people would not listen to
me;
Israel would not submit to me.[m]
12So I gave them over[n] to their
stubborn hearts
to follow their own devices.

13"If my people would but listen to
me,[o]
if Israel would follow my ways,
14how quickly would I subdue[p]
their enemies
and turn my hand against[q]
their foes!
15Those who hate the LORD would
cringe[r] before him,
and their punishment would last
forever.
16But you would be fed with the
finest of wheat;[s]
with honey from the rock I
would satisfy you."

Psalm 82

A psalm of Asaph.

1God presides in the great
assembly;
he gives judgment[t] among the
"gods":[u]

[i] *11* That is, the Euphrates [j] *15* Or *branch*
[k] Title: Probably a musical term [l] *5* Or / *and we heard a voice we had not known*

[2]"How long will you[m] defend the
unjust
and show partiality[v] to the
wicked?[w] *Selah*
[3]Defend the cause of the weak and
fatherless;[x]
maintain the rights of the poor[y]
and oppressed.
[4]Rescue the weak and needy;
deliver them from the hand of
the wicked.

[5]"They know nothing, they
understand nothing.[z]
They walk about in darkness;[a]
all the foundations[b] of the
earth are shaken.

[6]"I said, 'You are "gods";[c]
you are all sons of the Most
High.'
[7]But you will die[d] like mere men;
you will fall like every other
ruler."

[8]Rise up,[e] O God, judge[f] the
earth,
for all the nations are your
inheritance.[g]

Psalm 83

A song. A psalm of Asaph.

[1]O God, do not keep silent;[h]
be not quiet, O God, be not still.
[2]See how your enemies are astir,[i]
how your foes rear their
heads.[j]
[3]With cunning they conspire[k]
against your people;
they plot against those you
cherish.[l]
[4]"Come," they say, "let us destroy[m]
them as a nation,[n]
that the name of Israel be
remembered[o] no more."

[5]With one mind they plot
together;[p]
they form an alliance against
you—
[6]the tents of Edom[q] and the
Ishmaelites,
of Moab[r] and the Hagrites,[s]

82:2 [v]Dt 1:17 [w]Ps 58:1-2; Pr 18:5
82:3 [x]S Dt 24:17 [y]Ps 140:12; Jer 5:28; 22:16
82:5 [z]S Ps 14:4; S 53:2 [a]Job 30:26; Isa 5:30; 8:21-22; 9:2; 59:9; 60:2; Jer 13:16; 23:12; La 3:2 [b]S Jdg 5:4; S Ps 11:3
82:6 [c]Jn 10:34*
82:7 [d]Ps 49:12; Eze 31:14
82:8 [e]Ps 12:5 [f]S Ps 76:9 [g]Ps 2:8
83:1 [h]Ps 28:1; 35:22; Isa 42:14; 57:11; 62:1; 64:12
83:2 [i]Ps 2:1; Isa 17:12 [j]Jdg 8:28
83:3 [k]S Ex 1:10; S Ps 31:13 [l]Ps 17:14
83:4 [m]S Est 3:6 [n]Jer 33:24 [o]Jer 11:19
83:5 [p]Ps 2:2
83:6 [q]Ps 137:7; Isa 34:5; Jer 49:7; Am 1:11 [r]2Ch 20:1 [s]S Ge 25:16
83:7 [t]S Jos 13:5 [u]Ge 19:38 [v]S Ge 14:7; S Ex 17:14 [w]Ex 15:14 [x]Isa 23:3; Eze 27:3
83:8 [y]S Ge 10:11 [z]S Dt 2:9
83:9 [a]S Ge 25:2; Jdg 7:1-23 [b]S Jdg 4:2 [c]S Jos 11:1 [d]S Jdg 4:23-24
83:10 [e]S 1Sa 28:7 [f]S 2Ki 9:37; Isa 5:25; Jer 8:2; 9:22; 16:4; 25:33; Zep 1:17
83:11 [g]Jdg 7:25 [h]S Jdg 8:5
83:12 [i]2Ch 20:11; Eze 35:10
83:13 [j]S Job 13:25
83:14 [k]Dt 32:22; Isa 9:18
83:15 [l]S Ps 50:3 [m]S Job 9:17
83:16 [n]S Ps 34:5; 109:29; 132:18
83:17 [o]S 2Ki 19:26 [p]S Ps 35:4
83:18 [q]S Ps 68:4 [r]Ps 7:8; 18:13 [s]S Job 34:29
84:1 [t]S Dt 33:27; Ps 27:4; 43:3; 90:1; 132:5

[7]Gebal,[n][t] Ammon[u] and
Amalek,[v]
Philistia,[w] with the people of
Tyre.[x]
[8]Even Assyria[y] has joined them
to lend strength to the
descendants of Lot.[z] *Selah*

[9]Do to them as you did to Midian,[a]
as you did to Sisera[b] and
Jabin[c] at the river
Kishon,[d]
[10]who perished at Endor[e]
and became like refuse[f] on the
ground.
[11]Make their nobles like Oreb and
Zeeb,[g]
all their princes like Zebah and
Zalmunna,[h]
[12]who said, "Let us take
possession[i]
of the pasturelands of God."

[13]Make them like tumbleweed, O my
God,
like chaff[j] before the wind.
[14]As fire consumes the forest
or a flame sets the mountains
ablaze,[k]
[15]so pursue them with your
tempest[l]
and terrify them with your
storm.[m]
[16]Cover their faces with shame[n]
so that men will seek your
name, O LORD.

[17]May they ever be ashamed and
dismayed;[o]
may they perish in disgrace.[p]
[18]Let them know that you, whose
name is the LORD[q]—
that you alone are the Most
High[r] over all the earth.[s]

Psalm 84

For the director of music. According to *gittith*.[o] Of the Sons of Korah. A psalm.

[1]How lovely is your dwelling
place,[t]

[m]*2* The Hebrew is plural. [n]*7* That is, Byblos [o]Title: Probably a musical term

82:6 I SAID, YOU ARE GODS. The term "gods" (Heb *'elohim*) probably refers to human authorities and judges in Israel who were designated as God's representatives in administering justice, protecting the weak and helping deliver them from their oppressors. The term in no way means that mere humans are potentially gods, but only that they can become God's representatives with power and authority to bring judgment and carry out justice (see Jn 10:34, note).

84:1–12 HOW LOVELY IS YOUR DWELLING PLACE. This psalm describes believers who are

O LORD Almighty!
2My soul yearns,[u] even faints,
for the courts of the LORD;
my heart and my flesh cry out
for the living God.[v]

3Even the sparrow has found a home,
and the swallow a nest for herself,
where she may have her young—
a place near your altar,[w]
O LORD Almighty,[x] my King[y]
and my God.[z]
4Blessed are those who dwell in your house;
they are ever praising you. *Selah*

5Blessed are those whose strength[a] is in you,
who have set their hearts on pilgrimage.[b]
6As they pass through the Valley of Baca,
they make it a place of springs;[c]
the autumn[d] rains also cover it with pools.[p]
7They go from strength to strength,[e]
till each appears[f] before God in Zion.[g]

8Hear my prayer,[h] O LORD God Almighty;
listen to me, O God of Jacob. *Selah*
9Look upon our shield,[q][i] O God;
look with favor on your anointed one.[j]

10Better is one day in your courts
than a thousand elsewhere;
I would rather be a doorkeeper[k]
in the house of my God
than dwell in the tents of the wicked.
11For the LORD God is a sun[l] and shield;[m]
the LORD bestows favor and honor;
no good thing does he withhold[n]
from those whose walk is blameless.

12O LORD Almighty,
blessed[o] is the man who trusts in you.

Psalm 85

For the director of music. Of the Sons of Korah. A psalm.

1You showed favor to your land, O LORD;
you restored the fortunes[p] of Jacob.
2You forgave[q] the iniquity[r] of your people
and covered all their sins. *Selah*
3You set aside all your wrath[s]
and turned from your fierce anger.[t]

4Restore[u] us again, O God our Savior,[v]
and put away your displeasure toward us.
5Will you be angry with us forever?[w]
Will you prolong your anger through all generations?
6Will you not revive[x] us again,

84:2 [u] S Job 19:27 [v] S Jos 3:10 **84:3** [w] S Ps 43:4 [x] Jer 44:11 [y] Ps 2:6 [z] Ps 5:2 **84:5** [a] Ps 81:1 [b] Jer 31:6 **84:6** [c] S Job 38:26 [d] Joel 2:23 **84:7** [e] S Job 17:9 [f] S Dt 16:16 [g] 1Ki 8:1 **84:8** [h] Ps 4:1 **84:9** [i] S Ps 59:11 [j] 1Sa 16:6; Ps 2:2; 18:50; 132:17 **84:10** [k] 1Ch 23:5 **84:11** [l] Isa 60:19; Jer 43:13; Rev 21:23 [m] S Ge 15:1 [n] Ps 34:10 **84:12** [o] Ps 2:12 **85:1** [p] S Dt 30:3; Ps 14:7 **85:2** [q] S Nu 14:19 [r] S Ex 32:30; S Ps 78:38 **85:3** [s] Ps 106:23; Da 9:16 [t] Ex 32:12; Dt 13:17; Ps 78:38; Jnh 3:9 **85:4** [u] S Ps 71:20 [v] S Ps 65:5 **85:5** [w] S Ps 50:21 **85:6** [x] S Ps 80:18

[p] 6 Or *blessings* [q] 9 Or *sovereign*

so attached to God that they long above everything else to be in God's house and presence (cf. Ps 42). Their greatest desire is to experience God's nearness, to worship him with other faithful believers (v. 10) and to receive his blessings (see v. 4, note).

84:2 MY SOUL YEARNS ... FOR THE COURTS OF THE LORD. See 42:2,6, notes on hungering and thirsting for God's nearness.

84:4 BLESSED ARE THOSE WHO DWELL IN YOUR HOUSE. Those who go to the Lord's house seeking his presence will receive his blessing. This blessing includes the nearness of God, a renewed spiritual strength (vv. 5–7), answered prayer (v. 8), and favor and honor (v. 11; see Lk 24:50, note).

84:11 NO GOOD THING DOES HE WITHHOLD. This promise is specifically directed to believers who sincerely strive to live godly and righteous lives. What God regards as good relates directly to our fulfilling his purpose for our lives. Our task is to walk uprightly and to trust God to furnish everything that is good—physically and spiritually, temporally and eternally (see 34:10; Mt 6:33; Ro 8:28; 1Co 2:9; 1Ti 4:8).

85:6 WILL YOU NOT REVIVE US AGAIN? It is right for God's people to pray that he will revive them, both individually and corporately. Salvation and spiritual life are dependent on God imparting to us his mercy, forgiveness, power, life-giving Spirit and fervent desire to do his will (see Jn 3:16; 1Co 15:10; Php 2:13; 1Ti 1:15–16). When we are at a low point spiritually, not experiencing spiritual blessings as God intended, then we should honestly confess our inner poverty and pray that God will revive us again (see 2Ch 17:9, note; 29:5, note; 34:30, note).

that your people may rejoice[y]
in you?
[7]Show us your unfailing love,[z]
O LORD,
and grant us your salvation.[a]

Ps 98:1-3

[8]I will listen to what God the LORD
will say;
he promises peace[b] to his
people, his saints—
but let them not return to
folly.[c]
[9]Surely his salvation[d] is near those
who fear him,
that his glory[e] may dwell in our
land.

[10]Love and faithfulness[f] meet
together;
righteousness[g] and peace kiss
each other.
[11]Faithfulness springs forth from the
earth,
and righteousness[h] looks down
from heaven.
[12]The LORD will indeed give what is
good,[i]
and our land will yield[j] its
harvest.
[13]Righteousness goes before him
and prepares the way for his
steps.

Psalm 86

A prayer of David.

[1]Hear, O LORD, and answer[k] me,
for I am poor and needy.
[2]Guard my life, for I am devoted to
you.
You are my God; save your
servant
who trusts in you.[l]
[3]Have mercy[m] on me, O Lord,
for I call[n] to you all day long.
[4]Bring joy to your servant,
for to you, O Lord,
I lift[o] up my soul.

[5]You are forgiving and good,
O Lord,
abounding in love[p] to all who
call to you.

[6]Hear my prayer, O LORD;
listen to my cry[q] for mercy.
[7]In the day of my trouble[r] I will
call[s] to you,
for you will answer[t] me.

[8]Among the gods[u] there is none
like you,[v] O Lord;
no deeds can compare with
yours.
[9]All the nations you have made
will come[w] and worship[x]
before you, O Lord;
they will bring glory[y] to your
name.
[10]For you are great[z] and do
marvelous deeds;[a]
you alone[b] are God.
[11]Teach me your way,[c] O LORD,
and I will walk in your truth;[d]
give me an undivided[e] heart,
that I may fear[f] your name.
[12]I will praise you, O Lord my God,
with all my heart;[g]
I will glorify your name forever.
[13]For great is your love toward me;
you have delivered me[h] from
the depths of the grave.[r][i]
[14]The arrogant are attacking me,
O God;
a band of ruthless men seeks
my life—
men without regard for you.[j]
[15]But you, O Lord, are a
compassionate and
gracious[k] God,
slow to anger,[l] abounding[m] in
love and faithfulness.[n]
[16]Turn to me[o] and have mercy[p] on
me;
grant your strength[q] to your
servant
and save the son of your
maidservant.[s][r]
[17]Give me a sign[s] of your goodness,

85:6 [y]Php 3:1 **85:7** [z]S Ps 6:4 [a]Ps 27:1 **85:8** [b]S Lev 26:6; S Isa 60:17; S Jn 14:27; 2Th 3:16 [c]Pr 26:11; 27:22 **85:9** [d]Ps 27:1; Isa 43:3; 45:8; 46:13; 51:5; 56:1; 62:11 [e]S Ex 29:43; Isa 60:19; Hag 2:9; Zec 2:5 **85:10** [f]Ps 89:14; 115:1; Pr 3:3 [g]Ps 72:2-3; Isa 32:17 **85:11** [h]Isa 45:8 **85:12** [i]Ps 84:11; Jas 1:17 [j]Lev 26:4; S Ps 67:6; Zec 8:12 **86:1** [k]Ps 17:6 **86:2** [l]Ps 25:2; 31:14 **86:3** [m]Ps 4:1; S 9:13; 57:1 [n]Ps 88:9 **86:4** [o]Ps 46:5; 143:8 **86:5** [p]Ex 34:6; Ne 9:17; Ps 103:8; 145:8; Joel 2:13; Jnh 4:2 **86:6** [q]Ps 5:2; 17:1 **86:7** [r]Ps 27:5; S 50:15; 94:13; Hab 3:16 [s]Job 22:27; Ps 4:3; 80:18; 91:15; Isa 30:19; 58:9; 65:24; Zec 13:9 [t]Ps 3:4 **86:8** [u]S Ex 8:10; S Job 21:22 [v]S Ps 18:31 **86:9** [w]S Ps 65:2 [x]Ps 66:4; Isa 19:21; 27:13; 49:7; Zec 8:20-22; 14:16; Rev 15:4 [y]Isa 43:7; 44:23 **86:10** [z]S 2Sa 7:22; S Ps 48:1 [a]S Ex 3:20; S Ps 71:17; 72:18 [b]S Dt 6:4; S Isa 43:10; Mk 12:29; 1Co 8:4 **86:11** [c]S Ex 33:13; S 1Sa 12:23; Ps 25:5 [d]S Ps 26:3 [e]Jer 24:7; 32:39; Eze 11:19; 1Co 7:35 [f]S Dt 6:24 **86:12** [g]S Ps 9:1 **86:13** [h]S Ps 34:4; 49:15; 116:8 [i]S Ps 16:10; S 56:13 **86:14** [j]Ps 54:3 **86:15** [k]S Ps 51:1; 103:8; 111:4; 116:5; 145:8 [l]Nu 14:18 [m]ver 5 [n]S Ex 34:6; S Ne 9:17; Joel 2:13 **86:16** [o]S Ps 6:4 [p]S Ps 9:13 [q]Ps 18:1 [r]Ps 116:16 **86:17** [s]S Ex 3:12; Mt 24:3; S Jn 2:11

[r]13 Hebrew *Sheol* [s]16 Or *save your faithful son*

86:1 I AM POOR AND NEEDY. Prayer that arises out of humility, affliction and great need is prayer that God will hear and answer. He has a special care for his people who are broken and needy (cf. 35:10; 74:21; Mt 6:25–34; see Lk 11:3, note).

86:11 TEACH ME YOUR WAY. In the midst of his trouble, the psalmist humbly asks God to teach him his ways and his truth, that he might fear God from the heart. When we are experiencing trials and difficulties, we must cry out to God for wisdom to walk in his ways and for a heart that truly fears and delights in his truth.

that my enemies may see it and
be put to shame,
for you, O LORD, have helped me
and comforted me.

Psalm 87

Of the Sons of Korah. A psalm.
A song.

1He has set his foundation on the
holy mountain;[t]
2 the LORD loves the gates of Zion[u]
more than all the dwellings of
Jacob.
3Glorious things are said of you,
O city of God:[v] *Selah*
4"I will record Rahab[t][w] and
Babylon
among those who acknowledge
me—
Philistia[x] too, and Tyre[y], along
with Cush[u]—
and will say, 'This[v] one was
born in Zion.[z]' "
5Indeed, of Zion it will be said,
"This one and that one were
born in her,
and the Most High himself will
establish her."
6The LORD will write in the
register[a] of the peoples:
"This one was born in Zion."
Selah
7As they make music[b] they will
sing,
"All my fountains[c] are in you."

Psalm 88

A song. A psalm of the Sons of
Korah. For the director of music.
According to *mahalath leannoth.*[w] A
maskil[x] of Heman the Ezrahite.

1O LORD, the God who saves me,[d]
day and night I cry out[e] before
you.
2May my prayer come before you;
turn your ear to my cry.

3For my soul is full of trouble[f]
and my life draws near the
grave.[y][g]
4I am counted among those who go
down to the pit;[h]
I am like a man without
strength.[i]
5I am set apart with the dead,
like the slain who lie in the
grave,
whom you remember no more,
who are cut off[j] from your
care.

6You have put me in the lowest pit,
in the darkest depths.[k]
7Your wrath[l] lies heavily upon me;
you have overwhelmed me with
all your waves.[m] *Selah*
8You have taken from me my
closest friends[n]
and have made me repulsive to
them.
I am confined[o] and cannot
escape;[p]
9 my eyes[q] are dim with grief.

I call[r] to you, O LORD, every
day;
I spread out my hands[s] to
you.
10Do you show your wonders to the
dead?
Do those who are dead rise up
and praise you?[t] *Selah*

87:1 [t]S Ps 48:1 **87:2** [u]Ps 2:6 **87:3** [v]S Ps 46:4 **87:4** [w]S Job 9:13 [x]S 2Sa 8:1; Ps 83:7 [y]Ps 45:12; Joel 3:4 [z]Isa 19:25 **87:6** [a]Ex 32:32; Ps 69:28; Isa 4:3; Mal 3:16 **87:7** [b]Ps 149:3 [c]S Ps 36:9 **88:1** [d]S Ps 51:14 [e]Ps 3:4; 22:2; Lk 18:7 **88:3** [f]Ps 6:3; 25:17 [g]S Job 33:22 **88:4** [h]S Ps 31:12 [i]Ps 18:1 **88:5** [j]S Ps 31:22 **88:6** [k]Ps 30:1; S 69:15; La 3:55; Jnh 2:3 **88:7** [l]Ps 7:11 [m]S Ps 42:7 **88:8** [n]S Job 19:13; Ps 31:11 [o]Jer 32:2; 33:1 [p]S Job 3:23 **88:9** [q]S Ps 38:10 [r]Ps 5:2 [s]Job 11:13; Ps 143:6 **88:10** [t]S Ps 6:5

[t]*4* A poetic name for Egypt [u]*4* That is, the upper Nile region [v]*4* Or *"O Rahab and Babylon, / Philistia, Tyre and Cush, / I will record concerning those who acknowledge me: / 'This* [w]Title: Possibly a tune, "The Suffering of Affliction" [x]Title: Probably a literary or musical term [y]*3* Hebrew *Sheol*

88:1–18 DAY AND NIGHT I CRY OUT. Some regard this as the saddest of all psalms. The supplicant has suffered much (v. 3), perhaps as a leper (cf. v. 8). He feels that he is nearing death and that God has rejected him (vv. 7,14,16–18). He has cried out day and night to God and appears to have received no answer (vv. 1–2,13). He is dejected and has little hope. Yet in faith he will not let go of God; he confesses that the Lord is still the God who saves him (v. 1). (1) The psalmist's experience is much like that of Job, though in this case we are not told the reason behind his suffering and God's apparent silence.

(2) This psalm reveals that God occasionally permits times of sadness and despair in a believer's life. It is a dark experience when there is no apparent reason for our problems and when God seems far away. Throughout such suffering a measure of mystery will remain until we are with God in heaven. In the meantime, both faith in God as the One who saves us and a right relationship with him are essential to get us through, and we must never forget that in the final analysis, "neither death nor life . . . neither the present nor the future . . . will be able to separate us from the love of God that is in Christ Jesus our Lord" (Ro 8:38–39).

11 Is your love declared in the grave,
your faithfulness[u] in
Destruction[z]?
12 Are your wonders known in the
place of darkness,
or your righteous deeds in the
land of oblivion?

13 But I cry to you for help,[v]
O LORD;
in the morning[w] my prayer
comes before you.[x]
14 Why, O LORD, do you reject[y] me
and hide your face[z] from me?

15 From my youth[a] I have been
afflicted[b] and close to
death;
I have suffered your terrors[c]
and am in despair.[d]
16 Your wrath[e] has swept over me;
your terrors[f] have destroyed
me.
17 All day long they surround me like
a flood;[g]
they have completely engulfed
me.
18 You have taken my companions[h]
and loved ones from me;
the darkness is my closest
friend.

Psalm 89

A *maskil*[a] of Ethan the Ezrahite.

1 I will sing[i] of the LORD's great
love forever;
with my mouth I will make your
faithfulness known[j]
through all generations.
2 I will declare that your love stands
firm forever,
that you established your
faithfulness in heaven
itself.[k]

3 You said, "I have made a covenant
with my chosen one,
I have sworn to David my
servant,
4 'I will establish your line forever
and make your throne firm
through all generations.' "[l]
Selah

5 The heavens[m] praise your
wonders, O LORD,
your faithfulness too, in the
assembly[n] of the holy
ones.
6 For who in the skies above can
compare with the LORD?
Who is like the LORD among the
heavenly beings?[o]
7 In the council[p] of the holy ones[q]
God is greatly feared;
he is more awesome than all
who surround him.[r]
8 O LORD God Almighty,[s] who is
like you?[t]
You are mighty, O LORD, and
your faithfulness surrounds
you.

9 You rule over the surging sea;
when its waves mount up, you
still them.[u]
10 You crushed Rahab[v] like one of
the slain;
with your strong arm you
scattered[w] your enemies.
11 The heavens are yours,[x] and
yours also the earth;[y]
you founded the world and all
that is in it.[z]

88:11 [u] S Ps 30:9 **88:13** [v] S Ps 30:2 [w] Ps 5:3; S 55:17 [x] Ps 119:147 **88:14** [y] S Ps 43:2 [z] Ps 13:1 **88:15** [a] Ps 129:1; Jer 22:21; Eze 16:22; Hos 2:15 [b] Ps 9:12 [c] Job 6:4; S 18:11 [d] 2Co 4:8 **88:16** [e] Ps 7:11 [f] Job 6:4 **88:17** [g] Ps 124:4 **88:18** [h] ver 8; Ps 38:11 **89:1** [i] Ps 59:16 [j] S Ps 36:5; 40:10 **89:2** [k] S Ps 36:5
89:4 [l] 2Sa 7:12-16; 1Ki 8:16; Ps 132:11-12; Isa 9:7; Eze 37:24-25; S Mt 1:1; S Lk 1:33 **89:5** [m] S Ps 19:1 [n] S Ps 1:5 **89:6** [o] S Ge 1:26; S Ex 9:14; S Ps 18:31; 113:5 **89:7** [p] Ps 111:1 [q] S Job 5:1 [r] Ps 47:2 **89:8** [s] Isa 6:3 [t] S Ps 71:19 **89:9** [u] S Ps 65:7 **89:10** [v] S Job 9:13 [w] S Ps 59:11; S 68:1; 92:9 **89:11** [x] S Dt 10:14; Ps 115:16 [y] 1Ch 29:11; S Ps 24:1 [z] S Ge 1:1

[z] *11* Hebrew *Abaddon* [a] Title: Probably a literary or musical term

89:1–52 YOUR FAITHFULNESS. This psalm is a prayer dealing with Jerusalem's destruction and the fallen dynasty of David, and with God's promise that David's line would continue forever (vv. 29,34–37; cf. 2Sa 7:8–16). The author questions whether God has failed to keep his pledge. He prays that God would restore his people and David's throne and remove his wrath from Israel (vv. 46–52). What the psalmist did not know was that even though God had punished Israel for her sins, he would keep his promise through Jesus Christ, who was from the line of David, and whose kingdom will never end (Lk 1:31–33).

89:4 I WILL ESTABLISH YOUR LINE FOREVER. God's covenant promise to David was that his "line" would rule on the throne forever (see also vv. 29,36–37). (1) It is obvious that God's promise did not involve all of David's descendants. When the Davidic kings disobeyed God, he removed them just as he delivered the northern kingdom over to its enemies and to captivity when the people persisted in apostasy (see vv. 38–51).

(2) The NT sees the fulfillment of this verse in the Lord Jesus Christ. The apostle Peter states: "From this man's [David's] descendants God has brought to Israel the Savior Jesus, as he promised" (Ac 13:23). And the angel Gabriel revealed to Mary: "The Lord God will give him [Jesus] the throne of his father David . . . his kingdom will never end" (Lk 1:32–33; cf. 1:69).

[12]You created the north and the
south;
Tabor[a] and Hermon[b] sing for
joy[c] at your name.
[13]Your arm is endued with power;
your hand is strong, your right
hand exalted.[d]
[14]Righteousness and justice are the
foundation of your throne;[e]
love and faithfulness go before
you.[f]
[15]Blessed are those who have
learned to acclaim you,
who walk[g] in the light[h] of
your presence, O LORD.
[16]They rejoice in your name[i] all
day long;
they exult in your righteousness.
[17]For you are their glory and
strength,[j]
and by your favor you exalt our
horn.[b][k]
[18]Indeed, our shield[c][l] belongs to
the LORD,
our king[m] to the Holy One of
Israel.
[19]Once you spoke in a vision,
to your faithful people you said:
"I have bestowed strength on a
warrior;
I have exalted a young man
from among the people.
[20]I have found David[n] my
servant;[o]
with my sacred oil[p] I have
anointed[q] him.
[21]My hand will sustain him;
surely my arm will strengthen
him.[r]
[22]No enemy will subject him to
tribute;[s]
no wicked man will oppress[t]
him.
[23]I will crush his foes before him[u]
and strike down his
adversaries.[v]
[24]My faithful love will be with him,[w]
and through my name his horn[d]
will be exalted.
[25]I will set his hand over the sea,
his right hand over the rivers.[x]

89:12 [a] S Jos 19:22 [b] S Dt 3:8; S 4:48 [c] Ps 98:8 **89:13** [d] S Jos 4:24 **89:14** [e] Ps 97:2 [f] Ps 85:10-11 **89:15** [g] Ps 1:1 [h] Ps 44:3 **89:16** [i] Ps 30:4; 105:3 **89:17** [j] Ps 18:1 [k] ver 24; Ps 75:10; 92:10; 112:9; 148:14 **89:18** [l] Ps 18:2 [m] Ps 47:9; Isa 16:5; 33:17,22 **89:20** [n] Ac 13:22 [o] Ps 78:70 [p] S Ex 29:7; S 1Ki 1:39 [q] S 1Sa 2:35; S 2Sa 22:51 **89:21** [r] ver 13; Ps 18:35 **89:22** [s] S Jdg 3:15 [t] 2Sa 7:10 **89:23** [u] Ps 18:40 [v] 2Sa 7:9 **89:24** [w] S 2Sa 7:15 **89:25** [x] Ps 72:8

[26]He will call out to me, 'You are my
Father,[y]
my God, the Rock[z] my
Savior.'[a]
[27]I will also appoint him my
firstborn,[b]
the most exalted[c] of the
kings[d] of the earth.
[28]I will maintain my love to him
forever,
and my covenant with him will
never fail.[e]
[29]I will establish his line forever,
his throne as long as the
heavens endure.[f]
[30]"If his sons forsake my law
and do not follow my statutes,
[31]if they violate my decrees
and fail to keep my commands,
[32]I will punish their sin with the
rod,
their iniquity with flogging;[g]
[33]but I will not take my love from
him,[h]
nor will I ever betray my
faithfulness.
[34]I will not violate my covenant
or alter what my lips have
uttered.[i]
[35]Once for all, I have sworn by my
holiness—
and I will not lie to David—
[36]that his line will continue forever
and his throne endure before me
like the sun;[j]
[37]it will be established forever like
the moon,
the faithful witness in the
sky."[k] *Selah*
[38]But you have rejected,[l] you have
spurned,
you have been very angry with
your anointed one.
[39]You have renounced the covenant
with your servant
and have defiled his crown in
the dust.[m]

89:26 [y] S 2Sa 7:14; S Jer 3:4; Heb 1:5 [z] S Ps 62:2 [a] S 2Sa 22:47 **89:27** [b] S Col 1:18 [c] S Nu 24:7 [d] Ps 2:6; Rev 1:5; 19:16 **89:28** [e] ver 33-34; Isa 55:3 **89:29** [f] ver 4,36 **89:32** [g] 2Sa 7:14 **89:33** [h] S 2Sa 7:15 **89:34** [i] S Nu 23:19 **89:36** [j] ver 4 **89:37** [k] Jer 33:20-21 **89:38** [l] 1Ch 28:9; Ps 44:9; 78:59 **89:39** [m] La 5:16

[b] *17 Horn* here symbolizes strong one. [c] *18* Or *sovereign* [d] *24 Horn* here symbolizes strength.

89:19–37 I HAVE EXALTED A YOUNG MAN. The psalmist reminds God of his election of David's line to rule over Israel and of his promise that David's dynasty would endure forever (vv. 27–29) in spite of Israel's unfaithfulness (see previous note).

89:30 IF HIS SONS FORSAKE MY LAW. God's promises in vv. 30–37 did not ensure the reign of David's descendants as kings forever, nor do they address the issue of the personal salvation of these kings. Rather, the promises were given to David to assure him that the unfaithfulness of Israel and her kings would not interfere with God's purpose to establish one of his descendants (i.e., Jesus) upon an everlasting throne (vv. 36–37).

40You have broken through all his
walls[n]
and reduced his strongholds[o] to
ruins.
41All who pass by have plundered[p]
him;
he has become the scorn of his
neighbors.[q]
42You have exalted the right hand of
his foes;
you have made all his enemies
rejoice.[r]
43You have turned back the edge of
his sword
and have not supported him in
battle.[s]
44You have put an end to his
splendor
and cast his throne to the
ground.
45You have cut short[t] the days of
his youth;
you have covered him with a
mantle of shame.[u] *Selah*

46How long, O LORD? Will you hide
yourself forever?
How long will your wrath burn
like fire?[v]
47Remember how fleeting is my
life.[w]
For what futility you have
created all men!
48What man can live and not see
death,
or save himself from the power
of the grave[e]?[x] *Selah*
49O Lord, where is your former great
love,
which in your faithfulness you
swore to David?
50Remember, Lord, how your servant
has[f] been mocked,[y]
how I bear in my heart the
taunts of all the nations,
51the taunts with which your
enemies have mocked,
O LORD,
with which they have mocked
every step of your anointed
one.[z]

52Praise be to the LORD forever!
Amen and Amen.[a]

BOOK IV

Psalms 90–106

Psalm 90

A prayer of Moses the man of God.

1Lord, you have been our dwelling
place[b]
throughout all generations.
2Before the mountains were born[c]
or you brought forth the earth
and the world,
from everlasting to everlasting[d]
you are God.[e]

3You turn men back to dust,
saying, "Return to dust, O sons
of men."[f]
4For a thousand years in your sight
are like a day that has just gone
by,
or like a watch in the night.[g]
5You sweep men away[h] in the
sleep of death;
they are like the new grass of
the morning—
6though in the morning it springs
up new,
by evening it is dry and
withered.[i]

7We are consumed by your anger
and terrified by your indignation.
8You have set our iniquities before
you,
our secret sins[j] in the light of
your presence.[k]
9All our days pass away under your
wrath;

89:40 [n]S Ps 80:12 [o]Isa 22:5; La 2:2 **89:41** [p]S Jdg 2:14 [q]S Ps 44:13 **89:42** [r]Ps 13:2; 80:6 **89:43** [s]Ps 44:10 **89:45** [t]S Ps 39:5 [u]Ps 44:15; 109:29 **89:46** [v]Ps 79:5 **89:47** [w]S Ge 47:9; S Job 7:7; Ps 39:5; 1Pe 1:24 **89:48** [x]S Ge 5:24; Ps 22:29 **89:50** [y]Ps 69:19 **89:51** [z]Ps 74:10 **89:52** [a]S Ps 41:13; S 72:19 **90:1** [b]S Dt 33:27; Eph 2:22; Rev 21:3 **90:2** [c]S Job 15:7 [d]Isa 9:6; 57:15 [e]S Ge 21:33; S Job 10:5; Ps 102:24-27; Pr 8:23-26 **90:3** [f]S Ge 2:7; S Job 7:21; 34:15; 1Co 15:47 **90:4** [g]S Job 10:5; 2Pe 3:8 **90:5** [h]S Ge 19:15 **90:6** [i]Isa 40:6-8; Mt 6:30; Jas 1:10 **90:8** [j]S Ps 19:12; 2Co 4:2; Eph 5:12 [k]S Heb 4:13

[e]48 Hebrew *Sheol* [f]50 Or *your servants have*

90:1–17 YOU HAVE BEEN OUR DWELLING PLACE. This prayer, ascribed to Moses, was probably written during the forty years that God made Israel wander in the desert as punishment for their unfaithfulness (Dt 8:15). A generation of disobedient Israelites died during this time (cf. vv. 7–11; see Nu 14:22–33). After acknowledging their iniquities and God's punishment, Moses prays for the restoration of God's favor and blessing.

90:2 FROM EVERLASTING TO EVERLASTING. This phrase refers to God's eternal existence, having neither beginning nor end. (1) "Everlasting" (Heb *olam*) does not necessarily mean that God transcends time, but rather connotes his endless duration in time (cf. 48:14; Ge 21:33; Job 10:5; 36:26). Scripture does not teach that God exists in some kind of eternal present, where there is neither past nor future. (2) Those Bible passages that affirm God's eternity do so in terms of continuation, not timelessness. God knows the past as past, the present as present, and the future as future.

we finish our years with a
moan.[l]
10The length of our days is seventy
years[m]—
or eighty,[n] if we have the
strength;
yet their span[g] is but trouble and
sorrow,[o]
for they quickly pass, and we fly
away.[p]

11Who knows the power of your
anger?
For your wrath[q] is as great as
the fear that is due you.[r]
12Teach us to number our days[s]
aright,
that we may gain a heart of
wisdom.[t]

13Relent, O LORD! How long[u] will it
be?
Have compassion on your
servants.[v]
14Satisfy[w] us in the morning with
your unfailing love,[x]
that we may sing for joy[y] and
be glad all our days.[z]
15Make us glad for as many days as
you have afflicted us,
for as many years as we have
seen trouble.
16May your deeds be shown to your
servants,
your splendor to their
children.[a]

17May the favor[h] of the Lord our
God rest upon us;
establish the work of our hands
for us—
yes, establish the work of our
hands.[b]

Psalm 91

1He who dwells in the shelter[c] of
the Most High
will rest in the shadow[d] of the
Almighty.[i]
2I will say[j] of the LORD, "He is my
refuge[e] and my fortress,[f]
my God, in whom I trust."

3Surely he will save you from the
fowler's snare[g]
and from the deadly
pestilence.[h]
4He will cover you with his
feathers,
and under his wings you will
find refuge;[i]
his faithfulness will be your
shield[j] and rampart.
5You will not fear[k] the terror of
night,
nor the arrow that flies by day,
6nor the pestilence that stalks in
the darkness,
nor the plague that destroys at
midday.
7A thousand may fall at your side,
ten thousand at your right hand,
but it will not come near you.
8You will only observe with your
eyes
and see the punishment of the
wicked.[l]

90:9 [l]Ps 78:33 **90:10** [m]Isa 23:15,17; Jer 25:11 [n]2Sa 19:35 [o]S Job 5:7 [p]S Job 20:8; S 34:15 **90:11** [q]Ps 7:11 [r]Ps 76:7 **90:12** [s]Ps 39:4; 139:16; Pr 16:9; 20:24 [t]Dt 32:29 **90:13** [u]Ps 6:3 [v]S Dt 32:36 **90:14** [w]Ps 103:5; 107:9; 145:16,19 [x]S Ps 77:8; 143:8 [y]S Ps 5:11 [z]Ps 31:7 **90:16** [a]Ps 44:1; Hab 3:2 **90:17** [b]Isa 26:12 **91:1** [c]S Ex 33:22 [d]Ps 63:7; Isa 49:2; La 4:20 **91:2** [e]ver 9; S 2Sa 22:3; Ps 9:9 [f]S 2Sa 22:2 **91:3** [g]Ps 124:7; Pr 6:5 [h]1Ki 8:37 **91:4** [i]S Ru 2:12; Ps 17:8 [j]S Dt 32:10; Ps 35:2; Isa 27:3; 31:5; Zec 12:8 **91:5** [k]S Job 5:21 **91:8** [l]Ps 37:34; S 58:10

g *10* Or *yet the best of them* h *17* Or *beauty* i *1* Hebrew *Shaddai* j *2* Or *He says*

90:12 TEACH US TO NUMBER OUR DAYS ARIGHT. Our days on this earth, at best seventy to eighty years (cf. v. 10), are few when compared to eternity. We should pray for a sober understanding of the brevity of our lives so as to present to God a heart of wisdom in how we use each day he gives us (cf. 39:4). This life should be a preparation for the next life, and we should determine what God wants to accomplish for himself, our families and others through our faithful service. When our time here is over and we reach heaven, how we lived or did not live in dedication to God will be evaluated. In that light, we must pray for a heart of wisdom, a righteous fear of God (v. 11), and God's favor in our lives and in our work for him (vv. 13–17).

91:1–16 IN THE SHADOW OF THE ALMIGHTY. This psalm expresses the security of those who trust fully in God; it assures us that God will be our refuge and that we may seek his protection in times of spiritual and physical danger.

91:1 WHO DWELLS IN THE SHELTER OF THE MOST HIGH. This psalm offers security for God's children, i.e., those who commit themselves to the will and protection of the Almighty and daily seek to dwell in God's presence. The more fully we abide in Christ and his word, making him our life and our dwelling place, the fuller will be our peace and the greater our deliverance in times of danger (cf. 17:8; Mt 23:37; Jn 15:1–11).

91:1–2 THE MOST HIGH. The four names for God in this psalm describe different aspects of his protection. (1) "Most High" shows him to be greater than any threat we face (cf. Ge 14:19); (2) "Almighty" emphasizes his power to confront and destroy every enemy (cf. Ex 6:3); (3) "the LORD" assures us that his presence is always with us; and (4) "my God" expresses the truth that God has chosen to associate intimately with those who trust in him.

[9]If you make the Most High your dwelling—
even the LORD, who is my refuge—
[10]then no harm[m] will befall you,
no disaster will come near your tent.
[11]For he will command his angels[n] concerning you
to guard you in all your ways;[o]
[12]they will lift you up in their hands,
so that you will not strike your foot against a stone.[p]
[13]You will tread upon the lion and the cobra;
you will trample the great lion and the serpent.[q]

Isa 14:12-20

[14]"Because he loves me," says the LORD, "I will rescue him;
I will protect him, for he acknowledges my name.
[15]He will call upon me, and I will answer him;
I will be with him in trouble,
I will deliver him and honor him.[r]
[16]With long life[s] will I satisfy him
and show him my salvation.[t]"

Psalm 92

A psalm. A song. For the Sabbath day.

[1]It is good to praise the LORD
and make music[u] to your name,[v] O Most High,[w]
[2]to proclaim your love in the morning[x]
and your faithfulness at night,
[3]to the music of the ten-stringed lyre[y]
and the melody of the harp.[z]
[4]For you make me glad by your deeds, O LORD;
I sing for joy[a] at the works of your hands.[b]
[5]How great are your works,[c] O LORD,
how profound your thoughts![d]
[6]The senseless man[e] does not know,
fools do not understand,
[7]that though the wicked spring up like grass
and all evildoers flourish,
they will be forever destroyed.[f]
[8]But you, O LORD, are exalted forever.
[9]For surely your enemies[g], O LORD,
surely your enemies will perish;
all evildoers will be scattered.[h]
[10]You have exalted my horn[k][i] like that of a wild ox;[j]
fine oils[k] have been poured upon me.
[11]My eyes have seen the defeat of my adversaries;
my ears have heard the rout of my wicked foes.[l]
[12]The righteous will flourish[m] like a palm tree,
they will grow like a cedar of Lebanon;[n]
[13]planted in the house of the LORD,

91:10 [m]Pr 12:21
91:11 [n]S Ge 32:1; Heb 1:14 [o]Ps 34:7
91:12 [p]Mt 4:6*; Lk 4:10-11*
91:13 [q]Da 6:22; Lk 10:19
91:15 [r]S 1Sa 2:30; Jn 12:26
91:16 [s]Dt 6:2; S Ps 21:4 [t]S Ps 50:23
92:1 [u]S Ps 27:6 [v]S Ps 9:2; 147:1 [w]Ps 135:3
92:2 [x]S Ps 55:17
92:3 [y]S Ps 71:22 [z]S 1Sa 10:5; S Ne 12:27; S Ps 33:2; 81:2
92:4 [a]S Ps 5:11; 27:6 [b]S Ps 8:6; 111:7; 143:5
92:5 [c]S Job 36:24; Rev 15:3 [d]Ps 40:5; 139:17; Isa 28:29; 31:2; Ro 11:33
92:6 [e]S Ps 73:22
92:7 [f]S Ps 37:2
92:9 [g]S Ps 45:5 [h]S Ps 68:1; S 89:10
92:10 [i]S Ps 89:17 [j]S Ps 29:6 [k]S Ps 23:5
92:11 [l]S Ps 54:7; 91:8
92:12 [m]S Ps 72:7 [n]S Ps 1:3; 52:8; Jer 17:8; Hos 14:6

[k] *10 Horn* here symbolizes strength.

91:10 NO HARM WILL BEFALL YOU. Nothing can happen to a faithful servant except by God's permission (cf. vv. 7–10); this truth does not mean there will never be unpleasant or difficult times (cf. Ro 8:35–37), but that as long as we make God our Lord and refuge, in everything that happens to us God will work for our good (see Ro 8:28, note).

91:11 COMMAND HIS ANGELS CONCERNING YOU. God commissions angels to watch carefully over the lives and interests of the faithful. (1) They take special note of all who seek continually to dwell in God's presence, and they guard the body, soul and spirit of these believers. (2) The protection includes all our ways; there is no limit as long as we walk in the shadow of the Almighty. They lift us up in our troubles (v. 12) and give us support as we face our spiritual enemies (Eph 6:10–12; 1Pe 5:8; see Mt 18:10, note; see article on ANGELS AND THE ANGEL OF THE LORD, p. 340).

91:14 BECAUSE HE LOVES ME. Here the Lord himself addresses his faithful followers. Because they truly love him, he himself promises to come to their aid in times of trouble. The secret for receiving God's protective care is a heart that is intimately attached to the Lord in gratitude and affection. He knows who such believers are, and he will be with them in trouble, hear their prayers, and give them lives full of his divine presence and provision (see Jn 14:12–21; 15:1–10).

92:1 IT IS GOOD TO PRAISE THE LORD. Praise and thanksgiving are basic elements in the believer's life (cf. Php 4:6; Col 4:2; 1Ti 2:1). We must thank the Lord morning and evening for salvation through his Son, Jesus (Col 1:12), for his love and grace, and for his faithful guidance and care (v. 2). We should express our gratitude for the word of God (1Th 2:13) and for his spiritual gifts (1Co 14:18). NT believers must give thanks in the name of the Lord Jesus (Col 3:17).

they will flourish in the courts
of our God.[o]
14They will still bear fruit[p] in old
age,
they will stay fresh and green,
15proclaiming, "The LORD is upright;
he is my Rock, and there is no
wickedness in him.[q]"

Psalm 93

1The LORD reigns,[r] he is robed in
majesty;[s]
the LORD is robed in majesty
and is armed with strength.[t]
The world is firmly established;[u]
it cannot be moved.[v]
2Your throne was established[w] long
ago;
you are from all eternity.[x]
3The seas[y] have lifted up, O LORD,
the seas have lifted up their
voice;[z]
the seas have lifted up their
pounding waves.[a]
4Mightier than the thunder[b] of the
great waters,
mightier than the breakers[c] of
the sea—
the LORD on high is mighty.[d]

5Your statutes stand firm;
holiness[e] adorns your house[f]
for endless days, O LORD.

Psalm 94

1O LORD, the God who avenges,[g]
O God who avenges, shine
forth.[h]
2Rise up,[i] O Judge[j] of the earth;
pay back[k] to the proud what
they deserve.
3How long will the wicked, O LORD,
how long will the wicked be
jubilant?[l]

4They pour out arrogant[m] words;
all the evildoers are full of
boasting.[n]
5They crush your people,[o] O LORD;
they oppress your inheritance.[p]
6They slay the widow[q] and the
alien;
they murder the fatherless.[r]
7They say, "The LORD does not
see;[s]
the God of Jacob[t] pays no
heed."

8Take heed, you senseless ones[u]
among the people;
you fools, when will you become
wise?
9Does he who implanted the ear not
hear?
Does he who formed the eye not
see?[v]
10Does he who disciplines[w] nations
not punish?
Does he who teaches[x] man lack
knowledge?
11The LORD knows the thoughts[y] of
man;
he knows that they are futile.[z]

12Blessed is the man you
discipline,[a] O LORD,
the man you teach[b] from your
law;
13you grant him relief from days of
trouble,[c]
till a pit[d] is dug for the wicked.
14For the LORD will not reject his
people;[e]
he will never forsake his
inheritance.
15Judgment will again be founded on
righteousness,[f]
and all the upright in heart[g]
will follow it.

16Who will rise up[h] for me against
the wicked?
Who will take a stand for me
against evildoers?[i]
17Unless the LORD had given me
help,[j]
I would soon have dwelt in the
silence of death.[k]
18When I said, "My foot is
slipping,[l]"

92:13 [o]Ps 135:2 **92:14** [p]S Ps 1:3; S Jn 15:2 **92:15** [q]S Job 34:10 **93:1** [r]S 1Ch 16:31; S Ps 97:1 [s]S Job 40:10; S Ps 21:5 [t]S Ps 65:6 [u]Ps 24:2; 78:69; 119:90 [v]1Ch 16:30; Ps 96:10 **93:2** [w]S 2Sa 7:16 [x]S Ge 21:33 **93:3** [y]Ps 96:11; 98:7; Isa 5:30; 17:12-13; Jer 6:23 [z]S Ps 46:3 [a]Job 9:8; Ps 107:25,29; Isa 51:15; Jer 31:35; Hab 3:10 **93:4** [b]Ps 65:7; Jer 6:23 [c]S Ps 18:4; Jnh 1:15 [d]S Ne 9:32; S Job 9:4 **93:5** [e]Ps 29:2; 96:9 [f]Ps 5:7; 23:6 **94:1** [g]S Ge 4:24; Ro 12:19 [h]S Dt 33:2; Ps 80:1 **94:2** [i]S Nu 10:35 [j]S Ge 18:25; Heb 12:23; S Jas 5:9 [k]S Ps 31:23 **94:3** [l]Ps 13:2 **94:4** [m]Jer 43:2 [n]S Ps 52:1 **94:5** [o]Ps 44:2; 74:8; Isa 3:15; Jer 8:21 [p]Ps 28:9 **94:6** [q]S Dt 10:18; S Isa 1:17 [r]Dt 24:19 **94:7** [s]S Job 22:14 [t]S Ge 24:12 **94:8** [u]S Dt 32:6; S Ps 73:22 **94:9** [v]Ex 4:11; Pr 20:12 **94:10** [w]S Ps 39:11 [x]S Ex 35:34; Job 35:11; Isa 28:26 **94:11** [y]Ps 139:2; Pr 15:26; S Mt 9:4 [z]1Co 3:20* **94:12** [a]S Job 5:17; 1Co 11:32; Heb 12:5 [b]S Dt 8:3; S 1Sa 12:23 **94:13** [c]S Ps 86:7 [d]S Ps 7:15; S 55:23 **94:14** [e]S Dt 31:6; Ps 37:28; Ro 11:2 **94:15** [f]Ps 97:2 [g]Ps 7:10; 11:2; S 36:10 **94:16** [h]Nu 10:35; Ps 17:13; Isa 14:22 [i]S Ps 59:2 **94:17** [j]Ps 124:2 [k]S Ps 31:17 **94:18** [l]S Dt 32:35; S Job 12:5

94:1–23 THE GOD WHO AVENGES. Believers should be so grieved because of all the injustice, brutality and wickedness in the world that they pray continually for God to stop the triumph of evil and avenge the wrong. Jesus states that his chosen ones should cry out day and night to God that they might "get justice, and quickly" (Lk 18:7–8; see also Rev 6:10–11). Commitment to justice and sympathy for those who are wrongfully treated should cause us to pray for Christ's return that he might rule the earth in righteousness (Mt 6:10).

94:12 BLESSED IS THE MAN YOU DISCIPLINE. See Heb 12:5, note on God's discipline of his children.

your love, O LORD, supported me.
19When anxiety[m] was great within
me,
your consolation[n] brought joy
to my soul.

20Can a corrupt throne[o] be allied
with you—
one that brings on misery by its
decrees?[p]
21They band together[q] against the
righteous
and condemn the innocent[r] to
death.[s]
22But the LORD has become my
fortress,
and my God the rock[t] in whom
I take refuge.[u]
23He will repay[v] them for their sins
and destroy[w] them for their
wickedness;
the LORD our God will destroy
them.

Psalm 95

1Come,[x] let us sing for joy[y] to the
LORD;
let us shout aloud[z] to the
Rock[a] of our salvation.
2Let us come before him[b] with
thanksgiving[c]
and extol him with music[d] and
song.
3For the LORD is the great God,[e]
the great King[f] above all
gods.[g]
4In his hand are the depths of the
earth,[h]
and the mountain peaks belong
to him.
5The sea is his, for he made it,
and his hands formed the dry
land.[i]

94:19 [m] Ecc 11:10 [n] S Job 6:10 **94:20** [o] Jer 22:30; 36:30 [p] S Ps 58:2 **94:21** [q] S Ps 56:6 [r] Ps 106:38; Pr 17:15,26; 28:21; Isa 5:20, 23; Mt 27:4 [s] S Ge 18:23 **94:22** [t] S Ps 61:2 [u] S 2Sa 22:3; S Ps 18:2 **94:23** [v] S Ex 32:34; S Ps 54:5 [w] Ps 9:5; 37:38; 145:20 **95:1** [x] Ps 34:11; 80:2 [y] S Ps 5:11 [z] Ps 81:1; Isa 44:23; Zep 3:14 [a] S 2Sa 22:47 **95:2** [b] Ps 100:2; Mic 6:6 [c] S Ps 42:4 [d] Ps 81:2; S Eph 5:19 **95:3** [e] Ps 48:1; 86:10; 145:3; 147:5 [f] S Ps 47:2 [g] Ps 96:4; 97:9 **95:4** [h] S Ps 63:9 **95:5** [i] S Ge 1:9; Ps 146:6

95:6 [j] S 2Sa 12:16; Php 2:10 [k] S Ps 22:29 [l] 2Ch 6:13 [m] Ps 100:3; 149:2; Isa 17:7; 54:5; Da 6:10-11; Hos 8:14 **95:7** [n] S Ps 74:1 **95:8** [o] Mk 10:5; Heb 3:8 [p] S Ex 17:7; S Dt 33:8; Heb 3:15*; 4:7 [q] S Ps 78:40 **95:9** [r] S Nu 14:22; 1Co 10:9 **95:10** [s] S Ex 16:35; S Nu 14:34; Ac 7:36; Heb 3:17 [t] Ps 58:3; 119:67, 176; Pr 12:26; 16:29; Isa 53:6; Jer 31:19; 50:6; Eze 34:6 [u] S Dt 8:6 **95:11** [v] S Nu 14:23 [w] Dt 1:35; Heb 3:7-11*; 4:3* **96:1** [x] Ps 30:4 [y] Ps 33:3; S 40:3;

6Come, let us bow down[j] in
worship,[k]
let us kneel[l] before the LORD
our Maker;[m]
7for he is our God
and we are the people of his
pasture,[n]
the flock under his care.

Today, if you hear his voice,
8 do not harden your hearts[o] as
you did at Meribah,[1][p]
as you did that day at Massah[m]
in the desert,[q]
9where your fathers tested[r] and
tried me,
though they had seen what I
did.
10For forty years[s] I was angry with
that generation;
I said, "They are a people whose
hearts go astray,[t]
and they have not known my
ways."[u]
11So I declared on oath[v] in my
anger,
"They shall never enter my
rest."[w]

Psalm 96

96:1-13pp — 1Ch 16:23-33

1Sing to the LORD[x] a new song;[y]
sing to the LORD, all the earth.
2Sing to the LORD, praise his
name;[z]
proclaim his salvation[a] day
after day.
3Declare his glory[b] among the
nations,

98:1; 144:9; 149:1; Isa 42:10; S Rev 5:9 **96:2** [z] S Ps 68:4 [a] Ps 27:1; 71:15 **96:3** [b] Ps 8:1

[1] 8 *Meribah* means *quarreling.* [m] 8 *Massah* means *testing.*

95:1–11 COME, LET US SING. This psalm calls us to make sure that our worship and praise are accompanied by hearts that are obedient to the Lord. It sets forth Israel's rebellion in the desert as an example of those who err in what they desire, do not know God's righteous ways, and therefore fail to receive what he has promised (see Nu 14:22–23,28,30; Dt 1:34–35).

95:7–11 TODAY, IF YOU HEAR HIS VOICE. The NT applies these verses to believers in Christ; the "rest" mentioned in v. 11 is no longer Canaan, but our salvation in him (see Heb 3:7—4:12, notes).

95:8 DO NOT HARDEN YOUR HEARTS. Those who worship and praise the Lord must also hear and obey his voice (vv. 7,10). To ignore the voice of the Holy Spirit results in a hardening of our hearts so that we become less and less sensitive to the Spirit's desires (see Heb 3:8, note); the result is God's wrath coming on a church or individual (vv. 10–11).

96:2–3 DECLARE HIS GLORY AMONG THE NATIONS. Those of us who have received God's salvation and experienced his wonderful deeds must be eager to tell others that he can deliver and save them. The command to declare his glory among the nations looks forward to the Great Commission that Jesus gave, i.e., to go into all the world and preach the gospel to all nations (see Mt 28:19, note).

his marvelous deeds[c] among all
peoples.
4For great is the LORD and most
worthy of praise;[d]
he is to be feared[e] above all
gods.[f]
5For all the gods of the nations are
idols,[g]
but the LORD made the heavens.[h]
6Splendor and majesty[i] are before
him;
strength and glory[j] are in his
sanctuary.

7Ascribe to the LORD,[k] O families of
nations,[l]
ascribe to the LORD glory and
strength.
8Ascribe to the LORD the glory due
his name;
bring an offering[m] and come
into his courts.[n]
9Worship the LORD[o] in the splendor
of his[n] holiness;[p]
tremble[q] before him, all the
earth.[r]

10Say among the nations, "The LORD
reigns.[s]"
The world is firmly
established,[t] it cannot be
moved;[u]
he will judge[v] the peoples with
equity.[w]
11Let the heavens rejoice,[x] let the
earth be glad;[y]
let the sea resound, and all that
is in it;
12 let the fields be jubilant, and
everything in them.
Then all the trees of the forest[z]
will sing for joy;[a]
13 they will sing before the LORD,
for he comes,
he comes to judge[b] the earth.
He will judge the world in
righteousness[c]
and the peoples in his truth.[d]

96:3 [c]S Ps 71:17; Rev 15:3
96:4 [d]S Ps 48:1 [e]S Dt 28:58; S 1Ch 16:25; Ps 89:7 [f]S Ps 95:3
96:5 [g]S Lev 19:4 [h]S Ge 1:1; S 2Ch 2:12
96:6 [i]S Ps 21:5 [j]Ps 29:1; 89:17
96:7 [k]Ps 29:1 [l]Ps 22:27
96:8 [m]Ps 45:12; S 51:19; 72:10 [n]Ps 65:4; 84:10; 92:13; 100:4
96:9 [o]Ex 23:25; Jnh 1:9 [p]S Ps 93:5 [q]S Ex 15:14; Ps 114:7 [r]Ps 33:8
96:10 [s]Ps 97:1 [t]Ps 24:2; 78:69; 119:90 [u]S Ps 93:1 [v]Ps 58:11 [w]Ps 67:4; 98:9
96:11 [x]S Rev 12:12 [y]Ps 97:1; Isa 49:13
96:12 [z]Isa 44:23; 55:12; Eze 17:24 [a]Ps 65:13
96:13 [b]Rev 19:11 [c]S Ps 7:11; Ac 17:31 [d]Ps 86:11

97:1 [e]Ex 15:18; Ps 93:1; 96:10; 99:1; Isa 24:23; 52:7 [f]S Ps 96:11 [g]S Est 10:1
97:2 [h]S Job 22:14 [i]S Ex 19:9 [j]Ps 89:14
97:3 [k]Isa 9:19; Da 7:10; Joel 1:19; 2:3 [l]Hab 3:5 [m]S 2Sa 22:9
97:4 [n]S Job 36:30 [o]S 2Sa 22:8 [p]S Ps 18:7; 104:32; S Rev 6:12
97:5 [q]S Ps 46:2,6 [r]S Ps 22:14 [s]S Jos 3:11
97:6 [t]Ps 50:6; 98:2 [u]S Ps 19:1
97:7 [v]S Lev 26:1 [w]Isa 42:17; Jer 10:14 [x]S Dt 5:8 [y]Heb 1:6 [z]Ex 12:12; Ps 16:4
97:8 [a]S Ps 9:2 [b]Ps 48:11
97:9 [c]Ps 7:8 [d]S Job 34:29 [e]S Ps 47:9
97:10

Psalm 97

1The LORD reigns,[e] let the earth be
glad;[f]
let the distant shores[g] rejoice.
2Clouds[h] and thick darkness[i]
surround him;
righteousness and justice are
the foundation of his
throne.[j]
3Fire[k] goes before[l] him
and consumes[m] his foes on
every side.
4His lightning[n] lights up the world;
the earth[o] sees and trembles.[p]
5The mountains melt[q] like wax[r]
before the LORD,
before the Lord of all the
earth.[s]
6The heavens proclaim his
righteousness,[t]
and all the peoples see his
glory.[u]

7All who worship images[v] are put
to shame,[w]
those who boast in idols[x]—
worship him,[y] all you gods![z]

8Zion hears and rejoices
and the villages of Judah are
glad[a]
because of your judgments,[b]
O LORD.
9For you, O LORD, are the Most
High[c] over all the earth;[d]
you are exalted[e] far above all
gods.

10Let those who love the LORD hate
evil,[f]
for he guards[g] the lives of his
faithful ones[h]

[f]S Job 28:28; Am 5:15; Ro 12:9 [g]Ps 145:20 [h]Ps 31:23; 37:28; Pr 2:8

[n]9 Or *LORD with the splendor of*

97:1–12 THE LORD REIGNS. This psalm describes four elements of God's kingdom: righteousness and justice as the foundation of his throne (v. 2), his ruling power over all the earth (vv. 1–6,9), his victory over false gods (v. 7) and the subsequent joy of the righteous (vv. 8–12). It prophesies the ultimate revelation of Christ and his kingdom rule at the end of history (Rev 19—22), an event that will call forth great joy among the redeemed (cf. Isa 25:9; Rev 11:15–17; 18:20; 19:1–3).

97:10 LET THOSE WHO LOVE THE LORD HATE EVIL. Those who claim to love the Lord will be tested by how much they hate evil while living on this earth. A truly regenerated believer, made one with Christ and indwelt by the Holy Spirit, will love what God loves and hate what he hates. We should be vexed by the wickedness, brutality and ungodliness in the world, and grieved by the lives being destroyed by its evil; furthermore, we should be deeply distressed when sin and immorality are tolerated in God's house (see 1Co 5:2, note; Heb 1:9, note).

and delivers[i] them from the
hand of the wicked.[j]
11 Light is shed[k] upon the
righteous[l]
and joy on the upright in
heart.[m]
12 Rejoice in the LORD,[n] you who are
righteous,
and praise his holy name.[o]

Psalm 98

A psalm.

1 Sing to the LORD[p] a new song,[q]
for he has done marvelous
things;[r]
his right hand[s] and his holy
arm[t]
have worked salvation[u] for him.
2 The LORD has made his salvation
known[v]
and revealed his righteousness[w]
to the nations.[x]
3 He has remembered[y] his love
and his faithfulness to the house
of Israel;
all the ends of the earth[z] have
seen
the salvation of our God.[a]

Ps 116:1-13

4 Shout for joy[b] to the LORD, all the
earth,
burst into jubilant song with
music;
5 make music to the LORD with the
harp,[c]
with the harp and the sound of
singing,[d]
6 with trumpets[e] and the blast of
the ram's horn[f]—
shout for joy[g] before the LORD,
the King.[h]

7 Let the sea[i] resound, and
everything in it,
the world, and all who live in
it.[j]
8 Let the rivers clap their hands,[k]
let the mountains[l] sing
together for joy;
9 let them sing before the LORD,
for he comes to judge the earth.
He will judge the world in
righteousness
and the peoples with equity.[m]

Psalm 99

1 The LORD reigns,[n]
let the nations tremble;[o]
he sits enthroned[p] between the
cherubim,[q]
let the earth shake.
2 Great is the LORD[r] in Zion;[s]
he is exalted[t] over all the
nations.
3 Let them praise[u] your great and
awesome name[v]—
he is holy.[w]
4 The King[x] is mighty, he loves
justice[y]—
you have established equity;[z]
in Jacob you have done
what is just and right.[a]
5 Exalt[b] the LORD our God
and worship at his footstool;
he is holy.
6 Moses[c] and Aaron[d] were among
his priests,
Samuel[e] was among those who
called on his name;
they called on the LORD
and he answered[f] them.
7 He spoke to them from the pillar
of cloud;[g]

97:10 [i]S Ps 34:7; Da 3:28; 6:16 [j]Ps 37:40; Jer 15:21; 20:13 **97:11** [k]S Job 22:28 [l]Ps 11:5 [m]Ps 7:10 **97:12** [n]S Job 22:19; Ps 104:34; Isa 41:16; Php 4:4 [o]S Ex 3:15; S Ps 99:3 **98:1** [p]Ps 30:4 [q]S Ps 96:1 [r]Ex 15:1; Ps 96:3; Isa 12:5; Lk 1:51 [s]S Ex 15:6 [t]S Jos 4:24; Job 40:9; Isa 51:9; 52:10; 53:1; 63:5 [u]S Ps 44:3; Isa 59:16 **98:2** [v]Isa 52:10; Lk 3:6 [w]S Ps 97:6 [x]S Ps 67:2 **98:3** [y]S 1Ch 16:15 [z]S Ge 49:10; S Ps 48:10 [a]S Ps 50:23 **98:4** [b]Ps 20:5; Isa 12:6; 44:23; 52:9; 54:1; 55:12 **98:5** [c]Ps 33:2; 92:3; 147:7 [d]Isa 51:3 **98:6** [e]S Nu 10:2; S 2Sa 6:15 [f]S Ex 19:13 [g]Ps 20:5; 100:1; Isa 12:6 [h]Ps 2:6; 47:7 **98:7** [i]S Ps 93:3 [j]S Ps 24:1 **98:8** [k]S 2Ki 11:12 [l]Ps 148:9; Isa 44:23; 55:12 **98:9** [m]S Ps 96:10 **99:1** [n]S 1Ch 16:31; S Ps 97:1 [o]S Ex 15:14; S 1Ch 16:30 [p]S 2Sa 6:2 [q]S Ex 25:22 **99:2** [r]S Ps 48:1 [s]Ps 2:6 [t]Ex 15:1; Ps 46:10; 97:9; 113:4; 148:13 **99:3** [u]Ps 30:4; 33:21; 97:12; 103:1; 106:47; 111:9; 145:21; 148:5 [v]Ps 76:1 [w]S Ex 15:11; S Lev 11:44; Rev 4:8 **99:4** [x]Ps 2:6 [y]S 1Ki 10:9 [z]Ps 98:9 [a]S Ge 18:19; Rev 15:3 **99:5** [b]S Ex 15:2 **99:6** [c]S Ex 24:6 [d]S Ex 28:1 [e]1Sa 7:5 [f]Ps 4:3; 91:15 **99:7** [g]S Ex 13:21; S 19:9; S Nu 11:25

98:1–9 A NEW SONG. This psalm is a prophetic song of praise for the Lord's victory and for his salvation made known to Israel and all the nations (vv. 1–3). This prophecy is now being fulfilled through the outpouring of the Holy Spirit upon believers and the Spirit-empowered proclamation of the gospel (Ac 1:8; 2:4).

98:9 HE COMES TO JUDGE THE EARTH. This verse will find its ultimate fulfillment in our Lord's return to judge the world (see Rev 19—22), eliminate sin and sorrow, and renew the heavens and the earth. Nature itself will rejoice (v. 8) as it participates in the final redemption when Christ rules the earth in righteousness and justice (see Isa 55:12–13; Ro 8:19–22).

99:3 GREAT AND AWESOME NAME—HE IS HOLY. The Lord God is so awesome and holy that even his name must be treated with the utmost reverence and respect. God may never be treated lightly, for he is enthroned far above humans in strength, justice, purity and greatness. We must both love and fear God (vv. 1–3) and beware of adopting the world's casual use of his name (see Ex 20:7, note; Mt 6:9, note).

99:6 CALLED ON THE LORD, AND HE ANSWERED THEM. Although God is holy and to be feared (vv. 1–2), he has come down to us through Jesus Christ. He seeks our fellowship and delights in hearing and answering his people's prayers. Moses, Aaron and Samuel are listed as those who had a special relationship with God through their intercessory prayers.

they kept his statutes and the
decrees he gave them.

8O LORD our God,
you answered them;
you were to Israel[o] a forgiving
God,[h]
though you punished[i] their
misdeeds.[p]
9Exalt the LORD our God
and worship at his holy
mountain,
for the LORD our God is holy.

Psalm 100

A psalm. For giving thanks.

1Shout for joy[j] to the LORD, all the
earth.
2 Worship the LORD[k] with
gladness;
come before him[l] with joyful
songs.
3Know that the LORD is God.[m]
It is he who made us,[n] and we
are his[q];
we are his people,[o] the sheep
of his pasture.[p]
4Enter his gates with
thanksgiving[q]
and his courts[r] with praise;
give thanks to him and praise
his name.[s]
5For the LORD is good[t] and his love
endures forever;[u]
his faithfulness[v] continues
through all generations.

99:8 [h]S Ex 22:27; S Nu 14:20 [i]S Lev 26:18 **100:1** [j]S Ps 98:6 **100:2** [k]S Dt 10:12 [l]S Ps 95:2 **100:3** [m]S 1Ki 18:21; S Ps 46:10 [n]S Job 10:3 [o]Ps 79:13; Isa 19:25; 63:8, 17-19; 64:9 [p]S 2Sa 24:17; S Ps 74:1 **100:4** [q]S Ps 42:4 [r]S Ps 96:8 [s]Ps 116:17 **100:5** [t]S 1Ch 16:34 [u]S Ezr 3:11; Ps 106:1 [v]Ps 108:4; 119:90

101:1 [w]Ps 33:1; 51:14; 89:1; 145:7 **101:2** [x]S Ge 17:1; Php 1:10 [y]S 1Ki 3:14 **101:3** [z]Jer 16:18; Eze 11:21; Hos 9:10 [a]S Ps 5:5 **101:4** [b]Pr 3:32; 6:16-19; 11:20 **101:5** [c]S Ex 20:16; S Lev 19:16 [d]S Ps 10:5 **101:6** [e]ver 2; Ps 119:1

Psalm 101

Of David. A psalm.

1I will sing of your love[w] and
justice;
to you, O LORD, I will sing
praise.
2I will be careful to lead a
blameless life[x]—
when will you come to me?

I will walk[y] in my house
with blameless heart.
3I will set before my eyes
no vile thing.[z]

The deeds of faithless men I
hate;[a]
they will not cling to me.
4Men of perverse heart[b] shall be
far from me;
I will have nothing to do with
evil.
5Whoever slanders his neighbor[c] in
secret,
him will I put to silence;
whoever has haughty eyes[d] and a
proud heart,
him will I not endure.
6My eyes will be on the faithful in
the land,
that they may dwell with me;
he whose walk is blameless[e]
will minister to me.

[o]8 Hebrew *them* [p]8 Or / *an avenger of the wrongs done to them* [q]3 Or *and not we ourselves*

99:8 A FORGIVING GOD, THOUGH YOU PUNISHED THEIR MISDEEDS. God can pardon and punish an individual at the same time. We must distinguish between being restored in our relationship with God and still experiencing the consequences of sins we have committed (see 2Sa 12:13, note; 1Ch 21:14, note).

100:2 COME BEFORE HIM WITH JOYFUL SONGS. Individual and congregational singing should be done primarily "to the LORD" (v. 1), with joy and out of a conscious awareness of his presence. In song we remember that he created us and redeemed us, and that we are now his people and he is our shepherd (v. 3). We sing of his love and faithfulness that will continue forever (v. 5; see Eph 5:19, note).

101:1–8 LOVE AND JUSTICE. This psalm pictures the kind of heart that the king of Israel must have if he desires to rule according to God's will. The attitudes expressed in this psalm also apply to those who rule in God's church (cf. Ac 20:28; 24:16).

101:2 I WILL WALK IN MY HOUSE WITH BLAMELESS HEART. Faithful believers will make it a priority to please God in their own homes. Family relationships are where true godliness must first be manifested and developed. The very purpose and direction of our hearts must be to seek God in prayer, to study his Word, to have family devotions, to show love and care to the members of our family, to walk blamelessly and to have eyes that refuse to look at evil (see next note).

101:3 I WILL SET BEFORE MY EYES NO VILE THING. Today the ungodly are consumed with using their eyes to view immorality, wickedness, brutality, violence, pornography and all kinds of evil as a means to gratify their lust and desire for perverted pleasure. Through television, movies, videos, books and magazines, people can observe every kind of wickedness. However, those committed to God and his righteousness will hate and shun evil (see 97:10, note) and will guard their lives and families by setting nothing before their eyes that would displease or grieve the Holy Spirit (see previous note; Ro 1:32, note).

7 No one who practices deceit
will dwell in my house;
no one who speaks falsely
will stand in my presence.
8 Every morning[f] I will put to
silence
all the wicked[g] in the land;
I will cut off every evildoer[h]
from the city of the LORD.[i]

Psalm 102

A prayer of an afflicted man. When he is faint and pours out his lament before the LORD.

1 Hear my prayer,[j] O LORD;
let my cry for help[k] come to
you.
2 Do not hide your face[l] from me
when I am in distress.
Turn your ear[m] to me;
when I call, answer me quickly.
3 For my days vanish like smoke;[n]
my bones[o] burn like glowing
embers.
4 My heart is blighted and withered
like grass;[p]
I forget to eat my food.[q]
5 Because of my loud groaning[r]
I am reduced to skin and bones.
6 I am like a desert owl,[s]
like an owl among the ruins.
7 I lie awake;[t] I have become
like a bird alone[u] on a roof.
8 All day long my enemies[v] taunt
me;[w]
those who rail against me use
my name as a curse.[x]
9 For I eat ashes[y] as my food
and mingle my drink with
tears[z]
10 because of your great wrath,[a]
for you have taken me up and
thrown me aside.
11 My days are like the evening
shadow;[b]
I wither[c] away like grass.
12 But you, O LORD, sit enthroned
forever;[d]
your renown endures[e] through
all generations.[f]
13 You will arise[g] and have
compassion[h] on Zion,
for it is time[i] to show favor[j]
to her;
the appointed time[k] has come.
14 For her stones are dear to your
servants;
her very dust moves them to
pity.
15 The nations will fear[l] the name
of the LORD,
all the kings[m] of the earth will
revere your glory.
16 For the LORD will rebuild Zion[n]
and appear in his glory.[o]
17 He will respond to the prayer[p] of
the destitute;
he will not despise their plea.
18 Let this be written[q] for a future
generation,
that a people not yet created[r]
may praise the LORD:
19 "The LORD looked down[s] from his
sanctuary on high,
from heaven he viewed the
earth,
20 to hear the groans of the
prisoners[t]
and release those condemned to
death."
21 So the name of the LORD will be
declared[u] in Zion
and his praise[v] in Jerusalem
22 when the peoples and the
kingdoms
assemble to worship[w] the LORD.
23 In the course of my life[r] he broke
my strength;
he cut short my days.[x]
24 So I said:
"Do not take me away, O my
God, in the midst of my
days;
your years go on[y] through all
generations.
25 In the beginning[z] you laid the
foundations of the earth,

101:8 [f] Ps 5:3; Jer 21:12 [g] Ps 75:10 [h] S 2Sa 3:39; Ps 118:10-12 [i] S Ps 46:4 102:1 [j] Ps 4:1 [k] S Ex 2:23 102:2 [l] S Ps 22:24 [m] S 2Ki 19:16; Ps 31:2; 88:2 102:3 [n] S Ps 37:20; S Jas 4:14 [o] La 1:13 102:4 [p] S Ps 37:2; 90:5-6 [q] S 1Sa 1:7; S Ezr 10:6; S Job 33:20 102:5 [r] S Ps 6:6 102:6 [s] S Dt 14:15-17; Job 30:29; Isa 34:11; Zep 2:14 102:7 [t] Ps 77:4 [u] Ps 38:11 102:8 [v] S Ps 31:11 [w] S Ps 42:10; Lk 22:63-65; 23:35-37 [x] S Ex 22:28; Isa 65:15; Jer 24:9; 25:18; 42:18; 44:12; Eze 14:8; Zec 8:13 102:9 [y] Isa 44:20 [z] Ps 6:6; 42:3; 80:5 102:10 [a] Ps 7:11; 38:3 102:11 [b] S 1Ch 29:15; S Job 14:2; S Ps 39:6 [c] S Job 8:12; Jas 1:10 102:12 [d] S Ex 15:18 [e] Ps 135:13; Isa 55:13; 63:12 [f] S Ex 3:15 102:13 [g] S Ps 44:26 [h] S Dt 32:36; S 1Ki 3:26; Isa 54:8; 60:10; Zec 10:6 [i] Ps 119:126 [j] S Ps 77:7 [k] S Ex 13:10; Da 8:19; Ac 1:7 102:15 [l] 1Ki 8:43; Ps 67:7; Isa 2:2 [m] Ps 76:12; 138:4; 148:11 102:16 [n] S Ps 51:18 [o] Ps 8:1; Isa 60:1-2 102:17 [p] S 1Ki 8:29; Ps 4:1; 6:9 102:18 [q] S Ro 4:24 [r] S Ps 22:31 102:19 [s] Ps 53:2 102:20 [t] S Ps 68:6; S Lk 4:19 102:21 [u] Ps 22:22 [v] Ps 9:14 102:22 [w] S Ps 22:27; Isa 49:22-23; Zec 8:20-23 102:23 [x] S Ps 39:5 102:24 [y] S Ge 21:33; Job 36:26; Ps 90:2 102:25 [z] S Ge 1:1; Heb 1:10-12*

[r] 23 Or *By his power*

102:2 WHEN I AM IN DISTRESS. During times of great distress in life, when nearly everything seems to be going wrong and we find ourselves helpless to change the situation, our only hope is to call on God and place our lives and circumstances in his hands (cf. 39:12; 54:2; 61:1; 64:1). The psalmist does this by crying out to the Lord for mercy and asking for his intervention. He is confident that God will answer his prayer and not forsake him.

102:25–26 YOU LAID THE FOUNDATIONS. These verses, quoted in Heb 1:10–12, imply that

and the heavens[a] are the work
of your hands.[b]
26They will perish,[c] but you remain;
they will all wear out like a
garment.
Like clothing you will change them
and they will be discarded.
27But you remain the same,[d]
and your years will never end.[e]
28The children of your servants[f]
will live in your presence;
their descendants[g] will be
established before you."

Psalm 103

Of David.

1Praise the LORD,[h] O my soul;[i]
all my inmost being, praise his
holy name.[j]
2Praise the LORD,[k] O my soul,
and forget not[l] all his
benefits—
3who forgives all your sins[m]
and heals[n] all your diseases,
4who redeems your life[o] from the
pit
and crowns you with love and
compassion,[p]
5who satisfies[q] your desires with
good things
so that your youth is renewed[r]
like the eagle's.[s]
6The LORD works righteousness[t]
and justice for all the
oppressed.[u]
7He made known[v] his ways[w] to
Moses,
his deeds[x] to the people of
Israel:
8The LORD is compassionate and
gracious,[y]
slow to anger, abounding in
love.
9He will not always accuse,
nor will he harbor his anger
forever;[z]
10he does not treat us as our sins
deserve[a]
or repay us according to our
iniquities.
11For as high as the heavens are
above the earth,
so great is his love[b] for those
who fear him;[c]
12as far as the east is from the
west,
so far has he removed our
transgressions[d] from us.
13As a father has compassion[e] on
his children,
so the LORD has compassion on
those who fear him;
14for he knows how we are
formed,[f]

102:25 [a]S 2Ch 2:12 [b]S Ps 8:3 **102:26** [c]Isa 13:10,13; 34:4; 51:6; Eze 32:8; Joel 2:10; Mt 24:35; 2Pe 3:7-10; Rev 20:11 **102:27** [d]S Nu 23:19; Heb 13:8; Jas 1:17 [e]Ps 9:7 **102:28** [f]Ps 69:36 [g]Ps 25:13; 89:4 **103:1** [h]Ps 28:6 [i]Ps 104:1 [j]S Ps 30:4 **103:2** [k]Ps 106:1; 117:1 [l]S Dt 6:12; Ps 77:11 **103:3** [m]S Ex 34:7 [n]S Ex 15:26; Col 3:13; 1Pe 2:24; 1Jn 1:9 **103:4** [o]Ps 34:22; 56:13; Isa 43:1 [p]S Ps 8:5; 23:6 **103:5** [q]S Ps 90:14; S 104:28 [r]Job 33:25; Ps 119:25,93; 2Co 4:16 [s]S Ex 19:4 **103:6** [t]Ps 9:8; 65:5; Isa 9:7 [u]S Ps 74:21; S Lk 4:19 **103:7** [v]Ps 99:7; 147:19 [w]S Ex 33:13 [x]Ps 106:22 **103:8** [y]S Ex 22:27; S Ps 86:15; Mic 7:18-19; Jas 5:11 **103:9** [z]Ps 30:5; 79:5; Isa 57:16; Jer 3:5,12; Mic 7:18 **103:10** [a]S Ezr 9:13; Ro 6:23 **103:11** [b]Ps 13:5; 57:10; 100:5; 106:45; 117:2; La 3:22; Eph 3:18 [c]S 2Ch 6:31 **103:12** [d]S 2Sa 12:13; Ro 4:7; Eph 2:5 **103:13** [e]Mal 3:17; 1Jn 3:1 **103:14** [f]Ps 119:73; 139:13-15; Isa 29:16

the experiences of distress described by the psalmist apply to Jesus Christ as well (vv. 1–11). Vv. 12–28 speak about the Lord's kingdom on earth, his work in creation, and his eternity. The present heavens and earth will be exchanged for a brand new heaven and earth (as the figure of changing clothes shows). But God will not change; he remains the same.

103:1–2 PRAISE THE LORD, O MY SOUL. This psalm expresses thanksgiving and praise to the Lord for the benefits and blessings that he bestows on the believing covenant people. We must never forget God's goodness to us (cf. Dt 8:12–14; 2Ch 32:25) or fail to be thankful for his blessings showered on us through the Holy Spirit (see next note; cf. Ac 2:38–39; 9:17–18; see Jn 14:16, note).

103:3–16 FORGIVES . . . HEALS. The fall of Adam into sin led the human race into the universal experience of sin, sickness and death. In contrast, the psalmist lists God's blessings for his people: forgiveness of our sins, healing for our diseases, and the gifts of redemption and eternal life. Forgiveness is the first and most important gift we can receive from God. Through it we are restored to God and redeemed from destruction (v. 4). Healing of diseases that come to us because of sin and Satan is likewise part of the salvation that God makes available to his people (see Jas 5:15–16, notes; see article on DIVINE HEALING, p. 1420).

103:13 COMPASSION ON THOSE WHO FEAR HIM. God shows mercy to those who truly fear him. The fear of God is a redeeming fear that motivates us to turn away from evil, to keep God's precepts, and to seek the Lord's nearness and grace (see article on THE FEAR OF THE LORD, p. 260). The blessings God gives to those who fear him are: (1) his mercy, love and forgiveness (vv. 11–12,17; cf. Isa 1:18; 38:17; Jer 31:14); (2) his fatherly love and compassion (vv. 13–14); and (3) his faithfulness and goodness to their children (v. 17).

103:14 HE KNOWS HOW WE ARE FORMED. God has compassion on his children because he knows their weaknesses and infirmities. Even the best of his followers stand in need of his compassion. As a father has deep compassion for his children when they fail, suffer or are mistreated, so also the heavenly Father hurts when his own are hurting. In the midst of trouble, failure and struggle, we must not think that God is aloof or uncaring; rather, we must remember that his eyes look

he remembers that we are
dust.[g]
15As for man, his days are like
grass,[h]
he flourishes like a flower[i] of
the field;
16the wind blows[j] over it and it is
gone,
and its place[k] remembers it no
more.
17But from everlasting to everlasting
the LORD's love is with those
who fear him,
and his righteousness with their
children's children[l]—
18with those who keep his
covenant[m]
and remember[n] to obey his
precepts.[o]

19The LORD has established his
throne[p] in heaven,
and his kingdom rules[q] over
all.

20Praise the LORD,[r] you his
angels,[s]
you mighty ones[t] who do his
bidding,[u]
who obey his word.
21Praise the LORD, all his heavenly
hosts,[v]
you his servants[w] who do his
will.
22Praise the LORD, all his works[x]
everywhere in his dominion.

Praise the LORD, O my soul.[y]

Psalm 104

1Praise the LORD, O my soul.[z]

O LORD my God, you are very
great;
you are clothed with splendor
and majesty.[a]
2He wraps[b] himself in light[c] as
with a garment;
he stretches[d] out the heavens[e]
like a tent[f]
3 and lays the beams[g] of his
upper chambers on their
waters.[h]
He makes the clouds[i] his
chariot[j]
and rides on the wings of the
wind.[k]
4He makes winds his
messengers,[s][l]
flames of fire[m] his servants.

5He set the earth[n] on its
foundations;[o]
it can never be moved.
6You covered it[p] with the deep[q]
as with a garment;
the waters stood[r] above the
mountains.
7But at your rebuke[s] the waters
fled,
at the sound of your thunder[t]
they took to flight;
8they flowed over the mountains,
they went down into the valleys,
to the place you assigned[u] for
them.
9You set a boundary[v] they cannot
cross;
never again will they cover the
earth.

10He makes springs[w] pour water
into the ravines;
it flows between the mountains.
11They give water[x] to all the beasts
of the field;
the wild donkeys[y] quench their
thirst.
12The birds of the air[z] nest by the
waters;
they sing among the branches.[a]
13He waters the mountains[b] from
his upper chambers;[c]
the earth is satisfied by the fruit
of his work.[d]
14He makes grass grow[e] for the
cattle,
and plants for man to
cultivate—
bringing forth food[f] from the
earth:

103:14 [g]S Ge 2:7; S Ps 146:4
103:15 [h]Ps 37:2; 90:5; 102:11; Isa 40:6 [i]S Job 14:2; Jas 1:10
103:16 [j]Isa 40:7; Hag 1:9 [k]S Job 7:8
103:17 [l]S Ge 48:11; S Ezr 9:12
103:18 [m]S Dt 29:9 [n]Ps 119:52 [o]S Nu 15:40; Jn 14:15
103:19 [p]Ps 47:8; 80:1; 113:5 [q]Ps 22:28; 66:7; Da 4:17
103:20 [r]Ps 28:6 [s]S Ne 9:6; Lk 2:13; Heb 1:14 [t]S Ps 29:1 [u]Ps 107:25; 135:7; 148:8
103:21 [v]S 1Ki 22:19 [w]S Ne 7:73
103:22 [x]Ps 19:1; 67:3; 145:10; 150:6 [y]ver 1; Ps 104:1
104:1 [z]S Ps 103:22 [a]S Job 40:10
104:2 [b]Isa 49:18; Jer 43:12 [c]Ps 18:12; 1Ti 6:16 [d]Job 9:8; Jer 51:15 [e]Job 37:18; Isa 40:22; 42:5; 44:24; Zec 12:1 [f]S Ps 19:4
104:3 [g]Am 9:6 [h]S Ps 24:2 [i]S Dt 33:26; Isa 19:1; Na 1:3 [j]S 2Ki 2:11 [k]Ps 18:10
104:4 [l]Ps 148:8; Heb 1:7* [m]Ge 3:24; 2Ki 2:11
104:5 [n]Ex 31:17; Job 26:7; Ps 24:1-2; 102:25; 121:2 [o]S 1Sa 2:8
104:6 [p]Ge 7:19 [q]S Ge 1:2 [r]2Pe 3:6
104:7 [s]S Ps 18:15 [t]S Ex 9:23; Ps 29:3
104:8 [u]Ps 33:7
104:9 [v]S Ge 1:9; S Ps 16:6
104:10 [w]Ps 107:33; Isa 41:18
104:11 [x]ver 13 [y]S Ge 16:12; Isa 32:14; Jer 14:6
104:12 [z]ver 17; Mt 8:20 [a]Mt 13:32
104:13 [b]Ps 135:7; 147:8; Jer 10:13; Zec 10:1 [c]S Lev 26:4 [d]Am 9:6
104:14 [e]S Job 38:27; Ps 147:8 [f]S Ge 1:30; S Job 28:5

[s]4 Or *angels*

on us with compassion, and he will help us according to our need (cf. Lk 7:12–13).

104:1–35 GOD, YOU ARE VERY GREAT. This psalm is a hymn about God's creation of all things and his providential care over all his works. It emphasizes his involvement with all he has made, for he dwells in the world and sustains it (see article on THE PROVIDENCE OF GOD, p. 78). What God continues to do in the universe reflects his glory. Yet God's creation is marred because of sin and evil; thus the psalm ends with a prayer for God to remove from it all things that are wicked and all those who sin (cf. Ro 8:19–23; see Ge 1—2, notes).

15wine[g] that gladdens the heart of
man,
oil[h] to make his face shine,
and bread that sustains[i] his
heart.
16The trees of the LORD[j] are well
watered,
the cedars of Lebanon[k] that he
planted.
17There the birds[l] make their
nests;
the stork has its home in the
pine trees.
18The high mountains belong to the
wild goats;[m]
the crags are a refuge for the
coneys.[t][n]

19The moon marks off the seasons,[o]
and the sun[p] knows when to go
down.
20You bring darkness,[q] it becomes
night,[r]
and all the beasts of the forest[s]
prowl.
21The lions roar for their prey[t]
and seek their food from God.[u]
22The sun rises, and they steal
away;
they return and lie down in their
dens.[v]
23Then man goes out to his work,[w]
to his labor until evening.[x]

24How many are your works,[y]
O LORD!
In wisdom you made[z] them all;
the earth is full of your
creatures.[a]
25There is the sea,[b] vast and
spacious,
teeming with creatures beyond
number—
living things both large and
small.[c]
26There the ships[d] go to and fro,
and the leviathan,[e] which you
formed to frolic[f] there.[g]
27These all look to you
to give them their food[h] at the
proper time.
28When you give it to them,
they gather it up;
when you open your hand,
they are satisfied[i] with good
things.
29When you hide your face,[j]
they are terrified;
when you take away their breath,
they die and return to the
dust.[k]
30When you send your Spirit,[l]
they are created,
and you renew the face of the
earth.

31May the glory of the LORD[m] endure
forever;
may the LORD rejoice in his
works[n]—
32he who looks at the earth, and it
trembles,[o]
who touches the mountains,[p]
and they smoke.[q]

33I will sing[r] to the LORD all my
life;
I will sing praise to my God as
long as I live.
34May my meditation be pleasing to
him,
as I rejoice[s] in the LORD.
35But may sinners vanish[t] from the
earth
and the wicked be no more.[u]

Praise the LORD, O my soul.

Praise the LORD.[u][v]

Psalm 105

105:1–15pp — 1Ch 16:8–22

1Give thanks to the LORD,[w] call on
his name;[x]

104:15 [g] S Ge 14:18; S Jdg 9:13 [h] Ps 23:5; 92:10; Lk 7:46 [i] S Dt 8:3; Mt 6:11 **104:16** [j] Ge 1:11 [k] S Ps 72:16 **104:17** [l] ver 12 **104:18** [m] S Dt 14:5 [n] Pr 30:26 **104:19** [o] S Ge 1:14 [p] Ps 19:6 **104:20** [q] Isa 45:7; Am 5:8 [r] Ps 74:16 [s] S Ps 50:10 **104:21** [t] Am 3:4 [u] Ps 145:15; Joel 1:20; S Mt 6:26 **104:22** [v] S Job 37:8 **104:23** [w] S Ge 3:19 [x] Jdg 19:16 **104:24** [y] Ps 40:5 [z] S Ge 1:31 [a] Ps 24:1; 50:10-11 **104:25** [b] Ps 69:34 [c] Eze 47:10 **104:26** [d] Ps 107:23; Eze 27:9; Jnh 1:3 [e] S Job 3:8; 41:1 [f] Job 40:20 [g] S Ge 1:21 **104:27** [h] Job 36:31; Ps 145:15; 147:9 **104:28** [i] Ps 103:5; 145:16; Isa 58:11 **104:29** [j] S Dt 31:17 [k] S Job 7:21 **104:30** [l] S Ge 1:2 **104:31** [m] Ex 40:35; Ps 8:1; S Ro 11:36 [n] S Ge 1:4 **104:32** [o] S Ps 97:4 [p] S Ex 19:18 [q] Ps 144:5 **104:33** [r] S Ex 15:1; Ps 108:1 **104:34** [s] S Ps 2:11; 9:2; 32:11 **104:35** [t] Ps 37:38 [u] S Job 7:10 [v] Ps 28:6; 105:45; 106:48 **105:1** [w] S 1Ch 16:34 [x] Ps 80:18; 99:6; 116:13; Joel 2:32; Ac 2:21

[t] *18* That is, the hyrax or rock badger
[u] *35* Hebrew *Hallelu Yah*; in the Septuagint this line stands at the beginning of Psalm 105.

104:15 WINE THAT GLADDENS THE HEART. The word "wine" (Heb *yayin*) here refers to that which comes directly from "plants" (v. 14), not that which humans have permitted or caused to ferment. Natural grape juice is delicious in taste, nutritious as a food and fully approved by God (cf. Am 9:14; see article on WINE IN THE OLD TESTAMENT, p. 204).

105:1–45 GIVE THANKS TO THE LORD. This psalm calls Israel to worship, praise, obey and seek the Lord (vv. 1–4) because he has miraculously directed their personal and corporate history in order to create and preserve the nation of Israel as a holy people who observe his righteous laws (vv. 5–45). The psalmist intends to inspire in the people gratitude for the Lord's care in their lives, joy in their possession of the holy land, and faithfulness to him and his word. Likewise, we as believers should look back and remember God's history with us; to do so should elicit thankfulness and a greater loyalty to him who gave himself for us (Ro 8:32; Gal 2:20).

make known among the nations
what he has done.
2Sing to him,[y] sing praise[z] to
him;
tell of all his wonderful acts.[a]
3Glory in his holy name;[b]
let the hearts of those who seek
the LORD rejoice.
4Look to the LORD and his strength;
seek his face[c] always.

5Remember the wonders[d] he has
done,
his miracles, and the judgments
he pronounced,[e]
6O descendants of Abraham his
servant,[f]
O sons of Jacob, his chosen[g]
ones.
7He is the LORD our God;
his judgments are in all the
earth.

8He remembers his covenant[h]
forever,
the word he commanded, for a
thousand generations,
9the covenant he made with
Abraham,[i]
the oath he swore to Isaac.
10He confirmed it[j] to Jacob as a
decree,
to Israel as an everlasting
covenant:[k]
11"To you I will give the land of
Canaan[l]
as the portion you will
inherit."[m]

12When they were but few in
number,[n]
few indeed, and strangers in
it,[o]
13they wandered from nation to
nation,[p]
from one kingdom to another.
14He allowed no one to oppress[q]
them;
for their sake he rebuked
kings:[r]

105:2 [y]Ps 30:4; 33:3; 96:1 [z]Ps 7:17; 18:49; 27:6; 59:17; 71:22; 146:2 [a]S Ps 75:1
105:3 [b]S Ps 89:16
105:4 [c]S Ps 24:6
105:5 [d]S Ps 40:5 [e]S Dt 7:18
105:6 [f]ver 42 [g]S Dt 10:15; Ps 106:5
105:8 [h]S Ge 9:15; Ps 106:45; 111:5; Eze 16:60; S Lk 1:72
105:9 [i]Ge 12:7; S 15:18; S 22:16-18; Lk 1:73; Gal 3:15-18
105:10 [j]Ge 28:13-15 [k]Isa 55:3
105:11 [l]S Ge 12:7 [m]S Nu 34:2
105:12 [n]Dt 7:7 [o]Ge 23:4; Heb 11:9
105:13 [p]Ge 15:13-16; Nu 32:13; 33:3-49
105:14 [q]Ge 35:5 [r]Ge 12:17-20; S 20:3; S Ps 9:5
105:15 [s]S Ge 26:11; S 1Sa 12:3 [t]S Ge 20:7
105:16 [u]S Ge 12:10; S Lev 26:26; Isa 3:1; Eze 4:16
105:17 [v]S Ge 37:28; Ac 7:9
105:18 [w]S Ge 40:15
105:19 [x]S Ge 12:10; 40:20-22 [y]Ge 41:40
105:20 [z]Ge 41:14
105:22 [a]Ge 41:43-44 [b]S Ge 41:40
105:23 [c]Ge 46:6; Ac 7:15; 13:17 [d]Ge 47:28 [e]S Ps 78:51
105:24 [f]Ex 1:7, 9; Ac 7:17
105:25 [g]S Ex 4:21 [h]Ex 1:6-10; Ac 7:19
105:26 [i]S Ex 3:10 [j]S Ex 4:16;

15"Do not touch[s] my anointed ones;
do my prophets[t] no harm."

16He called down famine[u] on the
land
and destroyed all their supplies
of food;
17and he sent a man before them—
Joseph, sold as a slave.[v]
18They bruised his feet with
shackles,[w]
his neck was put in irons,
19till what he foretold[x] came to
pass,
till the word[y] of the LORD
proved him true.
20The king sent and released him,
the ruler of peoples set him
free.[z]
21He made him master of his
household,
ruler over all he possessed,
22to instruct his princes[a] as he
pleased
and teach his elders wisdom.[b]

23Then Israel entered Egypt;[c]
Jacob lived[d] as an alien in the
land of Ham.[e]
24The LORD made his people very
fruitful;
he made them too numerous[f]
for their foes,
25whose hearts he turned[g] to hate
his people,
to conspire[h] against his
servants.
26He sent Moses[i] his servant,
and Aaron,[j] whom he had
chosen.[k]
27They performed[l] his miraculous
signs[m] among them,
his wonders[n] in the land of
Ham.
28He sent darkness[o] and made the
land dark—

S Nu 33:1 [k]S Nu 16:5; 17:5-8 105:27 [l]ver 28-37; Ex 7:8-12:51 [m]S Ex 4:17; S 10:1 [n]S Ex 3:20; Da 4:3 105:28 [o]S Ge 1:4; S Ex 10:22

105:4 LOOK TO THE LORD AND HIS STRENGTH. We are invited not only to seek the Lord's presence but also the power and strength of his grace. (1) We all need divine strength in order to persevere in salvation, live a life pleasing to God, and witness in the power of the Holy Spirit (see Ac 1:8, note; 2:4, note; see article on FAITH AND GRACE, p. 1720). (2) We must daily look to God and his grace, or we will face spiritual weakness and defeat; thus we must stir ourselves up constantly to seek him earnestly with our whole heart (see Mt 7:7–8, note; Lk 18:1,7, notes) and to expect signs of his presence and power in our lives (see Dt 4:29, note; 2Ch 26:5, note; Mt 7:7; Heb 11:6).

105:15 DO NOT TOUCH MY ANOINTED ONES. In this context, the anointed ones are Abraham, Isaac, Jacob (with his new name, Israel) and Joseph (vv. 9–10,17); we may not conclude from this verse, however, that we should give heed to every person who claims to be anointed.

for had they not rebelled
against[p] his words?
29He turned their waters into
blood,[q]
causing their fish to die.[r]
30Their land teemed with frogs,[s]
which went up into the
bedrooms of their rulers.
31He spoke,[t] and there came
swarms of flies,[u]
and gnats[v] throughout their
country.
32He turned their rain into hail,[w]
with lightning throughout their
land;
33he struck down their vines[x] and
fig trees[y]
and shattered the trees of their
country.
34He spoke,[z] and the locusts
came,[a]
grasshoppers[b] without
number;[c]
35they ate up every green thing in
their land,
ate up the produce of their soil.
36Then he struck down all the
firstborn[d] in their land,
the firstfruits of all their
manhood.
37He brought out Israel, laden with
silver and gold,[e]
and from among their tribes no
one faltered.
38Egypt was glad when they left,
because dread of Israel[f] had
fallen on them.
39He spread out a cloud[g] as a
covering,
and a fire to give light at
night.[h]
40They asked,[i] and he brought
them quail[j]
and satisfied them with the
bread of heaven.[k]
41He opened the rock,[l] and water
gushed out;
like a river it flowed in the
desert.
42For he remembered his holy
promise[m]
given to his servant Abraham.

105:28 [p]S Ex 7:22 **105:29** [q]S Ps 78:44 [r]Ex 7:21 **105:30** [s]S Ex 8:2,6 **105:31** [t]Ps 107:25; 148:8 [u]Ex 8:21-24; S Ps 78:45 [v]Ex 8:16-18 **105:32** [w]Ex 9:22-25; S Job 38:22; S Ps 78:47 **105:33** [x]Ps 78:47 [y]Ex 10:5,12 **105:34** [z]Ps 107:25 [a]S Ex 10:4,12-15 [b]S 1Ki 8:37 [c]Joel 1:6 **105:36** [d]S Ex 4:23; S 12:12 **105:37** [e]S Ex 3:21,22 **105:38** [f]Ex 15:16 **105:39** [g]S Ex 13:21; 1Co 10:1 [h]S Ps 78:14 **105:40** [i]Ps 78:18,24 [j]S Ex 16:13 [k]S Ex 16:4; Jn 6:31 **105:41** [l]S Nu 20:11; 1Co 10:4 **105:42** [m]Ge 12:1-3; 13:14-17; 15:13-16 **105:43** [n]Ex 15:1-18; Ps 106:12 **105:44** [o]Ex 32:13; Jos 11:16-23; 12:8; 13:6-7; Ps 111:6 [p]Dt 6:10-11; Ps 78:55 **105:45** [q]S Dt 4:40; 6:21-24; Ps 78:5-7 [r]S Ps 104:35 **106:1** [s]S Ps 22:23; S 103:2 [t]S Ps 119:68 [u]S Ezr 3:11; Ps 136:1-26; Jer 33:11 **106:2** [v]S Ps 71:16 **106:3** [w]Ps 112:5; Hos 12:6 [x]Ps 15:2 **106:4** [y]Ps 25:6,7 [z]S Ps 77:7 [a]S Ge 50:24 **106:5** [b]S Dt 30:15; Ps 1:3 [c]S Ps 105:6 [d]Ps 20:5; 27:6; 47:5; 118:15

43He brought out his people with
rejoicing,[n]
his chosen ones with shouts of
joy;
44he gave them the lands of the
nations,[o]
and they fell heir to what others
had toiled[p] for—
45that they might keep his precepts
and observe his laws.[q]

Praise the LORD.[v][r]

Psalm 106

106:1,47–48pp — 1Ch 16:34–36

1Praise the LORD.[w][s]

Give thanks to the LORD, for he is
good;[t]
his love endures forever.[u]
2Who can proclaim the mighty
acts[v] of the LORD
or fully declare his praise?
3Blessed are they who maintain
justice,[w]
who constantly do what is
right.[x]
4Remember me,[y] O LORD, when you
show favor[z] to your
people,
come to my aid[a] when you save
them,
5that I may enjoy the prosperity[b]
of your chosen ones,[c]
that I may share in the joy[d] of
your nation
and join your inheritance[e] in
giving praise.

6We have sinned,[f] even as our
fathers[g] did;
we have done wrong and acted
wickedly.[h]
7When our fathers were in Egypt,
they gave no thought[i] to your
miracles;
they did not remember[j] your
many kindnesses,

[e]S Ex 34:9 **106:6** [f]S 1Ki 8:47; S Ro 3:9 [g]S 2Ch 30:7 [h]Ne 1:7 **106:7** [i]S Jdg 3:7 [j]Ps 78:11,42

[v]45 Hebrew *Hallelu Yah* [w]1 Hebrew *Hallelu Yah*; also in verse 48

106:1–48 HIS LOVE ENDURES FOREVER. This psalm recounts Israel's recurring rebellion and apostasy with respect to God's word and ways. The psalmist confesses their sins and unfaithfulness and prays that God will once again visit his repentant people with full salvation and blessings. God's people should individually and collectively confess their shortcomings before the Lord. When we recognize our spiritual failure and then repent, real revival and reformation can take place (see article on CHRIST'S MESSAGE TO THE SEVEN CHURCHES, p. 2008).

and they rebelled by the sea,[k]
the Red Sea.[x]
8Yet he saved them[l] for his
name's sake,[m]
to make his mighty power[n]
known.
9He rebuked[o] the Red Sea, and it
dried up;[p]
he led them through[q] the
depths as through a desert.
10He saved them[r] from the hand of
the foe;[s]
from the hand of the enemy he
redeemed them.[t]
11The waters covered[u] their
adversaries;
not one of them survived.
12Then they believed his promises
and sang his praise.[v]
13But they soon forgot[w] what he
had done
and did not wait for his
counsel.[x]
14In the desert[y] they gave in to
their craving;
in the wasteland[z] they put God
to the test.[a]
15So he gave them[b] what they
asked for,
but sent a wasting disease[c]
upon them.
16In the camp they grew envious[d]
of Moses
and of Aaron, who was
consecrated to the LORD.
17The earth opened[e] up and
swallowed Dathan;[f]
it buried the company of
Abiram.[g]
18Fire blazed[h] among their
followers;
a flame consumed the wicked.
19At Horeb they made a calf[i]
and worshiped an idol cast from
metal.
20They exchanged their Glory[j]
for an image of a bull, which
eats grass.
21They forgot the God[k] who saved
them,
who had done great things[l] in
Egypt,
22miracles in the land of Ham[m]
and awesome deeds[n] by the
Red Sea.
23So he said he would destroy[o]
them—
had not Moses, his chosen one,
stood in the breach[p] before him
to keep his wrath from
destroying them.
24Then they despised[q] the pleasant
land;[r]
they did not believe[s] his
promise.
25They grumbled[t] in their tents
and did not obey the LORD.
26So he swore[u] to them with
uplifted hand
that he would make them fall in
the desert,[v]
27make their descendants fall among
the nations
and scatter[w] them throughout
the lands.
28They yoked themselves to the Baal
of Peor[x]
and ate sacrifices offered to
lifeless gods;
29they provoked the LORD to anger[y]
by their wicked deeds,[z]
and a plague[a] broke out among
them.
30But Phinehas[b] stood up and
intervened,
and the plague was checked.[c]
31This was credited to him[d] as
righteousness
for endless generations[e] to
come.
32By the waters of Meribah[f] they
angered the LORD,
and trouble came to Moses
because of them;
33for they rebelled[g] against the
Spirit[h] of God,

106:7 [k]Ex 14:11-12 **106:8** [l]Ex 14:30; S Ps 80:3; 107:13; Isa 25:9; Joel 2:32 [m]S Ex 9:16; S Ps 23:3 [n]S Ex 14:31 **106:9** [o]Ps 18:15; Isa 50:2 [p]S Ex 14:21; Na 1:4 [q]Ps 78:13; Isa 63:11-14 **106:10** [r]Ex 14:30; Ps 107:13 [s]S Ps 78:53 [t]Ps 78:42; 107:2; Isa 35:9; 62:12 **106:11** [u]S Ex 14:28 **106:12** [v]Ex 15:1-21; S Ps 105:43 **106:13** [w]S Ex 15:24 [x]S Ex 16:28; S Nu 27:21 **106:14** [y]S Ps 78:40 [z]S Ps 68:7 [a]S Ex 17:2; 1Co 10:9 **106:15** [b]S Ex 16:13; Ps 78:29 [c]S Nu 11:33 **106:16** [d]Nu 16:1-3 **106:17** [e]Dt 11:6 [f]S Ex 15:12 [g]S Nu 16:1 **106:18** [h]S Lev 10:2 **106:19** [i]S Ex 32:4; Ac 7:41 **106:20** [j]Jer 2:11; Ro 1:23 **106:21** [k]Ps 78:11 [l]Dt 10:21; Ps 75:1 **106:22** [m]S Ps 78:51 [n]S Ex 3:20; S Dt 4:34 **106:23** [o]S Ex 32:10 [p]Ex 32:11-14; S Nu 11:2; S Dt 9:19 **106:24** [q]Nu 14:30-31 [r]S Dt 8:7; S Jer 3:19 [s]S Nu 14:11; Heb 3:18-19 **106:25** [t]S Ex 15:24; Dt 1:27; 1Co 10:10 **106:26** [u]S Nu 14:23; Heb 4:3 [v]S Dt 2:14; Heb 3:17 **106:27** [w]S Lev 26:33 **106:28** [x]S Nu 23:28 **106:29** [y]Nu 25:3 [z]S Ps 64:2; 141:4 [a]S Nu 16:46; 25:8 **106:30** [b]S Ex 6:25 [c]Nu 25:8 **106:31** [d]S Ge 15:6; S Nu 25:11-13 [e]Ps 49:11 **106:32** [f]S Ex 17:7; Nu 20:2-13 **106:33** [g]S Ex 23:21; Ps 107:11 [h]S Ps 51:11; Isa 63:10

x 7 Hebrew *Yam Suph*; that is, Sea of Reeds; also in verses 9 and 22

106:15 SENT A WASTING DISEASE. We must beware of desiring and pursuing what is not in God's will. When we insist on satisfying our selfish desires, God sometimes lets us have our own way, but with it comes spiritual leanness or physical calamity. God may allow us to pursue things contrary to his revealed will, such as an unholy vocational ambition, an unholy love affair, worldly pleasures, covetous desires or ungodly fellowship with unbelievers, but in the end those things have destructive consequences (e.g., Ge 13:12–13; 19; Hos 13:11).

and rash words came from
Moses' lips.[y][i]

34They did not destroy[j] the peoples
as the LORD had commanded[k]
them,
35but they mingled[l] with the
nations
and adopted their customs.
36They worshiped their idols,[m]
which became a snare[n] to
them.
37They sacrificed their sons[o]
and their daughters to
demons.[p]
38They shed innocent blood,
the blood of their sons[q] and
daughters,
whom they sacrificed to the idols
of Canaan,
and the land was desecrated by
their blood.
39They defiled themselves[r] by what
they did;
by their deeds they prostituted[s]
themselves.

40Therefore the LORD was angry[t]
with his people
and abhorred his inheritance.[u]
41He handed them over[v] to the
nations,
and their foes ruled over them.
42Their enemies oppressed[w] them
and subjected them to their
power.
43Many times he delivered them,[x]
but they were bent on
rebellion[y]
and they wasted away in their
sin.

44But he took note of their distress
when he heard their cry;[z]
45for their sake he remembered his
covenant[a]
and out of his great love[b] he
relented.[c]

46He caused them to be pitied[d]
by all who held them captive.
47Save us,[e] O LORD our God,
and gather us[f] from the
nations,
that we may give thanks[g] to your
holy name[h]
and glory in your praise.

48Praise be to the LORD, the God of
Israel,
from everlasting to everlasting.
Let all the people say, "Amen!"[i]

Praise the LORD.

106:33 [i]Ex 17:4-7; Nu 20:8-12 **106:34** [j]S Jos 9:15; Jdg 1:27-36 [k]Ex 23:24; S Dt 2:34; 7:16; 20:17 **106:35** [l]Jdg 3:5-6; Ezr 9:1-2 **106:36** [m]S Dt 7:16 [n]S Ex 10:7 **106:37** [o]S Lev 18:21; S Dt 12:31; Eze 16:20-21 [p]S Ex 22:20; S Dt 32:17; 1Co 10:20 **106:38** [q]S Lev 18:21; S Dt 18:10; S 2Ki 3:27 **106:39** [r]S Ge 3:17; Lev 18:24; Eze 20:18 [s]S Nu 15:39 **106:40** [t]S Lev 26:28 [u]S Ex 34:9; S Dt 9:29 **106:41** [v]S Jdg 2:14 **106:42** [w]S Jdg 4:3 **106:43** [x]S Jos 10:14; Jdg 7:1-25; S Ne 9:28; Ps 81:13-14 [y]S Jdg 2:16-19; 6:1-7 **106:44** [z]S Jdg 3:9 **106:45** [a]S Ge 9:15; Ps 105:8; S Lk 1:72 [b]S Ps 17:7; S 103:11 [c]S Ex 32:14 **106:46** [d]S Ex 3:21; S 1Ki 8:50 **106:47** [e]S Ps 28:9 [f]Ps 107:3; 147:2; Isa 11:12; 27:13; 56:8; 66:20; Jer 31:8; Eze 20:34; Mic 4:6 [g]Ps 105:1 [h]Ps 30:4; S 99:3 **106:48** [i]S Ps 41:13; S 72:19

BOOK V

Psalms 107–150

Psalm 107

1Give thanks to the LORD,[j] for he
is good;[k]
his love endures forever.
2Let the redeemed[l] of the LORD say
this—
those he redeemed from the
hand of the foe,
3those he gathered[m] from the
lands,
from east and west, from north
and south.[z]

4Some wandered in desert[n]
wastelands,
finding no way to a city[o] where
they could settle.
5They were hungry[p] and thirsty,[q]
and their lives ebbed away.

107:1 [j]S 1Ch 16:8; S 2Ch 5:13 [k]S 2Ch 7:3 **107:2** [l]S Ps 106:10; S Isa 35:9 **107:3** [m]S Ne 1:9 **107:4** [n]S Jos 5:6 [o]ver 36 **107:5** [p]Ex 16:3 [q]S Ex 15:22; S 17:2

[y]33 Or *against his spirit, / and rash words came from his lips* [z]3 Hebrew *north and the sea*

106:37 SACRIFICED THEIR SONS ... TO DEMONS. Those who served idols in OT times were in actuality dealing with demons, for behind all false religions are demonic manifestations, powers and influence (see article on THE NATURE OF IDOLATRY, p. 394). (1) Likewise, when a believer in Christ conforms to the world and adopts its ungodly customs and ways, he or she is in reality submitting to demonic influences (1Co 10:19–22; see Eph 2:2, note). (2) Today some in the church unknowingly sacrifice their children to demons by allowing them to be influenced by the ungodliness and immorality of the world through the entertainment media, unbelieving companions or instruction contrary to Biblical truth.

107:1–43 GIVE THANKS. This psalm exhorts the redeemed to praise the Lord for deliverance from desperate and dangerous situations. The psalmist uses four examples to illustrate that God responds to the extreme troubles of his people when they pray: hunger and thirst (vv. 4–9), bondage (vv. 10–16), illness almost to death (vv. 17–22), and the danger of storm (vv. 23–32). This psalm is relevant today for all believers who in misery and affliction cry out to the Lord; it builds up our faith and encourages us during those times when we need God to intervene specifically in our lives.

6Then they cried out[r] to the LORD
in their trouble,
and he delivered them from their
distress.
7He led them by a straight way[s]
to a city[t] where they could
settle.
8Let them give thanks[u] to the LORD
for his unfailing love[v]
and his wonderful deeds[w] for
men,
9for he satisfies[x] the thirsty
and fills the hungry with good
things.[y]

10Some sat in darkness[z] and the
deepest gloom,
prisoners suffering[a] in iron
chains,[b]
11for they had rebelled[c] against the
words of God
and despised[d] the counsel[e] of
the Most High.
12So he subjected them to bitter
labor;
they stumbled, and there was no
one to help.[f]
13Then they cried to the LORD in
their trouble,
and he saved them[g] from their
distress.
14He brought them out of darkness[h]
and the deepest gloom[i]
and broke away their chains.[j]
15Let them give thanks[k] to the LORD
for his unfailing love[l]
and his wonderful deeds[m] for
men,
16for he breaks down gates of
bronze
and cuts through bars of
iron.

17Some became fools[n] through their
rebellious ways[o]
and suffered affliction[p] because
of their iniquities.
18They loathed all food[q]
and drew near the gates of
death.[r]
19Then they cried[s] to the LORD in
their trouble,
and he saved them[t] from their
distress.
20He sent forth his word[u] and
healed them;[v]
he rescued[w] them from the
grave.[x]
21Let them give thanks[y] to the LORD
for his unfailing love[z]
and his wonderful deeds[a] for
men.
22Let them sacrifice thank
offerings[b]
and tell of his works[c] with
songs of joy.[d]

23Others went out on the sea[e] in
ships;[f]
they were merchants on the
mighty waters.
24They saw the works of the
LORD,[g]
his wonderful deeds in the
deep.
25For he spoke[h] and stirred up a
tempest[i]
that lifted high the waves.[j]
26They mounted up to the heavens
and went down to the
depths;
in their peril[k] their courage
melted[l] away.
27They reeled[m] and staggered like
drunken men;
they were at their wits'
end.
28Then they cried[n] out to the LORD
in their trouble,
and he brought them out of their
distress.[o]
29He stilled the storm[p] to a
whisper;
the waves[q] of the sea were
hushed.[r]

107:6 [r]S Ex 14:10
107:7 [s]S Ezr 8:21 [t]ver 36
107:8 [u]Ps 105:1 [v]Ps 6:4 [w]S Ps 75:1
107:9 [x]Ps 22:26; 63:5; Isa 58:11; Mt 5:6; Lk 1:53 [y]S Ps 23:1; Jer 31:25
107:10 [z]ver 14; Ps 88:6; 143:3; Isa 9:2; 42:7,16; 49:9; Mic 7:9 [a]Ps 102:20; Isa 61:1 [b]S Job 36:8
107:11 [c]S Ps 5:10 [d]S Nu 14:11 [e]S 1Ki 22:5; 2Ch 36:16
107:12 [f]S 2Ki 14:26; Ps 72:12
107:13 [g]S Ps 106:8
107:14 [h]S ver 10; Isa 9:2; 42:7; 50:10; 59:9; 60:2; S Lk 1:79 [i]Ps 86:13; Isa 29:18 [j]S Job 36:8; Ps 116:16; Ac 12:7
107:15 [k]ver 8, 21,31; Ps 105:1 [l]Ps 6:4 [m]S Ps 75:1
107:17 [n]S Ps 53:1 [o]S Ps 25:7 [p]S Lev 26:16; Isa 65:6-7; Jer 30:14-15; Gal 6:7-8
107:18 [q]S Job 3:24; S 6:6 [r]S Job 17:16; S 33:22
107:19 [s]ver 28; Ps 5:2 [t]ver 13; Ps 34:4
107:20 [u]S Dt 32:2; Ps 147:15; Mt 8:8; Lk 7:7 [v]S Ex 15:26 [w]S Job 33:28 [x]Ps 16:10; 30:3; S 56:13
107:21 [y]S ver 15 [z]Ps 6:4 [a]Ps 75:1
107:22 [b]S Lev 7:12 [c]Ps 9:11; 73:28; 118:17 [d]S Job 8:21; S Ps 65:8
107:23 [e]Isa 42:10 [f]S Ps 104:26
107:24 [g]Ps 64:9; 111:2; 143:5
107:25 [h]S Ps 105:31 [i]S Ps 50:3 [j]S Ps 93:3
107:26 [k]Lk 8:23 [l]S Jos 2:11
107:27 [m]Isa 19:14; 24:20; 28:7
107:28 [n]S ver 19 [o]Ps 4:1; Jnh 1:6
107:29 [p]Lk 8:24 [q]S Ps 93:3 [r]S Ps 65:7; Jnh 1:15

107:6 CRIED OUT TO THE LORD. Four times the psalmist uses this phrase, and four times it is stated that God delivered them "from their distress" (vv. 6,13,19,28). God frequently brings his children to a place where their own self-sufficiency fails and where no human being can help, in order that they might cry out to him in humble and childlike faith.

107:13 HE SAVED THEM FROM THEIR DISTRESS. Note that even when we have only ourselves to blame for our troubles, God desires to deliver us (vv. 1–13,17–22); thus, even if we are experiencing great distress, knowing that God may be judging us, we can still put our hope in his mercy and cry out to him in faith for his forgiveness and help.

30They were glad when it grew calm,
and he guided them[s] to their
desired haven.
31Let them give thanks[t] to the LORD
for his unfailing love[u]
and his wonderful deeds[v] for
men.
32Let them exalt[w] him in the
assembly[x] of the people
and praise him in the council of
the elders.
33He turned rivers into a desert,[y]
flowing springs[z] into thirsty
ground,
34and fruitful land into a salt
waste,[a]
because of the wickedness of
those who lived there.
35He turned the desert into pools of
water[b]
and the parched ground into
flowing springs;[c]
36there he brought the hungry to
live,
and they founded a city where
they could settle.
37They sowed fields and planted
vineyards[d]
that yielded a fruitful harvest;
38he blessed them, and their
numbers greatly
increased,[e]
and he did not let their herds
diminish.[f]
39Then their numbers decreased,[g]
and they were humbled[h]
by oppression, calamity and
sorrow;
40he who pours contempt on
nobles[i]
made them wander in a
trackless waste.[j]
41But he lifted the needy[k] out of
their affliction
and increased their families like
flocks.[l]
42The upright see and rejoice,[m]
but all the wicked shut their
mouths.[n]
43Whoever is wise,[o] let him heed
these things
and consider the great love[p] of
the LORD.

107:30 [s]ver 7
107:31 [t]S ver 15 [u]Ps 6:4 [v]Ps 75:1; 106:2
107:32 [w]Ps 30:1; 34:3; 99:5 [x]S Ps 1:5; 22:22,25; 26:12; 35:18
107:33 [y]1Ki 17:1; Ps 74:15; Isa 41:15; 42:15; 50:2 [z]S Ps 104:10
107:34 [a]S Ge 13:10
107:35 [b]S 2Ki 3:17; Ps 105:41; 126:4; Isa 43:19; 51:3 [c]S Job 38:26; S Isa 35:7
107:37 [d]S 2Ki 19:29; S Isa 37:30
107:38 [e]S Ge 12:2; S Dt 7:13 [f]S Ge 49:25
107:39 [g]S 2Ki 10:32; Eze 5:12 [h]S Ps 44:9
107:40 [i]S Job 12:18 [j]S Dt 32:10
107:41 [k]S 1Sa 2:8; Ps 113:7-9 [l]S Job 21:11
107:42 [m]S Job 22:19; Ps 97:10-12 [n]S Job 5:16; Ro 3:19
107:43 [o]Jer 9:12; Hos 14:9 [p]Ps 103:11

108:1 [q]Ps 112:7; 119:30,112 [r]S Ps 18:49
108:2 [s]S Job 21:12
108:4 [t]Nu 14:18; Ps 106:45 [u]S Ex 34:6 [v]S Ps 36:5
108:5 [w]S Ps 8:1 [x]S Ps 57:5
108:6 [y]S Job 40:14
108:7 [z]Ps 89:35 [a]Ps 68:35; 102:19 [b]S Ge 12:6 [c]S Ge 33:17
108:8 [d]S Ps 78:68
108:9 [e]S Ge 19:37 [f]S 2Sa 8:13-14 [g]S 2Sa 8:1
108:11 [h]S Ps 44:9
108:12 [i]Ps 118:8; 146:3; Isa 10:3; 30:5; 31:3; Jer 2:36; 17:5
108:13 [j]Ps 44:5; Isa 22:5; 63:3,6

Psalm 108

108:1-5pp — Ps 57:7-11
108:6-13pp — Ps 60:5-12

A song. A psalm of David.

1My heart is steadfast,[q] O God;
I will sing[r] and make music
with all my soul.
2Awake, harp and lyre![s]
I will awaken the dawn.
3I will praise you, O LORD, among
the nations;
I will sing of you among the
peoples.
4For great is your love,[t] higher
than the heavens;
your faithfulness[u] reaches to
the skies.[v]
5Be exalted, O God, above the
heavens,[w]
and let your glory be over all
the earth.[x]

6Save us and help us with your
right hand,[y]
that those you love may be
delivered.
7God has spoken[z] from his
sanctuary:[a]
"In triumph I will parcel out
Shechem[b]
and measure off the Valley of
Succoth.[c]
8Gilead is mine, Manasseh is mine;
Ephraim is my helmet,
Judah[d] my scepter.
9Moab[e] is my washbasin,
upon Edom[f] I toss my sandal;
over Philistia[g] I shout in
triumph."

10Who will bring me to the fortified
city?
Who will lead me to Edom?
11Is it not you, O God, you who have
rejected us
and no longer go out with our
armies?[h]
12Give us aid against the enemy,
for the help of man is
worthless.[i]
13With God we will gain the victory,
and he will trample down[j] our
enemies.

108:1–13 MY HEART IS STEADFAST. This psalm combines the words from 57:7–11 and 60:4–12. The psalmist is confident that ultimately God will deliver his people and give them victory over all their enemies.

108:9 MOAB . . . EDOM . . . PHILISTIA. Moab, Edom and Philistia were Israel's enemies on her eastern, southern and western borders, respectively.

Psalm 109

For the director of music. Of David.
A psalm.

1 O God, whom I praise,[k]
do not remain silent,[l]
2 for wicked and deceitful men[m]
have opened their mouths
against me;
they have spoken against me
with lying tongues.[n]
3 With words of hatred[o] they
surround me;
they attack me without cause.[p]
4 In return for my friendship they
accuse me,
but I am a man of prayer.[q]
5 They repay me evil for good,[r]
and hatred for my friendship.

6 Appoint[a] an evil man[b] to oppose
him;
let an accuser[c][s] stand at his
right hand.
7 When he is tried, let him be found
guilty,[t]
and may his prayers condemn[u]
him.
8 May his days be few;[v]
may another take his place[w] of
leadership.
9 May his children be fatherless
and his wife a widow.[x]
10 May his children be wandering
beggars;[y]
may they be driven[d] from their
ruined homes.
11 May a creditor[z] seize all he has;
may strangers plunder[a] the
fruits of his labor.[b]
12 May no one extend kindness to
him
or take pity[c] on his fatherless
children.
13 May his descendants be cut off,[d]
their names blotted out[e] from
the next generation.
14 May the iniquity of his fathers[f]
be remembered before the
LORD;
may the sin of his mother never
be blotted out.

109:1 [k]S Ex 15:2; Jer 17:14 [l]S Job 34:29
109:2 [m]S Ps 43:1 [n]S Ps 52:4
109:3 [o]Ps 69:4 [p]Ps 35:7; Jn 15:25
109:4 [q]Ps 69:13; 141:5
109:5 [r]S Ge 44:4
109:6 [s]1Ch 21:1; Job 1:6; Zec 3:1
109:7 [t]Ps 1:5 [u]Pr 28:9; Isa 41:24
109:8 [v]S Job 15:32 [w]Ac 1:20*
109:9 [x]Ex 22:24; Jer 18:21
109:10 [y]S Ge 4:12
109:11 [z]Ne 5:3 [a]S Nu 14:3; Isa 1:7; 6:11; 36:1; La 5:2 [b]Job 20:18
109:12 [c]S Job 5:4
109:13 [d]Job 18:19; Ps 21:10 [e]S Nu 14:12; Ps 9:5; Pr 10:7
109:14 [f]Ex 20:5; Nu 14:18; Isa 65:6-7; Jer 32:18
109:15 [g]Ps 90:8 [h]S Ex 17:14; S Dt 32:26
109:16 [i]S Job 20:19; S Ps 35:10 [j]S Ps 34:18
109:17 [k]Pr 28:27; S Mt 7:2
109:18 [l]Ps 10:7 [m]Nu 5:22
109:19 [n]ver 29; Ps 73:6; Eze 7:27
109:20 [o]S Ex 32:34; Ps 54:5; 94:23; Isa 3:11; 2Ti 4:14 [p]Ps 71:10
109:21 [q]S Ex 9:16; S Ps 23:3 [r]Ps 69:16 [s]S Ps 3:7
109:23 [t]S Job 14:2
109:24 [u]Heb 12:12 [v]S Ps 35:13 [w]S Job 16:8
109:25 [x]S Ps 22:6 [y]S Job 16:4; S Mt 27:39; Mk 15:29
109:26 [z]Ps 12:1; 119:86

15 May their sins always remain
before[g] the LORD,
that he may cut off the
memory[h] of them from the
earth.
16 For he never thought of doing a
kindness,
but hounded to death the poor
and the needy[i] and the
brokenhearted.[j]
17 He loved to pronounce a curse—
may it[e] come on him;[k]
he found no pleasure in blessing—
may it be[f] far from him.
18 He wore cursing[l] as his garment;
it entered into his body like
water,[m]
into his bones like oil.
19 May it be like a cloak wrapped[n]
about him,
like a belt tied forever around
him.
20 May this be the LORD's payment[o]
to my accusers,
to those who speak evil[p] of me.
21 But you, O Sovereign LORD,
deal well with me for your
name's sake;[q]
out of the goodness of your
love,[r] deliver me.[s]
22 For I am poor and needy,
and my heart is wounded within
me.
23 I fade away like an evening
shadow;[t]
I am shaken off like a locust.
24 My knees give[u] way from
fasting;[v]
my body is thin and gaunt.[w]
25 I am an object of scorn[x] to my
accusers;
when they see me, they shake
their heads.[y]

26 Help me,[z] O LORD my God;
save me in accordance with your
love.

[a]*6* Or ⌞*They say:*⌟ *"Appoint* (with quotation marks at the end of verse 19) [b]*6* Or *the Evil One* [c]*6* Or *let Satan* [d]*10* Septuagint; Hebrew *sought* [e]*17* Or *curse, / and it has* [f]*17* Or *blessing, / and it is*

109:1–31 DO NOT REMAIN SILENT. This psalm appeals to God to judge and punish those who are wicked and deceitful. This prayer reflects a concern that justice be done on earth through the righteous punishment of serious criminals who hurt others for personal gain. To carry out just retribution is the only way to protect the innocent and assure that lawlessness will be held in check in society (see Ro 13:1,4, notes). The psalmist's prayer will find ultimate fulfillment only when God again sends his Son Jesus to destroy all evil and to reign on earth (Rev 19—22; see also Ps 35:1–38, note).

27Let them know[a] that it is your
hand,
that you, O LORD, have done it.
28They may curse,[b] but you will
bless;
when they attack they will be
put to shame,
but your servant will rejoice.[c]
29My accusers will be clothed with
disgrace
and wrapped in shame[d] as in a
cloak.
30With my mouth I will greatly extol
the LORD;
in the great throng[e] I will
praise him.
31For he stands at the right hand[f]
of the needy one,
to save his life from those who
condemn him.

Psalm 110

Of David. A psalm.

1The LORD says[g] to my Lord:
"Sit at my right hand[h]
until I make your enemies
a footstool for your feet."[i]

2The LORD will extend your mighty
scepter[j] from Zion;[k]
you will rule[l] in the midst of
your enemies.
3Your troops will be willing
on your day of battle.
Arrayed in holy majesty,[m]
from the womb of the dawn
you will receive the dew of your
youth.[g][n]

4The LORD has sworn
and will not change his mind:[o]
"You are a priest forever,[p]
in the order of Melchizedek.[q]"
5The Lord is at your right hand;[r]
he will crush kings[s] on the day
of his wrath.[t]
6He will judge the nations,[u]
heaping up the dead[v]
and crushing the rulers[w] of the
whole earth.
7He will drink from a brook beside
the way[h];
therefore he will lift up his
head.[x]

Psalm 111[i]

1Praise the LORD.[j]

I will extol the LORD[y] with all my
heart[z]
in the council[a] of the upright
and in the assembly.[b]

2Great are the works[c] of the LORD;
they are pondered by all[d] who
delight in them.
3Glorious and majestic are his
deeds,
and his righteousness endures[e]
forever.
4He has caused his wonders to be
remembered;
the LORD is gracious and
compassionate.[f]
5He provides food[g] for those who
fear him;[h]
he remembers his covenant[i]
forever.
6He has shown his people the
power of his works,[j]
giving them the lands of other
nations.[k]
7The works of his hands[l] are
faithful and just;

109:27 [a]S Job 37:7 **109:28** [b]S 2Sa 16:12 [c]Ps 66:4; Isa 35:10; 51:11; 54:1; 65:14 **109:29** [d]S Ps 35:26 **109:30** [e]S Ps 35:18 **109:31** [f]Ps 16:8; 108:6 **110:1** [g]Mt 22:44*; Mk 12:36*; Lk 20:42*; Ac 2:34* [h]S Mk 16:19; Heb 1:13*; 12:2 [i]S Jos 10:24; S 1Ki 5:3; 1Co 15:25 **110:2** [j]S Ge 49:10; Ps 45:6; Isa 14:5; Jer 48:17 [k]S Ps 2:6 [l]Ps 72:8 **110:3** [m]S Ex 15:11 [n]Mic 5:7 **110:4** [o]S Nu 23:19 [p]Zec 6:13; Heb 5:6*; 7:21* [q]S Ge 14:18; Heb 5:10; 7:15-17* **110:5** [r]Ps 16:8 [s]S Dt 7:24; Ps 2:12; 68:21; 76:12; Isa 60:12; Da 2:44 [t]S Ps 2:5; Ro 2:5; Rev 6:17; 11:18 **110:6** [u]S Ps 9:19 [v]Isa 5:25; 34:3; 66:24 [w]S Ps 18:38 **110:7** [x]Ps 3:3; 27:6 **111:1** [y]Ps 34:1; 109:30; 115:18; 145:10 [z]S Ps 9:1 [a]Ps 89:7 [b]S Ps 1:5 **111:2** [c]S Job 36:24; Ps 143:5; Rev 15:3 [d]Ps 64:9 **111:3** [e]Ps 112:3, 9; 119:142 **111:4** [f]S Dt 4:31; S Ps 86:15 **111:5** [g]S Ge 1:30; S Ps 37:25; Mt 6:26,31-33 [h]Ps 103:11 [i]S 1Ch 16:15; S Ps 105:8 **111:6** [j]Ps 64:9; S 66:3,5 [k]S Ps 105:44 **111:7** [l]S Ps 92:4

[g]3 Or / *your young men will come to you like the dew* [h]7 Or / *The One who grants succession will set him in authority* [i]This psalm is an acrostic poem, the lines of which begin with the successive letters of the Hebrew alphabet. [j]1 Hebrew *Hallelu Yah*

110:1–7 THE LORD SAYS TO MY LORD. This psalm speaks of the lordship of the Messiah, his priesthood, his destruction of the wicked and his reign on earth. It clearly prophesies about Jesus Christ (the psalm is cited seven times in the NT). Jesus applied v. 1 to himself in making his claim to deity (Mt 22:44), and the apostle Peter quoted v. 1 to emphasize Christ's lordship (Ac 2:33–35; 5:30–31; cf. Ro 8:34; Heb 10:13). Heb 5:6 and 6:20—7:28 quote v. 4 to prove that God made Christ a priest forever.

110:4 YOU ARE A PRIEST FOREVER. See Heb 5:5–10; 6:19—7:28, for comments on how this is fulfilled in Christ.

110:6 HE WILL JUDGE THE NATIONS. This verse pictures Christ coming to the earth as a warrior to defeat and judge all those who oppose God's kingdom and his righteousness (see Rev 19:11–21).

111:1–10 I WILL EXTOL THE LORD. This psalm praises the Lord for his physical and spiritual blessings and for his providential care over those who love and fear him. The psalmist has determined to praise God not only privately, but also "in the assembly" (v. 1). It is Biblical to praise God spontaneously and aloud in church.

all his precepts are
trustworthy.[m]
8They are steadfast for ever[n] and
ever,
done in faithfulness and
uprightness.
9He provided redemption[o] for his
people;
he ordained his covenant
forever—
holy and awesome[p] is his
name.

10The fear of the LORD[q] is the
beginning of wisdom;[r]
all who follow his precepts have
good understanding.[s]
To him belongs eternal praise.[t]

Psalm 112[k]

1Praise the LORD.[l][u]

Blessed is the man[v] who fears
the LORD,[w]
who finds great delight[x] in his
commands.
2His children[y] will be mighty in
the land;
the generation of the upright
will be blessed.
3Wealth and riches[z] are in his
house,
and his righteousness endures[a]
forever.
4Even in darkness light dawns[b] for
the upright,
for the gracious and
compassionate and
righteous[c] man.[m]
5Good will come to him who is
generous and lends freely,[d]
who conducts his affairs with
justice.
6Surely he will never be shaken;[e]
a righteous man will be
remembered[f] forever.
7He will have no fear of bad news;
his heart is steadfast,[g] trusting
in the LORD.[h]
8His heart is secure, he will have
no fear;[i]
in the end he will look in
triumph on his foes.[j]
9He has scattered abroad his gifts
to the poor,[k]
his righteousness endures[l]
forever;
his horn[n] will be lifted[m] high
in honor.

10The wicked man will see[n] and be
vexed,
he will gnash his teeth[o] and
waste away;[p]
the longings of the wicked will
come to nothing.[q]

Psalm 113

1Praise the LORD.[o][r]

Praise, O servants of the LORD,[s]
praise the name of the LORD.
2Let the name of the LORD be
praised,[t]

111:7 [m]Ps 19:7; 119:128 **111:8** [n]Ps 119:89,152, 160; Isa 40:8; S Mt 5:18 **111:9** [o]Ps 34:22; S 103:4; 130:7; Lk 1:68 [p]Ps 30:4; 99:3; Lk 1:49 **111:10** [q]S Job 23:15; S Ps 19:9 [r]Dt 4:6 [s]S Dt 4:6; Ps 119:98,104,130 [t]Ps 28:6; 89:52 **112:1** [u]Ps 33:2; 103:1; 150:1 [v]Ps 1:1-2 [w]S Job 1:8; Ps 103:11; 115:13; 128:1 [x]S Ps 1:2; 119:14, 16,47,92 **112:2** [y]Ps 25:13; 37:26; 128:2-4 **112:3** [z]S Dt 8:18 [a]S Ps 37:6; S 111:3 **112:4** [b]S Ps 18:28 [c]Ps 5:12 **112:5** [d]S Ps 37:21,26; Lk 6:35 **112:6** [e]S Ps 15:5; S 55:22 [f]Pr 10:7; Ecc 2:16 **112:7** [g]Ps 57:7; 108:1 [h]S Ps 28:7; 56:3-4; S Isa 12:2 **112:8** [i]Ps 3:6; 27:1; 56:11; Pr 1:33; Isa 12:2 [j]S Ps 54:7 **112:9** [k]Lk 19:8; Ac 9:36; 2Co 9:9* [l]S Ps 111:3 [m]S Ps 75:10 **112:10** [n]Ps 86:17 [o]S Ps 37:12; S Mt 8:12 [p]S Ps 34:21 [q]S Job 8:13 **113:1** [r]S Ps 22:23 [s]Ps 34:22; S 103:21; 134:1 **113:2** [t]S Ps 30:4; 48:10; 145:21; 148:13; 149:3; Isa 12:4

[k] This psalm is an acrostic poem, the lines of which begin with the successive letters of the Hebrew alphabet. [l] *1* Hebrew *Hallelu Yah* [m] *4* Or / *for* ⌊*the* LORD⌋ *is gracious and compassionate and righteous* [n] *9* *Horn* here symbolizes dignity. [o] *1* Hebrew *Hallelu Yah;* also in verse 9

111:10 THE FEAR OF THE LORD IS THE BEGINNING OF WISDOM. This truth serves as the foundation for the OT wisdom literature (see Job 28:28; Pr 1:7; 9:10; Ecc 12:13; see article on THE FEAR OF THE LORD, p. 260).

112:1–10 BLESSED IS THE MAN. This psalm speaks of the blessings in store for a God-fearing and righteous person. God promises to bless those who fear him and find delight in his commands and written Word (v. 1; cf. Ps 119).

112:1 FINDS GREAT DELIGHT IN HIS COMMANDS. What matters most in the life of a God-fearing person is that God's will be done on earth (cf. Mt 6:10). Such people love God's laws because his commands represent the righteousness the world scorns (v. 10; see Heb 1:9, note).

112:3 WEALTH AND RICHES. See 3Jn 2, note on the well-being of God's faithful people.

112:7 WILL HAVE NO FEAR OF BAD NEWS. The psalmist is not moved by fear and anxiety in times of trouble because his trust is in the Lord and not in himself or in external circumstances (cf. Ps 37).

113—118 PASSOVER PSALMS. These psalms were used by Jews at the yearly Passover celebration. The first two were sung before the meal and the remaining four after the meal. Thus these were probably the last songs Jesus Christ sang before his death. Since these psalms begin in Hebrew with the word "Hallelu Yah" (113:1), Jews came to call them "The Hallel [Praise]."

113:1–9 PRAISE THE LORD. This psalm reiterates the twofold Biblical principle that God gives grace to the humble (cf. Jas 4:6,10; 1Pe 5:5–7) and has compassion on the poor and needy (see Lk 7:13, note; 1Ti 5:9, note; see article on THE CARE OF THE POOR AND NEEDY, p. 1316).

both now and forevermore.[u]
3From the rising of the sun[v] to the
place where it sets,
the name of the LORD is to be
praised.

4The LORD is exalted[w] over all the
nations,
his glory above the heavens.[x]
5Who is like the LORD our God,[y]
the One who sits enthroned[z] on
high,[a]
6who stoops down to look[b]
on the heavens and the earth?

7He raises the poor[c] from the dust
and lifts the needy[d] from the
ash heap;
8he seats them[e] with princes,
with the princes of their people.
9He settles the barren[f] woman in
her home
as a happy mother of children.

Praise the LORD.

Psalm 114

1When Israel came out of Egypt,[g]
the house of Jacob from a people
of foreign tongue,
2Judah[h] became God's sanctuary,[i]
Israel his dominion.

3The sea looked and fled,[j]
the Jordan turned back;[k]
4the mountains skipped[l] like
rams,
the hills like lambs.

5Why was it, O sea, that you fled,[m]
O Jordan, that you turned back,
6you mountains, that you skipped
like rams,
you hills, like lambs?

7Tremble, O earth,[n] at the
presence of the Lord,
at the presence of the God of
Jacob,
8who turned the rock into a pool,
the hard rock into springs of
water.[o]

113:2 [u]Ps 115:18; 131:3; Da 2:20 **113:3** [v]Isa 24:15; 45:6; 59:19; Mal 1:11 **113:4** [w]S Ps 99:2 [x]S Ps 8:1; S 57:11 **113:5** [y]S Ex 8:10; S Ps 35:10 [z]S Ps 103:19 [a]S Job 16:19 **113:6** [b]Ps 11:4; 138:6; Isa 57:15 **113:7** [c]1Sa 2:8; Ps 35:10; 68:10; 140:12 [d]Ps 107:41 **113:8** [e]S 2Sa 9:11 **113:9** [f]S 1Sa 2:5 **114:1** [g]S Ex 13:3; S 29:46 **114:2** [h]Ps 76:1 [i]S Ex 15:17; Ps 78:68-69 **114:3** [j]Ex 14:21; Ps 77:16 [k]S Ex 15:8; S Jos 3:16 **114:4** [l]S Jdg 5:5 **114:5** [m]S Ex 14:21 **114:7** [n]S Ex 15:14; S 1Ch 16:30 **114:8** [o]S Ex 17:6; S Nu 20:11

115:1 [p]Ps 29:2; 66:2; 96:8 [q]S Ex 34:6 **115:2** [r]S Ps 42:3 **115:3** [s]Ezr 5:11; Ne 1:4; Ps 103:19; 136:26; Mt 6:9 [t]Ps 135:6 **115:4** [u]Rev 9:20 [v]S 2Ki 19:18; S 2Ch 32:19; Jer 10:3-5; Ac 19:26 **115:5** [w]Jer 10:5 **115:9** [x]Ps 37:3; 62:8 **115:10** [y]Ex 30:30; Ps 118:3 **115:11** [z]Ps 22:23; 103:11; 118:4 **115:12** [a]S 1Ch 16:15 [b]S Ge 12:2 **115:13** [c]S Ps 112:1 **115:14** [d]Dt 1:11 **115:15** [e]S Ge 1:1; Ac 14:15; S Rev 10:6

Psalm 115

115:4–11pp — Ps 135:15–20

1Not to us, O LORD, not to us
but to your name be the glory,[p]
because of your love and
faithfulness.[q]

2Why do the nations say,
"Where is their God?"[r]
3Our God is in heaven;[s]
he does whatever pleases him.[t]
4But their idols are silver and
gold,[u]
made by the hands of men.[v]
5They have mouths, but cannot
speak,[w]
eyes, but they cannot see;
6they have ears, but cannot hear,
noses, but they cannot smell;
7they have hands, but cannot feel,
feet, but they cannot walk;
nor can they utter a sound with
their throats.
8Those who make them will be like
them,
and so will all who trust in
them.

9O house of Israel, trust[x] in the
LORD—
he is their help and shield.
10O house of Aaron,[y] trust in the
LORD—
he is their help and shield.
11You who fear him,[z] trust in the
LORD—
he is their help and shield.

12The LORD remembers[a] us and will
bless us:[b]
He will bless the house of
Israel,
he will bless the house of Aaron,
13he will bless those who fear[c] the
LORD—
small and great alike.

14May the LORD make you
increase,[d]
both you and your children.
15May you be blessed by the LORD,
the Maker of heaven[e] and
earth.

115:1 NOT TO US BUT TO YOUR NAME BE THE GLORY. We must never seek glory for ourselves, but rather always desire to manifest God's glory and honor his name before the world. We must determine to live in such a way that we will not bring shame or reproach on the name of Christ or his church (cf. Mt 5:14–16; 1Co 6:20).

115:9 TRUST IN THE LORD. Those who trust in the Lord rather than in things that can be seen (vv. 4–8) receive the Lord as their help and shield (vv. 9–11). He remembers those who fear him and promises to bless them (vv. 12–15). God rules in the heavens, but he has delegated the rule of the earth to humans (v. 16).

16The highest heavens belong to the LORD,[f]
but the earth he has given[g] to man.
17It is not the dead[h] who praise the LORD,
those who go down to silence;
18it is we who extol the LORD,[i]
both now and forevermore.[j]

Praise the LORD.[p][k]

Psalm 116

1I love the LORD,[l] for he heard my voice;
he heard my cry[m] for mercy.[n]
2Because he turned his ear[o] to me,
I will call on him as long as I live.
3The cords of death[p] entangled me,
the anguish of the grave[q] came upon me;
I was overcome by trouble and sorrow.
4Then I called on the name[q] of the LORD:
"O LORD, save me![r]"
5The LORD is gracious and righteous;[s]
our God is full of compassion.[t]
6The LORD protects the simplehearted;
when I was in great need,[u] he saved me.[v]
7Be at rest[w] once more, O my soul,
for the LORD has been good[x] to you.
8For you, O LORD, have delivered my soul[y] from death,
my eyes from tears,
my feet from stumbling,
9that I may walk before the LORD[z]
in the land of the living.[a]
10I believed;[b] therefore[r] I said,
"I am greatly afflicted."[c]
11And in my dismay I said,
"All men are liars."[d]
12How can I repay the LORD
for all his goodness[e] to me?
13I will lift up the cup of salvation
and call on the name[f] of the LORD.
14I will fulfill my vows[g] to the LORD
in the presence of all his people.
15Precious in the sight[h] of the LORD
is the death of his saints.[i]
16O LORD, truly I am your servant;[j]
I am your servant, the son of your maidservant[s];[k]
you have freed me from my chains.[l]
17I will sacrifice a thank offering[m] to you
and call on the name of the LORD.
18I will fulfill my vows[n] to the LORD
in the presence of all his people,
19in the courts[o] of the house of the LORD—
in your midst, O Jerusalem.[p]

Praise the LORD.[p]

Psalm 117

1Praise the LORD,[q] all you nations;[r]
extol him, all you peoples.
2For great is his love[s] toward us,
and the faithfulness of the LORD[t] endures forever.

Praise the LORD.[p]

115:16 [f]S Ps 89:11 [g]S Ge 1:28; Ps 8:6-8 **115:17** [h]Ps 88:10-12 **115:18** [i]S Ps 111:1 [j]S Ps 113:2 [k]Ps 28:6; 33:2; 103:1 **116:1** [l]Ps 18:1 [m]S Ps 31:22; S 40:1 [n]S Ps 6:9; S 28:2 **116:2** [o]S Ps 5:1 **116:3** [p]S 2Sa 22:6; Ps 18:4-5 **116:4** [q]Ps 80:18; 118:5 [r]S Ps 80:2 **116:5** [s]S Ex 9:27; S 2Ch 12:6; S Ezr 9:15 [t]S Ex 22:27; S Ps 86:15 **116:6** [u]S Ps 79:8 [v]Ps 18:3; 22:5; 107:13 **116:7** [w]Ps 46:10; 62:1; 131:2; Mt 11:29 [x]Ps 13:6; 106:1; 142:7 **116:8** [y]S Ps 86:13 **116:9** [z]S Ge 5:22; Ps 56:13; 89:15 [a]S Job 28:13; Ps 27:13; Isa 38:11; Jer 11:19 **116:10** [b]2Co 4:13* [c]Ps 9:18; 72:2; S 107:17; 119:67, 71,75 **116:11** [d]Jer 9:3-5; Hos 7:13; Mic 6:12; Ro 3:4 **116:12** [e]Ps 103:2; 106:1 **116:13** [f]S Ps 105:1 **116:14** [g]S Nu 30:2; S Ps 66:13 **116:15** [h]Ps 72:14 [i]S Nu 23:10 **116:16** [j]Ps 119:125; 143:12 [k]S Ps 86:16 [l]S Job 12:18 **116:17** [m]S Lev 7:12; S Ezr 1:4 **116:18** [n]ver 14; S Lev 22:18 **116:19** [o]Ps 92:13; 96:8; 100:4; 135:2 [p]Ps 102:21 **117:1** [q]S Ps 22:23; S 103:2 [r]Ro 15:11* **117:2** [s]S Ps 17:7; S 103:11 [t]Ps 119:90; 146:6

[p] *18,2* Hebrew *Hallelu Yah* [q] *3* Hebrew *Sheol* [r] *10* Or *believed even when* [s] *16* Or *servant, your faithful son*

116:1–19 I LOVE THE LORD. This psalm expresses thanksgiving to the Lord for deliverance from death and declares the praise of all afflicted believers who have been rescued by the Lord and have been spared death or great calamity.

116:12 HOW CAN I REPAY? Gratitude flows from the hearts of all those who have experienced salvation from the Lord; they will express it by their love (v. 1), loyalty (v. 2), righteous living (v. 9), thanksgiving and a firm resolve to obey the Lord (v. 14).

116:15 PRECIOUS ... IS THE DEATH OF HIS SAINTS. (1) The Lord carefully watches over the lives of his faithful people. (2) He exercises control over the circumstances of their death (Ro 8:28,35–39). (3) When they are dying, he is there with them. (4) Their death, which is of great value to him, is the occasion when they are delivered from all evil, are taken from this life to blessed victory and are brought into heaven to see Jesus face to face (see Php 1:21, note; see article on DEATH, p. 732).

117:1 ALL YOU NATIONS. Paul quotes this verse in Ro 15:11 to prove that the OT anticipated God's offer of salvation to people of all nations (cf. Ps 67).

Psalm 118

1Give thanks to the LORD,[u] for he
is good;[v]
his love endures forever.[w]

2Let Israel say:[x]
"His love endures forever."[y]
3Let the house of Aaron say:[z]
"His love endures forever."
4Let those who fear the LORD[a] say:
"His love endures forever."

5In my anguish[b] I cried to the
LORD,
and he answered[c] by setting
me free.
6The LORD is with me;[d] I will not
be afraid.
What can man do to me?[e]
7The LORD is with me; he is my
helper.[f]
I will look in triumph on my
enemies.[g]

8It is better to take refuge in the
LORD[h]
than to trust in man.[i]
9It is better to take refuge in the
LORD
than to trust in princes.[j]
10All the nations surrounded me,
but in the name of the LORD I
cut them off.[k]
11They surrounded me[l] on every
side,[m]
but in the name of the LORD I
cut them off.
12They swarmed around me like
bees,[n]
but they died out as quickly as
burning thorns;[o]
in the name of the LORD I cut
them off.[p]
13I was pushed back and about to
fall,
but the LORD helped me.[q]
14The LORD is my strength[r] and my
song;
he has become my salvation.[s]

15Shouts of joy[t] and victory
resound in the tents of the
righteous:
"The LORD's right hand[u] has done
mighty things![v]
16 The LORD's right hand is lifted
high;
the LORD's right hand has done
mighty things!"
17I will not die[w] but live,
and will proclaim[x] what the
LORD has done.
18The LORD has chastened[y] me
severely,
but he has not given me over to
death.[z]

19Open for me the gates[a] of
righteousness;
I will enter[b] and give thanks to
the LORD.
20This is the gate of the LORD[c]
through which the righteous may
enter.[d]
21I will give you thanks, for you
answered me;[e]
you have become my salvation.[f]
22The stone[g] the builders rejected
has become the capstone;[h]
23the LORD has done this,
and it is marvelous[i] in our
eyes.
24This is the day the LORD has made;
let us rejoice and be glad[j] in it.

25O LORD, save us;[k]
O LORD, grant us success.

118:1 [u]S 1Ch 16:8 [v]S 2Ch 5:13; S 7:3 [w]S Ezr 3:11 **118:2** [x]Ps 115:9 [y]Ps 106:1; 136:1-26 **118:3** [z]Ex 30:30; Ps 115:10 **118:4** [a]S Ps 115:11 **118:5** [b]Ps 18:6; 31:7; 77:2; 120:1 [c]ver 21; Ps 34:4; 86:7; 116:1; 138:3 **118:6** [d]S Dt 31:6; Heb 13:6* [e]S Ps 56:4 **118:7** [f]S Dt 33:29 [g]S Ps 54:7 **118:8** [h]Ps 2:12; 5:11; 9:9; 37:3; 40:4; Isa 25:4; 57:13 [i]2Ch 32:7-8; S Ps 108:12; S Isa 2:22 **118:9** [j]Ps 146:3 **118:10** [k]S Ps 37:9 **118:11** [l]Ps 88:17 [m]Ps 3:6 **118:12** [n]Dt 1:44 [o]S Ps 58:9 [p]Ps 37:9 **118:13** [q]ver 7; 2Ch 18:31; Ps 86:17 **118:14** [r]S Ex 15:2 [s]S Ps 62:2 **118:15** [t]S Job 8:21; S Ps 106:5 [u]S Ex 15:6; Ps 89:13; 108:6 [v]Lk 1:51 **118:17** [w]Hab 1:12 [x]S Dt 32:3; Ps 64:9; 71:16; 73:28 **118:18** [y]Jer 31:18; 1Co 11:32; Heb 12:5 [z]Ps 86:13 **118:19** [a]S Ps 24:7 [b]Ps 100:4 **118:20** [c]Ps 122:1-2 [d]Ps 15:1-2; 24:3-4; Rev 22:14 **118:21** [e]S ver 5 [f]Ps 27:1 **118:22** [g]Isa 8:14 [h]Isa 17:10; 19:13; 28:16; Zec 4:7; 10:4; Mt 21:42; Mk 12:10; Lk 20:17*; S Ac 4:11*; 1Pe 2:7* **118:23** [i]Mt 21:42*; Mk 12:11* **118:24** [j]S Ps 70:4 **118:25** [k]S Ps 28:9; 116:4

118:1–29 HIS LOVE ENDURES FOREVER. This psalm praises the Lord for his everlasting love for his people. It may have been the last words sung by Jesus and his disciples before he went to the Garden of Gethsemane, where he was arrested and led to his death (cf. Mt 26:30; Mk 14:26). It will also be sung before Christ's return at the end of the age (compare v. 26 with Mt 23:39). When reading this psalm, meditate on what might have been in Christ's mind when he sang it for the last time.

118:6 THE LORD IS WITH ME. Those who take refuge in the Lord are assured that he is with them to give help and strength (vv. 7,14; Jos 1:9; Jer 1:8; see Ex 3:14, note).

118:22–23 THE STONE ... REJECTED. Jesus applied these verses to himself because he was thrown aside by his own people, but afterwards became the principal stone of God's new house, the church (Mt 21:42; Mk 12:10; Lk 20:17; Ac 4:11; Eph 2:20; 1Pe 2:7).

118:24 THIS IS THE DAY. The context shows the day referred to here is a day of salvation or redemption.

118:25 SAVE US. This phrase (Heb *hosh'iana'*) becomes "Hosanna" in the Greek translation of the OT; it prophesies the salvation through Christ's sacrifice (cf. vv. 26–27) and was sung by the crowds during Jesus' triumphal entry into Jerusalem (cf. Mt 21:9).

[26]Blessed is he who comes[l] in the
name of the LORD.
From the house of the LORD we
bless you.[t][m]
[27]The LORD is God,[n]
and he has made his light
shine[o] upon us.
With boughs in hand,[p] join in the
festal procession
up[u] to the horns of the altar.[q]

[28]You are my God, and I will give
you thanks;
you are my God,[r] and I will
exalt[s] you.

[29]Give thanks to the LORD, for he is
good;
his love endures forever.

Psalm 119[v]

א Aleph

[1]Blessed are they whose ways are
blameless,[t]
who walk[u] according to the law
of the LORD.[v]
[2]Blessed[w] are they who keep his
statutes[x]
and seek him[y] with all their
heart.[z]
[3]They do nothing wrong;[a]
they walk in his ways.[b]
[4]You have laid down precepts[c]
that are to be fully obeyed.[d]
[5]Oh, that my ways were steadfast
in obeying your decrees![e]
[6]Then I would not be put to
shame[f]
when I consider all your
commands.[g]
[7]I will praise you with an upright
heart
as I learn your righteous laws.[h]
[8]I will obey your decrees;
do not utterly forsake me.[i]

ב Beth

[9]How can a young man keep his
way pure?[j]

118:26 [l]S Mt 11:3; 21:9*; 23:39*; Mk 11:9*; Lk 13:35*; 19:38*; Jn 12:13* [m]Ps 129:8 **118:27** [n]S 1Ki 18:21 [o]Ps 27:1; Isa 58:10; 60:1, 19,20; Mal 4:2; 1Pe 2:9 [p]S Lev 23:40 [q]Ex 27:2 **118:28** [r]S Ge 28:21; S Ps 16:2; 63:1; Isa 25:1 [s]S Ex 15:2 **119:1** [t]S Ge 17:1; S Dt 18:13; Pr 11:20 [u]Ps 128:1 [v]S Ps 1:2 **119:2** [w]Ps 112:1; Isa 56:2 [x]ver 146; Ps 99:7 [y]S 1Ch 16:11; S Ps 40:16 [z]S Dt 10:12 **119:3** [a]S Ps 59:4; 1Jn 3:9; 5:18 [b]Ps 128:1; Jer 6:16; 7:23 **119:4** [c]Ps 103:18 [d]S ver 56; S Dt 6:17 **119:5** [e]S Lev 19:37 **119:6** [f]ver 46,80 [g]ver 117 **119:7** [h]S Dt 4:8 **119:8** [i]S Ps 38:21 **119:9** [j]S Ps 39:1

[t]26 The Hebrew is plural. [u]27 Or *Bind the festal sacrifice with ropes / and take it* [v]This psalm is an acrostic poem; the verses of each stanza begin with the same letter of the Hebrew alphabet.

119:1–176 WAYS ARE BLAMELESS. This psalm expresses a majestic love for God's written Word. It deals with the Word as promise, command, guide, testimony, teaching, wisdom, truth, righteousness and rebuke. It is presented as the psalmist's comfort, protection, treasure, rule for life, delight to his heart and soul, and resource for all his needs. (1) The psalmist expresses a profound love for God by reading, meditating on and praying over his Word. He teaches us that we will grow in grace and righteousness only as love for that Word increases in us.

(2) This psalm is called an alphabetical acrostic because its 22 stanzas (or paragraphs) of eight verses each correspond to the 22 letters of the Hebrew alphabet. Each verse in the paragraphs begins with the letter characteristic of its stanza.

119:1 BLESSED. God promises to pour out his blessing on those who have chosen to live by his Word with all its standards and directives. They will have his personal presence (cf. Ge 26:3), bringing them strength, help and protection (Eph 3:16; Col 1:11; see Lk 24:50, note).

119:1 THE LAW. The law (Heb *torah*) represents God's entire instruction to his people; it can also refer to the Pentateuch (the first five OT books) or to the OT as a whole.

119:2 STATUTES. God's statutes (Heb *'edot*) represent the covenant stipulations or requirements that are declared as his will.

119:3 WAYS. God's ways (Heb *derek*) represent those principles and means of operation by which God relates to his people and advances his redemption in the earth. His ways are contrary to humanistic wisdom and values (see Isa 55:8–9).

119:4 PRECEPTS. God's precepts (Heb *piqqudim*) involve detailed instruction from the Lord.

119:5 DECREES. God's decrees (Heb *huqqim*) consist of regulations for his people individually and collectively.

119:5 STEADFAST IN OBEYING YOUR DECREES! Believers should ask God continually for the grace needed to do his will and be steadfast in his ways. Such a petition is necessary because we cannot remain faithful to God's laws without his sustaining help and the Holy Spirit's work in our hearts (see Mt 7:21, note).

119:6 COMMANDS. God's commands (Heb *miswot*) refer to rules and regulations that express God's authority and his will for his people and that he expects us to obey.

119:9 WORD. God's word (Heb *dabar*) represents both his revelation in general and his commands and promises.

119:9 HOW CAN A YOUNG MAN KEEP HIS WAY PURE? How may believers keep their lives pure, resisting the immoral influences that characterize the ungodly environment in which we live? The second stanza of this psalm lists the following eight ways, one in each verse: (1) by making an irreversible decision to remain loyal to God's written Word for the rest of our lives; (2) by seeking the Lord in prayer; (3) by committing God's Word to memory; (4) by looking to God for guidance; (5) by taking an open stand for God's truth; (6) by rejoicing and delighting in what God says; (7) by considering the outcome of God's ways as opposed to the world's ways; and (8) by never becoming too

By living according to your
word.[k]
10I seek you with all my heart;[l]
do not let me stray from your
commands.[m]
11I have hidden your word in my
heart[n]
that I might not sin[o] against
you.
12Praise be[p] to you, O LORD;
teach me[q] your decrees.[r]
13With my lips I recount
all the laws that come from your
mouth.[s]
14I rejoice in following your
statutes[t]
as one rejoices in great riches.
15I meditate on your precepts[u]
and consider your ways.
16I delight[v] in your decrees;
I will not neglect your
word.

ג Gimel

17Do good to your servant,[w] and I
will live;
I will obey your word.[x]
18Open my eyes that I may see
wonderful things in your
law.
19I am a stranger on earth;[y]
do not hide your commands from
me.
20My soul is consumed[z] with
longing
for your laws[a] at all times.
21You rebuke the arrogant,[b] who
are cursed[c]
and who stray[d] from your
commands.
22Remove from me scorn[e] and
contempt,
for I keep your statutes.[f]
23Though rulers sit together and
slander me,
your servant will meditate on
your decrees.
24Your statutes are my delight;
they are my counselors.

ד Daleth

25I am laid low in the dust;[g]
preserve my life[h] according to
your word.[i]
26I recounted my ways and you
answered me;
teach me your decrees.[j]
27Let me understand the teaching of
your precepts;
then I will meditate on your
wonders.[k]
28My soul is weary with sorrow;[l]
strengthen me[m] according to
your word.[n]
29Keep me from deceitful ways;[o]
be gracious to me[p] through
your law.
30I have chosen[q] the way of
truth;[r]
I have set my heart[s] on your
laws.
31I hold fast[t] to your statutes,
O LORD;
do not let me be put to shame.
32I run in the path of your
commands,
for you have set my heart free.

ה He

33Teach me,[u] O LORD, to follow your
decrees;
then I will keep them to the
end.
34Give me understanding,[v] and I
will keep your law[w]
and obey it with all my heart.[x]
35Direct me[y] in the path of your
commands,[z]
for there I find delight.[a]
36Turn my heart[b] toward your
statutes
and not toward selfish gain.[c]
37Turn my eyes away from worthless
things;
preserve my life[d] according to
your word.[w][e]

[w] *37* Two manuscripts of the Masoretic Text and Dead Sea Scrolls; most manuscripts of the Masoretic Text *life in your way*

119:9 [k] ver 65, 169
119:10 [l] S Ps 9:1 [m] ver 21,118
119:11 [n] S Dt 6:6; S Job 22:22 [o] ver 133,165; Ps 18:22-23; 19:13; Pr 3:23; Isa 63:13
119:12 [p] Ps 28:6 [q] Ps 143:8,10 [r] S Ex 18:20
119:13 [s] ver 72
119:14 [t] ver 111
119:15 [u] ver 97, 148; Ps 1:2
119:16 [v] S Ps 112:1
119:17 [w] Ps 13:6; 116:7 [x] ver 67; Ps 103:20
119:19 [y] S Ge 23:4; Heb 11:13
119:20 [z] Ps 42:2; 84:2 [a] ver 131; S Ps 63:1; Isa 26:9
119:21 [b] ver 51; Job 30:1; Ps 5:5; Jer 20:7; 50:32; Da 4:37; Mal 3:15 [c] Dt 27:26 [d] S ver 10
119:22 [e] Ps 39:8 [f] ver 2
119:25 [g] Ps 44:25 [h] ver 50,107; Ps 143:11 [i] ver 9
119:26 [j] Ps 25:4; 27:11; 86:11
119:27 [k] Ps 105:2; 145:5
119:28 [l] Ps 6:7; 116:3; Isa 51:11; Jer 45:3 [m] Ps 18:1; Isa 40:29; 41:10 [n] ver 9
119:29 [o] Ps 26:4 [p] S Nu 6:25
119:30 [q] S Jos 24:22 [r] S Ps 26:3 [s] S Ps 108:1
119:31 [t] S Dt 10:20
119:33 [u] ver 12
119:34 [v] ver 27, 73,144,169; S Job 32:8; Pr 2:6; Da 2:21; Jas 1:5 [w] S Dt 6:25 [x] ver 69
119:35 [y] Ps 25:4-5 [z] ver 32 [a] S Ps 1:2
119:36 [b] S Jos 24:23 [c] Eze 33:31
119:37 [d] ver 25; Ps 71:20 [e] ver 9

busy to read and study God's Word.

119:23 RULERS SIT TOGETHER AND SLANDER ME. The psalmist testifies that he has suffered much scorn, contempt and slander as he attempted to live a righteous life in accordance with God's Word; this opposition, however, did not deter him from following God's way. Today those who are faithful to Christ and his Word must also expect to be criticized and ridiculed; they may be called legalists or extremists by those who conform to the worldly ways of an ungodly society (see Mt 5:10, note; Lk 6:22, note).

119:27 UNDERSTAND THE TEACHING OF YOUR PRECEPTS. God's Word can only be understood fully with his help (vv. 26–27,29); thus we should continually pray for God, through his Holy Spirit, to draw near to us, to increase our understanding and to teach us his truth (see Jn 14:17, note; 1Jn 2:27, note).

38Fulfill your promise[f] to your
servant,
so that you may be feared.
39Take away the disgrace[g] I dread,
for your laws are good.
40How I long[h] for your precepts!
Preserve my life[i] in your
righteousness.

ו Waw

41May your unfailing love[j] come to
me, O LORD,
your salvation according to your
promise;[k]
42then I will answer[l] the one who
taunts me,[m]
for I trust in your word.
43Do not snatch the word of truth
from my mouth,[n]
for I have put my hope[o] in your
laws.
44I will always obey your law,[p]
for ever and ever.
45I will walk about in freedom,
for I have sought out your
precepts.[q]
46I will speak of your statutes before
kings[r]
and will not be put to shame,[s]
47for I delight[t] in your commands
because I love them.[u]
48I lift up my hands to[x] your
commands, which I love,
and I meditate[v] on your
decrees.

ז Zayin

49Remember your word[w] to your
servant,
for you have given me hope.[x]
50My comfort in my suffering is this:
Your promise preserves my
life.[y]
51The arrogant mock me[z] without
restraint,
but I do not turn[a] from your
law.
52I remember[b] your ancient laws,
O LORD,
and I find comfort in them.
53Indignation grips me[c] because of
the wicked,
who have forsaken your law.[d]
54Your decrees are the theme of my
song[e]
wherever I lodge.
55In the night I remember[f] your
name, O LORD,
and I will keep your law.[g]
56This has been my practice:
I obey your precepts.[h]

ח Heth

57You are my portion,[i] O LORD;
I have promised to obey your
words.[j]
58I have sought[k] your face with all
my heart;
be gracious to me[l] according to
your promise.[m]
59I have considered my ways[n]
and have turned my steps to
your statutes.
60I will hasten and not delay
to obey your commands.[o]
61Though the wicked bind me with
ropes,
I will not forget[p] your law.

119:38 [f]S Nu 23:19 **119:39** [g]ver 22; Ps 69:9; 89:51; Isa 25:8; 51:7; 54:4 **119:40** [h]ver 20 [i]ver 25,149,154 **119:41** [j]S Ps 6:4 [k]ver 76,116,154, 170 **119:42** [l]Pr 27:11 [m]S Ps 42:10 **119:43** [n]S 1Ki 17:24 [o]ver 74,81,114, 147 **119:44** [p]ver 33, 34,55; S Dt 6:25 **119:45** [q]ver 94, 155 **119:46** [r]Mt 10:18; Ac 26:1-2 [s]S ver 6 **119:47** [t]ver 77, 143; S Ps 112:1 [u]ver 97,127,159, 163,165 **119:48** [v]S Ge 24:63 **119:49** [w]ver 9 [x]ver 43 **119:50** [y]S ver 25 **119:51** [z]S ver 21; S Job 16:10; S 17:2 [a]S Job 23:11 **119:52** [b]Ps 103:18 **119:53** [c]S Ex 32:19; S 33:4 [d]Ps 89:30 **119:54** [e]ver 172; Ps 101:1; 138:5 **119:55** [f]ver 62, 72; Ps 1:2; 42:8; S 63:6; 77:2; Isa 26:9; Ac 16:25 [g]S ver 44 **119:56** [h]ver 4, 100,134,168; S Nu 15:40 **119:57** [i]S Dt 32:9; Jer 51:19; La 3:24 [j]ver 17,67,101 **119:58** [k]S Dt 4:29; S 1Ch 16:11; Ps 34:4 [l]S Ge 43:29; S Ezr 9:8 [m]ver 41 **119:59** [n]Jos 24:14-15; S Ps 39:1 **119:60** [o]ver 115 **119:61** [p]ver 83,109,153,176

[x]*48* Or *for*

119:47–48 I DELIGHT IN ... I LOVE ... YOUR COMMANDS. A major emphasis of Ps 119 is the psalmist's delight in and heartfelt love for the Word of God. (1) Joy comes to his heart as he reads and obeys God's Word. Likewise, when we read the Bible with an earnest desire to understand and obey Christ's commands (vv. 20,24,40, 60), the Holy Spirit imparts God's love to our hearts (see Jn 14:15–17,21,23; Ro 5:5, note), helps us to discern the truth of God's Word, and brings us great joy and delight (cf. Jn 15:10–11).

(2) Delighting in God's Word develops into an even deeper love for all God's ways. Because we have come to love him (v. 132), we love the Scriptures that reveal him and his will to us. As a result, we have been united with him (Ro 6:5), and our hearts now have a profound love and devotion for his revealed truth.

119:50 COMFORT IN MY SUFFERING ... YOUR PROMISE. God has ordained that his Word, made powerful by the Spirit, will bring comfort, hope and strength to his faithful as we experience trouble and sorrow. Because God's Word is living and active (cf. Heb 4:12), it has power to revive and restore us who abide in it and in God (cf. Jn 14:27). When in trouble, turn to the Lord and his Word and wait for his Spirit to give peace to your heart (cf. Php 4:6–9).

119:57 YOU ARE MY PORTION. The psalmist's life centers around God and his Word. If we desire to know God and his love (vv. 57–64), we must abide in his Word (v. 57), seek his face and his grace with our whole heart (v. 58), hasten to obey his Word (v. 60), pray often (v. 62), associate with those who fear him (v. 63), look for his love (v. 64), and pray to know and do his will (v. 64). We cannot remain in Christ without remaining in his Word (Jn 15:1–10).

[62]At midnight[q] I rise to give you thanks
for your righteous laws.[r]
[63]I am a friend to all who fear you,[s]
to all who follow your precepts.[t]
[64]The earth is filled with your love,[u] O LORD;
teach me your decrees.[v]

ט Teth

[65]Do good[w] to your servant according to your word,[x] O LORD.
[66]Teach me knowledge[y] and good judgment,
for I believe in your commands.
[67]Before I was afflicted[z] I went astray,[a]
but now I obey your word.[b]
[68]You are good,[c] and what you do is good;
teach me your decrees.[d]
[69]Though the arrogant have smeared me with lies,[e]
I keep your precepts with all my heart.
[70]Their hearts are callous[f] and unfeeling,
but I delight in your law.
[71]It was good for me to be afflicted[g]
so that I might learn your decrees.
[72]The law from your mouth is more precious to me
than thousands of pieces of silver and gold.[h]

י Yodh

[73]Your hands made me[i] and formed me;
give me understanding to learn your commands.
[74]May those who fear you rejoice[j] when they see me,
for I have put my hope in your word.[k]
[75]I know, O LORD, that your laws are righteous,[l]
and in faithfulness[m] you have afflicted me.
[76]May your unfailing love[n] be my comfort,
according to your promise[o] to your servant.
[77]Let your compassion[p] come to me that I may live,
for your law is my delight.[q]
[78]May the arrogant[r] be put to shame for wronging me without cause;[s]
but I will meditate on your precepts.
[79]May those who fear you turn to me,
those who understand your statutes.[t]
[80]May my heart be blameless[u] toward your decrees,[v]
that I may not be put to shame.[w]

כ Kaph

[81]My soul faints[x] with longing for your salvation,[y]
but I have put my hope[z] in your word.
[82]My eyes fail,[a] looking for your promise;[b]
I say, "When will you comfort me?"
[83]Though I am like a wineskin in the smoke,
I do not forget[c] your decrees.
[84]How long[d] must your servant wait?
When will you punish my persecutors?[e]
[85]The arrogant[f] dig pitfalls[g] for me,
contrary to your law.
[86]All your commands are trustworthy;[h]
help me,[i] for men persecute me[j] without cause.[k]
[87]They almost wiped me from the earth,
but I have not forsaken[l] your precepts.
[88]Preserve my life[m] according to your love,[n]
and I will obey the statutes[o] of your mouth.

ל Lamedh

[89]Your word, O LORD, is eternal;[p]
it stands firm in the heavens.

119:62 [q]S ver 55; Ac 16:25 [r]ver 7 **119:63** [s]Ps 15:4; 101:6-7; 103:11 [t]ver 56; Ps 111:10 **119:64** [u]Ps 33:5 [v]ver 12,108 **119:65** [w]ver 17; Ps 125:4; Isa 50:2; 59:1; Mic 2:7 [x]S ver 9 **119:66** [y]S Ps 51:6 **119:67** [z]S Ps 116:10 [a]S Ps 95:10; S Jer 8:4 [b]S ver 17 **119:68** [c]Ps 100:5; 106:1; 107:1; 135:3 [d]S Ex 18:20 **119:69** [e]Job 13:4; Ps 109:2 **119:70** [f]S Ps 17:10; Isa 29:13; Ac 28:27 **119:71** [g]ver 67, 75 **119:72** [h]S Job 28:17; S Ps 19:10 **119:73** [i]S Ge 1:27; S Job 4:17; 10:8; Ps 138:8; 139:13-16 **119:74** [j]S Ps 34:2 [k]ver 9; Ps 130:5 **119:75** [l]ver 7, 138,172 [m]Heb 12:5-11 **119:76** [n]Ps 6:4 [o]S ver 41 **119:77** [p]Ps 90:13; 103:13 [q]S ver 47 **119:78** [r]ver 51; Jer 50:32 [s]ver 86, 161; Ps 35:19 **119:79** [t]ver 27, 125 **119:80** [u]ver 1; S 1Ki 8:61 [v]S Ge 26:5 [w]S ver 6 **119:81** [x]ver 20; Ps 84:2 [y]ver 123 [z]S ver 43 **119:82** [a]S Ps 6:7; 69:3; La 2:11 [b]ver 41, 123 **119:83** [c]S ver 61 **119:84** [d]Ps 6:3; Rev 6:10 [e]ver 51; Jer 12:3; 15:15; 20:11 **119:85** [f]ver 51 [g]Ps 35:7; 57:6; Jer 18:20,22 **119:86** [h]ver 138 [i]S Ps 109:26 [j]S Ps 7:1 [k]S ver 78 **119:87** [l]ver 150; Isa 1:4,28; 58:2; 59:13 **119:88** [m]S Ps 41:2 [n]ver 124; Ps 51:1; 109:26 [o]ver 2, 100,129,134,168 **119:89** [p]ver 111,144; S Ps 111:8; Isa 51:6; S Mt 5:18; 1Pe 1:25

119:67 I WAS AFFLICTED . . . NOW I OBEY YOUR WORD. God sometimes allows us to experience hardships and troubles in order to draw us closer to his Word (cf. 94:12; Pr 3:11–12; see Heb 12:5, note).

119:89 YOUR WORD, O LORD IS ETERNAL.

90Your faithfulness[q] continues
through all generations;[r]
you established the earth, and it
endures.[s]
91Your laws endure[t] to this day,
for all things serve you.[u]
92If your law had not been my
delight,[v]
I would have perished in my
affliction.[w]
93I will never forget[x] your precepts,
for by them you have preserved
my life.[y]
94Save me,[z] for I am yours;
I have sought out your
precepts.[a]
95The wicked are waiting to destroy
me,[b]
but I will ponder your
statutes.[c]
96To all perfection I see a limit;
but your commands are
boundless.[d]

מ Mem

97Oh, how I love your law![e]
I meditate[f] on it all day long.
98Your commands make me wiser[g]
than my enemies,
for they are ever with me.
99I have more insight than all my
teachers,
for I meditate on your
statutes.[h]
100I have more understanding than
the elders,
for I obey your precepts.[i]
101I have kept my feet[j] from every
evil path
so that I might obey your
word.[k]
102I have not departed from your
laws,[l]
for you yourself have taught[m]
me.
103How sweet are your words to my
taste,
sweeter than honey[n] to my
mouth![o]
104I gain understanding[p] from your
precepts;
therefore I hate every wrong
path.[q]

נ Nun

105Your word is a lamp[r] to my feet
and a light[s] for my path.
106I have taken an oath[t] and
confirmed it,
that I will follow your righteous
laws.[u]
107I have suffered much;
preserve my life,[v] O LORD,
according to your word.
108Accept, O LORD, the willing praise
of my mouth,[w]
and teach me your laws.[x]
109Though I constantly take my life
in my hands,[y]
I will not forget[z] your law.
110The wicked have set a snare[a] for
me,
but I have not strayed[b] from
your precepts.
111Your statutes are my heritage
forever;
they are the joy of my heart.[c]
112My heart is set[d] on keeping your
decrees
to the very end.[e]

ס Samekh

113I hate double-minded men,[f]
but I love your law.[g]
114You are my refuge and my
shield;[h]
I have put my hope[i] in your
word.
115Away from me,[j] you evildoers,
that I may keep the commands
of my God!
116Sustain me[k] according to your
promise,[l] and I will live;
do not let my hopes be
dashed.[m]

119:90 [q] S Ps 36:5 [r] S Ps 45:17 [s] S Job 8:19; Ps 148:6 **119:91** [t] Jer 33:25 [u] Ps 104:2-4; Jer 31:35 **119:92** [v] Ps 37:4; S 112:1 [w] ver 50, 67 **119:93** [x] ver 83 [y] S Ps 103:5 **119:94** [z] ver 146; Ps 54:1; 116:4; Jer 17:14; 31:18; 42:11 [a] S ver 45 **119:95** [b] S Ps 69:4 [c] ver 99 **119:96** [d] Ps 19:7 **119:97** [e] S ver 47 [f] S ver 15 **119:98** [g] ver 130; S Dt 4:6; Ps 19:7; 2Ti 3:15 **119:99** [h] ver 15 **119:100** [i] S ver 56; S Dt 6:17 **119:101** [j] Pr 1:15 [k] S ver 57 **119:102** [l] S Dt 17:20 [m] S Dt 4:5 **119:103** [n] S Ps 19:10 [o] Pr 24:13-14 **119:104** [p] S Ps 111:10 [q] ver 128 **119:105** [r] Pr 20:27; 2Pe 1:19 [s] ver 130; Pr 6:23 **119:106** [t] S Ne 10:29 [u] ver 7 **119:107** [v] S ver 25 **119:108** [w] Ps 51:15; 63:5; 71:8; 109:30 [x] S ver 64 **119:109** [y] S Jdg 12:3 [z] S ver 61 **119:110** [a] Ps 25:15; S 64:5; Isa 8:14; Am 3:5 [b] ver 10 **119:111** [c] ver 14, 162 **119:112** [d] S Ps 108:1 [e] ver 33 **119:113** [f] S 1Ki 18:21; Jas 1:8; 4:8 [g] ver 47 **119:114** [h] S Ge 15:1; S Ps 18:2 [i] S ver 43 **119:115** [j] S Ps 6:8 **119:116** [k] S Ps 18:35; 41:3; 55:22; Isa 46:4 [l] S ver 41 [m] Ro 5:5

See article on THE INSPIRATION AND AUTHORITY OF SCRIPTURE, p. 1898.

119:98 COMMANDS MAKE ME WISER. Through our devotion to God's Word we learn to see life as God sees it, value what he values and love what he loves. We attune ourselves to the thoughts of God (see 1Co 2:16, note).

119:105 YOUR WORD IS . . . A LIGHT FOR MY PATH. God's Word contains the spiritual principles that will help us avoid many sorrows, pitfalls and tragedies brought on by wrong decisions and choices; consequently, we must treasure its wisdom and steadfastly hold on to its precepts in all life's situations (vv. 106,112).

119:113 HATE DOUBLE-MINDED MEN, BUT I LOVE YOUR LAW. We really cannot love God's Word without hating evil (vv. 113,115,119,128; see Heb 1:9, note) and maintaining a holy and reverent fear of God and his judgments.

117 Uphold me,[n] and I will be
delivered;[o]
I will always have regard for
your decrees.[p]
118 You reject all who stray[q] from
your decrees,
for their deceitfulness is in vain.
119 All the wicked of the earth you
discard like dross;[r]
therefore I love your statutes.[s]
120 My flesh trembles[t] in fear of
you;[u]
I stand in awe[v] of your laws.

ע Ayin

121 I have done what is righteous and
just;[w]
do not leave me to my
oppressors.
122 Ensure your servant's
well-being;[x]
let not the arrogant oppress
me.[y]
123 My eyes fail,[z] looking for your
salvation,[a]
looking for your righteous
promise.[b]
124 Deal with your servant according
to your love[c]
and teach me your decrees.[d]
125 I am your servant;[e] give me
discernment
that I may understand your
statutes.[f]
126 It is time for you to act, O LORD;
your law is being broken.[g]
127 Because I love your commands[h]
more than gold,[i] more than
pure gold,[j]
128 and because I consider all your
precepts right,[k]
I hate every wrong path.[l]

פ Pe

129 Your statutes are wonderful;[m]
therefore I obey them.[n]
130 The unfolding of your words gives
light;[o]
it gives understanding to the
simple.[p]
131 I open my mouth and pant,[q]
longing for your commands.[r]
132 Turn to me[s] and have mercy[t]
on me,
as you always do to those who
love your name.[u]
133 Direct my footsteps according to
your word;[v]
let no sin rule[w] over me.
134 Redeem me from the oppression
of men,[x]
that I may obey your precepts.[y]
135 Make your face shine[z] upon your
servant
and teach me your decrees.[a]
136 Streams of tears[b] flow from my
eyes,
for your law is not obeyed.[c]

צ Tsadhe

137 Righteous are you,[d] O LORD,
and your laws are right.[e]
138 The statutes you have laid down
are righteous;[f]
they are fully trustworthy.[g]
139 My zeal wears me out,[h]
for my enemies ignore your
words.
140 Your promises[i] have been
thoroughly tested,[j]
and your servant loves them.[k]
141 Though I am lowly and
despised,[l]
I do not forget your precepts.[m]
142 Your righteousness is everlasting
and your law is true.[n]
143 Trouble and distress have come
upon me,
but your commands are my
delight.[o]
144 Your statutes are forever right;
give me understanding[p] that I
may live.

ק Qoph

145 I call with all my heart;[q] answer
me, O LORD,
and I will obey your decrees.[r]
146 I call out to you; save me[s]

119:117 [n] Isa 41:10; 46:4 [o] Ps 34:4 [p] ver 6 **119:118** [q] S ver 10 **119:119** [r] Isa 1:22,25; Eze 22:18,19 [s] ver 47 **119:120** [t] S Job 4:14; S Isa 64:2 [u] S Jos 24:14 [v] Jer 10:7; Hab 3:2 **119:121** [w] S 2Sa 8:15; S Job 27:6 **119:122** [x] S Job 17:3 [y] ver 21,121,134; Ps 106:42 **119:123** [z] Isa 38:14 [a] ver 81 [b] S ver 82 **119:124** [c] S ver 88; S Ps 25:7 [d] ver 12 **119:125** [e] S Ps 116:16 [f] S ver 79 **119:126** [g] S Nu 15:31 **119:127** [h] S ver 47 [i] Ps 19:10 [j] S Job 3:21 **119:128** [k] S Ps 19:8 [l] ver 104,163; Ps 31:6; Pr 13:5 **119:129** [m] ver 18 [n] ver 22,S 88 **119:130** [o] S ver 105 [p] S Ps 19:7 **119:131** [q] Ps 42:1 [r] S ver 20 **119:132** [s] S Ps 6:4 [t] S 2Sa 24:14; S Ps 9:13 [u] S Ps 5:11 **119:133** [v] ver 9 [w] S ver 11; S Ro 6:16 **119:134** [x] S ver 122 [y] S ver 56,S 88 **119:135** [z] S Nu 6:25; Ps 4:6; 67:1; 80:3 [a] ver 12 **119:136** [b] Ps 6:6; Isa 22:4; Jer 9:1, 18; 13:17; 14:17; La 1:16; 3:48 [c] ver 158; Ps 106:25; Isa 42:24; Eze 9:4 **119:137** [d] S Ex 9:27; S Ezr 9:15 [e] S Ne 9:13 **119:138** [f] S ver 75; S Ps 19:7 [g] ver 86 **119:139** [h] Ps 69:9; Jn 2:17 **119:140** [i] S Jos 23:14 [j] Ps 12:6 [k] ver 47 **119:141** [l] S Ps 22:6 [m] ver 61,134 **119:142** [n] ver 151,160; Ps 19:7 **119:143** [o] ver 24,S 47 **119:144** [p] S ver 34 **119:145** [q] ver 10 [r] ver 22,55 **119:146** [s] S ver 94

119:121 DO NOT LEAVE ME TO MY OPPRESSORS. Like the psalmist, believers may appeal for God's help, based on (1) obedience to and love for his Word (vv. 121–122), (2) God's promises in his sure Word (v. 123), (3) God's mercy and steadfast love (v. 124), (4) our commitment to serve him (v. 125) and (5) the urgent needs we have in our lives (v. 126).

119:136 STREAMS OF TEARS FLOW FROM MY EYES. Those who love God's Word will experience grief and sorrow, even anger (v. 53), when they see God's laws rejected and scorned by the ungodly; these feelings will undoubtedly continue until Christ's return (see Lk 19:45, note; 2Pe 2:8, note).

and I will keep your statutes.
147I rise before dawn[t] and cry for help;
I have put my hope in your word.
148My eyes stay open through the watches of the night,[u]
that I may meditate on your promises.
149Hear my voice[v] in accordance with your love;[w]
preserve my life,[x] O LORD, according to your laws.
150Those who devise wicked schemes[y] are near,
but they are far from your law.
151Yet you are near,[z] O LORD,
and all your commands are true.[a]
152Long ago I learned from your statutes[b]
that you established them to last forever.[c]

ר Resh

153Look upon my suffering[d] and deliver me,[e]
for I have not forgotten[f] your law.
154Defend my cause[g] and redeem me;[h]
preserve my life[i] according to your promise.[j]
155Salvation is far from the wicked,
for they do not seek out[k] your decrees.
156Your compassion is great,[l] O LORD;
preserve my life[m] according to your laws.[n]
157Many are the foes who persecute me,[o]
but I have not turned[p] from your statutes.
158I look on the faithless with loathing,[q]
for they do not obey your word.[r]
159See how I love your precepts;
preserve my life,[s] O LORD, according to your love.
160All your words are true;
all your righteous laws are eternal.[t]

שׁ Sin and Shin

161Rulers persecute me[u] without cause,
but my heart trembles[v] at your word.
162I rejoice[w] in your promise
like one who finds great spoil.[x]
163I hate and abhor[y] falsehood
but I love your law.[z]
164Seven times a day I praise you
for your righteous laws.[a]
165Great peace[b] have they who love your law,
and nothing can make them stumble.[c]
166I wait for your salvation,[d] O LORD,
and I follow your commands.
167I obey your statutes,
for I love them[e] greatly.
168I obey your precepts[f] and your statutes,[g]
for all my ways are known[h] to you.

ת Taw

169May my cry come[i] before you, O LORD;
give me understanding[j] according to your word.[k]
170May my supplication come[l] before you;
deliver me[m] according to your promise.[n]
171May my lips overflow with praise,[o]
for you teach me[p] your decrees.
172May my tongue sing[q] of your word,
for all your commands are righteous.[r]
173May your hand be ready to help[s] me,
for I have chosen[t] your precepts.

119:147 [t]Ps 5:3; 57:8; 108:2 **119:148** [u]S Ps 63:6 **119:149** [v]S Ps 27:7 [w]ver 124 [x]S ver 40 **119:150** [y]S Ps 37:7 **119:151** [z]S Ps 34:18; Php 4:5 [a]S ver 142 **119:152** [b]ver 7, 73 [c]S ver 89; S Ps 111:8; Lk 21:33 **119:153** [d]S Ps 13:3 [e]S Ps 3:7 [f]S Ps 44:17 **119:154** [g]Ps 35:1; Jer 50:34; Mic 7:9 [h]S 1Sa 24:15 [i]ver 25 [j]S ver 41 **119:155** [k]ver 94, 118 **119:156** [l]S Ne 9:27; Jas 5:11 [m]ver 25 [n]ver 149 **119:157** [o]S Ps 7:1 [p]S Ps 44:18 **119:158** [q]ver 104; S Ex 32:19 [r]S ver 136 **119:159** [s]ver 25; S Ps 41:2 **119:160** [t]S ver 89; S Ps 111:8 **119:161** [u]ver 23, 122,157; 1Sa 24:14-15 [v]ver 120 **119:162** [w]S ver 111 [x]1Sa 30:16; Isa 9:3; 53:12 **119:163** [y]S ver 128 [z]ver 47 **119:164** [a]ver 7, 160 **119:165** [b]Ps 37:11; Isa 26:3,12; 27:5; 32:17; 57:19; 66:12 [c]S ver 11; S Ps 37:24; 1Jn 2:10 **119:166** [d]ver 81 **119:167** [e]ver 47 **119:168** [f]S ver 56,S 88 [g]ver 2,22 [h]S Job 10:4; S 23:10; Ps 139:3; Pr 5:21 **119:169** [i]S Job 16:18 [j]S ver 34 [k]S ver 9 **119:170** [l]1Ki 8:30; 2Ch 6:24; Ps 28:2; 140:6; 143:1 [m]Ps 3:7; 22:20; 59:1 [n]S ver 41 **119:171** [o]Ps 51:15; 63:3 [p]Ps 94:12; Isa 2:3; Mic 4:2 **119:172** [q]Ps 51:14 [r]ver 7,S 75 **119:173** [s]Ps 37:24; 73:23; Isa 41:10 [t]S Jos 24:22

119:151 YET YOU ARE NEAR. The psalmist experiences God's nearness in times of trouble because he loves the Lord and is devoted to meditating on his Word (v. 148; cf. vv. 153–160). The Lord is near to all who love him and his Word. If you have trouble in your life, take your Bible and in God's presence use it to revitalize your relationship with him.

174I long for your salvation,[u]
O LORD,
and your law is my delight.[v]
175Let me live[w] that I may praise
you,
and may your laws sustain me.
176I have strayed like a lost sheep.[x]
Seek your servant,
for I have not forgotten[y] your
commands.

Psalm 120

A song of ascents.

1I call on the LORD[z] in my
distress,[a]
and he answers me.
2Save me, O LORD, from lying lips[b]
and from deceitful tongues.[c]

3What will he do to you,
and what more besides,
O deceitful tongue?
4He will punish you with a warrior's
sharp arrows,[d]
with burning coals of the broom
tree.

5Woe to me that I dwell in
Meshech,
that I live among the tents of
Kedar![e]
6Too long have I lived
among those who hate peace.
7I am a man of peace;
but when I speak, they are for
war.

119:174 [u]ver 166 [v]ver 16,24 **119:175** [w]ver 116,159; Isa 55:3 **119:176** [x]ver 10; S Ps 95:10; Jer 50:17; Eze 34:11; S Lk 15:4 [y]S Ps 44:17 **120:1** [z]S Ps 18:6 [a]S 2Sa 22:7; S Ps 118:5 **120:2** [b]S Ps 31:18 [c]S Ps 52:4 **120:4** [d]S Dt 32:23 **120:5** [e]S Ge 25:13; Jer 2:10

121:2 [f]S Ge 1:1 [g]S Ps 104:5; Ps **121:4** [h]Ps 127:1 **121:5** [i]S Ps 1:6 **121:6** [j]Isa 49:10 **121:7** [k]S Ps 9:9 **121:8** [l]Dt 28:6

Psalm 121

A song of ascents.

1I lift up my eyes to the hills—
where does my help come from?
2My help comes from the LORD,
the Maker of heaven[f] and
earth.[g]

3He will not let your foot slip—
he who watches over you will
not slumber;
4indeed, he who watches[h] over
Israel
will neither slumber nor sleep.

5The LORD watches over[i] you—
the LORD is your shade at your
right hand;
6the sun[j] will not harm you by
day,
nor the moon by night.

7The LORD will keep you from all
harm[k]—
he will watch over your life;
8the LORD will watch over your
coming and going
both now and forevermore.[l]

Psalm 122

A song of ascents. Of David.

1I rejoiced with those who said to
me,

119:176 I HAVE STRAYED LIKE A LOST SHEEP. The writer cannot mean that he has departed from the Lord and rejected his Word, for he has declared the contrary over and over in this psalm; his concluding words remain, "I have not forgotten your commands." The psalmist here may simply be acknowledging that he is prone to error apart from being guided by God's Word.

120—134 SONGS OF ASCENTS. These fifteen psalms are entitled "Songs of Ascents" (i.e, of Steps). Some believe that this phrase refers to the steps on the stairlike sundial of King Ahaz where the shadow went back ten degrees as a guarantee that God would give King Hezekiah fifteen added years of peaceful reign; these psalms were then compiled to celebrate that promise (2Ki 20:6–10; Isa 38:5–8). Most believe the phrase "Songs of Ascents" refers to those psalms the Jews would sing together as they "went up" to Jerusalem as pilgrims to the sacred feasts.

120:1–7 HE ANSWERS ME. The grand thought of this pilgrim psalm is that the God who created the heavens and earth takes the time to watch over and care for all those who trust him and his word. No evil will be allowed to destroy their fellowship with him (see also Ro 8:28–39).

121:2 MY HELP COMES FROM THE LORD. Family, friends or wealth must never be viewed as our ultimate source of help in this life. That belongs to God, the only source for meeting our needs physically and spiritually. We must trust in him with all our hearts and seek him for grace to help us "in our time of need" (see Heb 4:16, note).

121:5 THE LORD WATCHES OVER YOU. The faithful child of God is always under the Lord's protection, defense and watchful care (see 1Pe 1:5, note). Jesus emphasized this truth when he said, "The very hairs of your head are all numbered. So don't be afraid" (Mt 10:30–31).

121:8 WATCH OVER YOUR COMING AND GOING. This text may be applied both to our Christian lives from spiritual birth until we leave this earth and to our physical lives as we go out in the morning to work and come home to rest. God will preserve us; he is our constant guard.

122:1 THE HOUSE OF THE LORD. God's house should be a place where the believer joyfully experiences intimate communion with the Lord, the fellowship of the Spirit and the love of fellow believers.

"Let us go to the house of the
LORD."
2Our feet are standing
in your gates, O Jerusalem.

3Jerusalem is built like a city
that is closely compacted
together.
4That is where the tribes go up,
the tribes of the LORD,
to praise the name of the LORD
according to the statute given to
Israel.
5There the thrones for judgment
stand,
the thrones of the house of
David.

6Pray for the peace of Jerusalem:
"May those who love[m] you be
secure.
7May there be peace[n] within your
walls
and security within your
citadels.[o]"
8For the sake of my brothers and
friends,
I will say, "Peace be within
you."
9For the sake of the house of the
LORD our God,
I will seek your prosperity.[p]

Psalm 123

A song of ascents.

1I lift up my eyes to you,
to you whose throne[q] is in
heaven.
2As the eyes of slaves look to the
hand of their master,
as the eyes of a maid look to
the hand of her mistress,
so our eyes look to the LORD[r] our
God,
till he shows us his mercy.

3Have mercy on us, O LORD, have
mercy on us,
for we have endured much
contempt.
4We have endured much ridicule
from the proud,
much contempt from the
arrogant.

Psalm 124

A song of ascents. Of David.

1If the LORD had not been on our
side—
let Israel say[s]—
2if the LORD had not been on our
side
when men attacked us,
3when their anger flared against us,
they would have swallowed us
alive;
4the flood[t] would have engulfed
us,
the torrent[u] would have swept
over us,
5the raging waters
would have swept us away.

6Praise be to the LORD,
who has not let us be torn by
their teeth.
7We have escaped like a bird
out of the fowler's snare;[v]
the snare has been broken,[w]
and we have escaped.
8Our help is in the name[x] of the
LORD,
the Maker of heaven[y] and
earth.

Psalm 125

A song of ascents.

1Those who trust in the LORD are
like Mount Zion,[z]
which cannot be shaken[a] but
endures forever.
2As the mountains surround
Jerusalem,[b]
so the LORD surrounds[c] his
people
both now and forevermore.
3The scepter[d] of the wicked will
not remain[e]

122:6 m S Ps 26:8 **122:7** n S 1Sa 25:6 o S Ps 48:3 **122:9** p Ps 128:5 **123:1** q S Ps 68:5; Isa 6:1; 63:15 **123:2** r S Ps 25:15 **124:1** s Ps 129:1 **124:4** t Ps 88:17 u S Ps 18:4 **124:7** v S Ps 91:3 w Ps 25:15 **124:8** x S 1Sa 17:45 y Ge 1:1; Ps 115:15; 121:2; 134:3 **125:1** z Ps 48:12; Isa 33:20 a Ps 46:5; 48:2-5 **125:2** b S 1Ch 21:15 c Ps 32:10; Zec 2:4-5 **125:3** d S Est 4:11 e Ps 89:22; Pr 22:8; Isa 13:11; 14:5

123:1 I LIFT UP MY EYES TO YOU. This psalm describes humble believers who look continually and expectantly to God to put an end to the contempt and scorn shown towards them. It expresses the cry of those who are always watching for and desiring Christ's return to save his people from an ungodly and hostile world (see Heb 12:2; 2Pe 3:12; see Mt 24:42, note; Tit 2:13, note).

124:1 IF THE LORD HAD NOT BEEN ON OUR SIDE. If God is not with us, we have no chance to escape the pitfalls of life or ward off our spiritual enemy. The dangers and troubles we face may seem so overwhelming that no one but God and his miraculous power can save us; yet, "If God is for us, who can be against us" (Ro 8:31)? No foe or situation can defeat us when God is on our side.

over the land allotted to the
righteous,
for then the righteous might use
their hands to do evil.[f]

4Do good, O LORD,[g] to those who
are good,
to those who are upright in
heart.[h]
5But those who turn[i] to crooked
ways[j]
the LORD will banish[k] with the
evildoers.

Peace be upon Israel.[l]

Psalm 126

A song of ascents.

1When the LORD brought back[m] the
captives to[y] Zion,
we were like men who
dreamed.[z]
2Our mouths were filled with
laughter,[n]
our tongues with songs of joy.[o]
Then it was said among the
nations,
"The LORD has done great
things[p] for them."
3The LORD has done great things[q]
for us,
and we are filled with joy.[r]

4Restore our fortunes,[a][s] O LORD,
like streams in the Negev.[t]
5Those who sow in tears[u]
will reap[v] with songs of joy.[w]
6He who goes out weeping,[x]
carrying seed to sow,
will return with songs of joy,
carrying sheaves with him.

Psalm 127

A song of ascents. Of Solomon.

1Unless the LORD builds[y] the
house,
its builders labor in vain.
Unless the LORD watches[z] over
the city,
the watchmen stand guard in
vain.
2In vain you rise early
and stay up late,
toiling for food[a] to eat—
for he grants sleep[b] to[b] those
he loves.[c]

3Sons are a heritage from the LORD,

125:3 [f] 1Sa 24:10 **125:4** [g] S Ps 119:65 [h] S Ps 36:10 **125:5** [i] S Job 23:11 [j] Pr 2:15; Isa 59:8 [k] Ps 92:7 [l] Ps 128:6; Gal 6:16 **126:1** [m] Ezr 1:1-3; Ps 85:1; Hos 6:11 **126:2** [n] S Ge 21:6 [o] S Job 8:21; S Ps 65:8 [p] S Dt 10:21; Ps 71:19; Lk 1:49 **126:3** [q] Ps 106:21; Joel 2:21,26 [r] S Ps 9:2; 16:11 **126:4** [s] S Dt 30:3 [t] S Ps 107:35; Isa 43:19; 51:3 **126:5** [u] Ps 6:6; 80:5; Jer 50:4 [v] Gal 6:9 [w] Ps 16:11; 20:5; 23:6; Isa 35:10; 51:11; 60:15; 61:7; Jer 31:6-7,12 **126:6** [x] S Nu 25:6; S Ps 30:5 **127:1** [y] Ps 78:69 [z] Ps 121:4 **127:2** [a] S Ge 3:17 [b] S Nu 6:26; S Job 11:18 [c] S Dt 33:12; Ecc 2:25

[y] *1* Or *LORD restored the fortunes of* [z] *1* Or *men restored to health* [a] *4* Or *Bring back our captives* [b] *2* Or *eat— / for while they sleep he provides for*

126:1 BROUGHT BACK THE CAPTIVES TO ZION. This is a technical phrase that also means, "restored the fortunes of Zion" (see NIV text note; cf. 14:7; Job 42:10). This restoration partially took place in 701 B.C., when Sennacherib's threat to take Jerusalem was turned back in fulfillment of prophecy, and the surrounding nations sent presents to Hezekiah (2Ch 32:22–23). The restoration was fulfilled in even greater measure when the Jews returned to Jerusalem from Babylon in 538 B.C.

126:5–6 SOW IN TEARS WILL REAP WITH SONGS OF JOY. Heartfelt brokenness and faithful sowing in agonizing prayer will bring from God the blessings of renewal, revival and miraculous works (cf. Mt 5:4; 2Co 9:6). Believers are assured that what they now diligently sow will be abundantly blessed by God in the future. So let us sow to God faithfulness, righteousness and intercession, regardless of whatever pain we may be experiencing, knowing that there will be a great harvest of God's blessings (cf. Jer 31:9).

127:1–5 UNLESS THE LORD BUILDS. Only what is from God and has his blessing is truly valuable in life; conversely, if God is not in our lives, activities, goals and families, then all is in vain and will end in frustration and disappointment. Thus we should seek God's blessing and guidance in all things from the very beginning of our lives (see Lk 24:50, note).

127:1 BUILDS THE HOUSE. As we labor to build God's house on earth, we must make sure we build it according to his pattern and by his Spirit, not according to mere human ideas, plans and efforts (cf. Ex 25:9,40; see Ac 7:44, note).

127:2 HE GRANTS SLEEP TO THOSE HE LOVES. It is God's will that we enjoy peaceful sleep and anxiety-free lives (see Mt 6:25–34; Php 4:6). The text also implies that God keeps on giving even when we are asleep.

127:3 SONS ARE A HERITAGE FROM THE LORD. Under the old covenant a large family was considered a blessing, while not having children was considered a curse (Ge 30:2,18; 33:5; 48:9; Dt 7:13). Under the new covenant the presence of many children is not necessarily evidence of divine favor, nor is their absence to be viewed as a curse. A large family may be a misfortune if the children are not properly cared for and brought to salvation in Christ; having no children can be a blessing if one dedicates his or her life and time to the Lord's service (1Co 7:7–8,32–33).

All children of believers must be viewed as gifts of God requiring wise and faithful stewardship. Only as the Lord's ways and commands are accepted, taught and followed by parents and children will they experience God's full blessing (see Ps 128; see article on PARENTS AND CHILDREN, p. 1854).

children a reward[d] from him.
4Like arrows[e] in the hands of a warrior
are sons born in one's youth.
5Blessed is the man
whose quiver is full of them.[f]
They will not be put to shame
when they contend with their enemies[g] in the gate.[h]

Psalm 128

A song of ascents.

1Blessed are all who fear the Lord,[i]
who walk in his ways.[j]
2You will eat the fruit of your labor;[k]
blessings and prosperity[l] will be yours.
3Your wife will be like a fruitful vine[m]
within your house;
your sons[n] will be like olive shoots[o]
around your table.
4Thus is the man blessed[p]
who fears the Lord.[q]
5May the Lord bless you from Zion[r]
all the days of your life;
may you see the prosperity of Jerusalem,[s]
6 and may you live to see your children's children.[t]

Peace be upon Israel.[u]

Psalm 129

A song of ascents.

1They have greatly oppressed[v] me
from my youth[w]—
let Israel say[x]—
2they have greatly oppressed me
from my youth,
but they have not gained the victory[y] over me.
3Plowmen have plowed my back
and made their furrows long.

127:3 [d]S Ge 1:28
127:4 [e]Ps 112:2
127:5 [f]Ps 128:2-3 [g]S Ge 24:60 [h]S Ge 23:10
128:1 [i]Ps 103:11; S 112:1 [j]Ps 119:1-3
128:2 [k]S Ps 58:11; 109:11; Isa 3:10 [l]S Ge 39:3; Pr 10:22
128:3 [m]S Ge 49:22 [n]S Job 29:5 [o]Ps 52:8; 144:12
128:4 [p]S Ps 1:1 [q]Ps 112:1
128:5 [r]S Ps 20:2 [s]Ps 122:9
128:6 [t]S Ge 48:11 [u]S Ps 125:5
129:1 [v]S Ex 1:13 [w]S Ps 88:15 [x]Ps 124:1
129:2 [y]Jer 1:19; 15:20; 20:11; Mt 16:18
129:4 [z]S Ex 9:27 [a]Ps 37:9 [b]Ps 140:5
129:5 [c]Mic 4:11 [d]S Ps 70:2
129:6 [e]Isa 37:27 [f]S 2Ki 19:26; Ps 102:11
129:7 [g]S Dt 28:38; Ps 79:12
129:8 [h]Ps 118:26
130:1 [i]S Job 30:19; Ps 42:7; La 3:55 [j]Ps 22:2; 55:17; 142:5
130:2 [k]S Ps 27:7; 28:2 [l]S 2Ch 6:40 [m]S Ps 28:6; 31:22; 86:6; 140:6
130:3 [n]S 1Sa 6:20; S Ezr 9:15; Ps 143:2; Na 1:6; Rev 6:17
130:4 [o]S Ex 34:7; S 2Sa 24:14; S Jer 31:34 [p]S 1Ki 8:40
130:5 [q]S Ps 27:14; Isa 8:17; 26:8; 30:18; 49:23 [r]S Ps 5:3 [s]S Ps 119:74
130:6 [t]Ps 63:6 [u]S 2Sa 23:4
130:7 [v]S Ps 25:5; S 71:14 [w]S 1Ch 21:13 [x]S Ps 111:9; S Ro 3:24
130:8 [y]Lk 1:68 [z]S Ex 34:7; S Mt 1:21

4But the Lord is righteous;[z]
he has cut me free[a] from the cords of the wicked.[b]
5May all who hate Zion[c]
be turned back in shame.[d]
6May they be like grass on the roof,[e]
which withers[f] before it can grow;
7with it the reaper cannot fill his hands,[g]
nor the one who gathers fill his arms.
8May those who pass by not say,
"The blessing of the Lord be upon you;
we bless you[h] in the name of the Lord."

Psalm 130

A song of ascents.

1Out of the depths[i] I cry to you,[j] O Lord;
2 O Lord, hear my voice.[k]
Let your ears be attentive[l]
to my cry for mercy.[m]
3If you, O Lord, kept a record of sins,
O Lord, who could stand?[n]
4But with you there is forgiveness;[o]
therefore you are feared.[p]

5I wait for the Lord,[q] my soul waits,[r]
and in his word[s] I put my hope.
6My soul waits for the Lord
more than watchmen[t] wait for the morning,
more than watchmen wait for the morning.[u]

7O Israel, put your hope[v] in the Lord,
for with the Lord is unfailing love[w]
and with him is full redemption.[x]
8He himself will redeem[y] Israel
from all their sins.[z]

130:1 OUT OF THE DEPTHS I CRY TO YOU. Those who reap the misery and torment of their own sins can cry out to God with assurance that God will forgive, heal and bring them back into fellowship with himself. God desires to show mercy to all who are in trouble, saving them from the slavery of sin in order that they might know his love, care and goodness (v. 4; see Mt 26:28, note).

Psalm 131

A song of ascents. Of David.

[1]My heart is not proud,[a] O LORD,
my eyes are not haughty;[b]
I do not concern myself with great matters[c]
or things too wonderful for me.[d]
[2]But I have stilled and quieted my soul;[e]
like a weaned child with its mother,
like a weaned child is my soul[f] within me.

[3]O Israel, put your hope[g] in the LORD
both now and forevermore.[h]

Psalm 132

132:8–10pp — 2Ch 6:41–42

A song of ascents.

[1]O LORD, remember David
and all the hardships he endured.[i]

[2]He swore an oath to the LORD
and made a vow to the Mighty One of Jacob:[j]
[3]"I will not enter my house[k]
or go to my bed—
[4]I will allow no sleep to my eyes,
no slumber to my eyelids,
[5]till I find a place[l] for the LORD,
a dwelling for the Mighty One of Jacob."

[6]We heard it in Ephrathah,[m]
we came upon it in the fields of Jaar[c:d][n]
[7]"Let us go to his dwelling place;[o]
let us worship at his footstool[p]—
[8]arise, O LORD,[q] and come to your resting place,
you and the ark of your might.
[9]May your priests be clothed with righteousness;[r]
may your saints[s] sing for joy."

[10]For the sake of David your servant,
do not reject your anointed one.

[11]The LORD swore an oath to David,[t]
a sure oath that he will not revoke:
"One of your own descendants[u]
I will place on your throne—
[12]if your sons keep my covenant[v]
and the statutes I teach them,
then their sons will sit
on your throne[w] for ever and ever."

[13]For the LORD has chosen Zion,[x]
he has desired it for his dwelling:[y]
[14]"This is my resting place for ever and ever;[z]
here I will sit enthroned,[a] for I have desired it—
[15]I will bless her with abundant provisions;
her poor will I satisfy with food.[b]
[16]I will clothe her priests[c] with salvation,
and her saints will ever sing for joy.[d]

[17]"Here I will make a horn[e] grow[e] for David
and set up a lamp[f] for my anointed one.[g]
[18]I will clothe his enemies with shame,[h]
but the crown on his head[i] will be resplendent."

131:1 [a]Ps 101:5; Isa 2:12; Ro 12:16 [b]S 2Sa 22:28; S Job 41:34 [c]Jer 45:5 [d]S Job 5:9; Ps 139:6 **131:2** [e]S Ps 116:7 [f]Mt 18:3; 1Co 13:11; 14:20 **131:3** [g]S Ps 25:5; 119:43; 130:7 [h]S Ps 113:2 **132:1** [i]1Sa 18:11; S 2Sa 15:14 **132:2** [j]S Ge 49:24; Isa 49:26; 60:16 **132:3** [k]S 2Sa 7:2,27 **132:5** [l]S 1Ki 8:17; Ac 7:46 **132:6** [m]S 1Sa 17:12 [n]S Jos 9:17; S 1Sa 7:2 **132:7** [o]S 2Sa 15:25; Ps 5:7; 122:1 [p]S 1Ch 28:2 **132:8** [q]S Nu 10:35 **132:9** [r]S Job 27:6; Isa 61:3,10; Zec 3:4; Mal 3:3; Eph 6:14 [s]Ps 16:3; 30:4; 149:5 **132:11** [t]S Ps 89:3-4,35 [u]S 1Ch 17:11-14; S Mt 1:1; Lk 3:31 **132:12** [v]2Ch 6:16; S Ps 25:10 [w]Lk 1:32; Ac 2:30 **132:13** [x]S Ex 15:17; Ps 48:1-2; S 68:16 [y]S 1Ki 8:13 **132:14** [z]ver 8; Ps 68:16 [a]S 2Sa 6:2; Ps 80:1 **132:15** [b]Ps 107:9; 147:14 **132:16** [c]S 2Ch 6:41 [d]S Job 8:21; Ps 149:5 **132:17** [e]S 1Sa 2:10; Ps 92:10; Eze 29:21; S Lk 1:69 [f]1Ki 11:36; 2Ki 8:19; 2Ch 21:7; Ps 18:28 [g]S Ps 84:9 **132:18** [h]S Job 8:22 [i]S 2Sa 12:30

[c]6 That is, Kiriath Jearim [d]6 Or *heard of it in Ephrathah, / we found it in the fields of Jaar.* (And no quotes around verses 7-9) [e]17 *Horn* here symbolizes strong one, that is, king.

132:1–18 REMEMBER DAVID. This psalm petitions God to bless David's sons as they rule Israel (cf. 2Sa 7:8–29; see article on GOD'S COVENANT WITH DAVID, p. 432). This blessing will become a reality only when God abides in his temple and among his people (vv. 13–18).

132:17 A HORN GROW FOR DAVID. The expectations of this prayer were never fulfilled through David's descendants who were kings of Israel and Judah. Because the Israelites rejected the Lord (cf. v. 12), God destroyed Jerusalem and the temple in 586 B.C. The longings of this prayer will be fulfilled only in Jesus Christ, the greatest Son of David, whose "kingdom will never end" (Lk 1:32–33; cf. Mt 1:1; Lk 1:68–79).

Psalm 133

A song of ascents. Of David.

[1]How good and pleasant it is
when brothers live together[j] in unity![k]
[2]It is like precious oil poured on the head,[l]
running down on the beard,
running down on Aaron's beard,
down upon the collar of his robes.
[3]It is as if the dew[m] of Hermon[n]
were falling on Mount Zion.[o]
For there the LORD bestows his blessing,[p]
even life forevermore.[q]

Psalm 134

A song of ascents.

[1]Praise the LORD, all you servants[r] of the LORD
who minister[s] by night[t] in the house of the LORD.
[2]Lift up your hands[u] in the sanctuary[v]
and praise the LORD.[w]

[3]May the LORD, the Maker of heaven[x] and earth,
bless you from Zion.[y]

Psalm 135

135:15–20pp — Ps 115:4–11

[1]Praise the LORD.[f]

Praise the name of the LORD;
praise him, you servants[z] of the LORD,
[2]you who minister in the house[a] of the LORD,
in the courts[b] of the house of our God.

[3]Praise the LORD, for the LORD is good;[c]
sing praise to his name,[d] for that is pleasant.[e]
[4]For the LORD has chosen Jacob[f] to be his own,
Israel to be his treasured possession.[g]

[5]I know that the LORD is great,[h]
that our Lord is greater than all gods.[i]
[6]The LORD does whatever pleases him,[j]
in the heavens and on the earth,[k]
in the seas and all their depths.
[7]He makes clouds rise from the ends of the earth;
he sends lightning with the rain[l]
and brings out the wind[m] from his storehouses.[n]

[8]He struck down the firstborn[o] of Egypt,
the firstborn of men and animals.
[9]He sent his signs[p] and wonders
into your midst, O Egypt,
against Pharaoh and all his servants.[q]
[10]He struck down many[r] nations
and killed mighty kings—
[11]Sihon[s] king of the Amorites,[t]
Og king of Bashan[u]
and all the kings of Canaan[v]—
[12]and he gave their land as an inheritance,[w]
an inheritance to his people Israel.

133:1 [j]S Ge 13:8; S Ro 12:10 [k]Jn 17:11 **133:2** [l]S Ex 29:7 **133:3** [m]Job 29:19; Pr 19:12; Isa 18:4; 26:19; 45:8; Hos 14:5; Mic 5:7 [n]S Dt 3:8; S 4:48 [o]S Ex 15:17; S Ps 2:6; 74:2 [p]S Lev 25:21 [q]S Ps 21:4 **134:1** [r]S Ps 113:1; 135:1-2; Rev 19:5 [s]S Nu 16:9; S 1Ch 15:2 [t]S 1Ch 23:30 **134:2** [u]S Ps 28:2; 1Ti 2:8 [v]Ps 15:1 [w]Ps 33:2; 103:1 **134:3** [x]S Ps 124:8 [y]S Lev 25:21; S Ps 20:2 **135:1** [z]Ne 7:73 **135:2** [a]S 1Ch 15:2; Lk 2:37 [b]S Ps 116:19 **135:3** [c]S 1Ch 16:34; S Ps 119:68 [d]S Ps 68:4 [e]S Ps 92:1; 147:1 **135:4** [f]S Dt 10:15 [g]Ex 19:5; Dt 7:6; Mal 3:17; S Tit 2:14 **135:5** [h]S Ps 48:1; 145:3 [i]S Ex 12:12; S 1Ch 16:25; S Job 21:22 **135:6** [j]Ps 115:3; Da 4:35 [k]Mt 6:10 **135:7** [l]S Job 5:10; Ps 68:9; Isa 30:23; Jer 10:13; 51:16; Joel 2:23; Zec 10:1 [m]Am 4:13 [n]S Dt 28:12 **135:8** [o]S Ex 4:23; S 12:12 **135:9** [p]S Ex 7:9 [q]Ps 136:10-15 **135:10** [r]Nu 21:21-25; Jos 24:8-11; Ps 44:2; 78:55; 136:17-21 **135:11** [s]S Nu 21:21 [t]S Nu 21:26 [u]S Nu 21:33 [v]S Jos 12:7-24; 24:12 **135:12** [w]S Dt 29:8

[f]*1* Hebrew *Hallelu Yah*; also in verses 3 and 21

133:1–3 WHEN BROTHERS LIVE TOGETHER IN UNITY! This psalm expresses the same spiritual truth as Jn 17, where Jesus prayed that his followers would be established in love, holiness and unity. He knew that the Holy Spirit could not operate among them if there were divisions based on sin and selfish ambitions (see 1Co 1:10–13; 3:1–3). But fervent love for God and for one another, along with sanctification in the truth of God's word, will bring God's nearness to and his anointing on his people (see Jn 17:21, note; Eph 4:3, note).

134:1–3 WHO MINISTER BY NIGHT IN THE HOUSE. This psalm speaks of all-night worship and intercession in God's house. Should not God's people under the new covenant be equally zealous for being involved in all-night services devoted to spiritual worship and earnest intercession for revival in the church and salvation for the lost?

135:1–21 PRAISE THE LORD. This call to praise God is based on three facts: (1) God has brought Israel into a saving covenant relationship with him (vv. 1–4; cf. Ex 19:5); (2) God is a living God, active in the affairs of the world and his people (vv. 5–13); (3) God is near his people, feeling compassion for those who serve him (v. 14).

13 Your name, O LORD, endures
forever,[x]
your renown,[y] O LORD, through
all generations.
14 For the LORD will vindicate his
people[z]
and have compassion on his
servants.[a]
15 The idols of the nations[b] are
silver and gold,
made by the hands of men.[c]
16 They have mouths, but cannot
speak,[d]
eyes, but they cannot see;
17 they have ears, but cannot hear,
nor is there breath[e] in their
mouths.
18 Those who make them will be like
them,
and so will all who trust in
them.
19 O house of Israel, praise the
LORD;[f]
O house of Aaron, praise the
LORD;
20 O house of Levi, praise the LORD;
you who fear him, praise the
LORD.
21 Praise be to the LORD from Zion,[g]
to him who dwells in
Jerusalem.[h]

Praise the LORD.

Psalm 136

1 Give thanks[i] to the LORD, for he
is good.[j]
His love endures forever.[k]
2 Give thanks[l] to the God of
gods.[m]
His love endures forever.
3 Give thanks[n] to the Lord of
lords:[o]
His love endures forever.

4 to him who alone does great
wonders,[p]
His love endures forever.
5 who by his understanding[q] made
the heavens,[r]
His love endures forever.
6 who spread out the earth[s] upon
the waters,[t]
His love endures forever.
7 who made the great lights[u]—
His love endures forever.
8 the sun to govern[v] the day,
His love endures forever.
9 the moon and stars to govern the
night;
His love endures forever.

10 to him who struck down the
firstborn[w] of Egypt
His love endures forever.
11 and brought Israel out[x] from
among them
His love endures forever.
12 with a mighty hand[y] and
outstretched arm;[z]
His love endures forever.

13 to him who divided the Red
Sea[g][a] asunder
His love endures forever.
14 and brought Israel through[b] the
midst of it,
His love endures forever.
15 but swept Pharaoh and his army
into the Red Sea;[c]
His love endures forever.

16 to him who led his people through
the desert,[d]
His love endures forever.
17 who struck down great kings,[e]
His love endures forever.
18 and killed mighty kings[f]—
His love endures forever.
19 Sihon king of the Amorites[g]
His love endures forever.
20 and Og king of Bashan[h]—
His love endures forever.
21 and gave their land[i] as an
inheritance,[j]
His love endures forever.
22 an inheritance[k] to his servant
Israel;[l]
His love endures forever.

23 to the One who remembered us[m]
in our low estate
His love endures forever.
24 and freed us[n] from our enemies,[o]
His love endures forever.

135:13 [x]S Ex 3:15 [y]S Ps 102:12 **135:14** [z]S 1Sa 24:15; Heb 10:30* [a]S Dt 32:36 **135:15** [b]Ps 96:5; Rev 9:20 [c]Isa 2:8; 31:7; 37:19; 40:19; Jer 1:16; 10:5 **135:16** [d]S 1Ki 18:26 **135:17** [e]Jer 10:14; Hab 2:19 **135:19** [f]S Ps 22:23 **135:21** [g]Ps 128:5; 134:3 [h]S 1Ki 8:13; S 2Ch 6:2 **136:1** [i]Ps 105:1 [j]Ps 100:5; 106:1; 145:9; Jer 33:11; Na 1:7 [k]ver 2-26; S 2Ch 5:13; S Ezr 3:11; Ps 118:1-4 **136:2** [l]Ps 105:1 [m]S Dt 10:17 **136:3** [n]Ps 105:1 [o]S Dt 10:17; S 1Ti 6:15 **136:4** [p]S Ex 3:20; S Job 9:10 **136:5** [q]Pr 3:19; Jer 51:15 [r]S Ge 1:1 **136:6** [s]S Ge 1:1; Isa 42:5; Jer 10:12; 33:2 [t]S Ge 1:6 **136:7** [u]Ge 1:14, 16; Ps 74:16; Jas 1:17 **136:8** [v]S Ge 1:16 **136:10** [w]S Ex 4:23; S 12:12 **136:11** [x]S Ex 6:6; 13:3; Ps 105:43 **136:12** [y]S Ex 3:20; S Dt 5:15 [z]S Dt 9:29 **136:13** [a]S Ps 78:13 **136:14** [b]Ex 14:22; Ps 106:9 **136:15** [c]S Ex 14:27 **136:16** [d]S Ex 13:18; Ps 78:52 **136:17** [e]Nu 21:23-25; Jos 24:8-11; Ps 78:55; 135:9-12 **136:18** [f]Dt 29:7; S Jos 12:7-24 **136:19** [g]Nu 21:21-25 **136:20** [h]Nu 21:33-35 **136:21** [i]Jos 12:1 [j]S Dt 1:38; S Jos 14:1 **136:22** [k]S Dt 29:8; Ps 78:55 [l]Isa 20:3; 41:8; 42:19; 43:10; 44:1,21; 45:4; 49:5-7 **136:23** [m]Ps 78:39; 103:14; 115:12 **136:24** [n]S Jos 10:14; S Ne 9:28 [o]S Dt 6:19

[g]13 Hebrew *Yam Suph*; that is, Sea of Reeds; also in verse 15

136:1–26 HIS LOVE ENDURES FOREVER. This repeated refrain teaches us that God's love is the foundation of all his actions on our behalf and the fountainhead of all our thanksgiving. His love includes his mercy, faithfulness and kindness.

[25]and who gives food[p] to every
creature.
His love endures forever.

[26]Give thanks[q] to the God of
heaven.[r]
His love endures forever.[s]

Psalm 137

[1]By the rivers of Babylon[t] we sat
and wept[u]
when we remembered Zion.[v]
[2]There on the poplars[w]
we hung our harps,[x]
[3]for there our captors[y] asked us
for songs,
our tormentors demanded[z]
songs of joy;
they said, "Sing us one of the
songs of Zion!"[a]

[4]How can we sing the songs of the
LORD[b]
while in a foreign land?
[5]If I forget you,[c] O Jerusalem,
may my right hand forget ⌊its
skill⌋.
[6]May my tongue cling to the roof[d]
of my mouth
if I do not remember[e] you,
if I do not consider Jerusalem[f]
my highest joy.

[7]Remember, O LORD, what the
Edomites[g] did
on the day Jerusalem fell.[h]
"Tear it down," they cried,
"tear it down to its
foundations!"[i]

[8]O Daughter of Babylon, doomed to
destruction,[j]
happy is he who repays you
for what you have done to us—
[9]he who seizes your infants
and dashes them[k] against the
rocks.

136:25 [p]S Ge 1:30; S Mt 6:26
136:26 [q]Ps 105:1 [r]S Ps 115:3 [s]S Ezr 3:11
137:1 [t]Eze 1:1,3; 3:15; 10:15 [u]Ne 1:4 [v]Isa 3:26; La 1:4
137:2 [w]S Lev 23:40 [x]Job 30:31; Isa 24:8; Eze 26:13; Am 6:5
137:3 [y]Ps 79:1-4; La 1:5 [z]S Job 30:9; Ps 80:6 [a]Eze 16:57; 22:4; 34:29
137:4 [b]S Ne 12:46
137:5 [c]Isa 2:3; 56:7; 65:11; 66:20
137:6 [d]S Ps 22:15 [e]Ne 2:3 [f]S Dt 4:29; Jer 51:50; Eze 6:9
137:7 [g]S Ge 25:30; S 2Ch 28:17; S Ps 83:6; La 4:21-22 [h]2Ki 25:1-10; Ob 1:11 [i]Ps 74:8
137:8 [j]Isa 13:1, 19; 47:1-15; Jer 25:12,26; 50:1; 50:2-51:58
137:9 [k]S 2Ki 8:12; S Isa 13:16; Lk 19:44

138:1 [l]Ps 95:3; 96:4 [m]Ps 27:6; 108:1
138:2 [n]S 1Ki 8:29; S Ps 5:7 [o]Ps 74:21; 97:12; 140:13 [p]Ps 108:4; 115:1 [q]Ps 119:9
138:3 [r]Ps 18:6; 30:2; 99:6; 116:4 [s]S Ps 118:5 [t]Pr 28:1; S Ac 4:29 [u]Ps 28:7
138:4 [v]Ps 72:11; 102:15
138:5 [w]S Ps 51:14; 71:16; 145:7 [x]Ps 21:5
138:6 [y]S Ps 113:6 [z]S Ps 40:4; S Mt 23:12
138:7 [a]Ps 23:4 [b]S Ps 41:2

Psalm 138

Of David.

[1]I will praise you, O LORD, with all
my heart;
before the "gods"[l] I will sing[m]
your praise.
[2]I will bow down toward your holy
temple[n]
and will praise your name[o]
for your love and your
faithfulness,[p]
for you have exalted above all
things
your name and your word.[q]
[3]When I called,[r] you answered
me;[s]
you made me bold[t] and
stouthearted.[u]

[4]May all the kings of the earth[v]
praise you, O LORD,
when they hear the words of
your mouth.
[5]May they sing[w] of the ways of the
LORD,
for the glory of the LORD[x] is
great.

[6]Though the LORD is on high, he
looks upon the lowly,[y]
but the proud[z] he knows from
afar.
[7]Though I walk[a] in the midst of
trouble,
you preserve my life;[b]
you stretch out your hand[c]
against the anger of my
foes,[d]
with your right hand[e] you save
me.[f]
[8]The LORD will fulfill ⌊his purpose⌋[g]
for me;
your love, O LORD, endures
forever[h]—

[c]S Ex 7:5 [d]Ps 7:6 [e]Ps 20:6; 60:5; 108:6 [f]Ps 17:7,14
138:8 [g]Php 1:6 [h]S Ezr 3:11; Ps 100:5

137:9 DASHES THEM AGAINST THE ROCKS. When the Babylonians captured Jerusalem in 586 B.C., they had taken helpless babies from their mothers and dashed them against the nearest wall. God will punish their cruelty by causing them to reap what they had sown (see Isa 13:16; Jer 23:2). The cruel violence they had unmercifully perpetrated on others will return to them. Note two things about this cry for appropriate retribution: (1) Divine retribution rests mostly on the cruel adults; they are the ones who will suffer the most. The innocent children who die in times of war or divine judgments are accepted by God and not condemned. God does not impute sin to an individual until he or she rejects God's law written in the human heart or in Scripture (see 1Sa 15:3, note; Ro 5:12,14, notes; 7:9–11, note).

(2) Although the NT emphasizes forgiving enemies and praying for their salvation (Mt 5:43–48), there will come a time at the end of history when the Holy Spirit will lead his people to pray for divine retribution on the arrogant, unrepentant and ungodly (see Rev 6:10).

do not abandon[i] the works of
your hands.[j]

Psalm 139

For the director of music. Of David.
A psalm.

1O LORD, you have searched me[k]
and you know[l] me.
2You know when I sit and when I
rise;[m]
you perceive my thoughts[n] from
afar.
3You discern my going out[o] and
my lying down;
you are familiar with all my
ways.[p]
4Before a word is on my tongue
you know it completely,[q]
O LORD.
5You hem me in[r]—behind and
before;
you have laid your hand upon
me.
6Such knowledge is too wonderful
for me,[s]
too lofty[t] for me to attain.
7Where can I go from your Spirit?
Where can I flee[u] from your
presence?
8If I go up to the heavens,[v] you
are there;
if I make my bed[w] in the
depths,[h] you are there.
9If I rise on the wings of the dawn,
if I settle on the far side of the
sea,
10even there your hand will guide
me,[x]
your right hand[y] will hold me
fast.
11If I say, "Surely the darkness will
hide me
and the light become night
around me,"
12even the darkness will not be
dark[z] to you;
the night will shine like the day,
for darkness is as light to you.
13For you created my inmost
being;[a]
you knit me together[b] in my
mother's womb.[c]
14I praise you[d] because I am
fearfully and wonderfully
made;
your works are wonderful,[e]
I know that full well.
15My frame was not hidden from you
when I was made[f] in the secret
place.
When I was woven together[g] in
the depths of the earth,[h]
16 your eyes saw my unformed
body.
All the days ordained[i] for me
were written in your book
before one of them came to be.
17How precious to[i] me are your
thoughts,[j] O God![k]
How vast is the sum of them!
18Were I to count them,[l]

138:8 [i]S Ps 51:11 [j]S Job 10:3,8 **139:1** [k]S Ps 17:3; Ro 8:27 [l]Ps 44:21 **139:2** [m]2Ki 19:27 [n]Ps 94:11; Pr 24:12; Jer 12:3 **139:3** [o]2Ki 19:27 [p]S Job 31:4 **139:4** [q]S Heb 4:13 **139:5** [r]S 1Sa 25:16; Ps 32:10; 34:7; 125:2 **139:6** [s]S Ps 131:1 [t]Ro 11:33 **139:7** [u]Jer 23:24; Jnh 1:3 **139:8** [v]Dt 30:12-15; Am 9:2-3 [w]Job 17:13 **139:10** [x]Ps 23:3 [y]Ps 108:6; Isa 41:10 **139:12** [z]Job 34:22; Da 2:22 **139:13** [a]Ps 119:73 [b]S Job 10:11 [c]Isa 44:2,24; 46:3; 49:5; Jer 1:5 **139:14** [d]Ps 119:164; 145:10 [e]S Job 40:19 **139:15** [f]Ecc 11:5 [g]S Job 10:11 [h]S Ps 63:9 **139:16** [i]S Job 33:29; S Ps 90:12 **139:17** [j]S Ps 92:5 [k]S Job 5:9 **139:18** [l]Ps 40:5

h *8* Hebrew *Sheol* **i** *17* Or *concerning*

139:1–24 YOU HAVE SEARCHED ME. This psalm describes various aspects of God's attributes, especially his omnipresence and omniscience as these characteristics relate to his care for his people (see article on THE ATTRIBUTES OF GOD, p. 882). The God of heaven and earth created us and has perfect knowledge of us; he is always with us, and his thoughts are always directed toward us in every situation.

139:1–6 YOU KNOW ME. God knows all our inward thoughts, motives, desires and fears, as well as our outward habits and actions. He knows all we do from the beginning of the day to its end. In everything we do, he encircles us with his care and lays his hand of favor upon our heads (v. 5).

139:7–12 WHERE CAN I GO FROM YOUR SPIRIT? The child of God can never move beyond God's care, guidance and supporting strength (see v. 10 as the key to understanding v. 7). He is with us in all situations, in whatever the present and the future brings.

139:13 YOU KNIT ME TOGETHER IN MY MOTHER'S WOMB. God is creatively and actively involved in the development of human life. He personally cares for a baby from the moment of its conception; his regard for a fetus extends to a plan for his or her life (see next note). For this reason God considers the abortion of an unborn infant as the murder of a human life (see Ex 21:22–23, note).

139:16 WERE WRITTEN IN YOUR BOOK. God does not bring us into life without a purpose. (1) The statement about the days ordained for us probably refers to our alloted time on earth, i.e., generally seventy or eighty years (see Ps 90:10), though one may die before his or her time (see 55:23; Job 22:16; Pr 10:27; Ecc 7:17).

(2) The time mentioned in this psalm refers not only to days, but also to God's plan for our lives as a whole. In his plan, he does not want "anyone to perish, but everyone to come to repentance" (2Pe 3:9; cf. 1Ti 2:4); thus God intends for us to accept Jesus as our Lord and Savior and fulfill his will in a life of service to him.

139:17 HOW PRECIOUS TO ME ARE YOUR THOUGHTS. We can be comforted knowing that

THE ATTRIBUTES OF GOD

***Ps 139:7–8** "Where can I go from your Spirit? Where can I flee from your presence? If I go up to the heavens, you are there; if I make my bed in the depths, you are there."*

The Bible does not seek to prove that God exists. Rather, it assumes his existence and describes numerous attributes that he possesses. Some of these attributes are unique to him as God; others we see in human beings as a result of their being created in God's image.

UNIQUE ATTRIBUTES OF GOD. (1) God is omnipresent—i.e., he is present everywhere at the same time. The psalmist states that no matter where we go, God is there (Ps 139:7–12; cf. Jer 23:23–24; Ac 17:27–28); God observes everything that we do.

(2) God is omniscient—i.e., he knows everything (Ps 139:1–6; 147:5). He knows not only our actions but also our very thoughts (1Sa 16:7; 1Ki 8:39; Ps 44:21; Jer 17:9–10). When the Bible speaks of God's foreknowledge (Isa 42:9; Ac 2:23; 1Pe 1:2), it means that he knows all things possible as possible, all things certain as certain, all things contingent as contingent, all things future as future, all things past as past, all things foreordained as predestined certainties (cf. 1Sa 23:10–13; Jer 38:17–20). Biblical foreknowledge does not entail philosophical determinism. God remains free to make decisions and alter his purposes in time and history, according to his own will and wisdom. In other words, God is not a prisoner of his own foreknowledge (see Nu 14:11–20; 2Ki 20:1–7; see article on ELECTION AND PREDESTINATION, p. 1824).

(3) God is omnipotent—i.e., he is all-powerful and has ultimate authority over all things and all creatures (Ps 147:13–18; Jer 32:17; Mt 19:26; Lk 1:37). This doesn't mean, however, that God uses all his power and authority at all times; for example, God has the power to destroy all sin, but he has chosen not to do so until the end of history (see 1Jn 5:19, note). In many cases, God limits his power, channeling it through his people (2Co 12:7–10); in these cases, his power is dependent on our degree of availability and submission to him (see Eph 3:20, note; see article on THE PROVIDENCE OF GOD, p. 78).

(4) God is transcendent—i.e., he is different and independent from his creation (see Ex 24:9–18; Isa 6:1–3; 40:12–26; 55:8–9). His being and existence are infinitely greater and higher than the created order (1Ki 8:27; Isa 66:1–2; Ac 17:24–25). He dwells in perfect and pure existence, far above what he has made; he himself is uncreated and exists apart from creation (see 1Ti 6:16, note). Transcendence does not entail, however, that God is incapable of living among his people as their God (Lev 26:11–12; Eze 37:27; 43:7; 2Co 6:16).

(5) God is eternal—i.e., he is from everlasting to everlasting (Ps 90:1–2; 102:12; Isa 57:15). There was never a time, either in the past or the future, when God did not or will not exist; he is not bound by human time (cf. Ps 90:4; 2Pe 3:8) and is, therefore, best described as "I am" (cf. Ex 3:14; Jn 8:58).

(6) God is unchangeable—i.e., there is no change in God's attributes, in his perfections or in his purpose for humankind (Nu 23:19; Ps 102:26–28; Isa 41:4; Mal 3:6; Heb 1:11–12; Jas 1:17); this doesn't mean, however, that God never alters his temporary purposes in response to the actions of humans. He may, for example, alter his intentions of judgment because of the sincere repentance of sinners (cf. Jnh 3:6–10). Furthermore, he remains free to respond to the needs of human beings and to the prayers of his people. The Bible often speaks of God changing his mind as a result of the diligent prayers of the righteous (e.g., Nu 14:1–20; 2Ki 20:2–6; Isa 38:2–6; Lk 18:1–8; see articles on ELECTION AND PREDESTINATION, p. 1824, and EFFECTIVE PRAYING, p. 496).

(7) God is perfect and holy—i.e., he is completely without sin and absolutely righteous (Lev 11:44–45; Ps 85:13; 145:17; Mt 5:48). Adam and Eve were created without

sin (cf. Ge 1:31) but with the capability of sinning. God, on the other hand, cannot sin (Nu 23:19; 2Ti 2:13; Tit 1:2; Heb 6:18). His holiness also includes his dedication to carrying out his purposes and plan.

(8) God is triune—i.e., he is one God (Dt 6:4; Isa 45:21; 1Co 8:5–6; Eph 4:6; 1Ti 2:5), who has manifested himself in three divine persons: Father, Son and Holy Spirit (e.g., Mt 28:19; 2Co 13:14; 1Pe 1:2). Each person is fully divine, equal with the other two; yet they are not three Gods, but one (see Mt 3:17, note; Mk 1:11, note).

MORAL ATTRIBUTES OF GOD. Many characteristics of the one true God, particularly his moral attributes, bear similarity to human qualities; however, his attributes all exist to a degree incomparably greater than they do in us. For example, even though both God and humans possess the ability to love, no human is able to love to the degree and intensity that God does. Moreover, it must be stressed that our ability to exercise these characteristics is related to our being created in God's image (Ge 1:26–27); in other words, we are like him, not he like us.

(1) God is good (Ps 25:8; 106:1; Mk 10:18). All that God originally created was good, an extension of his own nature (Ge 1:4,10,12,18,21,25,31). He continues to be good to his creation by sustaining it on behalf of all his creatures (Ps 104:10–28; 145:9; see article on THE PROVIDENCE OF GOD, p. 78); he even provides for the ungodly (Mt 5:45; Ac 14:17). God is especially good to his people who call on him in truth (Ps 145:18–20).

(2) God is love (1Jn 4:8). His love is a selfless love that embraces the entire world of sinful humankind (Jn 3:16; Ro 5:8). The chief expression of that love was his sending of his only Son Jesus to die for sinners (1Jn 4:9–10). In addition, God has a special family love for those who through Jesus are reconciled to him (see Jn 16:27, note).

(3) God is merciful and gracious (Ex 34:6; Dt 4:31; 2Ch 30:9; Ps 103:8; 145:8; Joel 2:13); he does not cut off and destroy humanity as our sins deserve (Ps 103:10), but offers forgiveness as a free gift to be received through faith in Jesus Christ (Ps 103:11–12; Ro 6:23; 1Co 1:3–4; Eph 2:8–9; Tit 2:11; 3:4–5; see article on FAITH AND GRACE, p. 1720).

(4) God is compassionate (2Ki 13:23; Ps 86:15; 111:4). To be compassionate means to feel sorrow for someone else's suffering, with a desire to help. Out of his compassion for humanity, God provided forgiveness and salvation (cf. Ps 78:38); likewise, Jesus, the Son of God, showed compassion for the crowds when he preached the gospel to the poor, proclaimed freedom for the prisoners and recovery of sight for the blind, and released the oppressed (Lk 4:18; cf. Mt 9:36; 14:14; 15:32; 20:34; Mk 1:41; see Mk 6:34, note).

(5) God is patient and slow to anger (Ex 34:6; Nu 14:18; Ro 2:4; 1Ti 1:16). God first expressed this characteristic in the Garden of Eden after Adam and Eve's sin, when he did not destroy the human race as he had a right to do (cf. Ge 2:16–17). God was also patient in the days of Noah, while the ark was being built (1Pe 3:20). And God is still patient with the sinful human race; he does not presently judge so as to destroy the world, because he is patiently giving everyone the opportunity to repent and be saved (2Pe 3:9).

(6) God is truth (Dt 32:4; Ps 31:5; Isa 65:16; Jn 3:33). Jesus called himself "the truth" (Jn 14:6), and the Spirit is known as the "Spirit of truth" (Jn 14:17; cf. 1Jn 5:6). Because God is entirely trustworthy and true in all he says and does, his word is also described as truth (2Sa 7:28; Ps 119:43; Isa 45:19; Jn 17:17). In keeping with this fact, the Bible makes it plain that God does not tolerate lies or falsehood of any kind (Nu 23:19; Tit 1:2; Heb 6:18).

(7) God is faithful (Ex 34:6; Dt 7:9; Isa 49:7; La 3:23; Heb 10:23); God will do what he has revealed in his Word, carrying out both his promises and his warnings (Nu 14:32–35; 2Sa 7:28; Job 34:12; Ac 13:23,32–33; see 2Ti 2:13, note). God's faithfulness should bring unspeakable comfort to believers and great fear of judgment to all who do not repent and believe in the Lord Jesus (Heb 6:4–8; 10:26–31).

(8) Finally, God is just (Dt 32:4; 1Jn 1:9); to be just means that God upholds the moral order of the universe, and is righteous and without sin in the manner in which he treats humankind (Ne 9:33; Da 9:14). God's determination to punish sinners with death (Ro 5:12; see article on DEATH, p. 732) proceeds from his justice (Ro 6:23; cf. Ge 2:16–17); he is angry at sin because of his love for righteousness (Ro 3:5–6; see Jdg 10:7, note). He reveals his wrath against every form of wickedness (Ro 1:18), especially idolatry (1Ki 14:9,15,22), unbelief (Ps 78:21–22; Jn 3:36) and unjust treatment of other people (Isa 10:1–4; Am 2:6–7). Jesus Christ, who is called the "Righteous One" (Ac 7:52; 22:14; cf. Ac 3:14), also loves righteousness and hates evil (see Mk 3:5; Ro 1:18, note; Heb 1:9, note). Note that God's justice is not opposed to his love. On the contrary, it was to satisfy his justice that he sent Jesus into the world as his gift of love (Jn 3:16; 1Jn 4:9–10) and as his sacrifice for sin on our behalf (Isa 53:5–6; Ro 4:25; 1Pe 3:18), in order to reconcile us to himself (see 2Co 5:18–21, notes).

God's final revelation of himself is in Jesus Christ (cf. Jn 1:18; Heb 1:1–4); in other words, if we want to understand completely the personhood of God, we must look at Christ, for in him all the fullness of the Deity lives (Col 2:9).

they would outnumber the grains
of sand.[m]
When I awake,[n]
I am still with you.

19If only you would slay the
wicked,[o] O God!
Away from me,[p] you
bloodthirsty men![q]
20They speak of you with evil intent;
your adversaries[r] misuse your
name.[s]
21Do I not hate those[t] who hate
you, O LORD,
and abhor[u] those who rise up
against you?
22I have nothing but hatred for
them;
I count them my enemies.[v]
23Search me,[w] O God, and know my
heart;[x]
test me and know my anxious
thoughts.
24See if there is any offensive way[y]
in me,
and lead me[z] in the way
everlasting.

Psalm 140

For the director of music. A psalm
of David.

1Rescue me,[a] O LORD, from evil
men;
protect me from men of
violence,[b]
2who devise evil plans[c] in their
hearts
and stir up war[d] every day.
3They make their tongues as sharp
as[e] a serpent's;
the poison of vipers[f] is on their
lips. *Selah*
4Keep me,[g] O LORD, from the hands
of the wicked;[h]
protect me from men of violence
who plan to trip my feet.
5Proud men have hidden a snare[i]
for me;
they have spread out the cords
of their net[j]
and have set traps[k] for me
along my path. *Selah*

6O LORD, I say to you, "You are my
God."[l]
Hear, O LORD, my cry for
mercy.[m]
7O Sovereign LORD,[n] my strong
deliverer,
who shields my head in the day
of battle—
8do not grant the wicked[o] their
desires, O LORD;
do not let their plans succeed,
or they will become proud. *Selah*

9Let the heads of those who
surround me
be covered with the trouble their
lips have caused.[p]
10Let burning coals fall upon them;
may they be thrown into the
fire,[q]
into miry pits, never to rise.
11Let slanderers not be established
in the land;
may disaster hunt down men of
violence.[r]

12I know that the LORD secures
justice for the poor[s]
and upholds the cause[t] of the
needy.[u]

139:18 [m]S Job 29:18 [n]S Ps 3:5
139:19 [o]Ps 5:6; Isa 11:4 [p]S Ps 6:8 [q]S Ps 59:2
139:20 [r]S Ps 65:7 [s]S Dt 5:11
139:21 [t]2Ch 19:2; Ps 31:6; 119:113 [u]S Ps 26:5
139:22 [v]Mt 5:43
139:23 [w]Job 31:6 [x]S 1Sa 16:7; S 1Ch 29:17; S Ps 7:9; Pr 17:3; Jer 11:20; S Rev 2:23
139:24 [y]Jer 25:5; 36:3 [z]Ps 5:8; 23:2; 143:10
140:1 [a]Ps 17:13; S 25:20; 59:2; 71:4; 142:6; 143:9 [b]ver 11; Ps 86:14
140:2 [c]Ps 36:4; 52:2; Pr 6:14; 16:27; Isa 59:4; Hos 7:15 [d]S Ps 68:30
140:3 [e]Ps 57:4 [f]Ps 58:4; Ro 3:13*; Jas 3:8
140:4 [g]Ps 141:9 [h]S Ps 36:11
140:5 [i]S Job 34:30; S Ps 119:110 [j]S Job 18:8 [k]Job 18:9; Ps 31:4; S 38:12
140:6 [l]S Ps 16:2 [m]S Ps 28:2,6
140:7 [n]Ps 68:20
140:8 [o]Ps 10:2-3; S 66:7
140:9 [p]Pr 18:7
140:10 [q]Ps 11:6; 21:9; S Mt 3:10; Lk 12:49; Rev 20:15
140:11 [r]S Ps 34:21
140:12 [s]S Ps 82:3 [t]S 1Ki 8:45 [u]S Ps 35:10

God is continually aware of our needs, troubles and suffering, and that he plans for our care, forgiveness, salvation and sanctification. His thoughts for us are unfathomable and immeasurable. As the apostle Paul writes, "No eye has seen, no ear has heard, no mind has conceived what God has prepared for those who love him" (1Co 2:9).

139:21 ABHOR THOSE WHO RISE UP AGAINST YOU? Having meditated on God's great love for him, the psalmist reciprocates with great love and loyalty to his Lord. His anger is stirred against those who oppose and blaspheme God's wonderful name. In deep sympathy with God and his cause, he so identifies himself with the Lord that he hates what God hates and loves what God loves (see Heb 1:9, note). He is grieved and distressed by all the evil and immorality around him (see 2Pe 2:7–8). We too who have truly seen the Lord's salvation, love and goodness should find no love within ourselves for the world and its ways (see 1Jn 2:15–16).

139:23–24 SEARCH ME, O GOD. This is an appropriate prayer for every believer. Not only must we hate unrighteousness in the world (vv. 19–22), but we must also be aware that there may be something in us that grieves God. We should be willing to ask God to put us through any test that would further his work of sanctification in us. If anything offensive is found, we must turn from it in repentance (see Col 3:17, note).

140:1–13 RESCUE ME, O LORD, FROM EVIL MEN. We should ask God to deliver us not only from evil people, but also from the "evil one," i.e., Satan. As our greatest enemy, he seeks to snare and destroy us (see Mt 4:10, note; Mt 6:13, note; see article on POWER OVER SATAN AND DEMONS, p. 1484).

[13]Surely the righteous will praise
your name[v]
and the upright will live[w] before
you.[x]

Psalm 141

A psalm of David.

[1]O LORD, I call to you; come
quickly[y] to me.
Hear my voice[z] when I call to
you.
[2]May my prayer be set before you
like incense;[a]
may the lifting up of my hands[b]
be like the evening
sacrifice.[c]

[3]Set a guard over my mouth,[d]
O LORD;
keep watch over the door of my
lips.[e]
[4]Let not my heart[f] be drawn to
what is evil,
to take part in wicked deeds[g]
with men who are evildoers;
let me not eat of their
delicacies.[h]

[5]Let a righteous man[j] strike
me—it is a kindness;
let him rebuke me[i]—it is oil on
my head.[j]
My head will not refuse it.

Yet my prayer is ever against the
deeds of evildoers;
[6] their rulers will be thrown down
from the cliffs,[k]
and the wicked will learn that
my words were well spoken.
[7]⌊They will say,⌋ "As one plows[l]
and breaks up the earth,[m]
so our bones have been
scattered at the mouth[n] of
the grave.[k]"

[8]But my eyes are fixed[o] on you,
O Sovereign LORD;
in you I take refuge[p]—do not
give me over to death.
[9]Keep me[q] from the snares they
have laid[r] for me,
from the traps set[s] by
evildoers.
[10]Let the wicked fall[t] into their
own nets,
while I pass by in safety.[u]

Psalm 142

A *maskil*[1] of David. When he was in
the cave.[v] A prayer.

[1]I cry aloud[w] to the LORD;
I lift up my voice to the LORD for
mercy.[x]
[2]I pour out my complaint[y] before
him;
before him I tell my trouble.[z]

[3]When my spirit grows faint[a]
within me,
it is you who know my way.
In the path where I walk
men have hidden a snare for me.
[4]Look to my right and see;
no one is concerned for me.
I have no refuge;[b]
no one cares[c] for my life.

[5]I cry to you, O LORD;
I say, "You are my refuge,[d]
my portion[e] in the land of the
living."[f]
[6]Listen to my cry,[g]
for I am in desperate need;[h]
rescue me[i] from those who
pursue me,
for they are too strong[j] for me.
[7]Set me free from my prison,[k]

j5 Or *Let the Righteous One* k7 Hebrew *Sheol* 1Title: Probably a literary or musical term

140:13 [v]S Ps 138:2 [w]S Ps 11:7 [x]Ps 16:11 **141:1** [y]S Ps 22:19 [z]S Ps 4:1; 5:1-2; 27:7; 143:1 **141:2** [a]S Lk 1:9; Rev 5:8; 8:3 [b]S Ps 28:2; 63:4; 1Ti 2:8 [c]S Ex 29:39,41; 30:8 **141:3** [d]S Ps 34:13; Jas 1:26; 3:8 [e]S Ps 12:2 **141:4** [f]S Jos 24:23 [g]S Ps 106:29 [h]Pr 23:1-3 **141:5** [i]Pr 9:8; 19:25; 25:12; Ecc 7:5 [j]S Ex 29:7; Ps 23:5 **141:6** [k]S 2Ch 25:12 **141:7** [l]Ps 129:3 [m]Nu 16:32-33 [n]S Nu 16:30 **141:8** [o]Ps 123:2 [p]Ps 2:12; 11:1 **141:9** [q]Ps 140:4 [r]S Ps 64:5 [s]S Ps 38:12 **141:10** [t]Ps 7:15; 35:8; 57:6 [u]Ps 124:7 **142:1** [v]142 Title 1Sa 22:1; 24:3; Ps 57 Title [w]S 1Ki 8:52; Ps 3:4 [x]Ps 30:8 **142:2** [y]Ps 64:1 [z]S Ps 50:15 **142:3** [a]Ps 6:2; 77:3; 84:2; 88:4; 143:4,7; Jer 8:18; La 1:22 **142:4** [b]Jer 25:35 [c]Jer 30:17 **142:5** [d]S Ps 46:1 [e]S Dt 32:9; Ps 16:5 [f]S Job 28:13; Ps 27:13 **142:6** [g]S Ps 17:1 [h]S Ps 79:8 [i]S Ps 25:20 [j]Jer 31:11 **142:7** [k]S Ps 66:11

141:4 LET NOT MY HEART BE DRAWN TO WHAT IS EVIL. Those who love the Lord should pray that God will keep them from desiring, speaking or doing any evil (cf. Mt 6:13; Jn 14:15,21). We must shun all compromise with wicked persons and refuse to be entertained by their "delicacies," i.e., seductive pleasures (see Ro 1:32, note; see article on SANCTIFICATION, p. 1956).

141:5 LET A RIGHTEOUS MAN STRIKE ME. If we sincerely desire to please our Lord, we will welcome rebuke that convicts us of anything contrary to God's holiness. When a righteous person cries out fervently against sin and compromise in the church, he or she should be supported, not rejected (see Pr 15:5,32; Jn 16:8; Eph 5:11; 2Ti 4:2). Our attitude towards such servants of God reveals our own spiritual state (see 2Ti 4:3–4, note).

142:1–7 I CRY ALOUD. This psalm comes from one who is deeply troubled and overwhelmed by a desperate situation. Although the psalmist is experiencing loneliness without any supporting human companionship or sympathy, the Lord still remains his refuge, friend and helper. When believers are afflicted and oppressed, rather than remaining silent, they should cry out to God, who has pledged himself to be our comforter and helper in time of need (see Jn 14:16–26; 2Co 1:4–5).

that I may praise your name.[l]

Then the righteous will gather
about me
because of your goodness to
me.[m]

Psalm 143

A psalm of David.

1O LORD, hear my prayer,[n]
listen to my cry for mercy;[o]
in your faithfulness[p] and
righteousness[q]
come to my relief.
2Do not bring your servant into
judgment,
for no one living is righteous[r]
before you.

3The enemy pursues me,
he crushes me to the ground;
he makes me dwell in darkness[s]
like those long dead.[t]
4So my spirit grows faint within me;
my heart within me is
dismayed.[u]

5I remember[v] the days of long ago;
I meditate[w] on all your works
and consider what your hands
have done.
6I spread out my hands[x] to you;
my soul thirsts for you like a
parched land. *Selah*

7Answer me quickly,[y] O LORD;
my spirit fails.[z]
Do not hide your face[a] from me
or I will be like those who go
down to the pit.
8Let the morning bring me word of
your unfailing love,[b]
for I have put my trust in you.
Show me the way[c] I should go,
for to you I lift up my soul.[d]

142:7 [l]Ps 7:17; 9:2 [m]S 2Ch 6:41
143:1 [n]S Ps 141:1 [o]S Ps 28:2; 130:2 [p]S Ex 34:6; Ps 89:1-2 [q]Ps 71:2
143:2 [r]S Ps 14:3; Ro 3:10
143:3 [s]S Ps 107:10 [t]La 3:6
143:4 [u]Ps 30:7
143:5 [v]Ps 77:6 [w]S Ge 24:63
143:6 [x]S Ex 9:29; S Job 11:13
143:7 [y]S Ps 69:17 [z]S Ps 142:3 [a]S Ps 22:24; 27:9; 30:7
143:8 [b]Ps 6:4; 90:14 [c]S Ex 33:13; S Job 34:32; Ps 27:11; 32:8 [d]Ps 25:1-2; S 86:4
143:9 [e]S Ps 140:1 [f]S Ps 18:17; 31:15
143:10 [g]S Ps 119:12 [h]Ps 31:14 [i]S Ne 9:20; Ps 25:4-5 [j]Ps 26:12
143:11 [k]Ps 25:11 [l]S Ps 41:2 [m]Ps 31:1; 71:2
143:12 [n]Ps 8:2 [o]Ps 54:5 [p]S Ps 116:16
144:1 [q]S Ge 49:24
144:2 [r]Ps 59:9; 91:2 [s]Ps 27:1; 37:39; 43:2 [t]S Ge 15:1; S Ps 18:2 [u]S Jdg 4:23; S Ps 18:39
144:3 [v]Heb 2:6
144:4 [w]S Job 7:7; 27:3; Isa 2:22 [x]S 1Ch 29:15; S Job 14:2; S Jas 4:14
144:5 [y]Ps 18:9; Isa 64:1 [z]S Ge 11:5; S Ps 57:3

9Rescue me[e] from my enemies,[f]
O LORD,
for I hide myself in you.
10Teach me[g] to do your will,
for you are my God;[h]
may your good Spirit
lead[i] me on level ground.[j]

11For your name's sake,[k] O LORD,
preserve my life;[l]
in your righteousness,[m] bring
me out of trouble.
12In your unfailing love, silence my
enemies;[n]
destroy all my foes,[o]
for I am your servant.[p]

Psalm 144

Of David.

1Praise be to the LORD my Rock,[q]
who trains my hands for war,
my fingers for battle.
2He is my loving God and my
fortress,[r]
my stronghold[s] and my
deliverer,
my shield,[t] in whom I take
refuge,
who subdues peoples[m][u] under
me.

3O LORD, what is man[v] that you
care for him,
the son of man that you think of
him?
4Man is like a breath;[w]
his days are like a fleeting
shadow.[x]

5Part your heavens,[y] O LORD, and
come down;[z]

[m]2 Many manuscripts of the Masoretic Text, Dead Sea Scrolls, Aquila, Jerome and Syriac; most manuscripts of the Masoretic Text *subdues my people*

143:1–12 HEAR MY PRAYER Like the preceding psalm, this one describes a believer who is facing overwhelming troubles and feels he has reached the end of his endurance (vv. 3–4,7; cf. 104:29). All he has left is prayerful hope that God will revive him again and deliver him out of his great trial (vv. 10–11; see previous note).

144:1–15 PRAISE BE TO THE LORD MY ROCK. God is an immovable rock, stronghold, shield and deliverer for those who take refuge in him (cf. Ps 140—143). He trains the hands of the righteous for war and their fingers for battle in all areas of spiritual conflict (see next note).

144:1 TRAINS MY HANDS FOR WAR. The psalmist was called on to wage war for the nation of Israel. We can apply this message to believers in Christ, whom God calls to wage spiritual battle against Satan, the world and the sinful nature. We must advance God's kingdom by proclaiming the gospel in the power of the Holy Spirit, by bringing down Satan's strongholds and by leading people to salvation in Christ (see Eph 6:11–18, notes). Warriors who depend on God's strength and training will be victorious.

144:5 O LORD . . . COME DOWN. God has trained the psalmist to trust him for the battle and for any time of crisis (vv. 1–2). Moreover, the psalmist must continue to trust God for the battle, as there are still many dangers to face (v. 7). After experiencing salvation in Christ and the baptism in

touch the mountains, so that
they smoke.[a]
6Send forth lightning[b] and
scatter[c] ⌊the enemies⌋;
shoot your arrows[d] and rout
them.
7Reach down your hand from on
high;[e]
deliver me and rescue me[f]
from the mighty waters,[g]
from the hands of foreigners[h]
8whose mouths are full of lies,[i]
whose right hands[j] are
deceitful.[k]

9I will sing a new song[l] to you,
O God;
on the ten-stringed lyre[m] I will
make music to you,
10to the One who gives victory to
kings,[n]
who delivers his servant David[o]
from the deadly sword.[p]

11Deliver me and rescue me[q]
from the hands of foreigners[r]
whose mouths are full of lies,[s]
whose right hands are
deceitful.[t]

12Then our sons in their youth
will be like well-nurtured
plants,[u]
and our daughters will be like
pillars[v]
carved to adorn a palace.
13Our barns will be filled[w]
with every kind of provision.
Our sheep will increase by
thousands,
by tens of thousands in our
fields;
14 our oxen[x] will draw heavy
loads.[n]
There will be no breaching of
walls,[y]
no going into captivity,
no cry of distress in our
streets.[z]
15Blessed are the people[a] of whom
this is true;
blessed are the people whose
God is the LORD.

Psalm 145[o]

A psalm of praise. Of David.

1I will exalt you,[b] my God the
King;[c]
I will praise your name[d] for
ever and ever.
2Every day I will praise[e] you
and extol your name[f] for ever
and ever.

3Great is the LORD[g] and most
worthy of praise;[h]
his greatness no one can
fathom.[i]
4One generation[j] will commend
your works to another;
they will tell[k] of your mighty
acts.[l]
5They will speak of the glorious
splendor[m] of your majesty,
and I will meditate on your
wonderful works.[p][n]
6They will tell[o] of the power of
your awesome works,[p]
and I will proclaim[q] your great
deeds.[r]
7They will celebrate your abundant
goodness[s]
and joyfully sing[t] of your
righteousness.[u]

8The LORD is gracious and
compassionate,[v]
slow to anger and rich in love.[w]

144:5 [a]Ps 104:32
144:6 [b]Hab 3:11; Zec 9:14 [c]S Ps 59:11; S 68:1 [d]Ps 7:12-13; 18:14
144:7 [e]S 2Sa 22:17 [f]Ps 3:7; S 57:3 [g]Ps 69:2 [h]S Ps 18:44
144:8 [i]Ps 12:2; 41:6 [j]Ge 14:22; Dt 32:40 [k]S Ps 36:3
144:9 [l]S Ps 28:7; S 96:1 [m]Ps 33:2-3; S 71:22
144:10 [n]S 2Sa 8:14 [o]Ps 18:50 [p]S Job 5:20
144:11 [q]Ps 3:7; S 25:20 [r]S Ps 18:44 [s]Ps 41:6-7 [t]Ps 12:2; S 36:3; 106:26; Isa 44:20
144:12 [u]Ps 92:12-14; S 128:3 [v]SS 4:4; 7:4
144:13 [w]Pr 3:10
144:14 [x]Pr 14:4 [y]2Ki 25:11 [z]Isa 24:11; Jer 14:2-3
144:15 [a]Dt 28:3
145:1 [b]Ps 30:1; 34:1 [c]Ps 2:6; 5:2 [d]S Ps 54:6
145:2 [e]S Ps 71:6 [f]Ps 34:1; Isa 25:1; 26:8
145:3 [g]S Ps 95:3 [h]S 2Sa 22:4; Ps 96:4 [i]S Job 5:9
145:4 [j]Ps 22:30 [k]S Dt 11:19 [l]S Ps 71:16
145:5 [m]Ps 96:6; 148:13 [n]S Ps 75:1
145:6 [o]Ps 78:4 [p]S Ps 66:3 [q]S Dt 32:3 [r]Ps 75:1; 106:22
145:7 [s]S Ex 18:9; S Ps 27:13 [t]S Ps 5:11; S 101:1 [u]S Ps 138:5
145:8 [v]S Ps 86:15; 103:8 [w]S Ps 86:5

[n] *14* Or *our chieftains will be firmly established*
[o] This psalm is an acrostic poem, the verses of which (including verse 13b) begin with the successive letters of the Hebrew alphabet.
[p] *5* Dead Sea Scrolls and Syriac (see also Septuagint); Masoretic Text *On the glorious splendor of your majesty / and on your wonderful works I will meditate*

the Holy Spirit, believers also continue to need God's daily strength and grace to face the battles of temptation and spiritual warfare encountered in following Christ. Seeking God's face for heaven's help is an ongoing need for all who are members of God's kingdom (Mt 6:33; Heb 7:25; 11:6).

145:2 EVERY DAY I WILL PRAISE YOU. No day should pass without praising and thanking God for his blessings and gifts to us. He is our Maker, Redeemer and Provider (cf. 34:1).

145:8 THE LORD IS GRACIOUS. This oft-repeated refrain expresses God's delight in showing mercy (cf. Ex 34:6–7). When he sees misery, it moves his heart to compassion; he is slow to become angry at our offenses and quickly shows love and mercy when forgiveness is requested (cf. Ex 3:7; Jdg 2:18).

9The LORD is good[x] to all;
he has compassion[y] on all he has made.
10All you have made will praise you,[z] O LORD;
your saints will extol[a] you.[b]
11They will tell of the glory of your kingdom[c]
and speak of your might,[d]
12so that all men may know of your mighty acts[e]
and the glorious splendor of your kingdom.[f]
13Your kingdom is an everlasting kingdom,[g]
and your dominion endures through all generations.

The LORD is faithful[h] to all his promises[i]
and loving toward all he has made.[q]
14The LORD upholds[j] all those who fall
and lifts up all[k] who are bowed down.[l]
15The eyes of all look to you,
and you give them their food[m] at the proper time.
16You open your hand
and satisfy the desires[n] of every living thing.

17The LORD is righteous[o] in all his ways
and loving toward all he has made.[p]
18The LORD is near[q] to all who call on him,[r]
to all who call on him in truth.
19He fulfills the desires[s] of those who fear him;[t]
he hears their cry[u] and saves them.[v]
20The LORD watches over[w] all who love him,[x]
but all the wicked he will destroy.[y]

21My mouth will speak[z] in praise of the LORD.
Let every creature[a] praise his holy name[b]
for ever and ever.

145:9 [x]S 1Ch 16:34; S Ps 136:1; Mt 19:17; Mk 10:18 [y]Ps 103:13-14 **145:10** [z]S Ps 8:6; S 103:22; S 139:14 [a]Ps 30:4; 148:14; 149:9 [b]Ps 115:17-18 **145:11** [c]ver 12-13; S Ex 15:2; Mt 6:33 [d]Ps 21:13 **145:12** [e]S Ps 75:1; 105:1 [f]ver 11; Ps 103:19; Isa 2:10,19,21 **145:13** [g]S Ex 15:18; 1Ti 1:17; 2Pe 1:11; Rev 11:15 [h]S Dt 7:9; S 1Co 1:9 [i]S Jos 23:14 **145:14** [j]S Ps 37:17 [k]S 1Sa 2:8; Ps 146:8 [l]S Ps 38:6 **145:15** [m]S Ge 1:30; S Job 28:5; S Ps 37:25; S Mt 6:26 **145:16** [n]S Ps 90:14; S 104:28 **145:17** [o]S Ex 9:27; S Ezr 9:15 [p]ver 13 **145:18** [q]S Nu 23:21; S Ps 46:1; Php 4:5 [r]Ps 18:6; 80:18 **145:19** [s]S Ps 20:4 [t]S Job 22:28 [u]S Ps 31:22; S 40:1 [v]S 1Sa 10:19; Ps 7:10; 34:18 **145:20** [w]S Ps 1:6 [x]Ps 31:23; 91:14; 97:10 [y]S Ps 94:23 **145:21** [z]Ps 71:8 [a]Ps 65:2; 150:6 [b]S Ex 3:15; S Ps 30:4; S 99:3

Psalm 146

1Praise the LORD.[r]

Praise the LORD,[c] O my soul.
2 I will praise the LORD all my life;[d]
I will sing praise[e] to my God as long as I live.[f]
3Do not put your trust in princes,[g]
in mortal men,[h] who cannot save.
4When their spirit departs, they return to the ground;[i]
on that very day their plans come to nothing.[j]
5Blessed is he[k] whose help[l] is the God of Jacob,
whose hope is in the LORD his God,
6the Maker of heaven[m] and earth,
the sea, and everything in them—
the LORD, who remains faithful[n] forever.
7He upholds[o] the cause of the oppressed[p]
and gives food to the hungry.[q]
The LORD sets prisoners free,[r]
8 the LORD gives sight[s] to the blind,[t]
the LORD lifts up those who are bowed down,[u]
the LORD loves the righteous.[v]
9The LORD watches over the alien[w]
and sustains the fatherless[x] and the widow,[y]
but he frustrates the ways of the wicked.

10The LORD reigns[z] forever,

146:1 [c]Ps 103:1; 104:1 **146:2** [d]Ps 104:33 [e]S Ps 105:2 [f]S Ps 63:4 **146:3** [g]Ps 118:9 [h]Ps 60:11; S 108:12; Isa 2:22 **146:4** [i]S Ge 3:19; S Job 7:21; Ps 103:14; Ecc 12:7 [j]Ps 33:10; 1Co 2:6 **146:5** [k]Ps 33:18; 37:9; 119:43; 144:15; Jer 17:7 [l]Ps 70:5; 71:5;121:2 **146:6** [m]S 2Ch 2:12; Ps 115:15; Ac 14:15; S Rev 10:6 [n]S Dt 7:9; S Ps 18:25; 108:4; 117:2 **146:7** [o]S Ps 37:17 [p]Ps 103:6 [q]Ps 107:9; 145:15 [r]S Ps 66:11; S 68:6 **146:8** [s]S Pr 20:12; Isa 29:18; 32:3; 35:5; 42:7,18-19; 43:8; Mt 11:5 [t]S Ex 4:11 [u]S Ps 38:6 [v]S Dt 7:13; S Job 23:10 **146:9** [w]S Lev 19:34 [x]S Ps 10:18 [y]S Ex 22:22; Jas 1:27 **146:10** [z]S Ge 21:33; S 1Ch 16:31; Ps 93:1; 99:1; Rev 11:15

[q]*13* One manuscript of the Masoretic Text, Dead Sea Scrolls and Syriac (see also Septuagint); most manuscripts of the Masoretic Text do not have the last two lines of verse 13. [r]*1* Hebrew *Hallelu Yah*; also in verse 10

145:18 NEAR TO ALL WHO CALL ON HIM. All who call on God in truth (i.e., with a sincere and upright heart) may be assured that he is near. He will hear their prayer, fulfill their desire for help and work for their deliverance (v. 19).

146—150 PRAISE THE LORD. These psalms begin and end with "Praise the LORD" (Heb *Hallelu Yah*), bringing the book of Psalms to a fitting climax. Note that the Jews called the entire book of Psalms *Tehillim* ("Praises"). Every worship service should include praise to God (see article on PRAISE, p. 770).

your God, O Zion, for all
generations.

Ps 150 Praise the LORD.

Psalm 147

1Praise the LORD.[s]

How good it is to sing praises to
our God,
how pleasant[a] and fitting to
praise him![b]

2The LORD builds up Jerusalem;[c]
he gathers the exiles[d] of Israel.
3He heals the brokenhearted[e]
and binds up their wounds.[f]

4He determines the number of the
stars[g]
and calls them each by name.
5Great is our Lord[h] and mighty in
power;[i]
his understanding has no limit.[j]
6The LORD sustains the humble[k]
but casts the wicked[l] to the
ground.

7Sing to the LORD[m] with
thanksgiving;[n]
make music[o] to our God on the
harp.[p]

8He covers the sky with clouds;[q]
he supplies the earth with rain[r]
and makes grass grow[s] on the
hills.
9He provides food[t] for the cattle
and for the young ravens[u] when
they call.
10His pleasure is not in the
strength[v] of the horse,[w]
nor his delight in the legs of a
man;
11the LORD delights[x] in those who
fear him,[y]
who put their hope[z] in his
unfailing love.[a]

12Extol the LORD, O Jerusalem;[b]
praise your God, O Zion,
13for he strengthens the bars of your
gates[c]
and blesses your people[d] within
you.
14He grants peace[e] to your borders
and satisfies you[f] with the
finest of wheat.[g]

15He sends his command[h] to the
earth;
his word runs[i] swiftly.
16He spreads the snow[j] like wool
and scatters the frost[k] like
ashes.
17He hurls down his hail[l] like
pebbles.
Who can withstand his icy blast?
18He sends his word[m] and melts
them;
he stirs up his breezes,[n] and
the waters flow.

19He has revealed his word[o] to
Jacob,[p]
his laws and decrees[q] to Israel.
20He has done this for no other
nation;[r]
they do not know[s] his laws.

Praise the LORD.[t]

Psalm 148

1Praise the LORD.[t][u]

Praise the LORD from the
heavens,[v]
praise him in the heights above.
2Praise him, all his angels,[w]
praise him, all his heavenly
hosts.[x]
3Praise him, sun[y] and moon,
praise him, all you shining stars.
4Praise him, you highest heavens[z]
and you waters above the
skies.[a]

5Let them praise the name[b] of the
LORD,

147:1 [a]S Ps 135:3 [b]Ps 33:1 **147:2** [c]S Ps 51:18 [d]S Ps 106:47 **147:3** [e]S Ps 34:18 [f]S Nu 12:13; S Job 5:18; Isa 1:6; Eze 34:16 **147:4** [g]S Ge 15:5 **147:5** [h]S Ps 48:1 [i]S Ex 14:31 [j]Ps 145:3; Isa 40:28 **147:6** [k]S 2Ch 33:23; Ps 146:8-9 [l]Ps 37:9-10; 145:20 **147:7** [m]Ps 30:4; 33:3 [n]S Ps 42:4 [o]S Ps 27:6 [p]S Ps 98:5 **147:8** [q]S Job 26:8 [r]S Dt 11:14; S 32:2; S 2Sa 1:21; S Job 5:10 [s]S Job 28:26; S Ps 104:14 **147:9** [t]S Ge 1:30; Ps 104:27-28; S Mt 6:26 [u]S Ge 8:7 **147:10** [v]S 1Sa 16:7 [w]S Job 39:11; Ps 33:16-17 **147:11** [x]S Ps 35:27 [y]Ps 33:18; 103:11 [z]Ps 119:43 [a]Ps 6:4 **147:12** [b]Ps 48:1 **147:13** [c]S Dt 33:25 [d]S Lev 25:21; Ps 128:5; 134:3 **147:14** [e]S Lev 26:6; S 2Sa 7:10; S Isa 48:18 [f]S Ps 132:15 [g]S Dt 32:14 **147:15** [h]Job 37:12; Ps 33:9; 148:5 [i]Isa 55:11 **147:16** [j]Ps 148:8 [k]S Job 37:12; 38:29 **147:17** [l]Ex 9:22-23; S Job 38:22; S Ps 78:47 **147:18** [m]ver 15; Ps 33:9; 107:20 [n]S Ps 50:3 **147:19** [o]S Ex 20:1; Ro 3:2 [p]Ps 78:5 [q]S Dt 33:4; Jos 1:8; 2Ki 22:8; Mal 4:4; Ro 9:4

147:20 [r]Dt 4:7-8,32-34 [s]S Ps 79:6 [t]Ps 33:2; 103:1 **148:1** [u]Ps 33:2; 103:1 [v]Ps 19:1; 69:34; 150:1 **148:2** [w]Ps 103:20 [x]S 1Ki 22:19 **148:3** [y]S Ps 19:1 **148:4** [z]S Dt 10:14 [a]S Ge 1:7 **148:5** [b]Ps 145:21

[s] *1* Hebrew *Hallelu Yah*; also in verse 20
[t] *1* Hebrew *Hallelu Yah*; also in verse 14

147:6 THE LORD SUSTAINS THE HUMBLE. The word "humble" (Heb *anawah*) often includes the idea of suffering and refers to those who are afflicted. Because such people cannot cope with all of life's problems and responsibilities by themselves, in humility they call on God for his help and strength. (1) God lifts up the humble and gives them support. The psalmist assures them of God's help and ultimate victory (cf. 22:26; 25:9; 37:11). (2) As God supported the humble in OT times, Jesus ministers to the afflicted and humble under the new covenant (Mt 11:28–30; cf. Isa 11:4; 29:19; Zep 2:3). (3) Since God delights in those who are of a humble spirit, all believers should earnestly pray for a spirit of humility so that they may please him (Gal 5:23; Eph 4:2; Col 3:12; Tit 3:2).

for he commanded[c] and they
were created.
6He set them in place for ever and
ever;
he gave a decree[d] that will
never pass away.

7Praise the LORD[e] from the earth,
you great sea creatures[f] and
all ocean depths,[g]
8lightning and hail,[h] snow and
clouds,
stormy winds that do his
bidding,[i]
9you mountains and all hills,[j]
fruit trees and all cedars,
10wild animals[k] and all cattle,
small creatures and flying birds,
11kings[l] of the earth and all
nations,
you princes and all rulers on
earth,
12young men and maidens,
old men and children.

13Let them praise the name of the
LORD,[m]
for his name alone is exalted;
his splendor[n] is above the earth
and the heavens.[o]
14He has raised up for his people a
horn,[u][p]
the praise[q] of all his saints,[r]
of Israel, the people close to his
heart.[s]

Praise the LORD.

Psalm 149

1Praise the LORD.[v][t]

Sing to the LORD a new song,[u]
his praise in the assembly[v] of
the saints.

148:5 [c]S Ps 147:15
148:6 [d]Jer 31:35-36; 33:25
148:7 [e]Ps 33:2 [f]S Ge 1:21; Ps 74:13-14 [g]S Dt 33:13
148:8 [h]S Ex 9:18; S Jos 10:11 [i]Job 37:11-12; S Ps 103:20; 147:15-18
148:9 [j]Isa 44:23; 49:13; 55:12
148:10 [k]Isa 43:20; Hos 2:18
148:11 [l]S Ps 102:15
148:13 [m]S Ps 113:2; 138:4 [n]S Ps 145:5 [o]S Ps 8:1
148:14 [p]S 1Sa 2:1 [q]S Ex 15:2; Ps 22:3 [r]S Ps 145:10 [s]S Dt 26:19
149:1 [t]Ps 33:2; 103:1 [u]S Ps 28:7; S 96:1; Rev 5:9 [v]S Ps 1:5
149:2 [w]Isa 13:3; Jer 51:48 [x]S Job 10:3; Ps 95:6; Isa 44:2; 45:11; 54:5 [y]Ps 10:16; 47:6; Isa 32:1; Zec 9:9
149:3 [z]S Ex 15:20 [a]S Ps 57:8
149:4 [b]Ps 35:27; 147:11 [c]Ps 132:16
149:5 [d]S Ps 132:16 [e]Job 35:10; Ps 42:8
149:6 [f]Ps 66:17 [g]Heb 4:12; Rev 1:16 [h]Ne 4:17
149:7 [i]S Nu 31:3; S Dt 32:41 [j]Ps 81:15
149:8 [k]S 2Sa 3:34; S Isa 14:1-2 [l]2Ch 33:11
149:9 [m]Dt 7:1; Eze 28:26 [n]S Ps 145:10

2Let Israel rejoice[w] in their
Maker;[x]
let the people of Zion be glad in
their King.[y]
3Let them praise his name with
dancing[z]
and make music to him with
tambourine and harp.[a]
4For the LORD takes delight[b] in his
people;
he crowns the humble with
salvation.[c]
5Let the saints rejoice[d] in this
honor
and sing for joy on their beds.[e]

6May the praise of God be in their
mouths[f]
and a double-edged[g] sword in
their hands,[h]
7to inflict vengeance[i] on the
nations
and punishment[j] on the
peoples,
8to bind their kings with fetters,[k]
their nobles with shackles of
iron,[l]
9to carry out the sentence written
against them.[m]
This is the glory of all his
saints.[n]

Praise the LORD.

Psalm 150

1Praise the LORD.[w][o]

Praise God in his sanctuary;[p]

150:1 [o]S Ps 112:1 [p]Ps 68:24-26; 73:17; 102:19

[u]14 *Horn* here symbolizes strong one, that is, king. [v]1 Hebrew *Hallelu Yah*; also in verse 9 [w]1 Hebrew *Hallelu Yah*; also in verse 6

149:6 PRAISE . . . DOUBLE-EDGED SWORD. This verse addresses the activity of the righteous in two areas: worship and spiritual warfare. Our desire to praise God must be accompanied by the desire to oppose aggressively Satan's kingdom and all evil. God's kingdom will never be fully realized until the hostile forces of darkness are destroyed. We must take our stand against the powers of evil by living a righteous life in faith, taking the sword of the Spirit (i.e., the word of God), and praying in the Spirit (see Eph 6:11–18, notes). At the end of the age we will, to the praise of God, participate in his judgment on the unrepentant world of the antichrist (1Co 6:2–3; Rev 18:20; 19:1–4,11–21).

150:1 PRAISE THE LORD. True praise of God will not be confined to the sanctuary (vv. 1–2,6). We can truly praise God only when we see his full greatness and goodness, and recall and meditate on all that he has done in creation and redemption and in our personal lives. In this way praise becomes a powerful response of the heart expressing joy, gratitude and the desire for communion with our Lord. In addition to praising God with our songs and instruments in the sanctuary, we can praise God with a life of love and joy (1Jn 4:19), with faith in Christ (Jn 1:7), with victory over the powers of Satan (Eph 6:10–18), with a spiritual hunger for his kingdom and his righteousness (Mt 6:33), with devotion to his Word (Ps 119), with the love of God poured into our hearts by the Holy Spirit (Ro 5:5), with the proclamation of his gospel (Ro 1:16) and with the expectation of his imminent return (Tit 2:13; see article on PRAISE, p. 770).

praise him in his mighty
heavens.[q]
2 Praise him for his acts of power;[r]
praise him for his surpassing
greatness.[s]
3 Praise him with the sounding of
the trumpet,[t]
praise him with the harp and
lyre,[u]
4 praise him with tambourine and
dancing,[v]
praise him with the strings[w]
and flute,[x]
5 praise him with the clash of
cymbals,[y]
praise him with resounding
cymbals.

6 Let everything[z] that has breath
praise the LORD.

Praise the LORD.

150:1 [q] S Ps 148:1 **150:2** [r] S Dt 3:24 [s] S Ex 15:7 **150:3** [t] S Nu 10:2 [u] S Ps 57:8 **150:4** [v] S Ex 15:20 [w] S Ps 45:8 [x] S Ge 4:21 **150:5** [y] S 2Sa 6:5 **150:6** [z] S Ps 103:22

OLD TESTAMENT PROPHECIES FULFILLED IN CHRIST

OT Text	NT Text	Subject
Ge 3:15	Lk 22:53	Satan against Jesus
Ge 3:15	Heb 2:14; 1Jn 3:8	Jesus' victory over Satan
Ge 12:3	Ac 3:25; Gal 3:8	Gentiles blessed through Christ as the offspring of Abraham
Ge 13:15	Gal 3:15–16,19	Messiah as the seed of Abraham
Ge 14:18–20	Heb 7	Jesus' priesthood according to the likeness of Melchizedek
Ge 18:18	Ac 3:25; Gal 3:8	Gentiles blessed through Christ as the offspring of Abraham
Ge 22:18	Ac 3:25; Gal 3:8	Gentiles blessed through Christ as the offspring of Abraham
Ge 26:4	Ac 3:25; Gal 3:8	Gentiles blessed through Christ as the offspring of Abraham
Ge 49:10	Lk 1:32–33	Coming ruler from Judah
Ex 12:1–14,46	Jn 19:31–36; 1Co 5:7; 1Pe 1:19	The Messiah as the Passover Lamb
Ex 16:4	Jn 6:31–33	Messiah to give true bread from heaven
Ex 24:8	Heb 9:11–28	The Messiah's blood to be shed as sacrifice
Lev 16:15–17	Ro 3:25; Heb 9:1–14,24; 1Jn 2:2	Atoning sacrifice of blood
Nu 21:8–9	Jn 3:14–15	Life through looking at one on a cross
Nu 24:17	Lk 1:32–33	Coming ruler from Jacob
Nu 24:17	Rev 22:16	Coming star out of Jacob
Dt 18:17	Jn 6:14; 12:49–50; Ac 3:22–23	Coming prophet sent from God
Dt 21:23	Gal 3:13	Messiah cursed for hanging on a tree
Dt 30:12–14	Ro 10:6–8	Jesus is God's word near to us
2Sa 7:14	Heb 1:5	Messiah to be God's Son
2Sa 7:16	Lk 1:32–33; Rev 19:11–16	David's Son as eternal king
1Ch 17:13	Heb 1:5	Messiah to be God's Son
1Ch 17:14	Lk 1:32–33; Rev 19:11–16	David's Son as eternal king
Ps 2:7	Mt 3:17; 17:5; Mk 1:11; 9:7; Lk 3:22; 9:35; Ac 13:33; Heb 1:5	God's address to his Son
Ps 2:9	Rev 2:27	Messiah to rule the nations with power
Ps 8:2	Mt 21:16	Children to praise God's Son
Ps 8:4–5	Heb 2:6–9	Jesus lower than the angels
Ps 8:6	1Co 15:27–28; Eph 1:22	Everything subject to God's Son

OT Text	NT Text	Subject
Ps 16:8–11	Ac 2:25–32; 13:35–37	David's Son to be raised from the dead
Ps 22:1	Mt 27:46; Mk 15:34	God-forsaken cry by the Messiah
Ps 22:7–8	Mt 27:29,41–44; Mk 15:18,29–32; Lk 23:35–39	Messiah mocked by a crowd
Ps 22:18	Mt 27:35; Mk 15:24; Lk 23:34; Jn 19:24	Casting lots for Jesus' clothes
Ps 22:22	Heb 2:12	Jesus to declare his name in the church
Ps 31:5	Lk 23:46	Messiah to commit his spirit to God
Ps 34:20	Jn 19:31–36	Messiah to have no broken bones
Ps 35:19	Jn 15:25	Messiah experiencing hatred for no reason
Ps 40:6–8	Jn 6:38; Heb 10:5–9	Messiah to do God's perfect will
Ps 41:9	Jn 13:18	The Messiah's betrayal by a friend
Ps 45:6–7	Heb 1:8–9	Characteristics of the coming King
Ps 68:18	Eph 4:7–11	Ascension and giving gifts to humans
Ps 69:4	Jn 15:25	Messiah experiencing hatred for no reason
Ps 69:9	Jn 2:14–22	The Messiah's zeal for God's house
Ps 69:21	Jn 19:29	The thirst of the suffering Messiah
Ps 69:25	Ac 1:20	Judgment on the Messiah's persecutor
Ps 78:2	Mt 13:34–35	Messiah to speak in parables
Ps 102:25–27	Heb 1:10–12	Characteristics of the coming King
Ps 110:1	Ac 2:34–35; 1Co 15:25; Eph 1:20–22; Heb 1:13; 10:12–13	Jesus exalted in power at God's right hand
Ps 110:1	Mt 22:41–45; Mk 12:35–37; Lk 20:41–44	Jesus as Son and Lord of David
Ps 110:4	Heb 5:6; 7:11–22	Jesus' priesthood after Melchizedek
Ps 118:22–23	Mt 21:42–44; Mk 12:10–12; Lk 20:17–19; Ac 4:10–11; 1Pe 2:7–8	Rejected stone to become capstone
Ps 118:26	Mt 21:9; Mk 11:9; Lk 19:38; Jn 12:13	Messiah to come in the name of the Lord
Isa 6:9–10	Mt 13:14–15; Mk 4:12; Lk 8:10; Jn 12:37–41	Hearts to be closed to the gospel
Isa 7:14	Mt 1:18–23; Lk 1:26–35	Virgin birth of the Messiah
Isa 8:14	Ro 9:32–33; 1Pe 2:7–8	A stone over which people stumble
Isa 9:1–2	Mt 4:13–16; Mk 1:14–15; Lk 4:14–15	Ministry to begin in Galilee
Isa 9:6–7	Lk 1:32–33	David's Son as eternal king

OT Text	NT Text	Subject
Isa 9:7	Jn 1:1,18	The Messiah to be God
Isa 9:7	Eph 2:14–17	The Messiah to be a man of peace
Isa 11:1–2	Mt 3:16; Mk 1:10; Lk 3:21–22	Branch of Jesse (David) to receive the Spirit
Isa 11:10	Lk 1:32–33	Root of Jesse (David) as coming ruler
Isa 11:10	Ro 15:12	Salvation to be available for Gentiles
Isa 22:22	Rev 3:7	Jesus to receive the key of David
Isa 25:8	1Co 15:54	Death to be swallowed up in victory
Isa 28:16	Ro 9:32–33; 1Pe 2:6	Messiah to be the chief cornerstone
Isa 35:5–6	Mt 11:4–6; Lk 7:22	Messiah to be a mighty worker of miracles
Isa 40:3–5	Mt 3:3; Mk 1:3; Lk 3:4–6; Jn 1:23	Jesus' forerunner, a voice in the desert
Isa 42:1–4	Mt 12:15–21	Messiah as the chosen servant of the Lord
Isa 45:23	Ro 14:11; Php 2:10	Every knee to bow before the Messiah
Isa 49:6	Ac 13:46–47	Messiah as a light to the Gentiles
Isa 50:6	Mt 27:26–30; Mk 14:65; 15:15,19; Lk 22:63; Jn 19:1,3	Beating God's servant
Isa 50:6	Mt 26:67; Mk 14:65	Spitting on God's servant
Isa 53:1	Jn 12:38; Ro 10:16	Israel not to believe in the Messiah
Isa 53:3	Jn 1:11	Messiah to be rejected by his own people
Isa 53:4–5	Mt 8:16–17; Mk 1:32–34; Lk 4:40–41; 1Pe 2:24	Healing ministry of God's servant
Isa 53:7–8	Jn 1:29,36; Ac 8:30–35; 1Pe 1:19; Rev 5:6,12	Suffering Lamb of God
Isa 53:9	Heb 4:15; 1Pe 2:22	The sinless servant of God
Isa 53:9	Mt 27:57–60	Messiah to be buried in a rich man's grave
Isa 53:12	Mt 27:38; Mk 15:27–28; Lk 22:37; 23:33; Jn 19:18	God's servant numbered with transgressors
Isa 55:3	Lk 22:20; 1Co 11:25	Everlasting covenant through the Messiah
Isa 55:3	Ac 13:33	Blessings of David given to the Messiah
Isa 59:20–21	Ro 11:26–27	Israel's Deliverer to come from Zion
Isa 60:1–3	Mt 2:11; Ro 15:8–12	Gentiles coming to worship the Messiah
Isa 61:1–2	Mt 3:16; Mk 1:10; Lk 4:18–21	The Messiah anointed by the Holy Spirit
Isa 65:1	Ro 10:20	Gentiles would believe in the Messiah
Isa 65:2	Ro 10:21	Israel would reject the Messiah
Jer 23:5	Lk 1:32–33	David's Son to be a great King
Jer 23:6	Mt 1:21	David's Son to be Savior
Jer 23:6	1Co 1:30	Messiah to be named "Our Righteousness"

OT Text	NT Text	Subject
Jer 31:15	Mt 2:16–18	Rachel weeping when God's Son is born
Jer 31:31–34	Lk 22:20; 1Co 11:25; Heb 8:8–12; 10:15–18	Jesus and the new covenant
Jer 32:40	Lk 22:20; 1Co 11:25	Everlasting covenant through the Messiah
Jer 33:15	Lk 1:32–33	David's Son to be a great King
Jer 33:16	Mt 1:21	David's Son to be Savior
Jer 33:16	1Co 1:30	Messiah to be named "Our Righteousness"
Eze 21:26–27	Lk 1:32–33	A rightful crown for the Messiah
Eze 34:23–24	Jn 10:11,14,16; Heb 13:20; 1Pe 5:4	The coming good shepherd
Eze 37:24–25	Lk 1:32–33	Messiah to be David's son and a king
Eze 37:24–25	Jn 10:11,14,16; Heb 13:20; 1Pe 5:4	The coming good shepherd
Eze 37:26	Lk 22:20; 1Co 11:25	Messiah's everlasting covenant of peace
Da 7:13–14	Mt 24:30; 26:64; Mk 13:26; 14:62; Lk 21:27; Rev 1:13; 14:14	The coming of the Son of Man
Da 7:27	Rev 11:15	The coming everlasting kingdom of the Messiah
Da 9:24–26	Gal 4:4	Timetable for the Messiah's coming
Hos 11:1	Mt 2:14–15	Jesus to return from Egypt
Joel 2:28–32	Ac 2:14–21	God's Spirit to be poured out
Am 9:11–12	Ac 15:13–18	Gentiles would believe in the Messiah
Jnh 1:17	Mt 12:39–40	Messiah to be three days and nights in grave
Mic 5:2	Mt 2:1–6	The Messiah to be born in Bethlehem
Mic 5:2	Lk 1:32–33	The Messiah as an eternal king
Mic 5:4	Jn 10:11,14	The coming shepherd of God's flock
Mic 5:5	Eph 2:14–17	The Messiah to be a man of peace
Zec 9:9	Mt 21:1–9; Mk 11:1–10; Lk 19:28–38; Jn 12:12–16	The coming ruler on a donkey
Zec 11:12–13	Mt 27:1–10	Thirty pieces of silver for a potter's field
Zec 12:10	Jn 19:37; Rev 1:7	Looking on the pierced Messiah
Zec 13:7	Mt 26:31; 26:55–56; Mk 14:27; 14:48–50	Striking the coming shepherd; the sheep flee
Mal 3:1	Mt 11:7–10; Mk 1:2–4; Lk 7:24–27	The forerunner to the Messiah
Mal 4:5–6	Mt 11:14; 17:11–13; Mk 9:11–13; Lk 1:16–17	The forerunner as Elijah returned

PROVERBS

Outline

I. Prologue: Purpose and Themes of Proverbs (1:1–7)
II. Thirteen Wisdom Discourses for Youth (1:8—9:18)
    A. Obey Your Parents and Heed Their Counsel (1:8–9)
    B. Say "No" to All Enticements of Sinners (1:10–19)
    C. Submit to Wisdom and the Fear of the Lord (1:20–33)
    D. Pursue Wisdom with Its Discernment and Virtue (2:1–22)
    E. Characteristics and Benefits of True Wisdom (3:1–35)
    F. Wisdom as a Family Treasure (4:1–13,20–27)
    G. Wisdom and the Two Paths in Life (4:14–19)
    H. The Enticement and Folly of Sexual Immorality (5:1–14)
    I. Exhortation Concerning Marital Faithfulness (5:15–23)
    J. Avoid Debt Responsibility of Another, Laziness and Deceit (6:1–19)
    K. The Crass Folly of All Forms of Sexual Immorality (6:20—7:27)
    L. Wisdom's Appeal (8:1–36)
    M. Wisdom and Folly Contrasted (9:1–18)
III. The Main Collection of Solomon's Proverbs (10:1—22:16)
    A. Proverbs Contrasting the Righteous and the Wicked (10:1—15:33)
    B. Proverbs Encouraging a Righteous Life (16:1—22:16)
IV. Additional Words of Wise Men (22:17—24:34)
V. Solomon's Proverbs Recorded by Hezekiah's Men (25:1—29:27)
    A. Proverbs Concerning Various Kinds of People (25:1—26:28)
    B. Proverbs Concerning Various Activities (27:1—29:27)
VI. Final Words of Wisdom (30:1—31:31)
    A. By Agur (30:1–33)
    B. By Lemuel (31:1–9)
    C. About a Wife of Noble Character (31:10–31)

Author: Solomon and Others

Theme: Wisdom for Right Living

Date of Writing: c. 970–700 B.C.

Background

The Hebrew OT was typically divided into three categories: The Law, the Prophets and the Writings (cf. Lk 24:44). Included under the third category were the Poetic and Wisdom books, such as Job, Psalms, Proverbs and Ecclesiastes. In a similar manner, ancient Israel had three categories of ministers: the priests, the prophets and the sages ("the wise men"). The latter were especially gifted with godly wisdom and counsel concerning both practical and philosophical issues of life. Proverbs represents the inspired wisdom of the sages.

The Hebrew term *mashal*, translated "proverb," variously means "oracle," "parable" or "wise saying." Thus there are some longer discourses (oracles) in the book of Proverbs (e.g., 1:20–33; 2:1–22; 5:1–14), as well as many short, pithy statements containing wisdom for living a prudent and righteous life. Whereas Proverbs represents a form of proverbial teaching common in the ancient Near East, its wisdom is distinctive in that it is given in the context of God and his righteous standards for his covenant people. Reasons for the popularity of proverbial teaching in ancient times were its crisp clarity and its capability of being easily memorized and passed on from generation to generation.

Just as David is the fountainhead of the psalmic tradition in Israel, so Solomon is the fountainhead of the wisdom tradition in Israel (see 1:1; 10:1; 25:1). According to 1Ki 4:32, Solomon produced 3,000 proverbs and 1,005 songs in his lifetime. Other authors mentioned by name in Proverbs are Agur (30:1–33) and King Lemuel (31:1–9), both of whom are unknown to us. Additional authors are implied in 22:17 and 24:23. Though most of the Proverbs originated in the 10th century B.C., the earliest possible date for completing this book would be during the reign of Hezekiah (i.e., c. 700 B.C.). The involvement of Hezekiah's men in compiling Solomon's proverbs (25:1—29:27) can be dated to 715–686 B.C., during a time of spiritual revival led by this God-fearing king. Most likely the proverbs of Agur, Lemuel and the additional "sayings of the wise" (i.e., the sages) were collected together at this time as well.

Purpose

The book's purpose is forthrightly stated in 1:2–7: to provide wisdom and understanding concerning wise behavior, righteousness, justice and equity (1:2–3), so that (1) simple people can be prudent (1:4), (2) youth can obtain knowledge and discretion (1:4), and (3) the wise might become wiser (1:5–6). Though Proverbs is essentially a wisdom handbook on living rightly and prudently, the necessary foundation of that wisdom is explicitly stated as being "the fear of the LORD" (1:7).

Survey

The unifying theme of Proverbs is "wisdom for right living," a wisdom that begins with humble submission to God and then flows to every area of life. The wisdom in Proverbs (1) admonishes concerning the family, youth, sexual purity, marital faithfulness, honesty, hard work, generosity, friendship, justice, righteousness and discipline; (2) warns about the folly of sin, strife, dangers of the tongue, foolishness, alcohol, gluttony, lust, immorality, falsehood, laziness and wrong company; (3) contrasts discretion and folly, the righteous and the wicked, pride and humility, laziness and diligence, poverty and wealth, love and lust, right and wrong, and life and death.

Although Proverbs, like Psalms, is not as easily summarized as other books of the Bible, there is some discernible structure (see "Outline"); this is especially true in chs. 1–9, which contain a series of 13 discourses such as a father would give to his son who is entering the teen years. Except for three discourses (see 1:30; 8:1; 9:1), each one begins with "my son" or "my sons." These 13 discourses contain numerous important precepts of wisdom for youth. Beginning with ch. 10, Proverbs contains important directives concerning family relationships (e.g., 10:1; 12:4; 17:21,25: 18:22; 19:14,26; 20:7; 21:9,19; 22:6,28; 23:13–14,22,24–25; 25:24; 27:15–16; 29:15–17; 30:11; 31:10–31). Although Proverbs is an intensely practical book, it also contains a profound view of God. God is wisdom personified (e.g., 8:22–31) and the Creator (e.g., 3:19–20; 8:22–31; 14:31; 22:2); he is characterized as omniscient (e.g., 5:21; 15:3,11; 21:2), just (e.g., 11:1; 15:25–27,29; 19:17; 21:2–3) and sovereign (e.g., 16:9,33; 19:21, 21:1). Proverbs concludes with an impressive tribute to a wife of noble character (31:10–31).

Special Features

Eight major features characterize Proverbs. (1) Wisdom, rather than being tied to intelligence or vast knowledge, is directly related to "the fear of the LORD" (1:7); thus the wise are those who know God and obey his commands. The fear of the Lord is a recurring emphasis in the book (1:7,29; 2:5; 3:7; 8:13; 9:10; 10:27; 14:26–27; 15:16,33; 16:6; 19:23; 22:4; 23:17; 24:21). (2) Much of the wise counsel presented in Proverbs is in the format of a father's godly advice to his young son or sons. (3) It is the most thoroughly practical book in the OT, as it touches on a broad range of basic principles for right relationships and behavior in everyday life—principles that are applicable to all generations and cultures. (4) Its practical wisdom, godly precepts and basic life principles are conveyed in short, pungent statements that are easily memorized and remembered by youth as guidelines for their lives. (5) The family occupies a place of pivotal importance in Proverbs, even as it did in God's covenant with Israel (cf. Ex 20:12,14,17; Dt 6:1–9). Sins that violate God's purpose for the family are especially exposed and warned against. (6) Prominent literary features of the proverbs are their prolific use of vivid, figurative language (e.g., similes and metaphors), comparisons and contrasts, concise precepts, and repetition. (7) The wise wife and mother portrayed at the book's end (ch. 31) is unique in ancient literature in terms of the high and noble manner in which a good woman is viewed. (8) Wisdom exhortations in Proverbs are the OT forerunner to the many practical exhortations in the NT letters.

New Testament Fulfillment

Wisdom is personified in ch. 8 in a way similar to the personification of *logos* ("Word") in the Gospel of John (ch. 1:1–18). Wisdom is (1) involved in creation (3:19–20); 8:22–31), (2) related to the origin of both biological and spiritual life (3:19; 8:35), (3) applicable to righteous and moral living (8:8–9), and (4) available to those who search for it (2:1–10; 3:13–18; 4:7–9; 8:35–36). The wisdom of Proverbs finds its ultimate expression in Jesus Christ, someone "greater than Solomon" (Lk 11:31), who "has become for us wisdom" (1Co 1:30) and "in whom are hidden all the treasures of wisdom and knowledge" (Col 2:3).

Reading Proverbs

In order to read the entire Old Testament in one year, the book of Proverbs should be read in 14 days, according to the following schedule: ☐ 1–2 ☐ 3–4 ☐ 5–7 ☐ 8–9 ☐ 10–11 ☐ 12–13 ☐ 14–15 ☐ 16–17 ☐ 18–19 ☐ 20–21 ☐ 22–23 ☐ 24–26 ☐ 27–28 ☐ 29–31

NOTES

Prologue: Purpose and Theme

1 The proverbs[a] of Solomon[b] son
of David, king of Israel:[c]

2for attaining wisdom and discipline;
for understanding words of
insight;
3for acquiring a disciplined and
prudent life,
doing what is right and just and
fair;
4for giving prudence to the simple,[d]
knowledge and discretion[e] to
the young—
5let the wise listen and add to their
learning,[f]
and let the discerning get
guidance—
6for understanding proverbs and
parables,[g]
the sayings and riddles[h] of the
wise.[i]

7The fear of the LORD[j] is the
beginning of knowledge,
but fools[a] despise wisdom[k]
and discipline.[l]

Exhortations to Embrace Wisdom

Warning Against Enticement

8Listen, my son,[m] to your
father's[n] instruction
and do not forsake your
mother's teaching.[o]
9They will be a garland to grace
your head
and a chain to adorn your
neck.[p]

10My son, if sinners entice[q]
you,
do not give in[r] to them.[s]
11If they say, "Come along with
us;
let's lie in wait[t] for someone's
blood,
let's waylay some harmless
soul;
12let's swallow[u] them alive, like the
grave,[b]
and whole, like those who go
down to the pit;[v]
13we will get all sorts of valuable
things
and fill our houses with
plunder;
14throw in your lot with us,
and we will share a common
purse[w]"—

1:1 [a] Mt 13:3 [b] 1Ki 4:29-34 [c] Pr 10:1; 25:1; Ecc 1:1 **1:4** [d] Pr 8:5 [e] Pr 8:12 **1:5** [f] Pr 9:9 **1:6** [g] S Ps 49:4; Mt 13:10-17 [h] S Nu 12:8; S Jdg 14:12 [i] Pr 22:17; 24:23 **1:7** [j] S Ex 20:20; S Job 23:15; Ps 34:4-22; S 112:1; Pr 9:10; 15:33; Isa 33:6; 50:10; 59:19 [k] S Dt 4:6; Jer 8:9 [l] Pr 8:33-36; 9:7-9; 12:1; 13:18; 15:32 **1:8** [m] ver 8-9; Pr 2:1; 3:1; 4:1; 5:1; 6:1; 7:1; 19:27; 22:17; 23:26-28 [n] Jer 35:8 [o] S Dt 21:18; Pr 6:20 **1:9** [p] Pr 3:21-22; 4:1-9 **1:10** [q] S Job 24:15 [r] Dt 13:8 [s] ver 15; Ps 1:1; Pr 16:29 **1:11** [t] S Ps 10:8 **1:12** [u] S Ps 35:25 [v] ver 16-18; S Job 33:18; S Ps 30:3 **1:14** [w] ver 19

[a] 7 The Hebrew words rendered *fool* in Proverbs, and often elsewhere in the Old Testament, denote one who is morally deficient. [b] *12* Hebrew *Sheol*

1:1 THE PROVERBS. A proverb is a short, compact saying, comparison or question that expresses a principle or an observation about human behavior from God's point of view. These proverbs were written to instruct God's people (especially young people) how to live to please him, have a happy and successful life, and avoid the tragedies resulting from sin (vv. 2–6,15–19).

1:1 SOLOMON. Solomon, Israel's third king, wrote many of these proverbs. Early in his reign he prayed for wisdom, and God granted his request (1Ki 3:5–14; 4:29–32). Later in life, however, Solomon himself did not follow the wisdom God gave him. Failing to persevere in the fear of the Lord, he turned his heart away from God (1Ki 11:1–11; see 11:1, note). Thus merely knowing or teaching moral principles from God's Word is not adequate to ensure spiritual life; there must also be an ongoing fear of, dependence on and responsibility to God (v. 7).

1:2 WISDOM. As used in this book, wisdom means living and thinking according to God's truth, ways and design. It means to approach all of life from God's point of view, believing that everything God says is right and true and the only worthy standard by which to live. Gaining wisdom is far better than possessing silver and gold (3:13–14). It comes only to those who seek it through a proper relationship with God (v. 7) and a diligent study of his Word (3:1–3). Christ, whom the NT says is the ultimate wisdom of God (1Co 1:30; Col 2:2–3), teaches us that we gain wisdom by remaining in his word, by allowing his words to remain in us (Jn 15:7), and by yielding our hearts and minds to the indwelling Holy Spirit (Jn 14:16–26).

1:7 THE FEAR OF THE LORD. A reverent awe of God's power, majesty and holiness produces in us a holy fear of transgressing his revealed will; such reverence is essential to gaining a heart of wisdom. The NT indicates that the sincere fear of the Lord in our hearts will be accompanied by the comfort of the Holy Spirit (see Ac 9:31, note; see article on THE FEAR OF THE LORD, p. 260).

1:10 MY SON, IF SINNERS ENTICE YOU. Early in life young people face enticements to sin. Peer pressure will tempt them to join with the majority and enjoy sinful pleasures. Young people can resist such temptations to turn from God and his way by developing a close relationship with God as their Lord, by a willingness to stand alone, if need be, in their commitment to God's righteous ways (vv. 15–16), and by knowing that the way of compromise and sinful pleasure leads to heartache, distress, calamity and destruction (v. 27; see Mt 4:1–11, note).

15my son, do not go along with
them,
do not set foot[x] on their
paths;[y]
16for their feet rush into sin,[z]
they are swift to shed blood.[a]
17How useless to spread a net
in full view of all the birds!
18These men lie in wait[b] for their
own blood;
they waylay only themselves![c]
19Such is the end of all who go after
ill-gotten gain;
it takes away the lives of those
who get it.[d]

Warning Against Rejecting Wisdom

20Wisdom calls aloud[e] in the street,
she raises her voice in the
public squares;
21at the head of the noisy streets[c]
she cries out,
in the gateways of the city she
makes her speech:

22"How long will you simple
ones[d][f] love your simple
ways?
How long will mockers delight
in mockery
and fools hate[g] knowledge?
23If you had responded to my
rebuke,
I would have poured out my
heart to you
and made my thoughts known to
you.
24But since you rejected[h] me when
I called[i]
and no one gave heed[j] when I
stretched out my hand,
25since you ignored all my advice
and would not accept my
rebuke,
26I in turn will laugh[k] at your
disaster;[l]
I will mock[m] when calamity
overtakes you[n] —
27when calamity overtakes you like
a storm,
when disaster[o] sweeps over you
like a whirlwind,
when distress and trouble
overwhelm you.

28"Then they will call to me but I
will not answer;[p]
they will look for me but will
not find me.[q]
29Since they hated knowledge
and did not choose to fear the
LORD,[r]
30since they would not accept my
advice
and spurned my rebuke,[s]
31they will eat the fruit of their ways
and be filled with the fruit of
their schemes.[t]
32For the waywardness of the simple
will kill them,
and the complacency of fools
will destroy them;[u]
33but whoever listens to me will live
in safety[v]
and be at ease, without fear of
harm."[w]

Moral Benefits of Wisdom

2 My son,[x] if you accept my
words
and store up my commands
within you,
2turning your ear to wisdom
and applying your heart to
understanding,[y]
3and if you call out for insight[z]
and cry aloud for understanding,
4and if you look for it as for silver

1:15 [x]S Ps 119:101 [y]S Ge 49:6; Pr 4:14 **1:16** [z]S Job 15:31 [a]Pr 6:18; Isa 59:7 **1:18** [b]S Ps 71:10 [c]S ver 11-12 **1:19** [d]S ver 13-14; Pr 4:14-17; 11:19 **1:20** [e]S Job 28:12; Pr 7:10-13; 9:1-3, 13-15 **1:22** [f]Pr 6:32; 7:7; 8:5; 9:4,16 [g]Ps 50:17 **1:24** [h]Jer 26:5; 35:17; 36:31 [i]Isa 65:12; 66:4; Jer 7:13 [j]S 1Sa 8:19 **1:26** [k]S Ps 2:4 [l]ver 33; S Ps 59:8 [m]S 2Ki 19:21 [n]Dt 28:63 **1:27** [o]S Ps 18:18; Pr 5:12-14 **1:28** [p]S Dt 1:45; S 1Sa 8:18; S Jer 11:11 [q]S Job 27:9; Pr 8:17; Eze 8:18; Hos 5:6; Zec 7:13 **1:29** [r]S Job 21:14 **1:30** [s]ver 25 **1:31** [t]S 2Ch 36:16; Pr 14:14; Jer 6:19; 14:16; 21:14; 30:15 **1:32** [u]Pr 5:22; 15:10; Isa 66:4 **1:33** [v]S Nu 24:21; S Dt 33:28; Pr 3:23 [w]S ver 21-26; S Ps 112:8 **2:1** [x]S Pr 1:8 **2:2** [y]Pr 22:17; 23:12 **2:3** [z]Jas 1:5

[c] *21* Hebrew; Septuagint / *on the tops of the walls* [d] *22* The Hebrew word rendered *simple* in Proverbs generally denotes one without moral direction and inclined to evil.

1:26 YOUR DISASTER. The book of Proverbs emphasizes that God has appointed absolute standards of right and wrong; to disregard them will bring tragic results in our lives. One of the greatest truths we can learn in our youth is that we will indeed reap what we sow (Gal 6:7–9). The eventual price we pay for sin is anguish, suffering and even disaster (v. 27).

2:1 STORE UP MY COMMANDS. Only by putting God's word into our minds will we learn to live wisely and righteously in our relationship with God (v. 5). We can become victorious over sin with God's commands in our hearts (Ps 119:11) and Christ's word remaining within us (Jn 15:7; Jas 1:21).

2:3 CALL OUT FOR INSIGHT. The study of God's word (see previous note) must be accompanied with a spirit of prayer that earnestly cries out for wisdom and insight. Study alone may make a Bible scholar, but prayer along with the study of God's word allows the Holy Spirit to take that revelation and transform us into spiritual people. Pray over the verses of Scripture you read, hungering for divine illumination and understanding (vv. 5–7).

and search for it as for hidden
treasure,[a]
5then you will understand the fear
of the LORD
and find the knowledge of
God.[b]
6For the LORD gives wisdom,[c]
and from his mouth come
knowledge and
understanding.[d]
7He holds victory in store for the
upright,
he is a shield[e] to those whose
walk is blameless,[f]
8for he guards the course of the
just
and protects the way of his
faithful ones.[g]

9Then you will understand[h] what
is right and just
and fair — every good path.
10For wisdom will enter your
heart,[i]
and knowledge will be pleasant
to your soul.
11Discretion will protect you,
and understanding will guard
you.[j]

12Wisdom will save[k] you from the
ways of wicked men,
from men whose words are
perverse,
13who leave the straight paths
to walk in dark ways,[l]
14who delight in doing wrong
and rejoice in the perverseness
of evil,[m]
15whose paths are crooked[n]
and who are devious in their
ways.[o]

16It will save you also from the
adulteress,[p]
from the wayward wife with her
seductive words,

2:4 [a] S Job 3:21; Mt 13:44
2:5 [b] S Dt 4:6
2:6 [c] S Job 12:13; S Ps 119:34 [d] S Job 9:4; S 22:22
2:7 [e] S Ge 15:1; Pr 30:5-6 [f] S Ge 6:9; Ps 84:11
2:8 [g] 1Sa 2:9; S Ps 18:25; S 97:10
2:9 [h] S Dt 1:16
2:10 [i] Pr 14:33
2:11 [j] Pr 4:6
2:12 [k] ver 16; Pr 3:13-18; 4:5
2:13 [l] Pr 4:19
2:14 [m] Pr 10:23; 15:21
2:15 [n] S Ps 125:5 [o] Pr 21:8
2:16 [p] Pr 5:1-6; 6:20-29; 7:5-27
2:17 [q] Mal 2:14
2:18 [r] Pr 5:5; 7:27; 9:18
2:19 [s] Pr 3:16-18; 5:8; Ecc 7:26
2:21 [t] S Ps 37:29
2:22 [u] S Ps 5:4 [v] S Job 18:17 [w] Dt 28:63; S 29:28; Ps 37:9, 28-29; Pr 10:30
3:1 [x] S Pr 1:8 [y] S Ps 44:17
3:2 [z] S Dt 11:21 [a] S Dt 5:16; S 30:15,16; S 1Ki 3:13,14; Pr 9:6,10-11
3:3 [b] S Ps 85:10 [c] S Ex 13:9; S Dt 6:6; Pr 6:21; 7:3; S 2Co 3:3
3:4 [d] S 1Sa 2:26; Lk 2:52
3:5 [e] S Ps 4:5

17who has left the partner of her
youth
and ignored the covenant she
made before God.[e][q]
18For her house leads down to death
and her paths to the spirits of
the dead.[r]
19None who go to her return
or attain the paths of life.[s]

20Thus you will walk in the ways of
good men
and keep to the paths of the
righteous.
21For the upright will live in the
land,[t]
and the blameless will remain in
it;
22but the wicked[u] will be cut off
from the land,[v]
and the unfaithful will be torn
from it.[w]

Further Benefits of Wisdom

3 My son,[x] do not forget my
teaching,[y]
but keep my commands in your
heart,
2for they will prolong your life
many years[z]
and bring you prosperity.[a]

3Let love and faithfulness[b] never
leave you;
bind them around your neck,
write them on the tablet of your
heart.[c]
4Then you will win favor and a
good name
in the sight of God and man.[d]

5Trust in the LORD[e] with all your
heart
and lean not on your own
understanding;

[e] *17* Or *covenant of her God*

2:10 WISDOM WILL ENTER YOUR HEART. Only when God's wisdom enters our hearts — i.e., our inward motives, desires and thoughts — will it produce life and power (cf. 4:23). To accomplish this, the Spirit of truth must work within our souls (Jn 16:13–14) to make God's commands and ways a delight to us (Ps 119:47–48).

2:20 WALK IN THE WAYS OF GOOD MEN. The blessings of gaining wisdom include: (1) learning to fear the Lord and thereby being guarded from evil along life's path (vv. 5–8); (2) having the ability to discern good from evil and thereby avoiding the tragedies of sin (v. 11); (3) desiring to avoid evil people and associating with those who are good and righteous (vv. 12–15,20); (4) abstaining from sexual immorality (vv. 16–19); and (5) gaining God's promised blessings (v. 21).

3:2 PROLONG YOUR LIFE ... BRING YOU PROSPERITY. Generally speaking, obeying God and living by his holy principles will result in better health (v. 8), a longer life, and a happier and more prosperous life (cf. v. 16). However, this general principle must not be taken as an absolute guarantee to which there are no exceptions. At times the righteous are afflicted (Job 1 — 2) and do not live long lives (Ac 7:59–60); conversely, sometimes it is the wicked who are healthy and prosperous (Ps 73:3,12; Jas 5:5), though their final judgment is sure (Ps 73:17–20: Jas 5:1–4).

3:5 TRUST IN THE LORD. Trusting in the

6in all your ways acknowledge him,
  and he will make your paths[f]
    straight.[f][g]

7Do not be wise in your own eyes;[h]
  fear the LORD[i] and shun evil.[j]
8This will bring health to your
    body[k]
  and nourishment to your
    bones.[l]

9Honor the LORD with your wealth,
  with the firstfruits[m] of all your
    crops;
10then your barns will be filled[n] to
    overflowing,
  and your vats will brim over
    with new wine.[o]

11My son,[p] do not despise the
    LORD's discipline[q]
  and do not resent his rebuke,
12because the LORD disciplines those
    he loves,[r]
  as a father[g] the son he delights
    in.[s]

13Blessed is the man who finds
    wisdom,
  the man who gains
    understanding,
14for she is more profitable than
    silver
  and yields better returns than
    gold.[t]

15She is more precious than
    rubies;[u]
  nothing you desire can compare
    with her.[v]
16Long life is in her right hand;[w]
  in her left hand are riches and
    honor.[x]
17Her ways are pleasant ways,
  and all her paths are peace.[y]
18She is a tree of life[z] to those who
    embrace her;
  those who lay hold of her will be
    blessed.[a]

19By wisdom[b] the LORD laid the
    earth's foundations,[c]
  by understanding he set the
    heavens[d] in place;
20by his knowledge the deeps were
    divided,
  and the clouds let drop the dew.

21My son,[e] preserve sound
    judgment and discernment,
  do not let them out of your
    sight;[f]
22they will be life for you,[g]
  an ornament to grace your
    neck.[h]
23Then you will go on your way in
    safety,[i]

3:6 *f* S Job 33:11; S Isa 30:11 *g* Ps 5:8; Pr 16:3; Isa 40:3; Jer 42:3
3:7 *h* Pr 26:5,12; Isa 5:21 *i* Ps 111:10 *j* S Ex 20:20; S Dt 4:6; S Job 1:1
3:8 *k* S Ps 38:3; Pr 4:22 *l* Job 21:24
3:9 *m* S Ex 22:29; Dt 26:1-15
3:10 *n* Ps 144:13 *o* S Job 22:21; Joel 2:24; Mal 3:10-12
3:11 *p* Pr 1:8-9 *q* S Job 5:17
3:12 *r* Pr 13:24; Rev 3:19 *s* S Dt 8:5; S Job 5:17; Heb 12:5-6*
3:14 *t* S Job 28:15; Pr 8:19; 16:16
3:15 *u* S Job 28:18 *v* S Job 28:17-19
3:16 *w* S Ge 15:15 *x* S 1Ki 3:13,14
3:17 *y* Mt 11:28-30
3:18 *z* S Ge 2:9; S Pr 10:11; S Rev 2:7 *a* S Pr 2:12; 4:3-9, 8; 8:17-21
3:19 *b* S Ge 1:31; Ps 136:5-9 *c* S Job 28:25-27 *d* Pr 8:27-29
3:21 *e* Pr 1:8-9; 6:20 *f* Pr 4:20-22
3:22 *g* S Dt 30:20; Pr 4:13 *h* S Pr 1:8-9
3:23 *i* S Pr 1:33

f 6 Or *will direct your paths* g 12 Hebrew; Septuagint / *and he punishes*

Lord with all our heart is the opposite of doubting God and his word. Such trust is fundamental to our relationship with God and is based on the premise that he is trustworthy. As God's children we can be assured that our heavenly Father loves us and will faithfully care for us (see Mt 10:31, note), guide us rightly, give us grace and keep his promises. In the most difficult times of our lives, we can commit our way to the Lord (cf. Ps 37:5) and trust him to work on our behalf.

3:5 YOUR OWN UNDERSTANDING. Our own understanding is limited, fallible and subject to error (Eph 4:18). It must therefore be enlightened by God's word and led by the Holy Spirit (Ro 8:9–16). Rather than relying on our own judgment (v. 7), we must pray for God's wisdom and will in all our decisions and goals of life (see 2:3, note).

3:6 IN ALL YOUR WAYS ACKNOWLEDGE HIM. In all our plans, decisions and activities, we should acknowledge God as Lord and his will as our supreme desire. Every day we must live in a close, trusting relationship with God, always looking to him for direction "by prayer and petition, with thanksgiving" (see Php 4:6, note). When we do this, God promises to make our paths straight; i.e., he will lead us to his goal for our lives, remove all obstacles and enable us to make the right choices (see 11:5; Isa 45:13).

3:9 HONOR THE LORD WITH YOUR WEALTH. The Israelites brought the first portion of their harvest to the Lord to acknowledge that he was owner of the land (Lev 23:10; 25:23; Nu 18:12–13). We also should give God the firstfruits of our income so that we may honor him as Lord of our lives and possessions. God will then open the way to pour out his blessings on us (see Mal 3:10, note; 2Co 9:6, note). "Those who honor me I will honor" (1Sa 2:30) is God's promise to all who faithfully and generously give of their finances.

3:11–12 DO NOT DESPISE THE LORD'S DISCIPLINE. At times God allows us to pass through trials and difficulties in order to conform us more perfectly to his holiness and to his will for our lives (cf. Job 5:17). The NT uses these verses to offer encouragement to believers who are enduring pain and affliction (see Heb 12:5, note).

3:16 RICHES AND HONOR. Earthly riches and honor do not always come to us even though we are living according to God's wisdom. But we can be sure that we will receive everlasting riches and honor from God as our future inheritance (Lk 16:11; Eph 1:18; 3:8).

3:23 GO ON YOUR WAY IN SAFETY. Wisdom gives security because it keeps us walking safely in God's good, pleasing and perfect will (cf. 10:9; Ro 12:2). God will not allow those who trust in him to be caught or destroyed by the traps set by the enemy (vv. 25–26).

and your foot will not stumble;[j]
24when you lie down,[k] you will not
be afraid;[l]
when you lie down, your sleep[m]
will be sweet.
25Have no fear of sudden disaster
or of the ruin that overtakes the
wicked,
26for the LORD will be your
confidence[n]
and will keep your foot[o] from
being snared.[p]

27Do not withhold good from those
who deserve it,
when it is in your power to act.
28Do not say to your neighbor,
"Come back later; I'll give it
tomorrow"—
when you now have it with
you.[q]
29Do not plot harm against your
neighbor,
who lives trustfully near you.[r]
30Do not accuse a man for no
reason—
when he has done you no harm.

31Do not envy[s] a violent man
or choose any of his ways,
32for the LORD detests a perverse
man[t]
but takes the upright into his
confidence.[u]
33The LORD's curse[v] is on the house
of the wicked,[w]
but he blesses the home of the
righteous.[x]
34He mocks[y] proud mockers[z]
but gives grace to the humble.[a]
35The wise inherit honor,
but fools he holds up to shame.

3:23 [j]S Ps 37:24; S 119:11; Pr 4:12 **3:24** [k]S Lev 26:6 [l]Ps 91:5; 112:8 [m]S Job 11:18; Jer 31:26 **3:26** [n]S 2Ki 18:5; S Job 4:6 [o]S 1Sa 2:9 [p]S Job 5:19 **3:28** [q]Lev 19:13; Dt 24:15; Lk 10:25-37 **3:29** [r]Zec 8:17 **3:31** [s]S Ps 37:1; Pr 24:1-2 **3:32** [t]S Ps 101:4 [u]S Job 29:4 **3:33** [v]S Job 5:3 [w]Zec 5:4 [x]Ps 37:22; Pr 14:11 **3:34** [y]S 2Ki 19:21 [z]S Ps 40:4 [a]S Ps 18:25-27; S Mt 23:12; Jas 4:6*; 1Pe 5:5*

Wisdom Is Supreme

4 Listen, my sons,[b] to a father's
instruction;[c]
pay attention and gain
understanding.[d]
2I give you sound learning,
so do not forsake my teaching.
3When I was a boy in my father's
house,
still tender, and an only child of
my mother,
4he taught me and said,
"Lay hold[e] of my words with all
your heart;
keep my commands and you will
live.[f]
5Get wisdom,[g] get understanding;
do not forget my words or
swerve from them.
6Do not forsake wisdom, and she
will protect you;[h]
love her, and she will watch
over you.[i]
7Wisdom is supreme; therefore get
wisdom.
Though it cost all[j] you have,[h]
get understanding.[k]
8Esteem her, and she will exalt
you;
embrace her, and she will honor
you.[l]
9She will set a garland of grace on
your head
and present you with a crown of
splendor."[m]

10Listen, my son,[n] accept what I
say,
and the years of your life will be
many.[o]

4:1 [b]S Pr 1:8 [c]Pr 19:20 [d]S Job 8:10 **4:4** [e]S 1Ki 9:4 [f]Pr 7:2 **4:5** [g]S Pr 2:12; 3:13-18 **4:6** [h]2Th 2:10 [i]S Pr 2:11 **4:7** [j]Mt 13:44-46 [k]Pr 23:23 **4:8** [l]S Pr 3:18 **4:9** [m]S Pr 1:8-9 **4:10** [n]Ps 34:11-16; Pr 1:8-9 [o]S Dt 11:21

h 7 Or *Whatever else you get*

4:1–4 LISTEN, MY SONS, TO A FATHER'S INSTRUCTION. Solomon had learned about God's ways from his father and was now passing instruction on to his sons. God wants true godliness and commitment to his ways to be learned primarily through the teaching of parents and the examples provided in the home, and not by delegating that responsibility exclusively to church education programs (Dt 6:7; see article on PARENTS AND CHILDREN, p. 1854).

4:5 GET WISDOM, GET UNDERSTANDING. The wisdom of God is essential for a meaningful and godly life (vv. 20–22; 3:21–22). Therefore, we must seek it above all things. However, to attain such wisdom is not easy, for it is given only to those who diligently pay the price for it. Wisdom comes through two avenues. (1) Instruction. Through instruction a person will experience a spiritual transformation that involves turning from evil and turning to a knowledge of God. A personal relationship with God is the first step in obtaining true wisdom. Believers must fear the Lord and hate evil (8:13; 9:10).

(2) Devotion. Wisdom is for the person who sees its value and therefore diligently seeks it (8:17). The wise person learns from instruction (9:9) and from God's discipline (3:11), accepts God's commands (10:8), listens to the godly counsel of parents and others (v. 1; 13:10), and treasures wisdom as more valuable than silver, gold or precious jewels (3:14–15; 23:23).

Jesus Christ is the supreme manifestation of the wisdom of God (1Co 1:30; Col 2:2–3); thus, this OT exhortation is equivalent to a call to commit our lives to Jesus Christ. We must turn from sin and self to him, sacrificing all that is necessary in order to follow him as his disciples (Mt 13:44–46; Lk 14:33).

11I guide[p] you in the way of
wisdom
and lead you along straight
paths.[q]
12When you walk, your steps will
not be hampered;
when you run, you will not
stumble.[r]
13Hold on to instruction, do not let it
go;
guard it well, for it is your
life.[s]
14Do not set foot on the path of the
wicked
or walk in the way of evil
men.[t]
15Avoid it, do not travel on it;
turn from it and go on your
way.
16For they cannot sleep till they
do evil;[u]
they are robbed of slumber till
they make someone fall.
17They eat the bread of wickedness
and drink the wine of violence.[v]
18The path of the righteous[w] is like
the first gleam of dawn,[x]
shining ever brighter till the full
light of day.[y]
19But the way of the wicked is like
deep darkness;[z]
they do not know what makes
them stumble.[a]

20My son,[b] pay attention to what I
say;
listen closely to my words.[c]
21Do not let them out of your
sight,[d]
keep them within your heart;
22for they are life to those who find
them
and health to a man's whole
body.[e]
23Above all else, guard[f] your heart,
for it is the wellspring of life.[g]
24Put away perversity from your
mouth;
keep corrupt talk far from your
lips.
25Let your eyes[h] look straight
ahead,
fix your gaze directly before you.
26Make level[1] paths for your feet[i]
and take only ways that are
firm.
27Do not swerve to the right or the
left;[j]
keep your foot from evil.

Warning Against Adultery

5 My son,[k] pay attention to my
wisdom,
listen well to my words[l] of
insight,
2that you may maintain discretion
and your lips may preserve
knowledge.
3For the lips of an adulteress drip
honey,
and her speech is smoother than
oil;[m]
4but in the end she is bitter as
gall,[n]
sharp as a double-edged sword.
5Her feet go down to death;
her steps lead straight to the
grave.[2][o]

4:11 [p]S 1Sa 12:23 [q]2Sa 22:37; Ps 5:8
4:12 [r]S Job 18:7; Pr 3:23
4:13 [s]S Pr 3:22
4:14 [t]Ps 1:1; S Pr 1:15
4:16 [u]Ps 36:4; Mic 7:3
4:17 [v]Ge 49:5; Ps 73:6; Pr 1:10-19; 14:22; Isa 59:6; Jer 22:3; Hab 1:2; Mal 2:16
4:18 [w]Job 17:9 [x]S Job 22:28 [y]S 2Sa 23:4; Da 12:3; Mt 5:14; Jn 8:12; Php 2:15
4:19 [z]S Pr 2:13 [a]S Dt 32:35; S Job 3:23; Pr 13:9; S Isa 8:15
4:20 [b]Ps 34:11-16; Pr 1:8-9 [c]Pr 5:1
4:21 [d]Pr 3:21
4:22 [e]S Pr 3:8
4:23 [f]S 2Ki 10:31 [g]Pr 10:11; Lk 6:45
4:25 [h]S Job 31:1
4:26 [i]Heb 12:13*
4:27 [j]S Lev 10:11; S Dt 5:32
5:1 [k]S Pr 1:8 [l]Pr 4:20
5:3 [m]S Ps 55:21; Pr 7:5
5:4 [n]Ecc 7:26
5:5 [o]S Ps 9:17; S Pr 2:18; 7:26-27

[1] 26 Or *Consider the* [2] 5 Hebrew *Sheol*

4:13 FOR IT IS YOUR LIFE. In Proverbs wisdom brings life and is life. To live as God has designed brings (1) a good and joyful life (15:23,27), (2) normally a longer physical life (v. 10; 3:2; 9:11), (3) a moral and spiritual life (8:35; 9:6; 10:16; 19:23), and (4) the hope of life after death (compare 11:7 with 14:32). Christ, who is our wisdom (see previous note), is the fulfillment of this OT ideal of wisdom; he is now our life (Jn 5:40; 11:25; 14:6), and those who have him have life (1Jn 5:12).

4:23 GUARD YOUR HEART. The heart is the wellspring of desire and decision (see article on THE HEART, p. 906). Following God and knowing his ways involve a resolute decision to remain committed to him, seeking first his kingdom and his righteousness (Mt 6:33). If we find that our hunger and thirst for God and his kingdom are declining, we should reevaluate our priorities, honestly acknowledge our lukewarmness, and earnestly pray for a renewed desire for God and his favor. Failure to "guard" our hearts results in a departure from the paths of safety and entrapment in a destructive snare (cf. 7:24–27); to watch over our hearts above all else results in a firm walk on a level path through his favor and grace (vv. 25–27).

5:3 LIPS OF AN ADULTERESS. The book of Proverbs repeatedly warns about the destructiveness of sexual immorality. Solomon emphasizes that though immorality's deceptive pleasures are attractive, giving in to them will lead to ruin (vv. 7–14). Violations of God's standards of sexual purity and chastity are found in this chapter and in 2:16–19; 6:20–35; 22:14; 23:27–28; 29:3; 30:20; 31:3. The alternative to sexual immorality is commitment to God (v. 1), disciplined restraint prior to marriage, and the fulfillment of natural sexual desire through a holy love life in marriage (vv. 15–23; see article on STANDARDS OF SEXUAL MORALITY, p. 1936).

THE HEART

Pr 4:23 "Above all else, guard your heart, for it is the wellspring of life."

DEFINITION OF THE HEART. Contemporary people generally consider the head with its brain to be the center and director of human activity. However, the Bible speaks of the heart as the center; "it is the wellspring of life" (Pr 4:23; cf. Lk 6:45). Biblically, the heart may be seen as containing the totality of one's intellect, emotion and volition (see Mk 7:20–23, note).

(1) The heart is the center of the intellect. People know things in their heart (Dt 8:5), pray in their heart (1Sa 1:12–13), meditate in their heart (Ps 19:14), hide God's word in their heart (Ps 119:11), devise plans in their heart (Ps 140:2), keep words within their heart (Pr 4:21), think in their heart (Mk 2:8), doubt in their heart (Mk 11:23), ponder in their heart (Lk 2:19), believe in their heart (Ro 10:9) and sing in their heart (Eph 5:19). All of these actions of the heart are primarily issues involving the mind.

(2) The heart is the center of the emotions. The Bible speaks about the glad heart (Ex 4:14), the loving heart (Dt 6:5), the fearful heart (Jos 5:1), the courageous heart (Ps 27:14), the repentant heart (Ps 51:17), the anxious heart (Pr 12:25), the angry heart (Pr 19:3), the revived heart (Isa 57:15), the anguished heart (Jer 4:19; Ro 9:2), the delighted heart (Jer 15:16), the grieving heart (La 2:18), the humble heart (Mt 11:29), the excited or burning heart (Lk 24:32) and the troubled heart (Jn 14:1). All of these actions of the heart are primarily emotional in character.

(3) Finally, the heart is the center of the human will. We read in Scripture about the hardened heart that refuses to do what God commands (Ex 4:21), the heart that is yielded to God (Jos 24:23), the heart that intends to do something (2Ch 6:7), the heart that is devoted to seeking the Lord (1Ch 22:19), the heart that decides (2Ch 6:7), the heart that desires to receive from the Lord (Ps 21:1–2), the heart that is turned toward God's statutes (Ps 119:36) and the heart that wants to do something (Ro 10:1). All of these activities take place in the human will.

THE NATURE OF THE HEART APART FROM GOD. When Adam and Eve chose to follow the serpent's temptation to eat from the tree of knowledge of good and evil, their decision drastically affected the human heart—it became filled with evil. At present, therefore, according to Jeremiah's testimony, "The heart is deceitful above all things and beyond cure. Who can understand it?" (Jer 17:9). Jesus confirmed Jeremiah's diagnosis when he said that what makes a person unclean before God is not the failure to follow some ceremonial law, but the willingness to listen to wicked inclinations lodged in one's heart such as "evil thoughts, sexual immorality, theft, murder, adultery, greed, malice, deceit, lewdness, envy, slander, arrogance and folly" (Mk 7:21–22). Jesus taught about the seriousness of sin in the heart when he said that the sin of anger is tantamount to murder (Mt 5:21–22) and the sin of lust is just as sinful as actual adultery (Mt 5:27–28; see Ex 20:14, note; Mt 5:28, note).

Hearts that are committed to doing evil run the grave risk of becoming hardened. Those who persistently refuse to listen to God's Word and to obey what he commands, and instead follow the wicked desires of their hearts, will find that God will eventually harden their hearts so that they lose all sensitivity to his Word and to the desires of the Holy Spirit (see Ex 7:3, note; Heb 3:8, note). The primary example of this in the Bible is Pharaoh's heart at the time of the exodus (see Ex 7:3,13,22–23; 8:15,32; 9:12; 10:1; 11:10; 14:17). Paul saw the same general principle operative in the Roman empire (cf. Ro 1:24,26,28) and predicted that it would also occur during the days of the antichrist (2Th 2:11–12). The writer of Hebrews filled his letter with warnings to believers not to harden their hearts (e.g., Heb 3:8–12; see article on PERSONAL APOSTASY, p. 1918, for a description of the steps leading to hardheartedness). Anyone who continues to reject God's word will eventually have a hardened heart.

THE REGENERATED HEART. God's answer to the sinfulness of the human heart is *regeneration*, which comes to all who repent of their sins, turn to God, and place a personal faith in Jesus as Lord and Savior. (1) Regeneration is a matter of the heart. Those who repent from their heart of all sin and confess in their heart that Jesus is Lord (Ro 10:9) are born again and receive a new heart from God (cf. Ps 51:10; Eze 11:19).

(2) Within the hearts of those who experience spiritual birth, God creates a desire to love him and to obey him (see article on REGENERATION, p. 1589). Repeatedly God emphasized to his people the necessity of a love that comes from the heart (see Dt 4:29, note; 6:6, note). Such love for and devotion to God cannot be separated from obedience to his law (cf. Ps 119:34,69,112); Jesus taught that love for God with the whole heart and love for one's neighbor summarize God's entire law (Mt 22:37–40).

(3) Love from the heart is the essential ingredient in obedience. All too often God's people tried to substitute obedience to mere outward religious forms (such as feast days, offerings and sacrifices) for genuine love from the heart (see Isa 1:10–17; Am 5:21–26; Mic 6:6–8; see Dt 10:12, note). Outward observance without an inner desire to serve God is hypocrisy and is severely condemned by our Lord (see Mt 23:13–28; see Lk 21:1–4, note).

(4) Many other spiritual activities take place in the hearts of regenerated believers. They praise God with all their heart (Ps 9:1), meditate in their heart (Ps 19:14), cry out to God from the heart (Ps 84:2), seek God with all their heart (Ps 119:2,10), hide God's word in their heart (Ps 119:11; see Dt 6:6, note), trust in the Lord with all their heart (Pr 3:5), experience God's love poured out into their heart (Ro 5:5) and sing to God in their heart (Eph 5:19; Col 3:16).

[6]She gives no thought to the way of life;
her paths are crooked, but she knows it not.[p]

[7]Now then, my sons, listen[q] to me;
do not turn aside from what I say.
[8]Keep to a path far from her,[r]
do not go near the door of her house,
[9]lest you give your best strength to others
and your years to one who is cruel,
[10]lest strangers feast on your wealth
and your toil enrich another man's house.[s]
[11]At the end of your life you will groan,
when your flesh and body are spent.
[12]You will say, "How I hated discipline!
How my heart spurned correction![t]
[13]I would not obey my teachers
or listen to my instructors.
[14]I have come to the brink of utter ruin[u]
in the midst of the whole assembly."[v]

[15]Drink water from your own cistern,
running water from your own well.
[16]Should your springs overflow in the streets,
your streams of water in the public squares?
[17]Let them be yours alone,
never to be shared with strangers.
[18]May your fountain[w] be blessed,
and may you rejoice in the wife of your youth.[x]
[19]A loving doe, a graceful deer[y]—
may her breasts satisfy you always,
may you ever be captivated by her love.
[20]Why be captivated, my son, by an adulteress?
Why embrace the bosom of another man's wife?

[21]For a man's ways are in full view[z] of the LORD,
and he examines[a] all his paths.[b]
[22]The evil deeds of a wicked man ensnare him;[c]
the cords of his sin hold him fast.[d]
[23]He will die for lack of discipline,[e]
led astray by his own great folly.[f]

Warnings Against Folly

6 My son,[g] if you have put up security[h] for your neighbor,[i]
if you have struck hands in pledge[j] for another,
[2]if you have been trapped by what you said,
ensnared by the words of your mouth,
[3]then do this, my son, to free yourself,
since you have fallen into your neighbor's hands:

5:6 [p] Pr 9:13; 30:20 **5:7** [q] Pr 1:8-9 **5:8** [r] S Pr 2:16-19; 6:20-29; 7:1-27 **5:10** [s] Pr 29:3 **5:12** [t] Pr 12:1 **5:14** [u] Pr 1:24-27; 6:33 [v] Pr 31:3 **5:18** [w] SS 4:12-15 [x] S Dt 20:7; Pr 2:17; Ecc 9:9; Mal 2:14 **5:19** [y] SS 4:5; 8:14 **5:21** [z] S Ps 119:168 [a] Jer 29:23 [b] S Job 10:4; S 14:16; Pr 15:3; Jer 32:19; S Heb 4:13 **5:22** [c] Ps 9:16 [d] Nu 32:23; S Job 18:9; Ps 7:15-16; S Pr 1:31-32 **5:23** [e] S Job 4:21; Pr 10:21 [f] Job 34:21-25; Pr 11:5 **6:1** [g] S Pr 1:8 [h] Job 17:3 [i] Pr 17:18 [j] Pr 11:15; 22:26-27

5:14 THE BRINK OF UTTER RUIN. God has ordained that those who give in to sexual immorality will experience regret and remorse—both in the breakdown of family life and in personal suffering. Premarital sex and marital infidelity have deadly consequences (vv. 5,11). What may begin as a taste of honey (v. 3) will end with the taste of bitterness. God will not be mocked (v. 21); what is sown will be reaped.

5:15 DRINK WATER FROM YOUR OWN CISTERN. A man's source of affectionate love (vv. 18–20) should be his own wife (cf. Ex 20:17). Note that sexual delight in marriage is legitimate and God-given (cf. Ge 2:20–25). A spouse should be considered a special gift from God and cherished with pleasure, purity and thanksgiving (19:14).

5:21 A MAN'S WAYS ARE IN FULL VIEW OF THE LORD. One reason Proverbs gives for resisting sexual immorality is that God sees and knows our ungodly ways (cf. 15:3; Job 31:4; 34:21; Jer 16:17) and will judge us accordingly. He "will be quick to testify against ... adulterers" (Mal 3:5). Because our activities are "in full view of the LORD," no one guilty of adultery will escape its terrible consequences (see 2Sa 12:9–13, notes).

6:1 IF YOU HAVE PUT UP SECURITY. This verse warns against putting up security for a friend (cf. 11:15; 17:18; 22:26), which means accepting responsibility for someone's debt if he or she fails to pay it. This makes the financial situation of a co-signer dependent on the actions of the friend and subject to events beyond his or her control. It can lead to poverty (cf. 22:26–27) and the loss of lifelong friendships. This does not mean, however, that we should refuse to help someone who is in real need of the basic necessities of life (Ex 22:14; Lev 25:35; Mt 5:42); but we should give to the poor rather than lend to them (cf. Mt 14:21; Mk 10:21; see Pr 19:17, note).

Go and humble yourself;
press your plea with your
neighbor!
4Allow no sleep to your eyes,
no slumber to your eyelids.[k]
5Free yourself, like a gazelle[l] from
the hand of the hunter,[m]
like a bird from the snare of the
fowler.[n]

6Go to the ant, you sluggard;[o]
consider its ways and be wise!
7It has no commander,
no overseer or ruler,
8yet it stores its provisions in
summer[p]
and gathers its food at
harvest.[q]

9How long will you lie there, you
sluggard?[r]
When will you get up from your
sleep?
10A little sleep, a little slumber,
a little folding of the hands to
rest[s]—
11and poverty[t] will come on you
like a bandit
and scarcity like an armed
man.[k]

12A scoundrel and villain,
who goes about with a corrupt
mouth,
13 who winks with his eye,[u]
signals with his feet
and motions with his fingers,[v]
14 who plots evil[w] with deceit in
his heart—
he always stirs up dissension.[x]
15Therefore disaster will overtake
him in an instant;[y]
he will suddenly[z] be
destroyed—without
remedy.[a]

16There are six things the LORD
hates,[b]
seven that are detestable to him:
17 haughty eyes,[c]
a lying tongue,[d]
hands that shed innocent
blood,[e]

6:4 [k]Ps 132:4
6:5 [l]S 2Sa 2:18
[m]Isa 13:14
[n]S Ps 91:3
6:6 [o]ver 6-11;
Pr 20:4
6:8 [p]Pr 30:24-25
[q]Pr 10:4
6:9 [r]Pr 24:30-34;
26:13-16
6:10 [s]Pr 24:33;
Ecc 4:5
6:11 [t]ver 10-11;
Pr 20:13;
24:30-34
6:13 [u]S Ps 35:19;
Pr 16:30 [v]Isa 58:9
6:14 [w]S Ps 140:2
[x]ver 16-19
6:15 [y]S Ps 55:15
[z]Job 5:3
[a]Pr 14:32; 29:1
6:16 [b]ver 16-19;
Pr 3:32; 8:13;
15:8,9,26; 16:5
6:17
[c]S Job 41:34;
S Ps 10:5
[d]Pr 12:22
[e]S Dt 19:10;
Pr 1:16; Isa 1:21;
59:7; Jer 2:34;
Mic 7:2

6:18 [f]S Job 15:31
6:19 [g]S Dt 19:16
[h]S Ps 12:2
[i]ver 12-15;
Pr 15:18; Zec 8:17
6:20 [j]S Pr 3:21
[k]Pr 1:8
6:21 [l]Dt 6:8;
S Pr 3:3; 7:1-3
6:23
[m]S Ps 119:105
[n]Pr 10:17
6:24 [o]Ge 39:8;
S Ps 55:21;
Pr 2:16; 7:5
6:26 [p]Pr 7:22-23
6:29 [q]S Ex 20:14
[r]Pr 2:16-19; S 5:8

18 a heart that devises wicked
schemes,
feet that are quick to rush
into evil,[f]
19 a false witness[g] who pours
out lies[h]
and a man who stirs up
dissension among
brothers.[i]

Warning Against Adultery

20My son,[j] keep your father's
commands
and do not forsake your
mother's teaching.[k]
21Bind them upon your heart forever;
fasten them around your neck.[l]
22When you walk, they will guide
you;
when you sleep, they will watch
over you;
when you awake, they will
speak to you.
23For these commands are a lamp,
this teaching is a light,[m]
and the corrections of discipline
are the way to life,[n]
24keeping you from the immoral
woman,
from the smooth tongue of the
wayward wife.[o]
25Do not lust in your heart after her
beauty
or let her captivate you with her
eyes,
26for the prostitute reduces you to a
loaf of bread,
and the adulteress preys upon
your very life.[p]
27Can a man scoop fire into his lap
without his clothes being
burned?
28Can a man walk on hot coals
without his feet being scorched?
29So is he who sleeps[q] with another
man's wife;[r]
no one who touches her will go
unpunished.

k 11 Or *like a vagrant / and scarcity like a beggar*

6:6 YOU SLUGGARD. The sluggard or lazy person is one who (1) puts off beginning what he or she should do (vv. 9–10; cf. 22:13), (2) does not finish what has been started (12:27), and (3) follows the least difficult course of action (20:4). Slothfulness, or laziness, is even more tempting in the spiritual realm than it is in the physical. God exhorts us to make our calling and election sure with all eagerness (2Pe 1:10; cf. 2Co 8:7; 2Pe 1:5).

6:20 SON . . . FATHER'S . . . MOTHER'S. The book of Proverbs places supreme value upon the family. (1) A family is made up of a father and a mother, with a child or children. (2) Both parents must share in the spiritual training of their children (1:8–9; 4:1–5). (3) Wise children will obey and honor their parents (1:8; 2:1; 3:1; 10:1). (4) Marital fidelity and mutual love are exalted (5:15–20).

30Men do not despise a thief if he
steals
to satisfy his hunger when he is
starving.
31Yet if he is caught, he must pay
sevenfold,[s]
though it costs him all the
wealth of his house.
32But a man who commits adultery[t]
lacks judgment;[u]
whoever does so destroys
himself.
33Blows and disgrace are his lot,
and his shame will never[v] be
wiped away;
34for jealousy[w] arouses a husband's
fury,[x]
and he will show no mercy when
he takes revenge.
35He will not accept any
compensation;
he will refuse the bribe, however
great it is.[y]

Warning Against the Adulteress

7 My son,[z] keep my words
and store up my commands
within you.
2Keep my commands and you will
live;[a]
guard my teachings as the apple
of your eye.
3Bind them on your fingers;
write them on the tablet of your
heart.[b]
4Say to wisdom, "You are my
sister,"
and call understanding your
kinsman;
5they will keep you from the
adulteress,
from the wayward wife with her
seductive words.[c]
6At the window of my house
I looked out through the lattice.
7I saw among the simple,
I noticed among the young men,
a youth who lacked judgment.[d]
8He was going down the street near
her corner,
walking along in the direction of
her house
9at twilight,[e] as the day was
fading,
as the dark of night set in.
10Then out came a woman to meet
him,
dressed like a prostitute and
with crafty intent.
11(She is loud[f] and defiant,
her feet never stay at home;
12now in the street, now in the
squares,
at every corner she lurks.)[g]
13She took hold of him[h] and kissed
him
and with a brazen face she
said:[i]
14"I have fellowship offerings[1][j] at
home;
today I fulfilled my vows.
15So I came out to meet you;
I looked for you and have found
you!
16I have covered my bed
with colored linens from Egypt.
17I have perfumed my bed[k]
with myrrh,[l] aloes and
cinnamon.
18Come, let's drink deep of love till
morning;
let's enjoy ourselves with love![m]
19My husband is not at home;
he has gone on a long journey.
20He took his purse filled with
money

6:31 [s] Ex 22:1-14 **6:32** [t] S Ex 20:14 [u] Pr 7:7; 9:4,16 **6:33** [v] Pr 5:9-14 **6:34** [w] S Nu 5:14 [x] S Ge 34:7 **6:35** [y] Job 31:9-11; SS 8:7 **7:1** [z] S Pr 1:8 **7:2** [a] Pr 4:4 **7:3** [b] S Pr 3:3 **7:5** [c] ver 21; S Job 31:9; S Pr 2:16; 6:24 **7:7** [d] S Pr 1:22; S 6:32 **7:9** [e] Job 24:15 **7:11** [f] Pr 9:13 **7:12** [g] Pr 8:1-36; 23:26-28 **7:13** [h] S Ge 39:12 [i] S Pr 1:20 **7:14** [j] S Lev 7:11-18 **7:17** [k] S Est 1:6; Isa 57:7; Eze 23:41; Am 6:4 [l] S Ge 37:25 **7:18** [m] S Ge 39:7

[1] *14* Traditionally *peace offerings*

6:32–33 HIS SHAME WILL NEVER BE WIPED AWAY. God's covenant children who commit adultery will experience trouble and disgrace; moreover, their shame will never be removed. (1) Adultery is a grave and heinous sin against God (2Sa 12:9–10) and against the innocent partner who has been defrauded; the shame and disgrace of that sin remain with the guilty party for life. Though the guilt of adultery may be forgiven by repentance, its shame will remain, for its scars are never completely removed; amends can never be adequately made (see 2Sa 12:10; 13:13,22; 1Ki 15:5; Ne 13:26; Mt 1:6).

(2) Because of the far-reaching and fearful consequences of adultery on all involved, we should run from every temptation and shun all associations that might lead to this sin. We should pray to be delivered from temptation (Mt 6:13) and soberly recall the words of Scripture when tempted: "So if you think you are standing firm, be careful that you don't fall" (1Co 10:12).

7:1–27 KEEP MY WORDS. Once more Proverbs warns against immorality committed in the name of love (v. 18), emphasizing its disastrous results (vv. 25–27; see 5:3,14, notes; 6:32–33, note). Sexual immorality can be avoided (1) by being firmly commited to all that God says is right and good (vv. 1–5), (2) by not allowing our thoughts to dwell on lustful pleasures (v. 25), and (3) by knowing that this sin leads to sorrow, regret and death (vv. 26–27).

and will not be home till full
moon."
21With persuasive words she led him
astray;
she seduced him with her
smooth talk.[n]
22All at once he followed her
like an ox going to the
slaughter,
like a deer[m] stepping into a
noose[n][o]
23 till an arrow pierces[p] his liver,
like a bird darting into a snare,
little knowing it will cost him
his life.[q]

24Now then, my sons, listen[r] to me;
pay attention to what I say.
25Do not let your heart turn to her
ways
or stray into her paths.[s]
26Many are the victims she has
brought down;
her slain are a mighty throng.
27Her house is a highway to the
grave,[o]
leading down to the chambers of
death.[t]

Wisdom's Call

8 Does not wisdom call out?[u]
Does not understanding raise
her voice?
2On the heights along the way,
where the paths meet, she takes
her stand;
3beside the gates leading into the
city,
at the entrances, she cries
aloud:[v]
4"To you, O men, I call out;[w]
I raise my voice to all mankind.
5You who are simple,[x] gain
prudence;[y]
you who are foolish, gain
understanding.
6Listen, for I have worthy things to
say;
I open my lips to speak what is
right.
7My mouth speaks what is true,[z]
for my lips detest wickedness.
8All the words of my mouth are
just;
none of them is crooked or
perverse.

9To the discerning all of them are
right;
they are faultless to those who
have knowledge.
10Choose my instruction instead of
silver,
knowledge rather than choice
gold,[a]
11for wisdom is more precious[b]
than rubies,
and nothing you desire can
compare with her.[c]

12"I, wisdom, dwell together with
prudence;
I possess knowledge and
discretion.[d]
13To fear the LORD[e] is to hate
evil;[f]
I hate[g] pride and arrogance,
evil behavior and perverse
speech.
14Counsel and sound judgment are
mine;
I have understanding and
power.[h]
15By me kings reign
and rulers[i] make laws that are
just;
16by me princes govern,[j]
and all nobles who rule on
earth.[p]
17I love those who love me,[k]
and those who seek me find
me.[l]
18With me are riches and honor,[m]
enduring wealth and
prosperity.[n]
19My fruit is better than fine gold;[o]
what I yield surpasses choice
silver.[p]
20I walk in the way of
righteousness,[q]
along the paths of justice,
21bestowing wealth on those who
love me
and making their treasuries
full.[r]

7:21 [n] S ver 5
7:22 [o] S Job 18:10
7:23 [p] S Job 15:22; S 16:13 [q] S Pr 6:26; Ecc 7:26
7:24 [r] Pr 1:8-9; 8:32
7:25 [s] Pr 5:7-8
7:27 [t] Jdg 16:19; S Pr 2:18; Rev 22:15
8:1 [u] S Job 28:12
8:3 [v] Pr 7:6-13
8:4 [w] Isa 42:2
8:5 [x] S Pr 1:22 [y] Pr 1:4
8:7 [z] Jn 8:14
8:10 [a] S Job 28:17; S Ps 19:10
8:11 [b] ver 19; S Job 28:17-19 [c] Pr 3:13-15
8:12 [d] Pr 1:4
8:13 [e] S Ge 22:12 [f] S Ex 20:20; S Job 28:28 [g] Jer 44:4
8:14 [h] S Job 9:4; Pr 21:22; Ecc 7:19
8:15 [i] S Ps 2:10
8:16 [j] S 2Ch 1:10; Pr 29:4
8:17 [k] S 1Sa 2:30; Jn 14:21-24 [l] S 1Ch 16:11; S Pr 1:28; 3:13-18; Mt 7:7-11
8:18 [m] S 1Ki 3:13 [n] S Dt 8:18
8:19 [o] S Job 28:17-19 [p] S Pr 3:13-14
8:20 [q] S Ps 5:8
8:21 [r] Pr 15:6; 24:4

[m] 22 Syriac (see also Septuagint); Hebrew *fool*
[n] 22 The meaning of the Hebrew for this line is uncertain. [o] 27 Hebrew *Sheol*
[p] 16 Many Hebrew manuscripts and Septuagint; most Hebrew manuscripts *and nobles—all righteous rulers*

8:13 TO FEAR THE LORD IS TO HATE EVIL. The fear of God should cause us to avoid evil (16:6) and to hate sin that displeases him and destroys us and those we love (see article on THE FEAR OF THE LORD, p. 260).

22"The LORD brought me forth as the
first of his works,[q,r]
before his deeds of old;
23I was appointed[s] from eternity,
from the beginning, before the
world began.
24When there were no oceans, I was
given birth,
when there were no springs
abounding with water;[s]
25before the mountains were settled
in place,[t]
before the hills, I was given
birth,[u]
26before he made the earth or its
fields
or any of the dust of the
world.[v]
27I was there when he set the
heavens in place,[w]
when he marked out the
horizon[x] on the face of the
deep,
28when he established the clouds
above[y]
and fixed securely the fountains
of the deep,[z]
29when he gave the sea its
boundary[a]
so the waters would not
overstep his command,[b]
and when he marked out the
foundations of the earth.[c]
30 Then I was the craftsman at his
side.[d]
I was filled with delight day after
day,
rejoicing always in his presence,
31rejoicing in his whole world
and delighting in mankind.[e]

32"Now then, my sons, listen[f] to
me;
blessed are[g] those who keep
my ways.[h]
33Listen to my instruction and be
wise;
do not ignore it.
34Blessed is the man who listens[i]
to me,
watching daily at my doors,
waiting at my doorway.
35For whoever finds me[j] finds life[k]
and receives favor from the
LORD.[l]
36But whoever fails to find me
harms himself;[m]
all who hate me love death."[n]

Invitations of Wisdom and of Folly

9 Wisdom has built[o] her house;
she has hewn out its seven
pillars.
2She has prepared her meat and
mixed her wine;[p]
she has also set her table.[q]
3She has sent out her maids, and
she calls[r]
from the highest point of the
city.[s]
4"Let all who are simple[t] come in
here!"
she says to those who lack
judgment.[u]
5"Come,[v] eat my food
and drink the wine I have
mixed.[w]
6Leave your simple ways and you
will live;[x]
walk in the way of
understanding.[y]

7"Whoever corrects a mocker invites
insult;
whoever rebukes a wicked man
incurs abuse.[z]
8Do not rebuke a mocker[a] or he
will hate you;
rebuke a wise man and he will
love you.[b]
9Instruct a wise man and he will be
wiser still;
teach a righteous man and he
will add to his learning.[c]

10"The fear of the LORD[d] is the
beginning of wisdom,
and knowledge of the Holy
One[e] is understanding.[f]
11For through me your days will be
many,
and years will be added to your
life.[g]
12If you are wise, your wisdom will
reward you;

8:24 [s]S Ge 7:11 **8:25** [t]S Job 38:6 [u]S Job 15:7 **8:26** [v]S Ps 90:2 **8:27** [w]S Job 26:7 [x]S Job 22:14 **8:28** [y]S Job 36:29 [z]S Ge 1:7; S Job 9:8; S 26:10 **8:29** [a]S Ge 1:9; S Ps 16:6 [b]S Job 38:8 [c]S 1Sa 2:8; S Job 38:5 **8:30** [d]Pr 3:19-20; Rev 3:14 **8:31** [e]S Job 28:25-27; 38:4-38; Ps 104:1-30; Pr 30:4; Jn 1:1-4; Col 1:15-20 **8:32** [f]S Pr 7:24 [g]Lk 11:28 [h]S 2Sa 22:22; S Ps 18:21 **8:34** [i]1Ki 10:8 **8:35** [j]Pr 3:13-18 [k]Pr 9:6; Jn 5:39-40 [l]S Job 33:26 **8:36** [m]Pr 15:32; Isa 3:9; Jer 40:2 [n]S Job 28:22 **9:1** [o]Eph 2:20-22; 1Pe 2:5 **9:2** [p]Isa 25:6; 62:8 [q]Lk 14:16-23 **9:3** [r]S Pr 1:20; 8:1-3 [s]ver 14 **9:4** [t]S Pr 1:22 [u]ver 16; S Pr 6:32 **9:5** [v]Jn 7:37-38 [w]S Ps 42:2; 63:1; 143:6; Isa 44:3; 55:1 **9:6** [x]S Pr 8:35 [y]S Pr 3:1-2 **9:7** [z]Pr 23:9; Mt 7:6 **9:8** [a]Pr 15:12 [b]Ps 141:5 **9:9** [c]Pr 1:5,7; 12:15; 13:10; 14:6; 15:31; 19:25 **9:10** [d]S Pr 1:7 [e]Ps 22:3; Pr 30:3 [f]S Dt 4:6 **9:11** [g]S Ge 15:15; S Dt 11:21; S Pr 3:1-2; 10:27

[q]*22* Or *way*; or *dominion* [r]*22* Or *The LORD possessed me at the beginning of his work*; or *The LORD brought me forth at the beginning of his work* [s]*23* Or *fashioned*

9:8 REBUKE A WISE MAN. If we are truly wise people who want to please God, we will welcome rebuke and criticism (27:6; 28:23). Admonition and correction from a friend, family member or pastor are some of the ways God uses to mold our character according to his holy will (see Jn 16:8; Eph 5:11; 2Ti 4:2; Tit 2:15; Rev 3:19). The church that receives with humility and obedience the rebuke of a loving pastor will indeed be blessed by the Holy Spirit.

if you are a mocker, you alone
will suffer."

13The woman Folly is loud;[h]
she is undisciplined and without
knowledge.[i]

14She sits at the door of her house,
on a seat at the highest point of
the city,[j]

15calling out[k] to those who pass by,
who go straight on their way.

16"Let all who are simple come in
here!"
she says to those who lack
judgment.[l]

17"Stolen water is sweet;
food eaten in secret is
delicious![m]"

18But little do they know that the
dead are there,
that her guests are in the depths
of the grave.[t][n]

Proverbs of Solomon

10 The proverbs[o] of Solomon:[p]

A wise son brings joy to his
father,[q]
but a foolish son grief to his
mother.

2Ill-gotten treasures are of no
value,[r]
but righteousness delivers from
death.[s]

3The LORD does not let the
righteous go hungry[t]
but he thwarts the craving of
the wicked.[u]

4Lazy hands make a man poor,[v]
but diligent hands bring
wealth.[w]

5He who gathers crops in summer
is a wise son,
but he who sleeps during
harvest is a disgraceful
son.[x]

6Blessings crown the head of the
righteous,
but violence overwhelms the
mouth of the wicked.[u][y]

7The memory of the righteous[z] will
be a blessing,
but the name of the wicked[a]
will rot.[b]

8The wise in heart accept
commands,
but a chattering fool comes to
ruin.[c]

9The man of integrity[d] walks
securely,[e]
but he who takes crooked paths
will be found out.[f]

10He who winks maliciously[g]
causes grief,
and a chattering fool comes to
ruin.

11The mouth of the righteous is a
fountain of life,[h]
but violence overwhelms the
mouth of the wicked.[i]

12Hatred stirs up dissension,
but love covers over all
wrongs.[j]

13Wisdom is found on the lips of the
discerning,[k]
but a rod is for the back of him
who lacks judgment.[l]

14Wise men store up knowledge,[m]
but the mouth of a fool invites
ruin.[n]

9:13 [h]Pr 7:11 [i]S Pr 5:6 9:14 [j]ver 3; Eze 16:25 9:15 [k]S Pr 1:20 9:16 [l]S Pr 1:22 9:17 [m]Pr 20:17 9:18 [n]S Pr 2:18; 7:26-27 10:1 [o]S 1Ki 4:32 [p]S Pr 1:1 [q]Pr 15:20; 17:21; 19:13; 23:22-25; 27:11; 29:3 10:2 [r]Pr 13:11; 21:6 [s]ver 16; Pr 11:4,19; 12:28 10:3 [t]Mt 6:25-34 [u]Pr 13:25 10:4 [v]Pr 6:6-8; 19:15; 24:30-34 [w]Pr 12:24; 21:5 10:5 [x]Pr 24:30-34 10:6 [y]ver 8,11, 14; Pr 12:13; 13:3; Ecc 10:12 10:7 [z]S Ps 112:6 [a]S Job 18:17; S Ps 109:13 [b]S Job 18:17; Ps 9:6 10:8 [c]ver 14; S Job 33:33; Mt 7:24-27 10:9 [d]S Ps 25:21 [e]S Ps 37:24 [f]Pr 28:18 10:10 [g]S Ps 35:19 10:11 [h]ver 27; S Pr 3:18; S 4:23; 11:30; 13:12,14, 19; 14:27; 15:4; 16:22 [i]S ver 6 10:12 [j]Pr 17:9; 1Co 13:4-7; 1Pe 4:8 10:13 [k]ver 31; S Ps 37:30; Pr 15:7 [l]S Dt 25:2; Pr 14:3; 26:3 10:14 [m]Pr 11:13; 12:23 [n]S ver 6; S Ps 59:12; S Pr 14:3; 18:6,7; S Mt 12:37

[t]18 Hebrew *Sheol* [u]6 Or *but the mouth of the wicked conceals violence*; also in verse 11

10:2–7 DELIVERS FROM DEATH. These verses contrast the blessings of righteous living with the unhappiness of wicked living.

10:3 DOES NOT LET THE RIGHTEOUS GO HUNGRY. This proverb describes God's general providence and provision in meeting the physical needs of his people (cf. Mt 6:11,33). This truth does not deny that there may be times when we will find it difficult to provide for the needs of ourselves or our families. Times of war, famine, or devastating economic or social conditions, as well as periods of persecution, may result in severe hardship for the righteous (see 3Jn 2, note); nevertheless, God will never abandon his children who trust fully in him.

10:5 WHO SLEEPS DURING HARVEST. How shameful it is to be lazy when there is physical work to be done (cf. 6:9–11; 19:15). How much more shameful is it to refuse selfishly to work for the harvest of souls. We must pay attention to the words of Jesus and work with him for the salvation of the world (Mt 9:37–38).

10:11 A FOUNTAIN OF LIFE. Those who know and follow God's ways will lead others into the full life given by God. Compare Eze 47:1–12 and Jn 4:14; 7:38, where the Spirit living in the believer is regarded as a source of living water. As this living water flows through the believer, it brings eternal life to others. Believers should pray that the Holy Spirit will enable them to carry out that great task (see 1Co 12:4–10; 14:1–40).

15The wealth of the rich is their
fortified city,[o]
but poverty is the ruin of the
poor.[p]

16The wages of the righteous bring
them life,[q]
but the income of the wicked
brings them punishment.[r]

17He who heeds discipline shows the
way to life,[s]
but whoever ignores correction
leads others astray.

18He who conceals his hatred has
lying lips,[t]
and whoever spreads slander is
a fool.

19When words are many, sin is not
absent,
but he who holds his tongue is
wise.[u]

20The tongue of the righteous is
choice silver,
but the heart of the wicked is of
little value.

21The lips of the righteous nourish
many,
but fools die for lack of
judgment.[v]

22The blessing of the LORD[w] brings
wealth,[x]
and he adds no trouble to it.[y]

23A fool finds pleasure in evil
conduct,[z]
but a man of understanding
delights in wisdom.

24What the wicked dreads[a] will
overtake him;[b]
what the righteous desire will be
granted.[c]

25When the storm has swept by, the
wicked are gone,
but the righteous stand firm[d]
forever.[e]

26As vinegar to the teeth and
smoke[f] to the eyes,
so is a sluggard to those who
send him.[g]

27The fear of the LORD adds length
to life,[h]
but the years of the wicked are
cut short.[i]

28The prospect of the righteous is
joy,
but the hopes of the wicked
come to nothing.[j]

29The way of the LORD is a refuge for
the righteous,
but it is the ruin of those who
do evil.[k]

30The righteous will never be
uprooted,
but the wicked will not remain
in the land.[l]

31The mouth of the righteous brings
forth wisdom,[m]
but a perverse tongue[n] will be
cut out.

32The lips of the righteous know
what is fitting,[o]
but the mouth of the wicked
only what is perverse.[p]

11

The LORD abhors dishonest
scales,[q]
but accurate weights are his
delight.[r]

2When pride comes, then comes
disgrace,[s]
but with humility comes
wisdom.[t]

10:15 [o]Pr 18:11 [p]Pr 19:7 **10:16** [q]S Dt 30:15 [r]Pr 11:18-19; 15:6; S Ro 6:23 **10:17** [s]Pr 6:23; 15:5 **10:18** [t]S Ps 31:18 **10:19** [u]S Job 1:22; S 6:24; Pr 17:28; S 20:25; 21:23; Jas 1:19; 3:2-12 **10:21** [v]Pr 5:22-23; Isa 5:13; Jer 5:4; Hos 4:1,6,14 **10:22** [w]S Ps 128:2 [x]S Ge 13:2; S 49:25; S Dt 8:18 [y]S 2Ch 25:9 **10:23** [z]S Pr 2:14 **10:24** [a]Isa 65:7; 66:4 [b]S Ge 42:36 [c]S Ps 37:4; 145:17-19; Eze 11:8 **10:25** [d]S Ps 20:8 [e]Pr 12:3,7; Mt 7:24-27 **10:26** [f]Isa 65:5 [g]Pr 13:17; 25:13; 26:6 **10:27** [h]S ver 11; Dt 11:9; Pr 9:10-11; 19:23; 22:4 [i]S Job 15:32 **10:28** [j]Est 7:10; S Job 8:13; Ps 112:10; Pr 11:7 **10:29** [k]Pr 21:15; Hos 14:9 **10:30** [l]Ps 37:9, 28-29; S Pr 2:20-22 **10:31** [m]S ver 13; S Pr 15:2; 31:26 [n]S Ps 52:4 **10:32** [o]Ecc 10:12 [p]S Ps 59:7 **11:1** [q]S Lev 19:36; Dt 25:13-16; S Job 6:2; Pr 20:10,23 [r]Pr 16:11; Eze 45:10 **11:2** [s]Pr 16:18 [t]Pr 18:12; 29:23

10:15 WEALTH OF THE RICH IS THEIR FORTIFIED CITY. This proverb observes the apparent advantages of riches (cf. 14:20; 19:4) and the disadvantages of poverty (cf. 18:23; 19:4,7). It may appear to the casual observer that the rich are secure (see 11:4). Yet in God's sight, "ill-gotten treasures are of no value" (v. 2). The NT sheds clearer light on the state of the rich and poor. "Has God not chosen those who are poor in the eyes of the world to be rich in faith and to inherit the kingdom?" (Jas 2:5; cf. Lk 2:7–12; 4:22). Like the other OT books, Proverbs must be read in the light of God's complete revelation in his Son recorded in the NT (Heb 1:1–3; see article on CHRIST IN THE OLD TESTAMENT, p. 518).

10:22 THE BLESSING OF THE LORD BRINGS WEALTH. All too often material wealth in this world is gained through wickedness and greed and is therefore not from God (v. 2). True riches consist in the blessing of the Lord. Whether we are poor or rich, the Lord's presence and favor are our greatest wealth.

11:1 THE LORD ABHORS DISHONEST SCALES. The use of inaccurate scales to cheat someone is condemned by God (cf. Lev 19:35). He commands that we deal honestly with all people, both in financial matters and in other circumstance where cheating is possible. We must always keep in mind that only the upright will see the Lord's face (Ps 11:7) and live before him (Ps 140:13; cf. 24:3–5).

[3]The integrity of the upright guides them,
but the unfaithful are destroyed by their duplicity.[u]

[4]Wealth[v] is worthless in the day of wrath,[w]
but righteousness delivers from death.[x]

[5]The righteousness of the blameless makes a straight way[y] for them,
but the wicked are brought down by their own wickedness.[z]

[6]The righteousness of the upright delivers them,
but the unfaithful are trapped by evil desires.[a]

[7]When a wicked man dies, his hope perishes;[b]
all he expected from his power comes to nothing.[c]

[8]The righteous man is rescued from trouble,
and it comes on the wicked instead.[d]

[9]With his mouth the godless destroys his neighbor,
but through knowledge the righteous escape.[e]

[10]When the righteous prosper, the city rejoices;[f]
when the wicked perish, there are shouts of joy.[g]

[11]Through the blessing of the upright a city is exalted,[h]
but by the mouth of the wicked it is destroyed.[i]

[12]A man who lacks judgment derides his neighbor,[j]
but a man of understanding holds his tongue.[k]

[13]A gossip betrays a confidence,[l]
but a trustworthy man keeps a secret.[m]

[14]For lack of guidance a nation falls,[n]
but many advisers make victory sure.[o]

[15]He who puts up security[p] for another will surely suffer,
but whoever refuses to strike hands in pledge is safe.[q]

[16]A kindhearted woman gains respect,[r]
but ruthless men gain only wealth.

[17]A kind man benefits himself,
but a cruel man brings trouble on himself.

[18]The wicked man earns deceptive wages,
but he who sows righteousness reaps a sure reward.[s]

[19]The truly righteous man attains life,[t]
but he who pursues evil goes to his death.[u]

[20]The LORD detests men of perverse heart[v]
but he delights[w] in those whose ways are blameless.[x]

[21]Be sure of this: The wicked will not go unpunished,
but those who are righteous will go free.[y]

[22]Like a gold ring in a pig's snout
is a beautiful woman who shows no discretion.

[23]The desire of the righteous ends only in good,
but the hope of the wicked only in wrath.

[24]One man gives freely, yet gains even more;

11:3 [u] ver 5; Pr 13:6 **11:4** [v] Eze 27:27 [w] S Job 20:20; S Eze 7:19 [x] S Pr 10:2 **11:5** [y] S 1Ki 8:36 [z] S ver 3; Pr 5:21-23; 13:6; 21:7 **11:6** [a] S Est 7:9 **11:7** [b] S Job 8:13 [c] S Pr 10:28 **11:8** [d] Pr 21:18 **11:9** [e] Pr 12:6; Jer 45:5 **11:10** [f] S 2Ki 11:20 [g] S Est 8:17 **11:11** [h] Pr 14:34 [i] Pr 29:8 **11:12** [j] Pr 14:21 [k] S Job 6:24 **11:13** [l] Pr 20:19 [m] S Pr 10:14 **11:14** [n] Pr 20:18 [o] S 2Sa 15:34; Pr 15:22; 24:6 **11:15** [p] S Pr 6:1 [q] Pr 17:18; 22:26-27 **11:16** [r] Pr 31:31 **11:18** [s] S Ex 1:20; S Job 4:8; Hos 10:12-13 **11:19** [t] S Dt 30:15; S Pr 10:2 [u] 1Sa 2:6; Ps 89:48; Pr 1:18-19; Ecc 7:2; Jer 43:11 **11:20** [v] Pr 3:32 [w] S Nu 14:8 [x] S 1Ch 29:17; S Ps 15:2; 101:1-4; S 119:1; Pr 12:2,22; 15:9 **11:21** [y] Pr 16:5

11:8 THE RIGHTEOUS MAN IS RESCUED FROM TROUBLE. As a general principle, righteous living results in less problems than wicked living (cf. vv. 3–9). This does not mean that those who follow God will never have any problems. But the righteous may be assured that when they are afflicted, they will ultimately be delivered in God's own time.

11:19 THE TRULY RIGHTEOUS MAN ATTAINS LIFE. See 10:11, note.

11:19 HE WHO PURSUES EVIL GOES TO HIS DEATH. God has decreed penalties for actions that violate his laws. The unrighteous will ultimately pay for their sins and their disregard of God and others (see 6:29; Ge 34:25–30; 49:7; Ro 6:23; Jas 1:15).

11:24–25 GIVES FREELY, YET GAINS. God promises that those who give generously will receive back more than they give. He blesses those who are kind and generous, whether it be in their financial giving or in giving of themselves. The NT teaches that we are stewards of God's gifts and must use them for his cause and for the benefit of those in need (Mt 25:26–27; see 2Co 8:2, note; 9:8, note).

another withholds unduly, but
comes to poverty.

25 A generous[z] man will prosper;
he who refreshes others will
himself be refreshed.[a]

26 People curse the man who hoards
grain,
but blessing crowns him who is
willing to sell.

27 He who seeks good finds goodwill,
but evil comes to him who
searches for it.[b]

28 Whoever trusts in his riches will
fall,[c]
but the righteous will thrive like
a green leaf.[d]

29 He who brings trouble on his
family will inherit only
wind,
and the fool will be servant to
the wise.[e]

Isa 6:8
30 The fruit of the righteous is a tree
of life,[f]
and he who wins souls is wise.

31 If the righteous receive their due[g]
on earth,
how much more the ungodly and
the sinner!

12 Whoever loves discipline
loves knowledge,
but he who hates correction is
stupid.[h]

2 A good man obtains favor from the
LORD,[i]
but the LORD condemns a crafty
man.[j]

3 A man cannot be established
through wickedness,
but the righteous cannot be
uprooted.[k]

4 A wife of noble character[l] is her
husband's crown,
but a disgraceful wife is like
decay in his bones.[m]

5 The plans of the righteous are
just,
but the advice of the wicked is
deceitful.

6 The words of the wicked lie in
wait for blood,
but the speech of the upright
rescues them.[n]

7 Wicked men are overthrown and
are no more,[o]
but the house of the righteous
stands firm.[p]

8 A man is praised according to his
wisdom,
but men with warped[q] minds
are despised.

9 Better to be a nobody and yet have
a servant
than pretend to be somebody
and have no food.

10 A righteous man cares for the
needs of his animal,[r]
but the kindest acts of the
wicked are cruel.

11 He who works his land will have
abundant food,
but he who chases fantasies
lacks judgment.[s]

12 The wicked desire the plunder of
evil men,
but the root of the righteous
flourishes.

13 An evil man is trapped by his
sinful talk,[t]
but a righteous man escapes
trouble.[u]

11:25 [z] 1Ch 29:17; Isa 32:8 [a] Pr 22:9; 2Co 9:6-9 **11:27** [b] Ps 7:15-16 **11:28** [c] Job 31:24-28; S Ps 49:6; S 52:7; 62:10; Jer 9:23; 48:7 [d] Ps 52:8; 92:12-14 **11:29** [e] Pr 14:19 **11:30** [f] S Ge 2:9; S Pr 10:11 **11:31** [g] Jer 25:29; 49:12; 1Pe 4:18 **12:1** [h] Pr 5:11-14; S 9:7-9; 13:1,18; 15:5,10,12,32 **12:2** [i] S Job 33:26; Ps 84:11 [j] 2Sa 15:3; S Pr 11:20 **12:3** [k] S Pr 10:25 **12:4** [l] S Ru 3:11; Pr 31:10-11 [m] Pr 18:22 **12:6** [n] S Pr 11:9; 14:3 **12:7** [o] S Ps 37:36 [p] S Pr 10:25; 14:11; 15:25 **12:8** [q] Isa 19:14; 29:24 **12:10** [r] S Nu 22:29 **12:11** [s] Pr 28:19 **12:13** [t] S Ps 59:12; S Pr 10:6; 18:7 [u] Pr 21:23

11:30 HE WHO WINS SOULS IS WISE. Influencing people for righteousness is wise. The NT emphasizes that believers should lead people to Christ, salvation and lives of righteousness (see Jn 14:6; 1Co 9:20–22; 10:33; 1Pe 3:1–2; Jas 5:19–20).

12:1 HE WHO HATES CORRECTION IS STUPID. At times we all need rebuke and correction. A proud person hates to be corrected, but the humble person will honestly receive criticism and profit from it (cf. 1:7; 6:23; 10:17).

12:4 WIFE OF NOBLE CHARACTER IS HER HUSBAND'S CROWN. Normally the most important human relationship we will ever have is with a wife or husband. A good spouse will help bring happiness, joy and success, while a bad spouse will cause much sorrow and misery. When seeking a marriage partner, we should consider the person's character and his or her commitment to Christ and his standards of holy living, so that we do not marry the wrong person and suffer a lifetime of regret (see 1Co 7:3,14, notes).

12:10 CARES FOR THE NEEDS OF HIS ANIMAL. God's way of righteous living includes kindness even to animals. Animals are useful to humans for companionship, work and food, and they should never be mistreated or used in a cruel manner (Ge 1:28; 9:3; 24:32; Dt 25:4).

14From the fruit of his lips a man is
filled with good things[v]
as surely as the work of his
hands rewards him.[w]

15The way of a fool seems right to
him,[x]
but a wise man listens to
advice.[y]

16A fool[z] shows his annoyance at
once,[a]
but a prudent man overlooks an
insult.[b]

17A truthful witness gives honest
testimony,
but a false witness tells lies.[c]

18Reckless words pierce like a
sword,[d]
but the tongue of the wise
brings healing.[e]

19Truthful lips endure forever,
but a lying tongue lasts only a
moment.

20There is deceit in the hearts of
those who plot evil,
but joy for those who promote
peace.[f]

21No harm befalls the righteous,[g]
but the wicked have their fill of
trouble.

22The LORD detests lying lips,[h]
but he delights[i] in men who
are truthful.[j]

23A prudent man keeps his
knowledge to himself,[k]
but the heart of fools blurts out
folly.[l]

24Diligent hands will rule,
but laziness ends in slave
labor.[m]

25An anxious heart weighs a man
down,[n]
but a kind word cheers him up.

26A righteous man is cautious in
friendship,[v]
but the way of the wicked leads
them astray.[o]

12:14 [v] Pr 13:2; 15:23; 18:20 [w] Pr 14:14
12:15 [x] Pr 14:12; 16:2,25 [y] S Pr 9:7-9; 19:20
12:16 [z] S 1Sa 25:25 [a] S Job 5:2 [b] Pr 29:11
12:17 [c] S Ps 12:2; Pr 14:5,25
12:18 [d] S Ps 55:21; Pr 25:18 [e] Pr 15:4
12:20 [f] S Ro 14:19
12:21 [g] S Job 4:7
12:22 [h] 1Ki 13:18; Pr 6:17 [i] Ps 18:19 [j] S Pr 11:20
12:23 [k] S Pr 10:14 [l] S Ps 38:5; S 59:7; Pr 18:2
12:24 [m] S Pr 10:4
12:25 [n] Pr 15:13
12:26 [o] S Ps 95:10
12:28 [p] S Dt 30:15; S Pr 10:2
13:1 [q] S Pr 12:1; 15:5
13:2 [r] S Pr 12:14
13:3 [s] S Ps 12:2; S 34:13 [t] S Pr 10:6; 21:23 [u] S Job 1:22; Pr 18:7,20-21
13:4 [v] Pr 21:25-26
13:5 [w] S Ps 119:128
13:6 [x] S Pr 11:3, 5; Jer 44:5
13:7 [y] Rev 3:17 [z] 2Co 6:10
13:8 [a] Pr 15:16
13:9 [b] S Job 18:5; S Pr 4:18-19

27The lazy man does not roast[w] his
game,
but the diligent man prizes his
possessions.

28In the way of righteousness there
is life;[p]
along that path is immortality.

13 A wise son heeds his father's
instruction,
but a mocker does not listen to
rebuke.[q]

2From the fruit of his lips a man
enjoys good things,[r]
but the unfaithful have a craving
for violence.

3He who guards his lips[s] guards
his life,[t]
but he who speaks rashly will
come to ruin.[u]

4The sluggard craves and gets
nothing,[v]
but the desires of the diligent
are fully satisfied.

5The righteous hate what is false,[w]
but the wicked bring shame and
disgrace.

6Righteousness guards the man of
integrity,
but wickedness overthrows the
sinner.[x]

7One man pretends to be rich, yet
has nothing;[y]
another pretends to be poor, yet
has great wealth.[z]

8A man's riches may ransom his
life,
but a poor man hears no
threat.[a]

9The light of the righteous shines
brightly,
but the lamp of the wicked is
snuffed out.[b]

10Pride only breeds quarrels,

[v] 26 Or *man is a guide to his neighbor*
[w] 27 The meaning of the Hebrew for this word is uncertain.

13:3 HE WHO GUARDS HIS LIPS GUARDS HIS LIFE. Careless speech and an unbridled tongue can undermine our influence for righteousness, cause us to sin (Ecc 5:6) and affect our relationship with God (Ecc 5:7). A perfect person carefully controls his or her speech (8:6–8; Jas 3:2). We should ask God for help in controlling our tongues (see Ps 141:3; cf. Pr 10:14,19; 18:7; 2Ti 3:3; Jas 3:2–13).

13:5 THE RIGHTEOUS HATE WHAT IS FALSE. A righteous person would rather experience pain by telling the truth than avoid suffering by lying (Da 3:16–18). Such people know that to give in to the habit of lying is to sin against the Lord (12:22); to do so will exclude them from God's kingdom (Jn 8:44; see Rev 22:15, note).

but wisdom is found in those
who take advice.[c]

11Dishonest money dwindles away,[d]
but he who gathers money little
by little makes it grow.

12Hope deferred makes the heart
sick,
but a longing fulfilled is a tree
of life.[e]

13He who scorns instruction will pay
for it,[f]
but he who respects[g] a
command is rewarded.[h]

14The teaching of the wise is a
fountain of life,[i]
turning a man from the snares
of death.[j]

15Good understanding wins favor,
but the way of the unfaithful is
hard.[x]

16Every prudent man acts out of
knowledge,
but a fool exposes[k] his folly.[l]

17A wicked messenger falls into
trouble,[m]
but a trustworthy envoy brings
healing.[n]

18He who ignores discipline comes
to poverty and shame,[o]
but whoever heeds correction is
honored.[p]

19A longing fulfilled is sweet to the
soul,[q]
but fools detest turning from
evil.

20He who walks with the wise grows
wise,
but a companion of fools suffers
harm.[r]

21Misfortune pursues the sinner,[s]
but prosperity[t] is the reward of
the righteous.[u]

22A good man leaves an inheritance
for his children's children,
but a sinner's wealth is stored
up for the righteous.[v]

23A poor man's field may produce
abundant food,
but injustice sweeps it away.

24He who spares the rod[w] hates his
son,
but he who loves him is careful
to discipline[x] him.[y]

25The righteous eat to their hearts'
content,
but the stomach of the wicked
goes hungry.[z]

14

The wise woman builds her
house,[a]
but with her own hands the
foolish one tears hers down.

2He whose walk is upright fears the
LORD,
but he whose ways are devious
despises him.

3A fool's talk brings a rod to his
back,[b]
but the lips of the wise protect
them.[c]

4Where there are no oxen, the
manger is empty,

13:10 [c]S Jdg 19:30; S Pr 9:9
13:11 [d]S Pr 10:2
13:12 [e]S Pr 10:11
13:13 [f]S Nu 15:31 [g]Ex 9:20 [h]Pr 16:20
13:14 [i]S Pr 10:11 [j]Pr 14:27
13:16 [k]Ecc 10:3 [l]Est 5:11; S Ps 38:5
13:17 [m]S Pr 10:26 [n]Pr 25:13
13:18 [o]S Pr 1:7; S 12:1 [p]Ps 141:5; Pr 25:12; Ecc 7:5
13:19 [q]S Pr 10:11
13:20 [r]2Ch 10:8
13:21 [s]2Sa 3:39; Jer 40:3; 50:7; Eze 14:13; 18:4 [t]Ps 25:13 [u]Ps 32:10
13:22 [v]S Est 8:2; S Job 27:17; Ecc 2:26
13:24 [w]S 2Sa 7:14 [x]S Pr 3:12 [y]Pr 19:18; 22:15; 23:13-14; 29:15, 17; Eph 6:4; Heb 12:7
13:25 [z]Pr 10:3
14:1 [a]S Ru 3:11; Pr 24:3
14:3 [b]S Pr 10:14; Ecc 10:12 [c]S Pr 10:13; S 12:6

[x]15 Or *unfaithful does not endure*

13:10 PRIDE ONLY BREEDS QUARRELS. Often people quarrel and fight for their own ideas because of pride. In so doing they may desire preeminence (Lk 22:24), be rebellious against authority (Nu 12:2) or Biblical truth (2Ti 4:3–4), or be driven by a spirit of sectarianism (1Co 3:3–4). When arguments occur, we need to ask ourselves whether pride is involved or whether we are honestly contending for the truth (Gal 2:4–5; 1Th 2:2; Jude 3).

13:23 INJUSTICE SWEEPS IT AWAY. Some people are poor and remain so because they are victims of injustice in society (cf. Ps 35:10; see Jas 5:1–6).

13:24 HE WHO SPARES THE ROD HATES HIS SON. Scripture instructs parents to discipline their children with "the rod" during their formative years. Spanking should be done only for willful disobedience or defiance; it has as its goal the elimination of folly, rebellion and disrespect for parents (22:15). Adequate parental discipline administered in a wise, loving and considerate manner helps children to learn that wrong behavior carries unpleasant consequences and may involve suffering (29:15). Such discipline is necessary so that children do not form attitudes that will later bring them to ruin and death (19:18; 23:13–14). Godly discipline in a family will bring happiness and peace to the home (29:17); it must always be administered out of love, just as our heavenly Father does (Heb 12:6–7; Rev 3:19).

14:1 THE WISE WOMAN BUILDS HER HOUSE. A wise and godly woman makes her home a place of refuge, peace and joy, whereas a foolish woman neglects her home and family (see 1Ti 2:15, note; Tit 2:4–5, note).

14:2 DESPISES HIM. To despise God is to sin against him and treat him with contempt.

but from the strength of an ox[d]
comes an abundant harvest.

5A truthful witness does not deceive,
but a false witness pours out lies.[e]

6The mocker seeks wisdom and finds none,
but knowledge comes easily to the discerning.[f]

7Stay away from a foolish man,
for you will not find knowledge on his lips.

8The wisdom of the prudent is to give thought to their ways,[g]
but the folly of fools is deception.[h]

9Fools mock at making amends for sin,
but goodwill is found among the upright.

10Each heart knows its own bitterness,
and no one else can share its joy.

11The house of the wicked will be destroyed,[i]
but the tent of the upright will flourish.[j]

12There is a way that seems right to a man,[k]
but in the end it leads to death.[l]

13Even in laughter[m] the heart may ache,
and joy may end in grief.

14The faithless will be fully repaid for their ways,[n]
and the good man rewarded for his.[o]

15A simple man believes anything,
but a prudent man gives thought to his steps.[p]

16A wise man fears the LORD and shuns evil,[q]
but a fool[r] is hotheaded and reckless.

17A quick-tempered[s] man does foolish things,[t]
and a crafty man is hated.[u]

18The simple inherit folly,
but the prudent are crowned with knowledge.

19Evil men will bow down in the presence of the good,
and the wicked at the gates of the righteous.[v]

20The poor are shunned even by their neighbors,
but the rich have many friends.[w]

21He who despises his neighbor sins,[x]
but blessed is he who is kind to the needy.[y]

22Do not those who plot evil go astray?[z]
But those who plan what is good find[y] love and faithfulness.

23All hard work brings a profit,
but mere talk leads only to poverty.

24The wealth of the wise is their crown,
but the folly of fools yields folly.[a]

25A truthful witness saves lives,
but a false witness is deceitful.[b]

26He who fears the LORD has a secure fortress,[c]
and for his children it will be a refuge.[d]

27The fear of the LORD is a fountain of life,[e]
turning a man from the snares of death.[f]

28A large population is a king's glory,

14:4 [d]Ps 144:14 **14:5** [e]S Ps 12:2; S Pr 12:17 **14:6** [f]S Pr 9:9 **14:8** [g]ver 15; Pr 15:28; 21:29 [h]ver 24 **14:11** [i]S Job 8:22; Pr 21:12 [j]S Ps 72:7; S Pr 3:33; S 12:7 **14:12** [k]S Pr 12:15 [l]Pr 16:25 **14:13** [m]Ecc 2:2; 7:3,6 **14:14** [n]S Pr 1:31 [o]S 2Ch 15:7; Pr 12:14 **14:15** [p]S ver 8 **14:16** [q]S Ex 20:20; Pr 22:3 [r]S 1Sa 25:25 **14:17** [s]S 2Ki 5:12 [t]ver 29; Pr 15:18; 16:28; 26:21; 28:25; 29:22 [u]S Est 5:9 **14:19** [v]Pr 11:29 **14:20** [w]Pr 19:4,7 **14:21** [x]Pr 11:12 [y]Pr 19:17 **14:22** [z]Pr 4:16-17 **14:24** [a]ver 8 **14:25** [b]S Pr 12:17 **14:26** [c]Pr 18:10 [d]Ps 9:9 **14:27** [e]S Pr 10:11 [f]Ps 18:5; Pr 13:14

[y]22 Or *show*

14:12 SEEMS RIGHT. Humanistic wisdom is a poor basis for determining what is true or false, right or wrong, worthy or unworthy. God's written revelation is the only infallible source for determining the right path of life. The human way has in it the seeds of death; God's way leads to eternal life.

14:14 THE FAITHLESS. The faithless are those who have turned their hearts away from God to go their own selfish way (see article on PERSONAL APOSTASY, p. 1918). Such persons will reap the fruit of their decision in heartache and misery (cf. 1:31; 12:14; Gal 6:7); those who remain faithful to God (i.e., the prudent, v. 15) will reap the rewards of righteousness, both in this life and in the next (see Rev 2:7, note).

but without subjects a prince is
ruined.[g]

29A patient man has great
understanding,[h]
but a quick-tempered man
displays folly.[i]

30A heart at peace gives life to the
body,
but envy rots the bones.[j]

31He who oppresses the poor shows
contempt for their Maker,[k]
but whoever is kind to the needy
honors God.[l]

32When calamity comes, the wicked
are brought down,[m]
but even in death the righteous
have a refuge.[n]

33Wisdom reposes in the heart of the
discerning[o]
and even among fools she lets
herself be known.[z]

34Righteousness exalts a nation,[p]
but sin is a disgrace to any
people.

35A king delights in a wise servant,
but a shameful servant incurs
his wrath.[q]

15

A gentle answer[r] turns away
wrath,[s]
but a harsh word stirs up anger.

2The tongue of the wise commends
knowledge,[t]
but the mouth of the fool gushes
folly.[u]

3The eyes[v] of the LORD are
everywhere,[w]
keeping watch on the wicked
and the good.[x]

4The tongue[y] that brings healing is
a tree of life,[z]
but a deceitful tongue crushes
the spirit.[a]

5A fool spurns his father's
discipline,
but whoever heeds correction
shows prudence.[b]

6The house of the righteous
contains great treasure,[c]
but the income of the wicked
brings them trouble.[d]

7The lips of the wise spread
knowledge;[e]
not so the hearts of fools.

8The LORD detests the sacrifice[f] of
the wicked,[g]
but the prayer of the upright
pleases him.[h]

9The LORD detests the way of the
wicked[i]
but he loves those who pursue
righteousness.[j]

10Stern discipline awaits him who
leaves the path;
he who hates correction will
die.[k]

11Death and Destruction[a] lie open
before the LORD[l]—
how much more the hearts of
men![m]

12A mocker resents correction;[n]
he will not consult the wise.

13A happy heart makes the face
cheerful,[o]

14:28 [g]S 2Sa 19:7
14:29 [h]S 2Ki 5:12; Pr 17:27 [i]S ver 17; Ecc 7:8-9
14:30 [j]Pr 17:22
14:31 [k]Pr 17:5 [l]S Dt 24:14; S Job 20:19; S Mt 10:42
14:32 [m]S Ps 34:21; S Pr 6:15 [n]S Job 13:15
14:33 [o]Pr 2:6-10
14:34 [p]Pr 11:11
14:35 [q]S Est 8:2; Mt 24:45-51; 25:14-30
15:1 [r]1Ki 12:7; 2Ch 10:7 [s]Pr 25:15
15:2 [t]ver 7; S Pr 10:31 [u]S Ps 59:7; Ecc 10:12
15:3 [v]S 2Ch 16:9 [w]S Job 10:4; S 31:4; S Heb 4:13 [x]S Job 34:21; Pr 5:21; Jer 16:17
15:4 [y]S Ps 5:9 [z]S Pr 10:11 [a]Pr 12:18
15:5 [b]S Pr 10:17; S 12:1; S 13:1
15:6 [c]S Pr 8:21 [d]S Pr 10:16
15:7 [e]S ver 2; S Pr 10:13
15:8 [f]S Ps 51:17; S Isa 1:13 [g]S Pr 6:16; 21:27 [h]ver 29; Job 35:13; Pr 28:9; S Jn 9:31
15:9 [i]S Pr 6:16 [j]S Dt 7:13; S Pr 11:20
15:10 [k]S Pr 1:31-32; S 12:1
15:11 [l]S Job 26:6 [m]S 1Sa 2:3; S 2Ch 6:30; S Ps 44:21; S Rev 2:23
15:12 [n]S Pr 9:8; S 12:1
15:13 [o]ver 15

[z]33 Hebrew; Septuagint and Syriac / *but in the heart of fools she is not known*
[a]11 Hebrew *Sheol and Abaddon*

14:31 HE WHO OPPRESSES THE POOR. Whosoever mistreats or takes advantage of a poor person offends God and shows contempt for him. The poor also are made in God's image (Ge 9:6) and are objects of his special mercy and concern (Dt 15:11). The NT reveals that the gospel must be proclaimed to the poor (Mt 11:5; Ac 4:13; Jas 2:5); note that Jesus Christ identified himself with the poor (Lk 2:7; 2Co 8:9; Php 2:7).

14:32 THE RIGHTEOUS HAVE A REFUGE. Although the OT contains no fully developed doctrine of what happens after death, Proverbs does reveal that the righteous have the hope of life after death. When the wicked die, they have no hope, only dread of final ruin. When the righteous die, they commit themselves to God as their refuge and hope beyond death (cf. 12:28; Ps 49:14–15; 73:24). Further revelation concerning the eternal destiny of the righteous and the wicked is given in the NT teachings of Christ and the apostles.

15:1 A GENTLE ANSWER. When facing anger, a gentle answer will encourage reconciliation and peace (cf. 1Sa 25:21–34), while harsh words stir up more anger and hostility (see Col 4:5–6).

15:6 HOUSE OF THE RIGHTEOUS CONTAINS GREAT TREASURE. Though the home of the righteous (individually or corporately) may lack earthly riches, it does contain spiritual treasures that greatly enrich and sustain the lives of God's people (cf. vv. 16–17). By contrast, the home of the wicked is filled with much trouble and strife (cf. v. 27; 1:10–19; 10:2).

15:8–9 THE SACRIFICE OF THE WICKED. Only those who are upright and who strive to follow God's ways are accepted by him (see 28:9, note).

but heartache crushes the
spirit.[p]

14The discerning heart seeks
knowledge,[q]
but the mouth of a fool feeds on
folly.

15All the days of the oppressed are
wretched,
but the cheerful heart has a
continual feast.[r]

16Better a little with the fear of the
LORD
than great wealth with
turmoil.[s]

17Better a meal of vegetables where
there is love
than a fattened calf with
hatred.[t]

18A hot-tempered man stirs up
dissension,[u]
but a patient man calms a
quarrel.[v]

19The way of the sluggard is blocked
with thorns,[w]
but the path of the upright is a
highway.

20A wise son brings joy to his
father,[x]
but a foolish man despises his
mother.

21Folly delights a man who lacks
judgment,[y]
but a man of understanding
keeps a straight course.

22Plans fail for lack of counsel,[z]
but with many advisers[a] they
succeed.[b]

23A man finds joy in giving an apt
reply[c]—
and how good is a timely
word![d]

15:13 [p] S Pr 12:25; 17:22; 18:14 **15:14** [q] Pr 18:15 **15:15** [r] ver 13 **15:16** [s] ver 17; Ps 37:16-17; Pr 13:8; 16:8; 17:1 **15:17** [t] S ver 16; Pr 17:1; Ecc 4:6 **15:18** [u] S Pr 6:16-19; S 14:17 [v] S Ge 13:8 **15:19** [w] Pr 22:5 **15:20** [x] S Pr 10:1 **15:21** [y] S Pr 2:14 **15:22** [z] S Ps 16:7 [a] 1Ki 1:12; Pr 24:6 [b] S Pr 11:14 **15:23** [c] S Pr 12:14 [d] Pr 25:11

15:25 [e] S Pr 12:7 [f] S Dt 19:14; Pr 23:10-11 **15:26** [g] S Ps 94:11 [h] S Pr 6:16 [i] S Ps 18:26 **15:27** [j] S Ex 23:8; S Ps 15:5; Isa 1:23; 33:15 **15:28** [k] S Pr 14:8 [l] S Ps 59:7 **15:29** [m] S ver 8; S Job 15:31; Ps 145:18-19; Isa 59:2; S Jn 9:31 **15:30** [n] Pr 25:25 **15:31** [o] S Pr 9:7-9; S 12:1 **15:32** [p] S Pr 1:7; S 12:1 [q] S Pr 9:7-9; S 12:1; Ecc 7:5 **15:33** [r] S Pr 1:7 [s] Pr 16:18; 18:12; 22:4; 29:23; Isa 66:2

24The path of life leads upward for
the wise
to keep him from going down to
the grave.[b]

25The LORD tears down the proud
man's house[e]
but he keeps the widow's
boundaries intact.[f]

26The LORD detests the thoughts[g] of
the wicked,[h]
but those of the pure[i] are
pleasing to him.

27A greedy man brings trouble to his
family,
but he who hates bribes will
live.[j]

28The heart of the righteous weighs
its answers,[k]
but the mouth of the wicked
gushes evil.[l]

29The LORD is far from the wicked
but he hears the prayer of the
righteous.[m]

30A cheerful look brings joy to the
heart,
and good news gives health to
the bones.[n]

31He who listens to a life-giving
rebuke
will be at home among the
wise.[o]

32He who ignores discipline despises
himself,[p]
but whoever heeds correction
gains understanding.[q]

33The fear of the LORD[r] teaches a
man wisdom,[c]
and humility comes before
honor.[s]

[b] *24* Hebrew *Sheol* [c] *33* Or *Wisdom teaches the fear of the LORD*

15:14 THE MOUTH OF A FOOL FEEDS ON FOLLY. In this day of high technology in communication media and entertainment, we must carefully guard our hearts and minds. We prove ourselves to be fools if we feed on what offends the Holy Spirit and profanes God's righteousness (see Ro 1:32, note). Wise persons will fill their thoughts only with what is noble, true and pure (Php 4:8).

15:22 LACK OF COUNSEL. Proverbs frequently emphasizes the wisdom of seeking the advice of others with regard to our plans and purposes (see also 11:14; 20:18; 24:6).

15:24 THE PATH OF LIFE LEADS UPWARD. Here is another OT glimpse of a future hope. The verse literally translates: "The path of life is to the place above for the wise, that he may avoid the grave (Heb *Sheol*) beneath." *Sheol* can also mean a place of punishment after death (cf. NT "Hades"; see Ps 16:10, note). Thus the godly will go to the place above (heaven) after death and avoid *Sheol* altogether (cf. Ps 23:6; 73:24–25).

15:29 HE HEARS THE PRAYER OF THE RIGHTEOUS. See 1Jn 3:22, note on prayer and obeying God's commands.

16 To man belong the plans of
the heart,
but from the LORD comes the
reply of the tongue.[t]

2All a man's ways seem innocent to
him,[u]
but motives are weighed[v] by
the LORD.[w]

3Commit to the LORD whatever you
do,
and your plans will succeed.[x]

4The LORD works out everything for
his own ends[y]—
even the wicked for a day of
disaster.[z]

5The LORD detests all the proud of
heart.[a]
Be sure of this: They will not go
unpunished.[b]

6Through love and faithfulness sin
is atoned for;
through the fear of the LORD[c] a
man avoids evil.[d]

Isa 44:24-25

7When a man's ways are pleasing
to the LORD,
he makes even his enemies live
at peace[e] with him.[f]

8Better a little with righteousness
than much gain[g] with
injustice.[h]

9In his heart a man plans his
course,
but the LORD determines his
steps.[i]

10The lips of a king speak as an
oracle,
and his mouth should not betray
justice.[j]

11Honest scales and balances are
from the LORD;
all the weights in the bag are of
his making.[k]

12Kings detest wrongdoing,
for a throne is established
through righteousness.[l]

13Kings take pleasure in honest
lips;
they value a man who speaks
the truth.[m]

14A king's wrath is a messenger of
death,[n]
but a wise man will appease
it.[o]

15When a king's face brightens, it
means life;[p]
his favor is like a rain cloud in
spring.[q]

16How much better to get wisdom
than gold,
to choose understanding[r]
rather than silver![s]

17The highway of the upright avoids
evil;
he who guards his way guards
his life.[t]

18Pride[u] goes before destruction,
a haughty spirit[v] before a
fall.[w]

19Better to be lowly in spirit and
among the oppressed
than to share plunder with the
proud.

20Whoever gives heed to instruction
prospers,[x]
and blessed is he who trusts in
the LORD.[y]

16:1 t ver 9; Pr 19:21 **16:2** u S Pr 12:15; 30:12 v S 1Sa 2:3 w S 2Ch 6:30; Pr 20:27; 21:2; Lk 16:15 **16:3** x S 2Ch 20:20; S Ps 20:4; 37:5-6; S Pr 3:5-6 **16:4** y Ex 9:16 z S 2Ch 34:24; S Ps 18:18; Ro 9:22 **16:5** a S Ps 40:4; S Pr 6:16 b Pr 11:20-21 **16:6** c S Ge 20:11; S Ex 1:17 d S Ex 20:20 **16:7** e S Ge 39:21 f Ps 105:15; Jer 39:12; 40:1; 42:12; Da 1:9 **16:8** g S Ps 37:16 h S Pr 15:16; 17:1; Ecc 4:6 **16:9** i S ver 1; S Job 33:29; S Ps 90:12 **16:10** j Pr 17:7

16:11 k S Pr 11:1; Eze 45:10 **16:12** l Pr 26:28; 25:5; 29:14; 31:5 **16:13** m Pr 22:11 **16:14** n S Ge 40:2; S Job 29:24; Pr 20:2 o Pr 25:15; 29:8; Ecc 10:4 **16:15** p S Ge 40:2; S Job 29:24 q Pr 19:12; 25:2-7 **16:16** r Ps 49:20 s S Job 28:15; S Pr 3:13-14 **16:17** t Pr 19:16 **16:18** u S 1Sa 17:42 v Ps 18:27; Isa 13:11; Jer 48:29 w S Est 5:12; Pr 11:2; S 15:33; 18:12; 29:23 **16:20** x Pr 13:13 y S Ps 32:10; 40:4; Pr 19:8; 29:25; Jer 17:7

16:1 THE REPLY OF THE TONGUE. We as humans may make plans, but the ability to carry out those plans rightly comes from God (cf. vv. 9,33; 21:31).

16:2 SEEM INNOCENT TO HIM. Believers are often blind to their own faults and their spiritual poverty. If we are honest when we come to God in prayer, he will reveal the real condition of our hearts so that we might be truly innocent and better follow the Holy Spirit (Lk 16:15; 1Co 4:4–5; Heb 4:12).

16:3 COMMIT TO THE LORD WHATEVER YOU DO. Believers should not undertake anything presumptuously, but in all things search for the Lord's will (Jas 4:14–16). If our deeds and motives are right, then we can commit them to the Lord and be assured that he will establish them and bless us (see 3:6; Ps 37:5; 90:16–17; 1Pe 5:7).

16:4 THE WICKED FOR A DAY OF DISASTER. Everything will meet with its proper end, and those who do evil will suffer God's just punishment (cf. v. 5). This passage stresses that God will deal justly with the wicked; he does not create or encourage wickedness (see Jas 1:13,17).

16:5 PROUD OF HEART. See Jas 4:6,16, notes.

16:7 ENEMIES LIVE AT PEACE WITH HIM. This verse applies to God's promise to Israel that their land would be preserved from hostile attack if they would do his will (Ex 34:24; 2Ch 17:10). NT believers, however, will experience the hostility of their enemies—Satan and the world—in many cases because they are doing God's will (cf. Mt 5:10; Lk 21:17–18; Jn 15:20; Ac 14:19).

[21]The wise in heart are called
discerning,
and pleasant words promote
instruction.[d z]

[22]Understanding is a fountain of life
to those who have it,[a]
but folly brings punishment to
fools.

[23]A wise man's heart guides his
mouth,[b]
and his lips promote
instruction.[e c]

[24]Pleasant words are a
honeycomb,[d]
sweet to the soul and healing to
the bones.[e]

[25]There is a way that seems right to
a man,[f]
but in the end it leads to
death.[g]

[26]The laborer's appetite works for
him;
his hunger drives him on.

[27]A scoundrel[h] plots evil,
and his speech is like a
scorching fire.[i]

[28]A perverse man stirs up
dissension,[j]
and a gossip separates close
friends.[k]

[29]A violent man entices his neighbor
and leads him down a path that
is not good.[l]

[30]He who winks[m] with his eye is
plotting perversity;
he who purses his lips is bent
on evil.

[31]Gray hair is a crown of splendor;[n]
it is attained by a righteous life.

[32]Better a patient man than a
warrior,
a man who controls his temper
than one who takes a city.

[33]The lot is cast[o] into the lap,
but its every decision[p] is from
the LORD.[q]

16:21 [z] ver 23
16:22 [a] S Pr 10:11
16:23 [b] Job 15:5 [c] ver 21
16:24 [d] S 1Sa 14:27 [e] Pr 24:13-14
16:25 [f] S Pr 12:15 [g] Est 3:6; Pr 14:12
16:27 [h] S Ps 140:2 [i] Jas 3:6
16:28 [j] S Pr 14:17 [k] Pr 17:9
16:29 [l] S Pr 1:10; 12:26
16:30 [m] S Pr 6:13
16:31 [n] Pr 20:29
16:33 [o] S Lev 16:8; S 1Sa 10:21; Eze 21:21 [p] 1Sa 14:41 [q] Jos 7:14; Pr 18:18; 29:26; Jnh 1:7

17:1 [r] S Pr 15:16, 17; S 16:8
17:3 [s] Pr 27:21 [t] S 1Ch 29:17; Ps 26:2; S 139:23; 1Pe 1:7
17:5 [u] S Job 5:16 [v] Pr 14:31 [w] S Job 31:29 [x] Eze 25:3; Ob 1:12
17:6 [y] S Ps 128:5-6
17:7 [z] Pr 16:10
17:8 [a] S Ex 23:8; Pr 19:6
17:9 [b] S Pr 10:12 [c] Pr 16:28

17

[1]Better a dry crust with peace
and quiet
than a house full of feasting,[f]
with strife.[r]

[2]A wise servant will rule over a
disgraceful son,
and will share the inheritance as
one of the brothers.

[3]The crucible for silver and the
furnace for gold,[s]
but the LORD tests the heart.[t]

[4]A wicked man listens to evil lips;
a liar pays attention to a
malicious tongue.

[5]He who mocks the poor[u] shows
contempt for their Maker;[v]
whoever gloats over disaster[w]
will not go unpunished.[x]

[6]Children's children[y] are a crown
to the aged,
and parents are the pride of
their children.

[7]Arrogant[g] lips are unsuited to a
fool—
how much worse lying lips to a
ruler![z]

[8]A bribe is a charm to the one who
gives it;
wherever he turns, he
succeeds.[a]

[9]He who covers over an offense
promotes love,[b]
but whoever repeats the matter
separates close friends.[c]

[10]A rebuke impresses a man of
discernment
more than a hundred lashes a
fool.

[11]An evil man is bent only on
rebellion;
a merciless official will be sent
against him.

[d] *21* Or *words make a man persuasive*
[e] *23* Or *mouth / and makes his lips persuasive*
[f] *1* Hebrew *sacrifices*
[g] *7* Or *Eloquent*

16:33 LOT IS CAST INTO THE LAP. Like vv. 1,9, this verse refers to God's providence and guidance in the life of the righteous. It does not mean that God directly controls and determines every flip of the coin in life; rather, it simply states the spiritual principle that a righteous person who commits his or her way to the Lord (vv. 3,9) and acknowledges him will be directed by the Lord (see 3:5–6, notes).

17:5 WHO MOCKS THE POOR. See 14:31, note.

17:8 A BRIBE. A bribe will sometimes bring temporary success and wealth. Bribery, however, is sin; it is therefore condemned in Scripture because it hinders justice from being realized (v. 23; 15:27; 1Sa 12:3; Isa 1:23; 1Ti 6:10).

12Better to meet a bear robbed of her cubs
than a fool in his folly.[d]

13If a man pays back evil[e] for good,[f]
evil will never leave his house.

14Starting a quarrel is like breaching a dam;
so drop the matter before a dispute breaks out.[g]

15Acquitting the guilty and condemning the innocent[h]—
the LORD detests them both.[i]

16Of what use is money in the hand of a fool,
since he has no desire to get wisdom?[j]

17A friend loves at all times,
and a brother is born for adversity.[k]

18A man lacking in judgment strikes hands in pledge
and puts up security for his neighbor.[l]

19He who loves a quarrel loves sin;
he who builds a high gate invites destruction.

20A man of perverse heart does not prosper;
he whose tongue is deceitful falls into trouble.

21To have a fool for a son brings grief;
there is no joy for the father of a fool.[m]

22A cheerful heart is good medicine,
but a crushed[n] spirit dries up the bones.[o]

23A wicked man accepts a bribe[p] in secret
to pervert the course of justice.[q]

24A discerning man keeps wisdom in view,
but a fool's eyes[r] wander to the ends of the earth.

25A foolish son brings grief to his father
and bitterness to the one who bore him.[s]

26It is not good to punish an innocent man,[t]
or to flog officials for their integrity.

27A man of knowledge uses words with restraint,[u]
and a man of understanding is even-tempered.[v]

28Even a fool is thought wise if he keeps silent,
and discerning if he holds his tongue.[w]

18 An unfriendly man pursues selfish ends;
he defies all sound judgment.

2A fool finds no pleasure in understanding
but delights in airing his own opinions.[x]

3When wickedness comes, so does contempt,
and with shame comes disgrace.

4The words of a man's mouth are deep waters,[y]
but the fountain of wisdom is a bubbling brook.

5It is not good to be partial to the wicked[z]
or to deprive the innocent of justice.[a]

6A fool's lips bring him strife,
and his mouth invites a beating.[b]

7A fool's mouth is his undoing,
and his lips are a snare[c] to his soul.[d]

8The words of a gossip are like choice morsels;
they go down to a man's inmost parts.[e]

17:12 [d]S 1Sa 25:25 17:13 [e]S 1Sa 19:4 [f]S Ge 44:4; S Ps 35:12 17:14 [g]Mt 5:25-26 17:15 [h]S Ps 94:21; S Pr 18:5 [i]Ex 23:6-7; Isa 5:23; La 3:34-36 17:16 [j]Pr 23:23 17:17 [k]S 2Sa 15:21; Pr 27:10 17:18 [l]Pr 6:1-5; S 11:15; 22:26-27 17:21 [m]S Pr 10:1 17:22 [n]S Ps 38:8 [o]S Ex 12:46; Pr 14:30; S 15:13; 18:14 17:23 [p]S Ex 18:21; S 23:8; S 1Sa 8:3 [q]S Job 34:33 17:24 [r]S Job 31:1 17:25 [s]S Pr 10:1 17:26 [t]S Ps 94:21 17:27 [u]S Job 6:24 [v]S Pr 14:29 17:28 [w]S Job 2:13; 13:5; S Pr 10:19 18:2 [x]S Pr 12:23 18:4 [y]S Ps 18:16 18:5 [z]Pr 24:23-25; 28:21 [a]S Ps 82:2; S Pr 17:15 18:6 [b]S Pr 10:14 18:7 [c]Ps 140:9 [d]S Ps 64:8; S Pr 10:14; S 12:13; S 13:3; Ecc 10:12 18:8 [e]Pr 26:22

17:13 EVIL WILL NEVER LEAVE HIS HOUSE. This truth is illustrated in David's life. He "rewarded" Uriah's integrity and faithfulness with evil. From that point on, evil never left David's own house (2Sa 12:10–12).

17:17 A BROTHER IS BORN FOR ADVERSITY. A brother is born to help us in time of need.

17:18 PUTS UP SECURITY. See 6:1, note.

17:27 A MAN OF KNOWLEDGE USES WORDS WITH RESTRAINT. The wise will restrain their speech and be cautious in what they say. They will not exaggerate the truth or harm others when speaking; rather, they will be careful to speak accurately and edify others (cf. Ps 39:1–2).

9One who is slack in his work
is brother to one who
destroys.[f]

10The name of the LORD is a strong
tower;[g]
the righteous run to it and are
safe.[h]

11The wealth of the rich is their
fortified city;[i]
they imagine it an unscalable
wall.

12Before his downfall a man's heart
is proud,
but humility comes before
honor.[j]

13He who answers before listening—
that is his folly and his shame.[k]

14A man's spirit sustains him in
sickness,
but a crushed spirit who can
bear?[l]

15The heart of the discerning
acquires knowledge;[m]
the ears of the wise seek it out.

16A gift[n] opens the way for the
giver
and ushers him into the
presence of the great.

17The first to present his case seems
right,
till another comes forward and
questions him.

18Casting the lot settles disputes[o]
and keeps strong opponents
apart.

19An offended[p] brother is more
unyielding than a fortified
city,
and disputes are like the barred
gates of a citadel.

20From the fruit of his mouth a
man's stomach is filled;
with the harvest from his lips he
is satisfied.[q]

21The tongue has the power of life
and death,[r]
and those who love it will eat its
fruit.[s]

22He who finds a wife finds what is
good[t]
and receives favor from the
LORD.[u]

23A poor man pleads for mercy,
but a rich man answers harshly.

24A man of many companions may
come to ruin,
but there is a friend who sticks
closer than a brother.[v]

19

Better a poor man whose
walk is blameless
than a fool whose lips are
perverse.[w]

2It is not good to have zeal without
knowledge,
nor to be hasty and miss the
way.[x]

3A man's own folly[y] ruins his
life,
yet his heart rages against the
LORD.[z]

4Wealth brings many friends,
but a poor man's friend deserts
him.[a]

5A false witness[b] will not go
unpunished,[c]
and he who pours out lies will
not go free.[d]

6Many curry favor with a ruler,[e]
and everyone is the friend of a
man who gives gifts.[f]

7A poor man is shunned by all his
relatives—
how much more do his friends
avoid him![g]

18:9 [f]Pr 28:24
18:10 [g]S Ps 61:3 [h]S Ps 20:1; Pr 14:26
18:11 [i]Pr 10:15
18:12 [j]S Pr 11:2; 15:33; S 16:18
18:13 [k]Pr 20:25
18:14 [l]S Pr 15:13; S 17:22
18:15 [m]S Pr 15:14
18:16 [n]S Ge 32:13; S 1Sa 10:4; Pr 19:6
18:18 [o]S Pr 16:33
18:19 [p]S 1Sa 17:28
18:20 [q]S Pr 12:14
18:21 [r]S Ps 12:4 [s]Pr 13:2-3; S Mt 12:37
18:22 [t]S Pr 12:4 [u]S Job 33:26; Pr 19:14; 31:10
18:24 [v]S 1Sa 20:42; Jn 15:13-15
19:1 [w]Pr 28:6
19:2 [x]Pr 29:20
19:3 [y]Ps 14:1; Pr 9:13; 24:9; Isa 32:6 [z]Jas 1:13-15
19:4 [a]ver 7; Pr 14:20
19:5 [b]S Ex 23:1 [c]S Ps 56:7 [d]ver 9; S Dt 19:19; Pr 21:28
19:6 [e]Pr 29:26 [f]S Pr 17:8; S 18:16
19:7 [g]Pr 10:15

18:10–11 THE NAME OF THE LORD. The name of the Lord represents his person, authority and character (cf. Ex 3:14–15; Ac 4:12). The righteous turn to the Lord for refuge and help in trouble. However, the misguided rich believe money is their source of security during life's storms (see article on RICHES AND POVERTY, p. 1562).

18:12 A MAN'S HEART IS PROUD. Pride is a spirit of self-importance that includes trusting in ourselves. Boasting and arrogance are sins associated with pride, and they will bring us to destruction (cf. 15:33; 16:18). Pride is deceptive (Jer 49:16), making a humble response to God and others impossible. God opposes the proud, but gives grace and honor to the humble (Jas 4:6).

19:4 WEALTH BRINGS MANY FRIENDS. This proverb speaks of what often is, not of the way things should be. Though superficial friends are attracted to the wealthy as flies are drawn to honey, a poor person has few friends because he or she cannot provide anyone with financial or personal gain (cf. v. 6). The NT warns against this attitude among believers (Jas 2:1–9).

Though he pursues them with pleading,
they are nowhere to be found.[h] [h]

8He who gets wisdom loves his own soul;
he who cherishes understanding prospers.[i]

9A false witness will not go unpunished,
and he who pours out lies will perish.[j]

10It is not fitting for a fool[k] to live in luxury—
how much worse for a slave to rule over princes![l]

11A man's wisdom gives him patience;[m]
it is to his glory to overlook an offense.

12A king's rage is like the roar of a lion,[n]
but his favor is like dew[o] on the grass.[p]

13A foolish son is his father's ruin,[q]
and a quarrelsome wife is like a constant dripping.[r]

14Houses and wealth are inherited from parents,[s]
but a prudent wife is from the LORD.[t]

15Laziness brings on deep sleep,
and the shiftless man goes hungry.[u]

16He who obeys instructions guards his life,
but he who is contemptuous of his ways will die.[v]

17He who is kind to the poor lends to the LORD,[w]
and he will reward him for what he has done.[x]

18Discipline your son, for in that there is hope;
do not be a willing party to his death.[y]

19A hot-tempered man must pay the penalty;
if you rescue him, you will have to do it again.

20Listen to advice and accept instruction,[z]
and in the end you will be wise.[a]

21Many are the plans in a man's heart,
but it is the LORD's purpose that prevails.[b]

22What a man desires is unfailing love[i];
better to be poor than a liar.

23The fear of the LORD leads to life:
Then one rests content, untouched by trouble.[c]

24The sluggard buries his hand in the dish;
he will not even bring it back to his mouth![d]

25Flog a mocker, and the simple will learn prudence;
rebuke a discerning man,[e] and he will gain knowledge.[f]

26He who robs his father and drives out his mother[g]
is a son who brings shame and disgrace.

27Stop listening to instruction, my son,[h]
and you will stray from the words of knowledge.

28A corrupt witness mocks at justice,

19:7 [h]S ver 4
19:8 [i]S Pr 16:20
19:9 [j]S ver 5; S Dt 19:19
19:10 [k]Pr 26:1 [l]Pr 30:21-23; Ecc 10:5-7
19:11 [m]S 2Ki 5:12
19:12 [n]Pr 20:2 [o]S Ps 133:3 [p]S Est 1:12; S 7:7; Ps 72:5-6; Pr 16:14-15
19:13 [q]S Pr 10:1 [r]S Est 1:18; Pr 21:9
19:14 [s]2Co 12:14 [t]S Pr 18:22
19:15 [u]S Pr 10:4; 20:13
19:16 [v]S Pr 16:17; S Ro 10:5
19:17 [w]S Dt 24:14 [x]S Dt 24:19; Pr 14:21; 22:9; S Mt 10:42
19:18 [y]S Pr 13:24; 23:13-14
19:20 [z]Pr 4:1 [a]S Pr 12:15
19:21 [b]Ps 33:11; Pr 16:9; 20:24; Isa 8:10; 14:24, 27; 31:2; 40:8; 46:10; 48:14; 55:11; Jer 44:29; La 3:37
19:23 [c]S Job 4:7; S Pr 10:27
19:24 [d]Pr 26:15
19:25 [e]S Ps 141:5 [f]S Pr 9:9; 21:11
19:26 [g]Pr 28:24
19:27 [h]S Pr 1:8

[h] 7 The meaning of the Hebrew for this sentence is uncertain. [i] 22 Or *A man's greed is his shame*

19:14 A PRUDENT WIFE IS FROM THE LORD. When seeking a marriage partner, prudence is more important than appearance. God's wisdom, guidance and blessing are essential if we want to have a happy marriage. A believer should seek to marry someone who is deeply committed to the Lord Jesus, his word, and the standards of his kingdom. Marriage to a person of godly character is a special blessing of God (cf. 18:22; Ge 24:14). To enter into marriage without God's guidance is to invite suffering, regret and disaster.

19:17 LENDS TO THE LORD. Graciously giving of what we have to help the poor is a way of serving the Lord. He will repay those who do this (see 6:1, note).

19:18 DISCIPLINE YOUR SON. Children should be disciplined at a young age while there is opportunity to mold their lives for good and to teach them godly ways. When parents fail to do so, they become partially responsible for subsequent ruin that comes to the lives of their children (see 13:24, note).

and the mouth of the wicked
gulps down evil.[i]

29Penalties are prepared for
mockers,
and beatings for the backs of
fools.[j]

20 Wine[k] is a mocker[l] and
beer a brawler;
whoever is led astray[m] by them
is not wise.[n]

2A king's wrath is like the roar of a
lion;[o]
he who angers him forfeits his
life.[p]

3It is to a man's honor to avoid
strife,
but every fool[q] is quick to
quarrel.[r]

4A sluggard[s] does not plow in
season;
so at harvest time he looks but
finds nothing.[t]

5The purposes of a man's heart are
deep waters,[u]
but a man of understanding
draws them out.

6Many a man claims to have
unfailing love,
but a faithful man who can
find?[v]

7The righteous man leads a
blameless life;[w]
blessed are his children after
him.[x]

8When a king sits on his throne to
judge,[y]
he winnows out all evil with his
eyes.[z]

9Who can say, "I have kept my
heart pure;[a]
I am clean and without sin"?[b]

10Differing weights and differing
measures—
the LORD detests them both.[c]

11Even a child is known by his
actions,
by whether his conduct is pure[d]
and right.

12Ears that hear and eyes that see—
the LORD has made them both.[e]

13Do not love sleep or you will grow
poor;[f]
stay awake and you will have
food to spare.

14"It's no good, it's no good!" says
the buyer;
then off he goes and boasts
about his purchase.

15Gold there is, and rubies in
abundance,
but lips that speak knowledge
are a rare jewel.

16Take the garment of one who puts
up security for a stranger;
hold it in pledge[g] if he does it
for a wayward woman.[h]

17Food gained by fraud tastes sweet
to a man,[i]
but he ends up with a mouth full
of gravel.[j]

18Make plans by seeking advice;
if you wage war, obtain
guidance.[k]

19A gossip betrays a confidence;[l]
so avoid a man who talks too
much.

19:28 [i]S Job 15:16 **19:29** [j]S Dt 25:2 **20:1** [k]S Lev 10:9; Hab 2:5 [l]S 1Sa 25:36 [m]1Ki 20:16 [n]Pr 31:4 **20:2** [o]S Pr 19:12 [p]S Est 7:7; S Pr 16:14 **20:3** [q]S 1Sa 25:25 [r]S Ge 13:8 **20:4** [s]S Pr 6:6 [t]Ecc 10:18 **20:5** [u]S Ps 18:16 **20:6** [v]Ps 12:1 **20:7** [w]S Ps 26:1 [x]Ps 37:25-26; 112:2 **20:8** [y]S 1Ki 7:7 [z]ver 26; Pr 25:4-5 **20:9** [a]S Job 15:14 [b]1Ki 8:46; Ecc 7:20; 1Jn 1:8 **20:10** [c]ver 23; S Pr 11:1 **20:11** [d]S Ps 39:1 **20:12** [e]S Ps 94:9 **20:13** [f]S Pr 6:11; S 19:15 **20:16** [g]S Ex 22:26 [h]Pr 27:13 **20:17** [i]Pr 9:17 [j]Job 20:14; La 3:16 **20:18** [k]Pr 11:14; 24:6 **20:19** [l]Pr 11:13

20:1 WINE IS A MOCKER AND BEER A BRAWLER. This verse describes the nature and potential evil of fermented drink. Note that the intoxicating drink itself is condemned along with its effects. (1) Wine as "a mocker" frequently leads to disdain for what is good (cf. 9:7–8; 13:1; 14:6; 15:12). Alcoholic beverages as "a brawler" often cause disturbances, hostility and conflict in families and society.

(2) Wine and intoxicating drinks are labeled a mocker and a brawler regardless of the quantity used.

(3) "Whoever is led astray" into thinking that intoxicating beverages are acceptable, good, healthy, or safe when taken moderately ignores Scripture's clear warning (23:29–35).

(4) This condemnation of intoxicating drinks does not mean the Bible condemns the use of all wine. *Yayin*, the common Hebrew word for "wine" in the OT, often refers to unfermented grape juice; the Bible does not condemn the consumption of unfermented wine (see 23:29–35, notes; see article on WINE IN THE OLD TESTAMENT, p. 204).

20:9 WHO CAN SAY . . . PURE . . . CLEAN. Apart from having been redeemed, no one has kept his or her heart pure and free from the guilt of sin (cf. Ro 3:9–12). Those who have come to God for forgiveness and cleansing have "clean hands and a pure heart" (Ps 24:4). Only by God's grace and redemption can anyone live a life with a clear conscience (see Ac 24:16, note).

[20]If a man curses his father or
mother,[m]
his lamp will be snuffed out in
pitch darkness.[n]

[21]An inheritance quickly gained at
the beginning
will not be blessed at the end.

[22]Do not say, "I'll pay you back for
this wrong!"[o]
Wait for the LORD, and he will
deliver you.[p]

[23]The LORD detests differing weights,
and dishonest scales do not
please him.[q]

[24]A man's steps are directed[r] by
the LORD.[s]
How then can anyone
understand his own way?[t]

[25]It is a trap for a man to dedicate
something rashly
and only later to consider his
vows.[u]

[26]A wise king winnows out the
wicked;
he drives the threshing wheel
over them.[v]

[27]The lamp of the LORD[w] searches
the spirit of a man[j];
it searches out his inmost
being.[x]

[28]Love and faithfulness keep a king
safe;
through love[y] his throne is
made secure.[z]

[29]The glory of young men is their
strength,
gray hair the splendor of the
old.[a]

[30]Blows and wounds cleanse[b] away
evil,
and beatings[c] purge the inmost
being.

21

[1]The king's heart is in the
hand of the LORD;
he directs it like a watercourse
wherever he pleases.[d]

[2]All a man's ways seem right to
him,
but the LORD weighs the heart.[e]

[3]To do what is right and just
is more acceptable to the LORD
than sacrifice.[f]

[4]Haughty eyes[g] and a proud heart,
the lamp of the wicked, are sin!

[5]The plans of the diligent lead to
profit[h]
as surely as haste leads to
poverty.

[6]A fortune made by a lying tongue
is a fleeting vapor and a deadly
snare.[k][i]

[7]The violence of the wicked will
drag them away,[j]
for they refuse to do what is
right.

[8]The way of the guilty is devious,[k]
but the conduct of the innocent
is upright.

20:20 [m]Pr 30:11 [n]Ex 21:17; S Job 18:5
20:22 [o]Pr 24:29 [p]Isa 37:20; Jer 1:19; 42:11; Ro 12:19
20:23 [q]S ver 10; S Dt 25:13
20:24 [r]S Ps 90:12 [s]S Job 33:29 [t]S Pr 19:21; Jer 10:23
20:25 [u]S Pr 10:19; 18:13; Ecc 5:2, 4-5; Jer 44:25
20:26 [v]S ver 8
20:27 [w]S Ps 119:105 [x]S Pr 16:2
20:28 [y]Ps 40:11 [z]S Pr 16:12; Isa 16:5
20:29 [a]Pr 16:31
20:30 [b]S Ps 51:2; Pr 22:15 [c]Isa 1:5
21:1 [d]Est 5:1; Jer 39:11-12
21:2 [e]S Pr 16:2
21:3 [f]S 1Sa 15:22; Isa 1:11; Mic 6:6-8
21:4 [g]S Job 41:34
21:5 [h]S Pr 10:4
21:6 [i]S Pr 10:2
21:7 [j]S Pr 11:5
21:8 [k]S Pr 2:15

[j] 27 Or *The spirit of man is the LORD's lamp*
[k] 6 Some Hebrew manuscripts, Septuagint and Vulgate; most Hebrew manuscripts *vapor for those who seek death*

20:22 I'LL PAY YOU BACK. When mistreated, we must not take vengeance into our own hands (cf. Dt 32:35; Ro 12:19; Heb 10:30). Rather, we must take our suffering to the Lord and entrust ourselves to our faithful God (cf. 1Pe 2:23; 4:19). He will in his own time avenge the injustices experienced by the righteous who cry out to him day and night (Lk 18:7–8).

20:24 HOW THEN CAN ANYONE UNDERSTAND HIS OWN WAY? God sometimes works in the lives of the righteous in such a way that they find it difficult to understand what is happening. We may be unable to see good in some circumstances, but the Bible encourages us to believe that God is nevertheless working behind the scenes for our good (see Ro 8:28, note; cf. Ps 37:23).

21:1 KING'S HEART IS IN THE HAND OF THE LORD. This verse does not mean that everything a national leader desires or does comes directly from the Lord; God is certainly not the author of the evil perpetrated by rulers (Jas 1:13–15). Rather, God has ultimate authority over the rulers of the world and at times chooses to influence their decisions so as to further his redemptive purpose in history (cf. Ex 10:1–2; Ezr 7:21; Isa 10:5–7; 45:1–6). The NT teaches that the prayers of God's people influence the Lord to direct the decisions of rulers more fully in accordance with his will (1Ti 2:1–3).

21:3 MORE ACCEPTABLE . . . THAN SACRIFICE. God wants his people to be righteous and just rather than merely to be involved in religious activities. Sacrifice, worship and offerings are unacceptable to him if we are not living according to his will (cf. Hos 6:6; Mic 6:7–8; Ro 12:1–2; Heb 10:5–9). Gifts offered to God should be accompanied by holy living; otherwise, they are detestable to him (v. 27).

9Better to live on a corner of the roof
than share a house with a quarrelsome wife.[l]

10The wicked man craves evil;
his neighbor gets no mercy from him.

11When a mocker is punished, the simple gain wisdom;
when a wise man is instructed, he gets knowledge.[m]

12The Righteous One[1] takes note of the house of the wicked
and brings the wicked to ruin.[n]

13If a man shuts his ears to the cry of the poor,
he too will cry out[o] and not be answered.[p]

14A gift given in secret soothes anger,
and a bribe concealed in the cloak pacifies great wrath.[q]

15When justice is done, it brings joy to the righteous
but terror to evildoers.[r]

16A man who strays from the path of understanding
comes to rest in the company of the dead.[s]

17He who loves pleasure will become poor;
whoever loves wine and oil will never be rich.[t]

18The wicked become a ransom[u] for the righteous,
and the unfaithful for the upright.

19Better to live in a desert
than with a quarrelsome and ill-tempered wife.[v]

20In the house of the wise are stores of choice food and oil,
but a foolish man devours all he has.

21He who pursues righteousness and love
finds life, prosperity[m][w] and honor.[x]

22A wise man attacks the city of the mighty[y]
and pulls down the stronghold in which they trust.

23He who guards his mouth[z] and his tongue
keeps himself from calamity.[a]

24The proud and arrogant[b] man—"Mocker" is his name;
he behaves with overweening pride.

25The sluggard's craving will be the death of him,[c]
because his hands refuse to work.

26All day long he craves for more,
but the righteous[d] give without sparing.[e]

27The sacrifice of the wicked is detestable[f]—
how much more so when brought with evil intent![g]

28A false witness[h] will perish,[i]
and whoever listens to him will be destroyed forever.[n]

29A wicked man puts up a bold front,
but an upright man gives thought to his ways.[j]

30There is no wisdom,[k] no insight, no plan
that can succeed against the LORD.[l]

31The horse is made ready for the day of battle,
but victory rests with the LORD.[m]

21:9 [l] ver 19; Pr 19:13; 25:24 **21:11** [m] S Pr 19:25 **21:12** [n] S Pr 14:11 **21:13** [o] S Ex 11:6 [p] S Job 29:12 **21:14** [q] S Ge 32:20 **21:15** [r] S Pr 10:29 **21:16** [s] Eze 18:24 **21:17** [t] Pr 23:20-21, 29-35 **21:18** [u] Pr 11:8; Isa 43:3 **21:19** [v] S ver 9 **21:21** [w] Ps 25:13 [x] Mt 5:6 **21:22** [y] S Pr 8:14 **21:23** [z] S Ps 34:13 [a] S Pr 10:19; 12:13; S 13:3 **21:24** [b] Jer 43:2 **21:25** [c] Pr 13:4 **21:26** [d] S 2Sa 17:27 [e] S Lev 25:35 **21:27** [f] S 1Ki 14:24 [g] S Pr 15:8 **21:28** [h] Isa 29:21 [i] S Pr 19:5 **21:29** [j] S Pr 14:8 **21:30** [k] S Job 12:13; S 15:25 [l] S 2Ch 13:12; S Job 5:13; Isa 8:10 **21:31** [m] Ps 33:12-19; Isa 31:1

[1] 12 Or *The righteous man* [m] 21 Or *righteousness* [n] 28 Or */ but the words of an obedient man will live on*

21:13 THE CRY OF THE POOR. If we want God to hear our prayers when we are in need, then we must also hear and respond in love to the needs of others (cf. Mt 25:31–46; Lk 16:19–31; Jas 2:13).

21:20 A FOOLISH MAN DEVOURS ALL HE HAS. Those who are wise and prudent will have the necessities of life, while the foolish spend all they have to acquire nonessential things for pleasure (v. 17). Today many foolishly use easy credit, which often proves to be their undoing. God is pleased with those who wisely accept a lower standard of living rather than go into debt and live beyond their means.

22 A good name is more
desirable than great riches;
to be esteemed is better than
silver or gold.[n]

2 Rich and poor have this in
common:
The LORD is the Maker of them
all.[o]

3 A prudent man sees danger and
takes refuge,[p]
but the simple keep going and
suffer for it.[q]

4 Humility and the fear of the LORD
bring wealth and honor[r] and
life.[s]

5 In the paths of the wicked lie
thorns and snares,[t]
but he who guards his soul
stays far from them.

6 Train[o][u] a child in the way he
should go,[v]
and when he is old he will not
turn from it.[w]

7 The rich rule over the poor,
and the borrower is servant to
the lender.

8 He who sows wickedness reaps
trouble,[x]
and the rod of his fury will be
destroyed.[y]

9 A generous man will himself be
blessed,[z]
for he shares his food with the
poor.[a]

22:1 [n]Ecc 7:1
22:2 [o]S Job 31:15; Pr 29:13; Mt 5:45
22:3 [p]S Pr 14:16 [q]Pr 27:12
22:4 [r]S Pr 15:33 [s]S Pr 10:27; Da 4:36
22:5 [t]Pr 15:19
22:6 [u]S Ge 14:14 [v]Eph 6:4 [w]S Dt 6:7
22:8 [x]S Ex 1:20; S Job 4:8; Gal 6:7-8 [y]Hos 8:7
22:9 [z]S Dt 14:29 [a]S Pr 11:25; S 19:17; 28:27

10 Drive out the mocker, and out
goes strife;
quarrels and insults are ended.[b]

11 He who loves a pure heart and
whose speech is gracious
will have the king for his
friend.[c]

12 The eyes of the LORD keep watch
over knowledge,
but he frustrates the words of
the unfaithful.

13 The sluggard says, "There is a lion
outside!"[d]
or, "I will be murdered in the
streets!"

14 The mouth of an adulteress is a
deep pit;[e]
he who is under the LORD's
wrath will fall into it.[f]

15 Folly is bound up in the heart of a
child,
but the rod of discipline will
drive it far from him.[g]

16 He who oppresses the poor to
increase his wealth
and he who gives gifts to the
rich—both come to poverty.

Sayings of the Wise

17 Pay attention[h] and listen to the
sayings of the wise;[i]
apply your heart to what I
teach,[j]

22:10 [b]Pr 26:20
22:11 [c]Pr 16:13; Mt 5:8
22:13 [d]Pr 26:13
22:14 [e]S Pr 5:3-5; 23:27 [f]Ecc 7:26
22:15 [g]S Pr 13:24; S 20:30
22:17 [h]S Pr 1:8 [i]S Pr 1:6; 30:1; 31:1 [j]S Pr 2:2

[o]6 Or *Start*

22:4 WEALTH AND HONOR AND LIFE. Those who remain faithful to God will receive these blessings at his own appointed time; all God's people will be among those who "inherit the earth" (Mt 5:5). Even now God's poor are considered rich in spiritual wealth and honor (Rev 2:9).

22:6 TRAIN A CHILD IN THE WAY HE SHOULD GO. Parents must commit themselves to the godly training and discipline of their children (cf. v. 15; 13:24; 19:18; 23:13–14; 29:17). (1) The Hebrew word for "train" means to "dedicate." Thus Christian training has as its purpose the dedication of our children to God and his will, accomplished by separating them from the world's evil influences and by instructing them in godly conduct. The same root word can also mean to "give or cultivate a taste for"; parents must encourage their children to seek God for themselves and thus to enjoy genuine spiritual experiences they will never forget.

(2) "He will not turn from it." The general principle is that a properly trained child will not turn from the godly ways taught by his or her parents. However, this is not an absolute guarantee that all children of God-fearing parents will remain true to God and his word. When living in an evil society where many of God's people are themselves unfaithful, the children of godly parents can be influenced to sin and to give in to temptation (see Eze 14:14–20, where God speaks of an apostasy so great that even righteous men like Noah, Daniel and Job could not save their own sons or daughters).

22:7 BORROWER IS SERVANT TO THE LENDER. Those who live beyond their means end up enslaved to their creditors (see 21:20, note).

22:9 GENEROUS MAN WILL HIMSELF BE BLESSED. God blesses those who are generous (see 11:24–25, note).

22:14 UNDER THE LORD'S WRATH. Those who turn from God, seek their own way and resent rebuke fall under God's wrath and curse. He gives them over to sexual impurity and sinful desires (see Ro 1:18–21, notes).

18for it is pleasing when you keep
them in your heart
and have all of them ready on
your lips.
19So that your trust may be in the
LORD,
I teach you today, even you.
20Have I not written thirty[p] sayings
for you,
sayings of counsel and
knowledge,
21teaching you true and reliable
words,[k]
so that you can give sound
answers
to him who sent you?

22Do not exploit the poor[l] because
they are poor
and do not crush the needy in
court,[m]
23for the LORD will take up their
case[n]
and will plunder those who
plunder them.[o]

24Do not make friends with a
hot-tempered man,
do not associate with one easily
angered,
25or you may learn his ways
and get yourself ensnared.[p]

26Do not be a man who strikes
hands in pledge[q]
or puts up security for debts;
27if you lack the means to pay,
your very bed will be snatched
from under you.[r]
28Do not move an ancient boundary
stone[s]
set up by your forefathers.

29Do you see a man skilled[t] in his
work?
He will serve[u] before kings;[v]
he will not serve before obscure
men.

23

1When you sit to dine with a
ruler,
note well what[q] is before you,
2and put a knife to your throat
if you are given to gluttony.
3Do not crave his delicacies,[w]
for that food is deceptive.

4Do not wear yourself out to get
rich;
have the wisdom to show
restraint.
5Cast but a glance at riches, and
they are gone,[x]
for they will surely sprout wings
and fly off to the sky like an
eagle.[y]

6Do not eat the food of a stingy
man,
do not crave his delicacies;[z]
7for he is the kind of man
who is always thinking about
the cost.[r]
"Eat and drink," he says to you,
but his heart is not with you.
8You will vomit up the little you
have eaten
and will have wasted your
compliments.

9Do not speak to a fool,
for he will scorn the wisdom of
your words.[a]

10Do not move an ancient boundary
stone[b]
or encroach on the fields of the
fatherless,
11for their Defender[c] is strong;[d]
he will take up their case
against you.[e]

12Apply your heart to instruction[f]
and your ears to words of
knowledge.

13Do not withhold discipline from a
child;
if you punish him with the rod,
he will not die.
14Punish him with the rod
and save his soul from
death.[s][g]

15My son, if your heart is wise,
then my heart will be glad;
16my inmost being will rejoice
when your lips speak what is
right.[h]

17Do not let your heart envy[i]
sinners,
but always be zealous for the
fear of the LORD.

22:21 [k]Ecc 12:10 **22:22** [l]S Lev 25:17; S Job 5:16 [m]S Ex 23:6 **22:23** [n]S Job 29:16; Ps 140:12 [o]Est 8:1; S 9:1; Pr 23:10-11 **22:25** [p]1Co 15:33 **22:26** [q]Pr 6:1-5 **22:27** [r]S Pr 11:15; S 17:18 **22:28** [s]S Dt 19:14 **22:29** [t]S 1Ki 11:28 [u]S Ge 41:46 [v]S Ge 39:4 **23:3** [w]ver 6-8; Ps 141:4 **23:5** [x]S Mt 6:19 [y]Pr 27:24 **23:6** [z]ver 1-3; Ps 141:4 **23:9** [a]S Pr 9:7 **23:10** [b]S Dt 19:14 **23:11** [c]S Job 19:25 [d]Ps 24:8 [e]Ex 22:22-24; Pr 15:25; 22:22-23 **23:12** [f]S Pr 2:2 **23:14** [g]S Pr 13:24; S 19:18 **23:16** [h]ver 24; Pr 27:11; 29:3 **23:17** [i]S Ps 37:1; S 73:3

[p] *20* Or *not formerly written*; or *not written excellent* [q] *1* Or *who* [r] *7* Or *for as he thinks within himself, / so he is*; or *for as he puts on a feast, / so he is* [s] *14* Hebrew *Sheol*

23:4 DO NOT WEAR YOURSELF OUT TO GET RICH. This command is repeated in the NT (Mt 6:19; 1Ti 6:9–11; Heb 13:5; see article on RICHES AND POVERTY, p. 1562).

18There is surely a future hope for
you,
and your hope will not be cut
off.[j]
19Listen, my son,[k] and be wise,
and keep your heart on the right
path.
20Do not join those who drink too
much wine[l]
or gorge themselves on meat,
21for drunkards and gluttons become
poor,[m]
and drowsiness clothes them in
rags.
22Listen to your father, who gave
you life,
and do not despise your mother
when she is old.[n]
23Buy the truth and do not sell it;
get wisdom, discipline and
understanding.[o]
24The father of a righteous man has
great joy;
he who has a wise son delights
in him.[p]
25May your father and mother be
glad;
may she who gave you birth
rejoice![q]
26My son,[r] give me your heart
and let your eyes keep to my
ways,[s]
27for a prostitute is a deep pit[t]
and a wayward wife is a narrow
well.
28Like a bandit she lies in wait,[u]
and multiplies the unfaithful
among men.
29Who has woe? Who has sorrow?
Who has strife? Who has
complaints?
Who has needless bruises? Who
has bloodshot eyes?
30Those who linger over wine,[v]
who go to sample bowls of
mixed wine.
31Do not gaze at wine when it is
red,
when it sparkles in the cup,
when it goes down smoothly!
32In the end it bites like a snake
and poisons like a viper.
33Your eyes will see strange sights
and your mind imagine confusing
things.
34You will be like one sleeping on
the high seas,
lying on top of the rigging.
35"They hit me," you will say, "but
I'm not hurt!
They beat me, but I don't feel it!
When will I wake up
so I can find another drink?"[w]

24 Do not envy[x] wicked men,
do not desire their company;
2for their hearts plot violence,[y]

23:18 [j] S Ps 9:18; 37:1-4; Pr 24:14, 19-20
23:19 [k] Dt 4:9; Pr 28:7
23:20 [l] Isa 5:11, 22; 56:12; Hab 2:15
23:21 [m] S Pr 21:17
23:22 [n] S Lev 19:32
23:23 [o] Pr 4:7; 17:16
23:24 [p] S ver 15-16
23:25 [q] S Pr 10:1
23:26 [r] Pr 5:1-6 [s] S Ps 18:21
23:27 [t] S Pr 22:14
23:28 [u] Pr 7:11-12
23:30 [v] ver 20-21; Isa 5:11
23:35 [w] Pr 20:1
24:1 [x] Pr 3:31-32; 23:17-18
24:2 [y] S Ps 2:1; Isa 32:6; 55:7-8; 59:7; 65:2; 66:18; Hos 4:1

23:29–35 MIXED WINE. These verses contain the first unambiguous commandment in God's progressive revelation that clearly forbids all his people to desire and to drink fermented wine (see next note). God instructs us here about alcoholic beverages and their corrupting influence (for an extended discussion of this issue, see article on WINE IN THE OLD TESTAMENT, p. 204).

23:31 DO NOT GAZE AT WINE. This verse warns of the danger of wine (Heb *yayin*) when it is in the process of fermentation; thus, the *yayin* spoken of in this passage must be distinguished from unfermented *yayin* (see Isa 16:10; see article on WINE IN THE OLD TESTAMENT, p. 204). Fermentation is the process whereby sugar in grape juice is converted into alcohol and carbon dioxide. (1) The word "gaze" (Heb *ra'ah*) is a common word meaning to "see, look at, examine" (cf. Ge 27:1); *ra'ah* can be used in the sense of to "choose," suggesting that fermented wine must not be looked on with desire. God instructs his people not even to think about drinking fermented wine; no allowance is made for moderate drinking. (2) The adjective "red" (Heb *'adem*) means "red, ruddy or rosy." According to Gesenius's *Lexicon*, it refers to the "sparkle" of wine in a cup, i.e., to the issue of fermentation.

23:32 IN THE END IT BITES LIKE A SNAKE. God commands his people not to gaze at wine when it is red because fermented wine destroys a person like a snake and poisons him or her like a viper. The effects of alcohol are demonic and destructive; they include bloodshot eyes, blurred vision, a confused mind, and perverse and deceitful words (vv. 29,33). Consuming alcohol opens one's life to drunkenness (v. 34), woe, sorrow, violence, strife, physical harm (vv. 29,35) and addiction (v. 35; see next note; see Ro 14:21, note).

23:35 SO I CAN FIND ANOTHER DRINK. This passage describes the addictive effects of fermented wine. Oftentimes, the one who drinks will seek more and more until he or she can no longer control the drinking. That is why God says, "Do not gaze at wine." Believers must not drink, or even think about drinking, any intoxicating beverage. This instruction is normative and authoritative for God's people today. We must not rationalize and relativize God's teaching in vv. 29–35 so that it doesn't apply to modern Christians. Beware of those who reinterpret v. 31 to mean, "Gaze at wine with self-control and moderation when it sparkles in the cup."

and their lips talk about making
trouble.[z]

3By wisdom a house is built,[a]
and through understanding it is
established;
4through knowledge its rooms are
filled
with rare and beautiful
treasures.[b]

5A wise man has great power,
and a man of knowledge
increases strength;
6for waging war you need guidance,
and for victory many advisers.[c]

7Wisdom is too high for a fool;
in the assembly at the gate he
has nothing to say.

8He who plots evil
will be known as a schemer.
9The schemes of folly are sin,
and men detest a mocker.

10If you falter in times of trouble,
how small is your strength![d]

11Rescue those being led away to
death;
hold back those staggering
toward slaughter.[e]
12If you say, "But we knew nothing
about this,"
does not he who weighs[f][g] the
heart perceive it?
Does not he who guards your life
know it?
Will he not repay[h] each person
according to what he has
done?[i]

13Eat honey, my son, for it is good;
honey from the comb is sweet to
your taste.
14Know also that wisdom is sweet to
your soul;
if you find it, there is a future
hope for you,
and your hope will not be cut
off.[j][k]

24:2 [z]Ps 10:7
24:3 [a]S Pr 14:1
24:4 [b]S Pr 8:21
24:6 [c]S Pr 11:14; S 20:18; Lk 14:31
24:10 [d]S Job 4:5
24:11 [e]Ps 82:4
24:12 [f]S Ps 139:2 [g]S 1Sa 2:3 [h]S Ps 54:5 [i]Job 34:11; Ps 62:12; S Mt 16:27; Ro 2:6*
24:14 [j]Ps 119:103; Pr 16:24 [k]Pr 23:18
24:16 [l]S Job 5:19; S Ps 34:21
24:17 [m]Ob 1:12 [n]S 2Sa 3:32; Mic 7:8
24:18 [o]S Job 31:29
24:19 [p]Ps 37:1
24:20 [q]S Job 18:5; S Pr 23:17-18
24:21 [r]Ro 13:1-5
24:22 [s]S Ps 73:19
24:23 [t]S Pr 1:6 [u]S Ex 18:16; S Lev 19:15 [v]Ps 72:2; Pr 28:21; 31:8-9; Jer 22:16
24:24 [w]S Pr 17:15

15Do not lie in wait like an outlaw
against a righteous man's
house,
do not raid his dwelling place;
16for though a righteous man falls
seven times, he rises again,
but the wicked are brought down
by calamity.[l]

17Do not gloat[m] when your enemy
falls;
when he stumbles, do not let
your heart rejoice,[n]
18or the LORD will see and
disapprove
and turn his wrath away from
him.[o]

19Do not fret[p] because of evil men
or be envious of the wicked,
20for the evil man has no future
hope,
and the lamp of the wicked will
be snuffed out.[q]

21Fear the LORD and the king,[r] my
son,
and do not join with the
rebellious,
22for those two will send sudden
destruction[s] upon them,
and who knows what calamities
they can bring?

Further Sayings of the Wise

23These also are sayings of the
wise:[t]

To show partiality[u] in judging is
not good:[v]
24Whoever says to the guilty, "You
are innocent"[w]—
peoples will curse him and
nations denounce him.
25But it will go well with those who
convict the guilty,
and rich blessing will come upon
them.

26An honest answer
is like a kiss on the lips.

24:10 TIMES OF TROUBLE. Trouble and distress will come to all of us at some time in this life (Job 7:7; Jas 1:3–4). When they do, we as believers must be strong in the Lord, look to him as our refuge (Dt 33:27) and call on him, confident that his promise never to forsake us is true (Heb 13:5). To those who faithfully trust in him, God gives sufficient strength and grace to endure the time of trouble (Isa 40:29; 2Co 12:9; Col 1:11).

24:16 A RIGHTEOUS MAN ... RISES AGAIN. When adversity, trials and setbacks occur in the lives of the righteous, they will bounce back because God's grace lifts them up (see previous note). God does not guarantee us trouble-free lives, but he does promise to sustain us no matter what happens. "We are hard pressed on every side, but not crushed; perplexed, but not in despair; persecuted, but not abandoned; struck down, but not destroyed" (2Co 4:8–9; see 4:7, note).

27Finish your outdoor work
and get your fields ready;
after that, build your house.

28Do not testify against your
neighbor without cause,[x]
or use your lips to deceive.
29Do not say, "I'll do to him as he
has done to me;
I'll pay that man back for what
he did."[y]

30I went past the field of the
sluggard,[z]
past the vineyard of the man
who lacks judgment;
31thorns had come up everywhere,
the ground was covered with
weeds,
and the stone wall was in ruins.
32I applied my heart to what I
observed
and learned a lesson from what
I saw:
33A little sleep, a little slumber,
a little folding of the hands to
rest[a]—
34and poverty will come on you like
a bandit
and scarcity like an armed
man.[t][b]

More Proverbs of Solomon

25 These are more proverbs[c] of
Solomon, copied by the men of
Hezekiah king of Judah:[d]

2It is the glory of God to conceal a
matter;
to search out a matter is the
glory of kings.[e]

3As the heavens are high and the
earth is deep,
so the hearts of kings are
unsearchable.

4Remove the dross from the silver,
and out comes material for[u] the
silversmith;
5remove the wicked from the king's
presence,[f]
and his throne will be
established[g] through
righteousness.[h]

6Do not exalt yourself in the king's
presence,
and do not claim a place among
great men;
7it is better for him to say to you,
"Come up here,"[i]
than for him to humiliate you
before a nobleman.

What you have seen with your eyes
8 do not bring[v] hastily to court,
for what will you do in the end
if your neighbor puts you to
shame?[j]

9If you argue your case with a
neighbor,
do not betray another man's
confidence,
10or he who hears it may shame you
and you will never lose your bad
reputation.

11A word aptly spoken
is like apples of gold in settings
of silver.[k]

12Like an earring of gold or an
ornament of fine gold
is a wise man's rebuke to a
listening ear.[l]

13Like the coolness of snow at
harvest time
is a trustworthy messenger to
those who send him;
he refreshes the spirit of his
masters.[m]

14Like clouds and wind without rain
is a man who boasts of gifts he
does not give.

15Through patience a ruler can be
persuaded,[n]
and a gentle tongue can break a
bone.[o]

16If you find honey, eat just
enough—
too much of it, and you will
vomit.[p]

24:28 [x]S Ps 7:4
24:29 [y]Pr 20:22; Mt 5:38-41
24:30 [z]Pr 6:6-11; 26:13-16
24:33 [a]S Pr 6:10
24:34 [b]S Pr 10:4; Ecc 10:18
25:1 [c]S 1Ki 4:32 [d]S Pr 1:1
25:2 [e]Pr 16:10-15
25:5 [f]S Pr 20:8 [g]S 2Sa 7:13 [h]S Pr 16:12; 29:14
25:7 [i]Lk 14:7-10
25:8 [j]Mt 5:25-26
25:11 [k]ver 12; Pr 15:23
25:12 [l]S ver 11; Ps 141:5; S Pr 13:18
25:13 [m]S Pr 10:26; 13:17
25:15 [n]Ecc 10:4 [o]Pr 15:1
25:16 [p]ver 27

[t]34 Or *like a vagrant / and scarcity like a beggar* [u]4 Or *comes a vessel from* [v]7,8 Or *nobleman / on whom you had set your eyes. / 8Do not go*

25:1 HEZEKIAH. Hezekiah ruled as king over Israel 200 years after Solomon (c. 715–686 B.C.); see 2 Ki 18—20; 2Ch 29—32; Isa 36—39 for information on his reign.

25:2 TO CONCEAL A MATTER. God has chosen not to reveal all things clearly (cf. Ro 11:33). He has left much concealed beneath a surface reading of the Scriptures that only those who pursue him diligently will discover. Leaders of God's people should eagerly search the depths of God's revelation in his Word (see 1Co 2:6–16).

17Seldom set foot in your neighbor's
house—
too much of you, and he will
hate you.

18Like a club or a sword or a sharp
arrow
is the man who gives false
testimony against his
neighbor.[q]

19Like a bad tooth or a lame foot
is reliance on the unfaithful in
times of trouble.

20Like one who takes away a
garment on a cold day,
or like vinegar poured on soda,
is one who sings songs to a
heavy heart.

21If your enemy is hungry, give him
food to eat;
if he is thirsty, give him water
to drink.

22In doing this, you will heap
burning coals[r] on his head,
and the LORD will reward you.[s]

23As a north wind brings rain,
so a sly tongue brings angry
looks.

24Better to live on a corner of the
roof
than share a house with a
quarrelsome wife.[t]

25Like cold water to a weary soul
is good news from a distant
land.[u]

26Like a muddied spring or a
polluted well
is a righteous man who gives
way to the wicked.

27It is not good to eat too much
honey,[v]
nor is it honorable to seek one's
own honor.[w]

28Like a city whose walls are broken
down
is a man who lacks self-control.

26

1Like snow in summer or
rain[x] in harvest,
honor is not fitting for a fool.[y]

2Like a fluttering sparrow or a
darting swallow,
an undeserved curse does not
come to rest.[z]

3A whip for the horse, a halter for
the donkey,[a]
and a rod for the backs of
fools![b]

4Do not answer a fool according to
his folly,
or you will be like him
yourself.[c]

5Answer a fool according to his
folly,
or he will be wise in his own
eyes.[d]

6Like cutting off one's feet or
drinking violence
is the sending of a message by
the hand of a fool.[e]

7Like a lame man's legs that hang
limp
is a proverb in the mouth of a
fool.[f]

8Like tying a stone in a sling
is the giving of honor to a
fool.[g]

9Like a thornbush in a drunkard's
hand
is a proverb in the mouth of a
fool.[h]

10Like an archer who wounds at
random
is he who hires a fool or any
passer-by.

11As a dog returns to its vomit,[i]
so a fool repeats his folly.[j]

12Do you see a man wise in his own
eyes?[k]

25:18 [q]S Pr 12:18 **25:22** [r]S Ps 18:8 [s]S 2Ch 28:15; Mt 5:44; Ro 12:20* **25:24** [t]S Pr 21:9 **25:25** [u]Pr 15:30 **25:27** [v]ver 16 [w]Pr 27:2; S Mt 23:12

26:1 [x]S 1Sa 12:17 [y]ver 8; Pr 19:10 **26:2** [z]S Dt 23:5 **26:3** [a]Ps 32:9 [b]S Pr 10:13 **26:4** [c]ver 5; Isa 36:21 **26:5** [d]ver 4; S Pr 3:7 **26:6** [e]S Pr 10:26 **26:7** [f]ver 9 **26:8** [g]S ver 1 **26:9** [h]ver 7 **26:11** [i]2Pe 2:22* [j]S Ps 85:8 **26:12** [k]S Pr 3:7

25:21–22 IF YOUR ENEMY IS HUNGRY. Doing good to our enemies may cause them to experience shame and eventually bring them to God and salvation (see Ro 12:20).

26:11 A DOG RETURNS TO HIS VOMIT. Peter applied this proverb to those who once followed Christ, knew the way of righteousness, and then turned back from God and his holy commands to live in sin again (2Pe 2:20–22).

26:12 WISE IN HIS OWN EYES. Pride and self-importance cause people to seem wise in their own estimation and therefore arrogantly confident in their own ideas. Wisdom and truth are formed not by human reasoning, however, but by accepting what God has said and revealed in all of Scripture. In honestly acknowledging the potential for deceit within our hearts, we must not automatically assume that our own standards of right and wrong are God's standards (see Jer 17:9, note); rather, God calls us humbly to bring all our thoughts into submission to the authority of his revelation and the ministry of the Holy Spirit (Jn

There is more hope for a fool
than for him.[l]

13The sluggard says,[m] "There is a
lion in the road,
a fierce lion roaming the
streets!"[n]

14As a door turns on its hinges,
so a sluggard turns on his
bed.[o]

15The sluggard buries his hand in
the dish;
he is too lazy to bring it back to
his mouth.[p]

16The sluggard is wiser in his own
eyes
than seven men who answer
discreetly.

17Like one who seizes a dog by the
ears
is a passer-by who meddles in a
quarrel not his own.

18Like a madman shooting
firebrands or deadly arrows
19is a man who deceives his
neighbor
and says, "I was only joking!"

20Without wood a fire goes out;
without gossip a quarrel dies
down.[q]

21As charcoal to embers and as
wood to fire,
so is a quarrelsome man for
kindling strife.[r]

22The words of a gossip are like
choice morsels;
they go down to a man's inmost
parts.[s]

23Like a coating of glaze[w] over
earthenware
are fervent lips with an evil
heart.

24A malicious man disguises himself
with his lips,[t]
but in his heart he harbors
deceit.[u]

25Though his speech is charming,[v]
do not believe him,
for seven abominations fill his
heart.[w]

26His malice may be concealed by
deception,
but his wickedness will be
exposed in the assembly.

27If a man digs a pit,[x] he will fall
into it;[y]
if a man rolls a stone, it will roll
back on him.[z]

28A lying tongue hates those it
hurts,
and a flattering mouth[a] works
ruin.

27 Do not boast[b] about
tomorrow,
for you do not know what a day
may bring forth.[c]

2Let another praise you, and not
your own mouth;
someone else, and not your own
lips.[d]

3Stone is heavy and sand[e] a
burden,
but provocation by a fool is
heavier than both.

4Anger is cruel and fury
overwhelming,
but who can stand before
jealousy?[f]

5Better is open rebuke
than hidden love.

6Wounds from a friend can be
trusted,
but an enemy multiplies
kisses.[g]

7He who is full loathes honey,
but to the hungry even what is
bitter tastes sweet.

8Like a bird that strays from its
nest[h]
is a man who strays from his
home.

26:12 [l]Pr 29:20 **26:13** [m]Pr 6:6-11; 24:30-34 [n]Pr 22:13 **26:14** [o]S Pr 6:9 **26:15** [p]Pr 19:24 **26:20** [q]Pr 22:10 **26:21** [r]S Pr 14:17 **26:22** [s]Pr 18:8 **26:24** [t]S Ps 31:18 [u]Ps 41:6 **26:25** [v]Ps 28:3 [w]Jer 9:4-8 **26:27** [x]S Ps 7:15 [y]S Est 6:13 [z]S Est 2:23; S 7:9; Ps 35:8; 141:10; Pr 28:10; 29:6; Isa 50:11 **26:28** [a]S Ps 12:3; Pr 29:5 **27:1** [b]S 1Ki 20:11 [c]Mt 6:34; Jas 4:13-16 **27:2** [d]S Pr 25:27 **27:3** [e]S Job 6:3 **27:4** [f]S Nu 5:14 **27:6** [g]Ps 141:5; Pr 28:23 **27:8** [h]Isa 16:2

[w]23 With a different word division of the Hebrew; Masoretic Text *of silver dross*

16:8–14), asking him to convict and correct us in the areas where we are wrong (cf. Rev 3:17).

27:1 DO NOT BOAST ABOUT TOMORROW. James may have had this verse in mind when he wrote, "You do not even know what will happen tomorrow. What is your life? You are a mist that appears for a little while and then vanishes" (Jas 4:14). Because of the brevity and uncertainty of life, our plans should always be contingent on what the Lord wills (Jas 4:15) and not on our assumptions. Christ applied this truth about the uncertainty of the future to the necessity of always being ready for the hour of his return (see Mk 13:35, note; Lk 12:35–40, note; 21:34, note).

9Perfume[i] and incense bring joy to
the heart,
and the pleasantness of one's
friend springs from his
earnest counsel.

10Do not forsake your friend and the
friend of your father,
and do not go to your brother's
house when disaster[j]
strikes you—
better a neighbor nearby than a
brother far away.

11Be wise, my son, and bring joy to
my heart;[k]
then I can answer anyone who
treats me with contempt.[l]

12The prudent see danger and take
refuge,
but the simple keep going and
suffer for it.[m]

13Take the garment of one who puts
up security for a stranger;
hold it in pledge if he does it for
a wayward woman.[n]

14If a man loudly blesses his
neighbor early in the
morning,
it will be taken as a curse.

15A quarrelsome wife is like
a constant dripping[o] on a rainy
day;
16restraining her is like restraining
the wind
or grasping oil with the hand.

17As iron sharpens iron,
so one man sharpens another.

18He who tends a fig tree will eat its
fruit,[p]
and he who looks after his
master will be honored.[q]

19As water reflects a face,
so a man's heart reflects the
man.

20Death and Destruction[x] are never
satisfied,[r]
and neither are the eyes of
man.[s]

27:9 [i]S Est 2:12; S Ps 45:8
27:10 [j]S Pr 17:17
27:11 [k]S Pr 10:1; S 23:15-16 [l]S Ge 24:60
27:12 [m]Pr 22:3
27:13 [n]Pr 20:16
27:15 [o]S Est 1:18
27:18 [p]1Co 9:7 [q]Lk 19:12-27
27:20 [r]Pr 30:15-16; Hab 2:5 [s]Ecc 1:8; 6:7

27:21 [t]S Pr 17:3
27:23 [u]Pr 12:10
27:24 [v]Pr 23:5
28:1 [w]S 2Ki 7:7 [x]S Lev 26:17 [y]S Ps 138:3

21The crucible for silver and the
furnace for gold,[t]
but man is tested by the praise
he receives.

22Though you grind a fool in a
mortar,
grinding him like grain with a
pestle,
you will not remove his folly
from him.

23Be sure you know the condition of
your flocks,[u]
give careful attention to your
herds;
24for riches do not endure forever,[v]
and a crown is not secure for all
generations.
25When the hay is removed and new
growth appears
and the grass from the hills is
gathered in,
26the lambs will provide you with
clothing,
and the goats with the price of a
field.
27You will have plenty of goats' milk
to feed you and your family
and to nourish your servant
girls.

28 The wicked man flees[w]
though no one pursues,[x]
but the righteous are as bold as
a lion.[y]

2When a country is rebellious, it
has many rulers,
but a man of understanding and
knowledge maintains order.

3A ruler[y] who oppresses the poor
is like a driving rain that leaves
no crops.

4Those who forsake the law praise
the wicked,
but those who keep the law
resist them.

5Evil men do not understand
justice,

[x]20 Hebrew *Sheol and Abaddon* [y]3 Or *A poor man*

27:21 MAN IS TESTED BY THE PRAISE. The praise we receive from others tests us as to how we will respond—either in pride or in humility. An attitude of pride reveals self-deception in our hearts, for we do not realize that what we are and what we have done are largely due to God and others (see Php 2:3, note). Our actions must never be done for praise or self-glory, but must flow from our commitment to God, his word, and his kingdom. When we pass the test of praise, it confirms that we are living to please God rather than other humans and that our hearts are pure and our spirits one with God.

28:5 THOSE WHO SEEK THE LORD. See

but those who seek the LORD
understand it fully.

6Better a poor man whose walk is
blameless
than a rich man whose ways are
perverse.[z]

7He who keeps the law is a
discerning son,
but a companion of gluttons
disgraces his father.[a]

8He who increases his wealth by
exorbitant interest[b]
amasses it for another,[c] who
will be kind to the poor.[d]

9If anyone turns a deaf ear to the
law,
even his prayers are
detestable.[e]

10He who leads the upright along an
evil path
will fall into his own trap,[f]
but the blameless will receive a
good inheritance.

11A rich man may be wise in his
own eyes,
but a poor man who has
discernment sees through
him.

12When the righteous triumph, there
is great elation;[g]
but when the wicked rise to
power, men go into
hiding.[h]

13He who conceals his sins[i] does
not prosper,
but whoever confesses[j] and
renounces them finds
mercy.[k]

14Blessed is the man who always
fears the LORD,
but he who hardens his heart
falls into trouble.

15Like a roaring lion or a charging
bear
is a wicked man ruling over a
helpless people.

16A tyrannical ruler lacks judgment,
but he who hates ill-gotten gain
will enjoy a long life.

17A man tormented by the guilt of
murder
will be a fugitive[l] till death;
let no one support him.

18He whose walk is blameless is
kept safe,[m]
but he whose ways are perverse
will suddenly fall.[n]

19He who works his land will have
abundant food,
but the one who chases
fantasies will have his fill
of poverty.[o]

20A faithful man will be richly
blessed,
but one eager to get rich will
not go unpunished.[p]

21To show partiality[q] is not
good[r]—
yet a man will do wrong for a
piece of bread.[s]

22A stingy man is eager to get rich
and is unaware that poverty
awaits him.[t]

23He who rebukes a man will in the
end gain more favor
than he who has a flattering
tongue.[u]

24He who robs his father or
mother[v]
and says, "It's not wrong"—
he is partner to him who
destroys.[w]

25A greedy man stirs up
dissension,[x]
but he who trusts in the LORD[y]
will prosper.

26He who trusts in himself is a
fool,[z]

28:6 [z] Pr 19:1 **28:7** [a] Pr 23:19-21 **28:8** [b] S Ex 18:21; Eze 18:8 [c] S Job 27:17 [d] S Job 3:15; Ps 112:9; Lk 14:12-14 **28:9** [e] S Ps 109:7; S Pr 15:8; S Isa 1:13 **28:10** [f] S Ps 57:6; S Pr 26:27 **28:12** [g] S 2Ki 11:20 [h] ver 28; Job 24:4; Pr 29:2 **28:13** [i] S 2Sa 12:13; S Job 31:33 [j] S Lev 5:5 [k] Ps 32:1-5; Da 4:27; 1Jn 1:9 **28:17** [l] 1Sa 30:17; 1Ki 20:20; Jer 41:15; 44:14 **28:18** [m] Jer 39:18 [n] S Est 6:13; Pr 10:9 **28:19** [o] Pr 12:11 **28:20** [p] ver 22 **28:21** [q] S Lev 19:15 [r] S Ps 94:21; S Pr 18:5 [s] Eze 13:19 **28:22** [t] ver 20 **28:23** [u] S Pr 27:5-6 **28:24** [v] Pr 19:26 [w] S Pr 18:9 **28:25** [x] S Pr 14:17 [y] Pr 29:25 **28:26** [z] S Ps 4:5; Pr 3:5

2Ch 14:4, note; 26:5, note.

28:9 HIS PRAYERS ARE DETESTABLE. God will not answer the prayers of those who have no sincere commitment to obey him and his word. To compromise our commitment to God and his word by participating in even a few sinful pleasures will render our prayers ineffective (cf. 15:29; Ps 66:18; Isa 59:2; see article on EFFECTIVE PRAYING, p. 496). Prayer without love for God's word and law is hypocrisy and is insulting to him (see 1Jn 3:22, note).

28:13 HE WHO CONCEALS HIS SINS. Those who attempt to deny their sin or keep it hidden rather than acknowledge, confess and forsake their sin will make no spiritual progress. God's forgiveness and mercy are available, however, for all who come to God in sincere repentance (see Mt 3:2, note).

28:20 A FAITHFUL MAN WILL BE RICHLY BLESSED. See Lk 24:50, note.

but he who walks in wisdom is
kept safe.[a]

27He who gives to the poor will lack
nothing,[b]
but he who closes his eyes to
them receives many
curses.[c]

28When the wicked rise to power,
people go into hiding;[d]
but when the wicked perish, the
righteous thrive.

29 A man who remains
stiff-necked[e] after many
rebukes
will suddenly be
destroyed[f]—without
remedy.[g]

2When the righteous thrive, the
people rejoice;[h]
when the wicked rule,[i] the
people groan.[j]

3A man who loves wisdom brings
joy to his father,[k]
but a companion of prostitutes
squanders his wealth.[l]

4By justice a king gives a country
stability,[m]
but one who is greedy for bribes
tears it down.

5Whoever flatters his neighbor
is spreading a net for his feet.[n]

6An evil man is snared by his own
sin,[o]
but a righteous one can sing and
be glad.

7The righteous care about justice
for the poor,[p]
but the wicked have no such
concern.

8Mockers stir up a city,
but wise men turn away anger.[q]

9If a wise man goes to court with a
fool,
the fool rages and scoffs, and
there is no peace.

10Bloodthirsty men hate a man of
integrity
and seek to kill the upright.[r]

11A fool gives full vent to his
anger,[s]
but a wise man keeps himself
under control.[t]

12If a ruler[u] listens to lies,
all his officials become wicked.[v]

13The poor man and the oppressor
have this in common:
The LORD gives sight to the eyes
of both.[w]

14If a king judges the poor with
fairness,
his throne will always be
secure.[x]

15The rod of correction imparts
wisdom,
but a child left to himself
disgraces his mother.[y]

16When the wicked thrive, so does
sin,
but the righteous will see their
downfall.[z]

17Discipline your son, and he will
give you peace;
he will bring delight to your
soul.[a]

28:26 [a] 1Co 3:18
28:27 [b] S Dt 24:19; S Pr 22:9 [c] S Ps 109:17
28:28 [d] S ver 12; S Job 20:19
29:1 [e] S Ex 32:9; S Dt 9:27 [f] Jer 19:15; 36:31; Hab 2:7 [g] S 2Ch 36:16; Pr 6:15
29:2 [h] S 2Ki 11:20 [i] Pr 30:22; Ecc 10:6 [j] S Pr 28:12
29:3 [k] S Pr 10:1; S 23:15-16 [l] Pr 5:8-10; Lk 15:11-32
29:4 [m] ver 14; S Pr 8:15-16
29:5 [n] S Job 32:21; S Pr 26:28
29:6 [o] S Job 5:13; S Pr 26:27; Ecc 9:12
29:7 [p] Pr 31:8-9
29:8 [q] Pr 11:11; S 16:14
29:10 [r] ver 27; 1Jn 3:12
29:11 [s] S Job 15:13 [t] Pr 12:16
29:12 [u] 2Ki 21:9 [v] S Job 34:30
29:13 [w] S Pr 22:2; Mt 5:45
29:14 [x] S ver 4; Ps 72:1-5; S Pr 16:12
29:15 [y] ver 17; S Pr 13:24
29:16 [z] S Ps 91:8; S 92:11
29:17 [a] S ver 15

28:27 GIVES TO THE POOR. God will take care of those who help the poor and needy (cf. 11:24–25; 14:21; 19:17; 21:26; see article on THE CARE OF THE POOR AND NEEDY, p. 1316). God's blessings abound to those who give to help meet the physical or spiritual needs of others (see 2Co 8:2, note; 9:6–8, notes).

29:1 DESTROYED—WITHOUT REMEDY. Those who repeatedly reject the clear rebuke and conviction of the Holy Spirit (Jn 16:8–11) and despise his discipline and correction (Heb 12:5–11,25) run the risk of hardening their hearts to the point of being cut off from God's mercy and of being judged by him. No one can continue in sin and reject God's grace, mercy and love without eventually suffering irreparably for it (cf. 1Sa 2:25; see article on PERSONAL APOSTASY, p. 1918).

29:7 CARE ABOUT JUSTICE FOR THE POOR. Concern for the poor and needy was revealed to Israel as God's standard of righteousness under the old covenant (see 28:27, note). True followers of Christ will likewise share his concern that the poor be treated fairly and compassionately (see Lk 6:20–21; Ac 4:34–35; 6:1–6; 20:38; 1Co 16:2; see Jas 1:27, note).

29:15 ROD OF CORRECTION. Children who are not trained, disciplined and restrained by their parents will later bring shame to them and harm to themselves. Sometimes words of rebuke alone are adequate; at other times they must be accompanied by the rod of correction (cf. v. 17; see 13:24, note). If physical discipline is used, it is important that it be accompanied by an explanation so that the child clearly understands why the rod was used and what conduct is required.

18Where there is no revelation, the
people cast off restraint;
but blessed is he who keeps the
law.[b]

19A servant cannot be corrected by
mere words;
though he understands, he will
not respond.

20Do you see a man who speaks in
haste?
There is more hope for a fool
than for him.[c]

21If a man pampers his servant from
youth,
he will bring grief[z] in the end.

22An angry man stirs up dissension,
and a hot-tempered one commits
many sins.[d]

23A man's pride brings him low,[e]
but a man of lowly spirit gains
honor.[f]

24The accomplice of a thief is his
own enemy;
he is put under oath and dare
not testify.[g]

25Fear[h] of man will prove to be a
snare,
but whoever trusts in the LORD[i]
is kept safe.[j]

26Many seek an audience with a
ruler,[k]
but it is from the LORD that man
gets justice.[l]

27The righteous detest the
dishonest;
the wicked detest the upright.[m]

Sayings of Agur

30 The sayings[n] of Agur son of Jakeh—an oracle[a]:

This man declared to Ithiel,
to Ithiel and to Ucal:[b]

2"I am the most ignorant of men;
I do not have a man's
understanding.

3I have not learned wisdom,
nor have I knowledge of the
Holy One.[o]

4Who has gone up[p] to heaven and
come down?
Who has gathered up the wind
in the hollow[q] of his
hands?
Who has wrapped up the waters[r]
in his cloak?[s]
Who has established all the ends
of the earth?
What is his name,[t] and the name
of his son?
Tell me if you know!

5"Every word of God is flawless;[u]
he is a shield[v] to those who
take refuge in him.

6Do not add[w] to his words,
or he will rebuke you and prove
you a liar.

7"Two things I ask of you, O LORD;
do not refuse me before I die:

8Keep falsehood and lies far from
me;
give me neither poverty nor
riches,
but give me only my daily
bread.[x]

9Otherwise, I may have too much
and disown[y] you
and say, 'Who is the LORD?'[z]
Or I may become poor and steal,
and so dishonor the name of my
God.[a]

10"Do not slander a servant to his
master,

29:18 [b] Ps 1:1-2; 19:11; 119:1-2 **29:20** [c] Pr 19:2; 26:12 **29:22** [d] S Pr 14:17 **29:23** [e] S Est 5:12 [f] S Pr 11:2; S 15:33; S 16:18 **29:24** [g] S Lev 5:1 **29:25** [h] S 1Sa 15:24 [i] Pr 28:25 [j] S Pr 16:20 **29:26** [k] Pr 19:6 [l] S Pr 16:33 **29:27** [m] S ver 10 **30:1** [n] S Pr 22:17

30:3 [o] S Pr 9:10 **30:4** [p] Dt 30:12; Ps 24:1-2; S Pr 8:22-31; Jn 3:13; Eph 4:7-10 [q] Isa 40:12 [r] Job 26:8 [s] S Ge 1:2 [t] Rev 19:12 **30:5** [u] S Ps 12:6; S 18:30 [v] S Ge 15:1 **30:6** [w] S Dt 4:2 **30:8** [x] Mt 6:11 **30:9** [y] Jos 24:27; Isa 1:4; 59:13 [z] Dt 6:12; 8:10-14; Hos 13:6 [a] S Dt 8:12

[z] *21* The meaning of the Hebrew for this word is uncertain. [a] *1* Or *Jakeh of Massa* [b] *1* Masoretic Text; with a different word division of the Hebrew *declared, "I am weary, O God; / I am weary, O God, and faint.*

29:18 WHERE THERE IS NO REVELATION. When there is no clear revelation and bold declaration of God's will and standards, God's people lose their Biblical convictions, cast off their moral restraints and subsequently perish (cf. Ex 32:25). God's revealed will and his righteous demands as expressed in Scripture must be repeatedly kept before the congregation, or many will begin to conform to the world (cf. Ro 12:1–2) and break God's law.

30:5 EVERY WORD OF GOD IS FLAWLESS. See article on THE INSPIRATION AND AUTHORITY OF SCRIPTURE, p. 1898.

30:6 DO NOT ADD TO HIS WORDS. God's Word must not be mixed with human ideas and speculations, such as those found in worldly philosophy, psychology, sorcery or spiritism. God's revealed truth is fully adequate to meet the spiritual needs of humankind. Those who teach that something must be added to Biblical truth in order to fulfill our lives in Christ are liars (cf. Rev 22:18; see 2Pe 1:3, note).

30:8 NEITHER POVERTY NOR RICHES. We should pray to have adequate income to meet personal and family needs, to support God's work and to give to those in need (see 2Co 9:8–12).

or he will curse you, and you
will pay for it.

11"There are those who curse their
fathers
and do not bless their
mothers;[b]
12those who are pure in their own
eyes[c]
and yet are not cleansed of their
filth;[d]
13those whose eyes are ever so
haughty,[e]
whose glances are so disdainful;
14those whose teeth[f] are swords
and whose jaws are set with
knives[g]
to devour[h] the poor[i] from the
earth,
the needy from among
mankind.[j]

15"The leech has two daughters.
'Give! Give!' they cry.

"There are three things that are
never satisfied,[k]
four that never say, 'Enough!':
16the grave,[c][l] the barren womb,
land, which is never satisfied
with water,
and fire, which never says,
'Enough!'

17"The eye that mocks[m] a father,
that scorns obedience to a
mother,
will be pecked out by the ravens of
the valley,
will be eaten by the vultures.[n]

18"There are three things that are
too amazing for me,
four that I do not understand:
19the way of an eagle in the sky,
the way of a snake on a rock,
the way of a ship on the high seas,
and the way of a man with a
maiden.

20"This is the way of an adulteress:
She eats and wipes her mouth
and says, 'I've done nothing
wrong.'[o]

21"Under three things the earth
trembles,
under four it cannot bear up:
22a servant who becomes king,[p]
a fool who is full of food,
23an unloved woman who is married,
and a maidservant who displaces
her mistress.

24"Four things on earth are small,
yet they are extremely wise:
25Ants are creatures of little
strength,
yet they store up their food in
the summer;[q]
26coneys[d][r] are creatures of little
power,
yet they make their home in the
crags;
27locusts[s] have no king,
yet they advance together in
ranks;
28a lizard can be caught with the
hand,
yet it is found in kings' palaces.

29"There are three things that are
stately in their stride,
four that move with stately
bearing:
30a lion, mighty among beasts,
who retreats before nothing;
31a strutting rooster, a he-goat,
and a king with his army around
him.[e]

32"If you have played the fool and
exalted yourself,
or if you have planned evil,
clap your hand over your
mouth![t]
33For as churning the milk produces
butter,
and as twisting the nose
produces blood,
so stirring up anger produces
strife."

Sayings of King Lemuel

31 The sayings[u] of King Lemuel—an oracle[f] his mother
taught him:

2"O my son, O son of my womb,
O son of my vows,[g][v]
3do not spend your strength on
women,

30:11 [b] S Pr 20:20 **30:12** [c] S Pr 16:2 [d] Jer 2:23,35 **30:13** [e] S 2Sa 22:28; S Job 41:34 **30:14** [f] S Job 4:11; S Ps 3:7 [g] Ps 57:4 [h] S Job 24:9 [i] Am 8:4; Mic 2:2 [j] S Job 19:22 **30:15** [k] Pr 27:20 **30:16** [l] Isa 5:14; 14:9,11; Hab 2:5 **30:17** [m] Dt 21:18-21 [n] S Job 15:23 **30:20** [o] Pr 5:6 **30:22** [p] S Pr 19:10; S 29:2

30:25 [q] Pr 6:6-8 **30:26** [r] S Ps 104:18 **30:27** [s] S Ex 10:4 **30:32** [t] S Job 29:9 **31:1** [u] S Pr 22:17 **31:2** [v] S Jdg 11:30

[c] *16* Hebrew *Sheol* [d] *26* That is, the hyrax or rock badger [e] *31* Or *king secure against revolt* [f] *1* Or *of Lemuel king of Massa, which* [g] *2* Or */ the answer to my prayers*

30:17 MOCKS A FATHER . . . A MOTHER. God requires of young people that they respect and obey their parents. To honor our fathers and mothers will bring God's blessing (Ex 20:12; Dt 5:16; Eph 6:1–3); to disobey and scorn them and their instruction will bring God's curse.

your vigor on those who ruin
kings.[w]

4"It is not for kings, O Lemuel—
not for kings to drink wine,[x]
not for rulers to crave beer,
5lest they drink[y] and forget what
the law decrees,[z]
and deprive all the oppressed of
their rights.
6Give beer to those who are
perishing,
wine[a] to those who are in
anguish;
7let them drink[b] and forget their
poverty
and remember their misery no
more.

8"Speak[c] up for those who cannot
speak for themselves,
for the rights of all who are
destitute.
9Speak up and judge fairly;
defend the rights of the poor
and needy."[d]

Epilogue: The Wife of Noble Character

10[h]A wife of noble character[e] who
can find?[f]
She is worth far more than
rubies.
11Her husband[g] has full confidence
in her
and lacks nothing of value.[h]
12She brings him good, not harm,
all the days of her life.
13She selects wool and flax
and works with eager hands.[i]
14She is like the merchant ships,
bringing her food from afar.
15She gets up while it is still dark;
she provides food for her family
and portions for her servant
girls.
16She considers a field and buys it;
out of her earnings she plants a
vineyard.
17She sets about her work
vigorously;
her arms are strong for her
tasks.
18She sees that her trading is
profitable,
and her lamp does not go out at
night.
19In her hand she holds the distaff

31:3 [w]S Dt 17:17; S 1Ki 11:3; Pr 5:1-14 **31:4** [x]S Pr 20:1; Ecc 10:16-17; Isa 5:22 **31:5** [y]S 1Ki 16:9 [z]S Pr 16:12 **31:6** [a]S Ge 14:18 **31:7** [b]S Est 1:10 **31:8** [c]S 1Sa 19:4 **31:9** [d]S Pr 24:23; 29:7 **31:10** [e]S Ru 3:11; S Pr 18:22 [f]Pr 8:35

31:11 [g]S Ge 2:18 [h]S Pr 12:4 **31:13** [i]1Ti 2:9-10

[h]*10* Verses 10-31 are an acrostic, each verse beginning with a successive letter of the Hebrew alphabet.

31:4–5 NOT FOR KINGS TO DRINK WINE. God had a high standard for the kings and rulers of his people, especially with respect to drinking fermented wine and intoxicating beverages. (1) The Hebrew literally says: "Let there be no drinking"; this passage makes no allowance for moderate drinking (see 20:1, note; 23:29–35, notes; see article on WINE IN THE OLD TESTAMENT, p. 204).

(2) The reason kings and rulers are not to drink intoxicating beverages is that they might otherwise forget what the law decrees; such drinking would weaken them morally and lead them to disobey God's law and pervert justice. This text led the Jewish rabbis to decree that a judge who drank a *renuth* (i.e., a glass of wine) was "not permitted to sit in judgment, nor in a school, or under similar circumstances permitted to teach" (Koplowitz, *Midrush*, *yayin*, p. 30).

(3) The same principle applied in the OT to priests and Levites who served before God on behalf of the people (Lev 10:8–11; see 10:9, note).

(4) All NT believers are regarded as kings and priests who rule in God's spiritual kingdom (1Pe 2:9). Therefore, God's standard for kings and priests with respect to intoxicating beverages applies equally to us (see Nu 6:1–3; Eph 5:18, note; 1Ti 3:3, note).

31:6–7 GIVE BEER TO THOSE WHO ARE PERISHING. It is improbable that the inspired writer intended to sanction or command intoxication as a way of forgetting one's troubles as death approaches. God's prescription for affliction is to turn to him in prayer, not to intoxicating drink (Ps 12; 25; 30; 34). (1) These words may be interpreted as an ironic expression that intoxicating drink is for those who have already ruined their lives and are without hope, unlike wise kings and rulers who must be total abstainers (vv. 4–5).

(2) Vv. 8–9 follow with the proper action to be taken toward those who are suffering because their rights have been violated (cf. v. 5): the righteous must defend the rights of the afflicted. To recommend drunkenness in order to help them forget their troubles would resolve no problems, but only create new ones. To attempt to alleviate problems through intoxication may be the world's way, but it is not God's way.

31:10–31 A WIFE OF NOBLE CHARACTER. These verses describe the ideal wife and mother. Her whole life is centered around a reverent fear of God (v. 30), compassion for those in need (vv. 19–20), and faithfulness and love toward her family (v. 27). All the ideals set forth here will probably not be fulfilled in any one wife and mother. But each wife can seek to serve God, her family and others with the ability and material resources that God has given her (see Eph 5:22, note; 1Ti 2:15, note).

and grasps the spindle with her
fingers.
20She opens her arms to the poor
and extends her hands to the
needy.[j]
21When it snows, she has no fear for
her household;
for all of them are clothed in
scarlet.
22She makes coverings for her bed;
she is clothed in fine linen and
purple.
23Her husband is respected at the
city gate,
where he takes his seat among
the elders[k] of the land.
24She makes linen garments and
sells them,
and supplies the merchants with
sashes.
25She is clothed with strength and
dignity;
she can laugh at the days to
come.
26She speaks with wisdom,
and faithful instruction is on her
tongue.[l]
27She watches over the affairs of her
household
and does not eat the bread of
idleness.
28Her children arise and call her
blessed;
her husband also, and he praises
her:
29"Many women do noble things,
but you surpass them all."
30Charm is deceptive, and beauty is
fleeting;
but a woman who fears the LORD
is to be praised.
31Give her the reward she has
earned,
and let her works bring her
praise[m] at the city gate.

31:20 [j] Dt 15:11
31:23 [k] S Ex 3:16
31:26 [l] S Pr 10:31
31:31 [m] Pr 11:16

ECCLESIASTES

Outline

Title (1:1)
- I. Introduction: The General Futility of Life (1:2–11)
- II. The Futility of a Self-centered Life Illustrated from Personal Experience (1:12—2:26)
  - A. The Uselessness of Human Wisdom and Philosophy (1:12–18)
  - B. The Emptiness of Pleasure and Wealth (2:1–11)
  - C. The Vanity of Great Accomplishments (2:12–17)
  - D. The Inequity of Hard Work (2:18–23)
  - E. Conclusion: Enjoyment Comes Only from God (2:24–26)
- III. Various Reflections on Life's Experiences (3:1—11:6)
  - A. Perspectives on the Created Order (3:1–22)
    1. A Time Created for Everything (3:1–8)
    2. The Beauty of Creation (3:9–14)
    3. God Is Judge of All (3:15–22)
  - B. Futile Experiences of Life (4:1–16)
    1. Experiencing Oppression (4:1–3)
    2. Competitive Work (4:4–6)
    3. Having No Friends (4:7–12)
    4. Failing to Accept Advice (4:13–16)
  - C. Warnings to the Reader (5:1—6:12)
    1. About Approaching God (5:1–7)
    2. About Accumulating Possessions (5:8–20)
    3. About Living and Dying (6:1–12)
  - D. Miscellaneous Proverbs on Wisdom (7:1—8:1)
  - E. Matters of Justice (8:2—9:12)
    1. Obedience to the King (8:2–8)
    2. Crime and Punishment (8:9–13)
    3. The Problem of True Justice (8:14–17)
    4. Ultimate Justice for Everyone (9:1–6)
    5. The Remedy of Faith (9:7–12)
  - F. More Miscellaneous Proverbs on Wisdom (9:13—11:6)
- IV. Concluding Exhortations (11:7—12:14)
  - A. Rejoice in Your Youth (11:7–10)
  - B. Remember God in Your Youth (12:1–8)
  - C. Cling to One Book (12:9–12)
  - D. Fear God and Keep His Commandments (12:13–14)

Author: Solomon

Theme: The Meaninglessness of Life Apart from God

Date of Writing: c. 935 B.C.

Background

The title of this book in the Hebrew OT is *qoheleth* (from Heb *qahal*, "to assemble"); literally, it means "one who holds and addresses an assembly." This word occurs seven times in the book (1:1,2,12; 7:27; 12:8–10) and is translated as "Teacher." The corresponding word in the Septuagint is *ekklesiastēs*, from which the English title Ecclesiastes is derived. The entire work, therefore, is a series of teachings by a well-known public speaker.

The author is generally believed to be Solomon, even though his name does not occur in this book as it does in Proverbs (e.g., Pr 1:1; 10:1; 25:1) and Song of Songs (cf. SS 1:1). Several passages, however, suggest his authorship. (1) The author identifies himself as a son of David who was king in Jerusalem (1:1,12). (2) He refers to himself as the wisest ruler of God's people (1:16) and the writer of many proverbs (12:9). (3) His kingdom was known for its wealth and affluent grandeur (2:4–9). All of these elements fit the Biblical description of King Solomon (cf. 1Ki 2:9; 3:12; 4:29–34; 5:12; 10:1–8). Furthermore, we know Solomon occasionally gathered an assembly of Israelites and addressed them (e.g., 1Ki 8:1). Jewish tradition ascribes the book to Solomon. On the other hand, the fact that his name is not explicitly recorded in Ecclesiastes (as in his other two books) may suggest that someone else was involved in putting the book together. It is best to regard the book as coming from the hand of Solomon, but perhaps as gathered together into its present form by some later person, similar to the way certain parts of the book of Proverbs were collated (cf. Pr 25:1).

Liturgically, the book of Ecclesiastes became one of the five scrolls from the third part of the Hebrew Bible, the *Hagiographa* ("Holy Writings"), each of which was read publicly each year at one of the Jewish feasts. Ecclesiastes was assigned to be read at the Feast of Tabernacles.

Purpose

According to Jewish tradition, Solomon wrote Song of Songs during his younger years, Proverbs in his middle years and Ecclesiastes during the last years of his life. The accumulative effect of Solomon's spiritual decline, idolatry and life of self-indulgence left him at the end disillusioned with pleasure and materialism as a way to happiness. Ecclesiastes records his cynical reflections about the futility and emptiness of seeking happiness in life apart from God and his Word. He had experienced wealth, power, honor, fame and sensual pleasure—all in great abundance—yet they added up in the end to emptiness and disillusionment: "Meaningless! Meaningless! . . . Everything is meaningless" (1:2). His primary purpose in writing Ecclesiastes may have been to share his regrets and his firsthand testimony with others before he died, especially with young people, so that they would not make the same mistakes he had. He establishes forever the utter futility of basing one's values in life on earthly possessions and personal ambition. Though young people should enjoy their youth (11:9–10), it is more important to commit themselves to their Creator (12:1) and to resolve to fear God and keep his commandments (12:13–14); such is the only path to meaning in life.

Survey

It is difficult to provide an orderly analysis of the contents of Ecclesiastes; no outline easily accounts for every verse or paragraph. In some ways, Ecclesiastes reads like excerpts from a philosopher's personal journal during the latter and disappointing years of his life. He begins by stating his underlying theme that all of life is meaningless and a chasing after the wind (1:1–11). The book's first major block of material is strictly autobiographical; Solomon describes the highlights of his intensely self-centered life of affluence, pleasure and worldly success (1:12—2:23). The pursuit of happiness through these means had ended for him in dissatisfaction and emptiness. The bulk of the book contains a series of random thoughts underscoring the futility and perplexity of life without God at its center.

Life "under the sun" (a phrase that occurs 29 times in the book) is life as seen through the eyes of the unredeemed, and it is characterized by inequities, uncertainties, unpredictable changes in fortune, and violations of justice. Solomon can find ultimate meaning in life only when he looks "above the sun" to God. Pleasure-seeking is superficial and foolish; one's youth is too brief and life too fleeting to be squandered foolishly. The unpredictability of life and the certainty of death cause Solomon to be cynical about God's purposes and ways. The book concludes by instructing youth to remember God while they are young, so that they do not grow old with bitter regrets and the sad task of giving an account to God for a wasted life.

Special Features

Five major features characterize Ecclesiastes. (1) It is an intensely personal book, with the author frequently using the personal pronoun "I" throughout the first ten chapters. (2) Through the underlying pessimism of the author, the book reveals that life apart from God is unpredictable and filled with meaninglessness (the word "meaningless" occurs 37 times). Solomon observes cynically the various paradoxes and perplexities of life (see, e.g., 2:23 and 2:24; 8:12 and 8:13; 7:3 and 8:15). (3) The heart of Solomon's advice in the book occurs in the last two verses: "Fear God and keep his commandments, for this is the whole ⌊duty⌋ of man" (12:13–14). (4) The literary style of the book is disjointed; its vocabulary and syntax are among the most difficult Hebrew in the OT and do not fit easily into any particular era of Hebrew literature. (5) It contains the most picturesque allegory in the Bible about a person growing older (12:2–7).

New Testament Fulfillment

Although only one passage from Ecclesiastes seems to be quoted in the NT (7:20 in Ro 3:10, on the universality of sin), yet there appear to be several allusions: Ecc 3:17; 11:9; 12:14 in Mt 16:27; Ro 2:6–8; 2Co 5:10; 2Th 1:6–7; Ecc 5:15 in 1Ti 6:7. The author's conclusion about the futility of pursuing worldly possessions was reiterated by Jesus when he said (1) that we should not store up treasures on earth (Mt 6:19–21,24), and (2) that it is senseless to gain the whole world and forfeit one's soul (Mt 16:26). The theme of Ecclesiastes, i.e., that life apart from God is meaningless and futile, sets the stage for the NT message of grace: joy, salvation and eternal life come only as a gift from God (cf. Jn 10:10; Ro 6:23).

In several ways, this book prepared the way for NT revelation in reverse fashion. Its frequent references to life's futility and death's certainty prepare the reader for God's answer to death and judgment, i.e., eternal life through Jesus Christ. Since the wisest man in the OT was unable to find satisfactory answers to life's problems through his pursuit of self-centered pleasure, wealth and accumulated knowledge, we must look for answers in One whom the NT says is "greater than Solomon" (Mt 12:42), even Jesus Christ, "in whom are hidden all the treasures of wisdom and knowledge" (Col 2:3).

Reading Ecclesiastes

In order to read the entire Old Testament in one year, the book of Ecclesiastes should be read in 4 days, according to the following schedule: □ 1–2 □ 3–5 □ 6–8 □ 9–12

NOTES

Everything Is Meaningless

1 The words of the Teacher,[a][a] son of David, king in Jerusalem:[b]

2"Meaningless! Meaningless!"
says the Teacher.
"Utterly meaningless!
Everything is meaningless."[c]
3What does man gain from all his labor
at which he toils under the sun?[d]
4Generations come and generations go,
but the earth remains forever.[e]
5The sun rises and the sun sets,
and hurries back to where it rises.[f]
6The wind blows to the south
and turns to the north;
round and round it goes,
ever returning on its course.
7All streams flow into the sea,
yet the sea is never full.
To the place the streams come from,
there they return again.[g]
8All things are wearisome,
more than one can say.
The eye never has enough of seeing,[h]
nor the ear its fill of hearing.
9What has been will be again,
what has been done will be done again;[i]
there is nothing new under the sun.
10Is there anything of which one can say,
"Look! This is something new"?
It was here already, long ago;
it was here before our time.
11There is no remembrance of men of old,[j]
and even those who are yet to come
will not be remembered
by those who follow.[k]

Wisdom Is Meaningless

12I, the Teacher,[l] was king over Israel in Jerusalem.[m] 13I devoted myself
to study and to explore by wisdom all
that is done under heaven.[n] What a
heavy burden God has laid on men![o]
14I have seen all the things that are
done under the sun; all of them are
meaningless, a chasing after the
wind.[p]

15What is twisted cannot be straightened;[q]
what is lacking cannot be counted.

16I thought to myself, "Look, I have
grown and increased in wisdom more
than anyone who has ruled over Jerusalem before me;[r] I have experienced
much of wisdom and knowledge."
17Then I applied myself to the understanding of wisdom,[s] and also of madness and folly,[t] but I learned that
this, too, is a chasing after the wind.

18For with much wisdom comes much sorrow;[u]
the more knowledge, the more grief.[v]

1:1 [a]ver 12; Ecc 7:27; 12:10 [b]S Pr 1:1
1:2 [c]Ps 39:5-6; 62:9; Ecc 12:8; Ro 8:20-21
1:3 [d]Ecc 2:11,22; 3:9; 5:15-16
1:4 [e]S Job 8:19
1:5 [f]Ps 19:5-6
1:7 [g]Job 36:28
1:8 [h]Pr 27:20
1:9 [i]Ecc 2:12; 3:15
1:11 [j]Ge 40:23; Ecc 9:15 [k]Ps 88:12; Ecc 2:16; 8:10; 9:5
1:12 [l]S ver 1 [m]Ecc 2:9
1:13 [n]S Job 28:3 [o]S Ge 3:17; Ecc 3:10
1:14 [p]Ecc 2:11, 17; 4:4; 6:9
1:15 [q]Ecc 7:13
1:16 [r]S 1Ki 3:12
1:17 [s]Ecc 7:23; 8:16 [t]Ecc 2:3,12; 7:25
1:18 [u]Jer 45:3 [v]Ecc 2:23; 12:12

[a] *1* Or *leader of the assembly*; also in verses 2 and 12

1:2 EVERYTHING IS MEANINGLESS. This verse states the theme of Ecclesiastes, i.e., all our activities on earth are meaningless and purposeless when carried out apart from God's will, his fellowship and his loving activity in our lives. The book also emphasizes that creation itself is subject to meaninglessness and corruption. (1) The author's concern is to destroy the false hopes that people place in a completely secular world; he wants them to see the solemn facts of evil, injustice and death, and to realize that life apart from God has no meaning and cannot produce true happiness.

(2) The solution to the problem is found in faith and trust in God; only this makes life worthwhile. We must look beyond earthly things into the heavenly realm to receive hope, joy and peace (3:12–17; 8:12–13; 12:13–14).

1:5–11 THE SUN RISES. The earth appears to go its own predetermined way with nothing changing. Human beings cannot look to nature to find meaning for their existence on earth, nor can they find total satisfaction in it.

1:9 THERE IS NOTHING NEW UNDER THE SUN. This verse does not mean that there are no new inventions, but only that there is no new type of activity. The pursuits, goals and desires of humankind remain the same.

1:12–18 I, THE TEACHER, . . . EXPLORE BY WISDOM. Humans cannot find purpose in life in and by themselves, nor can people use their own human achievement to set right all that appears wrong in the world (v. 15). The solution calls for something higher than human wisdom, philosophy or ideas. That wisdom is "from heaven" (Jas 3:17), "a wisdom that has been hidden and that God destined for our glory before time began" (1Co 2:7).

Pleasures Are Meaningless

2 I thought in my heart, "Come
now, I will test you with pleasure[w] to find out what is good." But
that also proved to be meaningless. 2"Laughter,"[x] I said, "is foolish. And what does pleasure accomplish?" 3I tried cheering myself with wine,[y] and embracing
folly[z]—my mind still guiding me
with wisdom. I wanted to see what
was worthwhile for men to do under
heaven during the few days of their
lives.

4I undertook great projects: I built
houses for myself[a] and planted vineyards.[b] 5I made gardens and parks
and planted all kinds of fruit trees in
them. 6I made reservoirs to water
groves of flourishing trees. 7I bought
male and female slaves and had other
slaves[c] who were born in my house.
I also owned more herds and flocks
than anyone in Jerusalem before
me. 8I amassed silver and gold[d] for
myself, and the treasure of kings
and provinces.[e] I acquired men
and women singers,[f] and a harem[b]
as well—the delights of the heart of
man. 9I became greater by far than
anyone in Jerusalem[g] before me.[h]
In all this my wisdom stayed with
me.

10I denied myself nothing my eyes
desired;
I refused my heart no
pleasure.
My heart took delight in all my
work,
and this was the reward for all
my labor.
11Yet when I surveyed all that my
hands had done
and what I had toiled to
achieve,
everything was meaningless, a
chasing after the wind;[i]
nothing was gained under the
sun.[j]

Wisdom and Folly Are Meaningless

12Then I turned my thoughts to
consider wisdom,
and also madness and folly.[k]
What more can the king's
successor do
than what has already been
done?[l]
13I saw that wisdom[m] is better than
folly,[n]
just as light is better than
darkness.
14The wise man has eyes in his
head,
while the fool walks in the
darkness;
but I came to realize
that the same fate overtakes
them both.[o]

15Then I thought in my heart,
"The fate of the fool will overtake
me also.
What then do I gain by being
wise?"[p]
I said in my heart,
"This too is meaningless."
16For the wise man, like the fool,
will not be long
remembered;[q]
in days to come both will be
forgotten.[r]
Like the fool, the wise man too
must die![s]

Toil Is Meaningless

17So I hated life, because the work
that is done under the sun was grievous to me. All of it is meaningless, a
chasing after the wind.[t] 18I hated all
the things I had toiled for under the
sun, because I must leave them to the
one who comes after me.[u] 19And who
knows whether he will be a wise man

2:1 [w] ver 24; Ecc 7:4; 8:15
2:2 [x] S Pr 14:13
2:3 [y] ver 24-25; S Jdg 9:13; Ru 3:3; Ecc 3:12-13; 5:18; 8:15 [z] S Ecc 1:17
2:4 [a] 2Ch 2:1; 8:1-6 [b] SS 8:11
2:7 [c] 2Ch 8:7-8
2:8 [d] S 1Ki 9:28 [e] S Jdg 3:15 [f] S 2Sa 19:35
2:9 [g] Ecc 1:12 [h] 1Ch 29:25
2:11 [i] S Ecc 1:14 [j] S Ecc 1:3
2:12 [k] S Ecc 1:17 [l] S Ecc 1:9
2:13 [m] Ecc 7:19; 9:18 [n] Ecc 7:11-12
2:14 [o] Ps 49:10; Ecc 3:19; 6:6; 7:2; 9:3,11-12
2:15 [p] ver 19; Ecc 6:8
2:16 [q] S Ps 112:6 [r] S Ecc 1:11 [s] Ps 49:10
2:17 [t] S Ecc 1:14
2:18 [u] Ps 39:6; 49:10

[b] *8* The meaning of the Hebrew for this phrase is uncertain.

2:1–11 PLEASURE ... PROVED TO BE MEANINGLESS. Solomon relates how he tried pleasure, wealth and cultural delights in an effort to find fulfillment and the good life; yet these things did not result in true happiness—life was still empty of satisfaction (v. 11). We can only find lasting peace, fulfillment and joy if we look for our happiness in God and his will.

2:12–17 WISDOM ... AND FOLLY. Solomon saw a temporary advantage of living wisely on earth, for the wise person has less trouble than the fool. But all advantages are canceled out at death. Thus earthly wisdom has no real permanent worth.

2:18–23 HATED ALL THE THINGS I HAD TOILED FOR. Human labor, if not dedicated to God, has no permanent value (see Col 3:23, note). Even what is left of one's possessions after death may be squandered foolishly by someone else.

or a fool?[v] Yet he will have control
over all the work into which I have
poured my effort and skill under the
sun. This too is meaningless. **20**So my
heart began to despair over all my toilsome labor under the sun. **21**For a man
may do his work with wisdom, knowledge and skill, and then he must leave
all he owns to someone who has not
worked for it. This too is meaningless
and a great misfortune. **22**What does a
man get for all the toil and anxious
striving with which he labors under the
sun?[w] **23**All his days his work is pain
and grief;[x] even at night his mind
does not rest.[y] This too is meaningless.

24A man can do nothing better than
to eat and drink[z] and find satisfaction
in his work.[a] This too, I see, is from
the hand of God,[b] **25**for without him,
who can eat or find enjoyment?[c] **26**To
the man who pleases him, God gives
wisdom,[d] knowledge and happiness,
but to the sinner he gives the task of
gathering and storing up wealth[e] to
hand it over to the one who pleases
God.[f] This too is meaningless, a chasing after the wind.

A Time for Everything

3 There is a time[g] for everything,
and a season for every activity
under heaven:

2 a time to be born and a time to
die,
a time to plant and a time to
uproot,[h]
3 a time to kill[i] and a time to
heal,
a time to tear down and a time
to build,
4 a time to weep and a time to
laugh,
a time to mourn and a time to
dance,
5 a time to scatter stones and a
time to gather them,
a time to embrace and a time to
refrain,
6 a time to search and a time to
give up,
a time to keep and a time to
throw away,
7 a time to tear and a time to
mend,
a time to be silent[j] and a time
to speak,
8 a time to love and a time to
hate,
a time for war and a time for
peace.

9What does the worker gain from his
toil?[k] **10**I have seen the burden God
has laid on men.[l] **11**He has made everything beautiful in its time.[m] He has
also set eternity in the hearts of men;
yet they cannot fathom[n] what God has
done from beginning to end.[o] **12**I
know that there is nothing better for
men than to be happy and do good
while they live. **13**That everyone may
eat and drink,[p] and find satisfaction[q]
in all his toil—this is the gift of God.[r]
14I know that everything God does will
endure forever; nothing can be added
to it and nothing taken from it. God
does it so that men will revere him.[s]

15Whatever is has already been,[t]
and what will be has been
before;[u]
and God will call the past to
account.[c]

16And I saw something else under
the sun:

2:19 [v] S ver 15
2:22 [w] S Ecc 1:3
2:23 [x] S Ecc 1:18 [y] S Ge 3:17; S Job 7:2
2:24 [z] ver 3; 1Co 15:32 [a] S ver 1; Ecc 3:22 [b] S Job 2:10; Ecc 3:12-13; 5:17-19; 7:14; 9:7-10; 11:7-10
2:25 [c] S Ps 127:2
2:26 [d] S Job 9:4 [e] S Job 27:17 [f] S Pr 13:22
3:1 [g] ver 11,17; Ecc 8:6
3:2 [h] Isa 28:24
3:3 [i] S Dt 5:17
3:7 [j] S Est 4:14
3:9 [k] S Ecc 1:3
3:10 [l] S Ecc 1:13
3:11 [m] S ver 1 [n] S Job 11:7 [o] S Job 28:23; Ro 11:33
3:13 [p] Ecc 2:3 [q] Ps 34:12 [r] S Dt 12:7,18; S Ecc 2:24
3:14 [s] S Job 23:15; Ecc 5:7; 7:18; 8:12-13
3:15 [t] Ecc 6:10 [u] S Ecc 1:9

[c] *15* Or *God calls back the past*

2:24–26 FROM THE HAND OF GOD. The author reaches two conclusions: (1) Eating, drinking and working—in fact, all activities in life—can bring satisfaction only if one has a personal relationship with God. Only he enables us to find enjoyment in life. (2) God gives true wisdom, knowledge and joy to those who in faith please him (cf. 3:12–13,22; 5:18–20; 8:15; 9:7). Thus we must see life as a gift from God and look to him to work out his purpose for us (see Php 2:13, note).

3:1–8 A TIME FOR EVERYTHING, AND A SEASON. God has an eternal plan that includes the purposes and activities of every person on earth. We must give ourselves to God as holy sacrifices, allow the Holy Spirit to accomplish God's plan for us, and be careful not to be out of God's will and miss his timing and purpose for our lives (see Ro 12:1–2, notes).

3:11 SET ETERNITY IN THE HEARTS OF MEN. God has placed within the human heart an inherent desire for more than just the earthly. Human beings want to live forever and find eternal value in the world and the activities of life. Consequently, material things, secular activities and the pleasures of this earth will never fully satisfy.

3:13 THE GIFT OF GOD. The ability to enjoy life and live it properly is a gift from God that comes only when we are brought into a right relationship with him and sincerely submit ourselves to him as our Lord and God. He then gives us joy in what we do.

3:16–17 WICKEDNESS WAS THERE. In this

In the place of
judgment—wickedness was there,
in the place of
justice—wickedness was there.

17I thought in my heart,

"God will bring to judgment[v]
both the righteous and the wicked,
for there will be a time for every activity,
a time for every deed."[w]

18I also thought, "As for men, God
tests them so that they may see that
they are like the animals.[x] 19Man's
fate[y] is like that of the animals; the
same fate awaits them both: As one
dies, so dies the other. All have the
same breath[d]; man has no advantage
over the animal. Everything is meaningless. 20All go to the same place; all
come from dust, and to dust all return.[z] 21Who knows if the spirit of
man rises upward[a] and if the spirit of
the animal[e] goes down into the
earth?"

22So I saw that there is nothing better for a man than to enjoy his work,[b]
because that is his lot.[c] For who can
bring him to see what will happen after
him?

Oppression, Toil, Friendlessness

4 Again I looked and saw all the oppression[d] that was taking place under the sun:

I saw the tears of the oppressed—
and they have no comforter;
power was on the side of their oppressors—
and they have no comforter.[e]
2And I declared that the dead,[f]
who had already died,
are happier than the living,
who are still alive.[g]
3But better than both
is he who has not yet been,[h]
who has not seen the evil
that is done under the sun.[i]

4And I saw that all labor and all
achievement spring from man's envy of
his neighbor. This too is meaningless,
a chasing after the wind.[j]

5The fool folds his hands[k]
and ruins himself.
6Better one handful with tranquillity
than two handfuls with toil[l]
and chasing after the wind.

7Again I saw something meaningless under the sun:

8There was a man all alone;
he had neither son nor brother.
There was no end to his toil,
yet his eyes were not content[m]
with his wealth.
"For whom am I toiling," he asked,
"and why am I depriving myself
of enjoyment?"
This too is meaningless—
a miserable business!

9Two are better than one,

[d] 19 Or *spirit* [e] 21 Or *Who knows the spirit of man, which rises upward, or the spirit of the animal, which*

3:17 [v] S Job 19:29; Ecc 11:9; 12:14 [w] ver 1 **3:18** [x] S Ps 73:22 **3:19** [y] S Ecc 2:14 **3:20** [z] S Ge 2:7; S Job 34:15 **3:21** [a] Ecc 12:7 **3:22** [b] S Ecc 2:24 [c] S Job 31:2 **4:1** [d] S Ps 12:5 [e] La 1:16 **4:2** [f] Jer 20:17-18; 22:10 [g] S Job 3:17; S 10:18 **4:3** [h] S Job 3:16 [i] S Job 3:22 **4:4** [j] S Ecc 1:14 **4:5** [k] S Pr 6:10 **4:6** [l] Pr 15:16-17; S 16:8 **4:8** [m] Pr 27:20

world the perfection of God's purposes is marred by injustice and wickedness. But, Solomon adds, we can be assured that God will, in his own time, judge the wicked and reward the righteous (cf. Ro 2:5–11).

3:19 SO DIES THE OTHER. Biologically, humans die just like the animals; this fact shows our weakness and frailty and should cause us to fear and obey God (12:13).

3:21 SPIRIT OF MAN RISES UPWARD. By physical observation no one can determine if a person's spirit goes "upward." Solomon revealed the meaning of this verse when he said in 12:7: "the spirit returns to God who gave it" (cf. Ps 16:9–11; 49:15; 73:23–26; Isa 26:19; Da 12:2–3).

4:1 THEY HAVE NO COMFORTER. Looking around at a world that was rejecting God's ways, Solomon saw oppression everywhere, and the oppressed had no comforter. It is still true that there is much oppression in the world—but comfort is available, for our God is "the God of all comfort" (2Co 1:3). God the Father comforted his people in OT times when they looked to him (Ps 86:17; Isa 51:3,12), Jesus brought comfort and healing while on earth (Mt 9:22) and the Holy Spirit was promised as another Counselor who stands by us to give comfort (Jn 14:16). Believers are also instructed to comfort one another (2Co 1:4).

4:4–8 ONE HANDFUL WITH TRANQUILITY THAN TWO HANDFULS WITH TOIL. Hard work and the development of skill are often spurred on by jealous rivalry with one's neighbor and the spirit of selfish competition; those motivations are self-destructive (v. 5). God wants us instead to seek a life of moderation—to do good work and to live in a quiet, godly manner. We must work together (v. 9) and help each other (vv. 10–11).

4:9–12 TWO ARE BETTER THAN ONE. Companionship has many advantages, for God did not create us to live without fellowship (Ge 2:18). We all need the love, help and support of friends, fami-

because they have a good return
for their work:
[10]If one falls down,
his friend can help him up.
But pity the man who falls
and has no one to help him up!
[11]Also, if two lie down together,
they will keep warm.
But how can one keep warm
alone?
[12]Though one may be overpowered,
two can defend themselves.
A cord of three strands is not
quickly broken.

Advancement Is Meaningless

[13]Better a poor but wise youth than
an old but foolish king who no longer
knows how to take warning. [14]The
youth may have come from prison to
the kingship, or he may have been born
in poverty within his kingdom. [15]I saw
that all who lived and walked under the
sun followed the youth, the king's successor. [16]There was no end to all the
people who were before them. But
those who came later were not pleased
with the successor. This too is meaningless, a chasing after the wind.

Stand in Awe of God

5 Guard your steps when you go to
the house of God. Go near to listen
rather than to offer the sacrifice of
fools, who do not know that they do
wrong.

[2]Do not be quick with your mouth,
do not be hasty in your heart
to utter anything before God.[n]
God is in heaven
and you are on earth,
so let your words be few.[o]
[3]As a dream[p] comes when there
are many cares,
so the speech of a fool when
there are many words.[q]

[4]When you make a vow to God, do
not delay in fulfilling it.[r] He has no
pleasure in fools; fulfill your vow.[s] [5]It
is better not to vow than to make a vow
and not fulfill it.[t] [6]Do not let your
mouth lead you into sin. And do not
protest to the ⌞temple⌟ messenger, "My
vow was a mistake." Why should God
be angry at what you say and destroy
the work of your hands? [7]Much dreaming and many words are meaningless.
Therefore stand in awe of God.[u]

Riches Are Meaningless

[8]If you see the poor oppressed[v] in
a district, and justice and rights denied, do not be surprised at such
things; for one official is eyed by a
higher one, and over them both are others higher still. [9]The increase from the
land is taken by all; the king himself
profits from the fields.

[10]Whoever loves money never has
money enough;
whoever loves wealth is never
satisfied with his income.
This too is meaningless.
[11]As goods increase,
so do those who consume them.

5:2 [n] S Jdg 11:35 [o] S Job 6:24; S Pr 20:25 **5:3** [p] S Job 20:8 [q] Ecc 10:14 **5:4** [r] S Dt 23:21; S Jdg 11:35; Ps 119:60 [s] S Nu 30:2; Ps 66:13-14 **5:5** [t] Nu 30:2-4; Jnh 2:9 **5:7** [u] Ecc 3:14 **5:8** [v] S Ps 12:5

ly and fellow believers (Ac 2:42); yet even this is insufficient without the daily companionship of God the Father, the Son and the Holy Spirit (1Co 1:9; 2Co 13:14; Php 2:1; 1Jn 1:3,6–7).

4:13–16 THOSE WHO CAME LATER WERE NOT PLEASED. This contrast between a wise youth and a foolish old king who refuses advice shows how sad it is when a ruler becomes arrogant and no longer knows how to be the servant-leader of his people (v. 13).

5:1 GUARD YOUR STEPS WHEN YOU GO TO THE HOUSE OF GOD. Entering God's house should be done reverently rather than carelessly. Be spiritually prepared before coming; then be ready to hear and obey what you hear.

5:4–6 FULFILL YOUR VOW. A vow is a solemn promise to God that must be kept. NT believers make a vow to live separated from sin and dedicated to God when they participate in the Lord's Supper (see 1Co 11:20, note). To seek the pleasures of sin after making this vow to God brings his anger and judgment, for it means that the vow was really a lie. Lying to God may bring severe punishment (e.g., Ananias and Sapphira, see Ac 5:1–11).

5:8 OTHERS STILL HIGHER. Observing again the oppression of the poor and the prevailing lack of justice, Solomon reminds the oppressors that God is the highest Judge. He is above everyone, and he will give the final verdict on the judgment day.

5:10–17 WHOEVER LOVES MONEY NEVER HAS MONEY ENOUGH. Money and the abundance of material things do not give life meaning and thus cannot bring real happiness. In general, the honest working person who comes in after a good day's work sleeps peacefully, while wealthy individuals can't sleep for fear that some calamity or a mistake on their part will cause them to lose everything. But even if they do not lose anything, they will take nothing with them when they die. It is sad that so many people work so hard for an abundance of possessions when it is much better to store up treasures in heaven (Mt 6:19–21).

And what benefit are they to the
owner
except to feast his eyes on
them?
12The sleep of a laborer is sweet,
whether he eats little or much,
but the abundance of a rich man
permits him no sleep.[w]

13I have seen a grievous evil under
the sun:[x]

wealth hoarded to the harm of its
owner,
14 or wealth lost through some
misfortune,
so that when he has a son
there is nothing left for him.
15Naked a man comes from his
mother's womb,
and as he comes, so he
departs.[y]
He takes nothing from his labor[z]
that he can carry in his hand.[a]

16This too is a grievous evil:

As a man comes, so he departs,
and what does he gain,
since he toils for the wind?[b]
17All his days he eats in darkness,
with great frustration, affliction
and anger.

18Then I realized that it is good and
proper for a man to eat and drink,[c]
and to find satisfaction in his toilsome
labor[d] under the sun during the few
days of life God has given him—for
this is his lot. 19Moreover, when God
gives any man wealth and possessions,[e] and enables him to enjoy
them,[f] to accept his lot[g] and be happy in his work—this is a gift of God.[h]
20He seldom reflects on the days of his
life, because God keeps him occupied
with gladness of heart.[i]

5:12 [w]Job 20:20
5:13 [x]Ecc 6:1-2
5:15 [y]S Job 1:21 [z]Ps 49:17; 1Ti 6:7 [a]Ecc 1:3
5:16 [b]S Ecc 1:3
5:18 [c]S Ecc 2:3 [d]Ecc 2:10,24
5:19 [e]S 1Ch 29:12 [f]Ecc 6:2 [g]S Job 31:2 [h]S Ecc 2:24
5:20 [i]S Dt 12:7, 18

6:2 [j]Ecc 5:19 [k]Ecc 5:13
6:3 [l]S Job 3:16 [m]S Job 3:3
6:6 [n]Ecc 2:14
6:7 [o]S Pr 27:20
6:8 [p]S Ecc 2:15
6:9 [q]S Ecc 1:14
6:10 [r]Ecc 3:15

6 I have seen another evil under the
sun, and it weighs heavily on men:
2God gives a man wealth, possessions
and honor, so that he lacks nothing his
heart desires, but God does not enable
him to enjoy them,[j] and a stranger enjoys them instead. This is meaningless, a grievous evil.[k]
3A man may have a hundred children
and live many years; yet no matter how
long he lives, if he cannot enjoy his
prosperity and does not receive proper
burial, I say that a stillborn[l] child is
better off than he.[m] 4It comes without
meaning, it departs in darkness, and in
darkness its name is shrouded.
5Though it never saw the sun or knew
anything, it has more rest than does
that man— 6even if he lives a thousand years twice over but fails to enjoy
his prosperity. Do not all go to the
same place?[n]
7All man's efforts are for his
mouth,
yet his appetite is never
satisfied.[o]
8What advantage has a wise man
over a fool?[p]
What does a poor man gain
by knowing how to conduct
himself before others?
9Better what the eye sees
than the roving of the appetite.
This too is meaningless,
a chasing after the wind.[q]

10Whatever exists has already been
named,[r]
and what man is has been
known;
no man can contend
with one who is stronger than
he.
11The more the words,
the less the meaning,

5:18–20 BE HAPPY IN HIS WORK—THIS IS A GIFT OF GOD. When God allows us to enjoy our work and to gain in a just manner more than we need for our necessities, we must consider that what we have is a gift from God to be used to help others and to advance God's cause on earth.
6:2 A STRANGER ENJOYS THEM. A person may have everything he or she needs to enjoy life, but still be unable to do so. The ability to enjoy what we have depends on a right relationship with God. If we are committed to him and to his kingdom, God will enable us to enjoy his material gifts.
6:3–6 IF HE LIVES A THOUSAND YEARS TWICE OVER. Death at an early age is sad; however, long life does not guarantee that a person will enjoy what God has given him or her. A life filled with trouble makes people wish they had died at birth and avoided all the suffering (cf. Job 3). In the light of eternity, the important thing is whether we live our lives for God (cf. 12:13–14).
6:10 NO MAN CAN CONTEND WITH ONE WHO IS STRONGER THAN HE. Almighty God knows everything that exists, and he knows all about us as human beings. How foolish it is to contend with him. We ourselves often do not know what is good for us, nor do we know what will happen after we die. How much better it is to trust God and humbly live for him.

and how does that profit
anyone?

12For who knows what is good for a
man in life, during the few and meaningless days[s] he passes through like
a shadow?[t] Who can tell him what
will happen under the sun after he is
gone?

Wisdom

7 A good name is better than fine
perfume,[u]
and the day of death better than
the day of birth.[v]
2It is better to go to a house of
mourning
than to go to a house of
feasting,
for death[w] is the destiny[x] of
every man;
the living should take this to
heart.
3Sorrow is better than laughter,[y]
because a sad face is good for
the heart.
4The heart of the wise is in the
house of mourning,
but the heart of fools is in the
house of pleasure.[z]
5It is better to heed a wise man's
rebuke[a]
than to listen to the song of
fools.
6Like the crackling of thorns[b]
under the pot,
so is the laughter[c] of fools.
This too is meaningless.
7Extortion turns a wise man into a
fool,
and a bribe[d] corrupts the heart.

6:12 [s]S Job 10:20; S 20:8 [t]S 1Ch 29:15; S Job 14:2; S Ps 39:6 **7:1** [u]Pr 22:1; SS 1:3 [v]S Job 10:18 **7:2** [w]S Pr 11:19 [x]S Ecc 2:14 **7:3** [y]S Pr 14:13 **7:4** [z]S Ecc 2:1; Jer 16:8 **7:5** [a]S Pr 13:18; 15:31-32 **7:6** [b]S Ps 58:9 [c]S Pr 14:13 **7:7** [d]S Ex 18:21; S 23:8

7:8 [e]Pr 14:29 **7:9** [f]S Mt 5:22 [g]S Pr 14:29 **7:10** [h]S Ps 77:5 **7:11** [i]Ecc 2:13 [j]Ecc 11:7 **7:13** [k]Ecc 2:24 [l]Ecc 1:15 **7:14** [m]S Job 1:21; S Ecc 2:24 **7:15** [n]S Job 7:7 [o]S Job 21:7; Ecc 8:12-14; Jer 12:1

8The end of a matter is better than
its beginning,
and patience[e] is better than
pride.
9Do not be quickly provoked[f] in
your spirit,
for anger resides in the lap of
fools.[g]
10Do not say, "Why were the old
days[h] better than these?"
For it is not wise to ask such
questions.
11Wisdom, like an inheritance, is a
good thing[i]
and benefits those who see the
sun.[j]
12Wisdom is a shelter
as money is a shelter,
but the advantage of knowledge is
this:
that wisdom preserves the life of
its possessor.

13Consider what God has done:[k]

Who can straighten
what he has made crooked?[l]
14When times are good, be happy;
but when times are bad,
consider:
God has made the one
as well as the other.[m]
Therefore, a man cannot discover
anything about his future.

15In this meaningless life[n] of mine
I have seen both of these:

a righteous man perishing in his
righteousness,
and a wicked man living long in
his wickedness.[o]
16Do not be overrighteous,

7:1 A GOOD NAME IS BETTER THAN FINE PERFUME. A good name means more than good social standing; it represents genuine goodness of character. Such a person has a more permanent influence on others than the person who is concerned only about social status.

7:1 THE DAY OF DEATH. The day of a believer's death is better than the day of his or her birth, for it marks the beginning of a far better life with God (2Co 5:1–10; Php 1:21–23; see article on DEATH, p. 732).

7:2–6 SORROW IS BETTER THAN LAUGHTER. Solomon contrasts the sober effects of sorrow and the grief caused by a wise rebuke with the silly laughter and frivolous joking of fools. Those who are reprimanded may feel sad, but such sorrow often results in their repentance. Because they are now confronted with the real issues of life, such sorrow is better than laughter and "good times."

7:8–14 CONSIDER WHAT GOD HAS DONE. Solomon calls for persevering toward God-given goals (cf. Php 3:13–14) while accepting the path God provides, whether it seems rough or smooth. By acknowledging that God is at work in us, we can rejoice in prosperity and learn to trust God in adversity. Like the apostle Paul we must learn to be content—whether living in plenty or in want (Php 4:12).

7:16 DO NOT BE OVERRIGHTEOUS, NEITHER BE OVERWISE. This verse must be interpreted in the light of Pr 3:7, "Do not be wise in your own eyes; fear the LORD and shun evil." Those who depend on their own good deeds for salvation and those who imagine themselves to be wise will only destroy themselves. We need true righteousness from God to regenerate our hearts and true wisdom from the Holy Spirit

neither be overwise—
why destroy yourself?
17Do not be overwicked,
and do not be a fool—
why die before your time?[p]
18It is good to grasp the one
and not let go of the other.
The man who fears God[q] will
avoid all ⌞extremes⌟.[f]

19Wisdom[r] makes one wise man
more powerful[s]
than ten rulers in a city.

20There is not a righteous man[t] on
earth
who does what is right and
never sins.[u]

21Do not pay attention to every word
people say,
or you[v] may hear your servant
cursing you—
22for you know in your heart
that many times you yourself
have cursed others.

23All this I tested by wisdom and I
said,

"I am determined to be wise"[w]—
but this was beyond me.
24Whatever wisdom may be,
it is far off and most profound—
who can discover it?[x]
25So I turned my mind to
understand,
to investigate and to search out
wisdom and the scheme of
things[y]
and to understand the stupidity of
wickedness
and the madness of folly.[z]

26I find more bitter than death
the woman who is a snare,[a]
whose heart is a trap
and whose hands are chains.
The man who pleases God will
escape her,
but the sinner she will
ensnare.[b]

27"Look," says the Teacher,[g][c]
"this is what I have discovered:

"Adding one thing to another to
discover the scheme of
things—
28 while I was still searching
but not finding—
I found one ⌞upright⌟ man among a
thousand,
but not one ⌞upright⌟ woman[d]
among them all.
29This only have I found:
God made mankind upright,
but men have gone in search of
many schemes."

8 Who is like the wise man?
Who knows the explanation of
things?
Wisdom brightens a man's face
and changes its hard
appearance.

Obey the King

2Obey the king's command, I say,
because you took an oath before God.
3Do not be in a hurry to leave the
king's presence.[e] Do not stand up for
a bad cause, for he will do whatever he
pleases. 4Since a king's word is supreme, who can say to him, "What are
you doing?[f]"

5Whoever obeys his command will
come to no harm,
and the wise heart will know the
proper time and procedure.
6For there is a proper time and
procedure for every
matter,[g]
though a man's misery weighs
heavily upon him.

7Since no man knows the future,

7:17 [p]Job 15:32
7:18 [q]S Ecc 3:14
7:19 [r]S Ecc 2:13 [s]S Pr 8:14
7:20 [t]S Ps 14:3 [u]S 2Ch 6:36; S Job 4:17; S Pr 20:9; Ro 3:12
7:21 [v]Pr 30:10
7:23 [w]S Ecc 1:17
7:24 [x]S Job 28:12
7:25 [y]S Job 28:3 [z]S Ecc 1:17
7:26 [a]S Ex 10:7; S Jdg 14:15 [b]S Pr 2:16-19; 5:3-5; S 7:23; 22:14
7:27 [c]S Ecc 1:1
7:28 [d]1Ki 11:3
8:3 [e]Ecc 10:4
8:4 [f]Est 1:19
8:6 [g]Ecc 3:1

[f]18 Or *will follow them both* [g]27 Or *leader of the assembly*

to understand God's Word.

7:20–22 WHO DOES WHAT IS RIGHT AND NEVER SINS. This verse does not contradict God's statement about Job's blamelessness (see Job 1:8; 2:3); rather, it states the truth that "all have sinned and fall short of the glory of God" (Ro 3:23; cf. 3:10–18).

7:23–28 DETERMINED TO BE WISE—BUT THIS WAS BEYOND ME. Those who seek wisdom by their own efforts and reasoning fail to find it. The hindrance comes from "the woman" (v. 26), who is the personification of the seduction of immorality and wickedness. She is the exact opposite of the woman personified as wisdom in Pr 8:1–4. Sinners cannot find wisdom because they are ensnared by wickedness, but those who please God by their faith and obedience receive God's wisdom and escape a life of sin.

8:2 OBEY THE KING'S COMMAND. The king here represents human government as instituted by God. Government officials who follow God's principles of living encourage righteous living. Our Lord wants us to obey the just laws of government (cf. Tit 3:1; 1Pe 2:13–18; see Ro 13:1, note).

who can tell him what is to
come?
[8]No man has power over the wind
to contain it[h];
so no one has power over the
day of his death.
As no one is discharged in time of
war,
so wickedness will not release
those who practice it.

[9]All this I saw, as I applied my mind
to everything done under the sun.
There is a time when a man lords it
over others to his own[i] hurt. [10]Then
too, I saw the wicked buried[h]—those
who used to come and go from the holy
place and receive praise[j] in the city
where they did this. This too is meaningless.
[11]When the sentence for a crime is
not quickly carried out, the hearts of
the people are filled with schemes to
do wrong. [12]Although a wicked man
commits a hundred crimes and still
lives a long time, I know that it will go
better[i] with God-fearing men,[j] who
are reverent before God.[k] [13]Yet because the wicked do not fear God,[l] it
will not go well with them, and their
days[m] will not lengthen like a shadow.
[14]There is something else meaningless that occurs on earth: righteous
men who get what the wicked deserve,
and wicked men who get what the righteous deserve.[n] This too, I say, is
meaningless.[o] [15]So I commend the
enjoyment of life[p], because nothing is
better for a man under the sun than to
eat and drink[q] and be glad.[r] Then joy
will accompany him in his work all the
days of the life God has given him under the sun.
[16]When I applied my mind to know
wisdom[s] and to observe man's labor
on earth[t]—his eyes not seeing sleep
day or night— [17]then I saw all that
God has done.[u] No one can comprehend what goes on under the sun. Despite all his efforts to search it out,
man cannot discover its meaning. Even
if a wise man claims he knows, he cannot really comprehend it.[v]

A Common Destiny for All

9 So I reflected on all this and concluded that the righteous and the
wise and what they do are in God's
hands, but no man knows whether love
or hate awaits him.[w] [2]All share a common destiny—the righteous and the
wicked, the good and the bad,[k] the
clean and the unclean, those who offer
sacrifices and those who do not.

As it is with the good man,
so with the sinner;
as it is with those who take oaths,
so with those who are afraid to
take them.[x]

[3]This is the evil in everything that
happens under the sun: The same destiny overtakes all.[y] The hearts of
men, moreover, are full of evil and
there is madness in their hearts while
they live,[z] and afterward they join the
dead.[a] [4]Anyone who is among the living has hope[l]—even a live dog is better off than a dead lion!

[5]For the living know that they will
die,
but the dead know nothing;[b]
they have no further reward,
and even the memory of them[c]
is forgotten.[d]
[6]Their love, their hate
and their jealousy have long
since vanished;
never again will they have a part
in anything that happens under
the sun.[e]

[7]Go, eat your food with gladness,

8:10 [h] S Ecc 1:11 **8:12** [i] S Dt 12:28 [j] S Ex 1:20 [k] Ecc 3:14 **8:13** [l] Ecc 3:14 [m] Dt 4:40; Job 5:26; Ps 34:12; Isa 65:20 **8:14** [n] S Job 21:7 [o] S Ecc 7:15 **8:15** [p] S Ps 42:8 [q] S Ex 32:6; S Ecc 2:3 [r] S Ecc 2:1 **8:16** [s] S Ecc 1:17 [t] Ecc 1:13 **8:17** [u] S Job 28:3 [v] S Job 28:23; Ro 11:33 **9:1** [w] Ecc 10:14 **9:2** [x] Job 9:22; Ecc 2:14 **9:3** [y] S Job 9:22; S Ecc 2:14 [z] Jer 11:8; 13:10; 16:12; 17:9 [a] S Job 21:26 **9:5** [b] S Job 14:21 [c] S Ps 9:6 [d] S Ecc 1:11 **9:6** [e] S Job 21:21

[h] *8* Or *over his spirit to retain it* [i] *9* Or *to their* [j] *10* Some Hebrew manuscripts and Septuagint (Aquila); most Hebrew manuscripts *and are forgotten* [k] *2* Septuagint (Aquila), Vulgate and Syriac; Hebrew does not have *and the bad.* [l] *4* Or *What then is to be chosen? With all who live, there is hope*

8:13 IT WILL NOT GO WELL WITH THEM. In the world it often seems that evil triumphs and sinners go unpunished (cf. Ps 73). Yet God assures us that he will eventually punish evildoers according to what they deserve.

8:17 NO ONE CAN COMPREHEND. Solomon recognized that no matter how wise we are, we cannot by our own wisdom explain all that God has done or the ways of his providence. Like Job, we do not have to know all the reasons; we simply need to trust in the Lord and believe that he does all things well. If we are his children, we are in his hands (9:1).

9:2 ALL SHARE A COMMON DESTINY. Solomon looks at the inevitability of death from the point of view of this life only. From that standpoint, it does not seem fair that death comes indiscriminately to all, both the righteous and the wicked.

9:7 FOOD WITH GLADNESS . . . WINE WITH

and drink your wine[f] with a joyful
heart,[g] for it is now that God favors
what you do. 8 Always be clothed in
white,[h] and always anoint your head
with oil. 9 Enjoy life with your wife,[i]
whom you love, all the days of this
meaningless life that God has given
you under the sun — all your meaningless days. For this is your lot[j] in life
and in your toilsome labor under the
sun. 10 Whatever[k] your hand finds to
do, do it with all your might,[l] for in
the grave,[m][m] where you are going,
there is neither working nor planning
nor knowledge nor wisdom.[n]

11 I have seen something else under
the sun:

The race is not to the swift
 or the battle to the strong,[o]
nor does food come to the wise[p]
 or wealth to the brilliant
 or favor to the learned;
but time and chance[q] happen to
 them all.[r]

12 Moreover, no man knows when his
hour will come:

As fish are caught in a cruel net,
 or birds are taken in a snare,
so men are trapped by evil times[s]
 that fall unexpectedly upon
 them.[t]

Wisdom Better Than Folly

13 I also saw under the sun this example of wisdom[u] that greatly impressed me: 14 There was once a small
city with only a few people in it. And a
powerful king came against it, surrounded it and built huge siegeworks
against it. 15 Now there lived in that
city a man poor but wise, and he saved
the city by his wisdom. But nobody remembered that poor man.[v] 16 So I
said, "Wisdom is better than strength."
But the poor man's wisdom is despised, and his words are no longer
heeded.[w]

17 The quiet words of the wise are
 more to be heeded
 than the shouts of a ruler of
 fools.
18 Wisdom[x] is better than weapons
 of war,
 but one sinner destroys much
 good.

10

As dead flies give perfume a
 bad smell,
 so a little folly[y] outweighs
 wisdom and honor.
2 The heart of the wise inclines to
 the right,
 but the heart of the fool to the
 left.
3 Even as he walks along the road,
 the fool lacks sense
 and shows everyone[z] how
 stupid he is.
4 If a ruler's anger rises against you,
 do not leave your post;[a]
 calmness can lay great errors to
 rest.[b]

5 There is an evil I have seen under
 the sun,
 the sort of error that arises from
 a ruler:
6 Fools are put in many high
 positions,[c]
 while the rich occupy the low
 ones.
7 I have seen slaves on horseback,
 while princes go on foot like
 slaves.[d]
8 Whoever digs a pit may fall
 into it;[e]

9:7 [f] S Nu 6:20 [g] S Ecc 2:24
9:8 [h] S Rev 3:4
9:9 [i] S Pr 5:18 [j] S Job 31:2
9:10 [k] S 1Sa 10:7 [l] Ecc 11:6 [m] Nu 16:33; S Ps 6:5; Isa 38:18 [n] S Ecc 2:24
9:11 [o] Am 2:14-15 [p] Job 32:13; Isa 47:10; Jer 9:23 [q] Ecc 2:14 [r] S Dt 8:18
9:12 [s] S Pr 29:6 [t] S Ps 73:22; S Ecc 2:14
9:13 [u] S 2Sa 20:22
9:15 [v] S Ge 40:14; S Ecc 1:11
9:16 [w] Est 6:3
9:18 [x] S Ecc 2:13
10:1 [y] Pr 13:16; 18:2
10:3 [z] Pr 13:16
10:4 [a] Ecc 8:3 [b] S Pr 16:14
10:6 [c] S Pr 29:2
10:7 [d] Pr 19:10
10:8 [e] S Ps 57:6

[m] 10 Hebrew *Sheol*

A JOYFUL HEART. Though death comes to all and time and chance happen to everyone (v. 11), we who are pleasing to God (cf. Ro 12:2) should not stop enjoying what he has given us. The "wine" (Heb *yayin*) referred to here undoubtedly means sweet, freshly squeezed grape juice (see article on WINE IN THE OLD TESTAMENT, p. 204).

9:10 DO IT WITH ALL YOUR MIGHT. Whatever work we do, we should undertake it with all our heart, as working for the Lord (see Col 3:23).

9:15 NOBODY REMEMBERED THAT POOR MAN. In this parable, a little city besieged by a great army seemed in a hopeless situation (v. 14). But a poor wise man devised a plan and the city was saved. Apparently someone else took the credit for saving the city, however, and the wise man, probably because he was poor, was forgotten. Believers should recognize that while they are on earth, justice and fairness will be imperfect at best, but in life after death, God will right all wrongs and reward all righteous deeds.

10:1 DEAD FLIES GIVE PERFUME A BAD SMELL. Just as dead flies by their decay spoil a batch of perfume, so a little foolishness can counteract the effects of great wisdom. Wise plans can be laid out, but someone who makes a foolish mistake can spoil them all (see 2Ki 20:12–19).

10:8–10 WHOEVER DIGS A PIT. Wisdom takes into account the risks and difficulties of life and its ordinary tasks. The wise person is kept

whoever breaks through a wall
may be bitten by a snake.[f]
9Whoever quarries stones may be
injured by them;
whoever splits logs may be
endangered by them.[g]

10If the ax is dull
and its edge unsharpened,
more strength is needed
but skill will bring success.

11If a snake bites before it is
charmed,
there is no profit for the
charmer.[h]

12Words from a wise man's mouth
are gracious,[i]
but a fool is consumed by his
own lips.[j]
13At the beginning his words are
folly;
at the end they are wicked
madness—
14 and the fool multiplies words.[k]

No one knows what is coming—
who can tell him what will
happen after him?[l]

15A fool's work wearies him;
he does not know the way to
town.

16Woe to you, O land whose king
was a servant[n][m]
and whose princes feast in the
morning.
17Blessed are you, O land whose
king is of noble birth
and whose princes eat at a
proper time—
for strength and not for
drunkenness.[n]

18If a man is lazy, the rafters sag;
if his hands are idle, the house
leaks.[o]

19A feast is made for laughter,
and wine[p] makes life merry,
but money is the answer for
everything.

20Do not revile the king[q] even in
your thoughts,
or curse the rich in your
bedroom,
because a bird of the air may carry
your words,
and a bird on the wing may
report what you say.

Bread Upon the Waters

11 Cast[r] your bread upon the
waters,
for after many days you will find
it again.[s]
2Give portions to seven, yes to
eight,
for you do not know what
disaster may come upon the
land.

3If clouds are full of water,
they pour rain upon the earth.
Whether a tree falls to the south
or to the north,
in the place where it falls, there
will it lie.
4Whoever watches the wind will not
plant;
whoever looks at the clouds will
not reap.
5As you do not know the path of
the wind,[t]
or how the body is formed[o] in a
mother's womb,[u]

10:8 [f]S Est 2:23; Ps 9:16; Am 5:19 10:9 [g]S Pr 26:27 10:11 [h]S Ps 58:5; S Isa 3:3 10:12 [i]Pr 10:32 [j]S Pr 10:6; S 14:3; S 15:2; S 18:7 10:14 [k]Ecc 5:3 [l]Ecc 9:1 10:16 [m]Isa 3:4-5, 12 10:17 [n]S Dt 14:26; S 1Sa 25:36; S Pr 31:4 10:18 [o]Pr 20:4; S 24:30-34 10:19 [p]S Ge 14:18; S Jdg 9:13 10:20 [q]S Ex 22:28 11:1 [r]ver 6; Isa 32:20; Hos 10:12 [s]S Dt 24:19 11:5 [t]Jn 3:8-10 [u]Ps 139:14-16

[n]16 Or *king is a child* [o]5 Or *know how life (or the spirit) / enters the body being formed*

---

from harm because he or she knows what could happen and is careful to avoid pitfalls.

10:16 WHOSE KING WAS A SERVANT. It is a sad state of affairs when rulers and leaders are childish (see NIV text note) and when their princes and their assistants begin the day by satisfying their appetites (probably in drinking parties). How tragic it is throughout history that intoxicating drink has flowed so freely in the capital cities of the world. We need godly leaders that set a good example (v. 17).

11:1 CAST YOUR BREAD UPON THE WATERS. One meaning of the Hebrew word for "bread" is "grain" that can be used for bread. The picture may be that of Egyptians scattering grain on the water that flooded their lands when the Nile rose every year. It would appear to sink down and be forgotten, but in due time there would be a harvest. We may apply this to our willingness to be generous and helpful (v. 2); we must give liberally, since one day we ourselves may be in great need (cf. 2Co 8:10–15).

11:4 WHOEVER WATCHES THE WIND WILL NOT PLANT. We are in a world where always waiting for the most favorable conditions will accomplish nothing (cf. Mt 24:7–14); conditions will never be ideal during this present age. We must persevere in praying and in reading our Bibles daily. We must live by God's righteous standards, even if everyone around us pursues sinful pleasures.

so you cannot understand the work
of God,
the Maker of all things.
6Sow your seed in the morning,
and at evening let not your
hands be idle,[v]
for you do not know which will
succeed,
whether this or that,
or whether both will do equally
well.

Remember Your Creator While Young

7Light is sweet,
and it pleases the eyes to see
the sun.[w]
8However many years a man may
live,
let him enjoy them all.
But let him remember[x] the days
of darkness,
for they will be many.
Everything to come is
meaningless.
9Be happy, young man, while you
are young,
and let your heart give you joy
in the days of your youth.
Follow the ways of your heart
and whatever your eyes see,
but know that for all these things
God will bring you to
judgment.[y]
10So then, banish anxiety[z] from
your heart
and cast off the troubles of your
body,
for youth and vigor are
meaningless.[a]

12 Remember[b] your Creator
in the days of your youth,
before the days of trouble[c] come
and the years approach when
you will say,
"I find no pleasure in them"—
2before the sun and the light
and the moon and the stars
grow dark,
and the clouds return after the
rain;
3when the keepers of the house
tremble,
and the strong men stoop,
when the grinders cease because
they are few,
and those looking through the
windows grow dim;
4when the doors to the street are
closed
and the sound of grinding fades;
when men rise up at the sound of
birds,
but all their songs grow
faint;[d]
5when men are afraid of heights
and of dangers in the streets;
when the almond tree blossoms
and the grasshopper drags
himself along
and desire no longer is stirred.
Then man goes to his eternal
home[e]
and mourners[f] go about the
streets.
6Remember him—before the silver
cord is severed,
or the golden bowl is broken;
before the pitcher is shattered at
the spring,
or the wheel broken at the
well,
7and the dust returns[g] to the
ground it came from,
and the spirit returns to God[h]
who gave it.[i]

11:6 [v]S Ecc 9:10 **11:7** [w]Ecc 7:11 **11:8** [x]Ecc 12:1 **11:9** [y]S Job 19:29; S Ecc 2:24; S 3:17 **11:10** [z]Ps 94:19 [a]S Ecc 2:24 **12:1** [b]Ecc 11:8 [c]S 2Sa 19:35 **12:4** [d]Jer 25:10 **12:5** [e]S Job 10:21 [f]Jer 9:17; Am 5:16 **12:7** [g]S Ge 2:7; S Ps 146:4 [h]Ecc 3:21 [i]S Job 20:8

11:9 FOR ALL THESE THINGS GOD WILL BRING YOU TO JUDGMENT. God wants his people to rejoice and young people to enjoy their youth. But all such rejoicing must be tempered with the recognition that God holds us accountable for our sinful actions. If we allow our lives to degenerate into superficial levity and the enjoyment of sinful things, the end result will be trouble and suffering in this life and judgment in the next.

12:1–7 REMEMBER YOUR CREATOR IN THE DAYS OF YOUR YOUTH. "Remember" in the Bible always implies action; e.g., when God "remembered" Abraham (Ge 19:29), he became involved in his life for his good. Therefore, remembering our Creator means acting in the way he intended us to act when he created us. He has given us life and the opportunities that come with youth. We can "remember" God only by the help of the Holy Spirit, as we "put on the new self, created to be like God in true righteousness and holiness" (Eph 4:24); and we must do so before death comes. Vv. 3–7 give a dramatic picture of the aging process of the physical body, leading to death. We can be comforted, however, by the fact that the inner person can still be "renewed day by day" (2Co 4:16).

12:7 DUST RETURNS TO THE GROUND . . . THE SPIRIT RETURNS TO GOD. This verse distinguishes between the aspect of the human person that remains at the time of death and the aspect that returns to God. For more on this, see article on HUMAN PERSONHOOD, p. 960.

[8]"Meaningless! Meaningless!" says
the Teacher.[p j]
"Everything is meaningless![k]"

The Conclusion of the Matter

[9]Not only was the Teacher wise, but
also he imparted knowledge to the people. He pondered and searched out and
set in order many proverbs.[l] [10]The
Teacher[m] searched to find just the
right words, and what he wrote was upright and true.[n]
[11]The words of the wise are like
goads, their collected sayings like
firmly embedded nails[o]—given by
one Shepherd. [12]Be warned, my son, of
anything in addition to them.

Of making many books there is no
end, and much study wearies the
body.[p]
[13]Now all has been heard;
here is the conclusion of the
matter:
Fear God[q] and keep his
commandments,[r]
for this is the whole ⌊duty⌋ of
man.[s]
[14]For God will bring every deed into
judgment,[t]
including every hidden thing,[u]
whether it is good or evil. Isa 2:3-5

12:8 [j]Ecc 1:1 [k]S Ecc 1:2 **12:9** [l]1Ki 4:32 **12:10** [m]S Ecc 1:1 [n]Pr 22:20-21 **12:11** [o]S Ezr 9:8; S Job 6:25 **12:12** [p]S Ecc 1:18 **12:13** [q]S Ex 20:20; S 1Sa 12:24; S Job 23:15; S Ps 19:9 [r]S Dt 4:2 [s]S Dt 4:6; S Job 37:24 **12:14** [t]S Job 19:29; S Ecc 3:17 [u]S Job 34:21; S Ps 19:12; Jer 16:17; 23:24

[p] 8 Or *the leader of the assembly*; also in verses 9 and 10

12:8 EVERYTHING IS MEANINGLESS. See 1:2, note.

12:11 WORDS OF THE WISE ARE LIKE GOADS. The wise words of truth that come from the one divine Shepherd act (1) as goads (i.e., pointed sticks) to prod us on in the right way, and (2) as nails to secure the truth in our minds. God's Word, therefore, is far more valuable than all the many books of human wisdom.

12:13 FEAR GOD AND KEEP HIS COMMANDMENTS. The entire book of Ecclesiastes must be understood in light of this concluding verse. Solomon began with a cynical appraisal of life as meaningless, but he ends with serious counsel about where meaning can be found. Fear of God, love for him and his Word, and obedience to his commandments bring purpose and satisfaction that cannot be found in any other way.

12:14 GOD WILL BRING EVERY DEED INTO JUDGMENT. As a final word, Solomon reminds us of a solemn and enduring truth: we are fully accountable to God for our deeds. The Lord will evaluate each of us, believer and unbeliever alike, and will judge all our deeds, whether they are good or evil (cf. Ro 14:10,12; 2Co 5:10; Rev 20:12–13). We will not be justified on the judgment day if we have neglected or rejected God's grace (see article on THE JUDGMENT OF BELIEVERS, p. 1791).

HUMAN PERSONHOOD

Ecc 12:6–7 "Remember him—before the silver cord is severed, or the golden bowl is broken; before the pitcher is shattered at the spring, or the wheel broken at the well, and the dust returns to the ground it came from, and the spirit returns to God who gave it."

Of all the creatures God made, the human being is by far the highest and most complex. Because of pride, however, humans often forget that God is their Creator, that they are created beings and that they are dependent on God. This article examines the Biblical perspective on human personhood.

HUMAN PERSONHOOD IN THE IMAGE OF GOD. (1) The Bible states clearly that the human race, by a special decision of God, was created in God's image and in his likeness (Ge 1:26–27). Thus both Adam and Eve were not products of evolution (Ge 1:27; Mt 19:4; Mk 10:6; see article on CREATION, p. 6). Because they were created in God's likeness, they were able to respond to and have fellowship with God, and to reflect his love, glory and holiness (see Ge 1:26, note).

(2) Note at least three different aspects of the image of God in humankind (see Ge 1:26, note): Adam and Eve possessed a *moral* likeness to God, in that they were righteous and holy (cf. Eph 4:24), with hearts capable of loving and of wanting to do what was right. They possessed a likeness to God in *intelligence*, for they were created with spirit, mind, emotions and power of choice (Ge 2:19–20; 3:6–7). In some sense their *physical* makeup was in God's image in a way not true of animals. God gave to human beings the image in which he was to appear visibly in the OT (Ge 18:1–2) and the form that his Son would one day assume (Lk 1:35; Php 2:7).

(3) When Adam and Eve sinned, this image of God in them was seriously corrupted, but not totally destroyed. (a) Certainly their moral likeness to God was corrupted when they sinned (cf. Ge 6:5), so that they were no longer perfect and holy, but now had a tendency toward sin, which they passed on to their children (cf. Ge 4; see Ro 5:12, note). The NT confirms the corruption of God's image when it says that redeemed believers must be renewed to the original moral likeness of God (cf. Eph 4:22–24; Col 3:10). (b) At the same time, sinful humans still have many of the aspects of the likeness to God in intelligence, with a capacity for fellowship and communication with him (cf. Ge 3:8–19; Ac 17:27–28). This dimension of the image of God was also marred but not totally obliterated when Adam and Eve sinned in the Garden of Eden (cf. Ge 9:6; Jas 3:9).

COMPONENTS OF HUMAN PERSONHOOD. The Bible reveals that human personhood, made in God's image, is a triunity involving the components of spirit, soul and body (1Th 5:23; Heb 4:12). (1) God formed Adam out of the dust of the ground (body) and breathed into his nostrils the breath of life (spirit), and he became "a living being" (soul; Ge 2:7). God intended that by eating from the tree of life and by obeying his command not to eat from the tree of knowledge of good and evil, humankind would never die but would live forever (cf. Ge 2:16–17; 3:22–24). Only after death entered the world as a result of human sin do we read about the separation of a person into the dust of the ground and the spirit that returns to God (Ge 3:19; 35:18; Ecc 12:7; Rev 6:9; see article on DEATH, p. 732). In other words, the separation of the body from the spirit and soul is the result of God's curse on the human race because of sin and will eventually be remedied only at the resurrection of the body on the last day (see article on THE RESURRECTION OF THE BODY, p. 1779).

(2) The soul (Heb *nephesh*; Gk *psychē*), often translated "life," may be briefly defined as the nonmaterial aspects of mind, emotions and will in human personhood that result from the union of spirit and body. The soul along with the human spirit will continue to live when an individual physically dies. The soul is so closely linked with one's inner personhood that it is sometimes used as a synonym for "person" (e.g., Lev 4:2; 7:20; Jos

20:3). The body (Heb *basar*; Gk *sōma*) may be briefly defined as that material element in an individual that returns to the dust when he or she dies (sometimes called "flesh"). The spirit (Heb *ruach*; Gk *pneuma*) may be briefly defined as the nonmaterial life component of the human being, wherein resides our spiritual capacity and conscience; that aspect is the one whereby we are most in contact with God's Spirit.

(3) Of the three components constituting the "whole" of human personhood, only the spirit and the soul are indestructible and survive death, either to live in heaven (Rev 6:9; 20:4) or in hell (cf. Ps 16:10; Mt 16:26). However, the Bible is insistent that as long as we are alive, believers must take good care of their bodies by keeping them free from immorality and evil (Ro 6:6,12–13; 1Co 6:13–20; 1Th 4:3–4) and by dedicating them to the service of God (Ro 6:13; 12:1; see article on STANDARDS OF SEXUAL MORALITY, p. 1936). The body will also experience transformation on the day of resurrection, so that human personhood is totally redeemed in the end for those who are in Christ Jesus.

THE RESPONSIBILITIES OF HUMAN PERSONHOOD. When God created human beings, he entrusted them with several responsibilities. (1) God made them in his own image so that he could develop a loving, personal relationship with them for all eternity and so that they would glorify him as Lord. So much did God desire a people to enjoy him, glorify him, and live in righteousness and holiness before him that when Satan succeeded in tempting Adam and Eve to rebel against and disobey God, the Lord promised to send a Savior to redeem the world (see Ge 3:15, note; see article on CREATION, p. 6).

(2) It was God's will that human beings love him above all and love their neighbors as themselves. This twofold commandment of love summarizes God's entire law (Lev 19:18; Dt 6:4–5; Mt 22:37–40; Ro 13:9–10).

(3) God also established the institution of marriage in the Garden of Eden (Ge 2:21–24). He intended that marriage should be monogamous, a lifelong relationship between husband and wife (cf. Mt 19:5–9; Eph 5:22–33). Within the context of marriage, God commanded that the human race "be fruitful and increase in number" (Ge 1:28; 9:7). Man and woman were to reproduce godly offspring in a family context. God considers a godly family and the raising of children within healthy family relationships as a high priority in the world (see Ge 1:28, note).

(4) God also charged Adam and all his descendants to "subdue" the earth and to "rule over the fish of the sea and the birds of the air and over every living creature that moves on the ground" (Ge 1:28). Already in the Garden of Eden Adam was given the responsibility of taking care of the garden and of naming the animals (Ge 2:15,19–20).

(5) Note that when Adam and Eve sinned by eating the forbidden fruit, some of their dominion over the world was lost to Satan, who now as "the god of this age" (2Co 4:4) controls this present evil age (see 1Jn 5:19, note; cf. Gal 1:4; Eph 6:12; see article on THE PROVIDENCE OF GOD, p. 78). But God still expects believers to fulfill his divine purpose by taking good care of his world, by consecrating all things in the earth to him and by managing his creation in a God-glorifying way (cf. Ps 8:6–8; Heb 2:7–8).

(6) Because of sin's presence in the world, God sent his Son Jesus to redeem the world. The awesome task of bringing that message of God's redemptive love has been given to God's people, whom he has called to be witnesses of Christ and his salvation to the ends of the earth (Mt 28:18–20; Ac 1:8) and to be the light of the world and the salt of the earth (Mt 5:13–16).

SONG OF SONGS

Outline

Title (1:1)

I. The First Poem: The Bride Longs for the Bridegroom (1:2—2:7)
   - A. Her Longing Expressed (1:2–4a)
   - B. Support from Her Friends (1:4b)
   - C. Her Question (1:5–7)
   - D. Advice from Her Friends (1:8)
   - E. The Bridegroom Appears and Speaks (1:9–11)
   - F. Exchange of Affection Between Bride and Bridegroom (1:12—2:7)

II. The Second Poem: The Lovers Seek and Find Each Other (2:8—3:5)
   - A. The Bride Spots Her Bridegroom Coming (2:8–9)
   - B. The Bridegroom's Overtures (2:10–15)
   - C. The Bride's Expression of Exclusive Love (2:16–17)
   - D. The Bridegroom Lost and Found Again (3:1–5)

III. The Third Poem: The Wedding Procession (3:6—5:1)
   - A. The Bridegroom Approaches (3:6–11)
   - B. The Bridegroom's Affection for His Bride (4:1–15)
   - C. The Bride and Bridegroom Come Together (4:16—5:1)

IV. The Fourth Poem: The Bride Fears Losing the Bridegroom (5:2—6:3)
   - A. The Bride's Dream at Night (5:2–7)
   - B. The Bride and Her Friends Discuss the Bridegroom (5:8–16)
   - C. The Place Where the Bridegroom Has Gone (6:1–3)

V. The Fifth Poem: The Beauty of the Bride (6:4—8:4)
   - A. The Bridegroom's Description of the Bride (6:4–9)
   - B. The Bridegroom and His Friends Discuss the Bride (6:10–13)
   - C. The Further Description of the Bride (7:1–8)
   - D. The Bride's Affection for the Bridegroom (7:9—8:4)

VI. The Sixth Poem: The Ultimate Beauty of Love (8:5–14)
   - A. The Intensity of Love (8:5–7)
   - B. The Expansion of Love (8:8–9)
   - C. The Contentment of Love (8:10–14)

Author: Solomon

Theme: Wedded Love

Date of Writing: c. 960 B.C.

Background

The Hebrew name for this book translates literally as "Song of Songs," an expression that means "The Greatest Song" (just as "King of kings" means "The Greatest King"); it was regarded, therefore, as the greatest of wedding songs ever penned. Solomon is believed to have written the "Song of Songs (1:1).

Solomon was a prolific songwriter of 1,005 songs (1Ki 4:32). His name appears in the title verse as the author (1:1), and at six other places throughout the song (1:5; 3:7,9,11;

8:11–12). He is also identified as the bridegroom (the "lover"); originally the book may have been a series of poems between himself and his bride. The book's eight chapters contain references to at least 15 different species of animals and 21 varieties of plant life; both of these groups were investigated and mentioned by Solomon in numerous songs (1Ki 4:33). Finally, geographical references in the book indicate places all throughout the land of Israel, suggesting that the book was composed before the division of the nation into the northern and southern kingdoms.

Solomon must have composed the book early in his life as the king of Israel, long before he had 700 wives and 300 concubines (1Ki 11:3); but the question arises: how could Solomon have used such monogamous language if he already may have had wives and concubines (6:8)? The answer may lie in the fact that the Shulammite maiden (6:13) was Solomon's first wife from his youth, before he became king (3:11); 6:8 may reflect only the state of things at the time the book was formally written for publication. The Shulammite is described in this song as a common girl from the countryside, attractive and beautiful, to whom Solomon was deeply and emotionally committed as one would be to his first love and bride.

Liturgically, Song of Songs became one of the five scrolls of the third part of the Hebrew Bible, the *Hagiographa* ("Holy Writings"), each of which was read publicly at one of the annual Jewish feasts; this one was assigned to be read at Passover.

Purpose

This book was inspired by the Holy Spirit and incorporated into the Scriptures to underscore the divine origin of the joy and dignity of human love in marriage. Genesis reveals that human sexuality and marriage preceded the fall of humankind into sin (Ge 2:18–25). Though sin has marred this important area of human experience, God wants us to know that it can be pure, wholesome and beautiful. Song of Songs, therefore, provides a corrective model between two extremes in history: (1) the abandonment of married love for sexual perversion (i.e., homosexual or lesbian relationships) and fleeting unmarried heterosexual encounters, and (2) an asceticism, often mistaken as the Christian view of sex, that denies the goodness of physical love in the marriage relationship.

Survey

The content of Song of Songs is not easily analyzed. Rather than moving in a methodical and logical manner from the first chapter to the last, it moves in a series of interlocking circles revolving around a central theme of love. As a song, it has six stanzas or poems, each one dealing with some aspect of the courtship and wedded love of Solomon and his bride (1:2—2:7; 2:8—3:5; 3:6—5:1; 5:2—6:3; 6:4—8:4; 8:5–14). The virginity of the bride is described as "a garden locked up" (4:12), and the consummation of the marriage as entering the garden to enjoy its choice fruits (4:16; 5:1). Most of the conversations are between the bride (a Shulammite maiden), Solomon the king, and a chorus of friends of the bride and bridegroom called the "daughters of Jerusalem." When the bride and bridegroom are together, they are mutually fulfilled; when they are apart, they experience a longing for each other's presence. The literary climax of the Song is 8:6–7.

Special Features

Four major features characterize the Song. (1) It is the only book in the Bible that deals exclusively with the unique love of a bride and a bridegroom. Throughout it describes courtship and married love, especially the bliss of newlyweds. (2) It is a unique literary masterpiece full of discreet but sensuous imagery, primarily drawn from the world of nature. The various metaphors and descriptive language portray the emotion, power and beauty of romantic and wedded love, which was considered pure and chaste in Bible times. (3) It is one of a small number of OT books that are neither quoted nor alluded to in the NT. (4) It is one of two books in the OT (cf. the book of Esther) that do not explicitly mention God in the text (though some manuscripts contain a reference to "the LORD" in 8:6).

New Testament Fulfillment

(1) Song of Songs prefigures a NT theme revealed to the writer of Hebrews: "Marriage should be honored by all, and the marriage bed kept pure" (Heb 13:4). Christians may, and even should, enjoy romantic love within the bonds of the marriage relationship. (2) Many past interpreters have seen this book as primarily or exclusively a prophetic allegory describing the love relationship between God and Israel, or between Christ and the church, his bride. Since the NT itself nowhere views Song of Songs in this manner, nor even quotes from it, this interpretation is highly unlikely. The Bible nowhere indicates that any aspect of Solomon's married life is a divinely intended "type" of Christ. However, since several crucial NT passages describe Christ's love for the church in terms of the marriage relationship (e.g., 2Co 11:2; Eph 5:22–33; Rev 19:7–9; 21:1–2,9), the Song may be viewed as *illustrating* the quality of love that exists between Christ and his bride, the church. It is an exclusive, committed and intensely personal love that allows for no other courtships.

Reading Song of Songs

In order to read the entire Old Testament in one year, the book of Song of Songs should be read in 3 days, according to the following schedule: ☐ 1–2 ☐ 3–5 ☐ 6–8

NOTES

1

Solomon's Song of Songs.[a]

Beloved[a]

²Let him kiss me with the kisses of
his mouth—
for your love[b] is more delightful
than wine.[c]
³Pleasing is the fragrance of your
perfumes;[d]
your name[e] is like perfume
poured out.
No wonder the maidens[f] love
you!
⁴Take me away with you—let us
hurry!
Let the king bring me into his
chambers.[g]

Friends

We rejoice and delight[h] in you[b];
we will praise your love[i] more
than wine.

Beloved

How right they are to adore you!

⁵Dark am I, yet lovely,[j]
O daughters of Jerusalem,[k]
dark like the tents of Kedar,[l]
like the tent curtains of
Solomon.[c]
⁶Do not stare at me because I am
dark,
because I am darkened by the
sun.
My mother's sons were angry with
me
and made me take care of the
vineyards;[m]
my own vineyard I have
neglected.

⁷Tell me, you whom I love, where
you graze your flock
and where you rest your sheep[n]
at midday.
Why should I be like a veiled[o]
woman
beside the flocks of your
friends?

Friends

⁸If you do not know, most beautiful
of women,[p]
follow the tracks of the sheep
and graze your young goats
by the tents of the shepherds.

Lover

⁹I liken you, my darling, to a mare
harnessed to one of the
chariots[q] of Pharaoh.
¹⁰Your cheeks[r] are beautiful with
earrings,
your neck with strings of
jewels.[s]
¹¹We will make you earrings of gold,
studded with silver.

Beloved

¹²While the king was at his table,
my perfume spread its
fragrance.[t]
¹³My lover is to me a sachet of
myrrh[u]

1:1 [a] S 1Ki 4:32; Ps 45 Title **1:2** [b] ver 4; SS 4:10; 8:6 [c] S Ge 14:18; S Jdg 9:13 **1:3** [d] S Est 2:12; S Ps 45:8 [e] S Ecc 7:1 [f] Ps 45:14 **1:4** [g] Ps 45:15 [h] SS 2:3 [i] S ver 2 **1:5** [j] SS 2:14; 4:3 [k] SS 5:16 [l] S Ge 25:13 **1:6** [m] SS 2:15; 7:12; 8:12 **1:7** [n] Isa 13:20 [o] S Ge 24:65 **1:8** [p] SS 5:9; 6:1 **1:9** [q] 2Ch 1:17 **1:10** [r] SS 5:13 [s] Isa 61:10 **1:12** [t] SS 4:11-14 **1:13** [u] S Ge 37:25

[a] Primarily on the basis of the gender of the Hebrew pronouns used, male and female speakers are indicated in the margins by the captions *Lover* and *Beloved* respectively. The words of others are marked *Friends.* In some instances the divisions and their captions are debatable. [b] *4* The Hebrew is masculine singular. [c] *5* Or *Salma*

1:1 SONG OF SONGS. This is the book's own title in the Hebrew text. It means the best or greatest song. Solomon wrote 1,005 songs (1Ki 4:32).

1:5 THE TENTS OF KEDAR. Tents were usually made of black goat hair. Kedar was an Arabian tribe descended from Ishmael (Ge 25:13; cf. Isa 21:16–17); thus some have suggested that the bride was an Arabian princess.

1:6 VINEYARD I HAVE NEGLECTED. The cruel brothers of the beloved forced her to guard and care for their vineyards, something she had not done for her own. This outdoor work may be the reason her skin was so dark, a marked contrast to the sun-bonnetted beauties of Jerusalem—though hard work had not destroyed her real beauty (v. 5). In light of these verses it is hard to see how some suppose the speaker here was Pharaoh's daughter (1Ki 3:1). This Shulammite maiden was probably the princess Solomon first loved and married before he began to enter marriages for the sake of political alliances.

1:9 MY DARLING. The Hebrew means "my companion" in the sense of "my friend" (see also 2:10, 4:1,7, etc.). It was a term of endearment used before marriage. The comparison to horses was considered a compliment in those days.

1:11 EARRINGS OF GOLD, STUDDED WITH SILVER. In contrast to her humble shepherd's attire, she would be decorated with jewels and strings of golden beads with points of silver.

1:12 MY PERFUME. This perfume is nard, an ointment from an aromatic Himalayan herb.

1:13 A SACHET OF MYRRH. Myrrh is an aromatic resin from the bark of a balsam tree found in Arabia and India. The bundle of myrrh was probably in a perfume bag. The Hebrew in the rest of the verse indicates that the myrrh, *not the lover,* would rest between her breasts; in other words, thoughts of him would be with her, refreshing her as myrrh would do.

resting between my breasts.
14My lover[v] is to me a cluster of
henna[w] blossoms
from the vineyards of En Gedi.[x]

Lover

15How beautiful[y] you are, my
darling!
Oh, how beautiful!
Your eyes are doves.[z]

Beloved

16How handsome you are, my
lover![a]
Oh, how charming!
And our bed is verdant.

Lover

17The beams of our house are
cedars;[b]
our rafters are firs.

Beloved[d]

2 I am a rose[e c] of Sharon,[d]
a lily[e] of the valleys.

Lover

2Like a lily among thorns
is my darling among the
maidens.

Beloved

3Like an apple tree among the trees
of the forest
is my lover[f] among the young
men.
I delight[g] to sit in his shade,
and his fruit is sweet to my
taste.[h]
4He has taken me to the banquet
hall,[i]
and his banner[j] over me is
love.
5Strengthen me with raisins,
refresh me with apples,[k]
for I am faint with love.[l]

6His left arm is under my head,
and his right arm embraces
me.[m]
7Daughters of Jerusalem, I charge
you[n]
by the gazelles and by the does
of the field:
Do not arouse or awaken love
until it so desires.[o]

8Listen! My lover!
Look! Here he comes,
leaping across the mountains,
bounding over the hills.[p]
9My lover is like a gazelle[q] or a
young stag.[r]
Look! There he stands behind
our wall,
gazing through the windows,
peering through the lattice.
10My lover spoke and said to me,
"Arise, my darling,
my beautiful one, and come with
me.
11See! The winter is past;
the rains are over and gone.
12Flowers appear on the earth;
the season of singing has come,
the cooing of doves
is heard in our land.
13The fig tree forms its early fruit;[s]
the blossoming[t] vines spread
their fragrance.
Arise, come, my darling;
my beautiful one, come with
me."

Lover

14My dove[u] in the clefts of the
rock,
in the hiding places on the
mountainside,
show me your face,
let me hear your voice;

1:14 [v] ver 16; SS 2:3,17; 5:8 [w] SS 4:13 [x] S 1Sa 23:29; S 2Ch 20:2
1:15 [y] SS 4:7; 7:6 [z] Ps 74:19; SS 2:14; 4:1; 5:2, 12; 6:9; Jer 48:28
1:16 [a] S ver 14
1:17 [b] 1Ki 6:9
2:1 [c] Isa 35:1 [d] S 1Ch 27:29 [e] SS 5:13; Hos 14:5
2:3 [f] S SS 1:14 [g] SS 1:4 [h] SS 4:16
2:4 [i] Est 1:11 [j] S Nu 1:52
2:5 [k] SS 7:8 [l] SS 5:8
2:6 [m] SS 8:3
2:7 [n] SS 5:8 [o] SS 3:5; 8:4
2:8 [p] ver 17; SS 8:14
2:9 [q] S 2Sa 2:18 [r] ver 17; SS 8:14
2:13 [s] Isa 28:4; Jer 24:2; Hos 9:10; Mic 7:1; Na 3:12 [t] SS 7:12
2:14 [u] S Ge 8:8; S SS 1:15

[d] *1* Or *Lover* [e] *1* Possibly a member of the crocus family

1:14 HENNA BLOSSOMS. The henna flowers produce an orange dye and have a pleasant fragrance.

1:15 YOUR EYES ARE DOVES. This comparison seems to refer to innocence. The Shulammite does not use seductive glances to try to stir up base emotions.

2:1 I AM A ROSE OF SHARON, A LILY OF THE VALLEYS. The Shulammite maiden compares herself to simple wild flowers of the fields, for she is not accustomed to Jerusalem's luxuries. Sharon is the coastal plain just south of Mount Carmel.

2:5 STRENGTHEN ME WITH RAISINS, REFRESH ME WITH APPLES. In a weakened, lovesick condition (possibly involving disappointment), the beloved wants to be strengthened with "raisins" (which were full of energy).

2:7 DO NOT AROUSE OR AWAKEN LOVE. This phrase occurs three times in Song of Songs (see 3:5; 8:4); it is spoken by the beloved and refers to physical intimacy between her and her lover. She does not want any intimacy to occur until the situation is appropriate, i.e., until she and Solomon are married. The Bible allows for sexual relations only between a husband and a wife (see 4:12, note; see article on STANDARDS OF SEXUAL MORALITY, p. 1936).

for your voice is sweet,
and your face is lovely.[v]
15 Catch for us the foxes,[w]
the little foxes
that ruin the vineyards,[x]
our vineyards that are in
bloom.[y]

Beloved

16 My lover is mine and I am his;[z]
he browses among the lilies.[a]
17 Until the day breaks
and the shadows flee,[b]
turn, my lover,[c]
and be like a gazelle
or like a young stag[d]
on the rugged hills.[f][e]

3 All night long on my bed
I looked[f] for the one my heart
loves;
I looked for him but did not find
him.
2 I will get up now and go about the
city,
through its streets and squares;
I will search for the one my heart
loves.
So I looked for him but did not
find him.
3 The watchmen found me
as they made their rounds in the
city.[g]
"Have you seen the one my
heart loves?"
4 Scarcely had I passed them
when I found the one my heart
loves.
I held him and would not let him
go
till I had brought him to my
mother's house,[h]
to the room of the one who
conceived me.[i]
5 Daughters of Jerusalem, I charge
you[j]
by the gazelles and by the does
of the field:
Do not arouse or awaken love
until it so desires.[k]
6 Who is this coming up from the
desert[l]
like a column of smoke,
perfumed with myrrh[m] and
incense
made from all the spices[n] of
the merchant?
7 Look! It is Solomon's carriage,
escorted by sixty warriors,[o]
the noblest of Israel,
8 all of them wearing the sword,
all experienced in battle,
each with his sword at his side,
prepared for the terrors of the
night.[p]
9 King Solomon made for himself the
carriage;
he made it of wood from
Lebanon.
10 Its posts he made of silver,
its base of gold.
Its seat was upholstered with
purple,
its interior lovingly inlaid
by[g] the daughters of Jerusalem.
11 Come out, you daughters of Zion,[q]
and look at King Solomon
wearing the crown,
the crown with which his mother
crowned him
on the day of his wedding,
the day his heart rejoiced.[r]

Lover

4 How beautiful you are, my
darling!
Oh, how beautiful!
Your eyes behind your veil[s] are
doves.[t]
Your hair is like a flock of goats
descending from Mount Gilead.[u]

2:14 [v]S SS 1:5 **2:15** [w]Jdg 15:4 [x]S SS 1:6 [y]SS 7:12 **2:16** [z]SS 7:10 [a]SS 4:5; 6:3 **2:17** [b]SS 4:6 [c]S SS 1:14 [d]S ver 9 [e]S ver 8 **3:1** [f]SS 5:6 **3:3** [g]SS 5:7 **3:4** [h]SS 8:2 [i]SS 6:9; 8:5 **3:5** [j]S SS 2:7 [k]SS 8:4 **3:6** [l]SS 8:5 [m]SS 4:6,14 [n]Ex 30:34 **3:7** [o]S 1Sa 8:11 **3:8** [p]S Job 15:22; Ps 91:5 **3:11** [q]Isa 3:16; 4:4; 32:9-13 [r]Isa 54:5; 62:5; Jer 3:14 **4:1** [s]S Ge 24:65 [t]S SS 1:15 [u]Ge 37:25; Nu 32:1; SS 6:5; Jer 22:6; Mic 7:14

[f] 17 Or *the hills of Bether* [g] 10 Or *its inlaid interior a gift of love / from*

2:16 MY LOVER IS MINE AND I AM HIS. The love the two lovers have for each other is genuine and monogamous. There is no desire or room for any other person. In marriage there must be such a love for and commitment to each other that faithfulness to a spouse is of highest importance in our lives.

3:1–4 ALL NIGHT LONG . . . I LOOKED FOR HIM. "Night" is plural in the Hebrew and means "night after night"; the Shulammite may have been dreaming (v. 5) night after night that she was searching for her lover but not finding him.

3:6 WHO IS THIS COMING UP. "This" is feminine in the Hebrew; the verbs that follow refer to the bride's coming.

3:11 COME OUT . . . AND LOOK AT KING SOLOMON. Because of the intercession of Bathsheba, Solomon's mother, and the prophet Nathan, Solomon was brought out and publicly anointed king (1Ki 1:22–40). It appears that when Solomon was anointed king, he was already married and was wearing the crown with which his mother crowned him. In view also are the covenant promises given by God (2Sa 7:13–16; see article on GOD'S COVENANT WITH DAVID, p. 432).

2Your teeth are like a flock of
sheep just shorn,
coming up from the washing.
Each has its twin;
not one of them is alone.[v]
3Your lips are like a scarlet ribbon;
your mouth[w] is lovely.[x]
Your temples behind your veil
are like the halves of a
pomegranate.[y]
4Your neck is like the tower[z] of
David,
built with elegance[h];
on it hang a thousand shields,[a]
all of them shields of warriors.
5Your two breasts[b] are like two
fawns,
like twin fawns of a gazelle[c]
that browse among the lilies.[d]
6Until the day breaks
and the shadows flee,[e]
I will go to the mountain of
myrrh[f]
and to the hill of incense.
7All beautiful[g] you are, my darling;
there is no flaw[h] in you.
8Come with me from Lebanon, my
bride,[i]
come with me from Lebanon.
Descend from the crest of Amana,
from the top of Senir,[j] the
summit of Hermon,[k]
from the lions' dens
and the mountain haunts of the
leopards.
9You have stolen my heart, my
sister, my bride;[l]
you have stolen my heart
with one glance of your eyes,
with one jewel of your
necklace.[m]
10How delightful[n] is your love[o], my
sister, my bride!
How much more pleasing is your
love than wine,[p]
and the fragrance of your
perfume[q] than any spice!
11Your lips drop sweetness as the
honeycomb, my bride;
milk and honey are under your
tongue.[r]
The fragrance of your garments
is like that of Lebanon.[s]
12You are a garden[t] locked up, my
sister, my bride;[u]
you are a spring enclosed, a
sealed fountain.[v]
13Your plants are an orchard of
pomegranates[w]
with choice fruits,
with henna[x] and nard,
14 nard and saffron,
calamus and cinnamon,[y]
with every kind of incense tree,
with myrrh[z] and aloes[a]
and all the finest spices.[b]
15You are[i] a garden[c] fountain,[d]
a well of flowing water
streaming down from Lebanon.

Beloved

16Awake, north wind,
and come, south wind!
Blow on my garden,[e]
that its fragrance[f] may spread
abroad.
Let my lover[g] come into his
garden
and taste its choice fruits.[h]

Lover

5 I have come into my garden,[i]
my sister, my bride;[j]
I have gathered my myrrh with
my spice.
I have eaten my honeycomb and
my honey;

4:2 [v] SS 6:6
4:3 [w] SS 5:16 [x] S SS 1:5 [y] SS 6:7
4:4 [z] S Ps 144:12 [a] Eze 27:10
4:5 [b] SS 7:3 [c] S Pr 5:19 [d] S SS 2:16
4:6 [e] SS 2:17 [f] S SS 3:6
4:7 [g] S SS 1:15 [h] SS 5:2
4:8 [i] ver 9,12; SS 5:1 [j] S Dt 3:9 [k] S 1Ch 5:23
4:9 [l] S ver 8 [m] S Ge 41:42; S Ps 73:6
4:10 [n] SS 7:6 [o] S SS 1:2 [p] S Jdg 9:13 [q] ver 16; S Ps 45:8; Isa 57:9
4:11 [r] S Ps 19:10; SS 5:1 [s] Hos 14:6
4:12 [t] ver 16; SS 5:1; 6:2; Isa 5:7 [u] S ver 8 [v] Pr 5:15-18
4:13 [w] SS 7:12 [x] SS 1:14
4:14 [y] S Ex 30:23 [z] S SS 3:6 [a] S Nu 24:6 [b] SS 1:12
4:15 [c] Isa 27:2; 58:11; Jer 31:12 [d] Pr 5:18
4:16 [e] S ver 12 [f] S ver 10 [g] SS 7:13 [h] SS 2:3
5:1 [i] S SS 4:12 [j] S SS 4:8

[h] *4* The meaning of the Hebrew for this word is uncertain. [i] *15* Or *I am* (spoken by the *Beloved*)

4:7 BEAUTIFUL YOU ARE . . . NO FLAW IN YOU. Everything about the Shulammite was beautiful and free from blemish. "Flaw" can also refer to moral blemishes; thus she is physically and morally pure.

4:8 AMANA . . . SENIR . . . HERMON. Amana is the name for a mountain in the Anti-Lebanon mountain range; at the southern end are the peaks of Senir and Mount Hermon, northeast of Galilee.

4:9 STOLEN MY HEART, MY SISTER, MY BRIDE. "Sister" here means "beloved." Solomon's beloved bride has captured his heart.

4:12 A GARDEN LOCKED UP. The three figures of speech in this verse emphasize the fact the Shulammite had retained her virginity and was sexually pure on her wedding night. Virginity until marriage is God's sexual standard of purity for all young people, male and female. To violate God's holy standard defiles one's spirit and conscience and cheapens the moment of marriage consummation (see article on STANDARDS OF SEXUAL MORALITY, p. 1936).

4:14 SAFFRON. Saffron is a plant whose violet flowers yielded a yellow dye; a fragrant ointment was made by mixing it with olive oil.

4:14 CALAMUS . . . ALOES. Calamus is an aromatic spice; aloes is an aromatic wood from Bangladesh and China.

I have drunk my wine and my
milk.[k]

Friends

Eat, O friends, and drink;
drink your fill, O lovers.

Beloved

2I slept but my heart was awake.
Listen! My lover is knocking:
"Open to me, my sister, my
darling,
my dove,[l] my flawless[m] one.[n]
My head is drenched with dew,
my hair with the dampness of
the night."
3I have taken off my robe—
must I put it on again?
I have washed my feet—
must I soil them again?
4My lover thrust his hand through
the latch-opening;
my heart began to pound for
him.
5I arose to open for my lover,
and my hands dripped with
myrrh,[o]
my fingers with flowing myrrh,
on the handles of the lock.
6I opened for my lover,[p]
but my lover had left; he was
gone.[q]
My heart sank at his
departure.[j]
I looked[r] for him but did not find
him.
I called him but he did not
answer.
7The watchmen found me
as they made their rounds in the
city.[s]
They beat me, they bruised me;
they took away my cloak,
those watchmen of the walls!
8O daughters of Jerusalem, I charge
you[t]—
if you find my lover,[u]
what will you tell him?
Tell him I am faint with love.[v]

Friends

9How is your beloved better than
others,
most beautiful of women?[w]
How is your beloved better than
others,
that you charge us so?

Beloved

10My lover is radiant and ruddy,
outstanding among ten
thousand.[x]
11His head is purest gold;
his hair is wavy
and black as a raven.
12His eyes are like doves[y]
by the water streams,
washed in milk,[z]
mounted like jewels.
13His cheeks[a] are like beds of
spice[b]
yielding perfume.
His lips are like lilies[c]
dripping with myrrh.[d]
14His arms are rods of gold
set with chrysolite.
His body is like polished ivory
decorated with sapphires.[k][e]
15His legs are pillars of marble
set on bases of pure gold.
His appearance is like Lebanon,[f]
choice as its cedars.
16His mouth[g] is sweetness itself;
he is altogether lovely.
This is my lover,[h] this my friend,
O daughters of Jerusalem.[i]

Friends

6 Where has your lover[j] gone,
most beautiful of women?[k]
Which way did your lover turn,
that we may look for him with
you?

Beloved

2My lover has gone[l] down to his
garden,[m]
to the beds of spices,[n]
to browse in the gardens
and to gather lilies.
3I am my lover's and my lover is
mine;[o]
he browses among the lilies.[p]

5:1 [k]S SS 4:11; Isa 55:1; Joel 3:18
5:2 [l]S SS 1:15 [m]SS 4:7 [n]SS 6:9
5:5 [o]ver 13
5:6 [p]SS 6:1 [q]SS 6:2 [r]SS 3:1
5:7 [s]SS 3:3
5:8 [t]SS 2:7 [u]S SS 1:14 [v]SS 2:5
5:9 [w]S SS 1:8
5:10 [x]Ps 45:2
5:12 [y]S SS 1:15 [z]Ge 49:12
5:13 [a]SS 1:10 [b]SS 6:2 [c]S SS 2:1 [d]ver 5
5:14 [e]S Job 28:6
5:15 [f]1Ki 4:33; SS 7:4
5:16 [g]SS 4:3 [h]SS 7:9 [i]SS 1:5
6:1 [j]SS 5:6 [k]S SS 1:8
6:2 [l]SS 5:6 [m]S SS 4:12 [n]SS 5:13
6:3 [o]SS 7:10 [p]S SS 2:16

[j]6 Or *heart had gone out to him when he spoke*
[k]14 Or *lapis lazuli*

5:4 MY HEART BEGAN TO POUND. The Hebrew *me'eh* here translated "heart" can also be translated "bowels" (i.e., the belly, intestines and inner parts); the bowels were considered the seat of emotions, especially feelings of affection. The beloved's entire body quivered when she thought of her lover.

5:14 SAPPHIRES. A sapphire is a semiprecious stone of rich azure blue.

5:16 HE IS ALTOGETHER LOVELY. Everything about the bridegroom is precious, desirable and delightful.

Lover

4You are beautiful, my darling, as
Tirzah,[q]
lovely as Jerusalem,[r]
majestic as troops with
banners.[s]
5Turn your eyes from me;
they overwhelm me.
Your hair is like a flock of goats
descending from Gilead.[t]
6Your teeth are like a flock of
sheep
coming up from the washing.
Each has its twin,
not one of them is alone.[u]
7Your temples behind your veil[v]
are like the halves of a
pomegranate.[w]
8Sixty queens[x] there may be,
and eighty concubines,[y]
and virgins beyond number;
9but my dove,[z] my perfect one,[a]
is unique,
the only daughter of her mother,
the favorite of the one who bore
her.[b]
The maidens saw her and called
her blessed;
the queens and concubines
praised her.

Friends

10Who is this that appears like the
dawn,
fair as the moon, bright as the
sun,
majestic as the stars in
procession?

Lover

11I went down to the grove of nut
trees
to look at the new growth in the
valley,
to see if the vines had budded
or the pomegranates were in
bloom.[c]
12Before I realized it,
my desire set me among the
royal chariots of my
people.[1]

Friends

13Come back, come back,
O Shulammite;
come back, come back, that we
may gaze on you!

Lover

Why would you gaze on the
Shulammite
as on the dance[d] of Mahanaim?

7 How beautiful your sandaled
feet,
O prince's[e] daughter!
Your graceful legs are like jewels,
the work of a craftsman's hands.
2Your navel is a rounded goblet
that never lacks blended wine.
Your waist is a mound of wheat
encircled by lilies.
3Your breasts[f] are like two fawns,
twins of a gazelle.
4Your neck is like an ivory tower.[g]
Your eyes are the pools of
Heshbon[h]
by the gate of Bath Rabbim.
Your nose is like the tower of
Lebanon[i]
looking toward Damascus.
5Your head crowns you like Mount
Carmel.[j]
Your hair is like royal tapestry;
the king is held captive by its
tresses.
6How beautiful[k] you are and how
pleasing,
O love, with your delights![l]
7Your stature is like that of the
palm,
and your breasts[m] like clusters
of fruit.
8I said, "I will climb the palm tree;
I will take hold of its fruit."

6:4 [q] S Jos 12:24; S 1Ki 15:33 [r] Ps 48:2; 50:2 [s] S Nu 1:52
6:5 [t] S SS 4:1
6:6 [u] SS 4:2
6:7 [v] S Ge 24:65 [w] SS 4:3
6:8 [x] Ps 45:9 [y] S Ge 22:24; S Est 2:14
6:9 [z] S SS 1:15 [a] SS 5:2 [b] S SS 3:4
6:11 [c] SS 7:12
6:13 [d] S Ex 15:20
7:1 [e] Ps 45:13
7:3 [f] SS 4:5
7:4 [g] S Ps 144:12 [h] Nu 21:26 [i] S SS 5:15
7:5 [j] Isa 35:2
7:6 [k] S SS 1:15 [l] SS 4:10
7:7 [m] SS 4:5

[1] 12 Or *among the chariots of Amminadab*; or *among the chariots of the people of the prince*

6:4 MAJESTIC AS TROOPS WITH BANNERS. The bridegroom regarded his darling to be as awe-inspiring as an army with banners; others take this to mean as awesome as a host of stars (such as the Milky Way).

6:8 QUEENS ... CONCUBINES, AND VIRGINS BEYOND NUMBER. The women of Jerusalem are classified as queens, concubines and virgins (Heb *alamoth*, virgins of marriageable age). But the Shulammite cannot be compared with any of them; she is one of a kind, in a class by herself.

6:13 COME BACK, O SHULAMMITE. Some take "Shulammite" to mean a woman of Shunem; others take it to be a feminine form of Solomon as a title, i.e., a "Solomonitess," or Solomon's girl.

7:4 POOLS OF HESHBON ... BATH RABBIM. These are reservoirs outside the walls of Heshbon, about five miles northeast of Mount Nebo. Bath Rabbim (lit. "daughter of multitudes") was probably the name of one of the gates of Heshbon.

May your breasts be like the
clusters of the vine,
the fragrance of your breath like
apples,[n]
9 and your mouth like the best
wine.

Beloved

May the wine go straight to my
lover,[o]
flowing gently over lips and
teeth.[m]
10 I belong to my lover,
and his desire[p] is for me.[q]
11 Come, my lover, let us go to the
countryside,
let us spend the night in the
villages.[n]
12 Let us go early to the vineyards[r]
to see if the vines have
budded,[s]
if their blossoms[t] have opened,
and if the pomegranates[u] are in
bloom[v]—
there I will give you my love.
13 The mandrakes[w] send out their
fragrance,
and at our door is every
delicacy,
both new and old,
that I have stored up for you,
my lover.[x]

8 If only you were to me like a
brother,
who was nursed at my mother's
breasts!
Then, if I found you outside,
I would kiss you,
and no one would despise me.
2 I would lead you
and bring you to my mother's
house[y]—
she who has taught me.
I would give you spiced wine to
drink,
the nectar of my pomegranates.

7:8 [n]SS 2:5
7:9 [o]S S 5:16
7:10 [p]Ps 45:11 [q]SS 2:16; 6:3
7:12 [r]S SS 1:6 [s]SS 2:15 [t]SS 2:13 [u]S SS 4:13 [v]SS 6:11
7:13 [w]S Ge 30:14 [x]SS 4:16
8:2 [y]SS 3:4

8:3 [z]SS 2:6
8:4 [a]SS 2:7; S 3:5
8:5 [b]SS 3:6 [c]S SS 3:4
8:6 [d]S SS 1:2 [e]S Nu 5:14
8:7 [f]S Pr 6:35

3 His left arm is under my head
and his right arm embraces
me.[z]
4 Daughters of Jerusalem, I charge
you:
Do not arouse or awaken love
until it so desires.[a]

Friends

5 Who is this coming up from the
desert[b]
leaning on her lover?

Beloved

Under the apple tree I roused you;
there your mother conceived[c]
you,
there she who was in labor gave
you birth.
6 Place me like a seal over your
heart,
like a seal on your arm;
for love[d] is as strong as death,
its jealousy[o][e] unyielding as
the grave.[p]
It burns like blazing fire,
like a mighty flame.[q]
7 Many waters cannot quench love;
rivers cannot wash it away.
If one were to give
all the wealth of his house for
love,
it[r] would be utterly scorned.[f]

Friends

8 We have a young sister,
and her breasts are not yet
grown.
What shall we do for our sister
for the day she is spoken for?
9 If she is a wall,

[m] *9* Septuagint, Aquila, Vulgate and Syriac; Hebrew *lips of sleepers* [n] *11* Or *henna bushes* [o] *6* Or *ardor* [p] *6* Hebrew *Sheol* [q] *6* Or / *like the very flame of the LORD* [r] *7* Or *he*

7:13 MANDRAKES. These herbs were considered to be an aphrodisiac, i.e., something that excites sexual desire (cf. Ge 30:14–17).

8:4 DO NOT AROUSE OR AWAKEN LOVE UNTIL IT SO DESIRES. See 2:7, note.

8:6–7 LOVE IS AS STRONG AS DEATH ... MANY WATERS CANNOT QUENCH LOVE. There is nothing more powerful and beautiful than the expression of mutual love between a man and woman who are truly committed to each other.

8:6 JEALOUSY UNYIELDING AS THE GRAVE. Jealousy here can be translated "ardent love." It is as inflexible as the grave (Heb *Sheol*), a place from which no one can escape (see Ps 16:10, note).

8:7 ALL THE WEALTH OF HIS HOUSE FOR LOVE, IT WOULD BE UTTERLY SCORNED. Trying to buy love for money is something to be scorned; it cannot be done. Similarly, any marriage that is based on the attractiveness of the earthly possessions of either the husband or the wife is doomed to failure.

8:9 IF SHE IS A WALL ... IF SHE IS A DOOR. If the young sister is a wall resisting temptation, the daughters of Jerusalem will adorn her (i.e., prepare her for marriage); if she is a door ready to succumb to temptation, they will do whatever is needed to protect her from such defilement.

we will build towers of silver on
her.
If she is a door,
we will enclose her with panels
of cedar.

Beloved

10 I am a wall,
and my breasts are like towers.
Thus I have become in his eyes
like one bringing contentment.
11 Solomon had a vineyard[g] in Baal
Hamon;
he let out his vineyard to
tenants.
Each was to bring for its fruit
a thousand shekels[s][h] of silver.
12 But my own vineyard[i] is mine to
give;
the thousand shekels are for
you, O Solomon,
and two hundred[t] are for those
who tend its fruit.

Lover

13 You who dwell in the gardens
with friends in attendance,
let me hear your voice!

Beloved

14 Come away, my lover,
and be like a gazelle[j]
or like a young stag[k]
on the spice-laden mountains.[l]

8:11 [g] Ecc 2:4 [h] Isa 7:23
8:12 [i] S SS 1:6
8:14 [j] S Pr 5:19 [k] S SS 2:9 [l] S SS 2:8,17

[s] *11* That is, about 25 pounds (about 11.5 kilograms); also in verse 12 [t] *12* That is, about 5 pounds (about 2.3 kilograms)

8:12 MY OWN VINEYARD IS MINE TO GIVE. In contrast to Solomon's many vineyards, she has her own single vineyard. Solomon can have the income from his, and those who tend it can have their portion, but her vineyard is something better.

ISAIAH

Outline

I. Prophecies of Judgment and Rebuke (1:1—35:10)
   A. The Setting for Isaiah's Prophecy (1:1-31)
   B. Isaiah's Early Prophecies (2:1—5:30)
      1. The Day of the Lord (2:1-22)
      2. Judgment Against Judah and Jerusalem (3:1—4:1)
      3. Predictions of Judgment and Glory (4:2-6)
      4. Parable About Judah's Judgment and Exile (5:1-30)
   C. Isaiah's Cleansing and Commissioning by God (6:1-13)
   D. Isaiah's Early Messianic Prophecies (7:1—12:6)
      1. The Sign of Immanuel (7:1-25)
      2. Foreshadowings of Messianic Deliverance (8:1—9:7)
      3. Prophecies of Judgment Against Israel (Northern Kingdom) and Assyria (9:8—10:34)
      4. The Davidic Messiah and His Kingdom (11:1—12:6)
   E. Isaiah's Prophecies of Judgment Against the Nations (13:1—23:18)
      1. Against Babylon (13:1—14:23)
      2. Against Assyria (14:24-27)
      3. Against Philistia (14:28-32)
      4. Against Moab (15:1—16:14)
      5. Against Damascus and Samaria (17:1-14)
      6. Against Cush (18:1-7)
      7. Against Egypt (19:1—20:6)
      8. Against Babylon (Second Oracle) (21:1-10)
      9. Against Edom (21:11-12)
      10. Against Arabia (21:13-17)
      11. Against Jerusalem (22:1-25)
      12. Against Tyre (23:1-18)
   F. Prophecies About the Consummation of History (24:1—27:13)
   G. Prophecies of Woe Intertwined with Prophetic Hope of Salvation (28:1—35:10)

II. Historical Interlude Concerning Hezekiah (36:1—39:8)
   A. Hezekiah's Deliverance from Assyria (36:1—37:38)
   B. Hezekiah's Sickness and Healing (38:1-22)
   C. Hezekiah's Foolish Pride (39:1-8)

III. Prophecies of Salvation and Hope (40:1—66:24)
   A. Prophetic Promises of Restoration for God's People (40:1—48:22)
      1. The Glory of the Lord and His Servant Will be Revealed (40:1—42:25)
      2. The Restoration of a Redeemed Remnant (43:1—45:25)
      3. Lessons of Faith for Judah When God Judges Babylon (46:1—48:22)
   B. Prophetic Promises Concerning the Suffering Servant Messiah (49:1—53:12)
      1. His Mission and Obedience (49:1—50:11)
      2. His Encouragement and Exhortation for the Remnant (51:1—52:12)
      3. His Suffering and His Atoning Death (52:13—53:12)
   C. Further Prophetic Revelation Concerning Restoration and Redemption (54:1—59:21)

D. Prophetic Visions of a Glorious Future for Zion (60:1—66:24)
   1. Zion's Prosperity and Peace (60:1–22)
   2. The Messiah's Anointing and Mission (61:1–11)
   3. Prophetic Intercession for Zion's Restoration and Glory (62:1—64:12)
   4. God's Answer of Mercy and Glorious Consummation (65:1—66:24)

Author: Isaiah

Theme: Judgment and Salvation

Date of Writing: c. 700–680 B.C.

Background

The historical setting for the prophetic ministry of Isaiah son of Amoz was Jerusalem during the reign of four kings of Judah: Uzziah, Jotham, Ahaz and Hezekiah (1:1). King Uzziah died in 740 B.C. (cf. 6:1) and Hezekiah in 687 B.C.; thus Isaiah's ministry spanned more than half a century of Judah's history. According to Hebrew tradition, Isaiah was martyred by being sawn in two (cf. Heb 11:37) by Hezekiah's wicked son and successor to the throne, King Manasseh (c. 680 B.C.).

Isaiah apparently came from an influential upper-class family in Jerusalem; he was educated, had gifts as a poet and prophet, was acquainted with royalty, and gave prophetic counsel to kings concerning Judah's foreign affairs. He is usually regarded as the most literary and influential of the writing prophets. He was married to a wife gifted as a prophetess, and they had two sons whose names contained a symbolic message for the nation.

Isaiah was a contemporary of Hosea and Micah; he prophesied during the threatening expansion of the Assyrian empire, the final collapse of Israel (the northern kingdom), and the spiritual and moral decline of Judah (the southern kingdom). Isaiah warned Judah's King Ahaz not to look to Assyria for help against Israel and Aram; he warned King Hezekiah, after Israel's fall in 722 B.C., not to make alliances with foreign nations against Assyria. He exhorted both kings to place their trust solely in the Lord as their security (7:3–7; 30:1–17). Isaiah enjoyed his greatest influence during King Hezekiah's reign.

Some scholars question whether Isaiah wrote the entire book that bears his name. These scholars assign only chs. 1—39 to Isaiah of Jerusalem; they typically attribute chs. 40—66 to another author or authors more than a century and a half later. There is no Biblical data, however, that requires rejecting Isaiah's authorship of the entire book. Isaiah's prophetic messages in chs. 40—66 for the Jewish exiles in Babylon long after his death emphasize God's ability to reveal specific future events through his prophets (e.g. 42:8–9; 44:6–8; 45:1; 47:1–11; 53:1–12). If one accepts the phenomena of prophetic visions and revelations (cf. Rev 1:1; 4:1—22:21), then the major obstacle to believing that Isaiah wrote the entire book is removed. Positive supporting evidence is plentiful and falls under two broad categories. (1) Internal evidence from the book itself includes the superscription in 1:1 (which stands for the entire book) and the numerous striking parallels of expression and thought between both major sections of the book. One notable example is the expression "the Holy One of Israel," which occurs 12 times in chs. 1—39, 14 times in chs. 40—66, and only six times in the rest of the OT combined. No less than 25 Hebrew word-forms appear in both major divisions of Isaiah but nowhere else in OT prophetic books. (2) External evidence includes the testimony of the Jewish Talmud and the NT itself, which attributes all parts of the book to the prophet Isaiah (e.g., cf. Mt 12:17–21 with Isa 42:1–4; Mt 3:3 and Lk 3:4 with Isa 40:3; Jn 12:37–41 with Isa 6:9–10 and 53:1; Ac 8:28–33 with Isa 53:7–9; Ro 9:27 and 10:16–21 with Isa 10, 53 and 65).

Purpose

A threefold purpose is apparent in Isaiah's writing. (1) The prophet first confronted his own nation and other contemporary nations with the word of the Lord concerning their sin and God's coming judgment. (2) Then, by revelatory visions and the Spirit of prophecy, Isaiah prophesied hope to a future generation of Jewish exiles who would in time be restored from captivity and whom God would redeem to be a light to the Gentiles. (3) Finally, Isaiah prophesied that God was going to send the Davidic Messiah, whose salvation would eventually encompass all the nations of the earth, thus providing hope for God's people under both the old and new covenants.

Survey

Most scholars agree that the 66 chapters of Isaiah divide naturally into two major sections: chs. 1—39 and chs. 40—66. In certain respects Isaiah is like the Bible in miniature: (1) Isaiah's twofold division stressed the general themes of judgment and salvation, corresponding to the overall general themes of the OT and NT; and (2) in both divisions of Isaiah and the Bible, the thread that ties them together is the redemptive work of Christ.

(1) Section one of Isaiah (chs. 1—39) contains four large blocks of material. (a) In chs. 1—12, Isaiah warns and denounces Judah for her idolatry, immorality and social injustices during a time of deceptive prosperity. Intertwined with the message of coming judgment are important Messianic prophecies (e.g. 2:4; 7:14; 9:6–7; 11:1–9), as well as Isaiah's testimony of his own cleansing from sin and divine commissioning for the prophetic ministry (ch. 6). (b) In chs. 13—23, Isaiah prophesies to nations contemporary with Judah about their sin and God's coming judgment. (c) Chs. 24—35 contain an assortment of prophetic promises of future salvation and judgment. (d) Chs. 36—39 record selective history from King Hezekiah's life, which parallels 2Ki 18:13—20:21.

(2) The second major section (chs. 40—66) contains some of the most profound prophecies in the Bible about God's greatness and the vastness of his redemptive plan. These chapters inspired hope and comfort in God's people during the remaining years of Hezekiah's reign (38:5) and for centuries afterward. They are full of prophetic revelation of God's glory and power and of his promises to restore a righteous and fruit-bearing remnant in Israel and among the nations in full demonstration of his redemptive love. These promises and their fulfillment are especially connected to the theme of suffering and contain Isaiah's "servant songs" (see 42:1–4; 49:1–6; 50:4–9; 52:13—53:12), which point beyond the experience of the Jewish exiles to the future coming of Jesus Christ and his atoning death (ch. 53). The prophet predicts that the coming Messiah will enable righteousness to shine brightly and salvation to go out to the nations like a torch that is burning (chs. 60—66). He condemns spiritual blindness concerning God's ways (42:18–25) and commends intercessory prayer and spiritual birth pains by God's people as necessary in order that all things may be fulfilled (cf. 56:6–8; 62:1–2,6–7; 66:7–18).

Special Features

Eight major features characterize the book of Isaiah. (1) It is largely written in Hebrew poetic form and stands unsurpassed as a literary gem in the beauty, power and versatility of its poetry. Isaiah's rich vocabulary surpasses that of all other OT writers. (2) Isaiah is called "the evangelical prophet" because, of all the OT books, his Messianic prophecies contain the fullest and clearest declaration of the gospel of Jesus Christ. (3) His vision of the cross in ch. 53 is the most specific and detailed prophecy in the whole Bible about Jesus' atoning death for sinners. (4) It is the most theological and comprehensive of all OT prophetic books; it reaches back in time to God's creation of the heavens and earth and human life (e.g., 42:5) and looks forward in time to God's consummation of history and the creation of new heavens and a new earth (e.g., 65:17; 66:22). (5) It contains more revelation about God's nature, majesty and holiness than any other OT prophetic book. Isaiah's God is holy and all-powerful, the One who will judge sin and unrighteousness among humans and the nations. His favorite expression for God is "the Holy One of Israel." (6) Isaiah—whose name means "The LORD saves"—is the prophet of salvation. He uses the specific term "salvation" nearly three times more than all other OT prophetic books combined. Isaiah reveals that God's full purpose of salvation will be realized only in connection with the Messiah. (7) Isaiah frequently refers back to earlier redemptive events in Israel's history: e.g., the exodus (4:5–6; 11:15; 31:5; 43:16–17), the destruction of Sodom and

Gomorrah (1:9), and Gideon's victory over the Midianites (9:4; 10:26; 28:21); he also draws from Moses' prophetic song in Dt 32 (1:2; 30:17; 43:11,13). (8) Isaiah joins Deuteronomy and Psalms as one of the three OT books most often quoted and referred to in the NT.

New Testament Fulfillment

Isaiah prophesies about John the Baptist as the appointed forerunner to the Messiah (40:3–5; cf. Mt 3:1–3). The following are some of Isaiah's many Messianic prophecies and their NT application in the life and ministry of Jesus Christ: his incarnation and deity (Isa 7:14; see Mt 1:22–23 and Lk 1:34–35; Isa 9:6–7; see Lk 1:32–33; 2:11); his youth (Isa 7:15–16 and 11:1; see Lk 3:23,32 and Ac 13:22–23); his mission (Isa 11:2–5; 42:1–4; 60:1–3 and 61:1; see Lk 4:17–19,21); his obedience (Isa 50:5; see Heb 5:8); his message and anointing by the Spirit (Isa 11:2; 42:1; and 61:1; see Mt 12:15–21); his miracles (Isa 35:5–6; see Mt 11:2–5); his suffering (Isa 50:6; see Mt 26:67 and 27:26,30; Isa 53:4–5,11; see Ac 8:28–33); his rejection (Isa 53:1–3; see Lk 23:18; Jn 1:11 and 7:5); his shame (Isa 52:14; see Php 2:7–8); his atoning death (Isa 53:4–12; see Ro 5:6); his ascension (Isa 52:13; see Php 2:9–11) and his second advent (Isa 26:20–21; see Jude 14; Isa 61:2–3; see 2Th 1:5–12; Isa 65:17–25; see 2Pe 3:13).

Reading Isaiah

In order to read the entire Old Testament in one year, the book of Isaiah should be read in 28 days, according to the following schedule: □ 1–2 □ 3–5 □ 6–8 □ 9–10 □ 11–12 □ 13–14 □ 15–18 □ 19–22 □ 23–24 □ 25–26 □ 27–28 □ 29–30 □ 31–32 □ 33–34 □ 35–37 □ 38–39 □ 40–41 □ 42–43 □ 44–45 □ 46–47 □ 48–49 □ 50–51 □ 52–53 □ 54–56 □ 57–58 □ 59–60 □ 61–63 □ 64–66

NOTES

1 The vision[a] concerning Judah and Jerusalem[b] that Isaiah son of Amoz saw[c] during the reigns of Uzziah,[d] Jotham,[e] Ahaz[f] and Hezekiah,[g] kings of Judah.

A Rebellious Nation

2 Hear, O heavens! Listen,
O earth![h]
For the LORD has spoken:[i]
"I reared children[j] and brought them up,
but they have rebelled[k] against me.
3 The ox knows[l] his master,
the donkey his owner's manger,[m]
but Israel does not know,[n]
my people do not understand.[o]"
4 Ah, sinful nation,
a people loaded with guilt,[p]
a brood of evildoers,[q]
children given to corruption![r]
They have forsaken[s] the LORD;
they have spurned the Holy One[t] of Israel
and turned their backs[u] on him.
5 Why should you be beaten[v] anymore?
Why do you persist[w] in rebellion?[x]
Your whole head is injured,
your whole heart[y] afflicted.[z]
6 From the sole of your foot to the top of your head[a]
there is no soundness[b]—
only wounds and welts[c]
and open sores,
not cleansed or bandaged[d]
or soothed with oil.[e]
7 Your country is desolate,[f]
your cities burned with fire;[g]
your fields are being stripped by foreigners[h]
right before you,
laid waste as when overthrown by strangers.[i]
8 The Daughter of Zion[j] is left[k]
like a shelter in a vineyard,
like a hut[l] in a field of melons,
like a city under siege.
9 Unless the LORD Almighty
had left us some survivors,[m]
we would have become like Sodom,

1:1 [a] 1Sa 3:1; Isa 22:1,5; Ob 1:1; Na 1:1 [b] Isa 40:9; 44:26 [c] Isa 2:1; 13:1 [d] S 2Ki 14:21; S 2Ch 26:22 [e] S 1Ch 3:12 [f] S 2Ki 16:1 [g] S 1Ch 3:13 **1:2** [h] S Dt 4:26 [i] Jdg 11:10; Jer 42:5; Mic 1:2 [j] Isa 23:4; 63:16 [k] ver 4,23; Isa 24:5,20; 30:1,9; 46:8; 48:8; 57:4; 65:2; 66:24; Eze 24:3; Hag 1:12; Mal 1:6; 3:5 **1:3** [l] Job 12:9 [m] S Ge 42:27 [n] Jer 4:22; 5:4; 9:3,6; Hos 2:8; 4:1 [o] S Dt 32:28; Isa 42:25; 48:8; Hos 4:6; 7:9 **1:4** [p] Isa 5:18 [q] S ver 2; Isa 9:17; 14:20; 31:2; Jer 23:14 [r] Ps 14:3 [s] S Dt 32:15; S Ps 119:87 [t] S 2Ki 19:22; Isa 5:19,24; 31:1; 37:23; 41:14; 43:14; 45:11; 47:4; Eze 39:7 [u] S Pr 30:9; Isa 59:13 **1:5** [v] Pr 20:30 [w] Jer 2:30; 5:3; 8:5 [x] S ver 2; Isa 31:6; Jer 44:16-17; Heb 3:16 [y] La 2:11; 5:17 [z] Isa 30:26; 33:6,24; 58:8; Jer 30:17 **1:6** [a] S Dt 28:35 [b] Ps 38:3 [c] Isa 53:5 [d] S Ps 147:3; Isa 30:26; Jer 8:22; 14:19; 30:17; La 2:13; Eze 34:4 [e] 2Sa 14:2; Ps 23:5; 45:7; 104:15; Isa 61:3; Lk 10:34 **1:7** [f] S Lev 26:34 [g] S Lev 26:31; S Dt 29:23 [h] Lev 26:16; Jdg 6:3-6; Isa 62:8; Jer 5:17 [i] S 2Ki 18:13; S Ps 109:11 **1:8** [j] S Ps 9:14; S Isa 10:32 [k] Isa 30:17; 49:21 [l] S Job 27:18 **1:9** [m] S Ge 45:7; S 2Ki 21:14; Isa 4:2; 6:13; 27:12; 28:5; 37:4,31-32; 45:25; 56:8; Jer 23:3; Joel 2:32

1:1 THE VISION. Isaiah did not prophesy about or record his own ideas; rather, he received visions from God inspired by the Holy Spirit (cf. 2Pe 1:20–21). He was allowed to see coming events in God's plan of salvation through an unerring communication from God himself.

1:1 ISAIAH. The name Isaiah means "the LORD saves." As a prophet commissioned by God, Isaiah began his ministry in 740 B.C., the year King Uzziah died (see 6:1). He prophesied forty or more years and probably died about 680 B.C. (see the introduction to Isaiah for more about him).

1:1 CONCERNING JUDAH. Isaiah's prophetic ministry took place during the time of the divided kingdom (see 1Ki 12:20, note; 2Ch 10:1, note). The northern kingdom—variously called "Israel," "Samaria" or "Ephraim"—included ten tribes of the Israelites. The southern kingdom—usually called "Judah," with its capital at Jerusalem—consisted of the tribes of Judah and Benjamin. Both kingdoms had turned from God and his law to foreign nations and their false gods to deliver them from their enemies. The northern kingdom was conquered and destroyed by Assyria in 722 B.C. Isaiah warned Judah that they too would be destroyed because of their sin and apostasy (39:6).

1:2 THEY HAVE REBELLED AGAINST ME. Judah and Israel had received God's covenant, his law, his temple and his many promises, yet they lived sinful lives, disregarded that covenant, and failed to acknowledge God as the source of their salvation and blessing; therefore, God was sending judgment (vv. 5–8).

1:3 ISRAEL. Here "Israel" refers to all twelve tribes, including Judah.

1:4 THE HOLY ONE OF ISRAEL. This expression as a title for God occurs 26 times in Isaiah; five additional times God is referred to simply as "the Holy One." By using this name for God, undoubtedly derived in part from Isaiah's powerful vision of God in his holiness (ch. 6), the prophet not only emphasizes God's distinctively holy character, but also that God's people must be holy if they are to continue in a covenant relationship with him.

1:7 YOUR COUNTRY IS DESOLATE. In an effort to bring Judah to repentance, God allowed their land to be plundered by foreigners (2Ch 28:5–18). The people's sin had cut them off from God's blessing and protection, and judgment had already begun. The land and people would ultimately be destroyed by Nebuchadnezzar and his Babylonian army (605–586 B.C.). Persistent sin by unrepentant sinners will always bring God's judgment and eventual destruction.

1:9–10 SODOM . . . GOMORRAH. The cities of Sodom and Gomorrah were completely destroyed because of their great sin (Ge 19:1–25). Isaiah equates Judah with these cities because of its great unfaithfulness.

we would have been like
Gomorrah.[n]

10 Hear the word of the LORD,[o]
you rulers of Sodom;[p]
listen to the law[q] of our God,
you people of Gomorrah![r]
11 "The multitude of your sacrifices—
what are they to me?" says the
LORD.
"I have more than enough of burnt
offerings,
of rams and the fat of fattened
animals;[s]
I have no pleasure[t]
in the blood of bulls[u] and lambs
and goats.[v]
12 When you come to appear before
me,
who has asked this of you,[w]
this trampling of my courts?
13 Stop bringing meaningless
offerings![x]
Your incense[y] is detestable[z] to
me.
New Moons,[a] Sabbaths and
convocations[b]—
I cannot bear your evil
assemblies.
14 Your New Moon[c] festivals and
your appointed feasts[d]
my soul hates.[e]
They have become a burden to
me;[f]
I am weary[g] of bearing them.
15 When you spread out your hands[h]
in prayer,
I will hide[i] my eyes from you;
even if you offer many prayers,
I will not listen.[j]
Your hands[k] are full of blood;[l]
16 wash[m] and make yourselves
clean.
Take your evil deeds
out of my sight![n]
Stop doing wrong,[o]
17 learn to do right![p]
Seek justice,[q]

1:9 [n] S Ge 19:24; Ro 9:29* **1:10** [o] Isa 28:14 [p] S Ge 13:13; S 18:20; Eze 16:49; Ro 9:29; Rev 11:8 [q] Isa 5:24; 8:20; 30:9 [r] Isa 13:19 **1:11** [s] Ps 50:8; Am 6:4 [t] S Job 22:3 [u] Isa 66:3; Jer 6:20 [v] 1Sa 15:22; S Ps 40:6; Mal 1:10; Heb 10:4 **1:12** [w] Ex 23:17; Dt 31:11 **1:13** [x] Pr 15:8; Isa 66:3; Hag 2:14 [y] Jer 7:9; 18:15; 44:8 [z] S 1Ki 14:24; Ps 115:8; Pr 28:9; Isa 41:24; Mal 2:11 [a] S Nu 10:10 [b] 1Ch 23:31 **1:14** [c] S Ne 10:33 [d] Ex 12:16; Lev 23:1-44; Nu 28:11-29:39; Dt 16:1-17; Isa 5:12; 29:1; Hos 2:11 [e] S Ps 11:5 [f] S Job 7:12 [g] Ps 69:3; Isa 7:13; 43:22, 24; Jer 44:22; Mal 2:17; 3:14 **1:15** [h] S Ex 9:29 [i] S Dt 31:17; Isa 57:17; 59:2 [j] S Dt 1:45; S 1Sa 8:18; S Job 15:31; S Jn 9:31 [k] S Job 9:30 [l] Isa 4:4; 59:3; Jer 2:34; Eze 7:23; Hos 4:2; Joel 3:21 **1:16** [m] S Ru 3:3; Mt 27:24; Jas 4:8 [n] Nu 19:11,16; Isa 52:11 [o] Isa 55:7; Jer 25:5 **1:17** [p] S Ps 34:14 [q] S Ps 72:1; Isa 11:4; 33:5; 56:1; 61:8; Am 5:14-15; Mic 6:8; Zep 2:3 [r] S Dt 14:29 [s] ver 23; Job 22:9; Ps 82:3; 94:6; Isa 10:2 [t] S Ex 22:22; Eze 18:31; 22:7; Lk 18:3; Jas 1:27 **1:18** [u] S 1Sa 2:25; Isa 41:1; 43:9,26 [v] S Ps 51:7;

encourage the oppressed.[a][r]
Defend the cause of the
fatherless,[s]
plead the case of the widow.[t]

18 "Come now, let us reason
together,"[u]
says the LORD.
"Though your sins are like scarlet,
they shall be as white as
snow;[v]
though they are red as crimson,
they shall be like wool.[w]
19 If you are willing and obedient,[x]
you will eat the best from the
land;[y]
20 but if you resist and rebel,[z]
you will be devoured by the
sword."[a]
For the mouth of the LORD
has spoken.[b]

21 See how the faithful city
has become a harlot![c]
She once was full of justice;
righteousness[d] used to dwell in
her—
but now murderers![e]
22 Your silver has become dross,[f]
your choice wine is diluted with
water.
23 Your rulers are rebels,[g]
companions of thieves;[h]
they all love bribes[i]
and chase after gifts.
They do not defend the cause of
the fatherless;
the widow's case does not come
before them.[j]

Rev 7:14 [w] Isa 55:7 **1:19** [x] S Job 36:11; S Isa 50:10 [y] Dt 30:15-16; Ezr 9:12; Ps 34:10; Isa 30:23; 55:2; 58:14; 62:9; 65:13,21-22 **1:20** [z] S 1Sa 12:15 [a] S Job 15:22; Isa 3:25; 27:1; 65:12; 66:16; Jer 17:27 [b] Nu 23:19; Isa 21:17; 34:16; 40:5; 58:14; Jer 49:13; Mic 4:4; Zec 1:6; Rev 1:16 **1:21** [c] Isa 57:3-9; Jer 2:20; 3:2,9; 13:27; Eze 23:3; Hos 2:1-13 [d] Isa 5:7; 46:13; 59:14; Am 6:12 [e] S Pr 6:17 **1:22** [f] S Ps 119:119 **1:23** [g] S ver 2 [h] S Dt 19:14; Mic 2:1-2; 6:12 [i] S Ex 23:8; Am 5:12 [j] Isa 10:2; Jer 5:28; Eze 22:6-7; Mic 3:9; Hab 1:4

[a] 17 Or / *rebuke the oppressor*

1:11 SACRIFICES—WHAT ARE THEY TO ME? Isaiah condemns the people for participating in evil deeds and injustices (vv. 16–17), while continuing to bring offerings and sacrifices to God and to pray to and worship him. Worship and praise become an abomination to him if our hearts are not sincerely devoted to him and to his holy ways (cf. 66:3; Jer 7:21–26; Hos 6:6; Am 5:21–24; Mic 6:6–8).

1:15 I WILL NOT LISTEN. Sin in our lives will cause God to turn away from our prayers (see Jas 4:3, note; 1Jn 3:22, note; see article on EFFECTIVE PRAYING, p. 496).

1:18 COME NOW, LET US REASON. God did not want to condemn and destroy his people. He offered full forgiveness and pardon if they would only repent, put away evil, strive to do right and obey his word (vv. 16–19). God's forgiveness is now available for all who, though they have sinned, confess their sins, repent and accept God's cleansing through the blood of Jesus Christ (Lk 24:46–47; 1Jn 1:9). Those who refuse God's mercy and choose instead to cling rebelliously to their own ways will be destroyed (v. 20).

24Therefore the Lord, the LORD Almighty,
the Mighty One[k] of Israel, declares:
"Ah, I will get relief from my foes
and avenge[l] myself on my enemies.[m]
25I will turn my hand against you;[n]
I will thoroughly purge[o] away your dross[p]
and remove all your impurities.[q]
26I will restore your judges as in days of old,[r]
your counselors as at the beginning.
Afterward you will be called[s]
the City of Righteousness,[t]
the Faithful City.[u]"

27Zion will be redeemed with justice,
her penitent[v] ones with righteousness.[w]
28But rebels and sinners[x] will both be broken,
and those who forsake[y] the LORD will perish.[z]

29"You will be ashamed[a] because of the sacred oaks[b]
in which you have delighted;
you will be disgraced because of the gardens[c]
that you have chosen.
30You will be like an oak with fading leaves,[d]
like a garden without water.
31The mighty man will become tinder
and his work a spark;
both will burn together,
with no one to quench the fire.[e]"

The Mountain of the LORD

2:1–4pp — Mic 4:1–3

2 This is what Isaiah son of Amoz saw concerning Judah and Jerusalem:[f]

2In the last days[g]

the mountain[h] of the LORD's temple will be established
as chief among the mountains;[i]
it will be raised[j] above the hills,
and all nations will stream to it.[k]

3Many peoples[l] will come and say,

"Come, let us go[m] up to the mountain[n] of the LORD,
to the house of the God of Jacob.
He will teach us his ways,
so that we may walk in his paths."
The law[o] will go out from Zion,
the word of the LORD from Jerusalem.[p]
4He will judge[q] between the nations
and will settle disputes[r] for many peoples.
They will beat their swords into plowshares

1:24 [k]S Ge 49:24 [l]Isa 34:2,8; 35:4; 47:3; 59:17; 61:2; 63:4; Jer 51:6; Eze 5:13 [m]S Dt 32:43; S Isa 10:3 **1:25** [n]Dt 28:63 [o]S Ps 78:38 [p]S Ps 119:119 [q]2Ch 29:15; Isa 48:10; Jer 6:29; 9:7; Eze 22:22; Mal 3:3 **1:26** [r]Jer 33:7,11; Mic 4:8 [s]S Ge 32:28 [t]Isa 32:16; 33:5; 46:13; 48:18; 61:11; 62:1; Jer 31:23; Zec 8:3 [u]Isa 4:3; 48:2; 52:1; 60:14; 62:2; 64:10; Da 9:24 **1:27** [v]Isa 30:15; 31:6; 59:20; Eze 18:30 [w]Isa 35:10; 41:14; 43:1; 52:3; 62:12; 63:4; Hos 2:19 **1:28** [x]Isa 33:14; 43:27; 48:8; 50:1; 59:2; Jer 4:18 [y]S Dt 32:15 [z]Ps 9:5; Isa 24:20; 66:24; Jer 16:4; 42:22; 44:12; 2Th 1:8-9 **1:29** [a]Ps 97:7; Isa 42:17; 44:9, 11; 45:16; Jer 10:14 [b]Isa 57:5; Eze 6:13; Hos 4:13 [c]Isa 65:3; 66:17 **1:30** [d]S Ps 1:3 **1:31** [e]Isa 4:4; 5:24; 9:18-19; 10:17; 24:6; 26:11; 30:27,33; 33:14; 34:10; 66:15-16,24; Jer 5:14; 7:20; 21:12; Ob 1:18; Mal 3:2; 4:1; S Mt 25:41 **2:1** [f]Isa 1:1 **2:2** [g]Ac 2:17; Heb 1:2 [h]Isa 11:9; 24:23; 25:6,10; 27:13; 56:7; 57:13; 65:25; 66:20; Jer 31:23; Da 11:45; Joel 3:17; Mic 4:7 [i]Isa 65:9 [j]Zec 14:10 [k]S Ps 102:15; Jer 16:19 **2:3** [l]Isa 45:23; 49:1; 60:3-6,14; 66:18; Jer 3:17; Joel 3:2; Zep 3:8; Zec 14:2 [m]Isa 45:14; 49:12,23; 55:5 [n]S Dt 33:19; S Ps 137:5 [o]S Isa 1:10; 33:22; 51:4,7 [p]Lk 24:47; S Jn 4:22 **2:4** [q]Ps 7:6; S 9:19; 96:13; 98:9; Isa 1:27; 3:13; 9:7; 42:4; 51:4; Joel 3:14 [r]S Ge 49:10

1:25 PURGE AWAY YOUR DROSS. God intended to purge away evil from his people and to restore a remnant who repented (vv. 18–19,26–27). He was not yet finished with Judah (cf. Ezr 1; 5:2,14–16), for the Redeemer of the entire human race still had to come through these chosen people. Although "Zion" (v. 27, i.e., Jerusalem) would be restored, only those who truly turned to God would be saved and not destroyed (cf. 65:8–16).

2:2 IN THE LAST DAYS. The NT defines the last days as the period of time between the first and second comings of Christ (see Ac 2:17, note). What Isaiah describes in vv. 1–5 will reach its complete fulfillment at Christ's second coming, when he establishes God's kingdom on earth.

2:2–5 MOUNTAIN ... WILL BE ESTABLISHED. Isaiah prophesies of a time when God's rule will be established over all the earth (cf. Mic 4:1–3). All evil, injustice and rebellion directed against God and his law will be put down, and righteousness will reign (cf. 59:20—60:3,14; Jer 33:14–16; Zec 2:10–12). "All nations," Jews and Gentiles, will worship and serve the Lord. This prophecy reflects God's final purpose for Israel and the human race; it is fulfilled in Jesus Christ himself, who executes justice and righteousness on the earth (9:1–7; 11:3–5).

2:3 TEACH US HIS WAYS ... HIS PATHS. The primary concern of all who come to the Lord should be to know and to obey God's will as citizens of his kingdom. It is important that we who proclaim God's message take supreme care that our preaching and teaching are the word of God—based on the inspired Scriptures as revealed through Christ, the OT prophets and the NT apostles (see Eph 2:20, note). All people, both the lost and the saved, need to hear God's truth proclaimed from the lips of those anointed by the Holy Spirit and committed to the righteousness of God's ways.

and their spears into pruning
hooks.[s]
Nation will not take up sword
against nation,[t]
nor will they train for war
anymore.

5 Come, O house of Jacob,[u]
let us walk in the light[v] of the
LORD.

Isa 35:8-9

The Day of the LORD

6 You have abandoned[w] your people,
the house of Jacob.[x]
They are full of superstitions from
the East;
they practice divination[y] like
the Philistines[z]
and clasp hands[a] with
pagans.[b]
7 Their land is full of silver and
gold;[c]
there is no end to their
treasures.[d]
Their land is full of horses;[e]
there is no end to their
chariots.[f]
8 Their land is full of idols;[g]
they bow down[h] to the work of
their hands,[i]
to what their fingers[j] have
made.
9 So man will be brought low[k]
and mankind humbled[l] —
do not forgive them.[b][m]

10 Go into the rocks,
hide[n] in the ground
from dread of the LORD
and the splendor of his
majesty![o]
11 The eyes of the arrogant[p] man
will be humbled[q]
and the pride[r] of men brought
low;[s]
the LORD alone will be exalted[t] in
that day.[u]

2:4 [s]Joel 3:10 [t]Ps 46:9; Isa 9:5; 11:6-9; 32:18; 57:19; 65:25; Jer 30:10; Da 11:45; Hos 2:18; Mic 4:3; Zec 9:10 **2:5** [u]Isa 58:1 [v]Isa 60:1,19-20; 1Jn 1:5,7 **2:6** [w]S Dt 31:17 [x]Jer 12:7 [y]S Dt 18:10; S Isa 44:25 [z]S 2Ki 1:2; S 2Ch 26:6 [a]Pr 6:1 [b]S 2Ki 16:7; Mic 5:12 **2:7** [c]S Dt 17:17 [d]S Ps 17:14 [e]S Dt 17:16 [f]S Ge 41:43; Isa 31:1; Mic 5:10 **2:8** [g]Isa 10:9-11; Rev 9:20 [h]Isa 44:17 [i]S 2Ch 32:19; S Ps 135:15; Mic 5:13 [j]Isa 17:8 **2:9** [k]Ps 62:9 [l]ver 11,17; Isa 5:15; 13:11 [m]S Ne 4:5 **2:10** [n]ver 19; Na 3:11 [o]S Ps 145:12; 2Th 1:9; Rev 6:15-16 **2:11** [p]S Ne 9:29; Hab 2:5 [q]S ver 9 [r]Isa 5:15; 10:12; 37:23; Eze 31:10 [s]S Job 40:11 [t]S Ps 46:10 [u]ver 17,20; Isa 3:7,18; 4:1,2; 5:30; 7:18; 17:4,7; 24:21; 25:9; 26:1; 27:1

2:12 [v]Isa 13:6,9; 22:5,8,12; 34:8; 61:2; Jer 30:7; La 1:12; Eze 7:7; 30:3; Joel 1:15; 2:11; Am 5:18; Zep 1:14 [w]S Ps 59:12 [x]S 2Sa 22:28 [y]Ps 76:12; Isa 24:4,21; 60:11; Mal 4:1 [z]S Job 40:11 **2:13** [a]S Jdg 9:15; Isa 10:34; 29:17; Eze 27:5 [b]Isa 10:33 [c]S Ps 22:12; Zec 11:2

12 The LORD Almighty has a day[v] in
store
for all the proud[w] and lofty,[x]
for all that is exalted[y]
(and they will be humbled),[z]
13 for all the cedars of Lebanon,[a]
tall and lofty,[b]
and all the oaks of Bashan,[c]
14 for all the towering mountains
and all the high hills,[d]
15 for every lofty tower[e]
and every fortified wall,[f]
16 for every trading ship[c][g]
and every stately vessel.
17 The arrogance of man will be
brought low[h]
and the pride of men humbled;[i]
the LORD alone will be exalted in
that day,[j]
18 and the idols[k] will totally
disappear.[l]

19 Men will flee to caves[m] in the
rocks
and to holes in the ground[n]
from dread[o] of the LORD
and the splendor of his
majesty,[p]
when he rises to shake the
earth.[q]
20 In that day[r] men will throw away
to the rodents and bats[s]
their idols of silver and idols of
gold,[t]
which they made to worship.[u]
21 They will flee to caverns in the
rocks[v]

2:14 [d]Isa 30:25; 40:4 **2:15** [e]Isa 30:25; 32:14; 33:18 [f]Isa 25:2,12; Zep 1:16 **2:16** [g]fn S Ge 10:4; S 1Ki 9:26 **2:17** [h]S 2Sa 22:28; S Job 40:11 [i]S ver 9 [j]S ver 11 **2:18** [k]S 1Sa 5:2; Eze 36:25 [l]S Dt 9:21; Isa 21:9; Jer 10:11; Mic 5:13 **2:19** [m]S Jdg 6:2; Isa 7:19 [n]S Jdg 6:2; S Job 30:6; Lk 23:30; Rev 6:15 [o]S Dt 2:25 [p]S Ps 145:12 [q]ver 21; S Job 9:6; S Isa 14:16; Heb 12:26 **2:20** [r]S ver 11 [s]Lev 11:19 [t]S Job 22:24; Eze 36:25; Rev 9:20 [u]Eze 7:19-20; 14:6 **2:21** [v]S Ex 33:22

[b]9 Or *not raise them up* [c]16 Hebrew *every ship of Tarshish*

2:6–9 YOU HAVE ABANDONED YOUR PEOPLE. These verses describe the apostasy and worldliness of the nation of Judah. They had rejected God, accepted idols and the occult, taken pleasure in the ungodly ways of pagans, and looked for their security in money, foreign alliances and military might. Thus Isaiah prayed that they would not be forgiven until God had dealt with them so severely that they genuinely repented (vv. 17–21). He knew that the superficial forgiveness of religious ritual would only make matters worse. True repentance must precede forgiveness (1:16–20).

2:11 PRIDE OF MEN BROUGHT LOW. One serious consequence of human pride is the belief that we can decide for ourselves, independent of God, how to live and what to consider as right and wrong. On the day of judgment, God will bring this arrogant attitude to the lowest shame.

2:12 HAS A DAY IN STORE. According to Isaiah, a time of judgment was coming. The immediate fulfillment of his prophecy was God's devastation of the land of Israel through the armies of the Assyrians and Babylonians as his agents of wrath (39:6). In the larger prophetic perspective, "the day of the LORD" refers to the time when God will defeat all evil on the earth (cf. Joel 2:31; see 1Th 5:2, notes; see Rev 4—19, notes; see article on THE GREAT TRIBULATION, p. 1456).

and to the overhanging crags
from dread of the LORD
and the splendor of his majesty,[w]
when he rises[x] to shake the
earth.[y]

22 Stop trusting in man,[z]
who has but a breath[a] in his
nostrils.
Of what account is he?[b]

Judgment on Jerusalem and Judah

3 See now, the Lord,
the LORD Almighty,
is about to take from Jerusalem
and Judah
both supply and support:[c]
all supplies of food[d] and all
supplies of water,[e]
2 the hero and warrior,[f]
the judge and prophet,
the soothsayer[g] and elder,[h]
3 the captain of fifty[i] and man of
rank,[j]
the counselor, skilled
craftsman[k] and clever
enchanter.[l]

4 I will make boys their officials;
mere children will govern
them.[m]
5 People will oppress each other—
man against man, neighbor
against neighbor.[n]
The young will rise up against the
old,
the base against the honorable.
6 A man will seize one of his
brothers
at his father's home, and say,
"You have a cloak, you be our
leader;
take charge of this heap of
ruins!"
7 But in that day[o] he will cry out,
"I have no remedy.[p]
I have no food[q] or clothing in my
house;
do not make me the leader of
the people."[r]

8 Jerusalem staggers,
Judah is falling;[s]
their words[t] and deeds[u] are
against the LORD,
defying[v] his glorious presence.
9 The look on their faces testifies[w]
against them;
they parade their sin like
Sodom;[x]
they do not hide it.
Woe to them!
They have brought disaster[y]
upon themselves.

10 Tell the righteous it will be well[z]
with them,
for they will enjoy the fruit of
their deeds.[a]
11 Woe to the wicked![b] Disaster[c] is
upon them!
They will be paid back[d] for what
their hands have done.[e]
12 Youths[f] oppress my people,
women rule over them.
O my people, your guides lead you
astray;[g]
they turn you from the path.
13 The LORD takes his place in court;[h]
he rises to judge[i] the people.
14 The LORD enters into judgment[j]
against the elders and leaders of
his people:
"It is you who have ruined my
vineyard;
the plunder[k] from the poor[l] is
in your houses.
15 What do you mean by crushing my
people[m]
and grinding[n] the faces of the
poor?"[o]
declares the Lord,
the LORD Almighty.[p]

Isa 27:6

2:21 [w] S Ps 145:12 [x] Isa 33:10 [y] S ver 19 **2:22** [z] Ps 118:6,8; 146:3; Isa 51:12; Jer 17:5 [a] S Ge 2:7; S Ps 144:4 [b] S Job 12:19; Ps 8:4; 18:42; 144:3; Isa 17:13; 29:5; 40:15; S Jas 4:14 **3:1** [c] S Ps 18:18 [d] S Lev 26:26; Am 4:6 [e] Isa 5:13; 65:13; Eze 4:16 **3:2** [f] Eze 17:13 [g] Dt 18:10 [h] Isa 9:14-15 **3:3** [i] S 2Ki 1:9 [j] S Job 22:8 [k] 2Ki 24:14 [l] S Ecc 10:11; Jer 8:17 **3:4** [m] ver 12; Ecc 10:16 fn **3:5** [n] Ps 28:3; Isa 9:19; Jer 9:8; Mic 7:2,6 **3:7** [o] S Isa 2:11 [p] Jer 30:12; Eze 34:4; Hos 5:13 [q] Joel 1:16 [r] Isa 24:2 **3:8** [s] Isa 1:7 [t] Isa 9:15,17; 28:15; 30:9; 59:3,13 [u] 2Ch 33:6 [v] S Job 1:11; Ps 73:9,11; Isa 65:7 **3:9** [w] Nu 32:23; Isa 59:12; Jer 14:7; Hos 5:5 [x] S Ge 13:13 [y] S 2Ch 34:24; S Pr 8:36; Ro 6:23 **3:10** [z] S Dt 5:33; S 12:28; 28:1-14; Ps 37:17; Jer 22:15 [a] S Ge 15:1; S Ps 128:2 **3:11** [b] S Job 9:13; Isa 57:20 [c] Dt 28:15-68 [d] S 2Ch 6:23 [e] Jer 21:14; La 5:16; Eze 24:14 **3:12** [f] S ver 4 [g] Isa 9:16; 19:14; 28:7; 29:9; Jer 23:13; 25:16; Mic 3:5 **3:13** [h] S Job 10:2 [i] S Ps 82:1; S Isa 2:4 **3:14** [j] S 1Sa 12:7; S Job 22:4 [k] S Job 24:9; Jas 2:6 [l] Isa 11:4; 25:4 **3:15** [m] S Ps 94:5 [n] S Job 24:14 [o] Isa 10:6; 11:4; 26:6; 29:19; 32:6; 51:23 [p] Isa 5:7

3:1 TAKE FROM JERUSALEM. As a result of the people's sins, God's judgment would touch every part of society and all classes of people would suffer (vv. 2–3).

3:5 OPPRESS EACH OTHER. The rejection of God's ways in a society opens the way for injustice, cruel oppression, violence, disrespect for parents by rebellious youth, and the throwing off of all moral restraint (see Mt 24:12, note; 2Ti 3:1–5, notes). All people suffer as society disintegrates.

3:10 TELL THE RIGHTEOUS. Isaiah was told to encourage those who remained faithful to God in the midst of an unrighteous people. Although now they might suffer because of righteousness, it would ultimately go well for them and God would richly reward them. To the wicked, however, God guarantees punishment (see Mt 5:10, note).

3:14 PLUNDER FROM THE POOR. God hates the mistreatment of the less fortunate in society. In the church too, he makes members accountable for the way they treat one another (see Col 3:25, note). God demands that we show love, justice and compassion in our relations with others.

[16]The LORD says,
"The women of Zion[q] are
haughty,
walking along with outstretched
necks,[r]
flirting with their eyes,
tripping along with mincing
steps,
with ornaments jingling on
their ankles.
[17]Therefore the Lord will bring sores
on the heads of the women
of Zion;
the LORD will make their scalps
bald.[s]"

[18]In that day[t] the Lord will snatch
away their finery: the bangles and
headbands and crescent necklaces,[u]
[19]the earrings and bracelets[v] and
veils,[w] [20]the headdresses[x] and ankle
chains and sashes, the perfume bottles
and charms, [21]the signet rings and
nose rings,[y] [22]the fine robes and the
capes and cloaks,[z] the purses [23]and
mirrors, and the linen garments[a] and
tiaras[b] and shawls.

[24]Instead of fragrance[c] there will
be a stench;[d]
instead of a sash,[e] a rope;
instead of well-dressed hair,
baldness;[f]
instead of fine clothing,
sackcloth;[g]
instead of beauty,[h] branding.[i]
[25]Your men will fall by the
sword,[j]
your warriors in battle.[k]
[26]The gates[l] of Zion will lament
and mourn;[m]
destitute,[n] she will sit on the
ground.[o]

3:16 [q]S SS 3:11 [r]S Job 15:25 **3:17** [s]ver 24; Eze 27:31; Am 8:10 **3:18** [t]S Isa 2:11 [u]Ge 41:42; S Jdg 8:21 **3:19** [v]S Ge 24:47 [w]Eze 16:11-12 **3:20** [x]Ex 39:28; Eze 24:17,23; 44:18 **3:21** [y]S Ge 24:22 **3:22** [z]Ru 3:15 **3:23** [a]Eze 16:10; 23:26 [b]S Ex 29:6; SS 3:11; Isa 61:3; 62:3 **3:24** [c]S Est 2:12 [d]Isa 4:4 [e]Pr 31:24 [f]S ver 17; S Lev 13:40; S Job 1:20 [g]S Ge 37:34; Job 16:15; Isa 20:2; Jer 4:8; La 2:10; Eze 27:30-31; Jnh 3:5-8 [h]1Pe 3:3 [i]S 2Sa 10:4; Isa 20:4 **3:25** [j]S Isa 1:20 [k]Jer 15:8 **3:26** [l]Isa 14:31; 24:12; 45:2 [m]S Ps 137:1; Isa 24:4,7; 29:2; 33:9; Jer 4:28; 14:2 [n]S Lev 26:31 [o]S Job 2:13; La 4:5

4:1 [p]S Isa 2:11 [q]Isa 13:12; 32:9 [r]2Th 3:12 [s]S Ge 30:23 **4:2** [t]S Isa 2:11 [u]Isa 11:1-5; 52:13; 53:2; Jer 23:5-6; 33:15-16; Eze 17:22; Zec 3:8; 6:12 [v]Isa 33:17; 53:2 [w]S Ps 72:16; Eze 36:8 [x]Isa 60:15; Eze 34:29 [y]S Isa 1:9 **4:3** [z]S Isa 1:26 [a]Isa 1:9; Ro 11:5 [b]S Ex 19:6; Isa 26:2; 45:25; 52:1; 60:21;

4 In that day[p] seven women
will take hold of one man[q]
and say, "We will eat our own
food[r]
and provide our own clothes;
only let us be called by your name.
Take away our disgrace!"[s]

The Branch of the LORD

[2]In that day[t] the Branch of the
LORD[u] will be beautiful[v] and glorious,
and the fruit[w] of the land will be the
pride and glory[x] of the survivors[y] in
Israel. [3]Those who are left in Zion,[z]
who remain[a] in Jerusalem, will be
called holy,[b] all who are recorded[c]
among the living in Jerusalem. [4]The
Lord will wash away the filth[d] of the
women of Zion;[e] he will cleanse[f] the
bloodstains[g] from Jerusalem by a spirit[d] of judgment[h] and a spirit[d] of
fire.[i] [5]Then the LORD will create[j]
over all of Mount Zion[k] and over those
who assemble there a cloud of smoke
by day and a glow of flaming fire by
night;[l] over all the glory[m] will be a
canopy.[n] [6]It will be a shelter[o] and
shade from the heat of the day, and a
refuge[p] and hiding place from the
storm[q] and rain.

The Song of the Vineyard

5 I will sing for the one I love
a song about his vineyard:[r]
My loved one had a vineyard

Joel 3:17; Ob 1:17; Zep 3:13 [c]S Ps 56:8; S 87:6; S Lk 10:20 **4:4** [d]Isa 3:24 [e]S SS 3:11 [f]S Ps 51:2 [g]S Isa 1:15 [h]Isa 28:6 [i]S Isa 1:31; S 30:30; S Zec 13:9; Mt 3:11; Lk 3:17 **4:5** [j]Isa 41:20; 65:18 [k]Rev 14:1 [l]S Ex 13:21 [m]Isa 35:2; 58:8; 60:1 [n]S Ps 18:11; Rev 7:15 **4:6** [o]Lev 23:34-43; Ps 27:5; Isa 8:14; 25:4; Eze 11:16 [p]Isa 14:32; 25:4; 30:2; 57:13 [q]S Ps 55:8 **5:1** [r]Ps 80:8-9; Isa 27:2; Jn 15:1

[d] *4* Or *the Spirit*

3:16–26 THE WOMEN OF ZION. In the midst of spiritual, moral and political decline, the women of Judah were characterized by their devotion to all kinds of things related to fashionable and external appearance rather than to inward holiness and love for God. They were self-centered women, searching for sexual attractiveness and thinking only of their wants, but showing no concern for the oppressed, the poor, or the tragic spiritual condition of their families and people. God threatened to bring them to shame and disgrace by making them miserable slaves of their conquerors (vv. 17, 24). God still demands humility, modesty and holiness in believing women (see 1Co 11:6, note; 1Ti 2:9, note; cf. 1Pe 3:3–4).

4:2 THE BRANCH OF THE LORD. This is a title for the Messiah (i.e., the Christ). He will come forth as a branch from the Root of David (see 11:1; 53:2; Jer 23:5; 33:15; Zec 3:8; 6:12; Ro 15:12; Rev 5:5; 22:16). Vv. 2–6 refer to a time of both judgment and salvation, a time when Christ will rule over his faithful remnant in Jerusalem (v. 4) and care for them with great concern and love (cf. 38:5–8,15–17; 65:18).

4:3 WILL BE CALLED HOLY. Those who survive the coming judgment will be "holy," i.e., they will have the character of God, who is "the Holy One of Israel" (1:4); in other words, they will be separated from the sinful world, cleansed from all defilement by Christ's blood and regenerated by the Holy Spirit. Over them will hover the glory of God like a canopy (v. 5).

5:1–7 A VINEYARD. This song of the vineyard demonstrates that God did everything possible to make Judah a righteous and fruitful nation. Only when they failed to become what he wanted them

on a fertile hillside.
2He dug it up and cleared it of stones
and planted it with the choicest vines.[s]
He built a watchtower[t] in it
and cut out a winepress[u] as well.
Then he looked for a crop of good grapes,
but it yielded only bad fruit.[v]

3"Now you dwellers in Jerusalem
and men of Judah,
judge between me and my vineyard.[w]
4What more could have been done
for my vineyard
than I have done for it?[x]
When I looked for good grapes,
why did it yield only bad?[y]
5Now I will tell you
what I am going to do to my vineyard:
I will take away its hedge,
and it will be destroyed;[z]
I will break down its wall,[a]
and it will be trampled.[b]
6I will make it a wasteland,[c]
neither pruned nor cultivated,
and briers and thorns[d] will grow there.
I will command the clouds
not to rain[e] on it."

7The vineyard[f] of the LORD Almighty
is the house of Israel,
and the men of Judah
are the garden of his delight.
And he looked for justice,[g] but saw bloodshed;
for righteousness,[h] but heard cries of distress.[i]

Woes and Judgments

8Woe[j] to you who add house to house
and join field to field[k]
till no space is left
and you live alone in the land.

9The LORD Almighty[l] has declared in my hearing:[m]

5:2 [s] S Ex 15:17; Isa 16:8 [t] 1Sa 2:9; Isa 27:3; 31:5; 49:8; Mt 21:33 [u] S Job 24:11 [v] Mt 21:19; Mk 11:13; Lk 13:6 **5:3** [w] Mt 21:40 **5:4** [x] S 2Ch 36:15; Jer 2:5-7; Mic 6:3-4; Mt 23:37 [y] Jer 2:21; 24:2; 29:17 **5:5** [z] 2Ch 36:21; Isa 6:12; 27:10 [a] S Ps 80:12; S Isa 22:5 [b] Isa 10:6; 26:6; 28:3,18; 41:25; 63:3; Jer 12:10; 34:22; La 1:15; Hos 2:12; Mic 7:10; Mal 4:3; S Lk 21:24 **5:6** [c] S Ge 6:13; S Lev 26:32; Isa 6:13; 49:17, 19; 51:3; Joel 1:10 [d] ver 10,17; S 2Sa 23:6; Isa 7:23,24; 32:13; 34:13; 55:13; Eze 28:24; Hos 2:12; Heb 6:8 [e] S Dt 28:24; S 2Sa 1:21; Am 4:7 **5:7** [f] Ps 80:8; Isa 17:10; 18:5; 37:30 [g] Isa 10:2; 29:21; 32:7; 59:15; 61:8; Eze 9:9; 22:29 [h] S Isa 1:21 [i] S Ps 12:5 **5:8** [j] ver 11,18,20; Isa 6:5; 10:1; 24:16; Jer 22:13 [k] Job 20:19; Mic 2:2; Hab 2:9-12 **5:9** [l] Jer 44:11 [m] Isa 22:14
[n] Isa 6:11-12; Mt 23:38 **5:10** [o] S ver 6; Lev 26:26; S Dt 28:38; Zec 8:10 **5:11** [p] S ver 8 [q] S 1Sa 25:36; S Pr 23:29-30 **5:12** [r] Ps 68:25; Isa 24:8 [s] S Job 21:12 [t] S 1Sa 12:24 [u] Ps 28:5; Eze 26:13 **5:13** [v] Isa 49:21 [w] S Pr 10:21; S Isa 1:3; Hos 4:6 [x] S Job 22:8 [y] S Isa 3:1 **5:14** [z] S Pr 30:16 [a] S Nu 16:30 [b] Isa 22:2,13; 23:7; 24:8 **5:15** [c] Isa 10:33 [d] S Isa 2:9

"Surely the great houses will become desolate,[n]
the fine mansions left without occupants.
10A ten-acre[e] vineyard will produce only a bath[f] of wine,
a homer[g] of seed only an ephah[h] of grain."[o]

11Woe[p] to those who rise early in the morning
to run after their drinks,
who stay up late at night
till they are inflamed with wine.[q]
12They have harps and lyres at their banquets,
tambourines[r] and flutes[s] and wine,
but they have no regard[t] for the deeds of the LORD,
no respect for the work of his hands.[u]
13Therefore my people will go into exile[v]
for lack of understanding;[w]
their men of rank[x] will die of hunger
and their masses will be parched with thirst.[y]
14Therefore the grave[i][z] enlarges its appetite
and opens its mouth[a] without limit;
into it will descend their nobles and masses
with all their brawlers and revelers.[b]
15So man will be brought low[c]
and mankind humbled,[d]
the eyes of the arrogant[e] humbled.
16But the LORD Almighty will be exalted[f] by his justice,[g]

[e] S Isa 2:11 **5:16** [f] Ps 97:9; Isa 33:10 [g] Isa 28:17; 30:18; 33:5; 61:8

[e] *10* Hebrew *ten-yoke,* that is, the land plowed by 10 yoke of oxen in one day [f] *10* That is, probably about 6 gallons (about 22 liters) [g] *10* That is, probably about 6 bushels (about 220 liters) [h] *10* That is, probably about 3/5 bushel (about 22 liters) [i] *14* Hebrew *Sheol*

to become did God destroy his vineyard (compare Jesus' parable of the tenants in Mt 21:33–44). Isaiah's parable points historically to the destruction of Jerusalem and the kingdom of Judah in 586 B.C.

5:8–32 WOE TO YOU. Six woes (i.e., statements of judgment) are pronounced on six types of sins: (1) selfish greed (v. 8), (2) drunken conduct (vv. 11–12), (3) mockery at God's power to judge their sin (vv. 18–19), (4) distortion of God's moral standards (v. 20), (5) arrogance and pride (v. 21), and (6) perversion of justice (vv. 22–23; cf. Christ's woes spoken to religious hypocrites; see Mt 23, notes).

and the holy God will show
himself holy[h] by his
righteousness.
17Then sheep will graze as in their
own pasture;[i]
lambs will feed[j] among the
ruins of the rich.

18Woe[j] to those who draw sin
along with cords[k] of
deceit,
and wickedness[l] as with cart
ropes,
19to those who say, "Let God hurry,
let him hasten[m] his work
so we may see it.
Let it approach,
let the plan of the Holy One[n] of
Israel come,
so we may know it."[o]

20Woe[p] to those who call evil
good[q]
and good evil,[r]
who put darkness for light
and light for darkness,[s]
who put bitter for sweet
and sweet for bitter.[t]

21Woe to those who are wise in their
own eyes[u]
and clever in their own sight.

22Woe to those who are heroes at
drinking wine[v]
and champions at mixing
drinks,[w]
23who acquit the guilty for a bribe,[x]
but deny justice[y] to the
innocent.[z]
24Therefore, as tongues of fire[a] lick
up straw[b]
and as dry grass sinks down in
the flames,
so their roots will decay[c]
and their flowers blow away like
dust;[d]
for they have rejected the law of
the LORD Almighty
and spurned the word[e] of the
Holy One[f] of Israel.
25Therefore the LORD's anger[g] burns
against his people;
his hand is raised and he strikes
them down.
The mountains shake,[h]
and the dead bodies[i] are like
refuse[j] in the streets.[k]
Yet for all this, his anger is not
turned away,[l]
his hand is still upraised.[m]

26He lifts up a banner[n] for the
distant nations,
he whistles[o] for those at the
ends of the earth.[p]
Here they come,
swiftly and speedily!
27Not one of them grows tired[q] or
stumbles,
not one slumbers or sleeps;
not a belt[r] is loosened at the
waist,[s]
not a sandal thong is broken.[t]
28Their arrows are sharp,[u]
all their bows[v] are strung;
their horses' hoofs[w] seem like
flint,
their chariot wheels like a
whirlwind.[x]
29Their roar is like that of the
lion,[y]

5:16 [h] S Lev 10:3; Isa 29:23; Eze 36:23 **5:17** [i] Isa 7:25; 17:2; 32:14; Zep 2:6,14 **5:18** [j] S ver 8 [k] Hos 11:4 [l] Isa 59:4-8; Jer 23:14 **5:19** [m] Isa 60:22 [n] S Isa 1:4; 29:23; 30:11,12 [o] Jer 17:15; Eze 12:22; 2Pe 3:4 **5:20** [p] S ver 8 [q] S Ge 18:25; S 1Ki 22:8 [r] S Ps 94:21 [s] S Job 24:13; Mt 6:22-23; Lk 11:34-35 [t] Am 5:7 **5:21** [u] S Pr 3:7; Isa 47:10; Ro 12:16; 1Co 3:18-20 **5:22** [v] S 1Sa 25:36; S Pr 23:20; S Isa 22:13 [w] S Pr 31:4; Isa 65:11; Jer 7:18 **5:23** [x] S Ex 23:8; S Eze 22:12 [y] ver 7; S Isa 1:17; 10:2; 29:21; 59:4, 13-15 [z] S Ps 94:21; Am 5:12; Jas 5:6 **5:24** [a] S Isa 1:31 [b] Isa 47:14; Na 1:10 [c] S 2Ki 19:30; S Job 18:16 [d] S Job 24:24; Isa 40:8 [e] Ps 107:11; Isa 8:6; 30:9,12 [f] Job 6:10; Isa 1:4; 10:20; 12:6 **5:25** [g] S 2Ki 22:13; S Job 40:11; Isa 10:17; 26:11; 31:9; 66:15; S Jer 6:12 [h] S Ex 19:18 [i] S Ps 110:6 [j] S 2Ki 9:37 [k] S 2Sa 22:43 [l] Jer 4:8; Da 9:16 [m] Isa 9:12,17,21; 10:4 **5:26** [n] S Ps 20:5 [o] Isa 7:18; Zec 10:8 [p] Dt 28:49; Isa 13:5; 18:3 **5:27** [q] Isa 14:31; 40:29-31 [r] Isa 22:21; Eze 23:15 [s] S Job 12:18 [t] Joel 2:7-8 **5:28** [u] S Job 39:23; Ps 45:5 [v] S Ps 7:12 [w] Eze 26:11 [x] S 2Ki 2:1; S Job 1:19 **5:29** [y] S 2Ki 17:25; Jer 51:38; Zep 3:3; Zec 11:3

j *17* Septuagint; Hebrew / *strangers will eat*

5:20 CALL EVIL GOOD. On the one hand, society often exalts sin by calling depravity manly strength, or calling immorality and perversion true virtue and commendable freedom; on the other hand, society opposes righteousness by calling it evil. Note these two common examples where this pattern occurs: (1) Sexual perversion (e.g., homosexuality and lesbianism) is called a legitimate alternative lifestyle that should be openly accepted, while opponents of such conduct who accept the Biblical standards of sexual morality are called bigots who perpetuate oppressive prejudice (see article on STANDARDS OF SEXUAL MORALITY, p. 1936). (2) Pro-abortion advocates are called "sensitive" persons with a deep commitment to the rights of women, while active pro-life supporters are called "extremists" or "religious fanatics." Believers, however, must commit themselves wholeheartedly and irreversibly to God's standards of good and evil as revealed in his written Word.

5:24 REJECTED THE LAW. Isaiah teaches the doctrine of just retribution for sin. Rejecting God's laws and despising his word will result in people being given over to the consequences of their sins and to divine punishment (v. 25; cf. Hos 4:6).

5:26 DISTANT NATIONS. Isaiah describes Judah's coming destruction by a distant nation. It was imminent and certain, and Judah would have no power to repel the enemy. Isaiah undoubtedly foresaw the invasions of the Assyrians, whose armies plundered Judah in 701 B.C., and the Babylonians, who began aggression in 605 B.C. God has often used other nations to punish the apostasy of his people (see also Mt 5:13, note).

they roar like young lions;
they growl as they seize[z] their
prey
and carry it off with no one to
rescue.[a]
30 In that day[b] they will roar over it
like the roaring of the sea.[c]
And if one looks at the land,
he will see darkness[d] and
distress;[e]
even the light will be darkened[f]
by the clouds.

Isaiah's Commission

6 In the year that King Uzziah[g]
died,[h] I saw the Lord[i] seated on
a throne,[j] high and exalted,[k] and the
train of his robe[l] filled the temple.
2 Above him were seraphs,[m] each with
six wings: With two wings they covered their faces, with two they covered
their feet,[n] and with two they were flying. 3 And they were calling to one another:

"Holy, holy[o], holy is the LORD
Almighty;[p]
the whole earth[q] is full of his
glory."[r]

4 At the sound of their voices the doorposts and thresholds shook and the
temple was filled with smoke.[s]
5 "Woe[t] to me!" I cried. "I am ruined![u] For I am a man of unclean
lips,[v w] and I live among a people of
unclean lips,[x] and my eyes have
seen[y] the King,[z] the LORD Almighty."[a]
6 Then one of the seraphs flew to me
with a live coal[b] in his hand, which he
had taken with tongs from the altar.
7 With it he touched my mouth and said,
"See, this has touched your lips;[c] your
guilt is taken away and your sin atoned
for.[d]"
8 Then I heard the voice[e] of the Lord
saying, "Whom shall I send?[f] And
who will go for us?[g]"
And I said, "Here am I.[h] Send me!" Isa 42:6-7
9 He said, "Go[i] and tell this people:

" 'Be ever hearing, but never
understanding;

5:29 [z] Isa 10:6; 49:24-25 [a] Isa 42:22; Mic 5:8 **5:30** [b] S Isa 2:11 [c] S Ps 93:3; Jer 50:42; Lk 21:25 [d] S 1Sa 2:9; S Job 21:30; Ps 18:28; 44:19; S 82:5 [e] S Jdg 6:2; Isa 22:5; 33:2; Jer 4:23-28 [f] Isa 13:10; 50:3; Joel 2:10 **6:1** [g] S 2Ch 26:22, 23 [h] S 2Ki 15:7 [i] S Ex 24:10; S Nu 12:8; Jn 12:41 [j] S 1Ki 22:19; S Ps 9:4; S 123:1; S Rev 4:2 [k] Isa 52:13; 53:12 [l] Rev 1:13 **6:2** [m] Eze 1:5; 10:15; Rev 4:8 [n] Eze 1:11 **6:3** [o] S Ex 15:11 [p] Ps 89:8 [q] Isa 11:9; 54:5; Mal 1:11 [r] S Ex 16:7; Nu 14:21; Ps 72:19; Rev 4:8 **6:4** [s] S Ex 19:18; S 40:34; Eze 43:5; 44:4; Rev 15:8 **6:5** [t] S Isa 5:8 [u] S Nu 17:12; S Dt 5:26 [v] Lk 5:8 [w] Ex 6:12 [x] Isa 59:3; Jer 9:3-8 [y] S Ex 24:10 [z] Ps 45:3; Isa 24:23; 32:1; 33:17; Jer 51:57 [a] S Job 42:5 **6:6** [b] S Lev 10:1; Eze 10:2 **6:7** [c] Jer 1:9; Da 10:16 [d] S Lev 26:41; Isa 45:25; Da 12:3; 1Jn 1:7 **6:8** [e] S Job 40:9; Ac 9:4 [f] Jer 26:12,15 [g] S Ge 1:26 [h] S Ge 22:1; S Ex 3:4 **6:9** [i] Eze 3:11; Am 7:15; Mt 28:19

6:1 THE YEAR THAT KING UZZIAH DIED. The year was approximately 740 B.C. (cf. 2Ch 26:16–21). Though Isaiah may have prophesied earlier (chs. 1–5), he now received a vision of God, was cleansed, and was given a specific commission to proclaim God's word to a spiritually blind, deaf and insensitive people (vv. 9–10).

6:1 I SAW THE LORD. This vision gave Isaiah a proper understanding of his message and call. It revealed one of this book's major concerns, namely, that God's glory, majesty and holiness demand that those who serve him also must be holy. Churches today likewise need a vision of God in their midst as the holy Lord and Judge of all. The recognition of the need for his sanctifying work in our lives will inevitably accompany such a vision; the result could well be similar to that of Isaiah—earnest confession, glorious cleansing, and powerful commissioning by God in regard to his will and call (vv. 5–8; cf. Rev 1:13–17).

6:2 SERAPHS. Seraphs are angelic beings of high order; the word may be another designation for the living creatures revealed elsewhere in Scripture (e.g., Rev 4:6–9). Their title (literally, "burning ones") may signify their purity as those who serve God around his throne; they so reflected God's glory that they seemed to be on fire.

6:3 HOLY, HOLY, HOLY. The foremost characteristic of God revealed to Isaiah is his holiness, signifying his purity of character, separation from sin and opposition to all that is evil (see article on THE ATTRIBUTES OF GOD, p. 882). God's absolute holiness must be proclaimed in the churches as it is proclaimed in the heavens.

6:5 WOE TO ME! In full view of God's holiness, Isaiah instantly realized his own imperfection and uncleanness, especially with respect to his speech (cf. Jas 3:1–6). He also recognized the consequences of seeing God face to face (cf. Ex 33:20) and was frightened. God then cleansed his mouth and heart (cf. Lev 16:12; Jer 1:9) and made him fit to remain in his presence as a servant and prophet of the Holy One of Israel. All who approach God must have their sins forgiven and their hearts cleansed by the Holy Spirit (cf. Heb 10:19–22), for only God can provide the purity that he demands (see article on REGENERATION, p. 1589).

6:8 WHOM SHALL I SEND? Only after receiving his cleansing was Isaiah commissioned as a prophet (see article on THE PROPHET IN THE OLD TESTAMENT, p. 986). This passage reminds us of the Great Commission of our risen Lord to proclaim the gospel of salvation to all the world (Mt 28:18–20). If that command to go out grips our hearts, we must respond in the same way as Isaiah did, "Here am I. Send me."

6:9 GO AND TELL THIS PEOPLE. God told Isaiah that the people would reject his message and remain indifferent to the prophetic call for repentance; his preaching would in fact turn hearts even more against the Lord (vv. 9–10; cf. Mt 13:14–15; Mk 4:12; Lk 8:10). Nevertheless, Isaiah had to preach faithfully the unpopular message of judgment (cf. Jer 1:8,19; Eze 2:3–4). There would be a limit, however, to his heartrending ministry. The judgments brought through Sennacherib in 701 B.C. (vv. 11–12) would bring Jerusalem to faith and obedience (36:21; 37:7); as a result

THE PROPHET IN THE OLD TESTAMENT

***Isa 6:8–9** "Then I heard the voice of the Lord saying, 'Whom shall I send? And who will go for us?' And I said, 'Here am I. Send me!' He said, 'Go and tell this people, "Be ever hearing but never understanding; be ever seeing, but never perceiving." ' "*

THE PLACE OF THE PROPHETS IN HEBREW HISTORY. (1) The OT prophets were men and women of God who towered spiritually over their contemporaries. No category of people in all literature presents a more dramatic picture than do the OT prophets. Priests, judges, kings, wise counselors and psalmists each had a distinctive place in Israel's history, but none of these ever rose to the stature of the prophets or continued to exert as much influence on the subsequent history of redemption.

(2) The prophets exerted a major influence in the composition of the OT itself. This is evident in the threefold division of the Hebrew Bible: The Torah, The Prophets and The Writings (cf. Lk 24:44). The category known as The Prophets included six historical books written from the prophetic perspective: Joshua, Judges, 1 and 2 Samuel, and 1 and 2 Kings. It is likely that the authors of these books were prophets. Secondly, there were the sixteen specific prophetic books (Isaiah to Malachi). Finally, Moses, the author of the first five books of the Bible (the Torah), was a prophet (Dt 18:15). Thus a full two-thirds of the OT was written by prophets.

HEBREW WORDS FOR THE PROPHETS. (1) *Ro'eh*. This Hebrew noun, translated "seer" in English, indicates a special ability to see in the spiritual realm and foresee future events. The title suggests that the prophet was not deceived by the external appearance of things, but that he saw issues as they really were from the perspective of God himself. As a seer, the prophet received dreams, visions and revelations from God that enabled him to convey spiritual realities to God's people.

(2) *Nabi'*. (a) This is the main Hebrew word for "prophet," occurring 316 times in the OT (*nabi'im* is its plural form). Although the origin of this word is unclear, the meaning of the Hebrew verb "to prophesy" meant: "to put forth words abundantly from God's mind and by God's Spirit" (Gesenius, *Hebrew Lexicon*). Thus a *nabi'* was a spokesperson who poured out words under the impelling power of God's Spirit. The Greek word *prophētēs*, from which the English word "prophet" is derived, means "one who speaks on behalf of another." The prophets spoke for God to the covenant people, based on what they heard, saw and received from him. (b) In the OT, the prophet was also designated by such terms as "man of God" (see 2Ki 4:21, note), "servant" of God (cf. Isa 20:3; Da 6:20), a man who has the "Spirit on him" (cf. Isa 61:1–3), "watchman" (Eze 3:17), and "the LORD's messenger" (Hag 1:13). Prophets also interpreted prophetic dreams (e.g., Joseph, Daniel) and provided an understanding of history—both present and future—from a prophetic perspective.

MEN OF THE SPIRIT AND THE WORD. The prophet was not simply another religious leader in Hebrew history, but one into whom God's Spirit and God's word had entered and taken possession (Eze 37:1,4). Because the Spirit and the word were in him, the OT prophet had the following three characteristics: (1) *Divinely revealed knowledge*. The prophet experienced God-given knowledge with respect to people, events and redemptive truth. The primary purpose of this knowledge was to encourage God's people to remain faithful to God and his covenant. OT prophecy's distinguishing feature was that it made clear God's will for his people by way of instruction, correction and warning. God used the prophets to pronounce his judgment before it occurred. Out of the soil of Israel's and Judah's dark history came specific prophecies about the Messiah and about God's kingdom, as well as predictions about future world events.

(2) *Divinely given powers*. The prophets were drawn into the sphere of the miraculous as they were filled with God's Spirit. Through the prophets God's life and power were demonstrated in supernatural ways in a world otherwise sealed against it.

(3) *A distinctive lifestyle*. The prophets by and large abandoned the ordinary pursuits of life to live exclusively for God. They protested intensely against idolatry, immorality and all kinds of evil among God's people, as well as against corruption in the lives of kings and priests; they were activists for holy and righteous changes in Israel. The prophets, always on the offense for God's kingdom and his righteousness, championed God's will without thought of personal risk.

EIGHT CHARACTERISTICS OF THE OLD TESTAMENT PROPHET. What sort of a person was the OT prophet? (1) He was a person who had a close relationship with God and who became God's confidant (Am 3:7). The prophet saw the world and the covenant people from God's perspective, not from a human point of view.

(2) Because he was close to God, the prophet was in sympathy with God and with what God was suffering because of his people's sins; because he understood God's purpose, will and desires better than anyone else, he experienced the same emotional reactions God did. In other words, the prophet not only heard God's voice but also felt his heart (Jer 6:11; 15:16–17; 20:9).

(3) Like God, the prophet deeply loved God's people. When the people hurt, the prophet felt deep pain (see the book of Lamentations). He wanted God's best for them (Eze 18:23), and thus his messages contained not only warnings but also words of hope and comfort.

(4) The prophet sought the highest good for the people, i.e., complete trust in and loyalty to God; therefore, he warned against trusting in other things, such as human wisdom, wealth, power or other gods (Jer 8:9–10; Hos 10:13–14; Am 6:8). The prophets continually urged the people to live by God's covenant obligations in order to receive God's redemptive blessings.

(5) The prophet had a deep sensitivity to sin and evil (Jer 2:12–13,19; 25:3–7; Am 8:4–7; Mic 3:8). He was impatient with cruelty, crime, immorality and injustice. What might appear as a slight deviation from God's law to the common people was seen as a disaster by the prophet. He had little tolerance for all their compromises, complacency, pretenses and excuses (Isa 32:11; Jer 6:20; 7:8–15,21–23; Am 4:1; 6:1). He shared better than anyone God's love of righteousness and hatred of wickedness (cf. Heb 1:9, note).

(6) The prophet constantly challenged the shallow, superficial holiness of God's people and tried desperately to encourage heartfelt obedience to every word God had revealed in his law. He was totally dedicated to God; he hated halfhearted commitment, shunned the middle road and demanded complete faithfulness to God. He accepted nothing less than the fullness of God's kingdom and his righteousness manifested among God's people.

(7) The prophet had a vision for the future—expressed in predictions of doom and destruction (e.g., Isa 63:1–6; Jer 11:22–23; 13:15–21; Eze 14:12–21; Am 5:16–20,27), as well as in visions of restoration and renewal (e.g., Isa 61—62; 65:17—66:24; Jer 33; Eze 37). The prophets spoke numerous prophecies regarding the coming of the Messiah (see chart on OLD TESTAMENT PROPHECIES FULFILLED IN CHRIST, p. 893).

(8) Finally, the prophet was often a man of loneliness and sorrow (Jer 14:17–18; 20:14–18; Am 7:10–13; Jnh 3—4), frequently persecuted by the false prophets who were predicting peace, prosperity and security for God's sinful people (Jer 15:15; 20:1–6; 26:8–11; Am 5:10; cf. Mt 23:29–36; Ac 7:51–53). At the same time, however, the true prophet was such a man of God that the people and their leaders could not ignore his character or his message (Eze 3:8–11).

THE PROPHET AND THE PRIEST. During most of Israel's history, priests and prophets invariably collided. God had intended them to work together, but the priests tended to compromise by not standing against the corruption of God's people. (1) The priests were usually tied to the status quo, finding it difficult to worship God except through ceremonies and liturgy. Though morality had a formal place in their theology, it was not emphasized in their practice.

(2) The prophet, on the other hand, placed great emphasis on lifestyle, conduct and moral issues. He constantly confronted those who depended on mere performance of religious duties. He irritated, prodded, denounced, stood alone in his righteous demands, and insisted on applying God's eternal principles to life. The prophet was an ethical teacher, a moral reformer and a disturber of the human mind; he exposed sin and apostasy, always seeking to stir the people to holy living.

THE MESSAGE OF THE OLD TESTAMENT PROPHETS. The prophets' message emphasized three major themes: (1) *The nature of God*. (a) They declared God to be the Creator and almighty Ruler of the universe (e.g., Isa 40:28), and the sovereign Lord of history who makes the events of history serve his ultimate purposes of salvation and judgment (cf. Isa 44:28; 45:1; Am 5:27; Hab 1:6). (b) They emphasized that God is a holy, righteous and just God who is repelled by sin, unrighteousness and injustice; because his holiness is tempered by mercy, he is patient and slow to act in wrath and judgment. Because God is holy by nature, he requires his people to be consecrated as HOLY TO THE LORD (Zec 14:20; cf. Isa 29:22–24; Jer 2:3). As the covenant-making God who entered into a unique relationship with Israel, he requires his people to obey his commands as part of that relational contract.

(2) *Sin and repentance*. The OT prophets shared God's grief at the continual disobedience, unfaithfulness, idolatry and immorality of his covenant people; they spoke stern words of righteous judgment against them. Their message was the same as the messages of John the Baptist and Jesus—"repent or perish." They predicted such major catastrophic judgments as Samaria's destruction by Assyria (e.g., Hos 5:8–12; 9:3–7; 10:6–15) and Jerusalem's destruction by Babylon (e.g., Jer 19:7–15; 32:28–36; Eze 5:5–12; 21:2,24–27).

(3) *Prediction and Messianic hope*. (a) Although the covenant people as a whole were unfaithful to God and to their covenant vows, the prophets never ceased to have a message of hope. They knew that God would fulfill the Abrahamic covenant and promises (see article on GOD'S COVENANT WITH ABRAHAM, ISAAC AND JACOB, p. 46) through a faithful and God-fearing remnant. Eventually the Messiah would come, and through him God would offer salvation to all the peoples of the earth. (b) The prophets stood between the spiritual collapse of their own generation and the emerging hope of a Messianic age. The prophetic dilemma was that they had to speak the word of God to an obstinate people, even though they knew it would be rejected and unheeded until the new order emerged (cf. Isa 6:9–13). The prophets were both champions of the old covenant and forerunners of the new covenant. They lived in the present but pointed to the future.

THE FALSE PROPHETS. There are numerous references to false prophets in the OT. For example, four hundred false prophets were brought together by King Ahab (2Ch 18:4–7); the Bible records that a lying spirit was in their mouths (2Ch 18:18–22). According to the OT, a prophet was considered false (1) if he turned people away from the true God toward some form of idolatry (Dt 13:1–5); (2) if he practiced divination, astrology, sorcery, witchcraft, and the like (see Dt 18:10–11, notes); (3) if his prophecies departed from or conflicted with God's clear message in Scripture (Dt 13:1–5); (4) if he did not expose the sins of God's people (Jer 23:9–18); or (5) if he predicted specific things that did not come to pass (Dt 18:20–22). Note that prophets under the new covenant did not speak with the same finality or infallibility as did the OT prophets, who were God's primary voice of revelation to Israel. In the NT, the prophet is only one of five major ministry gifts in the church (see article on THE MINISTRY GIFTS OF THE CHURCH, p. 1830). The NT prophets had limitations that the OT prophets did not (cf. 1Co 14:29–33) because of the multifaceted and interdependent nature of ministry in NT times (see article on SPIRITUAL GIFTS FOR BELIEVERS, p. 1770).

be ever seeing, but never
perceiving.'[j]
10Make the heart of this people
calloused;[k]
make their ears dull
and close their eyes.[k][l]
Otherwise they might see with
their eyes,
hear with their ears,[m]
understand with their hearts,
and turn and be healed."[n]

11Then I said, "For how long,
O Lord?"[o]
And he answered:

"Until the cities lie ruined[p]
and without inhabitant,
until the houses are left deserted[q]
and the fields ruined and
ravaged,[r]
12until the LORD has sent everyone
far away[s]
and the land is utterly
forsaken.[t]
13And though a tenth remains[u] in
the land,
it will again be laid waste.[v]
But as the terebinth and oak
leave stumps[w] when they are
cut down,
so the holy[x] seed will be the
stump in the land."[y]

The Sign of Immanuel

7 When Ahaz[z] son of Jotham, the
son of Uzziah, was king of Judah,
King Rezin[a] of Aram[b] and Pekah[c]
son of Remaliah[d] king of Israel
marched up to fight against Jerusalem,
but they could not overpower it.
2Now the house of David[e] was told,
"Aram has allied itself with[1] Ephraim[f]"; so the hearts of Ahaz and his
people were shaken,[g] as the trees of
the forest are shaken by the wind.
3Then the LORD said to Isaiah, "Go
out, you and your son Shear-Jashub,[m][h] to meet Ahaz at the end of
the aqueduct of the Upper Pool, on the
road to the Washerman's Field.[i] 4Say
to him, 'Be careful, keep calm[j] and
don't be afraid.[k] Do not lose heart[l]
because of these two smoldering
stubs[m] of firewood—because of the
fierce anger[n] of Rezin and Aram and
of the son of Remaliah.[o] 5Aram,
Ephraim and Remaliah's[p] son have
plotted[q] your ruin, saying, 6"Let us invade Judah; let us tear it apart and divide it among ourselves, and make the
son of Tabeel king over it." 7Yet this is
what the Sovereign LORD says:[r]

" 'It will not take place,
it will not happen,[s]
8for the head of Aram is
Damascus,[t]
and the head of Damascus is
only Rezin.[u]
Within sixty-five years
Ephraim will be too shattered[v]
to be a people.
9The head of Ephraim is Samaria,[w]
and the head of Samaria is only
Remaliah's son.

6:9 [j]Jer 5:21; S Mt 13:15*; Lk 8:10* **6:10** [k]S Ex 4:21; Dt 32:15; Ps 119:70 [l]Isa 29:9; 42:18-20; 43:8; 44:18 [m]S Dt 29:4; Eze 12:2; Mk 8:18 [n]S Dt 32:39; Mt 13:13-15; Mk 4:12*; Jn 12:40* **6:11** [o]Ps 79:5 [p]S Lev 26:31; S Jer 4:13 [q]S Lev 26:43; Isa 24:10 [r]Ps 79:1; S 109:11; Jer 35:17 **6:12** [s]S Dt 28:64 [t]S Isa 5:5,9; 60:15; 62:4; Jer 4:29; 30:17 **6:13** [u]S Isa 1:9; 10:22 [v]S Isa 5:6 [w]S Job 14:8 [x]S Lev 27:30; S Dt 14:2 [y]S Job 14:7 **7:1** [z]S 1Ch 3:13 [a]S ver 8; S 2Ki 15:37 [b]2Ch 28:5 [c]S 2Ki 15:25 [d]ver 5,9; Isa 8:6 **7:2** [e]ver 13; S 2Sa 7:11; Isa 16:5; 22:22; Jer 21:12; Am 9:11 [f]Isa 9:9; Hos 5:3 [g]Isa 6:4; Da 5:6 **7:3** [h]Isa 10:21-22 [i]2Ki 18:17; Isa 36:2 **7:4** [j]Isa 30:15; La 3:26 [k]S Ge 15:1; S Dt 3:2; Isa 8:12; 12:2; 35:4; 37:6; Mt 24:6 [l]S Dt 20:3; S Isa 21:4 [m]Am 4:11; Zec 3:2 [n]Isa 10:24; 51:13; 54:14 [o]S 2Ki 15:27 **7:5** [p]S ver 1 [q]ver 2 **7:7** [r]Isa 24:3; 25:8; 28:16 [s]Ps 2:1; Isa 8:10; 14:24; 28:18; 40:8; 46:10; Ac 4:25 **7:8** [t]S Ge 14:15 [u]ver 1; Isa 9:11 [v]2Ki 17:24; Isa 8:4; 17:1-3 **7:9** [w]S 2Ki 15:29; Isa 9:9; 28:1,3

k *9,10* Hebrew; Septuagint *'You will be ever hearing, but never understanding; / you will be ever seeing, but never perceiving.' / 10This people's heart has become calloused; / they hardly hear with their ears, / and they have closed their eyes* **1** *2* Or *has set up camp in* **m** *3 Shear-Jashub* means *a remnant will return.*

Isaiah would be able to have a new ministry during the additional 15 years granted to Hezekiah (38:5).

6:13 THE HOLY SEED. God encouraged Isaiah by telling him that a small remnant of people would believe and be preserved. A new Judah that could be called holy would come forth, through whom God would work out his plan of salvation for the world. Likewise, under the new covenant God will judge an apostate church and raise up a holy remnant that will remain faithful to him and his Word (see article on CHRIST'S MESSAGE TO THE SEVEN CHURCHES, p. 2008).

7:1–25 WHEN AHAZ ... WAS KING. About 735/734 B.C., the kings of Israel and Aram attacked Judah. King Ahaz of Judah was told by Isaiah to trust God for deliverance. Yet Ahaz refused to accept God's offer of a miraculous sign, and he sought help from Assyria instead (see 2Ki 16:5–18; 2Ch 28:16–21). God gave a sign anyway to the whole house of David—the birth of Immanuel (vv. 13–17). Though the Aramean and Israelite invasion was to fail, God would later send the Assyrians and Babylonians to devastate the land.

7:3 SHEAR-JASHUB. The name of Isaiah's oldest son means "a remnant will return." This name highlighted God's intention to preserve a faithful remnant of the people to carry out his plan of salvation (cf. 11:11–12,16; 37:4,31).

7:8 WITHIN SIXTY-FIVE YEARS. Israel (also called Ephraim) was defeated in 722 B.C. by Assyria, who brought foreigners to the land to intermarry with the few remaining Israelites; the resulting racial mixture came to be called Samaritans (see 2Ki 17:24–34; cf. Jn 4:7–42).

If you do not stand[x] firm in your
faith,[y]
you will not stand at all.' "[z]

10Again the LORD spoke to Ahaz,
11"Ask the LORD your God for a sign,[a]
whether in the deepest depths or in the
highest heights.[b]"
12But Ahaz said, "I will not ask; I
will not put the LORD to the test.[c]"
13Then Isaiah said, "Hear now, you
house of David![d] Is it not enough[e] to
try the patience of men? Will you try
the patience[f] of my God[g] also?
14Therefore the Lord himself will give
you[n] a sign:[h] The virgin[i] will be
with child and will give birth to a son,[j]
and[o] will call him Immanuel.[p][k] 15He
will eat curds[l] and honey[m] when he
knows enough to reject the wrong and
choose the right. 16But before the boy
knows[n] enough to reject the wrong
and choose the right,[o] the land of the
two kings you dread will be laid
waste.[p] 17The LORD will bring on you
and on your people and on the house of
your father a time unlike any since
Ephraim broke away[q] from Judah—
he will bring the king of Assyria.[r]"
18In that day[s] the LORD will whis-
tle[t] for flies from the distant streams
of Egypt and for bees from the land of
Assyria.[u] 19They will all come and
settle in the steep ravines and in the
crevices[v] in the rocks, on all the
thornbushes[w] and at all the water
holes. 20In that day[x] the Lord will
use[y] a razor hired from beyond the
River[q][z]—the king of Assyria[a]—to
shave your head and the hair of your
legs, and to take off your beards[b]
also.[c] 21In that day,[d] a man will keep
alive a young cow and two goats.[e]
22And because of the abundance of the
milk they give, he will have curds to
eat. All who remain in the land will eat
curds[f] and honey.[g] 23In that day,[h]
in every place where there were a thousand vines worth a thousand silver
shekels,[r][i] there will be only briers
and thorns.[j] 24Men will go there with
bow and arrow, for the land will be covered with briers[k] and thorns. 25As for
all the hills[l] once cultivated by the
hoe, you will no longer go there for fear
of the briers and thorns;[m] they will become places where cattle are turned
loose and where sheep run.[n]

Assyria, the LORD's Instrument

8 The LORD said to me, "Take a
large scroll[o] and write on it with
an ordinary pen: Maher-Shalal-Hash-
Baz.[s][p] 2And I will call in Uriah[q] the
priest and Zechariah son of Jeberekiah
as reliable witnesses[r] for me."
3Then I went to the prophetess,[s]
and she conceived and gave birth to a
son.[t] And the LORD said to me, "Name
him Maher-Shalal-Hash-Baz.[u] 4Be-
fore the boy knows[v] how to say 'My
father' or 'My mother,' the wealth of
Damascus[w] and the plunder of Samaria will be carried off by the king of Assyria.[x]"
5The LORD spoke to me again:

6"Because this people has
rejected[y]

7:9 [x]S Ps 20:8; Isa 8:10; 40:8 [y]2Ch 20:20 [z]Isa 8:6-8; 30:12-14 **7:11** [a]S Ex 7:9; S Dt 13:2 [b]Ps 139:8 **7:12** [c]Dt 4:34 **7:13** [d]S ver 2 [e]S Ge 30:15 [f]S Isa 1:14 [g]Ps 63:1; 118:28; Isa 25:1; 49:4; 61:10 **7:14** [h]S Ex 3:12; S Lk 2:12 [i]S Ge 24:43 [j]S Ge 3:15; Lk 1:31 [k]S Ge 21:22; Isa 8:8,10; Mt 1:23* **7:15** [l]S Ge 18:8 [m]ver 22 **7:16** [n]Isa 8:4 [o]Dt 1:39 [p]S Dt 13:16; Isa 17:3; Jer 7:15; Hos 5:9,13; Am 1:3-5 **7:17** [q]1Ki 12:16 [r]S ver 20; S 2Ch 28:20 **7:18** [s]ver 20,21; S Isa 2:11 [t]S Isa 5:26 [u]Isa 13:5 **7:19** [v]S Isa 2:19 [w]ver 25; Isa 17:9; 34:13; 55:13 **7:20** [x]S ver 18 [y]Isa 10:15; 29:16 [z]Isa 11:15; Jer 2:18 [a]ver 17; 2Ki 18:16; Isa 8:7; 10:5 [b]S 2Sa 10:4 [c]S Dt 28:49 **7:21** [d]ver 23; Isa 2:17 [e]Jer 39:10 **7:22** [f]S Ge 18:8 [g]ver 15; Isa 14:30 **7:23** [h]ver 21 [i]SS 8:11 [j]S Isa 5:6; Hos 2:12 **7:24** [k]S Isa 5:6 **7:25** [l]Hag 1:11 [m]S ver 19 [n]S Isa 5:17 **8:1** [o]S Dt 27:8; Job 19:23; Isa 30:8; Jer 51:60 [p]ver 3; Hab 2:2; Jer 20:3; Hos 1:4 **8:2** [q]S 2Ki 16:10 [r]ver 16; S Jos 24:22; S Ru 4:9; Jer 32:10,12,25,44 **8:3** [s]S Ex 15:20 [t]S Ge 3:15 [u]S ver 1 **8:4** [v]Isa 7:16 [w]S Ge 14:15 [x]S Isa 7:8 **8:6** [y]S Isa 5:24

[n]*14* The Hebrew is plural. [o]*14* Masoretic Text; Dead Sea Scrolls *and he* or *and they* [p]*14* *Immanuel* means *God with us.* [q]*20* That is, the Euphrates [r]*23* That is, about 25 pounds (about 11.5 kilograms) [s]*1* *Maher-Shalal-Hash-Baz* means *quick to the plunder, swift to the spoil*; also in verse 3.

7:12 I WILL NOT ASK. Ahaz rejected the prophet Isaiah's counsel to trust in God for deliverance; instead, he trusted his own limited understanding and sought Assyria's help (see 2Ki 16:5–18; 2Ch 28:16–21).

7:14 VIRGIN WILL BE WITH CHILD . . . IMMANUEL. "Virgin" (Heb *almah*) can mean either "virgin" or "a young woman before marriage." (1) The immediate application of this sign was to a new bride, who would have been a virgin until the time of her marriage. Before her son was old enough to know right from wrong, the kings of Aram and Israel would be destroyed (v. 16). (2) This prophecy's ultimate fulfillment was realized in the birth of Jesus Christ by the virgin Mary (Mt 1:23). Mary was a virgin and remained a virgin until after Jesus' birth (Mt 1:18,25). The conception of her son came about by a miracle of the Holy Spirit rather than through the act of a man (see Mt 1:16,23, notes; Lk 1:35, note). (3) The virgin's son was to be called "Immanuel," i.e., "God with us" (Mt 1:23); that name acquired a new depth of meaning in the personal coming into the world of God's one and only Son (cf. Jn 3:16).

8:1 MAHER-SHALAL-HASH-BAZ. The meaning of the name of Isaiah's second son (cf. 7:3, note) is "quick to the plunder, swift to the spoil." That name predicted not only Aram's destruction and fall (732 B.C.) at the hands of Assyria, but Israel's as well (722 B.C.).

8:6 WATERS OF SHILOAH. The "waters of Shiloah" (known in the NT as the pool of Siloam,

the gently flowing waters of
Shiloah[z]
and rejoices over Rezin
and the son of Remaliah,[a]
7therefore the Lord is about to
bring against them
the mighty floodwaters[b] of the
River[t]—
the king of Assyria[c] with all
his pomp.[d]
It will overflow all its channels,
run over all its banks[e]
8and sweep on into Judah, swirling
over it,[f]
passing through it and reaching
up to the neck.
Its outspread wings[g] will cover
the breadth of your land,
O Immanuel[u]!"[h]

9Raise the war cry,[v][i] you nations,
and be shattered![j]
Listen, all you distant lands.
Prepare[k] for battle, and be
shattered!
Prepare for battle, and be
shattered!
10Devise your strategy, but it will be
thwarted;[l]
propose your plan, but it will not
stand,[m]
for God is with us.[w][n]

Fear God

11The LORD spoke to me with his
strong hand upon me,[o] warning me
not to follow[p] the way of this people.
He said:

12"Do not call conspiracy[q]
everything that these people call
conspiracy[x];
do not fear what they fear,[r]
and do not dread it.[s]
13The LORD Almighty is the one you
are to regard as holy,[t]
he is the one you are to fear,[u]
he is the one you are to dread,[v]
14and he will be a sanctuary;[w]
but for both houses of Israel he
will be
a stone[x] that causes men to
stumble[y]
and a rock that makes them
fall.[z]
And for the people of Jerusalem he
will be
a trap and a snare.[a]
15Many of them will stumble;[b]
they will fall and be broken,
they will be snared and
captured."

16Bind up the testimony[c]
and seal[d] up the law among my
disciples.
17I will wait[e] for the LORD,
who is hiding[f] his face from
the house of Jacob.
I will put my trust in him.[g]

18Here am I, and the children the

[t]7 That is, the Euphrates [u]8 *Immanuel* means *God with us.* [v]9 Or *Do your worst* [w]10 Hebrew *Immanuel* [x]12 Or *Do not call for a treaty / every time these people call for a treaty*

8:6 [z]S Ne 3:15; Jn 9:7 [a]S Isa 7:1 **8:7** [b]Isa 17:12-13; 28:2,17; 30:28; 43:2; Da 11:40; Na 1:8 [c]S 2Ch 28:20; S Isa 7:20 [d]Isa 10:16 [e]S Jos 3:15 **8:8** [f]Isa 28:15 [g]Isa 18:6; 46:11; Jer 4:13; 48:40 [h]S Isa 7:14 **8:9** [i]S Jos 6:5; Isa 17:12-13 [j]S Job 34:24 [k]Jer 6:4; 46:3; 51:12,27-28; Eze 38:7; Joel 3:9; Zec 14:2-3 **8:10** [l]S Job 5:12 [m]S Pr 19:21; S 21:30; S Isa 7:7 [n]S Isa 7:14; Mt 1:23; Ro 8:31 **8:11** [o]Eze 1:3; 3:14 [p]Eze 2:8 **8:12** [q]Isa 7:2; 20:5; 30:1; 36:6 [r]S Isa 7:4; Mt 10:28 [s]1Pe 3:14* **8:13** [t]S Nu 20:12 [u]S Ex 20:20 [v]Isa 29:23 **8:14** [w]S Isa 4:6 [x]S Ps 118:22 [y]Jer 6:21; Eze 3:20; 14:3,7; Lk 20:18 [z]S Lk 2:34; Ro 9:33*; 1Pe 2:8* [a]S Ps 119:110; Isa 24:17-18 **8:15** [b]Pr 4:19; Isa 28:13; 59:10; Ro 9:32 **8:16** [c]S Ru 4:7 [d]Isa 29:11-12; Jer 32:14; Da 8:26; 12:4 **8:17** [e]S Ps 27:14 [f]S Dt 31:17 [g]S Ps 22:5; Heb 2:13*

Jn 9:7) were fed by a gentle spring that served as Jerusalem's underground source of water in times of siege by a hostile nation. They symbolized God's gracious and gentle rule over Israel through his kingly representatives—i.e., the godly Davidic kings. Since Judah and Jerusalem were rejecting God's beneficent rule, they would instead experience the "mighty floodwaters" from the region of the Euphrates, i.e., the mighty flood of invading Assyrian soldiers (vv. 7–10).

8:8 O IMMANUEL. In the midst of Isaiah's prophecy, the Spirit of prophecy pointed to a hope for the future. No matter what happened, those who were faithful to God did not need to fear, for Immanuel ("God with us," cf. v. 10) was the confidence of all who trusted in him. "Immanuel" is thus the enduring watchword for God's people throughout history—past, present and future (Mt 1:23).

8:12 A CONSPIRACY. Isaiah had been attempting to persuade Judah to seek God rather than foreign help. He was accused of conspiracy and treason. Likewise, throughout the history of the church, those who have attempted to call the church away from human programs and unbiblical Christianity and back to its original power, holiness and mission have often met with persecution and disfavor. Rather than fearing other people, the prophet was exhorted to fear only the Lord Almighty (vv. 12–13).

8:13 HE IS THE ONE YOU ARE TO FEAR. In times of danger and trial, God alone is the One whom we must fear and look to for our deliverance (cf. Mt 10:28). Through a proper reverence and love for him, he will be present with us and be our sanctuary and protection (v. 14).

8:16 SEAL UP THE LAW. The great majority of God's people were living in apostasy, but there remained a faithful remnant—disciples who followed the Lord's will. They were the ones called to preserve God's word. In every age, the true disciples of the Lord, those whose hearts have been set on his word, must contend for God's unalterable truth (see Jude 3) and pass it along to the next generation.

LORD has given me.[h] We are signs[i]
and symbols[j] in Israel from the LORD
Almighty, who dwells on Mount
Zion.[k]

19When men tell you to consult[l]
mediums and spiritists,[m] who whisper
and mutter,[n] should not a people inquire[o] of their God? Why consult the
dead on behalf of the living? 20To the
law[p] and to the testimony![q] If they
do not speak according to this word,
they have no light[r] of dawn. 21Dis-
tressed and hungry,[s] they will roam
through the land;[t] when they are famished, they will become enraged and,
looking upward, will curse[u] their king
and their God. 22Then they will look
toward the earth and see only distress
and darkness and fearful gloom,[v] and
they will be thrust into utter darkness.[w]

To Us a Child Is Born

9 Nevertheless, there will be no
more gloom[x] for those who were
in distress. In the past he humbled the
land of Zebulun and the land of Naphtali,[y] but in the future he will honor Galilee of the Gentiles, by the way of the
sea, along the Jordan—

2The people walking in darkness[z]
have seen a great light;[a]
on those living in the land of the
shadow of death[y][b]
a light has dawned.[c]
3You have enlarged the nation[d]
and increased their joy;[e]
they rejoice before you
as people rejoice at the harvest,
as men rejoice
when dividing the plunder.[f]
4For as in the day of Midian's
defeat,[g]
you have shattered[h]
the yoke[i] that burdens them,
the bar across their shoulders,[j]
the rod of their oppressor.[k]
5Every warrior's boot used in battle
and every garment rolled in
blood
will be destined for burning,[l]
will be fuel for the fire.
6For to us a child is born,[m]
to us a son is given,[n]
and the government[o] will be on
his shoulders.[p]
And he will be called
Wonderful Counselor,[z][q] Mighty
God,[r]
Everlasting[s] Father,[t] Prince of
Peace.[u]
7Of the increase of his
government[v] and peace[w]

8:18 [h] S Ge 33:5; Heb 2:13* [i] S Ex 3:12; Eze 4:3; 12:6; 24:24; Lk 2:34 [j] S Dt 28:46; S Eze 12:11 [k] Ps 9:11 8:19 [l] S 1Sa 28:8 [m] S Lev 19:31 [n] Isa 29:4 [o] S Nu 27:21 8:20 [p] S Isa 1:10; Lk 16:29 [q] S Ru 4:7 [r] ver 22; Isa 9:2; 59:9; 60:2; Mic 3:6 8:21 [s] S Job 18:12 [t] Job 30:3 [u] S Ex 22:28; Rev 16:11 8:22 [v] S Job 15:24 [w] S ver 20; S Job 3:13; S Isa 5:30; S Joel 2:2; Mt 25:30; Rev 16:10 9:1 [x] S Job 15:24 [y] S 2Ki 15:29 9:2 [z] S Ps 82:5; S 107:10,14; S Isa 8:20 [a] S Ps 36:9; Isa 42:6; 49:6; 60:19; Mal 4:2; Eph 5:8 [b] S Lk 1:79 [c] Isa 58:8; Mt 4:15-16* 9:3 [d] S Job 12:23 [e] S Ps 4:7; S Isa 25:9 [f] S Ex 15:9; S Jos 22:8; S Ps 119:162 9:4 [g] S Jdg 7:25 [h] S Job 34:24; Isa 37:36-38 [i] Isa 14:25; 58:6,9; Jer 2:20; 30:8; Eze 30:18; Na 1:13; Mt 11:30 [j] S Ps 81:6; S Isa 10:27 [k] Isa 14:4; 16:4; 29:5,20; 49:26; 51:13; 54:14; 60:18 9:5 [l] S Isa 2:4 9:6 [m] S Ge 3:15; Isa 53:2; Lk 2:11 [n] Jn 3:16 [o] S Mt 28:18 [p] Isa 22:22 [q] S Job 15:8; Isa 28:29 [r] S Dt 7:21; Ps 24:8; Isa 10:21; 11:2; 42:13 [s] S Ps 90:2 [t] S Ex 4:22; Isa 64:8; Jn 14:9-10 [u] Isa 26:3,12; 53:5; 66:12; Jer 33:6; Mic 5:5; S Lk 2:14 9:7 [v] S Isa 2:4 [w] S Ps 85:8; 119:165; Isa 11:9; 26:3,12; 32:17; 48:18

[y] 2 Or *land of darkness* [z] 6 Or *Wonderful, Counselor*

9:1–7 THERE WILL BE NO MORE GLOOM. Isaiah speaks of a coming deliverer who would one day lead God's people to joy, peace, righteousness and justice; this person is the Messiah—Jesus Christ, the Son of God. This prophecy reveals several important truths about the coming Messiah. (1) For the most part, he would minister in Galilee (v. 1; cf. Mt 4:13–14). (2) He would bring the light of salvation and hope (v. 2; cf. 42:6; 49:6; Mt 4:15–16). (3) He would enlarge the community of God's people, primarily by the inclusion of Gentiles in the household of faith (v. 3; cf. Ac 15:13–18). (4) He would bring peace by delivering his people from the yoke of oppression and crushing their enemies (vv. 4–5). (5) The Messiah would come from the nation of Israel and be called Wonderful Counselor, Mighty God, Everlasting Father, and Prince of Peace (see v. 6, note). (6) He would rule over God's people forever (v. 7; cf. 2Sa 7:16).

9:6 FOR TO US A CHILD IS BORN. This foretells the birth of the Messiah, Jesus Christ (see also 7:14, note). His birth would be at a definite time and place in history, and this Messianic Son would be born in a unique and marvelous way. Isaiah records four names that would characterize his function as Messiah. (1) Wonderful Counselor. The Messiah would himself be a supernatural wonder (the Hebrew word *pele'* is only used of God, never of humans or human work; cf. 28:29); he would show his character by his deeds and miracles. This Wonderful Counselor would be the incarnation of perfect wisdom and have the words of eternal life; as Counselor he would disclose the perfect plan of salvation (cf. ch. 11). (2) Mighty God. In the Messiah all the fullness of the Deity would exist in bodily form (Col 2:9; cf. Jn 1:1,14). (3) Everlasting Father. He not only would come to reveal the heavenly Father, but he himself would act toward his people eternally as a compassionate father who loves, protects and supplies the needs of his children (cf. Ps 103:13). (4) Prince of Peace. His rule would bring peace with God for humankind through deliverance from sin and death (11:6–9; cf. Ro 5:1; 8:2).

9:7 GOVERNMENT AND PEACE THERE WILL BE NO END. In this prophetic statement concerning the establishment of Christ's reign, no distinction is made between a first and second coming. At this point in human history, Christ's entire redemptive work and rule is viewed as oc-

there will be no end.[x]
He will reign[y] on David's throne
and over his kingdom,
establishing and upholding it
with justice[z] and
righteousness[a]
from that time on and forever.[b]
The zeal[c] of the LORD Almighty
will accomplish this.

The LORD's Anger Against Israel

8The Lord has sent a message[d]
against Jacob;
it will fall on Israel.
9All the people will know it—
Ephraim[e] and the inhabitants of
Samaria[f]—
who say with pride
and arrogance[g] of heart,
10"The bricks have fallen down,
but we will rebuild with dressed
stone;[h]
the fig[i] trees have been felled,
but we will replace them with
cedars.[j]"
11But the LORD has strengthened
Rezin's[k] foes against them
and has spurred their enemies
on.
12Arameans[l] from the east and
Philistines[m] from the west
have devoured[n] Israel with
open mouth.

Yet for all this, his anger[o] is not
turned away,
his hand is still upraised.[p]

13But the people have not returned[q]
to him who struck[r] them,
nor have they sought[s] the LORD
Almighty.
14So the LORD will cut off from Israel
both head and tail,
both palm branch and reed[t] in
a single day;[u]
15the elders[v] and prominent men[w]
are the head,
the prophets[x] who teach lies[y]
are the tail.
16Those who guide[z] this people
mislead them,
and those who are guided are
led astray.[a]

9:7 [x]Da 2:44; 4:3; S Lk 1:33; Jn 12:34 [y]Isa 1:26; 32:1; 60:17; 1Co 15:25 [z]Isa 11:4; 16:5; 32:1,16; 33:5; 42:1; Jer 23:5; 33:14 [a]S Ps 72:2 [b]S 2Sa 7:13 [c]2Ki 19:31; Isa 26:11; 37:32; 42:13; 59:17; 63:15
9:8 [d]S Dt 32:2
9:9 [e]S Isa 7:2 [f]S Isa 7:9 [g]Isa 46:12; 48:4; Eze 2:4; Zec 7:11
9:10 [h]S Ge 11:3 [i]Am 7:14; Lk 19:4 [j]1Ki 7:2-3
9:11 [k]S Isa 7:8
9:12 [l]2Ki 16:6 [m]S 2Ch 28:18 [n]S Ps 79:7 [o]S Job 40:11 [p]S Isa 5:25
9:13 [q]S 2Ch 28:22; Am 4:9; Zep 3:7; Hag 2:17 [r]Jer 5:3; Eze 7:9 [s]Isa 2:3; 17:7; 31:1; 55:6; Jer 50:4; Da 9:13; Hos 3:5; 7:7,10; Am 4:6,10; Zep 1:6
9:14 [t]ver 14-15; Isa 19:15 [u]Rev 18:8
9:15 [v]Isa 3:2-3 [w]S Isa 5:13 [x]Isa 28:7; Eze 13:2 [y]S Job 13:4; S Isa 3:8; 44:20; Eze 13:22; Mt 24:24
9:16 [z]Mt 15:14; 23:16,24 [a]S Isa 3:12
9:17 [b]Jer 9:21; 11:22; 18:21; 48:15; 49:26; Am 4:10; 8:13 [c]S Job 5:4; Isa 27:11; Jer 13:14 [d]Isa 10:6; 32:6; Mic 7:2 [e]S Isa 1:4 [f]S Isa 3:8; Mt 12:34; Ro 3:13-14 [g]S Isa 5:25
9:18 [h]S Dt 29:23; S Isa 1:31 [i]S Isa 5:6 [j]S Ps 83:14
9:19 [k]S Job 40:11; Isa 13:9,13 [l]Jer 17:27 [m]S Ps 97:3; S Isa 1:31 [n]S Isa 3:5
9:20 [o]S Lev 26:26; S Job 18:12 [p]Isa 49:26; Zec 11:9

17Therefore the Lord will take no
pleasure in the young
men,[b]
nor will he pity[c] the fatherless
and widows,
for everyone is ungodly[d] and
wicked,[e]
every mouth speaks vileness.[f]
Yet for all this, his anger is not
turned away,
his hand is still upraised.[g]

18Surely wickedness burns like a
fire;[h]
it consumes briers and thorns,[i]
it sets the forest thickets ablaze,[j]
so that it rolls upward in a
column of smoke.
19By the wrath[k] of the LORD
Almighty
the land will be scorched[l]
and the people will be fuel for the
fire;[m]
no one will spare his brother.[n]
20On the right they will devour,
but still be hungry;[o]
on the left they will eat,[p]
but not be satisfied.
Each will feed on the flesh of his
own offspring[a]:
21 Manasseh will feed on Ephraim,
and Ephraim on
Manasseh;[q]
together they will turn against
Judah.[r]

Yet for all this, his anger is not
turned away,
his hand is still upraised.[s]

10 Woe[t] to those who make
unjust laws,
to those who issue oppressive
decrees,[u]
2to deprive[v] the poor of their
rights
and withhold justice from the
oppressed of my people,[w]
making widows their prey

9:21 [q]S Jdg 7:22; S 12:4 [r]S 2Ch 28:6 [s]S Isa 5:25 10:1 [t]S Isa 5:8 [u]S Ps 58:2 10:2 [v]Isa 3:14 [w]S Isa 5:23

[a]20 Or *arm*

---

curring in one distant coming. Nowhere does the OT clearly reveal that Christ's rule on earth would involve a first and second advent in history. Likewise in the NT, time gaps between end-time events are not always clearly distinguished (see Mt 24:42–44, notes).

9:8—10:4 A MESSAGE AGAINST JACOB. These verses describe Israel's arrogance and persistent impenitence, and God's anger and judgment against them; even in great trouble they would not humble themselves and turn to God with a contrite and broken heart.

and robbing the fatherless.[x]
3What will you do on the day of
reckoning,[y]
when disaster[z] comes from
afar?
To whom will you run for help?[a]
Where will you leave your
riches?
4Nothing will remain but to cringe
among the captives[b]
or fall among the slain.[c]

Yet for all this, his anger is not
turned away,[d]
his hand is still upraised.

God's Judgment on Assyria

5"Woe[e] to the Assyrian,[f] the
rod[g] of my anger,
in whose hand is the club[h] of
my wrath![i]
6I send him against a godless[j]
nation,
I dispatch[k] him against a
people who anger me,[l]
to seize loot and snatch plunder,[m]
and to trample[n] them down like
mud in the streets.
7But this is not what he intends,[o]
this is not what he has in mind;
his purpose is to destroy,
to put an end to many nations.
8'Are not my commanders[p] all
kings?' he says.
9 'Has not Calno[q] fared like
Carchemish?[r]
Is not Hamath[s] like Arpad,[t]
and Samaria[u] like Damascus?[v]
10As my hand seized the kingdoms
of the idols,[w]
kingdoms whose images excelled
those of Jerusalem and
Samaria—
11shall I not deal with Jerusalem and
her images
as I dealt with Samaria and her
idols?[x]' "

12When the Lord has finished all his
work[y] against Mount Zion[z] and Jerusalem, he will say, "I will punish the
king of Assyria[a] for the willful pride[b]
of his heart and the haughty look[c] in
his eyes. 13For he says:

" 'By the strength of my hand[d] I
have done this,[e]
and by my wisdom, because I
have understanding.
I removed the boundaries of
nations,
I plundered their treasures;[f]
like a mighty one I subdued[b]
their kings.[g]
14As one reaches into a nest,[h]
so my hand reached for the
wealth[i] of the nations;
as men gather abandoned eggs,
so I gathered all the countries;[j]
not one flapped a wing,
or opened its mouth to
chirp.[k]' "

15Does the ax raise itself above him
who swings it,
or the saw boast against him
who uses it?[l]
As if a rod were to wield him who
lifts it up,
or a club[m] brandish him who is
not wood!
16Therefore, the Lord, the LORD
Almighty,
will send a wasting disease[n]
upon his sturdy warriors;[o]
under his pomp[p] a fire[q] will be
kindled
like a blazing flame.
17The Light of Israel will become a
fire,[r]
their Holy One[s] a flame;
in a single day it will burn and
consume
his thorns[t] and his briers.[u]
18The splendor of his forests[v] and
fertile fields
it will completely destroy,[w]
as when a sick man wastes
away.
19And the remaining trees of his
forests[x] will be so few[y]
that a child could write them
down.

10:2 [x]S Dt 10:18; S Job 6:27; S Isa 1:17 **10:3** [y]S Job 31:14 [z]ver 25; Ps 59:5; Isa 1:24; 13:6; 14:23; 24:6; 26:14; 47:11; Jer 5:9; 9:9; 50:15; Lk 19:44 [a]S Ps 108:12; Isa 20:6; 30:7; 31:3 **10:4** [b]Isa 24:22; Zec 9:11 [c]Isa 22:2; 34:3; 66:16; Jer 39:6; Na 3:3 [d]S Isa 5:25; 12:1; 63:10; 64:5; Jer 4:8; 30:24; La 1:12 **10:5** [e]S 2Ki 19:21; S Isa 28:1 [f]ver 12, 18; S Isa 7:20; 14:25; 31:8; 37:7; Zep 2:13 [g]Isa 14:5; 54:16 [h]ver 15,24; Isa 30:31; 41:15; 45:1; Jer 50:23; 51:20 [i]Isa 9:4; 13:3,5,13; 26:20; 30:30; 34:2; 63:6; 66:14; Eze 30:24-25 **10:6** [j]S Isa 9:17 [k]Hab 1:12 [l]S 2Ch 28:9; Isa 9:19 [m]S Jdg 6:4; S Isa 5:29; 8:1 [n]S 2Sa 22:43; S Ps 7:5; S Isa 5:5; 37:26-27 **10:7** [o]S Ge 50:20; Ac 4:23-28 **10:8** [p]2Ki 18:24 **10:9** [q]S Ge 10:10 [r]S 2Ch 35:20 [s]Nu 34:8; 2Ch 8:4; Isa 11:11 [t]2Ki 18:34 [u]2Ki 17:6 [v]S Ge 14:15; 2Ki 16:9; Jer 49:24 **10:10** [w]2Ki 19:18 **10:11** [x]S 2Ki 19:13; S Isa 2:8; 36:18-20; 37:10-13 **10:12** [y]Isa 28:21-22; 65:7; 66:4; Jer 5:29 [z]2Ki 19:31 [a]S ver 5; S 2Ki 19:7; Isa 30:31-33; 37:36-38; Jer 50:18 [b]S Isa 2:11; S Eze 28:17 [c]Ps 18:27 **10:13** [d]S Dt 8:17 [e]S Dt 32:26-27; Isa 47:7; Da 4:30 [f]Eze 28:4 [g]Isa 14:13-14 **10:14** [h]Jer 49:16; Ob 1:4; Hab 2:6-11 [i]S Job 31:25 [j]Isa 14:6 [k]2Ki 19:22-24; Isa 37:24-25 **10:15** [l]S Isa 7:20; 45:9; Ro 9:20-21 [m]S ver 5 **10:16** [n]ver 18; S Nu 11:33; Isa 17:4 [o]Ps 78:31 [p]S Isa 8:7 [q]Jer 21:14 **10:17** [r]S Job 41:21; S Isa 1:31; 31:9; Zec 2:5 [s]Isa 37:23 [t]S Nu 11:1-3; S 2Sa 23:6 [u]S Isa 9:18 **10:18** [v]S 2Ki 19:23 [w]S ver 5 **10:19** [x]ver 33-34; Isa 32:19 [y]Isa 17:6; 21:17; 27:13; Jer 44:28

[b]*13* Or */ I subdued the mighty,*

10:5 THE ASSYRIAN. God had used the Assyrians to punish his godless people. Now God would punish Assyria for their pride and arrogance (vv. 8–14). Thus Isaiah prophesied destruction for the Assyrians (vv. 16–19). This specific prophecy was fulfilled when God's angel put to death 185,000 soldiers in the Assyrian camp surrounding Jerusalem (see ch. 37).

The Remnant of Israel

20In that day[z] the remnant of
Israel,
the survivors[a] of the house of
Jacob,
will no longer rely[b] on him
who struck them down[c]
but will truly rely[d] on the LORD,
the Holy One of Israel.[e]
21A remnant[f] will return,[cg] a
remnant of Jacob
will return to the Mighty God.[h]
22Though your people, O Israel, be
like the sand[i] by the sea,
only a remnant will return.[j]
Destruction has been decreed,[k]
overwhelming and righteous.
23The Lord, the LORD Almighty, will
carry out
the destruction decreed[l] upon
the whole land.[m]

24Therefore, this is what the Lord,
the LORD Almighty, says:

"O my people who live in Zion,[n]
do not be afraid[o] of the
Assyrians,
who beat[p] you with a rod[q]
and lift up a club against you,
as Egypt did.
25Very soon[r] my anger against you
will end
and my wrath[s] will be directed
to their destruction.[t]"
26The LORD Almighty will lash[u]
them with a whip,
as when he struck down
Midian[v] at the rock of
Oreb;
and he will raise his staff[w] over
the waters,[x]
as he did in Egypt.
27In that day[y] their burden[z] will
be lifted from your
shoulders,
their yoke[a] from your neck;[b]
the yoke[c] will be broken
because you have grown so
fat.[d]
28They enter Aiath;
they pass through Migron;[d]
they store supplies[e] at
Micmash.[f]
29They go over the pass, and say,
"We will camp overnight at
Geba.[g]"
Ramah[h] trembles;
Gibeah[i] of Saul flees.[j]
30Cry out, O Daughter of Gallim![k]
Listen, O Laishah!
Poor Anathoth![l]
31Madmenah is in flight;
the people of Gebim take cover.
32This day they will halt at Nob;[m]
they will shake their fist[n]
at the mount of the Daughter of
Zion,[o]
at the hill of Jerusalem.
33See, the Lord, the LORD Almighty,
will lop off[p] the boughs with
great power.
The lofty trees will be felled,[q]
the tall[r] ones will be brought
low.[s]
34He will cut down[t] the forest
thickets with an ax;
Lebanon[u] will fall before the
Mighty One.[v]

The Branch From Jesse

11 A shoot[w] will come up from
the stump[x] of Jesse;[y]

10:20 [z] ver 27; Isa 11:10,11; 12:1,4; 19:18,19; 24:21; 28:5; 52:6; Zec 9:16 [a] S Isa 1:9; Eze 7:16 [b] S 2Ki 16:7 [c] 2Ch 28:20 [d] 2Ch 14:11; Isa 17:7; 48:2; 50:10; Jer 21:2; Hos 3:5; 6:1; Mic 3:11; 7:7 [e] S Isa 5:24 **10:21** [f] S Ge 45:7; Isa 6:13; Zep 3:13 [g] Isa 7:3 [h] S Isa 9:6 **10:22** [i] S Ge 12:2; Isa 48:19; Jer 33:22 [j] Ezr 1:4; Isa 11:11; 46:3 [k] ver 23; Isa 28:22; Jer 40:2; Da 9:27 **10:23** [l] S ver 22 [m] Isa 6:12; 28:22; Ro 9:27-28* **10:24** [n] Ps 87:5-6 [o] S Isa 7:4 [p] S Ex 5:14 [q] S ver 5 **10:25** [r] Isa 17:14; 29:17; Hag 2:6 [s] ver 5; Ps 30:5; Isa 13:5; 24:21; 26:20; 30:30; 34:2; 66:14; Da 8:19; 11:36 [t] S ver 3; Mic 5:6 **10:26** [u] Isa 37:36-38 [v] S Isa 9:4 [w] Isa 30:32 [x] S Ex 14:16 **10:27** [y] S ver 20 [z] S Ps 66:11 [a] S Lev 26:13; S Isa 9:4 [b] Isa 14:25; 47:6; 52:2 [c] Jer 30:8 **10:28** [d] S 1Sa 14:2 [e] S Jos 1:11 [f] 1Sa 13:2 **10:29** [g] S Jos 18:24; S Ne 11:31 [h] S Jos 18:25 [i] S Jdg 19:14 [j] Isa 15:5 **10:30** [k] 1Sa 25:44 [l] S Ne 11:32 **10:32** [m] S 1Sa 21:1 [n] S Job 15:25 [o] S Ps 9:14; Isa 16:1; Jer 6:23

10:33 [p] Isa 18:5; 27:11; Eze 17:4 [q] S Ex 12:12 [r] Isa 2:13; Am 2:9 [s] Isa 5:15 **10:34** [t] Na 1:12; Zec 11:2 [u] S 2Ki 19:23 [v] S Ge 49:24; Ps 93:4; Isa 33:21 **11:1** [w] S 2Ki 19:26; S Job 14:7 [x] S Job 14:8 [y] ver 10; Isa 9:7; S Mt 1:1; S Rev 5:5

[c] *21* Hebrew *shear-jashub*; also in verse 22
[d] *27* Hebrew; Septuagint *broken / from your shoulders*

10:20 THE REMNANT OF ISRAEL. Isaiah again assures the faithful believers that after God had judged Israel, a godly remnant who trusted in the Lord would be preserved and restored; this remnant would be the true Israel (cf. Ro 9:6–9). God's plan of salvation for the world will always be carried out by the remnant who truly believe and obey his word, not by those who merely profess to believe (see 6:13, note; 8:16, note; cf. Ro 4:16; 9:27; 11:5; Rev 3:4–5).

10:28–34 THEY ENTER AIATH. Isaiah foretells the route the Assyrian invaders would take as they sought to plunder Jerusalem. God himself would cut them down (cf. 37:33–38).

11:1 A BRANCH WILL BEAR FRUIT. Isaiah gives a glorious picture of a future new world governed by the Branch (i.e., Jesus Christ). The Hebrew word *netzer* ("Branch") is likely the root word from which the name Nazareth is derived. Jesus was called a Nazarene (Mt 2:23), which can mean either "a man of Nazareth" or "a man of the Branch." He would come up as a Branch from the root of Jesse, i.e., David's father (see 4:2, note; cf. 4:2–6; 7:14; 9:1–7; Ro 15:12) and would become ruler of a world restored to peace, righteousness and goodness. The initial fulfillment of this prophecy came 700 years later when Jesus Christ was born, while its completion awaits

from his roots a Branch[z] will
bear fruit.[a]
2The Spirit[b] of the LORD will rest
on him—
the Spirit of wisdom[c] and of
understanding,
the Spirit of counsel and of
power,[d]
the Spirit of knowledge and of
the fear of the LORD—
Isa 32:15 **3**and he will delight in the fear[e] of
the LORD.

He will not judge by what he sees
with his eyes,[f]
or decide by what he hears with
his ears;[g]
4but with righteousness[h] he will
judge the needy,[i]
with justice[j] he will give
decisions for the poor[k] of
the earth.
He will strike[l] the earth with the
rod of his mouth;[m]
with the breath[n] of his lips he
Isa 35:3-5 will slay the wicked.[o]
5Righteousness will be his belt[p]
and faithfulness[q] the sash
around his waist.[r]
6The wolf will live with the lamb,[s]
the leopard will lie down with
the goat,
the calf and the lion and the
yearling[e] together;
and a little child will lead them.
7The cow will feed with the bear,
their young will lie down
together,
and the lion will eat straw like
the ox.[t]
8The infant[u] will play near the
hole of the cobra,
and the young child put his hand
into the viper's[v] nest.
9They will neither harm nor
destroy[w]
on all my holy mountain,[x]
for the earth[y] will be full of the
knowledge[z] of the LORD
as the waters cover the sea.

10In that day[a] the Root of Jesse[b]

11:1 [z] S Isa 4:2 [a] S 2Ki 19:30; S Isa 27:6 **11:2** [b] S Jdg 3:10; Isa 32:15; 42:1; 44:3; 48:16; 59:21; 61:1; Eze 37:14; 39:29; Joel 2:28; Mt 3:16; Jn 1:32-33; 16:13 [c] S Ex 28:3; S Eph 1:17; S Col 2:3 [d] S Isa 9:6; 2Ti 1:7 **11:3** [e] Isa 33:6 [f] Jn 7:24 [g] Jn 2:25 **11:4** [h] S Ps 72:2 [i] S Ps 72:4; S Isa 14:30 [j] S Isa 9:7; Rev 19:11 [k] S Job 5:16; S Isa 3:14 [l] Isa 27:7; 30:31; Zec 14:12; Mal 4:6 [m] S Job 40:18; Ps 2:9; Rev 19:15 [n] S Job 4:9; Ps 18:8; Isa 30:28,33; 40:24; 59:19; Eze 21:31; 2Th 2:8 [o] S Ps 139:19 **11:5** [p] Ex 12:11; 1Ki 18:46 [q] Isa 25:1 [r] Eph 6:14
11:6 [s] Isa 65:25 **11:7** [t] S Job 40:15 **11:8** [u] Isa 65:20 [v] Isa 14:29; 30:6; 59:5 **11:9** [w] S Nu 25:12; S Isa 2:4; S 9:7 [x] S Ps 48:1; S Isa 2:2 [y] 1Sa 17:46; Ps 98:2-3; Isa 45:22; 48:20; 52:10 [z] Ex 7:5; Isa 19:21; 45:6,14; 49:26; Jer 24:7; 31:34; Hab 2:14 **11:10** [a] S Isa 10:20 [b] S ver 1

[e] 6 Hebrew; Septuagint *lion will feed*

Christ's second coming (see 9:7, note).

11:2 SPIRIT OF THE LORD WILL REST ON HIM. The Messiah would be mightily anointed by the Holy Spirit in order to carry out the Father's will and to bring full salvation to the nations (Isa 61:1; Mt 3:16–17; Jn 1:33–34; see article on JESUS AND THE HOLY SPIRIT, p. 1546). In order to carry out his plan of salvation, the Messiah would also baptize and anoint his followers in the Holy Spirit. This is an essential requirement in the ongoing work of redemption (see Mt 3:11, note; Lk 3:16, note; Ac 1:5, note; see article on BAPTISM IN THE HOLY SPIRIT, p. 1642).

11:2–3 THE SPIRIT. Isaiah mentions the Holy Spirit more often than any other OT prophet (11:2; 30:1; 32:15; 34:16; 40:13; 42:1; 44:3; 48:16; 59:21; 61:1; 63:10–11,14; see article on THE SPIRIT IN THE OLD TESTAMENT, p. 1302). This prophetic description of the Messiah's anointing relates to his spiritual character and stature (see 61:1–3, note). The Messiah is filled with the Spirit, and his charismatic gifts are described as (1) the Spirit (v. 1), (2) wisdom (v. 2), (3) understanding (v. 2), (4) counsel (v. 2), (5) power (v. 2), (6) knowledge (v. 2), and (7) the fear of the Lord. The fullness of this description is unprecedented in Scripture; the sevenfold gift signifies the fullness of the gift.

11:4 HE WILL STRIKE THE EARTH. This verse refers to Christ's return to earth in judgment and his destruction of all the wicked (cf. 2Th 1:6–10; 2:8; Rev 19). This return in just retribution is necessary in order to establish his perfect and righteous rule.

11:5 RIGHTEOUSNESS ... FAITHFULNESS. Righteousness and faithfulness are integral qualities of the Messiah's reign; they are also requirements for all who would rule in the Messiah's church (see article on MORAL QUALIFICATIONS FOR OVERSEERS, p. 1882).

11:6–9 THE WOLF WILL LIVE WITH THE LAMB. The Messianic age will be characterized by the absence of enmity, brutality and hostility, here symbolized by tranquility among animals. The Messiah will bring peace to earth and transform believers and nature as the final fruit of redemption (cf. 35:9; 65:20–25; Eze 34:25–29).

11:10–16 IN THAT DAY. The final days of the Messianic kingdom will be preceded by a regathering of Jews who accept Jesus Christ as the Messiah. This restoration of Israel and Judah will involve the following: (1) the faithful remnant that is left (vv. 11–12; cf. Dt 30:3–5; Jer 31:1,8,10; Eze 39:22,28); (2) a gathering to the Messiah (11:10, 12; Jer 23:5–8; Eze 37:21–25); (3) a total cleansing for Israel (Dt 30:3–6; Jer 32:37–41; Eze 11:17–20); (4) blessing and prosperity in the land (Jer 31:8,10,12–13,28; 32:37–41; Eze 28:25–26; 39:25–29; Am 9:11–15); (5) blessing for all people, Gentiles as well as Jews (v. 12; 55:3–5; 60:1–5,10–14; Jer 16:15,19- 21; Zec 2:10–12; Mic 4:1–4); (6) judgment on the ungodly (vv. 14–16; Jer 25:29–33; Joel 3:1- 2,12–14); and (7) ultimate restoration in "the last days" (Hos 3:4–5; see Ro 11:26, note; see article on ISRAEL IN GOD'S PLAN OF SALVATION, p. 1730).

will stand as a banner[c] for the peoples; the nations[d] will rally to him,[e] and his place of rest[f] will be glorious.[g] 11In that day[h] the Lord will reach out his hand a second time to reclaim the remnant[i] that is left of his people from Assyria,[j] from Lower Egypt, from Upper Egypt,[f][k] from Cush,[g][l] from Elam,[m] from Babylonia,[h] from Hamath[n] and from the islands[o] of the sea.[p]

12He will raise a banner[q] for the nations
and gather[r] the exiles of Israel;[s]
he will assemble the scattered people[t] of Judah
from the four quarters of the earth.[u]
13Ephraim's jealousy will vanish,
and Judah's enemies[i] will be cut off;
Ephraim will not be jealous of Judah,
nor Judah hostile toward Ephraim.[v]
14They will swoop down on the slopes of Philistia[w] to the west;
together they will plunder the people to the east.[x]
They will lay hands on Edom[y] and Moab,[z]
and the Ammonites[a] will be subject to them.[b]
15The LORD will dry up[c]
the gulf of the Egyptian sea;
with a scorching wind[d] he will sweep his hand[e]
over the Euphrates River.[j][f]
He will break it up into seven streams
so that men can cross over in sandals.[g]
16There will be a highway[h] for the remnant[i] of his people
that is left from Assyria,[j]
as there was for Israel
when they came up from Egypt.[k]

11:10 [c]S Ps 20:5; Isa 18:3; Jer 4:6; Jn 12:32 [d]Isa 2:4; 14:1; 49:23; 56:3, 6; 60:5,10; Lk 2:32; Ac 11:18 [e]Ro 15:12* [f]S Ps 116:7; Isa 14:3; 28:12; 32:17-18; 40:2; Jer 6:16; 30:10; 46:27 [g]Hag 2:9; Zec 2:5 **11:11** [h]S Isa 10:20 [i]S Dt 30:4; S Isa 1:9 [j]Isa 19:24; Hos 11:11; Mic 7:12; Zec 10:10 [k]Jer 44:1,15; Eze 29:14; 30:14 [l]S Ge 10:6; Ac 8:27 [m]S Ge 10:22 [n]S Isa 10:9 [o]Isa 24:15; 41:1, 5; 42:4,10,12; 49:1; 51:5; 59:18; 60:9; 66:19 [p]Isa 49:12; Jer 16:15; 46:27; Eze 38:8; Zec 8:7 **11:12** [q]S Ps 20:5 [r]Isa 14:2; 43:5; 49:22; 54:7; Jer 16:15; 31:10; 32:37 [s]S Ne 1:9; S Ps 106:47; Isa 14:1; 41:14; 49:5 [t]Eze 28:25; Zep 3:10 [u]S Ps 48:10; 67:7; Isa 41:5; Rev 7:1 **11:13** [v]S 2Ch 28:6; Jer 3:18; Eze 37:16-17,22; Hos 1:11 **11:14** [w]S 2Ch 26:6; S 28:18 [x]S Jdg 6:3 [y]S Nu 24:18; S Ps 137:7; Isa 34:5-6; 63:1; Jer 49:22; Eze 25:12; Da 11:41; Joel 3:19; Ob 1:1; Mal 1:4 [z]Isa 15:1; 16:14; 25:10; Jer 48:40; Zep 2:8-11 [a]Jdg 11:14-18 [b]Isa 25:3; 60:12 **11:15** [c]S Ex 14:22; S Dt 11:10; Isa 37:25; 42:15; Jer 50:38; 51:36 [d]S Ge 41:6 [e]Isa 19:16; 30:32 [f]S Isa 7:20 [g]S Ex 14:29 **11:16** [h]Isa 19:23; 35:8; 40:3; 49:11; 51:10; 57:14; 62:10; Jer 50:5

Songs of Praise

12 In that day[l] you will say:
"I will praise[m] you, O LORD.
Although you were angry with me,
your anger has turned away[n]
and you have comforted[o] me.
2Surely God is my salvation;[p]
I will trust[q] and not be afraid.
The LORD, the LORD,[r] is my strength[s] and my song;
he has become my salvation.[t]"
3With joy you will draw water[u]
from the wells[v] of salvation. Isa 25:9

4In that day[w] you will say:
"Give thanks to the LORD, call on his name;[x]
make known among the nations[y] what he has done,
and proclaim that his name is exalted.[z]
5Sing[a] to the LORD, for he has done glorious things;[b]
let this be known to all the world.
6Shout aloud and sing for joy,[c] people of Zion,
for great[d] is the Holy One of Israel[e] among you.[f]" Isa 26:1-4

A Prophecy Against Babylon

13 An oracle[g] concerning Babylon[h] that Isaiah son of Amoz[i] saw:[j]

[i]S Ge 45:7 [j]S ver 11 [k]Ex 14:26-31 **12:1** [l]S Isa 10:20 [m]Ps 9:1; Isa 25:1 [n]S Job 13:16 [o]S Ps 71:21 **12:2** [p]Isa 17:10; 25:9; 33:6; 45:17; 51:5,6; 54:8; 59:16; 61:10; 62:11 [q]S Job 13:15; S Ps 26:1; S 112:7; Isa 26:3; Da 6:23 [r]Isa 26:4; 38:11 [s]S Ps 18:1 [t]S Ex 15:2 **12:3** [u]S 2Ki 3:17; Ps 36:9; Jer 2:13; 17:13; Jn 4:10,14 [v]Ex 15:25 **12:4** [w]S Isa 10:20 [x]Ex 3:15; Ps 80:18; 105:1; Isa 24:15; 25:1; 26:8,13; Hos 12:5 [y]Isa 54:5; 60:3; Jer 10:7; Zep 2:11; Mal 1:11 [z]S Ps 113:2 **12:5** [a]S Ex 15:1 [b]S Ps 98:1 **12:6** [c]S Ge 21:6; S Ps 98:4; Isa 24:14; 48:20; 52:8; Jer 20:13; 31:7; Zec 2:10 [d]Ps 48:1 [e]S Ps 78:41; 99:2; Isa 1:24; 10:20; 17:7; 29:19; 37:23; 43:3,14; 45:11; 49:26; 55:5; Eze 39:7 [f]S Ps 46:5; Zep 3:14-17 **13:1** [g]Isa 14:28; 15:1; 21:1; Na 1:1; Hab 1:1; Zec 9:1; 12:1; Mal 1:1 [h]ver 19; S Ge 10:10; Isa 14:4; 21:9; 46:1-2; 48:14; Jer 24:1; 25:12; Rev 14:8 [i]Isa 20:2; 37:2 [j]S Isa 1:1

[f] 11 Hebrew *from Pathros* [g] 11 That is, the upper Nile region [h] 11 Hebrew *Shinar* [i] 13 Or *hostility* [j] 15 Hebrew *the River*

12:1–6 IN THAT DAY. God's people will praise him when the universal reign of the Messiah begins. Even now we must pray for and anticipate in faith and hope our Lord's return and the establishment of his eternal reign in righteousness. When that day comes, we will sing this song of praise.
13:1—23:18 ORACLE. These chapters record judgments pronounced on foreign nations and on apostate Jerusalem. Isaiah starts with Babylon (13:1—14:23) and Assyria (14:24–27) and continues with prophecies against smaller nations. These chapters teach that all nations and peoples are accountable to God; those who oppose him and his divine plan of salvation will be judged and destroyed, and those who believe in him will ultimately triumph.

2Raise a banner[k] on a bare hilltop,
shout to them;
beckon to them
to enter the gates[l] of the nobles.
3I have commanded my holy ones;
I have summoned my warriors[m]
to carry out my wrath[n]—
those who rejoice[o] in my triumph.

4Listen, a noise on the mountains,
like that of a great multitude![p]
Listen, an uproar[q] among the kingdoms,
like nations massing together!
The LORD Almighty[r] is mustering[s]
an army for war.
5They come from faraway lands,
from the ends of the heavens[t]—
the LORD and the weapons[u] of his wrath[v]—
to destroy[w] the whole country.

6Wail,[x] for the day[y] of the LORD is near;
it will come like destruction[z]
from the Almighty.[k][a]
7Because of this, all hands will go limp,[b]
every man's heart will melt.[c]
8Terror[d] will seize them,
pain and anguish will grip[e] them;
they will writhe like a woman in labor.[f]
They will look aghast at each other,
their faces aflame.[g]

9See, the day[h] of the LORD is coming
—a cruel[i] day, with wrath[j]
and fierce anger[k]—
to make the land desolate
and destroy the sinners within it.
10The stars of heaven and their constellations
will not show their light.[l]
The rising sun[m] will be darkened[n]
and the moon will not give its light.[o]
11I will punish[p] the world for its evil,
the wicked[q] for their sins.
I will put an end to the arrogance of the haughty[r]
and will humble[s] the pride of the ruthless.[t]
12I will make man[u] scarcer than pure gold,
more rare than the gold of Ophir.[v]
13Therefore I will make the heavens tremble;[w]
and the earth will shake[x] from its place
at the wrath[y] of the LORD Almighty,
in the day of his burning anger.[z]

14Like a hunted[a] gazelle,
like sheep without a shepherd,[b]
each will return to his own people,
each will flee[c] to his native land.[d]
15Whoever is captured will be thrust through;
all who are caught will fall[e] by the sword.[f]

13:2 [k]S Ps 20:5; Jer 50:2; 51:27 [l]Isa 24:12; 45:2; Jer 51:58 **13:3** [m]ver 17; Isa 21:2; Jer 51:11; Da 5:28,31; Joel 3:11 [n]S Job 40:11; S Isa 10:5 [o]S Ps 149:2 **13:4** [p]Joel 3:14 [q]S Ps 46:6 [r]Isa 47:4; 51:15 [s]Isa 42:13; Jer 50:41 **13:5** [t]S Isa 5:26 [u]Isa 45:1; 54:16; Jer 50:25 [v]S Isa 10:25 [w]S Jos 6:17; Isa 24:1; 30:25; 34:2 **13:6** [x]Isa 14:31; 15:2; 16:7; 23:1; Eze 30:2; Jas 5:1 [y]S Isa 2:12 [z]S Isa 10:3; S 14:15 [a]S Ge 17:1 **13:7** [b]S 2Ki 19:26; S Job 4:3; S Jer 47:3 [c]S Jos 2:11; Eze 21:7 **13:8** [d]S Ps 31:13; S 48:5; S Isa 21:4 [e]Ex 15:14 [f]S Ge 3:16; S Jn 16:21 [g]Joel 2:6; Na 2:10 **13:9** [h]S Isa 2:12; Jer 51:2 [i]Jer 6:23 [j]S Isa 9:19 [k]Isa 26:21; 66:16; Jer 25:31; Joel 3:2 **13:10** [l]S Job 9:7 [m]Isa 24:23; Zec 14:7 [n]S Ex 10:22; S Isa 5:30; Rev 8:12 [o]Eze 32:7; Am 5:20; 8:9; S Mt 24:29*; Mk 13:24* **13:11** [p]Isa 3:11; 11:4; 26:21; 65:6-7; 66:16 [q]S Ps 125:3 [r]S Ps 10:5; S Pr 16:18; Da 5:23 [s]S Isa 2:9; 23:9; Eze 28:2; Da 4:37 [t]Isa 25:3,5; 29:5, 20; 49:25,26 **13:12** [u]S Isa 4:1 [v]S Ge 10:29 **13:13** [w]S Ps 102:26; Isa 34:4; 51:6 [x]S Job 9:6; S Isa 14:16; Mt 24:7; Mk 13:8 [y]S Isa 9:19 [z]S Job 9:5 **13:14** [a]Pr 6:5 [b]S 1Ki 22:17; S Mt 9:36; S Jn 10:11 [c]S Ge 11:9; Isa 17:13; 21:15; 22:3; 33:3; Jer 4:9 [d]Jer 46:16; 50:16; 51:9; Na 3:7 **13:15** [e]Jer 51:4 [f]Isa 14:19; Jer 50:25

[k]6 Hebrew *Shaddai*

13:1 BABYLON. Isaiah prophesies that Babylon would be overthrown like Sodom and Gomorrah. Babylon was a center of pagan culture, opposing God and his ways from very early in human history (cf. Ge 11:1–9). Ironically it served as God's instrument of wrath against Jerusalem, taking its residents into captivity. In the NT Babylon symbolizes the world's religious and political center in opposition to God and his people (see Rev 17:1, note). Babylon's ruins are in modern-day Iraq.

13:4 AN ARMY FOR WAR. The fulfillment of the prophecy about Babylon's fall went through various stages. The first was the Assyrian attack on Babylon in 689 B.C., when Sennacherib overthrew it. After it rose to power again under Nebuchadnezzar, Babylon was captured in 539 B.C. by Cyrus of the Medo-Persian empire (cf. v. 17). In 518 B.C. the city was ravaged again; its walls were torn down, and it fell into total ruin.

13:6–13 DAY OF THE LORD IS NEAR. The destruction of Babylon is a type of the end-time destruction of all God's enemies and the final judgment to come over all the earth during the period of the tribulation; Isaiah puts them both together here (cf. Eze 32:7; Joel 2:10; 3:16; Hag 2:6–7,21–22; Zec 14:6–7).

16Their infants[g] will be dashed to
pieces before their eyes;
their houses will be looted and
their wives ravished.[h]
17See, I will stir up[i] against them
the Medes,[j]
who do not care for silver
and have no delight in gold.[k]
18Their bows[l] will strike down the
young men;[m]
they will have no mercy[n] on
infants
nor will they look with
compassion on children.[o]
19Babylon,[p] the jewel of
kingdoms,[q]
the glory[r] of the Babylonians'[1]
pride,
will be overthrown[s] by God
like Sodom and Gomorrah.[t]
20She will never be inhabited[u]
or lived in through all
generations;
no Arab[v] will pitch his tent there,
no shepherd will rest his flocks
there.
21But desert creatures[w] will lie
there,
jackals[x] will fill her houses;
there the owls[y] will dwell,
and there the wild goats[z] will
leap about.
22Hyenas[a] will howl in her
strongholds,[b]
jackals[c] in her luxurious
palaces.
Her time is at hand,[d]
and her days will not be
prolonged.[e]

14

The LORD will have
compassion[f] on Jacob;
once again he will choose[g]
Israel
and will settle them in their own
land.[h]
Aliens[i] will join them
and unite with the house of
Jacob.
2Nations will take them
and bring[j] them to their own
place.

13:16 [g]ver 18; S Nu 16:27; S 2Ki 8:12 [h]S Ge 34:29; S Hos 13:16 **13:17** [i]Jer 50:9, 41; 51:1 [j]S ver 3 [k]2Ki 18:14-16; Pr 6:34-35 **13:18** [l]S Ps 7:12; Isa 41:2; Jer 50:9, 14,29 [m]S Dt 32:25; Jer 49:26; 50:30; 51:4 [n]Isa 47:6; Jer 6:23; 50:42 [o]S ver 16; Isa 14:22; 47:9 **13:19** [p]S ver 1 [q]Isa 47:5; Da 2:37-38 [r]Da 4:30 [s]S Ps 137:8; S Rev 14:8 [t]S Ge 19:25; Isa 1:9-10; Ro 9:29 **13:20** [u]Isa 14:23; 34:10-15; Jer 51:29,37-43,62 [v]2Ch 17:11 **13:21** [w]S Ps 74:14; Rev 18:2 [x]Jer 14:6 [y]S Lev 11:16-18; S Dt 14:15-17 [z]Lev 17:7; 2Ch 11:15 **13:22** [a]Isa 34:14 [b]Isa 25:2; 32:14 [c]Isa 34:13; 35:7; 43:20; Jer 9:11; 49:33; 51:37; Mal 1:3 [d]Dt 32:35; Jer 48:16; 51:33 [e]Jer 50:39 **14:1** [f]Ps 102:13; Isa 49:10,13; 54:7-8,10; Jer 33:26; Zec 10:6 [g]Ge 18:19; 2Ch 6:6; Isa 41:8; 42:1; 44:1; 45:4; 49:7; 65:9,22; Zec 1:17; 2:12; 3:2 [h]Jer 3:18; 16:15; 23:8 [i]S Ex 12:43; S Isa 11:10; Eze 47:22; Zec 8:22-23; Eph 2:12-19 **14:2** [j]S Isa 11:12; 60:9 [k]S Ps 49:14; Isa 26:15; 43:14; 49:7,23; 54:3 [l]Ps 149:8; Isa 45:14; 49:25; 60:12; Jer 40:1 [m]Isa 60:14; 61:5; Jer 30:16; 49:2; Eze 39:10; Zep 3:19; Zec 2:9 **14:3** [n]S Isa 11:10 [o]S Job 3:17 [p]S Ex 1:14

And the house of Israel will
possess the nations[k]
as menservants and
maidservants in the LORD's
land.
They will make captives[l] of their
captors
and rule over their oppressors.[m]

3On the day the LORD gives you relief[n] from suffering and turmoil[o] and
cruel bondage,[p] 4you will take up this
taunt[q] against the king of Babylon:[r]

How the oppressor[s] has come to
an end!
How his fury[m] has ended!
5The LORD has broken the rod[t] of
the wicked,[u]
the scepter[v] of the rulers,
6which in anger struck down
peoples[w]
with unceasing blows,
and in fury subdued[x] nations
with relentless aggression.[y]
7All the lands are at rest and at
peace;[z]
they break into singing.[a]
8Even the pine trees[b] and the
cedars of Lebanon
exult over you and say,
"Now that you have been laid low,
no woodsman comes to cut us
down."[c]
9The grave[n][d] below is all astir
to meet you at your coming;
it rouses the spirits of the
departed[e] to greet you—
all those who were leaders[f] in
the world;
it makes them rise from their
thrones—

14:4 [q]Mic 2:4; Hab 2:6 [r]S Isa 13:1 [s]S Isa 9:4 **14:5** [t]S Isa 10:15 [u]S Ps 125:3 [v]S Ps 110:2 **14:6** [w]Isa 10:14 [x]S Ps 47:3 [y]S 2Ki 15:29; Isa 47:6; Hab 1:17 **14:7** [z]S Nu 6:26; Jer 50:34; Zec 1:11 [a]Ps 98:1; 126:1-3; Isa 12:6 **14:8** [b]S 1Ch 16:33; S Ps 65:13; Eze 31:16 [c]S 2Ki 19:23; Isa 37:24 **14:9** [d]S Pr 30:16; Eze 32:21 [e]S Job 26:5 [f]Zec 10:3

[1]*19* Or *Chaldeans'* [m]*4* Dead Sea Scrolls, Septuagint and Syriac; the meaning of the word in the Masoretic Text is uncertain. [n]*9* Hebrew *Sheol*; also in verses 11 and 15

13:20 SHE WILL NEVER BE INHABITED. This verse emphasizes that no monument to human glory and achievement has any permanence in itself. One day all things made by humans will rust or fade away (cf. Mt 6:19), while God's glory will fill the earth.

14:4–21 TAUNT AGAINST THE KING OF BABYLON. This taunting prophetic hymn was to be sung by those who saw the downfall of the king of Babylon. The king would be laid low and "brought down to the grave" (v. 15). These verses ultimately apply to all rulers and people who defy God and oppose the principles of his kingdom.

all those who were kings over the nations.[g]
10They will all respond,
they will say to you,
"You also have become weak, as we are;
you have become like us."[h]
11All your pomp has been brought down to the grave,[i]
along with the noise of your harps;[j]
maggots are spread out beneath you
and worms[k] cover you.[l]

12How you have fallen[m] from heaven,
O morning star,[n] son of the dawn!
You have been cast down to the earth,
you who once laid low the nations![o]
13You said in your heart,
"I will ascend[p] to heaven;
I will raise my throne[q]
above the stars of God;
I will sit enthroned on the mount of assembly,[r]
on the utmost heights[s] of the sacred mountain.°
14I will ascend above the tops of the clouds;[t]
I will make myself like the Most High."[u]
15But you are brought down[v] to the grave,[w]
to the depths[x] of the pit.[y]

16Those who see you stare at you,
they ponder your fate:[z]
"Is this the man who shook[a] the earth
and made kingdoms tremble,
17the man who made the world a desert,[b]
who overthrew[c] its cities
and would not let his captives go home?"[d]

18All the kings of the nations lie in state,
each in his own tomb.[e]
19But you are cast out[f] of your tomb
like a rejected branch;
you are covered with the slain,[g]
with those pierced by the sword,[h]
those who descend to the stones of the pit.[i]
Like a corpse trampled underfoot,
20 you will not join them in burial,[j]
for you have destroyed your land
and killed your people.

The offspring[k] of the wicked[l]
will never be mentioned[m] again.
21Prepare a place to slaughter his sons[n]
for the sins of their forefathers;[o]
they are not to rise to inherit the land
and cover the earth with their cities.

22"I will rise up[p] against them,"
declares the LORD Almighty.
"I will cut off from Babylon her name[q] and survivors,
her offspring and descendants,[r]"
declares the LORD.
23"I will turn her into a place for owls[s]
and into swampland;
I will sweep her with the broom of destruction,[t]"
declares the LORD Almighty.[u]

A Prophecy Against Assyria

24The LORD Almighty has sworn,[v]

"Surely, as I have planned,[w] so it will be,
and as I have purposed, so it will stand.[x]

14:9 [g]S Job 3:14 **14:10** [h]Eze 26:20; 32:21 **14:11** [i]S Nu 16:30; S Pr 30:16 [j]Isa 5:12; Eze 26:13; Am 6:5 [k]S Job 7:5; 24:20; Isa 51:8; 66:24 [l]S Job 21:26 **14:12** [m]Lk 10:18 [n]2Pe 1:19; Rev 2:28; 8:10; 9:1 [o]Eze 26:17 **14:13** [p]Da 5:23; 8:10; Ob 1:4; Mt 11:23 [q]Eze 28:2; 2Th 2:4 [r]Ps 82:1 [s]Isa 37:24 **14:14** [t]S Job 20:6 [u]S Ge 3:5; S Nu 24:16; Isa 10:13; 47:8; Jer 50:29; 51:53; Da 11:36; 2Th 2:4 **14:15** [v]Isa 13:6; 45:7; 47:11; Jer 51:8,43 [w]S Job 21:13 [x]Mt 11:23; Lk 10:15 [y]S Ps 55:23; Eze 31:16; 32:23 **14:16** [z]Jer 50:23; Rev 18:9 [a]S Isa 2:19; 13:13; Joel 3:16; Hag 2:6,21 **14:17** [b]Isa 15:6; Joel 2:3 [c]Ps 52:7 [d]Ex 7:14; S 2Ki 15:29; Jer 50:33; Rev 18:18 **14:18** [e]Job 21:32 **14:19** [f]Isa 22:16-18; Jer 8:1; 36:30 [g]Isa 34:3 [h]S Isa 13:15 [i]Jer 41:7-9 **14:20** [j]S 1Ki 21:19 [k]S Job 18:19 [l]S Isa 1:4 [m]S Dt 32:26 **14:21** [n]S Nu 16:27 [o]S Ge 9:25; S Lev 26:39 **14:22** [p]S Ps 94:16 [q]S Job 18:17; Ps 109:13; Na 1:14 [r]2Sa 18:18; 1Ki 14:10; Job 18:19; S Ps 9:6; S Isa 13:18 **14:23** [s]S Lev 11:16-18; Isa 34:11-15; Zep 2:14 [t]S Isa 10:3; Jer 25:12 [u]Jer 50:3; 51:62 **14:24** [v]Isa 45:23; 49:18; 54:9; 62:8 [w]Isa 19:12,17; 23:8-9; 25:1; Da 4:35 [x]S Job 9:3; S Isa 7:7; 46:10-11; Eze 12:25; Ac 4:28

° *13* Or *the north*; Hebrew *Zaphon*

14:12–15 O MORNING STAR. Some commentators believe that these verses not only refer to the king of Babylon, but also contain a veiled reference to Satan (cf. Christ's statement in Lk 10:18). Others think they may refer to the end-time antichrist who will rule over "Babylon" (see Rev 17:1–3, notes) in opposition to God and his people (cf. Rev 13:4; see article on THE AGE OF THE ANTICHRIST, p. 1872).

14:24–27 I WILL CRUSH THE ASSYRIAN. This prophecy concerns Judah's immediate threat from Assyria; God would crush the Assyrian army (see 37:21–36; 2Ki 19).

[25]I will crush the Assyrian[y] in my
land;
on my mountains I will trample
him down.
His yoke[z] will be taken from my
people,
and his burden removed from
their shoulders.[a]"

[26]This is the plan[b] determined for
the whole world;
this is the hand[c] stretched out
over all nations.
[27]For the LORD Almighty has
purposed,[d] and who can
thwart him?
His hand[e] is stretched out, and
who can turn it back?[f]

A Prophecy Against the Philistines

[28]This oracle[g] came in the year[h]
King Ahaz[i] died:

[29]Do not rejoice, all you
Philistines,[j]
that the rod that struck you is
broken;
from the root of that snake will
spring up a viper,[k]
its fruit will be a darting,
venomous serpent.[l]
[30]The poorest of the poor will find
pasture,
and the needy[m] will lie down in
safety.[n]
But your root I will destroy by
famine;[o]
it will slay[p] your survivors.[q]

[31]Wail,[r] O gate![s] Howl, O city!
Melt away, all you Philistines![t]
A cloud of smoke comes from the
north,[u]
and there is not a straggler in
its ranks.[v]
[32]What answer shall be given
to the envoys[w] of that nation?
"The LORD has established Zion,[x]
and in her his afflicted people
will find refuge.[y]"

14:25 [y]S Isa 10:5,12; 37:36-38 [z]S Isa 9:4 [a]S Isa 10:27 **14:26** [b]Isa 23:9 [c]Ex 15:12; S Job 30:21 **14:27** [d]Jer 49:20 [e]S Ex 14:21 [f]S 2Ch 20:6; Isa 43:13; Da 4:35 **14:28** [g]S Isa 13:1 [h]S 2Ki 15:7 [i]S 2Ki 16:1 **14:29** [j]S Jos 13:3; S 2Ki 1:2; S 2Ch 26:6 [k]S Isa 11:8 [l]S Dt 8:15 **14:30** [m]Isa 3:15; 25:4 [n]S Isa 7:21-22 [o]Isa 8:21; 9:20; 51:19 [p]Jer 25:16; Zec 9:5-6 [q]Eze 25:15-17; Zep 2:5 **14:31** [r]S Isa 13:6 [s]S Isa 3:26 [t]S Ge 10:14 [u]Isa 41:25; Jer 1:14; 4:6; 6:1, 22; 10:22; 13:20; 25:9; 46:20,24; 47:2; 50:41; Eze 32:30 [v]S Isa 5:27 **14:32** [w]Isa 37:9 [x]S Ps 51:18; 87:2, 5; Isa 2:2; 26:1; 28:16; 31:5; 33:5, 20; 44:28; 51:21; 54:11 [y]S Isa 4:6; Jas 2:5

15:1 [z]S Isa 13:1 [a]Nu 22:3-6; S Dt 23:6; S Isa 11:14 [b]S Nu 21:15 [c]S Nu 17:12; Isa 25:12; 26:5; Jer 48:24,41; 51:58 [d]S 2Ki 3:25 **15:2** [e]S Nu 21:30 [f]1Ki 11:7; Isa 16:12; Jer 48:35 [g]S Isa 13:6; 65:14 [h]S Nu 32:38 [i]S Lev 13:40; S Job 1:20 [j]S 2Sa 10:4 **15:3** [k]S Isa 3:24 [l]S Jos 2:8 [m]Jer 48:38 [n]Isa 14:31; Jer 47:2 [o]ver 5; Isa 16:9; 22:4; La 2:11; Eze 7:18; Mic 1:8 **15:4** [p]S Nu 21:25; S Jos 13:26 [q]S Nu 32:3 [r]S Nu 21:23

A Prophecy Against Moab

16:6–12pp — Jer 48:29–36

15 An oracle[z] concerning Moab:[a]

Ar[b] in Moab is ruined,[c]
destroyed in a night!
Kir[d] in Moab is ruined,
destroyed in a night!
[2]Dibon[e] goes up to its temple,
to its high places[f] to weep;
Moab wails[g] over Nebo[h] and
Medeba.
Every head is shaved[i]
and every beard cut off.[j]
[3]In the streets they wear
sackcloth;[k]
on the roofs[l] and in the public
squares[m]
they all wail,[n]
prostrate with weeping.[o]
[4]Heshbon[p] and Elealeh[q] cry out,
their voices are heard all the
way to Jahaz.[r]
Therefore the armed men of Moab
cry out,
and their hearts are faint.

[5]My heart cries out[s] over Moab;[t]
her fugitives[u] flee as far as
Zoar,[v]
as far as Eglath Shelishiyah.
They go up the way to Luhith,
weeping as they go;
on the road to Horonaim[w]
they lament their destruction.[x]
[6]The waters of Nimrim are dried
up[y]
and the grass is withered;[z]
the vegetation is gone[a]
and nothing green is left.[b]
[7]So the wealth they have acquired[c]
and stored up
they carry away over the Ravine
of the Poplars.
[8]Their outcry echoes along the
border of Moab;

15:5 [s]S ver 3 [t]Isa 16:11; Jer 48:31 [u]S Nu 21:29 [v]S Ge 13:10 [w]Jer 48:3,34 [x]Jer 4:20; 48:5 **15:6** [y]Isa 19:5-7; Jer 48:34 [z]Ps 37:2; Isa 16:8; 24:4,7,11; 33:9; 34:4; 37:27; 40:7; 51:6,12; Hos 4:3; Joel 1:12 [a]S Isa 14:17 [b]Jer 14:5 **15:7** [c]Isa 30:6; Jer 48:36

14:29 PHILISTINES. Isaiah prophesies the defeat of Philistia (v. 30). Judah should not accept the offer of the envoys of Philistia for an alliance, but must trust in the Lord instead (v. 32).

15:1 MOAB. Located immediately east of the Dead Sea, Moab had always been an enemy of Israel (cf. 25:10; 2Ki 3:4–5; 13:20; Eze 25:8–11). Like the other hostile nations, they too would be destroyed.

15:5 MY HEART CRIES OUT OVER MOAB. Seeing the terrible suffering of this enemy of God's people, Isaiah cried out in compassion for the Moabite victims (cf. 21:2–4; 22:4). In like manner, we should feel compassion and pity for those who destroy themselves by pursuing sin and evil (see Lk 19:41, note).

their wailing reaches as far as
Eglaim,
their lamentation as far as
Beer[d] Elim.
9Dimon's[p] waters are full of blood,
but I will bring still more upon
Dimon[p]—
a lion[e] upon the fugitives of
Moab[f]
and upon those who remain in
the land.

16 Send lambs[g] as tribute[h]
to the ruler of the land,
from Sela,[i] across the desert,
to the mount of the Daughter of
Zion.[j]
2Like fluttering birds
pushed from the nest,[k]
so are the women of Moab[l]
at the fords[m] of the Arnon.[n]

3"Give us counsel,
render a decision.
Make your shadow like night—
at high noon.
Hide the fugitives,[o]
do not betray the refugees.
4Let the Moabite fugitives stay with
you;
be their shelter[p] from the
destroyer."

The oppressor[q] will come to an
end,
and destruction will cease;[r]
the aggressor will vanish from
the land.
5In love a throne[s] will be
established;[t]
in faithfulness a man will sit on
it—
one from the house[q] of
David[u]—
one who in judging seeks justice[v]
and speeds the cause of
righteousness.

6We have heard of Moab's[w]
pride[x]—
her overweening pride and
conceit,
her pride and her insolence—
but her boasts are empty.
7Therefore the Moabites wail,[y]
they wail together for Moab.
Lament and grieve
for the men[r][z] of Kir
Hareseth.[a]
8The fields of Heshbon[b] wither,[c]
the vines of Sibmah[d] also.
The rulers of the nations
have trampled down the choicest
vines,[e]
which once reached Jazer[f]
and spread toward the desert.
Their shoots spread out[g]
and went as far as the sea.[h]
9So I weep,[i] as Jazer weeps,
for the vines of Sibmah.
O Heshbon, O Elealeh,[j]
I drench you with tears![k]
The shouts of joy[l] over your
ripened fruit
and over your harvests[m] have
been stilled.
10Joy and gladness are taken away
from the orchards;[n]
no one sings or shouts[o] in the
vineyards;
no one treads[p] out wine at the
presses,[q]
for I have put an end to the
shouting.
11My heart laments for Moab[r] like
a harp,[s]
my inmost being[t] for Kir
Hareseth.
12When Moab appears at her high
place,[u]
she only wears herself out;
when she goes to her shrine[v] to
pray,
it is to no avail.[w]

13This is the word the LORD has al-

15:8 [d]S Nu 21:16 15:9 [e]S 2Ki 17:25 [f]Eze 25:8-11 16:1 [g]S 2Ki 3:4 [h]S 2Ch 32:23 [i]S Jdg 1:36; Ob 3 *fn* [j]S Isa 10:32 16:2 [k]Pr 27:8 [l]Nu 21:29 [m]Jdg 12:5 [n]Nu 21:13-14; Jer 48:20 16:3 [o]S 1Ki 18:4 16:4 [p]Isa 58:7 [q]S Isa 9:4 [r]Isa 2:2-4 16:5 [s]S 1Sa 13:14; Da 7:14; Mic 4:7 [t]S Pr 20:28 [u]S Isa 7:2; Lk 1:32 [v]S Isa 9:7 16:6 [w]Jer 25:21; Eze 25:8; Am 2:1; Zep 2:8 [x]S Lev 26:19; S Job 20:6; Jer 49:16; Ob 1:3; Zep 2:10 16:7 [y]S Isa 13:6; Jer 48:20; 49:3 [z]S 1Ch 16:3 [a]S 2Ki 3:25 16:8 [b]S Nu 21:25 [c]S Isa 15:6 [d]S Nu 32:3 [e]S Isa 5:2 [f]S Nu 21:32 [g]S Job 8:16 [h]Ps 80:11 16:9 [i]S Isa 15:3; Eze 27:31 [j]S Nu 32:3 [k]S Job 7:3 [l]S Ezr 3:13 [m]Jer 40:12 16:10 [n]Isa 24:7-8 [o]Jer 25:30 [p]S Jdg 9:27 [q]S Job 24:11; S Isa 5:2 16:11 [r]S Isa 15:5 [s]S Job 30:31 [t]Isa 63:15; Hos 11:8; Php 2:1 16:12 [u]1Ki 11:7 [v]S Isa 15:2 [w]S 1Ki 18:29; Ps 115:4-7; Isa 44:17-18; 1Co 8:4

[p]9 Masoretic Text; Dead Sea Scrolls, some Septuagint manuscripts and Vulgate *Dibon*
[q]5 Hebrew *tent*
[r]7 Or *"raisin cakes,"* a wordplay

16:1–5 MOUNT OF THE DAUGHTER OF ZION. The fugitives and refugees of Moab were told to seek shelter in Judah and to submit to the king of Jerusalem.

16:4–5 OPPRESSOR WILL COME TO AN END. Looking to the future, Isaiah saw the Messianic kingdom and the end of all oppression.

16:6–13 MOAB'S PRIDE. Although war and destruction would someday cease (see previous note), the Moabites of Isaiah's day would face judgment because of their pride and their failure to acknowledge God and his righteousness.

16:10 NO ONE TREADS OUT WINE. Here the fresh, unfermented juice of the grape that is still in the presses is called "wine" (Heb *yayin*), as it is elsewhere in the OT (see article on WINE IN THE OLD TESTAMENT, p. 204). The NT Greek equivalent of *yayin* is *oinos* (see articles on WINE IN NEW TESTAMENT TIMES, (1) and (2), p. 1534, and p. 1586).

ready spoken concerning Moab. **14**But
now the LORD says: "Within three
years,[x] as a servant bound by contract[y] would count them,[z] Moab's
splendor and all her many people will
be despised,[a] and her survivors will
be very few and feeble."[b]

An Oracle Against Damascus

17 An oracle[c] concerning Damascus:[d]

"See, Damascus will no longer be
a city
but will become a heap of
ruins.[e]
2The cities of Aroer[f] will be
deserted
and left to flocks,[g] which will
lie down,[h]
with no one to make them
afraid.[i]
3The fortified[j] city will disappear
from Ephraim,
and royal power from Damascus;
the remnant of Aram will be
like the glory[k] of the
Israelites,"[l]
declares the LORD Almighty.

4"In that day[m] the glory[n] of Jacob
will fade;
the fat of his body will waste[o]
away.
5It will be as when a reaper gathers
the standing grain
and harvests[p] the grain with
his arm—
as when a man gleans heads of
grain[q]
in the Valley of Rephaim.[r]
6Yet some gleanings will remain,[s]
as when an olive tree is
beaten,[t]
leaving two or three olives on the
topmost branches,
four or five on the fruitful
boughs,"
declares the LORD, the God
of Israel.

7In that day[u] men will look[v] to
their Maker[w]
and turn their eyes to the Holy
One[x] of Israel.
8They will not look to the altars,[y]
the work of their hands,[z]
and they will have no regard for
the Asherah poles[s][a]
and the incense altars their
fingers[b] have made.

9In that day their strong cities,
which they left because of the Israelites, will be like places abandoned to
thickets and undergrowth.[c] And all
will be desolation.

10You have forgotten[d] God your
Savior;[e]
you have not remembered the
Rock,[f] your fortress.[g]
Therefore, though you set out the
finest plants
and plant imported vines,[h]
11though on the day you set them
out, you make them grow,
and on the morning[i] when you
plant them, you bring them
to bud,
yet the harvest[j] will be as
nothing[k]
in the day of disease and
incurable[l] pain.[m]

12Oh, the raging[n] of many
nations—
they rage like the raging sea![o]
Oh, the uproar[p] of the peoples—
they roar like the roaring of
great waters![q]
13Although the peoples roar[r] like
the roar of surging waters,
when he rebukes[s] them they
flee[t] far away,
driven before the wind like chaff[u]
on the hills,

16:14 [x]Isa 20:3; 37:30 [y]S Lev 25:50 [z]S Lev 19:13 [a]Isa 25:10; Jer 48:42 [b]Isa 21:17 **17:1** [c]Isa 13:1 [d]S Ge 14:15; Ac 9:2 [e]S Dt 13:16; S Isa 25:2 **17:2** [f]S 2Ki 10:33 [g]S Isa 5:17; 7:21; Eze 25:5 [h]Isa 27:10 [i]S Lev 26:6; Jer 7:33; Mic 4:4 **17:3** [j]Isa 25:2,12; Hos 10:14 [k]ver 4; Isa 21:16; Hos 9:11 [l]Isa 7:8, 16; 8:4 **17:4** [m]S Isa 2:11 [n]S ver 3 [o]S Isa 10:16 **17:5** [p]ver 11; Isa 33:4; Jer 51:33; Joel 3:13; Mt 13:30 [q]Job 24:24 [r]S Jos 17:15; S 1Ch 11:15 **17:6** [s]S Dt 4:27; S Isa 10:19; S 24:13 [t]ver 11; Isa 27:12
17:7 [u]S Isa 2:11 [v]S Isa 9:13; S 10:20 [w]S Ps 95:6 [x]S Isa 12:6 **17:8** [y]S Lev 26:30 [z]S 2Ch 32:19; Isa 2:18,20; 30:22; 46:6; Rev 9:20 [a]S Jdg 3:7; S 2Ki 17:10 [b]Isa 2:8 **17:9** [c]S Isa 7:19 **17:10** [d]S Dt 6:12; 8:11; Ps 50:22; 106:21; Isa 51:13; 57:11; Jer 2:32; 3:21; 13:25; 18:15; Eze 22:12; 23:35; Hos 8:14; 13:6 [e]S Isa 12:2; S Lk 1:47 [f]S Ge 49:24 [g]S Ps 18:2 [h]S Isa 5:7 **17:11** [i]Ps 90:6 [j]S ver 5 [k]S Lev 26:20; Hos 8:7; Joel 1:11; Hag 1:6 [l]Jer 10:19; 30:12 [m]S Dt 28:39; S Job 4:8 **17:12** [n]ver 13; Isa 41:11 [o]S Ps 18:4; Lk 21:25 [p]S Ps 46:6; Isa 8:9 [q]Isa 8:7 **17:13** [r]S Ps 46:3 [s]S Dt 28:20; S Ps 9:5 [t]S Ps 68:1; S Isa 13:14 [u]S Job 13:25; S Isa 2:22; 41:2,15-16; Da 2:35

[s]*8* That is, symbols of the goddess Asherah

17:1–6 DAMASCUS WILL NO LONGER BE A CITY. Damascus, the capital of Aram (v. 3), would be overthrown. Ephraim (i.e., Israel, or the northern kingdom) would also suffer because of its alliance with Damascus against Assyria.

17:7 LOOK TO THEIR MAKER. God's judgments on Israel would cause a remnant to turn away from idolatry back to the Lord God their Maker; they would realize how useless idols are in times of trouble and war.

17:10 YOU HAVE FORGOTTEN GOD YOUR SAVIOR. Forgetting God is not a sin limited to Israel. Jesus warns that the worries of this life, the deceitfulness of wealth, the pursuit of material things and the pleasure of sin can choke God's word in the lives of believers (cf. Mk 4:3–9,14–20) and cause them to forget him, to stop praying daily, and no longer to delight in him or in his word. When this happens, we lose God's blessing and presence.

like tumbleweed before a gale.[v]
14In the evening, sudden[w] terror![x]
Before the morning, they are
gone![y]
This is the portion of those who
loot us,
the lot of those who plunder us.

A Prophecy Against Cush

18 Woe[z] to the land of whirring
wings[t]
along the rivers of Cush,[u][a]
2which sends envoys[b] by sea
in papyrus[c] boats over the
water.

Go, swift messengers,
to a people tall and
smooth-skinned,[d]
to a people feared far and wide,
an aggressive[e] nation of strange
speech,
whose land is divided by
rivers.[f]

3All you people of the world,[g]
you who live on the earth,
when a banner[h] is raised on the
mountains,
you will see it,
and when a trumpet[i] sounds,
you will hear it.
4This is what the LORD says to me:
"I will remain quiet[j] and will
look on from my dwelling
place,[k]
like shimmering heat in the
sunshine,[l]
like a cloud of dew[m] in the heat
of harvest."
5For, before the harvest, when the
blossom is gone
and the flower becomes a
ripening grape,
he will cut off[n] the shoots with
pruning knives,
and cut down and take away the
spreading branches.[o]
6They will all be left to the
mountain birds of prey[p]
and to the wild animals;[q]
the birds will feed on them all
summer,
the wild animals all winter.

17:13 [v]Job 21:18; S Ps 65:7 **17:14** [w]Isa 29:5; 30:13; 47:11; 48:3 [x]Isa 33:18; 54:14 [y]S 2Ki 19:35 **18:1** [z]Isa 5:8 [a]S Ge 10:6; S Ps 68:31; S Eze 29:10 **18:2** [b]Ob 1:1 [c]Ex 2:3; Job 9:26 [d]S Ge 41:14 [e]S Ge 10:8-9; S 2Ch 12:3 [f]ver 7 **18:3** [g]S Ps 33:8 [h]S Ps 60:4; Isa 5:26; 11:10; 13:2; 31:9; Jer 4:21 [i]S Jos 6:20; S Jdg 3:27 **18:4** [j]Isa 62:1; 64:12 [k]Isa 26:21; Hos 5:15; Mic 1:3 [l]S Jdg 5:31; S Ps 18:12; Hab 3:4 [m]2Sa 1:21; S Ps 133:3; Isa 26:19; Hos 14:5 **18:5** [n]S Isa 10:33 [o]Isa 17:10-11; Eze 17:6 **18:6** [p]S Isa 8:8 [q]Isa 37:36; 56:9; Jer 7:33; Eze 32:4; 39:17

18:7 [r]S 2Ch 9:24; S Isa 60:7 [s]S Ge 41:14 [t]Hab 1:7 [u]ver 2 [v]Ps 68:31 **19:1** [w]Isa 13:1 [x]Isa 20:3; Joel 3:19 [y]S Ex 12:12; S Jer 44:3 [z]S Dt 10:14; S 2Sa 22:10; S Rev 1:7 [a]S Jos 2:11 **19:2** [b]S Jdg 7:22; S 12:4; Mt 10:21, 36 [c]S 2Ch 15:6; 20:23; Mt 24:7; Mk 13:8; Lk 21:10 **19:3** [d]Ps 18:45 [e]ver 11; S Job 5:12 [f]1Ch 10:13 [g]S Lev 19:31; Isa 47:13; Da 2:2, 10; 3:8; 5:7 **19:4** [h]Isa 20:4; Jer 46:26; Eze 29:19; 32:11 **19:5** [i]Isa 44:27; 50:2; Jer 50:38; 51:36 [j]S 2Sa 14:14 **19:6** [k]Ex 7:18

7At that time gifts[r] will be brought
to the LORD Almighty
from a people tall and
smooth-skinned,[s]
from a people feared[t] far and
wide,
an aggressive nation of strange
speech,
whose land is divided by
rivers[u]—
the gifts will be brought to Mount Zion,
the place of the Name of the LORD Almighty.[v]

A Prophecy About Egypt

19 An oracle[w] concerning
Egypt:[x][y]
See, the LORD rides on a swift
cloud[z]
and is coming to Egypt.
The idols of Egypt tremble before
him,
and the hearts of the Egyptians
melt[a] within them.

2"I will stir up Egyptian against
Egyptian—
brother will fight against
brother,[b]
neighbor against neighbor,
city against city,
kingdom against kingdom.[c]
3The Egyptians will lose heart,[d]
and I will bring their plans[e] to
nothing;[f]
they will consult the idols and the
spirits of the dead,
the mediums and the spiritists.[g]
4I will hand the Egyptians over
to the power of a cruel master,
and a fierce king[h] will rule over
them,"
declares the Lord, the LORD
Almighty.

5The waters of the river will dry
up,[i]
and the riverbed will be parched
and dry.[j]
6The canals will stink;[k]

[t]*1* Or *of locusts* [u]*1* That is, the upper Nile region

18:1 CUSH. Cush (ancient Ethiopia) was south of Egypt. Its king at that time ruled all of Egypt. He evidently had sent messengers to Israel in order to seek an alliance against Assyria (v. 2). God himself would defeat the Assyrian enemy in his own time (vv. 3–6). After the Assyrian defeat, the people of Cush would bring gifts to Jerusalem (v. 7).

19:1–15 EGYPT. Isaiah foretells a judgment of God coming on Egypt; consequently, it would do Judah no good to align herself with Egypt against the invading Assyrians.

the streams of Egypt will
dwindle and dry up.[l]
The reeds[m] and rushes will
wither,[n]
7 also the plants[o] along the Nile,
at the mouth of the river.
Every sown field[p] along the Nile
will become parched, will blow
away and be no more.[q]
8The fishermen[r] will groan and
lament,
all who cast hooks[s] into the
Nile;
those who throw nets on the water
will pine away.
9Those who work with combed
flax[t] will despair,
the weavers of fine linen[u] will
lose hope.
10The workers in cloth will be
dejected,
and all the wage earners will be
sick at heart.

11The officials of Zoan[v] are nothing
but fools;
the wise counselors[w] of
Pharaoh give senseless
advice.[x]
How can you say to Pharaoh,
"I am one of the wise men,[y]
a disciple of the ancient kings"?
12Where are your wise men[z] now?
Let them show you and make
known
what the LORD Almighty
has planned[a] against Egypt.
13The officials of Zoan[b] have
become fools,
the leaders of Memphis[v][c] are
deceived;
the cornerstones[d] of her peoples
have led Egypt astray.
14The LORD has poured into them
a spirit of dizziness;[e]
they make Egypt stagger in all
that she does,
as a drunkard staggers[f] around
in his vomit.
15There is nothing Egypt can do—
head or tail, palm branch or
reed.[g]

19:6 [l] Isa 37:25; Eze 30:12 [m] S Ge 41:2; S Job 8:11 [n] Isa 15:6 **19:7** [o] Nu 11:5 [p] Dt 29:23; Isa 23:3 [q] Zec 10:11 **19:8** [r] Nu 11:5; Eze 47:10 [s] Am 4:2; Hab 1:15 **19:9** [t] S Jos 2:6 [u] Pr 7:16; Eze 16:10; 27:7 **19:11** [v] S Nu 13:22 [w] S Ge 41:37 [x] S ver 3 [y] S 1Ki 4:30; Ac 7:22 **19:12** [z] 1Co 1:20 [a] S Isa 14:24; Ro 9:17 **19:13** [b] S Nu 13:22 [c] Jer 2:16; 44:1; 46:14,19; Eze 30:13,16; Hos 9:6 [d] S Ps 118:22 **19:14** [e] S Pr 12:8; Mt 17:17 [f] S Ps 107:27 **19:15** [g] S Isa 9:14 **19:16** [h] Isa 2:17; 11:10 [i] Jer 50:37; 51:30; Na 3:13 [j] S Dt 2:25; Heb 10:31 [k] S Isa 11:15 **19:17** [l] S Ge 35:5 [m] S Isa 14:24 **19:18** [n] S Isa 10:20 [o] Jer 44:1 [p] Ps 22:27; S 63:11; Isa 48:1; Jer 4:2; Zep 3:9 [q] Isa 17:1; 24:12; 32:19; fn Jer 43:13 **19:19** [r] S Isa 10:20 [s] S Jos 22:10 [t] S Ps 68:31 [u] S Ge 28:18 **19:20** [v] S Ge 21:30 [w] S Dt 28:29; S Jdg 2:18; S Isa 25:9 [x] Isa 49:24-26 **19:21** [y] S Isa 11:9; S 43:10 [z] ver 19; S Ge 27:29; S Ps 86:9; Isa 56:7; 60:7; Mal 1:11 [a] S Nu 30:2; S Dt 23:21 **19:22** [b] Ex 12:23; Heb 12:11 [c] Ex 11:10 [d] Isa 45:14; Eze 33:11; Hos 6:1; 10:12; 12:6; 14:1; Joel 2:13 [e] S Dt 32:39 **19:23** [f] S ver 16,24; Isa 20:6 [g] S Isa 11:16 [h] Mic 7:12 [i] S Ge 27:29; Isa 2:3; 27:13; 66:23 **19:24** [j] S ver 23 [k] S Isa 11:11 [l] S Ge 12:2 **19:25** [m] S Ge 12:3; Eph 2:11-14 [n] Ps 87:4; S 100:3

16In that day[h] the Egyptians will be
like women.[i] They will shudder with
fear[j] at the uplifted hand[k] that the
LORD Almighty raises against them.
17And the land of Judah will bring terror to the Egyptians; everyone to
whom Judah is mentioned will be terrified,[l] because of what the LORD Almighty is planning[m] against them.
18In that day[n] five cities[o] in Egypt
will speak the language of Canaan and
swear allegiance[p] to the LORD Almighty. One of them will be called the
City of Destruction.[w][q]
19In that day[r] there will be an altar[s] to the LORD in the heart of
Egypt,[t] and a monument[u] to the
LORD at its border. 20It will be a sign
and witness[v] to the LORD Almighty in
the land of Egypt. When they cry out to
the LORD because of their oppressors,
he will send them a savior[w] and defender, and he will rescue[x] them. 21So
the LORD will make himself known to
the Egyptians, and in that day they will
acknowledge[y] the LORD. They will
worship[z] with sacrifices and grain offerings; they will make vows to the
LORD and keep them.[a] 22The LORD will
strike[b] Egypt with a plague;[c] he will
strike them and heal them. They will
turn[d] to the LORD, and he will respond
to their pleas and heal[e] them.
23In that day[f] there will be a highway[g] from Egypt to Assyria.[h] The
Assyrians will go to Egypt and the
Egyptians to Assyria. The Egyptians
and Assyrians will worship[i] together.
24In that day[j] Israel will be the third,
along with Egypt and Assyria,[k] a
blessing[l] on the earth. 25The LORD Almighty will bless[m] them, saying,
"Blessed be Egypt my people,[n] Assyr-

[v] *13* Hebrew *Noph* [w] *18* Most manuscripts of the Masoretic Text; some manuscripts of the Masoretic Text, Dead Sea Scrolls and Vulgate *City of the Sun* (that is, Heliopolis)

19:16–25 IN THAT DAY. Isaiah gives four prophecies to be fulfilled "in that day." (1) The Egyptians would fear Judah when they realized their judgment had come from God (vv. 16–17). (2) After a time of affliction, cities in Egypt would worship the Lord, and altars would be erected to him (vv. 18–19). (3) The Egyptians would cry out to God, who would then send them a savior, and many would turn to the Lord (vv. 20–22). (4) Egypt, Assyria and Israel would all worship the Lord together (vv. 23–25). Though "that day" is not clearly identified here, other passages suggest that it refers to end-time events associated with the tribulation period (cf. Rev 4—19) and Christ's millennial rule (cf. Rev 20).

19:25 BLESS . . . EGYPT . . . ASSYRIA . . .

ia my handiwork,[o] and Israel my inheritance.[p]"

A Prophecy Against Egypt and Cush

20 In the year that the supreme commander,[q] sent by Sargon king of Assyria, came to Ashdod[r] and attacked and captured it— [2]at that time the LORD spoke through Isaiah son of Amoz.[s] He said to him, "Take off the sackcloth[t] from your body and the sandals[u] from your feet." And he did so, going around stripped[v] and barefoot.[w]

[3]Then the LORD said, "Just as my servant[x] Isaiah has gone stripped and barefoot for three years,[y] as a sign[z] and portent[a] against Egypt[b] and Cush,[x][c] [4]so the king[d] of Assyria will lead away stripped[e] and barefoot the Egyptian captives[f] and Cushite[g] exiles, young and old, with buttocks bared[h]—to Egypt's shame.[i] [5]Those who trusted[j] in Cush[k] and boasted in Egypt[l] will be afraid and put to shame.[m] [6]In that day[n] the people who live on this coast will say, 'See what has happened[o] to those we relied on,[p] those we fled to for help[q] and deliverance from the king of Assyria! How then can we escape?[r]' "

A Prophecy Against Babylon

21 An oracle[s] concerning the Desert[t] by the Sea:

Like whirlwinds[u] sweeping
through the southland,[v]
an invader comes from the desert,
from a land of terror.

[2]A dire[w] vision has been shown to me:
The traitor betrays,[x] the looter takes loot.
Elam,[y] attack! Media,[z] lay siege!
I will bring to an end all the groaning she caused.

[3]At this my body is racked with pain,[a]
pangs seize me, like those of a woman in labor;[b]
I am staggered by what I hear,
I am bewildered[c] by what I see.
[4]My heart[d] falters,
fear makes me tremble;[e]
the twilight I longed for
has become a horror[f] to me.

[5]They set the tables,
they spread the rugs,
they eat, they drink![g]
Get up, you officers,
oil the shields![h]

[6]This is what the Lord says to me:

"Go, post a lookout[i]
and have him report what he sees.
[7]When he sees chariots[j]
with teams of horses,
riders on donkeys
or riders on camels,[k]
let him be alert,
fully alert."

19:25 [o]Isa 29:23; 43:7; 45:11; 60:21; 64:8; Eph 2:10 [p]S Ex 34:9; Jer 30:22; Hos 2:23 **20:1** [q]2Ki 18:17 [r]S Jos 11:22; S 13:3 **20:2** [s]S Isa 13:1 [t]2Ki 1:8; S Isa 3:24; Zec 13:4; Mt 3:4 [u]Eze 24:17,23 [v]S 1Sa 19:24 [w]Eze 4:1-12; Mic 1:8 **20:3** [x]Isa 22:20; 41:8-9; 42:1; 43:10; 49:3,5-7; 50:10; 52:13; 53:11; Jer 7:25; Hag 2:23; Zec 4:14 [y]S Isa 16:14 [z]S Ex 3:12; S Isa 8:18; 37:30; 38:7; Ac 21:11 [a]S Dt 28:46 [b]S Isa 19:1 [c]ver 5; S Ge 10:6; Isa 37:9; 43:3 **20:4** [d]S Isa 19:4 [e]S Job 12:17 [f]Jer 46:19; Na 3:10 [g]Isa 18:1; Zep 2:12 [h]S Isa 3:24 [i]Isa 47:3; Jer 13:22,26; Na 3:5 **20:5** [j]S Isa 8:12 [k]S ver 3 [l]S 2Ki 18:21; S Isa 30:5 [m]Eze 29:16 **20:6** [n]Isa 2:11; S 19:23 [o]S 2Ki 18:21 [p]Jer 46:25 [q]S Isa 10:3 [r]Jer 30:15-17; 31:2; Mt 23:33; 1Th 5:3; Heb 2:3 **21:1** [s]S Isa 13:1 [t]Isa 13:21; Jer 50:12; 51:43 [u]S Job 1:19 [v]Da 11:40; Zec 9:14 **21:2** [w]Ps 60:3 [x]Isa 24:16; 33:1 [y]S Ge 10:22; Isa 22:6 [z]S Isa 13:3; Jer 25:25; 51:28 **21:3** [a]S Job 14:22 [b]S Ge 3:16; Ps 48:6; Isa 26:17; 37:3; Jer 30:6; 48:41; 49:22; Jn 16:21 [c]Da 7:28; 8:27; 10:16 **21:4** [d]Isa 7:4; 35:4 [e]S Isa 13:8; Da 5:9 [f]S Ps 55:5 **21:5** [g]Isa 5:12; 22:2,13; 23:7; 24:8; 32:13; Jer 25:16,27; 51:39, 57; Da 5:2 [h]2Sa 1:21; 1Ki 10:16-17; Jer 46:3; 51:11 **21:6** [i]S 2Ki 9:17 **21:7** [j]ver 9 [k]S Jdg 6:5

[x]*3* That is, the upper Nile region; also in verse 5

ISRAEL. This will ultimately be fulfilled at the end of the age when all nations of the earth will be blessed (Ge 12:3) during the righteous reign of the Messiah, Jesus Christ (cf. 2:2–4; 11:1–10). One day the God of Israel will be the God of Arabs, Jews, and all other peoples and nations.

20:1 ASHDOD. The attack on this Philistine city probably occurred in 711 B.C.

20:2 STRIPPED AND BAREFOOT. Isaiah was to appear in public stripped of his outer clothes for three years as an enacted parable or sign of what would happen to Egypt and Cush when Assyria carried them into captivity. The message was intended to warn Judah not to trust in an alliance with Egypt, but rather to look to the Lord their God. Isaiah may not have been completely naked (see 2Sa 6:20, note), but rather stripped to a loincloth; perhaps he conducted himself in this humiliating manner only a portion of each day.

20:3 A SIGN AND PORTENT. Isaiah obeyed God even though it meant shame and embarrassment to him for three years. If our obedience to God and our separation from ungodly ways are as they should be, then we can also expect at times to suffer reproach, embarrassment and humiliation. Righteousness and persecution often go together (see Mt 5:10, note).

21:1–10 THE DESERT BY THE SEA. God gives Isaiah a second vision of the downfall and destruction of Babylon, which lay just north of the Persian Gulf (see ch. 13, notes).

21:2 ELAM. Elam was located east of the Tigris River and Babylon, bordered on the north by Media and Assyria and on the south by the Persian Gulf. The Elamites were allied with the Medo-Persian army when Babylon was conquered in 539 B.C. The Elamite city of Susa became an important capital of the Persian empire.

8And the lookout[y][l] shouted,

"Day after day, my lord, I stand on
the watchtower;
every night I stay at my post.
9Look, here comes a man in a
chariot[m]
with a team of horses.
And he gives back the answer:
'Babylon[n] has fallen,[o] has
fallen!
All the images of its gods[p]
lie shattered[q] on the ground!' "

10O my people, crushed on the
threshing floor,[r]
I tell you what I have heard
from the LORD Almighty,
from the God of Israel.

A Prophecy Against Edom

11An oracle concerning Dumah[z]:[s]

Someone calls to me from Seir,[t]
"Watchman, what is left of the
night?
Watchman, what is left of the
night?"
12The watchman replies,
"Morning is coming, but also the
night.
If you would ask, then ask;
and come back yet again."

A Prophecy Against Arabia

13An oracle[u] concerning Arabia:[v]

You caravans of Dedanites,[w]
who camp in the thickets of
Arabia,
14 bring water for the thirsty;
you who live in Tema,[x]
bring food for the fugitives.
15They flee[y] from the sword,[z]
from the drawn sword,
from the bent bow
and from the heat of battle.

16This is what the Lord says to me:
"Within one year, as a servant bound
by contract[a] would count it, all the
pomp[b] of Kedar[c] will come to an end.
17The survivors of the bowmen, the
warriors of Kedar, will be few.[d]" The
LORD, the God of Israel, has spoken.[e]

A Prophecy About Jerusalem

22 An oracle[f] concerning the Valley[g] of Vision:[h]

What troubles you now,
that you have all gone up on the
roofs,[i]
2O town full of commotion,
O city of tumult[j] and revelry?[k]
Your slain[l] were not killed by the
sword,[m]
nor did they die in battle.
3All your leaders have fled[n]
together;
they have been captured[o]
without using the bow.
All you who were caught were
taken prisoner together,
having fled while the enemy was
still far away.
4Therefore I said, "Turn away from
me;
let me weep[p] bitterly.
Do not try to console me
over the destruction of my
people."[q]

21:8 [l]Mic 7:7; Hab 2:1 **21:9** [m]ver 7 [n]S Isa 13:1; 47:1, 5; S Rev 14:8 [o]Isa 47:11; Jer 51:8; Da 5:30 [p]S Lev 26:30; Isa 46:1; Jer 50:2; 51:44 [q]S Isa 2:18 **21:10** [r]Isa 27:12; 28:27,28; 41:15; Jer 51:33; Mic 4:13; Hab 3:12; Mt 3:12 **21:11** [s]S Ge 25:14; S Isa 34:11 [t]Ge 32:3 **21:13** [u]Isa 13:1 [v]S 2Ch 9:14 [w]S Ge 10:7; S 25:3 **21:14** [x]S Ge 25:15 **21:15** [y]S Isa 13:14 [z]Isa 31:8 **21:16** [a]S Lev 25:50 [b]S Isa 17:3 [c]S Ge 25:13 **21:17** [d]S Dt 4:27; S Isa 10:19 [e]S Isa 1:20; 16:14 **22:1** [f]Isa 13:1 [g]Ps 125:2; Jer 21:13; Joel 3:2, 12,14 [h]S Isa 1:1 [i]S Jos 2:8; Jer 48:38 **22:2** [j]Eze 22:5 [k]S Isa 5:14; S 21:5 [l]S Isa 10:4 [m]S 2Ki 25:3 **22:3** [n]S Isa 13:14 [o]S 2Ki 25:6 **22:4** [p]S Isa 15:3; S La 1:16; Eze 21:6; Lk 19:41 [q]Jer 9:1

[y] *8* Dead Sea Scrolls and Syriac; Masoretic Text *A lion* [z] *11 Dumah* means *silence* or *stillness,* a wordplay on *Edom.*

21:9 BABYLON HAS FALLEN. Babylon, the enemy of God's people, would fall, its reliance on false gods shattered; it first took place in 689 B.C., when Sennacherib smashed their idols (except for Bel and Nebo, see ch. 46). The apostle John heard the same words in his visions (Rev 14:8; 18:1–2), prophesying that the end-time Babylon, a symbol of all that opposes Christ and his people in this world, would be destroyed. At that time, Christ will complete the redemption of his people. Believers must pray for the fall and destruction of end-time Babylon (see Rev 17:1–5, notes; 18:2–21, notes).

21:11 DUMAH. Dumah is an alternate name for Edom, the land of Esau's descendants. Edom was located immediately south of Judah and the Dead Sea (see also 34:5–15).

21:13 ARABIA. Arabia was located between Edom and Babylon. It would experience warfare and defeat at the hands of invaders, fulfilled when the Assyrians attacked the Arabs in 732 and 725 B.C. (cf. Jer 25:17,24); Sennacherib also conquered Arabia in 688 B.C. and took the title "King of Arabia."

22:1 THE VALLEY OF VISION. This name refers to Jerusalem or to the valley near Jerusalem where God had revealed himself in prophetic visions. God here rebukes Jerusalem's inhabitants for their frivolous attitude in the midst of grave danger and apostasy (vv. 1–14).

22:4 LET ME WEEP BITTERLY. Isaiah, a true prophet, felt deeply the tragedy of a fallen and apostate people. God's people were being destroyed, and he grieved for them and for his betrayed God. While others were experiencing joy and revelry (vv. 12–13), the prophet had to share the sorrow of God (see next note).

[5]The Lord, the LORD Almighty, has
a day[r]
of tumult and trampling[s] and
terror[t]
in the Valley of Vision,[u]
a day of battering down walls[v]
and of crying out to the
mountains.
[6]Elam[w] takes up the quiver,[x]
with her charioteers and horses;
Kir[y] uncovers the shield.
[7]Your choicest valleys[z] are full of
chariots,
and horsemen are posted at the
city gates;[a]
[8] the defenses of Judah are
stripped away.

And you looked in that day[b]
to the weapons[c] in the Palace
of the Forest;[d]
[9]you saw that the City of David
had many breaches[e] in its
defenses;
you stored up water
in the Lower Pool.[f]
[10]You counted the buildings in
Jerusalem
and tore down houses[g] to
strengthen the wall.[h]
[11]You built a reservoir between the
two walls[i]
for the water of the Old Pool,[j]
but you did not look to the One
who made it,
or have regard[k] for the One
who planned[l] it long ago.

[12]The Lord, the LORD Almighty,
called you on that day[m]
to weep[n] and to wail,
to tear out your hair[o] and put
on sackcloth.[p]
[13]But see, there is joy and revelry,[q]
slaughtering of cattle and killing
of sheep,
eating of meat and drinking of
wine![r]
"Let us eat and drink," you say,
"for tomorrow we die!"[s]

[14]The LORD Almighty has revealed
this in my hearing:[t] "Till your dying
day this sin will not be atoned[u] for,"
says the Lord, the LORD Almighty.

[15]This is what the Lord, the LORD Almighty, says:

"Go, say to this steward,
to Shebna,[v] who is in charge[w]
of the palace:[x]
[16]What are you doing here and who
gave you permission
to cut out a grave[y] for
yourself[z] here,
hewing your grave on the height
and chiseling your resting place
in the rock?
[17]"Beware, the LORD is about to take
firm hold of you
and hurl[a] you away, O you
mighty man.
[18]He will roll you up tightly like a
ball
and throw[b] you into a large
country.
There you will die
and there your splendid
chariots[c] will remain—
you disgrace to your master's
house!
[19]I will depose you from your office,
and you will be ousted[d] from
your position.[e]

[20]"In that day[f] I will summon my
servant,[g] Eliakim[h] son of Hilkiah.
[21]I will clothe him with your robe and
fasten your sash[i] around him and
hand your authority[j] over to him. He
will be a father to those who live in Jerusalem and to the house of Judah. [22]I
will place on his shoulder[k] the key[l]
to the house of David;[m] what he opens
no one can shut, and what he shuts no
one can open.[n] [23]I will drive him like
a peg[o] into a firm place;[p] he will be
a seat[a] of honor[q] for the house of his
father. [24]All the glory of his family will
hang on him: its offspring and off-

22:5 [r]S Isa 2:12 [s]S Job 40:12; S Ps 108:13 [t]S 2Sa 22:43; Isa 13:3; Jer 30:7; La 1:5; Eze 8:17-18; 9:9-10; Joel 2:31; Am 5:18-20; Zep 1:15 [u]S Isa 1:1 [v]Ne 6:15; S Ps 89:40; Isa 5:5; Jer 39:8; Eze 13:14 **22:6** [w]S Isa 21:2 [x]Ps 46:9; Jer 49:35; 51:56 [y]S 2Ki 16:9 **22:7** [z]Jos 15:8 [a]S 2Ch 32:1-2 **22:8** [b]S Isa 2:12 [c]S 2Ch 32:5 [d]S 1Ki 7:2 **22:9** [e]S Ne 1:3 [f]S 2Ki 18:17; S 2Ch 32:4 **22:10** [g]Jer 33:4 [h]S 2Ch 32:5 **22:11** [i]2Ki 25:4; 2Ch 32:5; Jer 39:4 [j]S 2Ch 32:4 [k]S 1Sa 12:24 [l]2Ki 19:25 **22:12** [m]S Isa 2:12 [n]Joel 1:9; 2:17 [o]S Lev 13:40; Mic 1:16 [p]S Isa 3:24 **22:13** [q]S Isa 21:5 [r]S 1Sa 25:36; Ecc 8:15; Isa 5:22; 28:7-8; 56:12; Lk 17:26-29 [s]1Co 15:32* **22:14** [t]Isa 5:9 [u]S 1Sa 2:25; Isa 13:11; 26:21; 30:13-14; Eze 24:13 **22:15** [v]S 2Ki 6:30; S 18:18 [w]ver 21 [x]S Ge 41:40 **22:16** [y]Mt 27:60 [z]S Ge 50:5; S Nu 32:42 **22:17** [a]Jer 10:18; 13:18; 22:26 **22:18** [b]S Job 18:11; Isa 14:19; 17:13 [c]S Ge 41:43 **22:19** [d]S 1Sa 2:7; S Ps 52:5 [e]Lk 16:3 **22:20** [f]ver 25 [g]S Isa 20:3 [h]S 2Ki 18:18; S Isa 36:3 **22:21** [i]S Isa 5:27 [j]ver 15 **22:22** [k]Isa 9:6 [l]1Ch 9:27; Mt 16:19; Rev 3:7 [m]S Isa 7:2 [n]S Job 12:14 **22:23** [o]ver 25; Eze 15:3; Zec 10:4 [p]S Ezr 9:8; S Job 6:25 [q]S 1Sa 2:7-8; S Job 36:7

[a]23 Or *throne*

22:12–13 CALLED YOU . . . TO WEEP. When God's people compromise with the world and turn away from obeying God's righteous ways, he calls them to repent, confess their spiritual poverty and seek his face. Christ wants all churches to examine their spiritual state in the light of the NT and its standards (cf. Rev 2—3). Like Isaiah, today's prophets should call for repentance, humility, tears, prayer and fasting, rather than for frivolity.

22:15–25 SHEBNA. God pronounces judgment against a corrupt government official named Shebna, who was to be replaced by Eliakim, a godly ruler (cf. v. 20).

shoots—all its lesser vessels, from the
bowls to all the jars.

25"In that day,[r]" declares the LORD
Almighty, "the peg[s] driven into the
firm place will give way; it will be
sheared off and will fall, and the load
hanging on it will be cut down." The
LORD has spoken.[t]

A Prophecy About Tyre

23 An oracle concerning Tyre:[u]

Wail,[v] O ships[w] of
Tarshish![x]
For Tyre is destroyed[y]
and left without house or harbor.
From the land of Cyprus[b]
word has come to them.

2Be silent,[z] you people of the
island
and you merchants[a] of Sidon,[b]
whom the seafarers have
enriched.
3On the great waters
came the grain of the Shihor;[c]
the harvest of the Nile[c][d] was the
revenue of Tyre,[e]
and she became the marketplace
of the nations.

4Be ashamed, O Sidon,[f] and you,
O fortress of the sea,
for the sea has spoken:
"I have neither been in labor nor
given birth;[g]
I have neither reared sons nor
brought up daughters."
5When word comes to Egypt,
they will be in anguish[h] at the
report from Tyre.[i]

6Cross over to Tarshish;[j]
wail, you people of the island.
7Is this your city of revelry,[k]
the old, old city,
whose feet have taken her
to settle in far-off lands?
8Who planned this against Tyre,
the bestower of crowns,
whose merchants[l] are princes,
whose traders[m] are renowned in
the earth?
9The LORD Almighty planned[n] it,

22:25 [r]ver 20 [s]S ver 23 [t]Isa 46:11; Mic 4:4
23:1 [u]Jos 19:29; 1Ki 5:1; Jer 47:4; Joel 3:4-8; Am 1:9-10 [v]S Isa 13:6 [w]S 1Ki 10:22 [x]S Ge 10:4; Isa 2:16 *fn* [y]S Ge 1:2; Eze 26:4
23:2 [z]S Job 2:13 [a]Eze 27:5-24 [b]Jdg 1:31
23:3 [c]S Ge 41:5 [d]S Isa 19:7 [e]S Ps 83:7
23:4 [f]S Ge 10:15, 19 [g]Isa 54:1
23:5 [h]Eze 30:9 [i]Eze 26:17-18
23:6 [j]S Ge 10:4
23:7 [k]ver 12; S Isa 5:14; S 21:5; 32:13; Eze 26:13
23:8 [l]Na 3:16 [m]Eze 28:5; Rev 18:23
23:9 [n]S Isa 14:24 [o]S Job 40:11 [p]S Isa 13:11 [q]Isa 5:13; 9:15; Eze 27:3
23:11 [r]S Ex 14:21 [s]S Ps 46:6 [t]ver 14; Isa 25:2; Eze 26:4; Zec 9:3-4
23:12 [u]S ver 7; Rev 18:22 [v]Isa 37:22; 47:1; Jer 14:17; 46:11; La 2:13; Zep 3:14; Zec 2:10 [w]S Ge 10:4
23:13 [x]Isa 43:14; Jer 51:12 [y]Isa 10:5 [z]S Ps 74:14; Isa 18:6 [a]S 2Ki 25:1 [b]Isa 10:7
23:14 [c]S 1Ki 10:22 [d]S Ge 10:4; Isa 2:16 *fn* [e]S ver 11
23:15 [f]Jer 25:22 [g]S Ps 90:10
23:16 [h]Pr 7:10

to bring low[o] the pride of all
glory
and to humble[p] all who are
renowned[q] on the earth.

10Till[d] your land as along the Nile,
O Daughter of Tarshish,
for you no longer have a harbor.
11The LORD has stretched out his
hand[r] over the sea
and made its kingdoms
tremble.[s]
He has given an order concerning
Phoenicia[e]
that her fortresses be
destroyed.[t]
12He said, "No more of your
reveling,[u]
O Virgin Daughter[v] of Sidon,
now crushed!

"Up, cross over to Cyprus[b];[w]
even there you will find no rest."
13Look at the land of the
Babylonians,[f][x]
this people that is now of no
account!
The Assyrians[y] have made it
a place for desert creatures;[z]
they raised up their siege
towers,[a]
they stripped its fortresses bare
and turned it into a ruin.[b]

14Wail, you ships[c] of Tarshish;[d]
your fortress is destroyed![e]

15At that time Tyre[f] will be forgotten for seventy years,[g] the span of a
king's life. But at the end of these seventy years, it will happen to Tyre as in
the song of the prostitute:

16"Take up a harp, walk through the
city,
O prostitute[h] forgotten;
play the harp well, sing many a
song,
so that you will be remembered."

[b]*1* Hebrew *Kittim* [c]*2,3* Masoretic Text; one Dead Sea Scroll *Sidon, / who cross over the sea; / your envoys* *3are on the great waters. / The grain of the Shihor, / the harvest of the Nile,* [d]*10* Dead Sea Scrolls and some Septuagint manuscripts; Masoretic Text *Go through* [e]*11* Hebrew *Canaan* [f]*13* Or *Chaldeans*

23:1 TYRE. Tyre was a Phoenician center for world commerce on the east coast of the Mediterranean Sea just north of Palestine. Its citizens were wealthy, but also evil and full of pride. Thus Isaiah prophesied that God would bring that city down for seventy years and then restore it for a time (vv. 8–9,17–18). God's people would once again engage in trade with Tyre.

23:13 LAND OF THE BABYLONIANS. Nebuchadnezzar, one of Babylon's kings, invaded Tyre in 572 B.C., approximately one hundred years after Isaiah made this prophecy.

[17]At the end of seventy years,[i] the LORD will deal with Tyre. She will return to her hire as a prostitute[j] and will ply her trade with all the kingdoms on the face of the earth.[k] [18]Yet her profit and her earnings will be set apart for the LORD;[l] they will not be stored up or hoarded. Her profits will go to those who live before the LORD,[m] for abundant food and fine clothes.[n]

The LORD's Devastation of the Earth

24 See, the LORD is going to lay
waste the earth[o]
and devastate[p] it;
he will ruin its face
and scatter[q] its inhabitants—
[2]it will be the same
for priest as for people,[r]
for master as for servant,
for mistress as for maid,
for seller as for buyer,[s]
for borrower as for lender,
for debtor as for creditor.[t]
[3]The earth will be completely laid
waste[u]
and totally plundered.[v]
The LORD has spoken[w]
this word.

[4]The earth dries up[x] and
withers,[y]
the world languishes and
withers,
the exalted[z] of the earth
languish.[a]
[5]The earth is defiled[b] by its
people;
they have disobeyed[c] the laws,
violated the statutes
and broken the everlasting
covenant.[d]
[6]Therefore a curse[e] consumes the
earth;
its people must bear their guilt.
Therefore earth's inhabitants are
burned up,[f]
and very few are left.
[7]The new wine dries up[g] and the
vine withers;[h]
all the merrymakers groan.[i]
[8]The gaiety of the tambourines[j] is
stilled,
the noise[k] of the revelers[l] has
stopped,
the joyful harp[m] is silent.[n]
[9]No longer do they drink wine[o]
with a song;
the beer is bitter[p] to its
drinkers.
[10]The ruined city[q] lies desolate;[r]
the entrance to every house is
barred.
[11]In the streets they cry out[s] for
wine;[t]
all joy turns to gloom,[u]
all gaiety is banished from the
earth.
[12]The city is left in ruins,[v]
its gate[w] is battered to pieces.
[13]So will it be on the earth
and among the nations,
as when an olive tree is beaten,[x]
or as when gleanings are left
after the grape harvest.[y]

[14]They raise their voices, they shout
for joy;[z]

23:17 [i]S Ps 90:10 [j]Dt 23:17-18; Eze 16:26; Na 3:4; Rev 17:1; 18:3,9 [k]Jer 25:26 **23:18** [l]Ex 28:36; S 39:30; Jos 6:17-19; Ps 72:10 [m]Isa 18:7; 60:5-9; 61:6; Mic 4:13 [n]Am 1:9-10; Zec 14:1,14 **24:1** [o]ver 20; Isa 2:19-21; 33:9; Jer 25:29 [p]S Jos 6:17; S Isa 13:5 [q]S Ge 11:9 **24:2** [r]Hos 4:9 [s]Eze 7:12; 1Co 7:29-31 [t]S Lev 25:35-37; Dt 23:19-20; Isa 3:1-7 **24:3** [u]S Ge 6:13 [v]Isa 6:11-12; 10:6 [w]S Isa 7:7 **24:4** [x]Jer 12:11; 14:4; Joel 1:10 [y]S Isa 15:6 [z]S Isa 2:12 [a]S Isa 3:26 **24:5** [b]S Ge 3:17 [c]S Isa 1:2; 9:17; 10:6; 59:12; Jer 7:28 [d]S Ge 9:11; S Jer 11:10 **24:6** [e]S Jos 23:15 [f]S Isa 1:31 **24:7** [g]Jer 48:33; Joel 1:5 [h]Isa 7:23; S 15:6; 32:10 [i]S Isa 3:26; 16:8-10 **24:8** [j]S Ge 31:27; S Isa 5:12 [k]Jer 7:34; 16:9; 25:10; 33:11; Hos 2:11 [l]S Isa 5:14; S 21:5 [m]S Ps 137:2; Rev 18:22 [n]La 5:14; Eze 26:13 **24:9** [o]Isa 5:11,22 [p]Isa 5:20 **24:10** [q]Isa 25:2; 26:5 [r]S Ge 1:2; S Isa 6:11 **24:11** [s]S Ps 144:14 [t]La 2:12 [u]S Isa 15:6; 16:10; 32:13; Jer 14:3 **24:12** [v]S Isa 19:18 [w]S Isa 3:26; S 13:2 **24:13** [x]S Dt 30:4; S Isa 17:6 [y]Ob 1:5; Mic 7:1 **24:14** [z]S Isa 12:6

23:17 PLY HER TRADE. Tyre would ply her trade with the nations by using sinful and dishonest commercial practices, accompanied by immoral activity, to gain wealth from other nations.

24:1—27:13 SEE. These chapters deal with end-time events in apocalyptic language, the type of language used in the book of Revelation. They speak of God's judgment against the world for its sin and of the blessings he has prepared for his people.

24:1 LAY WASTE THE EARTH. This chapter describes God's coming judgment on the whole earth and its inhabitants; he will completely destroy most of the earth and its inhabitants. This time of world devastation is called the great tribulation in the NT (cf. Mt 24:15–21; 1Th 5:1–3; Rev 6; 8—9; 15—16; 18—19; see article on THE GREAT TRIBULATION, p. 1456). After this worldwide judgment, Christ will return to rule over the righteous of the earth (Rev 19—20).

24:5 THE EARTH IS DEFILED. God's wrath will come upon the world because humankind has defiled the earth with sin, immorality and wickedness. At the present time, sin predominates, but at the end time God ordains a dreadful and inescapable doom to come upon all who take pleasure in unrighteousness (see 1Th 5:2, note; 2Th 2:12, note).

24:6 INHABITANTS ARE BURNED UP. The wages of sin are death and destruction (cf. Ro 6:23). This truth is demonstrated on an international scale at the end of time when all who do not repent and turn to God will be destroyed. The devastation will be like that of a fire that burns and devours completely (cf. 1:31; 5:24; 9:18; 10:16–17; 29:6; 30:27; Zec 5:3–4; Rev 19:11–21).

24:14 RAISE THEIR VOICES. The righteous who remain faithful to God will rejoice and give him glory when they see the destruction of this

from the west[a] they acclaim the
LORD's majesty.
15Therefore in the east[b] give
glory[c] to the LORD;
exalt[d] the name[e] of the LORD,
the God of Israel,
in the islands[f] of the sea.
16From the ends of the earth[g] we
hear singing:[h]
"Glory[i] to the Righteous
One."[j]

But I said, "I waste away, I waste
away![k]
Woe[l] to me!
The treacherous[m] betray!
With treachery the treacherous
betray![n]"
17Terror[o] and pit and snare[p] await
you,
O people of the earth.[q]
18Whoever flees[r] at the sound of
terror
will fall into a pit;[s]
whoever climbs out of the pit
will be caught in a snare.[t]

The floodgates of the heavens[u]
are opened,
the foundations of the earth
shake.[v]
19The earth is broken up,[w]
the earth is split asunder,[x]
the earth is thoroughly shaken.
20The earth reels like a drunkard,[y]
it sways like a hut[z] in the
wind;
so heavy upon it is the guilt of its
rebellion[a]
that it falls[b]—never to rise
again.[c]

21In that day[d] the LORD will
punish[e]
the powers[f] in the heavens
above
and the kings[g] on the earth
below.
22They will be herded together
like prisoners[h] bound in a
dungeon;[i]
they will be shut up in prison
and be punished[g] after many
days.[j]
23The moon will be abashed, the
sun[k] ashamed;
for the LORD Almighty will
reign[l]
on Mount Zion[m] and in Jerusalem,
and before its elders,
gloriously.[n]

Da 10:11

24:14 [a]Isa 43:5; 49:12 **24:15** [b]S Ps 113:3 [c]Isa 42:12; 66:19; 2Th 1:12 [d]S Ex 15:2; Isa 25:3; 59:19; Mal 1:11 [e]S Isa 12:4 [f]S Isa 11:11 **24:16** [g]S Ps 48:10 [h]S Ps 65:8 [i]Isa 28:5; 60:1,19 [j]S Ezr 9:15 [k]S Lev 26:39 [l]1Sa 4:8; S Isa 5:8; Jer 10:19; 45:3 [m]S Ps 25:3 [n]Isa 21:2; 33:1; Jer 3:6,20; 5:11; 9:2; Hos 5:7; 9:1 **24:17** [o]Dt 32:23-25 [p]Isa 8:14; Jer 48:43 [q]Lk 21:35 **24:18** [r]S Job 20:24 [s]Isa 42:22 [t]S Job 18:9; S Isa 8:14; La 3:47; Eze 12:13 [u]S Ge 7:11 [v]S Jdg 5:4; S Job 9:6; S Ps 11:3; S Eze 38:19 **24:19** [w]S Ps 46:2 [x]S Dt 11:6 **24:20** [y]S Job 12:25 [z]S Job 27:18 [a]S Isa 1:2,28; 43:27; 58:1 [b]S Ps 46:2 [c]S Job 12:14 **24:21** [d]S Isa 2:11; S 10:20; Rev 16:14 [e]Isa 10:12; 13:11; Jer 25:29 [f]1Co 6:3; Eph 6:11-12 [g]S Isa 2:12 **24:22** [h]S Isa 10:4 [i]Isa 42:7,22; Lk 8:31; Rev 20:7-10 [j]Eze 38:8 **24:23** [k]S Isa 13:10 [l]S Ps 97:1; Rev 22:5

Praise to the LORD

25 O LORD, you are my God;[o]
I will exalt you and praise
your name,[p]
for in perfect faithfulness[q]
you have done marvelous
things,[r]
things planned[s] long ago.
2You have made the city a heap of
rubble,[t]
the fortified[u] town a ruin,[v]
the foreigners' stronghold[w] a city
no more;
it will never be rebuilt.[x]
3Therefore strong peoples will
honor you;[y]
cities of ruthless[z] nations will
revere you.
4You have been a refuge[a] for the
poor,[b]

[m]S Isa 2:2; Heb 12:22 [n]Isa 28:5; 41:16; 45:25; 60:19; Eze 48:35; Zec 2:5; Rev 21:23 **25:1** [o]S Isa 7:13 [p]S Ps 145:2; S Isa 12:1,4 [q]Isa 11:5 [r]Ps 40:5; 98:1; Joel 2:21,26 [s]Nu 23:19; S Isa 14:24; 37:26; 46:11; Eph 1:11 **25:2** [t]Isa 17:1; 26:5; 37:26 [u]S Isa 17:3 [v]S Dt 13:16 [w]S Isa 13:22 [x]S Job 12:14 **25:3** [y]S Ex 6:2; S Ps 22:23; S Isa 11:14 [z]S Isa 13:11 **25:4** [a]S 2Sa 22:3; S Ps 118:8; S Isa 4:6; 17:10; 27:5; 33:16; Joel 3:16 [b]S Isa 3:14

[g]22 Or *released*

corrupt world system. They will delight in the defeat of sin and evil (see Rev 18:20, where the angels and believers are commanded to rejoice in God's righteous judgment against Satan's system and the wickedness of humankind).

24:16 WOE TO ME! In contrast to the rejoicing about the coming victory over evil, Isaiah is distressed by all the sin and treachery around him.

24:17 TERROR AND PIT AND SNARE. Jesus taught that the only way believers can escape "all that is about to happen" (Lk 21:36) is by guarding against sin in their lives and persevering in prayer for God's grace (see Lk 21:34,36, notes).

24:21 PUNISH THE POWERS IN THE HEAVENS. These powers are satanic and demonic spiritual forces opposed to God (see Eph 6:11–12; Rev 20:1–3; see Rev 12:7–9, note). At the end of history, they will be shut up in prison (see Rev 20:1–3), judged and punished (Rev 20:11–15,20).

24:23 THE LORD ALMIGHTY WILL REIGN. After throwing down all evil powers, God's kingdom will come to the earth and the Lord will reign there (cf. Rev 20:1–4; 21:1–9). Only then will God receive the honor and glory due him.

25:1–12 PRAISE YOUR NAME. Isaiah praises the Lord for the defeat of everyone and everything that opposed his righteous purpose and kingdom, and for his role as the deliverer and comforter of his people.

a refuge for the needy[c] in his
distress,
a shelter from the storm[d]
and a shade from the heat.
For the breath of the ruthless[e]
is like a storm driving against a
wall
5 and like the heat of the desert.
You silence[f] the uproar of
foreigners;[g]
as heat is reduced by the
shadow of a cloud,
so the song of the ruthless[h] is
stilled.

6On this mountain[i] the LORD
Almighty will prepare
a feast[j] of rich food for all
peoples,
a banquet of aged wine—
the best of meats and the finest
of wines.[k]
7On this mountain he will destroy
the shroud[l] that enfolds all
peoples,[m]
the sheet that covers all nations;
8 he will swallow up death[n]
forever.
The Sovereign LORD will wipe away
the tears[o]
from all faces;
he will remove the disgrace[p] of
his people
from all the earth.
The LORD has spoken.[q]

9In that day[r] they will say,

"Surely this is our God;[s]
we trusted[t] in him, and he
saved[u] us.
This is the LORD, we trusted in
him;
let us rejoice[v] and be glad in
his salvation."[w]

10The hand of the LORD will rest on
this mountain;[x]
but Moab[y] will be trampled
under him
as straw is trampled down in
the manure.
11They will spread out their hands in
it,
as a swimmer spreads out his
hands to swim.
God will bring down[z] their pride[a]
despite the cleverness[h] of their
hands.
12He will bring down your high
fortified walls[b]
and lay them low;[c]
he will bring them down to the
ground,
to the very dust.

A Song of Praise

26 In that day[d] this song will be sung[e] in the land of Judah:

25:4 [c]S Isa 14:30; 29:19 [d]S Ps 55:8 [e]Isa 29:5; 49:25 25:5 [f]Jer 51:55 [g]S Ps 18:44 [h]S Isa 13:11 25:6 [i]S Isa 2:2 [j]S Ge 29:22; 1Ki 1:25; Isa 1:19; 55:1-2; 66:11; Joel 3:18; Mt 8:11; 22:4; Rev 19:9 [k]S Ps 36:8; S Pr 9:2 25:7 [l]2Co 3:15-16; Eph 4:18 [m]S Job 4:9 25:8 [n]Isa 26:19; Hos 13:14; 1Co 15:54-55* [o]Isa 15:3; 30:19; 35:10; 51:11; 65:19; Jer 31:16; Rev 7:17; 21:4 [p]S Ge 30:23; S Ps 119:39; Mt 5:11; 1Pe 4:14; Rev 7:14 [q]S Isa 7:7 25:9 [r]S Isa 2:11; S 10:20 [s]Isa 40:9 [t]S Ps 22:5; S Isa 12:2 [u]Ps 145:19; Isa 19:20; 33:22; 35:4; 43:3,11; 45:15,21; 49:25-26,26; 60:16; 63:8; Jer 14:8 [v]S Dt 32:43; S Ps 9:2; Isa 9:3; 35:2,10; 41:16; 51:3; 61:7,10; 66:14 [w]S Ps 13:5; S Isa 12:2 25:10 [x]S Isa 2:2 [y]S Ge 19:37; S Nu 21:29; S Dt 23:6; S Isa 11:14; Am 2:1-3 25:11 [z]Isa 5:25; 14:26; 16:14 [a]S Lev 26:19; S Job 40:12 25:12 [b]S Isa 2:15 [c]S Job 40:11; S Isa 15:1; S Jer 51:44 26:1 [d]S Isa 10:20 [e]Isa 30:29

[h] 11 The meaning of the Hebrew for this word is uncertain.

25:6 THIS MOUNTAIN. Isaiah prophesies about the future kingdom and salvation that will come after Christ's return to earth (vv. 6–12; cf. Rev 19—21). "This mountain" refers to Mount Zion, or Jerusalem (cf. 2:1–4; 24:23; Rev 21:1–2); "all peoples" indicates the success of the proclamation of the gospel around the world.

25:6 AGED WINE—THE BEST OF MEATS. The lavish banquet to be enjoyed in God's kingdom represents the wonderful blessings believers will experience in his presence. A banquet of "aged wine" (Heb *shemarim*) literally translates "a banquet of preserves," probably referring to the juice of the grape that had been preserved and kept for a long period of time. Note Jer 48:11–12, where God compares Moab to juice left on its dregs and therefore "she tastes as she did, and her aroma is unchanged"—meaning that God's blessings, which have been kept in store for centuries for his faithful people, will not change in purpose from his original intention (see article on WINE IN THE OLD TESTAMENT, p. 204).

25:8 SWALLOW UP DEATH FOREVER ... WIPE AWAY THE TEARS. In God's future kingdom all the sorrow, misery and death that now prevail on the earth will be removed and never again reappear (see the NT expression of this truth in 1Co 15:54; Rev 21:4). Like a caring parent, God himself will wipe away all the tears from the eyes of his children, and there will never again be a reason for tears and grief. These glorious blessings will occur only when Christ returns to earth, triumphs over evil and reigns over all creation. Such promises should lead us to see the Lord's great love and compassion for us and cause us to pray earnestly and ceaselessly for the glorious consummation of redemption through Christ (Rev 22:17,20).

25:9 WE TRUSTED IN HIM. Isaiah describes the faithful in God's kingdom as those who have trusted in the Lord. All believers should trust in the Lord, waiting expectantly for Christ's return and the fulfillment of all his promises (1Co 1:7; Tit 2:13; see Lk 2:25, note).

26:1–21 THIS SONG. Confident that God will accomplish his redemptive purpose, the saints break out into praise and prayer. Their song concerns God's triumphant destruction of all evil and the establishment of his kingdom.

We have a strong city;[f]
God makes salvation
its walls[g] and ramparts.[h]
2Open the gates[i]
that the righteous[j] nation may
enter,
the nation that keeps faith.
3You will keep in perfect peace[k]
him whose mind is steadfast,
because he trusts[l] in you.
4Trust[m] in the LORD forever,[n]
for the LORD, the LORD, is the
Rock[o] eternal.
5He humbles those who dwell on
high,
he lays the lofty city low;
he levels it to the ground[p]
and casts it down to the dust.[q]
6Feet trample[r] it down—
the feet of the oppressed,[s]
the footsteps of the poor.[t]
7The path of the righteous is
level;[u]
O upright One,[v] you make the
way of the righteous
smooth.[w]
8Yes, LORD, walking in the way of
your laws,[i][x]
we wait[y] for you;
your name[z] and renown
are the desire of our hearts.
9My soul yearns for you in the
night;[a]
in the morning my spirit longs[b]
for you.
When your judgments[c] come upon
the earth,
the people of the world learn
righteousness.[d]
10Though grace is shown to the
wicked,[e]
they do not learn righteousness;
even in a land of uprightness they
go on doing evil[f]
and regard[g] not the majesty of
the LORD.

26:1 [f] S Isa 14:32 [g] Isa 32:18; 60:18; Zec 2:5; 9:8 [h] S Ps 48:13 **26:2** [i] S Ps 24:7 [j] Ps 24:3-4; 85:13; S Isa 1:26; S 4:3; 9:7; 50:8; 53:11; 54:14; 58:8; 62:2 **26:3** [k] S Job 22:21; S Isa 9:6,7; Php 4:7 [l] S 1Ch 5:20; S Ps 22:5; S 28:7; S Isa 12:2 **26:4** [m] S Isa 12:2; 50:10 [n] S Ps 62:8 [o] S Ge 49:24 **26:5** [p] S Isa 25:12; Eze 26:11 [q] S Isa 25:2 **26:6** [r] S Isa 5:5 [s] Isa 49:26 [t] S Isa 3:15; S 14:30 **26:7** [u] S Ps 26:12 [v] S Ps 25:8 [w] S Ex 14:19; Isa 40:4; 42:16 **26:8** [x] S Dt 18:18; Ps 1:2; Isa 56:1; 64:5 [y] S Ps 37:9; S 130:5 [z] S Ps 145:2; S Isa 12:4 **26:9** [a] S Ps 119:55 [b] Ps 42:1-3; 63:1; 78:34; Isa 55:6 [c] S 1Ch 16:14 [d] Mt 6:33 **26:10** [e] Mt 5:45 [f] Isa 32:6; 59:7,13 [g] S 1Sa 12:24; Isa 22:12-13; Jer 2:19; Hos 11:7; Jn 5:37-38; Ro 2:4 **26:11** [h] S Ps 10:12 [i] Isa 18:3; 44:9,18 [j] S Isa 9:7; Joel 2:18; Zec 1:14 [k] Mic 7:16 [l] S Isa 1:31; Heb 10:27 **26:12** [m] S Ps 119:165; S Isa 9:6 [n] S Ps 68:28 **26:13** [o] Isa 2:8; 10:5,11 [p] S Isa 12:4 [q] Isa 42:8; 63:7 **26:14** [r] S Dt 4:28 [s] S Job 26:5 [t] S Ps 9:5; S Isa 10:3 [u] S Ps 9:6

11O LORD, your hand is lifted high,[h]
but they do not see[i] it.
Let them see your zeal[j] for your
people and be put to
shame;[k]
let the fire[l] reserved for your
enemies consume them.
12LORD, you establish peace[m] for us;
all that we have accomplished
you have done[n] for us.
13O LORD, our God, other lords[o]
besides you have ruled over
us,
but your name[p] alone do we
honor.[q]
14They are now dead,[r] they live no
more;
those departed spirits[s] do not
rise.
You punished them and brought
them to ruin;[t]
you wiped out all memory of
them.[u]
15You have enlarged the nation,
O LORD;
you have enlarged the nation.[v]
You have gained glory for yourself;
you have extended all the
borders[w] of the land.
16LORD, they came to you in their
distress;[x]
when you disciplined[y] them,
they could barely whisper[z] a
prayer.[j]
17As a woman with child and about
to give birth[a]
writhes and cries out in her
pain,
so were we in your presence,
O LORD.

26:15 [v] S Job 12:23; S Isa 14:2 [w] Isa 33:17 **26:16** [x] S Jdg 6:2; S Isa 5:30 [y] S Ps 39:11 [z] Isa 29:4 **26:17** [a] S Isa 21:3; S Jn 16:21; Rev 12:2

[i] 8 Or *judgments* [j] 16 The meaning of the Hebrew for this clause is uncertain.

26:3 PERFECT PEACE . . . MIND IS STEADFAST. As the trying and stressful days of the end of history occur, God will keep in perfect peace the remnant who remain steadfast and faithful to their Lord. In times of trouble we must continually strive to keep our minds turned to the Lord in prayer, trust and hope. We must place our trust in him because he is a Rock who endures forever (v. 4); he is a sure and firm foundation.

26:8–9 WE WAIT FOR YOU. During the final days of history the righteous will wait (i.e., long for) their Lord's appearing. (1) Isaiah describes that longing as an earnest yearning for the final manifestation of the presence of God and his righteousness on earth. (2) Faithful believers in Christ should long and pray for their Lord's return to catch them up from the earth so that they might be with him forever (see article on THE RAPTURE, p. 1864). They desire (a) the Lord's judgments to begin so that the ungodly will learn what justice and righteousness are, and (b) the Lord to reign triumphantly forever (cf. Rev 20—21).

26:16–19 WHISPER A PRAYER. Isaiah recalls the times when God disciplined Israel, and those who remained loyal to God called on him in earnest prayer. Although these faithful ones have died, they will rise from the dead and live again on the earth (see next note).

[18]We were with child, we writhed in pain,
but we gave birth[b] to wind.
We have not brought salvation[c] to the earth;
we have not given birth to people of the world.[d]

[19]But your dead[e] will live;
their bodies will rise.
You who dwell in the dust,[f]
wake up and shout for joy.
Your dew[g] is like the dew of the morning;
the earth will give birth to her dead.[h]

[20]Go, my people, enter your rooms
and shut the doors[i] behind you;
hide[j] yourselves for a little while
until his wrath[k] has passed by.[l]
[21]See, the LORD is coming[m] out of his dwelling[n]
to punish[o] the people of the earth for their sins.
The earth will disclose the blood[p] shed upon her;
she will conceal her slain no longer.

Deliverance of Israel

27 In that day,[q]
the LORD will punish with his sword,[r]
his fierce, great and powerful sword,
Leviathan[s] the gliding serpent,[t]
Leviathan the coiling serpent;
he will slay the monster[u] of the sea.

[2]In that day[v]—
"Sing[w] about a fruitful vineyard:[x]
[3] I, the LORD, watch over it;
I water[y] it continually.
I guard[z] it day and night
so that no one may harm[a] it.
[4] I am not angry.
If only there were briers and thorns confronting me!
I would march against them in battle;
I would set them all on fire.[b]
[5]Or else let them come to me for refuge;[c]
let them make peace[d] with me,
yes, let them make peace with me."

[6]In days to come Jacob will take root,[e]
Israel will bud and blossom[f]
and fill all the world with fruit.[g]

[7]Has ⌊the LORD⌋ struck her
as he struck[h] down those who struck her?
Has she been killed
as those were killed who killed her?
[8]By warfare[k] and exile[i] you contend with her—
with his fierce blast he drives her out,
as on a day the east wind[j] blows.
[9]By this, then, will Jacob's guilt be atoned[k] for,
and this will be the full fruitage of the removal of his sin:[l]
When he makes all the altar stones[m]
to be like chalk stones crushed to pieces,

26:18 [b]Isa 33:11; 59:4 [c]S Ge 49:10; Ps 17:14 [d]Isa 42:6; 49:6; 51:4; Jer 12:16 **26:19** [e]S Isa 25:8; Eph 5:14 [f]Ps 22:29 [g]S Ge 27:28; S Isa 18:4 [h]Isa 66:24; Eze 37:1-14; Da 12:2 **26:20** [i]Ex 12:23 [j]Ps 91:1,4 [k]S Isa 10:25; S 30:27 [l]S Job 14:13 **26:21** [m]Isa 29:6; Jude 1:14 [n]S Isa 18:4 [o]S Isa 13:9,11; 30:12-14 [p]S Job 16:18; Lk 11:50-51 **27:1** [q]ver 13; S Isa 2:11; 28:5 [r]S Ge 3:24; S Dt 32:41; Isa 31:8; 34:6; 65:12; 66:16; Eze 21:3; Na 3:15 [s]S Job 3:8 [t]Job 26:13 [u]S Ps 68:30; S 74:13; Rev 12:9 **27:2** [v]Isa 24:21 [w]S Isa 5:1 [x]Jer 2:21 **27:3** [y]Isa 58:11 [z]S Ps 91:4; S Isa 5:2 [a]S Jn 6:39 **27:4** [b]S ver 11; S Isa 10:17; Mt 3:12; Heb 6:8 **27:5** [c]S Isa 25:4 [d]S Job 22:21; S Ps 119:165; Ro 5:1; 2Co 5:20 **27:6** [e]S 2Ki 19:30; Isa 11:10 [f]S Ge 40:10 [g]S Ps 72:16; Isa 11:1; 37:31; Eze 17:23; 36:8; Hos 14:8 **27:7** [h]Isa 10:26; S 11:4; 37:36-38 **27:8** [i]Isa 49:14; 50:1; 54:7 [j]S Ge 41:6 **27:9** [k]S Ps 78:38 [l]Ro 11:27* [m]S Ex 23:24

[k]*8* See Septuagint; the meaning of the Hebrew for this word is uncertain.

26:19 THEIR BODIES WILL RISE. This is one of the strongest OT declarations of the doctrine of the resurrection of the body (cf. Job 19:26; Ps 16:10; Da 12:2). Those who have faithfully served God (vv. 2–3) will rise from the earth and live again after death (see Jn 5:28–29; 1Co 15:50–53; Php 3:21; see article on THE RESURRECTION OF THE BODY, p. 1779).

26:20–21 ENTER YOUR ROOMS. During the great tribulation, when God punishes the earth's inhabitants (cf. Mic 1:3), those who remain faithful to him will hide themselves and wait before the Lord in prayer until he has accomplished his purposes and the final redemption arrives (see article on THE GREAT TRIBULATION, p. 1456).

27:1 LEVIATHAN . . . SERPENT. This imagery symbolizes evil and the sinful world in revolt against God. At the end of time, all who oppose God will be destroyed (see Rev 19:11–20, notes).

27:2–6 A FRUITFUL VINEYARD. This prophetic song emphasizes God's desire to make Israel a fruitful vineyard. In the kingdom age, Israel will influence the whole earth for God and for righteousness (v. 6).

27:7–11 STRUCK HER. God promises not to destroy Israel completely as he will do to many of their enemies; yet punishment will surely come to many Israelites because of their sin and their need to be pruned in order to bear fruit again.

no Asherah poles[1][n] or incense
altars[o]
will be left standing.
10The fortified city stands
desolate,[p]
an abandoned settlement,
forsaken[q] like the desert;
there the calves graze,[r]
there they lie down;[s]
they strip its branches bare.
11When its twigs are dry, they are
broken off[t]
and women come and make
fires[u] with them.
For this is a people without
understanding;[v]
so their Maker has no
compassion on them,
and their Creator[w] shows them
no favor.[x]

12In that day the LORD will thresh[y]
from the flowing Euphrates[m] to the
Wadi of Egypt,[z] and you, O Israelites,
will be gathered[a] up one by one.
13And in that day[b] a great trumpet[c]
will sound. Those who were perishing
in Assyria and those who were exiled[d]
in Egypt[e] will come and worship[f] the
LORD on the holy mountain[g] in Jerusalem.

Woe to Ephraim

28 Woe[h] to that wreath, the
pride of Ephraim's[i]
drunkards,
to the fading flower, his glorious
beauty,
set on the head of a fertile
valley[j] —
to that city, the pride of those
laid low by wine![k]
2See, the Lord has one who is
powerful[l] and strong.
Like a hailstorm[m] and a
destructive wind,[n]
like a driving rain and a flooding[o]
downpour,
he will throw it forcefully to the
ground.
3That wreath, the pride of
Ephraim's[p] drunkards,
will be trampled[q] underfoot.
4That fading flower, his glorious
beauty,
set on the head of a fertile
valley,[r]
will be like a fig[s] ripe before
harvest —
as soon as someone sees it and
takes it in his hand,
he swallows it.

5In that day[t] the LORD Almighty
will be a glorious[u] crown,[v]
a beautiful wreath
for the remnant[w] of his people.
6He will be a spirit of justice[x]
to him who sits in judgment,[y]
a source of strength
to those who turn back the
battle[z] at the gate.

7And these also stagger[a] from
wine[b]
and reel[c] from beer:
Priests[d] and prophets[e] stagger
from beer
and are befuddled with wine;
they reel from beer,
they stagger when seeing
visions,[f]
they stumble when rendering
decisions.
8All the tables are covered with
vomit[g]
and there is not a spot without
filth.

9"Who is it he is trying to teach?[h]
To whom is he explaining his
message?[i]

27:9 [n] S Ex 34:13 [o] S Lev 26:30; S 2Ch 14:5 **27:10** [p] S Ge 1:2; S Dt 13:16; Isa 5:6; 32:14; Jer 10:22; 26:6; La 1:4; 5:18 [q] S Isa 5:5 [r] S Isa 5:17 [s] Isa 17:2 **27:11** [t] S Isa 10:33 [u] S ver 4; Isa 33:12 [v] S Dt 32:28; S Isa 1:3 [w] Dt 32:18; Isa 41:8; 43:1,7, 15; 44:1-2,21,24 [x] S Isa 9:17; Jer 11:16 **27:12** [y] S Isa 21:10; Mt 3:12 [z] S Ge 15:18 [a] S Dt 30:4; S Isa 1:9; S 11:12; S 17:6 **27:13** [b] S ver 1 [c] S Lev 25:9; S Jdg 3:27; S Mt 24:31 [d] S Ps 106:47 [e] S Isa 10:19; 19:21,25 [f] S Ge 27:29; S Ps 22:29; S 86:9 [g] S Isa 2:2 **28:1** [h] Isa 10:5; 29:1; 30:1; 31:1; 33:1 [i] ver 3; Isa 7:2; 9:9 [j] ver 4 [k] S Lev 10:9; Isa 5:11; Hos 7:5; Am 6:6 **28:2** [l] Isa 40:10 [m] S Jos 10:11 [n] Isa 29:6 [o] S Isa 8:7; S Da 9:26 **28:3** [p] S ver 1 [q] S Job 40:12; S Isa 5:5 **28:4** [r] ver 1 [s] S SS 2:13; Hos 9:10; Na 3:12 **28:5** [t] S Isa 10:20; S 27:1; 29:18; 30:23 [u] S Isa 24:16,23 [v] Isa 62:3; Jer 13:18; Eze 16:12; 21:26; Zec 9:16 [w] S Isa 1:9 **28:6** [x] S 2Sa 14:20; Isa 11:2-4; 32:1, 16; 33:5 [y] Isa 4:4; Jn 5:30 [z] Jdg 9:44-45; S 2Ch 32:8

28:7 [a] S Isa 3:12 [b] S Lev 10:9; S Isa 22:13; S Eph 5:18 [c] S Ps 107:27 [d] Isa 24:2 [e] S Isa 9:15 [f] S Isa 1:1; 29:11 **28:8** [g] Jer 48:26 **28:9** [h] ver 26; Ps 32:8; Isa 2:3; 30:20; 48:17; 50:4; 54:13; Jer 31:34; 32:33 [i] Isa 52:7; 53:1

[1]9 That is, symbols of the goddess Asherah
[m]12 Hebrew *River*

27:12–13 WILL BE GATHERED. At the end of time a remnant of Jews will accept Christ as the Messiah and will gather in Jerusalem to worship the Lord (cf. 11:11–16; see Mt 23:39, note; Ro 11:1,26, notes; Rev 12:6, note).

28:1–29 EPHRAIM'S. In chs. 28—33, Isaiah returns to his own day to prophesy about Israel (called Ephraim) and Judah. He denounces their sin and apostasy and reveals God's coming judgment. Yet the judgment will be no more severe than necessary to purify God's chosen people and bring forth a holy remnant.

28:7 STAGGER FROM WINE. Isaiah describes Israel's sin in terms of the despicable and shameful conduct resulting from their use of intoxicating wine (cf. Am 4:1; 6:1,6). Both the people and religious leaders had traded truth and righteousness for vomit and gross disorientation. Their drunken debauchery demonstrated a clear rejection of God's commands (see Pr 23:31, note). The righteous should be filled with the Spirit rather than with intoxicating wine (see Eph 5:18, note).

To children weaned[j] from their
milk,[k]
to those just taken from the
breast?
10For it is:
Do and do, do and do,
rule on rule, rule on rule[n];
a little here, a little there.[l]"

11Very well then, with foreign lips
and strange tongues[m]
God will speak to this people,[n]
12to whom he said,
"This is the resting place, let
the weary rest";[o]
and, "This is the place of
repose"—
but they would not listen.
13So then, the word of the LORD to
them will become:
Do and do, do and do,
rule on rule, rule on rule;
a little here, a little there[p]—
so that they will go and fall
backward,
be injured[q] and snared and
captured.[r]

14Therefore hear the word of the
LORD,[s] you scoffers[t]
who rule this people in
Jerusalem.
15You boast, "We have entered into a
covenant with death,[u]
with the grave[o] we have made
an agreement.
When an overwhelming scourge
sweeps by,[v]
it cannot touch us,
for we have made a lie[w] our
refuge
and falsehood[p] our hiding
place.[x]"

16So this is what the Sovereign LORD
says:
"See, I lay a stone in Zion,[y]
a tested stone,[z]
a precious cornerstone for a sure
foundation;[a]
the one who trusts will never be
dismayed.[b]
17I will make justice[c] the
measuring line
and righteousness the plumb
line;[d]
hail[e] will sweep away your
refuge, the lie,
and water will overflow[f] your
hiding place.
18Your covenant with death will be
annulled;
your agreement with the grave
will not stand.[g]
When the overwhelming scourge
sweeps by,[h]
you will be beaten down[i] by it.
19As often as it comes it will carry
you away;[j]
morning after morning,[k] by day
and by night,
it will sweep through."
The understanding of this message
will bring sheer terror.[l]
20The bed is too short to stretch out
on,
the blanket too narrow to wrap
around you.[m]
21The LORD will rise up as he did at
Mount Perazim,[n]
he will rouse himself as in the
Valley of Gibeon[o]—
to do his work,[p] his strange work,
and perform his task, his alien
task.
22Now stop your mocking,[q]
or your chains will become
heavier;

28:9 [j]Ps 131:2 [k]Heb 5:12-13; 1Pe 2:2 **28:10** [l]ver 13 **28:11** [m]S Ge 11:7; Isa 33:19; Jer 5:15 [n]Eze 3:5; 1Co 14:21* **28:12** [o]S Ex 14:14; S Jos 1:13; S Job 11:18; S Isa 11:10; Mt 11:28-29 **28:13** [p]ver 10 [q]Mt 21:44 [r]S Isa 8:15 **28:14** [s]Isa 1:10 [t]2Ch 36:16 **28:15** [u]S Job 5:23; Isa 8:19 [v]ver 2, 18; Isa 8:7-8; 10:26; 29:6; 30:28; Da 11:22 [w]S Isa 9:15 [x]S Jdg 9:35; Isa 29:15; Jer 23:24 **28:16** [y]S Isa 14:32 [z]Ps 118:22; Isa 8:14-15; Da 2:34-35,45; Zec 12:3; S Ac 4:11 [a]Jer 51:26; 1Co 3:11; 2Ti 2:19 [b]Isa 29:22; 45:17; 50:7; 54:4; Ro 9:33*; 10:11*; 1Pe 2:6* **28:17** [c]S Ps 11:7; S Isa 5:16 [d]S 2Ki 21:13 [e]S Jos 10:11 [f]S Isa 8:7 **28:18** [g]S Isa 7:7 [h]S ver 15 [i]S Isa 5:5; 63:18; Da 8:13 **28:19** [j]2Ki 24:2 [k]S Ps 5:3 [l]S Job 18:11 **28:20** [m]Isa 59:6 **28:21** [n]S Ge 38:29; S 1Ch 14:11 [o]S Jos 9:3 [p]Isa 10:12; 65:7; Lk 19:41-44 **28:22** [q]S 2Ch 36:16; Jer 29:18; La 2:15; Zep 2:15

[n] *10* Hebrew / *sav lasav sav lasav / kav lakav kav lakav* (possibly meaningless sounds; perhaps a mimicking of the prophet's words); also in verse 13 [o] *15* Hebrew *Sheol*; also in verse 18 [p] *15* Or *false gods*

28:11 STRANGE TONGUES. If the Israelites refused to listen to Isaiah, God would force them to listen through the military might of a foreign power, e.g., the Assyrians, who spoke a language they could not understand.

28:13 BE INJURED AND SNARED. Because they rejected the prophet's word, God would now use the message to harden them, thus ensuring their judgment and capture (see 6:9, note).

28:15 A COVENANT WITH DEATH. The people were choosing their own way by worshiping other gods (cf. 8:19). They felt secure in their agreement with these demonic powers (see article on THE NATURE OF IDOLATRY, p. 394), thinking these powers would provide immunity from harm; in reality, however, they were making a covenant with death.

28:16 I LAY A STONE IN ZION. The stone is the Lord himself (cf. 8:14; 17:10; Ge 49:24); faith in him alone provided hope for salvation. The NT declares that this verse's ultimate fulfillment is found in Jesus Christ (Ro 9:33; 1Co 3:11; Eph 2:20; 1Pe 2:4–6). On Christ as the foundation, God is building a new people, whose commitment must be to righteousness and justice (v. 17; cf. Ps 118:22).

the Lord, the LORD Almighty, has
told me
of the destruction decreed[r]
against the whole land.[s]
23Listen[t] and hear my voice;
pay attention and hear what I
say.
24When a farmer plows for
planting,[u] does he plow
continually?
Does he keep on breaking up
and harrowing the soil?
25When he has leveled the surface,
does he not sow caraway and
scatter cummin?[v]
Does he not plant wheat in its
place,[q]
barley[w] in its plot,[q]
and spelt[x] in its field?
26His God instructs him
and teaches[y] him the right way.
27Caraway is not threshed[z] with a
sledge,[a]
nor is a cartwheel rolled over
cummin;
caraway is beaten out with a
rod,[b]
and cummin with a stick.
28Grain must be ground to make
bread;
so one does not go on threshing
it forever.
Though he drives the wheels of his
threshing cart[c] over it,
his horses do not grind it.
29All this also comes from the LORD
Almighty,
wonderful in counsel[d] and
magnificent in wisdom.[e]

Woe to David's City

29 Woe[f] to you, Ariel, Ariel,[g]
the city[h] where David
settled!
Add year to year
and let your cycle of festivals[i]
go on.
2Yet I will besiege Ariel;[j]
she will mourn and lament,[k]
she will be to me like an altar
hearth.[r][l]
3I will encamp against you all
around;
I will encircle[m] you with towers
and set up my siege works[n]
against you.
4Brought low, you will speak from
the ground;
your speech will mumble[o] out
of the dust.[p]
Your voice will come ghostlike[q]
from the earth;
out of the dust your speech will
whisper.[r]
5But your many enemies will
become like fine dust,[s]
the ruthless[t] hordes like blown
chaff.[u]
Suddenly,[v] in an instant,
6 the LORD Almighty will come[w]
with thunder[x] and earthquake[y]
and great noise,
with windstorm and tempest[z]
and flames of a devouring
fire.[a]
7Then the hordes of all the
nations[b] that fight against
Ariel,[c]
that attack her and her fortress
and besiege her,
will be as it is with a dream,[d]
with a vision in the night—
8as when a hungry man dreams
that he is eating,
but he awakens,[e] and his
hunger remains;
as when a thirsty man dreams that
he is drinking,
but he awakens faint, with his
thirst unquenched.[f]

28:22 [r]S Isa 10:22 [s]S Isa 10:23 **28:23** [t]Isa 32:9 **28:24** [u]Ecc 3:2 **28:25** [v]Mt 23:23 [w]S Ex 9:31 [x]Ex 9:32; Eze 4:9 **28:26** [y]S Ps 94:10 **28:27** [z]S Isa 21:10 [a]S Job 41:30 [b]Isa 10:5 **28:28** [c]S Isa 21:10 **28:29** [d]S Isa 9:6 [e]S Ps 92:5; Ro 11:33 **29:1** [f]Isa 22:12-13; S 28:1 [g]ver 2,7 [h]S 2Sa 5:7 [i]S Isa 1:14 **29:2** [j]S ver 1 [k]S Isa 3:26; La 2:5 [l]Eze 43:15 **29:3** [m]Lk 19:43-44 [n]S 2Ki 25:1 **29:4** [o]Isa 8:19 [p]Isa 47:1; 52:2 [q]S Lev 19:31 [r]Isa 26:16 **29:5** [s]S Dt 9:21; Ps 78:39; 103:15; S Isa 2:22; 37:27; 40:6; 51:12 [t]S Isa 13:11 [u]S Isa 17:13 [v]S Ps 55:15; S Isa 17:14; 1Th 5:3 **29:6** [w]S Isa 26:21; Zec 14:1-5 [x]S Ex 19:16 [y]Mt 24:7; Mk 13:8; Lk 21:11; S Rev 6:12; 11:19 [z]S Ps 50:3; S 55:8; S Isa 28:15 [a]S Lev 10:2; Ps 83:13-15 **29:7** [b]Mic 4:11-12; Zec 12:9 [c]S ver 1 [d]S Job 20:8 **29:8** [e]S Ps 73:20 [f]ver 5,7; Isa 41:11,15; Jer 30:16; Zec 12:3

[q]25 The meaning of the Hebrew for this word is uncertain. [r]2 The Hebrew for *altar hearth* sounds like the Hebrew for *Ariel.*

28:23–29 HEAR MY VOICE. God would act in such a way that a righteous remnant would emerge from the crucible of judgment.

29:1–4 WOE TO YOU, ARIEL. Ariel (meaning "lion of God") is a symbolic name for Jerusalem. Although Jerusalem's inhabitants felt secure and continued their religious festivals as usual, God would bring devastating judgment on them because of their sin. When God's people do not recognize their spiritual poverty and their need to cry out to him in repentance and prayer, he eventually has to remove them from their place in his kingdom (see Rev 2:5, note).

29:5–8 MANY ENEMIES. Although terrible judgment was coming on Jerusalem, it would not involve total destruction. God would deliver his people and destroy Jerusalem's enemies. Isaiah's description likely refers to their deliverance from Assyria during Sennacherib's invasion (see 10:5–19). Unfortunately, even this miracle of God did not accomplish a thorough repentance and true obedience in his people; thus a more devastating judgment came later, during the Babylonian invasions (605, 597 and 586 B.C.).

So will it be with the hordes of all
the nations
that fight against Mount Zion.[g]

9 Be stunned and amazed,[h]
blind yourselves and be
sightless;[i]
be drunk,[j] but not from wine,[k]
stagger,[l] but not from beer.
10 The LORD has brought over you a
deep sleep:[m]
He has sealed your eyes[n] (the
prophets);[o]
he has covered your heads (the
seers).[p]

11 For you this whole vision[q] is
nothing but words sealed[r] in a scroll.
And if you give the scroll to someone
who can read, and say to him, "Read
this, please," he will answer, "I can't;
it is sealed." 12 Or if you give the scroll
to someone who cannot read, and say,
"Read this, please," he will answer, "I
don't know how to read."

13 The Lord says:

"These people[s] come near to me
with their mouth
and honor me with their lips,[t]
but their hearts are far from
me.[u]
Their worship of me
is made up only of rules taught
by men.[s][v]
14 Therefore once more I will astound
these people
with wonder upon wonder;[w]
the wisdom of the wise[x] will
perish,
the intelligence of the intelligent
will vanish.[y]"
15 Woe to those who go to great
depths
to hide[z] their plans from the
LORD,
who do their work in darkness and
think,
"Who sees us?[a] Who will
know?"[b]
16 You turn things upside down,
as if the potter were thought to
be like the clay![c]
Shall what is formed say to him
who formed[d] it,
"He did not make me"?
Can the pot say of the potter,[e]
"He knows nothing"?[f]
17 In a very short time,[g] will not
Lebanon[h] be turned into a
fertile field[i]
and the fertile field seem like a
forest?[j]
18 In that day[k] the deaf[l] will hear
the words of the scroll,
and out of gloom and darkness[m]
the eyes of the blind will see.[n]
19 Once more the humble[o] will
rejoice in the LORD;
the needy[p] will rejoice in the
Holy One[q] of Israel.
20 The ruthless[r] will vanish,[s]
the mockers[t] will disappear,
and all who have an eye for
evil[u] will be cut down—
21 those who with a word make a
man out to be guilty,
who ensnare the defender in
court[v]

29:8 [g] Isa 17:12-14; 54:17 **29:9** [h] ver 14; Jer 4:9; Hab 1:5 [i] S Isa 6:10 [j] Isa 51:17; 63:6; Jer 13:13; 25:27 [k] S Lev 10:9; Isa 28:1; 51:21-22 [l] S Ps 60:3; S Isa 3:12 **29:10** [m] S Jdg 4:21; Jnh 1:5 [n] Ps 69:23; S Isa 6:9-10; 44:18; Ro 11:8*; 2Th 2:9-11 [o] Mic 3:6 [p] S 1Sa 9:9 **29:11** [q] S Isa 28:7 [r] S Isa 8:16; Da 8:26; 12:9; Mt 13:11; Rev 5:1-2 **29:13** [s] Jer 14:11; Hag 1:2; 2:14 [t] S Ps 50:16 [u] S Ps 119:70; Isa 58:2; Jer 12:2; Eze 33:31 [v] Mt 15:8-9*; Mk 7:6-7*; Col 2:22 **29:14** [w] S Job 10:16 [x] S Job 5:13; Jer 8:9; 49:7 [y] Isa 6:9-10; 1Co 1:19* **29:15** [z] S Ge 3:8; S Isa 28:15 [a] S Job 8:3; Ps 10:11-13; 94:7; Isa 47:10; 57:12; Eze 8:12; 9:9 [b] S 2Ki 21:16; S Job 22:13 **29:16** [c] S Job 10:9; S Isa 10:15 [d] S Ge 2:7 [e] Isa 45:9; 64:8; Jer 18:6; Ro 9:20-21* [f] S Job 9:12 **29:17** [g] S Isa 10:25 [h] S Isa 2:13 [i] Ps 84:6; 107:33 [j] Isa 32:15 **29:18** [k] S Isa 28:5 [l] Mk 7:37 [m] S Ps 107:14 [n] S Ps 146:8; S Isa 32:3; Mt 11:5; Lk 7:22 **29:19** [o] Ps 25:9; 37:11; Isa 61:1; Mt 5:5; 11:29 [p] S Ps 72:4; S Isa 3:15; S 14:30; Mt 11:5; Lk 7:22; Jas 1:9; 2:5 [q] ver 23; Isa 1:4; S 5:19; S 12:6; 30:11 **29:20** [r] S Isa 9:4; S 13:11 [s] Isa 34:12 [t] S 2Ch 36:16; Isa 28:22 [u] S Job 15:35; Ps 7:14; Isa 32:7; 33:11; 59:4; Eze 11:2; Mic 2:1; Na 1:11 **29:21** [v] Am 5:10,15

[s] *13* Hebrew; Septuagint *They worship me in vain; / their teachings are but rules taught by men*

29:13 HEARTS ARE FAR FROM ME. God's people were coming before him in prayer, worship, song and praise, even though their hearts were not committed to him or his commands. They acted as if God's revelation and his righteous standards were not obligatory. Instead of cherishing God and his word, they filled their lives with the religious rituals and traditions taught by their leaders, and in false security they lived for themselves (cf. Jer 4:3–4; 24:7; 31:31–34). A similar destructive spiritual condition exists in some churches today. People praise and honor God with their lips, while having no real love for God or his righteous precepts. When their worship service is over, they seek the pleasures of sin and the world to satisfy their worldly desires (see Mk 7:6,8, notes); the result is spiritual blindness and deception (v. 14).

29:17–24 A FERTILE FIELD. Isaiah's prophecies of judgment are never without hope, for they characteristically include the theme of Israel's restoration. These verses envision the last days of this age when the humble and needy of Israel will turn to God (vv. 18–19) and the wicked will be destroyed (vv. 20–21). Israel's full restoration will occur shortly before Christ's return to earth to reign (see Ro 11:26, note; Rev 12:6, note; see article on ISRAEL IN GOD'S PLAN OF SALVATION, p. 1730). The blessings of sight for the blind and hearing for the deaf (v. 18; cf. 32:3; 35:5) accompanied Christ's first coming; God's people will receive full redemption at his second coming.

and with false testimony[w]
deprive the innocent of
justice.[x]

22Therefore this is what the LORD,
who redeemed[y] Abraham,[z] says to
the house of Jacob:

"No longer will Jacob be
ashamed;[a]
no longer will their faces grow
pale.[b]
23When they see among them their
children,[c]
the work of my hands,[d]
they will keep my name holy;[e]
they will acknowledge the
holiness of the Holy One[f]
of Jacob,
and will stand in awe of the God
of Israel.
24Those who are wayward[g] in spirit
will gain understanding;[h]
those who complain will accept
instruction."[i]

Woe to the Obstinate Nation

30 "Woe[j] to the obstinate
children,"[k]
declares the LORD,
"to those who carry out plans that
are not mine,
forming an alliance,[l] but not by
my Spirit,
heaping sin upon sin;
2who go down to Egypt[m]
without consulting[n] me;
who look for help to Pharaoh's
protection,[o]
to Egypt's shade for refuge.[p]
3But Pharaoh's protection will be to
your shame,
Egypt's shade[q] will bring you
disgrace.[r]
4Though they have officials in
Zoan[s]
and their envoys have arrived in
Hanes,
5everyone will be put to shame
because of a people[t] useless[u]
to them,
who bring neither help[v] nor
advantage,
but only shame and disgrace.[w]"

6An oracle[x] concerning the animals
of the Negev:[y]

Through a land of hardship and
distress,[z]
of lions[a] and lionesses,
of adders and darting snakes,[b]
the envoys carry their riches on
donkeys'[c] backs,
their treasures[d] on the humps
of camels,
to that unprofitable nation,
7 to Egypt, whose help is utterly
useless.[e]
Therefore I call her
Rahab[f] the Do-Nothing.

8Go now, write it on a tablet[g] for
them,
inscribe it on a scroll,[h]
that for the days to come
it may be an everlasting
witness.[i]
9These are rebellious[j] people,
deceitful[k] children,
children unwilling to listen to
the LORD's instruction.[l]
10They say to the seers,[m]
"See no more visions[n]!"
and to the prophets,
"Give us no more visions of
what is right!
Tell us pleasant things,[o]

29:21 [w] Pr 21:28 [x] S Isa 2:7; Hab 1:4 **29:22** [y] S Ex 6:6 [z] Ge 17:16; Isa 41:8; 51:2; 63:16 [a] Ps 22:5; 25:3; S Isa 28:16; 49:23; 61:7; Joel 2:26; Zep 3:11 [b] Jer 30:6,10; Joel 2:6,21; Na 2:10 **29:23** [c] Isa 49:20-26; 53:10; 54:1-3 [d] S Ps 8:6; S Isa 19:25 [e] Mt 6:9 [f] S ver 19; S Isa 5:19 **29:24** [g] Ps 95:10; S Pr 12:8; Isa 28:7; Heb 5:2 [h] Isa 1:3; 32:4; 41:20; 60:16 [i] Isa 30:21; 42:16 **30:1** [j] S Isa 28:1 [k] S Dt 21:18; S Isa 1:2 [l] S 2Ki 17:4; S Isa 8:12 **30:2** [m] 2Ki 25:26; Isa 31:1; 36:6; Jer 2:18,36; 42:14; Eze 17:15; 29:16 [n] S Ge 25:22; S Nu 27:21 [o] Isa 36:9 [p] S Isa 4:6 **30:3** [q] Jdg 9:8-15 [r] ver 5; S Ps 44:13; Isa 20:4-5; 36:6 **30:4** [s] S Nu 13:22 **30:5** [t] ver 7; Isa 20:5; 31:1; 36:6 [u] S 2Ki 18:21 [v] S Ps 108:12; Jer 37:3-5 [w] S ver 3; S 2Ki 18:21; Eze 17:15 **30:6** [x] Isa 13:1 [y] S Jdg 1:9 [z] S Ex 1:13; 5:10, 21; Isa 5:30; 8:22; Jer 11:4 [a] S Isa 5:29; 35:9 [b] S Dt 8:15 [c] S Ge 42:26; S 1Sa 25:18 [d] S Isa 15:7 **30:7** [e] S 2Ki 18:21; S Jer 2:36 [f] S Job 9:13 **30:8** [g] S Dt 27:8 [h] S Ex 17:14; S Isa 8:1; Jer 25:13; 30:2; 36:28; Hab 2:2 [i] Jos 24:26-27 **30:9** [j] S Ps 78:8; S Isa 1:2; S Eze 2:6 [k] Isa 28:15; 59:3-4 [l] S Isa 1:10 **30:10** [m] S 1Sa 9:9 [n] Jer 11:21; 32:3; Am 7:13 [o] S 1Ki 22:8; S Jer 4:10

30:1–5 PLANS THAT ARE NOT MINE. Judah had sought an alliance with Egypt to gain protection from Assyria (cf. 2Ki 18:21), thereby rejecting God's counsel, refusing to believe his promises and throwing aside his principles of holy living. They were guilty of despising the Lord and preferring the might of human achievement to the power of the Spirit (see Zec 4:6, note).

30:6–7 THE NEGEV. The Negev was the rugged and dangerous area of southern Palestine, filled with wild animals. Delegations from Judah had to pass through this region in order to take their merchandise and riches to Egypt. Isaiah prophesies that their journey to Egypt would do them no good; the Egyptians could not help them.

30:10 TELL US PLEASANT THINGS. The people could not bear to hear prophetic words that condemned their sinful lifestyle. (1) They were tired of hearing about God and the holy lifestyle he required. They wanted to hear encouraging, pleasant and inoffensive messages. (2) Paul states that in the last days a similar state of mind will prevail among some within the churches. These people will reject God's messengers who proclaim the truth and instead choose leaders who preach what they want to hear. They will insist on pleasant and flattering messages that do not expose their sin and worldliness, but rather assure them of their security and God's love no matter what they do (see 2Ti 4:3–4, note).

prophesy illusions.[p]
11 Leave this way,[q]
get off this path,
and stop confronting[r] us
with the Holy One[s] of Israel!"

12 Therefore, this is what the Holy
One[t] of Israel says:

"Because you have rejected this
message,[u]
relied on oppression[v]
and depended on deceit,
13 this sin will become for you
like a high wall,[w] cracked and
bulging,
that collapses[x] suddenly,[y] in
an instant.
14 It will break in pieces like
pottery,[z]
shattered so mercilessly
that among its pieces not a
fragment will be found
for taking coals from a hearth
or scooping water out of a
cistern."

15 This is what the Sovereign[a] LORD,
the Holy One[b] of Israel, says:

"In repentance and rest[c] is your
salvation,
in quietness and trust[d] is your
strength,
but you would have none of it.[e]
16 You said, 'No, we will flee[f] on
horses.'[g]
Therefore you will flee!
You said, 'We will ride off on swift
horses.'
Therefore your pursuers will be
swift!
17 A thousand will flee
at the threat of one;
at the threat of five[h]
you will all flee[i] away,
till you are left[j]
like a flagstaff on a
mountaintop,
like a banner[k] on a hill."

18 Yet the LORD longs[l] to be
gracious to you;
he rises to show you
compassion.[m]
For the LORD is a God of justice.[n]
Blessed are all who wait for
him![o]

19 O people of Zion, who live in Jerusalem, you will weep no more.[p] How
gracious he will be when you cry for
help![q] As soon as he hears, he will
answer[r] you. 20 Although the Lord
gives you the bread[s] of adversity and
the water of affliction, your teachers[t]
will be hidden[u] no more; with your
own eyes you will see them. 21 Whether
you turn to the right or to the left, your
ears will hear a voice[v] behind you,
saying, "This is the way;[w] walk in it."
22 Then you will defile your idols[x]
overlaid with silver and your images
covered with gold;[y] you will throw
them away like a menstrual[z] cloth
and say to them, "Away with you![a]"

23 He will also send you rain[b] for the
seed you sow in the ground, and the
food that comes from the land will be
rich[c] and plentiful.[d] In that day[e]
your cattle will graze in broad meadows.[f] 24 The oxen[g] and donkeys that
work the soil will eat fodder[h] and
mash, spread out with fork[i] and shov-
el. 25 In the day of great slaughter,[j]
when the towers[k] fall, streams of water will flow[l] on every high mountain
and every lofty hill. 26 The moon will
shine like the sun,[m] and the sunlight
will be seven times brighter, like the
light of seven full days, when the LORD
binds up the bruises of his people and
heals[n] the wounds he inflicted.

27 See, the Name[o] of the LORD comes
from afar,

30:10 [p] Jer 23:26; 25:9; 26:9; 36:29; Eze 13:7; Ro 16:18; 2Ti 4:3-4 **30:11** [q] ver 21; Pr 3:6; Isa 35:8-9; 48:17 [r] S Job 21:14 [s] S Isa 29:19 **30:12** [t] ver 15; S Isa 5:19; 31:1 [u] S Isa 5:24 [v] S Ps 10:7; S 12:5; S Isa 5:7 **30:13** [w] S Ne 2:17; Ps 62:3; S 80:12 [x] S 1Ki 20:30 [y] S Isa 17:14 **30:14** [z] S Ps 2:9 **30:15** [a] Jer 7:20; Eze 3:11 [b] S ver 12 [c] S Ex 14:14; S Jos 1:13 [d] S 2Ch 20:12; Isa 32:17 [e] Isa 8:6; 42:24; 57:17 **30:16** [f] Jer 46:6 [g] S Dt 17:16; 1Ki 10:28-29; S Ps 20:7; Isa 31:1,3; 36:8 **30:17** [h] S Lev 26:8 [i] Lev 26:36; Dt 28:25; S 2Ki 7:7 [j] S Isa 1:8 [k] S Ps 20:5 **30:18** [l] S Ge 43:31; Isa 42:14; 2Pe 3:9,15 [m] Ps 78:38; Isa 48:9; Jnh 3:10 [n] S Ps 11:7; S Isa 5:16 [o] S Ps 27:14; Isa 25:9; 33:2; 40:31; 64:4; La 3:25; Da 12:12 **30:19** [p] S Isa 25:8; 60:20; 61:3 [q] S Job 24:12 [r] Job 22:27; Ps 50:15; S 86:7; Isa 41:17; 58:9; 65:24; Zec 13:9; Mt 7:7-11 **30:20** [s] 1Ki 22:27 [t] S Isa 28:9 [u] Ps 74:9; Am 8:11 **30:21** [v] S Isa 29:24 [w] S ver 11; S Job 33:11 **30:22** [x] S Ex 32:4; S Isa 17:8 [y] S Job 22:24; Isa 31:7 [z] Lev 15:19-23 [a] Eze 7:19-20 **30:23** [b] S Dt 28:12; Isa 65:21-22 [c] Isa 25:6; 55:2; Jer 31:14 [d] S Job 36:31; Isa 62:8 [e] S Isa 28:5 [f] S Ps 65:13 **30:24** [g] Isa 32:14,20 [h] S Job 6:5 [i] Mt 3:12; Lk 3:17 **30:25** [j] S Isa 13:5; 34:6; 65:12; Jer 25:32; 50:27 [k] S Isa 2:15 [l] S Ex 17:6; Isa 32:2; 41:18; Joel 3:18; Zec 14:8 **30:26** [m] Isa 24:23; 60:19-20; Zec 14:7; Rev 21:23; 22:5 [n] S Dt 32:39; S 2Ch 7:14; Ps 107:20; S Isa 1:5; Jer 3:22; 17:14; Hos 14:4 **30:27** [o] 1Ki 18:24; Ps 20:1; Isa 59:19; 64:2

30:15 IN REPENTANCE . . . IS YOUR SALVATION. Judah could be saved if only its rulers and people would return to God and put their confidence in him. Since they would not, however, they would be defeated and stand alone like a banner on a hill, a stark example of the consequences of forsaking God (v. 17).

30:18–26 LONGS TO BE GRACIOUS. The Lord desires to be gracious to his people and to bless all who yearn for him (see Ps 42:2, note). He will pour out these blessings on the believing remnant when he restores them to a place of favor alongside the Messiah.

30:25 THE DAY OF GREAT SLAUGHTER. The long-range application of this prophecy may be to the battle of Armageddon, when God destroys all the wicked (see Rev 16:16, note; 19:17, note).

with burning anger[p] and dense
clouds of smoke;
his lips are full of wrath,[q]
and his tongue is a consuming
fire.[r]
28His breath[s] is like a rushing
torrent,[t]
rising up to the neck.[u]
He shakes the nations in the
sieve[v] of destruction;
he places in the jaws of the
peoples
a bit[w] that leads them astray.
29And you will sing
as on the night you celebrate a
holy festival;[x]
your hearts will rejoice[y]
as when people go up with
flutes[z]
to the mountain[a] of the LORD,
to the Rock[b] of Israel.
30The LORD will cause men to hear
his majestic voice[c]
and will make them see his
arm[d] coming down
with raging anger[e] and consuming
fire,[f]
with cloudburst, thunderstorm[g]
and hail.[h]
31The voice of the LORD will shatter
Assyria;[i]
with his scepter he will strike[j]
them down.
32Every stroke the LORD lays on
them
with his punishing rod[k]
will be to the music of
tambourines[l] and harps,
as he fights them in battle with
the blows of his arm.[m]
33Topheth[n] has long been prepared;
it has been made ready for the
king.
Its fire pit has been made deep
and wide,
with an abundance of fire and
wood;
the breath[o] of the LORD,
like a stream of burning
sulfur,[p]
sets it ablaze.[q]

30:27 [p] Isa 26:20; 66:14; Eze 22:31 [q] Isa 10:5; 13:5 [r] S ver 30; S Job 41:21
30:28 [s] S Isa 11:4 [t] S Ps 50:3; S Isa 28:15 [u] S Isa 8:8 [v] Am 9:9 [w] 2Ki 19:28
30:29 [x] Isa 25:6 [y] Isa 12:1 [z] S 1Sa 10:5 [a] S Ps 42:4; Mt 26:30 [b] S Ge 49:24
30:30 [c] S Ps 68:33 [d] Isa 9:12; 40:10; 51:9; 52:10; 53:1; 59:16; 62:8; 63:12 [e] S ver 27; S Isa 10:25 [f] S Isa 4:4; 47:14 [g] Ex 20:18; Ps 29:3 [h] S Ex 9:18
30:31 [i] S Isa 10:5,12 [j] S Isa 11:4
30:32 [k] Isa 10:26 [l] S Ex 15:20 [m] S Isa 11:15; Eze 32:10
30:33 [n] S 2Ki 23:10 [o] S Ex 15:10; S 2Sa 22:16 [p] S Ge 19:24; S Rev 9:17 [q] S Isa 1:31

31:1 [r] S Isa 28:1 [s] S Dt 17:16; S Isa 30:2,5; S Jer 37:5 [t] S Isa 30:16 [u] S Isa 2:7 [v] Job 6:10; S Isa 1:4; S 30:12 [w] S Dt 20:1; S Pr 21:31; S Isa 9:13; Jer 46:9; Eze 29:16
31:2 [x] S Ps 92:5; Ro 16:27 [y] Isa 45:7; 47:11; Am 3:6 [z] Nu 23:19; S Pr 19:21 [a] S Isa 1:4; 29:15; 32:6
31:3 [b] Isa 20:5; 36:9 [c] S Ps 9:20; Eze 28:9; 2Th 2:4 [d] S Isa 30:16 [e] Ne 1:10; S Job 30:21; Isa 9:17,21; Jer 51:25; Eze 20:34 [f] Isa 10:3; 30:5-7 [g] S Isa 20:6; Jer 17:5
31:4 [h] Nu 24:9; S 1Sa 17:34; Hos 11:10; Am 3:8

Woe to Those Who Rely on Egypt

31 Woe[r] to those who go down
to Egypt[s] for help,
who rely on horses,[t]
who trust in the multitude of their
chariots[u]
and in the great strength of
their horsemen,
but do not look to the Holy One[v]
of Israel,
or seek help from the LORD.[w]
2Yet he too is wise[x] and can bring
disaster;[y]
he does not take back his
words.[z]
He will rise up against the house
of the wicked,[a]
against those who help
evildoers.
3But the Egyptians[b] are men and
not God;[c]
their horses[d] are flesh and not
spirit.
When the LORD stretches out his
hand,[e]
he who helps will stumble,
he who is helped[f] will fall;
both will perish together.[g]

4This is what the LORD says to me:

"As a lion[h] growls,
a great lion over his prey—
and though a whole band of
shepherds[i]
is called together against him,
he is not frightened by their shouts
or disturbed by their clamor[j]—
so the LORD Almighty will come
down[k]
to do battle on Mount Zion and
on its heights.
5Like birds hovering[l] overhead,
the LORD Almighty will shield[m]
Jerusalem;
he will shield it and deliver[n] it,
he will 'pass over'[o] it and will
rescue it."

[i] Jer 3:15; 23:4; Eze 34:23; Na 3:18 [j] Ps 74:23 [k] Isa 42:13
31:5 [l] S Ge 1:2; S Mt 23:37 [m] S Ps 91:4; S Isa 5:2; S Zec 9:15 [n] S Ps 34:7; Isa 37:35; 38:6 [o] S Ex 12:23

30:27–33 WITH BURNING ANGER. This prophecy concerns the overthrow of the Assyrian army (v. 31; cf. 37:36).

31:1 WOE TO THEM. Isaiah pronounces a woe to the evildoers (v. 2) who were trusting in Egypt's horses and chariots rather than in the Lord (cf. Dt 17:16). Believers today must be careful not to commit the same sin as Judah; we must put our faith in God, revere his commands, and seek him daily for his grace and help in all our needs (cf. Heb 4:16).

31:4–9 TO DO BATTLE ON MOUNT ZION. God would come as a lion, fight the Assyrians as a champion warrior, and defend Jerusalem (cf. 37:36); thus Isaiah called on the Israelites to reject their idols and return to the Lord in faith.

6Return[p] to him you have so greatly revolted[q] against, O Israelites. 7For
in that day[r] every one of you will reject the idols of silver and gold[s] your
sinful hands have made.[t]

8"Assyria[u] will fall by a sword that
is not of man;
a sword, not of mortals, will
devour[v] them.
They will flee before the sword
and their young men will be put
to forced labor.[w]
9Their stronghold[x] will fall
because of terror;
at sight of the battle standard[y]
their commanders will
panic,[z]"
declares the LORD,
whose fire[a] is in Zion,
whose furnace[b] is in Jerusalem.

The Kingdom of Righteousness

32 See, a king[c] will reign in
righteousness
and rulers will rule with
justice.[d]
2Each man will be like a shelter[e]
from the wind
and a refuge from the storm,[f]
like streams of water[g] in the
desert[h]
and the shadow of a great rock
in a thirsty land.
3Then the eyes of those who see
will no longer be closed,[i]
and the ears[j] of those who
hear will listen.
4The mind of the rash will know
and understand,[k]
and the stammering tongue[l]
will be fluent and clear.
5No longer will the fool[m] be called
noble
nor the scoundrel be highly
respected.
6For the fool speaks folly,[n]
his mind is busy with evil:[o]
He practices ungodliness[p]
and spreads error[q] concerning
the LORD;

31:6 [p] S Job 22:23; S Isa 1:27 [q] S Isa 1:5 31:7 [r] Isa 29:18 [s] S Isa 30:22 [t] S Ps 135:15 31:8 [u] S Isa 10:12 [v] S Ex 12:12; Isa 10:12; 14:25; S 27:1; 33:1; 37:7; Jer 25:12; Hab 2:8 [w] S Ge 49:15; S Dt 20:11 31:9 [x] Dt 32:31, 37 [y] S Isa 18:3; S Jer 4:6 [z] Jer 51:9; Na 3:7 [a] S Isa 10:17 [b] Ps 21:9; Mal 4:1 32:1 [c] S Ps 149:2; S Isa 6:5; 55:4; Eze 37:24 [d] Ps 72:1-4; S Isa 9:7; S 28:6 32:2 [e] S 1Ki 18:4 [f] S Ps 55:8 [g] S Ps 23:2; S Isa 30:25; 49:10; Jer 31:9 [h] S Ps 107:35; Isa 44:3 32:3 [i] S Isa 29:18; 35:5; 42:7,16 [j] S Dt 29:4 32:4 [k] Isa 6:10; S 29:24 [l] Isa 35:6 32:5 [m] S 1Sa 25:25 32:6 [n] S Pr 19:3 [o] S Pr 24:2; S Isa 26:10 [p] S Isa 9:17 [q] Isa 3:12; 9:16 [r] S Isa 3:15 32:7 [s] Jer 5:26-28; Da 12:10 [t] S Isa 29:20; Mic 7:3 [u] S Ps 72:4; Isa 29:19; 61:1 [v] S Isa 29:21 32:8 [w] 1Ch 29:9; S Pr 11:25 [x] Isa 14:24 32:9 [y] S Isa 4:1 [z] Isa 28:23 [a] ver 11; Isa 47:8; Da 4:4; Am 6:1; Zep 2:15 32:10 [b] Isa 37:30 [c] Isa 5:5-6; S 24:7 32:11 [d] Isa 33:14 [e] S ver 9 [f] Isa 47:2; Mic 1:8; Na 3:5 [g] S Isa 3:24 32:12 [h] Na 2:7 [i] Isa 16:9 32:13 [j] S Isa 5:6; Hos 10:8 [k] S Isa 24:11 [l] S Isa 23:7 32:14 [m] S Isa 13:22 [n] S Isa 6:11; S 27:10 [o] S Isa 2:15; 34:13

the hungry he leaves empty[r]
and from the thirsty he
withholds water.
7The scoundrel's methods are
wicked,[s]
he makes up evil schemes[t]
to destroy the poor with lies,
even when the plea of the
needy[u] is just.[v]
8But the noble man makes noble
plans,
and by noble deeds[w] he
stands.[x]

The Women of Jerusalem

9You women[y] who are so
complacent,
rise up and listen[z] to me;
you daughters who feel secure,[a]
hear what I have to say!
10In little more than a year[b]
you who feel secure will
tremble;
the grape harvest will fail,[c]
and the harvest of fruit will not
come.
11Tremble,[d] you complacent women;
shudder, you daughters who feel
secure![e]
Strip off your clothes,[f]
put sackcloth[g] around your
waists.
12Beat your breasts[h] for the
pleasant fields,
for the fruitful vines[i]
13and for the land of my people,
a land overgrown with thorns
and briers[j]—
yes, mourn[k] for all houses of
merriment
and for this city of revelry.[l]
14The fortress[m] will be abandoned,
the noisy city deserted;[n]
citadel and watchtower[o] will
become a wasteland forever,
the delight of donkeys,[p] a
pasture for flocks,[q]
15till the Spirit[r] is poured upon us
from on high,

[p] S Ps 104:11 [q] S Isa 5:17 32:15 [r] S Isa 11:2; S Eze 37:9

32:1–8 A KING WILL REIGN IN RIGHTEOUSNESS. This prophecy foresees Christ's worldwide reign (cf. 9:7; 11:4; 16:5), characterized by righteousness and by people who live in accordance with God's word.

32:9–14 WOMEN WHO ARE SO COMPLACENT. Many Israelites were complacent about sin, even though it was destroying their families and their nation; instead, Isaiah told them they should beat their breasts (v. 12), tremble (v. 11), put on sackcloth (v. 11), and shudder (v. 11) as they cry out to God until he pours out the Spirit from heaven (v. 15). Today, whenever sin, Satan and the world gain inroads into the church, we too should mourn and cry out for God to restore righteousness and the fullness of the Spirit in his house (vv. 15–16; cf. ch. 35).

32:15–20 TILL THE SPIRIT IS POURED

and the desert becomes a fertile
field,[s]
and the fertile field seems like a
forest.[t]
16Justice[u] will dwell in the desert[v]
and righteousness[w] live in the
fertile field.
17The fruit of righteousness[x] will be
peace;[y]
the effect of righteousness will
be quietness and
confidence[z] forever.
18My people will live in peaceful[a]
dwelling places,
in secure homes,[b]
in undisturbed places of rest.[c]
19Though hail[d] flattens the forest[e]
and the city is leveled[f]
completely,
20how blessed you will be,
sowing[g] your seed by every
stream,[h]
and letting your cattle and
donkeys range free.[i]

Distress and Help

33 Woe[j] to you, O destroyer,
you who have not been
destroyed!
Woe to you, O traitor,
you who have not been betrayed!
When you stop destroying,
you will be destroyed;[k]
when you stop betraying,
you will be betrayed.[l]

2O LORD, be gracious[m] to us;
we long for you.
Be our strength[n] every morning,
our salvation[o] in time of
distress.[p]
3At the thunder of your voice,[q] the
peoples flee;[r]
when you rise up,[s] the nations
scatter.
4Your plunder,[t] O nations, is
harvested[u] as by young
locusts;[v]
like a swarm of locusts men
pounce on it.
5The LORD is exalted,[w] for he
dwells on high;[x]
he will fill Zion with justice[y]
and righteousness.[z]
6He will be the sure foundation for
your times,
a rich store of salvation[a] and
wisdom and knowledge;
the fear[b] of the LORD is the key
to this treasure.[t][c]

7Look, their brave men[d] cry aloud
in the streets;
the envoys[e] of peace weep
bitterly.
8The highways are deserted,
no travelers[f] are on the
roads.[g]
The treaty is broken,[h]
its witnesses[u] are despised,
no one is respected.
9The land mourns[v][i] and wastes
away,
Lebanon[j] is ashamed and
withers;[k]
Sharon[l] is like the Arabah,
and Bashan[m] and Carmel[n] drop
their leaves.

10"Now will I arise,[o]" says the LORD.
"Now will I be exalted;[p]
now will I be lifted up.
11You conceive[q] chaff,
you give birth[r] to straw;
your breath is a fire[s] that
consumes you.
12The peoples will be burned as if to
lime;[t]
like cut thornbushes[u] they will
be set ablaze.[v]"

32:15 [s]Ps 107:35; Isa 35:1-2 [t]Isa 29:17 **32:16** [u]S Isa 9:7; S 28:6 [v]Isa 35:1, 6; 42:11 [w]S Ps 48:1; S Isa 1:26 **32:17** [x]S Ps 85:10 [y]S Ps 119:165; S Isa 9:7; Ro 14:17; Heb 12:11; Jas 3:18 [z]S Isa 30:15 **32:18** [a]S Isa 2:4 [b]S Isa 26:1; 33:20; 37:33; 65:21; 66:14; Am 9:14 [c]S Jos 1:13; S Job 11:18; Hos 2:18-23 **32:19** [d]Isa 28:17 [e]S Isa 10:19; Zec 11:2 [f]S Job 40:11; S Isa 19:18; 24:10; 27:10 **32:20** [g]S Ecc 11:1 [h]S Dt 28:12 [i]Job 39:8; S Isa 30:24 **33:1** [j]S 2Ki 19:21; S Isa 28:1 [k]S Isa 31:8; S Mt 7:2 [l]S Isa 21:2; Jer 30:16; Eze 39:10 **33:2** [m]S Ge 43:29; S Ezr 9:8 [n]Isa 40:10; 51:9; 59:16; 63:5 [o]S Ps 13:5; S Isa 12:2 [p]S Isa 5:30 **33:3** [q]S Ps 46:6; S 68:33 [r]S Ps 68:1; S Isa 13:14 [s]ver 10; Nu 10:35; Ps 12:5; Isa 59:16-18 **33:4** [t]S Nu 14:3; S 2Ki 7:16 [u]S Isa 17:5; Joel 3:13 [v]Joel 1:4 **33:5** [w]S Isa 5:16 [x]S Job 16:19 [y]S Isa 9:7; S 28:6 [z]S Isa 1:26 **33:6** [a]S Isa 12:2; 26:1; 51:6; 60:18 [b]S Pr 1:7; Isa 11:2-3; Mt 6:33 [c]S Ge 39:3; S Job 22:25 **33:7** [d]Isa 10:34 [e]S 2Ki 18:37 **33:8** [f]Isa 60:15; Zec 7:14 [g]S Jdg 5:6; Isa 30:21; 35:8 [h]S 2Ki 18:14 **33:9** [i]S Isa 3:26 [j]S 2Ki 19:23; Isa 2:13; 35:2; 37:24; Jer 22:6 [k]S Isa 15:6 [l]S 1Ch 27:29 [m]Mic 7:14 [n]1Ki 18:19; Isa 35:2; Na 1:4 **33:10** [o]S ver 3; Isa 2:21 [p]S Isa 5:16 **33:11** [q]Ps 7:14; Isa 59:4; Jas 1:15 [r]S Isa 26:18 [s]Isa 1:31 **33:12** [t]Am 2:1 [u]S Isa 5:6 [v]S Isa 10:17; S 27:11

[t]6 Or *is a treasure from him* [u]8 Dead Sea Scrolls; Masoretic Text / *the cities* [v]9 Or *dries up*

UPON US. Isaiah returns to the theme of the righteous reign of the king (see vv. 1–8, note). (1) The righteousness and blessing of the kingdom age will come about because the Spirit will be poured out upon the people and will work in people's hearts (cf. 44:3). (2) In the present age, the blessings of redemption come to us through the Spirit, who has been poured out upon believers (cf. Joel 2:28–32; Ac 1:8 and 2:4, notes). Yet this outpouring is only partial; we await and pray for the fullness of redemption and the full outpouring of the Holy Spirit at the end of history.

33:1 O DESTROYER. The immediate application is to the Assyrians; the ultimate application is to the antichrist and to Satan himself (see Rev 19:20; 20:10).

33:2–9 O LORD, BE GRACIOUS TO US. This is the righteous remnant's prayer for deliverance from the hand of their enemy.

13You who are far away,[w] hear[x]
what I have done;
you who are near, acknowledge
my power!
14The sinners[y] in Zion are terrified;
trembling[z] grips the godless:
"Who of us can dwell with the
consuming fire?[a]
Who of us can dwell with
everlasting burning?"
15He who walks righteously[b]
and speaks what is right,[c]
who rejects gain from extortion[d]
and keeps his hand from
accepting bribes,[e]
who stops his ears against plots of
murder
and shuts his eyes[f] against
contemplating evil—
16this is the man who will dwell on
the heights,[g]
whose refuge[h] will be the
mountain fortress.[i]
His bread will be supplied,
and water will not fail[j] him.

17Your eyes will see the king[k] in
his beauty[l]
and view a land that stretches
afar.[m]
18In your thoughts you will ponder
the former terror:[n]
"Where is that chief officer?
Where is the one who took the
revenue?
Where is the officer in charge of
the towers?[o]"
19You will see those arrogant
people[p] no more,
those people of an obscure
speech,
with their strange,
incomprehensible tongue.[q]

20Look upon Zion,[r] the city of our
festivals;
your eyes will see Jerusalem,
a peaceful abode,[s] a tent[t] that
will not be moved;[u]
its stakes will never be pulled up,
nor any of its ropes broken.
21There the LORD will be our
Mighty[v] One.
It will be like a place of broad
rivers and streams.[w]
No galley with oars will ride them,
no mighty ship[x] will sail them.
22For the LORD is our judge,[y]
the LORD is our lawgiver,[z]
the LORD is our king;[a]
it is he who will save[b] us.

23Your rigging hangs loose:
The mast is not held secure,
the sail is not spread.
Then an abundance of spoils will
be divided
and even the lame[c] will carry
off plunder.[d]
24No one living in Zion will say, "I
am ill";[e]
and the sins of those who dwell
there will be forgiven.[f]

Judgment Against the Nations

34 Come near, you nations, and
listen;[g]
pay attention, you peoples![h]
Let the earth[i] hear, and all that
is in it,
the world, and all that comes
out of it![j]
2The LORD is angry with all nations;
his wrath[k] is upon all their
armies.
He will totally destroy[w][l] them,
he will give them over to
slaughter.[m]
3Their slain[n] will be thrown out,

33:13 [w]Ps 48:10; 49:1 [x]Isa 34:1; 48:16; 49:1
33:14 [y]S Isa 1:28 [z]S Isa 32:11 [a]S Isa 1:31; S 30:30; S Zec 13:9; Heb 12:29
33:15 [b]Isa 58:8 [c]Ps 15:2; 24:4 [d]Eze 22:13; 33:31 [e]S Pr 15:27 [f]Ps 119:37
33:16 [g]S Dt 32:13 [h]S Ps 46:1; S Isa 25:4 [i]Ps 18:1-2; Isa 26:1 [j]Isa 48:21; 49:10; 65:13
33:17 [k]S Isa 6:5 [l]S Isa 4:2 [m]S Isa 26:15
33:18 [n]S Isa 17:14 [o]S Isa 2:15
33:19 [p]S Ps 5:5 [q]S Ge 11:7; S Isa 28:11
33:20 [r]S Ps 125:1 [s]S Isa 32:18 [t]S Ge 26:22 [u]ver 6; Ps 46:5
33:21 [v]S Isa 10:34 [w]S Ex 17:6; S Ps 1:3; Isa 32:2; 41:18; 48:18; 49:10; 66:12; Na 3:8 [x]Isa 23:1
33:22 [y]Isa 11:4 [z]S Isa 2:3; Jas 4:12 [a]S Ps 89:18 [b]S Isa 25:9
33:23 [c]S 2Ki 7:8 [d]S 2Ki 7:16
33:24 [e]S Isa 30:26 [f]S Nu 23:21; S 2Ch 6:21; Isa 43:1; 48:20; Jer 31:34; 33:8; 1Jn 1:7-9
34:1 [g]S Isa 33:13 [h]Isa 41:1; 43:9 [i]S Dt 4:26; Ps 49:1 [j]Ps 24:1
34:2 [k]S Isa 10:25 [l]S Isa 13:5; S Zec 5:3 [m]S Isa 30:25
34:3 [n]S Isa 5:25; S 10:4

[w]2 The Hebrew term refers to the irrevocable giving over of things or persons to the LORD, often by totally destroying them; also in verse 5.

33:14–16 CAN DWELL WITH THE CONSUMING FIRE? Isaiah describes those among God's people who will come through the fire of his judgment. Note that it will only be those who live godly lives that flow from hearts that are right with God. That godly person is described as one who: (1) conforms to the righteous requirements of God's law, (2) speaks sincerely without deceit, (3) rejects making money by unjust means, (4) refuses to be involved in criminal violence, and (5) refuses to look at evil with pleasure or to delight in the wicked actions of others.

33:17–24 THE KING. This is probably a prophecy about God's future kingdom on earth; therefore, the reigning king will be the Messiah—Jesus Christ.

34:1–7 ALL NATIONS ... TOTALLY DESTROY. These verses depict the terrible judgment to fall on all nations at the end of time. They emphasize God's wrath against all sin and rebellion (vv. 2–3; see Rev 16:16, note; 19:17, note); this judgment will involve disturbances in the heavens (v. 4; cf. Mt 24:29; Rev 6:13–14) and is linked with Christ's return to set up his kingdom on earth (Rev 19—20). At the present time, nations may ridicule and reject God's way, but at a time known only to God, great tribulation and judgment will shake the nations.

their dead bodies[o] will send up
a stench;[p]
the mountains will be soaked
with their blood.[q]
4All the stars of the heavens will be
dissolved[r]
and the sky rolled up[s] like a
scroll;
all the starry host will fall[t]
like withered[u] leaves from the
vine,
like shriveled figs from the fig
tree.
5My sword[v] has drunk its fill in
the heavens;
see, it descends in judgment on
Edom,[w]
the people I have totally
destroyed.[x]
6The sword[y] of the LORD is bathed
in blood,
it is covered with fat—
the blood of lambs and goats,
fat from the kidneys of rams.
For the LORD has a sacrifice[z] in
Bozrah[a]
and a great slaughter[b] in
Edom.
7And the wild oxen[c] will fall with
them,
the bull calves and the great
bulls.[d]
Their land will be drenched with
blood,[e]
and the dust will be soaked with
fat.
8For the LORD has a day[f] of
vengeance,[g]
a year of retribution,[h] to uphold
Zion's cause.
9Edom's streams will be turned into
pitch,
her dust into burning sulfur;[i]
her land will become blazing
pitch!
10It will not be quenched[j] night
and day;
its smoke will rise forever.[k]
From generation to generation[l] it
will lie desolate;[m]
no one will ever pass through it
again.
11The desert owl[x][n] and screech
owl[x] will possess it;
the great owl[x] and the raven[o]
will nest there.
God will stretch out over Edom[p]
the measuring line of chaos[q]
and the plumb line[r] of
desolation.
12Her nobles will have nothing there
to be called a kingdom,
all her princes[s] will vanish[t]
away.
13Thorns[u] will overrun her citadels,
nettles and brambles her
strongholds.[v]
She will become a haunt for
jackals,[w]
a home for owls.[x]
14Desert creatures[y] will meet with
hyenas,[z]
and wild goats will bleat to each
other;
there the night creatures[a] will
also repose
and find for themselves places of
rest.
15The owl will nest there and lay
eggs,
she will hatch them, and care
for her young under the
shadow of her wings;[b]
there also the falcons[c] will
gather,
each with its mate.
16Look in the scroll[d] of the LORD
and read:

None of these will be missing,[e]
not one will lack her mate.
For it is his mouth[f] that has
given the order,[g]
and his Spirit will gather them
together.
17He allots their portions;[h]
his hand distributes them by
measure.
They will possess it forever
and dwell there from generation
to generation.[i]

34:3 [o]S Ps 110:6; Eze 39:11 [p]Joel 2:20; Am 4:10 [q]ver 7; S 2Sa 1:22; Isa 63:6; Eze 5:17; 14:19; 32:6; 35:6; 38:22 **34:4** [r]S Job 9:7; S Isa 13:13; 2Pe 3:10 [s]Isa 38:12; Heb 1:12 [t]S Mt 24:29*; Mk 13:25* [u]S Job 8:12; S Isa 15:6; Mt 21:19 **34:5** [v]Dt 32:41-42; Jer 47:6; Eze 21:5; Zec 13:7 [w]S 2Sa 8:13-14; S 2Ch 28:17; Am 1:11-12 [x]S Dt 13:15; S Jos 6:17; Isa 24:6; Am 3:14-15; 6:11 **34:6** [y]S Dt 32:41; S Isa 27:1 [z]S Lev 3:9 [a]S Ge 36:33 [b]S Isa 30:25; S Jer 25:34; Rev 19:17 **34:7** [c]S Nu 23:22 [d]S Ps 68:30 [e]S 2Sa 1:22 **34:8** [f]S Isa 2:12 [g]S Isa 1:24; 35:4; 47:3; 63:4 [h]Isa 59:18; Eze 25:12-17; Joel 3:4; Am 1:6-8, 9-10 **34:9** [i]S Ge 19:24 **34:10** [j]S Isa 1:31 [k]Rev 14:10-11; 19:3 [l]ver 17 [m]Isa 13:20; 24:1; Jer 49:18; Eze 29:12; 35:3; Mal 1:3 **34:11** [n]S Lev 11:16-18; S Dt 14:15-17; Rev 18:2 [o]S Ge 8:7 [p]Isa 21:11; Eze 35:15; Joel 3:19; Ob 1:1; Mal 1:4 [q]S Ge 1:2 [r]S 2Ki 21:13; Am 7:8 **34:12** [s]Job 12:21; Ps 107:40; Isa 40:23; Jer 21:7; 27:20; 39:6; Eze 24:5 [t]Isa 29:20; 41:11-12 **34:13** [u]S Isa 5:6; S 7:19 [v]S Isa 13:22 [w]Ps 44:19; S Isa 13:22; Jer 9:11; 10:22 [x]S Lev 11:16-18 **34:14** [y]S Ps 74:14 [z]Isa 13:22 [a]Rev 18:2 **34:15** [b]S Ps 17:8 [c]Dt 14:13 **34:16** [d]Isa 30:8 [e]Isa 40:26; 48:13 [f]Isa 1:20; 58:14 [g]S Isa 1:20 **34:17** [h]Isa 17:14; Jer 13:25 [i]ver 10

[x] *11* The precise identification of these birds is uncertain.

34:8–17 A YEAR OF RETRIBUTION. Though speaking in the context of a destruction coming from God on the Edomites as enemies of God and his people (cf. 2Sa 8:13–14; Ps 137:7; La 4:21), Isaiah prophesies a coming judgment on all the unregenerate, i.e., all those hostile to God and his word.

Joy of the Redeemed

35 The desert[j] and the parched
land will be glad;
the wilderness will rejoice and
blossom.[k]
Like the crocus,[l] **2**it will burst
into bloom;
it will rejoice greatly and shout
for joy.[m]
The glory of Lebanon[n] will be
given to it,
the splendor of Carmel[o] and
Sharon;[p]
they will see the glory[q] of the
LORD,
the splendor of our God.[r]

3Strengthen the feeble hands,
steady the knees[s] that give
way;
4say[t] to those with fearful
hearts,[u]
"Be strong, do not fear;[v]
your God will come,[w]
he will come with vengeance;[x]
with divine retribution
he will come to save[y] you."
5Then will the eyes of the blind be
opened[z]
Isa 40:10-11
and the ears of the deaf[a]
unstopped.
6Then will the lame[b] leap like a
deer,[c]
and the mute tongue[d] shout for
joy.[e]
Water will gush forth in the
wilderness
and streams[f] in the desert.
7The burning sand will become a
pool,
the thirsty ground[g] bubbling
springs.[h]
In the haunts where jackals[i] once
lay,
grass and reeds[j] and papyrus
will grow.
8And a highway[k] will be there;
it will be called the Way of
Holiness.[l]
The unclean[m] will not journey on
it;
it will be for those who walk in
that Way;
wicked fools will not go about
on it.[y]
9No lion[n] will be there,
nor will any ferocious beast[o]
get up on it;
they will not be found there.
But only the redeemed[p] will walk
there,
10 and the ransomed[q] of the LORD
will return.
They will enter Zion with
singing;[r]
everlasting joy[s] will crown their
heads.
Gladness[t] and joy will overtake
them,
and sorrow and sighing will flee
away.[u]

Sennacherib Threatens Jerusalem

36:1–22pp — 2Ki 18:13,17–37; 2Ch 32:9–19

36 In the fourteenth year of King
Hezekiah's[v] reign, Sennacher-

35:1 [j]Isa 27:10; 32:15,16; 41:18-19 [k]Isa 27:6; 51:3 [l]SS 2:1 **35:2** [m]S Ge 21:6; Ps 105:43; Isa 12:6; S 25:9; 44:23; 51:11; 52:9; 55:12 [n]S Ezr 3:7; S Isa 33:9 [o]SS 7:5 [p]S 1Ch 27:29; Isa 65:10 [q]S Ex 16:7; S Isa 4:5; S 59:19 [r]S Isa 25:9 **35:3** [s]S Job 4:4; Heb 12:12 **35:4** [t]2Ch 32:6; Isa 40:2; Zec 1:13 [u]S Dt 20:3; S Isa 21:4 [v]S Jos 1:9; S Isa 7:4; Da 10:19 [w]Isa 40:9,10-11; 51:5; 62:11; Rev 22:12 [x]S Isa 1:24; S 34:8 [y]S Isa 25:9 **35:5** [z]S Ps 146:8; Jn 9:6-7; Ac 26:18 [a]Isa 29:18; 42:18; 50:4 **35:6** [b]Mt 15:30; Lk 7:22; Jn 5:8-9; Ac 3:8 [c]S 2Sa 22:34 [d]Isa 32:4; Mt 9:32-33; 12:22; Mk 7:35; Lk 11:14 [e]Ps 20:5 [f]S Ex 17:6; Jn 7:38 **35:7** [g]S Ps 68:6; Isa 41:17; 44:3; 55:1 [h]Ps 107:35; Isa 49:10; 58:11 [i]S Isa 13:22 [j]S Job 8:11; S 40:21 **35:8** [k]S Isa 11:16; S 33:8; S Jer 31:21; Mt 7:13-14 [l]Isa 4:3; 1Pe 1:15 [m]Isa 52:1 **35:9** [n]S Isa 30:6 [o]Isa 11:6; 13:22; 34:14 [p]S Ex 6:6; Lev 25:47-55; Isa 51:11; 62:12; 63:4 **35:10** [q]S Job 19:25; S Isa 1:27 [r]Isa 30:29 [s]S Ps 4:7; S 126:5; S Isa 25:9 [t]S Ps 51:8; S Isa 51:3 [u]S Isa 30:19; Rev 7:17; 21:4 **36:1** [v]S 2Ki 18:9

[y] 8 Or / *the simple will not stray from it*

35:1 WILDERNESS WILL REJOICE. Whereas the preceding chapter described God's judgment through the destruction of the wicked, this chapter predicts a day of God's redemption when the earth will blossom profusely with righteousness and manifest his glory amidst great rejoicing by his people. This chapter has several levels of application, beginning with the first coming of Jesus Christ and reaching its full realization at his second coming (see Rev 19—22).

35:4 HE WILL COME WITH VENGEANCE. God will one day come to repay the world for its evil and to reward the righteous with his great salvation (cf. 2Th 1:6–10). At that time the redeemed will be completely saved from sin and all its consequences (see article on THE RAPTURE, p. 1864).

35:5–6 EYES OF THE BLIND BE OPENED. Jesus Christ refers to these verses as evidence of his Messiahship (Mt 11:4–5; Lk 7:22). When the church of Jesus Christ is truly empowered by the Holy Spirit to do the "greater things" (Jn 14:12), the signs and wonders of Isa 35 will again occur, just as they did during the time described in the book of Acts.

35:8–11 THE WAY OF HOLINESS. Whenever the Spirit is poured out from on high (32:15), resulting in a powerful revelation of God's glory and splendor (v. 2), the Way of Holiness will become clear; all the redeemed will then walk in complete holiness (v. 10).

36:1 KING HEZEKIAH. With chs. 36—39 (paralleling 2Ki 18—20), Isaiah moves from prophecy to the history of King Hezekiah. Hezekiah was a godly king of Judah who trusted in the Lord and served him (see 2Ki 18:5, note). "The fourteenth year" of his reign was 701 B.C., when Sennacherib, king of Assyria, invaded Judah with the intention of capturing Jerusalem.

ib[w] king of Assyria attacked all the fortified cities of Judah and captured them.[x] **2**Then the king of Assyria sent his field commander with a large army from Lachish[y] to King Hezekiah at Jerusalem. When the commander stopped at the aqueduct of the Upper Pool, on the road to the Washerman's Field,[z] **3**Eliakim[a] son of Hilkiah the palace administrator,[b] Shebna[c] the secretary,[d] and Joah[e] son of Asaph the recorder[f] went out to him.

4The field commander said to them, "Tell Hezekiah,

> " 'This is what the great king, the king of Assyria, says: On what are you basing this confidence of yours? **5**You say you have strategy and military strength—but you speak only empty words. On whom are you depending, that you rebel[g] against me? **6**Look now, you are depending[h] on Egypt,[ij] that splintered reed[k] of a staff, which pierces a man's hand and wounds him if he leans on it! Such is Pharaoh king of Egypt to all who depend on him. **7**And if you say to me, "We are depending[l] on the LORD our God"—isn't he the one whose high places and altars Hezekiah removed,[m] saying to Judah and Jerusalem, "You must worship before this altar"?[n]
>
> **8**" 'Come now, make a bargain with my master, the king of Assyria: I will give you two thousand horses[o]—if you can put riders on them! **9**How then can you repulse one officer of the least of my master's officials, even though you are depending on Egypt[p] for chariots[q] and horsemen?[r] **10**Furthermore, have I come to attack and destroy this land without the LORD? The LORD himself told[s] me to march against this country and destroy it.' "

11Then Eliakim, Shebna and Joah[t] said to the field commander, "Please speak to your servants in Aramaic,[u] since we understand it. Don't speak to us in Hebrew in the hearing of the people on the wall."

12But the commander replied, "Was it only to your master and you that my master sent me to say these things, and not to the men sitting on the wall—who, like you, will have to eat their own filth and drink their own urine?[v]"

13Then the commander stood and called out in Hebrew,[w] "Hear the words of the great king, the king of Assyria![x] **14**This is what the king says: Do not let Hezekiah deceive[y] you. He cannot deliver you! **15**Do not let Hezekiah persuade you to trust in the LORD when he says, 'The LORD will surely deliver[z] us; this city will not be given into the hand of the king of Assyria.'[a]

16"Do not listen to Hezekiah. This is what the king of Assyria says: Make peace with me and come out to me. Then every one of you will eat from his own vine and fig tree[b] and drink water from his own cistern,[c] **17**until I come and take you to a land like your own[d]—a land of grain and new wine,[e] a land of bread and vineyards.

18"Do not let Hezekiah mislead you when he says, 'The LORD will deliver us.' Has the god of any nation ever delivered his land from the hand of the king of Assyria? **19**Where are the gods of Hamath and Arpad?[f] Where are the gods of Sepharvaim?[g] Have they rescued Samaria[h] from my hand? **20**Who of all the gods[i] of these countries has been able to save his land from me? How then can the LORD deliver Jerusalem from my hand?"[j]

21But the people remained silent and said nothing in reply, because the king had commanded, "Do not answer him."[k]

22Then Eliakim[l] son of Hilkiah the palace administrator, Shebna the secretary, and Joah son of Asaph the recorder[m] went to Hezekiah, with their

36:1 [w]S 2Ch 32:1 [x]S Ps 109:11
36:2 [y]S Jos 10:3 [z]S Isa 7:3
36:3 [a]Isa 22:20-21; 37:2 [b]S Ge 41:40 [c]S 2Ki 18:18 [d]S 2Sa 8:17 [e]ver 11 [f]S 2Sa 8:16
36:5 [g]S 2Ki 18:7
36:6 [h]S 2Ki 17:4; S Isa 8:12 [i]Eze 17:17 [j]S Isa 30:2,5 [k]Isa 42:3; 58:5; Eze 29:6-7
36:7 [l]Ps 22:8; Mt 27:43 [m]S 2Ki 18:4 [n]Dt 12:2-5; S 2Ch 31:1
36:8 [o]S Ps 20:7; S Isa 30:16
36:9 [p]S Isa 31:3 [q]Isa 37:24 [r]S Ps 20:7; Isa 30:2-5
36:10 [s]S 1Ki 13:18; Isa 10:5-7
36:11 [t]ver 3 [u]S Ezr 4:7
36:12 [v]2Ki 6:25; Eze 4:12
36:13 [w]S 2Ch 32:18 [x]Isa 37:4
36:14 [y]S 2Ch 32:15
36:15 [z]S Ps 3:2,7 [a]Isa 37:10
36:16 [b]S 1Ki 4:25 [c]Pr 5:15
36:17 [d]S 2Ki 15:29 [e]S Ge 27:28; S Dt 28:51
36:19 [f]S 2Ki 18:34 [g]S 2Ki 17:24 [h]S 2Ki 15:29
36:20 [i]S 1Ki 20:23 [j]Ex 5:2; 2Ch 25:15; Isa 10:8-11; 37:10-13,18-20; 40:18; Da 3:15
36:21 [k]Pr 9:7-8; S 26:4
36:22 [l]S 2Ki 18:18 [m]S 2Sa 8:16

36:4–10 FIELD COMMANDER. The field commander of Sennacherib's army attempted to undermine the people's confidence in the Lord through intimidation, lies and arguments that Judah's God was not strong enough to deliver them (cf. 2Ki 19:6–13).

36:20 DELIVER JERUSALEM FROM MY HAND? The field commander mockingly suggested that the God of Judah was not powerful enough to deliver Jerusalem from his army. He implied that it would take a miracle and that this was no time to expect such a thing. Satan still uses such tactics on God's children; he tells them that when they are in great need, they should not expect or seek a miracle from God. Note, however, that God did work a miracle for Judah and defeated the commander and his army (37:36–38).

clothes torn,[n] and told him what the
field commander had said.

Jerusalem's Deliverance Foretold

37:1–13pp — 2Ki 19:1–13

37 When King Hezekiah heard
this, he tore his clothes[o] and
put on sackcloth[p] and went into the
temple[q] of the LORD. **2**He sent Eliakim[r] the palace administrator, Shebna[s] the secretary, and the leading
priests, all wearing sackcloth, to the
prophet Isaiah son of Amoz.[t] **3**They
told him, "This is what Hezekiah says:
This day is a day of distress[u] and rebuke and disgrace, as when children
come to the point of birth[v] and there
is no strength to deliver them. **4**It may
be that the LORD your God will hear the
words of the field commander, whom
his master, the king of Assyria, has
sent to ridicule[w] the living God,[x] and
that he will rebuke him for the words
the LORD your God has heard.[y] Therefore pray[z] for the remnant[a] that still
survives."

5When King Hezekiah's officials
came to Isaiah, **6**Isaiah said to them,
"Tell your master, 'This is what the
LORD says: Do not be afraid[b] of what
you have heard—those words with
which the underlings of the king of Assyria have blasphemed[c] me. **7**Listen!
I am going to put a spirit[d] in him so
that when he hears a certain report,[e]
he will return to his own country, and
there I will have him cut down[f] with
the sword.' "

8When the field commander heard
that the king of Assyria had left Lachish,[g] he withdrew and found the
king fighting against Libnah.[h]

9Now Sennacherib[i] received a report[j] that Tirhakah, the Cushite[z][k]
king ⌞of Egypt⌟, was marching out to
fight against him. When he heard it, he
sent messengers to Hezekiah with this
word: **10**"Say to Hezekiah king of Judah: Do not let the god you depend on
deceive[l] you when he says, 'Jerusalem will not be handed over to the king
of Assyria.'[m] **11**Surely you have heard
what the kings of Assyria have done to
all the countries, destroying them completely. And will you be delivered?[n]
12Did the gods of the nations that were
destroyed by my forefathers[o] deliver
them—the gods of Gozan, Haran,[p]
Rezeph and the people of Eden[q] who
were in Tel Assar? **13**Where is the king
of Hamath, the king of Arpad,[r] the
king of the city of Sepharvaim,[s] or of
Hena or Ivvah?"[t]

Hezekiah's Prayer

37:14–20pp — 2Ki 19:14–19

14Hezekiah received the letter[u]
from the messengers and read it. Then
he went up to the temple[v] of the LORD
and spread it out before the LORD.
15And Hezekiah prayed[w] to the LORD:
16"O LORD Almighty, God of Israel, enthroned[x] between the cherubim,[y]
you alone are God[z] over all the kingdoms[a] of the earth. You have made
heaven and earth.[b] **17**Give ear,
O LORD, and hear;[c] open your eyes,
O LORD, and see;[d] listen to all the
words Sennacherib[e] has sent to insult[f] the living God.[g]

18"It is true, O LORD, that the Assyrian kings have laid waste all these peoples and their lands.[h] **19**They have
thrown their gods into the fire[i] and
destroyed them,[j] for they were not
gods[k] but only wood and stone, fashioned by human hands.[l] **20**Now,
O LORD our God, deliver[m] us from his
hand, so that all kingdoms on earth[n]

36:22 [n]S Ge 37:29; S 2Ch 34:19 **37:1** [o]S Ge 37:29; S 2Ch 34:19 [p]S Ge 37:34 [q]S ver 14; S 1Ki 8:33; Mt 21:13 **37:2** [r]S 2Ki 18:18; S Isa 36:3 [s]S 2Ki 18:18 [t]ver 21; Isa 1:1; S 13:1; 38:1 **37:3** [u]S Jdg 6:2; S Isa 5:30 [v]Isa 26:18; 66:9; Hos 13:13 **37:4** [w]ver 23-24; S 2Ch 32:17 [x]S Jos 3:10 [y]Isa 36:13,18-20 [z]S 1Sa 7:8 [a]S Isa 1:9; Am 7:2 **37:6** [b]S Jos 1:9; S Isa 7:4 [c]S Nu 15:30 **37:7** [d]1Ch 5:26 [e]ver 9 [f]S Isa 31:8 **37:8** [g]S Jos 10:3 [h]S Nu 33:20 **37:9** [i]S 2Ch 32:1 [j]ver 7 [k]S Isa 20:3 **37:10** [l]2Ch 32:11,15 [m]Isa 36:15 **37:11** [n]Isa 36:18-20 **37:12** [o]2Ki 18:11 [p]Ge 11:31; 12:1-4; Ac 7:2 [q]Eze 27:23; Am 1:5 **37:13** [r]Isa 10:9 [s]S 2Ki 17:24 [t]S Isa 36:20 **37:14** [u]2Ch 32:17 [v]ver 1,38; S 1Ki 8:33 **37:15** [w]S 2Ch 32:20 **37:16** [x]S Ps 2:4 [y]S Ge 3:24 [z]Dt 10:17; S Ps 46:10; 86:10; 136:2-3 [a]Da 4:34 [b]S Ge 1:1; S Isa 11:12; 41:9; 43:6; Ac 4:24 **37:17** [c]S 1Ki 8:29; S 2Ch 6:40 [d]Jer 25:29; Da 9:18 [e]S 2Ch 32:1 [f]S 2Ch 32:17 [g]S Jos 3:10 **37:18** [h]S 2Ki 15:29; Na 2:11-12 **37:19** [i]S Jos 7:15 [j]Isa 26:14; 36:20 [k]2Ch 13:9; Isa 40:17; 41:24,29; Jer 2:11; 5:7; 16:20; Gal 4:8 [l]S 2Ch 32:19; S Ps 135:15; Isa 40:18-20; 44:9-11 **37:20** [m]S Ps 3:2,7; S Pr 20:22 [n]S Jos 4:24

[z]*9* That is, from the upper Nile region

37:1 HEZEKIAH . . . WENT INTO THE TEMPLE. The field commander's intimidation and accusations were unworthy of a response (36:21), but they were worthy of earnest intercession. Hezekiah, a man of God, turned to God in humble and contrite prayer and sought to know his word through the mouth of Isaiah the prophet (v. 2; see 2Ki 19:1, note). In times of trouble, the best thing we can do is seek God's face and ask him to speak to us through his written or prophetic word.

37:7 PUT A SPIRIT IN HIM. This phrase refers to an inner voice sent by God to influence a person's conduct and thought. Concerning the prediction that the king of Assyria would be "cut down with the sword," see vv. 37–38.

37:10 THE GOD YOU DEPEND ON. Sennacherib attempted in every way to destroy Hezekiah's confidence in the Lord. The Assyrian king arrogantly believed that his royal power surpassed that of Judah's God or of any god.

37:14–20 HEZEKIAH PRAYED. See 2Ki 19:15, note.

37:20 YOU ALONE, O LORD, ARE GOD. See 2Ki 19:19, note.

may know that you alone, O LORD, are God.[a][o]"

Sennacherib's Fall

37:21–38pp — 2Ki 19:20–37; 2Ch 32:20–21

21Then Isaiah son of Amoz[p] sent a
message to Hezekiah: "This is what
the LORD, the God of Israel, says: Because you have prayed to me concerning Sennacherib king of Assyria, 22this
is the word the LORD has spoken
against him:

"The Virgin Daughter[q] of Zion[r]
despises and mocks you.
The Daughter of Jerusalem
tosses her head[s] as you flee.
23Who is it you have insulted and
blasphemed?[t]
Against whom have you raised
your voice[u]
and lifted your eyes in pride?[v]
Against the Holy One[w] of
Israel!
24By your messengers
you have heaped insults on the
Lord.
And you have said,
'With my many chariots[x]
I have ascended the heights of the
mountains,
the utmost heights[y] of
Lebanon.[z]
I have cut down its tallest cedars,
the choicest of its pines.[a]
I have reached its remotest
heights,
the finest of its forests.
25I have dug wells in foreign lands[b]
and drunk the water there.
With the soles of my feet
I have dried up[b] all the streams
of Egypt.[c]'
26"Have you not heard?
Long ago I ordained[d] it.
In days of old I planned[e] it;
now I have brought it to pass,
that you have turned fortified cities
into piles of stone.[f]
27Their people, drained of power,
are dismayed and put to shame.
They are like plants in the field,
like tender green shoots,
like grass[g] sprouting on the
roof,[h]
scorched[c] before it grows up.
28"But I know where you stay
and when you come and go[i]
and how you rage[j] against me.

29Because you rage against me
and because your insolence[k]
has reached my ears,
I will put my hook[l] in your
nose[m]
and my bit in your mouth,
and I will make you return
by the way you came.[n]

30"This will be the sign[o] for you,
O Hezekiah:

"This year[p] you will eat what
grows by itself,
and the second year what
springs from that.
But in the third year[q] sow and
reap,
plant vineyards[r] and eat their
fruit.[s]
31Once more a remnant of the house
of Judah
will take root[t] below and bear
fruit[u] above.
32For out of Jerusalem will come a
remnant,[v]
and out of Mount Zion a band of
survivors.[w]
The zeal[x] of the LORD Almighty
will accomplish this.

33"Therefore this is what the LORD
says concerning the king of Assyria:

"He will not enter this city[y]
or shoot an arrow here.
He will not come before it with
shield
or build a siege ramp[z] against
it.
34By the way that he came he will
return;[a]
he will not enter this city,"
declares the LORD.
35"I will defend[b] this city and save
it,
for my sake[c] and for the sake
of David[d] my servant!"

36Then the angel[e] of the LORD went
out and put to death[f] a hundred and
eighty-five thousand men in the Assyrian[g] camp. When the people got up
the next morning—there were all the

37:20 [o]S 1Sa 17:46; S Ps 46:10 **37:21** [p]S ver 2 **37:22** [q]S Isa 23:12 [r]S Isa 10:32 [s]S Job 16:4 **37:23** [t]ver 4; S Nu 15:30; Isa 52:5; Eze 36:20,23; Da 7:25 [u]S Job 15:25 [v]S Isa 2:11 [w]S Isa 1:4; S 12:6 **37:24** [x]Isa 36:9 [y]Isa 14:13 [z]S 1Ki 7:2; S Isa 14:8; S 33:9 [a]1Ki 5:8-10; Isa 41:19; 55:13; 60:13; Hos 14:8 **37:25** [b]S Isa 19:6; 44:27 [c]S Dt 11:10; S Isa 10:14; Da 4:30 **37:26** [d]Ac 2:23; 4:27-28; 1Pe 2:8 [e]Isa 10:6; S 25:1 [f]S Dt 13:16; S Isa 25:2 **37:27** [g]S Isa 15:6 [h]Ps 129:6 **37:28** [i]Ps 139:1-3 [j]Ps 2:1

37:29 [k]Isa 10:12 [l]S 2Ch 33:11 [m]S Job 40:24 [n]ver 34 **37:30** [o]S Isa 20:3 [p]Isa 32:10 [q]S Isa 16:14 [r]S Lev 25:4 [s]S Ps 107:37; Isa 30:23; 65:21; Jer 31:5 **37:31** [t]Isa 11:10 [u]S Isa 27:6 **37:32** [v]S Isa 11:11 [w]S Isa 1:9 [x]S Isa 9:7 **37:33** [y]S Isa 32:18 [z]S 2Sa 20:15 **37:34** [a]ver 29 **37:35** [b]S Isa 31:5 [c]Isa 43:25; 48:9, 11; Eze 36:21-22 [d]S 1Ch 17:19 **37:36** [e]S Ex 12:23 [f]S Ex 12:12 [g]S Isa 10:12

[a] *20* Dead Sea Scrolls (see also 2 Kings 19:19); Masoretic Text *alone are the LORD* [b] *25* Dead Sea Scrolls (see also 2 Kings 19:24); Masoretic Text does not have *in foreign lands.* [c] *27* Some manuscripts of the Masoretic Text, Dead Sea Scrolls and some Septuagint manuscripts (see also 2 Kings 19:26); most manuscripts of the Masoretic Text *roof / and terraced fields*

dead bodies! 37So Sennacherib[h] king
of Assyria broke camp and withdrew.
He returned to Nineveh[i] and stayed
there.
38One day, while he was worshiping
in the temple[j] of his god Nisroch, his
sons Adrammelech and Sharezer cut
him down with the sword, and they escaped to the land of Ararat.[k] And
Esarhaddon[l] his son succeeded him
as king.[m]

Hezekiah's Illness

38:1–8pp — 2Ki 20:1–11; 2Ch 32:24–26

38 In those days Hezekiah became
ill and was at the point of
death. The prophet Isaiah son of
Amoz[n] went to him and said, "This is
what the LORD says: Put your house in
order,[o] because you are going to die;
you will not recover."[p]
2Hezekiah turned his face to the
wall and prayed to the LORD, 3"Remember, O LORD, how I have walked[q] before you faithfully and with wholehearted devotion[r] and have done
what is good in your eyes.[s]" And Hezekiah wept[t] bitterly.
4Then the word[u] of the LORD came
to Isaiah: 5"Go and tell Hezekiah, 'This
is what the LORD, the God of your father
David,[v] says: I have heard your prayer
and seen your tears;[w] I will add fifteen
years[x] to your life. 6And I will deliver
you and this city from the hand of the
king of Assyria. I will defend[y] this
city.
7" 'This is the LORD's sign[z] to you
that the LORD will do what he has promised: 8I will make the shadow cast by
the sun go back the ten steps it has
gone down on the stairway of Ahaz.' "
So the sunlight went back the ten steps
it had gone down.[a]
9A writing of Hezekiah king of Judah
after his illness and recovery:
10I said, "In the prime of my life[b]
must I go through the gates of
death[d][c]
and be robbed of the rest of my
years?[d]"
11I said, "I will not again see the
LORD,
the LORD,[e] in the land of the
living;[f]
no longer will I look on mankind,
or be with those who now dwell
in this world.[e]
12Like a shepherd's tent[g] my house
has been pulled down[h] and
taken from me.
Like a weaver I have rolled[i] up
my life,
and he has cut me off from the
loom;[j]
day and night[k] you made an
end of me.
13I waited patiently[l] till dawn,
but like a lion he broke[m] all my
bones;[n]
day and night[o] you made an
end of me.

37:37 [h]S 2Ch 32:1 [i]S Ge 10:11; S Na 1:1
37:38 [j]S ver 14 [k]Ge 8:4; Jer 51:27 [l]S 2Ki 17:24 [m]S Isa 9:4; 10:26; S 14:25
38:1 [n]S Isa 37:2 [o]2Sa 17:23 [p]2Ki 8:10
38:3 [q]Ps 26:3 [r]S 1Ki 8:61; S 1Ch 29:19 [s]S Dt 6:18; S 10:20 [t]Ps 6:8
38:4 [u]1Sa 13:13; Isa 39:5
38:5 [v]2Ki 18:3 [w]Ps 6:6 [x]S 2Ki 18:2
38:6 [y]S Isa 31:5
38:7 [z]S Ge 24:14; S 2Ch 32:31; Isa 7:11,14; S 20:3
38:8 [a]Jos 10:13
38:10 [b]Ps 102:24 [c]S Job 17:16; Ps 107:18; 2Co 1:9 [d]S Job 17:11
38:11 [e]S Isa 12:2 [f]S Job 28:13; S Ps 116:9
38:12 [g]Isa 33:20; 2Co 5:1,4; 2Pe 1:13-14 [h]S Job 4:21 [i]S Isa 34:4; Heb 1:12 [j]S Nu 11:15; S Job 7:6; S Ps 31:22 [k]ver 13; Ps 32:4; 73:14
38:13 [l]S Ps 37:7 [m]S Job 9:17; Ps 51:8 [n]S Job 10:16; Jer 34:17; La 3:4; Da 6:24 [o]S ver 12

[d] *10* Hebrew *Sheol* [e] *11* A few Hebrew manuscripts; most Hebrew manuscripts *in the place of cessation*

37:36 THE ANGEL OF THE LORD. This destruction of the Assyrian army was foretold in 10:3–34; 30:31; 31:8 (see 2Ki 19:35, note on this miraculous deliverance of God's people).

38:1 YOU ARE GOING TO DIE. Through Isaiah, God prophesied that Hezekiah would die as the inevitable physical consequence of his sickness. However, much prophecy is conditional (e.g., see Jer 18:7–10); God does not act deceitfully (Heb 6:18), but he can change his plans as a result of our response to his word. God's word to Hezekiah was a direct and unequivocable statement expressing a genuine possibility. But because Hezekiah responded in earnest prayer and in confidence in God's ability to heal his physical illness, God in mercy answered his prayer and added fifteen years to his life.

38:5 I HAVE HEARD YOUR PRAYER. God's statement that Hezekiah must prepare for death and Hezekiah's prayer to God (v. 2) have important implications for our relationship to God. (1) All the things that God declares about the future are not necessarily irrevocable (cf. Jnh 3:1–10). When believers are confronted with tragedy, we can rest assured that God cares about what happens to us; he is compassionate and sensitive to our experiences.

(2) Our prayers do have an effect on God, his purposes and the outworking of his sovereign plan; thus what happens in our lives or in the life of the church is determined by both God's plan and our prayers. We must always maintain the Scriptural conviction that prayer does change things (vv. 4–7; cf. 1Ki 21:29; Eze 33:13–16; Jas 5:14–15).

38:8 SUNLIGHT WENT BACK THE TEN STEPS. The exact nature of the sun's shadow being reversed on the stairway is not explained; what is clear is that it did occur by God's powerful word as a prophetic sign to Hezekiah that God had heard his prayer and seen his tears, and would heal him.

[14]I cried like a swift or thrush,
I moaned like a mourning dove.[p]
My eyes grew weak[q] as I looked to the heavens.
I am troubled; O Lord, come to my aid!"[r]

[15]But what can I say?[s]
He has spoken to me, and he himself has done this.[t]
I will walk humbly[u] all my years because of this anguish of my soul.[v]

[16]Lord, by such things men live;
and my spirit finds life in them too.
You restored me to health and let me live.[w]

[17]Surely it was for my benefit[x]
that I suffered such anguish.[y]
In your love you kept me
from the pit[z] of destruction;
you have put all my sins[a]
behind your back.[b]

[18]For the grave[f][c] cannot praise you,
death cannot sing your praise;[d]
those who go down to the pit[e]
cannot hope for your faithfulness.

[19]The living, the living—they praise[f] you,
as I am doing today;
fathers tell their children[g]
about your faithfulness.

[20]The LORD will save me,
and we will sing[h] with stringed instruments[i]
all the days of our lives[j]
in the temple[k] of the LORD.

[21]Isaiah had said, "Prepare a poultice of figs and apply it to the boil, and he will recover."

[22]Hezekiah had asked, "What will be the sign[l] that I will go up to the temple of the LORD?"

38:14 [p]S Ge 8:8; S Isa 59:11 [q]S Ps 6:7 [r]S Ge 50:24; S Job 17:3 **38:15** [s]2Sa 7:20 [t]S Ps 39:9 [u]1Ki 21:27 [v]S Job 7:11 **38:16** [w]Ps 119:25; Heb 12:9 **38:17** [x]Ro 8:28; Heb 12:11 [y]S Job 7:11; Ps 119:71,75 [z]S Job 17:16; S Ps 30:3 [a]Ps 103:3; Jer 31:34 [b]S Ps 103:12; Isa 43:25; Mic 7:19 **38:18** [c]S Nu 16:30; S Ecc 9:10 [d]Ps 6:5; 88:10-11; 115:17 [e]S Ps 30:9 **38:19** [f]Ps 118:17; 119:175 [g]S Dt 11:19 **38:20** [h]Ps 68:25 [i]S Ps 33:2; S 45:8 [j]Ps 23:6; S 63:4; 116:2 [k]Ps 116:17-19 **38:22** [l]S 2Ch 32:31

39:1 [m]S 2Ch 32:31 **39:2** [n]2Ch 32:31 [o]S 2Ki 18:15 [p]2Ch 32:27-29 **39:3** [q]S Dt 28:49 **39:5** [r]S Isa 38:4 **39:6** [s]S Jdg 6:4; S 2Ki 24:13 **39:7** [t]S 2Ki 24:15; Da 1:1-7 **39:8** [u]S Jdg 10:15; Job 1:21; Ps 39:9 [v]S 2Ch 32:26

Envoys From Babylon

39:1–8pp — 2Ki 20:12–19

39 At that time Merodach-Baladan son of Baladan king of Babylon[m] sent Hezekiah letters and a gift, because he had heard of his illness and recovery. [2]Hezekiah received the envoys[n] gladly and showed them what was in his storehouses—the silver, the gold,[o] the spices, the fine oil, his entire armory and everything found among his treasures.[p] There was nothing in his palace or in all his kingdom that Hezekiah did not show them.

[3]Then Isaiah the prophet went to King Hezekiah and asked, "What did those men say, and where did they come from?"

"From a distant land,[q]" Hezekiah replied. "They came to me from Babylon."

[4]The prophet asked, "What did they see in your palace?"

"They saw everything in my palace," Hezekiah said. "There is nothing among my treasures that I did not show them."

[5]Then Isaiah said to Hezekiah, "Hear the word[r] of the LORD Almighty: [6]The time will surely come when everything in your palace, and all that your fathers have stored up until this day, will be carried off to Babylon.[s] Nothing will be left, says the LORD. [7]And some of your descendants, your own flesh and blood who will be born to you, will be taken away, and they will become eunuchs in the palace of the king of Babylon.[t]"

[8]"The word of the LORD you have spoken is good,[u]" Hezekiah replied. For he thought, "There will be peace and security in my lifetime.[v]"

[f]18 Hebrew *Sheol*

39:1 KING OF BABYLON. Babylon was attempting to free itself from Assyrian domination at this time. Thus this visit by the king of Babylon to Jerusalem was clearly to seek political alliance with Judah. By his reaction to the gifts and the flattery of the delegation, Hezekiah demonstrated foolish presumption and a lack of faith in God. Isaiah later told him that the Babylonians would someday destroy Jerusalem (v. 6). We must remember that whatever we trust instead of God will one day turn on us and destroy us.

39:6 WILL BE CARRIED OFF TO BABYLON. When the Babylonians would conquer Jerusalem, they would carry off its people and treasures to their own country (cf. 14:3–4). In the final analysis, the cause of the Babylonian captivity was not Hezekiah's foolishness in showing the temple treasures, but the sins of the people and especially of Hezekiah's son Manasseh (cf. 2Ki 21). After Hezekiah's death the nation once again rebuilt the centers of idol worship (see 2Ch 33:11; 36:18, for this prophecy's fulfillment).

Comfort for God's People

40 Comfort, comfort[w] my
people,
says your God.
2Speak tenderly[x] to Jerusalem,
and proclaim to her
that her hard service[y] has been
completed,[z]
that her sin has been paid for,[a]
that she has received from the
LORD's hand
double[b] for all her sins.
3A voice of one calling:
"In the desert prepare
the way[c] for the LORD[g];
make straight[d] in the wilderness
a highway for our God.[h][e]
4Every valley shall be raised up,[f]
every mountain and hill[g] made
low;
the rough ground shall become
level,[h]
the rugged places a plain.
5And the glory[i] of the LORD will be
revealed,
and all mankind together will
see it.[j]
For the mouth of the LORD
has spoken."[k]
6A voice says, "Cry out."
And I said, "What shall I cry?"
"All men are like grass,[l]
and all their glory is like the
flowers of the field.
7The grass withers[m] and the
flowers fall,
because the breath[n] of the LORD
blows[o] on them.
Surely the people are grass.
8The grass withers and the
flowers[p] fall,
but the word[q] of our God
stands[r] forever.[s]"
9You who bring good tidings[t] to
Zion,
go up on a high mountain.
You who bring good tidings to
Jerusalem,[i][u]
lift up your voice with a shout,
lift it up, do not be afraid;
say to the towns of Judah,
"Here is your God!"[v]
10See, the Sovereign LORD comes[w]
with power,[x]

40:1 [w]Isa 12:1; 49:13; 51:3,12; 52:9; 57:18; 61:2; 66:13; Jer 31:13; Zep 3:14-17; Zec 1:17; 2Co 1:3 **40:2** [x]S Ge 34:3; S Isa 35:4 [y]S Job 7:1 [z]Isa 41:11-13; 49:25 [a]S Lev 26:41 [b]Isa 51:19; 61:7; Jer 16:18; 17:18; Zec 9:12; Rev 18:6 **40:3** [c]S Isa 11:16; 43:19; Mal 3:1 [d]S Pr 3:5-6 [e]Mt 3:3*; Mk 1:3*; Jn 1:23* **40:4** [f]Isa 49:11 [g]S Isa 2:14 [h]S Ps 26:12; S Isa 26:7; 45:2, 13; Jer 31:9 **40:5** [i]S Ex 16:7; S Nu 14:21; S Isa 59:19 [j]Isa 52:10; 62:2; Lk 2:30; 3:4-6* [k]S Isa 1:20; 58:14 **40:6** [l]S Ge 6:3; S Isa 29:5 **40:7** [m]S Job 8:12; S Isa 15:6 [n]S Ex 15:10; S Job 41:21 [o]S Ps 103:16; S Eze 22:21 **40:8** [p]S Isa 5:24; Jas 1:10 [q]Isa 55:11; 59:21 [r]S Pr 19:21; S Isa 7:7,9; S Jer 39:16 [s]S Ps 119:89; S Mt 5:18; 1Pe 1:24-25* **40:9** [t]Isa 41:27; 44:28; 52:7-10; 61:1; Na 1:15; S Ac 13:32; Ro 10:15; 1Co 15:1-4 [u]S Isa 1:1 [v]Isa 25:9 **40:10** [w]Isa 35:4; 59:20; Mt 21:5; Rev 22:7 [x]Isa 28:2

[g]3 Or *A voice of one calling in the desert: / "Prepare the way for the* LORD [h]3 Hebrew; Septuagint *make straight the paths of our God* [i]9 Or *O Zion, bringer of good tidings, / go up on a high mountain. / O Jerusalem, bringer of good tidings*

40—66 COMFORT. These chapters were written during the later years of Isaiah's life. God revealed these prophecies in order to offer hope and comfort to his people during their captivity in Babylon 150 years after the time of Isaiah (see 39:5–8); they are filled with prophetic revelation about the coming Messiah and his future kingdom on earth. Some predicted events were fulfilled in connection with Judah's Babylonian captivity and restoration, many relate more specifically to the appearing of Jesus Christ on earth, and still others await fulfillment. In general, chs. 40—48 emphasize deliverance, chs. 49—57 redemption, and chs. 58—66 glory.

40:1 COMFORT MY PEOPLE. Isaiah comforts God's people by prophesying to a future generation the good news that God's period of chastisement was nearly over and salvation and blessing were coming. If you are experiencing great difficulty in your life and you know that Christ is your Savior, you can pray for God either to deliver you from such trouble or to be with you and help you in the midst of it. To give us comfort is a task of the triune God: God the Father is called "the God of all comfort" (2Co 1:3), "to comfort all who mourn" is a characteristic of the ministry of the Son of God (Isa 61:2), and the Holy Spirit is called "the Counselor" (Jn 14:16,26; 15:26; 16:7), the One who stands alongside us to offer comfort and help.

40:3–8 A VOICE OF ONE CALLING. These verses, like much prophecy in Isaiah, have several levels of application: (1) to the Jews' restoration from exile, (2) to the coming of the Messiah and his salvation, and (3) to the consummation of redemption in the new heaven and the new earth. The NT sees the fulfillment of v. 3 in John the Baptist—the forerunner of the Messiah (Mt 3:1–4; Mk 1:1–4; Lk 1:76–78; Jn 1:23). John made clear that the way to prepare for the Lord's coming was through repentance (Mt 3:1–8).

40:5 GLORY OF THE LORD WILL BE REVEALED. Israel would see the glory of the Lord when he delivered them from Babylonian captivity. But God would reveal his glory and power in even greater ways in the person of Jesus Christ (Jn 1:14; 11:4,40; Heb 1:3) and at Christ's return from heaven (Mt 16:27; 24:30; Rev 1:7).

40:8 THE WORD OF OUR GOD STANDS FOREVER. All created life is frail and weak and will ultimately come to an end (cf. 37:27; Ps 90:5; 103:15), but God's word endures forever. God's promises will be fulfilled; his redemptive truth cannot be annulled or changed (see article on THE INSPIRATION AND AUTHORITY OF SCRIPTURE, p. 1898).

40:10 COMES WITH POWER. Salvation, blessing and comfort are all associated with the coming of the Lord to his faithful people. He comes

and his arm[y] rules[z] for him.
See, his reward[a] is with him,
and his recompense accompanies him.
11 He tends his flock like a shepherd:[b]
He gathers the lambs in his arms[c]
and carries them close to his heart;[d]
he gently leads[e] those that have young.[f]

12 Who has measured the waters[g] in the hollow of his hand,[h]
or with the breadth of his hand marked off the heavens?[i]
Who has held the dust of the earth in a basket,
or weighed the mountains on the scales
and the hills in a balance?[j]
13 Who has understood the mind[j][k] of the LORD,
or instructed him as his counselor?[l]
14 Whom did the LORD consult to enlighten him,
and who taught him the right way?
Who was it that taught him knowledge[m]
or showed him the path of understanding?[n]
15 Surely the nations are like a drop in a bucket;
they are regarded as dust on the scales;[o]
he weighs the islands as though they were fine dust.[p]
16 Lebanon[q] is not sufficient for altar fires,
nor its animals[r] enough for burnt offerings.
17 Before him all the nations[s] are as nothing;[t]
they are regarded by him as worthless

40:10 [y]S Ps 44:3; S Isa 30:30; S 33:2 [z]Isa 9:6-7 [a]S Isa 35:4; Rev 22:12
40:11 [b]S Ge 48:15; S Ps 28:9; S Mic 5:4; S Jn 10:11 [c]S Nu 11:12 [d]S Dt 26:19 [e]Isa 49:10 [f]S Ge 33:13; S Dt 30:4
40:12 [g]S Job 12:15; S 38:10 [h]Pr 30:4 [i]S Job 38:5; Heb 1:10-12 [j]S Job 38:18; Pr 16:11
40:13 [k]Isa 11:2; 42:1 [l]S Job 15:8; Ro 11:34*; 1Co 2:16*
40:14 [m]Job 21:22; Col 2:3 [n]S Job 12:13; S 34:13; Isa 55:9
40:15 [o]S Ps 62:9 [p]S Dt 9:21; Isa 2:22
40:16 [q]Isa 33:9; 37:24 [r]Ps 50:9-11; Mic 6:7; Heb 10:5-9
40:17 [s]Isa 30:28 [t]S Job 12:19; Isa 29:7
[u]S Isa 37:19; Da 4:35
40:18 [v]S Ex 8:10; S 1Sa 2:2 [w]S Dt 4:15; Ac 17:29
40:19 [x]S Ex 20:4; Ps 115:4; S Isa 37:19; 42:17; Jer 2:8,28; 10:8; 16:19; Hab 2:18; Zec 10:2 [y]Isa 41:7; 46:6; Jer 10:3 [z]Isa 2:20; 31:7
40:20 [a]Isa 44:19 [b]S 1Sa 12:21 [c]S 1Sa 5:3
40:21 [d]ver 28; 2Ki 19:25; Isa 41:22; 42:9; 44:8; 48:3,5 [e]Ps 19:1; 50:6; Ac 14:17 [f]S Ge 1:1 [g]Ro 1:19 [h]Isa 48:13; 51:13

and less than nothing.[u]

18 To whom, then, will you compare God?[v]
What image[w] will you compare him to?
19 As for an idol,[x] a craftsman casts it,
and a goldsmith[y] overlays it with gold[z]
and fashions silver chains for it.
20 A man too poor to present such an offering
selects wood[a] that will not rot.
He looks for a skilled craftsman
to set up an idol[b] that will not topple.[c]

21 Do you not know?
Have you not heard?[d]
Has it not been told[e] you from the beginning?[f]
Have you not understood[g] since the earth was founded?[h]
22 He sits enthroned[i] above the circle of the earth,
and its people are like grasshoppers.[j]
He stretches out the heavens[k] like a canopy,[l]
and spreads them out like a tent[m] to live in.[n]
23 He brings princes[o] to naught
and reduces the rulers of this world to nothing.[p]
24 No sooner are they planted,
no sooner are they sown,
no sooner do they take root[q] in the ground,
than he blows[r] on them and they wither,[s]

40:22 [i]S 2Ch 6:18; S Ps 2:4 [j]S Nu 13:33 [k]S Ge 1:1; S Isa 48:13 [l]S Ge 1:8; S Job 22:14 [m]S Job 36:29 [n]S Job 26:7 **40:23** [o]S Job 12:18; S Isa 34:12 [p]S Job 12:19; Am 2:3 **40:24** [q]S Job 5:3 [r]S 2Sa 22:16; S Isa 11:4; 41:16 [s]S Job 8:12; S 18:16

j *13* Or *Spirit*; or *spirit*

with power and authority like a mighty ruler, yet his presence is like that of a caring shepherd tending his lambs (v. 11; cf. Ge 49:24; Eze 34:23; 37:24; Jn 10:11,14; Heb 13:20; 1Pe 5:4). This truth should fill God's people with faith, hope and prayerful longing for his nearness and special visitation, while they look for the day of his return and of final redemption (1Th 4:14–18).

40:11 GATHERS THE LAMBS IN HIS ARMS. God is described as one who picks up an individual lamb in order to protect it and carry it close to his heart (cf. Mt 6:24–34). Although God is all-powerful (v. 10) and the nations are regarded by him as dust (v. 15), he still cares for each of his own in a personal way. We must never think that God is so majestic that he ignores the needs and problems of the individual believer.

40:12–31 WHO HAS MEASURED. These verses emphasize God's wisdom, greatness, majesty and creative power (see article on THE ATTRIBUTES OF GOD, p. 882). The truths expressed here inspire his people to trust in him, the One who can deliver them and establish his kingdom forever.

and a whirlwind sweeps them
away like chaff.[t]
25"To whom will you compare me?[u]
Or who is my equal?" says the
Holy One.[v]
26Lift your eyes and look to the
heavens:[w]
Who created[x] all these?
He who brings out the starry
host[y] one by one,
and calls them each by name.
Because of his great power and
mighty strength,[z]
not one of them is missing.[a]
27Why do you say, O Jacob,
and complain, O Israel,
"My way is hidden from the LORD;
my cause is disregarded by my
God"?[b]
28Do you not know?
Have you not heard?[c]
The LORD is the everlasting[d] God,
the Creator[e] of the ends of the
earth.[f]
He will not grow tired or weary,[g]
and his understanding no one
can fathom.[h]
29He gives strength[i] to the weary[j]
and increases the power of the
weak.
30Even youths grow tired and weary,
and young men[k] stumble and
fall;[l]
31but those who hope[m] in the LORD
will renew their strength.[n]
They will soar on wings like
eagles;[o]
they will run and not grow
weary,
they will walk and not be
faint.[p]

40:24 [t]S Job 24:24; S Isa 41:2 **40:25** [u]S 1Sa 2:2; S 1Ch 16:25 [v]Isa 1:4; 37:23 **40:26** [w]Isa 51:6 [x]ver 28; Ps 89:11-13; Isa 42:5; 66:2 [y]S 2Ki 17:16; S Ne 9:6; S Job 38:32 [z]S Job 9:4; S Isa 45:24; Eph 1:19 [a]S Isa 34:16 **40:27** [b]S Job 6:29; S 27:2; Lk 18:7-8 **40:28** [c]S ver 21 [d]S Dt 33:27; S Ps 90:2 [e]S ver 26 [f]S Isa 37:16 [g]Isa 44:12 [h]S Ps 147:5; Ro 11:33 **40:29** [i]S Ge 18:14; S Ps 68:35; S 119:28 [j]Isa 50:4; 57:19; Jer 31:25 **40:30** [k]Isa 9:17; Jer 6:11; 9:21 [l]S Ps 20:8; Isa 5:27 **40:31** [m]S Ps 37:9; 40:1; S Isa 30:18; Lk 18:1 [n]S 1Sa 2:4; S 2Ki 6:33; S 2Co 4:16 [o]S Ex 19:4 [p]2Co 4:1; Heb 12:1-3

41:1 [q]Ps 37:7; Hab 2:20; Zep 1:7; Zec 2:13 [r]S Isa 11:11 [s]S 1Sa 2:4 [t]Isa 48:16; 57:3 [u]S Isa 1:18; 34:1; 50:8 **41:2** [v]S Ezr 1:2 [w]ver 25; Isa 13:4, 17; 44:28; 45:1, 13; 48:14; Jer 50:3; 51:11 [x]Isa 45:8,13 [y]Isa 44:28; Jer 25:9

The Helper of Israel

41 "Be silent[q] before me, you
islands![r]
Let the nations renew their
strength![s]
Let them come forward[t] and
speak;
let us meet together[u] at the
place of judgment.
2"Who has stirred[v] up one from
the east,[w]
calling him in righteousness[x] to
his service[k]?[y]
He hands nations over to him
and subdues kings before him.
He turns them to dust[z] with his
sword,
to windblown chaff[a] with his
bow.[b]
3He pursues them and moves on
unscathed,[c]
by a path his feet have not
traveled before.
4Who has done this and carried it
through,
calling[d] forth the generations
from the beginning?[e]
I, the LORD—with the first of them
and with the last[f]—I am he.[g]"
5The islands[h] have seen it and
fear;
the ends of the earth[i] tremble.
They approach and come forward;
6 each helps the other
and says to his brother, "Be
strong![j]"

[z]S 2Sa 22:43 [a]Ps 1:4; Isa 40:24 [b]S Isa 13:18 **41:3** [c]Da 8:4 **41:4** [d]ver 9; Isa 43:7 [e]ver 26; S Ge 1:1; Isa 46:10 [f]Isa 44:6; 48:12; Rev 1:8,17 [g]S Dt 32:39 **41:5** [h]S Isa 11:11; Eze 26:17-18 [i]S Dt 30:4; S Isa 11:12 **41:6** [j]S Jos 1:6

[k]2 Or / *whom victory meets at every step*

40:26 WHO CREATED ALL THESE? See article on CREATION, p. 6.

40:31 HOPE IN THE LORD WILL RENEW THEIR STRENGTH. To hope in the Lord is to trust him fully with our lives; it involves looking to him as our source of help and grace in time of need (cf. Ps 25:3–5; 27:14; Lk 2:25,36–38). Those who hope in the Lord are promised: (1) God's strength to revive them in the midst of exhaustion and weakness, of suffering and trial; (2) the ability to rise above their difficulties like an eagle that soars into the sky; and (3) the ability to run spiritually without tiring and to walk steadily forward without fainting at God's delays. God promises that if his people will patiently trust him, he will provide whatever is needed to sustain them constantly (1Pe 1:5).

41:1 MEET TOGETHER AT THE PLACE OF JUDGMENT. In this chapter the nations are challenged to demonstrate that they have the same power, wisdom and foreknowledge as the God of Israel.

41:2 ONE FROM THE EAST. More than 150 years before Cyrus's birth, Isaiah foresaw that God would raise up a man to do his will by conquering the nations and protecting Israel; this man was Cyrus, the king of Persia (559–530 B.C.; see 44:28; 45:1), the one who freed the Jews from their Babylonian exile. He was called in righteousness, not because he himself was righteous, but because he would carry out God's righteous plan of redemption on the earth.

41:6 EACH HELPS THE OTHER. Alliances among nations would not stop the advance of Cyrus as the instrument of God's purpose.

[7]The craftsman[k] encourages the
goldsmith,[l]
and he who smooths with the
hammer
spurs on him who strikes the
anvil.
He says of the welding, "It is
good."
He nails down the idol so it will
not topple.[m]

[8]"But you, O Israel, my servant,[n]
Jacob, whom I have chosen,[o]
you descendants of Abraham[p]
my friend,[q]
[9]I took you from the ends of the
earth,[r]
from its farthest corners I
called[s] you.
I said, 'You are my servant';[t]
I have chosen[u] you and have
not rejected you.
[10]So do not fear,[v] for I am with
you;[w]
do not be dismayed, for I am
your God.
I will strengthen[x] you and help[y]
you;
I will uphold you[z] with my
righteous right hand.[a]

[11]"All who rage[b] against you
will surely be ashamed and
disgraced;[c]
those who oppose[d] you
will be as nothing and perish.[e]
[12]Though you search for your
enemies,
you will not find them.[f]
Those who wage war against you
will be as nothing[g] at all.
[13]For I am the LORD, your God,
who takes hold of your right
hand[h]
and says to you, Do not fear;
I will help[i] you.
[14]Do not be afraid,[j] O worm[k]
Jacob,
O little Israel,
for I myself will help[l] you,"
declares the LORD,
your Redeemer,[m] the Holy
One[n] of Israel.
[15]"See, I will make you into a
threshing sledge,[o]
new and sharp, with many teeth.
You will thresh the mountains[p]
and crush them,
and reduce the hills to chaff.[q]
[16]You will winnow[r] them, the wind
will pick them up,
and a gale[s] will blow them
away.[t]
But you will rejoice[u] in the LORD
and glory[v] in the Holy One[w] of
Israel.

[17]"The poor and needy search for
water,[x]
but there is none;
their tongues are parched with
thirst.[y]
But I the LORD will answer[z] them;
I, the God of Israel, will not
forsake[a] them.
[18]I will make rivers flow[b] on barren
heights,
and springs within the valleys.
I will turn the desert[c] into pools
of water,[d]
and the parched ground into
springs.[e]
[19]I will put in the desert[f]
the cedar and the acacia,[g] the
myrtle and the olive.
I will set pines[h] in the wasteland,
the fir and the cypress[i]
together,[j]
[20]so that people may see and
know,[k]
may consider and understand,[l]
that the hand[m] of the LORD has
done this,
that the Holy One[n] of Israel
has created[o] it.

41:7 [k]Isa 44:13; Jer 10:3-5 [l]S Isa 40:19 [m]S 1Sa 5:3; Isa 46:7 **41:8** [n]S Ps 136:22; S Isa 27:11 [o]S Isa 14:1 [p]S Isa 29:22; 51:2; 63:16 [q]2Ch 20:7; Jas 2:23 **41:9** [r]Isa 11:12; S 37:16 [s]S ver 4 [t]S Isa 20:3 [u]S Dt 7:6 **41:10** [v]S Ge 15:1 [w]S Dt 3:22; Jos 1:9; Isa 43:2, 5; Jer 30:10; 46:27-28; Ro 8:31 [x]S Ps 68:35; S 119:28 [y]ver 13-14; Isa 44:2; 49:8; 50:7,9 [z]S Ps 18:35; S 119:117 [a]S Ex 3:20; S Job 40:14 **41:11** [b]S Isa 17:12 [c]Isa 29:22; 45:24; 54:17 [d]S Ex 23:22 [e]S Isa 29:8; S Jer 2:3 **41:12** [f]Ps 37:35-36; S Isa 34:12 [g]S Job 7:8; Isa 17:14; 29:20 **41:13** [h]Ps 73:23; Isa 42:6; 45:1; 51:18 [i]ver 10 **41:14** [j]S Ge 15:1 [k]S Job 4:19; S Ps 22:6 [l]S ver 10 [m]S Ex 15:13; S Job 19:25; S Isa 1:27 [n]ver 16,20; S Isa 1:4 **41:15** [o]S Job 41:30; S Isa 10:5; S 21:10 [p]S Ex 19:18; S Ps 107:33; Jer 9:10; Eze 33:28 [q]S ver 2 **41:16** [r]Jer 15:7; 51:2 [s]S Isa 40:24 [t]Da 2:35 [u]S Isa 25:9 [v]Isa 45:25; 60:19 [w]S ver 14; S Mk 1:24 **41:17** [x]Isa 43:20 [y]S Isa 35:7 [z]S Isa 30:19 [a]S Dt 31:6; S Ps 27:9 **41:18** [b]S Isa 30:25 [c]Isa 43:19 [d]S 2Ki 3:17 [e]S Job 38:26; S Isa 35:7 **41:19** [f]S Isa 35:1; 51:3 [g]Ex 25:5,10,13 [h]S Isa 37:24 [i]Isa 44:14 [j]Isa 60:13 **41:20** [k]S Ex 6:7 [l]S Isa 29:24 [m]Ezr 7:6; 8:31; Isa 50:2; 51:9; 59:1; 66:14; Jer 32:17 [n]S ver 14; Isa 43:3, 14 [o]S Isa 4:5

41:8 JACOB, WHOM I HAVE CHOSEN. Israel must not fear destruction, because God had chosen them as his channel to carry out the promise of redemption he had made to their ancestors. Through the nation of Israel would come both the Messiah and the written revelation of God, by which salvation would go to all the nations of the earth (see article on GOD'S COVENANT WITH ABRAHAM, ISAAC AND JACOB, p. 46).

41:10–11 I AM WITH YOU. NT believers have also become God's chosen servants (Eph 1:3–12; 1Pe 2:9). We can therefore claim the promises of these verses for ourselves. We must not fear other humans, because God is with us (cf. 40:9; 43:2,5; Ge 15:1; Ac 18:9–10): (1) to impart the grace and strength needed to face all of life's circumstances; (2) to help us through times of crises as our source of peace; and (3) to sustain us and to be our advocate.

21"Present your case,[p]" says the
LORD.
"Set forth your arguments," says
Jacob's King.[q]
22"Bring in ⌞your idols⌟ to tell us
what is going to happen.[r]
Tell us what the former things[s]
were,
so that we may consider them
and know their final outcome.
Or declare to us the things to
come,[t]
23 tell us what the future holds,
so we may know[u] that you are
gods.
Do something, whether good or
bad,[v]
so that we will be dismayed[w]
and filled with fear.
24But you are less than nothing[x]
and your works are utterly
worthless;[y]
he who chooses you is
detestable.[z]

25"I have stirred[a] up one from the
north,[b] and he comes—
one from the rising sun who
calls on my name.
He treads[c] on rulers as if they
were mortar,
as if he were a potter treading
the clay.
26Who told of this from the
beginning,[d] so we could
know,
or beforehand, so we could say,
'He was right'?
No one told of this,
no one foretold[e] it,
no one heard any words[f] from
you.
27I was the first to tell[g] Zion,
'Look, here they are!'
I gave to Jerusalem a messenger
of good tidings.[h]
28I look but there is no one[i]—
no one among them to give
counsel,[j]
no one to give answer[k] when I
ask them.
29See, they are all false!
Their deeds amount to
nothing;[l]
their images[m] are but wind[n]
and confusion.

The Servant of the LORD

42 "Here is my servant,[o] whom
I uphold,
my chosen one[p] in whom I
delight;[q]
I will put my Spirit[r] on him
and he will bring justice[s] to the
nations.[t]
2He will not shout or cry out,[u]
or raise his voice in the streets.
3A bruised reed[v] he will not
break,[w]
and a smoldering wick he will
not snuff out.[x]
In faithfulness he will bring forth
justice;[y]
4 he will not falter or be
discouraged
till he establishes justice[z] on
earth.
In his law[a] the islands[b] will
put their hope."[c]

5This is what God the LORD says—
he who created the heavens[d] and
stretched them out,
who spread out the earth[e] and
all that comes out of it,[f]
who gives breath[g] to its people,

41:21 [p]S ver 1 [q]Isa 43:15; 44:6 **41:22** [r]ver 26; Isa 43:9; 44:7; 45:21; 48:14 [s]Isa 43:18,26; 46:9; 48:3 [t]Isa 42:9; 43:19; 46:10; 48:6; 65:17; Jn 13:19 **41:23** [u]Isa 45:3 [v]Jer 10:5 [w]S 2Ki 19:26 **41:24** [x]S Isa 37:19; 1Co 8:4 [y]S 1Sa 12:21; Jer 8:19; 10:5,8,15 [z]S Ps 109:7; S Isa 1:13; S 48:8 **41:25** [a]S Ezr 1:2 [b]S ver 2; Jer 50:9, 41; 51:48 [c]S 2Sa 22:43; S Isa 5:5; Na 3:14 **41:26** [d]S ver 4 [e]S ver 22; Isa 52:6 [f]S 1Ki 18:26; Hab 2:18-19 **41:27** [g]Isa 48:3, 16 [h]S Isa 40:9 **41:28** [i]Ps 22:11; Isa 50:2; 59:16; 63:5; 64:7; Eze 22:30 [j]Isa 40:13-14 [k]S 1Ki 18:26; Isa 65:12; 66:4; Jer 25:4 **41:29** [l]S 1Sa 12:21 [m]S Isa 37:19 [n]Jer 5:13 **42:1** [o]S Isa 20:3; S Mt 20:28 [p]S Isa 14:1; Lk 9:35; 23:35; 1Pe 2:4,6 [q]Mt 3:17 [r]S Isa 11:2; S 44:3; Mt 3:16-17; S Jn 3:34 [s]S Isa 9:7 [t]S Ge 49:10 **42:2** [u]Pr 8:1-4 **42:3** [v]S Isa 36:6 [w]S Job 30:24 [x]S Job 13:25 [y]Ps 72:2; 96:13 **42:4** [z]S Isa 2:4 [a]ver 21; Ex 34:29; Isa 51:4 [b]S Isa 11:11 [c]S Ge 49:10; Mt 12:18-21* **42:5** [d]S Ge 1:6; Ps 102:25; Isa 48:13 [e]S Ge 1:1 [f]Ps 24:2; Ac 17:24 [g]S Ge 2:7; Ac 17:25

41:21–24 PRESENT YOUR CASE. God challenges the nations to foretell the future by their idols as accurately as Isaiah has done by the Spirit of the Lord.

41:25 ONE FROM THE NORTH. This phrase describes Cyrus (see v. 2, note). North is the direction from which invasions into Israel usually came (cf. Jer 1:14; 6:22; 25:9; 46:20; 47:2; 50:3). Although Cyrus was not a worshiper of the Lord, he did use the Lord's name in his decree to allow the exiles to return to the promised land (Ezr 1:2).

42:1–7 HERE IS MY SERVANT. These verses are quoted in part in the NT (see Mt 12:18–21); clearly the servant about whom the prophet writes is Jesus Christ, the Messiah.

42:1 I WILL PUT MY SPIRIT ON HIM. The Messiah would be anointed with the Holy Spirit in order to perform his task of redemption (cf. 61:1; see article on JESUS AND THE HOLY SPIRIT, p. 1546). His followers, who would continue what Jesus had begun, also needed the Holy Spirit poured out upon them (Ac 1:8; 2:4). Only the Spirit can enable believers to minister with the necessary wisdom, revelation and power.

42:1 BRING JUSTICE TO THE NATIONS. By the power of the Holy Spirit, the Messiah would bring the standards of holy justice and the principles of divine truth to all the nations; his work was therefore missionary in nature. Today this same task is the responsibility of those who bear the name of Christ. He baptizes his followers in the Holy Spirit so that they may carry out this commission (see Ac 1:8, note).

and life to those who walk on it:
6"I, the LORD, have called[h] you in
righteousness;[i]
I will take hold of your hand.[j]
I will keep[k] you and will make
you
to be a covenant[l] for the
people
and a light[m] for the Gentiles,[n]
7to open eyes that are blind,[o]
to free[p] captives from prison[q]
and to release from the dungeon
those who sit in
darkness.[r]

8"I am the LORD;[s] that is my
name![t]
I will not give my glory to
another[u]
or my praise to idols.[v]
9See, the former things[w] have
taken place,
and new things I declare;
before they spring into being
I announce[x] them to you."

Song of Praise to the Lord

10Sing[y] to the LORD a new song,[z]
his praise[a] from the ends of the
earth,[b]
you who go down to the sea, and
all that is in it,[c]
you islands,[d] and all who live
in them.
11Let the desert[e] and its towns
raise their voices;
let the settlements where
Kedar[f] lives rejoice.
Let the people of Sela[g] sing for
joy;
let them shout from the
mountaintops.[h]
12Let them give glory[i] to the LORD
and proclaim his praise[j] in the
islands.[k]
13The LORD will march out like a
mighty[l] man,
like a warrior[m] he will stir up
his zeal;[n]
with a shout[o] he will raise the
battle cry
and will triumph over his
enemies.[p]

14"For a long time I have kept
silent,[q]
I have been quiet and held
myself back.[r]
But now, like a woman in
childbirth,
I cry out, I gasp and pant.[s]
15I will lay waste[t] the mountains[u]
and hills
and dry up all their vegetation;
I will turn rivers into islands
and dry up[v] the pools.
16I will lead[w] the blind[x] by ways
they have not known,
along unfamiliar paths I will
guide them;
I will turn the darkness into
light[y] before them
and make the rough places
smooth.[z]
These are the things I will do;
I will not forsake[a] them.
17But those who trust in idols,
who say to images, 'You are our
gods,'[b]
will be turned back in utter
shame.[c]

Israel Blind and Deaf

18"Hear, you deaf;[d]
look, you blind, and see!
19Who is blind[e] but my servant,[f]
and deaf like the messenger[g] I
send?
Who is blind like the one
committed[h] to me,
blind like the servant of the
LORD?

42:6 [h]Ex 31:2; S Jdg 4:10; Isa 41:9-10; 43:1 [i]Isa 45:24; Jer 23:6; Da 9:7 [j]Isa 41:13; 45:1 [k]Isa 26:3; 27:3 [l]Isa 49:8; 54:10; 59:21; 61:8; Jer 31:31; 32:40; Mal 3:1; S Lk 22:20 [m]S Isa 9:2 [n]S Isa 26:18; S Lk 2:32 **42:7** [o]S Ps 146:8; S Isa 32:3; Mt 11:5 [p]Isa 49:9; 51:14; 52:2; Zec 2:7 [q]S Ps 66:11; S Isa 24:22; 48:20; Zec 9:11; S Lk 4:19; 2Ti 2:26; Heb 2:14-15 [r]S Ps 107:10,14; Ac 26:18 **42:8** [s]Ps 81:10; Isa 43:3,11,15; 46:9; 49:23 [t]S Ex 3:15; S 6:3 [u]Isa 48:11 [v]S Ex 8:10; S 20:4 **42:9** [w]S Isa 41:22 [x]S Isa 40:21; Eze 2:4 **42:10** [y]S Ex 15:1 [z]S Ps 96:1 [a]1Ki 10:9; Isa 60:6 [b]S Dt 30:4; S Ps 48:10; 65:5; Isa 49:6 [c]S 1Ch 16:32; Ps 96:11 [d]S Isa 11:11 **42:11** [e]S Isa 32:16 [f]S Ge 25:13; Isa 60:7 [g]S Jdg 1:36 [h]Isa 52:7; Na 1:15 **42:12** [i]S 1Ch 16:24; S Isa 24:15 [j]S Ps 26:7; S 66:2; 1Pe 2:9 [k]S Isa 11:11 **42:13** [l]S Isa 9:6 [m]S Ex 14:14 [n]S Isa 26:11 [o]S Jos 6:5; Jer 25:30; Hos 11:10; Joel 3:16; Am 1:2; 3:4,8 [p]Isa 66:14 **42:14** [q]S Est 4:14; S Ps 50:21 [r]S Ge 43:31; Lk 18:7; 2Pe 3:9 [s]Jer 4:31

42:15 [t]Eze 38:20 [u]S Ps 107:33 [v]S Isa 11:15; 50:2; Na 1:4-6 **42:16** [w]S Isa 29:24; 40:11; 57:18; 58:11; Jer 31:8-9; Lk 1:78-79 [x]S Isa 32:3 [y]S Ps 18:28; Isa 58:8, 10; S Ac 26:18 [z]S Isa 26:7; Lk 3:5 [a]S Dt 4:31; Heb 13:5 **42:17** [b]S Ex 32:4 [c]S Ps 97:7; S Isa 1:29 **42:18** [d]S Isa 35:5 **42:19** [e]Isa 43:8; Eze 12:2 [f]Isa 41:8-9 [g]Isa 44:26; Hag 1:13 [h]Isa 26:3

42:6 A LIGHT FOR THE GENTILES. The Messiah's mission would include bringing the covenant of salvation to the Gentiles as well as to the Jews. The new covenant would be established by his death (Jer 31:31–34; Heb 8:6–13; 9:15; see article on THE OLD COVENANT AND THE NEW COVENANT, p. 1926).

42:7 TO OPEN EYES THAT ARE BLIND. By his death and the power of the Holy Spirit, the Messiah would free all believers from the darkness of sin and guilt (see Ro 5:12, note) and release them from the power of Satan (cf. 1Jn 3:8).

42:10–17 SING TO THE LORD. Isaiah foresees a time when the Gentiles and faithful Israel will sing the praise of their Lord from the ends of the earth because of the glorious redemption and victory they have experienced through him.

42:18–25 YOU DEAF ... YOU BLIND. Because of the spiritual blindness and deafness of God's people, they were being plundered and looted by their enemy; there was no one to deliver and restore them.

20 You have seen many things, but
have paid no attention;
your ears are open, but you hear
nothing."[i]
21 It pleased the LORD
for the sake[j] of his
righteousness
to make his law[k] great and
glorious.
22 But this is a people plundered[l]
and looted,
all of them trapped in pits[m]
or hidden away in prisons.[n]
They have become plunder,
with no one to rescue them;[o]
they have been made loot,
with no one to say, "Send them
back."
23 Which of you will listen to this
or pay close attention[p] in time
to come?
24 Who handed Jacob over to become
loot,
and Israel to the plunderers?[q]
Was it not the LORD,[r]
against whom we have sinned?
For they would not follow[s] his
ways;
they did not obey his law.[t]
25 So he poured out on them his
burning anger,[u]
the violence of war.
It enveloped them in flames,[v] yet
they did not understand;[w]
it consumed them, but they did
not take it to heart.[x]

Israel's Only Savior

43 But now, this is what the
LORD says—
he who created[y] you, O Jacob,
he who formed[z] you, O Israel:[a]
"Fear not, for I have redeemed[b]
you;
I have summoned you by
name;[c] you are mine.[d]
2 When you pass through the
waters,[e]
I will be with you;[f]
and when you pass through the
rivers,
they will not sweep over you.
When you walk through the fire,[g]
you will not be burned;
the flames will not set you
ablaze.[h]
3 For I am the LORD, your God,[i]
the Holy One[j] of Israel, your
Savior;[k]
I give Egypt[l] for your ransom,
Cush[1][m] and Seba[n] in your
stead.[o]
4 Since you are precious and
honored[p] in my sight,
and because I love[q] you,
I will give men in exchange for
you,
and people in exchange for your
life.
5 Do not be afraid,[r] for I am with
you;[s]
I will bring your children[t] from
the east
and gather[u] you from the
west.[v]
6 I will say to the north, 'Give them
up!'
and to the south,[w] 'Do not hold
them back.'
Bring my sons from afar
and my daughters[x] from the
ends of the earth[y]—
7 everyone who is called by my
name,[z]
whom I created[a] for my
glory,[b]
whom I formed and made.[c]"
8 Lead out those who have eyes but
are blind,[d]
who have ears but are deaf.[e]
9 All the nations gather together[f]
and the peoples assemble.

42:20 [i] Isa 6:9-10; 43:8; Jer 5:21; 6:10 **42:21** [j] Isa 43:25 [k] S ver 4; 2Co 3:7 **42:22** [l] S Jdg 6:4; S 2Ki 24:13 [m] S Isa 24:18 [n] S Ps 66:11; S Isa 24:22 [o] S Isa 5:29 **42:23** [p] Dt 32:29; Ps 81:13; Isa 47:7; 48:18; 57:11 **42:24** [q] S 2Ki 17:6; Isa 43:28; 47:6 [r] Isa 10:5-6 [s] S Isa 30:15 [t] S Jos 1:7; S Ps 119:136; Isa 5:24; Jer 44:10 **42:25** [u] S 2Ki 22:13; S Job 40:11; S Isa 51:17; S Eze 7:19 [v] 2Ki 25:9; Isa 66:15; Jer 4:4; 21:12; La 2:3; Na 1:6 [w] S Isa 1:3 [x] Isa 29:13; 47:7; 57:1,11; Hos 7:9 **43:1** [y] S Isa 27:11 [z] S ver 7; S Ge 2:7 [a] Ge 32:28; Isa 44:21 [b] S Ex 6:6; S Job 19:25 [c] S Isa 42:6; 45:3-4; 49:1 [d] S Dt 7:6; Mal 3:17 **43:2** [e] S Isa 8:7 [f] S Ge 26:3; S Ex 14:22 [g] Isa 29:6; 30:27 [h] Ps 66:12; Da 3:25-27 **43:3** [i] S Ex 20:2 [j] S Isa 41:20 [k] S Ex 14:30; S Jdg 2:18; S Ps 3:8; S Isa 25:9 [l] S Ps 68:31; Isa 19:1; Eze 29:20 [m] S Isa 20:3 [n] S Ge 10:7 [o] S Pr 21:18 **43:4** [p] Ex 19:5; Isa 49:5 [q] Isa 63:9; Rev 3:9 **43:5** [r] S Ge 15:1; Isa 44:2 [s] S Ge 21:22; S Ex 14:22; Jer 30:10-11 [t] Isa 41:8; 54:3; 61:9; 66:22 [u] S Isa 11:12; S 49:18 [v] S Isa 24:14; Zec 8:7; S Mt 8:11 **43:6** [w] Ps 107:3 [x] Isa 60:4; Eze 16:61; 2Co 6:18 [y] S Dt 30:4; S Isa 11:12; Jer 23:8; Eze 36:24 **43:7** [z] Isa 48:1; 56:5; 62:2; 63:19; 65:1; Jer 15:16; Jas 2:7 [a] S Isa 27:11 [b] S Ps 86:9 [c] ver 1,21; Ps 100:3; Eph 2:10; S Isa 19:25 **43:8** [d] S Isa 6:9-10 [e] S Isa 42:20; Eze 12:2 **43:9** [f] S Isa 41:1; 45:20; 48:14

1 3 That is, the upper Nile region

43:1–28 BUT NOW. This chapter speaks about Israel's deliverance from Babylonian captivity because of God's love for his people.

43:1–7 THIS IS WHAT THE LORD SAYS. In this section, God expresses his love for Israel and the benefits of that love. All the blessings mentioned here apply even more to those who are God's children through faith in Christ. God has created and redeemed us; we belong to him, and he knows each one of us by name (v. 1). When we pass through trouble and affliction, we will not be destroyed, for he is with us (vv. 2,5). We are precious and honored in his sight, objects of his great love (v. 4).

43:8–13 BUT ARE BLIND. Although Israel was still spiritually blind, God had a future for them in his plan of redemption; they would still be his witnesses and his servants (v. 10; see article on ISRAEL IN GOD'S PLAN OF SALVATION, p. 1730).

Which of them foretold[g] this
and proclaimed to us the former things?
Let them bring in their witnesses
to prove they were right,
so that others may hear and say,
"It is true."
10"You are my witnesses,[h]" declares the LORD,
"and my servant[i] whom I have chosen,
so that you may know[j] and believe me
and understand that I am he.
Before me no god[k] was formed,
nor will there be one after me.[l]
11I, even I, am the LORD,[m]
and apart from me there is no savior.[n]
12I have revealed and saved and proclaimed—
I, and not some foreign god[o] among you.
You are my witnesses,[p]" declares the LORD, "that I am God.
13 Yes, and from ancient days[q] I am he.[r]
No one can deliver out of my hand.
When I act, who can reverse it?"[s]

God's Mercy and Israel's Unfaithfulness

14This is what the LORD says—
your Redeemer,[t] the Holy One[u] of Israel:
"For your sake I will send to Babylon
and bring down as fugitives[v] all the Babylonians,[m][w]
in the ships in which they took pride.
15I am the LORD,[x] your Holy One,
Israel's Creator,[y] your King.[z]"
16This is what the LORD says—
he who made a way through the sea,
a path through the mighty waters,[a]
17who drew out[b] the chariots and horses,[c]
the army and reinforcements together,[d]
and they lay[e] there, never to rise again,
extinguished, snuffed out like a wick:[f]
18"Forget the former things;[g]
do not dwell on the past.
19See, I am doing a new thing![h]
Now it springs up; do you not perceive it?
I am making a way in the desert[i]
and streams in the wasteland.[j]
20The wild animals[k] honor me,
the jackals[l] and the owls,
because I provide water[m] in the desert
and streams in the wasteland,
to give drink to my people, my chosen,
21 the people I formed[n] for myself[o]
that they may proclaim my praise.[p]
22"Yet you have not called upon me, O Jacob,
you have not wearied[q] yourselves for me, O Israel.[r]
23You have not brought me sheep for burnt offerings,[s]
nor honored[t] me with your sacrifices.[u]
I have not burdened[v] you with grain offerings
nor wearied you with demands[w] for incense.[x]
24You have not bought any fragrant calamus[y] for me,
or lavished on me the fat[z] of your sacrifices.
But you have burdened me with your sins
and wearied[a] me with your offenses.[b]
25"I, even I, am he who blots out
your transgressions,[c] for my own sake,[d]

43:9 [g]S Isa 41:26 **43:10** [h]ver 12; S Jos 24:22 [i]S Isa 20:3; 41:8-9 [j]S Ex 6:7 [k]ver 11; S Ps 86:10; Isa 19:21; 44:6,8; 45:5-6,14 [l]S Dt 4:35; S 32:39; Jer 14:22 **43:11** [m]S Ex 6:2; S Isa 42:8 [n]S ver 10; S Ps 3:8; S 18:31; S Isa 25:9; 64:4 **43:12** [o]S Dt 32:12 [p]S ver 10 **43:13** [q]Ps 90:2 [r]S Dt 32:39; Isa 46:4; 48:12 [s]S Nu 23:8; S Job 9:12 **43:14** [t]S Ex 15:13; S Job 19:25 [u]S Isa 1:4; S 41:20 [v]Isa 13:14-15 [w]S Isa 23:13 **43:15** [x]S Isa 42:8 [y]S Isa 27:11; 45:11 [z]S Isa 41:21 **43:16** [a]S Ex 14:29; S 15:8; S Isa 11:15 **43:17** [b]Ps 118:12; Isa 1:31 [c]S Ex 14:22 [d]S Ex 14:9 [e]Ps 76:5-6 [f]S Job 13:25; Jer 51:21; Eze 38:4 **43:18** [g]S Isa 41:22 **43:19** [h]S Isa 41:22; Jer 16:14-15; 23:7-8; 2Co 5:17; Rev 21:5 [i]S Isa 40:3 [j]S Ps 126:4; S Isa 33:21; S 35:7 **43:20** [k]S Ps 148:10 [l]S Isa 13:22 [m]S Nu 20:8 **43:21** [n]S ver 7; S Ge 2:7 [o]Mal 3:17 [p]S Ps 66:2; 102:18; 1Pe 2:9 **43:22** [q]S Jos 22:5; S Isa 1:14 [r]Isa 30:11 **43:23** [s]S Ex 29:41 [t]Zec 7:5-6; Mal 1:6-8 [u]Am 5:25 [v]Mic 6:3; Mal 1:12-13 [w]Jer 7:22 [x]Ex 30:35; S Lev 2:1 **43:24** [y]S Ex 30:23 [z]Lev 3:9 [a]S Isa 1:14; S 7:13; S Jer 8:21 [b]Jer 44:22; Mal 2:17 **43:25** [c]S 2Sa 12:13; S 2Ch 6:21; Mk 2:7; Lk 5:21; Ac 3:19 [d]S Isa 37:35; S Eze 20:44

m *14* Or *Chaldeans*

43:14–21 BABYLON. God would judge the Babylonians and deliver his people. They would receive a "new thing" (v. 19), i.e., a new time of forgiveness, blessing, restoration and God's presence; for this they would praise their God (v. 21).

43:22–28 YET YOU HAVE NOT CALLED UPON ME. At the time of Isaiah's writing, Judah was not yet calling on God for forgiveness and help; they continued to wallow in their sins (v. 24). If they would not repent, they would be consigned to destruction and scorn (v. 28).

and remembers your sins[e] no
more.[f]
26Review the past for me,
let us argue the matter
together;[g]
state the case[h] for your
innocence.
27Your first father[i] sinned;
your spokesmen[j] rebelled[k]
against me.
28So I will disgrace the dignitaries of
your temple,
and I will consign Jacob to
destruction[n][l]
and Israel to scorn.[m]

Israel the Chosen

44 "But now listen, O Jacob, my
servant,[n]
Israel, whom I have chosen.[o]
2This is what the LORD says—
he who made[p] you, who formed
you in the womb,[q]
and who will help[r] you:
Do not be afraid,[s] O Jacob, my
servant,[t]
Jeshurun,[u] whom I have
chosen.
3For I will pour water[v] on the
thirsty land,
and streams on the dry
ground;[w]
I will pour out my Spirit[x] on your
offspring,
and my blessing[y] on your
descendants.[z]
4They will spring up like grass[a] in
a meadow,
like poplar trees[b] by flowing
streams.[c]
5One will say, 'I belong[d] to the
LORD';
another will call himself by the
name of Jacob;

Isa 59:21

43:25 [e]Isa 64:9; Mic 7:18 [f]S Job 7:21; S Isa 38:17 **43:26** [g]S Isa 1:18 [h]S Isa 41:1; 49:25; 50:8 **43:27** [i]S Ge 12:18 [j]Isa 9:15; 28:7; Jer 5:31 [k]S Isa 24:20; S 48:8 **43:28** [l]S Nu 5:27; S Dt 13:15; S Isa 42:24; S Zec 5:3 [m]S Ps 39:8; Jer 24:9; Eze 5:15 **44:1** [n]ver 21 [o]S Ge 16:11; S Isa 14:1 **44:2** [p]ver 21; S Ps 149:2 [q]S Ge 2:7; S Ps 139:13; S Isa 27:11 [r]S Isa 41:10 [s]S Isa 43:5 [t]Jer 30:10; 46:27 [u]S Nu 23:21; S Dt 32:15 **44:3** [v]Joel 3:18; Jn 4:10 [w]S Pr 9:5; S Isa 32:2; S 35:7 [x]S Isa 11:2; Eze 36:27; S Mk 1:8; S Ac 2:17 [y]Mal 3:10 [z]Isa 61:9; 65:23 **44:4** [a]S Job 5:25; S Ps 72:16 [b]S Lev 23:40 [c]S Job 40:22 **44:5** [d]Ps 116:16; Isa 19:21; Jer 50:5 [e]Ex 13:9 [f]Isa 60:3; 66:23; Zec 8:20-22; 13:9; 14:16 **44:6** [g]S Isa 41:21 [h]S Job 19:25; Isa 43:1 [i]S Isa 41:4; Rev 1:8,17 [j]S Dt 6:4; S 1Ch 17:20; S Ps 18:31; S Isa 43:10 **44:7** [k]S Dt 32:39 [l]S Isa 41:22,26 **44:8** [m]S Isa 40:21; S 42:9 [n]S Isa 43:10 [o]S Ge 49:24 **44:9** [p]S Ex 20:4; S Lev 19:4; Isa 40:19 [q]S Isa 41:24 [r]S Isa 26:11 [s]S Isa 1:29; 65:13; 66:5; Jer 22:22 **44:10** [t]S Isa 40:19 [u]Isa 41:29; Jer 10:5; Ac 19:26

still another will write on his
hand,[e] 'The LORD's,'[f]
and will take the name Israel.

The LORD, Not Idols

6"This is what the LORD says—
Israel's King[g] and Redeemer,[h]
the LORD Almighty:
I am the first and I am the last;[i]
apart from me there is no God.[j]
7Who then is like me?[k] Let him
proclaim it.
Let him declare and lay out
before me
what has happened since I
established my ancient
people,
and what is yet to come—
yes, let him foretell[l] what will
come.
8Do not tremble, do not be afraid.
Did I not proclaim[m] this and
foretell it long ago?
You are my witnesses. Is there any
God[n] besides me?
No, there is no other Rock;[o] I
know not one."
9All who make idols[p] are nothing,
and the things they treasure are
worthless.[q]
Those who would speak up for
them are blind;[r]
they are ignorant, to their own
shame.[s]
10Who shapes a god and casts an
idol,[t]
which can profit him nothing?[u]

[n] *28* The Hebrew term refers to the irrevocable giving over of things or persons to the LORD, often by totally destroying them.

44:3 POUR OUT MY SPIRIT ON YOUR OFFSPRING. Although Israel was largely an apostate nation in Isaiah's time, he prophesied that the day would come when the Holy Spirit would be poured out on a future generation (cf. 32:15; Jer 31:33–34; Eze 36:26–27; 39:29; Zec 12:10—13:1). This prophecy finds partial fulfillment on the day of Pentecost (cf. Joel 2:25–29; Ac 2:17–18; see Ac 1:8 and 2:4, notes) and awaits complete fulfillment for Israel after they accept Christ as the Messiah (see Ro 11:25–26, notes). The outpouring of God's Spirit upon his people is associated with restoration, blessing and fruitfulness (vv. 3–4).

44:5 I BELONG TO THE LORD. A prominent result of the Spirit being poured out upon us is our testimony that we belong to the Lord and that he is our heavenly Father. The Spirit creates in us the confidence that we belong to God and that we have all the rights and privileges of being his children (see Ro 8:16, note; Gal 4:6, note).

44:6–20 THIS IS WHAT THE LORD SAYS. God exposes the foolishness of making an idol or a god out of material substance and then praying to it for help (vv. 12,17); even today people make all kinds of statues and idols and bow before them in prayer and adoration, hoping that the spirit whom the image represents will help and deliver them (v. 17).

11He and his kind will be put to
shame;[v]
craftsmen are nothing but men.
Let them all come together and
take their stand;
they will be brought down to
terror and infamy.[w]

12The blacksmith[x] takes a tool
and works with it in the coals;
he shapes an idol with hammers,
he forges it with the might of
his arm.[y]
He gets hungry and loses his
strength;
he drinks no water and grows
faint.[z]

13The carpenter[a] measures with a
line
and makes an outline with a
marker;
he roughs it out with chisels
and marks it with compasses.
He shapes it in the form of man,[b]
of man in all his glory,
that it may dwell in a shrine.[c]

14He cut down cedars,
or perhaps took a cypress or
oak.
He let it grow among the trees of
the forest,
or planted a pine,[d] and the rain
made it grow.

15It is man's fuel[e] for burning;
some of it he takes and warms
himself,
he kindles a fire and bakes
bread.
But he also fashions a god and
worships[f] it;
he makes an idol and bows[g]
down to it.

16Half of the wood he burns in the
fire;
over it he prepares his meal,
he roasts his meat and eats his
fill.
He also warms himself and says,
"Ah! I am warm; I see the
fire.[h]"

17From the rest he makes a god, his
idol;
he bows down to it and
worships.[i]
He prays[j] to it and says,
"Save[k] me; you are my god."

18They know nothing, they
understand[l] nothing;

44:11 [v]S ver 9; S Isa 1:29 [w]S 2Ki 19:18; S Isa 37:19
44:12 [x]S Isa 40:19; 41:6-7; 54:16 [y]Ac 17:29 [z]Isa 40:28
44:13 [a]S Isa 41:7 [b]Ps 115:4-7 [c]S Jdg 17:4-5
44:14 [d]S Isa 41:19
44:15 [e]ver 19 [f]S Ex 20:5; Rev 9:20 [g]S 2Ch 25:14
44:16 [h]Isa 47:14
44:17 [i]S Ex 20:5; Isa 2:8; Jer 1:16 [j]S 1Ki 18:26 [k]S Jdg 10:14; Isa 45:20; 46:7; 47:15
44:18 [l]Isa 1:3; S 16:12; Jer 4:22; 10:8,14,14-15 [m]S Isa 6:9-10; S 29:10
44:19 [n]ver 18-19; Isa 5:13; 27:11; 45:20 [o]ver 15 [p]S Dt 27:15 [q]Isa 40:20
44:20 [r]Ps 102:9 [s]S Job 15:31; Ro 1:21-23,28; 2Th 2:11; 2Ti 3:13 [t]S Dt 4:28; Hos 10:5; 13:2 [u]Isa 59:3,4,13; Jer 9:3; 10:14; 51:17; Ro 1:25
44:21 [v]Isa 46:8; Zec 10:9 [w]S Isa 43:1 [x]S Ps 136:22; S Isa 27:11 [y]Ps 27:10; Isa 49:15; Jer 31:20
44:22 [z]S 2Sa 12:13; S 2Ch 6:21; Ac 3:19 [a]S Job 22:23; Isa 45:22; 55:7; Jer 36:3; Mal 3:7 [b]S Isa 33:24; S Mt 20:28; 1Co 6:20
44:23 [c]S Ps 98:4; S Isa 12:6 [d]S 1Ch 16:31; Ps 148:7 [e]S Ps 98:8 [f]S Ps 65:13 [g]S Ex 6:6; Isa 51:11; 62:12 [h]S Ex 16:7; S Lev 10:3; S Isa 4:2; 43:7; 46:13; 49:3; 52:1; 55:5; 60:9,21; 61:3; Jer 30:19
44:24 [i]S Job 19:25; Isa 43:14 [j]S Isa 27:11 [k]S Ps 139:13 [l]S Ge 2:1; S Isa 42:5 [m]S Ge 1:1
44:25 [n]Ps 33:10 [o]Lev 19:26; 1Sa 6:2; Isa 2:6; 8:19; 47:13; Jer 27:9; Da 2:2,10; 4:7; Mic 3:7; Zec 10:2

their eyes[m] are plastered over
so they cannot see,
and their minds closed so they
cannot understand.

19No one stops to think,
no one has the knowledge or
understanding[n] to say,
"Half of it I used for fuel;[o]
I even baked bread over its
coals,
I roasted meat and I ate.
Shall I make a detestable[p] thing
from what is left?
Shall I bow down to a block of
wood?"[q]

20He feeds on ashes,[r] a deluded[s]
heart misleads him;
he cannot save himself, or say,
"Is not this thing in my right
hand a lie?[t][u]"

21"Remember[v] these things,
O Jacob,
for you are my servant,
O Israel.[w]
I have made you, you are my
servant;[x]
O Israel, I will not forget you.[y]

22I have swept away[z] your offenses
like a cloud,
your sins like the morning mist.
Return[a] to me,
for I have redeemed[b] you."

23Sing for joy,[c] O heavens, for the
LORD has done this;
shout aloud, O earth[d] beneath.
Burst into song, you mountains,[e]
you forests and all your trees,[f]
for the LORD has redeemed[g] Jacob,
he displays his glory[h] in Israel.

Jerusalem to Be Inhabited

24"This is what the LORD says—
your Redeemer,[i] who formed[j]
you in the womb:[k]

I am the LORD,
who has made all things,
who alone stretched out the
heavens,[l]
who spread out the earth[m] by
myself,

25who foils[n] the signs of false
prophets
and makes fools of diviners,[o]

44:24 WHO HAS MADE ALL THINGS. See article on CREATION, p. 6.

Jer 1:18-19
who overthrows the learning of the
wise[p]
and turns it into nonsense,[q]
26who carries out the words[r] of his
servants
and fulfills[s] the predictions of
his messengers,

who says of Jerusalem,[t] 'It shall
be inhabited,'
of the towns of Judah, 'They
shall be built,'
and of their ruins,[u] 'I will
restore them,'[v]
27who says to the watery deep, 'Be
dry,
and I will dry up[w] your
streams,'
28who says of Cyrus,[x] 'He is my
shepherd
and will accomplish all that I
please;
he will say of Jerusalem,[y] "Let
it be rebuilt,"
and of the temple,[z] "Let its
foundations[a] be laid." '

45

"This is what the LORD says
to his anointed,[b]
to Cyrus,[c] whose right hand I
take hold[d] of
to subdue nations[e] before him
and to strip kings of their
armor,
to open doors before him
so that gates will not be shut:
2I will go before you[f]
and will level[g] the mountains[o];
I will break down gates[h] of
bronze
and cut through bars of iron.[i]
3I will give you the treasures[j] of
darkness,
riches stored in secret places,[k]
so that you may know[l] that I am
the LORD,
the God of Israel, who summons
you by name.[m]
4For the sake of Jacob my
servant,[n]
of Israel my chosen,
I summon you by name
and bestow on you a title of
honor,
though you do not
acknowledge[o] me.
5I am the LORD, and there is no
other;[p]
apart from me there is no God.[q]
I will strengthen you,[r]
though you have not
acknowledged me,
6so that from the rising of the sun
to the place of its setting[s]
men may know[t] there is none
besides me.[u]
I am the LORD, and there is no
other.
7I form the light and create
darkness,[v]
I bring prosperity and create
disaster;[w]
I, the LORD, do all these things.
8"You heavens above, rain[x] down
righteousness;[y]
let the clouds shower it down.
Let the earth open wide,
let salvation[z] spring up,
let righteousness grow with it;
I, the LORD, have created it.
9"Woe to him who quarrels[a] with
his Maker,[b]
to him who is but a potsherd[c]
among the potsherds on the
ground.
Does the clay say to the potter,[d]
'What are you making?'[e]
Does your work say,
'He has no hands'?[f]

44:25 [p] S Job 5:13; 1Co 1:27 [q] 2Sa 15:31; 1Co 1:19-20 **44:26** [r] Isa 59:21; Zec 1:6 [s] Isa 46:10; 55:11; Jer 23:20; 39:16; La 2:17; Da 9:12; S Mt 5:18 [t] S Isa 1:1 [u] S Ps 74:3; S Isa 51:3 [v] S Ezr 9:9; S Ps 51:18; Isa 49:8-21; S 61:4 **44:27** [w] S Isa 11:15; S 19:5; Rev 16:12 **44:28** [x] S 2Ch 36:22; S Isa 41:2 [y] S Isa 14:32 [z] Ezr 1:2-4 [a] S Isa 28:16; 58:12 **45:1** [b] S Ps 45:7 [c] S 2Ch 36:22; S Isa 41:2 [d] Ps 73:23; Isa 41:13; 42:6 [e] Isa 48:14; Jer 50:35; 51:20, 24; Mic 4:13 **45:2** [f] Ex 23:20 [g] S Isa 40:4 [h] S Isa 13:2 [i] Ps 107:16; 147:13; Jer 51:30; La 2:9; Na 3:13 **45:3** [j] S 2Ki 24:13; Jer 50:37; 51:13 [k] Jer 41:8 [l] Isa 41:23 [m] S Ex 33:12; S Isa 43:1 **45:4** [n] S Isa 14:1; 41:8-9 [o] Ac 17:23 **45:5** [p] S Isa 44:8 [q] S Dt 32:12; S Ps 18:31; S Isa 43:10 [r] S Ps 18:39; Eze 30:24-25 **45:6** [s] S Ps 113:3; Isa 43:5 [t] S Isa 11:9 [u] ver 5, 18; Isa 14:13-14; 47:8,10; Zep 2:15 **45:7** [v] S Ge 1:4; S Ex 10:22 [w] S Isa 14:15; S 31:2; La 3:38 **45:8** [x] Ps 72:6; S 133:3; Joel 3:18 [y] ver 24; Ps 85:11; S Isa 41:2; 46:13; 48:18; 60:21; 61:10,11; 62:1; Hos 10:12; Joel 2:23; Am 5:24; Mal 4:2 [z] S Ps 85:9; Isa 12:3 **45:9** [a] S Job 12:13; S 15:25; S 27:2; 1Co 10:22 [b] S Job 33:13 [c] Ps 22:15 [d] S Isa 29:16; Ro 9:20-21* [e] S Job 9:12; Da 4:35 [f] S Isa 10:15

[o] *2* Dead Sea Scrolls and Septuagint; the meaning of the word in the Masoretic Text is uncertain.

44:28 CYRUS ... TEMPLE. Isaiah identifies Cyrus by name as the very one who would initiate the Jews' release from captivity (v. 28). This prophecy was made 150 years before its fulfillment; in 538 B.C., Cyrus issued a decree permitting the Jews to return to Jerusalem to rebuild their city and temple (Ezr 1:1–2). God so ordered events in Cyrus's birth and life that God's own plans and purposes were fulfilled to the letter (see 41:2, note).

45:1 ANOINTED ... CYRUS. Although not a worshiper of God (vv. 4–5), Cyrus is called "his anointed," the same title God later gave to his Son (the Messiah, or Christ). Cyrus (550–530 B.C.) was anointed in the sense that he was used by God to perform the important task of setting Israel free from bondage so that God could complete his plan to use Israel to bring about the salvation of the human race. Cyrus founded the Persian empire, which lasted for two centuries. He captured Babylonia in 539 B.C. and then allowed the Jews to return to their land (see Ezr 1).

10Woe to him who says to his father,
'What have you begotten?'
or to his mother,
'What have you brought to birth?'

11"This is what the LORD says—
the Holy One[g] of Israel, and its Maker:[h]
Concerning things to come,
do you question me about my children,
or give me orders about the work of my hands?[i]
12It is I who made the earth[j]
and created mankind upon it.
My own hands stretched out the heavens;[k]
I marshaled their starry hosts.[l]
13I will raise up Cyrus[p][m] in my righteousness:
I will make all his ways straight.[n]
He will rebuild my city[o]
and set my exiles free,
but not for a price or reward,[p]
says the LORD Almighty."

14This is what the LORD says:

"The products[q] of Egypt and the merchandise of Cush,[q]
and those tall Sabeans[r]—
they will come over to you[s]
and will be yours;
they will trudge behind you,[t]
coming over to you in chains.[u]
They will bow down before you
and plead[v] with you, saying,
'Surely God is with you,[w] and there is no other;
there is no other god.[x]' "

15Truly you are a God who hides[y] himself,
O God and Savior[z] of Israel.
16All the makers of idols will be put to shame and disgraced;[a]
they will go off into disgrace together.
17But Israel will be saved[b] by the LORD
with an everlasting salvation;[c]
you will never be put to shame or disgraced,[d]
to ages everlasting.

18For this is what the LORD says—
he who created the heavens,
he is God;
he who fashioned and made the earth,[e]
he founded it;
he did not create it to be empty,[f]
but formed it to be inhabited[g]—
he says:
"I am the LORD,
and there is no other.[h]
19I have not spoken in secret,[i]
from somewhere in a land of darkness;[j]
I have not said to Jacob's descendants,[k]
'Seek[l] me in vain.'
I, the LORD, speak the truth;
I declare what is right.[m]

20"Gather together[n] and come;
assemble, you fugitives from the nations.
Ignorant[o] are those who carry[p] about idols of wood,
who pray to gods that cannot save.[q]
21Declare what is to be, present it—
let them take counsel together.
Who foretold[r] this long ago,
who declared it from the distant past?[s]
Was it not I, the LORD?
And there is no God apart from me,[t]
a righteous God[u] and a Savior;[v]
there is none but me.

22"Turn[w] to me and be saved,[x]
all you ends of the earth;[y]
for I am God, and there is no other.[z]
23By myself I have sworn,[a]

45:11 [g] S Isa 1:4 [h] S Ps 149:2; S Isa 51:13 [i] S Ps 8:6; S Isa 19:25 **45:12** [j] S Ge 1:1 [k] S Ge 2:1; S Isa 48:13 [l] S Ne 9:6; S Job 38:32 **45:13** [m] S 2Ch 36:22; S Isa 41:2 [n] S 1Ki 8:36; S Ps 26:12; S Isa 40:4 [o] S Ezr 1:2 [p] Isa 52:3 **45:14** [q] 2Sa 8:2; Isa 18:7; 60:5 [r] S Isa 2:3; 60:11; 62:2; Zec 8:20-22 [s] S Isa 2:3 [t] S Ge 27:29 [u] S 2Sa 3:34; S Isa 14:1-2 [v] Jer 16:19; Zec 8:20-23 [w] 1Co 14:25 [x] S Ps 18:31; S Isa 11:9; S 43:10 **45:15** [y] S Dt 31:17; Ps 44:24; S Isa 1:15 [z] S Isa 25:9 **45:16** [a] S Ps 35:4; S Isa 1:29 **45:17** [b] Jer 23:6; 33:16; Ro 11:26 [c] S Isa 12:2 [d] S Ge 30:23; S Isa 29:22; S 41:11 **45:18** [e] S Ge 1:1 [f] S Ge 1:2 [g] S Ge 1:26 [h] ver 5; Dt 4:35 **45:19** [i] Isa 48:16; 65:4 [j] Jer 2:31 [k] ver 25; Isa 41:8; 65:9; Jer 31:36 [l] S Dt 4:29; S 2Ch 15:2 [m] S Dt 30:11 **45:20** [n] S Isa 43:9 [o] S Isa 44:19 [p] Ps 115:7; Isa 46:1; Jer 10:5 [q] Dt 32:37; S Isa 44:17; Jer 1:16; 2:28 **45:21** [r] S Isa 41:22 [s] Isa 46:10 [t] ver 5; S Ps 46:10; Isa 46:9; Mk 12:32 [u] Ps 11:7 [v] S Ps 3:8; S Isa 25:9 **45:22** [w] S Isa 44:22; Zec 12:10 [x] Nu 21:8-9; S 2Ch 20:12 [y] S Ge 49:10; S Isa 11:9,12; 49:6,12 [z] Hos 13:4 **45:23** [a] S Ge 22:16; S Isa 14:24

[p] 13 Hebrew *him* [q] 14 That is, the upper Nile region

45:14–17 SURELY GOD IS WITH YOU. A day will come when all nations will acknowledge that the God of Israel is the only God and Israel will never again be put to shame (see Rev 20:4, note).

45:22 BE SAVED, ALL YOU ENDS OF THE EARTH. God gives an invitation to all individuals on the earth to repent and turn to him for salvation. The gospel of Christ contains the same invitation, and God has commanded that his church take this good news to all the world (Mt 28:19–20; Ac 1:8; see Isa 42:1, note). The Lord desires the conversion of all people (2Pe 3:9).

45:23 EVERY KNEE WILL BOW. Paul quotes this verse in Ro 14:11 and Php 2:10–11 to show that although not every person turns to the Lord in true repentance during this life, all people will

my mouth has uttered in all
integrity[b]
a word that will not be
revoked:[c]
Before me every knee will bow;[d]
by me every tongue will
swear.[e]
24They will say of me, 'In the LORD
alone
are righteousness[f] and
strength.[g]' "
All who have raged against him
will come to him and be put to
shame.[h]
25But in the LORD all the
descendants[i] of Israel
will be found righteous[j] and
will exult.[k]

Gods of Babylon

46 Bel[l] bows down, Nebo
stoops low;
their idols[m] are borne by beasts
of burden.[r]
The images that are carried[n]
about are burdensome,
a burden for the weary.
2They stoop and bow down
together;
unable to rescue the burden,
they themselves go off into
captivity.[o]
3"Listen[p] to me, O house of Jacob,
all you who remain[q] of the
house of Israel,
you whom I have upheld since you
were conceived,[r]
and have carried[s] since your
birth.[t]
4Even to your old age and gray
hairs[u]
I am he,[v] I am he who will
sustain you.
I have made you and I will carry
you;
I will sustain[w] you and I will
rescue you.
5"To whom will you compare me or
count me equal?
To whom will you liken me that
we may be compared?[x]
6Some pour out gold from their
bags
and weigh out silver on the
scales;
they hire a goldsmith[y] to make it
into a god,
and they bow down and worship
it.[z]
7They lift it to their shoulders and
carry[a] it;
they set it up in its place, and
there it stands.
From that spot it cannot move.[b]
Though one cries out to it, it does
not answer;[c]
it cannot save[d] him from his
troubles.
8"Remember[e] this, fix it in mind,
take it to heart, you rebels.[f]
9Remember the former things,[g]
those of long ago;[h]
I am God, and there is no other;
I am God, and there is none like
me.[i]
10I make known the end from the
beginning,[j]
from ancient times,[k] what is
still to come.[l]
I say: My purpose will stand,[m]
and I will do all that I please.
11From the east I summon[n] a bird
of prey;[o]
from a far-off land, a man to
fulfill my purpose.
What I have said, that will I bring
about;
what I have planned,[p] that will
I do.[q]
12Listen[r] to me, you
stubborn-hearted,[s]
you who are far from
righteousness.[t]
13I am bringing my righteousness[u]
near,
it is not far away;
and my salvation[v] will not be
delayed.

Isa 49:5-6

45:23 [b]S Dt 30:11; Heb 6:13 [c]Isa 55:11 [d]S ver 14 [e]S Ps 63:11; S Isa 19:18; Ro 14:11*; Php 2:10-11 **45:24** [f]S ver 8; Jer 33:16 [g]S Dt 33:29; S Ps 18:39; S Isa 40:26; 63:1 [h]S Isa 41:11 **45:25** [i]S ver 19 [j]S Isa 4:3; S 49:4 [k]S Isa 24:23; S 41:16 **46:1** [l]S Isa 21:9; Jer 50:2; 51:44 [m]S 1Sa 5:2 [n]ver 7; S Isa 45:20 **46:2** [o]S Jdg 18:17-18; S 2Sa 5:21; Jer 51:47 **46:3** [p]ver 12; Isa 48:12; 51:1 [q]S Isa 1:9 [r]S Ps 139:13; Isa 44:2 [s]S Dt 1:31; S Ps 28:9 [t]S Ps 22:10 **46:4** [u]Ps 71:18 [v]S Dt 32:39; S Isa 43:13 [w]S Ps 18:35; S 119:117 **46:5** [x]S Ex 15:11; Job 41:10; Isa 40:18,25; Jer 49:19 **46:6** [y]S Isa 40:19 [z]S Ex 20:5; Isa 44:17; Hos 13:2 **46:7** [a]S ver 1 [b]S 1Sa 5:3; S Isa 41:7 [c]S 1Ki 18:26 [d]S Isa 44:17; S 47:13 **46:8** [e]S Isa 44:21 [f]S Isa 1:2 **46:9** [g]S Isa 41:22 [h]S Dt 32:7 [i]S Ex 8:10; S Isa 45:5,21; Mk 12:32 **46:10** [j]S Isa 41:4 [k]S Isa 45:21 [l]S Isa 41:22 [m]S Pr 19:21; S Isa 7:7,9; S 44:26; Ac 5:39; Eph 1:11 **46:11** [n]S Jdg 4:10; S Ezr 1:2 [o]S Isa 8:8 [p]S Isa 25:1 [q]S Ge 41:25; Jer 44:28 **46:12** [r]S ver 3 [s]S Ex 32:9; S Isa 9:9 [t]Ps 119:150; Isa 48:1; Jer 2:5 **46:13** [u]S Isa 1:26; S 45:8; Ro 3:21 [v]S Ps 85:9

[r]*1* Or *are but beasts and cattle*

one day, either voluntarily or involuntarily, bow before Christ and confess that he is Lord.

46:1 BEL . . . NEBO. Bel, also called Marduk (cf. Jer 50:2) was the chief deity of Babylon; Nebo was the god of learning, writing and astronomy. These gods could not keep Babylon from being destroyed.

46:4 I WILL CARRY YOU. In contrast to gods made with human hands (44:12–17) which have to be carried by those who create them (v. 1), the Lord, our Creator, is able to carry us. He has cared for us from the beginning of our lives, continues to act on our behalf, and will sustain us even to the end.

I will grant salvation to Zion,[w]
my splendor[x] to Israel.

The Fall of Babylon

47 "Go down, sit in the dust,[y]
Virgin Daughter[z] of Babylon;
sit on the ground without a throne,
Daughter of the Babylonians.[s][a]
No more will you be called
tender or delicate.[b]
2Take millstones[c] and grind[d] flour;
take off your veil.[e]
Lift up your skirts,[f] bare your legs,
and wade through the streams.
3Your nakedness[g] will be exposed
and your shame[h] uncovered.
I will take vengeance;[i]
I will spare no one.[j]"

4Our Redeemer[k]—the LORD Almighty[l] is his name[m]—
is the Holy One[n] of Israel.

5"Sit in silence,[o] go into darkness,[p]
Daughter of the Babylonians;[q]
no more will you be called
queen[r] of kingdoms.[s]
6I was angry[t] with my people
and desecrated my inheritance;[u]
I gave them into your hand,[v]
and you showed them no mercy.[w]
Even on the aged
you laid a very heavy yoke.
7You said, 'I will continue forever[x]—
the eternal queen!'[y]
But you did not consider these things
or reflect[z] on what might happen.[a]

8"Now then, listen, you wanton creature,
lounging in your security[b]
and saying to yourself,
'I am, and there is none besides me.[c]
I will never be a widow[d]
or suffer the loss of children.'
9Both of these will overtake you
in a moment,[e] on a single day:
loss of children[f] and widowhood.[g]
They will come upon you in full measure,
in spite of your many sorceries[h]
and all your potent spells.[i]
10You have trusted[j] in your wickedness
and have said, 'No one sees me.'[k]
Your wisdom[l] and knowledge mislead[m] you
when you say to yourself,
'I am, and there is none besides me.'
11Disaster[n] will come upon you,
and you will not know how to conjure it away.
A calamity will fall upon you
that you cannot ward off with a ransom;
a catastrophe you cannot foresee
will suddenly[o] come upon you.

12"Keep on, then, with your magic spells
and with your many sorceries,[p]
which you have labored at since childhood.
Perhaps you will succeed,
perhaps you will cause terror.
13All the counsel you have received
has only worn you out![q]
Let your astrologers[r] come forward,
those stargazers who make predictions month by month,
let them save[s] you from what is coming upon you.
14Surely they are like stubble;[t]
the fire[u] will burn them up.
They cannot even save themselves
from the power of the flame.[v]
Here are no coals to warm anyone;
here is no fire to sit by.
15That is all they can do for you—
these you have labored with
and trafficked[w] with since childhood.

46:13 [w]S Ps 74:2; Joel 2:32 [x]S Isa 44:23 **47:1** [y]S Job 2:13; S Isa 29:4 [z]S Isa 21:9; S 23:12 [a]Ps 137:8; Jer 50:42; 51:33; Zec 2:7 [b]Dt 28:56 **47:2** [c]Ex 11:5; Mt 24:41 [d]S Jdg 16:21 [e]S Ge 24:65 [f]S Isa 32:11 **47:3** [g]S Ge 2:25; Eze 16:37; Na 3:5 [h]S Isa 20:4 [i]S Isa 1:24; S 34:8 [j]Isa 13:18-19 **47:4** [k]S Job 19:25 [l]S Isa 13:4 [m]Isa 48:2; Jer 50:34; Am 4:13 [n]S Isa 1:4; 48:17 **47:5** [o]S Job 2:13 [p]Isa 9:2; 13:10 [q]S Isa 21:9 [r]ver 7; La 1:1; Rev 18:7 [s]S Isa 13:19; Rev 17:18 **47:6** [t]S 2Ch 28:9 [u]S Dt 13:15; S Isa 42:24; Jer 2:7; 50:11 [v]Isa 10:13 [w]S Isa 14:6 **47:7** [x]S Isa 10:13; Da 4:30 [y]S ver 5; Rev 18:7 [z]S Isa 42:23,25 [a]S Dt 32:29 **47:8** [b]S Isa 32:9 [c]S Isa 45:6 [d]Isa 49:21; 54:4; La 1:1; Rev 18:7 **47:9** [e]S Ps 55:15; 73:19; 1Th 5:3; Rev 18:8-10 [f]S Isa 13:18 [g]Isa 4:1; Jer 15:8; 18:21 [h]ver 12; Na 3:4; Mal 3:5 [i]Dt 18:10-11; Rev 9:21; 18:23 **47:10** [j]S Job 15:31; Ps 52:7; 62:10 [k]S 2Ki 21:16; S Isa 29:15 [l]S Isa 5:21 [m]Isa 44:20 **47:11** [n]S Isa 10:3; S 14:15; S 21:9; S 31:2; Lk 17:27 [o]S Ps 55:15; S Isa 17:14; 1Th 5:3 **47:12** [p]S ver 9; S Ex 7:11 **47:13** [q]Isa 57:10; Jer 51:58; Hab 2:13 [r]S Isa 19:3; S 44:25 [s]ver 15; S Isa 5:29; 43:13; 46:7 **47:14** [t]S Isa 5:24 [u]S Isa 30:30 [v]Isa 10:17; Jer 51:30,32, 58 **47:15** [w]Rev 18:11

[s] 1 Or *Chaldeans*; also in verse 5

47:1–15 VIRGIN DAUGHTER OF BABYLON. This chapter prophesies Babylon's doom and fall. Babylon represented a pagan culture, self-centered and proud (vv. 8,10); its inhabitants lived in sensual pleasure and trusted in their own wisdom and knowledge and in magic (vv. 10,12–13). Such people were destined for a sudden and overwhelming judgment (vv. 9,11). In the last days of the tribulation, Babylon, representing all pagan and humanistic cultures of the unregenerate world, will be overthrown by God in his wrath (see Rev 17:1, notes; 18:2, note).

Each of them goes on in his error;
there is not one that can save[x]
you.

Stubborn Israel

48 "Listen to this, O house of
Jacob,
you who are called by the name
of Israel[y]
and come from the line of
Judah,[z]
you who take oaths[a] in the name
of the LORD[b]
and invoke[c] the God of Israel—
but not in truth[d] or
righteousness—
2you who call yourselves citizens of
the holy city[e]
and rely[f] on the God of
Israel—
the LORD Almighty is his name:[g]
3I foretold the former things[h] long
ago,
my mouth announced[i] them
and I made them known;
then suddenly[j] I acted, and
they came to pass.
4For I knew how stubborn[k] you
were;
the sinews of your neck[l] were
iron,
your forehead[m] was bronze.
5Therefore I told you these things
long ago;
before they happened I
announced[n] them to you
so that you could not say,
'My idols did them;[o]
my wooden image and metal god
ordained them.'
6You have heard these things; look
at them all.
Will you not admit them?
"From now on I will tell you of
new things,[p]
of hidden things unknown to
you.
7They are created[q] now, and not
long ago;[r]
you have not heard of them
before today.
So you cannot say,
'Yes, I knew[s] of them.'
8You have neither heard nor
understood;[t]
from of old your ear[u] has not
been open.
Well do I know how treacherous[v]
you are;
you were called a rebel[w] from
birth.
9For my own name's sake[x] I delay
my wrath;[y]
for the sake of my praise I hold
it back from you,
so as not to cut you off.[z]
10See, I have refined[a] you, though
not as silver;
I have tested[b] you in the
furnace[c] of affliction.
11For my own sake,[d] for my own
sake, I do this.
How can I let myself be
defamed?[e]
I will not yield my glory to
another.[f]

Israel Freed

12"Listen[g] to me, O Jacob,
Israel, whom I have called:[h]
I am he;[i]
I am the first and I am the
last.[j]
13My own hand laid the foundations
of the earth,[k]
and my right hand spread out
the heavens;[l]
when I summon them,
they all stand up together.[m]
14"Come together,[n] all of you, and
listen:
Which of ⌞the idols⌟ has
foretold[o] these things?
The LORD's chosen ally[p]

47:15 [x]S ver 13; S Isa 44:17 **48:1** [y]S Ge 17:5 [z]S Ge 29:35 [a]S Isa 19:18 [b]S 1Sa 20:42; S Isa 43:7 [c]Ex 23:13; 2Sa 14:11; Ps 50:16; Isa 58:2; Jer 7:9-10; 44:26 [d]Isa 59:14; Jer 4:2; 5:2; Da 8:12; Zec 8:3 **48:2** [e]S Ne 11:1; S Isa 1:26; S Mt 4:5 [f]S Isa 10:20; Ro 2:17 [g]S Isa 47:4 **48:3** [h]S Isa 41:22 [i]S Isa 40:21; 45:21 [j]S Isa 17:14; 30:13 **48:4** [k]S Isa 9:9 [l]S Ex 32:9; S Dt 9:27; Ac 7:51 [m]Eze 3:9 **48:5** [n]S Isa 40:21; S 42:9 [o]Jer 44:15-18 **48:6** [p]S Isa 41:22; S Ro 16:25 **48:7** [q]Isa 65:18 [r]Isa 45:21 [s]S Ex 6:7 **48:8** [t]S Isa 1:3 [u]S Dt 29:4 [v]Isa 41:24; Mal 2:11,14 [w]Dt 9:7,24; Ps 58:3; S Isa 1:2; 43:27; 58:1 **48:9** [x]S 1Sa 12:22; S Isa 37:35 [y]S Job 9:13; S Isa 30:18 [z]S Ne 9:31 **48:10** [a]S Isa 1:25; Zec 13:9; Mal 3:3; 1Pe 1:7 [b]S Ex 15:25 [c]S Ex 1:13; S 1Ki 8:51 **48:11** [d]S 1Sa 12:22; S Isa 37:35 [e]S Lev 18:21; Dt 32:27; Jer 14:7, 21; Eze 20:9,14, 22,44 [f]Isa 42:8 **48:12** [g]S Isa 46:3 [h]Isa 41:8; 42:6; 43:1 [i]S Isa 43:13 [j]S Isa 41:4; S Rev 1:17 **48:13** [k]Heb 1:10-12 [l]S Ge 2:1; Ex 20:11; Job 9:8; Isa 40:22; S 42:5; 45:18; 51:16; 65:17 [m]S Isa 34:16 **48:14** [n]S Isa 43:9 [o]S Isa 41:22 [p]S Isa 41:2

48:1–22 BUT NOT IN TRUTH OR RIGHTEOUSNESS. This chapter reveals that Judah was a people who professed to follow God and call on his name, but who in reality rejected the truths of his word and refused to live righteously before him. They had a form of religion, yet they denied God his rightful place in their lives (see Mt 23:13, note on hypocrisy; 2Ti 3:5, note).

48:5 LONG AGO. Through the prophets, God foretold Israel's captivity and release, proving that he is the one true God. No worshiper of idols or demons can accurately predict the future or foretell specific events as the God of Israel can.

48:6 NEW THINGS. The "new things" include the coming Messiah and the new heavens and new earth (ch. 53; 65:17).

48:12–15 LISTEN TO ME, O JACOB. This prophecy again alludes to Cyrus as God's chosen instrument to overthrow Babylon (see 41:2, note; 45:1, note).

will carry out his purpose[q]
against Babylon;[r]
his arm will be against the
Babylonians.[t]
15I, even I, have spoken;
yes, I have called[s] him.
I will bring him,
and he will succeed[t] in his
mission.

16"Come near[u] me and listen[v] to
this:

"From the first announcement I
have not spoken in
secret;[w]
at the time it happens, I am
there."

And now the Sovereign LORD[x] has
sent[y] me,
with his Spirit.[z]

17This is what the LORD says—
your Redeemer,[a] the Holy
One[b] of Israel:
"I am the LORD your God,
who teaches[c] you what is best
for you,
who directs[d] you in the way[e]
you should go.
18If only you had paid attention[f] to
my commands,
your peace[g] would have been
like a river,[h]
your righteousness[i] like the
waves of the sea.
19Your descendants[j] would have
been like the sand,[k]
your children like its numberless
grains;[l]
their name would never be cut
off[m]
nor destroyed from before me."

48:14 [q]Isa 46:10-11 [r]S Isa 21:9; S 45:1; Jer 50:45 **48:15** [s]S Jdg 4:10; Isa 45:1 [t]Isa 44:28-45:4 **48:16** [u]S Isa 41:1 [v]S Isa 33:13 [w]S Isa 45:19 [x]Isa 50:5,7,9 [y]Zec 2:9,11 [z]S Isa 11:2 **48:17** [a]S Job 19:25; Isa 49:7; 54:8 [b]S Isa 47:4 [c]S Isa 28:9; S Jer 7:13 [d]Isa 49:10; 57:18; 58:11 [e]S Isa 30:11 **48:18** [f]S Isa 42:23 [g]Ps 147:14; S Isa 9:7; 54:13; 66:12 [h]S Isa 33:21 [i]S Isa 1:26; S 45:8 **48:19** [j]Isa 43:5; 44:3; 61:9 [k]S Ge 12:2 [l]S Job 5:25 [m]Isa 56:5; 65:23; 66:22; Jer 35:19 **48:20** [n]Isa 52:11; Jer 48:6; 50:8; 51:6,45; Zec 2:6-7; Rev 18:4 [o]S Isa 12:6; 49:13; 51:11 [p]S Ge 49:10; S Dt 30:4; S Jer 25:22 [q]S Ex 6:6; S Isa 33:24; 52:9; 63:9; Mic 4:10 **48:21** [r]S Isa 33:16 [s]S Isa 30:25 [t]S Nu 20:11; S Isa 35:6 **48:22** [u]S Job 3:26 [v]S Isa 3:11; 57:21 **49:1** [w]S Isa 33:13 [x]S Isa 11:11 [y]Isa 44:24; 46:3; Mt 1:20 [z]Isa 7:14; 9:6; 44:2; Jer 1:5; Gal 1:15 [a]S Ex 33:12;

20Leave Babylon,
flee[n] from the Babylonians!
Announce this with shouts of joy[o]
and proclaim it.
Send it out to the ends of the
earth;[p]
say, "The LORD has redeemed[q]
his servant Jacob."
21They did not thirst[r] when he led
them through the deserts;
he made water flow[s] for them
from the rock;
he split the rock
and water gushed out.[t]

22"There is no peace," [u] says the
LORD, "for the wicked."[v]

The Servant of the LORD

49 Listen[w] to me, you islands;[x]
hear this, you distant nations:
Before I was born[y] the LORD
called[z] me;
from my birth he has made
mention of my name.[a]
2He made my mouth[b] like a
sharpened sword,[c]
in the shadow of his hand[d] he
hid me;
he made me into a polished
arrow[e]
and concealed me in his quiver.
3He said to me, "You are my
servant,[f]
Israel, in whom I will display my
splendor.[g]"
4But I said, "I have labored to no
purpose;

S Isa 43:1 **49:2** [b]S Job 40:18 [c]S Ps 64:3; Eph 6:17; S Rev 1:16 [d]S Ex 33:22; S Ps 91:1 [e]S Dt 32:23; Zec 9:13 **49:3** [f]S Isa 20:3; Zec 3:8 [g]S Lev 10:3; S Isa 44:23

t *14* Or *Chaldeans*; also in verse 20

48:16 SENT ME, WITH HIS SPIRIT. This verse refers to the coming Messiah, who is empowered by the Holy Spirit (cf. 61:1).

48:20 LEAVE BABYLON. This declaration would take on great importance for the Jews toward the end of their seventy-year captivity in Babylon (539 B.C.), as they prepared to leave that country and return to Judah according to Cyrus's decree (cf. Rev 18:4).

49—57 LISTEN TO ME. These chapters contain many prophecies about the "Servant of the LORD," who ultimately is Jesus Christ. His ministry brings atonement for sin, salvation to all the nations, the restoration of Israel and judgment on the ungodly.

49:1 THE LORD CALLED ME. Jesus' Messianic calling is pictured as coming before he was born to the virgin Mary (see Lk 1:31–33).

49:2 SWORD . . . ARROW. The words of the coming Messiah would be like a sharp sword that pierces the consciences of all who hear (cf. Rev 1:16; 2:12,16). The arrow may symbolize God's judgment on those who do not accept his word.

49:3 MY SERVANT, ISRAEL. This designation cannot be restricted to the nation of Israel, since the servant's task was that of bringing Jacob (i.e., Israel) back to God (v. 5). God's Servant-Son, Jesus, embodied the ideal Israel, and he fulfilled all that God had required from national Israel.

49:4 LABORED TO NO PURPOSE. The ministry of the prophets as God's servants was full of disappointments and hostile opposition from many in Israel. Likewise, the mission of *the* Servant, Jesus Christ, appeared to have failed when he died on the cross (see 50:6–9; 52:13—53:12 for more on the suffering of God's Servant).

I have spent my strength in
vain[h] and for nothing.
Yet what is due me is in the LORD's
hand,[i]
and my reward[j] is with my
God."[k]

5And now the LORD says—
he who formed me in the
womb[l] to be his servant
to bring Jacob back to him
and gather Israel[m] to himself,
for I am honored[n] in the eyes of
the LORD
and my God has been my
strength[o]—
6he says:
"It is too small a thing for you to
be my servant[p]
to restore the tribes of Jacob
and bring back those of Israel I
have kept.[q]
I will also make you a light[r] for
the Gentiles,[s]
that you may bring my salvation
to the ends of the earth."[t]

Isa 52:7-10

7This is what the LORD says—
the Redeemer and Holy One of
Israel[u]—
to him who was despised[v] and
abhorred by the nation,
to the servant of rulers:
"Kings[w] will see you and rise up,
princes will see and bow
down,[x]
because of the LORD, who is
faithful,[y]
the Holy One of Israel, who has
chosen[z] you."

Restoration of Israel

8This is what the LORD says:

"In the time of my favor[a] I will
answer you,
and in the day of salvation I will
help you;[b]
I will keep[c] you and will make
you
to be a covenant for the
people,[d]
to restore the land[e]
and to reassign its desolate
inheritances,[f]
9to say to the captives,[g] 'Come
out,'
and to those in darkness,[h] 'Be
free!'

"They will feed beside the roads
and find pasture on every barren
hill.[i]
10They will neither hunger nor
thirst,[j]
nor will the desert heat or the
sun beat upon them.[k]
He who has compassion[l] on them
will guide[m] them
and lead them beside springs[n]
of water.
11I will turn all my mountains into
roads,
and my highways[o] will be
raised up.[p]
12See, they will come from afar[q]—
some from the north, some from
the west,[r]
some from the region of
Aswan.[u]"
13Shout for joy,[s] O heavens;
rejoice, O earth;[t]
burst into song, O mountains![u]
For the LORD comforts[v] his people
and will have compassion[w] on
his afflicted ones.[x]
14But Zion[y] said, "The LORD has
forsaken[z] me,
the Lord has forgotten me."

49:4 [h]S Lev 26:20; Isa 55:2; 65:23 [i]Isa 45:25; 50:8; 53:10; 54:17 [j]S Isa 35:4 [k]S Job 27:2 **49:5** [l]S Ps 139:13; Gal 1:15 [m]S Dt 30:4; S Isa 11:12 [n]S Isa 43:4 [o]S Ps 18:1 **49:6** [p]S ver 3 [q]Isa 1:9 [r]S Isa 9:2; Jn 1:9 [s]S Isa 26:18; 55:5; Zec 8:22; S Lk 2:32 [t]S Dt 30:4; S Ps 48:10; S Mt 28:19; Jn 11:52; Ac 13:47* **49:7** [u]S Isa 48:17 [v]S Ps 22:6; 69:7-9 [w]S Ezr 1:2; Isa 52:15 [x]S Ge 27:29; S Ps 22:29; S 86:9 [y]S Dt 7:9; S 1Co 1:9 [z]S Isa 14:1 **49:8** [a]Ps 69:13; Isa 60:10; 61:2 [b]S Isa 41:10; 2Co 6:2* [c]S Isa 5:2; 26:3 [d]S Isa 42:6 [e]Lev 25:10; S Ps 37:9; Isa 44:26; 58:12; 61:4; Eze 36:10, 33; Am 9:11,14 [f]S Nu 34:13; S Isa 60:21 **49:9** [g]Isa 42:7; 61:1; S Lk 4:19 [h]S Ps 107:10 [i]Isa 41:18 **49:10** [j]S Isa 33:16 [k]Ps 121:6; Rev 7:16 [l]S Isa 14:1 [m]S Ps 48:14; S Isa 42:16; S 48:17 [n]S Isa 33:21; S 35:7 **49:11** [o]S Isa 11:16 [p]Isa 40:4; Jer 31:9 **49:12** [q]S Isa 2:3; S 11:11; 43:5-6 [r]Isa 59:19; S Mt 8:11 **49:13** [s]S Isa 48:20 [t]S Ps 96:11 [u]S Ps 65:12-13; 98:4; Isa 44:23 [v]S Ps 71:21; S Isa 40:1; S 2Co 1:4 [w]S Isa 14:1 [x]S Ps 9:12 **49:14** [y]Isa 40:9 [z]S Ps 9:10; S 71:11; S Isa 27:8

[u]*12* Dead Sea Scrolls; Masoretic Text *Sinim*

49:5–6 TO BRING JACOB BACK TO HIM. This prophecy describes two important aspects of Jesus' mission: (1) To bring Israel back to God—i.e., the Jewish converts of the NT church and of the present age, as well as the remnant of Israel to be restored in the final age; and (2) to bring God's light and message of salvation to all nations (see next note).

49:6 SALVATION TO THE ENDS OF THE EARTH. The Messiah's mission is that all nations hear the gospel and have an opportunity to believe in God's Servant-Son. This verse is sometimes called the "great commission of the Old Testament." This commission will not be fulfilled until the gospel is adequately preached throughout the whole world; when this occurs, "then the end will come" (see Mt 24:14, note). The task of NT believers is to preach the gospel faithfully, taking it to all nations until the Lord returns.

49:7 DESPISED AND ABHORRED. Christ would be despised and hated by many (cf. 53:3), yet his former enemies would bow down before him.

49:8–13 THIS IS WHAT THE LORD SAYS. These verses describe the joyful and blessed condition of those who find deliverance and salvation in Christ.

[15]"Can a mother forget the baby at
her breast
and have no compassion on the
child[a] she has borne?
Though she may forget,
I will not forget you![b]
[16]See, I have engraved[c] you on the
palms of my hands;
your walls[d] are ever before
me.
[17]Your sons hasten back,
and those who laid you waste[e]
depart from you.
[18]Lift up your eyes and look around;
all your sons gather[f] and come
to you.
As surely as I live,[g]" declares the
LORD,
"you will wear[h] them all as
ornaments;
you will put them on, like a
bride.

[19]"Though you were ruined and
made desolate[i]
and your land laid waste,[j]
now you will be too small for your
people,[k]
and those who devoured[l] you
will be far away.
[20]The children born during your
bereavement
will yet say in your hearing,
'This place is too small for us;
give us more space to live in.'[m]
[21]Then you will say in your heart,
'Who bore me these?[n]
I was bereaved[o] and barren;
I was exiled and rejected.[p]
Who brought these[q] up?
I was left[r] all alone,[s]
but these—where have they
come from?' "

[22]This is what the Sovereign LORD[t]
says:

"See, I will beckon to the Gentiles,
I will lift up my banner[u] to the
peoples;
they will bring[v] your sons in their
arms
and carry your daughters on
their shoulders.[w]
[23]Kings[x] will be your foster fathers,
and their queens your nursing
mothers.[y]
They will bow down[z] before you
with their faces to the
ground;
they will lick the dust[a] at your
feet.
Then you will know that I am the
LORD;[b]
those who hope[c] in me will not
be disappointed.[d]"

[24]Can plunder be taken from
warriors,[e]
or captives rescued from the
fierce[v]?

[25]But this is what the LORD says:

"Yes, captives[f] will be taken from
warriors,[g]
and plunder retrieved from the
fierce;[h]
I will contend with those who
contend with you,[i j]
and your children I will save.[k]
[26]I will make your oppressors[l]
eat[m] their own flesh;
they will be drunk on their own
blood,[n] as with wine.
Then all mankind will know[o]
that I, the LORD, am your
Savior,[p]
your Redeemer,[q] the Mighty
One of Jacob.[r]"

49:15 [a] S 1Ki 3:26; Isa 66:13 [b] S Isa 44:21 **49:16** [c] S Ge 38:18; S Ex 28:9 [d] Ps 48:12-13; Isa 62:6 **49:17** [e] S Isa 5:6; 10:6; 37:18 **49:18** [f] S Isa 11:12; 14:1; 43:5; 51:3; 54:7 [g] S Nu 14:21; Isa 45:23; 54:9; 62:8; Ro 14:11* [h] Isa 52:1; 61:10; Jer 2:32 **49:19** [i] S Lev 26:33; Isa 54:1,3; 60:18; 62:4 [j] S Isa 5:6 [k] Eze 36:10-11; Zec 10:10 [l] S Isa 1:20 **49:20** [m] Isa 54:1-3; Zec 2:4; 10:10 **49:21** [n] Isa 29:23; 66:7-8 [o] S Isa 47:8; 54:1 [p] Isa 5:13; 54:6 [q] Isa 60:8 [r] S Isa 1:8 [s] S Ps 142:4; Isa 51:18; Jer 10:20 **49:22** [t] S Ge 15:2 [u] S Isa 11:10 [v] S Isa 11:12; S 14:2 [w] Lk 15:5 **49:23** [x] Isa 60:3, 10-11 [y] S Nu 11:12; S Isa 60:16 [z] S Ge 27:29; Rev 3:9 [a] S Ge 3:14; Ps 72:9 [b] S Ex 6:2; S Ps 22:23; S Isa 42:8 [c] S Ps 37:9; S 130:5 [d] S Ps 22:5; S Isa 29:22; S 41:11 **49:24** [e] Mt 12:29; Mk 3:27; Lk 11:21 **49:25** [f] S Isa 14:2 [g] Jer 50:33-34; Mk 3:27 [h] S Isa 13:11; S 25:4 [i] Isa 25:5; S 43:26; 51:22; Jer 50:34 [j] S 1Sa 24:15 [k] Isa 25:9; 33:22; 35:4 **49:26** [l] S Isa 9:4; S 13:11 [m] S Isa 9:20 [n] Nu 23:24; Jer 25:27; Na 1:10; 3:11; Rev 16:6 [o] Ex 6:7; S Isa 11:9; Eze 39:7 [p] S Isa 25:9 [q] S Job 19:25; S Isa 48:17 [r] S Ge 49:24; S Ps 132:2

[v] *24* Dead Sea Scrolls, Vulgate and Syriac (see also Septuagint and verse 25); Masoretic Text *righteous*

49:14–17 THE LORD HAS FORSAKEN ME. These are the words of the Israelites, who experienced great adversity and thus felt abandoned and forgotten by God. God's response gives divine assurance to any believer going through trying times. (1) His love for us is greater than the natural affection of a loving mother for her children; it is therefore unthinkable that he will ever forget us, especially in our times of despair and grief (cf. Jer 31:20). (2) His compassion for us will never fail, regardless of life's circumstances; he watches over us with great tenderness and love, and we may rest in the conviction that he will never leave us. (3) The evidence of God's great love is that he has engraved us on the palms of his own hands, so that he can never forget us; the scars in his hands are always before his eyes as a reminder of the great love he has showered on us and of his desire to care for us.

49:22–26 GENTILES . . . WILL BRING YOUR SONS. These verses foresee a time when Israel would be restored to God and the Gentiles converted. The Gentiles would in fact lead a future generation of Jews back to the Lord (cf. 14:2; 43:6; 60:9; see article on ISRAEL IN GOD'S PLAN OF SALVATION, p. 1730).

Israel's Sin and the Servant's Obedience

50 This is what the LORD says:

"Where is your mother's
certificate of divorce[s]
with which I sent her away?
Or to which of my creditors
did I sell[t] you?
Because of your sins[u] you were
sold;[v]
because of your transgressions
your mother was sent away.
2 When I came, why was there no
one?
When I called, why was there no
one to answer?[w]
Was my arm too short[x] to ransom
you?
Do I lack the strength[y] to
rescue you?
By a mere rebuke[z] I dry up the
sea,[a]
I turn rivers into a desert;[b]
their fish rot for lack of water
and die of thirst.
3 I clothe the sky with darkness[c]
and make sackcloth[d] its
covering."

4 The Sovereign LORD[e] has given
me an instructed tongue,[f]
to know the word that sustains
the weary.[g]
He wakens me morning by
morning,[h]
wakens my ear to listen like one
being taught.[i]
5 The Sovereign LORD[j] has opened
my ears,[k]
and I have not been rebellious;[l]
I have not drawn back.
6 I offered my back to those who
beat[m] me,
my cheeks to those who pulled
out my beard;[n]
I did not hide my face
from mocking and spitting.[o]
7 Because the Sovereign LORD[p]
helps[q] me,
I will not be disgraced.
Therefore have I set my face like
flint,[r]
and I know I will not be put to
shame.[s]
8 He who vindicates[t] me is near.[u]
Who then will bring charges
against me?[v]
Let us face each other![w]
Who is my accuser?
Let him confront me!
9 It is the Sovereign LORD[x] who
helps[y] me.
Who is he that will condemn[z]
me?
They will all wear out like a
garment;
the moths[a] will eat them up.

10 Who among you fears[b] the LORD
and obeys[c] the word of his
servant?[d]
Let him who walks in the dark,
who has no light,[e]
trust[f] in the name of the LORD
and rely on his God.
11 But now, all you who light fires
and provide yourselves with
flaming torches,[g]
go, walk in the light of your fires[h]
and of the torches you have set
ablaze.
This is what you shall receive from
my hand:[i]
You will lie down in torment.[j]

Everlasting Salvation for Zion

51 "Listen[k] to me, you who
pursue righteousness[l]

50:1 [s] S Dt 24:1; Hos 2:2; Mt 19:7; Mk 10:4 [t] S Ne 5:5; S Mt 18:25 [u] S Isa 1:28 [v] S Dt 32:30; S Jdg 3:8 **50:2** [w] S 1Sa 8:19; S Isa 41:28 [x] Nu 11:23; Isa 59:1 [y] S Ge 18:14; S Ps 68:35; Jer 14:9 [z] S Ps 18:15 [a] S Ex 14:22 [b] S Ps 107:33 **50:3** [c] S Ex 10:22; S Isa 5:30 [d] Rev 6:12 **50:4** [e] ver 5; Isa 61:1 [f] S Ex 4:12 [g] S Isa 40:29; Mt 11:28 [h] Ps 5:3; 88:13; 119:147; 143:8 [i] S Isa 28:9 **50:5** [j] S Isa 48:16 [k] Isa 35:5 [l] Eze 2:8; 24:3; S Mt 26:39; Jn 8:29; 14:31; 15:10; Ac 26:19; Heb 5:8 **50:6** [m] Isa 53:5; Mt 27:30; Mk 14:65; 15:19; Lk 22:63; Jn 19:1 [n] S 2Sa 10:4 [o] S Nu 12:14; La 3:30; Mt 26:67; Mk 10:34 **50:7** [p] S Isa 48:16 [q] S Isa 41:10; 42:1 [r] Jer 1:18; 15:20; Eze 3:8-9 [s] S Isa 28:16; S 29:22 **50:8** [t] S Isa 26:2; S 49:4 [u] S Ps 34:18 [v] S Job 13:19; S Isa 43:26; Ro 8:32-34 [w] S Isa 41:1 **50:9** [x] S Isa 48:16 [y] S Isa 41:10 [z] Ro 8:1,34 [a] S Job 13:28; S Isa 51:8 **50:10** [b] S Pr 1:7 [c] Isa 1:19; Hag 1:12 [d] S Isa 49:3 [e] S Ps 107:14; Ac 26:18 [f] S Isa 10:20; S 26:4 **50:11** [g] Pr 26:18 [h] Isa 1:31; Jas 3:6 [i] S Dt 21:22-23; S Pr 26:27 [j] S Job 15:20; Isa 65:13-15 **51:1** [k] S Isa 46:3 [l] ver 7; S Dt 7:13; 16:20; Ps 94:15; Isa 63:8; Ro 9:30-31

50:4–11 SOVEREIGN LORD HAS GIVEN. Intertwined with the prophet's own experiences and exhortations in these verses are prophetic words of the Messiah's character and suffering.

50:4 WORD THAT SUSTAINS THE WEARY. The Messiah would comfort the weak and the troubled (cf. 42:3; Mt 11:28); he himself would commune "morning by morning" with his Father (cf. Mk 1:35).

50:6 TO THOSE WHO BEAT ME. The Messiah would endure suffering, humiliation and disgrace in fulfilling his task of redeeming the human race (cf. Mt 27:26,30; Mk 14:65; 15:16–20; Jn 19:1).

50:7 I SET MY FACE LIKE FLINT. Because Christ knew that his suffering and death would result in the redemption of all who would believe in him, he "resolutely set out for Jerusalem" (Lk 9:51).

50:10–11 FEARS THE LORD. The prophet Isaiah calls on those who trust in the Lord to remain faithful to him even though they may have to walk in the darkness of the nation's apostasy. Those who walk in the light of their own fires—their own ideas and ways—rather than submitting to God and the revelation of his word will "lie down in torment."

51:1–3 YOU WHO PURSUE RIGHTEOUSNESS. God encourages the faithful remnant who seek him and his righteousness (cf. Mt 5:6) to have full confidence that he will one day establish his

and who seek[m] the LORD:
Look to the rock[n] from which you were cut
and to the quarry from which you were hewn;
2look to Abraham,[o] your father,
and to Sarah, who gave you birth.
When I called him he was but one,
and I blessed him and made him many.[p]
3The LORD will surely comfort[q] Zion[r]
and will look with compassion on all her ruins;[s]
he will make her deserts like Eden,[t]
her wastelands[u] like the garden of the LORD.
Joy and gladness[v] will be found in her,
thanksgiving[w] and the sound of singing.

4"Listen to me, my people;[x]
hear me,[y] my nation:
The law[z] will go out from me;
my justice[a] will become a light to the nations.[b]
5My righteousness draws near speedily,
my salvation[c] is on the way,[d]
and my arm[e] will bring justice to the nations.
The islands[f] will look to me
and wait in hope[g] for my arm.
6Lift up your eyes to the heavens,
look at the earth beneath;
the heavens will vanish like smoke,[h]
the earth will wear out like a garment[i]
and its inhabitants die like flies.
But my salvation[j] will last forever,[k]
my righteousness will never fail.[l]

51:1 [m]Isa 55:6; 65:10 [n]Isa 17:10 **51:2** [o]S Ge 17:6; S Isa 29:22; Ro 4:16; Heb 11:11 [p]S Ge 12:2 **51:3** [q]S Isa 40:1 [r]S Ps 51:18; S Isa 61:4 [s]Isa 44:26; 52:9; 61:4 [t]S Ge 2:8 [u]S Isa 5:6; S 41:19 [v]S Isa 25:9; 35:10; 65:18; 66:10; Jer 16:9 [w]Jer 17:26; 30:19; 33:11 **51:4** [x]Ex 6:7; Ps 50:7; Isa 3:15; 63:8; 64:9 [y]S Ps 78:1 [z]S Dt 18:18 [a]S Isa 2:4 [b]S Isa 26:18; S 49:6 **51:5** [c]S Ps 85:9; S Isa 12:2 [d]S Isa 35:4 [e]Ps 98:1; Isa 40:10; 50:2; 52:10; 59:16; 63:1,5 [f]S Isa 11:11 [g]S Ge 49:10; S Ps 37:9 **51:6** [h]S Ps 37:20; S 102:26; Mt 24:35; Lk 21:33; 2Pe 3:10 [i]Ps 102:25-26; Heb 1:10-12 [j]S Isa 12:2 [k]ver 8; S Ps 119:89 [l]Ps 89:33; Isa 54:10

51:7 [m]S ver 1 [n]S Dt 6:6; Ps 119:11 [o]S Ps 119:39; Isa 50:7; 54:4; Mt 5:11; Lk 6:22; Ac 5:41 **51:8** [p]S Job 13:28; Jas 5:2 [q]S Isa 14:11 [r]S ver 6 **51:9** [s]S Jdg 5:12 [t]S Ge 18:14; S Ps 65:6; Isa 40:31; 52:1 [u]S Ps 98:1; S Isa 30:30; S 33:2 [v]Ex 6:6; Dt 4:34; S 32:7 [w]S Job 9:13 [x]S Ps 68:30; S 74:13 **51:10** [y]S Ex 14:22; Zec 10:11; Rev 16:12 [z]Ex 15:5,8 [a]S Job 36:30 [b]S Ex 15:13 **51:11** [c]S Isa 35:9; S 44:23 [d]S Ps 109:28; Isa 65:14; Jer 30:19; Zep 3:14 [e]S Isa 48:20; Jer 33:11 [f]S Isa 30:19; Jer 31:13; S Rev 7:17

7"Hear me, you who know what is right,[m]
you people who have my law in your hearts:[n]
Do not fear the reproach of men
or be terrified by their insults.[o]
8For the moth will eat them up like a garment;[p]
the worm[q] will devour them like wool.
But my righteousness will last forever,[r]
my salvation through all generations."

9Awake, awake![s] Clothe yourself with strength,[t]
O arm[u] of the LORD;
awake, as in days gone by,
as in generations of old.[v]
Was it not you who cut Rahab[w] to pieces,
who pierced that monster[x] through?
10Was it not you who dried up the sea,[y]
the waters of the great deep,[z]
who made a road in the depths of the sea[a]
so that the redeemed[b] might cross over?
11The ransomed[c] of the LORD will return.
They will enter Zion with singing;[d]
everlasting joy will crown their heads.
Gladness and joy[e] will overtake them,
and sorrow and sighing will flee away.[f]

---

kingdom on earth; this promise is repeated in the NT (Rev 11:15; 19—22). Although sin and Satan now have much of the world under their control (Jn 12:31; Eph 2:1–3), the Lord will return to destroy evil and establish his kingdom on this earth.

51:4–5 A LIGHT TO THE NATIONS. God's kingdom on earth at the end of time will bring salvation and righteousness to all the nations of the world (cf. 2:2–4; 42:4).

51:6 THE HEAVENS WILL VANISH. The establishment of God's eternal kingdom on earth will involve the destruction of the present heavens and earth and the death of all who oppose God and his righteousness (24:4; 34:4; 50:9; Heb 1:10–11; Rev 19); thereupon our Lord will create a new heaven and a new earth for the saints (65:17; 66:22; Rev 21:1), where he will dwell forever with those whom he has redeemed (2Pe 3:13).

51:9–11 AWAKE ... ARM OF THE LORD. We must respond to God's promises of the final redemption of his faithful people and the earth by fervently desiring and praying that those things come to pass. The apostle Peter teaches that our prayers can speed its coming: "In keeping with his promise, we are looking forward to a new heaven and a new earth, the home of righteousness" (2Pe 3:13; see 3:12, note).

12"I, even I, am he who comforts[g]
you.
Who are you that you fear[h]
mortal men,[i]
the sons of men, who are but
grass,[j]
13that you forget[k] the LORD your
Maker,[l]
who stretched out the heavens[m]
and laid the foundations of the
earth,
that you live in constant terror[n]
every day
because of the wrath of the
oppressor,
who is bent on destruction?
For where is the wrath of the
oppressor?[o]
14 The cowering prisoners will
soon be set free;[p]
they will not die in their dungeon,
nor will they lack bread.[q]
15For I am the LORD your God,
who churns up the sea[r] so that
its waves roar[s]—
the LORD Almighty[t] is his name.
16I have put my words in your
mouth[u]
and covered you with the
shadow of my hand[v]—
I who set the heavens in place,
who laid the foundations of the
earth,[w]
and who say to Zion, 'You are
my people.[x]' "

The Cup of the LORD's Wrath

17Awake, awake![y]
Rise up, O Jerusalem,
you who have drunk from the hand
of the LORD
the cup[z] of his wrath,[a]
you who have drained to its
dregs[b]
the goblet that makes men
stagger.[c]
18Of all the sons[d] she bore
there was none to guide her;[e]
of all the sons she reared
there was none to take her by
the hand.[f]
19These double calamities[g] have
come upon you—
who can comfort you?[h]—
ruin and destruction,[i] famine[j]
and sword[k]—
who can[w] console you?
20Your sons have fainted;
they lie at the head of every
street,[l]
like antelope caught in a net.[m]
They are filled with the wrath[n] of
the LORD
and the rebuke[o] of your God.
21Therefore hear this, you afflicted[p]
one,
made drunk,[q] but not with
wine.
22This is what your Sovereign LORD
says,
your God, who defends[r] his
people:
"See, I have taken out of your
hand
the cup[s] that made you
stagger;
from that cup, the goblet of my
wrath,
you will never drink again.
23I will put it into the hands of your
tormentors,[t]
who said to you,
'Fall prostrate[u] that we may
walk[v] over you.'
And you made your back like the
ground,
like a street to be walked
over."[w]

52 Awake, awake,[x] O Zion,
clothe yourself with
strength.[y]
Put on your garments of
splendor,[z]
O Jerusalem, the holy city.[a]
The uncircumcised[b] and defiled[c]
will not enter you again.[d]
2Shake off your dust;[e]
rise up,[f] sit enthroned,
O Jerusalem.

51:12 [g]S Isa 40:1; S 2Co 1:4 [h]S 2Ki 1:15 [i]S Isa 2:22 [j]S Isa 15:6; 40:6-7; 1Pe 1:24 **51:13** [k]S Job 8:13; S Isa 17:10 [l]S Job 4:17; Isa 17:7; 45:11; 54:5 [m]S Ge 1:1; S Isa 48:13 [n]S Isa 7:4 [o]S Isa 9:4 **51:14** [p]S Isa 42:7 [q]Isa 49:10 **51:15** [r]S Ex 14:21 [s]S Ps 93:3 [t]S Isa 13:4 **51:16** [u]S Ex 4:12,15 [v]S Ex 33:22 [w]S Isa 48:13 [x]Jer 7:23; 11:4; 24:7; Eze 14:11; Zec 8:8 **51:17** [y]S Jdg 5:12; Isa 52:1 [z]S ver 22; S Ps 16:5; S Mt 20:22 [a]ver 20; Job 21:20; Isa 42:25; 66:15; Rev 14:10; 16:19 [b]S Ps 75:8 [c]S ver 23; S Ps 60:3 **51:18** [d]Ps 88:18 [e]S Job 31:18; S Isa 49:21 [f]S Isa 41:13 **51:19** [g]S Isa 40:2; 47:9 [h]Isa 49:13; 54:11; Jer 15:5; Na 3:7 [i]Isa 60:18; 62:4; Jer 48:3; La 3:47 [j]S Isa 14:30 [k]Jer 14:12; 24:10 **51:20** [l]Isa 5:25; Jer 14:16; La 2:19 [m]S Job 18:10 [n]S ver 17; S Job 40:11; Jer 44:6 [o]S Dt 28:20 **51:21** [p]S Isa 14:32 [q]ver 17; S Isa 29:9 **51:22** [r]S Isa 49:25 [s]S ver 17; Jer 25:15; 51:7; Hab 2:16; S Mt 20:22 **51:23** [t]Isa 14:4; 49:26; Jer 25:15-17,26, 28; 49:12 [u]ver 17; Zec 12:2 [v]S Jos 10:24 [w]Ps 66:12; Mic 7:10 **52:1** [x]S Isa 51:17 [y]S 1Sa 2:4; S Isa 51:9 [z]Ex 28:2,40; Est 6:8; Ps 110:3; Isa 49:18; 61:10; Zec 3:4 [a]S Ne 11:1; S Isa 1:26; Mt 4:5; S Rev 21:2 [b]S Ge 34:14 [c]S Isa 35:8 [d]Joel 3:17; Na 1:15; Zec 9:8; Rev 21:27 **52:2** [e]S Isa 29:4 [f]Isa 60:1

[w] *19* Dead Sea Scrolls, Septuagint, Vulgate and Syriac; Masoretic Text / *how can I*

51:17–23 O JERUSALEM. In these verses Isaiah prophesies about Israel's exile because of God's wrath and goes on to proclaim God's promise of future deliverance. He foresees a time when God's judgment of his people would end and their anguish cease. God would then judge those who tormented them.

52:1–6 CLOTHE YOURSELF. Isaiah envisions a time when God would restore his exiled people for his name's sake and when Jerusalem would be rebuilt.

Free yourself from the chains on
your neck,[g]
O captive Daughter of Zion.[h]

3For this is what the LORD says:

"You were sold for nothing,[i]
and without money[j] you will be
redeemed.[k]"

4For this is what the Sovereign LORD
says:

"At first my people went down to
Egypt[l] to live;
lately, Assyria[m] has oppressed
them.

5"And now what do I have here?" declares the LORD.

"For my people have been taken
away for nothing,
and those who rule them
mock,[x]"
declares the LORD.

"And all day long
my name is constantly
blasphemed.[n]
6Therefore my people will know[o]
my name;[p]
therefore in that day[q] they will
know
that it is I who foretold[r] it.
Yes, it is I."

7How beautiful on the mountains[s]
are the feet of those who bring
good news,[t]
who proclaim peace,[u]
who bring good tidings,
who proclaim salvation,
who say to Zion,
"Your God reigns!"[v]
8Listen! Your watchmen[w] lift up
their voices;[x]
together they shout for joy.[y]
When the LORD returns[z] to Zion,[a]
they will see it with their own
eyes.
9Burst into songs of joy[b] together,
you ruins[c] of Jerusalem,
for the LORD has comforted[d] his
people,
he has redeemed Jerusalem.[e]
10The LORD will lay bare his holy
arm[f]
in the sight of all the nations,[g]
and all the ends of the earth[h] will
see
the salvation[i] of our God.

11Depart,[j] depart, go out from
there!
Touch no unclean thing![k]
Come out from it and be pure,[l]
you who carry the vessels[m] of
the LORD.
12But you will not leave in haste[n]
or go in flight;
for the LORD will go before you,[o]
the God of Israel will be your
rear guard.[p]

Eze 3:10-11

The Suffering and Glory of the Servant

13See, my servant[q] will act
wisely[y];
he will be raised and lifted up
and highly exalted.[r]
14Just as there were many who were
appalled[s] at him[z]—

52:2 [g] S Ps 81:6; S Isa 10:27 [h] Ps 9:14 **52:3** [i] S Ps 44:12 [j] Isa 45:13 [k] S Isa 1:27; 1Pe 1:18 **52:4** [l] S Ge 46:6 [m] Isa 10:24 **52:5** [n] S Isa 37:23; Ro 2:24* **52:6** [o] S Isa 49:23 [p] S Ex 6:3 [q] S Isa 10:20 [r] S Isa 41:26 **52:7** [s] S Isa 42:11 [t] S 2Sa 18:26; S Isa 40:9; Ro 10:15* [u] Na 1:15; Lk 2:14; Eph 6:15 [v] S 1Ch 16:31; S Ps 97:1; 1Co 15:24-25 **52:8** [w] S 1Sa 14:16; Isa 56:10; 62:6; Jer 6:17; 31:6; Eze 3:17; 33:7 [x] Isa 40:9 [y] S Isa 12:6 [z] S Nu 10:36 [a] Isa 59:20; Zec 8:3 **52:9** [b] S Ps 98:4; S Isa 35:2 [c] S Ps 74:3; S Isa 51:3 [d] S Isa 40:1; Lk 2:25 [e] S Ezr 9:9; S Isa 48:20 **52:10** [f] S 2Ch 32:8; S Ps 44:3; S Isa 30:30 [g] Isa 66:18 [h] S Jos 4:24; S Isa 11:9 [i] S Ps 67:2; Lk 2:30; 3:6 **52:11** [j] S Isa 48:20 [k] S Isa 1:16; 2Co 6:17* [l] S Nu 8:6; 2Ti 2:19 [m] S 2Ch 36:10 **52:12** [n] S Ex 12:11 [o] Mic 2:13; Jn 10:4 [p] S Ex 14:19 **52:13** [q] S Jos 1:8; S Isa 4:2; S 20:3 [r] S Isa 6:1; 57:15; Ac 3:13; S Php 2:9 **52:14** [s] S Lev 26:32; S Job 18:20

[x]*5* Dead Sea Scrolls and Vulgate; Masoretic Text *wail* [y]*13* Or *will prosper* [z]*14* Hebrew *you*

52:7 HOW BEAUTIFUL . . . ARE THE FEET. This verse refers first to those who proclaimed release to the captives in Babylon; it also foreshadows the announcement of salvation through the coming Messiah (see Ro 10:15; Eph 6:15). The focus of the proclaimed message is, "Your God reigns," i.e., the kingdom of God has come to earth (cf. Mk 1:14–15; see article on THE KINGDOM OF GOD, p. 1430).

52:11 DEPART . . . TOUCH NO UNCLEAN THING! The exodus from Babylon, like the exodus from Egypt, pictured deliverance from the world and all that is unclean. The redeemed people were specifically instructed to purify themselves from all uncleanness; likewise, when individuals accept Christ as Lord and Savior, they must separate themselves from the world and purify themselves from all evil (see article on SPIRITUAL SEPARATION FOR BELIEVERS, p. 1794).

52:13—53:12 THE SUFFERING SERVANT. This section speaks of the suffering and rejection of the Servant-Messiah, Jesus Christ. Isaiah prophesies that through his suffering many would be forgiven, justified, redeemed and healed. His suffering would also lead to his exaltation and glory. The NT quotes from this portion of Scripture more than from any other OT section.

52:13 SEE, MY SERVANT. Jesus the Messiah, the Servant of God, would do God's will perfectly and be highly exalted as a result (cf. Ac 2:33; Php 2:9; Col 3:1; Heb 1:3; 8:1).

52:14 APPEARANCE WAS SO DISFIGURED. This verse describes Jesus' mistreatment by the Jews and the Roman soldiers at his trial and crucifixion (cf. Ps 22:6–8; see Mt 26:67, note).

his appearance was so
disfigured[t] beyond that of
any man
and his form marred beyond
human likeness[u]—
15so will he sprinkle[v] many
nations,[a]
and kings[w] will shut their
mouths[x] because of him.
For what they were not told, they
will see,
and what they have not heard,
they will understand.[y]

53 Who has believed our
message[z]
and to whom has the arm[a] of
the LORD been revealed?[b]
2He grew up before him like a
tender shoot,[c]
and like a root[d] out of dry
ground.
He had no beauty or majesty to
attract us to him,
nothing in his appearance[e] that
we should desire him.
3He was despised and rejected by
men,
a man of sorrows,[f] and familiar
with suffering.[g]
Like one from whom men hide[h]
their faces
he was despised,[i] and we
esteemed him not.

4Surely he took up our infirmities
and carried our sorrows,[j]
yet we considered him stricken by
God,[k]
smitten by him, and afflicted.[l]
5But he was pierced[m] for our
transgressions,[n]
he was crushed[o] for our
iniquities;
the punishment[p] that brought us
peace[q] was upon him,
and by his wounds[r] we are
healed.[s]
6We all, like sheep, have gone
astray,[t]

52:14 [t]S 2Sa 10:4 [u]S Job 2:12; S 16:16
52:15 [v]S Lev 14:7; S 16:14-15 [w]S Isa 49:7 [x]S Jdg 18:19; Ps 107:42 [y]Ro 15:21*; Eph 3:4-5
53:1 [z]S Isa 28:9; Ro 10:16* [a]S Ps 98:1; S Isa 30:30 [b]Jn 12:38*
53:2 [c]S 2Ki 19:26; S Job 14:7; S Isa 4:2 [d]S Isa 11:10 [e]Isa 52:14
53:3 [f]Ps 69:29 [g]ver 4,10; S Ex 1:10; S Mt 16:21; Lk 18:31-33; Heb 5:8 [h]S Dt 31:17; Isa 1:15 [i]S 1Sa 2:30; S Ps 22:6; Mt 27:29; Jn 1:10-11
53:4 [j]Mt 8:17* [k]S Dt 5:24; S Job 4:5; Jer 23:5-6; 25:34; Eze 34:23-24; Mic 5:2-4; Zec 13:7; Jn 19:7 [l]S ver 3; S Ge 12:17; S Ru 1:21
53:5 [m]S Ps 22:16 [n]S Ex 28:38; S Ps 39:8; S Jn 3:17; Ro 4:25; 1Co 15:3; Heb 9:28 [o]Ps 34:18 [p]S Isa 50:6 [q]S Isa 9:6; Ro 5:1 [r]Isa 1:6; Mt 27:26; Jn 19:1 [s]S Dt 32:39; S 2Ch 7:14; 1Pe 2:24-25
53:6 [t]S Ps 95:10; 1Pe 2:24-25

[a] *15* Hebrew; Septuagint *so will many nations marvel at him*

52:15 SPRINKLE MANY NATIONS. This phrase refers to the spiritual cleansing and purification (cf. Ex 29:21; Lev 8:11,30) that people from all nations would experience when they received the message of the Servant-Messiah; this cleansing would come by the sprinkled blood of Christ.

53:1 WHO HAS BELIEVED OUR MESSAGE. Although Jesus is God's Messiah, many would choose not to believe in him and would therefore fail to receive the Lord's salvation (see Jn 12:38; Ro 10:16). There were relatively few true believers among the Jews at his first coming.

53:2 ROOT OUT OF DRY GROUND. Jesus not only had humble beginnings, but he came to earth at a time of great spiritual drought. John the Baptist began to awaken the people shortly before Jesus began his public ministry.

53:2 NO BEAUTY OR MAJESTY TO ATTRACT US. The Messiah would lack earthly grandeur and physical attractiveness. God's greatest concern is always a person's character, godliness and obedience, not earthly status or physical beauty (cf. 1Sa 16:7; see Lk 22:24–30, note).

53:3 DESPISED AND REJECTED. Instead of being accepted by Israel, Jesus Christ would be hated and rejected by its rulers (see 52:14, note; Mt 26:57, note).

53:3 A MAN OF SORROWS. Jesus' mission would involve great pain, suffering, disappointment and grief because of the sins of humankind. Likewise, all who follow Jesus will likely experience a measure of suffering and disappointment (see 2Co 11:23, note).

53:4 TOOK UP OUR INFIRMITIES. This verse is quoted in Mt 8:17 with reference to Jesus' ministry of healing the sick—both the physically and the spiritually sick. The Messiah would endure punishment in order that we may be delivered from our diseases and sicknesses as well as from our sins. It is therefore right and good for us to pray for physical healing. As he bore our sins, he also takes the sickness and grief that belong to us, lifts them upon himself and carries them (see next two notes).

53:5 PIERCED FOR OUR TRANSGRESSIONS. Christ was crucified because we have sinned and are guilty before God (cf. Ps 22:16; Zec 12:10; Jn 19:34). As our substitute, he took the punishment due us and paid the penalty for our sins—the penalty of death (Ro 6:23); therefore, we can be forgiven and have peace with God (Ro 5:1).

53:5 BY HIS WOUNDS WE ARE HEALED. This healing refers to salvation with all its benefits, spiritual and physical. Sickness and disease are the result of the fall and Satan's activity in the world (see article on DIVINE HEALING, p. 1420). "The reason the Son of God appeared was to destroy the devil's work" (1Jn 3:8). Christ gave gifts of healing to his church (1Co 12:9) and commanded his followers to heal the sick as part of their proclamation of God's kingdom (Lk 9:1–2,6; 10:1, 8–9,19).

53:6 WE ALL, LIKE SHEEP, HAVE GONE ASTRAY. Every person at one time or another has preferred following his or her own selfish and sinful way to obeying God's righteous commands (see Ro 6:1, notes); we are all guilty, and therefore we

each of us has turned to his own
way;[u]
and the LORD has laid on him
the iniquity[v] of us all.

7 He was oppressed[w] and afflicted,
yet he did not open his mouth;[x]
he was led like a lamb[y] to the
slaughter,[z]
and as a sheep before her
shearers is silent,
so he did not open his mouth.
8 By oppression[b] and judgment[a] he
was taken away.
And who can speak of his
descendants?
For he was cut off from the land of
the living;[b]
for the transgression[c] of my
people he was stricken.[c]
9 He was assigned a grave with the
wicked,[d]
and with the rich[e] in his death,
though he had done no violence,[f]
nor was any deceit in his
mouth.[g]

10 Yet it was the LORD's will[h] to
crush[i] him and cause him
to suffer,[j]
and though the LORD makes[d]
his life a guilt offering,[k]
he will see his offspring[l] and
prolong his days,
and the will of the LORD will
prosper[m] in his hand.

53:6 [u]S 1Sa 8:3; Isa 56:11; 57:17; Mic 3:5 [v]ver 12; S Ex 28:38; Ro 4:25 **53:7** [w]Isa 49:26 [x]S Mk 14:61; 1Pe 2:23 [y]Mt 27:31; S Jn 1:29 [z]S Ps 44:22 **53:8** [a]Mk 14:49 [b]Ps 88:5; Da 9:26; Ac 8:32-33* [c]ver 12; S Ps 39:8 **53:9** [d]Mt 27:38; Mk 15:27; Lk 23:32; Jn 19:18 [e]Mt 27:57-60; Mk 15:43-46; Lk 23:50-53; Jn 19:38-41 [f]Isa 42:1-3 [g]S Job 16:17; 1Pe 2:22*; 1Jn 3:5; Rev 14:5 **53:10** [h]Isa 46:10; 55:11; Ac 2:23 [i]ver 5 [j]S ver 3; S Ge 12:17 [k]S Lev 5:15; Jn 3:17 [l]S Ps 22:30 [m]S Jos 1:8; S Isa 49:4 **53:11** [n]Jn 10:14-18 [o]S Job 33:30 [p]S Isa 20:3; Ac 7:52 [q]S Isa 6:7; Jn 1:29; Ac 10:43; S Ro 4:25 [r]S Ex 28:38 **53:12** [s]S Isa 6:1; S Php 2:9 [t]S Ex 15:9; S Ps 119:162; Lk 11:22 [u]Mt 26:28,38,39, 42 [v]Mt 27:38; Mk 15:27*; Lk 22:37*; 23:32

11 After the suffering[n] of his soul,
he will see the light[o] ⌊of life⌋[e]
and be satisfied[f];
by his knowledge[g] my righteous
servant[p] will justify[q]
many,
and he will bear their
iniquities.[r]
12 Therefore I will give him a portion
among the great,[h][s]
and he will divide the spoils[t]
with the strong,[i]
because he poured out his life unto
death,[u]
and was numbered with the
transgressors.[v]
For he bore[w] the sin of many,[x]
and made intercession[y] for the
transgressors.

Isa 55:6-7

The Future Glory of Zion

54 "Sing, O barren woman,[z]
you who never bore a child;

[w]S ver 6; 1Pe 2:24 [x]Heb 9:28 [y]Isa 59:16; S Ro 8:34 **54:1** [z]S Ge 30:1

[b] *8* Or *From arrest* [c] *8* Or *away. / Yet who of his generation considered / that he was cut off from the land of the living / for the transgression of my people, / to whom the blow was due?* [d] *10* Hebrew *though you make* [e] *11* Dead Sea Scrolls (see also Septuagint); Masoretic Text does not have *the light ⌊of life⌋.* [f] *11* Or (with Masoretic Text) *11He will see the result of the suffering of his soul / and be satisfied* [g] *11* Or *by knowledge of him* [h] *12* Or *many* [i] *12* Or *numerous*

all need Christ to die in our place.

53:7 LIKE A LAMB TO THE SLAUGHTER. Jesus endured his suffering for us patiently and voluntarily (1Pe 2:23; cf. Jn 1:29,36; Rev 5:6).

53:9 A GRAVE WITH THE WICKED. This phrase may simply indicate that Jesus Christ would die alongside the wicked, or that the Roman soldiers intended to bury him with the two criminals. Yet, as here prophesied, he was buried in the grave of a rich man (Mt 27:57–60).

53:10 THE LORD'S WILL TO CRUSH HIM. It was the will of God the Father that his Son be sent to die on the cross for a lost world (see Jn 3:16, note; see article on THE WILL OF GOD, p. 1056). By making Christ an atoning sacrifice for all transgressions (cf. Lev 5:15; 6:5; 19:21; see article on THE DAY OF ATONEMENT, p. 174), God's redemptive purpose of bringing many people to salvation has been accomplished. He will "prolong his days" means he will "rise from the dead and live forever."

53:11 SUFFERING OF HIS SOUL. The suffering of the Messiah would accomplish God's purpose and result in salvation for the "many" who believe.

53:12 A PORTION AMONG THE GREAT. God promised to reward Christ for his atoning death, and Christ in turn promises to share his reward with all the "strong" who follow him in doing battle against sin and Satan through the power of the Spirit.

53:12 POURED OUT HIS LIFE UNTO DEATH. Because of Jesus' death on the cross, a great inheritance has been released to God's people. Any gospel proclamation that does not preach the cross of Christ and its demand for separation from sin is ultimately doomed to failure; all such efforts will be empty of the presence of Christ and his Spirit.

53:12 MADE INTERCESSION FOR THE TRANSGRESSORS. In his agony on the cross, Jesus interceded for sinners (Lk 23:34); his ministry of intercession still continues in heaven (cf. Ro 8:34; see Heb 7:25, note).

54:1–3 SING, O BARREN WOMEN. God encourages the exiles by promising new conditions that would bring blessing and joy. Though Jerusalem was barren and fruitless, a day was coming when true believers would be more numerous than before the exile. "Your descendants will dispossess nations" (v. 3) may refer to the faithful believers among the Jews who spread the gospel of

THE WILL OF GOD

***Isa 53:10** "Yet it was the LORD's will to crush him and cause him to suffer, and though the LORD makes his life a guilt offering, he will see his offspring and prolong his days, and the will of the LORD will prosper in his hand."*

DEFINING THE WILL OF GOD. In general, the Bible refers to the will of God in three different senses. (1) In some passages, "the will of God" is another way of saying "the law of God." For example, David parallels the phrase "your law" with "your will" in Ps 40:8. Similarly, the apostle Paul considers knowing God's law to be synonymous with knowing God's will (Ro 2:17–18). In other words, since in his law God instructs us in the way that he wants us to walk, the law may properly be called "the will of God." "Law" essentially means "instruction" and includes the whole word of God.

(2) "The will of God" is also used to designate anything that God expressly desires; this may properly be called God's "perfect will." For example, it is God's revealed will that everyone be saved (1Ti 2:4; 2Pe 3:9) and that no saved believer should fall from grace (see Jn 6:40, note). This truth does not mean that everyone will be saved, but only that God desires the salvation of everyone.

(3) Finally, the "will of God" may refer to what God permits or allows to happen, even though he does not specifically desire it to happen; this may properly be called God's "permissive will." Indeed, much that happens in the world is contrary to God's perfect will (e.g., sin, lust, violence, hatred and hardheartedness), yet he permits evil to continue for the time being. For example, the decision of many people to remain unsaved and thus lost for all eternity is permitted by God, for he does not force saving faith on those who refuse to accept his Son's salvation. Similarly, many troubles and evils that befall a person in life are permitted by God (1Pe 3:17; 4:19), but they are not necessarily his desire or ultimate will for that person (see 1Jn 5:19, note; see articles on THE PROVIDENCE OF GOD, p. 78, and THE SUFFERING OF THE RIGHTEOUS, p. 710).

RESPONDING TO THE WILL OF GOD. The Bible's teaching about the will of God expresses more than mere doctrine; it intersects with our lives as believers on an everyday basis. (1) First, we must learn what God's will is, i.e., his perfect will as revealed in Scripture (including his law). Because the days in which we live are evil, we must understand "what the Lord's will is" (Eph 5:17).

(2) Once we know from the revealed will of God how he desires us to live as believers, we must commit ourselves to do his will. The psalmist, for example, asks God to teach him "to do your will" (Ps 143:10). The parallel request, that the Spirit "lead me on level ground," indicates that he is essentially asking God for the ability to live a righteous life. Similarly, Paul expects the Thessalonian Christians to follow God's will by avoiding sexual immorality and by living in a holy and honorable way (1Th 4:3–4). Elsewhere he prays that Christians will be filled with the knowledge of God's will, in order that they "may live a life worthy of the Lord and may please him in every way" (Col 1:9–10).

(3) Believers are called to pray that God's will may be done (cf. Mt 6:10; 26:42; Lk 11:2; Ro 15:30–32; Jas 4:13–15); we must sincerely desire God's perfect will and intend to fulfill it in our lives and in the lives of our families (see Mt 6:10, note). If this is our prayer and commitment, then we can rest assured that our present and future are in the protective care of our heavenly Father (cf. Ac 18:21; 1Co 4:19; 16:7). However, if there is deliberate sin in our lives and rebellion against his word, then we must realize that God will not answer our prayers (see article on EFFECTIVE PRAYING, p. 496); we cannot expect God's will to be done on earth as it is in heaven unless we ourselves are attempting to do his will in our own lives.

(4) Finally, we must not use the will of God as an excuse for passivity or irresponsibility with respect to his call to battle sin, evil and spiritual lukewarmness. It is Satan, not God, who is responsible for this present evil age with its cruelty, evil and injustice (see 1Jn 5:19, note), and it is Satan who causes much of the pain and suffering in the world (cf. Job 1:6–12; 2:1–6; Lk 13:16; 2Co 12:7). Just as Jesus came to destroy the works of the devil (1Jn 3:8), so it is God's explicit will for believers to wage war against those spiritual hosts of wickedness through the Holy Spirit (Eph 6:10–20; 1Th 5:8; see article on THE CHRISTIAN'S RELATIONSHIP TO THE WORLD, p. 1976).

JERUSALEM DURING TIME OF THE PROPHETS

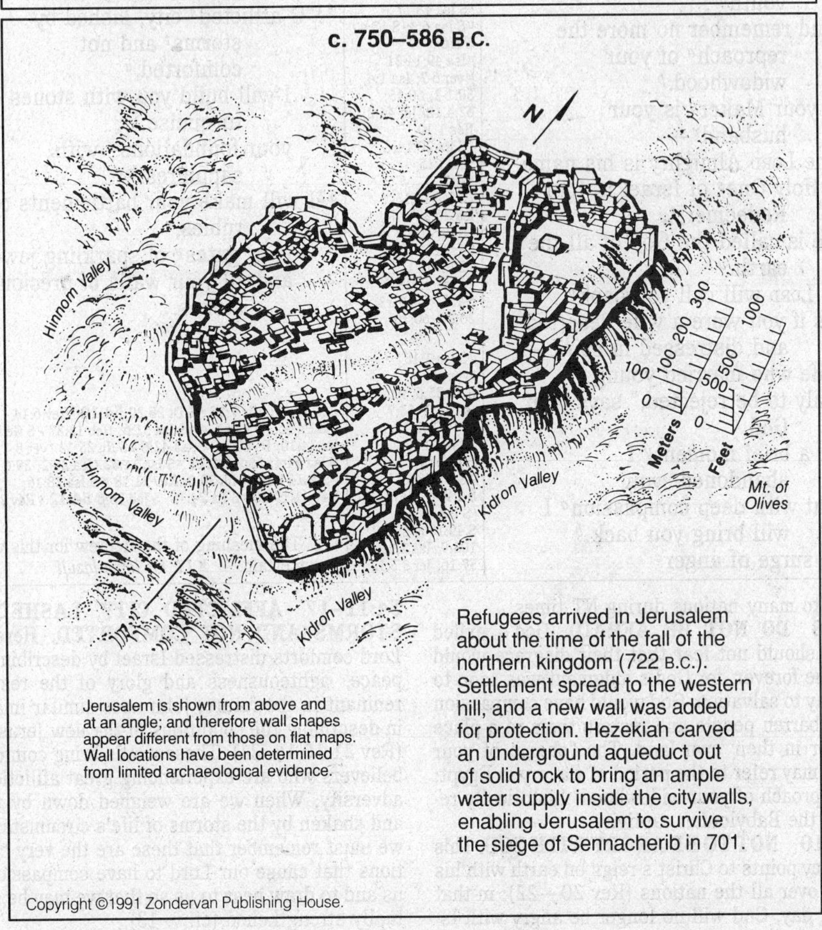

Jerusalem is shown from above and at an angle; and therefore wall shapes appear different from those on flat maps. Wall locations have been determined from limited archaeological evidence.

Refugees arrived in Jerusalem about the time of the fall of the northern kingdom (722 B.C.). Settlement spread to the western hill, and a new wall was added for protection. Hezekiah carved an underground aqueduct out of solid rock to bring an ample water supply inside the city walls, enabling Jerusalem to survive the siege of Sennacherib in 701.

burst into song, shout for joy,[a]
you who were never in labor;[b]
because more are the children[c] of
the desolate[d] woman
than of her who has a
husband,[e]"
says the LORD.
2"Enlarge the place of your tent,[f]
stretch your tent curtains wide,
do not hold back;
lengthen your cords,
strengthen your stakes.[g]
3For you will spread out to the
right and to the left;
your descendants[h] will
dispossess nations[i]
and settle in their desolate[j]
cities.

4"Do not be afraid;[k] you will not
suffer shame.[l]
Do not fear disgrace;[m] you will
not be humiliated.
You will forget the shame of your
youth[n]
and remember no more the
reproach[o] of your
widowhood.[p]
5For your Maker[q] is your
husband[r]—
the LORD Almighty is his name—
the Holy One[s] of Israel is your
Redeemer;[t]
he is called the God of all the
earth.[u]
6The LORD will call you back[v]
as if you were a wife deserted[w]
and distressed in spirit—
a wife who married young,[x]
only to be rejected," says your
God.
7"For a brief moment[y] I
abandoned[z] you,
but with deep compassion[a] I
will bring you back.[b]
8In a surge of anger[c]
I hid[d] my face from you for a
moment,
but with everlasting kindness[e]
I will have compassion[f] on
you,"
says the LORD your Redeemer.[g]

9"To me this is like the days of
Noah,
when I swore that the waters of
Noah would never again
cover the earth.[h]
So now I have sworn[i] not to be
angry[j] with you,
never to rebuke[k] you again.
10Though the mountains be
shaken[l][m]
and the hills be removed,
yet my unfailing love[n] for you will
not be shaken[o]
nor my covenant[p] of peace[q] be
removed,"
says the LORD, who has
compassion[r] on you.

11"O afflicted[s] city, lashed by
storms[t] and not
comforted,[u]
I will build you with stones of
turquoise,[j][v]
your foundations[w] with
sapphires.[k][x]
12I will make your battlements of
rubies,
your gates[y] of sparkling jewels,
and all your walls of precious
stones.

54:1 [a]S Ge 21:6; S Ps 98:4 [b]Isa 66:7 [c]Isa 49:20 [d]S Isa 49:19 [e]S 1Sa 2:5; Gal 4:27* **54:2** [f]S Ge 26:22; Isa 26:15; 49:19-20 [g]Ex 35:18; 39:40 **54:3** [h]S Ge 13:14; S Isa 48:19 [i]S Job 12:23; S Isa 14:2; 60:4-11 [j]S Isa 49:19 **54:4** [k]Jer 30:10; Joel 2:21 [l]S Isa 28:16; S 29:22 [m]S Ge 30:23; S Ps 119:39; S Isa 41:11 [n]S Ps 25:7; S Jer 2:2; S 22:21 [o]S Isa 51:7 [p]S Isa 47:8 **54:5** [q]S Ps 95:6; S 149:2; S Isa 51:13 [r]S SS 3:11; Jer 3:14; 31:32; Hos 2:7,16 [s]S Isa 1:4; 49:7; 55:5; 60:9 [t]S Isa 48:17 [u]S Isa 6:3; S 12:4 **54:6** [v]Isa 49:14-21 [w]ver 6-7; Isa 1:4; 50:1-2; 60:15; 62:4,12; Jer 44:2; Hos 1:10 [x]S Ex 20:14; Mal 2:15 **54:7** [y]S Job 14:13; Isa 26:20 [z]S Ps 71:11; S Isa 27:8 [a]S Ps 51:1 [b]S Isa 49:18 **54:8** [c]Isa 9:12; 26:20; 60:10 [d]S Isa 1:15 [e]ver 10; S Ps 25:6; 92:2; Isa 55:3; 63:7 [f]S Ps 102:13; S Isa 14:1; Hos 2:19 [g]S Isa 48:17 **54:9** [h]S Ge 8:21 [i]S Isa 14:24; S 49:18 [j]Ps 13:1; 103:9; Isa 12:1; 57:16; Jer 3:5,12; Eze 39:29; Mic 7:18 [k]S Dt 28:20 **54:10** [l]Rev 6:14 [m]S Ps 46:2 [n]S Ps 6:4 [o]S Isa 51:6; Heb 12:27 [p]S Ge 9:16; Ex 34:10; Ps 89:34; S Isa 42:6 [q]S Nu 25:12 [r]ver 8; S Isa 14:1; 55:7 **54:11** [s]S Isa 14:32 [t]Isa 28:2; 29:6 [u]S Isa 51:19 [v]1Ch 29:2; Rev 21:18 [w]S Isa 28:16; Rev 21:19-20 [x]S Ex 24:10; S Job 28:6 **54:12** [y]Rev 21:21

[j] *11* The meaning of the Hebrew for this word is uncertain. [k] *11* Or *lapis lazuli*

Christ to many nations during NT times.

54:4–8 DO NOT BE AFRAID. God's exiled people should not fear that their disgrace would continue forever, for God's judgment was soon to give way to salvation. God would have compassion on his barren people and restore them to a place of favor in their own land. The "shame of your youth" may refer to the period of slavery in Egypt; the "reproach of your widowhood" historically refers to the Babylonian captivity.

54:9–10 NOT TO BE ANGRY WITH YOU. This prophecy points to Christ's reign on earth with his people over all the nations (Rev 20—22); in that coming day, God will no longer be angry with Israel.

54:11–17 AFFLICTED CITY, LASHED BY STORMS AND NOT COMFORTED. Here the Lord comforts distressed Israel by describing the peace, righteousness and glory of the restored remnant in the future; John uses similar imagery in describing the conditions of the new Jerusalem (Rev 21:10,18–21). These words bring comfort to believers who are experiencing great affliction or adversity. When we are weighed down by trials and shaken by the storms of life's circumstances, we must remember that these are the very conditions that cause our Lord to have compassion on us and to draw near to us so that we may be spiritually strengthened (cf. v. 13).

13All your sons will be taught by the
LORD,[z]
and great will be your children's
peace.[a]
14In righteousness[b] you will be
established:[c]
Tyranny[d] will be far from you;
you will have nothing to fear.[e]
Terror[f] will be far removed;
it will not come near you.
15If anyone does attack you, it will
not be my doing;
whoever attacks you will
surrender[g] to you.

16"See, it is I who created the
blacksmith[h]
who fans the coals into flame
and forges a weapon[i] fit for its
work.
And it is I who have created the
destroyer[j] to work havoc;
17 no weapon forged against you
will prevail,[k]
and you will refute[l] every
tongue that accuses you.
This is the heritage of the
servants[m] of the LORD,
and this is their vindication[n]
from me,"
declares the LORD.

Invitation to the Thirsty

55 "Come, all you who are
thirsty,[o]
come to the waters;[p]
and you who have no money,
come, buy[q] and eat!
Come, buy wine and milk[r]
without money and without
cost.[s]
2Why spend money on what is not
bread,
and your labor on what does not
satisfy?[t]
Listen, listen to me, and eat what
is good,[u]
and your soul will delight in the
richest[v] of fare.
3Give ear and come to me;
hear[w] me, that your soul may
live.[x]
I will make an everlasting
covenant[y] with you,
my faithful love[z] promised to
David.[a]
4See, I have made him a witness[b]
to the peoples,
a leader and commander[c] of
the peoples.
5Surely you will summon nations[d]
you know not,
and nations that do not know
you will hasten to you,[e]
because of the LORD your God,
the Holy One[f] of Israel,
for he has endowed you with
splendor."[g]

6Seek[h] the LORD while he may be
found;[i]
call[j] on him while he is near.
7Let the wicked forsake[k] his way
and the evil man his thoughts.[l]
Let him turn[m] to the LORD, and he
will have mercy[n] on him,
and to our God, for he will freely
pardon.[o] ✝ Isa 59:15-17

8"For my thoughts[p] are not your
thoughts,
neither are your ways my
ways,"[q]
declares the LORD.
9"As the heavens are higher than
the earth,[r]

54:13 [z]S Isa 28:9; Mic 4:2; Jn 6:45*; Heb 8:11 [a]S Lev 26:6; S Isa 48:18 **54:14** [b]S Isa 26:2 [c]Jer 30:20 [d]S 2Sa 7:10; S Isa 9:4 [e]Zep 3:15; Zec 9:8 [f]S Isa 17:14 **54:15** [g]Isa 41:11-16 **54:16** [h]S Isa 44:12 [i]S Isa 10:5 [j]S Isa 13:5 **54:17** [k]S Isa 29:8 [l]S Isa 41:11 [m]Isa 56:6-8; 63:17; 65:8,9, 13-15; 66:14 [n]S Ps 17:2; Zec 1:20-21 **55:1** [o]S Pr 9:5; S Isa 35:7; Mt 5:6; Lk 6:21; Jn 4:14; 7:37 [p]Jer 2:13; Eze 47:1,12; Zec 14:8 [q]La 5:4; Mt 13:44; Rev 3:18 [r]S SS 5:1; 1Pe 2:2 [s]Hos 14:4; Mt 10:8; Rev 21:6; 22:17 **55:2** [t]Ps 22:26; Ecc 6:2; Isa 49:4; Jer 12:13; Hos 4:10; 8:7; Mic 6:14; Hag 1:6 [u]S Isa 1:19 [v]S Isa 30:23 **55:3** [w]S Ps 78:1 [x]S Lev 18:5; S Jn 6:27; Ro 10:5 [y]S Ge 9:16; S Isa 54:10; S Heb 13:20 [z]S Isa 54:8 [a]Ac 13:34* **55:4** [b]Rev 1:5 [c]S 1Sa 13:14; S 2Ch 7:18; S Isa 32:1 **55:5** [d]S Isa 49:6 [e]S Isa 2:3 [f]S Isa 12:6; S 54:5 [g]S Isa 44:23 **55:6** [h]S Dt 4:29; S 2Ch 15:2; S Isa 9:13 [i]Ps 32:6; Isa 49:8; Ac 17:27; 2Co 6:1-2 [j]S Ps 50:15; Isa 65:24; Jer 29:12; 33:3 **55:7** [k]S 2Ch 7:14; S 30:9; Eze 18:27-28 [l]Isa 32:7; 59:7 [m]S Isa 44:22; S Jer 26:3; S Eze 18:32 [n]S Isa 54:10 [o]S 2Ch 6:21; Isa 1:18; 40:2 **55:8** [p]Php 2:5; 4:8 [q]Isa 53:6; Mic 4:12 **55:9** [r]S Job 11:8; Ps 103:11

55:1–13 COME, ALL YOU. The Israelites, who have forsaken God and his righteousness, are invited by God to return to him and be restored to fellowship and blessing.

55:1 ALL YOU WHO ARE THIRSTY. An essential prerequisite for salvation is a genuine spiritual hunger and thirst for forgiveness and for a right relationship with God (cf. Jn 4:14; 7:37), based on the sacrificial death of the Servant-Messiah (ch. 53). We must repent of our sins and draw near to God in faith; furthermore, hunger and thirst for God's righteousness and the power of his kingdom continue to be vital conditions for receiving the fullness of his Spirit (see Mt 5:6, note).

55:6 SEEK THE LORD. We must seek God while there is still the promise of his response (cf. Jer 29:13–14; Hos 3:5; Am 5:4,6,14). God's time of salvation is limited (cf. 2Co 6:1–2); a day is coming when he will refuse to be found (see Heb 3:7–11).

55:8 MY THOUGHTS ARE NOT YOUR THOUGHTS. God's thoughts and ways are not those of the natural person. But human minds and hearts can be renewed and transformed by seeking him (cf. Ro 12:1–2); then our thoughts and ways will begin to conform to his. Our greatest desire should be to so live in conformity to the likeness of our Lord that everything we do pleases the God we serve. We can do this by abiding in his word and responding to the Holy Spirit's leading (see Ro 8:5–14, note; Jas 1:21, note).

so are my ways higher than your
ways
and my thoughts than your
thoughts.[s]
10As the rain[t] and the snow
come down from heaven,
and do not return to it
without watering the earth
and making it bud and flourish,[u]
so that it yields seed[v] for the
sower and bread for the
eater,[w]
11so is my word[x] that goes out
from my mouth:
It will not return to me empty,[y]
but will accomplish what I desire
and achieve the purpose[z] for
which I sent it.
12You will go out in joy[a]
and be led forth in peace;[b]
the mountains and hills
will burst into song[c] before
you,
and all the trees[d] of the field
will clap their hands.[e]
13Instead of the thornbush will grow
the pine tree,
and instead of briers[f] the
myrtle[g] will grow.
This will be for the LORD's
renown,[h]
for an everlasting sign,
which will not be destroyed."

Salvation for Others

56 This is what the LORD says:
"Maintain justice[i]
and do what is right,[j]
for my salvation[k] is close at hand
and my righteousness[l] will
soon be revealed.
2Blessed[m] is the man who does
this,
the man who holds it fast,
who keeps the Sabbath[n] without
desecrating it,
and keeps his hand from doing
any evil."
3Let no foreigner[o] who has bound
himself to the LORD say,
"The LORD will surely exclude
me from his people."[p]
And let not any eunuch[q]
complain,
"I am only a dry tree."
4For this is what the LORD says:
"To the eunuchs[r] who keep my
Sabbaths,
who choose what pleases me
and hold fast to my
covenant[s]—
5to them I will give within my
temple and its walls[t]
a memorial[u] and a name
better than sons and daughters;
I will give them an everlasting
name[v]
that will not be cut off.[w]
6And foreigners[x] who bind
themselves to the LORD
to serve[y] him,
to love the name[z] of the LORD,
and to worship him,
all who keep the Sabbath[a]
without desecrating it
and who hold fast to my
covenant—
7these I will bring to my holy
mountain[b]
and give them joy in my house
of prayer.
Their burnt offerings and
sacrifices[c]
will be accepted on my altar;
for my house will be called
a house of prayer for all
nations."[d][e]
8The Sovereign LORD declares—

55:9 [s]S Nu 23:19; S Isa 40:13-14 **55:10** [t]Isa 30:23 [u]S Lev 25:19; S Job 14:9; S Ps 67:6 [v]S Ge 47:23 [w]2Co 9:10 **55:11** [x]S Dt 32:2; Jn 1:1 [y]Isa 40:8; 45:23; S Mt 5:18; Heb 4:12 [z]S Pr 19:21; S Isa 44:26; Eze 12:25 **55:12** [a]S Ps 98:4; S Isa 35:2 [b]Isa 54:10,13 [c]S Ps 65:12-13; S 96:12-13 [d]S 1Ch 16:33 [e]Ps 98:8 **55:13** [f]S Nu 33:55; S Isa 5:6 [g]Isa 41:19 [h]S Ps 102:12; Isa 63:12; Jer 32:20; 33:9 **56:1** [i]S Ps 11:7; S Isa 1:17; S Jer 22:3 [j]S Isa 26:8 [k]S Ps 85:9 [l]Jer 23:6; Da 9:24 **56:2** [m]S Ps 119:2 [n]S Ex 20:8,10 **56:3** [o]S Ex 12:43; S 1Ki 8:41; S Isa 11:10; Zec 8:20-23 [p]Dt 23:3 [q]S Lev 21:20; Jer 38:7 *fn*; Ac 8:27 **56:4** [r]Jer 38:7 *fn* [s]S Ex 31:13 **56:5** [t]Isa 26:1; 60:18 [u]S Nu 32:42; 1Sa 15:12 [v]S Isa 43:7 [w]S Isa 48:19; 55:13 **56:6** [x]S Ex 12:43; S 1Ki 8:41 [y]S 1Ch 22:2; Isa 60:7,10; 61:5 [z]Mal 1:11 [a]ver 2,4 **56:7** [b]S Isa 2:2; Eze 20:40 [c]S Isa 19:21; Ro 12:1; Php 4:18; Heb 13:15 [d]Mt 21:13*; Lk 19:46* [e]Mk 11:17*

55:11 WORD . . . NOT RETURN TO ME EMPTY. The power and effect of God's word are never canceled or rendered void; his word will bring either spiritual life to those who receive it or just condemnation to those who reject it (see article on THE WORD OF GOD, p. 1062).

56:1–2 MAINTAIN JUSTICE . . . SALVATION IS CLOSE. Justice and righteousness are the fruit of salvation, directly linked to the influence of God's kingdom; they cannot be separated.

56:3–8 FOREIGNER . . . EUNUCH. In the Messiah's kingdom all foreigners and eunuchs who turn to the Lord are accepted with the same rights and privileges as the rest of the covenant community (see Ex 12:43; Dt 23:1, where they were once excluded from public worship). Regardless of one's nationality, societal status or personal disabilities, God loves and accepts each believer as one of his precious children.

56:7 A HOUSE OF PRAYER. The linking of prayer and God's house reveals that the central purpose of worship is to bring worshipers near to him in communion, praise, intercession and petition; to attend church without fervent and intense communion with God is to miss worship's essential nature and purpose. Jesus cited this verse when he drove the money changers out of God's temple (see Mk 11:17, note; Lk 19:45, note).

he who gathers the exiles of
Israel:
"I will gather[f] still others to them
besides those already gathered."

God's Accusation Against the Wicked

9Come, all you beasts of the field,[g]
come and devour, all you beasts
of the forest!
10Israel's watchmen[h] are blind,
they all lack knowledge;[i]
they are all mute dogs,
they cannot bark;
they lie around and dream,
they love to sleep.[j]
11They are dogs with mighty
appetites;
they never have enough.
They are shepherds[k] who lack
understanding;[l]
they all turn to their own way,[m]
each seeks his own gain.[n]
12"Come," each one cries, "let me
get wine![o]
Let us drink our fill of beer!
And tomorrow will be like today,
or even far better."[p]

57 The righteous perish,[q]
and no one ponders it in his
heart;[r]
devout men are taken away,
and no one understands
that the righteous are taken away
to be spared from evil.[s]
2Those who walk uprightly[t]
enter into peace;
they find rest[u] as they lie in
death.
3"But you—come here, you sons of
a sorceress,[v]
you offspring of adulterers[w] and
prostitutes![x]
4Whom are you mocking?
At whom do you sneer
and stick out your tongue?
Are you not a brood of rebels,[y]
the offspring of liars?
5You burn with lust among the
oaks[z]
and under every spreading
tree;[a]
you sacrifice your children[b] in the
ravines
and under the overhanging
crags.
6⌞The idols⌟[c] among the smooth
stones of the ravines are
your portion;
they, they are your lot.
Yes, to them you have poured out
drink offerings[d]
and offered grain offerings.
In the light of these things,
should I relent?[e]
7You have made your bed on a high
and lofty hill;[f]
there you went up to offer your
sacrifices.[g]
8Behind your doors and your
doorposts
you have put your pagan
symbols.
Forsaking me, you uncovered your
bed,
you climbed into it and opened it
wide;
you made a pact with those whose
beds you love,[h]
and you looked on their
nakedness.[i]
9You went to Molech[1][j] with olive
oil
and increased your perfumes.[k]
You sent your ambassadors[m][l] far
away;
you descended to the grave[n][m]
itself!
10You were wearied[n] by all your
ways,
but you would not say, 'It is
hopeless.'[o]
You found renewal of your
strength,[p]
and so you did not faint.

56:8 [f]S Dt 30:4; S Isa 1:9; S 11:12; 60:3-11; Eze 34:12; Jn 10:16 56:9 [g]Isa 18:6; Jer 12:9; Eze 34:5, 8; 39:17-20 56:10 [h]S Isa 52:8; 62:6; Jer 6:17; 31:6; Eze 3:17; 33:7 [i]Jer 2:8; 10:21; 14:13-14 [j]Na 3:18 56:11 [k]Jer 23:1; Eze 34:2 [l]Isa 1:3 [m]S Isa 53:6; Hos 4:7-8 [n]Isa 57:17; Jer 6:13; 8:10; 22:17; Eze 13:19; Mic 3:11 56:12 [o]S Lev 10:9; S Pr 23:20; S Isa 22:13 [p]Ps 10:6; Lk 12:18-19 57:1 [q]S Ps 12:1; Eze 21:3 [r]S Isa 42:25 [s]S 2Ki 22:20 57:2 [t]Isa 26:7 [u]Da 12:13 57:3 [v]S Ex 22:18; Mal 3:5 [w]ver 7-8; Mt 16:4; Jas 4:4 [x]Isa 1:21; Jer 2:20 57:4 [y]S Isa 1:2 57:5 [z]S Isa 1:29 [a]S Dt 12:2; 2Ki 16:4 [b]S Lev 18:21; S Dt 18:10; Ps 106:37-38; Eze 16:20 57:6 [c]S 2Ki 17:10; Jer 3:9; Hab 2:19 [d]Jer 7:18; 19:13; 44:18 [e]Jer 5:9,29; 9:9 57:7 [f]Jer 3:6; Eze 6:3; 16:16; 20:29 [g]Isa 65:7; Jer 13:27; Eze 6:13; 20:27-28 57:8 [h]Eze 16:26; 23:7 [i]Eze 16:15, 36; 23:18 57:9 [j]S Lev 18:21; S 1Ki 11:5 [k]S SS 4:10 [l]Eze 23:16,40 [m]S Isa 8:19 57:10 [n]S Isa 47:13 [o]Jer 2:25; 18:12; Mal 3:14 [p]S 1Sa 2:4

[1]9 Or *to the king* [m]9 Or *idols* [n]9 Hebrew *Sheol*

56:10–12 WATCHMEN ARE BLIND. God condemned Israel's corrupt leaders and priests, for they did not know his word, were greedy for selfish gain and could not stay away from alcoholic beverages.

57:1–2 THE RIGHTEOUS PERISH. Righteous believers were being mistreated at the hands of Judah's cruel and corrupt leaders and were perishing (cf. 2Ki 21:16). But by their death, these martyrs were spared the terrible horrors of God's judgment that would soon come upon his people.

57:3–14 YOU SONS OF A SORCERESS. The people of Judah forsook the Lord and chose instead to worship the gods of foreign nations. This worship involved immorality, prostitution, sorcery and human sacrifices. But God would let no one get away with sin; those who transgressed his law would reap what they had sown and lose much more than they had hoped to gain by their wickedness.

THE WORD OF GOD

Isa 55:10–11 "As the rain and the snow come down from heaven, and do not return to it without watering the earth and making it bud and flourish, so that it yields seed for the sower and bread for the eater, so is my word that goes out from my mouth: It will not return to me empty, but will accomplish what I desire and achieve the purpose for which I sent it."

THE NATURE OF THE WORD OF GOD. The phrase "the word of God" (also "the word of the LORD," or even simply "the Word") refers to a variety of situations in the Bible. (1) It obviously refers first of all to anything that God has spoken directly. When God spoke to Adam and Eve (e.g., Ge 2:16–17; Ge 3:9–19), what he said was the word of God. In a similar way, God spoke his word to Abraham (e.g., Ge 12:1–3), Isaac (e.g., Ge 26:1–5), Jacob (e.g., Ge 28:13–15) and Moses (e.g., Ex 3—4). God also spoke to the entire nation of Israel at Mount Sinai when he recited the Ten Commandments (see Ex 20:1–19); the words they heard were his words.

(2) In addition to direct speech, God also spoke through the prophets (see article on THE PROPHET IN THE OLD TESTAMENT, p. 986). When they addressed God's people, they usually prefaced their statements with "This is what the LORD says" or "The word of the LORD came to me." Thus, when the Israelites were listening to the words of a prophet, they were listening to the word of God.

(3) The same is true for what the apostles said in the NT. Even though they did not preface their comments with "This is what the Lord says," what they spoke and proclaimed was indeed the word of God. For example, Paul's sermon to the people of Pisidian Antioch (Ac 13:16–41) created such a stir that "on the next Sabbath day almost the whole city gathered to hear the word of the Lord" (Ac 13:44). Paul himself said to the Thessalonians that "when you received the word of God, which you heard from us, you accepted it not as the word of men, but as it actually is, the word of God" (1Th 2:13; cf. Ac 8:25).

(4) Furthermore, everything that Jesus spoke was the word of God, for he is, after all, God (Jn 1:1,18; 10:30; 1Jn 5:20). Luke, the writer of the third Gospel, states explicitly that when people heard Jesus, they heard the word of God (Lk 5:1). Note how in contrast to the OT prophets, who usually began with some form of "This is what the LORD says," Jesus introduced his sayings with "I tell you . . ." (e.g., Mt 5:18,20,22,32,39; 11:22,24; Mk 9:1; 10:15; Lk 10:12; 12:4; Jn 5:19; 6:26; 8:34); in other words, he had divine authority within himself to speak the word of God. So important is it to listen to Jesus' words that "whoever hears my word and believes him who sent me has eternal life and will not be condemned" (Jn 5:24). Indeed, Jesus is so closely identified with the word of God that he is actually called "the Word" (Jn 1:1,14; 1Jn 1:1; Rev 19:13–16; see Jn 1:1, note).

(5) The word of God is the written record of what the prophets, apostles and Jesus have spoken—i.e., the Scriptures. In the NT, whether a writer used the phrase "Moses said," "David said," "the Holy Spirit says," or "God says" made no difference (see Ac 3:22; Ro 10:5,19; Heb 3:7; 4:7); what was written in the Bible was the word of God (see article on THE INSPIRATION AND AUTHORITY OF SCRIPTURE, p. 1898).

(6) Though not on the same level of authority as Scripture itself, the spoken proclamation by preachers or prophets in the church today may be called the word of God. (a) Peter indicated that what his readers received through the preaching of the word was the word of God (1Pe 1:25), and Paul instructed Timothy to "preach the Word" (2Ti 4:2). Such preaching must never stand independent of the written Word of God, however. In fact, the test to determine whether God's word is being proclaimed in a sermon or message is whether it corresponds to God's written Word (see article on FALSE TEACH-

ERS, p. 1506). (b) What about a person who receives a prophecy or revelation in a worship setting (1Co 14:26–32); is he or she receiving the word of God? The answer to this question is a qualified "Yes." Paul asserts that such messages are subject to evaluation by other prophets; thus it is possible that such prophecies may not be the word of God (see 1Co 14:29, note). Only in a secondary sense can we speak of prophets today speaking under the inspiration of the Holy Spirit; the revelation of a prophet today must never be elevated to the point of inerrancy (see 1Co 14:31, note; see articles on SPIRITUAL GIFTS FOR BELIEVERS, p. 1770, and THE MINISTRY GIFTS OF THE CHURCH, p. 1830).

THE POWER OF THE WORD OF GOD. The word of God stands firm in the heavens (Ps 119:89; Isa 40:8; 1Pe 1:24–25). Yet it is not a static word; it is dynamic and powerful (cf. Heb 4:12), and it accomplishes great things (Isa 55:11). (1) The word of God is the creative word. According to the creation account, things came into being when God spoke his word (e.g., Ge 1:3–4,6–7,9). This process is summarized by the psalmist, who wrote, "By the word of the LORD were the heavens made" (Ps 33:6; cf. v. 9), and by the writer to Hebrews, "By faith we understand that the universe was formed at God's command" (Heb 11:3; cf. 2Pe 3:5). Note that according to John, the Word that God used to create all things was Jesus Christ (Jn 1:1–3; see article on CREATION, p. 6).

(2) The word of God also has the power to sustain creation. In the words of the writer to the Hebrews, God sustains "all things by his powerful word" (Heb 1:3; see also Ps 147:15–18). Like the creative word, this word is related to Jesus Christ, for Paul insists that "in him [Jesus] all things hold together" (Col 1:17).

(3) The word of God has the power to impart new life. Peter testifies that we are born again "through the living and enduring word of God" (1Pe 1:23; cf. 2Ti 3:15; Jas 1:18). It is for this reason that Jesus himself is called "the Word of life" (1Jn 1:1).

(4) The word of God also releases grace, power and revelation by which believers grow in their faith and in their commitment to Jesus Christ. Isaiah uses a powerful picture: just as water from the sky causes things to grow physically, so also the word that goes out from God's mouth causes us to grow spiritually (Isa 55:10–11). Peter echoes the same thought when he writes that by drinking the pure milk of the word of God, we grow up in our salvation (1Pe 2:2).

(5) The word of God is the sword God has given us by which we may fight Satan (Eph 6:17; cf. Rev 19:13–15). Note how in the story of Jesus' victory over Satan's temptations, each time he defeated Satan by declaring, "It is written" (i.e., "it stands as God's infallible Word"; cf. Lk 4:1–11; see Mt 4:1–11, note).

(6) Finally, the word of God has the power to judge us. The OT prophets and the NT apostles frequently spoke words of judgment received from the Lord. Jesus himself said his word will condemn those who reject him (Jn 12:48), and the author of Hebrews writes that the powerful word of God judges "the thoughts and attitudes of the heart" (see Heb 4:12, note); in other words, those who choose to ignore God's word will one day experience it as a word of condemnation.

OUR REACTION TO THE WORD OF GOD. The Bible describes in clear and unmistakable language how we should react to the word of God in all its different forms. We must eagerly hear God's word (Isa 1:10; Jer 7:1–2; Ac 17:11) and seek to understand it (Mt 13:23). We must praise God's word (Ps 56:4,10), love it (Ps 119:47,113), and let it be our joy and delight (Ps 119:16,47). We must accept what the word of God says (Mk 4:20; Ac 2:41; 1Th 2:13), hide it deep within our hearts (Ps 119:11), trust in it (Ps 119:42), and put our hope in its promises (Ps 119:74,81,114; 130:5). Above all, we must obey what it commands (Ps 119:17,67; Jas 1:22–24) and live according to it (Ps 119:9). God calls those who minister the word (cf. 1Ti 5:17) to handle it correctly (2Ti 2:15) and to preach it faithfully (2Ti 4:2). All believers are called to proclaim God's word wherever they go (Ac 8:4).

11“Whom have you so dreaded and
feared[q]
that you have been false to me,
and have neither remembered[r] me
nor pondered[s] this in your
hearts?
Is it not because I have long been
silent[t]
that you do not fear me?
12I will expose your righteousness
and your works,[u]
and they will not benefit you.
13When you cry out[v] for help,
let your collection ⌊of idols⌋
save[w] you!
The wind will carry all of them off,
a mere breath will blow[x] them
away.
But the man who makes me his
refuge[y]
will inherit the land[z]
and possess my holy
mountain.”[a]

Comfort for the Contrite

14And it will be said:

“Build up, build up, prepare the
road![b]
Remove the obstacles out of the
way of my people.”[c]
15For this is what the high and
lofty[d] One says—
he who lives forever,[e] whose
name is holy:
“I live in a high[f] and holy place,
but also with him who is
contrite[g] and lowly in
spirit,[h]
to revive the spirit of the lowly
and to revive the heart of the
contrite.[i]
16I will not accuse[j] forever,
nor will I always be angry,[k]
for then the spirit of man would
grow faint before me—
the breath[l] of man that I have
created.
17I was enraged by his sinful
greed;[m]
I punished him, and hid[n] my
face in anger,
yet he kept on in his willful
ways.[o]
18I have seen his ways, but I will
heal[p] him;
I will guide[q] him and restore
comfort[r] to him,
19 creating praise on the lips[s] of
the mourners in Israel.
Peace, peace,[t] to those far and
near,”[u]
says the LORD. “And I will heal
them.”
20But the wicked[v] are like the
tossing sea,[w]
which cannot rest,
whose waves cast up mire[x] and
mud.
21“There is no peace,”[y] says my
God, “for the wicked.”[z]

True Fasting

58 “Shout it aloud,[a] do not hold
back.
Raise your voice like a
trumpet.[b]
Declare to my people their
rebellion[c]
and to the house of Jacob their
sins.[d]
2For day after day they seek[e] me
out;

57:11 [q]S 2Ki 1:15; Pr 29:25; Isa 7:2 [r]S Isa 17:10; Jer 2:32; 3:21; 13:25; 18:15; Eze 22:12 [s]S Isa 42:23 [t]S Est 4:14; S Ps 50:21; S 83:1 **57:12** [u]Isa 29:15; 58:1; 59:6,12; 65:7; 66:18; Eze 16:2; Mic 3:2-4,8 **57:13** [v]Jer 22:20; 30:15 [w]S Jdg 10:14 [x]Isa 40:7,24 [y]S Ps 118:8 [z]S Ps 37:9 [a]Isa 2:2-3; 56:7; 65:9-11 **57:14** [b]S Isa 11:16 [c]Isa 62:10; Jer 18:15 **57:15** [d]S Isa 52:13 [e]S Dt 33:27; S Ps 90:2 [f]S Job 16:19 [g]Ps 147:3 [h]Ps 34:18; 51:17; Isa 66:2; Mic 6:8; Mt 5:3 [i]S 2Ki 22:19; S Job 5:18; S Mt 23:12 **57:16** [j]S Ps 50:21; Isa 3:13-14 [k]S Ps 103:9; S Isa 54:9 [l]S Ge 2:7; Zec 12:1 **57:17** [m]S Isa 56:11; Jer 8:10 [n]S Isa 1:15 [o]Isa 1:4; S 30:15; S 53:6; 66:3 **57:18** [p]S Dt 32:39; S 2Ch 7:14; S Isa 30:26 [q]S Ps 48:14; S Isa 42:16; S 48:17 [r]Isa 49:13; 61:1-3 **57:19** [s]Isa 6:7; 51:16; 59:21; Heb 13:15 [t]S Isa 2:4; 26:3, 12; 32:17; S Lk 2:14 [u]Ac 2:39 **57:20** [v]Job 18:5-21 [w]S Ge 49:4; Eph 4:14; Jude 1:13 [x]Ps 69:14 **57:21** [y]S Isa 26:3; 59:8; Eze 13:16 [z]S Isa 48:22 **58:1** [a]Isa 40:6 [b]S Ex 20:18 [c]S Isa 24:20; S 48:8 [d]S Isa 57:12; Eze 3:17 **58:2** [e]S Isa 48:1; Tit 1:16; Jas 4:8

57:15 CONTRITE AND LOWLY IN SPIRIT. To those who were humble and repentant, the Lord God came with a gracious promise: he who lives in “a high and holy place” would personally live with those who were “contrite and lowly in spirit.” “Contrite” refers to any who are oppressed by the burden of sin and want to find freedom from its enslavement; “lowly in spirit” refers to those who are brokenhearted because of life’s calamities and afflictions (cf. Ps 34:18–19). God comes to live with such people in order to revive their spirits, give new life and provide the comfort of his presence.

57:21 NO PEACE . . . FOR THE WICKED. God has so structured the human conscience that there will never be real peace for those who live wickedly—neither inward peace nor outward peace. As long as they sin, their lives will be like the troubled sea, full of mire and mud (v. 20). God is opposed to them, while desiring that they repent and be saved (cf. 2Pe 3:9).

58:1 SHOUT IT ALOUD. The prophet cries out against the people’s sins like a mighty trumpet blast; the transgressions and hypocrisy of God’s people must be revealed. If God’s messengers fail to point out the sins of his people, they are not faithful to God’s call.

58:2 DAY AFTER DAY THEY SEEK ME. Judah was seeking God every day as though they desired to know his ways; yet, at the same time, they were living in sin and in indifference to his righteous commands. Today congregations may worship the Lord outwardly, appear to delight in praising him and seem eager to know his ways; at

they seem eager to know my
ways,
as if they were a nation that does
what is right
and has not forsaken[f] the
commands of its God.
They ask me for just decisions
and seem eager for God to come
near[g] them.
3 'Why have we fasted,'[h] they say,
'and you have not seen it?
Why have we humbled[i] ourselves,
and you have not noticed?'[j]

"Yet on the day of your fasting,
you do as you please[k]
and exploit all your workers.
4 Your fasting ends in quarreling and
strife,[l]
and in striking each other with
wicked fists.
You cannot fast as you do today
and expect your voice to be
heard[m] on high.
5 Is this the kind of fast[n] I have
chosen,
only a day for a man to
humble[o] himself?
Is it only for bowing one's head
like a reed[p]
and for lying on sackcloth and
ashes?[q]
Is that what you call a fast,
a day acceptable to the LORD?

6 "Is not this the kind of fasting[r] I
have chosen:
to loose the chains of injustice[s]
and untie the cords of the yoke,
to set the oppressed[t] free
and break every yoke?[u]
7 Is it not to share your food with
the hungry[v]
and to provide the poor
wanderer with shelter[w]—
when you see the naked, to
clothe[x] him,
and not to turn away from your
own flesh and blood?[y]
8 Then your light will break forth
like the dawn,[z]
and your healing[a] will quickly
appear;
then your righteousness[o][b] will go
before you,
and the glory of the LORD will be
your rear guard.[c]
9 Then you will call,[d] and the LORD
will answer;[e]
you will cry for help, and he will
say: Here am I.

"If you do away with the yoke of
oppression,
with the pointing finger[f] and
malicious talk,[g]
10 and if you spend yourselves in
behalf of the hungry
and satisfy the needs of the
oppressed,[h]
then your light[i] will rise in the
darkness,
and your night will become like
the noonday.[j]
11 The LORD will guide[k] you always;
he will satisfy your needs[l] in a
sun-scorched land[m]
and will strengthen[n] your
frame.

Jer 11:1-5

58:2 [f] S Dt 32:15; S Ps 119:87 [g] Isa 29:13 **58:3** [h] S Lev 16:29 [i] S Ex 10:3; S 2Ch 6:37; Jer 44:10 [j] Mal 3:14 [k] Isa 22:13; Zec 7:5-6 **58:4** [l] 1Ki 21:9-13; Isa 59:6; Jer 6:7; Eze 7:11; Mal 2:16 [m] S 1Sa 8:18; Isa 59:2; La 3:44; Eze 8:18; Mic 3:4 **58:5** [n] Zec 7:5 [o] 1Ki 21:27; Mt 6:16 [p] S Isa 36:6 [q] S Job 2:8 **58:6** [r] Joel 2:12-14 [s] Ne 5:10-11 [t] S Dt 14:29; Isa 61:1; Jer 34:9; Am 4:1; S Lk 4:19 [u] S Isa 9:4 **58:7** [v] S Job 22:7; Eze 18:16; Lk 3:11 [w] Isa 16:4; Heb 13:2 [x] Job 31:19-20; S Mt 25:36 [y] S Ge 29:14; Lk 10:31-32 **58:8** [z] S Job 11:17; S Isa 9:2 [a] S Isa 1:5; S 30:26 [b] S Isa 26:2 [c] S Ex 14:19 **58:9** [d] S Ps 50:15 [e] S Job 8:6; S Isa 30:19; Da 9:20; S Zec 10:6 [f] S Pr 6:13 [g] Ps 12:2; Isa 59:13 **58:10** [h] Dt 15:7-8 [i] S Isa 42:16 [j] S Job 11:17 **58:11** [k] S Ps 48:14; S Isa 42:16; S 48:17 [l] S Ps 104:28; S 107:9 [m] S Ps 68:6 [n] S Ps 72:16

[o] 8 Or *your righteous One*

the same time, they may be conforming to the ways of the world and neglecting the diligent study of his written Word. Such "worship" is an insult and an abomination to God.

58:3 DAY OF YOUR FASTING. God's people were complaining that he would not help them. But God knew that their worship and fasting were hypocritical; he tells them that no religious act has any value to him if it does not come from those who humbly strive to obey his commands and who compassionately reach out to those in need.

58:6 FASTING I HAVE CHOSEN. The fast that God approves is one accompanied by love for him and genuine concern for those who are oppressed. Believers must understand that the giving of tithes and offerings to the church does not free them from their responsibility to give to the poor. We should share our food with the hungry and provide clothing for those who have none. We must make a sincere effort to determine the needs of others, especially within our local congregations, and to commit ourselves to helping in whatever way we can (cf. Gal 6:10; see article on THE CARE OF THE POOR AND NEEDY, p. 1316). The blessings of v. 8 (see next note) are given to those who have the heart of v. 6 and are committed to the course of action in v. 7.

58:8–12 YOUR LIGHT WILL BREAK FORTH. When there is true love for God and sincere concern for the welfare of others, a channel is opened for God's full blessing to come into our lives. The rewards for such love are stated here: (1) the light of God and the full joy of salvation and healing, (2) God's protection and presence manifested in our lives, (3) God's help in trouble through answered prayer, (4) the lifting of darkness and oppression, (5) God's guidance, strength and fruitfulness, and (6) true restoration, with the revival of God's standards and ideals.

You will be like a well-watered
garden,[o]
like a spring[p] whose waters
never fail.
12Your people will rebuild the
ancient ruins[q]
and will raise up the age-old
foundations;[r]
you will be called Repairer of
Broken Walls,[s]
Restorer of Streets with
Dwellings.

13"If you keep your feet from
breaking the Sabbath[t]
and from doing as you please on
my holy day,
if you call the Sabbath a delight[u]
and the LORD's holy day
honorable,
and if you honor it by not going
your own way
and not doing as you please or
speaking idle words,[v]
14then you will find your joy[w] in the
LORD,
and I will cause you to ride on
the heights[x] of the land
and to feast on the inheritance[y]
of your father Jacob."
The mouth of the LORD
has spoken.[z]

Sin, Confession and Redemption

59 Surely the arm[a] of the LORD
is not too short[b] to save,
nor his ear too dull to hear.[c]
2But your iniquities have
separated[d]
you from your God;
your sins have hidden his face
from you,
so that he will not hear.[e]
3For your hands are stained with
blood,[f]
your fingers with guilt.[g]
Your lips have spoken lies,[h]
and your tongue mutters wicked
things.
4No one calls for justice;[i]
no one pleads his case with
integrity.
They rely[j] on empty arguments
and speak lies;[k]
they conceive trouble and give
birth to evil.[l]
5They hatch the eggs of vipers[m]
and spin a spider's web.[n]
Whoever eats their eggs will die,
and when one is broken, an
adder is hatched.
6Their cobwebs are useless for
clothing;
they cannot cover themselves
with what they make.[o]
Their deeds are evil deeds,
and acts of violence[p] are in
their hands.
7Their feet rush into sin;
they are swift to shed innocent
blood.[q]
Their thoughts are evil thoughts;[r]
ruin and destruction mark their
ways.[s]
8The way of peace they do not
know;[t]
there is no justice in their paths.
They have turned them into
crooked roads;[u]
no one who walks in them will
know peace.[v]

9So justice is far from us,
and righteousness does not
reach us.
We look for light, but all is
darkness;[w]
for brightness, but we walk in
deep shadows.
10Like the blind[x] we grope along
the wall,
feeling our way like men without
eyes.
At midday we stumble[y] as if it
were twilight;

58:11 [o] S SS 4:15 [p] S Isa 35:7; Jn 4:14 **58:12** [q] S Isa 49:8 [r] S Isa 44:28 [s] Ne 2:17 **58:13** [t] S Ex 20:8 [u] Ps 37:4; 42:4; 84:2,10 [v] Isa 59:3 **58:14** [w] S Job 22:26 [x] S Dt 32:13 [y] Ps 105:10-11 [z] S Isa 1:20 **59:1** [a] S Isa 41:20 [b] S Isa 50:2 [c] Isa 30:19; 58:9; 65:24 **59:2** [d] Jer 5:25; Eze 39:23 [e] S Ps 18:41; S Isa 58:4; S Jer 11:11; S Jn 9:31 **59:3** [f] S 2Ki 21:16; S Isa 1:15; S Eze 22:9 [g] Ps 7:3 [h] S Isa 3:8 **59:4** [i] S Isa 5:23 [j] S Job 15:31 [k] S Isa 44:20 [l] S Job 4:8; S Isa 29:20; Jas 1:15 **59:5** [m] S Isa 11:8; Mt 3:7 [n] S Job 8:14 **59:6** [o] Isa 28:20 [p] S Ps 55:9; S Pr 4:17; S Isa 58:4 **59:7** [q] S 2Ki 21:16; S Pr 6:17; S Mic 3:10 [r] S Pr 24:2; S Isa 26:10; Mk 7:21-22 [s] Ro 3:15-17* **59:8** [t] Ro 3:15-17* [u] S Jdg 5:6 [v] S Isa 57:21; Lk 1:79 **59:9** [w] S Job 19:8; S Ps 107:14; S Isa 5:30; S 8:20; S Lk 1:79 **59:10** [x] Dt 28:29; S Isa 6:9-10; 56:10; La 4:14; Zep 1:17 [y] S Job 3:23; S Isa 8:15; Jn 11:9-10

58:13 THE SABBATH. God has ordained from creation that one day in seven should be set aside as "holy," a day for God's people to cease their usual activities and devote themselves to physical rest and spiritual renewal (see Ex 20:8, note; Mt 12:1, note); doing so will increase our joy in the Lord and enable us to attain new spiritual heights (v. 14).

59:1–8 ARM OF THE LORD IS NOT TOO SHORT. This passage describes additional sins that have prevented the people from receiving God's promised blessings (see previous two notes).

59:2 INIQUITIES HAVE SEPARATED YOU. Sin and wickedness in our lives put a wall between us and God. Because of this barrier, we can no longer experience God's favor, protection, help or salvation; thus our prayers will not be answered (Ps 66:18).

59:9–14 JUSTICE IS FAR FROM US. Isaiah describes true intercessors as those who know that they are sinners, who confess their sins, and who are deeply grieved over their seemingly hopeless condition.

among the strong, we are like
the dead.[z]
11We all growl like bears;
we moan mournfully like
doves.[a]
We look for justice, but find none;
for deliverance, but it is far
away.

12For our offenses[b] are many in
your sight,
and our sins testify[c] against us.
Our offenses are ever with us,
and we acknowledge our
iniquities:[d]
13rebellion[e] and treachery against
the LORD,
turning our backs[f] on our God,
fomenting oppression[g] and revolt,
uttering lies[h] our hearts have
conceived.
14So justice[i] is driven back,
and righteousness[j] stands at a
distance;
truth[k] has stumbled in the
streets,
honesty cannot enter.
15Truth[l] is nowhere to be found,
and whoever shuns evil becomes
a prey.

The LORD looked and was
displeased
that there was no justice.[m]
16He saw that there was no one,[n]
he was appalled that there was
no one to intervene;[o]
so his own arm worked salvation[p]
for him,
and his own righteousness[q]
sustained him.
17He put on righteousness as his
breastplate,[r]
and the helmet[s] of salvation on
his head;
he put on the garments[t] of
vengeance[u]
and wrapped himself in zeal[v] as
in a cloak.
18According to what they have done,
so will he repay[w]
wrath to his enemies
and retribution to his foes;
he will repay the islands[x] their
due.
19From the west,[y] men will fear the
name of the LORD,
and from the rising of the sun,[z]
they will revere his glory.[a]
For he will come like a pent-up
flood
that the breath[b] of the LORD
drives along.[p]

20"The Redeemer[c] will come to
Zion,[d]
to those in Jacob who repent of
their sins,"[e]
declares the LORD.

21"As for me, this is my covenant[f]
with them," says the LORD. "My Spirit,[g] who is on you, and my words that
I have put in your mouth[h] will not depart from your mouth,[i] or from the
mouths of your children, or from the
mouths of their descendants from this
time on and forever," says the LORD.

Isa 61:10

Eze 2:1-2

59:10 [z]La 3:6 **59:11** [a]S Ge 8:8; Ps 74:19; Isa 38:14; Jer 48:28; Eze 7:16; Na 2:7 **59:12** [b]S Ezr 9:6; S Isa 57:12 [c]S Ge 4:7; S Isa 3:9; S Jer 2:19 [d]Ps 51:3 **59:13** [e]Isa 46:8; 48:8 [f]S Nu 11:20; S Pr 30:9; Mt 10:33; Tit 1:16 [g]S Ps 12:5; S Isa 5:7 [h]S Isa 3:8; S 44:20; Mk 7:21-22 **59:14** [i]S Isa 29:21 [j]S Isa 1:21 [k]S Isa 48:1; S Jer 33:16 **59:15** [l]Jer 7:28; 9:5; Da 8:12 [m]S Isa 5:7 **59:16** [n]S Isa 41:28 [o]S Isa 53:12 [p]S Isa 51:5 [q]Isa 45:8,13; 46:13 **59:17** [r]Eph 6:14; 1Th 5:8 [s]Eph 6:17; 1Th 5:8 [t]S Job 27:6; Isa 63:3 [u]S Isa 1:24 [v]S Isa 9:7; Eze 5:13 **59:18** [w]S Lev 26:28; S Nu 10:35; S Isa 34:8; S Mt 16:27 [x]Isa 11:11; 41:5 **59:19** [y]S Isa 49:12; S Mt 8:11 [z]S Ps 113:3 [a]Ps 97:6; S Isa 24:15; 35:2; 40:5; 52:10; 66:18 [b]S Isa 11:4 **59:20** [c]S Job 19:25; Isa 60:16; 63:16 [d]S Isa 52:8; S Joel 3:21 [e]S Job 22:23; S Isa 1:27; S Jer 35:15; Ac 2:38-39; Ro 11:26-27* **59:21** [f]S Ge 9:16; S Dt 29:14; S Isa 42:6 [g]S Isa 11:2; S 44:3 [h]S Ex 4:15 [i]S Jos 1:8

[p] 19 Or *When the enemy comes in like a flood, / the Spirit of the LORD will put him to flight*

59:16 HE SAW THAT THERE WAS NO ONE. The Lord saw the magnitude of Israel's sins and recognized that there was no intercessor to turn the tide. Then he decided to stretch out "his own arm" to save his people, which ultimately happened in the coming of Jesus Christ. Even now it is Jesus himself who personally intercedes for us in heaven (Heb 7:25); he looks for intercessors on earth to join him in standing "in the gap" (Eze 22:30) on behalf of his church, which needs revival, and of the lost, who need salvation.

59:17–18 RIGHTEOUSNESS AS HIS BREASTPLATE. Paul cited two phrases from this verse in his description of the believer's armor: "the breastplate of righteousness" and "the helmet of salvation" (Eph 6:14–17). Isaiah's mention of "garments of vengeance" and "wrath to his enemies" (v. 18) envisions God's great day of wrath at the end of the age (see Rev 19, notes).

59:20 REDEEMER WILL COME TO ZION. This Redeemer is Jesus Christ (cf. 35:4; 40:9; 52:7); he will come to those who genuinely turn from their sins and serve the Lord, i.e., to the true Israel.

59:21 MY SPIRIT . . . MY WORDS. God promises those who turn from their sins and accept the Messiah that his Spirit will come upon them (cf. Jn 16:13; Ac 2:4) and his words will not depart from their mouths. The Spirit and the word of the Lord will endorse the witness of the true church and her descendants forever. God's people must declare the gospel in the power and righteousness of the Holy Spirit (see Ac 1:8, notes; see article on BAPTISM IN THE HOLY SPIRIT, p. 1642).

The Glory of Zion

60 "Arise,[j] shine, for your
light[k] has come,
and the glory[l] of the LORD rises
upon you.
2See, darkness[m] covers the earth
and thick darkness[n] is over the
peoples,
but the LORD rises upon you
and his glory appears over you.
3Nations[o] will come to your
light,[p]
and kings[q] to the brightness of
your dawn.

4"Lift up your eyes and look about
you:
All assemble[r] and come to you;
your sons come from afar,[s]
and your daughters[t] are carried
on the arm.[u]
5Then you will look and be
radiant,[v]
your heart will throb and swell
with joy;[w]
the wealth[x] on the seas will be
brought to you,
to you the riches of the nations
will come.
6Herds of camels[y] will cover your
land,
young camels of Midian[z] and
Ephah.[a]
And all from Sheba[b] will come,
bearing gold and incense[c]
and proclaiming the praise[d] of
the LORD.
7All Kedar's[e] flocks will be
gathered to you,
the rams of Nebaioth will serve
you;
they will be accepted as
offerings[f] on my altar,[g]
and I will adorn my glorious
temple.[h]

8"Who are these[i] that fly along
like clouds,[j]
like doves to their nests?
9Surely the islands[k] look to me;
in the lead are the ships of
Tarshish,[q][l]
bringing[m] your sons from afar,
with their silver and gold,[n]
to the honor[o] of the LORD your
God,
the Holy One[p] of Israel,
for he has endowed you with
splendor.[q]

10"Foreigners[r] will rebuild your
walls,
and their kings[s] will serve you.
Though in anger I struck you,
in favor[t] I will show you
compassion.[u]
11Your gates[v] will always stand
open,
they will never be shut, day or
night,
so that men may bring you the
wealth of the nations[w]—
their kings[x] led in triumphal
procession.
12For the nation or kingdom that
will not serve[y] you will
perish;
it will be utterly ruined.[z]

13"The glory of Lebanon[a] will come
to you,
the pine, the fir and the cypress
together,[b]
to adorn the place of my
sanctuary;[c]
and I will glorify the place of my
feet.[d]
14The sons of your oppressors[e] will
come bowing before you;
all who despise you will bow
down[f] at your feet
and will call you the City[g] of the
LORD,
Zion[h] of the Holy One[i] of
Israel.

60:1 [j]Isa 52:2 [k]S Ps 36:9; S 118:27; S Isa 9:2; Jn 8:12; Eph 5:14 [l]S Ex 16:7; S Isa 4:5; Rev 21:11 **60:2** [m]S 1Sa 2:9; S Ps 82:5; S 107:14; S Isa 8:20 [n]Jer 13:16; Col 1:13 **60:3** [o]S Isa 44:5; S 45:14; Mt 2:1-11; Rev 21:24 [p]S Isa 9:2; 42:6 [q]S Isa 49:23 **60:4** [r]S Isa 11:12 [s]S Isa 2:3; Jer 30:10 [t]S Isa 43:6 [u]Isa 49:20-22 **60:5** [v]S Ex 34:29 [w]Isa 35:2; 65:13; 66:14; Zec 10:7 [x]S Dt 33:19; S Jdg 3:15; Rev 21:26 **60:6** [y]S Jdg 6:5 [z]S Ge 25:2 [a]Ge 25:4 [b]S Ge 10:7,28 [c]Isa 43:23; Jer 6:20; Mt 2:11 [d]S 1Ki 5:7; S Isa 42:10 **60:7** [e]S Ge 25:13 [f]Isa 18:7; Eze 20:40; 43:27; Zep 3:10 [g]S Isa 19:21 [h]ver 13; Hag 2:3, 7,9 **60:8** [i]Isa 49:21 [j]Isa 19:1 **60:9** [k]S Isa 11:11 [l]S Ge 10:4; Isa 2:16*fn* [m]S Isa 14:2; S 43:6 [n]S 1Ki 10:22 [o]S Ps 22:23 [p]ver 14; Isa 1:4; S 54:5 [q]S Isa 44:23; 55:5; Jer 30:19 **60:10** [r]S Ex 1:11; S Isa 14:1-2; S 56:6 [s]S Ezr 1:2; Rev 21:24 [t]S Isa 49:8 [u]S Ps 102:13 **60:11** [v]ver 18; S Ps 24:7; Isa 62:10; Mic 2:13; Rev 21:25 [w]S ver 5; Isa 61:6; Rev 21:26 [x]Ps 149:8; S Isa 2:12 **60:12** [y]S Isa 11:14; S 14:2 [z]S Ge 27:29; S Ps 110:5; Da 2:34 **60:13** [a]S Ezr 3:7 [b]Isa 41:19 [c]S ver 7 [d]S 1Ch 28:2 **60:14** [e]S Isa 14:2 [f]S Ge 27:29; S Isa 2:3; Rev 3:9 [g]S Ge 32:28; S Isa 1:26 [h]Heb 12:22 [i]S ver 9

[q] 9 Or *the trading ships*

60:1–3 YOUR LIGHT HAS COME. This chapter prophesies that with the advent of the Messiah, the glory of the Lord would come among his people and many nations would come to the light. The NT applies these verses to Jesus' anointed ministry in Galilee (see Mt 4:16–17). Ever since the great missionary thrust of the gospel began in NT times, this prophecy is being fulfilled.

60:4–9 COME TO YOU. These verses describe the coming Messianic kingdom of our Lord. Isaiah sees God's glory coming to Israel and other nations coming to them to receive that light and salvation (cf. 49:23); these nations will bring offerings from their wealth to the Lord (cf. 61:6; 66:12).

60:10 REBUILD YOUR WALLS. The nations will contribute financially to the establishment of God's rule in Jerusalem. Those who oppose the Messianic kingdom will be destroyed (v. 12).

15"Although you have been
forsaken[j] and hated,
with no one traveling[k] through,
I will make you the everlasting
pride[l]
and the joy[m] of all generations.
16You will drink the milk of nations
and be nursed[n] at royal
breasts.
Then you will know[o] that I, the
LORD, am your Savior,[p]
your Redeemer,[q] the Mighty
One of Jacob.[r]
17Instead of bronze I will bring you
gold,[s]
and silver in place of iron.
Instead of wood I will bring you
bronze,
and iron in place of stones.
I will make peace[t] your governor
and righteousness your ruler.[u]
18No longer will violence[v] be heard
in your land,
nor ruin or destruction[w] within
your borders,
but you will call your walls
Salvation[x]
and your gates Praise.[y]
19The sun will no more be your light
by day,
nor will the brightness of the
moon shine on you,
for the LORD will be your
everlasting light,[z]
and your God will be your
glory.[a]
20Your sun[b] will never set again,
and your moon will wane no
more;
the LORD will be your everlasting
light,
and your days of sorrow[c] will
end.
21Then will all your people be
righteous[d]
and they will possess[e] the land
forever.
They are the shoot I have
planted,[f]
the work of my hands,[g]
for the display of my splendor.[h]
22The least of you will become a
thousand,
the smallest a mighty nation.[i]
I am the LORD;
in its time I will do this
swiftly."[j]

60:15 [j] Isa 1:7-9; S 6:12; S 54:6 [k] S Isa 33:8 [l] S Isa 4:2 [m] S Ps 126:5; Isa 65:18 **60:16** [n] S Ex 6:2; Isa 49:23; 66:11, 12 [o] S Ex 6:7 [p] S Ex 14:30; S Isa 25:9 [q] S Job 19:25; S Isa 59:20 [r] S Ge 49:24; S Ps 132:2 **60:17** [s] 1Ki 10:21 [t] S Ps 85:8; Isa 66:12; Hag 2:9 [u] S Isa 9:7 **60:18** [v] S Lev 26:6; S 2Sa 7:10; S Isa 9:4 [w] S Isa 49:19; S 51:19 [x] S Isa 33:6 [y] Isa 61:11; 62:7; Jer 33:9; Zep 3:20 **60:19** [z] S Ps 36:9; S 118:27; Rev 22:5 [a] S Ps 85:9; S Isa 24:16,23; Rev 21:23 **60:20** [b] Isa 30:26 [c] S Isa 30:19; S 35:10; S Rev 7:17 **60:21** [d] S Isa 4:3; S 26:2; Rev 21:27 [e] Ps 37:11,22; Isa 49:8; 57:13; 61:7; 65:9; Zec 8:12 [f] S Ex 15:17; Ps 44:2; 80:8-11; Jer 32:41; Am 9:15; Mt 15:13 [g] S Job 10:3; S Ps 8:6; S Isa 19:25; Eph 2:10 [h] S Lev 10:3; S Isa 44:23 **60:22** [i] S Ge 12:2; S Dt 1:10 [j] Isa 5:19 **61:1** [k] S Isa 11:2; 2Co 3:17 [l] S Isa 50:4

The Year of the LORD's Favor

61 The Spirit[k] of the Sovereign
LORD[l] is on me,
because the LORD has anointed[m]
me
to preach good news[n] to the
poor.[o]
He has sent me to bind up[p] the
brokenhearted,
to proclaim freedom[q] for the
captives[r]
and release from darkness for
the prisoners,[r]
2to proclaim the year of the LORD's
favor[s]
and the day of vengeance[t] of
our God,
to comfort[u] all who mourn,[v]

[m] S Ps 45:7; S Da 9:24-26; S Ac 4:26 [n] S 2Sa 18:26; S Isa 40:9 [o] S Job 5:16; S Mt 11:5; Lk 7:22 [p] S 2Ki 22:19; S Job 5:18 [q] S Lev 25:10 [r] S Ps 68:6; S Isa 49:9 **61:2** [s] S Isa 49:8; S Lk 4:18-19* [t] S Isa 1:24 [u] S Isa 40:1; Mt 5:4 [v] S Job 5:11; Lk 6:21

[r] *1* Hebrew; Septuagint *the blind*

60:19 SUN WILL NO MORE BE YOUR LIGHT. This verse looks forward to the Jerusalem of the new heaven and new earth, in which God and the Lamb will be the everlasting light of his people (see Rev 21:23; 22:3–5; cf. Zec 2:5).

60:21 ALL YOUR PEOPLE BE RIGHTEOUS. During the Messianic kingdom, Israel will be characterized by faithfulness and righteousness rather than by the unfaithfulness and apostasy of her past history.

61:1–3 THE SPIRIT . . . IS ON ME. This description of the Messiah and his anointing relate to the Messiah's mission or ministry (see 11:2–3, note, where Isaiah describes more directly his spiritual character and stature). When Jesus began his ministry, he quoted these verses and applied them to himself (Lk 4:18–19). In order to fulfill his ministry, Jesus was anointed with the Holy Spirit (cf. 11:2; 42:1). His anointed ministry involved (1) preaching the gospel to the poor, the meek and the afflicted; (2) healing and binding up the spiritually and physically sick and brokenhearted; (3) breaking the bonds of evil and proclaiming freedom from sin and satanic dominion; and (4) opening the spiritual eyes of the lost that they might see the light of the gospel and be saved. This fourfold purpose characterized Jesus Christ's entire ministry, and it will continue to be fulfilled by the church as long as it is on the earth.

61:1 SPIRIT . . . SOVEREIGN LORD . . . ME. There is a hint in this OT passage of the doctrine of the Trinity: the "Sovereign LORD," the "Spirit" and "me" (i.e., Jesus; see Mk 1:11, note).

61:2 THE DAY OF VENGEANCE. Jesus did not include this phrase when he quoted this prophecy (Lk 4:18–19), since the "day of vengeance" would not take place until his second coming. Final judgment on the wicked will take place during the great tribulation and at Christ's return to earth (Rev 5 – 19; cf. Isa 34:8; Mt 24:30).

3 and provide for those who grieve
in Zion—
to bestow on them a crown[w] of
beauty
instead of ashes,[x]
the oil[y] of gladness
instead of mourning,[z]
and a garment of praise
instead of a spirit of despair.
They will be called oaks of
righteousness,
a planting[a] of the LORD
for the display of his splendor.[b]

Eze 8:3-4

4They will rebuild the ancient
ruins[c]
and restore the places long
devastated;
they will renew the ruined cities
that have been devastated for
generations.
5Aliens[d] will shepherd your flocks;
foreigners will work your fields
and vineyards.
6And you will be called priests[e] of
the LORD,
you will be named ministers of
our God.
You will feed on the wealth[f] of
nations,
and in their riches you will
boast.
7Instead of their shame[g]
my people will receive a
double[h] portion,
and instead of disgrace
they will rejoice in their
inheritance;
and so they will inherit[i] a double
portion in their land,
and everlasting joy[j] will be
theirs.
8"For I, the LORD, love justice;[k]
I hate robbery and iniquity.
In my faithfulness I will reward
them
and make an everlasting
covenant[l] with them.

61:3 [w]S Isa 3:23 [x]S Job 2:8 [y]S Ru 3:3; S Isa 1:6; Heb 1:9 [z]Jer 31:13; Mt 5:4 [a]Ps 1:3; 92:12-13; Mt 15:13; 1Co 3:9 [b]S Isa 44:23
61:4 [c]S Isa 44:26; 51:3; 65:21; Eze 36:33; Am 9:14; Zec 1:16-17
61:5 [d]S Isa 14:1-2; S 56:6
61:6 [e]S Ex 19:6; 1Pe 2:5 [f]Dt 33:19; S Isa 60:11
61:7 [g]S Isa 29:22; S 41:11 [h]S Dt 21:17; S Isa 40:2 [i]S Isa 60:21 [j]S Ps 126:5; S Isa 25:9
61:8 [k]S Ps 11:7; S Isa 1:17; S 5:16 [l]S Ge 9:16; S Isa 42:6; S Heb 13:20
61:9 [m]S Isa 43:5; S 48:19 [n]S Ge 12:2; S Dt 28:3-12
61:10 [o]S Ps 2:11; S Isa 7:13; S 25:9; Hab 3:18; S Lk 1:47 [p]S Job 27:6; S Ps 132:9; S Isa 52:1; Rev 19:8 [q]S Ex 39:28 [r]S Isa 49:18; Rev 21:2
61:11 [s]S Ge 47:23; Isa 58:11 [t]S Isa 45:8
62:1 [u]S Est 4:14; S Ps 50:21; S 83:1 [v]S Isa 1:26; S 45:8 [w]S Job 11:17 [x]S Ps 67:2
62:2 [y]S Ps 67:2; S Isa 40:5; S 45:14; 52:10 [z]S Ge 32:28; S Isa 1:26; Rev 2:17; 3:12
62:3 [a]S Isa 28:5; 1Th 2:19
62:4 [b]S Lev 26:43; S Isa 6:12; S 54:6 [c]S Isa 49:19; S 51:19

9Their descendants[m] will be known
among the nations
and their offspring among the
peoples.
All who see them will acknowledge
that they are a people the LORD
has blessed."[n]

10I delight greatly in the LORD;
my soul rejoices[o] in my God.
For he has clothed me with
garments of salvation
and arrayed me in a robe of
righteousness,[p]
as a bridegroom adorns his head[q]
like a priest,
and as a bride[r] adorns herself
with her jewels.
11For as the soil makes the sprout
come up
and a garden[s] causes seeds to
grow,
so the Sovereign LORD will make
righteousness[t] and praise
spring up before all nations.

Zion's New Name

62 For Zion's sake I will not
keep silent,[u]
for Jerusalem's sake I will not
remain quiet,
till her righteousness[v] shines out
like the dawn,[w]
her salvation[x] like a blazing
torch.
2The nations[y] will see your
righteousness,
and all kings your glory;
you will be called by a new name[z]
that the mouth of the LORD will
bestow.
3You will be a crown[a] of splendor
in the LORD's hand,
a royal diadem in the hand of
your God.
4No longer will they call you
Deserted,[b]
or name your land Desolate.[c]

61:4–9 REBUILD THE ANCIENT RUINS. After Christ's second coming at the end of the age, Israel will be rebuilt and other nations will work among them and worship the Lord with them (vv. 5–6). Israelites will function as priests and ministers, teaching and mediating God's word to others (v. 6).

61:10–11 I DELIGHT GREATLY IN THE LORD. After Christ's return, all who are a part of his kingdom will rejoice. They will be clothed with "garments of salvation" (i.e., they will belong to God's redeemed) and "a robe of righteousness" (i.e., they will live by God's standards).

62:1–12 ZION'S ... JERUSALEM'S. This chapter speaks of a day when Jerusalem will be filled with the glory and righteousness of the Lord; God's people will live within its walls in peace and joy, and all the world will benefit from its exaltation. This day will take place after the Savior comes at the end of the age (v. 11).

62:4 HEPHZIBAH ... BEULAH. Hephzibah means "my delight is in her," and Beulah means

But you will be called
Hephzibah,[s][d]
and your land Beulah[t];
for the LORD will take delight[e] in
you,
and your land will be married.[f]
5As a young man marries a maiden,
so will your sons[u] marry you;
as a bridegroom[g] rejoices over his
bride,
so will your God rejoice[h] over
you.
6I have posted watchmen[i] on your
walls, O Jerusalem;
they will never be silent day or
night.
You who call on the LORD,
give yourselves no rest,[j]
7and give him no rest[k] till he
establishes Jerusalem
and makes her the praise[l] of
the earth.
8The LORD has sworn[m] by his right
hand
and by his mighty arm:
"Never again will I give your
grain[n]
as food for your enemies,
and never again will foreigners
drink the new wine
for which you have toiled;
9but those who harvest it will eat[o]
it
and praise the LORD,[p]
and those who gather the grapes
will drink it
in the courts of my sanctuary."[q]
10Pass through, pass through the
gates![r]
Prepare the way for the people.
Build up, build up the highway![s][t]
Remove the stones.
Raise a banner[u] for the nations.

62:4 [d] 2Ki 21:1 [e] Isa 65:19; Jer 32:41; Zep 3:17; Mal 3:12 [f] Isa 54:5; Jer 3:14; Hos 2:19 **62:5** [g] S SS 3:11 [h] S Dt 28:63; Isa 65:19; Jer 31:12; Zep 3:17 **62:6** [i] S Isa 52:8; Heb 13:17 [j] Ps 132:4 **62:7** [k] Mt 15:21-28; Lk 18:1-8 [l] S Dt 26:19; S Isa 60:18 **62:8** [m] S Ge 22:16; S Isa 14:24; S 49:18 [n] Dt 28:30-33; S Isa 1:7 **62:9** [o] S Isa 1:19; Am 9:14 [p] S Dt 12:7; Joel 2:26 [q] Lev 23:39 **62:10** [r] S Ps 24:7; S Isa 60:11 [s] Isa 57:14 [t] S Isa 11:16 [u] S Isa 11:10

62:11 [v] S Dt 30:4 [w] S Ps 9:14; Zec 9:9; Mt 21:5 [x] S Isa 35:4; Rev 22:12 [y] S Isa 40:10 **62:12** [z] S Ge 32:28 [a] S Ex 19:6; 1Pe 2:9 [b] S Ps 106:10; S Isa 35:9; S 44:23 [c] S Ps 27:9; Isa 42:16; S 54:6 **63:1** [d] S 2Ch 28:17; S Isa 11:14 [e] S Ge 36:33; Am 1:12 [f] Rev 19:13 [g] S Job 9:4; S Isa 45:24 [h] ver 5; Isa 46:13; S 51:5; Jer 42:11; Zep 3:17 **63:2** [i] S Ge 49:11 **63:3** [j] S Jdg 6:11; S Rev 14:20 [k] S Job 40:12; S Ps 108:13; S Isa 5:5 [l] S Isa 22:5 [m] Rev 19:13

11The LORD has made proclamation
to the ends of the earth:[v]
"Say to the Daughter of Zion,[w]
'See, your Savior comes![x]
See, his reward is with him,
and his recompense accompanies
him.' "[y]
12They will be called[z] the Holy
People,[a]
the Redeemed[b] of the LORD;
and you will be called Sought
After,
the City No Longer Deserted.[c]

Isa 66:15-16

God's Day of Vengeance and Redemption

63 Who is this coming from
Edom,[d]
from Bozrah,[e] with his
garments stained
crimson?[f]
Who is this, robed in splendor,
striding forward in the greatness
of his strength?[g]

"It is I, speaking in righteousness,
mighty to save."[h]

2Why are your garments red,
like those of one treading the
winepress?[i]

3"I have trodden the winepress[j]
alone;
from the nations no one was
with me.
I trampled[k] them in my anger
and trod them down in my
wrath;[l]
their blood spattered my
garments,[m]

[s] 4 *Hephzibah* means *my delight is in her.*
[t] 4 *Beulah* means *married.* [u] 5 Or *Builder*

"married"; these names signify that God has renewed his covenant with Jerusalem.

62:6 WATCHMEN . . . NEVER BE SILENT. God has appointed watchmen on the walls of Zion, i.e., prophets and faithful intercessors who never stop praying for the establishment of God's kingdom on earth and for the glory of Jerusalem. Similarly, NT believers must make it a practice to intercede unceasingly for the establishment of God's kingdom and Christ's righteous rule over the earth (see Mt 6:10, note). In all things that we know to be God's will, we must continually cry out to him and "give him no rest" (v. 7) till he brings to pass all that he has promised.

62:11 YOUR SAVIOR COMES. This verse refers to Christ's second coming to establish righteousness on the earth and bring praise to Jerusalem for his name's sake; "his reward is with him" (cf. Rev 22:12).

63:1–6 FROM EDOM. These verses depict God's future judgment on an ungodly world. "Edom" represents all the world powers that are opposed to God and his people. The Lord's garments are stained crimson with the blood of the wicked. Note Rev 19:13, where Christ's robe is pictured as "dipped in blood" as he returns to the earth to destroy the wicked.

63:3 TRODDEN THE WINEPRESS ALONE. God himself will wage war against the nations and defeat them; he will trample them as people trample grapes in the winepress (cf. Joel 3:13; Rev 14:17–20; 19:15).

and I stained all my clothing.
4For the day of vengeance[n] was in
my heart,
and the year of my redemption
has come.
5I looked, but there was no one[o]
to help,
I was appalled that no one gave
support;
so my own arm[p] worked salvation
for me,
and my own wrath sustained
me.[q]
6I trampled[r] the nations in my
anger;
in my wrath I made them
drunk[s]
and poured their blood[t] on the
ground."

Jer 23:5-6

Praise and Prayer

7I will tell of the kindnesses[u] of
the LORD,
the deeds for which he is to be
praised,
according to all the LORD has
done for us—
yes, the many good things[v] he
has done
for the house of Israel,
according to his compassion[w]
and many kindnesses.
8He said, "Surely they are my
people,[x]
sons who will not be false to
me";
and so he became their Savior.[y]
9In all their distress he too was
distressed,
and the angel[z] of his
presence[a] saved them.
In his love and mercy he
redeemed[b] them;
he lifted them up and carried[c]
them
all the days of old.[d]
10Yet they rebelled[e]
and grieved his Holy Spirit.[f]
So he turned and became their
enemy[g]
and he himself fought[h] against
them.
11Then his people recalled[v] the
days of old,
the days of Moses and his
people—
where is he who brought them
through the sea,[i]
with the shepherd of his flock?[j]
Where is he who set
his Holy Spirit[k] among them,
12who sent his glorious arm[l] of
power
to be at Moses' right hand,
who divided the waters[m] before
them,
to gain for himself everlasting
renown,[n]
13who led[o] them through the
depths?[p]
Like a horse in open country,
they did not stumble;[q]
14like cattle that go down to the
plain,
they were given rest[r] by the
Spirit of the LORD.
This is how you guided your
people
to make for yourself a glorious
name.
15Look down from heaven[s] and see
from your lofty throne,[t] holy
and glorious.
Where are your zeal[u] and your
might?
Your tenderness and
compassion[v] are
withheld[w] from us.
16But you are our Father,[x]
though Abraham does not know
us
or Israel acknowledge[y] us;
you, O LORD, are our Father,
our Redeemer[z] from of old is
your name.

63:4 [n] S Isa 1:24; S Jer 50:15
63:5 [o] S 2Ki 14:26; S Isa 41:28 [p] S Ps 44:3; S 98:1; S Isa 33:2 [q] Isa 59:16
63:6 [r] S Job 40:12; S Ps 108:13 [s] S Isa 29:9; La 4:21 [t] S Isa 34:3
63:7 [u] S Isa 54:8 [v] S Ex 18:9 [w] S Ps 51:1; Eph 2:4
63:8 [x] S Ps 100:3; S Isa 51:4 [y] S Ex 14:30; S Isa 25:9
63:9 [z] S Ex 14:19 [a] S Ex 33:14 [b] Dt 7:7-8; S Ezr 9:9; S Isa 48:20 [c] S Dt 1:31; S Ps 28:9 [d] S Dt 32:7; S Job 37:23
63:10 [e] S Ps 78:17; Eze 20:8; Ac 7:39-42 [f] S Ps 51:11; Ac 7:51; Eph 4:30 [g] Ps 106:40; S Isa 10:4 [h] S Jos 10:14
63:11 [i] S Ex 14:22,30 [j] S Ps 77:20 [k] S Nu 11:17
63:12 [l] S Ge 49:24; S Ex 3:20 [m] Ex 14:21-22; Isa 11:15 [n] S Ps 102:12; S Isa 55:13; S Jer 13:11
63:13 [o] S Dt 32:12 [p] S Ex 14:22 [q] S Ps 119:11; Jer 31:9
63:14 [r] S Ex 33:14; S Dt 12:9
63:15 [s] S Dt 26:15; La 3:50 [t] S 1Ki 22:19; S Ps 123:1 [u] S Isa 9:7; S 26:11 [v] S 1Ki 3:26; S Ps 25:6 [w] S Ge 43:31; Isa 64:12
63:16 [x] S Ex 4:22; S Jer 3:4; Jn 8:41 [y] S Job 14:21 [z] Isa 41:14; 44:6; S 59:20

[v] 11 Or *But may he recall*

63:7—64:12 KINDNESSES OF THE LORD. Isaiah praises God's compassion and kindness, confesses Israel's sin, and intercedes for their deliverance from judgment and for God's promised redemption.

63:9 ANGEL OF HIS PRESENCE. This angel is probably the angel of the Lord, who is really the Lord himself (see Ge 16:7, note; Ex 3:2, note; see article on ANGELS AND THE ANGEL OF THE LORD, p. 340).

63:10 GRIEVED HIS HOLY SPIRIT. "Grieved" suggests the violation of the Holy Spirit's love and a rebellion against his ways. The Spirit is a divine person who can be hurt and grieved (cf. Eph 4:30); "Holy" refers to his majestic holiness and spotless purity. The Holy Spirit has been given to all believers to bring them into God's grace, revelation, power, love, presence, guidance and holiness.

17Why, O LORD, do you make us
wander[a] from your ways
and harden our hearts[b] so we
do not revere[c] you?
Return[d] for the sake of your
servants,
the tribes that are your
inheritance.[e]
18For a little while[f] your people
possessed your holy place,
but now our enemies have
trampled[g] down your
sanctuary.[h]
19We are yours from of old;
but you have not ruled over
them,
they have not been called by
your name.[w][i]

64 Oh, that you would rend the
heavens[j] and come
down,[k]
that the mountains[l] would
tremble before you!
2As when fire sets twigs ablaze
and causes water to boil,
come down to make your name[m]
known to your enemies
and cause the nations to
quake[n] before you!
3For when you did awesome[o]
things that we did not
expect,
you came down, and the
mountains trembled[p]
before you.
4Since ancient times no one has
heard,
no ear has perceived,
no eye has seen any God besides
you,[q]
who acts on behalf of those who
wait for him.[r]
5You come to the help of those who
gladly do right,[s]
who remember your ways.
But when we continued to sin
against them,
you were angry.[t]
How then can we be saved?
6All of us have become like one
who is unclean,[u]
and all our righteous[v] acts are
like filthy rags;
we all shrivel up like a leaf,[w]
and like the wind our sins
sweep us away.[x]
7No one[y] calls on your name[z]
or strives to lay hold of you;
for you have hidden[a] your face
from us
and made us waste away[b]
because of our sins.

8Yet, O LORD, you are our Father.[c]
We are the clay, you are the
potter;[d]
we are all the work of your
hand.[e]
9Do not be angry[f] beyond
measure, O LORD;
do not remember our sins[g]
forever.
Oh, look upon us, we pray,
for we are all your people.[h]
10Your sacred cities[i] have become a
desert;
even Zion is a desert, Jerusalem
a desolation.[j]
11Our holy and glorious temple,[k]
where our fathers praised
you,
has been burned with fire,
and all that we treasured[l] lies
in ruins.
12After all this, O LORD, will you hold
yourself back?[m]
Will you keep silent[n] and
punish us beyond measure?

Judgment and Salvation

65 "I revealed myself to those
who did not ask for me;

[w] 19 Or *We are like those you have never ruled, / like those never called by your name*

63:17 [a] S Ge 20:13; La 3:9 [b] S Ex 4:21 [c] Isa 29:13 [d] S Nu 10:36 [e] S Ex 34:9 **63:18** [f] Dt 4:26; 11:17 [g] S Isa 28:18; Da 8:13; S Lk 21:24 [h] S Lev 26:31; S 2Ki 25:9 **63:19** [i] S Isa 43:7; S Jer 14:9 **64:1** [j] Ps 18:9; 144:5 [k] ver 3; Mic 1:3 [l] S Ex 19:18 **64:2** [m] S Isa 30:27 [n] Ps 99:1; 119:120; Jer 5:22; 33:9 **64:3** [o] S Ps 65:5 [p] S Ps 18:7 **64:4** [q] S Isa 43:10-11 [r] S Isa 30:18; 1Co 2:9* **64:5** [s] S Isa 26:8 [t] S Isa 10:4 **64:6** [u] S Lev 5:2; S 12:2 [v] Isa 46:12; 48:1 [w] S Ps 1:3; 90:5-6 [x] Ps 1:4; Jer 4:12 **64:7** [y] S Isa 41:28; 59:4; 63:5; Jer 8:6; Eze 22:30 [z] S Ps 14:4 [a] Dt 31:18; Isa 1:15; 54:8 [b] S Isa 9:18; Eze 22:18-22 **64:8** [c] S Ex 4:22; S Jer 3:4 [d] S Isa 29:16; Ro 9:20-21 [e] S Job 10:3; S Isa 19:25 **64:9** [f] Isa 54:8; 57:17; 60:10; La 5:22 [g] S Isa 43:25 [h] S Ps 100:3; S Isa 51:4 **64:10** [i] Ps 78:54; S Isa 1:26 [j] S Dt 29:23 **64:11** [k] S Lev 26:31; S 2Ki 25:9; Ps 74:3-7; La 2:7 [l] ver 10-11; La 1:7, 10 **64:12** [m] S Ge 43:31; Ps 74:10-11 [n] S Est 4:14; S Ps 50:21; S 83:1

64:1–4 REND THE HEAVENS AND COME DOWN. As a representative of God's people, Isaiah pleads with the Lord to intervene in the affairs of the world, to defeat his enemies and to save all who call on him. NT believers should pray this prayer daily. God promises to act on behalf of those who wait for him (v. 4).

64:4 THOSE WHO WAIT FOR HIM. God promises to do great things for those who wait for him. He can intervene in the events of human history so as to cause people to perform his will. Believers must look to him and persevere in hope, confidence and patience.

65:1–7 THOSE WHO DID NOT SEEK ME. In these verses, God responds to Isaiah's prayer by describing his continual appeal to the rebellious nation to return to him. Because of their wickedness, God would repay them with judgment (vv. 6–7), accomplished largely through the Assyrian invasion (chs. 1—37) and the Babylonian captivity (chs. 38—66).

I was found by those who did
not seek me.[o]
To a nation[p] that did not call on
my name,[q]
I said, 'Here am I, here am I.'
2All day long I have held out my
hands
to an obstinate people,[r]
who walk in ways not good,
pursuing their own
imaginations[s] —
3a people who continually provoke
me
to my very face,[t]
offering sacrifices in gardens[u]
and burning incense[v] on altars
of brick;
4who sit among the graves[w]
and spend their nights keeping
secret vigil;
who eat the flesh of pigs,[x]
and whose pots hold broth of
unclean meat;
5who say, 'Keep away; don't come
near me,
for I am too sacred[y] for you!'
Such people are smoke[z] in my
nostrils,
a fire that keeps burning all day.

6"See, it stands written before me:
I will not keep silent[a] but will
pay back[b] in full;
I will pay it back into their
laps[c]—
7both your sins[d] and the sins of
your fathers,"[e]
says the LORD.
"Because they burned sacrifices on
the mountains
and defied me on the hills,[f]
I will measure into their laps
the full payment[g] for their
former deeds."

8This is what the LORD says:

"As when juice is still found in a
cluster of grapes[h]
and men say, 'Don't destroy it,
there is yet some good in it,'
so will I do in behalf of my
servants;[i]
I will not destroy them all.
9I will bring forth descendants[j]
from Jacob,
and from Judah those who will
possess[k] my mountains;
my chosen[l] people will inherit
them,
and there will my servants
live.[m]
10Sharon[n] will become a pasture for
flocks,[o]
and the Valley of Achor[p] a
resting place for herds,
for my people who seek[q] me.
11"But as for you who forsake[r] the
LORD
and forget my holy mountain,[s]
who spread a table for Fortune
and fill bowls of mixed wine[t]
for Destiny,
12I will destine you for the sword,[u]
and you will all bend down for
the slaughter;[v]
for I called but you did not
answer,[w]
I spoke but you did not listen.[x]
You did evil in my sight
and chose what displeases
me."[y]

13Therefore this is what the Sovereign LORD says:

"My servants will eat,[z]
but you will go hungry;[a]
my servants will drink,[b]
but you will go thirsty;[c]
my servants will rejoice,[d]
but you will be put to shame.[e]
14My servants will sing[f]
out of the joy of their hearts,
but you will cry out[g]
from anguish of heart
and wail in brokenness of spirit.
15You will leave your name
to my chosen ones as a curse;[h]
the Sovereign LORD will put you to
death,

65:1 [o] Hos 1:10; Ro 9:24-26; 10:20* [p] Ro 9:30; Eph 2:12 [q] S Ps 14:4; S Isa 43:7 **65:2** [r] S Ps 78:8; S Isa 1:2,23; Ro 10:21* [s] Ps 81:11-12; S Pr 24:2; Isa 66:18 **65:3** [t] S Job 1:11 [u] S Isa 1:29 [v] S Lev 2:2; Jer 41:5; 44:17; Eze 23:41 **65:4** [w] S Lev 19:31; S Isa 8:19 [x] S Lev 11:7 **65:5** [y] S Ps 40:4; Mt 9:11; Lk 7:39; 18:9-12 [z] Pr 10:26 **65:6** [a] S Ps 50:3 [b] S 2Ch 6:23; Isa 59:18; Jer 16:18 [c] S Ps 79:12; Eze 9:10; Lk 6:38 **65:7** [d] S Isa 22:14 [e] Ex 20:5; Jer 32:18 [f] S Isa 57:7 [g] S Pr 10:24; S Isa 10:12 **65:8** [h] Isa 5:2 [i] S Isa 54:17 **65:9** [j] S Isa 45:19 [k] S Nu 34:13; S Isa 60:21; Jer 50:19; Am 9:11-15 [l] S Isa 14:1 [m] Isa 32:18 **65:10** [n] S 1Ch 27:29; S Isa 35:2; Ac 9:35 [o] Jer 31:12; 33:12; Eze 34:13-14 [p] S Jos 7:26 [q] S Isa 51:1 **65:11** [r] Dt 28:20; 29:24-25; S 32:15; Isa 1:28; Jer 2:13; 19:4 [s] S Dt 33:19; S Ps 137:5 [t] S Isa 5:22 **65:12** [u] S Isa 1:20; S 27:1 [v] S Isa 30:25 [w] S Pr 1:24-25; S Isa 41:28; 66:4; Jer 7:27 [x] 2Ch 36:15-16; Jer 7:13; 13:11; 25:3; 26:5 [y] Ps 149:7; Isa 1:24; 66:4; Mic 5:15 **65:13** [z] S Isa 1:19 [a] S Job 18:12; Lk 6:25 [b] S Isa 33:16 [c] S Isa 3:1; 41:17 [d] S Isa 60:5; 61:7 [e] S Isa 44:9 **65:14** [f] S Ps 109:28; Zep 3:14-20; Jas 5:13 [g] S Isa 15:2; Mt 8:12; Lk 13:28 **65:15** [h] S Nu 5:27; S Ps 102:8

65:8 JUICE. The Hebrew *tirosh* (usually translated "new wine," here translated "juice") generally refers to the unfermented fruit of the vine (see article on WINE IN THE OLD TESTAMENT, p. 204). Note that it is this type of wine that God says has "some good in it."

65:9 DESCENDANTS FROM JACOB. Although God would judge Israel (vv. 6–7), he would also save a remnant of true believers who would return to the land and carry on his redemptive mission in the world. They would experience his joy and blessings (vv. 13–16).

65:12 DESTINE YOU FOR THE SWORD. Those among God's people who refused to listen to God and persisted in sinning were destined for slaughter, famine and destruction.

but to his servants he will give
another name.[i]
16Whoever invokes a blessing[j] in
the land
will do so by the God of truth;[k]
he who takes an oath in the land
will swear[l] by the God of truth.
For the past troubles[m] will be
forgotten
and hidden from my eyes.

New Heavens and a New Earth

17"Behold, I will create
new heavens and a new earth.[n]
The former things will not be
remembered,[o]
nor will they come to mind.
18But be glad and rejoice[p] forever
in what I will create,
for I will create Jerusalem[q] to be
a delight
and its people a joy.
19I will rejoice[r] over Jerusalem
and take delight[s] in my people;
the sound of weeping and of
crying[t]
will be heard in it no more.

20"Never again will there be in it
an infant[u] who lives but a few
days,
or an old man who does not live
out his years;[v]
he who dies at a hundred
will be thought a mere youth;
he who fails to reach[x] a hundred
will be considered accursed.
21They will build houses[w] and dwell
in them;
they will plant vineyards and eat
their fruit.[x]
22No longer will they build houses
and others live in them,[y]
or plant and others eat.
For as the days of a tree,[z]
so will be the days[a] of my
people;
my chosen[b] ones will long enjoy
the works of their hands.
23They will not toil in vain[c]
or bear children doomed to
misfortune;[d]
for they will be a people blessed[e]
by the LORD,
they and their descendants[f]
with them.
24Before they call[g] I will answer;[h]
while they are still speaking[i] I
will hear.
25The wolf and the lamb[j] will feed
together,
and the lion will eat straw like
the ox,[k]
but dust will be the serpent's[l]
food.
They will neither harm nor destroy
on all my holy mountain,"[m]
says the LORD.

Judgment and Hope

66 This is what the LORD says:
"Heaven is my throne,[n]
and the earth is my footstool.[o]
Where is the house[p] you will
build for me?
Where will my resting place be?
2Has not my hand made all these
things,[q]
and so they came into being?"
declares the LORD.

"This is the one I esteem:
he who is humble and contrite in
spirit,[r]
and trembles at my word.[s]

65:15 [i]S Ge 32:28; Rev 2:17 **65:16** [j]S Dt 29:19 [k]Ps 31:5; Rev 3:14 [l]S Ps 63:11; S Isa 19:18 [m]S Job 11:16 **65:17** [n]S Isa 41:22; 66:22; 2Co 5:17; S 2Pe 3:13 [o]Isa 43:18; Jer 3:16; S Rev 7:17 **65:18** [p]S Dt 32:43; Ps 98:1-9; S Isa 25:9 [q]Rev 21:2 **65:19** [r]S Isa 35:10; S 62:5 [s]S Dt 30:9 [t]S Isa 25:8; Rev 7:17 **65:20** [u]Isa 11:8 [v]Ge 5:1-32; S 15:15; S Ecc 8:13; Zec 8:4 **65:21** [w]S Isa 32:18; S 61:4 [x]S 2Ki 19:29; S Isa 37:30; Eze 28:26; Am 9:14 **65:22** [y]S Dt 28:30 [z]Ps 1:3; 92:12-14 [a]Ps 21:4; 91:16 [b]S Isa 14:1 **65:23** [c]S Isa 49:4; 1Co 15:58 [d]Dt 28:32,41; Jer 16:3-4 [e]S Ge 12:2; S Dt 28:3-12 [f]S Isa 44:3; Ac 2:39 **65:24** [g]S Isa 55:6; Mt 6:8 [h]S Job 8:6; S Isa 30:19; S Zec 10:6 [i]Da 9:20-23; 10:12 **65:25** [j]Isa 11:6 [k]S Job 40:15 [l]Ge 3:14; Mic 7:17 [m]S Job 5:23; S Isa 2:4 **66:1** [n]S 2Ch 6:18; S Ps 2:4; S 9:7; Mt 23:22 [o]S 1Ki 8:27; Mt 5:34-35 [p]S 2Sa 7:7; Jn 4:20-21; Ac 7:49*; 17:24 **66:2** [q]S Isa 40:26; Ac 7:50*; 17:24 [r]S Isa 57:15; Mt 5:3-4; Lk 18:13-14 [s]S Ezr 9:4

[x]*20* Or / *the sinner who reaches*

65:17–25 CREATE NEW HEAVENS AND A NEW EARTH. This prophecy foresees God's future kingdom on earth. Isaiah blends the age of eternity where sin and death will be no more (vv. 17–19) with the Messianic age (i.e., the millennial kingdom) that precedes it (vv. 19–25; Rev 20:4–6). Note that v. 18 begins with a strong adversative ("But"): there will indeed be new heavens and a new earth, *but* God also has plans for the present Jerusalem in his millennial kingdom.

65:20 INFANT WHO LIVES BUT A FEW DAYS. Although death will exist in the Messianic kingdom, life spans will be much longer than they are now. A 100-year-old will still be considered a youth and those who die before that age will be considered accursed.

65:24 BEFORE THEY CALL I WILL ANSWER. No longer will God's people need to persevere in prayer for their daily needs; the Lord will answer their prayers without delay.

65:25 WOLF AND THE LAMB WILL FEED TOGETHER. Peace and safety will characterize the Messianic kingdom. Once-wild animals will be tame, and perfect harmony will exist (cf. 11:6–9).

66:2 THE ONE I ESTEEM. God is not impressed with the splendor of any building that humans construct for him, but he does delight in a certain kind of person (vv. 1–2) — those who are humble in spirit, who recognize their need for his continuing help and grace, and who seek to follow his word with all their heart (see 57:15, note).

[3]But whoever sacrifices a bull[t]
is like one who kills a man,
and whoever offers a lamb,
like one who breaks a dog's
neck;
whoever makes a grain offering
is like one who presents pig's[u]
blood,
and whoever burns memorial
incense,[v]
like one who worships an idol.
They have chosen their own
ways,[w]
and their souls delight in their
abominations;[x]
[4]so I also will choose harsh
treatment for them
and will bring upon them what
they dread.[y]
For when I called, no one
answered,[z]
when I spoke, no one listened.
They did evil[a] in my sight
and chose what displeases
me."[b]

[5]Hear the word of the LORD,
you who tremble at his word:[c]
"Your brothers who hate[d] you,
and exclude you because of my
name, have said,
'Let the LORD be glorified,
that we may see your joy!'
Yet they will be put to shame.[e]
[6]Hear that uproar from the city,
hear that noise from the temple!
It is the sound[f] of the LORD
repaying[g] his enemies all they
deserve.

[7]"Before she goes into labor,[h]
she gives birth;
before the pains come upon her,
she delivers a son.[i]
[8]Who has ever heard of such a
thing?
Who has ever seen[j] such
things?
Can a country be born in a day[k]
or a nation be brought forth in a
moment?
Yet no sooner is Zion in labor
than she gives birth to her
children.[l]
[9]Do I bring to the moment of
birth[m]
and not give delivery?" says the
LORD.
"Do I close up the womb
when I bring to delivery?" says
your God.
[10]"Rejoice[n] with Jerusalem and be
glad for her,
all you who love[o] her;
rejoice greatly with her,
all you who mourn[p] over her.
[11]For you will nurse[q] and be
satisfied
at her comforting breasts;[r]
you will drink deeply
and delight in her overflowing
abundance."[s]

[12]For this is what the LORD says:

"I will extend peace[t] to her like a
river,[u]
and the wealth[v] of nations like
a flooding stream;
you will nurse and be carried[w] on
her arm
and dandled on her knees.
[13]As a mother comforts her child,[x]
so will I comfort[y] you;
and you will be comforted over
Jerusalem."
[14]When you see this, your heart will
rejoice[z]
and you will flourish[a] like
grass;
the hand[b] of the LORD will be
made known to his
servants,[c]
but his fury[d] will be shown to
his foes.
[15]See, the LORD is coming with
fire,[e]
and his chariots[f] are like a
whirlwind;[g]
he will bring down his anger with
fury,

66:3 [t] S Isa 1:11 [u] S Lev 11:7 [v] S Lev 2:2 [w] S Isa 57:17 [x] ver 17; S Dt 27:15; Eze 8:9-13 **66:4** [y] S Pr 10:24; S Isa 10:12 [z] S 1Sa 8:19; S Isa 41:28 [a] 2Ki 21:2,4,6; Isa 59:12 [b] S Isa 65:12 **66:5** [c] S Ezr 9:4 [d] Ps 38:20; Isa 60:15; Jn 15:21 [e] S Isa 44:9; Lk 13:17 **66:6** [f] S 1Sa 2:10; S Ps 68:33 [g] S Lev 26:28; Isa 65:6; Joel 3:7 **66:7** [h] S Isa 54:1 [i] Rev 12:5 **66:8** [j] Isa 64:4; Jer 18:13 [k] S Isa 49:20 [l] S Isa 49:21 **66:9** [m] S Isa 37:3 **66:10** [n] S Dt 32:43; S Isa 25:9; Ro 15:10 [o] S Ps 26:8 [p] Isa 57:19; 61:2 **66:11** [q] S Nu 11:12; S Isa 60:16 [r] Ge 49:25 [s] S Nu 25:1; S Isa 25:6 **66:12** [t] S Ps 119:165; S Isa 9:6 [u] S Isa 33:21 [v] Ps 72:3; Isa 60:5; 61:6 [w] S Nu 11:12; Isa 60:4 **66:13** [x] S Isa 49:15; 1Th 2:7 [y] S Isa 40:1; S 2Co 1:4 **66:14** [z] S Isa 25:9; S 60:5; S Joel 2:23 [a] S Ps 72:16 [b] S Ezr 5:5; S Isa 41:20 [c] S Isa 54:17 [d] S Isa 10:5; S 30:27 **66:15** [e] S Isa 1:31; S 42:25 [f] S 2Ki 2:11; S Ps 68:17 [g] S 2Ki 2:1

66:3 SACRIFICES A BULL. Those who worship God while choosing to live in their own ways and not in accordance with his word (v. 2) are detestable to him; such people will receive harsh retribution from the Lord.

66:7–14 SHE GIVES BIRTH. Isaiah envisions the rebirth of Israel as God's people during the Messianic kingdom; the birth will be remarkably quick and will bring joy (v. 10), peace (v. 12; cf. 48:18) and prosperity (v. 11).

66:10–14 REJOICE WITH JERUSALEM. Jerusalem is compared to a mother who feeds and comforts her children. Jerusalem will have peace and be a comfort to all who love God, including the nations that come to her.

66:15 IS COMING WITH FIRE. When God establishes Jerusalem and the Messianic kingdom, he also will come with judgment upon his enemies (cf. Zec 14:3; 2Th 1:7–9; Rev 19:11–21).

and his rebuke[h] with flames of
fire.
16For with fire[i] and with his
sword[j]
the LORD will execute judgment[k]
upon all men,
and many will be those slain[l]
by the LORD.

17"Those who consecrate and purify
themselves to go into the gardens,[m]
following the one in the midst of[y]
those who eat the flesh of pigs[n] and
rats[o] and other abominable things—
they will meet their end[p] together,"
declares the LORD.
18"And I, because of their actions
and their imaginations,[q] am about to
come[z] and gather all nations[r] and
tongues, and they will come and see
my glory.[s]
19"I will set a sign[t] among them,
and I will send some of those who survive[u] to the nations—to Tarshish,[v]
to the Libyans[a] and Lydians[w] (famous as archers), to Tubal[x] and
Greece,[y] and to the distant islands[z]
that have not heard of my fame or seen
my glory.[a] They will proclaim my glory among the nations. 20And they will
bring[b] all your brothers, from all the
nations, to my holy mountain[c] in Jerusalem as an offering to the LORD—on
horses, in chariots and wagons, and on
mules and camels,"[d] says the LORD.
"They will bring them, as the Israelites
bring their grain offerings, to the temple of the LORD in ceremonially clean
vessels.[e] 21And I will select some of
them also to be priests[f] and Levites,"
says the LORD.

22"As the new heavens and the new
earth[g] that I make will endure before
me," declares the LORD, "so will your
name and descendants endure.[h]
23From one New Moon to another and
from one Sabbath[i] to another, all
mankind will come and bow down[j] before me," says the LORD. 24"And they
will go out and look upon the dead bodies[k] of those who rebelled[l] against
me; their worm[m] will not die, nor will
their fire be quenched,[n] and they will
be loathsome to all mankind."

66:15 [h]S Dt 28:20; S Ps 9:5; S 39:11 **66:16** [i]Isa 30:30; Am 7:4; Mal 4:1 [j]S Isa 1:20; S 27:1; S Eze 14:21 [k]S Isa 13:9,11; S Jer 2:35; S Eze 36:5 [l]S Isa 10:4 **66:17** [m]S Isa 1:29 [n]S Lev 11:7 [o]Lev 11:29 [p]Ps 37:20; Isa 1:28 **66:18** [q]S Pr 24:2; S Isa 65:2 [r]S Isa 2:3; S Zec 12:3 [s]S Ex 16:7; S Isa 59:19 **66:19** [t]Isa 11:10; 49:22; Mt 24:30 [u]S 2Ki 19:31 [v]S Isa 2:16 [w]Jer 46:9; Eze 27:10 [x]S Ge 10:2 [y]Jer 31:10; Da 11:18 [z]Isa 11:11 [a]S 1Ch 16:24; S Isa 24:15 **66:20** [b]S Isa 11:12; S Jer 25:22; Eze 34:13 [c]S Dt 33:19; S Isa 2:2; Jer 31:23 [d]S Ezr 2:66 [e]Isa 52:11 **66:21** [f]S Ex 19:6; 1Pe 2:5,9 **66:22** [g]S Isa 65:17; Heb 12:26-27; S 2Pe 3:13 [h]S Isa 48:19; Jn 10:27-29; 1Pe 1:4-5 **66:23** [i]Eze 46:1-3 [j]S Ps 22:29; S Isa 19:21; S 44:5; Rev 15:4 **66:24** [k]S Ps 110:6 [l]S Isa 1:2 [m]S Isa 14:11 [n]S Isa 1:31; S Mt 25:41; Mk 9:48*

[y] *17* Or *gardens behind one of your temples, and* [z] *18* The meaning of the Hebrew for this clause is uncertain. [a] *19* Some Septuagint manuscripts *Put* (Libyans); Hebrew *Pul*

66:18–21 GATHER ALL NATIONS AND TONGUES. Believers from all nations will be gathered to see God's glory. Having survived his judgment, they will be sent to the nations to bring all remaining Jews to the Lord, the God of Israel; this gathering will occur at the end of the age.

66:22–24 THE NEW HEAVENS AND THE NEW EARTH. At the end of history, i.e., at the end of the Messianic kingdom, God will create the new heavens and the new earth (see 65:17–25, note; Rev 21:1). All believers will be with the Lord forever (cf. Rev 21—22), while all those who rebelled against him and his word will spend eternity in hell (cf. 50:11; 57:21; Mk 9:45; 14:11; see Mt 10:28, note).

JEREMIAH

Outline

I. Jeremiah's Call and Commissioning (1:1–19)
II. Jeremiah's Prophetic Word to Judah (2:1—33:26)
   A. Prophecies About Judgment (2:1—29:32)
      1. Judah's Deliberate Apostasy and Approaching Destruction (2:1—6:30)
      2. Judah's Folly and Religious Hypocrisy (7:1—10:25)
      3. Judah's Unfaithfulness to the Covenant (11:1—13:27)
      4. Judgments Predicted, Intercession and Loneliness, and Judah's Sins (14:1—17:27)
      5. Two Prophetic Parables and a Lament (18:1—20:18)
      6. Condemnation of Wicked Kings, False Prophets and Rotten Judah (21:1—24:10)
      7. The Coming Babylonian Captivity (25:1—29:32)
   B. Prophecies About Restoration (30:1—33:26)
      1. Dimensions of God's Restoration of His People (30:1—31:26)
      2. Promise of a New Covenant and an Illustration of Faith (31:27—32:44)
      3. The Righteous Branch of David (33:1–26)
III. Jeremiah's Role as Prophetic Watchman (34:1—45:5)
   A. Declaration to King Zedekiah of Coming Captivity (34:1–22)
   B. The Lesson of the Recabites (35:1–19)
   C. Jeremiah's Scroll Burned and the Prophet Twice Incarcerated (36:1—38:28)
   D. Jeremiah's Prophecy Fulfilled About Jerusalem's Fall (39:1–18)
   E. Jeremiah's Ministry after the Fall of Jerusalem (40:1—45:5)
IV. Jeremiah's Prophetic Word to the Nations (46:1—51:64)
   A. Egypt (46:1–28)
   B. Philistia (47:1–7)
   C. Moab (48:1–47)
   D. Ammon (49:1–6)
   E. Edom (49:7–22)
   F. Damascus (49:23–27)
   G. Arabia (49:28–33)
   H. Elam (49:34–39)
   I. Babylon (50:1—51:64)
V. Historical Addendum About Jerusalem's Fall (52:1–34)

Author: Jeremiah

Theme: God's Inescapable Judgment for Unrepentant Judah

Date of Writing: c. 585–580 B.C.

Background

Jeremiah's prophetic ministry was directed to the southern kingdom of Judah during the last 40 years of its history (626–586 B.C.). He lived to witness the Babylonian invasions of Judah that resulted in the destruction of Jerusalem and the temple. Since it was Jeremiah's lot to prophesy to the nation during the final years of its decline and fall, his book is understandably filled with much gloom and foreboding.

Jeremiah, the son of a priest, was born and raised in the priestly village of Anathoth (four miles northeast of Jerusalem) during the reign of wicked King Manasseh. Jeremiah began his prophetic ministry during the 13th year of the reign of good King Josiah, and he supported Josiah's reform movement. He soon saw, however, that it was not resulting in a genuine change of heart among the people; Jeremiah warned that unless there was true national repentance, judgment and destruction would come suddenly.

In 612 B.C., Assyria was conquered by a Babylonian coalition. About four years after King Josiah's death, Egypt was defeated by Babylon at the battle of Carchemish (605 B.C.; see 46:2). That same year Nebuchadnezzar's Babylonian army invaded Palestine, captured Jerusalem and deported some of Jerusalem's choicest youth to Babylon, among whom were Daniel and his three friends. A second campaign against Jerusalem took place in 597 B.C., with 10,000 captives being taken to Babylon, among whom was Ezekiel. All this time Jeremiah's prophetic warning about God's impending judgment went unheeded. The final devastation came to Jerusalem, the temple and the entire kingdom of Judah in 586 B.C.

This prophetic book reveals that Jeremiah, often called "the weeping prophet," was a man with a harsh message but a sensitive and broken heart (e.g., 8:21—9:1). His tender spirit made his suffering more intense as God's prophetic word was spurned by family and friends, by priests and kings, and by the people of Judah as a whole. Though lonely and rejected all his life, Jeremiah was nevertheless one of the boldest and bravest of all the prophets. In spite of great opposition, he faithfully carried out his prophetic call to warn his fellow citizens that God's judgment was at hand. In summarizing Jeremiah's life, one writer says: "A more crushing burden was never laid upon mortal man. In the whole history of the Jewish race there has been no such example of intense sincerity, unrelieved suffering, fearless proclamation of God's message, and unwearying intercession of a prophet for his people as is found in the life of Jeremiah. But the tragedy of his life was this: he preached to deaf ears and reaped only hate in return for his love to his fellow countrymen" (Farley).

The book's author is clearly stated to be Jeremiah (1:1). After 20 years of prophesying to Judah, Jeremiah was instructed by God to put his messages in written form; he did so by dictating his prophecies to his faithful secretary, Baruch (36:1–4). Since Jeremiah was banned from appearing before the king, Jeremiah sent Baruch to read the prophecies in the temple, after which Jehudi read them to King Jehoiakim. The king demonstrated his contempt for Jeremiah and the Lord's word by cutting the scroll in pieces and throwing it into the fire (36:22–23). Jeremiah again dictated his prophecies to Baruch, this time including even more than were in the first scroll. Most likely, Baruch put Jeremiah's book in its final form shortly after Jeremiah's death (c. 585–580 B.C.).

Purpose

The book was written (1) to provide an enduring record of Jeremiah's prophetic ministry and message, (2) to reveal God's inevitable and inescapable judgment when his people broke the covenant and persisted in rebellion against God and his word, and (3) to demonstrate the authenticity and authority of the prophetic word. Many of Jeremiah's prophecies were fulfilled in his own lifetime (e.g., 16:9; 20:4; 25:1–14; 27:19–22; 28:15–17; 32:10–13; 34:1–5); other prophecies involving the far-distant future were fulfilled later or are yet to be fulfilled (e.g., 23:5–6; 30:8–9; 31:31–34; 33:14–16).

Survey

The book is essentially a collection of prophecies by Jeremiah, addressed primarily to Judah (chs. 2—29) but also to nine foreign nations (chs. 46—51); these prophecies focus mainly on judgment, though there are some that concern restoration (see especially chs. 30—33). These prophecies are not strictly arranged chronologically or thematically, though the book of Jeremiah has the overall structure indicated in the preceding outline. Part of the book is written in poetry, while other parts are written in a prose or narrative form. Its prophetic messages are interlaced with historical glimpses of (1) the prophet's personal life and ministry (e.g., chs. 1; 34—38; 40—45), (2) Judah's history primarily during the time of kings Josiah (chs. 1—6), Jehoiakim (chs. 7—20) and Zedekiah (chs. 21—25; 34), including the fall of Jerusalem (ch. 39), and (3) international events involving Babylon and other nations (chs. 25—29; 46—52).

Like Ezekiel, Jeremiah uses a variety of parabolic and symbolic actions to illustrate graphically his prophetic message: e.g., the useless belt (13:1–14), the drought (14:1–9), his being forbidden by God to marry or have children (16:1–9), the potter and the clay (18:1–11), the potter's smashed jar (19:1–13), the two baskets of figs (24:1–10), the yoke around his neck (27:1–11), buying a field in his hometown (32:6–15), and the large stones buried in Pharaoh's brick pavement (43:8–13). Jeremiah's clear understanding of his prophetic call (1:17), along with God's frequent reaffirmations (e.g., 3:12; 7:2,27–28; 11:2,6; 13:12–13; 17:19–20), enabled him to proclaim boldly and faithfully the prophetic word to Judah in spite of her continual response of hostility, rejection and persecution (e.g., 15:20–21). After the destruction of Jerusalem, Jeremiah was taken against his will to Egypt, where he continued to prophesy until his death (chs. 43—44).

Special Features

Seven major features characterize the book of Jeremiah. (1) It is the second longest book in the Bible, containing more words (not chapters) than any other book except the Psalms. (2) The personal life and struggles of Jeremiah as a prophet are revealed in greater depth and detail than those of any other OT prophet. (3) It is permeated with the sadness, heartache and sobs of the "weeping prophet" over Judah's rebellion. In spite of Jeremiah's harsh message, he felt deep grief and brokenness for God's people; yet his greatest loyalty was to God, and his deepest grief was God's hurt. (4) One of its key words is "backsliding" (used five times), or "unfaithful" (used 10 times), and its perpetual theme is God's inescapable judgment for rebellion and apostasy. (5) Its greatest single theological revelation is the concept of the "new covenant," which God would establish with his faithful people at a future time of restoration (31:31–34). (6) Its poetry is as eloquent and lyrical as any in the Bible, with an abundance of striking metaphors, vivid phrases and memorable passages. (7) There are more references to the nation of Babylon in Jeremiah's prophecies (164) than in the remainder of the Bible.

New Testament Fulfillment

The foremost use of Jeremiah in the NT concerns his prophecy of a "new covenant" (31:31–34). Though Israel and Judah repeatedly broke God's covenants and subsequently were broken in judgment for their backslidings, Jeremiah prophesied about a day when God would make a new covenant with them (31:31). The NT makes clear that this new covenant was instituted with the death and resurrection of Christ (Lk 22:20; cf. Mt 26:26–29; Mk 14:22–25), is now being fulfilled in the church as the new covenant people of God (Heb 8:8–13), and will reach its climax in the great salvation of Israel (Ro 11:27). Other Messianic passages from Jeremiah that are applied to Jesus Christ in the NT are: (1) the Messiah as the good shepherd and the righteous Branch of David (Jer 23:1–8; see Mt 21:8–9; Jn 10:1–18; 1Co 1:30; 2Co 5:21); (2) great weeping in Ramah (Jer 31:15), fulfilled at the time when Herod attempted to destroy the baby Jesus (see Mt 2:17–18); and (3) Messianic zeal for the purity of God's house (Jer 7:11), demonstrated in Jesus' cleansing of the temple (see Mt 21:13; Mk 11:17; Lk 19:46).

Reading Jeremiah

In order to read the entire Old Testament in one year, the book of Jeremiah should be read in 23 days, according to the following schedule: □ 1–2 □ 3–4 □ 5–6 □ 7–8 □ 9–10 □ 11–12 □ 13–14 □ 15–16 □ 17–18 □ 19–22 □ 23–25 □ 26–28 □ 29–30 □ 31–32 □ 33 □ 34–35 □ 36–37 □ 38–40 □ 41–43 □ 44–47 □ 48–49 □ 50–51 □ 52

NOTES

1 The words of Jeremiah son of Hilkiah, one of the priests at Anathoth[a] in the territory of Benjamin.
2 The word of the LORD came[b] to him
in the thirteenth year of the reign of
Josiah[c] son of Amon king of Judah,
3 and through the reign of Jehoiakim[d]
son of Josiah king of Judah, down to the
fifth month of the eleventh year of Zedekiah[e] son of Josiah king of Judah,
when the people of Jerusalem went into
exile.[f]

The Call of Jeremiah

4 The word of the LORD came to me,
saying,

5 "Before I formed you in the
womb[g] I knew[a][h] you,
before you were born[i] I set you
apart;[j]
I appointed you as a prophet to
the nations.[k]"

6 "Ah, Sovereign LORD," I said, "I do
not know how to speak;[l] I am only a
child."[m]

7 But the LORD said to me, "Do not
say, 'I am only a child.' You must go to
everyone I send you to and say whatever I command you. **8** Do not be afraid[n]
of them, for I am with you[o] and will
rescue[p] you," declares the LORD.[q]

9 Then the LORD reached out his hand
and touched[r] my mouth and said to
me, "Now, I have put my words in your
mouth.[s] **10** See, today I appoint you
over nations[t] and kingdoms to uproot[u] and tear down, to destroy and
overthrow, to build and to plant."[v]

11 The word of the LORD came to me:
"What do you see, Jeremiah?"[w]

"I see the branch of an almond tree,"
I replied.

12 The LORD said to me, "You have
seen correctly, for I am watching[b][x]
to see that my word is fulfilled."

13 The word of the LORD came to me
again: "What do you see?"[y]

"I see a boiling pot, tilting away from
the north," I answered.

14 The LORD said to me, "From the
north[z] disaster will be poured out on
all who live in the land. **15** I am about
to summon all the peoples of the northern kingdoms," declares the LORD.

"Their kings will come and set up
their thrones

1:1 [a] S Jos 21:18 **1:2** [b] Eze 1:3; Hos 1:1; Joel 1:1 [c] S 2Ki 22:1 **1:3** [d] S 2Ki 23:34 [e] S 2Ki 24:17 [f] Ezr 5:12; Jer 52:15 **1:5** [g] S Ps 139:13 [h] Ps 139:16 [i] S Isa 49:1 [j] Jn 10:36 [k] ver 10; Jer 25:15-26 **1:6** [l] S Ex 3:11; S 6:12 [m] 1Ki 3:7 **1:8** [n] S Ge 15:1; S Jos 8:1 [o] S Ge 26:3; S Jos 1:5; Jer 15:20 [p] ver 19; Jer 15:21; 26:24; 36:26; 42:11 [q] Jer 20:11 **1:9** [r] S Isa 6:7 [s] S Ex 4:12 **1:10** [t] Jer 25:17; 46:1 [u] Jer 12:17 [v] Jer 18:7-10; 24:6; 31:4,28 **1:11** [w] Jer 24:3; Am 7:8 **1:12** [x] S Job 29:2; Jer 44:27 **1:13** [y] Jer 24:3; Zec 4:2; 5:2 **1:14** [z] S Isa 14:31

[a] *5* Or *chose* [b] *12* The Hebrew for *watching* sounds like the Hebrew for *almond tree.*

1:1 JEREMIAH. Jeremiah was called by God to be a prophet to the southern kingdom of Judah; his ministry spanned its last forty years, including the days immediately before Jerusalem's destruction and the carrying away of God's people to Babylon (627–586 B.C.). He ministered during the reigns of Josiah, Jehoahaz, Jehoiakim, Jehoiachin and Zedekiah. During that time the nation was rebelling against God and relying on political alliances to gain deliverance from its enemies. Jeremiah urged the people to repent of their sins and warned them that they would indeed suffer punishment for rejecting God and his law. Because of his message and his devotion to the Lord, Jeremiah experienced much opposition and suffering.

1:5 BEFORE I FORMED YOU . . . I KNEW YOU. Before Jeremiah was born, God had already determined that he would be a prophet. Just as God had a life plan for Jeremiah, so he does for every person. His goal is for us to live in accordance with his will and to allow him to fulfill his plan in us. As with Jeremiah, living according to God's plan may involve suffering; nevertheless, God always works for our greatest good (see Ro 8:28, note).

1:8 DO NOT BE AFRAID. Jeremiah was only a youth at the time of his call; he experienced intense anxiety and fear at the awesome thought of speaking the word of the Lord to the elders of Judah (v. 7). God responded by promising to be with him and to empower him to fulfill that calling. No matter what your task is in life, God always promises his abiding presence and help if you remain steadfast in your faith.

1:9 MY WORDS IN YOUR MOUTH. God assures Jeremiah that his prophetic message would be inspired by God; his words would be God's words (cf. Ro 10:8). Convinced of this, Jeremiah never compromised or modified God's word (see 37:16–17).

1:10 TO UPROOT AND TEAR DOWN. Jeremiah's message contained elements of both judgment and restoration; however, because of his place in Judah's history, his message focused primarily on judgment and doom. The corrupt nation of Israel had to be torn down before God could plant and build anew.

1:11 BRANCH OF AN ALMOND TREE. The almond tree is the first tree to bud in spring. This vision implied two things: (1) God's spoken word through Jeremiah would be rapidly fulfilled, and (2) the people would recognize that God was alive and was guiding the course of history to fulfill his purposes (cf. Aaron's staff that produced almonds, Nu 17:1–10).

1:14 FROM THE NORTH DISASTER. This verse refers to the Babylonian campaigns against Judah and the siege of Jerusalem. A massive invasion would come from the north because God's people had forsaken him, offered sacrifices to other gods and worshiped what their own hands had made (v. 16).

in the entrance of the gates of
Jerusalem;
they will come against all her
surrounding walls
and against all the towns of
Judah.[a]
16 I will pronounce my judgments[b]
on my people
because of their wickedness[c] in
forsaking me,[d]
in burning incense to other gods[e]
and in worshiping[f] what their
hands have made.[g]

17 "Get yourself ready! Stand up and
say[h] to them whatever I command
you. Do not be terrified[i] by them, or
I will terrify you before them. 18 Today
I have made you[j] a fortified city, an
iron pillar and a bronze wall to stand
against the whole land—against the
kings of Judah, its officials, its priests
and the people of the land. 19 They will
fight against you but will not overcome[k] you, for I am with you[l] and
will rescue[m] you," declares the LORD.

Israel Forsakes God

2 The word[n] of the LORD came to
me: 2 "Go and proclaim in the hearing of Jerusalem:

" 'I remember the devotion of your
youth,[o]
how as a bride you loved me
and followed me through the
desert,[p]
through a land not sown.
3 Israel was holy[q] to the LORD,[r]
the firstfruits[s] of his harvest;
all who devoured[t] her were held
guilty,[u]
and disaster overtook them,' "
declares the LORD.

4 Hear the word of the LORD,
O house of Jacob,
all you clans of the house of
Israel.

5 This is what the LORD says:

"What fault did your fathers find in
me,
that they strayed so far from
me?
They followed worthless idols[v]
and became worthless[w]
themselves.
6 They did not ask, 'Where is the
LORD,
who brought us up out of
Egypt[x]
and led us through the barren
wilderness,
through a land of deserts[y] and
rifts,[z]
a land of drought and darkness,[c]
a land where no one travels[a]
and no one lives?'
7 I brought you into a fertile land
to eat its fruit and rich
produce.[b]
But you came and defiled my land
and made my inheritance
detestable.[c]
8 The priests did not ask,

c6 Or *and the shadow of death*

1:15 [a]Jer 4:16; 9:11; 10:22 **1:16** [b]Jer 4:12 [c]S Ge 6:5; Jer 44:5 [d]Jer 2:13; 17:13 [e]S Ex 20:3; Jer 7:9; 19:4; 44:3 [f]S Nu 25:3 [g]Ps 115:4-8; S 135:15 **1:17** [h]ver 7; Jer 7:27; 26:2,15; 42:4 [i]S Dt 31:6; S 2Ki 1:15 **1:18** [j]S Isa 50:7 **1:19** [k]S Ps 129:2 [l]S Ge 26:3; Isa 43:2; Jer 20:11 [m]S ver 8; S Pr 20:22; Ac 26:17 **2:1** [n]Isa 38:4; Eze 1:3; Mic 1:1 **2:2** [o]Ps 71:17; Isa 54:4; Jer 3:4; Eze 16:8-14,60; Hos 2:15; 11:1; Rev 2:4 [p]S Ex 13:21; S Dt 1:19 **2:3** [q]S Dt 7:6 [r]S Ex 19:6; S Dt 7:6 [s]Lev 23:9-14; Jas 1:18; Rev 14:4 [t]Isa 41:11; Jer 10:25; 30:16 [u]Jer 50:7 **2:5** [v]S Dt 32:21; S 1Sa 12:21; Ps 31:6 [w]2Ki 17:15 **2:6** [x]S Ex 6:6; Hos 13:4 [y]S Dt 1:19 [z]S Dt 32:10 [a]Jer 51:43 **2:7** [b]S Nu 13:27; Dt 8:7-9; 11:10-12 [c]Ps 106:34-39; Jer 3:9; 7:30; 16:18; Eze 11:21; 36:17

1:18 A FORTIFIED CITY, AN IRON PILLAR. Though Jeremiah was a sensitive young man, God put some spiritual iron into his backbone, enabling him to become the strongest, boldest and bravest of all the prophets. God can use us in ways far beyond our own natural tendencies and abilities.

1:19 THEY WILL FIGHT AGAINST YOU. Jeremiah was told that Judah's kings, officials, priests, and even the people would stand against him and the message he had been called to proclaim (v. 18). But the prophet was encouraged to speak out boldly and to stand firm in his convictions, for God promised to be with him; God assured him that his enemies would not overcome him. God always stands with his faithful servants who declare the truth to those who have departed from his word and are conformed to the world.

2:2 I REMEMBER THE DEVOTION. Early in Israel's history God's people trusted in the Lord with deep devotion. So intimate was their relationship that the nation was considered the Lord's wife (cf. 3:14; 31:32; Isa 54:5). But now the whole house of Israel had forsaken God and pursued other gods (vv. 4–5,25).

2:5 STRAYED SO FAR FROM ME. Israel had turned its back on the Lord, even though he had remained faithful to them. All believers are confronted with the same temptation of forgetting God's goodness and redemption while pursuing their own desires and the sinful pleasures of the world.

2:8 WHERE IS THE LORD? The priests were so insensitive to God's presence and power that they did not notice he had left them; they never wondered why the Lord's presence and blessing were missing in Israel. Today spiritual leaders should be greatly concerned when God's presence and the manifestations of the Holy Spirit are not evident in their congregations. A true servant of God will ask, "Where is the Lord?"

2:8 THOSE WHO DEAL WITH THE LAW. How sad it is that one can be a student or teacher of God's Word and yet not know the Lord as a personal Savior and an intimate friend (see article on BIBLE TRAINING FOR CHRISTIANS, p. 1894).

'Where is the LORD?'
Those who deal with the law did
not know me;[d]
the leaders[e] rebelled against
me.
The prophets prophesied by
Baal,[f]
following worthless idols.[g]

9"Therefore I bring charges[h]
against you again,"
declares the LORD.
"And I will bring charges
against your children's
children.
10Cross over to the coasts of
Kittim[d][i] and look,
send to Kedar[e][j] and observe
closely;
see if there has ever been
anything like this:
11Has a nation ever changed its
gods?
(Yet they are not gods[k] at all.)
But my people have exchanged
their[f] Glory[l]
for worthless idols.
12Be appalled at this, O heavens,
and shudder with great horror,"
declares the LORD.
13"My people have committed two
sins:
They have forsaken[m] me,
the spring of living water,[n]
and have dug their own cisterns,
broken cisterns that cannot hold
water.
14Is Israel a servant, a slave[o] by
birth?
Why then has he become
plunder?
15Lions[p] have roared;
they have growled at him.
They have laid waste[q] his land;
his towns are burned[r] and
deserted.[s]
16Also, the men of Memphis[g][t] and
Tahpanhes[u]
have shaved the crown of your
head.[h]
17Have you not brought this on
yourselves[v]
by forsaking[w] the LORD your
God
when he led you in the way?
18Now why go to Egypt[x]
to drink water from the
Shihor[i]?[y]
And why go to Assyria[z]
to drink water from the
River[j]?[a]
19Your wickedness will punish you;
your backsliding[b] will rebuke[c]
you.
Consider then and realize
how evil and bitter[d] it is for
you
when you forsake[e] the LORD your
God
and have no awe[f] of me,"
declares the Lord,
the LORD Almighty.

20"Long ago you broke off your
yoke[g]
and tore off your bonds;[h]

2:8 [d]S 1Sa 2:12; Jer 4:22 [e]Jer 3:15; 23:1; 25:34; 50:6 [f]S 1Ki 18:22 [g]ver 25; S Isa 40:19; S 56:10; Jer 5:19; 9:14; 16:19; 22:9 2:9 [h]Jer 25:31; Hos 4:1; Mic 6:2 2:10 [i]S Ge 10:4 [j]S Ge 25:13 2:11 [k]S Isa 37:19; Jer 16:20; Gal 4:8 [l]S 1Sa 4:21; Ro 1:23 2:13 [m]S Dt 31:16; S Isa 65:11 [n]S Isa 12:3; Jn 4:14 2:14 [o]Ex 4:22; Jer 31:9 2:15 [p]Jer 4:7; 50:17 [q]S Isa 1:7 [r]S 2Ki 25:9 [s]S Lev 26:43 2:16 [t]S Isa 19:13 [u]Jer 43:7-9 2:17 [v]Jer 4:18 [w]S Isa 1:28; Jer 17:13; 19:4 2:18 [x]S Isa 30:2 [y]S Jos 13:3 [z]S 2Ki 16:7; Hos 5:13; 7:11; 8:9 [a]S Isa 7:20 2:19 [b]Jer 3:11, 22; 7:24; 11:10; 14:7; Hos 14:4 [c]Isa 3:9; 59:12; Hos 5:5 [d]S Job 20:14; Am 8:10 [e]Jer 19:4 [f]S Ps 36:1 2:20 [g]S Lev 26:13 [h]Ps 2:3; Jer 5:5

[d] *10* That is, Cyprus and western coastlands
[e] *10* The home of Bedouin tribes in the Syro-Arabian desert
[f] *11* Masoretic Text; an ancient Hebrew scribal tradition *my*
[g] *16* Hebrew *Noph*
[h] *16* Or *have cracked your skull*
[i] *18* That is, a branch of the Nile
[j] *18* That is, the Euphrates

2:8 THE PROPHETS PROPHESIED BY BAAL. The prophets were expected to point the people back to God's word and to call for repentance (see article on THE PROPHET IN THE OLD TESTAMENT, p. 986); they were to speak only the word of God. Yet many of Judah's prophets were so backslidden that they prophesied by the demonic powers of idols (see article on THE NATURE OF IDOLATRY, p. 394). If pastors and leaders preach the humanistic ideas found in much contemporary psychology, philosophy and liberal theology rather than the word of God, they themselves become as guilty as the false prophets of Jeremiah's day.

2:13 COMMITTED TWO SINS. God's people under the old covenant committed two fundamental sins: (1) they forsook the Lord, the only One who could give them a truly abundant life (cf. 17:13; Ps 36:9; Jn 10:10), and (2) they sought life and pleasure in the idolatrous things of the world, things that had no real or lasting value. In doing so, they lost their purpose and destiny as a redeemed people (v. 11). True "living water" (cf. Jn 4:10–14; 7:37–39) is found only in a personal, devoted relationship with God through Christ.

2:19 YOUR WICKEDNESS WILL PUNISH YOU. Sin often brings its own punishment. When believers forsake the Lord, they lose God's protection and blessing and open themselves up to destructive temptations. Sin enslaves them, and many evil and bitter things may happen to them.

2:20–30 AS A PROSTITUTE. Jeremiah often used the analogy of an immoral, adulterous prostitute to illustrate the depth of Judah's unfaithfulness to God, her husband. Using a similar metaphor, the NT pictures the church as the bride of Christ (see 2Co 11:2; Eph 5:25–27; Rev 19:7). Believers should likewise be careful to remain faithful to their Lord and not to abandon him for other lovers (cf. v. 33).

you said, 'I will not serve
you!'[i]
Indeed, on every high hill[j]
and under every spreading
tree[k]
you lay down as a prostitute.[l]
21 I had planted[m] you like a choice
vine[n]
of sound and reliable stock.
How then did you turn against me
into a corrupt,[o] wild vine?
22 Although you wash[p] yourself with
soda[q]
and use an abundance of soap,
the stain of your guilt is still
before me,"
declares the Sovereign LORD.[r]
23 "How can you say, 'I am not
defiled;[s]
I have not run after the
Baals'?[t]
See how you behaved in the
valley;[u]
consider what you have done.
You are a swift she-camel
running[v] here and there,
24 a wild donkey[w] accustomed to the
desert,[x]
sniffing the wind in her
craving—
in her heat who can restrain
her?
Any males that pursue her need
not tire themselves;
at mating time they will find
her.
25 Do not run until your feet are bare
and your throat is dry.
But you said, 'It's no use![y]
I love foreign gods,[z]
and I must go after them.'[a]
26 "As a thief is disgraced[b] when he
is caught,
so the house of Israel is
disgraced—
they, their kings and their officials,
their priests[c] and their
prophets.[d]
27 They say to wood,[e] 'You are my
father,'
and to stone,[f] 'You gave me
birth.'
They have turned their backs[g] to
me
and not their faces;[h]
yet when they are in trouble,[i]
they say,
'Come and save[j] us!'
28 Where then are the gods[k] you
made for yourselves?
Let them come if they can save
you
when you are in trouble![l]
For you have as many gods
as you have towns,[m] O Judah.

29 "Why do you bring charges against
me?
You have all[n] rebelled against
me,"
declares the LORD.
30 "In vain I punished your people;
they did not respond to
correction.[o]
Your sword has devoured your
prophets[p]
like a ravening lion.
31 "You of this generation, consider
the word of the LORD:

"Have I been a desert to Israel
or a land of great darkness?[q]
Why do my people say, 'We are
free to roam;
we will come to you no more'?[r]
32 Does a maiden forget her jewelry,
a bride her wedding ornaments?
Yet my people have forgotten[s]
me,
days without number.
33 How skilled you are at pursuing[t]
love!
Even the worst of women can
learn from your ways.
34 On your clothes men find
the lifeblood[u] of the innocent
poor,
though you did not catch them
breaking in.[v]
Yet in spite of all this
35 you say, 'I am innocent;[w]
he is not angry with me.'
But I will pass judgment[x] on you
because you say, 'I have not
sinned.'[y]
36 Why do you go about so much,
changing[z] your ways?
You will be disappointed by
Egypt[a]
as you were by Assyria.
37 You will also leave that place
with your hands on your head,[b]

2:20 [i] S Job 21:14 [j] Isa 57:7; Jer 3:23; 17:2 [k] S Dt 12:2 [l] S Isa 1:21; Eze 16:15 **2:21** [m] S Ex 15:17 [n] S Ps 80:8 [o] S Isa 5:4 **2:22** [p] S Ps 51:2; La 1:8,17 [q] S Job 9:30 [r] Jer 17:1 **2:23** [s] S Pr 30:12 [t] ver 25; Jer 9:14; 23:27 [u] S 2Ki 23:10; Jer 7:31; 19:2; 31:40 [v] ver 33; Jer 31:22 **2:24** [w] S Ge 16:12; Jer 14:6 [x] S Job 39:6 **2:25** [y] S Isa 57:10 [z] Dt 32:16; Jer 3:13; 14:10 [a] S ver 8,S 23 **2:26** [b] Jer 48:27; La 1:7; Eze 16:54; 36:4 [c] Eze 22:26 [d] Jer 32:32; 44:17, 21 **2:27** [e] Jer 10:8 [f] Jer 3:9 [g] S 1Ki 14:9; S 2Ch 29:6; Ps 14:3; Eze 8:16 [h] Jer 18:17; 32:33; Eze 7:22 [i] Jdg 10:10; Isa 26:16 [j] Isa 37:20; Hos 5:15 **2:28** [k] S Isa 45:20 [l] S Dt 32:37; S Isa 40:19 [m] S 2Ki 17:29 **2:29** [n] Jer 5:1; 6:13; Da 9:11; Mic 3:11; 7:2 **2:30** [o] S Lev 26:23 [p] S Ne 9:26; S Jer 11:21; Ac 7:52; 1Th 2:15 **2:31** [q] Isa 45:19 [r] S Job 21:14 **2:32** [s] S Dt 32:18; S Isa 57:11 **2:33** [t] S ver 23 **2:34** [u] S 2Ki 21:16; S Pr 6:17 [v] S Ex 22:2 **2:35** [w] S Pr 30:12 [x] Isa 66:16; Jer 25:31; 39:7; 45:5; Eze 17:20; 20:35; Joel 3:2 [y] S 2Sa 12:13; 1Jn 1:8,10 **2:36** [z] Jer 31:22 [a] S Ps 108:12; S Isa 30:2,3,7; Jer 37:7 **2:37** [b] 2Sa 13:19

2:32 MY PEOPLE HAVE FORGOTTEN ME. Jeremiah reveals God's intense grief and sorrow because of his people's unfaithfulness. They had done the unthinkable in forgetting the One who had redeemed them from Egypt and cared for them in the desert.

for the LORD has rejected those you
trust;
you will not be helped[c] by
them.

3 "If a man divorces[d] his wife
and she leaves him and marries
another man,
should he return to her again?
Would not the land be
completely defiled?[e]
But you have lived as a prostitute
with many lovers[f]—
would you now return to me?"[g]
declares the LORD.
2"Look up to the barren heights[h]
and see.
Is there any place where you
have not been ravished?
By the roadside[i] you sat waiting
for lovers,
sat like a nomad**k** in the desert.
You have defiled the land[j]
with your prostitution[k] and
wickedness.
3Therefore the showers have been
withheld,[l]
and no spring rains[m] have
fallen.
Yet you have the brazen[n] look of
a prostitute;
you refuse to blush with
shame.[o]
4Have you not just called to me:
'My Father,[p] my friend from my
youth,[q]
5will you always be angry?[r]
Will your wrath continue
forever?'
This is how you talk,
but you do all the evil you can."

Unfaithful Israel

6During the reign of King Josiah,[s]
the LORD said to me, "Have you seen
what faithless[t] Israel has done? She
has gone up on every high hill and under every spreading tree[u] and has
committed adultery[v] there. **7**I thought
that after she had done all this she
would return to me but she did not, and
her unfaithful sister[w] Judah saw it.[x]
8I gave faithless Israel[y] her certificate of divorce[z] and sent her away because of all her adulteries. Yet I saw
that her unfaithful sister Judah had no
fear;[a] she also went out and committed adultery. **9**Because Israel's immorality mattered so little to her, she defiled the land[b] and committed
adultery[c] with stone[d] and wood.[e]
10In spite of all this, her unfaithful sister Judah did not return[f] to me with
all her heart, but only in pretense,[g]"
declares the LORD.[h]

11The LORD said to me, "Faithless Israel is more righteous[i] than unfaithful[j] Judah.[k] **12**Go, proclaim this message toward the north:[l]

" 'Return,[m] faithless[n] Israel,'
declares the LORD,
'I will frown on you no longer,
for I am merciful,'[o] declares the
LORD,
'I will not be angry[p] forever.
13Only acknowledge[q] your guilt—
you have rebelled against the
LORD your God,
you have scattered your favors to
foreign gods[r]
under every spreading tree,[s]
and have not obeyed[t] me,' "
declares the LORD.

14"Return,[u] faithless people," declares the LORD, "for I am your husband.[v] I will choose you—one from a
town and two from a clan—and bring
you to Zion. **15**Then I will give you
shepherds[w] after my own heart,[x]

2:37 [c]Jer 37:7 **3:1** [d]Dt 24:1-4 [e]S Ge 3:17 [f]S 2Ki 16:7; S Isa 1:21; Jer 2:20,25; 4:30; La 1:2; Eze 16:26, 29; Hos 2:5,12; 3:1 [g]Hos 2:7 **3:2** [h]ver 21 [i]Ge 38:14; Eze 16:25 [j]ver 9 [k]S Nu 15:39; S Isa 1:21 **3:3** [l]Lev 26:19; Jer 5:25; Am 4:7 [m]S Dt 11:14; Jer 14:4; Joel 1:10 [n]Eze 3:7; 16:30 [o]Jer 6:15; 8:12; Zep 2:1; 3:5 **3:4** [p]ver 19; S Dt 32:6; S Ps 89:26; Isa 63:16; 64:8; Jer 31:9 [q]S Jer 2:2 **3:5** [r]S Ps 103:9; S Isa 54:9 **3:6** [s]S 1Ch 3:14 [t]ver 12,22; S Isa 24:16; Jer 31:22; 49:4 [u]S Dt 12:2; Jer 17:2; Eze 20:28; Hos 4:13 [v]S Lev 17:7; Jer 2:20 **3:7** [w]Eze 16:46; 23:2,11 [x]Am 4:8 **3:8** [y]Jer 11:10 [z]S Dt 4:27; S 24:1 [a]Eze 16:47; 23:11 **3:9** [b]ver 2 [c]S Lev 17:7; S Isa 1:21 [d]S Isa 57:6 [e]Jer 2:27 **3:10** [f]Isa 31:6; Am 4:9; Hag 2:17 [g]Jer 12:2; Eze 33:31 [h]S 2Ki 17:19 **3:11** [i]Eze 16:52; 23:11 [j]ver 7 [k]S Jer 2:19 **3:12** [l]2Ki 17:3-6 [m]ver 14; S Dt 4:30; Jer 31:21,22; Eze 14:6; 33:11; Hos 14:1 [n]S ver 6 [o]S 1Ki 3:26; S Ps 6:2 [p]S Ps 103:9; S Isa 54:9 **3:13** [q]Dt 30:1-3; Jer 14:20; 1Jn 1:9 [r]S Jer 2:25 [s]S Dt 12:2 [t]ver 25; Jer 22:21 **3:14** [u]S ver 12; S Job 22:23; Jer 4:1 [v]S Isa 54:5 **3:15** [w]S Isa 31:4 [x]Ac 13:22

k *2* Or *an Arab*

3:1–5 LIVED AS A PROSTITUTE. Judah's turning to other gods is equivalent to spiritual adultery against the Lord; this unfaithfulness often came to expression in immorality in the natural realm as the people became involved in cult prostitution. In spite of God's word to them through his servant Jeremiah, the people continued in their evil ways. The NT often warns against idolatry and immorality, lest those who live under the new covenant repeat the mistakes of those who lived under the old (cf. 1Co 6:9–11).

3:6 WHAT FAITHLESS ISRAEL HAS DONE. Israel, the northern kingdom, had been unfaithful to God; as a result, they had been carried away into captivity by Assyria in 722–721 B.C. Judah, the southern kingdom, should have learned from her sister's tragic experience, but did not. She too gave herself to spiritual prostitution and wickedness.

3:12 THIS MESSAGE TOWARD THE NORTH. The remnant of Israel living in Assyrian captivity were told that they could still repent. God remains merciful and does not want to punish forever. Jeremiah went on to prophesy that a remnant would someday return to God and to the promised land (v. 14).

who will lead you with knowledge and
understanding. 16In those days, when
your numbers have increased greatly
in the land," declares the LORD, "men
will no longer say, 'The ark[y] of the
covenant of the LORD.' It will never enter their minds or be remembered;[z] it
will not be missed, nor will another one
be made. 17At that time they will call
Jerusalem The Throne[a] of the LORD,
and all nations[b] will gather in Jerusalem to honor[c] the name of the LORD.
No longer will they follow the stubbornness of their evil hearts.[d] 18In
those days the house of Judah will join
the house of Israel,[e] and together[f]
they will come from a northern[g] land
to the land[h] I gave your forefathers as
an inheritance.

19"I myself said,

" 'How gladly would I treat you
like sons
and give you a desirable land,[i]
the most beautiful inheritance[j]
of any nation.
I thought you would call me
'Father'[k]
and not turn away from
following me.
20But like a woman unfaithful to her
husband,
so you have been unfaithful[l] to
me, O house of Israel,"
declares the LORD.

21A cry is heard on the barren
heights,[m]
the weeping[n] and pleading of
the people of Israel,
because they have perverted their
ways
and have forgotten[o] the LORD
their God.

22"Return,[p] faithless people;
I will cure[q] you of
backsliding."[r]

"Yes, we will come to you,
for you are the LORD our God.
23Surely the ⌊idolatrous⌋ commotion
on the hills[s]
and mountains is a deception;
surely in the LORD our God
is the salvation[t] of Israel.
24From our youth shameful[u] gods
have consumed
the fruits of our fathers' labor—
their flocks and herds,
their sons and daughters.
25Let us lie down in our shame,[v]
and let our disgrace cover us.
We have sinned[w] against the LORD
our God,
both we and our fathers;[x]
from our youth[y] till this day
we have not obeyed[z] the LORD
our God."

4

1"If you will return[a], O Israel,
return to me,"
declares the LORD.
"If you put your detestable idols[b]
out of my sight
and no longer go astray,
2and if in a truthful, just and
righteous way
you swear,[c] 'As surely as the
LORD lives,'[d]
then the nations will be blessed[e]
by him
and in him they will glory.[f]"

3This is what the LORD says to the
men of Judah and to Jerusalem:

"Break up your unplowed ground[g]
and do not sow among thorns.[h]
4Circumcise yourselves to the LORD,
circumcise your hearts,[i]

3:16 [y] S Nu 3:31; S 1Ch 15:25 [z] S Isa 65:17
3:17 [a] S Ps 47:8; Jer 17:12; 33:16; Eze 1:26; 43:7; 48:35 [b] S Isa 2:3; Mic 4:1 [c] S Ps 22:23; Jer 13:11; 33:9 [d] Ps 81:12; Jer 7:24; 9:14; 11:8; 13:10; 16:12; 18:12
3:18 [e] Jer 30:3; Eze 37:19 [f] S Isa 11:13; Jer 50:4 [g] Jer 16:15; 31:8 [h] Dt 31:7; S Isa 14:1; Eze 11:17; 37:22; Am 9:15
3:19 [i] S Dt 8:7 [j] Ps 106:24; Eze 20:6 [k] S ver 4; S Ex 4:22; S 2Sa 7:14
3:20 [l] S Isa 24:16
3:21 [m] ver 2 [n] Jer 31:18 [o] S Isa 57:11
3:22 [p] S ver 12; S Job 22:23 [q] S Isa 30:26; 57:18; Jer 33:6; Hos 6:1 [r] S Jer 2:19
3:23 [s] S Jer 2:20 [t] Ps 3:8; Jer 17:14
3:24 [u] Jer 11:13; Hos 9:10
3:25 [v] S Ezr 9:6; Jer 31:19; Da 9:7 [w] S Jdg 10:10; S 1Ki 8:47 [x] Jer 14:20 [y] S Ps 25:7; S Jer 22:21 [z] S ver 13; Eze 2:3
4:1 [a] S Dt 4:30; S 2Ki 17:13; S Hos 12:6 [b] S 2Ki 21:4; Jer 16:18; 35:15; Eze 8:5
4:2 [c] Dt 10:20; S Isa 19:18; 65:16 [d] S Nu 14:21; Jer 5:2; 12:16; 44:26; Hos 4:15 [e] S Ge 12:2; Gal 3:8 [f] Jer 9:24
4:3 [g] Hos 10:12 [h] Mk 4:18
4:4 [i] S Lev 26:41

3:15 SHEPHERDS AFTER MY OWN HEART. Jeremiah pictures a day when Israel would have pastors who lived according to God's word and imparted life through their understanding of it. Because they knew God's heart, they would know how to shepherd God's people. That type of knowledge in leaders is essential for the spiritual vitality and ethical purity of God's people (see article on MORAL QUALIFICATIONS FOR OVERSEERS, p. 1882).

3:16–19 IN THOSE DAYS. Jeremiah prophesies here of the Messianic age when Christ will reign over his people. The ark, which had earlier symbolized God's presence, would no longer be needed, for the Messiah would be visibly present. Jerusalem would be called God's Throne, and all nations would worship him. (v. 17).

4:3–31 THIS IS WHAT THE LORD SAYS. Ch. 4 describes the disaster that would soon come upon God's people because of their sin and apostasy; they would learn how evil and bitter it was to forsake the Lord (cf. 2:19).

4:4 CIRCUMCISE YOUR HEARTS. To avoid the terrible disaster coming upon them, the people of Judah had to undergo a complete moral renewal by committing themselves to truth, justice and righteousness. They must be open to the conviction of the Spirit, repent of their sins and break up the hardened soil of their hearts (v. 3). The evil in their hearts must be removed as surely as the foreskin was removed in physical circumcision.

you men of Judah and people of
Jerusalem,
or my wrath[j] will break out and
burn like fire[k]
because of the evil[l] you have
done—
burn with no one to quench[m] it.

Disaster From the North

5"Announce in Judah and proclaim[n]
in Jerusalem and say:
'Sound the trumpet[o] throughout
the land!'
Cry aloud and say:
'Gather together!
Let us flee to the fortified
cities!'[p]
6Raise the signal[q] to go to Zion!
Flee for safety without delay!
For I am bringing disaster[r] from
the north,[s]
even terrible destruction."

7A lion[t] has come out of his lair;[u]
a destroyer[v] of nations has set
out.
He has left his place
to lay waste[w] your land.
Your towns will lie in ruins[x]
without inhabitant.
8So put on sackcloth,[y]
lament[z] and wail,
for the fierce anger[a] of the LORD
has not turned away from us.

9"In that day," declares the LORD,
"the king and the officials will
lose heart,[b]
the priests will be horrified,
and the prophets will be
appalled."[c]

10Then I said, "Ah, Sovereign LORD,
how completely you have deceived[d]
this people and Jerusalem by saying,
'You will have peace,'[e] when the
sword is at our throats."
11At that time this people and Jerusalem will be told, "A scorching wind[f]
from the barren heights in the desert
blows toward my people, but not to
winnow or cleanse; 12a wind[g] too
strong for that comes from me.[1] Now
I pronounce my judgments[h] against
them."

13Look! He advances like the
clouds,[i]
his chariots[j] come like a
whirlwind,[k]
his horses[l] are swifter than
eagles.[m]
Woe to us! We are ruined![n]
14O Jerusalem, wash[o] the evil from
your heart and be saved.[p]
How long[q] will you harbor
wicked thoughts?
15A voice is announcing from Dan,[r]
proclaiming disaster from the
hills of Ephraim.[s]
16"Tell this to the nations,
proclaim it to Jerusalem:
'A besieging army is coming from
a distant land,[t]
raising a war cry[u] against the
cities of Judah.[v]
17They surround[w] her like men
guarding a field,
because she has rebelled[x]
against me,'"
declares the LORD.
18"Your own conduct and actions[y]
have brought this upon you.[z]
This is your punishment.
How bitter[a] it is!
How it pierces to the heart!"

19Oh, my anguish, my anguish![b]
I writhe in pain.[c]
Oh, the agony of my heart!
My heart pounds[d] within me,
I cannot keep silent.[e]
For I have heard the sound of the
trumpet;[f]

4:4 [j]Zep 1:18; 2:2 [k]S Job 41:21 [l]S Ex 32:22 [m]Isa 1:31; Am 5:6 **4:5** [n]Jer 5:20; 11:2,6 [o]S ver 21; S Nu 10:2,7; S Job 39:24 [p]S Jos 10:20 **4:6** [q]ver 21; Ps 74:4; S Isa 11:10; 31:9; Jer 50:2 [r]Jer 11:11; 18:11 [s]S Isa 14:31; Jer 50:3 **4:7** [t]S 2Ki 24:1; S Jer 2:15 [u]Jer 25:38; Hos 5:14; 13:7; Na 2:12 [v]Jer 6:26; 15:8; 22:7; 48:8; 51:1,53; Eze 21:31; 25:7 [w]S Isa 1:7; Eze 12:20 [x]ver 29; S Lev 26:31; S Isa 6:11 **4:8** [y]1Ki 21:27; S Isa 3:24; Jer 6:26; Eze 7:18; Joel 1:8 [z]Jer 7:29; 9:20; Am 5:1 [a]S Isa 10:4; S Jer 30:24 **4:9** [b]S 1Sa 17:32 [c]S Isa 29:9 **4:10** [d]S Ex 5:23; 2Th 2:11 [e]Isa 30:10; Jer 6:14; 8:11; 14:13; 23:17; Eze 13:10; Mic 3:5; 1Th 5:3 **4:11** [f]S Ge 41:6; S Lev 26:33; S Job 1:19 **4:12** [g]S Isa 64:6 [h]Jer 1:16 **4:13** [i]S 2Sa 22:10; Isa 19:1 [j]Isa 66:15; Eze 26:10; Na 2:4 [k]S 2Ki 2:1 [l]Hab 3:8 [m]S Dt 28:49; Hab 1:8 [n]ver 20, 27; Isa 6:11; 24:3; Jer 7:34; 9:11,19; 12:11; 25:11; 44:6; Mic 2:4 **4:14** [o]S Ru 3:3; S Ps 51:2; Jas 4:8 [p]Isa 45:22 [q]S Ps 6:3 **4:15** [r]S Ge 30:6 [s]Jer 31:6 **4:16** [t]S Dt 28:49 [u]ver 19; Eze 21:22 [v]S Jer 1:15 **4:17** [w]S 2Ki 25:1, 4 [x]S 1Sa 12:15; Jer 5:23

4:18 [y]Ps 107:17; S Isa 1:28; Jer 5:25 [z]Jer 2:17 [a]Jer 2:19 **4:19** [b]Isa 22:4; Jer 6:24; 9:10; La 1:20 [c]S Job 6:10; S 14:22; Jer 10:19 [d]S Job 37:1; Jer 23:9 [e]S Job 4:2; Jer 20:9 [f]S ver 21; S Nu 10:2; S Job 39:24

[1]12 Or *comes at my command*

4:6 DISASTER FROM THE NORTH, EVEN TERRIBLE DESTRUCTION. In his anger against his people, God would cause the Babylonians to invade Judah and allow them to devastate the land (see 1:14, note).

4:10 YOU HAVE DECEIVED THIS PEOPLE. Many of Judah's prophets had spoken deceptively to God's people by giving them false hopes of peace and security, while ignoring their sinful ways (cf. 14:13–16; 23:17; 1Ki 22:20–23). God had permitted the people to believe a lie because they had no love for the truth and instead took pleasure in sin (cf. 2Th 2:9–12).

4:19–22 I WRITHE IN PAIN. Jeremiah experienced God's agony for Judah and expressed the pain and sorrow that the Lord felt at the coming desolation. Likewise, believers should feel sorrow at the thought of men and women being taken captive and destroyed by sin and Satan. The terrible future of the lost should cause us to lament as Jesus did when he expressed intense grief over the lost spiritual condition of Jerusalem (Lk 13:34).

I have heard the battle cry.[g]
20Disaster follows disaster;[h]
the whole land lies in ruins.[i]
In an instant my tents[j] are
destroyed,
my shelter in a moment.
21How long must I see the battle
standard[k]
and hear the sound of the
trumpet?[l]

22"My people are fools;[m]
they do not know me.[n]
They are senseless children;
they have no understanding.[o]
They are skilled in doing evil;[p]
they know not how to do
good."[q]

23I looked at the earth,
and it was formless and
empty;[r]
and at the heavens,
and their light[s] was gone.
24I looked at the mountains,
and they were quaking;[t]
all the hills were swaying.
25I looked, and there were no
people;
every bird in the sky had flown
away.[u]
26I looked, and the fruitful land was
a desert;[v]
all its towns lay in ruins[w]
before the LORD, before his fierce
anger.[x]

27This is what the LORD says:

"The whole land will be ruined,[y]
though I will not destroy[z] it
completely.
28Therefore the earth will mourn[a]
and the heavens above grow
dark,[b]
because I have spoken and will not
relent,[c]
I have decided and will not turn
back.[d]"

29At the sound of horsemen and
archers[e]
every town takes to flight.[f]
Some go into the thickets;
some climb up among the
rocks.[g]

4:19 [g]S ver 16; Nu 10:9; Jer 49:2; Zep 1:16
4:20 [h]S Dt 31:17 [i]S ver 13 [j]S Nu 24:5; Jer 10:20; La 2:4
4:21 [k]S ver 6; S Nu 2:2; S Isa 18:3 [l]ver 5, 19; S Jos 6:20; Jer 6:1; Hos 5:8; Am 3:6; Zep 1:16
4:22 [m]Jer 5:21; 10:8 [n]S Isa 1:3; 27:11; Jer 2:8; 8:7; Hos 5:4; 6:6 [o]S Ps 14:4; S 53:2 [p]Jer 13:23; S 1Co 14:20 [q]S Ps 36:3
4:23 [r]S Ge 1:2 [s]ver 28; S Job 9:7; 30:26; S Isa 5:30; 59:9; La 3:2
4:24 [t]S Ex 19:18; S Job 9:6
4:25 [u]Jer 7:20; 9:10; 12:4; Hos 4:3; Zep 1:3
4:26 [v]S Ge 13:10; Jer 12:4; 23:10 [w]S Isa 6:11 [x]Jer 12:13; 25:38
4:27 [y]S ver 13 [z]S Lev 26:44; Jer 5:10,18; 12:12; 30:11; 46:28; Eze 20:17; Am 9:8
4:28 [a]Jer 12:4, 11; 14:2; Hos 4:3 [b]S ver 23 [c]S Nu 23:19 [d]ver 8; Jer 23:20; 30:24
4:29 [e]S ver 13; Jer 6:23; 8:16 [f]2Ki 25:4 [g]S Ex 33:22; S 1Sa 26:20
4:30 [h]S ver 7; S Isa 6:12 [i]Isa 10:3-4 [j]Eze 16:11; 23:40 [k]S 2Ki 9:30 [l]Job 19:14; La 1:2; Eze 23:9,22 [m]S Ps 35:4
4:31 [n]S Ge 3:16; Jer 6:24; 13:21; 22:23; 30:6; Mic 4:10 [o]S Ps 9:14 [p]Isa 42:14 [q]Isa 1:15; La 1:17 [r]S Dt 32:25; La 2:21
5:1 [s]2Ch 16:9; Eze 22:30 [t]Ps 45:10 [u]Ge 18:32; S Jer 2:29 [v]ver 31; Jer 14:14; Eze 13:6 [w]S Ge 18:24
5:2 [x]S Jer 4:2 [y]S Lev 19:12
5:3 [z]2Ch 16:9 [a]S Isa 9:13 [b]S Lev 26:23 [c]Jer 7:26; 19:15; Eze 3:8-9; 36:26; Zec 7:12 [d]S 2Ch 28:22; S Isa 1:5; Eze 2:4-5; Am 4:6; Zec 7:11
5:4 [e]S ver 21; S Jer 4:22 [f]S Pr 10:21; S Isa 1:3

All the towns are deserted;[h]
no one lives in them.

30What are you doing,[i]
O devastated one?
Why dress yourself in scarlet
and put on jewels[j] of gold?
Why shade your eyes with paint?[k]
You adorn yourself in vain.
Your lovers[l] despise you;
they seek your life.[m]

31I hear a cry as of a woman in
labor,[n]
a groan as of one bearing her
first child—
the cry of the Daughter of Zion[o]
gasping for breath,[p]
stretching out her hands[q] and
saying,
"Alas! I am fainting;
my life is given over to
murderers."[r]

Not One Is Upright

5 "Go up and down[s] the streets
of Jerusalem,
look around and consider,[t]
search through her squares.
If you can find but one person[u]
who deals honestly[v] and seeks
the truth,
I will forgive[w] this city.
2Although they say, 'As surely as
the LORD lives,'[x]
still they are swearing
falsely.[y]"

3O LORD, do not your eyes[z] look for
truth?
You struck[a] them, but they felt
no pain;
you crushed them, but they
refused correction.[b]
They made their faces harder than
stone[c]
and refused to repent.[d]
4I thought, "These are only the
poor;
they are foolish,[e]
for they do not know[f] the way of
the LORD,

4:23 THE EARTH . . . FORMLESS AND EMPTY. Jeremiah's vision of the utter devastation coming upon his people made it appear as if the whole universe had been laid waste and changed into the same formlessness it had in the beginning before God began to shape the world (cf. Ge 1:2).

5:1–9 SEEKS THE TRUTH. Judah's corruption had reached such a degree that few could be found who loved God's truth and righteousness. The nation was guilty; therefore, God determined to bring judgment on his faithless people.

the requirements of their God.
5So I will go to the leaders[g]
and speak to them;
surely they know the way of the LORD,
the requirements of their God."
But with one accord they too had broken off the yoke
and torn off the bonds.[h]
6Therefore a lion from the forest[i]
will attack them,
a wolf from the desert will ravage[j] them,
a leopard[k] will lie in wait near their towns
to tear to pieces any who venture out,
for their rebellion is great
and their backslidings many.[l]

7"Why should I forgive you?
Your children have forsaken me
and sworn[m] by gods that are not gods.[n]
I supplied all their needs,
yet they committed adultery[o]
and thronged to the houses of prostitutes.[p]
8They are well-fed, lusty stallions,
each neighing for another man's wife.[q]
9Should I not punish them for this?"[r]
declares the LORD.
"Should I not avenge[s] myself
on such a nation as this?

10"Go through her vineyards and ravage them,
but do not destroy them completely.[t]
Strip off her branches,
for these people do not belong to the LORD.
11The house of Israel and the house of Judah
have been utterly unfaithful[u] to me,"
declares the LORD.

12They have lied[v] about the LORD;
they said, "He will do nothing!
No harm will come to us;[w]
we will never see sword or famine.[x]
13The prophets[y] are but wind[z]
and the word is not in them;
so let what they say be done to them."

14Therefore this is what the LORD God Almighty says:

"Because the people have spoken these words,
I will make my words in your mouth[a] a fire[b]
and these people the wood it consumes.[c]
15O house of Israel," declares the LORD,
"I am bringing a distant nation[d] against you—
an ancient and enduring nation,
a people whose language[e] you do not know,
whose speech you do not understand.
16Their quivers[f] are like an open grave;
all of them are mighty warriors.
17They will devour[g h] your harvests and food,
devour[i j] your sons and daughters;
they will devour[k] your flocks and herds,
devour your vines and fig trees.[l]
With the sword[m] they will destroy
the fortified cities[n] in which you trust.[o]

18"Yet even in those days," declares
the LORD, "I will not destroy[p] you completely. 19And when the people ask,[q]
'Why has the LORD our God done all this
to us?' you will tell them, 'As you have
forsaken me and served foreign gods[r]
in your own land, so now you will serve
foreigners[s] in a land not your own.'

20"Announce this to the house of Jacob
and proclaim[t] it in Judah:
21Hear this, you foolish and senseless people,[u]

5:5 [g] Mic 3:1,9 [h] S Jer 2:20 **5:6** [i] S Ps 17:12 [j] S Lev 26:22 [k] Hos 13:7 [l] Jer 14:7; 30:14 **5:7** [m] S Jos 23:7 [n] Dt 32:21; Jer 2:11; 16:20; Gal 4:8 [o] S Nu 25:1 [p] Jer 13:27 **5:8** [q] Jer 29:23; Eze 22:11; 33:26 **5:9** [r] ver 29; Jer 9:9 [s] S Isa 57:6 **5:10** [t] S Jer 4:27; Am 9:8 **5:11** [u] S 1Ki 19:10; S Ps 73:27; S Isa 24:16 **5:12** [v] Isa 28:15 [w] Jer 23:17 [x] Jer 14:13; 27:8 **5:13** [y] Jer 14:15 [z] S 2Ch 36:16; S Job 6:26 **5:14** [a] Hos 6:5 [b] S Ps 39:3; Jer 23:29 [c] S Isa 1:31 **5:15** [d] S Dt 28:49; S 2Ki 24:2 [e] S Ge 11:7; S Isa 28:11 **5:16** [f] S Job 39:23 **5:17** [g] S Isa 1:7; Jer 8:16; 30:16 [h] Lev 26:16 [i] Jer 50:7,17 [j] Dt 28:32 [k] Dt 28:31 [l] S Nu 16:14; Jer 8:13; Hos 2:12 [m] S Lev 26:25 [n] S Jos 10:20 [o] Dt 28:33 **5:18** [p] S Jer 4:27 **5:19** [q] S Dt 4:28; S 1Ki 9:9 [r] S Jer 2:8; 15:14; 16:13; 17:4 [s] Dt 28:48 **5:20** [t] S Jer 4:5 **5:21** [u] ver 4; S Dt 32:6; S Jer 4:22; Hab 2:18

5:10 DO NOT BELONG TO THE LORD. The people professed to be the Lord's (cf. 3:4), but God testified that they were not his people. Likewise, anyone who claims to be a born-again believer, yet is given over to the sins described in this chapter (e.g., lying, dishonesty, adultery), does not belong to the Lord; like many in Judah, such people have been deceived into believing that their unfaithfulness to God will not bring his ultimate condemnation.

5:12 NO HARM WILL COME TO US. The temptation is always strong to believe that God will overlook our sins and not send the judgment about which his Word warns. Many of God's people tend to claim the promises but doubt the warnings.

who have eyes[v] but do not
see,
who have ears but do not
hear:[w]
22Should you not fear[x] me?"
declares the LORD.
"Should you not tremble[y] in my
presence?
I made the sand a boundary for
the sea,[z]
an everlasting barrier it cannot
cross.
The waves may roll, but they
cannot prevail;
they may roar,[a] but they cannot
cross it.
23But these people have stubborn
and rebellious[b] hearts;
they have turned aside[c] and
gone away.
24They do not say to themselves,
'Let us fear[d] the LORD our God,
who gives autumn and spring
rains[e] in season,
who assures us of the regular
weeks of harvest.'[f]
25Your wrongdoings have kept these
away;
your sins have deprived you of
good.[g]
26"Among my people are wicked[h]
men
who lie in wait[i] like men who
snare birds
and like those who set traps[j]
to catch men.
27Like cages full of birds,
their houses are full of deceit;[k]
they have become rich[l] and
powerful
28 and have grown fat[m] and sleek.
Their evil deeds have no limit;
they do not plead the case of
the fatherless[n] to win it,
they do not defend the rights of
the poor.[o]
29Should I not punish them for
this?"
declares the LORD.
"Should I not avenge[p] myself
on such a nation as this?
30"A horrible[q] and shocking thing
has happened in the land:
31The prophets prophesy lies,[r]
the priests[s] rule by their own
authority,
and my people love it this way.
But what will you do in the
end?[t]

Jerusalem Under Siege

6 "Flee for safety, people of
Benjamin!
Flee from Jerusalem!
Sound the trumpet[u] in Tekoa![v]
Raise the signal over Beth
Hakkerem![w]
For disaster looms out of the
north,[x]
even terrible destruction.
2I will destroy the Daughter of
Zion,[y]
so beautiful and delicate.[z]
3Shepherds[a] with their flocks will
come against her;
they will pitch their tents
around[b] her,
each tending his own portion."
4"Prepare for battle against her!
Arise, let us attack at noon![c]
But, alas, the daylight is fading,
and the shadows of evening
grow long.
5So arise, let us attack at night
and destroy her fortresses!"

6This is what the LORD Almighty
says:

5:21 [v]Isa 6:10; Eze 12:2 [w]S Dt 29:4; S Isa 42:20; S Mt 13:15; Mk 8:18 5:22 [x]S Dt 28:58 [y]S Job 4:14; S Isa 64:2 [z]S Ge 1:9 [a]S Ps 46:3 5:23 [b]S Dt 21:18 [c]Ps 14:3 5:24 [d]Dt 6:24 [e]S Lev 26:4; S 2Sa 1:21; Jas 5:7 [f]S Ge 8:22; Ac 14:17 5:25 [g]Ps 84:11 5:26 [h]S Mt 7:15 [i]S Ps 10:8 [j]Ecc 9:12; Jer 9:8; Hos 5:1; Mic 7:2 5:27 [k]Jer 8:5; 9:6 [l]Jer 12:1 5:28 [m]S Dt 32:15 [n]Zec 7:10 [o]Ex 22:21-24; S Ps 82:3; S Isa 1:23; Jer 7:6; Eze 16:49; Am 5:12 5:29 [p]S Isa 57:6 5:30 [q]ver 30-31; Jer 18:13; 23:14; Hos 6:10 5:31 [r]S ver 1; Mic 2:11 [s]La 4:13 [t]Hos 9:5 6:1 [u]S Nu 10:7; S Jer 4:21 [v]2Ch 11:6; Am 1:1 [w]Ne 3:14 [x]S Jer 4:6 6:2 [y]S Ps 9:14 [z]La 4:5 6:3 [a]Jer 12:10 [b]S 2Ki 25:4; Lk 19:43 6:4 [c]Jer 15:8; 22:7

5:22 SHOULD YOU NOT FEAR ME? The people did not revere and obey God because they had no fear of him and did not tremble at the reality of his presence (see article on THE FEAR OF THE LORD, p. 260).

5:31 THE PROPHETS PROPHESY LIES. Those who had been entrusted with the spiritual well-being of the nation were guilty of treachery against their God. (1) The prophets had rejected God's word and prophesied only good things to come. They made few moral demands on the people, and the people were happy to have it that way. (2) The priests governed the people by their own ideas rather than by God's word. The prophets and priests thus lulled the nation into a false security. Jeremiah proclaimed that there was no real security before God apart from sincere repentance and a commitment to obey his word.

6:1–30 FLEE FROM JERUSALEM! This chapter describes the great destruction soon to be inflicted on Jerusalem and its impenitent people; this word was fulfilled in Jeremiah's lifetime. Jeremiah both warned Judah and Jerusalem and called them to repentance. If the people would only turn to God and renew their covenant with him, they would have an opportunity to escape disaster. Jeremiah's constant plea was rebuffed scornfully; thus judgment was imminent.

6:3 SHEPHERDS WITH THEIR FLOCKS. The Babylonian commanders are compared to shepherds and their troops to flocks who would devastate the land.

"Cut down the trees[d]
and build siege ramps[e] against
Jerusalem.
This city must be punished;
it is filled with oppression.[f]
7As a well pours out its water,
so she pours out her
wickedness.
Violence[g] and destruction[h]
resound in her;
her sickness and wounds are
ever before me.
8Take warning, O Jerusalem,
or I will turn away[i] from you
and make your land desolate
so no one can live in it."

9This is what the LORD Almighty
says:

"Let them glean the remnant[j] of
Israel
as thoroughly as a vine;
pass your hand over the branches
again,
like one gathering grapes."

10To whom can I speak and give
warning?
Who will listen[k] to me?
Their ears are closed[m][l]
so they cannot hear.[m]
The word[n] of the LORD is offensive
to them;
they find no pleasure in it.
11But I am full of the wrath[o] of the
LORD,
and I cannot hold it in.[p]

"Pour it out on the children in the
street
and on the young men[q]
gathered together;
both husband and wife will be
caught in it,
and the old, those weighed down
with years.[r]
12Their houses will be turned over to
others,[s]
together with their fields and
their wives,[t]
when I stretch out my hand[u]
against those who live in the
land,"
declares the LORD.
13"From the least to the greatest,
all[v] are greedy for gain;[w]
prophets and priests alike,
all practice deceit.[x]
14They dress the wound of my
people
as though it were not serious.
'Peace, peace,' they say,
when there is no peace.[y]
15Are they ashamed of their
loathsome conduct?
No, they have no shame at all;
they do not even know how to
blush.[z]
So they will fall among the fallen;
they will be brought down when
I punish[a] them,"
says the LORD.

16This is what the LORD says:

"Stand at the crossroads and look;
ask for the ancient paths,[b]
ask where the good way[c] is, and
walk in it,
and you will find rest[d] for your
souls.
But you said, 'We will not walk
in it.'
17I appointed watchmen[e] over you
and said,
'Listen to the sound of the
trumpet!'[f]
But you said, 'We will not
listen.'[g]
18Therefore hear, O nations;
observe, O witnesses,
what will happen to them.
19Hear, O earth:[h]
I am bringing disaster[i] on this
people,
the fruit of their schemes,[j]
because they have not listened to
my words[k]
and have rejected my law.[l]
20What do I care about incense from
Sheba[m]

6:6 [d]Dt 20:19-20 [e]S 2Sa 20:15; Jer 32:24; 52:4; Eze 26:8 [f]S Dt 28:33; Jer 25:38; Zep 3:1
6:7 [g]S Ps 55:9; S Isa 58:4 [h]Jer 20:8
6:8 [i]Eze 23:18
6:9 [j]S Ge 45:7
6:10 [k]Jer 7:13, 24; 35:15 [l]Jer 4:4; Ac 7:51 [m]S Isa 42:20 [n]Jer 15:10,15; 20:8
6:11 [o]Jer 7:20; 15:17 [p]Job 32:20; Jer 20:9 [q]S 2Ch 36:17; S Isa 40:30 [r]La 2:21
6:12 [s]S Dt 28:30; Mic 2:4 [t]1Ki 11:4; Jer 8:10; 29:23; 38:22; 43:6; 44:9, 15 [u]Isa 5:25; Jer 21:5; 32:21; Eze 6:14; 35:3; Zep 1:4
6:13 [v]S Jer 2:29 [w]S Isa 56:11 [x]La 4:13
6:14 [y]S Isa 30:10; S Jer 4:10
6:15 [z]Jer 3:3; 8:10-12; Mic 3:7; Zec 13:4 [a]2Ch 25:16; Jer 27:15
6:16 [b]Jer 18:15 [c]S 1Ki 8:36; S Ps 119:3 [d]S Jos 1:13; S Isa 11:10; Mt 11:29
6:17 [e]S Isa 52:8 [f]S Ex 20:18 [g]Jer 11:7-8; Eze 33:4; Zec 1:4
6:19 [h]S Dt 4:26; Jer 22:29; Mic 1:2 [i]S Jos 23:15; Jer 11:11; 19:3 [j]Pr 1:31 [k]Jer 29:19 [l]Jer 8:9; Eze 20:13; Am 2:4
6:20 [m]S Ge 10:7

[m]10 Hebrew *uncircumcised*

6:14 WHEN THERE IS NO PEACE. The false prophets were preaching a message of false security; instead of warning the people of coming judgment and of the need to repent, they told them there was nothing to fear.

6:16 ASK FOR THE ANCIENT PATHS. God's people had strayed from the way of righteousness into idolatry and wickedness, and he called them back to the former paths of the covenant and the law of Moses. Likewise, the church must always examine itself to see if it has strayed from the path of the Spirit's power and the righteousness proclaimed in the NT. God's full blessing will be enjoyed only by those who ask, seek and knock for his best (cf. Lk 11:5–13) and who are committed to live according to the pattern set forth in the NT (see Ac 7:44, note).

or sweet calamus[n] from a
distant land?
Your burnt offerings are not
acceptable;[o]
your sacrifices[p] do not please
me."[q]

21Therefore this is what the LORD
says:

"I will put obstacles before this
people.
Fathers and sons alike will
stumble[r] over them;
neighbors and friends will
perish."

22This is what the LORD says:

"Look, an army is coming
from the land of the north;[s]
a great nation is being stirred up
from the ends of the earth.[t]
23They are armed with bow and
spear;
they are cruel and show no
mercy.[u]
They sound like the roaring sea[v]
as they ride on their horses;[w]
they come like men in battle
formation
to attack you, O Daughter of
Zion.[x]"

24We have heard reports about them,
and our hands hang limp.[y]
Anguish[z] has gripped us,
pain like that of a woman in
labor.[a]
25Do not go out to the fields
or walk on the roads,
for the enemy has a sword,
and there is terror on every
side.[b]
26O my people, put on sackcloth[c]
and roll in ashes;[d]
mourn with bitter wailing[e]
as for an only son,[f]
for suddenly the destroyer[g]
will come upon us.

27"I have made you a tester[h] of
metals
and my people the ore,
that you may observe
and test their ways.
28They are all hardened rebels,[i]
going about to slander.[j]
They are bronze and iron;[k]
they all act corruptly.
29The bellows blow fiercely
to burn away the lead with fire,
but the refining[l] goes on in vain;
the wicked are not purged out.
30They are called rejected silver,[m]
because the LORD has rejected
them."[n]

False Religion Worthless

7 This is the word that came to Jeremiah from the LORD: 2"Stand[o] at
the gate of the LORD's house and there
proclaim this message:

" 'Hear the word of the LORD, all you
people of Judah who come through
these gates to worship the LORD. 3This
is what the LORD Almighty, the God of
Israel, says: Reform your ways[p] and
your actions, and I will let you live[q] in
this place. 4Do not trust[r] in deceptive[s] words and say, "This is the temple of the LORD, the temple of the LORD,
the temple of the LORD!" 5If you really
change[t] your ways and your actions
and deal with each other justly,[u] 6if
you do not oppress[v] the alien, the fatherless or the widow and do not shed
innocent blood[w] in this place, and if
you do not follow other gods[x] to your
own harm, 7then I will let you live in
this place, in the land[y] I gave your
forefathers[z] for ever and ever. 8But
look, you are trusting[a] in deceptive[b]
words that are worthless.

9" 'Will you steal[c] and murder,[d]
commit adultery[e] and perjury,[n][f]
burn incense to Baal[g][h] and follow
other gods[i] you have not known,
10and then come and stand[j] before
me in this house,[k] which bears my
Name, and say, "We are safe"—safe to
do all these detestable things?[l] 11Has

6:20 [n]S Ex 30:23 [o]Am 5:22; Mal 1:9 [p]Ps 50:8-10; Jer 7:21; Mic 6:7-8 [q]S Isa 1:11; Jer 14:12; Hos 8:13; 9:4
6:21 [r]S Lev 26:37; S Isa 8:14
6:22 [s]S Jer 4:6 [t]S Dt 28:49
6:23 [u]S Isa 13:18 [v]S Ps 18:4; S 93:3 [w]S Jer 4:29 [x]S Isa 10:32
6:24 [y]Isa 13:7 [z]S Jer 4:19 [a]S Jer 4:31; 50:41-43
6:25 [b]S Job 15:21; S Ps 31:13; Jer 49:29
6:26 [c]S Jer 4:8 [d]S Job 2:8; Jer 25:34; Eze 27:30; Jnh 3:6 [e]Jer 9:1; 18:22; 20:16; 25:36 [f]S Ge 21:16 [g]S Ex 12:23; S Jer 4:7
6:27 [h]Jer 9:7; Zec 13:9
6:28 [i]Jer 5:23 [j]S Lev 19:16 [k]Eze 22:18
6:29 [l]Mal 3:3
6:30 [m]Pr 17:3; Eze 22:18 [n]Ps 53:5; 119:119; Jer 7:29; La 5:22; Hos 9:17
7:2 [o]Jer 17:19
7:3 [p]Jer 18:11; 26:13; 35:15 [q]ver 7
7:4 [r]S Job 15:31 [s]ver 8; Jer 28:15; Mic 3:11
7:5 [t]ver 3; Jer 18:11; 26:13; 35:15 [u]S Ex 22:22; S Lev 25:17; S Isa 1:17
7:6 [v]S Jer 5:28; Eze 22:7 [w]S 2Ki 21:16; Jer 2:34; 19:4; 22:3 [x]S Ex 20:3; S Dt 8:19
7:7 [y]S Dt 4:40 [z]S Jos 1:6
7:8 [a]S Job 15:31 [b]S ver 4
7:9 [c]Ex 20:15 [d]Ex 20:13 [e]Ex 20:14; S Nu 25:1 [f]Ex 20:16; S Lev 19:12; Zec 8:17; Mal 3:5 [g]S Isa 1:13 [h]Jer 11:13,17; 32:29 [i]S Ex 20:3; Hos 2:13
7:10 [j]S Isa 48:1 [k]ver 30; 2Ki 21:4-5; Jer 23:11; 32:34; Eze 23:38-39 [l]Eze 33:25

[n]9 Or *and swear by false gods*

7:3 REFORM YOUR WAYS. God gives yet another call to the people to repent of their evil ways; however, as long as they believed they were secure simply because of the temple and its ritual, they saw no need to repent (v. 4; see next note).

7:9–10 STEAL AND MURDER . . . STAND BEFORE ME. The people were committing all kinds of sins (vv. 5–9); then on the Sabbath they came to the temple and stood before God, deluding themselves into thinking they were secure in God's love for them. This same sort of theology is in evidence today when people who live in rebellion against God and his commands feel secure because they believe in "the blood of Christ." In Jeremiah's words, they are trusting "in deceptive words that are worthless" (v. 8).

this house,[m] which bears my Name,
become a den of robbers[n] to you? But
I have been watching![o] declares the
LORD.
12" 'Go now to the place in Shiloh[p]
where I first made a dwelling[q] for my
Name,[r] and see what I did[s] to it because of the wickedness of my people
Israel. **13**While you were doing all
these things, declares the LORD, I
spoke[t] to you again and again,[u] but
you did not listen;[v] I called[w] you, but
you did not answer.[x] **14**Therefore,
what I did to Shiloh[y] I will now do to
the house that bears my Name,[z] the
temple[a] you trust in, the place I gave
to you and your fathers. **15**I will thrust
you from my presence,[b] just as I did
all your brothers, the people of Ephraim.'[c]
16"So do not pray for this people nor
offer any plea[d] or petition for them; do
not plead with me, for I will not listen[e]
to you. **17**Do you not see what they are
doing in the towns of Judah and in the
streets of Jerusalem? **18**The children
gather wood, the fathers light the fire,
and the women knead the dough and
make cakes of bread for the Queen of
Heaven.[f] They pour out drink offerings[g] to other gods to provoke[h] me to
anger. **19**But am I the one they are provoking?[i] declares the LORD. Are they
not rather harming themselves, to
their own shame?[j]
20" 'Therefore this is what the Sovereign[k] LORD says: My anger[l] and my
wrath will be poured[m] out on this
place, on man and beast, on the trees
of the field and on the fruit of the
ground, and it will burn and not be
quenched.[n]
21" 'This is what the LORD Almighty,
the God of Israel, says: Go ahead, add
your burnt offerings to your other sacrifices[o] and eat[p] the meat yourselves! **22**For when I brought your forefathers out of Egypt and spoke to
them, I did not just give them commands[q] about burnt offerings and sacrifices,[r] **23**but I gave them this command:[s] Obey[t] me, and I will be your
God and you will be my people.[u] Walk
in all the ways[v] I command you, that
it may go well[w] with you. **24**But they
did not listen[x] or pay attention;[y] instead, they followed the stubborn inclinations of their evil hearts.[z] They
went backward[a] and not forward.
25From the time your forefathers left
Egypt until now, day after day, again
and again[b] I sent you my servants[c]
the prophets.[d] **26**But they did not listen to me or pay attention.[e] They were
stiff-necked[f] and did more evil than
their forefathers.'[g]
27"When you tell[h] them all this,
they will not listen[i] to you; when you
call to them, they will not answer.[j]
28Therefore say to them, 'This is the
nation that has not obeyed the LORD its
God or responded to correction.[k]
Truth[l] has perished; it has vanished
from their lips. **29**Cut off[m] your hair
and throw it away; take up a lament[n]
on the barren heights, for the LORD has
rejected and abandoned[o] this generation that is under his wrath.

The Valley of Slaughter

30" 'The people of Judah have done
evil[p] in my eyes, declares the LORD.
They have set up their detestable
idols[q] in the house that bears my
Name and have defiled[r] it. **31**They
have built the high places of Topheth[s]
in the Valley of Ben Hinnom[t] to burn

7:11 [m] Isa 56:7 [n] Mt 21:13*; Mk 11:17*; Lk 19:46* [o] Ge 31:50; Jdg 11:10; Jer 29:23; 42:5 **7:12** [p] S Jos 18:1; S 1Sa 2:32 [q] S Ex 40:2; S Jos 18:10 [r] Da 9:18 [s] S 1Sa 4:10-11,22; Ps 78:60-64 **7:13** [t] Ps 71:17; Isa 48:17; Jer 32:33 [u] S 2Ch 36:15 [v] S ver 26; S Isa 65:12 [w] S Pr 1:24 [x] Jer 35:17 **7:14** [y] S Jdg 18:31; S 1Sa 2:32 [z] S 1Ki 9:7 [a] ver 4; Eze 24:21 **7:15** [b] S Ge 4:14; S Ex 33:15; S 2Ki 17:20; Jer 23:39 [c] S Ps 78:67 **7:16** [d] S Ex 32:10; Dt 9:14; Jer 15:1 [e] S Nu 23:19 **7:18** [f] Jer 44:17-19 [g] S Isa 57:6 [h] S Dt 31:17; S 1Ki 14:9 **7:19** [i] Dt 32:21, Jer 44:3 [j] S Job 7:20; Jer 9:19; 20:11; 22:22 **7:20** [k] S Isa 30:15 [l] S Job 40:11; Jer 42:18; La 2:3-5 [m] Jer 6:11-12; La 4:11 [n] S Isa 1:31; Jer 11:16; 13:14; 15:6,14; 17:4,27; Eze 20:47-48 **7:21** [o] S Jer 6:20; Am 5:21-22 [p] S 1Sa 2:12-17; Hos 8:13 **7:22** [q] Isa 43:23 [r] S 1Sa 15:22 **7:23** [s] 1Jn 3:23 [t] S Ex 19:5 [u] S Lev 26:12; S Isa 51:16 [v] S 1Ki 8:36; S Ps 119:3 [w] S Dt 5:33 **7:24** [x] S Jer 6:10 [y] Jer 11:8; 17:23; 34:14 [z] S Jer 3:17 [a] S Jer 2:19; Eze 37:23 **7:25** [b] S 2Ch 36:15 [c] S Isa 20:3 [d] S Nu 11:29; Jer 25:4; 35:15 **7:26** [e] ver 13,24; S 2Ch 36:16; Ps 81:11; Jer 13:11; 22:21; 25:3; 35:15; Eze 20:8,21 [f] S Ex 32:9; Ac 7:51 [g] Jer 16:12; Mal 3:7; Lk 11:47 **7:27** [h] Eze 2:7 [i] ver 13; Eze 3:7; Zec 7:13 [j] S Isa 65:12 **7:28** [k] S Lev 26:23; Zep 3:7 [l] S Ps 15:2; S Isa 59:15 **7:29** [m] S Lev 21:5; S Job 1:20 [n] S Jer 4:8; S Eze 19:1 [o] S Jer 6:30; 12:7; Hos 11:8; Mic 5:3 **7:30** [p] S ver 10; S Lev 18:21 [q] S Jer 2:7; S 4:1; Eze 7:20-22 [r] S Lev 20:3; Jer 32:34 **7:31** [s] S 2Ki 23:10 [t] S Jos 15:8; 2Ch 33:6

7:11 DEN OF ROBBERS. Robbers often used a den to hide in and plan their next crime. Jeremiah adopts this picture to depict people who were coming to the temple to offer sacrifices they thought would hide their sin from God; at the same time, they were planning to continue in their sinful ways. Jesus quoted part of this verse in his indictment of the Jewish leaders of his day (see Mt 21:13; Mk 11:17; Lk 19:46).

7:12 SHILOH. Shiloh, about eighteen miles north of Jerusalem, housed the tabernacle during the time of the judges (Jos 18:1). Jeremiah maintains that Shiloh was destroyed because of the sins of the people (7:12,14; 26:6); the same fate awaited Jerusalem and its temple if the people did not change their sinful ways.

7:18 QUEEN OF HEAVEN. The "Queen of Heaven" is either the the Babylonian fertility goddess Ishtar or the Phoenician goddess Ashtoreth; her images have been found in Palestine. Women were especially involved in her worship.

7:31 VALLEY OF BEN HINNOM. This valley on the southern perimeter of Jerusalem was used as a garbage dump and as a place to worship idols and sacrifice children by fire (a practice strictly forbidden under the Mosaic Law; see Lev 18:21;

their sons and daughters[u] in the
fire—something I did not command,
nor did it enter my mind.[v] 32So beware, the days are coming, declares
the LORD, when people will no longer
call it Topheth or the Valley of Ben
Hinnom, but the Valley of Slaughter,[w]
for they will bury[x] the dead in Topheth until there is no more room.
33Then the carcasses[y] of this people
will become food[z] for the birds of the
air and the beasts of the earth, and
there will be no one to frighten them
away.[a] 34I will bring an end to the
sounds[b] of joy and gladness and to the
voices of bride and bridegroom[c] in the
towns of Judah and the streets of Jerusalem,[d] for the land will become desolate.[e]

8 " 'At that time, declares the LORD,
the bones of the kings and officials
of Judah, the bones of the priests and
prophets, and the bones[f] of the people of Jerusalem will be removed[g]
from their graves. 2They will be exposed to the sun and the moon and all
the stars of the heavens, which they
have loved and served[h] and which
they have followed and consulted and
worshiped.[i] They will not be gathered
up or buried,[j] but will be like refuse
lying on the ground.[k] 3Wherever I
banish them,[l] all the survivors of this
evil nation will prefer death to life,[m]
declares the LORD Almighty.'

Sin and Punishment

4"Say to them, 'This is what the LORD says:

" 'When men fall down, do they not
get up?[n]
When a man turns away,[o] does
he not return?
5Why then have these people turned
away?
Why does Jerusalem always turn
away?
They cling to deceit;[p]
they refuse to return.[q]
6I have listened[r] attentively,
but they do not say what is
right.
No one repents[s] of his
wickedness,
saying, "What have I done?"
Each pursues his own course[t]
like a horse charging into battle.
7Even the stork in the sky
knows her appointed seasons,
and the dove, the swift and the
thrush
observe the time of their
migration.
But my people do not know[u]
the requirements of the LORD.

8" 'How can you say, "We are wise,
for we have the law[v] of the
LORD,"
when actually the lying pen of the
scribes
has handled it falsely?
9The wise[w] will be put to shame;
they will be dismayed[x] and
trapped.[y]
Since they have rejected the
word[z] of the LORD,
what kind of wisdom[a] do they
have?
10Therefore I will give their wives to
other men
and their fields to new owners.[b]
From the least to the greatest,
all are greedy for gain;[c]
prophets[d] and priests alike,
all practice deceit.[e]
11They dress the wound of my
people

7:31 [u]S Lev 18:21; Eze 16:20 [v]Jer 19:5; 32:35; Eze 20:31; Mic 6:7 **7:32** [w]Jer 19:6 [x]Jer 19:11 **7:33** [y]S Ge 15:11 [z]S Dt 28:26; Eze 29:5 [a]Jer 6:11; 14:16 **7:34** [b]S Isa 24:8 [c]Rev 18:23 [d]Isa 24:7-12; Jer 33:10 [e]S Lev 26:34; Zec 7:14; Mt 23:38 **8:1** [f]S Ps 53:5 [g]S Isa 14:19 **8:2** [h]S 2Ki 23:5; Jer 19:13; Zep 1:5; Ac 7:42 [i]S Job 31:27 [j]Jer 14:16; Eze 29:5; 37:1 [k]S 2Ki 9:37; Jer 31:40; 36:30 **8:3** [l]Dt 29:28 [m]S Job 3:22; Rev 9:6 **8:4** [n]Pr 24:16; Mic 7:8 [o]Ps 119:67; Jer 31:19 **8:5** [p]S Jer 5:27 [q]Zec 7:11 **8:6** [r]Mal 3:16 [s]Rev 9:20 [t]Ps 14:1-3 **8:7** [u]S Dt 32:28; S Jer 4:22 **8:8** [v]Ro 2:17 **8:9** [w]S Isa 29:14 [x]S 2Ki 19:26 [y]S Job 5:13 [z]S Jer 6:19 [a]Pr 1:7; 1Co 1:20 **8:10** [b]S Jer 6:12 [c]S Isa 56:11 [d]Jer 14:14; La 2:14 [e]Jer 23:11,15

20:2–5). Some of the worst sins in Jewish history were committed in this location. From the name "Valley of Hinnom" (Heb *ge'hinnom*) comes the Greek *geenna*, translated "hell" in the NT, the place of God's eternal judgment (Mt 18:9; Mk 9:47–48; see Mt 10:28, note).

8:1–22 AT THAT TIME. Jeremiah refers to the impending desolation of Judah and Jerusalem as if it had already occurred. Their fate would be the result of the people's stubborn rebellion and sin (cf. 7:24). Jeremiah's vision of desolation caused him great sorrow (vv. 18–22); yet while he was prophesying doom, false prophets were predicting peace (vv. 10–11).

8:1–2 BONES . . . THE STARS OF HEAVEN. In OT times, it was considered the ultimate sacrilege to leave the dead unburied. As a fitting punishment for their idolatry, God announced his intention of allowing the bones of the people to be exposed before the stars they loved to worship.

8:7 DO NOT KNOW THE REQUIREMENTS. The people were ignorant of God's law. Moreover, their leaders so distorted God's word and falsified its message that the people were assured they could sin without condemnation (v. 8). In a similar manner, the apostle Peter speaks of those who distort Scripture to their own destruction and to the destruction of others (cf. 2Pe 3:16). We must beware of ministers who teach that those who willfully continue in sin and rebellion against God will still inherit salvation and God's kingdom (see 1Co 6:9, note).

as though it were not serious.
"Peace, peace," they say,
when there is no peace.[f]
12Are they ashamed of their
loathsome conduct?
No, they have no shame[g] at all;
they do not even know how to
blush.
So they will fall among the fallen;
they will be brought down when
they are punished,[h]
says the LORD.[i]

13" 'I will take away their harvest,
declares the LORD.
There will be no grapes on the
vine.[j]
There will be no figs[k] on the tree,
and their leaves will wither.[l]
What I have given them
will be taken[m] from them.[o]' "

14"Why are we sitting here?
Gather together!
Let us flee to the fortified cities[n]
and perish there!
For the LORD our God has doomed
us to perish
and given us poisoned water[o]
to drink,
because we have sinned[p]
against him.
15We hoped for peace[q]
but no good has come,
for a time of healing
but there was only terror.[r]
16The snorting of the enemy's
horses[s]
is heard from Dan;[t]
at the neighing of their stallions
the whole land trembles.[u]
They have come to devour[v]
the land and everything in it,
the city and all who live there."

8:11 [f]ver 15; S Jer 4:10; Eze 7:25 **8:12** [g]S Jer 3:3 [h]Ps 52:5-7; Isa 3:9 [i]S Jer 6:15 **8:13** [j]Hos 2:12; Joel 1:7 [k]Lk 13:6 [l]Mt 21:19 [m]S Jer 5:17 **8:14** [n]S Jos 10:20; Jer 35:11 [o]S Dt 29:18; Jer 9:15; 23:15 [p]Jer 14:7,20; Da 9:5 **8:15** [q]S ver 11 [r]S Job 19:8; Jer 14:19 **8:16** [s]S Jer 4:29 [t]S Ge 30:6 [u]Jer 51:29 [v]S Jer 5:17

8:17 [w]Nu 21:6; S Dt 32:24 [x]S Ps 58:5; S Isa 3:3 **8:18** [y]La 5:17 **8:19** [z]Dt 28:64; Jer 9:16 [a]Mic 4:9 [b]Jer 44:3 [c]S Isa 41:24 [d]S Dt 32:21 **8:21** [e]S Ps 94:5 [f]Ps 78:40; Isa 43:24; Jer 4:19; 10:19; 14:17; 30:14; La 2:13; Eze 6:9 **8:22** [g]S Ge 37:25 [h]Job 13:4 [i]S Isa 1:6; Jer 30:12 **9:1** [j]S Ps 119:136 [k]Jer 13:17; 14:17; La 2:11,18; 3:48 [l]Isa 22:4 **9:2** [m]Ps 55:7 [n]S Nu 25:1; Jer 23:10; Hos 4:2; 7:4 [o]S 1Ki 19:10; S Isa 24:16

17"See, I will send venomous
snakes[w] among you,
vipers that cannot be charmed,[x]
and they will bite you,"
declares the LORD.

18O my Comforter[p] in sorrow,
my heart is faint[y] within me.
19Listen to the cry of my people
from a land far away:[z]
"Is the LORD not in Zion?
Is her King[a] no longer there?"
"Why have they provoked[b] me to
anger with their images,
with their worthless[c] foreign
idols?"[d]

20"The harvest is past,
the summer has ended,
and we are not saved."

21Since my people are crushed,[e] I
am crushed;
I mourn,[f] and horror grips me.
22Is there no balm in Gilead?[g]
Is there no physician[h] there?
Why then is there no healing[i]
for the wound of my people?

9 1Oh, that my head were a spring
of water
and my eyes a fountain of
tears![j]
I would weep[k] day and night
for the slain of my people.[l]
2Oh, that I had in the desert[m]
a lodging place for travelers,
so that I might leave my people
and go away from them;
for they are all adulterers,[n]
a crowd of unfaithful[o] people.

3"They make ready their tongue

[o] *13* The meaning of the Hebrew for this sentence is uncertain. [p] *18* The meaning of the Hebrew for this word is uncertain.

8:12 THEY HAVE NO SHAME AT ALL. The people had reached a stage of apostasy where they would never repent; all shame and remorse for sin was gone. Their impending judgment awaited only the day of God's visitation. Churches today reach this same stage of apostasy when they reject God's word and commit the sort of abominable sins described by Paul in Ro 1:24–32 (see Ro 1:27, note).

8:18–23 MY HEART IS FAINT. These words reveal the prophet's profound grief over the sin and the destruction of God's people. He is torn by his loyalty to God and his deep ties to the people; he is in such anguish that he wants to leave the people forever (9:2). Believers experience this same kind of grief when they see their loved ones live in rebellion against God and his righteous ways. Vicariously, they experience the suffering of God as they anticipate the disaster awaiting those who will not repent.

9:1–26 EYES A FOUNTAIN OF TEARS. Jeremiah continues to express his anguish over God's rebellious people and their refusal to repent and thereby find escape from the coming destruction. He wanted to weep, but his pain was too deep for tears. Cries of woe, charges of guilt and warnings of inescapable judgment are interspersed throughout the chapter. Jeremiah is often called the "weeping prophet" (cf. 14:17), weeping night and day for a people too hardhearted to realize the impending doom coming upon them; because of his intense emotions of sorrow, Jeremiah is traditionally considered to be the author of the book of Lamentations (see the introduction to Lamentations).

like a bow, to shoot lies;[p]
it is not by truth
that they triumph[q] in the land.
They go from one sin to another;
they do not acknowledge[q] me,"
declares the LORD.
4"Beware of your friends;[r]
do not trust your brothers.[s]
For every brother is a deceiver,[r][t]
and every friend a slanderer.[u]
5Friend deceives friend,[v]
and no one speaks the truth.[w]
They have taught their tongues to
lie;[x]
they weary themselves with
sinning.
6You[s] live in the midst of
deception;[y]
in their deceit they refuse to
acknowledge me,"
declares the LORD.

7Therefore this is what the LORD Almighty says:

"See, I will refine[z] and test[a]
them,
for what else can I do
because of the sin of my people?
8Their tongue[b] is a deadly arrow;
it speaks with deceit.
With his mouth each speaks
cordially to his neighbor,[c]
but in his heart he sets a trap[d]
for him.[e]
9Should I not punish them for this?"
declares the LORD.
"Should I not avenge[f] myself
on such a nation as this?"

10I will weep and wail for the
mountains
and take up a lament concerning
the desert pastures.[g]
They are desolate and untraveled,
and the lowing of cattle is not
heard.
The birds of the air[h] have fled
and the animals are gone.

11"I will make Jerusalem a heap[i] of
ruins,
a haunt of jackals;[j]
and I will lay waste the towns of
Judah[k]
so no one can live there."[l]

12What man is wise[m] enough to understand this? Who has been instructed by the LORD and can explain it? Why
has the land been ruined and laid

9:3 [p]ver 8; S Ex 20:16; Ps 64:3; S Isa 44:20; Jer 18:18; Mic 6:12
[q]S Isa 1:3
9:4 [r]S 2Sa 15:12
[s]Mic 7:5-6
[t]S Ge 27:35
[u]S Ex 20:16; S Lev 19:16
9:5 [v]S Lev 6:2
[w]S Ps 15:2; S Isa 59:15
[x]S Ps 52:3
9:6 [y]S Jer 5:27
9:7 [z]S Job 28:1; S Isa 1:25
[a]S Jer 6:27
9:8 [b]S ver 3; S Ps 35:20
[c]S Isa 3:5
[d]S Jer 5:26 [e]ver 4
9:9 [f]S Dt 32:43; S Isa 10:3
9:10 [g]Jer 23:10; Joel 1:19
[h]S Jer 4:25; 12:4; Hos 4:3; Joel 1:18
9:11 [i]Jer 26:18
[j]S Job 30:29; S Isa 34:13
[k]S Jer 1:15
[l]S Lev 26:31; Isa 25:2; S Jer 4:13; 26:9; 33:10; 50:3,13; 51:62; La 1:4
9:12 [m]S Ps 107:43
9:13 [n]S 2Ch 7:19; S Ps 89:30-32
9:14 [o]S Jer 2:8, 23; Am 2:4
[p]S Jer 3:17; S 7:24
9:15 [q]La 3:15
[r]S Jer 8:14
9:16 [s]S Lev 26:33
[t]S Dt 4:32; S Jer 8:19
[u]Jer 14:12; 24:10; Eze 5:2
[v]Jer 44:27; Eze 5:12
9:17 [w]S Ecc 12:5
9:18 [x]S Ps 119:136; La 3:48
9:19 [y]S Jer 4:13
9:20 [z]Jer 23:16
[a]Isa 32:9-13
9:21 [b]Joel 2:9
[c]S 2Ch 36:17; S Isa 40:30; S Jer 16:6
9:22 [d]S 2Ki 9:37

waste like a desert that no one can
cross?
13The LORD said, "It is because they
have forsaken my law, which I set before them; they have not obeyed me or
followed my law.[n] 14Instead, they
have followed[o] the stubbornness of
their hearts;[p] they have followed the
Baals, as their fathers taught them."
15Therefore, this is what the LORD Almighty, the God of Israel, says: "See,
I will make this people eat bitter food[q]
and drink poisoned water.[r] 16I will
scatter them among nations[s] that neither they nor their fathers have
known,[t] and I will pursue them with
the sword[u] until I have destroyed
them."[v]

17This is what the LORD Almighty
says:

"Consider now! Call for the wailing
women[w] to come;
send for the most skillful of
them.
18Let them come quickly
and wail over us
till our eyes overflow with tears
and water streams from our
eyelids.[x]
19The sound of wailing is heard from
Zion:
'How ruined[y] we are!
How great is our shame!
We must leave our land
because our houses are in
ruins.' "
20Now, O women, hear the word of
the LORD;
open your ears to the words of
his mouth.[z]
Teach your daughters how to wail;
teach one another a lament.[a]
21Death has climbed in through our
windows[b]
and has entered our fortresses;
it has cut off the children from the
streets
and the young men[c] from the
public squares.

22Say, "This is what the LORD declares:

" 'The dead bodies of men will lie
like refuse[d] on the open field,

[q]3 Or *lies; / they are not valiant for truth*
[r]4 Or *a deceiving Jacob* [s]6 That is,
Jeremiah (the Hebrew is singular)

like cut grain behind the reaper,
with no one to gather them.' "

23This is what the LORD says:

"Let not the wise man boast of his
wisdom[e]
or the strong man boast of his
strength[f]
or the rich man boast of his
riches,[g]
24but let him who boasts boast[h]
about this:
that he understands and
knows[i] me,
that I am the LORD,[j] who
exercises kindness,[k]
justice and righteousness[l] on
earth,
for in these I delight,"
declares the LORD.

25"The days are coming," declares
the LORD, "when I will punish all who
are circumcised only in the flesh[m]—
26Egypt, Judah, Edom, Ammon, Moab
and all who live in the desert in distant
places.[t][n] For all these nations are
really uncircumcised,[o] and even the
whole house of Israel is uncircumcised
in heart.[p]"

God and Idols

10:12–16pp — Jer 51:15–19

10 Hear what the LORD says to you, O house of Israel. 2This is what the LORD says:

"Do not learn the ways of the
nations[q]
or be terrified by signs[r] in the
sky,
though the nations are terrified
by them.
3For the customs of the peoples are
worthless;
they cut a tree out of the forest,
and a craftsman[s] shapes it with
his chisel.[t]
4They adorn it with silver[u] and gold;
they fasten it with hammer and
nails

9:23 [e]S Job 4:12; S Ecc 9:11 [f]S 1Ki 20:11 [g]Ps 62:10; S Pr 11:28; Jer 48:7; 49:4; Eze 28:4-5 **9:24** [h]S Ps 34:2; 1Co 1:31*; Gal 6:14 [i]S Ps 36:10 [j]2Co 10:17* [k]Ps 51:1 [l]Ps 36:6 **9:25** [m]S Lev 26:41; Ro 2:25 **9:26** [n]Jer 25:23; 49:32 [o]S 1Sa 14:6; Eze 31:18 [p]Ac 7:51 **10:2** [q]S Ex 23:24; S Lev 20:23 [r]S Ge 1:14 **10:3** [s]S Isa 40:19 [t]Dt 9:21; S 1Ki 8:36; Jer 44:8; Eze 7:20 **10:4** [u]Ps 135:15; Hos 13:2; Hab 2:19

[v]S 1Sa 5:3; Isa 41:7 **10:5** [w]S 1Ki 18:26; 1Co 12:2 [x]S Isa 45:20 [y]Isa 41:23 [z]S Isa 41:24; 44:9-20; 46:7; Ac 19:26 **10:6** [a]S Ex 8:10 [b]S 2Sa 7:22; S Ps 48:1 **10:7** [c]Jer 5:22 [d]Ps 22:28; S Isa 12:4; Rev 15:4 **10:8** [e]S Isa 44:18 [f]S Isa 40:19; S Jer 4:22 [g]S Dt 32:21 **10:9** [h]S Ge 10:4 [i]Ps 115:4; S Isa 40:19 **10:10** [j]S Jos 3:10; S Mt 16:16 [k]S Ge 21:33; Da 6:26 [l]S Ps 18:7 [m]S Jdg 5:4; S Job 9:6; Ps 29:8 [n]Ps 76:7; Jer 21:12; Na 1:6 **10:11** [o]S Isa 2:18 **10:12** [p]S 1Sa 2:8 [q]S ver 16

so it will not totter.[v]
5Like a scarecrow in a melon patch,
their idols cannot speak;[w]
they must be carried
because they cannot walk.[x]
Do not fear them;
they can do no harm[y]
nor can they do any good."[z]
6No one is like you,[a] O LORD;
you are great,[b]
and your name is mighty in
power.
7Who should not revere[c] you,
O King of the nations?[d]
This is your due.
Among all the wise men of the
nations
and in all their kingdoms,
there is no one like you.
8They are all senseless[e] and
foolish;[f]
they are taught by worthless
wooden idols.[g]
9Hammered silver is brought from
Tarshish[h]
and gold from Uphaz.
What the craftsman and goldsmith
have made[i]
is then dressed in blue and
purple—
all made by skilled workers.
10But the LORD is the true God;
he is the living God,[j] the
eternal King.[k]
When he is angry,[l] the earth
trembles;[m]
the nations cannot endure his
wrath.[n]

11"Tell them this: 'These gods, who
did not make the heavens and the
earth, will perish[o] from the earth and
from under the heavens.' "[u]

12But God made[p] the earth[q] by his
power;

[t]*26* Or *desert and who clip the hair by their foreheads* [u]*11* The text of this verse is in Aramaic.

9:24 LET HIM WHO BOASTS BOAST ABOUT THIS. We must not boast in worldly knowledge, human ability or earthly riches (v. 23); instead we must boast and rejoice only in our personal relationship with the Lord and in his grace, which enables us to live righteously. All earthly values pale in significance when compared to a knowledge of God. True worth consists in committing ourselves to the Lord God and his standards and in allowing him to fill us with his Holy Spirit.

10:2–16 DO NOT LEARN THE WAYS OF THE NATIONS. Because of the threat of the Babylonian invasion, the people turned more and more to idols and to the astrology and spiritism of the surrounding nations. Jeremiah warns the people against such action, declaring that the Lord God is the one true God who created all things (vv. 10–12).

he founded the world by his
wisdom[r]
and stretched out the heavens[s]
by his understanding.
13When he thunders,[t] the waters in
the heavens roar;
he makes clouds rise from the
ends of the earth.
He sends lightning[u] with the
rain[v]
and brings out the wind from his
storehouses.[w]
14Everyone is senseless and without
knowledge;
every goldsmith is shamed[x] by
his idols.
His images are a fraud;[y]
they have no breath in them.
15They are worthless,[z] the objects
of mockery;
when their judgment comes,
they will perish.
16He who is the Portion[a] of Jacob is
not like these,
for he is the Maker of all
things,[b]
including Israel, the tribe of his
inheritance[c]—
the LORD Almighty is his name.[d]

Coming Destruction

17Gather up your belongings[e] to
leave the land,
you who live under siege.
18For this is what the LORD says:
"At this time I will hurl[f] out
those who live in this land;
I will bring distress[g] on them
so that they may be captured."

19Woe to me because of my injury!
My wound[h] is incurable!
Yet I said to myself,
"This is my sickness, and I must
endure[i] it."
20My tent[j] is destroyed;
all its ropes are snapped.
My sons are gone from me and are
no more;[k]
no one is left now to pitch my
tent
or to set up my shelter.
21The shepherds[l] are senseless[m]
and do not inquire of the LORD;[n]
so they do not prosper[o]
and all their flock is scattered.[p]
22Listen! The report is coming—
a great commotion from the land
of the north![q]
It will make the towns of Judah
desolate,[r]
a haunt of jackals.[s]

Jeremiah's Prayer

23I know, O LORD, that a man's life
is not his own;
it is not for man to direct his
steps.[t]
24Correct me, LORD, but only with
justice—
not in your anger,[u]
lest you reduce me to
nothing.[v w]
25Pour out your wrath on the
nations[x]
that do not acknowledge you,
on the peoples who do not call
on your name.[y]
For they have devoured[z] Jacob;
they have devoured him
completely
and destroyed his homeland.[a]

The Covenant Is Broken

11 This is the word that came to
Jeremiah from the LORD: 2"Listen to the terms of this covenant[b] and
tell them to the people of Judah and to
those who live in Jerusalem. 3Tell them
that this is what the LORD, the God of
Israel, says: 'Cursed[c] is the man who
does not obey the terms of this covenant— 4the terms I commanded your
forefathers when I brought them out of
Egypt,[d] out of the iron-smelting furnace.[e]' I said, 'Obey[f] me and do everything I command you, and you will
be my people,[g] and I will be your God.
5Then I will fulfill the oath I swore[h]

10:12 [r]S Ge 1:31 [s]S Ge 1:1,8 **10:13** [t]S Job 36:29 [u]S Job 36:30 [v]S Ps 104:13; S 135:7 [w]S Dt 28:12 **10:14** [x]S Ps 97:7; S Isa 1:29 [y]S Isa 44:20 **10:15** [z]S Isa 41:24; S Jer 14:22 **10:16** [a]S Dt 32:9; S Ps 119:57 [b]ver 12; Jer 32:17; 33:2 [c]S Ex 34:9; Ps 74:2 [d]Jer 31:35; 32:18 **10:17** [e]Eze 12:3-12 **10:18** [f]S 1Sa 25:29; S Isa 22:17 [g]S Dt 28:52 **10:19** [h]Job 34:6; Jer 14:17; 15:18; 30:12,15; La 2:13; Mic 1:9; Na 3:19 [i]Mic 7:9 **10:20** [j]S Jer 4:20 [k]Jer 31:15; La 1:5 **10:21** [l]Jer 22:22; 23:1; 25:34; 50:6 [m]ver 8 [n]S Isa 56:10 [o]Jer 22:30 [p]Jer 23:2; Eze 34:6 **10:22** [q]Jer 6:22; 27:6; 49:28,30 [r]Eze 12:19 [s]S Isa 34:13 **10:23** [t]S Job 33:29; S Pr 3:5-6; 20:24 **10:24** [u]Ps 6:1; 38:1; S Jer 7:20; 18:23 [v]Jer 46:28 [w]Jer 30:11 **10:25** [x]S Ps 69:24; Zep 2:2; 3:8 [y]S Ps 14:4 [z]S Ps 79:7; S Jer 2:3 [a]Ps 79:6-7 **11:2** [b]S Dt 5:2 **11:3** [c]Dt 11:26-28; 27:26; 28:15-68; Gal 3:10 **11:4** [d]ver 7 [e]S 1Ki 8:51 [f]S Ex 24:8; Jer 7:23 [g]Jer 7:23; 31:33; Eze 11:20 **11:5** [h]S Ex 6:8; 13:5; Dt 7:12; Ps 105:8-11

10:17–22 GATHER UP YOUR BELONGINGS. The invasion of the Babylonians was so imminent and the accompanying disaster so real to Jeremiah that he uttered words of lament the people would wail in exile (vv. 19–20).

10:25 POUR OUT YOUR WRATH ON THE NATIONS. Jeremiah prays that the invaders who had so cruelly preyed on the Israelites would themselves experience the full tide of God's wrath, which they richly deserved (cf. Ps 79:6–7).

11:3 CURSED IS THE MAN WHO DOES NOT OBEY. Israel had made a covenant with God, promising to obey him as their Lord and God. In return he would be their God and would give them the deed to the land of Canaan and the protection that they needed (see article on GOD'S COVENANT WITH THE ISRAELITES, p. 290). But the people had persisted in disobedience and turned to other gods; thus the covenant curses pronounced for disobedience would go into effect (cf. Dt 28).

to your forefathers, to give them a land flowing with milk and honey'[i]—the land you possess today."

Eze 20:39-44

I answered, "Amen,[j] LORD."

6The LORD said to me, "Proclaim[k] all these words in the towns of Judah and in the streets of Jerusalem: 'Listen to the terms of this covenant and follow[l] them. 7From the time I brought your forefathers up from Egypt until today, I warned them again and again,[m] saying, "Obey me." 8But they did not listen or pay attention;[n] instead, they followed the stubbornness of their evil hearts.[o] So I brought on them all the curses[p] of the covenant I had commanded them to follow but that they did not keep.[q]' "

9Then the LORD said to me, "There is a conspiracy[r] among the people of Judah and those who live in Jerusalem. 10They have returned to the sins of their forefathers,[s] who refused to listen to my words.[t] They have followed other gods[u] to serve them.[v] Both the house of Israel and the house of Judah have broken the covenant[w] I made with their forefathers. 11Therefore this is what the LORD says: 'I will bring on them a disaster[x] they cannot escape.[y] Although they cry[z] out to me, I will not listen[a] to them. 12The towns of Judah and the people of Jerusalem will go and cry out to the gods to whom they burn incense,[b] but they will not help them at all when disaster[c] strikes. 13You have as many gods[d] as you have towns,[e] O Judah; and the altars you have set up to burn incense[f] to that shameful[g] god Baal are as many as the streets of Jerusalem.'

14"Do not pray[h] for this people nor offer any plea or petition for them, because I will not listen[i] when they call to me in the time of their distress.

15"What is my beloved doing in my temple
as she works out her evil schemes with many?
Can consecrated meat[j] avert ⌊your punishment⌋?[k]
When you engage in your wickedness,
then you rejoice.[v]"

16The LORD called you a thriving olive tree[l]
with fruit beautiful in form.
But with the roar of a mighty storm
he will set it on fire,[m]
and its branches will be broken.[n]

17The LORD Almighty, who planted[o] you, has decreed disaster[p] for you, because the house of Israel and the house of Judah have done evil and provoked[q] me to anger by burning incense to Baal.[r]

Plot Against Jeremiah

18Because the LORD revealed their plot to me, I knew it, for at that time he showed me what they were doing. 19I had been like a gentle lamb led to the slaughter;[s] I did not realize that they had plotted[t] against me, saying,

"Let us destroy the tree and its fruit;
let us cut him off from the land of the living,[u]
that his name be remembered[v] no more."

20But, O LORD Almighty, you who judge righteously[w]
and test the heart[x] and mind,[y]
let me see your vengeance[z] upon them,
for to you I have committed my cause.

11:5 [i]S Ex 3:8 [j]S Dt 27:26 **11:6** [k]S Jer 4:5 [l]S Ex 15:26; S Dt 15:5; Jas 1:22 **11:7** [m]S 2Ch 36:15 **11:8** [n]S Jer 7:26 [o]S Ecc 9:3; S Jer 3:17 [p]Lev 26:14-43; Dt 28:15-68; S Jos 23:15 [q]S 2Ch 7:19; Ps 78:10; Jer 26:4; 32:23; 44:10 **11:9** [r]Eze 22:25 **11:10** [s]Dt 9:7; S 2Ch 30:7 [t]Zec 7:11 [u]S Jdg 2:12-13; S 10:13 [v]Jer 16:11; Eze 20:8 [w]Isa 24:5; Jer 34:18; Hos 6:7; 8:1 **11:11** [x]S 2Ki 22:16; S Jer 4:6 [y]S Job 11:20; La 2:22 [z]S Job 27:9; Jer 14:12; Eze 8:18; Mal 2:13 [a]ver 14; S Ps 66:18; Pr 1:28; S Isa 1:15; 59:2; Eze 8:8; Zec 7:13 **11:12** [b]S Dt 32:38; S Jer 44:17 [c]S Dt 32:37; S Jdg 10:14 **11:13** [d]S Ex 20:3; Jer 19:4 [e]S 2Ki 17:29 [f]S Jer 7:9; 44:21 [g]S Jer 3:24 **11:14** [h]S Ex 32:10 [i]S ver 11 **11:15** [j]Hag 2:12 [k]S Jer 7:9-10 **11:16** [l]S Ps 1:3; Hos 14:6 [m]S Jer 7:20; 21:14 [n]S Isa 27:11; Ro 11:17-24 **11:17** [o]S Ex 15:17; Isa 5:2; Jer 12:2; 45:4 [p]ver 11 [q]Jer 7:18 [r]S Jer 7:9 **11:19** [s]S Ps 44:22 [t]ver 21; S Ps 44:16; 54:3; 71:10; Jer 18:18; 20:10 [u]S Job 28:13; S Ps 116:9; Isa 53:8 [v]Ps 83:4 **11:20** [w]Ps 7:11 [x]S 1Sa 2:3; S 1Ch 29:17 [y]S Ps 26:2 [z]S Ps 58:10; La 3:60

[v]*15* Or *Could consecrated meat avert your punishment? / Then you would rejoice*

11:14 DO NOT PRAY FOR THIS PEOPLE. Several times God instructed Jeremiah not to pray or intercede for the people (cf. 7:16; 14:11). The people so persisted in rebellion against the Lord and were so attached to their idols that prayer for them would do no good. God had resolved to give them no help when their time of destruction came. This passage warns us that our prayers might not be answered by God if we are not making a sincere effort to obey him and follow his ways (see article on EFFECTIVE PRAYING, p. 496).

11:19–23 PLOTTED AGAINST ME. A number of men of Anathoth (Jeremiah's hometown) plotted against Jeremiah; they wanted to kill him because he had remained faithful to the Lord Almighty and exposed their sins and idolatry. God assured the prophet that the conspirators would neither succeed in their plot nor survive the day of punishment. Jeremiah continued to proclaim God's word despite persecution.

21"Therefore this is what the LORD
says about the men of Anathoth[a] who
are seeking your life[b] and saying, 'Do
not prophesy[c] in the name of the LORD
or you will die[d] by our hands'—
22therefore this is what the LORD Almighty says: 'I will punish them. Their
young men[e] will die by the sword,
their sons and daughters by famine.
23Not even a remnant[f] will be left to
them, because I will bring disaster on
the men of Anathoth in the year of their
punishment.[g]' "

Jeremiah's Complaint

12 You are always righteous,[h]
O LORD,
when I bring a case[i] before
you.
Yet I would speak with you about
your justice:[j]
Why does the way of the wicked
prosper?[k]
Why do all the faithless live at
ease?
2You have planted[l] them, and they
have taken root;
they grow and bear fruit.[m]
You are always on their lips
but far from their hearts.[n]
3Yet you know me, O LORD;
you see me and test[o] my
thoughts about you.
Drag them off like sheep[p] to be
butchered!
Set them apart for the day of
slaughter![q]
4How long will the land lie
parched[w][r]
and the grass in every field be
withered?[s]
Because those who live in it are
wicked,
the animals and birds have
perished.[t]
Moreover, the people are saying,
"He will not see what happens
to us."

11:21 [a] S Jos 21:18 [b] S ver 19; Jer 12:6; 21:7; 34:20 [c] S Isa 30:10 [d] Jer 2:30; 18:23; 26:8,11; 38:4 **11:22** [e] S Isa 9:17; Jer 18:21 **11:23** [f] Jer 6:9 [g] Jer 23:12 **12:1** [h] S Ezr 9:15; Job 8:3; Da 9:14 [i] S Job 5:8 [j] Eze 18:25 [k] S Job 21:7,13; Ps 37:7; Jer 5:27-28 **12:2** [l] S Jer 11:17 [m] S Job 5:3 [n] S Isa 29:13; S Jer 3:10; S Eze 22:27; Mt 15:8; Mk 7:6; Tit 1:16 **12:3** [o] Ps 7:9; 11:5; 139:1-4 [p] S Ps 44:11 [q] Jer 16:18; 17:18; 20:11 **12:4** [r] S Jer 4:28 [s] S ver 11; S Jer 4:26; Joel 1:10-12; Am 1:2 [t] Dt 28:15-18; S Jer 4:25; S 9:10

12:5 [u] Jer 49:19; 50:44 **12:6** [v] S Pr 26:24-25; Jer 9:4 [w] Ps 12:2 **12:7** [x] S 2Ki 21:14 [y] S Jer 7:29 [z] Isa 5:1 [a] Jer 17:4 **12:8** [b] S Ps 17:12 [c] Ps 5:5; Hos 9:15; Am 6:8 **12:9** [d] S Dt 28:26; Isa 56:9; Jer 15:3; Eze 23:25; 39:17-20 **12:10** [e] Jer 23:1; 25:34; Eze 34:2-10 [f] Isa 5:1-7; Jer 9:10; 25:11 **12:11** [g] S Isa 5:6; S 24:4 [h] ver 4; Jer 9:12; 14:4; 23:10

God's Answer

5"If you have raced with men on
foot
and they have worn you out,
how can you compete with
horses?
If you stumble in safe country,[x]
how will you manage in the
thickets[u] by[y] the Jordan?
6Your brothers, your own family—
even they have betrayed you;
they have raised a loud cry
against you.[v]
Do not trust them,
though they speak well of you.[w]

7"I will forsake[x] my house,
abandon[y] my inheritance;
I will give the one I love[z]
into the hands of her enemies.[a]
8My inheritance has become to me
like a lion[b] in the forest.
She roars at me;
therefore I hate her.[c]
9Has not my inheritance become to
me
like a speckled bird of prey
that other birds of prey surround
and attack?
Go and gather all the wild beasts;
bring them to devour.[d]
10Many shepherds[e] will ruin my
vineyard
and trample down my field;
they will turn my pleasant field
into a desolate wasteland.[f]
11It will be made a wasteland,[g]
parched and desolate before
me;[h]
the whole land will be laid waste
because there is no one who
cares.
12Over all the barren heights in the
desert
destroyers will swarm,

[w]4 Or *land mourn* [x]5 Or *If you put your trust in a land of safety* [y]5 Or *the flooding of*

12:1–4 WHY DOES THE WAY OF THE WICKED PROSPER? Jeremiah contrasted his own suffering with the prosperity of the wicked. He was confused by the delay of God's judgment on such people. Coming to grips with the material success of the wicked was a recurring problem for OT saints, for they thought mainly in terms of temporal rewards and punishments (see Job 21:7–15; Ps 10; 37; 73; 94; Hab 1:5–13; Mal 3:15).

12:5 HAVE WORN YOU OUT. What Jeremiah endured at the hands of the priests in Anathoth was nothing compared to the persecutions yet to come; therefore, he was to prepare himself with faith and courage to face the greater trials ahead.

12:6 YOUR BROTHERS, YOUR OWN FAMILY. Evidently some of Jeremiah's own family had turned against him and dealt deceitfully with him.

12:7–13 I WILL FORSAKE MY HOUSE. The Lord himself laments the people's deplorable spiritual condition and the desolation coming upon the land. God experiences immense pain and sorrow whenever he must give his people over to the consequences of their sins.

for the sword[i] of the LORD[j] will
devour[k]
from one end of the land to the
other;[l]
no one will be safe.[m]
13They will sow wheat but reap
thorns;
they will wear themselves out
but gain nothing.[n]
So bear the shame of your harvest
because of the LORD's fierce
anger."[o]

14This is what the LORD says: "As for
all my wicked neighbors who seize the
inheritance[p] I gave my people Israel,
I will uproot[q] them from their lands
and I will uproot[r] the house of Judah
from among them. 15But after I uproot
them, I will again have compassion[s]
and will bring[t] each of them back to
his own inheritance and his own country. 16And if they learn[u] well the ways
of my people and swear by my name,
saying, 'As surely as the LORD
lives'[v]—even as they once taught my
people to swear by Baal[w]—then they
will be established among my people.[x]
17But if any nation does not listen, I
will completely uproot and destroy[y]
it," declares the LORD.

A Linen Belt

13 This is what the LORD said to
me: "Go and buy a linen belt
and put it around your waist, but do not
let it touch water." 2So I bought a belt,
as the LORD directed, and put it around
my waist.
3Then the word of the LORD came to
me a second time:[z] 4"Take the belt
you bought and are wearing around
your waist, and go now to Perath[z][a]
and hide it there in a crevice in the
rocks." 5So I went and hid it at Perath,
as the LORD told me.[b]
6Many days later the LORD said to
me, "Go now to Perath and get the belt

12:12 [i]Eze 21:3-4 [j]S Dt 32:41; Isa 31:8; Jer 46:10; 47:6; Eze 14:17; 21:28; 33:2 [k]S Dt 32:42 [l]Jer 3:2 [m]Jer 7:10
12:13 [n]S Lev 26:20; S Dt 28:38 [o]S Ex 15:7; S Jer 4:26
12:14 [p]S Dt 29:28; S 2Ch 7:20 [q]S Ps 9:6; Zec 2:7-9 [r]S Dt 28:63
12:15 [s]S Ps 6:2 [t]S Dt 30:3; Am 9:14-15
12:16 [u]Jer 18:8 [v]S Jer 4:2 [w]S Jos 23:7 [x]S Isa 26:18; 49:6; Jer 3:17
12:17 [y]S Ge 27:29
13:3 [z]Jer 33:1
13:4 [a]S Ge 2:14
13:5 [b]Ex 40:16
13:9 [c]S Lev 26:19; S Mt 23:12; S Lk 1:51
13:10 [d]Jer 22:21 [e]S Ecc 9:3; S Jer 3:17 [f]S Dt 8:19; Jer 9:14 [g]S Jdg 10:13 [h]Eze 15:3
13:11 [i]Isa 63:12; Jer 32:20 [j]Ex 19:5-6; Isa 43:21; S Jer 3:17 [k]S Isa 65:12; S Jer 7:26
13:13 [l]Ps 60:3; 75:8; S Isa 29:9; Jer 25:18; 51:57
13:14 [m]Eze 7:4; 8:18; 9:5,10; 24:14; Zec 11:6 [n]S Isa 9:17; Jer 16:5 [o]Dt 29:20; Isa 9:19-21; S Jer 7:20; 49:32, 36; La 2:21; Eze 5:10
13:15 [p]S Ex 23:21; Ps 95:7-8
13:16 [q]S Jos 7:19

I told you to hide there." 7So I went to
Perath and dug up the belt and took it
from the place where I had hidden it,
but now it was ruined and completely
useless.
8Then the word of the LORD came to
me: 9"This is what the LORD says: 'In
the same way I will ruin the pride of
Judah and the great pride[c] of Jerusalem. 10These wicked people, who refuse to listen[d] to my words, who follow the stubbornness of their hearts[e]
and go after other gods[f] to serve and
worship them,[g] will be like this belt—
completely useless![h] 11For as a belt is
bound around a man's waist, so I
bound the whole house of Israel and
the whole house of Judah to me,' declares the LORD, 'to be my people for my
renown[i] and praise and honor.[j] But
they have not listened.'[k]

Wineskins

12"Say to them: 'This is what the
LORD, the God of Israel, says: Every
wineskin should be filled with wine.'
And if they say to you, 'Don't we know
that every wineskin should be filled
with wine?' 13then tell them, 'This is
what the LORD says: I am going to fill
with drunkenness[l] all who live in this
land, including the kings who sit on
David's throne, the priests, the prophets and all those living in Jerusalem.
14I will smash them one against the
other, fathers and sons alike, declares
the LORD. I will allow no pity[m] or mercy
or compassion[n] to keep me from destroying[o] them.' "

Threat of Captivity

15Hear and pay attention,
do not be arrogant,
for the LORD has spoken.[p]
16Give glory[q] to the LORD your God

[z]4 Or possibly *the Euphrates;* also in verses 5-7

12:16–17 IF THEY LEARN WELL. Jeremiah has the Messianic age in view here. The nations will be given an inheritance among God's people if they learn the ways of God and worship him in truth; if they rebel, however, they will be destroyed.

13:1–11 A LINEN BELT. Jeremiah's symbolic act involving the linen belt gave the people a parabolic object lesson. Israel and Judah were the linen belt worn by the Lord, symbolizing the close relationship that he once had with them when they were faithful to him. Now the people had become useless and must be thrown off, just as Jeremiah did with the belt. During the people's exile in the area of the Euphrates, they would be useless because of their sin; all their pride and glory would disappear.

13:12–14 EVERY WINESKIN SHOULD BE FILLED WITH WINE. The empty wineskins are the people of Judah; they would be filled with "drunkenness," i.e., judgment and confusion (cf. 25:15–16; Isa 49:26; 63:6), and then they would be smashed and destroyed.

before he brings the darkness,
before your feet stumble[r]
on the darkening hills.
You hope for light,
but he will turn it to thick
darkness
and change it to deep gloom.[s]
17But if you do not listen,[t]
I will weep in secret
because of your pride;
my eyes will weep bitterly,
overflowing with tears,[u]
because the LORD's flock[v] will
be taken captive.[w]

18Say to the king[x] and to the queen
mother,[y]
"Come down from your thrones,
for your glorious crowns[z]
will fall from your heads."
19The cities in the Negev will be
shut up,
and there will be no one to open
them.
All Judah[a] will be carried into
exile,
carried completely away.

20Lift up your eyes and see
those who are coming from the
north.[b]
Where is the flock[c] that was
entrusted to you,
the sheep of which you boasted?
21What will you say when ⌊the LORD⌋
sets over you
those you cultivated as your
special allies?[d]
Will not pain grip you
like that of a woman in labor?[e]
22And if you ask yourself,
"Why has this happened to
me?"[f]—
it is because of your many sins[g]
that your skirts have been torn
off[h]
and your body mistreated.[i]
23Can the Ethiopian[a] change his
skin
or the leopard its spots?
Neither can you do good
who are accustomed to doing
evil.[j]

24"I will scatter you like chaff[k]
driven by the desert wind.[l]
25This is your lot,
the portion[m] I have decreed for
you,"
declares the LORD,
"because you have forgotten[n] me
and trusted in false gods.[o]
26I will pull up your skirts over your
face
that your shame may be
seen[p]—
27your adulteries and lustful
neighings,
your shameless prostitution![q]
I have seen your detestable acts
on the hills and in the fields.[r]
Woe to you, O Jerusalem!
How long will you be
unclean?"[s]

Drought, Famine, Sword

14 This is the word of the LORD to Jeremiah concerning the drought:[t]

2"Judah mourns,[u]
her cities languish;
they wail for the land,
and a cry goes up from
Jerusalem.
3The nobles send their servants for
water;
they go to the cisterns
but find no water.[v]
They return with their jars
unfilled;
dismayed and despairing,
they cover their heads.[w]
4The ground is cracked
because there is no rain in the
land;[x]
the farmers are dismayed
and cover their heads.
5Even the doe in the field
deserts her newborn fawn
because there is no grass.[y]
6Wild donkeys stand on the barren
heights[z]
and pant like jackals;

13:16 [r] S Lev 26:37; S Job 3:23; Isa 51:17; Jer 23:12 [s] S 1Sa 2:9; S Job 3:5; S Ps 82:5 **13:17** [t] Mal 2:2 [u] S Jer 9:1 [v] Ps 80:1; Jer 23:1 [w] Jer 14:18; 29:1 **13:18** [x] Jer 21:11; 22:1 [y] S 1Ki 2:19; S 2Ki 24:8; S Isa 22:17 [z] S 2Sa 12:30; La 5:16; Eze 16:12; 21:26 **13:19** [a] Jer 20:4; 52:30; La 1:3 **13:20** [b] Jer 6:22; Hab 1:6 [c] Jer 23:2 **13:21** [d] S Ps 41:9; Jer 4:30; 20:10; 38:22; Ob 1:7 [e] S Jer 4:31 **13:22** [f] S 1Ki 9:9 [g] Jer 9:2-6; 16:10-12 [h] S Isa 20:4 [i] La 1:8; Eze 16:37; 23:26; Na 3:5-6 **13:23** [j] S 2Ch 6:36 **13:24** [k] S Ps 1:4 [l] S Lev 26:33; S Job 1:19; S 27:21 **13:25** [m] S Job 20:29; Mt 24:51 [n] S Isa 17:10 [o] S Dt 31:20; S Ps 4:2; 106:19-21 **13:26** [p] La 1:8; Eze 16:37; Na 3:5 **13:27** [q] Eze 23:29 [r] S Isa 57:7; Eze 6:13 [s] Hos 8:5 **14:1** [t] S Dt 28:22; S Isa 5:6 **14:2** [u] S Isa 3:26 **14:3** [v] S Dt 28:48; S 2Ki 18:31; Job 6:19-20 [w] S Est 6:12 **14:4** [x] S Jer 3:3; S 12:11; Am 4:8; Zec 14:17 **14:5** [y] Isa 15:6 **14:6** [z] S Job 39:5-6; S Ps 104:11; S Jer 2:24

[a] 23 Hebrew *Cushite* (probably a person from the upper Nile region)

13:22 YOUR MANY SINS. When judgment came, the people had to know that it was happening to them because of their many sins; they were so accustomed to doing evil that they could not change (v. 23).

14:1 CONCERNING THE DROUGHT. This chapter speaks of the disastrous effects of a drought on the people and land. God sent this natural disaster on Judah during its final years because of their unfaithfulness to him and his covenant (cf. Lev 26:18–19; Dt 28:22–24). The people had rejected God—the spring of living water (2:13)—and now they would lose their supply of natural water.

their eyesight fails
for lack of pasture."[a]

7Although our sins testify[b] against us,
O LORD, do something for the sake of your name.[c]
For our backsliding[d] is great;
we have sinned[e] against you.
8O Hope[f] of Israel,
its Savior[g] in times of distress,[h]
why are you like a stranger in the land,
like a traveler who stays only a night?
9Why are you like a man taken by surprise,
like a warrior powerless to save?[i]
You are among[j] us, O LORD,
and we bear your name;[k]
do not forsake[l] us!

10This is what the LORD says about
this people:

"They greatly love to wander;
they do not restrain their feet.[m]
So the LORD does not accept[n] them;
he will now remember[o] their wickedness
and punish them for their sins."[p]

11Then the LORD said to me, "Do not
pray[q] for the well-being of this people.
12Although they fast, I will not listen
to their cry;[r] though they offer burnt
offerings[s] and grain offerings,[t] I will
not accept[u] them. Instead, I will destroy them with the sword,[v] famine[w]
and plague."[x]
13But I said, "Ah, Sovereign LORD,
the prophets[y] keep telling them, 'You
will not see the sword or suffer famine.[z] Indeed, I will give you lasting
peace[a] in this place.' "
14Then the LORD said to me, "The
prophets are prophesying lies[b] in my
name. I have not sent[c] them or appointed them or spoken to them. They
are prophesying to you false visions,[d]
divinations,[e] idolatries[b] and the delusions of their own minds. **15**Therefore, this is what the LORD says about
the prophets who are prophesying in
my name: I did not send them, yet they
are saying, 'No sword or famine will
touch this land.' Those same prophets
will perish[f] by sword and famine.[g]
16And the people they are prophesying
to will be thrown out into the streets of
Jerusalem because of the famine and
sword. There will be no one to bury[h]
them or their wives, their sons or their
daughters.[i] I will pour out on them
the calamity they deserve.[j]

17"Speak this word to them:

" 'Let my eyes overflow with tears[k]
night and day without ceasing;
for my virgin[l] daughter—my people—
has suffered a grievous wound,
a crushing blow.[m]
18If I go into the country,
I see those slain by the sword;
if I go into the city,
I see the ravages of famine.[n]
Both prophet and priest
have gone to a land they know not.[o]' "
19Have you rejected Judah completely?[p]
Do you despise Zion?
Why have you afflicted us
so that we cannot be healed?[q]
We hoped for peace
but no good has come,
for a time of healing
but there is only terror.[r]
20O LORD, we acknowledge[s] our wickedness
and the guilt of our fathers;[t]

14:6 [a]S Ge 47:4 **14:7** [b]S Isa 3:9; Hos 5:5 [c]S 1Sa 12:22; S Ps 79:9 [d]S Jer 2:19; 5:6 [e]S Jer 8:14 **14:8** [f]S Ps 9:18; Jer 17:13; 50:7 [g]Ps 18:46; S Isa 25:9 [h]Ps 46:1 **14:9** [i]S Isa 50:2 [j]S Ge 17:7; Jer 8:19 [k]Isa 63:19; Jer 15:16 [l]S Ps 27:9 **14:10** [m]Ps 119:101; Jer 2:25 [n]Jer 6:20; Am 5:22 [o]Hos 7:2; 9:9; Am 8:7 [p]Jer 44:21-23; Hos 8:13; Am 3:2 **14:11** [q]S Ex 32:10; S 1Sa 2:25 **14:12** [r]S Dt 1:45; S 1Sa 8:18; S Jer 11:11 [s]Lev 1:1-17; Jer 7:21 [t]S Lev 2:1-16 [u]Am 5:22 [v]S Isa 51:19; S Jer 9:16 [w]Jer 15:2; 16:4 [x]Jer 21:6; 27:8,13; 32:24; 34:17; Eze 14:21 **14:13** [y]Dt 18:22; Jer 27:14; 37:19 [z]S Jer 5:12 [a]S Isa 30:10; S Jer 4:10 **14:14** [b]S Jer 5:1; 23:25; 27:14; Eze 13:2 [c]Jer 23:21,32; 29:31; Eze 13:6 [d]Jer 23:16; La 2:9 [e]Eze 12:24 **14:15** [f]Jer 20:6; Eze 14:9 [g]Jer 5:12-13; 16:4; La 1:19 **14:16** [h]Ps 79:3 [i]S Jer 7:33 [j]S Pr 1:31; S Jer 17:10 **14:17** [k]S Ps 119:136 [l]S 2Ki 19:21; S Isa 23:12 [m]S Jer 8:21 **14:18** [n]Eze 7:15 [o]S 2Ch 36:10; S Jer 13:17 **14:19** [p]Jer 7:29 [q]S Isa 1:6; Jer 30:12-13 [r]S Job 19:8; S Jer 8:15 **14:20** [s]S Jer 3:13 [t]S Lev 26:40; S 1Ki 8:47; S Ezr 9:6

[b]*14* Or *visions, worthless divinations*

14:7–12 OUR SINS TESTIFY AGAINST US. The people cried out to God for rain, yet the Lord refused to answer these prayers as a testimony to the inescapable judgment they had to bear because of their sin. All who continue in sin should realize that a time may come when God refuses to hear their prayers and sends the punishment their sins deserve.

14:14 THE PROPHETS ARE PROPHESYING LIES. God's people must be aware that some prophets among them may prophesy lies and falsely claim to have received visions from the Lord; for this reason all prophets must be tested according to Biblical standards (see 1Co 14:29, note; see article on FALSE TEACHERS, p. 1506).

14:17 LET MY EYES OVERFLOW WITH TEARS. Once again, Jeremiah expresses deep sorrow over the coming judgment of God's people and the promised land (cf. 9:18; 13:17; see 9:1–26, note).

we have indeed sinned[u] against you.
21For the sake of your name[v] do not despise us;
do not dishonor your glorious throne.[w]
Remember your covenant[x] with us and do not break it.
22Do any of the worthless idols[y] of the nations bring rain?[z]
Do the skies themselves send down showers?
No, it is you, O LORD our God.
Therefore our hope is in you,
for you are the one who does all this.[a]

15 Then the LORD said to me:
"Even if Moses[b] and Samuel[c]
were to stand before me, my heart
would not go out to this people.[d] Send
them away from my presence![e] Let
them go! 2And if they ask you, 'Where
shall we go?' tell them, 'This is what
the LORD says:

" 'Those destined for death, to death;
those for the sword, to the sword;[f]
those for starvation, to starvation;[g]
those for captivity, to captivity.'[h]

3"I will send four kinds of destroyers[i] against them," declares the LORD,
"the sword[j] to kill and the dogs[k] to
drag away and the birds[l] of the air
and the beasts of the earth to devour
and destroy.[m] 4I will make them abhorrent[n] to all the kingdoms of the
earth[o] because of what Manasseh[p]
son of Hezekiah king of Judah did in
Jerusalem.

5"Who will have pity[q] on you, O Jerusalem?
Who will mourn for you?
Who will stop to ask how you are?
6You have rejected[r] me," declares the LORD.
"You keep on backsliding.
So I will lay hands[s] on you and destroy you;
I can no longer show compassion.[t]
7I will winnow[u] them with a winnowing fork
at the city gates of the land.
I will bring bereavement[v] and destruction on my people,[w]
for they have not changed their ways.[x]
8I will make their widows[y] more numerous
than the sand of the sea.
At midday I will bring a destroyer[z]
against the mothers of their young men;
suddenly I will bring down on them
anguish and terror.[a]
9The mother of seven will grow faint[b]
and breathe her last.[c]
Her sun will set while it is still day;
she will be disgraced[d] and humiliated.
I will put the survivors to the sword[e]
before their enemies,"[f]
declares the LORD.
10Alas, my mother, that you gave me birth,[g]
a man with whom the whole land strives and contends![h]
I have neither lent[i] nor borrowed,
yet everyone curses[j] me.
11The LORD said,

"Surely I will deliver you[k] for a good purpose;

14:20 [u]S Jdg 10:10; Da 9:7-8 **14:21** [v]ver 7; S Jos 7:9 [w]Isa 62:7; Jer 3:17 [x]S Ex 2:24 **14:22** [y]S Isa 41:24; S 44:10; Jer 10:15; 16:19; Hab 2:18 [z]S 1Ki 8:36; S Ps 135:7 [a]S Isa 43:10 **15:1** [b]S Ex 32:11; Nu 14:13-20 [c]S 1Sa 1:20; S 7:8 [d]S 1Sa 2:25; S Jer 7:16 [e]S 2Ki 17:20; Jer 16:13 **15:2** [f]Jer 42:22; 43:11; 44:13 [g]S Dt 28:26; S Jer 14:12; La 4:9 [h]Eze 12:11; Rev 13:10 **15:3** [i]S Nu 33:4 [j]S Lev 26:25 [k]S 1Ki 21:19; S 2Ki 9:36 [l]S Dt 28:26 [m]S Lev 26:22; Eze 14:21; 33:27 **15:4** [n]Jer 24:9; 29:18; 34:17 [o]S Dt 28:25; S Job 17:6 [p]S 2Ki 21:2; 23:26-27 **15:5** [q]Isa 27:11; 51:19; S Jer 13:14; 16:13; 21:7; Na 3:7 **15:6** [r]S Dt 32:15; Jer 6:19 [s]Isa 31:3; Zep 1:4 [t]S Jer 7:20; Am 7:8 **15:7** [u]S Isa 41:16 [v]Isa 3:26 [w]Jer 18:21 [x]S 2Ch 28:22 **15:8** [y]S Isa 47:9 [z]S Jer 4:7; S 6:4 [a]S Job 18:11 **15:9** [b]1Sa 2:5 [c]S Job 8:13 [d]Jer 7:19 [e]Jer 21:7; 25:31 [f]2Ki 25:7; Jer 19:7 **15:10** [g]S Job 3:1; S 10:18-19 [h]Jer 1:19 [i]S Lev 25:36; Ne 5:1-12 [j]S Jer 6:10 **15:11** [k]ver 21; Jer 40:4

15:1–9 THEN THE LORD SAID TO ME. God responds to Jeremiah's intercession in 14:19–22. Because the people had rejected God and kept on backsliding, the destruction of Jerusalem and the exile to Babylon were inevitable. God said he would ignore even the intercession of Moses and Samuel if they were to approach him on the people's behalf (see next note).

15:1 MOSES AND SAMUEL. Moses and Samuel were two great intercessors who in the past had pleaded with God on behalf of the children of Israel (cf. Ex 32:11–14,30–32; Nu 14:13–20; Dt 9:13–29; 1Sa 7:8–9; 12:19–25).

15:4 BECAUSE OF . . . MANASSEH. Manasseh was Judah's most evil king, the one who had led the people into great apostasy (2Ki 21:10–15; 23:26; 24:3). He was now dead, but the effects of his sins remained; judgment would come because of the people's willingness to persist in the unfaithfulness and rebellion inspired by Manasseh.

15:10 ALAS, MY MOTHER. Jeremiah complained to the Lord that he was being cursed by all the people of the land; the Lord responded (vv. 11–14) by telling him that when the judgment came, his enemies would plead with him for help (cf. 21:1–7; 37:1–10,17–20; 38:14–18).

surely I will make your enemies
plead[l] with you
in times of disaster and times of
distress.

12"Can a man break iron—
iron from the north[m]—or
bronze?
13Your wealth[n] and your treasures
I will give as plunder,[o] without
charge,[p]
because of all your sins
throughout your country.[q]
14I will enslave you to your enemies
in[c] a land you do not know,[r]
for my anger will kindle a fire[s]
that will burn against you."

15You understand, O LORD;
remember me and care for me.
Avenge me on my persecutors.[t]
You are long-suffering[u]—do not
take me away;
think of how I suffer reproach
for your sake.[v]
16When your words came, I ate[w]
them;
they were my joy and my heart's
delight,[x]
for I bear your name,[y]
O LORD God Almighty.
17I never sat[z] in the company of
revelers,
never made merry with them;
I sat alone because your hand[a]
was on me
and you had filled me with
indignation.
18Why is my pain unending
and my wound grievous and
incurable?[b]
Will you be to me like a deceptive
brook,
like a spring that fails?[c]

19Therefore this is what the LORD
says:

"If you repent, I will restore you
that you may serve[d] me;
if you utter worthy, not worthless,
words,
you will be my spokesman.[e]
Let this people turn to you,
but you must not turn to them.
20I will make you a wall[f] to this
people,
a fortified wall of bronze;
they will fight against you
but will not overcome[g] you,
for I am with you
to rescue and save you,"[h]
declares the LORD.
21"I will save[i] you from the hands
of the wicked[j]
and redeem[k] you from the
grasp of the cruel."[l]

Day of Disaster

16 Then the word of the LORD came
to me: 2"You must not marry[m]
and have sons or daughters in this
place." 3For this is what the LORD says
about the sons and daughters born in
this land and about the women who are
their mothers and the men who are
their fathers:[n] 4"They will die of deadly diseases. They will not be mourned
or buried[o] but will be like refuse lying
on the ground.[p] They will perish by
sword and famine,[q] and their dead
bodies will become food for the birds of
the air and the beasts of the earth."[r]
5For this is what the LORD says: "Do
not enter a house where there is a funeral meal; do not go to mourn or show
sympathy, because I have withdrawn
my blessing, my love and my pity[s]
from this people," declares the LORD.

15:11 [l]Jer 21:1-2; 37:3; 42:1-3 **15:12** [m]S Dt 28:48; Jer 28:14; La 1:14; Hos 10:11 **15:13** [n]S 2Ki 25:15 [o]S 2Ki 24:13; Eze 38:12-13 [p]S Ps 44:12 [q]Jer 17:3 **15:14** [r]S Dt 28:36; S Jer 5:19 [s]S Ps 21:9 **15:15** [t]Jdg 16:28; S Ps 119:84 [u]S Ex 34:6 [v]Ps 44:22; 69:7-9; S Jer 6:10 **15:16** [w]Eze 2:8; 3:3; Rev 10:10 [x]S Job 15:11; Ps 119:72,103 [y]S Isa 43:7; S Jer 14:9 **15:17** [z]Ru 3:3; Ps 1:1; 26:4-5; Jer 16:8 [a]S 2Ki 3:15 **15:18** [b]S Job 6:4; S Jer 10:19; 30:12; Mic 1:9 [c]S Job 6:15; S Ps 9:10 **15:19** [d]Zec 3:7 [e]S Ex 4:16 **15:20** [f]S Isa 50:7 [g]S Ps 129:2 [h]S Jer 1:8; 20:11; 42:11; Eze 3:8 **15:21** [i]S Jer 1:8 [j]S Ps 97:10 [k]Jer 50:34 [l]S Ge 48:16 **16:2** [m]Mt 19:12; 1Co 7:26-27 **16:3** [n]Jer 6:21 **16:4** [o]ver 6; Jer 25:33 [p]S Jer 9:22 [q]S Jer 14:15 [r]S Dt 28:26; Ps 79:1-3; S Jer 14:12; 19:7 **16:5** [s]S Jer 15:5

c *14* Some Hebrew manuscripts, Septuagint and Syriac (see also Jer. 17:4); most Hebrew manuscripts *I will cause your enemies to bring you / into*

15:16 YOUR WORDS ... JOY AND MY HEART'S DELIGHT. Jeremiah differed from the people in two fundamental ways. (1) He loved the word of the Lord; it was a joy and delight to his heart. One sure sign that we are children of God is an intense love for God's inspired Word (see Ps 119, notes; see article on THE WORD OF GOD, p. 1062). (2) He remained separated from the sinful actions of the wicked (v. 17); the resulting experience of isolation and loneliness was the price he had to pay for loyalty to God and his righteousness (cf. Ps 26:3–5).

15:19–21 IF YOU REPENT. Jeremiah accused God of not being as faithful to him as he should have been (v. 18). God told him to repent of such words and then went on to give him a promise and a renewal of his call.

16:2–10 YOU MUST NOT MARRY. Certain restrictions were put on Jeremiah's life and ministry that would serve as object lessons for the people when the hour of judgment arrived. (1) The first restriction was not to marry and have children, illustrating that in the coming affliction many families would die (vv. 1–4). (2) The second was not to mourn or show sympathy at a funeral meal, revealing that God had withdrawn his blessing, love and compassion from the people (vv. 5–7). (3) The third was not to take part in festive occasions, showing that God would bring an end to all joy and gladness in Judah (vv. 8–9).

6“Both high and low will die in this
land.[t] They will not be buried or
mourned,[u] and no one will cut[v] himself or shave[w] his head for them. 7No
one will offer food[x] to comfort those
who mourn[y] for the dead—not even
for a father or a mother—nor will anyone give them a drink to console[z]
them.

8“And do not enter a house where
there is feasting and sit down to eat
and drink.[a] 9For this is what the LORD
Almighty, the God of Israel, says: Before your eyes and in your days I will
bring an end to the sounds[b] of joy and
gladness and to the voices of bride[c]
and bridegroom in this place.[d]

10“When you tell these people all
this and they ask you, ‘Why has the
LORD decreed such a great disaster
against us? What wrong have we done?
What sin have we committed against
the LORD our God?’[e] 11then say to
them, ‘It is because your fathers forsook me,’ declares the LORD, ‘and followed other gods and served and worshiped[f] them. They forsook me and
did not keep my law.[g] 12But you have
behaved more wickedly than your fathers.[h] See how each of you is following the stubbornness of his evil heart[i]
instead of obeying me. 13So I will
throw you out of this land[j] into a land
neither you nor your fathers have
known,[k] and there you will serve other gods[l] day and night, for I will show
you no favor.’[m]

14“However, the days are coming,”[n] declares the LORD, “when men
will no longer say, ‘As surely as the
LORD lives, who brought the Israelites
up out of Egypt,’[o] 15but they will say,
‘As surely as the LORD lives, who
brought the Israelites up out of the
land of the north[p] and out of all the
countries where he had banished
them.’[q] For I will restore[r] them to
the land I gave their forefathers.[s]

16“But now I will send for many fishermen,” declares the LORD, “and they
will catch them.[t] After that I will send
for many hunters, and they will hunt[u]
them down on every mountain and hill
and from the crevices of the rocks.[v]
17My eyes are on all their ways; they
are not hidden[w] from me, nor is their
sin concealed from my eyes.[x] 18I will
repay[y] them double[z] for their wickedness and their sin, because they
have defiled my land[a] with the lifeless
forms of their vile images[b] and have
filled my inheritance with their detestable idols.[c]”[d]

19O LORD, my strength and my
fortress,
my refuge[e] in time of distress,
to you the nations will come[f]
from the ends of the earth and
say,
“Our fathers possessed nothing but
false gods,[g]
worthless idols[h] that did them
no good.[i]
20Do men make their own gods?
Yes, but they are not gods!”[j]

21“Therefore I will teach them—
this time I will teach them
my power and might.
Then they will know
that my name[k] is the LORD.

17 “Judah’s sin is engraved with
an iron tool,[l]
inscribed with a flint point,
on the tablets of their hearts[m]
and on the horns[n] of their
altars.
2Even their children remember
their altars and Asherah
poles[d][o]
beside the spreading trees
and on the high hills.[p]

16:6 [t]Jer 9:21; Eze 9:5-6 [u]S ver 4 [v]S Lev 19:28 [w]S Lev 21:5; S Job 1:20 **16:7** [x]S 2Sa 3:35 [y]Jer 22:10; Eze 24:17; Hos 9:4 [z]La 1:9, 16 **16:8** [a]S Ex 32:6; S Ecc 7:2-4; S Jer 15:17 **16:9** [b]S Isa 24:8; S 51:3; Eze 26:13; Am 6:4-7 [c]S Ps 78:63 [d]Isa 22:12-14; Rev 18:23 **16:10** [e]S Dt 29:24; Jer 5:19 **16:11** [f]S Job 31:27 [g]Dt 29:25-26; S 1Ki 9:9; Ps 106:35-43 **16:12** [h]S Ex 32:8; S Jer 7:26; Eze 20:30; Am 2:4 [i]S Ecc 9:3; S Jer 3:17 **16:13** [j]S 2Ch 7:20 [k]S Dt 28:36; S Jer 5:19 [l]S Dt 4:28; S 1Ki 9:9 [m]S Jer 15:5 **16:14** [n]Jer 29:10; 30:3; 31:27,38 [o]S Dt 15:15 **16:15** [p]S Jer 3:18 [q]S Isa 11:11; Jer 23:8 [r]Ps 53:6; S Isa 11:12; Jer 30:3; 32:44; Eze 38:14; Joel 3:1 [s]S Dt 30:3; S Isa 14:1 **16:16** [t]Am 4:2; Hab 1:14-15 [u]Am 9:3; Mic 7:2 [v]S 1Sa 26:20 **16:17** [w]S Ge 3:8; S Ecc 12:14; S Mk 4:22; 1Co 4:5; S Heb 4:13 [x]S Ps 51:9; Pr 15:3; Zep 1:12 **16:18** [y]S Isa 65:6 [z]S Isa 40:2; S Jer 12:3; Rev 18:6 [a]Nu 35:34; Jer 2:7 [b]S Ps 101:3 [c]S 1Ki 14:24 [d]S Jer 2:7; S 4:1; Eze 5:11; 8:10 **16:19** [e]S 2Sa 22:3; S Ps 46:1 [f]S Isa 2:2; Jer 3:17 [g]S Ps 4:2 [h]S Dt 32:21; S 1Sa 12:21 [i]S Isa 40:19; S Jer 14:22 **16:20** [j]Ps 115:4-7; S Jer 2:11; Ro 1:23 **16:21** [k]S Ex 3:15 **17:1** [l]Job 19:24 [m]S Dt 6:6; S 2Co 3:3 [n]S Ex 27:2 **17:2** [o]S 2Ch 24:18 [p]S Jer 2:20

[d]2 That is, symbols of the goddess Asherah

16:15 RESTORE THEM TO THE LAND. Although the people would be carried away into exile, their punishment would not be permanent. A remnant would again be restored to their homeland in order to carry out God’s plan of redemption centered in the coming Messiah.

16:18 REPAY THEM DOUBLE. The Hebrew term translated “double” can also mean “equivalent.” God would pay the people back in full for their sin and wickedness.

16:19 TO YOU THE NATIONS WILL COME. Jeremiah foresaw a day when the nations of the earth would come and worship the Lord and would renounce their false gods as worthless idols (cf. Isa 2:1–4; 45:14; Zec 8:20–23).

17:1 JUDAH’S SIN. Jeremiah indicts the nation for its great wickedness. The people’s sin was so deeply etched into their nature that idolatry and evil had become an integral part of their lives; for their infidelity they would lose their land and become slaves (v. 4).

3My mountain in the land
and your[e] wealth and all your treasures
I will give away as plunder,[q]
together with your high places,[r]
because of sin throughout your country.[s]
4Through your own fault you will lose
the inheritance[t] I gave you.
I will enslave you to your enemies[u]
in a land[v] you do not know,
for you have kindled my anger,
and it will burn[w] forever."

5This is what the LORD says:

"Cursed is the one who trusts in man,[x]
who depends on flesh for his strength
and whose heart turns away from the LORD.[y]
6He will be like a bush in the wastelands;
he will not see prosperity when it comes.
He will dwell in the parched places[z] of the desert,
in a salt[a] land where no one lives.

7"But blessed[b] is the man who trusts[c] in the LORD,
whose confidence is in him.
8He will be like a tree planted by the water
that sends out its roots by the stream.[d]
It does not fear when heat comes;
its leaves are always green.
It has no worries in a year of drought[e]
and never fails to bear fruit."[f]

17:3 [q]S 2Ki 24:13 [r]Jer 26:18; Mic 3:12 [s]Jer 15:13
17:4 [t]La 5:2 [u]Dt 28:48; S Jer 12:7 [v]Jer 16:13; 22:28 [w]S Jer 7:20
17:5 [x]S Ps 108:12; S Isa 2:22 [y]2Co 1:9
17:6 [z]Job 30:3 [a]Dt 29:23; S Job 39:6; Ps 107:34; Jer 48:9
17:7 [b]S Ps 146:5 [c]S Ps 26:1; 34:8; 40:4; Pr 16:20; Jer 39:18
17:8 [d]S Job 14:9 [e]Jer 14:1-6 [f]Ps 1:3; 92:12-14; Eze 19:10; 47:12
17:9 [g]S Ecc 9:3; Mt 13:15; Mk 7:21-22
17:10 [h]S Jos 22:22; S 2Ch 6:30; S Rev 2:23 [i]Ps 17:3; 139:23; Jer 11:20; 20:12; Eze 11:5; 38:10 [j]S Lev 26:28; Ps 62:12; Jer 32:19; S Mt 16:27 [k]Jer 12:13; 14:16; 21:14; 32:19
17:11 [l]Lk 12:20
17:12 [m]S Jer 3:17
17:13 [n]Ps 71:5; Jer 14:8 [o]S Jer 2:17 [p]S Ps 69:28; 87:6; Eze 13:9; Da 12:1 [q]S Isa 12:3; Jn 4:10
17:14 [r]S Isa 30:26; Jer 15:18 [s]S Ps 119:94 [t]S Ex 15:2; S Ps 109:1
17:15 [u]S Isa 5:19; 2Pe 3:4

9The heart[g] is deceitful above all things
and beyond cure.
Who can understand it?
10"I the LORD search the heart[h]
and examine the mind,[i]
to reward[j] a man according to his conduct,
according to what his deeds deserve."[k]

11Like a partridge that hatches eggs it did not lay
is the man who gains riches by unjust means.
When his life is half gone, they will desert him,
and in the end he will prove to be a fool.[l]

12A glorious throne,[m] exalted from the beginning,
is the place of our sanctuary.
13O LORD, the hope[n] of Israel,
all who forsake[o] you will be put to shame.
Those who turn away from you will be written in the dust[p]
because they have forsaken the LORD,
the spring of living water.[q]
14Heal me, O LORD, and I will be healed;[r]
save[s] me and I will be saved,
for you are the one I praise.[t]
15They keep saying to me,
"Where is the word of the LORD?
Let it now be fulfilled!"[u]
16I have not run away from being your shepherd;
you know I have not desired the day of despair.

[e] 2,3 Or *hills* / [3]*and the mountains of the land.* / *Your*

17:5–8 CURSED IS THE ONE. Those whose trust centers in themselves and in human resources are destined for disappointment, spiritual poverty and ultimate loss. On the contrary, those who fully trust in the Lord will be blessed and ultimately rewarded with a godly inheritance. They will not be afraid or anxious in any of life's circumstances because their roots go down deep into God.

17:9 THE HEART IS DECEITFUL. The heart is the inner being of a person and includes one's desires, feelings and thoughts (see article on THE HEART, p. 906). Above all, it is desperately evil and corrupt; as a result people turn to selfishness and evil rather than to God's way of righteousness. The corrupt human heart is beyond cure and cannot be changed by itself. The only remedy is to experience God's grace, be born again through faith in Christ and receive a new heart—one that hates evil and delights in doing God's will (cf. 24:7; Eze 11:19–20; Mt 5:8).

17:14–18 HEAL ME . . . SAVE ME. In the face of persecution and opposition, Jeremiah prays for God's grace to help him continue his prophetic ministry. The people and the false prophets had been taunting him and scoffing at his prophecies because his predictions had not yet been fulfilled (v. 15). In spite of this suffering, Jeremiah refused to turn from his ministry, but continued to look to God for strength and help.

What passes my lips[v] is open
before you.
17Do not be a terror[w] to me;
you are my refuge[x] in the day
of disaster.[y]
18Let my persecutors be put to
shame,
but keep me from shame;
let them be terrified,
but keep me from terror.
Bring on them the day of disaster;
destroy them with double
destruction.[z]

Keeping the Sabbath Holy

19This is what the LORD said to me:
"Go and stand at the gate of the people,
through which the kings of Judah go in
and out; stand also at all the other
gates of Jerusalem.[a] 20Say to them,
'Hear the word of the LORD, O kings of
Judah and all people of Judah and everyone living in Jerusalem[b] who come
through these gates.[c] 21This is what
the LORD says: Be careful not to carry
a load on the Sabbath[d] day or bring it
through the gates of Jerusalem. 22Do
not bring a load out of your houses or
do any work on the Sabbath, but keep
the Sabbath day holy, as I commanded
your forefathers.[e] 23Yet they did not
listen or pay attention;[f] they were
stiff-necked[g] and would not listen or
respond to discipline.[h] 24But if you
are careful to obey me, declares the
LORD, and bring no load through the
gates of this city on the Sabbath, but
keep the Sabbath day holy[i] by not doing any work on it, 25then kings who
sit on David's throne[j] will come
through the gates of this city with their

17:16 [v]Ps 139:4
17:17 [w]Ps 88:15-16 [x]S Ps 46:1; Jer 16:19; Na 1:7 [y]S Ps 18:18
17:18 [z]Ps 35:1-8; S Isa 40:2; S Jer 12:3
17:19 [a]Jer 7:2; 26:2
17:20 [b]Jer 19:3 [c]Jer 22:2
17:21 [d]Nu 15:32-36; S Dt 5:14; Ne 13:15-21; Jn 5:10
17:22 [e]S Ge 2:3; S Ex 20:8; Isa 56:2-6
17:23 [f]Jer 7:26 [g]Jer 19:15 [h]S 2Ch 28:22; S Jer 7:28; Zec 7:11
17:24 [i]ver 22
17:25 [j]S 2Sa 7:13; Isa 9:7; Jer 22:2,4; Lk 1:32
[k]Jer 30:10; 33:16; Eze 28:26
17:26 [l]Jer 32:44; 33:13; Zec 7:7
17:27 [m]S 1Ki 9:6; Jer 22:5 [n]S Ne 10:31 [o]S Jer 7:20 [p]S 2Ki 25:9; Hos 8:14; Am 2:5
18:6 [q]S Isa 29:16; 45:9; Ro 9:20-21 [r]S Ge 2:7
18:7 [s]Jer 1:10
18:8 [t]S Ex 32:14; Ps 25:11; Jer 26:13; 36:3; Jnh 3:8-10

officials. They and their officials will
come riding in chariots and on horses,
accompanied by the men of Judah and
those living in Jerusalem, and this city
will be inhabited forever.[k] 26People
will come from the towns of Judah and
the villages around Jerusalem, from
the territory of Benjamin and the western foothills, from the hill country and
the Negev,[l] bringing burnt offerings
and sacrifices, grain offerings, incense
and thank offerings to the house of the
LORD. 27But if you do not obey[m] me to
keep the Sabbath[n] day holy by not carrying any load as you come through the
gates of Jerusalem on the Sabbath day,
then I will kindle an unquenchable
fire[o] in the gates of Jerusalem that
will consume her fortresses.' "[p]

At the Potter's House

18 This is the word that came to
Jeremiah from the LORD: 2"Go
down to the potter's house, and there
I will give you my message." 3So I went
down to the potter's house, and I saw
him working at the wheel. 4But the pot
he was shaping from the clay was
marred in his hands; so the potter
formed it into another pot, shaping it
as seemed best to him.
5Then the word of the LORD came to
me: 6"O house of Israel, can I not do
with you as this potter does?" declares
the LORD. "Like clay[q] in the hand of
the potter, so are you in my hand,[r] O
house of Israel. 7If at any time I announce that a nation or kingdom is to
be uprooted,[s] torn down and destroyed, 8and if that nation I warned
repents of its evil, then I will relent[t]

17:19–23 STAND AT THE GATE. These verses on keeping the Sabbath holy demonstrate that even Jeremiah's prophecies of doom were conditional in nature. If the people would only turn to God, keep the Sabbath day holy, and do right, then they would avoid captivity (vv. 24–26); a way of salvation was still open for Judah.

18:2 THE POTTER'S HOUSE. Jeremiah was told to go to a potter's house, where he watched a potter fashioning a pot from clay. Because the vessel was not suitable for what the potter intended, he had to remold it into something other than what he had first designed. This parable contains several important principles for God's work in our lives. (1) Our submission to God as the One who molds both our character and our service to him determines to a large extent what he can do with us. (2) A lack of fervent commitment to God can frustrate his original purpose for us (cf. v. 10). (3) God remains free to change his intentions for our lives. If he has planned goodness and blessing for us and if we rebel against him, he may then shape us into pots destined for destruction (vv. 7–11; cf. 19:10–11; Ro 9:22); on the other hand, if we are, through our own stubbornness, pots headed for destruction, but then we repent, God will began to shape us into instruments of honor and blessing (cf. 2Ti 2:20–21).

18:8 I WILL RELENT. God remains free to change his pronounced decisions and to regulate his dealings with us according to our response to his offer of forgiveness or to his threat of judgment. Things are not predetermined and unalterable, not even in the mind of God; he takes into account spiritual changes in people. Although God does not change within himself (Nu 23:19; Jas 1:17), he retains the right to change his mind and alter his declared promises and threats. We should never accept a theology that denies God this sovereign freedom (cf. Eze 18:21–28; 33:13–16).

and not inflict on it the disaster[u] I had
planned. **9**And if at another time I announce that a nation or kingdom is to
be built[v] up and planted, **10**and if it
does evil[w] in my sight and does not
obey me, then I will reconsider[x] the
good I had intended to do for it.[y]

11"Now therefore say to the people
of Judah and those living in Jerusalem,
'This is what the LORD says: Look! I am
preparing a disaster[z] for you and de-
vising a plan[a] against you. So turn[b]
from your evil ways,[c] each one of you,
and reform your ways and your actions.'[d] **12**But they will reply, 'It's no
use.[e] We will continue with our own
plans; each of us will follow the stubbornness of his evil heart.[f]' "

13Therefore this is what the LORD
says:

"Inquire among the nations:
Who has ever heard anything like this?[g]
A most horrible[h] thing has been done
by Virgin[i] Israel.
14Does the snow of Lebanon
ever vanish from its rocky slopes?
Do its cool waters from distant sources
ever cease to flow?[f]
15Yet my people have forgotten[j] me;
they burn incense[k] to worthless idols,[l]
which made them stumble[m] in their ways
and in the ancient paths.[n]
They made them walk in bypaths
and on roads not built up.[o]
16Their land will be laid waste,[p]
an object of lasting scorn;[q]
all who pass by will be appalled[r]
and will shake their heads.[s]
17Like a wind[t] from the east,
I will scatter them before their enemies;
I will show them my back and not my face[u]
in the day of their disaster."

18They said, "Come, let's make
plans[v] against Jeremiah; for the
teaching of the law by the priest[w] will
not be lost, nor will counsel from the
wise,[x] nor the word from the prophets.[y] So come, let's attack him with
our tongues[z] and pay no attention to
anything he says."

19Listen to me, O LORD;
hear what my accusers[a] are saying!
20Should good be repaid with evil?[b]
Yet they have dug a pit[c] for me.
Remember that I stood[d] before you
and spoke in their behalf[e]
to turn your wrath away from them.
21So give their children over to famine;[f]
hand them over to the power of the sword.[g]
Let their wives be made childless and widows;[h]
let their men be put to death,
their young men[i] slain by the sword in battle.
22Let a cry[j] be heard from their houses
when you suddenly bring invaders against them,
for they have dug a pit[k] to capture me
and have hidden snares[l] for my feet.
23But you know, O LORD,
all their plots to kill[m] me.
Do not forgive[n] their crimes
or blot out their sins from your sight.
Let them be overthrown before you;
deal with them in the time of your anger.[o]

19 This is what the LORD says: "Go
and buy a clay jar from a potter.[p] Take along some of the elders[q]
of the people and of the priests **2**and go
out to the Valley of Ben Hinnom,[r]

18:8 [u] Jer 31:28; 42:10; Da 9:14; Hos 11:8-9; Joel 2:13; Jnh 4:2 **18:9** [v] Jer 1:10; 31:28 **18:10** [w] Eze 33:18 [x] 1Sa 2:29-30; 13:13 [y] S Jer 1:10 **18:11** [z] S 2Ki 22:16; S Jer 4:6 [a] ver 18 [b] S Dt 4:30; S 2Ki 17:13; Isa 1:16-19 [c] S Jer 7:3 [d] S Job 16:17 **18:12** [e] S Isa 57:10 [f] S Jer 3:17 **18:13** [g] S Isa 66:8 [h] S Jer 5:30 [i] S 2Ki 19:21 **18:15** [j] S Isa 17:10 [k] S Isa 1:13; Jer 44:15,19 [l] Jer 10:15; 51:18; Hos 11:2 [m] Eze 44:12; Mal 2:8 [n] Jer 6:16 [o] S Isa 57:14; 62:10 **18:16** [p] S Dt 28:37; Jer 25:9; Eze 33:28-29 [q] Jer 19:8; 42:18 [r] S Lev 26:32 [s] S 2Ki 19:21; S Job 16:4; Ps 22:7; La 1:12 **18:17** [t] S Job 7:10; Jer 13:24 [u] S 2Ch 29:6; S Jer 2:27 **18:18** [v] ver 11; Jer 11:19 [w] Jer 2:8; Hag 2:11; Mal 2:7 [x] S Job 5:13; Eze 7:26 [y] Jer 5:13 [z] Ps 52:2; 64:2-8; S Jer 9:3 **18:19** [a] Ps 71:13 **18:20** [b] S Ge 44:4 [c] Ps 35:7; 57:6; S 119:85 [d] Jer 15:1 [e] S Ge 20:7; S Dt 9:19; Ps 106:23; Jer 14:7-9 **18:21** [f] Jer 11:22; 14:16 [g] S Ps 63:10 [h] S 1Sa 15:33; Ps 109:9; S Isa 47:9; La 5:3 [i] S Isa 9:17 **18:22** [j] S Jer 6:26 [k] S Ps 119:85 [l] Ps 35:15; 140:5; Jer 5:26; 20:10 **18:23** [m] S Jer 11:21; 37:15 [n] S Ne 4:5 [o] Ps 59:5; S Jer 10:24 **19:1** [p] Jer 18:2 [q] S Nu 11:17; 1Ki 8:1 **19:2** [r] S Jos 15:8

[f] *14* The meaning of the Hebrew for this sentence is uncertain.

19:1–15 CLAY JAR FROM A POTTER. Through a dramatic parable, Jeremiah reveals that Jerusalem and Judah would experience such a devastating judgment that they would be smashed beyond repair.

19:2 VALLEY OF BEN HINNOM. God instructed Jeremiah to take some of the leaders (v. 1) to the place where they burned incense to other gods and sacrificed their children by fire (see 7:31, note); there he proclaimed the word of the Lord

near the entrance of the Potsherd Gate. There proclaim the words I tell you, 3 and say, 'Hear the word of the LORD, O kings[s] of Judah and people of Jerusalem. This is what the LORD Almighty, the God of Israel, says: Listen! I am going to bring a disaster[t] on this place that will make the ears of everyone who hears of it tingle.[u] 4 For they have forsaken[v] me and made this a place of foreign gods[w]; they have burned sacrifices[x] in it to gods that neither they nor their fathers nor the kings of Judah ever knew, and they have filled this place with the blood of the innocent.[y] 5 They have built the high places of Baal to burn their sons[z] in the fire as offerings to Baal—something I did not command or mention, nor did it enter my mind.[a] 6 So beware, the days are coming, declares the LORD, when people will no longer call this place Topheth[b] or the Valley of Ben Hinnom,[c] but the Valley of Slaughter.[d]

7 " 'In this place I will ruin[g] the plans[e] of Judah and Jerusalem. I will make them fall by the sword before their enemies,[f] at the hands of those who seek their lives, and I will give their carcasses[g] as food[h] to the birds of the air and the beasts of the earth. 8 I will devastate this city and make it an object of scorn;[i] all who pass by will be appalled[j] and will scoff because of all its wounds.[k] 9 I will make them eat[l] the flesh of their sons and daughters, and they will eat one another's flesh during the stress of the siege imposed on them by the enemies[m] who seek their lives.'

10 "Then break the jar[n] while those who go with you are watching, 11 and say to them, 'This is what the LORD Almighty says: I will smash[o] this nation and this city just as this potter's jar is smashed and cannot be repaired. They will bury[p] the dead in Topheth until there is no more room. 12 This is what I will do to this place and to those who live here, declares the LORD. I will make this city like Topheth. 13 The houses[q] in Jerusalem and those of the kings of Judah will be defiled[r] like this place, Topheth—all the houses where they burned incense on the roofs[s] to all the starry hosts[t] and poured out drink offerings[u] to other gods.' "

14 Jeremiah then returned from Topheth, where the LORD had sent him to prophesy, and stood in the court[v] of the LORD's temple and said to all the people, 15 "This is what the LORD Almighty, the God of Israel, says: 'Listen! I am going to bring on this city and the villages around it every disaster[w] I pronounced against them, because they were stiff-necked[x] and would not listen[y] to my words.' "

Jeremiah and Pashhur

20 When the priest Pashhur son of Immer,[z] the chief officer[a] in the temple of the LORD, heard Jeremiah prophesying these things, 2 he had Jeremiah the prophet beaten[b] and put in the stocks[c] at the Upper Gate of Benjamin[d] at the LORD's temple. 3 The next day, when Pashhur released him from the stocks, Jeremiah said to him, "The LORD's name[e] for you is not Pashhur, but Magor-Missabib.[h][f] 4 For this is what the LORD says: 'I will make you a terror to yourself and to all your friends; with your own eyes[g] you will see them fall by the sword of their enemies. I will hand[h] all Judah over to the king of Babylon, who will carry[i] them away to Babylon or put them to the sword. 5 I will hand over to their enemies all the wealth[j] of this city—all its products, all its valuables and all the treasures of the kings of Judah. They will take it away[k] as plunder and carry it off to Babylon. 6 And you, Pashhur, and all who live in your house will go into exile to Babylon. There you will

19:3 [s]Jer 17:20 [t]S Jer 6:19 [u]S 1Sa 3:11 **19:4** [v]S Dt 31:16; Dt 28:20; S Isa 65:11 [w]S Ex 20:3; S Jer 1:16 [x]S Lev 18:21 [y]S 2Ki 21:16 **19:5** [z]S Lev 18:21; S 2Ki 3:27; Ps 106:37-38 [a]S Jer 7:31; Eze 16:36 **19:6** [b]S 2Ki 23:10 [c]S Jos 15:8 [d]Jer 7:32 **19:7** [e]Ps 33:10-11 [f]S ver 9; S Lev 26:17; S Dt 28:25 [g]S Jer 16:4; 34:20 [h]S Dt 28:26 **19:8** [i]S Dt 28:37; S Jer 18:16; 25:9 [j]S Lev 26:32; La 2:15-16 [k]S Dt 29:22 **19:9** [l]S Lev 26:29; Dt 28:49-57; La 4:10 [m]S ver 7; Jer 21:7; 34:20 **19:10** [n]ver 1; S Ps 2:9; Jer 13:14 **19:11** [o]Ps 2:9; Isa 30:14 [p]Jer 7:32 **19:13** [q]Jer 32:29; 52:13; Eze 16:41 [r]Ps 74:7 [s]S 2Ki 23:12 [t]Dt 4:19; S 2Ki 17:16; S Job 38:32; Jer 8:2; Ac 7:42 [u]S Isa 57:6; Eze 20:28 **19:14** [v]2Ch 20:5; S Jer 7:2; 26:2 **19:15** [w]ver 3; Jer 11:11 [x]S Ne 9:16; Ac 7:51 [y]Jer 22:21 **20:1** [z]S 1Ch 24:14 [a]2Ki 25:18; Lk 22:52 **20:2** [b]Dt 25:2-3; S Jer 1:19; 15:15; 37:15; 2Co 11:24 [c]S Job 13:27; Jer 29:26; Ac 16:24; Heb 11:36 [d]S Job 29:7; Jer 37:13; 38:7; Zec 14:10 **20:3** [e]Hos 1:4 [f]S ver 10; S Ps 31:13 **20:4** [g]Jer 29:21 [h]Jer 21:10; 25:9 [i]Jer 13:19; 39:9; 52:27 **20:5** [j]S 2Ki 25:15; Jer 17:3 [k]S 2Ki 20:17

[g] 7 The Hebrew for *ruin* sounds like the Hebrew for *jar* (see verses 1 and 10).
[h] 3 *Magor-Missabib* means *terror on every side.*

---

concerning the coming disaster (v. 3).

19:9 EAT THE FLESH OF THEIR SONS. During the Babylonian siege in 586 B.C., some of the people resorted to cannibalism, thus showing the severity of the siege that God had brought on them and the depth of depravity to which they had fallen (see La 2:20; 4:10; Eze 5:10).

20:2–3 HAD JEREMIAH THE PROPHET BEATEN. Jeremiah was beaten, probably with forty lashes (see Dt 25:2–3), and imprisoned in the stocks. However, the prophet refused to yield to physical pain and continued to announce the nation's doom. He gave Pashhur a new name, "Magor-Missabib," meaning "terror on every side"; Pashhur and the nation would soon experience terror all around.

die and be buried, you and all your friends to whom you have prophesied[l] lies.' "

Jeremiah's Complaint

7O LORD, you deceived[i][m] me, and I
was deceived[i];
you overpowered[n] me and
prevailed.
I am ridiculed[o] all day long;
everyone mocks[p] me.
8Whenever I speak, I cry out
proclaiming violence and
destruction.[q]
So the word of the LORD has
brought me
insult and reproach[r] all day
long.
9But if I say, "I will not mention
him
or speak any more in his
name,"[s]
his word is in my heart like a
fire,[t]
a fire shut up in my bones.
I am weary of holding it in;[u]
indeed, I cannot.
10I hear many whispering,
"Terror[v] on every side!
Report[w] him! Let's report him!"
All my friends[x]
are waiting for me to slip,[y]
saying,
"Perhaps he will be deceived;
then we will prevail[z] over him
and take our revenge[a] on him."
11But the LORD[b] is with me like a
mighty warrior;
so my persecutors[c] will
stumble and not prevail.[d]
They will fail and be thoroughly
disgraced;[e]
their dishonor will never be
forgotten.
12O LORD Almighty, you who examine
the righteous
and probe the heart and mind,[f]
let me see your vengeance[g] upon
them,
for to you I have committed[h]
my cause.
13Sing[i] to the LORD!
Give praise to the LORD!
He rescues[j] the life of the needy
from the hands of the wicked.[k]
14Cursed be the day I was born![l]
May the day my mother bore me
not be blessed!
15Cursed be the man who brought
my father the news,
who made him very glad, saying,
"A child is born to you—a son!"
16May that man be like the towns[m]
the LORD overthrew without pity.
May he hear wailing[n] in the
morning,
a battle cry at noon.
17For he did not kill me in the
womb,[o]
with my mother as my grave,
her womb enlarged forever.
18Why did I ever come out of the
womb[p]
to see trouble[q] and sorrow
and to end my days in shame?[r]

God Rejects Zedekiah's Request

21 The word came to Jeremiah
from the LORD when King Zedekiah[s] sent to him Pashhur[t] son of
Malkijah and the priest Zephaniah[u]
son of Maaseiah. They said: 2"In-

20:6 [l]S Jer 14:15; La 2:14 **20:7** [m]S Ex 5:23; 22:16 [n]Isa 8:11; Am 3:8; 1Co 9:16 [o]Job 12:4 [p]S Job 17:2; S Ps 119:21 **20:8** [q]Jer 6:7; 28:8 [r]S 2Ch 36:16; S Jer 6:10 **20:9** [s]Jer 44:16 [t]S Ps 39:3; S Jer 4:19 [u]S Job 4:2; S Jer 6:11; Am 3:8; Ac 4:20 **20:10** [v]Jer 6:25 [w]Ne 6:6-13; Isa 29:21 [x]S Job 19:14; S Jer 13:21 [y]S Ps 57:4; S Jer 18:22; Lk 11:53-54 [z]S 1Ki 19:2 [a]S 1Sa 18:25; S Jer 11:19 **20:11** [b]Jer 1:8; Ro 8:31 [c]Jer 15:15; 17:18 [d]S Ps 129:2 [e]S Jer 7:19; 23:40 **20:12** [f]S Ps 7:9; S Jer 17:10 [g]Dt 32:35; S Ro 12:19 [h]Ps 62:8; Jer 11:20 **20:13** [i]S Isa 12:6 [j]Ps 34:6; 35:10 [k]S Ps 97:10 **20:14** [l]S Job 3:8, 16; Jer 15:10 **20:16** [m]S Ge 19:25 [n]S Jer 6:26 **20:17** [o]S Job 3:16; S 10:18-19 **20:18** [p]S Job 3:10-11; S Ecc 4:2 [q]S Ge 3:17; S Job 5:7 [r]S 1Ki 19:4; Ps 90:9; 102:3 **21:1** [s]2Ki 24:18; Jer 52:1 [t]S 1Ch 9:12 [u]S 2Ki 25:18

i 7 Or *persuaded*

20:7–18 O LORD. Jeremiah expresses to God the conflicting emotions of intense grief and deep depression on the one hand, and yet persistent faith and trust in God on the other.

20:7 YOU DECEIVED ME. Jeremiah was not accusing God of lying; the Hebrew word translated "deceived" means literally "reduced" or "overpowered." Jeremiah was maintaining that he had been forced into becoming a prophet by divine compulsion and that this had reduced him to shame and ridicule. His message, which had not yet been fulfilled, was continually being laughed at and mocked, and he himself was being treated with contempt by his fellow citizens.

20:9 HIS WORD . . . A FIRE. No matter how hard Jeremiah tried, he was unable to suppress the divine message within him. He sympathized fully with the divine anger against the people's sins. The prophet felt such a oneness with God and his cause that he had to proclaim God's word, even though it brought him excruciating pain and suffering.

20:14–18 CURSED BE THE DAY. Jeremiah's suffering and his feelings of frustration and failure made him wish he had never been born (cf. Job 3); yet he continued to declare God's word, sustained by God's grace in his darkest hours (vv. 11–13).

21:1 ZEDEKIAH. Zedekiah, the last king of Judah, was reigning when Jerusalem fell. His revolt against Babylon brought about the invasion of Judah and Jerusalem's subsequent destruction; the underlying spiritual cause behind the nation's fall, however, was God's decree against his people because of Manasseh's sin and Judah's apostasy (15:4).

quire[v] now of the LORD for us because
Nebuchadnezzar[j][w] king of Babylon[x]
is attacking us. Perhaps the LORD
will perform wonders[y] for us as in
times past so that he will withdraw
from us."

3But Jeremiah answered them, "Tell
Zedekiah, 4'This is what the LORD, the
God of Israel, says: I am about to
turn[z] against you the weapons of war
that are in your hands, which you are
using to fight the king of Babylon and
the Babylonians[k] who are outside the
wall besieging[a] you. And I will gather
them inside this city. 5I myself will
fight[b] against you with an outstretched hand[c] and a mighty arm[d]
in anger and fury and great wrath. 6I
will strike[e] down those who live in
this city—both men and animals—and
they will die of a terrible plague.[f] 7Af-
ter that, declares the LORD, I will hand
over Zedekiah[g] king of Judah, his officials and the people in this city who
survive the plague,[h] sword and famine, to Nebuchadnezzar king of Babylon[i] and to their enemies[j] who seek
their lives.[k] He will put them to the
sword;[l] he will show them no mercy
or pity or compassion.'[m]

8"Furthermore, tell the people, 'This
is what the LORD says: See, I am setting
before you the way of life[n] and the
way of death. 9Whoever stays in this
city will die by the sword, famine or
plague.[o] But whoever goes out and
surrenders[p] to the Babylonians who
are besieging you will live; he will escape with his life.[q] 10I have determined to do this city harm[r] and not
good, declares the LORD. It will be given
into the hands[s] of the king of Babylon,
and he will destroy it with fire.'[t]

11"Moreover, say to the royal
house[u] of Judah, 'Hear the word of the
LORD; 12O house of David, this is what
the LORD says:

" 'Administer justice[v] every
morning;
rescue from the hand of his
oppressor[w]
the one who has been robbed,
or my wrath will break out and
burn like fire[x]
because of the evil[y] you have
done—
burn with no one to quench[z] it.
13I am against[a] you, ⌞Jerusalem,⌟
you who live above this valley[b]
on the rocky plateau,
declares the LORD—
you who say, "Who can come
against us?
Who can enter our refuge?"[c]
14I will punish you as your deeds[d]
deserve,
declares the LORD.
I will kindle a fire[e] in your
forests[f]
that will consume everything
around you.' "

Judgment Against Evil Kings

22 This is what the LORD says: "Go
down to the palace of the

21:2 [v] S Ge 25:22; S 2Ki 22:18 [w] S 2Ki 25:1 [x] S Ge 10:10 [y] Ps 44:1-4; Jer 32:17 **21:4** [z] Jer 32:5 [a] Jer 37:8-10 **21:5** [b] S Jos 10:14; Eze 5:8 [c] S 2Ki 22:13; S Jer 6:12 [d] S Ex 3:20 **21:6** [e] S Jer 7:20 [f] S Jer 14:12 **21:7** [g] S 2Ki 25:7; Jer 52:9; Eze 12:14 [h] Jer 14:12; 27:8 [i] S 2Ch 36:10; Jer 27:6; 32:4; 34:3; 37:17; 38:18; 39:5; Eze 29:19 [j] S Lev 26:17; S Jer 19:9 [k] S Jer 11:21 [l] S Jer 15:9 [m] S 2Ch 36:17; S Jer 15:5; Eze 7:9; Hab 1:6 **21:8** [n] S Dt 30:15 **21:9** [o] Jer 14:12; Eze 5:12 [p] Jer 27:11; 40:9 [q] Jer 27:12; 38:2, 17; 39:18; 45:5 **21:10** [r] Jer 44:11, 27; Am 9:4 [s] S Jer 20:4; 32:28; 38:2-3 [t] S 2Ki 25:9; S 2Ch 36:19 **21:11** [u] S Jer 13:18 **21:12** [v] S Ex 22:22; S Lev 25:17 [w] S Ps 27:11 [x] S Isa 42:25; S Jer 10:10 [y] Jer 23:2 [z] S Isa 1:31 **21:13** [a] Jer 23:30; 50:31; 51:25; Eze 5:8; 13:8; 21:3; 29:10; 34:10; Na 2:13; 3:5 [b] Ps 125:2 [c] 2Sa 5:6-7; Jer 49:4; La 4:12; Ob 1:3-4 **21:14** [d] S Pr 1:31; S Isa 3:10-11; S Jer 17:10 [e] S 2Ch 36:19; La 2:3 [f] S 2Ki 19:23; Eze 20:47

[j] 2 Hebrew *Nebuchadrezzar,* of which *Nebuchadnezzar* is a variant; here and often in Jeremiah and Ezekiel [k] 4 Or *Chaldeans*; also in verse 9

21:5 I MYSELF WILL FIGHT AGAINST YOU. Zedekiah sent two priests to ask Jeremiah if God would cause Nebuchadnezzar to retreat (vv. 1–3). Through the prophet God declared an emphatic "No." In fact, God himself would fight against Judah and hand over his people into their enemies' hands. All their resistance would prove useless.

21:7 ZEDEKIAH . . . TO NEBUCHADNEZZAR. Jeremiah's prophecy was literally fulfilled in 586 B.C. (cf. 52:9–11,24–27). Zedekiah's sons were slaughtered before his eyes by Babylon's king; then Zedekiah's own eyes were blinded, and in pitiful humiliation he was led away in chains to Babylon, where he died in exile (39:5–7).

21:8–10 WAY OF LIFE . . . WAY OF DEATH. Jeremiah prophesied to the people that if they did not submit to God's decreed judgment and surrender to the Babylonians, they would die in the city.

21:11–14 HOUSE OF JUDAH. Jeremiah prophesies to the royal family of Judah that God had expected them to administer justice to the people. But because they had encouraged sin and done nothing for the oppressed, God's wrath would burn against them like fire.

22:1–30 THE KING OF JUDAH. Jeremiah's prophecies are not organized in strict chronological order. In this chapter he prophesies to the three kings who preceded King Zedekiah (see 21:1, note) about God's judgment against them. He predicted that God would punish the house of David (21:12) and judge the following kings: Shallum (vv. 1–12), Jehoiakim (vv. 13–23) and Jehoiachin (vv. 24–30).

22:1–6 GO DOWN TO . . . THE KING. Jeremiah exhorted Judah's King Shallum (v. 11; see next note) to do what is just and right and to help the oppressed and needy. If only the king would do this, he would not experience the desolation described in vv. 6–9.

king[g] of Judah and proclaim this message there: **2**‘Hear[h] the word of the
LORD, O king of Judah, you who sit on
David’s throne[i]—you, your officials
and your people who come through
these gates.[j] **3**This is what the LORD
says: Do what is just[k] and right. Rescue from the hand of his oppressor[l]
the one who has been robbed. Do no
wrong or violence to the alien, the fatherless or the widow,[m] and do not
shed innocent blood[n] in this place.
4For if you are careful to carry out
these commands, then kings[o] who sit
on David’s throne will come through
the gates of this palace, riding in chariots and on horses, accompanied by
their officials and their people. **5**But if
you do not obey[p] these commands, declares the LORD, I swear[q] by myself
that this palace will become a ruin.’ ”
6For this is what the LORD says about
the palace of the king of Judah:

“Though you are like Gilead[r] to me,
like the summit of Lebanon,[s]
I will surely make you like a
desert,[t]
like towns not inhabited.
7I will send destroyers[u] against
you,
each man with his weapons,
and they will cut[v] up your fine
cedar beams
and throw them into the fire.[w]

8“People from many nations will
pass by this city and will ask one another, ‘Why has the LORD done such a
thing to this great city?’[x] **9**And the answer will be: ‘Because they have forsaken the covenant of the LORD their
God and have worshiped and served
other gods.[y]’ ”

10Do not weep for the dead[z] ⌞king⌟
or mourn[a] his loss;
rather, weep bitterly for him
who is exiled,
because he will never return[b]
nor see his native land again.

11For this is what the LORD says about
Shallum[1c] son of Josiah, who succeeded his father as king of Judah but
has gone from this place: “He will never return. **12**He will die[d] in the place
where they have led him captive; he
will not see this land again.”

13“Woe[e] to him who builds[f] his
palace by unrighteousness,
his upper rooms by injustice,
making his countrymen work for
nothing,
not paying[g] them for their
labor.
14He says, ‘I will build myself a
great palace[h]
with spacious upper rooms.’
So he makes large windows in it,
panels it with cedar[i]
and decorates it in red.[j]

15“Does it make you a king
to have more and more cedar?
Did not your father have food and
drink?
He did what was right and
just,[k]
so all went well[l] with him.
16He defended the cause of the poor
and needy,[m]
and so all went well.
Is that not what it means to
know[n] me?”
declares the LORD.
17“But your eyes and your heart
are set only on dishonest
gain,[o]
on shedding innocent blood[p]
and on oppression and
extortion.”[q]

18Therefore this is what the LORD says
about Jehoiakim son of Josiah king of
Judah:

“They will not mourn[r] for him:
‘Alas, my brother! Alas, my
sister!’

[1] *11* Also called *Jehoahaz*

22:1 [g]S Jer 13:18; 34:2
22:2 [h]Am 7:16 [i]S Jer 17:25; Lk 1:32 [j]Jer 17:20
22:3 [k]S Lev 25:17; Isa 56:1; Jer 5:1; Eze 33:14; 45:9; Hos 12:6; Am 5:24; Mic 6:8; Zec 7:9 [l]Ps 72:4; Jer 21:12 [m]S Ex 22:22; S Isa 1:17; Jer 5:28 [n]S Jer 7:6
22:4 [o]S Jer 17:25
22:5 [p]S Jer 17:27 [q]S Ge 22:16; Heb 6:13
22:6 [r]S Ge 31:21; S SS 4:1 [s]S 1Ki 7:2; S Isa 33:9 [t]Mic 3:12
22:7 [u]S Jer 4:7; S 6:4 [v]Ps 74:5; Isa 10:34 [w]S 2Ch 36:19; Zec 11:1
22:8 [x]Dt 29:25-26; 1Ki 9:8-9; Jer 16:10-11
22:9 [y]S 1Ki 9:9; Jer 16:11; Eze 39:23
22:10 [z]S Ecc 4:2 [a]ver 18; Eze 24:16 [b]ver 27; Jer 24:9; 29:18; 42:18
22:11 [c]S 2Ki 23:31
22:12 [d]2Ki 23:34
22:13 [e]S Isa 5:8 [f]Mic 3:10; Hab 2:9 [g]S Lev 19:13; Jas 5:4
22:14 [h]Isa 5:8-9 [i]S 2Sa 7:2 [j]Eze 23:14
22:15 [k]2Ki 23:25 [l]Ps 128:2; S Isa 3:10
22:16 [m]Ps 72:1-4,12-13; S 82:3; S Pr 24:23 [n]S Ps 36:10
22:17 [o]S Isa 56:11 [p]S 2Ki 24:4 [q]S Dt 28:33; Eze 18:12; Mic 2:2
22:18 [r]S 2Sa 1:26

22:11–12 SHALLUM. Shallum, also called Jehoahaz (see 2Ki 23:31; 2Ch 36:1–4), was the fourth son of Josiah (1Ch 3:15); he was king for three months before being carried off to Egypt, where he died.

22:13–19 WOE TO HIM. This prophecy scathingly condemned King Jehoiakim (v. 18) for his sins of injustice and oppression. During Nebuchadnezzar’s first invasion of Jerusalem, Jehoiakim was taken captive to Babylon (see 2Ch 36:5–8); he was later released and given a dishonorable burial outside Jerusalem (vv. 18–19).

22:16 THE POOR AND NEEDY. The apostle James emphasizes this same truth: the kind of faith God accepts is one that expresses itself in a genuine care for those in need (see Jas 1:27, note). If we help the needy and the oppressed, we will receive God’s blessing and commendation (cf. Gal 6:10; see article on THE CARE OF THE POOR AND NEEDY, p. 1316).

They will not mourn for him:
'Alas, my master! Alas, his
splendor!'
19He will have the burial[s] of a
donkey—
dragged away and thrown[t]
outside the gates of Jerusalem."

20"Go up to Lebanon and cry out,[u]
let your voice be heard in
Bashan,[v]
cry out from Abarim,[w]
for all your allies[x] are crushed.
21I warned you when you felt
secure,[y]
but you said, 'I will not listen!'
This has been your way from your
youth;[z]
you have not obeyed[a] me.
22The wind[b] will drive all your
shepherds[c] away,
and your allies[d] will go into
exile.
Then you will be ashamed and
disgraced[e]
because of all your wickedness.
23You who live in 'Lebanon,[m][f]
who are nestled in cedar
buildings,
how you will groan when pangs
come upon you,
pain[g] like that of a woman in
labor!

24"As surely as I live," declares the
LORD, "even if you, Jehoiachin[n][h] son
of Jehoiakim king of Judah, were a signet ring[i] on my right hand, I would
still pull you off. 25I will hand you
over[j] to those who seek your life,
those you fear—to Nebuchadnezzar
king of Babylon and to the Babylonians.[o] 26I will hurl[k] you and the mother[l] who gave you birth into another
country, where neither of you was
born, and there you both will die. 27You
will never come back to the land you
long to return[m] to."

28Is this man Jehoiachin[n] a
despised, broken pot,[o]
an object no one wants?
Why will he and his children be
hurled[p] out,
cast into a land[q] they do not
know?
29O land,[r] land, land,
hear the word of the LORD!
30This is what the LORD says:
"Record this man as if childless,[s]
a man who will not prosper[t] in
his lifetime,
for none of his offspring[u] will
prosper,
none will sit on the throne[v] of
David
or rule anymore in Judah."

The Righteous Branch

23 "Woe to the shepherds[w] who
are destroying and scattering[x]
the sheep of my pasture!"[y] declares
the LORD. 2Therefore this is what the
LORD, the God of Israel, says to the
shepherds[z] who tend my people: "Because you have scattered my flock[a]
and driven them away and have not bestowed care on them, I will bestow
punishment on you for the evil[b] you
have done," declares the LORD. 3"I myself will gather the remnant[c] of my
flock out of all the countries where I
have driven them and will bring them
back to their pasture,[d] where they
will be fruitful and increase in number.
4I will place shepherds[e] over them
who will tend them, and they will no
longer be afraid[f] or terrified, nor will
any be missing,[g]" declares the LORD.

5"The days are coming," declares
the LORD,

22:19 [s]2Ki 24:6 [t]Jer 8:2; 36:30
22:20 [u]S Isa 57:13 [v]S Ps 68:15 [w]S Nu 27:12 [x]ver 22; Jer 30:14; La 1:19; Eze 16:33-34; Hos 8:9
22:21 [y]Zec 7:7 [z]Dt 9:7; Ps 25:7; Isa 54:4; Jer 3:25; 31:19; 32:30 [a]S Jer 3:13; 7:23-28; Zep 3:2
22:22 [b]S Dt 28:64; S Job 27:21 [c]S Jer 10:21 [d]S ver 20 [e]S Jer 7:19
22:23 [f]S 1Ki 7:2; Eze 17:3 [g]S Jer 4:31
22:24 [h]S 2Ki 24:6,8 [i]S Ge 38:18
22:25 [j]S 2Ki 24:16; S 2Ch 36:10
22:26 [k]S 1Sa 25:29; S 2Ki 24:8; 2Ch 36:10; S Isa 22:17; Eze 19:9-14 [l]S 1Ki 2:19
22:27 [m]S ver 10
22:28 [n]S 2Ki 24:6 [o]Ps 31:12; S Jer 19:10; 25:34; 48:38 [p]Jer 15:1 [q]S Jer 17:4
22:29 [r]S Jer 6:19
22:30 [s]1Ch 3:18; Jer 38:23; 52:10; Mt 1:12 [t]Jer 10:21 [u]S Job 18:19 [v]S Ps 94:20
23:1 [w]Jer 10:21; 12:10; 25:36; Eze 34:1-10; Zec 10:2; Zec 11:15-17 [x]S Isa 56:11 [y]Ps 100:3; S Jer 13:17; Eze 34:31
23:2 [z]Jn 10:8 [a]S Jer 10:21; 13:20 [b]Jer 21:12; Eze 34:8-10
23:3 [c]Isa 11:10-12; Jer 32:37; Eze 34:11-16 [d]S 1Ki 8:48
23:4 [e]S Ge 48:15; S Isa 31:4; Jer 31:10 [f]Jer 30:10; 46:27-28 [g]S Jn 6:39

[m]23 That is, the palace in Jerusalem (see 1 Kings 7:2) [n]24 Hebrew *Coniah,* a variant of *Jehoiachin;* also in verse 28 [o]25 Or *Chaldeans*

22:24–30 JEHOIACHIN. Jehoiachin ruled for only three months before he was taken to Babylon during Nebuchadnezzar's second invasion of Jerusalem (cf. 24:1; 29:2).

23:1 WOE TO THE SHEPHERDS. In this chapter Jeremiah prophesies woe and judgment on Judah's spiritual leaders (the priests and the false prophets), who were selfishly enriching themselves while not caring at all about the condition of the people (cf. Eze 34). They would be destroyed and the people sent into exile. What would God do then? He himself would "gather the remnant . . . and bring them back to their pasture" (v. 3) and give them shepherds who would rightly care for them; the ultimate Shepherd would be the "righteous Branch" (v. 5), i.e., the Messiah.

23:5–6 A RIGHTEOUS BRANCH. The branch (i.e., the kingly line) of David was cut off when God destroyed the Davidic monarchy in 586 B.C. (1) God did promise, however, to raise up a king from David's line who would be a righteous Branch; this King would finally and fully do what was just and right (cf. Zec 3:8). This prophecy points to the Messiah, Jesus Christ. (2) His full execution of

"when I will raise up to David[p]
a righteous Branch,[h]
a King[i] who will reign[j] wisely
and do what is just and right[k]
in the land.
6In his days Judah will be saved
and Israel will live in safety.[l]
This is the name[m] by which he
will be called:
The LORD Our Righteousness.[n]

Eze 3:16-21

7"So then, the days are coming,"[o] declares the LORD, "when people will no
longer say, 'As surely as the LORD lives,
who brought the Israelites up out of
Egypt,'[p] 8but they will say, 'As surely
as the LORD lives, who brought the
descendants of Israel up out of the
land of the north and out of all the
countries where he had banished
them.' Then they will live in their own
land."[q]

Lying Prophets

9Concerning the prophets:

My heart[r] is broken within me;
all my bones tremble.[s]
I am like a drunken man,
like a man overcome by wine,
because of the LORD
and his holy words.[t]
10The land is full of adulterers;[u]
because of the curse[q][v] the
land lies parched[r]
and the pastures[w] in the desert
are withered.[x]
The ⌞prophets⌟ follow an evil
course
and use their power unjustly.
11"Both prophet and priest are
godless;[y]
even in my temple[z] I find their
wickedness,"
declares the LORD.

12"Therefore their path will become
slippery;[a]
they will be banished to
darkness
and there they will fall.
I will bring disaster on them
in the year they are punished,[b]"
declares the LORD.

13"Among the prophets of Samaria
I saw this repulsive thing:
They prophesied by Baal[c]
and led my people Israel
astray.[d]
14And among the prophets of
Jerusalem
I have seen something
horrible:[e]
They commit adultery and live a
lie.[f]
They strengthen the hands of
evildoers,[g]
so that no one turns from his
wickedness.[h]
They are all like Sodom[i] to me;
the people of Jerusalem are like
Gomorrah."[j]

15Therefore, this is what the LORD
Almighty says concerning the prophets:

"I will make them eat bitter food
and drink poisoned water,[k]
because from the prophets of
Jerusalem
ungodliness[l] has spread
throughout the land."

16This is what the LORD Almighty
says:

23:5 [h]S 2Ki 19:26; S Isa 4:2; Eze 17:22 [i]S Mt 2:2 [j]Isa 9:7; S Mt 1:1 [k]S Ge 18:19 **23:6** [l]S Lev 25:18; S Dt 32:8; Hos 2:18 [m]Ex 23:21; Jer 33:16; Mt 1:21-23 [n]S Ezr 9:15; S Isa 42:6; Ro 3:21-22; S 1Co 1:30 **23:7** [o]Jer 30:3 [p]S Dt 15:15 **23:8** [q]S Isa 14:1; S 43:5-6; Jer 30:10; Eze 20:42; 34:13; Am 9:14-15 **23:9** [r]S Jer 4:19 [s]S Job 4:14 [t]Jer 20:8-9 **23:10** [u]S Jer 9:2 [v]Dt 28:23-24 [w]Ps 107:34; S Jer 9:10 [x]S Jer 4:26; S 12:11 **23:11** [y]Jer 6:13; S 8:10; Zep 3:4 [z]S 2Ki 21:4; S Jer 7:10 **23:12** [a]S Dt 32:35; S Job 3:23; Jer 13:16 [b]Jer 11:23 **23:13** [c]S 1Ki 18:22 [d]ver 32; S Isa 3:12; Eze 13:10 **23:14** [e]S Jer 5:30; Hos 6:10 [f]Jer 29:23 [g]ver 22 [h]S Isa 5:18 [i]S Ge 18:20; Mt 11:24 [j]Jer 20:16; Am 4:11 **23:15** [k]S Jer 8:14; 9:15 [l]S Jer 8:10

[p]5 Or *up from David's line* [q]10 Or *because of these things* [r]10 Or *land mourns*

judgment will occur after his second coming and before his millennial reign on the earth. (3) He will be called "The LORD Our Righteousness" (v. 6). The believing remnant will "be found in him, not having a righteousness of [their] own that comes from the law, but that which is through faith in Christ—the righteousness that comes from God and is by faith" (Php 3:9).

23:9–40 THE PROPHETS. Jeremiah denounces the sins of the false prophets, who had scorned his message of doom (6:13–14; 14:14–16; 29:8–9) and proclaimed only peace and prosperity (see 6:14, note). Jeremiah placed the responsibility for Judah's deplorable moral state on the shoulders of these wicked prophets.

23:14 AMONG THE PROPHETS ... SOMETHING HORRIBLE. God calls the spiritual adultery of the false prophets horrible. They were supposed to be his righteous representatives, but instead they lived like the people of Sodom and Gomorrah. The example of these "spiritual leaders" contributed greatly to the increase of immorality and the hardening of the people's hearts against repentance. When a minister of God commits adultery, it is especially detestable to God. Not only does such a sin show unfaithfulness to God but also contempt for him and his word (see 2Sa 12:9–12, notes), and it disqualifies this leader as a servant of the Lord and his flock (see article on MORAL QUALIFICATIONS FOR OVERSEERS, p. 1882).

"Do not listen[m] to what the
prophets are prophesying to
you;
they fill you with false hopes.
They speak visions[n] from their
own minds,
not from the mouth[o] of the
LORD.
17They keep saying[p] to those who
despise me,
'The LORD says: You will have
peace.'[q]
And to all who follow the
stubbornness[r] of their
hearts
they say, 'No harm[s] will come
to you.'
18But which of them has stood in
the council[t] of the LORD
to see or to hear his word?
Who has listened and heard his
word?
19See, the storm[u] of the LORD
will burst out in wrath,
a whirlwind[v] swirling down
on the heads of the wicked.
20The anger[w] of the LORD will not
turn back[x]
until he fully accomplishes
the purposes of his heart.
In days to come
you will understand it clearly.
21I did not send[y] these prophets,
yet they have run with their
message;
I did not speak to them,
yet they have prophesied.
22But if they had stood in my
council,[z]
they would have proclaimed[a]
my words to my people
and would have turned[b] them
from their evil ways
and from their evil deeds.[c]

23"Am I only a God nearby,[d]"
declares the LORD,
"and not a God far away?
24Can anyone hide[e] in secret places
so that I cannot see him?"
declares the LORD.
"Do not I fill heaven and
earth?"[f]
declares the LORD.

25"I have heard what the prophets
say who prophesy lies[g] in my name.
They say, 'I had a dream![h] I had a
dream!' 26How long will this continue
in the hearts of these lying prophets,
who prophesy the delusions[i] of their
own minds?[j] 27They think the dreams
they tell one another will make my people forget[k] my name, just as their fathers forgot[l] my name through Baal
worship.[m] 28Let the prophet who has
a dream[n] tell his dream, but let the
one who has my word[o] speak it faithfully. For what has straw to do with
grain?" declares the LORD. 29"Is not my
word like fire,"[p] declares the LORD,
"and like a hammer[q] that breaks a
rock in pieces?

30"Therefore," declares the LORD, "I
am against[r] the prophets[s] who steal
from one another words supposedly
from me. 31Yes," declares the LORD, "I
am against the prophets who wag their
own tongues and yet declare, 'The
LORD declares.'[t] 32Indeed, I am
against those who prophesy false
dreams,[u]" declares the LORD. "They
tell them and lead my people astray[v]
with their reckless lies,[w] yet I did not
send[x] or appoint them. They do not
benefit[y] these people in the least," declares the LORD.

False Oracles and False Prophets

33"When these people, or a prophet
or a priest, ask you, 'What is the oracle[s][z] of the LORD?' say to them, 'What
oracle?[t] I will forsake[a] you, declares
the LORD.' 34If a prophet or a priest or
anyone else claims, 'This is the oracle[b] of the LORD,' I will punish[c] that

23:16 [m] Jer 27:9-10,14; S Mt 7:15 [n] S Jer 14:14; Eze 13:3 [o] Jer 9:20 **23:17** [p] ver 31 [q] S 1Ki 22:8; S Jer 4:10 [r] S Jer 13:10 [s] Jer 5:12; Am 9:10; Mic 3:11 **23:18** [t] S 1Ki 22:19; S Ro 11:34 **23:19** [u] Isa 30:30; Jer 25:32; 30:23 [v] Zec 7:14 **23:20** [w] S 2Ki 23:26 [x] S Jer 4:28 **23:21** [y] S Jer 14:14; 27:15 **23:22** [z] S 1Ki 22:19 [a] S Dt 33:10 [b] S 2Ki 17:13; Jer 25:5; Zec 1:4 [c] ver 14; Am 3:7 **23:23** [d] Ps 139:1-10 **23:24** [e] S Ge 3:8; S Job 11:20; 22:12-14; S Ecc 12:14; S Isa 28:15; 1Co 4:5 [f] S 1Ki 8:27 **23:25** [g] ver 16; Jer 14:14; 27:10 [h] ver 28,32; S Dt 13:1; Jer 27:9; 29:8 **23:26** [i] S Isa 30:10; 1Ti 4:1-2 [j] Jer 14:14; Eze 13:2 **23:27** [k] Dt 13:1-3; Jer 29:8 [l] S Jdg 3:7; S 8:33-34 [m] S Jer 2:23 **23:28** [n] S ver 25 [o] S 1Sa 3:17 **23:29** [p] S Ps 39:3; Jer 5:14; S 1Co 3:13 [q] Heb 4:12 **23:30** [r] S Ps 34:16 [s] ver 2; Dt 18:20; Jer 14:15; S 21:13 **23:31** [t] ver 17 **23:32** [u] S ver 25 [v] S ver 13; S Jer 50:6 [w] S Job 13:4; Eze 13:3; 22:28 [x] S Jer 14:14 [y] Jer 7:8; La 2:14 **23:33** [z] Mal 1:1 [a] S 2Ki 21:14

23:34 [b] La 2:14 [c] Zec 13:3

[s] 33 Or *burden* (see Septuagint and Vulgate)
[t] 33 Hebrew; Septuagint and Vulgate *'You are the burden.'* (The Hebrew for *oracle* and *burden* is the same.)

23:17 YOU WILL HAVE PEACE. False prophets hold out to God's people a false hope and security (see vv. 9–40, note). (1) Those who maintain that the immoral and disobedient among God's people will not be condemned for their evil and do not need to fear God's wrath and judgment prove themselves to be false messengers. (2) Prophets with this message existed not only in OT times but also in NT times. The apostle Paul warned the Ephesians not to be deceived by such teachers (Eph 5:4–6; see 1Co 6:9, note; Gal 5:21, note).

23:31–32 I AM AGAINST THOSE. God's word to Jeremiah warns us how dangerous it is to declare, "This is the oracle of the LORD," if we are not sure that the word is from the Lord; the prophetic office must be undertaken only with the utmost seriousness (cf. vv. 33–40).

man and his household. **35**This is what each of you keeps on saying to his friend or relative: 'What is the LORD's answer?'[d] or 'What has the LORD spoken?' **36**But you must not mention 'the oracle of the LORD' again, because every man's own word becomes his oracle and so you distort[e] the words of the living God,[f] the LORD Almighty, our God. **37**This is what you keep saying to a prophet: 'What is the LORD's answer to you?' or 'What has the LORD spoken?' **38**Although you claim, 'This is the oracle of the LORD,' this is what the LORD says: You used the words, 'This is the oracle of the LORD,' even though I told you that you must not claim, 'This is the oracle of the LORD.' **39**Therefore, I will surely forget you and cast[g] you out of my presence along with the city I gave to you and your fathers. **40**I will bring upon you everlasting disgrace[h]—everlasting shame that will not be forgotten."

Two Baskets of Figs

24 After Jehoiachin[u][i] son of Jehoiakim king of Judah and the officials, the craftsmen and the artisans of Judah were carried into exile from Jerusalem to Babylon by Nebuchadnezzar king of Babylon, the LORD showed me two baskets of figs[j] placed in front of the temple of the LORD. **2**One basket had very good figs, like those that ripen early;[k] the other basket had very poor[l] figs, so bad they could not be eaten.

3Then the LORD asked me, "What do you see,[m] Jeremiah?"

"Figs," I answered. "The good ones are very good, but the poor ones are so bad they cannot be eaten."

4Then the word of the LORD came to me: **5**"This is what the LORD, the God of Israel, says: 'Like these good figs, I regard as good the exiles from Judah, whom I sent[n] away from this place to the land of the Babylonians.[v] **6**My eyes will watch over them for their good, and I will bring them back[o] to this land. I will build[p] them up and not tear them down; I will plant[q] them and not uproot them. **7**I will give them a heart to know[r] me, that I am the LORD. They will be my people,[s] and I will be their God, for they will return[t] to me with all their heart.[u]

8" 'But like the poor[v] figs, which are so bad they cannot be eaten,' says the LORD, 'so will I deal with Zedekiah[w] king of Judah, his officials[x] and the survivors[y] from Jerusalem, whether they remain in this land or live in Egypt.[z] **9**I will make them abhorrent[a] and an offense to all the kingdoms of the earth, a reproach and a byword,[b] an object of ridicule and cursing,[c] wherever I banish[d] them. **10**I will send the sword,[e] famine[f] and plague[g] against them until they are destroyed from the land I gave to them and their fathers.[h]' "

Seventy Years of Captivity

25 The word came to Jeremiah concerning all the people of Judah in the fourth year of Jehoiakim[i] son of Josiah king of Judah, which was the first year of Nebuchadnezzar[j] king of Babylon. **2**So Jeremiah the prophet said to all the people of Judah[k] and to all those living in Jerusalem: **3**For twenty-three years—from the thirteenth year of Josiah[l] son of Amon king of Judah until this very

23:35 [d]Jer 33:3; 42:4
23:36 [e]Gal 1:7-8; 2Pe 3:16 [f]S Jos 3:10
23:39 [g]S Jer 7:15
23:40 [h]S Jer 20:11; Eze 5:14-15
24:1 [i]S 2Ki 24:16; S 2Ch 36:9 [j]Ex 23:19; Dt 26:2; Am 8:1-2
24:2 [k]S SS 2:13 [l]S Isa 5:4
24:3 [m]Jer 1:11; Am 8:2
24:5 [n]Jer 29:4,20
24:6 [o]S Dt 30:3; Jer 27:22; 29:10; 30:3; Eze 11:17 [p]Jer 33:7; 42:10 [q]S Dt 30:9; S Jer 1:10; Am 9:14-15
24:7 [r]S Isa 11:9 [s]S Lev 26:12; S Isa 51:16; S Zec 2:11; Heb 8:10 [t]Jer 32:40 [u]S 2Ch 6:37; Eze 11:19
24:8 [v]Jer 29:17 [w]Jer 32:4-5; 38:18,23; 39:5; 44:30 [x]Jer 39:6 [y]Jer 39:9 [z]Jer 44:1,26; 46:14
24:9 [a]S Jer 15:4; 25:18 [b]S Dt 28:25; S 1Ki 9:7 [c]S 2Ki 22:19; S Jer 29:18 [d]S Dt 28:37; Da 9:7
24:10 [e]S Isa 51:19; S Jer 9:16; Rev 6:8 [f]Jer 15:2 [g]Jer 27:8 [h]S Dt 28:21
25:1 [i]S 2Ki 24:2 [j]S 2Ki 24:1
25:2 [k]Jer 18:11
25:3 [l]S 1Ch 3:14

[u]*1* Hebrew *Jeconiah,* a variant of *Jehoiachin*
[v]*5* Or *Chaldeans*

24:1–10 CARRIED INTO EXILE. The historical background for the parable of the two baskets of figs is the beginning of Zedekiah's reign. Nebuchadnezzar had just deported Jehoiachin and many other Israelites to Babylon (597 B.C.). Zedekiah and those who remained behind had been spared God's judgment; thus they believed Jeremiah's prophecies of total destruction were misguided. Jeremiah's parable warned that those left in Jerusalem would experience a far more devastating judgment than those who had already been carried into exile in Babylon.

24:1 TWO BASKETS OF FIGS. The first basket of figs (i.e., the exiles of 597 B.C.) was considered to contain good figs, good in that God would purify them through the suffering of the exile (v. 5). After their exile they would be brought back to the land (v. 6) and would turn from idolatry to God with all their hearts (v. 7); God would use them to accomplish his redemptive purpose in the world. The second basket of figs had bad figs (v. 2) and represented King Zedekiah and those who remained in Jerusalem after that recent deportation; they would continue to oppose Jeremiah and his message, and thus experience the incredible horrors of Jerusalem's fall in 586 B.C., bringing great disgrace.

25:1 FIRST YEAR OF NEBUCHADNEZZAR. This year was 605 B.C., an important date because Nebuchadnezzar's reign marks the beginning of four successive kingdoms that were to have world dominion (see Da 2; 7).

day—the word of the LORD has come to
me and I have spoken to you again and
again,[m] but you have not listened.[n]
4And though the LORD has sent all
his servants the prophets[o] to you
again and again, you have not listened
or paid any attention.[p] 5They said,
"Turn[q] now, each of you, from your
evil ways and your evil practices, and
you can stay in the land[r] the LORD
gave to you and your fathers for ever
and ever. 6Do not follow other gods[s]
to serve and worship them; do not provoke me to anger with what your hands
have made. Then I will not harm you."
7"But you did not listen to me," declares the LORD, "and you have provoked[t] me with what your hands have
made,[u] and you have brought harm[v]
to yourselves."
8Therefore the LORD Almighty says
this: "Because you have not listened to
my words, 9I will summon[w] all the
peoples of the north[x] and my servant[y] Nebuchadnezzar[z] king of Babylon," declares the LORD, "and I will
bring them against this land and its inhabitants and against all the surrounding nations. I will completely destroy[w][a] them and make them an
object of horror and scorn,[b] and an
everlasting ruin.[c] 10I will banish from
them the sounds[d] of joy and gladness,
the voices of bride and bridegroom,[e]
the sound of millstones[f] and the light
of the lamp.[g] 11This whole country
will become a desolate wasteland,[h]
and these nations will serve[i] the king
of Babylon seventy years.[j]
12"But when the seventy years[k] are
fulfilled, I will punish the king of Babylon[l] and his nation, the land of the
Babylonians,[x] for their guilt," declares the LORD, "and will make it desolate[m] forever. 13I will bring upon that
land all the things I have spoken
against it, all that are written[n] in this
book and prophesied by Jeremiah
against all the nations. 14They themselves will be enslaved[o] by many nations[p] and great kings; I will repay[q]
them according to their deeds and the
work of their hands."

The Cup of God's Wrath

15This is what the LORD, the God of
Israel, said to me: "Take from my hand
this cup[r] filled with the wine of my
wrath and make all the nations to
whom I send[s] you drink it. 16When
they drink[t] it, they will stagger[u] and
go mad[v] because of the sword[w] I will
send among them."
17So I took the cup from the LORD's
hand and made all the nations to whom
he sent[x] me drink it: 18Jerusalem[y]
and the towns of Judah, its kings and
officials, to make them a ruin[z] and an
object of horror and scorn[a] and cursing,[b] as they are today;[c] 19Pharaoh
king[d] of Egypt,[e] his attendants, his
officials and all his people, 20and all
the foreign people there; all the kings
of Uz;[f] all the kings of the Philistines[g] (those of Ashkelon,[h] Gaza,[i]
Ekron, and the people left at Ashdod);
21Edom,[j] Moab[k] and Ammon;[l]
22all the kings of Tyre[m] and Sidon;[n]
the kings of the coastlands[o] across

25:3 [m]Jer 11:7; 26:5 [n]S Isa 65:12; S Jer 7:26 **25:4** [o]Jer 6:17; S 7:25; 29:19 [p]S Jer 7:26; 34:14; 44:5 **25:5** [q]S Jdg 6:8; S 2Ch 7:14; S 30:9; S Jer 23:22 [r]S Ge 12:7; S Dt 4:40 **25:6** [s]S Ex 20:3; S Dt 8:19 **25:7** [t]Jer 30:14; 32:35; 44:5 [u]Dt 32:21 [v]2Ki 17:20; 21:15 **25:9** [w]Isa 13:3-5 [x]S Isa 14:31 [y]S Isa 41:2; Jer 27:6 [z]S 2Ch 36:6 [a]S Nu 21:2 [b]S 2Ch 29:8 [c]S Jer 19:8; S 20:4; Eze 12:20 **25:10** [d]S Isa 24:8; Eze 26:13 [e]Jer 7:34; 33:11 [f]Ecc 12:3-4 [g]S Job 18:5; La 5:15; Rev 18:22-23 **25:11** [h]S Lev 26:31,32; Jer 4:26-27; 12:11-12 [i]Jer 28:14 [j]S 2Ch 36:21 **25:12** [k]Jer 27:7; 29:10 [l]S Ge 10:10; S Ps 137:8 [m]S Isa 13:19-22; 14:22-23 **25:13** [n]S Isa 30:8 **25:14** [o]Isa 14:6; Jer 27:7 [p]Jer 50:9; 51:27-28 [q]S Dt 32:41; S Job 21:19; S Jer 51:6 **25:15** [r]S Isa 51:17; Jer 49:12; La 4:21; Eze 23:31; Rev 14:10 [s]Jer 1:5 **25:16** [t]ver 26 [u]S Ps 60:3 [v]Jer 51:7 [w]ver 27-29 **25:17** [x]Jer 1:10; 27:3 **25:18** [y]S Jer 13:13 [z]S Job 12:19 [a]S 2Ch 29:8 [b]S Jer 24:9 [c]S Ge 19:13; Jer 44:22 **25:19** [d]S 2Ki 18:21 [e]Isa 19:1; 20:3; Jer 44:30; Eze 29:2 **25:20** [f]S Ge 10:23 [g]S Jos 13:3; S 2Ch 26:6; S 28:18; Zep 2:4-7 [h]Jer 47:5; Am 1:7-8 [i]S Ge 10:19 **25:21** [j]S Ge 25:30 [k]S Ge 19:37; S Dt 23:6 [l]S Ge 19:38; Jer 27:3; 49:1 **25:22** [m]S Jos 19:29 [n]S Ge 10:15 [o]Isa 11:11; 48:20; 66:20; Jer 31:10; Eze 27:15; 39:6; Da 11:18

[w] *9* The Hebrew term refers to the irrevocable giving over of things or persons to the LORD, often by totally destroying them. [x] *12* Or *Chaldeans*

25:3 TWENTY-THREE YEARS. Jeremiah had preached earnestly for 23 years, but the people had not listened; he had exhorted them to turn from their worship of idols and from their sinful ways, but they had remained obstinate. God had even sent other prophets to warn Judah (v. 4), among whom were Uriah, Zephaniah and Habakkuk. Jeremiah's experience underscores the truth that no matter how faithful we are in witnessing to the saving gospel of Christ, some will refuse to hear and obey God's word and go on to their own destruction. Furthermore, in the last days, those in the church who remain faithful to God and his word will be grieved as they see many abandon Biblical faith and God's righteous standards (see 1Ti 4:1, note).

25:11 SEVENTY YEARS. Judah would remain in exile for approximately seventy years. The seventy years began in the fourth year of King Jehoiakim (605 B.C.), when the first set of exiles were carried off, and continued to the first return of exiles in 538 B.C., following Cyrus's decree (see Ezr 1:1, note; 2:1, note; cf. 2Ch 36:21–23; Da 9:2).

25:12 PUNISH THE KING OF BABYLON. Jeremiah prophesies that God would repay Babylon for its cruel and sinful deeds. Babylon was defeated by the Medes and Persians under Cyrus in 539 B.C. (cf. Da 5:30–31).

25:15 WINE OF MY WRATH. Intoxicating wine is often used in Scripture to signify God's wrath (see 49:12; 51:7; Job 21:20; Ps 60:3; Isa 51:17,22; Eze 23:31; Rev 14:8,10; 16:19; 18:6).

the sea; [23]Dedan,[p] Tema,[q] Buz[r] and all who are in distant places[y];[s] [24]all the kings of Arabia[t] and all the kings of the foreign people[u] who live in the desert; [25]all the kings of Zimri,[v] Elam[w] and Media;[x] [26]and all the kings of the north,[y] near and far, one after the other—all the kingdoms[z] on the face of the earth. And after all of them, the king of Sheshach[z][a] will drink it too.

[27]"Then tell them, 'This is what the LORD Almighty, the God of Israel, says: Drink, get drunk[b] and vomit, and fall to rise no more because of the sword[c] I will send among you.' [28]But if they refuse to take the cup from your hand and drink[d], tell them, 'This is what the LORD Almighty says: You must drink it! [29]See, I am beginning to bring disaster[e] on the city that bears my Name,[f] and will you indeed go unpunished?[g] You will not go unpunished, for I am calling down a sword[h] upon all[i] who live on the earth,[j] declares the LORD Almighty.'

[30]"Now prophesy all these words against them and say to them:

" 'The LORD will roar[k] from on high;
he will thunder[l] from his holy
dwelling[m]
and roar mightily against his
land.
He will shout like those who
tread[n] the grapes,
shout against all who live on the
earth.
[31]The tumult[o] will resound to the
ends of the earth,
for the LORD will bring charges[p]
against the nations;
he will bring judgment[q] on all[r]
mankind
and put the wicked to the
sword,[s]' "
declares the LORD.

[32]This is what the LORD Almighty says:

"Look! Disaster[t] is spreading
from nation to nation;[u]
a mighty storm[v] is rising
from the ends of the earth."[w]

[33]At that time those slain[x] by the LORD will be everywhere—from one end of the earth to the other. They will not be mourned or gathered[y] up or buried,[z] but will be like refuse lying on the ground.

[34]Weep and wail, you shepherds;[a]
roll[b] in the dust, you leaders of
the flock.
For your time to be slaughtered[c]
has come;
you will fall and be shattered
like fine pottery.[d]
[35]The shepherds will have nowhere
to flee,
the leaders of the flock no place
to escape.[e]
[36]Hear the cry[f] of the shepherds,[g]
the wailing of the leaders of the
flock,
for the LORD is destroying their
pasture.
[37]The peaceful meadows will be laid
waste
because of the fierce anger of
the LORD.
[38]Like a lion[h] he will leave his
lair,
and their land will become
desolate[i]
because of the sword[a] of the
oppressor[j]
and because of the LORD's fierce
anger.[k]

Jeremiah Threatened With Death

26 Early in the reign of Jehoiakim[l] son of Josiah king of Judah, this word came from the LORD: [2]"This is what the LORD says: Stand in the courtyard[m] of the LORD's house and speak to all the people of the towns of Judah who come to worship in the house of the LORD.[n] Tell[o] them everything I command you; do not omit[p] a word. [3]Perhaps they will lis-

25:23 [p]S Ge 25:3 [q]S Ge 25:15 [r]S Ge 22:21 [s]Jer 9:26; 49:32 **25:24** [t]S 2Ch 9:14 [u]ver 20 **25:25** [v]Ge 25:2 [w]S Ge 10:22 [x]S Isa 21:2 **25:26** [y]ver 9; Jer 50:3,9; 51:11, 48 [z]Isa 23:17 [a]Jer 51:41 **25:27** [b]ver 16,28; S Isa 29:9; S 49:26; Jer 51:57; Eze 23:32-34; Na 3:18; Hab 2:16 [c]S Jer 12:12; Eze 14:17; 21:4 **25:28** [d]S Isa 51:23 **25:29** [e]S 2Sa 5:7; Isa 10:12; Jer 13:12-14; 39:1 [f]S Dt 28:10; S Isa 37:17 [g]S Pr 11:31 [h]ver 27 [i]ver 30-31; Isa 34:2 [j]S Isa 24:1 **25:30** [k]Isa 16:10; S 42:13 [l]S Ps 46:6 [m]S Ps 68:5 [n]Isa 63:3; Joel 3:13; Rev 14:19-20 **25:31** [o]Jer 23:19 [p]S Jer 2:9 [q]S 1Sa 12:7; S Jer 2:35; S Eze 36:5 [r]S ver 29 [s]S Jer 15:9 **25:32** [t]S Isa 30:25 [u]Isa 34:2 [v]S Jer 23:19 [w]S Dt 28:49 **25:33** [x]Isa 66:16; Eze 39:17-20 [y]S Jer 8:2 [z]S Ps 79:3 **25:34** [a]S Jer 2:8; Zec 10:3 [b]S Jer 6:26 [c]S Ps 44:22; S Isa 34:6; Jer 50:27; 51:40; Zec 11:4,7 [d]S Jer 22:28 **25:35** [e]S Job 11:20 **25:36** [f]S Jer 6:26 [g]S Jer 23:1; Zec 11:3 **25:38** [h]S Job 10:16; S Jer 4:7 [i]Jer 44:22 [j]Jer 46:16; 50:16 [k]S Ex 15:7; S Jer 4:26 **26:1** [l]2Ki 23:36 **26:2** [m]Jer 19:14 [n]S Jer 17:19 [o]S ver 12; S Jer 1:17; Mt 28:20; Ac 20:27 [p]Dt 4:2

[y] *23* Or *who clip the hair by their foreheads*
[z] *26* *Sheshach* is a cryptogram for Babylon.
[a] *38* Some Hebrew manuscripts and Septuagint (see also Jer. 46:16 and 50:16); most Hebrew manuscripts *anger*

26:2 EVERYTHING I COMMAND YOU. Knowing that his prophecy would offend people and cause hostility and opposition, Jeremiah may have been tempted to hold back some particularly severe words given him by the Lord; the Lord told him not to omit a single word. God's entire message must be proclaimed. Faithful ministers should not avoid speaking the harsh words of God's commands and warnings, even though they know some will turn away from them. Those who ignore parts of God's word and accommodate the sins of the congregation are unworthy ministers.

ten and each will turn[q] from his evil way. Then I will relent[r] and not bring on them the disaster I was planning because of the evil they have done. [4]Say to them, 'This is what the LORD says: If you do not listen[s] to me and follow my law,[t] which I have set before you, [5]and if you do not listen to the words of my servants the prophets, whom I have sent to you again and again (though you have not listened[u]), [6]then I will make this house like Shiloh[v] and this city an object of cursing[w] among all the nations of the earth.' "

[7]The priests, the prophets and all the people heard Jeremiah speak these words in the house of the LORD. [8]But as soon as Jeremiah finished telling all the people everything the LORD had commanded[x] him to say, the priests, the prophets and all the people seized[y] him and said, "You must die![z] [9]Why do you prophesy in the LORD's name that this house will be like Shiloh and this city will be desolate and deserted?"[a] And all the people crowded[b] around Jeremiah in the house of the LORD.

[10]When the officials[c] of Judah heard about these things, they went up from the royal palace to the house of the LORD and took their places at the entrance of the New Gate[d] of the LORD's house. [11]Then the priests and the prophets said to the officials and all the people, "This man should be sentenced to death[e] because he has prophesied against this city. You have heard it with your own ears!"[f]

[12]Then Jeremiah said to all the officials[g] and all the people: "The LORD sent me to prophesy[h] against this house and this city all the things you have heard.[i] [13]Now reform[j] your ways and your actions and obey[k] the LORD your God. Then the LORD will relent[l] and not bring the disaster he has pronounced against you. [14]As for me, I am in your hands;[m] do with me whatever you think is good and right. [15]Be assured, however, that if you put me to death, you will bring the guilt of innocent blood[n] on yourselves and on this city and on those who live in it, for in truth the LORD has sent me to you to speak all these words[o] in your hearing."

[16]Then the officials[p] and all the people said to the priests and the prophets, "This man should not be sentenced to death![q] He has spoken to us in the name of the LORD our God."

[17]Some of the elders of the land stepped forward and said to the entire assembly of people, [18]"Micah[r] of Moresheth prophesied in the days of Hezekiah king of Judah. He told all the people of Judah, 'This is what the LORD Almighty says:

" 'Zion[s] will be plowed like a
field,
Jerusalem will become a heap of
rubble,[t]
the temple hill[u] a mound
overgrown with
thickets.'[b][v]

[19]"Did Hezekiah king of Judah or anyone else in Judah put him to death? Did not Hezekiah[w] fear the LORD and seek[x] his favor? And did not the LORD relent,[y] so that he did not bring the disaster[z] he pronounced against them? We are about to bring a terrible disaster[a] on ourselves!"

[20](Now Uriah son of Shemaiah from Kiriath Jearim[b] was another man who prophesied in the name of the LORD; he prophesied the same things against this city and this land as Jeremiah did. [21]When King Jehoiakim[c] and all his officers and officials[d] heard his words, the king sought to put him to

26:3 [q]Dt 30:2; 2Ch 33:12-13; Isa 55:7; Jer 35:15; 36:7 [r]S Jer 18:8 **26:4** [s]Lev 26:14; Jer 25:3 [t]Ex 20:1-23:33; S 1Ki 9:6; S Jer 11:8 **26:5** [u]S Pr 1:24; S Isa 65:12; Jer 25:4; 44:5 **26:6** [v]S Jos 18:1; S Jdg 18:31 [w]S Dt 28:25; S 2Ki 22:19 **26:8** [x]Jer 43:1 [y]Ac 6:12; 21:27 [z]Lev 24:15-16; S Ne 9:26; S Jer 11:21 **26:9** [a]S Lev 26:32; S Jer 9:11 [b]Ac 21:32 **26:10** [c]ver 16; Jer 34:19; Eze 22:27 [d]S Ge 23:10 **26:11** [e]Dt 18:20; S Jer 11:21; 18:23; Mt 26:66; Ac 6:11 [f]S Ps 44:1 **26:12** [g]Jer 1:18 [h]S Isa 6:8; Am 7:15; Ac 4:18-20; 5:29 [i]S ver 2,15 **26:13** [j]S Jer 7:5; Joel 2:12-14 [k]Jer 11:4 [l]S Jer 18:8 **26:14** [m]Jos 9:25; Jer 38:5 **26:15** [n]S Dt 19:10 [o]S ver 12; S Jer 1:17 **26:16** [p]S ver 10; S Ac 23:9 [q]Ac 23:29 **26:18** [r]Mic 1:1 [s]Isa 2:3 [t]S 2Ki 25:9; S Ne 4:2; Jer 9:11 [u]Mic 4:1; Zec 8:3 [v]S Jer 17:3 **26:19** [w]S 1Ch 3:13; 2Ch 32:24-26; Isa 37:14-20 [x]S 1Sa 13:12 [y]S Ex 32:14; S Jer 18:8 [z]Jer 44:7 [a]Hab 2:10 **26:20** [b]S Jos 9:17 **26:21** [c]S 1Ki 19:2 [d]ver 10

[b] *18* Micah 3:12

26:8 YOU MUST DIE! Because of his proclamation of the word of the Lord, Jeremiah was seized by the religious establishment (i.e., the priests and false prophets), who demanded his death. Religious leaders are often the ones who consistently oppose those who call for a return to Biblical faith and genuine righteousness; this was true in Jesus' day, and it will also be true in the last days before his return.

26:12–15 THEN JEREMIAH SAID. Jeremiah refused to retract his message of doom when threatened with death; rather, he emphasized that his authority came from God, and he then called on the sinful people to repent. He remained faithful to God and his word despite a possible dangerous outcome.

26:16–24 SHOULD NOT BE SENTENCED TO DEATH! After hearing Jeremiah's defense (vv. 12–15), the officials and people sided with him against the priests and prophets. Some elders defended Jeremiah by giving examples of the actions of a righteous king, Hezekiah, and an evil king, Jehoiakim.

death.[e] But Uriah heard of it and
fled[f] in fear to Egypt. 22King Jehoiakim, however, sent Elnathan[g] son of
Acbor to Egypt, along with some other
men. 23They brought Uriah out of
Egypt and took him to King Jehoiakim,
who had him struck down with a
sword[h] and his body thrown into the
burial place of the common people.)[i]
24Furthermore, Ahikam[j] son of
Shaphan supported Jeremiah, and so
he was not handed over to the people
to be put to death.

Judah to Serve Nebuchadnezzar

27 Early in the reign of Zedekiah[c][k] son of Josiah king of Judah, this word came to Jeremiah from
the LORD: 2This is what the LORD said
to me: "Make a yoke[l] out of straps
and crossbars and put it on your neck.
3Then send[m] word to the kings of
Edom, Moab, Ammon,[n] Tyre and Sidon[o] through the envoys who have
come to Jerusalem to Zedekiah king of
Judah. 4Give them a message for their
masters and say, 'This is what the LORD
Almighty, the God of Israel, says: "Tell
this to your masters: 5With my great
power and outstretched arm[p] I
made[q] the earth and its people and
the animals[r] that are on it, and I
give[s] it to anyone I please. 6Now I will
hand all your countries over to my servant[t] Nebuchadnezzar[u] king of Babylon; I will make even the wild animals
subject to him.[v] 7All nations will
serve[w] him and his son and his grandson until the time[x] for his land comes;
then many nations and great kings will
subjugate[y] him.
8" ' "If, however, any nation or kingdom will not serve Nebuchadnezzar
king of Babylon or bow its neck under
his yoke, I will punish[z] that nation
with the sword,[a] famine[b] and
plague,[c] declares the LORD, until I destroy it by his hand. 9So do not listen
to your prophets,[d] your diviners,[e]
your interpreters of dreams,[f] your
mediums[g] or your sorcerers[h] who
tell you, 'You will not serve[i] the king
of Babylon.' 10They prophesy lies[j] to
you that will only serve to remove[k]
you far from your lands; I will banish
you and you will perish. 11But if any
nation will bow its neck under the
yoke[l] of the king of Babylon and
serve him, I will let that nation remain
in its own land to till it and to live[m]
there, declares the LORD." ' "
12I gave the same message to Zedekiah king of Judah. I said, "Bow your
neck under the yoke[n] of the king of
Babylon; serve him and his people, and
you will live.[o] 13Why will you and your
people die[p] by the sword, famine and
plague[q] with which the LORD has
threatened any nation that will not
serve the king of Babylon? 14Do not listen[r] to the words of the prophets[s]
who say to you, 'You will not serve the
king of Babylon,' for they are prophesying lies[t] to you. 15'I have not sent[u]
them,' declares the LORD. 'They are
prophesying lies in my name.[v] Therefore, I will banish you and you will perish,[w] both you and the prophets who
prophesy to you.' "
16Then I said to the priests and all
these people, "This is what the LORD

26:21 [e] Jer 2:30; Mt 23:37 [f] S Ge 31:21; Mt 10:23
26:22 [g] Jer 36:12, 25
26:23 [h] Heb 11:37 [i] 2Ki 23:6
26:24 [j] S 2Ki 22:12
27:1 [k] S 2Ch 36:11
27:2 [l] S Lev 26:13; S 1Ki 22:11
27:3 [m] S Jer 25:17 [n] S Jer 25:21 [o] S Ge 10:15; S Jer 25:22
27:5 [p] S Dt 9:29 [q] S Ge 1:1 [r] S Ge 1:25 [s] Ps 115:16; Da 4:17
27:6 [t] S Jer 25:9 [u] S Jer 21:7 [v] Jer 28:14; Da 2:37-38
27:7 [w] S 2Ch 36:20; Da 5:18 [x] S Jer 25:12 [y] S Jer 25:14; 51:47; Da 5:28
27:8 [z] Jer 9:16 [a] Jer 21:9 [b] S Jer 5:12 [c] S Jer 14:12
27:9 [d] Eze 13:1-23 [e] S Ge 30:27; S Isa 44:25 [f] S Dt 13:1; S Jer 23:25 [g] S Dt 18:11 [h] S Ex 7:11 [i] Jer 6:14
27:10 [j] S Jer 23:25; S Mk 13:5 [k] S 2Ki 23:27
27:11 [l] S Jer 21:9 [m] Dt 6:2
27:12 [n] Jer 17:4 [o] S Jer 21:9
27:13 [p] Eze 18:31 [q] S Jer 14:12
27:14 [r] S Jer 23:16 [s] S Jer 14:13 [t] S Jer 14:14; S Mt 7:15
27:15 [u] S Jer 23:21 [v] Jer 29:9; 44:16 [w] S Jer 6:15; Mt 15:12-14

[c] *1* A few Hebrew manuscripts and Syriac (see also Jer. 27:3, 12 and 28:1); most Hebrew manuscripts *Jehoiakim* (Most Septuagint manuscripts do not have this verse.)

26:23 URIAH . . . STRUCK DOWN. Jeremiah was delivered from death, while another righteous prophet named Uriah was not. Why God allows some of his people to suffer a martyr's death and others to die a natural death is not explained in Scripture (cf. Ac 12:1–17). But we do know that God has an eternal purpose in what he permits to happen to his faithful followers and that in all things he works for their good (see Ro 8:28, note).

27:6 MY SERVANT NEBUCHADNEZZAR. Nebuchadnezzar is called God's servant, not because he was righteous, but because God would use him and his army to punish many nations, including God's nation of Judah, for their sins; however, God would also overthrow Babylon in his own set time (v. 7).

27:8 WILL NOT SERVE NEBUCHADNEZZAR. Jeremiah's prophetic counsel to Judah was to submit to Babylon's dominion and not resist God's will for them. However, if they rebelled and fought against Babylon, Jeremiah warned that they would experience great suffering and defeat.

27:9 DO NOT LISTEN TO YOUR PROPHETS. The false prophets were predicting a successful rebellion against their enemies and encouraging the people to throw off the yoke of Babylon. Jeremiah, on the other hand, instructed the people not to listen to them; he prophesied that Babylon would dominate Judah and the surrounding nations.

27:16 ARTICLES FROM THE LORD'S HOUSE. Some temple articles had been carried off to Babylon in 605 B.C. (see Da 1:1–2), others in 597 B.C. (2Ki 24:13).

says: Do not listen to the prophets who
say, 'Very soon now the articles[x] from
the LORD's house will be brought back
from Babylon.' They are prophesying
lies to you. **17**Do not listen[y] to them.
Serve the king of Babylon, and you will
live.[z] Why should this city become a
ruin? **18**If they are prophets and have
the word of the LORD, let them plead[a]
with the LORD Almighty that the furnishings remaining in the house of the
LORD and in the palace of the king of
Judah and in Jerusalem not be taken to
Babylon. **19**For this is what the LORD
Almighty says about the pillars, the
Sea,[b] the movable stands and the other furnishings[c] that are left in this
city, **20**which Nebuchadnezzar king of
Babylon did not take away when he
carried[d] Jehoiachin[d][e] son of Jehoiakim king of Judah into exile from Jerusalem to Babylon, along with all the
nobles of Judah and Jerusalem—
21yes, this is what the LORD Almighty,
the God of Israel, says about the things
that are left in the house of the LORD
and in the palace of the king of Judah
and in Jerusalem: **22**'They will be tak-
en[f] to Babylon and there they will remain until the day[g] I come for them,'
declares the LORD. 'Then I will bring[h]
them back and restore them to this
place.' "

The False Prophet Hananiah

28 In the fifth month of that same
year, the fourth year, early in
the reign of Zedekiah[i] king of Judah,
the prophet Hananiah son of Azzur,
who was from Gibeon,[j] said to me in
the house of the LORD in the presence
of the priests and all the people: **2**"This
is what the LORD Almighty, the God of
Israel, says: 'I will break the yoke[k] of
the king of Babylon. **3**Within two years
I will bring back to this place all the
articles[l] of the LORD's house that Nebuchadnezzar king of Babylon removed
from here and took to Babylon. **4**I will
also bring back to this place Jehoiachin[d][m] son of Jehoiakim king of Judah
and all the other exiles from Judah who
went to Babylon,' declares the LORD,
'for I will break the yoke of the king of
Babylon.' "[n]

5Then the prophet Jeremiah replied
to the prophet Hananiah before the
priests and all the people who were
standing in the house of the LORD. **6**He
said, "Amen! May the LORD do so! May
the LORD fulfill the words you have
prophesied by bringing the articles of
the LORD's house and all the exiles
back to this place from Babylon.[o]
7Nevertheless, listen to what I have to
say in your hearing and in the hearing
of all the people: **8**From early times the
prophets who preceded you and me
have prophesied war, disaster and
plague[p] against many countries and
great kingdoms. **9**But the prophet who
prophesies peace will be recognized as
one truly sent by the LORD only if his
prediction comes true.[q]"

10Then the prophet Hananiah took
the yoke[r] off the neck of the prophet
Jeremiah and broke it, **11**and he said[s]
before all the people, "This is what the
LORD says: 'In the same way will I
break the yoke of Nebuchadnezzar
king of Babylon off the neck of all the
nations within two years.' " At this, the
prophet Jeremiah went on his way.

12Shortly after the prophet Hananiah had broken the yoke off the neck of
the prophet Jeremiah, the word of the
LORD came to Jeremiah: **13**"Go and tell
Hananiah, 'This is what the LORD says:
You have broken a wooden yoke, but in
its place you will get a yoke of iron.
14This is what the LORD Almighty, the
God of Israel, says: I will put an iron

27:16 [x] 1Ki 7:48-50; S 2Ki 24:13 **27:17** [y] Jer 23:16 [z] Jer 42:11 **27:18** [a] S Nu 21:7; S 1Sa 7:8 **27:19** [b] 1Ki 7:23-26 [c] S 1Ki 7:51; Jer 52:17-23 **27:20** [d] S Dt 28:36; S 2Ch 36:10 [e] Jer 22:24; Mt 1:11 **27:22** [f] S 2Ki 20:17; 25:13 [g] S 2Ch 36:21; S Jer 24:6 [h] S Ezr 7:19 **28:1** [i] S 2Ch 36:11 [j] S Jos 9:3 **28:2** [k] Jer 27:12 **28:3** [l] S 2Ki 24:13 **28:4** [m] S 2Ki 25:30; Jer 22:24-27 [n] Hos 7:3 **28:6** [o] Zec 6:10 **28:8** [p] Lev 26:14-17; Isa 5:5-7; Na 1:14 **28:9** [q] S Dt 18:22; Eze 33:33 **28:10** [r] S Lev 26:13; S 1Ki 22:11 **28:11** [s] Jer 14:14; 27:10

[d] *20,4* Hebrew *Jeconiah,* a variant of *Jehoiachin*

28:1 THE PROPHET HANANIAH. Hananiah, who opposed Jeremiah's message of doom, was a false prophet who predicted Babylon's fall and the return of exiles and temple treasures within two years. False religious leaders often predict that God's blessings come unconditionally, without the need for repentance or holy living; such a message always has popular appeal.

28:6–9 AMEN! MAY THE LORD DO SO! Jeremiah's "Amen" shows he also desired the return of the captives; however, first he prophesied further disaster for the people. Time would show Hananiah to be a false prophet and Jeremiah a true one. Jeremiah here did not immediately give a new prophecy; he referred instead to the word of God already given through older prophets (like Isaiah).

28:13–17 GO AND TELL HANANIAH. Hananiah had deceived the people into believing lies; as a result, Jeremiah received a word from the Lord that predicted Hananiah's death; within two months the false prophet died, confirming Jeremiah's prophecy. The penalty for apostasy and false prophecy is high. All leaders within the church who are not genuine servants of God will someday encounter the same severe judgment.

yoke[t] on the necks of all these nations to make them serve[u] Nebuchadnezzar[v] king of Babylon, and they will
serve him. I will even give him control
over the wild animals.[w]' "
15Then the prophet Jeremiah said to
Hananiah the prophet, "Listen, Hananiah! The LORD has not sent[x] you, yet
you have persuaded this nation to trust
in lies.[y] **16**Therefore, this is what the
LORD says: 'I am about to remove you
from the face of the earth.[z] This very
year you are going to die,[a] because
you have preached rebellion[b] against
the LORD.' "
17In the seventh month of that same
year, Hananiah the prophet died.[c]

A Letter to the Exiles

29 This is the text of the letter[d]
that the prophet Jeremiah sent
from Jerusalem to the surviving elders
among the exiles and to the priests, the
prophets and all the other people Nebuchadnezzar had carried into exile
from Jerusalem to Babylon.[e] **2**(This
was after King Jehoiachin[e][f] and the
queen mother,[g] the court officials and
the leaders of Judah and Jerusalem, the
craftsmen and the artisans had gone
into exile from Jerusalem.) **3**He entrusted the letter to Elasah son of Shaphan and to Gemariah son of Hilkiah,
whom Zedekiah king of Judah sent to
King Nebuchadnezzar in Babylon. It
said:

4This is what the LORD Almighty, the God of Israel, says to
all those I carried[h] into exile
from Jerusalem to Babylon:
5"Build[i] houses and settle down;
plant gardens and eat what they
produce. **6**Marry and have sons
and daughters; find wives for your
sons and give your daughters in
marriage, so that they too may
have sons and daughters. Increase in number there; do not decrease.[j] **7**Also, seek[k] the peace
and prosperity of the city to which
I have carried you into exile.
Pray[l] to the LORD for it, because
if it prospers, you too will prosper." **8**Yes, this is what the LORD
Almighty, the God of Israel, says:
"Do not let the prophets[m] and diviners among you deceive[n] you.
Do not listen to the dreams[o] you
encourage them to have.[p] **9**They
are prophesying lies[q] to you in
my name. I have not sent[r] them,"
declares the LORD.
10This is what the LORD says:
"When seventy years[s] are completed for Babylon, I will come to
you[t] and fulfill my gracious
promise[u] to bring you back[v] to
this place. **11**For I know the
plans[w] I have for you," declares
the LORD, "plans to prosper[x] you
and not to harm you, plans to give
you hope and a future.[y] **12**Then
you will call[z] upon me and come
and pray[a] to me, and I will listen[b] to you. **13**You will seek[c] me
and find me when you seek me
with all your heart.[d] **14**I will be
found by you," declares the LORD,
"and will bring you back[e] from

28:14 [t] S Dt 28:48; S Jer 15:12 [u] Jer 25:11 [v] Jer 39:1; Da 1:1; 5:18 [w] S Jer 27:6
28:15 [x] Jer 29:31 [y] S Jer 7:4; 20:6; 29:21; La 2:14; Eze 13:6
28:16 [z] S Ge 7:4 [a] Dt 18:20; Zec 13:3 [b] Dt 13:5; Jer 29:32
28:17 [c] S 2Ki 1:17
29:1 [d] ver 28 [e] S 2Ch 36:10; S Jer 13:17
29:2 [f] S 2Ki 24:12 [g] S 2Ki 24:8
29:4 [h] S Jer 24:5
29:5 [i] ver 28
29:6 [j] Jer 30:19
29:7 [k] S Est 3:8 [l] 1Ti 2:1-2
29:8 [m] 1Jn 4:1 [n] Jer 37:9 [o] S Dt 13:1; S Jer 23:25 [p] S Jer 23:27
29:9 [q] S Jer 27:15; La 2:14; Eze 13:6 [r] Jer 23:21
29:10 [s] S 2Ch 36:21; S Da 9:2 [t] S Ru 1:6 [u] 1Ki 8:56; Jer 32:42; 33:14 [v] S Jer 16:14; S 24:6
29:11 [w] Ps 40:5 [x] Isa 55:12 [y] S Job 8:7; Zec 8:15
29:12 [z] Hos 2:23; Zep 3:12; Zec 13:9 [a] S 1Ki 8:30 [b] Ps 145:19; S Isa 55:6
29:13 [c] Mt 7:7 [d] S Dt 4:29; S 2Ch 6:37
29:14 [e] S Dt 30:3; Jer 30:3; Eze 39:25; Am 9:14; Zep 3:20

[e] *2* Hebrew *Jeconiah,* a variant of *Jehoiachin*

29:1–23 THE LETTER. Jeremiah's letter to the Jewish exiles taken captive in 597 B.C. was probably written a year or two after they arrived in Babylon. He gave them the following instructions: (1) They must live normal lives, build houses, marry, and seek the peace or well-being of the city where God had providentially placed them, for they would not be returning to the promised land until the end of seventy years (vv. 7,10). (2) They must not listen to the false prophets who were predicting the exile would be short (vv. 8–9). (3) Those who remained in Jerusalem would suffer greatly for their persistence in rebelling against God (vv. 15–19). (4) Two false prophets would be killed because they were living in adultery and falsely representing God's word (vv. 21–23). (5) At the end of the seventy years of captivity, the remnant would seek God earnestly for restoration; he would answer their intercession because of his plans for them (vv. 10–14).

29:10 SEVENTY YEARS. See 25:11, note.

29:12–13 YOU WILL CALL . . . AND I WILL LISTEN. Strategic timing is often involved in the fulfillment of God's promises (cf. Paul's reference to "when the time had fully come" in Gal 4:4). God fulfills his word and promises both in relation to the fullness of his redemptive purpose (cf. v. 10) and in response to his faithful people's earnest prayers (cf. Am 5:4–6; see Da 9:2,5, notes). Jeremiah prophesied that at the end of the seventy-year captivity, a new fullness of time would occur; God would then move within a holy remnant so that they would seek him in prayer with all their hearts. Thereupon God would listen, answer from heaven and fulfill his promises of restoration (vv. 13–14). Note two principles: (1) when God desires to do great things for his people, he moves his people to great praying; and (2) the timing of God's answers to their prayers is often linked to God's purposes for his people as a whole.

captivity.[t] I will gather you from
all the nations and places where I
have banished you," declares the
LORD, "and will bring you back to
the place from which I carried you
into exile."[f]
15You may say, "The LORD has
raised up prophets for us in Babylon," **16**but this is what the LORD
says about the king who sits on
David's throne and all the people
who remain in this city, your
countrymen who did not go with
you into exile— **17**yes, this is
what the LORD Almighty says: "I
will send the sword, famine and
plague[g] against them and I will
make them like poor figs[h] that
are so bad they cannot be eaten.
18I will pursue them with the
sword, famine and plague and will
make them abhorrent[i] to all the
kingdoms of the earth and an object of cursing[j] and horror,[k] of
scorn[l] and reproach, among all
the nations where I drive them.
19For they have not listened to my
words,"[m] declares the LORD,
"words that I sent to them again
and again[n] by my servants the
prophets.[o] And you exiles have
not listened either," declares the
LORD.
20Therefore, hear the word of
the LORD, all you exiles whom I
have sent[p] away from Jerusalem
to Babylon. **21**This is what the
LORD Almighty, the God of Israel,
says about Ahab son of Kolaiah
and Zedekiah son of Maaseiah,
who are prophesying lies[q] to you
in my name: "I will hand them
over to Nebuchadnezzar king of
Babylon, and he will put them to
death before your very eyes. **22**Because of them, all the exiles from
Judah who are in Babylon will use
this curse: 'The LORD treat you
like Zedekiah and Ahab, whom
the king of Babylon burned[r] in
the fire.' **23**For they have done
outrageous things in Israel; they
have committed adultery[s] with
their neighbors' wives and in my
name have spoken lies, which I
did not tell them to do. I know[t]
it and am a witness[u] to it," declares the LORD.

Message to Shemaiah

24Tell Shemaiah the Nehelamite,
25"This is what the LORD Almighty, the
God of Israel, says: You sent letters in
your own name to all the people in Jerusalem, to Zephaniah[v] son of Maaseiah the priest, and to all the other
priests. You said to Zephaniah, **26**'The
LORD has appointed you priest in place
of Jehoiada to be in charge of the house
of the LORD; you should put any madman[w] who acts like a prophet into the
stocks[x] and neck-irons. **27**So why
have you not reprimanded Jeremiah
from Anathoth, who poses as a prophet
among you? **28**He has sent this message[y] to us in Babylon: It will be a
long time.[z] Therefore build[a] houses
and settle down; plant gardens and eat
what they produce.' "
29Zephaniah[b] the priest, however,
read the letter to Jeremiah the prophet.
30Then the word of the LORD came to
Jeremiah: **31**"Send this message to all
the exiles: 'This is what the LORD says
about Shemaiah[c] the Nehelamite: Because Shemaiah has prophesied to
you, even though I did not send[d] him,
and has led you to believe a lie, **32**this
is what the LORD says: I will surely punish Shemaiah the Nehelamite and his
descendants.[e] He will have no one left
among this people, nor will he see the
good[f] things I will do for my people,
declares the LORD, because he has
preached rebellion[g] against me.' "

Restoration of Israel

30 This is the word that came to
Jeremiah from the LORD: **2**"This
is what the LORD, the God of Israel,

29:14 [f]Jer 23:3-4; 30:10; 46:27; Eze 37:21
29:17 [g]Jer 27:8 [h]S Isa 5:4
29:18 [i]S Jer 15:4 [j]S Nu 5:27; S Jer 18:16; S 22:10; 44:12 [k]S Dt 28:25 [l]S Dt 28:37; S Isa 28:22; S Mic 2:6
29:19 [m]Jer 6:19 [n]Jer 7:25 [o]S Jer 25:4
29:20 [p]S Jer 24:5
29:21 [q]ver 9; Jer 14:14
29:22 [r]Da 3:6
29:23 [s]S Jer 23:14 [t]S Heb 4:13 [u]S Ge 31:48; S Jer 7:11
29:25 [v]S 2Ki 25:18
29:26 [w]S 1Sa 10:11; Hos 9:7; S Jn 10:20 [x]Jer 20:2
29:28 [y]ver 1 [z]ver 10 [a]ver 5
29:29 [b]Jer 21:1
29:31 [c]ver 24 [d]S Jer 14:14
29:32 [e]S 1Sa 2:30-33 [f]ver 10 [g]S Jer 28:16

[t] 14 Or *will restore your fortunes*

29:23 OUTRAGEOUS THINGS IN ISRAEL. God considers it outrageous to proclaim his message and at the same time commit adultery and other immoral acts. For this reason, the two prophets Ahab and Zedekiah (v. 21) would be put to death before the people's very eyes. Church leaders today who proclaim God's word while living in adultery will also have to face his severe judgment (see article on MORAL QUALIFICATIONS FOR OVERSEERS, p. 1882).

29:24–32 SHEMAIAH. Shemaiah was a false prophet in Babylon who had written a letter to Zephaniah, a priest in Jerusalem, urging him to imprison Jeremiah. Evidently Jeremiah's letters to the exiles had angered the false prophets in Babylon. God responded by asserting that neither Shemaiah nor his descendants would participate in the return to Jerusalem.

says: 'Write[h] in a book all the words
I have spoken to you. [3]The days[i] are
coming,' declares the LORD, 'when I
will bring[j] my people Israel and Judah
back from captivity[g] and restore[k]
them to the land I gave their forefathers to possess,' says the LORD."
[4]These are the words the LORD spoke
concerning Israel and Judah: [5]"This is
what the LORD says:

" 'Cries of fear[l] are heard—
terror, not peace.
[6]Ask and see:
Can a man bear children?
Then why do I see every strong man
with his hands on his stomach
like a woman in labor,[m]
every face turned deathly pale?[n]
[7]How awful that day[o] will be!
None will be like it.
It will be a time of trouble[p] for Jacob,
but he will be saved[q] out of it.

[8]" 'In that day,' declares the LORD Almighty,
'I will break the yoke[r] off their necks
and will tear off their bonds;[s]
no longer will foreigners enslave them.[t]
[9]Instead, they will serve the LORD their God
and David[u] their king,[v]
whom I will raise up for them.

[10]" 'So do not fear,[w] O Jacob my servant;[x]
do not be dismayed, O Israel,'
declares the LORD.
'I will surely save[y] you out of a distant place,
your descendants from the land of their exile.
Jacob will again have peace and security,[z]
and no one will make him afraid.[a]
[11]I am with you[b] and will save you,'
declares the LORD.
'Though I completely destroy all the nations
among which I scatter you,
I will not completely destroy[c] you.
I will discipline[d] you but only with justice;
I will not let you go entirely unpunished.'[e]

[12]"This is what the LORD says:

" 'Your wound[f] is incurable,
your injury beyond healing.[g]
[13]There is no one to plead your cause,[h]
no remedy for your sore,
no healing[i] for you.
[14]All your allies[j] have forgotten you;
they care nothing for you.
I have struck you as an enemy[k] would

30:2 [h]S Isa 30:8; S Jer 36:2 30:3 [i]S Jer 16:14; S 24:6 [j]S Jer 29:14 [k]S Jer 16:15 30:5 [l]Jer 6:25 30:6 [m]S Jer 4:31 [n]S Isa 29:22 30:7 [o]S Isa 2:12 [p]S Isa 22:5; Zep 1:15 [q]ver 10; Jer 23:3 30:8 [r]S Isa 9:4 [s]Ps 107:14 [t]Jer 25:14; 27:7; Eze 34:27 30:9 [u]S Mt 1:1 [v]ver 21; S 1Sa 13:14; Jer 33:15; Eze 34:23-24; 37:24; Hos 1:11; 3:5 30:10 [w]S Isa 41:10 [x]S Isa 44:2 [y]S ver 7; S Jer 29:14 [z]Isa 35:9; S Jer 17:25 [a]S Isa 29:22; S 54:4; S Jer 23:4; Eze 34:25-28 30:11 [b]S Jos 1:5 [c]S Lev 26:44; S Jer 5:18; 46:28 [d]S Jer 10:24 [e]Hos 11:9; Am 9:8 30:12 [f]S Job 6:4; S Jer 10:19 [g]S Jer 8:22 30:13 [h]S Jdg 6:31 [i]S Jer 8:22; 14:19; 46:11; Na 3:19 30:14 [j]S Jer 22:20; La 1:2 [k]S Job 13:24

[g]3 Or *will restore the fortunes of my people Israel and Judah*

30:1—33:26 THE WORD ... FROM THE LORD. Chs. 30—33 contain prophecies about the future restoration and redemption of both Israel (the northern kingdom) and Judah (the southern kingdom). Jeremiah's prophecies encompass the near-at-hand restoration of the Jews from the Babylonian exile and the far-distant events related to the Messiah at the end of the age, when Christ will reign over his people. Jeremiah assures the Jewish exiles who were facing an apparently hopeless future that God's chosen people would not become extinct; a remnant would remain through whom God would accomplish his will for the world.

30:3 RESTORE THEM TO THE LAND. Jeremiah had good news for the exiles—the promise of restoration and repossession of their homeland. The promise was made to both the northern kingdom (Israel) and the southern kingdom (Judah). From the exiles who had been displaced and refined by their experience of deportation would come God's remnant, who would in turn give hope to all humankind.

30:7 A TIME OF TROUBLE FOR JACOB. The verses that follow this phrase indicate that Jeremiah is speaking about the time of future tribulation for the Jewish people (cf. Isa 2:12–21; Eze 30:3; Da 9:27; Joel 1:15; Zec 14:1–8,12–15; Mt 24:21). From this time of great trouble a remnant of Israel would be saved; they would be freed from their oppressors (v. 8) to serve God and the Messiah (v. 9). Jacob's trouble would end at the appearing of Christ to establish his kingdom on earth (Rev 19:11–21; 20:4–6).

30:9–10 DAVID THEIR KING. The person whom the people will serve is Jesus the Messiah, the descendant of David (cf. Hos 3:5; Eze 37:24–25). "Jacob" refers to a righteous remnant from both Israel and Judah; they will live in peace and security, and the nations that opposed God and persecuted those serving him will be destroyed (v. 11).

and punished you as would the
cruel,[l]
because your guilt is so great
and your sins[m] so many.
15Why do you cry out over your
wound,
your pain that has no cure?[n]
Because of your great guilt and
many sins
I have done these things to
you.[o]

16" 'But all who devour[p] you will be
devoured;
all your enemies will go into
exile.[q]
Those who plunder[r] you will be
plundered;
all who make spoil of you I will
despoil.
17But I will restore you to health
and heal[s] your wounds,'
declares the LORD,
'because you are called an
outcast,[t]
Zion for whom no one cares.'[u]

18"This is what the LORD says:

" 'I will restore the fortunes[v] of
Jacob's tents[w]
and have compassion[x] on his
dwellings;
the city will be rebuilt[y] on her
ruins,
and the palace will stand in its
proper place.
19From them will come songs[z] of
thanksgiving[a]
and the sound of rejoicing.[b]
I will add to their numbers,[c]
and they will not be decreased;
I will bring them honor,[d]
and they will not be disdained.
20Their children[e] will be as in days
of old,
and their community will be
established[f] before me;
I will punish[g] all who oppress
them.
21Their leader[h] will be one of their
own;
their ruler will arise from among
them.[i]
I will bring him near[j] and he will
come close to me,
for who is he who will devote
himself
to be close to me?'
declares the LORD.
22" 'So you will be my people,[k]
and I will be your God.[l]' "

23See, the storm[m] of the LORD
will burst out in wrath,
a driving wind swirling down
on the heads of the wicked.
24The fierce anger[n] of the LORD will
not turn back[o]
until he fully accomplishes
the purposes of his heart.
In days to come
you will understand[p] this.

31

"At that time," declares the LORD, "I will be the God[q] of all the clans of Israel, and they will be my people."

2This is what the LORD says:

"The people who survive the sword
will find favor[r] in the desert;
I will come to give rest[s] to
Israel."

3The LORD appeared to us in the past,[h] saying:

"I have loved[t] you with an
everlasting love;
I have drawn[u] you with
loving-kindness.
4I will build you up again

30:14 [l]S Job 30:21 [m]S Jer 25:7
30:15 [n]S Jer 10:19 [o]S Pr 1:31; La 1:5
30:16 [p]S Isa 29:8; S 33:1; S Jer 2:3 [q]S Isa 14:2; Joel 3:4-8 [r]Jer 49:2; 50:10
30:17 [s]S Isa 1:5; Hos 6:1 [t]S Isa 6:12; Jer 33:24 [u]Ps 142:4
30:18 [v]ver 3; S Dt 30:3; Jer 31:23; 32:44 [w]S Nu 24:5 [x]Ps 102:13; Jer 33:26; Eze 39:25 [y]Jer 31:4,24,38; 33:7; Eze 36:10, 33; Am 9:14
30:19 [z]S Ps 9:2; Isa 35:10; S 51:11 [a]S Isa 51:3 [b]Ps 126:1-2; Jer 31:4 [c]S Ge 15:5; 22:17; Jer 33:22; Eze 37:26; Zec 2:4 [d]S Isa 44:23; S 60:9
30:20 [e]Isa 54:13; Jer 31:17; Zec 8:5 [f]Isa 54:14 [g]S Ex 23:22
30:21 [h]S ver 9; Jer 23:5-6 [i]Dt 17:15 [j]Nu 16:5
30:22 [k]S Isa 19:25; Hos 2:23 [l]S Lev 26:12
30:23 [m]S Jer 23:19
30:24 [n]Jer 4:8; La 1:12 [o]S Jer 4:28 [p]Jer 23:19-20
31:1 [q]S Lev 26:12
31:2 [r]Nu 14:20 [s]S Ex 33:14; S Dt 12:9
31:3 [t]S Dt 4:37 [u]Hos 11:4; Jn 6:44

[h]3 Or *LORD has appeared to us from afar*

30:21 THEIR RULER. Jesus Christ is ultimately the new ruler who will lead the people to God. He will have intimate access to God; thus he will have a priestly ministry, resulting in the nation's restoration to the spiritual vitality and worship that God had always intended. But before this happens, God's anger will judge evil among the nations (vv. 23–24).

31:1–40 AT THAT TIME. This chapter concerns the restoration of Israel generally (vv. 2–22), and Judah specifically (vv. 23–26), to the promised land. God's people would again live together under his blessing (vv. 27–30). After assuring them of this regathering, Jeremiah reveals that God would make a new and better covenant with his people that would include spiritual power to obey his commands.

31:2 THE PEOPLE. These people are the remnant from all the families of Israel who would return from captivity. Many were carried away by the Assyrians in 722 B.C., others by the Babylonians in 605, 597 and 586 B.C. God would bring them back because of his everlasting love for his people (v. 3) and his commitment to the covenant he made with Abraham (see Ge 15:7–21) and with Israel (Ex 19:3–8; Dt 28:1—30:10). Israel would have renewed joy, peace, prosperity and fellowship in the Lord.

and you will be rebuilt,[v]
O Virgin[w] Israel.
Again you will take up your
tambourines[x]
and go out to dance[y] with the
joyful.[z]
5Again you will plant[a] vineyards
on the hills of Samaria;[b]
the farmers will plant them
and enjoy their fruit.[c]
6There will be a day when
watchmen[d] cry out
on the hills of Ephraim,
'Come, let us go up to Zion,
to the LORD our God.' "[e]

7This is what the LORD says:

"Sing[f] with joy for Jacob;
shout for the foremost[g] of the
nations.
Make your praises heard, and say,
'O LORD, save[h] your people,
the remnant[i] of Israel.'

Da 2:20-23

8See, I will bring them from the
land of the north[j]
and gather[k] them from the ends
of the earth.
Among them will be the blind[l]
and the lame,[m]
expectant mothers and women in
labor;
a great throng will return.
9They will come with weeping;[n]
they will pray as I bring them
back.
I will lead[o] them beside streams
of water[p]
on a level[q] path where they will
not stumble,
because I am Israel's father,[r]
and Ephraim is my firstborn son.

10"Hear the word of the LORD,
O nations;
proclaim it in distant
coastlands:[s]
'He who scattered[t] Israel will
gather[u] them
and will watch over his flock
like a shepherd.'[v]
11For the LORD will ransom Jacob
and redeem[w] them from the
hand of those stronger[x]
than they.
12They will come and shout for joy[y]
on the heights[z] of Zion;
they will rejoice in the bounty[a]
of the LORD—
the grain, the new wine and the
oil,[b]
the young of the flocks[c] and
herds.
They will be like a well-watered
garden,[d]
and they will sorrow[e] no more.
13Then maidens will dance and be
glad,
young men and old as well.
I will turn their mourning[f] into
gladness;
I will give them comfort[g] and
joy[h] instead of sorrow.
14I will satisfy[i] the priests[j] with
abundance,
and my people will be filled with
my bounty,[k]"
declares the LORD.

15This is what the LORD says:

"A voice is heard in Ramah,[l]
mourning and great weeping,
Rachel weeping for her children
and refusing to be comforted,[m]
because her children are no
more."[n]

16This is what the LORD says:

"Restrain your voice from weeping
and your eyes from tears,[o]
for your work will be rewarded,[p]"
declares the LORD.
"They will return[q] from the
land of the enemy.
17So there is hope[r] for your future,"
declares the LORD.
"Your children[s] will return to
their own land.

18"I have surely heard Ephraim's
moaning:

31:4 [v]S Jer 1:10; S 30:18 [w]S 2Ki 19:21 [x]S Ge 31:27 [y]S Ex 15:20 [z]S Jer 30:19 31:5 [a]S Dt 20:6 [b]Jer 33:13; 50:19; Ob 1:19 [c]S Isa 37:30; Am 9:14 31:6 [d]S Isa 52:8; S 56:10 [e]ver 12; S Dt 33:19; Jer 50:4-5; Mic 4:2 31:7 [f]S Isa 12:6 [g]Dt 28:13; Isa 61:9 [h]Ps 14:7; 28:9 [i]S Isa 37:31 31:8 [j]S Jer 3:18 [k]S Ge 33:13; S Dt 30:4; S Ps 106:47; Eze 34:12-14 [l]Isa 42:16 [m]Eze 34:16; Mic 4:6 31:9 [n]S Ezr 3:12; Ps 126:5 [o]Isa 63:13 [p]S Nu 20:8; S Ps 1:3; S Isa 32:2 [q]S Isa 40:4; S 49:11 [r]S Ex 4:22; S Jer 3:4 31:10 [s]Isa 49:1; S 66:19; S Jer 25:22 [t]S Lev 26:33 [u]S Dt 30:4; S Isa 11:12; Jer 50:19 [v]Isa 40:11; Eze 34:12
31:11 [w]S Ex 6:6; Zec 9:16 [x]Ps 142:6 31:12 [y]S Ps 126:5 [z]Eze 17:23; 20:40; 40:2; Mic 4:1 [a]S Ps 36:8; Joel 3:18 [b]S Nu 18:12; Hos 2:21-22; Joel 2:19 [c]ver 24; S Isa 65:10 [d]S SS 4:15 [e]S Isa 30:19; S 62:5; Jn 16:22; S Rev 7:17 31:13 [f]S Isa 61:3 [g]S Isa 40:1 [h]Ps 30:11; S Isa 51:11 31:14 [i]ver 25 [j]Lev 7:35-36 [k]S Ps 36:8; S Isa 30:23 31:15 [l]S Jos 18:25 [m]S Ge 37:35 [n]S Jer 10:20; Mt 2:17-18* 31:16 [o]S Ps 30:5; S Isa 25:8; 30:19 [p]S Ru 2:12; S 2Ch 15:7 [q]Jer 30:3; Eze 11:17 31:17 [r]S Job 8:7; La 3:29 [s]S Jer 30:20

31:15 HEARD IN RAMAH ... RACHEL WEEPING. Ramah was a town about five miles north of Jerusalem, probably the place where captives were held before deportation to Babylon (cf. 40:1–3). Rachel was one of Jacob's wives, and the mother of Joseph and Benjamin; she represents Israel weeping for those who were being deported into exile. God states that she did not need to weep any more, for the people would return (vv. 16–20). Matthew sees this passage as having a prophetic application to the time when Herod killed the children of Bethelem after Jesus' birth (Mt 2:16–18).

31:18 EPHRAIM'S MOANING. "Ephraim," a synonym for Israel (the northern kingdom), expressed grief for its sins and willingness to repent.

'You disciplined[t] me like an
unruly calf,[u]
and I have been disciplined.
Restore[v] me, and I will return,
because you are the LORD my
God.
19After I strayed,[w]
I repented;
after I came to understand,
I beat[x] my breast.
I was ashamed[y] and humiliated
because I bore the disgrace of
my youth.'[z]
20Is not Ephraim my dear son,
the child[a] in whom I delight?
Though I often speak against him,
I still remember[b] him.
Therefore my heart yearns for him;
I have great compassion[c] for
him,"
declares the LORD.

21"Set up road signs;
put up guideposts.[d]
Take note of the highway,[e]
the road that you take.
Return,[f] O Virgin[g] Israel,
return to your towns.
22How long will you wander,[h]
O unfaithful[i] daughter?
The LORD will create a new thing[j]
on earth—
a woman will surround[ik] a
man."

23This is what the LORD Almighty,
the God of Israel, says: "When I bring
them back from captivity,[jl] the people in the land of Judah and in its towns
will once again use these words: 'The
LORD bless[m] you, O righteous dwelling,[n] O sacred mountain.'[o] 24People
will live[p] together in Judah and all its
towns—farmers and those who move
about with their flocks.[q] 25I will refresh the weary[r] and satisfy the
faint."[s]

26At this I awoke[t] and looked
around. My sleep had been pleasant to
me.

27"The days are coming," declares
the LORD, "when I will plant[v] the
house of Israel and the house of Judah
with the offspring of men and of animals. 28Just as I watched[w] over them
to uproot[x] and tear down, and to overthrow, destroy and bring disaster,[y] so
I will watch over them to build and to
plant,"[z] declares the LORD. 29"In those
days people will no longer say,

'The fathers[a] have eaten sour
grapes,
and the children's teeth are set
on edge.'[b]

30Instead, everyone will die for his own
sin;[c] whoever eats sour grapes—his
own teeth will be set on edge.

31"The time is coming," declares the
LORD,
"when I will make a new
covenant[d]
with the house of Israel
and with the house of Judah.
32It will not be like the covenant[e]

31:18 [t]S Job 5:17 [u]Jer 50:11; Hos 4:16; 10:11 [v]S Ps 80:3 **31:19** [w]S Ps 95:10; S Jer 8:4; Eze 36:31 [x]Eze 21:12; Lk 18:13 [y]Ezr 9:6 [z]S Ps 25:7; S Jer 22:21 **31:20** [a]La 3:33 [b]S Isa 44:21 [c]S 1Ki 3:26; S Ps 6:2; Isa 55:7; Mic 7:18 **31:21** [d]Eze 21:19 [e]Isa 35:8; Jer 50:5 [f]Isa 52:11; S Jer 3:12 [g]ver 4 **31:22** [h]S Jer 2:23 [i]S Jer 3:6 [j]Isa 43:19 [k]S Dt 32:10 **31:23** [l]S Jer 30:18 [m]S Ge 28:3; S Nu 6:24 [n]S Isa 1:26 [o]S Ps 48:1; S Isa 2:2 **31:24** [p]S Jer 30:18; Zec 8:4-8 [q]S ver 12 **31:25** [r]S Isa 40:29 [s]Jn 4:14 **31:26** [t]Zec 4:1 **31:27** [u]S Jer 16:14 [v]Hos 2:23 **31:28** [w]S Job 29:2 [x]S Dt 29:28 [y]S Jer 18:8 [z]S Dt 28:63; S 30:9; S Jer 1:10; Eze 36:10-11; Am 9:14 **31:29** [a]S Ge 9:25; Dt 24:16; La 5:7 [b]Eze 18:2 **31:30** [c]S 2Ki 14:6; S Isa 3:11; Gal 6:7 **31:31** [d]S Dt 29:14; S Isa 42:6; S 54:10; S Lk 22:20; Heb 8:8-12*; 10:16-17 **31:32** [e]S Ex 24:8

[i]22 Or *will go about* ⌊*seeking*⌋; or *will protect*
[j]23 Or *I restore their fortunes*

31:23–30 JUDAH. Jeremiah prophesies that Judah, the southern kingdom, would be restored and the nation united through God's grace and blessing.

31:31–34 A NEW COVENANT. This is the only explicit statement referring to the "new covenant" in the OT. (1) These verses are quoted in Heb 8:8–12, revealing that NT believers saw the fulfillment of Jeremiah's words in the new covenant instituted by Jesus Christ for all who repent of their sins and believe in him (see article on THE OLD COVENANT AND THE NEW COVENANT, p. 1926). (2) However, the NT also teaches that Jeremiah's words will not be fulfilled completely until the last days of this age when a good portion of national Israel turns to the Lord Jesus as their true Messiah and Savior (Ro 11:25–27; cf. Eze 36:24–28; Zec 12:10—13:1; see article on ISRAEL IN GOD'S PLAN OF SALVATION, p. 1730).

31:31 HOUSE OF ISRAEL ... JUDAH. God promises to make a new covenant with all his people, both Israel and Judah, accomplished by Jesus Christ through his death and resurrection (Mt 26:28; Mk 14:24; 1Co 11:25; Heb 9:14–15; 10:29; 12:24) and the outpouring of the Holy Spirit on his followers (Jn 20:22; Ac 2:4). Furthermore, the NT makes it clear that Gentiles (i.e., all non-Jews) can participate in the new covenant if they believe in Jesus as God's Messiah and commit themselves to him as their Lord and Savior. Through faith in Christ, they become children of Abraham (Gal 3:7–9,29).

31:32 I MADE WITH THEIR FOREFATHERS. The new covenant was necessary because the old covenant was inadequate. Whereas the old covenant had been written in stone, Jeremiah prophesied that the new covenant would be written on the hearts of God's people (v. 33; cf. 2Co 3). Because of the indwelling of the Holy Spirit, the new covenant would be accompanied by sufficient power and grace for all the people to live righteously before God.

I made with their forefathers[f]
when I took them by the hand
to lead them out of Egypt,[g]
because they broke my covenant,
though I was a husband[h] to[k]
them,[1]"
declares the LORD.
33"This is the covenant I will make
with the house of Israel
after that time," declares the
LORD.
"I will put my law in their minds[i]
and write it on their hearts.[j]
I will be their God,
and they will be my people.[k]
34No longer will a man teach[l] his
neighbor,
or a man his brother, saying,
'Know the LORD,'
because they will all know[m] me,
from the least of them to the
greatest,"
declares the LORD.
"For I will forgive[n] their wickedness
and will remember their sins[o]
no more."
35This is what the LORD says,

he who appoints[p] the sun
to shine by day,
who decrees the moon and stars
to shine by night,[q]
who stirs up the sea[r]
so that its waves roar[s]—
the LORD Almighty is his name:[t]
36"Only if these decrees[u] vanish
from my sight,"
declares the LORD,
"will the descendants[v] of Israel
ever cease
to be a nation before me."

37This is what the LORD says:

"Only if the heavens above can be
measured[w]
and the foundations of the earth
below be searched out
will I reject[x] all the descendants
of Israel
because of all they have done,"
declares the LORD.

38"The days are coming," declares
the LORD, "when this city will be rebuilt[y] for me from the Tower of Hananel[z] to the Corner Gate.[a] 39The measuring line[b] will stretch from there
straight to the hill of Gareb and then
turn to Goah. 40The whole valley[c]
where dead bodies[d] and ashes are
thrown, and all the terraces out to the
Kidron Valley[e] on the east as far as
the corner of the Horse Gate,[f] will be
holy[g] to the LORD. The city will never
again be uprooted or demolished."

Jeremiah Buys a Field

32 This is the word that came to
Jeremiah from the LORD in the
tenth[h] year of Zedekiah king of Judah,
which was the eighteenth[i] year of
Nebuchadnezzar. 2The army of the
king of Babylon was then besieging[j]
Jerusalem, and Jeremiah the prophet
was confined[k] in the courtyard of the
guard[l] in the royal palace of Judah.
3Now Zedekiah king of Judah had
imprisoned him there, saying, "Why do
you prophesy[m] as you do? You say,

31:32 [f]Dt 5:3 [g]Jer 11:4 [h]S Isa 54:5 **31:33** [i]S Ex 4:15 [j]S Dt 6:6; S 2Co 3:3 [k]S Jer 11:4; Heb 10:16 **31:34** [l]1Jn 2:27 [m]S Isa 11:9; S Jn 6:45 [n]Ps 85:2; 130:4; Jer 33:8; 50:20 [o]S Job 7:21; S Isa 38:17; Mic 7:19; Heb 10:17* **31:35** [p]Ps 136:7-9 [q]S Ge 1:16 [r]S Ex 14:21 [s]S Ps 93:3 [t]S Jer 10:16 **31:36** [u]S Job 38:33; Jer 33:20-26 [v]Ps 89:36-37 **31:37** [w]S Job 38:5; Jer 33:22 [x]Jer 33:24-26; Ro 11:1-5 **31:38** [y]S Jer 30:18 [z]S Ne 3:1 [a]S 2Ki 14:13; S 2Ch 25:23 **31:39** [b]S 1Ki 7:23 **31:40** [c]S Jer 2:23; 7:31-32 [d]S Jer 8:2 [e]S 2Sa 15:23; Jn 18:1 [f]S 2Ki 11:16 [g]S Isa 4:3; Joel 3:17; Zec 14:21 **32:1** [h]2Ki 25:1 [i]Jer 25:1 **32:2** [j]S 2Ki 25:1 [k]S Ps 88:8 [l]S Ne 3:25 **32:3** [m]Jer 26:8-9

[k]*32* Hebrew; Septuagint and Syriac / *and I turned away from* [1]*32* Or *was their master*

31:33 PUT MY LAW IN THEIR MINDS. A distinctive feature of the new covenant is God's gift of a new heart and nature to all who believe in Christ so that they may spontaneously love and obey the Lord (Eze 11:19–20; Heb 8:10); the ability to respond to the Lord comes from the Holy Spirit living within the believer and the regeneration or new birth that results (see Eze 36:24–28; see article on REGENERATION, p. 1589). One sure way to know that we are saved people who participate in the new covenant is whether we possess a sincere desire to please God and to live by his righteous standards (cf. Ro 8:2–4).

31:34 THEY WILL ALL KNOW ME. In the age of the new covenant, every person who believes in Christ will personally know the Lord and have intimate fellowship with him. All will have direct access to God, and the Lord's presence will be imparted to believers through the Holy Spirit.

31:34 I WILL FORGIVE THEIR WICKEDNESS. Forgiveness of sins and the resulting reconciliation with God are foundational in the new covenant; they are based on Christ's atoning sacrifice on the cross (cf. Isa 53:4–6; Mt 26:27–28; Lk 22:20).

31:38 THIS CITY. Jeremiah foresaw that Jerusalem would be rebuilt and never again be destroyed (v. 40). This prophetic promise will have its ultimate fulfillment during Christ's reign on earth (Rev 19—22).

32:2 BESIEGING JERUSALEM. The siege occurred in 587 B.C. A year later, the city fell. Jeremiah's prophecies were coming true.

32:2 WAS CONFINED. Zedekiah had put Jeremiah in prison for persistently advising surrender to the Babylonian army (vv. 3–5; cf. 37:11–21). As far as the king was concerned, his preaching was having a demoralizing effect on the people and their will to resist. But Jeremiah knew that what he was proclaiming was the word of God.

'This is what the LORD says: I am about
to hand this city over to the king of
Babylon, and he will capture[n] it. 4Zed-
ekiah[o] king of Judah will not escape[p]
out of the hands of the Babylonians[m][q]
but will certainly be handed over to the
king of Babylon, and will speak with
him face to face and see him with his
own eyes. 5He will take[r] Zedekiah to
Babylon, where he will remain until I
deal with him,[s] declares the LORD. If
you fight against the Babylonians, you
will not succeed.' "[t]

6Jeremiah said, "The word of the
LORD came to me: 7Hanamel son of
Shallum your uncle is going to come to
you and say, 'Buy my field at Anathoth,[u] because as nearest relative it
is your right and duty[v] to buy it.'

8"Then, just as the LORD had said,
my cousin Hanamel came to me in the
courtyard of the guard and said, 'Buy
my field[w] at Anathoth in the territory
of Benjamin. Since it is your right to
redeem it and possess it, buy it for
yourself.'

"I knew that this was the word of the
LORD; 9so I bought the field[x] at Anathoth from my cousin Hanamel and
weighed out for him seventeen shekels[n] of silver.[y] 10I signed and sealed
the deed,[z] had it witnessed,[a] and
weighed out the silver on the scales.
11I took the deed of purchase—the
sealed copy containing the terms and
conditions, as well as the unsealed
copy— 12and I gave this deed to Baruch[b] son of Neriah,[c] the son of Mahseiah, in the presence of my cousin
Hanamel and of the witnesses who had
signed the deed and of all the Jews sitting in the courtyard of the guard.

13"In their presence I gave Baruch
these instructions: 14'This is what the
LORD Almighty, the God of Israel, says:
Take these documents, both the
sealed[d] and unsealed copies of the
deed of purchase, and put them in a
clay jar so they will last a long time.
15For this is what the LORD Almighty,
the God of Israel, says: Houses, fields
and vineyards will again be bought in
this land.'[e]

16"After I had given the deed of purchase to Baruch[f] son of Neriah, I
prayed to the LORD:

> 17"Ah, Sovereign LORD,[g] you
> have made the heavens and the
> earth[h] by your great power and
> outstretched arm.[i] Nothing is
> too hard[j] for you. 18You show
> love[k] to thousands but bring the
> punishment for the fathers' sins
> into the laps[l] of their children[m]
> after them. O great and powerful
> God,[n] whose name is the LORD Al-
> mighty,[o] 19great are your pur-
> poses and mighty are your
> deeds.[p] Your eyes are open to all
> the ways of men;[q] you reward ev-
> eryone according to his conduct
> and as his deeds deserve.[r] 20You
> performed miraculous signs and
> wonders[s] in Egypt[t] and have
> continued them to this day, both
> in Israel and among all mankind,
> and have gained the renown[u]
> that is still yours. 21You brought
> your people Israel out of Egypt
> with signs and wonders, by a
> mighty hand[v] and an out-
> stretched arm[w] and with great
> terror.[x] 22You gave them this
> land you had sworn to give their
> forefathers, a land flowing with
> milk and honey.[y] 23They came in
> and took possession[z] of it, but
> they did not obey you or follow
> your law;[a] they did not do what
> you commanded them to do. So
> you brought all this disaster[b]
> upon them.
>
> 24"See how the siege ramps[c]
> are built up to take the city. Be-
> cause of the sword, famine and

32:3 [n]ver 28; Jer 21:4; 34:2-3
32:4 [o]Jer 34:21; 44:30 [p]S Jer 21:7; 38:18,23; 39:5-7; 52:9 [q]ver 24
32:5 [r]Jer 39:7; Eze 12:13 [s]S 2Ki 25:7 [t]Jer 21:4; La 1:14
32:7 [u]S Jos 21:18 [v]Lev 25:24-25; S Ru 4:3-4; Mt 27:10*
32:8 [w]ver 25
32:9 [x]Jer 37:12 [y]S Ge 23:16
32:10 [z]Ge 23:20 [a]S Ru 4:9; S Isa 8:2
32:12 [b]ver 16; Jer 36:4; 43:3,6; 45:1 [c]Jer 51:59
32:14 [d]S Isa 8:16
32:15 [e]ver 43-44; Isa 44:26; Jer 30:18; Eze 28:26; Am 9:14-15
32:16 [f]S ver 12
32:17 [g]Jer 1:6 [h]S Ge 1:1; S Jer 10:16 [i]S Dt 9:29; 2Ki 19:15; Ps 102:25 [j]S 2Ki 3:18; Jer 51:15; S Mt 19:26
32:18 [k]S Dt 5:10 [l]S Ps 79:12 [m]S Ex 20:5; S Ps 109:14 [n]Jer 10:6 [o]S Jer 10:16
32:19 [p]S Job 12:13; Da 2:20 [q]S Job 14:16; S Pr 5:21; Jer 16:17 [r]S Job 34:11; S Mt 16:27
32:20 [s]S Ex 3:20; S Job 9:10 [t]Ex 9:16 [u]S Isa 55:13; S Jer 13:11
32:21 [v]S Ex 6:6; Da 9:15 [w]S Dt 5:15; S Jer 6:12 [x]S Dt 26:8
32:22 [y]S Ex 3:8; Eze 20:6
32:23 [z]S Ps 44:2; 78:54-55 [a]S Ex 16:28; S Jos 1:7; S 1Ki 9:6; S Jer 11:8 [b]S Dt 28:64; 31:29; Da 9:14
32:24 [c]S 2Sa 20:15; S Jer 6:6

[m] 4 Or *Chaldeans*; also in verses 5, 24, 25, 28, 29 and 43 [n] 9 That is, about 7 ounces (about 200 grams)

32:6–15 BUY MY FIELD. During his confinement (v. 2), Jeremiah was instructed by the Lord to buy a field in his hometown village of Anathoth, a place already controlled by Babylonian forces; it must have seemed foolish to buy land that was already in enemy hands. (1) By purchasing the land, Jeremiah demonstrated faith in God's promise that a remnant would return to the land and again buy land and build houses (v. 15); it was a prophetic sign of hope, despite Judah's present desperate situation. (2) In a similar manner, our situations may at times seem hopeless and desperate; yet if we belong to God, we have the promise and hope of a better future (Ro 8:28).

32:12 BARUCH. Baruch was Jeremiah's trusted friend and secretary (36:4–8). After the fall of Jerusalem, he was taken to Egypt along with Jeremiah (43:6).

plague,[d] the city will be handed
over to the Babylonians who are
attacking it. What you said[e] has
happened,[f] as you now see.
25And though the city will be
handed over to the Babylonians,
you, O Sovereign LORD, say to me,
'Buy the field[g] with silver and
have the transaction wit-
nessed.[h]' "

26Then the word of the LORD came to
Jeremiah: 27"I am the LORD, the God of
all mankind.[i] Is anything too hard for
me?[j] 28Therefore, this is what the
LORD says: I am about to hand this city
over to the Babylonians and to Nebuchadnezzar[k] king of Babylon, who will
capture it.[l] 29The Babylonians who
are attacking this city will come in and
set it on fire; they will burn it down,[m]
along with the houses[n] where the people provoked me to anger by burning
incense on the roofs to Baal and by
pouring out drink offerings[o] to other
gods.[p]
30"The people of Israel and Judah
have done nothing but evil in my sight
from their youth;[q] indeed, the people
of Israel have done nothing but provoke[r] me with what their hands have
made,[s] declares the LORD. 31From the
day it was built until now, this city[t]
has so aroused my anger and wrath
that I must remove[u] it from my sight.
32The people of Israel and Judah have
provoked[v] me by all the evil[w] they
have done—they, their kings and officials,[x] their priests and prophets, the
men of Judah and the people of Jerusalem. 33They turned their backs[y] to me
and not their faces; though I taught[z]
them again and again, they would not
listen or respond to discipline.[a]
34They set up their abominable idols[b]
in the house that bears my Name[c] and
defiled[d] it. 35They built high places
for Baal in the Valley of Ben Hinnom[e]
to sacrifice their sons and daughters[o]
to Molech,[f] though I never commanded, nor did it enter my mind,[g] that
they should do such a detestable[h]
thing and so make Judah sin.[i]
36"You are saying about this city,
'By the sword, famine and plague[j] it
will be handed over to the king of Babylon'; but this is what the LORD, the God
of Israel, says: 37I will surely gather[k]
them from all the lands where I banish
them in my furious anger[l] and great
wrath; I will bring them back to this
place and let them live in safety.[m]
38They will be my people,[n] and I will
be their God. 39I will give them singleness[o] of heart and action, so that they
will always fear[p] me for their own
good and the good of their children after them. 40I will make an everlasting
covenant[q] with them: I will never stop
doing good to them, and I will inspire[r]
them to fear me, so that they will never
turn away from me.[s] 41I will rejoice[t]
in doing them good[u] and will assuredly plant[v] them in this land with all my
heart and soul.[w]
42"This is what the LORD says: As I
have brought all this great calamity[x]
on this people, so I will give them all
the prosperity I have promised[y] them.
43Once more fields will be bought[z] in
this land of which you say, 'It is a desolate[a] waste, without men or animals,
for it has been handed over to the Babylonians.' 44Fields will be bought for
silver, and deeds[b] will be signed,
sealed and witnessed[c] in the territory
of Benjamin, in the villages around Jerusalem, in the towns of Judah and in
the towns of the hill country, of the
western foothills and of the Negev,[d]
because I will restore[e] their fortunes,[p] declares the LORD."

32:24 [d] S Jer 14:12 [e] Dt 4:25-26; Jos 23:15-16 [f] S Dt 28:2
32:25 [g] S ver 8 [h] S Isa 8:2
32:27 [i] S Nu 16:22 [j] S Ge 18:14; S 2Ki 3:18
32:28 [k] S 2Ch 36:17 [l] S ver 3; S Jer 21:10
32:29 [m] S 2Ch 36:19 [n] S Jer 19:13 [o] Jer 44:18 [p] S Jer 7:9
32:30 [q] S Ps 25:7; S Jer 22:21 [r] Jer 8:19 [s] Jer 25:7
32:31 [t] 1Ki 11:7-8; 2Ki 21:4-5; Mt 23:37 [u] S 2Ki 23:27
32:32 [v] S 1Ki 14:9 [w] Da 9:8 [x] S Jer 2:26; S 44:9
32:33 [y] S 1Ki 14:9; S Ps 14:3; Jer 2:27; Eze 8:16; Zec 7:11 [z] S Dt 4:5; S Isa 28:9; S Jer 7:13 [a] S Jer 7:28
32:34 [b] S 2Ki 21:4; Eze 8:3-16 [c] Jer 7:10; 34:15 [d] S Jer 7:30
32:35 [e] Jer 19:2 [f] S Lev 18:21 [g] S Jer 19:5 [h] S 1Ki 14:24 [i] S Jer 25:7
32:36 [j] ver 24
32:37 [k] S Isa 11:12 [l] Jer 21:5 [m] S Lev 25:18; Eze 34:28; 39:26
32:38 [n] Jer 24:7; 2Co 6:16*
32:39 [o] S 2Ch 30:12; S Ps 86:11; Jn 17:21; Ac 4:32 [p] S Dt 6:24; S 10:16
32:40 [q] S Ge 9:16; S Isa 42:6 [r] S Dt 4:10 [s] S Jer 24:7
32:41 [t] S Dt 28:63; S Isa 62:4 [u] S Dt 28:3-12 [v] Jer 24:6; 31:28 [w] Mic 7:18
32:42 [x] La 3:38 [y] S Jer 29:10
32:43 [z] ver 15 [a] Jer 33:12
32:44 [b] ver 10 [c] S Ru 4:9; S Isa 8:2 [d] S Jer 17:26 [e] S Ezr 9:9; Ps 14:7

[o] 35 Or *to make their sons and daughters pass through ⌊the fire⌋* [p] 44 Or *will bring them back from captivity*

32:25 YOU . . . SAY TO ME. Jeremiah was puzzled by God's instruction to buy land just when Jerusalem was about to fall; thus he prayed (v. 16) to God for understanding, while maintaining faith in his word.

32:27 IS ANYTHING TOO HARD FOR ME? With the Babylonians at the city walls, the future looked bleak; yet God assured Jeremiah that through his power the people would be restored to the land. God's word promises a blessed future for all believers in Christ. We can depend on his word even though we may not know the specific manner in which it will be accomplished.

32:37–44 SURELY GATHER THEM FROM ALL THE LANDS. Once again God told Jeremiah that the people would be restored to the land and to a right relationship with him (v. 38); thereafter God would make an everlasting covenant with them (see 31:31–34, notes).

Promise of Restoration

33 While Jeremiah was still confined[f] in the courtyard[g] of
the guard, the word of the LORD came
to him a second time:[h] 2"This is what
the LORD says, he who made the
earth,[i] the LORD who formed it and established it—the LORD is his name:[j]
3'Call[k] to me and I will answer you
and tell you great and unsearchable[l]
things you do not know.' 4For this is
what the LORD, the God of Israel, says
about the houses in this city and the
royal palaces of Judah that have been
torn down to be used against the
siege[m] ramps[n] and the sword 5in the
fight with the Babylonians[q]: 'They
will be filled with the dead bodies of the
men I will slay in my anger and
wrath.[o] I will hide my face[p] from this
city because of all its wickedness.
6" 'Nevertheless, I will bring health
and healing to it; I will heal[q] my people and will let them enjoy abundant
peace[r] and security. 7I will bring Judah[s] and Israel back from captivity[r][t] and will rebuild[u] them as they
were before.[v] 8I will cleanse[w] them
from all the sin they have committed
against me and will forgive[x] all their
sins of rebellion against me. 9Then this
city will bring me renown,[y] joy,
praise[z] and honor[a] before all nations
on earth that hear of all the good
things I do for it; and they will be in
awe and will tremble[b] at the abundant
prosperity and peace I provide for it.'
10"This is what the LORD says: 'You
say about this place, "It is a desolate
waste, without men or animals."[c] Yet
in the towns of Judah and the streets
of Jerusalem that are deserted,[d] inhabited by neither men nor animals,
there will be heard once more 11the
sounds of joy and gladness,[e] the
voices of bride and bridegroom, and the
voices of those who bring thank offerings[f] to the house of the LORD, saying,

"Give thanks to the LORD Almighty,
for the LORD is good;[g]
his love endures forever."[h]

For I will restore the fortunes[i] of the
land as they were before,[j]' says the
LORD.
12"This is what the LORD Almighty
says: 'In this place, desolate[k] and
without men or animals[l]—in all its
towns there will again be pastures for
shepherds to rest their flocks.[m] 13In
the towns of the hill[n] country, of the
western foothills and of the Negev,[o] in
the territory of Benjamin, in the villages around Jerusalem and in the
towns of Judah, flocks will again pass
under the hand[p] of the one who
counts them,' says the LORD.
14" 'The days are coming,' declares
the LORD, 'when I will fulfill the gracious promise[q] I made to the house of
Israel and to the house of Judah.

15" 'In those days and at that time
I will make a righteous[r]
Branch[s] sprout from
David's line;[t]
he will do what is just and right
in the land.
16In those days Judah will be
saved[u]
and Jerusalem will live in
safety.[v]
This is the name by which it[s] will
be called:[w]
The LORD Our Righteousness.'[x]

17For this is what the LORD says: 'David

33:1 [f]S Ps 88:8 [g]Jer 37:21; 38:28 [h]Jer 13:3 **33:2** [i]S Ps 136:6; S Jer 10:16 [j]S Ex 3:15 **33:3** [k]S Isa 55:6 [l]S Job 28:11 **33:4** [m]S 2Ki 25:1; Eze 4:2 [n]Jer 32:24; Eze 26:8; Hab 1:10 **33:5** [o]Jer 21:4-7 [p]S Dt 31:17; S Isa 8:17 **33:6** [q]S Dt 32:39; S Isa 30:26 [r]S Isa 9:6 **33:7** [s]Jer 32:44 [t]Jer 30:3; Eze 39:25; Am 9:14 [u]S Jer 24:6 [v]S Isa 1:26 **33:8** [w]S Lev 16:30; Heb 9:13-14 [x]S 2Sa 24:14; S Jer 31:34 **33:9** [y]S Isa 55:13 [z]S Isa 60:18 [a]S Jer 3:17 [b]S Isa 64:2 **33:10** [c]Jer 32:43 [d]S Lev 26:32; S Jer 9:11 **33:11** [e]S Ps 51:8; S Isa 24:8; S 51:3 [f]S Lev 7:12 [g]S 2Ch 7:3; Ps 25:8; S 136:1; Na 1:7 [h]S 1Ch 16:34; 2Ch 5:13; Ps 100:4-5 [i]Ps 14:7 [j]S Isa 1:26 **33:12** [k]Jer 32:43 [l]ver 10 [m]S Isa 65:10; Eze 34:11-15 **33:13** [n]S Jer 31:5 [o]S Jer 17:26; Ob 1:20 [p]S Lev 27:32 **33:14** [q]Dt 28:1-14; S Jos 23:15; S Jer 29:10 **33:15** [r]S Ps 72:2 [s]S Isa 4:2 [t]S 2Sa 7:12 **33:16** [u]S Isa 45:17 [v]S Jer 17:25; S 32:37 [w]Isa 59:14; Jer 3:17; Eze 48:35; Zep 3:13; Zec 8:3,16 [x]S 1Co 1:30

[q]5 Or *Chaldeans* [r]7 Or *will restore the fortunes of Judah and Israel* [s]16 Or *he*

33:1–26 A SECOND TIME. This chapter speaks again of Israel's and Judah's restoration to peace, prosperity and spiritual wholeness. Jeremiah's prophecy goes beyond the return of the exiles from Babylon; he foresees the days when Jesus the Messiah will establish his kingdom on earth.

33:6 ABUNDANT PEACE. In contrast to the false prophets who had been proclaiming a false peace (see 6:14, note; 23:17, note), Jeremiah offered the hope of true peace in the Lord. For more on peace, see article on THE PEACE OF GOD, p. 1134.

33:15 A RIGHTEOUS BRANCH. This "Branch" refers to Jesus Christ, who would come from the ancestral line of David (see next note). The initial fulfillment of this prophecy occurred at his first coming to earth. Through his death and resurrection he became King of all of God's people on earth. The final fulfillment will occur when he returns a second time to "do what is just and right" throughout the earth (cf. Rev 19; see Jer 23:5–6, note).

33:17 THRONE OF THE HOUSE OF ISRAEL. Through an unbroken line of descendants from David would come the righteous Branch, who would reign as King over God's people (cf. Lk 1:31–33). Jesus Christ fulfilled this promise; his *legal* lineage can be traced through Joseph to David (Mt 1:1–16), and his *physical* line through Mary back to David (Lk 3:23–31). Christ's reign will last

THE PEACE OF GOD

Jer 33:6 "Nevertheless, I will bring health and healing to it; I will heal my people and will let them enjoy abundant peace and security."

DEFINITION OF PEACE. The Hebrew word for peace is *shalom*; the word denotes far more than the absence of war and conflict. *Shalom's* basic meaning is harmony, wholeness, soundness, well-being and success in all areas of life. (1) Peace can refer to tranquility in international relationships, such as peace between warring nations (e.g., 1Sa 7:14; 1Ki 4:24; 1Ch 19:19). (2) It can also refer to a settled feeling within a nation, as during times of prosperity and no civil war (2Sa 3:21–23; 1Ch 22:9; Ps 122:6–7). (3) It can be experienced as wholeness and harmony in human relationships, both inside the home (Pr 17:1; 1Co 7:15) and outside the home (Ro 12:18; Heb 12:14; 1Pe 3:11). (4) It can refer to one's personal sense of wholeness and well-being, free from anxiety and at peace within our own souls (Ps 4:8; 119:165; cf. Job 3:26) and with God (Nu 6:26; Ro 5:1). (5) Finally, even though the word *shalom* is not used in Ge 1—2, *shalom* describes the original created world that existed in perfect harmony and wholeness. When God created the heavens and the earth, he created a world at peace. The total well-being of creation is reflected in the summary statement: "God saw all that he had made, and it was very good" (Ge 1:31).

THE DISRUPTION OF PEACE. When Adam and Eve listened to the voice of the serpent and ate from the forbidden tree (Ge 3:1–7), their disobedience introduced sin and disrupted creation's original harmony. (1) At that time, Adam and Eve experienced, for the first time, guilt and shame before God (Ge 3:8) and a loss of inner peace.

(2) Adam and Eve's sin in the Garden of Eden destroyed their harmonious relationship with God. Before eating that fruit, they had intimate fellowship with God in the garden (cf. Ge 3:8), but afterwards they "hid from the LORD God among the trees of the garden" (Ge 3:8). Instead of looking forward to talking with God, they were now afraid of his voice (Ge 3:10).

(3) Furthermore, the harmonious relationship between Adam and Eve as husband and wife was disrupted. When God began discussing their sin with them, Adam blamed Eve (Ge 3:12), and God pronounced that strife would continue between man and woman (Ge 3:16); thus began the social conflict that is now part of our human predicament, from arguments and violence in our homes (cf. 1Sa 1:1–8; Pr 15:18; 17:1) to international conflicts and wars.

(4) Finally, sin disrupted the harmony and unity between humankind and nature. Before Adam sinned, he joyfully worked in the Garden of Eden (Ge 2:15) and freely walked among the animals, giving each one a name (Ge 2:19–20). Part of God's curse after the fall included enmity between Adam and Eve and the serpent (Ge 3:15), as well as the reality that work would entail sweat and drudgery (Ge 3:17–19). Where there had been harmony between the human race and the environment, there was now struggle and conflict, so that "the whole creation has been groaning as in the pains of childbirth right up to the present time" (see Ro 8:22, note).

THE RESTORATION OF PEACE. Though the result of the fall was the destruction of peace and well-being for humankind and indeed for the entire created world, God has planned to restore *shalom*; thus the story of regaining peace is the story of redemption in Christ. (1) Insofar as Satan initiated the destruction of peace in our world, the reestablishment of peace must involve the destruction of Satan and his power. In fact, many of the OT promises regarding the coming of the Messiah were promises of a coming victory and peace. David prophesied that the Son of God would rule the nations (Ps 2:8–9; cf. Rev 2:26–27; 19:15). Isaiah prophesied that the Messiah would reign as the Prince of Peace (Isa 9:6–7). Ezekiel predicted that the new covenant God planned to establish through the Messiah would be a covenant of peace (Eze 34:25; 37:26). And Micah, in prophesying the birth of the coming ruler in Bethlehem, stated that "he will be their peace" (Mic 5:5).

(2) At Jesus' birth, the angels proclaimed that God's peace had now come to the earth (Lk 2:14). Jesus himself came to destroy the devil's work (1Jn 3:8) and to break down all barriers of conflict that are a part of our lives, thus making peace (Eph 2:12–17). Jesus gave his disciples his peace as a lasting legacy before he went to the cross (Jn 14:27; 16:33). By his death and resurrection, Jesus disarmed the hostile powers and authorities and thereby made peace possible (Col 1:20; 2:14–15; cf. Isa 53:4–5). Therefore, when we believe in Jesus Christ, we are justified through faith and have peace with God (Ro 5:1). The message that Christians proclaim is the good news of peace (Ac 10:36; cf. Isa 52:7).

(3) Merely knowing that Christ came as the Prince of Peace does not ensure that peace will automatically become part of our lives; to experience peace requires that we be united with Christ in an active faith. The first step is to believe in the Lord Jesus Christ. When we do, we are justified through faith (Ro 3:21–28; 4:1–13; Gal 2:16) and so have peace with God (Ro 5:1). Along with faith, we must walk in obedience to his commands in order to live in peace (Lev 26:3,6). The OT prophets frequently declare that there is no peace for the wicked (Isa 57:21; 59:8; Jer 6:14; 8:11; Eze 13:10,16). To know God's peace, he has given us the Holy Spirit, who begins to work his fruit in us—one aspect of which is peace (Gal 5:22; cf. Ro 14:17; Eph 4:3). With the Spirit's help, we must pray for peace (Ps 122:6–7; Jer 29:7; see Php 4:7, note), let peace rule in our hearts (Col 3:15), seek peace and pursue it (Ps 34:14; Jer 29:7; 2Ti 2:22; 1Pe 3:11), and do our best to live in peace with others (Ro 12:18; 2Co 13:11; 1Th 5:13; Heb 12:14).

will never fail[y] to have a man to sit on
the throne of the house of Israel, 18nor
will the priests,[z] who are Levites,[a]
ever fail to have a man to stand before
me continually to offer burnt offerings,
to burn grain offerings and to present
sacrifices.[b]' "

19The word of the LORD came to Jeremiah: 20"This is what the LORD says: 'If
you can break my covenant with the
day[c] and my covenant with the night,
so that day and night no longer come
at their appointed time,[d] 21then my
covenant[e] with David my servant—
and my covenant with the Levites[f]
who are priests ministering before
me—can be broken and David will no
longer have a descendant to reign on
his throne.[g] 22I will make the descendants of David my servant and the Levites who minister before me as countless[h] as the stars of the sky and as
measureless as the sand on the seashore.' "

23The word of the LORD came to Jeremiah: 24"Have you not noticed that
these people are saying, 'The LORD has
rejected the two kingdoms[t][i] he
chose'? So they despise[j] my people
and no longer regard them as a nation.[k] 25This is what the LORD says: 'If
I have not established my covenant
with day and night[l] and the fixed
laws[m] of heaven and earth,[n] 26then I
will reject[o] the descendants of Jacob[p] and David my servant and will
not choose one of his sons to rule over
the descendants of Abraham, Isaac
and Jacob. For I will restore their fortunes[u][q] and have compassion[r] on
them.' "

Warning to Zedekiah

34 While Nebuchadnezzar king of
Babylon and all his army and
all the kingdoms and peoples[s] in the
empire he ruled were fighting against
Jerusalem[t] and all its surrounding
towns, this word came to Jeremiah
from the LORD: 2"This is what the LORD,
the God of Israel, says: Go to Zedekiah[u] king of Judah and tell him, 'This
is what the LORD says: I am about to
hand this city over to the king of Babylon, and he will burn it down.[v] 3You
will not escape from his grasp but will
surely be captured and handed over[w]
to him. You will see the king of Babylon
with your own eyes, and he will speak
with you face to face. And you will go
to Babylon.

4" 'Yet hear the promise of the LORD,
O Zedekiah king of Judah. This is what
the LORD says concerning you: You will
not die by the sword;[x] 5you will die
peacefully. As people made a funeral
fire[y] in honor of your fathers, the former kings who preceded you, so they
will make a fire in your honor and lament, "Alas,[z] O master!" I myself
make this promise, declares the
LORD.' "

6Then Jeremiah the prophet told all
this to Zedekiah king of Judah, in Jerusalem, 7while the army of the king of
Babylon was fighting against Jerusalem and the other cities of Judah that
were still holding out—Lachish[a] and
Azekah.[b] These were the only fortified cities left in Judah.

Freedom for Slaves

8The word came to Jeremiah from
the LORD after King Zedekiah had made
a covenant with all the people[c] in Jerusalem to proclaim freedom[d] for the
slaves. 9Everyone was to free his Hebrew slaves, both male and female; no
one was to hold a fellow Jew in bondage.[e] 10So all the officials and people

33:17 [y] S 2Sa 7:13; S 2Ch 7:18; Ps 89:29-37; S Lk 1:33
33:18 [z] S Nu 25:11-13; Heb 7:17-22 [a] S Dt 18:1 [b] Heb 13:15
33:20 [c] Ps 89:36 [d] S Ge 1:14
33:21 [e] Ps 89:34 [f] S Dt 18:1 [g] S 2Sa 7:13; S 2Ch 7:18
33:22 [h] S Ge 12:2; S Jer 30:19; Hos 1:10
33:24 [i] Eze 37:22 [j] S Ne 4:4 [k] S Jer 30:17; Eze 36:20
33:25 [l] S Ge 1:18 [m] S Ps 148:6 [n] Ps 74:16-17
33:26 [o] S Lev 26:44 [p] S Isa 14:1 [q] ver 7; Ps 14:7 [r] S Jer 30:18
34:1 [s] Jer 27:7 [t] 2Ki 25:1; Jer 39:1
34:2 [u] S 2Ch 36:11 [v] ver 22; Jer 32:29; 37:8
34:3 [w] S 2Ki 25:7; S Jer 21:7
34:4 [x] Jer 52:11
34:5 [y] S 2Ch 16:14 [z] Jer 22:18
34:7 [a] S Jos 10:3 [b] Jos 10:10; 2Ch 11:9
34:8 [c] S 2Ki 11:17 [d] S Ex 21:2; Lev 25:10,39-41; Ne 5:5-8
34:9 [e] Dt 15:12-18

[t] 24 Or *families* [u] 26 Or *will bring them back from captivity*

throughout eternity.

33:18 PRIESTS, WHO ARE LEVITES. Jeremiah foresees an eternal priesthood through which God's people would enjoy access to and communion with him (cf. Nu 25:13). This prophecy is fulfilled in Jesus Christ, who as "a priest forever . . . is able to save completely those who come to God through him" (Heb 7:21–25; cf. Ps 110:4; Heb 5:6–10; 6:19–20; 7:11–28).

33:22 AS THE STARS OF THE SKY. Jeremiah envisions an innumerable host in the royal family of David and the priestly line of Levi; this prophecy will be fulfilled in those who will reign with Christ in his future kingdom (Ro 8:17; 1Co 6:3; 2Ti 2:12; Rev 3:21; 5:10; 19:6–16; 20:5–6; 22:5) and in those who in Christ have been made "a holy priesthood, offering spiritual sacrifices" (1Pe 2:5,9; cf. Rev 5:10).

34:8 TO PROCLAIM FREEDOM. The law of Moses stated that all Hebrew men or women sold into slavery because of debts were to be freed after six years (Ex 21:2–11; Dt 15:12–18). The king urged all the rulers and the people to obey this law by setting their slaves free. In this way he hoped to gain God's blessing; furthermore, the freed slaves would be more willing to help defend Jerusalem.

who entered into this covenant agreed
that they would free their male and female slaves and no longer hold them in
bondage. They agreed, and set them
free. 11But afterward they changed
their minds[f] and took back the slaves
they had freed and enslaved them
again.
12Then the word of the LORD came to
Jeremiah: 13"This is what the LORD, the
God of Israel, says: I made a covenant
with your forefathers[g] when I brought
them out of Egypt, out of the land of
slavery.[h] I said, 14'Every seventh year
each of you must free any fellow Hebrew who has sold himself to you. After he has served you six years, you
must let him go free.'[v][i] Your fathers,
however, did not listen to me or pay
attention[j] to me. 15Recently you repented and did what is right in my
sight: Each of you proclaimed freedom
to his countrymen.[k] You even made a
covenant before me in the house that
bears my Name.[l] 16But now you have
turned around[m] and profaned[n] my
name; each of you has taken back the
male and female slaves you had set
free to go where they wished. You have
forced them to become your slaves
again.
17"Therefore, this is what the LORD
says: You have not obeyed me; you
have not proclaimed freedom for your
fellow countrymen. So I now proclaim
'freedom' for you,[o] declares the
LORD—'freedom' to fall by the sword,
plague[p] and famine.[q] I will make you
abhorrent to all the kingdoms of the
earth.[r] 18The men who have violated
my covenant[s] and have not fulfilled
the terms of the covenant they made
before me, I will treat like the calf they
cut in two and then walked between its
pieces.[t] 19The leaders of Judah and
Jerusalem, the court officials,[u] the
priests and all the people of the land
who walked between the pieces of the
calf, 20I will hand over[v] to their enemies who seek their lives.[w] Their dead
bodies will become food for the birds of
the air and the beasts of the earth.[x]
21"I will hand Zedekiah[y] king of Judah and his officials[z] over to their enemies[a] who seek their lives, to the
army of the king of Babylon,[b] which
has withdrawn[c] from you. 22I am going to give the order, declares the LORD,
and I will bring them back to this city.
They will fight against it, take[d] it and
burn[e] it down. And I will lay waste[f]
the towns of Judah so no one can live
there."

The Recabites

35 This is the word that came to
Jeremiah from the LORD during
the reign of Jehoiakim[g] son of Josiah
king of Judah: 2"Go to the Recabite[h]
family and invite them to come to one
of the side rooms[i] of the house of the
LORD and give them wine to drink."
3So I went to get Jaazaniah son of
Jeremiah, the son of Habazziniah, and
his brothers and all his sons—the
whole family of the Recabites. 4I
brought them into the house of the
LORD, into the room of the sons of Hanan son of Igdaliah the man of God.[j]
It was next to the room of the officials,
which was over that of Maaseiah son of
Shallum[k] the doorkeeper.[l] 5Then I
set bowls full of wine and some cups
before the men of the Recabite family
and said to them, "Drink some wine."
6But they replied, "We do not drink
wine, because our forefather Jonadab[m]

34:11 [f] Ps 78:37 **34:13** [g] S Ex 24:8 [h] S Dt 15:15 **34:14** [i] S Ex 21:2 [j] 2Ki 17:14; S Jer 7:26 **34:15** [k] ver 8 [l] S Jer 32:34 **34:16** [m] Eze 3:20; 18:24 [n] S Lev 19:12 **34:17** [o] S Mt 7:2; Gal 6:7 [p] Jer 21:7 [q] S Jer 14:12 [r] Jer 15:4; S 24:9; S 29:18 **34:18** [s] S Jer 11:10 [t] S Ge 15:10 **34:19** [u] S Jer 26:10; Zep 3:3-4 **34:20** [v] Jer 21:7; Eze 16:27; 23:28 [w] S Jer 11:21 [x] S Dt 28:26 **34:21** [y] S Jer 32:4 [z] 2Ki 25:21; Jer 39:6; 52:24-27 [a] S Jer 21:7 [b] S 2Ch 36:10 [c] Jer 37:5 **34:22** [d] Jer 39:1-2 [e] S Ne 2:17; Jer 38:18; 39:8; Eze 23:47 [f] S Lev 26:32; S Isa 1:7 **35:1** [g] S 2Ch 36:5 **35:2** [h] S 2Ki 10:15 [i] S 1Ki 6:5 **35:4** [j] S Dt 33:1 [k] 1Ch 9:19 [l] S 2Ki 12:9; S 23:4 **35:6** [m] S 2Ki 10:15

[v] *14* Deut. 15:12

34:11 ENSLAVED THEM AGAIN. When the Babylonian siege of Jerusalem was temporarily interrupted by an Egyptian challenge to the Babylonian army (cf. vv. 21–22), the Jews forced their slaves back into bondage. This action showed that the previous freeing of the slaves (v. 8) had not been motivated by a concern for justice and God's law, but rather by selfishness. About these flagrant violaters of his law, God states: "Their dead bodies will become food for the birds of the air" (v. 20).

34:18 CALF THEY CUT IN TWO. Those involved in making a covenant would walk between two halves of a slain calf; this act may have signified that they deserved to be cut to pieces if they broke the covenant (cf. Ge 15:10).

35:2 RECABITES. These people were a nomadic tribe related to the Kenites and to Jethro, Moses' father-in-law (cf. Jdg 1:16; 1Ch 2:55). Their forefather, Jonadab (Jehonadab, cf. 2Ki 10:15–27), had commanded his sons more than two hundred years before not to drink any type of wine, not to live in permanent houses and not to plant crops. Instead, they were to live as nomads tending livestock. God instructed Jeremiah to test the Recabites in order to highlight their faithfulness to their forefather in contrast to Judah's unfaithfulness to its God. This all took place before the people in the house of the Lord.

35:6–11 WE DO NOT DRINK WINE. The Recabites remained true to their convictions, refusing to disobey the rules of their forefather (see previ-

son of Recab gave us this command:
'Neither you nor your descendants
must ever drink wine.[n] **7**Also you
must never build houses, sow seed or
plant vineyards; you must never have
any of these things, but must always
live in tents.[o] Then you will live a long
time in the land[p] where you are nomads.' **8**We have obeyed everything
our forefather[q] Jonadab son of Recab
commanded us. Neither we nor our
wives nor our sons and daughters have
ever drunk wine **9**or built houses to live
in or had vineyards, fields or crops.[r]
10We have lived in tents and have fully
obeyed everything our forefather Jonadab commanded us. **11**But when Nebuchadnezzar king of Babylon invaded[s]
this land, we said, 'Come, we must go
to Jerusalem[t] to escape the Babylonian[w] and Aramean armies.' So we have
remained in Jerusalem."

12Then the word of the LORD came to
Jeremiah, saying: **13**"This is what the
LORD Almighty, the God of Israel, says:
Go and tell[u] the men of Judah and the
people of Jerusalem, 'Will you not learn
a lesson[v] and obey my words?' declares the LORD. **14**'Jonadab son of Recab ordered his sons not to drink wine
and this command has been kept. To
this day they do not drink wine, because they obey their forefather's command.[w] But I have spoken to you
again and again,[x] yet you have not
obeyed[y] me. **15**Again and again I sent
all my servants the prophets[z] to you.
They said, "Each of you must turn[a]
from your wicked ways and reform[b]
your actions; do not follow other
gods[c] to serve them. Then you will
live in the land[d] I have given to you
and your fathers." But you have not
paid attention or listened[e] to me.
16The descendants of Jonadab son of
Recab have carried out the command
their forefather[f] gave them, but these
people have not obeyed me.'

17"Therefore, this is what the LORD
God Almighty, the God of Israel, says:
'Listen! I am going to bring on Judah
and on everyone living in Jerusalem every disaster[g] I pronounced against
them. I spoke to them, but they did not
listen;[h] I called to them, but they did
not answer.' "[i]

18Then Jeremiah said to the family
of the Recabites, "This is what the
LORD Almighty, the God of Israel, says:
'You have obeyed the command of your
forefather[j] Jonadab and have followed all his instructions and have
done everything he ordered.' **19**Therefore, this is what the LORD Almighty,
the God of Israel, says: 'Jonadab son of
Recab will never fail[k] to have a man
to serve[l] me.' "

Jehoiakim Burns Jeremiah's Scroll

36 In the fourth year of Jehoiakim[m] son of Josiah king of Judah, this word came to Jeremiah from
the LORD: **2**"Take a scroll[n] and write
on it all the words[o] I have spoken to
you concerning Israel, Judah and all
the other nations from the time I began
speaking to you in the reign of Josiah[p]
till now. **3**Perhaps[q] when the people
of Judah hear[r] about every disaster I

35:6 [n] S Lev 10:9; Nu 6:2-4; S Lk 1:15 **35:7** [o] Heb 11:9 [p] S Ex 20:12; Eph 6:2-3 **35:8** [q] Pr 1:8; Col 3:20 **35:9** [r] 1Ti 6:6 **35:11** [s] 2Ki 24:1 [t] S Jos 10:20; Jer 8:14 **35:13** [u] Jer 11:6 [v] Jer 6:10; 32:33 **35:14** [w] ver 6-10, 16 [x] S Jer 7:13 [y] Isa 30:9 **35:15** [z] S Jer 7:25 [a] S 2Ki 17:13; S Jer 26:3 [b] S Isa 1:16-17; S 59:20; Jer 4:1; 18:11; Eze 14:6; 18:30 [c] S Ex 20:3 [d] S Dt 4:40; Jer 25:5 [e] S Jer 6:10; S 7:26; 44:4-5 **35:16** [f] S Lev 20:9; Mal 1:6 **35:17** [g] S Jos 23:15; S 1Ki 13:34; Jer 21:4-7 [h] S Pr 1:24; Ro 10:21 [i] Jer 7:13 **35:18** [j] S Ge 31:35 **35:19** [k] S Isa 48:19; Jer 33:17 [l] Jer 15:19 **36:1** [m] S 2Ch 36:5 **36:2** [n] S ver 4; S Ex 17:14; S Ps 40:7; Jer 30:2; Hab 2:2 [o] Eze 2:7 [p] Jer 1:2; 25:3 **36:3** [q] ver 7; Eze 12:3; Am 5:15 [r] Isa 6:9; Mk 4:12

[w] *11* Or *Chaldean*

---

ous note). (1) Jonadab had given these rules so that his descendants might live lives of simplicity, stay separate from the Canaanites, and avoid conforming to the Israelites and their persistent apostasy. Abstinence from wine helped them escape the immorality and idolatry of Baal worship, which was often accompanied by drunkenness and carousing; the other prohibitions helped them sustain their simple nomadic lifestyle and remain untouched by the influences of spiritual, moral and social decay in their own nation.

(2) Although some of the Recabites' rules need not be followed by believers today, their goal to remain separated from evil must always be the goal of true followers of Christ. Like Jonadab, all parents should have standards for their children that help them remain faithful to God and his Word.

35:19 NEVER FAIL TO HAVE A MAN TO SERVE ME. The faithfulness of the Recabites to their forefather would be rewarded; they would always have descendants who would serve the Lord. All believers who have godly convictions and remain true to them out of honor for God, church and parents will receive God's blessing and rewards.

36:1 FOURTH YEAR OF JEHOIAKIM. The incident described in ch. 36 occurred in 605 B.C., after Nebuchadnezzar's army had defeated the Egyptians at Carchemish and was again advancing toward Jerusalem (cf. 25:1–38).

36:2 WRITE ON IT ALL THE WORDS. This is the first time that Jeremiah's prophecies were compiled into one book. Initially, all the prophecies were recorded so that they could be read aloud to the people. God intended that the people of Judah would respond to the written word by turning from their wicked way and receiving forgiveness, thus avoiding his wrath against them for their wickedness (vv. 3,6–7).

plan to inflict on them, each of them
will turn[s] from his wicked way; then
I will forgive[t] their wickedness and
their sin."
4So Jeremiah called Baruch[u] son of
Neriah,[v] and while Jeremiah dictated[w] all the words the LORD had spoken
to him, Baruch wrote them on the
scroll.[x] **5**Then Jeremiah told Baruch,
"I am restricted; I cannot go to the
LORD's temple. **6**So you go to the house
of the LORD on a day of fasting[y] and
read to the people from the scroll the
words of the LORD that you wrote as I
dictated.[z] Read them to all the people
of Judah[a] who come in from their
towns. **7**Perhaps they will bring their
petition[b] before the LORD, and each
will turn[c] from his wicked ways, for
the anger[d] and wrath pronounced
against this people by the LORD are
great."
8Baruch son of Neriah did everything Jeremiah the prophet told him to
do; at the LORD's temple he read the
words of the LORD from the scroll. **9**In
the ninth month[e] of the fifth year of
Jehoiakim son of Josiah king of Judah,
a time of fasting[f] before the LORD was
proclaimed for all the people in Jerusalem and those who had come from the
towns of Judah. **10**From the room of
Gemariah[g] son of Shaphan[h] the secretary,[i] which was in the upper courtyard at the entrance of the New Gate[j]
of the temple, Baruch read to all the
people at the LORD's temple the words
of Jeremiah from the scroll.
11When Micaiah son of Gemariah,
the son of Shaphan, heard all the
words of the LORD from the scroll, **12**he
went down to the secretary's[k] room in
the royal palace, where all the officials
were sitting: Elishama the secretary,
Delaiah son of Shemaiah, Elnathan[l]
son of Acbor, Gemariah son of Shaphan, Zedekiah son of Hananiah, and
all the other officials.[m] **13**After Micaiah told them everything he had heard
Baruch read to the people from the
scroll, **14**all the officials sent Jehudi[n]
son of Nethaniah, the son of Shelemiah, the son of Cushi, to say to Baruch,
"Bring the scroll[o] from which you
have read to the people and come." So
Baruch son of Neriah went to them
with the scroll in his hand. **15**They said
to him, "Sit down, please, and read it
to us."
So Baruch read it to them. **16**When
they heard all these words, they looked
at each other in fear[p] and said to Baruch, "We must report all these words
to the king." **17**Then they asked Baruch, "Tell us, how did you come to
write[q] all this? Did Jeremiah dictate
it?"
18"Yes," Baruch replied, "he dictated[r] all these words to me, and I wrote
them in ink on the scroll."
19Then the officials[s] said to Baruch, "You and Jeremiah, go and hide.[t]
Don't let anyone know where you are."
20After they put the scroll in the
room of Elishama the secretary, they
went to the king in the courtyard and
reported everything to him. **21**The king
sent Jehudi[u] to get the scroll, and Jehudi brought it from the room of Elishama the secretary and read it to the
king[v] and all the officials standing beside him. **22**It was the ninth month and
the king was sitting in the winter
apartment,[w] with a fire burning in the
firepot in front of him. **23**Whenever Jehudi had read three or four columns of
the scroll,[x] the king cut them off with
a scribe's knife and threw them into
the firepot, until the entire scroll was
burned in the fire.[y] **24**The king and all
his attendants who heard all these
words showed no fear,[z] nor did they
tear their clothes.[a] **25**Even though Elnathan, Delaiah[b] and Gemariah[c]
urged the king not to burn the scroll,
he would not listen to them. **26**Instead,
the king commanded Jerahmeel, a son
of the king, Seraiah son of Azriel and
Shelemiah son of Abdeel to arrest[d]
Baruch the scribe and Jeremiah the

36:3 [s] S 2Ki 17:13; S Isa 44:22; S Jer 26:3; Ac 3:19 [t] S Jer 18:8
36:4 [u] S Jer 32:12 [v] Jer 51:59 [w] ver 18 [x] ver 2; Eze 2:9; Da 7:1; Zec 5:1
36:6 [y] ver 9 [z] S Ex 4:16 [a] 2Ch 20:4
36:7 [b] Jer 37:20; 42:2 [c] S Jer 26:3 [d] S Dt 31:17
36:9 [e] ver 22 [f] S 2Ch 20:3
36:10 [g] ver 12, 25; Jer 29:3 [h] Jer 26:24 [i] Jer 52:25 [j] S Ge 23:10
36:12 [k] S 2Sa 8:17 [l] S Jer 26:22 [m] Jer 38:4
36:14 [n] ver 21 [o] ver 4
36:16 [p] S Ps 36:1
36:17 [q] Jer 30:2
36:18 [r] ver 4
36:19 [s] Jer 26:16 [t] S 1Ki 17:3
36:21 [u] ver 14 [v] 2Ki 22:10
36:22 [w] Am 3:15
36:23 [x] ver 2 [y] 1Ki 22:8
36:24 [z] S Ps 36:1 [a] S Ge 37:29; S Nu 14:6
36:25 [b] ver 12 [c] S ver 10
36:26 [d] Mt 23:34

36:16 WHEN THEY HEARD . . . IN FEAR. Evidently the officials believed the prophecies and knew they had to be read to the king; however, knowing the king's opposition to truth and righteousness, they suggested that Baruch and Jeremiah go into hiding.

36:23 CUT THEM OFF . . . THREW THEM INTO THE FIREPOT. As the king began destroying the scroll, he was revealing not only his open hostility to Jeremiah's warnings and pleas for repentance, but also his contempt for God's written Word and for the Lord himself. It is essential for our spiritual vitality that we strive to maintain a love and respect for God's written revelation. Even though we may not attempt to destroy it as did King Jehoiakim, we may still find ourselves throwing the Word behind our backs by neglecting to read, study and meditate on its inspired truths and by failing to live by its precepts.

prophet. But the LORD had hidden[e] them.

27After the king burned the scroll containing the words that Baruch had written at Jeremiah's dictation,[f] the word of the LORD came to Jeremiah: 28"Take another scroll[g] and write on it all the words that were on the first scroll, which Jehoiakim king of Judah burned up. 29Also tell Jehoiakim king of Judah, 'This is what the LORD says: You burned that scroll and said, "Why did you write on it that the king of Babylon would certainly come and destroy this land and cut off both men and animals[h] from it?"[i] 30Therefore, this is what the LORD says about Jehoiakim[j] king of Judah: He will have no one to sit on the throne of David; his body will be thrown out[k] and exposed[l] to the heat by day and the frost by night.[m] 31I will punish him and his children[n] and his attendants for their wickedness; I will bring on them and those living in Jerusalem and the people of Judah every disaster[o] I pronounced against them, because they have not listened.[p]' "

32So Jeremiah took another scroll and gave it to the scribe Baruch son of Neriah, and as Jeremiah dictated,[q] Baruch wrote[r] on it all the words of the scroll that Jehoiakim king of Judah had burned[s] in the fire. And many similar words were added to them.

Jeremiah in Prison

37 Zedekiah[t] son of Josiah was made king[u] of Judah by Nebuchadnezzar king of Babylon; he reigned in place of Jehoiachin[x][v] son of Jehoiakim. 2Neither he nor his attendants nor the people of the land paid any attention[w] to the words the LORD had spoken through Jeremiah the prophet.

3King Zedekiah, however, sent[x] Jehucal[y] son of Shelemiah with the priest Zephaniah[z] son of Maaseiah to Jeremiah the prophet with this message: "Please pray[a] to the LORD our God for us."

4Now Jeremiah was free to come and go among the people, for he had not yet been put in prison.[b] 5Pharaoh's army had marched out of Egypt,[c] and when the Babylonians[y] who were besieging Jerusalem heard the report about them, they withdrew[d] from Jerusalem.[e]

6Then the word of the LORD came to Jeremiah the prophet: 7"This is what the LORD, the God of Israel, says: Tell the king of Judah, who sent you to inquire[f] of me, 'Pharaoh's army, which has marched[g] out to support you, will go back to its own land, to Egypt.[h] 8Then the Babylonians will return and attack this city; they will capture[i] it and burn[j] it down.'

9"This is what the LORD says: Do not deceive[k] yourselves, thinking, 'The Babylonians will surely leave us.' They will not! 10Even if you were to defeat the entire Babylonian[z] army that is attacking you and only wounded men were left in their tents, they would come out and burn[l] this city down."

11After the Babylonian army had withdrawn[m] from Jerusalem because of Pharaoh's army, 12Jeremiah started to leave the city to go to the territory of Benjamin to get his share of the

36:26 [e]S 1Ki 17:3; Ps 11:1; S Jer 1:8; 15:21 **36:27** [f]ver 4 **36:28** [g]ver 2 **36:29** [h]Jer 33:12 [i]S Isa 30:10 **36:30** [j]Jer 52:2 [k]S Isa 14:19 [l]S 2Ki 24:6 [m]S Jer 8:2 **36:31** [n]Ex 20:5 [o]S Pr 29:1 [p]S Pr 1:24 **36:32** [q]ver 4 [r]Ex 34:1; Jer 30:2 [s]ver 23 **37:1** [t]S 2Ki 24:17 [u]1Sa 11:1; Eze 17:13 [v]S 2Ki 24:8,12; Jer 22:24 **37:2** [w]S 2Ki 24:19 **37:3** [x]ver 17; Jer 38:14 [y]Jer 38:1 [z]S 2Ki 25:18; Jer 29:25; 52:24 [a]S Ex 8:28; S Nu 21:7; 1Sa 12:19; 1Ki 13:6; 2Ki 19:4; Jer 42:2 **37:4** [b]ver 15; Jer 32:2 **37:5** [c]S Ge 15:18; Isa 31:1; Eze 17:15 [d]Jer 34:21 [e]S Isa 30:5; Jer 34:11 **37:7** [f]S Ge 25:22; S 2Ki 22:18 [g]ver 5 [h]S 2Ki 18:21; S Jer 2:36; La 1:7; 4:17 **37:8** [i]Jer 38:3 [j]Jer 21:10; 38:18; 39:8 **37:9** [k]Jer 29:8; S Mk 13:5 **37:10** [l]Jer 21:10 **37:11** [m]ver 5

[x]*1* Hebrew *Coniah,* a variant of *Jehoiachin* [y]*5* Or *Chaldeans;* also in verses 8, 9, 13 and 14 [z]*10* Or *Chaldean;* also in verse 11

36:30 NO ONE TO SIT ON THE THRONE. Jehoiakim's son Jehoiachin (2Ki 24:6,8) assumed the throne for only three months before he was carried away to Babylon in 597 B.C. No other descendant of Jehoiakim ascended the throne of David.

36:32 ANOTHER SCROLL. Jeremiah and Baruch prepared another scroll with some additions. As time passed, more was added, thus completing the book of Jeremiah as we know it today, a part of the inspired Scriptures.

37:1 ZEDEKIAH. Nebuchadnezzar placed Zedekiah on the throne in Jerusalem as a vassal of Babylon; previously King Jehoiachin had reigned for only three months before being deported to Babylon (see 36:30, note).

37:3 PRAY . . . FOR US. Though Zedekiah refused to pay attention to the words of the Lord (v. 2), he still wanted Jeremiah to pray for Judah, hoping in some way to gain the Lord's blessing. Zedekiah was like many today who want God's help, yet at the same time seek to enjoy the sinful pleasures of the world. Such people are superficial religionists who have no real relationship with God and yet believe that when trouble comes, they can call on him and receive his help; like Zedekiah, they will be disappointed (vv. 6–9).

37:9 THIS IS WHAT THE LORD SAYS. Jeremiah stood before the king and unwaveringly proclaimed God's word. He did not hesitate to announce the unpopular word that the city would be destroyed (vv. 8,10). Beatings, imprisonment and the threat of death did not cause him to waver from faithfulness to the Lord and to what God wanted him to say (vv. 11–17).

property[n] among the people there.
13But when he reached the Benjamin
Gate,[o] the captain of the guard, whose
name was Irijah son of Shelemiah, the
son of Hananiah, arrested him and
said, "You are deserting to the Babylonians!"[p]
14"That's not true!" Jeremiah said.
"I am not deserting to the Babylonians." But Irijah would not listen to
him; instead, he arrested[q] Jeremiah
and brought him to the officials.
15They were angry with Jeremiah and
had him beaten[r] and imprisoned[s] in
the house[t] of Jonathan the secretary,
which they had made into a prison.
16Jeremiah was put into a vaulted
cell in a dungeon, where he remained
a long time. 17Then King Zedekiah
sent[u] for him and had him brought to
the palace, where he asked[v] him privately,[w] "Is there any word from the
LORD?"
"Yes," Jeremiah replied, "you will be
handed over[x] to the king of Babylon."
18Then Jeremiah said to King Zedekiah, "What crime[y] have I committed
against you or your officials or this
people, that you have put me in prison?
19Where are your prophets[z] who
prophesied to you, 'The king of Babylon will not attack you or this land'?
20But now, my lord the king, please listen. Let me bring my petition before
you: Do not send me back to the house
of Jonathan the secretary, or I will die
there."[a]
21King Zedekiah then gave orders
for Jeremiah to be placed in the courtyard of the guard and given bread from
the street of the bakers each day until
all the bread[b] in the city was gone.[c]

37:12 [n] S Jer 32:9
37:13 [o] S Jer 20:2
[p] Jer 21:9
37:14 [q] Isa 58:6; Jer 40:4
37:15 [r] S Jer 20:2; Heb 11:36
[s] S 1Ki 22:27
[t] ver 20; Jer 38:26
37:17 [u] S ver 3
[v] S Ge 25:22; Jer 15:11
[w] Jer 38:16
[x] S Jer 21:7
37:18 [y] S 1Sa 26:18; Jn 10:32; Ac 25:8
37:19 [z] S Jer 14:13; Eze 13:2
37:20 [a] S ver 15
37:21 [b] S Lev 26:26; Isa 33:16; Jer 38:9; La 1:11
[c] S 2Ki 25:3
[d] Jer 32:2; 38:6,13, 28; 39:13-14
38:1 [e] S 1Ch 9:12
[f] Jer 37:3
38:2 [g] Jer 34:17
[h] ver 17; S Jer 21:9; 39:18; 45:5
38:3 [i] S Jer 21:4, 10
38:4 [j] S Jer 36:12
[k] S Jer 11:21
[l] S 1Sa 17:32
38:5 [m] S Jer 26:14
[n] 1Sa 15:24
38:6 [o] S Jer 37:21
[p] S Jos 2:15
[q] S Ge 37:24
[r] S Job 30:19; La 3:53
38:7 [s] Jer 39:16

So Jeremiah remained in the courtyard
of the guard.[d]

Jeremiah Thrown Into a Cistern

38 Shephatiah son of Mattan, Gedaliah son of Pashhur[e], Jehucal[a][f] son of Shelemiah, and Pashhur
son of Malkijah heard what Jeremiah
was telling all the people when he said,
2"This is what the LORD says: 'Whoever
stays in this city will die by the sword,
famine or plague,[g] but whoever goes
over to the Babylonians[b] will live. He
will escape with his life; he will live.'[h]
3And this is what the LORD says: 'This
city will certainly be handed over to the
army of the king of Babylon, who will
capture it.' "[i]
4Then the officials[j] said to the
king, "This man should be put to
death.[k] He is discouraging[l] the soldiers who are left in this city, as well
as all the people, by the things he is
saying to them. This man is not seeking the good of these people but their
ruin."
5"He is in your hands,"[m] King Zedekiah answered. "The king can do nothing[n] to oppose you."
6So they took Jeremiah and put him
into the cistern of Malkijah, the king's
son, which was in the courtyard of the
guard.[o] They lowered Jeremiah by
ropes[p] into the cistern; it had no water in it,[q] only mud, and Jeremiah
sank down into the mud.[r]
7But Ebed-Melech,[s] a Cushite,[c] an

[a] *1* Hebrew *Jucal,* a variant of *Jehucal* [b] *2* Or *Chaldeans;* also in verses 18, 19 and 23 [c] *7* Probably from the upper Nile region

37:15 BEATEN AND IMPRISONED. Some officials in the Judean army were hostile to Jeremiah because he had urged the people to surrender to the Babylonians (21:9; 38:2); thus they confined him to an underground dungeon (v. 16). He would likely have died in that dark and dangerous cell if he had remained there much longer (v. 20).

37:17 ANY WORD FROM THE LORD? Knowing that Jeremiah was a true prophet of the Lord, Zedekiah hoped for a more encouraging word from God. But Jeremiah's word remained the same—Jerusalem would fall and Zedekiah would be handed over to the king of Babylon. The prophet would not compromise the truth even in such desperate circumstances.

38:2 WHOEVER STAYS IN THIS CITY WILL DIE. Jeremiah's message was demoralizing the soldiers and weakening their will to resist the Babylonians; because of this, the officials wanted to put him to death (v. 4; see 32:2, note).

38:5 HE IS IN YOUR HANDS. King Zedekiah turned Jeremiah over to the officials because he feared their power and influence. His weakness and lack of moral fiber were evident throughout his reign.

38:6 PUT HIM INTO THE CISTERN. A cistern was used to catch rainwater during the winter and store it for summer use; shaped like a bell, the opening at the top was approximately three feet wide. The officials knew that Jeremiah would not live long confined to the cistern. Jeremiah suffered greatly for maintaining his faithfulness to God and his word. For those faithful to God's revelation and righteousness, opposition can be expected in this world; persecution because of righteousness will come from the world, and at times even from those within the church (see Mt 5:10, note).

38:7 EBED-MELECH. Acting on Jeremiah's be-

official[d][t] in the royal palace, heard that they had put Jeremiah into the cistern. While the king was sitting in the Benjamin Gate,[u] **8**Ebed-Melech went out of the palace and said to him, **9**"My lord the king, these men have acted wickedly in all they have done to Jeremiah the prophet. They have thrown him into a cistern,[v] where he will starve to death when there is no longer any bread[w] in the city."

10Then the king commanded Ebed-Melech the Cushite, "Take thirty men from here with you and lift Jeremiah the prophet out of the cistern before he dies."

11So Ebed-Melech took the men with him and went to a room under the treasury in the palace. He took some old rags and worn-out clothes from there and let them down with ropes[x] to Jeremiah in the cistern. **12**Ebed-Melech the Cushite said to Jeremiah, "Put these old rags and worn-out clothes under your arms to pad the ropes." Jeremiah did so, **13**and they pulled him up with the ropes and lifted him out of the cistern. And Jeremiah remained in the courtyard of the guard.[y]

Zedekiah Questions Jeremiah Again

14Then King Zedekiah sent[z] for Jeremiah the prophet and had him brought to the third entrance to the temple of the LORD. "I am going to ask you something," the king said to Jeremiah. "Do not hide[a] anything from me."

15Jeremiah said to Zedekiah, "If I give you an answer, will you not kill me? Even if I did give you counsel, you would not listen to me."

16But King Zedekiah swore this oath secretly[b] to Jeremiah: "As surely as the LORD lives, who has given us breath,[c] I will neither kill you nor hand you over to those who are seeking your life."[d]

17Then Jeremiah said to Zedekiah, "This is what the LORD God Almighty, the God of Israel, says: 'If you surrender[e] to the officers of the king of Babylon, your life will be spared and this city will not be burned down; you and your family will live.[f] **18**But if you will not surrender to the officers of the king of Babylon, this city will be handed over[g] to the Babylonians and they will burn[h] it down; you yourself will not escape[i] from their hands.' "

19King Zedekiah said to Jeremiah, "I am afraid[j] of the Jews who have gone over[k] to the Babylonians, for the Babylonians may hand me over to them and they will mistreat me."

20"They will not hand you over," Jeremiah replied. "Obey[l] the LORD by doing what I tell you. Then it will go well[m] with you, and your life[n] will be spared. **21**But if you refuse to surrender, this is what the LORD has revealed to me: **22**All the women[o] left in the palace of the king of Judah will be brought out to the officials of the king of Babylon. Those women will say to you:

" 'They misled you and overcame you—
those trusted friends[p] of yours.
Your feet are sunk in the mud;[q]
your friends have deserted you.'

23"All your wives and children[r] will be brought out to the Babylonians. You yourself will not escape[s] from their hands but will be captured[t] by the king of Babylon; and this city will[e] be burned down."[u]

24Then Zedekiah said to Jeremiah, "Do not let anyone know[v] about this conversation, or you may die. **25**If the officials hear that I talked with you, and they come to you and say, 'Tell us what you said to the king and what the king said to you; do not hide it from us or we will kill you,' **26**then tell[w] them, 'I was pleading with the king not to

38:7 [t] *fn* Isa 56:3-5; Ac 8:27 [u] S Job 29:7
38:9 [v] S Ge 37:20 [w] S Jer 37:21
38:11 [x] S Jos 2:15
38:13 [y] S Jer 37:21
38:14 [z] S Jer 37:3 [a] S 1Sa 3:17
38:16 [b] Jer 37:17 [c] Isa 42:5; 57:16 [d] ver 4
38:17 [e] Jer 27:8 [f] S Jer 21:9
38:18 [g] ver 3 [h] S Jer 37:8 [i] S Jer 24:8; S 32:4
38:19 [j] Isa 51:12; Jn 12:42 [k] Jer 39:9; 52:15
38:20 [l] Jer 11:4 [m] S Dt 5:33; Jer 40:9 [n] Isa 55:3
38:22 [o] S Jer 6:12 [p] S Job 19:14; S Jer 13:21 [q] S Job 30:19; Ps 69:14
38:23 [r] S 2Ki 25:6 [s] S Jer 32:4; Eze 17:15 [t] S Jer 24:8 [u] Jer 21:10; 37:8
38:24 [v] Jer 37:17
38:26 [w] 1Sa 16:2

[d] 7 Or *a eunuch* [e] 23 Or *and you will cause this city to*

half, this Cushite sought to rescue him by appealing to the king. Ebed-Melech showed both compassion for Jeremiah and courage in opposing the prophet's enemies. Believers should always try to help those who are being mistreated, even if it means standing against the majority. Because of his kindness to Jeremiah, Ebed-Melech's life was spared when Jerusalem fell; God did not forget this true servant (39:15–18).

38:20 OBEY THE LORD. Zedekiah believed Jeremiah's message, but his fear of others (v. 19), his weak character and his lack of faith in God kept him from firmly resolving to obey God. As a result, Zedekiah brought shame on himself and ruin on the nation. He was like many today who refuse to do right even though they know their actions will bring God's judgment on them and calamity to the lives of others.

send me back to Jonathan's house[x] to
die there.' "
27All the officials did come to Jeremiah and question him, and he told
them everything the king had ordered
him to say. So they said no more to
him, for no one had heard his conversation with the king.
28And Jeremiah remained in the
courtyard of the guard[y] until the day
Jerusalem was captured.

The Fall of Jerusalem

39:1–10pp — 2Ki 25:1–12; Jer 52:4–16

39 This is how Jerusalem[z] was
taken: 1In the ninth year of
Zedekiah[a] king of Judah, in the tenth
month, Nebuchadnezzar[b] king of Babylon marched against Jerusalem with
his whole army and laid siege[c] to it.
2And on the ninth day of the fourth[d]
month of Zedekiah's eleventh year, the
city wall[e] was broken through.[f]
3Then all the officials[g] of the king of
Babylon came and took seats in the
Middle Gate: Nergal-Sharezer of Sam-
gar, Nebo-Sarsekim[f] a chief officer,
Nergal-Sharezer a high official and all
the other officials of the king of Babylon. 4When Zedekiah king of Judah
and all the soldiers saw them, they
fled; they left the city at night by way
of the king's garden, through the gate
between the two walls,[h] and headed
toward the Arabah.[g][i]
5But the Babylonian[h] army pursued
them and overtook Zedekiah[j] in the
plains of Jericho. They captured[k] him
and took him to Nebuchadnezzar king
of Babylon at Riblah[l] in the land of
Hamath, where he pronounced sentence on him. 6There at Riblah the king
of Babylon slaughtered the sons of
Zedekiah before his eyes and also
killed all the nobles[m] of Judah. 7Then
he put out Zedekiah's eyes[n] and
bound him with bronze shackles to
take him to Babylon.[o]
8The Babylonians[i] set fire[p] to the
royal palace and the houses of the people and broke down the walls[q] of Jerusalem. 9Nebuzaradan commander of
the imperial guard carried into exile to
Babylon the people who remained in
the city, along with those who had
gone over to him,[r] and the rest of the
people.[s] 10But Nebuzaradan the commander of the guard left behind in the
land of Judah some of the poor people,
who owned nothing; and at that time
he gave them vineyards and fields.
11Now Nebuchadnezzar king of Babylon had given these orders about Jeremiah through Nebuzaradan commander of the imperial guard: 12"Take him
and look after him; don't harm[t] him
but do for him whatever he asks." 13So
Nebuzaradan the commander of the
guard, Nebushazban a chief officer,
Nergal-Sharezer a high official and all
the other officers[u] of the king of Babylon 14sent and had Jeremiah taken out
of the courtyard of the guard.[v] They
turned him over to Gedaliah[w] son of
Ahikam,[x] the son of Shaphan,[y] to
take him back to his home. So he remained among his own people.[z]
15While Jeremiah had been confined
in the courtyard of the guard, the word
of the LORD came to him: 16"Go and tell

38:26 [x]S Jer 37:15
38:28 [y]S Jer 37:21
39:1 [z]S Jer 25:29 [a]S 2Ch 36:11 [b]S 2Ki 24:1; S Jer 28:14 [c]S 2Ki 25:1; Jer 52:4; Eze 4:3; 24:2
39:2 [d]Zec 8:19 [e]S 2Ki 14:13 [f]Eze 33:21
39:3 [g]ver 13; Jer 21:4
39:4 [h]S Isa 22:11 [i]Eze 12:12
39:5 [j]S Jer 24:8; S 32:4 [k]S Jer 21:7 [l]S Nu 34:11
39:6 [m]S Isa 34:12
39:7 [n]S Nu 16:14; Eze 12:13 [o]S Jer 2:35
39:8 [p]S Jer 34:22 [q]S Ne 1:3; S Ps 80:12; S Isa 22:5; La 2:8
39:9 [r]Jer 21:9 [s]Jer 40:1; La 1:5
39:12 [t]S Pr 16:7; Jer 15:20-21; 1Pe 3:13
39:13 [u]S ver 3
39:14 [v]S Ne 3:25; Jer 37:21 [w]S 2Ki 25:22 [x]S 2Ki 22:12 [y]S 2Ki 22:3 [z]Jer 40:5

[f]3 Or *Nergal-Sharezer, Samgar-Nebo, Sarsekim*
[g]4 Or *the Jordan Valley*
[h]5 Or *Chaldean*
[i]8 Or *Chaldeans*

39:1 NINTH YEAR OF ZEDEKIAH ... TENTH MONTH. The siege against Jerusalem lasted about eighteen months, during which time the city was cut off from all outside help and supplies; after some time, severe famine set in. Jerusalem's fall is described in great detail in ch. 52 (cf. 2Ki 25; 2Ch 36); its defeat fulfilled Jeremiah's prophecies of God's judgment on an apostate people.

39:5–7 OVERTOOK ZEDEKIAH. Zedekiah suffered much because he refused to listen to God and obey his word (cf. 38:20–23). Grief and suffering will be the lot of all who persist in going their own sinful way while ignoring the voice of God, who seeks to save all who are perishing (Jn 3:16; Lk 19:10). If people could only understand that sin brings unhappiness and death, they might turn to God for mercy and grace. (Ro 6:16,23); however, Satan has so blinded the eyes of unbelievers that they cannot see their present condition or the awful fate that awaits them (2Co 4:4). Only through prayer, the proclamation of God's word, and the convicting work of the Holy Spirit (see Jn 16:8, note) will the unsaved recognize their true spiritual condition and the danger facing them.

39:11 JEREMIAH. Nebuchadnezzar had undoubtedly heard of Jeremiah's advice to submit to Babylon, and the Babylonians treated him kindly when they captured Jerusalem. He was put under the protection of Gedaliah, the appointed governor. After being freed, Jeremiah was apparently again arrested by mistake and put in chains, awaiting transport to Babylon; once again he was set free (40:1–6).

39:16 EBED-MELECH. See 38:7, note.

Ebed-Melech[a] the Cushite, 'This is what the LORD Almighty, the God of Israel, says: I am about to fulfill my words[b] against this city through disaster,[c] not prosperity. At that time they will be fulfilled before your eyes. 17But I will rescue[d] you on that day, declares the LORD; you will not be handed over to those you fear. 18I will save[e] you; you will not fall by the sword[f] but will escape with your life,[g] because you trust[h] in me, declares the LORD.' "

Jeremiah Freed

40 The word came to Jeremiah from the LORD after Nebuzaradan commander of the imperial guard had released him at Ramah.[i] He had found Jeremiah bound in chains among all the captives[j] from Jerusalem and Judah who were being carried into exile to Babylon. 2When the commander[k] of the guard found Jeremiah, he said to him, "The LORD your God decreed[l] this disaster[m] for this place.[n] 3And now the LORD has brought it about; he has done just as he said he would. All this happened because you people sinned[o] against the LORD and did not obey[p] him. 4But today I am freeing[q] you from the chains[r] on your wrists. Come with me to Babylon, if you like, and I will look after you; but if you do not want to, then don't come. Look, the whole country lies before you; go wherever you please."[s] 5However, before Jeremiah turned to go,[j] Nebuzaradan added, "Go back to Gedaliah[t] son of Ahikam,[u] the son of Shaphan, whom the king of Babylon has appointed[v] over the towns[w] of Judah, and live with him among the people, or go anywhere else you please."[x]

Then the commander gave him provisions and a present[y] and let him go. 6So Jeremiah went to Gedaliah son of Ahikam at Mizpah[z] and stayed with him among the people who were left behind in the land.

39:16 [a]Jer 38:7 [b]Ps 33:11; Isa 14:27; 40:8; Jer 44:28; La 2:17; S Mt 1:22 [c]S Jos 23:15; Jer 21:10 **39:17** [d]Ps 34:22; 41:1-2 **39:18** [e]S 1Sa 17:47; Ac 16:31 [f]S Job 5:20 [g]S Jer 21:9; S 38:2 [h]S Jer 17:7; Ro 10:11 **40:1** [i]S Jos 18:25; 1Sa 8:4; Mt 2:18 [j]S Dt 21:10; S 2Ki 24:1; S 2Ch 36:10; Na 3:10 **40:2** [k]Ro 13:4 [l]S Isa 10:22 [m]S 2Ch 34:24; S Ps 18:18; S Pr 8:36; Gal 6:7-8 [n]S Jos 23:15 **40:3** [o]S Pr 13:21; Ro 6:23; Jas 1:15 [p]S Lev 26:33; Dt 28:45-52; 29:24-28; 31:17-18; S 1Ki 9:9; Jer 22:8-9; Da 9:14; Ac 7:39; Ro 2:5-9 **40:4** [q]Ps 105:18-20; S Jer 37:14 [r]La 3:7 [s]S Ge 13:9 **40:5** [t]S 2Ki 25:22 [u]2Ki 22:12-14 [v]Ne 5:14; Jer 41:2 [w]Jer 44:2; Zec 1:12 [x]Jer 39:14 [y]S Ge 32:20; S 1Sa 9:7 **40:6** [z]ver 10; Jdg 20:1; 1Sa 7:5-17 **40:7** [a]S Ge 41:41; S Ne 5:14 [b]S 2Ki 24:14; S Ac 24:17; Jas 2:5 **40:8** [c]ver 13 [d]ver 14; Jer 41:1,2 [e]ver 15; Jer 41:11 [f]S 2Sa 23:28 [g]S Dt 3:14 **40:9** [h]Jer 5:19; 27:11; Ro 13:1-2; Eph 6:5-8 [i]Eze 23:23 [j]S Jer 38:20; La 1:1 **40:10** [k]S ver 6 [l]S Ge 27:28; S Ex 23:16 [m]Ex 7:19; 2Co 4:7 [n]Dt 1:39 **40:11** [o]S Nu 21:11; 25:1 [p]S Ge 25:30 [q]Jer 12:14

Gedaliah Assassinated

40:7-9; 41:1-3pp — 2Ki 25:22-26

7When all the army officers and their men who were still in the open country heard that the king of Babylon had appointed Gedaliah son of Ahikam as governor[a] over the land and had put him in charge of the men, women and children who were the poorest[b] in the land and who had not been carried into exile to Babylon, 8they came to Gedaliah at Mizpah[c]—Ishmael[d] son of Nethaniah, Johanan[e] and Jonathan the sons of Kareah, Seraiah son of Tanhumeth, the sons of Ephai the Netophathite,[f] and Jaazaniah[k] the son of the Maacathite,[g] and their men. 9Gedaliah son of Ahikam, the son of Shaphan, took an oath to reassure them and their men. "Do not be afraid to serve[h] the Babylonians,[l][i]" he said. "Settle down in the land and serve the king of Babylon, and it will go well with you.[j] 10I myself will stay at Mizpah[k] to represent you before the Babylonians who come to us, but you are to harvest the wine,[l] summer fruit and oil, and put them in your storage jars,[m] and live in the towns you have taken over."[n]

11When all the Jews in Moab,[o] Ammon, Edom[p] and all the other countries[q] heard that the king of Babylon had left a remnant in Judah and had appointed Gedaliah son of Ahikam, the son of Shaphan, as governor over them, 12they all came back to the land of Judah, to Gedaliah at Mizpah, from all the countries where they had been scattered.[r] And they harvested an abundance of wine and summer fruit.

13Johanan[s] son of Kareah and all the army officers still in the open country came to Gedaliah at Mizpah[t] 14and said to him, "Don't you know that Baalis king of the Ammonites[u]

40:12 [r]Jer 43:5 **40:13** [s]Jer 42:1 [t]ver 8 **40:14** [u]S Ge 19:38; 2Sa 10:1-19; Jer 25:21; 41:10; 49:1

[j]5 Or *Jeremiah answered* [k]8 Hebrew *Jezaniah,* a variant of *Jaazaniah* [l]9 Or *Chaldeans*; also in verse 10

40:1–44:30 CARRIED INTO EXILE. These chapters deal with events that occurred in Judah after Jerusalem's fall. Many of the people were carried off to Babylon, while a few of them were left behind. What happened after the fall of the city demonstrates that the people still refused to trust in God.

40:1 JEREMIAH BOUND IN CHAINS. See 39:11, note.

40:7–16 GEDALIAH ... GOVERNOR OVER THE LAND. Gedaliah, a good ruler, helped restore order and peace to the land; he served approximately five years before being assassinated by Ishmael, who wanted to continue opposition to Babylon. Gedaliah trusted Ishmael too much, even after being warned of an assassination plot.

has sent Ishmael[v] son of Nethaniah to
take your life?" But Gedaliah son of
Ahikam did not believe them.
15Then Johanan[w] son of Kareah
said privately to Gedaliah in Mizpah,
"Let me go and kill[x] Ishmael son of
Nethaniah, and no one will know it.
Why should he take your life and cause
all the Jews who are gathered around
you to be scattered[y] and the remnant[z] of Judah to perish?"
16But Gedaliah son of Ahikam said
to Johanan[a] son of Kareah, "Don't do
such a thing! What you are saying
about Ishmael is not true."
41 In the seventh month Ishmael[b] son of Nethaniah, the son
of Elishama, who was of royal blood
and had been one of the king's officers,
came with ten men to Gedaliah son of
Ahikam at Mizpah. While they were
eating together there, 2Ishmael[c] son
of Nethaniah and the ten men who
were with him got up and struck down
Gedaliah son of Ahikam, the son of
Shaphan, with the sword,[d] killing the
one whom the king of Babylon had appointed[e] as governor over the land.[f]
3Ishmael also killed all the Jews who
were with Gedaliah at Mizpah, as well
as the Babylonian[m] soldiers who were
there.
4The day after Gedaliah's assassination, before anyone knew about it,
5eighty men who had shaved off their
beards,[g] torn their clothes[h] and
cut[i] themselves came from Shechem,[j] Shiloh[k] and Samaria,[l]
bringing grain offerings and incense[m]
with them to the house of the LORD.[n]
6Ishmael son of Nethaniah went out
from Mizpah to meet them, weeping[o]
as he went. When he met them, he said,
"Come to Gedaliah son of Ahikam."[p]
7When they went into the city, Ishmael
son of Nethaniah and the men who
were with him slaughtered them and
threw them into a cistern.[q] 8But ten of
them said to Ishmael, "Don't kill us!
We have wheat and barley, oil and honey, hidden in a field."[r] So he let them
alone and did not kill them with the
others. 9Now the cistern where he
threw all the bodies of the men he had
killed along with Gedaliah was the one
King Asa[s] had made as part of his defense[t] against Baasha[u] king of Israel. Ishmael son of Nethaniah filled it
with the dead.
10Ishmael made captives of all the
rest of the people[v] who were in Mizpah—the king's daughters[w] along
with all the others who were left there,
over whom Nebuzaradan commander
of the imperial guard had appointed
Gedaliah son of Ahikam. Ishmael son
of Nethaniah took them captive and set
out to cross over to the Ammonites.[x]
11When Johanan[y] son of Kareah
and all the army officers who were with
him heard about all the crimes Ishmael
son of Nethaniah had committed,
12they took all their men and went to
fight[z] Ishmael son of Nethaniah. They
caught up with him near the great
pool[a] in Gibeon. 13When all the people[b] Ishmael had with him saw Johanan son of Kareah and the army officers who were with him, they were
glad. 14All the people Ishmael had tak-
en captive at Mizpah[c] turned and
went over to Johanan son of Kareah.
15But Ishmael son of Nethaniah and
eight of his men escaped[d] from Johanan and fled to the Ammonites.

Flight to Egypt

16Then Johanan son of Kareah and
all the army officers[e] who were with
him led away all the survivors[f] from
Mizpah whom he had recovered from
Ishmael son of Nethaniah after he had
assassinated Gedaliah son of Ahikam:
the soldiers, women, children and
court officials he had brought from Gibeon. 17And they went on, stopping at
Geruth Kimham[g] near Bethlehem[h]
on their way to Egypt[i] 18to escape the
Babylonians.[n] They were afraid[j] of
them because Ishmael son of Nethaniah had killed Gedaliah[k] son of Ahikam, whom the king of Babylon had appointed as governor over the land.

40:14 [v] S ver 8
40:15 [w] S ver 8 [x] S Dt 5:17; Mt 5:21-22 [y] S Ge 11:4; S Lev 26:33; Mt 26:31; Jn 11:52; Jas 1:1 [z] S 2Ki 21:14; S Isa 1:9; Ro 11:5
40:16 [a] Jer 43:2
41:1 [b] S Jer 40:8
41:2 [c] Ps 41:9; 109:5 [d] S Jos 11:10; Jer 40:15; Heb 11:37 [e] S Jer 40:5 [f] 2Sa 3:27; 20:9-10; S Jer 40:8
41:5 [g] S Lev 19:27; Jer 47:5; 48:37 [h] S Ge 37:29; S Lev 10:6; S Mk 14:63 [i] S Lev 19:28 [j] Ge 12:6; 33:18; Jdg 9:1-57; 1Ki 12:1 [k] S Jos 18:1 [l] 1Ki 16:24 [m] S Nu 16:40; S Lk 1:9 [n] 1Ki 3:2; 6:38; 2Ki 25:9
41:6 [o] 2Sa 3:16 [p] Ps 5:9; Hos 7:11; Rev 20:10
41:7 [q] S Ge 37:24; 2Ki 10:14
41:8 [r] Isa 45:3
41:9 [s] S 1Ki 15:22; S 2Ch 16:6 [t] S Jdg 6:2 [u] S 2Ch 16:1
41:10 [v] Jer 40:7, 12 [w] Jer 38:23 [x] S Jer 40:14
41:11 [y] S Jer 40:8
41:12 [z] S Ex 14:14; Jn 18:36 [a] S Jos 9:3; Jn 9:7
41:13 [b] ver 10
41:14 [c] Jer 40:6
41:15 [d] Job 21:30; S Pr 28:17
41:16 [e] Jer 42:1; 43:2 [f] Isa 1:9; Jer 43:4; Eze 7:16; 14:22; Zep 2:9
41:17 [g] 2Sa 19:37 [h] Ge 35:19; Mic 5:2 [i] Jer 42:14
41:18 [j] S Nu 14:9; Isa 51:12; Jer 42:16; Lk 12:4-5 [k] S 2Ki 25:22

[m] 3 Or *Chaldean* [n] 18 Or *Chaldeans*

41:2 STRUCK DOWN GEDALIAH. Because he was violently anti-Babylon, Ishmael killed Gedaliah, the governor appointed by Nebuchadnezzar; Ishmael may have believed that Gedaliah had supported the cruelty inflicted on Zedekiah (39:6–7).

41:7 SLAUGHTERED THEM. Ishmael slaughtered 70 of 80 pilgrims, evidently to get their supplies and money (cf. v. 8). He did not fear God or desire to do what was right; he failed to recognize that the Lord would one day judge his actions and punish him accordingly.

42 Then all the army officers, including Johanan[l] son of Kareah and Jezaniah[o] son of Hoshaiah,[m]
and all the people from the least to the
greatest[n] approached **2**Jeremiah the
prophet and said to him, "Please hear
our petition and pray[o] to the LORD
your God for this entire remnant.[p] For
as you now see, though we were once
many, now only a few[q] are left. **3**Pray
that the LORD your God will tell us
where we should go and what we
should do."[r]
4"I have heard you," replied Jeremiah the prophet. "I will certainly pray[s]
to the LORD your God as you have requested; I will tell[t] you everything the
LORD says and will keep nothing back
from you."[u]
5Then they said to Jeremiah, "May
the LORD be a true[v] and faithful[w] witness[x] against us if we do not act in
accordance with everything the LORD
your God sends you to tell us. **6**Whether it is favorable or unfavorable, we
will obey the LORD our God, to whom we
are sending you, so that it will go
well[y] with us, for we will obey[z] the
LORD our God."
7Ten days later the word of the LORD
came to Jeremiah. **8**So he called together Johanan son of Kareah and all the
army officers[a] who were with him and
all the people from the least to the
greatest.[b] **9**He said to them, "This is
what the LORD, the God of Israel, to
whom you sent me to present your petition,[c] says:[d] **10**'If you stay in this
land,[e] I will build[f] you up and not
tear you down; I will plant[g] you and
not uproot you,[h] for I am grieved over
the disaster I have inflicted on you.[i]
11Do not be afraid of the king of Babylon,[j] whom you now fear.[k] Do not
be afraid of him, declares the LORD, for
I am with you and will save[l] you and
deliver you from his hands.[m] **12**I will
show you compassion[n] so that he will
have compassion on you and restore
you to your land.'[o]
13"However, if you say, 'We will not
stay in this land,' and so disobey[p] the
LORD your God, **14**and if you say, 'No,
we will go and live in Egypt,[q] where
we will not see war or hear the trumpet[r] or be hungry for bread,'[s] **15**then
hear the word of the LORD,[t] O remnant
of Judah. This is what the LORD Almighty, the God of Israel, says: 'If you
are determined to go to Egypt and you
do go to settle there, **16**then the
sword[u] you fear[v] will overtake you
there, and the famine[w] you dread will
follow you into Egypt, and there you
will die.[x] **17**Indeed, all who are determined to go to Egypt to settle there will
die by the sword, famine and plague;[y]
not one of them will survive or escape
the disaster I will bring on them.'
18This is what the LORD Almighty, the
God of Israel, says: 'As my anger and
wrath[z] have been poured out on those
who lived in Jerusalem,[a] so will my
wrath be poured out on you when you
go to Egypt. You will be an object of
cursing[b] and horror,[c] of condemnation and reproach;[d] you will never see
this place again.'[e]
19"O remnant[f] of Judah, the LORD
has told you, 'Do not go to Egypt.'[g] Be
sure of this: I warn you today **20**that
you made a fatal mistake[p] when you
sent me to the LORD your God and said,
'Pray to the LORD our God for us; tell us
everything he says and we will do it.'[h]
21I have told you today, but you still
have not obeyed the LORD your God in
all he sent me to tell you.[i] **22**So now,
be sure of this: You will die by the
sword, famine[j] and plague[k] in the
place where you want to go to settle."[l]

43 When Jeremiah finished telling
the people all the words of the
LORD their God—everything the LORD
had sent him to tell them[m]— **2**Azariah
son of Hoshaiah[n] and Johanan[o] son
of Kareah and all the arrogant[p] men

42:1 [l]S Jer 40:13 [m]S Jer 41:16 [n]Jer 6:13; 44:12 **42:2** [o]S Ge 20:7; S Jer 36:7; Ac 8:24; Jas 5:16 [p]S Isa 1:9 [q]S Lev 26:22; La 1:1 **42:3** [r]ver 20; Ps 86:11; S Pr 3:6; S Jer 15:11 **42:4** [s]S Ex 8:29; 1Sa 12:23 [t]S Jer 1:17 [u]S Nu 22:18; S 1Sa 3:17 **42:5** [v]1Ki 22:16; Ps 119:160; Ro 3:4 [w]S Dt 7:9; Jn 8:26; S 1Co 1:9 [x]S Ge 31:48; S Dt 4:26; S Isa 1:2; S Ro 1:9; Rev 1:5 **42:6** [y]Dt 5:29; 6:3; Jer 7:23; 22:15 [z]S ver 19; S Ex 24:7; S Jos 24:24 **42:8** [a]ver 1 [b]Jer 41:16; S Mk 9:35; Lk 7:28; Heb 8:11 **42:9** [c]ver 2 [d]2Ki 22:15 **42:10** [e]Jer 43:4 [f]S Jer 24:6 [g]S Dt 30:9 [h]S Dt 29:28; Ecc 3:2; Jer 45:4; Eze 36:36; Da 11:4 [i]S 2Ch 34:24; Isa 30:26; S Jer 18:8 **42:11** [j]Jer 27:11 [k]S Nu 14:9; S 1Sa 15:24; Ps 23:4; Mt 10:28; 2Ti 1:7 [l]Ps 18:27; 69:35; S 119:94; S Isa 63:1; Heb 7:25 [m]S Ps 3:7; S Pr 20:22; S Jer 1:8; Ro 8:31 **42:12** [n]S Ex 3:21; S 2Sa 24:14; 2Co 1:3 [o]S Ge 31:3; S Ne 1:9; Ps 106:44-46 **42:13** [p]S Dt 11:28 **42:14** [q]Nu 11:4-5; S Dt 17:16; S Isa 30:2 [r]S Jos 6:20; S Mt 24:31 [s]S Dt 8:3; 1Sa 2:5; Pr 10:3; Isa 65:13; Mt 4:2-4 **42:15** [t]Jer 44:24 **42:16** [u]S Lev 26:33; Eze 11:8; 14:17 [v]S Jer 41:18 [w]S Ge 41:55 [x]S Ge 2:17; 2Ch 25:4; S Job 21:20; Eze 3:19; 18:4 **42:17** [y]ver 22; S Jer 21:7; 44:13 **42:18** [z]Dt 29:18-20; S 2Ch 12:7 [a]S 2Ch 36:19; Jer 39:1-9 [b]S Nu 5:27; S Jer 25:18 [c]S Dt 28:25,37 [d]S Ps 44:13 [e]S Jer 22:10 **42:19** [f]Jer 40:15 [g]S ver 6; Dt 17:16; Isa 30:7; Jer 43:2; 44:16 **42:20** [h]ver 2; Eze 14:7-8 **42:21** [i]S Ex 24:7; Jer 40:3; Eze 2:7; 12:2; Zec 7:11-12 **42:22** [j]S Isa 1:28 [k]S ver 17; Jer 24:10; Eze 6:11 [l]S Jer 15:2; Hos 9:6 **43:1** [m]Jer 26:8; 42:9-22 **43:2** [n]S Jer 41:16 [o]Jer 40:16 [p]S Ne 9:29; 1Co 4:18-21

[o] *1* Hebrew; Septuagint (see also 43:2) *Azariah*
[p] *20* Or *you erred in your hearts*

42:1–22 ALL THE PEOPLE ... APPROACHED. After Gedaliah was murdered, the people feared Babylon's wrath, and so they sought God's will from Jeremiah; however, having already made up their minds to flee to Egypt, they only wanted to hear God's word if it confirmed their intentions. God's answer was to "stay in this land" (v. 10). The leaders rejected God's word and went to Egypt anyway, taking Jeremiah along against his will (43:1–7).

said to Jeremiah, "You are lying![q] The LORD our God has not sent you to say, 'You must not go to Egypt to settle there.'[r] **3**But Baruch[s] son of Neriah is inciting you against us to hand us over to the Babylonians,[q] so they may kill us or carry us into exile to Babylon."[t]

4So Johanan son of Kareah and all the army officers and all the people[u] disobeyed the LORD's command[v] to stay in the land of Judah.[w] **5**Instead, Johanan son of Kareah and all the army officers led away all the remnant of Judah who had come back to live in the land of Judah from all the nations where they had been scattered.[x] **6**They also led away all the men, women[y] and children and the king's daughters whom Nebuzaradan commander of the imperial guard had left with Gedaliah son of Ahikam, the son of Shaphan, and Jeremiah the prophet and Baruch[z] son of Neriah. **7**So they entered Egypt[a] in disobedience to the LORD and went as far as Tahpanhes.[b]

8In Tahpanhes[c] the word of the LORD came to Jeremiah: **9**"While the Jews are watching, take some large stones[d] with you and bury them in clay in the brick[e] pavement at the entrance to Pharaoh's palace[f] in Tahpanhes. **10**Then say to them, 'This is what the LORD Almighty, the God of Israel, says: I will send for my servant[g] Nebuchadnezzar[h] king of Babylon, and I will set his throne[i] over these stones I have buried here; he will spread his royal canopy[j] above them. **11**He will come and attack Egypt,[k] bringing death[l] to those destined[m] for death, captivity to those destined for captivity,[n] and the sword to those destined for the sword.[o] **12**He[r] will set fire[p] to the temples[q] of the gods[r] of Egypt; he will burn their temples and take their gods captive.[s] As a shepherd wraps[t] his garment around him, so will he wrap Egypt around himself and depart from there unscathed. **13**There in the temple of the sun[s][u] in Egypt he will demolish the sacred pillars[v] and will burn down the temples of the gods of Egypt.' "

43:2 [q]S Ge 19:14; S Dt 13:3; Ro 9:1; 2Co 11:31; 1Ti 2:7 [r]S Ex 24:7; 2Ki 25:24; Jer 18:19; S 42:19; Eze 37:14 **43:3** [s]S Jer 32:12 [t]Jer 38:4; 41:18; 52:30 **43:4** [u]S Jer 41:16 [v]2Ch 25:16; Jer 42:5-6 [w]Jer 42:10 **43:5** [x]Jer 40:12 **43:6** [y]S Jer 6:12 [z]S Jer 32:12 **43:7** [a]S 2Ki 25:26 [b]Jer 2:16; 44:1; 46:14; Eze 30:18 **43:8** [c]Ps 139:7; Jer 2:16 **43:9** [d]Ge 31:45-53; Jos 4:1-7; 1Ki 18:31-32 [e]S Ge 11:3 [f]S Ge 47:14 **43:10** [g]Isa 44:28; 45:1; Jer 25:9; 27:6 [h]Jer 46:13 [i]Jer 49:38 [j]S Ps 18:11 **43:11** [k]Jer 46:13-26; Eze 29:19-20 [l]S Pr 11:19; Ro 6:23 [m]S Ps 49:14; Heb 9:27 [n]S Dt 28:64; Rev 13:10 [o]S Jer 15:2; Eze 32:11; Zec 11:9 **43:12** [p]S Jos 7:15 [q]S 1Ki 16:32 [r]ver 13; S Ex 12:12; S Isa 2:18; Jer 46:25; Eze 30:13; Zec 13:2 [s]Da 11:8 [t]S Ps 104:2; 109:18-19 **43:13** [u]S Ge 1:16; Isa 19:18 *fn*; S Dt 4:19 [v]Jer 52:17; Eze 26:11 **44:1** [w]S Dt 32:42; S Jer 24:8

Disaster Because of Idolatry

44 This word came to Jeremiah concerning all the Jews living in Lower Egypt[w]—in Migdol,[x] Tahpanhes[y] and Memphis[t][z]—and in Upper Egypt[u]:[a] **2**"This is what the LORD Almighty, the God of Israel, says: You saw the great disaster[b] I brought on Jerusalem and on all the towns of Judah.[c] Today they lie deserted and in ruins[d] **3**because of the evil[e] they have done. They provoked me to anger[f] by burning incense[g] and by worshiping other gods[h] that neither they nor you nor your fathers[i] ever knew. **4**Again and again[j] I sent my servants the prophets,[k] who said, 'Do not do this detestable[l] thing that I hate!' **5**But they did not listen or pay attention;[m][n] they did not turn from their wickedness[o] or stop burning incense[p] to other gods.[q] **6**Therefore, my fierce anger was poured out;[r] it

[x]S Ex 14:2 [y]S Jer 43:7,8 [z]S Isa 19:13 [a]S Isa 11:11 **44:2** [b]S 2Ch 34:24 [c]S Jer 40:5 [d]S Lev 26:31; S Dt 29:23; S Isa 6:11 **44:3** [e]S Ex 32:22 [f]S Nu 11:33 [g]S Nu 16:40 [h]ver 8; S Nu 25:3; Dt 13:6-11; 29:26; Isa 19:1 [i]S Jdg 2:19 **44:4** [j]S Jer 7:13 [k]S Nu 11:29 [l]S Dt 18:9; S 1Ki 14:24; 1Pe 4:3 **44:5** [m]Da 9:6 [n]S Jer 25:4 [o]S Ge 6:5; Ro 1:18; 2Ti 2:19 [p]ver 21; Jer 1:16; Eze 8:11; 16:18; 23:41 [q]Jer 11:8-10; S 25:7 **44:6** [r]Eze 8:18; 20:34

[q]3 Or *Chaldeans* [r]12 Or *I* [s]13 Or *in Heliopolis* [t]1 Hebrew *Noph* [u]1 Hebrew *in Pathros*

43:2 YOU ARE LYING! The people only pretended to want to obey God's will. Because of this folly, their punishment would include the sword, famine and plagues (42:22). It is a fatal mistake to pray, attend church and eat the Lord's Supper without sincerely desiring to follow the Lord (see 42:20); such persons will experience God's wrath and judgment (see 1Co 11:27, note).

43:7 ENTERED EGYPT. The people disobeyed the Lord's command (v. 4) and went to Egypt, taking Jeremiah with them (v. 6). Perhaps they thought Jeremiah's presence would guarantee God's protection. But this was not to be, for Jeremiah prophesied that God would send Nebuchadnezzar's army against Egypt and destroy its armies and all its gods (vv. 10–13). The country in which they sought security would be defeated. There is never divine security or protection outside of God's will.

44:1 ALL THE JEWS . . . EGYPT. Jeremiah delivered his last message to the unrepentant Jews in Egypt; God's judgment against them was certain (vv. 11–14) because of their persistent rejection of the Lord Almighty and their idolatry.

44:5 THEY DID NOT LISTEN. Judah sinned in failing to listen to God's word and to take seriously what he said. Many people continue to sin and to live selfishly because they ignore God's word or treat it lightly; they simply do not believe God means what he says. Even the church has members who are not afraid of God's warnings and who do not respect his commands (see v. 11, note).

raged against the towns of Judah and the streets of Jerusalem and made them the desolate ruins[s] they are today.

7"Now this is what the LORD God Almighty, the God of Israel, says: Why bring such great disaster[t] on yourselves by cutting off from Judah the men and women,[u] the children and infants, and so leave yourselves without a remnant?[v] 8Why provoke me to anger with what your hands have made,[w] burning incense[x] to other gods in Egypt,[y] where you have come to live?[z] You will destroy yourselves and make yourselves an object of cursing and reproach[a] among all the nations on earth. 9Have you forgotten the wickedness committed by your fathers[b] and by the kings[c] and queens[d] of Judah and the wickedness committed by you and your wives[e] in the land of Judah and the streets of Jerusalem?[f] 10To this day they have not humbled[g] themselves or shown reverence,[h] nor have they followed my law[i] and the decrees[j] I set before you and your fathers.[k]

11"Therefore, this is what the LORD Almighty,[l] the God of Israel, says: I am determined to bring disaster[m] on you and to destroy all Judah. 12I will take away the remnant[n] of Judah who were determined to go to Egypt to settle there. They will all perish in Egypt; they will fall by the sword or die from famine. From the least to the greatest,[o] they will die by sword or famine.[p] They will become an object of cursing and horror, of condemnation and reproach.[q] 13I will punish[r] those who live in Egypt with the sword,[s] famine and plague,[t] as I punished Jerusalem. 14None of the remnant of Judah who have gone to live in Egypt will escape or survive to return to the land of Judah, to which they long to return and live; none will return except a few fugitives."[u]

15Then all the men who knew that their wives[v] were burning incense[w] to other gods, along with all the women[x] who were present—a large assembly—and all the people living in Lower and Upper Egypt,▼[y] said to Jeremiah, 16"We will not listen[z] to the message you have spoken to us in the name of the LORD![a] 17We will certainly do everything we said we would:[b] We will burn incense[c] to the Queen of Heaven[d] and will pour out drink offerings to her just as we and our fathers, our kings and our officials[e] did in the towns of Judah and in the streets of Jerusalem.[f] At that time we had plenty of food[g] and were well off and suffered no harm.[h] 18But ever since we stopped burning incense to the Queen of Heaven and pouring out drink offerings[i] to her, we have had nothing and have been perishing by sword and famine.[j][k]"

19The women added, "When we burned incense[l] to the Queen of Heaven[m] and poured out drink offerings to her, did not our husbands[n] know that we were making cakes[o] like her image[p] and pouring out drink offerings to her?"

20Then Jeremiah said to all the people, both men and women, who were answering him, 21"Did not the LORD remember[q] and think about the incense[r] burned in the towns of Judah and the streets of Jerusalem[s] by you and your fathers,[t] your kings and your officials and the people of the land?[u] 22When the LORD could no

44:6 [s]S Lev 26:31,34; S Dt 29:23; La 1:13; Zec 7:14 **44:7** [t]Jer 26:19 [u]Jer 51:22 [v]S 2Ki 21:14 **44:8** [w]S Isa 40:18-20; S Jer 10:3; Ro 1:23 [x]ver 17-25; Jer 41:5 [y]S ver 3; S Ex 12:12 [z]S 1Co 10:22 [a]S Ps 44:13 **44:9** [b]S Jdg 2:19 [c]S 2Ki 23:11 [d]1Ki 21:25 [e]S Pr 31:10; S Jer 6:12 [f]ver 17, 21; Jer 11:12; 32:32 **44:10** [g]S Dt 8:3; S Mt 23:12; Php 2:8 [h]S Dt 6:13; S Ps 5:7 [i]S Jos 1:7; S Jer 11:8; Mt 5:17-20; Gal 3:19; 1Jn 3:4 [j]S Lev 18:4 [k]1Ki 9:6-9; 2Ki 17:17 **44:11** [l]Rev 4:8 [m]S 2Ch 34:24; Am 9:4 **44:12** [n]ver 7; Jer 40:15 [o]S Jer 42:1 [p]S Isa 1:28 [q]S Dt 28:25; S Jer 29:18 **44:13** [r]S Ex 32:34; Lev 26:14-17 [s]S Jer 15:2 [t]S Jer 42:17 **44:14** [u]Jer 22:24-27; 49:5; La 4:15; Eze 6:8; S Ro 9:27 **44:15** [v]S Pr 31:10; S Jer 6:12 [w]S Jer 18:15 [x]S Ge 3:6; 1Ti 2:14 [y]S Isa 11:11 **44:16** [z]S 1Sa 8:19; Job 15:25-26; Jer 11:8-10 [a]S Jer 42:19 **44:17** [b]ver 28; Dt 23:23; Zec 1:6 [c]S Isa 65:3 [d]ver 25; Jer 11:12 [e]Ne 9:34 [f]S ver 9; S Jer 2:26 [g]S Ex 16:3; Nu 11:4-6 [h]S Job 21:15; Isa 3:9; Hos 2:5-13; 9:1 **44:18** [i]Lev 23:18 [j]Mal 3:13-15 [k]Jer 42:16 **44:19** [l]S Jer 18:15 [m]Jer 7:18 [n]S Ge 3:6; Eph 5:22 [o]Lev 7:12 [p]S Lev 26:1; Ac 17:29 **44:21** [q]Isa 64:9; S Jer 14:10; Hos 8:13 [r]S Jer 11:13 [s]ver 9 [t]S Ps 79:8 [u]S Jer 2:26

▼*15* Hebrew *in Egypt and Pathros*

44:8 BURNING INCENSE TO OTHER GODS. The exiles in Egypt tossed aside their covenant with their God and turned to the gods of Egypt in hope of gaining the prosperity and protection they wanted. Jeremiah pleaded with them to turn back to the Lord and renew the covenant (vv. 7–10). Fundamental to Jeremiah's theology and practice is the truth that a person can only serve God by giving him total allegiance and devotion and by seeking to obey his revealed word.

44:11 DETERMINED TO BRING DISASTER. By their apostasy and disobedience, the Jews in Egypt spurned God's promises of help and restoration. Therefore, Jeremiah prophesied that God's judgment against them would be complete; they would all perish. Those who stubbornly determine to reject God's way and have their own way give him no other choice than to bring disaster on them.

44:17 QUEEN OF HEAVEN. See 7:18, note.

44:18 STOPPED BURNING INCENSE. The people attributed their latest problems to stopping the worship of the Queen of Heaven at the time of Josiah's reform. They felt idolatry had done more for them than the Lord God of Israel, and they were planning to continue their idolatrous worship (v. 23). Thus they would perish in Egypt (v. 27).

longer endure[v] your wicked actions
and the detestable things you did, your
land became an object of cursing[w] and
a desolate waste[x] without inhabitants, as it is today.[y] 23Because you
have burned incense and have sinned
against the LORD and have not obeyed
him or followed[z] his law or his decrees[a] or his stipulations, this disaster[b] has come upon you, as you now
see."[c]
24Then Jeremiah said to all the people, including the women,[d] "Hear the
word of the LORD, all you people of Judah in Egypt.[e] 25This is what the LORD
Almighty, the God of Israel, says: You
and your wives[f] have shown by your
actions what you promised when you
said, 'We will certainly carry out the
vows we made to burn incense and
pour out drink offerings to the Queen
of Heaven.'[g]

"Go ahead then, do what you promised! Keep your vows![h] 26But hear the
word of the LORD, all Jews living in
Egypt:[i] 'I swear[j] by my great name,'
says the LORD, 'that no one from Judah
living anywhere in Egypt will ever
again invoke my name or swear, "As
surely as the Sovereign[k] LORD
lives."[l] 27For I am watching[m] over
them for harm,[n] not for good; the Jews
in Egypt will perish[o] by sword and
famine[p] until they are all destroyed.[q]
28Those who escape the sword[r] and
return to the land of Judah from Egypt
will be very few.[s] Then the whole remnant[t] of Judah who came to live in
Egypt will know whose word will
stand[u]—mine or theirs.[v]
29" 'This will be the sign[w] to you
that I will punish[x] you in this place,'
declares the LORD, 'so that you will
know that my threats of harm against
you will surely stand.'[y] 30This is what
the LORD says: 'I am going to hand
Pharaoh[z] Hophra king of Egypt over
to his enemies who seek his life, just
as I handed Zedekiah[a] king of Judah
over to Nebuchadnezzar king of Babylon, the enemy who was seeking his
life.' "[b]

44:22 [v]S Isa 1:14 [w] S Jer 25:18 [x]S Lev 26:31,32 [y]S Ge 19:13; Ps 107:33-34; Eze 33:28-29 **44:23** [z]S 1Ki 9:6 [a]S Lev 18:4 [b]Jer 40:2 [c]S Lev 26:33; S 1Ki 9:9; Jer 7:13-15; Eze 39:23; Da 9:11-12 **44:24** [d]S Ge 3:6 [e]Jer 43:7 **44:25** [f]S Pr 31:10 [g]S ver 17; S Dt 32:38 [h]S Pr 20:25; Eze 20:39; Jas 1:13-15 **44:26** [i]S Jer 24:8 [j]S Ge 22:16; S Isa 48:1; Ac 19:13; Heb 6:13-17 [k]S Ge 15:2 [l]Dt 32:40; Ps 50:16; S Jer 4:2 **44:27** [m]S Jer 1:12 [n]S Jer 21:10 [o]S Lev 26:38; S Job 15:22; 2Pe 3:9 [p]S Ge 41:55 [q]S Jer 9:16; Da 9:14; Am 9:8 **44:28** [r]Jer 45:5; Eze 6:8 [s]ver 13-14; S Isa 10:19 [t]S 2Ki 21:14 [u]S Isa 7:9; S Jer 39:16; 42:15-18 [v]S ver 17,25-26 **44:29** [w]S Ge 24:14; S Ex 3:12; S Nu 16:38; S Mt 12:38; 24:3 [x]S Ex 32:34 [y]S Pr 19:21 **44:30** [z]S Jer 25:19; 46:26; Eze 30:21; 32:32 [a]2Ki 25:1-7; S Jer 24:8 [b]Jer 43:9-13 **45:1** [c]S Jer 32:12 [d]Jer 51:59 [e]S 2Ch 36:5 [f]S Ex 17:14; S Ps 40:7 **45:3** [g]S Isa 24:16; 1Co 9:16 [h]S Ps 119:28; Mk 14:34; Ro 9:2 [i]S Job 6:10 [j]S Job 23:2;

A Message to Baruch

45 This is what Jeremiah the
prophet told Baruch[c] son of
Neriah[d] in the fourth year of Jehoiakim[e] son of Josiah king of Judah, after
Baruch had written on a scroll[f] the
words Jeremiah was then dictating:
2"This is what the LORD, the God of Israel, says to you, Baruch: 3You said,
'Woe[g] to me! The LORD has added sorrow[h] to my pain;[i] I am worn out with
groaning[j] and find no rest.' "[k]
4⌊The LORD said,⌋ "Say this to him:
'This is what the LORD says: I will overthrow what I have built and uproot[l]
what I have planted,[m] throughout the
land.[n] 5Should you then seek great[o]
things for yourself? Seek them not.[p]
For I will bring disaster[q] on all people,[r] declares the LORD, but wherever
you go I will let you escape[s] with your
life.' "[t]

A Message About Egypt

46 This is the word of the LORD
that came to Jeremiah the
prophet concerning the nations:[u]

2Concerning Egypt:[v]

This is the message against the
army of Pharaoh Neco[w] king of Egypt,
which was defeated at Carchemish[x]
on the Euphrates[y] River by Nebuchadnezzar king of Babylon in the
fourth year of Jehoiakim[z] son of Josiah king of Judah:

3"Prepare your shields,[a] both large
and small,

Ps 69:3 [k]S Jos 1:13; Mt 11:28; Heb 4:3 **45:4** [l]S Jer 42:10 [m]S Jer 11:17 [n]S Dt 28:63; S 30:9; Isa 5:5-7; Jer 18:7-10 **45:5** [o]Ps 131:1 [p]Mt 6:25-27,33 [q]Jer 11:11; 40:2 [r]S Jer 2:35 [s]S Ps 68:20; S Jer 44:28 [t]S Jer 21:9 **46:1** [u]S Jer 1:10 **46:2** [v]S Ex 1:8 [w]S 2Ki 23:29 [x]S 2Ch 35:20 [y]S Ge 2:14 [z]Jer 1:3; 25:1; 35:1; 36:1; 45:1; Da 1:1 **46:3** [a]S Isa 21:5

45:1–5 BARUCH. Chronologically, this chapter goes back to the fourth year of King Jehoiakim's reign in Jerusalem. Its message was intended to strengthen the faith of Jeremiah's secretary Baruch, who had become discouraged because of the apparent failure of Jeremiah's ministry and the impending judgment on Judah (cf. ch. 36). God instructed him not to seek power or position for himself (cf. Mt 20:26–28). Because of his faithfulness to Jeremiah and to God's message, he would survive the destruction of Jerusalem.

46:1—51:64 CONCERNING THE NATIONS. These chapters contain prophecies of divine judgment against foreign nations. Jeremiah was ordained not only a prophet to Judah but also "a prophet to the nations" (1:5).

46:2 EGYPT ... CARCHEMISH. Carchemish, located in northern Syria some 300 miles north of Jerusalem, was the place where the Babylonians defeated the Egyptians in 605 B.C. At that time Babylon became the dominant world power.

and march out for battle!
4Harness the horses,
mount the steeds!
Take your positions
with helmets on!
Polish[b] your spears,
put on your armor![c]
5What do I see?
They are terrified,
they are retreating,
their warriors are defeated.
They flee[d] in haste
without looking back,
and there is terror[e] on every
side,"
declares the LORD.
6"The swift cannot flee[f]
nor the strong escape.
In the north by the River
Euphrates[g]
they stumble and fall.[h]
7"Who is this that rises like the
Nile,
like rivers of surging waters?[i]
8Egypt rises like the Nile,[j]
like rivers of surging waters.
She says, 'I will rise and cover the
earth;
I will destroy cities and their
people.'[k]
9Charge, O horses!
Drive furiously, O charioteers![l]
March on, O warriors—
men of Cush[w][m] and Put who
carry shields,
men of Lydia[n] who draw the
bow.
10But that day[o] belongs to the
Lord, the LORD Almighty—
a day of vengeance[p], for
vengeance on his foes.
The sword will devour[q] till it is
satisfied,
till it has quenched its thirst
with blood.[r]
For the Lord, the LORD Almighty,
will offer sacrifice[s]
in the land of the north by the
River Euphrates.[t]
11"Go up to Gilead and get balm,[u]
O Virgin[v] Daughter of Egypt.
But you multiply remedies in vain;
there is no healing[w] for you.
12The nations will hear of your
shame;
your cries will fill the earth.
One warrior will stumble over
another;
both will fall[x] down together."

13This is the message the LORD
spoke to Jeremiah the prophet about
the coming of Nebuchadnezzar king of
Babylon[y] to attack Egypt:[z]

14"Announce this in Egypt, and
proclaim it in Migdol;
proclaim it also in Memphis[x][a]
and Tahpanhes:[b]
'Take your positions and get ready,
for the sword devours[c] those
around you.'
15Why will your warriors be laid
low?
They cannot stand, for the LORD
will push them down.[d]
16They will stumble[e] repeatedly;
they will fall[f] over each other.
They will say, 'Get up, let us go
back
to our own people[g] and our
native lands,
away from the sword of the
oppressor.'[h]
17There they will exclaim,
'Pharaoh king of Egypt is only a
loud noise;[i]
he has missed his
opportunity.'[j]
18"As surely as I live," declares the
King,[k]
whose name is the LORD
Almighty,
"one will come who is like Tabor[l]
among the mountains,
like Carmel[m] by the sea.
19Pack your belongings for exile,[n]
you who live in Egypt,
for Memphis[o] will be laid waste[p]
and lie in ruins without
inhabitant.

46:4 [b] Eze 21:9-11 [c] 1Sa 17:5,38; 2Ch 26:14; Ne 4:16 **46:5** [d] ver 21; Jer 48:44 [e] S Ps 31:13; S 48:5 **46:6** [f] Isa 30:16 [g] Ge 2:14; 15:18 [h] ver 12,16; S Ps 20:8 **46:7** [i] Jer 47:2 **46:8** [j] Eze 29:3,9; 30:12; Am 8:8 [k] Da 11:10 **46:9** [l] Jer 47:3; Eze 26:10; Na 3:2 [m] S Ge 10:6 [n] S Isa 66:19 **46:10** [o] Eze 32:10; Joel 1:15; Ob 1:15 [p] S Nu 31:3; S Dt 32:41; 2Ki 23:29-30 [q] S Dt 32:42; S 2Sa 2:26; Zep 2:12 [r] S Dt 32:42 [s] S Lev 3:9; Zep 1:7 [t] Ge 2:14; 15:18 **46:11** [u] S Ge 37:25 [v] S 2Ki 19:21 [w] S Jer 30:13; S Mic 1:9 **46:12** [x] S ver 6; Isa 19:4; Na 3:8-10 **46:13** [y] ver 26; Eze 32:11 [z] Isa 19:1; Jer 27:7 **46:14** [a] S Isa 19:13 [b] S Jer 43:8 [c] S Dt 32:42; S 2Sa 2:26; S Jer 24:8 **46:15** [d] S Jos 23:5; Isa 66:15-16 **46:16** [e] S Lev 26:37 [f] S ver 6 [g] S Isa 13:14 [h] S Jer 25:38 **46:17** [i] 1Ki 20:10-11 [j] Isa 19:11-16 **46:18** [k] Jer 48:15 [l] S Jos 19:22 [m] 1Ki 18:42 **46:19** [n] S Isa 20:4 [o] S Isa 19:13 [p] Eze 29:10,12; 35:7

w *9* That is, the upper Nile region
x *14* Hebrew *Noph*; also in verse 19

46:10 DAY BELONGS TO THE LORD. Egypt's defeat was God's doing; it was "a day of vengeance" because of Egypt's oppression of Judah (e.g., 2Ki 23:29,33–35). Ultimately, God will punish all nations that have rejected his gospel and his righteous commands.

46:13 ATTACK EGYPT. Jeremiah prophesied that not only would the Babylonians defeat Egypt at Carchemish, but they would also defeat the Egyptian armies on their own land (568–567 B.C.). God would make it abundantly clear that Egypt's gods could not deliver them from defeat (vv. 25–26).

[20]"Egypt is a beautiful heifer,
but a gadfly is coming
against her from the north.[q]
[21]The mercenaries[r] in her ranks
are like fattened calves.[s]
They too will turn and flee[t]
together,
they will not stand their ground,
for the day[u] of disaster is coming
upon them,
the time[v] for them to be
punished.
[22]Egypt will hiss like a fleeing
serpent
as the enemy advances in force;
they will come against her with
axes,
like men who cut down trees.[w]
[23]They will chop down her forest,"
declares the LORD,
"dense though it be.
They are more numerous than
locusts,[x]
they cannot be counted.
[24]The Daughter of Egypt will be put
to shame,
handed over to the people of the
north.[y]"

[25]The LORD Almighty, the God of Israel, says: "I am about to bring punishment on Amon god of Thebes,[y][z] on
Pharaoh,[a] on Egypt and her gods[b]
and her kings, and on those who rely[c]
on Pharaoh. [26]I will hand them over[d]
to those who seek their lives, to Nebuchadnezzar king[e] of Babylon and his
officers. Later, however, Egypt will be
inhabited[f] as in times past," declares
the LORD.

[27]"Do not fear,[g] O Jacob[h] my
servant;[i]
do not be dismayed, O Israel.
I will surely save you out of a
distant place,
your descendants from the land
of their exile.[j]
Jacob will again have peace and
security,
and no one will make him
afraid.
[28]Do not fear, O Jacob my servant,
for I am with you,"[k] declares
the LORD.
"Though I completely destroy[l] all
the nations
among which I scatter you,
I will not completely destroy
you.
I will discipline you but only with
justice;
I will not let you go entirely
unpunished."

46:20 [q]ver 24; S Isa 14:31; Jer 47:2 46:21 [r]S 2Ki 7:6 [s]Lk 15:27 [t]S ver 5; S Job 20:24 [u]Ps 18:18; 37:13; Jer 18:17 [v]S Job 18:20 46:22 [w]Ps 74:5 46:23 [x]S Dt 28:42; S Jdg 7:12 46:24 [y]S 2Ki 24:7 46:25 [z]Eze 30:14; Na 3:8 [a]2Ki 24:7; Eze 30:22 [b]S Jer 43:12 [c]Isa 20:6 46:26 [d]S Jer 44:30 [e]S ver 13; S Isa 19:4 [f]Eze 29:11-16 46:27 [g]Isa 43:5; Jer 51:46 [h]Isa 41:8; 44:1; Mal 1:2 [i]S Isa 44:2 [j]S Isa 11:11; S Jer 29:14; 50:19

46:28 [k]S Ex 14:22; S Nu 14:9; Isa 8:9-10 [l]S Jer 4:27 47:1 [m]S Ge 10:14; S Jdg 3:31 [n]S Ge 10:19; Zec 9:5-7 47:2 [o]S Isa 14:31 [p]S Isa 15:3 47:3 [q]S Jer 46:9; S Eze 23:24 [r]Isa 13:7; Jer 50:43; Eze 7:17; 21:7 47:4 [s]S Isa 23:1; Am 1:9-10; Zec 9:2-4 [t]S Ge 10:15; S Jer 25:22 [u]S Ge 10:14; Joel 3:4 [v]S Dt 2:23 47:5 [w]S Jer 41:5 [x]S Jer 25:20

A Message About the Philistines

47 This is the word of the LORD that came to Jeremiah the prophet concerning the Philistines[m] before Pharaoh attacked Gaza:[n]

[2]This is what the LORD says:

"See how the waters are rising in
the north;[o]
they will become an overflowing
torrent.
They will overflow the land and
everything in it,
the towns and those who live in
them.
The people will cry out;
all who dwell in the land will
wail[p]
[3]at the sound of the hoofs of
galloping steeds,
at the noise of enemy chariots[q]
and the rumble of their wheels.
Fathers will not turn to help their
children;
their hands will hang limp.[r]
[4]For the day has come
to destroy all the Philistines
and to cut off all survivors
who could help Tyre[s] and
Sidon.[t]
The LORD is about to destroy the
Philistines,[u]
the remnant from the coasts of
Caphtor.[z][v]
[5]Gaza will shave[w] her head in
mourning;
Ashkelon[x] will be silenced.
O remnant on the plain,

[y]25 Hebrew *No* [z]4 That is, Crete

46:26 EGYPT WILL BE INHABITED. The destruction would not be forever; Egypt would be restored in the future and in the Messianic Age (cf. Isa 19:23–25; Eze 29:8–14).

46:27–28 DO NOT FEAR. Israel must not fear complete destruction. She would be punished for her sins, but a remnant would survive and be brought back to the promised land and to God's blessing (cf. 30:10–11; 31:1–6).

47:1–7 PHILISTINES. The Philistines occupied the coastal region of Judah. Hostility often existed between them and God's people. Other prophecies against the Philistines are found in Isa 14:28–31; Eze 25:15–17; Am 1:6–8; Zep 2:4–7.

how long will you cut[y]
yourselves?
6" 'Ah, sword[z] of the LORD,' ⌊you
cry,⌋
'how long till you rest?
Return to your scabbard;
cease and be still.'[a]
7But how can it rest
when the LORD has commanded
it,
when he has ordered it
to attack Ashkelon and the
coast?"[b]

A Message About Moab

48:29–36pp — Isa 16:6–12

48 Concerning Moab:[c]
This is what the LORD Almighty,
the God of Israel, says:

"Woe to Nebo,[d] for it will be
ruined.
Kiriathaim[e] will be disgraced
and captured;
the stronghold[a] will be
disgraced and shattered.
2Moab will be praised[f] no more;
in Heshbon[b][g] men will plot her
downfall:
'Come, let us put an end to that
nation.'[h]
You too, O Madmen,[c] will be
silenced;
the sword will pursue you.
3Listen to the cries from
Horonaim,[i]
cries of great havoc and
destruction.
4Moab will be broken;
her little ones will cry out.[d]
5They go up the way to Luhith,[j]
weeping bitterly as they go;
on the road down to Horonaim[k]
anguished cries over the
destruction are heard.
6Flee![l] Run for your lives;
become like a bush[e] in the
desert.[m]
7Since you trust in your deeds and
riches,[n]
you too will be taken captive,
and Chemosh[o] will go into exile,[p]
together with his priests and
officials.[q]
8The destroyer[r] will come against
every town,
and not a town will escape.
The valley will be ruined
and the plateau[s] destroyed,
because the LORD has spoken.
9Put salt[t] on Moab,
for she will be laid waste[f];[u]
her towns will become desolate,
with no one to live in them.
10"A curse on him who is lax in
doing the LORD's work!
A curse on him who keeps his
sword[v] from bloodshed![w]

11"Moab has been at rest[x] from
youth,
like wine left on its dregs,[y]
not poured from one jar to
another—
she has not gone into exile.
So she tastes as she did,
and her aroma is unchanged.
12But days are coming,"
declares the LORD,
"when I will send men who pour
from jars,
and they will pour her out;
they will empty her jars
and smash her jugs.
13Then Moab will be ashamed[z] of
Chemosh,[a]

47:5 [y]S Lev 19:28 47:6 [z]S Isa 34:5; Jer 12:12; 48:10; 50:35 [a]Eze 21:30 47:7 [b]Eze 25:15-17 48:1 [c]S Ge 19:37; S Dt 23:6 [d]S Nu 32:38 [e]S Nu 32:37; S Jos 13:19 48:2 [f]Isa 16:14 [g]S Nu 21:25; S Jos 13:26 [h]ver 42 48:3 [i]S Isa 15:5 48:5 [j]Isa 15:5 [k]ver 3 48:6 [l]S Ge 19:17 [m]Jer 17:6 48:7 [n]S Ps 49:6; S Pr 11:28 [o]S Nu 21:29 [p]Isa 46:1-2; Jer 49:3 [q]Am 2:3 48:8 [r]S Ex 12:23; S Jer 4:7 [s]S Jos 13:9 48:9 [t]Jdg 9:45 [u]Jer 51:29 48:10 [v]S Jer 47:6 [w]S 1Sa 15:11; 1Ki 20:42; 2Ki 13:15-19 48:11 [x]Zec 1:15 [y]Zep 1:12 48:13 [z]Hos 10:6 [a]ver 7

a *1* Or / *Misgab* b *2* The Hebrew for *Heshbon* sounds like the Hebrew for *plot*. c *2* The name of the Moabite town Madmen sounds like the Hebrew for *be silenced*. d *4* Hebrew; Septuagint / *proclaim it to Zoar* e *6* Or *like Aroer* f *9* Or *Give wings to Moab, / for she will fly away*

48:1 MOAB. The country of Moab was on the eastern shore of the Dead Sea. The Moabites were descendants of Lot, Abraham's nephew (Ge 19:30–37), and were often in conflict with Israel. During Jeremiah's time bands of Moabites attacked parts of Judah after Nebuchadnezzar invaded Palestine (2Ki 24:2). Jeremiah identified many of the Moabite cities that would be overthrown; Moab was conquered by the Babylonians and consequently disappeared as a nation (but see v. 47, note). Other prophecies against Moab are found in Isa 15—16; Jer 9:25–26; 25:14–21; 27:2–3; Eze 25:8–11; Am 2:1–3; Zep 2:8–11.

48:7 TRUST IN YOUR DEEDS AND RICHES. The tendency of all the nations of the world is to trust in their technology, military might, accomplishments and wealth; this misguided trust, along with ungodly behavior by their people, will cause their downfall. Just as God destroyed Moab, a day is coming when he will bring down all the nations of the world—a day called "the day of the Lord" (see 1Th 5:2–4, notes).

48:7 CHEMOSH. Chemosh was the chief god of the Moabites (see 1Ki 11:7,33; 2Ki 23:13).

48:10 A CURSE. This verse is addressed to those who were to destroy Moab.

as the house of Israel was
ashamed
when they trusted in Bethel.[b]

14"How can you say, 'We are
warriors,[c]
men valiant in battle'?
15Moab will be destroyed and her
towns invaded;
her finest young men[d] will go
down in the slaughter,[e]"
declares the King,[f] whose
name is the LORD
Almighty.[g]
16"The fall of Moab is at hand;[h]
her calamity will come quickly.
17Mourn for her, all who live around
her,
all who know her fame;[i]
say, 'How broken is the mighty
scepter,[j]
how broken the glorious staff!'

18"Come down from your glory
and sit on the parched ground,[k]
O inhabitants of the Daughter of
Dibon,[l]
for he who destroys Moab
will come up against you
and ruin your fortified cities.[m]
19Stand by the road and watch,
you who live in Aroer.[n]
Ask the man fleeing and the
woman escaping,
ask them, 'What has happened?'
20Moab is disgraced, for she is
shattered.
Wail[o] and cry out!
Announce by the Arnon[p]
that Moab is destroyed.
21Judgment has come to the
plateau[q]—
to Holon,[r] Jahzah[s] and
Mephaath,[t]
22 to Dibon,[u] Nebo[v] and Beth
Diblathaim,
23 to Kiriathaim,[w] Beth Gamul and
Beth Meon,[x]
24 to Kerioth[y] and Bozrah[z]—
to all the towns[a] of Moab, far
and near.
25Moab's horn[g][b] is cut off;
her arm[c] is broken,"
declares the LORD.

26"Make her drunk,[d]
for she has defied[e] the LORD.
Let Moab wallow in her vomit;[f]
let her be an object of ridicule.[g]
27Was not Israel the object of your
ridicule?[h]
Was she caught among
thieves,[i]
that you shake your head[j] in
scorn[k]
whenever you speak of her?
28Abandon your towns and dwell
among the rocks,
you who live in Moab.
Be like a dove[l] that makes its
nest
at the mouth of a cave.[m]

29"We have heard of Moab's
pride[n]—
her overweening pride and
conceit,
her pride and arrogance
and the haughtiness[o] of her
heart.
30I know her insolence but it is
futile,"
declares the LORD,
"and her boasts[p] accomplish
nothing.
31Therefore I wail[q] over Moab,
for all Moab I cry out,
I moan for the men of Kir
Hareseth.[r]
32I weep for you, as Jazer[s] weeps,
O vines of Sibmah.[t]
Your branches spread as far as the
sea;
they reached as far as the sea of
Jazer.
The destroyer has fallen
on your ripened fruit and grapes.
33Joy and gladness are gone
from the orchards and fields of
Moab.
I have stopped the flow of wine[u]
from the presses;
no one treads them with shouts
of joy.[v]
Although there are shouts,
they are not shouts of joy.

34"The sound of their cry rises
from Heshbon[w] to Elealeh[x] and
Jahaz,[y]
from Zoar[z] as far as Horonaim[a]
and Eglath Shelishiyah,
for even the waters of Nimrim
are dried up.[b]
35In Moab I will put an end
to those who make offerings on
the high places[c]
and burn incense[d] to their
gods,"
declares the LORD.

48:13 [b]S Jos 7:2 **48:14** [c]Ps 33:16 **48:15** [d]S Isa 9:17 [e]Jer 51:40 [f]S Jer 46:18 [g]Jer 51:57 **48:16** [h]Isa 13:22 **48:17** [i]2Ki 3:4-5 [j]S Ps 110:2 **48:18** [k]Isa 47:1 [l]S Nu 21:30; S Jos 13:9 [m]ver 8 **48:19** [n]S Nu 32:34 **48:20** [o]S Isa 16:7 [p]S Nu 21:13 **48:21** [q]S Jos 13:9,21 [r]S Jos 15:51 [s]S Nu 21:23; S Isa 15:4 [t]S Jos 13:18 **48:22** [u]S Nu 21:30; S Jos 13:9,17 [v]S Nu 32:38 **48:23** [w]S Nu 32:37; S Jos 13:19 [x]S Jos 13:17 **48:24** [y]Am 2:2 [z]Jer 49:13 [a]S Isa 15:1 **48:25** [b]Ps 75:10 [c]Ps 10:15; 37:17; Eze 30:21 **48:26** [d]Jer 25:16, 27; 51:39 [e]ver 42; 1Sa 17:26 [f]S Isa 28:8 [g]ver 39 **48:27** [h]S Jer 2:26 [i]2Ki 17:3-6 [j]S Job 16:4; Ps 44:14; Jer 18:16 [k]S Dt 28:37; Mic 7:8-10; Zep 2:8,10 **48:28** [l]S Ge 8:8; S SS 1:15 [m]S Jdg 6:2 **48:29** [n]S Lev 26:19; S Job 40:12 [o]S Ps 10:5; S Pr 16:18 **48:30** [p]S Ps 10:3 **48:31** [q]ver 36; Isa 15:5-8 [r]S 2Ki 3:25 **48:32** [s]S Jos 13:25 [t]S Nu 32:3 **48:33** [u]S Isa 24:7 [v]Joel 1:12; Am 5:17 **48:34** [w]S Nu 21:25; S Jos 13:26 [x]S Nu 32:3 [y]S Nu 21:23; S Isa 15:4 [z]S Ge 13:10 [a]S Isa 15:5 [b]S Isa 15:6 **48:35** [c]S Isa 15:2 [d]Jer 11:13

[g]25 *Horn* here symbolizes strength.

36"So my heart laments[e] for Moab
like a flute;
it laments like a flute for the
men of Kir Hareseth.[f]
The wealth they acquired[g] is
gone.
37Every head is shaved[h]
and every beard[i] cut off;
every hand is slashed
and every waist is covered with
sackcloth.[j]
38On all the roofs in Moab
and in the public squares[k]
there is nothing but mourning,
for I have broken Moab
like a jar[l] that no one wants,"
declares the LORD.
39"How shattered[m] she is! How they
wail!
How Moab turns her back in
shame!
Moab has become an object of
ridicule,[n]
an object of horror to all those
around her."

40This is what the LORD says:

"Look! An eagle is swooping[o]
down,
spreading its wings[p] over
Moab.
41Kerioth[h][q] will be captured
and the strongholds taken.
In that day the hearts of Moab's
warriors[r]
will be like the heart of a
woman in labor.[s]
42Moab will be destroyed[t] as a
nation[u]
because she defied[v] the LORD.
43Terror[w] and pit and snare[x] await
you,
O people of Moab,"
declares the LORD.
44"Whoever flees[y] from the terror
will fall into a pit,
whoever climbs out of the pit
will be caught in a snare;
for I will bring upon Moab
the year[z] of her punishment,"
declares the LORD.
45"In the shadow of Heshbon
the fugitives stand helpless,
for a fire has gone out from
Heshbon,
a blaze from the midst of
Sihon;[a]
it burns the foreheads of Moab,
the skulls[b] of the noisy
boasters.
46Woe to you, O Moab![c]
The people of Chemosh are
destroyed;
your sons are taken into exile
and your daughters into
captivity.
47"Yet I will restore[d] the fortunes
of Moab
in days to come,"
declares the LORD.

Here ends the judgment on Moab.

A Message About Ammon

49 Concerning the Ammonites:[e]

This is what the LORD says:
"Has Israel no sons?
Has she no heirs?
Why then has Molech[i][f] taken
possession of Gad?[g]
Why do his people live in its
towns?
2But the days are coming,"
declares the LORD,
"when I will sound the battle cry[h]
against Rabbah[i] of the
Ammonites;
it will become a mound of ruins,[j]
and its surrounding villages will
be set on fire.
Then Israel will drive out
those who drove her out,[k]"
says the LORD.
3"Wail, O Heshbon,[l] for Ai[m] is
destroyed!
Cry out, O inhabitants of
Rabbah!
Put on sackcloth[n] and mourn;
rush here and there inside the
walls,
for Molech[o] will go into exile,[p]
together with his priests and
officials.
4Why do you boast of your valleys,

48:36 [e] S ver 31 [f] S 2Ki 3:25 [g] S Isa 15:7 **48:37** [h] Isa 15:2; S Jer 41:5; Eze 27:31; 29:18 [i] S Lev 19:27; S 2Sa 10:4 [j] S Ge 37:34; S Isa 3:24; Jer 16:6; Am 8:10 **48:38** [k] S Isa 15:3 [l] S Jer 22:28 **48:39** [m] Jer 50:23 [n] ver 26 **48:40** [o] S Dt 28:49; Hab 1:8 [p] S Isa 8:8 **48:41** [q] S Isa 15:1 [r] Am 2:16 [s] S Isa 21:3 **48:42** [t] S Isa 16:14 [u] ver 2 [v] S ver 26 **48:43** [w] Jer 49:5 [x] S Isa 24:17 **48:44** [y] 1Ki 19:17; S Job 20:24; Isa 24:18; S Jer 46:5 [z] Jer 11:23; 23:12 **48:45** [a] S Nu 21:21, 26-28; S Jos 12:2 [b] Nu 24:17 **48:46** [c] S Nu 21:29 **48:47** [d] Ps 14:7; Isa 11:11; Jer 12:15; 49:6,39; Eze 16:53; Da 11:41 **49:1** [e] S Ge 19:38; S 1Sa 11:1-11; 2Sa 10:1-19 [f] S Lev 18:21 [g] Ge 30:11 **49:2** [h] S Jer 4:19 [i] S Dt 3:11 [j] S Dt 13:16 [k] S Isa 14:2; S Jer 30:16; Eze 21:28-32; 25:2-11 **49:3** [l] S Jos 13:26 [m] S Ge 12:8; S Jos 8:28 [n] S Ge 37:34 [o] Zep 1:5 [p] S Jer 48:7

h *41* Or *The cities* i *1* Or *their king*; Hebrew *malcam*; also in verse 3

48:47 IN DAYS TO COME. Not all Moabites would be destroyed; a remnant would survive. The phrase "in days to come" indicates that this restoration will occur in the Messianic age, i.e., when Christ reigns over the nations.

49:1 AMMONITES. These were descendants of Abraham's nephew, Lot (Ge 19:30–38), who lived east of the Jordan River and north of Moab. Their sins were idolatry, pride, trust in riches (vv. 3–4), and hostility toward Israel (v. 1).

boast of your valleys so fruitful?
O unfaithful daughter,[q]
you trust in your riches[r] and say,
'Who will attack me?'[s]
5I will bring terror on you
from all those around you,"
declares the Lord,
the LORD Almighty.
"Every one of you will be driven away,
and no one will gather the fugitives.[t]

6"Yet afterward, I will restore[u] the fortunes of the Ammonites,"
declares the LORD.

A Message About Edom

49:9–10pp — Ob 5–6
49:14–16pp — Ob 1–4

7Concerning Edom:[v]

This is what the LORD Almighty says:

"Is there no longer wisdom in Teman?[w]
Has counsel perished from the prudent?
Has their wisdom decayed?
8Turn and flee, hide in deep caves,[x]
you who live in Dedan,[y]
for I will bring disaster on Esau
at the time I punish him.
9If grape pickers came to you,
would they not leave a few grapes?
If thieves came during the night,
would they not steal only as much as they wanted?
10But I will strip Esau bare;
I will uncover his hiding places,[z]
so that he cannot conceal himself.
His children, relatives and neighbors will perish,
and he will be no more.[a]
11Leave your orphans;[b] I will protect their lives.
Your widows[c] too can trust in me."

12This is what the LORD says: "If
those who do not deserve to drink the
cup[d] must drink it, why should you go
unpunished?[e] You will not go unpunished, but must drink it. 13I swear[f] by
myself," declares the LORD, "that Bozrah[g] will become a ruin and an object
of horror,[h] of reproach[i] and of cursing; and all its towns will be in ruins
forever."[j]

14I have heard a message from the LORD:
An envoy was sent to the nations to say,
"Assemble yourselves to attack it!
Rise up for battle!"

15"Now I will make you small among the nations,
despised among men.
16The terror you inspire
and the pride[k] of your heart
have deceived you,
you who live in the clefts of the rocks,[l]
who occupy the heights of the hill.
Though you build your nest[m] as high as the eagle's,
from there I will bring you down,"
declares the LORD.
17"Edom will become an object of horror;[n]
all who pass by will be appalled
and will scoff
because of all its wounds.[o]
18As Sodom[p] and Gomorrah[q] were overthrown,
along with their neighboring towns,"
says the LORD,
"so no one will live there;
no man will dwell[r] in it.
19"Like a lion[s] coming up from Jordan's thickets[t]
to a rich pastureland,
I will chase Edom from its land in an instant.
Who is the chosen one I will appoint for this?

49:4 [q]S Jer 3:6 [r]S Jer 9:23; 1Ti 6:17 [s]S Jer 21:13 **49:5** [t]S Jer 44:14 **49:6** [u]Jer 12:14-17; S 48:47 **49:7** [v]S Ge 25:30; S Ps 83:6 [w]S Ge 36:11,15,34 **49:8** [x]S Jdg 6:2 [y]S Ge 10:7; S 25:3 **49:10** [z]S Ge 3:8 [a]Isa 34:10-12; S Jer 11:23; Eze 35:4; Ob 1:18; Mal 1:2-5 **49:11** [b]Hos 14:3 [c]S Dt 10:18; Jas 1:27 **49:12** [d]S Isa 51:23; S Jer 25:15; Mt 20:22 [e]S Pr 11:31 **49:13** [f]S Ge 22:16 [g]S Ge 36:33 [h]ver 17 [i]Jer 42:18 [j]S Jer 19:8; Eze 35:9 **49:16** [k]Eze 35:13; Ob 1:12 [l]S Job 39:28 [m]S Job 39:27 **49:17** [n]ver 13 [o]S Dt 29:22; Eze 35:7 **49:18** [p]Jer 23:14 [q]S Ge 19:24 [r]ver 33; S Isa 34:10 **49:19** [s]S 1Sa 17:34 [t]S Jer 12:5

49:7 EDOM. The Edomites were descendants of Jacob's twin brother Esau (Ge 36:1). Living in the mountainous region south of the Dead Sea, they had a history of enmity and conflict with Israel. Edom's great sins were its pride (v. 16) and its fervent hatred of Israel (cf. Ob 3,10–14).

49:16 PRIDE OF YOUR HEART. The Edomites' downfall was their pride, which had made them overly confident; they thought that because of their strong fortifications, they could never be defeated. Pride, overconfidence and material wealth can also deceive us into thinking we do not need to rely continually on God for his help and grace.

Who is like[u] me and who can
challenge me?[v]
And what shepherd[w] can stand
against me?"
20 Therefore, hear what the LORD has
planned against Edom,[x]
what he has purposed[y] against
those who live in Teman:[z]
The young of the flock[a] will be
dragged away;
he will completely destroy[b]
their pasture because of
them.[c]
21 At the sound of their fall the earth
will tremble;[d]
their cry[e] will resound to the
Red Sea.[j]
22 Look! An eagle will soar and
swoop[f] down,
spreading its wings over
Bozrah.[g]
In that day the hearts of Edom's
warriors[h]
will be like the heart of a
woman in labor.[i]

A Message About Damascus

23 Concerning Damascus:[j]

"Hamath[k] and Arpad[l] are
dismayed,
for they have heard bad news.
They are disheartened,
troubled like[k] the restless
sea.[m]
24 Damascus has become feeble,
she has turned to flee
and panic has gripped her;
anguish and pain have seized her,
pain like that of a woman in
labor.[n]
25 Why has the city of renown not
been abandoned,
the town in which I delight?
26 Surely, her young men[o] will fall
in the streets;
all her soldiers will be
silenced[p] in that day,"
declares the LORD Almighty.
27 "I will set fire[q] to the walls of
Damascus;[r]
it will consume[s] the fortresses
of Ben-Hadad.[t]"

49:19 [u] S Ex 8:10; S 2Ch 20:6; S Isa 46:5 [v] S Job 9:19; Jer 50:44 [w] 1Sa 17:35 **49:20** [x] Isa 34:5 [y] Isa 14:27 [z] ver 7; S Ge 36:11 [a] Jer 50:45 [b] ver 10; Ob 1:10; Mal 1:3-4 [c] Jer 50:45 **49:21** [d] Ps 114:7; Eze 26:15; 27:28; 31:16 [e] Jer 50:46; 51:29; Eze 26:18 **49:22** [f] S Dt 28:49; Hos 8:1; Hab 1:8 [g] S Ge 36:33 [h] Jer 50:36; Na 3:13 [i] Isa 13:8 **49:23** [j] S Ge 14:15; 2Ki 14:28; 2Ch 16:2; Ac 9:2 [k] 1Ki 8:65; Isa 10:9; Eze 47:16; Am 6:2; Zec 9:2 [l] S 2Ki 18:34; S 19:13 [m] S Ge 49:4 **49:24** [n] Jer 13:21 **49:26** [o] S Isa 9:17; S 13:18 [p] Isa 17:12-14 **49:27** [q] Jer 21:14; 43:12; 50:32; Eze 30:8; 39:6; Am 1:4 [r] S Ge 14:15 [s] Isa 17:1 [t] S 1Ki 15:18

A Message About Kedar and Hazor

28 Concerning Kedar[u] and the kingdoms of Hazor,[v] which Nebuchadnezzar[w] king of Babylon attacked:

This is what the LORD says:

"Arise, and attack Kedar
and destroy the people of the
East.[x]
29 Their tents and their flocks[y] will
be taken;
their shelters will be carried off
with all their goods and camels.
Men will shout to them,
'Terror[z] on every side!'
30 "Flee quickly away!
Stay in deep caves,[a] you who
live in Hazor,[b]"
declares the LORD.
"Nebuchadnezzar[c] king of Babylon
has plotted against you;
he has devised a plan against
you.
31 "Arise and attack a nation at ease,
which lives in confidence,"
declares the LORD,
"a nation that has neither gates
nor bars;[d]
its people live alone.
32 Their camels[e] will become
plunder,
and their large herds[f] will be
booty.
I will scatter to the winds[g] those
who are in distant
places[1][h]
and will bring disaster on them
from every side,"
declares the LORD.
33 "Hazor[i] will become a haunt of
jackals,[j]
a desolate[k] place forever.
No one will live there;
no man will dwell[l] in it."

A Message About Elam

34 This is the word of the LORD that

49:28 [u] S Ge 25:13 [v] S Jos 11:1 [w] S Jer 10:22 [x] S Jdg 6:3 **49:29** [y] ver 32 [z] S Jer 6:25 **49:30** [a] S Jdg 6:2 [b] Jos 11:1 [c] S Jer 10:22 **49:31** [d] Eze 38:11 **49:32** [e] S Jdg 6:5 [f] ver 29 [g] ver 36; Jer 13:24 [h] S Jer 9:26 **49:33** [i] S Jos 11:1 [j] S Isa 13:22 [k] Jer 48:9 [l] S ver 18; Jer 51:37

[j] *21* Hebrew *Yam Suph*; that is, Sea of Reeds
[k] *23* Hebrew *on* or *by*
[1] *32* Or *who clip the hair by their foreheads*

49:23–26 DAMASCUS. Damascus was the major city of Aram and was located in the southern part of that country. Amos also prophesied against the people of Damascus because of their cruelty (Am 1:3–5).

49:28–33 KEDAR . . . HAZOR. This section contains a prophecy against Arab tribes. The people of Kedar were descendants of Ishmael, Abraham's son by Hagar (Ge 25:13; cf. Isa 21:13,16).

49:34–39 ELAM. Elam was located 200 miles east of Babylon in what is now the country of Iran. After experiencing God's judgment, Elam would be restored. Several Elamites were in Jerusalem when the Holy Spirit was poured out on the disci-

came to Jeremiah the prophet concerning Elam,[m] early in the reign of Zedekiah[n] king of Judah:

35 This is what the LORD Almighty says:

"See, I will break the bow[o] of Elam,
the mainstay of their might.
36 I will bring against Elam the four winds[p]
from the four quarters of the heavens;[q]
I will scatter them to the four winds,
and there will not be a nation
where Elam's exiles do not go.
37 I will shatter Elam before their foes,
before those who seek their lives;
I will bring disaster upon them,
even my fierce anger,"[r]
declares the LORD.
"I will pursue them with the sword[s]
until I have made an end of them.
38 I will set my throne in Elam
and destroy her king and officials,"
declares the LORD.

39 "Yet I will restore[t] the fortunes of Elam
in days to come,"
declares the LORD.

A Message About Babylon

51:15–19pp — Jer 10:12–16

50 This is the word the LORD spoke through Jeremiah the prophet concerning Babylon[u] and the land of the Babylonians[m]:

2 "Announce and proclaim[v] among the nations,
lift up a banner[w] and proclaim it;
keep nothing back, but say,
'Babylon will be captured;[x]
Bel[y] will be put to shame,[z]
Marduk[a] filled with terror.
Her images will be put to shame
and her idols[b] filled with terror.'
3 A nation from the north[c] will attack her
and lay waste her land.
No one will live[d] in it;
both men and animals[e] will flee away.

4 "In those days, at that time,"
declares the LORD,
"the people of Israel and the people of Judah together[f]
will go in tears[g] to seek[h] the LORD their God.
5 They will ask the way[i] to Zion
and turn their faces toward it.
They will come[j] and bind themselves to the LORD
in an everlasting covenant[k]
that will not be forgotten.

6 "My people have been lost sheep;[l]
their shepherds[m] have led them astray[n]
and caused them to roam on the mountains.
They wandered over mountain and hill[o]
and forgot their own resting place.[p]
7 Whoever found them devoured[q] them;

49:34 [m] S Ge 10:22 [n] 2Ki 24:18 **49:35** [o] S Ps 37:15; S Isa 22:6 **49:36** [p] S ver 32 [q] Da 11:4 **49:37** [r] Jer 30:24 [s] Jer 9:16; Eze 32:24 **49:39** [t] S Jer 48:47 **50:1** [u] S Ge 10:10; S Ps 137:8 **50:2** [v] S Dt 30:4; Jer 4:16 [w] S Ps 20:5; S Isa 13:2 [x] ver 9; Jer 51:31 [y] S Isa 21:9; S 46:1 [z] Ps 97:7; Jer 51:52 [a] ver 38; Isa 46:6; Jer 51:47 [b] S Lev 26:30 **50:3** [c] S ver 26; S Isa 41:25; S Jer 25:26 [d] S ver 13; S Isa 14:22-23; S Jer 9:11 [e] Zep 1:3 **50:4** [f] S Jer 3:18; Eze 37:22 [g] S Ezr 3:12 [h] S Isa 9:13; Eze 37:17; Hos 3:5 **50:5** [i] S Isa 11:16; S Jer 31:21 [j] S 1Sa 29:1; Jer 33:7 [k] S Dt 29:14; Isa 55:3; Jer 32:40; Heb 8:6-10 **50:6** [l] S Ps 119:176; Mt 9:36; 10:6 [m] S Jer 2:8; S 10:21 [n] S Ps 95:10; Jer 23:32; Eze 13:10 [o] Jer 3:6; Eze 34:6 [p] ver 19 **50:7** [q] S Jer 5:17; 10:25; Eze 35:12

[m] *1* Or *Chaldeans*; also in verses 8, 25, 35 and 45

---

ples on the day of Pentecost (Ac 2:5–9).

50:1 BABYLON. Jeremiah also prophesied concerning Babylon's fall, an event that played an important part in the history of redemption. (1) When the prophet spoke these words, God's people were in exile in Babylon and in danger of being assimilated by another people and culture. Were that to occur, salvation through Abraham's descendants would be impossible. Babylon's grip on Israel had to be broken and God's people freed in order for God to work his will and prepare for the coming of the Messiah. Even though Babylon was the undisputed world power at this time, Jeremiah predicted its downfall five years before Jerusalem was taken (51:59–60).

(2) Jeremiah's prophecy, however, goes beyond Babylon's future defeat by Cyrus (see next note); it predicts a destruction of Babylon that will cause Israel and Judah to make an everlasting covenant with God that will never be broken (vv. 4–5). This destruction will occur at the end of the tribulation period (see Rev 17:1, note).

50:3 LAY WASTE HER LAND. Jeremiah foresaw that Babylon would experience a great destruction. In his day the nation from the north was the Medo-Persian coalition. Babylon fell in 539 B.C. at the hands of an army led by Cyrus of Persia.

50:4–5 IN THOSE DAYS. This passage speaks of the Jews' repentance and return to God in the last days (cf. 31:31; 32:40); they will turn to God and remain faithful to him forever (cf. vv. 19–20; see Rev 12:6, note).

their enemies said, 'We are not
guilty,[r]
for they sinned against the LORD,
their true pasture,
the LORD, the hope[s] of their
fathers.'

8"Flee[t] out of Babylon;[u]
leave the land of the
Babylonians,
and be like the goats that lead
the flock.
9For I will stir[v] up and bring
against Babylon
an alliance of great nations[w]
from the land of the
north.[x]
They will take up their positions
against her,
and from the north she will be
captured.[y]
Their arrows[z] will be like skilled
warriors
who do not return
empty-handed.
10So Babylonia[n] will be
plundered;[a]
all who plunder her will have
their fill,"
declares the LORD.

11"Because you rejoice and are
glad,
you who pillage my
inheritance,[b]
because you frolic like a heifer[c]
threshing grain
and neigh like stallions,
12your mother will be greatly
ashamed;
she who gave you birth will be
disgraced.[d]
She will be the least of the
nations—
a wilderness, a dry land, a
desert.[e]
13Because of the LORD's anger she
will not be inhabited
but will be completely
desolate.[f]
All who pass Babylon will be
horrified[g] and scoff[h]
because of all her wounds.[i]

50:7 [r]Jer 2:3 [s]S Jer 14:8
50:8 [t]S Isa 48:20 [u]ver 28
50:9 [v]S Isa 13:17 [w]S Jer 25:14 [x]S Isa 41:25; S Jer 25:26 [y]S ver 2 [z]S Isa 13:18
50:10 [a]Isa 47:11; S Jer 30:16
50:11 [b]S Isa 47:6 [c]S Jer 31:18
50:12 [d]Jer 51:47 [e]ver 13; S Isa 21:1; Jer 25:12; 51:26
50:13 [f]ver 3, S 12; S Jer 9:11; 48:9; 51:62 [g]Jer 51:41 [h]S Jer 18:16; 51:37; Eze 27:36; Hab 2:6 [i]S Dt 29:22
50:14 [j]ver 29,42 [k]S Isa 13:18
50:15 [l]Jer 51:14 [m]S 2Ki 25:4; S Jer 51:44,58 [n]ver 28; S Isa 10:3; 63:4; Jer 51:6 [o]ver 29; Ps 137:8; Rev 18:6 [p]Jer 51:24; Hab 2:7-8
50:16 [q]S Jer 25:38 [r]S Isa 13:14 [s]Jer 51:9
50:17 [t]S Lev 26:33; S Ps 119:176 [u]S 2Ki 24:1; S Jer 2:15 [v]S Jer 5:17 [w]S Dt 4:27; S 2Ki 15:29 [x]S Nu 24:8; La 3:4 [y]Jer 51:34 [z]S 2Ki 24:17; S 25:7
50:18 [a]S Isa 10:12 [b]Eze 31:3; Zep 2:13
50:19 [c]S Jer 31:10; Eze 34:13 [d]Jer 31:14 [e]S Jer 31:5 [f]Mic 7:14; Zec 10:10
50:20 [g]S Ps 17:3 [h]Ps 103:12; S Isa 38:17; Eze 33:16; Mic 7:18,19; Zec 3:4,9

14"Take up your positions around
Babylon,
all you who draw the bow.[j]
Shoot at her! Spare no arrows,[k]
for she has sinned against the
LORD.
15Shout[l] against her on every side!
She surrenders, her towers fall,
her walls[m] are torn down.
Since this is the vengeance[n] of
the LORD,
take vengeance on her;
do to her[o] as she has done to
others.[p]
16Cut off from Babylon the sower,
and the reaper with his sickle at
harvest.
Because of the sword[q] of the
oppressor
let everyone return to his own
people,[r]
let everyone flee to his own
land.[s]

17"Israel is a scattered flock[t]
that lions[u] have chased away.
The first to devour[v] him
was the king[w] of Assyria;
the last to crush his bones[x]
was Nebuchadnezzar[y] king[z] of
Babylon."

18Therefore this is what the LORD Almighty, the God of Israel, says:

"I will punish the king of Babylon
and his land
as I punished the king[a] of
Assyria.[b]
19But I will bring[c] Israel back to
his own pasture
and he will graze on Carmel and
Bashan;
his appetite will be satisfied[d]
on the hills[e] of Ephraim and
Gilead.[f]
20In those days, at that time,"
declares the LORD,
"search will be made for Israel's
guilt,
but there will be none,[g]
and for the sins[h] of Judah,

[n] 10 Or *Chaldea*

50:9 AN ALLIANCE OF GREAT NATIONS. These nations are named in 51:27–28.

50:11 BECAUSE YOU REJOICE. God would bring defeat on the Babylonians because they had rejoiced over their defeat of Judah and Jerusalem; what Babylon had done to others would now happen to her (v. 29).

50:17 ISRAEL IS A SCATTERED FLOCK. Assyria destroyed Israel, the northern kingdom, in 722 B.C. (2Ki 17:1–6), and Babylon destroyed Judah, the southern kingdom, in 586 B.C. (2Ki 24). Both nations took captives from among God's people and settled them far away from their homeland.

but none will be found,
for I will forgive[i] the
remnant[j] I spare.

21"Attack the land of Merathaim
and those who live in Pekod.[k]
Pursue, kill and completely
destroy[o] them,"
declares the LORD.
"Do everything I have
commanded you.
22The noise[l] of battle is in the
land,
the noise of great destruction!
23How broken and shattered
is the hammer[m] of the whole
earth![n]
How desolate[o] is Babylon
among the nations!
24I set a trap[p] for you, O Babylon,
and you were caught before you
knew it;
you were found and captured[q]
because you opposed[r] the LORD.
25The LORD has opened his arsenal
and brought out the weapons[s]
of his wrath,
for the Sovereign LORD Almighty
has work to do
in the land of the Babylonians.[t]
26Come against her from afar.[u]
Break open her granaries;
pile her up like heaps of grain.[v]
Completely destroy[w] her
and leave her no remnant.
27Kill all her young bulls;[x]
let them go down to the
slaughter![y]
Woe to them! For their day[z] has
come,
the time[a] for them to be
punished.
28Listen to the fugitives[b] and
refugees from Babylon
declaring in Zion[c]
how the LORD our God has taken
vengeance,[d]
vengeance for his temple.[e]
29"Summon archers against Babylon,
all those who draw the bow.[f]
Encamp all around her;
let no one escape.[g]
Repay[h] her for her deeds;[i]
do to her as she has done.
For she has defied[j] the LORD,
the Holy One[k] of Israel.
30Therefore, her young men[l] will
fall in the streets;
all her soldiers will be silenced
in that day,"
declares the LORD.
31"See, I am against[m] you,
O arrogant one,"
declares the Lord, the LORD
Almighty,
"for your day[n] has come,
the time for you to be punished.
32The arrogant[o] one will stumble
and fall[p]
and no one will help her up;[q]
I will kindle a fire[r] in her towns
that will consume all who are
around her."

33This is what the LORD Almighty
says:

"The people of Israel are
oppressed,[s]
and the people of Judah as well.
All their captors hold them fast,
refusing to let them go.[t]
34Yet their Redeemer[u] is strong;
the LORD Almighty[v] is his name.
He will vigorously defend their
cause[w]
so that he may bring rest[x] to
their land,
but unrest to those who live in
Babylon.

35"A sword[y] against the
Babylonians!"[z]
declares the LORD—
"against those who live in Babylon
and against her officials and
wise[a] men!
36A sword against her false
prophets!
They will become fools.
A sword against her warriors![b]
They will be filled with terror.[c]
37A sword against her horses and
chariots[d]
and all the foreigners in her
ranks!
They will become women.[e]

[o] 21 The Hebrew term refers to the irrevocable giving over of things or persons to the LORD, often by totally destroying them; also in verse 26.

50:20 [i] S Isa 33:24 [j] S Ge 45:7; Isa 1:9; 10:20-22; S Ro 9:27 **50:21** [k] Eze 23:23 **50:22** [l] Jer 4:19-21; 51:54 **50:23** [m] S Isa 10:5 [n] Jer 51:25 [o] S Isa 14:16 **50:24** [p] Jer 51:12 [q] Jer 51:31 [r] Job 9:4 **50:25** [s] S Isa 13:5 [t] Jer 51:25,55 **50:26** [u] ver 3,41; Jer 51:11 [v] S Ru 3:7 [w] S Isa 14:22-23 **50:27** [x] S Ps 68:30; Jer 48:15 [y] S Isa 30:25; S Jer 25:34 [z] S Job 18:20 [a] Jer 51:6 **50:28** [b] ver 8 [c] Isa 48:20; Jer 51:10 [d] S ver 15 [e] 2Ki 24:13; Jer 51:11; 52:13 **50:29** [f] S ver 14 [g] S Isa 13:18; Jer 51:3 [h] S Dt 32:41; S Job 21:19; S Jer 51:6; Rev 18:6 [i] Eze 35:11; Ob 1:15 [j] S Isa 14:13-14; 47:10; Da 5:23 [k] Ps 78:41; Isa 41:20; Jer 51:5 **50:30** [l] S Isa 13:18 **50:31** [m] S Jer 21:13 [n] S Job 18:20; Rev 18:7-8 **50:32** [o] S Ps 119:21 [p] S Ps 20:8 [q] Am 5:2 [r] S Jer 49:27 **50:33** [s] Isa 58:6 [t] S Isa 14:17 **50:34** [u] S Ex 6:6; S Job 19:25 [v] Jer 31:35; 51:19 [w] S Ps 119:154; S Isa 49:25; Jer 15:21; 51:36; La 3:58 [x] S Isa 14:7 **50:35** [y] S Jer 47:6 [z] S Isa 45:1 [a] Da 5:7 **50:36** [b] S Jer 49:22 [c] Jer 51:30,32 **50:37** [d] S 2Ki 19:23; Jer 51:21 [e] S Isa 19:16

50:32 THE ARROGANT ONE. Babylon defied the Lord and lived in pride; for this she would be brought low. Nothing is more odious than the pride of nations and people who live as they please while scorning the laws and righteous standards set forth in God's Word. What happened to ancient Babylon will happen to all the ungodly in the last days (see Rev 18:2–21, notes).

A sword against her treasures![f]
They will be plundered.
38A drought on[p] her waters![g]
They will dry[h] up.
For it is a land of idols,[i]
idols that will go mad with terror.

39"So desert creatures[j] and hyenas will live there,
and there the owl will dwell.
It will never again be inhabited
or lived in from generation to generation.[k]
40As God overthrew Sodom and Gomorrah[l]
along with their neighboring towns,"
declares the LORD,
"so no one will live there;
no man will dwell in it.[m]

41"Look! An army is coming from the north;[n]
a great nation and many kings
are being stirred[o] up from the ends of the earth.[p]
42They are armed with bows[q] and spears;
they are cruel[r] and without mercy.[s]
They sound like the roaring sea[t]
as they ride on their horses;
they come like men in battle formation
to attack you, O Daughter of Babylon.[u]
43The king of Babylon has heard reports about them,
and his hands hang limp.[v]
Anguish has gripped him,
pain like that of a woman in labor.[w]
44Like a lion coming up from Jordan's thickets[x]
to a rich pastureland,
I will chase Babylon from its land in an instant.
Who is the chosen[y] one I will appoint for this?
Who is like me and who can challenge me?[z]
And what shepherd can stand against me?"
45Therefore, hear what the LORD has planned against Babylon,
what he has purposed[a] against the land of the Babylonians:[b]
The young of the flock will be dragged away;
he will completely destroy their pasture because of them.
46At the sound of Babylon's capture
the earth will tremble;[c]
its cry[d] will resound among the nations.

51

This is what the LORD says:
"See, I will stir[e] up the spirit of a destroyer
against Babylon[f] and the people of Leb Kamai.[q]
2I will send foreigners[g] to Babylon
to winnow[h] her and to devastate her land;
they will oppose her on every side
in the day[i] of her disaster.
3Let not the archer string his bow,[j]
nor let him put on his armor.[k]
Do not spare her young men;
completely destroy[r] her army.
4They will fall[l] down slain in Babylon,[s]
fatally wounded in her streets.[m]
5For Israel and Judah have not been forsaken[n]
by their God, the LORD Almighty,
though their land[t] is full of guilt[o]
before the Holy One of Israel.

6"Flee[p] from Babylon!
Run for your lives!

50:37 [f]S Isa 45:3 50:38 [g]Ps 137:1; Jer 51:13 [h]S Isa 11:15; Jer 51:36 [i]S ver 2 50:39 [j]S Ps 74:14 [k]Isa 13:19-22; 34:13-15; Jer 51:37; Rev 18:2 50:40 [l]S Ge 19:24; S Mt 10:15 [m]Jer 51:62 50:41 [n]S ver 26; S Isa 41:25 [o]S Isa 13:17 [p]S Isa 13:4; Jer 51:22-28 50:42 [q]S ver 14 [r]S Job 30:21 [s]S Isa 13:18 [t]S Isa 5:30 [u]S Isa 47:1 50:43 [v]S Jer 47:3 [w]Jer 6:22-24 50:44 [x]S Jer 12:5 [y]S Nu 16:5 [z]S Job 41:10; Isa 46:9; S Jer 49:19 50:45 [a]Ps 33:11; Jer 51:11 [b]S Isa 48:14 50:46 [c]S Jdg 5:4; S Jer 49:21 [d]S Job 24:12; Rev 18:9-10 51:1 [e]S Isa 13:17 [f]Jer 25:12 51:2 [g]Isa 13:5 [h]S Isa 41:16; Mt 3:12 [i]S Isa 13:9 51:3 [j]S Jer 50:29 [k]Jer 46:4 51:4 [l]Isa 13:15 [m]S Isa 13:18 51:5 [n]S Lev 26:44; Isa 54:6-8 [o]Hos 4:1 51:6 [p]S Isa 48:20

[p]38 Or *A sword against* [q]1 *Leb Kamai* is a cryptogram for Chaldea, that is, Babylonia. [r]3 The Hebrew term refers to the irrevocable giving over of things or persons to the LORD, often by totally destroying them. [s]4 Or *Chaldea* [t]5 Or */ and the land of the Babylonians⌋*

51:1–64 AGAINST BABYLON. A second chapter concerning Babylon's doom prophesies that the Lord would bring about Babylon's complete overthrow in order to deliver his people from oppression. In the last days of this age, Christ will overthrow the whole world system, symbolically called "Babylon the Great" (Rev 18:2), with all its sin and immorality; this destruction will be God's righteous judgment of a world dominated by Satan and evil (see Rev 17:1, note).

51:6 FLEE FROM BABYLON. God calls on his people to flee from Babylon before its final destruction. Similarly, the NT exhorts believers to come out of the end-time Babylon (i.e., the ungodly world system), lest they participate in her sins and receive her judgment (see Rev 18:4, note; see article on SPIRITUAL SEPARATION FOR BELIEVERS, p. 1794).

Do not be destroyed because of
her sins.[q]
It is time[r] for the LORD's
vengeance;[s]
he will pay[t] her what she
deserves.
7Babylon was a gold cup[u] in the
LORD's hand;
she made the whole earth drunk.
The nations drank her wine;
therefore they have now gone
mad.
8Babylon will suddenly fall[v] and be
broken.
Wail over her!
Get balm[w] for her pain;
perhaps she can be healed.

9" 'We would have healed Babylon,
but she cannot be healed;
let us leave[x] her and each go to
his own land,
for her judgment[y] reaches to
the skies,
it rises as high as the clouds.'

10" 'The LORD has vindicated[z] us;
come, let us tell in Zion
what the LORD our God has
done.'[a]

11"Sharpen the arrows,[b]
take up the shields![c]
The LORD has stirred up the
kings[d] of the Medes,[e]
because his purpose[f] is to
destroy Babylon.
The LORD will take vengeance,[g]
vengeance for his temple.[h]
12Lift up a banner[i] against the
walls of Babylon!
Reinforce the guard,
station the watchmen,[j]
prepare an ambush![k]
The LORD will carry out his
purpose,[l]
his decree against the people of
Babylon.
13You who live by many waters[m]
and are rich in treasures,[n]
your end has come,
the time for you to be cut off.[o]
14The LORD Almighty has sworn by
himself:[p]
I will surely fill you with men,
as with a swarm of
locusts,[q]
and they will shout[r] in triumph
over you.

15"He made the earth by his power;
he founded the world by his
wisdom[s]
and stretched[t] out the heavens
by his understanding.[u]
16When he thunders,[v] the waters in
the heavens roar;
he makes clouds rise from the
ends of the earth.
He sends lightning with the rain[w]
and brings out the wind from his
storehouses.[x]

17"Every man is senseless and
without knowledge;
every goldsmith is shamed by
his idols.
His images are a fraud;[y]
they have no breath in them.
18They are worthless,[z] the objects
of mockery;
when their judgment comes,
they will perish.
19He who is the Portion[a] of Jacob is
not like these,
for he is the Maker of all things,
including the tribe of his
inheritance[b]—
the LORD Almighty is his name.

20"You are my war club,[c]
my weapon for battle—
with you I shatter[d] nations,[e]
with you I destroy kingdoms,
21with you I shatter horse and
rider,[f]
with you I shatter chariot[g] and
driver,
22with you I shatter man and
woman,
with you I shatter old man and
youth,
with you I shatter young man
and maiden,[h]
23with you I shatter shepherd and
flock,
with you I shatter farmer and
oxen,
with you I shatter governors and
officials.[i]

24"Before your eyes I will repay[j]
Babylon[k] and all who live in Babylonia[u] for all the wrong they have done
in Zion," declares the LORD.

51:6 [q]Nu 16:26; Rev 18:4 [r]Jer 50:27 [s]S Isa 1:24; S Jer 50:15 [t]ver 24,56; Dt 32:35; S Job 21:19; Jer 25:14; 50:29; La 3:64
51:7 [u]S Isa 51:22; Jer 25:15-16; 49:12; Rev 14:8-10
51:8 [v]S Isa 14:15; S 21:9; S Rev 14:8 [w]Jer 8:22; 46:11
51:9 [x]S Isa 13:14; S 31:9; Jer 50:16 [y]Rev 18:4-5
51:10 [z]Mic 7:9 [a]Ps 64:9; S Jer 50:28
51:11 [b]Jer 50:9 [c]S Isa 21:5 [d]S Isa 41:2 [e]ver 28; S Isa 13:3; S 41:25 [f]S Jer 50:45 [g]S Lev 26:25 [h]S Jer 50:28
51:12 [i]ver 27; S Ps 20:5 [j]2Sa 18:24; Eze 33:2 [k]Jer 50:24 [l]S Ps 33:11
51:13 [m]S Jer 50:38 [n]S Isa 45:3; Eze 22:27; Hab 2:9 [o]Jer 50:3
51:14 [p]S Ge 22:16; Am 6:8 [q]ver 27; Am 7:1; Na 3:15 [r]Jer 50:15
51:15 [s]Ps 104:24 [t]S Ge 1:1; S Ps 104:2 [u]S Ps 136:5
51:16 [v]Ps 18:11-13 [w]S Job 28:26 [x]S Dt 28:12; S Ps 135:7; Jnh 1:4
51:17 [y]S Isa 44:20; Hab 2:18-19
51:18 [z]S Jer 18:15
51:19 [a]S Ps 119:57 [b]S Ex 34:9
51:20 [c]S Isa 10:5; Zec 9:13 [d]S Job 34:24; Mic 4:13 [e]S Isa 45:1
51:21 [f]S Ex 15:1 [g]S Isa 43:17; S Jer 50:37
51:22 [h]S 2Ch 36:17; Isa 13:17-18
51:23 [i]ver 57
51:24 [j]S ver 6, 35; S Dt 32:41; S Jer 50:15; La 3:64 [k]S Isa 45:1

[u]24 Or *Chaldea*; also in verse 35

51:11 THE MEDES. The Medes, together with the Persians, overthrew Babylon in 539 B.C.

25"I am against[l] you, O destroying
mountain,
you who destroy the whole
earth,"[m]
declares the LORD.
"I will stretch out my hand[n]
against you,
roll you off the cliffs,
and make you a burned-out
mountain.[o]
26No rock will be taken from you for
a cornerstone,
nor any stone for a foundation,
for you will be desolate[p]
forever,"
declares the LORD.

27"Lift up a banner[q] in the land!
Blow the trumpet among the
nations!
Prepare the nations for battle
against her;
summon against her these
kingdoms:[r]
Ararat,[s] Minni and Ashkenaz.[t]
Appoint a commander against her;
send up horses like a swarm of
locusts.[u]
28Prepare the nations for battle
against her—
the kings of the Medes,[v]
their governors and all their
officials,
and all the countries they rule.[w]
29The land trembles[x] and writhes,
for the LORD's purposes[y]
against Babylon stand—
to lay waste[z] the land of Babylon
so that no one will live there.[a]
30Babylon's warriors[b] have stopped
fighting;
they remain in their strongholds.
Their strength is exhausted;
they have become like women.[c]
Her dwellings are set on fire;[d]
the bars[e] of her gates are
broken.
31One courier[f] follows another
and messenger follows
messenger
to announce to the king of Babylon
that his entire city is captured,[g]
32the river crossings seized,
the marshes set on fire,[h]
and the soldiers terrified.[i]"

33This is what the LORD Almighty, the God of Israel, says:

"The Daughter of Babylon[j] is like
a threshing floor[k]
at the time it is trampled;
the time to harvest[l] her will
soon come.[m]"

34"Nebuchadnezzar[n] king of Babylon
has devoured[o] us,[p]
he has thrown us into confusion,
he has made us an empty jar.
Like a serpent he has swallowed
us
and filled his stomach with our
delicacies,
and then has spewed[q] us out.
35May the violence[r] done to our
flesh[v] be upon Babylon,"
say the inhabitants of Zion.
"May our blood be on those who
live in Babylonia,"
says Jerusalem.[s]

36Therefore, this is what the LORD says:

"See, I will defend your cause[t]
and avenge[u] you;
I will dry up[v] her sea
and make her springs dry.
37Babylon will be a heap of ruins,
a haunt[w] of jackals,
an object of horror and scorn,[x]
a place where no one lives.[y]
38Her people all roar like young
lions,[z]
they growl like lion cubs.
39But while they are aroused,
I will set out a feast for them
and make them drunk,[a]
so that they shout with laughter—
then sleep forever[b] and not
awake,"
declares the LORD.[c]
40"I will bring them down
like lambs to the slaughter,
like rams and goats.[d]

41"How Sheshach[w][e] will be
captured,[f]

51:25 [l] S Jer 21:13 [m] Jer 50:23 [n] S Ex 3:20 [o] Zec 4:7 **51:26** [p] ver 29; S Isa 13:19-22; S Jer 50:12 **51:27** [q] S Ps 20:5; S Isa 13:2 [r] S Jer 25:14 [s] S Ge 8:4 [t] Ge 10:3 [u] S ver 14 **51:28** [v] S ver 11 [w] ver 48 **51:29** [x] S Jdg 5:4; S Jer 49:21 [y] S Ps 33:11 [z] Jer 48:9 [a] ver 43; S Isa 13:20 **51:30** [b] S Jer 50:36 [c] S Isa 19:16 [d] S Isa 47:14 [e] S Isa 45:2 **51:31** [f] 2Sa 18:19-31 [g] S Jer 50:2; Da 5:30 **51:32** [h] S Isa 47:14 [i] S Jer 50:36 **51:33** [j] S Isa 47:1 [k] S Isa 21:10 [l] S Isa 17:5 [m] S Isa 13:22 **51:34** [n] S Jer 50:17 [o] Na 2:12 [p] Hos 8:8 [q] ver 44; S Lev 18:25 **51:35** [r] Joel 3:19; Hab 2:17 [s] S ver 24; Ps 137:8 **51:36** [t] Ps 140:12; Jer 50:34; La 3:58 [u] ver 6; Jer 20:12; S Ro 12:19 [v] S Isa 11:15; S 19:5; Hos 13:15 **51:37** [w] S Isa 13:22; Rev 18:2 [x] Na 3:6; Mal 2:9 [y] S Jer 50:13,39 **51:38** [z] S Isa 5:29 **51:39** [a] S Isa 21:5 [b] S Ps 13:3 [c] ver 57; S Jer 50:24 **51:40** [d] Eze 39:18 **51:41** [e] S Jer 25:26 [f] Isa 13:19

[v] 35 Or *done to us and to our children*
[w] 41 *Sheshach* is a cryptogram for Babylon.

51:27 ARARAT. The people of Ararat were conquered by the Medes in the sixth century B.C. They joined with the Medes in overthrowing Babylon.

51:33 TIME TO HARVEST HER WILL SOON COME. Babylon had sown seeds of cruelty, idolatry and immorality; now she would reap the harvest of God's judgment. We must remember that sins are seeds from which a large and terrible harvest will eventually spring. "Do not be deceived: God cannot be mocked. A man reaps what he sows" (Gal 6:7).

the boast of the whole earth
seized!
What a horror[g] Babylon will be
among the nations!
42The sea will rise over Babylon;
its roaring waves[h] will cover
her.
43Her towns will be desolate,
a dry and desert[i] land,
a land where no one lives,
through which no man travels.[j]
44I will punish Bel[k] in Babylon
and make him spew out[l] what
he has swallowed.
The nations will no longer stream
to him.
And the wall[m] of Babylon will
fall.
45"Come out[n] of her, my people!
Run[o] for your lives!
Run from the fierce anger[p] of
the LORD.
46Do not lose heart[q] or be afraid[r]
when rumors[s] are heard in the
land;
one rumor comes this year,
another the next,
rumors of violence in the land
and of ruler against ruler.
47For the time will surely come
when I will punish the idols[t] of
Babylon;
her whole land will be disgraced[u]
and her slain will all lie fallen
within her.[v]
48Then heaven and earth and all
that is in them
will shout[w] for joy over
Babylon,
for out of the north[x]
destroyers[y] will attack her,"
declares the LORD.

49"Babylon must fall because of
Israel's slain,
just as the slain in all the earth
have fallen because of
Babylon.[z]
50You who have escaped the sword,
leave[a] and do not linger!
Remember[b] the LORD in a distant
land,[c]
and think on Jerusalem."

51"We are disgraced,[d]
for we have been insulted
and shame covers our faces,
because foreigners have entered
the holy places of the LORD's
house."[e]

52"But days are coming," declares
the LORD,
"when I will punish her idols,[f]
and throughout her land
the wounded will groan.[g]
53Even if Babylon reaches the sky[h]
and fortifies her lofty stronghold,
I will send destroyers[i] against
her,"
declares the LORD.

54"The sound of a cry[j] comes from
Babylon,
the sound of great destruction[k]
from the land of the
Babylonians.[x]
55The LORD will destroy Babylon;
he will silence[l] her noisy din.
Waves[m] ⌞of enemies⌟ will rage like
great waters;
the roar of their voices will
resound.
56A destroyer[n] will come against
Babylon;
her warriors will be captured,
and their bows will be broken.[o]
For the LORD is a God of
retribution;
he will repay[p] in full.
57I will make her officials[q] and
wise[r] men drunk,[s]
her governors, officers and
warriors as well;
they will sleep[t] forever and not
awake,"
declares the King,[u] whose
name is the LORD Almighty.

58This is what the LORD Almighty
says:

"Babylon's thick wall[v] will be
leveled
and her high gates[w] set on fire;
the peoples[x] exhaust[y]
themselves for nothing,
the nations' labor is only fuel for
the flames."[z]

59This is the message Jeremiah gave
to the staff officer Seraiah son of Neriah,[a] the son of Mahseiah, when he
went to Babylon with Zedekiah[b] king
of Judah in the fourth[c] year of his

51:41 [g] Jer 50:13
51:42 [h] S Ps 18:4; Isa 8:7
51:43 [i] S Isa 21:1 [j] S ver 29,62; S Isa 13:20; Jer 2:6
51:44 [k] S Isa 21:9; S 46:1 [l] S ver 34 [m] ver 58; S 2Ki 25:4; Isa 25:12; Jer 50:15
51:45 [n] ver 50 [o] S Isa 48:20 [p] Ps 76:10; 79:6
51:46 [q] Ps 18:45 [r] S Jer 46:27 [s] S 2Ki 19:7
51:47 [t] S Isa 46:1-2; S Jer 50:2 [u] Jer 50:12 [v] S Jer 27:7
51:48 [w] S Job 3:7; S Ps 149:2; Rev 18:20 [x] ver 11; S Isa 41:25; S Jer 25:26 [y] ver 53,56
51:49 [z] Ps 137:8; S Jer 50:29
51:50 [a] ver 45 [b] S Ps 137:6 [c] Jer 23:23
51:51 [d] Ps 44:13-16; 79:4
[e] La 1:10
51:52 [f] ver 47 [g] S Job 24:12
51:53 [h] S Ge 11:4; S Isa 14:13-14 [i] S ver 48; S Job 15:21
51:54 [j] S Job 24:12 [k] S Jer 50:22
51:55 [l] Isa 25:5 [m] S Ps 18:4
51:56 [n] S ver 48; S Job 15:21 [o] Ps 46:9 [p] S ver 6; S Ge 4:24; S Dt 32:41; Ps 94:1-2; Hab 2:8
51:57 [q] S ver 23 [r] S Job 5:13 [s] S Isa 21:5 [t] S ver 39; Ps 76:5; S Jer 25:27 [u] S Isa 6:5
51:58 [v] S ver 44; S 2Ki 25:4; S Isa 15:1 [w] S Isa 13:2 [x] ver 64 [y] S Isa 47:13 [z] S Isa 47:14
51:59 [a] Jer 36:4 [b] Jer 52:1 [c] Jer 28:1

[x] 54 Or *Chaldeans*

51:50 JERUSALEM. Having escaped the danger of Babylon's fall, the exiles had to consider that now was the time to return to Jerusalem and serve the Lord.

reign. **60**Jeremiah had written on a scroll[d] about all the disasters that would come upon Babylon—all that had been recorded concerning Babylon. **61**He said to Seraiah, "When you get to Babylon, see that you read all these words aloud. **62**Then say, 'O LORD, you have said you will destroy this place, so that neither man nor animal will live in it; it will be desolate[e] forever.' **63**When you finish reading this scroll, tie a stone to it and throw it into the Euphrates.[f] **64**Then say, 'So will Babylon sink to rise no more[g] because of the disaster I will bring upon her. And her people[h] will fall.' "[i]

The words of Jeremiah end[j] here.

The Fall of Jerusalem

52:1–3pp — 2Ki 24:18–20; 2Ch 36:11–16
52:4–16pp — Jer 39:1–10
52:4–21pp — 2Ki 25:1–21; 2Ch 36:17–20

52 Zedekiah[k] was twenty-one years old when he became king, and he reigned in Jerusalem eleven years. His mother's name was Hamutal daughter of Jeremiah; she was from Libnah.[l] **2**He did evil in the eyes of the LORD, just as Jehoiakim[m] had done. **3**It was because of the LORD's anger that all this happened to Jerusalem and Judah,[n] and in the end he thrust them from his presence.[o]

Now Zedekiah rebelled[p] against the king of Babylon.

4So in the ninth year of Zedekiah's reign, on the tenth[q] day of the tenth month, Nebuchadnezzar king of Babylon marched against Jerusalem[r] with his whole army. They camped outside the city and built siege works[s] all around it.[t] **5**The city was kept under siege until the eleventh year of King Zedekiah.

6By the ninth day of the fourth month the famine in the city had become so severe that there was no food for the people to eat.[u] **7**Then the city wall was broken through, and the whole army fled.[v] They left the city at night through the gate between the two walls near the king's garden, though the Babylonians[y] were surrounding the city. They fled toward the Arabah,[z] **8**but the Babylonian[a] army pursued King Zedekiah and overtook him in the plains of Jericho. All his soldiers were separated from him and scattered, **9**and he was captured.[w]

He was taken to the king of Babylon at Riblah[x] in the land of Hamath,[y] where he pronounced sentence on him. **10**There at Riblah the king of Babylon slaughtered the sons[z] of Zedekiah before his eyes; he also killed all the officials of Judah. **11**Then he put out Zedekiah's eyes, bound him with bronze shackles and took him to Babylon, where he put him in prison till the day of his death.[a]

12On the tenth day of the fifth[b] month, in the nineteenth year of Nebuchadnezzar king of Babylon, Nebuzaradan[c] commander of the imperial guard, who served the king of Babylon, came to Jerusalem. **13**He set fire[d] to the temple[e] of the LORD, the royal palace and all the houses[f] of Jerusalem. Every important building he burned down. **14**The whole Babylonian army under the commander of the imperial guard broke down all the walls[g] around Jerusalem. **15**Nebuzaradan the commander of the guard carried into exile[h] some of the poorest people and those who remained in the city, along with the rest of the craftsmen[b] and those who had gone over[i] to the king of Babylon. **16**But Nebuzaradan left behind[j] the rest of the poorest people of the land to work the vineyards and fields.

17The Babylonians broke up the bronze pillars,[k] the movable stands[l] and the bronze Sea[m] that were at the temple of the LORD and they carried all the bronze to Babylon.[n] **18**They also took away the pots, shovels, wick trimmers, sprinkling bowls,[o] dishes and all the bronze articles used in the temple service.[p] **19**The commander of the imperial guard took away the basins, censers,[q] sprinkling bowls, pots, lampstands,[r] dishes[s] and bowls used for drink offerings[t]—all that were made of pure gold or silver.[u]

20The bronze from the two pillars, the Sea and the twelve bronze bulls[v]

51:60 [d]S Ex 17:14; Jer 30:2; 36:2 **51:62** [e]S Isa 13:20; S Jer 9:11; S 50:13,39 **51:63** [f]S Ge 2:14 **51:64** [g]Eze 26:21; 28:19 [h]S ver 58 [i]Rev 18:21 [j]S Job 31:40 **52:1** [k]S 2Ki 24:17 [l]S Nu 33:20; Jos 10:29; 2Ki 8:22 **52:2** [m]S Jer 36:30 **52:3** [n]Isa 3:1 [o]S Ge 4:14; S Ex 33:15 [p]Eze 17:12-16 **52:4** [q]Zec 8:19 [r]Jer 34:1 [s]S Jer 6:6 [t]Eze 24:1-2 **52:6** [u]S Lev 26:26; S Isa 3:1; La 1:11 **52:7** [v]La 4:19

52:9 [w]S Jer 21:7; S 32:4 [x]S Nu 34:11 [y]S Nu 13:21 **52:10** [z]S Jer 22:30 **52:11** [a]Jer 34:4; Eze 12:13; 17:16 **52:12** [b]Zec 7:5; 8:19 [c]ver 26 **52:13** [d]S 2Ch 36:19; S Ps 74:8; La 2:6 [e]S Dt 29:24; Ps 79:1; Mic 3:12 [f]S Dt 13:16; S Jer 19:13 **52:14** [g]S Ne 1:3; La 2:8 **52:15** [h]S 2Ki 24:1; S Jer 1:3 [i]S Jer 38:19 **52:16** [j]Jer 40:6 **52:17** [k]S 1Ki 7:15 [l]1Ki 7:27-37 [m]S 1Ki 7:23 [n]Jer 27:19-22 **52:18** [o]S Nu 4:14 [p]S Ex 27:3; 1Ki 7:45 **52:19** [q]S Lev 10:1; S 1Ki 7:50 [r]S Nu 3:31 [s]Ex 25:29 [t]S Nu 4:7 [u]S Ezr 1:7; Da 5:2 **52:20** [v]1Ki 7:25

[y]7 Or *Chaldeans*; also in verse 17 [z]7 Or *the Jordan Valley* [a]8 Or *Chaldean*; also in verse 14 [b]15 Or *populace*

52:1–34 ZEDEKIAH. Jeremiah's last chapter shows that the prophet truly spoke God's word and that the doom he foretold had become a reality; this chapter is almost identical to 2Ki 24:18—25:30; cf. also Jer 39:1–10.

under it, and the movable stands,
which King Solomon had made for the
temple of the LORD, was more than
could be weighed.[w] 21Each of the pillars was eighteen cubits high and
twelve cubits in circumference[c]; each
was four fingers thick, and hollow.[x]
22The bronze capital[y] on top of the
one pillar was five cubits[d] high and
was decorated with a network and
pomegranates[z] of bronze all around.
The other pillar, with its pomegranates, was similar. 23There were ninety-
six pomegranates on the sides; the total number of pomegranates[a] above
the surrounding network was a hundred.[b]

24The commander of the guard took
as prisoners Seraiah[c] the chief priest,
Zephaniah[d] the priest next in rank
and the three doorkeepers.[e] 25Of
those still in the city, he took the officer in charge of the fighting men, and
seven royal advisers. He also took the
secretary[f] who was chief officer in
charge of conscripting the people of
the land and sixty of his men who were
found in the city. 26Nebuzaradan[g] the
commander took them all and brought
them to the king of Babylon at Riblah.
27There at Riblah,[h] in the land of Hamath, the king had them executed.

So Judah went into captivity, away[i]
from her land. 28This is the number of
the people Nebuchadnezzar carried
into exile:[j]

in the seventh year, 3,023 Jews;
29in Nebuchadnezzar's eighteenth
year,
832 people from Jerusalem;
30in his twenty-third year,
745 Jews taken into exile[k] by
Nebuzaradan the command-
er of the imperial guard.
There were 4,600 people in
all.[l]

Jehoiachin Released

52:31–34pp — 2Ki 25:27–30

31In the thirty-seventh year of the
exile of Jehoiachin[m] king of Judah, in
the year Evil-Merodach[e] became king
of Babylon, he released Jehoiachin
king of Judah and freed him from prison on the twenty-fifth day of the
twelfth month. 32He spoke kindly to
him and gave him a seat of honor higher than those of the other kings who
were with him in Babylon. 33So Jehoiachin put aside his prison clothes and
for the rest of his life ate regularly at
the king's table.[n] 34Day by day the
king of Babylon gave Jehoiachin a regular allowance[o] as long as he lived,
till the day of his death.

52:20 [w] S 1Ki 7:47 **52:21** [x] S 1Ki 7:15 **52:22** [y] S 1Ki 7:16 [z] S Ex 28:33 **52:23** [a] 1Ki 7:20 [b] S ver 17; S Jer 27:19 **52:24** [c] S 2Ki 25:18 [d] S 2Ki 25:18; S Jer 37:3 [e] S 2Ki 12:9 **52:25** [f] Jer 36:10 **52:26** [g] S ver 12 **52:27** [h] S Nu 34:11 [i] S Jer 20:4 **52:28** [j] S Dt 28:36; S 2Ch 36:20; S Ne 1:2 **52:30** [k] S Jer 43:3 [l] S Jer 13:19 **52:31** [m] S 2Ch 36:9 **52:33** [n] S 2Sa 9:7 **52:34** [o] 2Sa 9:10

[c] *21* That is, about 27 feet (about 8.1 meters) high and 18 feet (about 5.4 meters) in circumference [d] *22* That is, about 7 1/2 feet (about 2.3 meters) [e] *31* Also called *Amel-Marduk*

52:28–30 NUMBER OF THE PEOPLE ... INTO EXILE. The three deportations to Babylon mentioned here occurred in 597 B.C., in 586 B.C., and in 581 B.C. The number of Jews taken captive may refer to adult males only; the total number of exiles was probably much higher (see 2Ki 24:14,16).

LAMENTATIONS

Outline

I. Jerusalem's Devastation (1:1–22)
   A. Description of the Destroyed City (1:1–7)
   B. The Cause of the Destruction (1:8–11)
   C. The Agony of the People (1:12–22)
II. God's Anger and Jerusalem's Sorrow (2:1–22)
   A. God's Anger Against Zion (2:1–9)
   B. The People's Anguish (2:10–17)
   C. The Prophet's Appeal for Mercy (2:18–22)
III. God's Afflicted People and Their Hope (3:1–66)
   A. The Cry of Despair (3:1–18)
   B. The Confession of Hope (3:19–39)
   C. A Call to Repentance (3:40–42)
   D. The Prophet's Suffering (3:43–54)
   E. The Prophet's Prayer (3:55–66)
IV. Zion's Past, Present and Future (4:1–22)
   A. Zion's Past and Present Contrasted (4:1–12)
   B. The Cause of Zion's Devastation (4:13–20)
   C. Punishment for Edom and Restoration for Judah (4:21–22)
V. Prayer for Restoration (5:1–22)
   A. The Need for Mercy (5:1–15)
   B. The Confession of Sin (5:16–18)
   C. The Appeal for Restoration (5:19–22)

Author: Jeremiah

Theme: Present Sorrow and Future Hope

Date of Writing: 586–585 B.C.

Background

The title of this book is derived from the subtitle in the Greek and Latin versions of the OT—"The Lamentations of Jeremiah." The Hebrew OT includes the book as one of the five scrolls (with Ruth, Esther, Ecclesiastes and Song of Songs) of the third part of the Hebrew Bible, the *Hagiographa* ("Holy Writings"); each of these five books was traditionally read at a set time in the Jewish liturgical year. This one was assigned to be read on the ninth day of the month Ab (about mid-July), when the Jews commemorated the destruction of Jerusalem. The Septuagint placed Lamentations immediately after the prophet Jeremiah, where it is located in most Bibles today.

That Jeremiah was the author of Lamentations has long been the consensus of both Jewish and Christian traditions. Among the various evidences that support this conclusion are the following: (1) From 2Ch 35:25 we know that Jeremiah was familiar with composing laments; furthermore, the prophetic book of Jeremiah contains frequent references to his weeping about the coming devastation of Jerusalem (see Jer 7:29; 8:21; 9:1,10,20). (2) The vivid portrayal in Lamentations of that catastrophic event suggests an eyewitness account;

Jeremiah is the only known OT writer to have witnessed firsthand Jerusalem's tragedy in 586 B.C. (3) There are various thematic and linguistic parallels between the book of Jeremiah and Lamentations. For example, both books attribute Judah's suffering and Jerusalem's destruction to persistent sin and rebellion against God. In both books Jeremiah calls God's people his "virgin daughter" (Jer 14:17; 18:13; La 1:15; 2:13). These facts, along with similarities between the two books in their poetic style, point to the same human author.

Jerusalem's desolation is depicted in Lamentations so vividly and clearly that it indicates that it was experienced by the author as a recent event. Jeremiah himself was in his 50s when the city fell; he fully experienced its trauma and was forced against his will to go to Egypt in 585 B.C. (see Jer 41—44), where he died (perhaps as a martyr) in the decade thereafter. Thus the book was most likely written immediately after the destruction of Jerusalem (c. 586–585 B.C.).

Purpose

Jeremiah wrote a series of five laments to express his intense sorrow and emotional pain over Jerusalem's tragic devastation, involving (1) the humiliating downfall of the Davidic monarchy and kingdom, (2) the utter destruction of the city walls, the temple, the king's palace and the city generally, and (3) the pitiful deportation of most survivors far away to Babylon. "Jeremiah sat weeping and lamented with this lamentation over Jerusalem," says a superscription to the book in the Septuagint and the Latin Vulgate. In the book, the prophet's grief gushes out like the grief of a mourner at a funeral of a close relative who died tragically. The laments acknowledge that the tragedy was God's judgment on Judah for centuries of rebellion against him by its rulers and people; the day of reckoning had come and it was terrible indeed. In Lamentations, Jeremiah not only acknowledged that God was righteous and just in all his ways, but also that he is merciful and compassionate to those whose hope is in him (3:22–23,32). Thus Lamentations enabled the people to have hope in the midst of their despair and to look beyond the judgment of the moment to God's restoration of his people in the future.

Survey

The book is a series of five laments, each one complete in itself. The first one (ch. 1) describes Jerusalem's devastation and the prophet's lament over it as he cries out to God in anguish of soul; sometimes his lament is personified as the lament of Jerusalem (1:12–22). In his second lament (ch. 2), Jeremiah describes the cause of this devastation as God's wrath toward a rebellious people who refused to repent. Judah's enemy was God's instrument of judgment. The next poem (ch. 3) urges the nation to remember that God is indeed merciful and faithful, and that he is good to those whose hope is in him. The fourth one (ch. 4) reiterates the themes of the previous three. In the final poem (ch. 5), after a confession of Judah's sin and need for mercy, Jeremiah petitions God to restore his people to his favor.

The book's five laments, which correspond to its five chapters, each have 22 verses (except for ch. 3, which has 22 times 3, or 66, verses); the number 22 is the number of letters in the Hebrew alphabet. The first four poems are alphabetic acrostics, i.e., each verse (or in ch. 3, each set of three verses) begins with a different letter of the Hebrew alphabet in succession from Aleph to Taw. This alphabetizing structure, in addition to being an aid to memory, accomplishes two things. (1) It conveys the idea that the laments are complete, covering everything from A to Z (Heb *Aleph* to *Taw*). (2) By keeping the laments within this structure, the prophet is inhibited from going on and on with endless weeping and groaning; there is an end to the lament, just as there would someday be an end to the exile and a rebuilding of Jerusalem.

Special Features

Five major features characterize the book of Lamentations. (1) Although songs of individual and community lament occur in the psalms and in the prophetic books, only this Bible book is composed exclusively of grief-filled poems. (2) Its literary structure is entirely poetic, with four of the book's five poetic laments being acrostic (see the last paragraph under "Survey"). In keeping with the book's poetic structure, the fifth poem also has 22 verses. (3) While 2Ki 25 and Jer 52 describe the historical event of Jerusalem's destruction, only this book vividly portrays the emotions and feelings of those who actually experienced the catastrophe. (4) At the very heart of the book is one of the most powerful statements about God's faithfulness and salvation found in the Bible (3:21–26). Though Lamentations begins with a lament (1:1–2), it fittingly ends on a note of repentance and hope for restoration (5:16–22). (5) There are no quotations of this book in the NT and only a few possible allusions (cf. La 1:15 with Rev 14:19; La 2:1 with Mt 5:35; La 3:30 with Mt 5:39; La 3:45 with 1Co 4:13).

New Testament Fulfillment

Though Lamentations is nowhere quoted in the NT, it does have direct relevance for those who believe in Christ. Like Ro 1:18—3:20, these five chapters call believers to reflect on the seriousness of sin and the certainty of divine judgment. At the same time, they remind us that because of the compassion and mercy of the Lord, salvation is available for those who repent of their sins and turn to him. Furthermore, the prophet's tears call to mind the tears of Jesus Christ, who wept over the sins of Jerusalem as he foresaw its coming destruction at the hands of the Romans (Mt 23:37–38; Lk 13:34–35; 19:41–44).

Reading Lamentations

In order to read the entire Old Testament in one year, the book of Lamentations should be read in 2 days, according to the following schedule: □ 1–2 □ 3–5

NOTES

1 [a] How deserted[a] lies the city,
once so full of people![b]
How like a widow[c] is she,
who once was great[d] among
the nations!
She who was queen among the
provinces
has now become a slave.[e]

2 Bitterly she weeps[f] at night,
tears are upon her cheeks.
Among all her lovers[g]
there is none to comfort her.
All her friends have betrayed[h]
her;
they have become her
enemies.[i]

3 After affliction and harsh labor,
Judah has gone into exile.[j]
She dwells among the nations;
she finds no resting place.[k]
All who pursue her have overtaken
her[l]
in the midst of her distress.

4 The roads to Zion mourn,[m]
for no one comes to her
appointed feasts.
All her gateways are desolate,[n]
her priests groan,
her maidens grieve,
and she is in bitter anguish.[o]

5 Her foes have become her masters;
her enemies are at ease.
The LORD has brought her grief[p]
because of her many sins.[q]
Her children have gone into
exile,[r]
captive before the foe.[s]

6 All the splendor has departed
from the Daughter of Zion.[t]
Her princes are like deer
that find no pasture;
in weakness they have fled[u]
before the pursuer.

7 In the days of her affliction and
wandering
Jerusalem remembers all the
treasures
that were hers in days of old.
When her people fell into enemy
hands,
there was no one to help her.[v]
Her enemies looked at her
and laughed[w] at her
destruction.

8 Jerusalem has sinned[x] greatly
and so has become unclean.[y]
All who honored her despise her,
for they have seen her
nakedness;[z]
she herself groans[a]
and turns away.

9 Her filthiness clung to her skirts;
she did not consider her
future.[b]
Her fall[c] was astounding;
there was none to comfort[d] her.
"Look, O LORD, on my affliction,[e]
for the enemy has triumphed."

10 The enemy laid hands
on all her treasures;[f]
she saw pagan nations
enter her sanctuary[g]—
those you had forbidden[h]
to enter your assembly.

11 All her people groan[i]
as they search for bread;[j]
they barter their treasures for food
to keep themselves alive.
"Look, O LORD, and consider,
for I am despised."

12 "Is it nothing to you, all you who
pass by?[k]

1:1 [a] S Lev 26:43 [b] S Jer 42:2 [c] S Isa 47:8 [d] S 1Ki 4:21 [e] Isa 3:26; S Jer 40:9; Eze 5:5 **1:2** [f] Ps 6:6 [g] S Jer 3:1 [h] S Jer 4:30; Mic 7:5 [i] ver 16; S Jer 30:14 **1:3** [j] S Jer 13:19 [k] Dt 28:65 [l] S Ex 15:9 **1:4** [m] S Ps 137:1 [n] S Isa 27:10; S Jer 9:11 [o] ver 21; Joel 1:8-13 **1:5** [p] S Isa 22:5; S Jer 30:15 [q] S Ps 5:10 [r] S Jer 10:20; S 39:9; 52:28-30 [s] S Ps 137:3; La 2:17 **1:6** [t] S Ps 9:14; Jer 13:18 [u] S Lev 26:36 **1:7** [v] S 2Ki 14:26; S Jer 37:7; La 4:17 [w] S Jer 2:26 **1:8** [x] ver 20; Isa 59:2-13 [y] S Jer 2:22 [z] S Jer 13:22,26 [a] ver 21,22; S Ps 6:6; S 38:8 **1:9** [b] Dt 32:28-29; Eze 24:13 [c] Jer 13:18 [d] S Ecc 4:1; S Jer 16:7 [e] Ps 25:18 **1:10** [f] S Isa 64:11 [g] Ps 74:7-8; 79:1; Jer 51:51 [h] Dt 23:3 **1:11** [i] S Ps 6:6; S 38:8 [j] S Jer 37:21; S 52:6 **1:12** [k] S Jer 18:16

[a] This chapter is an acrostic poem, the verses of which begin with the successive letters of the Hebrew alphabet.

1:1 HOW DESERTED LIES THE CITY. Jeremiah expresses his deep sorrow because of Jerusalem's fall and the tragic circumstances that brought it about. The holy city is personified as a deserted widow who has lost her children and been betrayed by her friends; she is left completely alone with no one to comfort her.

1:5 BROUGHT HER GRIEF . . . MANY SINS. The catastrophe of suffering, devastation and loss is attributed to the peoples' sin (cf. vv. 8–9,14,18,20,22). It is they who have brought judgment upon themselves. Continuing in sin always results in punishment from God (Ro 6:23).

1:7 NO ONE TO HELP HER. Those who go their own way and ignore the conviction of the Holy Spirit in their hearts may find in their hour of need that there is no one to help them. Individuals can reach a point in rebellion against God where he will ordain calamity rather than good for them; such awful consequences can be avoided only by maintaining a holy fear of God and his judgment.

1:12 MY SUFFERING. In the first eleven verses Jeremiah is the one lamenting; in vv. 12–22 Jerusalem is personified as the one lamenting.

1:12 THE DAY OF HIS FIERCE ANGER. Some believers emphasize God's love and forgiveness and ignore his fierce anger against all who refuse to heed his call to righteousness. The view that Christ tolerates sin and immorality because of

Look around and see.
Is any suffering like my suffering[l]
that was inflicted on me,
that the LORD brought on me
in the day of his fierce anger?[m]

13"From on high he sent fire,
sent it down into my bones.[n]
He spread a net[o] for my feet
and turned me back.
He made me desolate,[p]
faint[q] all the day long.

14"My sins have been bound into a yoke[b];[r]
by his hands they were woven together.
They have come upon my neck
and the Lord has sapped my strength.
He has handed me over[s]
to those I cannot withstand.

15"The Lord has rejected
all the warriors in my midst;[t]
he has summoned an army[u]
against me
to[c] crush my young men.[v]
In his winepress[w] the Lord has trampled[x]
the Virgin Daughter[y] of Judah.

16"This is why I weep
and my eyes overflow with tears.[z]
No one is near to comfort[a] me,
no one to restore my spirit.
My children are destitute
because the enemy has prevailed."[b]

17Zion stretches out her hands,[c]
but there is no one to comfort her.
The LORD has decreed for Jacob
that his neighbors become his foes;[d]
Jerusalem has become
an unclean[e] thing[f] among them.

18"The LORD is righteous,[g]
yet I rebelled[h] against his command.
Listen, all you peoples;
look upon my suffering.[i]
My young men and maidens
have gone into exile.[j]

19"I called to my allies[k]
but they betrayed me.
My priests and my elders
perished[l] in the city
while they searched for food
to keep themselves alive.

20"See, O LORD, how distressed[m] I am!
I am in torment[n] within,
and in my heart I am disturbed,[o]
for I have been most rebellious.[p]
Outside, the sword bereaves;
inside, there is only death.[q]

21"People have heard my groaning,[r]
but there is no one to comfort me.[s]
All my enemies have heard of my distress;
they rejoice[t] at what you have done.
May you bring the day[u] you have announced
so they may become like me.

22"Let all their wickedness come before you;
deal with them
as you have dealt with me
because of all my sins.[v]
My groans[w] are many
and my heart is faint."

2[d] How the Lord has covered the Daughter of Zion
with the cloud of his anger[e]![x]
He has hurled down the splendor of Israel
from heaven to earth;

1:12 [l]ver 18 [m]S Isa 10:4; 13:13; S Jer 30:24 1:13 [n]S Job 30:30; Ps 102:3 [o]S Job 18:8 [p]S Jer 44:6 [q]Hab 3:16 1:14 [r]S Dt 28:48; S Isa 47:6; S Jer 15:12 [s]S Jer 32:5 1:15 [t]Jer 37:10 [u]Isa 41:2 [v]Isa 28:18; S Jer 18:21 [w]S Jdg 6:11 [x]S Isa 5:5 [y]Jer 14:17 1:16 [z]S Job 7:3; S Ps 119:136; S Isa 22:4; La 2:11,18; 3:48-49 [a]S Ps 69:20; Ecc 4:1; S Jer 16:7 [b]S ver 2; Jer 13:17; 14:17 1:17 [c]S Jer 4:31 [d]S Ex 23:21 [e]Jer 2:22 [f]S Lev 18:25-28 1:18 [g]S Ex 9:27; S Ezr 9:15 [h]S 1Sa 12:14 [i]ver 12 [j]Dt 28:32, 41 1:19 [k]S Jer 22:20 [l]S Jer 14:15; La 2:20 1:20 [m]S Jer 4:19 [n]La 2:11 [o]S Job 20:2 [p]S ver 8 [q]S Dt 32:25; Eze 7:15 1:21 [r]S ver 8; S Ps 6:6; S 38:8 [s]ver 4 [t]La 2:15 [u]Isa 47:11; Jer 30:16 1:22 [v]Ne 4:5 [w]S ver 8; S Ps 6:6 2:1 [x]La 3:44

[b] *14* Most Hebrew manuscripts; Septuagint *He kept watch over my sins* [c] *15* Or *has set a time for me / when he will* [d] This chapter is an acrostic poem, the verses of which begin with the successive letters of the Hebrew alphabet. [e] *1* Or *How the Lord in his anger / has treated the Daughter of Zion with contempt*

his love finds no support in Scripture (see Rev 19:15–17, notes). In order to gain insight into God's coming wrath, be sure to read and study the book of Revelation.

1:18 LOOK UPON MY SUFFERING. This verse expresses the main theme of Lamentations: sin brings sorrow. A person may enjoy the pleasures of sin and immorality for a time, but eventually slavery to Satan and the consequences of one's sinful desires will become evident (Jn 8:34; Ro 1:26–32). Distress, despair and destruction will come to all who do not turn to God in repentance.

1:22 WICKEDNESS COME BEFORE YOU. Prayer for God's judgment on evil nations and all who oppose God's work is appropriate if we are concerned about God's glory, the gospel and his righteous cause on earth.

he has not remembered his
footstool[y]
in the day of his anger.[z]

2 Without pity[a] the Lord has
swallowed[b] up
all the dwellings of Jacob;
in his wrath he has torn down
the strongholds[c] of the
Daughter of Judah.
He has brought her kingdom and
its princes
down to the ground[d] in
dishonor.

3 In fierce anger he has cut off
every horn[f][e] of Israel.
He has withdrawn his right hand[f]
at the approach of the enemy.
He has burned in Jacob like a
flaming fire
that consumes everything
around it.[g]

4 Like an enemy he has strung his
bow;[h]
his right hand is ready.
Like a foe he has slain
all who were pleasing to the
eye;[i]
he has poured out his wrath[j] like
fire[k]
on the tent[l] of the Daughter of
Zion.

5 The Lord is like an enemy;[m]
he has swallowed up Israel.
He has swallowed up all her
palaces
and destroyed her strongholds.[n]
He has multiplied mourning and
lamentation[o]
for the Daughter of Judah.[p]

6 He has laid waste his dwelling like
a garden;
he has destroyed[q] his place of
meeting.[r]
The LORD has made Zion forget
her appointed feasts and her
Sabbaths;[s]
in his fierce anger he has spurned
both king and priest.[t]

7 The Lord has rejected his altar
and abandoned his sanctuary.[u]
He has handed over to the enemy
the walls of her palaces;[v]
they have raised a shout in the
house of the LORD
as on the day of an appointed
feast.[w]

8 The LORD determined to tear down
the wall around the Daughter of
Zion.[x]
He stretched out a measuring
line[y]
and did not withhold his hand
from destroying.
He made ramparts[z] and walls
lament;
together they wasted away.[a]

9 Her gates[b] have sunk into the
ground;
their bars[c] he has broken and
destroyed.
Her king and her princes are
exiled[d] among the nations,
the law[e] is no more,
and her prophets[f] no longer find
visions[g] from the LORD.

10 The elders of the Daughter of Zion
sit on the ground in silence;[h]
they have sprinkled dust[i] on their
heads[j]
and put on sackcloth.[k]

2:1 [y]Ps 99:5; 132:7 [z]S Jer 12:7 **2:2** [a]ver 17; La 3:43 [b]Ps 21:9 [c]Ps 89:39-40; Mic 5:11 [d]S Isa 25:12 **2:3** [e]Ps 75:5,10 [f]Ps 74:11 [g]S Isa 42:25; Jer 21:4-5,14 **2:4** [h]S Job 3:23; 16:13; La 3:12-13 [i]S Ps 48:2; Eze 24:16,25 [j]S 2Ch 34:21; Eze 20:34 [k]Isa 42:25; S Jer 7:20 [l]S Jer 4:20 **2:5** [m]S Job 13:24 [n]ver 2 [o]S Isa 29:2 [p]S Jer 7:20; 9:17-20 **2:6** [q]2Ch 36:19 [r]S Jer 52:13 [s]Zep 3:18 [t]Isa 43:28; S Jer 7:14; La 4:16; 5:12 **2:7** [u]S Lev 26:31; S Eze 7:24 [v]Ps 74:7-8; S Isa 64:11; Jer 33:4-5; Eze 7:21-22 [w]Jer 21:4; 52:13 **2:8** [x]ver 18 [y]S 2Ki 21:13 [z]S Ps 48:13 [a]Isa 3:26; S Jer 39:8; S 52:14 **2:9** [b]S Ne 1:3 [c]S Isa 45:2; Hos 11:6 [d]Dt 28:36; S 2Ki 24:15; Jer 16:13; Hos 3:4 [e]S 2Ch 15:3 [f]S 1Sa 3:1 [g]S Jer 14:14 **2:10** [h]La 3:28 [i]S Jos 7:6 [j]Job 2:12 [k]S Isa 3:24

[f]3 Or *all the strength*; or *every king*; *horn* here symbolizes strength.

2:5 IS LIKE AN ENEMY. To have once known the Lord and then turned from him to the pleasures of sin is to make God an enemy; Israel and Judah did so, and they suffered greatly as a result. Believers cannot forsake the Lord and his word and expect that God will do nothing. A time will come when God will pour out his wrath on all who have unrepentant hearts (cf. Ro 2:8–9; Rev 2:16, 22–23).

2:7 HANDED OVER TO THE ENEMY. The Lord turned his apostate people over to their enemies for destruction. Likewise, under the new covenant, both churches and individuals who turn to lives of sin and persist in worldliness will be handed over to Satan (1Co 5:7). The sinful ways and values of ungodly society will bring destruction and retribution to all who forsake the Lord (see Mt 5:13, note).

2:9 NO LONGER FIND VISIONS. God was no longer communicating directly with his people, for sin had caused him to withdraw prophecies and visions. Likewise, under the new covenant, the Holy Spirit may cease to manifest his gifts and miraculous powers through believers (cf. 1Co 12—14) because of sin among God's leaders and people. This kind of judgment is a sure indication that God's people have departed from a lifestyle of seeking first God's kingdom and righteousness. The only remedy is to turn from all compromise with sin, to seek God earnestly, and to pray for the restoration of his favor and kingdom power (see article on SPIRITUAL GIFTS FOR BELIEVERS, p. 1770).

The young women of Jerusalem
have bowed their heads to the
ground.[l]

11My eyes fail from weeping,[m]
I am in torment within,[n]
my heart[o] is poured out[p] on the
ground
because my people are
destroyed,[q]
because children and infants
faint[r]
in the streets of the city.

12They say to their mothers,
"Where is bread and wine?"[s]
as they faint like wounded men
in the streets of the city,
as their lives ebb away[t]
in their mothers' arms.[u]

13What can I say for you?[v]
With what can I compare you,
O Daughter[w] of Jerusalem?
To what can I liken you,
that I may comfort you,
O Virgin Daughter of Zion?[x]
Your wound is as deep as the
sea.[y]
Who can heal you?

14The visions of your prophets
were false[z] and worthless;
they did not expose your sin
to ward off your captivity.[a]
The oracles they gave you
were false and misleading.[b]

15All who pass your way
clap their hands at you;[c]
they scoff[d] and shake their
heads[e]
at the Daughter of Jerusalem:[f]
"Is this the city that was called
the perfection of beauty,[g]
the joy of the whole earth?"[h]

16All your enemies open their
mouths
wide against you;[i]
they scoff and gnash their teeth[j]
and say, "We have swallowed
her up.[k]
This is the day we have waited for;
we have lived to see it."[l]

17The LORD has done what he
planned;
he has fulfilled[m] his word,
which he decreed long ago.[n]
He has overthrown you without
pity,[o]
he has let the enemy gloat over
you,[p]
he has exalted the horn[g] of
your foes.[q]

18The hearts of the people
cry out to the Lord.[r]
O wall of the Daughter of Zion,[s]
let your tears[t] flow like a river
day and night;[u]
give yourself no relief,
your eyes no rest.[v]

19Arise, cry out in the night,
as the watches of the night
begin;
pour out your heart[w] like water
in the presence of the Lord.[x]
Lift up your hands[y] to him
for the lives of your children,
who faint[z] from hunger
at the head of every street.

20"Look, O LORD, and consider:

2:10 [l]S Job 2:13; S Isa 3:26; Eze 27:30-31
2:11 [m]S Ps 119:82; S Isa 15:3; S La 1:16; 3:48-51 [n]S Job 30:27; La 1:20 [o]S Isa 1:5 [p]ver 19; Ps 22:14 [q]S Jer 9:1 [r]La 4:4
2:12 [s]Isa 24:11 [t]S Job 3:24 [u]La 4:4
2:13 [v]S Isa 1:6 [w]S 2Ki 19:21 [x]Isa 37:22 [y]Jer 14:17; 30:12-15; La 1:12
2:14 [z]S Jer 28:15 [a]Jer 8:11 [b]Jer 2:8; S 20:6; 23:25-32, 33-40; S 29:9; Eze 13:3; 22:28
2:15 [c]S Nu 24:10; Eze 25:6 [d]S Dt 28:37; S Isa 28:22; Jer 19:8; S Na 3:19 [e]S Job 16:4 [f]S La 1:21 [g]Ps 45:11; S 48:2; 50:2; Eze 16:14 [h]Ps 48:2
2:16 [i]Ps 22:13; La 3:46 [j]S Job 16:9 [k]S Ps 35:25 [l]Eze 36:3; Mic 4:11
2:17 [m]S Jer 39:16 [n]Dt 28:15-45 [o]S ver 2; Eze 5:11; 7:9; 8:18 [p]S Ps 22:17 [q]Ps 89:42; S Isa 44:26; S La 1:5; Zec 1:6
2:18 [r]S Ps 119:145 [s]ver 8 [t]S La 1:16 [u]S Jer 9:1 [v]La 3:49
2:19 [w]1Sa 1:15 [x]S ver 11; Isa 26:9 [y]S Ps 28:2 [z]S Isa 51:20

g 17 *Horn* here symbolizes strength.

2:11 MY EYES FAIL FROM WEEPING. Jeremiah weeps because of the tragic sorrow and suffering brought about by the people's rejection of their God. Jesus Christ himself wept for the people of Israel who would soon suffer terrible judgment for rejecting God's salvation (Lk 19:41–44), and the apostle Paul expressed deep sorrow and ceaseless concern over fellow Jews who did not accept Christ (Ro 9:1–3; 10:1). We who have experienced redemption and life in Christ should be heartbroken over the terrible suffering of people enslaved to sin and Satan. We should be grieved because of the moral breakdown in society, knowing the tragic pain and suffering that will result.

2:12 WHERE IS BREAD AND WINE? Infants and small children were crying out in famished distress to their mothers for basic physical nourishment. Here wine (Heb *yayin*) undoubtedly refers to nourishing grape juice rather than an intoxicating beverage (see article on WINE IN THE OLD TESTAMENT, p. 204).

2:14 DID NOT EXPOSE YOUR SIN. One mark of a false prophet was that his words and visions did not expose sin among the people (see article on THE PROPHET IN THE OLD TESTAMENT, p. 986). Those in the church who do not rebuke sin, thereby releasing the convicting work of the Holy Spirit (Jn 16:8–11), prove that they are false ministers; conversely, those who live holy lives and sincerely cry out against worldliness and sin in the congregation, just as Christ did (see Rev 2—3), prove themselves to be faithful ministers of their Lord.

2:18 LET YOUR TEARS FLOW. Jeremiah calls the people to prayer, weeping and repentance, with the hope that God would hear the intercessory cry of the remnant (cf. v. 19).

Whom have you ever treated like
 this?
Should women eat their
 offspring,[a]
 the children they have cared
 for?[b]
Should priest and prophet be
 killed[c]
 in the sanctuary of the Lord?[d]

21"Young and old lie together
 in the dust of the streets;
my young men and maidens
 have fallen by the sword.[e]
You have slain them in the day of
 your anger;
 you have slaughtered them
 without pity.[f]

22"As you summon to a feast day,
 so you summoned against me
 terrors[g] on every side.
In the day of the LORD's anger
 no one escaped[h] or survived;
those I cared for and reared,[i]
 my enemy has destroyed."

3

3[h] I am the man who has seen
 affliction[j]
 by the rod of his wrath.[k]
2He has driven me away and made
 me walk
 in darkness[l] rather than light;
3indeed, he has turned his hand
 against me[m]
 again and again, all day long.

4He has made my skin and my flesh
 grow old[n]
 and has broken my bones.[o]
5He has besieged me and
 surrounded me
 with bitterness[p] and hardship.[q]
6He has made me dwell in darkness
 like those long dead.[r]

7He has walled me in so I cannot
 escape;[s]
 he has weighed me down with
 chains.[t]
8Even when I call out or cry for
 help,[u]
 he shuts out my prayer.[v]
9He has barred[w] my way with
 blocks of stone;
 he has made my paths
 crooked.[x]

10Like a bear lying in wait,
 like a lion[y] in hiding,[z]
11he dragged me from the path and
 mangled[a] me
 and left me without help.
12He drew his bow[b]
 and made me the target[c] for
 his arrows.[d]

13He pierced[e] my heart
 with arrows from his quiver.[f]
14I became the laughingstock[g] of
 all my people;[h]
 they mock me in song[i] all day
 long.
15He has filled me with bitter herbs
 and sated me with gall.[j]

16He has broken my teeth with
 gravel;[k]
 he has trampled me in the
 dust.[l]
17I have been deprived of peace;
 I have forgotten what prosperity
 is.
18So I say, "My splendor is gone
 and all that I had hoped from
 the LORD."[m]

19I remember my affliction and my
 wandering,
 the bitterness[n] and the gall.[o]
20I well remember them,
 and my soul is downcast[p]
 within me.[q]
21Yet this I call to mind
 and therefore I have hope:

h This chapter is an acrostic poem; the verses of each stanza begin with the successive letters of the Hebrew alphabet, and the verses within each stanza begin with the same letter.

2:20 [a]S Dt 28:53; Jer 19:9; Eze 5:10 [b]La 4:10 [c]Ps 78:64; S Jer 14:15; 23:11-12 [d]S La 1:19 **2:21** [e]S Dt 32:25; S 2Ch 36:17; Ps 78:62-63; Jer 6:11 [f]S Jer 13:14; La 3:43; Zec 11:6 **2:22** [g]S Ps 31:13; S Jer 20:10 [h]S Jer 11:11 [i]Job 27:14; Hos 9:13 **3:1** [j]Jer 15:17-18 [k]S Job 19:21; Ps 88:7 **3:2** [l]S Job 19:8; S Ps 82:5; S Jer 4:23 **3:3** [m]Ps 38:2; Isa 5:25 **3:4** [n]S Job 30:30; La 4:8 [o]Ps 51:8; S Isa 38:13; S Jer 50:17 **3:5** [p]ver 19 [q]Jer 23:15 **3:6** [r]Ps 88:5-6; 143:3; Isa 59:10 **3:7** [s]S Job 3:23 [t]Jer 40:4 **3:8** [u]Ps 5:2 [v]ver 44; S Dt 1:45; S Job 30:20; Ps 22:2 **3:9** [w]S Job 19:8 [x]S Job 9:24; S Isa 63:17; Hos 2:6 **3:10** [y]S Job 10:16 [z]Hos 13:8; Am 5:18-19 **3:11** [a]Hos 6:1 **3:12** [b]S La 2:4 [c]Job 7:20 [d]S Job 16:12; Ps 7:12-13; 38:2 **3:13** [e]S Job 16:13 [f]Job 6:4 **3:14** [g]S Ge 38:23; Ps 22:6-7; Jer 20:7 [h]S Job 17:2 [i]S Job 30:9 **3:15** [j]ver 19; Jer 9:15 **3:16** [k]S Pr 20:17 [l]S Ps 7:5 **3:18** [m]S ver 54; S Job 17:15 **3:19** [n]ver 5 [o]S ver 15 **3:20** [p]S Ps 42:5 [q]Ps 42:11; 43:5

3:1 I AM THE MAN. In ch. 3 the afflicted people of Israel are portrayed as a human being who is under God's punishment, yet who has the hope of restoration. Such a person claims the truth that God's love and help will come to those who repent and continue to wait for the Lord (vv. 22–27).

3:8 HE SHUTS OUT MY PRAYER. For the ungodly, one of the terrible consequences of living in sin and immorality is that God refuses to hear their prayers (cf. v. 44; Ps 18:41; Pr 1:28; Jer 7:16; see article on EFFECTIVE PRAYING, p. 496).

3:21–33 THEREFORE I HAVE HOPE. Jeremiah wants the people to know that all is not lost. They may have hope for the following reasons: (1) The Lord's anger lasts only a brief time, but his great love never ceases (v. 22). God had not rejected Judah as his covenant people, and he still had a purpose for them. (2) The Lord is good and merciful to those who wait for him in humility and repentance (vv. 24–27). (3) The Lord desires to have compassion on sufferers when his chastisement has accomplished its purpose (vv. 28–33; see next note).

22 Because of the LORD's great love[r]
we are not consumed,[s]
for his compassions never fail.[t]
23 They are new every morning;
great is your faithfulness.[u]
24 I say to myself, "The LORD is my
portion;[v]
therefore I will wait for him."

25 The LORD is good to those whose
hope is in him,
to the one who seeks him;[w]
26 it is good to wait quietly[x]
for the salvation of the LORD.[y]
27 It is good for a man to bear the
yoke
while he is young.

28 Let him sit alone in silence,[z]
for the LORD has laid it on him.
29 Let him bury his face in the
dust[a]—
there may yet be hope.[b]
30 Let him offer his cheek to one who
would strike him,[c]
and let him be filled with
disgrace.[d]

31 For men are not cast off
by the Lord forever.[e]
32 Though he brings grief, he will
show compassion,
so great is his unfailing love.[f]
33 For he does not willingly bring
affliction
or grief to the children of men.[g]

34 To crush underfoot
all prisoners in the land,
35 to deny a man his rights
before the Most High,[h]
36 to deprive a man of justice—
would not the Lord see such
things?[i]

37 Who can speak and have it happen
if the Lord has not decreed it?[j]
38 Is it not from the mouth of the
Most High
that both calamities and good
things come?[k]

39 Why should any living man
complain
when punished for his sins?[l]

40 Let us examine our ways and test
them,[m]
and let us return to the LORD.[n]
41 Let us lift up our hearts and our
hands
to God in heaven,[o] and say:
42 "We have sinned and rebelled[p]
and you have not forgiven.[q]

43 "You have covered yourself with
anger and pursued[r] us;
you have slain without pity.[s]
44 You have covered yourself with a
cloud[t]
so that no prayer[u] can get
through.[v]
45 You have made us scum[w] and
refuse
among the nations.

46 "All our enemies have opened their
mouths
wide[x] against us.[y]
47 We have suffered terror and
pitfalls,[z]
ruin and destruction."[a]
48 Streams of tears[b] flow from my
eyes[c]
because my people are
destroyed.[d]

49 My eyes will flow unceasingly,
without relief,[e]
50 until the LORD looks down
from heaven and sees.[f]
51 What I see brings grief to my soul
because of all the women of my
city.

52 Those who were my enemies
without cause
hunted me like a bird.[g]
53 They tried to end my life in a pit[h]
and threw stones at me;
54 the waters closed over my head,[i]

3:22 [r] S Ps 103:11 [s] S Job 34:15; S Hos 11:9 [t] Ps 78:38; 130:7 **3:23** [u] S Ex 34:6; Zep 3:5 **3:24** [v] S Ps 119:57 **3:25** [w] S Ps 33:18; Isa 25:9; S 30:18 **3:26** [x] S Isa 7:4 [y] Ps 37:7; 40:1 **3:28** [z] Jer 15:17; La 2:10 **3:29** [a] S Job 2:8 [b] S Jer 31:17 **3:30** [c] S Job 16:10; S Isa 50:6 [d] Mic 5:1 **3:31** [e] Ps 94:14; Isa 54:7 **3:32** [f] Ps 78:38; 106:43-45; Hos 11:8; Na 1:12 **3:33** [g] S Job 37:23; S Jer 31:20; Eze 18:23; 33:11 **3:35** [h] Ge 14:18, 19,20,22 **3:36** [i] Ps 140:12; S Pr 17:15; S Jer 22:3; Hab 1:13 **3:37** [j] Ps 33:9-11; S Pr 19:21; S 21:30 **3:38** [k] S Job 2:10; S Isa 45:7; Jer 32:42

3:39 [l] S Jer 30:15; Mic 7:9 **3:40** [m] 2Co 13:5 [n] Ps 119:59; 139:23-24 **3:41** [o] S Ps 25:1; S 28:2 **3:42** [p] Jer 14:20; Da 9:5 [q] S 2Ki 24:4; Jer 5:7-9 **3:43** [r] ver 66; Ps 35:6 [s] S La 2:2, 17,21 **3:44** [t] Ps 97:2; La 2:1 [u] S ver 8; Zec 7:13 [v] S Isa 58:4 **3:45** [w] 1Co 4:13 **3:46** [x] Ps 22:13 [y] La 2:16 **3:47** [z] Jer 48:43 [a] S Isa 24:17-18; S 51:19 **3:48** [b] S Ps 119:136 [c] S Jer 9:1,18; La 1:16 [d] La 2:11 **3:49** [e] Jer 14:17; S La 2:18 **3:50** [f] S Ps 14:2; 80:14; S Isa 63:15 **3:52** [g] Ps 35:7

3:53 [h] Jer 37:16; S 38:6 **3:54** [i] Ps 69:2; Jnh 2:3-5

3:27–33 BEAR THE YOKE. God sometimes sends afflictions to those who have rebelled against him in order to accomplish a beneficial and purifying work in their lives. Those undergoing such trials should confess their sin, plead for pardon, and trust the Lord for forgiveness and restoration.

3:33 DOES NOT WILLINGLY BRING AFFLICTION. God does not delight in punishing people for their sins; he punishes because he has to maintain moral order in the world. God's ultimate hope is that his affliction will turn people back to him (see Eze 18:23,32; Hos 11:8; 2Pe 3:9).

3:40–41 LET US RETURN TO THE LORD. The prophet identifies with the people in a spiritual examination that would lead them to return to the Lord, obey his Word and exhibit a sincere change in their hearts. If they do this, God will hear them and redeem them (vv. 55–58).

and I thought I was about to be
cut off.[j]

55I called on your name, O LORD,
from the depths[k] of the pit.[l]
56You heard my plea:[m] "Do not
close your ears
to my cry for relief."
57You came near[n] when I called
you,
and you said, "Do not fear."[o]

58O Lord, you took up my case;[p]
you redeemed my life.[q]
59You have seen, O LORD, the wrong
done to me.[r]
Uphold my cause![s]
60You have seen the depth of their
vengeance,
all their plots against me.[t]

61O LORD, you have heard their
insults,[u]
all their plots against me—
62what my enemies whisper and
mutter
against me all day long.[v]
63Look at them! Sitting or standing,
they mock me in their songs.[w]

64Pay them back what they deserve,
O LORD,
for what their hands have
done.[x]
65Put a veil over their hearts,[y]
and may your curse be on them!
66Pursue[z] them in anger and
destroy them
from under the heavens of the
LORD.

4

[i] How the gold has lost its
luster,
the fine gold become dull!
The sacred gems are scattered
at the head of every street.[a]

2How the precious sons of Zion,[b]
once worth their weight in gold,
are now considered as pots of clay,
the work of a potter's hands!

3Even jackals offer their breasts
to nurse their young,
but my people have become
heartless
like ostriches in the desert.[c]
4Because of thirst[d] the infant's
tongue
sticks to the roof of its mouth;[e]
the children beg for bread,
but no one gives it to them.[f]

5Those who once ate delicacies
are destitute in the streets.
Those nurtured in purple[g]
now lie on ash heaps.[h]

6The punishment of my people
is greater than that of Sodom,[i]
which was overthrown in a
moment
without a hand turned to help
her.

7Their princes were brighter than
snow
and whiter than milk,
their bodies more ruddy than
rubies,
their appearance like
sapphires.[j]

8But now they are blacker[j] than
soot;
they are not recognized in the
streets.
Their skin has shriveled on their
bones;[k]
it has become as dry as a stick.

9Those killed by the sword are
better off
than those who die of famine;[l]
racked with hunger, they waste
away
for lack of food from the field.[m]

10With their own hands
compassionate women
have cooked their own
children,[n]
who became their food
when my people were destroyed.

11The LORD has given full vent to his
wrath;[o]
he has poured out[p] his fierce
anger.[q]
He kindled a fire[r] in Zion
that consumed her
foundations.[s]

12The kings of the earth did not
believe,

3:54 [j] ver 18; Ps 88:5; Eze 37:11
3:55 [k] S Ps 88:6 [l] Ps 130:1; Jnh 2:2
3:56 [m] S Ps 55:1; 116:1-2
3:57 [n] S Ps 46:1 [o] Isa 41:10
3:58 [p] S Jer 51:36 [q] Ps 34:22; S Jer 50:34
3:59 [r] Jer 18:19-20 [s] Ps 35:23; 43:1
3:60 [t] S Jer 11:20; 18:18
3:61 [u] Ps 89:50; Zep 2:8
3:62 [v] Eze 36:3
3:63 [w] S Job 30:9
3:64 [x] S Ps 28:4; S Jer 51:6
3:65 [y] Ex 14:8; Dt 2:30; Isa 6:10
3:66 [z] S ver 43
4:1 [a] Eze 7:19
4:2 [b] Isa 51:18
4:3 [c] S Job 39:16
4:4 [d] S Dt 28:48; S 2Ki 18:31 [e] S Ps 22:15 [f] La 2:11,12
4:5 [g] Jer 6:2 [h] S Isa 3:26; Am 6:3-7
4:6 [i] S Ge 19:25
4:8 [j] S Job 30:28 [k] Ps 102:3-5; S La 3:4
4:9 [l] S 2Ki 25:3 [m] S Jer 15:2; S 16:4; La 5:10
4:10 [n] S Lev 26:29; Dt 28:53-57; Jer 19:9; La 2:20; Eze 5:10
4:11 [o] S Job 20:23 [p] S 2Ch 34:21 [q] Na 1:6; Zep 2:2; 3:8 [r] Jer 17:27 [s] S Dt 32:22; S Jer 7:20; Eze 22:31

[i] This chapter is an acrostic poem, the verses of which begin with the successive letters of the Hebrew alphabet. [j] 7 Or *lapis lazuli*

4:1–12 GOLD BECOME DULL! Jeremiah compares Jerusalem's glories before the siege with the present devastation of the people brought on as a result of God's punishment.

nor did any of the world's
people,
that enemies and foes could enter
the gates of Jerusalem.[t]

13 But it happened because of the
sins of her prophets
and the iniquities of her
priests,[u]
who shed within her
the blood[v] of the righteous.

14 Now they grope through the
streets
like men who are blind.[w]
They are so defiled with blood[x]
that no one dares to touch their
garments.

15 "Go away! You are unclean!" men
cry to them.
"Away! Away! Don't touch us!"
When they flee and wander[y]
about,
people among the nations say,
"They can stay here no
longer."[z]

16 The LORD himself has scattered
them;
he no longer watches over
them.[a]
The priests are shown no honor,
the elders[b] no favor.[c]

17 Moreover, our eyes failed,
looking in vain[d] for help;[e]
from our towers we watched
for a nation[f] that could not
save us.

18 Men stalked us at every step,
so we could not walk in our
streets.
Our end was near, our days were
numbered,
for our end had come.[g]

19 Our pursuers were swifter
than eagles[h] in the sky;
they chased us[i] over the
mountains
and lay in wait for us in the
desert.[j]

20 The LORD's anointed,[k] our very
life breath,
was caught in their traps.[l]
We thought that under his
shadow[m]
we would live among the
nations.

21 Rejoice and be glad, O Daughter of
Edom,
you who live in the land of Uz.[n]
But to you also the cup[o] will be
passed;
you will be drunk and stripped
naked.[p]

22 O Daughter of Zion, your
punishment will end;[q]
he will not prolong your exile.
But, O Daughter of Edom, he will
punish your sin
and expose your wickedness.[r]

5 Remember, O LORD, what has
happened to us;
look, and see our disgrace.[s]

2 Our inheritance[t] has been turned
over to aliens,[u]
our homes[v] to foreigners.[w]

3 We have become orphans and
fatherless,
our mothers like widows.[x]

4 We must buy the water we
drink;[y]
our wood can be had only at a
price.[z]

5 Those who pursue us are at our
heels;
we are weary[a] and find no
rest.[b]

6 We submitted to Egypt and
Assyria[c]
to get enough bread.

7 Our fathers[d] sinned and are no
more,
and we bear their punishment.[e]

8 Slaves[f] rule over us,

4:12 [t] S 1Ki 9:9; S Jer 21:13 **4:13** [u] Jer 5:31; 6:13; Eze 22:28; Mic 3:11 [v] S 2Ki 21:16 **4:14** [w] S Isa 59:10 [x] Jer 19:4 **4:15** [y] S Jer 44:14 [z] Lev 13:46; Mic 2:10 **4:16** [a] Isa 9:14-16 [b] La 5:12 [c] S La 2:6 **4:17** [d] S Ge 15:18; S Isa 20:5; Eze 29:16 [e] S La 1:7 [f] Jer 37:7 **4:18** [g] Eze 7:2-12; Am 8:2 **4:19** [h] S Dt 28:49 [i] S Lev 26:36; Isa 5:26-28 [j] Jer 52:7 **4:20** [k] S 1Sa 26:9; 2Sa 19:21 [l] Jer 39:5; Eze 12:12-13; 19:4,8 [m] S Ps 91:1 **4:21** [n] S Ge 10:23 [o] S Ps 16:5; S Jer 25:15 [p] Isa 34:6-10; S 63:6; Eze 35:15; Am 1:11-12; Ob 1:16; Hab 2:16 **4:22** [q] Isa 40:2; Jer 33:8 [r] S Ps 137:7; Eze 25:12-14; Mal 1:4 **5:1** [s] Ps 44:13-16; 89:50 **5:2** [t] Ps 79:1 [u] S Ps 109:11 [v] Zep 1:13 [w] Jer 17:4 **5:3** [x] S Ex 22:24; Jer 15:8; S 18:21 **5:4** [y] S Isa 55:1; Eze 4:16-17 [z] Isa 3:1 **5:5** [a] S Ne 9:37; Isa 47:6 [b] S Jos 1:13 **5:6** [c] Jer 2:36; Hos 5:13; 7:11; 9:3 **5:7** [d] S Jer 31:29 [e] Jer 14:20; 16:12 **5:8** [f] Ne 5:15

4:13 SINS OF HER PROPHETS. Judah's tragic condition was brought on by her own sins, of which Jeremiah lists two key categories: (1) the corruption of those who claimed to be spiritual leaders (see Jer 26:7–11,16; Eze 22:26,28), and (2) the people's trust in human and political alliances rather than in God (v. 17).

4:22 YOUR PUNISHMENT WILL END. Jeremiah prophesies that Judah's captivity would come to an end when God's purpose for her affliction was achieved.

5:1–22 REMEMBER, O LORD. The last chapter of Lamentations is an intercessory prayer in which Jeremiah acknowledges that even though God is responsible for Jerusalem's judgment and calamity, he will yet listen to their cry, accept their sincere confession of sin, and respond in mercy and favor.

5:2–18 TURNED OVER TO ALIENS. The author vividly describes the desperate physical and emotional condition of the exiles. Persecution and fear were common experiences for them.

and there is none to free us
from their hands.[g]
9We get our bread at the risk of our
lives
because of the sword in the
desert.
10Our skin is hot as an oven,
feverish from hunger.[h]
11Women have been ravished[i] in
Zion,
and virgins in the towns of
Judah.
12Princes have been hung up by
their hands;
elders[j] are shown no respect.[k]
13Young men toil at the millstones;
boys stagger under loads of
wood.
14The elders are gone from the city
gate;
the young men have stopped
their music.[l]
15Joy is gone from our hearts;
our dancing has turned to
mourning.[m]
16The crown[n] has fallen from our
head.[o]
Woe to us, for we have sinned![p]
17Because of this our hearts[q] are
faint,[r]
because of these things our
eyes[s] grow dim[t]
18for Mount Zion,[u] which lies
desolate,[v]
with jackals prowling over
it.

19You, O LORD, reign forever;[w]
your throne endures[x] from
generation to generation.
20Why do you always forget us?[y]
Why do you forsake[z] us so
long?
21Restore[a] us to yourself, O LORD,
that we may return;
renew our days as of old
22unless you have utterly rejected
us[b]
and are angry with us beyond
measure.[c]

5:8 [g]Zec 11:6
5:10 [h]S Job 30:30; S La 4:8-9
5:11 [i]S Ge 34:29; Zec 14:2
5:12 [j]S Lev 19:32 [k]S La 2:6; 4:16
5:14 [l]S Isa 24:8; Jer 7:34
5:15 [m]S Jer 25:10; Am 8:10
5:16 [n]Ps 89:39; S Jer 13:18 [o]S Job 19:9 [p]S Isa 3:11; Jer 14:20
5:17 [q]S Isa 1:5 [r]S Jer 8:18 [s]Ps 6:7 [t]S Job 16:8
5:18 [u]Ps 74:2-3 [v]S Isa 27:10; Mic 3:12
5:19 [w]S 1Ch 16:31 [x]S Ps 45:6; 102:12,24-27
5:20 [y]S Ps 13:1; 44:24 [z]S Ps 71:11
5:21 [a]S Ps 80:3; Isa 60:20-22
5:22 [b]S Ps 53:5; 60:1-2; S Jer 6:30 [c]S Isa 64:9

5:21–22 RESTORE US TO YOURSELF. The book of Lamentations ends in a prayer that expresses hope for God's mercy. It teaches us to call on God in the worst of circumstances, even when we are under his chastising hand.

EZEKIEL

Outline

I. Ezekiel's Call and Commissioning (1:1—3:27)
  A. Envisioned by the Glory of God (1:1–28)
  B. Commissioned for the Prophetic Word (2:1—3:27)
II. The Prophetic Message of Judgment for Judah and Jerusalem (4:1—24:27)
  A. Prophetic Signs of Coming Judgment (4:1—5:17)
    1. A Clay Tablet (4:1–3)
    2. Ezekiel Lies on His Side (4:4–8)
    3. The Bread of Scarcity (4:9–17)
    4. The Divine Razor (5:1–17)
  B. Prophetic Messages of Coming Judgment (6:1—7:27)
  C. Prophetic Visions of Coming Judgment (8:1—11:25)
    1. Vision of Detestable Things in the Temple (8:1–18)
    2. Vision of Jerusalem's Destruction (9:1–11)
    3. Vision of God's Departing Glory (10:1–22)
    4. Vision of Wicked Rulers and Departed Glory (11:1–25)
  D. Prophetic Signs, Messages and Parables of Coming Judgment (12:1—24:27)
    1. Signs of Jerusalem's Exile (12:1–28)
    2. Message Against False Prophets (13:1–23)
    3. Message Against Idolatrous Elders (14:1–23)
    4. Parables of the Useless Vine (15:1–8), Adulterous Women (16:1–23) and Two Eagles (17:1–24)
    5. A Lesson (18:1–32) and a Lament (19:1–14)
    6. Further Messages and Signs of the Judgment of Jerusalem (20:1—24:27)
III. The Prophetic Message of Judgment for Foreign Nations (25:1—32:32)
  A. Ammon (25:1–7)
  B. Moab (25:8–11)
  C. Edom (25:12–14)
  D. Philistia (25:15–17)
  E. Tyre (26:1—28:19)
  F. Sidon (28:20–26)
  G. Egypt (29:1—32:32)
IV. The Prophetic Message of Restoration (33:1—48:35)
  A. The Watchman of Restoration (33:1–33)
  B. The Promises of Restoration (34:1—39:28)
  C. The Vision of Restoration (40:1—48:35)

Author: Ezekiel

Theme: God's Judgment and Glory

Date of Writing: 590–570 B.C.

Background

The historical setting for the book of Ezekiel is Babylon during the early years of the Babylonian exile (593–571 B.C.). Nebuchadnezzar took Jewish captives from Jerusalem to Babylon in three stages: (1) In 605 B.C., select Jewish youth were deported to Babylon, among whom were Daniel and his three friends; (2) in 597 B.C., 10,000 captives were taken to Babylon, among whom was Ezekiel; and (3) in 586 B.C., Nebuchadnezzar's forces totally destroyed both the city and the temple, with most of its surviving inhabitants carried off to Babylon. Ezekiel's prophetic ministry occurred during the darkest hour of OT history: the seven years preceding the 586 B.C. destruction (593–586 B.C.) and the 15 years following it (586–571 B.C.). The book was probably completed c. 570 B.C.

Ezekiel, whose name means "God strengthens," was from a priestly family (1:3) and spent his first 25 years in Jerusalem. He was in priestly training for service in the temple when he was taken captive to Babylon in 597 B.C. About five years later, at age 30 (1:2–3), Ezekiel received his prophetic call and divine commissioning, after which he faithfully ministered for at least 22 years (29:17); Ezekiel was about age 17 when Daniel was deported, making the two men virtually the same age. Both Ezekiel and Daniel were younger contemporaries of Jeremiah and most likely were influenced considerably by the older Jerusalem prophet (cf. Da 9:2). By the time Ezekiel arrived in Babylon, Daniel was already well known as a man of extraordinary prophetic wisdom; Ezekiel refers to him three times in his book (14:14,20; 28:3). Unlike Daniel, Ezekiel was married (24:15–18) and lived as a private citizen among the Jewish exiles by the Kebar River (1:1; 3:15,24; cf. Ps 137:1).

The book clearly attributes its prophecies to Ezekiel by name (1:3; 24:24). The use of the personal pronoun "I" throughout the book, along with the book's unity in style and language, point to sole authorship by Ezekiel. His prophecies can be dated with precision because of his orderly method of dating (cf. 1:1–2; 8:1; 20:1; 24:1; 26:1; 29:1,17; 30:20; 31:1; 32:1,17; 33:21; 40:1). His ministry began in July, 593 B.C. and continued at least until the last recorded prophecy in April, 571 B.C.

Purpose

The purpose of Ezekiel's prophecies was primarily twofold: (1) to deliver God's message of judgment to apostate Judah and Jerusalem (chs. 1—24) and to seven foreign nations around her (chs. 25—32) and (2) to sustain the faith of God's remnant in exile concerning the restoration of his covenant people and the final glory of his kingdom (chs. 33—48). The prophet also emphasized the personal responsibility of each individual before God rather than passing off the exilic judgment as simply the result of their ancestors' sins (18:1–32; 33:10–20).

Survey

Ezekiel's book is well-organized, and its 48 chapters divide naturally into four major sections. (1) The introductory section (chs. 1—3) describes Ezekiel's powerful vision of God's glory and throne (ch. 1) and the prophet's subsequent divine commissioning for the prophetic ministry (chs. 2—3); note Moses' experience at the burning bush (Ex 3—4) and Isaiah's vision in the temple (Isa 6) as similar momentous revelations of God at the outset of their prophetic missions.

(2) The second section (chs. 4—24) records Ezekiel's hard-hitting and hope-crushing message of Judah's and Jerusalem's inescapable approaching judgment because of their persistent rebellion and apostasy. During Jerusalem's last seven years (593–586 B.C.), Ezekiel warned the Jews in Jerusalem and the captives in Babylon against any false hope that Jerusalem would survive judgment. Jerusalem's past and present sins made her present doom certain. Ezekiel thunders this prophetic message of doom through various visions, parables and symbolic actions. Chs. 8—11 describe God's transporting Ezekiel to Jerusalem in a vision where he delivers prophecies to the city. In ch. 24, the death of Ezekiel's own beloved wife served as a parable and a sign of Jerusalem's end.

(3) The third section (chs. 25—32) contains prophecies of judgment against seven foreign nations that were rejoicing over Judah's calamity. In the exceptionally long prophecy against Tyre appears a veiled description of Satan (28:11–19) as the real power behind the king of Tyre.

(4) The book's final section (chs. 33—48) marks a transition in the prophet's message from gloomy judgment to comfort and future hope (cf. Isa 40—66). After Jerusalem's fall, Ezekiel prophesies about future revival and restoration, when God would be the true shepherd of his people (ch. 34) and give them a "new heart" and a "new spirit" (ch. 36). In this context occurs Ezekiel's famous vision of a whole army of dead bones being prophetically resurrected to life (ch. 37). The book concludes by describing the eschatological restoration of the holy temple, holy city and holy land (chs. 40—48).

Special Features

Seven major features characterize the book of Ezekiel. (1) It abounds in mysterious visions, daring parables and weird symbolic actions as media for God's prophetic revelation. (2) Its contents are carefully arranged and dated; it contains more dates than any other OT prophetic book. (3) Two distinctive phrases occur throughout the book: (a)"Then they will know that I am the LORD" (65 occurrences with its variations) and (b) "the glory of the LORD" (19 occurrences with its variations). (4) Ezekiel is characteristically addressed by God as "son of man" or "watchman." (5) This book records two extraordinary visions of the temple—one as desecrated and awaiting destruction (chs. 8—11) and the other as purified and perfectly restored (chs. 40—48). (6) More than any other prophet, Ezekiel was required by God to identify himself personally with the prophetic word by acting it out in prophetic symbolism. (7) Ezekiel emphasizes the individual's personal responsibility and accountability to God.

New Testament Fulfillment

The message of chs. 33—48 essentially concerns God's future redemptive work as revealed in the NT. It speaks not only of Israel's physical restoration to their land, but also of a final future restoration that involves the full realization of God's destiny for spiritual Israel in relation to God's glory and power in the temple (worship), and God's destiny for the nations as a result of missions. Important prophecies in Ezekiel about the NT Messiah are 17:22–24; 21:26–27; 34:23–24; 36:16–38 and 37:1–28.

Reading Ezekiel

In order to read the entire Old Testament in one year, the book of Ezekiel should be read in 22 days, according to the following schedule: ☐ 1–2 ☐ 3–4 ☐ 5–7 ☐ 8–10 ☐ 11–12 ☐ 13–15 ☐ 16 ☐ 17–19 ☐ 20–21 ☐ 22–23 ☐ 24–26 ☐ 27–28 ☐ 29–30 ☐ 31–32 ☐ 33–34 ☐ 35–36 ☐ 37–38 ☐ 39–40 ☐ 41–42 ☐ 43–44 ☐ 45–46 ☐ 47–48

NOTES

The Living Creatures and the Glory of the LORD

1 In the[a] thirtieth year, in the
fourth month on the fifth day,
while I was among the exiles[a] by the
Kebar River,[b] the heavens were
opened[c] and I saw visions[d] of God.
2On the fifth of the month—it was
the fifth year of the exile of King Jehoiachin[e]— 3the word of the LORD came
to Ezekiel[f] the priest, the son of
Buzi,[b] by the Kebar River in the land
of the Babylonians.[c] There the hand
of the LORD was upon him.[g]
4I looked, and I saw a windstorm[h]
coming out of the north[i]—an immense cloud with flashing lightning
and surrounded by brilliant light. The
center of the fire looked like glowing
metal,[j] 5and in the fire was what
looked like four living creatures.[k] In
appearance their form was that of a
man,[l] 6but each of them had four
faces[m] and four wings. 7Their legs
were straight; their feet were like
those of a calf and gleamed like burnished bronze.[n] 8Under their wings on
their four sides they had the hands of
a man.[o] All four of them had faces and
wings, 9and their wings touched one
another. Each one went straight
ahead; they did not turn as they
moved.[p]
10Their faces looked like this: Each
of the four had the face of a man, and
on the right side each had the face of
a lion, and on the left the face of an ox;
each also had the face of an eagle.[q]
11Such were their faces. Their wings[r]
were spread out upward; each had two
wings, one touching the wing of another creature on either side, and two
wings covering its body. 12Each one
went straight ahead. Wherever the
spirit would go, they would go, without
turning as they went.[s] 13The appearance of the living creatures was like
burning coals[t] of fire or like torches.
Fire moved back and forth among the
creatures; it was bright, and lightning[u] flashed out of it. 14The creatures sped back and forth like flashes
of lightning.[v]
15As I looked at the living creatures,[w] I saw a wheel[x] on the ground
beside each creature with its four
faces. 16This was the appearance and
structure of the wheels: They sparkled
like chrysolite,[y] and all four looked
alike. Each appeared to be made like a

1:1 [a] S Dt 21:10; Eze 11:24-25 [b] S Ps 137:1 [c] S Mt 3:16 [d] S Ex 24:10
1:2 [e] S 2Ki 24:15
1:3 [f] Eze 24:24 [g] S 2Ki 3:15; Isa 8:11; Eze 3:14, 22; 8:1; 33:22; 37:1; 40:1
1:4 [h] S Job 38:1 [i] Jer 1:14 [j] Eze 8:2
1:5 [k] S Isa 6:2; Rev 4:6 [l] ver 26; Da 7:13
1:6 [m] Eze 10:14
1:7 [n] Eze 40:3; Da 10:6; S Rev 1:15
1:8 [o] Eze 10:8
1:9 [p] Eze 10:22
1:10 [q] Eze 10:14; Rev 4:7
1:11 [r] Isa 6:2
1:12 [s] Eze 10:16-19
1:13 [t] S 2Sa 22:9 [u] Rev 4:5
1:14 [v] S Ps 29:7
1:15 [w] Eze 3:13 [x] Eze 10:2; Da 7:9
1:16 [y] S Ex 28:20

[a] *1* Or ⌞*my*⌟ [b] *3* Or *Ezekiel son of Buzi the priest* [c] *3* Or *Chaldeans*

1:1 THE THIRTIETH YEAR. This designation most likely refers to Ezekiel's age. At that time he was living among the exiles in Babylon, having been brought there in 597 B.C., nine years after Daniel had arrived and 11 years before Jerusalem was destroyed. Ezekiel was called to be a prophet during the captivity, proclaiming God's message to the exiles at the same time that Jeremiah was preaching in Jerusalem. Ezekiel ministered for at least 27 years; Judah's Babylonian captivity lasted approximately 70 years (from 605 to 538 B.C.).

1:3 WORD OF THE LORD CAME TO EZEKIEL. Ezekiel the priest received his prophetic calling in 593 B.C., four years after his arrival in Babylon. He evidently had settled by the Kebar River, possibly a ship canal on the Euphrates about fifty miles southeast of Babylon. His mission was to explain the reason for the captivity, foretell Jerusalem's fall, bring the exiled people back to God and give them hope through God's promise of restoration.

1:4 I LOOKED. Ezekiel is given a vision of God's glory and holiness (see v. 28, note). Visions were essential for his ministry to the exiles.

1:5 FOUR LIVING CREATURES. These creatures are later identified as cherubim (10:20). Cherubim are angelic beings who manifest the holiness and glory of God to humans (cf. 1Ch 28:18; Ps 18:10; see article on ANGELS AND THE ANGEL OF THE LORD, p. 340). They may accompany God at times of judgment or blessing; they guarded the Garden of Eden after the fall (Ge 3:22–24), and images of cherubim appeared on the atonement cover of the ark (Ex 25:18–22). In Ezekiel's vision the cherubim were manifesting God's glory and holiness to the exiles.

1:10 FACES LOOKED LIKE THIS. The faces of a man, a lion, an ox and an eagle represent God's living creation (cf. Rev 4:7). In the new heavens and new earth all of God's creation, having been fully redeemed from sin's curse, will manifest his glory.

1:12 THE SPIRIT. The cherubim are directed by "the spirit," which most likely refers to the Spirit of God (cf. v. 20).

1:13 BURNING COALS OF FIRE. These coals point to God's holiness (cf. Ex 3:1–5) and to his judgment that punishes sin (cf. Rev 20:14–15). The fire moving back and forth symbolizes the energy and power of the Spirit, who is always active and never rests.

1:16–25 STRUCTURE OF THE WHEELS. Ezekiel sees a supernatural throne-chariot in constant motion. God is pictured on an ever-moving mobile throne that goes wherever the Spirit commands; the imagery symbolizes both God's sovereignty over all things and his presence throughout his creation. He is present with the exiles by the Kebar River.

wheel intersecting a wheel. **17**As they
moved, they would go in any one of the
four directions the creatures faced; the
wheels did not turn[z] about[d] as the
creatures went. **18**Their rims were high
and awesome, and all four rims were
full of eyes[a] all around.
19When the living creatures moved,
the wheels beside them moved; and
when the living creatures rose from the
ground, the wheels also rose. **20**Wherever the spirit would go, they would
go,[b] and the wheels would rise along
with them, because the spirit of the living creatures was in the wheels.
21When the creatures moved, they also
moved; when the creatures stood still,
they also stood still; and when the
creatures rose from the ground, the
wheels rose along with them, because
the spirit of the living creatures was in
the wheels.[c]
22Spread out above the heads of the
living creatures was what looked like
an expanse,[d] sparkling like ice, and
awesome. **23**Under the expanse their
wings were stretched out one toward
the other, and each had two wings covering its body. **24**When the creatures
moved, I heard the sound of their
wings, like the roar of rushing[e] waters, like the voice[f] of the Almighty,[e]
like the tumult of an army.[g] When
they stood still, they lowered their
wings.
25Then there came a voice from
above the expanse over their heads as
they stood with lowered wings.
26Above the expanse over their heads
was what looked like a throne[h] of sapphire,[f][i] and high above on the
throne was a figure like that of a
man.[j] **27**I saw that from what appeared to be his waist up he looked like
glowing metal, as if full of fire, and that
from there down he looked like fire;
and brilliant light surrounded him.[k]
28Like the appearance of a rainbow[l]
in the clouds on a rainy day, so was the
radiance around him.[m]
This was the appearance of the likeness of the glory[n] of the LORD. When
I saw it, I fell facedown,[o] and I heard
the voice of one speaking.

Ezekiel's Call

2 He said to me, "Son of man,[p]
stand[q] up on your feet and I will
speak to you.[r]" **2**As he spoke, the
Spirit came into me and raised me[s] to
my feet, and I heard him speaking to
me.
3He said: "Son of man, I am sending
you to the Israelites, to a rebellious nation that has rebelled against me; they
and their fathers have been in revolt
against me to this very day.[t] **4**The
people to whom I am sending you are
obstinate and stubborn.[u] Say to them,
'This is what the Sovereign LORD
says.'[v] **5**And whether they listen or
fail to listen[w]—for they are a rebel-

1:17 [z] ver 9
1:18 [a] Rev 4:6
1:20 [b] ver 12
1:21 [c] Eze 10:9-12
1:22 [d] Eze 10:1
1:24 [e] S Ps 46:3; Eze 3:13 [f] Eze 10:5; 43:2; Da 10:6; Rev 1:15; 14:2; 19:6 [g] S 2Ki 7:6
1:26 [h] S 1Ki 22:19; Isa 6:1; S Jer 3:17 [i] S Ex 24:10 [j] S ver 5; S Eze 2:1; S Rev 1:13
1:27 [k] Eze 8:2
1:28 [l] S Ge 9:13; Rev 10:1 [m] S Rev 4:2 [n] S Ex 16:7; S 24:16; Lk 2:9 [o] S Ge 17:3; S Nu 14:5
2:1 [p] S Job 25:6; Ps 8:4; S Eze 1:26; Da 7:13; 8:15 [q] Da 10:11; Ac 14:10; 26:16 [r] Ac 9:6
2:2 [s] Eze 3:24; Da 8:18
2:3 [t] S Jer 3:25; Eze 5:6; 20:8-24; 24:3
2:4 [u] S Ex 32:9; S Isa 9:9; Eze 3:7 [v] Am 7:15
2:5 [w] Eze 3:11

[d] *17* Or *aside* [e] *24* Hebrew *Shaddai* [f] *26* Or *lapis lazuli*

1:26 FIGURE LIKE THAT OF A MAN. Ezekiel sees God sitting on the throne in the likeness of a man; this vision points to the fact that when God chose to reveal himself fully, he did so in human form—through Jesus Christ (cf. Php 2:5–7; Col 2:9).

1:28 THE GLORY OF THE LORD. This verse gives the significance of the entire vision: it was a vision of God's glory (see article on THE GLORY OF GOD, p. 1192). (1) God revealed his glory and power to Ezekiel to prepare him for the work to which he was calling him. The Lord would continue to appear to Ezekiel throughout his life in order to sustain him in that ministry (3:12,23–24; 8:2–4; 9:3; 10:1–22; 11:22–23; 43:2–4). (2) The appearance of God's glory to Ezekiel indicated that it had left the temple in Jerusalem (cf. 1Ki 8:11; Ps 26:8; 63:2) and was now being manifested to the exiles. Ezekiel later prophesied that God's glory would return to Canaan and Jerusalem (see 43:2–3,7). (3) Just as Ezekiel needed a vision of God's glory to prepare him to serve the Lord, so we too must experience the power of God's glory and holiness (cf. Isa 6) before we can actively enter into his work. We receive an understanding of God in all his glory through Jesus Christ (cf. Jn 1:14), through the Holy Spirit (1Pe 4:14) and through God's Word (2Co 3:7–11; see Ac 1:8, notes).

2:1 SON OF MAN. God refers to Ezekiel more than 90 times as "son of man." This title emphasized the prophet's humanity and weakness and reminded him that he was dependent on the Spirit's enabling power to fulfill his ministry. Jesus also used this title to refer to himself (Mt 8:20; 9:6; 11:19; Mk 2:28; 8:31,38; 9:9; Lk 5:24; Jn 3:13), emphasizing his relationship with humankind and his dependence on the Holy Spirit (cf. Da 8:17).

2:2 THE SPIRIT CAME INTO ME. Ezekiel is empowered by the Spirit of God in order to proclaim God's message. Then and now, God requires that his people be empowered by the Holy Spirit in order to preach the gospel effectively to all nations (see Ac 1:8, 2:4).

2:5 A PROPHET HAS BEEN AMONG THEM. God wants genuine and faithful servants to proclaim his word to the people. They must speak all

lious house[x]—they will know that a prophet has been among them.[y] **6**And you, son of man, do not be afraid[z] of them or their words. Do not be afraid, though briers and thorns[a] are all around you and you live among scorpions. Do not be afraid of what they say or terrified by them, though they are a rebellious house.[b] **7**You must speak[c] my words to them, whether they listen or fail to listen, for they are rebellious.[d] **8**But you, son of man, listen to what I say to you. Do not rebel[ef] like that rebellious house;[g] open your mouth and eat[h] what I give you."

9Then I looked, and I saw a hand[i] stretched out to me. In it was a scroll,[j] **10**which he unrolled before me. On both sides of it were written words of lament and mourning and woe.[k]

3 And he said to me, "Son of man, eat what is before you, eat this scroll; then go and speak to the house of Israel." **2**So I opened my mouth, and he gave me the scroll to eat.

3Then he said to me, "Son of man, eat this scroll I am giving you and fill your stomach with it." So I ate[l] it, and it tasted as sweet as honey[m] in my mouth.

4He then said to me: "Son of man, go now to the house of Israel and speak my words to them.[n] **5**You are not being sent to a people of obscure speech and difficult language,[o] but to the house of Israel— **6**not to many peoples of obscure speech and difficult language, whose words you cannot understand. Surely if I had sent you to them, they would have listened to you.[p] **7**But the house of Israel is not willing to listen[q] to you because they are not willing to listen to me, for the whole house of Israel is hardened and obstinate.[r] **8**But I will make you as unyielding and hardened as they are.[s] **9**I will make your forehead[t] like the hardest stone, harder than flint.[u] Do not be afraid of them or terrified by them, though they are a rebellious house.[v]"

10And he said to me, "Son of man, listen carefully and take to heart[w] all the words I speak to you. **11**Go[x] now to your countrymen in exile and speak to them. Say to them, 'This is what the Sovereign LORD says,'[y] whether they listen or fail to listen.[z]" Eze 33:7-11

12Then the Spirit lifted me up,[a] and I heard behind me a loud rumbling sound—May the glory of the LORD be praised in his dwelling place!— **13**the sound of the wings of the living creatures[b] brushing against each other and the sound of the wheels beside them, a loud rumbling sound.[c] **14**The Spirit[d] then lifted me up[e] and took me away, and I went in bitterness and in the anger of my spirit, with the strong hand of the LORD[f] upon me. **15**I came to the exiles who lived at Tel Abib near the Kebar River.[g] And there, where they were living, I sat among them for seven days[h]—overwhelmed.

Warning to Israel

16At the end of seven days the word of the LORD came to me:[i] **17**"Son of man, I have made you a watchman[j] for the house of Israel; so hear the word I speak and give them warning from me.[k] **18**When I say to a wicked man, 'You will surely die,[l]' and you do

2:5 [x]Eze 3:27 [y]S Jer 5:3; Eze 33:33; Jn 15:22
2:6 [z]S Dt 31:6; S 2Ki 1:15 [a]S Nu 33:55; Isa 9:18; Mic 7:4 [b]S Isa 1:2; 30:9; Eze 24:3; 44:6
2:7 [c]Jer 7:27 [d]Jer 1:7; S 42:21; Eze 3:10-11
2:8 [e]Nu 20:10-13 [f]Isa 8:11 [g]S Isa 50:5 [h]Ps 81:10; S Jer 15:16; Rev 10:9
2:9 [i]Eze 8:3 [j]S Ps 40:7; S Jer 36:4; Rev 5:1-5; 10:8-10
2:10 [k]Isa 3:11; Rev 8:13
3:3 [l]S Jer 15:16 [m]S Ps 19:10; Rev 10:9-10
3:4 [n]Eze 11:4,25
3:5 [o]S Isa 28:11; Jnh 1:2
3:6 [p]Jnh 3:5-10; Mt 11:21-23; Ac 13:46-48
3:7 [q]S Jer 7:27 [r]Isa 48:4; Jer 3:3; S Eze 2:4; Jn 15:20-23
3:8 [s]Jer 1:18; S 15:20
3:9 [t]S Isa 48:4 [u]S Jer 5:3 [v]Isa 50:7; Eze 2:6; 44:6; Mic 3:8
3:10 [w]S Job 22:22
3:11 [x]S Isa 6:9 [y]ver 27 [z]Eze 2:4-5,7; 11:24-25
3:12 [a]ver 14; Eze 8:3; 43:5
3:13 [b]Eze 1:15 [c]Eze 1:24; 10:5, 16-17
3:14 [d]S 1Ki 18:12 [e]S ver 12 [f]ver 22; S Isa 8:11; Eze 37:1
3:15 [g]S Ps 137:1 [h]S Ge 50:10
3:16 [i]Jer 42:7
3:17 [j]S Isa 52:8 [k]S Isa 58:1; Jer 1:17; Eze 11:4; Hab 2:1
3:18 [l]S Ge 2:17; Jn 8:21,24

---

that God wants them to speak without fear or compromise; their message must not be determined by the people's response, but rather be spoken out of an absolute loyalty to God and his truth (v. 7). If some in their audience are determined to resist God and his law, so be it; the prophets must continue to speak God's words, rebuke sin and rebellion, and call the people to faithfulness to the Lord.

2:10 WORDS OF LAMENT. Ezekiel's initial message was to be one of judgment, which would produce lament in the people who heard.

3:1 EAT THIS SCROLL. On the scroll were the words and judgments of God for his people. Ezekiel's eating the scroll symbolized that he had to receive God's message and commit himself to it before proclaiming it.

3:3 AS HONEY IN MY MOUTH. Although Ezekiel was to bring a message of destruction and lament, God caused it to be as sweet as honey to the prophet himself. The word of God, simply because it is his word, will be loved and valued by all who are committed to God and his cause.

3:7 NOT WILLING TO LISTEN. The people would not believe Ezekiel's prophetic message of judgment on Jerusalem, for they were still hardened to the truth. To enable Ezekiel to face that coming rejection, God promised to give him courage and the determination to proclaim God's prophetic word in all circumstances (vv. 8–9).

3:14 I WENT IN BITTERNESS. Ezekiel shows great sadness because of the impending calamities God had commissioned him to announce. Though deeply disturbed, he remained faithful to his calling. One sure sign that we are in a right relation-

not warn him or speak out to dissuade
him from his evil ways in order to save
his life, that wicked man will die for[g]
his sin, and I will hold you accountable
for his blood.[m] 19But if you do warn
the wicked man and he does not turn[n]
from his wickedness[o] or from his evil
ways, he will die[p] for his sin; but you
will have saved yourself.[q]

20"Again, when a righteous man
turns[r] from his righteousness and
does evil, and I put a stumbling block[s]
before him, he will die. Since you did
not warn him, he will die for his sin.
The righteous things he did will not be
remembered, and I will hold you accountable for his blood.[t] 21But if you
do warn the righteous man not to sin
and he does not sin, he will surely live
Eze 18:21-23 because he took warning, and you will
have saved yourself.[u]"

22The hand of the LORD[v] was upon
me there, and he said to me, "Get up
and go[w] out to the plain,[x] and there
I will speak to you." 23So I got up and
went out to the plain. And the glory of
the LORD was standing there, like the
glory I had seen by the Kebar River,[y]
and I fell facedown.[z]

24Then the Spirit came into me and
raised me[a] to my feet. He spoke to me
and said: "Go, shut yourself inside your
house.[b] 25And you, son of man, they
will tie with ropes; you will be bound so
that you cannot go out among the people.[c] 26I will make your tongue stick
to the roof[d] of your mouth so that you
will be silent and unable to rebuke
them, though they are a rebellious
house.[e] 27But when I speak to you, I
will open your mouth and you shall say
to them, 'This is what the Sovereign
LORD says.'[f] Whoever will listen let
him listen, and whoever will refuse let
him refuse; for they are a rebellious
house.[g]

Siege of Jerusalem Symbolized

4 "Now, son of man, take a clay tablet, put it in front of you and draw
the city of Jerusalem on it. 2Then lay
siege to it: Erect siege works against
it, build a ramp[h] up to it, set up camps
against it and put battering rams
around it.[i] 3Then take an iron pan,[j]
place it as an iron wall between you
and the city and turn your face toward[k] it. It will be under siege, and
you shall besiege it. This will be a
sign[l] to the house of Israel.[m]

4"Then lie on your left side and put
the sin of the house of Israel upon

3:18 [m] ver 20 **3:19** [n] S Ps 7:12 [o] S Ge 6:5 [p] S Jer 42:16 [q] S 2Ki 17:13; Eze 14:14,20; Ac 18:6; 20:26; 1Ti 4:14-16 **3:20** [r] S Jer 34:16 [s] S Lev 26:37; S Isa 8:14; S Eze 7:19 [t] ver 18; Ps 125:5; Eze 18:24; 33:12, 18 **3:21** [u] Ac 20:31 **3:22** [v] S ver 14; S Eze 1:3 [w] Ac 9:6 [x] Eze 8:4 **3:23** [y] Eze 1:1 [z] S Ge 17:3 **3:24** [a] S Eze 2:2 [b] Jer 15:17 **3:25** [c] Eze 4:8 **3:26** [d] S Ps 22:15 [e] Eze 2:5; 24:27; 33:22; Hos 4:4 **3:27** [f] ver 11 [g] Eze 2:5; 12:3; 24:27; 29:21; 33:22; Rev 22:11 **4:2** [h] S Jer 6:6; Eze 17:17; Da 11:15 [i] S Jer 33:4; Eze 21:22 **4:3** [j] S Lev 2:5 [k] ver 7; Eze 20:46; 21:2 [l] S Isa 8:18; S 20:3; Jer 13:1-7; 18:1-4; 19:1-2; Eze 5:1-4; 12:3-6 [m] S Jer 39:1

[g] *18* Or *in*; also in verses 19 and 20

ship to God is that we begin to love righteousness and hate wickedness to the same extent that God does (see Heb 1:9, note).

3:18 THAT WICKED MAN WILL DIE. Ezekiel was to be a watchman, warning his countrymen that those who persisted in sin and in rejection of God would be punished with death. If Ezekiel failed to warn the wicked, he would be held accountable for their death. (1) Under the new covenant, faithful ministers of God must likewise warn those in their congregations who are living unrighteous lives that they will be excluded from God's kingdom and salvation if they do not repent (see 1Co 6:9, note; Gal 5:21, note; Eph 5:5, note). Those who teach that believers may live immoral and unrighteous lives without jeopardizing their eternal salvation will themselves face God's severe judgment.

(2) We must always remember that God has given us the commission to go into all the world and proclaim the gospel (Mt 28:18–20; Ac 1:8), which includes the warning of eternal death for all who refuse to repent and believe in Christ (cf. Ac 17:22–31); God has thus made the church a watchman (see Mt 18:15, note).

3:20 HE WILL DIE. A righteous person who turns from God, begins to live wickedly, and refuses to repent will experience God's judgment and die. Note the words of the apostle Paul: "If you live according to the sinful nature, you will die," i.e., receive eternal death (Ro 8:13).

3:26 YOU WILL BE SILENT. Ezekiel was restrained from speaking to the people except when he received a direct message from the Lord. Because the people had refused to hear and obey what the prophets were saying, God deprived them of his word by imposing silence on Ezekiel. Denying his people the divine oracle was a powerful manifestation of God's judgment on them for their persistent wickedness (see Am 8:11, note). Ezekiel's muteness lasted approximately seven and one-half years, until the fall of Jerusalem (24:27; 33:22).

4:1 TAKE A CLAY TABLET. Ezekiel was commanded to symbolize the siege of Jerusalem and the resulting exile by specific actions. He portrayed these events by making a small model of the siege. The iron pan (v. 3) may represent the unbreakable strength of the Babylonians. Through this action, Ezekiel impressed on the people that God himself would bring the Babylonians against Jerusalem.

4:4 LIE ON YOUR LEFT SIDE. God instructed Ezekiel to bear, in a symbolic way, the punishment God intended for Israel's and Judah's sin (see next note). Each day that Ezekiel lay on his side represented one year of their sin. He did not lie on his side all day long, however, for he had other duties to perform (vv. 9–17).

yourself.[h] You are to bear their sin for
the number of days you lie on your
side. 5I have assigned you the same
number of days as the years of their
sin. So for 390 days you will bear the
sin of the house of Israel.
6"After you have finished this, lie
down again, this time on your right
side, and bear the sin[n] of the house of
Judah. I have assigned you 40 days, a
day for each year.[o] 7Turn your face[p]
toward the siege of Jerusalem and with
bared arm prophesy against her. 8I will
tie you up with ropes so that you cannot turn from one side to the other until you have finished the days of your
siege.[q]
9"Take wheat and barley, beans and
lentils, millet and spelt;[r] put them in
a storage jar and use them to make
bread for yourself. You are to eat it during the 390 days you lie on your side.
10Weigh out twenty shekels[i][s] of food
to eat each day and eat it at set times.
11Also measure out a sixth of a hin[j]
of water and drink it at set times.[t]
12Eat the food as you would a barley
cake; bake it in the sight of the people,
using human excrement[u] for fuel."
13The LORD said, "In this way the people of Israel will eat defiled food among
the nations where I will drive them."[v]
14Then I said, "Not so, Sovereign
LORD![w] I have never defiled myself.
From my youth until now I have never
eaten anything found dead[x] or torn by
wild animals. No unclean meat has
ever entered my mouth.[y]"
15"Very well," he said, "I will let you
bake your bread over cow manure instead of human excrement."
16He then said to me: "Son of man,
I will cut off[z] the supply of food in
Jerusalem. The people will eat rationed
food in anxiety and drink rationed water in despair,[a] 17for food and water
will be scarce.[b] They will be appalled
at the sight of each other and will
waste away because of[k] their sin.[c]

5 "Now, son of man, take a sharp
sword and use it as a barber's razor[d] to shave[e] your head and your
beard.[f] Then take a set of scales and
divide up the hair. 2When the days of
your siege come to an end, burn a
third[g] of the hair with fire[h] inside the
city. Take a third and strike it with the
sword all around the city. And scatter
a third to the wind.[i] For I will pursue
them with drawn sword.[j] 3But take a
few strands of hair and tuck them away
in the folds of your garment.[k] 4Again,
take a few of these and throw them into
the fire[l] and burn them up. A fire will
spread from there to the whole house
of Israel.
5"This is what the Sovereign LORD
says: This is Jerusalem, which I have
set in the center of the nations, with
countries all around her.[m] 6Yet in her
wickedness she has rebelled against
my laws and decrees more than the nations and countries around her. She
has rejected my laws and has not followed my decrees.[n]
7"Therefore this is what the Sovereign LORD says: You have been more
unruly than the nations around you
and have not followed my decrees or
kept my laws. You have not even[l] conformed to the standards of the nations
around you.[o]
8"Therefore this is what the Sovereign LORD says: I myself am against
you, Jerusalem, and I will inflict punishment on you in the sight of the nations.[p] 9Because of all your detestable idols, I will do to you what I have

4:6 [n] S Ex 28:38 [o] Nu 14:34; Da 9:24-26; 12:11-12 **4:7** [p] S ver 3; Eze 6:2; S 13:17 **4:8** [q] Eze 3:25 **4:9** [r] S Isa 28:25 **4:10** [s] S Ex 30:13 **4:11** [t] ver 16 **4:12** [u] S Isa 36:12 **4:13** [v] Hos 9:3; Am 7:17 **4:14** [w] Jer 1:6; Eze 9:8; 20:49 [x] S Lev 11:39 [y] S Ex 22:31; Dt 14:3; 32:37-38; Da 1:8; Hos 9:3-4 **4:16** [z] S Ps 105:16 [a] ver 10-11; S Lev 26:26; Isa 3:1; Eze 12:19 **4:17** [b] La 5:4; Eze 5:16; 12:18-19; Am 4:8 [c] S Lev 26:39; Eze 24:23; 33:10 **5:1** [d] S Nu 6:5 [e] Eze 44:20 [f] S Lev 21:5; S 2Sa 10:4 **5:2** [g] Zec 13:8 [h] Jer 21:10; Eze 15:7 [i] ver 10; Jer 13:24 [j] ver 12; S Lev 26:33; S Jer 9:16; S 39:1-2 **5:3** [k] 2Ki 25:12; S Ps 74:11; Jer 39:10 **5:4** [l] Eze 10:7; 15:7 **5:5** [m] S Dt 4:6; S La 1:1; Eze 16:14 **5:6** [n] S 2Ki 17:15; Ne 9:17; Jer 11:10; S Eze 2:3; 16:47-51; Zec 7:11 **5:7** [o] S 2Ki 21:9; S 2Ch 33:9; Jer 2:10-11; Eze 16:47 **5:8** [p] S Jer 21:5, 13; 24:9; Eze 11:9; 15:7; Zec 14:2

[h] *4* Or *your side* [i] *10* That is, about 8 ounces (about 0.2 kilogram) [j] *11* That is, about 2/3 quart (about 0.6 liter) [k] *17* Or *away in* [l] *7* Most Hebrew manuscripts; some Hebrew manuscripts and Syriac *You have*

4:5 FOR 390 DAYS. The number of days assigned to Ezekiel for lying on his side corresponded to the years of Israel's and Judah's sin. The 390 years appear to encompass the period of the monarchy from Solomon to the fall of Jerusalem. The 40 additional years that were applied to Judah (v. 6) may represent the exceedingly wicked reign of Manasseh, which influenced Judah for the rest of its history (2Ki 21:11–15).

4:9–11 MAKE BREAD. The purpose of the meager food and drink was to symbolize the scarcity of provisions in Jerusalem during the siege (vv. 16–17); famine would be severe.

5:1–2 TAKE A SHARP SWORD. Ezekiel's shaved hair and beard, divided into three portions, symbolized the fate of Jerusalem's inhabitants. The third that was set on fire represented those who would die by plague or by famine; another third would die by the sword, and the final third would be scattered in exile (v. 12).

5:3 A FEW STRANDS. The few hairs tucked inside Ezekiel's garment represented a remnant of the people whom God would preserve; even some of these, however, would be burned and experience God's judgment (v. 4).

never done before and will never do
again.[q] **10**Therefore in your midst fathers will eat their children, and children will eat their fathers.[r] I will inflict punishment on you and will
scatter all your survivors to the
winds.[s] **11**Therefore as surely as I
live,[t] declares the Sovereign[u] LORD,
because you have defiled my sanctuary[v] with all your vile images[w] and
detestable practices,[x] I myself will
withdraw my favor; I will not look on
you with pity or spare you.[y] **12**A third
of your people will die of the plague or
perish by famine inside you; a third will
fall by the sword outside your walls;
and a third I will scatter to the winds[z]
and pursue with drawn sword.[a]

13"Then my anger will cease and my
wrath[b] against them will subside, and
I will be avenged.[c] And when I have
spent my wrath upon them, they will
know that I the LORD have spoken in
my zeal.[d]

14"I will make you a ruin and a reproach among the nations around you,
in the sight of all who pass by.[e] **15**You
will be a reproach[f] and a taunt, a
warning[g] and an object of horror to
the nations around you when I inflict
punishment on you in anger and in
wrath and with stinging rebuke.[h] I the
LORD have spoken.[i] **16**When I shoot at
you with my deadly and destructive arrows of famine, I will shoot to destroy
you. I will bring more and more famine
upon you and cut off your supply of
food.[j] **17**I will send famine and wild
beasts[k] against you, and they will
leave you childless. Plague and bloodshed[l] will sweep through you, and I
will bring the sword against you. I the
LORD have spoken.[m]"

A Prophecy Against the Mountains of Israel

6 The word of the LORD came to me:
2"Son of man, set your face[n]
against the mountains[o] of Israel;
prophesy against them[p] **3**and say: 'O
mountains of Israel, hear the word of
the Sovereign LORD. This is what the
Sovereign LORD says to the mountains
and hills, to the ravines and valleys:[q]
I am about to bring a sword against
you, and I will destroy your high
places.[r] **4**Your altars will be demolished and your incense altars[s] will be
smashed; and I will slay your people in
front of your idols.[t] **5**I will lay the
dead bodies of the Israelites in front of
their idols, and I will scatter your
bones[u] around your altars.[v] **6**Wherever you live,[w] the towns will be laid
waste and the high places[x] demolished, so that your altars will be laid
waste and devastated, your idols[y]
smashed and ruined, your incense altars[z] broken down, and what you have
made wiped out.[a] **7**Your people will
fall slain[b] among you, and you will
know that I am the LORD.[c]

8" 'But I will spare some, for some of
you will escape[d] the sword when you
are scattered among the lands and nations.[e] **9**Then in the nations where
they have been carried captive, those

5:9 [q]Da 9:12; S Mt 24:21 **5:10** [r]S Lev 26:29; S La 2:20 [s]S Lev 26:33; S Ps 44:11; S Jer 13:14; Eze 12:14 **5:11** [t]S Nu 14:21 [u]S Ge 15:2 [v]S Lev 15:31 [w]Eze 7:20; 11:18 [x]2Ch 36:14; Eze 8:6 [y]S Job 27:22; S Jer 16:18; S La 2:17; Eze 7:4,9; 8:18; 9:5 **5:12** [z]ver 10; Jer 13:24 [a]S ver 2, 17; S Ps 107:39; S Jer 15:2; S 21:9; Eze 6:11-12; 7:15; 12:14; Am 9:4; Zec 13:8; Rev 6:8 **5:13** [b]S 2Ch 12:7; S Job 20:23; Eze 21:17; 24:13 [c]S Isa 1:24 [d]S Isa 59:17; Eze 16:42; 38:19; Hos 10:10; Zec 6:8 **5:14** [e]S Lev 26:32; Ne 2:17; Ps 74:3-10; 79:1-4; Isa 64:11; Eze 6:6; 22:4; Da 9:16; Mic 3:12 **5:15** [f]S Isa 43:28 [g]S Dt 28:46 [h]S Dt 28:20; S 1Ki 9:7; S Jer 22:8-9; 24:9; Eze 14:8 [i]S Jer 23:40 **5:16** [j]S Lev 26:26; S Dt 32:24 **5:17** [k]Eze 14:15 [l]Eze 38:22 [m]S ver 12; S Lev 26:25; Eze 14:21; 28:23 **6:2** [n]S Eze 4:7 [o]Eze 18:6; Mic 6:1 [p]ver 13 **6:3** [q]Eze 36:4 [r]S Lev 26:30

6:4 [s]S 2Ch 14:5 [t]Eze 9:6; 14:3; 20:16 **6:5** [u]S Nu 19:16; S Ps 53:5; Jer 8:1-2 [v]ver 13; S Lev 26:30 **6:6** [w]S Ex 12:20 [x]Hos 10:8 [y]Eze 30:13; Mic 1:7; Zec 13:2 [z]S Lev 26:30 [a]S 1Sa 5:4; Isa 6:11; S Eze 5:14 **6:7** [b]Eze 9:7 [c]ver 10,13, 14; Eze 11:10-12 **6:8** [d]S Ps 68:20; S Jer 44:28 [e]S Ge 11:4; S Ps 44:11; Isa 6:13; S Jer 44:14; Eze 7:16; 12:16; 14:22

5:11 YOU HAVE DEFILED MY SANCTUARY. One of the major reasons God's anger was directed against Jerusalem was her defilement of the temple through idol worship (see chs. 8–11). The NT warns believers against this same terrible sin. The apostle Paul states that "if anyone destroys God's temple, God will destroy him" (1Co 3:17); in this passage, the temple refers to a local church or group of churches. People defile God's church by participating in its worship while living in sin and immorality, or by promoting unbiblical doctrines.

5:17 I THE LORD HAVE SPOKEN. Statements about God's determination to carry out his judgment against Judah occur some 60 times in the book of Ezekiel. We must not make God out to be One who is unwilling to punish those who defile his church (see previous note) or reject his ways. God keeps his word, and his threats of judgment will be fulfilled. For a more complete understanding of the outpouring of God's wrath in the future, see the book of Revelation.

6:4 YOUR IDOLS. The Israelites' chief sin against the Lord was their idolatry. They repeatedly spurned God's goodness and gave their worship and allegiance to other gods. Today people become guilty of idolatry whenever they seek satisfaction, pleasure, meaning or help in the sinful and secular things of this world (see Mt 6:19–24; Col 3:5) rather than place their trust in God alone as the hope of their lives. For more on idolatry, see article on THE NATURE OF IDOLATRY, p. 394.

6:9 HOW I HAVE BEEN GRIEVED. God was genuinely grieved and hurt by the spiritual adultery (i.e., idolatry) of his people (see Eph 4:30, note); their unfaithfulness broke his heart.

6:9 THEY WILL LOATHE THEMSELVES. God's punishment would cause some to recognize the seriousness of their sin, to experience true sorrow for their transgression, and consequently to return to God. Note that repentance is not merely

who escape will remember[f] me—how
I have been grieved[g] by their adulterous hearts, which have turned away
from me, and by their eyes, which have
lusted after their idols.[h] They will
loathe themselves for the evil[i] they
have done and for all their detestable
practices.[j] **10**And they will know that
I am the LORD;[k] I did not threaten in
vain to bring this calamity on them.[l]
11"This is what the Sovereign LORD
says: Strike your hands together and
stamp your feet and cry out "Alas!" because of all the wicked and detestable
practices of the house of Israel, for
they will fall by the sword, famine and
plague.[m] **12**He that is far away will die
of the plague, and he that is near will
fall by the sword, and he that survives
and is spared will die of famine. So will
I spend my wrath[n] upon them.[o]
13And they will know that I am the
LORD, when their people lie slain
among their idols[p] around their altars, on every high hill and on all the
mountaintops, under every spreading
tree and every leafy oak[q]—places
where they offered fragrant incense to
all their idols.[r] **14**And I will stretch
out my hand[s] against them and make
the land a desolate waste from the
desert to Diblah[m]—wherever they
live. Then they will know that I am the
LORD.[t]' "

The End Has Come

7 The word of the LORD came to me:
2"Son of man, this is what the Sovereign LORD says to the land of Israel:
The end![u] The end has come upon the
four corners[v] of the land. **3**The end is
now upon you and I will unleash my
anger against you. I will judge you according to your conduct[w] and repay
you for all your detestable practices.[x]
4I will not look on you with pity[y] or
spare you; I will surely repay you for
your conduct and the detestable practices among you. Then you will know
that I am the LORD.[z]
5"This is what the Sovereign LORD
says: Disaster![a] An unheard-of[n] disaster is coming. **6**The end[b] has come!
The end has come! It has roused itself
against you. It has come! **7**Doom has
come upon you—you who dwell in the
land. The time has come, the day[c] is
near;[d] there is panic, not joy, upon the
mountains. **8**I am about to pour out my
wrath[e] on you and spend my anger
against you; I will judge you according
to your conduct and repay you for all
your detestable practices.[f] **9**I will not
look on you with pity or spare you;[g] I
will repay you in accordance with your
conduct and the detestable practices
among you.[h] Then you will know that
it is I the LORD who strikes the blow.[i]
10"The day is here! It has come!
Doom has burst forth, the rod[j] has
budded, arrogance has blossomed!
11Violence[k] has grown into[o] a rod to
punish wickedness; none of the people
will be left, none of that crowd—no
wealth, nothing of value.[l] **12**The time
has come, the day has arrived. Let not
the buyer[m] rejoice nor the seller
grieve, for wrath is upon the whole
crowd.[n] **13**The seller will not recover
the land he has sold as long as both of
them live, for the vision concerning the
whole crowd will not be reversed. Because of their sins, not one of them will
preserve his life.[o] **14**Though they blow
the trumpet[p] and get everything
ready, no one will go into battle, for my
wrath[q] is upon the whole crowd.
15"Outside is the sword, inside are
plague and famine; those in the country will die by the sword, and those in
the city will be devoured by famine and

6:9 [f] S Ps 137:6; Zec 10:9 [g] S Isa 7:13; S Jer 8:21 [h] S Ex 22:20; Eze 20:7,24; Mic 5:13 [i] S Ex 32:22 [j] S Job 42:6; Eze 20:43; 23:14-16; 36:31
6:10 [k] S ver 7 [l] S Dt 28:52; Jer 40:2
6:11 [m] S Jer 42:22; Eze 21:14,17; 22:13; 25:6
6:12 [n] S Job 20:23 [o] S Eze 5:12; 7:15
6:13 [p] S Lev 26:30 [q] S Isa 1:29 [r] S 1Ki 14:23; S Jer 2:20; Eze 18:6; 20:28; Hos 4:13
6:14 [s] S Ex 7:5; S Job 30:21; S Jer 6:12; 51:25; Eze 20:34 [t] Eze 12:19; 14:13
7:2 [u] Am 8:2,10 [v] Rev 7:1; 20:8
7:3 [w] Eze 18:30 [x] S Ge 6:13
7:4 [y] S Jer 13:14; S Eze 5:11 [z] S Eze 5:11; 23:49
7:5 [a] S 2Ki 21:12
7:6 [b] Eze 39:8
7:7 [c] S Job 18:20; S Isa 2:12; Am 5:18-20 [d] Eze 12:23; 30:3; Zep 1:14; Mal 3:2
7:8 [e] Isa 42:25; Eze 9:8; 14:19; 22:22; Hos 5:10; Na 1:6 [f] Eze 20:8, 21; 36:19
7:9 [g] S Jer 21:7; S Eze 5:11 [h] Eze 22:31 [i] Dt 32:35; S Ps 39:10; S Isa 9:13
7:10 [j] Ps 89:32; Isa 10:5
7:11 [k] S Ps 55:9; S Isa 58:4 [l] Jer 16:6; Zep 1:18
7:12 [m] S Isa 24:2 [n] ver 7; Isa 5:13-14; Eze 30:3
7:13 [o] Lev 25:24-28
7:14 [p] S Job 39:24 [q] Jer 25:38

[m] *14* Most Hebrew manuscripts; a few Hebrew manuscripts *Riblah* [n] *5* Most Hebrew manuscripts; some Hebrew manuscripts and Syriac *Disaster after* [o] *11* Or *The violent one has become*

---

a change of mind, but also a change of feeling; it is a godly sorrow and regret because of personal sin (Ps 51:17; 2Co 7:9–10).

6:11 STRIKE YOUR HANDS TOGETHER. Those loyal to God and dedicated to serving him would grieve and lament because of the sinful practices occurring in the world, even among those who professed the name of the Lord (see 9:4, note).

7:7 THE DAY IS NEAR. The day of wrath and destruction was soon to come for the Israelites. Their rebellion against God would come to an abrupt end (vv. 2–3,6) when he punished them for their detestable practices; few would survive. Today, it may seem that God is ignoring the evil and immorality of the nations; nevertheless, the Bible assures us over and over again that the day of the Lord is coming (cf. Am 5:18–20), a day of great judgment bringing destruction and God's wrath on the entire world (see 1Pe 4:7,17). Just as the day of God's wrath finally came on Judah, so it will come on all the wicked, immoral and arrogant of this world (see 1Th 5:2, note).

plague.[r] **16**All who survive[s] and escape will be in the mountains, moaning
like doves[t] of the valleys, each because of his sins.[u] **17**Every hand will
go limp,[v] and every knee will become
as weak as water.[w] **18**They will put on
sackcloth[x] and be clothed with terror.[y] Their faces will be covered with
shame and their heads will be
shaved.[z] **19**They will throw their silver into the streets,[a] and their gold
will be an unclean thing. Their silver
and gold will not be able to save them
in the day of the LORD's wrath.[b] They
will not satisfy[c] their hunger or fill
their stomachs with it, for it has made
them stumble[d] into sin.[e] **20**They
were proud of their beautiful jewelry
and used it to make[f] their detestable
idols and vile images.[g] Therefore I
will turn these into an unclean thing
for them.[h] **21**I will hand it all over as
plunder[i] to foreigners and as loot to
the wicked of the earth, and they will
defile it.[j] **22**I will turn my face[k] away
from them, and they will desecrate my
treasured place; robbers will enter it
and desecrate it.[l]

23"Prepare chains, because the land
is full of bloodshed[m] and the city is full
of violence.[n] **24**I will bring the most
wicked of the nations to take possession of their houses; I will put an end
to the pride of the mighty, and their
sanctuaries[o] will be desecrated.[p]
25When terror comes, they will seek
peace, but there will be none.[q] **26**Calamity upon calamity[r] will come, and
rumor upon rumor. They will try to get
a vision from the prophet;[s] the teaching of the law by the priest will be lost,
as will the counsel of the elders.[t]
27The king will mourn, the prince will
be clothed with despair,[u] and the
hands of the people of the land will
tremble. I will deal with them according to their conduct,[v] and by their own
standards I will judge them. Then they
will know that I am the LORD.[w]"

Idolatry in the Temple

8 In the sixth year, in the sixth
month on the fifth day, while I was
sitting in my house and the elders[x] of
Judah were sitting before[y] me, the
hand of the Sovereign LORD came upon
me there.[z] **2**I looked, and I saw a figure like that of a man.[p] From what
appeared to be his waist down he was
like fire, and from there up his appearance was as bright as glowing metal.[a]
3He stretched out what looked like a
hand[b] and took me by the hair of my
head. The Spirit lifted me up[c] between earth and heaven and in visions[d] of God he took me to Jerusalem, to the entrance to the north gate
of the inner court,[e] where the idol that
provokes to jealousy[f] stood. **4**And
there before me was the glory[g] of the
God of Israel, as in the vision I had
seen in the plain.[h]

5Then he said to me, "Son of man,
look toward the north." So I looked,
and in the entrance north of the gate of
the altar I saw this idol[i] of jealousy.

6And he said to me, "Son of man, do
you see what they are doing—the ut-

7:15 [r] S Dt 32:25; Jer 14:18; S La 1:20; S Eze 5:12; 33:27
7:16 [s] S Isa 10:20; S Jer 41:16; 42:17 [t] S Ge 8:8; S Isa 59:11 [u] S Ezr 9:15; Jer 9:19; S Eze 6:8
7:17 [v] S 2Ki 19:26; S Jer 47:3; Eze 21:7; 22:14 [w] Da 5:6
7:18 [x] S Jer 4:8; 48:37; 49:3 [y] S Ps 55:5 [z] S Isa 15:2-3; Eze 27:31; Am 8:10
7:19 [a] S La 4:1 [b] Isa 42:25; Eze 13:5; 30:3; Joel 1:15; 2:1; Zep 1:7,18; 2:2 [c] Isa 55:2 [d] Eze 3:20; 14:3; Hos 4:5 [e] S Pr 11:4
7:20 [f] S Jer 10:3 [g] S Eze 5:11 [h] S Isa 2:20; 30:22; Eze 16:17
7:21 [i] S Nu 14:3 [j] S 2Ki 24:13
7:22 [k] S Jer 2:27; Eze 39:23-24 [l] Ps 74:7-8; Jer 19:13; S La 2:7
7:23 [m] S 2Ki 21:16; S Isa 1:15; S Eze 22:9 [n] S Ge 6:11; Eze 11:6
7:24 [o] La 2:7; Eze 24:21 [p] 2Ch 7:20; Eze 28:7
7:25 [q] Jer 6:14; S 8:11; Eze 13:10, 16
7:26 [r] S Dt 29:21; S 31:17 [s] S 1Sa 3:1 [t] Isa 47:11; S Jer 18:18; Eze 20:1-3; Am 8:11; Mic 3:6
7:27 [u] S Ps 109:19; Eze 26:16 [v] S Isa 3:11; Eze 18:20 [w] S ver 4
8:1 [x] S 2Ki 6:32; Eze 14:1 [y] Eze 33:31 [z] Eze 1:1-3; 24:1; 40:1
8:2 [a] Eze 1:4,26-27
8:3 [b] S Eze 2:9 [c] S Eze 3:12; 11:1 [d] S Ex 24:10 [e] ver 16 [f] ver 5; Ex 20:5; Dt 32:16
8:4 [g] S Ex 24:16 [h] Eze 3:22
8:5 [i] Ps 78:58; S Jer 4:1; 32:34

[p] 2 Or *saw a fiery figure*

7:19 THEIR SILVER AND GOLD. When God's coming wrath falls on this world, the wealth and the abundant possessions of the unrighteous will not be able to deliver them. God's people must be careful not to strive selfishly for excessive material gain; if we do, we will find that worldly goods do not satisfy (cf. Ecc 2), and we will become subject to God's severe judgment.

7:25 TERROR COMES. At first sin may seem pleasant and pleasurable; when it has run its course, however, it brings destruction, anguish and despair. The only hope for deliverance is to turn to God in repentance and faith and to trust in the atoning death of Jesus Christ.

8:1 HAND OF THE SOVEREIGN LORD. Ezekiel experienced an awesome visitation of God's presence and power as he was transported to Jerusalem "in visions of God" (v. 3; cf. 2Co 12:1–4). NT believers likewise experienced the presence and power of God when they were filled with the Holy Spirit (Ac 4:29–31) and received visions and dreams (Ac 2:16–18). Believers today should ask, seek and knock for the Holy Spirit to come upon them in power (Lk 11:5–13) and to pour out his spiritual gifts, so that they may witness for Christ (Ac 1:8; 2:4,16–18). In this way, the word of God will go out to God's house and to the world in boldness, with miraculous power and with full conviction (Ac 2:1–12,37–41; 1Th 1:5; Heb 2:4).

8:3 TOOK ME TO JERUSALEM. Ezekiel was taken to the temple in Jerusalem in order to see the detestable things the people were doing. This revelation disclosed clearly why God would judge the holy city.

8:6 DRIVE ME FAR FROM MY SANCTUARY? God revealed to Ezekiel that he would not dwell in the temple if idolatry and sin were tolerated. Jesus likewise stated that churches that com-

terly detestable[j] things the house of
Israel is doing here, things that will
drive me far from my sanctuary?[k] But
you will see things that are even more
detestable."
7Then he brought me to the entrance
to the court. I looked, and I saw a hole
in the wall. 8He said to me, "Son of
man, now dig into the wall." So I dug
into the wall and saw a doorway there.
9And he said to me, "Go in and see
the wicked and detestable things they
are doing here." 10So I went in and
looked, and I saw portrayed all over
the walls[l] all kinds of crawling things
and detestable[m] animals and all the
idols of the house of Israel.[n] 11In front
of them stood seventy elders[o] of the
house of Israel, and Jaazaniah son of
Shaphan was standing among them.
Each had a censer[p] in his hand, and
a fragrant cloud of incense[q] was rising.[r]
12He said to me, "Son of man, have
you seen what the elders of the house
of Israel are doing in the darkness,[s]
each at the shrine of his own idol? They
say, 'The LORD does not see[t] us; the
LORD has forsaken the land.' " 13Again,
he said, "You will see them doing
things that are even more detestable."
14Then he brought me to the entrance to the north gate of the house of
the LORD, and I saw women sitting
there, mourning for Tammuz.[u] 15He
said to me, "Do you see this, son of
man? You will see things that are even
more detestable than this."
16He then brought me into the inner
court[v] of the house of the LORD, and
there at the entrance to the temple, between the portico and the altar,[w] were
about twenty-five men. With their

8:6 [j]Ps 78:60; S Eze 5:11 [k]Hos 5:6 **8:10** [l]S Jdg 17:4-5; Eze 23:14 [m]Jer 44:4 [n]Ex 20:4; Dt 4:15-18; S Jer 16:18; Eze 11:12 **8:11** [o]S Ex 3:16 [p]S Lev 10:1; Nu 16:17 [q]Nu 16:35; S Jer 44:5 [r]Eze 11:1-2 **8:12** [s]S Job 22:13 [t]S 2Ki 21:16; Ps 10:11; S Isa 29:15; Eze 9:9; Zep 1:12 **8:14** [u]Eze 11:12 **8:16** [v]ver 3 [w]Joel 2:17

[x]S Ge 1:16 [y]Dt 4:19; S 17:3; S Job 31:28; S Jer 2:27; Eze 9:6; 11:1,12; 40:6; 43:1 **8:17** [z]Eze 16:2 [a]S Ge 6:11 [b]S Nu 11:33; S 1Ki 14:9; Eze 16:26 **8:18** [c]S Jer 44:6 [d]S Jer 13:14; S Eze 5:11; 9:10; 24:14 [e]S 1Sa 8:18; S Isa 58:4; S Jer 11:11 **9:2** [f]S Lev 16:4; Eze 10:2; Da 10:5; 12:6; Rev 15:6 **9:3** [g]S 1Sa 4:21; Eze 10:4 [h]Eze 11:22 **9:4** [i]Jer 25:29 [j]S Ge 4:15; Ex 12:7; 2Co 1:22; S Rev 7:3 [k]Ps 119:136; Jer 7:29; 13:17; Eze 21:6; Am 6:6 [l]Ps 119:53 **9:5** [m]S Jer 13:14; S Eze 5:11 [n]S Ex 32:27; Isa 13:18 **9:6** [o]Jer 7:32

backs toward the temple of the LORD
and their faces toward the east, they
were bowing down to the sun[x] in the
east.[y]
17He said to me, "Have you seen
this, son of man? Is it a trivial matter
for the house of Judah to do the detestable things[z] they are doing here?
Must they also fill the land with violence[a] and continually provoke me to
anger?[b] Look at them putting the
branch to their nose! 18Therefore I will
deal with them in anger;[c] I will not
look on them with pity[d] or spare them.
Although they shout in my ears, I will
not listen[e] to them."

Idolaters Killed

9 Then I heard him call out in a loud
voice, "Bring the guards of the city
here, each with a weapon in his hand."
2And I saw six men coming from the
direction of the upper gate, which faces
north, each with a deadly weapon in his
hand. With them was a man clothed in
linen[f] who had a writing kit at his
side. They came in and stood beside
the bronze altar.
3Now the glory[g] of the God of Israel
went up from above the cherubim,[h]
where it had been, and moved to the
threshold of the temple. Then the LORD
called to the man clothed in linen who
had the writing kit at his side 4and said 
to him, "Go throughout the city of Jeru-
salem[i] and put a mark[j] on the foreheads of those who grieve and la- Da
ment[k] over all the detestable things 1:8-
that are done in it.[l]" 20
5As I listened, he said to the others,
"Follow him through the city and kill,
without showing pity[m] or compassion.[n] 6Slaughter[o] old men, young

promise with the world, forsake apostolic teaching or tolerate immorality will lose his presence and their place in God's kingdom (see Rev 2—3).

8:14 TAMMUZ. Tammuz was the Babylonian god of vegetation. When plant life died in the fall, the people mourned what they thought was his death. Judah's women had forsaken the Sovereign Lord, turning to gods such as these for help and blessing.

8:17 THE BRANCH TO THEIR NOSE. This act may have been a ritual of the worship of the sun or of nature.

9:2 SIX MEN. The six men are six angels assigned by God to carry out his judgment against the city. They were each carrying a weapon (v. 1) by which to kill all the wicked. With them appeared a seventh angel clothed in linen, with a writing kit at his side; his task was to put a mark on the foreheads of those who remained faithful to God (cf. Rev 7:3; 9:4; 14:1; 22:4; see next note).

9:4 LAMENT OVER ALL THE DETESTABLE THINGS. God commanded that only those who remained faithful to him and his word were to be spared the coming judgment. (1) Their loyalty to God was determined by their love for righteousness and their grief and hatred over the sins committed around them. They were to receive a special mark of identification from God—the Hebrew letter *taw* (the final letter of the Hebrew alphabet, which took the form of a cross). (2) Grief over sin is evidence of true saving faith; those who genuinely belong to the Lord will grieve just as he does when they see sin and immorality in the world and in the church (see Heb 1:9, note).

men and maidens, women and children,[p] but do not touch anyone who
has the mark.[q] Begin at my sanctuary." So they began with the elders[r]
who were in front of the temple.[s]
7Then he said to them, "Defile the
temple and fill the courts with the
slain.[t] Go!" So they went out and began killing throughout the city. **8**While
they were killing and I was left alone,
I fell facedown,[u] crying out, "Ah, Sovereign LORD![v] Are you going to destroy
the entire remnant of Israel in this outpouring of your wrath[w] on Jerusalem?[x]"
9He answered me, "The sin of the
house of Israel and Judah is exceedingly great; the land is full of bloodshed
and the city is full of injustice.[y] They
say, 'The LORD has forsaken the land;
the LORD does not see.'[z] **10**So I will not
look on them with pity[a] or spare them,
but I will bring down on their own
heads what they have done.[b]"
11Then the man in linen with the
writing kit at his side brought back
word, saying, "I have done as you commanded."

The Glory Departs From the Temple

10 I looked, and I saw the likeness
of a throne[c] of sapphire[q][d]
above the expanse[e] that was over the
heads of the cherubim.[f] **2**The LORD
said to the man clothed in linen,[g] "Go
in among the wheels[h] beneath the
cherubim. Fill[i] your hands with burning coals[j] from among the cherubim
and scatter them over the city." And as
I watched, he went in.
3Now the cherubim were standing
on the south side of the temple when
the man went in, and a cloud filled the
inner court. **4**Then the glory of the
LORD[k] rose from above the cherubim
and moved to the threshold of the temple. The cloud filled the temple, and
the court was full of the radiance of the
glory of the LORD. **5**The sound of the
wings of the cherubim could be heard
as far away as the outer court, like the
voice[l] of God Almighty[r] when he
speaks.[m]
6When the LORD commanded the
man in linen, "Take fire from among
the wheels,[n] from among the cherubim," the man went in and stood beside
a wheel. **7**Then one of the cherubim
reached out his hand to the fire[o] that
was among them. He took up some of
it and put it into the hands of the man
in linen, who took it and went out.
8(Under the wings of the cherubim
could be seen what looked like the
hands of a man.)[p]
9I looked, and I saw beside the cherubim four wheels, one beside each of
the cherubim; the wheels sparkled like
chrysolite.[q] **10**As for their appearance, the four of them looked alike;
each was like a wheel intersecting a
wheel. **11**As they moved, they would go
in any one of the four directions the

9:6 [p] S Jer 16:6 [q] S Ge 4:15; S Ex 12:7 [r] Eze 8:11-13,16 [s] S 2Ch 36:17; Jer 25:29; S Eze 6:4; 1Pe 4:17 **9:7** [t] Eze 6:7 **9:8** [u] S Jos 7:6 [v] S Eze 4:14 [w] S Eze 7:8 [x] Eze 11:13; Am 7:1-6 **9:9** [y] S Ps 58:2; Jer 12:1; Eze 22:29; Hab 1:4 [z] S Job 22:13; S Eze 8:12; 14:23 **9:10** [a] S Jer 13:14; S Eze 8:18 [b] S Isa 22:5; S 65:6; Eze 11:21; 23:49 **10:1** [c] S Rev 4:2 [d] S Ex 24:10 [e] Eze 1:22 [f] S Ge 3:24 **10:2** [g] S Eze 9:2 [h] S Eze 1:15 [i] Rev 8:5 [j] S 2Sa 22:9 **10:4** [k] S Ex 24:16; Eze 9:3; 44:4 **10:5** [l] S Job 40:9 [m] S Eze 3:13 **10:6** [n] Da 7:9 **10:7** [o] S Eze 5:4 **10:8** [p] Eze 1:8 **10:9** [q] S Ex 28:20; Rev 21:20

[q] *1* Or *lapis lazuli* [r] *5* Hebrew *El-Shaddai*

9:6 BEGIN AT MY SANCTUARY ... WITH THE ELDERS. God's judgment begins with his own people (see 1Pe 4:17), especially with the spiritual leaders of his congregations. Leaders and overseers in the church are particularly accountable to God for their faithfulness to his Word and for their perseverance in righteous and holy living (Jas 3:1); if they fail to be good examples, they will lead many away from God and his word.

10:2 BURNING COALS. The burning coals scattered over the city symbolized judgment and destruction. The Babylonians destroyed Jerusalem by fire shortly after this vision (2Ch 36:19; 2Ki 25:8–9).

10:4 THE GLORY OF THE LORD ROSE. The focus of chs. 10—11 is the departure of God's glory and presence from the temple and the city (see article on THE GLORY OF GOD, p. 1192). God's glory first left the Most Holy Place and moved to the threshold of the temple (v. 4); the glory then departed from the temple and rested on the cherubim throne-chariot (v. 18). The cherubim moved the glory of God to the east gate of the temple (v. 19), and then it departed from the temple area altogether. Finally, the divine glory left the city of Jerusalem and rested on the Mount of Olives (11:23).

(1) The glory of God left the temple because of the people's sin and idolatry. God left his house reluctantly and gradually, but because of his holiness, he knew he had to separate himself from the idolatry in the temple.

(2) What happened to Israel and the temple can also happen to churches. If leaders permit sin, Satan and worldliness to gain a foothold, then God's glory and presence will depart from that congregation; as a result, the church will become an empty shell and the manifestations of the Spirit will be absent (see 1Co 14).

(3) We must fervently desire God's glory and presence and at the same time intensely hate sin and immorality (see Heb 1:9, note); any other attitude will lead to spiritual compromise and God's judgment (see Rev 2—3; cf. Dt 31:17; 1Sa 4:21; Hos 9:12).

cherubim faced; the wheels did not
turn about[s] as the cherubim went.
The cherubim went in whatever direction the head faced, without turning as
they went. **12**Their entire bodies, including their backs, their hands and
their wings, were completely full of
eyes,[r] as were their four wheels.[s] **13**I
heard the wheels being called "the
whirling wheels." **14**Each of the cherubim[t] had four faces:[u] One face was
that of a cherub, the second the face of
a man, the third the face of a lion,[v]
and the fourth the face of an eagle.[w]
15Then the cherubim rose upward.
These were the living creatures[x] I had
seen by the Kebar River.[y] **16**When the
cherubim moved, the wheels beside
them moved; and when the cherubim
spread their wings to rise from the
ground, the wheels did not leave their
side. **17**When the cherubim stood still,
they also stood still; and when the
cherubim rose, they rose with them,
because the spirit of the living creatures was in them.[z]
18Then the glory[a] of the LORD departed from over the threshold of the
temple and stopped above the cherubim.[b] **19**While I watched, the cherubim spread their wings and rose from
the ground, and as they went, the
wheels went with them.[c] They
stopped at the entrance to the east
gate of the LORD's house, and the glory[d] of the God of Israel was above
them.
20These were the living creatures I
had seen beneath the God of Israel by
the Kebar River,[e] and I realized that
they were cherubim. **21**Each had four
faces[f] and four wings,[g] and under
their wings was what looked like the
hands of a man. **22**Their faces had the
same appearance as those I had seen
by the Kebar River.[h] Each one went
straight ahead.

10:12 r Rev 4:6-8 s Eze 1:15-21 **10:14** t 1Ki 7:36 u Eze 1:6 v 1Ki 7:29 w Eze 1:10; 41:19; Rev 4:7 **10:15** x S Isa 6:2 y S Ps 137:1 **10:17** z S Eze 3:13 **10:18** a S 1Sa 4:21 b S Ps 18:10 **10:19** c Eze 11:1, 22 d Eze 43:4 **10:20** e Eze 1:1 **10:21** f Eze 41:18 g Eze 1:6 **10:22** h Eze 1:1

11:1 i ver 13 j Jer 5:5 k S Eze 8:16; S 10:19; 43:4-5 **11:2** l S Isa 29:20; Na 1:11 m Eze 8:11 **11:3** n Jer 1:13; Eze 24:3 o ver 7, 11; Eze 12:22,27; Mic 3:3 **11:4** p S Eze 3:4, 17 **11:5** q S Ps 26:2; S Jer 17:10 **11:6** r S Eze 7:23; 22:6 **11:7** s Jer 1:13 t ver 3; Eze 24:3-13; Mic 3:2-3 **11:8** u S Lev 26:25; S Jer 42:16 v S Pr 10:24; Isa 66:4 **11:9** w Ps 106:41 x Dt 28:36; S Eze 5:8 **11:10** y 2Ki 14:25 **11:11** z ver 3; Eze 24:6 **11:12** a S Eze 6:7 b S Lev 18:4; Eze 18:9

Judgment on Israel's Leaders

11 Then the Spirit lifted me up and
brought me to the gate of the
house of the LORD that faces east.
There at the entrance to the gate were
twenty-five men, and I saw among
them Jaazaniah son of Azzur and Pelatiah[i] son of Benaiah, leaders[j] of the
people.[k] **2**The LORD said to me, "Son
of man, these are the men who are
plotting evil[l] and giving wicked
advice in this city.[m] **3**They say, 'Will
it not soon be time to build houses?[t]
This city is a cooking pot,[n] and we
are the meat.'[o] **4**Therefore prophesy[p]
against them; prophesy, son of man."
5Then the Spirit of the LORD came
upon me, and he told me to say: "This
is what the LORD says: That is what you
are saying, O house of Israel, but I
know what is going through your
mind.[q] **6**You have killed many people
in this city and filled its streets with
the dead.[r]
7"Therefore this is what the Sovereign LORD says: The bodies you have
thrown there are the meat and this city
is the pot,[s] but I will drive you out of
it.[t] **8**You fear the sword,[u] and the
sword is what I will bring against you,
declares the Sovereign LORD.[v] **9**I will
drive you out of the city and hand you
over[w] to foreigners and inflict punishment on you.[x] **10**You will fall by the
sword, and I will execute judgment on
you at the borders of Israel.[y] Then
you will know that I am the LORD.
11This city will not be a pot[z] for you,
nor will you be the meat in it; I will
execute judgment on you at the borders of Israel. **12**And you will know
that I am the LORD,[a] for you have not
followed my decrees[b] or kept my laws

[s] *11* Or *aside* [t] *3* Or *This is not the time to build houses.*

11:3 TIME TO BUILD HOUSES? Those who remained in Jerusalem after the Babylonian invasion of 597 B.C. felt secure and favored by God. They thought of themselves as choice portions of meat in a cooking pot (Jerusalem), while the exiles were the bones. They refused to believe the prophet's message that because of their sins God would destroy them as well.

11:7 DRIVE YOU OUT OF IT. God threatened to pour the people out of the pot (Jerusalem) and allow them to be destroyed by Babylon (vv. 8–11).

11:12 CONFORMED TO THE STANDARDS OF THE NATIONS. Just as Judah adopted the religious practices of the surrounding nations, so God's people are constantly tempted to conform to the ways of the evil societies around them. We must firmly resist the desire to copy the ways and customs of the wicked. Since we belong to God, he calls us to be a holy people separated from our evil generation (see Ro 12:1–2, notes; see articles on SPIRITUAL SEPARATION FOR BELIEVERS, p. 1794, and THE CHRISTIAN'S RELATIONSHIP TO THE WORLD, p. 1976). The determination to resist the spirit of the world must be accompanied by a bold proclamation of the eternal truth and righteous standards of the gospel.

THE GLORY OF GOD

Eze 10:4 "Then the glory of the LORD rose from above the cherubim and moved to the threshold of the temple. The cloud filled the temple, and the court was full of the radiance of the glory of the LORD."

THE GLORY OF GOD DEFINED. The phrase "the glory of God" is used several ways in the Bible. (1) Sometimes it describes God's splendor and majesty (cf. 1Ch 29:11; Hab 3:3–5), a glory so great that no human being can see it and live (see Ex 33:18–23). At best one can see only an "appearance of the likeness of the glory of the LORD" (cf. Ezekiel's vision of God's throne, Eze 1:26–28). In this sense, the glory of God designates his uniqueness, his holiness (cf. Isa 6:1–3) and his transcendence (cf. Ro 11:36; Heb 13:21). Peter uses the term "the Majestic Glory" as a name for God (2Pe 1:17).

(2) The glory of God also refers to God's visible presence among his people, called by later rabbis the "*shekinah*" glory. *Shekinah* is a Hebrew word meaning "dwelling [of God]," employed to describe a visible manifestation of God's presence and glory. Moses saw God's *shekinah* glory in the pillars of cloud and fire (Ex 13:21); in Ex 29:43 it is called "my glory" (cf. Isa 60:2). It covered Sinai when God gave the law (see Ex 24:16–17, note), filled the tabernacle (Ex 40:34), guided Israel in the desert (Ex 40:36–38) and later filled Solomon's temple (2Ch 7:1; 1Ki 8:11–13). More specifically, God lived between the cherubim in the Most Holy Place (1Sa 4:4; 2Sa 6:2; Ps 80:1). Ezekiel saw the glory of the Lord rise and depart from the temple because of rampant idolatry there (Eze 10:4,18–19). The NT equivalent of the *shekinah* glory is Jesus Christ, who as the glory of God in human flesh came to make his dwelling among us (Jn 1:14). The shepherds of Bethlehem saw the glory of the Lord at Jesus' birth (Lk 2:9), the disciples saw it at Christ's transfiguration (Mt 17:2; 2Pe 1:16–18), and Stephen saw it at the time of his martyrdom (Ac 7:55).

(3) A third aspect of God's glory is his spiritual presence and power. Even though the heavens declare the glory of God (Ps 19:1; cf. Ro 1:19–20) and the whole earth is full of his glory (Isa 6:3; cf. Hab 2:14), the brightness of his majesty is not now visibly evident and often goes unnoticed. However, believers experience God's glory and presence in his nearness, love, righteousness and manifestations through the power of the Holy Spirit (see 2Co 3:18, note; Eph 3:16–19, note; 1Pe 4:14, note).

(4) Finally, the OT warns that any kind of idolatry encroaches on God's glory and brings reproach to his name. Whenever God manifests himself as our Redeemer, his name is glorified (see Ps 79:9; Jer 14:21). Christ's entire ministry on earth brought glory to our God (Jn 14:13; 17:1,4–5).

THE GLORY OF GOD REVEALED IN JESUS CHRIST. When Isaiah spoke about the coming of Jesus Christ, he prophesied that in him the glory of God would be revealed for all mankind to see (Isa 40:5). Both John (Jn 1:14) and the writer to the Hebrews (Heb 1:3) testify that Jesus Christ fulfilled this prophecy. Christ's glory was the same glory he had with his Father before the world began (Jn 1:14; 17:5). The glory of his ministry far surpassed the glory of the OT's ministry (2Co 3:7–11). Paul calls Jesus "the Lord of glory" (1Co 2:8), and James calls him "our glorious Lord Jesus Christ" (Jas 2:1).

Repeatedly the NT refers to the relationship between Jesus Christ and the glory of God. His miracles revealed his glory (Jn 2:11; 11:40–44). Christ was transfigured in a "bright cloud" (Mt 17:5) where he received glory (cf. 2Pe 1:16–19). The hour of his death was the hour of his glorification (Jn 12:23–24; cf. 17:2–5). He ascended into heaven in glory (cf. Ac 1:9; 1Ti 3:16), is now exalted in glory (Rev 5:12–13), and will someday return "on the clouds of the sky, with power and great glory" (Mt 24:30; cf. 25:31; Mk 14:62; 1Th 4:17).

THE GLORY OF GOD EXPERIENCED IN THE LIVES OF BELIEVERS. How does the glory of God apply to believers personally? (1) Regarding God's majestic heavenly glory, it is still true that no one can see that glory and live. We know it is there, but we do not see it. Because God lives in unapproachable light and glory, no mortal human can see him face to face (1Ti 6:16).

(2) God's *shekinah* glory, however, was experienced by God's people in Bible times. Throughout history to the present time there have been believers who have had visions of God similar to those of Isaiah (Isa 6) and Ezekiel (Eze 1), though this was not common then or now. The experience of God's glory, however, is something that all believers will have at the consummation, when we see Jesus face to face. We will be brought into God's glorious presence (Heb 2:10; 1Pe 5:10; Jude 24), share in Christ's glory (Ro 8:17–18) and be given a crown of glory (1Pe 5:4). Even our resurrection bodies will bear the glory of the risen Christ (1Co 15:42–43; Php 3:21).

(3) On a more immediate basis, sincere believers experience the spiritual presence of God. The Holy Spirit brings the presence of God and the Lord Jesus near to us (2Co 3:17; 1Pe 4:14). When the Spirit becomes powerfully active in the church through his supernatural manifestations (1Co 12:1–12), believers experience God's glory in their midst, i.e., an awesome feeling of God's presence, similar to what the shepherds felt in the fields of Bethlehem (Lk 2:8–20).

(4) Believers who forsake sin and shun idolatry may be filled with both Christ's glory (see Jn 17:22, note) and the Spirit of glory (1Pe 4:14); indeed, one reason Jesus came into the world was to fill believers with glory (Lk 2:29–32). As believers, we must live our entire lives to the glory of God, so that he is glorified in us (Jn 17:10; 1Co 10:31; 2Co 3:18).

but have conformed to the standards of the nations around you.[c]"

13 Now as I was prophesying, Pelatiah[d] son of Benaiah died. Then I fell facedown and cried out in a loud voice, "Ah, Sovereign LORD! Will you completely destroy the remnant of Israel?[e]"

14 The word of the LORD came to me: 15 "Son of man, your brothers—your brothers who are your blood relatives[u] and the whole house of Israel—are those of whom the people of Jerusalem have said, 'They are[v] far away from the LORD; this land was given to us as our possession.'[f]

Promised Return of Israel

16 "Therefore say: 'This is what the Sovereign LORD says: Although I sent them far away among the nations and scattered them among the countries, yet for a little while I have been a sanctuary[g] for them in the countries where they have gone.'

17 "Therefore say: 'This is what the Sovereign LORD says: I will gather you from the nations and bring you back from the countries where you have been scattered, and I will give you back the land of Israel again.'[h]

18 "They will return to it and remove all its vile images[i] and detestable idols.[j] 19 I will give them an undivided heart[k] and put a new spirit in them; I will remove from them their heart of stone[l] and give them a heart of flesh.[m] 20 Then they will follow my decrees and be careful to keep my laws.[n] They will be my people,[o] and I will be their God.[p] 21 But as for those whose hearts are devoted to their vile images and detestable idols,[q] I will bring down on their own heads what they have done, declares the Sovereign LORD.[r]"

22 Then the cherubim, with the wheels beside them, spread their wings, and the glory[s] of the God of Israel was above them.[t] 23 The glory[u] of the LORD went up from within the city and stopped above the mountain[v] east of it. 24 The Spirit[w] lifted me up and brought me to the exiles in Babylonia[w] in the vision[x] given by the Spirit of God.

Then the vision I had seen went up from me, 25 and I told the exiles everything the LORD had shown me.[y]

The Exile Symbolized

12 The word of the LORD came to me: 2 "Son of man, you are living among a rebellious people.[z] They have eyes to see but do not see and ears to hear but do not hear, for they are a rebellious people.[a]

3 "Therefore, son of man, pack your belongings for exile and in the daytime, as they watch, set out and go from where you are to another place. Perhaps[b] they will understand,[c] though

11:12 [c] Eze 8:10
11:13 [d] ver 1 [e] S Eze 9:8; Am 7:2
11:15 [f] Eze 33:24
11:16 [g] Ps 31:20; 90:1; 91:9; S Isa 4:6
11:17 [h] S Ne 1:9; S Jer 3:18; 24:5-6; S 31:16; Eze 20:41; 28:25; 34:13; 36:28
11:18 [i] S Eze 5:11 [j] Eze 37:23
11:19 [k] S 2Ch 30:12; S Ps 86:11 [l] Zec 7:12; Ro 2:5 [m] Eze 18:31; S 2Co 3:3
11:20 [n] S Ps 1:2 [o] S Jer 11:4; 32:38 [p] S Ex 6:7; Eze 14:11; 34:30; 36:26-28; Hos 1:9; Zec 8:8; Heb 8:10
11:21 [q] Jer 16:18 [r] Jer 16:11; S Eze 9:10; 16:43
11:22 [s] S Ex 24:16 [t] Eze 9:3; S 10:19
11:23 [u] Eze 1:28; S 10:4 [v] Zec 14:4
11:24 [w] Eze 37:1; 43:5 [x] 2Co 12:2-4
11:25 [y] S Eze 3:4, 11
12:2 [z] Ps 78:40; S Jer 42:21 [a] S Isa 6:10; S Mt 13:15; Mk 4:12; 8:18
12:3 [b] S Jer 36:3 [c] Jer 26:3

[u] *15* Or *are in exile with you* (see Septuagint and Syriac) [v] *15* Or *those to whom the people of Jerusalem have said, 'Stay* [w] *24* Or *Chaldea*

11:16 A SANCTUARY. God answers Ezekiel's question about the remnant of Israel (v. 13) by stating that he still cared for the exiles; he would be a sanctuary for them and would bring them back to the promised land (vv. 16–20).

11:17–21 GIVE YOU BACK THE LAND. This prophecy was partially fulfilled when a remnant returned after the Babylonian captivity (beginning in 538 B.C.). Furthermore, these verses point to a future gathering of Israel at the end of this age (see Rev 12:6, note).

11:19 A NEW SPIRIT IN THEM. This was initially fulfilled at the time of Jesus' resurrection (see article on THE REGENERATION OF THE DISCIPLES, p. 1627) and the outpouring of the Holy Spirit on Pentecost (see Ac 2:4, note; cf. Joel 2:28–29). Ezekiel prophesied that the people would be empowered by the Holy Spirit to live in accordance with God's will and law. God's Holy Spirit, with all his gifts and activity, is available today to all who put their faith in Jesus Christ.

11:23 THE GLORY OF THE LORD WENT UP. God's glory departed from Jerusalem and stopped at the Mount of Olives (see 10:4, note); later, Ezekiel had a vision of God's glory returning at a time when the Lord sets up his eternal kingdom (43:1–4).

12:2 A REBELLIOUS PEOPLE. Judah refused to believe that God would destroy Jerusalem and eliminate the Davidic king. Because they were God's chosen people, they felt the Lord would protect them regardless of their sinful actions. Thus the Lord appointed Ezekiel to be a sign to the nation (v. 6), portraying in symbolic actions what the people would experience as a result of their rebellion; here Ezekiel gives two further dramatic demonstrations (vv. 3–7 and vv. 17–20) of God's coming judgment on the people of Judah.

12:3–7 PACK YOUR BELONGINGS FOR EXILE. Ezekiel was to play out the role of a captive heading to another place while leaving everything behind except the absolute essentials needed for the journey. This action portrayed that another wave of exiles from Jerusalem would be brought to Babylon; it also discouraged the exiles from unrealistically expecting to return soon to Jerusalem.

they are a rebellious house.[d] 4During
the daytime, while they watch, bring
out your belongings packed for exile.
Then in the evening, while they are
watching, go out like those who go into
exile.[e] 5While they watch, dig through
the wall[f] and take your belongings
out through it. 6Put them on your
shoulder as they are watching and carry them out at dusk. Cover your face so
that you cannot see the land, for I have
made you a sign[g] to the house of
Israel."

7So I did as I was commanded.[h]
During the day I brought out my things
packed for exile. Then in the evening I
dug through the wall with my hands. I
took my belongings out at dusk, carrying them on my shoulders while they
watched.

8In the morning the word of the LORD
came to me: 9"Son of man, did not that
rebellious house of Israel ask you,
'What are you doing?'[i]

10"Say to them, 'This is what the
Sovereign LORD says: This oracle concerns the prince in Jerusalem and
the whole house of Israel who are
there.' 11Say to them, 'I am a sign[j]
to you.'

"As I have done, so it will be done to
them. They will go into exile as captives.[k]

12"The prince among them will put
his things on his shoulder at dusk[l]
and leave, and a hole will be dug in the
wall for him to go through. He will cover his face so that he cannot see the
land.[m] 13I will spread my net[n] for
him, and he will be caught in my
snare;[o] I will bring him to Babylonia,
the land of the Chaldeans,[p] but he will
not see[q] it, and there he will die.[r] 14I
will scatter to the winds all those
around him—his staff and all his
troops—and I will pursue them with
drawn sword.[s]

15"They will know that I am the
LORD, when I disperse them among the
nations[t] and scatter them through
the countries. 16But I will spare a few
of them from the sword, famine and
plague, so that in the nations where
they go they may acknowledge all their
detestable practices. Then they will
know that I am the LORD.[u]"

17The word of the LORD came to me:
18"Son of man, tremble as you eat your
food,[v] and shudder in fear as you
drink your water. 19Say to the people
of the land: 'This is what the Sovereign
LORD says about those living in Jerusalem and in the land of Israel: They will
eat their food in anxiety and drink their
water in despair, for their land will be
stripped of everything[w] in it because
of the violence of all who live there.[x]
20The inhabited towns will be laid
waste and the land will be desolate.
Then you will know that I am the
LORD.[y]' "

21The word of the LORD came to me:
22"Son of man, what is this proverb[z]
you have in the land of Israel: 'The
days go by and every vision comes to
nothing'?[a] 23Say to them, 'This is
what the Sovereign LORD says: I am going to put an end to this proverb, and
they will no longer quote it in Israel.'
Say to them, 'The days are near[b]
when every vision will be fulfilled.[c]
24For there will be no more false visions or flattering divinations[d] among
the people of Israel. 25But I the LORD
will speak what I will, and it shall be
fulfilled without delay.[e] For in your
days, you rebellious house, I will fulfill[f] whatever I say, declares the Sovereign LORD.[g]' "

26The word of the LORD came to me:
27"Son of man, the house of Israel is
saying, 'The vision he sees is for many
years from now, and he prophesies
about the distant future.'[h]

28"Therefore say to them, 'This is
what the Sovereign LORD says: None of
my words will be delayed any longer;
whatever I say will be fulfilled, declares the Sovereign LORD.' "

12:3 [d] ver 11; S Eze 3:27; 2Ti 2:25-26
12:4 [e] ver 12; 2Ki 25:4; S Jer 39:4
12:5 [f] Jer 52:7; Am 4:3
12:6 [g] ver 12; S Isa 8:18; S 20:3
12:7 [h] Eze 24:18; 37:10
12:9 [i] Eze 17:12; 20:49; 24:19
12:11 [j] Isa 8:18; Zec 3:8 [k] S 2Ki 25:7; S Jer 15:2; 52:15
12:12 [l] S Jer 39:4 [m] Jer 52:7
12:13 [n] Eze 17:20; 19:8; 32:3; Hos 7:12 [o] S Isa 24:17-18 [p] Eze 1:3 [q] S Jer 39:7 [r] S Jer 24:8; S 52:11; S La 4:20; Eze 17:16
12:14 [s] S 2Ki 25:5; S Jer 21:7; S Eze 5:10,12; 17:21
12:15 [t] S Lev 26:33
12:16 [u] S Jer 22:8-9; Eze 6:8-10; 14:22; 36:20
12:18 [v] La 5:9
12:19 [w] Jer 10:22; S Eze 6:6-14; Mic 7:13; Zec 7:14 [x] S Eze 4:16; 23:33
12:20 [y] Isa 7:23-24; S Jer 4:7; S 25:9
12:22 [z] S Ps 49:4 [a] S Isa 5:19; Eze 11:3; Am 6:3; 2Pe 3:4
12:23 [b] S Eze 7:7 [c] S Ps 37:13; Eze 18:3; Joel 2:1; Zep 1:14
12:24 [d] Jer 14:14; Eze 13:23; Mic 3:6; Zec 13:2-4
12:25 [e] Hab 2:3 [f] S Nu 11:23; Eze 13:6 [g] Nu 14:28-34; S Isa 14:24; S 55:11; Jer 16:9; Hab 1:5
12:27 [h] S Eze 11:3; Da 10:14; Mt 24:48-50; 2Pe 3:4

12:5 DIG THROUGH THE WALL. This action illustrated the Jews' desperate attempt to escape captivity.

12:6 COVER YOUR FACE. This action probably refers to the disgrace and grief that would be experienced by the captives.

12:10–13 THE PRINCE IN JERUSALEM. The "prince" is Judah's last king, Zedekiah, a resident of Jerusalem. Ezekiel prophesied that God had destined him for judgment. He would be taken captive to Babylon, yet he would never see it (v. 13), for he would be blinded by his captors (see 2Ki 25:7; Jer 39:6–7).

12:21–28 THE DAYS GO BY. The Jewish exiles refused to believe that Ezekiel's messages were true. So far nothing had happened, and thus they continued to expect that a time of peace was at hand; God declared, however, that judgment was imminent.

False Prophets Condemned

13 The word of the LORD came to
me: **2**“Son of man, prophesy
against the prophets[i] of Israel who
are now prophesying. Say to those who
prophesy out of their own imagination:[j] ‘Hear the word of the LORD![k]
3This is what the Sovereign LORD says:
Woe to the foolish[x] prophets[l] who
follow their own spirit and have seen
nothing![m] **4**Your prophets, O Israel,
are like jackals among ruins. **5**You
have not gone up to the breaks in the
wall to repair[n] it for the house of Israel so that it will stand firm in the battle
on the day of the LORD.[o] **6**Their visions
are false[p] and their divinations a lie.
They say, “The LORD declares,” when
the LORD has not sent[q] them; yet they
expect their words to be fulfilled.[r]
7Have you not seen false visions[s] and
uttered lying divinations when you say,
“The LORD declares,” though I have not
spoken?
8“ ‘Therefore this is what the Sovereign LORD says: Because of your false
words and lying visions, I am against
you,[t] declares the Sovereign LORD.
9My hand will be against the prophets
who see false visions and utter lying[u]
divinations. They will not belong to the
council of my people or be listed in the
records[v] of the house of Israel, nor
will they enter the land of Israel. Then
you will know that I am the Sovereign
LORD.[w]
10“ ‘Because they lead my people
astray,[x] saying, “Peace,”[y] when
there is no peace, and because, when
a flimsy wall is built, they cover it with
whitewash,[z] **11**therefore tell those
who cover it with whitewash that it is
going to fall. Rain will come in torrents, and I will send hailstones[a] hur-
tling down,[b] and violent winds will
burst forth.[c] **12**When the wall collapses, will people not ask you, “Where
is the whitewash you covered it with?”
13“ ‘Therefore this is what the Sovereign LORD says: In my wrath I will
unleash a violent wind, and in my anger hailstones[d] and torrents of rain[e]
will fall with destructive fury.[f] **14**I will
tear down the wall[g] you have covered
with whitewash and will level it to the
ground so that its foundation[h] will be
laid bare. When it[y] falls,[i] you will be
destroyed in it; and you will know that
I am the LORD. **15**So I will spend my
wrath against the wall and against
those who covered it with whitewash.
I will say to you, “The wall is gone and
so are those who whitewashed it,
16those prophets of Israel who prophesied to Jerusalem and saw visions of
peace for her when there was no peace,
declares the Sovereign LORD.[j]” ’
17“Now, son of man, set your face[k]
against the daughters[l] of your people
who prophesy out of their own imagination. Prophesy against them[m] **18**and
say, ‘This is what the Sovereign LORD
says: Woe to the women who sew magic charms on all their wrists and make
veils of various lengths for their heads
in order to ensnare people. Will you ensnare the lives of my people but preserve your own? **19**You have profaned[n] me among my people for a few
handfuls of barley and scraps of
bread.[o] By lying to my people, who listen to lies, you have killed those who
should not have died and have spared
those who should not live.[p]
20“ ‘Therefore this is what the Sovereign LORD says: I am against your
magic charms with which you ensnare
people like birds and I will tear them
from your arms; I will set free the people that you ensnare like birds.[q] **21**I

[x] 3 Or *wicked* [y] 14 Or *the city*

13:2 [i] S Isa 9:15 [j] Jer 28:15 [k] ver 17; S Jer 23:16; S 37:19; Eze 22:28 **13:3** [l] S La 2:14; Hos 9:7 [m] S Jer 23:25-32 **13:5** [n] Isa 58:12; Eze 22:30 [o] S Eze 7:19; 30:3 **13:6** [p] S Jer 5:1; 23:16 [q] S Jer 14:14 [r] S Jer 28:15; S 29:9; Eze 12:24-25; 22:28 **13:7** [s] S Isa 30:10 **13:8** [t] S Jer 21:13 **13:9** [u] S Dt 13:3 [v] S Ex 32:32; S Jer 17:13 [w] S Ex 6:2; Jer 20:3-6; Eze 20:38 **13:10** [x] S Jer 23:13; S 50:6 [y] S Jer 4:10 [z] S Eze 7:25; 22:28 **13:11** [a] S Jos 10:11 [b] S Job 38:23 [c] Ps 11:6; Eze 38:22

13:13 [d] S Jos 10:11; Rev 11:19; 16:21 [e] Job 14:19 [f] S Ex 9:25; S Job 38:23; Isa 30:30 **13:14** [g] S Isa 22:5 [h] Mic 1:6 [i] Jer 6:15 **13:16** [j] S Isa 57:21; Jer 6:14; S Eze 7:25 **13:17** [k] S Eze 4:7; 25:2; 28:21 [l] S Ex 15:20; Rev 2:20 [m] S ver 2 **13:19** [n] Jer 44:26; Eze 20:39; 22:26; 36:20; 39:7 [o] S Isa 56:11 [p] Pr 28:21; Mic 3:11 **13:20** [q] Ps 124:7

13:2–23 PROPHESY AGAINST THE PROPHETS. God condemns the false prophets of Israel who were prophesying that there would be no coming judgment. They were falsely predicting that the people were secure even though they were living in sin and idolatry (see Jer 6:14, note; 23:17, note). God was against such prophets (v. 8).

13:10 WHEN THERE IS NO PEACE. The false prophets seduced the people into a false sense of security by proclaiming God's peace and salvation to them while they continued in rebellion against his laws; for this God would cut them off from the nation of Israel and from his salvation (see previous note). (1) Today, there are false prophets in the church who teach that a person can be a genuine believer and possess eternal life in Christ, yet at the same time participate in and enjoy the sins of immorality, greed, homosexuality, sorcery or any other kind of detestable evil. (2) The apostle Paul states that believers must not be deceived by such lying words (Eph 5:6), for those who do such things will not inherit God's kingdom (see 1Co 6:9, note; Gal 5:21, note; Eph 5:5, note).

13:18 WOE TO THE WOMEN. These women were involved in sorcery, spiritism and black magic; they were even using the powers of evil to bring death to certain individuals (v. 19).

will tear off your veils and save my people from your hands, and they will no
longer fall prey to your power. Then
you will know that I am the LORD.[r]
22Because you disheartened the righteous with your lies,[s] when I had
brought them no grief, and because
you encouraged the wicked not to turn
from their evil ways and so save their
lives,[t] 23therefore you will no longer
see false visions[u] or practice divination.[v] I will save[w] my people from
your hands. And then you will know
that I am the LORD.[x]' "

Idolaters Condemned

14 Some of the elders of Israel
came to me and sat down in
front of me.[y] 2Then the word of the
LORD came to me: 3"Son of man, these
men have set up idols in their hearts[z]
and put wicked stumbling blocks[a] before their faces. Should I let them inquire of me at all?[b] 4Therefore speak
to them and tell them, 'This is what the
Sovereign LORD says: When any Israelite sets up idols in his heart and puts
a wicked stumbling block before his
face and then goes to a prophet, I the
LORD will answer him myself in keeping
with his great idolatry. 5I will do this
to recapture the hearts of the people of
Israel, who have all deserted[c] me for
their idols.'[d]
6"Therefore say to the house of Israel, 'This is what the Sovereign LORD
says: Repent![e] Turn from your idols
and renounce all your detestable practices![f]
7" 'When any Israelite or any alien[g]
living in Israel separates himself from
me and sets up idols in his heart and
puts a wicked stumbling block[h] before his face and then goes to a prophet
to inquire[i] of me, I the LORD will answer him myself. 8I will set my face
against[j] that man and make him an
example[k] and a byword.[l] I will cut
him off from my people. Then you will
know that I am the LORD.[m]
9" 'And if the prophet[n] is enticed[o]
to utter a prophecy, I the LORD have enticed that prophet, and I will stretch
out my hand against him and destroy
him from among my people Israel.[p]
10They will bear their guilt—the
prophet will be as guilty as the one who
consults him. 11Then the people of Israel will no longer stray[q] from me, nor
will they defile themselves anymore
with all their sins. They will be my people,[r] and I will be their God, declares
the Sovereign LORD.[s]' "

Judgment Inescapable

12The word of the LORD came to me:
13"Son of man, if a country sins[t]
against me by being unfaithful and I
stretch out my hand against it to cut off
its food supply[u] and send famine upon
it and kill its men and their animals,[v]
14even if these three men—Noah,[w]
Daniel[z][x] and Job[y]—were in it, they
could save only themselves by their
righteousness,[z] declares the Sovereign LORD.
15"Or if I send wild beasts[a] through
that country and they leave it childless
and it becomes desolate so that no one
can pass through it because of the
beasts,[b] 16as surely as I live, declares
the Sovereign LORD, even if these three

13:21 [r]Ps 91:3
13:22 [s]S Isa 9:15 [t]Jer 23:14; Eze 18:21; 33:14-16
13:23 [u]Ne 6:12 [v]S Eze 12:24 [w]S Ps 72:14 [x]Mic 3:6
14:1 [y]S Eze 8:1; 20:1
14:3 [z]S Eze 6:4 [a]S ver 7; S Eze 7:19 [b]Isa 1:15; Eze 20:31
14:5 [c]S Dt 32:15; Eze 16:45; Hos 5:7; Zec 11:8 [d]Jer 2:11
14:6 [e]Ne 1:9; S Jer 3:12; S 35:15 [f]S Isa 2:20; S 30:22
14:7 [g]Ex 12:48; 20:10 [h]ver 3; S Isa 8:14; Hos 4:5; 5:5
[i]S Ge 25:22
14:8 [j]Eze 15:7 [k]S Nu 16:38 [l]S Ps 102:8; S Eze 5:15 [m]S Jer 42:20
14:9 [n]S Jer 14:15 [o]Isa 63:17; Jer 4:10 [p]1Ki 22:23; S 2Ch 18:22; Zec 13:3
14:11 [q]Eze 48:11 [r]S Isa 51:16 [s]S Eze 11:19-20; 37:23
14:13 [t]S Pr 13:21 [u]S Lev 26:26 [v]S Eze 5:16; 6:14; 15:8
14:14 [w]Ge 6:8 [x]ver 20; Eze 28:3; Da 1:6; 6:13 [y]S Job 1:1 [z]S Ge 6:9; S Job 42:9; Jer 15:1; S Eze 3:19; 18:20
14:15 [a]Eze 5:17 [b]S Lev 26:22

[z]14 Or *Danel*; the Hebrew spelling may suggest a person other than the prophet Daniel; also in verse 20.

14:3 IDOLS IN THEIR HEARTS. The elders of Israel (v. 1) were guilty of idolatry in their hearts, i.e., they were not loyal to God and his word. They spurned God's will and desired an ungodly way of life; therefore, God refused to guide them by answering their prayers. In a similar manner, those today who look for guidance from God will find no help from his Spirit if their hearts are filled with ungodly desires for the sinful things of the world (see article on THE NATURE OF IDOLATRY, p. 394).

14:7 SEPARATES HIMSELF FROM ME. Believers who forsake God to pursue sinful and immoral lives while continuing to seek religious comfort, assurance and guidance from him make God their enemy (v. 8); he will judge and punish such people. They should either repent of and forsake their sinful ways or leave the fellowship of believers (see 1Co 5:5, note; 11:27, note).

14:9–10 THE PROPHET . . . DESTROY HIM. God would destroy any prophet who tolerated, supported or encouraged the Israelites' idolatry. Likewise, ministers of the church who tolerate immoral members and refuse to condemn their persistent wickedness by expelling them from the congregation (see previous note) will be considered as guilty as the hypocritical members themselves.

14:14 NOAH, DANIEL AND JOB. The judgment coming against Jerusalem was so certain that even these three men of God known for their righteousness (Ge 6:9; Job 1:1,8; 2:3; Da 6:4–5,22) could not deliver anyone by their intercessory prayers.

14:16 NOT SAVE THEIR OWN SONS OR DAUGHTERS. Judah's moral climate had become so sinful that the righteous prayers of Noah, Dan-

men were in it, they could not save
their own sons or daughters. They
alone would be saved, but the land
would be desolate.[c]
17"Or if I bring a sword[d] against
that country and say, 'Let the sword
pass throughout the land,' and I kill its
men and their animals,[e] 18as surely
as I live, declares the Sovereign LORD,
even if these three men were in it, they
could not save their own sons or
daughters. They alone would be saved.
19"Or if I send a plague into that
land and pour out my wrath[f] upon it
through bloodshed,[g] killing its men
and their animals,[h] 20as surely as I
live, declares the Sovereign LORD, even
if Noah, Daniel and Job were in it, they
could save neither son nor daughter.
They would save only themselves by
their righteousness.[i]
21"For this is what the Sovereign
LORD says: How much worse will it be
when I send against Jerusalem my four
dreadful judgments[j]—sword[k] and
famine[l] and wild beasts and
plague[m]—to kill its men and their animals![n] 22Yet there will be some survivors[o]—sons and daughters who will
be brought out of it.[p] They will come
to you, and when you see their conduct[q] and their actions, you will be
consoled[r] regarding the disaster I
have brought upon Jerusalem—every
disaster I have brought upon it. 23You
will be consoled when you see their
conduct and their actions, for you will
know that I have done nothing in it
without cause, declares the Sovereign
LORD.[s]"

Jerusalem, A Useless Vine

15 The word of the LORD came to
me: 2"Son of man, how is the
wood of a vine[t] better than that of a
branch on any of the trees in the forest? 3Is wood ever taken from it to
make anything useful?[u] Do they make
pegs[v] from it to hang things on? 4And
after it is thrown on the fire as fuel and
the fire burns both ends and chars the
middle, is it then useful for anything?[w]
5If it was not useful for anything when
it was whole, how much less can it be
made into something useful when the
fire has burned it and it is charred?
6"Therefore this is what the Sovereign LORD says: As I have given the
wood of the vine among the trees of the
forest as fuel for the fire, so will I treat
the people living in Jerusalem. 7I will
set my face against[x] them. Although
they have come out of the fire[y][z], the
fire will yet consume them. And when
I set my face against them, you will
know that I am the LORD.[a] 8I will make
the land desolate[b] because they have
been unfaithful,[c] declares the Sovereign LORD."

An Allegory of Unfaithful Jerusalem

16 The word of the LORD came to
me: 2"Son of man, confront[d]
Jerusalem with her detestable practices[e] 3and say, 'This is what the Sovereign LORD says to Jerusalem: Your
ancestry[f] and birth were in the land of
the Canaanites; your father[g] was an
Amorite[h] and your mother a Hittite.[i]
4On the day you were born[j] your cord
was not cut, nor were you washed with
water to make you clean, nor were you
rubbed with salt or wrapped in cloths.
5No one looked on you with pity or had
compassion enough to do any of these
things for you. Rather, you were
thrown out into the open field, for on
the day you were born you were despised.
6" 'Then I passed by and saw you
kicking about in your blood, and as you

14:16 [c]S Ge 19:29; Eze 18:20 **14:17** [d]S Lev 26:25; S Jer 25:27; S 42:16 [e]Eze 25:13; Zep 1:3 **14:19** [f]S Eze 7:8 [g]S Isa 34:3 [h]Jer 14:12; Eze 38:22 **14:20** [i]S ver 14 **14:21** [j]S Nu 33:4 [k]Isa 31:8; 34:6; 66:16; Eze 21:3, 19 [l]S 2Sa 24:13 [m]S Jer 14:12; 27:8 [n]S Jer 15:3; S Eze 5:17; 33:27; Am 4:6-10; Rev 6:8 **14:22** [o]S Jer 41:16 [p]S Eze 12:16 [q]Eze 20:43 [r]Eze 31:16; 32:31 **14:23** [s]S Jer 22:8-9; Eze 8:6-18; S 9:9 **15:2** [t]Ps 80:8-16; Isa 5:1-7; 27:2-6; Jer 2:21; Hos 10:1; S Jn 15:2 **15:3** [u]Jer 13:10 [v]S Isa 22:23 **15:4** [w]Eze 17:3-10; 19:14; Jn 15:6 **15:7** [x]S Lev 26:17; Ps 34:16; Eze 14:8 [y]S Eze 5:2 [z]S Eze 5:4 [a]Isa 24:18; Am 9:1-4 **15:8** [b]S Eze 14:13 [c]Eze 17:20; 18:24 **16:2** [d]S Isa 57:12; Eze 23:36 [e]Eze 8:17; 20:4; 22:2 **16:3** [f]Ge 11:25-29; Eze 21:30 [g]S Ge 12:18 [h]S Ge 15:16 [i]ver 45; S Ge 10:15; S Dt 7:1; Jos 24:14-15 **16:4** [j]Hos 2:3

iel and Job would not be sufficient to save even their own children. Believers must be very careful about the social and educational environment in which they place their children; it may become so ungodly that neither our righteous living nor our fervent prayers will be enough to bring them to accept Christ as their Lord and Savior.

15:2–8 A VINE. The people of Jerusalem are compared to a vine that does not bear fruit and is therefore useless. The fruit of righteousness and faithfulness to the Lord could not be found in them (v. 8); thus they would be burned in the fire (v. 6). Jesus likewise taught that all believers who fail to remain faithfully in him and to bear fruit will be cut off and thrown into the fire (see Jn 15:1–7, notes).

16:1–63 JERUSALEM. This chapter portrays Jerusalem as a wife and God as her husband (see Hos 1:2, note). In the beginning Jerusalem had no natural endowments that would entitle her to be God's chosen city. But God in love lifted her up, took care of her, and made her into a city of beauty and splendor; yet she was ungrateful to her husband, became unfaithful and began committing adultery with anyone who passed by. Because of her prostitution, she would be put to death.

16:3 LAND OF THE CANAANITES. Jerusalem was originally founded not by Hebrews but by the pagan people of Canaan (cf. Ge 14:18; Jos 15:63).

lay there in your blood I said to you,
"Live!"[a][k] **7**I made you grow[l] like a
plant of the field. You grew up and developed and became the most beautiful
of jewels.[b] Your breasts were formed
and your hair grew, you who were naked and bare.[m]
8" 'Later I passed by, and when I
looked at you and saw that you were
old enough for love, I spread the corner
of my garment[n] over you and covered
your nakedness. I gave you my solemn
oath and entered into a covenant[o]
with you, declares the Sovereign LORD,
and you became mine.[p]
9" 'I bathed[c] you with water and
washed[q] the blood from you and put
ointments on you. **10**I clothed you with
an embroidered[r] dress and put leather sandals on you. I dressed you in fine
linen[s] and covered you with costly
garments.[t] **11**I adorned you with jewelry:[u] I put bracelets[v] on your arms
and a necklace[w] around your neck,
12and I put a ring on your nose,[x] earrings[y] on your ears and a beautiful
crown[z] on your head.[a] **13**So you were
adorned with gold and silver; your
clothes[b] were of fine linen and costly
fabric and embroidered cloth. Your
food was fine flour, honey and olive
oil.[c] You became very beautiful and
rose to be a queen.[d] **14**And your
fame[e] spread among the nations on
account of your beauty,[f] because the
splendor I had given you made your
beauty perfect, declares the Sovereign
LORD.[g]
15" 'But you trusted in your beauty
and used your fame to become a prostitute. You lavished your favors on anyone who passed by[h] and your beauty
became his.[d][i] **16**You took some of
your garments to make gaudy high
places,[j] where you carried on your
prostitution.[k] Such things should not
happen, nor should they ever occur.
17You also took the fine jewelry I gave
you, the jewelry made of my gold and
silver, and you made for yourself male
idols and engaged in prostitution with
them.[l] **18**And you took your embroidered clothes to put on them, and you
offered my oil and incense[m] before
them. **19**Also the food I provided for
you—the fine flour, olive oil and honey
I gave you to eat—you offered as fragrant incense before them. That is
what happened, declares the Sovereign LORD.[n]
20" 'And you took your sons and
daughters[o] whom you bore to me[p]
and sacrificed them as food to the
idols. Was your prostitution not
enough?[q] **21**You slaughtered my children and sacrificed them[e] to the
idols.[r] **22**In all your detestable practices and your prostitution you did not
remember the days of your youth,[s]
when you were naked and bare,[t] kicking about in your blood.[u]
23" 'Woe![v] Woe to you, declares the
Sovereign LORD. In addition to all your
other wickedness, **24**you built a mound
for yourself and made a lofty shrine[w]
in every public square.[x] **25**At the head

16:6 [k]ver 22; S Ex 19:4; Eze 18:23,32 **16:7** [l]S Dt 1:10 [m]S Ex 1:7 **16:8** [n]Ru 3:9 [o]ver 59; S Jer 11:10; Mal 2:14 [p]Jer 2:2; Hos 2:7,19-20 **16:9** [q]S Ru 3:3 **16:10** [r]S Ex 26:36; S Isa 19:9 [s]Eze 27:16 [t]ver 18; S Isa 3:23 **16:11** [u]S Jer 4:30; Eze 23:40 [v]Isa 3:19; Eze 23:42 [w]S Ge 41:42; S Ps 73:6 **16:12** [x]Isa 3:21 [y]S Ge 35:4 [z]S Isa 28:5; S Jer 13:18 [a]Pr 1:9; S Isa 3:19 **16:13** [b]Est 5:1 [c]1Sa 10:1 [d]Dt 32:13-14; S 1Ki 4:21; S Est 2:9,17 **16:14** [e]1Ki 10:24 [f]S Est 1:11; S Ps 48:2; S La 2:15 [g]S Eze 5:5 **16:15** [h]ver 25 [i]S Isa 57:8; S Jer 2:20; Eze 23:3; 27:3 **16:16** [j]S Isa 57:7 [k]S 2Ki 23:7 **16:17** [l]S Eze 7:20; Hos 2:13 **16:18** [m]S Jer 44:5 **16:19** [n]Hos 2:8 **16:20** [o]S Jer 7:31 [p]Ex 13:2 [q]Ps 106:37-38; S Isa 57:5; Eze 23:37 **16:21** [r]S 2Ki 17:17; S Jer 19:5 **16:22** [s]S Ps 25:7; S 88:15; Jer 2:2; Hos 2:15; 11:1 [t]Hos 2:3 [u]ver 6 **16:23** [v]Eze 24:6 **16:24** [w]ver 31; Isa 57:7

[x]Ps 78:58; S Jer 2:20; 3:2; S 44:21; Eze 20:28

[a]*6* A few Hebrew manuscripts, Septuagint and Syriac; most Hebrew manuscripts *"Live!" And as you lay there in your blood I said to you, "Live!"* [b]*7* Or *became mature* [c]*9* Or *I had bathed* [d]*15* Most Hebrew manuscripts; one Hebrew manuscript (see some Septuagint manuscripts) *by. Such a thing should not happen* [e]*21* Or *and made them pass through* ⌊*the fire*⌋

16:6 LIVE! God gave Jerusalem life, choosing it to be the holy city and inspiring David to capture it from the Jebusites (2Sa 5:6–10).

16:8–14 ENTERED INTO A COVENANT. As chosen by God, Jerusalem received blessings and gifts from the Lord. Under his care she grew to full maturity, and the Lord gave her great beauty and claimed her for himself. After the marriage her fame spread throughout the ancient world (especially during the reigns of David and Solomon).

16:8 CORNER OF MY GARMENT OVER YOU. This metaphor is symbolic of protection and of entering into a marriage contract (see Ru 3:9, note).

16:15 LAVISHED YOUR FAVORS. Jerusalem began to trust in her beauty and riches (cf. Dt 6:10–12) rather than in God. She became a prostitute in the sense of spiritually becoming unfaithful to and forsaking the Lord. She entered into alliances with other nations (cf. 1Ki 11:1–13) and began to worship their gods. Today spiritual adultery is committed by those churches or individuals who turn from the Lord and give themselves to sinful pleasures and worldly values rather than to God and his kingdom.

16:17 ENGAGED IN PROSTITUTION. The people of Jerusalem not only committed spiritual adultery, but they also participated in physical sexual immorality in the fertility rites of the Canaanite religions.

16:20 SONS AND DAUGHTERS ... SACRIFICED. Ultimately Jerusalem's apostasy resulted in their participation in child sacrifice (cf. 2Ki 16:3; 21:6) and all kinds of detestable pagan practices (vv. 21–25).

of every street[y] you built your lofty
shrines and degraded your beauty, offering your body with increasing promiscuity to anyone who passed by.[z]
26You engaged in prostitution[a] with
the Egyptians,[b] your lustful neighbors, and provoked[c] me to anger with
your increasing promiscuity.[d] **27**So I
stretched out my hand[e] against you
and reduced your territory; I gave you
over[f] to the greed of your enemies,
the daughters of the Philistines,[g] who
were shocked by your lewd conduct.
28You engaged in prostitution with the
Assyrians[h] too, because you were insatiable; and even after that, you still
were not satisfied.[i] **29**Then you increased your promiscuity to include
Babylonia,[f][j] a land of merchants,
but even with this you were not satisfied.[k]

30" 'How weak-willed you are, declares the Sovereign LORD, when you do
all these things, acting like a brazen
prostitute![l] **31**When you built your
mounds at the head of every street and
made your lofty shrines[m] in every public square, you were unlike a prostitute, because you scorned payment.

32" 'You adulterous wife! You prefer
strangers to your own husband! **33**Every prostitute receives a fee,[n] but you
give gifts[o] to all your lovers, bribing
them to come to you from everywhere
for your illicit favors.[p] **34**So in your
prostitution you are the opposite of
others; no one runs after you for your
favors. You are the very opposite, for
you give payment and none is given to
you.

35" 'Therefore, you prostitute, hear
the word of the LORD! **36**This is what
the Sovereign LORD says: Because you
poured out your wealth[g] and exposed
your nakedness in your promiscuity
with your lovers, and because of all
your detestable idols, and because you
gave them your children's blood,[q]
37therefore I am going to gather all
your lovers, with whom you found pleasure, those you loved as well as those
you hated. I will gather them against
you from all around and will strip[r] you
in front of them, and they will see all
your nakedness.[s] **38**I will sentence
you to the punishment of women who
commit adultery and who shed
blood;[t] I will bring upon you the blood
vengeance of my wrath and jealous anger.[u] **39**Then I will hand you over[v] to
your lovers, and they will tear down
your mounds and destroy your lofty
shrines. They will strip you of your
clothes and take your fine jewelry and
leave you naked and bare.[w] **40**They
will bring a mob against you, who will
stone[x] you and hack you to pieces
with their swords. **41**They will burn
down[y] your houses and inflict punishment on you in the sight of many wom-
en.[z] I will put a stop[a] to your prostitution, and you will no longer pay your
lovers. **42**Then my wrath against you
will subside and my jealous anger will
turn away from you; I will be calm and
no longer angry.[b]

43" 'Because you did not remember[c] the days of your youth but enraged me with all these things, I will
surely bring down[d] on your head what
you have done, declares the Sovereign
LORD. Did you not add lewdness to all
your other detestable practices?[e]

44" 'Everyone who quotes proverbs[f] will quote this proverb about
you: "Like mother, like daughter."
45You are a true daughter of your
mother, who despised[g] her husband[h]
and her children; and you are a true
sister of your sisters, who despised
their husbands and their children. Your
mother was a Hittite and your father an
Amorite.[i] **46**Your older sister[j] was
Samaria, who lived to the north of you
with her daughters; and your younger
sister, who lived to the south of you
with her daughters, was Sodom.[k]
47You not only walked in their ways
and copied their detestable practices,
but in all your ways you soon became

16:25 [y] S Jer 3:2 [z] ver 15; S Pr 9:14 **16:26** [a] S Isa 23:17 [b] S Jer 3:1 [c] S 1Ki 14:9; S Eze 8:17 [d] S Isa 57:8; Jer 11:15; Eze 20:8; 23:19-21 **16:27** [e] Eze 20:33; 25:13 [f] S Jer 34:20 [g] S 2Ch 28:18 **16:28** [h] S 2Ki 16:7 [i] Isa 57:8 **16:29** [j] S Jer 3:1; Eze 23:14-17 [k] Na 3:4 **16:30** [l] S Jer 3:3 **16:31** [m] S ver 24 **16:33** [n] S Ge 30:15 [o] Isa 30:6; 57:9 [p] Hos 8:9-10 **16:36** [q] S Jer 19:5; Eze 23:10 **16:37** [r] Hos 2:3 [s] S Isa 47:3; S Jer 13:22; Eze 23:22; Hos 2:10; 8:10; Rev 17:16 **16:38** [t] S Ge 38:24 [u] S Lev 20:10; Ps 79:3,5; Eze 23:25; Zep 1:17 **16:39** [v] S 2Ki 18:11 [w] Eze 21:31; Hos 2:3 **16:40** [x] Jn 8:5,7 **16:41** [y] S Dt 13:16; S Jer 19:13 [z] Eze 23:10 [a] Eze 22:15; 23:27,48 **16:42** [b] 2Sa 24:25; Isa 40:1-2; 54:9; S Eze 5:13; 39:29 **16:43** [c] S Ex 15:24; Ps 78:42 [d] Eze 22:31 [e] Eze 11:21 **16:44** [f] S Ps 49:4 **16:45** [g] S Eze 14:5 [h] Jer 44:19 [i] ver 3; Eze 23:2 **16:46** [j] S Jer 3:7 [k] Ge 13:10-13; S 18:20; Jer 3:8-11; Eze 23:4; Rev 11:8

[f] 29 Or *Chaldea* [g] 36 Or *lust*

16:37–42 GATHER ALL YOUR LOVERS. Jerusalem had engaged in spiritual adultery with other nations and their gods (see v. 15, note); now God would use those very nations to punish her. They would bring such devastating destruction that further punishment would not be needed.

16:43 THE DAYS OF YOUR YOUTH. In her formative days, Jerusalem had been dependent on the Lord and on his blessings; but she had forgotten those days and was now pursuing other gods. This same tragic error is committed by churches or denominations when they no longer hunger for God's presence or seek first his kingdom in the righteousness, peace, joy and power in the Holy Spirit (cf. Ro 14:17); instead, they tolerate worldly practices and the absence of genuine spiritual life and of the Spirit's manifestation.

more depraved than they.[l] 48 As surely as I live, declares the Sovereign[m] LORD, your sister Sodom[n] and her daughters never did what you and your daughters have done.[o]

49 " 'Now this was the sin of your sister Sodom:[p] She and her daughters were arrogant,[q] overfed and unconcerned;[r] they did not help the poor and needy.[s] 50 They were haughty[t] and did detestable things before me. Therefore I did away with them as you have seen.[u] 51 Samaria did not commit half the sins you did. You have done more detestable things than they, and have made your sisters seem righteous by all these things you have done.[v] 52 Bear your disgrace, for you have furnished some justification for your sisters. Because your sins were more vile than theirs, they appear more righteous[w] than you. So then, be ashamed and bear[x] your disgrace, for you have made your sisters appear righteous.

53 " 'However, I will restore[y] the fortunes of Sodom and her daughters and of Samaria and her daughters, and your fortunes along with them,[z] 54 so that you may bear your disgrace[a] and be ashamed of all you have done in giving them comfort. 55 And your sisters, Sodom with her daughters and Samaria with her daughters, will return to what they were before; and you and your daughters will return to what you were before.[b] 56 You would not even mention your sister Sodom in the day of your pride, 57 before your wickedness was uncovered. Even so, you are now scorned[c] by the daughters of Edom[h][d] and all her neighbors and the daughters of the Philistines—all those around you who despise you. 58 You will bear the consequences of your lewdness and your detestable practices, declares the LORD.[e]

59 " 'This is what the Sovereign LORD says: I will deal with you as you deserve, because you have despised my oath by breaking the covenant.[f] 60 Yet I will remember the covenant[g] I made with you in the days of your youth,[h] and I will establish an everlasting covenant[i] with you. 61 Then you will remember your ways and be ashamed[j] when you receive your sisters, both those who are older than you and those who are younger. I will give them to you as daughters,[k] but not on the basis of my covenant with you. 62 So I will establish my covenant[l] with you, and you will know that I am the LORD.[m] 63 Then, when I make atonement[n] for you for all you have done, you will remember and be ashamed[o] and never again open your mouth[p] because of your humiliation, declares the Sovereign LORD.[q]' "

Two Eagles and a Vine

17 The word of the LORD came to me: 2 "Son of man, set forth an allegory and tell the house of Israel a parable.[r] 3 Say to them, 'This is what the Sovereign LORD says: A great eagle[s] with powerful wings, long feathers and full plumage of varied colors came to Lebanon.[t] Taking hold of the top of a cedar, 4 he broke off[u] its topmost shoot and carried it away to a land of merchants, where he planted it in a city of traders.

5 " 'He took some of the seed of your land and put it in fertile soil. He planted it like a willow by abundant water,[v] 6 and it sprouted and became a low, spreading vine. Its branches[w] turned toward him, but its roots remained under it. So it became a vine and produced branches and put out leafy boughs.[x]

7 " 'But there was another great eagle with powerful wings and full plumage. The vine now sent out its roots

16:47 [l] S Eze 5:7 **16:48** [m] S Ge 15:2 [n] S Ge 19:25 [o] Mt 10:15; 11:23-24 **16:49** [p] S Isa 1:10 [q] Ps 138:6; Eze 28:2 [r] Isa 22:13 [s] S Ge 13:13; 19:9; S Jer 5:28; Eze 18:7,12,16; Am 6:4-6; Lk 12:16-20; 16:19; Jas 5:5 **16:50** [t] Ps 18:27 [u] Ge 18:20-21; S 19:5 **16:51** [v] Jer 3:8-11; Eze 5:6-7; 23:11 **16:52** [w] S Jer 3:11 [x] Eze 23:35 **16:53** [y] S Dt 30:3; Isa 19:24-25; S Jer 48:47 [z] Eze 39:25 **16:54** [a] S Jer 2:26 **16:55** [b] Eze 36:11; Mal 3:4 **16:57** [c] S Ps 137:3 [d] 2Ki 16:6 **16:58** [e] Eze 23:49 **16:59** [f] S ver 8; Eze 17:19 **16:60** [g] S Ge 6:18; S 9:15 [h] S Ps 25:7; S Jer 2:2 [i] S Ge 9:16; Eze 37:26 **16:61** [j] ver 63; Eze 20:43; 43:10; 44:13 [k] S Isa 43:6 **16:62** [l] S Dt 29:14 [m] S Jer 24:7; Eze 20:37,43-44; 34:25; 37:26; Hos 2:19-20 **16:63** [n] Ps 65:3; 78:38; 79:9 [o] Eze 36:31-32 [p] Ro 3:19 [q] Ps 39:9; Da 9:7-8 **17:2** [r] S Jdg 14:12; S Eze 20:49 **17:3** [s] S Dt 28:49; Jer 49:22; Da 7:4; Hos 8:1 [t] S Jer 22:23 **17:4** [u] S Isa 10:33 **17:5** [v] Dt 8:7-9; Ps 1:3; Isa 44:4; Eze 31:5 **17:6** [w] S Isa 18:5 [x] S Job 5:3

[h] *57* Many Hebrew manuscripts and Syriac; most Hebrew manuscripts, Septuagint and Vulgate *Aram*

16:60 I WILL REMEMBER THE COVENANT. After God's judgment against Jerusalem and the whole house of Israel, he would remember his promise to Abraham (cf. Ge 17:7–8; Lev 26:42; see article on GOD'S COVENANT WITH ABRAHAM, ISAAC AND JACOB, p. 46) and restore them to the land of Canaan and to fellowship with him. This "new covenant" spoken of by Jeremiah (Jer 31:31–34) and Ezekiel (Eze 11:18–20; 36:26–28; 37:26–28) would involve Jesus Christ's atoning sacrifice and death on the cross.

17:3 A GREAT EAGLE. Ezekiel expresses God's message in a parable. The great eagle refers to King Nebuchadnezzar of Babylon (see v. 12); "Lebanon" refers to Jerusalem (see v. 12).

17:4 TOPMOST SHOOT. This designation refers to King Jehoiachin of Judah, who was carried away to Babylon (see 2Ki 24:11–16).

17:7 ANOTHER GREAT EAGLE. This eagle pictures the pharaoh of Egypt. King Zedekiah of Judah rebelled against Nebuchadnezzar and turned to Egypt for military aid (2Ki 24:20).

toward him from the plot where it was
planted and stretched out its branches
to him for water.[y] **8**It had been planted in good soil by abundant water so
that it would produce branches,[z] bear
fruit and become a splendid vine.'
9"Say to them, 'This is what the Sovereign LORD says: Will it thrive? Will it
not be uprooted and stripped of its fruit
so that it withers? All its new growth
will wither. It will not take a strong
arm or many people to pull it up by the
roots.[a] **10**Even if it[b] is transplanted,
will it thrive? Will it not wither completely when the east wind strikes it—
wither away in the plot where it
grew?[c]' "
11Then the word of the LORD came to
me: **12**"Say to this rebellious house,
'Do you not know what these things
mean?[d]' Say to them: 'The king of
Babylon went to Jerusalem and carried
off her king and her nobles,[e] bringing
them back with him to Babylon.[f]
13Then he took a member of the royal
family and made a treaty[g] with him,
putting him under oath.[h] He also carried away the leading men[i] of the
land, **14**so that the kingdom would be
brought low,[j] unable to rise again,
surviving only by keeping his treaty.
15But the king rebelled[k] against him
by sending his envoys to Egypt[l] to get
horses and a large army.[m] Will he succeed? Will he who does such things escape? Will he break the treaty and yet
escape?[n]
16" 'As surely as I live, declares the
Sovereign LORD, he shall die[o] in Babylon, in the land of the king who put
him on the throne, whose oath he despised and whose treaty he broke.[p]
17Pharaoh[q] with his mighty army and
great horde will be of no help to him in
war, when ramps[r] are built and siege
works erected to destroy many lives.[s]
18He despised the oath by breaking the
covenant. Because he had given his
hand in pledge[t] and yet did all these
things, he shall not escape.
19" 'Therefore this is what the Sovereign LORD says: As surely as I live, I
will bring down on his head my oath
that he despised and my covenant that
he broke.[u] **20**I will spread my net[v] for
him, and he will be caught in my snare.
I will bring him to Babylon and execute
judgment[w] upon him there because he
was unfaithful[x] to me. **21**All his fleeing troops will fall by the sword,[y] and
the survivors[z] will be scattered to the
winds.[a] Then you will know that I the
LORD have spoken.[b]
22" 'This is what the Sovereign LORD
says: I myself will take a shoot[c] from
the very top of a cedar and plant it; I
will break off a tender sprig from its
topmost shoots and plant it on a high
and lofty mountain.[d] **23**On the mountain heights[e] of Israel I will plant it;
it will produce branches and bear
fruit[f] and become a splendid cedar.
Birds of every kind will nest in it; they
will find shelter in the shade of its
branches.[g] **24**All the trees of the
field[h] will know that I the LORD bring
down[i] the tall tree and make the low
tree grow tall. I dry up the green tree
and make the dry tree flourish.[j]
" 'I the LORD have spoken, and I will
do it.[k]' "

The Soul Who Sins Will Die

18 The word of the LORD came to
me: **2**"What do you people mean
by quoting this proverb about the land
of Israel:

17:7 [y] Eze 31:4 **17:8** [z] Job 18:19; Mal 4:1 **17:9** [a] Jer 42:10; Am 2:9 **17:10** [b] S Job 1:19; Hos 12:1; 13:15 [c] S Eze 15:4 **17:12** [d] S Eze 12:9 [e] S 2Ki 24:15 [f] S Dt 21:10; S 2Ch 36:10; Eze 24:19 **17:13** [g] S Ex 23:32; S Jer 37:1 [h] 2Ch 36:13 [i] Isa 3:2 **17:14** [j] Eze 29:14 **17:15** [k] Jer 52:3 [l] S Isa 30:2; S Jer 37:5 [m] S Dt 17:16 [n] S Ps 56:7; S Isa 30:5; Jer 34:3; 38:18; Eze 29:16 **17:16** [o] S Jer 52:11; Eze 12:13 [p] S 2Ki 24:17 **17:17** [q] Jer 37:7 [r] S Eze 4:2 [s] S Isa 36:6; Jer 37:5; Eze 29:6-7 **17:18** [t] S 2Ki 10:15; 1Ch 29:24 **17:19** [u] Jer 7:9; S Eze 16:59; 21:23; Hos 10:4 **17:20** [v] S Eze 12:13; 32:3 [w] S Jer 2:35 [x] S Eze 15:8 **17:21** [y] S Eze 12:14 [z] 2Ki 25:11 [a] S Lev 26:33; S 2Ki 25:5; Zec 2:6 [b] S Jer 27:8 **17:22** [c] S 2Ki 19:30; S Isa 4:2 [d] ver 23; Isa 2:2; S Jer 23:5; Eze 20:40; 36:1, 36; 37:22; 40:2; 43:12 **17:23** [e] S ver 22; S Jer 31:12 [f] S Isa 27:6 [g] Ps 92:12; S Isa 2:2; Eze 31:6; Da 4:12; Hos 14:5-7; S Mt 13:32 **17:24** [h] S Ps 96:12; Isa 2:13 [i] S Ps 52:5 [j] S Nu 17:8; Da 5:21 [k] S 1Sa 2:7-8; Eze 19:12; 21:26; 22:14; 37:13; Am 9:11

17:10 THE EAST WIND. The "east wind" refers to the Babylonian army. Because Judah's last king, Zedekiah, broke the oath of allegiance that he had made in the Lord's name with Nebuchadnezzar, he would be carried away captive to Babylon and would die there (vv. 16–21; see 2Ki 25:7).

17:22 SHOOT FROM THE VERY TOP. God himself would plant a branch, the Messiah, Jesus Christ; his kingdom would be established throughout the whole earth (see 34:23, note; Isa 11:1, note; Jer 23:5–6, note).

18:1–32 WHAT DO YOU PEOPLE MEAN. Apparently many Jews believed that they were being punished for the sins of their forefathers and that therefore God was unjust; they failed to recognize that their own sins were even worse than those of their fathers. This chapter teaches the basic truths that each person is accountable to God for his or her own life, and that each person who persists in sin will die spiritually and experience eternal judgment.

18:2–4 THIS PROVERB. This proverb was probably based on Ex 20:5 and Dt 5:9, both of which teach that children are affected by the sins of their parents; however, Ezekiel makes it clear that these passages were not intended to teach that children were to be punished for their fathers' sins. All are accountable for their own sins and their own unwillingness to trust in Christ as Savior and to live righteous lives (see v. 4). The apostle

“ ‘The fathers eat sour grapes,
and the children’s teeth are set
on edge’?[l]

3“As surely as I live, declares the
Sovereign LORD, you will no longer
quote this proverb[m] in Israel. 4For every living soul belongs to me, the father as well as the son—both alike belong to me. The soul who sins[n] is the
one who will die.[o]

5“Suppose there is a righteous man
who does what is just and right.
6He does not eat at the mountain[p]
shrines
or look to the idols[q] of the
house of Israel.
He does not defile his neighbor’s
wife
or lie with a woman during her
period.[r]
7He does not oppress[s] anyone,
but returns what he took in
pledge[t] for a loan.
He does not commit robbery[u]
but gives his food to the
hungry[v]
and provides clothing for the
naked.[w]
8He does not lend at usury
or take excessive interest.[i][x]
He withholds his hand from doing
wrong
and judges fairly[y] between man
and man.
9He follows my decrees[z]
and faithfully keeps my laws.
That man is righteous;[a]
he will surely live,[b]
declares the Sovereign LORD.

10“Suppose he has a violent son,
who sheds blood[c] or does any of these
other things[j] 11(though the father has
done none of them):

“He eats at the mountain
shrines.[d]
He defiles his neighbor’s wife.
12He oppresses the poor[e] and
needy.
He commits robbery.
He does not return what he took
in pledge.[f]
He looks to the idols.
He does detestable things.[g]
13He lends at usury and takes
excessive interest.[h]
Will such a man live? He will not! Because he has done all these detestable
things, he will surely be put to death
and his blood will be on his own
head.[i]

14“But suppose this son has a son
who sees all the sins his father commits, and though he sees them, he does
not do such things:[j]

15“He does not eat at the mountain
shrines[k]
or look to the idols[l] of the
house of Israel.
He does not defile his neighbor’s
wife.
16He does not oppress anyone
or require a pledge for a loan.
He does not commit robbery
but gives his food to the
hungry[m]
and provides clothing for the
naked.[n]
17He withholds his hand from sin[k]
and takes no usury or excessive
interest.
He keeps my laws[o] and follows
my decrees.
He will not die for his father’s sin; he
will surely live. 18But his father will die
for his own sin, because he practiced
extortion, robbed his brother and did
what was wrong among his people.
19“Yet you ask, ‘Why does the son
not share the guilt of his father?’ Since
the son has done what is just and right

18:2 [l]S Job 21:19; Isa 3:15; Jer 31:29 **18:3** [m]S Ps 49:4 **18:4** [n]S 2Ki 14:6; S Pr 13:21 [o]ver 20; S Ge 18:23; S Ex 17:14; S Job 21:20; Isa 42:5; Eze 33:8; S Ro 6:23 **18:6** [p]S Eze 6:2 [q]Dt 4:19; S Eze 6:13; 20:24; Am 5:26 [r]S Lev 12:2; S 15:24 **18:7** [s]Ex 22:21; Mal 3:5; Jas 5:4 [t]S Ex 22:26 [u]S Ex 20:15 [v]S Job 22:7 [w]Dt 15:11; S Eze 16:49; S Mt 25:36; Lk 3:11 **18:8** [x]S Ex 18:21; 22:25; S Lev 25:35-37; Dt 23:19-20 [y]S Jer 22:3; Zec 8:16 **18:9** [z]S Lev 19:37 [a]Hab 2:4 [b]S Lev 18:5; S Eze 11:12; 20:11; Am 5:4 **18:10** [c]Ex 21:12; Eze 22:6 **18:11** [d]Eze 22:9 **18:12** [e]S Ex 22:22; S Job 24:9; Am 4:1 [f]S Ex 22:27 [g]2Ki 21:11; Isa 59:6-7; S Jer 22:17; S Eze 16:49; Hab 2:6 **18:13** [h]Ex 22:25 [i]S Lev 20:9; Eze 33:4-5; Hos 12:14 **18:14** [j]2Ch 34:21; S Pr 23:24 **18:15** [k]Eze 22:9 [l]S Ps 24:4 **18:16** [m]Isa 58:7 [n]S Ex 22:27; Ps 41:1; Isa 58:10; S Eze 16:49 **18:17** [o]S Ps 1:2

[i]*8* Or *take interest*; similarly in verses 13 and 17 [j]*10* Or *things to a brother* [k]*17* Septuagint (see also verse 8); Hebrew *from the poor*

Paul restates the principle with these words: “For the wages of sin is death, but the gift of God is eternal life in Christ Jesus our Lord” (Ro 6:23).

18:5–9 A RIGHTEOUS MAN. These verses describe a person who has a right relationship with the Lord and who demonstrates that commitment to God by loving righteousness and justice. It is this individual who will live eternally in communion and favor with the Lord. Paul emphasized this same truth when he said, “to those who by persistence in doing good seek glory, honor and immortality, he will give eternal life” (Ro 2:7); this lifestyle is now made possible by grace through faith in Christ (Eph 2:8–10).

18:10–13 A VIOLENT SON. The unrighteous children of a godly father will be held accountable for their own sins. As a result of their refusal to repent and turn to God, they will experience spiritual and eternal death (see Ro 2:8).

and has been careful to keep all my decrees, he will surely live.[p] **20**The soul
who sins is the one who will die.[q] The
son will not share the guilt of the father, nor will the father share the guilt
of the son. The righteousness of the
righteous man will be credited to him,
and the wickedness of the wicked will
be charged against him.[r]
21"But if[s] a wicked man turns away
from all the sins he has committed and
keeps all my decrees[t] and does what
is just and right, he will surely live; he
will not die.[u] **22**None of the offenses
he has committed will be remembered
against him. Because of the righteous
things he has done, he will live.[v] **23**Do
I take any pleasure in the death of the
wicked? declares the Sovereign LORD.
Eze 33:14-16 Rather, am I not pleased[w] when they
turn from their ways and live?[x]
24"But if a righteous man turns[y]
from his righteousness and commits
sin and does the same detestable
things the wicked man does, will he
live? None of the righteous things he
has done will be remembered. Because
of the unfaithfulness[z] he is guilty of
and because of the sins he has committed, he will die.[a]
25"Yet you say, 'The way of the Lord
is not just.'[b] Hear, O house of Israel:
Is my way unjust?[c] Is it not your ways
that are unjust? **26**If a righteous man
turns from his righteousness and commits sin, he will die for it; because of
the sin he has committed he will die.
27But if a wicked man turns away from
the wickedness he has committed and
does what is just and right, he will save
his life.[d] **28**Because he considers all
the offenses he has committed and
turns away from them, he will surely
live; he will not die.[e] **29**Yet the house
of Israel says, 'The way of the Lord is
not just.' Are my ways unjust, O house
of Israel? Is it not your ways that are
unjust?
30"Therefore, O house of Israel, I
will judge you, each one according to
his ways, declares the Sovereign LORD.
Repent![f] Turn away from all your offenses; then sin will not be your downfall.[g] **31**Rid[h] yourselves of all the offenses you have committed, and get a
new heart[i] and a new spirit. Why[j]
will you die, O house of Israel?[k] **32**For
I take no pleasure in the death of anyone, declares the Sovereign LORD. Repent[l] and live![m]

18:19 [p] Ex 20:5; Dt 5:9; Jer 15:4; Zec 1:3-6 **18:20** [q] S Nu 15:31 [r] Dt 24:16; S 1Ki 8:32; 2Ki 14:6; Isa 3:11; S Eze 7:27; S 14:14; S Mt 16:27; Jn 9:2 **18:21** [s] Jer 18:8 [t] S Ge 26:5 [u] S Eze 13:22; 36:27 **18:22** [v] Ps 18:20-24; S Isa 43:25; Da 4:27; Mic 7:19 **18:23** [w] Ps 147:11 [x] S Job 37:23; S La 3:33; S Eze 16:6; Mic 7:18; S 1Ti 2:4 **18:24** [y] S Jer 34:16 [z] S Eze 15:8 [a] S 1Sa 15:11; 2Ch 24:17-20; S Job 35:8; Pr 21:16; S Eze 3:20; 20:27; 2Pe 2:20-22 **18:25** [b] Jer 2:29 [c] S Ge 18:25; Jer 12:1; Eze 33:17; Zep 3:5; Mal 2:17; 3:13-15 **18:27** [d] S Isa 1:18; S Eze 13:22 **18:28** [e] S Isa 55:7 **18:30** [f] S Isa 1:27; S Jer 35:15; Mt 3:2 [g] Eze 7:3; 24:14; 33:20; Hos 12:6; 1Pe 1:17 **18:31** [h] S Jdg 6:8 [i] Ps 51:10 [j] Jer 27:13 [k] S Isa 1:16-17; S Eze 11:19; 36:26 **18:32** [l] S Job 22:23; Isa 55:7; Mal 3:7 [m] S 2Ch 7:14; S Job 37:23; S Eze 16:6; 33:11 **19:1** [n] ver 14; Jer 7:29; 9:10,20; Eze 26:17; 27:2, 32; 28:12; 32:2, 16; Am 5:1 [o] S 2Ki 24:6

A Lament for Israel's Princes

19 "Take up a lament[n] concerning the princes[o] of Israel **2**and
say:

" 'What a lioness[p] was your
mother
among the lions!
She lay down among the young
lions
and reared her cubs.[q]
3She brought up one of her cubs,
and he became a strong lion.
He learned to tear the prey
and he devoured men.
4The nations heard about him,
and he was trapped in their pit.
They led him with hooks[r]
to the land of Egypt.[s]

5" 'When she saw her hope
unfulfilled,
her expectation gone,
she took another of her cubs[t]
and made him a strong lion.[u]
6He prowled among the lions,
for he was now a strong lion.
He learned to tear the prey
and he devoured men.[v]

19:2 [p] S Nu 23:24 [q] S Ge 49:9 **19:4** [r] S Job 41:2 [s] 2Ki 23:33-34; 2Ch 36:4; S La 4:20 **19:5** [t] S Ge 49:9 [u] 2Ki 23:34 **19:6** [v] 2Ki 24:9; 2Ch 36:9

18:21–23 A WICKED MAN TURNS AWAY. God promises salvation to any of the wicked who choose to forsake their sins and turn to God. No one is forced to follow the sins of his or her family. God desires to bring each sinner into fellowship with himself and is never pleased when a wicked person dies in sin (cf. 1Ti 2:4).

18:24 A RIGHTEOUS MAN TURNS FROM. The righteous who trust in God and follow his way must not think they are eternally secure if they later become unfaithful and rebellious against God. Such people also will die, just like the one who has always lived in sin. Paul warns believers: "if you live according to the sinful nature, you will die" (Ro 8:13; see also Heb 2:3; 3:6; 2Pe 2:20–22; see article on PERSONAL APOSTASY, p. 1918).

19:1–14 A LAMENT. The lament in this chapter compares Judah's last king to a caged lion and the nation to a ruined vine.

19:3–4 ONE OF HER CUBS. Young King Jehoahaz (see 2Ki 23:31–34) reigned for three months; then he was taken captive to Egypt, where he eventually died.

19:5–9 ANOTHER OF HER CUBS. This designation refers either to Jehoiachin or to Zedekiah; both were taken captive to Babylon (see 2Ki 24:8—25:7).

7He broke down[l] their strongholds
and devastated[w] their towns.
The land and all who were in it
were terrified by his roaring.
8Then the nations[x] came against
him,
those from regions round about.
They spread their net[y] for him,
and he was trapped in their
pit.[z]
9With hooks[a] they pulled him into
a cage
and brought him to the king of
Babylon.[b]
They put him in prison,
so his roar[c] was heard no
longer
on the mountains of Israel.[d]

10" 'Your mother was like a vine in
your vineyard[me]
planted by the water;[f]
it was fruitful and full of branches
because of abundant water.[g]
11Its branches were strong,
fit for a ruler's scepter.
It towered high
above the thick foliage,
conspicuous for its height
and for its many branches.[h]
12But it was uprooted[i] in fury
and thrown to the ground.
The east wind[j] made it shrivel,
it was stripped of its fruit;
its strong branches withered
and fire consumed them.[k]
13Now it is planted in the desert,[l]
in a dry and thirsty land.[m]
14Fire spread from one of its main[n]
branches
and consumed[n] its fruit.
No strong branch is left on it
fit for a ruler's scepter.'[o]

This is a lament[p] and is to be used as
a lament."

Rebellious Israel

20 In the seventh year, in the fifth
month on the tenth day, some
of the elders of Israel came to inquire[q]
of the LORD, and they sat down in front
of me.[r]
2Then the word of the LORD came to
me: 3"Son of man, speak to the elders[s] of Israel and say to them, 'This
is what the Sovereign LORD says: Have
you come to inquire[t] of me? As surely
as I live, I will not let you inquire of me,
declares the Sovereign LORD.[u]'
4"Will you judge them? Will you
judge them, son of man? Then confront
them with the detestable practices of
their fathers[v] 5and say to them: 'This
is what the Sovereign LORD says: On
the day I chose[w] Israel, I swore with
uplifted hand[x] to the descendants of
the house of Jacob and revealed myself
to them in Egypt. With uplifted hand I
said to them, "I am the LORD your
God.[y]" 6On that day I swore[z] to them
that I would bring them out of Egypt
into a land I had searched out for them,
a land flowing with milk and honey,[a]
the most beautiful of all lands.[b] 7And
I said to them, "Each of you, get rid of
the vile images[c] you have set your
eyes on, and do not defile yourselves
with the idols[d] of Egypt. I am the LORD
your God.[e]"
8" 'But they rebelled against me and
would not listen to me;[f] they did not
get rid of the vile images they had set
their eyes on, nor did they forsake the
idols of Egypt.[g] So I said I would pour
out my wrath on them and spend my
anger against them in Egypt.[h] 9But
for the sake of my name I did what
would keep it from being profaned[i] in
the eyes of the nations they lived
among and in whose sight I had revealed myself to the Israelites by
bringing them out of Egypt.[j] 10There-
fore I led them out of Egypt and
brought them into the desert.[k] 11I
gave them my decrees and made
known to them my laws, for the man

[l] 7 Targum (see Septuagint); Hebrew *He knew*
[m] 10 Two Hebrew manuscripts; most Hebrew manuscripts *your blood*
[n] 14 Or *from under its*

19:7 [w] Eze 29:10; 30:12
19:8 [x] 2Ki 24:2 [y] S Eze 12:13 [z] 2Ki 24:11; S La 4:20
19:9 [a] S 2Ki 19:28 [b] S 2Ki 25:7; S 2Ch 36:6 [c] Zec 11:3 [d] S 2Ki 24:15
19:10 [e] S Ge 49:22 [f] S Jer 17:8 [g] Ps 80:8-11
19:11 [h] Eze 31:3; Da 4:11
19:12 [i] S Dt 29:28 [j] S Ge 41:6 [k] S Isa 27:11; S Eze 17:24; 28:17; Hos 13:15
19:13 [l] Eze 20:35; Hos 2:14 [m] Hos 2:3
19:14 [n] Eze 20:47 [o] S Eze 15:4 [p] S ver 1
20:1 [q] S Ge 25:22 [r] Eze 1:1-2; S 8:1; 21:1
20:3 [s] S Eze 7:26 [t] S Ge 25:22; Eze 14:3 [u] S 1Sa 28:6; Isa 1:15; Am 8:12; Mic 3:7
20:4 [v] S Eze 16:2; 22:2; Mt 23:32
20:5 [w] S Dt 7:6 [x] S Ge 14:22; S Nu 14:30 [y] S Lev 11:44
20:6 [z] S Ex 6:8 [a] S Ex 3:8 [b] S Dt 8:7; Da 8:9; 11:41; Mal 3:12
20:7 [c] Ex 20:4 [d] S Eze 6:9 [e] S Ex 20:2; Lev 18:3; Dt 29:18
20:8 [f] S Jer 7:26 [g] S Jer 11:10; S Eze 7:8; S 16:26 [h] S Ex 32:7; Dt 9:7; S Isa 63:10
20:9 [i] S Isa 48:11 [j] Eze 36:22; 39:7
20:10 [k] S Ex 13:18; 19:1

19:10–14 YOUR MOTHER. The lioness (Israel, see vv. 1–2) is here pictured as a fruitful vine that was uprooted and its branches burned; what was left of the vine was planted in a desert (i.e., the Babylonian captivity).

20:1–49 SOME OF THE ELDERS. This chapter expresses the sad truth that Israel's history had been one of continual idol worship and moral failure. Ezekiel told the elders of his day that they themselves had not yet removed their love for idols from their hearts; thus they too were guilty before God.

20:9 THE SAKE OF MY NAME. God did not totally destroy the Israelites in the desert after the exodus because he wanted to uphold the honor of his name. He made himself known to them by bringing them out of Egypt, so that he could fulfill his promise of universal blessing through his chosen people (see Ge 12:1–3).

who obeys them will live by them.[l]
12Also I gave them my Sabbaths[m] as
a sign[n] between us,[o] so they would
know that I the LORD made them
holy.[p]
13" 'Yet the people of Israel rebelled[q] against me in the desert. They
did not follow my decrees but rejected
my laws[r]—although the man who
obeys them will live by them—and
they utterly desecrated my Sabbaths.[s] So I said I would pour out my
wrath[t] on them and destroy[u] them in
the desert.[v] **14**But for the sake of my
name I did what would keep it from being profaned[w] in the eyes of the nations in whose sight I had brought
them out.[x] **15**Also with uplifted hand
I swore[y] to them in the desert that I
would not bring them into the land I
had given them—a land flowing with
milk and honey, most beautiful of all
lands[z]— **16**because they rejected my
laws[a] and did not follow my decrees
and desecrated my Sabbaths. For their
hearts[b] were devoted to their idols.[c]
17Yet I looked on them with pity and
did not destroy[d] them or put an end to
them in the desert. **18**I said to their
children in the desert, "Do not follow
the statutes of your fathers[e] or keep
their laws or defile yourselves[f] with
their idols. **19**I am the LORD your God;[g]
follow my decrees and be careful to
keep my laws.[h] **20**Keep my Sabbaths[i] holy, that they may be a sign[j]
between us. Then you will know that I
am the LORD your God.[k]"
21" 'But the children rebelled
against me: They did not follow my decrees, they were not careful to keep my
laws[l]—although the man who obeys
them will live by them—and they desecrated my Sabbaths. So I said I would
pour out my wrath on them and spend
my anger[m] against them in the
desert.[n] **22**But I withheld[o] my hand,
and for the sake of my name[p] I did
what would keep it from being profaned in the eyes of the nations in
whose sight I had brought them out.
23Also with uplifted hand I swore to
them in the desert that I would disperse them among the nations and
scatter[q] them through the countries,
24because they had not obeyed my
laws but had rejected my decrees[r]
and desecrated my Sabbaths,[s] and
their eyes ⌞lusted⌟ after[t] their fathers'
idols.[u] **25**I also gave them over[v] to
statutes that were not good and laws
they could not live by;[w] **26**I let them
become defiled through their gifts—
the sacrifice[x] of every firstborn[o]—
that I might fill them with horror so
they would know that I am the LORD.[y]'
27"Therefore, son of man, speak to
the people of Israel and say to them,
'This is what the Sovereign LORD says:
In this also your fathers[z] blasphemed[a] me by forsaking me:[b]
28When I brought them into the land[c]
I had sworn to give them and they saw
any high hill or any leafy tree, there
they offered their sacrifices, made offerings that provoked me to anger, presented their fragrant incense and
poured out their drink offerings.[d]
29Then I said to them: What is this
high place[e] you go to?' " (It is called
Bamah[p] to this day.)

Judgment and Restoration

30"Therefore say to the house of Israel: 'This is what the Sovereign LORD
says: Will you defile yourselves[f] the
way your fathers did and lust after
their vile images?[g] **31**When you offer
your gifts—the sacrifice of your sons[h]
in[q] the fire—you continue to defile
yourselves with all your idols to this
day. Am I to let you inquire of me, O
house of Israel? As surely as I live, declares the Sovereign LORD, I will not let
you inquire of me.[i]
32" 'You say, "We want to be like the

20:11 [l]Ex 20:1-23; Lev 18:5; Dt 4:7-8; S Eze 18:9; S Ro 10:5 **20:12** [m]S Ex 20:10 [n]S Ex 31:13 [o]Jer 17:22 [p]S Lev 20:8 **20:13** [q]Ps 78:40 [r]S Jer 6:19; 11:8 [s]ver 24 [t]S Dt 9:8 [u]S Ex 32:10 [v]Lev 26:15,43; S Nu 14:29; Ps 95:8-10; Isa 56:6 **20:14** [w]S Isa 48:11 [x]Eze 36:23 **20:15** [y]S Dt 1:34 [z]Nu 14:22-23; Ps 95:11; 106:26; Heb 3:11 **20:16** [a]Jer 11:8; Am 2:4 [b]S Nu 15:39 [c]ver 24; S Eze 6:4; Am 5:26 **20:17** [d]S Jer 4:27 **20:18** [e]S 2Ch 30:7; Zec 1:4 [f]S Ps 106:39 **20:19** [g]S Ex 20:2 [h]Dt 5:32-33; 6:1-2; S 8:1; 11:1; S 12:1 **20:20** [i]S Ex 20:10 [j]S Ex 31:13 [k]Jer 17:22 **20:21** [l]S Jer 7:26 [m]Nu 25:3 [n]S Eze 7:8 **20:22** [o]Ps 78:38 [p]S Isa 48:11 **20:23** [q]S Lev 26:33; S Ps 9:11 **20:24** [r]Am 2:4 [s]ver 13 [t]S Eze 6:9 [u]S ver 16; S Eze 2:3; S 18:6 **20:25** [v]S Ps 81:12; Ro 1:28 [w]Isa 66:4; 2Th 2:11 **20:26** [x]S Lev 18:21 [y]Lev 20:2-5; 2Ki 17:17 **20:27** [z]S Ps 78:57 [a]S Nu 15:30; Ro 2:24 [b]S Eze 18:24 **20:28** [c]Ne 9:23; Ps 78:55,58 [d]S Jer 2:7; S 3:6; S 19:13; S Eze 6:13 **20:29** [e]Eze 16:16; 43:7 **20:30** [f]ver 43 [g]S Jdg 2:16-19; S Jer 16:12 **20:31** [h]S Eze 16:20 [i]Ps 106:37-39; S Jer 7:31; S Eze 14:3; Am 8:12; Zec 7:13

[o]*26* Or *—making every firstborn pass through ⌞the fire⌟* [p]*29* *Bamah* means *high place.* [q]*31* Or *—making your sons pass through*

20:12 MY SABBATHS. Israel's observance of the weekly and annual Sabbaths was intended to remind her that she had been set apart as a holy nation in order to manifest God's righteousness and glory before the world (see Ex 31:13–17; Lev 23:32).

20:30 WILL YOU DEFILE YOURSELVES. The crucial question of this chapter is: "Will you Israelites continue to defile yourselves?" Believers today face daily decisions on whether to surrender to the sinful desires of their human nature or to yield themselves to the Holy Spirit and serve the cause of Christ (Ro 6:11–14; Gal 5:16–25).

20:32 TO BE LIKE THE NATIONS. God's people are constantly tempted to conform to the customs and ways of the world and thereby cease being God's special people. We must always ask ourselves two basic questions: (1) Do I give

nations, like the peoples of the world, who serve wood and stone." But what you have in mind will never happen. **33**As surely as I live, declares the Sovereign LORD, I will rule over you with a mighty hand and an outstretched arm[j] and with outpoured wrath.[k] **34**I will bring you from the nations[l] and gather[m] you from the countries where you have been scattered—with a mighty hand[n] and an outstretched arm and with outpoured wrath.[o] **35**I will bring you into the desert[p] of the nations and there, face to face, I will execute judgment[q] upon you. **36**As I judged your fathers in the desert of the land of Egypt, so I will judge you, declares the Sovereign LORD.[r] **37**I will take note of you as you pass under my rod,[s] and I will bring you into the bond of the covenant.[t] **38**I will purge[u] you of those who revolt and rebel against me. Although I will bring them out of the land where they are living, yet they will not enter the land of Israel. Then you will know that I am the LORD.[v]

39" 'As for you, O house of Israel, this is what the Sovereign LORD says: Go and serve your idols,[w] every one of you! But afterward you will surely listen to me and no longer profane my holy name[x] with your gifts and idols.[y] **40**For on my holy mountain, the high mountain of Israel,[z] declares the Sovereign LORD, there in the land the entire house of Israel will serve me, and there I will accept them. There I will require your offerings[a] and your choice gifts,[r] along with all your holy sacrifices.[b] **41**I will accept you as fragrant incense[c] when I bring you out from the nations and gather[d] you from the countries where you have been scattered, and I will show myself holy[e] among you in the sight of the nations.[f] **42**Then you will know that I am the LORD,[g] when I bring you into the land of Israel,[h] the land I had sworn with uplifted hand to give to your fathers.[i] **43**There you will remember your conduct[j] and all the actions by which you have defiled yourselves, and you will loathe yourselves[k] for all the evil you have done.[l] **44**You will know that I am the LORD, when I deal with you for my name's sake[m] and not according to your evil ways and your corrupt practices, O house of Israel, declares the Sovereign LORD.[n]' "

Da 9:4-6

Prophecy Against the South

45The word of the LORD came to me: **46**"Son of man, set your face toward[o] the south; preach against the south and prophesy against[p] the forest of the southland.[q] **47**Say to the southern forest:[r] 'Hear the word of the LORD. This is what the Sovereign LORD says: I am about to set fire to you, and it will consume[s] all your trees, both green and dry. The blazing flame will not be quenched, and every face from south to north[t] will be scorched by it.[u] **48**Everyone will see that I the LORD have kindled it; it will not be quenched.[v]' "

49Then I said, "Ah, Sovereign LORD![w] They are saying of me, 'Isn't he just telling parables?[x]' "

Babylon, God's Sword of Judgment

21 The word of the LORD came to me:[y] **2**"Son of man, set your face against[z] Jerusalem and preach against the sanctuary.[a] Prophesy against[b] the land of Israel **3**and say to her: 'This is what the LORD says: I am against you.[c] I will draw my sword[d]

20:33 [j] S Eze 16:27 [k] Jer 21:5; Eze 25:16 **20:34** [l] 2Co 6:17* [m] S Dt 30:4; S Ps 106:47 [n] S Isa 31:3 [o] Isa 27:12-13; S Jer 44:6; S La 2:4; S Eze 6:14 **20:35** [p] S Eze 19:13 [q] S 1Sa 12:7; S Job 22:4; S Jer 2:35 **20:36** [r] Nu 11:1-35; 14:28-30; 1Co 10:5-10 **20:37** [s] S Lev 27:32 [t] S Eze 16:62 **20:38** [u] Eze 34:17-22; Am 9:9-10 [v] Ps 95:11; Jer 44:14; S Eze 13:9; 23:49; Hos 2:14; Zec 13:8-9; Mal 3:3; 4:1-3; Heb 4:3 **20:39** [w] S Jer 44:25 [x] S Ex 20:7; S Eze 13:19 [y] Eze 43:7; Am 4:4 **20:40** [z] S Eze 17:22; 34:14 [a] S Isa 60:7 [b] S Isa 56:7; Mal 3:4 **20:41** [c] S 2Co 2:14 [d] S Dt 30:4 [e] Eze 28:25; 36:23 [f] S Isa 5:16; S Eze 11:17; 2Co 6:17 **20:42** [g] Eze 38:23 [h] S Jer 23:8; Eze 34:13; 36:24 [i] Jer 30:3; Eze 34:27; 37:21 **20:43** [j] Eze 14:22 [k] S Lev 26:41 [l] S Eze 6:9; S 16:61; Hos 5:15 **20:44** [m] Ps 109:21; Isa 43:25; Eze 36:22 [n] S Eze 16:62; 36:32 **20:46** [o] S Eze 4:3; S 13:17 [p] Eze 21:2; Am 7:16 [q] Isa 30:6; Jer 13:19 **20:47** [r] S 2Ki 19:23 [s] Eze 19:14 [t] Eze 21:4 [u] Isa 9:18-19; S 13:8 **20:48** [v] S Jer 7:20; Eze 21:5,32; 23:25 **20:49** [w] S Eze 4:14 [x] S Jdg 14:12; S Ps 78:2; S Eze 12:9; Mt 13:13; S Jn 16:25 **21:1** [y] S Eze 20:1 **21:2** [z] S Eze 13:17 [a] Eze 9:6 [b] Jer 26:11-12; S Eze 20:46 **21:3** [c] S Jer 21:13 [d] S Isa 27:1; S Eze 14:21

[r] 40 Or *and the gifts of your firstfruits*

---

in to peer pressure at school, on the job or among friends? (2) Am I different in my ways and actions or do I instead conform to the ways and expectations of the ungodly (see Ro 12:1–2, notes)?

20:34–44 I WILL BRING YOU FROM. God promised to bring Israel back from their captivity after he had purged out the rebels and evildoers (cf. 11:17,21; Mal 3:2–5). A faithful remnant would return to the land (cf. Isa 10:21–23) and would no longer profane God's name by disobedience or idol worship (v. 39); they would enjoy the blessings of the "new covenant" (see Jer 31:31–34; Heb 8:1—10:18).

21:3–32 MY SWORD. The judgment against Jerusalem and the nation of Judah would come by the sword (i.e., by the Babylonian army) that God was going to use to destroy them.

21:3 THE RIGHTEOUS AND THE WICKED. In natural catastrophies or national disasters, the righteous and the wicked often suffer alike. Note, however, that Ezekiel had earlier made it clear that the righteous would not experience the eternal judgment of the wicked (see 18:1–24).

from its scabbard and cut off from you
both the righteous and the wicked.[e]
4Because I am going to cut off the righteous and the wicked, my sword[f] will
be unsheathed against everyone from
south to north.[g] 5Then all people will
know that I the LORD have drawn my
sword[h] from its scabbard; it will not
return[i] again.'[j]

6"Therefore groan, son of man!
Groan before them with broken heart
and bitter grief.[k] 7And when they ask
you, 'Why are you groaning?[l]' you
shall say, 'Because of the news that is
coming. Every heart will melt[m] and every hand go limp;[n] every spirit will become faint[o] and every knee become as
weak as water.'[p] It is coming! It will
surely take place, declares the Sovereign LORD."

8The word of the LORD came to me:
9"Son of man, prophesy and say, 'This
is what the Lord says:

" 'A sword, a sword,
sharpened and polished—
10sharpened for the slaughter,[q]
polished to flash like lightning!

" 'Shall we rejoice in the scepter of
my son ⌊Judah⌋? The sword despises
every such stick.[r]

11" 'The sword is appointed to be
polished,[s]
to be grasped with the hand;
it is sharpened and polished,
made ready for the hand of the
slayer.
12Cry out and wail, son of man,
for it is against my people;
it is against all the princes of
Israel.
They are thrown to the sword
along with my people.
Therefore beat your breast.[t]

13" 'Testing will surely come. And
what if the scepter ⌊of Judah⌋, which the
sword despises, does not continue? declares the Sovereign LORD.'

14"So then, son of man, prophesy
and strike your hands[u]
together.
Let the sword strike twice,
even three times.
It is a sword for slaughter—
a sword for great slaughter,
closing in on them from every
side.[v]
15So that hearts may melt[w]
and the fallen be many,
I have stationed the sword for
slaughter[s]
at all their gates.
Oh! It is made to flash like
lightning,
it is grasped for slaughter.[x]
16O sword, slash to the right,
then to the left,
wherever your blade is turned.
17I too will strike my hands[y]
together,
and my wrath[z] will subside.
I the LORD have spoken.[a]"

18The word of the LORD came to me:
19"Son of man, mark out two roads for
the sword[b] of the king of Babylon to
take, both starting from the same
country. Make a signpost[c] where the
road branches off to the city. 20Mark
out one road for the sword to come
against Rabbah of the Ammonites[d]
and another against Judah and fortified
Jerusalem. 21For the king of Babylon
will stop at the fork in the road, at the
junction of the two roads, to seek an
omen: He will cast lots[e] with arrows,
he will consult his idols,[f] he will examine the liver.[g] 22Into his right hand
will come the lot for Jerusalem, where
he is to set up battering rams, to give
the command to slaughter, to sound
the battle cry,[h] to set battering rams
against the gates, to build a ramp[i]
and to erect siege works.[j] 23It will
seem like a false omen to those who
have sworn allegiance to him, but he
will remind[k] them of their guilt[l] and
take them captive.

24"Therefore this is what the Sovereign LORD says: 'Because you people
have brought to mind your guilt by your

21:3 [e]ver 9-11; S Job 9:22; S Isa 57:1; Jer 47:6-7 **21:4** [f]S Lev 26:25; S Jer 25:27 [g]Eze 20:47 **21:5** [h]S Isa 34:5 [i]ver 30 [j]S Eze 20:47-48; Na 1:9 **21:6** [k]ver 12; S Isa 22:4; Jer 30:6; S Eze 9:4 **21:7** [l]S Job 23:2 [m]S Jos 7:5 [n]S Jer 47:3; Eze 22:14 [o]S Ps 6:2 [p]S Lev 26:36; S Job 11:16 **21:10** [q]Ps 110:5-6; Isa 34:5-6 [r]Dt 32:41 **21:11** [s]Jer 46:4 **21:12** [t]Jer 31:19 **21:14** [u]ver 17; S Nu 24:10 [v]S Eze 6:11; 30:24 **21:15** [w]S 2Sa 17:10 [x]Ps 22:14 **21:17** [y]ver 14; Eze 22:13 [z]S Eze 5:13 [a]S Eze 6:11; S 16:42 **21:19** [b]S Eze 14:21; 32:11 [c]Jer 31:21 **21:20** [d]S Dt 3:11 **21:21** [e]S Pr 16:33 [f]Zec 10:2 [g]Nu 22:7; S 23:23 **21:22** [h]S Jer 4:16 [i]Jer 32:24 [j]S 2Ki 25:1; S Eze 4:2; 26:9 **21:23** [k]S Nu 5:15 [l]S Eze 17:19

[s] *15* Septuagint; the meaning of the Hebrew for this word is uncertain.

21:12 THROWN TO THE SWORD. Because God's people had not accepted his chastising correction, God had no choice but to deliver them to the sword. To remain stubborn and self-willed while being chastened by the Lord results in being condemned along with the world (see Heb 12:5, note).

21:19–23 THE KING OF BABYLON. Spiritists believed they could tell the future by examining the livers of slain animals (v. 21); Ezekiel insists, however, that God controlled the pagan practices of King Nebuchadnezzar in order to accomplish his will (cf. Jer 27:6).

open rebellion, revealing your sins in
all that you do—because you have
done this, you will be taken captive.
25" 'O profane and wicked prince of
Israel, whose day has come,[m] whose
time of punishment has reached its climax,[n] **26**this is what the Sovereign
LORD says: Take off the turban, remove
the crown.[o] It will not be as it was:
The lowly will be exalted and the exalted will be brought low.[p] **27**A ruin! A
ruin! I will make it a ruin! It will not be
restored until he comes to whom it
rightfully belongs;[q] to him I will give
it.'[r]
28"And you, son of man, prophesy
and say, 'This is what the Sovereign
LORD says about the Ammonites[s] and
their insults:

" 'A sword,[t] a sword,
drawn for the slaughter,
polished to consume
and to flash like lightning!
29Despite false visions concerning
you
and lying divinations[u] about
you,
it will be laid on the necks
of the wicked who are to be
slain,
whose day has come,
whose time of punishment has
reached its climax.[v]
30Return the sword to its
scabbard.[w]
In the place where you were
created,
in the land of your ancestry,[x]
I will judge you.
31I will pour out my wrath upon you
and breathe[y] out my fiery
anger[z] against you;
I will hand you over to brutal men,
men skilled in destruction.[a]
32You will be fuel for the fire,[b]
your blood will be shed in your
land,
you will be remembered[c] no more;
for I the LORD have spoken.' "

Jerusalem's Sins

22 The word of the LORD came to
me: **2**"Son of man, will you
judge her? Will you judge this city of
bloodshed?[d] Then confront her with
all her detestable practices[e] **3**and say:
'This is what the Sovereign LORD says:
O city that brings on herself doom by
shedding blood[f] in her midst and defiles herself by making idols, **4**you have
become guilty because of the blood you
have shed[g] and have become defiled
by the idols you have made. You have
brought your days to a close, and the
end of your years has come.[h] Therefore I will make you an object of
scorn[i] to the nations and a laughingstock to all the countries.[j] **5**Those
who are near and those who are far
away will mock you, O infamous city,
full of turmoil.[k]
6" 'See how each of the princes of
Israel who are in you uses his power to
shed blood.[l] **7**In you they have treated
father and mother with contempt;[m] in
you they have oppressed the alien[n]
and mistreated the fatherless and the
widow.[o] **8**You have despised my holy
things and desecrated my Sabbaths.[p]
9In you are slanderous men[q] bent on
shedding blood;[r] in you are those who
eat at the mountain shrines[s] and commit lewd acts.[t] **10**In you are those
who dishonor their fathers' bed;[u] in
you are those who violate women during their period,[v] when they are ceremonially unclean.[w] **11**In you one man
commits a detestable offense with his
neighbor's wife,[x] another shamefully
defiles his daughter-in-law,[y] and another violates his sister,[z] his own father's daughter.[a] **12**In you men accept
bribes[b] to shed blood; you take usu-

21:25 [m] Eze 22:4 [n] Eze 35:5 **21:26** [o] S Isa 28:5; S Jer 13:18 [p] S Ps 75:7; Isa 40:4; S Eze 17:24; S Mt 23:12 **21:27** [q] Ge 49:10 [r] Ps 2:6; Jer 23:5-6; Eze 37:24; Hag 2:21-22 **21:28** [s] S Ge 19:38; Zep 2:8 [t] S Jer 12:12 **21:29** [u] Jer 27:9 [v] ver 25; Eze 22:28; 35:5 **21:30** [w] ver 5; Jer 47:6 [x] S Eze 16:3 **21:31** [y] Ps 18:15; S Isa 11:4 [z] Ps 79:6; Eze 22:20-21 [a] S Jer 4:7; 51:20-23; S Eze 16:39 **21:32** [b] S Eze 20:47-48; Mal 4:1 **22:2** [c] Eze 25:10 [d] Eze 24:6,9; Hos 4:2; Na 3:1; Hab 2:12 [e] S Eze 16:2; 23:36 **22:3** [f] ver 6,13,27; Eze 23:37,45; 24:6 **22:4** [g] S 2Ki 21:16 [h] Eze 21:25 [i] S Ps 137:3 [j] Ps 44:13-14; S Eze 5:14 **22:5** [k] S Isa 22:2 **22:6** [l] S Eze 11:6; 18:10; 33:25 **22:7** [m] S Dt 5:16; Mic 7:6 [n] S Ex 23:9 [o] S Ex 22:21-22 **22:8** [p] S Ex 20:8; Eze 23:38-39 **22:9** [q] S Lev 19:16 [r] Isa 59:3; S Eze 11:6; Hos 4:2; 6:9 [s] Eze 18:11 [t] Eze 23:29; Hos 4:10,14 **22:10** [u] Lev 18:7 [v] S Lev 12:2 [w] S Lev 18:8,19 **22:11** [x] S Jer 5:8 [y] S Ge 11:31; Lev 18:15 [z] S Lev 18:9; S 2Sa 13:14 [a] Eze 18:6 **22:12** [b] S Ex 18:21; Dt 27:25; Ps 26:10; Isa 5:23; Am 5:12; Mic 7:3

21:27 UNTIL HE COMES. Ezekiel prophesies that though the Davidic line would continue, the Davidic throne would not be reinstituted until the Messianic King came to establish his rule (cf. Ge 49:10; Zec 9:9; Mt 21:1–11; Rev 19:11–16; 20:4). Jesus Christ, the Messiah, will yet rule over Israel.

22:2–12 BY SHEDDING BLOOD. Jerusalem had become a city of violence and all sorts of wickedness. There was no longer any respect for holy things, family, or the poor and needy. Sexual immorality was rampant, and cheating and bribery were commonplace. All this happened because the people had turned from God and his word. Therefore, God was giving the city over to severe judgment and destruction. Today the social and spiritual condition of cities throughout the world is similar to that of ancient Jerusalem. Unless these cities repent, they will perish just as Jerusalem did. Nations, cities and people cannot despise God and his ways without ultimately reaping the consequences.

ry[c] and excessive interest[t] and make
unjust gain from your neighbors[d] by
extortion. And you have forgotten[e]
me, declares the Sovereign LORD.[f]
13" 'I will surely strike my hands[g]
together at the unjust gain[h] you have
made and at the blood[i] you have shed
in your midst.[j] 14Will your courage
endure[k] or your hands[l] be strong in
the day I deal with you? I the LORD have
spoken,[m] and I will do it.[n] 15I will disperse you among the nations and scatter[o] you through the countries; and I
will put an end to[p] your uncleanness.[q] 16When you have been defiled[u] in the eyes of the nations, you
will know that I am the LORD.' "
17Then the word of the LORD came to
me: 18"Son of man, the house of Israel
has become dross[r] to me; all of them
are the copper, tin, iron and lead left
inside a furnace.[s] They are but the
dross of silver.[t] 19Therefore this is
what the Sovereign LORD says: 'Because you have all become dross,[u] I
will gather you into Jerusalem. 20As
men gather silver, copper, iron, lead
and tin into a furnace to melt it with a
fiery blast, so will I gather you in my
anger and my wrath and put you inside
the city and melt you.[v] 21I will gather
you and I will blow[w] on you with my
fiery wrath, and you will be melted inside her.[x] 22As silver is melted[y] in a
furnace, so you will be melted inside
her, and you will know that I the LORD
have poured out my wrath[z] upon
you.' "[a]
23Again the word of the LORD came
to me: 24"Son of man, say to the land,
'You are a land that has had no rain or
showers[v] in the day of wrath.'[b]
25There is a conspiracy[c] of her
princes[w] within her like a roaring
lion[d] tearing its prey; they devour
people,[e] take treasures and precious
things and make many widows[f] within her. 26Her priests do violence to my
law[g] and profane my holy things; they
do not distinguish between the holy
and the common;[h] they teach that
there is no difference between the unclean and the clean;[i] and they shut
their eyes to the keeping of my Sabbaths, so that I am profaned[j] among
them.[k] 27Her officials[l] within her are
like wolves[m] tearing their prey; they
shed blood and kill people[n] to make
unjust gain.[o] 28Her prophets whitewash[p] these deeds for them by false
visions and lying divinations.[q] They
say, 'This is what the Sovereign LORD
says'—when the LORD has not spoken.[r] 29The people of the land practice extortion and commit robbery;[s]
they oppress the poor and needy and
mistreat the alien,[t] denying them justice.[u]
30"I looked for a man among them
who would build up the wall[v] and
stand before me in the gap on behalf of
the land so I would not have to destroy
it, but I found none.[w] 31So I will pour
out my wrath on them and consume

22:12 [c]S Eze 18:8 [d]Lev 19:13 [e]Ps 106:21; S Isa 17:10; S 57:11 [f]S Eze 11:6 **22:13** [g]S Nu 24:10; S Eze 21:17 [h]S ver 27; S Isa 33:15 [i]S ver 3 [j]S Eze 6:11 **22:14** [k]Ps 76:7; Joel 2:11; Na 1:6; Mal 3:2 [l]S Eze 7:17 [m]Eze 24:14 [n]S Eze 17:24 **22:15** [o]S Lev 26:33; Dt 4:27; Zec 7:14 [p]S Eze 16:41 [q]Eze 24:11 **22:18** [r]S Ps 119:119 [s]Isa 48:10 [t]Jer 6:28-30 **22:19** [u]S Ps 119:119 **22:20** [v]Hos 8:10; Mal 3:2 **22:21** [w]Isa 40:7; Hag 1:9 [x]Ps 68:2; Eze 21:31 **22:22** [y]S Isa 1:25 [z]S Eze 7:8 [a]S Isa 64:7 **22:24** [b]Eze 24:13 **22:25** [c]Jer 11:9 [d]S Ps 22:13 [e]Hos 6:9 [f]Jer 15:8; 18:21 **22:26** [g]Hos 9:7-8; Zep 3:4; Mal 2:7-8 [h]Eze 42:20; 44:23 [i]S Lev 20:25 [j]S Lev 18:21; S Eze 13:19 [k]ver 8; S 1Sa 2:12-17; Jer 2:8,26; Hag 2:11-14 **22:27** [l]S Jer 26:10; Zep 3:3 [m]Mt 7:15 [n]S ver 3; S Eze 11:6; 33:25; 34:2-3; Mic 3:2,10 [o]ver 13; S Ge 37:24; S Isa 1:23; S Jer 12:2; S 51:13; Eze 33:31 **22:28** [p]S Eze 13:10 [q]S La 2:14; S 4:13; S Eze 21:29 [r]S Eze 13:2, 6-7 **22:29** [s]S Ps 62:10 [t]S Ex 22:21 [u]S Isa 5:7 **22:30** [v]S Eze 13:5 [w]Ps 106:23; S Isa 64:7; Jer 5:1

[t]*12* Or *usury and interest* [u]*16* Or *When I have allotted you your inheritance* [v]*24* Septuagint; Hebrew *has not been cleansed or rained on* [w]*25* Septuagint; Hebrew *prophets*

22:25–28 HER PRIESTS. Instead of being loyal to God and to their holy calling, the people's spiritual leaders used their offices for personal financial gain and gave themselves to sinful gratification. Some so-called Christian leaders today are guilty of the same sins, bringing incalculable harm to the church.

22:28 HER PROPHETS WHITEWASH. As a result of this whitewashing by the prophets, the people did not fear God or his judgment as they persisted in sin. Today some ministers comfort people in their sins by assuring them that: (1) everyone sins that way; (2) we live in an age when it is impossible to live above sin and immorality because of a tidal wave of evil; (3) we are only human and cannot expect to live up to God's holy standards; (4) God loves us just the way we are, no matter what we do, so that there is no reason to fear him or his judgment; and (5) God does not see our sin if we are believers, for he sees only Christ's righteousness.

22:30 I LOOKED FOR A MAN. Corruption among leaders (vv. 25–28) and the people (v. 29) was so widespread in Judah that God could not find even one person who would attempt to lead the people back to God. It is a tragedy when some churches are so gripped by worldliness and spiritual compromise that God can find no one in the congregation who is willing to intercede by building up the wall and standing "in the gap" of the collapsing situation, no one to cry out against spiritual and moral decay, no one to lead the way in humble prayer, true repentance and an earnest seeking of God for revival (cf. 2Ch 7:14). All too often many good people remain silent out of a spirit of fear or compromise rather than risk becoming fervent intercessors for revival and for turning away God's wrath and judgment.

them with my fiery anger,[x] bringing
down[y] on their own heads all they
have done, declares the Sovereign
LORD.[z]"

Two Adulterous Sisters

23 The word of the LORD came to
me: 2"Son of man, there were
two women, daughters of the same
mother.[a] 3They became prostitutes in
Egypt,[b] engaging in prostitution[c]
from their youth.[d] In that land their
breasts were fondled and their virgin
bosoms caressed.[e] 4The older was
named Oholah, and her sister was
Oholibah. They were mine and gave
birth to sons and daughters. Oholah is
Samaria, and Oholibah is Jerusalem.[f]
5"Oholah engaged in prostitution
while she was still mine; and she lusted after her lovers, the Assyrians[g]—
warriors[h] 6clothed in blue, governors
and commanders, all of them handsome young men, and mounted horsemen. 7She gave herself as a prostitute
to all the elite of the Assyrians and defiled herself with all the idols of everyone she lusted after.[i] 8She did not
give up the prostitution she began in
Egypt,[j] when during her youth men
slept with her, caressed her virgin bosom and poured out their lust upon
her.[k]
9"Therefore I handed her over[l] to
her lovers,[m] the Assyrians, for whom
she lusted.[n] 10They stripped[o] her naked, took away her sons and daughters
and killed her with the sword. She became a byword among women,[p] and
punishment was inflicted[q] on her.[r]
11"Her sister Oholibah saw this,[s]
yet in her lust and prostitution she was
more depraved than her sister.[t] 12She
too lusted after the Assyrians—governors and commanders, warriors in full
dress, mounted horsemen, all handsome young men.[u] 13I saw that she
too defiled herself; both of them went
the same way.[v]
14"But she carried her prostitution
still further. She saw men portrayed on
a wall,[w] figures of Chaldeans[x] portrayed in red,[x] 15with belts[y] around
their waists and flowing turbans on
their heads; all of them looked like
Babylonian chariot officers, natives of
Chaldea.[y] 16As soon as she saw them,
she lusted after them and sent messengers[z] to them in Chaldea.[a] 17Then
the Babylonians[b] came to her, to the
bed of love, and in their lust they defiled her. After she had been defiled by
them, she turned away from them in
disgust.[c] 18When she carried on her
prostitution openly and exposed her
nakedness,[d] I turned away[e] from her
in disgust, just as I had turned away
from her sister.[f] 19Yet she became
more and more promiscuous as she recalled the days of her youth, when she
was a prostitute in Egypt. 20There she
lusted after her lovers, whose genitals
were like those of donkeys and whose
emission was like that of horses. 21So
you longed for the lewdness of your
youth, when in Egypt your bosom was
caressed and your young breasts fondled.[z][g]
22"Therefore, Oholibah, this is what
the Sovereign LORD says: I will stir up
your lovers[h] against you, those you
turned away from in disgust, and I will
bring them against you from every
side[i]— 23the Babylonians[j] and all
the Chaldeans,[k] the men of Pekod[l]
and Shoa and Koa, and all the Assyrians with them, handsome young men,
all of them governors and commanders, chariot officers and men of high
rank, all mounted on horses.[m] 24They
will come against you with weapons,[a]
chariots and wagons[n] and with a
throng of people; they will take up positions against you on every side with
large and small shields and with helmets. I will turn you over to them for
punishment,[o] and they will punish

22:31 [x]Ex 32:10; S Isa 30:27; S La 4:11 [y]Eze 16:43 [z]Eze 7:8-9; Ro 2:8
23:2 [a]S Jer 3:7; S Eze 16:45
23:3 [b]Jos 24:14 [c]S Lev 17:7; S Isa 1:21 [d]S Ps 25:7 [e]S Eze 16:15
23:4 [f]S Eze 16:46
23:5 [g]S 2Ki 16:7; Hos 5:13 [h]Hos 8:9
23:7 [i]Isa 57:8; Hos 5:3; 6:10
23:8 [j]Ex 32:4 [k]S Eze 16:15
23:9 [l]S 2Ki 18:11 [m]S Jer 4:30 [n]Hos 11:5
23:10 [o]Hos 2:10 [p]Eze 16:41 [q]Jer 42:10 [r]Eze 16:36
23:11 [s]S Jer 3:7 [t]Jer 3:8-11; S Eze 16:51
23:12 [u]2Ki 16:7-15; S 2Ch 28:16; S Eze 16:15,28
23:13 [v]S 2Ki 17:19; Hos 12:2
23:14 [w]S Eze 8:10 [x]Jer 22:14; Na 2:3
23:15 [y]S Isa 5:27
23:16 [z]S Isa 57:9 [a]S Eze 6:9
23:17 [b]Jer 40:9 [c]S Eze 16:29
23:18 [d]S Isa 57:8 [e]Ps 78:59; 106:40; Jer 6:8 [f]Jer 12:8; Am 5:21
23:21 [g]S Eze 16:26
23:22 [h]S Jer 4:30 [i]S Eze 16:37
23:23 [j]2Ki 20:14-18; S Jer 40:9 [k]S Ge 11:28 [l]Jer 50:21 [m]S 2Ki 24:2
23:24 [n]Jer 47:3; Eze 26:7,10; Na 2:4 [o]Jer 39:5-6

[x] *14* Or *Babylonians* [y] *15* Or *Babylonia*; also in verse 16 [z] *21* Syriac (see also verse 3); Hebrew *caressed because of your young breasts* [a] *24* The meaning of the Hebrew for this word is uncertain.

23:2 TWO WOMEN. God's people are pictured as two sisters—Samaria (representing the northern kingdom of Israel) and Jerusalem (representing the southern kingdom of Judah). Ezekiel describes them as those who are unfaithful to God and who have committed spiritual adultery by engaging in prostitution with other nations. Prostitution here represents Israel's and Judah's seeking alliances with ungodly nations instead of trusting in God alone as their source of strength and protection.

23:5–9 ENGAGED IN PROSTITUTION. Israel entered into alliances first with Assyria (2Ki 15:19–29) and then with Egypt (2Ki 17:3–6); eventually they began conforming to the pagan practices and idolatry of these nations. The younger "sister" Judah later did the same thing (cf. 2Ki 24:1; Isa 7:1–25; 30—31).

you according to their standards. 25I
will direct my jealous anger[p] against
you, and they will deal with you in fury.
They will cut off your noses and your
ears, and those of you who are left will
fall by the sword. They will take away
your sons and daughters,[q] and those
of you who are left will be consumed by
fire.[r] 26They will also strip[s] you of
your clothes and take your fine jewelry.[t] 27So I will put a stop[u] to the
lewdness and prostitution you began in
Egypt. You will not look on these
things with longing or remember Egypt
anymore.

28"For this is what the Sovereign
LORD says: I am about to hand you
over[v] to those you hate, to those you
turned away from in disgust. 29They
will deal with you in hatred and take
away everything you have worked for.
They will leave you naked[w] and bare,
and the shame of your prostitution will
be exposed.[x] Your lewdness[y] and
promiscuity[z] 30have brought this
upon you, because you lusted after the
nations and defiled yourself with their
idols.[a] 31You have gone the way of
your sister; so I will put her cup[b] into
your hand.[c]

32"This is what the Sovereign LORD
says:

"You will drink your sister's cup,
a cup large and deep;
it will bring scorn and derision,[d]
for it holds so much.[e]
33You will be filled with drunkenness
and sorrow,
the cup of ruin and desolation,
the cup of your sister Samaria.[f]
34You will drink it[g] and drain it
dry;
you will dash it to pieces
and tear your breasts.
I have spoken, declares the Sovereign
LORD.[h]

35"Therefore this is what the Sovereign LORD says: Since you have forgotten[i] me and thrust me behind your
back,[j] you must bear[k] the consequences of your lewdness and prostitution."

36The LORD said to me: "Son of man,
will you judge Oholah and Oholibah?
Then confront[l] them with their detestable practices,[m] 37for they have
committed adultery and blood is on
their hands. They committed adultery
with their idols; they even sacrificed
their children, whom they bore to
me,[b] as food for them.[n] 38They have
also done this to me: At that same time
they defiled my sanctuary[o] and desecrated my Sabbaths.[p] 39On the very
day they sacrificed their children to
their idols, they entered my sanctuary
and desecrated[q] it. That is what they
did in my house.[r]

40"They even sent messengers for
men who came from far away,[s] and
when they arrived you bathed yourself
for them, painted your eyes[t] and put
on your jewelry.[u] 41You sat on an elegant couch,[v] with a table[w] spread before it on which you had placed the incense[x] and oil that belonged to me.[y]

42"The noise of a carefree[z] crowd
was around her; Sabeans[c][a] were
brought from the desert along with
men from the rabble, and they put
bracelets[b] on the arms of the woman
and her sister and beautiful crowns on
their heads.[c] 43Then I said about the
one worn out by adultery, 'Now let
them use her as a prostitute,[d] for that
is all she is.' 44And they slept with her.
As men sleep with a prostitute, so they
slept with those lewd women, Oholah
and Oholibah. 45But righteous men will
sentence them to the punishment of
women who commit adultery and shed
blood,[e] because they are adulterous
and blood is on their hands.[f]

46"This is what the Sovereign LORD
says: Bring a mob[g] against them and
give them over to terror and plunder.[h]
47The mob will stone them and cut
them down with their swords; they will
kill their sons and daughters[i] and
burn[j] down their houses.[k]

48"So I will put an end[l] to lewdness
in the land, that all women may take
warning and not imitate you.[m] 49You

23:25 [p]S Dt 29:20 [q]ver 47; Eze 24:21 [r]S Jer 12:9; S Eze 16:38; S 20:47-48
23:26 [s]S Jer 13:22 [t]S Isa 3:18-23; S Eze 16:39
23:27 [u]S Eze 16:41
23:28 [v]S Jer 34:20
23:29 [w]Mic 1:11 [x]S Jer 13:27 [y]S Eze 22:9 [z]Dt 28:48; S Eze 16:36
23:30 [a]Ps 106:37-38; Zep 3:1
23:31 [b]S Jer 25:15 [c]2Ki 21:13
23:32 [d]Ps 44:13; Hos 7:16 [e]Ps 60:3; Isa 51:17; Jer 25:15
23:33 [f]Jer 25:15-16; S Eze 12:19
23:34 [g]S Ps 16:5 [h]S Jer 25:27
23:35 [i]S Dt 32:18; S Isa 17:10 [j]S 1Ki 14:9; S 2Ch 29:6 [k]Eze 16:52
23:36 [l]S Eze 16:2 [m]Isa 58:1; S Eze 22:2; Mic 3:8
23:37 [n]S Eze 16:36
23:38 [o]S Lev 15:31 [p]S Ne 10:31
23:39 [q]S 2Ki 21:4 [r]S Jer 7:10; Eze 22:8
23:40 [s]S Isa 57:9 [t]2Ki 9:30 [u]S Jer 4:30; Eze 16:13-19; Hos 2:13
23:41 [v]S Est 1:6; S Pr 7:17 [w]Isa 65:11; Eze 41:22; 44:16; Mal 1:7,12 [x]Isa 57:9; S 65:3; S Jer 44:5 [y]S Nu 18:12
23:42 [z]S Ps 73:5 [a]S 2Ch 9:1 [b]S Ge 24:30 [c]S Eze 16:11-12
23:43 [d]ver 3
23:45 [e]S Eze 22:3 [f]S Lev 20:10; S Eze 16:38; Hos 2:2; 6:5
23:46 [g]Eze 16:40 [h]S Dt 28:25; S Jer 25:9
23:47 [i]S ver 25 [j]2Ch 36:19; S Jer 34:22 [k]S 2Ch 36:17
23:48 [l]Eze 16:41 [m]2Pe 2:6

[b]37 Or *even made the children they bore to me pass through ⌊the fire⌋* [c]42 Or *drunkards*

23:35 THRUST ME BEHIND YOUR BACK. To revert to the ungodly ways and values of the world after having experienced God's salvation and deliverance is equivalent to despising the Lord and throwing him away as though he were useless (cf. Heb 6:1–8). Believers must never abandon the Lord; instead, we must show love and gratitude to him who has redeemed us by the death of his Son Jesus.

will suffer the penalty for your lewdness and bear the consequences of your sins of idolatry.[n] Then you will know that I am the Sovereign LORD.[o]"

The Cooking Pot

24 In the ninth year, in the tenth month on the tenth day, the word of the LORD came to me:[p] 2"Son of man, record[q] this date, this very date, because the king of Babylon has laid siege to Jerusalem this very day.[r] 3Tell this rebellious house[s] a parable[t] and say to them: 'This is what the Sovereign LORD says:

" 'Put on the cooking pot;[u] put it on
and pour water into it.
4Put into it the pieces of meat,
all the choice pieces—the leg
and the shoulder.
Fill it with the best of these
bones;[v]
5 take the pick of the flock.[w]
Pile wood beneath it for the bones;
bring it to a boil
and cook the bones in it.[x]

6" 'For this is what the Sovereign LORD says:

" 'Woe[y] to the city of bloodshed,[z]
to the pot now encrusted,
whose deposit will not go away!
Empty it piece by piece
without casting lots[a] for
them.[b]

7" 'For the blood she shed is in her
midst:
She poured it on the bare rock;
she did not pour it on the ground,
where the dust would cover it.[c]
8To stir up wrath and take revenge
I put her blood on the bare rock,
so that it would not be covered.

9" 'Therefore this is what the Sovereign LORD says:

" 'Woe to the city of bloodshed!
I, too, will pile the wood high.
10So heap on the wood
and kindle the fire.
Cook the meat well,
mixing in the spices;
and let the bones be charred.
11Then set the empty pot on the
coals
till it becomes hot and its
copper glows
so its impurities may be melted
and its deposit burned away.[d]
12It has frustrated all efforts;
its heavy deposit has not been
removed,
not even by fire.

13" 'Now your impurity is lewdness. Because I tried to cleanse you but you would not be cleansed[e] from your impurity, you will not be clean again until my wrath against you has subsided.[f]

14" 'I the LORD have spoken.[g] The time has come for me to act.[h] I will not hold back; I will not have pity,[i] nor will I relent.[j] You will be judged according to your conduct and your actions,[k] declares the Sovereign LORD.[l]' "

Ezekiel's Wife Dies

15The word of the LORD came to me:
16"Son of man, with one blow[m] I am about to take away from you the delight of your eyes.[n] Yet do not lament or weep or shed any tears.[o] 17Groan quietly;[p] do not mourn for the dead.

23:49 [n] Eze 24:13 [o] S Eze 7:4; S 9:10; 16:58; S 20:38
24:1 [p] S Eze 8:1; 26:1; 29:17
24:2 [q] Isa 30:8; Hab 2:2 [r] 2Ki 25:1; S Jer 39:1
24:3 [s] S Isa 1:2; S Eze 2:3,6 [t] S Eze 20:49 [u] S Eze 11:3
24:4 [v] S Eze 11:7
24:5 [w] S Isa 34:12; Jer 52:10 [x] Jer 52:24-27; Mic 3:2-3
24:6 [y] S Eze 16:23 [z] S Eze 22:2 [a] S Job 6:27; Joel 3:3; Ob 1:11; Na 3:10 [b] S Eze 11:11
24:7 [c] S Lev 17:13
24:11 [d] Jer 21:10
24:13 [e] S Isa 22:14 [f] Jer 6:28-30; La 1:9; S Eze 16:42; 22:24; 23:36-49; Hos 7:1; Zec 6:8
24:14 [g] Eze 22:14 [h] S Nu 11:23 [i] S Eze 8:18 [j] S Job 27:22 [k] Eze 36:19; Zec 8:14 [l] S Isa 3:11; S Eze 18:30
24:16 [m] S Ps 39:10 [n] ver 21; Ps 84:1; S La 2:4 [o] Jer 13:17; 16:5; S 22:10
24:17 [p] Ps 39:9

24:2 RECORD THIS DATE. "This date" was Jan. 15, 588 B.C. Ezekiel received his message on the same day that the Babylonian siege of Jerusalem began. The attack lasted nearly two years and brought total destruction to Jerusalem.

24:3–12 PUT ON THE COOKING POT. God gives Ezekiel a parable to speak to his rebellious people. Jerusalem would be like a cooking pot and its inhabitants like pieces of meat and choice bones. The meat and bones would be consumed by the Babylonians; after the pot's contents were emptied, the pot would be further purified by the fire of judgment until its copper glowed, its impurities melted and its rust burned away (v. 11).

24:13 NOT BE CLEAN AGAIN UNTIL. Because Jerusalem refused to let God cleanse her from her impurity, she had to face his furious wrath. Likewise, all the nations will face God's wrath at the end of time. Only by God's righteous judgment will the world be cleansed of sin (Rev 5—22).

24:16 THE DELIGHT OF YOUR EYES. God told Ezekiel that he would lose his wife, whom he loved dearly, yet he was not to lament her death publicly or to engage in the usual customs of mourning. By this command, however, God did not forbid Ezekiel the right to grieve privately over the loss of his wife. Ezekiel's refusal to show any outward expression of grief was meant to be a sign to the exiles that the fall of Jerusalem and the temple would be so devastating that the people would be unable to make the usual expressions of sorrow.

Keep your turban[q] fastened and your
sandals[r] on your feet; do not cover
the lower part of your face[s] or eat the
customary food ⌞of mourners⌟.[t]"
18So I spoke to the people in the
morning, and in the evening my wife
died. The next morning I did as I had
been commanded.[u]
19Then the people asked me, "Won't
you tell us what these things have to
do with us?[v]"
20So I said to them, "The word of the
LORD came to me: **21**Say to the house of
Israel, 'This is what the Sovereign
LORD says: I am about to desecrate my
sanctuary[w]—the stronghold in which
you take pride,[x] the delight of your
eyes,[y] the object of your affection.
The sons and daughters[z] you left behind will fall by the sword.[a] **22**And you
will do as I have done. You will not cover the lower part of your face[b] or eat
the customary food ⌞of mourners⌟.[c]
23You will keep your turbans[d] on your
heads and your sandals[e] on your feet.
You will not mourn[f] or weep but will
waste away[g] because of[d] your sins
and groan among yourselves.[h]
24Ezekiel[i] will be a sign[j] to you; you
will do just as he has done. When this
happens, you will know that I am the
Sovereign LORD.'
25"And you, son of man, on the day
I take away their stronghold, their joy
and glory, the delight of their eyes,[k]
their heart's desire,[l] and their sons
and daughters[m] as well— **26**on that
day a fugitive will come to tell you[n]
the news. **27**At that time your mouth
will be opened; you will speak with him
and will no longer be silent.[o] So you
will be a sign to them, and they will
know that I am the LORD.[p]"

24:17 [q]S Ex 28:39; S Isa 3:20 [r]S Isa 20:2 [s]S Lev 13:45 [t]ver 22; S Jer 16:7
24:18 [u]S Eze 12:7
24:19 [v]Eze 12:9; 37:18
24:21 [w]S Lev 26:31; S Eze 7:24 [x]S Lev 26:19 [y]S ver 16; Ps 27:4 [z]S Eze 23:25 [a]Jer 7:14,15; Hos 9:12,16; Mal 2:12
24:22 [b]S Lev 13:45 [c]Jer 16:7
24:23 [d]S Ex 28:39; S Isa 3:20 [e]S Isa 20:2 [f]Ex 33:4 [g]S Lev 26:16 [h]Ps 78:64
24:24 [i]Eze 1:3 [j]S Isa 20:3; Eze 12:11
24:25 [k]S La 2:4 [l]S Ps 20:4 [m]Dt 28:32; Jer 11:22
24:26 [n]S 1Sa 4:12; Job 1:15-19
24:27 [o]Da 10:15 [p]S Eze 3:26; 33:22

25:2 [q]S Eze 13:17; 29:2 [r]S Eze 21:28 [s]Jer 49:1-6
25:3 [t]S Ps 35:21; Eze 26:2; 36:2 [u]Zep 2:8 [v]S Pr 17:5
25:4 [w]S Ge 25:6; S Jdg 6:3 [x]S Nu 31:10 [y]Dt 28:33,51; S Jdg 6:33
25:5 [z]S Dt 3:11 [a]S S Isa 17:2
25:6 [b]S Nu 24:10 [c]S Eze 6:11; Ob 1:12; Zep 2:8
25:7 [d]Zep 1:4 [e]S Nu 14:3 [f]Eze 21:31 [g]ver 13-14,17; Am 1:14-15

A Prophecy Against Ammon

25 The word of the LORD came to
me: **2**"Son of man, set your face
against[q] the Ammonites[r] and prophesy against them.[s] **3**Say to them,
'Hear the word of the Sovereign LORD.
This is what the Sovereign LORD says:
Because you said "Aha![t]" over my
sanctuary when it was desecrated[u]
and over the land of Israel when it was
laid waste and over the people of Judah
when they went into exile,[v] **4**therefore
I am going to give you to the people of
the East[w] as a possession. They will
set up their camps[x] and pitch their
tents among you; they will eat your
fruit and drink your milk.[y] **5**I will turn
Rabbah[z] into a pasture for camels and
Ammon into a resting place for
sheep.[a] Then you will know that I am
the LORD. **6**For this is what the Sovereign LORD says: Because you have
clapped your hands[b] and stamped
your feet, rejoicing with all the malice
of your heart against the land of Israel,[c] **7**therefore I will stretch out my
hand[d] against you and give you as
plunder[e] to the nations. I will cut you
off from the nations and exterminate
you from the countries. I will destroy[f]
you, and you will know that I am the
LORD.[g]' "

A Prophecy Against Moab

8"This is what the Sovereign LORD
says: 'Because Moab[h] and Seir[i] said,
"Look, the house of Judah has become
like all the other nations," **9**therefore I
will expose the flank of Moab, beginning at its frontier towns—Beth Jeshi-

25:8 [h]S Ge 19:37; S Dt 23:6; S Isa 16:6 [i]S Ge 14:6

[d]23 Or *away in*

24:18 DID AS I HAD BEEN COMMANDED. Ezekiel's obedience in this situation must have been one of his most difficult tasks as a prophet. Though experiencing great sorrow over the loss of his wife, he still had to keep on prophesying day after day to a rebellious people. He was sharing in God's sufferings, for God himself was about to lose his people, his city and his temple, just as the faithful prophet had lost his precious wife. Being faithful to God can be very costly. In a similar manner, NT believers are called on to share the sufferings of Christ (see 2Co 1:7; 4:10–11).

25:1—32:32 SET YOUR FACE AGAINST. These chapters contain prophecies against seven nations that were hostile to God, his commands and his people. Ezekiel reveals in these eight chapters that all nations are ultimately answerable to God and that worldly powers will never destroy his plan of salvation. Though the ungodly forces of the world sometimes seem victorious, the day is coming when God will bring all evil into judgment, the wicked nations will perish and his faithful people will receive full salvation.

25:2–3 AMMONITES. The Ammonites were a people living east of Israel whom God chastised for taking great delight in Jerusalem's fall and the temple's devastation.

25:4 PEOPLE OF THE EAST. These people are most likely the Babylonian army.

25:8 LIKE ALL THE OTHER NATIONS. Ezekiel prophesies that Moab would be punished because they believed that Israel's God was no greater than the gods of other nations (cf. v. 11).

moth[j], Baal Meon[k] and Kiriathaim[l]—the glory of that land. 10I will
give Moab along with the Ammonites
to the people of the East as a possession, so that the Ammonites will not be
remembered[m] among the nations;
11and I will inflict punishment on
Moab. Then they will know that I am
the LORD.' "[n]

A Prophecy Against Edom

12"This is what the Sovereign LORD
says: 'Because Edom[o] took revenge
on the house of Judah and became very
guilty by doing so, 13therefore this is
what the Sovereign LORD says: I will
stretch out my hand[p] against Edom
and kill its men and their animals.[q] I
will lay it waste, and from Teman[r] to
Dedan[s] they will fall by the sword.[t]
14I will take vengeance on Edom by the
hand of my people Israel, and they will
deal with Edom in accordance with my
anger[u] and my wrath; they will know
my vengeance, declares the Sovereign
LORD.' "[v]

A Prophecy Against Philistia

15"This is what the Sovereign LORD
says: 'Because the Philistines[w] acted
in vengeance and took revenge with
malice[x] in their hearts, and with ancient hostility sought to destroy Judah,
16therefore this is what the Sovereign
LORD says: I am about to stretch out my
hand against the Philistines,[y] and I
will cut off the Kerethites[z] and destroy those remaining along the
coast.[a] 17I will carry out great vengeance[b] on them and punish[c] them
in my wrath. Then they will know that
I am the LORD,[d] when I take vengeance on them.[e][f] "

A Prophecy Against Tyre

26 In the eleventh year, on the
first day of the month, the word
of the LORD came to me:[g] 2"Son of
man, because Tyre[h] has said of Jerusalem, 'Aha![i] The gate to the nations
is broken, and its doors have swung
open to me; now that she lies in ruins
I will prosper,' 3therefore this is what
the Sovereign LORD says: I am against
you, O Tyre, and I will bring many nations against you, like the sea[j] casting up its waves. 4They will destroy[k]
the walls of Tyre[l] and pull down her
towers; I will scrape away her rubble
and make her a bare rock. 5Out in the
sea[m] she will become a place to spread
fishnets,[n] for I have spoken, declares
the Sovereign LORD. She will become
plunder[o] for the nations,[p] 6and her
settlements on the mainland will be
ravaged by the sword. Then they will
know that I am the LORD.
7"For this is what the Sovereign
LORD says: From the north I am going
to bring against Tyre Nebuchadnezzar[e][q] king of Babylon, king of
kings,[r] with horses and chariots,[s]
with horsemen and a great army. 8He
will ravage your settlements on the
mainland with the sword; he will set up
siege works[t] against you, build a
ramp[u] up to your walls and raise his
shields against you. 9He will direct the
blows of his battering rams against
your walls and demolish your towers
with his weapons.[v] 10His horses will
be so many that they will cover you
with dust. Your walls will tremble at
the noise of the war horses, wagons
and chariots[w] when he enters your
gates as men enter a city whose walls
have been broken through. 11The
hoofs[x] of his horses will trample all
your streets; he will kill your people
with the sword, and your strong pillars[y] will fall to the ground.[z] 12They
will plunder your wealth and loot your
merchandise; they will break down
your walls and demolish your fine
houses and throw your stones, timber
and rubble into the sea.[a] 13I will put
an end[b] to your noisy songs,[c] and the
music of your harps[d] will be heard no

25:9 [j] S Nu 33:49 [k] S Nu 32:3; S Jos 13:17 [l] S Nu 32:37; S Jos 13:19
25:10 [m] Eze 21:32
25:11 [n] Isa 15:9; 16:1-14; Jer 48:1; Am 2:1-3
25:12 [o] S 2Sa 8:13-14; S 2Ch 28:17; S Isa 11:14
25:13 [p] S Ex 7:5; S Eze 16:27 [q] Eze 29:8 [r] S Ge 36:11,15,34 [s] Jer 25:23 [t] S Jer 49:10; S Eze 14:17
25:14 [u] Eze 35:11 [v] S Ps 137:7; Eze 32:29; 35:2-3; 36:5; Am 1:11; Ob 1:1,10-16; Mal 1:4
25:15 [w] S Jos 13:3; S 2Ch 28:18 [x] S Ps 73:8
25:16 [y] S 2Ch 26:6; Am 1:8 [z] S 1Sa 30:14 [a] S Eze 20:33
25:17 [b] S Nu 31:3 [c] Jer 44:13 [d] S Ex 6:2; S 8:22 [e] S Isa 11:14 [f] S Isa 14:30; Jer 47:7; Joel 3:4
26:1 [g] S Eze 24:1; 29:1; 30:20
26:2 [h] S Jos 19:29; 2Sa 5:11 [i] S Eze 25:3
26:3 [j] ver 19; Isa 5:30; Jer 50:42; 51:42
26:4 [k] S Isa 23:1, 11 [l] Am 1:10
26:5 [m] Eze 27:32 [n] Eze 47:10 [o] S Nu 14:3; Eze 29:19 [p] Zec 9:2-4
26:7 [q] Jer 27:6; 39:1 [r] S Ezr 7:12 [s] S Eze 23:24; Na 2:3-4
26:8 [t] S Jer 6:6 [u] S Jer 33:4
26:9 [v] S Eze 21:22
26:10 [w] S Jer 4:13; S 46:9; S Eze 23:24
26:11 [x] Isa 5:28 [y] S Jer 43:13 [z] S Isa 26:5
26:12 [a] Isa 23:8; S Jer 4:7; Eze 27:3-27; 28:8; Hab 1:8
26:13 [b] S Jer 7:34 [c] S Isa 23:7 [d] S Ps 137:2; S Isa 14:11

[e] 7 Hebrew *Nebuchadrezzar,* of which *Nebuchadnezzar* is a variant; here and often in Ezekiel and Jeremiah

25:12 REVENGE. The Edomites would be punished for their intense hatred of Israel.

26:2 TYRE. Tyre, the capital of Phoenicia, was located sixty miles northwest of Nazareth on the Mediterranean coast. Part of the city was an island and part was coastland at the foot of the Lebanon mountains. Tyre rejoiced over Jerusalem's fall because it believed it would gain financially from trade advantages now that Judah was out of the picture. Tyre's desire for wealth with no thought of the suffering it caused others brought God's judgment (see also Isa 23). The city was subjugated by "many nations" (v. 3), i.e., the Babylonians, next the Persians, and then the Greeks, led by Alexander the Great (332 B.C.).

more.[e] 14I will make you a bare rock,
and you will become a place to spread
fishnets. You will never be rebuilt,[f]
for I the LORD have spoken, declares
the Sovereign LORD.
15"This is what the Sovereign LORD
says to Tyre: Will not the coastlands[g]
tremble[h] at the sound of your fall,
when the wounded groan[i] and the
slaughter takes place in you? 16Then
all the princes of the coast will step
down from their thrones and lay aside
their robes and take off their embroidered[j] garments. Clothed[k] with terror, they will sit on the ground,[l] trembling[m] every moment, appalled[n] at
you. 17Then they will take up a lament[o] concerning you and say to you:

" 'How you are destroyed, O city of
renown,
peopled by men of the sea!
You were a power on the seas,
you and your citizens;
you put your terror
on all who lived there.[p]
18Now the coastlands tremble[q]
on the day of your fall;
the islands in the sea
are terrified at your collapse.'[r]

19"This is what the Sovereign LORD
says: When I make you a desolate city,
like cities no longer inhabited, and
when I bring the ocean depths[s] over
you and its vast waters cover you,[t]
20then I will bring you down with those
who go down to the pit,[u] to the people
of long ago. I will make you dwell in
the earth below, as in ancient ruins,
with those who go down to the pit, and
you will not return or take your place[f]
in the land of the living.[v] 21I will bring
you to a horrible end and you will be no
more.[w] You will be sought, but you
will never again be found, declares the
Sovereign LORD."[x]

A Lament for Tyre

27 The word of the LORD came to
me: 2"Son of man, take up a lament[y] concerning Tyre. 3Say to
Tyre,[z] situated at the gateway to the
sea,[a] merchant of peoples on many
coasts, 'This is what the Sovereign
LORD says:

" 'You say, O Tyre,
"I am perfect in beauty.[b]"
4Your domain was on the high seas;
your builders brought your
beauty to perfection.[c]
5They made all your timbers
of pine trees from Senir[g];[d]
they took a cedar from Lebanon[e]
to make a mast for you.
6Of oaks[f] from Bashan
they made your oars;
of cypress wood[h] from the coasts
of Cyprus[i][g]
they made your deck, inlaid with
ivory.
7Fine embroidered linen[h] from
Egypt was your sail
and served as your banner;
your awnings were of blue and
purple[i]
from the coasts of Elishah.[j]
8Men of Sidon and Arvad[k] were
your oarsmen;
your skilled men, O Tyre, were
aboard as your seamen.[l]
9Veteran craftsmen of Gebal[j][m]
were on board
as shipwrights to caulk your
seams.
All the ships of the sea[n] and their
sailors
came alongside to trade for your
wares.
10" 'Men of Persia,[o] Lydia[p] and
Put[q]
served as soldiers in your army.
They hung their shields[r] and
helmets on your walls,
bringing you splendor.
11Men of Arvad and Helech
manned your walls on every
side;
men of Gammad
were in your towers.

26:13 [e]S Job 30:31; S Jer 16:9; S 25:10; Rev 18:22 **26:14** [f]S Job 12:14; Mal 1:4 **26:15** [g]Isa 41:5; Eze 27:35 [h]S Jer 49:21 [i]S Job 24:12 **26:16** [j]S Ex 26:36 [k]S Job 8:22 [l]S Job 2:8,13 [m]Hos 11:10 [n]S Lev 26:32; Eze 32:10 **26:17** [o]S Eze 19:1 [p]Isa 14:12 **26:18** [q]S Ps 46:6; S Jer 49:21 [r]Isa 23:5; S 41:5; Eze 27:35 **26:19** [s]S Ge 7:11 [t]S ver 3; Isa 8:7-8 **26:20** [u]Nu 16:30; Ps 28:1; 88:6; Eze 31:14; 32:18; Am 9:2; Jnh 2:2,6 [v]S Job 28:13; S Isa 14:9-10; Eze 32:24,30 **26:21** [w]S Jer 51:64; Da 11:19 [x]Jer 20:4; Eze 27:36; 28:19; Rev 18:21 **27:2** [y]S Eze 19:1 **27:3** [z]S Ps 83:7 [a]ver 33; Hos 9:13 [b]S Isa 23:9; S Eze 16:15 **27:4** [c]Eze 28:12 **27:5** [d]S Dt 3:9 [e]S Isa 2:13 **27:6** [f]Nu 21:33; S Ps 29:9; Jer 22:20; Zec 11:2 [g]S Ge 10:4; Isa 23:12 **27:7** [h]S Ex 26:36; S Isa 19:9 [i]Ex 25:4; Jer 10:9 [j]Ge 10:4 **27:8** [k]Ge 10:18 [l]1Ki 9:27 **27:9** [m]S Jos 13:5 [n]S Ps 104:26 **27:10** [o]2Ch 36:20; Ezr 1:1; Eze 38:5; Da 8:20 [p]S Isa 66:19 [q]S Ge 10:6; Eze 30:5; Na 3:9 [r]SS 4:4

[f]20 Septuagint; Hebrew *return, and I will give glory* [g]5 That is, Hermon [h]6 Targum; the Masoretic Text has a different division of the consonants. [i]6 Hebrew *Kittim* [j]9 That is, Byblos

27:1–36 LAMENT CONCERNING TYRE. Tyre had a great fleet of merchant ships; this chapter pictures her as a great and beautiful ship bringing merchandise and treasures to many nations. Yet God in his judgment would break the ship to pieces, and many would lament its destruction. Compare this chapter with Rev 18, where God destroys the world's commercial center (see Rev 18:2–9, notes).

They hung their shields around
your walls;
they brought your beauty to
perfection.[s]

12 "'Tarshish[t] did business with
you because of your great wealth of
goods;[u] they exchanged silver, iron,
tin and lead for your merchandise.
13 "'Greece,[v] Tubal and Meshech[w]
traded with you; they exchanged
slaves[x] and articles of bronze for your
wares.
14 "'Men of Beth Togarmah[y] exchanged work horses, war horses and
mules for your merchandise.
15 "'The men of Rhodes[k][z] traded
with you, and many coastlands[a] were
your customers; they paid you with ivory[b] tusks and ebony.
16 "'Aram[l][c] did business with you
because of your many products; they
exchanged turquoise,[d] purple fabric,
embroidered work, fine linen,[e] coral[f]
and rubies for your merchandise.
17 "'Judah and Israel traded with
you; they exchanged wheat[g] from
Minnith[h] and confections,[m] honey, oil
and balm[i] for your wares.[j]
18 "'Damascus,[k] because of your
many products and great wealth of
goods,[l] did business with you in wine
from Helbon and wool from Zahar.
19 "'Danites and Greeks[m] from
Uzal[n] bought your merchandise; they
exchanged wrought iron, cassia[o] and
calamus for your wares.
20 "'Dedan[p] traded in saddle blankets with you.
21 "'Arabia[q] and all the princes of
Kedar[r] were your customers; they did
business with you in lambs, rams and
goats.
22 "'The merchants of Sheba[s] and
Raamah traded with you; for your merchandise they exchanged the finest of
all kinds of spices[t] and precious
stones, and gold.[u]
23 "'Haran,[v] Canneh and Eden[w]
and merchants of Sheba, Asshur[x] and
Kilmad traded with you. 24 In your marketplace they traded with you beautiful
garments, blue fabric, embroidered
work and multicolored rugs with cords
twisted and tightly knotted.

25 "'The ships of Tarshish[y] serve
as carriers for your wares.
You are filled with heavy cargo
in the heart of the sea.[z]
26 Your oarsmen take you
out to the high seas.
But the east wind[a] will break you
to pieces
in the heart of the sea.
27 Your wealth,[b] merchandise and
wares,
your mariners, seamen and
shipwrights,
your merchants and all your
soldiers,
and everyone else on board
will sink into the heart of the
sea[c]
on the day of your shipwreck.
28 The shorelands will quake[d]
when your seamen cry out.
29 All who handle the oars
will abandon their ships;
the mariners and all the seamen
will stand on the shore.
30 They will raise their voice
and cry bitterly over you;
they will sprinkle dust[e] on their
heads
and roll[f] in ashes.[g]
31 They will shave their heads[h]
because of you
and will put on sackcloth.
They will weep[i] over you with
anguish of soul
and with bitter mourning.[j]
32 As they wail and mourn over you,
they will take up a lament[k]
concerning you:
"Who was ever silenced like Tyre,
surrounded by the sea?[l]"
33 When your merchandise went out
on the seas,[m]
you satisfied many nations;
with your great wealth[n] and your
wares
you enriched the kings of the
earth.
34 Now you are shattered by the sea
in the depths of the waters;
your wares and all your company
have gone down with you.[o]
35 All who live in the coastlands[p]
are appalled[q] at you;
their kings shudder with horror
and their faces are distorted
with fear.[r]
36 The merchants among the nations
hiss at you;[s]

27:11 [s] ver 27
27:12 [t] S Ge 10:4 [u] ver 18,33
27:13 [v] Joel 3:6 [w] Ge 10:2; Isa 66:19; Eze 32:26; 38:2; 39:1 [x] Rev 18:13
27:14 [y] S Ge 10:3
27:15 [z] S Ge 10:7 [a] S Jer 25:22 [b] 1Ki 10:22; Rev 18:12
27:16 [c] Jdg 10:6; Isa 7:1-8 [d] Ex 28:18; 39:11; Eze 28:13 [e] S Eze 16:10 [f] Job 28:18
27:17 [g] S 1Ki 5:9 [h] Jdg 11:33 [i] S Ge 43:11 [j] Ac 12:20
27:18 [k] S Ge 14:15; Eze 47:16-18 [l] S ver 12
27:19 [m] S Ge 10:2 [n] Ge 10:27 [o] S Ex 30:24
27:20 [p] S Ge 10:7
27:21 [q] S 2Ch 9:14 [r] S Ge 25:13; Isa 21:17
27:22 [s] S Ge 10:7,28 [t] S Ge 43:11 [u] Rev 18:12
27:23 [v] S Ge 11:26 [w] S Isa 37:12 [x] S Ge 10:22; S Nu 24:24
27:25 [y] S Ge 10:4; Isa 2:16 *fn* [z] Rev 18:3
27:26 [a] S Ge 41:6; Jer 18:17
27:27 [b] Pr 11:4 [c] Eze 28:8
27:28 [d] S Jer 49:21
27:30 [e] S Jos 7:6; S 2Sa 1:2 [f] S Jer 6:26 [g] Rev 18:18-19
27:31 [h] S Lev 13:40; S Job 1:20; S Isa 3:17; S Jer 48:37 [i] S Isa 16:9; Rev 18:15 [j] S Est 4:1; Job 3:20; Isa 22:12; Jer 6:26; S La 2:10; S Eze 7:18
27:32 [k] S Eze 19:1 [l] Isa 23:1-6; Eze 26:5
27:33 [m] S ver 3 [n] S ver 12; Eze 28:4-5
27:34 [o] Zec 9:4
27:35 [p] S Eze 26:15 [q] S Lev 26:32; S Job 18:20 [r] S Eze 26:17-18; 32:10
27:36 [s] Jer 19:8; S 49:17; S 50:13; Zep 2:15

[k] *15* Septuagint; Hebrew *Dedan* [l] *16* Most Hebrew manuscripts; some Hebrew manuscripts and Syriac *Edom* [m] *17* The meaning of the Hebrew for this word is uncertain.

you have come to a horrible end
and will be no more.[t]' "

A Prophecy Against the King of Tyre

28 The word of the LORD came to
me: 2"Son of man[u], say to the
ruler of Tyre, 'This is what the Sovereign LORD says:

" 'In the pride of your heart
you say, "I am a god;
I sit on the throne[v] of a god
in the heart of the seas."[w]
But you are a man and not a god,
though you think you are as
wise as a god.[x]
3Are you wiser than Daniel[n]?[y]
Is no secret hidden from you?
4By your wisdom and understanding
you have gained wealth for
yourself
and amassed gold and silver
in your treasuries.[z]
5By your great skill in trading[a]
you have increased your
wealth,[b]
and because of your wealth
your heart has grown proud.[c]

6" 'Therefore this is what the Sovereign LORD says:

" 'Because you think you are wise,
as wise as a god,
7I am going to bring foreigners
against you,
the most ruthless of nations;[d]
they will draw their swords against
your beauty and wisdom[e]
and pierce your shining
splendor.[f]
8They will bring you down to the
pit,[g]
and you will die a violent
death[h]
in the heart of the seas.[i]
9Will you then say, "I am a god,"
in the presence of those who kill
you?
You will be but a man, not a god,[j]
in the hands of those who slay
you.[k]
10You will die the death of the
uncircumcised[l]
at the hands of foreigners.
I have spoken, declares the Sovereign
LORD.' "

11The word of the LORD came to me:
12"Son of man, take up a lament[m] concerning the king of Tyre and say to
him: 'This is what the Sovereign LORD
says:

" 'You were the model of
perfection,
full of wisdom and perfect in
beauty.[n]
13You were in Eden,[o]
the garden of God;[p]
every precious stone[q] adorned
you:
ruby, topaz and emerald,
chrysolite, onyx and jasper,
sapphire,[o] turquoise[r] and
beryl.[p]
Your settings and mountings[q]
were made of gold;
on the day you were created
they were prepared.[s]
14You were anointed[t] as a guardian
cherub,[u]
for so I ordained you.
You were on the holy mount of
God;
you walked among the fiery
stones.
15You were blameless in your ways
from the day you were created
till wickedness was found in
you.
16Through your widespread trade
you were filled with violence,[v]
and you sinned.

27:36 [t]S Ps 37:10,36; S Eze 26:21 28:2 [u]S Isa 13:11 [v]S Isa 14:13 [w]Zep 2:15 [x]S Ge 3:5; S Ps 9:20; 82:6-7; S Eze 16:49; 2Th 2:4 28:3 [y]S Eze 14:14; Da 1:20; 2:20-23, 28; 5:11-12 28:4 [z]Isa 10:13; Zec 9:3 28:5 [a]S Isa 23:8 [b]S Jer 9:23; S Eze 27:33 [c]S Job 31:25; Ps 52:7; 62:10; Hos 12:8; 13:6 28:7 [d]Eze 30:11; 31:12; 32:12; Hab 1:6 [e]Jer 9:23 [f]S Eze 7:24 28:8 [g]S Ps 55:23; Eze 32:30 [h]Rev 18:7 [i]S Eze 26:12; 27:27 28:9 [j]S Isa 31:3 [k]S Eze 16:49 28:10 [l]S 1Sa 14:6; S Jer 9:26; Eze 32:19,24 28:12 [m]S Eze 19:1 [n]Eze 27:2-4 28:13 [o]S Ge 2:8 [p]Eze 31:8-9 [q]Rev 17:4 [r]S Eze 27:16 [s]Isa 14:11; Rev 21:20 28:14 [t]Ex 30:26; 40:9 [u]Ex 25:17-20 28:16 [v]S Ge 6:11; Hab 2:17

[n] *3* Or *Danel*; the Hebrew spelling may suggest a person other than the prophet Daniel. [o] *13* Or *lapis lazuli* [p] *13* The precise identification of some of these precious stones is uncertain. [q] *13* The meaning of the Hebrew for this phrase is uncertain.

28:1–10 RULER OF TYRE. The king of Tyre's fundamental sin was pride, which led him to exalt himself as a deity. For this he would face the Sovereign Lord's judgment and be brought down to the pit like all mortals (v. 8). Many today, especially those caught up in New Age thinking, actually believe that we are gods or at least are becoming gods; such deceivers and their victims will receive the same condemnation as the ruler of Tyre.

28:12 KING OF TYRE. In its context, Ezekiel's prophecy against Tyre's ruler appears to contain a veiled description of Satan as the true ruler of Tyre and as the god of this world (cf. 1Jn 5:19). The king is described as having been a visitor to the Garden of Eden (v. 13), a "guardian cherub," or angel (v. 14), and a blameless creature in all his ways till wickedness was found in him (v. 15). Because of his sinful pride (v. 17), he was driven out from the mount of God (vv. 16–17; cf. Isa 14:13–15).

So I drove you in disgrace from
the mount of God,
and I expelled you, O guardian
cherub,[w]
from among the fiery stones.
17Your heart became proud[x]
on account of your beauty,
and you corrupted your wisdom
because of your splendor.
So I threw you to the earth;
I made a spectacle of you before
kings.[y]
18By your many sins and dishonest
trade
you have desecrated your
sanctuaries.
So I made a fire[z] come out from
you,
and it consumed you,
and I reduced you to ashes[a] on
the ground
in the sight of all who were
watching.[b]
19All the nations who knew you
are appalled[c] at you;
you have come to a horrible end
and will be no more.[d]' "

A Prophecy Against Sidon

20The word of the LORD came to me:
21"Son of man, set your face against[e]
Sidon;[f] prophesy against her 22and
say: 'This is what the Sovereign LORD
says:

" 'I am against you, O Sidon,
and I will gain glory[g] within
you.
They will know that I am the LORD,
when I inflict punishment[h] on
her
and show myself holy[i] within
her.
23I will send a plague upon her
and make blood flow in her
streets.
The slain will fall within her,
with the sword against her on
every side.
Then they will know that I am the
LORD.[j]

24" 'No longer will the people of Israel have malicious neighbors who are
painful briers and sharp thorns.[k]
Then they will know that I am the Sovereign LORD.
25" 'This is what the Sovereign LORD
says: When I gather[l] the people of Israel from the nations where they have
been scattered,[m] I will show myself
holy[n] among them in the sight of the
nations. Then they will live in their
own land, which I gave to my servant
Jacob.[o] 26They will live there in safety[p] and will build houses and plant[q]
vineyards; they will live in safety when
I inflict punishment[r] on all their
neighbors who maligned them. Then
they will know that I am the LORD their
God.[s]' "

A Prophecy Against Egypt

29 In the tenth year, in the tenth
month on the twelfth day, the
word of the LORD came to me:[t] 2"Son
of man, set your face against[u] Pharaoh king of Egypt[v] and prophesy
against him and against all Egypt.[w]
3Speak to him and say: 'This is what
the Sovereign LORD says:

" 'I am against you, Pharaoh[x]
king of Egypt,
you great monster[y] lying among
your streams.
You say, "The Nile[z] is mine;
I made it for myself."
4But I will put hooks[a] in your jaws
and make the fish of your
streams stick to your
scales.
I will pull you out from among
your streams,
with all the fish sticking to your
scales.[b]
5I will leave you in the desert,
you and all the fish of your
streams.
You will fall on the open field
and not be gathered[c] or picked
up.
I will give you as food
to the beasts of the earth and
the birds of the air.[d]

28:16 [w] S Ge 3:24 **28:17** [x] Isa 10:12; Eze 16:49; 31:10 [y] S Eze 19:12 **28:18** [z] Ob 1:18 [a] Mal 4:3 [b] Zec 9:2-4 **28:19** [c] S Lev 26:32 [d] S Jer 51:64; S Eze 26:21 **28:21** [e] S Eze 13:17 [f] S Ge 10:15; S Jer 25:22 **28:22** [g] Eze 39:13 [h] Eze 30:19 [i] S Lev 10:3 **28:23** [j] S Eze 5:17; 38:22 **28:24** [k] S Isa 5:6; S Eze 2:6 **28:25** [l] Ps 106:47; Jer 32:37 [m] S Isa 11:12 [n] S Eze 20:41 [o] Jer 12:15; 23:8; S Eze 11:17; 34:27; 37:25 **28:26** [p] S Lev 25:18; S 1Ki 4:25; S Jer 17:25 [q] S Dt 20:6 [r] S Ps 149:9 [s] S Isa 65:21; S Jer 32:15; Eze 38:8; 39:26-27; Hos 2:15; 11:11; Am 9:14-15 **29:1** [t] ver 17; S Eze 26:1 **29:2** [u] S Eze 25:2 [v] S Jer 25:19 [w] Isa 19:1-17; Jer 46:2; Eze 30:1-26; 31:1-18; 32:1-32 **29:3** [x] Jer 44:30 [y] S Ps 68:30; S 74:13; Eze 32:2 [z] S Jer 46:8 **29:4** [a] S 2Ki 19:28; S Job 41:2 [b] Eze 38:4 **29:5** [c] S Jer 8:2 [d] S Jer 7:33; 34:20; Eze 31:13; 32:4-6; 39:4

28:25 GATHER THE PEOPLE OF ISRAEL. Ezekiel frequently emphasizes the promise to restore Israel (11:17; 20:34,41–42; 34:13; 36:24; 37:21; 38:8; 39:27). This restoration will not fully take place until God executes judgment on all the nations in the end times. By regathering Israel to serve him in righteousness, God will demonstrate that he is indeed a holy God who will accomplish all his purposes in this world (Ge 12:7; 26:3; 35:12).

29:1—32:32 EGYPT. These chapters give seven prophecies of judgment against Egypt. Egypt was judged because it was a world power that worshiped many gods and arrogantly boasted of its might.

6Then all who live in Egypt will know
that I am the LORD.

" 'You have been a staff of reed[e] for
the house of Israel. 7When they
grasped you with their hands, you
splintered[f] and you tore open their
shoulders; when they leaned on you,
you broke and their backs were
wrenched.[r][g]

8" 'Therefore this is what the Sovereign LORD says: I will bring a sword
against you and kill your men and their
animals.[h] 9Egypt will become a desolate wasteland. Then they will know
that I am the LORD.

" 'Because you said, "The Nile[i] is
mine; I made it,[j]" 10therefore I am
against you[k] and against your
streams, and I will make the land of
Egypt[l] a ruin and a desolate waste[m]
from Migdol[n] to Aswan,[o] as far as
the border of Cush.[s][p] 11No foot of
man or animal will pass through it; no
one will live there for forty years.[q] 12I
will make the land of Egypt desolate[r]
among devastated lands, and her cities
will lie desolate forty years among ruined cities. And I will disperse the
Egyptians among the nations and scatter them through the countries.[s]

13" 'Yet this is what the Sovereign
LORD says: At the end of forty years I
will gather the Egyptians from the nations where they were scattered. 14I
will bring them back from captivity and
return them to Upper Egypt,[t][t] the
land of their ancestry. There they will
be a lowly[u] kingdom.[v] 15It will be the
lowliest of kingdoms and will never
again exalt itself above the other nations.[w] I will make it so weak that it
will never again rule over the nations.
16Egypt will no longer be a source of
confidence[x] for the people of Israel
but will be a reminder[y] of their sin in
turning to her for help.[z] Then they
will know that I am the Sovereign
LORD.[a]' "

17In the twenty-seventh year, in the
first month on the first day, the word
of the LORD came to me:[b] 18"Son of
man, Nebuchadnezzar[c] king of Babylon drove his army in a hard campaign
against Tyre; every head was rubbed
bare[d] and every shoulder made raw.[e]
Yet he and his army got no reward from
the campaign he led against Tyre.
19Therefore this is what the Sovereign
LORD says: I am going to give Egypt to
Nebuchadnezzar king[f] of Babylon,
and he will carry off its wealth. He will
loot and plunder[g] the land as pay for
his army.[h] 20I have given him Egypt[i]
as a reward for his efforts because he
and his army did it for me, declares the
Sovereign LORD.[j]

21"On that day I will make a
horn[u][k] grow for the house of Israel,
and I will open your mouth[l] among
them. Then they will know that I am
the LORD.[m]"

A Lament for Egypt

30 The word of the LORD came to
me: 2"Son of man, prophesy
and say: 'This is what the Sovereign
LORD says:

" 'Wail[n] and say,
"Alas for that day!"
3For the day is near,[o]
the day of the LORD[p] is near—
a day of clouds,
a time of doom for the nations.
4A sword will come against
Egypt,[q]
and anguish will come upon
Cush.[v][r]
When the slain fall in Egypt,
her wealth will be carried away
and her foundations torn
down.[s]

5Cush and Put,[t] Lydia and all Arabia,[u] Libya[w] and the people[v] of the
covenant land will fall by the sword
along with Egypt.[w]

6" 'This is what the LORD says:

" 'The allies of Egypt will fall
and her proud strength will fail.
From Migdol to Aswan[x]

29:6 [e]S 2Ki 18:21
29:7 [f]2Ki 18:21; Isa 36:6 [g]Jer 17:5; Eze 17:15-17
29:8 [h]Eze 25:13; 32:11-13
29:9 [i]S Jer 46:8 [j]Eze 30:7-8,13-19
29:10 [k]S Jer 21:13 [l]S Ex 3:22 [m]S Jer 46:19 [n]S Ex 14:2 [o]Eze 30:6 [p]Isa 18:1; Eze 30:4
29:11 [q]Eze 32:13
29:12 [r]S Isa 34:10 [s]S Jer 46:19; Eze 30:7,23,26
29:14 [t]S Isa 11:11; Eze 30:14 [u]Eze 17:14 [v]S Isa 19:22; Jer 46:26
29:15 [w]Zec 10:11
29:16 [x]2Ch 32:10 [y]S Nu 5:15 [z]S La 4:17 [a]Isa 20:5; S 30:2; Hos 8:13
29:17 [b]S ver 1; S Eze 24:1; 30:20; 40:1
29:18 [c]Jer 27:6; 39:1 [d]S Lev 13:40; S Job 1:20; S Jer 48:37 [e]Ge 49:15
29:19 [f]S Isa 19:4 [g]S Eze 26:5 [h]Jer 43:10-13; Eze 30:4,10,24-25; 32:11
29:20 [i]S Isa 43:3 [j]Isa 10:6-7; 45:1; S Jer 25:9
29:21 [k]S Ps 132:17; S Lk 1:69 [l]Eze 33:22 [m]S Eze 3:27
30:2 [n]S Isa 13:6; Jas 5:1
30:3 [o]S Eze 7:7; Joel 1:15; 2:1,11; Ob 1:15 [p]ver 18; S Eze 7:12,19; 32:7; 34:12
30:4 [q]Jer 25:19; Da 11:43 [r]S Ge 10:6; S Eze 29:10 [s]S Eze 29:19
30:5 [t]S Eze 27:10 [u]S 2Ch 9:14 [v]Jer 25:20 [w]Na 3:9
30:6 [x]Eze 29:10

[r] *7* Syriac (see also Septuagint and Vulgate); Hebrew *and you caused their backs to stand*
[s] *10* That is, the upper Nile region
[t] *14* Hebrew *to Pathros*
[u] *21* *Horn* here symbolizes strength.
[v] *4* That is, the upper Nile region; also in verses 5 and 9
[w] *5* Hebrew *Cub*

29:8 BRING A SWORD AGAINST YOU. God would send Nebuchadnezzar, the Babylonian king, against Egypt and reduce it to "the lowliest of kingdoms" (v. 15; cf. vv. 19–20); Babylon attacked Egypt in 572 and 568 B.C.

30:3 THE DAY OF THE LORD. Egypt's doom foreshadows the coming "day of the LORD" when God will bring judgment on all the ungodly nations of the world (see 1Th 5:2,4, notes).

they will fall by the sword
within her,
declares the Sovereign LORD.
7" 'They will be desolate
among desolate lands,
and their cities will lie
among ruined cities.[y]
8Then they will know that I am the
LORD,
when I set fire[z] to Egypt
and all her helpers are
crushed.[a]

9" 'On that day messengers will go
out from me in ships to frighten Cush[b]
out of her complacency. Anguish[c] will
take hold of them on the day of Egypt's
doom, for it is sure to come.[d]
10" 'This is what the Sovereign LORD
says:

" 'I will put an end to the hordes
of Egypt
by the hand of
Nebuchadnezzar[e] king of
Babylon.[f]
11He and his army—the most
ruthless of nations[g]—
will be brought in to destroy the
land.
They will draw their swords
against Egypt
and fill the land with the
slain.[h]
12I will dry up[i] the streams of the
Nile[j]
and sell the land to evil men;
by the hand of foreigners
I will lay waste[k] the land and
everything in it.

I the LORD have spoken.

13" 'This is what the Sovereign LORD
says:

" 'I will destroy the idols[l]
and put an end to the images in
Memphis.[x][m]
No longer will there be a prince in
Egypt,[n]
and I will spread fear
throughout the land.
14I will lay[o] waste Upper Egypt,[y]
set fire to Zoan[p]
and inflict punishment on
Thebes.[z][q]
15I will pour out my wrath on
Pelusium,[a]
the stronghold of Egypt,
and cut off the hordes of
Thebes.
16I will set fire[r] to Egypt;
Pelusium will writhe in agony.
Thebes will be taken by storm;
Memphis[s] will be in constant
distress.
17The young men of Heliopolis[b][t]
and Bubastis[c]
will fall by the sword,
and the cities themselves will go
into captivity.
18Dark will be the day at
Tahpanhes[u]
when I break the yoke of
Egypt;[v]
there her proud strength will
come to an end.
She will be covered with clouds,
and her villages will go into
captivity.[w]
19So I will inflict punishment[x] on
Egypt,
and they will know that I am
the LORD.' "

20In the eleventh year, in the first
month on the seventh day, the word of
the LORD came to me:[y] 21"Son of man,
I have broken the arm[z] of Pharaoh[a]
king of Egypt. It has not been bound up
for healing[b] or put in a splint so as to
become strong enough to hold a sword.
22Therefore this is what the Sovereign
LORD says: I am against Pharaoh king
of Egypt.[c] I will break both his arms,
the good arm as well as the broken
one, and make the sword fall from his
hand.[d] 23I will disperse the Egyptians
among the nations and scatter them
through the countries.[e] 24I will
strengthen[f] the arms of the king of
Babylon and put my sword[g] in his
hand, but I will break the arms of Pharaoh, and he will groan[h] before him
like a mortally wounded man. 25I will
strengthen the arms of the king of Babylon, but the arms of Pharaoh will fall
limp. Then they will know that I am the
LORD, when I put my sword[i] into the
hand of the king of Babylon and he
brandishes it against Egypt.[j] 26I will
disperse the Egyptians among the nations and scatter them through the
countries. Then they will know that I
am the LORD.[k]"

30:7 [y]S Eze 29:12
30:8 [z]S Jer 49:27; Eze 39:6; Am 1:4, 7,10; Na 1:6 [a]S Eze 29:9
30:9 [b]S Ge 10:6 [c]Isa 23:5 [d]Eze 32:9-10; Zep 2:12
30:10 [e]Jer 39:1 [f]S Eze 29:19
30:11 [g]S Eze 28:7 [h]ver 24-25
30:12 [i]S Isa 19:6 [j]S Jer 46:8; Eze 29:9 [k]S Eze 19:7
30:13 [l]S Jer 43:12; S Eze 6:6 [m]S Isa 19:13 [n]Zec 10:11
30:14 [o]S Eze 29:14 [p]S Nu 13:22 [q]S Jer 46:25
30:16 [r]S Jos 7:15 [s]S Isa 19:13
30:17 [t]Ge 41:45
30:18 [u]S Jer 43:7 [v]S Lev 26:13; S Isa 9:4 [w]S ver 3
30:19 [x]Eze 28:22
30:20 [y]S Eze 26:1; S 29:17; 31:1; 32:1
30:21 [z]S Jer 48:25 [a]S Jer 44:30 [b]Jer 30:13; 46:11
30:22 [c]S Ge 15:18; S Jer 46:25 [d]Ps 37:17; Zec 11:17
30:23 [e]S Eze 29:12
30:24 [f]Zec 10:6, 12; 12:5 [g]S Eze 21:14; Zep 2:12 [h]Jer 51:52
30:25 [i]1Ch 21:12 [j]S Isa 10:5; 45:1, 5; S Eze 29:19
30:26 [k]S Eze 29:12

[x]*13* Hebrew *Noph;* also in verse 16 [y]*14* Hebrew *waste Pathros* [z]*14* Hebrew *No;* also in verses 15 and 16 [a]*15* Hebrew *Sin;* also in verse 16 [b]*17* Hebrew *Awen* (or *On*) [c]*17* Hebrew *Pi Beseth*

A Cedar in Lebanon

31 In the eleventh year,[l] in the
third month on the first day, the
word of the LORD came to me:[m] **2**"Son
of man, say to Pharaoh king of Egypt
and to his hordes:

" 'Who can be compared with you
in majesty?
3Consider Assyria,[n] once a cedar
in Lebanon,[o]
with beautiful branches
overshadowing the forest;
it towered on high,
its top above the thick foliage.[p]
4The waters[q] nourished it,
deep springs made it grow tall;
their streams flowed
all around its base
and sent their channels
to all the trees of the field.[r]
5So it towered higher[s]
than all the trees of the field;
its boughs increased
and its branches grew long,
spreading because of abundant
waters.[t]
6All the birds of the air
nested in its boughs,
all the beasts of the field
gave birth[u] under its branches;
all the great nations
lived in its shade.[v]
7It was majestic in beauty,
with its spreading boughs,
for its roots went down
to abundant waters.[w]
8The cedars[x] in the garden of God
could not rival it,
nor could the pine trees
equal its boughs,
nor could the plane trees[y]
compare with its branches—
no tree in the garden of God
could match its beauty.[z]
9I made it beautiful
with abundant branches,
the envy of all the trees of Eden[a]
in the garden of God.[b]

10" 'Therefore this is what the Sovereign LORD says: Because it towered
on high, lifting its top above the thick
foliage, and because it was proud[c] of
its height, **11**I handed it over to the ruler of the nations, for him to deal with
according to its wickedness. I cast it
aside,[d] **12**and the most ruthless of foreign nations[e] cut it down and left it.
Its boughs fell on the mountains and in
all the valleys;[f] its branches lay broken in all the ravines of the land. All
the nations of the earth came out from
under its shade and left it.[g] **13**All the
birds of the air settled on the fallen
tree, and all the beasts of the field were
among its branches.[h] **14**Therefore no
other trees by the waters are ever to
tower proudly on high, lifting their tops
above the thick foliage. No other trees
so well-watered are ever to reach such
a height; they are all destined[i] for
death,[j] for the earth below, among
mortal men, with those who go down to
the pit.[k]

15" 'This is what the Sovereign LORD
says: On the day it was brought down
to the grave[d] I covered the deep
springs with mourning for it; I held
back its streams, and its abundant waters were restrained. Because of it I
clothed Lebanon with gloom, and all
the trees of the field withered away.[l]
16I made the nations tremble[m] at the
sound of its fall when I brought it down
to the grave with those who go down to
the pit. Then all the trees[n] of Eden,[o]
the choicest and best of Lebanon, all
the trees that were well-watered, were
consoled[p] in the earth below.[q]
17Those who lived in its shade, its allies among the nations, had also gone
down to the grave with it, joining those
killed by the sword.[r]

18" 'Which of the trees of Eden can
be compared with you in splendor and
majesty? Yet you, too, will be brought
down with the trees of Eden to the
earth below; you will lie among the uncircumcised,[s] with those killed by the
sword.

" 'This is Pharaoh and all his hordes,
declares the Sovereign LORD.' "

A Lament for Pharaoh

32 In the twelfth year, in the
twelfth month on the first day,

31:1 [l]Jer 52:5 [m]S Eze 30:20; 32:17 **31:3** [n]S Jer 50:18 [o]S 2Ki 19:23; Hab 2:17; Zec 11:1 [p]Isa 10:34; S Eze 19:11 **31:4** [q]Eze 17:7 [r]Da 4:10 **31:5** [s]ver 10 [t]S Nu 24:6; S Eze 17:5 **31:6** [u]S Ge 31:7-9 [v]S Eze 17:23; S Mt 13:32 **31:7** [w]S Job 14:9 **31:8** [x]Ps 80:10 [y]S Ge 30:37 [z]Ge 2:8-9 **31:9** [a]S Ge 2:8 [b]S Ge 13:10; Eze 28:13 **31:10** [c]S Isa 2:11; S 14:13-14; S Eze 28:17 **31:11** [d]Da 5:20 **31:12** [e]S Eze 28:7 [f]Eze 32:5; 35:8 [g]Eze 32:11-12; Da 4:14 **31:13** [h]S Isa 18:6; S Eze 29:5; 32:4 **31:14** [i]S Ps 49:14 [j]S Ps 82:7 [k]S Nu 14:11; Ps 63:9; S Eze 26:20; 32:24 **31:15** [l]S 2Sa 1:21 **31:16** [m]S Jer 49:21 [n]S Isa 14:8 [o]S Ge 2:8 [p]S Eze 14:22 [q]S Isa 14:15; Eze 32:18 **31:17** [r]Ps 9:17 **31:18** [s]S Jer 9:26

[d] *15* Hebrew *Sheol*; also in verses 16 and 17

31:3 ASSYRIA. Ezekiel compares Egypt's situation to Assyria's days of glory and to its fall. Once a world power, Assyria had been destroyed by Babylon, the same nation that would defeat Egypt.

31:11 ACCORDING TO ITS WICKEDNESS. God's judgments are not arbitrary; they are always in accordance with the wickedness of individuals or nations. At the present time, God desires not to exercise judgment but to offer forgiveness to all who turn to him through his Son Jesus Christ.

the word of the LORD came to me:[t]
2"Son of man, take up a lament[u] concerning Pharaoh king of Egypt and say
to him:

" 'You are like a lion[v] among the
nations;
you are like a monster[w] in the
seas[x]
thrashing about in your streams,
churning the water with your
feet
and muddying the streams.[y]

3" 'This is what the Sovereign LORD
says:

" 'With a great throng of people
I will cast my net over you,
and they will haul you up in my
net.[z]
4I will throw you on the land
and hurl you on the open field.
I will let all the birds of the air
settle on you
and all the beasts of the earth
gorge themselves on you.[a]
5I will spread your flesh on the
mountains
and fill the valleys[b] with your
remains.
6I will drench the land with your
flowing blood[c]
all the way to the mountains,
and the ravines will be filled
with your flesh.[d]
7When I snuff you out, I will cover
the heavens
and darken their stars;
I will cover the sun with a cloud,
and the moon will not give its
light.[e]
8All the shining lights in the
heavens
I will darken[f] over you;
I will bring darkness over your
land,[g]
declares the Sovereign LORD.
9I will trouble the hearts of many
peoples
when I bring about your
destruction among the
nations,
among[e] lands you have not
known.

32:1 [t]S Eze 31:1; 33:21 **32:2** [u]2Sa 1:17; 3:33; 2Ch 35:25; S Eze 19:1 [v]S 2Ki 24:1; Na 2:11-13 [w]S Job 3:8; S Ps 74:13 [x]S Ge 1:21 [y]ver 13; Job 41:31; S Eze 29:3; 34:18 **32:3** [z]S Eze 12:13; Hab 1:15 **32:4** [a]S Isa 18:6; Eze 31:12-13; 39:4-5,17 **32:5** [b]S Eze 31:12 **32:6** [c]S Isa 34:3 [d]S Eze 29:5 **32:7** [e]S Isa 13:10; 34:4; S Eze 30:3; Joel 2:2,31; 3:15; S Mt 24:29; Rev 8:12 **32:8** [f]S Ps 102:26 [g]S Job 9:7; S Jer 4:23; Joel 2:10

32:10 [h]S Isa 30:32 [i]S Jer 46:10 [j]S Eze 26:16; S 27:35; 30:9; Rev 18:9-10 **32:11** [k]S Eze 21:19 [l]S Isa 19:4; S Jer 46:13 [m]S Eze 29:19 **32:12** [n]S Eze 28:7 [o]Eze 31:11-12 **32:13** [p]S ver 2; S Eze 29:8,11 **32:15** [q]Ex 7:5; S 14:4,18; Ps 107:33-34 **32:16** [r]S Ge 50:10; S Eze 19:1 **32:17** [s]S ver 1 **32:18** [t]Jer 1:10

10I will cause many peoples to be
appalled at you,
and their kings will shudder
with horror because of you
when I brandish my sword[h]
before them.
On the day[i] of your downfall
each of them will tremble
every moment for his life.[j]

11" 'For this is what the Sovereign
LORD says:

" 'The sword[k] of the king of
Babylon[l]
will come against you.[m]
12I will cause your hordes to fall
by the swords of mighty men—
the most ruthless of all
nations.[n]
They will shatter the pride of
Egypt,
and all her hordes will be
overthrown.[o]
13I will destroy all her cattle
from beside abundant waters
no longer to be stirred by the foot
of man
or muddied by the hoofs of
cattle.[p]
14Then I will let her waters settle
and make her streams flow like
oil,
declares the Sovereign LORD.
15When I make Egypt desolate
and strip the land of everything
in it,
when I strike down all who live
there,
then they will know that I am
the LORD.[q]'

16"This is the lament[r] they will
chant for her. The daughters of the nations will chant it; for Egypt and all her
hordes they will chant it, declares the
Sovereign LORD."

17In the twelfth year, on the fifteenth day of the month, the word of
the LORD came to me:[s] 18"Son of man,
wail for the hordes of Egypt and consign[t] to the earth below both her and

[e] 9 Hebrew; Septuagint *bring you into captivity among the nations, / to*

32:2 LAMENT CONCERNING PHARAOH. This lament mocks Pharaoh, who believed that he was as strong as a lion or a great sea monster; however, he would have to answer to the Sovereign Lord, as all world leaders will eventually have to do.

32:18–31 THE EARTH BELOW. Egypt is pictured as joining in the grave other nations that had been punished for their cruelty and injustice (v. 27); other mighty leaders who had died would speak about Egypt there (v. 21).

the daughters of mighty nations, with those who go down to the pit.[u] **19**Say to them, 'Are you more favored than others? Go down and be laid among the uncircumcised.'[v] **20**They will fall among those killed by the sword. The sword is drawn; let her be dragged[w] off with all her hordes.[x] **21**From within the grave[f][y] the mighty leaders will say of Egypt and her allies, 'They have come down and they lie with the uncircumcised,[z] with those killed by the sword.'

22"Assyria is there with her whole army; she is surrounded by the graves of all her slain, all who have fallen by the sword. **23**Their graves are in the depths of the pit[a] and her army lies around her grave.[b] All who had spread terror in the land of the living are slain, fallen by the sword.

24"Elam[c] is there, with all her hordes around her grave. All of them are slain, fallen by the sword.[d] All who had spread terror in the land of the living[e] went down uncircumcised to the earth below. They bear their shame with those who go down to the pit.[f] **25**A bed is made for her among the slain, with all her hordes around her grave. All of them are uncircumcised,[g] killed by the sword. Because their terror had spread in the land of the living, they bear their shame with those who go down to the pit; they are laid among the slain.

26"Meshech and Tubal[h] are there, with all their hordes around their graves. All of them are uncircumcised, killed by the sword because they spread their terror in the land of the living. **27**Do they not lie with the other uncircumcised[i] warriors who have fallen, who went down to the grave with their weapons of war, whose swords were placed under their heads? The punishment for their sins rested on their bones, though the terror of these warriors had stalked through the land of the living.

28"You too, O Pharaoh, will be broken and will lie among the uncircumcised, with those killed by the sword.

29"Edom[j] is there, her kings and all her princes; despite their power, they are laid with those killed by the sword. They lie with the uncircumcised, with those who go down to the pit.[k]

30"All the princes of the north[l] and all the Sidonians[m] are there; they went down with the slain in disgrace despite the terror caused by their power. They lie uncircumcised[n] with those killed by the sword and bear their shame with those who go down to the pit.[o]

31"Pharaoh—he and all his army—will see them and he will be consoled[p] for all his hordes that were killed by the sword, declares the Sovereign LORD. **32**Although I had him spread terror in the land of the living, Pharaoh[q] and all his hordes will be laid among the uncircumcised, with those killed by the sword, declares the Sovereign LORD."[r]

Ezekiel a Watchman

33 The word of the LORD came to me: **2**"Son of man, speak to your countrymen and say to them: 'When I bring the sword[s] against a land, and the people of the land choose one of their men and make him their watchman,[t] **3**and he sees the sword coming against the land and blows the trumpet[u] to warn the people, **4**then if anyone hears the trumpet but does not take warning[v] and the sword comes and takes his life, his blood will be on his own head.[w] **5**Since he heard the sound of the trumpet but did not take warning, his blood will be on his own head.[x] If he had taken warning, he would have saved himself.[y] **6**But if the watchman sees the sword coming and does not blow the trumpet to warn the people and the sword comes and takes the life of one of them, that man will be taken away because of his sin, but I

32:18 [u]Eze 26:20; S 31:14,16; Mic 1:8 **32:19** [v]ver 29-30; S Eze 28:10 **32:20** [w]Ps 28:3 [x]Eze 31:17-18 **32:21** [y]S Isa 14:9 [z]Eze 28:10 **32:23** [a]S Isa 14:15 [b]Na 1:14 **32:24** [c]S Ge 10:22 [d]S Jer 49:37 [e]S Job 28:13 [f]S Eze 26:20 **32:25** [g]Eze 28:10 **32:26** [h]S Eze 27:13 **32:27** [i]Eze 28:10 **32:29** [j]S Ps 137:7; Isa 34:5-15; Jer 49:7; Eze 35:15; Ob 1:1 [k]Eze 25:12-14 **32:30** [l]S Isa 14:31; Jer 25:26; Eze 38:6; 39:2 [m]S Ge 10:15; S Jer 25:22 [n]Eze 28:10 [o]S Eze 26:20; S 28:8 **32:31** [p]S Eze 14:22 **32:32** [q]S Jer 44:30 [r]S Job 3:14 **33:2** [s]S Lev 26:25; S Jer 12:12 [t]S 1Sa 14:16; Isa 21:6-9; S Jer 51:12 **33:3** [u]S Ex 20:18; S Nu 10:7; Hos 5:8; 8:1 **33:4** [v]2Ch 25:16 [w]S Lev 20:9; S Jer 6:17; Zec 1:4; Ac 18:6 **33:5** [x]S Lev 20:9 [y]S Ex 9:21

[f] *21* Hebrew *Sheol*; also in verse 27

32:31 WILL BE CONSOLED. The pharaoh would be somewhat "consoled" upon discovering that he was not the only one in the grave, reflecting the truths that misery loves company and that the judged do not want to suffer alone.

33:6 HOLD THE WATCHMAN ACCOUNTABLE. The watchman who saw destruction coming and did not warn the people would be held responsible for their blood. (1) Likewise, in God's kingdom, a prophet or preacher who does not warn a lukewarm church of coming judgment will be held accountable for the people's blood. (2) To a great extent all believers have the responsibility to witness to the lost and to help fulfill the mission task given to the church by Jesus (see Mt 28:19, note). We will have to give an account to God if we refuse to obey Jesus' Great Commission (see Ac 20:26, note).

will hold the watchman accountable for his blood.'[z]

7“Son of man, I have made you a watchman[a] for the house of Israel; so hear the word I speak and give them warning from me.[b] 8When I say to the wicked, ‘O wicked man, you will surely die,[c]’ and you do not speak out to dissuade him from his ways, that wicked man will die for[g] his sin, and I will hold you accountable for his blood.[d] 9But if you do warn the wicked man to turn from his ways and he does not do so,[e] he will die for his sin, but you will have saved yourself.[f]

10“Son of man, say to the house of Israel, ‘This is what you are saying: “Our offenses and sins weigh us down, and we are wasting away[g] because of[h] them. How then can we live?[h]” ’ 11Say to them, ‘As surely as I live, declares the Sovereign LORD, I take no pleasure in the death of the wicked, but rather that they turn from their ways and live.[i] Turn![j] Turn from your evil ways! Why will you die, O house of Israel?'[k]

12“Therefore, son of man, say to your countrymen,[l] ‘The righteousness of the righteous man will not save him when he disobeys, and the wickedness of the wicked man will not cause him to fall when he turns from it. The righteous man, if he sins, will not be allowed to live because of his former righteousness.'[m] 13If I tell the righteous man that he will surely live, but then he trusts in his righteousness and does evil, none of the righteous things he has done will be remembered; he will die for the evil he has done.[n] 14And if I say to the wicked man, ‘You will surely die,’ but he then turns away from his sin and does what is just[o] and right— 15if he gives back what he took in pledge[p] for a loan, returns what he has stolen,[q] follows the decrees that give life, and does no evil, he will surely live; he will not die.[r] 16None of the sins[s] he has committed will be remembered against him. He has done what is just and right; he will surely live.[t]

Joel 2:32

17“Yet your countrymen say, ‘The way of the Lord is not just.’ But it is their way that is not just. 18If a righteous man turns from his righteousness and does evil,[u] he will die for it.[v] 19And if a wicked man turns away from his wickedness and does what is just and right, he will live by doing so.[w] 20Yet, O house of Israel, you say, ‘The way of the Lord is not just.’ But I will judge each of you according to his own ways.”[x]

Jerusalem's Fall Explained

21In the twelfth year of our exile, in the tenth month on the fifth day, a man who had escaped[y] from Jerusalem came to me and said, “The city has fallen![z]” 22Now the evening before the man arrived, the hand of the LORD was upon me,[a] and he opened my mouth[b] before the man came to me in the morning. So my mouth was opened and I was no longer silent.[c]

23Then the word of the LORD came to me: 24“Son of man, the people living in those ruins[d] in the land of Israel are saying, ‘Abraham was only one man, yet he possessed the land. But we are many;[e] surely the land has been given to us as our possession.'[f] 25Therefore

[g] *8* Or *in*; also in verse 9 [h] *10* Or *away in*

33:6 [z] Isa 56:10-11; S Eze 3:18 **33:7** [a] S Isa 52:8 [b] Jer 1:17; 26:2 **33:8** [c] ver 14 [d] S Isa 3:11; S Eze 18:4 **33:9** [e] S Ps 7:12 [f] Eze 3:17-19 **33:10** [g] S Lev 26:16 [h] S Lev 26:39; S Eze 4:17 **33:11** [i] S La 3:33 [j] S 2Ch 30:9; S Isa 19:22; S Jer 3:12 [k] Jer 44:7-8; S Eze 18:23; Hos 11:8; Joel 2:12; S 1Ti 2:4 **33:12** [l] ver 2 [m] 2Ch 7:14; S Eze 3:20; S 18:21 **33:13** [n] Heb 10:38; 2Pe 2:20-21 **33:14** [o] S Jer 22:3 **33:15** [p] S Ex 22:26 [q] Ex 22:1-4; S Lev 6:2-5 [r] Isa 55:7; Jer 18:7-8; S Lk 19:8 **33:16** [s] S Jer 50:20 [t] S Isa 43:25 **33:18** [u] Jer 18:10 [v] S Eze 3:20 **33:19** [w] S ver 14-15 **33:20** [x] S Job 34:11 **33:21** [y] Eze 24:26 [z] S 2Ki 25:4,10; Jer 39:1-2; 52:4-7; S Eze 32:1 **33:22** [a] S Eze 1:3 [b] Eze 29:21; Lk 1:64 [c] Eze 3:26-27; S 24:27 **33:24** [d] Eze 36:4 [e] S Dt 1:10 [f] Isa 51:2; Jer 40:7; Eze 11:15; Lk 3:8; Ac 7:5

33:7 MADE YOU A WATCHMAN. God emphasizes again that Ezekiel was to be a faithful prophet to the people, warning them to turn from sin and to accept God's salvation. Today the church and its ministers must witness to all nations about salvation in Jesus Christ (see 3:18, note).

33:11 NO PLEASURE IN THE DEATH OF THE WICKED. God wants everyone to turn to him for salvation so that they will not die in their sins (see 2Pe 3:9, note). Believers should share God's desire for the repentance of the wicked.

33:12–20 WHEN HE DISOBEYS. God judges everyone righteously and justly. (1) The righteous who turn away from God and back to sin will be held accountable for their sins and will die in them if they do not repent; they cannot count on their past righteous deeds to save them (vv. 12–13). (2) On the other hand, the wicked who turn to God and away from sin will be saved, and none of their sins will be remembered against them (vv. 14–16); they will receive the gift of eternal life. (3) This passage, therefore, emphasizes the importance of our present relationship with God. To turn away from God and his word while assuming that our past faith and good deeds will save us is spiritually fatal. Conversely, if we turn to God in sincere repentance and true faith, he will accept us, regardless of our past sins (see 18:21–24, notes).

33:21 THE CITY HAS FALLEN! News came to Ezekiel and the exiles in Babylon that Jerusalem had fallen, fulfilling his prophecies and vindicating his message to the people. His ministry changed at this point, for he now began to prophesy redemption and restoration for Judah at some future time.

say to them, 'This is what the Sovereign LORD says: Since you eat[g]
meat with the blood[h] still in it and
look to your idols and shed blood,
should you then possess the land?[i]
26You rely on your sword,
you do detestable things,[j] and
each of you defiles his neighbor's
wife.[k] Should you then possess the
land?'

27"Say this to them: 'This is what
the Sovereign LORD says: As surely as
I live, those who are left in the ruins
will fall by the sword, those out in the
country I will give to the wild animals
to be devoured, and those in strongholds and caves will die of a plague.[l]
28I will make the land a desolate
waste, and her proud strength will
come to an end, and the mountains[m] of
Israel will become desolate so that no
one will cross them.[n] 29Then they will
know that I am the LORD, when I have
made the land a desolate[o] waste because of all the detestable things they
have done.'[p]

30"As for you, son of man, your
countrymen are talking together about
you by the walls and at the doors of the
houses, saying to each other, 'Come
and hear the message that has come
from the LORD.' 31My people come to
you, as they usually do, and sit before[q] you to listen to your words, but
they do not put them into practice.
With their mouths they express devotion, but their hearts are greedy[r] for
unjust gain.[s] 32Indeed, to them you
are nothing more than one who sings
love songs[t] with a beautiful voice and
plays an instrument well, for they hear
your words but do not put them into
practice.[u]

33"When all this comes true—and it
surely will—then they will know that
a prophet has been among them.[v]"

33:25 [g] Jer 7:21 [h] S Ge 9:4 [i] Jer 7:9-10; S Eze 22:6,27 **33:26** [j] Jer 41:7 [k] Eze 22:11 **33:27** [l] 1Sa 13:6; Isa 2:19; S Jer 42:22; S Eze 7:15; S 14:21; 39:4 **33:28** [m] S Isa 41:15 [n] S Ge 6:7; Jer 9:10 **33:29** [o] S Lev 26:34 [p] S Jer 18:16; S 44:22; Eze 36:4; Mic 7:13 **33:31** [q] S Eze 8:1 [r] Ps 119:36 [s] Ps 78:36-37; S Isa 29:13; S 33:15; S Jer 3:10; S 6:17; S Eze 22:27; Mt 13:22; 1Jn 3:18 **33:32** [t] S 1Ki 4:32 [u] Mk 6:20 **33:33** [v] S 1Sa 3:20; S Jer 28:9; S Eze 2:5

34:2 [w] Ps 78:70-72; Isa 40:11; Jer 3:15; S 23:1; Mic 3:11; Jn 10:11; 21:15-17; Jude 1:12 **34:3** [x] Isa 56:11; S Eze 22:27; Am 6:4; Zec 11:5 **34:4** [y] S Isa 3:7 [z] S Isa 1:6 [a] ver 16; S Lev 25:43; Mic 3:3; Zec 11:15-17 **34:5** [b] S Nu 27:17 [c] ver 28; S Isa 56:9; Ac 20:29 **34:6** [d] S Jer 50:6 [e] S Lev 26:33; S Ps 95:10; S Jer 10:21 [f] 2Ch 18:16; Ps 142:4; Hos 7:13; S Mt 9:36; 18:12-13; Lk 15:5; 1Pe 2:25 **34:8** [g] S Jdg 2:14 [h] S Isa 56:9 [i] Jude 1:12 **34:10** [j] S Jer 21:13

Shepherds and Sheep

34 The word of the LORD came to
me: 2"Son of man, prophesy
against the shepherds of Israel; prophesy and say to them: 'This is what the
Sovereign LORD says: Woe to the shepherds of Israel who only take care of
themselves! Should not shepherds
take care of the flock?[w] 3You eat the
curds, clothe yourselves with the wool
and slaughter the choice animals, but
you do not take care of the flock.[x]
4You have not strengthened the weak
or healed[y] the sick or bound up[z] the
injured. You have not brought back the
strays or searched for the lost. You
have ruled them harshly and brutally.[a] 5So they were scattered because
there was no shepherd,[b] and when
they were scattered they became food
for all the wild animals.[c] 6My sheep
wandered over all the mountains and
on every high hill.[d] They were scattered[e] over the whole earth, and no
one searched or looked for them.[f]

7" 'Therefore, you shepherds, hear
the word of the LORD: 8As surely as I
live, declares the Sovereign LORD, because my flock lacks a shepherd and so
has been plundered[g] and has become
food for all the wild animals,[h] and because my shepherds did not search for
my flock but cared for themselves rather than for my flock,[i] 9therefore, O
shepherds, hear the word of the LORD:
10This is what the Sovereign LORD
says: I am against[j] the shepherds and
will hold them accountable for my
flock. I will remove them from tending
the flock so that the shepherds can no
longer feed themselves. I will rescue[k]
my flock from their mouths, and it will
no longer be food for them.[l]

11" 'For this is what the Sovereign

[k] S Ps 72:14 [l] 1Sa 2:29-30; S Jer 23:2; Zec 10:3

33:31 SIT BEFORE YOU. The people were listening to Ezekiel, but they were not obeying God's word; their hearts were still far from the Lord. They viewed Ezekiel as a performer on stage and God's message as entertainment (v. 32). NT believers must be careful not to turn worship services into performances staged for entertainment. God and his word are not honored by such activity, and the Holy Spirit will not manifest his presence in such worship (see article on WORSHIP, p. 680). Believers must not only be hearers but also doers of God's word (see Jas 1:22).

34:1–31 THE SHEPHERDS OF ISRAEL. Ezekiel prophesies against the leaders of Israel, i.e., its kings, priests and prophets. By greed, corruption and selfishness, they had failed to lead God's people in the way he wanted. They were exploiting the people (v. 3) and using them for personal gain instead of helping them spiritually (v. 4); thus, they were responsible for Judah's captivity, and God would bring them into judgment. In contrast to the faithless shepherds, Ezekiel went on to prophesy a day when God would send a Shepherd after his own heart (i.e., the Messiah), who would truly care for the people. Rather than being exploited and manipulated, the flock would then receive "showers of blessing" (v. 26).

34:11 SEARCH FOR MY SHEEP AND LOOK

LORD says: I myself will search for my
sheep[m] and look after them. **12**As a
shepherd[n] looks after his scattered
flock when he is with them, so will I
look after my sheep. I will rescue them
from all the places where they were
scattered on a day of clouds and darkness.[o] **13**I will bring them out from the
nations and gather[p] them from the
countries, and I will bring them into
their own land.[q r s t] I will pasture
them on the mountains of Israel, in the
ravines and in all the settlements in
the land.[u v w] **14**I will tend them in a
good pasture, and the mountain
heights of Israel[x] will be their grazing
land. There they will lie down in good
grazing land, and there they will feed
in a rich pasture[y] on the mountains of
Israel.[z] **15**I myself will tend my sheep
and have them lie down,[a] declares the
Sovereign LORD.[b] **16**I will search for
the lost and bring back the strays. I
will bind up[c] the injured and strength-
en the weak,[d] but the sleek and the
strong I will destroy.[e] I will shepherd
the flock with justice.[f]
17" 'As for you, my flock, this is what
the Sovereign LORD says: I will judge
between one sheep and another, and
between rams and goats.[g] **18**Is it not
enough[h] for you to feed on the good
pasture? Must you also trample the
rest of your pasture with your feet?[i]
Is it not enough for you to drink clear
water? Must you also muddy the rest
with your feet? **19**Must my flock feed
on what you have trampled and drink
what you have muddied with your feet?
20" 'Therefore this is what the Sovereign LORD says to them: See, I myself
will judge between the fat sheep and
the lean sheep.[j] **21**Because you shove
with flank and shoulder, butting all the
weak sheep with your horns[k] until
you have driven them away, **22**I will
save my flock, and they will no longer
be plundered. I will judge between one
sheep and another.[l] **23**I will place
over them one shepherd, my servant
David, and he will tend[m] them; he will
tend them and be their shepherd.[n] **24**I
the LORD will be their God,[o] and my
servant David[p] will be prince among
them.[q] I the LORD have spoken.[r]
25" 'I will make a covenant[s] of
peace[t] with them and rid the land of
wild beasts[u] so that they may live in
the desert and sleep in the forests in
safety.[v] **26**I will bless[w] them and the
places surrounding my hill.[i] I will
send down showers in season;[x] there
will be showers of blessing.[y] **27**The
trees of the field will yield their fruit[z]
and the ground will yield its crops;[a]
the people will be secure[b] in their
land. They will know that I am the
LORD, when I break the bars of their
yoke[c] and rescue them from the
hands of those who enslaved them.[d]
28They will no longer be plundered by
the nations, nor will wild animals devour them. They will live in safety,[e]
and no one will make them afraid.[f] **29**I
will provide for them a land renowned[g] for its crops, and they will no
longer be victims of famine[h] in the
land or bear the scorn[i] of the nations.[j] **30**Then they will know that I,
the LORD their God, am with them and
that they, the house of Israel, are my
people, declares the Sovereign LORD.[k]
31You my sheep,[l] the sheep of my
pasture,[m] are people, and I am your
God, declares the Sovereign LORD.' "

34:11 [m] S Ps 119:176 **34:12** [n] Isa 40:11; S Jer 31:10; Zec 10:3; Lk 19:10 [o] S Eze 32:7 **34:13** [p] S Ge 48:21; S Dt 30:4 [q] Mic 4:6 [r] S Eze 11:17 [s] S Jer 23:8 [t] S Isa 66:20 [u] S Eze 28:25; 36:24 [v] S Jer 50:19 [w] Jer 23:3 **34:14** [x] S Eze 20:40 [y] Ps 23:2; S 37:3 [z] S Isa 65:10; Eze 36:29-30; 37:22; Am 9:14; Mic 7:14 **34:15** [a] Zep 3:13 [b] Ps 23:1-2; S Jer 33:12; Mic 5:4 **34:16** [c] S Ps 147:3 [d] Mic 4:6; Zep 3:19 [e] Lk 19:10 [f] Isa 10:16; S Jer 31:8; Lk 5:32 **34:17** [g] Mt 25:32-33 **34:18** [h] S Ge 30:15 [i] S Eze 32:2 **34:20** [j] Mt 25:32 **34:21** [k] S Dt 33:17 **34:22** [l] Ps 72:12-14; Jer 23:2-3; Eze 20:37-38 **34:23** [m] Isa 40:11 [n] S Isa 31:4; Mic 5:4 **34:24** [o] Eze 36:28 [p] Ps 89:49 [q] S Isa 53:4; Zec 13:7 [r] Jer 23:4-5; S 30:9; S 33:14; Jn 10:16; Rev 7:17 **34:25** [s] S Eze 16:62 [t] S Nu 25:12 [u] Lev 26:6 [v] S Lev 25:18; Isa 11:6-9; Hos 2:18 **34:26** [w] S Ge 12:2 [x] Ps 68:9; Joel 2:23 [y] Dt 11:13-15; S 28:12; Isa 44:3 **34:27** [z] S Ps 72:16 [a] S Job 14:9; S Ps 67:6 [b] S Nu 24:21 [c] S Lev 26:13 [d] S Jer 30:8; S Eze 20:42; S 28:25 **34:28** [e] S Jer 32:37 [f] S Jer 30:10; S Eze 28:26; 39:26; Hos 11:11; Am 9:15; Zep 3:13; Zec 14:11 **34:29** [g] S Isa 4:2 [h] Eze 36:29 [i] S Ps 137:3; Eze 36:6; Joel 2:19 [j] Eze 36:15 **34:30** [k] S Eze 14:11; 37:27 **34:31** [l] S Ps 28:9 [m] S Jer 23:1

[i] 26 Or *I will make them and the places surrounding my hill a blessing*

AFTER THEM. Because of the failure of Israel's leaders, the Lord himself would take charge of his people. He would care for his flock (vv. 11–16), judge between the sheep, rams and goats (vv. 17–24), and make a covenant of peace with the people (vv. 25–31).

34:23 PLACE OVER THEM ONE SHEPHERD. This shepherd is Jesus the Messiah, who came from David's line (cf. Ps 89:4,20,29; Jer 23:5–6). He shepherded God's people as a righteous priest, prophet and king. He is "the good shepherd" (Jn 10:14), who laid down his life for the sheep (Jn 10:1–18; 1Jn 3:1; cf. 1Pe 2:25; 5:4). In the future, when God's people are restored to their land, the Messiah will set up his kingdom of peace and justice (see next note).

34:25 A COVENANT OF PEACE. The Messiah-Shepherd will restore the peace and perfection that characterized life before sin entered the world (Ge 1—3). This covenant, also called the "new covenant" (see Jer 31:31–34), will reach its full realization only when God's kingdom is forever established in the new heaven and the new earth (Rev 21—22). Then there will be "showers of blessing" for the redeemed (v. 26) and the full presence of God among his people (v. 30).

A Prophecy Against Edom

35 The word of the LORD came to
me: 2“Son of man, set your face
against Mount Seir;[n] prophesy
against it 3and say: ‘This is what the
Sovereign LORD says: I am against you,
Mount Seir, and I will stretch out my
hand[o] against you and make you a
desolate waste.[p] 4I will turn your
towns into ruins[q] and you will be desolate. Then you will know that I am the
LORD.[r]
5“ ‘Because you harbored an ancient
hostility and delivered the Israelites
over to the sword[s] at the time of their
calamity,[t] the time their punishment
reached its climax,[u] 6therefore as
surely as I live, declares the Sovereign
LORD, I will give you over to bloodshed[v] and it will pursue you.[w] Since
you did not hate bloodshed, bloodshed
will pursue you. 7I will make Mount
Seir a desolate waste[x] and cut off
from it all who come and go.[y] 8I will
fill your mountains with the slain;
those killed by the sword will fall on
your hills and in your valleys and in all
your ravines.[z] 9I will make you desolate forever;[a] your towns will not be
inhabited. Then you will know that I
am the LORD.[b]
10“ ‘Because you have said, “These
two nations and countries will be ours
and we will take possession[c] of
them,” even though I the LORD was
there, 11therefore as surely as I live,
declares the Sovereign LORD, I will
treat you in accordance with the anger[d] and jealousy you showed in your
hatred of them and I will make myself
known among them when I judge
you.[e] 12Then you will know that I the
LORD have heard all the contemptible
things you have said against the mountains of Israel. You said, “They have
been laid waste and have been given
over to us to devour.[f]” 13You boasted[g] against me and spoke against me
without restraint, and I heard it.[h]
14This is what the Sovereign LORD
says: While the whole earth rejoices, I
will make you desolate.[i] 15Because
you rejoiced[j] when the inheritance of
the house of Israel became desolate,
that is how I will treat you. You will be
desolate, O Mount Seir,[k] you and all
of Edom.[l] Then they will know that I
am the LORD.’ ”

A Prophecy to the Mountains of Israel

36 “Son of man, prophesy to the
mountains of Israel[m] and say,
‘O mountains of Israel, hear the word
of the LORD. 2This is what the Sovereign LORD says:[n] The enemy said of
you, “Aha![o] The ancient heights[p]
have become our possession.[q]” ’
3Therefore prophesy and say, ‘This is
what the Sovereign LORD says: Because
they ravaged[r] and hounded you from
every side so that you became the possession of the rest of the nations and
the object of people’s malicious talk
and slander,[s] 4therefore, O mountains
of Israel, hear the word of the Sovereign LORD: This is what the Sovereign
LORD says to the mountains and hills,
to the ravines and valleys,[t] to the desolate ruins[u] and the deserted[v] towns
that have been plundered and ridiculed[w] by the rest of the nations
around you[x]— 5this is what the Sovereign LORD says: In my burning[y] zeal
I have spoken against the rest of the
nations, and against all Edom, for with
glee and with malice in their hearts
they made my land their own possession so that they might plunder its pastureland.’[z] 6Therefore prophesy concerning the land of Israel and say to
the mountains and hills, to the ravines
and valleys: ‘This is what the Sovereign LORD says: I speak in my jealous
wrath because you have suffered the
scorn of the nations.[a] 7Therefore this
is what the Sovereign LORD says: I
swear with uplifted hand[b] that the nations around you will also suffer
scorn.[c]
8“ ‘But you, O mountains of Israel,

35:2 [n] S Ge 14:6 **35:3** [o] S Jer 6:12 [p] S Isa 34:10; Eze 25:12-14 **35:4** [q] Jer 44:2 [r] ver 9; S Jer 49:10 **35:5** [s] S Ps 63:10 [t] Ob 1:13 [u] Ps 137:7; S Eze 21:29 **35:6** [v] S Isa 34:3 [w] Isa 63:2-6 **35:7** [x] S Jer 46:19 [y] S Jer 49:17 **35:8** [z] S Eze 31:12 **35:9** [a] Ob 1:10 [b] S Isa 34:5-6; S Jer 49:13 **35:10** [c] S Ps 83:12; Eze 36:2,5 **35:11** [d] Eze 25:14 [e] S Ps 9:16; Ob 1:15; S Mt 7:2 **35:12** [f] S Jer 50:7 **35:13** [g] S Jer 49:16 [h] Da 11:36

35:14 [i] Jer 51:48 **35:15** [j] Eze 36:5; Ob 1:12 [k] ver 3 [l] S Isa 34:5-6,11; Jer 50:11-13; S La 4:21; S Eze 32:29 **36:1** [m] S Eze 17:22 **36:2** [n] Eze 6:2-3 [o] S Eze 25:3 [p] S Dt 32:13 [q] S Eze 35:10 **36:3** [r] Ob 1:13 [s] Ps 44:13-14; S La 2:16; 3:62 **36:4** [t] Eze 6:3 [u] Eze 33:24 [v] S Lev 26:43 [w] S Jer 2:26 [x] Dt 11:11; S Ps 79:4; S Eze 33:28-29 **36:5** [y] S Dt 29:20 [z] Isa 66:16; Jer 25:31; 50:11; Eze 25:12-14; S 35:10,15; 38:22; Joel 3:2,14 **36:6** [a] Ps 123:3-4; Eze 34:29 **36:7** [b] S Nu 14:30 [c] S Jer 25:9

35:2 AGAINST YOU, MOUNT SEIR. Ezekiel prophesies against Edom (Mount Seir, cf. v. 15), the descendants of Esau. They had been Israel's perpetual enemies (v. 5). After the fall of Israel and Judah, they hoped to possess the promised land (v. 10); but all their attempts to gain the land would fail, for God would bring them to ruin (vv. 10–15). They would not be able to prevent God from carrying out his plan to restore Israel.

35:10 THESE TWO NATIONS. This designation refers to Israel and Judah.

36:2–7 THE ENEMY. Israel's enemies would be punished for their slander (v. 3), their plunder of Israel (vv. 4–5), and their attempt to take over the promised land (v. 2).

36:8–15 O MOUNTAINS OF ISRAEL. In these verses, God personifies the promised land and speaks directly to it. He promises to restore the

will produce branches and fruit[d] for
my people Israel, for they will soon
come home. 9I am concerned for you
and will look on you with favor; you
will be plowed and sown,[e] 10and I will
multiply the number of people upon
you, even the whole house of Israel.
The towns will be inhabited and the ruins[f] rebuilt.[g] 11I will increase the
number of men and animals upon you,
and they will be fruitful[h] and become
numerous. I will settle people[i] on you
as in the past[j] and will make you
prosper more than before.[k] Then you
will know that I am the LORD. 12I will
cause people, my people Israel, to walk
upon you. They will possess you, and
you will be their inheritance;[l] you will
never again deprive them of their children.

13" 'This is what the Sovereign LORD
says: Because people say to you, "You
devour men[m] and deprive your nation
of its children," 14therefore you will no
longer devour men or make your nation
childless, declares the Sovereign LORD.
15No longer will I make you hear the
taunts of the nations, and no longer
will you suffer the scorn of the peoples
or cause your nation to fall, declares
the Sovereign LORD.[n]' "

16Again the word of the LORD came
to me: 17"Son of man, when the people
of Israel were living in their own land,
they defiled it by their conduct and
their actions. Their conduct was like a
woman's monthly uncleanness[o] in my
sight.[p] 18So I poured out[q] my wrath
on them because they had shed blood
in the land and because they had defiled it with their idols. 19I dispersed
them among the nations, and they
were scattered[r] through the countries; I judged them according to their
conduct and their actions.[s] 20And
wherever they went among the nations
they profaned[t] my holy name, for it
was said of them, 'These are the LORD's
people, and yet they had to leave his
land.'[u] 21I had concern for my holy
name, which the house of Israel profaned among the nations where they
had gone.[v]

22"Therefore say to the house of Israel, 'This is what the Sovereign LORD
says: It is not for your sake, O house
of Israel, that I am going to do these
things, but for the sake of my holy
name,[w] which you have profaned[x]
among the nations where you have
gone.[y] 23I will show the holiness of
my great name,[z] which has been profaned[a] among the nations, the name
you have profaned among them. Then
the nations will know that I am the
LORD,[b] declares the Sovereign LORD,
when I show myself holy[c] through you
before their eyes.[d]

24" 'For I will take you out of the nations; I will gather you from all the
countries and bring you back into your
own land.[e] 25I will sprinkle[f] clean
water on you, and you will be clean; I
will cleanse[g] you from all your impurities[h] and from all your idols.[i] 26I will
give you a new heart[j] and put a new
spirit in you; I will remove from you
your heart of stone[k] and give you a
heart of flesh.[l] 27And I will put my
Spirit[m] in you and move you to follow
my decrees[n] and be careful to keep
my laws.[o] 28You will live in the land
I gave your forefathers; you will be my
people,[p] and I will be your God.[q] 29I

Eze 37:14

36:8 [d]S Isa 4:2; S 27:6; Eze 47:12 36:9 [e]ver 34-36; Jer 31:27 36:10 [f]S Isa 49:8 [g]Isa 49:17-23; S Jer 30:18 36:11 [h]S Ge 1:22 [i]S Isa 49:19 [j]Mic 7:14 [k]Lev 26:9; Job 42:13; S Jer 31:28; S Eze 16:55; Zec 10:8 36:12 [l]Eze 47:14,22 36:13 [m]S Nu 13:32 36:15 [n]Ps 89:50-51; Isa 54:4; S Eze 34:29 36:17 [o]S Lev 5:2; S 12:2 [p]Ps 106:37-38; S Jer 2:7 36:18 [q]S 2Ch 34:21 36:19 [r]Dt 28:64 [s]Lev 18:24-28; S Eze 7:8; S 24:14; 39:24 36:20 [t]S Lev 18:21; S Eze 13:19; Ro 2:24 [u]Isa 52:5; S Jer 33:24; S Eze 12:16 36:21 [v]Ps 74:18; Isa 48:9 36:22 [w]S Isa 37:35; S Eze 20:44 [x]Ro 2:24* [y]Dt 9:5-6; Ps 106:8; S Eze 20:9 36:23 [z]S Nu 6:27 [a]S Isa 37:23 [b]S Ps 46:10 [c]S Eze 20:41 [d]Ps 126:2; S Isa 5:16; Eze 20:14; 38:23; 39:7,27-28 36:24 [e]S Isa 43:5-6; S Eze 34:13; 37:21 36:25 [f]S Lev 14:7; S 16:14-15; Heb 9:13 [g]S Ps 51:2,7 [h]S Ezr 6:21 [i]Isa 2:18; Joel 3:21; Zec 3:4; 13:2; S Ac 22:16 36:26 [j]Jer 24:7 [k]S Jer 5:3 [l]S Ps 51:10; S Eze 18:31; S 2Co 3:3 36:27 [m]S Isa 44:3; Joel 2:29; Jn 3:5 [n]S Eze 18:21 [o]Jer 50:20; 1Th 4:8 36:28 [p]Jer 30:22; 31:33 [q]S Eze 11:17; S 14:11; 34:24; 37:14,27; Zec 8:8

---

devoured land as a place of blessing (vv. 13–14). This prophecy will be most fully realized when Israel possesses the land of Palestine during Christ's millennial reign.

36:20–22 THEY PROFANED MY HOLY NAME. Israel had profaned God's name through their wickedness, and they were destroyed; as a result, the nations viewed that defeat as a sign of the Lord's weakness. God therefore intended to restore Israel to the land, not primarily for their sake, but to vindicate the holiness of his great name. When that time came, all nations would know that the Sovereign Lord of Israel is the only true God (v. 23; cf. 1Ki 18:20–39).

36:26–27 A NEW HEART. God promises to restore Israel not only physically, but also spiritually; this restoration involves giving them a new heart that is as tender as flesh so that they will respond to God's word. Also, God will put his Holy Spirit in them (cf. 11:19–20; Ps 51:7–11; see Ro 11:26, note; see article on ISRAEL IN GOD'S PLAN OF SALVATION, p. 1730). This work of God encompasses the new covenant established by Christ (see Jer 31:31–34).

36:27 MY SPIRIT IN YOU. Apart from the indwelling of the Holy Spirit, it is impossible for a person to have true life and to follow God's ways. It is essential that we remain open to the voice and guidance of the Holy Spirit (see articles on BAPTISM IN THE HOLY SPIRIT, p. 1642, and THE DOCTRINE OF THE HOLY SPIRIT, p. 1654).

will save you from all your uncleanness. I will call for the grain and make
it plentiful and will not bring famine[r]
upon you. **30**I will increase the fruit of
the trees and the crops of the field, so
that you will no longer suffer disgrace
among the nations because of famine.[s] **31**Then you will remember your
evil ways and wicked deeds, and you
will loathe yourselves for your sins and
detestable practices.[t] **32**I want you to
know that I am not doing this for your
sake, declares the Sovereign LORD. Be
ashamed[u] and disgraced for your conduct, O house of Israel![v]

33" 'This is what the Sovereign LORD
says: On the day I cleanse[w] you from
all your sins, I will resettle your towns,
and the ruins[x] will be rebuilt.[y] **34**The
desolate land will be cultivated instead
of lying desolate in the sight of all who
pass through it. **35**They will say, "This
land that was laid waste has become
like the garden of Eden;[z] the cities
that were lying in ruins, desolate and
destroyed, are now fortified and inhabited.[a]" **36**Then the nations around you
that remain will know that I the LORD
have rebuilt what was destroyed and
have replanted what was desolate. I
the LORD have spoken, and I will do
it.'[b]

37"This is what the Sovereign LORD
says: Once again I will yield to the
plea[c] of the house of Israel and do this
for them: I will make their people as
numerous as sheep,[d] **38**as numerous
as the flocks for offerings[e] at Jerusalem during her appointed feasts. So
will the ruined cities be filled with
flocks of people. Then they will know
that I am the LORD.[f]"

The Valley of Dry Bones

37 The hand of the LORD was upon
me,[g] and he brought me out by

36:29 [r] Eze 34:29
36:30 [s] Lev 26:4-5; S Eze 34:13-14; Hos 2:21-22
36:31 [t] Isa 6:5; S Jer 31:19; S Eze 6:9
36:32 [u] Eze 16:63 [v] Dt 9:5
36:33 [w] S Lev 16:30 [x] S Lev 26:31 [y] S Isa 49:8
36:35 [z] S Ge 2:8 [a] Am 9:14
36:36 [b] S Jer 42:10; S Eze 17:22; 37:14; 39:27-28
36:37 [c] Zec 10:6; 13:9 [d] Ps 102:17; Jer 29:12-14
36:38 [e] 1Ki 8:63; 2Ch 35:7-9 [f] S Ex 6:2
37:1 [g] S Eze 1:3 [h] S Eze 11:24; Lk 4:1; Ac 8:39 [i] Jer 7:32 [j] S Jer 8:2; Eze 40:1
37:3 [k] Dt 32:39; S 1Sa 2:6; Isa 26:19; 1Co 15:35
37:4 [l] Jer 22:29
37:5 [m] S Ge 2:7; Ps 104:29-30; Rev 11:11
37:6 [n] S Ex 6:2; Eze 38:23
37:9 [o] ver 14; Ps 104:30; Isa 32:15; Eze 39:29; Zec 12:10 [p] Jer 49:36; Da 7:2; 8:8; 11:4; Zec 2:6; 6:5; Rev 7:1
37:10 [q] S Eze 12:7 [r] Rev 11:11
37:11 [s] S Job 17:15; S La 3:54

the Spirit[h] of the LORD and set me in
the middle of a valley;[i] it was full of
bones.[j] **2**He led me back and forth
among them, and I saw a great many
bones on the floor of the valley, bones
that were very dry. **3**He asked me, "Son
of man, can these bones live?"

I said, "O Sovereign LORD, you alone
know.[k]"

4Then he said to me, "Prophesy to
these bones and say to them, 'Dry
bones, hear the word of the LORD![l]
5This is what the Sovereign LORD says
to these bones: I will make breath[j]
enter you, and you will come to life.[m]
6I will attach tendons to you and make
flesh come upon you and cover you
with skin; I will put breath in you, and
you will come to life. Then you will
know that I am the LORD.[n]' "

7So I prophesied as I was commanded. And as I was prophesying, there
was a noise, a rattling sound, and the
bones came together, bone to bone. **8**I
looked, and tendons and flesh appeared on them and skin covered them,
but there was no breath in them.

9Then he said to me, "Prophesy to
the breath;[o] prophesy, son of man,
and say to it, 'This is what the Sovereign LORD says: Come from the four
winds,[p] O breath, and breathe into
these slain, that they may live.' " **10**So
I prophesied as he commanded[q] me,
and breath entered them; they came to
life and stood up on their feet—a vast
army.[r]

11Then he said to me: "Son of man,
these bones are the whole house of Israel. They say, 'Our bones are dried up
and our hope is gone; we are cut off.'[s]
12Therefore prophesy and say to them:
'This is what the Sovereign LORD says:
O my people, I am going to open your

j5 The Hebrew for this word can also mean *wind* or *spirit* (see verses 6-14).

37:1–14 HAND OF THE LORD . . . BONES. By the Holy Spirit Ezekiel sees in a vision a valley full of bones. The bones represent "the whole house of Israel" (v. 11), i.e., both Israel and Judah in exile, whose hope had died when they were dispersed among foreigners. God instructed Ezekiel to prophesy to the bones (vv. 4–6). The bones were then raised to life in two stages: (1) a political restoration to the land (vv. 7–8), and (2) a spiritual restoration to faith (vv. 9–10). This vision was given to assure the exiles that they would be restored by God's power and again become a living community in the promised land in spite of their seemingly hopeless circumstances (vv. 11–14). The time between these two stages is not given.

37:10 BREATH ENTERED . . . LIFE. Israel's restoration to life reminds us of the creation of man as recorded in Ge 2:7. Adam was first formed physically, after which God gave him "the breath of life." In like manner, dead Israel would first be restored physically, and then God would give them his breath of life (i.e., pour out his Spirit on them).

37:12–14 THE LAND OF ISRAEL. The vision of the revived bones would be fulfilled at the time of Israel's restoration, not only physically but also spiritually. This restoration was initially fulfilled in Cyrus's time (cf. Ezr 1), but it will be fully realized only when God gathers the Israelites to their

graves and bring you up from them; I
will bring you back to the land of Israel.[t] 13Then you, my people, will know
that I am the LORD,[u] when I open your
graves and bring you up from them.[v]
14I will put my Spirit[w] in you and you
will live, and I will settle[x] you in your
own land. Then you will know that I
the LORD have spoken, and I have done
it, declares the LORD.[y]' "

One Nation Under One King

15The word of the LORD came to me:
16"Son of man, take a stick of wood
and write on it, 'Belonging to Judah
and the Israelites[z] associated with
him.[a]' Then take another stick of
wood, and write on it, 'Ephraim's stick,
belonging to Joseph and all the house
of Israel associated with him.' 17Join
them together into one stick so that
they will become one in your hand.[b]
18"When your countrymen ask you,
'Won't you tell us what you mean by
this?'[c] 19say to them, 'This is what
the Sovereign LORD says: I am going to
take the stick of Joseph—which is in
Ephraim's hand—and of the Israelite
tribes associated with him, and join it
to Judah's stick, making them a single
stick of wood, and they will become
one in my hand.'[d] 20Hold before their
eyes the sticks you have written on
21and say to them, 'This is what the
Sovereign LORD says: I will take the Israelites out of the nations where they
have gone. I will gather them from all
around and bring them back into their
own land.[e] 22I will make them one nation in the land, on the mountains of
Israel.[f] There will be one king over all
of them and they will never again be

37:12 [t]ver 21; Dt 32:39; 1Sa 2:6; Isa 26:19; Jer 29:14; Hos 13:14; Am 9:14-15; Zep 3:20; Zec 8:8 **37:13** [u]S Ex 6:2 [v]S Eze 17:24; Hos 13:14 **37:14** [w]S ver 9; S Isa 11:2; Joel 2:28-29 [x]S Jer 43:2 [y]Eze 36:27-28,36; Rev 11:11 **37:16** [z]S 1Ki 12:20; 2Ch 10:17-19 [a]Nu 17:2-3; 2Ch 15:9 **37:17** [b]ver 24; Isa 11:13; S Jer 50:4; Hos 1:11 **37:18** [c]S Eze 24:19 **37:19** [d]Zec 10:6 **37:21** [e]S ver 12; S Isa 43:5-6; S Eze 20:42; 39:27; Mic 4:6 **37:22** [f]S Eze 17:22; S 34:13-14

[g]Isa 11:13; Jer 33:24; S 50:4; Hos 1:11 **37:23** [h]Eze 43:7 [i]S Jer 7:24 [j]Eze 11:18; S 36:28; Na 2:2 **37:24** [k]Isa 55:4; Hos 3:5 [l]S 1Sa 13:14; S Isa 32:1 [m]Zec 13:7 [n]Ps 78:70-71; S Jer 30:21; S Eze 21:27 **37:25** [o]S Eze 28:25 [p]S Ezr 9:12; Am 9:15 [q]S Ps 89:3-4; Isa 11:1; S Eze 34:23-24 **37:26** [r]S Nu 25:12 [s]S Ge 9:16; S Dt 29:14; S Heb 13:20 [t]S Jer 30:19

two nations or be divided into two kingdoms.[g] 23They will no longer defile[h]
themselves with their idols and vile images or with any of their offenses, for
I will save them from all their sinful
backsliding,[k][i] and I will cleanse
them. They will be my people, and I
will be their God.[j]
24" 'My servant David[k] will be
king[l] over them, and they will all
have one shepherd.[m] They will follow
my laws and be careful to keep my decrees.[n] 25They will live in the land I
gave to my servant Jacob, the land
where your fathers lived.[o] They and
their children and their children's children will live there forever,[p] and David my servant will be their prince forever.[q] 26I will make a covenant of
peace[r] with them; it will be an everlasting covenant.[s] I will establish
them and increase their numbers,[t]
and I will put my sanctuary among
them[u] forever.[v] 27My dwelling
place[w] will be with them; I will be
their God, and they will be my people.[x] 28Then the nations will know
that I the LORD make Israel holy,[y]
when my sanctuary is among them forever.[z][a]' "

A Prophecy Against Gog

38 The word of the LORD came to
me: 2"Son of man, set your face
against Gog,[b] of the land of Magog,[c]

[u]Lev 26:11 [v]S Eze 16:62 **37:27** [w]S Lev 26:11 [x]S Eze 34:30; S 36:28; S 2Co 6:16* **37:28** [y]S Ex 31:13 [z]Hos 1:10-11 [a]Eze 43:9; Zep 3:15 **38:2** [b]ver 14; Eze 39:11 [c]S Ge 10:2

k23 Many Hebrew manuscripts (see also Septuagint); most Hebrew manuscripts *all their dwelling places where they sinned*

land in the end time and a great spiritual awakening occurs. Many Jews will believe in and accept Jesus Christ as their Messiah before he returns to establish his kingdom (cf. Ro 11:15,25–26; see article on ISRAEL IN GOD'S PLAN OF SALVATION, p. 1730).

37:16–23 TAKE A STICK OF WOOD. After Solomon's death, God's people were divided into two kingdoms (see 1Ki 12)—one was called Judah, and the other Israel (or sometimes Ephraim). God now promises that the two kingdoms will be reunited as one kingdom, with one King to rule over them.

37:24 MY SERVANT DAVID. The coming Messiah is called "David" because he would be *the* descendant of David and the fulfillment of the Davidic covenant (cf. 2Sa 7:16; see article on GOD'S COVENANT WITH DAVID, p. 432). He would cleanse Israel, and the people would receive forgiveness and obey God's law. These benefits would become effective through his death on the cross and the ministry of the Holy Spirit (cf. 36:16–32; Jer 31:31–34).

38:1–23 GOG ... MAGOG. In this chapter Ezekiel describes a coalition of nations that will make a final assault on Israel after the people's restoration to their homeland, attempting to destroy the nation and possess the land. The leader of these nations is named Gog. In the end, however, the invading nations will not succeed; they will be defeated by God himself.

38:2 GOG. Gog was king of the land of Magog and chief ruler over Meshech and Tubal. In Ge 10:2, Magog, Meshech and Tubal are the names of the sons of Japheth; thus the future battle described here will be led by a descendant of Japheth. Gog may also be a name symbolizing evil and opposition to God (see Rev 20:7–9). These countries

the chief prince of[1] Meshech and Tubal;[d] prophesy against him **3**and say:
'This is what the Sovereign LORD says:
I am against you, O Gog, chief prince
of[m] Meshech and Tubal.[e] **4**I will turn
you around, put hooks[f] in your jaws
and bring you out with your whole
army—your horses, your horsemen
fully armed, and a great horde with
large and small shields, all of them
brandishing their swords.[g] **5**Persia,
Cush[n][h] and Put[i] will be with them,
all with shields and helmets, **6**also Gomer[j] with all its troops, and Beth Togarmah[k] from the far north[l] with all
its troops—the many nations with you.

7" 'Get ready; be prepared,[m] you
and all the hordes gathered about you,
and take command of them. **8**After
many days[n] you will be called to arms.
In future years you will invade a land
that has recovered from war, whose
people were gathered from many nations[o] to the mountains of Israel,
which had long been desolate. They
had been brought out from the nations,
and now all of them live in safety.[p]
9You and all your troops and the many
nations with you will go up, advancing
like a storm;[q] you will be like a
cloud[r] covering the land.[s]

10" 'This is what the Sovereign LORD
says: On that day thoughts will come
into your mind[t] and you will devise an
evil scheme.[u] **11**You will say, "I will
invade a land of unwalled villages; I
will attack a peaceful and unsuspecting people[v]—all of them living without walls and without gates and
bars.[w] **12**I will plunder and loot and
turn my hand against the resettled ruins and the people gathered from the
nations, rich in livestock and goods,
living at the center of the land." **13**Sheba[x] and Dedan[y] and the merchants
of Tarshish[z] and all her villages[o] will
say to you, "Have you come to plunder?
Have you gathered your hordes to loot,
to carry off silver and gold, to take
away livestock and goods and to seize
much plunder?[a]" '

14"Therefore, son of man, prophesy
and say to Gog: 'This is what the Sovereign LORD says: In that day, when my
people Israel are living in safety,[b] will
you not take notice of it? **15**You will
come from your place in the far
north,[c] you and many nations with
you, all of them riding on horses, a
great horde, a mighty army.[d] **16**You
will advance against my people Israel
like a cloud[e] that covers the land.[f] In
days to come, O Gog, I will bring you
against my land, so that the nations
may know me when I show myself
holy[g] through you before their eyes.[h]

17" 'This is what the Sovereign LORD
says: Are you not the one I spoke of in
former days by my servants the prophets of Israel? At that time they prophesied for years that I would bring you
against them. **18**This is what will happen in that day: When Gog attacks the
land of Israel, my hot anger will be
aroused, declares the Sovereign LORD.
19In my zeal and fiery wrath I declare
that at that time there shall be a great
earthquake[i] in the land of Israel.[j]
20The fish of the sea, the birds of the
air, the beasts of the field, every creature that moves along the ground, and
all the people on the face of the earth
will tremble[k] at my presence. The
mountains will be overturned,[l] the
cliffs will crumble[m] and every wall will
fall to the ground.[n] **21**I will summon a
sword[o] against Gog on all my mountains, declares the Sovereign LORD. Every man's sword will be against his
brother.[p] **22**I will execute judgment[q]
upon him with plague and bloodshed;[r]
I will pour down torrents of rain, hailstones[s] and burning sulfur[t] on him
and on his troops and on the many nations with him.[u] **23**And so I will show
my greatness and my holiness, and I
will make myself known in the sight of

38:2 [d] S Eze 27:13
38:3 [e] Eze 39:1
38:4 [f] S 2Ki 19:28 [g] S Isa 43:17; Eze 29:4; 39:2; Da 11:40
38:5 [h] S Ge 10:6 [i] S Ge 10:6; S Eze 27:10
38:6 [j] S Ge 10:2 [k] S Ge 10:3 [l] S Eze 32:30
38:7 [m] S Isa 8:9
38:8 [n] Isa 24:22 [o] S Isa 11:11 [p] ver 14; Jer 23:6; S Eze 28:26; Joel 3:1
38:9 [q] Isa 25:4; 28:2 [r] ver 16; Jer 4:13; Joel 2:2 [s] Rev 20:8
38:10 [t] S Jer 17:10 [u] Ps 36:4; Mic 2:1
38:11 [v] S Ge 34:25 [w] Jer 49:31; Zec 2:4
38:13 [x] S Ge 10:7 [y] S Ge 25:3 [z] S Ge 10:4 [a] Isa 10:6; 33:23; S Jer 15:13
38:14 [b] S ver 8; S Lev 25:18; S Jer 16:15; Zec 2:5
38:15 [c] Eze 32:30 [d] Eze 39:2; Rev 20:8
38:16 [e] S ver 9 [f] Joel 3:11 [g] S Lev 10:3 [h] Isa 29:23; Eze 39:21
38:19 [i] Isa 24:18; Joel 2:10; 3:16; S Rev 6:12 [j] Ps 18:7; S Eze 5:13; Hag 2:6,21
38:20 [k] S Ex 15:14 [l] Isa 42:15 [m] Job 14:18 [n] S Ps 76:8; Hos 4:3; Na 1:5
38:21 [o] Isa 66:16; Jer 25:29 [p] S 1Sa 14:20; S 2Ch 20:23; Hag 2:22
38:22 [q] Isa 66:16; Jer 25:31; S Eze 36:5 [r] S Eze 14:19; S 28:23 [s] S Ex 9:18; Ps 18:12; Rev 16:21 [t] S Ge 19:24; S Rev 9:17 [u] S Eze 13:11

[1] 2 Or *the prince of Rosh,* [m] 3 Or *Gog, prince of Rosh,* [n] 5 That is, the upper Nile region [o] 13 Or *her strong lions*

are probably located to the far north of Israel (vv. 6,15; 39:2). They will be joined by armies from the east and south (v. 5). The time of this battle is difficult to establish, but most likely it is not identical with the battle of Gog and Magog in Rev 20:7–9, which will occur at the end of the millennium.

38:5 PERSIA, CUSH AND PUT. These countries are allies of Gog's armies: Persia, Cush (Ethiopia), Put (Libya or some other north African country), Gomer (people north of the Black Sea) and Beth Togarmah (Armenia).

38:21–22 EVERY MAN'S SWORD. God will confuse the invading army so that some nations will turn against their allies. He will also directly destroy the armies by earthquakes, disease and other catastrophic events.

many nations. Then they will know
that I am the LORD.[v]'

39 "Son of man, prophesy against
Gog[w] and say: 'This is what
the Sovereign LORD says: I am against
you, O Gog, chief prince of[p] Meshech[x] and Tubal.[y] **2**I will turn you
around and drag you along. I will bring
you from the far north[z] and send you
against the mountains of Israel.[a]
3Then I will strike your bow[b] from
your left hand and make your arrows[c]
drop from your right hand. **4**On the
mountains of Israel you will fall, you
and all your troops and the nations
with you. I will give you as food to all
kinds of carrion birds[d] and to the wild
animals.[e] **5**You will fall in the open
field, for I have spoken, declares the
Sovereign LORD.[f] **6**I will send fire[g] on
Magog[h] and on those who live in safety in the coastlands,[i] and they will
know[j] that I am the LORD.

7" 'I will make known my holy name
among my people Israel. I will no longer let my holy name be profaned,[k] and
the nations will know[l] that I the LORD
am the Holy One in Israel.[m] **8**It is coming! It will surely take place, declares
the Sovereign LORD. This is the day[n] I
have spoken of.

9" 'Then those who live in the towns
of Israel will go out and use the weapons for fuel and burn them up—the
small and large shields, the bows and
arrows,[o] the war clubs and spears.
For seven years they will use them for
fuel.[p] **10**They will not need to gather
wood from the fields or cut it from the
forests, because they will use the
weapons for fuel. And they will plunder[q] those who plundered them and
loot those who looted them, declares
the Sovereign LORD.[r]

11" 'On that day I will give Gog a
burial place in Israel, in the valley of
those who travel east toward[q] the
Sea.[r] It will block the way of travelers, because Gog and all his hordes
will be buried[s] there. So it will be
called the Valley of Hamon Gog.[s][t]

12" 'For seven months the house of
Israel will be burying them in order to
cleanse the land.[u] **13**All the people of
the land will bury them, and the day I
am glorified[v] will be a memorable day
for them, declares the Sovereign LORD.

14" 'Men will be regularly employed
to cleanse the land. Some will go
throughout the land and, in addition to
them, others will bury those that remain on the ground. At the end of the
seven months they will begin their
search. **15**As they go through the land
and one of them sees a human bone, he
will set up a marker beside it until the
gravediggers have buried it in the Valley of Hamon Gog. **16**(Also a town
called Hamonah[t] will be there.) And
so they will cleanse the land.'

17"Son of man, this is what the Sovereign LORD says: Call out to every kind
of bird[w] and all the wild animals: 'Assemble and come together from all
around to the sacrifice I am preparing
for you, the great sacrifice on the
mountains of Israel. There you will eat
flesh and drink blood.[x] **18**You will eat
the flesh of mighty men and drink the
blood of the princes of the earth as if
they were rams and lambs, goats and
bulls—all of them fattened animals
from Bashan.[y] **19**At the sacrifice[z] I
am preparing for you, you will eat fat
till you are glutted and drink blood till
you are drunk. **20**At my table you will
eat your fill of horses and riders,
mighty men and soldiers of every kind,'
declares the Sovereign LORD.[a]

21"I will display my glory among the
nations, and all the nations will see the
punishment I inflict and the hand I lay
upon them.[b] **22**From that day forward
the house of Israel will know that I am
the LORD their God. **23**And the nations
will know that the people of Israel
went into exile for their sin, because
they were unfaithful to me. So I hid my

38:23 [v]Eze 20:42; S 36:23; S 37:6
39:1 [w]Rev 20:8 [x]S Ge 10:2 [y]S Eze 27:13; S 38:2,3
39:2 [z]S Eze 32:30 [a]S Eze 38:4,15
39:3 [b]Hos 1:5; Am 2:15 [c]Ps 76:3
39:4 [d]S Ge 40:19 [e]ver 17-20; S Jer 25:33; S Eze 29:5; S 33:27
39:5 [f]S Eze 32:4
39:6 [g]S Eze 30:8; Rev 20:9 [h]S Ge 10:2 [i]S Jer 25:22 [j]S Ex 6:7
39:7 [k]S Ex 20:7; S Eze 13:19 [l]S Isa 49:26 [m]S Isa 12:6; S 54:5; S Eze 20:9; S 36:16,23
39:8 [n]Eze 7:6
39:9 [o]Ps 76:3 [p]S Ps 46:9
39:10 [q]S Ex 3:22 [r]S Isa 14:2; S 33:1; Hab 2:8
39:11 [s]S Isa 34:3 [t]S Eze 38:2
39:12 [u]Dt 21:23
39:13 [v]Eze 28:22
39:17 [w]S Job 15:23 [x]S Eze 32:4
39:18 [y]S Ps 22:12; Jer 51:40
39:19 [z]S Lev 3:9
39:20 [a]S Isa 56:9; S Jer 12:9; Rev 19:17-18
39:21 [b]Ex 9:16; Isa 37:20; S Eze 38:16

[p]1 Or *Gog, prince of Rosh,* [q]11 Or *of* [r]11 That is, the Dead Sea [s]11 *Hamon Gog* means *hordes of Gog.* [t]16 *Hamonah* means *horde.*

39:1–29 PROPHESY AGAINST GOG. This chapter reiterates God's judgment against Gog and portrays the total annihilation of Israel's enemy. It emphasizes God's miraculous intervention on behalf of his people.

39:6 THAT I AM THE LORD. By destroying the armies of the invading evil nations, the Lord will manifest his glory so that everyone will know that he alone is Lord.

39:9 SEVEN YEARS. The "seven years" (see also v. 12) may mean a literal seven years, or it may be a symbolic number signifying the completeness of the enemies' destruction. In either case, the message of this chapter is clear: God's people will ultimately be victorious, and all evil and suffering will be abolished.

face from them and handed them over
to their enemies, and they all fell by the
sword.[c] 24I dealt with them according
to their uncleanness and their offenses, and I hid my face from them.[d]
25"Therefore this is what the Sovereign LORD says: I will now bring Jacob
back from captivity[u][e] and will have
compassion[f] on all the people of Israel, and I will be zealous for my holy
name.[g] 26They will forget their shame
and all the unfaithfulness they showed
toward me when they lived in safety[h]
in their land with no one to make them
afraid.[i] 27When I have brought them
back from the nations and have gathered them from the countries of their
enemies, I will show myself holy
through them in the sight of many nations.[j] 28Then they will know that I
am the LORD their God, for though I
sent them into exile among the nations, I will gather them[k] to their own
land, not leaving any behind.[l] 29I will
no longer hide my face[m] from them, for
I will pour out my Spirit[n] on the house
of Israel, declares the Sovereign
LORD.[o]"

Joel 2:28-29

The New Temple Area

40 In the twenty-fifth year of our
exile, at the beginning of the
year, on the tenth of the month, in the
fourteenth year after the fall of the
city[p]—on that very day the hand of
the LORD was upon me[q] and he took
me there. 2In visions[r] of God he took
me to the land of Israel and set me on
a very high mountain,[s] on whose
south side were some buildings that
looked like a city. 3He took me there,
and I saw a man whose appearance
was like bronze;[t] he was standing in
the gateway with a linen cord and a
measuring rod[u] in his hand. 4The man
said to me, "Son of man, look with your
eyes and hear with your ears and pay
attention to everything I am going to
show you,[v] for that is why you have
been brought here. Tell[w] the house of
Israel everything you see.[x]"

The East Gate to the Outer Court

5I saw a wall completely surrounding the temple area. The length of the
measuring rod in the man's hand was
six long cubits, each of which was a
cubit[v] and a handbreadth.[w] He measured[y] the wall; it was one measuring
rod thick and one rod high.
6Then he went to the gate facing
east.[z] He climbed its steps and measured the threshold of the gate; it was
one rod deep.[x] 7The alcoves[a] for the
guards were one rod long and one rod
wide, and the projecting walls between
the alcoves were five cubits thick. And
the threshold of the gate next to the
portico facing the temple was one rod
deep.
8Then he measured the portico of
the gateway; 9it[y] was eight cubits
deep and its jambs were two cubits
thick. The portico of the gateway faced
the temple.
10Inside the east gate were three alcoves on each side; the three had the
same measurements, and the faces of
the projecting walls on each side had
the same measurements. 11Then he
measured the width of the entrance to
the gateway; it was ten cubits and its
length was thirteen cubits. 12In front

39:23 [c]Isa 1:15; 59:2; S Jer 22:8-9; S 44:23 **39:24** [d]2Ki 17:23; Jer 2:17,19; 4:18; S Eze 7:22; Da 9:7 **39:25** [e]S Jer 33:7 [f]S Jer 30:18 [g]Isa 27:12-13; S Eze 16:53 **39:26** [h]S 1Ki 4:25; S Jer 32:37; S Eze 38:8 [i]Isa 17:2; Eze 34:28; Mic 4:4 **39:27** [j]S Eze 37:21 **39:28** [k]Ps 147:2 [l]S Eze 36:23,36 **39:29** [m]S Dt 31:17 [n]S Isa 11:2; S Eze 37:9; S Ac 2:17 [o]S Eze 16:42 **40:1** [p]S 2Ki 25:7; Jer 39:1-10; 52:4-11 [q]S Eze 1:3; S 29:17 **40:2** [r]S Ex 24:10; Da 7:1,7 [s]S Jer 31:12; S Eze 17:22; Rev 21:10 **40:3** [t]S Eze 1:7; Rev 1:15 [u]Eze 47:3; Zec 2:1-2; Rev 11:1; 21:15 **40:4** [v]S Dt 6:6 [w]Jer 26:2 [x]Eze 44:5 **40:5** [y]Eze 42:20 **40:6** [z]S Eze 8:16 **40:7** [a]ver 36

[u]25 Or *now restore the fortunes of Jacob*
[v]5 The common cubit was about 1 1/2 feet (about 0.5 meter).
[w]5 That is, about 3 inches (about 8 centimeters)
[x]6 Septuagint; Hebrew *deep, the first threshold, one rod deep*
[y]8,9 Many Hebrew manuscripts, Septuagint, Vulgate and Syriac; most Hebrew manuscripts *gateway facing the temple; it was one rod deep. 9Then he measured the portico of the gateway; it*

40:1—43:27 VISIONS OF GOD. The vision of the temple came to Ezekiel in 573 B.C., 25 years after his exile had begun. Its purpose was to encourage the people that there would be a full restoration of God's glory in the future, resulting in an anointing and blessing that would endure forever.

40:5 TEMPLE AREA. There are three main interpretations of Ezekiel's temple vision: (1) a symbolic temple picturing the eternal state described in Rev 21—22; (2) a symbolic temple describing the blessings of the millennial kingdom; or (3) a future literal temple that will be built during the millennial kingdom. Regardless of which interpretation is adopted, the main teachings are (1) that someday God's presence and his glory will be restored to his people forever (43:7), and (2) that Christ's blessings will flow out in an ever-deepening stream (47:1–12).

40:5 A WALL COMPLETELY SURROUNDING. This wall would mark the temple area and set it apart from the rest of the city. Believers, whose bodies are now the living temples of the Holy Spirit (1Co 6:19), must keep themselves separated from the sinful society around them and set apart for God and his holy purposes (see article on SPIRITUAL SEPARATION FOR BELIEVERS, p. 1794).

of each alcove was a wall one cubit high, and the alcoves were six cubits square. **13**Then he measured the gateway from the top of the rear wall of one alcove to the top of the opposite one; the distance was twenty-five cubits from one parapet opening to the opposite one. **14**He measured along the faces of the projecting walls all around the inside of the gateway—sixty cubits. The measurement was up to the portico[z] facing the courtyard.[a][b] **15**The distance from the entrance of the gateway to the far end of its portico was fifty cubits. **16**The alcoves and the projecting walls inside the gateway were surmounted by narrow parapet openings all around, as was the portico; the openings all around faced inward. The faces of the projecting walls were decorated with palm trees.[c]

The Outer Court

17Then he brought me into the outer court.[d] There I saw some rooms and a pavement that had been constructed all around the court; there were thirty rooms[e] along the pavement.[f] **18**It abutted the sides of the gateways and was as wide as they were long; this was the lower pavement. **19**Then he measured the distance from the inside of the lower gateway to the outside of the inner court;[g] it was a hundred cubits[h] on the east side as well as on the north.

The North Gate

20Then he measured the length and width of the gate facing north, leading into the outer court. **21**Its alcoves[i]—three on each side—its projecting walls and its portico[j] had the same measurements as those of the first gateway. It was fifty cubits long and twenty-five cubits wide. **22**Its openings, its portico[k] and its palm tree decorations had the same measurements as those of the gate facing east. Seven steps led up to it, with its portico opposite them.[l] **23**There was a gate to the inner court facing the north gate, just as there was on the east. He measured from one gate to the opposite one; it was a hundred cubits.[m]

The South Gate

24Then he led me to the south side and I saw a gate facing south. He measured its jambs and its portico, and they had the same measurements[n] as the others. **25**The gateway and its portico had narrow openings all around, like the openings of the others. It was fifty cubits long and twenty-five cubits wide.[o] **26**Seven steps led up to it, with its portico opposite them; it had palm tree decorations on the faces of the projecting walls on each side.[p] **27**The inner court[q] also had a gate facing south, and he measured from this gate to the outer gate on the south side; it was a hundred cubits.[r]

Gates to the Inner Court

28Then he brought me into the inner court through the south gate, and he measured the south gate; it had the same measurements[s] as the others. **29**Its alcoves,[t] its projecting walls and its portico had the same measurements as the others. The gateway and its portico had openings all around. It was fifty cubits long and twenty-five cubits wide.[u] **30**(The porticoes[v] of the gateways around the inner court were twenty-five cubits wide and five cubits deep.) **31**Its portico[w] faced the outer court; palm trees decorated its jambs, and eight steps led up to it.[x]

32Then he brought me to the inner court on the east side, and he measured the gateway; it had the same measurements[y] as the others. **33**Its alcoves,[z] its projecting walls and its portico had the same measurements as the others. The gateway and its portico had openings all around. It was fifty cubits long and twenty-five cubits wide. **34**Its portico[a] faced the outer court; palm trees decorated the jambs on either side, and eight steps led up to it.

35Then he brought me to the north gate[b] and measured it. It had the same measurements[c] as the others, **36**as did its alcoves,[d] its projecting walls and its portico, and it had openings all around. It was fifty cubits long and twenty-five cubits wide. **37**Its portico[b][e] faced the outer court; palm trees decorated the jambs on either side, and eight steps led up to it.[f]

40:14 [b] S Ex 27:9
40:16 [c] ver 21-22; 2Ch 3:5; Eze 41:26
40:17 [d] Rev 11:2 [e] Eze 41:6 [f] Eze 42:1
40:19 [g] Eze 46:1 [h] ver 23,27
40:21 [i] ver 7 [j] ver 30
40:22 [k] ver 49 [l] S ver 16,26
40:23 [m] S ver 19
40:24 [n] ver 32,35
40:25 [o] ver 33
40:26 [p] S ver 22
40:27 [q] ver 32 [r] S ver 19
40:28 [s] ver 35
40:29 [t] ver 7 [u] ver 25
40:30 [v] ver 21
40:31 [w] ver 22 [x] ver 34,37
40:32 [y] S ver 24
40:33 [z] ver 7
40:34 [a] ver 22
40:35 [b] Eze 44:4; 47:2 [c] S ver 24
40:36 [d] ver 7
40:37 [e] ver 22 [f] ver 34

[z] *14* Septuagint; Hebrew *projecting wall*
[a] *14* The meaning of the Hebrew for this verse is uncertain.
[b] *37* Septuagint (see also verses 31 and 34); Hebrew *jambs*

The Rooms for Preparing Sacrifices

38 A room with a doorway was by the portico in each of the inner gateways, where the burnt offerings[g] were washed. 39 In the portico of the gateway were two tables on each side, on which the burnt offerings,[h] sin offerings[i] and guilt offerings[j] were slaughtered.[k] 40 By the outside wall of the portico of the gateway, near the steps at the entrance to the north gateway were two tables, and on the other side of the steps were two tables. 41 So there were four tables on one side of the gateway and four on the other—eight tables in all—on which the sacrifices were slaughtered. 42 There were also four tables of dressed stone[l] for the burnt offerings, each a cubit and a half long, a cubit and a half wide and a cubit high. On them were placed the utensils for slaughtering the burnt offerings and the other sacrifices.[m] 43 And double-pronged hooks, each a handbreadth long, were attached to the wall all around. The tables were for the flesh of the offerings.

Rooms for the Priests

44 Outside the inner gate, within the inner court, were two rooms, one[c] at the side of the north gate and facing south, and another at the side of the south[d] gate and facing north. 45 He said to me, "The room facing south is for the priests who have charge of the temple,[n] 46 and the room facing north[o] is for the priests who have charge of the altar.[p] These are the sons of Zadok,[q] who are the only Levites who may draw near to the LORD to minister before him.[r]"

47 Then he measured the court: It was square—a hundred cubits long and a hundred cubits wide. And the altar was in front of the temple.[s]

The Temple

48 He brought me to the portico of the temple[t] and measured the jambs of the portico; they were five cubits wide on either side. The width of the entrance was fourteen cubits and its projecting walls were[e] three cubits wide on either side. 49 The portico[u] was twenty cubits wide, and twelve[f] cubits from front to back. It was reached by a flight of stairs,[g] and there were pillars[v] on each side of the jambs.

41 Then the man brought me to the outer sanctuary[w] and measured the jambs; the width of the jambs was six cubits[h] on each side.[i] 2 The entrance was ten cubits wide, and the projecting walls on each side of it were five cubits wide. He also measured the outer sanctuary; it was forty cubits long and twenty cubits wide.[x]

3 Then he went into the inner sanctuary and measured the jambs of the entrance; each was two cubits wide. The entrance was six cubits wide, and the projecting walls on each side of it were seven cubits wide. 4 And he measured the length of the inner sanctuary; it was twenty cubits, and its width was twenty cubits across the end of the outer sanctuary.[y] He said to me, "This is the Most Holy Place.[z]"

5 Then he measured the wall of the temple; it was six cubits thick, and each side room around the temple was four cubits wide. 6 The side rooms were on three levels, one above another, thirty[a] on each level. There were ledges all around the wall of the temple to serve as supports for the side rooms, so that the supports were not inserted into the wall of the temple.[b] 7 The side rooms all around the temple were wider at each successive level. The structure surrounding the temple was built in ascending stages, so that the rooms widened as one went upward. A stairway[c] went up from the lowest floor to the top floor through the middle floor.

8 I saw that the temple had a raised base all around it, forming the foundation of the side rooms. It was the length of the rod, six long cubits. 9 The

40:38 [g] S 2Ch 4:6; Eze 42:13 **40:39** [h] Eze 46:2 [i] Lev 4:3,28 [j] S Lev 7:1 [k] ver 42 **40:42** [l] Ex 20:25 [m] ver 39 **40:45** [n] 1Ch 9:23 **40:46** [o] Eze 42:13 [p] Nu 18:5 [q] S 2Sa 8:17; S Ezr 7:2 [r] Nu 16:5; Eze 43:19; 44:15; 45:4; 48:11 **40:47** [s] Eze 41:13-14 **40:48** [t] 1Ki 6:2

40:49 [u] ver 22; 1Ki 6:3 [v] S 1Ki 7:15 **41:1** [w] ver 23 **41:2** [x] 2Ch 3:3 **41:4** [y] 1Ki 6:20 [z] S Ex 26:33; Heb 9:3-8 **41:6** [a] Eze 40:17 [b] S 1Ki 6:5 **41:7** [c] 1Ki 6:8

[c] *44* Septuagint; Hebrew *were rooms for singers, which were* [d] *44* Septuagint; Hebrew *east* [e] *48* Septuagint; Hebrew *entrance was* [f] *49* Septuagint; Hebrew *eleven* [g] *49* Hebrew; Septuagint *Ten steps led up to it* [h] *1* The common cubit was about 1 1/2 feet (about 0.5 meter). [i] *1* One Hebrew manuscript and Septuagint; most Hebrew manuscripts *side, the width of the tent*

40:38 BURNT OFFERINGS. See 43:18–27, note.

41:1 THE OUTER SANCTUARY. The temple Ezekiel saw is somewhat different than Solomon's temple. Nothing is said about the altar of incense, the lampstand, or the ark of the covenant. The reason for the difference is not explained.

outer wall of the side rooms was five
cubits thick. The open area between
the side rooms of the temple **10**and the
⌞priests'⌟ rooms was twenty cubits
wide all around the temple. **11**There
were entrances to the side rooms from
the open area, one on the north and
another on the south; and the base adjoining the open area was five cubits
wide all around.
12The building facing the temple
courtyard on the west side was seventy
cubits wide. The wall of the building
was five cubits thick all around, and its
length was ninety cubits.
13Then he measured the temple; it
was a hundred cubits long, and the
temple courtyard and the building with
its walls were also a hundred cubits
long. **14**The width of the temple courtyard on the east, including the front of
the temple, was a hundred cubits.[d]
15Then he measured the length of
the building facing the courtyard at the
rear of the temple, including its galleries[e] on each side; it was a hundred
cubits.
The outer sanctuary, the inner sanctuary and the portico facing the court,
16as well as the thresholds and the
narrow windows[f] and galleries
around the three of them—everything
beyond and including the threshold
was covered with wood. The floor, the
wall up to the windows, and the windows were covered.[g] **17**In the space
above the outside of the entrance to
the inner sanctuary and on the walls at
regular intervals all around the inner
and outer sanctuary **18**were carved[h]
cherubim[i] and palm trees.[j] Palm
trees alternated with cherubim. Each
cherub had two faces:[k] **19**the face of a
man toward the palm tree on one side
and the face of a lion toward the palm
tree on the other. They were carved all
around the whole temple.[l] **20**From the
floor to the area above the entrance,
cherubim and palm trees were carved
on the wall of the outer sanctuary.
21The outer sanctuary[m] had a rectangular doorframe, and the one at the
front of the Most Holy Place was similar. **22**There was a wooden altar[n]
three cubits high and two cubits
square[j]; its corners, its base[k] and its
sides were of wood. The man said to
me, "This is the table[o] that is before
the LORD." **23**Both the outer sanctuary[p] and the Most Holy Place had
double doors.[q] **24**Each door had two
leaves—two hinged leaves[r] for each
door. **25**And on the doors of the outer
sanctuary were carved cherubim and
palm trees like those carved on the
walls, and there was a wooden over-
hang on the front of the portico. **26**On
the sidewalls of the portico were narrow windows with palm trees carved
on each side. The side rooms of the
temple also had overhangs.[s]

Rooms for the Priests

42 Then the man led me northward into the outer court and
brought me to the rooms[t] opposite
the temple courtyard[u] and opposite
the outer wall on the north side.[v]
2The building whose door faced north
was a hundred cubits[l] long and fifty
cubits wide. **3**Both in the section twenty cubits from the inner court and in
the section opposite the pavement of
the outer court, gallery[w] faced gallery
at the three levels.[x] **4**In front of the
rooms was an inner passageway ten
cubits wide and a hundred cubits[m]
long. Their doors were on the north.[y]
5Now the upper rooms were narrower,
for the galleries took more space from
them than from the rooms on the lower
and middle floors of the building. **6**The
rooms on the third floor had no pillars,
as the courts had; so they were smaller
in floor space than those on the lower
and middle floors. **7**There was an outer
wall parallel to the rooms and the outer court; it extended in front of the
rooms for fifty cubits. **8**While the row
of rooms on the side next to the outer
court was fifty cubits long, the row on
the side nearest the sanctuary was a
hundred cubits long. **9**The lower rooms
had an entrance[z] on the east side as
one enters them from the outer court.
10On the south side[n] along the
length of the wall of the outer court,
adjoining the temple courtyard[a] and
opposite the outer wall, were rooms[b]
11with a passageway in front of them.
These were like the rooms on the
north; they had the same length and
width, with similar exits and dimensions. Similar to the doorways on the

41:14 [d]Eze 40:47
41:15 [e]Eze 42:3
41:16 [f]1Ki 6:4
[g]ver 25-26; 1Ki 6:15; Eze 42:3
41:18 [h]S 1Ki 6:18
[i]Ex 37:7; S 2Ch 3:7;
[j]S 1Ki 6:29; 7:36
[k]Eze 10:21
41:19 [l]S Eze 10:14
41:21 [m]ver 1
41:22 [n]S Ex 30:1
[o]S Ex 25:23; S Eze 23:41
41:23 [p]ver 1
[q]1Ki 6:32
41:24 [r]1Ki 6:34
41:26 [s]ver 15-16; Eze 40:16
42:1 [t]ver 13
[u]S Ex 27:9; Eze 41:12-14
[v]Eze 40:17
42:3 [w]Eze 41:15
[x]Eze 41:16
42:4 [y]Eze 46:19
42:9 [z]Eze 44:5; 46:19
42:10 [a]Eze 41:12-14
[b]ver 1

[j]22 Septuagint; Hebrew *long*
[k]22 Septuagint; Hebrew *length* [l]2 The common cubit was about 1 1/2 feet (about 0.5 meter). [m]4 Septuagint and Syriac; Hebrew *and one cubit* [n]10 Septuagint; Hebrew *Eastward*

north **12**were the doorways of the rooms on the south. There was a doorway at the beginning of the passageway that was parallel to the corresponding wall extending eastward, by which one enters the rooms.

13Then he said to me, "The north[c] and south rooms[d] facing the temple courtyard[e] are the priests' rooms, where the priests who approach the LORD will eat the most holy offerings. There they will put the most holy offerings—the grain offerings,[f] the sin offerings[g] and the guilt offerings[h]—for the place is holy.[i] **14**Once the priests enter the holy precincts, they are not to go into the outer court until they leave behind the garments[j] in which they minister, for these are holy. They are to put on other clothes before they go near the places that are for the people.[k]"

15When he had finished measuring what was inside the temple area, he led me out by the east gate[l] and measured the area all around: **16**He measured the east side with the measuring rod; it was five hundred cubits.[o] **17**He measured the north side; it was five hundred cubits[p] by the measuring rod. **18**He measured the south side; it was five hundred cubits by the measuring rod. **19**Then he turned to the west side and measured; it was five hundred cubits by the measuring rod. **20**So he measured[m] the area[n] on all four sides. It had a wall around it,[o] five hundred cubits long and five hundred cubits wide,[p] to separate the holy from the common.[q]

The Glory Returns to the Temple

Joel 1:15

43 Then the man brought me to the gate facing east,[r] **2**and I saw the glory of the God of Israel coming from the east. His voice was like the roar of rushing waters,[s] and the land was radiant with his glory.[t] **3**The vision I saw was like the vision I had seen when he[q] came to destroy the city and like the visions I had seen by the Kebar River, and I fell facedown. **4**The glory[u] of the LORD entered the temple through the gate facing east.[v] **5**Then the Spirit[w] lifted me up[x] and brought me into the inner court, and the glory[y] of the LORD filled the temple.[z]

6While the man was standing beside me, I heard someone speaking to me from inside the temple. **7**He said: "Son of man, this is the place of my throne[a] and the place for the soles of my feet. This is where I will live among the Israelites forever. The house of Israel will never again defile[b] my holy name—neither they nor their kings—by their prostitution[r] and the lifeless idols[s] of their kings at their high places.[c] **8**When they placed their threshold next to my threshold and their doorposts beside my doorposts, with only a wall between me and them, they defiled my holy name by their detestable practices. So I destroyed them in my anger. **9**Now let them put away from me their prostitution and the lifeless idols of their kings, and I will live among them forever.[d]

10"Son of man, describe the temple to the people of Israel, that they may be ashamed[e] of their sins. Let them consider the plan, **11**and if they are ashamed of all they have done, make known to them the design of the temple—its arrangement, its exits and entrances—its whole design and all its regulations[t] and laws. Write these down before them so that they may be faithful to its design and follow all its regulations.[f]

12"This is the law of the temple: All

42:13 [c]Eze 40:46 [d]ver 1 [e]Eze 41:12-14 [f]Jer 41:5 [g]S Lev 10:17 [h]Lev 14:13 [i]S Ex 29:31; S Lev 6:29; 7:6; 10:12-13; Nu 18:9-10 **42:14** [j]Lev 16:23; Eze 44:19 [k]Ex 29:9; S Lev 8:7-9 **42:15** [l]Eze 43:1 **42:20** [m]Eze 40:5 [n]Eze 43:12 [o]Zec 2:5 [p]Eze 45:2; Rev 21:16 [q]S Eze 22:26 **43:1** [r]S 1Ch 9:18; S Eze 8:16; 42:15; 44:1 **43:2** [s]S Ps 18:4; S Rev 1:15 [t]Isa 6:3; Rev 18:1; 21:11 **43:4** [u]Eze 1:28 [v]Eze 10:19; 44:2 **43:5** [w]S Eze 11:24 [x]S Eze 3:12 [y]S Ex 16:7 [z]S Isa 6:4 **43:7** [a]S Jer 3:17 [b]S Eze 37:23 [c]S Lev 26:30; S Eze 20:29,39 **43:9** [d]Eze 37:26-28 **43:10** [e]S Eze 16:61 **43:11** [f]Eze 44:5

[o] *16* See Septuagint of verse 17; Hebrew *rods*; also in verses 18 and 19. [p] *17* Septuagint; Hebrew *rods* [q] *3* Some Hebrew manuscripts and Vulgate; most Hebrew manuscripts *I* [r] *7* Or *their spiritual adultery*; also in verse 9 [s] *7* Or *the corpses*; also in verse 9 [t] *11* Some Hebrew manuscripts and Septuagint; most Hebrew manuscripts *regulations and its whole design*

43:5 GLORY OF THE LORD FILLED THE TEMPLE. The book of Ezekiel began with an awe-inspiring vision of God's glory. Chs. 8–11 described how God's glory progressively departed from the temple and the city because of the people's sins. Ezekiel concludes with another awe-inspiring vision: God's glory, power and love filling the temple again. We should desire above all else to see God's glory manifested within the church through the operation of the Holy Spirit (see article on THE GLORY OF GOD, p. 1192). The absence of such holy and burning desire is evidence of spiritual decline among God's people.

43:7 LIVE AMONG THE ISRAELITES FOREVER. God's eternal plan is to live in a caring fellowship with his people forever. The blessing and joy he has in store for us will be far beyond what we can perceive (cf. 1Co 2:9; Rev 21—22).

43:12 LAW OF THE TEMPLE. The fundamental law of God's temple is holiness, which requires

the surrounding area[g] on top of the
mountain will be most holy.[h] Such is
the law of the temple.

The Altar

13"These are the measurements of
the altar[i] in long cubits, that cubit being a cubit[u] and a handbreadth[v]: Its
gutter is a cubit deep and a cubit wide,
with a rim of one span[w] around the
edge. And this is the height of the altar: **14**From the gutter on the ground
up to the lower ledge it is two cubits
high and a cubit wide, and from the
smaller ledge up to the larger ledge it
is four cubits high and a cubit wide.
15The altar hearth[j] is four cubits
high, and four horns[k] project upward
from the hearth. **16**The altar hearth is
square, twelve cubits long and twelve
cubits wide.[l] **17**The upper ledge[m]
also is square, fourteen cubits long and
fourteen cubits wide, with a rim of half
a cubit and a gutter of a cubit all
around. The steps[n] of the altar face
east.[o]"

18Then he said to me, "Son of man,
this is what the Sovereign LORD says:
These will be the regulations for sacrificing burnt offerings[p] and sprinkling
blood[q] upon the altar when it is built:
19You are to give a young bull[r] as a
sin offering to the priests, who are Levites, of the family of Zadok,[s] who
come near[t] to minister before me, declares the Sovereign LORD. **20**You are to
take some of its blood and put it on the
four horns of the altar[u] and on the
four corners of the upper ledge[v] and
all around the rim, and so purify the
altar[w] and make atonement for it.
21You are to take the bull for the sin
offering and burn it in the designated
part of the temple area outside the
sanctuary.[x]

22"On the second day you are to offer
a male goat without defect for a sin offering, and the altar is to be purified as
it was purified with the bull. **23**When
you have finished purifying it, you are
to offer a young bull and a ram from the
flock, both without defect.[y] **24**You are
to offer them before the LORD, and the
priests are to sprinkle salt[z] on them
and sacrifice them as a burnt offering
to the LORD.

25"For seven days[a] you are to provide a male goat daily for a sin offering;
you are also to provide a young bull
and a ram from the flock, both without
defect.[b] **26**For seven days they are to
make atonement for the altar and
cleanse it; thus they will dedicate it.
27At the end of these days, from the
eighth day[c] on, the priests are to
present your burnt offerings[d] and fellowship offerings[x][e] on the altar.
Then I will accept you, declares the
Sovereign LORD."

The Prince, the Levites, the Priests

44 Then the man brought me back
to the outer gate of the sanctuary, the one facing east,[f] and it was
shut. **2**The LORD said to me, "This gate
is to remain shut. It must not be
opened; no one may enter through it.[g]
It is to remain shut because the LORD,
the God of Israel, has entered through
it. **3**The prince himself is the only one
who may sit inside the gateway to eat
in the presence[h] of the LORD. He is to
enter by way of the portico of the gateway and go out the same way.[i]"

4Then the man brought me by way of
the north gate[j] to the front of the temple. I looked and saw the glory of the
LORD filling the temple[k] of the LORD,
and I fell facedown.[l]

5The LORD said to me, "Son of man,

43:12 [g] Eze 42:20 [h] S Eze 17:22
43:13 [i] S Ex 20:24; 2Ch 4:1
43:15 [j] Isa 29:2 [k] S Ex 27:2
43:16 [l] Rev 21:16
43:17 [m] ver 20; Eze 45:19 [n] Ex 20:26 [o] S Ex 27:1
43:18 [p] Ex 40:29 [q] Lev 1:5,11; Heb 9:21-22
43:19 [r] S Lev 4:3 [s] S 2Sa 8:17; S Ezr 7:2 [t] Nu 16:40; S Eze 40:46
43:20 [u] S Lev 4:7 [v] S ver 17 [w] Lev 16:19
43:21 [x] Ex 29:14; Heb 13:11
43:23 [y] Ex 29:1; S Lev 22:20
43:24 [z] S Lev 2:13; Mk 9:49-50
43:25 [a] S Lev 8:33 [b] S Ex 29:37
43:27 [c] Lev 9:1 [d] S Isa 60:7 [e] S Ex 32:6; S Lev 17:5
44:1 [f] S Eze 43:1
44:2 [g] Eze 43:4-5
44:3 [h] S Ex 24:9-11 [i] Eze 46:2,8
44:4 [j] S Eze 40:35 [k] S Isa 6:4; S Eze 10:4; Rev 15:8 [l] Da 8:17

[u] *13* The common cubit was about 1 1/2 feet (about 0.5 meter). [v] *13* That is, about 3 inches (about 8 centimeters) [w] *13* That is, about 9 inches (about 22 centimeters)
[x] *27* Traditionally *peace offerings*

separation from all sin and evil. Similarly, believers, as the temple of the Holy Spirit (1Co 6:19), must live in accordance with the Spirit of holiness (Ro 1:4) and remain cleansed from all sin (1Co 6:18–20; see article on SPIRITUAL SEPARATION FOR BELIEVERS, p. 1794).

43:18–27 SACRIFICING BURNT OFFERINGS. The issue of resuming animal sacrifices after the final and ultimate sacrifice of Christ has perplexed interpreters. Some insist that Ezekiel's temple with its sacrifices cannot be literal because Jesus' atoning sacrifice fulfilled and made obsolete OT sacrifices (see Heb 9:10–15; 10:1–4,8). Perhaps Ezekiel was describing in OT terms the benefits of Christ's atoning sacrifice, which avails for all time. Some believe that the sacrifices will be literal, offered as memorials of Christ's sacrifice on the cross.

44:3 THE PRINCE. Only the prince is allowed to enter the east gate. His function seems to be to lead the people in worship (45:17). The identity of the prince is unknown, though he cannot be the Messiah because he makes a sin offering for himself (45:22) and has biological children (46:16).

look carefully, listen closely and give attention to everything I tell you concerning all the regulations regarding the temple of the LORD. Give attention to the entrance[m] of the temple and all the exits of the sanctuary.[n] **6**Say to the rebellious house[o] of Israel, 'This is what the Sovereign LORD says: Enough of your detestable practices, O house of Israel! **7**In addition to all your other detestable practices, you brought foreigners uncircumcised in heart[p] and flesh into my sanctuary, desecrating my temple while you offered me food, fat and blood, and you broke my covenant.[q] **8**Instead of carrying out your duty in regard to my holy things, you put others in charge of my sanctuary.[r] **9**This is what the Sovereign LORD says: No foreigner uncircumcised in heart and flesh is to enter my sanctuary, not even the foreigners who live among the Israelites.[s]

10" 'The Levites who went far from me when Israel went astray[t] and who wandered from me after their idols must bear the consequences of their sin.[u] **11**They may serve in my sanctuary, having charge of the gates of the temple and serving in it; they may slaughter the burnt offerings[v] and sacrifices for the people and stand before the people and serve them.[w] **12**But because they served them in the presence of their idols and made the house of Israel fall[x] into sin, therefore I have sworn with uplifted hand[y] that they must bear the consequences of their sin, declares the Sovereign LORD.[z] **13**They are not to come near to serve me as priests or come near any of my holy things or my most holy offerings; they must bear the shame[a] of their detestable practices.[b] **14**Yet I will put them in charge of the duties of the temple and all the work that is to be done in it.[c]

15" 'But the priests, who are Levites and descendants of Zadok[d] and who faithfully carried out the duties of my sanctuary when the Israelites went astray from me, are to come near to minister before me; they are to stand before me to offer sacrifices of fat[e] and blood, declares the Sovereign LORD.[f] **16**They alone are to enter my sanctuary; they alone are to come near my table[g] to minister before me and perform my service.[h]

17" 'When they enter the gates of the inner court, they are to wear linen clothes;[i] they must not wear any woolen garment while ministering at the gates of the inner court or inside the temple. **18**They are to wear linen turbans[j] on their heads and linen undergarments[k] around their waists. They must not wear anything that makes them perspire.[l] **19**When they go out into the outer court where the people are, they are to take off the clothes they have been ministering in and are to leave them in the sacred rooms, and put on other clothes, so that they do not consecrate[m] the people by means of their garments.[n]

20" 'They must not shave[o] their heads or let their hair grow long, but they are to keep the hair of their heads trimmed.[p] **21**No priest is to drink wine when he enters the inner court.[q] **22**They must not marry widows or divorced women; they may marry only virgins of Israelite descent or widows of priests.[r] **23**They are to teach my people the difference between the holy and the common[s] and show them how to distinguish between the unclean and the clean.[t]

24" 'In any dispute, the priests are to serve as judges[u] and decide it according to my ordinances. They are to keep my laws and my decrees for all my appointed feasts,[v] and they are to keep my Sabbaths holy.[w]

25" 'A priest must not defile himself by going near a dead person; however, if the dead person was his father or mother, son or daughter, brother or unmarried sister, then he may defile himself.[x] **26**After he is cleansed, he must wait seven days.[y] **27**On the day he goes into the inner court of the sanctuary[z] to minister in the sanctuary, he

44:5 [m]S Eze 42:9 [n]Eze 40:4; 43:10-11
44:6 [o]S Eze 3:9
44:7 [p]S Lev 26:41 [q]Ge 17:14; Ex 12:48; Lev 22:25
44:8 [r]Lev 22:2; Nu 18:7
44:9 [s]Joel 3:17; Zec 14:21
44:10 [t]Ps 95:10 [u]Nu 18:23
44:11 [v]2Ch 29:34 [w]Nu 3:5-37; S 16:9; S 1Ch 26:12-19
44:12 [x]S Jer 18:15 [y]Ps 106:26 [z]2Ki 16:10-16; Jer 14:10
44:13 [a]S Eze 16:61 [b]Nu 18:3; Hos 5:1
44:14 [c]1Sa 2:36; 2Ki 23:9; S 1Ch 23:28-32
44:15 [d]S 2Sa 8:17; S Ezr 7:2 [e]S Ex 29:13 [f]S Jer 33:18; S Eze 40:46; Zec 3:7
44:16 [g]S Eze 41:22 [h]Lev 3:16-17; 17:5-6; Nu 18:5; S 1Sa 2:35; Zec 3:7
44:17 [i]Rev 19:8
44:18 [j]S Ex 28:39; S Isa 3:20 [k]S Ex 28:42 [l]S Lev 16:4
44:19 [m]S Lev 6:27 [n]Ex 39:27-29; Lev 6:10-11; S Eze 42:14
44:20 [o]Eze 5:1 [p]S Lev 21:5; Nu 6:5
44:21 [q]S Lev 10:9
44:22 [r]Lev 21:7
44:23 [s]S Eze 22:26 [t]S Ge 7:2; Lev 13:50; 15:31; Jer 15:19; Hag 2:11-13
44:24 [u]Dt 17:8-9; 19:17; 21:5; S 1Ch 23:4 [v]S Lev 23:2 [w]2Ch 19:8
44:25 [x]Lev 21:1-4
44:26 [y]Nu 19:14
44:27 [z]S Nu 3:28

44:15 DESCENDANTS OF ZADOK. Zadok had remained faithful to God when other Levites had abandoned God's way (1Ki 1). Because of his loyalty, he and his descendants were granted the privilege of ministering before the Lord in the future temple. This honor reveals that the extent of our faithfulness to God during our earthly lives will determine our place in God's eternal kingdom (see article on THE JUDGMENT OF BELIEVERS, p. 1791).

44:17–31 ENTER THE GATES. This regulation for the priests indicates that God must be worshiped with holy reverence.

is to offer a sin offering[a] for himself,
declares the Sovereign LORD.
28“ ‘I am to be the only inheritance[b]
the priests have. You are to give them
no possession in Israel; I will be their
possession. **29**They will eat[c] the grain
offerings, the sin offerings and the
guilt offerings; and everything in Israel
devoted[y] to the LORD[d] will belong to
them.[e] **30**The best of all the firstfruits[f] and of all your special gifts will
belong to the priests. You are to give
them the first portion of your ground
meal[g] so that a blessing[h] may rest on
your household.[i] **31**The priests must
not eat anything, bird or animal, found
dead[j] or torn by wild animals.[k]

Division of the Land

45 “ ‘When you allot the land as
an inheritance,[l] you are to
present to the LORD a portion of the
land as a sacred district, 25,000 cubits
long and 20,000[z] cubits wide; the entire area will be holy.[m] **2**Of this, a section 500 cubits square[n] is to be for the
sanctuary, with 50 cubits around it for
open land. **3**In the sacred district, measure off a section 25,000 cubits[a] long
and 10,000 cubits[b] wide. In it will be
the sanctuary, the Most Holy Place. **4**It
will be the sacred portion of the land
for the priests,[o] who minister in the
sanctuary and who draw near to minister before the LORD. It will be a place for
their houses as well as a holy place for
the sanctuary.[p] **5**An area 25,000 cubits long and 10,000 cubits wide will
belong to the Levites, who serve in the
temple, as their possession for towns
to live in.[c][q]
6“ ‘You are to give the city as its
property an area 5,000 cubits wide and
25,000 cubits long, adjoining the sacred portion; it will belong to the whole
house of Israel.[r]
7“ ‘The prince will have the land bordering each side of the area formed by
the sacred district and the property of
the city. It will extend westward from
the west side and eastward from the
east side, running lengthwise from the
western to the eastern border parallel
to one of the tribal portions.[s] **8**This
land will be his possession in Israel.
And my princes will no longer oppress
my people but will allow the house of
Israel to possess the land according to
their tribes.[t]
9“ ‘This is what the Sovereign LORD
says: You have gone far enough, O
princes of Israel! Give up your violence
and oppression[u] and do what is just
and right.[v] Stop dispossessing my
people, declares the Sovereign LORD.
10You are to use accurate scales,[w] an
accurate ephah[d][x] and an accurate
bath.[e] **11**The ephah[y] and the bath are
to be the same size, the bath containing a tenth of a homer[f] and the ephah
a tenth of a homer; the homer is to be
the standard measure for both. **12**The
shekel[g] is to consist of twenty gerahs.[z] Twenty shekels plus twenty-
five shekels plus fifteen shekels equal
one mina.[h]

Offerings and Holy Days

13“ ‘This is the special gift you are to
offer: a sixth of an ephah from each homer of wheat and a sixth of an ephah
from each homer of barley. **14**The prescribed portion of oil, measured by the
bath, is a tenth of a bath from each cor
(which consists of ten baths or one homer, for ten baths are equivalent to a
homer). **15**Also one sheep is to be tak-
en from every flock of two hundred
from the well-watered pastures of Israel. These will be used for the grain offerings, burnt offerings[a] and fellowship offerings[i] to make atonement[b]
for the people, declares the Sovereign
LORD. **16**All the people of the land will
participate in this special gift for the

44:27 [a]S Lev 4:28; Nu 6:11 **44:28** [b]S Nu 18:20; Dt 18:1-2; S Jos 13:33 **44:29** [c]Lev 6:16 [d]S Lev 27:21 [e]Nu 18:9,14; S Jos 13:14 **44:30** [f]Nu 18:12-13; S 2Ch 31:5 [g]S Nu 15:18-21 [h]S Lev 25:21 [i]S 2Ch 31:10; Ne 10:35-37 **44:31** [j]S Lev 11:39 [k]S Ex 22:31; S Lev 11:40 **45:1** [l]S Nu 34:13 [m]Eze 48:8-9,29 **45:2** [n]Eze 42:20 **45:4** [o]S Eze 40:46 [p]Eze 48:10-11 **45:5** [q]Eze 48:13 **45:6** [r]Eze 48:15-18 **45:7** [s]Eze 48:21 **45:8** [t]S Nu 26:53; Eze 46:18 **45:9** [u]Ps 12:5 [v]S Jer 22:3; Zec 7:9-10; 8:16 **45:10** [w]Dt 25:15; S Pr 11:1; Am 8:4-6; Mic 6:10-11 [x]S Lev 19:36 **45:11** [y]Isa 5:10 **45:12** [z]Ex 30:13; Lev 27:25; Nu 3:47 **45:15** [a]S Lev 1:4 [b]Lev 6:30

[y] *29* The Hebrew term refers to the irrevocable giving over of things or persons to the LORD. [z] *1* Septuagint (see also verses 3 and 5 and 48:9); Hebrew *10,000* [a] *3* That is, about 7 miles (about 12 kilometers) [b] *3* That is, about 3 miles (about 5 kilometers) [c] *5* Septuagint; Hebrew *temple; they will have as their possession 20 rooms* [d] *10* An ephah was a dry measure. [e] *10* A bath was a liquid measure. [f] *11* A homer was a dry measure. [g] *12* A shekel weighed about 2/5 ounce (about 11.5 grams). [h] *12* That is, 60 shekels; the common mina was 50 shekels. [i] *15* Traditionally *peace offerings*; also in verse 17

45:1–8 LAND AS AN INHERITANCE. These verses speak of the land that was to be set apart as the inheritance for the priests who minister before the Lord in his holy temple. These ministers will no longer exploit the people financially, but will be satisfied with their "sacred portion" (v. 4).

45:9–12 GIVE UP YOUR VIOLENCE. Ezekiel exhorts the leaders to stop their oppression and violence, and instead to do what is right and honest.

use of the prince in Israel. 17It will be
the duty of the prince to provide the
burnt offerings, grain offerings and
drink offerings at the festivals, the
New Moons[c] and the Sabbaths[d]—at
all the appointed feasts of the house of
Israel. He will provide the sin offerings, grain offerings, burnt offerings
and fellowship offerings to make
atonement for the house of Israel.[e]

18" 'This is what the Sovereign LORD
says: In the first month[f] on the first
day you are to take a young bull without defect[g] and purify the sanctuary.[h] 19The priest is to take some of
the blood of the sin offering and put it
on the doorposts of the temple, on the
four corners of the upper ledge[i] of the
altar[j] and on the gateposts of the inner court. 20You are to do the same on
the seventh day of the month for anyone who sins unintentionally[k] or
through ignorance; so you are to make
atonement for the temple.

21" 'In the first month on the fourteenth day you are to observe the Passover,[l] a feast lasting seven days, during which you shall eat bread made
without yeast. 22On that day the prince
is to provide a bull as a sin offering for
himself and for all the people of the
land.[m] 23Every day during the seven
days of the Feast he is to provide seven
bulls and seven rams[n] without defect
as a burnt offering to the LORD, and a
male goat for a sin offering.[o] 24He is
to provide as a grain offering[p] an
ephah for each bull and an ephah for
each ram, along with a hin[j] of oil for
each ephah.[q]

25" 'During the seven days of the
Feast,[r] which begins in the seventh
month on the fifteenth day, he is to
make the same provision for sin offerings, burnt offerings, grain offerings
and oil.[s]

46 " 'This is what the Sovereign
LORD says: The gate of the inner
court[t] facing east[u] is to be shut on
the six working days, but on the Sabbath day and on the day of the New
Moon[v] it is to be opened. 2The prince
is to enter from the outside through the
portico[w] of the gateway and stand by
the gatepost. The priests are to sacrifice his burnt offering[x] and his fellowship offerings.[k] He is to worship at the
threshold of the gateway and then go
out, but the gate will not be shut until
evening.[y] 3On the Sabbaths[z] and
New Moons the people of the land are
to worship in the presence of the LORD
at the entrance to that gateway.[a]
4The burnt offering the prince brings to
the LORD on the Sabbath day is to be six
male lambs and a ram, all without defect. 5The grain offering given with the
ram is to be an ephah,[l] and the grain
offering with the lambs is to be as
much as he pleases, along with a hin[j]
of oil for each ephah.[b] 6On the day of
the New Moon[c] he is to offer a young
bull, six lambs and a ram, all without
defect.[d] 7He is to provide as a grain
offering one ephah with the bull, one
ephah with the ram, and with the
lambs as much as he wants to give,
along with a hin of oil with each
ephah.[e] 8When the prince enters, he
is to go in through the portico[f] of the
gateway, and he is to come out the
same way.[g]

9" 'When the people of the land come
before the LORD at the appointed
feasts,[h] whoever enters by the north
gate to worship is to go out the south
gate; and whoever enters by the south
gate is to go out the north gate. No one
is to return through the gate by which
he entered, but each is to go out the
opposite gate. 10The prince is to be
among them, going in when they go in
and going out when they go out.[i]

11" 'At the festivals and the appointed feasts, the grain offering is to be an
ephah with a bull, an ephah with a ram,
and with the lambs as much as one
pleases, along with a hin of oil for each
ephah.[j] 12When the prince provides[k]
a freewill offering[l] to the LORD—
whether a burnt offering or fellowship
offerings—the gate facing east is to be
opened for him. He shall offer his burnt

45:17 [c]S Nu 10:10 [d]S Lev 23:38; Isa 66:23 [e]S 1Ki 8:62; S 2Ch 31:3; Eze 46:4-12 **45:18** [f]Ex 12:2 [g]S Lev 22:20; Heb 9:14 [h]S Lev 16:16,33 **45:19** [i]S Eze 43:17 [j]Lev 16:18-19 **45:20** [k]Lev 4:27 **45:21** [l]S Ex 12:11 **45:22** [m]Lev 4:14 **45:23** [n]S Nu 22:40; S Job 42:8 [o]Nu 28:16-25 **45:24** [p]Nu 28:12-13 [q]Eze 46:5-7 **45:25** [r]Dt 16:13 [s]Lev 23:34-43; Nu 29:12-38 **46:1** [t]S Eze 40:19 [u]S 1Ch 9:18 [v]ver 6; Isa 66:23 **46:2** [w]ver 8 [x]Eze 40:39 [y]ver 12; S Eze 44:3 **46:3** [z]S Isa 66:23 [a]Lk 1:10 **46:5** [b]ver 11 **46:6** [c]ver 1; S Nu 10:10 [d]S Lev 22:20 **46:7** [e]Eze 45:24 **46:8** [f]ver 2 [g]Eze 44:3 **46:9** [h]S Ex 23:14; S 34:20 **46:10** [i]2Sa 6:14-15; Ps 42:4 **46:11** [j]ver 5 **46:12** [k]S Eze 45:17 [l]S Lev 7:16

[j] *24,5* That is, probably about 4 quarts (about 4 liters) [k] *2* Traditionally *peace offerings;* also in verse 12 [l] *5* That is, probably about 3/5 bushel (about 22 liters)

45:21 THE PASSOVER. The seven-day Passover feast commemorated Israel's deliverance from slavery in Egypt (see article on THE PASSOVER, p. 104). The exodus was the most significant OT event involving Israel's redemption.

46:1–24 SABBATH DAY . . . THE NEW MOON. This chapter deals with Sabbath offerings and worship, the day of the New Moon (vv. 1–8), the appointed feasts (vv. 9–12) and the daily offerings (vv. 13–15).

offering or his fellowship offerings as
he does on the Sabbath day. Then he
shall go out, and after he has gone out,
the gate will be shut.[m]
13" 'Every day you are to provide a
year-old lamb without defect for a
burnt offering to the LORD; morning by
morning[n] you shall provide it.[o] **14**You
are also to provide with it morning by
morning a grain offering, consisting of
a sixth of an ephah with a third of a hin
of oil[p] to moisten the flour. The presenting of this grain offering to the
LORD is a lasting ordinance.[q] **15**So the
lamb and the grain offering and the oil
shall be provided morning by morning
for a regular[r] burnt offering.[s]
16" 'This is what the Sovereign LORD
says: If the prince makes a gift from
his inheritance to one of his sons, it
will also belong to his descendants; it
is to be their property by inheritance.[t]
17If, however, he makes a gift from his
inheritance to one of his servants, the
servant may keep it until the year of
freedom;[u] then it will revert to the
prince. His inheritance belongs to his
sons only; it is theirs. **18**The prince
must not take[v] any of the inheritance[w] of the people, driving them off
their property. He is to give his sons
their inheritance out of his own property, so that none of my people will be
separated from his property.' "
19Then the man brought me through
the entrance[x] at the side of the gate
to the sacred rooms facing north,[y]
which belonged to the priests, and
showed me a place at the western end.
20He said to me, "This is the place
where the priests will cook the guilt
offering and the sin offering and bake
the grain offering, to avoid bringing
them into the outer court and consecrating[z] the people."[a]
21He then brought me to the outer
court and led me around to its four corners, and I saw in each corner another
court. **22**In the four corners of the outer
court were enclosed[m] courts, forty cubits long and thirty cubits wide; each of
the courts in the four corners was the
same size. **23**Around the inside of each
of the four courts was a ledge of stone,
with places for fire built all around under the ledge. **24**He said to me, "These
are the kitchens where those who minister at the temple will cook the sacrifices of the people."

The River From the Temple

47 The man brought me back to
the entrance of the temple, and
I saw water[b] coming out from under
the threshold of the temple toward the
east (for the temple faced east). The
water was coming down from under
the south side of the temple, south of
the altar.[c] **2**He then brought me out
through the north gate[d] and led me
around the outside to the outer gate
facing east, and the water was flowing
from the south side.
3As the man went eastward with a
measuring line[e] in his hand, he measured off a thousand cubits[n] and then
led me through water that was ankle-
deep. **4**He measured off another thousand cubits and led me through water
that was knee-deep. He measured off
another thousand and led me through
water that was up to the waist. **5**He
measured off another thousand, but
now it was a river[f] that I could not
cross, because the water had risen and
was deep enough to swim in—a river
that no one could cross.[g] **6**He asked
me, "Son of man, do you see this?"
Then he led me back to the bank of
the river. **7**When I arrived there, I saw
a great number of trees on each side of
the river.[h] **8**He said to me, "This water
flows toward the eastern region and
goes down into the Arabah,[o][i] where
it enters the Sea.[p] When it empties
into the Sea,[p] the water there be-

46:12 [m]ver 2
46:13 [n]S Ps 5:3 [o]Ex 29:38; S Nu 28:3
46:14 [p]Nu 15:6 [q]Da 8:11
46:15 [r]S Ex 29:42 [s]S Ex 29:38; Nu 28:5-6
46:16 [t]2Ch 21:3
46:17 [u]S Lev 25:10
46:18 [v]1Sa 8:14 [w]S Lev 25:23; Eze 45:8; Mic 2:1-2
46:19 [x]S Eze 42:9 [y]Eze 42:4
46:20 [z]S Lev 6:27 [a]ver 24; Zec 14:20
47:1 [b]S Isa 55:1 [c]Ps 46:4; Joel 3:18; Rev 22:1
47:2 [d]S Eze 40:35
47:3 [e]S Eze 40:3
47:5 [f]S Ge 2:10 [g]Isa 11:9; Hab 2:14
47:7 [h]ver 12; Rev 22:2
47:8 [i]S Dt 1:1; S 3:17

[m]*22* The meaning of the Hebrew for this word is uncertain. [n]*3* That is, about 1,500 feet (about 450 meters) [o]*8* Or *the Jordan Valley* [p]*8* That is, the Dead Sea

47:1–12 WATER COMING OUT FROM ... THE TEMPLE. In his vision, Ezekiel sees a life-giving river coming out from the temple. As it flows, it grows in depth and width (vv. 2–5), giving life and fruitfulness to everything it touches (vv. 9–12). The river flows into the Dead Sea area and rids it of death (vv. 8–9). The purpose of the river is to bring abundant life and healing from God to the land and people (v. 12). (1) This river is similar to the river flowing from the Garden of Eden (Ge 2:8–10) and the river of life in the new Jerusalem (Rev 22:1–2; cf. Zec 14:8), which flows from the throne of God.

(2) This river also is similar to the one mentioned by Jesus: "Whoever believes in me, as the Scripture has said, streams of living water will flow from within him" (Jn 7:38). The "living water" is the Holy Spirit and the blessings of life he has come to bring.

comes fresh.[j] **9**Swarms of living creatures will live wherever the river flows. There will be large numbers of fish, because this water flows there and makes the salt water fresh; so where the river flows everything will live.[k] **10**Fishermen[l] will stand along the shore; from En Gedi[m] to En Eglaim there will be places for spreading nets.[n] The fish will be of many kinds[o]—like the fish of the Great Sea.[q][p] **11**But the swamps and marshes will not become fresh; they will be left for salt.[q] **12**Fruit trees of all kinds will grow on both banks of the river.[r] Their leaves will not wither, nor will their fruit[s] fail. Every month they will bear, because the water from the sanctuary[t] flows to them. Their fruit will serve for food and their leaves for healing.[u]"

Hos 11:3-4

The Boundaries of the Land

13This is what the Sovereign LORD says: "These are the boundaries[v] by which you are to divide the land for an inheritance among the twelve tribes of Israel, with two portions for Joseph.[w] **14**You are to divide it equally among them. Because I swore with uplifted hand to give it to your forefathers, this land will become your inheritance.[x]

15"This is to be the boundary of the land:[y]

"On the north side it will run from the Great Sea[z] by the Hethlon road[a] past Lebo[r] Hamath to Zedad, **16**Berothah[s][b] and Sibraim (which lies on the border between Damascus and Hamath),[c] as far as Hazer Hatticon, which is on the border of Hauran. **17**The boundary will extend from the sea to Hazar Enan,[t] along the northern border of Damascus, with the border of Hamath to the north. This will be the north boundary.[d]

18"On the east side the boundary will run between Hauran and Damascus, along the Jordan between Gilead and the land of Israel, to the eastern sea and as far as Tamar.[u] This will be the east boundary.[e]

19"On the south side it will run from Tamar as far as the waters of Meribah Kadesh,[f] then along the Wadi ⌞of Egypt⌟[g] to the Great Sea.[h] This will be the south boundary.

20"On the west side, the Great Sea will be the boundary to a point opposite Lebo[v] Hamath.[i] This will be the west boundary.[j]

21"You are to distribute this land among yourselves according to the tribes of Israel. **22**You are to allot it as an inheritance[k] for yourselves and for the aliens[l] who have settled among you and who have children. You are to consider them as native-born Israelites; along with you they are to be allotted an inheritance among the tribes of Israel.[m] **23**In whatever tribe the alien settles, there you are to give him his inheritance," declares the Sovereign LORD.[n]

The Division of the Land

48 "These are the tribes, listed by name: At the northern frontier, Dan[o] will have one portion; it will follow the Hethlon road[p] to Lebo[w] Hamath;[q] Hazar Enan and the northern border of Damascus next to Hamath will be part of its border from the east side to the west side.

2"Asher[r] will have one portion; it will border the territory of Dan from east to west.

3"Naphtali[s] will have one portion; it will border the territory of Asher from east to west.

47:8 [j] Isa 41:18 **47:9** [k] Isa 12:3; 55:1; Jn 4:14; 7:37-38 **47:10** [l] S Isa 19:8; Mt 4:19 [m] S Jos 15:62 [n] Eze 26:5 [o] S Ps 104:25; Mt 13:47 [p] S Nu 34:6 **47:11** [q] S Dt 29:23 **47:12** [r] ver 7; Rev 22:2 [s] S Ps 1:3 [t] S Isa 55:1 [u] S Ge 2:9; S Jer 17:8; Eze 36:8 **47:13** [v] Nu 34:2-12 [w] S Ge 48:16; S 49:26 **47:14** [x] S Ge 12:7; S Dt 1:8; S Eze 36:12 **47:15** [y] Nu 34:2 [z] ver 19; S Nu 34:6 [a] Eze 48:1 **47:16** [b] 2Sa 8:8 [c] Nu 13:21; S Jer 49:23; Eze 48:1 **47:17** [d] Eze 48:1 **47:18** [e] S Eze 27:18 **47:19** [f] Dt 32:51 [g] S Ge 15:18; Isa 27:12 [h] S ver 15; Eze 48:28 **47:20** [i] S Nu 13:21; Eze 48:1 [j] Nu 34:6 **47:22** [k] S Eze 36:12 [l] S Dt 24:19; S Isa 14:1; Mal 3:5 [m] S Lev 24:22; Nu 15:29; 26:55-56; Isa 56:6-7; Ro 10:12; Eph 2:12-16; 3:6; Col 3:11 **47:23** [n] S Dt 10:19 **48:1** [o] S Ge 30:6 [p] Eze 47:15-17 [q] S Eze 47:20 **48:2** [r] Jos 19:24-31 **48:3** [s] Jos 19:32-39

[q] *10* That is, the Mediterranean; also in verses 15, 19 and 20 [r] *15* Or *past the entrance to* [s] *15,16* See Septuagint and Ezekiel 48:1; Hebrew *road to go into Zedad, 16Hamath, Berothah* [t] *17* Hebrew *Enon,* a variant of *Enan* [u] *18* Septuagint and Syriac; Hebrew *Israel. You will measure to the eastern sea* [v] *20* Or *opposite the entrance to* [w] *1* Or *to the entrance to*

47:21–23 INHERITANCE FOR YOURSELVES AND FOR THE ALIENS. Though the land is redivided in east-west strips among the tribes of Israel, God's purpose is not to build up again the "dividing wall of hostility" (Eph 2:14) between Jews and Gentiles. Resident aliens will also be given an inheritance among the tribes. Some believe that the children mentioned here are spiritual children, and that those Gentiles who have had a ministry among the people of Israel will share in their inheritance in the restored millennial land.

48:1–29 ITS BORDER. Ezekiel's final chapter continues designating the boundaries of the restored land and the location of the tribes (47:13—48:29).

4“Manasseh[t] will have one portion; it will border the territory of Naphtali from east to west.

5“Ephraim[u] will have one portion; it will border the territory of Manasseh[v] from east to west.[w]

6“Reuben[x] will have one portion; it will border the territory of Ephraim from east to west.

7“Judah[y] will have one portion; it will border the territory of Reuben from east to west.

8“Bordering the territory of Judah from east to west will be the portion you are to present as a special gift. It will be 25,000 cubits[x] wide, and its length from east to west will equal one of the tribal portions; the sanctuary will be in the center of it.[z]

9“The special portion you are to offer to the LORD will be 25,000 cubits long and 10,000 cubits[y] wide.[a] 10This will be the sacred portion for the priests. It will be 25,000 cubits long on the north side, 10,000 cubits wide on the west side, 10,000 cubits wide on the east side and 25,000 cubits long on the south side. In the center of it will be the sanctuary of the LORD.[b] 11This will be for the consecrated priests, the Zadokites,[c] who were faithful in serving me[d] and did not go astray as the Levites did when the Israelites went astray.[e] 12It will be a special gift to them from the sacred portion of the land, a most holy portion, bordering the territory of the Levites.

13“Alongside the territory of the priests, the Levites will have an allotment 25,000 cubits long and 10,000 cubits wide. Its total length will be 25,000 cubits and its width 10,000 cubits.[f] 14They must not sell or exchange any of it. This is the best of the land and must not pass into other hands, because it is holy to the LORD.[g]

15“The remaining area, 5,000 cubits wide and 25,000 cubits long, will be for the common use of the city, for houses and for pastureland. The city will be in the center of it 16and will have these measurements: the north side 4,500 cubits, the south side 4,500 cubits, the east side 4,500 cubits, and the west side 4,500 cubits.[h] 17The pastureland for the city will be 250 cubits on the north, 250 cubits on the south, 250 cubits on the east, and 250 cubits on the west. 18What remains of the area, bordering on the sacred portion and running the length of it, will be 10,000 cubits on the east side and 10,000 cubits on the west side. Its produce will supply food for the workers of the city.[i] 19The workers from the city who farm it will come from all the tribes of Israel. 20The entire portion will be a square, 25,000 cubits on each side. As a special gift you will set aside the sacred portion, along with the property of the city.

21“What remains on both sides of the area formed by the sacred portion and the city property will belong to the prince. It will extend eastward from the 25,000 cubits of the sacred portion to the eastern border, and westward from the 25,000 cubits to the western border. Both these areas running the length of the tribal portions will belong to the prince, and the sacred portion with the temple sanctuary will be in the center of them.[j] 22So the property of the Levites and the property of the city will lie in the center of the area that belongs to the prince. The area belonging to the prince will lie between the border of Judah and the border of Benjamin.

23“As for the rest of the tribes: Benjamin[k] will have one portion; it will extend from the east side to the west side.

24“Simeon[l] will have one portion; it will border the territory of Benjamin from east to west.

25“Issachar[m] will have one portion; it will border the territory of Simeon from east to west.

26“Zebulun[n] will have one portion; it will border the territory of Issachar from east to west.

27“Gad[o] will have one portion; it

48:4 [t] Jos 17:1-11 **48:5** [u] Jos 16:5-9 [v] Jos 17:7-10 [w] Jos 17:17 **48:6** [x] Jos 13:15-21 **48:7** [y] Jos 15:1-63 **48:8** [z] ver 21 **48:9** [a] S Eze 45:1 **48:10** [b] ver 21; S Eze 45:3-4 **48:11** [c] S 2Sa 8:17 [d] S Lev 8:35 [e] Eze 14:11; S 44:15 **48:13** [f] Eze 45:5 **48:14** [g] S Lev 25:34; 27:10,28

48:16 [h] Rev 21:16 **48:18** [i] Eze 45:6 **48:21** [j] ver 8,10; Eze 45:7 **48:23** [k] Jos 18:11-28 **48:24** [l] S Ge 29:33; Jos 19:1-9 **48:25** [m] Jos 19:17-23 **48:26** [n] Jos 19:10-16 **48:27** [o] Jos 13:24-28

[x] *8* That is, about 7 miles (about 12 kilometers) [y] *9* That is, about 3 miles (about 5 kilometers)

48:11–12 DID NOT GO ASTRAY. Once again God emphasizes that those who remain faithful to his will and righteous standards while on earth will be rewarded in the future kingdom. Here the gift for the Zadokites is the privilege of living near God's sanctuary (see 44:15, note). It is eternally important to strive with all our heart to remain faithful to God and to spurn the influences of this evil generation.

will border the territory of Zebulun
from east to west.
28"The southern boundary of Gad
will run south from Tamar[p] to the waters of Meribah Kadesh, then along the
Wadi ⌞of Egypt⌟ to the Great Sea.[z][q]
29"This is the land you are to allot as
an inheritance to the tribes of Israel,
and these will be their portions," declares the Sovereign LORD.[r]

The Gates of the City

30"These will be the exits of the city:
Beginning on the north side, which is
4,500 cubits long, 31the gates of the
city will be named after the tribes of
Israel. The three gates on the north
side will be the gate of Reuben, the
gate of Judah and the gate of Levi.
32"On the east side, which is 4,500
cubits long, will be three gates: the
gate of Joseph, the gate of Benjamin
and the gate of Dan.
33"On the south side, which measures 4,500 cubits, will be three gates:
the gate of Simeon, the gate of Issachar and the gate of Zebulun.
34"On the west side, which is 4,500
cubits long, will be three gates: the
gate of Gad, the gate of Asher and the
gate of Naphtali.[s]
35"The distance all around will be
18,000 cubits.
"And the name of the city from that
time on will be:

THE LORD IS THERE.[t]"

48:28 [p] S Ge 14:7 [q] S Nu 34:6; Eze 47:19
48:29 [r] S Eze 45:1
48:34 [s] S 2Ch 4:4; Rev 21:12-13
48:35 [t] S Isa 12:6; S 24:23; S Jer 3:17; 14:9; Joel 3:21; Rev 3:12; S 21:3

[z] *28* That is, the Mediterranean

48:35 THE LORD IS THERE. The book of Ezekiel ends with the great promise that one day God will live eternally with his people, a promise that is repeated in Rev 21:3: "Now the dwelling of God is with men, and he will live with them." The greatest blessing for us as God's people is to have God in our midst; this is the essence of joy and happiness. As a result of God's enduring presence, we will never again experience the sorrows, disappointments and troubles of our former life (Rev 21:4); this is our ultimate vision and hope as we look for the day of the appearing of our Lord and Savior, Jesus Christ.

DANIEL

Outline

I. The Historical Setting of Daniel (1:1–21)
  A. Daniel and His Friends Deported to Babylon (1:1–7)
  B. The Faithfulness of Daniel and His Friends in Babylon (1:8–16)
  C. The Promotion of Daniel and His Friends in the King's Court (1:17–21)
II. Daniel's Message Concerning God's Sovereignty Over the Nations (2:1—7:28)
  A. Nebuchadnezzar's Prophetic Dream and Daniel's Revelation About It (2:1–49)
  B. The Image of Gold and the Fiery Furnace (3:1–30)
  C. The Prophetic Dream of Nebuchadnezzar's Insanity and Its Fulfillment (4:1–37)
  D. Belshazzar's Feast and Babylon's Downfall (5:1–31)
  E. Darius's Decree and Daniel's Deliverance (6:1–28)
  F. Daniel's Prophetic Dream of Four World Empires and the Ancient of Days (7:1–28)
III. Daniel's Visions Concerning the Nation of Israel (8:1—12:13)
  A. Daniel's Vision of a Ram, a Goat and a Small Horn (8:1–27)
  B. Daniel's Intercession for Restoration and His Vision of the Seventy "Sevens" (9:1–27)
  C. Daniel's Vision of Israel's Future (10:1—12:13)
    1. Daniel's Revelation and Angelic Encounter (10:1—11:1)
    2. Prophetic Revelation About Persia and Greece (11:2–4), Egypt and Aram (11:5–35), and the Coming Antichrist (11:36–45)
    3. Prophetic Revelation About Other End-Time Events (12:1–13)

Author: Daniel

Theme: God's Sovereignty in History

Date of Writing: c. 536–530 B.C.

Background

Daniel, whose name means "God is (my) Judge," is both the chief character and the author of the book that bears his name. Authorship by Daniel is not only explicitly stated in 12:4, but also implied by the numerous autobiographical references in chs. 7—12. Jesus attributes the book to "the prophet Daniel" (Mt 24:15) when quoting from 9:27.

The book records events from Nebuchadnezzar's first invasion of Jerusalem (605 B.C.) to the third year of Cyrus (536 B.C.); thus the historical setting for the book is Babylon during the 70-year Babylonian captivity prophesied by Jeremiah (cf. Jer 25:11). Daniel would have been a teenager when the events of ch. 1 began and in his late 80s when receiving his visions in chs. 9—12. He may have lived until c. 530 B.C., completing the book as an old man during the last decade of his life (cf. John and the apocalyptic book of Revelation). Modern critics who regard the book of Daniel as a 2nd century B.C. pseudepigraphon are guided by their philosophical presuppositions rather than by facts.

Our knowledge of the prophet Daniel comes almost entirely from this book (cf. Eze 14:14,20). Perhaps Daniel was a descendant of King Hezekiah (cf. 2Ki 20:17–18;

Isa 39:6–7); certainly he was from an upper-class educated family in Jerusalem (1:3–6), for Nebuchadnezzar would not have selected young foreigners from a lower class for his royal court (1:4,17). Daniel may have been made a eunuch in Babylon, as was common in those days when a male served in a royal court (cf. 1:3; 2Ki 20:18; Mt 19:12). Daniel's success in Babylon is attributed to his integrity of character, his prophetic gifts, and God's interventions that resulted in his rapid advancement to places of prominence and responsibility (2:46–49; 6:1–3).

Chronologically, Daniel is one of the last OT prophets. Only Haggai, Zechariah and Malachi come after him in the prophetic stream of OT history. He was a younger contemporary of Jeremiah and probably the same age as Ezekiel.

Purpose

There is a twofold purpose for the writing of Daniel: (1) to reassure the OT covenant people that their judgment of captivity under Gentile nations was not to be their permanent fate; and (2) to bequeath to God's people throughout history the prophetic visions of God's sovereignty over nations and the final triumph of his kingdom in the earth. This twofold purpose is demonstrated throughout the book in the lives of Daniel and his three friends and illustrated in Daniel's prophetic message and ministry. The book affirms that God's promises to preserve and restore his covenant people are as sure as the coming Messianic kingdom that will last forever.

Survey

The content of Daniel is a blend of autobiography, history and prophecy. Its literary form is apocalyptic literature, meaning that its prophetic message unveils God's revelation (1) through visions and dreams and symbolism, (2) for the purpose of encouraging God's people during a crisis period of history, and (3) for the envisioning of Israel's hope concerning the eventual triumph of God's kingdom and righteousness in the earth (see the introduction to the book of Revelation).

The book divides naturally into three major parts. (1) Ch. 1 is written in Hebrew and introduces the historical setting for the book. (2) Chs. 2—7, beginning at 2:4, were written in Aramaic, describing the rise and fall of four mighty successive world kingdoms and followed by the establishment of God's kingdom as an everlasting one (especially chs. 2; 7). These chapters emphasize God's sovereignty over and intervention in the affairs of humans and nations by describing: (a) Daniel's rise to prominence in Nebuchadnezzar's court (ch. 2); (b) one looking like "a son of the gods" in the fiery furnace with Daniel's three friends (ch. 3); (c) Nebuchadnezzar's temporary insanity as God's judgment (ch. 4); (d) Daniel's role at Belshazzar's banquet, declaring the end of the Babylonian kingdom (ch. 5); (e) Daniel's miraculous deliverance from the lions' den (ch. 6); and (f) the vision of the four successive world kingdoms being judged by the "Ancient of Days" (ch. 7). (3) In chs. 8—12, Daniel once again writes in Hebrew and describes unusual revelations and angelic visitations from God concerning (a) the Jewish people under future Gentile domination (chs. 8—11), (b) the period of seventy "sevens" as the time set by God for the accomplishment of the Messiah's mission on their behalf (ch. 9), and (c) their ultimate deliverance from all tribulation at the end of time (ch. 12).

Daniel's prophetic messages involve two dimensions: (1) the close-at-hand future and (2) the far-distant future, though these two dimensions often blend together. For example, in chs. 8 and 11, Daniel prophesies about the "antichrist"-type figure of Antiochus IV Epiphanes, who desecrated the Jerusalem temple in 168 B.C., while he also prophesied about the antichrist of the end time (8:23–26; 11:36–45; cf. Rev 13:1–10). This interplay between these two futures characterizes Biblical prophecy generally and Daniel specifically. God reveals to Daniel that the far-distant prophecy is a concealed message until "the time of the end" (12:4,9), when insight will be given to God's people who in purity and wisdom seek him for understanding just as Daniel did (12:3,10).

Special Features

Eight special features characterize the book of Daniel. (1) It is the shortest of the four major prophetic books and the most read and studied of all the OT prophets. (2) In prophetic passages of the NT, Daniel is quoted or alluded to more often than any other OT book. (3) It is "the Apocalypse" of the OT, as the book of Revelation is of the NT, revealing great themes of prophecy that are vitally important to the end-time church. (4) It contains the most detailed prophetic summary of history in the OT. It is the only OT prophecy to set the time of the Messiah's first advent (9:24–27). (5) It discloses more about its author than any other OT prophetic writing (with the possible exception of Jeremiah). Note especially that Daniel was a man characterized by deep integrity of character, great prophetic wisdom, and diligence in prayer and fasting. (6) It contains the Bible's foremost model of intercession for the restoration of God's people, based on the inspired promises of God's word (see ch. 9, inspired by Jer 25:11–16; 29:7,10–14). (7) The stories about Daniel and his friends are among the best-loved stories in the Bible (especially chs. 3; 6). (8) The drama of "the handwriting on the wall" at Belshazzar's banquet has made that phrase a proverbial part of our language to this day.

New Testament Fulfillment

The influence of Daniel on the NT goes far beyond the five or six times the book is directly quoted. Much of Daniel's history and prophecy reappears in prophetic passages in the Gospels, Letters, and Revelation. Daniel's prophecy about the coming Messiah includes a description of him as (1) the huge rock that would crush earthly kingdoms (2:34–35,45), (2) the Son of Man, who would be given dominion, glory and a kingdom by the Ancient of Days (7:13–14), and (3) "the Anointed One, the ruler," who would come and then be cut off (9:25–26). Some interpreters believe that Daniel's vision in 10:5–9 is a preincarnate appearance of Christ (cf. Rev 1:12–16).

Daniel contains numerous prophetic themes that are more fully developed in the NT: e.g., the great tribulation and the antichrist, the second advent of our Lord, the triumph of God's kingdom, the resurrection of the righteous and the wicked, and the day of judgment. The lives of Daniel and his three friends demonstrate the NT teaching about personal separation from sin and the world, i.e., living in the unbelieving world but not participating in its spirit and ways (1:8; 3:12; 6:10; cf. Jn 17:6,15–16,18; 2Co 6:14—7:1).

Reading Daniel

In order to read the entire Old Testament in one year, the book of Daniel should be read in 6 days, according to the following schedule: ☐ 1–2 ☐ 3–4 ☐ 5–6 ☐ 7–8 ☐ 9–10 ☐ 11–12

NOTES

Daniel's Training in Babylon

1 In the third year of the reign of Jehoiakim[a] king of Judah, Nebuchadnezzar[b] king of Babylon[c] came
to Jerusalem and besieged it.[d] **2**And
the Lord delivered Jehoiakim king of
Judah into his hand, along with some of
the articles from the temple of God.
These he carried[e] off to the temple of
his god in Babylonia[a] and put in the
treasure house of his god.[f]
3Then the king ordered Ashpenaz,
chief of his court officials, to bring in
some of the Israelites from the royal
family and the nobility[g]— **4**young
men without any physical defect, handsome,[h] showing aptitude for every
kind of learning,[i] well informed,
quick to understand, and qualified to
serve in the king's palace. He was to
teach them the language[j] and literature of the Babylonians.[b] **5**The king
assigned them a daily amount of food
and wine[k] from the king's table.[l]
They were to be trained for three
years,[m] and after that they were to enter the king's service.[n]
6Among these were some from Judah: Daniel,[o] Hananiah, Mishael and
Azariah.[p] **7**The chief official gave
them new names: to Daniel, the name
Belteshazzar;[q] to Hananiah, Shadrach; to Mishael, Meshach; and to Azariah, Abednego.[r]
8But Daniel resolved not to defile[s]
himself with the royal food and wine,
and he asked the chief official for permission not to defile himself this way.
9Now God had caused the official to
show favor[t] and sympathy[u] to Daniel, **10**but the official told Daniel, "I am
afraid of my lord the king, who has assigned your[c] food and drink.[v] Why
should he see you looking worse than
the other young men your age? The
king would then have my head because
of you."
11Daniel then said to the guard
whom the chief official had appointed
over Daniel, Hananiah, Mishael and
Azariah, **12**"Please test[w] your servants for ten days: Give us nothing but
vegetables to eat and water to drink.
13Then compare our appearance with
that of the young men who eat the roy-

1:1 [a]S Jer 46:2 [b]S 2Ki 24:1; S Jer 28:14 [c]Jer 50:1 [d]2Ki 24:1; S 2Ch 36:6; Jer 35:11 **1:2** [e]S 2Ki 24:13 [f]S 2Ch 36:7; Jer 27:19-20; Zec 5:5-11 **1:3** [g]S 2Ki 20:18; S 24:15; Isa 39:7 **1:4** [h]S Ge 39:6 [i]ver 17 [j]S Ezr 4:7 **1:5** [k]ver 8,10 [l]S Est 2:9 [m]ver 18 [n]ver 19; S Est 2:5-6 **1:6** [o]S Eze 14:14 [p]Da 2:17,25 **1:7** [q]Da 2:26; 4:8; 5:12; 10:1 [r]S Isa 39:7; Da 2:49; 3:12 **1:8** [s]S Eze 4:13-14 **1:9** [t]S Ge 39:21; S Pr 16:7 [u]S 1Ki 8:50 **1:10** [v]ver 5 **1:12** [w]Rev 2:10

[a] *2* Hebrew *Shinar* [b] *4* Or *Chaldeans* [c] *10* The Hebrew for *your* and *you* in this verse is plural.

1:4 QUALIFIED TO SERVE IN THE KING'S PALACE. When God gave Nebuchadnezzar the victory over Jehoiakim in 605 B.C., the Babylonian monarch took some of the temple articles and also some of the choice princes. Since Nineveh's destruction seven years earlier, the Babylonian empire had grown so fast that they did not have enough of their own educated men needed to run the government; so Nebuchadnezzar took good-looking, healthy, well-educated young men to Babylon in order to teach them the Babylonian culture and language and thus to make them useful in the king's royal service. Among them were Daniel and his three friends.

1:7 GAVE THEM NEW NAMES. In order for Daniel and his friends to enter the king's service, they needed to have Babylonian citizenship; this was accomplished by giving them Babylonian names. The young prince Daniel ("God is my Judge") was named Belteshazzar ("Bel [chief god of Babylon], protect his life"); Hananiah ("The LORD shows grace") was named Shadrach ("Servant of Aku", i.e., the moon-god); Mishael ("Who is equal to God?") was named Meshach ("The shadow of the prince" or "Who is this?"); Azariah ("The LORD helps") was named Abednego ("Servant of Nego", i.e., the god of wisdom, or the morning star). As citizens of Babylon, they now carried official responsibilities. Despite having these new names, these Jewish men resolved that they would remain loyal to the one true God (see next note).

1:8 DANIEL RESOLVED NOT TO DEFILE HIMSELF. Babylon's moral climate was totally pagan. We can be sure that what Daniel and his friends were being taught often contradicted God's law and righteous principles. The same food and wine served to King Nebuchadnezzar was served to them—food and wine that may have been offered to idols. To eat such food would have disobeyed God's laws; to drink the wine would have dulled their minds because of its intoxicating effect. (1) Daniel made up his mind from the start not to defile himself; he would not compromise his convictions even if it meant death. Note that Daniel no longer had his parents around to guide him in his decisions; his love for God and his law had been so instilled in him as a child that he desired to serve the Lord from the heart (see Dt 6:7, note; see article on PARENTS AND CHILDREN, p. 1854).

(2) Those who are determined to remain faithful to God when confronted with temptation will be given the strength to stand firm for God. Conversely, those who have not previously decided to remain true to God and his word will find it difficult to resist sin or avoid conforming to the ways of the world.

1:12 TEST YOUR SERVANTS FOR TEN DAYS. Because Daniel and his friends were objects of the king's special attention, the king's wrath could fall on the official if he agreed to Daniel's request; thus he refused (v. 10). Daniel did not argue; instead, with grace and dignity he went to the guard who actually served their food and proposed an experimental ten-day diet.

al food, and treat your servants in accordance with what you see."[x] 14So
he agreed to this and tested[y] them for
ten days.
15At the end of the ten days they
looked healthier and better nourished
than any of the young men who ate the
royal food.[z] 16So the guard took away
their choice food and the wine they
were to drink and gave them vegetables instead.[a]
17To these four young men God gave
knowledge and understanding[b] of all
kinds of literature and learning.[c] And
Daniel could understand visions and
dreams of all kinds.[d]
18At the end of the time[e] set by the
king to bring them in, the chief official
presented them to Nebuchadnezzar.
19The king talked with them, and he
found none equal to Daniel, Hananiah,
Mishael and Azariah; so they entered
the king's service.[f] 20In every matter
of wisdom and understanding about
which the king questioned them, he
found them ten times better than all
the magicians[g] and enchanters in his
6 whole kingdom.[h]
21And Daniel remained there until
the first year of King Cyrus.[i]

Nebuchadnezzar's Dream

2 In the second year of his reign,
Nebuchadnezzar had dreams;[j]
his mind was troubled[k] and he could
not sleep.[l] 2So the king summoned
the magicians,[m] enchanters, sorcerers[n] and astrologers[d][o] to tell him
what he had dreamed.[p] When they
came in and stood before the king, 3he
said to them, "I have had a dream that
troubles[q] me and I want to know what
it means.[e]"
4Then the astrologers answered the
king in Aramaic,[f][r] "O king, live forever![s] Tell your servants the dream,
and we will interpret it."
5The king replied to the astrologers,
"This is what I have firmly decided:[t]
If you do not tell me what my dream
was and interpret it, I will have you cut
into pieces[u] and your houses turned
into piles of rubble.[v] 6But if you tell
me the dream and explain it, you will
receive from me gifts and rewards and
great honor.[w] So tell me the dream
and interpret it for me."
7Once more they replied, "Let the
king tell his servants the dream, and
we will interpret it."
8Then the king answered, "I am certain that you are trying to gain time,
because you realize that this is what I
have firmly decided: 9If you do not tell
me the dream, there is just one penalty[x] for you. You have conspired to tell
me misleading and wicked things, hoping the situation will change. So then,
tell me the dream, and I will know that
you can interpret it for me."[y]
10The astrologers[z] answered the
king, "There is not a man on earth who
can do what the king asks! No king,
however great and mighty, has ever
asked such a thing of any magician or
enchanter or astrologer.[a] 11What the
king asks is too difficult. No one can
reveal it to the king except the gods,[b]
and they do not live among men."

[d] *2* Or *Chaldeans*; also in verses 4, 5 and 10
[e] *3* Or *was* [f] *4* The text from here through chapter 7 is in Aramaic.

1:13 [x]ver 16
1:14 [y]Rev 2:10
1:15 [z]Ex 23:25
1:16 [a]ver 12-13
1:17 [b]S Job 12:13 [c]Da 2:23; Col 1:9; Jas 1:5 [d]Da 2:19, 30; 5:11; 7:1; 8:1
1:18 [e]ver 5
1:19 [f]S Ge 41:46
1:20 [g]S Ge 41:8 [h]S 1Ki 4:30; Est 2:15; S Eze 28:3; Da 2:13,28; 4:18; 6:3
1:21 [i]S 2Ch 36:22; Da 6:28; 10:1
2:1 [j]ver 3; S Ge 20:3; S Job 33:15,18; Da 4:5 [k]Ge 41:8 [l]S Est 6:1
2:2 [m]S Ge 41:8 [n]Ex 7:11; Jer 27:9 [o]S ver 10; S Isa 19:3; S 44:25 [p]Da 4:6
2:3 [q]Da 4:5
2:4 [r]S Ezr 4:7 [s]S Ne 2:3
2:5 [t]Ge 41:32 [u]ver 12 [v]Ezr 6:11; Da 3:29
2:6 [w]ver 48; Da 5:7,16
2:9 [x]Est 4:11 [y]Isa 41:22-24
2:10 [z]ver 2; Da 3:8; 4:7 [a]ver 27; Da 5:8
2:11 [b]S Ge 41:38

1:17 GOD GAVE KNOWLEDGE AND UNDERSTANDING. Because the four young men were committed to God, God committed himself to help them. If you are striving to be faithful to God and his ways, rest assured that he will remain with you and give you the help and grace needed to accomplish his will.

1:20 IN EVERY MATTER OF WISDOM . . . TEN TIMES BETTER. At the final examination, Daniel and his friends stood healthy and unafraid before the king. They had remained faithful to the Lord, and by their demonstration of wisdom and knowledge they gave testimony to God's power.

1:21 FIRST YEAR OF KING CYRUS. This date (539 B.C.) was 66 years after Daniel was deported to Babylon. Daniel lived to see the first exiles return to Judah from the Babylonian captivity in 538 B.C., since he was still alive in 537 B.C. (cf. 10:1).

2:1 NEBUCHADNEZZAR HAD DREAMS. The king was greatly troubled about his dream and undoubtedly believed that the gods were trying to communicate something to him; thus he called for the diviners to tell him the dream and its meaning.

2:4 IN ARAMAIC. Up to this point, the book of Daniel is written in Hebrew. Here it changes to Aramaic, which was the language of trade and of government communication at that time. The use of Aramaic in Daniel continues through ch. 7; chs. 8—12 are again in Hebrew.

2:5 I HAVE FIRMLY DECIDED. The king sensed the importance of his dream and wanted to put the Babylonian wise men to the test. If they could tell him the dream (which he probably remembered very well), then he would know they could give him the correct interpretation; if they could not give him both, then he would destroy them.

12This made the king so angry and
furious[c] that he ordered the execution[d] of all the wise men of Babylon.
13So the decree was issued to put the
wise men to death, and men were sent
to look for Daniel and his friends to put
them to death.[e]
14When Arioch, the commander of
the king's guard, had gone out to put
to death the wise men of Babylon, Daniel spoke to him with wisdom and tact.
15He asked the king's officer, "Why did
the king issue such a harsh decree?"
Arioch then explained the matter to
Daniel. **16**At this, Daniel went in to the
king and asked for time, so that he
might interpret the dream for him.
17Then Daniel returned to his house
and explained the matter to his friends
Hananiah, Mishael and Azariah.[f]
18He urged them to plead for mercy[g]
from the God of heaven[h] concerning
this mystery,[i] so that he and his
friends might not be executed with the
rest of the wise men of Babylon. **19**During the night the mystery[j] was revealed to Daniel in a vision.[k] Then
Daniel praised the God of heaven[l]
20and said:

"Praise be to the name of God for
ever and ever;[m]
wisdom and power[n] are his.
21He changes times and seasons;[o]
he sets up kings[p] and
deposes[q] them.
He gives wisdom[r] to the wise
and knowledge to the
discerning.[s]
22He reveals deep and hidden
things;[t]
he knows what lies in
darkness,[u]
and light[v] dwells with him.
23I thank and praise you, O God of
my fathers:[w]
You have given me wisdom[x]
and power,
you have made known to me what
we asked of you,
you have made known to us the
dream of the king.[y]"

Daniel Interprets the Dream

24Then Daniel went to Arioch,[z]
whom the king had appointed to execute the wise men of Babylon, and said
to him, "Do not execute the wise men
of Babylon. Take me to the king, and
I will interpret his dream for him."
25Arioch took Daniel to the king at
once and said, "I have found a man
among the exiles[a] from Judah[b] who
can tell the king what his dream
means."
26The king asked Daniel (also called
Belteshazzar),[c] "Are you able to tell
me what I saw in my dream and interpret it?"
27Daniel replied, "No wise man, enchanter, magician or diviner can explain to the king the mystery he has
asked about,[d] **28**but there is a God in
heaven who reveals mysteries.[e] He
has shown King Nebuchadnezzar what
will happen in days to come.[f] Your
dream and the visions that passed
through your mind[g] as you lay on your
bed[h] are these:[i]
29"As you were lying there, O king,
your mind turned to things to come,
and the revealer of mysteries showed
you what is going to happen.[j] **30**As for
me, this mystery has been revealed[k]
to me, not because I have greater wisdom than other living men, but so that
you, O king, may know the interpretation and that you may understand what
went through your mind.
31"You looked, O king, and there before you stood a large statue — an enormous, dazzling statue,[l] awesome[m] in
appearance. **32**The head of the statue
was made of pure gold, its chest and
arms of silver, its belly and thighs of

2:12 [c] Da 3:13,19 [d] ver 5 **2:13** [e] S Da 1:20; 5:19 **2:17** [f] S Da 1:6 **2:18** [g] S Isa 37:4 [h] Ezr 1:2; Ne 1:4; Jnh 1:9; Rev 11:13 [i] ver 23; Jer 33:3 **2:19** [j] ver 28 [k] S Job 33:15; S Da 1:17 [l] S Jos 22:33 **2:20** [m] S Ps 113:2; 145:1-2 [n] S Job 9:4; S Jer 32:19 **2:21** [o] Da 7:25 [p] Da 4:17 [q] S Job 12:19; Ps 75:6-7; Ro 13:1 [r] S Ps 119:34; Jas 1:5 [s] S 2Sa 14:17 **2:22** [t] S Ge 40:8; S Job 12:22; Da 5:11; 1Co 2:10 [u] Job 12:22; Ps 139:11-12; Jer 23:24; S Heb 4:13 [v] Isa 45:7; Jas 1:17 **2:23** [w] S Ge 31:5; S Ex 3:15 [x] S Da 1:17 [y] S Eze 28:3 **2:24** [z] ver 14 **2:25** [a] S Dt 21:10 [b] S Da 1:6; 5:13; 6:13 **2:26** [c] S Da 1:7 **2:27** [d] S ver 10; S Ge 41:8 **2:28** [e] S Ge 40:8; Jer 10:7; Am 4:13 [f] S Ge 49:1; Da 10:14; Mt 24:6; Rev 1:1; 22:6 [g] Da 4:5 [h] S Ps 4:4 [i] S Eze 28:3; S Da 1:20 **2:29** [j] S Ge 41:25 **2:30** [k] Isa 45:3; S Da 1:17; Am 4:13 **2:31** [l] Hab 1:7 [m] Isa 25:3-5

2:16 ASKED FOR TIME. Being recent graduates, Daniel and his three friends were not called in before the king with the rest of the wise men, but the decree to kill all of them included those four as well. Daniel then approached the king and asked for time to interpret the dream. He needed time to pray and to receive God's assistance; so the four Hebrew men sought the Lord earnestly in prayer and waited for his revelation.

2:19–23 DANIEL PRAISED THE GOD OF HEAVEN. Daniel's first thought after God revealed the dream and its interpretation was to praise the Lord for his goodness and power. To break out in spontaneous expressions of praise to God is characteristic of those who truly love and serve him.

2:28–30 A GOD IN HEAVEN WHO REVEALS MYSTERIES. Daniel took no personal credit for making the dream and its interpretation known to the king. We must be careful never to take the credit and glory for what God does through us (cf. Dt 8:11–20). Because Daniel was humble, straightforward and honest about God, Nebuchadnezzar was able to make a proper response of acknowledging Daniel's God (v. 47).

bronze, 33its legs of iron, its feet partly
of iron and partly of baked clay.
34While you were watching, a rock was
cut out, but not by human hands.[n] It
struck the statue on its feet of iron and
clay and smashed[o] them.[p] 35Then
the iron, the clay, the bronze, the silver
and the gold were broken to pieces at
the same time and became like chaff on
a threshing floor in the summer. The
wind swept them away[q] without leaving a trace. But the rock that struck
the statue became a huge mountain[r]
and filled the whole earth.[s]

36"This was the dream, and now we
will interpret it to the king.[t] 37You, O
king, are the king of kings.[u] The God
of heaven has given you dominion[v]
and power and might and glory; 38in
your hands he has placed mankind and
the beasts of the field and the birds of
the air. Wherever they live, he has
made you ruler over them all.[w] You
are that head of gold.

39"After you, another kingdom will
rise, inferior to yours. Next, a third
kingdom, one of bronze, will rule over
the whole earth.[x] 40Finally, there will
be a fourth kingdom, strong as iron—
for iron breaks and smashes everything—and as iron breaks things to
pieces, so it will crush and break all
the others.[y] 41Just as you saw that the
feet and toes were partly of baked clay
and partly of iron, so this will be a divided kingdom; yet it will have some of
the strength of iron in it, even as you
saw iron mixed with clay. 42As the toes
were partly iron and partly clay, so this
kingdom will be partly strong and partly brittle. 43And just as you saw the
iron mixed with baked clay, so the people will be a mixture and will not remain united, any more than iron mixes
with clay.

44"In the time of those kings, the
God of heaven will set up a kingdom
that will never be destroyed, nor will it
be left to another people. It will
crush[z] all those kingdoms[a] and
bring them to an end, but it will itself
endure forever.[b] 45This is the meaning of the vision of the rock[c] cut out
of a mountain, but not by human
hands[d]—a rock that broke the iron,
the bronze, the clay, the silver and the
gold to pieces.

"The great God has shown the king
what will take place in the future.[e]
The dream is true[f] and the interpretation is trustworthy."

46Then King Nebuchadnezzar fell
prostrate[g] before Daniel and paid him
honor and ordered that an offering[h]
and incense be presented to him. 47The
king said to Daniel, "Surely your God
is the God of gods[i] and the Lord of
kings[j] and a revealer of mysteries,[k]
for you were able to reveal this mystery.[l]"

2:34 [n]S Job 12:19; Zec 4:6 [o]S Job 34:24 [p]ver 44-45; Ps 2:9; S Isa 60:12; Da 8:25 **2:35** [q]Ps 1:4; 37:10; S Isa 17:13; 41:15-16 [r]Isa 2:3; Mic 4:1 [s]Zec 12:3 **2:36** [t]S Ge 40:12 **2:37** [u]S Ezr 7:12 [v]S Jer 27:7; Da 4:26 **2:38** [w]S Jer 27:6; Da 4:21-22; 5:18 **2:39** [x]Da 7:5 **2:40** [y]Da 7:7,23

2:44 [z]S Ge 27:29; Ps 2:9; S 110:5; Mt 21:43-44; 1Co 15:24 [a]S 1Sa 9:20; Hag 2:22 [b]Ps 145:13; S Isa 9:7; Da 4:34; 6:26; 7:14,27; Ob 1:21; Mic 4:7, 13; S Lk 1:33; Rev 11:15 **2:45** [c]S Isa 28:16 [d]Da 8:25 [e]S Ge 41:25 [f]Rev 22:6 **2:46** [g]Da 8:17; Ac 10:25 [h]Ac 14:13 **2:47** [i]S Dt 10:17; Da 11:36 [j]Da 4:25; 1Ti 6:15 [k]S ver 22,28 [l]Da 4:9; 1Co 14:25

2:37–38 YOU ARE THAT HEAD OF GOLD. Nebuchadnezzar was the head of gold, representing the Neo-Babylonian empire (605–539 B.C.). After he died, the empire soon began to disintegrate.

2:39 INFERIOR TO YOURS. Nebuchadnezzar's kingdom would be followed by an inferior kingdom, represented by the silver chest and arms (v. 32); this kingdom would be the Medo-Persian empire established by Cyrus (539 B.C.). A third kingdom, symbolized by the bronze belly and thighs, represented the Greek empire established by Alexander the Great (330 B.C.).

2:40 A FOURTH KINGDOM, STRONG AS IRON. The iron kingdom (v. 33) represents the Roman empire, which began about 67 B.C. and subdued the world to a degree no empire had done previously.

2:41–43 PARTLY STRONG AND PARTLY BRITTLE. The feet of iron and clay probably represent the nationalistic states that have existed in the area of the Roman empire since that empire fell. Some of them have been strong and lasted a long time; others are brittle, breaking up again and again.

2:44–45 KINGDOM THAT WILL NEVER BE DESTROYED. In the dream, a rock cut out of the mountain, not by human hands, (i.e., supernaturally) struck the image on the feet. Not only were the feet destroyed, but the gold, silver, bronze, iron and clay all turned to powder and were swept away. (1) When Babylon gave way to Medo-Persia, the latter coalition remained part of the same image; the same was true of Greece and Rome and is still true of the modern nationalistic states. All are part of the same world system. Furthermore, we still have around us Babylonian astrology, Medo-Persian ethics, Greek art and philosophy, and both Roman law and the Roman idea that peace can be obtained by military might. According to Nebuchadnezzar's dream, the world order with its philosophy and values must be completely destroyed in order that Christ's kingdom may be fully established.

(2) The rock became a kingdom that filled the whole earth (v. 35). This fifth kingdom is God's kingdom established by Jesus the Messiah. It will fill the whole earth and extend to the new heaven and new earth (cf. Rev 21:1). We can be sure that the present world order will not last forever, but that God's kingdom will last forever (cf. 2Pe 3:10–13).

48Then the king placed Daniel in a
high[m] position and lavished many
gifts on him. He made him ruler over
the entire province of Babylon and
placed him in charge of all its wise
men.[n] **49**Moreover, at Daniel's request the king appointed Shadrach,
Meshach and Abednego administrators over the province of Babylon,[o]
while Daniel himself remained at the
royal court.[p]

The Image of Gold and the Fiery Furnace

3 King Nebuchadnezzar made an image[q] of gold, ninety feet high and
nine feet[g] wide, and set it up on the
plain of Dura in the province of Babylon. **2**He then summoned the satraps,[r] prefects, governors, advisers,
treasurers, judges, magistrates and all
the other provincial officials[s] to come
to the dedication of the image he had
set up. **3**So the satraps, prefects, governors, advisers, treasurers, judges,
magistrates and all the other provincial officials assembled for the dedication of the image that King Nebuchadnezzar had set up, and they stood
before it.

4Then the herald loudly proclaimed,
"This is what you are commanded to
do, O peoples, nations and men of every language:[t] **5**As soon as you hear
the sound of the horn, flute, zither,
lyre, harp,[u] pipes and all kinds of music, you must fall down and worship
the image[v] of gold that King Nebuchadnezzar has set up.[w] **6**Whoever
does not fall down and worship will immediately be thrown into a blazing furnace."[x]

7Therefore, as soon as they heard
the sound of the horn, flute, zither,
lyre, harp and all kinds of music, all
the peoples, nations and men of every
language fell down and worshiped the
image of gold that King Nebuchadnezzar had set up.[y]

8At this time some astrologers[h][z]
came forward and denounced the Jews.
9They said to King Nebuchadnezzar,
"O king, live forever![a] **10**You have issued a decree,[b] O king, that everyone
who hears the sound of the horn, flute,
zither, lyre, harp, pipes and all kinds of
music must fall down and worship the
image of gold,[c] **11**and that whoever
does not fall down and worship will be
thrown into a blazing furnace. **12**But
there are some Jews whom you have
set over the affairs of the province of
Babylon—Shadrach, Meshach and
Abednego[d]—who pay no attention[e]
to you, O king. They neither serve your
gods nor worship the image of gold you
have set up."[f]

13Furious[g] with rage, Nebuchadnezzar summoned Shadrach, Meshach
and Abednego. So these men were
brought before the king, **14**and Nebuchadnezzar said to them, "Is it true,
Shadrach, Meshach and Abednego,
that you do not serve my gods[h] or worship the image[i] of gold I have set up?
15Now when you hear the sound of the
horn, flute, zither, lyre, harp, pipes and
all kinds of music, if you are ready to
fall down and worship the image I
made, very good. But if you do not worship it, you will be thrown immediately
into a blazing furnace. Then what
god[j] will be able to rescue[k] you from
my hand?"

16Shadrach, Meshach and Abedne-

2:48 [m] S 2Ki 25:28 [n] S ver 6; S Est 8:2; S Da 1:20; 4:9; 5:11; 8:27 **2:49** [o] S Da 1:7; 3:30 [p] Da 6:2 **3:1** [q] ver 14; S Isa 46:6; Jer 16:20; Hab 2:19 **3:2** [r] S Est 1:1 [s] ver 27; Da 6:7 **3:4** [t] Da 4:1; 6:25; Rev 10:11 **3:5** [u] S Ge 4:21 [v] Rev 13:12 [w] ver 10,15 **3:6** [x] ver 11,15, 21; Jer 29:22; Da 5:19; 6:7; Mt 13:42,50; Rev 13:15 **3:7** [y] S ver 5 **3:8** [z] S Isa 19:3; S Da 2:10 **3:9** [a] S Ne 2:3; Da 5:10; 6:6 **3:10** [b] Da 6:12 [c] ver 4-6 **3:12** [d] S Da 2:49 [e] Da 6:13 [f] S Est 3:3 **3:13** [g] S Da 2:12 **3:14** [h] Isa 46:1; Jer 50:2 [i] S ver 1 **3:15** [j] S Isa 36:18-20 [k] S 2Ch 32:15

[g] 1 Aramaic *sixty cubits high and six cubits wide* (about 27 meters high and 2.7 meters wide) [h] 8 Or *Chaldeans*

3:1 AN IMAGE OF GOLD. Nebuchadnezzar may have carried out this proud act because, as had been revealed through Daniel (2:37–38), he was the head of gold on the statue in his dream. Nebuchadnezzar's empire had just risen to power, and he was undoubtedly trying to use religion to consolidate the many provinces he had added to his empire; he demanded worship of the image as a means of promoting loyalty to himself. He was not the first, nor will he be the last, world leader to try to use religion for political purposes or for self-exaltation.

3:2 THE DEDICATION OF THE IMAGE. At Daniel's request, his three friends were appointed by the king to positions of responsibility in Babylon's administration, while Daniel served in the king's court (2:49). Daniel may not have been present among the officials commanded to fall down and worship the gold image; he could have been traveling in the provinces at the time on a business trip for the king, or his responsibilities may have differed from those mentioned in this verse.

3:12 NEITHER SERVE YOUR GODS. Though the Bible teaches us to obey, honor and pray for those who rule over us (Ro 13:1–7; 1Ti 2:1–2; 1Pe 2:13–17), our first duty is to God himself. If we obey the first and greatest commandment—to love the one true God with all our hearts, souls, minds and strength (Dt 6:5; Mt 22:37–38)—we cannot worship or give divine honor to any false god or any image representing a god.

go[l] replied to the king, "O Nebuchadnezzar, we do not need to defend ourselves before you in this matter. **17**If
we are thrown into the blazing furnace,
the God we serve is able to save[m] us
from it, and he will rescue[n] us from
your hand, O king. **18**But even if he
does not, we want you to know, O king,
that we will not serve your gods or worship the image of gold you have set
up.[o]"
19Then Nebuchadnezzar was furious
with Shadrach, Meshach and Abednego, and his attitude toward them
changed. He ordered the furnace heat-
ed seven[p] times hotter than usual
20and commanded some of the strongest soldiers in his army to tie up Shadrach, Meshach and Abednego[q] and
throw them into the blazing furnace.
21So these men, wearing their robes,
trousers, turbans and other clothes,
were bound and thrown into the blazing furnace. **22**The king's command
was so urgent and the furnace so hot
that the flames of the fire killed the
soldiers who took up Shadrach, Meshach and Abednego,[r] **23**and these
three men, firmly tied, fell into the
blazing furnace.
24Then King Nebuchadnezzar
leaped to his feet in amazement and
asked his advisers, "Weren't there
three men that we tied up and threw
into the fire?"
They replied, "Certainly, O king."
25He said, "Look! I see four men
walking around in the fire, unbound
and unharmed, and the fourth looks
like a son of the gods."

3:16 [l]S Da 1:7
3:17 [m]S Ge 48:16; S Ps 18:48; 27:1-2 [n]S Job 5:19; Jer 1:8; Da 6:20
3:18 [o]ver 28; S Ex 1:17; S Jos 24:15
3:19 [p]Lev 26:18-28
3:20 [q]S Da 1:7
3:22 [r]S Da 1:7
3:26 [s]Da 4:2,34
3:27 [t]ver 2; Da 6:7 [u]Ps 91:3-11; S Isa 43:2; Heb 11:32-34 [v]Da 6:23
3:28 [w]S Ps 34:7; Da 6:22; Ac 5:19 [x]S Ps 97:10; Ac 12:11 [y]S Dt 31:20; S Job 13:15; S Ps 26:1; 84:12 [z]S ver 18
3:29 [a]Da 6:26 [b]S Ezr 6:11 [c]Da 6:27
3:30 [d]S Da 2:49
4:1 [e]S Da 3:4

26Nebuchadnezzar then approached
the opening of the blazing furnace and
shouted, "Shadrach, Meshach and
Abednego, servants of the Most High
God,[s] come out! Come here!"
So Shadrach, Meshach and Abedne-
go came out of the fire, **27**and the satraps, prefects, governors and royal
advisers[t] crowded around them.[u]
They saw that the fire[v] had not
harmed their bodies, nor was a hair of
their heads singed; their robes were
not scorched, and there was no smell
of fire on them. Da 6:1-23
28Then Nebuchadnezzar said,
"Praise be to the God of Shadrach, Meshach and Abednego, who has sent his
angel[w] and rescued[x] his servants!
They trusted[y] in him and defied the
king's command and were willing to
give up their lives rather than serve or
worship any god except their own
God.[z] **29**Therefore I decree[a] that the
people of any nation or language who
say anything against the God of Shadrach, Meshach and Abednego be cut
into pieces and their houses be turned
into piles of rubble,[b] for no other god
can save[c] in this way."
30Then the king promoted Shadrach, Meshach and Abednego in the
province of Babylon.[d]

Nebuchadnezzar's Dream of a Tree

4 King Nebuchadnezzar,
To the peoples, nations and
men of every language,[e] who live
in all the world:

3:17–18 GOD WE SERVE IS ABLE TO SAVE US. Neither the jealous insinuations of the astrologers nor the ugly threats of King Nebuchadnezzar frightened these three young men into compromising their personal convictions. Instead, they gave bold and unhesitating witness to their allegiance to the one true God. They had a hope and a faith that were fixed on him who was their refuge and strength (Ps 46:1; 56:4). They also knew that God's wrath against sin and disobedience was far worse than human wrath (cf. Lev 26; Dt 28). Thus, as an expression of unconditional faith, complete trust and total loyalty to God, they said, "But even if he does not." They possessed a faith that trusted and obeyed God regardless of the consequences. Obedience and persevering trust in God, and not necessarily the experience of deliverance, give true evidence of Biblical faith. Like many of the great saints of the Bible, these three friends had their faith greatly tested.

3:24–25 THE FOURTH LOOKS LIKE A SON OF THE GODS. The fourth man could have been an angel or a preincarnate manifestation of Christ sent to protect Daniel's three friends and be with them in their time of great trial. Note that the meaning of the three youths' Hebrew names correspond to the deliverance God gave them. "The LORD showed grace" (Hananiah) to them and "the LORD helped" (Azariah) them. The form of the fourth man in the fire was as one "who is equal to God" (Mishael; see 1:7, note).

3:30 SHADRACH, MESHACH AND ABEDNEGO. These three men who remained true to God even at the possible cost of their lives serve to condemn the spiritual and moral compromise of those who use contemporary influences and customs as an excuse for their worldly actions. God does not accept the reasoning that we may do something simply because "everyone is doing it." We should diligently ask God to put a firm determination within our hearts to remain true to him and his Word, regardless of the consequences.

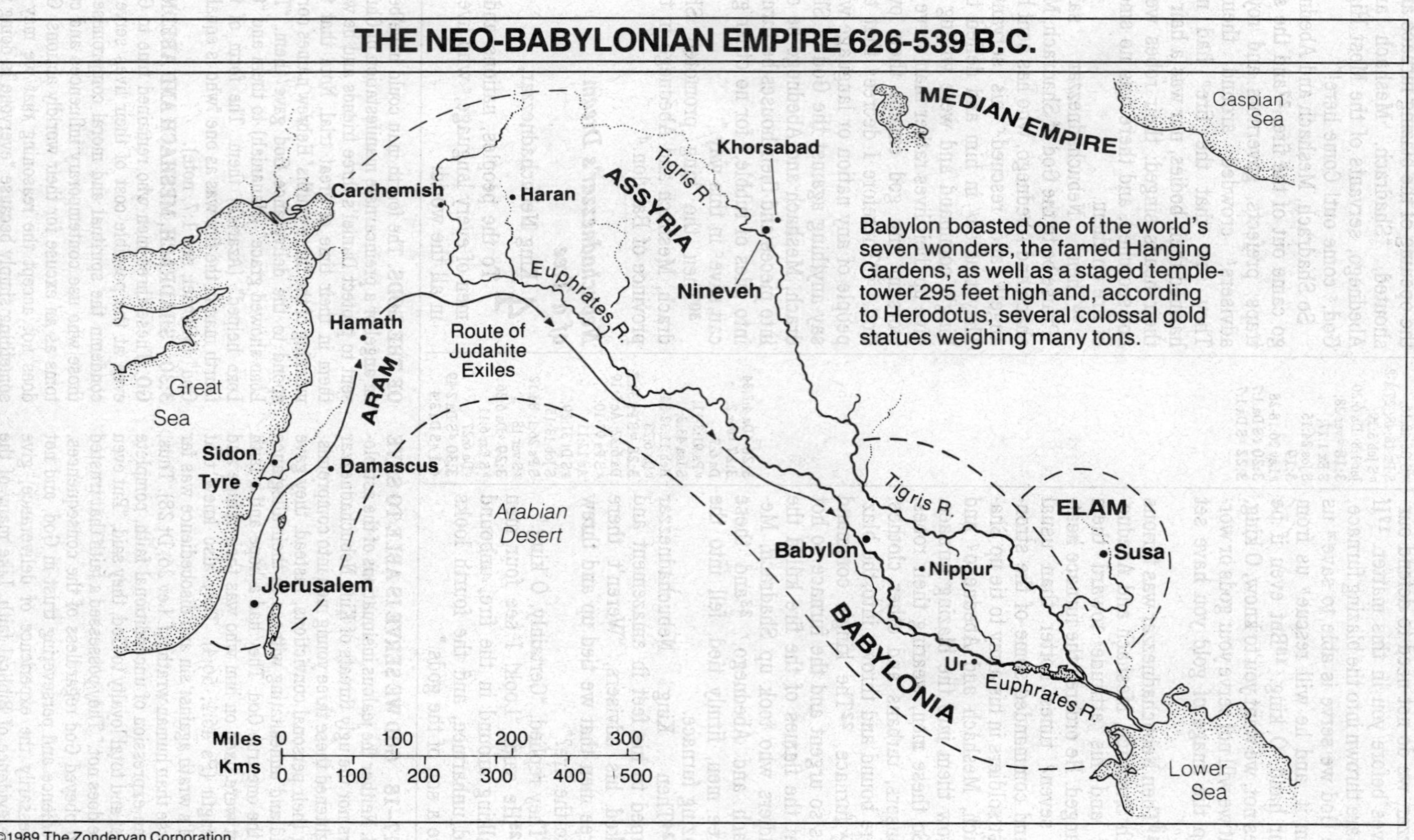
THE NEO-BABYLONIAN EMPIRE 626-539 B.C.
Caspian Sea
MEDIAN EMPIRE
Khorsabad
Tigris R.
ASSYRIA
Carchemish
Haran
Nineveh
Babylon boasted one of the world's seven wonders, the famed Hanging Gardens, as well as a staged temple-tower 295 feet high and, according to Herodotus, several colossal gold statues weighing many tons.
Euphrates R.
Hamath
Route of Judahite Exiles
ARAM
Great Sea
Sidon
Tyre
Damascus
Arabian Desert
Tigris R.
ELAM
Babylon
Nippur
Susa
Jerusalem
BABYLONIA
Ur
Euphrates R.
Miles 0 100 200 300
Kms 0 100 200 300 400 500
Lower Sea

May you prosper greatly![f]

[2]It is my pleasure to tell you
about the miraculous signs[g] and
wonders that the Most High
God[h] has performed for me.

[3]How great are his signs,
how mighty his wonders![i]
His kingdom is an eternal
kingdom;
his dominion endures[j]
from generation to
generation.

[4]I, Nebuchadnezzar, was at
home in my palace, contented[k]
and prosperous. [5]I had a dream[l]
that made me afraid. As I was lying in my bed,[m] the images and
visions that passed through my
mind[n] terrified me.[o] [6]So I commanded that all the wise men of
Babylon be brought before me to
interpret[p] the dream for me.
[7]When the magicians,[q] enchanters, astrologers[i] and diviners[r]
came, I told them the dream, but
they could not interpret it for
me.[s] [8]Finally, Daniel came into
my presence and I told him the
dream. (He is called Belteshazzar,[t] after the name of my god,
and the spirit of the holy gods[u] is
in him.)

[9]I said, "Belteshazzar, chief[v]
of the magicians, I know that the
spirit of the holy gods[w] is in you,
and no mystery is too difficult for
you. Here is my dream; interpret
it for me. [10]These are the visions
I saw while lying in my bed:[x] I
looked, and there before me stood
a tree in the middle of the land. Its
height was enormous.[y] [11]The
tree grew large and strong and its
top touched the sky; it was visible
to the ends of the earth.[z] [12]Its
leaves were beautiful, its fruit
abundant, and on it was food for
all. Under it the beasts of the field
found shelter, and the birds of the
air lived in its branches;[a] from it
every creature was fed.

[13]"In the visions I saw while lying in my bed,[b] I looked, and
there before me was a messenger,[j] a holy one,[c] coming down
from heaven. [14]He called in a loud
voice: 'Cut down the tree[d] and
trim off its branches; strip off its
leaves and scatter its fruit. Let
the animals flee from under it and
the birds from its branches.[e]
[15]But let the stump and its roots,
bound with iron and bronze, remain in the ground, in the grass of
the field.

" 'Let him be drenched with the
dew of heaven, and let him live
with the animals among the
plants of the earth. [16]Let his mind
be changed from that of a man and
let him be given the mind of an
animal, till seven times[k] pass by
for him.[f]

[17]" 'The decision is announced
by messengers, the holy ones declare the verdict, so that the living
may know that the Most High[g] is
sovereign[h] over the kingdoms of
men and gives them to anyone he
wishes and sets over them the
lowliest[i] of men.'

[18]"This is the dream that I,
King Nebuchadnezzar, had. Now,
Belteshazzar, tell me what it
means, for none of the wise men
in my kingdom can interpret it for
me.[j] But you can,[k] because the

4:1 [f]Da 6:25
4:2 [g]Ps 74:9
[h]S Da 3:26
4:3 [i]S Ps 105:27; Da 6:27 [j]Da 2:44
4:4 [k]Ps 30:6; S Isa 32:9
4:5 [l]S Da 2:1
[m]Ps 4:4 [n]Da 2:28
[o]ver 19; S Ge 41:8; S Job 3:26; Da 2:3; 5:6
4:6 [p]Da 2:2
4:7 [q]S Ge 41:8
[r]S Isa 44:25; S Da 2:2
[s]S Da 2:10
4:8 [t]S Da 1:7
[u]S Ge 41:38
4:9 [v]Da 2:48
[w]Da 5:11-12
4:10 [x]S ver 5; Ps 4:4
[y]Eze 31:3-4
4:11
[z]S Eze 19:11; 31:5
4:12
[a]S Eze 17:23; S Mt 13:32
4:13 [b]ver 10; Da 7:1 [c]S ver 23; S Dt 33:2
4:14 [d]S Job 24:20
[e]S Eze 31:12; S Mt 3:10
4:16 [f]ver 23,32
4:17 [g]ver 2,25; Ps 83:18
[h]S Ps 103:19; Jer 27:5-7; Da 2:21; 5:18-21; Ro 13:1
[i]Da 11:21; Mt 23:12
4:18 [j]S Ge 41:8; Da 5:8,15
[k]S Ge 41:15

[i]7 Or *Chaldeans* [j]13 Or *watchman*; also in verses 17 and 23 [k]16 Or *years*; also in verses 23, 25 and 32

4:1–3 SIGNS AND WONDERS. Nebuchadnezzar testifies to God's greatness and power. He came to this conviction after his humbling experience of insanity described in this chapter.

4:9 CHIEF OF THE MAGICIANS. "Magicians" (Aramaic, *hartumaya*) actually refers to the learned scribes who copied and understood the most ancient cuneiform writings; some of these people did make use of magic formulas. However, the king recognized that Daniel's knowledge and ability were supernaturally given and not derived from the things he may have read in ancient pagan lore.

4:10 A TREE. See v. 22 for the symbolism Daniel saw in this tree.

4:16 THE MIND OF AN ANIMAL, TILL SEVEN TIMES PASS BY. At this point the picture changes from that of a felled tree to that of a living being. This being was to lose his own mind, or reasoning powers, and be given the mind of an animal. This loss of reason was to last "seven times," which probably means seven seasons (i.e., three and one-half years, since there were essentially only two seasons, a wet season and a dry one).

4:17 THE MOST HIGH IS SOVEREIGN. The king needed to learn that the Lord God is all-powerful and can place whomever he wants over the kingdoms of the world.

spirit of the holy gods[l] is in
you."[m]

Daniel Interprets the Dream

19Then Daniel (also called Belteshazzar) was greatly perplexed
for a time, and his thoughts terrified[n] him. So the king said, "Belteshazzar, do not let the dream or
its meaning alarm you."[o]
Belteshazzar answered, "My
lord, if only the dream applied to
your enemies and its meaning to
your adversaries! 20The tree you
saw, which grew large and strong,
with its top touching the sky, visible to the whole earth, 21with
beautiful leaves and abundant
fruit, providing food for all, giving
shelter to the beasts of the field,
and having nesting places in its
branches for the birds of the
air[p]— 22you, O king, are that
tree![q] You have become great
and strong; your greatness has
grown until it reaches the sky,
and your dominion extends to distant parts of the earth.[r]
23"You, O king, saw a messenger, a holy one,[s] coming down
from heaven and saying, 'Cut
down the tree and destroy it, but
leave the stump, bound with iron
and bronze, in the grass of the
field, while its roots remain in the
ground. Let him be drenched with
the dew of heaven; let him live
like the wild animals, until seven
times pass by for him.'[t][u]
24"This is the interpretation, O
king, and this is the decree[v] the
Most High has issued against my
lord the king: 25You will be driven
away from people and will live
with the wild animals; you will eat
grass like cattle and be
drenched[w] with the dew of heav-
en. Seven times will pass by for
you until you acknowledge that
the Most High[x] is sovereign over
the kingdoms of men and gives
them to anyone he wishes.[y]
26The command to leave the
stump of the tree with its roots[z]
means that your kingdom will be
restored to you when you acknowledge that Heaven rules.[a]
27Therefore, O king, be pleased to
accept my advice: Renounce your
sins by doing what is right, and
your wickedness by being kind to
the oppressed.[b] It may be that
then your prosperity[c] will continue.[d]"

The Dream Is Fulfilled

28All this happened[e] to King
Nebuchadnezzar. 29Twelve
months later, as the king was
walking on the roof of the royal
palace of Babylon, 30he said, "Is
not this the great Babylon I have
built as the royal residence, by my
mighty power and for the glory[f]
of my majesty?"[g]
31The words were still on his
lips when a voice came from heav-
en, "This is what is decreed for
you, King Nebuchadnezzar: Your
royal authority has been taken
from you.[h] 32You will be driven
away from people and will live
with the wild animals; you will eat
grass like cattle. Seven times will
pass by for you until you acknowledge that the Most High is sovereign over the kingdoms of men
and gives them to anyone he
wishes."[i]
33Immediately what had been
said about Nebuchadnezzar was
fulfilled. He was driven away from
people and ate grass like cattle.
His body was drenched[j] with the
dew of heaven until his hair grew
like the feathers of an eagle and
his nails like the claws of a bird.[k]
34At the end of that time, I,
Nebuchadnezzar, raised my eyes
toward heaven, and my sanity[l]
was restored. Then I praised the
Most High; I honored and glorified him who lives forever.[m]

4:18 [l]S Ge 41:38 [m]ver 7-9; S Da 1:20 **4:19** [n]S ver 5; S Ge 41:8; Da 7:15,28; 8:27; 10:16-17 [o]S Ge 40:12 **4:21** [p]S Eze 31:6 **4:22** [q]S 2Sa 12:7 [r]Jer 27:7; Da 5:18-19 **4:23** [s]ver 13; Da 8:13 [t]Da 5:21 [u]S Eze 31:3-4 **4:24** [v]Job 40:12; Ps 107:40; Jer 40:2 **4:25** [w]S Job 24:8 [x]S ver 17 [y]Jer 27:5; S Da 2:47; 5:21 **4:26** [z]ver 15 [a]S Da 2:37 **4:27** [b]Isa 55:6-7 [c]Jer 29:7 [d]S Dt 24:13; 1Ki 21:29; S Ps 41:3; S Pr 28:13; S Eze 18:22 **4:28** [e]Nu 23:19 **4:30** [f]Isa 13:19 [g]S Isa 10:13; S 37:24-25; Da 5:20; Hab 1:11; 2:4 **4:31** [h]S 2Sa 22:28; Da 5:20 **4:32** [i]S Job 9:12 **4:33** [j]S Job 24:8 [k]Da 5:20-21 **4:34** [l]S Job 12:20 [m]Da 12:7

4:27 RENOUNCE YOUR SINS BY DOING WHAT IS RIGHT. The very fact that Daniel called for the king to repent indicates that God's terrible judgment could be avoided. If Nebuchadnezzar would forsake his sins and turn to a righteous lifestyle, being kind to the poor and downtrodden whom he had oppressed, God would not carry out what he had revealed in the dream.

4:34–37 MY SANITY WAS RESTORED. Seven is a number of completion, so at the end of the seven seasons, Nebuchadnezzar's sanity was restored. He not only understood what had happened to him, but he also recognized the power, greatness and sovereignty of Daniel's God, the Lord God of Israel.

His dominion is an eternal
dominion;
his kingdom[n] endures from
generation to generation.[o]
35All the peoples of the earth
are regarded as nothing.[p]
He does as he pleases[q]
with the powers of heaven
and the peoples of the earth.
No one can hold back[r] his hand[s]
or say to him: "What have you
done?"[t]

36At the same time that my
sanity was restored, my honor
and splendor were returned to me
for the glory of my kingdom.[u] My
advisers and nobles sought me
out, and I was restored to my
throne and became even greater
than before. **37**Now I, Nebuchadnezzar, praise and exalt[v] and
glorify[w] the King of heaven, because everything he does is right
and all his ways are just.[x] And
those who walk in pride[y] he is
able to humble.[z]

The Writing on the Wall

5 King Belshazzar[a] gave a great
banquet[b] for a thousand of his nobles[c] and drank wine with them.
2While Belshazzar was drinking[d] his
wine, he gave orders to bring in the
gold and silver goblets[e] that Nebuchadnezzar his father[1] had taken
from the temple in Jerusalem, so that
the king and his nobles, his wives and
his concubines[f] might drink from
them.[g] **3**So they brought in the gold
goblets that had been taken from the
temple of God in Jerusalem, and the
king and his nobles, his wives and his
concubines drank from them. **4**As they
drank the wine, they praised the
gods[h] of gold and silver, of bronze,
iron, wood and stone.[i]

5Suddenly the fingers of a human
hand appeared and wrote on the plaster of the wall, near the lampstand in
the royal palace. The king watched the

4:34 [n]Isa 37:16 [o]Ps 145:13; S Da 2:44; 5:21; 6:26; Lk 1:33
4:35 [p]S Isa 40:17 [q]Dt 21:8; Ps 115:3; S 135:6; Jnh 1:14 [r]S Isa 14:27 [s]S Dt 32:39 [t]S Job 9:4; S Isa 14:24; S 45:9; Da 5:21; Ro 9:20
4:36 [u]S Pr 22:4; Da 5:18
4:37 [v]S Ex 15:2 [w]S Ps 34:3 [x]Dt 32:4; Ps 33:4-5 [y]Ps 18:27; S 119:21 [z]S Job 31:4; 40:11-12; S Isa 13:11; Da 5:20,23; Mt 23:12
5:1 [a]ver 30; Da 7:1; 8:1 [b]S 1Ki 3:15 [c]Jer 50:35
5:2 [d]S Isa 21:5 [e]S 2Ki 24:13; S 2Ch 36:10; S Jer 52:19 [f]S Est 2:14 [g]S Est 1:7; Da 1:2
5:4 [h]Jdg 16:24 [i]S Est 1:10; Ps 135:15-18; Hab 2:19; Rev 9:20
5:6 [j]S Job 4:15 [k]S Da 4:5 [l]S Isa 7:2 [m]S Ps 22:14; Eze 7:17
5:7 [n]S Ge 41:8 [o]S Isa 19:3 [p]Isa 44:25 [q]Jer 50:35; Da 4:6-7 [r]S Ge 41:42 [s]Est 10:3 [t]Da 2:5-6,48
5:8 [u]S Ex 8:18 [v]S Da 2:10,27; S 4:18
5:9 [w]S Ps 48:5; S Isa 21:4
5:10 [x]S Ne 2:3; S Da 3:9
5:11 [y]S Ge 41:38 [z]ver 14; S Da 1:17 [a]S Da 2:22 [b]Da 2:47-48
5:12 [c]S Da 1:7 [d]S Nu 12:8 [e]ver 14-16; Da 6:3 [f]S Eze 28:3
5:13 [g]S Est 2:5-6; Da 6:13
5:14 [h]S Ge 41:38

hand as it wrote. **6**His face turned
pale[j] and he was so frightened[k] that
his knees knocked[l] together and his
legs gave way.[m]

7The king called out for the enchanters,[n] astrologers[m][o] and diviners[p]
to be brought and said to these wise[q]
men of Babylon, "Whoever reads this
writing and tells me what it means will
be clothed in purple and have a gold
chain placed around his neck,[r] and he
will be made the third[s] highest ruler
in the kingdom."[t]

8Then all the king's wise men[u]
came in, but they could not read the
writing or tell the king what it
meant.[v] **9**So King Belshazzar became
even more terrified[w] and his face grew
more pale. His nobles were baffled.

10The queen,[n] hearing the voices of
the king and his nobles, came into the
banquet hall. "O king, live forever!"[x]
she said. "Don't be alarmed! Don't look
so pale! **11**There is a man in your kingdom who has the spirit of the holy
gods[y] in him. In the time of your father he was found to have insight and
intelligence and wisdom[z] like that of
the gods.[a] King Nebuchadnezzar your
father—your father the king, I say—
appointed him chief of the magicians,
enchanters, astrologers and diviners.[b] **12**This man Daniel, whom the
king called Belteshazzar,[c] was found
to have a keen mind and knowledge
and understanding, and also the ability
to interpret dreams, explain riddles[d]
and solve difficult problems.[e] Call for
Daniel, and he will tell you what the
writing means.[f]"

13So Daniel was brought before the
king, and the king said to him, "Are
you Daniel, one of the exiles my father
the king brought from Judah?[g] **14**I
have heard that the spirit of the gods[h]
is in you and that you have insight, in-

[1] *2* Or *ancestor*; or *predecessor*; also in verses 11, 13 and 18 [m] *7* Or *Chaldeans*; also in verse 11 [n] *10* Or *queen mother*

5:1 BELSHAZZAR GAVE A GREAT BANQUET. Nebuchadnezzar's brilliant reign lasted 44 years; after his death, Babylon's glory began to decline. Though the empire lasted another 22 years, revolutions and assassinations weakened it. The last Babylonian kings were Nabonidus and his oldest son Belshazzar, who served together as co-regents.

5:2 NEBUCHADNEZZAR HIS FATHER. "Father" is used here in the general sense of an ancestor or predecessor, not one's biological parent (see NIV text note).

5:3 GOLD GOBLETS THAT HAD BEEN TAKEN FROM THE TEMPLE. By drinking from the Lord's sacred vessels in honor of Babylon's pagan gods, Belshazzar and his nobles dishonored the one true God and brought final judgment upon themselves (vv. 22–24).

telligence and outstanding wisdom.[i]
15The wise men and enchanters were
brought before me to read this writing
and tell me what it means, but they
could not explain it.[j] 16Now I have
heard that you are able to give interpretations and to solve difficult problems.[k] If you can read this writing and
tell me what it means, you will be
clothed in purple and have a gold chain
placed around your neck,[l] and you
will be made the third highest ruler in
the kingdom."
17Then Daniel answered the king,
"You may keep your gifts for yourself
and give your rewards to someone
else.[n] Nevertheless, I will read the
writing for the king and tell him what
it means.
18"O king, the Most High God gave
your father Nebuchadnezzar[o] sovereignty and greatness and glory and
splendor.[p] 19Because of the high position he gave him, all the peoples and
nations and men of every language
dreaded and feared him. Those the
king wanted to put to death, he put to
death;[q] those he wanted to spare, he
spared; those he wanted to promote,
he promoted; and those he wanted to
humble, he humbled.[r] 20But when his
heart became arrogant and hardened
with pride,[s] he was deposed from his
royal throne[t] and stripped[u] of his
glory.[v] 21He was driven away from
people and given the mind of an animal; he lived with the wild donkeys and
ate grass like cattle; and his body was
drenched with the dew of heaven, until
he acknowledged that the Most High
God is sovereign[w] over the kingdoms
of men and sets over them anyone he
wishes.[x]

5:14 [i] S Da 2:22
5:15 [j] S Da 4:18
5:16 [k] S Ge 41:15 [l] S Ge 41:42
5:17 [m] S Est 5:3; S Da 2:6 [n] S 2Ki 5:16
5:18 [o] S Jer 28:14 [p] S Jer 27:7; S Da 2:37-38; S 4:36
5:19 [q] Da 2:12-13; S 3:6 [r] S Da 4:22
5:20 [s] Da 4:30 [t] Jer 43:10 [u] Jer 13:18; S Da 4:31 [v] S Job 40:12; Isa 14:13-15; Eze 31:10-11; Da 8:8
5:21 [w] S Eze 17:24 [x] Da 4:16-17,35
5:22 [y] S Ex 10:3
5:23 [z] S Isa 14:13; S Jer 50:29 [a] Jer 44:9 [b] Ps 115:4-8; Hab 2:19; Rev 9:20 [c] Job 12:10; Ac 17:28 [d] S Job 31:4; S Isa 13:11; Jer 10:23; S 48:26
5:26 [e] Jer 27:7 [f] Isa 13:6
5:27 [g] S Job 6:2 [h] Ps 62:9
5:28 [i] Isa 13:17 [j] S Jer 27:7; 50:41-43; Da 6:28
5:29 [k] S Ge 41:42 [l] S Da 2:6

22"But you his son,[o] O Belshazzar,
have not humbled[y] yourself, though
you knew all this. 23Instead, you have
set yourself up against[z] the Lord of
heaven. You had the goblets from his
temple brought to you, and you and
your nobles, your wives[a] and your
concubines drank wine from them. You
praised the gods of silver and gold, of
bronze, iron, wood and stone, which
cannot see or hear or understand.[b]
But you did not honor the God who
holds in his hand your life[c] and all
your ways.[d] 24Therefore he sent the
hand that wrote the inscription.
25"This is the inscription that was
written:

MENE, MENE, TEKEL, PARSIN[p]

26"This is what these words mean:

Mene[q]: God has numbered
the days[e] of your reign
and brought it to an
end.[f]
27*Tekel*[r]: You have been
weighed on the scales[g]
and found wanting.[h]
28*Peres*[s]: Your kingdom is
divided and given to
the Medes[i] and Per-
sians."[j]

29Then at Belshazzar's command,
Daniel was clothed in purple, a gold
chain was placed around his neck,[k]
and he was proclaimed the third highest ruler in the kingdom.[l]

[o] 22 Or *descendant*; or *successor*
[p] 25 Aramaic *UPARSIN* (that is, *AND PARSIN*)
[q] 26 *Mene* can mean *numbered* or *mina* (a unit of money).
[r] 27 *Tekel* can mean *weighed* or *shekel*.
[s] 28 *Peres* (the singular of *Parsin*) can mean *divided* or *Persia* or *a half mina* or *a half shekel*.

5:22 NOT HUMBLED YOURSELF, THOUGH YOU KNEW ALL THIS. Daniel reminded Belshazzar of how God had humbled Nebuchadnezzar. Though Belshazzar surely had heard about this tragic event, he refused to learn anything from it. His desecration of the Lord's holy articles was a deliberate act of defiance toward the living God. Few people learn the lessons of history. Allegiance to the things of this world—the cravings of the sinful nature, the lust of the eyes, and the spirit of arrogance and independence (cf. 1Jn 2:15–17; see article on THE CHRISTIAN'S RELATIONSHIP TO THE WORLD, p. 1976)—lead them along the same broad road to destruction that others before them have taken (cf. Mt 7:13–14).

5:26 GOD HAS NUMBERED THE DAYS. "MENE" was written twice by the hand, for it had a twofold meaning: "numbered" and "tested." Daniel's interpretation was surprisingly simple: God had tested the kingdom of Babylon and found it to be wanting, and therefore numbered its days.

5:27 WEIGHED ON THE SCALES AND FOUND WANTING. The term "wanting" here means "defective" or "of poor quality." Belshazzar had been weighed on heaven's scales and was found seriously defective according to God's standard of measurement.

5:28 DIVIDED AND GIVEN TO THE MEDES AND PERSIANS. Note that v. 25 has "PARSIN" (see NIV text note—"UPARSIN"). "U" is Aramaic for "and"; "parsin" is the Aramaic plural of "peres," which has two meanings: "division" and "Persia." It signified the division of the kingdom of Babylon and its conquest by the Persians and the Medes.

30That very night Belshazzar,[m]
king[n] of the Babylonians,[t] was
slain,[o] 31and Darius[p] the Mede[q]
took over the kingdom, at the age of
sixty-two.

Daniel in the Den of Lions

6 It pleased Darius[r] to appoint 120
satraps[s] to rule throughout the
kingdom, 2with three administrators
over them, one of whom was Daniel.[t]
The satraps were made accountable[u]
to them so that the king might not suffer loss. 3Now Daniel so distinguished
himself among the administrators and
the satraps by his exceptional qualities
that the king planned to set him over
the whole kingdom.[v] 4At this, the administrators and the satraps tried to
find grounds for charges[w] against
Daniel in his conduct of government affairs, but they were unable to do so.
They could find no corruption in him,
because he was trustworthy and neither corrupt nor negligent. 5Finally
these men said, "We will never find any
basis for charges against this man
Daniel unless it has something to do
with the law of his God."[x]
6So the administrators and the satraps went as a group to the king and
said: "O King Darius, live forever![y]
7The royal administrators, prefects,
satraps, advisers and governors[z]
have all agreed that the king should
issue an edict and enforce the decree
that anyone who prays to any god or
man during the next thirty days, except to you, O king, shall be thrown
into the lions' den.[a] 8Now, O king, issue the decree and put it in writing so
that it cannot be altered—in accordance with the laws of the Medes and
Persians, which cannot be repealed."[b]
9So King Darius put the decree in writing.
10Now when Daniel learned that the
decree had been published, he went
home to his upstairs room where the
windows opened toward[c] Jerusalem.
Three times a day he got down on his
knees[d] and prayed, giving thanks to
his God, just as he had done before.[e]
11Then these men went as a group and
found Daniel praying and asking God
for help.[f] 12So they went to the king
and spoke to him about his royal decree: "Did you not publish a decree that

5:30 [m] S ver 1 [n] Jer 50:35 [o] S Isa 21:9; S Jer 51:31
5:31 [p] Jer 50:41; Da 6:1; 9:1; 11:1 [q] S Isa 13:3
6:1 [r] S Da 5:31 [s] S Est 1:1
6:2 [t] Da 2:48-49 [u] Ezr 4:22
6:3 [v] S Ge 41:41; S Est 10:3; S Da 1:20; 5:12-14
6:4 [w] Jer 20:10
6:5 [x] Ac 24:13-16
6:6 [y] S Ne 2:3
6:7 [z] S Da 3:2 [a] Ps 59:3; 64:2-6; S Da 3:6
6:8 [b] S Est 1:19
6:10 [c] S 1Ki 8:29 [d] Ps 95:6 [e] Mt 6:6; Ac 5:29
6:11 [f] 1Ki 8:48-50; Ps 55:17; 1Th 5:17-18

[t] 30 Or *Chaldeans*

5:30 BELSHAZZAR . . . WAS SLAIN. Both Babylonian and Persian records indicate that when the Medo-Persian army approached Babylon, the people swung open the gates to admit his army without resistance. Belshazzar may have been the only one killed. A little later Cyrus entered the city and was hailed as the deliverer from the tyranny of Nabonidus and Belshazzar.

5:31 DARIUS THE MEDE TOOK OVER THE KINGDOM. It is possible that "Darius" was a title Cyrus adopted when he took over Babylon; alternatively, it may have been another name for Gubaru, whom Cyrus appointed as his subordinate and who continued to rule in Babylon for some time after Cyrus died.

6:3 TO SET HIM OVER THE WHOLE KINGDOM. Daniel was the foremost of three administrators who assisted Darius in ruling the empire. Because of Daniel's "exceptional qualities," which included an extraordinary intelligence, the king planned to give him a new position above all the other administrators and satraps. It was due to God's goodness that at 80 years of age his mind was still sharp and his abilities undiminished (cf. Moses, Caleb and Joshua at age 80—Ex 7:7; Dt 34:7; Jos 14:10–11; 24:29).

6:5 AGAINST THIS MAN DANIEL UNLESS. Daniel's enemies had no hope of accusing him of wrongdoing; their only hope of condemning him would be to require something that had official government sanction and conflicted with Daniel's loyalty to God and his word. This same strategy will be used by Satan against God's faithful people during the antichrist's rule at the end of time. In order to find any ground on which to accuse God's people, he will create a situation where there is conflict between God's laws and official government requirements; thus the antichrist will set up an image and command that it be worshiped as deity (cf. 3:1–6; see 2Th 2:1–12; see article on THE AGE OF THE ANTICHRIST, p. 1872).

6:7 HAVE ALL AGREED. Jealous because of Daniel's promotion, those under him plotted to make an issue of Daniel's faithfulness to the law of his God. They agreed together to get Darius to issue a decree that they knew Daniel would not obey; his act of disobedience would force the king to command the death penalty. Daniel's uncompromising loyalty to God and his word is a good example for all believers. We should demonstrate integrity and do superior work even in the most difficult situations without compromising our Biblical convictions; in this way God will be honored.

6:10 DANIEL . . . PRAYED, GIVING THANKS. The king's decree did not cause Daniel to become timid and change his habit of praying; his windows remained open toward Jerusalem where the temple once stood (cf. 2Ch 6:21). Though he knew of the danger, he did not let anything keep him from presenting his petitions to God (cf. Php 4:6). Likewise, we must not let anything cause us to neglect our daily prayer and devotion to God.

during the next thirty days anyone who
prays to any god or man except to you,
O king, would be thrown into the lions'
den?"
The king answered, "The decree
stands—in accordance with the laws
of the Medes and Persians, which cannot be repealed."[g]
13Then they said to the king, "Daniel, who is one of the exiles from Judah,[h] pays no attention[i] to you, O
king, or to the decree you put in writing. He still prays three times a day."
14When the king heard this, he was
greatly distressed;[j] he was determined to rescue Daniel and made every
effort until sundown to save him.
15Then the men went as a group to
the king and said to him, "Remember,
O king, that according to the law of the
Medes and Persians no decree or edict
that the king issues can be changed."[k]
16So the king gave the order, and
they brought Daniel and threw him into
the lions' den.[l] The king said to Daniel, "May your God, whom you serve
continually, rescue[m] you!"
17A stone was brought and placed
over the mouth of the den, and the king
sealed[n] it with his own signet ring and
with the rings of his nobles, so that
Daniel's situation might not be
changed. **18**Then the king returned to
his palace and spent the night without
eating[o] and without any entertainment being brought to him. And he
could not sleep.[p]
19At the first light of dawn, the king
got up and hurried to the lions' den.
20When he came near the den, he
called to Daniel in an anguished voice,
"Daniel, servant of the living God, has
your God, whom you serve continually,
been able to rescue you from the lions?"[q]
21Daniel answered, "O king, live forever![r] **22**My God sent his angel,[s] and
he shut the mouths of the lions.[t] They
have not hurt me, because I was found
innocent in his sight.[u] Nor have I ever
done any wrong before you, O king."
23The king was overjoyed and gave
orders to lift Daniel out of the den. And
when Daniel was lifted from the den,
no wound[v] was found on him, because
he had trusted[w] in his God.
24At the king's command, the men
who had falsely accused Daniel were
brought in and thrown into the lions'
den,[x] along with their wives and children.[y] And before they reached the
floor of the den, the lions overpowered
them and crushed all their bones.[z]
25Then King Darius wrote to all the
peoples, nations and men of every language[a] throughout the land:

"May you prosper greatly![b]

26"I issue a decree that in every
part of my kingdom people must
fear and reverence[c] the God of
Daniel.[d]

"For he is the living God[e]
and he endures forever;[f]
his kingdom will not be destroyed,
his dominion will never end.[g]
27He rescues and he saves;[h]
he performs signs and
wonders[i]
in the heavens and on the earth.
He has rescued Daniel
from the power of the lions."[j]

28So Daniel prospered during the
reign of Darius and the reign of Cyrus[u][k] the Persian.[l]

Daniel's Dream of Four Beasts

7 In the first year of Belshazzar[m]
king of Babylon, Daniel had a

6:12 [g]S Est 1:19; Da 3:8-12 **6:13** [h]S Eze 14:14; Da 2:25 [i]S Est 3:8 **6:14** [j]Mk 6:26 **6:15** [k]S Est 8:8 **6:16** [l]S ver 7 [m]S Job 5:19; Ps 37:39-40; S 97:10 **6:17** [n]Mt 27:66 **6:18** [o]S 2Sa 12:17; Da 10:3 [p]S Est 6:1 **6:20** [q]S Da 3:17 **6:21** [r]S Ne 2:3; Da 3:9 **6:22** [s]S Ge 32:1; S Da 3:28 [t]ver 27; Ps 91:11-13; Heb 11:33 [u]Ac 12:11; 2Ti 4:17 **6:23** [v]Da 3:27 [w]S 1Ch 5:20; S Isa 12:2 **6:24** [x]Dt 19:18-19; Est 7:9-10; Ps 54:5 [y]Dt 24:16; 2Ki 14:6 [z]S Isa 38:13 **6:25** [a]S Da 3:4 [b]Da 4:1 **6:26** [c]S Ps 5:7 [d]S Est 8:17; Ps 99:1-3; Da 3:29 [e]S Jos 2:11; S 3:10 [f]S Jer 10:10; Da 12:7; Rev 1:18 [g]S Da 2:44 **6:27** [h]Da 3:29 [i]S Da 4:3 [j]S ver 22 **6:28** [k]S 2Ch 36:22; S Da 1:21 [l]S Da 5:28 **7:1** [m]S Da 5:1

[u]28 Or *Darius, that is, the reign of Cyrus*

6:17 A STONE ... PLACED OVER THE MOUTH OF THE DEN. The den of lions was underground, with an opening at the top. A large flat stone was laid over the opening, and the king's seal meant it could not be opened without his authorization. Because of Daniel's integrity (v. 4) and his "exceptional qualities" (v. 3), the king had come to admire Daniel and to respect Daniel's God. Thus, as the king dutifully fulfilled the letter of his decree, he expressed the hope that God would deliver Daniel (v. 16); perhaps he had heard accounts of God's deliverance of Daniel's three friends from the fiery furnace (ch. 3).

6:23 BECAUSE HE HAD TRUSTED IN HIS GOD. Though the king tried to encourage Daniel to trust his God (v. 16), his voice the next morning did not express expectation that Daniel had been delivered (v. 20); but God's angel had shut the lions' mouths before the faithful prophet, and he was alive and well. This deliverance prompted Darius to testify to the power of a God who is greater than the power of lions (vv. 26–27). Note also that Daniel's name, meaning "God is my Judge," had been shown to be true in his own experience. He was vindicated by the Lord and judged to be right with respect to his choosing the purity of God's law (ch. 1) and to his faithfulness in prayer (ch. 6).

7:1 DANIEL HAD A DREAM, AND VISIONS.

dream, and visions[n] passed through
his mind[o] as he was lying on his
bed.[p] He wrote[q] down the substance
of his dream.
2Daniel said: "In my vision at night
I looked, and there before me were the
four winds of heaven[r] churning up the
great sea. 3Four great beasts,[s] each
different from the others, came up out
of the sea.
4"The first was like a lion,[t] and
it had the wings of an eagle.[u] I
watched until its wings were torn off
and it was lifted from the ground so
that it stood on two feet like a man,
and the heart of a man was given
to it.
5"And there before me was a second
beast, which looked like a bear. It was
raised up on one of its sides, and it had
three ribs in its mouth between its
teeth. It was told, 'Get up and eat your
fill of flesh!'[v]
6"After that, I looked, and there before me was another beast, one that
looked like a leopard.[w] And on its
back it had four wings like those of a
bird. This beast had four heads, and it
was given authority to rule.
7"After that, in my vision[x] at night
I looked, and there before me was a
fourth beast—terrifying and frightening and very powerful. It had large
iron[y] teeth; it crushed and devoured
its victims and trampled[z] underfoot
whatever was left.[a] It was different
from all the former beasts, and it had
ten horns.[b]
8"While I was thinking about the
horns, there before me was another
horn, a little[c] one, which came up
among them; and three of the first
horns were uprooted before it. This
horn had eyes like the eyes of a
man[d] and a mouth that spoke boast-
fully.[e]
9"As I looked,

"thrones were set in place,
 and the Ancient of Days[f] took
  his seat.[g]
His clothing was as white as
  snow;[h]
 the hair of his head was white
  like wool.[i]
His throne was flaming with fire,
 and its wheels[j] were all ablaze.
10A river of fire[k] was flowing,
 coming out from before him.[l]
Thousands upon thousands
  attended him;

7:1 [n]S Eze 40:2 [o]S Da 1:17 [p]Ps 4:4; S Da 4:13 [q]S Jer 36:4
7:2 [r]S Eze 37:9; Da 8:8; 11:4; Rev 7:1
7:3 [s]Rev 13:1
7:4 [t]S 2Ki 24:1; Ps 7:2; Jer 4:7; Rev 13:2 [u]S Eze 17:3
7:5 [v]Da 2:39
7:6 [w]Rev 13:2
7:7 [x]S Eze 40:2 [y]S Da 2:40 [z]Da 8:10 [a]Da 8:7 [b]S Rev 12:3
7:8 [c]Da 8:9 [d]Rev 9:7 [e]S Ps 12:3; Rev 13:5-6
7:9 [f]ver 22 [g]S 1Ki 22:19; 2Ch 18:18; Mt 19:28; Rev 4:2; 20:4 [h]S Mt 28:3 [i]Rev 1:14 [j]S Eze 1:15; 10:6
7:10 [k]Ps 50:3; 97:3; Isa 30:27 [l]S Dt 33:2; Ps 68:17; Jude 1:14; Rev 5:11

The words "dream" and "vision" are sometimes used interchangeably in the Bible. Daniel interpreted the prophetic dreams of others; God also gave Daniel himself unusual dreams and visions. He was probably close to 70 years old by this time. Prophetic dreams and visions are also among the manifestations that will characterize God's people in the last days when the Holy Spirit's ministry and activity are fully manifested in believers (cf. Joel 2:28; Ac 2:16, note; see article on SPIRITUAL GIFTS FOR BELIEVERS, p. 1770).

7:3 FOUR GREAT BEASTS. Some modern writers take these beasts to represent nations existing in the end times. Most Bible expositors, however, take this vision to parallel Nebuchadnezzar's dream in ch. 2 (see 2:37–43, notes) but to reveal the bestial, i.e., the inner characteristics of the kingdoms. (1) The lion, a symbol of royal power, represents the Neo-Babylonian empire. The eagle, the king of birds, may specifically represent King Nebuchadnezzar's power, and the tearing off of the wings represents what happened in ch. 4.

(2) The bear raised up on one side represents Medo-Persia, with Persia dominating Media. The three ribs in its mouth may represent its conquests of Babylon, Lydia and Egypt.

(3) The leopard, a powerful and swift animal, with its four wings, represents Alexander's Greek empire and his rapid conquests. The four heads are the four kingdoms that came out of his empire when he died, for it was divided among his generals: Lysimachus (who took Thrace and Bithynia), Cassander (who took Greece and Macedon), Seleucus (who took Babylonia and Syria) and Ptolemy (who took Palestine, Egypt and Arabia).

(4) The fourth beast, dreadful and terrible, and with iron teeth, represents Rome, as does the remainder of the image, including the ten toes.

7:8 HORN, A LITTLE ONE. The little horn symbolizes the last great ruler in the world—the antichrist (1Jn 2:18), the man of lawlessness (2Th 2:3,8), the beast who subdues three of the ten kings (vv. 11,24; Rev 13:7; 19:19–20). He will wage war against God's saints, defeat them (vv.21–22,25), and speak against God (v. 25). When Jesus Christ comes (v. 9), the saints will possess the kingdom (vv.22,27; cf. Rev 11:15–18; 20:4–6); the antichrist will be destroyed (vv. 11, 26) and thrown into the fiery lake (Rev 19:20). See also 7:13, note.

7:9 THE ANCIENT OF DAYS TOOK HIS SEAT. "Ancient of Days" is another way of recognizing God as the Eternal One, the One Abraham acknowledged as "the Judge of all the earth" (Ge 18:25). He is pictured as judging all people and all kingdoms at the end of time. The description of God in this verse also reveals his holiness ("his clothing was as white as snow"), majesty ("the hair of his head was white like wool") and fiery justice ("his throne was flaming with fire, and its wheels were all ablaze").

ten thousand times ten thousand
stood before him.
The court was seated,
and the books[m] were opened.

11"Then I continued to watch because of the boastful words the horn
was speaking.[n] I kept looking until
the beast was slain and its body destroyed and thrown into the blazing
fire.[o] 12(The other beasts had been
stripped of their authority, but were allowed to live for a period of time.)
13"In my vision at night I looked,
and there before me was one like a son
of man,[p] coming[q] with the clouds of
heaven.[r] He approached the Ancient
of Days and was led into his presence.
14He was given authority,[s] glory and
sovereign power; all peoples, nations
and men of every language worshiped
him.[t] His dominion is an everlasting
dominion that will not pass away, and
his kingdom[u] is one that will never be
destroyed.[v]

The Interpretation of the Dream

15"I, Daniel, was troubled in spirit,
and the visions that passed through my
mind disturbed me.[w] 16I approached
one of those standing there and asked
him the true meaning of all this.

"So he told me and gave me the interpretation[x] of these things: 17'The
four great beasts are four kingdoms
that will rise from the earth. 18But the
saints[y] of the Most High will receive
the kingdom[z] and will possess it forever—yes, for ever and ever.'[a]

19"Then I wanted to know the true
meaning of the fourth beast, which was
different from all the others and most
terrifying, with its iron teeth and
bronze claws—the beast that crushed
and devoured its victims and trampled
underfoot whatever was left. 20I also
wanted to know about the ten horns[b]
on its head and about the other horn
that came up, before which three of
them fell—the horn that looked more
imposing than the others and that had
eyes and a mouth that spoke boastful-
ly.[c] 21As I watched, this horn was
waging war against the saints and defeating them,[d] 22until the Ancient of
Days came and pronounced judgment
in favor of the saints of the Most High,
and the time came when they possessed the kingdom.[e]

23"He gave me this explanation:
'The fourth beast is a fourth kingdom
that will appear on earth. It will be different from all the other kingdoms and
will devour the whole earth, trampling
it down and crushing it.[f] 24The ten
horns[g] are ten kings who will come
from this kingdom. After them another
king will arise, different from the earlier ones; he will subdue three kings.
25He will speak against the Most
High[h] and oppress his saints[i] and
try to change the set times[j] and the
laws. The saints will be handed over to

7:10 [m] S Ex 32:32; S Ps 56:8; Rev 20:11-15 **7:11** [n] Rev 13:5-6 [o] Rev 19:20 **7:13** [p] S Eze 1:5; S 2:1; Mt 8:20*; Rev 1:13*; 14:14* [q] Isa 13:6; Zep 1:14; Mal 3:2; 4:1 [r] S Dt 33:26; S Rev 1:7 **7:14** [s] S Mt 28:18 [t] Ps 72:11; 102:22 [u] S Isa 16:5 [v] S Da 2:44; Heb 12:28; Rev 11:15 **7:15** [w] S Job 4:15; S Da 4:19 **7:16** [x] Da 8:16; 9:22; Zec 1:9 **7:18** [y] S Ps 16:3 [z] S Ps 49:14 [a] Isa 60:12-14; Lk 12:32; Heb 12:28; Rev 2:26; 20:4 **7:20** [b] Rev 17:12 [c] Rev 13:5-6 **7:21** [d] Rev 13:7 **7:22** [e] Mk 8:35 **7:23** [f] S Da 2:40 **7:24** [g] Rev 17:12 **7:25** [h] S Isa 37:23; Da 11:36 [i] Rev 16:6 [j] Da 2:21; Mk 1:15; Lk 21:8; Ac 1:6-7

7:13 ONE LIKE A SON OF MAN. This majestic being is presented before God the Father as a person separate and distinct from him in order to receive an eternal kingdom that will never be given to others (as were the preceding kingdoms). The clouds of heaven are probably clouds of glory (cf. Ex 40:34,38; Ac 1:9,11; 1Th 4:17; Rev 1:7), indicating that he is the divine Son (Mt 26:64), our Lord Jesus Christ (cf. Lk 21:27; Jn 1:51).

7:17 FOUR KINGDOMS ... FROM THE EARTH. "From the earth" does not contradict "out of the sea" (v. 3), since in the Bible the sea is symbolic of the peoples or nations of the earth (cf. Rev 13:1).

7:18 SAINTS. . . RECEIVE THE KINGDOM. The kingdom belongs to the Son of Man (vv. 13–14), but the saints (who here probably include the saints of all ages) receive the kingdom (cf. Mt 5:3,10) and share in Christ's rule (cf. Rev 3:21). Saints are those who are holy (1) because in their relationship to the holy God, they are sanctified by his holy presence, and (2) because they have separated themselves from sin and the corrupt world and consecrated themselves instead to the service and worship of God.

7:24–25 ANOTHER KING WILL ARISE. The little horn (see v. 8, note) will appear after the ten horns (ten kingdoms, or nations), i.e., at the end of this present age in the area of the old Roman empire. The little horn here is different from the horn that "started small" of 8:9, which comes out of the Greek kingdom and represents Antiochus Epiphanes, a type of the antichrist. This little horn comes out of the Roman beast and takes control of three kingdoms by force; the remaining kingdoms seem to delegate their powers to him. He speaks blasphemy against the Most High, i.e., the Ancient of Days, God the Father (cf. 2Th 2:4). He will "oppress his [God's] saints" by persecution as he tries to change "the set times" (seasons for special religious worship) and God's laws; he will continue to persecute the saints for a period of three and one-half years until he is destroyed (cf. 9:27; Rev 11:2–3; 12:11; 13:5). All this serves to identify the little horn with the first beast of the book of Revelation (see Rev 13), the one who is usually called the antichrist (see articles on THE GREAT TRIBULATION, p. 1456, and THE AGE OF THE ANTICHRIST, p. 1872).

him for a time, times and half a
time.[v][k]
26" 'But the court will sit, and his
power will be taken away and completely destroyed[l] forever. 27Then
the sovereignty, power and greatness
of the kingdoms[m] under the whole
heaven will be handed over to the
saints,[n] the people of the Most
High.[o] His kingdom will be an everlasting[p] kingdom, and all rulers will
worship[q] and obey him.'
28"This is the end of the matter. I,
Daniel, was deeply troubled[r] by my
thoughts,[s] and my face turned pale,[t]
but I kept the matter to myself."

Daniel's Vision of a Ram and a Goat

8 In the third year of King Belshazzar's[u] reign, I, Daniel, had a vision,[v] after the one that had already
appeared to me. 2In my vision I saw
myself in the citadel of Susa[w] in the
province of Elam;[x] in the vision I was
beside the Ulai Canal. 3I looked up,[y]
and there before me was a ram[z] with
two horns, standing beside the canal,
and the horns were long. One of the
horns was longer than the other but
grew up later. 4I watched the ram as he
charged toward the west and the north
and the south. No animal could stand
against him, and none could rescue
from his power.[a] He did as he
pleased[b] and became great.
5As I was thinking about this, suddenly a goat with a prominent horn between his eyes came from the west,
crossing the whole earth without
touching the ground. 6He came toward
the two-horned ram I had seen standing beside the canal and charged at
him in great rage. 7I saw him attack
the ram furiously, striking the ram and
shattering his two horns. The ram was
powerless to stand against him; the
goat knocked him to the ground and
trampled on him,[c] and none could rescue the ram from his power.[d] 8The
goat became very great, but at the
height of his power his large horn was
broken off,[e] and in its place four
prominent horns grew up toward the
four winds of heaven.[f]
9Out of one of them came another
horn, which started small[g] but grew
in power to the south and to the east
and toward the Beautiful Land.[h] 10It
grew until it reached[i] the host of the
heavens, and it threw some of the starry host down to the earth[j] and trampled[k] on them. 11It set itself up to be
as great as the Prince[l] of the host;[m]
it took away the daily sacrifice[n] from
him, and the place of his sanctuary was
brought low.[o] 12Because of rebellion,
the host ⌊of the saints⌋[w] and the daily
sacrifice were given over to it. It prospered in everything it did, and truth
was thrown to the ground.[p]
13Then I heard a holy one[q] speaking, and another holy one said to him,
"How long will it take for the vision to
be fulfilled[r]—the vision concerning
the daily sacrifice, the rebellion that
causes desolation, and the surrender
of the sanctuary and of the host that
will be trampled[s] underfoot?"
14He said to me, "It will take 2,300
evenings and mornings; then the sanctuary will be reconsecrated."[t]

The Interpretation of the Vision

15While I, Daniel, was watching the
vision[u] and trying to understand it,
there before me stood one who looked
like a man.[v] 16And I heard a man's
voice from the Ulai[w] calling, "Gabri-

7:25 [k]Da 8:24; 12:7; S Rev 11:2 7:26 [l]Rev 19:20 7:27 [m]S Isa 14:2 [n]1Co 6:2 [o]Ge 14:18 [p]S 2Sa 7:13; Ps 145:13; S Da 2:44; S 4:34; S Lk 1:33; Rev 11:15; 22:5 [q]S Ps 22:27; 72:11; 86:9 7:28 [r]S Isa 21:3; S Da 4:19 [s]S Ps 13:2 [t]S Job 4:15 8:1 [u]S Da 5:1 [v]S Da 1:17 8:2 [w]S Ezr 4:9; S Est 2:8 [x]S Ge 10:22 8:3 [y]Da 10:5 [z]Rev 13:11 8:4 [a]Isa 41:3 [b]Da 11:3,16 8:7 [c]S Da 7:7 [d]Da 11:11,16 8:8 [e]2Ch 26:16-21; S Da 5:20 [f]S Da 7:2; Rev 7:1 8:9 [g]Da 7:8 [h]S Eze 20:6; Da 11:16 8:10 [i]S Isa 14:13 [j]Rev 8:10; 12:4 [k]S Da 7:7 8:11 [l]ver 25 [m]Da 11:36-37 [n]Eze 46:13-14 [o]Da 11:31; 12:11 8:12 [p]S Isa 48:1 8:13 [q]S Dt 33:2; S Da 4:23 [r]Da 12:6 [s]S Isa 28:18; S Lk 21:24; Rev 11:2 8:14 [t]Da 12:11-12 8:15 [u]ver 1 [v]S Eze 2:1; Da 10:16-18 8:16 [w]ver 2

v25 Or *for a year, two years and half a year*
w12 Or *rebellion, the armies*

8:1 THE THIRD YEAR. The third year is 551 B.C. The remainder of the book of Daniel is written in Hebrew (cf. 2:4, note).

8:3 A RAM WITH TWO HORNS. This ram represents the Medo-Persian empire (see v. 20).

8:5 A GOAT. The goat from the west is the Greek empire and its prominent horn represents Alexander the Great (see vv. 21–22), who died prematurely at the height of his power; subsequently, his empire was divided among his four generals (see 7:3, note).

8:9 ANOTHER HORN. Out of one of the horns came a horn that "started small"; it refers to Antiochus Epiphanes, who in 168 B.C. set up an image of the Greek god Zeus in the temple and sacrificed a pig on the altar (see vv. 23–25). Judas Maccabeus later recaptured Jerusalem and reconsecrated the temple and altar (165 B.C.).

8:14 THE SANCTUARY WILL BE RECONSECRATED. The reconsecrating of the sanctuary took place three years and two months (2,300 evenings and mornings, or 1,150 days) after the Lord's altar had been removed by Antiochus.

8:16 TELL THIS MAN THE MEANING. Gabriel (literally, "mighty man of God" or "God has shown himself mighty") is a leading angel who also appears to Daniel in 9:21, to Zechariah in Lk 1:19 and to the virgin Mary in Lk 1:26 (see article

el,[x] tell this man the meaning of the
vision."[y]
17As he came near the place where
I was standing, I was terrified and fell
prostrate.[z] "Son of man," he said to
me, "understand that the vision concerns the time of the end."[a]
18While he was speaking to me, I
was in a deep sleep, with my face to the
ground.[b] Then he touched me and
raised me to my feet.[c]
19He said: "I am going to tell you
what will happen later in the time of
wrath,[d] because the vision concerns
the appointed time[e] of the end.[x][f]
20The two-horned ram that you saw
represents the kings of Media and Persia.[g] 21The shaggy goat is the king of
Greece,[h] and the large horn between
his eyes is the first king.[i] 22The four
horns that replaced the one that was
broken off represent four kingdoms
that will emerge from his nation but
will not have the same power.
23"In the latter part of their reign,
when rebels have become completely
wicked, a stern-faced king, a master of
intrigue, will arise. 24He will become
very strong, but not by his own power.
He will cause astounding devastation
and will succeed in whatever he does.
He will destroy the mighty men and the
holy people.[j] 25He will cause deceit[k]
to prosper, and he will consider himself superior. When they feel secure,
he will destroy many and take his
stand against the Prince of princes.[l]
Yet he will be destroyed, but not by human power.[m]
26"The vision of the evenings and
mornings that has been given you is
true,[n] but seal[o] up the vision, for it
concerns the distant future."[p]
27I, Daniel, was exhausted and lay
ill[q] for several days. Then I got up and
went about the king's business.[r] I
was appalled[s] by the vision; it was beyond understanding.

Daniel's Prayer

9 In the first year of Darius[t] son of
Xerxes[y][u] (a Mede by descent),
who was made ruler over the Babylonian[z] kingdom— 2in the first year of his
reign, I, Daniel, understood from the
Scriptures, according to the word of
the LORD given to Jeremiah the prophet,
that the desolation of Jerusalem would
last seventy[v] years. 3So I turned to
the Lord God and pleaded with him in
prayer and petition, in fasting,[w] and in
sackcloth and ashes.[x]
4I prayed to the LORD my God and
confessed:[y]

"O Lord, the great and awesome God,[z] who keeps his covenant of love[a] with all who love
him and obey his commands, 5we
have sinned[b] and done wrong.[c]
We have been wicked and have rebelled; we have turned away[d]
from your commands and laws.[e]
6We have not listened[f] to your
servants the prophets,[g] who
spoke in your name to our kings,

8:16 [x]Da 9:21; S Lk 1:19 [y]S Da 7:16 **8:17** [z]Eze 1:28; 44:4; S Da 2:46; Rev 1:17 [a]ver 19; Hab 2:3 **8:18** [b]Da 10:9 [c]S Eze 2:2; Da 10:16-18; Zec 4:1 **8:19** [d]S Isa 10:25 [e]S Ps 102:13 [f]Hab 2:3 **8:20** [g]S Eze 27:10 **8:21** [h]Da 10:20 [i]Da 11:3 **8:24** [j]S Da 7:25; 11:36 **8:25** [k]Da 11:23 [l]Da 11:36 [m]S Da 2:34; 11:21 **8:26** [n]Da 10:1 [o]S Isa 8:16; S 29:11; Rev 10:4; 22:10 [p]Da 10:14 **8:27** [q]Da 10:8 [r]S Da 2:48 [s]S Isa 21:3; S Da 4:19 **9:1** [t]S Da 5:31 [u]S Ezr 4:6 **9:2** [v]S 2Ch 36:21; Jer 29:10; Zec 1:12; 7:5 **9:3** [w]S 2Ch 20:3 [x]S 2Sa 13:19; S Ne 1:4; Jer 29:12; Da 10:12; Jnh 3:6 **9:4** [y]S 1Ki 8:30 [z]S Dt 7:21 [a]Dt 7:9; S 1Ki 8:23 **9:5** [b]S Jer 8:14 [c]Ps 106:6 [d]Isa 53:6 [e]ver 11; La 1:20; S 3:42 **9:6** [f]S 2Ki 18:12 [g]S 2Ch 36:16; S Jer 44:5; Jas 5:10; Rev 10:7

[x]*19* Or *because the end will be at the appointed time* [y]*1* Hebrew *Ahasuerus* [z]*1* Or *Chaldean*

---

on ANGELS AND THE ANGEL OF THE LORD, p. 340).

8:23 A STERN-FACED KING. Because of the mention of "the latter part," some believe Gabriel is speaking here of the antichrist; however, the reference is more likely to the latter time of the four kingdoms that came out of Alexander's kingdom (see v. 5, note). Thus, the stern-faced king is Antiochus Epiphanes, who is a type of the antichrist; the reference to "the evenings and the mornings" (v. 26; see v. 14, note) indicates that the time is still that of Antiochus.

9:2 SEVENTY YEARS. Jeremiah had prophesied that restoration would begin for Jerusalem in 70 years (Jer 25:11–12; 29:10–14). The 70 years were just about up, and still there was no indication of the promised return and restoration; thus Daniel was severely troubled. From this verse, it is clear that Daniel expected a literal fulfillment of Jeremiah's prophecy. In general, prophecies should be interpreted literally unless there is something in the context to show that a prophecy or vision is symbolic; even then, the symbols represent literal historical realities (cf. 7:3, note; 8:3,5, notes).

9:5 WE HAVE SINNED. Daniel did not sit back and passively wait for the promised restoration to come about (see previous note); instead, he began to plead earnestly in prayer and fasting (v. 3) for the fulfillment of God's word. Daniel began his intercessory prayer by recognizing God's awe-inspiring greatness, his faithful love, and his covenant mercy shown to those who love and obey him. Then he made his confession, identifying himself with the people of Israel who had sinned and rebelled against God. He asked for Jerusalem's restoration not because of any righteousness on the part of Daniel or of Israel, but for the Lord's sake (9:17–18). When God responded, he demonstrated his great mercy and loving compassion as a God who fulfills his promises.

our princes and our fathers,[h] and
to all the people of the land.
7“Lord, you are righteous,[i]
but this day we are covered with
shame[j]—the men of Judah and
people of Jerusalem and all Israel,
both near and far, in all the countries where you have scattered[k]
us because of our unfaithfulness[l] to you.[m] 8O LORD, we and
our kings, our princes and our fathers are covered with shame because we have sinned against
you.[n] 9The Lord our God is merciful and forgiving,[o] even though
we have rebelled against him;[p]
10we have not obeyed the LORD our
God or kept the laws he gave us
through his servants the prophets.[q] 11All Israel has transgressed[r] your law[s] and turned
away, refusing to obey you.
“Therefore the curses[t] and
sworn judgments[u] written in the
Law of Moses, the servant of God,
have been poured out on us, because we have sinned[v] against
you. 12You have fulfilled[w] the
words spoken against us and
against our rulers by bringing
upon us great disaster.[x] Under
the whole heaven nothing has
ever been done like[y] what has
been done to Jerusalem.[z] 13Just
as it is written in the Law of Moses, all this disaster has come
upon us, yet we have not sought
the favor of the LORD[a] our God by
turning from our sins and giving
attention to your truth.[b] 14The
LORD did not hesitate to bring the
disaster[c] upon us, for the LORD
our God is righteous in everything
he does;[d] yet we have not obeyed
him.[e]
15“Now, O Lord our God, who
brought your people out of Egypt
with a mighty hand[f] and who
made for yourself a name[g] that
endures to this day, we have
sinned, we have done wrong.
16O Lord, in keeping with all your
righteous acts,[h] turn away[i]
your anger and your wrath[j] from
Jerusalem,[k] your city, your holy
hill.[l] Our sins and the iniquities
of our fathers have made Jerusalem and your people an object of
scorn[m] to all those around us.
17“Now, our God, hear the
prayers and petitions of your servant. For your sake, O Lord, look
with favor[n] on your desolate
sanctuary. 18Give ear,[o] O God,
and hear;[p] open your eyes and
see[q] the desolation of the city
that bears your Name.[r] We do
not make requests of you because
we are righteous, but because of
your great mercy.[s] 19O Lord, listen! O Lord, forgive![t] O Lord,
hear and act! For your sake,[u]
O my God, do not delay, because
your city and your people bear
your Name.”

The Seventy “Sevens”

20While I was speaking and praying,
confessing[v] my sin and the sin of my
people Israel and making my request
to the LORD my God for his holy hill[w]—
21while I was still in prayer, Gabriel,[x]
the man I had seen in the earlier vision,
came to me in swift flight about the
time of the evening sacrifice.[y] 22He
instructed me and said to me, “Daniel,
I have now come to give you insight
and understanding.[z] 23As soon as you
began to pray,[a] an answer was given,
which I have come to tell you, for you
are highly esteemed.[b] Therefore, consider the message and understand the
vision:[c]
24“Seventy ‘sevens’[a] are decreed

9:6 [h] S 2Ch 29:6
9:7 [i] S Ezr 9:15; S Isa 42:6 [j] Ezr 9:7; Ps 44:15 [k] Dt 4:27; Am 9:9 [l] S Dt 7:3 [m] S Jer 3:25; S 24:9; S Eze 39:23-24
9:8 [n] S Ne 9:33; S Jer 14:20; S Eze 16:63
9:9 [o] S Ex 34:7; S 2Sa 24:14; Jer 42:12 [p] S Ne 9:17; Jer 14:7
9:10 [q] 2Ki 17:13-15; S 18:12; Rev 10:7
9:11 [r] S Jer 2:29 [s] 2Ki 22:16 [t] S Dt 11:26; S 13:15; S 28:15 [u] 2Ki 17:23 [v] Isa 1:4-6; Jer 8:5-10
9:12 [w] S Isa 44:26; Zec 1:6 [x] S Jer 44:23 [y] Jer 30:7 [z] Jer 44:2-6; Eze 5:9; Da 12:1; Joel 2:2; Zec 7:12
9:13 [a] S Dt 4:29; S Isa 31:1 [b] S Isa 9:13; Jer 2:30
9:14 [c] S Jer 18:8; S 44:27 [d] S Ge 18:25; S 2Ch 12:6; S Jer 12:1 [e] S Ne 9:33; S Jer 32:23; S 40:3
9:15 [f] S Ex 3:20; S Jer 32:21 [g] S Ne 9:10
9:16 [h] S Jdg 5:11; Ps 31:1 [i] S Isa 5:25 [j] S Ps 85:3 [k] Jer 32:32 [l] S Ex 15:17; S Ps 48:1 [m] S Ps 39:8; S Eze 5:14
9:17 [n] Nu 6:24-26; Ps 80:19
9:18 [o] S Ps 5:1 [p] Ps 116:1 [q] Ps 80:14 [r] S Dt 28:10; S Isa 37:17; Jer 7:10-12; 25:29 [s] Lk 18:13
9:19 [t] Ps 44:23 [u] S 1Sa 12:22
9:20 [v] S Ezr 10:1 [w] S ver 3; Ps 145:18; S Isa 58:9
9:21 [x] S Da 8:16; S Lk 1:19 [y] S Ex 29:39
9:22 [z] S Da 7:16; 10:14; Am 3:7
9:23 [a] S Isa 65:24 [b] Da 10:19; Lk 1:28 [c] Da 10:11-12; Mt 24:15

[a] 24 Or *‘weeks’*; also in verses 25 and 26

9:24 SEVENTY “SEVENS”. Daniel’s prophecy here concerning Israel and the holy city is crucial for the last days of this age. The word translated “sevens” here means a unit of seven years; thus, “seventy ‘sevens’” is a period of 490 years. Six specific things would be accomplished for Israel during the 490 years. (1) An atonement for wickedness will be made, accomplished in the atoning death of Jesus.

(2) There will be “an end to sin.” All Israel (i.e., the remnant) will return to God in righteousness (see Ro 11:26, note; see article on ISRAEL IN GOD’S PLAN OF SALVATION, p. 1730).

(3) The “transgression” will be finished; i.e., the national transgression of unbelief will cease (cf. Jer 33:7–8; Eze 37:21–23).

(4) A rule of “everlasting righteousness” will be brought in (cf. Isa 59:2–21; Jer 31:31–34).

(5) Prophecy will be fulfilled and completed (cf. Ac 3:19–26).

INTERCESSION

Da 9:3 "So I turned to the Lord God and pleaded with him in prayer and petition, in fasting, and in sackcloth and ashes."

Intercession may be defined as holy, believing, persevering prayer whereby someone pleads with God on behalf of another or others who desperately need God's intervention. Daniel's prayer in Da 9 is an intercessory prayer, as he prays earnestly for Jerusalem's restoration and for the entire nation. The Bible records the intercession of Christ and the Holy Spirit, and of numerous godly men and women under both the old and new covenants.

THE INTERCESSION OF CHRIST AND THE HOLY SPIRIT. (1) During his earthly ministry, Jesus prayed for the lost he came to seek and to save (Lk 19:10). He wept in brokenness over the city of Jerusalem (Lk 19:41). He prayed for his disciples, both individually (see Lk 22:32) and as a group (Jn 17:6–26). He even prayed for his enemies while hanging on the cross (Lk 23:34).

(2) A present aspect of Christ's ministry is to intercede on our behalf before God's throne (Ro 8:34; Heb 7:25; 9:24; see 7:25, note); John calls Jesus the "one who speaks to the Father in our defense" (see 1Jn 2:1, note). Christ's intercession is essential to our salvation (cf. Isa 53:12); without his grace, mercy and help mediated to us through his intercession, we would fall away from God and once again become enslaved to sin.

(3) The Holy Spirit is also involved in intercession. Paul states, "We do not know what we ought to pray for, but the Spirit himself intercedes for us with groans that words cannot express" (Ro 8:26, see note). The Holy Spirit through the human spirit of the believer intercedes "in accordance with God's will" (Ro 8:27). Thus, Christ intercedes for the believer in heaven, and the Spirit intercedes within the believer on earth.

THE INTERCESSION OF THE BELIEVER. The Bible often refers to believers' intercessory prayers and records numerous examples of remarkable, powerful prayers. (1) In the OT, the leaders of God's people, such as kings (1Ch 21:17; 2Ch 6:14–42), prophets (1Ki 18:41–45; Da 9) and priests (Ezr 9:5–15; Joel 1:13; 2:17–18), were to lead the way in intercessory prayer for the nation. Superb examples of OT intercession include Abraham's prayers for Ishmael (Ge 17:18) and for Sodom and Gomorrah (Ge 18:23–32), David's prayers for a son (2Sa 12:16; 1Ch 29:19), and Job's for his children (Job 1:5). In Moses' life we see the supreme OT example of the power of intercessory prayer. On several occasions he prayed intensely to God to change his declared will, even when God had told Moses his course of action. For example, after the Israelites rebelled against the Lord and refused to go into Canaan, God told Moses that he would destroy them and make Moses into a greater nation (Nu 14:1–12). Moses then took the matter to the Lord in prayer and pleaded for them (Nu 14:13–19); at the conclusion of his prayer God said, "I have forgiven them, as you asked" (Nu 14:20; see also Ex 32:11–14; Nu 11:2; 12:13; 21:7; 27:5; see article on EFFECTIVE PRAYING, p. 496). Other powerful OT intercessors include Elijah (1Ki 18:21–46; Jas 5:16–18), Daniel (Da 9:2–23) and Nehemiah (Ne 1:3–11).

(2) The NT presents even more examples of intercessory prayers. The Gospels record how parents and others interceded with Jesus on behalf of loved ones. Parents pleaded with Jesus to heal their sick children (Mk 5:22–43; Jn 4:47–53); a group of mothers asked Jesus to bless their children (Mk 10:13); a man pleaded for his servant to be healed (Mt 8:6–13); and the mother of James and John interceded with Jesus on their behalf (Mt 20:20–21).

(3) The NT church frequently interceded on behalf of various individuals. For example, the church in Jerusalem gathered to pray for Peter's release from prison (Ac 12:5,12). The church in Antioch prayed for the success of the ministry of Barnabas and Paul (Ac 13:3). James specifically instructs the elders of the church to pray for the sick (Jas 5:14) and for all Christians to "pray for each other" (Jas 5:16; cf. Heb 13:18–19). Paul goes one step further and asks that prayers be offered for *everyone* (1Ti 2:1–3).

(4) The apostle Paul deserves special mention. In many of his letters he tells of his own prayers for various churches or individuals (e.g., Ro 1:9–10; 2Co 13:7; Php 1:4–11; Col 1:3,9–12; 1Th 1:2–3; 2Th 1:11–12; 2Ti 1:3; Phm 4–6). Occasionally he records his prayers (e.g., Eph 1:15–19; 3:14–19; 1Th 3:11–13). At the same time, Paul frequently asks churches to pray for him, knowing that only through their prayers will his ministry have its fullest effect (Ro 15:30–32; 2Co 1:11; Eph 6:18–20; Php 1:19; Col 4:3–4; 1Th 5:25; 2Th 3:1–2).

PURPOSES OF INTERCESSORY PRAYERS. In the numerous intercessory prayers in the Bible, God-fearing saints pleaded with God to turn aside his judgment (Ge 18:23–32; Nu 14:13–19; Joel 2:17), to restore his people (Ne 1; Da 9), to deliver individuals from danger (Ac 12:5,12; Ro 15:31) and to bless his people (Nu 6:24–26; 1Ki 18:41–45; Ps 122:6–8). Intercessors also prayed for the Holy Spirit's power to come (Ac 8:15–17; Eph 3:14–17), for someone to be healed (1Ki 17:20–21; Ac 28:8; Jas 5:14–16), for the forgiveness of sins (Ezr 9:5–15; Da 9; Ac 7:60), for the ability of people in authority to rule well (1Ch 29:19; 1Ti 2:1–2), for Christian growth (Php 1:9–11; Col 1:10–11), for effective pastors (2Ti 1:3–7), for effective mission work (Mt 9:38; Eph 6:19–20), for the salvation of others (Ro 10:1) and for people to praise God (Ps 67:3–5). Anything that the Bible reveals as God's perfect will for his people (see article on THE WILL OF GOD, p. 1056) can appropriately be the focus of intercessory prayer.

for your people and your holy city[d] to
finish[b] transgression, to put an end to
sin, to atone[e] for wickedness, to bring
in everlasting righteousness,[f] to seal
up vision and prophecy and to anoint
the most holy.[c]
25 "Know and understand this: From
the issuing of the decree[d] to restore
and rebuild[g] Jerusalem until the
Anointed One,[e][h] the ruler,[i] comes,
there will be seven 'sevens,' and sixty-
two 'sevens.' It will be rebuilt with
streets and a trench, but in times of
trouble.[j] 26 After the sixty-two 'sevens,' the Anointed One will be cut off[k]
and will have nothing.[f] The people of
the ruler who will come will destroy
the city and the sanctuary. The end
will come like a flood:[l] War will continue until the end, and desolations[m]
have been decreed.[n] 27 He will confirm
a covenant with many for one 'sev-
en.'[g] In the middle of the 'seven'[g] he
will put an end to sacrifice and offering. And on a wing ⌞of the temple⌟ he
will set up an abomination that causes

9:24 [d] S Isa 1:26 [e] S Isa 53:10 [f] S Isa 56:1; Heb 9:12 9:25 [g] S Ezr 4:24; S 6:15 [h] Mt 1:17; Jn 4:25 [i] S 1Sa 13:14 [j] S Ezr 3:3 9:26 [k] S Isa 53:8; Mt 16:21 [l] Isa 28:2; Da 11:10; Na 1:8 [m] S Ps 46:8 [n] Isa 61:1; S Eze 4:5-6; Hag 2:23; Zec 4:14

[b] *24* Or *restrain* [c] *24* Or *Most Holy Place*; or *most holy One* [d] *25* Or *word* [e] *25* Or *an anointed one*; also in verse 26 [f] *26* Or *off and will have no one*; or *off, but not for himself* [g] *27* Or *'week'*

(6) Jesus Christ will be anointed as King (cf. 1Sa 9:16; 10:1; Eze 21:26–27).

9:25 SEVEN "SEVENS" AND SIXTY-TWO "SEVENS". God revealed to Daniel that sixty-nine periods of sevens, i.e., 483 years, would occur between the time of the decree to rebuild Jerusalem and the coming of the Messiah, the Anointed One. There are differences of opinion as to the exact time when the 483 years began. Some say 538 B.C., when Cyrus's decree was given; that decree, however, was for the rebuilding of the temple, not the city. Most likely it began in 457 B.C., when Ezra returned and began rebuilding the city (Ezr 4:12–13,16; see 4:11,23, notes); that would bring the 483 years to an end in A.D. 27, about the time Jesus began his ministry.

9:26 ANOINTED ONE WILL BE CUT OFF. After the "seven 'sevens' " (v. 25) and after "the sixty-two 'sevens,' " i.e., a total of 69 "sevens" (483 years), two things would happen: (1) The Messiah would be "cut off," or crucified (cf. Isa 53:8). (2) The "people of the ruler who will come" would destroy Jerusalem and the temple. The "people" are the Roman army, which destroyed Jerusalem in A.D. 70 (see Lk 21:20, note); the "ruler" refers to the end-time antichrist. (3) Note that the destruction of Jerusalem did not follow immediately after Christ's crucifixion; thus, the conclusion of the 69 "sevens" are separated from the beginning 70th "seven" by an interval of time. Many interpreters say that the church age is the interval between the 69th and 70th "sevens."

9:27 CONFIRM A COVENANT . . . FOR ONE "SEVEN". The making of a covenant between "the ruler who will come" (v. 26) and Israel will signal the beginning of the 70th "seven," the final seven years of this age. Concerning this event, the Bible teaches the following: (1) The ruler who will make the covenant with Israel is the antichrist, but he will be unrevealed at the time (cf. 2Th 2:3–10; 1Jn 2:18). Evidently a peace treaty will be negotiated by the antichrist between Israel and its enemies concerning a land dispute (11:39).

(2) In the middle of the seven years (i.e., after three and one-half years), the ruler will break his covenant with Israel, declare himself to be God, take over the temple in Jerusalem, forbid the worship of the Lord (cf. 2Th 2:4), and devastate Palestine; he will reign for three and one-half years (Rev 11:1–2; 13:4–6; see article on THE AGE OF THE ANTICHRIST, p. 1872).

(3) The prophetic significance of "an abomination that causes desolation" will be known only to God's faithful (12:10–11). Jesus said that believers must watch for this pivotal sign, for it will bring the final three and one-half year countdown to his coming to earth in glory (see Mt 24:15). By careful watching, believers in the tribulation will know that Christ's coming is near, right at the door (Mt 24:33; see article on THE GREAT TRIBULATION, p. 1456). The coming of the Messiah (2Th 2:8; Rev 19:11–20) will occur at the end of the seven years or the second three and one-half years. Revelation confirms the time by stating twice that the antichrist (i.e., "the beast") will have power for only 42 months (Rev 11:1–2; 13:4–6). Daniel later states again that it will be three and one-half years ("a time, times and half a time") from the time of great distress to the end (12:7).

(4) In the three and one-half years allotted to the antichrist, Jerusalem will continue to be trampled on by the Gentiles (Rev 11:2).

(5) The "abomination that causes desolation" is the unmistakable sign that the great tribulation has begun (12:11; Mt 24:15–21; cf. Dt 4:30–31; Jer 30:5–7; Zec 13:8–9).

(6) The tribulation and the rule of the antichrist will end with Christ's coming in power to judge the wicked (Mt 25:31–46), to destroy the antichrist and to begin his millennial reign (Jer 23:5–6; Mt 24:27,30).

9:27 AN ABOMINATION THAT CAUSES DESOLATION. Jesus referred to Daniel's vision when he said: "when you see standing in the holy place the abomination that causes desolation, spoken of through the prophet Daniel" (Mt 24:15); Jesus' remark may refer to the future desecration of the temple in Jerusalem by the antichrist (cf. 2Th 2:3–4; Rev 13:14–15; see article on THE AGE OF THE ANTICHRIST, p. 1872).

desolation, until the end that is decreed[o] is poured out on him.[h][i]

Daniel's Vision of a Man

10 In the third year of Cyrus[p]
king of Persia, a revelation was
given to Daniel (who was called Belteshazzar).[q] Its message was true[r]
and it concerned a great war.[j] The understanding of the message came to
him in a vision.
2 At that time I, Daniel, mourned[s]
for three weeks. 3 I ate no choice food;
no meat or wine touched my lips;[t] and
I used no lotions at all until the three
weeks were over.
4 On the twenty-fourth day of the
first month, as I was standing on the
bank[u] of the great river, the Tigris,[v]
5 I looked up[w] and there before me was
a man dressed in linen,[x] with a belt of
the finest gold[y] around his waist. 6 His
body was like chrysolite,[z] his face like
lightning,[a] his eyes like flaming
torches,[b] his arms and legs like the
gleam of burnished bronze,[c] and his
voice[d] like the sound of a multitude.
7 I, Daniel, was the only one who saw
the vision; the men with me did not see
it,[e] but such terror overwhelmed them
that they fled and hid themselves. 8 So
I was left alone,[f] gazing at this great
vision; I had no strength left,[g] my face
turned deathly pale[h] and I was helpless.[i] 9 Then I heard him speaking,
and as I listened to him, I fell into a
deep sleep, my face to the ground.[j]
10 A hand touched me[k] and set me
trembling on my hands and knees.[l]
11 He said, "Daniel, you who are highly
esteemed,[m] consider carefully the
words I am about to speak to you, and
stand up,[n] for I have now been sent to
you." And when he said this to me, I
stood up trembling. Mt 4:1-11
12 Then he continued, "Do not be
afraid,[o] Daniel. Since the first day
that you set your mind to gain understanding and to humble[p] yourself before your God, your words[q] were
heard, and I have come in response to
them.[r] 13 But the prince[s] of the Persian kingdom resisted me twenty-one
days. Then Michael,[t] one of the chief
princes, came to help me, because I
was detained there with the king of
Persia. 14 Now I have come to explain[u]
to you what will happen to your people
in the future,[v] for the vision concerns
a time yet to come.[w]"
15 While he was saying this to me, I
bowed with my face toward the ground
and was speechless.[x] 16 Then one who
looked like a man[k] touched my lips,
and I opened my mouth and began to
speak.[y] I said to the one standing before me, "I am overcome with anguish[z] because of the vision, my lord,
and I am helpless. 17 How can I, your
servant, talk with you, my lord? My
strength is gone and I can hardly
breathe."[a]
18 Again the one who looked like a
man touched[b] me and gave me

9:27 [o] S Isa 10:22 **10:1** [p] S Da 1:21 [q] S Da 1:7 [r] Da 8:26 **10:2** [s] S Ezr 9:4 **10:3** [t] S Da 6:18 **10:4** [u] Da 12:5 [v] S Ge 2:14 **10:5** [w] Da 8:3 [x] S Eze 9:2; Rev 15:6 [y] Jer 10:9 **10:6** [z] S Ex 28:20 [a] Mt 17:2; S 28:3 [b] Job 41:19; Rev 19:12 [c] S Eze 1:7; S Rev 1:15 [d] S Eze 1:24 **10:7** [e] 2Ki 6:17-20; Ac 9:7 **10:8** [f] Ge 32:24 [g] S Job 4:14; Da 8:27 [h] S Job 4:15 [i] Hab 3:16 **10:9** [j] Da 8:18; Mt 17:6 **10:10** [k] Jer 1:9 [l] Rev 1:17 **10:11** [m] S Ge 6:9; Da 9:23 [n] S Eze 2:1 **10:12** [o] S Mt 14:27 [p] S Lev 16:31; S Da 9:3 [q] S Isa 65:24 [r] Da 9:20 **10:13** [s] Isa 24:21 [t] ver 21; Da 12:1; S Jude 1:9 **10:14** [u] S Da 9:22 [v] S Eze 12:27 [w] S Da 2:28; 8:26; Hab 2:3 **10:15** [x] Eze 24:27; Lk 1:20 **10:16** [y] S Isa 6:7; Jer 1:9; Da 8:15-18 [z] S Isa 21:3 **10:17** [a] S Da 4:19 **10:18** [b] ver 16

[h] 27 Or *it* [i] 27 Or *And one who causes desolation will come upon the pinnacle of the abominable ⌊temple⌋, until the end that is decreed is poured out on the desolated ⌊city⌋* [j] 1 Or *true and burdensome* [k] 16 Most manuscripts of the Masoretic Text; one manuscript of the Masoretic Text, Dead Sea Scrolls and Septuagint *Then something that looked like a man's hand*

10:5 A MAN DRESSED IN LINEN. Daniel was visited by a heavenly being, probably an angel, for the messenger spoke of being resisted by the prince of the Persian kingdom (i.e., a demon) and of needing the help of Michael (see v. 13, note).

10:11 YOU WHO ARE HIGHLY ESTEEMED. The glory and awesomeness of the vision drained Daniel's strength; then the hand of an angel touched him and raised him to his hands and knees. Daniel was encouraged as this angel called him "you who are highly esteemed" and told him, "Do not be afraid" (v. 12). God loves the world (Jn 3:16), but he responds in a special way to the love and faithfulness of people who, like Daniel, are his true servants. God's faithful people never need to be afraid when God speaks to them.

10:13 PRINCE OF THE PERSIAN KINGDOM RESISTED ME. While Daniel was fasting and praying, a spiritual battle of great magnitude was occurring. (1) The prince of Persia prevented Daniel from receiving God's message from the angel. Because of this conflict, he had to wait 21 days for the revelation. This Persian prince was not a human king, but a demon from Satan's kingdom. He was defeated only when Michael, Israel's prince (v. 21), came to help the angel. Though satanic forces wished to hinder the reception of this vision about Israel, Israel's angelic prince (12:1) proved stronger (cf. Rev 12:7–12).

(2) This incident gives us a glimpse of the unseen battles going on in the spiritual realm on our behalf. Note that God had responded to Daniel's prayer, but the answer was delayed for 21 days by satanic forces. Because we know Satan always seeks to hinder our prayers (2Co 2:11), we must persevere in prayer (cf. Lk 18:1–8) in spite of the spiritual forces of the evil one arrayed against us (see Eph 6:11–12, notes; see article on POWER OVER SATAN AND DEMONS, p. 1484).

strength.[c] 19"Do not be afraid, O man
highly esteemed,"[d] he said. "Peace![e]
Be strong now; be strong."[f]

When he spoke to me, I was
strengthened and said, "Speak, my
lord, since you have given me
strength."[g]

20So he said, "Do you know why I
have come to you? Soon I will return to
fight against the prince of Persia, and
when I go, the prince of Greece[h] will
come; 21but first I will tell you what is
written in the Book of Truth.[i] (No one
supports me against them except Mi-
11 chael,[j] your prince. 1And in
the first year of Darius[k] the
Mede, I took my stand to support and
protect him.)

The Kings of the South and the North

2"Now then, I tell you the truth:[l]
Three more kings will appear in Persia, and then a fourth, who will be far
richer than all the others. When he has
gained power by his wealth, he will stir
up everyone against the kingdom of
Greece.[m] 3Then a mighty king will appear, who will rule with great power
and do as he pleases.[n] 4After he has
appeared, his empire will be broken up
and parceled out toward the four winds
of heaven.[o] It will not go to his
descendants, nor will it have the power
he exercised, because his empire will
be uprooted[p] and given to others.

5"The king of the South will become
strong, but one of his commanders will
become even stronger than he and will
rule his own kingdom with great power. 6After some years, they will become
allies. The daughter of the king of the
South will go to the king of the North
to make an alliance, but she will not
retain her power, and he and his power[1] will not last. In those days she will
be handed over, together with her royal
escort and her father[m] and the one
who supported her.

7"One from her family line will arise
to take her place. He will attack the
forces of the king of the North[q] and
enter his fortress; he will fight against
them and be victorious. 8He will also
seize their gods,[r] their metal images
and their valuable articles of silver and
gold and carry them off to Egypt.[s] For
some years he will leave the king of the
North alone. 9Then the king of the
North will invade the realm of the king
of the South but will retreat to his own
country. 10His sons will prepare for
war and assemble a great army, which
will sweep on like an irresistible
flood[t] and carry the battle as far as
his fortress.

10:18 [c]S Da 8:18
10:19 [d]S Da 9:23 [e]Jdg 6:23; S Isa 35:4 [f]Jos 1:9 [g]Isa 6:1-8
10:20 [h]Da 8:21; 11:2
10:21 [i]Da 11:2 [j]S ver 13; S Jude 1:9
11:1 [k]S Da 5:31
11:2 [l]Da 10:21 [m]S Da 10:20
11:3 [n]S Da 8:4, 21
11:4 [o]S Da 7:2; 8:22
[p]S Jer 42:10
11:7 [q]ver 6
11:8 [r]Isa 37:19; S 46:1-2 [s]Jer 43:12
11:10 [t]Isa 8:8; Jer 46:8; S Da 9:26

[1]6 Or *offspring* [m]6 Or *child* (see Vulgate and Syriac)

10:20 PRINCE OF PERSIA . . . GREECE. The nations of the world have powerful demons assigned to them to oppose God's forces and to promote evil and ungodliness among the people.

11:2 I TELL YOU THE TRUTH. "The truth" is a prophecy that outlined the key events leading to the rise of Antiochus Epiphanes, the Greek ruler who profaned the temple (vv. 2–35). Persia would have three more kings, Cambyses (530–522 B.C.), Pseudo-Smerdis or Gaumata (522 B.C.) and Darius I (522–486 B.C.). Then a fourth king, Xerxes (486–465 B.C.), would fight against Greece. With the mention of Greece (the next kingdom), no more is said about Persia, though Persia continued for a time.

11:3 A MIGHTY KING. The mighty king who would appear was Alexander the Great (336–323 B.C.), who died at the height of his power; instead of his kingdom going to his heirs, it was divided among his four generals (v. 4; see 7:3, note).

11:5 THE KING OF THE SOUTH. This first king of the South is Ptolemy I Soter of Egypt (323–285 B.C.); the commander referred to is Seleucus I Nicator (311–280 B.C.).

11:6 DAUGHTER OF THE KING OF THE SOUTH. After several years, Berenice, the daughter of Ptolemy II Philadelphus of Egypt (285–246 B.C.), married Antiochus II Theos (261–246 B.C.), the king of the North, who had divorced Laodice to marry Berenice. In 246 B.C. Ptolemy II died; about the same time Laodice murdered Berenice and Antiochus and their son.

11:7–9 ONE FROM HER FAMILY LINE. The "one from her family line" is Berenice's brother, Ptolemy III Euergetes of Egypt (246–221 B.C.), who won a victory over the king of the North, Seleucus II Callinicus (246–226 B.C.). Ptolemy III entered the "fortress" (probably Syrian Antioch) and took to Egypt both Syrian images and the Egyptian images that had been taken by the Persian King Cambyses when he conquered Egypt in 525 B.C. Ptolemy III returned to Egypt with much plunder, but he refrained from any further attacks on Seleucus. After a time Seleucus attempted to invade Egypt to recoup his losses, but he failed and was forced to go back to his own land.

11:10–12 HIS SONS WILL PREPARE FOR WAR. The two sons of Seleucus II were Seleucus III Ceraunus (226–223 B.C.) and Antiochus III the Great (223–187 B.C.). Antiochus III was defeated by Ptolemy IV Philopater (221–203 B.C.), with the loss of nearly 10,000 Syrian soldiers at the fortress of Raphia in southern Palestine.

11"Then the king of the South will
march out in a rage and fight against
the king of the North, who will raise a
large army, but it will be defeated.[u]
12When the army is carried off, the
king of the South will be filled with
pride and will slaughter many thousands, yet he will not remain triumphant. 13For the king of the North will
muster another army, larger than the
first; and after several years, he will
advance with a huge army fully
equipped.
14"In those times many will rise
against the king of the South. The violent men among your own people will
rebel in fulfillment of the vision, but
without success. 15Then the king of
the North will come and build up siege
ramps[v] and will capture a fortified
city. The forces of the South will be
powerless to resist; even their best
troops will not have the strength to
stand. 16The invader will do as he
pleases;[w] no one will be able to stand
against him.[x] He will establish himself in the Beautiful Land and will have
the power to destroy it.[y] 17He will determine to come with the might of his
entire kingdom and will make an alliance with the king of the South. And he
will give him a daughter in marriage in
order to overthrow the kingdom, but
his plans[n] will not succeed[z] or help
him. 18Then he will turn his attention
to the coastlands[a] and will take many
of them, but a commander will put an
end to his insolence and will turn his
insolence back upon him.[b] 19After
this, he will turn back toward the fortresses of his own country but will
stumble and fall,[c] to be seen no
more.[d]

20"His successor will send out a tax
collector to maintain the royal splendor.[e] In a few years, however, he will
be destroyed, yet not in anger or in battle.
21"He will be succeeded by a contemptible[f] person who has not been
given the honor of royalty.[g] He will
invade the kingdom when its people
feel secure, and he will seize it through
intrigue. 22Then an overwhelming
army will be swept away[h] before him;
both it and a prince of the covenant will
be destroyed.[i] 23After coming to an
agreement with him, he will act deceitfully,[j] and with only a few people he
will rise to power. 24When the richest
provinces feel secure, he will invade
them and will achieve what neither his
fathers nor his forefathers did. He will
distribute plunder, loot and wealth
among his followers.[k] He will plot the
overthrow of fortresses — but only for a
time.
25"With a large army he will stir up
his strength and courage against the
king of the South. The king of the
South will wage war with a large and
very powerful army, but he will not be
able to stand because of the plots devised against him. 26Those who eat
from the king's provisions will try to
destroy him; his army will be swept
away, and many will fall in battle.
27The two kings, with their hearts bent
on evil,[l] will sit at the same table and
lie[m] to each other, but to no avail, because an end will still come at the appointed time.[n] 28The king of the North
will return to his own country with

11:11 [u]Da 8:7-8
11:15 [v]S Eze 4:2
11:16 [w]S Da 8:4 [x]S Jos 1:5; S Da 8:7 [y]S Da 8:9
11:17 [z]S Ps 20:4
11:18 [a]S Isa 66:19; S Jer 25:22 [b]Hos 12:14
11:19 [c]S Ps 27:2; S 46:2 [d]S Ps 37:36; S Eze 26:21
11:20 [e]Isa 60:17
11:21 [f]Da 4:17 [g]S Da 8:25
11:22 [h]S Isa 28:15 [i]Da 8:10-11
11:23 [j]Da 8:25
11:24 [k]Ne 9:25
11:27 [l]Ps 64:6 [m]Ps 12:2; Jer 9:5 [n]Hab 2:3

[n] 17 Or *but she*

11:16 THE BEAUTIFUL LAND. Antiochus III attacked Egypt in 200 B.C., but was crushed by the king of the South, Ptolemy V Epiphanes (203–181 B.C.); Antiochus then gained new strength and conquered the well-fortified city of Sidon (v. 15). By 197 B.C., Antiochus had taken control of the "Beautiful Land," Palestine.

11:19 WILL STUMBLE AND FALL. After several years Antiochus III made a peace treaty with Egypt (194 B.C.) and gave his daughter Cleopatra I as wife to Ptolemy V. Then Antiochus III moved north but was defeated at Magnesia in Asia Minor in 190 B.C. Later (187 B.C.) he attempted to plunder a pagan temple in the province of Elymais, but died in the attempt.

11:20 HE WILL BE DESTROYED. The murder of Seleucus IV Philopater (187–175 B.C.) was arranged by his finance minister, Heliodorus.

11:21 A CONTEMPTIBLE PERSON. This chapter has been leading up to the coming of the "contemptible person," Antiochus IV Epiphanes (175–164 B.C.), the brother of Seleucus IV. He took the throne that really belonged to Demetrius, the young son of Seleucus IV. Antiochus (the horn that "started small" of 8:9–14,23–25) made several campaigns against Egypt. He murdered the "prince of the covenant" (a prophecy of the murder of the high priest Onias in 170 B.C., v. 22). His treaties with other nations were full of intrigue and deceit. He supported Ptolemy Philometor against Ptolemy Euergetes for selfish reasons and he made unexpected attacks on rich cities in times of peace (v. 24). His attacks on Egypt were successful because those who should have helped Egypt did not, and Antiochus was able to return home with great wealth (vv. 25–28).

great wealth, but his heart will be set
against the holy covenant. He will take
action against it and then return to his
own country.
29"At the appointed time he will invade the South again, but this time the
outcome will be different from what it
was before. **30**Ships of the western
coastlands[o][o] will oppose him, and he
will lose heart.[p] Then he will turn
back and vent his fury[q] against the
holy covenant. He will return and show
favor to those who forsake the holy
covenant.
31"His armed forces will rise up to
desecrate the temple fortress and will
abolish the daily sacrifice.[r] Then they
will set up the abomination that causes
desolation.[s] **32**With flattery he will
corrupt those who have violated the
covenant, but the people who know
their God will firmly resist[t] him.
33"Those who are wise will instruct[u] many, though for a time they
will fall by the sword or be burned or
captured or plundered.[v] **34**When they
fall, they will receive a little help, and
many who are not sincere[w] will join
them. **35**Some of the wise will stumble,
so that they may be refined,[x] purified
and made spotless until the time of the
end, for it will still come at the appointed time.

The King Who Exalts Himself

36"The king will do as he pleases. He
will exalt and magnify himself[y] above
every god and will say unheard-of
things[z] against the God of gods.[a] He
will be successful until the time of
wrath[b] is completed, for what has
been determined must take place.[c]
37He will show no regard for the gods
of his fathers or for the one desired by
women, nor will he regard any god, but
will exalt himself above them all. **38**Instead of them, he will honor a god of
fortresses; a god unknown to his fathers he will honor with gold and silver, with precious stones and costly
gifts. **39**He will attack the mightiest
fortresses with the help of a foreign
god and will greatly honor those who
acknowledge him. He will make them
rulers over many people and will distribute the land at a price.[p]
40"At the time of the end the king of
the South[d] will engage him in battle,
and the king of the North will storm[e]

11:30 [o]S Ge 10:4 [p]S 1Sa 17:32 [q]S Job 15:13 **11:31** [r]Hos 3:4 [s]S Jer 19:4; Da 8:11-13; S 9:27; Mt 24:15*; Mk 13:14* **11:32** [t]Mic 5:7-9 **11:33** [u]Da 12:3; Mal 2:7 [v]Mt 24:9; Jn 16:2; Heb 11:32-38 **11:34** [w]Mt 7:15; Ro 16:18 **11:35** [x]S Job 28:1; S Ps 78:38; S Isa 48:10; Da 12:10; Zec 13:9; Jn 15:2 **11:36** [y]Jude 1:16 [z]Rev 13:5-6 [a]S Dt 10:17; S Isa 14:13-14; S Da 7:25; 8:11-12,25; 2Th 2:4 [b]S Isa 10:25; 26:20 [c]Eze 35:13; S Da 8:24 **11:40** [d]S Isa 21:1 [e]Isa 5:28

[o] *30* Hebrew *of Kittim* [p] *39* Or *land for a reward*

11:28 HEART WILL BE SET AGAINST THE HOLY COVENANT. Antiochus developed a hatred of the Jews and their holy covenant law. He was persuaded that Greek culture and language were superior to any other culture and language, and he hated the Jews because their religion was exclusivistic. About 168 B.C. he invaded Egypt again, but the ships of the western coastlands (v. 30) headed by the Roman consul Laenas defeated him, and he withdrew to his own land. There he took out his frustration against the Jews, though some Jews forsook the holy covenant and joined him; these apostate Jews invited Antiochus to bring in Greek culture and religion (v. 30). Thus Antiochus marched to Jerusalem, offered a pig on the temple altar, stopped the daily sacrifices required by God's law, and set up in the holy place an image of the Greek god Zeus; this altar to Zeus is "the abomination that causes desolation" (v. 31), prefiguring another abomination that Jesus prophesied will occur in the last days of this age (see article on THE GREAT TRIBULATION, p. 1456).

11:32 WHO KNOW THEIR GOD WILL FIRMLY RESIST. Flattery corrupted some Jews and caused them to join Antiochus, but God always had a faithful remnant among the Jews in OT times (see 1Ki 19:18; see Isa 6:13, note; 8:16, note; 10:20, note). In this situation too, there were Jews who knew God and remained loyal to him. Though the persecution by Antiochus continued, the faithful Jews under the leadership of Judas Maccabeus of the Hasmonean priestly family offered strong resistance and carried on a guerrilla-type warfare that eventually wore down Antiochus and caused him to take his armies home; thereupon the temple was reconsecrated and the lamps relit, an event still celebrated by the Jews as the Feast of Hanukkah. God has not yet completed his dealings with the Jews, however (see v. 35); a purging process will continue to the time of the end.

11:36–45 EXALT AND MAGNIFY HIMSELF. The prophecies in these verses do not fit Antiochus. The mention of "the time of the end" (vv. 35,40) indicates that this prophecy is jumping ahead to the end of the age and to the one of whom Antiochus was the type, i.e., to the antichrist (see 7:8, note; 9:27, note). The antichrist will be a dictatorial ruler who will present himself as greater than any god and will speak "unheard-of things" (blasphemies) against the true God; he will be allowed to prosper for a time, thus bringing the fulfillment of this prophecy. He will show no regard for "the gods [God] of his fathers" (v. 37; Heb *'elohim*, which can mean either "gods" or "God"); neither will he show regard for what is desired by women (some take this to be Tammuz, a Babylonian fertility god; see Eze 8:14). The only god he will honor will be "a god of fortresses" (v. 38), which may refer to his own ability to wage war. He will also redivide territories he conquers in order to promote his own gain (v. 39).

out against him with chariots and cavalry and a great fleet of ships. He will
invade many countries and sweep
through them like a flood.[f] **41**He will
also invade the Beautiful Land.[g]
Many countries will fall, but Edom,[h]
Moab[i] and the leaders of Ammon will
be delivered from his hand. **42**He will
extend his power over many countries;
Egypt will not escape. **43**He will gain
control of the treasures of gold and silver and all the riches of Egypt,[j] with
the Libyans[k] and Nubians in submission. **44**But reports from the east and
the north will alarm him, and he will
set out in a great rage to destroy and
annihilate many. **45**He will pitch his
royal tents between the seas at[q] the
beautiful holy mountain.[l] Yet he will
come to his end, and no one will help
him.

The End Times

12 "At that time Michael,[m] the
great prince who protects your
people, will arise. There will be a time
of distress[n] such as has not happened
from the beginning of nations until
then. But at that time your people — everyone whose name is found written in
the book[o] — will be delivered.[p] **2**Multitudes who sleep in the dust of the
earth will awake:[q] some to everlasting life, others to shame and everlasting contempt.[r] **3**Those who are
wise[r][s] will shine[t] like the brightness of the heavens, and those who
lead many to righteousness,[u] like the
stars for ever and ever.[v] **4**But you,
Daniel, close up and seal[w] the words
of the scroll until the time of the end.[x]
Many will go here and there[y] to increase knowledge."

5Then I, Daniel, looked, and there
before me stood two others, one on this
bank of the river and one on the opposite bank.[z] **6**One of them said to the
man clothed in linen,[a] who was above
the waters of the river, "How long will
it be before these astonishing things
are fulfilled?"[b]

7The man clothed in linen, who was
above the waters of the river, lifted his
right hand[c] and his left hand toward
heaven, and I heard him swear by him
who lives forever,[d] saying, "It will be
for a time, times and half a time.[s][e]
When the power of the holy people[f]
has been finally broken, all these
things will be completed.[g]"

8I heard, but I did not understand.
So I asked, "My lord, what will the outcome of all this be?"

9He replied, "Go your way, Daniel,
because the words are closed up and
sealed[h] until the time of the end.[i]
10Many will be purified, made spotless

11:40 [f] S Isa 8:7; S Eze 38:4 **11:41** [g] S Eze 20:6; Mal 3:12 [h] S Isa 11:14 [i] S Jer 48:47 **11:43** [j] S Eze 30:4 [k] 2Ch 12:3; Na 3:9 **11:45** [l] S Isa 2:2, 4; Da 8:9 **12:1** [m] S Da 10:13; Jude 1:9 [n] S Da 9:12; S Mt 24:21; Mk 13:19; Rev 16:18 [o] S Ex 32:32; S Ps 56:8; S Jer 17:13; S Lk 10:20 [p] Jer 30:7 **12:2** [q] Jn 11:24 [r] S Isa 26:19; Mt 25:46 **12:3** [s] S Da 11:33 [t] Mt 13:43; Jn 5:35; Php 2:15 [u] S Isa 6:7 [v] S Pr 4:18; 1Co 15:42 **12:4** [w] S Isa 8:16 [x] ver 9,13; Rev 22:10 [y] Jer 5:1 **12:5** [z] Da 10:4 **12:6** [a] S Eze 9:2 [b] Da 8:13 **12:7** [c] S Ge 14:22 [d] S Da 6:26; Rev 10:5-6 [e] S Da 7:25; S Rev 11:2 [f] S Da 8:24 [g] Lk 21:24; Rev 10:7 **12:9** [h] S Isa 29:11 [i] S ver 4

[q] *45* Or *the sea and* [r] *3* Or *who impart wisdom* [s] *7* Or *a year, two years and half a year*

11:45 HE WILL COME TO HIS END. Though the antichrist will be successful for a time, there will be further battles with another king of the North and another king of the South, culminating in the battle of Armageddon, where the antichrist will be finally defeated by the sword coming out of Christ's mouth (i.e., by his word) and be thrown into the fiery lake (Rev 19:20).

12:1 A TIME OF DISTRESS. Daniel prophesies a time of trouble for Israel, fulfilling Jer 30:7 (see also Mt 24:15,21; Rev 6:17), but God's purpose is still to deliver those of Daniel's people whose names are written "in the book" (i.e., "the book of life," see Php 4:3; Rev 3:5; 21:27). They will have finally placed their faith in Jesus as their Messiah, Savior and Lord.

12:2 MULTITUDES . . . WILL AWAKE. This verse contains the clearest OT reference to the resurrection of the righteous and the wicked (cf. Job 19:25–26; Ps 16:10; Isa 26:19), revealing that there are two, and only two, destinies for all humankind. Jesus indicates that there are two distinct resurrections (Jn 5:28–29).

12:3 WISE WILL SHINE. The wise, as described in the OT, are the godly. They show their wisdom not only by how they live but by the effect of their lives and testimony, for they lead many to a righteous way of life. Their shining means they will be transformed, and God's glory will be reflected in and through them.

12:4 SEAL THE WORDS. Daniel is told to seal the book; the prophecies are not merely for his own time, but for the time of the end, to encourage those who will be alive at the end of the age. Daniel then sees two angels, one on each side of the river, asking how long it would be until the time of the end. The man clothed in linen (cf. 10:5–6) swore by God that the time would be three and one-half years, probably referring to the last half of the 70th period of seven years (see 9:27, note).

12:10 WISE WILL UNDERSTAND. Daniel is told that the full understanding of his prophecy will not come until the time of the end. At that time, some will be purified through testing; these will be the wise who understand. No wicked or rebellious person will be among them. Furthermore, there will be an "abomination that causes desolation" (cf. Mt 24:15; see article on THE GREAT TRIBULATION, p. 1456), which will be followed

and refined,[j] but the wicked will continue to be wicked.[k] None of the wicked will understand, but those who are
wise will understand.[l]
11"From the time that the daily sacrifice[m] is abolished and the abomination that causes desolation[n] is set up,
there will be 1,290 days.[o] 12Blessed
is the one who waits[p] for and reaches
the end of the 1,335 days.[q]
13"As for you, go your way till the
end.[r] You will rest,[s] and then at the
end of the days you will rise to receive
your allotted inheritance.[t][u]"

12:10 [j] S Isa 1:25; S Da 11:35 [k] S Isa 32:7; Rev 22:11 [l] Hos 14:9 **12:11** [m] S Ex 29:38 [n] S Da 8:11; S 9:27; Mt 24:15*; Mk 13:14* [o] Rev 11:2 **12:12** [p] S Isa 30:18 [q] S Eze 4:5-6; Da 8:14 **12:13** [r] S ver 4 [s] Isa 57:2 [t] Ps 16:5; Rev 14:13 [u] Mt 10:22; Jas 1:12

by a period of 1,290 days, corresponding to the last three and one-half years of the tribulation plus 45 days. A special blessing will also be pronounced on those who come through the 1,335 days. The significance of these days is not explained to Daniel, but this vision does let us know that there will be a period of time between the battle of Armageddon and the full establishment of the millennial kingdom. The important thing for us is that the wise (the godly) will understand; even if they do not understand everything, they will understand enough about end-time events to cause them to believe in Jesus and his kingdom and to enter into its final form.

HOSEA

Outline

Title (1:1)

I. Hosea's Marriage Illustrates Israel's Unfaithfulness, Rejection and Restoration (1:2—3:5)
   - A. Marriage to Gomer (1:2)
   - B. Birth of Their Three Children (1:3–9)
   - C. A Prophecy of Restoration (1:10—2:1)
   - D. Gomer as a Symbol of Israel (2:2–23)
     1. Israel's Adultery (2:2–5)
     2. God's Judgment (2:6–13)
     3. God's Promised Restoration of Israel (2:14–23)
   - E. Hosea's Redemption of Gomer (3:1–5)

II. Hosea's Message Describes Israel's Unfaithfulness, Rejection and Restoration (4:1—14:9)
   - A. Israel's Spiritual Adultery (4:1–19)
   - B. God's Judgment Against Israel (5:1–14)
   - C. Israel's Insincere Repentance (5:15—6:3)
   - D. Record of Israel's Sins (6:4—8:6)
     1. Breaking the Covenant (6:4–10)
     2. Refusal to Trust and Obey God (6:11—7:16)
     3. Going after False Gods (8:1–6)
   - E. Israel's Judgment Predicted (8:7—10:15)
     1. To Be Swallowed Up by the Nations (8:7–14)
     2. Prosperity to Evaporate (9:1–9)
     3. Wombs to Miscarry (9:10–17)
     4. Nation to Be Destroyed (10:1–15)
   - F. God's Persistent Love for Israel (11:1–11)
   - G. Israel's Sins Repeated (11:12—12:14)
   - H. God's Past Care and Present Anger (13:1–16)
     1. Israel's Idolatry (13:1–3)
     2. God's Care in the Exodus (13:4–6)
     3. God's Plan to Destroy Israel (13:7–13)
     4. God's Plan for Israel's Ultimate Restoration (13:14)
     5. Israel's Coming Destruction Reemphasized (13:15–16)
   - I. God's Promise to Restore Israel (14:1–9)
     1. Call to Repentance (14:1–3)
     2. Abundant Blessings Promised (14:4–9)

Author: Hosea

Theme: God's Judgment and Redeeming Love

Date of Writing: 715–710 B.C.

Background

Hosea, whose name means "salvation," is identified as the son of Beeri (1:1). Nothing else is known about the prophet apart from the autobiographical glimpses in the book itself. That Hosea was a native of Israel, not Judah, who prophesied to his own nation is apparent from (1) his numerous references to "Israel" and "Ephraim" (the two foremost designations for the northern kingdom) and to "Samaria" (the capital of the northern kingdom), (2) his reference to Israel's king at Samaria as "our king" (7:5), and (3) his intense concern about Israel's spiritual, moral, political and social corruption. Hosea's ministry to the northern kingdom followed closely on the heels of Amos's ministry (a prophet from Judah who prophesied to Israel). Amos and Hosea are the only two OT prophets whose prophetic books addressed entirely the northern kingdom and its coming destruction.

Hosea was called by God to prophesy to the crumbling kingdom of Israel during its last 30-plus years, just as Jeremiah was later required to do in Judah. When Hosea began his ministry during the latter years of Jeroboam II, Israel was enjoying a temporary period of economic prosperity and political peace that produced a false sense of security. Immediately after Jeroboam II died (753 B.C.), however, the nation began to deteriorate rapidly and ran swiftly to its destruction in 722 B.C. Within 15 years following his death, four of Israel's kings were assassinated; in 15 more years Samaria was a smoking ruin and the Israelites were deported to Assyria and later dispersed among the nations. Hosea's tragic marriage and prophetic word combined together as God's message to Israel during these final chaotic years of its slide to destruction.

God commanded Hosea to take "an adulterous wife" (1:2) to illustrate Israel's spiritual infidelity to God. Although some have interpreted Hosea's marriage as a fictitious allegory, most conservative Bible scholars view it as literal. It seems unlikely, however, that God would command a godly prophet to marry a prostitute in order to illustrate his message to Israel; it seems more likely that Hosea married Gomer when she was chaste, and she became a prostitute afterwards. Thus the command to take "an adulterous wife" was in prophetic anticipation of what was to be.

The historical setting of Hosea's ministry is identified as the reigns of Jeroboam II of Israel and four kings of Judah (Uzziah, Jotham, Ahaz and Hezekiah; see 1:1)—i.e., about 755–715 B.C.—making him not only a younger contemporary of Amos, but also of Isaiah and Micah. The fact that Hosea dates much of his ministry by referring to four kings in Judah rather than the brief reigns of Israel's last six kings, may indicate that he fled from the northern kingdom to live in the land of Judah shortly before Samaria was destroyed by Assyria (722 B.C.); there he compiled his prophecies into the book that now bears his name.

Purpose

The prophecy of Hosea was God's last attempt to call the Israelites to repent of their persistent idolatry and wickedness before giving them over to the full judgment of their sins. The book was written to reveal (1) that God maintained his love for his covenant people and intensely desired to redeem them from their iniquity, and (2) that tragic consequences follow when a people persist in disobeying God and in rejecting his redeeming love. The infidelity of Hosea's wife is recorded as an illustration of Israel's unfaithfulness to God. Gomer runs after other men, while Israel runs after other gods; Gomer commits physical adultery, while Israel commits spiritual adultery.

Survey

Chs. 1—3 describe Hosea's marriage to Gomer. The names of their three children are prophetic signs to Israel : Jezreel ("God Scatters"), Lo-Ruhamah ("Not Loved"), and Lo-Ammi ("Not My People"). Hosea's persevering love for his adulterous wife symbolizes God's steadfast love for Israel.

Chs. 4—14 contain a series of prophecies by Hosea that parallel Israel's unfaithfulness to that of his wife. Gomer's desertion of Hosea for other lovers (ch. 1) represents Israel's departure from God (chs. 4—7). Gomer's degradation (ch. 2) represents Israel's shame and judgment (chs. 8—10). Hosea's redemption of Gomer from the slave market (ch. 3) represents God's desire and intention to restore Israel in the future (chs. 11—14). The book emphasizes that because Israel has spurned God's love and his call to repentance, judgment can no longer be delayed.

Special Features

Seven major features characterize the book of Hosea. (1) It stands first in that part of the OT called "The Book of the Twelve," also known as the "Minor Prophets" ("minor" because of their brevity when compared with Isaiah, Jeremiah and Ezekiel). (2) Hosea is one of only two prophets from the north with a prophetic book in the OT (the other is Jonah). (3) As with Jeremiah and Ezekiel, Hosea's personal experiences illustrated his prophetic message. (4) It contains about 150 statements concerning Israel's sins, more than half of which relate to idolatry. (5) More than any other OT prophet, Hosea reminded the Israelites that the Lord had been patient and faithful in his love for them. (6) There is no discernible order among Hosea's prophecies in the main body of the book (chs. 4–14); it is difficult to tell where one prophecy ends and another begins. (7) Its prophecies are filled with vivid figures of speech, many of them taken from the rural scene.

New Testament Fulfillment

Hosea contains several verses that the NT quotes as being fulfilled in Jesus Christ: (1) the call of God's son out of Egypt (11:1; cf. Mt 2:15); (2) Christ's victory over death (13:14; cf. 1Co 15:55); (3) God's desire for mercy and not sacrifice (6:6; cf. Mt 9:13; 12:7); and (4) the Gentiles, who were not God's people, now becoming his people (1:6,9–10; 2:23; cf. Ro 9:25–26; 1Pe 1:10). In addition to specific passages, the NT expands the book's theme of God being the husband of his people, in that Christ is the bridegroom/husband of his redeemed bride, the church (see 1Co 11:2; Eph 5:22–32; Rev 19:6–9; 21:1–2,9–10). Hosea emphasizes the NT message of truly knowing God in order to enter into life (2:20; 4:6; 5:15; 6:3,6; cf. Jn 17:1–3). Coupled with this message, Hosea shows clearly the direct relationship between persistent sin and inescapable judgment. The two main emphases in Hosea are summed up by Paul in Ro 6:23: "For the wages of sin is death, but the gift of God is eternal life in Christ Jesus our Lord."

Reading Hosea

In order to read the entire Old Testament in one year, the book of Hosea should be read in 4 days, according to the following schedule: ☐ 1–2 ☐ 3–6 ☐ 7–10 ☐ 11–14

NOTES

1 The word of the LORD that came[a]
to Hosea son of Beeri during the
reigns of Uzziah,[b] Jotham,[c] Ahaz[d]
and Hezekiah,[e] kings of Judah,[f] and
during the reign of Jeroboam[g] son of
Jehoash[a] king of Israel:[h]

Hosea's Wife and Children

2When the LORD began to speak
through Hosea, the LORD said to him,
"Go, take to yourself an adulterous[i]
wife and children of unfaithfulness, because the land is guilty of the vilest
adultery[j] in departing from the LORD."
3So he married Gomer[k] daughter of
Diblaim, and she conceived and bore
him a son.
4Then the LORD said to Hosea, "Call
him Jezreel,[l] because I will soon punish the house of Jehu for the massacre
at Jezreel, and I will put an end to the
kingdom of Israel. 5In that day I will
break Israel's bow in the Valley of Jezreel.[m]"
6Gomer[n] conceived again and gave
birth to a daughter. Then the LORD said
to Hosea, "Call her Lo-Ruhamah,[b][o]
for I will no longer show love to the
house of Israel,[p] that I should at all
forgive them. 7Yet I will show love to
the house of Judah; and I will save
them—not by bow,[q] sword or battle,
or by horses and horsemen, but by the
LORD their God.[r]"
8After she had weaned Lo-Ruhamah,[s] Gomer had another son. 9Then
the LORD said, "Call him Lo-Ammi,[c] for
you are not my people, and I am not
your God.[t]
10"Yet the Israelites will be like the
sand on the seashore, which cannot be
measured or counted.[u] In the place
where it was said to them, 'You are not
my people,' they will be called 'sons of
the living God.'[v][w] 11The people of Judah and the people of Israel will be reunited,[x] and they will appoint one
leader[y] and will come up out of the

1:1 [a]S Jer 1:2 [b]S 2Ki 14:21 [c]S 1Ch 3:12 [d]S 1Ch 3:13 [e]S 1Ch 3:13 [f]Isa 1:1; Mic 1:1 [g]S 2Ki 13:13 [h]Am 1:1
1:2 [i]S Jer 3:1; Hos 2:2,5; 3:1 [j]Dt 31:16; Jer 3:14; Eze 23:3-21; Hos 5:3
1:3 [k]ver 6
1:4 [l]ver 11; S 1Sa 29:1; 1Ki 18:45; 2Ki 10:1-14; Hos 2:22
1:5 [m]S Jos 15:56; S 1Sa 29:1; 2Ki 15:29
1:6 [n]ver 3 [o]ver 8; Hos 2:23 [p]Hos 2:4
1:7 [q]S Ps 44:6 [r]Zec 4:6
1:8 [s]S ver 6
1:9 [t]ver 10; S Eze 11:19-20; 1Pe 2:10
1:10 [u]S Ge 22:17; S Jer 33:22 [v]S ver 9; Hos 2:23; Ro 9:26* [w]S Jos 3:10
1:11 [x]S Isa 11:12,13 [y]Jer 23:5-8; 30:9

[a] *1* Hebrew *Joash,* a variant of *Jehoash*
[b] *6 Lo-Ruhamah* means *not loved.*
[c] *9 Lo-Ammi* means *not my people.*

1:2 AN ADULTEROUS WIFE. God's relationship with Israel is frequently compared to a marriage contract (e.g., Isa 54:5; Jer 3:14; cf. Eph 5:22–32); Israel's "*departing* from the LORD" in order to worship idols was treated by God as spiritual infidelity or prostitution. Hosea's marriage was to be an object lesson for the unfaithful northern kingdom. Gomer was likely not a prostitute at the time of her marriage, but she would later turn to physical adultery and immorality, perhaps as a prostitute in the temple of Baal. Her departure from the Lord led not only to false worship, but also to lower moral standards. The same pattern of immoral living can be seen today wherever God's people turn away from true commitment to him (see Pr 5:3, note).

1:4 SOON PUNISH THE HOUSE OF JEHU. This verse very likely refers back to the killing of Ahab's 70 sons by Jehu (2Ki 10:1–8). Though Jehu was commended for bringing God's just judgment on Ahab's family, Jehu was too severe (2Ki 10:30–31).

1:4 AN END TO THE KINGDOM OF ISRAEL. God would soon bring judgment and destruction upon the northern kingdom of Israel. Hosea probably lived to see this prophecy fulfilled in 722 B.C., when the Assyrians took Samaria, carried off about 10 percent of the people and made the remaining people part of a province under the Assyrian empire.

1:6 I WILL NO LONGER SHOW LOVE. The name "Lo-Ruhamah" (literally, "not loved") means that God in his holiness had said it was time for his patience to come to an end; judgment must eventually come to a sinful and rebellious people.

1:7 I WILL SAVE THEM. The southern kingdom (Judah) would not come to an end at the same time as the northern kingdom (Israel). Because King Hezekiah was leading his nation in faith and repentance, the Lord saved them from Samaria's fate at that time (2Ki 19:32–36; Isa 37:36). Judah's kingdom lasted for another 136 years.

1:9 YOU ARE NOT MY PEOPLE. Gomer's third child, a boy named "Lo-Ammi" (meaning "not my people"), is not thought to be Hosea's. The child's name symbolized the breaking of the covenant relationship through ongoing rebellion against God and through idolatry; the people of the northern kingdom could no longer expect God to bless them and deliver their nation. Hosea was learning through his own anguish how God's heart was broken over his people's sins.

1:10–11 LIKE THE SAND ON THE SEASHORE. God's rejection of the northern kingdom as a separate nation did not mean God would forget his promise to Abraham, Isaac and Jacob concerning the land and the nation. In spite of Israel's sin, God would find a way to restore them to sonship; he would bring all twelve tribes together into one nation and under one leader. This promise of reuniting points to the reign of the coming Messiah.

1:11 GREAT WILL BE THE DAY OF JEZREEL. Jezreel means "God scatters," and it is used in a slightly different sense here from v. 4. God would scatter his people (see v. 4), but later he would bring them out of the lands where they were scattered and would sow them in their own land again, as a farmer scatters seeds.

land,[z] for great will be the day of Jezreel.[a]

2 "Say of your brothers, 'My people,' and of your sisters, 'My loved one.'[b]

Israel Punished and Restored

2"Rebuke your mother,[c] rebuke her,
for she is not my wife,
and I am not her husband.
Let her remove the adulterous[d] look from her face
and the unfaithfulness from between her breasts.
3Otherwise I will strip[e] her naked
and make her as bare as on the day she was born;[f]
I will make her like a desert,[g]
turn her into a parched land,
and slay her with thirst.
4I will not show my love to her children,[h]
because they are the children of adultery.[i]
5Their mother has been unfaithful
and has conceived them in disgrace.
She said, 'I will go after my lovers,[j]
who give me my food and my water,
my wool and my linen, my oil and my drink.'[k]
6Therefore I will block her path with thornbushes;
I will wall her in so that she cannot find her way.[l]
7She will chase after her lovers but not catch them;
she will look for them but not find them.[m]
Then she will say,
'I will go back to my husband[n] as at first,[o]
for then I was better off[p] than now.'
8She has not acknowledged[q] that I was the one
who gave her the grain, the new wine and oil,[r]
who lavished on her the silver and gold[s]—
which they used for Baal.[t]

9"Therefore I will take away my grain[u] when it ripens,
and my new wine[v] when it is ready.
I will take back my wool and my linen,
intended to cover her nakedness.
10So now I will expose[w] her lewdness
before the eyes of her lovers;[x]
no one will take her out of my hands.[y]
11I will stop[z] all her celebrations:[a]
her yearly festivals, her New Moons,
her Sabbath days—all her appointed feasts.[b]
12I will ruin her vines[c] and her fig trees,[d]
which she said were her pay from her lovers;[e]
I will make them a thicket,[f]
and wild animals will devour them.[g]
13I will punish her for the days
she burned incense[h] to the Baals;[i]
she decked herself with rings and jewelry,[j]
and went after her lovers,[k]
but me she forgot,[l]"
declares the LORD.[m]

1:11 [z]S Eze 37:15-28 [a]S ver 4
2:1 [b]ver 23; 1Pe 2:10
2:2 [c]ver 5; S Isa 50:1; S Hos 1:2; 4:5 [d]S Isa 1:21; S Eze 23:45
2:3 [e]S Eze 16:37 [f]Eze 16:4,22 [g]Isa 32:13-14
2:4 [h]S Eze 8:18; Hos 1:6 [i]Hos 5:7
2:5 [j]S Jer 3:6; S Hos 1:2 [k]Jer 44:17-18
2:6 [l]S Job 3:23; S 19:8; S La 3:9
2:7 [m]Hos 5:13 [n]S Isa 54:5 [o]Jer 2:2; S 3:1 [p]S Eze 16:8
2:8 [q]S Isa 1:3 [r]S Nu 18:12 [s]S Dt 8:18 [t]ver 13; Eze 16:15-19; Hos 8:4
2:9 [u]Hos 8:7 [v]Hos 9:2
2:10 [w]Eze 23:10 [x]Jer 13:26 [y]S Eze 16:37
2:11 [z]Jer 7:34 [a]S Isa 24:8 [b]S Isa 1:14; Jer 16:9; Hos 3:4; 9:5; Am 5:21; 8:10
2:12 [c]S Isa 7:23; S Jer 8:13 [d]S Jer 5:17 [e]S Jer 3:1 [f]S Isa 5:6 [g]Hos 5:7; 13:8
2:13 [h]Isa 65:7 [i]ver 8; S Jer 7:9; Hos 11:2 [j]S Eze 16:17; S 23:40 [k]Hos 4:13 [l]Hos 4:6; 8:14; 13:6 [m]S Jer 44:17; Hos 13:1

2:2–7 REBUKE YOUR MOTHER. Hosea returns again to warnings of judgment. "Rebuke" is a legal term used for presenting a case against someone with complaints and reproaches. The nation is the wife and mother; the individual Israelites are the children who have turned to idolatry. They must repent and turn from their "lovers" (2:5), i.e., from the various Canaanite gods.

2:6 THEREFORE I WILL BLOCK HER PATH. God promised to put obstacles in the Israelites' way—not to destroy them, but to make them realize it would be better for them to return to God. It is always appropriate to pray that God will bring difficulties into the lives of our unsaved loved ones, so that they will learn that it is far better to turn to the Lord and his goodness than to remain in the sorrow of sin.

2:8 HAS NOT ACKNOWLEDGED. Israel attributed their good harvest to the Baals (Canaanite gods), when in reality it was God's mercy and grace that brought good things to them. We must be careful always to acknowledge God's grace and the blessings that he gives us, and to thank him with grateful hearts. To fail to do so is to take a first step away from him.

2:11 STOP ALL HER CELEBRATIONS. God intended Israel's holy days and holy festivals to be times for rejoicing in his blessings; yet their rejoicing had turned to mere mirth and the hollow laughter of people trying to have a good time. The feasts God commanded were no longer his feasts; rather, they had become "her" (i.e., Israel's) feasts, mere social gatherings celebrated with empty ritual.

14“Therefore I am now going to
allure her;
I will lead her into the desert[n]
and speak tenderly to her.
15There I will give her back her
vineyards,
and will make the Valley of
Achor[d][o] a door of hope.
There she will sing[e][p] as in the
days of her youth,[q]
as in the day she came up out of
Egypt.[r]
16“In that day,” declares the LORD,
“you will call me ‘my
husband’;[s]
you will no longer call me ‘my
master.[f]’
17I will remove the names of the
Baals from her lips;[t]
no longer will their names be
invoked.[u]
18In that day I will make a covenant
for them
with the beasts of the field and
the birds of the air
and the creatures that move
along the ground.[v]
Bow and sword and battle
I will abolish[w] from the land,
so that all may lie down in
safety.[x]
19I will betroth[y] you to me forever;
I will betroth you in[g]
righteousness and justice,[z]
in[h] love and compassion.[a]
20I will betroth you in faithfulness,
and you will acknowledge[b] the
LORD.[c]

21“In that day I will respond,”
declares the LORD—
“I will respond[d] to the skies,
and they will respond to the
earth;
22and the earth will respond to the
grain,
the new wine and oil,[e]
and they will respond to
Jezreel.[i][f]
23I will plant[g] her for myself in the
land;
I will show my love to the one I
called ‘Not my loved
one.[j][h]’
I will say to those called ‘Not my
people,[k]’ ‘You are my
people’;[i]
and they will say, ‘You are my
God.[j]’ ”

2:14 [n]S Eze 19:13 **2:15** [o]S Jos 7:24, 26 [p]Ex 15:1-18 [q]S Jer 2:2; S Eze 16:22 [r]S Eze 28:26; Hos 12:9 **2:16** [s]S Isa 54:5 **2:17** [t]Ex 23:13; Ps 16:4 [u]S Jos 23:7; Zec 13:2 **2:18** [v]S Job 5:22 [w]S Ps 46:9; S Isa 2:4; Zec 9:10 [x]S Job 5:23; S Jer 23:6; Eze 34:25 **2:19** [y]S Isa 62:4; 2Co 11:2 [z]S Isa 1:27 [a]S Isa 54:8 **2:20** [b]Jer 31:34; Hos 4:1; 6:6; 13:4 [c]S Eze 16:8 **2:21** [d]Isa 55:10; Zec 8:12; Mal 3:10-11 **2:22** [e]S Jer 31:12; Hos 14:7; Joel 2:19 [f]S Eze 36:29-30; S Hos 1:4 **2:23** [g]S Jer 31:27 [h]S Hos 1:6 [i]S ver 1; S Isa 19:25; S Hos 1:10 [j]S Jer 29:12; Ro 9:25*; 1Pe 2:10 **3:1** [k]S Hos 1:2 [l]S 2Sa 6:19

Hosea’s Reconciliation With His Wife

3 The LORD said to me, “Go, show
your love to your wife again,
though she is loved by another and is
an adulteress.[k] Love her as the LORD
loves the Israelites, though they turn
to other gods and love the sacred raisin
cakes.[l]”
2So I bought her for fifteen shekels[1] of silver and about a homer and

[d]*15 Achor* means *trouble.* [e]*15* Or *respond* [f]*16* Hebrew *baal* [g]*19* Or *with*; also in verse 20 [h]*19* Or *with* [i]*22 Jezreel* means *God plants.* [j]*23* Hebrew *Lo-Ruhamah* [k]*23* Hebrew *Lo-Ammi* [1]*2* That is, about 6 ounces (about 170 grams)

2:14 THEREFORE ... ALLURE HER. Hosea alternates between warnings of judgment and promises of hope and restoration. The two preceding “therefores” (vv. 6,9) spoke of judgment; now God reveals a great and marvelous contrast. In his grace he would still call Israel to return. As in the exodus when God brought his people out of Egypt into the desert to give them his law and to lead them to the promised land, so he would again bring them out of the Egypt of their sin into a new desert, where he would guide, teach and restore them.

2:20 I WILL BETROTH YOU IN FAITHFULNESS. In Bible times, betrothal was a covenant commitment as binding as marriage itself. God here promised to restore Israel to a covenant relationship by his redeeming love and to cause them to know him in a real and personal way. In return, God was looking for righteousness, justice, steadfast love, kindness and faithfulness in his people. Likewise, he wants us to demonstrate faithfulness to him and sincere love and compassion for others.

2:23 PLANT HER FOR MYSELF IN THE LAND. God’s purpose for his people in bringing them out of Egypt was to establish a covenant relationship with them (Ex 19:4); that has always been his purpose with humankind. The NT applies the latter part of this verse to the inclusion of Gentiles into the church as his new Israel (Ro 9:25–26; 1Pe 2:10).

3:1 SHOW YOUR LOVE TO YOUR WIFE ... AN ADULTERESS. Hosea must now illustrate God’s love for Israel in a new way. Gomer had apparently deserted her husband in order to continue her immoral Baal worship, but Hosea had never given up his love for her, even though his heart was broken. He must go and express his love and care for her again, just as God would do for Israel, even though they have broken his heart by turning to other gods and loving “sacred raisin cakes.”

3:2 I BOUGHT HER. Though Gomer was most likely now in debt and about to be sold as a slave, as the laws allowed, Hosea came and bought her back at great cost to himself. This response of Hosea illustrates God’s redeeming love for sinners, who have no way to redeem, deliver or save themselves; our only hope is his grace.

a lethek[m] of barley. 3 Then I told her,
"You are to live with[n] me many days;
you must not be a prostitute or be intimate with any man, and I will live
with[n] you."
4 For the Israelites will live many
days without king or prince,[m] without
sacrifice[n] or sacred stones,[o] without
ephod[p] or idol.[q] 5 Afterward the Israelites will return and seek[r] the LORD
their God and David their king.[s] They
will come trembling[t] to the LORD and
to his blessings in the last days.[u]

The Charge Against Israel

4 Hear the word of the LORD, you
Israelites,
because the LORD has a charge[v]
to bring
against you who live in the
land:[w]
"There is no faithfulness,[x] no
love,
no acknowledgment[y] of God in
the land.[z]
2 There is only cursing,[o] lying[a]
and murder,[b]
stealing[c] and adultery;[d]
they break all bounds,
and bloodshed follows
bloodshed.[e]
3 Because of this the land
mourns,[p][f]
and all who live in it waste
away;[g]
the beasts of the field and the
birds of the air
and the fish of the sea are
dying.[h]

4 "But let no man bring a charge,
let no man accuse another,
for your people are like those
who bring charges against a
priest.[i]
5 You stumble[j] day and night,
and the prophets stumble with
you.
So I will destroy your mother[k]—
6 my people are destroyed from
lack of knowledge.[l]

"Because you have rejected
knowledge,
I also reject you as my priests;
because you have ignored the
law[m] of your God,
I also will ignore your children.
7 The more the priests increased,
the more they sinned against
me;
they exchanged[q] their[r] Glory[n]
for something disgraceful.[o]
8 They feed on the sins of my people
and relish their wickedness.[p]
9 And it will be: Like people, like
priests.[q]
I will punish both of them for
their ways
and repay them for their
deeds.[r]

10 "They will eat but not have
enough;[s]
they will engage in
prostitution[t] but not
increase,
because they have deserted[u] the
LORD
to give themselves 11 to
prostitution,[v]
to old wine[w] and new,

3:4 [m] Hos 13:11 [n] Da 11:31; S Hos 2:11 [o] Hos 10:1 [p] S Ex 25:7 [q] Jdg 17:5-6; 18:14-17; S La 2:9; Zec 10:2 **3:5** [r] S Dt 4:29; S Isa 9:13; S 10:20; Hos 5:15; Mic 4:1-2 [s] S 1Sa 13:14 [t] S Ps 18:45 [u] S Dt 4:30; S Jer 50:4-5; Hos 11:10 **4:1** [v] S Job 10:2; S Jer 2:9 [w] Joel 1:2,14 [x] S Pr 24:2 [y] S Pr 10:21; S Isa 1:3; Jer 7:28; S Hos 2:20 [z] S Jer 51:5 **4:2** [a] Isa 59:3; Hos 7:3; 10:4; 11:12 [b] Hos 5:2; 6:9 [c] Hos 7:1 [d] S Jer 9:2 [e] S 2Ki 21:16; S Isa 1:15; S Eze 22:2,9; Hos 5:2; 10:13 **4:3** [f] S Jer 4:28 [g] S Isa 15:6; S 33:9 [h] S Jer 4:25; S 9:10; S Eze 38:20; Zep 1:3 **4:4** [i] Dt 17:12; S Eze 3:26

4:5 [j] S Eze 7:19; S 14:7 [k] S Hos 2:2 **4:6** [l] S Pr 10:21; S Isa 1:3; S Hos 2:13; Mal 2:7-8 [m] Hos 8:1,12 **4:7** [n] Hab 2:16 [o] Hos 9:11; 10:1,6; 13:6 **4:8** [p] S Isa 56:11; Hos 14:1; Mic 3:11 **4:9** [q] S Isa 24:2 [r] Jer 5:31; Hos 8:13; 9:9,15; 10:10; 12:2 **4:10** [s] S Lev 26:26; S Isa 55:2; Mic 6:14 [t] S Eze 22:9 [u] Hos 7:14; 9:17 **4:11** [v] ver 14; Hos 5:4 [w] S Lev 10:9; S 1Sa 25:36

[m] *2* That is, probably about 10 bushels (about 330 liters) [n] *3* Or *wait for* [o] *2* That is, to pronounce a curse upon [p] *3* Or *dries up* [q] *7* Syriac and an ancient Hebrew scribal tradition; Masoretic Text *I will exchange* [r] *7* Masoretic Text; an ancient Hebrew scribal tradition *my*

3:5 AFTERWARD THE ISRAELITES WILL RETURN. After many days without a king or prince and without the sacrifices, Israel would return to God and to their Davidic King, i.e., the Messiah. They would humble themselves, come with godly sorrow (2Co 7:10) and recognize their need for the Savior, Jesus.

4:1 HAS A CHARGE TO BRING. This chapter begins a section dealing in great detail with Israel's sin, the root of which was a lack of knowledge of God and the Scriptures (see next note). Crime and violence had reached a critical point; fear and misery prevailed in the land (v. 2). An increase in crimes of violence always follows when a nation does not acknowledge God and his Word as its ultimate authority.

4:6 YOU HAVE REJECTED KNOWLEDGE. Lack of personal knowledge of God was destroying the people, but not because knowledge wasn't available. The people were willfully rejecting the truth God had given them through the prophets and his written Word. Even today within the church some are being destroyed by the sinful ways of the world because they do not know God and his inspired Word.

4:9 LIKE PEOPLE, LIKE PRIESTS. Instead of leading the people into paths of truth and righteousness, the priests were following the people, telling them what they wanted to hear and no longer rebuking their sins. God would therefore punish both the spiritual leaders and the people for their wickedness.

which take away the
understanding[x] 12of my
people.
They consult a wooden idol[y]
and are answered by a stick of
wood.[z]
A spirit of prostitution[a] leads
them astray;[b]
they are unfaithful[c] to their
God.
13They sacrifice on the mountaintops
and burn offerings on the hills,
under oak,[d] poplar and terebinth,
where the shade is pleasant.[e]
Therefore your daughters turn to
prostitution[f]
and your daughters-in-law to
adultery.[g]
14"I will not punish your daughters
when they turn to prostitution,
nor your daughters-in-law
when they commit adultery,
because the men themselves
consort with harlots[h]
and sacrifice with shrine
prostitutes[i]—
a people without
understanding[j] will come
to ruin![k]

15"Though you commit adultery,
O Israel,
let not Judah become guilty.

"Do not go to Gilgal;[l]
do not go up to Beth Aven.[s][m]
And do not swear, 'As surely as
the LORD lives!'[n]
16The Israelites are stubborn,[o]
like a stubborn heifer.[p]
How then can the LORD pasture
them
like lambs[q] in a meadow?
17Ephraim is joined to idols;
leave him alone!
18Even when their drinks are gone,
they continue their prostitution;
their rulers dearly love shameful
ways.
19A whirlwind[r] will sweep them
away,
and their sacrifices will bring
them shame.[s]

Judgment Against Israel

5 "Hear this, you priests!
Pay attention, you Israelites!
Listen, O royal house!
This judgment[t] is against you:
You have been a snare[u] at
Mizpah,
a net[v] spread out on Tabor.
2The rebels are deep in slaughter.[w]
I will discipline all of them.[x]
3I know all about Ephraim;
Israel is not hidden[y] from me.
Ephraim, you have now turned to
prostitution;
Israel is corrupt.[z]

4"Their deeds do not permit them
to return[a] to their God.
A spirit of prostitution[b] is in their
heart;
they do not acknowledge[c] the
LORD.
5Israel's arrogance testifies[d]
against them;
the Israelites, even Ephraim,
stumble[e] in their sin;
Judah also stumbles with
them.[f]
6When they go with their flocks and
herds
to seek the LORD,[g]

4:11 [x]S Pr 20:1 **4:12** [y]Jer 2:27 [z]Hab 2:19 [a]S Nu 15:39 [b]S Isa 44:20 [c]S Ps 73:27 **4:13** [d]S Isa 1:29 [e]S Jer 3:6; Hos 10:8; 11:2 [f]Jer 2:20; Am 7:17 [g]Hos 2:13 **4:14** [h]S ver 11 [i]S Ge 38:21; Hos 9:10 [j]S Pr 10:21 [k]ver 19 **4:15** [l]Hos 9:15; 12:11; Am 4:4; 5:5 [m]S Jos 7:2; S Hos 5:8 [n]S Jer 4:2 **4:16** [o]S Ex 32:9 [p]S Jer 31:18 [q]Isa 5:17; 7:25 **4:19** [r]Hos 12:1; 13:15 [s]ver 13-14; Isa 1:29 **5:1** [t]S Job 10:2 [u]Hos 6:9; 9:8 [v]S Jer 5:26 **5:2** [w]S Hos 4:2 [x]Hos 9:15 **5:3** [y]Am 5:12 [z]S Eze 23:7; S Hos 1:2; 6:10 **5:4** [a]Hos 7:10 [b]S Hos 4:11 [c]S Jer 4:22; S Hos 4:6 **5:5** [d]S Isa 3:9; S Jer 2:19; Hos 7:10 [e]S Eze 14:7 [f]Hos 14:1 **5:6** [g]Mic 6:6-7

[s]15 *Beth Aven* means *house of wickedness* (a name for Bethel, which means *house of God*).

4:11 OLD WINE AND NEW. The spirit of prostitution, whether associated with old wine or new wine, was destroying sound judgment and the discernment of God's ways. By itself, new, unfermented wine (i.e., *tirosh*) is a blessing (see Isa 65:8, note), but it stops being a blessing when it is associated with evil practices such as prostitution and idolatry (v. 12; see article on WINE IN THE OLD TESTAMENT, p. 204).

4:15 THE LORD LIVES. The priests were using religious and pious language to deceive the people and turn them away from the pure worship of the Lord. False teachers know how to use Biblical language to communicate unscriptural teachings. We must listen carefully to what is preached in order to evaluate whether the ideas being expressed are a proper exposition of the written Word of God (see article on FALSE TEACHERS, p. 1506).

5:1 YOU HAVE BEEN A SNARE. The people were snared, or trapped, into idolatry by the same religious and political leaders who should have been drawing them to the Lord.

5:6 HE HAS WITHDRAWN HIMSELF. The Israelites were coming with their flocks and herds to offer sacrifices and to seek the Lord, but they would not find him. He had withdrawn himself from them because their deeds were evil. There was no love, no faith, no faithfulness and no real repentance; their hearts had been given over to sinful pleasures. Sometimes when people seek help from the Lord, they do not find it because they keep holding on to the immoral and sinful attractions of the world (cf. Jas 4:1–4; see article on

they will not find him;
he has withdrawn[h] himself from them.
7They are unfaithful[i] to the LORD;
they give birth to illegitimate[j] children.
Now their New Moon festivals[k]
will devour[l] them and their fields.

8"Sound the trumpet[m] in Gibeah,[n]
the horn in Ramah.[o]
Raise the battle cry in Beth Aven[t];[p]
lead on, O Benjamin.
9Ephraim will be laid waste[q]
on the day of reckoning.[r]
Among the tribes of Israel
I proclaim what is certain.[s]
10Judah's leaders are like those
who move boundary stones.[t]
I will pour out my wrath[u] on them
like a flood of water.
11Ephraim is oppressed,
trampled in judgment,
intent on pursuing idols.[u][v]
12I am like a moth[w] to Ephraim,
like rot[x] to the people of Judah.

13"When Ephraim[y] saw his sickness,
and Judah his sores,
then Ephraim turned to Assyria,[z]
and sent to the great king for help.[a]
But he is not able to cure[b] you,
not able to heal your sores.[c]
14For I will be like a lion[d] to Ephraim,
like a great lion to Judah.
I will tear them to pieces[e] and go away;
I will carry them off, with no one to rescue them.[f]
15Then I will go back to my place[g]
until they admit their guilt.[h]
And they will seek my face;[i]
in their misery[j] they will
earnestly seek me.[k]"

Israel Unrepentant

6 "Come, let us return[l] to the LORD.
He has torn us to pieces[m]
but he will heal us;[n]
he has injured us
but he will bind up our wounds.[o]
2After two days he will revive us;[p]
on the third day[q] he will
restore[r] us,
that we may live in his presence.
3Let us acknowledge the LORD;
let us press on to acknowledge him.
As surely as the sun rises,
he will appear;
he will come to us like the winter rains,[s]
like the spring rains that water the earth.[t]"

4"What can I do with you,
Ephraim?[u]

Hos 14:4-8

5:6 [h]S Pr 1:28; Isa 1:15; Eze 8:6; Mal 1:10 5:7 [i]S Isa 24:16; Hos 6:7 [j]Hos 2:4 [k]Isa 1:14 [l]S Hos 2:11-12 5:8 [m]S Nu 10:2; S Jer 4:21; S Eze 33:3 [n]Jdg 19:12; Hos 9:9; 10:9 [o]S Isa 10:29 [p]S Jos 7:2; Hos 4:15; 10:5 5:9 [q]S Isa 7:16 [r]Isa 37:3; Hos 9:11-17 [s]Isa 46:10; Zec 1:6 5:10 [t]S Dt 19:14 [u]S Eze 7:8 5:11 [v]Hos 9:16; Mic 6:16 5:12 [w]S Job 13:28; S Isa 51:8 [x]S Job 18:16 5:13 [y]S Isa 7:16 [z]S Eze 23:5; Hos 7:11; 8:9; 12:1 [a]S La 5:6; Hos 7:8; 10:6 [b]S Isa 3:7; Hos 14:3 [c]Hos 2:7 5:14 [d]S Job 10:16; S Jer 4:7; Am 3:4 [e]Hos 6:1 [f]S Dt 32:39; Mic 5:8 5:15 [g]S Isa 18:4 [h]S Lev 26:40 [i]S Nu 21:7; S Ps 24:6; S Hos 3:5 [j]Ps 50:15; S Jer 2:27 [k]Isa 64:9; S Eze 20:43 6:1 [l]S Isa 10:20; S 19:22 [m]S Job 16:9; La 3:11; Hos 5:14 [n]S Nu 12:13; S Jer 3:22 [o]S Dt 32:39; S Job 5:18; S Jer 30:17; Hos 14:4 6:2 [p]Ps 30:5; S 80:18 [q]S Mt 16:21 [r]S Ps 71:20 6:3 [s]S Job 4:3; Joel 2:23 [t]Ps 72:6; Hos 11:10; 12:6 6:4 [u]Hos 11:8

[t]8 *Beth Aven* means *house of wickedness* (a name for Bethel, which means *house of God*).
[u]11 The meaning of the Hebrew for this word is uncertain.

EFFECTIVE PRAYING, p. 496).
5:10 WHO MOVE BOUNDARY STONES. The effect of moving the boundary stones of your neighbor's property is to steal a strip of his land (Dt 19:14; 27:17).
5:12 LIKE A MOTH . . . LIKE ROT. Because of their rebellion, God would give his people sickness and disease. Ephraim (the northern Israel) and Judah would decay. Sin brings God's judgment; there is only one cure for sin, the cure God has provided—the blood of Jesus.
5:15 I WILL GO BACK TO MY PLACE. God would not hear Israel's prayer for help until they admitted their guilt, bore their punishment and genuinely sought his help. The next chapter records the prophetic words that a future repentant generation would pray (6:1–3).
6:1 HE WILL HEAL US. In yet another call to repentance, Hosea gives assurance that though God must judge sin, he always desires to heal and restore.
6:2–3 AFTER TWO DAYS HE WILL REVIVE US. Genuine repentance by God's people would bring renewed spiritual life. Then as they began to know the Lord better, he would come like the rain, bringing further spiritual life and blessing. Water is often used as a symbol or type of the Holy Spirit (see Jn 7:37–39; see Ps 1:3, note). The spring rains are the rains that come in the time of plowing and planting; they symbolize the Holy Spirit's work in OT times (see article on THE SPIRIT IN THE OLD TESTAMENT, p. 1302). The winter rains are the rains that come in the time of harvest; they symbolize the Holy Spirit's work in the age of the church.
6:4 YOUR LOVE IS LIKE THE MORNING MIST. "Love" (Heb *hesed*) refers to a covenant love that is holy, steadfast and loyal. Israel claimed to have a deep love for God; but just as the morning mist and the early dew vanish in the heat

What can I do with you, Judah?
Your love is like the morning mist,
like the early dew that
disappears.[v]
5Therefore I cut you in pieces with
my prophets,
I killed you with the words of
my mouth;[w]
my judgments flashed like
lightning upon you.[x]
6For I desire mercy, not sacrifice,[y]
and acknowledgment[z] of God
rather than burnt
offerings.[a]
7Like Adam,▼ they have broken the
covenant[b] —
they were unfaithful[c] to me
there.
8Gilead is a city of wicked men,[d]
stained with footprints of blood.
9As marauders lie in ambush for a
man,[e]
so do bands of priests;
they murder[f] on the road to
Shechem,
committing shameful crimes.[g]
10I have seen a horrible[h] thing
in the house of Israel.
There Ephraim is given to
prostitution
and Israel is defiled.[i]

11"Also for you, Judah,
a harvest[j] is appointed.

"Whenever I would restore the
fortunes[k] of my people,

7

1whenever I would heal Israel,
the sins of Ephraim are exposed
and the crimes of Samaria
revealed.[l]
They practice deceit,[m]
thieves break into houses,[n]
bandits rob in the streets;[o]
2but they do not realize
that I remember[p] all their evil
deeds.[q]
Their sins engulf them;[r]
they are always before me.

3"They delight the king with their
wickedness,
the princes with their lies.[s]
4They are all adulterers,[t]
burning like an oven
whose fire the baker need not stir
from the kneading of the dough
till it rises.
5On the day of the festival of our
king
the princes become inflamed
with wine,[u]
and he joins hands with the
mockers.[v]
6Their hearts are like an oven;[w]
they approach him with intrigue.
Their passion smolders all night;
in the morning it blazes like a
flaming fire.
7All of them are hot as an oven;
they devour their rulers.
All their kings fall,[x]
and none of them calls[y] on me.

8"Ephraim mixes[z] with the nations;
Ephraim is a flat cake not
turned over.
9Foreigners sap his strength,[a]
but he does not realize it.
His hair is sprinkled with gray,
but he does not notice.
10Israel's arrogance testifies against
him,[b]
but despite all this
he does not return[c] to the LORD
his God
or search[d] for him.

11"Ephraim is like a dove,[e]

6:4 [v] Hos 7:1; 13:3
6:5 [w] Jer 1:9-10; 5:14; 23:29 [x] Heb 4:12
6:6 [y] S 1Sa 15:22; S Isa 1:11; Mt 9:13*; 12:7*; Mk 12:33 [z] S Jer 4:22; S Hos 2:20 [a] S Ps 40:6; Mic 6:8
6:7 [b] S Ge 9:11; S Jer 11:10; Hos 8:1 [c] S Hos 5:7
6:8 [d] Hos 12:11
6:9 [e] Ps 10:8 [f] S Hos 4:2 [g] Jer 5:30-31; 7:9-10; S Eze 22:9; S Hos 5:1; 7:1
6:10 [h] S Jer 5:30 [i] S Jer 23:14; S Eze 23:7; S Hos 5:3
6:11 [j] Jer 51:33; Joel 3:13 [k] S Ps 126:1; Zep 2:7
7:1 [l] S Eze 24:13; S Hos 6:4 [m] ver 13 [n] S Ex 22:2; Hos 4:2 [o] S Hos 6:9; 12:1
7:2 [p] S Jer 14:10; S 44:21; S Hos 8:13 [q] S Job 35:15; Hos 9:15 [r] Jer 2:19; 4:18
7:3 [s] Jer 28:1-4; S Hos 4:2; 10:13; Mic 7:3
7:4 [t] S Jer 9:2
7:5 [u] S Isa 28:1,7 [v] S Ps 1:1
7:6 [w] Ps 21:9
7:7 [x] Hos 13:10 [y] ver 16; S Ps 14:4; S Isa 9:13; Zep 1:6
7:8 [z] ver 11; Ps 106:35; S Hos 5:13
7:9 [a] Isa 1:7; Hos 8:7
7:10 [b] Hos 5:5 [c] Hos 5:4 [d] ver 14; S Isa 9:13
7:11 [e] S Ge 8:8

▼7 Or *As at Adam*; or *Like men*

of the day, so did that love, for it was superficial and selfish. We must always test our love for God by our loyalty to Jesus Christ and our commitment to his righteous law and to his purposes on earth.

6:6 I DESIRE MERCY . . . AND ACKNOWLEDGMENT OF GOD. What God really wanted from his people was "mercy" (Heb *hesed*, cf. previous note), i.e., a steadfast and loyal love that responded to his love; he also wanted a personal acknowledgment of him as Lord of their lives. God wants the same from us.

7:2 EVIL DEEDS . . . ALWAYS BEFORE ME. We must remember that God observes all our thoughts and actions and records them in his book. A keen awareness of his presence will keep us from evil. Satan's goal, on the other hand, is to make us forget that God is always there watching us.

7:8 MIXES WITH THE NATIONS. The Israelites had entered into close fellowship with unbelievers, adopting many of their ways; as a result they were now as worthless as a half-cooked piece of bread. It is true that God calls us to witness to the lost and help them as we are able, but we must not enter into close fellowship with the world, for we run the risk of adopting their ways and attitudes and thereby turning to sin and away from God (cf. Jude 23; see articles on SPIRITUAL SEPARATION FOR BELIEVERS, p. 1794, and THE CHRISTIAN'S RELATIONSHIP TO THE WORLD, p. 1976).

easily deceived and senseless—
now calling to Egypt,[f]
now turning to Assyria.[g]
12When they go, I will throw my
net[h] over them;
I will pull them down like birds
of the air.
When I hear them flocking
together,
I will catch them.
13Woe[i] to them,
because they have strayed[j]
from me!
Destruction to them,
because they have rebelled
against me!
I long to redeem them
but they speak lies[k] against
me.[l]
14They do not cry out to me from
their hearts[m]
but wail upon their beds.
They gather together[w] for grain
and new wine[n]
but turn away from me.[o]
15I trained[p] them and strengthened
them,
but they plot evil[q] against me.
16They do not turn to the Most
High;[r]
they are like a faulty bow.[s]
Their leaders will fall by the sword
because of their insolent[t]
words.
For this they will be ridiculed[u]
in the land of Egypt.[v]

Israel to Reap the Whirlwind

8 "Put the trumpet[w] to your lips!
An eagle[x] is over the house of
the LORD
because the people have broken
my covenant[y]
and rebelled against my law.[z]
2Israel cries out to me,
'O our God, we acknowledge
you!'
3But Israel has rejected what is
good;
an enemy will pursue him.[a]
4They set up kings without my
consent;
they choose princes without my
approval.[b]
With their silver and gold
they make idols[c] for
themselves
to their own destruction.
5Throw out your calf-idol,
O Samaria![d]
My anger burns against them.
How long will they be incapable of
purity?[e]
6 They are from Israel!
This calf—a craftsman has made
it;
it is not God.[f]
It will be broken in pieces,
that calf[g] of Samaria.[h]
7"They sow the wind
and reap the whirlwind.[i]
The stalk has no head;
it will produce no flour.[j]
Were it to yield grain,
foreigners would swallow it
up.[k]
8Israel is swallowed up;[l]
now she is among the nations
like a worthless[m] thing.
9For they have gone up to Assyria[n]
like a wild donkey[o] wandering
alone.
Ephraim has sold herself to
lovers.[p]

7:11 [f]ver 16; Hos 9:6 [g]S ver 8; S Jer 2:18; S La 5:6; Hos 9:3; 12:1 **7:12** [h]S Eze 12:13; S 32:3 **7:13** [i]Hos 9:12 [j]Jer 14:10; S Eze 34:4-6; Hos 9:17 [k]S Ps 116:11 [l]ver 1; Jer 51:9; Mt 23:37 **7:14** [m]Jer 3:10 [n]Am 2:8 [o]S ver 10; S Hos 4:10; 9:1; 13:16 **7:15** [p]Hos 11:3 [q]Ps 2:1; S 140:2; Na 1:9,11 **7:16** [r]S ver 7 [s]S Ps 78:9,57 [t]Mal 3:14 [u]S Eze 23:32 [v]S ver 11; Hos 9:3; 11:5 **8:1** [w]S Nu 10:2; S Eze 33:3 [x]S Dt 28:49; Jer 4:13 [y]S Jer 11:10 [z]S Hos 4:6; S 6:7 **8:3** [a]S Mt 7:23; Tit 1:16 **8:4** [b]Hos 13:10 [c]S Hos 2:8; 13:1-2 **8:5** [d]ver 6; Hos 10:5 [e]Jer 13:27 **8:6** [f]S Jer 16:20; Hos 14:3 [g]S Ex 32:4 [h]S ver 5 **8:7** [i]S Job 4:8; Pr 22:8; Isa 66:15; Hos 10:12-13; Na 1:3; Gal 6:8 [j]S Dt 28:38; S Isa 17:11; Hos 9:16 [k]Hos 2:9; S 7:9 **8:8** [l]Jer 51:34 [m]Jer 22:28 **8:9** [n]S Jer 2:18 [o]S Ge 16:12 [p]S Jer 22:20; Eze 23:5; S Hos 5:13

w *14* Most Hebrew manuscripts; some Hebrew manuscripts and Septuagint *They slash themselves*

7:13–16 THEY HAVE STRAYED FROM ME. Israel rebelled against God by refusing to turn to him as the One who could help them; they felt that Egypt and Assyria offered more security than the Lord their God (v. 11). People commit the same sort of sin today when they seek personal fulfillment in possessions, activities or sinful pleasures rather than in God's will and word.

8:2–3 ISRAEL CRIES OUT TO ME. Israel would keep calling on God and claiming to serve him, but their profession would do them no good. Their worship of God was corrupted by their worldly and sinful lives. They were praising God while at the same time rejecting his righteous ways.

8:4 SET UP KINGS WITHOUT MY CONSENT. The people were choosing leaders who did not meet with God's approval. The apostle Paul warns of a time when churches will choose pastors who are not qualified according to God's righteous standards (see 2Ti 4:3–4, note; see article on MORAL QUALIFICATIONS FOR OVERSEERS, p. 1882).

8:7 SOW THE WIND AND REAP THE WHIRLWIND. Israel had sown the wind of sin and idolatry; now they would reap the whirlwind of the Assyrian attack. We must remember that sinful actions and attitudes sow seeds that will yield evil fruit in our lives (see Job 4:8; Gal 6:7; cf. Ps 126:5–6; Pr 11:18; 2Co 9:6).

10Although they have sold
themselves among the
nations,
I will now gather them
together.[q]
They will begin to waste away[r]
under the oppression of the
mighty king.

11"Though Ephraim built many altars
for sin offerings,
these have become altars for
sinning.[s]
12I wrote for them the many things
of my law,
but they regarded them as
something alien.[t]
13They offer sacrifices given to me
and they eat[u] the meat,
but the LORD is not pleased with
them.[v]
Now he will remember[w] their
wickedness
and punish their sins:[x]
They will return to Egypt.[y]
14Israel has forgotten[z] his Maker[a]
and built palaces;
Judah has fortified many towns.
But I will send fire upon their
cities
that will consume their
fortresses."[b]

Punishment for Israel

9 Do not rejoice, O Israel;
do not be jubilant[c] like the
other nations.
For you have been unfaithful[d] to
your God;
you love the wages of a
prostitute[e]
at every threshing floor.
2Threshing floors and winepresses
will not feed the people;
the new wine[f] will fail them.
3They will not remain[g] in the
LORD's land;
Ephraim will return to Egypt[h]
and eat unclean[x] food in
Assyria.[i]
4They will not pour out wine
offerings[j] to the LORD,
nor will their sacrifices please[k]
him.
Such sacrifices will be to them like
the bread of mourners;[l]
all who eat them will be
unclean.[m]
This food will be for themselves;
it will not come into the temple
of the LORD.[n]

5What will you do[o] on the day of
your appointed feasts,[p]
on the festival days of the LORD?
6Even if they escape from
destruction,
Egypt will gather them,[q]
and Memphis[r] will bury
them.[s]
Their treasures of silver[t] will be
taken over by briers,
and thorns[u] will overrun their
tents.
7The days of punishment[v] are
coming,
the days of reckoning[w] are at
hand.
Let Israel know this.
Because your sins[x] are so many
and your hostility so great,
the prophet is considered a fool,[y]
the inspired man a maniac.[z]
8The prophet, along with my God,
is the watchman over Ephraim,[y]

8:10 [q]S Eze 16:37; S 22:20 [r]Jer 42:2 **8:11** [s]Hos 10:1; 12:11 **8:12** [t]S ver 1 **8:13** [u]S Jer 7:21 [v]S Jer 6:20; Hos 9:4 [w]Hos 7:2; 9:9; Am 8:7 [x]S Hos 4:9 [y]Hos 9:3,6 **8:14** [z]S Dt 32:18; S Isa 17:10; S Hos 2:13 [a]S Ps 95:6 [b]Jer 5:17; S 17:27; Am 2:5 **9:1** [c]Isa 22:12-13 [d]S Ps 73:27; S Isa 24:16; S Hos 7:14; 10:5 [e]S Ge 30:15 **9:2** [f]Isa 24:7; Hos 2:9; Joel 1:10 **9:3** [g]Lev 25:23 [h]S Hos 7:16; S 8:13 [i]Eze 4:13; S Hos 7:11; 10:5; Am 7:17 **9:4** [j]Joel 1:9,13; 2:14 [k]S Hos 8:13 [l]S Jer 16:7 [m]S Dt 26:14; Hag 2:13-14 [n]S Eze 4:13-14 **9:5** [o]Isa 10:3; Jer 5:31 [p]S Hos 2:11 **9:6** [q]S Hos 7:11; S 8:13 [r]S Isa 19:13 [s]S Jer 42:22 [t]Zep 1:11 [u]Isa 5:6; Hos 10:8 **9:7** [v]Isa 34:8; Jer 10:15; Mic 7:4; Lk 21:22 [w]S Job 31:14 [x]Jer 16:18 [y]S 1Sa 10:11; Isa 44:25; S La 2:14; Eze 14:9-10 [z]S Jer 29:26; Hos 14:1

[x]3 That is, ceremonially unclean [y]8 Or *The prophet is the watchman over Ephraim, / the people of my God*

8:11 ALTARS FOR SINNING. The altars Israel built in the north were not commanded by God; their sacrifices thus expressed their selfish ambitions and desires. Our worship of the Lord must be based on the teachings of Scripture and follow the practices of the NT church. False worship may appear beautiful to our senses and may entertain us, but it is still sinful, for it substitutes worldly ways of worship for the true worship in the Spirit of God (cf. Jn 4:23–24; see article on WORSHIP, p. 680).

8:12 MY LAW . . . SOMETHING ALIEN. Long before Hosea's day, God had given the Israelites his laws and commands. But the people were treating God's word as a strange or alien thing. Many people in the church today rarely read their Bibles or cherish God's laws; the commands of his Word do not suit them because they want to continue in their sin.

9:3 EPHRAIM WILL RETURN TO EGYPT. Hosea prophesies that Ephraim (i.e., the northern kingdom) would go into exile. Egypt symbolized the slavery and oppression they once endured; the Egypt they were now about to go to was Assyria (see 11:5, note).

9:7 PROPHET IS CONSIDERED A FOOL. Many Israelites regarded God's prophets as foolish and insane (cf. 2Ki 9:1–3,11). They were hostile toward any prophet who preached against their sins and warned them of God's coming judgment. Frequently today those ministers who challenge the lifestyles of church members and confront them with their conformity to the world will find themselves ridiculed by some within the church.

yet snares[a] await him on all his
paths,
and hostility in the house of his
God.[b]
9They have sunk deep into
corruption,[c]
as in the days of Gibeah.[d]
God will remember[e] their
wickedness
and punish them for their sins.[f]

10"When I found Israel,
it was like finding grapes in the
desert;
when I saw your fathers,
it was like seeing the early
fruit[g] on the fig[h] tree.
But when they came to Baal
Peor,[i]
they consecrated themselves to
that shameful idol[j]
and became as vile as the thing
they loved.
11Ephraim's glory[k] will fly away
like a bird[l]—
no birth, no pregnancy, no
conception.[m]
12Even if they rear children,
I will bereave[n] them of every
one.
Woe[o] to them
when I turn away from them![p]
13I have seen Ephraim,[q] like Tyre,
planted in a pleasant place.[r]
But Ephraim will bring out
their children to the slayer."[s]

14Give them, O LORD—
what will you give them?
Give them wombs that miscarry
and breasts that are dry.[t]

15"Because of all their wickedness in
Gilgal,[u]
I hated them there.
Because of their sinful deeds,[v]
I will drive them out of my
house.
I will no longer love them;[w]
all their leaders are rebellious.[x]
16Ephraim[y] is blighted,
their root is withered,
they yield no fruit.[z]
Even if they bear children,
I will slay[a] their cherished
offspring."

17My God will reject[b] them
because they have not obeyed[c]
him;
they will be wanderers among
the nations.[d]

10 Israel was a spreading vine;[e]
he brought forth fruit for
himself.
As his fruit increased,
he built more altars;[f]
as his land prospered,[g]
he adorned his sacred stones.[h]
2Their heart is deceitful,[i]
and now they must bear their
guilt.[j]
The LORD will demolish their
altars[k]
and destroy their sacred
stones.[l]

3Then they will say, "We have no
king
because we did not revere the
LORD.
But even if we had a king,
what could he do for us?"
4They make many promises,
take false oaths[m]
and make agreements;[n]
therefore lawsuits spring up
like poisonous weeds[o] in a
plowed field.
5The people who live in Samaria
fear
for the calf-idol[p] of Beth
Aven.[z][q]
Its people will mourn over it,
and so will its idolatrous
priests,[r]
those who had rejoiced over its
splendor,
because it is taken from them
into exile.[s]
6It will be carried to Assyria[t]

9:8 [a]S Hos 5:1 [b]S Eze 22:26 9:9 [c]Zep 3:7 [d]Jdg 19:16-30; S Hos 5:8 [e]S Hos 8:13 [f]S Hos 4:9 9:10 [g]S SS 2:13 [h]S Isa 28:4 [i]Nu 25:1-5; Ps 106:28-29 [j]Jer 11:13; S Hos 4:14 9:11 [k]S Isa 17:3 [l]S Hos 4:7; 10:5 [m]ver 14 9:12 [n]ver 16; S Eze 24:21 [o]Hos 7:13 [p]S Dt 31:17 9:13 [q]S Ps 78:67 [r]S Eze 27:3 [s]S Job 15:22; S La 2:22 9:14 [t]ver 11; Lk 23:29 9:15 [u]S Hos 4:15 [v]S Hos 7:2 [w]S Jer 12:8 [x]S Isa 1:23; S Hos 4:9; 5:2 9:16 [y]S Hos 5:11 [z]S Job 15:32; S Hos 8:7 [a]S ver 12 9:17 [b]S Jer 6:30 [c]S Hos 4:10 [d]S Dt 28:65; S Hos 7:13 10:1 [e]S Eze 15:2 [f]S 1Ki 14:23 [g]Hos 13:15 [h]Hos 3:4; S 4:7; S 8:11; 12:11 10:2 [i]1Ki 18:21 [j]Hos 13:16 [k]ver 8 [l]Mic 5:13 10:4 [m]S Hos 4:2 [n]S Eze 17:19; Am 5:7 [o]Am 6:12 10:5 [p]S Ex 32:4; S Isa 44:17-20 [q]ver 8; S Hos 5:8 [r]S 2Ki 23:5; Zep 1:4 [s]S Jdg 18:17-18; S Hos 8:5; S 9:1,3, 11 10:6 [t]S 2Ki 16:7; Hos 11:5

[z]5 *Beth Aven* means *house of wickedness* (a name for Bethel, which means *house of God*).

9:15 I WILL NO LONGER LOVE THEM. God's love is not unconditional for those who repeatedly reject his grace and word. The teaching that God will love us forever no matter what evil we do is contrary to Biblical revelation.

9:17 THEY WILL BE WANDERERS. In fulfillment of Dt 28:65–66, Israel was to become a disbanded nation of homeless vagabonds because they had not listened to the warnings of God's word through the prophets.

10:1 AS HIS FRUIT INCREASED. The more Israel's land had prospered and brought forth fruit, the more the Israelites engaged in idolatry. Great prosperity is not necessarily a blessing. The more money some people have, the more they spend on themselves; they forget God and the needs of his kingdom, becoming self-centered rather than God-centered.

as tribute[u] for the great king.[v]
Ephraim will be disgraced;[w]
Israel will be ashamed[x] of its
wooden idols.[a]
7Samaria and its king will float
away[y]
like a twig on the surface of the
waters.
8The high places[z] of
wickedness[b][a] will be
destroyed—
it is the sin of Israel.
Thorns[b] and thistles will grow up
and cover their altars.[c]
Then they will say to the
mountains, "Cover us!"[d]
and to the hills, "Fall on us!"[e]
9"Since the days of Gibeah,[f] you
have sinned,[g] O Israel,
and there you have remained.[c]
Did not war overtake
the evildoers in Gibeah?
10When I please, I will punish[h]
them;
nations will be gathered against
them
to put them in bonds for their
double sin.
11Ephraim is a trained heifer
that loves to thresh;
so I will put a yoke[i]
on her fair neck.
I will drive Ephraim,
Judah must plow,
and Jacob must break up the
ground.
12Sow[j] for yourselves
righteousness,[k]
reap the fruit of unfailing love,
and break up your unplowed
ground;[l]
for it is time to seek[m] the LORD,
until he comes
and showers righteousness[n] on
you.
13But you have planted wickedness,
you have reaped evil,[o]
you have eaten the fruit of
deception.[p]
Because you have depended on
your own strength
and on your many warriors,[q]
14the roar of battle will rise against
your people,
so that all your fortresses will
be devastated[r]—
as Shalman[s] devastated Beth
Arbel on the day of battle,
when mothers were dashed to
the ground with their
children.[t]
15Thus will it happen to you,
O Bethel,
because your wickedness is
great.
When that day dawns,
the king of Israel will be
completely destroyed.[u]

God's Love for Israel

11 "When Israel was a child,[v] I
loved[w] him,
and out of Egypt I called my
son.[x]
2But the more I[d] called Israel,
the further they went from
me.[e][y]
They sacrificed to the Baals[z]
and they burned incense to
images.[a]

10:6 [u] S Jdg 3:15 [v] S Hos 5:13 [w] Isa 30:3; S Hos 4:7 [x] Jer 48:13 **10:7** [y] ver 15; Hos 13:11 **10:8** [z] S Eze 6:6 [a] S ver 5; 1Ki 12:28-30; S Hos 4:13 [b] S Hos 9:6 [c] ver 2; S Isa 32:13 [d] S Job 30:6; Am 3:14-15 [e] Am 7:9; Lk 23:30*; Rev 6:16 **10:9** [f] S Hos 5:8 [g] S Jos 7:11 **10:10** [h] S Eze 5:13; S Hos 4:9 **10:11** [i] S Jer 15:12; S 31:18 **10:12** [j] S Ecc 11:1 [k] S Pr 11:18; Jas 3:18 [l] Jer 4:3 [m] S Isa 19:22; Hos 12:6 [n] S Isa 45:8 **10:13** [o] S Job 4:8; S Hos 7:3; 11:12; Gal 6:7-8 [p] S Pr 11:18; S Hos 8:7 [q] Ps 33:16 **10:14** [r] S Isa 17:3; Mic 5:11 [s] S 2Ki 17:3 [t] S Isa 13:16; Hos 13:16 **10:15** [u] S ver 7 **11:1** [v] S Jer 2:2; S Eze 16:22 [w] S Dt 4:37 [x] S Ex 4:22; Hos 12:9,13; 13:4; Mt 2:15* **11:2** [y] ver 7 [z] S Hos 2:13 [a] S 2Ki 17:15; Isa 65:7; S Jer 18:15; S Hos 4:13; 13:1

[a] *6* Or *its counsel* [b] *8* Hebrew *aven,* a reference to Beth Aven (a derogatory name for Bethel) [c] *9* Or *there a stand was taken* [d] *2* Some Septuagint manuscripts; Hebrew *they* [e] *2* Septuagint; Hebrew *them*

10:8 COVER US! Those who had trusted in false gods and adopted sensual pagan lifestyles would call on the mountains and hills to fall on them and hide them from God's wrath once his judgment began. Backsliders and the enemies of God and his people will do the same when the present world system collapses and they see the wrath of God poured out on this world (see Lk 23:30; Rev 6:16; see article on THE GREAT TRIBULATION, p. 1456).

10:12 BREAK UP YOUR UNPLOWED GROUND. Unplowed ground is soil that has been so neglected and hardened that it cannot receive seed. The peoples' hearts had become like that spiritually (v. 13). They needed to break up their own hearts and minds by sorrow for sin and a repentance that would open them to the word and will of God; they had to begin sowing seeds of righteousness by earnestly seeking God, until they once again experienced his faithful love and mercy.

10:14 SHALMAN. This name probably refers to Shalmaneser (2Ki 17:3), who took Samaria in 722 B.C. and made the northern kingdom of Israel an Assyrian province. His son Sargon later claimed that victory, but he may have simply been present with his father.

11:1 OUT OF EGYPT I CALLED MY SON. God points to Israel's history when they were brought out of Egypt to become an independent nation. He calls them his "son" (cf. Ex 4:22), yet they soon became a wayward and disobedient child (v. 2). Mt 2:14–15 applies this verse to Jesus, who was taken by Joseph and Mary to Egypt and was then called back to Palestine after Herod's death.

3It was I who taught Ephraim to
walk,
taking them by the arms;[b]
but they did not realize
it was I who healed[c] them.
4I led them with cords of human
kindness,
with ties of love;[d]
I lifted the yoke[e] from their neck
and bent down to feed[f] them.[g]

5"Will they not return to Egypt[h]
and will not Assyria[i] rule over
them
because they refuse to repent?[j]
6Swords[k] will flash in their cities,
will destroy the bars[l] of their
gates
and put an end to their plans.
7My people are determined to
turn[m] from me.[n]
Even if they call to the Most
High,
he will by no means exalt them.

8"How can I give you up,[o]
Ephraim?[p]
How can I hand you over,
Israel?
How can I treat you like Admah?
How can I make you like
Zeboiim?[q]
My heart is changed within me;
all my compassion[r] is
aroused.[s]
9I will not carry out my fierce
anger,[t]
nor will I turn and devastate[u]
Ephraim.
For I am God, and not man[v]—
the Holy One[w] among you.
I will not come in wrath.[f]
10They will follow the LORD;
he will roar[x] like a lion.[y]
When he roars,
his children will come
trembling[z] from the
west.[a]
11They will come trembling
like birds from Egypt,
like doves[b] from Assyria.[c]
I will settle them in their
homes,"[d]
declares the LORD.

Israel's Sin

12Ephraim has surrounded me with
lies,[e]
the house of Israel with deceit.
And Judah is unruly against God,
even against the faithful[f] Holy
One.[g]

12 1Ephraim[h] feeds on the
wind;[i]
he pursues the east wind all day
and multiplies lies and
violence.[j]
He makes a treaty with Assyria[k]
and sends olive oil to Egypt.[l]
2The LORD has a charge[m] to bring
against Judah;[n]
he will punish[o] Jacob[g]
according to his ways

11:3 [b]S Dt 1:31; S 32:11; Hos 7:15 [c]S Ex 15:26; Jer 30:17 **11:4** [d]Jer 31:2-3 [e]S Lev 26:13 [f]Ex 16:32; Ps 78:25 [g]Jer 31:20 **11:5** [h]S Hos 7:16 [i]S Hos 10:6 [j]S Ex 13:17 **11:6** [k]Hos 13:16 [l]S La 2:9 **11:7** [m]S Isa 26:10 [n]ver 2; Jer 3:6-7; 8:5 **11:8** [o]S Jer 7:29 [p]Hos 6:4 [q]S Ge 14:8; S La 3:32 [r]S 1Ki 3:26; S Ps 25:6 [s]S Eze 33:11; Am 7:3 **11:9** [t]Dt 13:17; S Jer 18:8; S 30:11 [u]La 3:22; Mal 3:6 [v]S Nu 23:19 [w]S 2Ki 19:22; S Isa 31:1 **11:10** [x]S Isa 42:13 [y]S Isa 31:4 [z]S Ps 18:45 [a]S Hos 3:5; S 6:1-3 **11:11** [b]S Ge 8:8 [c]S Isa 11:11 [d]S Eze 28:26; S 34:25-28 **11:12** [e]S Hos 4:2 [f]S Dt 7:9 [g]S Hos 10:13 **12:1** [h]S Ps 78:67 [i]S Ge 41:6; S Eze 17:10 [j]S Hos 4:19; S 7:1 [k]Hos 5:13; S 7:11 [l]S 2Ki 17:4 **12:2** [m]S Job 10:2; Mic 6:2 [n]Am 2:4 [o]S Ex 32:34

f9 Or *come against any city* g2 *Jacob* means *he grasps the heel* (figuratively, *he deceives*).

11:4 TIES OF LOVE. God's care was seen in the way he led his people with cords of kindness and with ties of his divine love and compassion. He as Father and Physician was always caring for, healing, and guiding them, yet they did not acknowledge his love and blessing. We ought always to be thankful for God's love demonstrated to us in our salvation and in many other ways, both in the past and in the present. We must work hard at developing grateful hearts that love him in response.

11:5 WILL NOT ASSYRIA RULE OVER THEM. "Egypt" represents the place of slavery (see 9:3, note); the Egypt to which the northern kingdom (Israel) would go because of its idolatry would be Assyria. This exile took place when Samaria was destroyed in 722 B.C. Northern Israel was never restored as a separate nation, though a remnant did return (Ezr 8:35; Eze 47:13). Note that in the NT, Anna was of the tribe of Asher (Lk 2:36), one of the northern tribes. Thus, the idea of "ten lost tribes" is fictitious; they were never lost. Some members of the northern kingdom rejected Israel's idolatry and joined the nation of Judah, both before and after Samaria's fall (cf. 2Ch 15:9; 34:9; see 2Ki 17:18, note), while others intermarried with people from other nations and became the Samaritans (see 2Ki 17:24, note).

11:8 HOW CAN I GIVE YOU UP, EPHRAIM? This is one of the Bible's most powerful verses that shows the intense love, compassion and grief experienced by the Lord for the plight of sinners. It demonstrates so clearly that his love and compassion are like that of a caring Father (Jer 31:9). He does not want to give up his wayward people, and it grieves him to be forced to punish them.

11:9 CARRY OUT MY FIERCE ANGER. Israel would not experience God's full anger. They would not be completely destroyed when he punished them; rather, he would save a remnant by which he would rebuild the nation.

12:1 EPHRAIM FEEDS ON THE WIND. Feeding on or pursuing the wind symbolized Israel's foreign alliances with Egypt and Assyria. This foreign policy would be worthless in gaining protection from their enemies.

and repay him according to his
deeds.[p]
3In the womb he grasped his
brother's heel;[q]
as a man he struggled[r] with
God.
4He struggled with the angel and
overcame him;
he wept and begged for his
favor.
He found him at Bethel[s]
and talked with him there—
5the LORD God Almighty,
the LORD is his name[t] of
renown!
6But you must return[u] to your
God;
maintain love and justice,[v]
and wait for your God always.[w]
7The merchant uses dishonest
scales;[x]
he loves to defraud.
8Ephraim boasts,[y]
"I am very rich; I have become
wealthy.[z]
With all my wealth they will not
find in me
any iniquity or sin."
9"I am the LORD your God,
⌊who brought you⌋ out of[h]
Egypt;[a]
I will make you live in tents[b]
again,
as in the days of your appointed
feasts.
10I spoke to the prophets,
gave them many visions
and told parables[c] through
them."[d]
11Is Gilead wicked?[e]
Its people are worthless!
Do they sacrifice bulls in Gilgal?[f]
Their altars will be like piles of
stones
on a plowed field.[g]
12Jacob fled to the country of
Aram[i];[h]
Israel served to get a wife,
and to pay for her he tended
sheep.[i]
13The LORD used a prophet to bring
Israel up from Egypt,[j]
by a prophet he cared for him.[k]
14But Ephraim has bitterly provoked
him to anger;
his Lord will leave upon him the
guilt of his bloodshed[l]
and will repay him for his
contempt.[m]

The LORD's Anger Against Israel

13 When Ephraim spoke, men
trembled;[n]
he was exalted[o] in Israel.
But he became guilty of Baal
worship[p] and died.
2Now they sin more and more;
they make[q] idols for
themselves from their
silver,[r]
cleverly fashioned images,
all of them the work of
craftsmen.[s]
It is said of these people,
"They offer human sacrifice
and kiss[j][t] the calf-idols.[u]"
3Therefore they will be like the
morning mist,

12:2 [p]S Hos 4:9; S 9:15 12:3 [q]Ge 25:26 [r]Ge 32:24-29 12:4 [s]S Ge 12:8; S 35:15 12:5 [t]S Ex 3:15 12:6 [u]S Isa 19:22; Jer 4:1; Joel 2:12 [v]S Ps 106:3; S Jer 22:3 [w]S Eze 18:30; Hos 6:1-3; 10:12; Mic 7:7 12:7 [x]S Lev 19:36; Am 8:5 12:8 [y]S Eze 28:5 [z]Ps 62:10; Rev 3:17 12:9 [a]Lev 23:43; S Hos 2:15; S 11:1 [b]S Ne 8:17 12:10 [c]S Jdg 14:12; S Eze 20:49 [d]2Ki 17:13; Jer 7:25 12:11 [e]S Hos 6:8 [f]S Hos 4:15 [g]S Hos 8:11 12:12 [h]Ge 28:5 [i]S Ge 29:18 12:13 [j]S Hos 11:1 [k]Ex 13:3; 14:19-22; Isa 63:11-14 12:14 [l]S Eze 18:13 [m]Da 11:18 13:1 [n]Jdg 12:1 [o]S Jdg 8:1 [p]S Hos 11:2 13:2 [q]Jer 44:8 [r]S Isa 46:6; S Jer 10:4 [s]Hos 14:3 [t]1Ki 19:18 [u]S Isa 44:17-20; S Hos 8:4

h 9 Or *God / ever since you were in* i 12 That is, Northwest Mesopotamia j 2 Or *"Men who sacrifice / kiss*

12:6 RETURN TO YOUR GOD. Though God's people were unfaithful, he kept reminding them that they must return to him, maintain love and justice, and keep waiting for him. Returning to the Lord and repenting of sin mean more than merely being sorry for sin. We must earnestly follow the Lord in love and righteousness according to the Scriptures and persistently seek his face in prayer.

12:7 THE MERCHANT. Hosea implies that the Israelites were using Canaanite business practices that were contrary to the honesty God required. At the same time the merchants felt that they would not be called to account for their dishonesty. God's people must always be told that he will judge them if they follow sinful practices and worldly ways.

12:10 SPOKE TO THE PROPHETS. God had been faithful in sending numerous prophets to speak his message in a variety of ways and to drive home the truth of his word. The people could therefore not plead ignorance of his requirements; they were rejecting divine revelation, and God would repay them for the contempt they were showing to his messengers. Those who have heard God's word have no excuse if they fail to obey what he has said.

13:2 THEY SIN MORE AND MORE. The Israelites suffered spiritual death when they turned to Baal worship; they in turn engaged in ever-increasing sin and idolatry. Kissing the calf-idols was a picture of the false worship of the Lord that they had mixed with their worship of idols. The threefold picture of dew, chaff and smoke (v. 3) emphasized that God's judgment would soon come and the people would disappear. Those who pervert the worship of the Lord by allegiance to the ways of the world make their worship worthless, and they cannot expect God to help them.

like the early dew that
disappears,[v]
like chaff[w] swirling from a
threshing floor,[x]
like smoke[y] escaping through a
window.

4"But I am the LORD your God,
⌊who brought you⌋ out of[k]
Egypt.[z]
You shall acknowledge[a] no God
but me,[b]
no Savior[c] except me.
5I cared for you in the desert,[d]
in the land of burning heat.
6When I fed them, they were
satisfied;
when they were satisfied, they
became proud;[e]
then they forgot[f] me.[g]
7So I will come upon them like a
lion,[h]
like a leopard I will lurk by the
path.
8Like a bear robbed of her cubs,[i]
I will attack them and rip them
open.
Like a lion[j] I will devour them;
a wild animal will tear them
apart.[k]

9"You are destroyed, O Israel,
because you are against me,[l]
against your helper.[m]
10Where is your king,[n] that he may
save you?
Where are your rulers in all your
towns,
of whom you said,
'Give me a king and princes'?[o]
11So in my anger I gave you a
king,[p]
and in my wrath I took him
away.[q]
12The guilt of Ephraim is stored up,
his sins are kept on record.[r]
13Pains as of a woman in
childbirth[s] come to him,
but he is a child without
wisdom;
when the time[t] arrives,
he does not come to the opening
of the womb.[u]

14"I will ransom them from the
power of the grave[l];[v]
I will redeem them from
death.[w]
Where, O death, are your plagues?
Where, O grave,[l] is your
destruction?[x]

"I will have no compassion,
15 even though he thrives[y] among
his brothers.
An east wind[z] from the LORD will
come,
blowing in from the desert;
his spring will fail
and his well dry up.[a]
His storehouse will be plundered[b]
of all its treasures.
16The people of Samaria[c] must bear
their guilt,[d]
because they have rebelled[e]
against their God.
They will fall by the sword;[f]
their little ones will be dashed[g]
to the ground,
their pregnant women[h] ripped
open."

Repentance to Bring Blessing

14 Return,[i] O Israel, to the
LORD your God.

13:3 [v]S Hos 6:4 [w]S Job 13:25; Ps 1:4; S Isa 17:13 [x]Da 2:35 [y]Ps 68:2 13:4 [z]S Jer 2:6; S Hos 12:9 [a]S Hos 2:20 [b]S Ex 20:3 [c]S Dt 28:29; Ps 18:46; Isa 43:11; 45:21-22 13:5 [d]S Dt 1:19 13:6 [e]S Eze 28:5 [f]S Dt 32:18; S Isa 17:10 [g]Dt 32:12-15; S Pr 30:7-9; S Jer 5:7; S Hos 2:13; S 4:7 13:7 [h]S Job 10:16; S Jer 4:7 13:8 [i]2Sa 17:8 [j]S 1Sa 17:34; Ps 17:12 [k]Ps 50:22; S La 3:10; S Hos 2:12 13:9 [l]Jer 2:17-19 [m]S Dt 33:29 13:10 [n]2Ki 17:4; Hos 7:7 [o]1Sa 8:6; Hos 8:4 13:11 [p]S Nu 11:20 [q]S Jos 24:20; S 1Sa 13:14; S 1Ki 14:10; Hos 3:4; S 10:7 13:12 [r]S Dt 32:34 13:13 [s]Isa 13:8; Mic 4:9-10 [t]2Ki 19:3 [u]Isa 66:9 13:14 [v]S Ps 16:10; 49:15; S Eze 37:12-13 [w]S Isa 25:8 [x]1Co 15:55* 13:15 [y]S Hos 10:1 [z]S Job 1:19; S Eze 19:12; S Hos 4:19 [a]S Jer 51:36 [b]Jer 20:5 13:16 [c]2Ki 17:5 [d]Hos 10:2 [e]S Hos 7:14 [f]Hos 11:6 [g]S 2Ki 8:12; S Hos 10:14 [h]2Ki 15:16; Isa 13:16; Am 1:13 14:1 [i]S Isa 19:22; S Jer 3:12

[k]4 Or *God / ever since you were in*
[l]14 Hebrew *Sheol*

13:6 THEY WERE SATISFIED. God had blessed the land, and the people had prospered. Because of their wealth and success, they had become satisfied and self-sufficient, thinking that they did not need God or his word. Likewise, when we have an abundance of blessings, we are often tempted to feel that we do not need to seek God and his help; our hearts and minds are prone to turn to earthly matters (cf. Dt 6:10–15; 8:11–20). The Lord will punish us as he did the Israelites if we forget him in our pride.

13:14 I WILL REDEEM THEM FROM DEATH. God's promise to redeem the nation from death means that a remnant would be saved (see 11:5, note). God's purpose has not changed. He is the Redeemer from death, the grave and hell, and he stands ready to deliver now. The ultimate deliverance will be on the day of resurrection. Death and the grave are cruel tyrants, but they cannot frustrate God's purpose for his people. The NT points to Christ's resurrection as the guarantee of God's victory (1Co 15:54–55; see article on THE RESURRECTION OF THE BODY, p. 1779).

14:1 RETURN, O ISRAEL. Though their sins were their downfall, the Israelites still had opportunity to repent and return to the Lord. But God wanted more than the meaningless sacrifices they had been offering; he wanted them to offer words that came from their hearts—words of submission, words of praise, words showing a changed attitude of heart, words of complete trust in the Lord. Words such as these would lead to deeds

Your sins[j] have been your
downfall![k]

2Take words with you
and return to the LORD.
Say to him:
"Forgive[l] all our sins
and receive us graciously,[m]
that we may offer the fruit of
our lips.[m n]

3Assyria cannot save us;[o]
we will not mount war-horses.[p]
We will never again say 'Our
gods'[q]
to what our own hands have
made,[r]
for in you the fatherless[s] find
compassion."

4"I will heal[t] their waywardness[u]
and love them freely,[v]
for my anger has turned away[w]
from them.
5I will be like the dew[x] to Israel;
he will blossom like a lily.[y]
Like a cedar of Lebanon[z]
he will send down his roots;[a]
6 his young shoots will grow.
His splendor will be like an olive
tree,[b]
his fragrance like a cedar of
Lebanon.[c]
7Men will dwell again in his
shade.[d]
He will flourish like the grain.
He will blossom[e] like a vine,
and his fame will be like the
wine[f] from Lebanon.[g]
8O Ephraim, what more have I[n] to
do with idols?[h]
I will answer him and care for
him.
I am like a green pine[i] tree;
your fruitfulness comes from
me."

9Who is wise?[j] He will realize
these things.
Who is discerning? He will
understand them.[k]
The ways of the LORD are right;[l]
the righteous walk[m] in them,
but the rebellious stumble in
them.

14:1 [j]S Hos 4:8 [k]S Hos 5:5; S 9:7 **14:2** [l]S Ex 34:9 [m]Ps 51:16-17; Mic 7:18-19 [n]Heb 13:15 **14:3** [o]S Hos 5:13 [p]Ps 33:17; S Isa 31:1; Mic 5:10 [q]Hos 8:6 [r]ver 28; Hos 13:2 [s]Ps 10:14; 68:5; Jer 49:11 **14:4** [t]S Isa 30:26; S Hos 6:1 [u]S Jer 2:19 [v]S Isa 55:1; Jer 31:20; Zep 3:17 [w]S Job 13:16 **14:5** [x]S Ge 27:28; S Isa 18:4 [y]S SS 2:1 [z]Isa 35:2 [a]Job 29:19 **14:6** [b]Ps 52:8; S Jer 11:16 [c]S Ps 92:12; S SS 4:11 **14:7** [d]Ps 91:1-4 [e]S Ge 40:10 [f]S Hos 2:22 [g]S Eze 17:23 **14:8** [h]S ver 3 [i]S Isa 37:24 **14:9** [j]S Ps 107:43 [k]S Pr 10:29; S Isa 1:28; Da 12:10 [l]Ps 111:7-8; Zep 3:5; Ac 13:10 [m]Isa 26:7

[m]2 Or *offer our lips as sacrifices of bulls*
[n]8 Or *What more has Ephraim*

---

that would please the Lord.

14:4–7 LOVE THEM FREELY. After the people bore their punishment, God would heal and restore them, caring for them as a father cares for his children. Their lifestyle would be beautiful and pure like the lily; like the cedars of Lebanon the people would be strong, highly prized and deeply rooted in God's word. All the figures of speech in these verses show how precious God's restored people will be to him.

14:9 WHO IS WISE? True wisdom involves understanding God and his ways; it is expressed through a lifestyle in accordance with his standards of righteousness (Dt 4:3–9; Ps 111:10; Pr 1:7; 8:10,32–36). Wisdom in the Bible is never merely the possession of intellectual skill; it is always practical and includes a right relationship with the Lord (see Pr 1:2, note).

JOEL

Outline

Introduction (1:1)
- I. Judah's Present Calamity (1:2–20)
  - A. A Devastating Plague of Locusts (1:2–12)
  - B. The Prophet's Call to National Repentance (1:13–14)
  - C. Judah's Desperate Situation (1:15–20)
- II. The Imminence of Even Greater Judgment (2:1–17)
  - A. A Foreboding Army Prepared to March Against Judah (2:1–11)
  - B. The Prophet's Call to National Repentance (2:12–17)
- III. The Future Day of the Lord (2:18—3:21)
  - A. Prophetic Promise of Restoration (2:18–27)
  - B. Prophetic Promise of the Outpouring of the Holy Spirit (2:28–32)
  - C. Prophetic Promise of Judgment and Salvation (3:1–21)
    1. For the Nations (3:1–15)
    2. For Zion (3:16–21)

Author: Joel

Theme: The Great and Awesome Day of the Lord

Date of Writing: 835–830 B.C.(?)

Background

Joel, whose name means "The LORD is God", identifies himself as "son of Pethuel" (1:1). His numerous references throughout the book to Zion and the ministry of the temple indicate that he was a prophet to Judah and Jerusalem. His familiarity with the priests has caused some to think he was a "priestly" prophet (cf. Jer 28:1,5) who spoke the true word of the Lord.

Since Joel mentions no king or datable historical events, the time of his prophetic message and ministry is uncertain. Some believe Joel's ministry occurred after the Jewish exiles returned to Jerusalem and rebuilt the temple (c. 510–400 B.C.). At this time there was no king in Judah and the most prominent spiritual leaders were priests. Others believe Joel's message occurred during the early days of young King Joash (835–830 B.C.), who ascended Judah's throne at age seven (2Ki 11:21) and remained under the regency of the high priest Jehoiada while a minor; that situation would account for the priests' prominence in Joel and the absence of any reference to the king. Joel's prophetic theme and literary style are closer to those of the 8th-century prophets Amos, Micah and Isaiah than to the post-exilic prophets Haggai, Zechariah and Malachi. These and other facts favor a 9th-century setting for the book.

The immediate occasion for the book was an invasion of locusts and a severe drought, the combination of which devastated the people of Judah at nearly every level of society. The ability of a large locust plague to strip bare everything green over many square miles is well-documented as occurring in that part of the world in both ancient and modern times.

Purpose

Joel spoke and wrote because of two recent natural disasters and the imminent potential of a foreign military invasion of Judah. His purpose was threefold: (1) to bring the people together before the Lord in a great sacred assembly (1:14; 2:15–16); (2) to exhort the people to repent and humbly return to the Lord God with fasting, weeping, mourning and intercession for God's mercy (2:12–17); and (3) to record God's prophetic word to his people on the occasion of their sincere repentance (2:18—3:21).

Survey

The book's contents divide into three sections. (1) Section one (1:2–20) describes the devastation of Judah when a large invasion of locusts stripped the foliage from vineyards, trees and fields (1:7,10), thereby bringing great hardship to the people. In the midst of this disaster, the prophet Joel called Judah's spiritual leaders to lead the people in national repentance (1:13–14).

(2) Section two (2:1–17) records the imminence of an even greater judgment of God from the north (1:1–11), either in the form of (a) another locust plague described metaphorically as an army of destroyers, or (b) an actual foreign military invasion. Again the prophet sounded a spiritual alarm in Zion (2:1,15), calling for a great sacred assembly in which the priests and all the people would earnestly seek God's mercy in repentance, fasting, intercession and true brokenness before him (2:12–17).

(3) The final section (2:18—3:21) begins by declaring that God had pity on his people when he saw their sincere repentance (the Hebrew verbs in 2:18–19a indicate completed action). Judah's humble repentance and God's great mercy became the occasion for Joel's prophecies about the future, encompassing promises of restoration (2:19b-27), the outpouring of the Holy Spirit on all humankind (2:28–31), and God's end-time judgments and salvation (3:1–21).

Special Features

Five major features characterize the book of Joel. (1) It is one of the most polished literary masterpieces in the OT. (2) It contains the most profound OT prophecy about the Pentecostal outpouring of the Holy Spirit on all humankind. (3) It records numerous national disasters—locust plagues, drought and famine, raging fires, foreign military invasions, celestial calamities—as God's judgments for spiritual and moral disintegration. (4) It emphasizes that God sometimes sovereignly works in history through such natural disasters and military invasions in order to bring about repentance, revival and redemption. (5) It models a prophetic preacher who, because of his close communion with God and his spiritual stature, is able to call God's people decisively to repent as a nation at a critical hour in their history and to achieve positive results through that repentance.

New Testament Fulfillment

Several verses in Joel contributed powerfully to the NT message. (1) The prophecy about the coming of the Holy Spirit (2:28–32) is specifically quoted by Peter in his message at Pentecost (Ac 2:16–21), after the Holy Spirit had descended from heaven with power on the 120 charter members of the early church and with the spiritual manifestations of speaking in tongues, prophesying and praising God (Ac 2:4,6–8,11,17–18). (2) Moreover, Peter's invitation to the multitudes at that Jewish feast regarding their need to call on the name of the Lord and be saved was inspired (in part) by what Joel had said (2:32a; 3:14; see Ac 2:21,37–41); Paul also quotes this same verse from Joel (see Ro 10:13). (3) The apocalyptic signs in the heavens that Joel prophesied would occur at the end of time (2:30–31) are not only quoted by Peter (Ac 2:19–20) but also referred to by Jesus (e.g., Mt 24:29) and by John on Patmos (Rev 6:12–14). (4) Finally, Joel's prophecy about God judging the nations in the Valley of Jehoshaphat (3:2,12–14) is further developed in the last book of the Bible (Rev 14:18–20; 16:12–16; 19:19–21: 20:7–9).

There are both present and future dimensions to all these NT applications of Joel. The gifts of the Spirit that began to flow through God's people at Pentecost are still available today to believers (cf. 1Co 12:1—14:40). Also, the verses immediately preceding Joel's prophecy about the Holy Spirit (i.e., the harvest analogy of the autumn and spring rains, 2:23–27) and those immediately following (i.e., the end-time celestial signs, 2:30–32) indicate that the prophecy about the outpouring of the Holy Spirit (2:28–29) includes not only the initial rain of the Holy Spirit at Pentecost, but also a final climactic outpouring of the Spirit on all humankind at the end of the age.

Reading Joel

In order to read the entire Old Testament in one year, the book of Joel should be read in 1 day: ☐ Joel

NOTES

1 The word of the LORD that came[a] to Joel[b] son of Pethuel.

An Invasion of Locusts

2Hear this,[c] you elders;[d]
listen, all who live in the land.[e]
Has anything like this ever
happened in your days
or in the days of your
forefathers?[f]
3Tell it to your children,[g]
and let your children tell it to
their children,
and their children to the next
generation.[h]
4What the locust[i] swarm has left
the great locusts have eaten;
what the great locusts have left
the young locusts have eaten;
what the young locusts have left[j]
other locusts[a] have eaten.[k]

5Wake up, you drunkards, and
weep!
Wail, all you drinkers of wine;[l]
wail because of the new wine,
for it has been snatched[m] from
your lips.
6A nation has invaded my land,
powerful and without number;[n]
it has the teeth[o] of a lion,
the fangs of a lioness.
7It has laid waste[p] my vines
and ruined my fig trees.[q]
It has stripped off their bark
and thrown it away,
leaving their branches white.

8Mourn like a virgin[b] in
sackcloth[r]
grieving for the husband[c] of her
youth.
9Grain offerings and drink
offerings[s]
are cut off from the house of the
LORD.
The priests are in mourning,[t]
those who minister before the
LORD.
10The fields are ruined,
the ground is dried up[d];[u]
the grain is destroyed,
the new wine[v] is dried up,
the oil fails.[w]
11Despair, you farmers,[x]
wail, you vine growers;
grieve for the wheat and the
barley,[y]
because the harvest of the field
is destroyed.[z]
12The vine is dried up
and the fig tree is withered;[a]
the pomegranate,[b] the palm and
the apple tree—
all the trees of the field—are
dried up.[c]
Surely the joy of mankind
is withered away.

A Call to Repentance

13Put on sackcloth,[d] O priests, and
mourn;
wail, you who minister[e] before
the altar.
Come, spend the night in
sackcloth,
you who minister before my God;
for the grain offerings and drink
offerings[f]
are withheld from the house of
your God.
14Declare a holy fast;[g]
call a sacred assembly.

[a] *4* The precise meaning of the four Hebrew words used here for locusts is uncertain.
[b] *8* Or *young woman*
[c] *8* Or *betrothed*
[d] *10* Or *ground mourns*

1:1 [a] S Jer 1:2 [b] Ac 2:16 **1:2** [c] Hos 5:1 [d] Joel 2:16 [e] S Hos 4:1 [f] Joel 2:2 **1:3** [g] S Ex 10:2 [h] S Ps 71:18 **1:4** [i] S Ex 10:14 [j] S Ex 10:5 [k] S Ex 10:15; S Dt 28:39; Am 7:1; Na 3:15 **1:5** [l] Joel 3:3 [m] S Isa 24:7 **1:6** [n] Ps 105:34; Joel 2:2,11,25 [o] Rev 9:8 **1:7** [p] Isa 5:6 [q] Am 4:9 **1:8** [r] ver 13; Isa 22:12; Am 8:10 **1:9** [s] S Hos 9:4 [t] S Isa 22:12 **1:10** [u] S Isa 5:6; S 24:4; S Jer 3:3 [v] S Hos 9:2 [w] S Nu 18:12 **1:11** [x] S Job 6:20; Am 5:16 [y] S Ex 9:31 [z] S Isa 17:11 **1:12** [a] S Isa 15:6 [b] S Ex 28:33 [c] S Isa 16:8; Hag 2:19 **1:13** [d] S Ge 37:34; S Jer 4:8 [e] Joel 2:17 [f] ver 9; S Hos 9:4; Joel 2:14 **1:14** [g] S 2Ch 20:3

1:1 THE WORD OF THE LORD. The prophet indicates that his message is the very word he received from the Lord. Thus it has relevance for all generations of believers.

1:2 HEAR THIS, YOU ELDERS. God's people had been overwhelmed by a terrible catastrophe. To Joel, this crisis was sent by God, and the elders and the people needed to turn to the Lord and cry out for his help.

1:4 LOCUSTS. The nature of the crisis was a severe locust plague that had swept over the land; the countryside and all vegetation were destroyed, and the people were facing a severe famine. The precise meaning of the four words used for locusts here is uncertain; they may represent the successive stages in the growth of the locust.

1:5 WAKE UP, YOU DRUNKARDS. Drunkenness is the only specific sin mentioned in Joel. Perhaps its inclusion indicates that the people's moral sensitivity to sin and evil was so dulled that they could not recognize when they were offending God's holiness. The church must be careful that it does not slowly accept the world's ways and become oblivious to that which grieves the Holy Spirit (see Eph 4:30, note; see article on SPIRITUAL SEPARATION FOR BELIEVERS, p. 1794).

1:6 A NATION. The locusts are compared to the powerful army of a great nation, with its innumerable soldiers.

1:14 A HOLY FAST . . . CRY OUT. Because of the land's serious desolation and the distress among God's people, Joel calls on them to intensify their mourning, to intercede with God through fasting and prayer night and day, and to repent of

Summon the elders
and all who live in the land[h]
to the house of the LORD your God,
and cry out[i] to the LORD.[j]

[15]Alas for that[k] day!
For the day of the LORD[l] is near;
it will come like destruction
5 from the Almighty.[e][m]

[16]Has not the food been cut off[n]
before our very eyes—
joy and gladness[o]
from the house of our God?[p]
[17]The seeds are shriveled
beneath the clods.[f][q]
The storehouses are in ruins,
the granaries have been broken down,
for the grain has dried up.
[18]How the cattle moan!
The herds mill about
because they have no pasture;[r]
even the flocks of sheep are suffering.[s]

[19]To you, O LORD, I call,[t]
for fire[u] has devoured the open pastures[v]
and flames have burned up all
the trees of the field.
[20]Even the wild animals pant for you;[w]
the streams of water have dried up[x]
and fire has devoured the open pastures.[y]

An Army of Locusts

2 Blow the trumpet[z] in Zion;[a]
sound the alarm on my holy hill.[b]
Let all who live in the land tremble,
for the day of the LORD[c] is coming.
It is close at hand[d]—
[2]a day of darkness[e] and gloom,[f][g]
a day of clouds[h] and blackness.[i]
Like dawn spreading across the mountains
a large and mighty army[j] comes,
such as never was of old[k]
nor ever will be in ages to come.

[3]Before them fire[l] devours,
behind them a flame blazes.
Before them the land is like the garden of Eden,[m]
behind them, a desert waste[n]—
nothing escapes them.
[4]They have the appearance of horses;[o]
they gallop along like cavalry.
[5]With a noise like that of chariots[p]
they leap over the mountaintops,
like a crackling fire[q] consuming stubble,
like a mighty army drawn up for battle.

[6]At the sight of them, nations are in anguish;[r]
every face turns pale.[s]
[7]They charge like warriors;[t]
they scale walls like soldiers.
They all march in line,[u]
not swerving[v] from their course.
[8]They do not jostle each other;
each marches straight ahead.
They plunge through defenses
without breaking ranks.
[9]They rush upon the city;
they run along the wall.
They climb into the houses;[w]
like thieves they enter through the windows.[x]

1:14 [h] S Hos 4:1 [i] Jnh 3:8 [j] 2Ch 20:4 **1:15** [k] S Isa 2:12; Jer 30:7; S 46:10; S Eze 30:3; Mal 4:5 [l] Joel 2:1, 11,31; 3:14; Am 5:18; Zep 1:14; Zec 14:1 [m] S Ge 17:1 **1:16** [n] Isa 3:7 [o] S Ps 51:8 [p] Dt 12:7 **1:17** [q] S Isa 17:10-11 **1:18** [r] S Ge 47:4 [s] S Jer 9:10 **1:19** [t] Ps 50:15 [u] S Ps 97:3; Am 7:4 [v] S Jer 9:10 **1:20** [w] S Ps 42:1; S 104:21 [x] 1Ki 17:7 [y] Joel 2:22 **2:1** [z] S Nu 10:2,7 [a] ver 15 [b] S Ex 15:17 [c] S Joel 1:15; Zep 1:14-16 [d] S Eze 12:23; S 30:3; Ob 1:15
2:2 [e] ver 10,31; S Job 9:7; S Isa 8:22; S 13:10; Am 5:18 [f] S Da 9:12; S Mt 24:21 [g] S Eze 34:12 [h] S Eze 38:9 [i] Zep 1:15; Rev 9:2 [j] S Joel 1:6 [k] Joel 1:2 **2:3** [l] S Ps 97:3; S Isa 1:31 [m] S Ge 2:8 [n] Ex 10:12-15; Ps 105:34-35; S Isa 14:17 **2:4** [o] Rev 9:7 **2:5** [p] Rev 9:9 [q] Isa 5:24; 30:30 **2:6** [r] S Isa 13:8 [s] S Isa 29:22 **2:7** [t] S Job 16:14 [u] Pr 30:27 [v] Isa 5:27 **2:9** [w] Ex 10:6 [x] Jer 9:21

[e] *15* Hebrew *Shaddai* [f] *17* The meaning of the Hebrew for this word is uncertain.

all sin. Today God's people may not experience literal locust plagues, but they may find their congregations plagued by overwhelming trouble, sin and sickness that devastate family after family (cf. 1Co 11:30–32). The Biblical pattern for resolving such situations is for ministers and laypeople alike to recognize that God's help, power and blessing are severely lacking. They must turn to him with the kind of sincerity, intensity, repentance and intercession described by Joel (vv. 13–14; 2:12–17).

1:15 THE DAY OF THE LORD. This "day" is the major theme in the book of Joel (cf. 2:1,11,31; 3:14); it can refer (1) to a present judgment of God on his people or on foreign nations; or (2) to God's final judgment on all evil at the end of this age, which will include the seven-year tribulation and Christ's return to reign on earth (see 1Th 5:2, note). At this point in Joel, it refers primarily to God's present judgment, though it is a reminder of that coming day as well. Joel speaks more of the final day of the Lord in the next two chapters.

2:1–2 BLOW THE TRUMPET. Joel intensifies his warning by referring to "darkness and gloom," symbols of judgment and destruction. The appropriate response to God's day of judgment is fear and trembling.

10Before them the earth shakes,[y]
the sky trembles,[z]
the sun and moon are darkened,[a]
and the stars no longer shine.[b]
11The LORD[c] thunders[d]
at the head of his army;[e]
his forces are beyond number,
and mighty are those who obey
his command.
The day of the LORD is great;[f]
it is dreadful.
Who can endure it?[g]

Rend Your Heart

12"Even now," declares the LORD,
"return[h] to me with all your
heart,[i]
with fasting and weeping and
mourning."

13Rend your heart[j]
and not your garments.[k]
Return[l] to the LORD your God,
for he is gracious and
compassionate,[m]
slow to anger and abounding in
love,[n]
and he relents from sending
calamity.[o]
14Who knows? He may turn[p] and
have pity[q]
and leave behind a blessing[r]—
grain offerings and drink
offerings[s]
for the LORD your God.

15Blow the trumpet[t] in Zion,[u]
declare a holy fast,[v]
call a sacred assembly.[w]
16Gather the people,
consecrate[x] the assembly;
bring together the elders,[y]
gather the children,
those nursing at the breast.
Let the bridegroom[z] leave his
room
and the bride her chamber.

2:10 [y]Ps 18:7; Na 1:5 [z]S Eze 38:19 [a]S ver 2; S Isa 5:30; S Mt 24:29; Mk 13:24; Rev 9:2 [b]S Job 9:7; S Ps 102:26; Isa 13:10; S Eze 32:8 **2:11** [c]S Isa 2:12; S Eze 30:3; S Joel 1:15; Ob 1:15 [d]S Ps 29:3 [e]S ver 2,25 [f]Zep 1:14 [g]S Eze 22:14; Zep 2:11; Rev 6:17 **2:12** [h]S Dt 4:30; S Eze 33:11; S Hos 12:6 [i]S 1Sa 7:3 **2:13** [j]Ps 51:17; Isa 57:15 [k]S Ge 37:29; S Nu 14:6; Job 1:20 [l]S Isa 19:22 [m]S Dt 4:31 [n]Ex 34:6; S Ps 86:5,15 [o]S Jer 18:8; Jnh 4:2 **2:14** [p]Jer 26:3; Jnh 3:9 [q]Am 5:15; Jnh 1:6 [r]Jer 31:14; Hag 2:19; Zec 8:13; Mal 3:10 [s]S Joel 1:13 **2:15** [t]S Nu 10:2 [u]ver 1 [v]S 2Ch 20:3; Jer 36:9 [w]S Ex 32:5; Nu 10:3 **2:16** [x]S Ex 19:10, 22 [y]Joel 1:2 [z]Ps 19:5 **2:17** [a]Joel 1:13 [b]S Isa 22:12 [c]Eze 8:16; Mt 23:35 [d]Dt 9:26-29; Ps 44:13 [e]S 1Ki 9:7; S Job 17:6 [f]S Ps 42:3 **2:18** [g]S Isa 26:11; Zec 1:14; 8:2 [h]S Ps 72:13 **2:19** [i]Ps 4:7 [j]S Jer 31:12 [k]S Lev 26:5 [l]S Eze 34:29 **2:20** [m]Jer 1:14-15 [n]Zec 14:8

17Let the priests, who minister[a]
before the LORD,
weep[b] between the temple
porch and the altar.[c]
Let them say, "Spare your people,
O LORD.
Do not make your inheritance an
object of scorn,[d]
a byword[e] among the nations.
Why should they say among the
peoples,
'Where is their God?'[f]"

The LORD's Answer

18Then the LORD will be jealous[g] for
his land
and take pity[h] on his people.
19The LORD will reply[g] to them:

"I am sending you grain, new
wine[i] and oil,[j]
enough to satisfy you fully;[k]
never again will I make you
an object of scorn[l] to the
nations.

20"I will drive the northern army[m]
far from you,
pushing it into a parched and
barren land,
with its front columns going into
the eastern[n] sea[h]
and those in the rear into the
western sea.[i]
And its stench[o] will go up;
its smell will rise."

Surely he has done great things.[j]
21 Be not afraid,[p] O land;
be glad and rejoice.[q]

[o]S Isa 34:3 **2:21** [p]S Isa 29:22; S 54:4; Zep 3:16-17 [q]S Ps 9:2

[g]*18,19* Or *LORD was jealous . . . / and took pity . . . / 19The LORD replied* [h]*20* That is, the Dead Sea [i]*20* That is, the Mediterranean [j]*20* Or *rise. / Surely it has done great things."*

2:13 REND YOUR HEART. The prophet calls for broken and contrite hearts (Ps 51:17). If the people would turn from their sins to God, he would have pity on them. It is God's character to show mercy and compassion to his people if they sincerely repent (see article on THE ATTRIBUTES OF GOD, p. 882).

2:17 MINISTER BEFORE THE LORD. When ministers and church leaders see hurt and devastation among God's people, they are the ones who should lead the way in turning to God with a broken heart, with weeping and with intense prayer. God expects them to intercede earnestly for him to spare his people from physical and spiritual calamity; he wants them to plead night and day for the outpouring of his favor and Spirit upon them (vv. 18–29). Only then will the people be restored and renewed in their love for and dedication to God.

2:18 TAKE PITY ON HIS PEOPLE. When God's people humble themselves, seek his face in prayer and turn from their wicked ways (see 2Ch 7:14, notes), God hears from heaven, reverses his temporal judgment, renews the land and pours out his blessing (vv. 18–20). In other words, God answers his people's humble prayers that come from repentant hearts. Furthermore, persistent and sincere prayer for revival will result in the outpouring of God's Spirit upon his people (see vv. 28–32).

Surely the LORD has done great
things.[r]
22 Be not afraid, O wild animals,
for the open pastures are
becoming green.[s]
The trees are bearing their fruit;
the fig tree[t] and the vine[u]
yield their riches.[v]
23Be glad, O people of Zion,
rejoice[w] in the LORD your God,
for he has given you
the autumn rains in
righteousness.[k][x]
He sends you abundant showers,[y]
both autumn[z] and spring
rains,[a] as before.
24The threshing floors will be filled
with grain;
the vats will overflow[b] with
new wine[c] and oil.

25"I will repay you for the years the
locusts[d] have eaten[e]—
the great locust and the young
locust,
the other locusts and the locust
swarm[l]—
my great army[f] that I sent among
you.
26You will have plenty to eat, until
you are full,[g]
and you will praise[h] the name
of the LORD your God,
who has worked wonders[i] for
you;
never again will my people be
shamed.[j]
27Then you will know[k] that I am in
Israel,
that I am the LORD[l] your God,
and that there is no other;
never again will my people be
shamed.[m]

The Day of the LORD

28"And afterward,
I will pour out my Spirit[n] on all
people.[o]
Your sons and daughters will
prophesy,[p]
your old men will dream
dreams,[q]
your young men will see visions.
29Even on my servants,[r] both men
and women,
I will pour out my Spirit in
those days.[s]
30I will show wonders in the
heavens[t]
and on the earth,[u]
blood and fire and billows of
smoke.
31The sun will be turned to
darkness[v]
and the moon to blood
before the coming of the great
and dreadful day of the
LORD.[w]
32And everyone who calls
on the name of the LORD[x] will
be saved;[y]

Hab 3:3

Mic 3:8

2:21 [r]S Ps 126:3; S Isa 25:1 2:22 [s]S Ps 65:12 [t]S 1Ki 4:25 [u]S Nu 16:14 [v]Joel 1:18-20; Zec 8:12 2:23 [w]Ps 33:21; 97:12; 149:2; Isa 12:6; 41:16; 66:14; Hab 3:18; Zec 10:7 [x]S Isa 45:8 [y]S Job 36:28; S Eze 34:26 [z]Ps 84:6 [a]S Lev 26:4; S Ps 135:7; Jas 5:7 2:24 [b]Lev 26:10; Mal 3:10 [c]S Pr 3:10; Joel 3:18; Am 9:13 2:25 [d]S Ex 10:14; Am 4:9 [e]S Dt 28:39 [f]S Joel 1:6 2:26 [g]S Lev 26:5 [h]S Lev 23:40; S Isa 62:9 [i]S Ps 126:3; S Isa 25:1 [j]S Isa 29:22 2:27 [k]S Ex 6:7 [l]S Ex 6:2; S Isa 44:8; Joel 3:17 [m]Isa 45:17; 54:4; Zep 3:11 2:28 [n]S Isa 11:2; S 44:3 [o]S Nu 11:17; S Mk 1:8; Gal 3:14 [p]S 1Sa 19:20 [q]Jer 23:25 2:29 [r]1Co 12:13; Gal 3:28 [s]S Eze 36:27 2:30 [t]Lk 21:11 [u]Mk 13:24-25 2:31 [v]S ver 2; S Isa 22:5; S Jer 4:23; S Mt 24:29 [w]S Joel 1:15; Ob 1:15; Mal 3:2; 4:1,5 2:32 [x]S Ge 4:26; S Ps 105:1 [y]S Ps 106:8; Ac 2:17-21*; Ro 10:13*

[k]23 Or / *the teacher for righteousness:*
[l]25 The precise meaning of the four Hebrew words used here for locusts is uncertain.

2:26 NEVER AGAIN WILL MY PEOPLE BE SHAMED. This promise is contingent on God's people remaining humble and faithful to him. If they become arrogant and return to the paths of sin, God's blessings will be withheld and his judgment will follow.

2:28–29 POUR OUT MY SPIRIT. Joel predicts a day when God would pour out his Spirit on "everyone who calls on the name of the LORD" (v. 32). This outpouring will result in a charismatic flow of the Spirit of prophecy among God's people. Peter quoted this passage on the day of Pentecost, explaining that the outpouring of the Spirit on that day was the beginning of the fulfillment of Joel's prophecy (Ac 2:14–21). This prophecy is an ongoing promise to all who accept Christ as Lord, for all believers can and should be filled with the Holy Spirit (cf. Ac 2:38–39; 10:44–48; 11:15–18; see article on BAPTISM IN THE HOLY SPIRIT, p. 1642). For more on the Holy Spirit, see articles on THE SPIRIT IN THE OLD TESTAMENT, p. 1302, and THE DOCTRINE OF THE HOLY SPIRIT, p. 1654.

2:28 YOUR SONS AND DAUGHTERS WILL PROPHESY. Joel envisions that one of the primary results of the outpouring of the Holy Spirit will be the impartation and release of prophetic gifts. The manifestation of the Spirit through his gifts makes known God's presence among his people. The apostle Paul declared that if the church prophesies, an unbelieving visitor will be compelled to exclaim, "God is really among you!" (1Co 14:24–25).

2:30–31 WONDERS IN THE HEAVENS. The full realization of this outpouring of the Spirit and the offer of salvation to all people will someday be followed by the end-time cosmic signs and the "day of the LORD" (cf. Mt 24:29–31). At that time, God's enemies will experience his wrath (cf. Rev 6:12–17). When examined in the light of Biblical prophecy, worldwide conditions indicate that the time for these future events is near (see article on THE AGE OF THE ANTICHRIST, p. 1872).

THE SPIRIT IN THE OLD TESTAMENT

Joel 2:28–29 *"And afterward, I will pour out my Spirit on all people. Your sons and your daughters will prophesy, your old men will dream dreams, your young men will see visions. Even on my servants, both men and women, I will pour out my Spirit in those days."*

The Holy Spirit is one of the three persons of the eternal triune God (see Mk 1:11, note; see article on THE DOCTRINE OF THE HOLY SPIRIT, p. 1654). Although his full power was not revealed to God's people until the ministry of Jesus (see article on JESUS AND THE HOLY SPIRIT, p. 1546) and, later, at Pentecost (see Ac 2), there are OT passages that refer to him and his work. This article examines the OT teachings about the Holy Spirit.

TERM USED. The Hebrew word for "Spirit" is *ruah*, a word that is sometimes translated as "wind" and "breath." Thus, the OT references to the breath of God or a wind from God (e.g., Ge 2:7; Eze 37:9–10,14) can also refer to the work of God's Spirit.

THE WORK OF THE HOLY SPIRIT IN THE OLD TESTAMENT. The Bible describes various activities of the Holy Spirit during the OT times. (1) The Holy Spirit had an active role in creation. The Bible's second verse says that "the Spirit of God was hovering over the waters" (Ge 1:2), preparing for the creative word of God to shape the world. Both the Word of God (i.e., the second person of the Trinity) and the Spirit of God were agents in creation (see Job 26:13; Ps 33:6; see article on CREATION, p. 6). The Spirit is also the author of life. When God created Adam, it was undoubtedly his Spirit that breathed into him the breath of life (Ge 2:7; cf. Job 27:3), and the Holy Spirit continues to be involved in giving life to God's creatures (Job 33:4; Ps 104:30).

(2) The Spirit was active in communicating God's message to his people. For example, it was the Spirit who instructed the Israelites in the desert (Ne 9:20). When the psalmists of Israel sang their songs, they did so by the Spirit of the Lord (2Sa 23:2; cf. Ac 1:16,20). Similarly, the prophets were inspired by God's Spirit to declare his word to the people (Nu 11:29; 1Sa 10:5–6,10; 2Ch 20:14; 24:19–20; Ne 9:30; Isa 61:1–3; Mic 3:8; Zec 7:12; cf. 2Pe 1:20–21). According to Ezekiel, one clue to detecting false prophets is that they "follow their own spirit" rather than the Spirit of God (Eze 13:2–3); note, though, that it was possible for God's Spirit to come upon someone who was not in a right relationship with God in order to speak a true message regarding God's people (see Nu 24:2, note).

(3) The leadership of God's OT people was energized by the Spirit of the Lord. Moses, for example, was one with the Spirit of God to such an extent that he shared God's very feelings, suffering when he suffered and becoming angry at sin when he became angry (see Ex 33:11, note; cf. Ex 32:19). When Moses obediently chose seventy elders to help him lead the Israelites, God took the Spirit that was on Moses and put it on them (Nu 11:16–17; see 11:12, note). Similarly, when Joshua was commissioned to succeed Moses as leader, God indicated that "the spirit" (i.e., the Holy Spirit) was in him (Nu 27:18, note). The same Spirit came upon Gideon (Jdg 6:34), David (1Sa 16:13) and Zerubbabel (Zec 4:6). In other words, in the OT the greatest qualification needed for leadership was the presence of the Spirit of God.

(4) The Spirit of God could also come upon individuals to equip them for special service. A notable OT example was Joseph, who was given the Spirit to enable him to function effectively in Pharaoh's cabinet (Ge 41:38). Also note Bezalel and Oholiab, whom God filled with his Spirit in order to do the artistic work needed for the tabernacle construction and also to teach others (see Ex 31:1–11; 35:30–35). The idea of "being filled with the Holy Spirit" here is not precisely the same as the baptism in the Holy

Spirit in the NT (see article on BAPTISM IN THE HOLY SPIRIT, p. 1642). In the OT, in other words, the Holy Spirit came upon and empowered only a few select individuals chosen for special service to God (see Ex 31:3, note). The Spirit of the Lord came upon many of the judges, such as Othniel (Jdg 3:9–10), Gideon (Jdg 6:34), Jephthah (Jdg 11:29) and Samson (Jdg 14:5–6; 15:14–16); these examples reveal God's enduring principle that when he chooses to use people greatly, the Spirit of the Lord comes upon them.

(5) There was also an awareness in the OT that the Spirit desired to lead a person on the level ground of righteous living; David testified to this in some of his psalms (Ps 51:10–13; 143:10). God's people who followed their own way instead of listening to God were really refusing to follow the way of the Spirit (see Ge 16:2, note). Those who failed to live by God's Spirit inevitably experienced some form of God's judgment (see Nu 14:29, note; Dt 1:26, note).

(6) Note that in OT times the Holy Spirit came upon or filled only a few people, empowering them for service or prophecy. There was no general outpouring of the Holy Spirit on all Israel (cf. Joel 2:28–29; Ac 2:4,16–18); the outpouring of the Spirit in this larger sense did not begin until the great day of Pentecost (Ac 2).

THE PROMISE OF THE FULL POWER OF THE SPIRIT. The OT looks forward to the coming age of the Spirit, i.e., the NT age. (1) On several occasions, the prophets prophesied about the role that the Spirit would play in the life of the coming Messiah. Isaiah especially characterized the coming King and Servant of the Lord as one on whom the Spirit of God would rest in a special way (see Isa 11:1–2; 42:1; 61:1–3). When Jesus read the words from Isa 61 in his hometown synagogue at Nazareth, he ended with: "Today this scripture is fulfilled in your hearing" (Lk 4:21).

(2) Other OT prophecies looked forward to the time when there would be a general outpouring of the Holy Spirit on all God's people. Most prominent among these passages is Joel 2:28–29, a text quoted on the day of Pentecost by Peter (Ac 2:17–18); but the same message can also be found in Isa 32:15–17; 44:3–5; 59:20–21; Eze 11:19–20; 36:26–27; 37:14; 39:29. God promised that when the life and power of his Spirit would come upon his people, they would be enabled to prophesy, see visions, have prophetic dreams, live lives of obedience, holiness and righteousness, and witness with great power. Thus the OT prophets foresaw and prophesied about the Messianic age when the outpouring and filling of the Holy Spirit on all humanity would take place; it finally did happen on Pentecost Sunday (ten days after Jesus ascended into heaven), with a subsequent great harvest of salvation (cf. Joel 2:28,32; Ac 2:41; 4:4; 13:44,48–49).

Mic 7:7 for on Mount Zion[z] and in
Jerusalem
there will be deliverance,[a]
as the LORD has said,
among the survivors[b]
whom the LORD calls.[c]

The Nations Judged

3 "In those days and at that time,
when I restore the fortunes[d] of
Judah[e] and Jerusalem,
2 I will gather[f] all nations
and bring them down to the
Valley of Jehoshaphat.[m][g]
There I will enter into judgment[h]
against them
concerning my inheritance, my
people Israel,
for they scattered[i] my people
among the nations
and divided up my land.
3 They cast lots[j] for my people
and traded boys for prostitutes;
they sold girls for wine[k]
that they might drink.

4 "Now what have you against me, O
Tyre and Sidon[l] and all you regions of
Philistia?[m] Are you repaying me for
something I have done? If you are paying me back, I will swiftly and speedily
return on your own heads what you
have done.[n] 5 For you took my silver
and my gold and carried off my finest
treasures to your temples.[o] 6 You sold
the people of Judah and Jerusalem to
the Greeks,[p] that you might send
them far from their homeland.
7 "See, I am going to rouse them out
of the places to which you sold them,[q]

2:32 [z]S Isa 46:13 [a]Ob 1:17 [b]S Isa 1:9; 11:11; Mic 4:7; 7:18; S Ro 9:27 [c]Ac 2:39 **3:1** [d]S Dt 30:3; S Jer 16:15; S Eze 38:8; Zep 3:20 [e]Jer 40:5 **3:2** [f]Zep 3:8 [g]ver 12; S Isa 22:1 [h]S Isa 13:9; S Jer 2:35; S Eze 36:5 [i]S Ge 11:4; S Lev 26:33 **3:3** [j]S Job 6:27; S Eze 24:6 [k]Joel 1:5; Am 2:6 **3:4** [l]S Ge 10:15; S Mt 11:21 [m]S Ps 87:4; Isa 14:29-31; Jer 47:1-7 [n]S Lev 26:28; S Isa 34:8; S Eze 25:15-17; Zec 9:5-7 **3:5** [o]S 1Ki 15:18; S 2Ch 21:16-17 **3:6** [p]Eze 27:13; Zec 9:13 **3:7** [q]S Isa 43:5-6; Jer 23:8 [r]S Isa 66:6 **3:8** [s]Isa 60:14 [t]Isa 14:2 [u]S Ge 10:7; S 2Ch 9:1 [v]S Isa 23:1; S Jer 30:16 **3:9** [w]S Isa 8:9 [x]Jer 46:4 **3:10** [y]Isa 2:4 [z]S Nu 25:7 [a]Zec 12:8 [b]S Jos 1:6 **3:11** [c]Eze 38:15-16; Zep 3:8 [d]S Isa 13:3 **3:12** [e]S ver 2 [f]S Ps 82:1; S Isa 2:4 **3:13** [g]Mk 4:29 [h]S Isa 17:5; S Hos 6:11; Mt 13:39; Rev 14:15-19

and I will return[r] on your own heads
what you have done. 8 I will sell your
sons[s] and daughters to the people of
Judah,[t] and they will sell them to the
Sabeans,[u] a nation far away." The
LORD has spoken.[v]

9 Proclaim this among the nations:
Prepare for war![w]
Rouse the warriors![x]
Let all the fighting men draw
near and attack.
10 Beat your plowshares into swords
and your pruning hooks[y] into
spears.[z]
Let the weakling[a] say,
"I am strong!"[b]
11 Come quickly, all you nations from
every side,
and assemble[c] there.

Bring down your warriors,[d]
O LORD!

12 "Let the nations be roused;
let them advance into the Valley
of Jehoshaphat,[e]
for there I will sit
to judge[f] all the nations on
every side.
13 Swing the sickle,[g]
for the harvest[h] is ripe.
Come, trample the grapes,[i]
for the winepress[j] is full
and the vats overflow—
so great is their wickedness!"

14 Multitudes,[k] multitudes

[i]S Jer 25:30 [j]S Jdg 6:11; S Rev 14:20 **3:14** [k]Isa 13:4

[m] 2 *Jehoshaphat* means *the LORD judges*; also in verse 12.

3:1–21 IN THOSE DAYS. This chapter deals with Israel's future restoration and God's judgment on all nations of the world; this judgment will include the great battle of Armageddon that precedes Christ's reign over all the earth (see Rev 16:16, note).

3:2 THE VALLEY OF JEHOSHAPHAT. The Valley of Jehoshaphat, meaning "valley where the LORD judges," is also called "the valley of decision" (v. 14); it may be the valley of Megiddo in north-central Palestine. More important than its physical location, however, is the message that God will one day destroy all evil and will vindicate and rescue his faithful people.

3:3 CAST LOTS FOR MY PEOPLE. God will judge the nations for their cruelty and for treating people as if they were possessions to be traded for money and pleasure. We must be careful how we treat other people, for God will hold us accountable on his judgment day for mistreating another person (see Col 3:25, note).

3:4–8 TYRE AND SIDON. The Lord addresses cities and a region that had been especially cruel to Israel. The prophecy of judgment was at least partly fulfilled in the fourth century when they were subjugated by Alexander the Great and later by Antiochus III (see also Isa 23; Eze 26—28; Am 1:9–10).

3:9–16 PREPARE FOR WAR! The nations are told to prepare for war, for the Lord will come against them with a great destruction. Those who stand against God and his word will be called to account for their sins (see Rev 14:19, note; 16:16, note; cf. Rev 19:11–21). Believers must remember that ungodliness, lawlessness and evil will prevail only for a limited time; God's people will ultimately inherit the earth (cf. Ps 37:11; Mt 5:5).

3:13 THE HARVEST IS RIPE. The harvest of God's judgment on the nations is about to occur, for "great is their wickedness." When sin reaches a certain measure of fullness, judgment is unavoidable (cf. Ge 15:16).

in the valley[l] of decision!
For the day of the LORD[m] is near
in the valley of decision.[n]
15The sun and moon will be
darkened,
and the stars no longer shine.[o]
16The LORD will roar[p] from Zion
and thunder from Jerusalem;[q]
the earth and the sky will
tremble.[r]
But the LORD will be a refuge[s] for
his people,
a stronghold[t] for the people of
Israel.

Blessings for God's People

17"Then you will know[u] that I, the
LORD your God,[v]
dwell in Zion,[w] my holy hill.[x]
Jerusalem will be holy;[y]
never again will foreigners
invade her.[z]

18"In that day the mountains will
drip new wine,[a]
and the hills will flow with
milk;[b]
all the ravines of Judah will run
with water.[c]
A fountain will flow out of the
LORD's house[d]
and will water the valley of
acacias.[n][e]
19But Egypt[f] will be desolate,
Edom[g] a desert waste,
because of violence[h] done to the
people of Judah,
in whose land they shed
innocent blood.
20Judah will be inhabited forever[i]
and Jerusalem through all
generations.
21Their bloodguilt,[j] which I have
not pardoned,
I will pardon.[k]"

The LORD dwells in Zion![l]

3:14 [l] S Isa 22:1 [m] Isa 34:2-8; S Joel 1:15; S Zep 1:7 [n] S Isa 2:4; S Eze 36:5 **3:15** [o] S Job 9:7; S Eze 32:7 **3:16** [p] S Isa 42:13 [q] Am 1:2 [r] S Jdg 5:4; S Isa 14:16; S Eze 38:19 [s] S Ps 46:1; S Isa 25:4; Zec 12:8 [t] S 2Sa 22:3; Jer 16:19; Zec 9:12 **3:17** [u] S Ex 6:7 [v] S Joel 2:27 [w] S Ps 74:2; S Isa 4:3 [x] Ps 2:6; S Isa 2:2; S Eze 17:22 [y] S Jer 31:40 [z] S Isa 52:1; S Eze 44:9; Zec 9:8 **3:18** [a] S Joel 2:24 [b] Ex 3:8; S SS 5:1 [c] S Isa 30:25; 35:6; S 44:3 [d] Rev 22:1-2 [e] S Nu 25:1; S Isa 25:6; S Jer 31:12; S Eze 47:1; Am 9:13 **3:19** [f] S Isa 19:1 [g] S Isa 11:14; S 34:11 [h] S Jer 51:35; Ob 1:10 **3:20** [i] S Ezr 9:12; Am 9:15 **3:21** [j] S Isa 1:15 [k] S Eze 36:25 [l] S Ps 74:2; Isa 59:20; S Eze 48:35; Zec 8:3

[n] *18* Or *Valley of Shittim*

3:17–21 DWELL IN ZION. The book of Joel ends with a promise that Jerusalem will someday be delivered from her enemies and God's blessing will be showered upon his people. This blessing consists first of all in God himself living among his people and showing them his love and care. With the destruction of the ungodly in all nations, God's kingdom will prevail. Joel's conclusion shows Israel that those who remain unrepentant will face God's wrath, while those who repent and seek the Lord will experience his blessings and have a glorious future for all eternity.

AMOS

Outline

Introduction (1:1–2)

I. Eight Oracles of Judgment on Nations (1:3—2:16)
   - A. Damascus (Aram) (1:3–5)
   - B. Gaza (Philistia) (1:6–8)
   - C. Tyre (Phoenicia) (1:9–10)
   - D. Edom (1:11–12)
   - E. Ammon (1:13–15)
   - F. Moab (2:1–3)
   - G. Judah (2:4–5)
   - H. Israel (2:6–16)

II. Three Prophetic Messages for Israel (3:1—6:14)
   - A. Israel's Sin Assures Her of Coming Judgment (3:1–15)
   - B. Israel's Corruption Is at Every Level (4:1–13)
   - C. Israel's Just Judgment Will Be Destruction and Exile (5:1—6:14)
     1. The Death Dirge (5:1–3)
     2. Israel's Refusal to Seek the Lord (5:4–17)
     3. Israel's Perverted Religion (5:18–27)
     4. Israel's Reprimand and Woe (6:1–14)

III. Five Visions of Coming Retribution for Sin (7:1—9:10)
   - A. Vision of Devouring Locusts (7:1–3)
   - B. Vision of a Devouring Fire (7:4–6)
   - C. Vision of a Plumb Line (7:7–9)
   - D. Historical Parenthesis: Amaziah and His Punishment (7:10–17)
   - E. Vision of a Basket of Ripe Fruit (8:1–14)
   - F. Vision of the Lord Judging (9:1–10)

Epilogue: Future Restoration of Israel (9:11–15)

Author: Amos

Theme: Justice, Righteousness and Divine Retribution for Sin

Date of Writing: c. 760–755 B.C.

Background

Amos was an 8th-century B.C. prophet, a contemporary of Isaiah and Micah in Judah, and Jonah and Hosea in Israel. He reveals four important facts about himself in 1:1. (1) He was a shepherd (who also "took care of sycamore-fig trees," see 7:14) from Tekoa, a village in Judah about 12 miles south of Jerusalem. (2) He "saw" his message (i.e., he had prophetic visions; cf. 7:1,4,7; 8:1–2; 9:1) concerning Israel, the northern kingdom. Though he was a layman without the official status of a prophet, God nevertheless gave him a prophetic burden and ministry for rebellious Israel (cf. 7:14–15); his name means "burdened" or "burden bearer." (3) Amos's ministry to Israel occurred during the days when Uzziah was king of Judah and Jeroboam II was king of Israel. The reign of these two kings overlapped during the years 767–753 B.C. Most likely his ministry was c. 760–755 B.C. (4) Amos prophesied during the two years before "the earthquake." Archaeologists have found evidence of a major destructive earthquake from this time period at sites in Israel, including its capital, Samaria. Zechariah mentioned the same earthquake (Zec 14:5) more than 200 years later, further indicating that it was a massive quake. The reference by Amos suggests that he saw it as a confirmation of his prophetic message and ministry to Israel (cf. 9:1).

When Amos prophesied to the northern kingdom in the mid-8th century B.C., the nation outwardly was at its zenith in territorial expansion, political peace and national prosperity, but inwardly it was rotten. Hypocrisy and idolatrous religion were popular, society extravagantly indulgent, immorality rampant, the judicial system corrupt and the oppression of the poor commonplace. In response to God's call, Amos went to Bethel, the residential home of King Jeroboam II and a religious center crowded with worshipers. There Amos courageously proclaimed his message of justice, righteousness and divine retribution for sin to a people who did not want to hear what the Lord had to say to them.

Purpose

Israel's prosperity served only to deepen her corruption. When God mercifully sent Amos to Bethel to proclaim the message "repent or perish," the prophet was expelled from the city and commanded not to prophesy there again (cf. Nineveh's contrasting response to Jonah's message). Then, or soon afterwards, Amos apparently returned to his home in Judah and committed his message to writing. His purpose in doing so was (1) to deliver a written copy of his prophetic warning to King Jeroboam II, and (2) to spread the message widely in Israel (and Judah) about the certainty of God's approaching judgment on Israel and the nations around her unless they repented of their idolatry, immorality and injustice. Israel's destruction occurred only three decades later.

Survey

The book divides naturally into three major sections. (1) In section one (1:3—2:16), Amos first addresses his message of judgment to seven nations surrounding the land of Israel, including Judah. Having drawn Israel at the outset into pleasant agreement concerning God's judgment of other nations (1:3—2:5), Amos then vividly describes Israel's sins and God's judgment against her (2:6–16). This section sets the tone for the book's message of judgment, resulting in national destruction and exile.

(2) Section two (3:1—6:14) records three bold messages, each beginning with the phrase "Hear this word" (3:1; 4:1; 5:1). In the first, God indicts Israel as a privileged people whom he delivered from Egypt: "You only have I chosen of all the families of the earth; therefore I will punish you for all your sins" (3:2). The second message begins by addressing Israel's affluent women at Samaria as "you cows of Bashan . . . who oppress the poor and crush the needy and say to your husbands, 'Bring us some drinks!' " (4:1). Amos prophesied that they would be led into captivity with hooks and fishhooks as their just judgment from God (4:2–3). Amos had similar words for dishonest merchants, corrupt rulers, opportunistic lawyers and judges, and compromising priests and prophets. The third message (chs. 5—6) lists Israel's abhorrent sins, and Amos called the people to repent. "Woe to you who are complacent in Zion" (6:1); terrible ruin and retribution for sin were coming.

(3) The final major section (7:1—9:10) records five prophetic visions of Amos about God's approaching judgment. The fourth vision graphically describes Israel as a basket of overripe summer fruit, soon to be exposed as rotten in the heat of God's judgment (8:1–14). The last vision sees God standing by the altar, ready to strike the capital city of Samaria and the decadent kingdom (9:1–10). The book closes with a brief but powerful promise of future restoration for the surviving remnant (9:11–15).

Special Features

Six major features characterize the book of Amos. (1) It is primarily a prophetic cry for justice and righteousness, based on God's character. Whereas Hosea was crushed by Israel's unfaithfulness to God, Amos is outraged at Israel's violation of God's standards of justice and righteousness for his people. (2) It vividly illustrates how abhorrent religion is to God when divorced from righteous conduct in daily living. (3) It is thoroughly and vigorously confrontational. Amos's confrontation with the priest Amaziah (7:10–17) is a classic scene in Hebrew prophecy. (4) Its bold and vigorous style reflects the prophet's strong, unbending loyalty to God and to his righteous standards for the covenant people. (5) It demonstrates God's willingness and readiness to use God-fearing people without formal ministerial credentials to proclaim his message in an age of professionalism. (6) It has numerous well-known passages, some of which are 3:3,7; 4:6–12; 5:14–15,21–24; 6:1a; 7:8; 8:11; 9:13.

New Testament Fulfillment

The message of Amos is most clearly seen in Jesus' teaching and in the NT book of James. Jesus and James both applied Amos's message that true worship of God is not the formal observance of religious ritual, but "hearing" and "doing" God's will, demonstrated in a just and righteous treatment of one's fellow human beings (e.g., Mt 7:15–27; 23; Jas 2). Also, both Amos and James emphasize the principle that "true religion demands righteous behavior." Finally, James quoted 9:11–12 at the Council at Jerusalem (see Ac 15:16–18) with respect to the inclusion of Gentiles into the church.

Reading Amos

In order to read the entire Old Testament in one year, the book of Amos should be read in 2 days, according to the following schedule: ☐ 1–4 ☐ 5–9

NOTES

1 The words of Amos, one of the shepherds of Tekoa[a]—what he saw concerning Israel two years before the earthquake,[b] when Uzziah[c] was king of Judah and Jeroboam[d] son of Jehoash[a] was king of Israel.[e]

2He said:

"The LORD roars[f] from Zion
and thunders[g] from
Jerusalem;[h]
the pastures of the shepherds dry
up,[b]
and the top of Carmel[i]
withers."[j]

Judgment on Israel's Neighbors

3This is what the LORD says:

"For three sins of Damascus,[k]
even for four, I will not turn
back ⌊my wrath⌋.[l]
Because she threshed Gilead
with sledges having iron teeth,
4I will send fire[m] upon the house
of Hazael[n]
that will consume the
fortresses[o] of
Ben-Hadad.[p]
5I will break down the gate[q] of
Damascus;
I will destroy the king who is
in[c] the Valley of Aven[d]
and the one who holds the scepter
in Beth Eden.[r]
The people of Aram will go into
exile to Kir,[s]"
says the LORD.[t]

6This is what the LORD says:

"For three sins of Gaza,[u]
even for four, I will not turn
back ⌊my wrath⌋.[v]
Because she took captive whole
communities
and sold them to Edom,[w]
7I will send fire upon the walls of
Gaza
that will consume her fortresses.
8I will destroy the king[e] of
Ashdod[x]
and the one who holds the
scepter in Ashkelon.
I will turn my hand[y] against
Ekron,
till the last of the Philistines[z]
is dead,"[a]
says the Sovereign LORD.[b]

9This is what the LORD says:

"For three sins of Tyre,[c]
even for four, I will not turn
back ⌊my wrath⌋.[d]
Because she sold whole
communities of captives to
Edom,
disregarding a treaty of
brotherhood,[e]
10I will send fire upon the walls of
Tyre
that will consume her
fortresses.[f]"

11This is what the LORD says:

"For three sins of Edom,[g]
even for four, I will not turn
back ⌊my wrath⌋.
Because he pursued his brother
with a sword,[h]
stifling all compassion,[f]
because his anger raged
continually
and his fury flamed
unchecked,[i]
12I will send fire upon Teman[j]

1:1 [a]S 2Sa 14:2 [b]Zec 14:5 [c]S 2Ki 14:21; S 2Ch 26:23 [d]S 2Ki 14:23 [e]S Hos 1:1
1:2 [f]S Isa 42:13 [g]S Ps 29:3 [h]Joel 3:16 [i]Am 9:3 [j]S Jer 12:4
1:3 [k]Isa 7:8; 8:4; 17:1-3 [l]ver 6,9,11, 13; Am 2:6
1:4 [m]S Jer 49:27; S Eze 30:8 [n]S 1Ki 19:17; 2Ki 8:7-15 [o]Jer 17:27 [p]1Ki 20:1; 2Ki 6:24; Jer 49:23-27
1:5 [q]Jer 51:30 [r]S Isa 37:12 [s]S 2Ki 16:9; S Isa 22:6; Zec 9:1 [t]S Isa 7:16; Jer 49:27
1:6 [u]S Ge 10:19; 1Sa 6:17; Zep 2:4 [v]S ver 3 [w]S Ge 14:6; Ob 1:11
1:8 [x]S 2Ch 26:6 [y]Ps 81:14 [z]S Eze 25:16 [a]S Isa 34:8 [b]Isa 14:28-32; Zep 2:4-7
1:9 [c]1Ki 5:1; 9:11-14; Jer 25:22; Joel 3:4; S Mt 11:21 [d]ver 3 [e]S 1Ki 5:12
1:10 [f]Isa 23:1-18; S 34:8; S Jer 47:4; Eze 26:2-4; Zec 9:1-4
1:11 [g]Nu 20:14-21; S 2Ch 28:17; S Ps 83:6 [h]S Ps 63:10 [i]S Eze 25:12-14; Zec 1:15
1:12 [j]S Ge 36:11, 15

[a] *1* Hebrew *Joash,* a variant of *Jehoash*
[b] *2* Or *shepherds mourn*
[c] *5* Or *the inhabitants of*
[d] *5* *Aven* means *wickedness.*
[e] *8* Or *inhabitants*
[f] *11* Or *sword / and destroyed his allies*

1:1 AMOS. Amos was a prophet whose home was in Judah, the southern kingdom, yet whose message was to Israel, the northern kingdom. He was a godly layman who earned his living as a shepherd and a grower of sycamore figs (cf. 7:14). God called this faithful man to deliver a message of judgment to Israel and to give them a final warning. His ministry took place most likely in the years 760–750 B.C. Other prophets who probably ministered during this time were Jonah and Hosea.

1:3–2:5 FOR THREE SINS . . . EVEN FOR FOUR. Amos begins by pronouncing judgment on Israel's seven neighboring nations. He lists each nation's particular sins, even Judah's, placing all of them under the same formula, "for three sins . . . even for four" (i.e., for their many sins, and especially the one named).

1:4 I WILL SEND FIRE. This phrase (used also in vv. 7,10,12,14; 2:2,5) alludes to God's judgment by the fiery destruction carried out by an invading army. Major cities would be burned to the ground.

1:6 BECAUSE SHE TOOK CAPTIVE. The majority of the sins listed are sins of brutality and cruelty (see vv. 6,9,11,13). God especially hates sins of mistreatment of other human beings, and he will severely judge violent and inhumane acts that are void of all compassion (cf. Ro 1:18–32). In the light of God's hatred of cruelty, it is essential that God's people strive always to treat others with kindness, justice and love.

that will consume the fortresses
of Bozrah.[k]"

13This is what the LORD says:

"For three sins of Ammon,[l]
even for four, I will not turn
back ⌊my wrath⌋.
Because he ripped open the
pregnant women[m] of Gilead
in order to extend his borders,
14I will set fire to the walls of
Rabbah[n]
that will consume[o] her
fortresses
amid war cries[p] on the day of
battle,
amid violent winds[q] on a
stormy day.
15Her king[g] will go into exile,
he and his officials together,[r]"
says the LORD.[s]

2 This is what the LORD says:
"For three sins of Moab,[t]
even for four, I will not turn
back ⌊my wrath⌋.
Because he burned, as if to lime,[u]
the bones of Edom's king,
2I will send fire upon Moab
that will consume the fortresses
of Kerioth.[h][v]
Moab will go down in great tumult
amid war cries[w] and the blast
of the trumpet.[x]
3I will destroy her ruler[y]
and kill all her officials with
him,"[z]
says the LORD.[a]

4This is what the LORD says:

"For three sins of Judah,[b]
even for four, I will not turn
back ⌊my wrath⌋.
Because they have rejected the
law[c] of the LORD
and have not kept his decrees,[d]
because they have been led
astray[e] by false gods,[i][f]
the gods[j] their ancestors
followed,[g]
5I will send fire[h] upon Judah
that will consume the
fortresses[i] of
Jerusalem.[j]"

Judgment on Israel

6This is what the LORD says:

"For three sins of Israel,
even for four, I will not turn
back ⌊my wrath⌋.[k]
They sell the righteous for silver,
and the needy for a pair of
sandals.[l]
7They trample on the heads of the
poor
as upon the dust of the ground
and deny justice to the
oppressed.
Father and son use the same girl
and so profane my holy name.[m]
8They lie down beside every altar
on garments taken in pledge.[n]
In the house of their god
they drink wine[o] taken as
fines.[p]

9"I destroyed the Amorite[q] before
them,
though he was tall[r] as the
cedars
and strong as the oaks.[s]
I destroyed his fruit above
and his roots[t] below.

10"I brought you up out of Egypt,[u]

1:12 [k] S Isa 34:5; 63:1-6; Jer 25:21; Eze 25:12-14; 35:1-15; Ob 1:1; Mal 1:2-5 **1:13** [l] S Ge 19:38; S Eze 21:28 [m] S Ge 34:29; S 2Ki 8:12; S Hos 13:16 **1:14** [n] S Dt 3:11 [o] Isa 30:30 [p] S Job 39:25 [q] Jer 23:19 **1:15** [r] S Jer 25:21 [s] 1Ch 20:1; S Jer 49:1; Eze 21:28-32; 25:2-7 **2:1** [t] S Isa 16:6 [u] Isa 33:12 **2:2** [v] Jer 48:24 [w] S Job 39:25 [x] S Jos 6:20 **2:3** [y] S Ps 2:10 [z] S Isa 40:23 [a] Isa 15:1-9; 16:1-14; S 25:10; Jer 48:1; S Eze 25:8-11; Zep 2:8-9 **2:4** [b] 2Ki 17:19; Hos 12:2 [c] S Jer 6:19 [d] S Eze 20:24 [e] Isa 9:16 [f] S Ex 34:15; S Dt 31:20; S Ps 4:2 [g] S 2Ki 22:13; S Jer 9:14; S 16:12 **2:5** [h] S 2Ki 25:9; S 2Ch 36:19 [i] Am 3:11 [j] S Jer 17:27; S Hos 8:14 **2:6** [k] S Am 1:3 [l] S Joel 3:3; Am 8:6 **2:7** [m] S Lev 18:21; Am 5:11-12; 8:4 **2:8** [n] S Ex 22:26; Dt 24:12-13 [o] Hos 7:14; Am 4:1; 6:6 [p] Hab 2:6 **2:9** [q] Nu 21:23-26; Jos 10:12 [r] S Isa 10:33 [s] S Ps 29:9 [t] S 2Ki 19:30; S Job 18:16; S Eze 17:9 **2:10** [u] S Ex 6:6; 20:2; Am 3:1

[g] *15* Or / *Molech*; Hebrew *malcam* [h] *2* Or *of her cities* [i] *4* Or *by lies* [j] *4* Or *lies*

2:4 SINS OF JUDAH. The nations of Judah and Israel were God's chosen people, but they too would come under his judgment for their sins. Judah's sins centered in their rejection of God's law and their refusal to keep his decrees. They had been led astray into idolatry, i.e., the worship of the false gods of other nations. God's people always face the temptation of being led astray by the customs and beliefs of the surrounding society.

2:6 SINS OF ISRAEL. Having addressed the sins of Israel's neighbors, Amos now reaches his climax and focuses on the sins and the coming judgment of Israel, the northern kingdom. Instead of following the word of God, they were mistreating the poor (vv. 6–7), living immorally (v. 7) and corrupting the worship of God (vv. 7–8); elsewhere it is made clear that they opposed the ministry of God's true prophets (cf. 7:10–17).

2:10 I BROUGHT YOU UP. Despite having received God's covenant love and blessings, the Israelites turned their backs on the covenant and forgot all that God had done for them; this rejection made their sin worse and their guilt greater. Likewise, we as NT believers must never forget God's love for us through Christ. Remembering his blessings should lead us to remain faithful to him throughout our lives.

and I led[v] you forty years in
the desert[w]
to give you the land of the
Amorites.[x]
11I also raised up prophets[y] from
among your sons
and Nazirites[z] from among your
young men.
Is this not true, people of Israel?"
declares the LORD.
12"But you made the Nazirites drink
wine
and commanded the prophets
not to prophesy.[a]

13"Now then, I will crush you
as a cart crushes when loaded
with grain.[b]
14The swift will not escape,[c]
the strong[d] will not muster
their strength,
and the warrior will not save his
life.[e]
15The archer[f] will not stand his
ground,
the fleet-footed soldier will not
get away,
and the horseman[g] will not
save his life.[h]
16Even the bravest warriors[i]
will flee naked on that day,"
declares the LORD.

2:10 [v]S Dt 8:2 [w]S Dt 2:7 [x]S Ex 3:8; S Nu 21:25; S Jos 13:4; Am 9:7 **2:11** [y]Dt 18:18; Jer 7:25 [z]S Jdg 13:5 **2:12** [a]Isa 30:10; Jer 11:21; Am 7:12-13; Mic 2:6 **2:13** [b]Am 7:16-17 **2:14** [c]S Job 11:20 [d]S 1Ki 20:11 [e]Ps 33:16; Isa 30:16-17 **2:15** [f]S Eze 39:3 [g]S Ex 15:21; Zec 10:5 [h]Ecc 9:11 **2:16** [i]Jer 48:41

3:1 [j]Zep 2:5 [k]S Am 2:10 **3:2** [l]S Ex 19:6; Dt 7:6; Lk 12:47 [m]ver 14 [n]S Jer 14:10; Mic 2:3; 1Pe 4:17 **3:4** [o]S Isa 42:13 [p]Ps 104:21; S Hos 5:14 **3:5** [q]S Ps 119:110 **3:6** [r]S Nu 10:2; S Job 39:24; S Jer 4:21 [s]S Isa 31:2 [t]Isa 14:24-27 **3:7** [u]Ge 18:17; S 1Sa 3:7; S Da 9:22; Jn 15:15; Rev 10:7

Witnesses Summoned Against Israel

3 Hear this word the LORD has spoken against you,[j] O people of Israel—against the whole family I brought up out of Egypt:[k]

2"You only have I chosen[l]
of all the families of the earth;
therefore I will punish[m] you
for all your sins.[n]"

3Do two walk together
unless they have agreed to do
so?
4Does a lion roar[o] in the thicket
when he has no prey?[p]
Does he growl in his den
when he has caught nothing?
5Does a bird fall into a trap on the
ground
where no snare[q] has been set?
Does a trap spring up from the
earth
when there is nothing to catch?
6When a trumpet[r] sounds in a city,
do not the people tremble?
When disaster[s] comes to a city,
has not the LORD caused it?[t]
7Surely the Sovereign LORD does
nothing
without revealing his plan[u]

2:12 MADE THE NAZIRITES DRINK WINE. God had consecrated the Nazirites to be the highest examples of dedication and righteousness in Israel (see Nu 6:2, note). Part of their consecration was to abstain from all types of wine (see article on WINE IN THE OLD TESTAMENT, p. 204). Many Israelites loved intoxicating drink (6:6), and they subverted the faithfulness of the Nazirites by making them abandon their pledge of abstinence. Because they placed this temptation before the Nazirites, God would bring judgment on them (2:12–16). Those who influence others to a life of sin, including the sin of drinking intoxicating beverages, should listen to God's warning in these verses.

2:13–16 CRUSH YOU. Because of Israel's sin, God's wrath would come upon that wicked nation. Those who thought themselves strong, independent and brave would collapse in fear and be crushed. Likewise, when God's judgment comes against the earth at the end of time, all the ungodly who thought they were strong and tough will cringe in fear as they see their coming destruction.

3:1 THE WHOLE FAMILY. Both Israel and Judah are in mind here. They were God's chosen people who had to be brought to accountability.

3:2 YOU ONLY HAVE I CHOSEN. The Israelites were objecting to Amos's message, for they believed that God would not punish them; they were, after all, his elect whom he had called and redeemed. They felt that God's past salvation meant their present security, even if they turned from God and his ways, forgetting that election established a relationship with God that brought with it the responsibility to remain faithful in their obedience to God (see articles on GOD'S COVENANT WITH THE ISRAELITES, p. 290, and ELECTION AND PREDESTINATION, p. 1824). The punishment that Israel would receive was the result of her failure to fulfill her part in election.

3:3–8 DO TWO WALK TOGETHER UNLESS. The examples in these verses show that a second event happens only when it is preceded by a first event. Thus, as surely as God had spoken, Amos had to pronounce divine judgment; he was not simply speaking his own opinions (vv. 7–8).

3:3 DO TWO WALK TOGETHER. No real fellowship can exist between two people unless they agree on fundamental truths; thus we can have no genuine relationship with God unless we accept his Word and agree with it. It is impossible to call yourself a believer and at the same time not believe God's Word.

3:7–8 WITHOUT REVEALING HIS PLAN. The Lord did nothing with regard to his people Israel without first revealing his plans to the prophets. When God did so, they were compelled to prophesy and to warn the people of God's threatened judgments.

to his servants the prophets.[v]

8The lion[w] has roared[x]—
who will not fear?
The Sovereign LORD has spoken—
who can but prophesy?[y]

9Proclaim to the fortresses of
Ashdod[z]
and to the fortresses of Egypt:
"Assemble yourselves on the
mountains of Samaria;[a]
see the great unrest within her
and the oppression among her
people."

10"They do not know how to do
right,[b]" declares the LORD,
"who hoard plunder[c] and loot
in their fortresses."[d]

11Therefore this is what the Sovereign LORD says:

"An enemy will overrun the land;
he will pull down your
strongholds
and plunder your fortresses.[e]"

12This is what the LORD says:

"As a shepherd saves from the
lion's[f] mouth
only two leg bones or a piece of
an ear,
so will the Israelites be saved,
those who sit in Samaria
on the edge of their beds
and in Damascus on their
couches.[k][g]"

13"Hear this and testify[h] against the house of Jacob," declares the Lord, the LORD God Almighty.

14"On the day I punish[i] Israel for
her sins,
I will destroy the altars of
Bethel;[j]
the horns[k] of the altar will be cut
off
and fall to the ground.
15I will tear down the winter
house[l]
along with the summer house;[m]
the houses adorned with ivory[n]
will be destroyed
and the mansions[o] will be
demolished,[p]"
declares the LORD.[q]

Israel Has Not Returned to God

4 Hear this word, you cows of
Bashan[r] on Mount
Samaria,[s]
you women who oppress the
poor[t] and crush the
needy[u]
and say to your husbands,[v]
"Bring us some drinks![w]"
2The Sovereign LORD has sworn by
his holiness:
"The time[x] will surely come
when you will be taken away[y]
with hooks,[z]
the last of you with fishhooks.
3You will each go straight out
through breaks in the wall,[a]
and you will be cast out toward
Harmon,[l]"
declares the LORD.

4"Go to Bethel[b] and sin;
go to Gilgal[c] and sin yet more.
Bring your sacrifices every
morning,[d]
your tithes[e] every three
years.[m][f]
5Burn leavened bread[g] as a thank
offering

3:7 [v]S Jer 23:22 3:8 [w]S Isa 31:4 [x]S Isa 42:13 [y]S Jer 20:9; Jnh 1:1-3; 3:1-3; Ac 4:20 3:9 [z]S Jos 13:3; S 2Ch 26:6 [a]Am 4:1; 6:1 3:10 [b]Am 5:7; 6:12 [c]Hab 2:8 [d]S Ps 36:3; Mic 6:10; Zep 1:9 3:11 [e]Am 2:5; 6:14 3:12 [f]S 1Sa 17:34 [g]S Est 1:6; Am 6:4 3:13 [h]Eze 2:7 3:14 [i]S ver 2; S Lev 26:18 [j]S Ge 12:8; Am 5:5-6 [k]S Ex 27:2 3:15 [l]Jer 36:22 [m]Jdg 3:20 [n]S 1Ki 22:39 [o]Am 5:11; 6:11 [p]S Isa 34:5 [q]Hos 10:5-8,14-15 4:1 [r]S Ps 22:12 [s]S Am 3:9 [t]S Isa 58:6; S Eze 18:12 [u]S Dt 24:14 [v]Jer 44:19 [w]S Am 2:8; 5:11; 8:6 4:2 [x]Jer 31:31 [y]Am 6:8 [z]S 2Ki 19:28; S 2Ch 33:11; S Isa 19:8 4:3 [a]S Eze 12:5 4:4 [b]S Jos 7:2 [c]S Hos 4:15 [d]S Nu 28:3 [e]Dt 14:28 [f]S Eze 20:39; Am 5:21-22 4:5 [g]S Lev 7:13

[k] *12* The meaning of the Hebrew for this line is uncertain. [l] *3* Masoretic Text; with a different word division of the Hebrew (see Septuagint) *out, O mountain of oppression* [m] *4* Or *tithes on the third day*

3:9–15 ASSEMBLE YOURSELVES. Amos called on Israel's neighbors to witness the guilt, sin and judgment of Israel. They would recognize that this judgment was well-deserved.
3:11–12 AN ENEMY WILL OVERRUN. The enemy was Assyria, the nation God used to destroy Israel. Only a small remnant in Israel would survive to tell the story of God's judgment (v. 12).
4:1 YOU COWS OF BASHAN. The upper-class women are called "cows of Bashan" (i.e. the highly bred and well-fed cattle of Canaan, cf. Ps 22:12). As these women drank their wine, they would urge their husbands to get more money by oppressing the poor so that they could drink even more and bask in luxury.

4:2 TAKEN AWAY WITH HOOKS. Assyrian pictures engraved on stone portray prisoners being led away with ropes tied to hooks in their nose or lips. The wealthy women of Israel's capital would be led away in judgment like cattle.
4:4–5 SIN YET MORE. Many Israelites were adding to their sins by going to worship and bringing sacrifices and tithes while continuing to live in sin. Those who profess to be saved and to worship the Lord and give offerings while loving the world's sinful pleasures are detestable to the Lord. God accepts only the worship and devotion of those who love him and are committed to his ways and word.

and brag about your freewill
offerings[h]—
boast about them, you Israelites,
for this is what you love to do,"
declares the Sovereign LORD.

6"I gave you empty stomachs[n] in
every city
and lack of bread in every town,
yet you have not returned to
me,"
declares the LORD.[i]

7"I also withheld[j] rain from you
when the harvest was still three
months away.
I sent rain on one town,
but withheld it from another.[k]
One field had rain;
another had none and dried up.
8People staggered from town to
town for water[l]
but did not get enough[m] to
drink,
yet you have not returned[n] to
me,"
declares the LORD.[o]

9"Many times I struck your gardens
and vineyards,
I struck them with blight and
mildew.[p]
Locusts[q] devoured your fig and
olive trees,[r]
yet you have not returned[s] to
me,"
declares the LORD.

10"I sent plagues[t] among you
as I did to Egypt.[u]
I killed your young men[v] with the
sword,
along with your captured horses.
I filled your nostrils with the
stench[w] of your camps,
yet you have not returned to
me,"[x]
declares the LORD.[y]

11"I overthrew some of you
as I[o] overthrew Sodom and
Gomorrah.[z]
You were like a burning stick[a]
snatched from the fire,
yet you have not returned to
me,"
declares the LORD.[b]

12"Therefore this is what I will do to
you, Israel,
and because I will do this to
you,
prepare to meet your God,
O Israel."

13He who forms the mountains,[c]
creates the wind,[d]
and reveals his thoughts[e] to
man,
he who turns dawn to darkness,
and treads the high places of
the earth[f]—
the LORD God Almighty is his
name.[g]

A Lament and Call to Repentance

5 Hear this word, O house of Israel,
this lament[h] I take up concerning
you:

2"Fallen is Virgin[i] Israel,
never to rise again,
deserted in her own land,
with no one to lift her up.[j]"

3This is what the Sovereign LORD
says:

"The city that marches out a
thousand strong for Israel
will have only a hundred left;
the town that marches out a
hundred strong
will have only ten left.[k]"

4This is what the LORD says to the
house of Israel:

4:5 [h]S Lev 22:18-21 **4:6** [i]S Isa 3:1; S 9:13; S Jer 5:3; Hag 2:17 **4:7** [j]S Jer 3:3; Zec 14:17 [k]Ex 9:4,26; Dt 11:17; S 2Ch 7:13; S Isa 5:6 **4:8** [l]S Eze 4:16-17 [m]Hag 1:6 [n]S Jer 3:7 [o]S Job 36:31; S Jer 14:4 **4:9** [p]S Dt 28:22 [q]S Ex 10:13; S Joel 2:25 [r]Joel 1:7 [s]S Isa 9:13; S Jer 3:10 **4:10** [t]S Ex 9:3 [u]Ex 11:5 [v]S Isa 9:17 [w]S Isa 34:3 [x]S Dt 28:21 [y]S Isa 9:13 **4:11** [z]S Ge 19:24; S Jer 23:14 [a]S Isa 7:4; Jude 1:23 [b]S Job 36:13 **4:13** [c]Ps 65:6 [d]Ps 135:7 [e]S Da 2:28 [f]Mic 1:3 [g]S Isa 47:4; Am 5:8,27; 9:6 **5:1** [h]S Jer 4:8; S Eze 19:1 **5:2** [i]S 2Ki 19:21; Jer 14:17 [j]Jer 50:32; Am 8:14 **5:3** [k]Isa 6:13; Am 6:9

[n] 6 Hebrew *you cleanness of teeth*
[o] 11 Hebrew *God*

4:6–11 YET YOU HAVE NOT RETURNED TO ME. God had sent disaster after disaster on the people in order to urge them to repent and return to him; however, nothing availed to lead the people out of their corrupt lifestyle. For this they would ultimately face God's judgment (v. 12).

4:12 PREPARE TO MEET YOUR GOD. Israel would meet God's judgment at the hands of the Assyrians, an ultimate judgment that would be terrible. This passage reminds us that all God's people will one day be judged for their deeds (see Jn 5:29, notes; see article on THE JUDGMENT OF BELIEVERS, p. 1791).

5:1–27 THIS LAMENT. In this lament, Amos communicates the Lord's sorrow because of Israel's sins. The song maintains that their doom was certain, speaking as if it had already taken place; yet Amos appeals to the people to turn to God so that at least a "remnant" might be saved (v. 15).

5:4 SEEK ME AND LIVE. If the people would seek the Lord, a remnant could be spared the doom of which Amos spoke (see v. 15). In this life, seeking the Lord daily is essential to receiving his grace and mercy. You should be alarmed if you find yourself neglecting prayer and meditation on God's Word.

"Seek[l] me and live;[m]
5 do not seek Bethel,
do not go to Gilgal,[n]
do not journey to Beersheba.[o]
For Gilgal will surely go into exile,
and Bethel will be reduced to
nothing.[p][p]"
6Seek[q] the LORD and live,[r]
or he will sweep through the
house of Joseph like a
fire;[s]
it will devour,
and Bethel[t] will have no one to
quench it.[u]

7You who turn justice into
bitterness[v]
and cast righteousness[w] to the
ground[x]
8(he who made the Pleiades and
Orion,[y]
who turns blackness into dawn[z]
and darkens day into night,[a]
who calls for the waters of the sea
and pours them out over the
face of the land—
the LORD is his name[b]—
9he flashes destruction on the
stronghold
and brings the fortified city to
ruin),[c]
10you hate the one who reproves in
court[d]
and despise him who tells the
truth.[e]

11You trample on the poor[f]
and force him to give you grain.
Therefore, though you have built
stone mansions,[g]
you will not live in them;[h]
though you have planted lush
vineyards,
you will not drink their wine.[i]
12For I know how many are your
offenses
and how great your sins.[j]

You oppress the righteous and
take bribes[k]
and you deprive the poor[l] of
justice in the courts.[m]
13Therefore the prudent man keeps
quiet[n] in such times,
for the times are evil.[o]

14Seek good, not evil,
that you may live.[p]
Then the LORD God Almighty will
be with you,
just as you say he is.
15Hate evil,[q] love good;[r]
maintain justice in the courts.[s]
Perhaps[t] the LORD God Almighty
will have mercy[u]
on the remnant[v] of Joseph.

16Therefore this is what the Lord,
the LORD God Almighty, says:

"There will be wailing[w] in all the
streets[x]
and cries of anguish in every
public square.
The farmers[y] will be summoned
to weep
and the mourners to wail.
17There will be wailing[z] in all the
vineyards,
for I will pass through[a] your
midst,"
says the LORD.[b]

The Day of the LORD

18Woe to you who long
for the day of the LORD![c]
Why do you long for the day of the
LORD?[d]

5:4 [l]S Dt 4:29 [m]Dt 32:46-47; Isa 55:3; Jer 29:13; S Eze 18:9 **5:5** [n]1Sa 11:14; S Hos 4:15 [o]Ge 21:31; Am 8:14 [p]S 1Sa 7:16; S 8:2 **5:6** [q]Ps 22:26; 105:4; S Isa 31:1; 55:6; Zep 2:3 [r]ver 14; S Lev 18:5 [s]Dt 4:24 [t]S Am 3:14 [u]S Jer 4:4 **5:7** [v]Isa 5:20; Am 6:12 [w]S Am 3:10 [x]S Hos 10:4 **5:8** [y]S Ge 1:16; S Job 38:31 [z]S Job 38:12; Isa 42:16 [a]S Ps 104:20; Am 8:9 [b]Ps 104:6-9; Jer 16:21; S Am 4:13 **5:9** [c]Mic 5:11 **5:10** [d]S Isa 29:21 [e]1Ki 22:8; Gal 4:16 **5:11** [f]Am 8:6 [g]S Am 3:15 [h]S Dt 28:30; Mic 1:6 [i]S Jdg 9:27; S Am 4:1; 9:14; Mic 6:15; Zep 1:13 **5:12** [j]Hos 5:3 [k]S Job 36:18; S Isa 1:23; S Eze 22:12 [l]S Jer 5:28 [m]S Job 5:4; S Isa 5:23; S Am 2:6-7 **5:13** [n]S Est 4:14 [o]Mic 2:3 **5:14** [p]S ver 6 **5:15** [q]S Ps 52:3; S 97:10; Ro 12:9 [r]S Ge 18:25 [s]S Isa 1:17; S 29:21; Zec 8:16 [t]S Jer 36:3 [u]S Joel 2:14 [v]Mic 5:7,8; 7:18 **5:16** [w]Jer 9:17; Am 8:3; Zep 1:10 [x]Jer 7:34 [y]S Joel 1:11 **5:17** [z]S Ex 11:6 [a]Ex 12:12 [b]Isa 16:10; S Jer 48:33 **5:18** [c]S Isa 2:12; S Joel 1:15 [d]S Jer 30:5

[p]5 Or *grief*; or *wickedness*; Hebrew *aven*, a reference to Beth Aven (a derogatory name for Bethel)

5:7 CAST RIGHTEOUSNESS TO THE GROUND. True spirituality does not exist where there is no desire for righteousness. We all must have an intense concern for righteousness in our own lives and in the society in which we live (cf. Mt 6:33). Righteousness comes to expression by following the direction of the Holy Spirit, by hating evil and by loving good (see v. 15, note).

5:12 YOU OPPRESS THE RIGHTEOUS. Of all the sins that Amos pointed out, prominent were the people's social sins—the rich taking advantage of the poor and exploiting them. It is God's will that we have a special love and compassion for the needy (see article on THE CARE OF THE POOR AND NEEDY, p. 1316).

5:15 HATE EVIL, LOVE GOOD. If God's people would only hate evil and love good, God would have mercy on the remnant, i.e., those who survived the coming judgment. A sure sign that we have committed ourselves to God is a sincere hatred of all sin and a deep love for God's righteous standards (see Heb 1:9, note).

5:18 DAY OF THE LORD. The Israelites believed that "the day of the LORD" would be a day when God would judge all their enemies and they themselves would be exalted. Amos shocked them by insisting that when that day came, it would mean judgment for the sinful nation of Israel (see Joel 1:15, note).

That day will be darkness,[e] not
light.[f]
19It will be as though a man fled
from a lion
only to meet a bear,[g]
as though he entered his house
and rested his hand on the
wall
only to have a snake bite him.[h]
20Will not the day of the LORD be
darkness,[i] not light—
pitch-dark, without a ray of
brightness?[j]
21"I hate,[k] I despise your religious
feasts;[l]
I cannot stand your
assemblies.[m]
22Even though you bring me burnt
offerings[n] and grain
offerings,
I will not accept them.[o][p]
Though you bring choice fellowship
offerings,[q]
I will have no regard for
them.[q][r]
23Away with the noise of your
songs!
I will not listen to the music of
your harps.[s]
24But let justice[t] roll on like a
river,
righteousness[u] like a
never-failing stream![v]
25"Did you bring me sacrifices[w] and
offerings
forty years[x] in the desert,
O house of Israel?
26You have lifted up the shrine of
your king,
the pedestal of your idols,[y]
the star of your god[r]—
which you made for yourselves.
27Therefore I will send you into
exile[z] beyond Damascus,"
says the LORD, whose name is
God Almighty.[a]

Woe to the Complacent

6 Woe to you[b] who are
complacent[c] in Zion,
and to you who feel secure[d] on
Mount Samaria,[e]
you notable men of the foremost
nation,
to whom the people of Israel
come![f]
2Go to Calneh[g] and look at it;
go from there to great
Hamath,[h]
and then go down to Gath[i] in
Philistia.
Are they better off than[j] your two
kingdoms?
Is their land larger than yours?
3You put off the evil day
and bring near a reign of
terror.[k]
4You lie on beds inlaid with ivory
and lounge on your couches.[l]
You dine on choice lambs
and fattened calves.[m]
5You strum away on your harps[n]
like David
and improvise on musical
instruments.[o]
6You drink wine[p] by the bowlful
and use the finest lotions,
but you do not grieve[q] over the
ruin of Joseph.[r]
7Therefore you will be among the
first to go into exile;[s]
your feasting and lounging will
end.[t]

5:18 [e] S 1Sa 2:9; S Joel 2:2 [f] S Job 20:28; Isa 5:19,30; Jer 30:7 **5:19** [g] S La 3:10 [h] S Dt 32:24; Job 20:24; S Ecc 10:8; Isa 24:17-18; Jer 15:2-3; 48:44 **5:20** [i] S 1Sa 2:9 [j] S Isa 13:10; S Eze 7:7; Ob 1:15; Zep 1:15 **5:21** [k] Jer 44:4 [l] S Lev 26:31; S Hos 2:11 [m] S Eze 23:18 **5:22** [n] Lev 26:31 [o] S Jer 7:21 [p] S Ps 40:6 [q] Jer 14:12; S Am 4:4; Mic 6:6-7 [r] Isa 1:11-16; S 66:3 **5:23** [s] Am 6:5 **5:24** [t] S Jer 22:3 [u] S Isa 45:8 [v] Mic 6:8 **5:25** [w] S Isa 43:23 [x] S Ex 16:35 **5:26** [y] S Eze 18:6; S 20:16 **5:27** [z] Am 6:7; 7:11,17; Mic 1:16 [a] Dt 32:17-19; Jer 38:17; S Am 4:13; Ac 7:42-43* **6:1** [b] Lk 6:24 [c] Zep 1:12 [d] S Job 24:23 [e] S Am 3:9 [f] Isa 32:9-11 **6:2** [g] S Ge 10:10 [h] S 2Ki 17:24; S Jer 49:23 [i] S Jos 11:22; 2Ch 26:6 [j] Na 3:8 **6:3** [k] S Isa 56:12; S Eze 12:22; Am 9:10 **6:4** [l] S Est 1:6; S Pr 7:17 [m] S Isa 1:11; S Eze 34:2-3; S Am 3:12 **6:5** [n] S Ps 137:2; S Isa 14:11; Am 5:23 [o] S 1Ch 15:16 **6:6** [p] S Isa 28:1; S Am 2:8 [q] S Eze 9:4 [r] S Eze 16:49 **6:7** [s] S Am 5:27 [t] S Jer 16:9; S La 4:5

[q] *22* Traditionally *peace offerings* [r] *26* Or *lifted up Sakkuth your king / and Kaiwan your idols, / your star-gods*; Septuagint *lifted up the shrine of Molech / and the star of your god Rephan, / their idols*

5:21–27 I DESPISE YOUR RELIGIOUS FEASTS. God hates worship rituals, church attendance and songs of praise by those who profess to be believers while seeking the sinful pleasures of the world. (1) God desires worship and praise only from those whose hearts are turned toward him in sincere love and adoration and who seek to live godly lives (see article on WORSHIP, p. 680). (2) Religious hypocrisy is detestable to God, and it will bring special condemnation on those who are guilty of it (see 1Co 11:27, note).

6:1–7 WOE TO YOU WHO ARE COMPLACENT. God's people in both Israel (Samaria) and Judah (Zion) are addressed here. (1) They possessed power and prosperity, but had become complacent about their sins. They believed that their material success proved they were living under God's blessing; they felt confident that God's judgment would never come. (2) Likewise, prosperity and a comfortable lifestyle can cause us to drift into a worldly lifestyle where a deep and abiding hunger for God no longer exists (see article on RICHES AND POVERTY, p. 1562).

6:6 YOU DO NOT GRIEVE. Rather than happily living in material luxury, the Israelites should have been grieving over the sins of the nation and its impending doom. Those who experience sorrow for the people's sins will escape God's judgment (see Eze 9:4) and experience his blessing instead (Mt 5:4).

THE CARE OF THE POOR AND NEEDY

***Am 5:12–14** "For I know how many are your offenses and how great your sins. You oppress the righteous and take bribes and you deprive the poor of justice in the courts. Therefore the prudent man keeps quiet in such times, for the times are evil. Seek good, not evil, that you may live. Then the LORD God Almighty will be with you, just as you say he is."*

In this world where there are both rich and poor, haves and have-nots, frequently those who have material wealth take advantage of those who have little, often gaining more at the expense of the exploited poor (see Ps 10:2,9–10; Isa 3:14–15; Jer 2:34; Am 2:6–7; 5:12–13; Jas 2:6). The Bible has much to say about how believers are to treat the poor and needy.

GOD'S CONCERN FOR THE POOR AND NEEDY. In various ways God has expressed his great concern for the poor, the needy and the oppressed. (1) The Lord God is the champion of the poor and the needy. He reveals himself as their refuge (Ps 14:6; Isa 25:4), their help (Ps 40:17; 70:5), their deliverer (1Sa 2:8; Ps 12:5; 34:6; 35:10; 113:7; cf. Lk 1:52–53) and their provider (Ps 10:14; 68:10; 132:15).

(2) When God revealed his law to the Israelites, he provided a number of ways to eliminate poverty among them (see Dt 15:7–11, note). He stated his overall goal for them as follows: "there should be no poor among you, for in the land the LORD your God is giving you to possess as your inheritance, he will richly bless you" (Dt 15:4). Thus in his law God forbade the charging of interest on loans to the poor (Ex 22:25; Lev 25:35–36). If the poor gave something as security ("a pledge") for a loan (such as his cloak), the person loaning the money had to return the cloak by sunset. If a poor person was hired to work for a rich man, he was to receive his pay every day so that he could buy food for himself and his family (Dt 24:14–15). During the harvest season, grain that dropped was to be left so that the poor could glean it for themselves (Lev 19:10; Dt 24:19–21); in fact, the edges of the field were specifically to be left unharvested for gleaning (Lev 19:9). Even more striking was God's command that every seven years, all debts of poor Israelites were to be canceled (Dt 15:1–6); neither could a man with means refuse to loan a poor person something simply because it was too close to that seventh year (Dt 15:7–11). In addition to providing the year for canceling debts, God provided a year for return of property—the Year of Jubilee (every fifty years), when he commanded that all land that had traded hands since the previous Year of Jubilee was to be returned to its original family owner (see Lev 25:8–55). And most important of all, justice was to be impartial; neither the rich nor the poor were to receive any favoritism in the law courts (Ex 23:2–3,6; Dt 1:17; cf. Pr 31:9). Thus, God sought to protect the poor from being exploited by those with material means and to ensure justice for them (see Dt 24:14, note).

(3) Unfortunately, the Israelites did not always keep these laws. Instead, many of the rich took advantage of the poor and increased their misery. For such actions the Lord through the prophets spoke severe words of judgment against the wealthy Israelites (see Isa 1:21–25; Jer 17:11; Am 4:1–3; 5:11–13; Mic 2:1–5; Hab 2:6–8; Zec 7:8–14).

THE NEW TESTAMENT BELIEVER'S RESPONSIBILITY TO THE POOR AND NEEDY. In the NT, God also instructed his people to show a deep concern for the poor and needy, especially for those within the Christian church. (1) Much of Jesus' ministry was to the poor and disadvantaged in Jewish society whom no one else seemed to care about—such as the oppressed and downtrodden (Lk 4:18–19), Samaritans (Lk 17:11–19; Jn 4:1–42), those with leprosy (Mt 8:2–4; Lk 17:11–19), widows (Lk 7:11–15; 20:45–47), and the like. He had harsh words of judgment for those who clung tightly to worldly possessions and ignored the poor (Mk 10:17–25; Lk 6:24–25; 12:16–20; 16:13–15,19–31; see article on RICHES AND POVERTY, p. 1562).

(2) Jesus assumed and expected that his people would give generously to the poor and needy (see Mt 6:1–4). Jesus himself practiced what he preached, keeping a money bag from which he and his disciples would give to the poor (see Jn 12:5–6; 13:29). On more than one occasion he instructed those who wanted to be his followers to care about the poor, to help them and to give them money (Mt 19:21; Lk 12:33; 14:12–14,16–24; 18:22). Such giving was not regarded as optional by Jesus; in fact, one of his requirements for entrance into his eternal kingdom is whether we have been kind to our brothers and sisters who are hungry, thirsty and naked (Mt 25:31–46).

(3) The apostle Paul and the early church likewise demonstrated deep concern for those in need. Very early in Paul's ministry, he and Barnabas, representing the church in Antioch of Syria, brought an offering to Jerusalem for the needy Christians in Judea (Ac 11:28–30). When the council met at Jerusalem, the leaders there refused to declare that circumcision was necessary for salvation, but they did suggest that Paul and his associates "continue to remember the poor, the very thing I was eager to do" (Gal 2:10). One of his goals on his third missionary journey was to gather money for "the poor among the saints in Jerusalem" (Ro 15:26). He instructed his churches both in Galatia and in Corinth to give for this cause (1Co 16:1–4). When the church in Corinth did not give as he thought they should, he exhorted them at great length about helping the poor and needy (2Co 8—9). He praised the Macedonian churches that had urgently pleaded with Paul to let them participate in this collection (2Co 8:1–4; 9:2). Paul regarded giving so highly that he states in the book of Romans that one of the gifts that the Holy Spirit gives to Christians is the ability to give generously for the needs of God's work or people (see Ro 12:8, note; cf. 1Ti 6:17–19).

(4) Our first priority in the care of the poor and needy is those who are brothers and sisters in Christ. Jesus equated gifts given to our fellow believers with gifts given to him (Mt 25:40,45). The early church established a caring community that shared their possessions to help meet each other's needs (Ac 2:44–45; 4:34–37). When the increased size of the church made it impossible for the apostles to care for the needy in a fair and equitable manner, seven men full of the Holy Spirit were chosen for that task (Ac 6:1–6). Paul states the principle of a caring community explicitly: "Therefore as we have opportunity, let us do good to all people, especially to those who belong to the family of believers" (Gal 6:10). God wants those who have plenty to share with those who have needs, so that there may be equality among God's people (2Co 8:14–15; cf. Eph 4:28; Tit 3:14). In summary, then, the Bible gives us no choice but to be sensitive to the material needs of those around us, especially our brothers and sisters in Christ.

The Lord Abhors the Pride of Israel

8The Sovereign Lord has sworn by
himself[u]—the Lord God Almighty declares:

"I abhor[v] the pride of Jacob[w]
and detest his fortresses;[x]
I will deliver up[y] the city
and everything in it.[z]"

9If ten[a] men are left in one house,
they too will die. **10**And if a relative
who is to burn the bodies[b] comes to
carry them out of the house and asks
anyone still hiding there, "Is anyone
with you?" and he says, "No," then he
will say, "Hush![c] We must not mention the name of the Lord."

11For the Lord has given the
command,
and he will smash[d] the great
house[e] into pieces
and the small house into
bits.[f]
12Do horses run on the rocky
crags?
Does one plow there with
oxen?
But you have turned justice into
poison[g]
and the fruit of righteousness[h]
into bitterness[i]—
13you who rejoice in the conquest of
Lo Debar[s]
and say, "Did we not take
Karnaim[t] by our own
strength?[j]"
14For the Lord God Almighty
declares,
"I will stir up a nation[k] against
you, O house of Israel,
that will oppress you all the way
from Lebo[u] Hamath[l] to the
valley of the Arabah.[m]"

Locusts, Fire and a Plumb Line

7 This is what the Sovereign Lord
showed me:[n] He was preparing
swarms of locusts[o] after the king's
share had been harvested and just as
the second crop was coming up. **2**When
they had stripped the land clean,[p] I
cried out, "Sovereign Lord, forgive!
How can Jacob survive?[q] He is so
small![r]"

3So the Lord relented.[s]
"This will not happen," the Lord
said.[t]

4This is what the Sovereign Lord
showed me: The Sovereign Lord was
calling for judgment by fire;[u] it dried
up the great deep and devoured[v] the
land. **5**Then I cried out, "Sovereign
Lord, I beg you, stop! How can Jacob
survive? He is so small![w]"

6So the Lord relented.[x]
"This will not happen either," the
Sovereign Lord said.[y]

7This is what he showed me: The
Lord was standing by a wall that had
been built true to plumb, with a plumb
line in his hand. **8**And the Lord asked
me, "What do you see,[z] Amos?[a]"
"A plumb line,[b]" I replied.
Then the Lord said, "Look, I am setting a plumb line among my people Israel; I will spare them no longer.[c]

9"The high places[d] of Isaac will be
destroyed
and the sanctuaries[e] of Israel
will be ruined;
with my sword I will rise
against the house of
Jeroboam.[f]"

6:8 [u] S Ge 22:16; Heb 6:13 [v] S Lev 26:30 [w] S Ps 47:4 [x] S Jer 12:8 [y] Am 4:2 [z] S Lev 26:19; Dt 32:19 **6:9** [a] S Am 5:3 **6:10** [b] S 1Sa 31:12 [c] Am 8:3 **6:11** [d] S Isa 34:5 [e] S Am 3:15 [f] Isa 55:11 **6:12** [g] Hos 10:4 [h] S Am 3:10 [i] S Isa 1:21; S Am 5:7 **6:13** [j] S Job 8:15; Isa 28:14-15 **6:14** [k] Jer 5:15 [l] S Nu 13:21 [m] S Am 3:11
7:1 [n] ver 7; Am 8:1 [o] Ps 78:46; S Jer 51:14; S Joel 1:4 **7:2** [p] S Ex 10:15 [q] S Isa 37:4 [r] S Eze 11:13; S Am 4:9 **7:3** [s] S Ex 32:14; Dt 32:36; S Jer 18:8; 26:19 [t] S Hos 11:8 **7:4** [u] S Isa 66:16; S Joel 1:19 [v] Dt 32:22 **7:5** [w] S ver 1-2; Joel 2:17 **7:6** [x] S Ex 32:14; S Jer 18:8; Jnh 3:10 [y] Jer 42:10; S Eze 9:8 **7:8** [z] Jer 1:11,13 [a] Am 8:2 [b] S 2Ki 21:13 [c] S Jer 15:6; Eze 7:2-9 **7:9** [d] S Lev 26:30 [e] S Lev 26:31 [f] S 1Ki 13:34; 2Ki 15:9; Isa 63:18; S Hos 10:8

[s] 13 *Lo Debar* means *nothing.* [t] 13 *Karnaim* means *horns*; *horn* here symbolizes strength. [u] 14 Or *from the entrance to*

6:8 I WILL DELIVER UP THE CITY. Because the people had refused to return to the Lord, their cities would be destroyed. Their doom was certain, for God Almighty had declared it by a solemn oath.

6:10 HUSH! When the day of the Lord came, the place of disaster would be filled with the fear of God. People would not even dare to mention his name, lest it bring further destruction and death on them.

7:1–6 THE SOVEREIGN LORD SHOWED ME. Amos was given two visions of God's imminent judgment on Israel; judgment would come in the form of locusts (v. 1) and intense heat (v. 4), causing the land to be devoured and mass starvation to result. The prophet interceded for the people, and the Lord delayed his judgment (vv. 3,6). God does not desire the death of sinners (1Ti 2:4; 2Pe 3:9), and he promises to respond to the prayers of a righteous person (Jas 5:16).

7:7–9 A PLUMB LINE. Amos's third vision revealed God measuring Israel with a plumb line. A plumb line was a string with a weight tied on the end by which builders ascertained the straightness of a wall. Israel was found to be out of plumb and in danger of collapsing because they had rejected God's word (vv. 12–17); therefore, God's judgment would certainly come.

Amos and Amaziah

10Then Amaziah the priest of Bethel[g] sent a message to Jeroboam[h]
king of Israel: "Amos is raising a conspiracy[i] against you in the very heart
of Israel. The land cannot bear all his
words.[j] 11For this is what Amos is
saying:

" 'Jeroboam will die by the sword,
and Israel will surely go into
exile,[k]
away from their native land.' "[l]

12Then Amaziah said to Amos, "Get
out, you seer![m] Go back to the land of
Judah. Earn your bread there and do
your prophesying there.[n] 13Don't
prophesy anymore at Bethel,[o] because this is the king's sanctuary and
the temple[p] of the kingdom.[q]"

14Amos answered Amaziah, "I was
neither a prophet[r] nor a prophet's
son, but I was a shepherd, and I also
took care of sycamore-fig trees.[s]
15But the LORD took me from tending
the flock[t] and said to me, 'Go,[u]
prophesy[v] to my people Israel.'[w]
16Now then, hear[x] the word of the
LORD. You say,

" 'Do not prophesy against[y]
Israel,
and stop preaching against the
house of Isaac.'

17"Therefore this is what the LORD
says:

" 'Your wife will become a
prostitute[z] in the city,
and your sons and daughters
will fall by the sword.
Your land will be measured and
divided up,
and you yourself will die in a
pagan[v] country.
And Israel will certainly go into
exile,[a]
away from their native
land.[b]' "

7:10 [g] S Jos 7:2 [h] S 2Ki 14:23 [i] Jer 38:4 [j] 2Ki 14:24; Jer 26:8-11 7:11 [k] S Am 5:27 [l] Jer 36:16 7:12 [m] S 1Sa 9:9 [n] Mt 8:34 7:13 [o] S Jos 7:2; S 1Ki 12:29 [p] Jer 36:5 [q] S Jer 20:2; S Am 2:12; Ac 4:18 7:14 [r] S 1Sa 10:5; 2Ki 2:5; 4:38; Zec 13:5 [s] S 1Ki 10:27; S Isa 9:10 7:15 [t] S Ge 37:2; S 2Sa 7:8 [u] S Isa 6:9 [v] S Jer 26:12 [w] Jer 7:1-2; S Eze 2:3-4 7:16 [x] Jer 22:2 [y] S Eze 20:46; Mic 2:6 7:17 [z] S Hos 4:13 [a] S Am 5:27 [b] S 2Ki 17:6; S Eze 4:13; S Hos 9:3; Am 2:12-13

8:1 [c] S Am 7:1 8:2 [d] Jer 1:13; 24:3 [e] Am 7:8 [f] S Ge 40:16 [g] S La 4:18; Eze 7:2-9 8:3 [h] S Am 5:16 [i] Am 6:10 8:4 [j] S Pr 30:14 [k] S Job 20:19; S Ps 14:4; S Am 2:7 8:5 [l] S Nu 10:10 [m] Isa 58:13 [n] S Ne 10:31 [o] S Ge 31:7 [p] Dt 25:15; 2Ki 4:23; Ne 13:15-16; Eze 45:10-12; S Hos 12:7; Mic 6:10-11; Zec 5:6 8:6 [q] Am 5:11 [r] S Am 2:6; S 4:1 8:7 [s] S Ps 47:4 [t] S Hos 8:13 [u] S Job 35:15 8:8 [v] S Job 9:6; Jer 51:29 [w] Ps 18:7; S Jer 46:8; Am 9:5

A Basket of Ripe Fruit

8 This is what the Sovereign LORD
showed me:[c] a basket of ripe
fruit. 2"What do you see,[d] Amos?[e]"
he asked.

"A basket[f] of ripe fruit," I answered.

Then the LORD said to me, "The time
is ripe for my people Israel; I will spare
them no longer.[g]

3"In that day," declares the Sovereign LORD, "the songs in the temple will
turn to wailing.[w][h] Many, many bodies—flung everywhere! Silence![i]"

4Hear this, you who trample the
needy
and do away with the poor[j] of
the land,[k]

5saying,

"When will the New Moon[l] be
over
that we may sell grain,
and the Sabbath be ended
that we may market[m]
wheat?"[n]—
skimping the measure,
boosting the price
and cheating[o] with dishonest
scales,[p]
6buying the poor[q] with silver
and the needy for a pair of
sandals,
selling even the sweepings with
the wheat.[r]

7The LORD has sworn by the Pride of
Jacob:[s] "I will never forget[t] anything
they have done.[u]

8"Will not the land tremble[v] for this,
and all who live in it mourn?
The whole land will rise like the
Nile;
it will be stirred up and then
sink
like the river of Egypt.[w]

[v] *17* Hebrew *an unclean* [w] *3* Or *"the temple singers will wail*

7:12–17 GET OUT, YOU SEER! These verses reveal one of the main reasons God would spare the people no longer. Amaziah the priest, representing the people and especially their leaders, openly rejected God's prophet and his message. Those who consciously reject God's word are dooming themselves to eternal death; a time will come when intercession will do no good.

8:1 A BASKET OF RIPE FRUIT. The ripe fruit signifies that the people were ripe for judgment; their end was at hand.

8:5 THE SABBATH. The merchants were so materialistic that they were anxious for the Sabbath to be over so they might resume selling their products. We must ask ourselves: Am I so caught up in making money that I have little or no concern for God's word and the advancement of his kingdom? According to the Lord Jesus himself, we cannot serve both God and Money at the same time (see Mt 6:24, note).

9"In that day," declares the Sovereign LORD,

"I will make the sun go down at
noon
and darken the earth in broad
daylight.[x]
10I will turn your religious feasts[y]
into mourning
and all your singing into
weeping.[z]
I will make all of you wear
sackcloth[a]
and shave[b] your heads.
I will make that time like
mourning for an only son[c]
and the end of it like a bitter
day.[d]

11"The days are coming,"[e] declares
the Sovereign LORD,
"when I will send a famine
through the land—
not a famine of food or a thirst for
water,
but a famine[f] of hearing the
words of the LORD.[g]
12Men will stagger from sea to sea
and wander from north to
east,
searching for the word of the
LORD,
but they will not find it.[h]

13"In that day

"the lovely young women and
strong young men[i]
will faint because of thirst.[j]
14They who swear by the shame[x] of
Samaria,[k]
or say, 'As surely as your god
lives, O Dan,'[l]
or, 'As surely as the god[y] of
Beersheba[m] lives'—
they will fall,[n]
never to rise again.[o]"

Israel to Be Destroyed

9 I saw the Lord standing by the altar, and he said:

"Strike the tops of the pillars
so that the thresholds shake.
Bring them down on the heads[p] of
all the people;
those who are left I will kill
with the sword.
Not one will get away,
none will escape.[q]
2Though they dig down to the
depths of the grave,[z r]
from there my hand will take
them.
Though they climb up to the
heavens,[s]
from there I will bring them
down.[t]
3Though they hide themselves on
the top of Carmel,[u]
there I will hunt them down and
seize them.[v]
Though they hide from me at the
bottom of the sea,[w]
there I will command the
serpent[x] to bite them.[y z]
4Though they are driven into exile
by their enemies,
there I will command the
sword[a] to slay them.
I will fix my eyes upon them
for evil[b] and not for good.[c]"[d]

5The Lord, the LORD Almighty,
he who touches the earth and it
melts,[e]
and all who live in it mourn—
the whole land rises like the Nile,
then sinks like the river of
Egypt[f]—
6he who builds his lofty palace[a g]
in the heavens
and sets its foundation[b] on the
earth,
who calls for the waters of the sea

x *14* Or *by Ashima;* or *by the idol* y *14* Or *power* z *2* Hebrew *to Sheol* a *6* The meaning of the Hebrew for this phrase is uncertain. b *6* The meaning of the Hebrew for this word is uncertain.

8:9 [x]S Job 5:14; Isa 59:9-10; Jer 13:16; 15:9; S Eze 32:7; S Am 5:8; Mic 3:6; Mt 27:45; Mk 15:33; Lk 23:44-45
8:10 [y]S Lev 26:31 [z]S La 5:15; S Hos 2:11 [a]S Joel 1:8 [b]S Lev 13:40; S Isa 3:17 [c]S Ge 21:16 [d]S Jer 2:19; S Eze 7:18
8:11 [e]Jer 30:3; 31:27 [f]S Isa 30:20 [g]S 1Sa 3:1; S 28:6; S 2Ch 15:3
8:12 [h]S Eze 20:3, 31
8:13 [i]S Isa 9:17 [j]Isa 41:17; Hos 2:3
8:14 [k]Mic 1:5 [l]S 1Ki 12:29 [m]S Am 5:5 [n]S Ps 46:2 [o]S Am 5:2
9:1 [p]Ps 68:21 [q]Jer 11:11
9:2 [r]S Job 7:9; S Eze 26:20 [s]Jer 51:53 [t]Ob 1:4
9:3 [u]Am 1:2 [v]Ps 139:8-10 [w]Ps 68:22 [x]Isa 27:1 [y]Jer 16:16-17 [z]S Ge 49:17; S Job 11:20
9:4 [a]S Lev 26:33; S Eze 5:12 [b]S Jer 21:10 [c]Jer 39:16; S Eze 15:7 [d]S Jer 44:11
9:5 [e]S Ps 46:2 [f]S Am 8:8
9:6 [g]Jer 43:9

8:11 FAMINE OF HEARING THE WORDS OF THE LORD. Israel had repeatedly rejected the word of God spoken to them (2:11–12; 7:10–13,16); now they would receive what they desired. (1) God would send no prophet to them, and no word of God would come to them; in other words, whenever they might seek God's guidance during the coming calamity, they would find only silence. (2) No judgment is worse than God giving a person over to his or her own sinful desires; such a person will plunge into degradation and perversion and end up becoming a slave to the demonic (Ro 1:21–32; see Ro 1:24, note).

9:1–10 I SAW THE LORD. In his fifth vision, Amos saw the Lord standing by the altar in his sanctuary, ready to destroy all the worshipers by bringing the temple down on their heads. Those who escaped would be killed by the sword; all the sinners among his people would die (v. 10). Likewise, when Christ returns, he will severely judge all within his churches who are living a sinful lifestyle; none of them will escape God's wrath.

and pours them out over the
face of the land—
the LORD is his name.[h]

7"Are not you Israelites
the same to me as the
Cushites[c]?"[i]
declares the LORD.
"Did I not bring Israel up from
Egypt,
the Philistines[j] from
Caphtor[d][k]
and the Arameans from Kir?[l]

8"Surely the eyes of the Sovereign
LORD
are on the sinful kingdom.
I will destroy[m] it
from the face of the earth—
yet I will not totally destroy
the house of Jacob,"
declares the LORD.[n]
9"For I will give the command,
and I will shake the house of
Israel
among all the nations
as grain[o] is shaken in a sieve,[p]
and not a pebble will reach the
ground.[q]
10All the sinners among my people
will die by the sword,[r]
all those who say,
'Disaster will not overtake or
meet us.'[s]

Israel's Restoration

11"In that day I will restore
David's[t] fallen tent.[u]
I will repair its broken places,
restore its ruins,[v]
and build it as it used to be,[w]
12so that they may possess the
remnant of Edom[x]
and all the nations that bear my
name,[e][y]"
declares the LORD, who will do
these things.[z]

13"The days are coming,"[a] declares
the LORD,

"when the reaper[b] will be
overtaken by the plowman[c]
and the planter by the one
treading[d] grapes.
New wine[e] will drip from the
mountains
and flow from all the hills.[f]
14I will bring[g] back my exiled[f][h]
people Israel;
they will rebuild the ruined
cities[i] and live in them.
They will plant vineyards[j] and
drink their wine;
they will make gardens and eat
their fruit.[k]
15I will plant[l] Israel in their own
land,[m]
never again to be uprooted[n]
from the land I have given
them,"[o]

says the LORD your God.[p]

9:6 [h] Ps 104:1-3, 5-6,13; S Am 5:8 **9:7** [i] S 2Ch 12:3; Isa 20:4; 43:3 [j] S Ge 10:14 [k] S Dt 2:23 [l] S 2Ki 16:9; S Isa 22:6; S Am 2:10 **9:8** [m] S Jer 4:27 [n] S Jer 44:27 **9:9** [o] Lk 22:31 [p] Isa 30:28 [q] S Jer 31:36; S Da 9:7 **9:10** [r] Jer 49:37 [s] Jer 5:12; S 23:17; S Eze 20:38; S Am 6:3 **9:11** [t] S Isa 7:2 [u] S Ge 26:22 [v] Ps 53:6; S Isa 49:8 [w] Ps 80:12; S Eze 17:24; Mic 7:8,11; Zec 12:7; 14:10 **9:12** [x] S Nu 24:18 [y] Isa 43:7; Jer 25:29 [z] Ac 15:16-17* **9:13** [a] Jer 31:38; 33:14 [b] S Ru 2:3 [c] Lev 26:5 [d] S Jdg 9:27 [e] S Joel 2:24 [f] S Joel 3:18 **9:14** [g] S Jer 29:14 [h] S Jer 33:7 [i] S Isa 32:18; S 49:8; S 61:4 [j] S 2Ki 19:29 [k] S Isa 62:9; S Jer 30:18; S 31:28; Eze 28:25-26; S 34:13-14; S Am 5:11 **9:15** [l] S Ex 15:17; S Isa 60:21 [m] S Jer 23:8 [n] S Joel 3:20 [o] S Isa 65:9; S Jer 3:18; Ob 1:17 [p] S Jer 18:9; S 24:6; S 32:15; S Eze 28:26; S 34:25-28; S 37:12,25

[c] 7 That is, people from the upper Nile region [d] 7 That is, Crete [e] *12* Hebrew; Septuagint *so that the remnant of men / and all the nations that bear my name may seek* ⌊*the Lord*⌋ [f] *14* Or *will restore the fortunes of my*

9:11–15 IN THAT DAY. The book of Amos ends with a promise that Israel would not be totally destroyed (cf. v. 8). The prophet envisions a day when the nation would be restored to its land and would bless all the nations of the earth; the Lord will be their God (v. 15). This day refers to the Messianic kingdom when Christ reigns over all the earth. James quotes vv. 11–12 to show that God's plan of salvation was designed to include non-Jews in his kingdom (see Ac 15:16, note).

9:11 DAVID'S FALLEN TENT. This phrase refers to all twelve tribes of Israel living under the Messiah's rule.

9:12 ALL THE NATIONS. The Messiah will reign over all nations, and Israel will be a blessing to them; this is the ultimate fulfillment of God's covenant with Abraham and with David (see articles on GOD'S COVENANT WITH ABRAHAM, ISAAC AND JACOB, p. 46, and GOD'S COVENANT WITH DAVID, p. 432).

9:13–15 REAPER WILL BE OVERTAKEN BY THE PLOWMAN. Amos prophesies a transformed and glorious earth where God's people can continually plant and reap at the same time. The land will be abundantly productive, and God's blessings will never end. Israel will finally be restored to the Lord and will never again abandon him; they will be secure in the land.

OBADIAH

Outline

I. The Judgment on Edom (1–14)
  A. Destruction to Come on Edom (1–4)
  B. Devastation Will Be Complete (5–9)
  C. Reason: Their Joy at Judah's Troubles (10–14)
II. The Day of the Lord (15–21)
  A. Judgment on Edom and Other Nations (15–16)
  B. Israel's Place in "The Day of the LORD" (17–21)
    1. Salvation for Israel (17–18a)
    2. Destruction for Edom (18b)
    3. Israel's Borders Enlarged As Part of God's Kingdom (19–21)

Author: Obadiah

Theme: Judgment on Edom

Date of Writing: c. 840 B.C.

Background

The author of this short book is a prophet named Obadiah; in the book, neither ancestry nor any other details about his life are given. The name "Obadiah" is rather common, meaning "servant of the LORD"; 12 or 13 people are mentioned in the Bible with that name (e.g., 1Ki 18:3–16; 2Ch 17:7; 34:12–13).

Whether the Obadiah who wrote this book is mentioned elsewhere in the OT depends on the date of this prophecy. Since no king is mentioned, we do not know for certain the date of its origin. The only historical allusion in the text is to a time when the Edomites rejoiced at an invasion in Jerusalem and even participated in its plunder (vv. 11–14); however, it is not clear what invasion of Jerusalem Obadiah had in mind. There were five significant ones during OT times: (1) by Shishak, king of Egypt, in 926 B.C., during Rehoboam's reign (1Ki 14:25–26); (2) by the Philistines and Arabs during the reign of Jehoram c. 848–841 B.C. (see 2Ch 21:16–17); (3) by King Jehoash of Israel during the reign of Amaziah c. 790 B.C. (2Ki 14:13–14); (4) by Sennacherib, king of Assyria, during Hezekiah's reign, in 701 B.C. (2Ki 18:13); and (5) by the Babylonians during the years 605–586 B.C. (2Ki 24—25). Most scholars believe Obadiah prophesied in connection with either (2) or (5). The destruction of Jerusalem by Nebuchadnezzar seems the less likely of the two, since there is no hint of Jerusalem's complete destruction or the deportation of its people into exile. Other prophets who refer to Jerusalem's destruction always identify the enemy as Nebuchadnezzar and Babylon, not just "strangers" and "foreigners" (v. 11). Thus the occasion for Obadiah's prophecy is more likely the second one, when the Philistines and Arabs pillaged the city. Just prior to that event, the Edomites (who had been under Jerusalem's control) had managed to free themselves (2Ch 21:8–10). Their rejoicing at Jerusalem's downfall shortly thereafter is quite understandable. Since the dates for Jehoram's reign are 848–841 B.C., and since the pillaging of Jerusalem had already occurred when Obadiah wrote, 840 B.C. is a likely date for this book.

Part of the background of this prophecy recalls Ge 25:19–34; 27:1—28:9, i.e., the long-standing rivalry between Esau (the father of the Edomites) and Jacob (the father of Israel's twelve tribes). Though we read in Genesis about the reconciliation of these two brothers (Ge 33), the hatred between their descendants often erupted into war throughout Biblical history (cf. Nu 20:14–21; 1Sa 14:47; 2Sa 8:14; 1Ki 11:14–22). In keeping with their history of hostility, the Edomites rejoiced at Jerusalem's troubles.

Purpose

This prophetic book was written (1) to reveal God's intense anger at Edom for their rejoicing at Judah's suffering, and (2) to deliver the word of God's coming judgment against Edom. Obadiah prophesies the end result of God's dealings: for the Edomites—destruction; for God's people Israel—deliverance in a coming day of the Lord.

Survey

The book of Obadiah has two main sections. In the first (vv. 1–14), God expresses through the prophet his hot displeasure with Edom and calls them to accountability for their sins, especially the sin of pride (because of their geographical security) and the sin of rejoicing at Judah's downfall. The foreboding judgment of God is coming against them, and the prophet offers no hope of reprieve based on an invitation to repent and turn to the Lord; they will be destroyed forever (v. 10). The second section (vv. 15–21) refers prophetically to a coming day of the Lord when Edom and all God's enemies will be destroyed, while God's people will be saved and his kingdom triumph.

Special Features

Four major features characterize Obadiah's prophecy. (1) It is the shortest OT book. (2) Obadiah is one of three prophets who were called by God to direct their written message almost exclusively to a nation other than Israel or Judah (the other two are Jonah and Nahum). (3) There are many similarities between the book of Obadiah and Jer 49:7–22. (4) This book is neither quoted nor alluded to in the NT.

New Testament Fulfillment

Although the NT does not refer to Obadiah directly, the feud between Esau and Jacob underlying this book is also played out in the NT. Paul refers to the Esau-Jacob rivalry in Ro 9:10–13, but goes on to remind us of God's message of hope: all who repent of their sins, both Jews and Gentiles, and call on the name of the Lord will be saved (Ro 10:9–13; 15:7–12).

Reading Obadiah

In order to read the entire Old Testament in one year, the book of Obadiah should be read in 1 day: ☐ Obadiah

NOTES

1The vision[a] of Obadiah.

1-4pp — Jer 49:14-16
5-6pp — Jer 49:9-10

This is what the Sovereign LORD says about Edom[b]—

We have heard a message from the
LORD:
An envoy[c] was sent to the
nations to say,
"Rise, and let us go against her for
battle"[d]—

2"See, I will make you small[e]
among the nations;
you will be utterly despised.
3The pride[f] of your heart has
deceived you,
you who live in the clefts of the
rocks[a][g]
and make your home on the
heights,
you who say to yourself,
'Who can bring me down to the
ground?'[h]
4Though you soar like the eagle
and make your nest[i] among the
stars,
from there I will bring you
down,"[j]
declares the LORD.[k]
5"If thieves came to you,
if robbers in the night—
Oh, what a disaster awaits you—
would they not steal only as
much as they wanted?
If grape pickers came to you,
would they not leave a few
grapes?[l]
6But how Esau will be ransacked,
his hidden treasures pillaged!
7All your allies[m] will force you to
the border;
your friends will deceive and
overpower you;
those who eat your bread[n] will
set a trap for you,[b]
but you will not detect it.

8"In that day," declares the LORD,
"will I not destroy[o] the wise
men of Edom,
men of understanding in the
mountains of Esau?
9Your warriors, O Teman,[p] will be
terrified,
and everyone in Esau's
mountains
will be cut down in the
slaughter.
10Because of the violence[q] against
your brother Jacob,[r]
you will be covered with shame;
you will be destroyed forever.[s]
11On the day you stood aloof
while strangers carried off his
wealth
and foreigners entered his gates
and cast lots[t] for Jerusalem,
you were like one of them.[u]
12You should not look down[v] on
your brother
in the day of his misfortune,[w]
nor rejoice[x] over the people of
Judah
in the day of their destruction,[y]

1:1 [a]S Isa 1:1 [b]S Ge 25:14; S Isa 11:14; S 34:11; 63:1-6; Jer 49:7-22; S Eze 25:12-14; S 32:29; S Am 1:11-12 [c]Isa 18:2 [d]Jer 6:4-5 **1:2** [e]Nu 24:18 **1:3** [f]S Isa 16:6 [g]*fn* Isa 16:1 [h]S 2Ch 25:11-12 **1:4** [i]S Isa 10:14 [j]S Isa 14:13 [k]S Job 20:6 **1:5** [l]S Dt 4:27; 24:21; S Isa 24:13 **1:7** [m]Jer 30:14 [n]S Ps 41:9 **1:8** [o]Job 5:12; Isa 29:14 **1:9** [p]S Ge 36:11, 34 **1:10** [q]S Joel 3:19 [r]Ps 137:7; Am 1:11-12 [s]S Ps 137:7; S Eze 25:12-14; 35:9 **1:11** [t]S Job 6:27; S Eze 24:6 [u]S Am 1:6 **1:12** [v]Pr 24:17 [w]S Job 31:29 [x]S Eze 35:15 [y]S Pr 17:5

[a] *3* Or *of Sela* [b] *7* The meaning of the Hebrew for this clause is uncertain.

1 OBADIAH. Obadiah was a prophet to Judah who prophesied about God's judgment against Edom (see the introduction).

1 ABOUT EDOM. The Edomites, Judah's southern neighbors, were descendants of Esau (v. 6), Jacob's brother; thus, they were related to Israel (v. 10). However, that nation had become a perpetual enemy of God's people, often giving aid to foreign armies attacking Israel. Because of Edom's long hostility toward and hatred of the Israelites, God's wrath would come upon them.

3 THE PRIDE OF YOUR HEART. (1) The Edomites lived in a rocky range of mountains. They arrogantly regarded their homeland as secure and were proud of their self-sufficiency and power; yet God would bring them down. (2) The Bible teaches that pride and haughtiness lead to self-deception, go before a fall (v. 4; Pr 16:18) and cause God to become one's enemy (v. 8; Jas 4:6; 1Pe 5:5).

5–6 IF THIEVES CAME TO YOU. The Edomites had made it a practice to plunder other people, robbing and killing them; now they would experience the same thing, for God would bring another nation against them.

10 DESTROYED FOREVER. Obadiah prophesies that the Edomites would be completely destroyed because of their violence and cruelty (cf. vv. 16,18), whereas Judah would be restored and God's kingdom would prevail (vv. 17,19,21). In 582 B.C., four years after Jerusalem was destroyed, the Edomite people were nearly destroyed by the Babylonians and forced to live in southern Judah. In A.D. 70, after Jerusalem's destruction by Rome, they were never heard of again.

11–14 YOU STOOD ALOOF. (1) Edom refused to help Israel, its neighbor and relative, when they were in trouble; for this God would judge them. (2) God is concerned that his people who have received his help and mercy show mercy to others in their time of need. Indifference and self-centeredness demonstrate that God's love and grace do not abide in us (1Jn 3:15–17; see article on THE CARE OF THE POOR AND NEEDY, p. 1316).

nor boast[z] so much
in the day of their trouble.[a]
13You should not march through the gates of my people
in the day of their disaster,
nor look down on them in their calamity[b]
in the day of their disaster,
nor seize their wealth
in the day of their disaster.
14You should not wait at the crossroads
to cut down their fugitives,[c]
nor hand over their survivors
in the day of their trouble.

15"The day of the LORD is near[d]
for all nations.
As you have done, it will be done to you;
your deeds[e] will return upon your own head.
16Just as you drank[f] on my holy hill,[g]
so all the nations will drink[h] continually;
they will drink and drink
and be as if they had never been.[i]
17But on Mount Zion will be deliverance;[j]
it will be holy,[k]
and the house of Jacob
will possess its inheritance.[l]
18The house of Jacob will be a fire
and the house of Joseph a flame;
the house of Esau will be stubble,
and they will set it on fire[m] and consume[n] it.
There will be no survivors[o]
from the house of Esau."
The LORD has spoken.

19People from the Negev will occupy
the mountains of Esau,
and people from the foothills will possess
the land of the Philistines.[p]
They will occupy the fields of Ephraim and Samaria,[q]
and Benjamin[r] will possess Gilead.
20This company of Israelite exiles
who are in Canaan
will possess ⌊the land⌋ as far as Zarephath;[s]
the exiles from Jerusalem who are in Sepharad
will possess the towns of the Negev.[t]
21Deliverers[u] will go up on[c] Mount Zion
to govern the mountains of Esau.
And the kingdom will be the LORD's.[v]

1:12 [z] Ps 137:7 [a] S Eze 25:6; Mic 4:11; 7:8 **1:13** [b] S Eze 35:5 **1:14** [c] S 1Ki 18:4 **1:15** [d] S Jer 46:10; S Eze 30:3; S Joel 2:31; S Am 5:18 [e] S Jer 50:29; Hab 2:8 **1:16** [f] Isa 51:17 [g] S Ex 15:17 [h] Jer 25:15; 49:12; S La 4:21-22 [i] S La 4:21; S Eze 25:12-14 **1:17** [j] S Ps 69:35; S Isa 14:1-2; Joel 2:32; S Am 9:11-15 [k] S Ps 74:2; S Isa 4:3 [l] Zec 8:12 **1:18** [m] S Isa 1:31 [n] Zec 12:6 [o] S Jer 49:10 **1:19** [p] Isa 11:14 [q] S Jer 31:5 [r] S Nu 1:36 **1:20** [s] 1Ki 17:9-10; Lk 4:26 [t] S Jer 33:13 **1:21** [u] S Dt 28:29; S Jdg 3:9 [v] S Ps 22:28; 47:9; 66:4; S Da 2:44; Zec 14:9,16; Mal 1:14; Rev 11:15

[c] *21* Or *from*

15 IT WILL BE DONE TO YOU. Obadiah prophesies that God would repay Edom and all other nations according to their treatment of others; this same principle applies to NT believers (see Col 3:25, note).

17–21 ON MOUNT ZION WILL BE DELIVERANCE. Mount Zion represents Jerusalem under the old covenant and the heavenly abode of the church under the new covenant (Heb 12:22–24; see article on THE CITY OF JERUSALEM, p. 576). The Bible prophesies that Israel and all of God's faithful people will be delivered from their enemies, inherit the earth and reign with Christ. This fulfillment awaits the return of Jesus the Messiah to earth, at which time evil will be defeated; then "the kingdom will be the LORD's" (v. 21).

JONAH

Outline

I. God's First Call to Jonah (1:1—2:10)
   A. Jonah's Call: Go to Nineveh (1:1–2)
   B. Jonah's Disobedience (1:3)
   C. Consequences of Jonah's Disobedience (1:4–17)
      1. To Others (1:4–11)
      2. To Himself (1:12–17)
   D. Jonah's Prayer Amidst Calamity (2:1–9)
   E. Jonah's Deliverance (2:10)

II. God's Second Call to Jonah (3:1—4:11)
   A. Jonah's Call: Go to Nineveh (3:1–2)
   B. Jonah's Obedient Mission (3:3–4)
   C. Consequences of Jonah's Obedience (3:5–10)
      1. The Ninevites Repent (3:5–9)
      2. The Ninevites Spared God's Judgment (3:10)
   D. Jonah's Complaint (4:1–3)
   E. Jonah's Rebuke and Lesson (4:4–11)

Author: Jonah

Theme: The Breadth of God's Saving Mercy

Date of Writing: c. 760 B.C.

Background

Jonah, whose name means "dove," is introduced as the son of Amittai (1:1). He is mentioned in 2Ki 14:25 as (1) a prophet to the northern kingdom of Israel during the reign of Jeroboam II (793–753 B.C.); (2) he was from Gath Hepher, two to three miles north of Nazareth in Galilee. Thus the Pharisees were mistaken when they suggested that no prophet ever came from Galilee (Jn 7:52). Jonah's prophetic ministry occurred shortly after that of Elisha (cf. 2Ki 13:14–19), overlapped that of Amos (cf. Am 1:1) and was followed by that of Hosea (cf. Hos 1:1). Though the book makes no claim as to its author, most likely the author was Jonah himself.

Nineveh's repentance in response to Jonah's preaching most likely occurred during the reign of one of two Assyrian monarchs: (1) Adad-nirari III (810–783 B.C.), whose reign was marked by a swing toward monotheism, or (2) Ashurdan III (733–755 B.C.), whose reign experienced two major plagues (765 and 759 B.C.) and an eclipse of the sun (763 B.C.), both of which may have been interpreted as signs of divine judgment and thus prepared Assyria's capital city for Jonah's prophetic message. Nineveh was about 500 miles northeast of Galilee.

Purpose

This book appears to have been written for a threefold purpose: (1) to demonstrate to Israel and the nations the magnitude and breadth of God's saving mercy and activity through the preaching of repentance; (2) to show through Jonah's experience how far Israel had fallen from its original missionary calling to be a light of redemption to those who dwell in darkness (Ge 12:1–3; Isa 42:6–7; 49:6); and (3) to remind backslidden Israel that God in love and mercy had sent her not just one prophet but many faithful prophets who delivered his message of repentance so as to avert inevitable judgment for sin. Yet unlike Nineveh, Israel had rejected God's prophets and his offer to repent and receive mercy.

Survey

The book of Jonah tells the story of the prophet's call to go to Nineveh and of his reactions. Ch. 1 describes Jonah's initial disobedience and God's subsequent judgment. Instead of going northeast to Nineveh, Jonah boarded a westbound ship going to Tarshish (in Spain), the farthest possible destination in the opposite direction from God's will. Jonah soon faced God's countermeasure of a severe storm on the Mediterranean Sea, with the disgrace of being found out by the sailors and thrown overboard. God providentially had "a great fish" ready to spare his life. Ch. 2 recounts Jonah's prayer from his unique chamber inside the fish, in which he thanked God for sparing his life, vowed to obey God's call, and was then vomited by the fish onto dry land. Ch. 3 records Jonah's second chance to go to Nineveh and his preaching of God's message to that city's inhabitants. In one of the most remarkable city-wide spiritual awakenings in all of history, the king called the entire city to fasting and repentance, through which they were spared God's judgment. Ch. 4 contains Jonah's complaint against God for sparing this enemy city of Israel. Using a vine, a worm and an east wind, God taught his angry prophet that he delights in making his grace available to everyone, not just to Israel and Judah.

Special Features

Four major features characterize the book of Jonah. (1) It is one of only two OT prophetic books written by a prophet born and raised in the northern kingdom of Israel (Hosea is the other one). (2) It is a masterpiece of condensed prose narrative; only Jonah's prayer of thanksgiving (2:2–9) is in poetry. (3) It is full of God's supernatural activity: in addition to the providential timing of the storm and the appearance of the great fish, there are the vine, the worm, the east wind, and (greatest of all) the repentance of the entire city of Nineveh. (4) It contains the clearest OT message that God's saving grace is for Gentiles as well as for Jews.

New Testament Fulfillment

Jesus compared himself to Jonah as follows: "A wicked and adulterous generation asks for a miraculous sign! But none will be given it except the sign of the prophet Jonah. For as Jonah was three days and three nights in the belly of a huge fish, so the Son of Man will be three days and three nights in the heart of the earth. The men of Nineveh will stand up at the judgment with this generation and condemn it; for they repented at the preaching of Jonah, and now one greater than Jonah is here" (Mt 12:39–41).

Historical Reliability

Liberal theologians and unbelievers regard this book as a fictional story coming out of the 5th to the 3rd century B.C., designed to counter the narrow Jewish nationalism of post-exilic Judaism. According to this view, the book of Jonah does not represent actual historical events. However, the OT elsewhere mentions Jonah as an accredited prophet from the 8th century B.C. (2Ki 14:25). In the NT, Jesus himself refers to Jonah (1) as being the foremost OT prophetic sign of his being three days in the grave and his subsequent resurrection (Mt 12:39–40; Lk 11:29), (2) as having historically preached repentance to the Ninevites who repented (Mt 12:41; Lk 11:30,32), and (3) as being as much a part of OT history as Solomon and his visit from the Queen of the South (Mt 12:42; Lk 11:31). Jesus clearly regarded the book as historically reliable; to view the book otherwise not only implies we have a fallible Bible, but also a fallible Savior.

Reading Jonah

In order to read the entire Old Testament in one year, the book of Jonah should be read in 1 day: □ Jonah

NOTES

THE BOOK OF JONAH

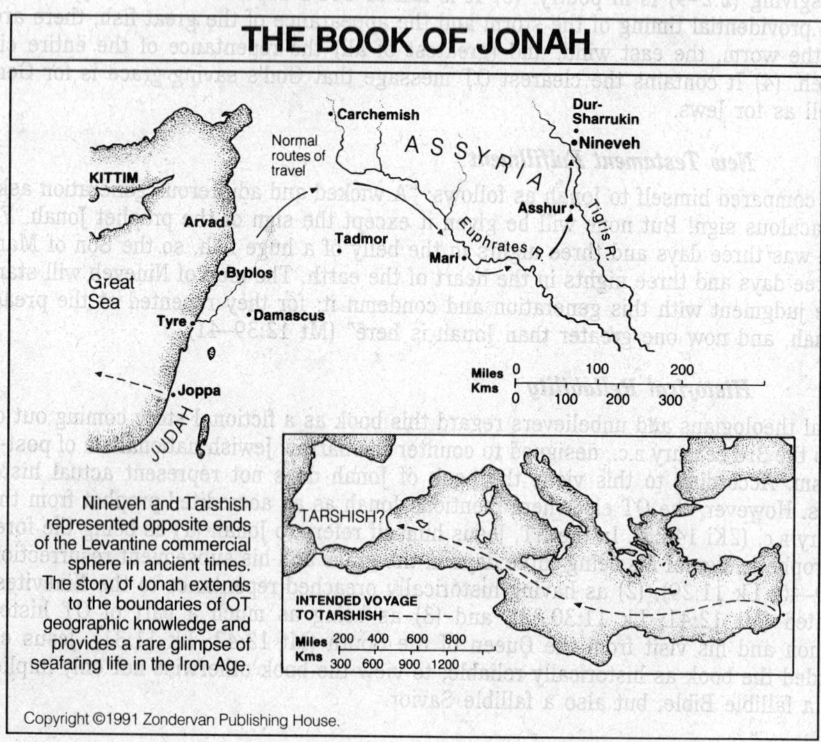

Nineveh and Tarshish represented opposite ends of the Levantine commercial sphere in ancient times. The story of Jonah extends to the boundaries of OT geographic knowledge and provides a rare glimpse of seafaring life in the Iron Age.

Jonah Flees From the LORD

1 The word of the LORD came to Jonah[a] son of Amittai:[b] **2**"Go to the
great city of Nineveh[c] and preach
against it, because its wickedness has
come up before me."
3But Jonah ran[d] away from the LORD
and headed for Tarshish[e]. He went
down to Joppa,[f] where he found a ship
bound for that port. After paying the
fare, he went aboard and sailed for Tarshish to flee from the LORD.[g]
4Then the LORD sent a great wind on
the sea, and such a violent storm arose
that the ship threatened to break up.[h]
5All the sailors were afraid and each
cried out to his own god. And they
threw the cargo into the sea to lighten
the ship.[i]
But Jonah had gone below deck,
where he lay down and fell into a deep
sleep. **6**The captain went to him and
said, "How can you sleep? Get up and
call[j] on your god! Maybe he will take
notice of us, and we will not perish."[k]
7Then the sailors said to each other,
"Come, let us cast lots to find out who
is responsible for this calamity."[l]
They cast lots and the lot fell on Jonah.[m]
8So they asked him, "Tell us, who is
responsible for making all this trouble
for us? What do you do? Where do you
come from? What is your country?
From what people are you?"
9He answered, "I am a Hebrew and
I worship the LORD,[n] the God of heav-
en,[o] who made the sea[p] and the
land.[q]"
10This terrified them and they
asked, "What have you done?" (They
knew he was running away from the
LORD, because he had already told them
so.)
11The sea was getting rougher and
rougher. So they asked him, "What
should we do to you to make the sea
calm down for us?"
12"Pick me up and throw me into the
sea," he replied, "and it will become
calm. I know that it is my fault that this
great storm has come upon you."[r]
13Instead, the men did their best to
row back to land. But they could not,
for the sea grew even wilder than before.[s] **14**Then they cried to the LORD,
"O LORD, please do not let us die for
taking this man's life. Do not hold us
accountable for killing an innocent
man,[t] for you, O LORD, have done as
you pleased."[u] **15**Then they took Jonah and threw him overboard, and the
raging sea grew calm.[v] **16**At this the
men greatly feared[w] the LORD, and
they offered a sacrifice to the LORD and
made vows[x] to him.
17But the LORD provided[y] a great

1:1 [a] Mt 12:39-41; 16:4; Lk 11:29-32 [b] 2Ki 14:25
1:2 [c] S Ge 10:11; S Na 1:1
1:3 [d] Ps 139:7 [e] S Ge 10:4 [f] S Jos 19:46; Ac 9:36,43 [g] Ex 4:13; S Jer 20:9; S Am 3:8
1:4 [h] Ps 107:23-26
1:5 [i] Ac 27:18-19
1:6 [j] Jnh 3:8 [k] S Ps 107:28
1:7 [l] Nu 32:23; Jos 7:10-18; S 1Sa 14:42 [m] S Pr 16:33
1:9 [n] S Ps 96:9 [o] S Da 2:18; Ac 17:24 [p] S Ne 9:6 [q] S Ge 1:9
1:12 [r] 2Sa 24:17; 1Ch 21:17
1:13 [s] S Pr 21:30
1:14 [t] Dt 21:8 [u] S Da 4:35
1:15 [v] S Ps 107:29; Lk 8:24
1:16 [w] Mk 4:41 [x] S Nu 30:2; Ps 66:13-14
1:17 [y] Jnh 4:6,7

1:1 JONAH. Jonah was a prophet to the northern kingdom of Israel during the reign of Jeroboam II (2Ki 14:23–25; see the introduction).

1:2 GO TO . . . NINEVEH. Jonah was called by God to warn Nineveh about his judgment on that city for its sins. Nineveh was the capital of Assyria, a very wicked, brutal and immoral nation (see Na 1:11; 2:12–13; 3:1,4,16,19). Israel hated the Assyrians and saw them as a great threat.

1:3 JONAH RAN AWAY. Jonah ran away from God's call, refusing to deliver God's message to Nineveh for fear that they might repent and be spared God's judgment (see 4:1–2). (1) He did not want God to have mercy on any nation but Israel, and especially not on Assyria. Jonah had forgotten that God's ultimate purpose for Israel was to be a blessing to the Gentiles and help bring them to a knowledge of God (Ge 12:1–3; cf. Isa 49:3). (2) Christ has called the church to fulfill an even greater missionary task than that of Jonah—to go out into the whole world with the gospel (cf. Mt 28:18–20; Ac 1:8). Like Jonah, however, many churches have little interest in missionary work; they are concerned only with building their own kingdom at home.

1:3 TARSHISH. Tarshish was a city in southwest Spain, about 2,500 miles from Israel; as such, it was one of the farthest places in the opposite direction of Nineveh that Jonah could go.

1:4 A GREAT WIND. God sent a great storm on the Mediterranean Sea in order to persuade Jonah to obey his call. Because of Jonah's disobedience, the lives of the sailors aboard the ship were imperiled. If we are not fully committed to God and his will for our lives, our family and others will ultimately suffer as well.

1:5 FELL INTO A DEEP SLEEP. While the sailors' lives were in great danger, God's servant was sleeping. Today some within the church are asleep and unconcerned, even though all around them people are perishing spiritually in the storms of life.

1:7 LET US CAST LOTS. The sailors probably put marked sticks or stones in a container and one was taken out. God directed the choosing of the lot, and Jonah was identified as the guilty one.

1:12 THROW ME INTO THE SEA. Jonah's willingness to die to save the sailors indicates how guilty he felt for disobeying God and for putting their lives in peril.

1:17 PROVIDED A GREAT FISH TO SWALLOW JONAH. God provided a great fish, perhaps a large whale, to save Jonah's life. God miraculously kept Jonah alive for three days in the stomach of the fish. (1) Unbelievers in the world and false teachers in the church have rejected this miracle,

fish to swallow Jonah,[z] and Jonah was inside the fish three days and three nights.

Jonah's Prayer

2 From inside the fish Jonah prayed
to the LORD his God. 2He said:

"In my distress I called[a] to the
LORD,[b]
and he answered me.
From the depths of the grave[a c] I
called for help,
and you listened to my
cry.
3You hurled me into the deep,[d]
into the very heart of the seas,
and the currents swirled about
me;
all your waves[e] and breakers
swept over me.[f]
4I said, 'I have been banished
from your sight;[g]
yet I will look again
toward your holy temple.'[h]
5The engulfing waters threatened
me,[b]
the deep surrounded me;
seaweed was wrapped around
my head.[i]
6To the roots of the mountains[j] I
sank down;
the earth beneath barred me in
forever.
But you brought my life up from
the pit,[k]
O LORD my God.
7"When my life was ebbing away,
I remembered[l] you, LORD,
and my prayer[m] rose to you,
to your holy temple.[n]
8"Those who cling to worthless
idols[o]
forfeit the grace that could be
theirs.
9But I, with a song of
thanksgiving,[p]
will sacrifice[q] to you.
What I have vowed[r] I will make
good.
Salvation[s] comes from the
LORD."
10And the LORD commanded the fish,
and it vomited Jonah onto dry land.

Jonah Goes to Nineveh

3 Then the word of the LORD came to
Jonah[t] a second time: 2"Go to the
great city of Nineveh and proclaim to it
the message I give you."

1:17 [z]Mt 12:40; 16:4; Lk 11:30
2:2 [a]La 3:55 [b]Ps 18:6; 120:1 [c]Ps 86:13
2:3 [d]S Ps 88:6 [e]S 2Sa 22:5 [f]S Ps 42:7
2:4 [g]Ps 31:22; Jer 7:15 [h]S 1Ki 8:48
2:5 [i]Ps 69:1-2
2:6 [j]Job 28:9 [k]S Job 17:16; S 33:18; S Ps 30:3
2:7 [l]Ps 77:11-12 [m]2Ch 30:27 [n]S Ps 11:4; 18:6
2:8 [o]S Dt 32:21; S 1Sa 12:21
2:9 [p]S Ps 42:4 [q]Ps 50:14,23; Heb 13:15 [r]S Nu 30:2; Ps 116:14; S Ecc 5:4-5 [s]S Ex 15:2; S Ps 3:8
3:1 [t]Jnh 1:1

[a]2 Hebrew *Sheol* [b]5 Or *waters were at my throat*

calling it fiction. Jesus, however, regarded it as historical fact; he used the incident of Jonah and the fish to illustrate his own death, burial and resurrection (see Mt 12:39–41). (2) In other words, Jesus put Jonah's experience with the great fish in the same category as his death and resurrection. Jesus accepted it as a miracle of God occurring according to his purpose in redemptive history. For all true believers, that should settle the question of its authenticity (see also the introduction to this book).

2:1–10 JONAH PRAYED. This is Jonah's prayer for deliverance from death and his subsequent thanksgiving. (1) Inside the fish, he found himself still alive and called out to the Lord. Although he thought himself as good as dead (v. 6), the Lord heard his prayer and spared his life. (2) Believers should never give up hope in seemingly impossible situations. Like Jonah, we must cry out to God for mercy and help and put our lives into his hands.

2:3 YOU HURLED ME. Jonah knew he had been disobedient and recognized that it was God who threw him into the sea. His greatest sorrow and fear was to be banished forever from God's presence (v. 4).

2:7 I REMEMBERED YOU. To "remember" the Lord means that God becomes such a living presence within us and around us that we can call out to him at any time in faith, hope and love (cf. Dt 8:18).

2:7 MY PRAYER ROSE TO YOU. When we pray, we must believe that our prayers go to God's very presence in heaven.

2:9 THANKSGIVING ... SACRIFICE. At the very moment when Jonah was offering to God a sincere sacrifice of thanksgiving and praise (v. 9), God intervened on his behalf (v. 10).

2:10 VOMITED JONAH ONTO DRY LAND. So far in the narrative of Jonah seven miracles have occurred: God (1) sent a great storm (1:4); (2) directed the lot to implicate Jonah (1:7); (3) calmed the sea (1:15); (4) arranged for a great fish to swallow Jonah (1:17); (5) kept him alive inside the fish for three days (v. 6; 1:17); (6) caused the fish to transport him to land and (7) made the fish vomit Jonah onto dry land.

3:2 PROCLAIM TO IT THE MESSAGE. (1) Jonah was called a second time to preach doom and judgment (see v. 4). It was his responsibility to deliver that message whether the Ninevites received it or not. (2) Preachers of the gospel are similarly called to proclaim the whole counsel of God (Ac 20:27; 2Ti 4:2). They must preach both God's mercy and God's wrath, both forgiveness and condemnation; they must be careful not to water down the gospel so as to avoid the difficult doctrines and ethics of God's Word. They must preach in such a way that people turn from their sins (see Ac 14:15).

[3]Jonah obeyed the word of the LORD and went to Nineveh. Now Nineveh was a very important city—a visit required three days. [4]On the first day, Jonah started into the city. He proclaimed:[u] "Forty more days and Nineveh will be overturned." [5]The Ninevites believed God. They declared a fast, and all of them, from the greatest to the least, put on sackcloth.[v]

[6]When the news reached the king of Nineveh, he rose from his throne, took off his royal robes, covered himself with sackcloth and sat down in the dust.[w] [7]Then he issued a proclamation in Nineveh:

"By the decree of the king and his nobles:

Do not let any man or beast, herd or flock, taste anything; do not let them eat or drink.[x] [8]But let man and beast be covered with sackcloth. Let everyone call[y] urgently on God. Let them give up[z] their evil ways[a] and their violence.[b] [9]Who knows?[c] God may yet relent[d] and with compassion turn[e] from his fierce anger[f] so that we will not perish."

[10]When God saw what they did and how they turned from their evil ways, he had compassion[g] and did not bring upon them the destruction[h] he had threatened.[i]

3:4 [u]S Jer 18:7-10 3:5 [v]Da 9:3; Mt 11:21; 12:41; Lk 11:32 3:6 [w]Est 4:1-3; S Job 2:8,13; S Eze 27:30-31 3:7 [x]S 2Ch 20:3; S Ezr 10:6 3:8 [y]Ps 130:1; Jnh 1:6 [z]Jer 25:5 [a]Jer 7:3 [b]S Job 16:17 3:9 [c]2Sa 12:22 [d]S Jer 18:8 [e]S Joel 2:14 [f]S Ps 85:3 3:10 [g]S Am 7:6 [h]S Jer 18:8 [i]S Ex 32:14

Jonah's Anger at the LORD's Compassion

4 But Jonah was greatly displeased and became angry.[j] [2]He prayed to the LORD, "O LORD, is this not what I said when I was still at home? That is why I was so quick to flee to Tarshish. I knew[k] that you are a gracious[l] and compassionate God, slow to anger and abounding in love,[m] a God who relents[n] from sending calamity.[o] [3]Now, O LORD, take away my life,[p] for it is better for me to die[q] than to live."[r]

[4]But the LORD replied, "Have you any right to be angry?"[s]

[5]Jonah went out and sat down at a place east of the city. There he made himself a shelter, sat in its shade and waited to see what would happen to the city. [6]Then the LORD God provided[t] a vine and made it grow up over Jonah to give shade for his head to ease his discomfort, and Jonah was very happy about the vine. [7]But at dawn the next day God provided a worm, which chewed the vine so that it withered.[u] [8]When the sun rose, God provided a scorching east wind, and the sun blazed on Jonah's head so that he grew

4:1 [j]ver 4; Mt 20:11; Lk 15:28 4:2 [k]Jer 20:7-8 [l]S Dt 4:31; Ps 103:8 [m]S Ex 22:27; Ps 86:5,15 [n]S Nu 14:18 [o]S Joel 2:13 4:3 [p]S Nu 11:15 [q]S Job 7:15 [r]Jer 8:3 4:4 [s]Ge 4:6; Mt 20:11-15 4:6 [t]S Jnh 1:17 4:7 [u]Joel 1:12

3:3 A VERY IMPORTANT CITY. The city of Nineveh had more than 120,000 inhabitants (see 4:11).

3:5 THE NINEVITES BELIEVED GOD. (1) The Ninevites accepted Jonah's message, believing that they were doomed unless they repented. As an outward expression of their true repentance and humility, they fasted (cf. 1Sa 7:6; 2Sa 1:12) and put on sackcloth (a coarse cloth, usually made of goats' hair; cf. 2Sa 3:31; 2Ki 19:1–2). (2) Jesus stated that Nineveh would stand up at the judgment to condemn Israel for their failure to repent and believe in him (Mt 12:41).

3:10 NOT BRING UPON THEM THE DESTRUCTION. Because the people repented, God canceled his plan of judgment. (1) God's primary desire is to have compassion, not to execute his threatened punishment. The Lord is a God who is moved with compassion for sinners who sincerely repent. (2) This book illustrates the Biblical truth that God does not want anyone to perish, but everyone to come to repentance, forgiveness and eternal life (see 2Pe 3:9).

4:1 JONAH WAS GREATLY DISPLEASED. Jonah was angry that God had decided to forgive the Ninevites; he did not want God to spare this enemy of Israel. (1) Jonah's fundamental problem was that he was not dedicated first and foremost to God's will; he was more concerned about Israel's physical security. (2) People today can be committed to the "success" of the church, yet not really be committed to God's will, purposes and holy standards as revealed in the Bible.

4:2 A GRACIOUS AND COMPASSIONATE GOD. God is "gracious" (i.e., he longs to help others); "compassionate" (i.e., he hurts with those who hurt); "slow to anger" (i.e., he does not desire to punish the wicked); "abounding in love" (i.e., he is kind and sympathetic); "a God who relents from sending calamity" (i.e., he delights in canceling his plans of judgment when people repent). These characteristics of God are revealed throughout the Bible (see Ps 103:8; 111:4; 112:4; 145:8; see article on THE ATTRIBUTES OF GOD, p. 882).

4:3 IT IS BETTER FOR ME TO DIE. Jonah was so disappointed and emotionally distraught that he preferred to die. In some way he felt God had turned against him and his people by sparing the Ninevites.

4:6 GOD PROVIDED A VINE. Rather than rejecting Jonah because of his wrong response, God compassionately attempted to convince him, by the use of a fast-growing vine, that he was concerned for both Israel and other nations.

faint. He wanted to die,[v] and said, "It
would be better for me to die than to
live."
9But God said to Jonah, "Do you
have a right to be angry about the
vine?"[w]
"I do," he said. "I am angry enough
to die."
10But the LORD said, "You have been
concerned about this vine, though you
did not tend it or make it grow. It
sprang up overnight and died overnight. 11But Nineveh[x] has more than
a hundred and twenty thousand people
who cannot tell their right hand from
their left, and many cattle as well.
Should I not be concerned[y] about that
great city?"

4:8 [v] S 1Ki 19:4
4:9 [w] ver 4
4:11 [x] Jnh 1:2; 3:2 [y] Jnh 3:10

4:9 DO YOU HAVE A RIGHT TO BE ANGRY. God's action with the vine and the scorching east wind (vv. 6–9) was intended to show Jonah's selfish concern for his own physical welfare in contrast to his lack of concern for the Ninevites. Jonah cared more for his own physical comfort than he did for God's will for this lost nation.

4:11 SHOULD I NOT BE CONCERNED ABOUT THAT GREAT CITY? God expresses his love for Nineveh. (1) It is the love of the Creator for his creatures even though they have lived in sin and rebellion against his laws; it is a love that goes far beyond any human love (cf. Ro 5:8). (2) God's love for humankind extends beyond his own people to lost people everywhere. This truth was fully seen (a) when God sent his Son Jesus to die for all people (Jn 3:16), and (b) when Jesus sent out his disciples into all the world to preach the gospel and make disciples of all nations (Mt 28:18–20).

MICAH

Outline

I. Judgment Against Israel and Judah (1:1—3:12)
   A. Introduction (1:1)
   B. Destruction Predicted for Samaria (1:2–7)
   C. Destruction Predicted for Judah (1:8–16)
   D. Specific Sins Among God's People Requiring Judgment (2:1–11)
      1. Greed and Pride (2:1–5)
      2. False Prophets (2:6–11)
   E. First Glimpse of Promised Deliverance (2:12–13)
   F. Specific Sins Among the Leaders of God's People (3:1–12)
      1. Injustice and Oppression (3:1–4)
      2. False Prophecy (3:5–7)
      3. Micah As a True Prophet (3:8)
      4. Summary of the Sins of the Leaders (3:9–12)
II. Prophetic Message of Hope (4:1—5:15)
   A. The Promise of the Coming Kingdom (4:1–8)
   B. Defeat of Israel's Enemies (4:9–13)
   C. The Coming King from Bethlehem (5:1–5)
   D. The Nature of the New Kingdom (5:6–15)
III. God's Lawsuit Against Israel and His Final Mercy (6:1—7:20)
   A. God's Case Against His People (6:1–8)
   B. Israel's Guilt and God's Judgment (6:9–16)
   C. The Prophet's Painful Lament (7:1–6)
   D. The Prophet's Personal Hope (7:7)
   E. Israel Will Rise Again (7:8–13)
   F. God's Final Blessings for His People (7:14–20)

Author: Micah

Theme: Judgment and Messianic Salvation

Date of Writing: c. 740–710 B.C.

Background

The prophet Micah was from the small town of Moresheth Gath (1:14) in southern Judah, a productive agricultural area about 25 miles southwest of Jerusalem. Like Amos, he came from the countryside, probably from a family of humble standing. While Isaiah, his contemporary in Jerusalem, addressed the king and international situations, Micah was a country prophet who condemned Judah's corrupt rulers, false prophets, ungodly priests, dishonest merchants and bribed judges. He preached against the sins of injustice, oppression of the peasants and villagers, greed, avarice, immorality and idolatry, and he warned of severe consequences if the people and their leaders persisted in their evil ways. He predicted the fall of Israel and its capital, Samaria (1:6–7), as well as that of Judah and its capital, Jerusalem (1:9–16; 3:9–12).

Micah's prophetic ministry took place during the reigns of three kings of Judah: Jotham (751–736 B.C.), Ahaz (736–716) and Hezekiah (716–687). Though some of Micah's prophecies were spoken during King Hezekiah's time (cf. Jer 26:18), most of them reflect Judah's condition during the reigns of Jotham and Ahaz prior to Hezekiah's religious reforms. Undoubtedly his ministry, along with that of Isaiah, helped to bring about the revival and reforms under the righteous King Hezekiah.

Purpose

Micah wrote to warn his nation of the certainty of divine judgment, to specify the sins that were provoking God's anger, and to summarize God's prophetic word to Samaria and Jerusalem (1:1). He accurately predicted Israel's downfall before it happened in 722 B.C.; he prophesied that a similar destruction would come to Judah and Jerusalem because of their flagrant sin and rebellion. This book thus preserves Micah's serious prophetic message for Judah's last generations before the Babylonians came against the nation; it also makes an important contribution to the total OT revelation about the coming Messiah.

Survey

The book of Micah consists of a three-part message: (1) it indicts Israel (Samaria) and Judah (Jerusalem) for specific sins including idolatry, pride, oppression of the poor, bribery among leaders, covetousness and greed, immorality, and empty religion; (2) it warns that God's judgment is coming because of these sins; and (3) it promises that true peace, righteousness and justice will prevail in the future when the Messiah reigns. Amost equal attention is given to these three themes throughout the book.

Viewed another way, chs. 1—3 record the Lord's denunciation of Israel's and Judah's sins, their corrupt leaders, and the impending doom awaiting these nations and their capitals. Chs. 4—5 offer hope and comfort to the remnant concerning days to come when God's house will be established in peace and righteousness, and idolatry and oppression will be purged from the land. Chs. 6—7 describe God's grievance with his people in terms of a great court scene: God presents his case against Israel; this is followed by Israel's confession of guilt and a prophetic prayer and promise. Micah concludes with a wordplay on the meaning of his own name: "Who is a God like you?" (7:18). Answer: He alone is merciful and can render the final verdict of "pardoned" (7:18–20).

Special Features

Five major features characterize the book of Micah. (1) It champions the cause of the humble peasants who face exploitation by the arrogant wealthy, similar to James's message in the NT (cf. 6:6–8 and Jas 1:27); in this connection, Micah gives his most memorable exhortation of the Lord's requirement for his people: "to act justly and to love mercy and to walk humbly with your God" (6:8). (2) Some of Micah's language is rugged and direct; other times it is eloquently poetic, with intricate use of wordplays (as in 1:10–15). (3) Like the prophet Isaiah (cf. Isa 48:16; 59:21), Micah expresses a keen awareness of God's call and his prophetic anointing by the Holy Spirit: "I am filled with power, with the Spirit of the LORD, and with justice and might, to declare to Jacob his transgression, to Israel his sin" (3:8). (4) The book contains one of the grandest expressions in the Bible about God's mercy and forgiving grace (7:18–20). (5) It has three important prophecies quoted elsewhere in the Bible: one that saved Jeremiah's life (3:12; Jer 26:18), one about the Messiah's birthplace (5:2; Mt 2:5–6), and one used by Jesus himself (7:6; Mt 10:35–36).

New Testament Fulfillment

Like other OT prophets, Micah saw beyond God's judgment of Israel and Judah to the coming Messiah and his righteous reign on earth. Seven hundred years before Christ's incarnation, Micah prophesied that he would be born in Bethlehem (5:2). Mt 2:4–6 records that the priests and the teachers of the law quoted this verse in reply to Herod's inquiry about the Messiah's birthplace. Micah also revealed that the Messianic kingdom would be a kingdom of peace (5:5; cf. Eph 2:14–18), and that the Messiah would shepherd God's people justly (5:4; cf. Jn 10:1–16; Heb 13:20). Micah's frequent references to future redemption reveal that God's enduring desire and purpose for his people is salvation, not judgment; this truth is magnified in the NT (e.g., Jn 3:16).

Reading Micah

In order to read the entire Old Testament in one year, the book of Micah should be read in 3 days, according to the following schedule: ☐ 1–3 ☐ 4–5 ☐ 6–7

NOTES

1 The word of the LORD that came to Micah of Moresheth[a] during the reigns of Jotham,[b] Ahaz[c] and Hezekiah,[d] kings of Judah[e]—the vision[f] he saw concerning Samaria and Jerusalem.

2Hear,[g] O peoples, all of you,[h]
listen, O earth[i] and all who are in it,
that the Sovereign LORD may witness[j] against you,
the Lord from his holy temple.[k]

Judgment Against Samaria and Jerusalem

3Look! The LORD is coming from his dwelling[l] place;
he comes down[m] and treads the high places of the earth.[n]
4The mountains melt[o] beneath him[p]
and the valleys split apart,[q]
like wax before the fire,
like water rushing down a slope.
5All this is because of Jacob's transgression,
because of the sins of the house of Israel.
What is Jacob's transgression?
Is it not Samaria?[r]
What is Judah's high place?
Is it not Jerusalem?

6"Therefore I will make Samaria a heap of rubble,
a place for planting vineyards.[s]
I will pour her stones[t] into the valley
and lay bare her foundations.[u]
7All her idols[v] will be broken to pieces;[w]
all her temple gifts will be burned with fire;
I will destroy all her images.[x]
Since she gathered her gifts from the wages of prostitutes,[y]
as the wages of prostitutes they will again be used."

Weeping and Mourning

8Because of this I will weep[z] and wail;
I will go about barefoot[a] and naked.
I will howl like a jackal
and moan like an owl.
9For her wound[b] is incurable;[c]
it has come to Judah.[d]
It[a] has reached the very gate[e] of my people,
even to Jerusalem itself.
10Tell it not in Gath[b];
weep not at all.[c]
In Beth Ophrah[d]
roll in the dust.
11Pass on in nakedness[f] and shame,
you who live in Shaphir.[e]
Those who live in Zaanan[f]
will not come out.
Beth Ezel is in mourning;
its protection is taken from you.
12Those who live in Maroth[g] writhe in pain,
waiting for relief,[g]

1:1 [a]ver 14; Jer 26:18 [b]S 1Ch 3:12 [c]S 1Ch 3:13 [d]S 1Ch 3:13 [e]Hos 1:1 [f]Isa 1:1 1:2 [g]S Dt 32:1 [h]Ps 50:7 [i]S Jer 6:19 [j]S Ge 31:50; S Dt 4:26; S Isa 1:2 [k]S Ps 11:4 1:3 [l]S Isa 18:4 [m]S Isa 64:1 [n]S Am 4:13 1:4 [o]S Ps 46:2,6 [p]S Job 9:5 [q]S Nu 16:31; Na 1:5 1:5 [r]Am 8:14 1:6 [s]S Dt 20:6 [t]S Am 5:11 [u]Eze 13:14 1:7 [v]S Eze 6:6 [w]S Ex 32:20 [x]S Dt 9:21 [y]Dt 23:17-18 1:8 [z]S Isa 15:3 [a]S Isa 20:2 1:9 [b]Jer 46:11 [c]S Jer 10:19 [d]S 2Ki 18:13 [e]Isa 3:26 1:11 [f]Eze 23:29 1:12 [g]Jer 14:19

[a]9 Or *He* [b]10 *Gath* sounds like the Hebrew for *tell.* [c]10 Hebrew; Septuagint may suggest *not in Acco.* The Hebrew for *in Acco* sounds like the Hebrew for *weep.* [d]10 *Beth Ophrah* means *house of dust.* [e]11 *Shaphir* means *pleasant.* [f]11 *Zaanan* sounds like the Hebrew for *come out.* [g]12 *Maroth* sounds like the Hebrew for *bitter.*

1:1 MICAH. Micah, from southern Judah, prophesied sometime between 750–687 B.C. He was a contemporary of Isaiah (cf. Isa 1:1) and Hosea (cf. Hos 1:1; see the introduction to Micah). His message was directed mainly to Judah (the southern kingdom), though he also had revelation concerning Israel (the northern kingdom). While Micah's predominant theme was judgment, he also stressed the restoration of God's people.

1:1 SAMARIA AND JERUSALEM. Samaria was the capital of Israel; Jerusalem was Judah's capital. Both represented apostate nations that would be judged by God (vv. 5–7).

1:5 TRANSGRESSION . . . SINS. The people would be judged because of their sins, especially idolatry (v. 7), immorality (v. 7), crime and injustice (2:1–2). The sins prevalent in the capital cities were typical of the sins being committed throughout the nations.

1:6 SAMARIA A HEAP OF RUBBLE. This prophecy was fulfilled in 722 B.C., when the Assyrians completely destroyed the city (see 2Ki 17:1–5); the fulfillment came shortly after Micah prophesied it.

1:8–9 I WILL WEEP AND WAIL. Micah mourned Samaria's fall (cf. v. 6). He was heartbroken that they had rejected God and had to be punished. Do we experience regret and grief when people persist in sinning against God and are heading toward their own destruction and doom?

1:9 IT HAS COME TO JUDAH. Judah was equally guilty of transgression and rebellion against God. Thus, Micah called on certain towns in Judah (vv. 10–16) to mourn for the destruction that was coming upon them. Micah's prophecy was fulfilled when Sennacherib took walled cities of Judah (2Ki 18:13); according to Assyrian records, he took 46 of them.

because disaster[h] has come from
the LORD,
even to the gate of Jerusalem.
13You who live in Lachish,[h][i]
harness the team to the chariot.
You were the beginning of sin
to the Daughter of Zion,[j]
for the transgressions of Israel
were found in you.
14Therefore you will give parting
gifts[k]
to Moresheth[l] Gath.
The town of Aczib[i][m] will prove
deceptive[n]
to the kings of Israel.
15I will bring a conqueror against
you
who live in Mareshah.[j][o]
He who is the glory of Israel
will come to Adullam.[p]
16Shave[q] your heads in mourning
for the children in whom you
delight;
make yourselves as bald as the
vulture,
for they will go from you into
exile.[r]

Man's Plans and God's

2 Woe to those who plan iniquity,
to those who plot evil[s] on their
beds![t]
At morning's light they carry it out
because it is in their power to
do it.
2They covet fields[u] and seize
them,[v]
and houses, and take them.
They defraud[w] a man of his home,
a fellowman of his inheritance.[x]
3Therefore, the LORD says:

"I am planning disaster[y] against
this people,
from which you cannot save
yourselves.
You will no longer walk proudly,[z]
for it will be a time of calamity.
4In that day men will ridicule you;
they will taunt you with this
mournful song:
'We are utterly ruined;[a]
my people's possession is
divided up.[b]
He takes it from me!
He assigns our fields to
traitors.' "
5Therefore you will have no one in
the assembly of the LORD
to divide the land[c] by lot.[d]

False Prophets

6"Do not prophesy," their prophets
say.
"Do not prophesy about these
things;
disgrace[e] will not overtake
us.[f]"
7Should it be said, O house of
Jacob:
"Is the Spirit of the LORD angry?
Does he do such things?"

"Do not my words do good[g]
to him whose ways are
upright?[h]
8Lately my people have risen up

1:12 [h]Jer 40:2 1:13 [i]S Jos 10:3 [j]S Ps 9:14 1:14 [k]2Ki 16:8 [l]S ver 1 [m]S Jos 15:44 [n]Jer 15:18 1:15 [o]Jos 15:44 [p]S Jos 12:15 1:16 [q]S Lev 13:40; S Job 1:20 [r]S Dt 4:27; S Am 5:27 2:1 [s]S Isa 29:20 [t]Ps 36:4 2:2 [u]Isa 5:8 [v]S Pr 30:14 [w]S Jer 22:17 [x]S 1Sa 8:14; S Isa 1:23; S Eze 46:18 2:3 [y]Jer 18:11; S Am 3:1-2 [z]Isa 2:12 2:4 [a]S Lev 26:31; S Jer 4:13 [b]S Jer 6:12 2:5 [c]Dt 32:13; Jos 18:4 [d]S Nu 34:13 2:6 [e]Ps 44:13; Jer 18:16; 19:8; 25:18; 29:18; Mic 6:16 [f]S Am 2:12 2:7 [g]S Ps 119:65 [h]Ps 15:2; 84:11

[h]13 *Lachish* sounds like the Hebrew for *team.* [i]14 *Aczib* means *deception.* [j]15 *Mareshah* sounds like the Hebrew for *conqueror.*

1:16 SHAVE YOUR HEADS. Shaving one's head was an external sign of sorrow; thus Micah called on God's people to anticipate intense mourning. (1) Judgment would be severe; their children would be taken from them and carried away into captivity. Micah emphasized that God's people could not turn from him without suffering terrible consequences. (2) Those who leave God and his Word to align themselves with the world and its sinful activities will find that God is against them and may bring disaster into their lives.

2:1–5 WOE TO THOSE WHO PLAN INIQUITY. Micah pronounces doom on certain people who were powerful enough to exploit others in order to achieve their own selfish aims. (1) They were land barons, who either bought or stole farm after farm; they did not hesitate to defraud others in order to gain more property. Having devoted their hearts to greed, they did not care about the suffering they inflicted on others. (2) God had a plan for them; they would reap what they sowed. God would send Assyria to take their land away from them and carry them into captivity. (3) We must be careful that we do not become greedy and mistreat others to gain money or possessions (see article on RICHES AND POVERTY, p. 1562).

2:6 DO NOT PROPHESY. Judah's false prophets were condemning Micah for bringing a message of judgment (cf. Isa 30:10). (1) They rejected his prophecy of gloom and doom, insisting that shame and disgrace would not overtake the people, for God was a God of love and forgiveness, and not anger. (2) Their optimistic message allowed the people to continue in their sinful ways of disregarding God's righteous demands. (3) Sometimes the church manifests this same insistence on the positive message of God's love, mercy and forgiveness while ignoring his righteous standards and his call for holy living. A church that tolerates any kind of sin among its people should listen again to the clear message of both the OT prophets and the NT apostles (cf. 1Co 5—6).

like an enemy.
You strip off the rich robe
from those who pass by without
a care,
like men returning from battle.
9You drive the women of my people
from their pleasant homes.[i]
You take away my blessing
from their children forever.
10Get up, go away!
For this is not your resting
place,[j]
because it is defiled,[k]
it is ruined, beyond all remedy.
11If a liar and deceiver[l] comes and
says,
'I will prophesy for you plenty of
wine and beer,'[m]
he would be just the prophet for
this people![n]

Deliverance Promised

12"I will surely gather all of you,
O Jacob;
I will surely bring together the
remnant[o] of Israel.
I will bring them together like
sheep in a pen,
like a flock in its pasture;
the place will throng with
people.[p]
13One who breaks open the way will
go up before[q] them;
they will break through the
gate[r] and go out.
Their king will pass through before
them,
the LORD at their head."

2:9 [i]Jer 10:20
2:10 [j]S Dt 12:9 [k]Lev 18:25-29; Ps 106:38-39; S La 4:15
2:11 [l]S 2Ch 36:16; Jer 5:31 [m]S Lev 10:9 [n]Isa 30:10
2:12 [o]Mic 4:7; 5:7; 7:18 [p]S Ne 1:9
2:13 [q]S Isa 52:12 [r]S Isa 60:11

3:1 [s]S Jer 5:5
3:2 [t]Ps 53:4; S Eze 22:27
3:3 [u]S Ps 14:4 [v]S Eze 34:4; Zep 3:3 [w]S Job 24:14 [x]S Eze 11:7; S 24:4-5
3:4 [y]S Dt 1:45; S 1Sa 8:18; S Isa 58:4; S Jer 11:11 [z]S Dt 31:17 [a]S Job 15:31; S Eze 8:18
3:5 [b]S Isa 3:12; S 9:16; S 53:6 [c]S Jer 4:10
3:6 [d]Isa 8:19-22; S Eze 12:24 [e]Isa 29:10

Leaders and Prophets Rebuked

3 Then I said,
"Listen, you leaders[s] of Jacob,
you rulers of the house of Israel.
Should you not know justice,
2 you who hate good and love evil;
who tear the skin from my people
and the flesh from their bones;[t]
3who eat my people's flesh,[u]
strip off their skin
and break their bones in
pieces;[v]
who chop[w] them up like meat for
the pan,
like flesh for the pot?[x]"

4Then they will cry out to the LORD,
but he will not answer them.[y]
At that time he will hide his face[z]
from them
because of the evil they have
done.[a]

5This is what the LORD says:

"As for the prophets
who lead my people astray,[b]
if one feeds them,
they proclaim 'peace';[c]
if he does not,
they prepare to wage war
against him.
6Therefore night will come over
you, without visions,
and darkness, without
divination.[d]
The sun will set for the
prophets,[e]

2:11 WINE AND BEER. Micah sarcastically declares that if Judah's false prophets were prophesying prosperity and plenty of intoxicating drink for everyone who wanted it, the people would eagerly accept such a prophet. Today there are still pastors who refuse to warn God's people about the consequences of adopting the drinking customs of the society in which they live (see article on WINE IN THE OLD TESTAMENT, p. 204).

2:12–13 THE REMNANT OF ISRAEL. Micah adds a word of hope by proclaiming that God would spare a remnant of Israel and Judah, who would return to the promised land (see Isa 6:13, note; 10:20, note; 17:7, note). The land would again be filled with the hustle and bustle of people coming and going.

3:1–12 LEADERS OF JACOB. This passage prophesies against the cruelty of the ruling classes (vv. 1–4), the deceit of false prophets (vv. 5–7), and the perversion of Judah's apostate leaders, priests and prophets (vv. 9–12). God would judge all of them accordingly.

3:2 HATE GOOD AND LOVE EVIL. The nation's leaders had abandoned the godly standards of the past and substituted their own legal codes. They purposely loved evil and injustice in their pursuit of material gain. God calls us to do the opposite: to love righteousness and hate wickedness (see Am 5:15; Ro 12:9; Heb 1:9).

3:3 EAT MY PEOPLE'S FLESH. This vivid expression describes the severe oppression and exploitation of the common folk.

3:4 HE WILL NOT ANSWER THEM. Because of the evil and cruel behavior of the leaders, God would refuse to answer their prayers, and they themselves would come to a God-forsaken end.

3:5–7 AS FOR THE PROPHETS. God longed to lead his people back to the paths of righteousness and truth, yet the false prophets cared for none of this. They made the people feel comfortable in their sinful lifestyles by proclaiming a false hope and security. Instead of taking an uncompromising stand against sin among God's people, they actually encouraged it. Because of their refusal to lead the people back to God's ways, the false prophets would be abandoned by God.

and the day will go dark for
them.[f]
7The seers will be ashamed[g]
and the diviners disgraced.[h]
They will all cover[i] their faces[j]
because there is no answer from
God.[k]"

8But as for me, I am filled with
power,
with the Spirit of the LORD,
and with justice and might,
to declare to Jacob his
transgression,
to Israel his sin.[l]
9Hear this, you leaders of the house
of Jacob,
you rulers of the house of Israel,
who despise justice
and distort all that is right;[m]
10who build[n] Zion with bloodshed,[o]
and Jerusalem with
wickedness.[p]
11Her leaders judge for a bribe,[q]
her priests teach for a price,[r]
and her prophets tell fortunes
for money.[s]
Yet they lean[t] upon the LORD and
say,
"Is not the LORD among us?
No disaster will come upon
us."[u]
12Therefore because of you,
Zion will be plowed like a field,
Jerusalem will become a heap of
rubble,[v]
the temple[w] hill a mound
overgrown with thickets.[x]

The Mountain of the LORD

4:1–3pp — Isa 2:1–4

4 In the last days
the mountain[y] of the LORD's
temple will be established
as chief among the mountains;
it will be raised above the hills,[z]
and peoples will stream to it.[a]
2Many nations will come and say,
"Come, let us go up to the
mountain of the LORD,[b]
to the house of the God of
Jacob.[c]
He will teach us[d] his ways,[e]
so that we may walk in his
paths."
The law[f] will go out from Zion,
the word of the LORD from
Jerusalem.
3He will judge between many
peoples
and will settle disputes for
strong nations far and
wide.[g]
They will beat their swords into
plowshares
and their spears into pruning
hooks.[h]
Nation will not take up sword
against nation,
nor will they train for war[i]
anymore.[j]
4Every man will sit under his own
vine
and under his own fig tree,[k]
and no one will make them
afraid,[l]
for the LORD Almighty has
spoken.[m]
5All the nations may walk
in the name of their gods;[n]
we will walk in the name of the
LORD
our God for ever and ever.[o]

The LORD's Plan

6"In that day," declares the LORD,
"I will gather the lame;[p]
I will assemble the exiles[q]
and those I have brought to
grief.[r]
7I will make the lame a remnant,[s]

3:6 [f] S Eze 7:26; S Am 8:11 **3:7** [g] S Jer 6:15; Mic 7:16 [h] S Isa 44:25 [i] S Est 6:12 [j] S Lev 13:45 [k] S Eze 20:3 **3:8** [l] S Isa 57:12; 61:2 **3:9** [m] Ps 58:1-2; S Isa 1:23 **3:10** [n] S Jer 22:13 [o] Isa 59:7; Mic 7:2; Na 3:1; Hab 2:12 [p] Jer 22:17; S Eze 22:27 **3:11** [q] S Ex 23:8; S Lev 19:15; Mal 2:9 [r] S Eze 13:19 [s] Isa 1:23; S 56:11; Jer 6:13; S La 4:13; S Hos 4:8,18 [t] S Isa 10:20 [u] Jer 7:4; S Eze 34:2 **3:12** [v] S 2Ki 25:9; S Isa 6:11 [w] S Jer 52:13 [x] S Lev 26:31; S Jer 17:3; S 22:6; S La 5:18; S Eze 5:14 **4:1** [y] S Ps 48:1; Zec 8:3 [z] S Eze 17:22

[a] S Ps 22:27; 86:9; S Jer 3:17; S 31:12; S Da 2:35 **4:2** [b] S Jer 31:6; S Eze 20:40 [c] Zec 2:11; 14:16 [d] S Ps 119:171 [e] Ps 25:8-9; S Isa 54:13 [f] S Dt 18:18 **4:3** [g] S Isa 11:4 [h] Joel 3:10; Zec 9:10 [i] S Ps 46:9 [j] Zec 8:20-22 **4:4** [k] S 1Ki 4:25 [l] S Lev 26:6; S Eze 39:26 [m] S Isa 1:20 **4:5** [n] 2Ki 17:29; Ac 14:16 [o] Jos 24:14-15; Isa 26:8; Zec 10:12 **4:6** [p] S Jer 31:8 [q] S Ps 106:47 [r] S Eze 34:13,16; S 37:21; Zep 3:19 **4:7** [s] S Joel 2:32; S Mic 2:12

3:8 FILLED WITH POWER, WITH THE SPIRIT. Micah had been called to be a spokesman for God. (1) He spoke by the power and inspiration of the Holy Spirit (cf. Jer 20:9; Eph 3:7). The Spirit moved him to condemn sin in God's house. It was his task to reflect the heart of God, to encourage right and to discourage wrong. (2) Pastors and prophets today have the same task. They must not bend to pressures within the church to conform to the ways of the world. Instead, they must be God's voice for truth, godliness and righteousness (see article on THE CHRISTIAN'S RELATIONSHIP TO THE WORLD, p. 1976).

4:1 IN THE LAST DAYS. Micah prophesies a time when God will rule over the entire world. (1) It will be a time of peace, happiness and godliness. God will be honored and worshiped not only by Israel but also by all the nations of the world. (2) The "mountain of the LORD's temple" (i.e., Jerusalem) will be the center of God's government. This future kingdom of God will begin when Christ returns to destroy all evil and to establish his righteous reign on earth (see Rev 20:4, note).

4:5 WALK IN THE NAME OF THE LORD. How should we live while we wait for God's kingdom to come to the earth in all its fullness? We must live for God, walk in his righteous ways and witness to all the nations (cf. 2Pe 3:11–12).

those driven away a strong
nation.[t]
The LORD will rule over them in
Mount Zion[u]
from that day and forever.[v]
8As for you, O watchtower of the
flock,
O stronghold[k] of the Daughter
of Zion,
the former dominion will be
restored[w] to you;
kingship will come to the
Daughter of Jerusalem.[x]"

9Why do you now cry aloud—
have you no king?[y]
Has your counselor perished,
that pain seizes you like that of
a woman in labor?[z]
10Writhe in agony, O Daughter of
Zion,
like a woman in labor,
for now you must leave the city
to camp in the open field.
You will go to Babylon;[a]
there you will be rescued.
There the LORD will redeem[b] you
out of the hand of your enemies.

11But now many nations
are gathered against you.
They say, "Let her be defiled,
let our eyes gloat[c] over Zion!"
12But they do not know
the thoughts of the LORD;
they do not understand his plan,[d]
he who gathers them like
sheaves to the threshing
floor.
13"Rise and thresh,[e] O Daughter of
Zion,
for I will give you horns of iron;
I will give you hoofs of bronze
and you will break to pieces
many nations."[f]
You will devote their ill-gotten
gains to the LORD,[g]
their wealth to the Lord of all
the earth.

A Promised Ruler From Bethlehem

5 Marshal your troops, O city of
troops,[1]
for a siege is laid against us.
They will strike Israel's ruler
on the cheek[h] with a rod.

2"But you, Bethlehem[i]
Ephrathah,[j]
though you are small among the
clans[m] of Judah,
out of you will come for me
one who will be ruler[k] over
Israel,
whose origins[n] are from of old,[l]
from ancient times.[o]"[m]

3Therefore Israel will be
abandoned[n]
until the time when she who is
in labor gives birth
and the rest of his brothers return
to join the Israelites.

4He will stand and shepherd his
flock[o]
in the strength of the LORD,
in the majesty of the name of
the LORD his God.
And they will live securely, for
then his greatness[p]
will reach to the ends of the
earth.
5 And he will be their peace.[q]

4:7 [t]S Ge 12:2 [u]S Isa 2:2 [v]S Da 2:44; S 7:14; S Lk 1:33; Rev 11:15
4:8 [w]S Isa 1:26 [x]Zec 9:9
4:9 [y]Jer 8:19 [z]S Ge 3:16; Jer 30:6; 48:41
4:10 [a]S Dt 21:10; 2Ki 20:18; Isa 43:14 [b]S Isa 48:20
4:11 [c]S La 2:16; S Ob 1:12; Mic 7:8
4:12 [d]S Ge 50:20; S Isa 55:8; Ro 11:33-34
4:13 [e]S Isa 21:10 [f]S Isa 45:1; S Da 2:44 [g]S Isa 23:18
5:1 [h]La 3:30
5:2 [i]S Jn 7:42 [j]S Ge 35:16; S 48:7 [k]S Nu 24:19; S 1Sa 13:14; S 2Sa 6:21; S 2Ch 7:18 [l]Ps 102:25 [m]Mt 2:6*
5:3 [n]S Jer 7:29
5:4 [o]Isa 40:11; 49:9; S Eze 34:11-15,23; Mic 7:14 [p]Isa 52:13; Lk 1:32
5:5 [q]S Isa 9:6; S Lk 2:14; Col 1:19-20

[k]8 Or *hill* [1]1 Or *Strengthen your walls, O walled city* [m]2 Or *rulers* [n]2 Hebrew *goings out* [o]2 Or *from days of eternity*

4:9–13 WHY DO YOU NOW CRY ALOUD. The prophet returns to the doom of the present Jerusalem, stating that the people would be carried away to Babylon. He spoke this prophecy 100 years before the Babylonian empire became the dominant world power (the Babylonians destroyed Jerusalem in 586 B.C.). Micah also foresaw the restoration of Judah from Babylon (v. 10).

5:2 BUT YOU, BETHLEHEM. Micah prophesies that a ruler would come out of Bethlehem who would fulfill God's promises to his people. This verse refers to Jesus the Messiah (see Mt 2:1, 3–6), whose origin is "from ancient times" (i.e., from eternity; see Jn 1:1; Col 1:17; Rev 1:8); yet he would be born as a human (v. 3; see Jn 1:14; Php 2:7–8).

5:3 THEREFORE ISRAEL WILL BE ABANDONED. Israel would be abandoned by God until the birth of the Messiah. "She who is in labor" refers physically to the virgin Mary, the mother of Jesus, and spiritually to the godly remnant. All hope for Israel, indeed for all nations, lies with the birth, life, death and resurrection of Jesus the Messiah. "The rest of his brothers" refers to the northern tribes, showing that the Messiah would be for all of Israel's twelve tribes.

5:4 TO THE ENDS OF THE EARTH. Like Isaiah (see Isa 9:6–7; 61:1–2), Micah did not distinguish between the first and second advents of Jesus Christ. When Christ returns to destroy all evil, Israel will live securely and Christ will reign over all the world.

Deliverance and Destruction

When the Assyrian invades[r] our
land
and marches through our
fortresses,
we will raise against him seven
shepherds,
even eight leaders of men.[s]
6They will rule[p] the land of
Assyria with the sword,
the land of Nimrod[t] with drawn
sword.[q][u]
He will deliver us from the
Assyrian
when he invades our land
and marches into our borders.[v]

7The remnant[w] of Jacob will be
in the midst of many peoples
like dew[x] from the LORD,
like showers on the grass,[y]
which do not wait for man
or linger for mankind.
8The remnant of Jacob will be
among the nations,
in the midst of many peoples,
like a lion among the beasts of the
forest,[z]
like a young lion among flocks
of sheep,
which mauls and mangles[a] as it
goes,
and no one can rescue.[b]
9Your hand will be lifted up[c] in
triumph over your enemies,
and all your foes will be
destroyed.

10"In that day," declares the LORD,

"I will destroy your horses from
among you
and demolish your chariots.[d]
11I will destroy the cities[e] of your
land
and tear down all your
strongholds.[f]
12I will destroy your witchcraft
and you will no longer cast
spells.[g]
13I will destroy your carved
images[h]
and your sacred stones from
among you;[i]
you will no longer bow down
to the work of your hands.[j]
14I will uproot from among you your
Asherah poles[r][k]
and demolish your cities.
15I will take vengeance[l] in anger
and wrath
upon the nations that have not
obeyed me."

The LORD's Case Against Israel

6 Listen to what the LORD says:
"Stand up, plead your case
before the mountains;[m]
let the hills hear what you have
to say.
2Hear,[n] O mountains, the LORD's
accusation;[o]
listen, you everlasting
foundations of the earth.
For the LORD has a case[p] against
his people;
he is lodging a charge[q] against
Israel.

3"My people, what have I done to
you?

5:5 [r]Isa 8:7 [s]Isa 10:24-27
5:6 [t]Ge 10:8 [u]Zep 2:13 [v]Na 2:11-13
5:7 [w]S Am 5:15; S Mic 2:12 [x]S Ps 133:3 [y]Isa 44:4
5:8 [z]S Ge 49:9 [a]Mic 4:13; Zec 10:5 [b]S Ps 50:22; S Isa 5:29; S Hos 5:14
5:9 [c]S Ps 10:12
5:10 [d]Ex 15:4,19; S Hos 14:3; Hag 2:22; Zec 9:10
5:11 [e]S Dt 29:23; Isa 6:11 [f]S La 2:2; S Hos 10:14; Am 5:9
5:12 [g]Dt 18:10-12; Isa 2:6; 8:19
5:13 [h]Na 1:14 [i]Hos 10:2 [j]S Isa 2:18; S Eze 6:9; Zec 13:2
5:14 [k]S Ex 34:13; S Jdg 3:7; S 2Ki 17:10
5:15 [l]S Isa 65:12
6:1 [m]S Ps 50:1; S Eze 6:2
6:2 [n]Dt 32:1 [o]S Hos 12:2 [p]S Isa 3:13 [q]Ps 50:7; S Jer 2:9

[p]6 Or *crush* [q]6 Or *Nimrod in its gates*
[r]14 That is, symbols of the goddess Asherah

5:5 HE WILL BE THEIR PEACE. Only Jesus the Messiah will bring everlasting peace to Israel. Even with his first coming, he gives peace with God, forgiveness of sin, and the assurance of eternal life to those who repent and receive him by faith (see Ro 5:1–11). Because they believe in his atoning death, true believers will not face condemnation (see Jn 14:27; Eph 2:14).

5:5 ASSYRIAN. Assyria represents all God's enemies. The Messiah will one day deliver his people from those who oppose them and their worship of God.

5:10–14 DEMOLISH YOUR CHARIOTS. When the Messiah returns to judge the world's evil, he will also purge Israel of her military power (vv. 10–11) and her sin, witchcraft and idolatry (vv. 12–14). All those in Israel not loyal to God and his ways will be destroyed.

6:1–5 LISTEN TO WHAT THE LORD SAYS. The Lord had an accusation against his people, so he summoned them to listen to his complaint and to justify their evil actions if they could. What right did they have to reject their covenant God and to disobey his laws? The charges against the people are given in vv. 9–16.

6:3–5 WHAT HAVE I DONE TO YOU? God asks his people if he had failed them in some way. (1) Could it be his fault that they had disobeyed his word? Had he neglected the people or failed to love them sufficiently? The answer is obvious. Israel had no excuse; God had treated his people with kindness and patience throughout their history. (2) Today God could ask the very same questions of all who turn their backs on him. If we become disloyal to him and his righteous standards and accept the world's ungodly ways, it will not be because God has been unfaithful to us; rather, it will be due to our own selfish desires and our ingrati-

How have I burdened[r] you?[s]
Answer me.
[4]I brought you up out of Egypt[t]
and redeemed you from the land
of slavery.[u]
I sent Moses[v] to lead you,
also Aaron[w] and Miriam.[x]
[5]My people, remember
what Balak[y] king of Moab
counseled
and what Balaam son of Beor
answered.
Remember ⌊your journey⌋ from
Shittim[z] to Gilgal,[a]
that you may know the
righteous acts[b] of the
LORD."

[6]With what shall I come before[c]
the LORD
and bow down before the exalted
God?
Shall I come before him with burnt
offerings,
with calves a year old?[d]
[7]Will the LORD be pleased with
thousands of rams,[e]
with ten thousand rivers of
oil?[f]
Shall I offer my firstborn[g] for my
transgression,
the fruit of my body for the sin
of my soul?[h]
[8]He has showed you, O man, what
is good.
And what does the LORD require
of you?
To act justly[i] and to love mercy
and to walk humbly[j] with your
God.[k]

Mal 2:5-6

Israel's Guilt and Punishment

[9]Listen! The LORD is calling to the
city—
and to fear your name is
wisdom—
"Heed the rod[l] and the One
who appointed it.[s]

6:3 [r]Jer 2:5 [s]Jer 2:5
6:4 [t]S Ex 3:10; S 6:6 [u]Dt 7:8 [v]S Ex 4:16 [w]S Nu 33:1; Ps 77:20 [x]S Ex 15:20
6:5 [y]S Nu 22:2 [z]S Nu 25:1 [a]S Dt 11:30; Jos 5:9-10 [b]Jdg 5:11; 1Sa 12:7
6:6 [c]S Ps 95:2 [d]Ps 40:6-8; 51:16-17
6:7 [e]S Isa 1:11; S 40:16 [f]Ps 50:8-10 [g]S Lev 18:21; S 2Ki 3:27 [h]Hos 5:6; S Am 5:22
6:8 [i]S Isa 1:17; S Jer 22:3 [j]S 2Ki 22:19; S Isa 57:15 [k]S Ge 5:22; Dt 10:12-13; 1Sa 15:22; Hos 6:6; Zec 7:9-10; Mt 9:13; 23:23; Mk 12:33; Lk 11:42
6:9 [l]S Ge 17:1; Isa 11:4
6:10 [m]Eze 45:9-10; S Am 3:10; 8:4-6
6:11 [n]S Lev 19:36 [o]S Dt 25:13
6:12 [p]S Isa 1:23 [q]S Ps 116:11; Isa 3:8 [r]S Ps 35:20; S Jer 9:3
6:13 [s]Isa 1:7; 6:11
6:14 [t]S Isa 9:20; S Hos 4:10 [u]Isa 30:6
6:15 [v]S Dt 28:38; Jer 12:13 [w]Job 24:11; S Am 5:11; Zep 1:13
6:16 [x]S 1Ki 16:25 [y]1Ki 16:29-33 [z]Jer 7:24 [a]S Jer 25:9 [b]S Dt 28:37; S Jer 51:51; S Mic 2:6

[10]Am I still to forget, O wicked
house,
your ill-gotten treasures
and the short ephah,[t] which is
accursed?[m]
[11]Shall I acquit a man with
dishonest scales,[n]
with a bag of false weights?[o]
[12]Her rich men are violent;[p]
her people are liars[q]
and their tongues speak
deceitfully.[r]
[13]Therefore, I have begun to
destroy[s] you,
to ruin you because of your sins.
[14]You will eat but not be satisfied;[t]
your stomach will still be
empty.[u]
You will store up but save
nothing,[u]
because what you save I will
give to the sword.
[15]You will plant but not harvest;[v]
you will press olives but not use
the oil on yourselves,
you will crush grapes but not
drink the wine.[w]
[16]You have observed the statutes of
Omri[x]
and all the practices of Ahab's[y]
house,
and you have followed their
traditions.[z]
Therefore I will give you over to
ruin[a]
and your people to derision;
you will bear the scorn[b] of the
nations.[v]"

Israel's Misery

7 What misery is mine!
I am like one who gathers
summer fruit

[s]*9* The meaning of the Hebrew for this line is uncertain. [t]*10* An ephah was a dry measure. [u]*14* The meaning of the Hebrew for this word is uncertain. [v]*16* Septuagint; Hebrew *scorn due my people*

tude for his grace and love.

6:8 WHAT DOES THE LORD REQUIRE OF YOU? Micah gives a threefold definition of what God's standard of goodness and what our commitment to him involve: (1) we must act justly, i.e., be fair and honest in our dealings with others (cf. Mt 7:12); (2) we must love mercy, i.e., show genuine compassion and kindness to individuals in need; (3) we must walk humbly with our God, i.e., humble ourselves daily before him in godly fear and reverence for his will (cf. Jas 4:6–10; 1Pe 5:5–6). Public worship is only a small part of our total commitment to Christ. A genuine love for the Lord must come to expression in an abiding concern for people in need (see article on THE CARE OF THE POOR AND NEEDY, p. 1316).

6:9–16 THE LORD IS CALLING. The Lord lists some of Israel's sins and announces the judgment they had to face.

7:1–7 WHAT MISERY IS MINE! Micah laments the corruption of the society in which he lived. Violence, dishonesty and immorality ran rampant in Israel. Few people were really godly (v. 2), and family love had nearly disappeared (v. 6).

at the gleaning of the vineyard;
there is no cluster of grapes to eat,
none of the early figs[c] that I crave.
2The godly have been swept from the land;[d]
not one[e] upright man remains.
All men lie in wait[f] to shed blood;[g]
each hunts his brother[h] with a net.[i]
3Both hands are skilled in doing evil;[j]
the ruler demands gifts,
the judge accepts bribes,[k]
the powerful dictate what they desire—
they all conspire together.
4The best of them is like a brier,[l]
the most upright worse than a thorn[m] hedge.
The day of your watchmen has come,
the day God visits you.
Now is the time of their confusion.[n]
5Do not trust a neighbor;
put no confidence in a friend.[o]
Even with her who lies in your embrace
be careful of your words.
6For a son dishonors his father,
a daughter rises up against her mother,[p]
a daughter-in-law against her mother-in-law—
a man's enemies are the members of his own household.[q]

7But as for me, I watch[r] in hope[s] for the LORD,
I wait for God my Savior;
my God will hear[t] me.

Israel Will Rise

8Do not gloat over me,[u] my enemy!
Though I have fallen, I will rise.[v]
Though I sit in darkness,
the LORD will be my light.[w]
9Because I have sinned against him,
I will bear the LORD's wrath,[x]
until he pleads my case[y]
and establishes my right.
He will bring me out into the light;[z]
I will see his righteousness.[a]
10Then my enemy will see it
and will be covered with shame,[b]
she who said to me,
"Where is the LORD your God?"[c]
My eyes will see her downfall;[d]
even now she will be trampled[e] underfoot
like mire in the streets.

11The day for building your walls[f] will come,
the day for extending your boundaries.
12In that day people will come to you
from Assyria[g] and the cities of Egypt,
even from Egypt to the Euphrates
and from sea to sea
and from mountain to mountain.[h]
13The earth will become desolate
because of its inhabitants,
as the result of their deeds.[i]

Prayer and Praise

14Shepherd[j] your people with your staff,[k]
the flock of your inheritance,
which lives by itself in a forest,

7:1 [c]S SS 2:13 7:2 [d]S Ps 12:1 [e]S Jer 2:29; 8:6 [f]Ps 10:8 [g]S Pr 6:17; S Mic 3:10 [h]S Isa 3:5 [i]S Jer 5:26 7:3 [j]S Pr 4:16 [k]S Ex 23:8; S Eze 22:12 7:4 [l]S Nu 33:55; S Eze 2:6 [m]S 2Sa 23:6 [n]S Job 31:14; Isa 22:5; S Hos 9:7 7:5 [o]Jer 9:4 7:6 [p]S Eze 22:7 [q]Mt 10:35-36*; S Mk 13:12 7:7 [r]S Isa 21:8 [s]Ps 130:5; Isa 25:9 [t]S Ps 4:3 7:8 [u]S Ps 22:17; S Pr 24:17; S Mic 4:11 [v]Ps 20:8; 37:24; S Am 9:11 [w]S 2Sa 22:29; Isa 9:2 7:9 [x]La 3:39-40 [y]S Ps 119:154 [z]S Ps 107:10 [a]Isa 46:13 7:10 [b]S Ps 35:26 [c]S Ps 42:3 [d]S Isa 51:23 [e]S 2Sa 22:43; S Job 40:12; S Isa 5:5; Zec 10:5 7:11 [f]Isa 54:11; S Am 9:11 7:12 [g]S Isa 11:11 [h]Isa 19:23-25; 60:4 7:13 [i]Isa 3:10-11; S Eze 12:19; S 33:28-29 7:14 [j]S Ps 28:9; S Mic 5:4 [k]Ps 23:4

If we are truly committed to the Lord and his ways, we will also mourn over the evil that is so prevalent around us. We will intensify our intercession and pray for the intervention of God our Savior (vv. 7–9).

7:7 I WATCH IN HOPE FOR THE LORD. In the midst of a morally sick society, Micah put his faith in God and his promises. He knew that God would sustain him, execute justice one day against all evil, and cause righteousness to reign (v. 9). (1) God calls believers in Christ to live "without fault in a crooked and depraved generation, in which you shine like stars" (Php 2:15). (2) Although evil may increase and society may disintegrate, we can offer God's gift of salvation to all who will listen, while we pray and watch for the day when he will set things right (cf. vv. 15–20).

7:8–13 I WILL RISE. The righteous remnant of Judah was facing dark days ahead because of God's judgment for the nation's sins; however, Micah trumpeted words of faith on their behalf and looked beyond the temporary triumph of their enemies to the glorious day of their restoration by God. "I will rise" is an affirmation of faith comparable to Job's (see Job 19:25–27, notes).

7:14–20 SHEPHERD YOUR PEOPLE. These verses are a prayer of supplication, asking God to fulfill the words of vv. 8–13. Micah's chief concern was that God would once again care for Israel as a shepherd cares for his sheep.

in fertile pasturelands.[w] [l]
Let them feed in Bashan[m] and
Gilead[n]
as in days long ago.[o]

15 "As in the days when you came
out of Egypt,
I will show them my wonders.[p]"

16 Nations will see and be
ashamed,[q]
deprived of all their power.
They will lay their hands on their
mouths[r]
and their ears will become deaf.
17 They will lick dust[s] like a snake,
like creatures that crawl on the
ground.
They will come trembling[t] out of
their dens;
they will turn in fear[u] to the
LORD our God
and will be afraid of you.
18 Who is a God[v] like you,
who pardons sin[w] and
forgives[x] the transgression
of the remnant[y] of his
inheritance?[z]
You do not stay angry[a] forever
but delight to show mercy.[b]
19 You will again have compassion on
us;
you will tread our sins underfoot
and hurl all our iniquities[c] into
the depths of the sea.[d]
20 You will be true to Jacob,
and show mercy to Abraham,[e]
as you pledged on oath to our
fathers[f]
in days long ago.[g]

7:14 [l] Ps 95:7 [m] S Isa 33:9 [n] S SS 4:1; S Jer 50:19 [o] Eze 36:11
7:15 [p] S Ex 3:20; Ps 78:12
7:16 [q] Isa 26:11 [r] S Jdg 18:19
7:17 [s] S Ge 3:14 [t] 2Sa 22:46 [u] Isa 25:3; 59:19
7:18 [v] S Ex 8:10; S 1Sa 2:2 [w] S Isa 43:25; S Jer 50:20; Zec 3:4 [x] S 2Ch 6:21; Ps 103:8-13 [y] S Joel 2:32; S Am 5:15; S Mic 2:12 [z] S Ex 34:9 [a] S Ps 103:9; S Isa 54:9 [b] S 2Ch 30:9; S Jer 31:20; 32:41; S Eze 18:23
7:19 [c] S Isa 43:25 [d] S Jer 31:34
7:20 [e] Gal 3:16 [f] Dt 7:8; Lk 1:72 [g] Ps 108:4

[w] 14 Or *in the middle of Carmel*

NAHUM

Outline

Title (1:1)
- I. The Nature of God and His Judgment (1:2–15)
  - A. Characteristics of God's Administration of Justice (1:2–7)
  - B. The Impending Doom of Nineveh (1:8–11,14)
  - C. Comfort for Judah (1:12–13,15)
- II. Oracle Concerning the Fall of Nineveh (2:1–13)
  - A. Introduction (2:1–2)
  - B. The Soldiers Clash (2:3–5)
  - C. The City Devastated (2:6–12)
  - D. The Voice of the Lord (2:13)
- III. Reasons for Nineveh's Fall (3:1–19)
  - A. Nineveh's Sins of Cruelty (3:1–4)
  - B. The Just Retribution of God (3:5–19)

Author: Nahum

Theme: Nineveh's Approaching Destruction

Date of Writing: c. 630–620 B.C.

Background

This brief prophetic book about Nineveh's coming destruction was written by a prophet whose name means "comfort." Nothing is known about Nahum except that he came from Elkosh (1:1), a town whose location is uncertain. Jerome believed it to be near Ramah in Galilee, some have suggested the vicinity of Capernaum, and still others believe it was in southern Judah. Most likely Nahum was a prophet in Judah, since the northern kingdom (Israel) had already been dissolved at the time of this book.

Nahum uttered his prophecy before the fall of Nineveh in 612 B.C. He refers in 3:8–10 to the fall of Thebes as a past event (this occurred in 663 B.C.). Thus Nahum's prophecy occurred sometime between 663 and 612, more likely nearer the latter date, during the time of King Josiah and his reform movement (c. 630–620 B.C.).

The Assyrians were known in the ancient world for their extreme cruelty to people whom they conquered. After attacking a city, they would ruthlessly slaughter hundreds of people and deport the remaining population to other parts of their empire; many more would die as a result of the brutal marches into exile (cf. 3:3). Leaders of conquered cities and nations were tortured without mercy and finally executed. A century earlier, Jonah had been sent to preach to Assyria's capital city of Nineveh. For a brief time the Assyrians repented of their sins, but sometime thereafter returned to their wicked ways. God used the wicked Assyrians as his instrument of judgment to destroy Israel's capital city of Samaria and to deport the northern kingdom into exile. Now the day of Assyria's own judgment was fast approaching.

Purpose

Nahum had a twofold purpose in this prophetic book. (1) God used him to pronounce the impending destruction of the wicked and cruel Assyrian capital of Nineveh. No nation as wicked as the Assyrians could expect to go unpunished by God. (2) At the same time, Nahum delivered a message of comfort for God's own people. The comfort derives not from seeing the bloodshed of their enemies, but from knowing that God was upholding justice in the world and would someday establish his kingdom of peace.

Survey

The book of Nahum is a series of three separate oracles against Assyria, especially the capital city of Nineveh; the three oracles correspond to the book's three chapters. Ch. 1 contains a clear and bold description of God's nature—especially his wrath, justice and power, which make inevitable the judgment of the wicked generally and the doom of Nineveh specifically. Ch. 2 predicts Nineveh's approaching judgment and describes in vivid language what it would be like. Ch. 3 lists briefly the sins of Nineveh, declares that God is just in his judgment and concludes by envisioning the completed judgment.

Special Features

Three major features characterize the book of Nahum. (1) Nahum is one of three OT prophetic books whose message is almost exclusively addressed to a foreign nation (the other two are Obadiah and Jonah). (2) Its prophetic content and poetic imagery is punctuated with some of the most graphic metaphors, vivid word pictures and blunt language found anywhere in the Bible. (3) There is a conspicuous absence of any prophetic message to Judah about her sins or idolatry, perhaps because it was written during the time of King Josiah's reforms (2Ki 22:8—23:5). It does contain a few words of hope and comfort for Judah (e.g., 1:12–13,15).

New Testament Fulfillment

The NT makes no direct use of this book. The only verse that may appear in the NT is 1:15, a verse that Nahum himself borrowed from Isa 52:7. Paul used its imagery of "beautiful feet" to emphasize that just as a messenger in the OT was joyfully received by God's people when bearing the good news of peace and deliverance from their enemies Assyria (1:15) and Babylon (Isa 52:7), so new covenant preachers bear the good news of deliverance from sin's bondage and Satan's power through Jesus Christ (Ro 10:15). The book of Nahum also underscores the NT message that God will not allow guilty sinners to go unpunished (1:3).

Reading Nahum

In order to read the entire Old Testament in one year, the book of Nahum should be read in 1 day: ☐ Nahum

NOTES

1 An oracle[a] concerning Nineveh.[b] The book of the vision[c] of Nahum the Elkoshite.

The LORD's Anger Against Nineveh

2The LORD is a jealous[d] and
avenging God;
the LORD takes vengeance[e] and
is filled with wrath.
The LORD takes vengeance on his
foes
and maintains his wrath against
his enemies.[f]
3The LORD is slow to anger[g] and
great in power;
the LORD will not leave the guilty
unpunished.[h]
His way is in the whirlwind[i] and
the storm,[j]
and clouds[k] are the dust of his
feet.
4He rebukes[l] the sea and dries it
up;[m]
he makes all the rivers run dry.
Bashan and Carmel[n] wither
and the blossoms of Lebanon
fade.
5The mountains quake[o] before him
and the hills melt away.[p]
The earth trembles[q] at his
presence,
the world and all who live in
it.[r]
6Who can withstand[s] his
indignation?
Who can endure[t] his fierce
anger?[u]
His wrath is poured out like fire;[v]
the rocks are shattered[w] before
him.
7The LORD is good,[x]
a refuge in times of trouble.[y]
He cares for[z] those who trust in
him,[a]
8 but with an overwhelming
flood[b]
he will make an end of ⌊Nineveh⌋;
he will pursue his foes into
darkness.
9Whatever they plot[c] against the
LORD
he[a] will bring to an end;
trouble will not come a second
time.
10They will be entangled among
thorns[d]
and drunk[e] from their wine;
they will be consumed like dry
stubble.[b][f]
11From you, ⌊O Nineveh,⌋ has one
come forth
who plots evil against the LORD
and counsels wickedness.

12This is what the LORD says:

"Although they have allies and are
numerous,
they will be cut off[g] and pass
away.
Although I have afflicted you,
⌊O Judah,⌋
I will afflict you no more.[h]
13Now I will break their yoke[i] from
your neck
and tear your shackles away."[j]

14The LORD has given a command
concerning you, ⌊Nineveh⌋:
"You will have no descendants
to bear your name.[k]
I will destroy the carved images[l]
and cast idols
that are in the temple of your
gods.
I will prepare your grave,[m]
for you are vile."

1:1 [a] S Isa 13:1; 19:1; Jer 23:33-34 [b] S Ge 10:11; S Jer 50:18; Na 2:8; 3:7 [c] S Isa 1:1
1:2 [d] S Ex 20:5 [e] S Ge 4:24; S Dt 32:41; Ps 94:1 [f] S Dt 7:10
1:3 [g] S Ne 9:17 [h] S Ex 34:7 [i] S Ex 14:21; S 2Ki 2:1 [j] S Ps 50:3 [k] S 2Sa 22:10; S Ps 104:3
1:4 [l] S 2Sa 22:16 [m] S Ex 14:22 [n] S Isa 33:9
1:5 [o] S Ex 19:18; S Job 9:6 [p] S Mic 1:4 [q] S Joel 2:10 [r] S Eze 38:20
1:6 [s] S Ps 130:3 [t] S Eze 22:14 [u] S Ps 76:7 [v] S Isa 5:24-25; S 42:25; S Jer 10:10 [w] 1Ki 19:11
1:7 [x] S Jer 33:11 [y] S Jer 17:17 [z] S Ps 1:6 [a] S Ps 22:9
1:8 [b] S Isa 8:7; S Da 9:26
1:9 [c] S Hos 7:15
1:10 [d] S 2Sa 23:6 [e] S Isa 49:26 [f] S Isa 5:24; Mal 4:1
1:12 [g] S Isa 10:34 [h] Isa 54:6-8; S La 3:31-32
1:13 [i] S Isa 9:4 [j] S Job 12:18; S Ps 107:14
1:14 [k] S Isa 14:22 [l] Mic 5:13 [m] S Jer 28:8; Eze 32:22-23

[a] 9 Or *What do you foes plot against the LORD? / He* [b] 10 The meaning of the Hebrew for this verse is uncertain.

1:1 NINEVEH. Prophesying sometime between 663–612 B.C., Nahum predicts the downfall of Assyria's capital city, Nineveh (see the introduction). Nineveh had repented under Jonah's preaching more than 100 years earlier, but the people had returned to their idolatry, cruelty and oppression. The Assyrians had conquered the northern kingdom of Israel and were now plundering parts of Judah. Nahum comforts God's people by telling them that God would destroy the Assyrians; Nineveh's fall occurred in 612 B.C., when it was conquered by a coalition of the Babylonians, Medes and Scythians.

1:2 A JEALOUS AND AVENGING GOD. "Jealous" is used here in the sense of the Lord's zeal for the protection of his people (cf. Dt 4:24; 5:9). He would take revenge on those who opposed his word and kingdom by justly repaying them for their hostility and sins (see Dt 32:35,41).

1:3 THE LORD IS SLOW TO ANGER. God desires to give sinners time to repent (2Pe 3:9), but there is a limit to his kindness and patience; those who persist in wickedness will eventually encounter his wrath (cf. Ro 11:22).

1:9 PLOT AGAINST THE LORD. The Assyrians were plotting ways to destroy Jerusalem and Judah, but God would not allow their plans to be carried out.

[15]Look, there on the mountains,
the feet of one who brings good news,[n]
who proclaims peace![o]
Celebrate your festivals,[p] O Judah,
and fulfill your vows.
No more will the wicked invade you;[q]
they will be completely destroyed.

Nineveh to Fall

2 An attacker[r] advances against you, ⌞Nineveh⌟.
Guard the fortress,
watch the road,
brace yourselves,
marshal all your strength!

[2]The LORD will restore[s] the splendor[t] of Jacob
like the splendor of Israel,
though destroyers have laid them waste
and have ruined their vines.

[3]The shields of his soldiers are red;
the warriors are clad in scarlet.[u]
The metal on the chariots flashes
on the day they are made ready;
the spears of pine are brandished.[c]
[4]The chariots[v] storm through the streets,
rushing back and forth through the squares.
They look like flaming torches;
they dart about like lightning.

[5]He summons his picked troops,
yet they stumble[w] on their way.
They dash to the city wall;
the protective shield is put in place.
[6]The river gates[x] are thrown open
and the palace collapses.
[7]It is decreed[d] that ⌞the city⌟
be exiled and carried away.
Its slave girls moan[y] like doves
and beat upon their breasts.[z]
[8]Nineveh is like a pool,
and its water is draining away.
"Stop! Stop!" they cry,
but no one turns back.
[9]Plunder the silver!
Plunder the gold!
The supply is endless,
the wealth from all its treasures!
[10]She is pillaged, plundered, stripped!
Hearts melt,[a] knees give way,
bodies tremble, every face grows pale.[b]

[11]Where now is the lions' den,[c]
the place where they fed their young,
where the lion and lioness went,
and the cubs, with nothing to fear?
[12]The lion killed[d] enough for his cubs
and strangled the prey for his mate,
filling his lairs[e] with the kill
and his dens with the prey.[f]

[13]"I am against[g] you,"
declares the LORD Almighty.

1:15 [n]Isa 40:9; Ro 10:15 [o]S Isa 52:7; Ac 10:36 [p]Lev 23:2-4 [q]S Isa 52:1
2:1 [r]Jer 51:20
2:2 [s]S Eze 37:23 [t]Isa 60:15
2:3 [u]S Eze 23:14-15
2:4 [v]S Jer 4:13; S Eze 23:24
2:5 [w]Jer 46:12
2:6 [x]Isa 45:1; Na 3:13
2:7 [y]S Ge 8:8; S Isa 59:11 [z]Isa 32:12
2:10 [a]S Jos 2:11; S 7:5 [b]S Isa 29:22
2:11 [c]Isa 5:29
2:12 [d]S Jer 51:34 [e]S Jer 4:7 [f]S Isa 37:18
2:13 [g]Isa 10:5-13; S Jer 21:13; Na 3:5

[c] 3 Hebrew; Septuagint and Syriac / *the horsemen rush to and fro* [d] 7 The meaning of the Hebrew for this word is uncertain.

1:15 GOOD NEWS. This passage parallels Isa 52:7 (see note there). (1) The good news for Judah was that the Assyrians would be completely destroyed so they could no longer attack their cities. (2) Likewise, NT preachers bring the good news of deliverance from sin's bondage and Satan's power through faith in the Lord Jesus Christ (Ro 10:15). At an appointed time in the future, sickness, sorrow, the ungodly world and Satan himself will be completely destroyed (see Rev 19—21).

2:1–13 AN ATTACKER. This chapter gives a detailed prediction of the attack on and the destruction of Nineveh by the Babylonian coalition in 612 B.C.

2:3 SHIELDS OF HIS SOLDIERS. The appearance of the attackers (v. 1) would be fearsome.

2:5 HE SUMMONS. "He" is probably the Assyrian king, summoning his soldiers to resist the attackers.

2:6 THE RIVER GATES. These gates apparently are the flood gates or dams that controlled the Khoser River, which ran through the city. They may have been closed to gather a large body of water and then released to damage the walls of the city.

2:8 ITS WATER IS DRAINING AWAY. Some commentators see a vivid picture here of people fleeing from the city, like water draining from a pool.

2:11–12 THE LIONS' DEN. The Assyrians had mercilessly plundered other nations as a lion kills its prey. They had had no compassion or mercy for other people; now they themselves would be plundered and killed (v. 10). Jesus articulates this principle when he said, "all who draw the sword will die by the sword" (Mt 26:52; cf. Rev 13:10).

2:13 I AM AGAINST YOU. God himself stood against Nineveh. Their brutality, cruelty and inhumane atrocities had been so great that the almighty God of the universe declared war against

"I will burn up your chariots in
smoke,[h]
and the sword[i] will devour
your young lions.
I will leave you no prey on the
earth.
The voices of your messengers
will no longer be heard."[j]

Woe to Nineveh

3 Woe to the city of blood,[k]
full of lies,[l]
full of plunder,
never without victims!
2The crack of whips,
the clatter of wheels,
galloping horses
and jolting chariots!
3Charging cavalry,
flashing swords
and glittering spears!
Many casualties,
piles of dead,
bodies without number,
people stumbling over the
corpses[m]—
4all because of the wanton lust of a
harlot,
alluring, the mistress of
sorceries,[n]
who enslaved nations by her
prostitution[o]
and peoples by her witchcraft.

5"I am against[p] you," declares the
LORD Almighty.
"I will lift your skirts[q] over
your face.
I will show the nations your
nakedness[r]
and the kingdoms your shame.
6I will pelt you with filth,[s]
I will treat you with contempt[t]
and make you a spectacle.[u]
7All who see you will flee[v] from
you and say,
'Nineveh[w] is in ruins[x]—who
will mourn for her?'[y]
Where can I find anyone to
comfort[z] you?"

8Are you better than[a] Thebes,[e][b]
situated on the Nile,[c]
with water around her?
The river was her defense,
the waters her wall.
9Cush[f][d] and Egypt were her
boundless strength;
Put[e] and Libya[f] were among
her allies.
10Yet she was taken captive[g]
and went into exile.
Her infants were dashed[h] to
pieces
at the head of every street.
Lots[i] were cast for her nobles,
and all her great men were put
in chains.[j]
11You too will become drunk;[k]
you will go into hiding[l]
and seek refuge from the enemy.

12All your fortresses are like fig
trees
with their first ripe fruit;[m]
when they are shaken,
the figs[n] fall into the mouth of
the eater.
13Look at your troops—
they are all women![o]
The gates[p] of your land
are wide open to your enemies;
fire has consumed their bars.[q]

14Draw water for the siege,[r]
strengthen your defenses![s]
Work the clay,

2:13 [h]Ps 46:9 [i]S 2Sa 2:26 [j]S Mic 5:6
3:1 [k]S Eze 22:2; S Mic 3:10 [l]Ps 12:2
3:3 [m]2Ki 19:35; Isa 34:3; Jer 47:3
3:4 [n]S Isa 47:9 [o]S Isa 23:17; Eze 16:25-29
3:5 [p]S Na 2:13 [q]S Isa 20:4; Jer 13:22 [r]S Isa 47:3
3:6 [s]S Ex 29:14; S Job 9:31 [t]S 1Sa 2:30; S Jer 51:37 [u]Isa 14:16
3:7 [v]S Isa 13:14; S 31:9 [w]S Na 1:1 [x]S Job 3:14 [y]S Jer 15:5 [z]S Isa 51:19
3:8 [a]Am 6:2 [b]S Jer 46:25 [c]Isa 19:6-9
3:9 [d]S Ge 10:6; S 2Ch 12:3 [e]S Eze 27:10 [f]Eze 30:5
3:10 [g]S Isa 20:4 [h]S 2Ki 8:12; S Isa 13:16; Hos 13:16 [i]S Job 6:27; S Eze 24:6 [j]S Jer 40:1
3:11 [k]S Isa 49:26 [l]S Isa 2:10
3:12 [m]S SS 2:13 [n]S Isa 28:4
3:13 [o]S Isa 19:16 [p]S Na 2:6 [q]S Isa 45:2
3:14 [r]S 2Ch 32:4 [s]Na 2:1

[e]8 Hebrew *No Amon* [f]9 That is, the upper Nile region

them. The time for their repentance was past; they would now receive the torture and grief they deserved (cf. Rev 18:6–8).

3:1 THE CITY OF BLOOD. Nineveh is called "the city of blood" because she had cruelly massacred large numbers of conquered peoples.

3:4 PROSTITUTION ... WITCHCRAFT. Sin never exists in isolation. Not only were the Assyrians brutally cruel, but they were also extremely immoral. (1) Externally Nineveh appeared attractive, but internally she was full of cult prostitution, degrading immorality and sensual activity. The city was also given over to witchcraft, black magic and spiritism; demons and evil spirits controlled the people's lives. (2) The relationship between these two elements is clear. Those who give themselves over to sin and immorality are opening up their lives to being controlled by demonic spirits.

3:5 I AM AGAINST YOU. Because of Nineveh's great sin, God himself would personally expose the depravity of its residents and destroy them. No power on earth can protect a nation that God has determined to oppose. When sin reaches a certain level in any society, God will expose the people to shame by bringing down all their means of security; such a society will collapse.

3:8 ARE YOU BETTER THAN THEBES. If Nineveh thought it was invincible, it should remember how God had brought down other great cities, such as the city of Thebes in Egypt, conquered by the Assyrians in 663 B.C.

tread the mortar,
repair the brickwork!
15There the fire[t] will devour you;
the sword[u] will cut you down
and, like grasshoppers, consume you.
Multiply like grasshoppers,
multiply like locusts![v]
16You have increased the number of your merchants
till they are more than the stars of the sky,
but like locusts[w] they strip the land
and then fly away.
17Your guards are like locusts,[x]
your officials like swarms of locusts
that settle in the walls on a cold day—
but when the sun appears they fly away,
and no one knows where.
18O king of Assyria, your shepherds[g] slumber;[y]
your nobles lie down to rest.[z]
Your people are scattered[a] on the mountains
with no one to gather them.
19Nothing can heal your wound;[b]
your injury is fatal.
Everyone who hears the news about you
claps his hands[c] at your fall,
for who has not felt
your endless cruelty?[d]

3:15 [t] S Isa 27:1 [u] S 2Sa 2:26 [v] S Jer 51:14; S Joel 1:4 3:16 [w] S Ex 10:13 3:17 [x] Jer 51:27 3:18 [y] Ps 76:5-6; S Jer 25:27 [z] Isa 56:10 [a] S 1Ki 22:17 3:19 [b] S Jer 30:13; S Mic 1:9 [c] S Job 27:23; S La 2:15; Zep 2:15 [d] Isa 37:18

[g] 18 Or *rulers*

3:19 NOTHING CAN HEAL YOUR WOUND. Nineveh would be destroyed and never again rebuilt. After the city fell in 612 B.C., it became a desolate area for animals and birds (see Zep 2:13–15).

HABAKKUK

Outline

Introduction (1:1)

I. The Questions of Habakkuk (1:2—2:20)
   A. Question 1: How Can God Allow Wicked Judah To Go Unpunished? (1:2–4)
   B. Answer 1: God Will Use Babylon to Punish Judah (1:5–11)
   C. Question 2: How Can God Use a More Wicked Nation Than Judah As the Instrument of His Judgment? (1:12—2:1)
   D. Answer 2: God Will Also Judge Babylon (2:2–20)
      1. Introduction of the Answer (2:2–3)
      2. Sins of Babylon (2:4–5)
      3. Series of Five Woes to Babylon (2:6–19)
      4. The Lord of the Whole Earth (2:20)

II. The Song of Habakkuk (3:1–19)
   A. Habakkuk's Prayer for Mercy (3:1–2)
   B. The Power of the Lord (3:3–7)
   C. The Saving Acts of the Lord (3:8–15)
   D. Habakkuk's Unwavering Faith (3:16–19)

Author: Habakkuk

Theme: Living By Faith

Date of Writing: c. 606 B.C.

Background

The author of this book identifies himself as "Habakkuk the prophet" (1:1; 3:1). Otherwise he gives no personal or family background, nor does his name (which means "embrace") appear elsewhere in the Scriptures. Habakkuk's reference to "the director of music" (3:19) suggests that he may have also been a Levite and a musician in Jerusalem.

Unlike other OT prophets, Habakkuk does not date his prophecy by referring to contemporary kings. However, the fact that he was perplexed about God using the Babylonians as an instrument of his judgment against Judah suggests a time when Babylon was already a world power and an invasion of Judah was imminent (c. 608–598 B.C.). Nebuchadnezzar defeated the Egyptians at the battle of Carchemish (605 B.C.), the last strong nation to oppose Babylonian expansion. If the description of the Babylonian army in 1:6–11 refers to the Babylonian march towards Carchemish, as many interpret it, then the date for Habakkuk's prophecy is c. 606–605 B.C., during the early years of Judah's King Jehoiakim.

The results of Babylon's rise to world power were devastating for apostate Judah (see 2Ki 24—25). As Nebuchadnezzar was returning from Egypt, he invaded Judah and took a significant number of captives to Babylon, among whom were Daniel and his three friends (605 B.C.). In 597 B.C. the Babylonian forces again invaded Jerusalem, ransacked the temple and took 10,000 captives back to Babylon, among whom was the prophet Ezekiel. When King Zedekiah tried to free Judah from Babylonian control 11 years later (586 B.C.), Nebuchadnezzar angrily laid siege to Jerusalem, burned the temple, totally destroyed the city and brought back to Babylon as captives most of the surviving inhabitants. Habakkuk probably lived through most or all of this time of Judah's judgment.

Purpose

Unlike his contemporary, Jeremiah, Habakkuk does not prophesy to backslidden Judah; he writes instead to help the godly remnant in Judah comprehend God's ways with regard to their sinful nation and its approaching judgment. Having himself wrestled with the profoundly disturbing problem of God using a deplorably wicked people like the Babylonians to swallow up his people in judgment (1:6–13), Habakkuk assures fellow believers that God will deal with all wickedness at the appointed time. In the meantime, "the righteous will live by his faith" (2:4) and not by his understanding, and will "rejoice in the LORD," in God his Savior (3:18).

Survey

Chs. 1—2 constitute Habakkuk's perplexing questions about God's ways and the answers God gave to him. Having seen so much wickedness and idolatry in Judah, his first question was how God could allow his rebellious people to get away with so much sin without being punished. God answered by showing the prophet that he would soon be using the Babylonians to punish the nation of Judah. Habakkuk's second question followed immediately: how could God allow a nation even more wicked and cruel than Judah to punish her? God answered by assuring the prophet that a day of reckoning would also come for the Babylonians. Throughout the entire book, Habakkuk expresses his faith in God's sovereignty and in the certainty that God is just in all his ways. The revelation of God's love for the righteous and his purpose to destroy wicked Babylon evoked a prophetic hymn of praise and promise concerning salvation in Zion (ch. 3).

Special Features

Five major features characterize the prophecy of Habakkuk. (1) Rather than prophesying to apostate Judah, the book records from the prophet's personal journal his conversations with God and subsequent prophetic revelation. (2) It contains at least three distinct literary forms: "dialogue" between the prophet and God (1:2—2:5), classic "prophetic woes" (2:6–20) and a prophetic song (ch. 3)—all with vigorous diction and graphic metaphors. (3) The prophet manifests three characteristics in the midst of adverse times: honest inquiry of the Lord (ch. 1), unshakable faith (2:4; 3:18–19) and concern for revival (3:2). (4) The prophet's vision of God in ch. 3 is one of the loftiest in the Bible, reminiscent of the theophany to the Israelites at Mount Sinai; other memorable passages in Habakkuk are 1:5; 2:3–4,20; 3:2,17–19. (5) No prophet in the OT is more eloquent on the issue of faith than Habakkuk—not only in his declaration that "the righteous will live by his faith" (2:4), but also in his personal testimony (3:17–19).

New Testament Fulfillment

Habakkuk's declaration that the righteous will live by faith (2:4) is the key OT text used by Paul in his theology of justification by faith; the apostle of faith quotes this verse both in Ro 1:17 and Gal 3:11 (cf. also Heb 10:37–38).

Reading Habakkuk

In order to read the entire Old Testament in one year, the book of Habakkuk should be read in 1 day: ☐ Habakkuk

NOTES

1 The oracle[a] that Habakkuk the prophet received.

Habakkuk's Complaint

2How long,[b] O LORD, must I call
for help,
but you do not listen?[c]
Or cry out to you, "Violence!"
but you do not save?[d]
3Why do you make me look at
injustice?
Why do you tolerate[e] wrong?[f]
Destruction and violence[g] are
before me;
there is strife,[h] and conflict
abounds.
4Therefore the law[i] is paralyzed,
and justice never prevails.
The wicked hem in the righteous,
so that justice[j] is perverted.[k]

The LORD's Answer

5"Look at the nations and watch—
and be utterly amazed.[l]
For I am going to do something in
your days
that you would not believe,
even if you were told.[m]
6I am raising up the
Babylonians,[a][n]
that ruthless and impetuous
people,
who sweep across the whole
earth[o]
to seize dwelling places not their
own.[p]
7They are a feared and dreaded
people;[q]
they are a law to themselves
and promote their own honor.
8Their horses are swifter[r] than
leopards,
fiercer than wolves[s] at dusk.
Their cavalry gallops headlong;
their horsemen come from afar.
They fly like a vulture swooping to
devour;
9 they all come bent on violence.
Their hordes[b] advance like a
desert wind
and gather prisoners[t] like
sand.
10They deride kings
and scoff at rulers.[u]
They laugh at all fortified cities;
they build earthen ramps[v] and
capture them.
11Then they sweep past like the
wind[w] and go on—
guilty men, whose own strength
is their god."[x]

Habakkuk's Second Complaint

12O LORD, are you not from
everlasting?[y]
My God, my Holy One,[z] we will
not die.[a]
O LORD, you have appointed[b] them
to execute judgment;
O Rock,[c] you have ordained
them to punish.
13Your eyes are too pure[d] to look
on evil;

1:1 [a] S Na 1:1 **1:2** [b] S Ps 6:3 [c] Ps 13:1-2; 22:1-2 [d] Jer 14:9; Zec 1:12 **1:3** [e] ver 13 [f] S Job 9:23 [g] Jer 20:8 [h] S Ps 55:9 **1:4** [i] Ps 119:126 [j] S Isa 29:21 [k] S Job 19:7; S Isa 1:23; 5:20; S Eze 9:9 **1:5** [l] S Isa 29:9 [m] Ac 13:41* **1:6** [n] S Dt 28:49; S 2Ki 24:2 [o] Rev 20:9 [p] S Jer 13:20; S 21:7 **1:7** [q] Isa 18:7; Jer 39:5-9 **1:8** [r] S Jer 4:13 [s] S Ge 49:27 **1:9** [t] Hab 2:5 **1:10** [u] S 2Ch 36:6 [v] S Jer 33:4 **1:11** [w] Jer 4:11-12 [x] S Da 4:30 **1:12** [y] S Ge 21:33 [z] Isa 31:1; 37:23 [a] Ps 118:17 [b] Isa 10:6 [c] S Ge 49:24; S Ex 33:22 **1:13** [d] Ps 18:26

[a] *6* Or *Chaldeans* [b] *9* The meaning of the Hebrew for this word is uncertain.

1:1 HABAKKUK. Habakkuk prophesied to Judah between the defeat of the Assyrians at Nineveh and the invasion of Jerusalem by the Babylonians (605–597 B.C.; see the introduction to Habakkuk). (1) The book is unique in that it is not a prophecy addressed directly to Israel, but rather a dialogue between the prophet and God. Habakkuk asked the question: "Why doesn't God do something about the evil so dominant in Judah?" God responded by stating that he was sending the Babylonians to punish Judah. (2) This answer only confused the prophet more, and he wanted to know, "Why does God punish his people with a nation more wicked than they?" In the end, Habakkuk learned to trust God and to live by faith in God's way, regardless of the circumstances.

1:2–4 HOW LONG ... MUST I CALL FOR HELP. Habakkuk had been praying to God to stop the wrong he saw among the covenant people; yet God seemed to be doing nothing but tolerating violence, injustice and the destruction of the righteous. His questions dealt with the age-old theme: "Why does God wait so long to punish evil?" and "Why are our prayers generally not answered quickly?" Note, however, that these complaints came out of a heart of faith in a righteous God.

1:5–11 I AM GOING TO DO SOMETHING. God answered Habakkuk by telling him he already had plans to chastise Judah for its sins. He would use the ruthless and pagan Babylonians to correct Judah. That God would use such a wicked, pagan people to punish Judah was astonishing to the prophet and unbelievable to God's people (see next note).

1:12 ARE YOU NOT FROM EVERLASTING? Habakkuk was appalled that God would use such a wicked nation to attack Judah, yet he was confident that God would not allow them to annihilate his own people and by that destruction cancel his redemptive purpose for the human race.

1:13 YOUR EYES ARE TOO PURE. This verse does not mean that God does not see evil, for he observes everything; he is omniscient (see article on THE ATTRIBUTES OF GOD, p. 882). God does not, however, look on evil to condone or tolerate it. What perplexed Habakkuk was this: God's use

you cannot tolerate wrong.[e]
Why then do you tolerate[f] the
treacherous?[g]
Why are you silent while the
wicked
swallow up those more righteous
than themselves?[h]
14You have made men like fish in
the sea,
like sea creatures that have no
ruler.
15The wicked[i] foe pulls all of them
up with hooks,[j]
he catches them in his net,[k]
he gathers them up in his dragnet;
and so he rejoices and is glad.
16Therefore he sacrifices to his net
and burns incense[l] to his
dragnet,
for by his net he lives in luxury
and enjoys the choicest food.
17Is he to keep on emptying his net,
destroying nations without
mercy?[m]

2 I will stand at my watch[n]
and station myself on the
ramparts;[o]
I will look to see what he will
say[p] to me,
and what answer I am to give to
this complaint.[c][q]

The LORD*'s Answer*

2Then the LORD replied:

"Write[r] down the revelation
and make it plain on tablets
so that a herald[d] may run with
it.
3For the revelation awaits an
appointed time;[s]
it speaks of the end[t]
and will not prove false.
Though it linger, wait[u] for it;
it[e] will certainly come and will
not delay.[v]

4"See, he is puffed up;
his desires are not upright—
but the righteous[w] will live by
his faith[f][x]—
5indeed, wine[y] betrays him;
he is arrogant[z] and never at
rest.
Because he is as greedy as the
grave[g]
and like death is never
satisfied,[a]
he gathers to himself all the
nations
and takes captive[b] all the
peoples.

6"Will not all of them taunt[c] him
with ridicule and scorn, saying,

" 'Woe to him who piles up stolen
goods
and makes himself wealthy by
extortion![d]
How long must this go on?'
7Will not your debtors[h] suddenly
arise?

1:13 [e]S La 3:34-36 [f]ver 3 [g]S Ps 25:3 [h]S Job 21:7 **1:15** [i]Jer 5:26 [j]S Isa 19:8 [k]S Job 18:8; Jer 16:16 **1:16** [l]Jer 44:8 **1:17** [m]S Isa 14:6; 19:8 **2:1** [n]S Isa 21:8 [o]S Ps 48:13 [p]Ps 85:8 [q]S Ps 5:3; S Eze 3:17 **2:2** [r]S Isa 30:8; S Jer 36:2; S Eze 24:2; S Ro 4:24; Rev 1:19 **2:3** [s]Da 11:27 [t]Da 8:17 [u]S Ps 27:14 [v]S Eze 12:25 **2:4** [w]S Eze 18:9 [x]Ro 1:17*; Gal 3:11*; Heb 10:37-38* **2:5** [y]S Pr 20:1 [z]S Isa 2:11 [a]S Pr 27:20; S 30:15-16 [b]Hab 1:9 **2:6** [c]S Isa 14:4 [d]Am 2:8

[c]1 Or *and what to answer when I am rebuked* [d]2 Or *so that whoever reads it* [e]3 Or *Though he linger, wait for him; / he* [f]4 Or *faithfulness* [g]5 Hebrew *Sheol* [h]7 Or *creditors*

of the wicked Babylonians made it seem like he was tolerating *their* sin while punishing Judah, who, in spite of all their evil, was still a more righteous nation than Babylon.

2:2–20 WRITE DOWN THE REVELATION. In ch. 2 God gave Habakkuk an answer to his questions about evil's dominance in the world and the possible annihilation of the righteous. The Lord stated that a time was coming when all the wicked would be destroyed and the only people not shaken would be the righteous, those who are related to God by their faith (see v. 4, note).

2:3 AWAITS AN APPOINTED TIME. The final solution to Habakkuk's problem would come only in the future, at God's "appointed time." (1) There would be a termination point to wickedness in the world. God's faithful people had to "wait for it," even though it seemed to take such a long time. (2) Like Habakkuk, we must wait for the Lord's righteous intervention at the end of this age. Ultimately, Christ will take away the righteous from the earth and bring destruction on all evil (see 1Th 4:16–17; see article on THE RAPTURE, p. 1864).

2:4 THE RIGHTEOUS WILL LIVE BY HIS FAITH. It is "the righteous" who at the end will emerge victorious. (1) The righteous are contrasted with the proud and the ungodly, whose lives are not upright. The hearts of the righteous are turned to God, and they want to be his children, to have close fellowship with him and to obey his will. (2) The righteous must live in this world by faith in God. Here "faith" means a steadfast trust in God that his ways are right, a personal loyalty to him as Savior and Lord, and a moral steadfastness to follow his ways. Paul develops this theme in Ro 1:17 and Gal 3:11 (cf. Heb 10:38; see article on FAITH AND GRACE, p. 1720).

2:6–20 WOE TO HIM. These verses pronounce woes of judgment on any whose "desires are not upright" (v. 4). Such people will be judged because of their aggression (vv. 6–8), injustice (vv. 9–11), violence and crime (vv. 12–14), immorality (vv. 15–17) and idolatry (vv. 18–20).

Will they not wake up and make
you tremble?
Then you will become their
victim.[e]
8Because you have plundered many
nations,
the peoples who are left will
plunder you.[f]
For you have shed man's blood;[g]
you have destroyed lands and
cities and everyone in
them.[h]

9"Woe to him who builds[i] his
realm by unjust gain[j]
to set his nest[k] on high,
to escape the clutches of ruin!
10You have plotted the ruin[l] of
many peoples,
shaming[m] your own house and
forfeiting your life.
11The stones[n] of the wall will cry
out,
and the beams of the woodwork
will echo it.

12"Woe to him who builds a city with
bloodshed[o]
and establishes a town by crime!
13Has not the LORD Almighty
determined
that the people's labor is only
fuel for the fire,[p]
that the nations exhaust
themselves for nothing?[q]
14For the earth will be filled with
the knowledge of the
glory[r] of the LORD,
as the waters cover the sea.[s]

15"Woe to him who gives drink[t] to
his neighbors,
pouring it from the wineskin till
they are drunk,
so that he can gaze on their
naked bodies.
16You will be filled with shame[u]
instead of glory.[v]
Now it is your turn! Drink[w] and
be exposed[i]![x]
The cup[y] from the LORD's right
hand is coming around to
you,
and disgrace will cover your
glory.
17The violence[z] you have done to
Lebanon will overwhelm
you,
and your destruction of animals
will terrify you.[a]
For you have shed man's blood;[b]
you have destroyed lands and
cities and everyone in them.

18"Of what value[c] is an idol,[d] since
a man has carved it?
Or an image[e] that teaches lies?
For he who makes it trusts in his
own creation;
he makes idols that cannot
speak.[f]
19Woe to him who says to wood,
'Come to life!'
Or to lifeless stone, 'Wake up!'[g]
Can it give guidance?
It is covered with gold and
silver;[h]
there is no breath in it.[i]
20But the LORD is in his holy
temple;[j]
let all the earth be silent[k]
before him."

Habakkuk's Prayer

3 A prayer of Habakkuk the prophet.
On *shigionoth*.[j][l]

2LORD, I have heard[m] of your fame;
I stand in awe[n] of your deeds,
O LORD.[o]
Renew[p] them in our day,
in our time make them known;
in wrath remember mercy.[q]

3God came from Teman,[r]

2:7 [e]S Pr 29:1 **2:8** [f]Isa 33:1; Jer 50:17-18; S Ob 1:15; Zec 2:8-9 [g]ver 17 [h]S Eze 39:10 **2:9** [i]S Jer 22:13 [j]S Jer 51:13 [k]S Job 39:27; S Isa 10:14 **2:10** [l]Jer 26:19 [m]ver 16; S Na 3:6 **2:11** [n]S Jos 24:27; Zec 5:4; Lk 19:40 **2:12** [o]S Eze 22:2; S Mic 3:10 **2:13** [p]Isa 50:11 [q]S Isa 47:13 **2:14** [r]S Ex 16:7; S Nu 14:21 [s]S Isa 11:9 **2:15** [t]S Pr 23:20 **2:16** [u]S ver 10 [v]S Eze 23:32-34; Hos 4:7 [w]S Lev 10:9 [x]S La 4:21 [y]S Ps 16:5; S Isa 51:22 **2:17** [z]S Jer 51:35 [a]S Jer 50:15 [b]ver 8 **2:18** [c]S 1Sa 12:21 [d]S Jdg 10:14; S Isa 40:19; S Jer 5:21; S 14:22 [e]S Lev 26:1 [f]Ps 115:4-5; Jer 10:14; 1Co 12:2 **2:19** [g]1Ki 18:27 [h]S Jer 10:4 [i]S Da 5:4,23; S Hos 4:12 **2:20** [j]S Ps 11:4 [k]S Isa 41:1 **3:1** [l]Ps 7 Title **3:2** [m]S Job 26:14; Ps 44:1 [n]S Ps 119:120 [o]S Ps 90:16 [p]Ps 85:6 [q]Isa 54:8 **3:3** [r]S Ge 36:11, 15

i *16* Masoretic Text; Dead Sea Scrolls, Aquila, Vulgate and Syriac (see also Septuagint) *and stagger* j *1* Probably a literary or musical term

3:1–19 A PRAYER. This chapter is Habakkuk's response to God's answer of ch. 2. In the midst of the world's sin and God's judgment, he has learned to live by faith in God and to trust in the wisdom of God's ways.

3:2 RENEW THEM IN OUR DAY. Habakkuk knew God's people had sinned and would experience his judgment. In this situation he made two petitions. (1) He prayed for God to come among his people with a fresh manifestation of his power. Habakkuk knew that God's people would not survive if the Lord did not intervene in their lives with an outpouring of his grace and Spirit; only then would there be true spiritual life among them. (2) Habakkuk prayed that in times of distress for the Lord's people, God would remember to be merciful; without mercy his people would not be sustained. As the foundation of the church is being shaken today and trouble seems to be on every hand, we too need to plead with the Lord to manifest himself, his mercy and his power anew, in order that life and renewal might come to his people.

the Holy One[s] from Mount
Paran.[t] *Selah*[k]
Zep 3:19-20
His glory covered the heavens[u]
and his praise filled the earth.[v]
4His splendor was like the
sunrise;[w]
rays flashed from his hand,
where his power[x] was hidden.
5Plague[y] went before him;
pestilence followed his steps.
6He stood, and shook the earth;
he looked, and made the nations
tremble.
The ancient mountains crumbled[z]
and the age-old hills[a]
collapsed.[b]
His ways are eternal.[c]
7I saw the tents of Cushan in
distress,
the dwellings of Midian[d] in
anguish.[e]

8Were you angry with the rivers,[f]
O LORD?
Was your wrath against the
streams?
Did you rage against the sea[g]
when you rode with your horses
and your victorious chariots?[h]
9You uncovered your bow,
you called for many arrows.[i]
Selah
You split the earth with rivers;
10 the mountains saw you and
writhed.[j]
Torrents of water swept by;
the deep roared[k]
and lifted its waves[l] on high.

11Sun and moon stood still[m] in the
heavens
at the glint of your flying
arrows,[n]
at the lightning[o] of your
flashing spear.
12In wrath you strode through the
earth
and in anger you threshed[p] the
nations.

13You came out[q] to deliver[r] your
people,
to save your anointed[s] one.
You crushed[t] the leader of the
land of wickedness,
you stripped him from head to
foot. *Selah*
14With his own spear you pierced his
head
when his warriors stormed out
to scatter us,[u]
gloating as though about to devour
the wretched[v] who were in
hiding.
15You trampled the sea[w] with your
horses,
churning the great waters.[x]

16I heard and my heart pounded,
my lips quivered at the sound;
decay crept into my bones,
and my legs trembled.[y]
Yet I will wait patiently[z] for the
day of calamity
to come on the nation invading
us.
17Though the fig tree does not bud
and there are no grapes on the
vines,
though the olive crop fails
and the fields produce no food,[a]
though there are no sheep in the
pen
and no cattle in the stalls,[b]
18yet I will rejoice in the LORD,[c]
I will be joyful in God my
Savior.[d]

19The Sovereign LORD is my
strength;[e]
he makes my feet like the feet
of a deer,
he enables me to go on the
heights.[f]

For the director of music. On my stringed instruments.

3:3 [s]S Isa 31:1 [t]S Nu 10:12 [u]S Ps 8:1 [v]Ps 48:10 3:4 [w]S Isa 18:4 [x]S Job 9:6 3:5 [y]S Lev 26:25 3:6 [z]S Ps 46:2 [a]Ge 49:26 [b]S Ex 19:18; Ps 18:7; 114:1-6 [c]S Ge 21:33 3:7 [d]S Ge 25:2; S Nu 25:15; Jdg 7:24-25 [e]Ex 15:14 3:8 [f]S Ex 7:20 [g]S Ps 77:16 [h]S 2Ki 2:11; S Ps 68:17 3:9 [i]S Dt 32:23; Ps 7:12-13 3:10 [j]S Ps 77:16 [k]Ps 98:7 [l]S Ps 93:3 3:11 [m]Jos 10:13 [n]Ps 18:14 [o]S Ps 144:6; Zec 9:14 3:12 [p]S Isa 41:15 3:13 [q]S Ex 13:21 [r]S Ps 20:6; S 28:8 [s]S 2Sa 23:1 [t]Ps 68:21; 110:6 3:14 [u]Jdg 7:22 [v]Ps 64:2-5 3:15 [w]S Job 9:8 [x]Ex 15:8 3:16 [y]S Job 4:14 [z]S Ps 37:7 3:17 [a]Joel 1:10-12,18 [b]Jer 5:17 3:18 [c]Ps 97:12; S Isa 61:10; Php 4:4 [d]S Ex 15:2; S Lk 1:47 3:19 [e]S Dt 33:29; Ps 46:1-5 [f]S Dt 32:13; Ps 18:33

[k]3 A word of uncertain meaning; possibly a musical term; also in verses 9 and 13

3:3–16 GOD CAME. In these verses Habakkuk refers to the time God delivered his people from Egypt (see Ex 14). The same God who came with salvation in the past would come again in all his glory. All who were waiting for that coming would live and see his triumph over empires and nations.

3:18–19 I WILL REJOICE IN THE LORD. Habakkuk testifies that he served God not for what he gave, but because he was God. Even in the midst of God's judgment on Judah (v. 16), Habakkuk chose to rejoice in the Lord; God would be his Savior and an unfailing source of strength. He knew beyond a doubt that a righteous remnant would survive the Babylonian invasion, and he proclaimed with confidence the ultimate victory of all who live by faith in God (cf. 2:4).

ZEPHANIAH

Outline

Introduction (1:1)

- I. Judgment and the Day of the Lord (1:2—3:8)
  - A. Judgment on the Whole Earth (1:2–3)
  - B. Judgment Against the People of Judah (1:4–18)
    - 1. Description of Judah's Sins (1:4–9)
    - 2. Warning to Jerusalem (1:10–13)
    - 3. The Great Day of the Lord (1:14–18)
  - C. Call to Repentance (2:1–3)
  - D. Judgment Against the Nations (2:4–15)
    - 1. The Philistines (2:4–7)
    - 2. The Ammonites and Moabites (2:8–11)
    - 3. The Cushites (2:12)
    - 4. The Assyrians (2:13–15)
  - E. Judgment Against Jerusalem (3:1–7)
    - 1. Sins of Jerusalem (3:1–4)
    - 2. God's Justice Against Jerusalem (3:5–7)
  - F. Judgment on the Whole Earth (3:8)
- II. Salvation and the Day of the Lord (3:9–20)
  - A. The Remnant Restored and Jerusalem Purified (3:9–13)
  - B. The Jubilant People with God in Their Midst (3:14–17)
  - C. Final Promises Concerning Restoration (3:18–20)

Author: Zephaniah

Theme: The Day of the Lord

Date of Writing: c. 630 B.C.

Background

Zephaniah, whose name means "the LORD hides," was a great-great-grandson of King Hezekiah and prophesied during the reign of Josiah (639–609 B.C.), Judah's last godly ruler (1:1). His reference to Jerusalem as "this place" (1:4), as well as his precise description of its topography and its sins, indicates that he resided in the capital. Being a descendant of royalty and related to King Josiah meant that he had access to the royal palace. Understandably, his prophecies focused on the word of the Lord for Judah and the nations.

The sins that Zephaniah charged against Jerusalem and Judah (1:4–13; 3:1–7) indicate that he prophesied before Josiah's revival and reform, at a time when the terrible sins of Josiah's wicked predecessors (Manasseh and Amon) were still rampant in society. It was not until the 12th year of Josiah's reign (i.e., 627 B.C.) that the king set out to purge the nation of idolatry and to reinstitute the true worship of the Lord; eight years later he ordered the repair and purification of Solomon's temple, during which time a copy of the law of the Lord was discovered (cf. 2Ki 22:1–10). The description that Zephaniah gave of Judah's pathetic spiritual and moral condition must have been written about 630 B.C.. Most likely Zephaniah's prophetic preaching had a direct influence on the king and helped to inspire his reforms. A date of 630 B.C. is further indicated by Zephaniah's total lack of reference to Babylon as a power to be reckoned with on the international scene; Babylon began its rise to prominence with the ascendancy of Nabopolassar in 625 B.C.. However, Zephaniah did prophesy the destruction of mighty Assyria, an event that occurred in 612 B.C. with Nineveh's downfall. Jeremiah was a younger contemporary of Zephaniah.

Purpose

Zephaniah prophesied and wrote to warn Judah and Jerusalem of the impending ominous judgment of God called "the great day of the LORD" (1:14). The imminent application of this prophetic word was that apostate Judah would receive just retribution for her wickedness, as would the pagan nations around her, whom he listed by name. The far-distant dimension of the prophecy applies to the church and the world at the end of history. Zephaniah also wrote to encourage the godly that God would one day restore his people; then Judah would sing the praises of their just God, who was living in their midst.

Survey

For the most part, the book is a sober warning about the coming day of God's judgment for sin. Zephaniah saw a worldwide judgment coming for the sins of all humanity (1:2; 3:8), but he especially focused on the judgment coming on Judah for her sins (1:4–18; 3:1–7). Zephaniah made a prophetic appeal for the nation to repent and to seek the Lord in humility before the decree took effect (2:1–3); this national repentance happened in part during Josiah's revival (627–609 B.C.).

Zephaniah also prophesied coming judgment on five foreign nations: Philistia, Ammon, Moab, Cush and Assyria (2:4–15). After addressing again the sins of Jerusalem (3:1–7), the prophet predicted a time when God would regather, redeem and restore his people. They would shout for joy as true worshipers of the Lord God; he would be in their midst as a victorious warrior (3:9–20).

Special Features

Five major features characterize the book of Zephaniah. (1) Zephaniah is the only prophet to give an extended list of his ancestry, going back four generations to King Hezekiah. (2) It has the most extensive revelation in the OT about the future "day of the LORD." (3) It demonstrates that God's people need to be confronted by his warnings as well as comforted by his promises. (4) It contains a rather well-developed teaching about the faithful remnant that would be restored in the day of the Lord's visitation (3:9–20). (5) Zephaniah's revelation about the coming day of God's wrath for the wicked and the great day of salvation for his people contributed to the NT revelation about the end of time.

New Testament Fulfillment

Jesus may have alluded to Zephaniah twice (1:2–3, cf. Mt 13:40–42; 1:15, cf. Mt 24:29); both references are associated with Jesus' second coming. NT writers understood Zephaniah's message about the "day of the LORD" as a description of the eschatological events that begin with the great tribulation and conclude with Jesus' return to judge the living and the dead (compare 1:14 with Rev 6:17; 3:8 with Rev 16:1). Frequently the NT refers to Christ's second coming and the day of judgment as "the Day" (e.g., 1Co 3:13; cf. 2Ti 1:12,18; 4:8).

Reading Zephaniah

In order to read the entire Old Testament in one year, the book of Zephaniah should be read in 1 day: ☐ Zephaniah

NOTES

1 The word of the LORD that came to Zephaniah son of Cushi, the son of Gedaliah, the son of Amariah, the son of Hezekiah, during the reign of Josiah[a] son of Amon[b] king of Judah:

Warning of Coming Destruction

2"I will sweep away everything
 from the face of the earth,"[c]
 declares the LORD.
3"I will sweep away both men and
 animals;[d]
 I will sweep away the birds of
 the air[e]
 and the fish of the sea.
The wicked will have only heaps of
 rubble[a]
 when I cut off man from the
 face of the earth,"[f]
 declares the LORD.[g]

Against Judah

4"I will stretch out my hand[h]
 against Judah
 and against all who live in
 Jerusalem.
I will cut off from this place every
 remnant of Baal,[i]
 the names of the pagan and the
 idolatrous priests[j]—
5those who bow down on the roofs
 to worship the starry host,[k]
those who bow down and swear by
 the LORD
 and who also swear by
 Molech,[b][l]
6those who turn back from
 following[m] the LORD
 and neither seek[n] the LORD nor
 inquire[o] of him.
7Be silent[p] before the Sovereign
 LORD,
 for the day of the LORD[q] is near.
The LORD has prepared a
 sacrifice;[r]
 he has consecrated those he has
 invited.
8On the day of the LORD's sacrifice
 I will punish[s] the princes
 and the king's sons[t]
and all those clad
 in foreign clothes.
9On that day I will punish
 all who avoid stepping on the
 threshold,[c][u]
who fill the temple of their gods
 with violence and deceit.[v]
10"On that day,[w]" declares the LORD,
 "a cry will go up from the Fish
 Gate,[x]
 wailing[y] from the New Quarter,
 and a loud crash from the hills.
11Wail,[z] you who live in the market
 district[d];
 all your merchants will be wiped
 out,
 all who trade with[e] silver will
 be ruined.[a]

1:1 [a] 2Ki 22:1; 2Ch 34:1-35:25 [b] S 1Ch 3:14 **1:2** [c] S Ge 6:7 **1:3** [d] Jer 50:3 [e] S Jer 4:25 [f] ver 18; S Hos 4:3 [g] S Eze 14:17 **1:4** [h] S Jer 6:12 [i] Mic 5:13; Zep 2:11 [j] S Jer 15:6; S Hos 10:5 **1:5** [k] S Jer 8:2 [l] S Lev 18:21; Jer 5:7 **1:6** [m] Isa 1:4; Jer 2:13 [n] S Isa 9:13 [o] S Hos 7:7 **1:7** [p] S Isa 41:1 [q] ver 14; Isa 13:6; S Eze 7:19; S Joel 3:14; S Am 5:18-20 [r] S Lev 3:9; S Jer 46:10 **1:8** [s] Isa 24:21 [t] Jer 39:6 **1:9** [u] 1Sa 5:5 [v] S Am 3:10 **1:10** [w] Isa 22:5 [x] S 2Ch 33:14 [y] S Am 5:16 **1:11** [z] Jas 5:1 [a] Hos 9:6

[a] *3* The meaning of the Hebrew for this line is uncertain. [b] *5* Hebrew *Malcam,* that is, Milcom [c] *9* See 1 Samuel 5:5. [d] *11* Or *the Mortar* [e] *11* Or *in*

1:1 ZEPHANIAH. Zephaniah prophesied during the reign of Josiah, king of Judah (640–609 B.C.). The nation was entangled in violence and idolatry, and scornfully indifferent to the Lord. His message to the nation was probably given before the reform movement led by Josiah and may have been a motivating force encouraging the king to call for renewed obedience to God and his law (see the introduction).

1:2–3 SWEEP AWAY EVERYTHING. Zephaniah begins by announcing God's coming judgment on the entire world. Because the majority of humankind will refuse to turn from their sins to the Lord, God has appointed a day when he will destroy all the wicked as well as the world itself; it will be a time of distress, anguish, trouble and ruin (v. 15; see article on THE GREAT TRIBULATION, p. 1456).

1:4 AGAINST JUDAH. Judah, God's people of Zephaniah's day, would soon experience God's wrath for turning from the Lord, worshiping other gods, and engaging in violence, corruption and deceit (vv. 4–9).

1:5 WORSHIP THE STARRY HOST. This form of idolatry is prevalent among us today in those who seek comfort or direction for their lives by astrological signs and horoscope readings (cf. Dt 4:19).

1:5 SWEAR BY THE LORD. Many in Judah were participating in other forms of religion while at the same time worshiping the Sovereign Lord; this mixture was both idolatrous and flagrantly evil. God will not tolerate those who claim to be his followers, and yet at the same time participate in idolatrous, sinful and immoral activity. Condemnation awaits all who fail to separate themselves as holy to the Lord (see article on SPIRITUAL SEPARATION FOR BELIEVERS, p. 1794).

1:7 THE DAY OF THE LORD. This prophecy applies first of all to Judah's destruction by the Babylonians in 605 B.C., and secondly to God's worldwide judgment on all nations at the end of time (cf. Isa 2:12; 13:6,9; Jer 46:10; Eze 13:5; Joel 1:15; 2:1; see Joel 1:15, note; Am 5:18, note). The latter day of wrath is yet to come (Ro 2:5), associated with the final return of Jesus Christ (Mt 24:29–33; see 1Th 5:2, note).

12At that time I will search
Jerusalem with lamps
and punish those who are
complacent,[b]
who are like wine left on its
dregs,[c]
who think, 'The LORD will do
nothing,[d]
either good or bad.'[e]
13Their wealth will be plundered,[f]
their houses demolished.
They will build houses
but not live in them;
they will plant vineyards
but not drink the wine.[g]

The Great Day of the LORD

14"The great day of the LORD[h] is
near[i]—
near and coming quickly.
Listen! The cry on the day of the
LORD will be bitter,
the shouting of the warrior
there.
15That day will be a day of wrath,
a day of distress and anguish,
a day of trouble and ruin,
a day of darkness[j] and gloom,
a day of clouds and blackness,[k]
16a day of trumpet and battle
cry[l]
against the fortified cities
and against the corner towers.[m]
17I will bring distress[n] on the
people
and they will walk like blind[o]
men,
because they have sinned
against the LORD.
Their blood will be poured out[p]
like dust
and their entrails like filth.[q]
18Neither their silver nor their
gold
will be able to save them
on the day of the LORD's
wrath.[r]
In the fire of his jealousy[s]
the whole world will be
consumed,[t]
for he will make a sudden end
of all who live in the earth.[u]"

2 Gather together,[v] gather
together,
O shameful[w] nation,
2before the appointed time arrives
and that day sweeps on like
chaff,[x]
before the fierce anger[y] of the
LORD comes upon you,
before the day of the LORD's
wrath[z] comes upon you.
3Seek[a] the LORD, all you humble of
the land,
you who do what he commands.
Seek righteousness,[b] seek
humility;[c]
perhaps you will be sheltered[d]
on the day of the LORD's anger.

Against Philistia

4Gaza[e] will be abandoned
and Ashkelon[f] left in ruins.
At midday Ashdod will be emptied
and Ekron uprooted.
5Woe to you who live by the sea,
O Kerethite[g] people;

1:12 [b] Am 6:1 [c] Jer 48:11 [d] S 2Ki 21:16; S Eze 8:12 [e] S Job 22:13
1:13 [f] S 2Ki 24:13; Jer 15:13 [g] Dt 28:30,39; La 5:2; S Am 5:11
1:14 [h] S ver 7; S Joel 1:15 [i] S Eze 7:7; S Da 7:13
1:15 [j] S 1Sa 2:9 [k] S Isa 22:5; Joel 2:2; Mk 13:24-25
1:16 [l] S Jer 4:19 [m] S Dt 28:52; S Isa 2:15; S Joel 2:1
1:17 [n] S Dt 28:52 [o] S Isa 59:10 [p] Ps 79:3 [q] S Ps 83:10
1:18 [r] S Job 20:20; S 40:11; S Jer 4:4; S Eze 7:19 [s] S Dt 29:20 [t] S ver 2-3; Zep 3:8 [u] S Ge 6:7; S Eze 7:11
2:1 [v] 2Ch 20:4; Joel 1:14 [w] S Jer 3:3; 6:15
2:2 [x] Isa 17:13; Hos 13:3 [y] S Jer 10:25; S La 4:11 [z] S Jer 4:4; S Eze 7:19
2:3 [a] S Am 5:6 [b] S Isa 1:17 [c] Ps 45:4 [d] Ps 57:1
2:4 [e] S Ge 10:19; S Am 1:6,7-8; Zec 9:5-7 [f] Jer 47:5
2:5 [g] S 1Sa 30:14

1:12 WILL DO NOTHING, EITHER GOOD OR BAD. Some in Judah had a deistic view of God (i.e., the view that God was not actively involved in the everyday affairs of people's lives); they believed that God would not punish sin among his people. (1) Those who had this attitude would fearfully discover on the day of judgment that God did indeed hold them accountable for those sins they refused to abandon. (2) We too need to know that God is not distant from or uninvolved in the affairs of humans; he will reward those who seek him and judge those who turn from him and follow evil (see Ro 2:5–11).

2:1–3 GATHER TOGETHER, O SHAMEFUL NATION. Zephaniah had declared the coming day of God's wrath upon Judah, a day that would not be canceled. The time and certainty of judgment had been set, and the nation had to be punished for its apostasy and sin. Nevertheless, God offered hope for those who repented before that day; the truly righteous would be sheltered by the Lord on the day of his fierce anger (see next note).

2:3 SEEK RIGHTEOUSNESS, SEEK HUMILITY. The prophet offers hope to those who had already turned to the Lord. He exhorted them to deepen their commitment to God and his ways; perhaps God would shelter them when he came to punish his people. They had to seek three things if they hoped to experience revival and renewed blessing from the Lord, three things equally essential today for NT believers. (1) First, they had to seek God himself. Their hearts were to be turned toward him with a deep desire to know and love him as their covenant Lord and protector (cf. Jer 29:13). (2) They had to seek righteousness according to God's Word as their way of life (cf. Isa 1:21; Am 5:24; Mt 6:33). (3) They had to seek humility, realizing their helplessness and their need to submit in obedience to God (cf. Nu 12:3; Ps 45:4; Pr 15:33).

2:4–15 GAZA WILL BE ABANDONED. After warning Judah, Zephaniah prophesies that God's judgment would also come on their sinful and idolatrous neighbors.

the word of the LORD is against
you,[h]
O Canaan, land of the
Philistines.
"I will destroy you,
and none will be left."[i]

6The land by the sea, where the
Kerethites[f] dwell,
will be a place for shepherds
and sheep pens.[j]
7It will belong to the remnant[k] of
the house of Judah;
there they will find pasture.
In the evening they will lie down
in the houses of Ashkelon.
The LORD their God will care for
them;
he will restore their
fortunes.[g][l]

Against Moab and Ammon

8"I have heard the insults[m] of
Moab[n]
and the taunts of the
Ammonites,[o]
who insulted[p] my people
and made threats against their
land.[q]
9Therefore, as surely as I live,"
declares the LORD Almighty, the
God of Israel,
"surely Moab[r] will become like
Sodom,[s]
the Ammonites[t] like
Gomorrah—
a place of weeds and salt pits,
a wasteland forever.
The remnant of my people will
plunder[u] them;
the survivors[v] of my nation will
inherit their land.[w]"
10This is what they will get in return
for their pride,[x]
for insulting[y] and mocking the
people of the LORD
Almighty.[z]

2:5 [h]S Lev 26:31; Am 3:1 [i]S Isa 14:30 **2:6** [j]S Isa 5:17 **2:7** [k]S Ge 45:7 [l]S Dt 30:3; Ps 126:4; Jer 32:44; S Hos 6:11; S Joel 3:1; Am 1:6-8 **2:8** [m]S Jer 48:27 [n]S Ge 19:37; S Isa 16:6 [o]S Eze 21:28 [p]Eze 25:3 [q]S La 3:61 **2:9** [r]S Dt 23:6; Isa 15:1-16:14; Jer 48:1-47; Eze 25:8-11 [s]Dt 29:23; Isa 13:19; Jer 49:18 [t]Jer 49:1-6; Eze 25:1-7 [u]S Isa 11:14 [v]S 2Ki 19:31 [w]S Am 2:1-3 **2:10** [x]S Job 40:12; S Isa 16:6 [y]S Jer 48:27 [z]S Ps 9:6

2:11 [a]S Joel 2:11 [b]S Zep 1:4 [c]S 1Ch 19:1; Eze 25:6-7 [d]Ps 86:9; S Isa 12:4; Zep 3:9 **2:12** [e]S Ge 10:6; S Isa 20:4 [f]S Jer 46:10 **2:13** [g]S Isa 10:5 [h]S Ge 10:11; S Na 1:1 [i]S Mic 5:6; Zec 10:11 **2:14** [j]S Isa 5:17 [k]S Isa 14:23 [l]Rev 18:2 [m]S Ps 102:6 **2:15** [n]S Isa 32:9 [o]Isa 47:8 [p]Eze 28:2 [q]Jer 49:33 [r]S Isa 28:22; S Na 3:19 [s]S Eze 27:36 **3:1** [t]S Jer 6:6 [u]S Dt 21:18 [v]S Eze 23:30 **3:2** [w]S Jer 22:21 [x]S Lev 26:23; S Jer 7:28 [y]S Dt 1:32

11The LORD will be awesome[a] to
them
when he destroys all the gods[b]
of the land.[c]
The nations on every shore will
worship him,[d]
every one in its own land.

Against Cush

12"You too, O Cushites,[h][e]
will be slain by my sword.[f]"

Against Assyria

13He will stretch out his hand
against the north
and destroy Assyria,[g]
leaving Nineveh[h] utterly desolate
and dry as the desert.[i]
14Flocks and herds[j] will lie down
there,
creatures of every kind.
The desert owl[k] and the screech
owl[l][m]
will roost on her columns.
Their calls will echo through the
windows,
rubble will be in the doorways,
the beams of cedar will be
exposed.
15This is the carefree[n] city
that lived in safety.[o]
She said to herself,
"I am, and there is none besides
me."[p]
What a ruin she has become,
a lair for wild beasts![q]
All who pass by her scoff[r]
and shake their fists.[s]

The Future of Jerusalem

3 Woe to the city of oppressors,[t]
rebellious[u] and defiled![v]
2She obeys[w] no one,
she accepts no correction.[x]
She does not trust[y] in the LORD,

[f]6 The meaning of the Hebrew for this word is uncertain. [g]7 Or *will bring back their captives* [h]12 That is, people from the upper Nile region

2:10 INSULTING AND MOCKING THE PEOPLE. The unbelieving world insults and mocks God's people, those who are committed to the righteous and holy standards of his Word. (1) This kind of treatment is unavoidable in a world under Satan's control and dominated by people whose minds are blinded (cf. 2Co 4:4; Eph 2:2–3; 4:18). Jesus himself experienced mocking and insults while on earth (see Mt 27:39–44; cf. Ps 69:10). (2) The persecution of the righteous will not last forever. God has appointed a day when he will vindicate those who have remained loyal to his ways and will bring just punishment on those who have mocked the faithful.

3:1–7 WOE TO THE CITY OF OPPRESSORS. After condemning the other nations, Zephaniah turned again to the sins of Jerusalem and God's people. They had become a people who were opposed to God and his law. Moral decay had penetrated every stratum of society, and people everywhere were refusing to listen to God's true prophets.

she does not draw near[z] to her
God.
3Her officials are roaring lions,[a]
her rulers are evening wolves,[b]
who leave nothing for the
morning.[c]
4Her prophets are arrogant;
they are treacherous[d] men.
Her priests profane the sanctuary
and do violence to the law.[e]
5The LORD within her is righteous;[f]
he does no wrong.[g]
Morning by morning[h] he
dispenses his justice,
and every new day he does not
fail,[i]
yet the unrighteous know no
shame.[j]
6"I have cut off nations;
their strongholds are
demolished.
I have left their streets deserted,
with no one passing through.
Their cities are destroyed;[k]
no one will be left—no one at
all.
7I said to the city,
'Surely you will fear me
and accept correction!'[l]
Then her dwelling would not be
cut off,
nor all my punishments come
upon her.
But they were still eager
to act corruptly[m] in all they did.
8Therefore wait[n] for me," declares
the LORD,

3:2 [z]S Ps 73:28
3:3 [a]S Ps 22:13
[b]S Ge 49:27
[c]S Mic 3:3
3:4 [d]S Ps 25:3; S Isa 48:8; Jer 3:20; 9:4; Mal 2:10
[e]S Jer 23:11; S Eze 22:26
3:5 [f]S Ezr 9:15
[g]Dt 32:4
[h]S Ps 5:3
[i]S La 3:23
[j]S Jer 3:3; S Eze 18:25
3:6 [k]S Lev 26:31
3:7 [l]S Jer 7:28
[m]S Hos 9:9
3:8 [n]S Ps 27:14

"for the day I will stand up to
testify.[i]
I have decided to assemble[o] the
nations,[p]
to gather the kingdoms
and to pour out my wrath[q] on
them—
all my fierce anger.[r]
The whole world will be
consumed[s]
by the fire of my jealous anger.
9"Then will I purify the lips of the
peoples,
that all of them may call[t] on
the name of the LORD[u]
and serve[v] him shoulder to
shoulder.
10From beyond the rivers of
Cush[j][w]
my worshipers, my scattered
people,
will bring me offerings.[x]
11On that day you will not be put to
shame[y]
for all the wrongs you have done
to me,[z]
because I will remove from this
city
those who rejoice in their
pride.[a]
Never again will you be haughty
on my holy hill.[b]
12But I will leave within you
the meek[c] and humble,

[o]S Joel 3:11
[p]S Isa 2:3
[q]Ps 79:6; Rev 16:1
[r]S Jer 10:25; S La 4:11
[s]S Zep 1:18
3:9 [t]S Zep 2:11
[u]S Ge 4:26
[v]S Isa 19:18
3:10 [w]S Ge 10:6; S Ps 68:31
[x]S 2Ch 32:23; S Isa 60:7
3:11 [y]S Isa 29:22; S Joel 2:26-27
[z]S Ge 50:15
[a]S Ps 59:12
[b]S Ex 15:17; S Lev 26:19
3:12 [c]Isa 14:32

[i]*8* Septuagint and Syriac; Hebrew *will rise up to plunder* [j]*10* That is, the upper Nile region

3:3–4 OFFICIALS ... RULERS ... PROPHETS ... PRIESTS. These were the four main categories of leadership in Judah. God condemned these spiritual leaders for failing to be holy and righteous. (1) The officials and rulers perverted the law and unjustly used their positions to gain money and property for themselves. (2) The prophets altered God's message so as to gain popularity and approval. (3) The priests profaned God's house by violating his precepts and living immoral lives. (4) We must resist leaders who tolerate or promote worldliness and immorality in God's name and replace them with leaders and laypeople who insist that God's holy standards be followed. God's standards must never be lowered to accommodate the sins of some leaders (see article on MORAL QUALIFICATIONS FOR OVERSEERS, p. 1882).

3:5 HE DOES NO WRONG. Though humans fail and fall into sin, God himself will remain righteous and never do wrong; that truth is inherent in his very nature (see article on THE ATTRIBUTES OF GOD, p. 882). (1) The Lord God is truthful, righteous and just in all his ways (cf. Dt 32:4). We must maintain faith in his never-failing righteousness. (2) Although things may happen to us that we cannot understand (see article on THE SUFFERING OF THE RIGHTEOUS, p. 710), we must remain convinced that his love and his faithfulness to us will never cease. Every day he will work in our lives that which is right; he cannot fail.

3:9–20 ALL OF THEM MAY CALL ON THE NAME. Zephaniah now turns to God's plan to redeem the nations after they have been purified by judgment. The nations will someday be reconciled to God, will call on him and will serve him. These promises will be fulfilled during the millennium, when Christ rules over the entire world (see Rev 20:4, note).

3:10 BEYOND THE RIVERS OF CUSH. Cush represents one of the most distant lands known at that time. The nations will bring offerings to God in Jerusalem (cf. Isa 66:18,20).

3:11 ON THAT DAY. When God brings the nations to a true knowledge of him, he will restore the fortunes of his own people (v. 20).

who trust[d] in the name of the
LORD.
13The remnant[e] of Israel will do no
wrong;[f]
they will speak no lies,[g]
nor will deceit be found in their
mouths.[h]
They will eat and lie down[i]
and no one will make them
afraid.[j]"

14Sing, O Daughter of Zion;[k]
shout aloud,[l] O Israel!
Be glad and rejoice[m] with all your
heart,
O Daughter of Jerusalem!
15The LORD has taken away your
punishment,
he has turned back your enemy.
The LORD, the King of Israel, is
with you;[n]
never again will you fear[o] any
harm.[p]
16On that day they will say to
Jerusalem,
"Do not fear, O Zion;
do not let your hands hang
limp.[q]
17The LORD your God is with you,
he is mighty to save.[r]
He will take great delight[s] in you,
he will quiet you with his love,[t]
he will rejoice over you with
singing."[u]

18"The sorrows for the appointed
feasts
I will remove from you;
they are a burden and a
reproach to you.[k]
19At that time I will deal
with all who oppressed[v] you;
I will rescue the lame
and gather those who have been
scattered.[w]
I will give them praise[x] and honor
in every land where they were
put to shame.
20At that time I will gather you;
at that time I will bring[y] you
home.
I will give you honor[z] and
praise[a]
among all the peoples of the
earth
when I restore your fortunes[1b]
before your very eyes,"
says the LORD.

Mt 9:8

3:12 [d]S Jer 29:12; Na 1:7 **3:13** [e]S Isa 10:21 [f]Ps 119:3; S Isa 4:3 [g]S Jer 33:16; Rev 14:5 [h]S Job 16:17 [i]Eze 34:15; Zep 2:7 [j]S Lev 26:6; S Eze 34:25-28 **3:14** [k]S Ps 9:14; Zec 2:10 [l]S Ps 95:1; Isa 12:6; Zec 2:10 [m]S Ps 9:2; S Isa 51:11 **3:15** [n]Eze 37:26-28 [o]S Isa 54:14 [p]Zec 9:9 **3:16** [q]S 2Ki 19:26; S Job 4:3; Isa 35:3-4; Heb 12:12 **3:17** [r]S Isa 63:1; S Joel 2:21 [s]S Dt 28:63; S Isa 62:4 [t]S Hos 14:4 [u]S Isa 40:1 **3:19** [v]S Isa 14:2 [w]S Eze 34:16; S Mic 4:6 [x]Isa 60:18 **3:20** [y]S Jer 29:14; S Eze 37:12 [z]Isa 56:5; 66:22 [a]S Dt 26:19; S Isa 60:18 [b]S Joel 3:1

[k]*18* Or *"I will gather you who mourn for the appointed feasts; / your reproach is a burden to you* [1]*20* Or *I bring back your captives*

3:14–17 BE GLAD AND REJOICE. God's people must rejoice over their salvation. Joy in one's heart is not a natural response; it is a supernatural response resulting from God's redemptive activity in our lives. Note that joy comes to us because: (1) we are forgiven and no longer punished for our sins (v. 15); (2) our enemy has been defeated, i.e., we are set free from the bondage of Satan and sin (v. 15); (3) God is with us, giving us his fellowship, grace and help throughout our lives (v. 15–17; cf. Heb 4:16); and (4) we are objects of God's great love and delight (v. 17). These conditions for joy exist now for those who have a full knowledge of what God has done for us in his Son (see Eph 1:17–18; 3:16–20). Our joy will reach its pinnacle in that day when God manifests his full glory and majesty on the earth (cf. Isa 35:1–10).

HAGGAI

Outline

I. The First Message: Finish Building the Temple (1:1–15)
   A. Date: 1 Elul (Aug. 29), 520 B.C. (1:1)
   B. The Prophet's Rebuke for the Unfinished Temple (1:2–11)
   C. The People's Response (1:12–15)
II. The Second Message: The Promise of Greater Glory (2:1–9)
   A. Date: 21 Tishri (Oct. 17), 520 B.C. (2:1)
   B. The Latter Temple Compared with the Former (2:2–4)
   C. The Glory of the Latter Temple to Be Greater (2:5–9)
III. The Third Message: The Call to Holiness with Blessing (2:10–19)
   A. Date: 24 Kislev (Dec. 18), 520 B.C. (2:10)
   B. The Corrupting Effect of Sin (2:11–14)
   C. The Blessing of Obedience (2:15–19)
IV. The Fourth Message: A Prophetic Promise (2:20–23)
   A. Date: 24 Kislev (Dec. 18), 520 B.C. (2:20)
   B. The Future Overthrow of Nations (2:21–22)
   C. The Prophetic Significance of Zerubbabel (2:23)

Author: Haggai

Theme: Rebuilding the Temple

Date of Writing: 520 B.C.

Background

Haggai is the first of three post-exilic prophetic books in the OT (Haggai, Zechariah and Malachi). Haggai is mentioned by name twice in Ezra (5:1; 6:14) and nine times in this book. He is called "the prophet" (1:1; 2:1,10; Ezr 6:14) and "the LORD's messenger" (1:13). He may have been one of a small handful of exiles who, upon returning to resettle Jerusalem, could remember Solomon's temple before it was destroyed by Nebuchadnezzar's army in 586 B.C. (2:3). If so, Haggai would have been in his 70s or 80s at the time of this writing. The book is dated precisely: the second year of King Darius of Persia (520 B.C.; 1:1).

The book's historical setting is important for understanding its message. In 538 B.C., King Cyrus of Persia issued a decree permitting the Jewish exiles to return to their homeland to rebuild Jerusalem and the temple in fulfillment of Isaiah's and Jeremiah's prophecies (Isa. 45:1–3; Jer 25:11–12; 29:10–14) and Daniel's intercession (Da 9). The first company of Jews to return to Jerusalem laid the foundation for a new temple in 536 B.C. amid great excitement and expectation (Ezr 3:8–10). However, soon afterwards the Samaritans and other neighbors physically opposed the building project and discouraged the workers so that work on the temple stopped in 534 B.C. Spiritual lethargy set in, and the people turned to rebuilding their own houses. In 520 B.C., Haggai, accompanied by the younger prophet Zechariah (see the introduction to Zechariah), began urging Zerubbabel and the people to resume building God's house. Four years later the temple was completed and dedicated (cf. Ezr 4—6).

Purpose

During a four-month period in 520 B.C., Haggai delivered the four terse messages recorded in this book (see the outline). These messages had a twofold purpose: (1) to exhort Zerubbabel (the governor) and Joshua (the high priest) to mobilize the people to rebuild the temple, and (2) to motivate the people to reorder their lives and priorities so as to resume the work in a dedicated way with God's blessing.

Survey

The book contains four messages, each of which is introduced by the phrase, "the word of the LORD" (1:1; 2:1; 2:10; 2:20). (1) Haggai first rebuked the former exiles for being preoccupied with their own paneled houses while God's house remained a ruin (1:4). The prophet twice exhorted them to "give careful thought" to their ways (1:5,7), revealing that God had withdrawn his blessing from them because of their ways (1:6,9–11). In response to Haggai's words, Zerubbabel, Joshua and all the people feared God and began the work (1:12–15).

(2) A few weeks later, the evaluation of some returned exiles discouraged the people, i.e., persons who had seen the glory of the former temple and regarded the present efforts at rebuilding as nothing in comparison with it (2:3). Haggai exhorted the leaders to take courage because (a) their efforts were part of a larger prophetic picture (2:4–7) and (b) "the glory of this present house will be greater than the glory of the former house" (2:9).

(3) Haggai's third message, which called the people to lives of holy obedience (2:10–19), and his (4) fourth message (2:20–23) were both delivered on the same day. The latter message prophesied that Zerubbabel represented the continuation of the Messianic lineage and promise (2:23).

Special Features

Four major features characterize the book of Haggai. (1) It was the first clear prophetic word heard in Judah after the Babylonian exile. (2) It is the second shortest OT book (a total of 38 verses); Obadiah is the shortest. (3) The phrase "this is what the LORD Almighty says" (and its variations) occurs 29 times and underscores the urgency of its message for the returned remnant in Jerusalem. (4) It contains one of the boldest prophecies in the OT about God's future visitation (2:6–9).

New Testament Fulfillment

Several verses in ch. 2 speak of the coming of the Messiah (vv. 6–9,21–23). The future shaking of the heavens and the earth and of nations and kingdoms is referred to by the author of Hebrews (Heb 12:26–28). Also, Haggai prophesies that Zerubbabel will be like a "signet ring" or official seal; in the two NT genealogies of Jesus Christ (Mt 1:12–13; Lk 3:27), Zerubbabel is the center that ties the two branches of the Messianic line together: from Solomon (son of David) to Zerubbabel to Joseph, and from Nathan (son of David) to Zerubbabel to Mary.

Reading Haggai

In order to read the entire Old Testament in one year, the book of Haggai should be read in 1 day: ☐ Haggai

NOTES

A Call to Build the House of the L*ORD*

1 In the second year of King Darius,[a] on the first day of the sixth
month, the word of the LORD came
through the prophet Haggai[b] to Zerubbabel[c] son of Shealtiel, governor[d]
of Judah, and to Joshua[a][e] son of Jehozadak,[f] the high priest:[g]
2This is what the LORD Almighty[h]
says: "These people[i] say, 'The time
has not yet come for the LORD's house
to be built.[j]' "
3Then the word of the LORD came
through the prophet Haggai:[k] **4**"Is it a
time for you yourselves to be living in
your paneled houses,[l] while this
house remains a ruin?[m]"
5Now this is what the LORD Almighty
says: "Give careful thought[n] to your
ways. **6**You have planted much, but
have harvested little.[o] You eat, but
never have enough.[p] You drink, but
never have your fill.[q] You put on
clothes, but are not warm. You earn
wages,[r] only to put them in a purse
with holes in it."
7This is what the LORD Almighty
says: "Give careful thought[s] to your
ways. **8**Go up into the mountains and
bring down timber[t] and build the
house, so that I may take pleasure[u] in
it and be honored,[v]" says the LORD.
9"You expected much, but see, it
turned out to be little.[w] What you
brought home, I blew[x] away. Why?"
declares the LORD Almighty. "Because
of my house, which remains a ruin,[y]
while each of you is busy with his own
house. **10**Therefore, because of you the
heavens have withheld[z] their dew[a]
and the earth its crops.[b] **11**I called for
a drought[c] on the fields and the mountains,[d] on the grain, the new wine,[e]
the oil[f] and whatever the ground produces, on men and cattle, and on the
labor of your hands.[g]"

12Then Zerubbabel[h] son of Shealtiel, Joshua son of Jehozadak, the high
priest, and the whole remnant[i] of the
people obeyed[j] the voice of the LORD
their God and the message of the
prophet Haggai, because the LORD their
God had sent him. And the people
feared[k] the LORD.
13Then Haggai,[l] the LORD's messenger,[m] gave this message of the
LORD to the people: "I am with[n] you,"
declares the LORD. **14**So the LORD
stirred up[o] the spirit of Zerubbabel[p]
son of Shealtiel, governor of Judah, and
the spirit of Joshua son of Jehozadak,[q]
the high priest, and the spirit of the
whole remnant[r] of the people. They
came and began to work on the house
of the LORD Almighty, their God, **15**on
the twenty-fourth day of the sixth
month[s] in the second year of King Darius.[t]

1:1 [a]S Ezr 4:24 [b]S Ezr 5:1 [c]S 1Ch 3:19; Mt 1:12-13 [d]Ezr 5:3; S Ne 5:14 [e]S Ezr 2:2 [f]S 1Ch 6:15; S Ezr 3:2 [g]Zec 3:8 **1:2** [h]Isa 13:4 [i]S Isa 29:13 [j]Ezr 1:2 **1:3** [k]S Ezr 5:1 **1:4** [l]S 2Sa 7:2 [m]ver 9; Jer 33:12 **1:5** [n]ver 7; La 3:40; Hag 2:15, 18 **1:6** [o]S Lev 26:20; S Isa 5:10 [p]S Isa 9:20; S 55:2 [q]Am 4:8 [r]Hag 2:16; Zec 8:10 **1:7** [s]S ver 5 **1:8** [t]S 1Ch 14:1 [u]S Job 22:3; Ps 132:13-14 [v]S Ex 29:43; Jer 13:11 **1:9** [w]S Dt 28:38; S Isa 5:10 [x]S Ps 103:16; S Eze 22:21 [y]S ver 4; S Ne 13:11 **1:10** [z]S Dt 28:24 [a]S Ge 27:28; 1Ki 17:1 [b]Lev 26:19; Dt 28:23 **1:11** [c]S Dt 11:26; S 28:22; S Ru 1:1; S 1Ki 17:1; S Isa 5:6 [d]Isa 7:25 [e]S Dt 28:51; Ps 4:7 [f]S Nu 18:12 [g]Hag 2:17 **1:12** [h]ver 1 [i]ver 14; Isa 1:9; Hag 2:2 [j]S Job 36:11; S Isa 50:10; Mt 28:20 [k]S Dt 31:12; S Isa 1:2 **1:13** [l]ver 1 [m]S Nu 27:21; S 2Ch 36:15 [n]S Ge 26:3; S Nu 14:9; S Mt 28:20; Ro 8:31 **1:14** [o]S Ezr 1:5 [p]S Ezr 5:2 [q]S 1Ch 6:15 [r]S ver 12 **1:15** [s]ver 1; Hag 2:10, 20 [t]S Ezr 4:24

[a] *1* A variant of *Jeshua*; here and elsewhere in Haggai

1:1 THE WORD OF THE LORD CAME. King Cyrus of Persia permitted 50,000 exiled Jews to return to Jerusalem under the leadership of Zerubbabel as governor and Joshua the high priest (see Ezr 1:2–4; 2:64–65; 3:2; 5:1). During the second year of the return (536/535 B.C.), the foundation of the temple was laid (see Ezr 3:8–10). However, Samaritan opposition halted work on the temple (see Ezr 4:1–5,24), after which the Jewish people became spiritually apathetic and stopped building the temple for 16 years. God then sent the prophets Haggai and Zechariah to encourage his people to resume work on the temple (see the introduction to Haggai).

1:4 PANELED HOUSES. Having become so busy with their own interests, the returned Jews were neglecting the construction of God's house. Their own houses were paneled with beautiful cedar, while the temple remained in ruins. Haggai insisted that God and his work had to come first. Likewise for us, God's kingdom and righteous concerns must be the first and highest priority in our lives (Mt 6:33). Note how zealous the Lord Jesus was for God's house and work (Jn 2:17; 4:34; 6:38; 9:4). What we set as a priority indicates the love we have for our Lord.

1:6–11 PLANTED MUCH, BUT HAVE HARVESTED LITTLE. God's people had lost his blessing because they were living self-seeking lives; they showed minimal interest in his goals and purposes. We too can expect God's blessing and help in our lives to decline if we are not vitally concerned for his work, both at home and among the nations.

1:12 THE PEOPLE OBEYED. The leaders and the people responded to Haggai's message by obeying and fearing the Lord; they took God's word seriously and committed themselves to resuming work on God's house.

1:13 I AM WITH YOU. God responded to his obedient people by promising to be with them. He strengthened their resolve and helped them accomplish the work (cf. Zec 4:6). To be "with you" is the greatest commitment the Lord can make to any believer (see Ge 26:24; 28:15; 39:2–3,21,23; Ex 3:12; Mt 28:20).

The Promised Glory of the New House

2 On the twenty-first day of the seventh month,[u] the word of the LORD
came through the prophet Haggai:[v]
2"Speak to Zerubbabel[w] son of Shealtiel, governor of Judah, to Joshua son of
Jehozadak,[x] the high priest, and to
the remnant[y] of the people. Ask them,
3'Who of you is left who saw this
house[z] in its former glory? How does
it look to you now? Does it not seem to
you like nothing?[a] 4But now be
strong, O Zerubbabel,' declares the
LORD. 'Be strong,[b] O Joshua son of Jehozadak,[c] the high priest. Be strong,
all you people of the land,' declares the
LORD, 'and work. For I am with[d] you,'
declares the LORD Almighty. 5'This is
what I covenanted[e] with you when
you came out of Egypt.[f] And my
Spirit[g] remains among you. Do not
fear.'[h]
6"This is what the LORD Almighty
says: 'In a little while[i] I will once
more shake the heavens and the
earth,[j] the sea and the dry land. 7I
will shake all nations, and the desired[k] of all nations will come, and I
will fill this house[l] with glory,[m]' says
the LORD Almighty. 8'The silver is mine
and the gold[n] is mine,' declares the
LORD Almighty. 9'The glory[o] of this
present house[p] will be greater than
the glory of the former house,' says the
LORD Almighty. 'And in this place I will
grant peace,[q]' declares the LORD Almighty."

Blessings for a Defiled People

10On the twenty-fourth day of the
ninth month,[r] in the second year of
Darius, the word of the LORD came to
the prophet Haggai: 11"This is what
the LORD Almighty says: 'Ask the
priests[s] what the law says: 12If a person carries consecrated meat[t] in the
fold of his garment, and that fold
touches some bread or stew, some
wine, oil or other food, does it become
consecrated?[u]' "

The priests answered, "No."

13Then Haggai said, "If a person defiled by contact with a dead body
touches one of these things, does it become defiled?"

"Yes," the priests replied, "it becomes defiled.[v]"

14Then Haggai said, " 'So it is with
this people[w] and this nation in my
sight,' declares the LORD. 'Whatever
they do and whatever they offer[x]
there is defiled.

15" 'Now give careful thought[y] to
this from this day on[b]—consider how
things were before one stone was
laid[z] on another in the LORD's temple.[a] 16When anyone came to a heap[b]

2:1 [u]ver 10,20; S Lev 23:34; Jn 7:37 [v]S Ezr 5:1 **2:2** [w]Hag 1:1 [x]S 1Ch 6:15 [y]S Hag 1:12 **2:3** [z]S Ezr 3:12; S Isa 60:7 [a]Zec 4:10 **2:4** [b]S 1Ch 28:20; Zec 8:9; S Eph 6:10 [c]S 1Ch 6:15 [d]S Ex 33:14; S Nu 14:9; S 2Sa 5:10; Ac 7:9 **2:5** [e]S Ge 6:18 [f]S Ex 29:46 [g]S Ne 9:20 [h]S Ge 15:1; 1Ch 28:20; S Ezr 5:2; Zec 8:13 **2:6** [i]S Isa 10:25 [j]S Ex 19:18; S Job 9:6; S Isa 14:16; S Eze 38:19; Heb 12:26* **2:7** [k]S 1Sa 9:20 [l]S Isa 60:7 [m]S Ex 16:7; S 29:43; Lk 2:32 **2:8** [n]S 1Ch 29:2 **2:9** [o]S Ps 85:9; S Isa 11:10 [p]S Ezr 3:12; S Isa 60:7 [q]S Lev 26:6; S Isa 60:17 **2:10** [r]S ver 1; S Hag 1:15 **2:11** [s]S Lev 10:10-11; Dt 17:8-11; 33:8; S Jer 18:18 **2:12** [t]Jer 11:15 [u]S Ge 7:2; S Lev 6:27; Mt 23:19 **2:13** [v]Lev 22:4-6; Nu 19:13 **2:14** [w]S Isa 29:13 [x]S Ps 51:17; S Isa 1:13 **2:15** [y]S Hag 1:5 [z]S Ezr 3:10 [a]Ezr 4:24 **2:16** [b]S Ru 3:7

[b]15 Or *to the days past*

2:3 THIS HOUSE IN ITS FORMER GLORY. When the post-exilic temple was completed, some people were discouraged and disillusioned because they viewed the present temple as "nothing" in comparison with the magnificence of the first temple built by Solomon. Thus God encouraged the people with three promises: (1) God himself would be with them to fulfill all his covenant promises (v. 4; see previous note), (2) God's Spirit would remain among the people (v. 5), and (3) the latter glory of God's house would be greater than the former because of the great demonstration of his power there (v. 9; cf. the ministry of Jesus and the apostles as recorded in the Gospels and the book of Acts).

It is not the beauty of church buildings that will ultimately yield fruit for God's kingdom. The one essential thing in our congregations is the presence of God manifested through the Holy Spirit and his gifts, ministries and power (see article on SPIRITUAL GIFTS FOR BELIEVERS, p. 1770). We must ask ourselves: Is the Holy Spirit manifested greatly in our gatherings, or is there little or no evidence of his presence and power among us?

2:6–9 ONCE MORE SHAKE THE HEAVENS AND THE EARTH. These verses refer to God's judgment on the world preceding and accompanying Christ's return to earth (cf. Heb 12:26–27): "The earth and the sky will tremble" (Joel 3:16; cf. Mt 24:29–30). God's glory will then fill the temple more than ever before, and he will dwell among his people in peace as the glorious Savior.

2:10–14 ASK THE PRIESTS. God explains to the people that whereas holiness could not be transmitted by contact, the corrupting influence of sin could; in other words, living in the holy land would not make them holy, but sin in their lives would defile everything they did, including their worship.

2:15–19 GIVE CAREFUL THOUGHT. God asked the people to consider why they had not been blessed by him in the past; it was because of their disobedience (see 1:9–11). Now, however, because of their willingness to build the temple, God would cause all that they did to succeed. This principle is expressed also in the NT: God's favor, love and fellowship come to us only as we continue to seek him and obey his commands (see Jn 14:21–23).

of twenty measures, there were only
ten. When anyone went to a wine vat[c]
to draw fifty measures, there were only
twenty.[d] **17**I struck all the work of
your hands[e] with blight,[f] mildew and
hail,[g] yet you did not turn[h] to me,'
declares the LORD.[i] **18**'From this day
on, from this twenty-fourth day of the
ninth month, give careful thought[j] to
the day when the foundation[k] of the
LORD's temple was laid. Give careful
thought: **19**Is there yet any seed left in
the barn? Until now, the vine and the
fig tree, the pomegranate[l] and the olive tree have not borne fruit.[m]
" 'From this day on I will bless[n]
you.' "

Zerubbabel the LORD's Signet Ring

20The word of the LORD came to Haggai[o] a second time on the twenty-
fourth day of the month:[p] **21**"Tell Zerubbabel[q] governor of Judah that I
will shake[r] the heavens and the
earth. **22**I will overturn[s] royal thrones
and shatter the power of the foreign
kingdoms.[t] I will overthrow chariots[u] and their drivers; horses and
their riders[v] will fall, each by the
sword of his brother.[w]
23" 'On that day,[x]' declares the
LORD Almighty, 'I will take you, my servant[y] Zerubbabel[z] son of Shealtiel,'
declares the LORD, 'and I will make you
like my signet ring,[a] for I have chosen
you,' declares the LORD Almighty."

2:16 [c] S Job 24:11; S Isa 5:2 [d] S Dt 28:38; S Isa 5:10; S Hag 1:6 **2:17** [e] Hag 1:11 [f] S Dt 28:22 [g] S Ex 9:18; Ps 78:48 [h] S Isa 9:13; S Jer 3:10 [i] S Am 4:6 **2:18** [j] S Hag 1:5 [k] S Ezr 3:11 **2:19** [l] S Ex 28:33 [m] S Joel 1:12 [n] S Ge 12:2; S Lev 25:21; Ps 128:1-6; S Joel 2:14 **2:20** [o] S Ezr 5:1 [p] S ver 1; S Hag 1:15 **2:21** [q] S Ezr 5:2 [r] S Isa 14:16; Eze 38:19-20 **2:22** [s] S Ge 19:25; S Job 2:13 [t] S Da 2:44 [u] S Mic 5:10 [v] S Ex 15:21 [w] S Jdg 7:22; S Eze 38:21 **2:23** [x] Isa 2:11; 10:20; Zec 4:10 [y] S Isa 20:3; S Da 9:24-26 [z] Mt 1:12 [a] S Ge 38:18; S Ex 28:9; 2Co 1:22

2:21 SHAKE THE HEAVENS AND THE EARTH. The prophet encouraged Zerubbabel, the governor of God's people, by saying that one day God would destroy the power of kingdoms and nations throughout the earth; that day is the time Jesus Christ will reign over all the world's inhabitants (see Rev 19:11–21).

2:23 LIKE MY SIGNET RING. When the time came for God to shake the heavens and the earth, he would make Zerubbabel like a signet ring. This ring was the official mark of supreme authority and a pledge of favor towards God's people. Haggai may have been prophesying that Jesus Christ, a descendant of Zerubbabel (see Mt 1:12–13), would "on that day" be the supreme ruler who would have absolute and universal reign.

ZECHARIAH

Outline

I. Part One: Prophetic Words in the Context of Rebuilding the Temple (520–518 B.C.) (1:1—8:23)
  A. Introduction (1:1–6)
  B. A Series of Eight Night Visions (1:7—6:8)
    1. Vision of the Horseman Among the Myrtle Trees (1:7–17)
    2. Vision of the Four Horns and Four Craftsmen (1:18–21)
    3. Vision of a Man Measuring Jerusalem (2:1–13)
    4. Vision of the Cleansing of Joshua the High Priest (3:1–10)
    5. Vision of the Gold Lampstand and Two Olive Trees (4:1–14)
    6. Vision of the Flying Scroll (5:1–4)
    7. Vision of the Woman in a Basket (5:5–11)
    8. Vision of the Four Chariots (6:1–8)
  C. The Crowning of Joshua as High Priest and Its Prophetic Significance (6:9–15)
  D. Two Messages (7:1—8:23)
    1. Fasting and Social Justice (7:1–14)
    2. The Restoration of Zion (8:1–23)

II. Part Two: Prophetic Words Concerning Israel and the Coming Messiah (undated) (9:1—14:21)
  A. First Oracle of the Lord (9:1—11:17)
    1. The Triumphant Intervention of the Lord (9:1–10)
    2. Announcement of Messianic Salvation (9:11—10:12)
    3. Rejection of the Messiah (11:1–17)
  B. Second Oracle of the Lord (12:1—14:21)
    1. The Mourning and Conversion of Israel (12:1—13:9)
    2. The Enthronement of the Messiah-King (14:1–21)

Author: Zechariah

Theme: Finishing the Temple, and Messianic Promises

Date of Writing: 520–470 B.C.

Background

The opening verse identifies the prophet Zechariah son of Berekiah and grandson of Iddo (1:1) as the book's author; the book of Nehemiah further states that Zechariah was the head of the priestly family of Iddo (Ne 12:16), indicating he was from the tribe of Levi and served in Jerusalem after the exile as both a priest and a prophet.

Zechariah was a younger contemporary of the prophet Haggai. Ezr 5:1 states that both were prophets who stirred up the Jews in Judah and Jerusalem to resume rebuilding the temple in the days of Zerubbabel (the governor) and Joshua (the high priest). Thus the historical setting for chs. 1–8 (dated 520–518 B.C.) is identical to that of Haggai (see the introduction to Haggai). As a result of Zechariah's and Haggai's prophetic ministries, the temple was completed and dedicated in 516/515 B.C.

Whereas Zechariah was a young man (cf. 2:4) when he prophesied alongside Haggai, he apparently was an old man when he wrote chs. 9—14 (dated by most scholars between 480–470 B.C.). All of Zechariah's prophecy occurred in Jerusalem for the 50,000 Jewish exiles who had returned to Judah in the first stage of the restoration. The NT indicates that in the end, Zechariah son of Berekiah was "murdered between the temple and the altar" (i.e., the place of intercession) by hostile temple officials (Mt 23:35), in a manner similar to the death of an earlier man of God by the same name (see 2Ch 24:20–21).

Purpose

Zechariah's twofold purpose in writing corresponds to the two major parts of the book. (1) Chs. 1–8 were given to encourage the Jewish remnant in Judah to resume building the temple and to stick with it until the task was completed. (2) Chs. 9–14 were given to encourage the same people who, having completed the temple, were disheartened when the Messiah did not appear immediately, and to reveal what it will mean when the Messiah does come.

Survey

The book divides into two major parts. (1) Part one (chs. 1—8) begins by exhorting the Jews to return to the Lord so that he might return to them (1:1–6). While encouraging the people to finish rebuilding the temple, the prophet Zechariah received a series of eight visions (1:7—6:8), which assured the Jewish community in Judah and Jerusalem that God cared for his people and ruled over their future destiny. The first five visions conveyed hope and consolation; the last three visions involved judgment. The fourth vision contains an important Messianic prophecy (3:8–9). The coronation scene in 6:9–15 is a classic OT Messianic prophecy. Two messages (chs. 7—8) provided both present and future perspectives for the original readers.

(2) Part two (chs. 9—14) contains two blocks of apocalyptic prophecy, each of which is introduced with the words, "An oracle" (9:1; 12:1). The first oracle (9:1—11:17) included promises of Messianic salvation for Israel, revealing that the future Messiah-Shepherd who would accomplish this salvation would first be rejected and struck (11:4–17; cf. 13:7). The second oracle (12:1—14:21) focused on the restoration and conversion of Israel. In an amazing prophecy, God predicted that Israel would mourn over God himself, "the one they have pierced" (12:10). In that day a fountain for cleansing from sin would be opened to the house of David (13:1); Israel would say, "The LORD is our God" (13:9), and the Messiah would reign as King over Jerusalem (ch. 14).

Special Features

Six special features characterize the book of Zechariah. (1) It is the most Messianic of all the OT books in that its many clear references to the Messiah occur in 14 chapters. Only Isaiah (in 66 chapters) contains more prophecies about the Messiah than Zechariah. (2) Among the minor prophets, it contains the most specific and comprehensive prophecies concerning end-time events. (3) It represents the most successful merger of the priestly and the prophetic roles in Israel's history. (4) More than any other OT book, its visions and highly symbolic language resemble the apocalyptic books of Daniel and Revelation. (5) It records a bold example of divine sarcasm in the prophecy about the Messiah's betrayal for thirty pieces of silver, referring to it as the "handsome price at which they priced me" (11:13). (6) Zechariah's prophecy of the Messiah in ch. 14 as the great Warrior-King reigning over Jerusalem is an awe-inspiring OT prophecy.

New Testament Fulfillment

There is profound NT application in Zechariah. The merger in Zechariah's personal life of the priestly and the prophetic may have contributed to the NT understanding of Christ as both priest and prophet. Also, Zechariah prophesied about the atoning death of Jesus at the hands of the Jews, which at the end of time will cause Israel to mourn, repent and be saved (12:10—13:9; Ro 11:25–27). But Zechariah's most obvious contribution relates to his numerous prophecies about the Messiah, which the NT writers cite as being fulfilled in Jesus Christ. Among these are: (1) he will come in a humble and lowly fashion (9:9; 13:7; Mt 21:5; 26:31,56); (2) he will restore Israel by the blood of his covenant (9:11; Mk 14:24); (3) he will be a Shepherd to God's scattered and wandering sheep (10:2; Mt 9:36); (4) he will be betrayed and rejected (11:12–13; Mt 26:15; 27:9–10); (5) he will be pierced and struck down (12:10; 13:7; Mt 26:31,56; Jn 19:37); (6) he will return in glory to deliver Israel from its enemies (14:1–6; Mt 24:30–31; Rev 19:15); (7) he will rule as King in peace and righteousness (9:9–10; 14:9,16; Ro 14:17; Rev 11:15); and (8) he will establish his glorious kingdom forever over all the nations (14:6–19; Rev 11:15; 21:24–26; 22:1–5).

Reading Zechariah

In order to read the entire Old Testament in one year, the book of Zechariah should be read in 5 days, according to the following schedule: ☐ 1–3 ☐ 4–6 ☐ 7–8 ☐ 9–11 ☐ 12–14

NOTES

A Call to Return to the LORD

1 In the eighth month of the second
year of Darius,[a] the word of the
LORD came to the prophet Zechariah[b]
son of Berekiah,[c] the son of Iddo:[d]
2“The LORD was very angry[e] with
your forefathers. **3**Therefore tell the
people: This is what the LORD Almighty
says: ‘Return[f] to me,’ declares the
LORD Almighty, ‘and I will return to
you,’[g] says the LORD Almighty. **4**Do
not be like your forefathers,[h] to whom
the earlier prophets[i] proclaimed:
This is what the LORD Almighty says:
‘Turn from your evil ways[j] and your
evil practices.’ But they would not listen or pay attention to me,[k] declares
the LORD.[l] **5**Where are your forefathers now? And the prophets, do they
live forever? **6**But did not my words[m]
and my decrees, which I commanded
my servants the prophets, overtake
your forefathers?[n]

“Then they repented and said, ‘The
LORD Almighty has done to us what our
ways and practices deserve,[o] just as
he determined to do.’ ”[p]

The Man Among the Myrtle Trees

7On the twenty-fourth day of the
eleventh month, the month of Shebat,
in the second year of Darius, the word
of the LORD came to the prophet Zechariah son of Berekiah, the son of Iddo.[q]

8During the night I had a vision—
and there before me was a man riding
a red[r] horse! He was standing among
the myrtle trees in a ravine. Behind
him were red, brown and white
horses.[s]

9I asked, “What are these, my lord?”

The angel[t] who was talking with
me answered, “I will show you what
they are.”[u]

10Then the man standing among the
myrtle trees explained, “They are the
ones the LORD has sent to go throughout the earth.”[v]

11And they reported to the angel of
the LORD,[w] who was standing among
the myrtle trees, “We have gone
throughout the earth and found the
whole world at rest and in peace.”[x]

12Then the angel of the LORD said,
“LORD Almighty, how long[y] will you
withhold mercy[z] from Jerusalem and
from the towns of Judah,[a] which you
have been angry with these seventy[b]
years?” **13**So the LORD spoke[c] kind
and comforting words[d] to the angel
who talked with me.[e]

14Then the angel who was speaking

1:1 [a] S Ezr 4:24; S 6:15 [b] S Ezr 5:1 [c] Mt 23:35; Lk 11:51 [d] ver 7; S Ne 12:4
1:2 [e] S 2Ch 36:16
1:3 [f] S Job 22:23 [g] Mal 3:7; Jas 4:8
1:4 [h] S 2Ch 36:15 [i] Zec 7:7 [j] S 2Ki 17:13; S 2Ch 7:14; Ps 106:6; S Jer 23:22 [k] S 2Ch 24:19; Ps 78:8; S Jer 6:17; 17:23 [l] S Eze 20:18; S 33:4
1:6 [m] S Isa 44:26 [n] S Dt 28:2; S Da 9:12; S Hos 5:9 [o] Jer 12:14-17; La 2:17 [p] Jer 23:20; 39:16; S 44:17
1:7 [q] S ver 1
1:8 [r] Rev 6:4 [s] Zec 6:2-7
1:9 [t] Zec 4:1,4-5; 5:5 [u] S Da 7:16
1:10 [v] Zec 6:5-8
1:11 [w] Ge 16:7 [x] S Isa 14:7
1:12 [y] S Ps 6:3 [z] Ps 40:11 [a] S Jer 40:5 [b] S 2Ch 36:21; S Da 9:2
1:13 [c] S Isa 35:4 [d] S Job 15:11 [e] Zec 4:1

1:1 IN THE EIGHTH MONTH ... THE PROPHET ZECHARIAH. In November of 520 B.C., about a month after Haggai's second prophecy (see Hag 2:1), God raised up Zechariah, a younger man, to help Haggai encourage the people to rebuild the temple. The first six chapters contain a series of eight night visions given during the first two years of the rebuilding. These visions encouraged the people to look at what they were doing in the light of God's plan to bring a greater restoration, a spiritual one, in the future. Both Christ's first and second comings are in view in these prophecies.

1:3 RETURN TO ME . . . I WILL RETURN TO YOU. God's message through Zechariah begins with a call for the people to return to God, i.e., to repent. God was waiting for them to obey, and he in turn promised to bless and protect them.

1:4 DO NOT BE LIKE YOUR FOREFATHERS. God reminds the people of how he had given the same call to their forefathers through the earlier prophets, but they had not repented. (1) Because they had not turned from their evil ways, the forefathers missed their opportunities and suffered the consequences; the warnings of Dt 28 were fulfilled. (2) Likewise, if we live for the sinful pleasures of the present world system, we too will miss God's plan for our lives and be forever denied the ultimate blessings and good that he intends for us.

1:8–11 I HAD A VISION. In February of 519 B.C., God gave Zechariah a vision of a man on a red horse among myrtle trees, with various other horses behind him. Some believe this man was a manifestation of Christ as the angel of the Lord (cf. v. 12; see article on ANGELS AND THE ANGEL OF THE LORD, p. 340). An interpreting angel explained that these horses had patrolled the whole world and found it at rest and in peace (v. 11), yet God's people in Judah were still oppressed and insecure. The Lord would change the world situation by restoring and blessing Jerusalem and the towns of Judah.

1:9 THE ANGEL WHO WAS TALKING WITH ME. The interpreting angel continued to explain things to Zechariah (vv. 3–14,19; 2:3; 4:1,4–5; 5:5,10; 6:4–5). This angel is not, however, the same as the angel of the Lord (see previous note).

1:12 ANGEL OF THE LORD SAID. The rider on the red horse is now identified as the angel of the Lord, interceding on behalf of Israel and Jerusalem to bring an end to the 70 years of God's judgment on Jerusalem and the temple, which were destroyed in 586 B.C. The rebuilding of the temple was finished in 516 B.C., 70 years later. The angel of the Lord is probably Christ (see vv. 8–11, note; cf. Ex 23:20–21; Isa 63:9), who is still the One who speaks in our defense (1Jn 2:1).

1:14 VERY JEALOUS FOR JERUSALEM. God's love was behind his choice of Jerusalem and the nation of Israel. That love, however, was not

to me said, "Proclaim this word: This
is what the LORD Almighty says: 'I am
very jealous[f] for Jerusalem and Zion,
15but I am very angry with the nations
that feel secure.[g] I was only a little
angry,[h] but they added to the calamity.'[i]
16"Therefore, this is what the LORD
says: 'I will return[j] to Jerusalem with
mercy, and there my house will be rebuilt. And the measuring line[k] will be
stretched out over Jerusalem,' declares the LORD Almighty.[l]
17"Proclaim further: This is what
the LORD Almighty says: 'My towns will
again overflow with prosperity, and the
LORD will again comfort[m] Zion and
choose[n] Jerusalem.' "[o]

Four Horns and Four Craftsmen

18Then I looked up—and there before me were four horns! 19I asked the
angel who was speaking to me, "What
are these?"
He answered me, "These are the
horns[p] that scattered Judah, Israel
and Jerusalem."
20Then the LORD showed me four
craftsmen. 21I asked, "What are these
coming to do?"
He answered, "These are the horns
that scattered Judah so that no one
could raise his head, but the craftsmen
have come to terrify them and throw
down these horns of the nations who
lifted up their horns[q] against the land
of Judah to scatter its people."[r]

A Man With a Measuring Line

2 Then I looked up—and there before me was a man with a measuring line in his hand! 2I asked, "Where
are you going?"
He answered me, "To measure Jerusalem, to find out how wide and how
long it is."[s]
3Then the angel who was speaking
to me left, and another angel came to
meet him 4and said to him: "Run, tell
that young man, 'Jerusalem will be a
city without walls[t] because of the
great number[u] of men and livestock in
it.[v] 5And I myself will be a wall[w] of
fire[x] around it,' declares the LORD,
'and I will be its glory[y] within.'[z][a]
6"Come! Come! Flee from the land of
the north," declares the LORD, "for I
have scattered[b] you to the four winds
of heaven,"[c] declares the LORD.[d]
7"Come, O Zion! Escape,[e] you who
live in the Daughter of Babylon!"[f]
8For this is what the LORD Almighty
says: "After he has honored me and
has sent me against the nations that

1:14 [f] S Isa 26:11; S Joel 2:18 **1:15** [g] Jer 48:11 [h] S 2Ch 28:9 [i] S Ps 69:26; 123:3-4; S Am 1:11 **1:16** [j] Zec 8:3 [k] S Job 38:5; Zec 2:1-2 [l] S Ezr 1:1 **1:17** [m] S Isa 40:1 [n] S Isa 14:1 [o] S Ezr 9:9; S Ps 51:18; Isa 54:8-10; S 61:4 **1:19** [p] Am 6:13 **1:21** [q] S 1Ki 22:11; Ps 75:4 [r] S Ps 75:10; S Isa 54:16-17; Zec 12:9 **2:2** [s] S Eze 40:3; S Zec 1:16; Rev 21:15 **2:4** [t] S Eze 38:11 [u] S Isa 49:20; S Jer 30:19; S 33:22 [v] Zec 14:11 **2:5** [w] S Isa 26:1; Eze 42:20 [x] S Isa 10:17 [y] S Ps 85:9; S Isa 11:10; S 24:23; Rev 21:23 [z] S Ps 125:2 [a] S Ps 46:5; S Eze 38:14 **2:6** [b] S Ps 44:11 [c] S Eze 17:21; S 37:9 [d] Mt 24:31; Mk 13:27 **2:7** [e] S Isa 42:7 [f] S Isa 48:20; Jer 3:18

---

meant to stay just with the Israelites; it was intended to reach out to all people. God desired to bless all the families of the earth through Abram and his descendants (see Ge 12:3, note).

1:15 NATIONS . . . ADDED TO THE CALAMITY. God used pagan nations to bring his judgment on Jerusalem (Isa 10:5–6; Hab 1:6). In their greed for wealth and power, however, these nations went too far. Now they would be judged by God for their proud self-sufficiency.

1:18–19 HORNS THAT SCATTERED JUDAH, ISRAEL AND JERUSALEM. The animal horns represent Assyria, Egypt, Babylon and Medo-Persia.

1:20–21 FOUR CRAFTSMEN. These craftsmen probably are four empires that brought God's judgment on the horns (v. 18). All the oppressors of God's people must eventually come under his judgment (cf. Ps 2:5,9).

2:1 MAN WITH A MEASURING LINE. Jerusalem was still in pitiful condition at the end of the Babylonian exile. The number of the returnees was comparatively small. God encouraged them by telling them that he was not through with Jerusalem; it would become the most glorious place on earth. This third vision looks ahead to the millennial kingdom, when the city will have no walls and will overflow with a great crowd of people (see next note).

2:5 I MYSELF WILL BE A WALL . . . ITS GLORY. In the millennial kingdom, the city will not need walls, for the Lord himself will be a wall of fire around it (cf. Isa 4:5). Even more important, God's glory in the midst of the people will make the whole city a temple filled with his presence (cf. Eze 43:1–7). Even now, the presence and glory of God among his people is something the church must desire and seek above all else (see article on THE GLORY OF GOD, p. 1192).

2:6 FLEE FROM THE LAND OF THE NORTH. Zechariah's instruction here can be interpreted on several different levels. (1) The rebuilding of the temple was a signal for more of the exiled Jews to return from Babylon (v. 7). (2) The OT prophets also saw a future return of Jews at the end of the age that will climax in the millennial kingdom (vv. 7–9). (3) We can apply this in our own day as a call to flee from the idolatry, immorality, wickedness, occult practices and sinful ways of today's world system.

2:8 TOUCHES THE APPLE OF HIS EYE. Zion (v. 7) represents the godly remnant of Israel; they are the apple (pupil) of God's eye, precious and important to him (see Ps 17:8, note). Believers today are as important and loved as were God's people of OT times; we are under his protective care and concern.

have plundered you—for whoever
touches you touches the apple of his
eye[g]— **9**I will surely raise my hand
against them so that their slaves will
plunder them.[a][h] Then you will know
that the LORD Almighty has sent me.[i]
10"Shout[j] and be glad, O Daughter
of Zion.[k] For I am coming,[l] and I will
live among you,"[m] declares the
LORD.[n] **11**"Many nations will be joined
with the LORD in that day and will become my people.[o] I will live among
you and you will know that the LORD
Almighty has sent me to you.[p] **12**The
LORD will inherit[q] Judah[r] as his portion in the holy land and will again
choose[s] Jerusalem. **13**Be still[t] before
the LORD, all mankind, because he has
roused himself from his holy dwelling.[u]"

Clean Garments for the High Priest

3 Then he showed me Joshua[b][v] the
high priest standing before the angel of the LORD, and Satan[c][w] standing
at his right side to accuse him. **2**The
LORD said to Satan, "The LORD rebuke
you,[x] Satan! The LORD, who has chosen[y] Jerusalem, rebuke you! Is not
this man a burning stick[z] snatched
from the fire?"[a]
3Now Joshua was dressed in filthy
clothes as he stood before the angel.
4The angel said to those who were
standing before him, "Take off his
filthy clothes."
Then he said to Joshua, "See, I have
taken away your sin,[b] and I will put
rich garments[c] on you."
5Then I said, "Put a clean turban[d]
on his head." So they put a clean turban on his head and clothed him, while
the angel of the LORD stood by.
6The angel of the LORD gave this
charge to Joshua: **7**"This is what the
LORD Almighty says: 'If you will walk in
my ways and keep my requirements,[e]
then you will govern my house[f] and
have charge[g] of my courts, and I will
give you a place among these standing
here.[h]
8" 'Listen, O high priest[i] Joshua
and your associates seated before you,
who are men symbolic[j] of things to
come: I am going to bring my servant,
the Branch.[k] **9**See, the stone I have
set in front of Joshua![l] There are sev-

2:8 [g]S Dt 32:10 **2:9** [h]S Isa 14:2; S Jer 12:14; S Hab 2:8 [i]S Isa 48:16; Zec 4:9; 6:15 **2:10** [j]S Zep 3:14 [k]S Isa 23:12; S Zep 3:14 [l]Zec 9:9 [m]S Ex 25:8; Lev 26:12; S Nu 23:21; Zec 8:3 [n]S Rev 21:3 **2:11** [o]S Jer 24:7; S Mic 4:2; Zec 8:8, 20-22 [p]Zec 4:9; 6:15 **2:12** [q]S Ex 34:9; Ps 33:12; Jer 10:16 [r]Jer 40:5 [s]S Dt 12:5; S Isa 14:1 **2:13** [t]S Ex 14:14; S Isa 41:1 [u]S Dt 26:15 **3:1** [v]S Ezr 2:2; Zec 6:11 [w]S 2Sa 24:1; S 2Ch 18:21; S Ps 109:6; S Mt 4:10 **3:2** [x]Jude 1:9 [y]S Isa 14:1 [z]S Isa 7:4 [a]Jude 1:23 **3:4** [b]S 2Sa 12:13; S Eze 36:25; S Mic 7:18 [c]S Ge 41:42; S Ps 132:9; S Isa 52:1; Rev 19:8 **3:5** [d]S Ex 29:6 **3:7** [e]S Lev 8:35 [f]Dt 17:8-11; S Eze 44:15-16 [g]2Ch 23:6 [h]Jer 15:19; Zec 6:15 **3:8** [i]Hag 1:1 [j]S Dt 28:46; S Eze 12:11 [k]S Isa 4:2; S 49:3; S Eze 17:22 **3:9** [l]S Ezr 2:2

[a] *8,9* Or *says after . . . eye:* [9]*"I . . . plunder them."* [b] *1* A variant of *Jeshua*; here and elsewhere in Zechariah [c] *1 Satan* means *accuser.*

2:10–12 JOINED WITH THE LORD IN THAT DAY. "That day" refers to the time when Jesus Christ will reign on earth. Then Zion, the godly remnant of Israel, along with the Gentiles, will all be God's people. They will have the blessing of God's presence among them as well as the blessing of God's choice of Jerusalem as his holy city.

3:1 SATAN STANDING AT HIS RIGHT SIDE TO ACCUSE HIM. Joshua was representing the nation of Israel before God. Satan, "the accuser" (see Mt 4:10, note), stood to oppose him, signifying that the hindrances and opposition to the temple rebuilding were really coming from Satan. He is still our adversary, the "accuser of our brothers" (Rev 12:10), who seeks to take advantage of us.

3:2 REBUKE YOU, SATAN! As Israel's representative, Joshua could not resist Satan, for the high priest was dressed in filthy clothes (i.e., sin). (1) God himself resisted Satan and rebuked him, for God had chosen Israel to carry out his purposes. (2) Israel was a "burning stick snatched from the fire." The fire represents Israel's sufferings in the Babylonian exile. God had brought Israel through these sufferings, not to destroy them, but to discipline them and prepare them for greater things.

3:4 I WILL PUT RICH GARMENTS ON YOU. God had Joshua's filthy clothes removed, symbolizing the removal of his (and Israel's) sin. He was then clothed in costly festive robes and had a clean turban placed on his head, indicating full restoration to priestly office. Israel's sin was cleansed and they were clothed with divine righteousness; this same cleansing is available to us through Christ (Eph 1:7; Ro 1:16–17; 3:22,25–26).

3:7 IF YOU WILL WALK IN MY WAYS. God's personal word to Joshua strongly encouraged him to follow the Lord and keep his requirements; if Joshua did so, he would govern in the temple, have charge of God's courts on earth, and have free access to God's throne room in heaven, where the angels minister. We too can have free access to heaven's courts through prayer if we walk in God's ways.

3:8 MY SERVANT, THE BRANCH. Joshua and the other priests were prophetic types, pointing to the work of God's servant, the Branch (see Isa 4:2, note; 11:1, note; Jer 23:5, note). The angel of the Lord (i.e., Christ), standing by during Joshua's cleansing and restoration (v. 5), is now identified as the Branch, the new shoot who would bear our sins as a sin offering and accomplish our redemption (cf. Isa 53:1–6). He would defeat Satan by taking the filthy clothes of the world's sins on himself and by dying in our place.

3:9 SEVEN EYES ON THAT ONE STONE. The stone is another figure of the Messiah (cf. Isa 28:16; 1Pe 2:6). The seven eyes represent a full-

en eyes[d][m] on that one stone,[n] and I will engrave an inscription on it,' says the LORD Almighty, 'and I will remove the sin[o] of this land in a single day.

10" 'In that day each of you will invite his neighbor to sit[p] under his vine and fig tree,[q]' declares the LORD Almighty."

The Gold Lampstand and the Two Olive Trees

4 Then the angel who talked with me returned and wakened[r] me, as a man is wakened from his sleep.[s] **2**He asked me, "What do you see?"[t]

I answered, "I see a solid gold lampstand[u] with a bowl at the top and seven lights[v] on it, with seven channels to the lights. **3**Also there are two olive trees[w] by it, one on the right of the bowl and the other on its left."

4I asked the angel who talked with me, "What are these, my lord?"

5He answered, "Do you not know what these are?"

"No, my lord," I replied.[x]

6So he said to me, "This is the word of the LORD to Zerubbabel:[y] 'Not[z] by might nor by power,[a] but by my Spirit,'[b] says the LORD Almighty.

7"What[e] are you, O mighty mountain? Before Zerubbabel you will become level ground.[c] Then he will bring out the capstone[d] to shouts[e] of 'God bless it! God bless it!' "

8Then the word of the LORD came to me: **9**"The hands of Zerubbabel have laid the foundation[f] of this temple; his hands will also complete it.[g] Then you will know that the LORD Almighty has sent me[h] to you.

10"Who despises the day[i] of small things?[j] Men will rejoice when they see the plumb line in the hand of Zerubbabel.[k]

"(These seven are the eyes[l] of the LORD, which range throughout the earth.)"

11Then I asked the angel, "What are these two olive trees[m] on the right and the left of the lampstand?"

12Again I asked him, "What are these two olive branches beside the two gold pipes that pour out golden oil?"

13He replied, "Do you not know what these are?"

"No, my lord," I said.

14So he said, "These are the two who are anointed[n] to[f] serve the Lord of all the earth."

The Flying Scroll

5 I looked again—and there before me was a flying scroll![o]

3:9 [m]S 2Ch 16:9 [n]Isa 28:16 [o]S 2Sa 12:13; S Jer 50:20 **3:10** [p]S Job 11:18 [q]S Nu 16:14; S 1Ki 4:25; Mic 4:4 **4:1** [r]S Da 8:18 [s]Jer 31:26 **4:2** [t]S Jer 1:13 [u]S Ex 25:31; Rev 1:12 [v]Rev 4:5 **4:3** [w]ver 11; S Ps 1:3; S Rev 11:4 **4:5** [x]S Zec 1:9 **4:6** [y]S 1Ch 3:19; S Ezr 5:2 [z]S 1Sa 13:22; S 1Ki 19:12 [a]S 1Sa 2:9 [b]S Ne 9:20; Isa 11:2-4; S Da 2:34; Hos 1:7 **4:7** [c]S Ps 26:12; Jer 51:25 [d]S Ps 118:22 [e]S 1Ch 15:28 **4:9** [f]S Ezr 3:11 [g]Ezr 3:8; S 6:15; Zec 6:12 [h]S Zec 2:9 **4:10** [i]S Hag 2:23 [j]Hag 2:3 [k]S Ezr 5:1; S Ne 12:1; S Job 38:5 [l]S 2Ch 16:9; Rev 5:6 **4:11** [m]S ver 3; S Rev 11:4 **4:14** [n]Ex 29:7; 40:15; S Ps 45:7; S Isa 20:3; S Da 9:24-26 **5:1** [o]S Ps 40:7; S Jer 36:4; Rev 5:1

[d] 9 Or *facets* [e] 7 Or *Who* [f] 14 Or *two who bring oil and*

---

ness of insight, omniscience and divine intelligence (cf. Rev 5:6). Christ would remove sin in a single day, i.e., on the day he atoned for sin on the cross.

4:2 SOLID GOLD LAMPSTAND. This lampstand is an olive oil lampstand. (1) It had seven lights all on the same level, arranged under a reservoir bowl. Oil flowed from the bowl to keep the lamps full. The bowl of oil symbolized God's inexhaustible and abundant power through the Holy Spirit. (2) Each light had seven channels or lips with a wick, thus giving forty-nine lights in all. These lamps represent God's people giving fullness of light to the world because of the abundant flow of the Holy Spirit.

4:3 TWO OLIVE TREES. The two olive trees represent the royal and priestly ministries of Zerubbabel and Joshua (see Hag 1:1, note). (1) The trees symbolize a continual source of oil; the two leaders were to lead the people into a life made possible by the power of the Spirit (v. 12). (2) Thus the trees represent the kingly and priestly ministries of Jesus Christ himself. He is the One who baptizes in the Holy Spirit, and all further fillings come from Christ.

4:6 NOT BY MIGHT NOR BY POWER, BUT BY MY SPIRIT. Though this message was spoken to Zerubbabel, it applies to all believers (cf. 2Ti 3:16). Military might, political power or human strength cannot accomplish God's work; we can only do his work if we are enabled by the Holy Spirit (cf. Jdg 6:34; Isa 31:3). Jesus entered his ministry in the power of the Spirit (Lk 4:1,18), and the church was empowered by the Holy Spirit at Pentecost (Ac 1:8; 2:4; see article on BAPTISM IN THE HOLY SPIRIT, p. 1642). Only if the Spirit continues to govern and empower our lives will we accomplish God's will for us; this is why Jesus baptizes his followers in the Holy Spirit (see Lk 3:16, note).

4:7 O MIGHTY MOUNTAIN. Difficulties that seem as large as a mountain can be overcome by the power of the Spirit working through us. Conversely, when the manifestations of the Spirit are not present among God's people, opposition to his work and spiritual problems will overwhelm them (see article on SPIRITUAL GIFTS FOR BELIEVERS, p. 1770).

4:10 WHO DESPISES THE DAY OF SMALL THINGS? What the people were doing seemed unimportant to some; however, no work done in the power and with the blessing of God's Spirit is ever insignificant, but has eternal value and importance.

2 He asked me, "What do you see?"[p]
I answered, "I see a flying scroll,
thirty feet long and fifteen feet
wide.[g]"
3 And he said to me, "This is the
curse[q] that is going out over the
whole land; for according to what it
says on one side, every thief[r] will be
banished, and according to what it
says on the other, everyone who
swears falsely[s] will be banished. 4 The
LORD Almighty declares, 'I will send it
out, and it will enter the house of the
thief and the house of him who swears
falsely[t] by my name. It will remain in
his house and destroy it, both its timbers and its stones.[u]' "

The Woman in a Basket

5 Then the angel who was speaking
to me came forward and said to me,
"Look up and see what this is that is
appearing."
6 I asked, "What is it?"
He replied, "It is a measuring basket.[h][v]" And he added, "This is the iniquity[i] of the people throughout the
land."
7 Then the cover of lead was raised,
and there in the basket sat a woman!
8 He said, "This is wickedness," and he
pushed her back into the basket and
pushed the lead cover down over its
mouth.[w]
9 Then I looked up—and there before me were two women, with the
wind in their wings! They had wings
like those of a stork,[x] and they lifted
up the basket between heaven and
earth.
10 "Where are they taking the basket?" I asked the angel who was speaking to me.
11 He replied, "To the country of Babylonia[j][y] to build a house[z] for it.
When it is ready, the basket will be set
there in its place."[a]

Four Chariots

6 I looked up again—and there before me were four chariots[b] coming out from between two mountains—
mountains of bronze! 2 The first chariot
had red horses, the second black,[c]
3 the third white,[d] and the fourth dappled—all of them powerful. 4 I asked
the angel who was speaking to me,
"What are these, my lord?"
5 The angel answered me, "These are
the four spirits[k][e] of heaven, going
out from standing in the presence of
the Lord of the whole world.[f] 6 The
one with the black horses is going toward the north country, the one with
the white horses toward the west,[l]
and the one with the dappled horses
toward the south."
7 When the powerful horses went
out, they were straining to go throughout the earth.[g] And he said, "Go
throughout the earth!" So they went
throughout the earth.
8 Then he called to me, "Look, those
going toward the north country have

5:2 [p] S Jer 1:13
5:3 [q] Isa 24:6; 34:2; 43:28; Mal 3:9; 4:6 [r] Ex 20:15; Mal 3:8 [s] Ex 20:7; Isa 48:1
5:4 [t] Zec 8:17 [u] Lev 14:34-45; S Pr 3:33; S Hab 2:9-11; Mal 3:5
5:6 [v] Mic 6:10
5:8 [w] Mic 6:11
5:9 [x] Lev 11:19
5:11 [y] S Ge 10:10 [z] Jer 29:5,28 [a] S Da 1:2
6:1 [b] ver 5; S 2Ki 2:11
6:2 [c] Rev 6:5
6:3 [d] Rev 6:2
6:5 [e] S Eze 37:9; Mt 24:31; Rev 7:1 [f] S Jos 3:11
6:7 [g] Isa 43:6; Zec 1:8

[g] 2 Hebrew *twenty cubits long and ten cubits wide* (about 9 meters long and 4.5 meters wide) [h] 6 Hebrew *an ephah*; also in verses 7-11 [i] 6 Or *appearance* [j] 11 Hebrew *Shinar* [k] 5 Or *winds* [l] 6 Or *horses after them*

5:1–4 A FLYING SCROLL. This flying scroll represented God's curse or judgment against sinners in the land of Israel. Though God is merciful and patient (see 2Pe 3:9), a time for judgment is coming that will quickly consume the wicked. The age of grace will someday come to an end. Judgment's ultimate fulfillment will come during the great tribulation.

5:5–11 A MEASURING BASKET. The measuring basket represents the sin and immorality of the people. (1) The woman represents idolatry and all kinds of wickedness; she was imprisoned in the basket by a heavy lead cover and was then taken to Babylonia, which represents the godless world system dominated by Satan (see Rev 17:1, note). The wicked among God's people not only had to be punished but also removed from the land. (2) Sin and wickedness must be removed from our churches or God will remove his Spirit from us (see Rev 2–3). In the end time God will remove sin from the whole earth, and Jesus Christ will reign in glory with his people (Rev 19—22).

6:1–5 THE FOUR SPIRITS OF HEAVEN. In his eighth vision, Zechariah saw four war chariots between two bronze mountains. (1) The colors of the horses pulling the chariots were red (signifying war), black (signifying famine and death) and dappled (signifying pestilence; cf. Rev 6:2–8). Most interpreters believe the chariot drawn by white horses represents the glorious victory of God's agents of judgment. (2) The four spirits are actually angelic beings (cf. Ps 104:4; Rev 7:1–3). (3) Both the war chariots and the bronze mountains speak of judgment against God's enemies. The riders and chariots go toward the north and the south, i.e., toward Babylon and Egypt, which also represent the northern and southern powers at the end of time, which God will destroy.

6:8 HAVE GIVEN MY SPIRIT REST. By bringing God's judgment, these angelic beings had satisfied his justice and caused his anger to cease (see alternate translation in NIV text note). God

given my Spirit[m] rest[h] in the land of the north."[i]

A Crown for Joshua

9The word of the LORD came to me: **10**"Take ⌊silver and gold⌋ from the exiles Heldai, Tobijah and Jedaiah, who have arrived from Babylon.[j] Go the same day to the house of Josiah son of Zephaniah. **11**Take the silver and gold and make a crown,[k] and set it on the head of the high priest, Joshua[l] son of Jehozadak.[m] **12**Tell him this is what the LORD Almighty says: 'Here is the man whose name is the Branch,[n] and he will branch out from his place and build the temple of the LORD.[o] **13**It is he who will build the temple of the LORD, and he will be clothed with majesty and will sit and rule on his throne. And he will be a priest[p] on his throne. And there will be harmony between the two.' **14**The crown will be given to Heldai,[n] Tobijah, Jedaiah and Hen[o] son of Zephaniah as a memorial[q] in the temple of the LORD. **15**Those who are far away will come and help to build the temple of the LORD,[r] and you will know that the LORD Almighty has sent me to you.[s] This will happen if you diligently obey[t] the LORD your God."

Justice and Mercy, Not Fasting

7 In the fourth year of King Darius, the word of the LORD came to Zechariah[u] on the fourth day of the ninth month, the month of Kislev.[v] **2**The people of Bethel had sent Sharezer and Regem-Melech, together with their men, to entreat[w] the LORD[x] **3**by asking the priests of the house of the LORD Almighty and the prophets, "Should I mourn[y] and fast in the fifth[z] month, as I have done for so many years?"

4Then the word of the LORD Almighty came to me: **5**"Ask all the people of the land and the priests, 'When you fasted[a] and mourned in the fifth and seventh[b] months for the past seventy years,[c] was it really for me that you fasted? **6**And when you were eating and drinking, were you not just feasting for yourselves?[d] **7**Are these not the words the LORD proclaimed through the earlier prophets[e] when Jerusalem and its surrounding towns were at rest[f] and prosperous, and the Negev and the western foothills[g] were settled?' "[h]

8And the word of the LORD came again to Zechariah: **9**"This is what the LORD Almighty says: 'Administer true justice;[i] show mercy and compassion to one another.[j] **10**Do not oppress the widow[k] or the fatherless, the alien[l] or the poor.[m] In your hearts do not think evil of each other.'[n]

11"But they refused to pay attention; stubbornly[o] they turned their backs[p] and stopped up their ears.[q] **12**They made their hearts as hard as flint[r] and would not listen to the law or to

6:8 [h] S Eze 5:13; S 24:13 [i] S Zec 1:10
6:10 [j] Ezr 7:14-16; Jer 28:6
6:11 [k] Ps 21:3 [l] S Ezr 2:2; S Zec 3:1 [m] S 1Ch 6:15; S Ezr 3:2
6:12 [n] S Isa 4:2; S Eze 17:22 [o] Ezr 3:8-10; Zec 4:6-9
6:13 [p] S Ps 110:4
6:14 [q] S Ex 28:12
6:15 [r] Isa 60:10 [s] Zec 2:9-11 [t] Isa 58:12; Jer 7:23; S Zec 3:7
7:1 [u] S Ezr 5:1 [v] Ne 1:1
7:2 [w] Jer 26:19; Zec 8:21 [x] Hag 2:10-14
7:3 [y] Zec 12:12-14 [z] 2Ki 25:9; Jer 52:12-14
7:5 [a] Isa 58:5 [b] 2Ki 25:25 [c] S Da 9:2
7:6 [d] S Isa 43:23
7:7 [e] Isa 1:11-20; Zec 1:4 [f] Jer 22:21 [g] S Jer 17:26 [h] Jer 44:4-5
7:9 [i] S Jer 22:3; 42:5; Zec 8:16 [j] S Dt 22:1
7:10 [k] Jer 49:11 [l] S Ex 22:21 [m] S Lev 25:17; Isa 1:23 [n] S Ex 22:22; S Job 35:8; S Isa 1:17; S Eze 45:9; S Mic 6:8
7:11 [o] S Isa 9:9 [p] S Jer 32:33 [q] S Jer 5:3; 8:5; 11:10; S 17:23; S Eze 5:6
7:12 [r] S Jer 5:3; 17:1; S Eze 11:19

[m] 8 Or *spirit* [n] 14 Syriac; Hebrew *Helem* [o] 14 Or *and the gracious one, the*

would see to it that his purposes were carried out in his own time.

6:13 WILL BE A PRIEST ON HIS THRONE. The Lord commanded Zechariah to make a crown of silver and gold and set it on the head of Joshua the high priest. (1) The crowning of Joshua foreshadows the crowning and the reign of Jesus, who is the "Branch," the Messiah (Isa 11:1; Jer 33:15; cf. Isa 53:2; see Zec 3:8, note). Jesus would be both priest and king; he would first do his priestly work, and then reign (cf. Isa 53:10; Lk 24:26). (2) At the present time, Jesus is our peace (Eph 2:14–15), and in him we find God's kingdom, which exists in righteousness, peace and joy in the Holy Spirit (Ro 14:17). The ultimate fulfillment of Christ's reign begins in the millennium, when he will rule on earth in a reign of peace (cf. Isa 9:6).

6:15 THOSE WHO ARE FAR AWAY WILL COME. This phrase refers to the Gentiles (cf. Eph 2:11–13).

7:1–5 WAS IT REALLY FOR ME THAT YOU FASTED? The law of God called for only one fast day each year, the Day of Atonement in the seventh month. The Jews at this time had added a fast in the fifth month to commemorate the destruction of the temple by Nebuchadnezzar's armies (2Ki 25:8–9). Now that the temple was being rebuilt (518 B.C.), they wanted to know if they had to continue observing that fast day. (1) The word of the Lord was that they were not fasting in the right way (see Mt 6:16, note); their fasting was mere formalism, empty of real hunger and thirst for God and his righteousness. (2) The people needed to pay attention to prophets such as Isaiah (cf. Isa 58:3–5) and to respond by fasting and by praying for grace to live holy and just lives before God and others (vv. 8–10).

7:12 MADE THEIR HEARTS AS HARD AS FLINT. Flint was one of the hardest substances known in OT times (see Jer 17:1; Eze 3:8–9). (1) God's call by his Spirit through the earlier prophets was for justice, mercy and compassion, but the people stubbornly refused to obey. Then when judgment came, it was too late to repent. (2) What God expects from his people has not changed, for he desires that we show love and compassion to those who experience various needs (see article on THE CARE OF THE POOR AND NEEDY, p. 1316).

the words that the LORD Almighty had sent by his Spirit through the earlier
Mk 16:17-18 prophets.[s] So the LORD Almighty was very angry.[t]

13"'When I called, they did not listen;[u] so when they called, I would not listen,'[v] says the LORD Almighty.[w] **14**'I scattered[x] them with a whirlwind[y] among all the nations, where they were strangers. The land was left so desolate behind them that no one could come or go.[z] This is how they made the pleasant land desolate.[a]' "

The LORD Promises to Bless Jerusalem

8 Again the word of the LORD Almighty came to me. **2**This is what the LORD Almighty says: "I am very jealous[b] for Zion; I am burning with jealousy for her."

3This is what the LORD says: "I will return[c] to Zion[d] and dwell in Jerusalem.[e] Then Jerusalem will be called the City of Truth,[f] and the mountain[g] of the LORD Almighty will be called the Holy Mountain.[h]"

4This is what the LORD Almighty says: "Once again men and women of ripe old age will sit in the streets of Jerusalem,[i] each with cane in hand because of his age. **5**The city streets will be filled with boys and girls playing there.[j]"

6This is what the LORD Almighty says: "It may seem marvelous to the remnant of this people at that time,[k] but will it seem marvelous to me?[l]" declares the LORD Almighty.

7This is what the LORD Almighty says: "I will save my people from the countries of the east and the west.[m] **8**I will bring them back[n] to live[o] in Jerusalem; they will be my people,[p] and I will be faithful and righteous to them as their God.[q]"

9This is what the LORD Almighty says: "You who now hear these words spoken by the prophets[r] who were there when the foundation[s] was laid for the house of the LORD Almighty, let your hands be strong[t] so that the temple may be built. **10**Before that time there were no wages[u] for man or beast. No one could go about his business safely[v] because of his enemy, for I had turned every man against his neighbor. **11**But now I will not deal with the remnant of this people as I did in the past,"[w] declares the LORD Almighty.

12"The seed will grow well, the vine will yield its fruit,[x] the ground will produce its crops,[y] and the heavens will drop their dew.[z] I will give all these things as an inheritance[a] to the remnant of this people.[b] **13**As you have been an object of cursing[c] among the nations, O Judah and Israel, so will I save[d] you, and you will be a blessing.[e] Do not be afraid,[f] but let your hands be strong.[g]"

14This is what the LORD Almighty says: "Just as I had determined to bring disaster[h] upon you and showed no pity when your fathers angered me," says the LORD Almighty, **15**"so now I have determined to do good[i] again to Jerusalem and Judah.[j] Do not be afraid. **16**These are the things you are to do: Speak the truth[k] to each other, and render true and sound judgment[l] in your courts;[m] **17**do not plot evil[n] against your neighbor, and do not love

7:12 [s]S Ne 9:29 [t]S Jer 42:21; S Da 9:12 **7:13** [u]S Jer 7:27 [v]Isa 1:15; S Jer 11:11; 14:12; S Mic 3:4 [w]S Pr 1:28; S La 3:44; S Eze 20:31 **7:14** [x]S Lev 26:33; Dt 4:27; 28:64-67; S Ps 44:11 [y]Jer 23:19 [z]S Isa 33:8 [a]S Jer 7:34; S 44:6; S Eze 12:19 **8:2** [b]S Joel 2:18 **8:3** [c]Zec 1:16 [d]S Isa 52:8; S Joel 3:21 [e]S Zec 2:10 [f]S Ps 15:2; S Isa 1:26; S 48:1; S Jer 33:16 [g]S Jer 26:18 [h]S Isa 1:26; S Mic 4:1 **8:4** [i]S Isa 65:20 **8:5** [j]S Jer 30:20; 31:13 **8:6** [k]Ps 118:23; 126:1-3 [l]Jer 32:17,27 **8:7** [m]Ps 107:3; S Isa 11:11; S 43:5 **8:8** [n]S Eze 37:12; Zec 10:10 [o]S Jer 31:24 [p]S Isa 51:16; S Eze 11:19-20; S 36:28; S Zec 2:11; Heb 8:10 [q]Jer 11:4; Zec 10:6 **8:9** [r]S Ezr 5:1 [s]S Ezr 3:11 [t]S Hag 2:4 **8:10** [u]S Isa 5:10; S Hag 1:6 [v]S 2Ch 15:5 **8:11** [w]Isa 12:1 **8:12** [x]S Ps 85:12; S Joel 2:22 [y]S Ps 67:6 [z]S Ge 27:28 [a]S Ps 65:13; S Isa 60:21; Ob 1:17 [b]S Hos 2:21 **8:13** [c]S Nu 5:27; S Dt 13:15; S Ps 102:8; Jer 42:18 [d]S Ps 48:8 [e]S Ge 12:2; S Joel 2:14 [f]S Hag 2:5 [g]ver 9 **8:14** [h]S Eze 24:14 **8:15** [i]ver 13; S Jer 29:11; Mic 7:18-20 [j]Jer 31:28; 32:42 **8:16** [k]S Ps 15:2; S Jer 33:16; S Eph 4:25 [l]S Eze 18:8 [m]S Eze 45:9; S Am 5:15; S Zec 7:9 **8:17** [n]Pr 3:29

8:3 I WILL RETURN TO ZION. The key to Israel's full restoration is God's return to Zion, pointing to the time when Christ returns in glory and begins his earthly reign over the nations. At that time God's presence will make Jerusalem a city of truth and faithfulness, and the mountain of the Lord will be holy, i.e., set apart for his worship. This chapter gives ten blessings that will accompany that earthly reign, each one beginning with the phrase, "This is what the LORD Almighty says."

8:4–5 RIPE OLD AGE . . . BOYS AND GIRLS. These verses picture the peace, prosperity and happiness in the future millennial Jerusalem.

8:7–8 I WILL SAVE MY PEOPLE. The restoration after the Babylonian exile was only from the east; thus, this section refers to a future restoration from the east and the west, i.e., from the whole earth (cf. Isa 43:5–6). God will truly become the God of his people, and they will partake of his righteousness through Christ.

8:16–17 THE THINGS YOU ARE TO DO. In view of God's return to his people and of the hope contained within these millennial prophecies, the people of Zechariah's day were to respond with conduct worthy of the Lord they served (cf. 7:9–10). Prophecy has never been given merely to satisfy our curiosity. God expects our hope for the future to cause us to seek him and his kingdom with greater intensity and commitment (cf. Jas 1:22; 1Jn 3:2–3).

to swear falsely.[o] I hate all this," declares the LORD.
18Again the word of the LORD Almighty came to me. 19This is what the
LORD Almighty says: "The fasts of the
fourth,[p] fifth,[q] seventh[r] and tenth[s]
months will become joyful[t] and glad
occasions and happy festivals for Judah. Therefore love truth[u] and
peace."
20This is what the LORD Almighty
says: "Many peoples and the inhabitants of many cities will yet come,
21and the inhabitants of one city will
go to another and say, 'Let us go at
once to entreat[v] the LORD and seek[w]
the LORD Almighty. I myself am going.'
22And many peoples and powerful nations will come to Jerusalem to seek
the LORD Almighty and to entreat
him."[x]
23This is what the LORD Almighty
says: "In those days ten men from all
languages and nations will take firm
hold of one Jew by the hem of his robe
and say, 'Let us go with you, because
we have heard that God is with
you.' "[y]

Judgment on Israel's Enemies

An Oracle[z]

9 The word of the LORD is against
the land of Hadrach
and will rest upon
Damascus[a] —
for the eyes of men and all the
tribes of Israel
are on the LORD —[p]
2and upon Hamath[b] too, which
borders on it,
and upon Tyre[c] and Sidon,[d]
though they are very
skillful.
3Tyre has built herself a stronghold;
she has heaped up silver like
dust,
and gold like the dirt of the
streets.[e]
4But the Lord will take away her
possessions
and destroy[f] her power on the
sea,
and she will be consumed by
fire.[g]
5Ashkelon[h] will see it and fear;
Gaza will writhe in agony,
and Ekron too, for her hope will
wither.
Gaza will lose her king
and Ashkelon will be deserted.
6Foreigners will occupy Ashdod,
and I will cut off[i] the pride of
the Philistines.
7I will take the blood from their
mouths,
the forbidden food from between
their teeth.
Those who are left will belong to
our God[j]
and become leaders in Judah,
and Ekron will be like the
Jebusites.[k]
8But I will defend[l] my house
against marauding forces.[m]
Never again will an oppressor
overrun my people,
for now I am keeping watch.[n]

The Coming of Zion's King

9Rejoice greatly, O Daughter of
Zion![o]
Shout,[p] Daughter of Jerusalem!
See, your king[q] comes to you,[q]
righteous and having
salvation,[r]

8:17 [o] S Pr 6:16-19; S Jer 7:9; Zec 5:4 **8:19** [p] S 2Ki 25:7; Jer 39:2 [q] S Jer 52:12 [r] 2Ki 25:25 [s] Jer 52:4 [t] Ps 30:11 [u] ver 16 **8:21** [v] S Zec 7:2 [w] Jer 26:19 **8:22** [x] S Ps 86:9; 117:1; Isa 2:2-3; S 44:5; S 45:14; 49:6; S Zec 2:11 **8:23** [y] S Ps 102:22; S Isa 14:1; S 45:14; S 56:3; 1Co 14:25 **9:1** [z] S Isa 13:1; Jer 23:33 [a] Isa 17:1; S Am 1:5 **9:2** [b] S Jer 49:23 [c] Eze 28:1-19 [d] S Ge 10:15

9:3 [e] Job 27:16; S Eze 28:4 **9:4** [f] S Isa 23:11 [g] S Isa 23:1; Jer 25:22; Eze 26:3-5; 27:32-36; 28:18 **9:5** [h] Jer 47:5 **9:6** [i] S Isa 14:30 **9:7** [j] S Job 25:2 [k] S Jer 47:1; S Joel 3:4; S Zep 2:4 **9:8** [l] S Isa 26:1 [m] Zec 14:21 [n] S Isa 52:1; S 54:14; S Joel 3:17 **9:9** [o] S Isa 62:11 [p] S 1Ki 1:39 [q] S Ps 24:7; S 149:2; Mic 4:8 [r] Isa 9:6-7; 43:3-11; Jer 23:5-6; Zep 3:14-15; Zec 2:10

[p] *1* Or *Damascus. / For the eye of the LORD is on all mankind, / as well as on the tribes of Israel,*
[q] *9* Or *King*

8:22 TO SEEK THE LORD ALMIGHTY. Incomparable joy will come as many Gentiles join Jews in seeking the Lord in Jerusalem, for the Lord will be there (see Eze 48:35); this pictures the final fulfillment of the promise in the Abrahamic covenant that Gentiles would be brought to the Lord (Ge 12:3; Gal 3:8,26–29; see article on GOD'S COVENANT WITH ABRAHAM, ISAAC AND JACOB, p. 46).

9:1 THE EYES OF MEN ... ARE ON THE LORD. Because of God's promises, Israel would turn to the Lord for deliverance, as would many others. The result would be judgment on the various nations around Israel who had caused them so much suffering in the past. Alexander the Great brought a partial fulfillment of this prophecy in 332 B.C.

9:8 NEVER AGAIN WILL AN OPPRESSOR OVERRUN. Ultimate peace will come to earthly Jerusalem during the Messiah's millennial reign. God will not allow his people to be totally destroyed. The same assurance is given to the church, for the gates of hell will never overcome it (see Mt 16:18, note).

9:9 YOUR KING COMES ... HAVING SALVATION. A still greater cause for rejoicing is the coming of the King, not in royal splendor but in humility (cf. Php 2:5–8), riding on a donkey. Zechariah's prophecy foresees Jesus' triumphal entry into Jerusalem (Mt 21:1–5). By riding into the holy city in this way, Jesus declared himself to be Messiah and Savior, ready to go to the cross.

gentle and riding on a donkey,[s]
on a colt, the foal of a donkey.[t]
10I will take away the chariots from
Ephraim
and the war-horses from
Jerusalem,
and the battle bow will be
broken.[u]
He will proclaim peace[v] to the
nations.
His rule will extend from sea to
sea
Zec 14:3-9 and from the River[r] to the ends
of the earth.[s][w]
11As for you, because of the blood of
my covenant[x] with you,
I will free your prisoners[y] from
the waterless pit.[z]
12Return to your fortress,[a]
O prisoners of hope;
even now I announce that I will
restore twice[b] as much to
you.
13I will bend Judah as I bend my
bow[c]
and fill it with Ephraim.[d]
I will rouse your sons, O Zion,
against your sons, O Greece,[e]
and make you like a warrior's
sword.[f]

The LORD Will Appear

14Then the LORD will appear over
them;[g]
his arrow will flash like
lightning.[h]
The Sovereign LORD will sound the
trumpet;[i]
he will march in the storms[j] of
the south,
15 and the LORD Almighty will
shield[k] them.
They will destroy
and overcome with
slingstones.[l]
They will drink and roar as with
wine;[m]
they will be full like a bowl[n]
used for sprinkling[t] the
corners[o] of the altar.
16The LORD their God will save them
on that day[p]
as the flock of his people.
They will sparkle in his land
like jewels in a crown.[q]
17How attractive and beautiful they
will be!
Grain will make the young men
thrive,
and new wine the young women.

The LORD Will Care for Judah

10 Ask the LORD for rain in the
springtime;
it is the LORD who makes the
storm clouds.
He gives showers of rain[r] to men,
and plants of the field[s] to
everyone.
2The idols[t] speak deceit,
diviners[u] see visions that lie;
they tell dreams[v] that are false,
they give comfort in vain.[w]
Therefore the people wander like
sheep
oppressed for lack of a
shepherd.[x]
3"My anger burns against the
shepherds,
and I will punish the leaders;[y]
for the LORD Almighty will care

9:9 [s] S Ge 49:11; S 1Ki 1:33 [t] Mt 21:5*; Jn 12:15* **9:10** [u] Hos 1:7; 2:18; Mic 4:3; 5:10; Zec 10:4 [v] S Isa 2:4 [w] Ps 72:8 **9:11** [x] S Ex 24:8; S Mt 26:28; S Lk 22:20 [y] S Isa 10:4; S 42:7 [z] Jer 38:6 **9:12** [a] S Joel 3:16 [b] S Dt 21:17; S Isa 40:2 **9:13** [c] S 2Sa 22:35 [d] S Isa 49:2 [e] S Joel 3:6 [f] S Jer 51:20 **9:14** [g] Isa 31:5 [h] Ps 18:14; S Hab 3:11 [i] S Lev 25:9; S Mt 24:31 [j] Isa 21:1; 66:15 **9:15** [k] Isa 31:5; 37:35; Zec 12:8 [l] Zec 14:3 [m] Zec 10:7 [n] Zec 14:20 [o] S Ex 27:2 **9:16** [p] S Isa 10:20 [q] S Jer 31:11 **10:1** [r] S Lev 26:4; S 1Ki 8:36; S Ps 104:13; S 135:7 [s] S Job 14:9 **10:2** [t] Eze 21:21 [u] S Isa 44:25 [v] Jer 23:16 [w] S Isa 40:19 [x] S Nu 27:17; S Jer 23:1; S Hos 3:4; S Mt 9:36 **10:3** [y] Isa 14:9; S Jer 25:34

[r] *10* That is, the Euphrates [s] *10* Or *the end of the land* [t] *15* Or *bowl, / like*

9:10 PROCLAIM PEACE . . . RULE WILL EXTEND. Without referring to the period of time between Christ's resurrection and his second coming, Zechariah jumps ahead to his second coming at the end of the age. After Christ's triumph over the antichrist and his armies, there will be no more need for battle chariots, war-horses or any war instruments; his rule will extend over the entire earth.

9:12 RETURN TO YOUR FORTRESS, O PRISONERS OF HOPE. The future of the scattered Israelites is not hopeless; God promises to restore them with his double blessing because of all they have suffered.

9:13 GREECE. Greece came into prominence in 480–479 B.C., when the Greeks defeated Xerxes. Fulfillment of the prophecy in this verse came in the defeat of Antiochus Epiphanes about 168 B.C.

9:16–17 THEIR GOD WILL SAVE THEM. God's salvation will reach a climax when he makes Israel his flock, his people. Their salvation will be a crowning work, lifted up for the rest of the world to see. This result is guaranteed by the Lord's great goodness and beauty. All that the Lord does for his people reflects his goodness and the beauty of his holiness.

10:1 FOR RAIN IN THE SPRINGTIME. See Hos 6:2–3, note.

10:2 DIVINERS SEE VISIONS THAT LIE. Because the people had no true shepherd to lead them in the right paths, i.e., the paths of trust in God, they had turned to reliance on idols, fortune tellers, and other occult practices. Pastors and teachers who destroy confidence in the Bible by denying its divine inspiration and infallibility indirectly influence people to turn to such practices today.

for his flock, the house of Judah,
and make them like a proud
horse in battle.[z]
4From Judah will come the
cornerstone,[a]
from him the tent peg,[b]
from him the battle bow,[c]
from him every ruler.
5Together they[u] will be like mighty
men
trampling the muddy streets in
battle.[d]
Because the LORD is with them,
they will fight and overthrow the
horsemen.[e]

6"I will strengthen[f] the house of
Judah
and save the house of Joseph.
I will restore them
because I have compassion[g] on
them.[h]
They will be as though
I had not rejected them,
for I am the LORD their God
and I will answer[i] them.
7The Ephraimites will become like
mighty men,
and their hearts will be glad as
with wine.[j]
Their children will see it and be
joyful;
their hearts will rejoice[k] in the
LORD.
8I will signal[l] for them
and gather them in.
Surely I will redeem them;
they will be as numerous[m] as
before.
9Though I scatter them among the
peoples,
yet in distant lands they will
remember me.[n]
They and their children will
survive,
and they will return.
10I will bring them back from Egypt
and gather them from Assyria.[o]
I will bring them to Gilead[p] and
Lebanon,
and there will not be room[q]
enough for them.
11They will pass through the sea of
trouble;
the surging sea will be subdued
and all the depths of the Nile
will dry up.[r]
Assyria's pride[s] will be brought
down
and Egypt's scepter[t] will pass
away.[u]
12I will strengthen[v] them in the
LORD
and in his name they will
walk,[w]"
declares the LORD.

11 Open your doors,
O Lebanon,[x]
so that fire[y] may devour your
cedars!
2Wail, O pine tree, for the cedar has
fallen;
the stately trees are ruined!
Wail, oaks[z] of Bashan;
the dense forest[a] has been cut
down![b]
3Listen to the wail of the
shepherds;
their rich pastures are
destroyed!
Listen to the roar of the lions;[c]
the lush thicket of the Jordan is
ruined![d]

Two Shepherds

4This is what the LORD my God says:
"Pasture the flock marked for slaughter.[e] 5Their buyers slaughter them
and go unpunished. Those who sell
them say, 'Praise the LORD, I am rich!'
Their own shepherds do not spare
them.[f] 6For I will no longer have pity
on the people of the land," declares the
LORD. "I will hand everyone over to his

[u]4,5 Or *ruler, all of them together. / 5They*

10:3 [z]S Eze 34:8-10
10:4 [a]S Ps 118:22; S Ac 4:11 [b]S Isa 22:23 [c]S Zec 9:10
10:5 [d]S 2Sa 22:43; S Mic 7:10 [e]S Am 2:15; S Mic 5:8; Hag 2:22; Zec 12:4
10:6 [f]S Eze 30:24 [g]S Ps 102:13; S Isa 14:1 [h]S Eze 36:37; 37:19; S Zec 8:7-8 [i]Ps 34:17; Isa 58:9; 65:24; Zec 13:9
10:7 [j]Zec 9:15 [k]S 1Sa 2:1; S Isa 60:5; S Joel 2:23
10:8 [l]Isa 5:26 [m]S Jer 33:22; S Eze 36:11
10:9 [n]S Isa 44:21; S Eze 6:9
10:10 [o]S Isa 11:11; S Zec 8:8 [p]S Jer 50:19 [q]S Isa 49:19
10:11 [r]Isa 19:5-7; S 51:10 [s]Zep 2:13 [t]Eze 30:13 [u]Eze 29:15
10:12 [v]S Eze 30:24 [w]S Mic 4:5
11:1 [x]S Eze 31:3 [y]S 2Ch 36:19; Zec 12:6
11:2 [z]S Isa 2:13 [a]Isa 32:19 [b]S Isa 10:34
11:3 [c]S Isa 5:29 [d]Jer 2:15; 50:44; Eze 19:9
11:4 [e]S Jer 25:34
11:5 [f]Jer 50:7; S Eze 34:2-3

10:4 FROM JUDAH WILL COME THE CORNERSTONE. Out of the tribe of Judah came the cornerstone (Ps 118:22; Isa 28:16), Jesus the Messiah, who would be like the tent peg, indicating security (cf. Isa 22:22–23); he would be the victorious King (cf. Rev 19:11–16).

10:6–8 JUDAH ... JOSEPH. God's purpose was to redeem and save all twelve tribes of Israel. Judah represents the southern two tribes and Joseph the northern ten tribes.

10:11 ASSYRIA'S ... EGYPT'S. Assyria represented Israel's enemies to the north and east, while Egypt represented the enemies to the south. God promised to remove all opposition to Israel's restoration.

11:4–17 PASTURE THE FLOCK. Zechariah was instructed to represent God's appointed Shepherd of Israel, the Messiah (vv. 4–14). Next he was to portray Israel's wicked shepherd (vv. 15–17), which may prefigure the end-time antichrist.

11:4 FLOCK MARKED FOR SLAUGHTER. The flock is Israel, marked for punishment because they would reject the Messiah; the slaughter would be carried out by the Romans in A.D. 70.

neighbor[g] and his king. They will oppress the land, and I will not rescue
them from their hands."[h]
7So I pastured the flock marked for
slaughter,[i] particularly the oppressed of the flock. Then I took two
staffs and called one Favor and the other Union, and I pastured the flock. 8In
one month I got rid of the three shepherds.
The flock detested[j] me, and I grew
weary of them 9and said, "I will not be
your shepherd. Let the dying die, and
the perishing perish.[k] Let those who
are left eat[l] one another's flesh."
10Then I took my staff called Favor[m] and broke it, revoking[n] the covenant I had made with all the nations.
11It was revoked on that day, and so
the afflicted of the flock who were
watching me knew it was the word of
the LORD.
12I told them, "If you think it best,
give me my pay; but if not, keep it." So
they paid me thirty pieces of silver.[o]
13And the LORD said to me, "Throw
it to the potter"—the handsome price
at which they priced me! So I took the
thirty pieces of silver[p] and threw
them into the house of the LORD to the
potter.[q]
14Then I broke my second staff
called Union, breaking the brotherhood
between Judah and Israel.
15Then the LORD said to me, "Take
again the equipment of a foolish shepherd. 16For I am going to raise up a
shepherd over the land who will not
care for the lost, or seek the young, or
heal the injured, or feed the healthy,
but will eat the meat of the choice
sheep, tearing off their hoofs.

17"Woe to the worthless shepherd,[r]
who deserts the flock!
May the sword strike his arm[s]
and his right eye!
May his arm be completely
withered,
his right eye totally blinded!"[t]

Jerusalem's Enemies to Be Destroyed

An Oracle[u]

12 This is the word of the LORD
concerning Israel. The LORD,
who stretches out the heavens,[v] who
lays the foundation of the earth,[w] and
who forms the spirit of man[x] within
him, declares: 2"I am going to make
Jerusalem a cup[y] that sends all the
surrounding peoples reeling.[z] Judah[a] will be besieged as well as Jerusalem. 3On that day, when all the nations[b] of the earth are gathered
against her, I will make Jerusalem an
immovable rock[c] for all the nations.
All who try to move it will injure[d]
themselves. 4On that day I will strike
every horse with panic and its rider
with madness," declares the LORD. "I
will keep a watchful eye over the house
of Judah, but I will blind all the horses
of the nations.[e] 5Then the leaders of
Judah will say in their hearts, 'The people of Jerusalem are strong,[f] because
the LORD Almighty is their God.'
6"On that day I will make the leaders
of Judah like a firepot[g] in a woodpile,
like a flaming torch among sheaves.

11:6 [g] Zec 14:13 [h] Isa 9:19-21; S Jer 13:14; S La 2:21; 5:8; S Mic 5:8; 7:2-6 **11:7** [i] S Jer 25:34 **11:8** [j] S Eze 14:5 **11:9** [k] S Jer 43:11 [l] S Isa 9:20 **11:10** [m] ver 7 [n] S Ps 89:39; Jer 14:21 **11:12** [o] S Ge 23:16; Mt 26:15 **11:13** [p] S Ex 21:32 [q] Mt 27:9-10*; Ac 1:18-19 **11:17** [r] Jer 23:1 [s] S Eze 30:21-22 [t] S Jer 23:1 **12:1** [u] S Isa 13:1 [v] S Ge 1:8; S Ps 104:2; S Jer 51:15 [w] Ps 102:25; Heb 1:10 [x] S Isa 57:16 **12:2** [y] S Ps 75:8 [z] S Ps 60:3; S Isa 51:23 [a] Zec 14:14 **12:3** [b] Isa 66:18; Zec 14:2 [c] S Isa 28:16; Da 2:34-35 [d] S Isa 29:8 **12:4** [e] Ps 76:6; S Zec 10:5 **12:5** [f] S Eze 30:24 **12:6** [g] Isa 10:17-18; S Zec 11:1

11:7 TWO STAFFS. Zechariah, representing the Messiah, uses two staffs to pasture his flock. The staffs represent God's favor toward Israel and his plan to unite Israel and Judah as a single nation. These blessings would become reality if the people would follow the Messiah.

11:9 I WILL NOT BE YOUR SHEPHERD. Because the flock despised the Shepherd-Messiah, he would turn from his role as Shepherd and give the people over to their doom.

11:10 REVOKING THE COVENANT. God had made a covenant to restrain the nations from attacking Israel. Zechariah vividly describes God removing that protection and Israel being destroyed and dispersed; this occurred in 70 A.D. when the Romans destroyed Jerusalem.

11:12 THIRTY PIECES OF SILVER. Zechariah, still representing the Messiah, asked the leaders to pay him what they thought his services were worth. They insulted him by offering him the price of a slave (Ex 21:32). Thirty pieces of silver was also the price paid to Judas for betraying Jesus (Mt 27:3–10).

11:14 BREAKING THE BROTHERHOOD. Part of God's judgment was the destruction of Israel's unity; the covenant nation would break up into hostile factions.

11:15–16 A FOOLISH SHEPHERD. Zechariah was now to take again the equipment of a shepherd and impersonate a godless shepherd, who used that equipment to hurt the sheep rather than help them (see vv. 4–17, note). The foolish shepherd will have its final fulfillment in the antichrist (cf. Eze 34:2–4; Da 11:36–39; Jn 5:43; 2Th 2:3–10; Rev 13:1–8).

12:3–9 ALL THE NATIONS . . . GATHERED AGAINST HER. At the end of time, many nations will gather against Jerusalem and Israel. God will intervene and destroy her enemies, and the world powers will be overthrown at the battle called Armageddon (see Rev 16:16, note; 19:19).

They will consume[h] right and left all
the surrounding peoples, but Jerusalem will remain intact[i] in her place.
7"The LORD will save the dwellings of
Judah first, so that the honor of the
house of David and of Jerusalem's inhabitants may not be greater than that
of Judah.[j] **8**On that day the LORD will
shield[k] those who live in Jerusalem,
so that the feeblest[l] among them will
be like David, and the house of David
will be like God,[m] like the Angel of the
LORD going before[n] them. **9**On that day
I will set out to destroy all the nations[o] that attack Jerusalem.[p]

Mourning for the One They Pierced

10"And I will pour out on the house
of David and the inhabitants of Jerusalem a spirit[v][q] of grace and supplication.[r] They will look on[w] me, the one
they have pierced,[s] and they will
mourn for him as one mourns for an
only child,[t] and grieve bitterly for him
as one grieves for a firstborn son.[u]
11On that day the weeping[v] in Jerusalem will be great, like the weeping of
Hadad Rimmon in the plain of Megiddo.[w] **12**The land will mourn,[x] each
clan by itself, with their wives by themselves: the clan of the house of David
and their wives, the clan of the house
of Nathan and their wives, **13**the clan of
the house of Levi and their wives, the
clan of Shimei and their wives, **14**and
all the rest of the clans and their
wives.[y]

12:6 [h] Ob 1:18 [i] Zec 14:10
12:7 [j] Jer 30:18; S Am 9:11
12:8 [k] S Ps 91:4; S Joel 3:16; S Zec 9:15 [l] Joel 3:10 [m] Ps 82:6 [n] Mic 7:8
12:9 [o] S Isa 29:7 [p] S Zec 1:21; 14:2-3
12:10 [q] S Eze 37:9 [r] Isa 44:3; S Eze 39:29; Joel 2:28-29 [s] S Ps 22:16; Jn 19:34,37* [t] Jdg 11:34 [u] S Ge 21:16; Jer 31:19
12:11 [v] Jer 50:4 [w] 2Ki 23:29
12:12 [x] Mt 24:30; Rev 1:7
12:14 [y] Zec 7:3
13:1 [z] Jer 17:13 [a] S Lev 16:30; S Ps 51:2; Heb 9:14
13:2 [b] S Jer 43:12; S Eze 6:6; S 36:25; S Hos 2:17 [c] S Mic 5:13 [d] 1Ki 22:22; Jer 23:14-15
13:3 [e] S Jer 28:16 [f] Dt 13:6-11; 18:20; S Ne 6:14; Jer 23:34; S Eze 14:9
13:4 [g] S Jer 6:15 [h] Mt 3:4 [i] S 1Ki 18:7; S Isa 20:2 [j] S Eze 12:24
13:5 [k] S Am 7:14
13:7 [l] S Isa 34:5; Jer 47:6 [m] Isa 40:11; S 53:4; Eze 37:24

Cleansing From Sin

13 "On that day a fountain[z] will
be opened to the house of David
and the inhabitants of Jerusalem, to
cleanse[a] them from sin and impurity.
2"On that day, I will banish the
names of the idols[b] from the land, and
they will be remembered no more,"[c]
declares the LORD Almighty. "I will remove both the prophets[d] and the spirit of impurity from the land. **3**And if
anyone still prophesies, his father and
mother, to whom he was born, will say
to him, 'You must die, because you
have told lies[e] in the LORD's name.'
When he prophesies, his own parents
will stab him.[f]
4"On that day every prophet will be
ashamed[g] of his prophetic vision. He
will not put on a prophet's garment[h]
of hair[i] in order to deceive.[j] **5**He will
say, 'I am not a prophet. I am a farmer;
the land has been my livelihood since
my youth.[x][k] **6**If someone asks him,
'What are these wounds on your
body[y]?' he will answer, 'The wounds
I was given at the house of my friends.'

The Shepherd Struck, the Sheep Scattered

7"Awake, O sword,[l] against my
shepherd,[m]
against the man who is close to
me!"
declares the LORD Almighty.

[v] *10 Or the Spirit* [w] *10 Or to* [x] *5 Or farmer; a man sold me in my youth* [y] *6 Or wounds between your hands*

12:10–14 A SPIRIT OF GRACE. These verses speak of the conversion of individual Jews who, in danger of being defeated by their enemies, come to believe in Jesus as the true Messiah.

12:10 THEY WILL MOURN FOR HIM. In the midst of danger on that day of battle, the people will cry out to God for his help. God will pour out his Holy Spirit to bring his grace and to answer their prayers. (1) The repentant people will then recognize that they were guilty for the Roman sword that pierced the side of Jesus the Messiah (cf. Ps 22:16; Isa 53:5; Jn 19:34) and for his death. (2) Their mourning will be bitter. Each family will mourn separately, as will husbands and wives. Thus, each individual will have to repent personally of his or her sin and rejection of Jesus Christ (cf. Ro 3:23; 6:23; Ac 16:31; 1Pe 2:24).

13:1–6 FOUNTAIN WILL BE OPENED TO THE HOUSE OF DAVID. This fountain pictures the cleansing from sin brought about by Christ's death on the cross. The Jewish people will be cleansed from sin in the same way that all believers in Christ are (cf. 1Jn 1:7,9).

13:4 EVERY PROPHET WILL BE ASHAMED. In those days God will expose all false prophets, who will be so afraid and ashamed that each will say, "I am not a prophet. I am a farmer." Until that time we must recognize that there will be many false prophets among the churches; in that light God calls us to test the spirits (1Jn 4:1, note; see article on FALSE TEACHERS, p. 1506).

13:6 WOUNDS ON YOUR BODY. These wounds are probably self-inflicted wounds associated with idol worship (vv. 2–5).

13:7 SWORD . . . STRIKE THE SHEPHERD. In this prophetic view of the future, the shepherd is the Messiah. (1) God calls the shepherd a "man who is close to me" (i.e., my equal, my associate), and thus a divine Messiah. (2) The Shepherd-Messiah would be struck, i.e., crucified. His disciples would then be scattered like sheep (see Mt 26:31, 56; Mk 14:27). This prophecy may also foreshadow the scattering of the Jewish nation in A.D. 70.

"Strike the shepherd,
and the sheep will be
scattered,[n]
and I will turn my hand against
the little ones.
8In the whole land," declares the
LORD,
"two-thirds will be struck down
and perish;
yet one-third will be left in it.[o]
9This third I will bring into the
fire;[p]
I will refine them like silver[q]
and test them like gold.[r]
They will call[s] on my name[t]
and I will answer[u] them;
I will say, 'They are my people,'[v]
and they will say, 'The LORD is
our God.[w]' "

The LORD Comes and Reigns

14 A day of the LORD[x] is coming
when your plunder[y] will be divided among you.
2I will gather all the nations[z] to Jerusalem to fight against it;[a] the city
will be captured, the houses ransacked, and the women raped.[b] Half
of the city will go into exile, but the
rest of the people will not be taken
from the city.[c]
3Then the LORD will go out and
fight[d] against those nations, as he
fights in the day of battle.[e] 4On that
day his feet will stand on the Mount of
Olives,[f] east of Jerusalem, and the
Mount of Olives will be split[g] in two
from east to west, forming a great valley, with half of the mountain moving
north and half moving south. 5You will
flee by my mountain valley, for it will
extend to Azel. You will flee as you fled
from the earthquake[z][h] in the days of
Uzziah king of Judah. Then the LORD my
God will come,[i] and all the holy ones
with him.[j]
6On that day there will be no light,[k]
no cold or frost. 7It will be a unique[l]
day, without daytime or nighttime[m]—
a day known to the LORD. When evening
comes, there will be light.[n]
8On that day living water[o] will
flow[p] out from Jerusalem, half to the
eastern[q] sea[a] and half to the western
sea,[b] in summer and in winter.[r]
9The LORD will be king[s] over the
whole earth.[t] On that day there will
be one LORD, and his name the only
name.[u]
10The whole land, from Geba[v] to
Rimmon,[w] south of Jerusalem, will become like the Arabah. But Jerusalem
will be raised up[x] and remain in its
place,[y] from the Benjamin Gate[z] to
the site of the First Gate, to the Corner

13:7 [n] S 2Sa 17:2; Mt 26:31*; Mk 14:27* **13:8** [o] S Eze 5:2-4,12; Zec 14:2 **13:9** [p] S Isa 4:4; 33:14; Mal 3:2 [q] S Ps 12:6; S Da 11:35; 1Pe 1:6-7 [r] S Job 6:29; S Jer 6:27 [s] S Ps 50:15 [t] Ps 105:1 [u] S Ps 86:7; S Isa 30:19; S Zec 10:6 [v] S Lev 26:12; S Jer 30:22 [w] S Isa 44:5; S Jer 29:12; S Eze 20:38 **14:1** [x] Isa 13:6; S Joel 1:15; Mal 4:1 [y] S Isa 23:18 **14:2** [z] S Isa 2:3; S Zec 12:3 [a] S Eze 5:8 [b] S Ge 34:29; S La 5:11 [c] Isa 13:6; S Zec 13:8 **14:3** [d] Zec 9:14-15 [e] S Isa 8:9; S Zec 12:9 **14:4** [f] Eze 11:23 [g] S Nu 16:31 **14:5** [h] Am 1:1 [i] Isa 29:6; 66:15-16 [j] S Dt 33:2; Mt 16:27; 25:31; Jude 14 **14:6** [k] S Isa 13:10; S Jer 4:23 **14:7** [l] Jer 30:7 [m] Rev 21:23-25; 22:5 [n] S Isa 13:10; S 30:26 **14:8** [o] Eze 47:1-12; Jn 7:38; Rev 22:1-2 [p] S Isa 30:25 [q] Joel 2:20 [r] S Ge 8:22 **14:9** [s] S Ps 22:28; S Ob 1:21 [t] S Dt 6:4; Ps 47:7; Isa 45:24; Rev 11:15 [u] Hab 2:14; Eph 4:5-6 **14:10** [v] 1Ki 15:22 [w] S Jos 15:32 [x] Isa 2:2; Jer 30:18; S Am 9:11 [y] Zec 12:6 [z] S Jer 20:2

[z] 5 Or *5My mountain valley will be blocked and will extend to Azel. It will be blocked as it was blocked because of the earthquake* [a] 8 That is, the Dead Sea [b] 8 That is, the Mediterranean

13:8–9 THIS THIRD I WILL BRING INTO THE FIRE. These verses probably refer to the tribulation period at the end of time (see article on THE GREAT TRIBULATION, p. 1456). The unbelieving Jews (two-thirds) will be killed (v. 8); only one-third will be left. These people are the ones who will "look on . . . the one they have pierced" (12:10–14); thus, only a remnant of Israel will be saved (Rev 11—18).

14:1 A DAY OF THE LORD IS COMING. The "day of the LORD" is a time of both judgment and restoration. Here it refers to the time when Christ will return to judge the nations and establish his earthly reign.

14:2 GATHER ALL THE NATIONS TO JERUSALEM. The nations will appear to gain a military victory, but they will ultimately be destroyed (see 12:3–9, note).

14:3 THEN THE LORD WILL GO OUT. The Lord will intervene in the battle and defeat the nations.

14:4 HIS FEET WILL STAND ON THE MOUNT OF OLIVES. This prophecy will be fulfilled by Jesus Christ at his final coming when he returns to the place from which he left (Lk 24:50–51; Ac 1:9–12). The topography of that area will be dramatically changed as the mountain splits in two, half moving north, half south, leaving a valley between.

14:8 LIVING WATER WILL FLOW OUT FROM JERUSALEM. Living water (in contrast to stagnant water) will flow out of Jerusalem (cf. Ps 46:4; Eze 47:1–12; Joel 3:18). Instead of drying up in summer, as most Palestinian streams do, its flow will be constant to the Mediterranean Sea and to the Dead Sea. This passage envisions God's blessings flowing from the millennial Jerusalem (Rev 22:1).

14:9 THE LORD WILL BE KING OVER THE WHOLE EARTH. When Christ establishes his kingdom, he will be worshiped by all the people of the earth (cf. 4:14; 6:5; Mic 4:13; Rev 17:14; 19:16).

14:10 WILL BECOME LIKE THE ARABAH. As a result of our Lord's return, the land around Jerusalem will be flattened, even though Jerusalem itself will be a plateau, elevated a little above the surrounding area so that it stands out.

Gate,[a] and from the Tower of Hananel[b] to the royal winepresses. **11**It will
be inhabited;[c] never again will it be
destroyed. Jerusalem will be secure.[d]
12This is the plague with which the
LORD will strike[e] all the nations that
fought against Jerusalem: Their flesh
will rot while they are still standing on
their feet, their eyes will rot in their
sockets, and their tongues will rot in
their mouths.[f] **13**On that day men will
be stricken by the LORD with great panic.[g] Each man will seize the hand of
another, and they will attack each other.[h] **14**Judah[i] too will fight at Jerusalem. The wealth of all the surrounding
nations will be collected[j]—great
quantities of gold and silver and clothing. **15**A similar plague[k] will strike
the horses and mules, the camels and
donkeys, and all the animals in those
camps.
16Then the survivors[l] from all the
nations that have attacked Jerusalem
will go up year after year to worship[m]
the King,[n] the LORD Almighty, and to
celebrate the Feast of Tabernacles.[o]
17If any of the peoples of the earth do
not go up to Jerusalem to worship[p] the
King, the LORD Almighty, they will have
no rain.[q] **18**If the Egyptian people do
not go up and take part, they will have
no rain. The LORD[c] will bring on them
the plague[r] he inflicts on the nations
that do not go up to celebrate the Feast
of Tabernacles.[s] **19**This will be the
punishment of Egypt and the punishment of all the nations that do not go
up to celebrate the Feast of Tabernacles.[t]
20On that day HOLY TO THE LORD[u] will
be inscribed on the bells of the horses,
and the cooking pots[v] in the LORD's
house will be like the sacred bowls[w] in
front of the altar. **21**Every pot in Jerusalem and Judah will be holy[x] to the
LORD Almighty, and all who come to
sacrifice will take some of the pots and
cook in them. And on that day[y] there
will no longer be a Canaanite[d][z] in the
house[a] of the LORD Almighty.[b]

14:10 [a] S 2Ki 14:13 [b] S Ne 3:1
14:11 [c] Zec 2:4 [d] S Ps 48:8; S Eze 34:25-28
14:12 [e] S Isa 11:4 [f] ver 18; S Lev 26:16; S Dt 28:22; Job 18:13
14:13 [g] S Ge 35:5 [h] S Jdg 7:22; S Zec 11:6
14:14 [i] Zec 12:2 [j] S Isa 23:18
14:15 [k] ver 12
14:16 [l] S 2Ki 19:31 [m] S Ps 22:29; S 86:9; S Isa 19:21 [n] S Ob 1:21 [o] S Ex 23:16; Isa 60:6-9; S Mic 4:2
14:17 [p] S 2Ch 32:23 [q] S Jer 14:4; S Am 4:7
14:18 [r] S Ge 27:29 [s] S ver 12
14:19 [t] S Ezr 3:4
14:20 [u] S Ex 39:30 [v] S Eze 46:20 [w] Zec 9:15
14:21 [x] S Jer 31:40; Ro 14:6-7; 1Co 10:31 [y] Ne 8:10 [z] Zec 9:8 [a] S Ne 11:1 [b] S Eze 44:9

[c] *18* Or *part, then the LORD* [d] *21* Or *merchant*

14:12–15 THE LORD WILL STRIKE. These verses give more details about the judgment on the nations (see v. 3, note).

14:16 THE SURVIVORS ... WORSHIP THE KING. After the return of Christ and the destruction of the antichrist and his armies (cf. Rev 19), the survivors from the nations will come annually to Jerusalem at the Feast of Tabernacles to worship the Messianic King, the Lord Jesus. The survivors are most likely civilian personnel who had remained in their homeland and who accepted Christ as Lord.

14:17 WILL HAVE NO RAIN. A total absence of rain will be the punishment of nations that do not go up to worship the Lord and celebrate the Feast of Tabernacles.

14:20 HOLY TO THE LORD. No longer will there be separation between the holy and the common. Everything and everyone will be holy, consecrated and dedicated to the worship and service of the Lord.

14:21 NO LONGER BE A CANAANITE IN THE HOUSE. The term "Canaanite" was synonymous with immorality and wickedness. God will establish holiness and righteousness as the prevailing and all-pervasive characteristics of his kingdom.

MALACHI

Outline

Introduction (1:1)

I. The Oracle of the Lord and Israel's Questions (1:2—3:18)
   - A. First Oracle: God Has Loved Israel (1:2–5)
     Israel's Question: "How have you loved us?" (1:2)
   - B. Second Oracle: Israel Has Dishonored the Lord (1:6—2:9)
     Israel's Questions: "How have we shown contempt for your name?" (1:6); "How have we defiled you?" (1:7)
   - C. Third Oracle: God Does Not Accept Israel's Offerings (2:10–16)
     Israel's Question: "Why?" (2:14)
   - D. Fourth Oracle: The Lord Will Come Suddenly (2:17—3:6)
     Israel's Questions: "How have we wearied him?"; "Where is the God of justice?" (2:17)
   - E. Fifth Oracle: Return to the Lord (3:7–12)
     Israel's Questions: "How are we to return?" (3:7); "How do we rob you?" (3:8)
   - F. Sixth Oracle: Israel's Unwarranted Assertions Against God (3:13–18)
     Israel's Questions: "What have we said against you?" (3:13); "What did we gain by carrying out his requirements?" (3:14)

II. The Day of the Lord (4:1–6)
   - A. Will Be a Day of Judgment for the Arrogant and Evildoer (4:1)
   - B. Will Be a Day of Triumph for the Righteous (4:2–3)
   - C. Will Be Preceded by a Supernatural Restoration of Father/Child Relationships Among God's People (4:4–6)

Author: Malachi

Theme: God's Indictments Against Post-exilic Judaism

Date of Writing: c. 430–420 B.C.

Background

The name Malachi means "my messenger"; it may be an abbreviation of "Malachiah," which means "the messenger of the LORD." The view that "Malachi" in 1:1 is a descriptive title rather than a personal name is highly unlikely. Though we are told nothing about the prophet elsewhere in the OT, his personality is quite visible in this book. He was a devout Jew in post-exilic Judah, a contemporary of Nehemiah, and most likely a priestly prophet. His staunch convictions in favor of faithfulness to the covenant (2:4,5,8,10) and against hypocritical and perfunctory worship (1:7—2:9), idolatry (2:10–12), divorce (2:13–16), and robbing God of tithes and offerings (3:8–10) all speak of a man of strict integrity and intense devotion to God.

The content of the book indicates that (1) the temple had been rebuilt (516/515 B.C.) and the sacrifices and feasts reinstituted, (2) a general knowledge of the law had been reintroduced by Ezra (c. 457–455 B.C.; see Ezr 7:10,14,25–26), and (3) a subsequent backsliding had occurred among the priests and the people (c. 433 B.C.). In addition, the spiritual climate and neglect that Malachi addressed closely resembles the situation Nehemiah found when he returned from a stay in Persia (c. 433–425 B.C.) to serve as governor a second time in Jerusalem (cf. Ne 13:4–30). At that time, (a) the priests had become corrupt (1:6—2:9; Ne 13:1–9), (b) tithes and offerings were being neglected (3:7–12; Ne 13:10–13), and (c) the marriage covenant was being violated as men divorced their Hebrew wives to marry (probably younger and prettier) pagan women (2:10–16; Ne 13:23–28). It is likely, therefore, that Malachi proclaimed his message sometime between 430–420 B.C.

Purpose

When Malachi wrote, the post-exilic Jews in Palestine were again experiencing adversity and spiritual decline. The people had become cynical, doubting God's love and promises, questioning his justice and disbelieving there was any profit in obeying his commands. As their faith dimmed, they became mechanical and insensitive in their worship observances, indifferent to the law's requirements and guilty of all kinds of sins against the covenant. Malachi confronted both the priests and the people with the prophetic summons (1) to repent of their sins and religious hypocrisy before God suddenly came in judgment, (2) to remove the obstacles of disobedience that were blocking the flow of God's favor and blessing, and (3) to return to the Lord and his covenant with sincere and obedient hearts.

Survey

The book consists of a sixfold "oracle: the word of the LORD to Israel through Malachi" (1:1), intermingled with a series of 10 rhetorical, sarcastic questions by Israel and God's response through the prophet. Though the use of debate-like questions and answers is not unique to Malachi among the OT prophets, his use of this style is distinctive in that it is central to the book's literary structure (see the outline).

The Lord's "oracle" through Malachi is as follows. (1) First, God affirmed his covenant love for Israel (1:2–5). (2) The second oracle indicted the priests for being unfaithful guardians of the covenant relationship between God and Israel (1:6—2:9). (3) The third rebuked the people for breaking the covenant of their fathers (2:10–16). (4) The fourth reminded Israel of the certainty of God's judgment for sinning against the covenant (2:17—3:6). (5) The fifth called the entire post-exilic Jewish community in Palestine to repent and return to the Lord, in order that they might once again be blessed by him (3:7–12). (6) The final oracle refers to God's "scroll of remembrance" concerning those who fear him and honor his name (3:13–18). Malachi concludes with a prophetic warning and promise concerning the coming "day of the LORD" (4:1–6).

Special Features

Five special features characterize the book of Malachi. (1) In a simple, direct and forceful manner, it vividly pictures an encounter between God and his people, largely using the first person. (2) It features a question-and-answer method of presenting the prophetic word, with no fewer than 23 questions asked back and forth between God and the people. One scholar suggests Malachi's "method" of writing may have originated because of questioning by hecklers when Malachi first delivered his prophetic message on the streets of Jerusalem or in the temple courts. (3) Malachi, the last of the OT prophets, is followed by 400 years without a major prophetic voice in Israel. The long absence of a major prophet of the Lord finally ended when John the Baptist appeared, whom Malachi foresaw and prophesied would precede the Messiah (3:1). (4) The phrase "the LORD Almighty" occurs 20 times in this brief book. (5) Significantly, the final prophecy (which concludes the OT prophetic message) predicted that God would someday send the spirit of Elijah to restore strong godly fathers in Zion, contrary to prevailing societal trends toward family disintegration (4:5–6).

New Testament Fulfillment

Three specific passages from Malachi are quoted in the NT. (1) The phrases "I have loved Jacob" and "Esau I have hated" (1:2–3) are quoted by Paul in his discourse on election (Ro 9:13; see article on ELECTION AND PREDESTINATION, p. 1824). (2) Malachi's prophecy about "the messenger, who will prepare the way before me" (3:1; cf. Isa 40:3) is quoted by Jesus as referring to John the Baptist and his ministry (Mt 11:7–15). (3) Likewise, Jesus understood that Malachi's prophecy about God sending "the prophet Elijah before that great and dreadful day of the LORD comes" (4:5) applied to John the Baptist (Mt 11:14; 17:10–13; Mk 9:11–13). The last book of the Bible adds that the spirit of Elijah will appear again before the second coming of Christ (Rev 11:3–6).

In addition to these three clear NT references to Malachi, the prophet's condemnation of unjust divorce (2:14–16) anticipates the strict NT teaching on this topic (Mt 5:31–32; 19:3–10; Mk 10:2–12; Ro 7:1–3; 1Co 7:10–16,39). Malachi's prophecy about the appearance of the future Messiah (3:1–6; 4:1–3) encompasses both the first and second comings of Christ.

Reading Malachi

In order to read the entire Old Testament in one year, the book of Malachi should be read in 2 days, according to the following schedule: ☐ 1–2 ☐ 3–4

NOTES

1 An oracle:[a] The word[b] of the
LORD to Israel through Malachi.[a]

Jacob Loved, Esau Hated

2"I have loved[c] you," says the LORD.
"But you ask,[d] 'How have you loved
us?'
"Was not Esau Jacob's brother?" the
LORD says. "Yet I have loved Jacob,[e]
3but Esau I have hated,[f] and I have
turned his mountains into a wasteland[g] and left his inheritance to the
desert jackals.[h]"
4Edom[i] may say, "Though we have
been crushed, we will rebuild[j] the ruins."
But this is what the LORD Almighty
says: "They may build, but I will demolish.[k] They will be called the Wicked
Land, a people always under the wrath
of the LORD.[l] 5You will see it with your
own eyes and say, 'Great[m] is the
LORD—even beyond the borders of Israel!'[n]

Blemished Sacrifices

6"A son honors his father,[o] and a
servant his master.[p] If I am a father,
where is the honor due me? If I am a
master, where is the respect[q] due
me?" says the LORD Almighty.[r] "It is
you, O priests, who show contempt for
my name.
"But you ask,[s] 'How have we
shown contempt for your name?'
7"You place defiled food[t] on my altar.
"But you ask,[u] 'How have we defiled you?'
"By saying that the LORD's table[v] is
contemptible. 8When you bring blind
animals for sacrifice, is that not
wrong? When you sacrifice crippled or
diseased animals,[w] is that not wrong?
Try offering them to your governor!
Would he be pleased[x] with you?
Would he accept you?" says the LORD
Almighty.[y]
9"Now implore God to be gracious to
us. With such offerings[z] from your
hands, will he accept[a] you?"—says
the LORD Almighty.
10"Oh, that one of you would shut
the temple doors,[b] so that you would
not light useless fires on my altar! I am
not pleased[c] with you," says the LORD
Almighty, "and I will accept[d] no offering[e] from your hands. 11My name will
be great[f] among the nations,[g] from
the rising to the setting of the sun.[h] In
every place incense[i] and pure offerings[j] will be brought to my name, because my name will be great among the
nations," says the LORD Almighty.
12"But you profane it by saying of
the Lord's table,[k] 'It is defiled,' and of

1:1 [a] S Na 1:1 [b] Ac 7:38; Ro 3:1-2; 1Pe 4:11 **1:2** [c] S Dt 4:37 [d] ver 6,7; Mal 2:14,17; 3:7, 13 [e] S Jer 46:27; Ro 9:13* **1:3** [f] Lk 14:26 [g] S Isa 34:10 [h] S Isa 13:22 **1:4** [i] S Isa 11:14; S 34:11 [j] Isa 9:10 [k] S Isa 34:5 [l] S La 4:22; S Eze 25:12-14; S 26:14 **1:5** [m] Ps 35:27; 48:1; Mic 5:4 [n] Isa 45:22; 52:10; S Am 1:11-12 **1:6** [o] S Lev 20:9; Mt 15:4; 23:9 [p] Lk 6:46 [q] S Dt 31:12; S Isa 1:2 [r] Job 5:17 [s] S ver 2 **1:7** [t] ver 12; Lev 21:6 [u] S ver 2 [v] S Eze 23:41 **1:8** [w] S Lev 1:3; S Dt 15:21 [x] S Ge 32:20 [y] S Isa 43:23 **1:9** [z] Lev 23:33-44; Ps 51:17; Mic 6:6-8; Ro 12:1; Heb 13:16 [a] S Jer 6:20 **1:10** [b] 2Ch 28:24 [c] S Hos 5:6 [d] Lev 22:20 [e] ver 13; Isa 1:11-14; Jer 14:12; Mal 2:12 **1:11** [f] S Isa 24:15; 56:6 [g] S Isa 6:3; S 12:4 [h] S Ps 113:3; S Mt 8:11 [i] Isa 60:6-7; Rev 5:8; 8:3 [j] S Isa 19:21; Heb 13:15 **1:12** [k] S Eze 41:22

[a] 1 *Malachi* means *my messenger.*

1:1 MALACHI. Malachi prophesied about 100 years after the first exiles had returned from Babylon to their homeland. Although the people had initially responded to their restoration with a zeal for God, their commitment to him diminished as the years went by. About 430 B.C. Malachi confronted the people with their lack of trust in God, their insincere worship and their refusal to obey God's law.

1:2 I HAVE LOVED YOU. The people were doubting that God really loved them; having experienced trouble, they accused God of being unfaithful to his covenant promises. The Lord insisted that he had cared for them over the years in a special way. In reality, it was Israel who had failed to love and honor God by their disobedience to his law (vv. 6–8).

1:3 ESAU I HAVE HATED. The term "hated" means only that God chose Esau's brother Jacob, and not Esau himself, to inherit the covenant promises and to be one of the forefathers of the chosen people from whom the Messiah would come. God's rejection of Esau and his descendants as progenitors of the Messiah had nothing to do with their eternal destiny. God's desire was that Esau and his people would serve him and thus also receive his blessing (see Ge 25:23, note; Ro 9:13, note).

1:6–8 PRIESTS, WHO SHOW CONTEMPT FOR MY NAME. Malachi brings an accusation against the priests of the land. (1) They were showing contempt for God by offering to him animals that were crippled or diseased, contrary to God's law (Lev 22:22). (2) As believers in Christ we must give to God the best we have. Our whole life should be a living sacrifice to him (Ro 12:1). The time we spend in prayer and Bible study should be at the choice time of the day, not when we are too tired to do anything else. (3) "The LORD's table" was the table used for slaughtering the sacrifices.

1:11 MY NAME WILL BE GREAT AMONG THE NATIONS. Malachi predicts a time when people from the nations of the world would worship God in sincerity and truth (cf. Isa 45:22–25; 49:5–7; 59:19). The God of the Scriptures would be known around the world. This prophecy is being partially fulfilled now as churches send missionaries into all the world to preach the gospel. One way to demonstrate the genuineness of our faith is by assisting in God's worldwide missionary outreach.

its food,[l] 'It is contemptible.' 13 And
you say, 'What a burden!'[m] and you
sniff at it contemptuously,[n]" says the
LORD Almighty.
"When you bring injured, crippled or
diseased animals and offer them as
sacrifices,[o] should I accept them from
your hands?"[p] says the LORD.
14 "Cursed is the cheat who has an acceptable male in his flock and vows to
give it, but then sacrifices a blemished
animal[q] to the Lord. For I am a great
king,[r]" says the LORD Almighty,[s]
"and my name is to be feared[t] among
the nations.[u]

Admonition for the Priests

2 "And now this admonition is for
you, O priests.[v] 2 If you do not listen,[w] and if you do not set your heart
to honor[x] my name," says the LORD Almighty, "I will send a curse[y] upon
you, and I will curse your blessings.[z]
Yes, I have already cursed them, because you have not set your heart to
honor me.
3 "Because of you I will rebuke[b]
your descendants[c]; I will spread on
your faces the offal[a] from your festival sacrifices, and you will be carried
off with it.[b] 4 And you will know that
I have sent you this admonition so that
my covenant with Levi[c] may continue," says the LORD Almighty. 5 "My covenant was with him, a covenant[d] of
life and peace,[e] and I gave them to
him; this called for reverence[f] and he
revered me and stood in awe of my
name. 6 True instruction[g] was in his
mouth and nothing false was found on
his lips. He walked[h] with me in
peace[i] and uprightness,[j] and turned
many from sin.[k]
7 "For the lips of a priest[l] ought to
preserve knowledge, and from his
mouth men should seek instruction[m]—because he is the messenger[n] of the LORD Almighty. 8 But you
have turned from the way[o] and by
your teaching have caused many to
stumble;[p] you have violated the covenant[q] with Levi,"[r] says the LORD Almighty. 9 "So I have caused you to be
despised[s] and humiliated[t] before all
the people, because you have not followed my ways but have shown partiality[u] in matters of the law."[v]

Judah Unfaithful

10 Have we not all one Father[d]?[w]
Did not one God create us?[x] Why do
we profane the covenant[y] of our fathers by breaking faith[z] with one another?
11 Judah has broken faith. A detestable[a] thing has been committed in Israel and in Jerusalem: Judah has desecrated the sanctuary the LORD loves,[b]
by marrying[c] the daughter of a foreign
god.[d] 12 As for the man who does this,
whoever he may be, may the LORD cut

1:12 [l] S ver 7 **1:13** [m] Isa 43:22-24 [n] S Nu 14:11 [o] S ver 10 [p] S Dt 15:21 **1:14** [q] Ex 12:5; S Lev 22:18-21 [r] Ps 95:3; S Ob 1:21; 1Ti 6:15 [s] Jer 46:18 [t] S Dt 28:58 [u] Ps 72:8-11 **2:1** [v] ver 7 **2:2** [w] Jer 13:17 [x] Mt 15:7-9; Jn 5:23; 1Ti 6:16; Rev 5:12-13 [y] S Dt 11:26; S 28:20 [z] Nu 6:23-27 **2:3** [a] S Ex 29:14; S Lev 4:11; S Job 9:31 [b] 1Ki 14:10 **2:4** [c] S Nu 3:12 **2:5** [d] Dt 33:9; Ps 25:10; 103:18; S Mt 26:28; S Lk 22:20; Heb 7:22 [e] S Nu 25:12 [f] S Dt 14:23; S 28:58; Ps 119:161; Heb 12:28 **2:6** [g] S Dt 33:10 [h] S Ge 5:22 [i] Lk 2:14; S Jn 14:27; Gal 5:22 [j] S Ps 25:21 [k] S Ro 11:14; Jas 5:19-20 **2:7** [l] S Jer 18:18 [m] S Lev 10:11; S 2Ch 17:7 [n] S Nu 27:21; S 2Ch 36:15; Mt 11:10; Mk 1:2 **2:8** [o] S Ex 32:8; Jer 2:8 [p] S Jer 18:15 [q] Jer 33:21; S Eze 22:26 [r] S Hos 4:6 **2:9** [s] S 1Sa 2:30; S Ps 22:6; S Jer 51:37 [t] S Ps 35:4; Jer 3:25; Ac 8:32-33 [u] S Ex 18:16; S Lev 19:15; Ac 10:34; Ro 2:11 [v] S 1Sa 2:17 **2:10** [w] S Ex 4:22; Mt 5:16; 6:4,18; Lk 11:2; 1Co 8:6 [x] S Job 4:17; Isa 43:1 [y] Ex 19:5; S 2Ki 17:15; Jer 31:32 [z] S Zep 3:3-4 **2:11** [a] S Isa 1:13; S 48:8 [b] S Dt 4:37 [c] S Ne 13:23 [d] S Ex 34:16; Jer 3:7-9

b *3* Or *cut off* (see Septuagint) c *3* Or *will blight your grain* d *10* Or *father*

2:1–4 O PRIESTS. The priests had corrupted the ministry to which God had called them. They did not fear him or revere his name, and they failed to proclaim his word and to live a good and righteous life. For this God would send terrible punishment on them; he would curse them and their ministry.

2:4–6 MY COVENANT WITH LEVI. The priests were to be chosen from the tribe of Levi. Here God used Levi and his faithful descendants as examples of what ministers should be. Ministers today must have the same qualities mentioned in these verses. They must show love and respect for God, live honestly and righteously, preach the truth, and by their example and word turn many from sin (see article on MORAL QUALIFICATIONS FOR OVERSEERS, p. 1882).

2:9 PARTIALITY IN MATTERS OF THE LAW. The priests were showing partiality to the rich and influential, allowing them to continue in their unjust and sinful ways and failing to confront them with God's word of warning. Pastoral leaders must preach the whole counsel of God (see Ac 20:27), proclaiming his righteous demands to all the people. To preach the blessings of the Lord Almighty and omit his righteous requirements for us is detestable to him.

2:11–16 A DETESTABLE THING. Malachi rebukes the people for a serious double transgression of God's law: divorcing their wives and marrying pagan women (see next two notes).

2:11 MARRYING THE DAUGHTER OF A FOREIGN GOD. The men were marrying pagan women who served other gods, a practice forbidden in the law of Moses (see Ex 34:15–16; Dt 7:3–4; 1Ki 11:1–6). The NT states that believers are to marry only believers (see 1Co 7:39). For a Christian to marry someone not committed to the Lord opens him or her to the possibility of being influenced to depart from the Lord and the children influenced against commitment to him.

him off[e] from the tents of Jacob[e][f]—
even though he brings offerings[g] to
the LORD Almighty.
13Another thing you do: You flood
the LORD's altar with tears.[h] You weep
and wail[i] because he no longer pays
attention[j] to your offerings or accepts
them with pleasure from your hands.[k]
14You ask,[l] "Why?" It is because the
LORD is acting as the witness[m] between you and the wife of your youth,[n]
because you have broken faith with
her, though she is your partner, the
wife of your marriage covenant.[o]
15Has not ⌊the LORD⌋ made them
one?[p] In flesh and spirit they are his.
And why one? Because he was seeking
godly offspring.[f][q] So guard yourself[r] in your spirit, and do not break
faith[s] with the wife of your youth.
16"I hate divorce,[t]" says the LORD
God of Israel, "and I hate a man's covering himself[g] with violence[u] as well
as with his garment," says the LORD Almighty.
So guard yourself in your spirit,[v]
and do not break faith.

The Day of Judgment

17You have wearied[w] the LORD with
your words.
"How have we wearied him?" you
ask.[x]
By saying, "All who do evil are good
in the eyes of the LORD, and he is
pleased[y] with them" or "Where is the
God of justice?[z]"

3 "See, I will send my messenger,[a]
who will prepare the way before
me.[b] Then suddenly the Lord[c] you
are seeking will come to his temple;
the messenger of the covenant,[d]
whom you desire,[e] will come," says
the LORD Almighty.

2:12 [e]S 1Sa 2:30-33; S Eze 24:21 [f]S Nu 24:5; 2Sa 20:1 [g]S Mal 1:10 **2:13** [h]S Jer 11:11 [i]Ps 39:12 [j]Ps 66:18; Jer 14:12 [k]Isa 58:2 **2:14** [l]S Mal 1:2 [m]S Ge 21:30; S Jos 24:22 [n]S Pr 5:18 [o]S Eze 16:8; Heb 13:4 **2:15** [p]S Ge 2:24; Mt 19:4-6 [q]S Dt 14:2; 1Co 7:14 [r]S Dt 4:15 [s]S Isa 54:6; 1Co 7:10; Heb 13:4 **2:16** [t]S Dt 24:1; Mt 5:31-32; 19:4-9; Mk 10:4-5 [u]S Ge 6:11; 34:25; S Pr 4:17; S Isa 58:4 [v]Ps 51:10 **2:17** [w]S Isa 1:14 [x]S Mal 1:2 [y]Ps 5:4 [z]S Ge 18:25; S Job 8:3; S Eze 18:25 **3:1** [a]S Nu 27:21; S 2Ch 36:15 [b]S Isa 40:3; S Mt 3:3; 11:10*; Mk 1:2*; Lk 7:27* [c]Mic 5:2 [d]S Isa 42:6 [e]S 1Sa 9:20

3:2 [f]S Eze 22:14; Rev 6:17 [g]S Eze 7:7; S Da 7:13; S Joel 2:31; S Mt 16:27; Jas 5:8; 2Pe 3:4; S Rev 1:7 [h]S 1Sa 6:20 [i]S Isa 1:31; S 30:30; S Zec 13:9; Mt 3:10-12 [j]S Job 9:30 **3:3** [k]S Da 12:10; S 1Co 3:13 [l]S 1Ch 23:28; S Isa 1:25 [m]S Job 28:1; S Ps 12:6; 1Pe 1:7; Rev 3:18

2But who can endure[f] the day of his
coming?[g] Who can stand[h] when he
appears? For he will be like a refiner's
fire[i] or a launderer's soap.[j] **3**He will
sit as a refiner and purifier of silver;[k]
he will purify[l] the Levites and refine
them like gold and silver.[m] Then the
LORD will have men who will bring offerings in righteousness,[n] **4**and the offerings[o] of Judah and Jerusalem will
be acceptable to the LORD, as in days
gone by, as in former years.[p]
5"So I will come near to you for judgment. I will be quick to testify against
sorcerers,[q] adulterers[r] and perjurers,[s] against those who defraud laborers of their wages,[t] who oppress the
widows[u] and the fatherless, and deprive aliens[v] of justice, but do not
fear[w] me," says the LORD Almighty.

Robbing God

6"I the LORD do not change.[x] So you,
O descendants of Jacob, are not destroyed.[y] **7**Ever since the time of your
forefathers you have turned away[z]
from my decrees and have not kept
them. Return[a] to me, and I will return
to you,"[b] says the LORD Almighty.
"But you ask,[c] 'How are we to return?'

[n]S Ps 132:9 **3:4** [o]2Ch 7:12; Ps 51:19; Mal 1:11 [p]S 2Ch 7:3; S Eze 20:40 **3:5** [q]S Ex 7:11; S Isa 47:9 [r]Ex 20:14; Jas 2:11; 2Pe 2:12-14 [s]Lev 19:11-12; S Jer 7:9 [t]S Lev 19:13; Jas 5:4 [u]S Ex 22:22 [v]S Ex 22:21; S Dt 24:19; S Eze 22:7 [w]S Dt 31:12; S Isa 1:2 **3:6** [x]S Nu 23:19; S Heb 7:21; Jas 1:17 [y]S Job 34:15; S Hos 11:9 **3:7** [z]S Ex 32:8; S Jer 7:26; Ac 7:51 [a]S Isa 44:22; S Eze 18:32 [b]S Zec 1:3; Jas 4:8 [c]S Mal 1:2

[e]12 Or [12]*May the LORD cut off from the tents of Jacob anyone who gives testimony in behalf of the man who does this* [f]15 Or [15]*But the one ⌊who is our father⌋ did not do this, not as long as life remained in him. And what was he seeking? An offspring from God* [g]16 Or *his wife*

2:14 THE WIFE OF YOUR YOUTH. Many men were being unfaithful to the wives whom they had married when they were young. They were seeking to divorce them, only because they wanted to marry someone else. The Lord detested this kind of selfish action, stating that he had made a husband and wife one (v. 15). Because of this sin, God had turned his back on the sinners and refused to hear their prayers (vv. 13–14).

2:16 I HATE DIVORCE. God hates divorce that is initiated for selfish purposes; this kind of divorce is like one "covering himself with violence," indicating that unjust divorce is equal in God's sight to gross injustice, cruelty and murder (see Mt 19:9, note on the NT teaching on divorce).

3:1 I WILL SEND MY MESSENGER. In answer to the people's skepticism, Malachi emphasizes the certainty of the Messiah's coming. Before the Messiah came, he would send a messenger to prepare the way. This prophecy was fulfilled when John the Baptist came as the forerunner of Jesus Christ (see Mt 11:10; Mk 1:2; Lk 1:76; 7:27).

3:1–5 THE MESSENGER OF THE COVENANT. This "messenger" is Jesus the Messiah. Christ's first and second comings are united in this passage.

3:2 THE DAY OF HIS COMING. The ultimate fulfillment of this verse will be at Christ's second coming, when he will purify (v. 3) and judge (v. 5) Israel. He will purge out all the wicked in the land; only the righteous will remain (cf. Isa 1:25; Eze 22:17–22).

TITHES AND OFFERINGS

***Mal 3:10** "Bring the whole tithe into the storehouse, that there may be food in my house. Test me in this, says the* LORD *Almighty, and see if I will not throw open the floodgates of heaven and pour out so much blessing that you will not have room enough for it."*

DEFINITION OF TITHES AND OFFERINGS. The Hebrew word for "tithe" (*ma'ser*) literally means "a tenth part." (1) In God's law, the Israelites were required to give one-tenth of the livestock and the land's produce, as well as of their income, as a recognition that God had blessed them (see Lev 27:30–32; Nu 18:21,26; Dt 14:22–29; see Lev 27:30, note); the tithe was used primarily for the expenses of worship and for the support of the priests. God held his people responsible to manage the resources he had given them in the promised land (cf. Mt 25:15, note; Lk 19:13, note).

(2) At the heart of tithing was the notion that God owns everything (Ex 19:5; Ps 24:1; 50:10–12; Hag 2:8). Humans are created by him, and they owe to him every breath they take (Ge 1:26–27; Ac 17:28); thus, no one has anything that he or she has not first of all received from the Lord (Job 1:21; Jn 3:27; 1Co 4:7). In the laws about tithing, God was simply commanding them to return to him what he had first given them.

(3) In addition to tithes, the Israelites were required to bring numerous offerings to the Lord, mostly in the form of sacrifices. The book of Leviticus describes various ritual offerings: the burnt offering (Lev 1; 6:8–13), the grain offering (Lev 2; 6:14–23), the fellowship offering (Lev 3; 7:11–21), the sin offering (Lev 4:1—5:13; 6:24–30) and the guilt offering (Lev 5:14—6:7; 7:1–10).

(4) In addition to prescribed offerings, the Israelites could present freewill offerings to the Lord. Some of these were repeated (see Lev 22:18–23; Nu 15:3; Dt 12:6,17), while others were one-time occasions. For example, when the Israelites undertook the building of the tabernacle at Mount Sinai, the people gave freely for this tent and its furnishings (see Ex 35:20–29); they were so excited about this project that Moses had to tell them to stop making anything else as an offering (Ex 36:3–7). In Joash's time, the high priest Jehoiada made a chest into which people could put freewill offerings to finance needed repairs on the temple, and they gave generously (2Ki 12:9–10). Similarly, in Hezekiah's time, people gave freely for the reconstruction work required on the temple (2Ch 31:5–19).

(5) There were also numerous times in OT history that God's people selfishly held on to their money rather than give it to the Lord in regular tithes and offerings. During the building of the second temple, the Jews seemed more interested in building up their own property, while leaving God's house in ruins. As a result, said Haggai, many of them were suffering financial reverses (Hag 1:3–6). A similar thing was happening in the prophet Malachi's time, and once again God was judging his people for refusing to bring in the tithe (Mal 3:9–12).

STEWARDSHIP OF OUR MONEY. These OT examples of tithes and offerings contain important principles about the stewardship of money that are valid for NT believers. (1) We must remember that everything we have belongs to the Lord, so that what we do possess is not our own but what God has entrusted to us; we have no rightful ownership of our possessions.

(2) We must decide within our hearts to serve God and not Money (Mt 6:19–24; cf. 2Co 8:1–5). The Bible makes it plain that any greed is a form of idolatry (Col 3:5).

(3) Our giving must be to advance God's kingdom, especially the work of the local church and the spread of the gospel throughout the world (1Co 9:4–14; Php 4:15–18; 1Ti 5:17–18), to help those who are in need (Pr 19:17; Gal 2:10; 2Co 8:14; see article on THE CARE OF THE POOR AND NEEDY, p. 1316), to store up treasures in heaven (Mt 6:20) and to learn to fear the Lord (Dt 14:22–23).

(4) Our giving should always be in proportion to our income. In the OT the tithe amounted to one-tenth. Giving less than that was disobedience to God's law and was in effect robbing God (Mal 3:8–10). Similarly, the NT requires that our giving be in proportion to what God has given us (1Co 16:2; 2Co 8:3,12; see 2Co 8:2, note).

(5) Our giving should be voluntary and generous; this practice is taught in both the OT (see Ex 25:1–2; 2Ch 24:8–11) and in the NT (see 2Co 8:1–5,11–12). We should not hesitate to give sacrificially (2Co 8:3), for that is the spirit in which the Lord Jesus gave himself for us (see 2Co 8:9, note). Far more important to God than the monetary value of the gift is the sacrifice involved (see Lk 21:1–4, note).

(6) Our giving should be cheerful (2Co 9:7). Both the example of the Israelites in the OT (Ex 35:21–29; 2Ch 24:10) and the Macedonian Christians in the NT (2Co 8:1–5) serve as models for us.

(7) God has promised to reward us according to how we have given to him (see Dt 15:4; Mal 3:10–12; Mt 19:21; 1Ti 6:18-19; see 2Co 9:6, note).

[8]"Will a man rob[d] God? Yet you rob
me.
"But you ask, 'How do we rob you?'
"In tithes[e] and offerings. [9]You are
under a curse[f]—the whole nation of
you—because you are robbing me.
[10]Bring the whole tithe[g] into the
storehouse,[h] that there may be food in
my house. Test me in this," says the
LORD Almighty, "and see if I will not
throw open the floodgates[i] of heaven
and pour out[j] so much blessing[k] that
you will not have room enough for it.[l]
[11]I will prevent pests from devouring[m]
your crops, and the vines in your fields
will not cast their fruit,[n]" says the
LORD Almighty. [12]"Then all the nations
will call you blessed,[o] for yours will be
a delightful land,"[p] says the LORD Almighty.[q]
[13]"You have said harsh things[r]
against me," says the LORD.
"Yet you ask,[s] 'What have we said
against you?'
[14]"You have said, 'It is futile[t] to
serve[u] God. What did we gain by carrying out his requirements[v] and going
about like mourners[w] before the LORD
Almighty? [15]But now we call the arrogant[x] blessed. Certainly the evildoers[y] prosper,[z] and even those who
challenge God escape.' "
[16]Then those who feared the LORD
talked with each other, and the LORD
listened and heard.[a] A scroll[b] of remembrance was written in his presence concerning those who feared[c]
the LORD and honored his name.
[17]"They will be mine,[d]" says the
LORD Almighty, "in the day when I
make up my treasured possession.[h][e]
I will spare[f] them, just as in compassion a man spares his son[g] who serves
him. [18]And you will again see the distinction between the righteous[h] and
the wicked, between those who serve
God and those who do not.[i]

The Day of the LORD

4 "Surely the day is coming;[j] it will
burn like a furnace.[k] All the arrogant[l] and every evildoer will be stubble,[m] and that day that is coming will
set them on fire,[n]" says the LORD Almighty. "Not a root or a branch[o] will
be left to them. [2]But for you who revere
my name,[p] the sun of righteousness[q]
will rise with healing[r] in its wings.
And you will go out and leap[s] like
calves released from the stall. [3]Then

3:8 [d]S Zec 5:3 [e]S Lev 27:30; Nu 18:21; S Ne 13:10-12; Lk 18:12 **3:9** [f]S Dt 11:26; 28:15-68; S Zec 5:3 **3:10** [g]S Ex 22:29 [h]S Ne 13:12 [i]S 2Ki 7:2 [j]Isa 44:3 [k]S Lev 25:21; S Joel 2:14; 2Co 9:8-11 [l]S Joel 2:24 **3:11** [m]S Ex 10:15; S Dt 28:39 [n]S Ex 23:26 **3:12** [o]S Dt 28:3-12; Isa 61:9 [p]S Isa 62:4; S Eze 20:6 [q]S 2Ch 31:10 **3:13** [r]Mal 2:17 [s]S Mal 1:2 **3:14** [t]Ps 73:13; S Isa 57:10 [u]Ps 100:2; Jn 12:26; Ro 12:11 [v]S Jos 22:5; S Isa 1:14 [w]Isa 58:3 **3:15** [x]S Ps 119:21 [y]Ps 14:1; 36:1-2; Jer 7:10 [z]S Job 21:7 **3:16** [a]S Ps 34:15 [b]S Ex 32:32; S Ps 56:8; S 87:6; S Lk 10:20 [c]S Dt 28:58; S 31:12; Ps 33:18; S Pr 1:7; Rev 11:18 **3:17** [d]Isa 43:21 [e]S Ex 8:22; S Dt 7:6; S Ro 8:14; S Tit 2:14 [f]Ne 13:22; Ps 103:13; Isa 26:20; Lk 15:1-32 [g]Ro 8:32 **3:18** [h]S Ge 18:25 [i]Dt 32:4; Mt 25:32-33,41 **4:1** [j]S Da 7:13; S Joel 2:31; Mt 11:14; Ac 2:20 [k]S Isa 31:9 [l]S Isa 2:12 [m]S Isa 5:24; S Na 1:10 [n]S Isa 1:31 [o]S 2Ki 10:11; S Eze 17:8; S Mt 3:10 **4:2** [p]S Dt 28:58; Ps 61:5; 111:9; Rev 14:1 [q]S Ps 118:27; S Isa 9:2; S 45:8; Lk 1:78; Eph 5:14 [r]S 2Ch 7:14; S Isa 30:26; S Mt 4:23; Rev 22:2 [s]S Isa 35:6

[h]17 Or *Almighty, "my treasured possession, in the day when I act*

3:8 WILL A MAN ROB GOD? The people were robbing God by failing to bring him their tithes (one-tenth of their income). Tithing was required of the people in the law of Moses (Lev 27:30). (1) God threatened to curse those who selfishly refused to give (vv. 8–9) and to bless those who supported his work (vv. 10–12; see next note). (2) NT believers are obligated to give in order to support the Lord's work both at home and on the mission field (see 2Co 8:2, note).

3:10 POUR OUT SO MUCH BLESSING. If the people would repent, return to God, and, as a sign of their repentance, begin to support God's work and ministers with their tithes and offerings, God would abundantly bless them. God expects his people to demonstrate their love for and devotion to him and his work by giving tithes and offerings to further his kingdom (see article on TITHES AND OFFERINGS, p. 1392). The blessings that accompany faithfulness in financial giving will come both in this life and in the hereafter.

3:14 FUTILE TO SERVE GOD. The people believed that mere external worship of God was enough to gain his blessing, but it was not; thus they felt it was useless to serve him. They failed to see that their hearts weren't right before him (see article on WORSHIP, p. 680).

3:16 THOSE WHO FEARED THE LORD. In contrast to the majority, there were still a few who honored God. (1) The Lord promises to keep in heaven a permanent record of those who honor and fear him by living faithfully before him; they will not be forgotten. (2) This passage assures us that God observes and records our faithfulness to and love for him. When we stand before him in heaven, he will remember our devoted commitment and will treat us accordingly.

4:1 THE DAY IS COMING. "The day" refers both to Christ's first coming and second coming. The prophet speaks as though the two comings would occur as a single event; this blending is seen often in OT prophecy (see Zec 9:9–10, notes). Those committed to pride and evildoing will be excluded from God's kingdom (cf. 3:2–3; Isa 66:15; Zep 1:18; 3:8; 1Co 6:9–11).

4:2 FOR YOU WHO REVERE MY NAME. The day of the Lord will also mean salvation and deliverance for all who love and serve him. In his kingdom God's glory and righteousness will shine like the sun, bringing to his faithful people the ultimate in goodness, blessing, salvation and healing. Everything will be made right, and God's people will leap for joy like calves released from the stall.

you will trample[t] down the wicked;
they will be ashes[u] under the soles of
your feet on the day when I do these
things," says the LORD Almighty.
4"Remember the law[v] of my servant Moses, the decrees and laws I
gave him at Horeb[w] for all Israel.[x]
5"See, I will send you the prophet
Elijah[y] before that great and dreadful
day of the LORD comes.[z] 6He will turn
the hearts of the fathers to their children,[a] and the hearts of the children
to their fathers; or else I will come and
strike[b] the land with a curse."[c]

4:3 [t] S Job 40:12; Ps 18:40-42 [u] Eze 28:18 4:4 [v] S Dt 28:61; S Ps 147:19; Mt 5:17; 7:12; Ro 2:13; 4:15; Gal 3:24 [w] S Ex 3:1 [x] S Ex 20:1 4:5 [y] S 1Ki 17:1; S Mt 11:14; 16:14 [z] S Joel 2:31

4:6 [a] Lk 1:17 [b] S Isa 11:4; Rev 19:15 [c] S Dt 11:26; S 13:15; S Jos 6:17; S 23:15; S Zec 5:3

4:4 REMEMBER THE LAW. Malachi tells God's people that to survive the day of the Lord, they must obey his laws. Faith in God always includes an attitude of obedience to the Lord from the heart. Believers in Christ are still required to follow the moral demands of the OT law as well as the commands of Christ (see Mt 5:17, note; see article on THE OLD TESTAMENT LAW, p. 118).

4:5 SEND YOU THE PROPHET ELIJAH. Malachi prophesies that Elijah would come and minister before the coming of the day of the Lord; the NT reveals that this prophecy refers to John the Baptist (Mt 11:7–14), who, "in the spirit and power of Elijah" (see Lk 1:17, note), prepared the way for the Messiah. Some also believe that Elijah will again come during the tribulation period and will be one of the two witnesses mentioned in Revelation (see Rev 11:3, note).

4:6 TURN THE HEARTS OF THE FATHERS TO THEIR CHILDREN. The future ministry of the coming prophet is described in terms of putting families right with God and each other; John the Baptist preached to this end (see Lk 1:17). (1) There can be no blessing from God or abundant life in the Spirit if God's people do not make family authority, love and faithfulness absolute priorities in the church. The purity and righteousness of the home must be maintained or our congregations will fail.

(2) The one most responsible for accomplishing this task is the father of the family. Fathers must love their children by praying for them (see Jn 17:1, note), spending time with them, pointing out the ungodly ways of the world, and diligently teaching them God's Word and righteous standards (see article on PARENTS AND CHILDREN, p. 1854).

(3) Pastors must also make this goal of John the Baptist their own purpose for their ministry, thus preparing the church for the Lord's coming (see Lk 1:17, note).

FROM MALACHI TO CHRIST

THE PERSIAN PERIOD 450-330 B.C.

For about 100 years after Nehemiah's time the Persians controlled Judah, but the Jews were allowed to carry on their religious observances and were not interfered with. During this time Judah was ruled by high priests who were responsible to the Jewish government.

Rule of Alexander the Great

THE HELLENISTIC PERIOD 330-166 B.C.

In 333 B.C. the Persian armies stationed in Macedonia were defeated by Alexander the Great. He was convinced that Greek culture was the one force that could unify the world. Alexander permitted the Jews to observe their laws and even granted them exemption from tribute or tax during their sabbath years. The Greek conquest prepared the way for the translation of the OT into Greek (Septuagint version) c. 250 B.C.

Rule of the Ptolemies of Egypt

Malachi c. 430 B.C.

410

400 B.C.

390

380

370

360

350

340

330

334-323 Alexander the Great conquers the East

330-328 Alexander's years of power

320

320 Ptolemy (I) Soter conquers Jerusalem

310

311 Seleucus conquers Babylon; Seleucid dynasty begins

300

290

280

270

260

250

240

230

226 Antiochus III (the Great) of Syria overpowers Palestine

220

223-187 Antiochus becomes Seleucid ruler of Syria

210

200

198 Antiochus defeats Egypt and gains control of Palestine

190

THE HASMONEAN PERIOD 166-63 B.C.

When this historical period began, the Jews were being greatly oppressed. The Ptolemies had been tolerant of the Jews and their religious practices but the Seleucid rulers were determined to force Hellenism on them. Copies of the Scriptures were ordered destroyed and laws were enforced with extreme cruelty. The oppressed Jews revolted, led by Judas the Maccabee.

THE ROMAN PERIOD 63 B.C. . . .

In the year 63 B.C. Pompey, the Roman general, captured Jerusalem, and the provinces of Palestine became subject to Rome. The local government was entrusted part of the time to princes and the rest of the time to procurators who were appointed by the emperors. Herod the Great was ruler of all Palestine at the time of Christ's birth.

Rule of the Seleucids of Syria
Hasmonean Dynasty
Herod the Great rules as king; subject to Rome
180
170
160
150
140
130
120
110
100
90
80
70
60
50
40
30
20
10
10
20
A.D. 30
175-164 Antiochus (IV) Epiphanes rules Syria; Judaism is prohibited
167 Mattathias and his sons rebel against Antiochus; Maccabean revolt begins
166-160 Judas Maccabeus's leadership
160-143 Jonathan is high priest
142 Tower of Jerusalem cleansed
142-134 Simon becomes high priest; establishes Hasmonean dynasty
134-104 John Hyrcanus enlarges the independent Jewish state
103 Aristobulus's rule
102-76 Alexander Janneus's rule
75-67 Rule of Salome Alexandra with Hyrcanus II as high priest
66-63 Battle between Aristobulus II and Hyrcanus II
63 Pompey invades Palestine; Roman rule begins
63-40 Hyrcanus II rules but is subject to Rome
40-37 Parthians conquer Jerusalem
37 Jerusalem besieged for six months
32 Herod defeated
19 Herod's temple begun
16 Herod visits Agrippa
4 Herod dies; Archelaus succeeds

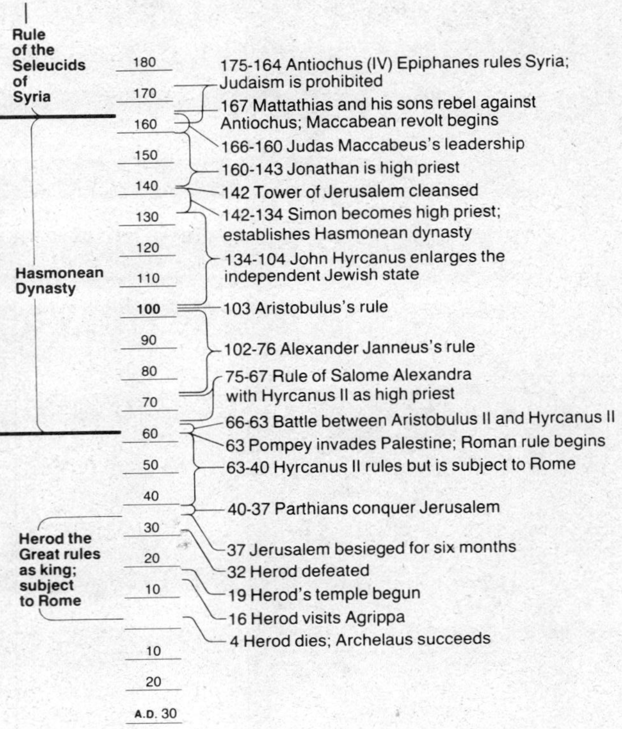

THE NEW TESTAMENT

MATTHEW

Outline

I. Introduction to the Messiah (1:1—4:11)
   A. The Jewish Lineage of Jesus (1:1–17)
   B. His Birth and Flight to Egypt (1:18—2:23)
   C. Prophetic Forerunner to the Messiah (3:1–12)
   D. Baptism of the Messiah (3:13–17)
   E. Temptation of the Messiah (4:1–11)
II. Jesus' Messianic Ministry in and Around Galilee (4:12—18:35)
   A. Summary of His Early Galilean Ministry (4:12–25)
   B. Discourse About Discipleship in the Kingdom (5:1—7:29)
   C. Narrative I: Mighty Deeds of the Kingdom (8:1—9:38)
   D. Discourse About the Proclamation of the Kingdom (10:1–42)
   E. Narrative II: The Presence of the Kingdom (11:1—12:50)
   F. Discourse About the Mystery of the Kingdom (13:1–58)
   G. Narrative III: Crisis of the Kingdom (14:1—17:27)
   H. Discourse About Membership in the Kingdom (18:1–35)
III. The Climax of Jesus' Messianic Mission in Judea/Perea and Jerusalem (19:1—26:46)
   A. Jesus' Journey to Jerusalem (19:1—20:34)
   B. Jesus' Last Week at Jerusalem (21:1—26:46)
      1. Triumphal Entry and Cleansing the Temple (21:1–22)
      2. Controversies With the Jews (21:23—22:46)
      3. Denunciations of the Teachers of the Law and the Pharisees (23:1–39)
      4. Olivet Discourse About the Future of the Kingdom (24:1—25:46)
      5. The Plot to Betray Jesus (26:1–16)
      6. The Last Supper (26:17–30)
      7. Gethsemane (26:31–46)
IV. Jesus' Arrest, Trial and Crucifixion (26:47—27:66)
   A. The Arrest (26:47–56)
   B. The Trial (26:57—27:26)
   C. The Crucifixion (27:27–56)
   D. The Burial (27:57–66)
V. The Resurrection (28:1–20)
   A. The Women's Glorious Discovery (28:1–10)
   B. False Witnesses (28:11–15)
   C. The Risen Lord's Commission (28:16–20)

Author: Matthew

Theme: Jesus, the Messianic King

Date of Writing: A.D. 60s

Background

This Gospel is appropriately placed first as an introduction to the NT and to "the Christ, the Son of the living God" (16:16). Although the author is not identified by name in the Biblical text, the unanimous testimony of all early church fathers (beginning c. A.D. 130) is that this Gospel was written by Matthew, one of Jesus' twelve disciples.

Whereas Mark's Gospel was written for the Romans (see the introduction to Mark) and Luke's Gospel for Theophilus and for all Gentile believers (see the introduction to Luke), Matthew's Gospel was written for Jewish believers. The Jewish background of this Gospel is evident in many ways, including (1) its reliance on OT revelation, promises and prophecy to prove that Jesus was the long-awaited Messiah; (2) its tracing of Jesus' lineage, starting from Abraham (1:1–17); (3) its repeated declaration that Jesus is the "Son of David" (1:1; 9:27; 12:23; 15:22; 20:30–31; 21:9,15; 22:41–45); (4) its use of preferred Jewish terminology such as "kingdom of heaven" (a synonym for "kingdom of God") because of the Jews' reverential reluctance to say the name of God directly; and (5) its reference to Jewish customs without any explanation (unlike the other Gospels).

However, this Gospel is not exclusively Jewish. Like the message of Jesus himself, Matthew's Gospel was intended ultimately for the whole church, faithfully revealing the universal scope of the gospel (e.g., 2:1–12; 8:11–12; 13:38; 21:43; 28:18–20).

The date and location of its origin are uncertain. However, there are good reasons for believing that Matthew wrote prior to A.D. 70 while in Palestine or Syrian Antioch. Some Bible scholars believe Matthew was the first of the four Gospels to be written; others ascribe that place to the Gospel of Mark.

Purpose

Matthew wrote this Gospel (1) to provide his readers with an eyewitness account of Jesus' life, (2) to assure his readers that Jesus was God's Son and the long-awaited Messiah foretold by the OT prophets, and (3) to show that God's kingdom was manifested in and through Jesus in an unprecedented way. Matthew is concerned that his readers understand (1) that Israel for the most part rejected Jesus and his kingdom, refusing to believe because he came as a spiritual rather than as a political Messiah, and (2) that only at the end of the age will Jesus come in glory as the King of kings to judge and rule the nations.

Survey

Matthew presents Jesus as the fulfillment of Israel's prophetic hope. He fulfills OT prophecy in his birth (1:22–23), birthplace (2:5–6), return from Egypt (2:15) and residence in Nazareth (2:23); as the one for whom the Messianic forerunner was sent (3:1–3); in the primary location of his public ministry (4:14–16), his healing ministry (8:17), his role as God's servant (12:17–21), his teaching in parables (13:34–35), his triumphal entry into Jerusalem (21:4–5) and his arrest (26:50).

Chs. 5–25 record five major discourses by Jesus and five major narratives about his mighty deeds as Messiah. The five major discourses are: (1) Sermon on the Mount (chs. 5–7); (2) instruction for itinerant proclaimers of the kingdom (ch. 10); (3) parables about the kingdom (ch. 13); (4) the character of true disciples (ch. 18); and (5) the Olivet discourse about the end of the age (chs. 24–25). The five major narratives in this Gospel are: (1) Jesus performs mighty deeds and miracles, which testify about the reality of the kingdom (chs. 8–9); (2) Jesus further demonstrates the presence of the kingdom (chs. 11–12); (3) proclamation of the kingdom provokes various crises (chs. 14–17); (4) Jesus journeys to Jerusalem and spends his last week there (19:1—26:46); (5) Jesus is arrested, tried, crucified and raised from the dead (26:47—28:20). The last three verses of the Gospel record Jesus' "Great Commission."

Special Features

Seven major features characterize this Gospel. (1) It is the most Jewish of the NT Gospels. (2) It contains the most systematic arrangement of Jesus' teaching and ministry of healing and deliverance. This led the church in the second century to rely heavily on it for instructing new converts. (3) The five major discourses contain the most extensive blocks of material in the Gospels on Jesus' teaching (a) during his Galilean ministry, and (b) on the subject of eschatology (the last things). (4) This Gospel specifically identifies events in Jesus' life as fulfilling the OT far more often than any other NT book. (5) It mentions the kingdom of heaven/kingdom of God twice as often as any other Gospel. (6) Matthew emphasizes (a) the righteous standards of the kingdom (chs. 5–7); (b) the present power of the kingdom over sin, sickness, demons, and even death; and (c) the future triumph of the kingdom in that final victory at the end of the age. (7) It is the only Gospel to mention or predict the church as a future entity belonging to Jesus (16:18; 18:17).

Reading Matthew

In order to read the entire New Testament in one year, the book of Matthew should be read in 44 days, according to the following schedule:
☐ 1 ☐ 2 ☐ 3 ☐ 4 ☐ 5:1–20 ☐ 5:21–48 ☐ 6:1–18 ☐ 6:19—7:6 ☐ 7:7–29 ☐ 8:1–27 ☐ 8:28–9:17 ☐ 9:18–38 ☐ 10:1–23 ☐ 10:24–42 ☐ 11 ☐ 12:1–21 ☐ 12:22–50 ☐ 13:1–23 ☐ 13:24–43 ☐ 13:44—14:12 ☐ 14:13–36 ☐ 15:1–28 ☐ 15:29—16:12 ☐ 16:13—17:13 ☐ 17:14—18:14 ☐ 18:15–35 ☐ 19:1–15 ☐ 19:16—20:16 ☐ 20:17–34 ☐ 21:1–32 ☐ 21:33—22:14 ☐ 22:15–46 ☐ 23 ☐ 24:1–35 ☐ 24:36–51 ☐ 25:1–30 ☐ 25:31–46 ☐ 26:1–30 ☐ 26:31–56 ☐ 26:57–75 ☐ 27:1–26 ☐ 27:26–44 ☐ 27:45–66 ☐ 28

NOTES

The Genealogy of Jesus

1:1–17pp — Lk 3:23–38
1:3–6pp — Ru 4:18–22
1:7–11pp — 1Ch 3:10–17

1 A record of the genealogy of Jesus
Christ the son of David,[a] the son
of Abraham:[b]

2 Abraham was the father of
Isaac,[c]
Isaac the father of Jacob,[d]
Jacob the father of Judah and
his brothers,[e]
3 Judah the father of Perez and
Zerah, whose mother was
Tamar,[f]
Perez the father of Hezron,
Hezron the father of Ram,
4 Ram the father of Amminadab,
Amminadab the father of Nahshon,
Nahshon the father of Salmon,
5 Salmon the father of Boaz,
whose mother was Rahab,[g]
Boaz the father of Obed, whose
mother was Ruth,
Obed the father of Jesse,
6 and Jesse the father of King David.[h]

David was the father of Solomon,
whose mother had been Uriah's wife,[i]
7 Solomon the father of Rehoboam,
Rehoboam the father of Abijah,
Abijah the father of Asa,
8 Asa the father of Jehoshaphat,
Jehoshaphat the father of Jehoram,
Jehoram the father of Uzziah,
9 Uzziah the father of Jotham,
Jotham the father of Ahaz,
Ahaz the father of Hezekiah,
10 Hezekiah the father of Manasseh,[j]
Manasseh the father of Amon,
Amon the father of Josiah,
11 and Josiah the father of Jeconiah[a] and his brothers at the
time of the exile to Babylon.[k]

12 After the exile to Babylon:
Jeconiah was the father of Shealtiel,[l]
Shealtiel the father of Zerubbabel,[m]
13 Zerubbabel the father of Abiud,
Abiud the father of Eliakim,
Eliakim the father of Azor,
14 Azor the father of Zadok,
Zadok the father of Akim,
Akim the father of Eliud,
15 Eliud the father of Eleazar,
Eleazar the father of Matthan,
Matthan the father of Jacob,
16 and Jacob the father of Joseph,
the husband of Mary,[n] of
whom was born Jesus, who is
called Christ.[o]

17 Thus there were fourteen generations in all from Abraham to David,
fourteen from David to the exile to

1:1 [a] 2Sa 7:12-16; Isa 9:6,7; 11:1; Jer 23:5,6; S Mt 9:2_ 7; Lk 1:32,69; Rev 22:16 [b] Ge 22:18; S Gal 3:16 **1:2** [c] Ge 21:3,12 [d] Ge 25:26 [e] Ge 29:35; 49:10 **1:3** [f] Ge 38:27-30 **1:5** [g] S Heb 11:31 **1:6** [h] 1Sa 16:1; 17:12 [i] 2Sa 12:24 **1:10** [j] 2Ki 20:21 **1:11** [k] 2Ki 24:14-16; Jer 27:20; 40:1; Da 1:1,2 **1:12** [l] 1Ch 3:17 [m] 1Ch 3:19; Ezr 3:2 **1:16** [n] Lk 1:27 [o] Mt 27:17

[a] *11* That is, Jehoiachin; also in verse 12

1:1 GENEALOGY OF JESUS CHRIST. Matthew's Gospel opens with this genealogy, which traces Jesus' ancestral lineage through the paternal line (the line of Joseph), as was Jewish custom (v. 16). Although Joseph was not Jesus' biological father (v. 20), he was his legal father. Since God had promised that the Messiah would be a descendant of Abraham (Ge 12:3; 22:18; Gal 3:16) and David (2Sa 7:12–19; Jer 23:5), Matthew traces Jesus' legal lineage back to these two men in order to demonstrate to the Jews that Jesus had the proper genealogy to qualify as the Messiah.

1:1 CHRIST. The word "Christ" (Gk *christos*) means "anointed"; it is the Greek equivalent of the Hebrew term "Messiah" (Da 9:25–26). (1) From the beginning Matthew affirms that Jesus is God's Anointed One, anointed with the Holy Spirit (cf. Isa 61:1; Lk 4:18; Jn 3:34; Ac 10:38). (2) He was anointed as Prophet to bring knowledge and truth (Dt 18:15), as Priest to offer the sacrifice and cancel the guilt (Ps 110:4; Heb 10:10–14), and as King to rule, guide and establish the kingdom of righteousness (Zec 9:9).

1:1 SON OF DAVID. (1) Matthew establishes that Jesus was a legal descendant of David by tracing the genealogy of Joseph, who was from the house of David. Although Jesus was conceived by the Holy Spirit, he was still formally registered as Joseph's son and legally a son of David. (2) Luke's genealogy (Lk 3:23ff) traces the lineage of Jesus through the males in Mary's line (she was also from the Davidic line). Luke stresses that Jesus is the flesh and blood (i.e., offspring) of Mary and therefore one of us (cf. Ro 1:3). Thus, the Gospel writers assert both Jesus' legal and biological right to the Messiahship.

1:16 MARY . . . JESUS. The virgin birth of Jesus is safeguarded in the genealogy. Notice the words "the father of" are used of all the names down to Joseph, but then the statement is altered. It is not said that Joseph "was the father of" Jesus, but rather that Joseph was the "husband of Mary, of whom was born Jesus" (see Mt 1:23, note).

Babylon, and fourteen from the exile to
the Christ.[b]

The Birth of Jesus Christ

18This is how the birth of Jesus
Christ came about: His mother Mary
was pledged to be married to Joseph,
but before they came together, she was
found to be with child through the Holy
Spirit.[p] 19Because Joseph her husband was a righteous man and did not
want to expose her to public disgrace,
he had in mind to divorce[q] her quietly.
20But after he had considered this,
an angel[r] of the Lord appeared to him
in a dream[s] and said, "Joseph son of
David, do not be afraid to take Mary
home as your wife, because what is
conceived in her is from the Holy Spirit. 21She will give birth to a son, and
you are to give him the name Jesus,[c][t]
because he will save his people from
their sins."[u]
22All this took place to fulfill[v] what
the Lord had said through the prophet:

1:18 [p]Lk 1:35
1:19 [q]Dt 24:1
1:20 [r]S Ac 5:19
[s]S Mt 27:19
1:21 [t]S Lk 1:31
[u]Ps 130:8; S Lk 2:11; S Jn 3:17; Ac 5:31; S Ro 11:14; Tit 2:14
1:22 [v]Mt 2:15,17, 23; 4:14; 8:17; 12:17; 21:4; 26:54,56; 27:9; Lk 4:21; 21:22; 24:44; Jn 13:18; 19:24,28,36
1:23 [w]Isa 7:14; 8:8,10
1:24 [x]S Ac 5:19
1:25 [y]ver 21; S Lk 1:31
2:1 [z]Lk 2:4-7
[a]Lk 1:5
2:2 [b]Jer 23:5; Mt 27:11; Mk 15:2; Lk 23:38; Jn 1:49; 18:33-37
[c]Nu 24:17

23"The virgin will be with child and will
give birth to a son, and they will call
him Immanuel"[d][w]—which means,
"God with us."
24When Joseph woke up, he did what
the angel[x] of the Lord had commanded him and took Mary home as his wife.
25But he had no union with her until
she gave birth to a son. And he gave
him the name Jesus.[y]

The Visit of the Magi

2 After Jesus was born in Bethlehem
in Judea,[z] during the time of King
Herod,[a] Magi[e] from the east came to
Jerusalem 2and asked, "Where is the
one who has been born king of the
Jews?[b] We saw his star[c] in the east[f]
and have come to worship him."
3When King Herod heard this he was

[b] 17 Or *Messiah.* "The Christ" (Greek) and "the Messiah" (Hebrew) both mean "the Anointed One." [c] 21 *Jesus* is the Greek form of *Joshua,* which means *the LORD saves.* [d] 23 Isaiah 7:14 [e] 1 Traditionally *Wise Men* [f] 2 Or *star when it rose*

1:21 JESUS. Jesus is the Greek form of the Hebrew word *yeshua* (Joshua), meaning "the LORD saves" (see Jos 1:1, note). This describes the future task of Mary's son and is the initial promise of the gospel. Jesus as Savior "will save his people from their sins." Sin is the greatest enemy of the human race, destroying one's soul and life. Through the atoning death of Jesus and the sanctifying power of the Holy Spirit, those who turn to Jesus will be set free from the guilt and slavery of sin (see Jn 8:31–36; Ac 26:18; Ro 6; 8:1–16).

1:23 VIRGIN . . . GIVE BIRTH TO A SON. Both Matthew and Luke agree unequivocally that Jesus Christ was conceived by the Holy Spirit (v. 18; Lk 1:34–35) and born of a virgin mother without the intervention of a human father. The doctrine of Jesus' virgin birth has been opposed by liberal theologians for years. However, it is undeniable that the prophet Isaiah promised a virgin-born child who would be called "Immanuel," a Hebrew term meaning "God with us" (Isa 7:14). This prediction was made 700 years before the birth of Christ.

(1) The word "virgin" in Mt 1:23 is the correct translation of the Greek *parthenos* found in the Septuagint in Isa 7:14. The Hebrew word for virgin (*almah*) used by Isaiah means a virgin of marriageable age, and is never used in the OT for any state other than virginity (cf. Ge 24:43; SS 1:3; 6:8). Therefore, Isaiah in the OT and both Matthew and Luke in the NT ascribe virginity to the mother of Jesus (see Isa 7:14, note).

(2) The importance of the virgin birth cannot be overemphasized. In order for our Redeemer to qualify to pay for our sins and bring salvation, he must be, in one person, fully human, sinless and fully divine (Heb 7:25–26). The virgin birth satisfies all three of these requirements. (a) The only way Jesus could be born a human being was to be born of a woman. (b) The only way he could be sinless was to be conceived by the Holy Spirit (1:20; cf. Heb 4:15). (c) The only way he could be divine was to have God as his Father. As a result, his conception was not by natural but by supernatural means: "the holy one to be born will be called the Son of God" (Lk 1:35). Jesus Christ is therefore revealed to us as one divine person with two natures—divine and sinless human.

(3) In living and suffering as a human person, Jesus sympathizes with our weaknesses (Heb 4:15–16). As the divine Son of God, he has the power to deliver us from sin's bondage and Satan's power (Ac 26:18; Col 2:15; Heb 2:14; 7:25). As both divine and human, he qualifies to serve as a sacrifice for the sins of every person, and as a high priest to intercede for all who come to God (Heb 2:9–18; 5:1–9; 7:24–28; 10:4–12).

1:25 NO UNION WITH HER UNTIL. The word "until" draws attention to the fact that after Christ's birth, Joseph and Mary entered into the full physical union commonly associated with marriage. We are told that Jesus had brothers and sisters (12:46–47; Mk 3:31–32; 6:3; Lk 8:19–20).

2:1 MAGI. These men were probably members of a learned religious class from the region now called Iran. They specialized in astrology, medicine and natural science. Their visit occurred when Jesus was between 40 days (cf. Lk 2:22) and 2 years old (cf. v. 16). The importance of this story is that (1) Jesus is worthy of royal honor from all humanity, and (2) Gentiles as well as Jews are included in God's redemptive plan (cf. 8:11; 28:19; Ro 10:12).

disturbed, and all Jerusalem with him.
4When he had called together all the
people's chief priests and teachers of
the law, he asked them where the
Christ[g] was to be born. **5**"In Bethlehem[d] in Judea," they replied, "for this
is what the prophet has written:

6" 'But you, Bethlehem, in the land
of Judah,
are by no means least among
the rulers of Judah;
for out of you will come a ruler
who will be the shepherd of my
people Israel.'[h]"[e]

7Then Herod called the Magi secretly and found out from them the exact
time the star had appeared. **8**He sent
them to Bethlehem and said, "Go and
make a careful search for the child. As
soon as you find him, report to me, so
that I too may go and worship him."
9After they had heard the king, they
went on their way, and the star they
had seen in the east[i] went ahead of
them until it stopped over the place
where the child was. **10**When they saw
the star, they were overjoyed. **11**On
coming to the house, they saw the child
with his mother Mary, and they bowed
down and worshiped him.[f] Then they
opened their treasures and presented
him with gifts[g] of gold and of incense
and of myrrh. **12**And having been
warned[h] in a dream[i] not to go back
to Herod, they returned to their country by another route.

The Escape to Egypt

13When they had gone, an angel[j] of
the Lord appeared to Joseph in a
dream.[k] "Get up," he said, "take the
child and his mother and escape to
Egypt. Stay there until I tell you, for
Herod is going to search for the child
to kill him."[l]
14So he got up, took the child and
his mother during the night and left for
Egypt, **15**where he stayed until the
death of Herod. And so was fulfilled[m]
what the Lord had said through the
prophet: "Out of Egypt I called my
son."[j][n]
16When Herod realized that he had
been outwitted by the Magi, he was furious, and he gave orders to kill all the
boys in Bethlehem and its vicinity who
were two years old and under, in accordance with the time he had learned
from the Magi. **17**Then what was said
through the prophet Jeremiah was fulfilled:[o]

18"A voice is heard in Ramah,
weeping and great mourning,
Rachel[p] weeping for her children
and refusing to be comforted,
because they are no more."[k][q]

The Return to Nazareth

19After Herod died, an angel[r] of the
Lord appeared in a dream[s] to Joseph
in Egypt **20**and said, "Get up, take the
child and his mother and go to the land
of Israel, for those who were trying to
take the child's life are dead."[t]
21So he got up, took the child and
his mother and went to the land of Israel. **22**But when he heard that Archelaus

2:5 *d* Jn 7:42
2:6 *e* Mic 5:2; 2Sa 5:2
2:11 *f* Isa 60:3 *g* Ps 72:10
2:12 *h* Heb 11:7 *i* ver 13,19,22; S Mt 27:19
2:13 *j* S Ac 5:19 *k* ver 12,19,22; S Mt 27:19 *l* Rev 12:4
2:15 *m* ver 17,23; S Mt 1:22 *n* Hos 11:1; Ex 4:22,23
2:17 *o* ver 15,23; S Mt 1:22
2:18 *p* Ge 35:19 *q* Jer 31:15
2:19 *r* S Ac 5:19 *s* ver 12,13,22; S Mt 27:19
2:20 *t* Ex 4:19

g *4* Or *Messiah* **h** *6* Micah 5:2 **i** *9* Or *seen when it rose* **j** *15* Hosea 11:1 **k** *18* Jer. 31:15

2:4 CHIEF PRIESTS AND TEACHERS OF THE LAW. Chief priests were the temple ministers in charge of worship; the teachers of the law were copyists of Scripture in post-exilic times. They were trained to teach and apply OT law and were considered experts "in the Law" (22:35). Together the teachers of the law and the chief priests constituted the Sanhedrin, or the Jewish Senate and Supreme Court. This body was composed of 70 or 71 men who were in charge of the civil and religious affairs of the Jews and who were given considerable authority under the Romans.

2:13 ESCAPE TO EGYPT. Herod's attempt to kill Jesus and God's way of protecting the child reveal several truths about God's method of guiding and protecting his people. (1) God did not protect Joseph and Mary and their child without their cooperation (vv. 13,19–20,22). Protection required obedience to God's guidance, which in this case involved fleeing the country (v. 14).

(2) God may allow some things that are hard to understand to enter our lives in order to accomplish his will (see article on THE SUFFERING OF THE RIGHTEOUS, p. 710). In a real sense Christ began life as a refugee and stranger in another country (vv. 14–15). To our limited understanding it would have been easier if God had removed Herod immediately, thus avoiding the escape to Egypt and all the trials involved in that circumstance.

(3) Even after a particular trial is resolved, there may be other problems to face (vv. 19–23). God's protection and providential care will always be needed, for the believer's enemy never ceases his attack on the faithful (Eph 6:10–18; 1Pe 5:8; see article on THE PROVIDENCE OF GOD, p. 78).

2:16 KILL ALL THE BOYS. Bethlehem and its vicinity were not large. It most likely contained between one and two thousand inhabitants; in this case the number of male children slain would have been around twenty.

was reigning in Judea in place of his
father Herod, he was afraid to go there.
Having been warned in a dream,[u] he
withdrew to the district of Galilee,[v]
23 and he went and lived in a town
called Nazareth.[w] So was fulfilled[x]
what was said through the prophets:
"He will be called a Nazarene."[y]

John the Baptist Prepares the Way

3:1–12pp — Mk 1:3–8; Lk 3:2–17

3 In those days John the Baptist[z]
came, preaching in the Desert of
Judea 2 and saying, "Repent, for the
kingdom of heaven[a] is near." 3 This is
he who was spoken of through the
prophet Isaiah:

"A voice of one calling in the
desert,
'Prepare the way for the Lord,
make straight paths for
him.' "[1b]

4 John's[c] clothes were made of camel's hair, and he had a leather belt
around his waist.[d] His food was locusts[e] and wild honey. 5 People went
out to him from Jerusalem and all Judea and the whole region of the Jordan.
6 Confessing their sins, they were baptized[f] by him in the Jordan River.

7 But when he saw many of the Pharisees and Sadducees coming to where
he was baptizing, he said to them: "You
brood of vipers![g] Who warned you to
flee from the coming wrath?[h] 8 Produce fruit in keeping with repentance.[i] 9 And do not think you can say
to yourselves, 'We have Abraham as
our father.'[j] I tell you that out of
these stones God can raise up children
for Abraham. 10 The ax is already at the
root of the trees, and every tree that
does not produce good fruit will be cut
down and thrown into the fire.[k]

Jesus Will Baptize in the Spirit

11 "I baptize you with[m] water for re-

2:22 [u] ver 12,13, 19; S Mt 27:19 [v] Lk 2:39 **2:23** [w] Mk 1:9; 6:1; S 1:24; Lk 1:26; 2:39,51; 4:16,23; Jn 1:45, 46 [x] ver 15,17; S Mt 1:22 [y] S Mk 1:24 **3:1** [z] ver 13,14; Mt 9:14; 11:2-14; 14:1-12; Lk 1:13, 57-66; 3:2-19; Ac 19:3,4 **3:2** [a] Da 7:14; Mt 4:17; 6:10; 7:21; S 25:34; Lk 11:20; 17:20, 21; 19:11; 21:31; Jn 3:3,5; Ac 1:3,6 **3:3** [b] Isa 40:3; Mal 3:1; Lk 1:76; Jn 1:23 **3:4** [c] S Mt 3:1 [d] 2Ki 1:8 [e] Lev 11:22 **3:6** [f] ver 11; S Mk 1:4 **3:7** [g] Mt 12:34; 23:33 [h] S Ro 1:18 **3:8** [i] Ac 26:20 **3:9** [j] S Lk 3:8 **3:10** [k] Mt 7:19; Lk 3:9; 13:6-9; Jn 15:2,6

[1] 3 Isaiah 40:3 [m] 11 Or *in*

2:22 WARNED IN A DREAM. From the two warnings of God (vv. 12,22) we learn that God watches over those whom he loves, and that he knows best how to frustrate the plans of the wicked and how to deliver his faithful out of the hands of those who would harm them.

3:2 REPENT. The basic meaning of repentance (Gk *metanoeō*) is "to turn around." It is a turning from evil ways and a turning to Christ, and through him to God (Jn 14:1,6; Ac 8:22; 26:18; 1Pe 2:25).

(1) The decision to turn from sin and to salvation in Christ involves accepting Christ not only as Savior from the penalty of sin, but also as Lord of one's life. Thus, repentance involves a change of lords—from the lordship of Satan (Eph 2:2) to the lordship of Christ and his Word (Ac 26:18).

(2) Repentance is a free decision on the part of sinners, made possible by the enabling grace given to them as they hear and believe the gospel (Ac 11:21; see article on FAITH AND GRACE, p. 1720).

(3) The definition of saving faith as "mere trust" in Christ as Savior is wholly inadequate in the light of Christ's demand for repentance. To define saving faith in a way that does not necessarily involve a radical break with sin is to dangerously distort the Biblical view of redemption. Faith that includes repentance is always a condition for salvation (cf. Mk 1:15; Lk 13:3,5; Ac 2:38; 3:19; 11:21).

(4) Repentance was a basic message of the OT prophets (Jer 7:3; Eze 18:30; Joel 2:12–14; Mal 3:7), John the Baptist (Mt 3:2), Jesus Christ (Mt 4:17; 18:3; Lk 5:32) and NT Christians (Ac 2:38; 8:22; 11:18; 2Pe 3:9). The preaching of repentance must always accompany the gospel message (Lk 24:47).

3:7 PHARISEES AND SADDUCEES. Two of the most prominent religious groups in Judaism were the Pharisees and Sadducees.

(1) The Pharisees were a Jewish religious group that adhered to both the entire OT and their own human interpretations of it. They especially emphasized that salvation came by obeying the letter of God's law and their interpretations of that law. They taught that the coming Messiah would be an earthly ruler who would help Israel dominate the nations and force all people to obey God's law. However, their religion was outward in form with no inward godliness of heart (23:25), and they refused to acknowledge the depravity of their own nature. By and large they opposed Jesus and his message that religion is a matter of the heart and spirit and not simply a legalistic obedience to the commands of Scripture (cf. 9:14; 23:2–4; Lk 18:9–14).

(2) The Sadducees were the theological liberals and anti-supernaturalists of their day. While appearing to hold to the law of God, they really denied many of its teachings. They rejected the doctrines of the resurrection, angels, miracles, immortality and the judgment to come. Their lives were morally lax and worldly. They also were persecutors of Jesus Christ (16:1–4).

3:8 FRUIT IN KEEPING WITH REPENTANCE. Genuine repentance will be accompanied by the fruit of righteousness (cf. 23:23; Lk 3:10–14; Ac 26:20). True saving faith and conversion must become evident through lives that forsake sin and bear godly fruit (see Jn 15:16, note). Those who say they believe in Christ and are God's children, and yet do not live lives that produce good fruit, are like trees that will be cut down and thrown into the fire (vv. 8–10,12).

3:11 WILL BAPTIZE YOU WITH THE HOLY

pentance.[l] But after me will come one
who is more powerful than I, whose
sandals I am not fit to carry. He will
baptize you with the Holy Spirit[m] and
Mk 1:7-8 with fire.[n] 12His winnowing fork is in
his hand, and he will clear his threshing floor, gathering his wheat into the
barn and burning up the chaff with unquenchable fire."[o]

The Baptism of Jesus

3:13–17pp — Mk 1:9–11; Lk 3:21,22; Jn 1:31–34

13Then Jesus came from Galilee to
the Jordan to be baptized by John.[p]
14But John tried to deter him, saying,
"I need to be baptized by you, and do
you come to me?"
15Jesus replied, "Let it be so now; it
is proper for us to do this to fulfill
all righteousness." Then John consented.
16As soon as Jesus was baptized, he
went up out of the water. At that moment heaven was opened,[q] and he
saw the Spirit of God[r] descending like
a dove and lighting on him. 17And a
voice from heaven[s] said, "This is my
Son,[t] whom I love; with him I am well
pleased."[u]

The Temptation of Jesus

4:1–11pp — Mk 1:12,13; Lk 4:1–13

4 Then Jesus was led by the Spirit
into the desert to be tempted[v] by
the devil.[w] 2After fasting forty days
and forty nights,[x] he was hungry.

3:11 [l] ver 6; S Mk 1:4 [m] S Mk 1:8 [n] Isa 4:4; Ac 2:3,4 **3:12** [o] Mt 13:30; S 25:41 **3:13** [p] S Mt 3:1; S Mk 1:4 **3:16** [q] Eze 1:1; Jn 1:51; Ac 7:56; 10:11; Rev 4:1; 19:11 [r] Isa 11:2; 42:1 **3:17** [s] Dt 4:12; Mt 17:5; Jn 12:28 [t] Ps 2:7; Ac 13:33; Heb 1:1-5; 5:5; 2Pe 1:17,18 [u] Isa 42:1; Mt 12:18; 17:5; Mk 1:11; 9:7; Lk 3:22; 9:35; 2Pe 1:17 **4:1** [v] Heb 4:15 [w] Ge 3:1-7 **4:2** [x] Ex 34:28; 1Ki 19:8

SPIRIT. John teaches that the work of the coming Messiah will involve baptizing his followers with the Holy Spirit and fire—a baptism that gives great power to live and witness for Christ (see Lk 3:16, note on the baptism in the Holy Spirit).

3:13 JESUS ... BAPTIZED. Jesus was baptized by John for the following reasons: (1) "To fulfill all righteousness" (v. 15; cf. Lev 16:4; Gal 4:4–5). Christ, through baptism, publicly consecrated himself to God and his kingdom and thus fulfilled God's righteous requirement. (2) To identify himself with sinners—although Jesus himself did not need to repent of sin (2Co 5:21; 1Pe 2:24). (3) To associate himself with the new movement of God that was calling everyone to repentance; note the message of John the Baptist as the forerunner of the Messiah (Jn 1:23,32–33).

3:16 SPIRIT ... ON HIM. Everything Jesus did—his preaching, his healings, his suffering, his victory over sin—he did by the power of the Holy Spirit. If Jesus could do nothing apart from the working of the Holy Spirit, how much more do we need the Spirit's enablement (cf. Lk 4:1,14,18; Jn 3:34; Ac 1:2; 10:38). The Spirit came on Jesus to equip him with power for his work of redemption (see Lk 3:22, note). Jesus himself would later baptize his followers with the Holy Spirit so that they too might have the Spirit's enablement (see Mt 3:11, notes; Ac 1:5,8; 2:4).

3:17 THE TRINITY IN EXAMPLE. The baptism of Jesus is a striking manifestation of the fact of the Trinity. (1) Jesus Christ, declared to be equal with God (Jn 10:30), is baptized in the Jordan. (2) The Holy Spirit, who is also equal with the Father (Ac 5:3–4), descends on Jesus like a dove. (3) The Father declares that he is well pleased with Jesus. Thus, we have three equal divine persons; it is contrary to the whole of Scripture to explain this event in any other manner. The trinitarian understanding of God teaches that these three divine persons exist in such unity that they are one God (see Mk 1:11, note on the Trinity; cf. Mt 28:19; Jn 15:26; 1Co 12:4–13; Eph 2:18; 1Pe 1:2).

4:1–11 JESUS ... TEMPTED. The temptation of Jesus by Satan was an attempt to entice Jesus from the pathway of perfect obedience to the will of God. Notice that in each temptation, Jesus submitted himself to the authority of the Word of God rather than to the desires of Satan (vv. 4,7,10). What can we learn from the temptation of Christ?

(1) Satan is our greatest enemy. As Christians, we must be aware that we are engaged in a spiritual warfare with unseen but very real powers of evil (see Eph 6:12, note).

(2) Without the Holy Spirit and the proper use of God's Word, the Christian cannot overcome sin and temptation. The following are suggestions on how to use God's Word in overcoming temptation: (a) Realize that through the Word you have the power to resist any appeal Satan can make (Jn 15:3,7). (b) Engraft (i.e., memorize) the Word of God into your heart and mind (see Jas 1:21, note). (c) Meditate day and night on the verses you have memorized (see Dt 6:6, note; Ps 1:2, notes; 119:47–48, note). (d) Say the memorized passage to yourself and God the instant you are tempted (vv. 4,7,10). (e) Recognize and obey the prompting of the Holy Spirit to obey God's Word (Ro 8:12–14; Gal 5:18). (f) Surround all these steps with prayer (Eph 6:18).

Some passages to memorize in facing temptation: General (Ro 6 and 8); Specific: concerning immorality (Ro 13:14), lying (Jn 8:44; Col 3:9), gossiping (Jas 4:11), disobeying parents (Heb 13:17), discouragement (Gal 6:9), fear of the future (2Ti 1:7), lust (Mt 5:28; 2Ti 2:22), desire for revenge (Mt 6:15), neglect of God's Word (Mt 4:4), worry over finances (Mt 6:24–34; Php 4:6).

4:2 FASTING FORTY DAYS. After fasting "forty days and forty nights," Jesus "was hungry" and was tempted by Satan to eat. This seems to indicate that Christ abstained from food but not from water (see Lk 4:2). To abstain from water for forty days would have required a miracle. Christ, insofar as he had to encounter temptation as our human representative (cf. Heb 2:17; 4:15), could not have used any other means of resisting temptation than is available to the Spirit-filled believer (see Ex 34:28, note; 1Ki 19:8, note; Mt 6:16, note on fasting). During the forty-day fast it is reasonable to

3The tempter[y] came to him and said,
"If you are the Son of God,[z] tell these
stones to become bread."
4Jesus answered, "It is written:
'Man does not live on bread alone, but
on every word that comes from the
mouth of God.'[n]"[a]
5Then the devil took him to the holy
city[b] and had him stand on the highest point of the temple. 6"If you are the
Son of God," he said, "throw yourself
down. For it is written:

" 'He will command his angels
concerning you,
and they will lift you up in their
hands,
so that you will not strike your
foot against a stone.'[o]"[d]

7Jesus answered him, "It is also
written: 'Do not put the Lord your God
to the test.'[p]"[e]
8Again, the devil took him to a very
high mountain and showed him all the
kingdoms of the world and their splendor. 9"All this I will give you," he said,
"if you will bow down and worship me."
10Jesus said to him, "Away from me,
Satan![f] For it is written: 'Worship the
Lord your God, and serve him
only.'[q]"[g]
11Then the devil left him,[h] and an- Mt 8:28-33
gels came and attended him.[i]

Jesus Begins to Preach

12When Jesus heard that John had
been put in prison,[j] he returned to
Galilee.[k] 13Leaving Nazareth, he went
and lived in Capernaum,[l] which was
by the lake in the area of Zebulun and
Naphtali— 14to fulfill[m] what was said
through the prophet Isaiah:

15"Land of Zebulun and land of
Naphtali,
the way to the sea, along the
Jordan,
Galilee of the Gentiles—
16the people living in darkness
have seen a great light;
on those living in the land of the
shadow of death
a light has dawned."[r][n]

4:3 [y] 1Th 3:5 [z] S Mt 3:17; 14:33; 16:16; 27:54; Mk 3:11; Lk 1:35; 22:70; Jn 1:34,49; 5:25; 11:27; 20:31; Ac 9:20; Ro 1:4; 1Jn 5:10-13,20; Rev 2:18 **4:4** [a] Dt 8:3; Jn 4:34 **4:5** [b] Ne 11:1; Da 9:24; Mt 27:53 **4:6** [c] S ver 3 [d] Ps 91:11,12 **4:7** [e] Dt 6:16 **4:10** [f] 1Ch 21:1; Job 1:6-9; Mt 16:23; Mk 4:15; Lk 10:18; 13:16; 22:3,31; Ro 16:20; 2Co 2:11; 11:14; 2Th 2:9; Rev 12:9 [g] Dt 6:13 **4:11** [h] Jas 4:7 [i] Mt 26:53; Lk 22:43; Heb 1:14 **4:12** [j] Mt 14:3 [k] Mk 1:14 **4:13** [l] Mk 1:21; 9:33; Lk 4:23,31; Jn 2:12; 4:46,47 **4:14** [m] S Mt 1:22 **4:16** [n] Isa 9:1,2; Lk 2:32; Jn 1:4,5,9

[n] *4* Deut. 8:3 [o] *6* Psalm 91:11,12 [p] *7* Deut. 6:16 [q] *10* Deut. 6:13 [r] *16* Isaiah 9:1,2

---

assume that he was preparing himself by means of prayer and meditation on God's Word for the work the Father sent him to do.

4:6 IT IS WRITTEN. Satan used the Word of God to tempt Christ to sin. At times worldly people will use Scripture in an attempt to persuade believers to do something they know is wrong or unwise. Some Scripture texts, when taken out of context or not compared with other passages of God's Word, may even appear to condone sinful behavior (see, e.g., 1Co 6:12). Believers must know God's Word thoroughly and beware of those who pervert Scripture in order to fulfill the desires of the sinful human nature. The apostle Peter speaks of those who distort the Scriptures to their own destruction (2Pe 3:16).

4:8 ALL THE KINGDOMS OF THE WORLD. See Lk 4:5, note.

4:10 SATAN. Satan (Heb, meaning "accuser" or "adversary") was a great angel created perfect and good. He was appointed to be a minister at the throne of God; yet before the world began, he rebelled and became the chief antagonist of God and humanity (Eze 28:12–15).

(1) In his rebellion against God, Satan drew with him a multitude of lesser angels (Rev 12:4) who are probably to be identified, after their fall, with demons or evil spirits (see article on POWER OVER SATAN AND DEMONS, p. 1484). Satan and many of these lesser angels were exiled to the earth and the atmosphere around it, and operate within this sphere under God's permissive will.

(2) Satan, also called "the serpent," caused the fall of the human race (Ge 3:1–6; see 1Jn 5:19, note).

(3) Satan's kingdom (12:26) is a highly systematized empire of evil that has authority over the kingdom of the air (Eph 2:2), fallen angels (25:41; Rev 12:7), unregenerate humanity (vv. 8–9; Jn 12:31; Eph 2:2) and the world (Lk 4:5–6; 2Co 4:4; see 1Jn 5:19, note). Satan is not omnipresent, omnipotent or omniscient; therefore, most of his activity is delegated to demons (8:28; Rev 16:13–14; see Job 1:12, note).

(4) Jesus came to earth to destroy the works of Satan (1Jn 3:8), establish God's kingdom and deliver us from Satan's dominion (12:28; Lk 4:18; 13:16; Ac 26:18). By his death and resurrection, Christ initiated the defeat of Satan and thereby ensured God's ultimate victory over him (Heb 2:14).

(5) At the end of the age Satan is to be confined to the Abyss for a thousand years (Rev 20:1–3). After his release he will make a final attempt to overthrow God; this will result in Satan's final defeat and his being thrown into the lake of fire (Rev 20:7–10).

(6) Satan presently wars against God and his people (Job 1—2; Eph 6:11–18), seeking to draw them away from loyalty to Christ (2Co 11:3) and into sin and bondage to this present world system (cf. 2Co 11:3; 1Ti 5:15; 1Jn 5:16). Believers must pray constantly for deliverance from Satan (Mt 6:13), be on the alert concerning his schemes and temptations (Eph 6:11), and resist him through spiritual warfare, while remaining firm in the faith (Eph 6:10–18; 1Pe 5:8–9).

17From that time on Jesus began to
preach, "Repent, for the kingdom of
heaven[o] is near."

The Calling of the First Disciples

4:18–22pp — Mk 1:16–20; Lk 5:2–11; Jn 1:35–42

18As Jesus was walking beside the
Sea of Galilee,[p] he saw two brothers,
Simon called Peter[q] and his brother
Andrew. They were casting a net into
the lake, for they were fishermen.
19"Come, follow me,"[r] Jesus said,
"and I will make you fishers of men."
20At once they left their nets and followed him.[s]
21Going on from there, he saw two
other brothers, James son of Zebedee
and his brother John.[t] They were in a
boat with their father Zebedee, preparing their nets. Jesus called them, 22and
immediately they left the boat and
their father and followed him.[u]

Jesus Heals the Sick

23Jesus went throughout Galilee,[v]
teaching in their synagogues,[w]
preaching the good news[x] of the kingdom,[y] and healing every disease and
sickness among the people.[z] 24News
about him spread all over Syria,[a] and
people brought to him all who were ill
with various diseases, those suffering
severe pain, the demon-possessed,[b]
those having seizures,[c] and the paralyzed,[d] and he healed them. 25Large
crowds from Galilee, the Decapolis,[s]
Jerusalem, Judea and the region across
the Jordan followed him.[e]

The Beatitudes

5:3–12pp — Lk 6:20–23

5 Now when he saw the crowds, he
went up on a mountainside and sat
down. His disciples came to him, 2and
he began to teach them, saying:

3"Blessed are the poor in
spirit,
for theirs is the kingdom of
heaven.[f]
4Blessed are those who mourn,
for they will be comforted.[g]
5Blessed are the meek,
for they will inherit the earth.[h]
6Blessed are those who hunger and
thirst for righteousness,
for they will be filled.[i]

4:17 [o] S Mt 3:2 **4:18** [p] Mt 15:29; Mk 7:31; Jn 6:1 [q] Mt 16:17,18 **4:19** [r] ver 20,22; Mt 8:22; Mk 10:21,28,52; Lk 5:28; Jn 1:43; 21:19,22 **4:20** [s] S ver 19 **4:21** [t] Mt 17:1; 20:20; 26:37; Mk 3:17; 13:3; Lk 8:51; Jn 21:2 **4:22** [u] S ver 19 **4:23** [v] Mk 1:39; Lk 4:15,44 [w] Mt 9:35; 13:54; Mk 1:21; Lk 4:15; Jn 6:59; 18:20 [x] Mk 1:14 [y] S Mt 3:2; Ac 20:25; 28:23, 31 [z] Mt 8:16; 14:14; 15:30; Mk 3:10; Lk 7:22; Ac 10:38 **4:24** [a] S Lk 2:2 [b] Mt 8:16,28; 9:32; 12:22; 15:22; Mk 1:32; 5:15,16, 18 [c] Mt 17:15 [d] Mt 8:6; 9:2; Mk 2:3 **4:25** [e] Mk 3:7,8; Lk 6:17 **5:3** [f] ver 10,19; S Mt 25:34 **5:4** [g] Isa 61:2,3; Rev 7:17 **5:5** [h] Ps 37:11; Ro 4:13 **5:6** [i] Isa 55:1,2

[s] *25* That is, the Ten Cities

4:19 FISHERS OF MEN. One may be a pastor, evangelist, missionary, writer, teacher, deacon or layperson, but if he or she is not actually striving to bring others to Christ, they are not fulfilling their work for God (see 28:19; Lk 5:10; Jn 15:16; Ac 1:8; 1Co 9:19).

4:23 THE KINGDOM, AND HEALING. In the Gospels, the kingdom of God is closely associated with healing, the performing of miracles and the driving out of demons (4:23–24; 9:35; 10:7–8; 12:28; Lk 9:1–2; cf. Ac 8:6–7,12). The kingdom includes blessings for the body as well as for the soul (see article on DIVINE HEALING, p. 1420).

5–7 SERMON ON THE MOUNT. Chs. 5–7, commonly called Christ's Sermon on the Mount, contain a revelation of God's principles of righteousness by which all Christians are to live through faith in the Son of God (Gal 2:20) and through the power of the indwelling Spirit (cf. Ro 8:2–14; Gal 5:16–25). All who belong to the kingdom of God are to have an intense hunger and thirst for the righteousness taught in Christ's sermon (see 5:6, note).

5:3 BLESSED . . . POOR IN SPIRIT. The word "blessed" refers to the well-being of those who, because of their relationship to Christ and his Word, receive God's kingdom, which includes his love, care, salvation and daily presence (see 14:19, note; Lk 24:50, note). There are certain requirements if we wish to receive the blessings of God's kingdom; we must be guided by God's ways and values revealed in Scripture and not by the ways and values of the world. The first of these requirements is to be "poor in spirit." We must recognize that we are not spiritually self-sufficient; we need the Holy Spirit's life, power and sustaining grace in order to inherit God's kingdom.

5:4 THOSE WHO MOURN. To "mourn" is to grieve over our own weakness in relation to God's standard of righteousness and his kingdom power (v. 6; 6:33). It is also to mourn over the things that grieve God, to have our feelings in sympathy with the feelings of God, and to be afflicted in our spirits over the sin, immorality and cruelty manifested in the world (see Lk 19:41, note; Ac 20:19; 2Pe 2:8, note). Those who mourn are comforted by receiving from the Father "righteousness, peace and joy in the Holy Spirit" (Ro 14:17).

5:5 THE MEEK. The "meek" are those who are humble and submissive before God. They find their refuge in him and commit their way entirely to him. They are more concerned about God's work and God's people than about what might happen to them personally (cf. Ps 37:11). The meek, rather than the aggressors, ultimately inherit the earth.

5:6 HUNGER AND THIRST FOR RIGHTEOUSNESS. This is one of the most important verses in the Sermon on the Mount. (1) The foundational requirement for all godly living is to "hunger and thirst for righteousness" (cf. 6:33). Such hunger is seen in Moses (Ex 33:13,18), the psalmist (see Ps 42:2,6, notes; 63:1, note) and the apostle Paul (Php 3:10). The spiritual condition of Christians all throughout their lives will depend on

7Blessed are the merciful,
for they will be shown
mercy.[j]
8Blessed are the pure in heart,[k]
for they will see God.[l]
9Blessed are the peacemakers,[m]
for they will be called sons of
God.[n]
10Blessed are those who are
persecuted because of
righteousness,[o]
for theirs is the kingdom of
heaven.[p]

11"Blessed are you when people insult you,[q] persecute you and falsely
say all kinds of evil against you because of me.[r] 12Rejoice and be glad,[s]
because great is your reward in heav-
en, for in the same way they persecuted the prophets who were before you.[t]

5:7 [j] S Jas 2:13
5:8 [k] Ps 24:3,4; 73:1 [l] Ps 17:15; 42:2; Heb 12:14; Rev 22:4
5:9 [m] Jas 3:18; S Ro 14:19 [n] ver 44,45; S Ro 8:14
5:10 [o] S 1Pe 3:14 [p] ver 3,19; S Mt 25:34
5:11 [q] Isa 51:7 [r] S Jn 15:21
5:12 [s] Ps 9:2; Ac 5:41; S 2Co 6:10; 12:10; Col 1:24; Jas 1:2; 1Pe 1:6; 4:13,16 [t] 2Ch 36:16; Mt 23:31,37; Ac 7:52; 1Th 2:15; Heb 11:32-38
5:13 [u] Mk 9:50; Lk 14:34,35
5:14 [v] Jn 8:12
5:15 [w] Mk 4:21; Lk 8:16; 11:33
5:16 [x] 1Co 10:31; Php 1:11 [y] S Tit 2:14 [z] S Mt 9:8

Salt and Light

13"You are the salt of the earth. But
if the salt loses its saltiness, how can
it be made salty again? It is no longer
good for anything, except to be thrown
out and trampled by men.[u]
14"You are the light of the world.[v]
A city on a hill cannot be hidden. 15Nei-
ther do people light a lamp and put it
under a bowl. Instead they put it on its
stand, and it gives light to everyone in
the house.[w] 16In the same way, let
your light shine before men,[x] that
they may see your good deeds[y] and Mt 6:19-24
praise[z] your Father in heaven.

The Fulfillment of the Law

17"Do not think that I have come to

their hunger and thirst for (a) the presence of God (Dt 4:29), (b) the Word of God (Ps 119), (c) the communion of Christ (Php 3:8–10), (d) the fellowship of the Spirit (Jn 7:37–39; 2Co 13:14), (e) righteousness (5:6), (f) kingdom power (6:33) and (g) the return of the Lord (2Ti 4:8).

(2) The Christian's hunger for the things of God is destroyed by worldly anxiety, deceitfulness of wealth (13:22), desire for things (Mk 4:19) and life's pleasures (Lk 8:14), and failure to remain in Christ (see Jn 15:4, note). When the hunger of believers for God and his righteousness is destroyed, they will die spiritually. For this reason it is essential that we be sensitive to the Holy Spirit's convicting work in our lives (see Jn 16:8–13; Ro 8:5–16).

5:7 THE MERCIFUL. The "merciful" are full of compassion and pity toward those who are suffering either from sin or sorrow. The merciful sincerely want to make such suffering less by bringing those people to the grace and help of God through Jesus Christ (cf. 18:23–35; Lk 10:30–37; Heb 2:17). In showing mercy to others, we "will be shown mercy."

5:8 THE PURE IN HEART. The "pure in heart" are those who have been delivered from sin's power by God's grace and now strive without deceit to please and glorify God and to be like him. (1) They seek to have the same attitude of heart that God has—a love of righteousness and a hatred of evil (see Heb 1:9, note). Their heart (which includes mind, will and emotions; see article on THE HEART, p. 906) is in tune with the heart of God (1Sa 13:14; Mt 22:37; 1Ti 1:5). (2) Only the pure in heart "will see God." To see God means to be his child and to dwell in his presence, both now and in the future kingdom (Ex 33:11; Rev 21:7; 22:4).

5:9 THE PEACEMAKERS. The "peacemakers" are those who have been reconciled to God. They have peace with him through the cross (Ro 5:1; Eph 2:14–16; see article on THE PEACE OF GOD, p. 1134). They now strive by their witness and life to bring others, including their enemies, to peace with God.

5:10 PERSECUTED BECAUSE OF RIGHTEOUSNESS. Persecution will be the lot of all who seek to live in harmony with God's Word for the sake of righteousness. (1) Those who uphold God's standards of truth, justice and purity, and who at the same time refuse to compromise with the present evil society or the lifestyles of lukewarm believers (Rev 2; 3:1–4,14–22), will undergo unpopularity, rejection and criticism. Persecution and opposition will come from the world (10:22; 24:9; Jn 15:19) and at times from those within the professing church (Ac 20:28–31; 2Co 11:3–15; 2Ti 1:15; 3:8–14; 4:16). When they experience this suffering, Christians are to rejoice (v. 12), for to those who suffer most God imparts the highest blessing (2Co 1:5; 2Ti 2:12; 1Pe 1:7; 4:13). (2) Christians must beware of the temptation to compromise God's will in order to avoid shame, embarrassment or loss (10:33; Mk 8:38; Lk 9:26; 2Ti 2:12). The principles of God's kingdom never change: ". . . everyone who wants to live a godly life in Christ Jesus will be persecuted" (2Ti 3:12). Those who suffer and endure persecution because of righteousness are promised the kingdom and heavenly rewards.

5:13 SALT OF THE EARTH. As salt is valuable to give flavor and to preserve from corruption, believers and the church must be godly examples in the world and must resist the moral decay and corruption evident in society. (1) Churches that become lukewarm, quench the power of the Holy Spirit and cease to resist the prevailing spirit in the world will be "thrown out" by God (see Rev 3:15–16, note). (2) They consequently will be "trampled by men"; i.e., those who are lukewarm, together with their families, will be destroyed by the ways and values of an ungodly society (cf. Dt 28:13,43,48; Jdg 2:20–22).

5:17 THE LAW . . . TO FULFILL. It is Christ's intention that the spiritual requirement of God's law be fulfilled in the lives of his followers (Ro

abolish the Law or the Prophets; I have
not come to abolish them but to fulfill
them.[a] 18 I tell you the truth, until
heaven and earth disappear, not the
smallest letter, not the least stroke of
a pen, will by any means disappear
from the Law until everything is accomplished.[b] 19 Anyone who breaks
one of the least of these commandments[c] and teaches others to do the
same will be called least in the kingdom of heaven, but whoever practices
and teaches these commands will be
called great in the kingdom of heaven.
20 For I tell you that unless your righteousness surpasses that of the Pharisees and the teachers of the law, you
will certainly not enter the kingdom of
heaven.[d]

Murder

5:25,26pp — Lk 12:58,59

21 "You have heard that it was said to
the people long ago, 'Do not murder,[t][e] and anyone who murders will
be subject to judgment.' 22 But I tell
you that anyone who is angry[f] with
his brother[u] will be subject to judgment.[g] Again, anyone who says to his
brother, 'Raca,[v]' is answerable to the
Sanhedrin.[h] But anyone who says,
'You fool!' will be in danger of the fire
of hell.[i]

23 "Therefore, if you are offering your
gift at the altar and there remember
that your brother has something
against you, 24 leave your gift there in
front of the altar. First go and be reconciled to your brother; then come and
offer your gift.

25 "Settle matters quickly with your
adversary who is taking you to court.
Do it while you are still with him on the
way, or he may hand you over to the
judge, and the judge may hand you
over to the officer, and you may be
thrown into prison. 26 I tell you the

5:17 [a] Jn 10:34,35; Ro 3:31
5:18 [b] Ps 119:89; Isa 40:8; 55:11; Mt 24:35; Mk 13:31; Lk 16:17; 21:33
5:19 [c] Jas 2:10
5:20 [d] Isa 26:2; Mt 18:3; Jn 3:5
5:21 [e] Ex 20:13; 21:12; Dt 5:17
5:22 [f] Ecc 7:9; 1Co 13:5; Eph 4:26; Jas 1:19,20 [g] 1Jn 3:15 [h] Mt 26:59; Jn 11:47; Ac 5:21,27,34,41; 6:12 [i] Mt 18:9; Mk 9:43,48; Lk 16:24; Jas 3:6

[t] *21* Exodus 20:13 [u] *22* Some manuscripts *brother without cause* [v] *22* An Aramaic term of contempt

3:31; 8:4). The believer's relation to the law of God involves the following:

(1) The law that the believer is obliged to keep consists of the ethical and moral principles of the OT (7:12; 22:36–40; Ro 3:31; Gal 5:14; see article on THE OLD TESTAMENT LAW, p. 118) as well as the teachings of Christ and the apostles (28:20; 1Co 7:19; 9:21; Gal 6:2). These laws reveal the nature and will of God for all people and still apply today. OT laws that applied directly to the nation of Israel, such as the sacrificial, ceremonial, social or civil laws, are no longer binding (Heb 10:1–4; e.g., Lev 1:2–3; 24:10).

(2) Believers must not view the law as a system of legal commandments by which to obtain merit for forgiveness and salvation (Gal 2:16,19). Rather, the law must be seen as a moral code for those who are already in a saved relationship with God and who, by obeying it, express the life of Christ within themselves (Ro 6:15–22).

(3) Faith in Christ is the point of departure for the fulfilling of the law. Through faith in Christ, God becomes our Father (cf. Jn 1:12). Therefore, our obedience as believers is done not only out of a relationship to God as sovereign Lawgiver, but also out of a relationship of children to their Father (Gal 4:6).

(4) Through faith in Christ, believers, by God's grace (Ro 5:21) and the indwelling Holy Spirit (Ro 8:13; Gal 3:5,14), are given an inner compulsion and power to fulfill God's law (Ro 16:25–26; Heb 10:16). We fulfill it by living according to the Spirit (Ro 8:4–14). The Spirit helps us put to death the misdeeds of the body and to fulfill God's will (Ro 8:13; see Mt 7:21, note). Thus, external conformity to God's law must be accompanied by the inner transformation of our hearts and spirits (cf. vv. 21–28).

(5) Having been freed from sin's power, and now being enslaved to God (Ro 6:18–22), believers follow the principle of "faith" by being "under Christ's law" (1Co 9:21). In so doing we fulfill "the law of Christ" (Gal 6:2) and are thus faithful to the requirement of the law (see Ro 7:4, note; 8:4, note; Gal 3:19, note; 5:16–25).

(6) Jesus emphatically taught that doing the will of his heavenly Father is an ongoing condition of entering the kingdom of heaven (see 7:21, note).

5:19 GREAT IN THE KINGDOM. The position of believers in the kingdom of heaven will be determined by our attitude toward God's law and by our teaching and practice of it. Our degree of faithfulness in this respect will determine our degree of glory in heaven (see article on THE JUDGMENT OF BELIEVERS, p. 1791).

5:20 UNLESS YOUR RIGHTEOUSNESS. The righteousness of the Pharisees and the teachers of the law was external only. They kept many rules, prayed, praised, fasted, read God's Word and attended worship services. However, they substituted the outward acts for the correct inner attitudes. Jesus said the righteousness that God requires of the believer is more. The heart and spirit, not only the outward deeds, must conform to God's will in faith and love (see Mk 7:6, note on legalism.)

5:22 ANGRY . . . RACA . . . FOOL. Jesus is not speaking of a righteous anger at those who are wicked and unjust (cf. Jn 2:13–17), but is condemning the vindictive anger that would unjustly desire the death of another. "Raca" is a term of contempt and probably means "empty-headed fool." To call a person a "godless fool" in anger and contempt may indicate a heart attitude that places one "in danger of the fire of hell."

truth, you will not get out until you
have paid the last penny.[w]

Adultery

27"You have heard that it was said,
'Do not commit adultery.'[x][j] **28**But I
tell you that anyone who looks at a
woman lustfully has already committed adultery with her in his heart.[k]
29If your right eye causes you to sin,[l]
gouge it out and throw it away. It is
better for you to lose one part of your
body than for your whole body to be
thrown into hell. **30**And if your right
hand causes you to sin,[m] cut it off and
throw it away. It is better for you to
lose one part of your body than for your
whole body to go into hell.

Divorce

31"It has been said, 'Anyone who divorces his wife must give her a certificate of divorce.'[y][n] **32**But I tell you
that anyone who divorces his wife, except for marital unfaithfulness, causes
her to become an adulteress, and anyone who marries the divorced woman
commits adultery.[o]

Oaths

33"Again, you have heard that it was
said to the people long ago, 'Do not
break your oath,[p] but keep the oaths
you have made to the Lord.'[q] **34**But I
tell you, Do not swear at all:[r] either
by heaven, for it is God's throne;[s] **35**or
by the earth, for it is his footstool; or
by Jerusalem, for it is the city of the
Great King.[t] **36**And do not swear by
your head, for you cannot make even
one hair white or black. **37**Simply let

5:27 *j* Ex 20:14; Dt 5:18
5:28 *k* Pr 6:25; 2Pe 2:14
5:29 *l* ver 30; Mt 18:6,8,9; Mk 9:42-47; Lk 17:2; Ro 14:21; 1Co 8:13; S 2Co 6:3; 11:29
5:30 *m* S ver 29
5:31 *n* Dt 24:1-4
5:32 *o* S Lk 16:18
5:33 *p* Lev 19:12 *q* Nu 30:2; Dt 23:21; Mt 23:16-22
5:34 *r* Jas 5:12 *s* Isa 66:1; Mt 23:22
5:35 *t* Ps 48:2
5:37 *u* Jas 5:12 *v* Mt 6:13; 13:19, 38; Jn 17:15; Eph 6:16; 2Th 3:3; 1Jn 2:13,14; 3:12; 5:18,19
5:38 *w* Ex 21:24; Lev 24:20; Dt 19:21
5:39 *x* Lk 6:29; Ro 12:17,19; 1Pe 3:9
5:42 *y* Dt 15:8; Lk 6:30
5:43 *z* Lev 19:18; Mt 19:19; 22:39; Mk 12:31; Lk 10:27; Ro 13:9; Gal 5:14; Jas 2:8 *a* Dt 23:6; Ps 139:21,22
5:44 *b* Lk 6:27,28; 23:34; Jn 15:20; Ac 7:60; Ro 8:35; 12:14; 1Co 4:12; 1Pe 2:23
5:45 *c* ver 9; Lk 6:35; S Ro 8:14 *d* Job 25:3
5:46 *e* Lk 6:32
5:48 *f* Lev 19:2; 1Pe 1:16

your 'Yes' be 'Yes,' and your 'No,'
'No';[u] anything beyond this comes
from the evil one.[v]

An Eye for an Eye

38"You have heard that it was said,
'Eye for eye, and tooth for tooth.'[z][w]
39But I tell you, Do not resist an evil
person. If someone strikes you on the
right cheek, turn to him the other
also.[x] **40**And if someone wants to sue
you and take your tunic, let him have
your cloak as well. **41**If someone forces
you to go one mile, go with him two
miles. **42**Give to the one who asks you,
and do not turn away from the one who
wants to borrow from you.[y]

Love for Enemies

43"You have heard that it was said,
'Love your neighbor[a][z] and hate your
enemy.'[a] **44**But I tell you: Love your
enemies[b] and pray for those who persecute you,[b] **45**that you may be sons[c]
of your Father in heaven. He causes his
sun to rise on the evil and the good,
and sends rain on the righteous and
the unrighteous.[d] **46**If you love those
who love you, what reward will you
get?[e] Are not even the tax collectors
doing that? **47**And if you greet only
your brothers, what are you doing
more than others? Do not even pagans
do that? **48**Be perfect, therefore, as
your heavenly Father is perfect.[f]

w *26* Greek *kodrantes* **x** *27* Exodus 20:14 **y** *31* Deut. 24:1 **z** *38* Exodus 21:24; Lev. 24:20; Deut. 19:21 **a** *43* Lev. 19:18 **b** *44* Some late manuscripts *enemies, bless those who curse you, do good to those who hate you*

5:28 LOOKS ... LUSTFULLY. What Christ condemns is not the sudden thought that Satan may place in a person's mind or an improper desire that arises suddenly. Rather it is a wrong thought or desire that is accompanied by the approval of one's will. It is having an immoral desire that would seek fulfillment if the opportunity arose. The inner desire for illicit sexual pleasure, if contemplated and not resisted, is sin (see article on STANDARDS OF SEXUAL MORALITY, p. 1936).

(1) The Christian must be particularly careful to abstain from taking pleasure in scenes of immorality such as those shown in films or pornographic literature (cf. 1Co 6:15,18; Gal 5:19,21; Eph 5:5; Col 3:5; 2Ti 2:22; Tit 2:12; Heb 13:4; Jas 1:14; 1Pe 2:11; 2Pe 3:3; 1Jn 2:16).

(2) In the area of maintaining sexual purity, the woman as well as the man has a responsibility. The Christian woman must be careful not to dress in a way that attracts attention to her body, thereby creating temptation for men and encouraging lust. Dressing immodestly or sensually is sinful (1Ti 2:9; 1Pe 3:2–3).

5:29 HELL. See Mk 9:43, note.

5:32 EXCEPT FOR MARITAL UNFAITHFULNESS. See 19:9, note.

5:39 DO NOT RESIST AN EVIL PERSON. Jesus is not speaking against the administration of proper justice toward those who are evil (cf. Ro 13:1–4). The verses that follow (vv. 43–48) indicate that he is referring to loving one's enemies (v. 44; Lk 6:27). When we are wronged, we are not to react in a spirit of hatred but in a way that shows we have values that are centered in Christ and his kingdom. Our actions toward those who are unkind to us should be such that it might lead them to accept Christ as their Savior. As examples of this spirit, compare Ge 13:1–13 with Ge 14:14, and Ge 50:19–21 with Ge 37:18–28; see also 1Sa 24 and 26; Lk 23:34; Ac 7:60.

Giving to the Needy

6 "Be careful not to do your 'acts of
righteousness' before men, to be
seen by them.[g] If you do, you will have
no reward from your Father in heaven.
2"So when you give to the needy, do
not announce it with trumpets, as the
hypocrites do in the synagogues and on
the streets, to be honored by men. I tell
you the truth, they have received their
reward in full. **3**But when you give to
the needy, do not let your left hand
know what your right hand is doing,
4so that your giving may be in secret.
Then your Father, who sees what is
done in secret, will reward you.[h]

Prayer

6:9–13pp — Lk 11:2–4

5"And when you pray, do not be like
the hypocrites, for they love to pray
standing[i] in the synagogues and on
the street corners to be seen by men.
I tell you the truth, they have received
their reward in full. **6**But when you
pray, go into your room, close the door
and pray to your Father,[j] who is unseen. Then your Father, who sees what
is done in secret, will reward you. **7**And
when you pray, do not keep on babbling[k] like pagans, for they think they
will be heard because of their many
words.[l] **8**Do not be like them, for your
Father knows what you need[m] before
you ask him.
9"This, then, is how you should pray:

" 'Our Father[n] in heaven,
hallowed be your name,
10your kingdom[o] come,
your will be done[p]
on earth as it is in heaven.

6:1 [g] Mt 5:16; 23:5
6:4 [h] ver 6,18; Col 3:23,24
6:5 [i] Mk 11:25; Lk 18:10-14
6:6 [j] 2Ki 4:33
6:7 [k] Ecc 5:2 [l] 1Ki 18:26-29
6:8 [m] ver 32
6:9 [n] Jer 3:19; Mal 2:10; 1Pe 1:17
6:10 [o] S Mt 3:2 [p] S Mt 26:39

6:1 'ACTS OF RIGHTEOUSNESS' BEFORE MEN. The principle stated here concerns our motives for acting righteously. (1) If believers, whether laypersons or ministers, do good for the admiration of others or for selfish reasons, they will lose their reward and praise from God. Instead they will stand exposed as hypocrites who, under the guise of giving glory to God, are really seeking glory for themselves.

(2) Jesus speaks of acts of righteousness in three areas: giving (vv. 2–4), prayer (vv. 5–8) and fasting (vv. 16–18). His condemnation of doing acts of righteousness to be seen by others challenges much of contemporary Christian activity, including competing for bigness, advertising one's success, performing and entertaining in the church, and wanting to be first (see 1Co 3:13–15; 4:5).

6:6 PRAY . . . IN SECRET. Every child of God should have some place to be alone with God. Unless such a place exists, secret prayer will not be long or consistently maintained. Jesus had his secret places (14:23; Mk 1:35; Lk 4:42; 5:16; 6:12). Secret prayer is especially important: (1) in the morning to commit our day to God; (2) in the evening to give thanks for his mercies; (3) in times when the Holy Spirit prompts us to pray. Our Father promises to reward us openly—with answered prayer, with his intimate presence and with true honor for eternity (see 6:9, note on God as Father).

6:9 THIS, THEN, IS HOW YOU SHOULD PRAY. With this model prayer, Christ indicates areas of concern that should occupy a Christian's prayer. The prayer contains six petitions: three concerned with the holiness and will of God; three concerned with our personal needs. The brevity of the prayer does not mean we should pray only briefly about our concerns. At times Christ prayed all night long (Lk 6:12).

6:9 OUR FATHER IN HEAVEN. Prayer involves worship of the heavenly Father. (1) As Father, God loves us, cares for us, and welcomes our fellowship and intimacy; through Christ we have access to him at any time to worship him and communicate our needs to him (vv. 25–34). (2) God as Father does not mean that he is like an earthly father who tolerates evil in his children or fails to discipline them correctly. God is a Father of holiness who must oppose sin. He will not tolerate evil, even in those who name him as Father. His name must be "hallowed." (3) As a heavenly Father he can punish as well as bless, withhold as well as give, act with justice as well as with mercy. How he responds to his children depends on our faith in and obedience to him.

6:9 HALLOWED BE YOUR NAME. The greatest concern in our prayers and in our lives should be the hallowing of the name of God. It is of utmost importance that God himself be reverenced, glorified and exalted (cf. Ps 34:3). In our prayer and daily walk we must be intensely concerned with the reputation of God, his church, his gospel and his kingdom. To do something that brings scandal on the Lord's name and character is a hideous sin that puts God to open shame.

6:10 YOUR KINGDOM COME. Prayer must be concerned with the kingdom of God on earth now and with its ultimate fulfillment in the future. (1) We must pray for Christ's return and the establishment of God's eternal kingdom in the new heaven and the new earth (Rev 21:1; cf. 2Pe 3:10–12; Rev 20:11; 22:20). (2) We must pray for the spiritual presence and manifestation of the kingdom of God now. This includes asserting God's power among his people in order to destroy the works of Satan, heal the sick, save the lost, promote righteousness and pour out the Holy Spirit on his people (see article on THE KINGDOM OF GOD, p. 1430).

6:10 YOUR WILL BE DONE. To pray "your will be done" means that we sincerely desire God's will and purpose to be fulfilled in our lives and the lives of our families, according to his eternal plan. We can determine what God's will is primarily in his

[11]Give us today our daily bread.[q]
[12]Forgive us our debts,
as we also have forgiven our debtors.[r]
[13]And lead us not into temptation,[s]
but deliver us from the evil one.[c] [t]

[14]For if you forgive men when they sin against you, your heavenly Father will also forgive you.[u] [15]But if you do not forgive men their sins, your Father will not forgive your sins.[v]

Fasting

[16]"When you fast,[w] do not look somber[x] as the hypocrites do, for they disfigure their faces to show men they are fasting. I tell you the truth, they have received their reward in full. [17]But when you fast, put oil on your head and wash your face, [18]so that it will not be obvious to men that you are fasting, but only to your Father, who is unseen; and your Father, who sees what is done in secret, will reward you.[y]

6:11 [q]Pr 30:8
6:12 [r]Mt 18:21-35
6:13 [s]Jas 1:13 [t]S Mt 5:37
6:14 [u]Mt 18:21-35; Mk 11:25,26; Eph 4:32; Col 3:13
6:15 [v]Mt 18:35
6:16 [w]Lev 16:29, 31; 23:27-32; Nu 29:7 [x]Isa 58:5; Zec 7:5; 8:19
6:18 [y]ver 4,6
6:19 [z]Pr 23:4; Lk 12:16-21; Heb 13:5 [a]S Jas 5:2,3
6:20 [b]Mt 19:21; Lk 12:33; 16:9; 18:22; 1Ti 6:19 [c]Lk 12:33
6:21 [d]Lk 12:34

Treasures in Heaven

6:22,23pp — Lk 11:34–36

[19]"Do not store up for yourselves treasures on earth,[z] where moth and rust destroy,[a] and where thieves break in and steal. [20]But store up for yourselves treasures in heaven,[b] where moth and rust do not destroy, and where thieves do not break in and steal.[c] [21]For where your treasure is, there your heart will be also.[d]

[22]"The eye is the lamp of the body. If your eyes are good, your whole body will be full of light. [23]But if your eyes are bad, your whole body will be full of darkness. If then the light within you is darkness, how great is that darkness!

[c]*13* Or *from evil*; some late manuscripts *one, / for yours is the kingdom and the power and the glory forever. Amen.*

---

revealed Word, the Bible, and through the Holy Spirit's leading in our hearts (cf. Ro 8:4–14; see article on THE WILL OF GOD, p. 1056). God's will is accomplished when we pray for "his kingdom and his righteousness" to come among us (v. 33; see article on THE KINGDOM OF GOD, p. 1430).

6:11 DAILY BREAD. Prayer should contain requests concerned with the individual's daily needs (Php 4:19; see Lk 11:3, note).

6:12 FORGIVE . . . AS WE ALSO HAVE FORGIVEN. Prayer must be concerned with sins and a willingness to forgive those who have harmed us (vv. 14–15; Heb 9:14; 1Jn 1:9).

6:13 DELIVER US FROM THE EVIL ONE. All believers are the special object of Satan's enmity and evil purpose. For this reason, we must never forget to pray for deliverance from his power and schemes (see Lk 11:26, note; 18:1, note; 22:31; Jn 17:15; 2Co 2:11; see article on POWER OVER SATAN AND DEMONS, p. 1484).

6:15 IF YOU DO NOT FORGIVE. Jesus here emphasizes that Christians must be ready and willing to forgive the offenses of others. If they do not forgive repenting offenders, God will not forgive them, and their prayers will be to no avail. This is an important principle by which God forgives (18:35; Mk 11:26; Lk 11:4).

6:16 WHEN YOU FAST. In the Bible fasting refers to the discipline of abstaining from food for spiritual purposes. Although it was often linked with prayer, it should be considered a spiritual exercise all its own. In fact, fasting can be called "prayer without words."

(1) There are three main forms of fasting presented in the Bible. (a) The normal fast: abstaining from all food, solid or liquid, but not from water (see 4:2, note). (b) The absolute fast: abstaining from both food and water (Est 4:16; Ac 9:9). Normally this kind of fast should not be for more than three days, for the body then begins to dehydrate. Moses and Elijah undertook the absolute fast for 40 days, but only under supernatural conditions (Ex 34:28; Dt 9:9,18; 1Ki 19:8). (c) The partial fast: a restriction of diet rather than complete abstention (Da 10:3).

(2) Christ himself practiced this discipline and taught that it should be a part of Christian devotion and an act of preparation for his return (see 9:15, note). The NT church practiced fasting (Ac 13:2–3; 14:23; 27:33).

(3) Fasting with prayer has several purposes: (a) to honor God (vv. 16–18; Zec 7:5; Lk 2:37; Ac 13:2); (b) to humble ourselves before God (Ezr 8:21; Ps 69:10; Isa 58:3) in order to experience more grace (1Pe 5:5) and God's intimate presence (Isa 57:15; 58:6–9); (c) to mourn over personal sin and failure (1Sa 7:6; Ne 9:1–2); (d) to mourn over the sins of the church, nation and world (1Sa 7:6; Ne 9:1–2); (e) to seek grace for a new task and to reaffirm our consecration to God (4:2); (f) to seek God by drawing near to him and persisting in prayer against opposing spiritual forces (Jdg 20:26; Ezr 8:21,23,31; Jer 29:12–14; Joel 2:12; Lk 18:3; Ac 9:10–19); (g) to show repentance and so make a way for God to change his declared intentions of judgment (2Sa 12:16,22; 1Ki 21:27–29; Jer 18:7–8; Joel 2:12–14; Jnh 3:5,10); (h) to save people from bondage to evil (Isa 58:6; Mt 17:14–21; Lk 4:18); (i) to gain revelation and wisdom concerning God's will (Isa 58:5–6,11; Da 9:3, 21–22; Ac 13:2–3); (j) to open the way for the outpouring of the Spirit and Christ's return to earth for his people (see 9:15, note).

24"No one can serve two masters. Either he will hate the one and love the
other, or he will be devoted to the one
Jn 15:18-20 and despise the other. You cannot
serve both God and Money.[e]

Do Not Worry

6:25–33pp — Lk 12:22–31

25"Therefore I tell you, do not worry[f] about your life, what you will eat
or drink; or about your body, what you
will wear. Is not life more important
than food, and the body more important than clothes? 26Look at the birds
of the air; they do not sow or reap or
store away in barns, and yet your heavenly Father feeds them.[g] Are you not
much more valuable than they?[h]
27Who of you by worrying can add a
single hour to his life[d]?[i]
28"And why do you worry about
clothes? See how the lilies of the field
grow. They do not labor or spin. 29Yet
I tell you that not even Solomon in all
his splendor[j] was dressed like one of
these. 30If that is how God clothes the
grass of the field, which is here today
and tomorrow is thrown into the fire,
will he not much more clothe you, O
you of little faith?[k] 31So do not worry,
saying, 'What shall we eat?' or 'What
shall we drink?' or 'What shall we
wear?' 32For the pagans run after all
these things, and your heavenly Father
knows that you need them.[l] 33But
seek first his kingdom[m] and his righteousness, and all these things will be
given to you as well.[n] 34Therefore do
not worry about tomorrow, for tomorrow will worry about itself. Each day
has enough trouble of its own.

Judging Others

7:3–5pp — Lk 6:41,42

7 "Do not judge, or you too will be
judged.[o] 2For in the same way
you judge others, you will be judged,
and with the measure you use, it will
be measured to you.[p]
3"Why do you look at the speck of
sawdust in your brother's eye and pay
no attention to the plank in your own
eye? 4How can you say to your brother,
'Let me take the speck out of your eye,'
when all the time there is a plank in
your own eye? 5You hypocrite, first
take the plank out of your own eye, and

6:24 [e]Lk 16:13
6:25 [f]ver 27,28, 31,34; Lk 10:41; 12:11,22
6:26 [g]Job 38:41; Ps 104:21; 136:25; 145:15; 147:9 [h]Mt 10:29-31
6:27 [i]Ps 39:5
6:29 [j]1Ki 10:4-7
6:30 [k]Mt 8:26; 14:31; 16:8; Lk 12:28
6:32 [l]ver 8
6:33 [m]S Mt 3:2 [n]Ps 37:4; Mt 19:29
7:1 [o]Lk 6:37; Ro 14:4,10,13; 1Co 4:5; 5:12; Jas 4:11,12
7:2 [p]Eze 35:11; Mk 4:24; Lk 6:38; Ro 2:1

[d]27 Or *single cubit to his height*

6:24 MONEY. (1) To serve money is to place such a high value on it that we (a) place our trust and faith in it, (b) look to it for our ultimate security and happiness, (c) expect it to guarantee our future, and (d) desire it more than we desire God's righteousness and kingdom. (2) The accumulation of wealth soon dominates one's mind and life so that God's glory will no longer be first (see article on RICHES AND POVERTY, p. 1562).

6:25 DO NOT WORRY. Jesus does not mean that it is wrong to make provisions for future physical needs (cf. 2Co 12:14; 1Ti 5:8). What he does forbid is anxiety or worry that shows a lack of faith in God's fatherly care and love (Eze 34:12; 1Pe 5:7; see next note).

6:30 IF THAT IS HOW GOD CLOTHES. These words contain God's promise to all his children in this age of trouble and uncertainty. God has promised to provide for our food, clothing and necessities. We need not worry; if we seek to let God reign in our lives (v. 33), we can be sure that he will assume full responsibility for those wholly yielded to him (Php 4:6; 1Pe 5:7; see article on THE PROVIDENCE OF GOD, p. 78).

6:33 SEEK . . . KINGDOM . . . RIGHTEOUSNESS. Those who follow Christ are urged to seek above all else God's kingdom and his righteousness. The verb "seek" implies being continually absorbed in a search for something, or making a strenuous and diligent effort to obtain something (cf. 13:45). Christ refers to two objects of our seeking: (1) "His kingdom"—we must seek earnestly to have the rule and power of God demonstrated in our lives and assemblies. We must pray that God's kingdom will come in the mighty power of the Holy Spirit to save sinners, to destroy the demonic, to heal the sick and to magnify the name of the Lord Jesus (see article on THE KINGDOM OF GOD, p. 1430).

(2) "His righteousness"—through the Holy Spirit we must seek to obey the commands of Christ, possess Christ's righteousness, remain separated from the world and show Christ's love toward everyone (cf. Php 2:12–13).

7:1 DO NOT JUDGE. Jesus condemns the habit of criticizing others while ignoring one's own faults. Believers must first submit themselves to God's righteous standard before attempting to examine and influence the conduct of other Christians (vv. 3–5). Judging in an unjust manner also includes condemning a wrongdoer without desiring to see the offender return to God and his ways (Lk 6:36–37).

(1) Christ is not denying the necessity of exercising a certain degree of discernment or of making value judgments with respect to sin in others. Elsewhere we are commanded to identify false ministers within the church (v. 15) and to evaluate the character of individuals (v. 6; cf. Jn 7:24; 1Co 5:12; see Gal 1:9, note; 1Ti 4:1, note; 1Jn 4:1).

(2) This verse must not be used as an excuse for laxity in exercising church discipline (see 18:15, note).

then you will see clearly to remove the
speck from your brother's eye.
6"Do not give dogs what is sacred;
do not throw your pearls to pigs. If you
do, they may trample them under their
feet, and then turn and tear you to
pieces.

Ask, Seek, Knock

7:7–11pp — Lk 11:9–13

7"Ask and it will be given to you;[q]
seek and you will find; knock and the
door will be opened to you. 8For everyone who asks receives; he who seeks
finds;[r] and to him who knocks, the
door will be opened.
9"Which of you, if his son asks for
bread, will give him a stone? 10Or if he
asks for a fish, will give him a snake?
11If you, then, though you are evil,
know how to give good gifts to your
children, how much more will your Father in heaven give good gifts[s] to
those who ask him! 12So in everything,
do to others what you would have them
do to you,[t] for this sums up the Law
and the Prophets.[u]

The Narrow and Wide Gates

13"Enter through the narrow gate.[v]
For wide is the gate and broad is the
road that leads to destruction, and
many enter through it. 14But small is
the gate and narrow the road that leads
to life, and only a few find it.

A Tree and Its Fruit

15"Watch out for false prophets.[w]
They come to you in sheep's clothing,
but inwardly they are ferocious
wolves.[x] 16By their fruit you will recognize them.[y] Do people pick grapes
from thornbushes, or figs from thistles?[z] 17Likewise every good tree
bears good fruit, but a bad tree bears
bad fruit. 18A good tree cannot bear
bad fruit, and a bad tree cannot bear
good fruit.[a] 19Every tree that does not
bear good fruit is cut down and thrown

7:7 [q] 1Ki 3:5; Mt 18:19; 21:22; Jn 14:13,14; 15:7, 16; 16:23,24; Jas 1:5-8; 4:2,3; 5:16; 1Jn 3:22; 5:14,15
7:8 [r] Pr 8:17; Jer 29:12,13
7:11 [s] Jas 1:17
7:12 [t] Lk 6:31 [u] Ro 13:8-10; Gal 5:14
7:13 [v] Lk 13:24; Jn 10:7,9
7:15 [w] Jer 23:16; Mt 24:24; Lk 6:26; 2Pe 2:1; 1Jn 4:1; Rev 16:13 [x] Eze 22:27; Ac 20:29
7:16 [y] Mt 12:33; Lk 6:44 [z] Jas 3:12
7:18 [a] Lk 6:43

7:7–8 ASK . . . SEEK . . . KNOCK. Jesus encourages perseverance in prayer. The tense of the Greek verbs in v. 8 designates continued action. This means we must keep on asking, seeking and knocking. Asking implies consciousness of need and the belief that God hears our prayer. Seeking implies earnest petitioning along with obedience to God's will. Knocking implies perseverance in coming to God even when he does not respond quickly. Christ's assurance that those who ask will receive what they ask is based on: (1) seeking first the kingdom of God (see 6:33, note); (2) recognizing God's fatherly goodness and love (6:8; 7:11; Jn 15:16; 16:23,26f; Col 1:9–12); (3) praying according to God's will (Mk 11:24; Jn 21:22; 1Jn 5:14); (4) maintaining fellowship with Christ (Jn 15:7); and (5) obeying Christ (1Jn 3:22; see article on EFFECTIVE PRAYING, p. 496).

7:11 YOUR FATHER . . . GIVE GOOD GIFTS. Christ promises that the Father in heaven will not disappoint his children. He loves us even more than a good earthly father loves his children, and he wants us to ask him for whatever we need, promising to give us what is good. He desires to provide solutions for our problems and bread for our daily needs. And most of all, he gives the Holy Spirit to his children as their Counselor and Helper (Lk 11:13; Jn 14:16–18).

7:14 SMALL IS THE GATE . . . AND ONLY A FEW FIND IT. Christ taught that we are not to expect a majority of people to follow him on the road that leads to life. (1) Comparatively few will enter the humble gate of true repentance and deny themselves to follow Jesus, sincerely endeavor to obey his commands, earnestly seek his kingdom and his righteousness, and persevere until the end in true faith, purity and love.

(2) Jesus in his Sermon on the Mount describes the great blessings that accompany discipleship in his kingdom (5:3–12), but he also insists that his disciples will not escape persecution (5:10–12). Furthermore, contrary to some evangelists who preach that "getting saved" is one of the easiest things in the world, Jesus taught that following him involves heavy obligations concerning righteousness, acceptance of persecution, love for enemies and self-denial.

7:15 WATCH OUT FOR FALSE PROPHETS. See article on FALSE TEACHERS, p. 1506.

7:16 BY THEIR FRUIT YOU WILL RECOGNIZE THEM. False teachers who outwardly appear righteous but "inwardly . . . are ferocious wolves" (v. 15) can, at times, be identified by their "fruit." The fruit of false teachers will be unwholesome characteristics evident in the lives of their followers (see 1Jn 4:5–6), such as those listed below. (1) They will be professing Christians whose loyalty is more to personalities than to the Word of God (v. 21). They worship the creature more than the Creator (cf. Ro 1:25).

(2) They will be more concerned with their own desires than with God's glory and honor. Their doctrine will be self-centered rather than God-centered (vv. 21–23; see 2Ti 4:3, note).

(3) They will accept human teachings and traditions even when those teachings contradict the Word of God (vv. 24–27; 1Jn 4:6).

(4) They will seek and respond to religious experiences and supernatural manifestations as their final authority in validating truth (vv. 22–23), rather than grounding themselves in the whole counsel of God's Word.

(5) They will not put up with sound doctrine but will seek teachers who offer salvation with the "broad road" of unrighteousness (vv. 13–14,23; see 2Ti 4:3, note).

Mt 12:33
into the fire.[b] 20Thus, by their fruit
you will recognize them.

The Saved Do God's Will

21"Not everyone who says to me,
'Lord, Lord,'[c] will enter the kingdom
of heaven,[d] but only he who does the
will of my Father who is in heaven.[e]
22Many will say to me on that day,[f]
'Lord, Lord, did we not prophesy in
your name, and in your name drive out
demons and perform many mira-
cles?'[g] 23Then I will tell them plainly,
'I never knew you. Away from me, you
evildoers!'[h]

Mt 19:16-26

The Wise and Foolish Builders

7:24–27pp — Lk 6:47–49

24"Therefore everyone who hears
these words of mine and puts them into
practice[i] is like a wise man who built
his house on the rock. 25The rain came
down, the streams rose, and the winds
blew and beat against that house; yet
it did not fall, because it had its foundation on the rock. 26But everyone who
hears these words of mine and does not
put them into practice is like a foolish
man who built his house on sand.
27The rain came down, the streams
rose, and the winds blew and beat
against that house, and it fell with a
great crash."

28When Jesus had finished saying
these things,[j] the crowds were
amazed at his teaching,[k] 29because
he taught as one who had authority,
and not as their teachers of the law.

The Man With Leprosy

8:2–4pp — Mk 1:40–44; Lk 5:12–14

8 When he came down from the
mountainside, large crowds fol-

7:19 [b]S Mt 3:10 **7:21** [c]Hos 8:2; Mt 25:11; S Jn 13:13; 1Co 12:3 [d]S Mt 3:2 [e]Mt 12:50; Ro 2:13; Jas 1:22; 1Jn 3:18 **7:22** [f]S Mt 10:15 [g]Lk 10:20; Ac 19:13; 1Co 13:1-3 **7:23** [h]Ps 6:8; Mt 25:12,41; Lk 13:25-27 **7:24** [i]ver 21; Jas 1:22-25

7:28 [j]Mt 11:1; 13:53; 19:1; 26:1 [k]Mt 13:54; 22:33; Mk 1:22; 6:2; 11:18; Lk 4:32; Jn 7:46

7:21 DOES THE WILL OF MY FATHER. Jesus emphatically taught that carrying out the will of his heavenly Father was a condition of entering the kingdom of heaven (cf. vv. 22–27; 19:16–26; 25:31–46). However, this does not mean that we can gain or merit salvation by our own efforts or works alone. This is true for the following reasons: (1) God's forgiveness comes to us through faith and repentance made possible by the grace and sacrificial death of Christ (see 26:28, note; Lk 15:11–32; 18:9–14).

(2) The obedience to God's will demanded by Christ is indeed an ongoing condition for salvation, but Christ also declares that it is a grace belonging to the salvation of the kingdom. As such we must continually pray for it, receive it and put it into effect by sincere faith and earnest endeavor. Note the Lord's Prayer (6:9–13) and the many admonitions directed toward believers to put sin to death and to present themselves to God as living sacrifices (cf. Ro 6:1–23; 8:1–17; 12:1–2; see Mt 5:6, note on hungering and thirsting for righteousness; see article on THE WILL OF GOD, p. 1056).

(3) We are capable of doing God's will and living righteous lives by virtue of this gift, i.e., God's grace, power and spiritual life continually given to us through Christ (Eph 2:5). Scripture declares that "by grace you have been saved, through faith—and this not from yourselves, it is the gift of God . . . . For we are God's workmanship" (Eph 2:8–10).

(4) God always makes available the obedience he demands of us. It is ascribed to God's redemptive action. "For it is God who works in you to will and to act according to his good purpose" (see Php 2:13, note). Yet God's gift of grace does not annul human responsibility or action. We must respond positively to God's gift of obedience (Eph 4:22–32; Jude 20–21,24; see Php 2:12, note), for we remain free to reject God's grace, to refuse to draw near to God through Christ (see Heb 7:25, note), and to refuse to pray for and accept the life of obedience (see 5:6, note; see article on FAITH AND GRACE, p. 1720).

7:22 MANY WILL SAY . . . LORD, LORD. Jesus emphatically states that there will be "many" in the church who will minister in his name and believe they are his servants, yet in reality he never knew them (v. 23). To escape the deceit of the last days, church leaders (or any disciple) must be totally committed to the truth and the righteousness revealed in God's Word (see Rev 22:19, note) and not consider "ministerial success" as the standard by which to judge their relationship to Christ.

7:23 I NEVER KNEW YOU. These words of Christ make it unmistakably clear that preachers may proclaim the gospel in the name of Christ, drive out demons and perform miracles while they themselves have no genuine saving faith in Christ. (1) Scripture teaches that fervent gospel preaching, an apparent zeal for righteousness and the working of miracles can be performed in this age under the influence and power of Satan. Paul warns that "Satan himself masquerades as an angel of light. It is not surprising, then, if his servants masquerade as servants of righteousness" (2Co 11:14–15; cf. Mt 24:24). Paul makes it clear that an apparent powerful anointing can be "the work of Satan" (see 2Th 2:9–10; Rev 13:3,12; see article on FALSE TEACHERS, p. 1506).

(2) Many times God overrides Satan's activity in false preachers in order to bring salvation or healing to those who sincerely respond to God's Word (see Php 1:15–18). It is always God's desire that those who proclaim the gospel be righteous (see 1Ti 3:1–7); yet when an evil or immoral person preaches God's Word, God can still work in the hearts of those who receive his Word with commitment to Christ. God does not endorse any unrighteous preacher of the gospel, but he will endorse Biblical truth and those who accept it in faith.

lowed him. **2**A man with leprosy[e][l]
came and knelt before him[m] and said,
"Lord, if you are willing, you can make
me clean."
3Jesus reached out his hand and
touched the man. "I am willing," he
said. "Be clean!" Immediately he was
cured[f] of his leprosy. **4**Then Jesus
said to him, "See that you don't tell
anyone.[n] But go, show yourself to the
priest[o] and offer the gift Moses commanded,[p] as a testimony to them."

The Faith of the Centurion

8:5–13pp — Lk 7:1–10

5When Jesus had entered Capernaum, a centurion came to him, asking
for help. **6**"Lord," he said, "my servant
lies at home paralyzed[q] and in terrible
suffering."
7Jesus said to him, "I will go and
heal him."
8The centurion replied, "Lord, I do
not deserve to have you come under my
roof. But just say the word, and my servant will be healed.[r] **9**For I myself am
a man under authority, with soldiers
under me. I tell this one, 'Go,' and he
goes; and that one, 'Come,' and he
comes. I say to my servant, 'Do this,'
and he does it."
10When Jesus heard this, he was astonished and said to those following
him, "I tell you the truth, I have not
found anyone in Israel with such great
faith.[s] **11**I say to you that many will
come from the east and the west,[t] and
will take their places at the feast with
Abraham, Isaac and Jacob in the kingdom of heaven.[u] **12**But the subjects of
the kingdom[v] will be thrown outside,
into the darkness, where there will be
weeping and gnashing of teeth."[w]
13Then Jesus said to the centurion,
"Go! It will be done just as you believed
it would."[x] And his servant was
healed at that very hour.

Jesus Heals Many

8:14–16pp — Mk 1:29–34; Lk 4:38–41

14When Jesus came into Peter's
house, he saw Peter's mother-in-law
lying in bed with a fever. **15**He touched
her hand and the fever left her, and she
got up and began to wait on him.
16When evening came, many who
were demon-possessed were brought
to him, and he drove out the spirits
with a word and healed all the sick.[y]
17This was to fulfill[z] what was spoken through the prophet Isaiah:

"He took up our infirmities
and carried our diseases."[g][a]

Mt 10:1

The Cost of Following Jesus

8:19–22pp — Lk 9:57–60

18When Jesus saw the crowd around
him, he gave orders to cross to the other side of the lake.[b] **19**Then a teacher
of the law came to him and said,
"Teacher, I will follow you wherever
you go."
20Jesus replied, "Foxes have holes
and birds of the air have nests, but the
Son of Man[c] has no place to lay his
head."
21Another disciple said to him,
"Lord, first let me go and bury my father."
22But Jesus told him, "Follow me,[d]
and let the dead bury their own dead."

Jesus Calms the Storm

8:23–27pp — Mk 4:36–41; Lk 8:22–25
8:23–27Ref — Mt 14:22–33

23Then he got into the boat and his
disciples followed him. **24**Without
warning, a furious storm came up on
the lake, so that the waves swept over
the boat. But Jesus was sleeping.
25The disciples went and woke him,
saying, "Lord, save us! We're going to
drown!"
26He replied, "You of little faith,[e]
why are you so afraid?" Then he got up
and rebuked the winds and the waves,
and it was completely calm.[f]
27The men were amazed and asked,

[e]*2* The Greek word was used for various diseases affecting the skin—not necessarily leprosy. [f]*3* Greek *made clean* [g]*17* Isaiah 53:4

8:2 [l]Lev 13:45; Mt 10:8; 11:5; 26:6; Lk 5:12; 17:12 [m]Mt 9:18; 15:25; 18:26; 20:20
8:4 [n]Mt 9:30; 12:16; Mk 5:43; 7:36; S 8:30; Lk 4:41 [o]Lk 17:14 [p]Lev 14:2-32
8:6 [q]S Mt 4:24
8:8 [r]Ps 107:20
8:10 [s] Mt 15:28
8:11 [t]Ps 107:3; Isa 49:12; 59:19; Mal 1:11 [u]Lk 13:29
8:12 [v]Mt 13:38 [w]Mt 13:42,50; 22:13; 24:51; 25:30; Lk 13:28
8:13 [x]S Mt 9:22
8:16 [y]S Mt 4:23, 24
8:17 [z]S Mt 1:22 [a]Isa 53:4
8:18 [b]Mk 4:35
8:20 [c]Da 7:13; Mt 12:8,32,40; 16:13,27,28; 17:9; 19:28; Mk 2:10; 8:31
8:22 [d]S Mt 4:19
8:26 [e]S Mt 6:30 [f]Ps 65:7; 89:9; 107:29

8:10 GREAT FAITH. The centurion's faith surpassed anything that Jesus found among the Jews, for it combined a loving concern for another person with great trust in Christ. This story, along with Christ's application to the unbelieving Jews (vv. 11–12), warns us that we may be excluded from what God is doing by adhering to human traditions or by failing to believe in the power of his kingdom.

8:16–17 HEALED ALL THE SICK. See article on DIVINE HEALING, p. 1420.

8:22 LET THE DEAD BURY THEIR OWN DEAD. Christ's saying means, "Let the spiritually dead bury the physically dead." The disciple of v. 21 probably wanted to stay with his elderly father until his father died.

DIVINE HEALING

Mt 8:16–17 "When evening came, many who were demon-possessed were brought to him, and he drove out the spirits with a word and healed all the sick. This was to fulfill what was spoken through the prophet Isaiah: 'He took up our infirmities and carried our diseases.' "

GOD'S REDEMPTIVE PROVISION. (1) The problem of sickness and disease is intertwined with the problem of sin and death — i.e., the consequences of the fall. Whereas medical science views the causes of sickness and disease in physiological or psychosomatic terms, the Bible presents spiritual causes as the underlying or basic problem: (a) *sin,* which has affected our spiritual and physical makeup (e.g., Jn 5:5,14), and (b) *Satan* (e.g., Ac 10:38; cf. Mk 9:17,20,25; Lk 13:11; Ac 19:11–12).

(2) God's provision in redemption is as extensive as the consequences of the fall. For sin, God provides forgiveness; for death, God provides eternal and resurrection life; and for sickness, God provides healing (cf. Ps 103:1–5; Lk 4:18; 5:17–26; Jas 5:14–15). Thus, during Jesus' earthly life, his threefold ministry was *teaching* God's word, *preaching* repentance (the sin problem) and the blessings of God's kingdom (life), and *healing* every kind of sickness, disease and infirmity among the people (Mt 4:23–24).

REVELATION CONCERNING GOD'S WILL. God's will concerning healing is revealed in four main ways in Scripture. (1) *God's own pronouncement.* In Ex 15:26 God promised health and healing for his people if they remained faithful to his covenant and commands (see Ex 15:26, note). His pronouncement was twofold: (a) "I will not bring on you any of the diseases [as judgment] I brought on the Egyptians" and (b) "I am the LORD, who heals you [as Redeemer]." God continued to be the doctor or healer of his OT people whenever they earnestly sought his face and obeyed his word (cf. 2Ki 20:5; Ps 103:3).

(2) *Jesus' ministry.* Jesus as the incarnate Son of God was and is the exact representation of God's nature and character (Heb 1:3; cf. Col 1:15; 2:9). In his earthly ministry (Mt 4:23–24; 8:14–16; 9:35; 15:28; Mk 1:32–34,40–41; Lk 4:40; Ac 10:38), Jesus revealed God's will in action (Jn 6:38; 14:10), proving that it is in God's heart, nature and purpose to heal all who are sick and oppressed by the devil.

(3) *The provision of Christ's atonement* (Isa 53:4–5; Mt 8:16–17; 1Pe 2:24). Jesus' atoning death was complete and adequate for redeeming the whole person—spirit, soul and body. As sin and sickness have become the twin giants designed by Satan to destroy us, so forgiveness and healing are twin blessings designed by God to redeem us and make us whole (cf. Ps 103:3; Jas 5:14–16). The believer should press on in humility and faith to possess the full provision of Christ's atonement, including the healing of the body.

(4) *The ongoing ministry of the church.* Jesus commissioned his twelve disciples to heal the sick as part of their proclamation of God's kingdom (Lk 9:1–2,6). Later, he commissioned seventy disciples to do the same (Lk 10:1,8–9,19). After Pentecost, the early church carried on Jesus' healing ministry as part of preaching the gospel (Ac 3:1–10; 4:30; 5:16; 8:7; 9:34; 14:8–10; 19:11–12; cf. Mk 16:18; 1Co 12:9,28,30; Jas 5:14–16). The NT records three ways that God's healing power and faith were imparted through the church: (a) the laying on of hands (Mk 16:15–18; Ac 9:17), (b) confession of known sin, followed by anointing the sick with oil and the prayer of faith (Jas 5:14–16), and (c) spiritual gifts of healings given to the church (1Co 12:9). Note that it is the elders who are to pray the prayer of faith.

HINDRANCES TO HEALING. Sometimes there are hindrances to receiving divine healing, such as, (1) unconfessed sin (Jas 5:16), (2) demonic oppression or bondage (Lk 13:11–13), (3) fear or acute anxiety (Pr 3:5–8; Php 4:6–7), (4) past disappointments that undermine present faith (Mk 5:26; Jn 5:5–7), (5) people (Mk 10:48), (6) unbiblical teaching (Mk 3:1–5; 7:13), (7) failure of the elders to pray the prayer of faith (Mk 11:22–24; Jas 5:14–16), (8) failure of the church to seek and obtain the gifts of miracles and healings as God intended (Ac 4:29–30; 6:8; 8:5–6; 1Co 12:9–10,29–31; Heb 2:4), (9) unbelief (Mk 6:3–6; 9:19,23–24), and (10) self-centered behavior (1Co 11:29–30). At other times, the reason for the persistence of physical affliction in godly people is not readily apparent (e.g., Gal 4:13; 1Ti 5:23; 2Ti 4:20). In still other instances, God chooses to take his beloved saints to heaven during an illness (cf. 2Ki 13:14).

STEPS TO TAKE. What can you do when praying for and seeking God's healing of your body? (1) Be sure you are in a right relationship with God and others (Mt 6:33; 1Co 11:27–30; Jas 5:16; see Jn 15:7, note).

(2) Seek the presence of Jesus in your life, for it is he who will give your heart the faith you need (Ro 12:3; 1Co 12:9; Php 2:13; see Mt 17:20, note on true faith).

(3) Saturate your life with God's Word (Jn 15:7; Ro 10:17).

(4) If you are not finding healing, continue to remain in him (Jn 15:1–7). Examine your life to see what changes God may desire to work in you.

(5) Call for the prayers of the elders of the church with the anointing of oil, as well as the prayers of family members and friends (Jas 5:14–16).

(6) Attend a service where a person with a respected healing ministry is present (cf. Ac 5:15–16; 8:5–7).

(7) Expect a miracle—trust in Christ's power (Mt 7:8; 19:26).

(8) Rejoice if healing comes this day. Rejoice if it does not come in the present hour (Php 4:4,11–13).

(9) Know that God's delays in answering prayers are not necessarily denials of those requests. Sometimes God has a larger purpose in mind that, when realized, results in his greater glory (cf. Jn 9:3; 11:4,14–15,45; 2Co 12:7–10) and in good for us (Ro 8:28).

(10) Realize that if you are a committed Christian, God will never forsake you or forget you. He loves you so much that he has engraved you on the palms of his hands (Isa 49:15–16).

Note: The Bible acknowledges the proper use of medical care (Mt 9:12; Lk 10:34; Col 4:14).

"What kind of man is this? Even the winds and the waves obey him!"

The Healing of Two Demon-possessed Men

8:28–34pp — Mk 5:1–17; Lk 8:26–37

28When he arrived at the other side in the region of the Gadarenes,[h] two demon-possessed[g] men coming from the tombs met him. They were so violent that no one could pass that way. 29"What do you want with us,[h] Son of God?" they shouted. "Have you come here to torture us before the appointed time?"[i]

30Some distance from them a large herd of pigs was feeding. 31The demons begged Jesus, "If you drive us out, send us into the herd of pigs."

32He said to them, "Go!" So they came out and went into the pigs, and the whole herd rushed down the steep bank into the lake and died in the water. 33Those tending the pigs ran off, went into the town and reported all
Mt 17:14-18 this, including what had happened to the demon-possessed men. 34Then the whole town went out to meet Jesus. And when they saw him, they pleaded with him to leave their region.[j]

Jesus Heals a Paralytic

9:2–8pp — Mk 2:3–12; Lk 5:18–26

9 Jesus stepped into a boat, crossed over and came to his own town.[k] 2Some men brought to him a paralytic,[l] lying on a mat. When Jesus saw their faith,[m] he said to the paralytic,
Mt 9:29-30 "Take heart,[n] son; your sins are forgiven."[o]

3At this, some of the teachers of the law said to themselves, "This fellow is blaspheming!"[p]

4Knowing their thoughts,[q] Jesus said, "Why do you entertain evil thoughts in your hearts? 5Which is easier: to say, 'Your sins are forgiven,' or to say, 'Get up and walk'? 6But so that you may know that the Son of Man[r] has authority on earth to forgive sins. . . ." Then he said to the paralytic, "Get up, take your mat and go home." 7And the man got up and went home. 8When the crowd saw this, they were filled with awe; and they praised God,[s] who had given such authority to men.

The Calling of Matthew

9:9–13pp — Mk 2:14–17; Lk 5:27–32

9As Jesus went on from there, he saw a man named Matthew sitting at the tax collector's booth. "Follow me,"[t] he told him, and Matthew got up and followed him.

10While Jesus was having dinner at Matthew's house, many tax collectors and "sinners" came and ate with him and his disciples. 11When the Pharisees saw this, they asked his disciples, "Why does your teacher eat with tax collectors and 'sinners'?"[u]

12On hearing this, Jesus said, "It is not the healthy who need a doctor, but the sick. 13But go and learn what this means: 'I desire mercy, not sacrifice.'[i][v] For I have not come to call the righteous, but sinners."[w]

Jesus Questioned About Fasting

9:14–17pp — Mk 2:18–22; Lk 5:33–39

14Then John's[x] disciples came and asked him, "How is it that we and the Pharisees fast,[y] but your disciples do not fast?"

15Jesus answered, "How can the guests of the bridegroom mourn while he is with them?[z] The time will come when the bridegroom will be taken from them; then they will fast.[a]

16"No one sews a patch of unshrunk cloth on an old garment, for the patch will pull away from the garment, mak-

8:28 [g] S Mt 4:24 **8:29** [h] Jdg 11:12; 2Sa 16:10; 1Ki 17:18; Mk 1:24; Lk 4:34; Jn 2:4 [i] 2Pe 2:4 **8:34** [j] Lk 5:8; Ac 16:39 **9:1** [k] Mt 4:13 **9:2** [l] S Mt 4:24 [m] S ver 22 [n] Jn 16:33 [o] Lk 7:48 **9:3** [p] Mt 26:65; Jn 10:33 **9:4** [q] Ps 94:11; Mt 12:25; Lk 6:8; 9:47; 11:17; Jn 2:25 **9:6** [r] S Mt 8:20 **9:8** [s] Mt 5:16; 15:31; Lk 7:16; 13:13; 17:15; 23:47; Jn 15:8; Ac 4:21; 11:18; 21:20 **9:9** [t] S Mt 4:19 **9:11** [u] Mt 11:19; Lk 5:30; 15:2; 19:7; Gal 2:15 **9:13** [v] Hos 6:6; Mic 6:6-8; Mt 12:7 [w] Lk 19:10; 1Ti 1:15 **9:14** [x] S Mt 3:1 [y] Mt 11:18,19; Lk 18:12 **9:15** [z] Jn 3:29 [a] Ac 13:2,3; 14:23

[h] *28* Some manuscripts *Gergesenes*; others *Gerasenes* [i] *13* Hosea 6:6

8:28 DEMON-POSSESSED MEN. See 17:17, note; see article on POWER OVER SATAN AND DEMONS, p. 1484.

9:11 EAT WITH . . . 'SINNERS'. In vv. 11–13 Jesus gives the rule to guide us in our contact with nonbelievers: It should not be for pleasure or intimate friendship, but in order to do good to them and to show them the way of salvation (v. 12; Ps 1:1). At no time should a believer date or marry a nonbeliever (1Co 7:39; see article on SPIRITUAL SEPARATION FOR BELIEVERS, p. 1794).

9:15 THEN THEY WILL FAST. It is clear that Jesus expected believers to fast after he was gone. This age is the time of the "bridegroom's" absence, from the time of his ascension until his return. The church awaits this return of the bridegroom (25:6; see Jn 14:3, note). Therefore, fasting in this age is (1) a sign of the believer's longing for the Lord's return, (2) a preparation for Christ's coming, (3) a mourning of Christ's absence, and (4) a sign of sorrow for the sin and decay of the world (see 6:16, note).

ing the tear worse. 17Neither do men
pour new wine into old wineskins. If
they do, the skins will burst, the wine
will run out and the wineskins will be
ruined. No, they pour new wine into
new wineskins, and both are preserved."

A Dead Girl and a Sick Woman

9:18–26pp — Mk 5:22–43; Lk 8:41–56

18While he was saying this, a ruler
came and knelt before him[b] and said,
"My daughter has just died. But come
and put your hand on her,[c] and she
will live." 19Jesus got up and went with
him, and so did his disciples.
20Just then a woman who had been
subject to bleeding for twelve years
came up behind him and touched the
edge of his cloak.[d] 21She said to herself, "If I only touch his cloak, I will be
healed."
22Jesus turned and saw her. "Take
heart,[e] daughter," he said, "your faith
has healed you."[f] And the woman was
healed from that moment.[g]
23When Jesus entered the ruler's
house and saw the flute players and
the noisy crowd,[h] 24he said, "Go
away. The girl is not dead[i] but
asleep."[j] But they laughed at him.
25After the crowd had been put outside, he went in and took the girl by the
hand, and she got up.[k] 26News of this
spread through all that region.[l]

9:18 [b] S Mt 8:2 [c] S Mk 5:23
9:20 [d] Mt 14:36; Mk 3:10; 6:56; Lk 6:19
9:22 [e] ver 2; Jn 16:33 [f] ver 29; Mt 8:13; Mk 10:52; Lk 7:50; 17:19; 18:42 [g] Mt 15:28
9:23 [h] 2Ch 35:25; Jer 9:17,18
9:24 [i] Ac 20:10 [j] Da 12:2; Ps 76:5; Jn 11:11-14; Ac 7:60; 13:36; 1Co 11:30; 15:6, 18,20; 1Th 4:13-16
9:25 [k] S Lk 7:14
9:26 [l] ver 31; Mt 4:24; 14:1; Mk 1:28,45; Lk 4:14,37; 5:15; 7:17

9:27 [m] S Mt 1:1; 12:23; 15:22; 20:30,31; 21:9,15; 22:42; Mk 10:47
9:28 [n] Ac 14:9
9:29 [o] S ver 22
9:30 [p] S Mt 8:4
9:31 [q] S ver 26; Mk 7:36
9:32 [r] S Mt 4:24 [s] Mt 12:22-24
9:33 [t] Mk 2:12
9:34 [u] Mt 12:24
9:35 [v] S Mt 4:23
9:36 [w] Mt 14:14; 15:32; Mk 8:2

Jesus Heals the Blind and Mute

27As Jesus went on from there, two
blind men followed him, calling out,
"Have mercy on us, Son of David!"[m]
28When he had gone indoors, the
blind men came to him, and he asked
them, "Do you believe that I am able to
do this?"
"Yes, Lord," they replied.[n]
29Then he touched their eyes and
said, "According to your faith will it be
done to you";[o] 30and their sight was
restored. Jesus warned them sternly,
"See that no one knows about this."[p] Mt 17:20
31But they went out and spread the
news about him all over that region.[q]
32While they were going out, a man
who was demon-possessed[r] and could
not talk[s] was brought to Jesus. 33And
when the demon was driven out, the
man who had been mute spoke. The
crowd was amazed and said, "Nothing
like this has ever been seen in Israel."[t]
34But the Pharisees said, "It is by
the prince of demons that he drives out
demons."[u]

The Workers Are Few

35Jesus went through all the towns
and villages, teaching in their synagogues, preaching the good news of
the kingdom and healing every disease
and sickness.[v] 36When he saw the
crowds, he had compassion on them,[w]

9:17 NEW WINE INTO OLD WINESKINS. This verse has been interpreted in various ways by commentators. Two views are: (1) The "new wine" was fresh grape juice. As it began to ferment, new wineskins would stretch and not break, whereas old wineskins would break. The "new wine" represented the gospel as fermenting change that the old forms of Judaism could not contain. This view is questionable, however, because those familiar with the process of fermentation say that even the newest and strongest of wineskins, if sealed, would burst from the violent action of fermentation (see Job 32:19).

(2) A second interpretation sees the parable as emphasizing the importance of preserving both the new wine and the new wineskins. (a) The "new wine" was fresh unfermented grape juice, representing the original saving message of Jesus Christ and the power of the Holy Spirit thrust forth at Pentecost. Jesus' overriding concern was that the original gospel and redemptive power of the Spirit be preserved from all change, corruption or loss. This interpretation is supported by Christ's concern that the gospel (new wine) not be altered by the teachings (yeast) of the Pharisees and Judaism (yeast being a fermenting/altering agent, cf. 16:6,12; Ex 12:19; 1Co 5:7).

(b) In ancient times, in order to preserve the sweetness of the juice for an adequate period of time, people would strain or boil the juice, bottle it and place it in a cool area (see articles on WINE IN NEW TESTAMENT TIMES (1) and (2), p. 1534 and p. 1586). New wineskins were required because they would be free from all residual fermenting matter such as mature yeast cells. If placed in old wineskins, new wine would more easily begin to ferment because of the yeast cells that remained in the old wineskins. The subsequent fermentation would then cause the loss of both the new wine and the wineskins (which would burst from pressure). Columella, the great Roman authority on agriculture in the first century A.D., wrote that in order to keep new wine "always sweet" it must be put into a new sealed container (*On Agriculture*, 12.29).

9:17 NEW WINE . . . PRESERVED. Christ's emphasis here is on preserving the new wine for as long a time as possible (see previous note). For the various methods used in Bible times of keeping wine in a sweet and unfermented state, see articles on WINE IN NEW TESTAMENT TIMES (1) and (2), p. 1534 and p. 1586.

because they were harassed and helpless, like sheep without a shepherd.[x] 37Then he said to his disciples, "The harvest[y] is plentiful but the workers are few.[z] 38Ask the Lord of the harvest, therefore, to send out workers into his harvest field."

Jesus Sends Out the Twelve

10:2–4pp — Mk 3:16–19; Lk 6:14–16; Ac 1:13
10:9–15pp — Mk 6:8–11; Lk 9:3–5; 10:4–12
10:19–22pp — Mk 13:11–13; Lk 21:12–17
10:26–33pp — Lk 12:2–9
10:34,35pp — Lk 12:51–53

Mt 12:22

10 He called his twelve disciples to him and gave them authority to drive out evil[j] spirits[a] and to heal every disease and sickness.[b]

2These are the names of the twelve apostles: first, Simon (who is called Peter) and his brother Andrew; James son of Zebedee, and his brother John; 3Philip and Bartholomew; Thomas and Matthew the tax collector; James son of Alphaeus, and Thaddaeus; 4Simon the Zealot and Judas Iscariot, who betrayed him.[c]

5These twelve Jesus sent out with the following instructions: "Do not go among the Gentiles or enter any town of the Samaritans.[d] 6Go rather to the lost sheep of Israel.[e] 7As you go, preach this message: 'The kingdom of heaven[f] is near.' 8Heal the sick, raise the dead, cleanse those who have leprosy,[k] drive out demons. Freely you have received, freely give. 9Do not take along any gold or silver or copper in your belts;[g] 10take no bag for the journey, or extra tunic, or sandals or a staff; for the worker is worth his keep.[h] 11"Whatever town or village you enter, search for some worthy person there and stay at his house until you leave. 12As you enter the home, give it your greeting.[i] 13If the home is deserving, let your peace rest on it; if it is not, let your peace return to you. 14If anyone will not welcome you or listen to your words, shake the dust off your feet[j] when you leave that home or town. 15I tell you the truth, it will be more bearable for Sodom and Gomorrah[k] on the day of judgment[l] than for that town.[m] 16I am sending you out like sheep among wolves.[n] Therefore be as shrewd as snakes and as innocent as doves.[o]

Discipleship and Suffering

17"Be on your guard against men; they will hand you over to the local councils[p] and flog you in their synagogues.[q] 18On my account you will be brought before governors and kings[r] as witnesses to them and to the Gentiles. 19But when they arrest you, do not worry about what to say or how to say it.[s] At that time you will be given what to say, 20for it will not be you speaking, but the Spirit of your Father[t] speaking through you.

21"Brother will betray brother to death, and a father his child; children will rebel against their parents[u] and

9:36 [x]Nu 27:17; 1Ki 22:17; Eze 34:5,6; Zec 10:2
9:37 [y]Jn 4:35 [z]Lk 10:2
10:1 [a]Mk 3:13-15; 6:7; Lk 4:36; 9:1 [b]S Mt 4:23
10:4 [c]Mt 26:14-16,25, 47; 27:3; Mk 14:10; Jn 6:71; 12:4; 13:2,26,27; Ac 1:16
10:5 [d]1Ki 16:24; 2Ki 17:24; Lk 9:52; 10:33; 17:16; Jn 4:4-26, 39,40; 8:48; Ac 8:5,25
10:6 [e]Jer 50:6; Mt 15:24
10:7 [f]S Mt 3:2
10:9 [g]Lk 22:35
10:10 [h]S 1Ti 5:18
10:12 [i]1Sa 25:6
10:14 [j]Ne 5:13; Mk 6:11; Lk 9:5; 10:11; Ac 13:51; 18:6
10:15 [k]Ge 18:20; 19:24; 2Pe 2:6; Jude 7 [l]Mt 12:36; Ac 17:31; 2Pe 2:9; 3:7; 1Jn 4:17; Jude 6 [m]Mt 11:22, 24
10:16 [n]Lk 10:3; Ac 20:29 [o]S 1Co 14:20
10:17 [p]S Mt 5:22 [q]Mt 23:34; Mk 13:9; Ac 5:40; 22:19; 26:11
10:18 [r]Ac 25:24-26
10:19 [s]Ex 4:12
10:20 [t]Lk 12:11, 12; Ac 4:8
10:21 [u]ver 35, 36; Mic 7:6

j *1* Greek *unclean* k *8* The Greek word was used for various diseases affecting the skin—not necessarily leprosy.

9:37 THE HARVEST IS PLENTIFUL. Jesus admonishes all believers to always remember that the lost have an invaluable, everlasting soul and must spend eternity in heaven or in hell, and that many of them can be saved if only someone presents the gospel to them (see 10:28, note).

9:38 ASK THE LORD . . . TO SEND. This verse expresses one of God's own spiritual principles. Before he acts, he usually calls his people to prayer. Only after his people have prayed does God accomplish that work. In other words, God has limited himself to the prayers of his people. It is clear from the context (9:35—10:1,8) that the kind of workers Jesus desires in his kingdom are those who (1) teach and preach the gospel of the kingdom (9:35), (2) heal the sick (9:35; 10:1,8) and (3) drive out evil spirits (10:1,8).

10:1 AUTHORITY TO DRIVE OUT EVIL SPIRITS. Jesus wants his followers to wage war against the forces of evil by driving out evil spirits and healing the sick. This demonstration of authority in spiritual confrontation is considered a continuing manifestation of the kingdom of God on earth (see article on THE KINGDOM OF GOD, p. 1430).

10:7 PREACH . . . THE KINGDOM. The context (vv. 1,8) makes clear that the preaching of the kingdom is to be accompanied by God asserting his power against the forces of sin, sickness and Satan (see article on THE KINGDOM OF GOD, p. 1430). It is Christ's purpose that the kingdom of heaven and its power be "near" to bring salvation, grace and healing to God's people. When the "kingdom of heaven" is not being manifested among God's people, they should turn from the spirit of the world and all that is not pleasing to God, "seek first his kingdom and his righteousness" (6:33) and pray "your kingdom come, your will be done" (6:10; cf. Mk 9:29).

10:19 GIVEN WHAT TO SAY. Christ's promise is seen in operation in Ac 4:8–12,19–20; 21:39—22:21; 23:1,6; 24:10–21; 26:1–29. After Pentecost the Spirit was poured out in all his fullness to give power to witness (Ac 1:8).

have them put to death.[v] 22"All men
will hate you because of me,[w] but he
who stands firm to the end will be
saved.[x] 23When you are persecuted in
one place, flee to another. I tell you the
truth, you will not finish going through
the cities of Israel before the Son of
Man comes.[y]

24"A student is not above his teacher, nor a servant above his master.[z]
25It is enough for the student to be like
his teacher, and the servant like his
master. If the head of the house has
been called Beelzebub,[1a] how much
more the members of his household!

26"So do not be afraid of them. There
is nothing concealed that will not be
disclosed, or hidden that will not be
made known.[b] 27What I tell you in the
dark, speak in the daylight; what is
whispered in your ear, proclaim from
the roofs. 28Do not be afraid of those
who kill the body but cannot kill the
soul. Rather, be afraid of the One[c]
who can destroy both soul and body in
hell. 29Are not two sparrows sold for a
penny[m]? Yet not one of them will fall
to the ground apart from the will of
your Father. 30And even the very hairs
of your head are all numbered.[d] 31So
don't be afraid; you are worth more
than many sparrows.[e]

32"Whoever acknowledges me before men,[f] I will also acknowledge
him before my Father in heaven. 33But
whoever disowns me before men, I will
disown him before my Father in heav-
en.[g]

34"Do not suppose that I have come

10:21 [v] Mk 13:12
10:22 [w] S Jn 15:21 [x] Mt 24:13; Mk 13:13; Lk 21:19; Rev 2:10
10:23 [y] S Lk 17:30
10:24 [z] S Jn 13:16
10:25 [a] S Mk 3:22
10:26 [b] Mk 4:22; Lk 8:17
10:28 [c] Isa 8:12,13; Heb 10:31
10:30 [d] 1Sa 14:45; 2Sa 14:11; 1Ki 1:52; Lk 21:18; Ac 27:34
10:31 [e] Mt 6:26; 12:12
10:32 [f] Ro 10:9
10:33 [g] Mk 8:38; 2Ti 2:12

[1] 25 Greek *Beezeboul* or *Beelzeboul*
[m] 29 Greek *an assarion*

10:23 CITIES OF ISRAEL. Christ may have been telling his disciples that the gospel would continue to be proclaimed to the Jews until his return.

10:26 DO NOT BE AFRAID OF THEM. The disciples' work for Christ and their battle against Satan will expose them to Satan's counterattack (vv. 16–25); yet they do not need to be afraid, because the Holy Spirit and the Father will sustain them (vv. 20,29–31). They must remain faithful to the Word of Christ, preaching openly, frankly and courageously.

10:28 HELL. The word here translated "hell" (Gk *geenna*; see Jer 7:31, note) refers to a place of eternal torment reserved for the ungodly (cf. Mk 9:43,48). The Bible teaches that one's existence does not end at death but continues on forever, either in the presence of God or in a place of punishment. Note the following about the state of the lost:

(1) Jesus teaches that there is a place of eternal punishment for those condemned before God (see 5:22,29–30; 18:9; 23:15,33; Mk 9:43,45,47; Lk 10:15; 12:5). It is the terrifying reality of continuous punishment, the place of a "fire that never goes out" (Mk 9:43), of "eternal fire, prepared for the devil and his angels" (25:41), of "weeping and gnashing of teeth" (13:42,50), of binding and darkness (22:13), and of torment and agony and separation from heaven (Lk 16:23).

(2) The teaching of the letters is essentially the same. The apostles speak of a coming judgment of God to inflict vengeance on those who disobey the gospel (2Th 1:5–9), of a separation from the presence and majesty of the Lord (2Th 1:9) and of the destruction of God's enemies (Php 3:18–19; see also Ro 9:22; 1Co 16:22; Gal 1:9; 2Ti 2:12; Heb 10:27; 2Pe 2:4; Jude 1:7; Rev 14:10; 19:20; 20:10, 14).

(3) The Bible teaches that judgment on evildoers is certain. The main idea is condemnation, suffering and separation from God with no time limit. Christians may find this doctrine unpleasant or hard to understand. Yet we must submit to the authority of God's Word and trust God's decision and justice.

(4) We must always keep in mind that God sent his Son to die in order that no one should perish (Jn 3:16). It is not God's intention or desire to send anyone to hell (2Pe 3:9). Those who enter hell do so by resisting the salvation provided by God (Ro 1:16—2:10). The fact and reality of hell should cause all of God's people to hate sin fervently, to seek continually the salvation of the lost and to warn everyone of God's future righteous judgment (see Rev 20:14, note).

10:31 YOU ARE WORTH MORE. Jesus teaches that God's faithful children are of great worth to their heavenly Father. (1) God values you and your personal needs; he desires your love and fellowship so much that he sent Jesus to die on the cross for you (see Jn 3:16, note). You are never away from his presence, care and concern. He knows all your needs, trials and sorrows (6:8). (2) You are so important to God that he treasures your faithfulness, love and loyalty above all earthly things. Your unwavering faith in Christ, proved genuine in the midst of trials and trouble, is his glory and honor. Read the assurances found in Ps 91:14–16; 116:15; Isa 49:16; Mt 11:28–29; Lk 12:32; Jn 13:1; 14:3; 17:24; Ro 8:28; 1Jn 4:19.

10:32 ACKNOWLEDGES ME BEFORE MEN. To "acknowledge" (Gk *homologeō*) Christ means to confess him as Lord of one's life, and to do so openly before others, even before those who oppose him, his ways and his standards.

10:34 I DID NOT COME TO BRING PEACE. Although Jesus Christ is called the "Prince of Peace" (Isa 9:6; cf. Mt 5:9; Ro 5:1), and truth must always be proclaimed in love (Eph 4:15), there is a sense in which his coming and the proclamation of the gospel will bring division, and do so intentionally. (1) Faith in Christ separates the believer from the sinner and the world (vv. 32–37; Lk

to bring peace to the earth. I did not
come to bring peace, but a sword.
35For I have come to turn

"'a man against his
father,
a daughter against her
mother,
a daughter-in-law against her
mother-in-law[h]—
36 a man's enemies will be the
members of his own
household.'[n][i]

37"Anyone who loves his father or
mother more than me is not worthy of
me; anyone who loves his son or
daughter more than me is not worthy
of me;[j] 38and anyone who does not
take his cross and follow me is not worthy of me.[k] 39Whoever finds his life
will lose it, and whoever loses his life
for my sake will find it.[l]

40"He who receives you receives
me,[m] and he who receives me receives
the one who sent me.[n] 41Anyone who
receives a prophet because he is a
prophet will receive a prophet's reward, and anyone who receives a righteous man because he is a righteous
man will receive a righteous man's reward. 42And if anyone gives even a cup
of cold water to one of these little ones
because he is my disciple, I tell you the
truth, he will certainly not lose his reward."[o]

10:35 [h] ver 21 **10:36** [i] Mic 7:6 **10:37** [j] Lk 14:26 **10:38** [k] Mt 16:24; Lk 14:27 **10:39** [l] S Jn 12:25 **10:40** [m] Ex 16:8; Mt 18:5; Gal 4:14 [n] Lk 9:48; 10:16; Jn 12:44; 13:20 **10:42** [o] Pr 14:31; 19:17; Mt 25:40; Mk 9:41; Ac 10:4; Heb 6:10

11:1 [p] S Mt 7:28 **11:2** [q] S Mt 3:1 [r] Mt 14:3 **11:3** [s] Ps 118:26; Jn 11:27; Heb 10:37 **11:5** [t] Isa 35:4-6; 61:1; Mt 15:31; Lk 4:18,19 **11:6** [u] Mt 13:21; 26:31 **11:7** [v] S Mt 3:1 [w] Mt 3:1 **11:9** [x] Mt 14:5; 21:26; Lk 1:76; 7:26

Jesus and John the Baptist

11:2–19pp — Lk 7:18–35

11 After Jesus had finished instructing his twelve disci-
ples,[p] he went on from there to teach
and preach in the towns of Galilee.[o]
2When John[q] heard in prison[r]
what Christ was doing, he sent his disciples 3to ask him, "Are you the one
who was to come,[s] or should we expect someone else?"
4Jesus replied, "Go back and report
to John what you hear and see: 5The
blind receive sight, the lame walk,
those who have leprosy[p] are cured,
the deaf hear, the dead are raised, and
the good news is preached to the
poor.[t] 6Blessed is the man who does
not fall away on account of me."[u]
7As John's[v] disciples were leaving,
Jesus began to speak to the crowd
about John: "What did you go out into
the desert[w] to see? A reed swayed by
the wind? 8If not, what did you go out
to see? A man dressed in fine clothes?
No, those who wear fine clothes are in
kings' palaces. 9Then what did you go
out to see? A prophet?[x] Yes, I tell you,
and more than a prophet. 10This is the
one about whom it is written:

[n] *36* Micah 7:6 [o] *1* Greek *in their towns*
[p] *5* The Greek word was used for various diseases affecting the skin—not necessarily leprosy.

12:51–53; see article on SPIRITUAL SEPARATION FOR BELIEVERS, p. 1794). (2) The proclamation of God's Word and its truth will bring opposition, division and persecution (12:24; 14:4–12; 27:1; Ac 5:17; 7:54–60; 14:22). (3) A life lived according to Christ's righteous standards will bring ridicule and scorn (5:10–11). (4) The defense of the NT apostolic faith against heresy will bring division (2Co 11:12–15; Gal 1:9; Php 1:15–17; see 2Ti 1:15, note). (5) The teaching of Christ about peace and unity must be faithfully held in tension with the truth that he "did not come to bring peace, but a sword" (see Jn 17:21, note).

10:38 TAKE HIS CROSS. See Mk 8:34, note.

10:41 PROPHET ... RIGHTEOUS MAN. Jesus speaks of receiving a prophet and a righteous man, those who are the most frequently rejected and persecuted because of their stand for godliness and their proclamation of the truth (see 5:10). For this reason those who accept prophets or righteous men and receive their messages will receive God's special reward. (1) If your commitment to truth and righteousness is so firm that you devote your life to providing for, cooperating with and encouraging God's ministers who are righteous, then your reward will be the same as that of the prophet or righteous person you help.

(2) Conversely, one should not support, encourage or cooperate with ministers and preachers who do not proclaim God's truth according to the NT revelation or who do not live godly lives according to God's righteous standards. Supporting such people will bring one into their condemnation (see 2Jn).

11:7 JOHN. When Christ stated that John was not "a reed swayed by the wind," he was referring to John's righteous character and to his reputation as a preacher who refused to compromise his convictions. John preached God's commandments without fear of others, never yielding to popular opinion. Herod's sin was ignored in silence by all the Jewish authorities, but never for a moment by John. He rose against it as a rock, showing absolute fidelity to God and to his Word. He stood with God against sin, even though it cost him his life (14:3–12). Let every preacher of God's Word take note, for Christ will evaluate each one's ministry, character and stand against sin (see Lk 1:17, notes).

" 'I will send my messenger ahead
of you,[y]
who will prepare your way
before you.'[q][z]

11I tell you the truth: Among those
born of women there has not risen anyone greater than John the Baptist; yet
he who is least in the kingdom of heav-
en is greater than he. 12From the days
of John the Baptist until now, the kingdom of heaven has been forcefully advancing, and forceful men lay hold of it.
13For all the Prophets and the Law
prophesied until John.[a] 14And if you
are willing to accept it, he is the Elijah
who was to come.[b] 15He who has
ears, let him hear.[c]
16"To what can I compare this generation? They are like children sitting
in the marketplaces and calling out to
others:

17" 'We played the flute for you,
and you did not dance;
we sang a dirge,
and you did not mourn.'

18For John came neither eating[d] nor
drinking,[e] and they say, 'He has a demon.' 19The Son of Man came eating
and drinking, and they say, 'Here is a
glutton and a drunkard, a friend of tax
collectors and "sinners." '[f] But wisdom is proved right by her actions."

Woe to Unrepentant Cities

11:21–23pp — Lk 10:13–15

20Then Jesus began to denounce the
cities in which most of his miracles had
been performed, because they did not
repent. 21"Woe to you, Korazin! Woe to
you, Bethsaida![g] If the miracles that
were performed in you had been performed in Tyre and Sidon,[h] they
would have repented long ago in sackcloth and ashes.[i] 22But I tell you, it
will be more bearable for Tyre and Sidon on the day of judgment than for
you.[j] 23And you, Capernaum,[k] will
you be lifted up to the skies? No, you
will go down to the depths.[r][l] If the
miracles that were performed in you
had been performed in Sodom, it would
have remained to this day. 24But I tell
you that it will be more bearable for
Sodom on the day of judgment than for
you."[m]

Rest for the Weary

11:25–27pp — Lk 10:21,22

25At that time Jesus said, "I praise
you, Father,[n] Lord of heaven and
earth, because you have hidden these
things from the wise and learned, and
revealed them to little children.[o]
26Yes, Father, for this was your good
pleasure.
27"All things have been committed
to me[p] by my Father.[q] No one knows
the Son except the Father, and no one
knows the Father except the Son and
those to whom the Son chooses to reveal him.[r]
28"Come to me,[s] all you who are
weary and burdened, and I will give
you rest.[t] 29Take my yoke upon you
and learn from me,[u] for I am gentle
and humble in heart, and you will find
rest for your souls.[v] 30For my yoke is
easy and my burden is light."[w]

Lord of the Sabbath

12:1–8pp — Mk 2:23–28; Lk 6:1–5
12:9–14pp — Mk 3:1–6; Lk 6:6–11

12 At that time Jesus went
through the grainfields on the
Sabbath. His disciples were hungry

11:10 [y]Jn 3:28 [z]Mal 3:1; Mk 1:2; Lk 7:27 **11:13** [a]Lk 16:16 **11:14** [b]Mal 4:5; Mt 17:10-13; Mk 9:11-13; Lk 1:17; Jn 1:21 **11:15** [c]Mt 13:9, 43; Mk 4:23; Lk 14:35; S Rev 2:7 **11:18** [d]Mt 3:4 [e]S Lk 1:15 **11:19** [f]S Mt 9:11 **11:21** [g]Mk 6:45; 8:22; Lk 9:10; Jn 1:44; 12:21 [h]Joel 3:4; Am 1:9; Mt 15:21; Mk 3:8; Lk 6:17; Ac 12:20

[i]Jnh 3:5-9 **11:22** [j]ver 24; Mt 10:15 **11:23** [k]S Mt 4:13 [l]Isa 14:13-15 **11:24** [m]S Mt 10:15 **11:25** [n]Mt 16:17; Lk 22:42; 23:34; Jn 11:41; 12:27,28 [o]S Mt 13:11; 1Co 1:26-29 **11:27** [p]S Mt 28:18 [q]S Jn 3:35 [r]Jn 10:15; 17:25, 26 **11:28** [s]Jn 7:37 [t]Ex 33:14 **11:29** [u]Jn 13:15; Php 2:5; 1Pe 2:21; 1Jn 2:6 [v]Ps 116:7; Jer 6:16 **11:30** [w]1Jn 5:3

[q] *10* Mal. 3:1 [r] *23* Greek *Hades*

11:11 GREATER THAN HE. This statement may mean that the privileges of the least of those who belong to the age of the new covenant are greater than John the Baptist (see article on THE OLD COVENANT AND THE NEW COVENANT, p. 1926). They have greater treasures of revelation given to them by God (cf. 13:16–17) and will experience greater miracles (11:5), see the death and resurrection of Christ, and receive the Pentecostal outpouring of the Holy Spirit (Ac 2:4).

11:12 FORCEFUL MEN LAY HOLD OF IT. See article on THE KINGDOM OF GOD, p. 1430.

11:19 GLUTTON AND A DRUNKARD. See Lk 7:34, note.

11:28 COME TO ME. Jesus' gracious invitation comes to all "who are weary and burdened" with the troubles of life and the sins of their own human nature. By coming to Jesus, becoming his servant and obeying his direction, he will free you from your insurmountable burdens and give you rest, peace and his Holy Spirit to lead you through life. What trials and cares you carry will be borne with his help and grace (see Heb 4:16).

12:1 SABBATH. The weekly Sabbath (Gk *sabbaton*, meaning rest, ceasing) was the seventh day of the week set apart by the Law of Moses as a day for ceasing from normal work and for giving of oneself to rest and to the worship of the Lord (Ex 20:10; Dt 5:14; see Ex 20:8, note). There are strong reasons to believe that the principles of the Sabbath have permanent validity for Christians and that we should still set aside one

and began to pick some heads of
grain[x] and eat them. **2**When the Pharisees saw this, they said to him, "Look!
Your disciples are doing what is unlawful on the Sabbath."[y]
3He answered, "Haven't you read
what David did when he and his companions were hungry?[z] **4**He entered
the house of God, and he and his companions ate the consecrated bread—
which was not lawful for them to do,
but only for the priests.[a] **5**Or haven't
you read in the Law that on the Sabbath the priests in the temple desecrate the day[b] and yet are innocent?
6I tell you that one[s] greater than the
temple is here.[c] **7**If you had known
what these words mean, 'I desire mercy, not sacrifice,'[t][d] you would not
have condemned the innocent. **8**For the
Son of Man[e] is Lord of the Sabbath."
9Going on from that place, he went
into their synagogue, **10**and a man with
a shriveled hand was there. Looking
for a reason to accuse Jesus,[f] they
asked him, "Is it lawful to heal on the
Sabbath?"[g]
11He said to them, "If any of you has
a sheep and it falls into a pit on the
Sabbath, will you not take hold of it
and lift it out?[h] **12**How much more
valuable is a man than a sheep![i]
Therefore it is lawful to do good on the
Sabbath."
13Then he said to the man, "Stretch
out your hand." So he stretched it out
and it was completely restored, just as
sound as the other. **14**But the Pharisees went out and plotted how they
might kill Jesus.[j]

God's Chosen Servant

15Aware of this, Jesus withdrew
from that place. Many followed him,
and he healed all their sick,[k] **16**warning them not to tell who he was.[l]
17This was to fulfill[m] what was spoken through the prophet Isaiah:

18"Here is my servant whom I have chosen,
the one I love, in whom I delight;[n]
I will put my Spirit on him,[o]
and he will proclaim justice to the nations.
19He will not quarrel or cry out;
no one will hear his voice in the streets.
20A bruised reed he will not break,
and a smoldering wick he will not snuff out,
till he leads justice to victory.
21 In his name the nations will put their hope."[u][p]

Jesus and Beelzebub

12:25–29pp — Mk 3:23–27; Lk 11:17–22

22Then they brought him a demon-
possessed man who was blind and
mute, and Jesus healed him, so that he
could both talk and see.[q] **23**All the

12:1 [x]Dt 23:25 **12:2** [y]ver 10; Ex 20:10; 23:12; Dt 5:14; Lk 13:14; 14:3; Jn 5:10; 7:23; 9:16 **12:3** [z]1Sa 21:6 **12:4** [a]Lev 24:5,9 **12:5** [b]Nu 28:9,10; Jn 7:22,23 **12:6** [c]ver 41,42 **12:7** [d]Hos 6:6; Mic 6:6-8; Mt 9:13 **12:8** [e]S Mt 8:20 **12:10** [f]Mk 3:2; 12:13; Lk 11:54; 14:1; 20:20 [g]S ver 2 **12:11** [h]Lk 14:5 **12:12** [i]Mt 6:26; 10:31

12:14 [j]Ge 37:18; Ps 71:10; Mt 26:4; 27:1; Mk 3:6; Lk 6:11; Jn 5:18; 7:1,19; 11:53 **12:15** [k]S Mt 4:23 **12:16** [l]S Mt 8:4 **12:17** [m]S Mt 1:22 **12:18** [n]S Mt 3:17 [o]S Jn 3:34 **12:21** [p]Isa 42:1-4 **12:22** [q]S Mt 4:24

[s] *6* Or *something*; also in verses 41 and 42
[t] *7* Hosea 6:6 [u] *21* Isaiah 42:1-4

day in seven as a day of rest and worship.

(1) The concept of a sacred day of rest was instituted before the Jewish law: "God blessed the seventh day and made it holy" (see Ge 2:3, note; cf. Ex 20:11). This indicates that from the time of creation God wanted one day in seven to be a source of blessing for everyone, and not just for the Jewish race.

(2) Jesus never abrogated the principle of a day of rest, only the misuse of it by Jewish leaders (vv. 1–8; Lk 13:10–17; 14:1–6). He stated that the day of rest was given for our spiritual and physical well-being (Mk 2:27). Nowhere does the Bible indicate that this principle has been done away with.

(3) The spiritual purpose of a seventh day of rest benefits Christians. In the OT it was used as a day to rest from work and to dedicate oneself to God—a special time to get to know God, to worship him and to concentrate in private and in public on the things of God (Lev 24:8; Nu 28:9). Today it provides us an opportunity to reaffirm that our trust and delight is in the Lord and not in the world, our own selfish ways, our material goods or our pleasure (cf. Ex 20:10; 34:21; Isa 38:13). We can use this day to renew our initial commitment to Christ and our oneness with other believers, and to acknowledge that our entire lives, not just one-seventh, belong to God (see Heb 4:9–10).

(4) As the Sabbath was a covenant sign that the Israelites were the people of God (Ex 31:16–17), so the Christian day of worship (Sunday) can be seen as a sign to the world that we belong to Christ and that he is our Lord. Christians in the NT set aside the first day of the week to worship God and to commemorate the resurrection of Christ (Ac 20:7; 1Co 16:2).

(5) The Sabbath was set apart by God as a holy day (Ge 2:3; Ex 16:23; 20:11; 31:14; Isa 58:13). Thus believers who set aside one day in seven as holy are reminded that they themselves are set apart by God to live lives of holiness in the midst of a perverse generation (cf. Ex 31:13; 1Pe 2:9).

(6) Finally, the Sabbath can be seen as God's commitment to believers that he will carry out his will for them and that he is constantly available to act to meet their needs. He is always open to their prayers and devoted to their interest (cf. Ex 31:13; Eze 20:12).

people were astonished and said,
"Could this be the Son of David?"[r]
24But when the Pharisees heard
this, they said, "It is only by Beelzebub,[v][s] the prince of demons, that
this fellow drives out demons."[t]
25Jesus knew their thoughts[u] and
said to them, "Every kingdom divided
against itself will be ruined, and every
city or household divided against itself
will not stand. 26If Satan[v] drives out
Satan, he is divided against himself.
How then can his kingdom stand?
27And if I drive out demons by Beelzebub,[w] by whom do your people[x] drive
them out? So then, they will be your
judges. 28But if I drive out demons by
the Spirit of God, then the kingdom of
God[y] has come upon you.
29"Or again, how can anyone enter a
strong man's house and carry off his
possessions unless he first ties up the
strong man? Then he can rob his
house.
30"He who is not with me is against
me, and he who does not gather with
me scatters.[z] 31And so I tell you, every sin and blasphemy will be forgiven
men, but the blasphemy against the
Spirit will not be forgiven.[a] 32Anyone
who speaks a word against the Son of
Man will be forgiven, but anyone who
speaks against the Holy Spirit will not
be forgiven, either in this age[b] or in
the age to come.[c]
33"Make a tree good and its fruit will
be good, or make a tree bad and its
fruit will be bad, for a tree is recognized by its fruit.[d] 34You brood of vipers,[e] how can you who are evil say
anything good? For out of the overflow
of the heart the mouth speaks.[f] 35The
good man brings good things out of the
good stored up in him, and the evil man
brings evil things out of the evil stored
up in him. 36But I tell you that men will
have to give account on the day of judgment for every careless word they have
spoken. 37For by your words you will
be acquitted, and by your words you
will be condemned."[g]

The Sign of Jonah

12:39–42pp — Lk 11:29–32
12:43–45pp — Lk 11:24–26

38Then some of the Pharisees and
teachers of the law said to him,
"Teacher, we want to see a miraculous
sign[h] from you."[i]
39He answered, "A wicked and adulterous generation asks for a miraculous sign! But none will be given it except the sign of the prophet Jonah.[j]
40For as Jonah was three days and
three nights in the belly of a huge
fish,[k] so the Son of Man[l] will be
three days and three nights in the
heart of the earth.[m] 41The men of Nineveh[n] will stand up at the judgment
with this generation and condemn it;
for they repented at the preaching of
Jonah,[o] and now one[w] greater than
Jonah is here. 42The Queen of the
South will rise at the judgment with
this generation and condemn it; for she
came[p] from the ends of the earth to
listen to Solomon's wisdom, and now
one greater than Solomon is here.

12:23 [r] S Mt 9:27 **12:24** [s] S Mk 3:22 [t] Mt 9:34 **12:25** [u] S Mt 9:4 **12:26** [v] S Mt 4:10 **12:27** [w] ver 24 [x] Ac 19:13 **12:28** [y] S Mt 3:2 **12:30** [z] Mk 9:40; Lk 11:23 **12:31** [a] Mk 3:28, 29; Lk 12:10 **12:32** [b] Tit 2:12 [c] Mk 10:30; Lk 20:34,35; Eph 1:21; Heb 6:5 **12:33** [d] Mt 7:16, 17; Lk 6:43,44 **12:34** [e] Mt 3:7; 23:33
[f] Mt 15:18; Lk 6:45 **12:37** [g] Job 15:6; Pr 10:14; 18:21; Jas 3:2 **12:38** [h] S Jn 2:11; S 4:48 [i] Mt 16:1; Mk 8:11,12; Lk 11:16; Jn 2:18; 6:30; 1Co 1:22 **12:39** [j] Mt 16:4; Lk 11:29 **12:40** [k] Jnh 1:17 [l] S Mt 8:20 [m] S Mt 16:21 **12:41** [n] Jnh 1:2 [o] Jnh 3:5 **12:42** [p] 1Ki 10:1; 2Ch 9:1

[v] *24* Greek *Beezeboul* or *Beelzeboul*; also in verse 27 [w] *41* Or *something*; also in verse 42

12:28 THE KINGDOM OF GOD. See article on THE KINGDOM OF GOD, p. 1430.

12:29 TIES UP THE STRONG MAN. See article on POWER OVER SATAN AND DEMONS, p. 1484.

12:31 BLASPHEMY AGAINST THE SPIRIT. Blasphemy against the Spirit is the continual and deliberate rejection of the Holy Spirit's witness to Christ, to his Word and to his convicting work against sin (cf. Jn 16:7–11). Those who reject and oppose the voice of the Spirit remove themselves from the only force that can lead them to forgiveness. The process leading to blasphemy against the Spirit is as follows: (1) Grieving the Spirit (Eph 4:30), if ongoing, leads to resisting the Spirit (Ac 7:51); (2) Resisting the Spirit leads to putting out the Spirit's fire (1Th 5:19); (3) Putting out the Spirit's fire leads to hardening the heart (Heb 3:8–13); (4) Hardening the heart leads to a depraved mind and to a labeling of good as evil and evil as good (Isa 5:20; Ro 1:28). When this hardening of the heart reaches a certain fullness of development, determined only by God, the Spirit will no longer strive to lead that person to repentance (cf. Ge 6:3; see Dt 29:18–21, note; 1Sa 2:25, note; Pr 29:1, note). For those who are worried about having committed the unpardonable sin, the very fact of wanting to be forgiven and the willingness to repent of sin is evidence that one has not committed the unpardonable sin (see article on PERSONAL APOSTASY, p. 1918).

12:36 THE DAY OF JUDGMENT. See article on THE JUDGMENT OF BELIEVERS, p. 1791).

12:37 BY YOUR WORDS ... ACQUITTED. See Lk 13:34, note.

12:40 JONAH. It is clear that Jesus accepted the OT account of Jonah as historical fact (see Jnh 1:17, note). The modern skeptics who deny the possibility of OT miracles must reckon with and be judged by the words of Jesus.

THE KINGDOM OF GOD

Mt 12:28 "But if I drive out demons by the Spirit of God, then the kingdom of God has come upon you."

THE NATURE OF THE KINGDOM. The kingdom of God (or heaven) carries the idea of God coming into the world to assert his power, glory and rights against Satan's dominion and the present course of this world. It is more than salvation or the church; it is God expressing himself powerfully in all his works.

(1) The kingdom is primarily an assertion of divine power in action. God is beginning his spiritual rule on earth in the hearts of and among his people (Jn 14:23; 20:22). He comes into the world with power (Isa 64:1; Mk 9:1; 1Co 4:20). We must not conceive of this power as material or political, but as spiritual. The kingdom is not a religio-political theocracy; it is not a matter of social or political dominion over the kingdoms of this world (Jn 18:36). God does not intend at this time to redeem and reform the world through social or political activism, or through violent action (Mt 26:52; see Jn 18:36, note). The world throughout this age will remain an enemy of God and his people (Jn 15:19; Ro 12:1–2; Jas 4:4; 1Jn 2:15–17; 4:4). God's rule by direct judgment and force will occur only at the end of this age (Rev 19:11–21).

(2) Because God asserts himself with power, the world enters into a crisis. God's expression of power fills the devil's empire with alarm (Mt 4:3ff; 12:29; Mk 1:24), and everyone is confronted with the decision whether or not to submit to God's rule (Mt 3:1–2; 4:17; Mk 1:14–15). The necessary and fundamental condition of entry into God's kingdom is, "Repent and believe the good news" (Mk 1:15).

(3) This breaking into the world with divine power involves: (a) spiritual power over Satan's rule and dominion (Mt 12:28; Jn 18:36)—the coming of the kingdom is the beginning of the destruction of Satan's rule (Jn 12:31; 16:11) and of humanity's deliverance from the demonic (Mk 1:34,39; 3:14–15; Ac 26:18) and from sin (Ro 6); (b) power to work miracles and to heal the sick (Mt 4:23; 9:35; Ac 4:30; 8:7; see article on DIVINE HEALING, p. 1420); (c) the preaching of the gospel, accompanied by conviction with regard to sin, righteousness and judgment (Mt 11:5; Jn 16:8–11; Ac 4:33); (d) the salvation and sanctification of those who repent and believe the gospel (see Jn 3:3; 17:17; Ac 2:38–40; 2Co 6:14–18; see article on SPIRITUAL SEPARATION FOR BELIEVERS, p. 1794); and (e) the baptism in the Holy Spirit for power to witness for Christ (see Ac 1:8, notes; 2:4, notes).

(4) An essential evidence that one is experiencing God's kingdom is a life of "righteousness, peace and joy in the Holy Spirit" (Ro 14:17).

(5) This kingdom has both a present and a future aspect. It is a present reality in the world today (Mk 1:15; Lk 18:16–17; Col 1:13; Heb 12:28), yet God's rule and power are not completely realized. The work and influence of Satan and evil people will continue until the end of the age (1Ti 4:1; 2Ti 3:1–5; Rev 19:19–20:10). The future manifestation of God's glory, power and kingdom will occur when Jesus returns to judge the world (Mt 24:30; Lk 21:27; Rev 19:11–20; 20:1–6). The ultimate fulfillment of the kingdom comes when Christ finally triumphs over all evil and opposition and hands over the kingdom to God the Father (1Co 15:24–28; Rev 20:7—21:8; see also Mk 1:15, note concerning the various manifestations of the kingdom in redemptive history.)

THE ROLE OF BELIEVERS IN THE KINGDOM. The NT has much to say about the role of believers in God's kingdom.

(1) It is the responsibility of believers to seek unceasingly God's kingdom in all its manifestations, hungering and thirsting for God's presence and power both in their own lives and within the Christian community (see Mt 5:10, notes; 6:33, note).

(2) In Mt 11:12 Jesus gives additional information on the nature of kingdom people. There he indicates that the kingdom of heaven is taken hold of only by forceful people who are committed to breaking away from the sinful practices of the human race and who turn to Christ, his Word and his righteous ways. No matter what the cost may be, such people vigorously seek the kingdom in all its power. In other words, experiencing the kingdom of heaven and all its blessings requires earnest endeavor and constant exertion—a fight of faith accompanied by a strong will to resist Satan, sin and an often corrupt society.

(3) The kingdom of God is not for those who seldom pray or who compromise with the world, neglect the Word and have little spiritual hunger. It is for men like Joseph (Ge 39:9), Nathan (2Sa 12:7), Elijah (1 Ki 18:21), Daniel and his three friends (Da 1:8, 3:16–18), Mordecai (Est 3:4–5), Peter and John (Ac 4:19–20), Stephen (Ac 6:8, 7:51) and Paul (Php 3:13–14); it is for women like Deborah (Jdg 4:9), Ruth (Ru 1:16–18), Esther (Est 4:16), Mary (Lk 1:26–35), Anna (Lk 2:36–38) and Lydia (Ac 16:14–15,40).

JEWISH SECTS

PHARISEES

Their roots can be traced to the second century B.C. — to the Hasidim.

1. Along with the Torah, they accepted as equally inspired and authoritative, all material contained within the oral tradition.
2. On free will and determination, they held to a mediating view that made it impossible for either free will or the sovereignty of God to cancel out the other.
3. They accepted a rather developed hierarchy of angels and demons.
4. They taught that there was a future for the dead.
5. They believed in the immortality of the soul and in reward and retribution after death.
6. They were champions of human equality.
7. The emphasis of their teaching was ethical rather than theological.

SADDUCEES

They probably had their beginning during the Hasmonean period (166-63 B.C.). Their demise occurred C. A.D. 70 with the fall of Jerusalem.

1. They denied that the oral law was authoritative and binding.
2. They interpreted Mosaic law more literally than did the Pharisees.
3. They were very exacting in Levitical purity.
4. They attributed all to free will.
5. They argued there is neither resurrection of the dead nor a future life.
6. They rejected a belief in angels and demons.
7. They rejected the idea of a spiritual world.
8. Only the books of Moses were canonical Scripture.

43“When an evil[x] spirit comes out
of a man, it goes through arid places
seeking rest and does not find it.
44Then it says, ‘I will return to the
house I left.’ When it arrives, it finds
the house unoccupied, swept clean and
put in order. 45Then it goes and takes
with it seven other spirits more wicked
than itself, and they go in and live
there. And the final condition of that
man is worse than the first.[q] That is
how it will be with this wicked generation.”

Jesus’ Mother and Brothers

12:46–50pp — Mk 3:31–35; Lk 8:19–21

46While Jesus was still talking to the
crowd, his mother[r] and brothers[s]
stood outside, wanting to speak to him.
47Someone told him, “Your mother and
brothers are standing outside, wanting
to speak to you.”[y]
48He replied to him, “Who is my
mother, and who are my brothers?”
49Pointing to his disciples, he said,
“Here are my mother and my brothers.
50For whoever does the will of my Father
in heaven[t] is my brother and sister
and mother.”

The Parable of the Sower

13:1–15pp — Mk 4:1–12; Lk 8:4–10
13:16,17pp — Lk 10:23,24
13:18–23pp — Mk 4:13–20; Lk 8:11–15

13 That same day Jesus went out
of the house[u] and sat by the
lake. 2Such large crowds gathered
around him that he got into a boat[v]
and sat in it, while all the people stood
on the shore. 3Then he told them many
things in parables, saying: “A farmer
went out to sow his seed. 4As he was
scattering the seed, some fell along the
path, and the birds came and ate it up.
5Some fell on rocky places, where it
did not have much soil. It sprang up
quickly, because the soil was shallow.
6But when the sun came up, the plants
were scorched, and they withered because
they had no root. 7Other seed fell
among thorns, which grew up and
choked the plants. 8Still other seed fell
on good soil, where it produced a
crop—a hundred,[w] sixty or thirty
times what was sown. 9He who has
ears, let him hear.”[x]
10The disciples came to him and
asked, “Why do you speak to the people
in parables?”
11He replied, “The knowledge of the
secrets of the kingdom of heaven[y] has
been given to you,[z] but not to them.
12Whoever has will be given more, and
he will have an abundance. Whoever
does not have, even what he has will be
taken from him.[a] 13This is why I
speak to them in parables:

> “Though seeing, they do not see;
> though hearing, they do not hear
> or understand.[b]

14In them is fulfilled[c] the prophecy of
Isaiah:

> “ ‘You will be ever hearing but
> never understanding;

12:45 [q] 2Pe 2:20
12:46 [r] Mt 1:18; 2:11,13,14,20; Lk 1:43; 2:33,34, 48,51; Jn 2:1,5; 19:25,26
[s] Mt 13:55; Jn 2:12; 7:3,5; Ac 1:14; 1Co 9:5; Gal 1:19
12:50 [t] Mt 6:10; Jn 15:14
13:1 [u] ver 36; Mt 9:28
13:2 [v] Lk 5:3
13:8 [w] Ge 26:12
13:9 [x] S Mt 11:15
13:11 [y] S Mt 3:2
[z] Mt 11:25; 16:17; 19:11; Jn 6:65; 1Co 2:10,14; Col 1:27; 1Jn 2:20, 27
13:12 [a] S Mt 25:29
13:13 [b] Dt 29:4; Jer 5:21; Eze 12:2
13:14 [c] ver 35; S Mt 1:22

[x] 43 Greek *unclean* [y] 47 Some manuscripts do not have verse 47.

12:43 AN EVIL SPIRIT. Vv. 43–45 teach three important truths concerning demon-possession. (1) Evil spirits desire to return to one formerly possessed (v. 44). (2) Evil spirits cannot return if that person’s heart is occupied by the Holy Spirit (v. 44; cf. 1Co 6:19; 2Co 6:15–16, note). (3) A whole nation or society may seek the pleasure of evil to such an extent that the society itself can become demon-possessed (v. 45; cf. Rev 16:14).

13:3 PARABLES OF THE KINGDOM. In ch. 13 we have the parables of the kingdom of heaven, describing both the results of preaching the gospel and the spiritual conditions that will prevail on earth within the visible manifestation of the kingdom of heaven (i.e., the churches) until the end of the age.

(1) In most of these parables, Christ teaches that there will be good and evil in his visible kingdom throughout the entire age. Among those who profess his name, there will be compromise and worldliness that lead to apostasy, as well as faithfulness and godliness that lead to eternal life. At the end of the age the wicked will be destroyed (vv. 41,49); “Then the righteous will shine like the sun in the kingdom of their Father” (v. 43).

(2) Christ speaks these parables in order to alert his true disciples to expect evil within the kingdom and to teach them how to overcome the influence and opposition of Satan and his followers. The only way to do so is through wholehearted devotion to Christ (vv. 44,46) and lives committed to righteousness (v. 43; see Rev 2–3 for examples of good and evil within the churches of the kingdom).

(3) Parables are stories from everyday life that relate and illustrate certain spiritual truths. Their uniqueness is found in revealing truth to those who are spiritual while at the same time concealing it from the unbeliever (v. 11). Parables may at times demand a decision (e.g., Lk 10:30–37).

13:3 FARMER WENT OUT TO SOW. See Mk 4:3, note.

13:12 WHOEVER HAS WILL BE GIVEN MORE. See 25:29, note; Mk 4:25, note.

you will be ever seeing but
never perceiving.
15For this people's heart has become
calloused;
they hardly hear with their ears,
and they have closed their eyes.
Otherwise they might see with
their eyes,
hear with their ears,
understand with their hearts
and turn, and I would heal
them.'[z][d]

16But blessed are your eyes because
they see, and your ears because they
hear.[e] 17For I tell you the truth, many
prophets and righteous men longed to
see what you see[f] but did not see it,
and to hear what you hear but did not
hear it.

18"Listen then to what the parable of
the sower means: 19When anyone
hears the message about the kingdom[g] and does not understand it, the
evil one[h] comes and snatches away
what was sown in his heart. This is the
seed sown along the path. 20The one
who received the seed that fell on
rocky places is the man who hears the
word and at once receives it with joy.
21But since he has no root, he lasts
only a short time. When trouble or persecution comes because of the word,
he quickly falls away.[i] 22The one who
received the seed that fell among the
thorns is the man who hears the word,
but the worries of this life and the deceitfulness of wealth[j] choke it, making it unfruitful. 23But the one who received the seed that fell on good soil is
the man who hears the word and understands it. He produces a crop, yielding a hundred, sixty or thirty times
what was sown."[k]

The Parable of the Weeds

24Jesus told them another parable:
"The kingdom of heaven is like[l] a
man who sowed good seed in his field.
25But while everyone was sleeping, his
enemy came and sowed weeds among
the wheat, and went away. 26When the
wheat sprouted and formed heads,
then the weeds also appeared.

27"The owner's servants came to
him and said, 'Sir, didn't you sow good
seed in your field? Where then did the
weeds come from?'

28" 'An enemy did this,' he replied.

"The servants asked him, 'Do you
want us to go and pull them up?'

29" 'No,' he answered, 'because
while you are pulling the weeds, you
may root up the wheat with them.
30Let both grow together until the harvest. At that time I will tell the harvesters: First collect the weeds and tie
them in bundles to be burned; then
gather the wheat and bring it into my
barn.' "[m]

13:15 [d] Isa 6:9, 10; Jn 12:40; Ac 28:26,27; Ro 11:8 **13:16** [e] Mt 16:17 **13:17** [f] Jn 8:56; Heb 11:13; 1Pe 1:10-12 **13:19** [g] Mt 4:23 [h] S Mt 5:37 **13:21** [i] Mt 11:6; 26:31
13:22 [j] Mt 19:23; 1Ti 6:9,10,17 **13:23** [k] ver 8 **13:24** [l] ver 31,33, 45,47; Mt 18:23; 20:1; 22:2; 25:1; Mk 4:26,30 **13:30** [m] Mt 3:12

[z] *15* Isaiah 6:9,10

13:19 EVIL ONE . . . SNATCHES AWAY. See Mk 4:15, note.

13:24–25 GOOD SEED . . . WEEDS. The parable of the wheat and weeds emphasizes that Satan will sow alongside those who sow the Word of God. The "field" represents the world, and the "good seed" represents the faithful of the kingdom (v. 38). (1) The gospel and true believers will be planted throughout the world (v. 38). Satan also will plant his followers, "the sons of the evil one" (v. 38), among God's people to counteract God's truth (vv. 25,38–39).

(2) The principal work of Satan's emissaries within the visible kingdom of heaven will be undermining the authority of God's Word (see Ge 3:4) and promoting unrighteousness and false doctrine (cf. Ac 20:29–30; 2Th 2:7,12). Christ later spoke of a great deception among his people because of these professed Christians who are really false teachers (see 24:11, note; see article on THE GREAT TRIBULATION, p. 1456).

(3) The condition of Satan's people existing among God's people will terminate with God's final destruction of all the wicked at the end of the age (vv. 38–43). For other parables emphasizing the mixed condition of believers with unbelievers, see 22:11–14; 25:1–30; Lk 18:10–14; see article on CHRIST'S MESSAGE TO THE SEVEN CHURCHES, p. 2008.

13:30 LET BOTH GROW TOGETHER. Concerning the growing together of Christ's true followers and Satan's children who masquerade as believers (v. 38; cf. 2Co 11:13–15), three points should be noted. (1) Throughout the age of the gospel such coexistence will occur. God will not command his angels to destroy the children of the evil one until the end of the age (vv. 30,38–41).

(2) The above parable does not contradict Biblical instructions found elsewhere that command believers to discipline sinning members and expel unrepentant and false members from their fellowship (see 18:15, note; Ac 20:28, note; 1Co 5:1, note). However, it must be understood that church discipline at its best will be only a partial solution to evil individuals in the kingdom. God and his angels will make the final separation.

(3) Faithful believers must always be alert to the subversive elements and individuals that Satan is planting within all parts of God's work. They will in many ways look like true children of God (see 2Co 11:13, note; see article on FALSE TEACHERS, p. 1506).

The Parables of the Mustard Seed and the Yeast

13:31,32pp — Mk 4:30–32
13:31–33pp — Lk 13:18–21

31 He told them another parable: "The kingdom of heaven is like[n] a mustard seed,[o] which a man took and planted in his field. 32 Though it is the smallest of all your seeds, yet when it grows, it is the largest of garden plants and becomes a tree, so that the birds of the air come and perch in its branches."[p]

33 He told them still another parable: "The kingdom of heaven is like[q] yeast that a woman took and mixed into a large amount[a] of flour[r] until it worked all through the dough."[s]

34 Jesus spoke all these things to the crowd in parables; he did not say anything to them without using a parable.[t] 35 So was fulfilled[u] what was spoken through the prophet:

"I will open my mouth in parables,
I will utter things hidden since
the creation of the
world."[b][v]

The Parable of the Weeds Explained

36 Then he left the crowd and went into the house. His disciples came to him and said, "Explain to us the parable[w] of the weeds in the field."

37 He answered, "The one who sowed the good seed is the Son of Man.[x] 38 The field is the world, and the good seed stands for the sons of the kingdom. The weeds are the sons of the evil one,[y] 39 and the enemy who sows them is the devil. The harvest[z] is the end of the age,[a] and the harvesters are angels.[b]

40 "As the weeds are pulled up and burned in the fire, so it will be at the end of the age. 41 The Son of Man[c] will send out his angels,[d] and they will weed out of his kingdom everything that causes sin and all who do evil. 42 They will throw them into the fiery furnace, where there will be weeping and gnashing of teeth.[e] 43 Then the righteous will shine like the sun[f] in the kingdom of their Father. He who has ears, let him hear.[g]

The Parables of the Hidden Treasure and the Pearl

44 "The kingdom of heaven is like[h] treasure hidden in a field. When a man found it, he hid it again, and then in his joy went and sold all he had and bought that field.[i]

45 "Again, the kingdom of heaven is like[j] a merchant looking for fine pearls. 46 When he found one of great value, he went away and sold everything he had and bought it.

The Parable of the Net

47 "Once again, the kingdom of heaven is like[k] a net that was let down into

13:31 [n] S ver 24 [o] Mt 17:20; Lk 17:6
13:32 [p] Ps 104:12; Eze 17:23; 31:6; Da 4:12
13:33 [q] S ver 24 [r] Ge 18:6 [s] Gal 5:9
13:34 [t] S Jn 16:25
13:35 [u] ver 14; S Mt 1:22 [v] Ps 78:2; Ro 16:25,26; 1Co 2:7; Eph 3:9; Col 1:26
13:36 [w] Mt 15:15
13:37 [x] S Mt 8:20
13:38 [y] Jn 8:44, 45; 1Jn 3:10
13:39 [z] Joel 3:13 [a] Mt 24:3; 28:20 [b] Rev 14:15
13:41 [c] S Mt 8:20 [d] Mt 24:31
13:42 [e] S Mt 8:12
13:43 [f] Da 12:3 [g] S Mt 11:15
13:44 [h] S ver 24 [i] Isa 55:1; Mt 19:21; Php 3:7, 8
13:45 [j] S ver 24
13:47 [k] S ver 24

[a] *33* Greek *three satas* (probably about 1/2 bushel or 22 liters) [b] *35* Psalm 78:2

13:31 A MUSTARD SEED. See Lk 13:19, note.

13:33 YEAST. See Lk 13:21, note.

13:41 WEED OUT ... EVERYTHING THAT CAUSES SIN. At the return of Christ to earth after the tribulation and at the end of the age (Rev 19:11–21), there will be a time of harvest of both the wicked and the righteous living on earth (vv. 30,40–42; see article on THE GREAT TRIBULATION, p. 1456). (1) The wicked are first gathered and taken out from among the righteous (vv. 30, 41,49). (2) The righteous are gathered next (vv. 30b,41–43,49); this gathering will be from "out of his kingdom." (3) After the harvest and the destruction of the wicked, "then the righteous will shine like the sun in the kingdom of their Father" (v. 43; cf. 25:31–34; see Rev 20:4, notes).

13:42 THE FIERY FURNACE. Jesus describes what will happen to all who cause sin and do evil (v. 41). They will be tormented with fire and experience great suffering (cf. Rev 14:9–11; 20:10). No one accepting the Bible as the Word of God can reject this doctrine. The wicked are not annihilated, but are thrown into "the fiery furnace" (see 10:28, note).

13:44–46 KINGDOM ... TREASURE. The parables of the hidden treasure and the pearl teach two truths: (1) The kingdom is a priceless treasure that is to be desired above all else. (2) The kingdom is to be acquired by giving up everything that would prevent our being part of it. "Selling all" means that we must transfer our whole heart from other interests to the one supreme interest, Christ (Ro 12:1).

13:47 KINGDOM ... A NET. The parable of the net reveals once again the truth Christ has so greatly emphasized: not all who are in the visible kingdom are truly children of God. Churches and Christian organizations are not synonymous with the true people of God, who consist of all believers living in true faith and righteousness (cf. 24:11,24; Gal 5:19–21; see Lk 13:21, note).

the lake and caught all kinds[l] of fish.
48When it was full, the fishermen
pulled it up on the shore. Then they sat
down and collected the good fish in
baskets, but threw the bad away.
49This is how it will be at the end of the
age. The angels will come and separate
the wicked from the righteous[m] 50and
throw them into the fiery furnace,
where there will be weeping and
gnashing of teeth.[n]
51"Have you understood all these
things?" Jesus asked.
"Yes," they replied.
52He said to them, "Therefore every
teacher of the law who has been instructed about the kingdom of heaven
is like the owner of a house who brings
out of his storeroom new treasures as
well as old."

A Prophet Without Honor

13:54–58pp — Mk 6:1–6

53When Jesus had finished these
parables,[o] he moved on from there.
54Coming to his hometown, he began
teaching the people in their synagogue,[p] and they were amazed.[q]
"Where did this man get this wisdom
and these miraculous powers?" they
asked. 55"Isn't this the carpenter's
son?[r] Isn't his mother's[s] name
Mary, and aren't his brothers[t] James,
Joseph, Simon and Judas? 56Aren't all
his sisters with us? Where then did this
man get all these things?" 57And they
took offense[u] at him.
But Jesus said to them, "Only in his
hometown and in his own house is a
prophet without honor."[v]
58And he did not do many miracles
there because of their lack of faith.

13:47 [l] Mt 22:10
13:49 [m] Mt 25:32
13:50 [n] S Mt 8:12
13:53 [o] S Mt 7:28
13:54 [p] S Mt 4:23 [q] S Mt 7:28
13:55 [r] Lk 3:23; Jn 6:42 [s] S Mt 12:46 [t] S Mt 12:46
13:57 [u] Jn 6:61 [v] Lk 4:24; Jn 4:44

John the Baptist Beheaded

14:1–12pp — Mk 6:14–29

14 At that time Herod[w] the tetrarch heard the reports about
Jesus,[x] 2and he said to his attendants,
"This is John the Baptist;[y] he has ris-
en from the dead! That is why miraculous powers are at work in him."
3Now Herod had arrested John and
bound him and put him in prison[z] because of Herodias, his brother Philip's
wife,[a] 4for John had been saying to
him: "It is not lawful for you to have
her."[b] 5Herod wanted to kill John, but
he was afraid of the people, because
they considered him a prophet.[c]
6On Herod's birthday the daughter
of Herodias danced for them and
pleased Herod so much 7that he promised with an oath to give her whatever
she asked. 8Prompted by her mother,
she said, "Give me here on a platter the
head of John the Baptist." 9The king
was distressed, but because of his
oaths and his dinner guests, he ordered that her request be granted
10and had John beheaded[d] in the prison. 11His head was brought in on a
platter and given to the girl, who carried it to her mother. 12John's disciples
came and took his body and buried it.[e]
Then they went and told Jesus.

Jesus Feeds the Five Thousand

14:13–21pp — Mk 6:32–44; Lk 9:10–17; Jn 6:1–13
14:13–21Ref — Mt 15:32–38

13When Jesus heard what had happened, he withdrew by boat privately to
a solitary place. Hearing of this, the
crowds followed him on foot from the
towns. 14When Jesus landed and saw a

14:1 [w] Mk 8:15; Lk 3:1,19; 13:31; 23:7,8; Ac 4:27; 12:1 [x] Lk 9:7-9
14:2 [y] S Mt 3:1
14:3 [z] Mt 4:12; 11:2 [a] Lk 3:19,20
14:4 [b] Lev 18:16; 20:21
14:5 [c] S Mt 11:9
14:10 [d] Mt 17:12
14:12 [e] Ac 8:2

13:49 SEPARATE THE WICKED FROM THE RIGHTEOUS. In the parable of the net, the separating of the wicked from the righteous at the end of the age is in the same order as that given in the parable of the weeds and wheat (vv. 30,41,43): all who do evil are gathered first and the righteous are gathered second (cf. Rev 19:11—20:4). This order clearly shows that the separation occurs at the end of the tribulation (24:29–31; Rev 19:11—20:4) and not at the rapture, at which time the faithful of Christ's churches are gathered from among the wicked (see 1Th 4:13–18; Rev 3:10). In this parable Christ again stresses that among God's people there will be many who are not truly loyal to him and his Word.

14:6 DANCED FOR THEM. The public dancing of an ungodly girl for Herod and his guests led to the death of one of the holiest of men. (1) Worldly parties, dancing and ungodly films lead to a forgetfulness of God, an inciting of passion, and a hardening of one's ability to discern sin, righteousness or judgment. In these things true children of God will not participate (see article on THE CHRISTIAN'S RELATIONSHIP TO THE WORLD, p. 1976).

(2) According to Scripture spontaneous dancing by Hebrew women and girls was done on exceptionally joyful occasions (cf. Jer 31:4), and especially after victory in battle as they sang to the Lord (Ex 15:19–21). There is no Scriptural record, however, that Jewish men danced with women, nor is there any indication that Jewish women ever danced publicly for an audience. The dancing of the daughter of Herodias at Herod's birthday party was a pagan practice.

large crowd, he had compassion on
them[f] and healed their sick.[g]
15As evening approached, the disciples came to him and said, "This is a
remote place, and it's already getting
late. Send the crowds away, so they
can go to the villages and buy themselves some food."
16Jesus replied, "They do not need to
go away. You give them something to
eat."
17"We have here only five loaves[h]
of bread and two fish," they answered.
18"Bring them here to me," he said.
19And he directed the people to sit
down on the grass. Taking the five
loaves and the two fish and looking up
to heaven, he gave thanks and broke
the loaves.[i] Then he gave them to the
disciples, and the disciples gave them
to the people. 20They all ate and were
satisfied, and the disciples picked up
twelve basketfuls of broken pieces that
were left over. 21The number of those
who ate was about five thousand men,
besides women and children.

Jesus Walks on the Water

14:22–33pp — Mk 6:45–51; Jn 6:15–21
14:34–36pp — Mk 6:53–56

22Immediately Jesus made the disciples get into the boat and go on ahead
of him to the other side, while he dismissed the crowd. 23After he had dismissed them, he went up on a mountainside by himself to pray.[j] When
evening came, he was there alone,
24but the boat was already a considerable distance[c] from land, buffeted by
the waves because the wind was
against it.
25During the fourth watch of the
night Jesus went out to them, walking
on the lake. 26When the disciples saw
him walking on the lake, they were terrified. "It's a ghost,"[k] they said, and
cried out in fear.
27But Jesus immediately said to
them: "Take courage![l] It is I. Don't be
afraid."[m]
28"Lord, if it's you," Peter replied,
"tell me to come to you on the water."
29"Come," he said.
Then Peter got down out of the boat,
walked on the water and came toward
Jesus. 30But when he saw the wind, he
was afraid and, beginning to sink, cried
out, "Lord, save me!"
31Immediately Jesus reached out his
hand and caught him. "You of little
faith,"[n] he said, "why did you doubt?"
32And when they climbed into the
boat, the wind died down. 33Then those
who were in the boat worshiped him,
saying, "Truly you are the Son of
God."[o]
34When they had crossed over, they
landed at Gennesaret. 35And when the
men of that place recognized Jesus,
they sent word to all the surrounding
country. People brought all their sick
to him 36and begged him to let the sick
just touch the edge of his cloak,[p] and
all who touched him were healed.

Tradition and God's Commands

15:1–20pp — Mk 7:1–23

15 Then some Pharisees and
teachers of the law came to
Jesus from Jerusalem and asked,
2"Why do your disciples break the tradition of the elders? They don't wash
their hands before they eat!"[q]
3Jesus replied, "And why do you

14:14 [f]S Mt 9:36 [g]S Mt 4:23
14:17 [h]Mt 16:9
14:19 [i]1Sa 9:13; Mt 26:26; Mk 8:6; Lk 9:16; 24:30; Ac 2:42; 20:7,11; 27:35; 1Co 10:16; 1Ti 4:4
14:23 [j]S Lk 3:21
14:26 [k]Lk 24:37
14:27 [l]Mt 9:2; Ac 23:11 [m]Da 10:12; Mt 17:7; 28:10; Lk 1:13,30; 2:10; Ac 18:9; 23:11; Rev 1:17
14:31 [n]S Mt 6:30
14:33 [o]Ps 2:7; S Mt 4:3
14:36 [p]S Mt 9:20
15:2 [q]Lk 11:38

[c]*24* Greek *many stadia*

14:19 LOAVES AND . . . FISH. The miracle of the feeding of the five thousand is recorded in all four Gospels (Mk 6:34–44; Lk 9:10–17; Jn 6:1–14). The significance of the miracle includes the following. (1) It points to Jesus as the bread of life (cf. Jn 6), the one who provides for both body and soul. (2) It is proof of the Lord's power to perform miracles. (3) It is an example of Jesus' compassion for needy people (v. 14; cf. Ex 34:6; Mic 7:18). (4) It teaches that the little we have can be made into much if put into the Lord's hands and blessed.

14:23 PRAY . . . ALONE. While on earth, Jesus often sought time to be alone with God (cf. Mk 1:35; 6:46; Lk 5:16; 6:12; 9:18; 22:41–42; Heb 5:7). Time alone with God is essential to the spiritual well-being of every believer. The lack of desire for solitary prayer to and communion with our heavenly Father is an unmistakable sign that the spiritual life within us is in a process of decline. If this is happening, we must turn from all that offends the Lord and renew our commitment to persevere in seeking God and his saving grace (see Lk 18:1, note).

14:27 DON'T BE AFRAID. In this life there are many things to fear, yet Jesus wants us to look to him and not be afraid. His words of encouragement are founded on his limitless power and intense personal love for all who truly belong to him. Often in Scripture, God or Jesus Christ encourages his people, "do not be afraid" (see, for example, Jos 1:9; 11:6; 2Ki 19:6; 2Ch 20:15; 32:7; Ne 4:14; Ps 49:16; 91:5; Isa 10:24; 37:6; 44:8; Mt 17:7; 28:10; Mk 5:36; Lk 12:4; Jn 14:1,27; Ac 18:9; 1Pe 3:14).

break the command of God for the sake
of your tradition? 4For God said, 'Hon-
or your father and mother'[d][r] and
'Anyone who curses his father or mother must be put to death.'[e][s] 5But you
say that if a man says to his father or
mother, 'Whatever help you might otherwise have received from me is a gift
devoted to God,' 6he is not to 'honor his
father[f]' with it. Thus you nullify the
word of God for the sake of your tradition. 7You hypocrites! Isaiah was right
when he prophesied about you:

8" 'These people honor me with
their lips,
but their hearts are far from me.
9They worship me in vain;
their teachings are but rules
taught by men.'[t][g][u]"

Clean and Unclean

10Jesus called the crowd to him and
said, "Listen and understand. 11What
goes into a man's mouth does not
make him 'unclean,'[v] but what comes
out of his mouth, that is what makes
him 'unclean.' "[w]
12Then the disciples came to him
and asked, "Do you know that the
Pharisees were offended when they
heard this?"
13He replied, "Every plant that my
heavenly Father has not planted[x] will
be pulled up by the roots. 14Leave
them; they are blind guides.[h][y] If a
blind man leads a blind man, both will
fall into a pit."[z]
15Peter said, "Explain the parable to
us."[a]
16"Are you still so dull?"[b] Jesus
asked them. 17"Don't you see that
whatever enters the mouth goes into
the stomach and then out of the body?
18But the things that come out of the
mouth come from the heart,[c] and
these make a man 'unclean.' 19For out
of the heart come evil thoughts, murder, adultery, sexual immorality, theft,
false testimony, slander.[d] 20These
are what make a man 'unclean';[e] but
eating with unwashed hands does not
make him 'unclean.' "

The Faith of the Canaanite Woman

15:21–28pp — Mk 7:24–30

21Leaving that place, Jesus withdrew to the region of Tyre and Sidon.[f]
22A Canaanite woman from that vicinity came to him, crying out, "Lord, Son
of David,[g] have mercy on me! My
daughter is suffering terribly from demon-possession."[h]
23Jesus did not answer a word. So
his disciples came to him and urged
him, "Send her away, for she keeps crying out after us."
24He answered, "I was sent only to
the lost sheep of Israel."[i]
25The woman came and knelt before
him.[j] "Lord, help me!" she said.
26He replied, "It is not right to take
the children's bread and toss it to their
dogs."
27"Yes, Lord," she said, "but even
the dogs eat the crumbs that fall from
their masters' table."
28Then Jesus answered, "Woman,
you have great faith![k] Your request is
granted." And her daughter was healed
from that very hour.

Jesus Feeds the Four Thousand

15:29–31pp — Mk 7:31–37
15:32–39pp — Mk 8:1–10
15:32–39Ref — Mt 14:13–21

29Jesus left there and went along the
Sea of Galilee. Then he went up on a
mountainside and sat down. 30Great
crowds came to him, bringing the lame,
the blind, the crippled, the mute and
many others, and laid them at his feet;
and he healed them.[l] 31The people
were amazed when they saw the mute
speaking, the crippled made well, the

15:4 [r] Ex 20:12; Dt 5:16; Eph 6:2 [s] Ex 21:17; Lev 20:9
15:9 [t] Col 2:20-22 [u] Isa 29:13; Mal 2:2
15:11 [v] S Ac 10:14,15 [w] ver 18
15:13 [x] Isa 60:21; 61:3
15:14 [y] Mt 23:16, 24; Ro 2:19 [z] Lk 6:39
15:15 [a] Mt 13:36
15:16 [b] Mt 16:9
15:18 [c] Mt 12:34; Lk 6:45; Jas 3:6
15:19 [d] Gal 5:19-21
15:20 [e] Ro 14:14
15:21 [f] S Mt 11:21
15:22 [g] S Mt 9:27 [h] S Mt 4:24
15:24 [i] Mt 10:6, 23; Ro 15:8
15:25 [j] S Mt 8:2
15:28 [k] S Mt 9:22
15:30 [l] S Mt 4:23

[d] *4* Exodus 20:12; Deut. 5:16 [e] *4* Exodus 21:17; Lev. 20:9 [f] *6* Some manuscripts *father or his mother* [g] *9* Isaiah 29:13 [h] *14* Some manuscripts *guides of the blind*

15:6 FOR THE SAKE OF YOUR TRADITION. Some Pharisees invalidated the commands of God for the sake of their traditions and the ideas of humans. Believers today must be on the alert that they do not "nullify the word of God" because of tradition, popular ideas or present-day cultural norms. To do so is to fall into this sin of the Pharisees and Jewish leaders (see Mk 7:8, note).

15:8 THEIR HEARTS ARE FAR FROM ME. See Mk 7:6, note.

15:11 THAT IS WHAT MAKES HIM 'UNCLEAN'. See Mk 7:18, note.

15:19 OUT OF THE HEART. See Mk 7:21, note.

15:28 YOU HAVE GREAT FAITH. To persevere in true faith is to trust God in all circumstances and remain true to him, even when you are in great trouble and he does not seem to answer or to care. This is "the test of faith" (Lk 18:1–7; 1Pe 1:7; see Mk 7:27, note).

Mk 2:3-12 lame walking and the blind seeing. And they praised the God of Israel.[m]

32Jesus called his disciples to him and said, "I have compassion for these people;[n] they have already been with me three days and have nothing to eat. I do not want to send them away hungry, or they may collapse on the way."

33His disciples answered, "Where could we get enough bread in this remote place to feed such a crowd?"

34"How many loaves do you have?" Jesus asked.

"Seven," they replied, "and a few small fish."

35He told the crowd to sit down on the ground. **36**Then he took the seven loaves and the fish, and when he had given thanks, he broke them[o] and gave them to the disciples, and they in turn to the people. **37**They all ate and were satisfied. Afterward the disciples picked up seven basketfuls of broken pieces that were left over.[p] **38**The number of those who ate was four thousand, besides women and children. **39**After Jesus had sent the crowd away, he got into the boat and went to the vicinity of Magadan.

The Demand for a Sign

16:1–12pp — Mk 8:11–21

16 The Pharisees and Sadducees[q] came to Jesus and tested him by asking him to show them a sign from heaven.[r]

2He replied,[i] "When evening comes, you say, 'It will be fair weather, for the sky is red,' **3**and in the morning, 'Today it will be stormy, for the sky is red and overcast.' You know how to interpret the appearance of the sky, but you cannot interpret the signs of the times.[s] **4**A wicked and adulterous generation looks for a miraculous sign, but none will be given it except the sign of Jonah."[t] Jesus then left them and went away.

The Yeast of the Pharisees and Sadducees

5When they went across the lake, the disciples forgot to take bread. **6**"Be careful," Jesus said to them. "Be on your guard against the yeast of the Pharisees and Sadducees."[u]

7They discussed this among themselves and said, "It is because we didn't bring any bread."

8Aware of their discussion, Jesus asked, "You of little faith,[v] why are you talking among yourselves about having no bread? **9**Do you still not understand? Don't you remember the five loaves for the five thousand, and how many basketfuls you gathered?[w] **10**Or the seven loaves for the four thousand, and how many basketfuls you gathered?[x] **11**How is it you don't understand that I was not talking to you about bread? But be on your guard against the yeast of the Pharisees and Sadducees." **12**Then they understood that he was not telling them to guard against the yeast used in bread, but against the teaching of the Pharisees and Sadducees.[y]

Peter's Confession of Christ

16:13–16pp — Mk 8:27–29; Lk 9:18–20

13When Jesus came to the region of Caesarea Philippi, he asked his disciples, "Who do people say the Son of Man is?"

14They replied, "Some say John the Baptist;[z] others say Elijah; and still others, Jeremiah or one of the prophets."[a]

15"But what about you?" he asked. "Who do you say I am?"

16Simon Peter answered, "You are the Christ,[j] the Son of the living God."[b]

17Jesus replied, "Blessed are you, Simon son of Jonah, for this was not revealed to you by man,[c] but by my Father in heaven.[d] **18**And I tell you that you are Peter,[k][e] and on this rock I will build my church,[f] and the gates

15:31 [m] S Mt 9:8 **15:32** [n] S Mt 9:36 **15:36** [o] S Mt 14:19 **15:37** [p] Mt 16:10 **16:1** [q] S Ac 4:1 [r] S Mt 12:38 **16:3** [s] Lk 12:54-56 **16:4** [t] Mt 12:39

16:6 [u] Lk 12:1 **16:8** [v] S Mt 6:30 **16:9** [w] Mt 14:17-21 **16:10** [x] Mt 15:34-38 **16:12** [y] S Ac 4:1 **16:14** [z] S Mt 3:1 [a] Mk 6:15; Jn 1:21 **16:16** [b] S Mt 4:3; Ps 42:2; Jer 10:10; Ac 14:15; 2Co 6:16; 1Th 1:9; 1Ti 3:15; Heb 10:31; 12:22 **16:17** [c] 1Co 15:50; Eph 6:12; Heb 2:14 [d] S Mt 13:11 **16:18** [e] Jn 1:42 [f] S Eph 2:20

[i] *2* Some early manuscripts do not have the rest of verse 2 and all of verse 3. [j] *16* Or *Messiah;* also in verse 20 [k] *18 Peter* means *rock.*

16:6 BE ON YOUR GUARD AGAINST THE YEAST. Here "yeast," a symbol of evil and corruption, refers to the teaching of the Pharisees and Sadducees. Christ calls their teaching "yeast" because even a small amount can penetrate and influence a large group of people to believe the wrong thing (see Mk 8:15, note).

16:18 PETER ... ROCK ... CHURCH. In these words Christ promises to build his church on the truth of Peter's and the other disciples' confession that Jesus is the Christ, the Son of the living God (v. 16; cf. Ac 2:14–26). Jesus uses a play on words here. He calls his disciple "Peter" (Gk *Petros,* meaning a small stone), but goes on to say,

THE CHURCH

Mt 16:18 "And I tell you that you are Peter, and on this rock I will build my church, and the gates of Hades will not overcome it."

The Greek word *ekklēsia* (church) refers to a meeting of a people called out and summoned together. In the NT it designates primarily the congregation of God's people in Christ, who come together as citizens of God's kingdom (Eph 2:19) for the purpose of worshiping God. The word "church" can refer to a local church (Mt 18:17; Ac 15:4) or the universal church (Mt 16:18; Ac 20:28; Eph 2:21–22).

(1) The church is presented as the people of God (1Co 1:2; 10:32; 1Pe 2:4–10), the company of redeemed believers made possible by Christ's death (1Pe 1:18–19). It is a pilgrim people no longer belonging to this earth (Heb 13:12–14), whose first function is to stand as a community in a living, personal relationship with God (1Pe 2:5; see Heb 11:6, note).

(2) The church is a people called out (Gk *ekkaleō*) of the world and into God's kingdom. Separation from the world is inherent to the church's nature and is rewarded by having the Lord as one's God and Father (2Co 6:16–18; see article on SPIRITUAL SEPARATION FOR BELIEVERS, p. 1794).

(3) The church is the temple of God and of the Holy Spirit (see 1Co 3:16, note; 2Co 6:14—7:1; Eph 2:11–22; 1Pe 2:4–10). This truth about the church demands separation from unrighteousness and from worldly immorality.

(4) The church is the body of Christ (1Co 6:15–16; 10:16–17; 12:12–27). This image indicates that no true church exists apart from vital union of the members with Christ. The head of the body is Christ (Eph 1:22; 4:15; 5:23; Col 1:18).

(5) The church is the bride of Christ (2Co 11:2; Eph 5:22–27; Rev 19:7–9). This marriage image emphasizes the devotion and faithfulness of the church to Christ, as well as Christ's love for and intimacy with his church.

(6) The church is a spiritual fellowship (Gk *koinōnia*) (2Co 13:14; Php 2:1). This involves the indwelling of the Spirit (Lk 11:13; Jn 7:37–39; 20:22), the unity of the Spirit (Eph 4:4) and the baptism in the Spirit (Ac 1:5; 2:4; 8:14–17; 10:44; 19:1–7). The fellowship is to demonstrate observable love and care for one another (Jn 13:34–35).

(7) The church is a spiritual ministry (Gk *diakonia*). It serves through the use of gifts (Gk *charismata*) bestowed by the Holy Spirit (Ro 12:6; 1Co 1:7; 12:4–11,28–31; Eph 4:11).

(8) The church is an army involved in spiritual conflict. It fights by the sword and power of the Spirit (Eph 6:17). The church is in a spiritual struggle against Satan and sin (see article on THE KINGDOM OF GOD, p. 1430). The Spirit, with which the church is filled, is like a warrior wielding the living Word of God, delivering people from Satan's dominion and conquering every power of this dark world (Ac 26:18; Eph 6:10–18; Heb 4:12; Rev 1:16; 2:16; 19:15,21).

(9) The church is the pillar and ground of the truth (1Ti 3:15), supporting the truth as a foundation supports a building. It must uphold the truth and keep it safe, defending it against distorters and false teachers (see Php 1:16, note; Jude 3, note).

(10) The church is a people with a future hope. This hope centers in Christ's return for his people (see Jn 14:3, note; 1Ti 6:14; 2Ti 4:8; Tit 2:13; Heb 9:28; see article on THE RAPTURE, p. 1864).

(11) The church is both invisible and visible. (a) The church invisible is the body of true believers united by their living faith in Christ (see article on FAITH AND GRACE, p. 1720). (b) The visible church consists of local congregations containing faithful overcomers (Rev 2:11,17,26; see 2:7, note) as well as those professed Christians who are false (Rev 2:2), "fallen" (Rev 2:5), spiritually "dead" (Rev 3:1) and "lukewarm" (Rev 3:16; see Mt 13:24, note; Ac 12:5, note on essential characteristics of a NT church).

of Hades[l] will not overcome it.[m] **19**I
will give you the keys[g] of the kingdom
of heaven; whatever you bind on earth
will be[n] bound in heaven, and whatever you loose on earth will be[n] loosed
in heaven."[h] **20**Then he warned his
disciples not to tell anyone[i] that he
was the Christ.

Jesus Predicts His Death

16:21–28pp — Mk 8:31–9:1; Lk 9:22–27

21From that time on Jesus began to
explain to his disciples that he must go
to Jerusalem[j] and suffer many
things[k] at the hands of the elders,
chief priests and teachers of the law,[l]
and that he must be killed[m] and on the
third day[n] be raised to life.[o]
22Peter took him aside and began
to rebuke him. "Never, Lord!" he
said. "This shall never happen to
you!"
23Jesus turned and said to Peter,
"Get behind me, Satan![p] You are a
stumbling block to me; you do not have
in mind the things of God, but the
things of men."

16:19 [g] Isa 22:22; Rev 3:7 [h] Mt 18:18; Jn 20:23
16:20 [i] S Mk 8:30
16:21 [j] S Lk 9:51 [k] Ps 22:6; Isa 53:3; Mt 26:67,68; Mk 10:34; Lk 17:25; Jn 18:22,23; 19:3 [l] Mt 27:1,2 [m] Ac 2:23; 3:13 [n] Hos 6:2; Mt 12:40; Lk 24:21,46; Jn 2:19; 1Co 15:3,4 [o] Mt 17:22,23; 27:63; Mk 9:31; Lk 9:22; 18:31-33; 24:6,7
16:23 [p] S Mt 4:10
16:24 [q] Mt 10:38; Lk 14:27
16:25 [r] S Jn 12:25
16:27 [s] S Mt 8:20 [t] S Lk 17:30; Jn 14:3; Ac 1:11; S 1Co 1:7; S 1Th 2:19; 4:16; S Rev 1:7; 22:7, 12,20 [u] 2Ch 6:23; Job 34:11; Ps 62:12; Jer 17:10; Eze 18:20; 1Co 3:12-15; 2Co 5:10; Rev 22:12

24Then Jesus said to his disciples,
"If anyone would come after me, he
must deny himself and take up his
cross and follow me.[q] **25**For whoever
wants to save his life[o] will lose it, but
whoever loses his life for me will find
it.[r] **26**What good will it be for a man
if he gains the whole world, yet forfeits
his soul? Or what can a man give in
exchange for his soul? **27**For the Son of
Man[s] is going to come[t] in his Father's glory with his angels, and
then he will reward each person according to what he has done.[u] **28**I tell
you the truth, some who are standing
here will not taste death before they
see the Son of Man coming in his kingdom."

[l] *18* Or *hell* [m] *18* Or *not prove stronger than it* [n] *19* Or *have been* [o] *25* The Greek word means either *life* or *soul*; also in verse 26.

"on this rock [Gk *Petra*, meaning a massive rock or a rocky cliff] I will build my church," i.e., he will build his church on Peter's solid confession.

(1) It is Jesus Christ who is the Rock, the first and great foundation of the church (1Co 3:11). Peter states in his first letter that Jesus is the "living Stone, . . . a chosen and precious cornerstone . . . the stone the builders rejected" (1Pe 2:4,6–7). At the same time, Peter and all other Christians are living stones who become part of the structure of the spiritual house that God is building (1Pe 2:5).

(2) Nowhere in Scripture is it stated that Peter would be the supreme and infallible authority above all other disciples (cf. Ac 15; Gal 2:11). Nor is it stated that Peter should have infallible successors who would represent Christ and function as the official head of the church.

For a discussion of the doctrine of the church as seen here and elsewhere in Scripture, see article on THE CHURCH, p. 1439.

16:18 THE GATES OF HADES WILL NOT OVERCOME IT. The "gates of Hades" represent Satan and all the world's evil striving to destroy the church of Jesus Christ. (1) This passage does not mean that any particular believer, local church, fellowship of churches, or denomination will never fall into immorality, doctrinal error or apostasy. Jesus himself predicted that many will fall from the faith, and he warns churches that are abandoning the NT faith to turn from their sins or face removal from his kingdom (24:10–11; Rev 2:5,12–29; 3:1–6,14–16; see 1Ti 4:1, note; see article on PERSONAL APOSTASY, p. 1918). The promise of v. 18 does not apply to either those who deny the faith or to lukewarm churches.

(2) What Christ means is that in spite of Satan doing his worst, apostasy occurring among believers, churches becoming lukewarm, and false teachers infiltrating God's kingdom, the church will not be destroyed. By his sovereign grace, wisdom and power, God will always have a remnant of believers and churches throughout redemptive history that will remain faithful to the original gospel of Christ and the apostles and who experience his fellowship, the lordship of Christ and the power of the Holy Spirit. As God's true people, they will demonstrate the kingdom power of the Holy Spirit against Satan, sin, disease, the world and the demonic. It is this church that Satan and all his host can never destroy or resist.

16:19 KEYS OF THE KINGDOM. The "keys" represent God's delegated authority to Peter and the church. By these keys they (1) rebuke sin and carry out church discipline (18:15–18); (2) pray effectively for God's cause on earth (18:19–20); (3) tie up the demonic and set free the captives (see article on POWER OVER SATAN AND DEMONS, p. 1484); (4) announce the guilt of sin, God's standard of righteousness and the judgment to come (Ac 2:23; 5:3,9); (5) proclaim salvation and the forgiveness of sin for all who repent and believe in Christ (Jn 20:23; Ac 2:37–40; 15:7–9).

16:24 TAKE UP HIS CROSS. See Mk 8:34, note.

16:28 COMING IN HIS KINGDOM. The "Son of Man coming in his kingdom" probably refers to the event of Pentecost when Christ baptized his followers with the Holy Spirit and great power (cf. Mk 9:1; Ac 1:8; 2:4).

The Transfiguration

17:1–8pp — Lk 9:28–36
17:1–13pp — Mk 9:2–13

17 After six days Jesus took with him Peter, James and John[v] the brother of James, and led them up a high mountain by themselves. **2**There he was transfigured before them. His face shone like the sun, and his clothes became as white as the light. **3**Just then there appeared before them Moses and Elijah, talking with Jesus.

4Peter said to Jesus, "Lord, it is good for us to be here. If you wish, I will put up three shelters—one for you, one for Moses and one for Elijah."

5While he was still speaking, a bright cloud enveloped them, and a voice from the cloud said, "This is my Son, whom I love; with him I am well pleased.[w] Listen to him!"[x]

6When the disciples heard this, they fell facedown to the ground, terrified. **7**But Jesus came and touched them. "Get up," he said. "Don't be afraid."[y] **8**When they looked up, they saw no one except Jesus.

9As they were coming down the mountain, Jesus instructed them, "Don't tell anyone[z] what you have seen, until the Son of Man[a] has been raised from the dead."[b]

10The disciples asked him, "Why then do the teachers of the law say that Elijah must come first?"

17:1 [v] S Mt 4:21
17:5 [w] S Mt 3:17
[x] Ac 3:22,23
17:7 [y] S Mt 14:27
17:9 [z] S Mk 8:30
[a] S Mt 8:20
[b] S Mt 16:21

11Jesus replied, "To be sure, Elijah comes and will restore all things.[c] **12**But I tell you, Elijah has already come,[d] and they did not recognize him, but have done to him everything they wished.[e] In the same way the Son of Man is going to suffer[f] at their hands." **13**Then the disciples understood that he was talking to them about John the Baptist.[g]

The Healing of a Boy With a Demon

17:14–19pp — Mk 9:14–28; Lk 9:37–42

14When they came to the crowd, a man approached Jesus and knelt before him. **15**"Lord, have mercy on my son," he said. "He has seizures[h] and is suffering greatly. He often falls into the fire or into the water. **16**I brought him to your disciples, but they could not heal him."

17"O unbelieving and perverse generation," Jesus replied, "how long shall I stay with you? How long shall I put up with you? Bring the boy here to me." **18**Jesus rebuked the demon, and it came out of the boy, and he was healed from that moment.

Mk 1:23-28

19Then the disciples came to Jesus in private and asked, "Why couldn't we drive it out?"

20He replied, "Because you have so little faith. I tell you the truth, if you have faith[i] as small as a mustard

17:11 [c] Mal 4:6; Lk 1:16,17
17:12 [d] S Mt 11:14
[e] Mt 14:3,10
[f] S Mt 16:21
17:13 [g] S Mt 3:1
17:15 [h] Mt 4:24
17:20 [i] S Mt 21:21

17:2 WAS TRANSFIGURED. See Lk 9:29, note.

17:17 UNBELIEVING AND PERVERSE. This text reflects Jesus' estimation of disciples and churches who fail to minister to others in the real power of God's kingdom (see article on THE KINGDOM OF GOD, p. 1430). (1) Failure to deliver those oppressed by Satan or demons (vv. 15–21) demonstrates a lack of faith, understanding and spiritual authority (vv. 17,20–21; Mk 9:29). (2) The Holy Spirit's purpose in recording the narratives in vv. 14–21 emphasizes not only that Jesus drove out demons, but also that he desires his disciples to do the same thing through faith (vv. 20–21; see article on POWER OVER SATAN AND DEMONS, p. 1484). Jesus is intensely disappointed and pained when his people fail to share in his ministry against the forces of Satan (see 10:1, note; 10:8; Mk 9:28–29; Lk 9:1; Jn 14:12, note).

17:20 FAITH . . . NOTHING WILL BE IMPOSSIBLE. Jesus frequently comments on the nature of true faith. He speaks of a faith that can move mountains, cause miracles and healing, and accomplish great things for God. Just what is this faith that Jesus speaks of? (1) True faith is an effective faith that produces results: "it will move" mountains.

(2) True faith is not a belief in "faith" as a force or power, but it is a "faith in God" (Mk 11:22).

(3) True faith is a work of God within the hearts of Christians (Mk 9:24; Php 2:13). It involves an awareness divinely imparted to our hearts that our prayers are answered (Mk 11:23). It is created within us by the Holy Spirit; we cannot produce it in our own minds (Ro 12:3; 1Co 12:9; see article on FAITH AND GRACE, p. 1720).

(4) Since true faith is a gift imparted to us by Christ, it is important to draw near to Christ and his Word and to deepen our commitment to, and confidence in, him (Ro 10:17; Php 3:8–15). We are dependent on him for everything; "apart from me you can do nothing" (Jn 15:5; see also Jn 3:27; Heb 4:16; 7:25). In other words, we must seek Christ as the author and perfecter of our faith (Heb 12:2). His close presence and our obedience to his Word are the source and the secret of faith (9:21; Jn 15:7).

(5) True faith is under God's control. Faith is given on the basis of his love, wisdom, grace and kingdom purpose. It is given to accomplish his will and to express his love for us. It is not to be used for our own selfish interest (Jas 4:3).

seed,[j] you can say to this mountain, 'Move from here to there' and it will move.[k] Nothing will be impossible for you.[p]"

Mt 21:21-22

22 When they came together in Galilee, he said to them, "The Son of Man[l] is going to be betrayed into the hands of men. 23 They will kill him,[m] and on the third day[n] he will be raised to life."[o] And the disciples were filled with grief.

The Temple Tax

24 After Jesus and his disciples arrived in Capernaum, the collectors of the two-drachma tax[p] came to Peter and asked, "Doesn't your teacher pay the temple tax[q]?"

25 "Yes, he does," he replied.

When Peter came into the house, Jesus was the first to speak. "What do you think, Simon?" he asked. "From whom do the kings of the earth collect duty and taxes[q]—from their own sons or from others?"

26 "From others," Peter answered.

"Then the sons are exempt," Jesus said to him. 27 "But so that we may not offend[r] them, go to the lake and throw out your line. Take the first fish you catch; open its mouth and you will find a four-drachma coin. Take it and give it to them for my tax and yours."

The Greatest in the Kingdom of Heaven

18:1–5pp — Mk 9:33–37; Lk 9:46–48

18 At that time the disciples came to Jesus and asked, "Who is the greatest in the kingdom of heaven?"

2 He called a little child and had him stand among them. 3 And he said: "I tell you the truth, unless you change and become like little children,[s] you will never enter the kingdom of heaven.[t] 4 Therefore, whoever humbles himself like this child is the greatest in the kingdom of heaven.[u]

5 "And whoever welcomes a little child like this in my name welcomes me.[v] 6 But if anyone causes one of these little ones who believe in me to sin,[w] it would be better for him to have a large millstone hung around his neck and to be drowned in the depths of the sea.[x]

7 "Woe to the world because of the things that cause people to sin! Such things must come, but woe to the man

17:20 [j] Mt 13:31; Lk 17:6 [k] 1Co 13:2
17:22 [l] S Mt 8:20
17:23 [m] Ac 2:23; 3:13 [n] S Mt 16:21 [o] S Mt 16:21
17:24 [p] Ex 30:13
17:25 [q] Mt 22:17-21; Ro 13:7
17:27 [r] Jn 6:61
18:3 [s] Mt 19:14; 1Pe 2:2 [t] S Mt 3:2
18:4 [u] S Mk 9:35
18:5 [v] Mt 10:40
18:6 [w] S Mt 5:29 [x] Mk 9:42; Lk 17:2

p 20 Some manuscripts *you.* [21] *But this kind does not go out except by prayer and fasting.*
q 24 Greek *the two drachmas*

18:1 WHO IS THE GREATEST. See Lk 22:24–30, note.

18:3 UNLESS YOU CHANGE. The change required by Jesus in conversion begins with becoming like little children—i.e., in being humble, unpretentious, dependent, weak and ready to be molded by the heavenly Father. Theologically, after the initial childlike step of humility, the conversion or change required by Jesus consists of two parts: radically turning away from everything that is ungodly, and turning to God and doing the works of righteousness (i.e., producing fruit in keeping with repentance; see 3:8, note).

(1) Conversion does not denote merely a single act of sorrow or penitence but an all-embracing attitude of life (see 2Co 7:10, note). This is necessary because by nature we follow a way of life that leads away from God and toward eternal death (Ro 1:18–32; Eph 2:2–3). Conversion is the human response to God's gift of salvation, accomplished by the grace and power of the Holy Spirit received through faith (Ac 11:18).

(2) Because of our new relation to God, conversion involves changes in the areas of relationships, habits, commitments, pleasures and our whole view of life. Conversion is a part of genuine saving faith and a basic requirement of salvation and sanctification (Ac 26:18).

18:6 MILLSTONE . . . AROUND HIS NECK. This verse means that whoever spiritually destroys a child or a childlike believer will incur the greatest wrath of Christ. (1) Pastors, teachers and especially parents should give special attention to these words of Christ. The parents' responsibility is to instruct their children in the ways of God (see Dt 6:1–9; Lk 1:17, note; Eph 6:4; 1Ti 4:16; see article on PARENTS AND CHILDREN, p. 1854) and to protect them from the influence of the world and Satan (Tit 1:10–11; 2:11–12; 1Jn 2:15–17). (2) Christian parents must not allow their children to be influenced by ungodly friends. They must be especially careful about what they allow the world to put into their children's minds and hearts by means of public education or the entertainment media (cf. Ps 101:3; Eph 6:4; Col 3:21).

18:7 WOE TO THE MAN. Jesus warns that those who are instrumental in placing sinful things before others and especially before children will receive the ultimate condemnation (vv. 2,5–7). (1) To place "things that cause people to sin" in the path of others—such as worldly entertainment, humanistic teaching, immoral films, pornographic literature, drugs, alcoholic beverages, wicked examples, false teaching and unrighteous companions—is to join oneself with Satan who is the great tempter (cf. 4:1; Ge 3:1–6; Jn 8:44; Jas 1:12). (2) The godly way of the faithful is to remove from the lives of our family, our homes, our churches and our own selves any and all things that might lead others into temptation and sin (vv. 7–9).

through whom they come![y] 8If your
hand or your foot causes you to sin,[z]
cut it off and throw it away. It is better
for you to enter life maimed or crippled
than to have two hands or two feet and
be thrown into eternal fire. 9And if your
eye causes you to sin,[a] gouge it out
and throw it away. It is better for you
to enter life with one eye than to have
two eyes and be thrown into the fire of
hell.[b]

The Parable of the Lost Sheep

18:12–14pp — Lk 15:4–7

10"See that you do not look down on
one of these little ones. For I tell you
that their angels[c] in heaven always
see the face of my Father in heaven.[r]
12"What do you think? If a man owns
a hundred sheep, and one of them wanders away, will he not leave the ninety-
nine on the hills and go to look for the
one that wandered off? 13And if he
finds it, I tell you the truth, he is happier about that one sheep than about the
ninety-nine that did not wander off.
14In the same way your Father in heav-
en is not willing that any of these little
ones should be lost.

A Brother Who Sins Against You

15"If your brother sins against
you,[s] go and show him his fault,[d] just
between the two of you. If he listens to
you, you have won your brother over.
16But if he will not listen, take one or
two others along, so that 'every matter
may be established by the testimony of
two or three witnesses.'[t][e] 17If he refuses to listen to them, tell it to the
church;[f] and if he refuses to listen
even to the church, treat him as you
would a pagan or a tax collector.[g]
18"I tell you the truth, whatever you
bind on earth will be[u] bound in heav-
en, and whatever you loose on earth
will be[u] loosed in heaven.[h]
19"Again, I tell you that if two of you

18:7 [y]Lk 17:1 **18:8** [z]S Mt 5:29 **18:9** [a]S Mt 5:29 [b]S Mt 5:22 **18:10** [c]Ge 48:16; Ps 34:7; Ac 12:11, 15; Heb 1:14

18:15 [d]Lev 19:17; Lk 17:3; Gal 6:1; Jas 5:19,20 **18:16** [e]Nu 35:30; Dt 17:6; 19:15; Jn 8:17; 2Co 13:1; 1Ti 5:19; Heb 10:28 **18:17** [f]1Co 6:1-6 [g]S Ro 16:17 **18:18** [h]Mt 16:19; Jn 20:23

[r] *10* Some manuscripts *heaven. 11The Son of Man came to save what was lost.* [s] *15* Some manuscripts do not have *against you.* [t] *16* Deut. 19:15 [u] *18* Or *have been*

18:10 ANGELS. Scripture teaches that God often takes care of his faithful by means of angels. These angels carry a sincere interest and love for God's children (cf. Ps 34:7; 91:11; Lk 15:10; 16:22; Heb 1:14; Rev 5:11–12; see article on ANGELS AND THE ANGEL OF THE LORD, p. 340).

18:15 IF YOUR BROTHER SINS. In vv. 15–17 Jesus sets forth the method of restoring or disciplining a professing Christian who sins against another member of the church in a private manner. To neglect Christ's instruction will bring spiritual compromise and ultimate destruction to the church as a holy people of God (cf. 1Pe 2:9; see Mt 5:13, note).

(1) The purpose of church discipline is to protect God's reputation (6:9; Ro 2:23–24), to guard the moral purity and doctrinal integrity of the church (1Co 5:6–7; 2Jn 7–11), and to attempt to save wayward members and restore them to full Christlikeness (1Co 5:5; Jas 5:19–20).

(2) The offender must first be dealt with and admonished in private. If he listens, he must be forgiven (v. 15). If the offender refuses to respond to his Christian brother (vv. 15–16), and after that to one or two members (v. 16) and finally to the local church, he must be treated as "a pagan," i.e., as one outside the kingdom of God, severed from Christ and fallen from grace (v. 17; cf. Gal 5:4). He has no right to church membership and must be removed from the fellowship of the church.

(3) This practice of the purity of the church is to operate not only in areas of sin and immorality, but also in cases of doctrinal heresy and unfaithfulness to the original and fundamental NT faith (see Gal 1:9, note; Jude 3, note; see articles on FALSE TEACHERS, p. 1506, and OVERSEERS AND THEIR DUTIES, p. 1690).

(4) Church discipline must be carried out in a spirit of humility, love, regret and self-examination (see 22:37, note; 2Co 2:6–7; Gal 6:1).

(5) Sins within the church involving sexual immorality must be dealt with according to 1Co 5:1–5 and 2Co 2:6–11. These types of grave sins require regret and mourning by the whole congregation (1Co 5:2), "punishment . . . sufficient" for the transgressor (2Co 2:6) and expulsion from the church (1Co 5:2,13). Later, after a period of evident repentance, the individual may be forgiven, receive a reaffirmation of love and be restored to fellowship (2Co 2:6–8).

(6) Sins of an elder, after being dealt with privately, must also involve public exposure and discipline, i.e., "rebuked publicly, so that the others may take warning" (Gal 2:11–18; 1Ti 5:19–20, note; see article on MORAL QUALIFICATIONS FOR OVERSEERS, p. 1882).

(7) Leaders within the church and pastors of local congregations do well to remember that they are charged to "keep watch over . . . all the flock" (see article on OVERSEERS AND THEIR DUTIES, p. 1690). The Lord will require of them a personal accounting of "the blood of all men" (Ac 20:26) who are lost because leaders failed to restore, discipline or expel according to God's will and purpose (cf. Eze 3:20–21; Ac 20:26–27; see Eze 3:18, note).

18:19 IF TWO . . . AGREE. There is great authority in corporate and agreeing prayer. The reason is that where two or three are gathered together in faith and commitment to Christ, he is in their midst (v. 20). His presence will impart faith,

on earth agree about anything you ask
for, it will be done for you[i] by my Father in heaven. 20For where two or
three come together in my name, there
am I with them."[j]

The Parable of the Unmerciful Servant

21Then Peter came to Jesus and
asked, "Lord, how many times shall I
forgive my brother when he sins
against me?[k] Up to seven times?"[l]
22Jesus answered, "I tell you,
not seven times, but seventy-seven
times.[v][m]
23"Therefore, the kingdom of heav-
en is like[n] a king who wanted to settle
accounts[o] with his servants. 24As he
began the settlement, a man who owed
him ten thousand talents[w] was
brought to him. 25Since he was not
able to pay,[p] the master ordered that
he and his wife and his children and all
that he had be sold[q] to repay the debt.
26"The servant fell on his knees before him.[r] 'Be patient with me,' he
begged, 'and I will pay back everything.' 27The servant's master took
pity on him, canceled the debt and let
him go.
28"But when that servant went out,
he found one of his fellow servants who
owed him a hundred denarii.[x] He
grabbed him and began to choke him.
'Pay back what you owe me!' he demanded.
29"His fellow servant fell to his
knees and begged him, 'Be patient with
me, and I will pay you back.'
30"But he refused. Instead, he went
off and had the man thrown into prison
until he could pay the debt. 31When the
other servants saw what had happened, they were greatly distressed
and went and told their master everything that had happened.

18:19 [i]S Mt 7:7
18:20 [j]S Mt 28:20
18:21 [k]S Mt 6:14 [l]Lk 17:4
18:22 [m]Ge 4:24
18:23 [n]S Mt 13:24 [o]Mt 25:19
18:25 [p]Lk 7:42 [q]Lev 25:39; 2Ki 4:1; Ne 5:5,8
18:26 [r]S Mt 8:2
18:35 [s]S Mt 6:14; S Jas 2:13
19:1 [t]S Mt 7:28
19:2 [u]S Mt 4:23
19:3 [v]Mt 5:31
19:4 [w]Ge 1:27; 5:2
19:5 [x]Ge 2:24; 1Co 6:16; Eph 5:31
19:7 [y]Dt 24:1-4; Mt 5:31

32"Then the master called the servant in. 'You wicked servant,' he said,
'I canceled all that debt of yours because you begged me to. 33Shouldn't
you have had mercy on your fellow servant just as I had on you?' 34In anger
his master turned him over to the jailers to be tortured, until he should pay
back all he owed.
35"This is how my heavenly Father
will treat each of you unless you forgive your brother from your heart."[s]

Divorce

19:1–9pp — Mk 10:1–12

19 When Jesus had finished saying
these things,[t] he left Galilee
and went into the region of Judea to the
other side of the Jordan. 2Large crowds
followed him, and he healed them[u]
there.
3Some Pharisees came to him to test
him. They asked, "Is it lawful for a man
to divorce his wife[v] for any and every
reason?"
4"Haven't you read," he replied,
"that at the beginning the Creator
'made them male and female,'[y][w] 5and
said, 'For this reason a man will leave
his father and mother and be united to
his wife, and the two will become one
flesh'[z]?[x] 6So they are no longer two,
but one. Therefore what God has joined
together, let man not separate."
7"Why then," they asked, "did Moses
command that a man give his wife a
certificate of divorce and send her
away?"[y]
8Jesus replied, "Moses permitted
you to divorce your wives because your
hearts were hard. But it was not this
way from the beginning. 9I tell you that
anyone who divorces his wife, except

[v] 22 Or *seventy times seven* [w] 24 That is, millions of dollars [x] 28 That is, a few dollars [y] 4 Gen. 1:27 [z] 5 Gen. 2:24

strength, direction, grace and consolation (cf. Ps 46:5; Isa 12:6).

18:35 UNLESS YOU FORGIVE. In this parable, Jesus teaches that the forgiveness of God, though freely given to repentant sinners, nevertheless remains conditional, according to a person's willingness to forgive others. In other words, one may forfeit God's forgiveness by maintaining a bitter and unforgiving heart (see 6:14–15; Heb 12:15; Jas 3:11,14; note especially Eph 4:31–32, where Paul maintains that bitterness, resentment and animosity are totally incompatible with the Christian profession and must be done away with).

19:9 FOR MARITAL UNFAITHFULNESS. God's will for marriage is one mate, one marriage for life (vv. 5–6; see Ge 2:24, note; SS 2:7, note; 4:12, note; Mal 2:14, note). To this Jesus gives an exception, namely, "marital unfaithfulness." Marital unfaithfulness (Gk *porneia*) includes adultery or any kind of sexual immorality (cf. 5:32). Therefore, divorce is to be permitted when sexual immorality is involved. The following are important Biblical facts concerning divorce. (1) When Jesus criticizes divorce in vv. 7–8, he is not criticizing a separation because of adultery, but a divorce permitted in the OT in those cases where a husband discovered premarital unchastity after the marriage ceremony had taken place (Dt

for marital unfaithfulness, and marries another woman commits adultery."[z]

10The disciples said to him, "If this is the situation between a husband and wife, it is better not to marry."

11Jesus replied, "Not everyone can accept this word, but only those to whom it has been given.[a] **12**For some are eunuchs because they were born that way; others were made that way by men; and others have renounced marriage[a] because of the kingdom of heaven. The one who can accept this should accept it."

The Little Children and Jesus

19:13–15pp — Mk 10:13–16; Lk 18:15–17

13Then little children were brought to Jesus for him to place his hands on them[b] and pray for them. But the disciples rebuked those who brought them.

14Jesus said, "Let the little children come to me, and do not hinder them, for the kingdom of heaven belongs[c] to such as these."[d] **15**When he had placed his hands on them, he went on from there.

The Rich Young Man

19:16–29pp — Mk 10:17–30; Lk 18:18–30

16Now a man came up to Jesus and asked, "Teacher, what good thing must I do to get eternal life[e]?"[f]

17"Why do you ask me about what is good?" Jesus replied. "There is only One who is good. If you want to enter life, obey the commandments."[g]

18"Which ones?" the man inquired.

Jesus replied, " 'Do not murder, do not commit adultery,[h] do not steal, do not give false testimony, **19**honor your father and mother,'[b][i] and 'love your neighbor as yourself.'[c]"[j]

20"All these I have kept," the young man said. "What do I still lack?"

21Jesus answered, "If you want to be perfect,[k] go, sell your possessions and give to the poor,[l] and you will have treasure in heaven.[m] Then come, follow me."

22When the young man heard this, he went away sad, because he had great wealth.

23Then Jesus said to his disciples, "I tell you the truth, it is hard for a rich man[n] to enter the kingdom of heaven. **24**Again I tell you, it is easier for a camel to go through the eye of a needle than for a rich man to enter the kingdom of God."

25When the disciples heard this, they were greatly astonished and asked, "Who then can be saved?"

26Jesus looked at them and said, "With man this is impossible, but with God all things are possible."[o] Mk 9:42-48

27Peter answered him, "We have left everything to follow you![p] What then will there be for us?"

28Jesus said to them, "I tell you the truth, at the renewal of all things, when the Son of Man sits on his glorious throne,[q] you who have followed me will also sit on twelve thrones, judging the twelve tribes of Israel.[r] **29**And everyone who has left houses or brothers or sisters or father or moth-

19:9 [z] S Lk 16:18
19:11 [a] S Mt 13:11; 1Co 7:7-9,17
19:13 [b] S Mk 5:23
19:14 [c] S Mt 25:34 [d] Mt 18:3; 1Pe 2:2
19:16 [e] S Mt 25:46 [f] Lk 10:25
19:17 [g] Lev 18:5
19:18 [h] Jas 2:11
19:19 [i] Ex 20:12-16; Dt 5:16-20 [j] Lev 19:18; S Mt 5:43
19:21 [k] Mt 5:48 [l] S Ac 2:45 [m] S Mt 6:20
19:23 [n] Mt 13:22; 1Ti 6:9,10
19:26 [o] Ge 18:14; Job 42:2; Jer 32:17; Lk 1:37; 18:27; Ro 4:21
19:27 [p] S Mt 4:19
19:28 [q] Mt 20:21; 25:31 [r] Lk 22:28-30; Rev 3:21; 4:4; 20:4

a *12* Or *have made themselves eunuchs*
b *19* Exodus 20:12-16; Deut. 5:16-20
c *19* Lev. 19:18

24:1–4). God's desire in such cases was that the two remain together. However, he permitted divorce due to premarital unchastity because of the hardness of the people's hearts (vv. 7–8).

(2) In the case of immorality after marriage, the OT law prescribed the dissolving of the marriage by executing both the offending parties (Lev 20:10; Dt 22:22). This, of course, would leave the innocent person free to remarry (Ro 7:2; 1Co 7:39).

(3) Under the new covenant the privileges of the believer are no less. Although divorce is a tragedy, marital unfaithfulness is such a cruel sin against one's mate that Christ states that the innocent party has a proper right to end the marriage by a divorce. He or she is free to remarry another believer (1Co 7:27–28).

(4) Paul's treatment of marriage and desertion in 1Co 7:12–16 indicates that a marriage also may be dissolved by the desertion of an unbelieving spouse. He further indicates that remarriage by the believer in such cases is not sin (see 1Co 7:15, note; 7:27–28).

19:13 LITTLE CHILDREN. See Mk 10:16, note.

19:21 GO, SELL YOUR POSSESSIONS. Jesus tested the rich young man at his weakest area, his wealth. He was not willing to put Christ above his possessions. Does Christ's statement mean that all believers should sell everything they own? No, for we must care for the needs of our families and others. However, we must be willing to give up anything that Christ asks of us. Our commitment to him can be nothing less.

19:23 A RICH MAN . . . THE KINGDOM. See article on RICHES AND POVERTY, p. 1562.

19:29 RECEIVE A HUNDRED TIMES. See Mk 10:30, note.

er[d] or children or fields for my sake
will receive a hundred times as much
and will inherit eternal life.[s] **30**But
many who are first will be last, and
many who are last will be first.[t]

The Parable of the Workers in the Vineyard

20 "For the kingdom of heaven is
like[u] a landowner who went
out early in the morning to hire men to
work in his vineyard.[v] **2**He agreed to
pay them a denarius for the day and
sent them into his vineyard.
3"About the third hour he went out
and saw others standing in the marketplace doing nothing. **4**He told them,
'You also go and work in my vineyard,
and I will pay you whatever is right.'
5So they went.
"He went out again about the sixth
hour and the ninth hour and did the
same thing. **6**About the eleventh hour
he went out and found still others
standing around. He asked them, 'Why
have you been standing here all day
long doing nothing?'
7" 'Because no one has hired us,'
they answered.
"He said to them, 'You also go and
work in my vineyard.'
8"When evening came,[w] the owner
of the vineyard said to his foreman,
'Call the workers and pay them their
wages, beginning with the last ones
hired and going on to the first.'
9"The workers who were hired about
the eleventh hour came and each received a denarius. **10**So when those
came who were hired first, they expected to receive more. But each one of
them also received a denarius. **11**When
they received it, they began to grumble[x] against the landowner. **12**'These
men who were hired last worked only
one hour,' they said, 'and you have
made them equal to us who have borne
the burden of the work and the heat[y]
of the day.'
13"But he answered one of them,
'Friend,[z] I am not being unfair to you.
Didn't you agree to work for a denarius? **14**Take your pay and go. I want to
give the man who was hired last the
same as I gave you. **15**Don't I have the
right to do what I want with my own
money? Or are you envious because I
am generous?'[a]
16"So the last will be first, and the
first will be last."[b]

Jesus Again Predicts His Death

20:17–19pp — Mk 10:32–34; Lk 18:31–33

17Now as Jesus was going up to Jerusalem, he took the twelve disciples
aside and said to them, **18**"We are going up to Jerusalem,[c] and the Son of
Man[d] will be betrayed to the chief
priests and the teachers of the law.[e]
They will condemn him to death **19**and
will turn him over to the Gentiles to be
mocked and flogged[f] and crucified.[g]
On the third day[h] he will be raised to
life!"[i]

A Mother's Request

20:20–28pp — Mk 10:35–45

20Then the mother of Zebedee's
sons[j] came to Jesus with her sons
and, kneeling down,[k] asked a favor of
him.
21"What is it you want?" he asked.
She said, "Grant that one of these
two sons of mine may sit at your right
and the other at your left in your kingdom."[l]
22"You don't know what you are asking," Jesus said to them. "Can you
drink the cup[m] I am going to drink?"
"We can," they answered.
23Jesus said to them, "You will indeed drink from my cup,[n] but to sit at

19:29 [s] Mt 6:33; S 25:46
19:30 [t] Mt 20:16; Mk 10:31; Lk 13:30
20:1 [u] S Mt 13:24 [v] Mt 21:28,33
20:8 [w] Lev 19:13; Dt 24:15
20:11 [x] Jnh 4:1
20:12 [y] Jnh 4:8; Lk 12:55; Jas 1:11
20:13 [z] Mt 22:12; 26:50
20:15 [a] Dt 15:9; Mk 7:22
20:16 [b] S Mt 19:30
20:18 [c] S Lk 9:51 [d] S Mt 8:20 [e] Mt 27:1,2
20:19 [f] S Mt 16:21 [g] S Ac 2:23 [h] S Mt 16:21 [i] S Mt 16:21
20:20 [j] S Mt 4:21 [k] S Mt 8:2
20:21 [l] Mt 19:28
20:22 [m] Isa 51:17,22; Jer 49:12; Mt 26:39,42; Mk 14:36; Lk 22:42; Jn 18:11
20:23 [n] Ac 12:2; Rev 1:9

[d] *29* Some manuscripts *mother or wife*

19:30 FIRST WILL BE LAST. The "first" are those who because of their wealth, education, status or talents are held in esteem by the world and sometimes even by the church. The "last" are those who are unknown and considered unimportant. In the age to come, "many" who were thought to be great leaders in the church will be given positions behind others, and many who were unknown will be exalted to glorious positions (cf. 1Co 15:41–42). This is because God values people not by outward appearance, but by the sincerity, purity and love of their hearts (1Sa 16:7). Read the stories of the poor widow (Mk 12:42–44) and Mary of Bethany (26:7–13) to see Christ's attitude toward the humble.

20:1 MEN TO WORK IN HIS VINEYARD. The parable of the workers in the vineyard teaches that entrance into God's kingdom is a matter of privilege, not merit. Christ here warns against three wrong attitudes: (1) Do not feel superior because of a fortunate position or assignment. (2) Do not fail to share God's concern in offering his grace to all. (3) Avoid the spirit of envy toward the spiritual blessings of others.

my right or left is not for me to grant.
These places belong to those for whom
they have been prepared by my Father."
24When the ten heard about this,
they were indignant[o] with the two
brothers. 25Jesus called them together
and said, "You know that the rulers of
the Gentiles lord it over them, and
their high officials exercise authority
over them. 26Not so with you. Instead,
whoever wants to become great among
you must be your servant,[p] 27and
whoever wants to be first must be your
slave— 28just as the Son of Man[q] did
not come to be served, but to serve,[r]
and to give his life as a ransom[s] for
many."

Two Blind Men Receive Sight

20:29–34pp — Mk 10:46–52; Lk 18:35–43

29As Jesus and his disciples were
leaving Jericho, a large crowd followed
him. 30Two blind men were sitting by
the roadside, and when they heard that
Jesus was going by, they shouted,
"Lord, Son of David,[t] have mercy on
us!"
31The crowd rebuked them and told
them to be quiet, but they shouted all
the louder, "Lord, Son of David, have
mercy on us!"
32Jesus stopped and called them.
"What do you want me to do for you?"
he asked.
33"Lord," they answered, "we want
our sight."
34Jesus had compassion on them
and touched their eyes. Immediately
they received their sight and followed
him.

The Triumphal Entry

21:1–9pp — Mk 11:1–10; Lk 19:29–38
21:4–9pp — Jn 12:12–15

21 As they approached Jerusalem
and came to Bethphage on the
Mount of Olives,[u] Jesus sent two disciples, 2saying to them, "Go to the village ahead of you, and at once you will
find a donkey tied there, with her colt
by her. Untie them and bring them to
me. 3If anyone says anything to you,
tell him that the Lord needs them, and
he will send them right away."
4This took place to fulfill[v] what
was spoken through the prophet:

5"Say to the Daughter of Zion,
'See, your king comes to you,
gentle and riding on a donkey,
on a colt, the foal of a
donkey.'"[e][w]

6The disciples went and did as Jesus
had instructed them. 7They brought
the donkey and the colt, placed their
cloaks on them, and Jesus sat on them.
8A very large crowd spread their
cloaks[x] on the road, while others cut
branches from the trees and spread
them on the road. 9The crowds that
went ahead of him and those that followed shouted,

"Hosanna[f] to the Son of David!"[y]

"Blessed is he who comes in the
name of the Lord!"[g][z]

"Hosanna[f] in the highest!"[a]

10When Jesus entered Jerusalem,
the whole city was stirred and asked,
"Who is this?"
11The crowds answered, "This is
Jesus, the prophet[b] from Nazareth in
Galilee."

Jesus at the Temple

21:12–16pp — Mk 11:15–18; Lk 19:45–47

12Jesus entered the temple area and

20:24 [o] Lk 22:24, 25
20:26 [p] S Mk 9:35
20:28 [q] S Mt 8:20 [r] Isa 42:1; Lk 12:37; 22:27; Jn 13:13-16; 2Co 8:9; Php 2:7 [s] Ex 30:12; Isa 44:22; 53:10; Mt 26:28; 1Ti 2:6; Tit 2:14; Heb 9:28; 1Pe 1:18,19
20:30 [t] S Mt 9:27
21:1 [u] Mt 24:3; 26:30; Mk 14:26; Lk 19:37; 21:37; 22:39; Jn 8:1; Ac 1:12
21:4 [v] S Mt 1:22
21:5 [w] Zec 9:9; Isa 62:11
21:8 [x] 2Ki 9:13
21:9 [y] ver 15; S Mt 9:27 [z] Ps 118:26; Mt 23:39 [a] Lk 2:14
21:11 [b] Dt 18:15; Lk 7:16,39; 24:19; Jn 1:21,25; 6:14; 7:40

[e] *5* Zech. 9:9 [f] *9* A Hebrew expression meaning "Save!" which became an exclamation of praise; also in verse 15 [g] *9* Psalm 118:26

20:26 NOT SO WITH YOU. In this world those who "lord it over" and "exercise authority" are considered great men and women. Jesus says that in the kingdom of God greatness will not be measured by authority over others, but by giving one's self in service. Believers must not try to reach the top in order to exert their authority or rule. Rather they must give their lives in helping others, and especially in laboring for the spiritual good of all people (v. 28; cf. Jn 13:34; 1Co 13; Col 3:14; 1Jn 3:14; 4:8).

20:28 RANSOM FOR MANY. Ransom conveys the meaning of a price paid to obtain the freedom of others. In the redemptive work of Christ, his death is the price paid for the release of men and women from sin's dominion (see article on BIBLICAL WORDS FOR SALVATION, p. 1710). The release is from condemnation (Ro 3:25–26), sin (Eph 1:7) and death (Ro 8:2). "Many" is used in the sense of "all people" (1Ti 2:5–6; see Ro 3:25, note on the meaning of the cross of Christ).

21:12 JESUS ... OVERTURNED THE TABLES. This is the second time that Jesus entered the temple and cleansed it from unrighteousness (for the temple cleansing at the beginning of his ministry, see Lk 19:45, note; Jn 2:13–22). Those

drove out all who were buying[c] and selling there. He overturned the tables of the money changers[d] and the benches of those selling doves.[e] 13“It is written,” he said to them, “ ‘My house will be called a house of prayer,’[h][f] but you are making it a ‘den of robbers.’[i]”[g]

14The blind and the lame came to him at the temple, and he healed them.[h] 15But when the chief priests and the teachers of the law saw the wonderful things he did and the children shouting in the temple area, “Hosanna to the Son of David,”[i] they were indignant.[j]

16“Do you hear what these children are saying?” they asked him.

“Yes,” replied Jesus, “have you never read,

“ ‘From the lips of children and
infants
you have ordained praise’[j]?”[k]

Lk 1:42-47

17And he left them and went out of the city to Bethany,[l] where he spent the night.

The Fig Tree Withers

21:18–22pp — Mk 11:12–14,20–24

18Early in the morning, as he was on his way back to the city, he was hungry. 19Seeing a fig tree by the road, he went up to it but found nothing on it except leaves. Then he said to it, “May you never bear fruit again!” Immediately the tree withered.[m]

20When the disciples saw this, they were amazed. “How did the fig tree wither so quickly?” they asked.

21Jesus replied, “I tell you the truth, if you have faith and do not doubt,[n] not only can you do what was done to the fig tree, but also you can say to this mountain, ‘Go, throw yourself into the sea,’ and it will be done. 22If you believe, you will receive whatever you ask for[o] in prayer.”

Mk 4:40

21:12 [c]Dt 14:26 [d]Ex 30:13 [e]Lev 1:14
21:13 [f]Isa 56:7 [g]Jer 7:11
21:14 [h]S Mt 4:23
21:15 [i]ver 9; S Mt 9:27 [j]Lk 19:39
21:16 [k]Ps 8:2
21:17 [l]Mt 26:6; Mk 11:1; Lk 24:50; Jn 11:1, 18; 12:1
21:19 [m]Isa 34:4; Jer 8:13
21:21 [n]Mt 17:20; Lk 17:6; 1Co 13:2; Jas 1:6
21:22 [o]S Mt 7:7

The Authority of Jesus Questioned

21:23–27pp — Mk 11:27–33; Lk 20:1–8

23Jesus entered the temple courts, and, while he was teaching, the chief priests and the elders of the people came to him. “By what authority[p] are you doing these things?” they asked. “And who gave you this authority?”

24Jesus replied, “I will also ask you one question. If you answer me, I will tell you by what authority I am doing these things. 25John’s baptism—where did it come from? Was it from heaven, or from men?”

They discussed it among themselves and said, “If we say, ‘From heaven,’ he will ask, ‘Then why didn’t you believe him?’ 26But if we say, ‘From men’—we are afraid of the people, for they all hold that John was a prophet.”[q]

27So they answered Jesus, “We don’t know.”

Then he said, “Neither will I tell you by what authority I am doing these things.

The Parable of the Two Sons

28“What do you think? There was a man who had two sons. He went to the first and said, ‘Son, go and work today in the vineyard.’[r]

29“ ‘I will not,’ he answered, but later he changed his mind and went.

30“Then the father went to the other son and said the same thing. He answered, ‘I will, sir,’ but he did not go.

31“Which of the two did what his father wanted?”

“The first,” they answered.

Jesus said to them, “I tell you the truth, the tax collectors[s] and the prostitutes[t] are entering the kingdom of God ahead of you. 32For John came to you to show you the way of righteousness,[u] and you did not believe

21:23 [p]Ac 4:7; 7:27
21:26 [q]S Mt 11:9
21:28 [r]ver 33; Mt 20:1
21:31 [s]Lk 7:29 [t]Lk 7:50
21:32 [u]Mt 3:1-12

[h]13 Isaiah 56:7 [i]13 Jer. 7:11
[j]16 Psalm 8:2

who bear Christ’s name must know that hypocrisy, greed, self-serving interest, immorality and irreverence in the house of God will bring God’s judgment and righteous indignation. Christ is Lord of his church and demands that it be a “house of prayer” (v. 13).

21:13 A HOUSE OF PRAYER. See Mk 11:17, note.

21:21 IF YOU HAVE FAITH. Jesus speaks of faith and prayer (v. 22), stating that answers to prayer are related to our faith. Everything that is in harmony with God’s will is possible to perform or receive for those who do not doubt (see 17:20, note; Mk 11:24, note; cf. 1Ki 17:1,7; 18:42–45; Lk 17:5–6; see article on EFFECTIVE PRAYING, p. 496). This does not exclude other variables in receiving answers to prayer (e.g., Da 10:12–14; Jas 4:3).

him, but the tax collectors[v] and the
prostitutes[w] did. And even after you
saw this, you did not repent[x] and believe him.

The Parable of the Tenants

21:33–46pp — Mk 12:1–12; Lk 20:9–19

33"Listen to another parable: There
was a landowner who planted[y] a vineyard. He put a wall around it, dug a
winepress in it and built a watchtower.[z] Then he rented the vineyard to
some farmers and went away on a journey.[a] **34**When the harvest time approached, he sent his servants[b] to the
tenants to collect his fruit.

35"The tenants seized his servants;
they beat one, killed another, and
stoned a third.[c] **36**Then he sent other
servants[d] to them, more than the first
time, and the tenants treated them the
same way. **37**Last of all, he sent his son
to them. 'They will respect my son,' he
said.

38"But when the tenants saw the
son, they said to each other, 'This is
the heir.[e] Come, let's kill him[f] and
take his inheritance.'[g] **39**So they took
him and threw him out of the vineyard
and killed him.

40"Therefore, when the owner of the
vineyard comes, what will he do to
those tenants?"

41"He will bring those wretches to a
wretched end,"[h] they replied, "and he
will rent the vineyard to other tenants,[i] who will give him his share of
the crop at harvest time."

42Jesus said to them, "Have you never read in the Scriptures:

" 'The stone the builders rejected
has become the capstone[k];
the Lord has done this,
and it is marvelous in our
eyes'[l]?[j]

43"Therefore I tell you that the kingdom of God will be taken away from
you[k] and given to a people who will
produce its fruit. **44**He who falls on this
stone will be broken to pieces, but he
on whom it falls will be crushed."[m][l]

45When the chief priests and the
Pharisees heard Jesus' parables, they
knew he was talking about them.
46They looked for a way to arrest him,
but they were afraid of the crowd because the people held that he was a
prophet.[m]

The Parable of the Wedding Banquet

22:2–14Ref — Lk 14:16–24

22 Jesus spoke to them again in
parables, saying: **2**"The kingdom of heaven is like[n] a king who prepared a wedding banquet for his son.
3He sent his servants[o] to those who
had been invited to the banquet to tell
them to come, but they refused to
come.

4"Then he sent some more servants[p] and said, 'Tell those who have
been invited that I have prepared my
dinner: My oxen and fattened cattle
have been butchered, and everything is
ready. Come to the wedding banquet.'

5"But they paid no attention and
went off—one to his field, another to
his business. **6**The rest seized his servants, mistreated them and killed
them. **7**The king was enraged. He sent
his army and destroyed those murderers[q] and burned their city.

8"Then he said to his servants, 'The
wedding banquet is ready, but those I
invited did not deserve to come. **9**Go to
the street corners[r] and invite to the
banquet anyone you find.' **10**So the servants went out into the streets and
gathered all the people they could find,
both good and bad,[s] and the wedding
hall was filled with guests.

11"But when the king came in to see
the guests, he noticed a man there who

21:32 [v]Lk 3:12, 13; 7:29 [w]Lk 7:36-50 [x]Lk 7:30 **21:33** [y]Ps 80:8 [z]Isa 5:1-7 [a]Mt 25:14,15 **21:34** [b]Mt 22:3 **21:35** [c]2Ch 24:21; Mt 23:34,37; Heb 11:36,37 **21:36** [d]Mt 22:4 **21:38** [e]Heb 1:2 [f]S Mt 12:14 [g]Ps 2:8 **21:41** [h]Mt 8:11, 12 [i]S Ac 13:46 **21:42** [j]Ps 118:22,23; S Ac 4:11 **21:43** [k]Mt 8:12

21:44 [l]S Lk 2:34 **21:46** [m]S ver 11, 26 **22:2** [n]S Mt 13:24 **22:3** [o]Mt 21:34 **22:4** [p]Mt 21:36 **22:7** [q]Lk 19:27 **22:9** [r]Eze 21:21 **22:10** [s]Mt 13:47, 48

[k] *42* Or *cornerstone* [l] *42* Psalm 118:22,23
[m] *44* Some manuscripts do not have verse 44.

21:33–44 THE TENANTS. This parable pictures Israel's rejection of God's beloved Son (cf. Mk 12:1, note; Lk 20:9).

21:43 KINGDOM . . . TAKEN AWAY FROM YOU. Israel rejects the Messiah and his kingdom. As a result, the kingdom of God and its power are given to others, to those who respond to the gospel, whether they are Jew or Gentile (1Pe 2:9). This principle is still in operation. The kingdom and its power will be taken away from those who fail to remain faithful to Christ, rejecting his righteous ways (Ro 11:19–22); instead, it will be given to a people who separate themselves from the world and seek first God's kingdom and righteousness (see 5:6; 6:33).

21:44 WILL BE BROKEN TO PIECES. See Lk 20:18, note.

22:11 WEDDING CLOTHES. Many who claim to be members of the kingdom of heaven on earth will not be wearing wedding clothes and therefore are not among the chosen (v. 14). The "wedding clothes" symbolize a condition of readiness—

was not wearing wedding clothes.
12'Friend,'[t] he asked, 'how did you
get in here without wedding clothes?'
The man was speechless.
13"Then the king told the attendants, 'Tie him hand and foot, and
throw him outside, into the darkness,
where there will be weeping and
gnashing of teeth.'[u]
14"For many are invited, but few are
chosen."[v]

Paying Taxes to Caesar

22:15–22pp — Mk 12:13–17; Lk 20:20–26

15Then the Pharisees went out and
laid plans to trap him in his words.
16They sent their disciples to him
along with the Herodians.[w] "Teacher,"
they said, "we know you are a man of
integrity and that you teach the way of
God in accordance with the truth. You
aren't swayed by men, because you pay
no attention to who they are. **17**Tell us
then, what is your opinion? Is it right
to pay taxes[x] to Caesar or not?"
18But Jesus, knowing their evil intent, said, "You hypocrites, why are
you trying to trap me? **19**Show me the
coin used for paying the tax." They
brought him a denarius, **20**and he
asked them, "Whose portrait is this?
And whose inscription?"
21"Caesar's," they replied.
Then he said to them, "Give to Caesar what is Caesar's,[y] and to God
what is God's."
22When they heard this, they were
amazed. So they left him and went
away.[z]

Marriage at the Resurrection

22:23–33pp — Mk 12:18–27; Lk 20:27–40

23That same day the Sadducees,[a]
who say there is no resurrection,[b]
came to him with a question. **24**"Teacher," they said, "Moses told us that if a
man dies without having children, his
brother must marry the widow and
have children for him.[c] **25**Now there
were seven brothers among us. The
first one married and died, and since he
had no children, he left his wife to his
brother. **26**The same thing happened to
the second and third brother, right on
down to the seventh. **27**Finally, the
woman died. **28**Now then, at the resurrection, whose wife will she be of the
seven, since all of them were married
to her?"
29Jesus replied, "You are in error because you do not know the Scriptures[d] or the power of God. **30**At the
resurrection people will neither marry
nor be given in marriage;[e] they will be
like the angels in heaven. **31**But about
the resurrection of the dead—have you
not read what God said to you, **32**'I am
the God of Abraham, the God of Isaac,
and the God of Jacob'[n]?[f] He is not the
God of the dead but of the living."
33When the crowds heard this, they
were astonished at his teaching.[g]

The Greatest Commandment

22:34–40pp — Mk 12:28–31

34Hearing that Jesus had silenced
the Sadducees,[h] the Pharisees got together. **35**One of them, an expert in the
law,[i] tested him with this question:
36"Teacher, which is the greatest commandment in the Law?"
37Jesus replied: " 'Love the Lord
your God with all your heart and with
all your soul and with all your

22:12 [t]Mt 20:13; 26:50
22:13 [u]S Mt 8:12
22:14 [v]Rev 17:14
22:16 [w]Mk 3:6
22:17 [x]Mt 17:25
22:21 [y]Ro 13:7
22:22 [z]Mk 12:12
22:23 [a]S Ac 4:1
[b]Ac 23:8; 1Co 15:12
22:24 [c]Dt 25:5,6
22:29 [d]Jn 20:9
22:30 [e]Mt 24:38
22:32 [f]Ex 3:6; Ac 7:32
22:33 [g]S Mt 7:28
22:34 [h]S Ac 4:1
22:35 [i]Lk 7:30; 10:25; 11:45; 14:3

[n] *32* Exodus 3:6

---

present possession of true faith in Christ and continued obedience made possible through the grace of Christ (cf. 24:44; 25:21). Christ refers to the man who was not wearing wedding clothes in order to make all of us examine ourselves and ask, "Lord, is it I?"

22:14 FEW ARE CHOSEN. The call to salvation goes out to the many. However, the few who are chosen to inherit the kingdom of heaven are those who respond to God's call, repent of their sins and believe in Christ. Responding to God's grace by the free exercise of our will brings us into the chosen people of God (see article on ELECTION AND PREDESTINATION, p. 1824).

22:30 PEOPLE WILL NEITHER MARRY. See Mk 12:25, note.

22:35 AN EXPERT IN THE LAW. An "expert in the law" (Gk *nomikos*) was an interpreter and teacher of the Law of Moses.

22:37 LOVE THE LORD YOUR GOD. What God asks of all those who believe in Christ and receive his salvation is devoted love (cf. Dt 6:5; Ro 13:9–10; 1Co 13). (1) This love requires an attitude of heart where God is so valued and esteemed that we truly long for his fellowship, strive to obey him, and sincerely care for his honor and will on earth. Those who truly love God will desire to share his suffering (Php 3:10), promote his kingdom (1Co 9:23), and live for his honor and righteous standards on earth (6:9–10,33).

(2) Our love for God must be a wholehearted and dominating love, a love inspired by his love for us whereby he gave his Son for our sake (see Jn 3:16, note; Ro 8:32). Our love is to be the kind of love

mind.'[o][j] **38**This is the first and greatest commandment. **39**And the second
is like it: 'Love your neighbor as yourself.'[p][k] **40**All the Law and the Prophets hang on these two command-
ments."[l]

Whose Son Is the Christ?

22:41–46pp — Mk 12:35–37; Lk 20:41–44

41While the Pharisees were gathered together, Jesus asked them,
42"What do you think about the
Christ[q]? Whose son is he?"

"The son of David,"[m] they replied.
43He said to them, "How is it then
that David, speaking by the Spirit,
calls him 'Lord'? For he says,

44" 'The Lord said to my Lord:
"Sit at my right hand
until I put your enemies
under your feet." '[r][n]

45If then David calls him 'Lord,' how
can he be his son?" **46**No one could say
a word in reply, and from that day on
no one dared to ask him any more
questions.[o]

The Sin of the Pharisees

23:1–7pp — Mk 12:38,39; Lk 20:45,46
23:37–39pp — Lk 13:34,35

23 Then Jesus said to the crowds
and to his disciples: **2**"The
teachers of the law[p] and the Pharisees sit in Moses' seat. **3**So you must
obey them and do everything they tell
you. But do not do what they do, for
they do not practice what they preach.
4They tie up heavy loads and put them
on men's shoulders, but they themselves are not willing to lift a finger to
move them.[q]

5"Everything they do is done for men
to see:[r] They make their phylacteries[s][s] wide and the tassels on their
garments[t] long; **6**they love the place
of honor at banquets and the most important seats in the synagogues;[u]
7they love to be greeted in the marketplaces and to have men call them 'Rabbi.'[v]

8"But you are not to be called 'Rabbi,' for you have only one Master and
you are all brothers. **9**And do not call
anyone on earth 'father,' for you have
one Father,[w] and he is in heaven.
10Nor are you to be called 'teacher,' for
you have one Teacher, the Christ.[q]
11The greatest among you will be your
servant.[x] **12**For whoever exalts himself will be humbled, and whoever
humbles himself will be exalted.[y]

Seven Woes

13"Woe to you, teachers of the law
and Pharisees, you hypocrites![z] You

22:37 [j]Dt 6:5
22:39 [k]Lev 19:18; S Mt 5:43
22:40 [l]Mt 7:12; Lk 10:25-28
22:42 [m]S Mt 9:27
22:44 [n]Ps 110:1; 1Ki 5:3; Ac 2:34, 35; 1Co 15:25; Heb 1:13; 10:13
22:46 [o]Mk 12:34; Lk 20:40
23:2 [p]Ezr 7:6,25
23:4 [q]Lk 11:46; Ac 15:10; Gal 6:13
23:5 [r]Mt 6:1,2,5, 16 [s]Ex 13:9; Dt 6:8 [t]Nu 15:38; Dt 22:12
23:6 [u]Lk 11:43; 14:7; 20:46
23:7 [v]ver 8; Mt 26:25,49; Mk 9:5; 10:51; Jn 1:38,49; 3:2,26; 20:16
23:9 [w]Mal 1:6; Mt 6:9; 7:11
23:11 [x]S Mk 9:35
23:12 [y]1Sa 2:8; Ps 18:27; Pr 3:34; Isa 57:15; Eze 21:26; Lk 1:52; 14:11
23:13 [z]ver 15,23, 25,27,29

[o]*37* Deut. 6:5 [p]*39* Lev. 19:18 [q]*42* Or *Messiah* [r]*44* Psalm 110:1 [s]*5* That is, boxes containing Scripture verses, worn on forehead and arm

---

expressed in Ro 12:1–2; 1Co 6:20; 10:31; 2Co 9:15; Eph 4:30; 5:1–2; Col 3:12–17.

(3) Love for God includes: (a) a personal attachment of allegiance and loyalty to him; (b) faith as a firm, unswerving adherence to the One to whom we are united by a Father-child relationship; (c) faithfulness to our commitment to him; (d) heartfelt devotion, expressed in our dedication to his righteous standards in the midst of a God-rejecting world; and (e) a desire for his presence and fellowship.

22:39 LOVE YOUR NEIGHBOR. Children of God are required to love all people (cf. Gal 6:10; 1Th 3:12), including their enemies (5:44). They are also commanded to love all true born-again Christians in a special way (see Jn 13:34, note; Gal 6:10; cf. 1Th 3:12; 1Jn 3:11). (1) The love of believers for their Christian brothers and sisters, their neighbors and their enemies must be subordinated to, and controlled and directed by, their love and devotion for God. (2) Love for God is the "first and greatest commandment" (vv. 37–38). Therefore, God's holiness, his desire for purity, and his will and standard as revealed in Scripture must never be compromised in our practice of love for all people.

23:13 WOE TO YOU . . . PHARISEES. Jesus' words in ch. 23 constitute his most severe denunciation. His words were directed against religious leaders and false teachers who had rejected at least a part of the revealed Word of God and replaced it with their own ideas and interpretations (vv. 23,28; 15:3,6–9; Mk 7:6–9). (1) The spirit of Jesus should be noted. It is not the tolerant, permissive and accommodative spirit of someone who is unconcerned about faithfulness to God and his Word. Jesus was not a weak preacher who tolerated sin. Being true to his calling caused him to be angry with evil (cf. 21:12–17; Jn 2:13–16) and to denounce sin and corruption in high places (vv. 23,25).

(2) Jesus' love for the inspired Scriptures of his Father, as well as his concern for those who were being destroyed by its distortion (see 15:2–3; 18:6–7; 23:13,15), was so great that it caused him to use words like "hypocrites" (v. 15), "son of hell" (v. 15), "blind guides" (v. 16), "fools" (v. 17), "greed and self-indulgence" (v. 25), "whitewashed tombs . . . unclean" (v. 27), "full of . . . wickedness" (v. 28), "snakes," "brood of vipers" (v. 33) and murderers (v. 34). These words, though severe and condemning, were spoken with a

shut the kingdom of heaven in men's
faces. You yourselves do not enter, nor
will you let those enter who are trying
to.[t][a]
15“Woe to you, teachers of the law
and Pharisees, you hypocrites! You
travel over land and sea to win a single
convert,[b] and when he becomes one,
you make him twice as much a son of
hell[c] as you are.
16“Woe to you, blind guides![d] You
say, ‘If anyone swears by the temple,
it means nothing; but if anyone swears
by the gold of the temple, he is bound
by his oath.’[e] 17You blind fools! Which
is greater: the gold, or the temple that
makes the gold sacred?[f] 18You also
say, ‘If anyone swears by the altar, it
means nothing; but if anyone swears
by the gift on it, he is bound by his
oath.’ 19You blind men! Which is greater: the gift, or the altar that makes the
gift sacred?[g] 20Therefore, he who
swears by the altar swears by it and by
everything on it. 21And he who swears
by the temple swears by it and by
the one who dwells[h] in it. 22And he
who swears by heaven swears by
God's throne and by the one who sits
on it.[i]
23“Woe to you, teachers of the law
and Pharisees, you hypocrites! You
give a tenth[j] of your spices—mint,
dill and cummin. But you have neglected the more important matters of the
law—justice, mercy and faithfulness.[k] You should have practiced the
latter, without neglecting the former.
24You blind guides![l] You strain out a
gnat but swallow a camel.
25“Woe to you, teachers of the law
and Pharisees, you hypocrites! You
clean the outside of the cup and dish,[m]
but inside they are full of greed and
self-indulgence.[n] 26Blind Pharisee!
First clean the inside of the cup and
dish, and then the outside also will be
clean.
27“Woe to you, teachers of the law
and Pharisees, you hypocrites! You are
like whitewashed tombs,[o] which look
beautiful on the outside but on the inside are full of dead men's bones and
everything unclean. 28In the same
way, on the outside you appear to people as righteous but on the inside
you are full of hypocrisy and wickedness.
29“Woe to you, teachers of the law
and Pharisees, you hypocrites! You
build tombs for the prophets[p] and decorate the graves of the righteous.
30And you say, ‘If we had lived in the
days of our forefathers, we would not
have taken part with them in shedding
the blood of the prophets.’ 31So you
testify against yourselves that you are
the descendants of those who murdered the prophets.[q] 32Fill up, then,
the measure[r] of the sin of your forefathers![s]
33“You snakes! You brood of vipers![t] How will you escape being condemned to hell?[u] 34Therefore I am
sending you prophets and wise men
and teachers. Some of them you will
kill and crucify;[v] others you will flog
in your synagogues[w] and pursue from
town to town.[x] 35And so upon you will

23:13 [a] Lk 11:52
23:15 [b] Ac 2:11; 6:5; 13:43 [c] S Mt 5:22
23:16 [d] ver 24; Isa 9:16; Mt 15:14 [e] Mt 5:33-35
23:17 [f] Ex 30:29
23:19 [g] Ex 29:37
23:21 [h] 1Ki 8:13; Ps 26:8
23:22 [i] Ps 11:4; Mt 5:34
23:23 [j] Lev 27:30 [k] Mic 6:8; Lk 11:42
23:24 [l] ver 16
23:25 [m] Mk 7:4 [n] Lk 11:39
23:27 [o] Lk 11:44; Ac 23:3
23:29 [p] Lk 11:47, 48
23:31 [q] S Mt 5:12
23:32 [r] 1Th 2:16 [s] Eze 20:4
23:33 [t] Mt 3:7; 12:34 [u] S Mt 5:22
23:34 [v] 2Ch 36:15,16; Lk 11:49 [w] S Mt 10:17 [x] Mt 10:23

[t] *13* Some manuscripts *to.* *14Woe to you, teachers of the law and Pharisees, you hypocrites! You devour widows' houses and for a show make lengthy prayers. Therefore you will be punished more severely.*

broken heart (v. 37) by One who died for those to whom they were addressed (cf. Jn 3:16; Ro 5:6,8).

(3) Jesus describes the character of false teachers and preachers as those ministers who seek to be popular, important and noticed by others (v. 5), who love honor (v. 6) and titles (v. 7), and who keep people out of heaven by their distorted gospel (v. 13; see article on FALSE TEACHERS, p. 1506). They are professional religionists who appear spiritual and godly, but are really unrighteous (vv. 14, 25–27). They speak well of godly spiritual leaders of the past, but do not follow their practices or their commitment to God and his Word and righteousness (vv. 29–30).

(4) The Bible commands believers to beware of such false religious leaders (7:15; 24:11), consider them to be unbelievers (see Gal 1:9, note) and refuse to support their ministry or have fellowship with them (2Jn 9–11).

(5) Those in the church who, in the name of love, toleration or unity, refuse to share Jesus' attitude toward those who distort the original teaching of Christ and the Scriptures (7:15; Gal 1:6–7; 2Jn 9), are participating in the evil deeds of false prophets and teachers (2Jn 10–11).

23:28 ON THE OUTSIDE ... RIGHTEOUS. Jesus continues his speech about religious leaders and ministers of his day whose public conduct appeared righteous but whose hearts were full of hypocrisy, pride, lust and wickedness. They were like painted tombs, beautiful and attractive on the outside, yet with foulness and corruption hidden inside. For more on what the Bible has to say about false teachers, see article on FALSE TEACHERS, p. 1506.

come all the righteous blood that has
been shed on earth, from the blood of
righteous Abel[y] to the blood of Zechariah son of Berekiah,[z] whom you murdered between the temple and the altar.[a] 36I tell you the truth, all this will
come upon this generation.[b]

Jesus' Sorrow for Jerusalem

37"O Jerusalem, Jerusalem, you who
kill the prophets and stone those sent
to you,[c] how often I have longed to
gather your children together, as a hen
gathers her chicks under her wings,[d]
but you were not willing. 38Look, your
house is left to you desolate.[e] 39For I
tell you, you will not see me again until
you say, 'Blessed is he who comes in
the name of the Lord.'[u]"[f]

23:35 [y]Ge 4:8; Heb 11:4 [z]Zec 1:1 [a]2Ch 24:21
23:36 [b]Mt 10:23; 24:34; Lk 11:50, 51
23:37 [c]2Ch 24:21; S Mt 5:12 [d]Ps 57:1; 61:4; Isa 31:5
23:38 [e]1Ki 9:7,8; Jer 22:5
23:39 [f]Ps 118:26; Mt 21:9

Signs of the End of the Age

24:1-51pp — Mk 13:1-37; Lk 21:5-36

24 Jesus left the temple and was
walking away when his disciples came up to him to call his attention to its buildings. 2"Do you see all
these things?" he asked. "I tell you the
truth, not one stone here will be left on
another;[g] every one will be thrown
down."

3As Jesus was sitting on the Mount
of Olives,[h] the disciples came to him
privately. "Tell us," they said, "when
will this happen, and what will be the
sign of your coming[i] and of the end of
the age?"[j]

4Jesus answered: "Watch out that no

24:2 [g]Lk 19:44
24:3 [h]S Mt 21:1 [i]S Lk 17:30 [j]Mt 13:39; 28:20

[u]39 Psalm 118:26

23:37 O JERUSALEM, JERUSALEM. See Lk 13:34, note; Lk 19:41, note.

23:39 YOU WILL NOT SEE ME AGAIN UNTIL. The city of Jerusalem repeatedly rejected Jesus' message. Therefore, in sorrow (vv. 37–38) Christ must withdraw and would not be seen by Israel again until they acknowledge their offense and call for the Messiah to come as their Deliverer. (1) This will occur only when Israel (i.e., a remnant, see Isa 6:13, note; 10:20, note; 17:7, note) experiences the dreadful days of the tribulation and are in their greatest peril (Hos 5:15—6:3; see article on THE GREAT TRIBULATION, p. 1456).

(2) When Israel experiences intense tribulation at the end of the age (Am 9:9), the nations of the world will gather against Jerusalem (Zec 12:1–4) and two-thirds of Israel will be killed (Zec 13:8–9). At the point when Israel is nearly destroyed, the remnant will turn in repentance and mourning (Isa 26:16–17; 64:1,6; Hos 5:15; Zec 12:4–5,10; Ro 11:26; see Rev 11:2, note; 12:6, note; see article on ISRAEL IN GOD'S PLAN OF SALVATION, p. 1730).

24:3—25:46 THE OLIVET DISCOURSE. Jesus' prophecy was primarily a reply to the disciples' question: "What will be the sign of your coming and of the end of the age?" Jesus gave them: (1) general signs of the course of the age leading up to the last days (24:4–14); (2) special signs to indicate the final days of the age, the great tribulation (24:15–28); (3) spectacular signs to occur at his triumphant coming with power and great glory (24:29–31); (4) admonition to tribulation saints to be alert to the signs leading up to Christ's expected coming immediately after the tribulation (24:32–35); (5) admonition to believers living before the tribulation to be spiritually ready for the unexpected and unknown time of Christ's coming for his faithful (24:36–51; 25:1–30; see Jn 14:3, note; see article on THE RAPTURE, p. 1864); (6) a description of the judgment of nations after his return to earth (25:31–46).

Note that many details of Christ's coming are not disclosed in Mt 24. Furthermore, no one has so far deciphered all the prophecies concerning the end time with complete certainty. There remains in Jesus' discourse an element of mystery requiring humility and a heart fixed on the Lord Jesus himself. We can expect additional unfolding of revelatory understanding at the time of the end (cf. Da 12:9).

24:4–51 JESUS ANSWERED. Jesus' words in the Olivet discourse are addressed to his disciples and to all of God's faithful people until the end of the age and his triumphant return to reign on earth. (1) Concerning believers living before the tribulation period, Christ tells them they cannot calculate or even estimate the time of his return for them (vv. 42–44). Therefore they must be ready at any time, for he will return to take them to heaven (i.e., his "Father's house," see Jn 14:2–3, notes) at a time when they do not think he will (see v. 44, note; see article on THE RAPTURE, p. 1864).

(2) For those converted to Christ during the great tribulation, they can know the time of his coming for them with a high degree of certainty, for Christ gives them signs by which to expect and know that his return is very near (vv. 15–29). When they see these signs they will "know that it is near, right at the door" (see v. 33, note).

24:4 SIGNS OF THE END OF THIS AGE. In vv. 4–14 Jesus gives the signs (cf. v. 3) that will characterize the whole course of the last days and that will intensify as the end draws nearer. (1) False prophets and religious compromisers within the visible church will increase and deceive many (vv. 4–5,11). (2) The increase of wars, famines and earthquakes (vv. 6–7) will be "the beginning of birth pains" (v. 8) of the new Messianic age. (3) As the end draws nearer, the persecution of God's people will become more severe (v. 9), and many will forsake their loyalty to Christ (vv. 9–10). (4) Violence, crime and disregard for God's law will increase rapidly, and natural love and family affection will decrease (v. 12; cf. Mk 13:12; 2Ti 3:3). (5) In spite of this intensification of trouble, the gospel will be preached in the whole world (v. 14).

one deceives you.[k] 5For many will
come in my name, claiming, 'I am the
Christ,[v]' and will deceive many.[l]
6You will hear of wars and rumors of
wars, but see to it that you are not
alarmed. Such things must happen, but
the end is still to come. 7Nation will
rise against nation, and kingdom
against kingdom.[m] There will be famines[n] and earthquakes in various
places. 8All these are the beginning of
birth pains.
9"Then you will be handed over to be
persecuted[o] and put to death,[p] and
you will be hated by all nations because of me.[q] 10At that time many will
turn away from the faith and will betray and hate each other, 11and many
false prophets[r] will appear and deceive many people.[s] 12Because of the
increase of wickedness, the love of
most will grow cold, 13but he who
stands firm to the end will be saved.[t]
14And this gospel of the kingdom[u]
will be preached in the whole world[v]
as a testimony to all nations, and then
the end will come.
15"So when you see standing in the

24:4 [k] S Mk 13:5 **24:5** [l] ver 11,23, 24; 1Jn 2:18 **24:7** [m] Isa 19:2 [n] Ac 11:28 **24:9** [o] Mt 10:17 [p] Jn 16:2 [q] S Jn 15:21 **24:11** [r] S Mt 7:15 [s] S Mk 13:5 **24:13** [t] S Mt 10:22 **24:14** [u] S Mt 4:23 [v] S Ro 10:18; Lk 2:1; 4:5; Ac 11:28; 17:6; Rev 3:10; 16:14

v *5* Or *Messiah;* also in verse 23

(6) The saved will be those who stand firm in their faith through all the end-time distress (v. 13). (7) The faithful, as they see the intensification of these signs, will know that the day of the Lord's return for them is "approaching" (Heb 10:25; see Jn 14:3, note).

24:5 MANY WILL ... DECEIVE MANY. This first major sign has special importance. Toward the end of this age religious deception will be rampant on the earth. Christ is so concerned that his followers be aware of the coming worldwide spiritual deception to occur just before the end that he repeats his warning twice more in the Olivet discourse (see v. 11, note; v. 24; see article on THE AGE OF THE ANTICHRIST, p. 1872).

24:9 YOU WILL BE HATED. All believers in Christ may expect trouble during their pilgrimage on earth. Suffering for Christ because of our loyalty to him and his Word is an intrinsic part of the Christian faith (cf. Jn 15:20; 16:33; Ac 14:22; Ro 5:3; see Mt 5:10, note; 2Ti 3:12, note).

24:11 MANY FALSE PROPHETS WILL APPEAR. As the last days draw to a close, false teachers and preachers will be exceedingly prevalent (see article on FALSE TEACHERS, p. 1506). Much of Christendom will be in an apostate condition. Those who are totally committed to the truth of God's Word and Biblical righteousness will be in the minority.

(1) Professing believers will accept "new revelation" even though it conflicts with the revealed Word of God. This will lead to opposition to Biblical truth within the churches (see 1Ti 4:1, notes; 2Ti 3:8; 4:3, note). Those who preach a distorted gospel may even gain strategic leadership positions in denominations and theological schools (see 7:22, note), enabling them to deceive and mislead many within the church (see Gal 1:9, note; 2Ti 4:3, note; 2Pe 3:3–4).

(2) Throughout the world millions will be involved in the occult, astrology, witchcraft, spiritism and Satanism. The influence of demons and evil spirits will multiply greatly (see 1Ti 4:1, note).

(3) Protection against being deceived is found in an enduring faith and love for Christ, in a commitment to the absolute authority of his Word (vv. 4,11,13,25) and in a thorough knowledge of that Word (see 1Ti 4:16, note).

24:12 INCREASE OF WICKEDNESS. An unbelievable increase in immorality, shamelessness, rebellion against God and a throwing off of moral restraint will characterize the last days. Sexual perversion, immorality, adultery, pornography, drugs, ungodly music and lustful entertainment will abound. It will be "as it was in the days of Noah" (v. 37), when the thoughts of human hearts were evil continually (see Ge 6:5). It will be as "in the days of Lot" (Lk 17:28,30), when homosexuality, lesbianism and all kinds of sexual perversion permeated society (see Ge 19:5, note; 1Ti 4:1, note; 2Ti 3:1–8, notes). Jesus goes on to indicate that true love will be in short supply.

24:14 THIS GOSPEL OF THE KINGDOM ... THE END. The end will come only after the "gospel of the kingdom" has been adequately preached in the whole world. (1) This "gospel of the kingdom" refers to the apostolic gospel preached in the power and righteousness of the Holy Spirit and accompanied by the major signs of the gospel (see article on THE KINGDOM OF GOD, p. 1430).

(2) Only God will know when this task is accomplished according to his purpose. The believer's task is to faithfully and continually press on "to all nations" till the Lord returns to take his church to heaven (see 28:19–20, notes; Jn 14:3, note; 1Th 4:13, note).

(3) Many interpreters believe "the end" refers to the time when "the dead in Christ will rise" and the faithful of Christ's churches "will be caught up together with them in the clouds to meet the Lord in the air" (1Th 4:16–17; see article on THE RAPTURE, p. 1864). Christ gives more details about his unexpected appearance for the faithful church in vv. 37–44.

24:14 THEN THE END WILL COME. Christ speaks to the disciples as though everything he predicts could be fulfilled within their generation. This, therefore, was the hope of the NT church. It must also be the hope of all who believe in Jesus Christ throughout the ages. We are to hope that the Lord will return and that the end of the age will occur in our generation (see 1Co 15:51, note). We must live in a tension between the imminency of Christ's coming and the fact that Christ has commanded us to keep on spreading the gospel.

24:15–28 THE GREAT TRIBULATION. This entire section deals with the great tribulation. For a study of this material, see article on THE

holy place[w] 'the abomination that
causes desolation,'[wx] spoken of
through the prophet Daniel—let the
reader understand— **16**then let those
who are in Judea flee to the mountains.
17Let no one on the roof of his house[y]
go down to take anything out of the
house. **18**Let no one in the field go back
to get his cloak. **19**How dreadful it will
be in those days for pregnant women
and nursing mothers![z] **20**Pray that
your flight will not take place in winter
or on the Sabbath. **21**For then there will
be great distress, unequaled from the
beginning of the world until now—and
never to be equaled again.[a] **22**If those
days had not been cut short, no one
would survive, but for the sake of the
elect[b] those days will be shortened.
23At that time if anyone says to you,
'Look, here is the Christ!' or, 'There he
is!' do not believe it.[c] **24**For false
Christs and false prophets will appear
and perform great signs and miracles[d] to deceive even the elect—if
that were possible. **25**See, I have told
you ahead of time.

26"So if anyone tells you, 'There he
is, out in the desert,' do not go out; or,
'Here he is, in the inner rooms,' do not
believe it. **27**For as lightning[e] that
comes from the east is visible even in
the west, so will be the coming[f] of the
Son of Man.[g] **28**Wherever there is a
carcass, there the vultures will gather.[h]

29"Immediately after the distress of
those days

" 'the sun will be darkened,
and the moon will not give its
light;
the stars will fall from the sky,
and the heavenly bodies will be
shaken.'[x][i]

30"At that time the sign of the Son
of Man will appear in the sky, and all
the nations of the earth will mourn.[j]
They will see the Son of Man coming
on the clouds of the sky,[k] with power
and great glory. **31**And he will send his
angels[l] with a loud trumpet call,[m]
and they will gather his elect from the
four winds, from one end of the heavens to the other.

32"Now learn this lesson from the fig
tree: As soon as its twigs get tender
and its leaves come out, you know that
summer is near. **33**Even so, when you
see all these things, you know that it[y]
is near, right at the door.[n] **34**I tell you
the truth, this generation[z] will certainly not pass away until all these

24:15 [w] S Ac 6:13 [x] Da 9:27; 11:31; 12:11
24:17 [y] 1Sa 9:25; Mt 10:27; Lk 12:3; Ac 10:9
24:19 [z] Lk 23:29
24:21 [a] Eze 5:9; Da 12:1; Joel 2:2
24:22 [b] ver 24,31
24:23 [c] Lk 17:23; 21:8
24:24 [d] Ex 7:11, 22; 2Th 2:9-11; Rev 13:13; 16:14; 19:20
24:27 [e] Lk 17:24 [f] S Lk 17:30
[g] S Mt 8:20
24:28 [h] Lk 17:37
24:29 [i] Isa 13:10; 34:4; Eze 32:7; Joel 2:10,31; Zep 1:15; Rev 6:12,13; 8:12
24:30 [j] Rev 1:7 [k] S Rev 1:7
24:31 [l] Mt 13:41 [m] Isa 27:13; Zec 9:14; 1Co 15:52; 1Th 4:16; Rev 8:2; 10:7; 11:15
24:33 [n] Jas 5:9

[w] *15* Daniel 9:27; 11:31; 12:11 [x] *29* Isaiah 13:10; 34:4 [y] *33* Or *he* [z] *34* Or *race*

GREAT TRIBULATION, p. 1456.

24:29 THE SUN WILL BE DARKENED. Immediately after the tribulation, there will occur spectacular cosmic signs that will precede the appearing of Christ and give clear warning of his return (v. 30). Christ's return to earth with power and great glory will not take by surprise any tribulation believer who heeds God's Word and observes the cosmic signs related to the sun, moon, stars and the shaking of the powers of the heavens (see Isa 13:6–13, note).

24:30 SON OF MAN COMING. This verse portrays Christ's appearing in the sky after the tribulation and the cosmic signs. He will come to judge the wicked (Rev 19:11—20:3), to deliver his faithful people and to establish righteousness on earth (Rev 20:4). All Christians, both the living and the dead who had been taken from the earth at the rapture (see Jn 14:3, note; see article on THE RAPTURE, p. 1864), will return with Christ at his coming with power and great glory (see Rev 19:14, note). The "sign" is probably Christ himself coming on the clouds of glory, surrounded by brilliant light.

24:31 GATHER HIS ELECT. When Jesus Christ returns to earth after the tribulation, the following events will take place: (1) God's judgment on the wicked (v. 30; Rev 19:11–21), the antichrist (Rev 19:20) and Satan (Rev 20:1–3); (2) the judgment and the separation of people on earth alive at Christ's coming (see 13:41, note; 25:32, note); (3) the gathering of the saints of all ages, including the saints already in heaven (cf. Mk 13:27; see Jn 14:3, note; Rev 19:14, note; 20:4,6) and those alive on earth at Christ's advent (see 13:40); (4) the thousand-year reign of Christ on earth (see Rev 20:4, notes).

24:32 THE FIG TREE. The coming out of the leaves of the fig tree (cf. Lk 21:29–31) refers to events occurring during the tribulation (vv. 15–29). Some interpret the fig tree to represent the restoration of Israel as a political state (cf. Hos 9:10; Lk 13:6–9).

24:33 ALL THESE THINGS. This refers to all the signs that will occur during the great tribulation (vv. 15–29), the pivotal sign being the "abomination that causes desolation" (v. 15; see article on THE GREAT TRIBULATION, p. 1456). As the prophetic events unfold, the tribulation faithful who search the Scriptures will "see all these things" and know that the Lord's return "is near, right at the door."

24:34 THIS GENERATION. "This generation" may refer to the generation that begins to see the intensification of the general signs of the age (vv. 4–14) that consummate with the signs of the tribulation (see v. 5, note), or it may refer to the Jewish people as a race.

THE GREAT TRIBULATION

***Mt 24:21** "For then there will be great distress, unequaled from the beginning of the world until now—and never to be equaled again."*

Beginning with Mt 24:15, Jesus speaks about special signs that will occur during the great tribulation (Rev 7:14; cf. "great distress" in Mt 24:21—the phrase in Greek is the same), signs to indicate that the end of the age is very near (Mt 24:15–29). These signs will lead up to and signal Christ's return to earth after the tribulation (Mt 24:30–31; cf. Rev 19:11—20:4).

The major sign is "the abomination that causes desolation" (Mt 24:15), a specific observable event that tells the faithful who are alive during the tribulation that Christ's coming to earth at the end of the age will occur very shortly. This visible sign-event refers primarily to the future desecration of the Jewish temple in Jerusalem by the antichrist (see Da 9:27, note; 1Jn 2:18; see article on THE AGE OF THE ANTICHRIST, p. 1872). The antichrist, or man of lawlessness, will set up an image of himself in God's temple, declaring himself to be God (2Th 2:3–4; Rev 13:14–15). The following are important facts concerning this pivotal event.

(1) The "abomination that causes desolation" will mark the beginning of the final stage of the tribulation, which culminates in Christ's return to earth and his judgment on the ungodly at Armageddon (Mt 24:21,29–30; see Da 9:27; Rev 19:11–21).

(2) By noting the time of this event ("So when you see" Mt 24:15), tribulation saints can know with a high degree of certainty when the tribulation will end and Christ will come to reign on earth (see Mt 24:33, note). The time span between this event and the end is given four times in Scripture as three and a half years, or 1,260 days (see Da 9:25–27; Rev 11:1–2; 12:6; 13:5–7; see Da 9:25–27, note).

(3) Because of this strong expectancy of Christ's coming (Mt 24:33), the faithful must be aware that any report that Christ has returned is deceptive (Mt 24:23–27). The "coming of the Son of Man" after the tribulation will be observable and known to all who are in the world (Mt 24:27–30).

Another sign will be the appearance of false prophets who, as ministers of Satan, will perform "great signs and miracles" (Mt 24:24).

(1) Jesus admonishes all believers to be especially alert for these professed Christian prophets, teachers and preachers who are, in reality, false, and yet who perform miracles, healings, signs and wonders and who appear to have great success in their ministries. At the same time, these false prophets will distort and reject the truth found in God's Word (see Mt 7:22, note; Gal 1:9, note; see article on THE AGE OF THE ANTICHRIST, p. 1872).

(2) Elsewhere Scripture urges believers to continually test the spirit energizing all teachers, leaders and preachers (see 1Jn 4:1, note). God allows deception accompanied by miracles in order to test believers as to their love for him and their loyalty to the truth of Scripture (see Dt 13:3). This period of deception will not be easy, for Jesus states in Mt 24:24 that during the last days religious deceit will be so widespread that it will be difficult even for "the elect" (i.e., committed Christians) to discern truth from error (see 1Ti 4:16, note; Jas 1:21, note; see article on ELECTION AND PREDESTINATION, p. 1824).

(3) Those among God's people who do not love the truth will be deceived. They will be given no further opportunity to believe the truth of the gospel after the antichrist comes (see 2Th 2:11, note).

Finally, the great tribulation will be a specific period of terrible suffering and distress for all the people in the world. Observe:

(1) It will be worldwide (see Rev 3:10, note). (2) It will be the worst time of affliction and distress ever to occur in the history of humanity (Da 12:1; Mt 24:21). (3) It will be a terrible time of suffering for the Jews (Jer 30:5–7). (4) The period will be dominated by the "man of lawlessness" (i.e., antichrist; cf. Da 9:27; Rev 13:12; see article on THE AGE OF THE ANTICHRIST, p. 1872). (5) The faithful of Christ's churches are promised deliverance and "escape" from the tribulation time (see Lk 21:36, note; 1Th 5:8–10; Rev 3:10, note). (6) During this time, there will be both Jews and Gentiles who believe in Jesus Christ and are saved (Dt 4:30–31; Hos 5:15; Rev 7:9–17; 14:6–7). (7) It will be a time of great suffering and dreadful persecution for all who remain faithful to God (Rev 12:17; 13:15). (8) It will be a time of God's wrath and judgment upon the ungodly (1Th 5:1–11; Rev 6:16–17). (9) Jesus' statement that those days will be shortened (Mt 24:22) must not be understood to imply that there will be any reduction of the predicted three and a half years or 1,260 days. Rather, it seems to refer to the fact that the period is so awful that if it were not confined to a limited period of time, the whole human race would be destroyed. (10) The great tribulation will end with the coming of Jesus Christ in glory with his bride (Rev 19:7–8,14) to bring deliverance to the faithful and judgment and destruction to the wicked (Eze 20:34–38; Mt 24:29–31; Lk 19:11–27; Rev 19:11–21). (11) We must not confuse this coming at the end of the great tribulation with Jesus' reference to his unexpected descent from heaven in Mt 24:42,44 (see notes on those verses, which demonstrate that this coming refers to the rapture of believers occurring at a time different from that of Christ's final return at the end of the tribulation). (12) The major Scripture passage describing the whole seven-year tribulation is found in Rev 6–18.

things have happened.[o] 35Heaven and
earth will pass away, but my words will
never pass away.[p]

The Unexpected Coming of the Son of Man

24:37–39pp — Lk 17:26,27
24:45–51pp — Lk 12:42–46

36"No one knows about that day or
hour, not even the angels in heaven,
nor the Son,[a] but only the Father.[q]
37As it was in the days of Noah,[r] so
it will be at the coming of the Son of
Man. 38For in the days before the flood,
people were eating and drinking, marrying and giving in marriage,[s] up to
the day Noah entered the ark; 39and
they knew nothing about what would
happen until the flood came and took
them all away. That is how it will be at
the coming of the Son of Man.[t] 40Two
men will be in the field; one will be tak-
en and the other left.[u] 41Two women
will be grinding with a hand mill; one
will be taken and the other left.[v]
42"Therefore keep watch, because
you do not know on what day your Lord

24:34 [o] Mt 16:28; S 23:36
24:35 [p] S Mt 5:18
24:36 [q] Ac 1:7
24:37 [r] Ge 6:5; 7:6-23
24:38 [s] Mt 22:30
24:39 [t] S Lk 17:30
24:40 [u] Lk 17:34
24:41 [v] Lk 17:35

[a] *36* Some manuscripts do not have *nor the Son.*

24:36 ONLY THE FATHER. This verse speaks of only the Father knowing the time of Christ's return. We must understand this as referring to the time when Christ was on earth. Certainly now Jesus, who has returned to his former glory (Jn 17:5), has future knowledge of his return. Tribulation saints can also know the time of his final return by observing the signs of the tribulation that Christ described (see article on THE GREAT TRIBULATION, p. 1456).

24:37 THE COMING OF THE SON OF MAN. Jesus' statements concerning "the coming of the Son of Man" have a double reference: to the first stage of his return at an unknown and unexpected time (i.e., the rapture of the church saints: see v. 42, notes; Jn 14:3, note; Rev 3:10, note; see article on THE RAPTURE, p. 1864), and to the second stage of his coming after the tribulation, when he will destroy the wicked and gather all the righteous into his kingdom (Rev 19:11—20:4). We encounter this double reference when Christ describes three different categories of people in his illustration of "the days of Noah" (vv. 37–44). These three categories and their relation to Christ's coming are as follows:

(1) The tribulation unbelievers, represented by the flood victims of Noah's day. They do not know the time of Christ's return, are unprepared and are thus destroyed at the end time (vv. 38–39,43; cf. Lk 17:26–28). This is the second stage of his return, the one occurring after the tribulation.

(2) The tribulation believers, represented by Noah. Because of the signs of the end time, tribulation saints know almost the precise time of the Lord's return and are prepared and saved. Christ returns for them at the expected time (v. 27; cf. Ge 7:4; see article on THE GREAT TRIBULATION, p. 1456). This too refers to the second stage of Christ's return.

(3) Present-day believers or church saints living before the tribulation, represented by Jesus' disciples. They will not know the time of Christ's return to take them to heaven (vv. 42,44; see Jn 14:3, note; cf. 1Th 4:14). There will be no definite signs preceding the Lord's return for them, for Christ states that it will occur unexpectedly (vv. 42,44). Notice that Jesus likens the disciples (i.e., church saints) not to Noah (i.e., tribulation believers) but to the flood victims (compare "they knew nothing," v. 39, with "you do not know," v. 42). That is, the church saints will be like the flood victims in one sense: they will not know the time of Christ's return for them and will be surprised when he comes, just as the flood victims did not know the time of the flood and were surprised when it came. Therefore, church saints must be ready at any time (v. 44).

24:40 ONE ... TAKEN ... THE OTHER LEFT. Christ's statement that "one will be taken and the other left" comes before his exhortation to church saints (vv. 42–44). Therefore, these words likely refer to church saints who are taken out from among the wicked when Christ calls the faithful to himself at the rapture (see Jn 14:3, note; see article on THE RAPTURE, p. 1864). He emphasizes the surprise element for the church believers (see v. 37, note).

24:42 THEREFORE KEEP WATCH. "Keep watch" (Gk *grēgoreō*) is a present imperative, indicating a constant vigil at the present time. The reason for this vigil today instead of only in the future is that present-day believers do not know when the Lord will come for them (see Jn 14:3, note). There will be no warning signs, and they may never assume that he cannot come today. In other words, they must be committed to the historical possibility of Christ returning at any time (see v. 44, note; cf. Mk 13:33–37). His return for the church is possible any day.

24:42 YOU DO NOT KNOW ON WHAT DAY. Christ's warning that his disciples must always be ready must be understood as referring to his return from heaven to take church saints out of the world, i.e., the rapture (see Jn 14:3, note; see article on THE RAPTURE, p. 1864). (1) Jesus explicitly states that his coming for the saints living before the tribulation will be at an unexpected time and without warning. He declares that they not only "do not know" the time, but that he will return at a time when they "do not expect him" (v. 44). This clearly points to an element of surprise, amazement and unexpectedness for the faithful at this particular return of Christ. This is sometimes referred to as the first stage of Christ's second coming.

(2) With regard to Christ's coming with power and glory to judge the world after the tribulation (v. 30; Rev 19:11–21), his coming will be expect-

will come.[w] **43**But understand this: If
the owner of the house had known at
what time of night the thief was coming,[x] he would have kept watch and
would not have let his house be broken
into. **44**So you also must be ready,[y]
because the Son of Man will come at an
hour when you do not expect him.
45"Who then is the faithful and wise
servant,[z] whom the master has put in
charge of the servants in his household
to give them their food at the proper
time? **46**It will be good for that servant
whose master finds him doing so when
he returns.[a] **47**I tell you the truth, he
will put him in charge of all his possessions.[b] **48**But suppose that servant is
wicked and says to himself, 'My master is staying away a long time,' **49**and
he then begins to beat his fellow servants and to eat and drink with drunkards.[c] **50**The master of that servant
will come on a day when he does not
expect him and at an hour he is not
aware of. **51**He will cut him to pieces
and assign him a place with the hypocrites, where there will be weeping and
gnashing of teeth.[d] Mt 25:31-46

24:42 [w]Mt 25:13; Lk 12:40
24:43 [x]S Lk 12:39
24:44 [y]1Th 5:6
24:45 [z]Mt 25:21, 23
24:46 [a]Rev 16:15
24:47 [b]Mt 25:21, 23

The Parable of the Ten Virgins

25 "At that time the kingdom of
heaven will be like[e] ten virgins who took their lamps[f] and went
out to meet the bridegroom.[g] **2**Five of
them were foolish and five were
wise.[h] **3**The foolish ones took their
lamps but did not take any oil with
them. **4**The wise, however, took oil in

24:49 [c]Lk 21:34
24:51 [d]S Mt 8:12
25:1 [e]S Mt 13:24 [f]Lk 12:35-38; Ac 20:8; Rev 4:5 [g]Rev 19:7; 21:2
25:2 [h]Mt 24:45

---

ed, anticipated and foreseen (Lk 21:28; see v. 33, note; see article on THE GREAT TRIBULATION, p. 1456). The events and signs during the tribulation will create an attitude of certainty and expectancy for tribulation saints, and not the attitude of surprise that the present-day church saints will have at the time of the rapture (see v. 44, note; Jn 14:3, note). Christ's coming after the tribulation is sometimes regarded as the second stage of Christ's second coming.

24:43 THE THIEF. Christ's coming at an unknown time is to be as unexpected as that of a thief who breaks into a house. Thus the devoted disciple must be ready at any time for the Lord's appearance (v. 44).

24:44 AN HOUR WHEN YOU DO NOT EXPECT HIM. Once again Christ refers to his return for the faithful of his churches at an unexpected and unknown time. (1) This warning is not for tribulation saints (see article on THE GREAT TRIBULATION, p. 1456). The only way to harmonize Christ's teaching about his unexpected coming (vv. 42,44) with his statement concerning his expected coming (v. 33) is to assume two phases to his second coming. The first stage involves Christ's return at an unexpected time to take believers from earth (cf. 1Th 4:17; see Jn 14:3, note; Rev 3:10, note; see article on THE RAPTURE, p. 1864), and the second stage is his coming at the end of the age at an expected time (i.e., after the tribulation and cosmic signs, vv. 29–30) to destroy the wicked and begin his reign on earth (see v. 42, notes; Rev 19:11–21; 20:4).

(2) This second coming of Christ as one event consisting of two phases parallels Christ's coming predicted in the OT; the OT speaks of one coming of the Messiah, but sees its fulfillment in two phases: his coming to die for sin and his coming to reign (see Isa 9:2–7; 40:3–5; compare Isa 61:1–3 with Lk 4:18–19; see Isa 9:7, note).

(3) Christ's urgent warning to be always spiritually ready for his unexpected coming (i.e., the rapture) applies to all generations of Christians before the tribulation (vv. 15–29). It is a motive for perseverance in the faith.

24:48 MY MASTER IS STAYING AWAY. Concerning those within the church who are unfaithful to the Lord, Christ's unexpected return cannot be a motive for present vigilance if they believe it is impossible for Christ to come now. (1) Any professed believer living in sin who believes that Christ will delay his coming for a few years can be compared to the wicked servant. Such a person will feel no impending threat that the Lord's return will overtake him or her (see v. 44, note; Lk 12:45–46, notes). (2) It is significant that Jesus associates unfaithfulness and hypocrisy with the belief and desire that Christ will delay his return.

25:1 PARABLE OF THE TEN VIRGINS. The parable of the ten virgins emphasizes that all believers must constantly look to their own spiritual condition in light of Christ's coming at an unknown and unexpected time. They must persevere in faith so that when the day and hour arrive they will be received by the returning Lord (v. 10). Failure to be in a personal relationship with the Lord at his return means being excluded from his presence and kingdom.

(1) What differentiates the foolish from the wise is the failure of the foolish to recognize that the returning Lord (see Jn 14:3, note) will come at an unexpected time, a time not preceded with unmistakable and specific observable signs (v. 13; see 24:36,44, notes).

(2) Christ indicates here and elsewhere (Lk 18:8) that a large portion of the church will be unprepared at the time of his return (vv. 8–13). Thus Christ makes it clear he will not wait until all churches are prepared for his coming.

(3) It should be noticed that all the virgins (both faithful and unfaithful) were taken by surprise at the bridegroom's coming (vv. 5–7). This suggests that the parable of the ten virgins applies to believers living before the tribulation and not to those living during the tribulation, who will have adequate signs preceding Christ's return at the end of the tribulation (see article on THE GREAT TRIBULATION, p. 1456).

jars along with their lamps. **5**The bridegroom was a long time in coming, and
they all became drowsy and fell
asleep.[i]
6"At midnight the cry rang out:
'Here's the bridegroom! Come out to
meet him!'
7"Then all the virgins woke up and
trimmed their lamps. **8**The foolish ones
said to the wise, 'Give us some of your
oil; our lamps are going out.'[j]
9" 'No,' they replied, 'there may not
be enough for both us and you. Instead,
go to those who sell oil and buy some
for yourselves.'
10"But while they were on their way
to buy the oil, the bridegroom arrived.
The virgins who were ready went in
with him to the wedding banquet.[k]
And the door was shut.
11"Later the others also came. 'Sir!
Sir!' they said. 'Open the door for us!'
12"But he replied, 'I tell you the
truth, I don't know you.'[l]
13"Therefore keep watch, because
you do not know the day or the hour.[m]

The Parable of the Talents

25:14–30Ref — Lk 19:12–27

14"Again, it will be like a man going
on a journey,[n] who called his servants
and entrusted his property to them.
15To one he gave five talents[b] of money, to another two talents, and to another one talent, each according to his
ability.[o] Then he went on his journey.
16The man who had received the five
talents went at once and put his money
to work and gained five more. **17**So
also, the one with the two talents
gained two more. **18**But the man who
had received the one talent went off,
dug a hole in the ground and hid his
master's money.
19"After a long time the master of
those servants returned and settled accounts with them.[p] **20**The man who
had received the five talents brought
the other five. 'Master,' he said, 'you
entrusted me with five talents. See, I
have gained five more.'
21"His master replied, 'Well done,
good and faithful servant! You have
been faithful with a few things; I will
put you in charge of many things.[q]
Come and share your master's happiness!'
22"The man with the two talents
also came. 'Master,' he said, 'you entrusted me with two talents; see, I
have gained two more.'
23"His master replied, 'Well done,
good and faithful servant! You have
been faithful with a few things; I will
put you in charge of many things.[r]
Come and share your master's happiness!'
24"Then the man who had received
the one talent came. 'Master,' he said,
'I knew that you are a hard man, harvesting where you have not sown and
gathering where you have not scattered seed. **25**So I was afraid and went
out and hid your talent in the ground.
See, here is what belongs to you.'
26"His master replied, 'You wicked,
lazy servant! So you knew that I harvest where I have not sown and gather
where I have not scattered seed?
27Well then, you should have put my
money on deposit with the bankers, so
that when I returned I would have received it back with interest.
28" 'Take the talent from him and
give it to the one who has the ten talents. **29**For everyone who has will be
given more, and he will have an abundance. Whoever does not have, even

25:5 [i] 1Th 5:6
25:8 [j] Lk 12:35
25:10 [k] Rev 19:9
25:12 [l] ver 41; S Mt 7:23
25:13 [m] Mt 24:42,44; Mk 13:35; Lk 12:40
25:14 [n] Mt 21:33; Lk 19:12
25:15 [o] Mt 18:24, 25
25:19 [p] Mt 18:23
25:21 [q] ver 23; Mt 24:45,47; Lk 16:10
25:23 [r] ver 21

[b] *15* A talent was worth more than a thousand dollars.

25:4 OIL. Jesus, in a series of illustrations (ch. 25), stresses the requirement of faithfulness and watchfulness until he returns. The parable of the ten virgins stresses the necessity of perseverance in the faith and spiritual preparedness because of the danger of Christ's coming at an unforeseeable date (see Lk 21:19, note). The oil in the parable represents true faith, righteousness and the abiding presence of the Holy Spirit. Five other parables that teach the lesson of perseverance are the sower (Lk 8:4–15), the owner of the house (Lk 12:35–40), the manager (Lk 12:42–48), the tower builder (Lk 14:28–30) and the tasteless salt (Lk 14:34–35).

25:15 TALENTS. The parable of the talents warns us that our place and service in heaven will depend on the faithfulness of our lives and service here (cf. v. 29). A talent represents our abilities, time, resources and opportunities to serve God while on earth. These things are considered by God as a trust that we are responsible to administer in the wisest possible way.

25:29 EVERYONE WHO HAS. Jesus gives an important principle with regard to the believer's reward and state in heaven. What believers receive in the future kingdom of God will depend on what they possess of it now. Their position and inheritance in heaven will be in proportion to their present commitment to God's ways and kingdom (see Lk 22:24–30, note).

what he has will be taken from him.[s]
30And throw that worthless servant
outside, into the darkness, where there
will be weeping and gnashing of
teeth.'[t]

The Sheep and the Goats

31"When the Son of Man comes[u] in
his glory, and all the angels with him,
he will sit on his throne[v] in heavenly
glory. **32**All the nations will be gathered before him, and he will separate[w]
the people one from another as a shepherd separates the sheep from the
goats.[x] **33**He will put the sheep on his
right and the goats on his left.
34"Then the King will say to those
on his right, 'Come, you who are
blessed by my Father; take your inheritance, the kingdom[y] prepared for you
since the creation of the world.[z] **35**For
I was hungry and you gave me something to eat, I was thirsty and you gave
me something to drink, I was a stranger and you invited me in,[a] **36**I needed
clothes and you clothed me,[b] I was
sick and you looked after me,[c] I was
in prison and you came to visit me.'[d]
37"Then the righteous will answer
him, 'Lord, when did we see you hungry and feed you, or thirsty and give
you something to drink? **38**When did
we see you a stranger and invite you in,
or needing clothes and clothe you?
39When did we see you sick or in prison
and go to visit you?'
40"The King will reply, 'I tell you the
truth, whatever you did for one of the
least of these brothers of mine, you did
for me.'[e]

25:29 [s]Mt 13:12; Mk 4:25; Lk 8:18; 19:26 **25:30** [t]S Mt 8:12 **25:31** [u]S Lk 17:30 [v]Mt 19:28 **25:32** [w]Mal 3:18 [x]Eze 34:17,20 **25:34** [y]S Mt 3:2; 5:3,10,19; 19:14; S Ac 20:32; 1Co 15:50; Gal 5:21; Jas 2:5 [z]Heb 4:3; 9:26; Rev 13:8; 17:8 **25:35** [a]Job 31:32; Heb 13:2 **25:36** [b]Isa 58:7; Eze 18:7; Jas 2:15, 16 [c]Jas 1:27 [d]2Ti 1:16 **25:40** [e]S Mt 10:40,42; Heb 13:2

25:41 [f]S Mt 7:23 [g]Isa 66:24; Mt 3:12; S 5:22; Mk 9:43,48; Lk 3:17; Jude 7 [h]2Pe 2:4 **25:45** [i]Pr 14:31; 17:5 **25:46** [j]Mt 19:29; Jn 3:15,16,36; 17:2,3; Ro 2:7; Gal 6:8; 1Jn 1:2; 5:11,13,20 [k]Da 12:2; Jn 5:29; Ac 24:15; Ro 2:7, 8; Gal 6:8 **26:1** [l]S Mt 7:28 **26:2** [m]S Jn 11:55 **26:3** [n]Ps 2:2 [o]ver 57; Lk 3:2; Jn 11:47-53; 18:13,14,24,28; Ac 4:6 **26:4** [p]S Mt 12:14 **26:5** [q]Mt 27:24

41"Then he will say to those on his
left, 'Depart from me,[f] you who are
cursed, into the eternal fire[g] prepared
for the devil and his angels.[h] **42**For I
was hungry and you gave me nothing
to eat, I was thirsty and you gave me
nothing to drink, **43**I was a stranger
and you did not invite me in, I needed
clothes and you did not clothe me, I
was sick and in prison and you did not
look after me.'
44"They also will answer, 'Lord,
when did we see you hungry or thirsty
or a stranger or needing clothes or sick
or in prison, and did not help you?'
45"He will reply, 'I tell you the truth,
whatever you did not do for one
of the least of these, you did not do
for me.'[i]
46"Then they will go away to eternal
punishment, but the righteous to eternal life."[j][k] Mt 26:64

The Plot Against Jesus

26:2-5pp — Mk 14:1,2; Lk 22:1,2

26 When Jesus had finished saying
all these things,[l] he said to his
disciples, **2**"As you know, the Passover[m] is two days away—and the Son
of Man will be handed over to be crucified."
3Then the chief priests and the elders of the people assembled[n] in the
palace of the high priest, whose name
was Caiaphas,[o] **4**and they plotted to
arrest Jesus in some sly way and kill
him.[p] **5**"But not during the Feast,"
they said, "or there may be a riot[q]
among the people."

25:32 SHEEP FROM THE GOATS. The sheep and goat judgment occurs after the tribulation and Christ's return to earth but before the beginning of his earthly reign (cf. Da 7:9–14; Rev 5:10; 19:11—20:4). (1) At the time of Christ's coming the saved and the lost who are living on earth and who survived the tribulation are still mingled together. (2) The judgment involves the separation of the wicked from the righteous (vv. 32–33; see 13:41, note). (3) The judgment will be based on outward works of love and kindness to those belonging to Christ and who are suffering. The expression of love and compassion is taken as an inherent part of true faith and salvation (vv. 35–46). (4) The wicked will not be allowed to enter Christ's kingdom, but will go into eternal punishment (vv. 41,46; Rev 14:11). (5) The righteous will inherit eternal life (v. 46) and the kingdom of God (v. 34; see Rev 20:4, notes).

25:41 DEVIL AND HIS ANGELS. Satan's initial rebellion against God (see 4:10, note) drew with him a third of the heavenly angels (Rev 12:4). A part of these are bound in hell (2Pe 2:4; Jude 6), while the rest are free and exist under Satan's dominion and control (12:24; 25:41; Eph 2:2; Rev 12:7). These free angels are his highly organized emissaries (Eph 6:11–12) and are probably identical with the demons referred to in the Bible (see article on POWER OVER SATAN AND DEMONS, p. 1484).

26:2 PASSOVER. The Passover (Gk *pascha*) was a spring festival associated with the historical episode of Israel's departure from Egypt. It celebrated the "passing over" of the Hebrews' houses by the destroying angel because of the blood of the lamb that had been put on the doorposts and frames of the houses (see Ex 12:7; see article on THE PASSOVER, p. 104). Christ's crucifixion occurred on "the day of Preparation of Passover Week" (Jn 19:14). He is "our Passover . . . sacrificed" (1Co 5:7).

Jesus Anointed at Bethany

26:6–13pp — Mk 14:3–9
26:6–13Ref — Lk 7:37,38; Jn 12:1–8

6While Jesus was in Bethany[r] in the home of a man known as Simon the Leper, **7**a woman came to him with an alabaster jar of very expensive perfume, which she poured on his head as he was reclining at the table.

8When the disciples saw this, they were indignant. "Why this waste?" they asked. **9**"This perfume could have been sold at a high price and the money given to the poor."

10Aware of this, Jesus said to them, "Why are you bothering this woman? She has done a beautiful thing to me. **11**The poor you will always have with you,[s] but you will not always have me. **12**When she poured this perfume on my body, she did it to prepare me for burial.[t] **13**I tell you the truth, wherever this gospel is preached throughout the world, what she has done will also be told, in memory of her."

Judas Agrees to Betray Jesus

26:14–16pp — Mk 14:10,11; Lk 22:3–6

14Then one of the Twelve—the one called Judas Iscariot[u]—went to the chief priests **15**and asked, "What are you willing to give me if I hand him over to you?" So they counted out for him thirty silver coins.[v] **16**From then on Judas watched for an opportunity to hand him over.

The Lord's Supper

26:17–19pp — Mk 14:12–16; Lk 22:7–13
26:20–24pp — Mk 14:17–21
26:26–29pp — Mk 14:22–25; Lk 22:17–20; 1Co 11:23–25

17On the first day of the Feast of Unleavened Bread,[w] the disciples came to Jesus and asked, "Where do you want us to make preparations for you to eat the Passover?"[x]

18He replied, "Go into the city to a certain man and tell him, 'The Teacher says: My appointed time[y] is near. I am going to celebrate the Passover with my disciples at your house.' " **19**So the disciples did as Jesus had directed them and prepared the Passover.

20When evening came, Jesus was reclining at the table with the Twelve. **21**And while they were eating, he said, "I tell you the truth, one of you will betray me."[z]

22They were very sad and began to say to him one after the other, "Surely not I, Lord?"

23Jesus replied, "The one who has dipped his hand into the bowl with me will betray me.[a] **24**The Son of Man will go just as it is written about him.[b] But woe to that man who betrays the Son of Man! It would be better for him if he had not been born."

25Then Judas, the one who would betray him,[c] said, "Surely not I, Rabbi?"[d]

Jesus answered, "Yes, it is you."[c]

26While they were eating, Jesus took bread, gave thanks and broke it,[e] and gave it to his disciples, saying, "Take and eat; this is my body."

27Then he took the cup,[f] gave thanks and offered it to them, saying, "Drink from it, all of you. **28**This is my blood of the[d] covenant,[g] which is poured out for many for the forgiveness of sins.[h] **29**I tell you, I will not

26:6 [r] S Mt 21:17 **26:11** [s] Dt 15:11 **26:12** [t] Jn 19:40 **26:14** [u] ver 25, 47; S Mt 10:4 **26:15** [v] Ex 21:32; Zec 11:12
26:17 [w] Ex 12:18-20 [x] Dt 16:5-8 **26:18** [y] Mk 14:35,41; Jn 7:6,8,30; 8:20; 12:23; 13:1; 17:1 **26:21** [z] Lk 22:21-23; Jn 13:21 **26:23** [a] Ps 41:9; Jn 13:18 **26:24** [b] ver 31,54, 56; Isa 53; Da 9:26; Mk 9:12; Lk 24:25-27,46; Ac 17:2,3; 26:22, 23; 1Pe 1:10,11 **26:25** [c] S Mt 10:4 [d] S Mt 23:7 **26:26** [e] S Mt 14:19 **26:27** [f] 1Co 10:16 **26:28** [g] Ex 24:6-8; Zec 9:11; Mal 2:5; Heb 9:20; 10:29; S 13:20 [h] S Mt 20:28; Mk 1:4

[c] *25* Or *"You yourself have said it"*
[d] *28* Some manuscripts *the new*

26:13 IN MEMORY OF HER. The Lord has ordained that this story of Mary (vv. 6–13) should always accompany the preaching of the gospel. This is because she exemplifies better than anyone else the dedication that all followers of Christ should have. Her act was the expression of her deep devotion to and profound love for the Master. The Christian faith is first of all a personal ministering to him. We learn here that our heartfelt attachment to and love for Jesus is the most valuable aspect of our relationship to him (see Jn 21:15, note).

26:26 TAKE AND EAT; THIS IS MY BODY. See 1Co 11:24–25, note on the Lord's Supper.

26:28 THE COVENANT. See article on THE OLD COVENANT AND THE NEW COVENANT, p. 1926.

26:28 FORGIVENESS OF SINS. Forgiveness is necessary because we have sinned, destroyed our relationship with God and become subject to condemnation (Ro 1:18–32). Forgiveness is the means by which this relationship is restored (Eph 1:7; Col 2:13).

(1) The Hebrew and Greek words for forgiveness denote the ideas of "to cover," "to pardon," "to cancel," "to send away." God's forgiveness involves making of no account the sin that has been committed (Mk 2:5; Jn 8:11), saving sinners from eternal punishment (Ro 5:9; 1Th 1:10), accepting them (Lk 15:20ff), delivering them from the dominion of sin and transferring them into Christ's kingdom (Col 1:13), and renewing the whole person and promising eternal life (Lk 23:43; Jn 14:19b).

(2) In order to receive forgiveness, there must

drink of this fruit of the vine from
now on until that day when I drink it
anew with you[i] in my Father's kingdom."
30When they had sung a hymn, they
went out to the Mount of Olives.[j]

Jesus Predicts Peter's Denial

26:31–35pp — Mk 14:27–31; Lk 22:31–34

31Then Jesus told them, "This very
night you will all fall away on account
of me,[k] for it is written:

" 'I will strike the shepherd,
and the sheep of the flock will
be scattered.'[e][l]

32But after I have risen, I will go ahead
of you into Galilee."[m]
33Peter replied, "Even if all fall away
on account of you, I never will."
34"I tell you the truth," Jesus answered, "this very night, before the
rooster crows, you will disown me
three times."[n]
35But Peter declared, "Even if I have
to die with you,[o] I will never disown
you." And all the other disciples said
the same.

Gethsemane

26:36–46pp — Mk 14:32–42; Lk 22:40–46

36Then Jesus went with his disciples
to a place called Gethsemane, and he
said to them, "Sit here while I go over
there and pray." 37He took Peter and
the two sons of Zebedee[p] along with
him, and he began to be sorrowful and
troubled. 38Then he said to them, "My
soul is overwhelmed with sorrow[q] to
the point of death. Stay here and keep
watch with me."[r]
39Going a little farther, he fell with
his face to the ground and prayed, "My
Father, if it is possible, may this cup[s]
be taken from me. Yet not as I will, but
as you will."[t]
40Then he returned to his disciples
and found them sleeping. "Could you
men not keep watch with me[u] for one
hour?" he asked Peter. 41"Watch and
pray so that you will not fall into temptation.[v] The spirit is willing, but the
body is weak."
42He went away a second time and
prayed, "My Father, if it is not possible
for this cup to be taken away unless I
drink it, may your will be done."[w]
43When he came back, he again
found them sleeping, because their
eyes were heavy. 44So he left them and
went away once more and prayed the
third time, saying the same thing.
45Then he returned to the disciples
and said to them, "Are you still sleeping and resting? Look, the hour[x] is
near, and the Son of Man is betrayed
into the hands of sinners. 46Rise, let us
go! Here comes my betrayer!"

Jesus Arrested

26:47–56pp — Mk 14:43–50; Lk 22:47–53

47While he was still speaking, Judas,[y] one of the Twelve, arrived. With
him was a large crowd armed with
swords and clubs, sent from the chief
priests and the elders of the people.
48Now the betrayer had arranged a signal with them: "The one I kiss is the
man; arrest him." 49Going at once to
Jesus, Judas said, "Greetings, Rabbi!"[z] and kissed him.

26:29 [i]Ac 10:41 26:30 [j]S Mt 21:1 26:31 [k]Mt 11:6; 13:21 [l]Zec 13:7; Jn 16:32 26:32 [m]Mt 28:7, 10,16 26:34 [n]ver 75; Jn 13:38 26:35 [o]Jn 13:37 26:37 [p]S Mt 4:21 26:38 [q]S Jn 12:27 [r]ver 40,41
26:39 [s]S Mt 20:22 [t]ver 42; Ps 40:6-8; Isa 50:5; Mt 6:10; Jn 4:34; 5:30; 6:38 26:40 [u]ver 38 26:41 [v]Mt 6:13 26:42 [w]S ver 39 26:45 [x]S ver 18 26:47 [y]S Mt 10:4 26:49 [z]ver 25; S Mt 23:7

[e]*31* Zech. 13:7

be repentance, faith and confession of sin (Lk 17:3–4; Ac 2:38; 5:31; 20:21; 1Jn 1:9). For God to be able to extend forgiveness, the shedding of blood was required (Heb 9:22). Thus, forgiveness is based on Jesus' death on the cross (v. 28; Jn 1:29; 3:16; Ro 8:32). Divine forgiveness is an ongoing need for believers, so that we might maintain our saving relationship with God (6:12,14–15; 1Jn 1:9).

26:37 HE BEGAN TO BE SORROWFUL. The sufferings of Christ, stage one. The physical and spiritual sufferings of Christ begin in Gethsemane. "His sweat was like drops of blood" (Lk 22:44). Under great stress, the small capillaries in the sweat glands can break and mix blood with sweat (see next note for further insights into this stage of Christ's sufferings; for the second stage of Christ's sufferings, see v. 67, note).

26:39 MAY THIS CUP BE TAKEN. What Christ meant by "this cup" has been the subject of much discussion. (1) It is doubtful that Christ was praying to be saved from physical death, for he had resolutely set himself to die for the sin of humanity (cf. Mk 10:33–34; Lk 9:51; Jn 12:24,27; Heb 10:5–9).

(2) It is more probable that he was praying to be delivered from the punishment of separation from God, the ultimate penalty for sin. Christ prayed that his physical death might be accepted as full payment for the sin of sinners. However, he prayed, "yet not as I will, but as you will." He then committed himself to undergo both physical death and spiritual separation from his heavenly Father in order to achieve our salvation (cf. 27:46). His prayer was "heard," for he was strengthened by his Father to drink the appointed cup (see Heb 5:7).

50Jesus replied, "Friend,[a] do what
you came for."[f]
Then the men stepped forward,
seized Jesus and arrested him. 51With
that, one of Jesus' companions reached
for his sword,[b] drew it out and struck
the servant of the high priest, cutting
off his ear.[c]
52"Put your sword back in its place,"
Jesus said to him, "for all who draw the
sword will die by the sword.[d] 53Do
you think I cannot call on my Father,
and he will at once put at my disposal
more than twelve legions of angels?[e]
54But how then would the Scriptures
be fulfilled[f] that say it must happen in
this way?"
55At that time Jesus said to the
crowd, "Am I leading a rebellion, that
you have come out with swords and
clubs to capture me? Every day I sat in
the temple courts teaching,[g] and you
did not arrest me. 56But this has all
taken place that the writings of the
prophets might be fulfilled."[h] Then all
the disciples deserted him and fled.

Before the Sanhedrin

26:57–68pp — Mk 14:53–65; Jn 18:12,13,19–24

57Those who had arrested Jesus
took him to Caiaphas,[i] the high
priest, where the teachers of the law
and the elders had assembled. 58But
Peter followed him at a distance, right
up to the courtyard of the high priest.[j]
He entered and sat down with the
guards[k] to see the outcome.
59The chief priests and the whole
Sanhedrin[l] were looking for false evidence against Jesus so that they could
put him to death. 60But they did not
find any, though many false witnesses[m] came forward.
Finally two[n] came forward 61and
declared, "This fellow said, 'I am able
to destroy the temple of God and rebuild it in three days.' "[o]
62Then the high priest stood up and
said to Jesus, "Are you not going to answer? What is this testimony that
these men are bringing against you?"
63But Jesus remained silent.[p]
The high priest said to him, "I
charge you under oath[q] by the living
God:[r] Tell us if you are the Christ,[g][s]
the Son of God."[t]
64"Yes, it is as you say,"[u] Jesus replied. "But I say to all of you: In the
future you will see the Son of Man sitting at the right hand of the Mighty
One[v] and coming on the clouds of
heaven."[w]
65Then the high priest tore his
clothes[x] and said, "He has spoken
blasphemy! Why do we need any more
witnesses? Look, now you have heard
the blasphemy. 66What do you think?"
"He is worthy of death,"[y] they answered.
67Then they spit in his face and
struck him with their fists.[z] Others
slapped him 68and said, "Prophesy to
us, Christ. Who hit you?"[a]

Peter Disowns Jesus

26:69–75pp — Mk 14:66–72; Lk 22:55–62; Jn 18:16–18,25–27

69Now Peter was sitting out in the
courtyard, and a servant girl came to
him. "You also were with Jesus of Galilee," she said.
70But he denied it before them all. "I
don't know what you're talking about,"
he said.
71Then he went out to the gateway,
where another girl saw him and said to
the people there, "This fellow was with
Jesus of Nazareth."

26:50 [a] Mt 20:13; 22:12
26:51 [b] Lk 22:36,38 [c] Jn 18:10
26:52 [d] Ge 9:6; Ex 21:12; Rev 13:10
26:53 [e] 2Ki 6:17; Da 7:10; Mt 4:11
26:54 [f] S ver 24; S Mt 1:22
26:55 [g] Mk 12:35; Lk 21:37; Jn 7:14,28; 18:20
26:56 [h] S ver 24; S Mt 1:22
26:57 [i] S ver 3
26:58 [j] ver 69; Mk 14:66; Lk 22:55; Jn 18:15 [k] Mk 15:16; Lk 11:21; Jn 7:32,45,46
26:59 [l] S Mt 5:22
26:60 [m] Ps 27:12; 35:11; Ac 6:13 [n] Dt 19:15
26:61 [o] S Jn 2:19
26:63 [p] S Mk 14:61 [q] Lev 5:1 [r] S Mt 16:16 [s] Lk 22:67 [t] S Mt 4:3
26:64 [u] Mt 27:11; Lk 22:70 [v] S Mk 16:19 [w] S Rev 1:7
26:65 [x] S Mk 14:63
26:66 [y] Lev 24:16; Jn 19:7
26:67 [z] S Mt 16:21
26:68 [a] Lk 22:63-65

[f] 50 Or *"Friend, why have you come?"*
[g] 63 Or *Messiah*; also in verse 68

26:57 ARRESTED JESUS. A study of the events from Christ's arrest to his crucifixion can be very rewarding. The order is as follows: (1) the arrest (26:47–56; Mk 14:43–52; Lk 22:47–53; Jn 18:2–12); (2) the religious trial before Annas (Jn 18:12–14,19–24) and before Caiaphas (26:57, 59–68; Mk 14:53,55–65; Lk 22:54,63–65; Jn 18:24); (3) the denial by Peter (26:58,69–75; Mk 14:54,66–72; Lk 22:54–62; Jn 18:15–18, 25–27); (4) the condemnation by the Sanhedrin (27:1; Mk 15:1; Lk 22:66–71); (5) the death of Judas (27:3–10); (6) the civil trial before Pilate (27:2,11–14; Mk 15:2–5; Lk 23:1–5; Jn 18:28–38); (7) the trial before Herod (Lk 23:6–12), who sent him back to Pilate (27:11–26; Mk 15:6–15; Lk 23:11–25; Jn 18:28—19:1, 4–16); (8) the mockery (27:27–30; Mk 15:16–19; Jn 19:2–3), after which he was beaten and then led away to be crucified (27:31); (9) the procession to Golgotha (27:32–34; Mk 15:20–23; Lk 23:26–33); (10) the crucifixion (27:35, note).

26:67 SPIT . . . STRUCK . . . SLAPPED. The sufferings of Christ, stage two. After the arrest at night and abandonment by his disciples (vv. 55–57), Jesus is brought before Caiaphas and the Jewish council. He is blindfolded, mocked repeatedly, spat on and struck in the face. (For the third stage of Christ's sufferings, see 27:2, note.)

72He denied it again, with an oath: "I
don't know the man!"
73After a little while, those standing
there went up to Peter and said, "Surely you are one of them, for your accent
gives you away."
74Then he began to call down curses
on himself and he swore to them, "I
don't know the man!"
Immediately a rooster crowed.
75Then Peter remembered the word
Jesus had spoken: "Before the rooster
crows, you will disown me three
times."[b] And he went outside and
wept bitterly.

Judas Hangs Himself

27 Early in the morning, all the
chief priests and the elders of
the people came to the decision to put
Jesus to death.[c] 2They bound him, led
him away and handed him over[d] to Pilate, the governor.[e]
3When Judas, who had betrayed
him,[f] saw that Jesus was condemned,
he was seized with remorse and returned the thirty silver coins[g] to the
chief priests and the elders. 4"I have
sinned," he said, "for I have betrayed
innocent blood."
"What is that to us?" they replied.
"That's your responsibility."[h]
5So Judas threw the money into the
temple[i] and left. Then he went away
and hanged himself.[j]
6The chief priests picked up the
coins and said, "It is against the law to
put this into the treasury, since it is
blood money." 7So they decided to use
the money to buy the potter's field as
a burial place for foreigners. 8That is
why it has been called the Field of
Blood[k] to this day. 9Then what was
spoken by Jeremiah the prophet was
fulfilled:[l] "They took the thirty silver
coins, the price set on him by the people of Israel, 10and they used them to
buy the potter's field, as the Lord commanded me."[h][m]

Jesus Before Pilate

27:11–26pp — Mk 15:2–15; Lk 23:2,3, 18–25; Jn 18:29–19:16

11Meanwhile Jesus stood before the
governor, and the governor asked him,
"Are you the king of the Jews?"[n]
"Yes, it is as you say," Jesus replied.
12When he was accused by the chief
priests and the elders, he gave no answer.[o] 13Then Pilate asked him,
"Don't you hear the testimony they are
bringing against you?"[p] 14But Jesus
made no reply,[q] not even to a single
charge—to the great amazement of
the governor.
15Now it was the governor's custom
at the Feast to release a prisoner[r]
chosen by the crowd. 16At that time
they had a notorious prisoner, called
Barabbas. 17So when the crowd had
gathered, Pilate asked them, "Which
one do you want me to release to you:
Barabbas, or Jesus who is called
Christ?"[s] 18For he knew it was out of
envy that they had handed Jesus over
to him.
19While Pilate was sitting on the
judge's seat,[t] his wife sent him this
message: "Don't have anything to do
with that innocent[u] man, for I have
suffered a great deal today in a
dream[v] because of him."
20But the chief priests and the elders persuaded the crowd to ask for
Barabbas and to have Jesus executed.[w]
21"Which of the two do you want me
to release to you?" asked the governor.
"Barabbas," they answered.
22"What shall I do, then, with Jesus

26:75 [b]ver 34; Jn 13:38 **27:1** [c]S Mt 12:14; Mk 15:1; Lk 22:66 **27:2** [d]Mt 20:19 [e]Mk 15:1; Lk 13:1; Ac 3:13; 1Ti 6:13 **27:3** [f]S Mt 10:4 [g]Mt 26:14,15 **27:4** [h]ver 24 **27:5** [i]Lk 1:9,21 [j]Ac 1:18 **27:8** [k]Ac 1:19 **27:9** [l]S Mt 1:22 **27:10** [m]Zec 11:12,13; Jer 32:6-9 **27:11** [n]S Mt 2:2 **27:12** [o]S Mk 14:61 **27:13** [p]Mt 26:62 **27:14** [q]S Mk 14:61 **27:15** [r]Jn 18:39 **27:17** [s]ver 22; Mt 1:16 **27:19** [t]Jn 19:13 [u]ver 24 [v]Ge 20:6; Nu 12:6; 1Ki 3:5; Job 33:14-16; Mt 1:20; 2:12,13, 19,22 **27:20** [w]Ac 3:14

[h]*10* See Zech. 11:12,13; Jer. 19:1-13; 32:6-9.

27:2 HANDED HIM OVER TO PILATE. The sufferings of Christ, stage three. In the morning, Jesus, battered and exhausted, is taken across Jerusalem to be interrogated by Pilate. Barabbas is released (v. 21) and Jesus is scourged and handed over to be crucified (v. 26). (For the fourth stage of Christ's sufferings, see v. 26, note.)

27:3 JUDAS'S REMORSE. Judas learned that his sinful actions would lead to the death of Jesus. Likewise, our actions inevitably affect others for good or for evil. Many things we set in motion cannot be stopped, and their evil and destructive results will be experienced by us and others. It is of utmost importance to avoid all actions and plans that may have potentially harmful consequences.

27:5 JUDAS'S DEATH. Matthew states that Judas "hanged himself"; Ac 1:18 records that he died by falling. What Judas probably did was to throw himself on a sharpened stake. Hanging in those days was done by crucifixion or impalement.

27:9 JEREMIAH THE PROPHET. Matthew here combines and summarizes elements of prophetic symbolism, one from Jeremiah (Jer 32:6–9) and one from Zechariah (Zec 11:12–13). Then he mentions the older and more prominent prophet as the source, a custom frequently used in alluding to passages from the prophets.

who is called Christ?"[x] Pilate asked.
They all answered, "Crucify him!"
23"Why? What crime has he committed?" asked Pilate.
But they shouted all the louder,
"Crucify him!"
24When Pilate saw that he was getting nowhere, but that instead an uproar[y] was starting, he took water and
washed his hands[z] in front of the
crowd. "I am innocent of this man's
blood,"[a] he said. "It is your responsibility!"[b]
25All the people answered, "Let his
blood be on us and on our children!"[c]
26Then he released Barabbas to
them. But he had Jesus flogged,[d] and
handed him over to be crucified.

The Soldiers Mock Jesus

27:27–31pp — Mk 15:16–20

27Then the governor's soldiers took
Jesus into the Praetorium[e] and gathered the whole company of soldiers
around him. 28They stripped him and
put a scarlet robe on him,[f] 29and then
twisted together a crown of thorns and
set it on his head. They put a staff in
his right hand and knelt in front of him
and mocked him. "Hail, king of the
Jews!" they said.[g] 30They spit on him,
and took the staff and struck him on
the head again and again.[h] 31After
they had mocked him, they took off the
robe and put his own clothes on him.
Then they led him away to crucify
him.[i]

The Crucifixion

27:33–44pp — Mk 15:22–32; Lk 23:33–43; Jn 19:17–24

32As they were going out,[j] they
met a man from Cyrene,[k] named Simon, and they forced him to carry the
cross.[l] 33They came to a place called
Golgotha (which means The Place of
the Skull).[m] 34There they offered
Jesus wine to drink, mixed with gall;[n]
but after tasting it, he refused to drink
it. 35When they had crucified him, they
divided up his clothes by casting
lots.[i][o] 36And sitting down, they kept
watch[p] over him there. 37Above his
head they placed the written charge
against him: THIS IS JESUS, THE KING OF THE
JEWS. 38Two robbers were crucified with
him,[q] one on his right and one on his
left. 39Those who passed by hurled insults at him, shaking their heads[r]

27:22 [x] Mt 1:16
27:24 [y] Mt 26:5 [z] Ps 26:6 [a] Dt 21:6-8 [b] ver 4
27:25 [c] Jos 2:19; S Ac 5:28
27:26 [d] Isa 53:5; Jn 19:1
27:27 [e] Jn 18:28, 33; 19:9
27:28 [f] Jn 19:2
27:29 [g] Isa 53:3; Jn 19:2,3
27:30 [h] S Mt 16:21
27:31 [i] Isa 53:7
27:32 [j] Heb 13:12 [k] Ac 2:10; 6:9; 11:20; 13:1 [l] Mk 15:21; Lk 23:26
27:33 [m] Jn 19:17
27:34 [n] ver 48; Ps 69:21
27:35 [o] Ps 22:18
27:36 [p] ver 54
27:38 [q] Isa 53:12
27:39 [r] Ps 22:7; 109:25; La 2:15

i 35 A few late manuscripts *lots that the word spoken by the prophet might be fulfilled: "They divided my garments among themselves and cast lots for my clothing"* (Psalm 22:18)

27:24 PILATE. Pilate's greatest sin was compromising what he knew to be true and right for the sake of position, status and personal gain. Pilate knew Christ was innocent, and declared so on several occasions (v. 18; Jn 19:4,6).

27:26 HAD JESUS FLOGGED. The sufferings of Christ, stage four. (1) The Roman flogging consisted of the victim being stripped and stretched against a pillar or bent over a low post, and the hands tied. The instrument of torture was a short wooden handle to which several leather thongs were attached, with bits of iron or bone tied to the thongs. The blows were laid on the victim's back by two men, one lashing the victim from one side, one from the other side. This resulted in the flesh being cut to such an extent that veins, arteries and sometimes even inner organs were exposed. Often the victim died during the flogging.

(2) Flogging was hideous torture. The inability of Jesus to bear his own cross is no doubt due to this severe infliction (v. 32; Lk 23:26). "But he was pierced for our transgressions, he was crushed for our iniquities; the punishment that brought us peace was upon him, and by his wounds we are healed" (Isa 53:5; 1Pe 2:24). (For the fifth stage of the sufferings of Christ, see v. 28, note.)

27:28–29 A SCARLET ROBE . . . A CROWN OF THORNS. The sufferings of Christ, stage five. Jesus is untied and placed in the middle of the Roman company (v. 27). The soldiers put a robe across his shoulders, place a stick in his hand and press a circle of branches covered with long thorns on his head (v. 29). The soldiers mock him and strike him across the face and head, driving the thorns deeper into his scalp (vv. 30–31). (For the sixth stage of the sufferings of Christ, see v. 31, note.)

27:31 LED HIM AWAY TO CRUCIFY HIM. The sufferings of Christ, stage six. The heavy beam of the cross is tied to Christ's shoulder. He begins the slow journey to Golgotha. The weight of the wooden beam, together with sheer physical exhaustion, cause him to fall. He tries to rise, but cannot. Simon is then pressed into service to bear Christ's cross. (For the seventh stage of the sufferings of Christ, see v. 35, note.)

27:35 THEY . . . CRUCIFIED HIM. The sufferings of Christ, stage seven. At Golgotha the cross beam is placed on the ground and Jesus is laid on it. His arms are stretched along the beams and a heavy, square, wrought-iron nail is driven through his hand (or wrist), first into the right, then into the left hand, and deep into the wood. Next Christ is lifted up by means of ropes or ladders, the cross beam is bound or nailed to the upright beam and a support for the body is fastened on it. Lastly, his feet are extended and a larger piece of iron is driven through them. (For the eighth stage of the sufferings of Christ, see v. 39, note.)

27:39 HURLED INSULTS AT HIM. The suf-

40and saying, "You who are going to
destroy the temple and build it in three
days,[s] save yourself![t] Come down
from the cross, if you are the Son of
God!"[u]
41In the same way the chief priests,
the teachers of the law and the elders
mocked him. **42**"He saved others," they
said, "but he can't save himself! He's
the King of Israel![v] Let him come
down now from the cross, and we will
believe[w] in him. **43**He trusts in God.
Let God rescue him[x] now if he wants
him, for he said, 'I am the Son of
God.' " **44**In the same way the robbers
who were crucified with him also
heaped insults on him.

The Death of Jesus

27:45–56pp — Mk 15:33–41; Lk 23:44–49

45From the sixth hour until the ninth
hour darkness[y] came over all the
land. **46**About the ninth hour Jesus
cried out in a loud voice, *"Eloi, Eloi,*[j]
lama sabachthani?"—which means,
"My God, my God, why have you forsaken me?"[k][z]
47When some of those standing
there heard this, they said, "He's calling Elijah."
48Immediately one of them ran and
got a sponge. He filled it with wine vinegar,[a] put it on a stick, and offered it
to Jesus to drink. **49**The rest said, "Now
leave him alone. Let's see if Elijah
comes to save him."
50And when Jesus had cried out
again in a loud voice, he gave up his
spirit.[b]
51At that moment the curtain of the
temple[c] was torn in two from top to
bottom. The earth shook and the rocks
split.[d] **52**The tombs broke open and
the bodies of many holy people who
had died were raised to life. **53**They
came out of the tombs, and after Jesus'
resurrection they went into the holy
city[e] and appeared to many people.
54When the centurion and those
with him who were guarding[f] Jesus
saw the earthquake and all that had
happened, they were terrified, and exclaimed, "Surely he was the Son[l] of
God!"[g]
55Many women were there, watching from a distance. They had followed
Jesus from Galilee to care for his
needs.[h] **56**Among them were Mary
Magdalene, Mary the mother of James
and Joses, and the mother of Zebedee's
sons.[i]

The Burial of Jesus

27:57–61pp — Mk 15:42–47; Lk 23:50–56; Jn 19:38–42

57As evening approached, there

27:40 [s]S Jn 2:19 [t]ver 42 [u]Mt 4:3,6 **27:42** [v]Jn 1:49; 12:13 [w]S Jn 3:15 **27:43** [x]Ps 22:8 **27:45** [y]Am 8:9 **27:46** [z]Ps 22:1 **27:48** [a]ver 34; Ps 69:21 **27:50** [b]Jn 19:30 **27:51** [c]Ex 26:31-33; Heb 9:3,8; 10:19, 20 [d]ver 54 **27:53** [e]S Mt 4:5 **27:54** [f]ver 36 [g]S Mt 4:3; 17:5 **27:55** [h]Lk 8:2,3 **27:56** [i]Mk 15:47; Lk 24:10; Jn 19:25

[j]*46* Some manuscripts *Eli, Eli* [k]*46* Psalm 22:1 [l]*54* Or *a son*

ferings of Christ, stage eight. Jesus is now a pathetic spectacle, blood-streaked, covered with wounds and exposed to the view of the people. He experiences hours of pain in his entire body, fatigue in his arms, great waves of cramps in the muscles and skin torn from his back. Then another agony begins—a crushing pain deep in the chest as fluid begins to compress the heart. He feels an intense thirst (Jn 19:28) and is aware of the abuse and ridicule of those who pass by the cross (vv. 39–44). (For the ninth stage of the sufferings of Christ, see v. 46, note.)

27:46 WHY HAVE YOU FORSAKEN ME? The sufferings of Christ, stage nine. These words mark the climax of the sufferings of Christ for a lost world. His cry in Aramaic, "My God, my God, why have you forsaken me," testifies that he experiences separation from God as the sinner's substitute. Here the sorrow, grief and pain are at their worst. He is pierced for our transgressions (Isa 53:5) and gives himself a "ransom for many" (20:28; 1Ti 2:6). Him who had no sin God makes "to be sin for us" (2Co 5:21); he dies forsaken, that we might never be forsaken (cf. Ps 22). Thus we are redeemed by the sufferings of Christ (1Pe 1:19). (For the tenth stage of the sufferings of Christ, see v. 50, note.)

27:50 JESUS . . . CRIED OUT AGAIN. The sufferings of Christ, stage ten. Christ utters his final words with a loud voice, "It is finished" (Jn 19:30). This cry signifies the end of his sufferings and the completion of the work of redemption. The debt for our sin has been paid in full, and the plan of salvation established. Only then does he offer a final prayer, "Father, into your hands I commit my spirit" (Lk 23:46). (For the first stage of Christ's sufferings, see 26:37, note.)

27:51 THE CURTAIN ... WAS TORN. The tearing of the "curtain of the temple" (see Ex 26:33, note) signified that a way was now open into the presence of God. The curtain separating the Holy Place from the Most Holy Place barred the way into the presence of God. Through the death of Christ, the curtain was removed and the way into the Most Holy Place (i.e., God's presence) was open for all who believe in Christ and his saving word (cf. Heb 9:1–14; 10:19–22).

27:52 MANY HOLY PEOPLE ... WERE RAISED. The significance of this event is the prophetic indication that Christ's death and resurrection guarantee our glorious resurrection at his return. His resurrection marked the defeat of death (see 1Co 15:50–58; 1Th 4:14).

came a rich man from Arimathea,
named Joseph, who had himself become a disciple of Jesus. 58Going to
Pilate, he asked for Jesus' body,
and Pilate ordered that it be giv-
en to him. 59Joseph took the body,
wrapped it in a clean linen cloth,
60and placed it in his own new tomb[j]
that he had cut out of the rock. He
rolled a big stone in front of the
entrance to the tomb and went away.
61Mary Magdalene and the other
Mary were sitting there opposite the
tomb.

The Guard at the Tomb

62The next day, the one after Preparation Day, the chief priests and the
Pharisees went to Pilate. 63"Sir," they
said, "we remember that while he was
still alive that deceiver said, 'After
three days I will rise again.'[k] 64So
give the order for the tomb to be made
secure until the third day. Otherwise,
his disciples may come and steal the
body[l] and tell the people that he has
been raised from the dead. This last
deception will be worse than the
first."

65"Take a guard,"[m] Pilate answered. "Go, make the tomb as secure
as you know how." 66So they went and
made the tomb secure by putting a
seal[n] on the stone[o] and posting the
guard.[p]

27:60 [j] Mt 27:66; 28:2; Mk 16:4; Ac 13:29
27:63 [k] S Mt 16:21
27:64 [l] Mt 28:13
27:65 [m] ver 66; Mt 28:11
27:66 [n] Da 6:17 [o] ver 60; Mt 28:2 [p] Mt 28:11

The Resurrection

28:1-8pp — Mk 16:1-8; Lk 24:1-10

28 After the Sabbath, at dawn on
the first day of the week, Mary
Magdalene[q] and the other Mary[r]
went to look at the tomb.

2There was a violent earthquake,[s]
for an angel[t] of the Lord came down
from heaven and, going to the tomb,
rolled back the stone[u] and sat on it.
3His appearance was like lightning,
and his clothes were white as snow.[v]
4The guards were so afraid of him
that they shook and became like dead
men.

5The angel said to the women, "Do
not be afraid,[w] for I know that you are
looking for Jesus, who was crucified.
6He is not here; he has risen, just as he
said.[x] Come and see the place where
he lay. 7Then go quickly and tell his
disciples: 'He has risen from the dead
and is going ahead of you into Galilee.[y] There you will see him.' Now I
have told you."

8So the women hurried away
from the tomb, afraid yet filled with
joy, and ran to tell his disciples.
9Suddenly Jesus met them.[z] "Greetings," he said. They came to him,
clasped his feet and worshiped him.
10Then Jesus said to them, "Do not
be afraid. Go and tell my brothers[a]
to go to Galilee; there they will
see me."

28:1 [q] Lk 8:2 [r] Mt 27:56
28:2 [s] Mt 27:51 [t] Jn 20:12; S Ac 5:19 [u] Mt 27:60
28:3 [v] Da 7:9; 10:6; Mk 9:3; S Jn 20:12
28:5 [w] ver 10; S Mt 14:27
28:6 [x] S Mt 16:21
28:7 [y] ver 10,16; Mt 26:32
28:9 [z] Jn 20:14-18
28:10 [a] Mt 12:50; 25:40; Mk 3:34; Jn 20:17; Ro 8:29; Heb 2:11-13,17

28:6 HE HAS RISEN. The resurrection of Jesus is one of the central truths of the gospel (1Co 15:1–8). What is the importance of Christ's resurrection to those who believe in him? (1) It proves he is the Son of God (Jn 10:17–18; Ro 1:4). (2) It guarantees the efficacy of his redemptive death (Ro 6:4; 1Co 15:17). (3) It verifies the truth of Scripture (Ps 16:10; Lk 24:44–47; Ac 2:31). (4) It is proof of future judgment on the wicked (Ac 17:30–31). (5) It is the foundation for Christ's gift of the Holy Spirit and spiritual life to his people (Jn 20:22; Ro 5:10; 1Co 15:45) and for his heavenly ministry of intercession for the believer (Heb 7:23–28). (6) It assures believers of their future heavenly inheritance (1Pe 1:3–4) and of their resurrection or translation when the Lord returns (see Jn 14:3, note; 1Th 4:14ff). (7) It makes available the presence of Christ and his power over sin in our everyday experience (Gal 2:20; Eph 1:18–20).

28:9 JESUS MET THEM. The resurrection is well verified historically. After his resurrection, Christ remained on earth for forty days, appearing and talking to the apostles and many of his followers. The resurrection appearances are as follows: (1) Mary Magdalene (Jn 20:11–18); (2) the women returning from the tomb (vv. 9–10); (3) Peter (Lk 24:34); (4) two travelers on the Emmaus road (Lk 24:13–32); (5) all the disciples except Thomas, and others with them (Lk 24:36–43); (6) all the disciples on Sunday night one week later (Jn 20:26–31); (7) seven disciples by the Sea of Galilee (Jn 21:1–25); (8) five hundred people in Galilee (compare vv. 16–20 with 1Co 15:6); (9) James (1Co 15:7); (10) the disciples receiving the Great Commission (vv. 16–20); (11) the apostles at the ascension (Ac 1:3–11); and (12) the apostle Paul (1Co 15:8).

28:10 DO NOT BE AFRAID. Why were these women not to be afraid? The angel's response gives us the answer: "for I know that you are looking for Jesus" (v. 5). The women had remained loyal friends of Jesus when the world despised and crucified him. At Christ's return, his faithful will have no reason to fear if they also have remained loyal to him in the midst of a world that rejects his love, salvation and holy Word. John expresses this truth in 1Jn 2:28: "And now, dear children, continue in him, so that when he appears we may be confident and unashamed before him at his coming."

The Guards' Report

11While the women were on their
way, some of the guards[b] went into
the city and reported to the chief
priests everything that had happened.
12When the chief priests had met with
the elders and devised a plan, they
gave the soldiers a large sum of money,
13telling them, "You are to say, 'His
disciples came during the night and
stole him away[c] while we were
asleep.' 14If this report gets to the governor,[d] we will satisfy him and keep
you out of trouble." 15So the soldiers
took the money and did as they were
instructed. And this story has been
widely circulated among the Jews to
this very day.

28:11 [b] Mt 27:65, 66
28:13 [c] Mt 27:64
28:14 [d] S Mt 27:2
28:16 [e] ver 7,10; Mt 26:32
28:18 [f] Da 7:13, 14; Lk 10:22; Jn 3:35; S 13:13; 17:2; 1Co 15:27; Eph 1:20-22; Php 2:9,10
28:19 [g] Isa 49:6; Mk 16:15,16; Lk 24:47; Ac 1:8; 14:21 [h] Ac 1:8; 2:38; 8:16; Ro 6:3,4; Gal 3:27; Col 2:12
28:20 [i] Jn 14:26; Ac 2:42 [j] Dt 31:6; 1Ki 8:57; Hag 1:13; Mt 18:20; Ac 18:10 [k] Mt 13:39; 24:3

The Great Commission

16Then the eleven disciples went to
Galilee, to the mountain where Jesus
had told them to go.[e] 17When they
saw him, they worshiped him; but
some doubted. 18Then Jesus came to
them and said, "All authority in heaven
and on earth has been given to me.[f]
19Therefore go and make disciples of
all nations,[g] baptizing them in[m] the
name of the Father and of the Son and
of the Holy Spirit,[h] 20and teaching[i]
them to obey everything I have commanded you. And surely I am with
you[j] always, to the very end of the
age."[k]

Mk 16:15-16

[m] *19* Or *into*; see Acts 8:16; 19:5; Romans 6:3; 1 Cor. 1:13; 10:2 and Gal. 3:27.

28:18 ALL AUTHORITY. God's people are promised authority and power to proclaim the gospel throughout the world (vv. 19–20). But first they must obey Jesus' command to wait for the promise of the Father, which is the power of the Holy Spirit at Pentecost. We cannot expect the power of Ac 1:8 to accompany our going to the nations without first following the pattern of Ac 1:4 (see Lk 24:47–49; Ac 1:8; 2:4).

28:19 GO . . . MAKE DISCIPLES . . . BAPTIZING. These words are Christ's Great Commission to all his followers of every generation. They state the goal, responsibility and commissioning of the church's missionary task. (1) The church is to go into all the world and preach the gospel to all people according to the NT revelation of Christ and the apostles (see Eph 2:20, note). This task includes the primary responsibility of sending missionaries into every nation (Ac 13:1–4).

(2) The preaching of the gospel is centered on "repentance and forgiveness of sins" (Lk 24:47), the promise of receiving "the gift of the Holy Spirit" (Ac 2:38) and the exhortation to separate from this corrupt generation (Ac 2:40) while waiting for the return of Jesus from heaven (Ac 3:19–20; 1Th 1:10).

(3) The purpose is to make disciples who will observe Christ's commands. This is the only direct imperative in this passage. Christ does not intend that evangelism and missionary witness result only in conversion decisions. Spiritual energies must not be concentrated in merely enlarging church membership, but in making disciples who separate themselves from the world, observe the commands of Christ, and follow him with all their heart, mind and will (cf. Jn 8:31).

(4) Furthermore, note that Christ commands us to concentrate on reaching lost men and women, not on Christianizing society or taking over the world. Those who believe must come out of the current evil world system and be separated from its immorality (Ro 13:12; 2Co 6:14; see article on SPIRITUAL SEPARATION FOR BELIEVERS, p. 1794), while exposing its evil (Eph 5:11).

(5) Those who believe in Christ and the gospel are to be "baptized" with water. This represents their covenant pledge to renounce immorality, the world and their own sinful nature, and to unreservedly commit themselves to Christ and his kingdom purposes (see Ac 22:16, note).

(6) Christ will be with his obedient followers in the presence and power of the Holy Spirit (cf. v. 20; 1:23; 18:20). They are to go to all nations and witness only after they are "clothed with power from on high" (Lk 24:49; see Ac 1:8, notes).

28:20 I AM WITH YOU. This promise is Christ's assurance to those involved in winning the lost and teaching them to obey his righteous standards. Jesus arose, is now alive and is personally interested in each one of his children. He is with you in the person of the Holy Spirit (Jn 14:16, 26) and through his Word (Jn 14:23). No matter what your condition is—weak, poor, humble, apparently unimportant—he cares for you, watches with concern every detail of life's trials and struggles, and gives both the grace that is sufficient (2Co 12:9) and his presence to lead you home (18:20; Ac 18:10). This is the Christian's answer to every fear, every doubt, every trouble, every heartache and every discouragement.

THE KINGDOM OF GOD VERSUS THE KINGDOM OF SATAN

A. The Nature of the Kingdoms

Item	Kingdom of God: Description	Kingdom of God: Reference	Kingdom of Satan: Description	Kingdom of Satan: Reference
1. Rulership	a. Rule by God—Theocracy	2Ch 20:6; Ps 95:3; Da 4:17,32; 1Ti 1:17	a. Rule by Satan—the god of this age	Jn 12:31; 14:30; 2Co 4:4; Eph 2:2; 1Jn 5:19
	b. God's rule through his Son	Ps 110:1; Isa 9:6–7; Da 7:13–14; Mt 28:18; Lk 1:32–33; Eph 1:20–22; Heb 1:3–8; Rev 1:5; 19:13–16	b. Satan assisted by principalities, powers and rulers of this dark world	Eph 1:21; 6:12; Col 1:16; 2:15; cf. Da 10:13
2. Character	a. Righteousness, peace and joy in the Holy Spirit	Mt 6:33; Jn 18:36; Ro 14:17	a. Centered in the things of this world	1Jn 2:15–17; 5:19; Rev 2:9,13
	b. Divine power	Lk 11:20–22; 1Co 2:4; 4:20; 1Th 1:5	b. Disease, sickness, slavery	Mt 10:1; Lk 9:1
	c. Truth	Jn 8:31–32; 14:6,16–17; 15:26; 16:13; 17:17	c. Deception	Ge 3:4–5,13; Jn 8:44; Ro 1:25; 2Co 4:4; 2Th 2:10–12
	d. Holiness	1Co 1:2,30; 2Co 6:17—7:1; Eph 4:24; Heb 12:10,14; 1Pe 1:15–16	d. Sin and evil	Ro 1:28–32; 1Co 6:9–10; Eph 2:1–3; 1Jn 3:7–10,12
	e. Light	Jn 1:4–9; 3:19; Ac 26:18; Col 1:12–13; 1Ti 6:16; 1Jn 1:5,7	e. Darkness	Lk 22:53; Ac 26:18; Eph 6:12; Col 1:13; 1Jn 1:6; cf. 2Co 11:14
	f. Eternal life	Jn 1:4; 3:16; Ro 5:17; 6:4,12; 8:2; 1Jn 5:12; Rev 1:18	f. Eternal death	Ro 5:12,14; 6:23; Eph 2:1; Rev 20:14–15; 21:8
3. Manifestation	a. Salvation	Mk 1:15; Ac 8:12; 1Co 5:10–11	a. Destruction	Jn 10:10; 1Pe 5:8

Item	Kingdom of God		Kingdom of Satan	
	Description	Reference	Description	Reference
3. Manifestation (cont.)	b. Baptism in the Holy Spirit	Mt 3:2,11–12; Ac 1:3–8	b. Filled with the spirit of the world	1Co 2:12; Jas 4:4; 1Jn 2:15
	c. Miracles and driving out demons	Mt 4:23–24; 10:7–8; 12:28; Lk 9:1–2,11; 11:20–22; 13:11–16	c. By counterfeit miracles and demon-possession	Mt 4:24; 8:28; 24:24; 2Th 2:9; Rev 13:13–14
	d. The presence of Jesus	Mt 3:1–3; 4:17; Mk 1:14–15	d. The presence of evil spirits	Mt 8:28; 12:22–29; Mk 5:2–5,9; 6:7; Ac 19:16; Rev 18:2
	e. Gifts of the Spirit	Ro 12:6–8; 1Co 12:1–31	e. Sorcery, witchcraft, drugs, occult activity	Ac 16:16; 19:18–19; 1Co 10:20; Gal 5:20; Rev 2:24
	f. Fruit of the Spirit	Gal 5:22–23	f. Acts of the sinful nature	Gal 5:19–21

B. The People of the Kingdoms

Item	Kingdom of God		Kingdom of Satan	
	Description	Reference	Description	Reference
1. Entrance	a. Repentance and forgiveness	Mk 1:15; Ac 2:37–38; 1Jn 1:9	a. All unregenerate humanity	Ro 3:23; 5:12; Eph 2:2–3; Col 1:13
	b. Humility	Mt 18:3; Mk 10:15	b. Pride, independence	Ps 2:1–2; Pr 16:18; Eze 16:40–50; Da 4:30; Ob 3; Ro 1:30; 2Ti 3:2; Jude 16
	c. Confession and faith	Ro 10:8–13; Heb 4:2	c. Rebellion and unbelief	Ro 1:18–32; Heb 3:19; 12:25
	d. New birth	Jn 3:3,5	d. Spiritual death	Ro 5:12,17; 6:23; Eph 2:1; Col 2:13
	e. Union with Christ	Ro 6:3–8	e. Separation from God	Eph 2:12

Item	Kingdom of God: Description	Kingdom of God: Reference	Kingdom of Satan: Description	Kingdom of Satan: Reference
2. Characteristics of Members	a. Children of God	Jn 1:12–13; 3:3–5; Ro 8:15; Gal 4:5; Eph 1:5	a. Children of Satan	Jn 8:44; 1Jn 3:8–10
	b. Faith and obedience	Mt 6:25–32; Jn 14:21; Ro 1:5; 16:26; Heb 11:6	b. Unbelief and rebellion	Mt 17:17; Lk 12:46; 2Th 3:2; Tit 1:15; Rev 21:8
	c. Eternal life	Jn 3:16,36; 5:24; 6:40; 1Jn 2:25; 5:11; Rev 2:7	c. Eternal death	Jn 3:18,36; Ro 5:12; 6:23; Jas 1:15; 1Jn 5:12; Rev 20:14–15; 21:8
	d. Walk in the light	Ro 13:13; Eph 5:8; Php 2:15; 1Th 5:5,8	d. Walk in darkness	Jn 3:19; Ro 13:12–13; Eph 5:11–12; 1Jn 1:6; 2:9,11
	e. Devoted to the truth	2Th 2:13; 1Ti 3:15; 3Jn 3–5	e. Speak lies and oppose truth	Jn 8:44; Ro 1:18,25; 2Ti 2:18; 3:8; 4:4
	f. Strangers in the world	Heb 11:13; 1Pe 2:11	f. Love things of the world	1Co 6:9; 2Ti 3:4; 2Pe 2:3; Jude 11; Rev 3:17–19
	g. Live by the Spirit	Ro 8:9–11; 1Co 2:10–13; Gal 5:16–26	g. Live by the sinful nature	Ro 8:5–6; Gal 5:16–26
	h. Humble and childlike, living righteously	Mt 5:6,20; 6:33; 18:1–4; Lk 18:16–17; 1Th 2:12; Eph 4:24	h. Wicked, disobedient and immoral	Gal 5:19–21; Eph 2:2–3; 5:5–6; Jas 1:14–15; 1Jn 2:15–17; 3:8
	i. Meekness and submission	Pr 16:19; Mt 5:5; Eph 5:21–22; Jas 3:17; 1Pe 2:13—3:9	i. Arrogance and self-assertion	2Ti 3:2; Jas 4:6
	j. Freedom in Christ	Ro 6:6,18,22; 1Pe 2:16	j. Bondage to sin and Satan	Ro 7:14–24
	k. Honesty	Ex 20:15–16; Eph 4:25,28	k. Deceit	Pr 12:5,20a; Ro 1:29; Eph 4:22; Rev 21:8

Item	Kingdom of God: Description	Kingdom of God: Reference	Kingdom of Satan: Description	Kingdom of Satan: Reference
2. Characteristics of Members (cont.)	l. Love	Mt 5:43–48; 7:12; 1Co 13; Eph 5:2	l. Hatred and hostility	Lk 21:17; Jn 15:18–19; 18:14; Ro 1:30; Tit 3:3; Jas 4:4
	m. Forgiveness	Mt 5:14–15; Eph 4:32	m. Bitterness	Ro 3:14; Eph 4:31
	n. Godly influence	Mt 5:13–16; Tit 2:12; 1Pe 2:12; 2Pe 3:11	n. Corrupting influence	Ge 19:1–38; Pr 2:12–22; 1Co 15:33
	o. Sexual purity and marital faithfulness	Eph 5:3; 1Th 4:3–8	o. Lust and immorality	Ro 1:24–27; 1Co 6:9–10; Gal 5:19; Eph 5:5–6
	p. Generosity	Lk 12:33–34; 6:38; 2Co 8:2–5	p. Greed and covetousness	Lk 12:15–21; Col 3:5; 2Pe 2:14
	q. Holy	Mt 5:8; 1Pe 1:15–16; Rev 22:11	q. Unholy	2Ti 3:2; 2Pe 2:5–6; Jude 15; Rev 22:11
	r. Upright speech	Ex 20:16; Pr 10:19–21; Ecc 5:2,6–7; Eph 4:29; 5:4; Jas 1:26; 3:1–2	r. Corrupt speech	Pr 10:18; 15:28; Ro 3:13–14
	s. Inherit the kingdom	Mt 25:34–40; Jn 3:3–5; 1Co 6:11; Rev 21:7	s. Do not inherit the kingdom	1Co 6:9–11; Gal 5:21; Eph 5:5
3. Duties	a. Worship only God	Ex 20:2–6; Mt 4:10; Jn 4:23–24; 1Th 1:9	a. Idolatry; living for self; ultimately worshiping Satan and antichrist	Da 11:30–33; 2Th 2:4; Rev 13:4,8,12,15
	b. Hate sin and Satan	Ps 139:21; Ro 12:9; Heb 1:9; 1Jn 2:15	b. Hate and persecute believers; hate Christ and righteousness	Jn 15:19; 16:3; 17:14; 2Ti 3:12; Rev 12:13,17
	c. Seek to advance God's kingdom and his righteousness	Mt 6:31–33; 11:12; 28:19–20; Ac 1:6–8; 19:8; 28:23,31; Col 4:11	c. Promote evil and corrupt God's kingdom and righteousness	Mt 7:15; 13:24–28,36–43; 24:23–24; Lk 21:8; Ac 20:29–30; Gal 1:8–9; 1Jn 2:18–19; 2Jn 7–11

Item	Kingdom of God: Description	Kingdom of God: Reference	Kingdom of Satan: Description	Kingdom of Satan: Reference
3. Duties (cont.)	d. Do not love the world	Mt 6:19–24; Jn 17:15–16; Ro 12:1–2; 1Co 10:21–22; 2Co 6:14–18; 2Ti 3:1–5; Jas 4:4; 1Jn 2:15–17	d. Love the world	Ps 17:14; Mk 8:36; Php 3:19; 2Ti 4:10; 1Jn 2:15–16
	e. Wait for Christ's return from heaven	1Th 1:10; 4:13–18; 1Ti 4:8; Tit 2:13	e. Do not watch for Christ's return	Mt 24:45–51; Lk 12:42–46; 1Th 5:4–6
4. Power and dominion	a. Personal level	Lk 10:17; Jn 16:33; Ro 6:12,14	a. Personal level	Jn 8:23; Eph 2:1; 1Jn 3:8
	b. Family level	Dt 6:1–9; 1Co 11:3; Eph 5:22—6:4	b. Family level	Lk 16:27–31; 21:16; 2Ti 3:2–3,6
	c. Church level	Mt 5:13–20; 18:15–20	c. Organizational level	Jn 12:31; Eph 6:12; Rev 13:1–11; 17—18
	d. Business level	Lk 16:1–13; Col 3:23–25	d. Business level	Ac 16:16–21; 19:23–28; Rev 18:3,11–24

C. The Warfare of the Kingdoms

Item	Kingdom of God: Description	Kingdom of God: Reference	Kingdom of Satan: Description	Kingdom of Satan: Reference
1. Christ's Warfare with Satan	a. Christ came to destroy Satan's kingdom	Lk 4:18–21; Jn 12:31; Ac 26:15–18; 1Jn 3:8	a. Satan intent on destroying Christ's kingdom	Mt 4:1–11; 16:22–23
	b. Christ overcame temptation	Mt 4:1–11; Lk 4:1–11; Heb 4:15	b. Satan tempted Christ	Mt 4:1–11; Lk 4:1–11; Heb 4:15
	c. Christ drove out demons	Mk 1:25–26,32–34,39; 3:12; 5:12–15; 7:24–30; 9:14–29; Lk 11:20–22	c. Demons challenged Christ	Mk 1:24,34; 3:11; 5:7
	d. All power belongs eternally to Christ	Mt 28:18; 1Jn 4:4	d. Satan has only temporary and limited power	Job 1:6–12; 2:1–6; Lk 22:53; Rev 20:7–9

Item	Kingdom of God		Kingdom of Satan	
	Description	Reference	Description	Reference
1. Christ's Warfare with Satan (cont.)	e. Deliverance from sin and disease provided through the cross	Isa 53; 1Pe 2:24	e. Satan cannot withstand the power of the cross	2Co 4:10; Rev 12:10–11
	f. Final victory belongs to Christ	2Th 2:7–8; 2Pe 3:10–13; Rev 17:14; 19:11–21	f. Satan will be finally defeated and destroyed	Mt 25:41,46; Jn 16:11; Rev 20:10,14–15
2. Believers' warfare with Satan	a. Believers hate sin and seek to destroy the works of the devil	Mt 12:29–30; Mk 3:27; Lk 11:21–23	a. Satan hates and persecutes believers	Jn 15:19; 17:14; Rev 12:13,17
	b. The weapons of believers are spiritual and not worldly	Mt 26:52; 2Co 10:4–5; Eph 6:10–17	b. Satan uses the world, the sinful nature and the demonic against believers	2Co 11:3,14–15; Gal 5:17–21; Eph 6:11–12; 1Pe 2:11; 5:8; Rev 12:13,17; 13:15–18
	c. Believers are given authority to drive out demons	Mk 3:14–15; 6:7; 16:17; Lk 9:1–2; 10:17; Ac 5:16; 8:7; 16:18; 19:12	c. Demons try to destroy believers spiritually	Mk 9:17–18; Ac 8:7; 16:16–17;1Pe 5:8
	d. Believers must overcome the world	Gal 6:14; 1Jn 2:13–14; 4:4; 5:4; Rev 2:7,11,17,26; 3:5,12,21; 12:11; 21:7,11	d. Satan seeks to overcome believers	Jer 1:19; Lk 10:19; Ro 12:21; 1Ti 5:11; 2Pe 2:20
	e. By the cross believers are dead to the world	Gal 6:14; Heb 11:25–26	e. Satan entices to sinful pleasures of the world	Php 3:19; 2Ti 3:4; 1Jn 2:16–17

MARK

Outline

I. Preparation for Jesus' Ministry (1:1–13)
  A. The Ministry of John the Baptist (1:2–8)
  B. The Baptism of Jesus (1:9–11)
  C. The Temptation of Jesus (1:12–13)
II. Early Galilean Ministry (1:14—3:6)
  A. The First Four Disciples (1:14–20)
  B. A Sabbath in Capernaum (1:21–34)
  C. First Preaching Tour (1:35–45)
  D. Conflicts With the Pharisees (2:1—3:6)
III. Later Galilean Ministry (3:7—7:23)
  A. Withdrawal to the Seaside (3:7–12)
  B. Appointment of the Twelve Disciples (3:13–19)
  C. Friends and Foes (3:20–35)
  D. Teaching in Parables (4:1–34)
  E. Teaching Through Mighty Works (4:35—5:43)
  F. Jesus at Nazareth (6:1–6)
  G. The Mission of the Twelve (6:7–13)
  H. Herod and John the Baptist (6:14–29)
  I. Miracles and Teaching Around the Sea of Galilee (6:30–56)
  J. Conflict With Tradition (7:1–23)
IV. Ministry Beyond Galilee (7:24–9:29)
  A. Two Gentiles' Healings (7:24–37)
  B. More Miracles (8:1–26)
  C. The Caesarea Philippi Episode (8:27—9:1)
  D. The Transfiguration Episode (9:2–29)
V. The Road Toward Jerusalem (9:30—10:52)
  A. En Route Through Galilee (9:30–50)
  B. Ministry in Perea (10:1–52)
VI. Passion Week (11:1—15:47)
  A. Sunday: Triumphal Entry to Jerusalem (11:1–11)
  B. Monday: 1. Cursing the Fig Tree (11:12–14)
    2. Cleansing the Temple (11:15–19)
  C. Tuesday: 1. Faith and Fear (11:20–33)
    2. Parable and Controversy (12:1–44)
    3. The Olivet Discourse (13:1–37)
    4. The Anointing at Bethany (14:1–11)
  D. Thursday: The Last Supper (14:12–25)
  E. Friday: 1. Jesus in Gethsemane (14:26–52)
    2. The Jewish Trial (14:53–72)
    3. The Roman Trial (15:1–20)
    4. The Crucifixion and Burial (15:21–47)
VII. The Resurrection (16:1–20)
  A. The Resurrection Discovery (16:1–8)
  B. Post-Resurrection Appearances (16:9–18)
  C. Ascension and Apostolic Mission (16:19–20)

Author: Mark

Theme: Jesus, the Servant-Son

Date of Writing: A.D. 55–65

Background

Among the four Gospels, Mark is the most concise account of "the beginning of the gospel about Jesus Christ, the Son of God" (1:1). Although the author is not identified by name in the book itself (true of all the Gospels), the early and unanimous testimony of the church is that John Mark was responsible for its writing. This man grew up in Jerusalem and was among the first generation Christians (Ac 12:12). He had the unique opportunity of being associated in ministry with three NT apostles: Paul (Ac 13:1–13; Col 4:10; Phm 24), Barnabas (Ac 15:39) and Peter (1Pe 5:13). According to Papias (c. A.D. 130) and other second-century church fathers, Mark derived the content of his Gospel from his association with Peter, wrote it in Rome and designed it for Roman believers. Although the specific date for the writing of Mark's Gospel is uncertain, most scholars date it in the late 50s or the 60s; it may have been the first of the four Gospels to be written.

Purpose

In the 60s of the first century A.D., believers in Rome were treated cruelly by the populace, and many were tortured and put to death by the Roman emperor Nero. According to tradition, among the Christian martyrs in Rome during this decade were the apostles Peter and Paul. As one of the church leaders in Rome, John Mark was moved by the Holy Spirit to write this Gospel as a prophetic anticipation of, or a pastoral response to, this time of persecution. His intention was to strengthen the foundations of faith in Roman believers and, if need be, to inspire them to suffer faithfully for the gospel, placing before them the life, suffering, death and resurrection of Jesus their Lord.

Survey

In a fast-moving narrative, Mark presents Jesus as the Son of God and the suffering servant Messiah. The watershed of the book is the episode in Caesarea Philippi, followed by the transfiguration (8:27—9:10), where both Jesus' identity and his mission of suffering are fully disclosed to his twelve disciples. The first half of Mark focuses primarily both on Jesus' mighty miracles and on his authority over sickness and demons as signs that God's kingdom is at hand. At Caesarea Philippi, however, Jesus tells his disciples openly that he "must suffer many things and be rejected by the elders, chief priests and teachers of the law, and that he must be killed and after three days rise again" (8:31). There are numerous references throughout Mark to suffering as the cost of discipleship (e.g., 3:21–22,30; 8:34–38; 10:30,33–34,45; 13:8,11–13). God's vindication, however, will follow righteous suffering, as demonstrated in Jesus' resurrection.

Special Features

Four major features characterize Mark's Gospel: (1) It is a Gospel of action, emphasizing what Jesus did rather than what he said. (Mark records eighteen miracles but only four of his parables, not including parabolic statements.) (2) It is distinctively a Gospel for the Romans—explaining Jewish customs, omitting all Jewish genealogies and birth narratives, translating Aramaic words and using Latin terms. (3) It is a Gospel that begins abruptly and proceeds rapidly from one episode to another with the frequent use of the Greek adverb for "immediately" (42 times). (4) It is a Gospel of vividness, describing the events of Jesus' life succinctly, vividly and with the picturesque skill of a literary artist.

Reading Mark

In order to read the entire New Testament in one year, the book of Mark should be read in 29 days, according to the following schedule:
☐ 1:1–20 ☐ 1:21–45 ☐ 2:1–22 ☐ 2:23—3:12 ☐ 3:13–35 ☐ 4:1–20 ☐ 4:21–41 ☐ 5:1–20 ☐ 5:21–43 ☐ 6:1–29 ☐ 6:30–56 ☐ 7:1–23 ☐ 7:24—8:13 ☐ 8:14–26 ☐ 8:27—9:13 ☐ 9:14–32 ☐ 9:33–50 ☐ 10:1–31 ☐ 10:32–52 ☐ 11:1–26 ☐ 11:27—12:17 ☐ 12:18–44 ☐ 13 ☐ 14:1–26 ☐ 14:27–52 ☐ 14:53–72 ☐ 15:1–20 ☐ 15:21–47 ☐ 16

NOTES

John the Baptist Prepares the Way

1:2–8pp — Mt 3:1–11; Lk 3:2–16

1 The beginning of the gospel about
Jesus Christ, the Son of God.[a][a]

2It is written in Isaiah the prophet:

"I will send my messenger ahead
of you,
who will prepare your
way"[b][b]—
3"a voice of one calling in the
desert,
'Prepare the way for the Lord,
make straight paths for
him.' "[c][c]

4And so John[d] came, baptizing in the
desert region and preaching a baptism
of repentance[e] for the forgiveness of
sins.[f] 5The whole Judean countryside
and all the people of Jerusalem went
out to him. Confessing their sins, they
were baptized by him in the Jordan River. 6John wore clothing made of camel's hair, with a leather belt around his
waist,[g] and he ate locusts[h] and wild
honey. 7And this was his message: "After me will come one more powerful
than I, the thongs of whose sandals I
am not worthy to stoop down and untie.[i] 8I baptize you with[d] water, but
he will baptize you with the Holy Spir- Lk 1:15
it."[j]

The Baptism and Temptation of Jesus

1:9–11pp — Mt 3:13–17; Lk 3:21,22
1:12,13pp — Mt 4:1–11; Lk 4:1–13

9At that time Jesus came from Nazareth[k] in Galilee and was baptized by
John[l] in the Jordan. 10As Jesus was
coming up out of the water, he saw
heaven being torn open and the Spirit
descending on him like a dove.[m]
11And a voice came from heaven: "You
are my Son,[n] whom I love; with you I
am well pleased."[o]

12At once the Spirit sent him out
into the desert, 13and he was in the
desert forty days,[p] being tempted by
Satan.[q] He was with the wild animals,
and angels attended him.

The Calling of the First Disciples

1:16–20pp — Mt 4:18–22; Lk 5:2–11; Jn 1:35–42

14After John[r] was put in prison,
Jesus went into Galilee,[s] proclaiming
the good news of God.[t] 15"The time
has come,"[u] he said. "The kingdom of

1:1 [a] S Mt 4:3
1:2 [b] Mal 3:1; Mt 11:10; Lk 7:27
1:3 [c] Isa 40:3; Jn 1:23
1:4 [d] S Mt 3:1 [e] ver 8; Jn 1:26,33; Ac 1:5,22; 11:36; 13:24; 18:25; 19:3,4 [f] Lk 1:77
1:6 [g] 2Ki 1:8 [h] Lev 11:22
1:7 [i] Ac 13:25
1:8 [j] Isa 44:3; Joel 2:28; Jn 1:33; Ac 1:5; 2:4; 11:16; 19:4-6
1:9 [k] S Mt 2:23 [l] S Mt 3:1
1:10 [m] Jn 1:32
1:11 [n] S Mt 3:17 [o] S Mt 3:17
1:13 [p] Ex 24:18; 1Ki 19:8 [q] S Mt 4:10; Heb 4:15
1:14 [r] S Mt 3:1 [s] Mt 4:12 [t] Mt 4:23
1:15 [u] Ro 5:6; Gal 4:4; Eph 1:10

[a] *1* Some manuscripts do not have *the Son of God.* [b] *2* Mal. 3:1 [c] *3* Isaiah 40:3 [d] *8* Or *in*

1:4 REPENTANCE. See Mt 3:2, note.

1:5 THE WHOLE JUDEAN COUNTRYSIDE. There was a general spiritual awakening in Judea and Galilee that accompanied the ministry of John the Baptist. Israel's spiritual climate changed among the common people as a result, helping to prepare the way for the full revelation of God in his incarnate Son, Jesus Christ.

1:8 BAPTIZE YOU WITH THE HOLY SPIRIT. John the Baptist was the first one who preached the good news concerning Jesus; his preaching is condensed by Mark into one single theme: the proclamation of Jesus Christ, who would come and baptize his followers in the Holy Spirit. All those who accept Christ as Lord and Savior should proclaim that Jesus is still the One who baptizes in the Holy Spirit (see Ac 1:8; 2:4,38–39; see Lk 3:16, note on the promised baptism in the Holy Spirit; Ac 1:5, note).

1:9 JESUS . . . WAS BAPTIZED. See Mt 3:13, note.

1:10 THE SPIRIT . . . DESCENDING ON HIM. See Mt 3:16, note.

1:11 MY SON, WHOM I LOVE. All three persons of the Trinity are involved in Jesus' baptism (see Mt 3:17, note). Here and elsewhere in Scripture God is revealed as one essence existing in three distinct persons who share a common divine nature: Father, Son and Holy Spirit (cf. Mt 3:16–17; 28:19; 2Co 13:14; Eph 4:4–6; 1Pe 1:2; Jude 20–21). Thus, God is singular (i.e., a unity) in one sense and plural (i.e., three) in another (see article on THE ATTRIBUTES OF GOD, p. 882). (1) Scripture declares that God is one being—a perfect unity of one nature and essence (12:29; Dt 6:4; Gal 3:20). Of the persons in the Godhead none is God without the others and each with the others is God.

(2) The one God exists in a plurality of three identifiable and distinct, though not separate, persons. The three are not three gods, or three parts or expressions of God, but are three persons so completely united that they form the one true and eternal God. Both the Son and the Holy Spirit possess attributes that can only be true of God (see Ge 1:2; Isa 61:1; Jn 1:1,14, note; 5:18, note; 14:16; 16:8,13; 20:28, note; Ac 5:3–4; Ro 8:2,26–27; 1Co 2:10–11; 2Th 2:13; Heb 9:14). None of the three persons was ever made or created, but each exists equal in essential being, attributes, power and glory.

(3) This one God existing in three persons made possible from all eternity reciprocal love, fellowship, the exercise of divine attributes, mutual communion in knowledge, and interrelationship within the Godhead (cf. Jn 10:15; 11:27; 17:24; 1Co 2:10).

1:13 TEMPTED BY SATAN. See Mt 4:1, note.

1:14 THE GOOD NEWS. See 14:9, note.

God is near. Repent and believe[v] the
good news!"[w]

16As Jesus walked beside the Sea of
Galilee, he saw Simon and his brother
Andrew casting a net into the lake, for
they were fishermen. 17"Come, follow
me," Jesus said, "and I will make you
fishers of men." 18At once they left
their nets and followed him.[x]

19When he had gone a little farther,
he saw James son of Zebedee and his
brother John in a boat, preparing their
nets. 20Without delay he called them,
and they left their father Zebedee in
the boat with the hired men and followed him.

Jesus Drives Out an Evil Spirit

1:21–28pp — Lk 4:31–37

21They went to Capernaum, and
when the Sabbath came, Jesus went
into the synagogue and began to
teach.[y] 22The people were amazed at
his teaching, because he taught them
as one who had authority, not as the
teachers of the law.[z] 23Just then a
man in their synagogue who was possessed by an evil[e] spirit cried out,
24"What do you want with us,[a] Jesus
of Nazareth?[b] Have you come to destroy us? I know who you are—the
Holy One of God!"[c]

25"Be quiet!" said Jesus sternly.
"Come out of him!"[d] 26The evil spirit
shook the man violently and came out
of him with a shriek.[e]

27The people were all so amazed[f]
that they asked each other, "What is
this? A new teaching—and with authority! He even gives orders to evil
spirits and they obey him." 28News
about him spread quickly over the Mk 3:1–
whole region[g] of Galilee. 15

Jesus Heals Many

1:29–31pp — Mt 8:14,15; Lk 4:38,39
1:32–34pp — Mt 8:16,17; Lk 4:40,41

29As soon as they left the synagogue,[h] they went with James and
John to the home of Simon and Andrew. 30Simon's mother-in-law was in
bed with a fever, and they told Jesus
about her. 31So he went to her, took
her hand and helped her up.[i] The fever left her and she began to wait on
them.

32That evening after sunset the people brought to Jesus all the sick and
demon-possessed.[j] 33The whole town
gathered at the door, 34and Jesus
healed many who had various diseases.[k] He also drove out many demons, but he would not let the demons
speak because they knew who he
was.[l]

1:15 [v] S Jn 3:15 [w] Ac 20:21 **1:18** [x] S Mt 4:19 **1:21** [y] ver 39; S Mt 4:23; S Mk 10:1 **1:22** [z] S Mt 7:28, 29 **1:24** [a] S Mt 8:29 [b] Mt 2:23; Lk 24:19; Jn 1:45, 46; Ac 4:10; 24:5 [c] Ps 16:10; Isa 41:14,16,20; Lk 1:35; Jn 6:69; Ac 3:14; 1Jn 2:20
1:25 [d] ver 34 **1:26** [e] Mk 9:20 **1:27** [f] Mk 10:24, 32 **1:28** [g] S Mt 9:26 **1:29** [h] ver 21,23 **1:31** [i] S Lk 7:14 **1:32** [j] S Mt 4:24 **1:34** [k] S Mt 4:23 [l] Mk 3:12; Ac 16:17,18

[e] 23 Greek *unclean*; also in verses 26 and 27

1:15 KINGDOM OF GOD. Christ came to proclaim and bring to completion the kingdom of God. This was the theme of his earthly message (Mt 4:17). About the form of its appearing, we should be aware of several aspects of the kingdom:

(1) The kingdom in Israel. The kingdom in the OT was God's redemptive action within Israel in order to prepare the way for the salvation of the human race (see article on GOD'S COVENANT WITH ABRAHAM, ISAAC AND JACOB, p. 46). Because Israel rejected Jesus, the Messiah, the kingdom was taken away from them (see Mt 21:43, note).

(2) The kingdom in Christ. The kingdom and its power were present in the person and work of Jesus the King (Lk 11:20).

(3) The kingdom in the church. This involves the present manifestation of God's power and rule in the hearts and lives of all who repent and believe the gospel (Jn 3:3,5; Ro 14:17; Col 1:13). Its presence comes with great spiritual power, asserting itself against the dominion of Satan, sin and evil. It is not a political or material kingdom, but a powerful and forceful presence and activity of God among his people (see 1:27; 9:1; see article on THE KINGDOM OF GOD, p. 1430, for a detailed description of the kingdom of God in the church age).

(4) The kingdom in the consummation. This is the Messianic kingdom foretold by the prophets (Ps 89:36–37; Isa 11:1–9; Da 7:13–14). Christ will reign on earth for a thousand years (Rev 20:4–6), and the church will reign with him over the nations (1Co 6:2–3; 2Ti 2:12; Rev 2:26–27; see 20:4, notes).

(5) The kingdom in eternity. The Messianic kingdom will terminate after a thousand years and God's eternal kingdom will be established in the new heaven and new earth (Rev 21:1–4). The center of the new earth is the Holy City, the new Jerusalem (Rev 21:9–11). Its inhabitants are the redeemed from the OT (Rev 21:12) and the NT (Rev 21:14). Their greatest blessing is, "they will see his face" (Rev 22:4; see 21:1, note).

1:17 COME, FOLLOW ME. The first calling of the disciples is to follow Jesus and to know him personally (Php 3:8–10). As a result of this relationship, they must then lead others to a saving knowledge of Jesus (cf. Pr 11:30; Da 12:3; 1Co 9:22).

1:27 EVIL SPIRITS . . . OBEY HIM. See article on POWER OVER SATAN AND DEMONS, p. 1484, for comments on this text.

1:34 DROVE OUT MANY DEMONS. See article on POWER OVER SATAN AND DEMONS, p. 1484.

Jesus Prays in a Solitary Place

1:35–38pp — Lk 4:42,43

35Very early in the morning, while it
was still dark, Jesus got up, left the
house and went off to a solitary place,
where he prayed.[m] **36**Simon and his
companions went to look for him,
37and when they found him, they exclaimed: "Everyone is looking for you!"
38Jesus replied, "Let us go somewhere else—to the nearby villages—
so I can preach there also. That is why
I have come."[n] **39**So he traveled
throughout Galilee, preaching in their
synagogues[o] and driving out demons.[p]

A Man With Leprosy

1:40–44pp — Mt 8:2–4; Lk 5:12–14

40A man with leprosy[f] came to him
and begged him on his knees,[q] "If you
are willing, you can make me clean."
41Filled with compassion, Jesus
reached out his hand and touched the
man. "I am willing," he said. "Be
clean!" **42**Immediately the leprosy left
him and he was cured.
43Jesus sent him away at once with
a strong warning: **44**"See that you don't
tell this to anyone.[r] But go, show
yourself to the priest[s] and offer the
sacrifices that Moses commanded for
your cleansing,[t] as a testimony to
them." **45**Instead he went out and began to talk freely, spreading the news.
As a result, Jesus could no longer enter
a town openly but stayed outside in
lonely places.[u] Yet the people still
came to him from everywhere.[v]

Jesus Heals a Paralytic

2:3–12pp — Mt 9:2–8; Lk 5:18–26

2 A few days later, when Jesus again
entered Capernaum, the people
heard that he had come home. **2**So
many[w] gathered that there was no
room left, not even outside the door,
and he preached the word to them.
3Some men came, bringing to him a
paralytic,[x] carried by four of them.
4Since they could not get him to Jesus
because of the crowd, they made an
opening in the roof above Jesus and,
after digging through it, lowered the
mat the paralyzed man was lying on.
5When Jesus saw their faith, he said to
the paralytic, "Son, your sins are forgiven."[y]
6Now some teachers of the law were
sitting there, thinking to themselves,
7"Why does this fellow talk like that?
He's blaspheming! Who can forgive
sins but God alone?"[z]
8Immediately Jesus knew in his spirit that this was what they were thinking in their hearts, and he said to them,
"Why are you thinking these things?
9Which is easier: to say to the paralytic, 'Your sins are forgiven,' or to say,
'Get up, take your mat and walk'?
10But that you may know that the Son
of Man[a] has authority on earth to forgive sins . . . ." He said to the paralytic,
11"I tell you, get up, take your mat and
go home." **12**He got up, took his mat
and walked out in full view of them all.
This amazed everyone and they
praised God,[b] saying, "We have never
seen anything like this!"[c] Mk 5:25-34

The Calling of Levi

2:14–17pp — Mt 9:9–13; Lk 5:27–32

13Once again Jesus went out beside
the lake. A large crowd came to him,[d]
and he began to teach them. **14**As he
walked along, he saw Levi son of Alphaeus sitting at the tax collector's
booth. "Follow me,"[e] Jesus told him,
and Levi got up and followed him.
15While Jesus was having dinner at
Levi's house, many tax collectors and
"sinners" were eating with him and his
disciples, for there were many who followed him. **16**When the teachers of the
law who were Pharisees[f] saw him
eating with the "sinners" and tax collectors, they asked his disciples: "Why
does he eat with tax collectors and
'sinners'?"[g]
17On hearing this, Jesus said to
them, "It is not the healthy who need

1:35 [m] S Lk 3:21 **1:38** [n] Isa 61:1 **1:39** [o] S Mt 4:23 [p] S Mt 4:24 **1:40** [q] Mk 10:17 **1:44** [r] S Mt 8:4 [s] Lev 13:49 [t] Lev 14:1-32 **1:45** [u] Lk 5:15,16 [v] Mk 2:13; Lk 5:17; Jn 6:2 **2:2** [w] ver 13; Mk 1:45 **2:3** [x] S Mt 4:24

2:5 [y] Lk 7:48 **2:7** [z] Isa 43:25 **2:10** [a] S Mt 8:20 **2:12** [b] S Mt 9:8 [c] Mt 9:33 **2:13** [d] Mk 1:45; Lk 5:15; Jn 6:2 **2:14** [e] S Mt 4:19 **2:16** [f] Ac 23:9 [g] S Mt 9:11

[f] *40* The Greek word was used for various diseases affecting the skin—not necessarily leprosy.

2:10 SON OF MAN. See Lk 5:24, note.

2:11 HEALING THE PARALYTIC. It was never God's intention that people should live with sickness, disease and infirmity. These things are the results of the sinfulness of the human race and the activity of Satan in the world. Consequently, every healing through Christ involves God invading the realm of Satan to destroy his work (1Jn 3:8; see article on DIVINE HEALING, p. 1420).

2:17 TO CALL . . . SINNERS. See Mt 9:11, note.

a doctor, but the sick. I have not come to call the righteous, but sinners."[h]

Jesus Questioned About Fasting

2:18–22pp — Mt 9:14–17; Lk 5:33–38

18Now John's disciples and the Pharisees were fasting.[i] Some people came and asked Jesus, "How is it that John's disciples and the disciples of the Pharisees are fasting, but yours are not?"

19Jesus answered, "How can the guests of the bridegroom fast while he is with them? They cannot, so long as they have him with them. **20**But the time will come when the bridegroom will be taken from them,[j] and on that day they will fast.

21"No one sews a patch of unshrunk cloth on an old garment. If he does, the new piece will pull away from the old, making the tear worse. **22**And no one pours new wine into old wineskins. If he does, the wine will burst the skins, and both the wine and the wineskins will be ruined. No, he pours new wine into new wineskins."

Lord of the Sabbath

2:23–28pp — Mt 12:1–8; Lk 6:1–5
3:1–6pp — Mt 12:9–14; Lk 6:6–11

23One Sabbath Jesus was going through the grainfields, and as his disciples walked along, they began to pick some heads of grain.[k] **24**The Pharisees said to him, "Look, why are they doing what is unlawful on the Sabbath?"[l]

25He answered, "Have you never read what David did when he and his companions were hungry and in need? **26**In the days of Abiathar the high priest,[m] he entered the house of God and ate the consecrated bread, which is lawful only for priests to eat.[n] And he also gave some to his companions."[o]

2:17 [h] Lk 19:10; 1Ti 1:15
2:18 [i] S Mt 6:16-18; Ac 13:2
2:20 [j] Lk 17:22
2:23 [k] Dt 23:25
2:24 [l] S Mt 12:2
2:26 [m] 1Ch 24:6; 2Sa 8:17 [n] Lev 24:5-9 [o] 1Sa 21:1-6

2:27 [p] Ex 23:12; Dt 5:14 [q] Col 2:16
2:28 [r] S Mt 8:20
3:1 [s] S Mt 4:23; Mk 1:21
3:2 [t] S Mt 12:10 [u] Lk 14:1
3:6 [v] Mt 22:16; Mk 12:13 [w] S Mt 12:14
3:7 [x] Mt 4:25
3:8 [y] S Mt 11:21
3:10 [z] S Mt 4:23 [a] S Mt 9:20
3:11 [b] S Mt 4:3; Mk 1:23,24
3:12 [c] S Mt 8:4; Mk 1:24,25,34; Ac 16:17,18

27Then he said to them, "The Sabbath was made for man,[p] not man for the Sabbath.[q] **28**So the Son of Man[r] is Lord even of the Sabbath."

3

Another time he went into the synagogue,[s] and a man with a shriveled hand was there. **2**Some of them were looking for a reason to accuse Jesus, so they watched him closely[t] to see if he would heal him on the Sabbath.[u] **3**Jesus said to the man with the shriveled hand, "Stand up in front of everyone."

4Then Jesus asked them, "Which is lawful on the Sabbath: to do good or to do evil, to save life or to kill?" But they remained silent.

5He looked around at them in anger and, deeply distressed at their stubborn hearts, said to the man, "Stretch out your hand." He stretched it out, and his hand was completely restored. **6**Then the Pharisees went out and began to plot with the Herodians[v] how they might kill Jesus.[w]

Crowds Follow Jesus

3:7–12pp — Mt 12:15,16; Lk 6:17–19

7Jesus withdrew with his disciples to the lake, and a large crowd from Galilee followed.[x] **8**When they heard all he was doing, many people came to him from Judea, Jerusalem, Idumea, and the regions across the Jordan and around Tyre and Sidon.[y] **9**Because of the crowd he told his disciples to have a small boat ready for him, to keep the people from crowding him. **10**For he had healed many,[z] so that those with diseases were pushing forward to touch him.[a] **11**Whenever the evil[g] spirits saw him, they fell down before him and cried out, "You are the Son of God."[b] **12**But he gave them strict orders not to tell who he was.[c]

[g] *11* Greek *unclean*; also in verse 30

2:20 ON THAT DAY THEY WILL FAST. See Mt 9:15, note.

2:22 NEW WINE INTO OLD WINESKINS. See Mt 9:17, note.

2:23 SABBATH. See Mt 12:1, note.

2:27 THE SABBATH WAS MADE FOR MAN. The Sabbath was instituted by God as a blessing for humans (see Ex 20:8, note). On this day we are to refrain from our daily work. Instead we must worship God and seek fellowship with him, in order to keep ourselves physically healthy and spiritually strong and refreshed (Isa 58:13–14). Those who ignore the principle of the Sabbath do so to their own ruin (see Mt 12:1, note).

3:5 LOOKED ... IN ANGER. The anger of Jesus indicates his hatred and disapproval of all unrighteousness and injustice (see Heb 1:9, note). Though Christians must resist unrighteous anger (Gal 5:20; Col 3:8), it is thoroughly Christlike to be angry at evil (Ex 32:19; 1Sa 11:6; 2Sa 12:5; Ne 5:6). Indignation at the sins of one's generation is evidence of believers placing themselves on God's side against evil (Ex 32:19; 1Sa 11:6; Ps 94:16; Jer 6:11; Ac 17:16).

3:10 HEALED MANY. See article on DIVINE HEALING, p. 1420.

The Appointing of the Twelve Apostles

3:16–19pp — Mt 10:2–4; Lk 6:14–16; Ac 1:13

13Jesus went up on a mountainside
and called to him those he wanted, and
they came to him.[d] **14**He appointed
twelve—designating them apostles[h][e]—that they might be with him
and that he might send them out to
preach **15**and to have authority to drive
out demons.[f] **16**These are the twelve
he appointed: Simon (to whom he gave
the name Peter);[g] **17**James son of Zebedee and his brother John (to them he
gave the name Boanerges, which
means Sons of Thunder); **18**Andrew,
Philip, Bartholomew, Matthew, Thomas, James son of Alphaeus, Thaddaeus,
Simon the Zealot **19**and Judas Iscariot,
who betrayed him.

Jesus and Beelzebub

3:23–27pp — Mt 12:25–29; Lk 11:17–22

20Then Jesus entered a house, and
again a crowd gathered,[h] so that he
and his disciples were not even able to
eat.[i] **21**When his family heard about
this, they went to take charge of him,
for they said, "He is out of his mind."[j]

22And the teachers of the law who
came down from Jerusalem[k] said, "He
is possessed by Beelzebub[i]![l] By the
prince of demons he is driving out demons."[m]

23So Jesus called them and spoke to
them in parables:[n] "How can Satan[o]
drive out Satan? **24**If a kingdom is divided against itself, that kingdom cannot stand. **25**If a house is divided
against itself, that house cannot stand.
26And if Satan opposes himself and is
divided, he cannot stand; his end has
come. **27**In fact, no one can enter a
strong man's house and carry off his
possessions unless he first ties up the
strong man. Then he can rob his
house.[p] **28**I tell you the truth, all the Mk 5:1-16
sins and blasphemies of men will be
forgiven them. **29**But whoever blasphemes against the Holy Spirit will
never be forgiven; he is guilty of an
eternal sin."[q]

30He said this because they were
saying, "He has an evil spirit."

Jesus' Mother and Brothers

3:31–35pp — Mt 12:46–50; Lk 8:19–21

31Then Jesus' mother and brothers
arrived.[r] Standing outside, they sent
someone in to call him. **32**A crowd was
sitting around him, and they told him,
"Your mother and brothers are outside
looking for you."

33"Who are my mother and my
brothers?" he asked.

34Then he looked at those seated in
a circle around him and said, "Here are
my mother and my brothers! **35**Whoever does God's will is my brother and
sister and mother."

The Parable of the Sower

4:1–12pp — Mt 13:1–15; Lk 8:4–10
4:13–20pp — Mt 13:18–23; Lk 8:11–15

4 Again Jesus began to teach by the
lake.[s] The crowd that gathered
around him was so large that he got
into a boat and sat in it out on the lake,
while all the people were along the
shore at the water's edge. **2**He taught
them many things by parables,[t] and

3:13 [d]Mt 5:1
3:14 [e]S Mk 6:30
3:15 [f]S Mt 10:1
3:16 [g]Jn 1:42
3:20 [h]ver 7
[i]Mk 6:31
3:21 [j]Jn 10:20; Ac 26:24
3:22 [k]Mt 15:1
[l]Mt 10:25; 11:18; 12:24; Jn 7:20; 8:48,52; 10:20
[m]Mt 9:34
3:23 [n]Mk 4:2
[o]S Mt 4:10
3:27 [p]Isa 49:24, 25
3:29 [q]Mt 12:31, 32; Lk 12:10
3:31 [r]ver 21
4:1 [s]Mk 2:13; 3:7
4:2 [t]ver 11; Mk 3:23

[h] *14* Some manuscripts do not have *designating them apostles.* [i] *22* Greek *Beezeboul* or *Beelzeboul*

3:15 AUTHORITY TO DRIVE OUT DEMONS. In coming to earth Jesus' purpose was to destroy the works of the devil (1:27; 1Jn 3:8) and release those oppressed by Satan and sin (Lk 4:18; see article on POWER OVER SATAN AND DEMONS, p. 1484). Jesus gave his followers power and authority to continue his battle against the forces of darkness. This truth is verified by the following observations. (1) It is recorded that after Jesus appointed the twelve disciples, he gave them "authority to drive out demons" (vv. 14–15; cf. Mt 10:1). After he appointed the seventy-two, he gave them "authority . . . to overcome all the power of the enemy" (Lk 10:1,17–19; cf. Mt 10:1–8; Mk 6:7,13).

(2) The disciples were not only to go out and preach (v. 14; Mt 10:7), but also to manifest the kingdom's rule, power and authority by doing battle against Satan, driving out demons, and healing every kind of disease and sickness (Mt 10:1,7–8, notes).

(3) Mark teaches that Jesus, after his resurrection, reemphasized to his followers their task of preaching the gospel and their authority over Satan and his demons (see article on SIGNS OF BELIEVERS, p. 1513).

3:27 TIES UP THE STRONG MAN. See article on POWER OVER SATAN AND DEMONS, p. 1484.

3:29 BLASPHEMES AGAINST THE HOLY SPIRIT. See Mt 12:31, note.

4:2 PARABLES. Jesus often taught in parables. A parable is a simple story from everyday life that reveals truth about God's kingdom to those whose hearts are prepared to hear and conceals this truth from those whose hearts are unprepared (cf. Isa 6:9–10; see Mt 13:3, note).

POWER OVER SATAN AND DEMONS

***Mk 3:27** "No one can enter a strong man's house and carry off his possessions unless he first ties up the strong man. Then he can rob his house."*

One of the primary emphases in Mark's Gospel is Jesus' overriding concern to defeat Satan and his demonic powers; in 3:27, this is phrased as "tying up the strong man" (i.e., Satan) and "robbing his house" (i.e., setting free those who are enslaved to Satan). This power over Satan is especially evident in the driving out of demons (Gk *daimonion*) or evil spirits.

DEMONS. (1) The NT frequently refers to those who are suffering from Satan's oppression and influence because of the indwelling of an evil spirit, and to Jesus' conflict with demons. In the Gospel of Mark, for example, numerous such encounters are described: 1:23–28,32–34,39; 3:10–12,14–15; 5:1–20; 6:7,13; 7:24–30; 9:14–29; 16:17.

(2) Demons are spirit beings who have personality and intelligence. As members of Satan's kingdom and as enemies of God and humans (Mt 12:43–45), they are evil, malicious and under Satan's authority (see Mt 4:10, note).

(3) Demons are the power behind idol gods, so that to worship false gods is essentially to worship demons (see 1Co 10:20, note; see article on THE NATURE OF IDOLATRY, p. 394).

(4) The NT presents the world as estranged from God and seized by Satan (see Jn 12:31, note; 2Co 4:4; Eph 6:10–12; see article on THE CHRISTIAN'S RELATIONSHIP TO THE WORLD, p. 1976). Demons are within the hierarchy of the rulers of this age; Christians must wage continual warfare with them (see Eph 6:12, note).

(5) Demons can, and often do, live in the bodies of unbelievers (see Mk 5:15; Lk 4:41; 8:27–28; Ac 16:18) and use their voices to talk. They enslave such individuals and influence them toward evil, immorality and destruction.

(6) Demons can cause physical illness in the human body (Mt 9:32–33; 12:22; 17:14–18; Mk 9:20–22; Lk 13:11,16), although not all sickness and disease are the result of evil spirits (Mt 4:24; Lk 5:12–13).

(7) Those involved in spiritism and magic (i.e., sorcery) are dealing with evil spirits; this can easily lead to demonic bondage (cf. Ac 13:8–10; 19:19; Gal 5:20; Rev 9:20).

(8) Evil spirits will be especially active in the last days of this age, promoting the occult, immorality, violence and cruelty; they will assault God's Word and sound doctrine (Mt 24:24; 2Co 11:14–15; 1Ti 4:1). The ultimate outpouring of demonic activity will be in the antichrist and his followers (2Th 2:9; Rev 13:2–8; 16:13–14).

JESUS AND DEMONS. (1) In his miracles, Jesus often attacks the power of Satan and the demonic (e.g., 1:26,34,39; 3:10–11; 5:1–20; 9:17–29; cf. Lk 13:16). One of Jesus' clearly stated purposes in coming to earth was to bind Satan and to set free those enslaved by him (Mt 12:29; Mk 1:27; Lk 4:18).

(2) Jesus' binding of Satan, accomplished in part through his driving out of demons and more completely in his death and resurrection (Jn 12:31), shatters the power of Satan's realm and restores the power of God's kingdom (see article on THE KINGDOM OF GOD, p. 1430).

(3) Hell (Gk *Gehenna*), the place of torment, has been prepared by our Lord for the devil and his demons (Mt 8:29; 25:41).

BELIEVERS AND DEMONS. (1) Scripture teaches that no true believer who is indwelt by the Holy Spirit can be demon-possessed; the Spirit and demons can never live in the same body (see 2Co 6:15–16, note). Demons may, however, influence the thoughts, emotions and actions of Christians who fail to follow the leading of the Spirit (Mt 16:23; 2Co 11:3,14).

(2) Jesus promised true believers authority over the power of Satan and his cohorts. As we confront them, we must break the power they want to exert over us and others by waging intense spiritual warfare through the power of the Holy Spirit (see Lk 4:14–19). In this way we can be set free from the powers of darkness.

(3) According to the parable in Mk 3:27, spiritual conflict against Satan involves three aspects: (a) declaring war against Satan according to God's purpose (see Lk 4:14–19); (b) entering Satan's house (any place where he has a stronghold), attacking and overpowering him by prayer and proclamation of the Word and destroying his weapons of demonic deception and temptation (cf. Lk 11:20–22); (c) carrying off his possessions, i.e., delivering those who have been held captive by Satan's power and giving them over to God so that they may receive forgiveness and sanctification through faith in Christ (Lk 11:22; Ac 26:18).

(4) The following are the individual steps we should take in this process: (a) Recognize that we are not in a conflict against flesh and blood but against spiritual forces and powers of evil (Eph 6:12). (b) Live before God, fervently committed to his truth and righteousness (Ro 12:1–2; Eph 6:14). (c) Have faith that Satan's power can be broken in any specific area of his domain (Ac 26:18; Eph 6:16; 1Th 5:8), and realize that the believer has powerful spiritual weapons given by God for the destruction of Satan's strongholds (2Co 10:4–5). (d) Proclaim the gospel of the kingdom in the fullness of the Holy Spirit (Mt 4:23; Lk 1:15–17; Ac 1:8; 2:4; 8:12; Ro 1:16; Eph 6:15). (e) Challenge Satan and his power directly by believing in Jesus' name (Ac 16:16–18), by using God's Word (Eph 6:17), by praying in the Spirit (Ac 6:4; Eph 6:18), by fasting (see Mt 6:16, note) and by driving out demons (see Mt 10:1, note; 12:28; 17:17–21; Mk 16:17; Lk 10:17; Ac 5:16; 8:7; 16:18; 19:12; see article on SIGNS OF BELIEVERS, p. 1513). (f) Pray especially for the Holy Spirit to convict the lost concerning sin, righteousness and the coming judgment (Jn 16:7–11). (g) Pray for and eagerly desire the manifestation of the Spirit through gifts of healing, tongues, miracles, signs and wonders (Ac 4:29–33; 10:38; 1Co 12:7–11).

in his teaching said: 3"Listen! A farmer
went out to sow his seed.[u] 4As he was
scattering the seed, some fell along the
path, and the birds came and ate it up.
5Some fell on rocky places, where it
did not have much soil. It sprang up
quickly, because the soil was shallow.
6But when the sun came up, the plants
were scorched, and they withered because they had no root. 7Other seed fell
among thorns, which grew up and
choked the plants, so that they did not
bear grain. 8Still other seed fell on
good soil. It came up, grew and produced a crop, multiplying thirty, sixty,
or even a hundred times."[v]

9Then Jesus said, "He who has ears
to hear, let him hear."[w]

10When he was alone, the Twelve
and the others around him asked him
about the parables. 11He told them,
"The secret of the kingdom of God[x]
has been given to you. But to those on
the outside[y] everything is said in parables 12so that,

"'they may be ever seeing but
never perceiving,
and ever hearing but never
understanding;
otherwise they might turn and be
forgiven!'[j]"[z]

13Then Jesus said to them, "Don't
you understand this parable? How then
will you understand any parable?
14The farmer sows the word.[a] 15Some
people are like seed along the path,
where the word is sown. As soon as
they hear it, Satan[b] comes and takes
away the word that was sown in them.
16Others, like seed sown on rocky
places, hear the word and at once receive it with joy. 17But since they have
no root, they last only a short time.
When trouble or persecution comes because of the word, they quickly fall
away. 18Still others, like seed sown
among thorns, hear the word; 19but the
worries of this life, the deceitfulness of
wealth[c] and the desires for other
things come in and choke the word,
making it unfruitful. 20Others, like
seed sown on good soil, hear the word,
accept it, and produce a crop—thirty,
sixty or even a hundred times what
was sown."

A Lamp on a Stand

21He said to them, "Do you bring in
a lamp to put it under a bowl or a bed?
Instead, don't you put it on its stand?[d]
22For whatever is hidden is meant to
be disclosed, and whatever is concealed is meant to be brought out into
the open.[e] 23If anyone has ears to
hear, let him hear."[f]

24"Consider carefully what you
hear," he continued. "With the measure you use, it will be measured to
you—and even more.[g] 25Whoever has
will be given more; whoever does not

4:3 [u]ver 26 **4:8** [v]Jn 15:5; Col 1:6 **4:9** [w]ver 23; S Mt 11:15 **4:11** [x]S Mt 3:2 [y]1Co 5:12,13; Col 4:5; 1Th 4:12; 1Ti 3:7 **4:12** [z]Isa 6:9,10; S Mt 13:13-15 **4:14** [a]Mk 16:20; Lk 1:2; Ac 4:31; 8:4; 16:6; 17:11; Php 1:14 **4:15** [b]S Mt 4:10 **4:19** [c]Mt 19:23; 1Ti 6:9,10,17; 1Jn 2:15-17 **4:21** [d]S Mt 5:15 **4:22** [e]Jer 16:17; Mt 10:26; Lk 8:17; 12:2 **4:23** [f]ver 9; S Mt 11:15 **4:24** [g]S Mt 7:2

j *12* Isaiah 6:9,10

4:3 A FARMER WENT OUT TO SOW. Jesus uses this parable to tell how the gospel will be received in the world. Three truths may be learned: (1) Conversion and fruitfulness depend on how one responds to God's Word (v. 14; cf. Jn 15:1–10). (2) There will be a mixed reaction to the gospel by the world. Some who hear will not understand (v. 15); others will believe unto salvation, but will later fall away (vv. 16–19); still others will believe unto salvation, persevere and bear fruit in varying degrees (v. 20). (3) The enemies of God's Word are Satan, worldly concerns, riches and pleasures (vv. 15,19).

4:15–17 TAKES AWAY THE WORD. Christ speaks here about an incomplete conversion—one in which individuals seek forgiveness but fall short of actual regeneration by the Holy Spirit (see article on REGENERATION, p. 1589). They do not receive salvation and the new birth and never enter into fellowship with believers; or if they do become church members, they fail to show genuine commitment to Christ and true separation from the world.

Halfway conversions result from the following: (1) The church deals with seekers quickly without communicating a proper understanding of the gospel and its demands. (2) The church fails to deal with the demonic bondage of seekers (16:15–17; Mt 10:1,8; 12:22–29). (3) Seekers believe in Christ only with their mind, not heart (i.e., with their innermost being, their whole personality; cf. Ac 2:37; 2Co 4:6). (4) They fail to repent in true sincerity or to turn from sin (cf. Mt 3:2; Ac 8:18–23). (5) Seekers want to accept Christ as Savior but not as Lord (Mt 13:20–21). (6) Their faith is based on the persuasiveness of human words rather than on the demonstration of the Spirit and the power of God (1Co 2:4–5).

4:25 EVEN WHAT HE HAS WILL BE TAKEN. Jesus states here a principle of his kingdom: believers must continue to acquire truth and grace or they will lose even what they have. Growth in grace or spiritual decline may be hardly perceptible in the lives of many. Nevertheless, it is a fact that a Christian either grows or degenerates (2Pe 3:17–18). The peril of final apostasy increases in proportion as one declines spiritually (Heb 3:12–15; 4:11; 6:11–12; 10:23–39; 12:15; see ar-

have, even what he has will be taken
from him."[h]

The Parable of the Growing Seed

26He also said, "This is what the
kingdom of God is like.[i] A man scatters seed on the ground. 27Night and
day, whether he sleeps or gets up, the
seed sprouts and grows, though he
does not know how. 28All by itself the
soil produces grain—first the stalk,
then the head, then the full kernel in
the head. 29As soon as the grain is
ripe, he puts the sickle to it, because
the harvest has come."[j]

The Parable of the Mustard Seed

4:30–32pp — Mt 13:31,32; Lk 13:18,19

30Again he said, "What shall we say
the kingdom of God is like,[k] or what
parable shall we use to describe it? 31It
is like a mustard seed, which is the
smallest seed you plant in the ground.
32Yet when planted, it grows and becomes the largest of all garden plants,
with such big branches that the birds
of the air can perch in its shade."

33With many similar parables Jesus
spoke the word to them, as much as
they could understand.[l] 34He did not
say anything to them without using a
parable.[m] But when he was alone with
his own disciples, he explained everything.

Jesus Calms the Storm

4:35–41pp — Mt 8:18,23–27; Lk 8:22–25

35That day when evening came, he
said to his disciples, "Let us go over to
the other side." 36Leaving the crowd
behind, they took him along, just as he
was, in the boat.[n] There were also
other boats with him. 37A furious
squall came up, and the waves broke
over the boat, so that it was nearly
swamped. 38Jesus was in the stern,
sleeping on a cushion. The disciples
woke him and said to him, "Teacher,
don't you care if we drown?"

39He got up, rebuked the wind and
said to the waves, "Quiet! Be still!"
Then the wind died down and it was
completely calm.

4:25 [h]S Mt 25:29
4:26 [i] S Mt 13:24
4:29 [j]Rev 14:15
4:30 [k]S Mt 13:24
4:33 [l]Jn 16:12
4:34 [m]S Jn 16:25
4:36 [n]ver 1; Mk 3:9; 5:2,21; 6:32,45

4:40 [o]Mt 14:31; Mk 16:14
5:2 [p]Mk 4:1 [q]Mk 1:23
5:7 [r]S Mt 8:29 [s]S Mt 4:3; Lk 1:32; 6:35; Ac 16:17; Heb 7:1
5:9 [t]ver 15

40He said to his disciples, "Why are
you so afraid? Do you still have no
faith?"[o]

Mk 9:23-24

41They were terrified and asked
each other, "Who is this? Even the
wind and the waves obey him!"

The Healing of a Demon-possessed Man

5:1–17pp — Mt 8:28–34; Lk 8:26–37
5:18–20pp — Lk 8:38,39

5 They went across the lake to the
region of the Gerasenes.[k] 2When
Jesus got out of the boat,[p] a man with
an evil[1] spirit[q] came from the tombs
to meet him. 3This man lived in the
tombs, and no one could bind him any
more, not even with a chain. 4For he
had often been chained hand and foot,
but he tore the chains apart and broke
the irons on his feet. No one was strong
enough to subdue him. 5Night and day
among the tombs and in the hills he
would cry out and cut himself with
stones.

6When he saw Jesus from a distance,
he ran and fell on his knees in front of
him. 7He shouted at the top of his
voice, "What do you want with me,[r]
Jesus, Son of the Most High God?[s]
Swear to God that you won't torture
me!" 8For Jesus had said to him, "Come
out of this man, you evil spirit!"

9Then Jesus asked him, "What is
your name?"

"My name is Legion,"[t] he replied,
"for we are many." 10And he begged
Jesus again and again not to send them
out of the area.

11A large herd of pigs was feeding
on the nearby hillside. 12The demons
begged Jesus, "Send us among the
pigs; allow us to go into them." 13He
gave them permission, and the evil
spirits came out and went into the pigs.
The herd, about two thousand in number, rushed down the steep bank into
the lake and were drowned.

14Those tending the pigs ran off and
reported this in the town and country-

[k] 1 Some manuscripts *Gadarenes*; other manuscripts *Gergesenes* [1] 2 Greek *unclean*; also in verses 8 and 13

ticle on PERSONAL APOSTASY, p. 1918).
4:31 MUSTARD SEED. See Lk 13:19, note.
5:2 A MAN WITH AN EVIL SPIRIT. Demon-possessed people suffer from satanic oppression (Ac 10:38) or influence (Mt 12:45; Ac 16:16–18) because an evil spirit dwells in them (see Lk 13:11, note). Scripture records many occasions in which Jesus drove out demons (for a full discussion on demons and the Christian's power over them, see article on POWER OVER SATAN AND DEMONS, p. 1484).

side, and the people went out to see what had happened. 15When they came to Jesus, they saw the man who had been possessed by the legion[u] of demons,[v] sitting there, dressed and in his right mind; and they were afraid. 16Those who had seen it told the people what had happened to the demon-possessed man—and told about the pigs as well. 17Then the people began to plead with Jesus to leave their region.

Lk 4:2-13

18As Jesus was getting into the boat, the man who had been demon-possessed begged to go with him. 19Jesus did not let him, but said, "Go home to your family and tell them[w] how much the Lord has done for you, and how he has had mercy on you." 20So the man went away and began to tell in the Decapolis[m][x] how much Jesus had done for him. And all the people were amazed.

A Dead Girl and a Sick Woman

5:22–43pp — Mt 9:18–26; Lk 8:41–56

21When Jesus had again crossed over by boat to the other side of the lake,[y] a large crowd gathered around him while he was by the lake.[z] 22Then one of the synagogue rulers,[a] named Jairus, came there. Seeing Jesus, he fell at his feet 23and pleaded earnestly with him, "My little daughter is dying. Please come and put your hands on[b] her so that she will be healed and live." 24So Jesus went with him.

A large crowd followed and pressed around him. 25And a woman was there who had been subject to bleeding[c] for twelve years. 26She had suffered a great deal under the care of many doctors and had spent all she had, yet instead of getting better she grew worse. 27When she heard about Jesus, she came up behind him in the crowd and touched his cloak, 28because she thought, "If I just touch his clothes,[d] I will be healed." 29Immediately her bleeding stopped and she felt in her body that she was freed from her suffering.[e]

30At once Jesus realized that power[f] had gone out from him. He turned around in the crowd and asked, "Who touched my clothes?"

31"You see the people crowding against you," his disciples answered, "and yet you can ask, 'Who touched me?' "

32But Jesus kept looking around to see who had done it. 33Then the woman, knowing what had happened to her, came and fell at his feet and, trembling with fear, told him the whole truth. 34He said to her, "Daughter, your faith has healed you.[g] Go in peace[h] and be freed from your suffering."

Mk 6:

35While Jesus was still speaking, some men came from the house of Jairus, the synagogue ruler.[i] "Your daughter is dead," they said. "Why bother the teacher any more?"

36Ignoring what they said, Jesus told the synagogue ruler, "Don't be afraid; just believe."

37He did not let anyone follow him except Peter, James and John the brother of James.[j] 38When they came to the home of the synagogue ruler,[k] Jesus saw a commotion, with people crying and wailing loudly. 39He went in and said to them, "Why all this commotion and wailing? The child is not dead but asleep."[l] 40But they laughed at him.

After he put them all out, he took the child's father and mother and the disciples who were with him, and went in where the child was. 41He took her by the hand[m] and said to her, *"Talitha koum!"* (which means, "Little girl, I say to you, get up!").[n] 42Immediately the girl stood up and walked around (she

5:15 [u] ver 9 [v] ver 16,18; S Mt 4:24 **5:19** [w] S Mt 8:4 **5:20** [x] Mt 4:25; Mk 7:31 **5:21** [y] Mt 9:1 [z] Mk 4:1 **5:22** [a] ver 35,36, 38; Lk 13:14; Ac 13:15; 18:8,17 **5:23** [b] Mt 19:13; Mk 6:5; 7:32; 8:23; 16:18; Lk 4:40; 13:13; S Ac 6:6 **5:25** [c] Lev 15:25-30 **5:28** [d] S Mt 9:20

5:29 [e] ver 34 **5:30** [f] Lk 5:17; 6:19 **5:34** [g] S Mt 9:22 [h] S Ac 15:33 **5:35** [i] S ver 22 **5:37** [j] S Mt 4:21 **5:38** [k] S ver 22 **5:39** [l] S Mt 9:24 **5:41** [m] Mk 1:31 [n] S Lk 7:14

[m] *20* That is, the Ten Cities

5:28 JUST TOUCH HIS CLOTHES. The Gospels often speak of the sick touching Jesus (3:10; 5:27–34; 6:56) or of Jesus touching the sick (1:41–42; 7:33–35; Mt 8:3,15; 9:29–30; 20:34; Lk 5:13; 7:14–15; 22:51). It was the contact and presence of Jesus that mattered. His touch has healing power because he sympathizes with our weaknesses and is the source of life and grace (Heb 4:16). Our responsibility in seeking healing is to draw near to Jesus and to live in his presence (see Mt 17:20, note on true faith).

5:36 JUST BELIEVE. The daughter of the synagogue ruler had died (v. 35). Jesus' response was to encourage the father's faith, even in this seemingly hopeless situation. Throughout redemptive history, believers have placed their trust in God even when it seemed as if all was lost. In such times, God gave the necessary faith and delivered his people according to his will and purpose (cf. Ps 22:4; Isa 26:3–4; 43:2). This was true for Abraham (Ge 22:2; Jas 2:21–22), Moses (Ex 14:10–22; 32:10–14), David (1Sa 17:44–47), Jehoshaphat (2Ch 20:1–2,12) and Jairus (vv. 21–23,35–42).

was twelve years old). At this they
were completely astonished. 43He gave
strict orders not to let anyone know
about this,[o] and told them to give her
something to eat.

A Prophet Without Honor

6:1–6pp — Mt 13:54–58

6 Jesus left there and went to his
hometown,[p] accompanied by his
disciples. 2When the Sabbath came,[q]
he began to teach in the synagogue,[r]
and many who heard him were
amazed.[s]

"Where did this man get these
things?" they asked. "What's this wisdom that has been given him, that he
even does miracles! 3Isn't this the carpenter? Isn't this Mary's son and the
brother of James, Joseph,[n] Judas and
Simon?[t] Aren't his sisters here with
us?" And they took offense at him.[u]

4Jesus said to them, "Only in his
hometown, among his relatives and in
his own house is a prophet without
honor."[v] 5He could not do any miracles there, except lay his hands on[w] a
few sick people and heal them. 6And he
was amazed at their lack of faith.

Jesus Sends Out the Twelve

6:7–11pp — Mt 10:1,9–14; Lk 9:1,3–5

Then Jesus went around teaching
from village to village.[x] 7Calling the
Twelve to him,[y] he sent them out two
by two[z] and gave them authority over
evil[o] spirits.[a]

8These were his instructions: "Take
nothing for the journey except a

5:43 [o] S Mt 8:4
6:1 [p] S Mt 2:23
6:2 [q] Mk 1:21 [r] S Mt 4:23 [s] S Mt 7:28
6:3 [t] S Mt 12:46 [u] Mt 11:6; Jn 6:61
6:4 [v] Lk 4:24; Jn 4:44
6:5 [w] S Mk 5:23
6:6 [x] Mt 9:35; Mk 1:39; Lk 13:22
6:7 [y] Mk 3:13 [z] Dt 17:6; Lk 10:1 [a] S Mt 10:1

staff—no bread, no bag, no money in
your belts. 9Wear sandals but not an
extra tunic. 10Whenever you enter a
house, stay there until you leave that
town. 11And if any place will not welcome you or listen to you, shake the
dust off your feet[b] when you leave, as
a testimony against them."

12They went out and preached that
people should repent.[c] 13They drove
out many demons and anointed many
sick people with oil[d] and healed them. Mk 7:32-37

John the Baptist Beheaded

6:14–29pp — Mt 14:1–12
6:14–16pp — Lk 9:7–9

14King Herod heard about this, for
Jesus' name had become well known.
Some were saying,[p] "John the Baptist[e] has been raised from the dead,
and that is why miraculous powers are
at work in him."

15Others said, "He is Elijah."[f]

And still others claimed, "He is a
prophet,[g] like one of the prophets of
long ago."[h]

16But when Herod heard this, he
said, "John, the man I beheaded, has
been raised from the dead!"

17For Herod himself had given orders to have John arrested, and he had
him bound and put in prison.[i] He did
this because of Herodias, his brother
Philip's wife, whom he had married.
18For John had been saying to Herod,
"It is not lawful for you to have

6:11 [b] S Mt 10:14
6:12 [c] Lk 9:6
6:13 [d] S Jas 5:14
6:14 [e] S Mt 3:1
6:15 [f] Mal 4:5 [g] S Mt 21:11 [h] Mt 16:14; Mk 8:28
6:17 [i] Mt 4:12; 11:2; Lk 3:19,20

[n] 3 Greek *Joses*, a variant of *Joseph*
[o] 7 Greek *unclean*
[p] 14 Some early manuscripts *He was saying*

6:4 JESUS . . . A PROPHET. Jesus is portrayed in the Gospels as a prophet (vv. 4,15; Mt 21:11; Lk 4:24; cf. Ac 3:20–23) in keeping with the calling of a prophet in the OT (see article on THE PROPHET IN THE OLD TESTAMENT, p. 986). The following characteristics identify him as a prophet: (1) He was a man of the Spirit and the Word (Mt 21:42; 22:29; Lk 4:1,18; 24:27; Jn 3:34). (2) He was in intimate communion with God (see Lk 5:16, note). (3) He gave prophetic predictions (Mt 24; Lk 19:43–44). (4) He performed symbolic actions that expressed a zeal for God's honor (Mt 21:12–13; Jn 2:13–17). (5) He exposed the hypocrisy of the religious leaders and criticized their adherence to traditions rather than God's Word (7:7–9,13). (6) He shared the pathos and suffering of God over the lost condition of those who refused to repent (Lk 13:34; 19:41). (7) He emphasized the ethical teaching of God's Word (holiness, justice, righteousness, love, mercy) in contrast to ceremonial observance (12:38–40; Mt 23:1–36). (8) He proclaimed the impending reign and judgment of God (Mt 11:22,24; 10:15; Lk 10:12,14). (9) He was a preacher of repentance, calling people to turn from sin and the world to God (v. 12; Mt 4:17).

6:6 LACK OF FAITH. As lack of faith hindered the working of miracles in Jesus' hometown, so unbelief in the church still hinders the working of his power. Failure to believe Biblical truth, denial of the possibility of the gifts of the Spirit for today, or rejection of God's righteous standards will prevent our Lord from demonstrating his kingdom power among his people. Believers must maintain a hunger for the Word and pray, "increase our faith" (Lk 17:5).

6:7 EVIL SPIRITS. See 3:15, note.

6:13 ANOINTED . . . WITH OIL. Healing by anointing with oil is mentioned only here and in Jas 5:14. The oil was probably used as a symbol of the presence and power of the Holy Spirit (see Zec 4:3–6, notes) and as a point of contact to encourage faith.

6:17 JOHN . . . IN PRISON. See Mt 11:7, note.

your brother's wife."[j] **19**So Herodias
nursed a grudge against John and
wanted to kill him. But she was not
able to, **20**because Herod feared John
and protected him, knowing him to be
a righteous and holy man.[k] When Herod heard John, he was greatly puzzled[q]; yet he liked to listen to him.

21Finally the opportune time came.
On his birthday Herod gave a banquet[l] for his high officials and military commanders and the leading men
of Galilee.[m] **22**When the daughter of
Herodias came in and danced, she
pleased Herod and his dinner guests.

The king said to the girl, "Ask me for
anything you want, and I'll give it to
you." **23**And he promised her with an
oath, "Whatever you ask I will give
you, up to half my kingdom."[n]

24She went out and said to her mother, "What shall I ask for?"

"The head of John the Baptist," she
answered.

25At once the girl hurried in to the
king with the request: "I want you to
give me right now the head of John the
Baptist on a platter."

26The king was greatly distressed,
but because of his oaths and his dinner
guests, he did not want to refuse her.
27So he immediately sent an execu-
tioner with orders to bring John's head.
The man went, beheaded John in the
prison, **28**and brought back his head on
a platter. He presented it to the girl,
and she gave it to her mother. **29**On
hearing of this, John's disciples came
and took his body and laid it in a tomb.

Jesus Feeds the Five Thousand

6:32–44pp — Mt 14:13–21; Lk 9:10–17;
Jn 6:5–13
6:32–44Ref — Mk 8:2–9

30The apostles[o] gathered around
Jesus and reported to him all they had
done and taught.[p] **31**Then, because so
many people were coming and going
that they did not even have a chance to
eat,[q] he said to them, "Come with me
by yourselves to a quiet place and get
some rest."

32So they went away by themselves
in a boat[r] to a solitary place. **33**But
many who saw them leaving recognized them and ran on foot from all the
towns and got there ahead of them.
34When Jesus landed and saw a large
crowd, he had compassion on them, because they were like sheep without a
shepherd.[s] So he began teaching
them many things.

35By this time it was late in the day,
so his disciples came to him. "This is
a remote place," they said, "and it's already very late. **36**Send the people
away so they can go to the surrounding
countryside and villages and buy themselves something to eat."

37But he answered, "You give them
something to eat."[t]

They said to him, "That would take
eight months of a man's wages[r]! Are
we to go and spend that much on bread
and give it to them to eat?"

38"How many loaves do you have?"
he asked. "Go and see."

When they found out, they said,
"Five—and two fish."[u]

39Then Jesus directed them to have
all the people sit down in groups on the
green grass. **40**So they sat down in
groups of hundreds and fifties. **41**Taking the five loaves and the two fish and
looking up to heaven, he gave thanks
and broke the loaves.[v] Then he gave
them to his disciples to set before the
people. He also divided the two fish
among them all. **42**They all ate and
were satisfied, **43**and the disciples
picked up twelve basketfuls of broken
pieces of bread and fish. **44**The number

6:18 [j] Lev 18:16; 20:21
6:20 [k] S Mt 11:9
6:21 [l] Est 1:3; 2:18 [m] Lk 3:1
6:23 [n] Est 5:3,6; 7:2
6:30 [o] Mt 10:2; Lk 9:10; 17:5; 22:14; 24:10; Ac 1:2,26 [p] Lk 9:10
6:31 [q] Mk 3:20
6:32 [r] ver 45; S Mk 4:36
6:34 [s] S Mt 9:36
6:37 [t] 2Ki 4:42-44
6:38 [u] Mt 15:34; Mk 8:5
6:41 [v] S Mt 14:19

[q] *20* Some early manuscripts *he did many things* [r] *37* Greek *take two hundred denarii*

6:22 DANCED. See Mt 14:6, note.

6:34 COMPASSION. Compassion is an emotion that moves people to the very depths of their being. It involves a sorrow felt for another's suffering and misfortune, accompanied by an intense desire to help. It is a characteristic both of God (Dt 30:3; 2Ki 13:23; Ps 78:38; 111:4) and of his Son Jesus (1:41; 8:2, note; Mt 9:36; 14:14; 15:32; Lk 7:13). In all ages, and particularly in this present age of indifference to the physical and spiritual suffering of others, Jesus wants and expects this attitude to characterize his followers (Mt 18:33; Lk 10:33).

6:41 FIVE LOAVES . . . TWO FISH. See Mt 14:19, note.

6:41 THANKSGIVING AT MEALTIMES. Before eating, Christ gave thanks to his heavenly Father for the food. Believers ought to follow his example and give thanks at every meal. To eat with thanksgiving is to recognize God's care and provision for us. Every meal should be an act of worship, done to the glory of God. On giving thanks before meals, see 1Sa 9:13; Mt 14:19; 15:36; 26:26; Ro 14:6; 1Co 10:31; 1Ti 4:4–5.

of the men who had eaten was five
thousand.

Jesus Walks on the Water

6:45–51pp — Mt 14:22–32; Jn 6:15–21
6:53–56pp — Mt 14:34–36

45 Immediately Jesus made his disciples get into the boat[w] and go on
ahead of him to Bethsaida,[x] while he
dismissed the crowd. 46 After leaving
them, he went up on a mountainside to
pray.[y]
47 When evening came, the boat was
in the middle of the lake, and he was
alone on land. 48 He saw the disciples
straining at the oars, because the wind
was against them. About the fourth
watch of the night he went out to them,
walking on the lake. He was about to
pass by them, 49 but when they saw him
walking on the lake, they thought he
was a ghost.[z] They cried out, 50 because they all saw him and were terrified.
Immediately he spoke to them and
said, "Take courage! It is I. Don't be
afraid."[a] 51 Then he climbed into the
boat[b] with them, and the wind died
down.[c] They were completely
amazed, 52 for they had not understood
about the loaves; their hearts were
hardened.[d]
53 When they had crossed over, they
landed at Gennesaret and anchored
there.[e] 54 As soon as they got out of
the boat, people recognized Jesus.
55 They ran throughout that whole region and carried the sick on mats to
wherever they heard he was. 56 And
wherever he went—into villages,
towns or countryside—they placed the
sick in the marketplaces. They begged
him to let them touch even the edge of
his cloak,[f] and all who touched him
were healed.

Tradition and God's Commands

7:1–23pp — Mt 15:1–20

7 The Pharisees and some of the
teachers of the law who had come
from Jerusalem gathered around Jesus
and 2 saw some of his disciples eating
food with hands that were "unclean,"[g]
that is, unwashed. 3 (The Pharisees
and all the Jews do not eat unless they
give their hands a ceremonial washing,
holding to the tradition of the elders.[h]
4 When they come from the marketplace they do not eat unless they wash.
And they observe many other traditions, such as the washing of cups,
pitchers and kettles.[s])[i]
5 So the Pharisees and teachers of
the law asked Jesus, "Why don't your
disciples live according to the tradition
of the elders[j] instead of eating their
food with 'unclean' hands?"
6 He replied, "Isaiah was right when
he prophesied about you hypocrites; as
it is written:

" 'These people honor me with
their lips,
but their hearts are far from me.
7 They worship me in vain;
their teachings are but rules
taught by men.'[t][k]

8 You have let go of the commands of

6:45 [w] ver 32 [x] S Mt 11:21 **6:46** [y] S Lk 3:21 **6:49** [z] Lk 24:37 **6:50** [a] S Mt 14:27 **6:51** [b] ver 32 [c] Mk 4:39 **6:52** [d] Mk 8:17-21 **6:53** [e] Jn 6:24,25 **6:56** [f] S Mt 9:20 **7:2** [g] Ac 10:14,28; 11:8; Ro 14:14 **7:3** [h] ver 5,8,9,13; Lk 11:38 **7:4** [i] Mt 23:25; Lk 11:39 **7:5** [j] S ver 3; Gal 1:14; Col 2:8 **7:7** [k] Isa 29:13

[s] *4* Some early manuscripts *pitchers, kettles and dining couches* [t] *6,7* Isaiah 29:13

7:6 THEIR HEARTS ARE FAR FROM ME. The Pharisees and the teachers of the law were guilty of the sin of legalism. A legalist substitutes outward acts or words for proper inner attitudes that come from being born of God and the Spirit (see Mt 5:20, note; 5:27–28; 6:1–7; Jn 1:13; 3:3–6; see Isa 1:11, note; Am 4:4–5, note). Such people honor God with their lips, while their hearts are far from him; they appear righteous outwardly, but inwardly have no real love for God. (1) Legalism does not refer to the mere existence of laws or standards within the Christian community. Rather, it has to do with motives—the motives by which the Christian approaches God's will as expressed in his Word. Any motive for keeping commands or regulations that does not stem from a living faith in Christ, the regenerating power of the Holy Spirit, and the sincere desire to obey and please God is legalism (Mt 6:1–7; Jn 14:21).

(2) Even in this day of grace Christians remain under the instruction, discipline and duty of obeying Christ's law and his Word. The NT speaks of the "perfect law that gives freedom" (Jas 1:25), "the royal law" (Jas 2:8), the "law of Christ" (Gal 6:2) and the "law of the Spirit" (Ro 8:2). In God's Word we find (a) positive commands (1Th 5:16–18), (b) negative commands (Ro 12:2), (c) basic principles (1Co 8:13) and (d) words spoken by spiritual leaders who have been given authority to rule in spiritual matters (Eph 4:11–12; 1Ti 3:5; Heb 13:7,17).

7:8 THE TRADITIONS OF MEN. The Pharisees and the teachers of the law were guilty of placing human tradition above divine revelation. Jesus is not condemning all traditions here, but only those that conflict with God's Word. Traditions or rules must be based on corresponding truths found in Scripture (cf. 2Th 2:15). Churches must resist the tendency to exalt religious traditions, human wisdom or contemporary customs

DECAPOLIS AND LANDS BEYOND THE JORDAN

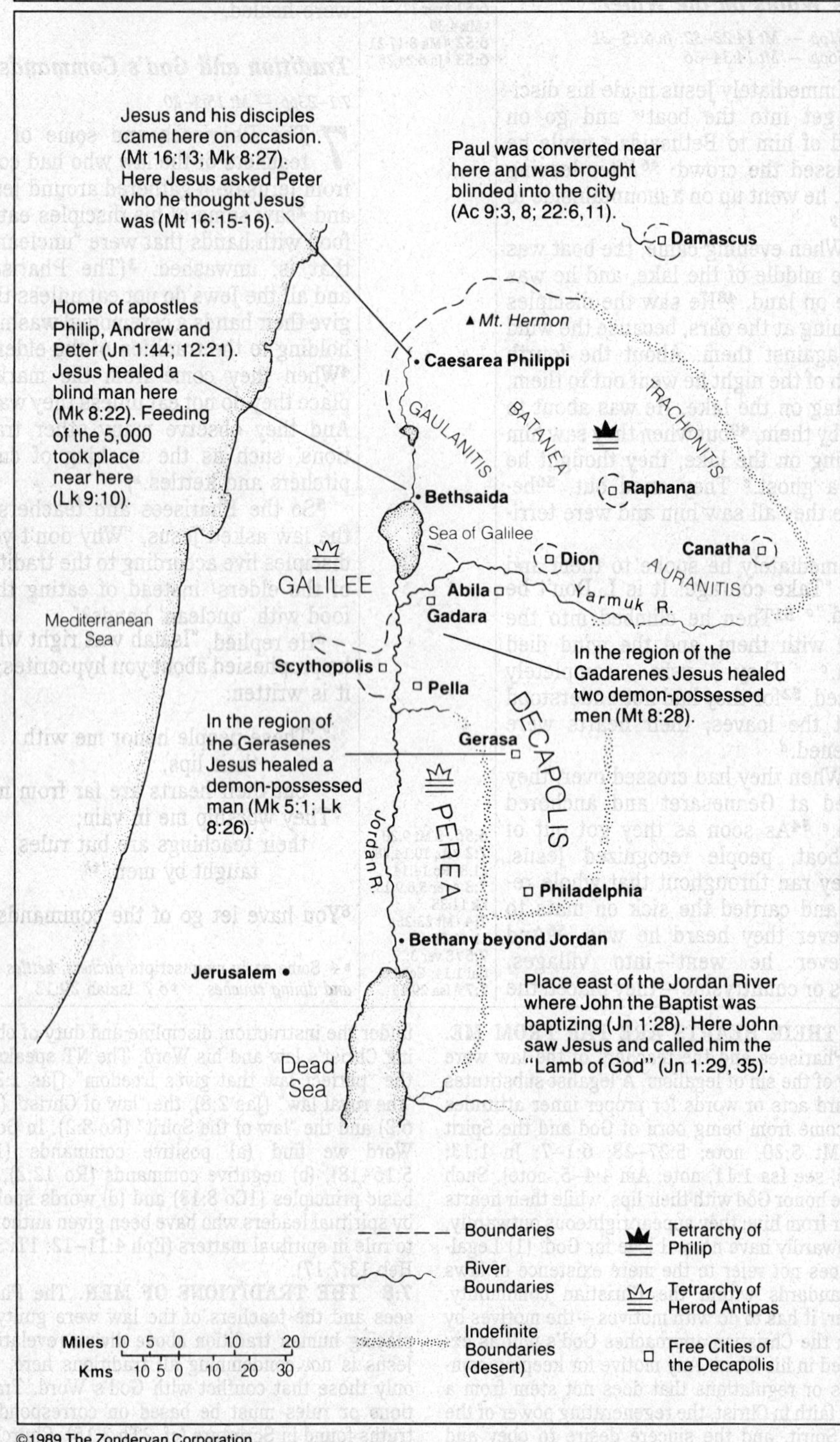

Jesus and his disciples came here on occasion. (Mt 16:13; Mk 8:27). Here Jesus asked Peter who he thought Jesus was (Mt 16:15-16).
Paul was converted near here and was brought blinded into the city (Ac 9:3, 8; 22:6,11).
Damascus
Mt. Hermon
Home of apostles Philip, Andrew and Peter (Jn 1:44; 12:21). Jesus healed a blind man here (Mk 8:22). Feeding of the 5,000 took place near here (Lk 9:10).
Caesarea Philippi
GAULANITIS
BATANEA
TRACHONITIS
Raphana
Bethsaida
Sea of Galilee
Canatha
Dion
AURANITIS
GALILEE
Abila
Yarmuk R.
Gadara
Mediterranean Sea
In the region of the Gadarenes Jesus healed two demon-possessed men (Mt 8:28).
Scythopolis
Pella
DECAPOLIS
In the region of the Gerasenes Jesus healed a demon-possessed man (Mk 5:1; Lk 8:26).
Gerasa
PEREA
Jordan R.
Philadelphia
Bethany beyond Jordan
Jerusalem
Place east of the Jordan River where John the Baptist was baptizing (Jn 1:28). Here John saw Jesus and called him the "Lamb of God" (Jn 1:29, 35).
Dead Sea
Boundaries
River Boundaries
Indefinite Boundaries (desert)
Tetrarchy of Philip
Tetrarchy of Herod Antipas
Free Cities of the Decapolis
Miles 10 5 0 10 20
Kms 10 5 0 10 20 30

God and are holding on to the traditions of men."[l]
9 And he said to them: "You have a
fine way of setting aside the commands
of God in order to observe[u] your own
traditions![m] 10 For Moses said, 'Honor
your father and your mother,'[v][n] and,
'Anyone who curses his father or mother must be put to death.'[w][o] 11 But you
say[p] that if a man says to his father
or mother: 'Whatever help you might
otherwise have received from me is
Corban' (that is, a gift devoted to God),
12 then you no longer let him do anything for his father or mother. 13 Thus
you nullify the word of God[q] by your
tradition[r] that you have handed down.
And you do many things like that."

Clean and Unclean

14 Again Jesus called the crowd to
him and said, "Listen to me, everyone, and understand this. 15 Nothing
outside a man can make him 'unclean'
by going into him. Rather, it is what
comes out of a man that makes him
'unclean.'[x]"

17 After he had left the crowd and entered the house, his disciples asked
him[s] about this parable. 18 "Are you so
dull?" he asked. "Don't you see that
nothing that enters a man from the outside can make him 'unclean'? 19 For it
doesn't go into his heart but into his
stomach, and then out of his body." (In
saying this, Jesus declared all foods[t]
"clean.")[u]

20 He went on: "What comes out of a
man is what makes him 'unclean.'
21 For from within, out of men's hearts,
come evil thoughts, sexual immorality,
theft, murder, adultery, 22 greed,[v]
malice, deceit, lewdness, envy, slander, arrogance and folly. 23 All these
evils come from inside and make a man
'unclean.'"

The Faith of a Syrophoenician Woman

7:24–30pp — Mt 15:21–28

24 Jesus left that place and went to
the vicinity of Tyre.[y][w] He entered a
house and did not want anyone to
know it; yet he could not keep his presence secret. 25 In fact, as soon as she
heard about him, a woman whose little
daughter was possessed by an evil[z]
spirit[x] came and fell at his feet. 26 The
woman was a Greek, born in Syrian
Phoenicia. She begged Jesus to drive
the demon out of her daughter.

27 "First let the children eat all they
want," he told her, "for it is not right
to take the children's bread and toss it
to their dogs."

28 "Yes, Lord," she replied, "but even
the dogs under the table eat the children's crumbs."

29 Then he told her, "For such a reply, you may go; the demon has left
your daughter."

30 She went home and found her
child lying on the bed, and the demon
gone.

The Healing of a Deaf and Mute Man

7:31–37pp — Mt 15:29–31

31 Then Jesus left the vicinity of
Tyre[y] and went through Sidon, down
to the Sea of Galilee[z] and into the re-

7:8 [l] S ver 3
7:9 [m] S ver 3
7:10 [n] Ex 20:12; Dt 5:16 [o] Ex 21:17; Lev 20:9
7:11 [p] Mt 23:16, 18
7:13 [q] S Heb 4:12 [r] S ver 3
7:17 [s] Mk 9:28
7:19 [t] Ro 14:1-12; Col 2:16; 1Ti 4:3-5 [u] S Ac 10:15
7:22 [v] Mt 20:15
7:24 [w] S Mt 11:21
7:25 [x] S Mt 4:24
7:31 [y] ver 24; S Mt 11:21 [z] S Mt 4:18

[u] *9* Some manuscripts *set up* [v] *10* Exodus 20:12; Deut. 5:16 [w] *10* Exodus 21:17; Lev. 20:9 [x] *15* Some early manuscripts *'unclean.' 16If anyone has ears to hear, let him hear.* [y] *24* Many early manuscripts *Tyre and Sidon* [z] *25* Greek *unclean*

above the Bible. Scripture is the only infallible rule of faith and practice; it must never be nullified by human ideas (v. 13; see Mt 15:6, note).

7:18 MAKE HIM 'UNCLEAN'. Jesus is speaking of foods that enter a person but do not affect his or her heart (v. 19). This verse cannot be used to justify using harmful drugs or alcoholic beverages, for such use has resulted in all the sins listed in vv. 21–22 (see Pr 23:31, note).

7:20–23 MEN'S HEARTS. In this passage "makes . . . 'unclean' " (v. 20) means being separated from the life, salvation and fellowship of Christ because of sins that come from the heart. The "heart" in Scripture is the totality of intellect, emotion, desire and volition (see article on THE HEART, p. 906). An impure heart will corrupt one's thoughts, feelings, words and actions (Pr 4:23; Mt 12:34; 15:19). What is needed is a new, transformed heart, refashioned after the image of Christ (see Lk 6:45; see article on REGENERATION, p. 1589).

7:27 CHILDREN'S BREAD. The word "children" refers to Israel. Jesus indicates that the gospel must be taken first to Israel. The woman understands this, yet responds to Christ in wisdom, perseverance and faith. She argues that it is God's purpose for Gentiles to receive blessings indirectly when he blesses Israel. Christ rewards her diligent faith by healing her child (vv. 28–30). Believers, in prayer for themselves or others, must persevere in prayer, and occasionally even reason with God (see Mt 15:28, note).

gion of the Decapolis.[a][a] 32There some people brought to him a man who was deaf and could hardly talk,[b] and they begged him to place his hand on[c] the man.

33After he took him aside, away from the crowd, Jesus put his fingers into the man's ears. Then he spit[d] and touched the man's tongue. 34He looked up to heaven[e] and with a deep sigh[f] said to him, *"Ephphatha!"* (which means, "Be opened!"). 35At this, the man's ears were opened, his tongue was loosened and he began to speak plainly.[g]

36Jesus commanded them not to tell anyone.[h] But the more he did so, the more they kept talking about it. 37People were overwhelmed with amazement. "He has done everything well," they said. "He even makes the deaf hear and the mute speak."

Lk 6:17-19

Jesus Feeds the Four Thousand

8:1–9pp — Mt 15:32–39
8:1–9Ref — Mk 6:32–44
8:11–21pp — Mt 16:1–12

8 During those days another large crowd gathered. Since they had nothing to eat, Jesus called his disciples to him and said, 2"I have compassion for these people;[i] they have already been with me three days and have nothing to eat. 3If I send them home hungry, they will collapse on the way, because some of them have come a long distance."

4His disciples answered, "But where in this remote place can anyone get enough bread to feed them?"

5"How many loaves do you have?" Jesus asked.

"Seven," they replied.

6He told the crowd to sit down on the ground. When he had taken the seven loaves and given thanks, he broke them and gave them to his disciples to set before the people, and they did so. 7They had a few small fish as well; he gave thanks for them also and told the disciples to distribute them.[j] 8The people ate and were satisfied. Afterward the disciples picked up seven basketfuls of broken pieces that were left over.[k] 9About four thousand men were present. And having sent them away, 10he got into the boat with his disciples and went to the region of Dalmanutha.

11The Pharisees came and began to question Jesus. To test him, they asked him for a sign from heaven.[l] 12He sighed deeply[m] and said, "Why does this generation ask for a miraculous sign? I tell you the truth, no sign will be given to it." 13Then he left them, got back into the boat and crossed to the other side.

The Yeast of the Pharisees and Herod

14The disciples had forgotten to bring bread, except for one loaf they had with them in the boat. 15"Be careful," Jesus warned them. "Watch out for the yeast[n] of the Pharisees[o] and that of Herod."[p]

16They discussed this with one another and said, "It is because we have no bread."

17Aware of their discussion, Jesus asked them: "Why are you talking about having no bread? Do you still not see or understand? Are your hearts hardened?[q] 18Do you have eyes but fail to see, and ears but fail to hear? And don't you remember? 19When I broke the five loaves for the five thousand, how many basketfuls of pieces did you pick up?"

"Twelve,"[r] they replied.

20"And when I broke the seven loaves for the four thousand, how

7:31 [a]Mt 4:25; Mk 5:20
7:32 [b]Mt 9:32; Lk 11:14
[c]S Mk 5:23
7:33 [d]Mk 8:23
7:34 [e]Mk 6:41; Jn 11:41 [f]Mk 8:12
7:35 [g]Isa 35:5,6
7:36 [h] S Mt 8:4
8:2 [i]S Mt 9:36
8:7 [j]Mt 14:19
8:8 [k]ver 20
8:11 [l]S Mt 12:38
8:12 [m]Mk 7:34
8:15 [n]1Co 5:6-8
[o]Lk 12:1
[p]S Mt 14:1; Mk 12:13
8:17 [q]Isa 6:9,10; Mk 6:52
8:19 [r]Mt 14:20; Mk 6:41-44; Lk 9:17; Jn 6:13

[a]*31* That is, the Ten Cities

8:2 I HAVE COMPASSION. Jesus was touched with compassion for the needs and suffering of humanity (see 1:41). Jesus is still moved today with a deep and earnest sympathy by the needs and hurts of each child of God. This assures us that in our troubles we can come to him in prayer in order to receive grace, mercy and help (Mt 6:31–32; Heb 4:14–16; 7:25).

8:15 YEAST. In the NT "yeast" is usually a symbol for evil or corruption (see Mt 13:33; 16:6,11; Lk 12:1; 1Co 5:6–8; Gal 5:9; see Ex 13:7, note). A small amount of yeast will ferment and affect the whole. (1) The yeast of the Pharisees refers to their religious traditions by which they set aside God's righteous commands and invalidated portions of his word and will (see 7:5–8, notes). (2) The yeast of Herod is identical with that of the Sadducees; it refers to a spirit of secularism and worldliness (see Mt 3:7, note). Followers of Christ must always guard against accepting the views of those who preach human ideas, unbiblical traditions or a secular, humanistic type of gospel. To accept the "yeast . . . of Herod" will cause the church to turn against Christ and his Word.

many basketfuls of pieces did you pick
up?"
They answered, "Seven."[s]
21He said to them, "Do you still not
understand?"[t]

The Healing of a Blind Man at Bethsaida

22They came to Bethsaida,[u] and
some people brought a blind man[v] and
begged Jesus to touch him. 23He took
the blind man by the hand and led him
outside the village. When he had spit[w]
on the man's eyes and put his hands
on[x] him, Jesus asked, "Do you see
anything?"
24He looked up and said, "I see people; they look like trees walking
around."
25Once more Jesus put his hands on
the man's eyes. Then his eyes were
opened, his sight was restored, and he
saw everything clearly. 26Jesus sent
him home, saying, "Don't go into the
village.[b]"

Peter's Confession of Christ

8:27–29pp — Mt 16:13–16; Lk 9:18–20

27Jesus and his disciples went on to
the villages around Caesarea Philippi.
On the way he asked them, "Who do
people say I am?"
28They replied, "Some say John the
Baptist;[y] others say Elijah;[z] and still
others, one of the prophets."
29"But what about you?" he asked.
"Who do you say I am?"
Peter answered, "You are the
Christ.[c]"[a]

8:20 [s] ver 6-9; Mt 15:37
8:21 [t] Mk 6:52
8:22 [u] S Mt 11:21 [v] Mk 10:46; Jn 9:1
8:23 [w] Mk 7:33 [x] S Mk 5:23
8:28 [y] S Mt 3:1 [z] Mal 4:5
8:29 [a] Jn 6:69; 11:27
8:30 [b] S Mt 8:4; 16:20; 17:9; Mk 9:9; Lk 9:21
8:31 [c] S Mt 8:20 [d] S Mt 16:21 [e] Mt 27:1,2 [f] Ac 2:23; 3:13 [g] S Mt 16:21 [h] S Mt 16:21
8:32 [i] Jn 18:20
8:33 [j] S Mt 4:10
8:34 [k] Mt 10:38; Lk 14:27
8:35 [l] S Jn 12:25
8:38 [m] S Mt 8:20 [n] Mt 10:33; Lk 12:9

30Jesus warned them not to tell anyone about him.[b]

Jesus Predicts His Death

8:31 — 9:1pp — Mt 16:21–28; Lk 9:22–27

31He then began to teach them that
the Son of Man[c] must suffer many
things[d] and be rejected by the elders,
chief priests and teachers of the law,[e]
and that he must be killed[f] and after
three days[g] rise again.[h] 32He spoke
plainly[i] about this, and Peter took
him aside and began to rebuke him.
33But when Jesus turned and looked
at his disciples, he rebuked Peter. "Get
behind me, Satan!"[j] he said. "You do
not have in mind the things of God, but
the things of men."
34Then he called the crowd to him
along with his disciples and said: "If
anyone would come after me, he must
deny himself and take up his cross and
follow me.[k] 35For whoever wants to
save his life[d] will lose it, but whoever
loses his life for me and for the gospel
will save it.[l] 36What good is it for a
man to gain the whole world, yet forfeit
his soul? 37Or what can a man give in
exchange for his soul? 38If anyone is
ashamed of me and my words in this
adulterous and sinful generation, the
Son of Man[m] will be ashamed of him[n]

[b] *26* Some manuscripts *Don't go and tell anyone in the village* [c] *29* Or *Messiah.* "The Christ" (Greek) and "the Messiah" (Hebrew) both mean "the Anointed One." [d] *35* The Greek word means either *life* or *soul*; also in verse 36.

8:25 HIS SIGHT WAS RESTORED. This healing in Bethsaida is the only instance of a gradual cure by Jesus. It teaches that not every healing has to be instantaneous, for in some cases the victory of divine power over sickness will be gradual.

8:34 TAKE UP HIS CROSS. The cross of Christ is a symbol of suffering (1Pe 2:21; 4:13), death (Ac 10:39), shame (Heb 12:2), ridicule (Mt 27:39), rejection (1Pe 2:4) and self-denial (Mt 16:24). When we as believers take up our cross and follow Christ, we deny our own selves (Lk 14:26–27) and commit ourselves to four areas of struggle and suffering:

(1) We suffer in a lifelong battle against sin (Ro 6; 1Pe 4:1–2) by crucifying our own sinful desires (Ro 6; 8:13; Gal 2:20; 6:14; Tit 2:12; 1Pe 2:11, 21–24).

(2) We suffer in a war against Satan and the powers of darkness as we advance the kingdom of God (2Co 10:4–5; 6:7; Eph 6:12; 1Ti 6:12). We experience both the hostility of the adversary with his demonic host (2Co 6:3–7; 11:23–29; 1Pe 5:8–10) and the persecution that comes from standing against false teachers who distort the true gospel (Mt 23:1–36; Gal 1:9; Php 1:15–17).

(3) We suffer the hatred and ridicule of the world (Jn 15:18–25; Heb 11:25–26) by testifying in love that its deeds are evil (Jn 7:7), by separating ourselves from it both morally and spiritually (see article on SPIRITUAL SEPARATION FOR BELIEVERS, p. 1794), and by refusing to accept its standards or philosophies as our own (1Co 1:21–27).

(4) Like Jesus, we may also suffer ridicule and persecution from the religious world (v. 31; see v. 15, note).

8:38 ASHAMED OF ME AND MY WORDS. Jesus sees the world and society in which we live as an "adulterous and sinful generation." All those who seek to be popular in or accepted by their present evil generation rather than follow Christ and his righteous standards will be rejected by Christ at his return (cf. Mt 7:23; 25:41–46; Lk 9:26, note; 13:27).

when he comes[o] in his Father's glory
with the holy angels."

9 And he said to them, "I tell you the
truth, some who are standing here
will not taste death before they see the
kingdom of God come[p] with power."[q]

The Transfiguration

9:2–8pp — Lk 9:28–36
9:2–13pp — Mt 17:1–13

[2]After six days Jesus took Peter,
James and John[r] with him and led
them up a high mountain, where they
were all alone. There he was transfigured before them. [3]His clothes became
dazzling white,[s] whiter than anyone
in the world could bleach them. [4]And
there appeared before them Elijah and
Moses, who were talking with Jesus.
[5]Peter said to Jesus, "Rabbi,[t] it is
good for us to be here. Let us put up
three shelters—one for you, one for
Moses and one for Elijah." [6](He did not
know what to say, they were so frightened.)
[7]Then a cloud appeared and enveloped them, and a voice came from the
cloud:[u] "This is my Son, whom I love.
Listen to him!"[v]
[8]Suddenly, when they looked
around, they no longer saw anyone
with them except Jesus.
[9]As they were coming down the
mountain, Jesus gave them orders not
to tell anyone[w] what they had seen until the Son of Man[x] had risen from the
dead. [10]They kept the matter to themselves, discussing what "rising from
the dead" meant.
[11]And they asked him, "Why do the
teachers of the law say that Elijah
must come first?"
[12]Jesus replied, "To be sure, Elijah
does come first, and restores all
things. Why then is it written that the
Son of Man[y] must suffer much[z] and
be rejected?[a] [13]But I tell you, Elijah

8:38 [o]S 1Th 2:19
9:1 [p]Mk 13:30; Lk 22:18 [q]Mt 24:30; 25:31
9:2 [r]S Mt 4:21
9:3 [s]S Mt 28:3
9:5 [t]S Mt 23:7
9:7 [u]Ex 24:16 [v]S Mt 3:17
9:9 [w]S Mk 8:30 [x]S Mt 8:20
9:12 [y]S Mt 8:20 [z]S Mt 16:21 [a]Lk 23:11

9:13 [b]S Mt 11:14
9:20 [c]Mk 1:26
9:23 [d]S Mt 21:21; Mk 11:23; Jn 11:40

has come,[b] and they have done to him
everything they wished, just as it is
written about him."

The Healing of a Boy With an Evil Spirit

9:14–28; 30–32pp — Mt 17:14–19; 22,23; Lk 9:37–45

[14]When they came to the other disciples, they saw a large crowd around
them and the teachers of the law arguing with them. [15]As soon as all the people saw Jesus, they were overwhelmed
with wonder and ran to greet him.
[16]"What are you arguing with them
about?" he asked.
[17]A man in the crowd answered,
"Teacher, I brought you my son, who is
possessed by a spirit that has robbed
him of speech. [18]Whenever it seizes
him, it throws him to the ground. He
foams at the mouth, gnashes his teeth
and becomes rigid. I asked your disciples to drive out the spirit, but they
could not."
[19]"O unbelieving generation," Jesus
replied, "how long shall I stay with
you? How long shall I put up with you?
Bring the boy to me."
[20]So they brought him. When the
spirit saw Jesus, it immediately threw
the boy into a convulsion. He fell to the
ground and rolled around, foaming at
the mouth.[c]
[21]Jesus asked the boy's father,
"How long has he been like this?"
"From childhood," he answered.
[22]"It has often thrown him into fire or
water to kill him. But if you can do anything, take pity on us and help us."
[23]" 'If you can'?" said Jesus. "Everything is possible for him who believes."[d]
[24]Immediately the boy's father exclaimed, "I do believe; help me overcome my unbelief!"
[25]When Jesus saw that a crowd was

9:1 KINGDOM OF GOD . . . WITH POWER. See Mt 16:28, note.

9:2 HE WAS TRANSFIGURED. See Lk 9:29, note.

9:19 UNBELIEVING GENERATION. Failure to wage effective warfare against demons is seen as a spiritual weakness on the part of Christ's disciples (see Mt 17:17, note).

9:23 EVERYTHING IS POSSIBLE. Jesus' statement must not be taken as an unqualified promise. (1) The "everything" does not mean everything we can think of. The prayer of faith must be based on God's will; it never asks for anything foolish or wrong (Jas 4:3). (2) The faith required here must be received as a gift of God. He implants it in the heart of a sincere seeker who lives faithfully according to his will (see Mt 17:20, note).

9:24 HELP ME OVERCOME MY UNBELIEF. In this life our faith is often mixed with doubt. This weakness does not mean, however, that Christ will not respond to our petitions, for he understands and sympathizes with our weaknesses (Heb 4:15). We should confess our lack of faith and pray that he would give us the faith that is needed (see Mt 17:20, note).

running to the scene,[e] he rebuked the
evil[e] spirit. "You deaf and mute spirit," he said, "I command you, come out
of him and never enter him again."
26The spirit shrieked, convulsed him
violently and came out. The boy looked
so much like a corpse that many said,
"He's dead." **27**But Jesus took him by
the hand and lifted him to his feet, and
he stood up.
28After Jesus had gone indoors, his
disciples asked him privately,[f] "Why
couldn't we drive it out?"
29He replied, "This kind can come
out only by prayer.[f]"
30They left that place and passed
through Galilee. Jesus did not want
anyone to know where they were, **31**because he was teaching his disciples.
He said to them, "The Son of Man[g] is
going to be betrayed into the hands of
men. They will kill him,[h] and after
three days[i] he will rise."[j] **32**But they
did not understand what he meant[k]
and were afraid to ask him about it.

Who Is the Greatest?

9:33–37pp — Mt 18:1–5; Lk 9:46–48

33They came to Capernaum.[l] When
he was in the house,[m] he asked them,
"What were you arguing about on the
road?" **34**But they kept quiet because
on the way they had argued about who
was the greatest.[n]
35Sitting down, Jesus called the
Twelve and said, "If anyone wants to
be first, he must be the very last, and
the servant of all."[o]
36He took a little child and had him
stand among them. Taking him in his
arms,[p] he said to them, **37**"Whoever
welcomes one of these little children in
my name welcomes me; and whoever
welcomes me does not welcome me but
the one who sent me."[q]

9:25 *e* ver 15
9:28 *f* Mk 7:17
9:31 *g* S Mt 8:20 *h* ver 12; Ac 2:23; 3:13 *i* S Mt 16:21 *j* S Mt 16:21
9:32 *k* Lk 2:50; 9:45; 18:34; Jn 12:16
9:33 *l* S Mt 4:13 *m* Mk 1:29
9:34 *n* Lk 22:24
9:35 *o* Mt 18:4; Mk 10:43; Lk 22:26
9:36 *p* Mk 10:16
9:37 *q* S Mt 10:40

Whoever Is Not Against Us Is for Us

9:38–40pp — Lk 9:49,50

38"Teacher," said John, "we saw a
man driving out demons in your name
and we told him to stop, because he
was not one of us."[r]
39"Do not stop him," Jesus said. "No
one who does a miracle in my name can
in the next moment say anything bad
about me, **40**for whoever is not against
us is for us.[s] **41**I tell you the truth,
anyone who gives you a cup of water in
my name because you belong to Christ
will certainly not lose his reward.[t]

Causing to Sin

42"And if anyone causes one of these
little ones who believe in me to sin,[u]
it would be better for him to be thrown
into the sea with a large millstone tied
around his neck.[v] **43**If your hand
causes you to sin,[w] cut it off. It is better for you to enter life maimed than
with two hands to go into hell,[x] where
the fire never goes out.[g][y] **45**And if
your foot causes you to sin,[z] cut it off.
It is better for you to enter life crippled
than to have two feet and be thrown
into hell.[h][a] **47**And if your eye causes
you to sin,[b] pluck it out. It is better for
you to enter the kingdom of God with
one eye than to have two eyes and be
thrown into hell,[c] **48**where

"'their worm does not die,
and the fire is not
quenched.'[i][d]

49Everyone will be salted[e] with fire.

Lk 6:46-49

9:38 *r* Nu 11:27-29
9:40 *s* Mt 12:30; Lk 11:23
9:41 *t* S Mt 10:42
9:42 *u* S Mt 5:29 *v* Mt 18:6; Lk 17:2
9:43 *w* S Mt 5:29 *x* Mt 5:30; 18:8 *y* S Mt 25:41
9:45 *z* S Mt 5:29 *a* Mt 18:8
9:47 *b* S Mt 5:29 *c* Mt 5:29; 18:9
9:48 *d* Isa 66:24; S Mt 25:41
9:49 *e* Lev 2:13

e 25 Greek *unclean* f 29 Some manuscripts *prayer and fasting* g 43 Some manuscripts *out,* 44*where / " 'their worm does not die, / and the fire is not quenched.'* h 45 Some manuscripts *hell,* 46*where / " 'their worm does not die, / and the fire is not quenched.'* i 48 Isaiah 66:24

9:29 ONLY BY PRAYER. Jesus does not mean that a time of prayer was necessary before this kind of evil spirit could be driven out. Rather, a principle is implied here: where there is little faith, there is little prayer. Where there is much prayer, founded on true commitment to God and his Word, there is much faith. Had the disciples been maintaining, as Jesus did, a life of prayer, they could have dealt successfully with this case.

9:34 THE GREATEST. See Lk 22:24–30, note.

9:42 CAUSES . . . LITTLE ONES. One of the highest priorities for believers is to set an example for their children by life and teaching. In doing so, they demonstrate a sincere love for them. Christian parents must also do their best to keep their children from the ungodly influences of the world (see Mt 18:6, note; see article on PARENTS AND CHILDREN, p. 1854).

9:43 HELL. "Hell," the place of unquenchable fire, is so terrible that every influence of sin must be opposed and rejected, whatever the cost. Sin must be put to death (Col 3:5); we must never stop waging war against it through the Spirit (Ro 8:13; Eph 6:10).

9:49 SALTED WITH FIRE. Everyone will be salted with fire in one of two ways: (1) either by fiery tribulation in this life, which comes to those who genuinely follow Jesus Christ (Lk 14:33–34;

50"Salt is good, but if it loses its saltiness, how can you make it salty
again?[f] Have salt in yourselves,[g]
and be at peace with each other."[h]

Divorce

10:1–12pp — Mt 19:1–9

10 Jesus then left that place and
went into the region of Judea
and across the Jordan.[i] Again crowds
of people came to him, and as was his
custom, he taught them.[j]
2Some Pharisees[k] came and tested
him by asking, "Is it lawful for a man
to divorce his wife?"
3"What did Moses command you?"
he replied.
4They said, "Moses permitted a man
to write a certificate of divorce and
send her away."[l]
5"It was because your hearts were
hard[m] that Moses wrote you this law,"
Jesus replied. 6"But at the beginning of
creation God 'made them male and female.'[j][n] 7'For this reason a man will
leave his father and mother and be
united to his wife,[k] 8and the two will
become one flesh.'[l][o] So they are no
longer two, but one. 9Therefore what
God has joined together, let man not
separate."
10When they were in the house
again, the disciples asked Jesus about
this. 11He answered, "Anyone who divorces his wife and marries another
woman commits adultery against
her.[p] 12And if she divorces her husband and marries another man, she
commits adultery."[q]

The Little Children and Jesus

10:13–16pp — Mt 19:13–15; Lk 18:15–17

13People were bringing little children to Jesus to have him touch them,
but the disciples rebuked them.
14When Jesus saw this, he was indignant. He said to them, "Let the little
children come to me, and do not hinder
them, for the kingdom of God belongs
to such as these.[r] 15I tell you the
truth, anyone who will not receive the
kingdom of God like a little child will
never enter it."[s] 16And he took the
children in his arms,[t] put his hands
on them and blessed them.

The Rich Young Man

10:17–31pp — Mt 19:16–30; Lk 18:18–30

17As Jesus started on his way, a man
ran up to him and fell on his knees[u]
before him. "Good teacher," he asked,
"what must I do to inherit eternal
life?"[v]
18"Why do you call me good?" Jesus
answered. "No one is good—except
God alone. 19You know the commandments: 'Do not murder, do not commit
adultery, do not steal, do not give false
testimony, do not defraud, honor your
father and mother.'[m]"[w]
20"Teacher," he declared, "all these
I have kept since I was a boy."
21Jesus looked at him and loved him.
"One thing you lack," he said. "Go, sell
everything you have and give to the
poor,[x] and you will have treasure in
heaven.[y] Then come, follow me."[z]
22At this the man's face fell. He
went away sad, because he had great
wealth.
23Jesus looked around and said

9:50 [f]Mt 5:13; Lk 14:34,35 [g]Col 4:6 [h]Ro 12:18; 2Co 13:11; 1Th 5:13
10:1 [i]Mk 1:5; Jn 10:40; 11:7 [j]S Mt 4:23; Mk 2:13; 4:2; 6:6, 34
10:2 [k]Mk 2:16
10:4 [l]Dt 24:1-4; Mt 5:31
10:5 [m]Ps 95:8; Heb 3:15
10:6 [n]Ge 1:27; 5:2
10:8 [o]Ge 2:24; 1Co 6:16
10:11 [p]S Lk 16:18
10:12 [q]Ro 7:3; 1Co 7:10,11
10:14 [r]S Mt 25:34
10:15 [s]Mt 18:3
10:16 [t]Mk 9:36
10:17 [u]Mk 1:40 [v]Lk 10:25; S Ac 20:32
10:19 [w]Ex 20:12-16; Dt 5:16-20
10:21 [x]S Ac 2:45 [y]Mt 6:20; Lk 12:33 [z]S Mt 4:19

[j] *6* Gen. 1:27 [k] *7* Some early manuscripts do not have *and be united to his wife.*
[l] *8* Gen. 2:24 [m] *19* Exodus 20:12-16; Deut. 5:16-20

Jn 15:18–21), or (2) by the fire of hell in the next life, which comes to those who reject Jesus in this life (cf. vv. 47–48).

9:50 SALT. See Mt 5:13, note.

10:11 COMMITS ADULTERY. Anyone who divorces for other than Biblical reasons and then remarries sins against God by committing adultery (see Mal 2:14, note; Mt 19:9, note; 1Co 7:15). In other words, a divorce is not necessarily recognized as right or legitimate by God merely because the state (or any human institution) legalizes it.

10:14 KINGDOM OF GOD. Mark uses the term "kingdom of God" while Matthew generally uses the preferred Jewish expression "kingdom of heaven." The meaning, however, is the same; compare the following parallel passages: Mt 4:17 with Mk 1:15; Mt 5:3 with Lk 6:20; Mt 11:11 with Lk 7:28; Mt 10:7 with Lk 10:9 (see article on THE KINGDOM OF GOD, p. 1430).

10:15 LIKE A LITTLE CHILD. Receiving the kingdom of God like a child means accepting it in a simple, humble, trustful and wholehearted manner so as to turn from sin and receive Christ as your Lord and Savior, and God as your heavenly Father (see Mt 18:3, note).

10:16 AND BLESSED THEM. Christ is deeply concerned about the salvation and the spiritual upbringing of children. Christian parents should use every means of grace available to bring their children to Christ, for he longs to receive them, love them and bless them (vv. 13–16; see article on PARENTS AND CHILDREN, p. 1854).

10:23 THE RICH. See article on RICHES AND POVERTY, p. 1562.

to his disciples, "How hard it is for the rich[a] to enter the kingdom of God!"

24The disciples were amazed at his words. But Jesus said again, "Children, how hard it is[n] to enter the kingdom of God![b] **25**It is easier for a camel to go through the eye of a needle than for a rich man to enter the kingdom of God."[c]

26The disciples were even more amazed, and said to each other, "Who then can be saved?"

27Jesus looked at them and said, "With man this is impossible, but not with God; all things are possible with God."[d]

28Peter said to him, "We have left everything to follow you!"[e]

29"I tell you the truth," Jesus replied, "no one who has left home or brothers or sisters or mother or father or children or fields for me and the gospel **30**will fail to receive a hundred times as much[f] in this present age (homes, brothers, sisters, mothers, children and fields—and with them, persecutions) and in the age to come,[g] eternal life.[h] **31**But many who are first will be last, and the last first."[i]

Jesus Again Predicts His Death

10:32–34pp — Mt 20:17–19; Lk 18:31–33

32They were on their way up to Jerusalem, with Jesus leading the way, and the disciples were astonished, while those who followed were afraid. Again he took the Twelve[j] aside and told them what was going to happen to him. **33**"We are going up to Jerusalem,"[k] he said, "and the Son of Man[l] will be betrayed to the chief priests and teachers of the law.[m] They will condemn him to death and will hand him over to the Gentiles, **34**who will mock him and spit on him, flog him[n] and kill him.[o] Three days later[p] he will rise."[q]

10:23 [a] Ps 52:7; 62:10; Mk 4:19; 1Ti 6:9,10,17
10:24 [b] Mt 7:13, 14; Jn 3:5
10:25 [c] Lk 12:16-20; 16:19-31
10:27 [d] S Mt 19:26
10:28 [e] S Mt 4:19
10:30 [f] Mt 6:33 [g] S Mt 12:32 [h] S Mt 25:46
10:31 [i] S Mt 19:30
10:32 [j] Mk 3:16-19
10:33 [k] S Lk 9:51 [l] S Mt 8:20 [m] Mt 27:1,2
10:34 [n] S Mt 16:21 [o] Ac 2:23; 3:13 [p] S Mt 16:21 [q] S Mt 16:21

The Request of James and John

10:35–45pp — Mt 20:20–28

35Then James and John, the sons of Zebedee, came to him. "Teacher," they said, "we want you to do for us whatever we ask."

36"What do you want me to do for you?" he asked.

37They replied, "Let one of us sit at your right and the other at your left in your glory."[r]

38"You don't know what you are asking,"[s] Jesus said. "Can you drink the cup[t] I drink or be baptized with the baptism I am baptized with?"[u]

39"We can," they answered.

Jesus said to them, "You will drink the cup I drink and be baptized with the baptism I am baptized with,[v] **40**but to sit at my right or left is not for me to grant. These places belong to those for whom they have been prepared."

41When the ten heard about this, they became indignant with James and John. **42**Jesus called them together and said, "You know that those who are regarded as rulers of the Gentiles lord it over them, and their high officials exercise authority over them. **43**Not so with you. Instead, whoever wants to become great among you must be your servant,[w] **44**and whoever wants to be first must be slave of all. **45**For even the Son of Man did not come to be served, but to serve,[x] and to give his life as a ransom for many."[y]

Blind Bartimaeus Receives His Sight

10:46–52pp — Mt 20:29–34; Lk 18:35–43

46Then they came to Jericho. As Jesus and his disciples, together with a large crowd, were leaving the city, a blind man, Bartimaeus (that is, the Son

10:37 [r] Mt 19:28
10:38 [s] Job 38:2 [t] S Mt 20:22 [u] Lk 12:50
10:39 [v] Ac 12:2; Rev 1:9
10:43 [w] S Mk 9:35
10:45 [x] S Mt 20:28 [y] S Mt 20:28

[n] *24* Some manuscripts *is for those who trust in riches*

10:30 RECEIVE A HUNDRED TIMES. The rewards promised here are not to be understood in a literal way. Rather, the blessings and joy inherent in the relationships listed here will be experienced by the true disciple who sacrifices for Christ's sake.

10:31 FIRST WILL BE LAST. See Mt 19:30, note.

10:43 WHOEVER WANTS TO BECOME GREAT. True greatness is not a matter of leadership, authority or high personal achievement (v. 42), but of an attitude of heart that sincerely desires to live for God and others. We must be so committed to God that we identify with his will on earth without desiring glory, position or material rewards. Accomplishing God's will, bringing others to salvation in Christ, and pleasing God are the rewards of the truly great (see Lk 22:24–30, note on greatness).

10:45 A RANSOM. See Mt 20:28, note; Ro 3:25, note on the meaning of Christ's death for humankind.

of Timaeus), was sitting by the roadside begging. **47**When he heard that it
was Jesus of Nazareth,[z] he began to
shout, "Jesus, Son of David,[a] have
mercy on me!"
48Many rebuked him and told him to
be quiet, but he shouted all the more,
"Son of David, have mercy on me!"
49Jesus stopped and said, "Call
him."
So they called to the blind man,
"Cheer up! On your feet! He's calling
you." **50**Throwing his cloak aside, he
jumped to his feet and came to Jesus.
51"What do you want me to do for
you?" Jesus asked him.
The blind man said, "Rabbi,[b] I want
to see."
52"Go," said Jesus, "your faith has
healed you."[c] Immediately he re-
Mk 11:22-24 ceived his sight and followed[d] Jesus
along the road.

The Triumphal Entry

11:1–10pp — Mt 21:1–9; Lk 19:29–38
11:7–10pp — Jn 12:12–15

11 As they approached Jerusalem
and came to Bethphage and
Bethany[e] at the Mount of Olives,[f]
Jesus sent two of his disciples, **2**saying
to them, "Go to the village ahead of
you, and just as you enter it, you will
find a colt tied there, which no one has
ever ridden.[g] Untie it and bring it
here. **3**If anyone asks you, 'Why are
you doing this?' tell him, 'The Lord
needs it and will send it back here
shortly.' "
4They went and found a colt outside
in the street, tied at a doorway.[h] As
they untied it, **5**some people standing
there asked, "What are you doing, untying that colt?" **6**They answered as
Jesus had told them to, and the people
let them go. **7**When they brought the
colt to Jesus and threw their cloaks
over it, he sat on it. **8**Many people
spread their cloaks on the road, while
others spread branches they had cut in
the fields. **9**Those who went ahead and
those who followed shouted,

"Hosanna![o]"

"Blessed is he who comes in the
name of the Lord!"[p][i]

10"Blessed is the coming kingdom of
our father David!"

"Hosanna in the highest!"[j]

11Jesus entered Jerusalem and went
to the temple. He looked around at everything, but since it was already late,
he went out to Bethany with the
Twelve.[k]

Jesus Cleanses the Temple

11:12–14pp — Mt 21:18–22
11:15–18pp — Mt 21:12–16; Lk 19:45–47; Jn 2:13–16

12The next day as they were leaving
Bethany, Jesus was hungry. **13**Seeing
in the distance a fig tree in leaf, he
went to find out if it had any fruit.
When he reached it, he found nothing
but leaves, because it was not the season for figs.[l] **14**Then he said to the
tree, "May no one ever eat fruit from
you again." And his disciples heard
him say it.
15On reaching Jerusalem, Jesus entered the temple area and began driving out those who were buying and
selling there. He overturned the tables
of the money changers and the benches
of those selling doves, **16**and would not
allow anyone to carry merchandise
through the temple courts. **17**And as he
taught them, he said, "Is it not written:

" 'My house will be called

10:47 [z]S Mk 1:24 [a]S Mt 9:27
10:51 [b]S Mt 23:7
10:52 [c]S Mt 9:22 [d]S Mt 4:19
11:1 [e]S Mt 21:17 [f]S Mt 21:1
11:2 [g]Nu 19:2; Dt 21:3; 1Sa 6:7
11:4 [h]Mk 14:16
11:9 [i]Ps 118:25, 26; Mt 23:39
11:10 [j]Lk 2:14
11:11 [k]Mt 21:12, 17
11:13 [l]Lk 13:6-9

[o] *9* A Hebrew expression meaning "Save!" which became an exclamation of praise; also in verse 10 [p] *9* Psalm 118:25,26

11:1 PASSION WEEK. At this point in the Gospel of Mark, the events of Passion Week begin (chs. 11–15), followed by the account of the resurrection (ch. 16).

11:9 BLESSED IS HE WHO COMES. The crowd believed that the Messiah would restore Israel nationally and rule the nations politically. They failed to understand the purpose that Jesus expressed regarding his coming into the world. Later the crowd shouted "crucify him" when they saw he was not the Messiah they wanted (15:13).

11:15 JESUS ENTERED THE TEMPLE AREA. Christ's driving out those who were buying and selling in the temple shows his zeal for true holiness and prayer among those who claim to worship God (see Isa 56:7, note; Lk 19:45, note).

11:17 A HOUSE OF PRAYER. Jesus makes clear that God's house was meant to be a "house of prayer," a place where God's people could meet with him in spiritual devotion, prayer and worship (see Lk 19:45, note). It must not be profaned by making it a means for social advancement, monetary gain, entertainment or showmanship. Whenever God's house is so used by worldly-minded people, it once again becomes "a den of robbers."

a house of prayer for all
nations'[q]?[m]

But you have made it 'a den of robbers.'[r]"[n]

18 The chief priests and the teachers of the law heard this and began looking for a way to kill him, for they feared him,[o] because the whole crowd was amazed at his teaching.[p]

19 When evening came, they[s] went out of the city.[q]

The Withered Fig Tree

11:20–24pp — Mt 21:19–22

20 In the morning, as they went along, they saw the fig tree withered from the roots. 21 Peter remembered and said to Jesus, "Rabbi,[r] look! The fig tree you cursed has withered!"

22 "Have[t] faith in God," Jesus answered. 23 "I tell you the truth, if anyone says to this mountain, 'Go, throw yourself into the sea,' and does not doubt in his heart but believes that what he says will happen, it will be done for him.[s] 24 Therefore I tell you, whatever you ask for in prayer, believe that you have received it, and it will be yours.[t] 25 And when you stand praying, if you hold anything against anyone, forgive him, so that your Father in heaven may forgive you your sins.[u]"[u]

The Authority of Jesus Questioned

11:27–33pp — Mt 21:23–27; Lk 20:1–8

27 They arrived again in Jerusalem, and while Jesus was walking in the temple courts, the chief priests, the teachers of the law and the elders came to him. 28 "By what authority are you doing these things?" they asked. "And who gave you authority to do this?"

29 Jesus replied, "I will ask you one question. Answer me, and I will tell you by what authority I am doing these things. 30 John's baptism—was it from heaven, or from men? Tell me!"

31 They discussed it among themselves and said, "If we say, 'From heaven,' he will ask, 'Then why didn't you believe him?' 32 But if we say, 'From men' ...." (They feared the people, for everyone held that John really was a prophet.)[v]

33 So they answered Jesus, "We don't know."

Jesus said, "Neither will I tell you by what authority I am doing these things."

The Parable of the Tenants

12:1–12pp — Mt 21:33–46; Lk 20:9–19

12 He then began to speak to them in parables: "A man planted a vineyard.[w] He put a wall around it, dug a pit for the winepress and built a watchtower. Then he rented the vineyard to some farmers and went away on a journey. 2 At harvest time he sent a servant to the tenants to collect from them some of the fruit of the vineyard. 3 But they seized him, beat him and sent him away empty-handed. 4 Then he sent another servant to them; they struck this man on the head and treated him shamefully. 5 He sent still another, and that one they killed. He sent many others; some of them they beat, others they killed.

6 "He had one left to send, a son, whom he loved. He sent him last of all,[x] saying, 'They will respect my son.'

7 "But the tenants said to one another, 'This is the heir. Come, let's kill him, and the inheritance will be ours.'

11:17 [m] Isa 56:7 [n] Jer 7:11
11:18 [o] Mt 21:46; Mk 12:12; Lk 20:19 [p] S Mt 7:28
11:19 [q] Lk 21:37
11:21 [r] S Mt 23:7
11:23 [s] S Mt 21:21
11:24 [t] S Mt 7:7
11:25 [u] S Mt 6:14
11:32 [v] S Mt 11:9
12:1 [w] Isa 5:1-7
12:6 [x] Heb 1:1-3

[q] *17* Isaiah 56:7 [r] *17* Jer. 7:11
[s] *19* Some early manuscripts *he* [t] *22* Some early manuscripts *If you have* [u] *25* Some manuscripts *sins.* *26 But if you do not forgive, neither will your Father who is in heaven forgive your sins.*

11:24 BELIEVE ... WILL BE YOURS. Believing that receives is not something humanly produced; rather, it is a believing faith imparted to the believer's heart by God himself (see 9:23, note). Sometimes the fulfillment that true faith desires is granted immediately; at other times it is not. Yet God gives the faith that the prayer has been heard and the request will be granted. The uncertainty concerns the time of the fulfillment, not the granting of the request (see Mt 17:20, note; 21:21, note).

11:25 WHEN YOU STAND PRAYING ... FORGIVE. Let no Christians delude themselves that they have faith sufficient for answered prayer if they secretly hold animosity or bitterness in their hearts against anyone (see Mt 18:35, note).

12:1 PARABLE OF THE TENANTS. This parable points out the guilt of the Jewish nation. They turned God's kingdom into a private possession, showed contempt for his Word and refused to obey his Son, Jesus Christ. Churches today show the same attitude as the wicked landowner whenever they reject Christ's Word and his true messengers, and create a church after their own ideas.

8So they took him and killed him, and
threw him out of the vineyard.
9"What then will the owner of the
vineyard do? He will come and kill
those tenants and give the vineyard to
others. 10Haven't you read this scripture:

" 'The stone the builders rejected
has become the capstone[v];[y]
11the Lord has done this,
and it is marvelous in our
eyes'[w]?"[z]

12Then they looked for a way to arrest him because they knew he had
spoken the parable against them. But
they were afraid of the crowd;[a] so
they left him and went away.[b]

Paying Taxes to Caesar

12:13–17pp — Mt 22:15–22; Lk 20:20–26

13Later they sent some of the Pharisees and Herodians[c] to Jesus to catch
him[d] in his words. 14They came to
him and said, "Teacher, we know you
are a man of integrity. You aren't
swayed by men, because you pay no attention to who they are; but you teach
the way of God in accordance with the
truth. Is it right to pay taxes to Caesar
or not? 15Should we pay or shouldn't
we?"

But Jesus knew their hypocrisy.
"Why are you trying to trap me?" he
asked. "Bring me a denarius and let me
look at it." 16They brought the coin,
and he asked them, "Whose portrait is
this? And whose inscription?"

"Caesar's," they replied.

17Then Jesus said to them, "Give to
Caesar what is Caesar's and to God
what is God's."[e]

And they were amazed at him.

Marriage at the Resurrection

12:18–27pp — Mt 22:23–33; Lk 20:27–38

18Then the Sadducees,[f] who say
there is no resurrection,[g] came to him
with a question. 19"Teacher," they
said, "Moses wrote for us that if a
man's brother dies and leaves a wife
but no children, the man must marry
the widow and have children for his
brother.[h] 20Now there were seven
brothers. The first one married and
died without leaving any children.
21The second one married the widow,
but he also died, leaving no child. It
was the same with the third. 22In fact,
none of the seven left any children.
Last of all, the woman died too. 23At
the resurrection[x] whose wife will she
be, since the seven were married to
her?"

24Jesus replied, "Are you not in error
because you do not know the Scriptures[i] or the power of God? 25When
the dead rise, they will neither marry
nor be given in marriage; they will be
like the angels in heaven.[j] 26Now
about the dead rising—have you not
read in the book of Moses, in the account of the bush, how God said to him,
'I am the God of Abraham, the God of
Isaac, and the God of Jacob'[y]?[k] 27He
is not the God of the dead, but of the
living. You are badly mistaken!"

The Greatest Commandment

12:28–34pp — Mt 22:34–40

28One of the teachers of the law[l]
came and heard them debating. Noticing that Jesus had given them a good
answer, he asked him, "Of all the commandments, which is the most important?"

29"The most important one," answered Jesus, "is this: 'Hear, O Israel,
the Lord our God, the Lord is one.[z]
30Love the Lord your God with all your
heart and with all your soul and with
all your mind and with all your
strength.'[a][m] 31The second is this:
'Love your neighbor as yourself.'[b][n]

12:10 [y] S Ac 4:11 **12:11** [z] Ps 118:22,23 **12:12** [a] S Mk 11:18 [b] Mt 22:22 **12:13** [c] Mt 22:16; Mk 3:6 [d] S Mt 12:10 **12:17** [e] Ro 13:7 **12:18** [f] S Ac 4:1 [g] Ac 23:8; 1Co 15:12 **12:19** [h] Dt 25:5 **12:24** [i] 2Ti 3:15-17 **12:25** [j] 1Co 15:42,49,52 **12:26** [k] Ex 3:6 **12:28** [l] Lk 10:25-28; 20:39 **12:30** [m] Dt 6:4,5 **12:31** [n] Lev 19:18; S Mt 5:43

[v] 10 Or *cornerstone* [w] 11 Psalm 118:22,23 [x] 23 Some manuscripts *resurrection, when men rise from the dead,* [y] 26 Exodus 3:6 [z] 29 Or *the Lord our God is one Lord* [a] 30 Deut. 6:4,5 [b] 31 Lev. 19:18

12:10 HAS BECOME THE CAPSTONE. Christ is the "rejected" stone, thrown away by Israel but about to become the capstone or cornerstone of God's new people, the church (Ac 4:11–12; see Ps 118:22, note). He is the most important stone in this new structure that God is building.

12:25 THEY WILL NEITHER MARRY. Jesus' teaching does not mean that a husband or wife will lose their particular identity and thus not recognize each other. Rather, the relationship with our earthly partners then will be a deeper, spiritual one, though no longer governed by the marriage union as on earth.

12:30 LOVE THE LORD YOUR GOD. See Mt 22:37, note.

12:31 LOVE YOUR NEIGHBOR. See Mt 22:39, note.

There is no commandment greater
than these."
32"Well said, teacher," the man replied. "You are right in saying that God
is one and there is no other but him.[o]
33To love him with all your heart, with
all your understanding and with all
your strength, and to love your neighbor as yourself is more important than
all burnt offerings and sacrifices."[p]
34When Jesus saw that he had answered wisely, he said to him, "You are
not far from the kingdom of God."[q]
And from then on no one dared ask him
any more questions.[r]

Whose Son Is the Christ?

12:35–37pp — Mt 22:41–46; Lk 20:41–44
12:38–40pp — Mt 23:1–7; Lk 20:45–47

35While Jesus was teaching in the
temple courts,[s] he asked, "How is it
that the teachers of the law say that
the Christ[c] is the son of David?[t]
36David himself, speaking by the Holy
Spirit,[u] declared:

" 'The Lord said to my Lord:
"Sit at my right hand
until I put your enemies
under your feet." '[d][v]

37David himself calls him 'Lord.' How
then can he be his son?"
The large crowd[w] listened to him
with delight.
38As he taught, Jesus said, "Watch
out for the teachers of the law. They
like to walk around in flowing robes
and be greeted in the marketplaces,
39and have the most important seats in
the synagogues and the places of hon-
or at banquets.[x] **40**They devour widows' houses and for a show make
lengthy prayers. Such men will be punished most severely."

The Widow's Offering

12:41–44pp — Lk 21:1–4

41Jesus sat down opposite the place
where the offerings were put[y] and
watched the crowd putting their money
into the temple treasury. Many rich
people threw in large amounts. **42**But
a poor widow came and put in two very
small copper coins,[e] worth only a
fraction of a penny.[f]
43Calling his disciples to him, Jesus
said, "I tell you the truth, this poor widow has put more into the treasury than
all the others. **44**They all gave out of
their wealth; but she, out of her poverty, put in everything—all she had to
live on."[z]

Signs of the End of the Age

13:1–37pp — Mt 24:1–51; Lk 21:5–36

13 As he was leaving the temple,
one of his disciples said to him,
"Look, Teacher! What massive stones!
What magnificent buildings!"
2"Do you see all these great buildings?" replied Jesus. "Not one stone
here will be left on another; every one
will be thrown down."[a]
3As Jesus was sitting on the Mount
of Olives[b] opposite the temple, Peter,
James, John[c] and Andrew asked him
privately, **4**"Tell us, when will these
things happen? And what will be the
sign that they are all about to be fulfilled?"
5Jesus said to them: "Watch out that

12:32 o Dt 4:35, 39; Isa 45:6,14; 46:9
12:33 p 1Sa 15:22; Hos 6:6; Mic 6:6-8; Heb 10:8
12:34 q S Mt 3:2 r Mt 22:46; Lk 20:40
12:35 s S Mt 26:55 t S Mt 9:27
12:36 u 2Sa 23:2 v Ps 110:1; S Mt 22:44
12:37 w Jn 12:9
12:39 x Lk 11:43
12:41 y 2Ki 12:9; Jn 8:20
12:44 z 2Co 8:12
13:2 a Lk 19:44
13:3 b S Mt 21:1 c S Mt 4:21

c 35 Or *Messiah* d 36 Psalm 110:1
e 42 Greek *two lepta* f 42 Greek *kodrantes*

12:38–39 LIKE . . . THE MOST IMPORTANT SEATS. Jesus warns his followers to watch out for religious leaders who seek recognition and honor from others. He calls such leaders hypocrites (Mt 23:13–15,23,25,29) and describes them as frauds and deceivers in the area of observable righteousness (cf. Mt 23:25–28). Such persons do not possess the indwelling Holy Spirit and his regenerating grace (cf. Ro 8:5–14). While remaining in this condition, they cannot "escape being condemned to hell" (Mt 23:33; see Mt 23:13, note; see article on FALSE TEACHERS, p. 1506).

12:40 DEVOUR WIDOWS' HOUSES. Some of the Jewish religious leaders took advantage of unsuspecting and lonely widows. They would seek and receive exorbitant offerings from them, exploiting the widows' willingness to help those whom the widows believed to be men of God. By deceit and fraud these leaders persuaded the widows to give more than they could afford, and then lived in luxury on these misguided offerings. This same pattern has occurred throughout the history of the church, right up to today; each age has its experts in the art of religious extortion.

12:42 POOR WIDOW. See Lk 7:13, note on God's special care and love for women who are alone, abandoned or widowed.

12:42 TWO . . . COPPER COINS. God measures giving not by the amount but by the love, devotion and sacrifice represented in the gift (see Lk 21:1–4, note).

13:5 WATCH OUT. Jesus' Olivet discourse contains repeated warnings that, as the end draws near, his people must be on constant alert to the danger of religious deception. Jesus admonishes, "Watch out" (v. 5), "You must be on your guard" (v. 9), "So be on your guard" (v. 23), "Be on guard! Be alert!" (v. 33), "Therefore, keep watch" (v. 35),

no one deceives you.[d] **6**Many will
come in my name, claiming, 'I am he,'
and will deceive many. **7**When you hear
of wars and rumors of wars, do not be
alarmed. Such things must happen, but
the end is still to come. **8**Nation will
rise against nation, and kingdom
against kingdom. There will be earthquakes in various places, and famines.
These are the beginning of birth pains.
9"You must be on your guard. You
will be handed over to the local councils and flogged in the synagogues.[e]
On account of me you will stand before
governors and kings as witnesses to
them. **10**And the gospel must first be
preached to all nations. **11**Whenever
you are arrested and brought to trial,
do not worry beforehand about what to
say. Just say whatever is given you at
the time, for it is not you speaking, but
the Holy Spirit.[f]
12"Brother will betray brother to
death, and a father his child. Children
will rebel against their parents and
have them put to death.[g] **13**All men
will hate you because of me,[h] but he
who stands firm to the end will be
saved.[i]
14"When you see 'the abomination
that causes desolation'[g][j] standing
where it[h] does not belong—let the
reader understand—then let those
who are in Judea flee to the mountains.
15Let no one on the roof of his house
go down or enter the house to take anything out. **16**Let no one in the field go
back to get his cloak. **17**How dreadful
it will be in those days for pregnant
women and nursing mothers![k] **18**Pray
that this will not take place in winter,
19because those will be days of distress unequaled from the beginning,
when God created the world,[l] until
now—and never to be equaled again.[m]
20If the Lord had not cut short those
days, no one would survive. But for the
sake of the elect, whom he has chosen,
he has shortened them. **21**At that time
if anyone says to you, 'Look, here is the
Christ[i]!' or, 'Look, there he is!' do not
believe it.[n] **22**For false Christs and
false prophets[o] will appear and perform signs and miracles[p] to deceive
the elect—if that were possible. **23**So
be on your guard;[q] I have told you everything ahead of time.
24"But in those days, following that
distress,

" 'the sun will be darkened,
and the moon will not give its
light;
25the stars will fall from the sky,
and the heavenly bodies will be
shaken.'[j][r]

26"At that time men will see the Son
of Man coming in clouds[s] with great
power and glory. **27**And he will send his
angels and gather his elect from the

13:5 [d]ver 22; Jer 29:8; Eph 5:6; 2Th 2:3,10-12; 1Ti 4:1; 2Ti 3:13; 1Jn 4:6
13:9 [e]S Mt 10:17
13:11 [f]Mt 10:19, 20; Lk 12:11,12
13:12 [g]Mic 7:6; Mt 10:21; Lk 12:51-53
13:13 [h]S Jn 15:21 [i]S Mt 10:22
13:14 [j]Da 9:27; 11:31; 12:11
13:17 [k]Lk 23:29
13:19 [l]Mk 10:6 [m]Da 9:26; 12:1; Joel 2:2
13:21 [n]Lk 17:23; 21:8
13:22 [o]S Mt 7:15 [p]S Jn 4:48; 2Th 2:9,10
13:23 [q]2Pe 3:17
13:25 [r]Isa 13:10; 34:4; S Mt 24:29
13:26 [s]S Rev 1:7

[g] *14* Daniel 9:27; 11:31; 12:11 [h] *14* Or *he;* also in verse 29 [i] *21* Or *Messiah*
[j] *25* Isaiah 13:10; 34:4

and "Watch!" (v. 37). These warnings indicate that many unbiblical teachings will be prominent among the churches. The believer, more than ever, must know and obey only the Word of God (see Mt 24:5, note).

13:6 MANY . . . WILL DECEIVE MANY. See Mt 24:11, note.

13:10 GOSPEL . . . PREACHED TO ALL NATIONS. See Mt 24:14, notes.

13:13 STANDS FIRM TO THE END. Perseverance in the faith and endurance in our loyalty to Christ is a Scriptural condition for final salvation (cf. Heb 3:14; 6:11–12; 10:36). The glory of final salvation is described in Rev 2:7,17,26–28; 3:5, 12,20–21; 7:9–17; 14:13; 21:1–7.

13:14 ABOMINATION THAT CAUSES DESOLATION. The abomination that causes desolation refers to that which defames or pollutes what is holy (see Da 9:25–27). (1) Christ's statement may prophetically refer both to the Roman invasion of Jerusalem when the temple was destroyed (A.D. 70) and to the placing of the image of the antichrist in Jerusalem just before Christ returns to judge the wicked (see 2Th 2:2–3; Rev 13:14–15; 19:11–21). (2) This is sometimes called "prophetic foreshadowing," a term used when two or more events are viewed as if they are one. Examples would be the combining of Christ's first coming to preach the gospel with his second coming to bring judgment in Isa 11:1–4, 61:1–2 and Zec 9:9–10 (see notes on those passages; see Mt 24:44, note). Likewise, the Pentecostal outpouring of the Spirit and "the great and dreadful day of the LORD" are combined and spoken of as one event in Joel 2:28–31. Christ here describes Jerusalem's destruction as a type of the great tribulation that occurs at the end of the age (see article on THE GREAT TRIBULATION, p. 1456).

13:19–22 DISTRESS. See article on THE GREAT TRIBULATION, p. 1456, for the interpretation of these verses.

13:22 FALSE PROPHETS. See article on FALSE TEACHERS, p. 1506.

13:24 THE SUN . . . DARKENED. See Mt 24:29, note.

13:26 SON OF MAN COMING. See Mt 24:30, note.

13:27 HIS ELECT. See Mt 24:31, note.

four winds, from the ends of the earth
to the ends of the heavens.[t]
28"Now learn this lesson from the fig
tree: As soon as its twigs get tender
and its leaves come out, you know that
summer is near. **29**Even so, when you
see these things happening, you know
that it is near, right at the door. **30**I tell
you the truth, this generation[k][u] will
certainly not pass away until all these
things have happened.[v] **31**Heaven and
earth will pass away, but my words will
never pass away.[w]

The Day and Hour Unknown

32"No one knows about that day or
hour, not even the angels in heaven,
nor the Son, but only the Father.[x]
33Be on guard! Be alert[l]![y] You do not
know when that time will come. **34**It's
like a man going away: He leaves his
house and puts his servants[z] in
charge, each with his assigned task,
and tells the one at the door to keep
watch.
35"Therefore keep watch because
you do not know when the owner of the
house will come back—whether in the
evening, or at midnight, or when
the rooster crows, or at dawn. **36**If he
comes suddenly, do not let him find
you sleeping. **37**What I say to you, I say
to everyone: 'Watch!' "[a]

Jesus Anointed at Bethany

14:1–11pp — Mt 26:2–16
14:1,2,10,11pp — Lk 22:1–6
14:3–8Ref — Jn 12:1–8

14 Now the Passover[b] and the
Feast of Unleavened Bread
were only two days away, and the chief
priests and the teachers of the law
were looking for some sly way to arrest
Jesus and kill him.[c] **2**"But not during
the Feast," they said, "or the people
may riot."
3While he was in Bethany,[d] reclining at the table in the home of a man
known as Simon the Leper, a woman
came with an alabaster jar of very expensive perfume, made of pure nard.
She broke the jar and poured the perfume on his head.[e]
4Some of those present were saying
indignantly to one another, "Why this
waste of perfume? **5**It could have been
sold for more than a year's wages[m]
and the money given to the poor." And
they rebuked her harshly.
6"Leave her alone," said Jesus. "Why
are you bothering her? She has done a
beautiful thing to me. **7**The poor you
will always have with you, and you can
help them any time you want.[f] But
you will not always have me. **8**She did
what she could. She poured perfume on
my body beforehand to prepare for my
burial.[g] **9**I tell you the truth, wherever
the gospel is preached throughout the
world,[h] what she has done will also be
told, in memory of her."
10Then Judas Iscariot, one of the
Twelve,[i] went to the chief priests to
betray Jesus to them.[j] **11**They were
delighted to hear this and promised to

13:27 [t]Zec 2:6
13:30 [u]Lk 17:25
[v]Mk 9:1
13:31
[w]S Mt 5:18
13:32 [x]Ac 1:7; 1Th 5:1,2
13:33 [y]1Th 5:6
13:34 [z]Mt 25:14
13:37
[a]Lk 12:35-40
14:1 [b]S Jn 11:55
[c]S Mt 12:14
14:3 [d]S Mt 21:17
[e]Lk 7:37-39
14:7 [f]Dt 15:11
14:8 [g]Jn 19:40
14:9
[h]S Mt 24:14; Mk 16:15
14:10
[i]Mk 3:16-19
[j]S Mt 10:4

[k]*30* Or *race* [l]*33* Some manuscripts *alert and pray* [m]*5* Greek *than three hundred denarii*

13:28 THE FIG TREE. See Mt 24:32, note.

13:29 SEE THESE THINGS. See Mt 24:33, note.

13:30 THIS GENERATION. See Mt 24:34, note.

13:32 NO ONE KNOWS ABOUT THAT DAY OR HOUR. See Mt 24:36, note.

13:33 BE ALERT! See Mt 24:42, notes.

13:35 IN THE EVENING ... MIDNIGHT ... AT DAWN. Christ affirms that his return for the faithful of his churches could occur at four possible times during the night or early morning. This points to the fact that his coming for them could be at any time and emphasizes the unexpectedness and hiddenness of the first stage of his second coming, when the faithful will be caught up from the earth (i.e., the rapture; see article on THE RAPTURE, p. 1864). Since it is imminent and unexpected, all believers must be spiritually alert and faithful (see Mt 24:42, notes; 24:44, note; cf. Lk 12:35–36,38–40,46; 21:34–36).

14:9 THE GOSPEL. Gospel (Gk *euangelion*) means good news—the good news that God has acted to save the perishing human race through the incarnation, death and resurrection of Jesus Christ (Lk 4:18–21; 7:22; Jn 3:16). Wherever this is proclaimed in the power of the Spirit (1Co 2:4; Gal 1:11), (1) it comes with authority (Mt 28:18–20); (2) it reveals God's righteousness (Ro 1:16–17); (3) it demands repentance (1:15; Mt 3:2; 4:17); (4) it convicts of sin, righteousness and judgment (Jn 16:8; cf. Ac 24:25); (5) it creates faith (Ro 10:17; Php 1:27); (6) it brings salvation, life and the gift of the Holy Spirit (Ac 2:33,38–39; Ro 1:16; 1Co 15:22; 1Pe 1:23); (7) it delivers from the dominion of sin and Satan (Mt 12:28; Ac 26:18; Ro 6); (8) it brings hope (Col 1:5,23), peace (Eph 2:17; 6:15) and immortality (2Ti 1:10); (9) it warns of judgment (Ro 2:16); and (10) it brings condemnation and eternal death when refused (Jn 3:18).

14:9 IN MEMORY OF HER. See Mt 26:13, note.

FALSE TEACHERS

Mk 13:22 "For false Christs and false prophets will appear and perform signs and miracles to deceive the elect—if that were possible."

DESCRIPTION. Believers today must be aware that within the churches there may be ministers of God's Word who are of the same spirit and life as the corrupt teachers of God's law in Jesus' day (Mt 24:11,24). Jesus warns that not everyone who professes Christ is a true believer, nor are all Christian writers, missionaries, pastors, evangelists, teachers, deacons and workers what they claim to be.

(1) These ministers will on the outside "appear to people as righteous" (Mt 23:28). They come "in sheep's clothing" (Mt 7:15). They may base their message solidly on God's Word and proclaim high righteous standards. They may appear sincerely concerned for God's work and kingdom and show great interest in the salvation of the lost while professing love for all people. They may appear to be great ministers of God, commendable spiritual leaders anointed by the Holy Spirit. They may perform miracles and have great success, and multitudes may follow them (see Mt 7:21–23, notes; 24:11,24; 2Co 11:13–15).

(2) Nevertheless, these people find their spiritual ancestors in the false prophets of the OT (see Dt 13:3, note; 1Ki 18:40, note; Ne 6:12, note; Jer 14:14, note; Hos 4:15, note; see article on THE PROPHET IN THE OLD TESTAMENT, p. 986) and in the Pharisees of the NT. Away from the crowds and in their hidden lives, the Pharisees were given over to "greed and self-indulgence" (Mt 23:25), "full of dead men's bones and everything unclean" (23:27), "full of hypocrisy and wickedness" (23:28). Their lives behind closed doors involved such things as lust, immorality, adultery, greed and self-centered indulgence.

(3) These imposters gain a place of influence in the church in two ways. (a) Some false teachers/preachers begin their ministry in sincerity, truth, purity and genuine faith in Christ. Then because of their pride and their own immoral desires, personal commitment to and love for Christ gradually die. Consequently, they are severed from God's kingdom (1Co 6:9–10; Gal 5:19–21; Eph 5:5–6) and become instruments of Satan while disguising themselves as ministers of righteousness (see 2Co 11:15). (b) Other false teachers/preachers have never been genuine believers in Christ. Satan has planted them within the church from the very beginning of their ministry (Mt 13:24–28,36–43), using their ability and charisma and aiding in their success. His strategy is to place them in influential positions so that they can undermine the genuine work of Christ. If they are discovered or exposed, Satan knows that great damage will come to the gospel and that the name of Christ will be put to open shame.

TESTING. Jesus warned his disciples fourteen times in the Gospels to watch out for leaders who would mislead (Mt 7:15; 16:6,11; 24:4,24; Mk 4:24; 8:15; 12:38–40; 13:5; Lk 12:1; 17:23; 20:46; 21:8). Elsewhere believers are exhorted to test teachers, preachers and leaders in the church (1Th 5:21; 1Jn 4:1). The following steps can be taken in testing false teachers or false prophets:

(1) Discern character. Do they have diligent prayer lives and do they show a sincere and pure devotion to God? Do they manifest the fruit of the Spirit (Gal 5:22–23), love sinners (Jn 3:16), hate wickedness and love righteousness (Heb 1:9, note), and cry out against sin (Mt 23; Lk 3:18–20)?

(2) Discern motives. True Christian leaders will seek to do four things: (a) honor Christ (2Co 8:23; Php 1:20); (b) lead the church into sanctification (Ac 26:18; 1Co 6:18; 2Co 6:16–18); (c) save the lost (1Co 9:19–22); and (d) proclaim and defend the gospel of Christ and the apostles (see Php 1:16, note; Jude 3, note).

(3) Test fruit in life and message. The fruit of false preachers will often consist in converts not totally committed to all of God's Word (see Mt 7:16, note).

(4) Discern level of reliance on Scripture. This is a key issue. Do they believe and teach that the original writings of both the OT and NT are fully inspired by God, and that we are to submit to all its teachings (2Jn 9–11; see article on THE INSPIRATION AND AUTHORITY OF SCRIPTURE, p. 1898)? If not, we can be sure that they and their message are not from God.

(5) Finally, test integrity with respect to the Lord's money. Do they refuse to take large amounts for themselves, handle all finances with integrity and responsibility, and seek to promote God's work in ways consistent with NT standards for leaders (1Ti 3:3; 6:9–10)?

It must be understood that in spite of all that faithful believers do in evaluating a person's life and message, there will still be false teachers within the churches who, with Satan's help, remain undetected until God determines to expose those persons for what they are.

give him money. So he watched for an
opportunity to hand him over.

The Lord's Supper

14:12–26pp — Mt 26:17–30; Lk 22:7–23
14:22–25pp — 1Co 11:23–25

12On the first day of the Feast of Unleavened Bread, when it was customary to sacrifice the Passover lamb,[k]
Jesus' disciples asked him, "Where do you want us to go and make preparations for you to eat the Passover?"
13So he sent two of his disciples, telling them, "Go into the city, and a man carrying a jar of water will meet you. Follow him.
14Say to the owner of the house he enters, 'The Teacher asks: Where is my guest room, where I may eat the Passover with my disciples?'
15He will show you a large upper room,[l] furnished and ready. Make preparations for us there."
16The disciples left, went into the city and found things just as Jesus had told them. So they prepared the Passover.
17When evening came, Jesus arrived with the Twelve.
18While they were reclining at the table eating, he said, "I tell you the truth, one of you will betray me—one who is eating with me."
19They were saddened, and one by one they said to him, "Surely not I?"
20"It is one of the Twelve," he replied, "one who dips bread into the bowl with me.[m]
21The Son of Man[n] will go just as it is written about him. But woe to that man who betrays the Son of Man! It would be better for him if he had not been born."
22While they were eating, Jesus took bread, gave thanks and broke it,[o] and gave it to his disciples, saying, "Take it; this is my body."
23Then he took the cup, gave thanks and offered it to them, and they all drank from it.[p]
24"This is my blood of the[n] covenant,[q] which is poured out for many," he said to them.
25"I tell you the truth, I will not drink again of the fruit of the vine until that day when I drink it anew in the kingdom of God."[r]
26When they had sung a hymn, they went out to the Mount of Olives.[s]

Jesus Predicts Peter's Denial

14:27–31pp — Mt 26:31–35

27"You will all fall away," Jesus told them, "for it is written:

> " 'I will strike the shepherd,
> and the sheep will be
> scattered.'[o][t]

28But after I have risen, I will go ahead of you into Galilee."[u]
29Peter declared, "Even if all fall away, I will not."
30"I tell you the truth," Jesus answered, "today—yes, tonight—before the rooster crows twice[p] you yourself will disown me three times."[v]
31But Peter insisted emphatically, "Even if I have to die with you,[w] I will never disown you." And all the others said the same.

Gethsemane

14:32–42pp — Mt 26:36–46; Lk 22:40–46

32They went to a place called Gethsemane, and Jesus said to his disciples, "Sit here while I pray."
33He took Peter, James and John[x] along with him, and he began to be deeply distressed and troubled.
34"My soul is over-

14:12 [k]Ex 12:1-11; Dt 16:1-4; 1Co 5:7 **14:15** [l]Ac 1:13 **14:20** [m]Jn 13:18-27 **14:21** [n]S Mt 8:20 **14:22** [o]S Mt 14:19 **14:23** [p]1Co 10:16 **14:24** [q]S Mt 26:28 **14:25** [r]S Mt 3:2 **14:26** [s]S Mt 21:1 **14:27** [t]Zec 13:7 **14:28** [u]Mk 16:7 **14:30** [v]ver 66-72; Lk 22:34; Jn 13:38 **14:31** [w]Lk 22:33; Jn 13:37 **14:33** [x]S Mt 4:21

[n]24 Some manuscripts *the new* [o]27 Zech. 13:7 [p]30 Some early manuscripts do not have *twice*.

14:14 PASSOVER. See Mt 26:2, note.

14:21 HAD NOT BEEN BORN. Jesus always judges and evaluates life from a spiritual and eternal viewpoint. He affirms that it would be better that a person never be born than to come into this world, fail to accept Jesus as Lord and Savior, and consequently perish eternally in hell (see Jn 6:64, note).

14:22 BREAD ... MY BODY. See Lk 22:20, notes; 1Co 11:24–25,27 notes.

14:24 BLOOD OF THE COVENANT. Christ's blood was shed for us in order to bring us forgiveness and salvation. His death on the cross established a new covenant between God and all who receive Christ as Lord and Savior (see Jer 31:31–34, notes). Those who repent and turn to God through faith in Christ will be forgiven, be delivered from the power of Satan, receive new spiritual life, be made children of God, be baptized with the Holy Spirit, and have access to God at any time in order to receive mercy, grace, strength and help (see Mt 26:28, note; Heb 4:16; 7:25).

14:32 GETHSEMANE . . . PRAY. Jesus' action is an example of what believers ought to do in times of great distress or grief. (1) Turn to God in prayer (vv. 32,35–36,39). (2) Seek the support of friends (vv. 33–34,42). (3) Affirm in your heart that God is your heavenly Father who cares for you (v. 36). (4) Trust God and commit yourself to his will (v. 36). See Mt 26:37ff, notes on the ten stages of the sufferings of Christ.

whelmed with sorrow to the point of
death,"[y] he said to them. "Stay here
and keep watch."
35 Going a little farther, he fell to the
ground and prayed that if possible the
hour[z] might pass from him.
36 "*Abba*,[q] Father,"[a] he said, "everything is possible for you. Take this
cup[b] from me. Yet not what I will, but
what you will."[c]
37 Then he returned to his disciples
and found them sleeping. "Simon," he
said to Peter, "are you asleep? Could
you not keep watch for one hour?
38 Watch and pray so that you will not
fall into temptation.[d] The spirit is
willing, but the body is weak."[e]
39 Once more he went away and
prayed the same thing. 40 When he
came back, he again found them sleeping, because their eyes were heavy.
They did not know what to say to him.
41 Returning the third time, he said
to them, "Are you still sleeping and
resting? Enough! The hour[f] has
come. Look, the Son of Man is betrayed
into the hands of sinners. 42 Rise! Let
us go! Here comes my betrayer!"

Jesus Arrested

14:43–50pp — Mt 26:47–56; Lk 22:47–50; Jn 18:3–11

43 Just as he was speaking, Judas,[g]
one of the Twelve, appeared. With him
was a crowd armed with swords and
clubs, sent from the chief priests, the
teachers of the law, and the elders.
44 Now the betrayer had arranged a
signal with them: "The one I kiss is the
man; arrest him and lead him away under guard." 45 Going at once to Jesus,
Judas said, "Rabbi!"[h] and kissed him.
46 The men seized Jesus and arrested
him. 47 Then one of those standing near
drew his sword and struck the servant
of the high priest, cutting off his ear.
48 "Am I leading a rebellion," said
Jesus, "that you have come out with
swords and clubs to capture me? 49 Every day I was with you, teaching in the
temple courts,[i] and you did not arrest
me. But the Scriptures must be fulfilled."[j] 50 Then everyone deserted
him and fled.[k]
51 A young man, wearing nothing but
a linen garment, was following Jesus.
When they seized him, 52 he fled naked,
leaving his garment behind.

Before the Sanhedrin

14:53–65pp — Mt 26:57–68; Jn 18:12,13,19–24
14:61–63pp — Lk 22:67–71

53 They took Jesus to the high priest,
and all the chief priests, elders and
teachers of the law came together.
54 Peter followed him at a distance,
right into the courtyard of the high
priest.[l] There he sat with the guards
and warmed himself at the fire.[m]
55 The chief priests and the whole
Sanhedrin[n] were looking for evidence
against Jesus so that they could put
him to death, but they did not find any.
56 Many testified falsely against him,
but their statements did not agree.
57 Then some stood up and gave this
false testimony against him: 58 "We
heard him say, 'I will destroy this man-

14:34 y Jn 12:27 **14:35** z ver 41; S Mt 26:18 **14:36** a Ro 8:15; Gal 4:6 b S Mt 20:22 c S Mt 26:39 **14:38** d Mt 6:13 e Ro 7:22,23 **14:41** f ver 35; S Mt 26:18 **14:43** g S Mt 10:4 **14:45** h S Mt 23:7 **14:49** i S Mt 26:55 j Isa 53:7-12; S Mt 1:22 **14:50** k ver 27 **14:54** l S Mt 26:3 m Jn 18:18 **14:55** n S Mt 5:22

q 36 Aramaic for *Father*

14:35 HOUR MIGHT PASS FROM HIM. See Mt 26:39, note.

14:37 KEEP WATCH FOR ONE HOUR. Peter and the disciples neglected to keep watch and pray, the only thing that could have saved them from failure at this time of testing (v. 50). Failure in our Christian life is absolutely certain without prayer (see Ac 10:9, note on the commitment to pray for one hour).

14:46 ARRESTED HIM. See Mt 26:57, note, for the order of events from Christ's arrest to his crucifixion.

14:50 EVERYONE DESERTED HIM. We should never compare the failure of Peter and the other disciples at Jesus' arrest to the spiritual and moral failure of pastors or overseers after Christ's death and resurrection. This is so for the following reasons: (1) Peter and the disciples at the time of their failure were not yet under the new covenant. The new covenant did not go into effect until Christ shed his blood on the cross (Heb 9:15–20).

(2) Peter and the disciples had not yet experienced the new birth or regeneration by the Holy Spirit in the full NT sense. The Holy Spirit was not imparted to them in his indwelling and sanctifying presence until the day of Christ's resurrection when Christ "breathed on them and said, 'Receive the Holy Spirit' " (Jn 20:22). The disciples' failure was an act of weakness rather than wickedness.

(3) When Peter and the disciples forsook Christ, they did not possess the advantage of those who are conscious of the moral implications of Christ's sacrificial death on the cross (see Ro 6), nor did they have a sustaining faith inspired by his resurrection from the dead.

In other words, this passage should not be used to justify restoring leaders to ministry who, because of their own sins and moral laxity, have voluntarily thrown aside in their personal and spiritual lives the qualifications necessary for the office of overseer (see article on MORAL QUALIFICATIONS FOR OVERSEERS, p. 1882).

made temple and in three days will
build another,[o] not made by man.' "
59 Yet even then their testimony did not
agree.
60 Then the high priest stood up before them and asked Jesus, "Are you
not going to answer? What is this testimony that these men are bringing
against you?" 61 But Jesus remained silent and gave no answer.[p]
Again the high priest asked him,
"Are you the Christ,[r] the Son of the
Blessed One?"[q]
62 "I am," said Jesus. "And you will
see the Son of Man sitting at the right
hand of the Mighty One and coming on
the clouds of heaven."[r]
63 The high priest tore his clothes.[s]
"Why do we need any more witnesses?"
he asked. 64 "You have heard the blasphemy. What do you think?"
They all condemned him as worthy
of death.[t] 65 Then some began to spit
at him; they blindfolded him, struck
him with their fists, and said, "Prophesy!" And the guards took him and beat
him.[u]

Peter Disowns Jesus

14:66–72pp — Mt 26:69–75; Lk 22:56–62; Jn 18:16–18,25–27

66 While Peter was below in the
courtyard,[v] one of the servant girls of
the high priest came by. 67 When she
saw Peter warming himself,[w] she
looked closely at him.
"You also were with that Nazarene,
Jesus,"[x] she said.
68 But he denied it. "I don't know or
understand what you're talking
about,"[y] he said, and went out into the
entryway.[s]
69 When the servant girl saw him
there, she said again to those standing
around, "This fellow is one of them."
70 Again he denied it.[z]
After a little while, those standing
near said to Peter, "Surely you are one
of them, for you are a Galilean."[a]
71 He began to call down curses on
himself, and he swore to them, "I don't
know this man you're talking about."[b]
72 Immediately the rooster crowed
the second time.[t] Then Peter remembered the word Jesus had spoken to
him: "Before the rooster crows twice[u]
you will disown me three times."[c] And
he broke down and wept.

Jesus Before Pilate

15:2–15pp — Mt 27:11–26; Lk 23:2,3,18–25; Jn 18:29–19:16

15 Very early in the morning, the
chief priests, with the elders,
the teachers of the law[d] and the whole
Sanhedrin,[e] reached a decision. They
bound Jesus, led him away and handed
him over to Pilate.[f]
2 "Are you the king of the Jews?"[g]
asked Pilate.
"Yes, it is as you say," Jesus replied.
3 The chief priests accused him of
many things. 4 So again Pilate asked
him, "Aren't you going to answer? See
how many things they are accusing you
of."
5 But Jesus still made no reply,[h] and
Pilate was amazed.
6 Now it was the custom at the Feast
to release a prisoner whom the people
requested. 7 A man called Barabbas
was in prison with the insurrectionists
who had committed murder in the up-
rising. 8 The crowd came up and asked
Pilate to do for them what he usually
did.
9 "Do you want me to release to you
the king of the Jews?"[i] asked Pilate,
10 knowing it was out of envy that the
chief priests had handed Jesus over to
him. 11 But the chief priests stirred up
the crowd to have Pilate release Barabbas[j] instead.
12 "What shall I do, then, with the
one you call the king of the Jews?" Pilate asked them.
13 "Crucify him!" they shouted.
14 "Why? What crime has he committed?" asked Pilate.
But they shouted all the louder,
"Crucify him!"
15 Wanting to satisfy the crowd, Pilate released Barabbas to them. He had

14:58 [o] S Jn 2:19 **14:61** [p] Isa 53:7; Mt 27:12,14; Mk 15:5; Lk 23:9; Jn 19:9 [q] Mt 16:16; Jn 4:25,26 **14:62** [r] S Rev 1:7 **14:63** [s] Lev 10:6; 21:10; Nu 14:6; Ac 14:14 **14:64** [t] Lev 24:16 **14:65** [u] S Mt 16:21 **14:66** [v] ver 54 **14:67** [w] ver 54 [x] S Mk 1:24 **14:68** [y] ver 30,72 **14:70** [z] ver 30,68, 72 [a] Ac 2:7 **14:71** [b] ver 30,72
14:72 [c] ver 30,68 **15:1** [d] Mt 27:1; Lk 22:66 [e] S Mt 5:22 [f] S Mt 27:2 **15:2** [g] ver 9,12, 18,26; S Mt 2:2 **15:5** [h] S Mk 14:61 **15:9** [i] S ver 2 **15:11** [j] Ac 3:14

[r] *61* Or *Messiah* [s] *68* Some early manuscripts *entryway and the rooster crowed*
[t] *72* Some early manuscripts do not have *the second time.* [u] *72* Some early manuscripts do not have *twice.*

14:65 STRUCK HIM. See Mt 26:67, note.

14:71 TO CALL DOWN CURSES . . . AND HE SWORE. Peter affirmed what he was saying with an oath and called the curse of God down on himself if his statements should prove to be false.

15:1 HANDED HIM OVER TO PILATE. See Mt 27:2, note.

15:15 HAD JESUS FLOGGED. See Mt 27:26, note.

Jesus flogged,[k] and handed him over
to be crucified.

The Soldiers Mock Jesus

15:16–20pp — Mt 27:27–31

16 The soldiers led Jesus away into
the palace[l] (that is, the Praetorium)
and called together the whole company
of soldiers. 17 They put a purple robe on
him, then twisted together a crown of
thorns and set it on him. 18 And they
began to call out to him, "Hail, king of
the Jews!"[m] 19 Again and again they
struck him on the head with a staff and
spit on him. Falling on their knees,
they paid homage to him. 20 And when
they had mocked him, they took off the
purple robe and put his own clothes on
him. Then they led him out[n] to crucify
him.

The Crucifixion

15:22–32pp — Mt 27:33–44; Lk 23:33–43; Jn 19:17–24

21 A certain man from Cyrene,[o] Simon, the father of Alexander and Rufus,[p] was passing by on his way in
from the country, and they forced him
to carry the cross.[q] 22 They brought
Jesus to the place called Golgotha
(which means The Place of the Skull).
23 Then they offered him wine mixed
with myrrh,[r] but he did not take it.
24 And they crucified him. Dividing up
his clothes, they cast lots[s] to see
what each would get.
25 It was the third hour when they
crucified him. 26 The written notice of
the charge against him read: THE KING OF
THE JEWS.[t] 27 They crucified two robbers with him, one on his right and one
on his left.[v] 29 Those who passed by
hurled insults at him, shaking their
heads[u] and saying, "So! You who are
going to destroy the temple and build
it in three days,[v] 30 come down from
the cross and save yourself!"
31 In the same way the chief priests
and the teachers of the law mocked
him[w] among themselves. "He saved
others," they said, "but he can't save
himself! 32 Let this Christ,[w][x] this
King of Israel,[y] come down now from
the cross, that we may see and believe." Those crucified with him also
heaped insults on him.

The Death of Jesus

15:33–41pp — Mt 27:45–56; Lk 23:44–49

33 At the sixth hour darkness came
over the whole land until the ninth
hour.[z] 34 And at the ninth hour Jesus
cried out in a loud voice, *"Eloi, Eloi,
lama sabachthani?"*—which means,
"My God, my God, why have you forsaken me?"[x][a]
35 When some of those standing near
heard this, they said, "Listen, he's calling Elijah."
36 One man ran, filled a sponge with
wine vinegar,[b] put it on a stick, and
offered it to Jesus to drink. "Now leave
him alone. Let's see if Elijah comes to
take him down," he said.
37 With a loud cry, Jesus breathed his
last.[c]
38 The curtain of the temple was torn
in two from top to bottom.[d] 39 And
when the centurion,[e] who stood there
in front of Jesus, heard his cry and[y]
saw how he died, he said, "Surely this
man was the Son[z] of God!"[f]
40 Some women were watching from
a distance.[g] Among them were Mary
Magdalene, Mary the mother of James
the younger and of Joses, and Salome.[h] 41 In Galilee these women had
followed him and cared for his needs.
Many other women who had come up
with him to Jerusalem were also
there.[i]

The Burial of Jesus

15:42–47pp — Mt 27:57–61; Lk 23:50–56; Jn 19:38–42

42 It was Preparation Day (that is,
the day before the Sabbath).[j] So as

15:15 [k] Isa 53:6
15:16 [l] Jn 18:28, 33; 19:9
15:18 [m] S ver 2
15:20 [n] Heb 13:12
15:21 [o] S Mt 27:32 [p] Ro 16:13 [q] Mt 27:32; Lk 23:26
15:23 [r] ver 36; Ps 69:21; Pr 31:6
15:24 [s] Ps 22:18
15:26 [t] S ver 2
15:29 [u] Ps 22:7; 109:25 [v] S Jn 2:19
15:31 [w] Ps 22:7
15:32 [x] S Mk 14:61 [y] S ver 2
15:33 [z] Am 8:9
15:34 [a] Ps 22:1
15:36 [b] ver 23; Ps 69:21
15:37 [c] Jn 19:30
15:38 [d] Heb 10:19,20
15:39 [e] ver 45 [f] Mk 1:1,11; 9:7; S Mt 4:3
15:40 [g] Ps 38:11 [h] Mk 16:1; Lk 24:10; Jn 19:25
15:41 [i] Mt 27:55, 56; Lk 8:2,3
15:42 [j] Mt 27:62; Jn 19:31

[v] 27 Some manuscripts *left,* [28] *and the scripture was fulfilled which says, "He was counted with the lawless ones"* (Isaiah 53:12) [w] 32 Or *Messiah* [x] 34 Psalm 22:1 [y] 39 Some manuscripts do not have *heard his cry and* [z] 39 Or *a son*

15:17 CROWN OF THORNS. See Mt 27:28–29, note.
15:20 LED HIM OUT TO CRUCIFY HIM. See Mt 27:31, note.
15:24 CRUCIFIED HIM. See Mt 27:35, note.
15:29 HURLED INSULTS. See Mt 27:39, note.
15:34 WHY HAVE YOU FORSAKEN ME? See Mt 27:46, note.
15:36 WINE VINEGAR. See Jn 19:29, note.
15:37 BREATHED HIS LAST. See Mt 27:50, note.

evening approached, **43**Joseph of Arimathea, a prominent member of the
Council,[k] who was himself waiting for
the kingdom of God,[l] went boldly to
Pilate and asked for Jesus' body. **44**Pilate was surprised to hear that he was
already dead. Summoning the centurion, he asked him if Jesus had already
died. **45**When he learned from the centurion[m] that it was so, he gave the
body to Joseph. **46**So Joseph bought
some linen cloth, took down the body,
wrapped it in the linen, and placed it in
a tomb cut out of rock. Then he rolled
a stone against the entrance of the
tomb.[n] **47**Mary Magdalene and Mary
the mother of Joses[o] saw where he
was laid.

The Resurrection

16:1–8pp — Mt 28:1–8; Lk 24:1–10

16 When the Sabbath was over,
Mary Magdalene, Mary the
mother of James, and Salome bought
spices[p] so that they might go to
anoint Jesus' body. **2**Very early on the
first day of the week, just after sunrise,
they were on their way to the tomb
3and they asked each other, "Who will
roll the stone away from the entrance
of the tomb?"[q]

4But when they looked up, they saw
that the stone, which was very large,
had been rolled away. **5**As they entered
the tomb, they saw a young man
dressed in a white robe[r] sitting on the
right side, and they were alarmed.

6"Don't be alarmed," he said. "You
are looking for Jesus the Nazarene,[s]
who was crucified. He has risen! He is
not here. See the place where they laid
him. **7**But go, tell his disciples and Peter, 'He is going ahead of you into Galilee. There you will see him,[t] just as he
told you.' "[u]

8Trembling and bewildered, the
women went out and fled from the
tomb. They said nothing to anyone, because they were afraid.

15:43 [k]S Mt 5:22 [l]S Mt 3:2; Lk 2:25,38
15:45 [m]ver 39
15:46 [n]Mk 16:3
15:47 [o]ver 40
16:1 [p]Lk 23:56; Jn 19:39,40
16:3 [q]Mk 15:46
16:5 [r]S Jn 20:12
16:6 [s]S Mk 1:24
16:7 [t]Jn 21:1-23 [u]Mk 14:28

[The earliest manuscripts and some other ancient witnesses do not have Mark 16:9–20.]

Resurrection Appearances of Jesus

9When Jesus rose early on the
first day of the week, he appeared
first to Mary Magdalene,[v] out of
whom he had driven seven demons.
10She went and told those who had
been with him and who were mourning and weeping. **11**When they heard
that Jesus was alive and that she
had seen him, they did not believe
it.[w]

12Afterward Jesus appeared in a
different form to two of them while
they were walking in the country.[x]
13These returned and reported it to the
rest; but they did not believe them either.

14Later Jesus appeared to the
Eleven as they were eating; he rebuked them for their lack of faith and
their stubborn refusal to believe
those who had seen him after he had
risen.[y]

Go and Preach

15He said to them, "Go into all the
world and preach the good news to all
creation.[z] **16**Whoever believes and is
baptized will be saved, but whoever
does not believe will be condemned.[a]
17And these signs[b] will accompany
those who believe: In my name they
will drive out demons;[c] they will
speak in new tongues;[d] **18**they will
pick up snakes[e] with their hands; and
when they drink deadly poison, it will
not hurt them at all; they will place
their hands on[f] sick people, and they
will get well."

16:9 [v]Mk 15:47; Jn 20:11-18
16:11 [w]ver 13, 14; Lk 24:11
16:12 [x]Lk 24:13-32
16:14 [y]Lk 24:36-43
16:15 [z]Mt 28:18-20; Lk 24:47,48; Ac 1:8
16:16 [a]Jn 3:16, 18,36; Ac 16:31
16:17 [b]S Jn 4:48 [c]Mk 9:38; Lk 10:17; Ac 5:16; 8:7; 16:18; 19:13-16 [d]Ac 2:4; 10:46; 19:6; 1Co 12:10,28,30; 13:1; 14:2-39
16:18 [e]Lk 10:19; Ac 28:3-5 [f]S Ac 6:6

16:6 HE HAS RISEN. See Mt 28:6, note.

16:9–20 JESUS' APPEARANCES. Although vv. 9–20 are omitted from two of the oldest Greek manuscripts, they do appear in other old manuscripts, as well as in the majority of Greek manuscripts from all over the ancient world. Many scholars conclude, therefore, that any reading attested to by the majority of ancient manuscripts is likely to be part of the original writing of the Biblical author; Vv. 9–20 should thus be considered part of the inspired Word of God.

16:17 THESE SIGNS WILL ACCOMPANY. See article on SIGNS OF BELIEVERS, p. 1513.

16:18 PICK UP SNAKES. Picking up snakes or drinking poison is not to be ritualized and made into a "trial by ordeal" in order to prove one's spirituality. These are promises given to believers who encounter such dangers in their normal work for Christ. It is a sin to test God by initiating unnecessary danger or trials (Mt 4:5–7; 10:23; 24:16–18).

SIGNS OF BELIEVERS

***Mk 16:17–18** "And these signs will accompany those who believe: In my name they will drive out demons; they will speak in new tongues; they will pick up snakes with their hands; and when they drink deadly poison, it will not hurt them at all; they will place their hands on sick people, and they will get well."*

Scripture clearly teaches that Christ wants his followers to perform miraculous deeds as they announce the gospel of the kingdom of God (see Mt 10:1; Mk 3:14–15; Lk 9:2, note; 10:17; Jn 14:12, note).

(1) These signs (Gk *sēmeion*), done by true disciples, confirm that the gospel message is genuine, that God's kingdom has come to earth in power (see article on THE KINGDOM OF GOD, p. 1430), and that the living and risen Jesus is present with his people and working through them (see Jn 10:25; Ac 10:38).

(2) Every one of these signs (except for drinking poison) occurred in the recorded history of the early church: (a) speaking in new tongues (see Ac 2:4; 10:46; 19:6; 1Co 12:30; 14; see article on SPEAKING IN TONGUES, p. 1646); (b) driving out demons (Ac 5:15–16; 16:18; 19:11–12); (c) escaping death from snakebites (Ac 28:3–5); and (d) healing the sick (Ac 3:1–7; 8:7; 9:33–34; 14:8–10; 28:7–8).

(3) These spiritual manifestations are intended to continue within Christ's churches until Jesus returns. Scripture never suggests that these signs were restricted to the period immediately following Jesus' ascension (see 1Co 1:7, note; 12:28; Gal 3:5).

(4) Christ's followers were not only to preach the gospel of the kingdom and bring salvation to those who believe (Mt 28:19–20; Mk 16:15–16; Lk 24:47), but were also to bring in that kingdom, just as Jesus did (Ac 10:38), by driving out demons and healing the sick (see article on THE KINGDOM OF GOD, p. 1430).

(5) Jesus indicates in Mk 16:15–20 that these signs are not special gifts for a few, but were to be given to *all* believers who, in obedience to Christ, witness to the gospel and claim his promises.

(6) The failure of these "signs" to occur in the church today is not Christ's failure to keep his promises. Failure, Jesus states, lies within the hearts of his followers (see Mt 17:17, note).

(7) Christ has promised that his authority, power and presence will accompany us as we battle Satan's kingdom (Mt 28:18–20; Lk 24:47–49). We must liberate people from their captivity by preaching the gospel, by living righteous lives (Mt 6:33; Ro 6:13; 14:17), and by performing signs and miracles through the power of the Spirit (see Mt 10:1, note; Mk 16:16–20; Ac 4:31–33; see article on POWER OVER SATAN AND DEMONS, p. 1484).

19 After the Lord Jesus had spoken to
them, he was taken up into heaven[g]
and he sat at the right hand of God.[h]
20 Then the disciples went out and
preached everywhere, and the Lord
worked with them and confirmed his
word by the signs[i] that accompanied
it.

16:19 [g] Lk 24:50, 51; Jn 6:62; Ac 1:9-11; 1Ti 3:16 [h] Ps 110:1; Mt 26:64; Ac 2:33; 5:31; Ro 8:34; Col 3:1; Heb 1:3; 12:2 **16:20** [i] S Jn 4:48

LUKE

Outline

I. Preface to Luke's Gospel (1:1–4)
II. The Coming of the Savior (1:5—2:52)
  A. Announcement of John's Coming Birth (1:5–25)
  B. Announcement of Jesus' Coming Birth (1:26–56)
  C. Birth of John the Baptist (1:57–80)
  D. Birth of Jesus (2:1–20)
  E. Jesus at the Temple as an Infant (2:21–39)
  F. Jesus' Visit to the Temple as a Boy (2:40–52)
III. Preparation for the Savior's Ministry (3:1—4:13)
  A. Preaching of John the Baptist (3:1–20)
  B. Baptism of Jesus (3:21–22)
  C. Genealogy of Jesus (3:23–38)
  D. Temptation of Jesus (4:1–13)
IV. Ministry in Galilee (4:14—9:50)
  A. Beginning of Jesus' Ministry, and Rejection at Nazareth (4:14–30)
  B. Capernaum: Jesus' Divine Authority Manifested (4:31–44)
  C. Miraculous Catch of Fish (5:1–11)
  D. Healing the Man With Leprosy (5:12–16)
  E. Jesus' Authority Is Challenged (5:17–26)
  F. The Savior of Sinners (5:27–32)
  G. Inauguration of the New Order (5:33—6:49)
  H. Demonstration of Divine Power (7:1—8:56)
  I. Jesus Gives Power to His Disciples (9:1–6)
  J. Herod and John the Baptist (9:7–9)
  K. Feeding of the Five Thousand (9:10–17)
  L. Peter's Confession and Jesus' Response (9:18–27)
  M. The Savior's Glory Revealed (9:28–50)
V. Ministry During the Final Journey Toward Jerusalem (9:51—19:28)
  A. The Savior's Mission of Redemption (9:51—10:37)
  B. Jesus' Special Instruction on Service and Prayer (10:38—11:13)
  C. Jesus' Warnings to Both Enemies and Followers (11:14—14:35)
  D. Parables About the Lost and Found (15:1–32)
  E. Jesus' Commands to His Followers (16:1—17:10)
  F. Ingratitude of Nine Men With Leprosy Who Were Healed (17:11–19)
  G. Suddenness of Jesus' Return Predicted (17:20—18:14)
  H. The Savior, Little Children and the Rich Ruler (18:15–30)
  I. Toward the End of the Journey (18:31—19:28)
VI. Passion Week (19:29—23:56)
  A. Jesus Enters Jerusalem (19:29–48)
  B. Jesus Teaches Daily in the Temple (20:1—21:4)
  C. Jesus Foretells the Destruction of the Temple and His Return (21:5–38)
  D. Final Preparations and the Last Supper (22:1–38)
  E. Gethsemane and the Betrayal (22:39–53)
  F. The Jewish Trial (22:54–71)

G. The Roman Trial (23:1–25)
H. The Crucifixion (23:26–49)
I. The Burial (23:50–56)
VII. Resurrection to Ascension (24:1–53)
A. The Resurrection Morning (24:1–12)
B. The Risen Lord's Appearances (24:13–43)
C. The Farewell Instructions (24:44–53)

Author: Luke

Theme: Jesus, the Divine-Human Savior

Date of Writing: A.D. 60–63

Background

Luke's Gospel is the first of two books addressed to a man named Theophilus (1:3; Ac 1:1). Although the author is not identified by name in either book, the unanimous testimony of early Christianity and the corroborating internal evidence of the two books point to common authorship by Luke.

Apparently Luke was a Gentile convert, the only non-Jewish author of a Bible book. The Holy Spirit prompted him to write to Theophilus (whose name means "one who loves God") in order to fill a need in the Gentile church for a full account of the beginnings of Christianity. This included two parts: (1) Jesus' birth, life and ministry, death, resurrection and ascension (Luke's Gospel), and (2) the outpouring of the Spirit at Jerusalem and the subsequent development of the early church (book of Acts). These two books comprise more than one-fourth of the NT.

From Paul's letters we learn that Luke was a "dear friend . . . the doctor" (Col 4:14) and a loyal co-worker with Paul (2Ti 4:11; Phm 24; cf. "we" passages in Acts, see the introduction to Acts). From Luke's own writings we know he was well-educated, a skilled writer, a careful historian and an inspired theologian. When he wrote his Gospel, the Gentile church apparently had no complete or widely circulated Gospel about Jesus. Matthew wrote initially for the Jews, and Mark wrote a concise Gospel for the church in Rome. The Greek-speaking Gentile world did have oral accounts about Jesus by eyewitnesses, as well as short written digests, but no complete and orderly Gospel (see 1:1–4). Thus Luke set about to investigate everything carefully "from the beginning" (1:3), probably doing research in Palestine while Paul was in prison at Caesarea (Ac 21:17; 23:23—26:32) and completing his Gospel toward the end of that time or soon after arriving in Rome with Paul (Ac 28:16).

Purpose

Luke wrote this Gospel to the Gentiles to provide a full and accurate record "about all that Jesus began to do and to teach until the day he was taken up to heaven" (Ac 1:1b-2a). Writing under the inspiration of the Holy Spirit, Luke wanted Theophilus and other Gentile inquirers and converts to know with certainty the exact truth about which they had been orally instructed (1:3–4). That Luke wrote for Gentiles is apparent throughout the Gospel; for example, he traces Jesus' human genealogy back *to Adam* (3:23–38) and not just *to Abraham* as did Matthew (cf. Mt 1:1–17). In Luke, Jesus is clearly seen as the divine-human Savior who was God's provision of salvation for all of Adam's descendants.

Survey

Luke's Gospel begins with the most complete infancy narratives (1:5—2:40) and gives the only glimpse in the Gospels of Jesus' boyhood (2:41–52). After describing John the Baptist's ministry and giving Jesus' genealogy, Luke divides Jesus' ministry into three major sections: (1) his ministry in and around Galilee (4:14—9:50), (2) his ministry during the final journey to Jerusalem (9:51—19:27) and (3) his last week in Jerusalem (19:28—24:43).

While Jesus' miracles are prominent in Luke's record of the Galilean ministry, the main focus in this Gospel is on Jesus' teaching and parables during his extended ministry on the way to Jerusalem (9:51—19:27). This section comprises the greatest block of material unique to Luke, and includes many well-loved stories and parables. The pivotal verse (9:51) and the key verse (19:10) of the Gospel occur at the beginning and toward the end of this special Lukan material.

Special Features

Eight major emphases characterize Luke's Gospel. (1) It is the most comprehensive Gospel, recording events in Jesus' life from pre-birth to his ascension, and it is the longest NT book. (2) It is the most literary of the Gospels, demonstrating exceptional style and content, a rich vocabulary and an excellent command of Greek. (3) It emphasizes the universal scope of the gospel—that Jesus came to bring salvation for Jews and Gentiles alike. (4) It stresses Jesus' concern for the underprivileged, including women, children, poor people and social outcasts. (5) It emphasizes Jesus' prayer life and his teaching about prayer. (6) The prominent title for Jesus in this Gospel is "Son of Man." (7) The response of joy characterizes those who accept Jesus and his message. (8) The Holy Spirit is given a place of great importance in the life of Jesus and of his people (e.g., 1:15,41,67; 2:25–27; 4:1,14,18; 10:21; 12:12; 24:49).

Reading Luke

In order to read the entire New Testament in one year, the book of Luke should be read in 49 days, according to the following schedule:
☐ 1:1–25 ☐ 1:26–56 ☐ 1:57–80 ☐ 2:1–20 ☐ 2:21–52 ☐ 3 ☐ 4:1–13 ☐ 4:14–44 ☐ 5:1–16 ☐ 5:17–39 ☐ 6:1–16 ☐ 6:17–49 ☐ 7:1–35 ☐ 7:36–50 ☐ 8:1–21 ☐ 8:22–39 ☐ 8:40–56 ☐ 9:1–17 ☐ 9:18–36 ☐ 9:37–62 ☐ 10:1–24 ☐ 10:25–42 ☐ 11:1–13 ☐ 11:14–36 ☐ 11:37–54 ☐ 12:1–21 ☐ 12:22–48 ☐ 12:49–59 ☐ 13:1–21 ☐ 13:22–35 ☐ 14:1–24 ☐ 14:25—15:10 ☐ 15:11–32 ☐ 16 ☐ 17:1–19 ☐ 17:20—18:14 ☐ 18:15–43 ☐ 19:1–27 ☐ 19:28–48 ☐ 20:1–19 ☐ 20:20—21:4 ☐ 21:5–38 ☐ 22:1–38 ☐ 22:39–65 ☐ 22:66—23:25 ☐ 23:26–49 ☐ 23:50—24:12 ☐ 24:13–35 ☐ 24:36–53

NOTES

Introduction

1:1–4Ref — Ac 1:1

1 Many have undertaken to draw up
an account of the things that have
been fulfilled[a] among us, **2**just as they
were handed down to us by those who
from the first[a] were eyewitnesses[b]
and servants of the word.[c] **3**Therefore, since I myself have carefully investigated everything from the beginning, it seemed good also to me to
write an orderly account[d] for you,
most excellent[e] Theophilus,[f] **4**so
that you may know the certainty of the
things you have been taught.[g]

The Birth of John the Baptist Foretold

5In the time of Herod king of Judea[h]
there was a priest named Zechariah,
who belonged to the priestly division of
Abijah;[i] his wife Elizabeth was also a
descendant of Aaron. **6**Both of them
were upright in the sight of God, observing all the Lord's commandments
and regulations blamelessly.[j] **7**But
they had no children, because Elizabeth was barren; and they were both
well along in years.
8Once when Zechariah's division
was on duty and he was serving as
priest before God,[k] **9**he was chosen by
lot,[l] according to the custom of the
priesthood, to go into the temple of the
Lord and burn incense.[m] **10**And when
the time for the burning of incense
came, all the assembled worshipers
were praying outside.[n]
11Then an angel[o] of the Lord appeared to him, standing at the right
side of the altar of incense.[p] **12**When
Zechariah saw him, he was startled
and was gripped with fear.[q] **13**But the
angel said to him: "Do not be afraid,[r]
Zechariah; your prayer has been heard.
Your wife Elizabeth will bear you a son,
and you are to give him the name
John.[s] **14**He will be a joy and delight
to you, and many will rejoice because
of his birth,[t] **15**for he will be great in
the sight of the Lord. He is never to
take wine or other fermented drink,[u]
and he will be filled with the Holy Spirit[v] even from birth.[b][w] **16**Many of the
people of Israel will he bring back to
the Lord their God. **17**And he will go on
before the Lord,[x] in the spirit and
power of Elijah,[y] to turn the hearts of

1:2 [a] Mk 1:1; Jn 15:27; Ac 1:21, 22 [b] Heb 2:3; 1Pe 5:1; 2Pe 1:16; 1Jn 1:1 [c] S Mk 4:14
1:3 [d] Ac 11:4 [e] Ac 24:3; 26:25 [f] Ac 1:1
1:4 [g] Jn 20:31; Ac 2:42
1:5 [h] Mt 2:1 [i] 1Ch 24:10
1:6 [j] Ge 6:9; Dt 5:33; 1Ki 9:4; Lk 2:25
1:8 [k] 1Ch 24:19; 2Ch 8:14
1:9 [l] Ac 1:26 [m] Ex 30:7,8; 1Ch 23:13; 2Ch 29:11; Ps 141:2
1:10 [n] Lev 16:17
1:11 [o] S Ac 5:19 [p] Ex 30:1-10
1:12 [q] Jdg 6:22, 23; 13:22
1:13 [r] ver 30; S Mt 14:27 [s] ver 60,63; S Mt 3:1
1:14 [t] ver 58
1:15 [u] Nu 6:3; Lev 10:9; Jdg 13:4; Lk 7:33 [v] ver 41,67; Ac 2:4; 4:8,31; 6:3,5; 9:17; 11:24; Eph 5:18; S Ac 10:44 [w] Jer 1:5; Gal 1:15
1:17 [x] ver 76 [y] S Mt 11:14

[a] *1* Or *been surely believed* [b] *15* Or *from his mother's womb*

1:6 UPRIGHT IN THE SIGHT OF GOD. See Lk 2:25, note.

1:15 FILLED WITH THE HOLY SPIRIT. Notice the outcome of John's Spirit-filled life and ministry. Through the power of the Holy Spirit (1) his preaching convicts people of their sins, brings them to repentance and turns them back to God (vv. 15–17; see Jn 16:8, note); (2) he preaches in the spirit and power of Elijah (v. 17; see Ac 1:8, notes); (3) he reconciles families and turns many to a life of righteousness (v. 17).

1:15 WINE . . . FERMENTED DRINK. The literal translation of the Greek text here is "He will never drink wine [*oinos*] or strong drink [*sikera*]." The word "other" ("other fermented drink") does not appear in the Greek. (1) The Greek word used for "fermented drink" is *sikera*. Its exact meaning has not been determined, but it undoubtedly corresponds to the OT word *shekar* (see articles on WINE IN THE OLD TESTAMENT, p. 204, and WINE IN NEW TESTAMENT TIMES (1) and (2), p. 1534 and 1586).

1:17 SPIRIT AND POWER OF ELIJAH. In many ways John will be like the fearless prophet Elijah (see Mal 4:5, note). Because he is filled with the Holy Spirit (v. 15), John will be a preacher of moral righteousness (3:7–14; Mt 3:1–10). He will demonstrate the Holy Spirit's ministry by preaching about sin, righteousness and judgment (see Jn 16:8, note). He will turn the hearts of "the disobedient to the wisdom of the righteous" (see Mt 11:7, note). He will not compromise his conscience or bend Biblical principles for the sake of status or security (3:19–20; Mt 14:1–11). He will obey God and remain loyal to all truth. In short, John will be a "man of God."

1:17 THE FATHERS TO THEIR CHILDREN. One of the greatest sins of God's OT people had been the failure of the fathers to love their sons and daughters enough to teach them the ways and commands of God (see Mal 4:6, note). With the coming of John and the gospel of Christ, the hearts of the fathers will return to their children.

(1) This is a clear statement that one of the key goals of the gospel is to reestablish God's will for the family in a correct relationship between fathers and children. Through the preaching of repentance and the lordship of Christ, fathers will become dedicated to their children in an attitude of righteousness.

(2) If the church today fails to become what God wants it to be, one factor may be that once again the fathers' hearts have forsaken their children by failing to love them, spend time with them, and teach them God's Word and righteous standards. As a result, the children will reject God's ways (Mal 4:6).

(3) The following are important passages related to fathers and children: (a) teaching children faithfulness to God's ways: Ex 10:2; 13:8; Dt 4:9–10; 6:6–25; 11:18–21; Ps 78:5–8; Isa 38:19; Joel 1:3; Eph 6:4; 1Th 2:11; (b) loving and correct-

the fathers to their children[z] and the
disobedient to the wisdom of the righteous—to make ready a people prepared for the Lord."[a]
18 Zechariah asked the angel, "How
can I be sure of this?[b] I am an old man
and my wife is well along in years."[c]
19 The angel answered, "I am Gabriel.[d] I stand in the presence of God,
and I have been sent to speak to you
and to tell you this good news. 20 And
now you will be silent and not able to
speak[e] until the day this happens, because you did not believe my words,
which will come true at their proper
time."
21 Meanwhile, the people were waiting for Zechariah and wondering why
he stayed so long in the temple.
22 When he came out, he could not
speak to them. They realized he had
seen a vision in the temple, for he kept
making signs[f] to them but remained
unable to speak.
23 When his time of service was completed, he returned home. 24 After this
his wife Elizabeth became pregnant
and for five months remained in seclusion. 25 "The Lord has done this for
me," she said. "In these days he has
shown his favor and taken away my
disgrace[g] among the people."

The Birth of Jesus Foretold

26 In the sixth month, God sent the
angel Gabriel[h] to Nazareth,[i] a town
in Galilee, 27 to a virgin pledged to be
married to a man named Joseph,[j] a
descendant of David. The virgin's
name was Mary. 28 The angel went to
her and said, "Greetings, you who are
highly favored! The Lord is with you."
29 Mary was greatly troubled at his
words and wondered what kind of
greeting this might be. 30 But the angel
said to her, "Do not be afraid,[k] Mary,
you have found favor with God.[l]
31 You will be with child and give birth
to a son, and you are to give him the
name Jesus.[m] 32 He will be great and
will be called the Son of the Most
High.[n] The Lord God will give him the
throne of his father David,[o] 33 and he
will reign over the house of Jacob forever; his kingdom[p] will never end."[q]
34 "How will this be," Mary asked the
angel, "since I am a virgin?"
35 The angel answered, "The Holy
Spirit will come upon you,[r] and the
power of the Most High[s] will overshadow you. So the holy one[t] to be
born will be called[c] the Son of God.[u]
36 Even Elizabeth your relative is going
to have a child[v] in her old age, and she
who was said to be barren is in her
sixth month. 37 For nothing is impossible with God."[w]
38 "I am the Lord's servant," Mary
answered. "May it be to me as you have
said." Then the angel left her.

Mary Visits Elizabeth

39 At that time Mary got ready and
hurried to a town in the hill country of
Judea,[x] 40 where she entered Zechariah's
home and greeted Elizabeth. 41 When
Elizabeth heard Mary's greeting,
the baby leaped in her womb, and Elizabeth was filled with the Holy Spirit.[y] Lk 1:67

1:17 [z] Mal 4:5,6 [a] S Mt 3:3
1:18 [b] Ge 15:8 [c] ver 34; Ge 17:17
1:19 [d] ver 26; Da 8:16; 9:21
1:20 [e] Ex 4:11; Eze 3:26
1:22 [f] ver 62
1:25 [g] Ge 30:23; Isa 4:1
1:26 [h] S ver 19 [i] S Mt 2:23
1:27 [j] Mt 1:16,18,20; Lk 2:4
1:30 [k] ver 13; S Mt 14:27 [l] Ge 6:8
1:31 [m] Isa 7:14; Mt 1:21,25; Lk 2:21
1:32 [n] ver 35,76; S Mk 5:7 [o] S Mt 1:1
1:33 [p] Mt 28:18 [q] 2Sa 7:16; Ps 89:3,4; Isa 9:7; Jer 33:17; Da 2:44; 7:14,27; Mic 4:7; Heb 1:8
1:35 [r] Mt 1:18 [s] ver 32,76; S Mk 5:7 [t] S Mk 1:24 [u] S Mt 4:3
1:36 [v] ver 24
1:37 [w] S Mt 19:26
1:39 [x] ver 65
1:41 [y] S ver 15

[c] *35 Or So the child to be born will be called holy,*

ing children: Ps 103:13; Pr 3:12; 13:24; 23:13–14; Mal 4:6; Lk 11:11–13; 2Co 12:14; Eph 6:4; Col 3:21; 1Th 2:11; 1Ti 3:4–5,12; 5:8; Tit 2:4; Heb 12:7; (c) fathers praying for their children: Ge 17:18; 2Sa 12:16; 1Ch 22:11–12; 29:19; Job 1:5; Eph 3:14–19. See Jn 17:1, note on a model prayer of a father for his children; see also article on PARENTS AND CHILDREN, p. 1854.

1:28 YOU WHO ARE HIGHLY FAVORED. While Mary was favored above all women in being chosen as the mother of Jesus, the NT writers never indicate that she is to be worshiped, prayed to or given special titles. Mary merits our respect, but only her son merits our worship. (1) Note that Mary was chosen because she found favor with God (cf. Ge 6:8). Her humble and godly life pleased God to such an extent that he chose her for this most important task (cf. 2Ti 2:21). (2) Mary's blessing not only brought her great joy, but also much suffering and pain (see 2:35), for her son would be rejected and crucified. In this world God's calling will always involve blessing and suffering, joy and sadness, successes and disappointments.

1:35 THE HOLY ONE. Both Luke and Matthew state explicitly and unmistakably that Jesus was born of a virgin (v. 27; Mt 1:18,23, note). The Holy Spirit would come upon Mary and the child would be conceived solely by a miraculous deed of God. As a result, Jesus would be "holy" (i.e., free from all taint of sin). For more on this, see article on JESUS AND THE HOLY SPIRIT, p. 1546.

1:38 AS YOU HAVE SAID. Mary submitted herself completely to God's will and trusted his message. She willingly accepted the honor and the reproach that being the mother of the holy child would bring. Young women in the church should follow Mary's example in sexual purity, love for God, faith in his Word and a willingness to obey the Holy Spirit.

42 In a loud voice she exclaimed:
"Blessed are you among women,[z] and
blessed is the child you will bear! 43 But
why am I so favored, that the mother
of my Lord[a] should come to me? 44 As
soon as the sound of your greeting
reached my ears, the baby in my womb
leaped for joy. 45 Blessed is she who
has believed that what the Lord has
said to her will be accomplished!"

Mary's Song

1:46–53pp — 1Sa 2:1–10

46 And Mary said:

"My soul glorifies the Lord[b]
47 and my spirit rejoices in God my Savior,[c] (Lk 2:13-14)
48 for he has been mindful
of the humble state of his servant.[d]
From now on all generations will call me blessed,[e]
49 for the Mighty One has done great things[f] for me—
holy is his name.[g]
50 His mercy extends to those who fear him,
from generation to generation.[h]
51 He has performed mighty deeds with his arm;[i]
he has scattered those who are proud in their inmost thoughts.[j]
52 He has brought down rulers from their thrones
but has lifted up the humble.[k]
53 He has filled the hungry with good things[l]
but has sent the rich away empty.
54 He has helped his servant Israel,
remembering to be merciful[m]
55 to Abraham and his descendants[n] forever,
even as he said to our fathers."

56 Mary stayed with Elizabeth for
about three months and then returned
home.

The Birth of John the Baptist

57 When it was time for Elizabeth to
have her baby, she gave birth to a son.

1:42 [z] Jdg 5:24
1:43 [a] S Jn 13:13
1:46 [b] Ps 34:2,3
1:47 [c] Ps 18:46; Isa 17:10; 61:10; Hab 3:18; 1Ti 1:1; 2:3; 4:10
1:48 [d] ver 38; Ps 138:6 [e] Lk 11:27
1:49 [f] Ps 71:19 [g] Ps 111:9
1:50 [h] Ex 20:6; Ps 103:17
1:51 [i] Ps 98:1; Isa 40:10 [j] Ge 11:8; Ex 18:11; 2Sa 22:28; Jer 13:9; 49:16
1:52 [k] S Mt 23:12
1:53 [l] Ps 107:9
1:54 [m] Ps 98:3
1:55 [n] S Gal 3:16
1:59 [o] Ge 17:12; Lev 12:3; Lk 2:21; Php 3:5
1:60 [p] ver 13,63; S Mt 3:1
1:62 [q] ver 22
1:63 [r] ver 13,60; S Mt 3:1
1:64 [s] ver 20; Eze 24:27
1:65 [t] ver 39
1:66 [u] Ge 39:2; Ac 11:21
1:67 [v] S ver 15 [w] Joel 2:28
1:68 [x] Ge 24:27; 1Ki 8:15; Ps 72:18 [y] Ps 111:9; Lk 7:16
1:69 [z] 1Sa 2:1,10; 2Sa 22:3; Ps 18:2; 89:17; 132:17; Eze 29:21 [a] S Mt 1:1
1:70 [b] Jer 23:5; Ac 3:21; Ro 1:2
1:72 [c] Mic 7:20 [d] Ps 105:8,9; 106:45; Eze 16:60
1:73 [e] Ge 22:16-18

58 Her neighbors and relatives heard
that the Lord had shown her great mercy, and they shared her joy.
59 On the eighth day they came to circumcise[o] the child, and they were going to name him after his father Zechariah, 60 but his mother spoke up and
said, "No! He is to be called John."[p]
61 They said to her, "There is no one
among your relatives who has that
name."
62 Then they made signs[q] to his father, to find out what he would like to
name the child. 63 He asked for a writing tablet, and to everyone's astonishment he wrote, "His name is John."[r]
64 Immediately his mouth was opened
and his tongue was loosed, and he began to speak,[s] praising God. 65 The
neighbors were all filled with awe, and
throughout the hill country of Judea[t]
people were talking about all these
things. 66 Everyone who heard this
wondered about it, asking, "What then
is this child going to be?" For the
Lord's hand was with him.[u]

Zechariah's Song

67 His father Zechariah was filled
with the Holy Spirit[v] and prophesied:[w]

68 "Praise be to the Lord, the God of Israel,[x]
because he has come and has redeemed his people.[y]
69 He has raised up a horn[d z] of salvation for us
in the house of his servant David[a]
70 (as he said through his holy prophets of long ago),[b]
71 salvation from our enemies
and from the hand of all who hate us—
72 to show mercy to our fathers[c]
and to remember his holy covenant,[d]
73 the oath he swore to our father Abraham:[e]
74 to rescue us from the hand of our enemies,

[d] 69 *Horn* here symbolizes strength.

1:47 GOD MY SAVIOR. In these words Mary recognizes her own need of salvation. She was a sinner who needed Christ as "Savior." The idea that Mary was immaculately conceived and lived without sin is nowhere taught in Scripture (cf. Ro 3:9,23).

1:67 FILLED WITH THE HOLY SPIRIT. Luke records how the Holy Spirit empowered many of the important people associated with the birth of Christ (vv. 15,35,41,67; 2:25). After Christ's ascension, the way was opened for all believers to be filled with the Holy Spirit (Ac 1–2).

and to enable us to serve him[f]
without fear[g]
75 in holiness and righteousness[h]
before him all our days.

76 And you, my child, will be called a
prophet[i] of the Most
High;[j]
for you will go on before the
Lord to prepare the way for
him,[k]
77 to give his people the knowledge
of salvation
through the forgiveness of their
sins,[l]
78 because of the tender mercy of our
God,
by which the rising sun[m] will
come to us from heaven
79 to shine on those living in
darkness
and in the shadow of death,[n]
to guide our feet into the path of
peace."[o]

80 And the child grew and became
strong in spirit;[p] and he lived in the
desert until he appeared publicly to Israel.

The Birth of Jesus

2 In those days Caesar Augustus[q]
issued a decree that a census
should be taken of the entire Roman
world.[r] 2 (This was the first census
that took place while Quirinius was
governor of Syria.)[s] 3 And everyone
went to his own town to register.
4 So Joseph also went up from the
town of Nazareth in Galilee to Judea, to
Bethlehem[t] the town of David, because he belonged to the house and
line of David. 5 He went there to register with Mary, who was pledged to be
married to him[u] and was expecting a
child. 6 While they were there, the time
came for the baby to be born, 7 and she
gave birth to her firstborn, a son. She
wrapped him in cloths and placed him
in a manger, because there was no
room for them in the inn.

The Shepherds and the Angels

8 And there were shepherds living
out in the fields nearby, keeping watch
over their flocks at night. 9 An angel[v]
of the Lord appeared to them, and the
glory of the Lord shone around them,
and they were terrified. 10 But the angel said to them, "Do not be afraid.[w]
I bring you good news of great joy that
will be for all the people. 11 Today in
the town of David a Savior[x] has been
born to you; he is Christ[e][y] the
Lord.[z] 12 This will be a sign[a] to you:
You will find a baby wrapped in cloths
and lying in a manger."
13 Suddenly a great company of the
heavenly host appeared with the angel,
praising God and saying,

14 "Glory to God in the highest,
and on earth peace[b] to men on
whom his favor rests." Lk 2:20

15 When the angels had left them and
gone into heaven, the shepherds said
to one another, "Let's go to Bethlehem
and see this thing that has happened,
which the Lord has told us about."
16 So they hurried off and found Mary
and Joseph, and the baby, who was lying in the manger.[c] 17 When they had
seen him, they spread the word concerning what had been told them about
this child, 18 and all who heard it were
amazed at what the shepherds said to
them. 19 But Mary treasured up all
these things and pondered them in her
heart.[d] 20 The shepherds returned,
glorifying and praising God[e] for all

[e] 11 Or *Messiah.* "The Christ" (Greek) and "the Messiah" (Hebrew) both mean "the Anointed One"; also in verse 26.

1:74 [f] Heb 9:14 [g] 1Jn 4:18
1:75 [h] Eph 4:24
1:76 [i] S Mt 11:9 [j] ver 32,35; S Mk 5:7 [k] ver 17; S Mt 3:3
1:77 [l] Jer 31:34; Mt 1:21; Mk 1:4
1:78 [m] Mal 4:2
1:79 [n] Ps 107:14; Isa 9:2; 59:9; Mt 4:16; S Ac 26:18 [o] S Lk 2:14
1:80 [p] Lk 2:40,52
2:1 [q] Lk 3:1; Mt 22:17 [r] S Mt 24:14
2:2 [s] Mt 4:24; Ac 15:23,41; 21:3; Gal 1:21
2:4 [t] S Jn 7:42
2:5 [u] Lk 1:27
2:9 [v] S Ac 5:19
2:10 [w] S Mt 14:27
2:11 [x] S Mt 1:21; S Jn 3:17; 4:42; Ac 5:31; 13:23; S Ro 11:14; 1Ti 4:10; 1Jn 4:14 [y] Mt 1:16; 16:16, 20; Jn 11:27; Ac 2:36; 3:20; S 9:22 [z] S Jn 13:13
2:12 [a] 1Sa 2:34; 10:7; 2Ki 19:29; Ps 86:17; Isa 7:14
2:14 [b] Isa 9:6; 52:7; 53:5; Mic 5:5; Lk 1:79; S Jn 14:27; Ro 5:1; Eph 2:14, 17
2:16 [c] ver 7
2:19 [d] ver 51
2:20 [e] S Mt 9:8

1:75 HOLINESS AND RIGHTEOUSNESS. The ultimate aim of our redemption is to be delivered from Satan's kingdom (Ac 26:18) in order to serve God "in holiness and righteousness before him all our days" (cf. Eph 1:4). Every child of God must aim at a life of holiness and righteousness in an evil world. This holy life is "before him," i.e., in God's presence.

2:7 A MANGER. Christ was born in a stable, a place where animals were kept. The stable was probably a cave and the manger a feeding trough for animals. The birth of the Savior, the greatest event in all history, occurred in the most humble of circumstances. Jesus was the King of kings, but he was neither born nor did he live like a king in this life. God's people are kings and priests, but in this life we must be as he was—humble and simple.

2:11 A SAVIOR . . . CHRIST THE LORD. At his birth, Jesus is called "a Savior." (1) As Savior, he has come to deliver us from sin, Satan's domain, the ungodly world, fear, death and the condemnation of our transgressions (see Mt 1:21, note). (2) The Savior is also "Christ the Lord." He has been anointed as the Messiah of God and the Lord who rules over his people (see Mt 1:1, note on the name of Christ). No person can have Jesus as Savior while not submitting to his lordship.

Lk 18:43 the things they had heard and seen, which were just as they had been told.

Jesus Presented in the Temple

[21]On the eighth day, when it was time to circumcise him,[f] he was named Jesus, the name the angel had given him before he had been conceived.[g]

[22]When the time of their purification according to the Law of Moses[h] had been completed, Joseph and Mary took him to Jerusalem to present him to the Lord [23](as it is written in the Law of the Lord, "Every firstborn male is to be consecrated to the Lord"[f]),[i] [24]and to offer a sacrifice in keeping with what is said in the Law of the Lord: "a pair of doves or two young pigeons."[g][j]

Simeon and Anna Praise God

[25]Now there was a man in Jerusalem called Simeon, who was righteous and devout.[k] He was waiting for the consolation of Israel,[l] and the Holy Spirit was upon him. [26]It had been revealed to him by the Holy Spirit that he would not die before he had seen the Lord's Christ. [27]Moved by the Spirit, he went into the temple courts. When the parents brought in the child Jesus to do for him what the custom of the Law required,[m] [28]Simeon took him in his arms and praised God, saying:

[29]"Sovereign Lord, as you have promised,[n]
you now dismiss[h] your servant in peace.[o]
[30]For my eyes have seen your salvation,[p]
[31] which you have prepared in the sight of all people,
[32]a light for revelation to the Gentiles
and for glory to your people Israel."[q]

[33]The child's father and mother marveled at what was said about him. [34]Then Simeon blessed them and said to Mary, his mother:[r] "This child is destined to cause the falling[s] and rising of many in Israel, and to be a sign that will be spoken against, [35]so that the thoughts of many hearts will be revealed. And a sword will pierce your own soul too."

[36]There was also a prophetess,[t] Anna, the daughter of Phanuel, of the tribe of Asher. She was very old; she had lived with her husband seven years

2:21 [f]S Lk 1:59 [g]S Lk 1:31
2:22 [h]Lev 12:2-8
2:23 [i]Ex 13:2,12, 15; Nu 3:13
2:24 [j]Lev 12:8
2:25 [k]Lk 1:6 [l]ver 38; Isa 52:9; Lk 23:51
2:27 [m]ver 22
2:29 [n]ver 26 [o]Ac 2:24
2:30 [p]Isa 40:5; 52:10; Lk 3:6
2:32 [q]Isa 42:6; 49:6; Ac 13:47; 26:23
2:34 [r]S Mt 12:46 [s]Isa 8:14; Mt 21:44; 1Co 1:23; 2Co 2:16; Gal 5:11; 1Pe 2:7, 8
2:36 [t]S Ac 21:9

[f]*23* Exodus 13:2,12 [g]*24* Lev. 12:8
[h]*29* Or *promised, / now dismiss*

2:22 PRESENT HIM TO THE LORD. As Joseph and Mary presented Jesus to the Lord, so all parents should sincerely consecrate their children to the Lord. They should pray constantly that from the beginning to the end of each child's life, he or she will be found doing the Lord's will, serving and glorifying God with complete devotion.

2:24 A PAIR OF DOVES. The offering of a pair of doves indicates that Joseph and Mary were poor (Lev 12:8). From the very beginning Christ was identified with the underprivileged (9:58; Mt 8:20; see Rev 2:9, note).

2:25 RIGHTEOUS AND DEVOUT. "Righteous" or "upright" (cf. 1:6) translates the Greek word *dikaios* (Heb *yasher*), meaning "straight." In the OT this word did not mean mere conformity to the commandments, but indicated a person was right with God both in heart and in action (see Ps 32:2, note). (1) The righteousness that God sought in the OT was one that came from the heart, based on true faith in, love for and fear of God (Dt 4:10, 29; 5:29). This condition of the heart was seen in the parents of John the Baptist, who observed "all the Lord's commandments and regulations blamelessly" (1:6; see Ge 7:1; 17:1; 1Ki 9:4, where the term includes "integrity of heart"). Simeon manifested the same characteristic in his life. (2) OT righteous persons were not perfect. When sin entered their lives they obtained forgiveness by presenting an animal sacrifice to God in an attitude of sincere repentance and faith (Lev 4:27–35; see article on THE DAY OF ATONEMENT, p. 174).

2:25 WAITING FOR THE CONSOLATION. In a time of deplorable spiritual conditions righteous Simeon was devoted to God and filled with the Holy Spirit, waiting in faith, patience and great longing for the coming of the Messiah. Likewise, in the last days of this present age, when many are abandoning the NT apostolic faith and the blessed hope for the coming of Christ (Tit 2:13), there will always be the faithful Simeons. Others may place their hope in this life and this world, but the faithful will be like the loyal slave who keeps watch through the long, dark night, waiting for the return of his master (Mt 24:45–47). Our greatest blessing is to see face to face "the Lord's Christ" (v. 26; cf. Rev 22:4), to be ready when he comes and to live forever in his presence (Rev 21–22).

2:36–37 ANNA . . . WORSHIPED. Anna was a prophetess who earnestly hoped for the coming of Christ. She remained a widow for many years, never remarrying, but devoting herself to the Lord, "fasting and praying" night and day. The Bible teaches that the unmarried state can be a greater blessing than the married. Paul states that the unmarried have greater opportunity to be concerned about the things of the Lord—how to please him and give him undistracted devotion (see 1Co 7:32–35).

after her marriage, 37and then was a widow until she was eighty-four.[i][u] She never left the temple but worshiped night and day, fasting and praying.[v] 38Coming up to them at that very moment, she gave thanks to God and spoke about the child to all who were looking forward to the redemption of Jerusalem.[w]

39When Joseph and Mary had done everything required by the Law of the Lord, they returned to Galilee to their own town of Nazareth.[x] 40And the child grew and became strong; he was filled with wisdom, and the grace of God was upon him.[y]

The Boy Jesus at the Temple

41Every year his parents went to Jerusalem for the Feast of the Passover.[z] 42When he was twelve years old, they went up to the Feast, according to the custom. 43After the Feast was over, while his parents were returning home, the boy Jesus stayed behind in Jerusalem, but they were unaware of it. 44Thinking he was in their company, they traveled on for a day. Then they began looking for him among their relatives and friends. 45When they did not find him, they went back to Jerusalem to look for him. 46After three days they found him in the temple courts, sitting among the teachers, listening to them and asking them questions. 47Everyone who heard him was amazed[a] at his understanding and his answers. 48When his parents saw him, they were astonished. His mother[b] said to him, "Son, why have you treated us like this? Your father[c] and I have been anxiously searching for you."

49"Why were you searching for me?" he asked. "Didn't you know I had to be in my Father's house?"[d] 50But they did not understand what he was saying to them.[e]

51Then he went down to Nazareth with them[f] and was obedient to them. But his mother treasured all these things in her heart.[g] 52And Jesus grew in wisdom and stature, and in favor with God and men.[h]

John the Baptist Prepares the Way

3:2–10pp — Mt 3:1–10; Mk 1:3–5
3:16,17pp — Mt 3:11,12; Mk 1:7,8

3 In the fifteenth year of the reign of Tiberius Caesar—when Pontius Pilate[i] was governor of Judea, Herod[j] tetrarch of Galilee, his brother Philip tetrarch of Iturea and Traconitis, and Lysanias tetrarch of Abilene— 2during the high priesthood of Annas and Caiaphas,[k] the word of God came to John[l] son of Zechariah[m] in the desert. 3He went into all the country around the Jordan, preaching a baptism of repentance for the forgiveness of sins.[n] 4As is written in the book of the words of Isaiah the prophet:

"A voice of one calling in the
desert,
'Prepare the way for the Lord,
make straight paths for him.
5Every valley shall be filled in,
every mountain and hill made
low.
The crooked roads shall become
straight,
the rough ways smooth.
6And all mankind will see God's
salvation.' "[j][o]

7John said to the crowds coming out to be baptized by him, "You brood of vipers![p] Who warned you to flee from the coming wrath?[q] 8Produce fruit in keeping with repentance. And do not begin to say to yourselves, 'We have

2:37 [u] 1Ti 5:9 [v] Ac 13:3; 14:23; 1Ti 5:5
2:38 [w] ver 25; Isa 40:2; 52:9; Lk 1:68; 24:21
2:39 [x] ver 51; S Mt 2:23
2:40 [y] ver 52; Lk 1:80
2:41 [z] Ex 23:15; Dt 16:1-8; Lk 22:8
2:47 [a] S Mt 7:28
2:48 [b] S Mt 12:46 [c] Lk 3:23; 4:22
2:49 [d] Jn 2:16
2:50 [e] S Mk 9:32
2:51 [f] ver 39; S Mt 2:23 [g] ver 19
2:52 [h] ver 40; 1Sa 2:26; Pr 3:4; Lk 1:80
3:1 [i] S Mt 27:2 [j] S Mt 14:1
3:2 [k] S Mt 26:3 [l] S Mt 3:1 [m] Lk 1:13
3:3 [n] ver 16; S Mk 1:4
3:6 [o] Isa 40:3-5; Ps 98:2; Isa 42:16; 52:10; Lk 2:30
3:7 [p] Mt 12:34; 23:33 [q] S Ro 1:18

[i] 37 Or *widow for eighty-four years* [j] 6 Isaiah 40:3-5

2:40 THE CHILD GREW. As a true human child, Jesus experienced the process of physical and spiritual development. He kept increasing in wisdom as the grace of God was upon him. He was perfect in his human nature, developing perfectly as God desired.

2:52 JESUS GREW IN WISDOM. Between 2:52 and 3:1, approximately eighteen years of Jesus' life passed without comment. What was his life like during those years? From Mt 13:55 and Mk 6:3, we learn that he grew up in a large family, that his father was a carpenter and that Jesus learned the trade. Since Joseph is never mentioned again in the Gospels, it is likely that Joseph died before Jesus began his public ministry and that Jesus provided for his mother and younger brothers and sisters. The carpenter's trade included household repairs, furniture making, and construction of agricultural implements such as plows and yokes. During all these years he grew and developed both physically and spiritually according to God's will, fully conscious that God was his Father (v. 49).

3:8 FRUIT IN KEEPING WITH REPENTANCE. See Mt 3:8, note.

Abraham as our father.'[r] For I tell you that out of these stones God can raise up children for Abraham. **9**The ax is already at the root of the trees, and every tree that does not produce good fruit will be cut down and thrown into the fire."[s]

10"What should we do then?"[t] the crowd asked.

11John answered, "The man with two tunics should share with him who has none, and the one who has food should do the same."[u]

12Tax collectors also came to be baptized.[v] "Teacher," they asked, "what should we do?"

13"Don't collect any more than you are required to,"[w] he told them.

14Then some soldiers asked him, "And what should we do?"

He replied, "Don't extort money and don't accuse people falsely[x]—be content with your pay."

15The people were waiting expectantly and were all wondering in their hearts if John[y] might possibly be the Christ.[k][z] **16**John answered them all, "I baptize you with[1] water.[a] But one more powerful than I will come, the thongs of whose sandals I am not worthy to untie. He will baptize you with
Lk 4:1 the Holy Spirit and with fire.[b] **17**His winnowing fork[c] is in his hand to clear his threshing floor and to gather the wheat into his barn, but he will burn up the chaff with unquenchable fire."[d] **18**And with many other words John exhorted the people and preached the good news to them.

19But when John rebuked Herod[e] the tetrarch because of Herodias, his brother's wife, and all the other evil things he had done, **20**Herod added this to them all: He locked John up in prison.[f]

The Baptism and Genealogy of Jesus

3:21,22pp — Mt 3:13–17; Mk 1:9–11
3:23–38pp — Mt 1:1–17

21When all the people were being baptized, Jesus was baptized too. And as he was praying,[g] heaven was opened **22**and the Holy Spirit descended on him[h] in bodily form like a dove. And a voice came from heaven: "You are my Son,[i] whom I love; with you I am well pleased."[j]

23Now Jesus himself was about thirty years old when he began his ministry.[k] He was the son, so it was thought, of Joseph,[l]

the son of Heli, **24**the son of Matthat,
the son of Levi, the son of Melki,
the son of Jannai, the son of Joseph,
25the son of Mattathias, the son of Amos,
the son of Nahum, the son of Esli,
the son of Naggai, **26**the son of Maath,
the son of Mattathias, the son of Semein,
the son of Josech, the son of Joda,
27the son of Joanan, the son of Rhesa,
the son of Zerubbabel,[m] the son of Shealtiel,
the son of Neri, **28**the son of Melki,
the son of Addi, the son of Cosam,
the son of Elmadam, the son of Er,

3:8 [r]Isa 51:2; Lk 19:9; Jn 8:33, 39; Ac 13:26; Ro 4:1,11,12,16, 17; 9:7,8; Gal 3:7
3:9 [s]S Mt 3:10
3:10 [t]ver 12,14; Ac 2:37; 16:30
3:11 [u]Isa 58:7; Eze 18:7
3:12 [v]Lk 7:29
3:13 [w]Lk 19:8
3:14 [x]Ex 23:1; Lev 19:11
3:15 [y]S Mt 3:1 [z]Jn 1:19,20; Ac 13:25
3:16 [a]ver 3; S Mk 1:4 [b]Jn 1:26, 33; Ac 1:5; 2:3; 11:16; 19:4
3:17 [c]Isa 30:24 [d]Mt 13:30; S 25:41
3:19 [e]ver 1; S Mt 14:1
3:20 [f]S Mt 14:3,4
3:21 [g]Mt 14:23; Mk 1:35; 6:46; Lk 5:16; 6:12; 9:18,28; 11:1
3:22 [h]Isa 42:1; Jn 1:32,33; Ac 10:38 [i]S Mt 3:17 [j]S Mt 3:17
3:23 [k]Mt 4:17; Ac 1:1 [l]Lk 1:27
3:27 [m]Mt 1:12

[k]*15* Or *Messiah* [1]*16* Or *in*

3:16 BAPTIZE YOU WITH THE HOLY SPIRIT. Christ's baptizing his followers with [or in] the Holy Spirit (cf. Mt 3:11) is the new sign by which to identify God's people. (1) This was promised in Joel 2:28 and reaffirmed after Christ's resurrection (24:49; Ac 1:4–8). This prediction was initially fulfilled on the day of Pentecost (see Ac 2:4, notes).

(2) Christ's ministry of baptizing in the Holy Spirit is a continuing ministry throughout this present age (see article on BAPTISM IN THE HOLY SPIRIT, p. 1642). This is made clear by the Greek text of Jn 1:33 ("he who will baptize with the Holy Spirit"); this phrase uses the present participle (*ho baptizōn*), meaning "he who will continue to baptize." Therefore, the references in Luke and John are not only to the first outpouring of the Holy Spirit at Pentecost, but to the important role and ministry of Jesus as the Baptizer in the Holy Spirit throughout this age. "The promise is for you and your children and for all who are far off" (Ac 2:39).

3:17 HE WILL BURN UP THE CHAFF. Those who turn from sin and receive Christ and his Word will be baptized with the Holy Spirit. Those who cling to their sins will be punished with unquenchable fire (see Mt 10:28, note).

3:22 HOLY SPIRIT DESCENDED ON HIM. Jesus, who from the beginning had been conceived and indwelt by the Holy Spirit (1:35), is now personally anointed and empowered by the Spirit for his ministry. For more on the significance of Jesus' baptism in the Holy Spirit, see article on JESUS AND THE HOLY SPIRIT, p. 1546.

3:23 JESUS' GENEALOGY. See Mt 1:1, notes.

[29]the son of Joshua, the son of Eliezer,
the son of Jorim, the son of Matthat,
the son of Levi, [30]the son of Simeon,
the son of Judah, the son of Joseph,
the son of Jonam, the son of Eliakim,
[31]the son of Melea, the son of Menna,
the son of Mattatha, the son of Nathan,[n]
the son of David, [32]the son of Jesse,
the son of Obed, the son of Boaz,
the son of Salmon,[m] the son of Nahshon,
[33]the son of Amminadab, the son of Ram,[n]
the son of Hezron, the son of Perez,[o]
the son of Judah, [34]the son of Jacob,
the son of Isaac, the son of Abraham,
the son of Terah, the son of Nahor,[p]
[35]the son of Serug, the son of Reu,
the son of Peleg, the son of Eber,
the son of Shelah, [36]the son of Cainan,
the son of Arphaxad,[q] the son of Shem,
the son of Noah, the son of Lamech,[r]
[37]the son of Methuselah, the son of Enoch,
the son of Jared, the son of Mahalalel,
the son of Kenan,[s] [38]the son of Enosh,
the son of Seth, the son of Adam,
the son of God.[t]

3:31 [n]2Sa 5:14; 1Ch 3:5
3:33 [o]Ru 4:18-22; 1Ch 2:10-12
3:34 [p]Ge 11:24, 26
3:36 [q]Ge 11:12 [r]Ge 5:28-32
3:37 [s]Ge 5:12-25
3:38 [t]Ge 5:1,2, 6-9
4:1 [u]ver 14,18; S Lk 1:15,35; 3:16,22; 10:21 [v]Lk 3:3,21 [w]Eze 37:1; Lk 2:27
4:2 [x]Ex 34:28; 1Ki 19:8 [y]Heb 4:15
4:3 [z]S Mt 4:3
4:4 [a]Dt 8:3

The Temptation of Jesus

4:1–13pp — Mt 4:1–11; Mk 1:12,13

4 Jesus, full of the Holy Spirit,[u]
returned from the Jordan[v] and
was led by the Spirit[w] in the desert, Lk 24:49
[2]where for forty days[x] he was
tempted by the devil.[y] He ate nothing
during those days, and at the end of
them he was hungry.
[3]The devil said to him, "If you are
the Son of God,[z] tell this stone to become bread."
[4]Jesus answered, "It is written:
'Man does not live on bread
alone.'[o]"[a]
[5]The devil led him up to a high place

[m]32 Some early manuscripts *Sala*
[n]33 Some manuscripts *Amminadab, the son of Admin, the son of Arni*; other manuscripts vary widely.
[o]4 Deut. 8:3

4:1 JESUS, FULL OF THE HOLY SPIRIT. Jesus was empowered and led by the Spirit when he encountered Satan's temptation. For comments on the role of the Spirit in Jesus' life, see article on JESUS AND THE HOLY SPIRIT, p. 1546.

4:2 TEMPTED BY THE DEVIL. One essential feature of Jesus' temptation revolved around what kind of Messiah he would be and how he would use his anointing from God. (1) Jesus was tempted to use his anointing and position to serve his own self-interest (vv. 3–4), to attain glory and power over the nations instead of accepting the cross and the way of suffering (vv. 5–8), and to accommodate himself to the people's popular expectation for a sensational Messiah (vv. 9–11). (2) Satan still tempts Christian leaders to use their anointing, position and ability for their own self-interest, to establish their own glory and kingdom, and to please people rather than God. Those who selfishly compromise with Satan have in reality surrendered to Satan's lordship.

4:2 HE ATE NOTHING. See Mt 4:2, note on fasting.

4:4 DOES NOT LIVE ON BREAD ALONE. Jesus meets Satan's temptation by declaring that he will live by God's Word above all else (cf. Dt 8:3). (1) Jesus is saying that everything important in life depends on God and his will (Jn 4:34). To strive for success, happiness or material things apart from God's way and purpose will lead to bitter disappointment and end in failure. (2) Jesus emphasized this truth when he taught that we must seek first the kingdom of God (i.e., God's rule, activity and power in our lives); only then will other necessary things be given according to his will and way (see Mt 5:6, note; 6:33, note).

4:5 THE KINGDOMS OF THE WORLD. Satan tempts Jesus with the offer of dominion over all the kingdoms of the world, a proposal that Jesus rejects. (1) Jesus' kingdom in this age is *not* a kingdom of this world (Jn 18:36–37). He refuses to seek a kingdom for himself by the worldly methods of compromise, earthly power, political maneuvering, external violence, popularity, honor and glory. (2) Jesus' kingdom is a spiritual kingdom ruling in the hearts of his people, who have been taken out of the kingdoms of the world. As a heavenly kingdom, (a) it is gained through suffering, self-denial, humility and meekness; (b) it requires giving our bodies as living and holy sacrifices (Ro 12:1) in complete devotion and obedience to God; (c) it involves struggling with spiritual weapons against sin, temptation and Satan (Eph 6:10–20); (d) it means resisting conformity to this world (Ro 12:2). See article on THE KINGDOM OF GOD, p. 1430.

and showed him in an instant all the kingdoms of the world.[b] 6And he said to him, "I will give you all their authority and splendor, for it has been given to me,[c] and I can give it to anyone I want to. 7So if you worship me, it will all be yours."

8Jesus answered, "It is written: 'Worship the Lord your God and serve him only.'[p]"[d]

9The devil led him to Jerusalem and had him stand on the highest point of the temple. "If you are the Son of God," he said, "throw yourself down from here. 10For it is written:

" 'He will command his angels
concerning you
to guard you carefully;
11they will lift you up in their hands,
so that you will not strike your
foot against a stone.'[q]"[e]

12Jesus answered, "It says: 'Do not put the Lord your God to the test.'[r]"[f]

Lk 4:33-36 13When the devil had finished all this tempting,[g] he left him[h] until an opportune time.

Jesus and the Power of the Spirit

14Jesus returned to Galilee[i] in the power of the Spirit, and news about him spread through the whole countryside.[j] 15He taught in their synagogues,[k] and everyone praised him.

Jesus Rejected at Nazareth

16He went to Nazareth,[l] where he had been brought up, and on the Sabbath day he went into the synagogue,[m] as was his custom. And he stood up to read.[n] 17The scroll of the prophet Isaiah was handed to him. Unrolling it, he found the place where it is written:

18"The Spirit of the Lord is on me,[o]
because he has anointed me
to preach good news[p] to the
poor.
He has sent me to proclaim
freedom for the prisoners
and recovery of sight for the
blind,
to release the oppressed,
19 to proclaim the year of the
Lord's favor."[s][q]

20Then he rolled up the scroll, gave it back to the attendant and sat down.[r] The eyes of everyone in the synagogue were fastened on him, 21and he began by saying to them, "Today this scripture is fulfilled[s] in your hearing."

22All spoke well of him and were amazed at the gracious words that came from his lips. "Isn't this Joseph's son?" they asked.[t]

23Jesus said to them, "Surely you will quote this proverb to me: 'Physician, heal yourself! Do here in your hometown[u] what we have heard that you did in Capernaum.' "[v]

24"I tell you the truth," he continued, "no prophet is accepted in his hometown.[w] 25I assure you that there were many widows in Israel in Elijah's time, when the sky was shut for three and a half years and there was a severe famine throughout the land.[x] 26Yet Elijah was not sent to any of them, but to a widow in Zarephath in the region of Sidon.[y] 27And there were many in Israel with leprosy[t] in the time of Elisha the prophet, yet not one of them was cleansed—only Naaman the Syrian."[z]

28All the people in the synagogue were furious when they heard this. 29They got up, drove him out of the town,[a] and took him to the brow of the

4:5 [b] S Mt 24:14
4:6 [c] Jn 12:31; 14:30; 1Jn 5:19
4:8 [d] Dt 6:13
4:11 [e] Ps 91:11, 12
4:12 [f] Dt 6:16
4:13 [g] Heb 4:15 [h] Jn 14:30
4:14 [i] Mt 4:12 [j] S Mt 9:26
4:15 [k] S Mt 4:23
4:16 [l] S Mt 2:23 [m] Mt 13:54 [n] S 1Ti 4:13
4:18 [o] S Jn 3:34 [p] Mk 16:15
4:19 [q] Isa 61:1,2; Lev 25:10; Ps 102:20; 103:6; Isa 42:7; 49:8,9; 58:6
4:20 [r] ver 17; S Mt 26:55
4:21 [s] S Mt 1:22
4:22 [t] Mt 13:54, 55; Jn 6:42; 7:15
4:23 [u] ver 16; S Mt 2:23 [v] Mk 1:21-28; 2:1-12
4:24 [w] Mt 13:57; Jn 4:44
4:25 [x] 1Ki 17:1; 18:1; Jas 5:17,18; Rev 11:6
4:26 [y] 1Ki 17:8-16; S Mt 11:21
4:27 [z] 2Ki 5:1-14
4:29 [a] Nu 15:35; Ac 7:58; Heb 13:12

[p] *8* Deut. 6:13 [q] *11* Psalm 91:11,12
[r] *12* Deut. 6:16 [s] *19* Isaiah 61:1,2
[t] *27* The Greek word was used for various diseases affecting the skin—not necessarily leprosy.

4:9 THE DEVIL. See Mt 4:10, note on Satan.

4:10 SATAN'S USE OF SCRIPTURE. See Mt 4:6, note.

4:18 THE SPIRIT . . . ON ME. See article on JESUS AND THE HOLY SPIRIT, p. 1546.

4:18 HE HAS ANOINTED ME. Jesus gives the purpose of his Spirit-anointed ministry here: (1) To preach the gospel to the poor, the destitute, the afflicted, the humble, those crushed in spirit, the brokenhearted and those who "tremble at his word" (see Isa 61:1–3, note; 66:2, note). (2) To heal those who are bruised and oppressed. This healing involves the whole person, both physical and spiritual. (3) To open the spiritual eyes of those blinded by the world and Satan in order that they might see the truth of God's good news (cf. Jn 9:39). (4) To proclaim the time of true freedom and salvation from Satan's domain, sin, fear and guilt (cf. Jn 8:36; Ac 26:18).

All those who are filled with the Spirit are called to share Jesus' ministry in these ways. To do so we must gain a deep realization of the terrible need and misery that has resulted from sin and the power of Satan—a condition of bondage to evil, brokenheartedness, spiritual blindness and physical distress.

hill on which the town was built, in order to throw him down the cliff. **30**But
he walked right through the crowd and
went on his way.[b]

Jesus Drives Out an Evil Spirit

4:31–37pp — Mk 1:21–28

31Then he went down to Capernaum,[c] a town in Galilee, and on the
Sabbath began to teach the people.
32They were amazed at his teaching,[d]
because his message had authority.[e]
33In the synagogue there was a man
possessed by a demon, an evil[u] spirit.
He cried out at the top of his voice,
34"Ha! What do you want with us,[f]
Jesus of Nazareth?[g] Have you come to
destroy us? I know who you are[h]—
the Holy One of God!"[i]
35"Be quiet!" Jesus said sternly.[j]
"Come out of him!" Then the demon
threw the man down before them all
and came out without injuring him.
36All the people were amazed[k] and
said to each other, "What is this teaching? With authority[l] and power he
gives orders to evil spirits and they
come out!" **37**And the news about him
spread throughout the surrounding
area.[m]

Jesus Heals Many

4:38–41pp — Mt 8:14–17
4:38–43pp — Mk 1:29–38

38Jesus left the synagogue and went
to the home of Simon. Now Simon's
mother-in-law was suffering from a
high fever, and they asked Jesus to
help her. **39**So he bent over her and rebuked[n] the fever, and it left her. She
got up at once and began to wait on
them.
40When the sun was setting, the
people brought to Jesus all who had
various kinds of sickness, and laying
his hands on each one,[o] he healed
them.[p] **41**Moreover, demons came out
of many people, shouting, "You are
the Son of God!"[q] But he rebuked[r]
them and would not allow them to
speak,[s] because they knew he was
the Christ.[v]
42At daybreak Jesus went out to a
solitary place. The people were looking
for him and when they came to where
he was, they tried to keep him from
leaving them. **43**But he said, "I must
preach the good news of the kingdom
of God[t] to the other towns also, because that is why I was sent." **44**And he
kept on preaching in the synagogues of
Judea.[w][u]

The Calling of the First Disciples

5:1–11pp — Mt 4:18–22; Mk 1:16–20; Jn 1:40–42

5 One day as Jesus was standing by
the Lake of Gennesaret,[x] with the
people crowding around him and listening to the word of God,[v] **2**he saw at
the water's edge two boats, left there
by the fishermen, who were washing
their nets. **3**He got into one of the
boats, the one belonging to Simon, and
asked him to put out a little from
shore. Then he sat down and taught
the people from the boat.[w]
4When he had finished speaking, he
said to Simon, "Put out into deep water, and let down[y] the nets for a
catch."[x]
5Simon answered, "Master,[y] we've
worked hard all night and haven't
caught anything.[z] But because you
say so, I will let down the nets."
6When they had done so, they
caught such a large number of fish that
their nets began to break.[a] **7**So they
signaled their partners in the other
boat to come and help them, and they
came and filled both boats so full that
they began to sink.
8When Simon Peter saw this, he fell
at Jesus' knees and said, "Go away
from me, Lord; I am a sinful man!"[b]
9For he and all his companions were

4:30 [b]Jn 8:59; 10:39
4:31 [c]ver 23; S Mt 4:13
4:32 [d]S Mt 7:28 [e]ver 36; Mt 7:29
4:34 [f]S Mt 8:29 [g]S Mk 1:24 [h]Jas 2:19 [i]ver 41; S Mk 1:24
4:35 [j]ver 39,41; Mt 8:26; Lk 8:24
4:36 [k]S Mt 7:28 [l]ver 32; Mt 7:29; S Mt 10:1
4:37 [m]ver 14; S Mt 9:26
4:39 [n]ver 35,41
4:40 [o]S Mk 5:23 [p]S Mt 4:23
4:41 [q]S Mt 4:3 [r]S ver 35 [s]S Mt 8:4
4:43 [t]S Mt 3:2
4:44 [u]S Mt 4:23
5:1 [v]S Mk 4:14; S Heb 4:12
5:3 [w]Mt 13:2
5:4 [x]Jn 21:6
5:5 [y]Lk 8:24,45; 9:33,49; 17:13 [z]Jn 21:3
5:6 [a]Jn 21:11
5:8 [b]Ge 18:27; Job 42:6; Isa 6:5

[u] *33* Greek *unclean*; also in verse 36
[v] *41* Or *Messiah*
[w] *44* Or *the land of the Jews*; some manuscripts *Galilee*
[x] *1* That is, Sea of Galilee
[y] *4* The Greek verb is plural.

4:33 AN EVIL SPIRIT. Luke records that one of Jesus' first acts after announcing his Messiahship was to enter into direct conflict with the demonic. (1) Jesus' foremost concern in his ministry was to destroy the devil's works (1Jn 3:8). There can be no realization of the kingdom of God without confronting the kingdom of Satan (see Mt 12:28; see article on THE KINGDOM OF GOD, p. 1430). (2) One unmistakable sign that the kingdom has ceased to be manifested among God's people is the failure to confront directly the power of evil by setting sinners free from the bondage of sin and the demonic (see article on POWER OVER SATAN AND DEMONS, p. 1484).

4:40 HEALED THEM. See Mt 4:23, note; see article on DIVINE HEALING, p. 1420.

astonished at the catch of fish they had
taken, **10**and so were James and
John, the sons of Zebedee, Simon's
partners.
Then Jesus said to Simon, "Don't be
afraid;[c] from now on you will catch
men." **11**So they pulled their boats up
on shore, left everything and followed
him.[d]

The Man With Leprosy

5:12–14pp — Mt 8:2–4; Mk 1:40–44

12While Jesus was in one of the
towns, a man came along who was covered with leprosy.[z][e] When he saw
Jesus, he fell with his face to the
ground and begged him, "Lord, if you
are willing, you can make me clean."
13Jesus reached out his hand and
touched the man. "I am willing," he
said. "Be clean!" And immediately the
leprosy left him.
14Then Jesus ordered him, "Don't
tell anyone,[f] but go, show yourself to
the priest and offer the sacrifices that
Moses commanded[g] for your cleansing, as a testimony to them."
15Yet the news about him spread all
the more,[h] so that crowds of people
came to hear him and to be healed
of their sicknesses. **16**But Jesus
often withdrew to lonely places and
prayed.[i]

Jesus Heals a Paralytic

5:18–26pp — Mt 9:2–8; Mk 2:3–12

17One day as he was teaching, Pharisees and teachers of the law,[j] who
had come from every village of Galilee
and from Judea and Jerusalem, were
sitting there. And the power of the
Lord was present for him to heal the
sick.[k] **18**Some men came carrying a
paralytic on a mat and tried to take him
into the house to lay him before Jesus.
19When they could not find a way to do
this because of the crowd, they went up
on the roof and lowered him on his mat
through the tiles into the middle of the
crowd, right in front of Jesus.
20When Jesus saw their faith, he
said, "Friend, your sins are forgiv-
en."[l]
21The Pharisees and the teachers of
the law began thinking to themselves,
"Who is this fellow who speaks blasphemy? Who can forgive sins but God
alone?"[m]
22Jesus knew what they were thinking and asked, "Why are you thinking
these things in your hearts? **23**Which is
easier: to say, 'Your sins are forgiven,'
or to say, 'Get up and walk'? **24**But that
you may know that the Son of Man[n]

[z] 12 The Greek word was used for various diseases affecting the skin—not necessarily leprosy.

5:10 [c] S Mt 14:27
5:11 [d] ver 28; S Mt 4:19
5:12 [e] S Mt 8:2
5:14 [f] S Mt 8:4 [g] Lev 14:2-32
5:15 [h] S Mt 9:26
5:16 [i] S Lk 3:21
5:17 [j] Mt 15:1; Lk 2:46 [k] Mk 5:30; Lk 6:19
5:20 [l] Lk 7:48,49
5:21 [m] Isa 43:25
5:24 [n] S Mt 8:20

5:10 YOU WILL CATCH MEN. See Mt 4:19, note.

5:16 PRAYERS OF JESUS. (1) Luke stresses more than the other Gospel writers the place of prayer in the life and work of Jesus. When the Holy Spirit descended upon Jesus at the Jordan, he was "praying" (3:21); at times he withdrew from the multitudes "and prayed" (5:16), and he "spent the night praying" before choosing the twelve disciples (6:12). He was "praying in private" before he asked his disciples an important question (9:18); at his transfiguration he climbed the mountain "to pray" (9:28); the actual transfiguration occurred while "he was praying" (9:29); and he "was praying" just before he taught the disciples the Lord's Prayer (11:1). In Gethsemane he "prayed more earnestly" (22:44); on the cross he prayed for others (23:34); and the last words he uttered before his death were a prayer (23:46). Luke also records that Jesus prayed after his resurrection (24:30). (2) In examining the life of Jesus in the other Gospels, we note that he prayed before extending the invitation, "Come to me, all you who are weary and burdened." (Mt 11:25–28); he prayed at Lazarus's tomb (Jn 11:41–42) and during the institution of the Lord's Supper (Jn 17). For more on prayer in Jesus' life, see Mt 14:23, note.

5:18 CARRYING A PARALYTIC. The friends of the paralyzed man had strong faith that Jesus could heal him, as seen by their determination to present him to Jesus. We too must believe that Christ can meet the needs of those we know, using every opportunity to bring them to Jesus. God's Spirit will open up such opportunities if we desire to lead others to Christ.

5:22 JESUS KNEW WHAT THEY WERE THINKING. Believers must remember that God knows and evaluates their every thought, desire and imagination (see Ps 139; Mt 17:25; Jn 1:48; 2:25; 21:17; Heb 4:13).

5:24 SON OF MAN. The "Son of Man" is Jesus' favorite expression by which he refers to himself; Da 7:13 seems to be the background for Jesus' use of the expression. Daniel used the title to describe a person he saw in a vision, one "like a son of man" coming with the clouds of heaven, who is given an everlasting kingdom (see Da 7:13, note). Thus Jesus expresses the truth that he is the predicted Messiah, sent by God. Jesus uses the term (1) as a substitute for "I" (Mt 11:19); (2) when making important claims (Mt 20:28; Mk 10:45); (3) when foretelling his death on the cross (9:44; Mt 17:22; Mk 8:31); (4) when speaking about his resurrection (Mt 17:9); (5) when referring to his glorious return to earth (Mt 24:27; Mk 13:26; 14:62); (6) when speaking of his role in judgment (Mt 13:41).

has authority on earth to forgive
sins. . . ." He said to the paralyzed
man, "I tell you, get up, take your mat
and go home." 25 Immediately he stood
up in front of them, took what he had
been lying on and went home praising
God. 26 Everyone was amazed and gave
praise to God.[o] They were filled with
awe and said, "We have seen remarkable things today."

The Calling of Levi

5:27–32pp — Mt 9:9–13; Mk 2:14–17

27 After this, Jesus went out and saw
a tax collector by the name of Levi sitting at his tax booth. "Follow me,"[p]
Jesus said to him, 28 and Levi got up,
left everything and followed him.[q]
29 Then Levi held a great banquet for
Jesus at his house, and a large crowd
of tax collectors[r] and others were eating with them. 30 But the Pharisees and
the teachers of the law who belonged
to their sect[s] complained to his disciples, "Why do you eat and drink with
tax collectors and 'sinners'?"[t]
31 Jesus answered them, "It is not
the healthy who need a doctor, but the
sick. 32 I have not come to call the righteous, but sinners to repentance."[u]

Jesus Questioned About Fasting

5:33–39pp — Mt 9:14–17; Mk 2:18–22

33 They said to him, "John's disciples[v] often fast and pray, and so do
the disciples of the Pharisees, but
yours go on eating and drinking."
34 Jesus answered, "Can you make
the guests of the bridegroom[w] fast
while he is with them? 35 But the time
will come when the bridegroom will be
taken from them;[x] in those days they
will fast."
36 He told them this parable: "No one
tears a patch from a new garment and
sews it on an old one. If he does, he will
have torn the new garment, and the
patch from the new will not match the
old. 37 And no one pours new wine into
old wineskins. If he does, the new wine
will burst the skins, the wine will run
out and the wineskins will be ruined.
38 No, new wine must be poured into
new wineskins. 39 And no one after
drinking old wine wants the new, for he
says, 'The old is better.' "

Lord of the Sabbath

6:1–11pp — Mt 12:1–14; Mk 2:23–3:6

6 One Sabbath Jesus was going
through the grainfields, and his
disciples began to pick some heads of
grain, rub them in their hands and eat
the kernels.[y] 2 Some of the Pharisees
asked, "Why are you doing what is unlawful on the Sabbath?"[z]
3 Jesus answered them, "Have you
never read what David did when he and
his companions were hungry?[a] 4 He
entered the house of God, and taking
the consecrated bread, he ate what is

5:26 [o] S Mt 9:8
5:27 [p] S Mt 4:19
5:28 [q] ver 11; S Mt 4:19
5:29 [r] Lk 15:1
5:30 [s] Ac 23:9 [t] S Mt 9:11
5:32 [u] S Jn 3:17
5:33 [v] Lk 7:18; Jn 1:35; 3:25,26
5:34 [w] Jn 3:29
5:35 [x] Lk 9:22; 17:22; Jn 16:5-7
6:1 [y] Dt 23:25
6:2 [z] S Mt 12:2
6:3 [a] 1Sa 21:6

5:30 EAT AND DRINK WITH . . . 'SINNERS'. See Mt 9:11, note.

5:35 IN THOSE DAYS THEY WILL FAST. See Mt 9:15, note.

5:37 NEW WINE INTO OLD WINESKINS. See Mt 9:17, notes.

5:39 'THE OLD IS BETTER'. This is probably an ironic comment about the Jews who rejected the "new wine" of the gospel and held that the "old wine" (first-century Judaism) was good enough. Jesus suggests here that those who are accustomed to drinking fermented wine acquire a desire for it and do not want unfermented wine (see articles on WINE IN THE OLD TESTAMENT, p. 204, and WINE IN NEW TESTAMENT TIMES (1), p. 1534). He recognizes the habit-forming, addictive effect of alcoholic beverages. It is not Jesus but the one drinking the old wine who thinks "the old is better."

(1) We may not interpret this verse to state that old wine (i.e., Judaism) is better than new wine (i.e., Christ's gospel), for this would invert the parable's meaning. What Jesus is stating is that the Pharisees and their followers will not even recognize the merits of the new; they feel that "the old" is good enough. The Pharisees prefer the rabbinical interpretation of the law to the pure, new, sweet wine of the gospel of Christ.

(2) The Pharisees have no desire for the best wine. They refuse to accept the fresh revelation of God and instead seek only what humans have altered (i.e., fermented). Yet for those who receive Jesus, the fresh new juice of the grape (gospel) is preferable to old fermented wine (Pharisaic religion).

6:1 SABBATH. See Mt 12:1, note on Sabbath.

6:2–10 JESUS AND THE SABBATH. Though the Pharisees accuse Jesus of breaking the Sabbath, in reality he broke only their extreme interpretation of it. Jesus states that Sabbath observance must not degenerate into a ritual to be kept at the cost of the essential needs of humans. Christ is the Lord of the Sabbath (v. 5); the Sabbath should be used to come away from our daily work and pursuit of material gain and turn to God as a pledge that he is Lord over all of life. Furthermore, Jesus' words and actions (vv. 6–10) teach us that the Lord's Day should be an opportunity to help those in need, spiritually as well as physically.

lawful only for priests to eat.[b] And he
also gave some to his companions."
5Then Jesus said to them, "The Son of
Man[c] is Lord of the Sabbath."
6On another Sabbath[d] he went into
the synagogue and was teaching, and
a man was there whose right hand was
shriveled. 7The Pharisees and the
teachers of the law were looking for a
reason to accuse Jesus, so they
watched him closely[e] to see if he
would heal on the Sabbath.[f] 8But
Jesus knew what they were thinking[g]
and said to the man with the shriveled
hand, "Get up and stand in front of everyone." So he got up and stood there.
9Then Jesus said to them, "I ask you,
which is lawful on the Sabbath: to do
good or to do evil, to save life or to
destroy it?"
10He looked around at them all, and
then said to the man, "Stretch out your
hand." He did so, and his hand was
completely restored. 11But they were
furious[h] and began to discuss with
one another what they might do to
Jesus.

The Twelve Apostles

6:13–16pp — Mt 10:2–4; Mk 3:16–19; Ac 1:13

12One of those days Jesus went out
to a mountainside to pray, and spent
the night praying to God.[i] 13When
morning came, he called his disciples
to him and chose twelve of them, whom
he also designated apostles:[j] 14Si-
mon (whom he named Peter), his
brother Andrew, James, John, Philip,

6:4 [b]Lev 24:5,9
6:5 [c]S Mt 8:20
6:6 [d]ver 1
6:7 [e]S Mt 12:10 [f]S Mt 12:2
6:8 [g]S Mt 9:4
6:11 [h]Jn 5:18
6:12 [i]S Lk 3:21
6:13 [j]S Mk 6:30
6:15 [k]Mt 9:9
6:17 [l]Mt 4:25; S Mt 11:21; Mk 3:7,8
6:19 [m]S Mt 9:20 [n]Mk 5:30; Lk 5:17
6:20 [o]S Mt 25:34
6:21 [p]Isa 55:1,2; Mt 5:6 [q]Isa 61:2,3; Mt 5:4; Rev 7:17
6:22 [r]Jn 9:22; 16:2 [s]Isa 51:7 [t]S Jn 15:21

Bartholomew, 15Matthew,[k] Thomas,
James son of Alphaeus, Simon who
was called the Zealot, 16Judas son of
James, and Judas Iscariot, who became
a traitor.

Blessings and Woes

6:20–23pp — Mt 5:3–12

17He went down with them and
stood on a level place. A large crowd of
his disciples was there and a great
number of people from all over Judea,
from Jerusalem, and from the coast of
Tyre and Sidon,[l] 18who had come to
hear him and to be healed of their diseases. Those troubled by evil[a] spirits
were cured, 19and the people all tried
to touch him,[m] because power was
coming from him and healing them
all.[n]
20Looking at his disciples, he said:

"Blessed are you who are poor,
for yours is the kingdom of
God.[o]
21Blessed are you who hunger now,
for you will be satisfied.[p]
Blessed are you who weep now,
for you will laugh.[q]
22Blessed are you when men hate
you,
when they exclude you[r] and
insult you[s]
and reject your name as evil,
because of the Son of Man.[t]

23"Rejoice in that day and leap for

[a] *18* Greek *unclean*

6:12 SPENT THE NIGHT PRAYING. Again and again Jesus sought to be alone with his Father in prayer, especially at times of momentous decisions (see 5:16, note). (1) His entire night of earnest prayer produced tremendous results (see Jas 5:16, note). Following this night of prayer, Jesus chose the twelve to become his apostles (vv. 13–16), healed many who were sick (vv. 17–19) and preached his most quoted sermon (vv. 20–49). (2) If Jesus, the perfect Son of God, spent a whole night in prayer to the Father in order to make an important decision, how much more do we, with all our weaknesses and failings, need to spend nights in prayer and in intimate communion with our heavenly Father.

6:17 SERMON ON THE PLAIN. See Mt 5–7, note on the Sermon on the Mount.

6:20 BLESSED. See Mt 5:3, note.

6:20 YOU WHO ARE POOR. See article on RICHES AND POVERTY, p. 1562, for comments on this verse.

6:21 YOU WHO WEEP. See Mt 5:4, note.

6:22 WHEN MEN HATE YOU. Followers of Jesus should "rejoice" and "leap for joy" (v. 23) when, because of faithfulness to Christ and his godly standards, they are criticized and scorned. Persecution because of righteousness is proof that believers are in true fellowship with the Lord, since Jesus was also ill-treated and hated by the world (Jn 15:18–21; see Mt 5:10, note).

6:23 HOW THEIR FATHERS TREATED THE PROPHETS. The OT people of Israel rejected the prophets and their messages many times (1Ki 19:10; Mt 5:12; 23:31,37; Ac 7:51–52). (1) Churches today should bear in mind that God sends them prophets (1Co 12:28; Eph 4:11) for the purpose of calling both leaders and people to lives of righteousness, faithfulness to all Scripture, and separation from the world (see Rev 2–3).

(2) Churches can do the same thing as Israel of old by rejecting the words of their prophets and losing the blessing and salvation of God. On the other hand, they can accept God's message, draw back from sin, deepen their loyalty to God and his Word, and continue as God's people. Those churches that reject God's true prophets will ulti-

joy,[u] because great is your reward in
heaven. For that is how their fathers
treated the prophets.[v]

24"But woe to you who are rich,[w]
for you have already received
your comfort.[x]
25Woe to you who are well fed now,
for you will go hungry.[y]
Woe to you who laugh now,
for you will mourn and weep.[z]
26Woe to you when all men speak
well of you,
for that is how their fathers
treated the false prophets.[a]

Love for Enemies

6:29,30pp — Mt 5:39–42

27"But I tell you who hear me: Love
your enemies, do good to those who
hate you,[b] **28**bless those who curse
you, pray for those who mistreat you.[c]
29If someone strikes you on one cheek,
turn to him the other also. If someone
takes your cloak, do not stop him from
taking your tunic. **30**Give to everyone
who asks you, and if anyone takes
what belongs to you, do not demand it
back.[d] **31**Do to others as you would
have them do to you.[e]
32"If you love those who love you,
what credit is that to you?[f] Even 'sinners' love those who love them. **33**And
if you do good to those who are good
to you, what credit is that to you? Even
'sinners' do that. **34**And if you lend to
those from whom you expect repayment, what credit is that to you?[g]
Even 'sinners' lend to 'sinners,' expecting to be repaid in full. **35**But love
your enemies, do good to them,[h] and
lend to them without expecting to get
anything back. Then your reward will
be great, and you will be sons[i] of the
Most High,[j] because he is kind to the
ungrateful and wicked. **36**Be merciful,[k] just as your Father[l] is merciful.

Judging Others

6:37–42pp — Mt 7:1–5

37"Do not judge, and you will not be
judged.[m] Do not condemn, and you
will not be condemned. Forgive, and
you will be forgiven.[n] **38**Give, and it
will be given to you. A good measure,
pressed down, shaken together and
running over, will be poured into your
lap.[o] For with the measure you use, it
will be measured to you."[p]
39He also told them this parable:
"Can a blind man lead a blind man? Will
they not both fall into a pit?[q] **40**A student is not above his teacher, but everyone who is fully trained will be like
his teacher.[r]
41"Why do you look at the speck of
sawdust in your brother's eye and pay

6:23 [u] S Mt 5:12 [v] S Mt 5:12
6:24 [w] Jas 5:1 [x] Lk 16:25
6:25 [y] Isa 65:13 [z] Pr 14:13
6:26 [a] S Mt 7:15
6:27 [b] ver 35; Mt 5:44; Ro 12:20
6:28 [c] S Mt 5:44
6:30 [d] Dt 15:7,8,10; Pr 21:26
6:31 [e] Mt 7:12
6:32 [f] Mt 5:46
6:34 [g] Mt 5:42
6:35 [h] ver 27 [i] S Ro 8:14 [j] S Mk 5:7
6:36 [k] Jas 2:13 [l] Mt 5:48; 6:1; Lk 11:2; 12:32; Ro 8:15; Eph 4:6; 1Pe 1:17; 1Jn 1:3; 3:1
6:37 [m] S Mt 7:1 [n] Mt 6:14
6:38 [o] Ps 79:12; Isa 65:6,7 [p] S Mt 7:2
6:39 [q] Mt 15:14
6:40 [r] S Jn 13:16

---

mately be rejected by God himself (13:34–35; Rev 2–3).

(3) Satan will deliberately send false prophets into the churches (Mt 13:24–30,36–43), prophets who reject the absolute authority of God's Word, claim to have authority equal to God's Word, and maintain that their revelation is infallible and their words immune from judgment by the churches (see article on FALSE TEACHERS, p. 1506). These false prophets must be firmly rejected.

6:24 WOE TO YOU WHO ARE RICH. Jesus is speaking of those who center their lives, purpose, happiness or goals primarily in material things or in the pursuit of great wealth (see article on RICHES AND POVERTY, p. 1562).

6:26 WOE TO YOU WHEN ALL MEN SPEAK WELL. When a large portion of the unbelieving world speaks well of a believer or a professed minister of God, it may be evidence that he or she is not a true follower of Christ, since false prophets are often popular with those who are not loyal to Christ. Prophets or ministers who serve God will have the same thing happen to them as happened to Christ; their lives and message will come into collision with the sins of the ungodly and will consequently be rejected by those unbelievers.

6:27 LOVE YOUR ENEMIES. In vv. 27–42, Jesus tells us how we are to live with other persons. As members of the new covenant, we are obligated to follow the demands set forth here. (1) Loving our enemies does not mean an emotional love, such as liking our enemies, but rather a genuine concern for their good and for their eternal salvation. Since we know the terrible fate awaiting those who are hostile to God and his people, we must pray for them and attempt, by repaying good for evil, to bring them to Christ and the faith of the gospel (cf. Pr 20:22; 24:29; Mt 5:39–45; Ro 12:17; 1Th 5:15; 1Pe 3:9).

(2) Loving our enemies does not mean standing by idly while evildoers continue their wicked deeds. When it is necessary for God's honor, the good or safety of others, or the ultimate good of the wicked, severe action must be taken to stop evil (see Mk 11:15; Jn 2:13–17).

6:29 DO NOT STOP HIM FROM TAKING YOUR TUNIC. See Mt 5:39, note.

6:37 DO NOT JUDGE. See Mt 7:1, note.

6:38 GIVE. In conformity with the principle of love, we must give to those in need (see 2Co 8:2, note; see article on THE CARE OF THE POOR AND NEEDY, p. 1316). God himself will measure our giving and in return will give to us. The measure of blessing and reward we receive will be in proportion to our concern for and help given to others (see 2Co 9:6).

no attention to the plank in your own eye? 42 How can you say to your brother, 'Brother, let me take the speck out of your eye,' when you yourself fail to see the plank in your own eye? You hypocrite, first take the plank out of your eye, and then you will see clearly to remove the speck from your brother's eye.

A Tree and Its Fruit

6:43,44pp — Mt 7:16,18,20

43 "No good tree bears bad fruit, nor does a bad tree bear good fruit. 44 Each tree is recognized by its own fruit.[s] People do not pick figs from thornbushes, or grapes from briers. 45 The good man brings good things out of the good stored up in his heart, and the evil man brings evil things out of the evil stored up in his heart. For out of the overflow of his heart his mouth speaks.[t]

Jn 15:1-8

The Wise and Foolish Builders

6:47–49pp — Mt 7:24–27

46 "Why do you call me, 'Lord, Lord,'[u] and do not do what I say?[v] 47 I will show you what he is like who comes to me and hears my words and puts them into practice.[w] 48 He is like a man building a house, who dug down deep and laid the foundation on rock. When a flood came, the torrent struck that house but could not shake it, because it was well built. 49 But the one who hears my words and does not put them into practice is like a man who built a house on the ground without a foundation. The moment the torrent struck that house, it collapsed and its destruction was complete."

Lk 10:25-37

The Faith of the Centurion

7:1–10pp — Mt 8:5–13

7 When Jesus had finished saying all this[x] in the hearing of the people, he entered Capernaum. 2 There a centurion's servant, whom his master valued highly, was sick and about to die. 3 The centurion heard of Jesus and sent some elders of the Jews to him, asking him to come and heal his servant. 4 When they came to Jesus, they pleaded earnestly with him, "This man deserves to have you do this, 5 because he loves our nation and has built our synagogue." 6 So Jesus went with them.

He was not far from the house when the centurion sent friends to say to him: "Lord, don't trouble yourself, for I do not deserve to have you come under my roof. 7 That is why I did not even consider myself worthy to come to you. But say the word, and my servant will be healed.[y] 8 For I myself am a man under authority, with soldiers under me. I tell this one, 'Go,' and he goes; and that one, 'Come,' and he comes. I say to my servant, 'Do this,' and he does it."

9 When Jesus heard this, he was amazed at him, and turning to the crowd following him, he said, "I tell you, I have not found such great faith even in Israel." 10 Then the men who had been sent returned to the house and found the servant well.

Jesus Raises a Widow's Son

7:11–16Ref — 1Ki 17:17–24; 2Ki 4:32–37; Mk 5:21–24,35–43; Jn 11:1–44

11 Soon afterward, Jesus went to a town called Nain, and his disciples and a large crowd went along with him. 12 As he approached the town gate, a dead person was being carried out—the only son of his mother, and she was a widow. And a large crowd from the town was with her. 13 When the Lord[z] saw her, his heart went out to her and he said, "Don't cry."

14 Then he went up and touched the coffin, and those carrying it stood still. He said, "Young man, I say to you, get

6:44 [s] Mt 12:33
6:45 [t] Pr 4:23; Mt 12:34,35; Mk 7:20
6:46 [u] S Jn 13:13 [v] Mal 1:6; Mt 7:21
6:47 [w] Lk 8:21; 11:28; Jas 1:22-25
7:1 [x] Mt 7:28
7:7 [y] Ps 107:20
7:13 [z] ver 19; Lk 10:1; 13:15; 17:5; 22:61; 24:34; Jn 11:2

6:45 HIS HEART. The heart, the center of our being, determines our outward behavior and must be changed or converted (see Mk 7:20–23, note; see articles on THE HEART, p. 906, and REGENERATION, p. 1589). Without that inward change, no one can do God's will (cf. Jer 24:7; 31:33; 32:39; Eze 36:23,27; Mt 7:16–20; 12:33–35; 15:18–19; 21:43; Lk 1:17; Ro 6:17).

6:46 DO NOT DO WHAT I SAY. See Mt 7:21, note.

7:9 SUCH GREAT FAITH. See Mt 8:10, note.

7:13 HIS HEART WENT OUT TO HER. Jesus' compassion for this widow shows that God has a special love and care for widows or for any person who is left alone in the world. Scripture teaches the following: (1) God is a Father to the fatherless and a defender of widows (see Ps 68:5, note). They are under his special care and protection (Ex 22:22–23; Dt 10:18; Ps 146:9; Pr 15:25). (2) By means of the tithe and the abundance of his people, God provides for the fatherless and the widows (Dt 14:28–29; 24:19–21; 26:12–13). (3) He blesses those who help and honor them (Isa 1:17, 19; Jer 7:6–7; 22:3–4). (4) He is against those who

up!"[a] 15The dead man sat up and began to talk, and Jesus gave him back to
his mother.
16They were all filled with awe[b]
and praised God.[c] "A great prophet[d]
has appeared among us," they said.
"God has come to help his people."[e]
17This news about Jesus spread
throughout Judea[b] and the surrounding country.[f]

Jesus and John the Baptist

7:18–35pp — Mt 11:2–19

18John's[g] disciples[h] told him
about all these things. Calling two of
them, 19he sent them to the Lord to
ask, "Are you the one who was to
come, or should we expect someone
else?"
20When the men came to Jesus, they
said, "John the Baptist sent us to you
to ask, 'Are you the one who was to
come, or should we expect someone
else?' "
21At that very time Jesus cured
many who had diseases, sicknesses[i]
and evil spirits, and gave sight to many
who were blind. 22So he replied to the
messengers, "Go back and report to
John what you have seen and heard:
The blind receive sight, the lame walk,
those who have leprosy[c] are cured,
the deaf hear, the dead are raised, and
the good news is preached to the
poor.[j] 23Blessed is the man who does
not fall away on account of me."
24After John's messengers left,
Jesus began to speak to the crowd
about John: "What did you go out into
the desert to see? A reed swayed by the
wind? 25If not, what did you go out to
see? A man dressed in fine clothes? No,

7:14 [a]Mt 9:25; Mk 1:31; Lk 8:54; Jn 11:43; Ac 9:40
7:16 [b]Lk 1:65 [c]S Mt 9:8 [d]ver 39; S Mt 21:11 [e]Lk 1:68
7:17 [f]S Mt 9:26
7:18 [g]S Mt 3:1 [h]S Lk 5:33
7:21 [i]S Mt 4:23
7:22 [j]Isa 29:18, 19; 35:5,6; 61:1,2; Lk 4:18
7:26 [k]S Mt 11:9
7:27 [l]Mal 3:1; Mt 11:10; Mk 1:2
7:28 [m]S Mt 3:2
7:29 [n]Mt 21:32; Mk 1:5; Lk 3:12
7:30 [o]S Mt 22:35
7:33 [p]Lk 1:15

those who wear expensive clothes and
indulge in luxury are in palaces. 26But
what did you go out to see? A prophet?[k] Yes, I tell you, and more than a
prophet. 27This is the one about whom
it is written:

" 'I will send my messenger ahead
of you,
who will prepare your way
before you.'[d][l]

28I tell you, among those born of wom-
en there is no one greater than John;
yet the one who is least in the kingdom
of God[m] is greater than he."
29(All the people, even the tax collectors, when they heard Jesus' words,
acknowledged that God's way was
right, because they had been baptized
by John.[n] 30But the Pharisees and experts in the law[o] rejected God's purpose for themselves, because they had
not been baptized by John.)
31"To what, then, can I compare the
people of this generation? What are
they like? 32They are like children sitting in the marketplace and calling out
to each other:

" 'We played the flute for you,
and you did not dance;
we sang a dirge,
and you did not cry.'

33For John the Baptist came neither
eating bread nor drinking wine,[p] and
you say, 'He has a demon.' 34The Son
of Man came eating and drinking, and
you say, 'Here is a glutton and a drunk-

[b]*17* Or *the land of the Jews* [c]*22* The Greek word was used for various diseases affecting the skin—not necessarily leprosy. [d]*27* Mal. 3:1

take advantage of or hurt widows or orphans (Ex 22:22–24; Dt 24:17; 27:19; Job 24:3; Ps 94:6,16; Zec 7:10). (5) Widows are recipients of God's tender love and compassion (vv. 11–17; 18:2–8; 21:2–4; Mk 12:42–43). (6) The early church made it a priority to care for widows (Ac 6:1–6). (7) One aspect of true faith is to look after orphans and widows in their distress (Jas 1:27; cf. 1Ti 5:3–8).

7:24 A REED SWAYED. See Mt 11:7, note.

7:28 JOHN. See Mt 11:11, note.

7:33 WINE. For an examination of Biblical words for wine and for its use in NT times, see 1:15, note; see articles on WINE IN NEW TESTAMENT TIMES (1) and (2), p. 1534 and p. 1586.

7:34 GLUTTON AND A DRUNKARD. Wine (Gk *oinos*) in the NT referred to all kinds of wine, both unfermented and fermented (see article on WINE IN NEW TESTAMENT TIMES (1), p. 1534). Jesus' statement indicates that he drank some types of wine, whereas John did not. However, it cannot be determined from this passage what types of wine he drank, for the allegation of the Pharisees concerning Jesus' character is clearly false. They accuse Jesus of being a glutton and a drunkard, but these were characteristically slanderous lies designed to destroy his influence as a teacher of righteousness (see Mt 12:24; Jn 7:20; 8:48). Jesus himself implies that those who "eat and drink with drunkards" are wicked servants who are not rightly preparing for the return of their Master (Mt 24:48–49). Therefore, it can in no way be proven from this passage that Jesus drank intoxicating wine. For a discussion on the kind of wine Jesus may have used, see articles on WINE IN NEW TESTAMENT TIMES (1) and (2), p. 1534 and p. 1586; cf. Pr 23:31.

WINE IN NEW TESTAMENT TIMES (1)

***Lk 7:33–34** "For John the Baptist came neither eating bread nor drinking wine, and you say, 'He has a demon.' The Son of Man came eating and drinking, and you say, 'Here is a glutton and a drunkard, a friend of tax collectors and "sinners."'"*

WINE: FERMENTED OR UNFERMENTED? The following is an examination of the most common Biblical word for wine. The Greek word for "wine" in Lk 7:33 is *oinos*. *Oinos* can refer to two distinctly different types of juice of the grape: (1) unfermented juice, and (2) fermented or intoxicating wine. This is supported by the following data.

(1) The Greek word *oinos* was used by secular and religious authors in pre-Christian and early church times to refer to fresh grape juice (see Aristotle, *Metereologica*, 387.b.9–13). (a) Anacreon (c. 500 B.C.) writes, "Squeeze the grape, let out the wine [*oinos*]" (Ode 5). (b) Nicander (second century B.C.) writes of squeezing grapes and refers to the produced juice as *oinos* (*Georgica*, fragment 86). (c) Papias (A.D. 60–130), an early church father, mentions that when grapes are crushed they yield "jars of wine [*oinos*]" (cited by Irenaeus, *Against Heresies*, 5.33.3–4). (d) A Greek papyrus letter (P. Oxy. 729; A.D. 137) speaks of "fresh wine [*oinos*] from the treading vat" (see Moulton and Milligan, *The Vocabulary of the Greek Testament*, p. 10). (e) Athenaeus (A.D. 200) speaks of a "sweet wine [*oinos*]" that "does not make the head heavy" (Athenaeus, *Banquet*, 1.54). In another place, he writes of a man gathering grapes who "went about, and took wine [*oinos*] from the field" (1.54). For more detailed discussions on the use of *oinos* by ancient writers, see Robert P. Teachout, "The Use of 'Wine' in the Old Testament" (Th.D. dissertation, Dallas Theological Seminary, 1979).

(2) The Jewish scholars who translated the OT into Greek about 200 B.C. used *oinos* to translate several Hebrew words for wine (see article on WINE IN THE OLD TESTAMENT, p. 204). In other words, the NT writers undoubtedly knew that *oinos* could be either fermented or unfermented juice from the grape.

(3) As with secular and religious Greek sources, an examination of NT passages also reveals that *oinos* may mean either fermented or unfermented wine. In Eph 5:18 the command, "do not get drunk on wine [*oinos*]," refers to alcoholic wine. On the other hand, in Rev 19:15 Christ is pictured as treading the winepress. The Greek text reads: "He treads the winepress of the wine [*oinos*]"; the *oinos* that comes from the winepress would be grape juice (see Isa 16:10, note; Jer 48:32–33, note). In Rev 6:6 *oinos* refers to grapes on the vine as a crop not to be destroyed. Thus, for believers in NT times, "wine" (*oinos*) was a general word that could be used for two distinctly different grape beverages—fermented and unfermented wine.

(4) Finally, ancient Roman writers have explained in detail various processes used in dealing with freshly squeezed grape juice, especially ways to preserve it from fermenting. (a) Columella (*On Agriculture*, 12.29), knowing that grape juice would not ferment if kept cool (under 50 degrees) and oxygen free, writes as follows: "That your grape juice may be always as sweet as when it is new, thus proceed. After you apply the press to the grapes, take the newest must [i.e., fresh juice], put it in a new container (*amphora*), bung it up, and cover it up very carefully with pitch lest any water should enter; then sink it in a cistern or pond of cold water and allow no part of the amphora to remain above the surface. After forty days take it out. It will remain sweet for a year" (see also Columella, *Agriculture and Trees*; Cato, *On Agriculture*). The Roman writer Pliny (first century A.D.) writes: "as soon as the must [grape juice] is taken from the vat and put into casks, they plunge the casks in water till midwinter passes and regular cold weather sets in" (Pliny, *Natural History*, 14.11.83). This method would have worked well in the land of Israel (see Dt 8:7; 11:11–12; Ps 65:9–13).

(b) Another method to keep grapes from fermenting was to boil them into a syrup (for more details, see article on WINE IN NEW TESTAMENT TIMES (2), p. 1586). Ancient historians actually referred to this product as wine (*oinos*). Canon Farrar (*Smith's Bible Dictionary*, p. 747) states that "the wines of antiquity were more like syrups; many of them were not intoxicant." Also, *The New Bible Dictionary* (p. 1332) notes that "there were means of keeping wine sweet all year round."

USE OF WINE IN LORD'S SUPPER. Did Jesus use fermented or unfermented grape drink when he instituted the Lord's Supper (Mt 26:26–29; Mk 14:22–25; Lk 22:17–20; 1Co 11:23–26)? The following data support the conclusion that Jesus and his disciples drank unfermented grape juice.

(1) Neither Luke nor any other Biblical writer uses the word "wine" (Gk *oinos*) with regard to the Lord's Supper. The first three Gospel writers use "fruit of the vine" (Mt 26:29; Mk 14:25; Lk 22:18). Unfermented wine is the only truly natural "fruit of the vine," containing approximately 20 percent sugar and no alcohol. Fermentation destroys much of the sugar and alters what the vine produced. Fermented wine is not the product of the vine.

(2) The Lord's Supper was instituted when Jesus and his disciples were eating the Passover. The Passover law in Ex 12:14–20 prohibited, during Passover week, the presence and use of *seor* (Ex 12:15), a word referring to yeast or any agent of fermentation. *Seor* in the ancient world was often obtained from the thick scum on top of fermenting wine. Furthermore, all *hametz* (i.e., anything that contained any type of fermentation) was forbidden (Ex 12:19; 13:7; see 13:7, note). God had given these laws because fermentation symbolized corruption and sin (cf. Mt 16:6,12; 1Co 5:7–8). Jesus, the Son of God, fulfilled the law in every requirement (Mt 5:17). Thus, he would have followed God's law for the Passover and not used fermented wine.

(3) A rather lively debate has taken place over the centuries among Jewish rabbis and scholars as to whether fermented products of the vine were allowed in the Passover. Those who held to a stricter and more literal interpretation of the Hebrew Scriptures, especially Ex 13:7, insisted that no fermented wine could be used on this occasion.

(4) Some Jewish sources affirm that the use of unfermented wine at the Passover was common in NT times. For example, "According to the Synoptic Gospels, it would appear that on the Thursday evening of the last week of his life Jesus with his disciples entered Jerusalem in order to eat the Passover meal with them in the sacred city; if so, the wafer and the wine of . . . the communion service then instituted by him as a memorial would be the unleavened bread and the unfermented wine of the Seder service" (see "Jesus," *The Jewish Encyclopedia*, 1904 edition, V.165).

(5) In the OT, fermented drink was never to be used in the house of God, nor were the priests allowed to draw near to God in worship while drinking intoxicating beverages (see Lev 10:9, note). Jesus Christ was God's high priest of the new covenant, drawing near to God for the sake of his people (Heb 3:1; 5:1–10).

(6) The value of a symbol is determined by its capacity to conceptualize the spiritual reality. Therefore, just as the bread represented Christ's pure body and had to be unleavened (i.e., uncorrupted with fermentation), the fruit of the vine, representing the incorruptible blood of Christ, would have been best represented by juice that was unfermented (cf. 1Pe 1:18–19). Since Scripture states explicitly that the process of corruption was not allowed to work in either the body or blood of Christ (Ps 16:10; Ac 2:27; 13:37), both Christ's body and blood are properly symbolized by that which is uncorrupted and unfermented.

(7) Paul instructed the Corinthians to put away spiritual yeast, i.e., the fermenting agent of "malice and wickedness," because Christ is our Passover (1Co 5:6–8). It would be inconsistent with the goal and spiritual requirement of the Lord's Supper to use something that was a symbol of evil, i.e., something with yeast.

For more on wine in NT times, see article on WINE IN NEW TESTAMENT TIMES (2), p. 1586.

ard, a friend of tax collectors and "sinners." '[q] 35But wisdom is proved right by all her children."

Jesus Anointed by a Sinful Woman

7:37–39Ref — Mt 26:6–13; Mk 14:3–9; Jn 12:1–8
7:41,42Ref — Mt 18:23–34

36Now one of the Pharisees invited Jesus to have dinner with him, so he went to the Pharisee's house and reclined at the table. 37When a woman who had lived a sinful life in that town learned that Jesus was eating at the Pharisee's house, she brought an alabaster jar of perfume, 38and as she stood behind him at his feet weeping, she began to wet his feet with her tears. Then she wiped them with her hair, kissed them and poured perfume on them.

39When the Pharisee who had invited him saw this, he said to himself, "If this man were a prophet,[r] he would know who is touching him and what kind of woman she is—that she is a sinner."

40Jesus answered him, "Simon, I have something to tell you."

"Tell me, teacher," he said.

41"Two men owed money to a certain moneylender. One owed him five hundred denarii,[e] and the other fifty. 42Neither of them had the money to pay him back, so he canceled the debts of both. Now which of them will love him more?"

43Simon replied, "I suppose the one who had the bigger debt canceled."

"You have judged correctly," Jesus said.

44Then he turned toward the woman and said to Simon, "Do you see this woman? I came into your house. You did not give me any water for my feet,[s] but she wet my feet with her tears and wiped them with her hair. 45You did not give me a kiss,[t] but this woman, from the time I entered, has not stopped kissing my feet. 46You did not put oil on my head,[u] but she has poured perfume on my feet. 47Therefore, I tell you, her many sins have been forgiven—for she loved much. But he who has been forgiven little loves little."

48Then Jesus said to her, "Your sins are forgiven."[v]

49The other guests began to say among themselves, "Who is this who even forgives sins?"

50Jesus said to the woman, "Your faith has saved you;[w] go in peace."[x]

The Parable of the Sower

8:4–15pp — Mt 13:2–23; Mk 4:1–20

8 After this, Jesus traveled about from one town and village to another, proclaiming the good news of the kingdom of God.[y] The Twelve were with him, 2and also some women who had been cured of evil spirits and diseases: Mary (called Magdalene)[z] from whom seven demons had come out; 3Joanna the wife of Cuza, the manager of Herod's[a] household; Susanna; and many others. These women were helping to support them out of their own means.

4While a large crowd was gathering and people were coming to Jesus from town after town, he told this parable:

7:34 q Lk 5:29,30; 15:1,2
7:39 r ver 16; S Mt 21:11
7:44 s Ge 18:4; 19:2; 43:24; Jdg 19:21; Jn 13:4-14; 1Ti 5:10
7:45 t Lk 22:47, 48; S Ro 16:16
7:46 u Ps 23:5; Ecc 9:8
7:48 v Mt 9:2
7:50 w S Mt 9:22 x S Ac 15:33
8:1 y S Mt 4:23
8:2 z Mt 27:55,56
8:3 a S Mt 14:1

e 41 A denarius was a coin worth about a day's wages.

7:38 WEEPING. Because of her love for Jesus, this woman wets his feet with her tears. Weeping can be an expression of sorrow and grief or of grateful love for Christ. (1) By weeping in prayer and faith, believers express to God what is in their hearts; such tears are valued as an offering and service to him (vv. 37–50; Ps 126:5–6; Jer 9:1; 14:17; 31:15–16; Ac 20:19,31; 2Co 2:4; see Ne 8:9, note). In this manner believers also participate in the sufferings of Christ (2Co 1:5; Php 3:10; 1Pe 4:13).

(2) Christ himself wept while praying and was heard (Heb 5:7); likewise, the apostle Paul served the Lord with many tears (Ac 20:19; 2Co 2:4). Even today those who weep in Christ are considered blessed (6:21). In Christ's future kingdom God will wipe away all tears from the eyes of his people (Rev 7:17; 21:4; concerning prayer and tears, read 2Ki 20:5; Ps 39:12; see Ps 56:8, note).

7:47 SHE LOVED MUCH. Real love for and devotion to Jesus must come from a deep awareness of the sinfulness of our past condition, his love for us revealed when he gave himself on the cross, and the inner assurance that we are now forgiven and cared for. Faith that is not based on these foundations will not endure.

8:3 HELPING TO SUPPORT THEM. These women who had received healing and special care from Jesus honored him by faithfully contributing to the support of Jesus and his disciples. Their service and devotion continue to be an example for every woman who believes in him. To the extent that you minister to him, the words of Mt 25:34–40 apply to you.

8:4 PARABLE. See Mt 13:3, note.

5"A farmer went out to sow his seed.
As he was scattering the seed, some
fell along the path; it was trampled on,
and the birds of the air ate it up. 6Some
fell on rock, and when it came up, the
plants withered because they had no
moisture. 7Other seed fell among
thorns, which grew up with it and
choked the plants. 8Still other seed fell
on good soil. It came up and yielded a
crop, a hundred times more than was
sown."

When he said this, he called out, "He
who has ears to hear, let him hear."[b]

9His disciples asked him what this
parable meant. 10He said, "The knowledge of the secrets of the kingdom of
God has been given to you,[c] but to
others I speak in parables, so that,

" 'though seeing, they may not see;
though hearing, they may not
understand.'[f][d]

11"This is the meaning of the parable: The seed is the word of God.[e]
12Those along the path are the ones
who hear, and then the devil comes and
takes away the word from their hearts,
so that they may not believe and be
saved. 13Those on the rock are the
ones who receive the word with joy
when they hear it, but they have no
root. They believe for a while, but in
the time of testing they fall away.[f]
14The seed that fell among thorns
stands for those who hear, but as they
go on their way they are choked by
life's worries, riches[g] and pleasures,
and they do not mature. 15But the seed
on good soil stands for those with a
noble and good heart, who hear the
word, retain it, and by persevering produce a crop.

8:8 [b]S Mt 11:15
8:10 [c]S Mt 13:11 [d]Isa 6:9; S Mt 13:13,14
8:11 [e]S Heb 4:12
8:13 [f]Mt 11:6
8:14 [g]Mt 19:23; 1Ti 6:9,10,17

A Lamp on a Stand

16"No one lights a lamp and hides it
in a jar or puts it under a bed. Instead,
he puts it on a stand, so that those who
come in can see the light.[h] 17For there
is nothing hidden that will not be disclosed, and nothing concealed that will
not be known or brought out into the
open.[i] 18Therefore consider carefully
how you listen. Whoever has will be
given more; whoever does not have,
even what he thinks he has will be tak-
en from him."[j]

Jesus' Mother and Brothers

8:19–21pp — Mt 12:46–50; Mk 3:31–35

19Now Jesus' mother and brothers
came to see him, but they were not able
to get near him because of the crowd.
20Someone told him, "Your mother and
brothers[k] are standing outside, wanting to see you."

21He replied, "My mother and brothers are those who hear God's word and
put it into practice."[l]

Jesus Calms the Storm

8:22–25pp — Mt 8:23–27; Mk 4:36–41
8:22–25Ref — Mk 6:47–52; Jn 6:16–21

22One day Jesus said to his disciples,
"Let's go over to the other side of the
lake." So they got into a boat and set
out. 23As they sailed, he fell asleep. A
squall came down on the lake, so that
the boat was being swamped, and they
were in great danger.

24The disciples went and woke him,
saying, "Master, Master,[m] we're going
to drown!"

He got up and rebuked[n] the wind
and the raging waters; the storm sub-

[f]10 Isaiah 6:9

8:16 [h]S Mt 5:15
8:17 [i]Mt 10:26; Mk 4:22; Lk 12:2
8:18 [j]S Mt 25:29
8:20 [k]Jn 7:5
8:21 [l]Lk 6:47; 11:28; Jn 14:21
8:24 [m]S Lk 5:5 [n]Lk 4:35,39,41

8:5 PARABLE OF THE SOWER. See Mk 4:3, note.

8:12 TAKES AWAY THE WORD. See Mk 4:15, note on halfway conversions.

8:13 BELIEVE FOR A WHILE ... FALL AWAY. In Christ's interpretation of this parable, he explicitly affirms the possibility of a person believing (i.e., making a sincere beginning in the life of faith), but subsequently falling away because of a failure to resist temptation. In contrast are those who "hear the word, retain it, and by persevering produce a crop" (v. 15). Jesus teaches that it is essential that those who hear the Word "hold firmly" to it (11:28; Jn 8:51; 1Co 15:1–2; Col 1:21–23; 1Ti 4:1,16; 2Ti 3:13–15; 1Jn 2:24–25; see Jn 15:6, note on remaining in Christ).

8:14 CHOKED BY LIFE'S WORRIES. We who believe in Jesus must always be careful that worldly responsibilities, abundance or pleasures do not absorb our thoughts until our spiritual life is altogether destroyed. These kinds of thorns/weeds can slowly but surely choke the Word from our lives. Let each of us ask: What is happening in my life? Am I being caught up more and more in the temporal things of life? Or are the Word of God and heavenly things becoming more important as time goes by?

8:18 WHOEVER HAS WILL BE GIVEN MORE. See Mt 25:29, note.

8:21 MY MOTHER AND BROTHERS. Only those who hear and obey the Word of God are personally related to Jesus and are a part of God's family. Faith without obedience is not an option in God's spiritual family.

sided, and all was calm.[o] **25**“Where is
your faith?” he asked his disciples.

In fear and amazement they asked
one another, “Who is this? He commands even the winds and the water,
and they obey him.”

The Healing of a Demon-possessed Man

8:26–37pp — Mt 8:28–34
8:26–39pp — Mk 5:1–20

26They sailed to the region of the
Gerasenes,[g] which is across the lake
from Galilee. **27**When Jesus stepped
ashore, he was met by a demon-possessed man from the town. For a long
time this man had not worn clothes or
lived in a house, but had lived in the
tombs. **28**When he saw Jesus, he cried
out and fell at his feet, shouting at the
top of his voice, “What do you want
with me,[p] Jesus, Son of the Most High
God?[q] I beg you, don’t torture me!”
29For Jesus had commanded the evil[h]
spirit to come out of the man. Many
times it had seized him, and though he
was chained hand and foot and kept
under guard, he had broken his chains
and had been driven by the demon into
solitary places.

30Jesus asked him, “What is your
name?”

“Legion,” he replied, because many
demons had gone into him. **31**And they
begged him repeatedly not to order
them to go into the Abyss.[r]

32A large herd of pigs was feeding
there on the hillside. The demons
begged Jesus to let them go into them,
and he gave them permission. **33**When
the demons came out of the man, they
went into the pigs, and the herd rushed
down the steep bank into the lake[s]
and was drowned.

34When those tending the pigs saw
what had happened, they ran off and
reported this in the town and countryside, **35**and the people went out to see
what had happened. When they came
to Jesus, they found the man from
whom the demons had gone out, sitting
at Jesus’ feet,[t] dressed and in his
right mind; and they were afraid.
36Those who had seen it told the people how the demon-possessed[u] man
had been cured. **37**Then all the people
of the region of the Gerasenes asked
Jesus to leave them,[v] because they
were overcome with fear. So he got
into the boat and left.

38The man from whom the demons
had gone out begged to go with him,
but Jesus sent him away, saying,
39“Return home and tell how much
God has done for you.” So the man
went away and told all over town how
much Jesus had done for him.

A Dead Girl and a Sick Woman

8:40–56pp — Mt 9:18–26; Mk 5:22–43

40Now when Jesus returned, a crowd
welcomed him, for they were all expecting him. **41**Then a man named Jairus, a ruler of the synagogue,[w] came
and fell at Jesus’ feet, pleading with
him to come to his house **42**because his
only daughter, a girl of about twelve,
was dying.

As Jesus was on his way, the crowds
almost crushed him. **43**And a woman
was there who had been subject to
bleeding[x] for twelve years,[i] but no
one could heal her. **44**She came up behind him and touched the edge of his
cloak,[y] and immediately her bleeding
stopped.

45“Who touched me?” Jesus asked.

When they all denied it, Peter said,
“Master,[z] the people are crowding
and pressing against you.”

46But Jesus said, “Someone touched
me;[a] I know that power has gone out
from me.”[b]

47Then the woman, seeing that she
could not go unnoticed, came trembling and fell at his feet. In the presence of all the people, she told why she
had touched him and how she had been
instantly healed. **48**Then he said to her,
“Daughter, your faith has healed
you.[c] Go in peace.”[d]

49While Jesus was still speaking,
someone came from the house of Jairus, the synagogue ruler.[e] “Your

8:24 [o] Ps 107:29; Jnh 1:15
8:28 [p] S Mt 8:29 [q] S Mk 5:7
8:31 [r] Rev 9:1,2, 11; 11:7; 17:8; 20:1,3
8:33 [s] ver 22,23
8:35 [t] Lk 10:39
8:36 [u] S Mt 4:24
8:37 [v] Ac 16:39
8:41 [w] ver 49; S Mk 5:22
8:43 [x] Lev 15:25-30
8:44 [y] S Mt 9:20
8:45 [z] S Lk 5:5
8:46 [a] Mt 14:36; Mk 3:10 [b] Lk 5:17; 6:19
8:48 [c] S Mt 9:22 [d] S Ac 15:33
8:49 [e] ver 41

[g] *26* Some manuscripts *Gadarenes;* other manuscripts *Gergesenes;* also in verse 37
[h] *29* Greek *unclean*
[i] *43* Many manuscripts *years, and she had spent all she had on doctors*

8:27–33 A DEMON-POSSESSED MAN. Demon-possession (or the indwelling of demons within a human personality) is one of the means used by Satan and the kingdom of evil in their struggle against the kingdom of God. For more on this subject, see article on POWER OVER SATAN AND DEMONS, p. 1484.

8:44 TOUCHED . . . HIS CLOAK. See Mk 5:28, note.

daughter is dead," he said. "Don't bother the teacher any more."
50Hearing this, Jesus said to Jairus,
"Don't be afraid; just believe, and she
will be healed."
51When he arrived at the house of
Jairus, he did not let anyone go in with
him except Peter, John and James,[f]
and the child's father and mother.
52Meanwhile, all the people were wailing and mourning[g] for her. "Stop wailing," Jesus said. "She is not dead but
asleep."[h]
53They laughed at him, knowing
that she was dead. 54But he took her
by the hand and said, "My child, get
up!"[i] 55Her spirit returned, and at
once she stood up. Then Jesus told
them to give her something to eat.
56Her parents were astonished, but he
ordered them not to tell anyone what
had happened.[j]

Jesus Sends Out the Twelve

9:3–5pp — Mt 10:9–15; Mk 6:8–11
9:7–9pp — Mt 14:1,2; Mk 6:14–16

9 When Jesus had called the Twelve
together, he gave them power and
authority to drive out all demons[k] and
to cure diseases,[l] 2and he sent them
out to preach the kingdom of God[m]
and to heal the sick. 3He told them:
"Take nothing for the journey—no
staff, no bag, no bread, no money, no
extra tunic.[n] 4Whatever house you enter, stay there until you leave that
town. 5If people do not welcome you,
shake the dust off your feet when you
leave their town, as a testimony
against them."[o] 6So they set out and
went from village to village, preaching
the gospel and healing people everywhere.

8:51 [f]S Mt 4:21
8:52 [g]Lk 23:27 [h]S Mt 9:24
8:54 [i]S Lk 7:14
8:56 [j]S Mt 8:4
9:1 [k]S Mt 10:1 [l]S Mt 4:23; Lk 5:17
9:2 [m]S Mt 3:2
9:3 [n]Lk 10:4; 22:35
9:5 [o]S Mt 10:14

7Now Herod[p] the tetrarch heard
about all that was going on. And he
was perplexed, because some were
saying that John[q] had been raised
from the dead,[r] 8others that Elijah
had appeared,[s] and still others that
one of the prophets of long ago had
come back to life.[t] 9But Herod said, "I
beheaded John. Who, then, is this I
hear such things about?" And he tried
to see him.[u]

Jesus Feeds the Five Thousand

9:10–17pp — Mt 14:13–21; Mk 6:32–44; Jn 6:5–13
9:13–17Ref — 2Ki 4:42–44

10When the apostles[v] returned,
they reported to Jesus what they had
done. Then he took them with him and
they withdrew by themselves to a town
called Bethsaida,[w] 11but the crowds
learned about it and followed him. He
welcomed them and spoke to them
about the kingdom of God,[x] and
healed those who needed healing.
12Late in the afternoon the Twelve
came to him and said, "Send the crowd
away so they can go to the surrounding
villages and countryside and find food
and lodging, because we are in a remote place here."
13He replied, "You give them something to eat."
They answered, "We have only five
loaves of bread and two fish—unless
we go and buy food for all this crowd."
14(About five thousand men were
there.)
But he said to his disciples, "Have
them sit down in groups of about fifty
each." 15The disciples did so, and everybody sat down. 16Taking the five
loaves and the two fish and looking up
to heaven, he gave thanks and broke

9:7 [p]S Mt 14:1 [q]S Mt 3:1 [r]ver 19
9:8 [s]S Mt 11:14 [t]ver 19; Jn 1:21
9:9 [u]Lk 23:8
9:10 [v]S Mk 6:30 [w]S Mt 11:21
9:11 [x]ver 2; S Mt 3:2

8:50 DON'T BE AFRAID; JUST BELIEVE. See Mk 5:36, note.

9:1 AUTHORITY TO DRIVE OUT ALL DEMONS. See Mt 10:1, note.

9:2 PREACH THE KINGDOM . . . HEAL THE SICK. (1) This is the first time Jesus sent out the twelve disciples to represent him by word and deed. The instruction given to the twelve, according to the parallel passage in Matthew, was to go to "the lost sheep of Israel" (Mt 10:6). After his resurrection, however, Jesus changed the scope to encompass all nations, in a commission that is to continue "to the very end of the age" (Mt 28:18–20; Mk 16:15–20).

(2) The Gospel writers make it clear that Jesus' command to preach the kingdom of God (see article on THE KINGDOM OF GOD, p. 1430) was seldom given apart from the command to heal the sick and to drive out demons (Mt 9:35–38; 10:7–8; Mk 3:14–15; 6:7–13; 16:15,17; Lk 9:2,6; 10:1,9; cf. 4:17–19). God intends that the presentation of the gospel today be accompanied by the same demonstration of the Spirit and of power (Mt 10:1, note; Mk 16:15–18; Ac 1:8; Ro 15:18–19; 1Co 2:4–5; 4:20; see article on SIGNS OF BELIEVERS, p. 1513) in order to meet Satan's challenge in these last days (1Ti 4:1; 2Ti 3:1–5).

(3) Churches today should not compare themselves with other churches, but with this NT message and pattern. Are we seeing and experiencing the kingdom of God as did the early Christians? Is the kingdom of God near us? If not, why not?

9:12–17 FEEDING OF THE FIVE THOUSAND. See Mt 14:19, note.

them.[y] Then he gave them to the disciples to set before the people. 17They
all ate and were satisfied, and the
disciples picked up twelve basketfuls of broken pieces that were left
over.

Peter's Confession of Christ

9:18–20pp — Mt 16:13–16; Mk 8:27–29
9:22–27pp — Mt 16:21–28; Mk 8:31–9:1

18Once when Jesus was praying[z] in
private and his disciples were with
him, he asked them, "Who do the
crowds say I am?"

19They replied, "Some say John the
Baptist;[a] others say Elijah; and still
others, that one of the prophets of long
ago has come back to life."[b]

20"But what about you?" he asked.
"Who do you say I am?"

Peter answered, "The Christ[j] of
God."[c]

21Jesus strictly warned them not to
tell this to anyone.[d] 22And he said,
"The Son of Man[e] must suffer many
things[f] and be rejected by the elders,
chief priests and teachers of the law,[g]
and he must be killed[h] and on the
third day[i] be raised to life."[j]

23Then he said to them all: "If anyone would come after me, he must deny
himself and take up his cross daily and
follow me.[k] 24For whoever wants to
save his life will lose it, but whoever
loses his life for me will save it.[l]
25What good is it for a man to gain the
whole world, and yet lose or forfeit his
very self? 26If anyone is ashamed of me
and my words, the Son of Man will be
ashamed of him[m] when he comes in
his glory and in the glory of the Father
and of the holy angels.[n] 27I tell you
the truth, some who are standing here
will not taste death before they see the
kingdom of God."

The Transfiguration

9:28–36pp — Mt 17:1–8; Mk 9:2–8

28About eight days after Jesus said
this, he took Peter, John and James[o]
with him and went up onto a mountain
to pray.[p] 29As he was praying, the appearance of his face changed, and his
clothes became as bright as a flash of
lightning. 30Two men, Moses and Elijah, 31appeared in glorious splendor,
talking with Jesus. They spoke about
his departure,[q] which he was about to
bring to fulfillment at Jerusalem. 32Pe-
ter and his companions were very
sleepy,[r] but when they became fully
awake, they saw his glory and the two
men standing with him. 33As the men
were leaving Jesus, Peter said to him,
"Master,[s] it is good for us to be here.
Let us put up three shelters — one for
you, one for Moses and one for Elijah."
(He did not know what he was saying.)

34While he was speaking, a cloud
appeared and enveloped them, and
they were afraid as they entered the
cloud. 35A voice came from the cloud,
saying, "This is my Son, whom I have
chosen;[t] listen to him."[u] 36When the
voice had spoken, they found that
Jesus was alone. The disciples kept
this to themselves, and told no one at
that time what they had seen.[v]

9:16 [y] S Mt 14:19
9:18 [z] S Lk 3:21
9:19 [a] S Mt 3:1 [b] ver 7,8
9:20 [c] Jn 1:49; 6:66-69; 11:27
9:21 [d] S Mk 8:30
9:22 [e] S Mt 8:20 [f] S Mt 16:21 [g] Mt 27:1,2 [h] Ac 2:23; 3:13 [i] S Mt 16:21 [j] S Mt 16:21
9:23 [k] Mt 10:38; Lk 14:27
9:24 [l] S Jn 12:25
9:26 [m] Mt 10:33; Lk 12:9; 2Ti 2:12 [n] S Mt 16:27
9:28 [o] S Mt 4:21 [p] S Lk 3:21
9:31 [q] 2Pe 1:15
9:32 [r] Mt 26:43
9:33 [s] S Lk 5:5
9:35 [t] Isa 42:1 [u] S Mt 3:17
9:36 [v] Mt 17:9

[j] 20 Or *Messiah*

9:23 TAKE UP HIS CROSS DAILY. Accepting Jesus as Lord and Savior demands not only believing the truth of the gospel, but also committing ourselves to sacrificially follow him (see Mk 8:34, note). The choice between denying ourselves or living for our own selfish desires must be made daily. That choice will determine our eternal destiny.

9:24 WHOEVER LOSES HIS LIFE. Making the achievement of happiness and pleasure our goal in life instead of living in God's will and by his principles will end in disappointment and loss. To renounce our own ways and live in fellowship with Jesus, basing our lives on the teachings of his Word, is to find true life and joy, here and hereafter.

9:26 ASHAMED OF ME. To be ashamed of Jesus means to feel shame or embarrassment before the world when we identify with the ways, values and goals that Jesus taught. It is to be ashamed of his Word, ashamed to claim its full divine inspiration, ashamed to live by it and defend it. Such people Christ will reject and condemn (Mt 10:33; Mk 8:34, note; Ro 1:16; 2Ti 1:8,12,16; Rev 3:14–16).

9:27 SEE THE KINGDOM OF GOD. See Mt 16:28, note.

9:29 THE TRANSFIGURATION. In his transfiguration, Jesus was transformed in the presence of three disciples, and they saw his heavenly glory as he really was — God in human flesh. The experience of the transfiguration was: (1) an encouragement to Jesus as he faced death on the cross (cf. Mt 16:21); (2) an announcement to the disciples that Jesus had to suffer on the cross (v. 31); (3) an endorsement by God that Jesus was his true Son qualified to redeem the human race (v. 35).

The Healing of a Boy With an Evil Spirit

9:37–42,43–45pp — Mt 17:14–18, 22,23; Mk 9:14–27, 30–32

37 The next day, when they came down from the mountain, a large crowd met him. **38** A man in the crowd called out, "Teacher, I beg you to look at my son, for he is my only child. **39** A spirit seizes him and he suddenly screams; it throws him into convulsions so that he foams at the mouth. It scarcely ever leaves him and is destroying him. **40** I begged your disciples to drive it out, but they could not."

41 "O unbelieving and perverse generation,"[w] Jesus replied, "how long shall I stay with you and put up with you? Bring your son here."

42 Even while the boy was coming, the demon threw him to the ground in a convulsion. But Jesus rebuked the evil[k] spirit, healed the boy and gave him back to his father. **43** And they were all amazed at the greatness of God.

While everyone was marveling at all that Jesus did, he said to his disciples, **44** "Listen carefully to what I am about to tell you: The Son of Man is going to be betrayed into the hands of men."[x] **45** But they did not understand what this meant. It was hidden from them, so that they did not grasp it,[y] and they were afraid to ask him about it.

Who Will Be the Greatest?

9:46–48pp — Mt 18:1–5
9:46–50pp — Mk 9:33–40

46 An argument started among the disciples as to which of them would be the greatest.[z] **47** Jesus, knowing their thoughts,[a] took a little child and had him stand beside him. **48** Then he said to them, "Whoever welcomes this little child in my name welcomes me; and whoever welcomes me welcomes the one who sent me.[b] For he who is least among you all—he is the greatest."[c]

49 "Master,"[d] said John, "we saw a man driving out demons in your name and we tried to stop him, because he is not one of us."

50 "Do not stop him," Jesus said, "for whoever is not against you is for you."[e]

Samaritan Opposition

51 As the time approached for him to be taken up to heaven,[f] Jesus resolutely set out for Jerusalem.[g] **52** And he sent messengers on ahead, who went into a Samaritan[h] village to get things ready for him; **53** but the people there did not welcome him, because he was heading for Jerusalem. **54** When the disciples James and John[i] saw this, they asked, "Lord, do you want us to call fire down from heaven to destroy them[l]?"[j] **55** But Jesus turned and rebuked them, **56** and[m] they went to another village.

The Cost of Following Jesus

9:57–60pp — Mt 8:19–22

57 As they were walking along the road,[k] a man said to him, "I will follow you wherever you go."

58 Jesus replied, "Foxes have holes and birds of the air have nests, but the Son of Man[l] has no place to lay his head."

59 He said to another man, "Follow me."[m]

But the man replied, "Lord, first let me go and bury my father."

60 Jesus said to him, "Let the dead bury their own dead, but you go and proclaim the kingdom of God."[n]

61 Still another said, "I will follow you, Lord; but first let me go back and say good-by to my family."[o]

62 Jesus replied, "No one who puts his hand to the plow and looks back is fit for service in the kingdom of God."

Jesus Sends Out the Seventy-two

10:4–12pp — Lk 9:3–5
10:13–15,21,22pp — Mt 11:21–23,25–27
10:23,24pp — Mt 13:16,17

10 After this the Lord[p] appointed seventy-two[n] others[q] and

9:41 [w] Dt 32:5
9:44 [x] S ver 22
9:45 [y] S Mk 9:32
9:46 [z] Lk 22:24
9:47 [a] S Mt 9:4
9:48 [b] S Mt 10:40 [c] S Mk 9:35
9:49 [d] S Lk 5:5
9:50 [e] Mt 12:30; Lk 11:23
9:51 [f] S Mk 16:19 [g] Lk 13:22; 17:11; 18:31; 19:28
9:52 [h] S Mt 10:5
9:54 [i] S Mt 4:21 [j] 2Ki 1:10,12
9:57 [k] ver 51
9:58 [l] S Mt 8:20
9:59 [m] S Mt 4:19
9:60 [n] S Mt 3:2
9:61 [o] 1Ki 19:20
10:1 [p] S Lk 7:13 [q] Lk 9:1,2,51,52

[k] 42 Greek *unclean* [l] 54 Some manuscripts *them, even as Elijah did* [m] 55,56 Some manuscripts *them. And he said, "You do not know what kind of spirit you are of, for the Son of Man did not come to destroy men's lives, but to save them."* 56*And* [n] 1 Some manuscripts *seventy;* also in verse 17

9:41 UNBELIEVING . . . GENERATION. See Mt 17:17, note.

9:55 REBUKED THEM. We must be careful that our loyalty to and zeal for Christ do not conceal a spirit of revenge or violence against the unsaved who live in darkness and sin.

10:1 SENT THEM TWO BY TWO. The principle of sending out workers two by two is very important in the work of the Lord, for it provides each one with double faith and wisdom; in addition, a

sent them two by two[r] ahead of him to every town and place where he was about to go.[s] **2**He told them, "The harvest is plentiful, but the workers are few. Ask the Lord of the harvest, therefore, to send out workers into his harvest field.[t] **3**Go! I am sending you out like lambs among wolves.[u] **4**Do not take a purse or bag or sandals; and do not greet anyone on the road.

5"When you enter a house, first say, 'Peace to this house.' **6**If a man of peace is there, your peace will rest on him; if not, it will return to you. **7**Stay in that house, eating and drinking whatever they give you, for the worker deserves his wages.[v] Do not move around from house to house.

8"When you enter a town and are welcomed, eat what is set before you.[w] **9**Heal the sick who are there and tell them, 'The kingdom of God[x] is near you.' **10**But when you enter a town and are not welcomed, go into its streets and say, **11**'Even the dust of your town that sticks to our feet we wipe off against you.[y] Yet be sure of this: The kingdom of God is near.'[z] **12**I tell you, it will be more bearable on that day for Sodom[a] than for that town.[b]

Lk 13:10-17

13"Woe to you,[c] Korazin! Woe to you, Bethsaida! For if the miracles that were performed in you had been performed in Tyre and Sidon, they would have repented long ago, sitting in sackcloth[d] and ashes. **14**But it will be more bearable for Tyre and Sidon at the judgment than for you. **15**And you, Capernaum,[e] will you be lifted up to the skies? No, you will go down to the depths.[o]

16"He who listens to you listens to me; he who rejects you rejects me; but he who rejects me rejects him who sent me."[f]

17The seventy-two[g] returned with joy and said, "Lord, even the demons submit to us in your name."[h]

18He replied, "I saw Satan[i] fall like lightning from heaven.[j] **19**I have given you authority to trample on snakes[k] and scorpions and to overcome all the power of the enemy; nothing will harm you. **20**However, do not rejoice that the spirits submit to you, but rejoice that your names are written in heaven."[l]

21At that time Jesus, full of joy through the Holy Spirit, said, "I praise you, Father, Lord of heaven and earth, because you have hidden these things from the wise and learned, and revealed them to little children.[m] Yes, Father, for this was your good pleasure.

22"All things have been committed to me by my Father.[n] No one knows who the Son is except the Father, and no one knows who the Father is except the Son and those to whom the Son chooses to reveal him."[o]

23Then he turned to his disciples and said privately, "Blessed are the eyes that see what you see. **24**For I tell you that many prophets and kings wanted to see what you see but did not see it, and to hear what you hear but did not hear it."[p]

10:1 [r]Mk 6:7 [s]Mt 10:1
10:2 [t]Mt 9:37,38; Jn 4:35
10:3 [u]Mt 10:16
10:7 [v]S 1Ti 5:18
10:8 [w]1Co 10:27
10:9 [x]S Mt 3:2
10:11 [y]S Mt 10:14 [z]ver 9
10:12 [a]S Mt 10:15 [b]Mt 11:24
10:13 [c]Lk 6:24-26 [d]S Rev 11:3
10:15 [e]S Mt 4:13
10:16 [f]S Mt 10:40
10:17 [g]ver 1 [h]S Mk 16:17
10:18 [i]S Mt 4:10 [j]Isa 14:12; Rev 9:1; 12:8,9
10:19 [k]Mk 16:18; Ac 28:3-5
10:20 [l]S Rev 20:12
10:21 [m]1Co 1:26-29
10:22 [n]S Mt 28:18 [o]Jn 1:18
10:24 [p]1Pe 1:10-12

[o]15 Greek *Hades*

companion helps bolster courage. Other passages dealing with the two by two principle are: Ecc 4:9–12; Mt 18:16; Mk 6:7; 14:13; Lk 7:19; Jn 1:35–41; 8:17; Ac 9:38; 10:7; 15:36–41; 19:22; 2Co 13:1; 1Ti 5:19; Heb 10:28; Rev 11:3–6, 10–12.

10:2 THE HARVEST IS PLENTIFUL. See Mt 9:37, note.

10:3 LAMBS AMONG WOLVES. Believers who faithfully follow the will of God will be threatened by many dangers. They will be like defenseless lambs among wolves. Knowing this, we must pray for God's presence, protection and provision.

10:9 HEAL THE SICK . . . THE KINGDOM OF GOD. Jesus once again emphasizes that the "kingdom of God" is associated with healing the sick. For more on this, see 9:2, note.

10:19 SNAKES AND SCORPIONS. "Snakes and scorpions" are terms representing the most dangerous forces of spiritual evil. Christians have power over evil spirits because Christ has given us his authority over Satan (see article on POWER OVER SATAN AND DEMONS, p. 1484).

10:20 DO NOT REJOICE. Christ warns the disciples that they must not make power over demons or success in ministry a fundamental source of their joy. Their rejoicing must come from the fact that they are redeemed from sin and destined for heaven (see Mt 7:22–23, notes).

10:21 THE WISE . . . LITTLE CHILDREN. Jesus rejoices that his heavenly Father has given the understanding of spiritual truths not to those who are intellectually wise in their own eyes, but to those who accept in childlike humility the truth revealed in his Word. Those who believe themselves wise enough to question the teachings of Scripture by their own "superior" knowledge, and use that as a basis for accepting or rejecting God's Word, are excluded from the fellowship and knowledge of the Son (v. 22).

The Parable of the Good Samaritan

10:25–28pp — Mt 22:34–40; Mk 12:28–31

25On one occasion an expert in the law stood up to test Jesus. "Teacher," he asked, "what must I do to inherit eternal life?"[q]
26"What is written in the Law?" he replied. "How do you read it?"
27He answered: " 'Love the Lord your God with all your heart and with all your soul and with all your strength and with all your mind'[p];[r] and, 'Love your neighbor as yourself.'[q]"[s]
28"You have answered correctly," Jesus replied. "Do this and you will live."[t]
29But he wanted to justify himself,[u] so he asked Jesus, "And who is my neighbor?"
30In reply Jesus said: "A man was going down from Jerusalem to Jericho, when he fell into the hands of robbers. They stripped him of his clothes, beat him and went away, leaving him half dead.
31A priest happened to be going down the same road, and when he saw the man, he passed by on the other side.[v]
32So too, a Levite, when he came to the place and saw him, passed by on the other side.
33But a Samaritan,[w] as he traveled, came where the man was; and when he saw him, he took pity on him.
34He went to him and bandaged his wounds, pouring on oil and wine. Then he put the man on his own donkey, took him to an inn and took care of him.
35The next day he took out two silver coins[r] and gave them to the innkeeper. 'Look after him,' he said, 'and when I return, I will reimburse you for any extra expense you may have.'
36"Which of these three do you think was a neighbor to the man who fell into the hands of robbers?"
37The expert in the law replied, "The one who had mercy on him."
Jesus told him, "Go and do likewise."

10:25 [q]Mt 19:16; Lk 18:18
10:27 [r]Dt 6:5 [s]Lev 19:18; S Mt 5:43
10:28 [t]S Ro 7:10
10:29 [u]Lk 16:15
10:31 [v]Lev 21:1-3
10:33 [w]S Mt 10:5

At the Home of Martha and Mary

Lk 12:42-48

38As Jesus and his disciples were on their way, he came to a village where a woman named Martha[x] opened her home to him.
39She had a sister called Mary,[y] who sat at the Lord's feet[z] listening to what he said.
40But Martha was distracted by all the preparations that had to be made. She came to him and asked, "Lord, don't you care[a] that my sister has left me to do the work by myself? Tell her to help me!"
41"Martha, Martha," the Lord answered, "you are worried[b] and upset about many things,
42but only one thing is needed.[s][c] Mary has chosen what is better, and it will not be taken away from her."

Jesus' Teaching on Prayer

11:2–4pp — Mt 6:9–13
11:9–13pp — Mt 7:7–11

11 One day Jesus was praying[d] in a certain place. When he finished, one of his disciples said to him, "Lord,[e] teach us to pray, just as John taught his disciples."
2He said to them, "When you pray, say:

" 'Father,[t]
hallowed be your name,
your kingdom[f] come.[u]
3Give us each day our daily bread.

10:38 [x]Jn 11:1; 12:2
10:39 [y]Jn 11:1; 12:3 [z]Lk 8:35
10:40 [a]Mk 4:38
10:41 [b]Mt 6:25-34; Lk 12:11,22
10:42 [c]Ps 27:4
11:1 [d]S Lk 3:21 [e]S Jn 13:13
11:2 [f]S Mt 3:2

[p]27 Deut. 6:5 [q]27 Lev. 19:18 [r]35 Greek *two denarii* [s]42 Some manuscripts *but few things are needed—or only one* [t]2 Some manuscripts *Our Father in heaven* [u]2 Some manuscripts *come. May your will be done on earth as it is in heaven.*

10:27 LOVE THE LORD . . . AND LOVE YOUR NEIGHBOR. See Mt 22:37,39, notes.

10:30 THE PARABLE OF THE GOOD SAMARITAN. This parable emphasizes that inherent in true saving faith and obedience is compassion for those in need. The call to love God is a call to love others. (1) The new life and grace that Christ gives to those who accept him will produce love, mercy and compassion for those who are distressed and afflicted. It is the responsibility of all believers to act on the Holy Spirit's love within them and not to harden their hearts. (2) Those who are professed Christians, yet whose hearts are insensitive to the suffering and needs of others, give sure evidence that they do not have eternal life in them (vv. 25–28,31–37; cf. Mt 25:41–46; 1Jn 3:16–20).

10:42 ONE THING IS NEEDED. Although active, practical service to God is essential and good, our first and most important task is a love and devotion that expresses itself in quiet worship, prayer and fellowship with the Lord (see Mt 26:13, note). Are we so busy doing the work of the Lord, attending church services and performing good deeds that we forget spiritual communion with our Savior?

11:2–4 THE LORD'S PRAYER. See Mt 6:9–15, notes on the Lord's Prayer.

11:3 OUR DAILY BREAD. Believers should learn to pray for life's necessary provisions (cf. Mt

4 Forgive us our sins,
for we also forgive everyone who
sins against us.[v][g]
And lead us not into
temptation.[w]'"[h]

5 Then he said to them, "Suppose one
of you has a friend, and he goes to him
at midnight and says, 'Friend, lend me
three loaves of bread, 6 because a
friend of mine on a journey has come
to me, and I have nothing to set before
him.'
7 "Then the one inside answers,
'Don't bother me. The door is already
locked, and my children are with me in
bed. I can't get up and give you anything.' 8 I tell you, though he will not
get up and give him the bread because he is his friend, yet because
of the man's boldness[x] he will get
up and give him as much as he
needs.[i]
9 "So I say to you: Ask and it will be
given to you;[j] seek and you will find;
knock and the door will be opened to
you. 10 For everyone who asks receives; he who seeks finds; and to
him who knocks, the door will be
opened.
11 "Which of you fathers, if your son
asks for[y] a fish, will give him a snake
instead? 12 Or if he asks for an egg, will
give him a scorpion? 13 If you then,
though you are evil, know how to give
good gifts to your children, how much
more will your Father in heaven
give the Holy Spirit to those who ask
him!"

11:4 [g] Mt 18:35; Mk 11:25 [h] Mt 26:41; Jas 1:13
11:8 [i] Lk 18:1-6
11:9 [j] S Mt 7:7

Jesus and Beelzebub

11:14,15, 17–22, 24–26pp — Mt 12:22,24–29, 43–45
11:17–22pp — Mk 3:23–27

14 Jesus was driving out a demon
that was mute. When the demon left,
the man who had been mute spoke, and
the crowd was amazed.[k] 15 But some
of them said, "By Beelzebub,[z][l] the
prince of demons, he is driving out demons."[m] 16 Others tested him by asking for a sign from heaven.[n]
17 Jesus knew their thoughts[o] and
said to them: "Any kingdom divided
against itself will be ruined, and a
house divided against itself will fall.
18 If Satan[p] is divided against himself,
how can his kingdom stand? I say this
because you claim that I drive out demons by Beelzebub. 19 Now if I drive
out demons by Beelzebub, by whom do
your followers drive them out? So then,
they will be your judges. 20 But if I drive
out demons by the finger of God,[q]
then the kingdom of God[r] has come to
you.
21 "When a strong man, fully armed,
guards his own house, his possessions
are safe. 22 But when someone stronger
attacks and overpowers him, he takes
away the armor in which the man trusted and divides up the spoils.
23 "He who is not with me is against

11:14 [k] Mt 9:32, 33
11:15 [l] S Mk 3:22 [m] Mt 9:34
11:16 [n] S Mt 12:38
11:17 [o] S Mt 9:4
11:18 [p] S Mt 4:10
11:20 [q] Ex 8:19 [r] S Mt 3:2

[v] *4* Greek *everyone who is indebted to us*
[w] *4* Some manuscripts *temptation but deliver us from the evil one*
[x] *8* Or *persistence*
[y] *11* Some manuscripts *for bread, will give him a stone; or if he asks for*
[z] *15* Greek *Beezeboul* or *Beelzeboul*; also in verses 18 and 19

6:11) based on four principles. (1) We must pray such petitions according to God's will and his glory (Mt 6:10,33; 1Co 10:31; 1Jn 5:14–15). (2) We must want God to demonstrate his fatherly love for us (Mt 6:9,25–34). (3) The provisions we pray for must supply our basic needs and give us the ability to perform Christian service (2Co 9:8; 1Ti 6:8; Heb 13:5). (4) We may ask for things only after we have faithfully given to God and to others (2Co 9:6; see 8:2, note).

11:9 ASK . . . SEEK . . . KNOCK. See Mt 7:7, note.

11:11 GIVE HIM A SNAKE. See Mt 7:11, note on God's care for his children.

11:13 GIVE THE HOLY SPIRIT TO THOSE WHO ASK. This verse probably does not refer to the impartation of the Spirit at the new birth (Jn 3:3), since at conversion all believers are automatically given the indwelling presence of the Holy Spirit (Ro 8:9–10; 1Co 6:19–20; see article on THE REGENERATION OF THE DISCIPLES, p. 1627). Rather, the verse most likely refers to the baptism in the Holy Spirit that Christ promised to his followers (see article on JESUS AND THE HOLY SPIRIT, p. 1546).

11:20 DEMONS . . . THE KINGDOM OF GOD. This passage reveals three things: (1) The success of God's kingdom on earth is in direct proportion to the destruction of the devil's work and the deliverance of sinners from bondage to sin and the demonic; (2) Satan will resist the coming of Christ's kingdom on earth (vv. 24–26; cf. Mt 13:18–30; Rev 12:12); (3) Jesus demonstrates divine power and authority in driving out demons, overpowering Satan and plundering his possessions (vv. 20–22). For more on this, see articles on THE KINGDOM OF GOD, p. 1430, and POWER OVER SATAN AND DEMONS, p. 1484.

11:23 WHO IS NOT WITH ME IS AGAINST ME. It is impossible to remain neutral in the spiritual conflict between Christ's kingdom and the power of evil. (1) Those who do not, along with

me, and he who does not gather with
me, scatters.[s]
24"When an evil[a] spirit comes out
of a man, it goes through arid places
seeking rest and does not find it. Then
it says, 'I will return to the house I
left.' 25When it arrives, it finds the
house swept clean and put in order.
26Then it goes and takes seven other
spirits more wicked than itself, and
they go in and live there. And the final
condition of that man is worse than the
first."[t]

27As Jesus was saying these things,
a woman in the crowd called out,
"Blessed is the mother who gave you
birth and nursed you."[u]
28He replied, "Blessed rather are
those who hear the word of God[v] and
obey it."[w]

The Sign of Jonah

11:29–32pp — Mt 12:39–42

29As the crowds increased, Jesus
said, "This is a wicked generation. It
asks for a miraculous sign,[x] but none
will be given it except the sign of Jonah.[y] 30For as Jonah was a sign to the
Ninevites, so also will the Son of Man
be to this generation. 31The Queen of
the South will rise at the judgment
with the men of this generation and
condemn them; for she came from the
ends of the earth to listen to Solomon's
wisdom,[z] and now one[b] greater than

11:23 [s]Mt 12:30; Mk 9:40; Lk 9:50
11:26 [t]2Pe 2:20
11:27 [u]Lk 23:29
11:28 [v]S Heb 4:12 [w]Pr 8:32; Lk 6:47; 8:21; Jn 14:21
11:29 [x]ver 16; S Mt 12:38 [y]Jnh 1:17; Mt 16:4
11:31 [z]1Ki 10:1; 2Ch 9:1
11:32 [a]Jnh 3:5
11:33 [b]S Mt 5:15
11:37 [c]Lk 7:36; 14:1
11:38 [d]Mk 7:3,4
11:39 [e]S Lk 7:13

Solomon is here. 32The men of Nineveh
will stand up at the judgment with this
generation and condemn it; for they repented at the preaching of Jonah,[a] and
now one greater than Jonah is here.

The Lamp of the Body

11:34,35pp — Mt 6:22,23

33"No one lights a lamp and puts it
in a place where it will be hidden, or
under a bowl. Instead he puts it on its
stand, so that those who come in may
see the light.[b] 34Your eye is the lamp
of your body. When your eyes are good,
your whole body also is full of light.
But when they are bad, your body also
is full of darkness. 35See to it, then,
that the light within you is not darkness. 36Therefore, if your whole body
is full of light, and no part of it dark,
it will be completely lighted, as when
the light of a lamp shines on you."

Six Woes

37When Jesus had finished speaking, a Pharisee invited him to eat with
him; so he went in and reclined at the
table.[c] 38But the Pharisee, noticing
that Jesus did not first wash before the
meal,[d] was surprised.
39Then the Lord[e] said to him, "Now
then, you Pharisees clean the outside
of the cup and dish, but inside you are

[a] *24* Greek *unclean* [b] *31* Or *something*; also in verse 32

Christ, oppose Satan and evil have in reality set themselves against Jesus Christ. Every person is fighting either on the side of Christ and righteousness, or on the side of Satan and the ungodly. (2) Jesus' words condemn any attempted neutrality or compromise with unrighteousness, or any partial obedience.

11:26 SEVEN OTHER SPIRITS ... LIVE THERE. The point of this passage is made clear in its parallel in Mt 12:43–45 (see note), which speaks of the house left unoccupied. (1) In conversion and salvation (Jn 3:3) believers must not only be delivered from sin, but also commit themselves to radical obedience, prayer, righteousness, the Word and being filled with the Holy Spirit (see Ac 2:4; Ro 8). (2) After conversion, Satan's power does not end but continues as a never-ceasing menace (22:31; see Mt 6:13, note). There is safety from sin and Satan only by full commitment to Christ and by using all the means of grace available through Christ (see Eph 6:11, note). (3) Believers who have been delivered from the demonic but have still not completely renounced sin or opened their lives to the Spirit of God are inviting the evil spirits to come back with renewed power to live in those persons.

11:34 YOUR EYE IS THE LAMP OF YOUR BODY. The eye is the body's means of receiving light. If the eye is healthy, then one can fully receive and use light. If the eye is defective, then darkness prevails and one cannot see in order to walk or work. (1) Likewise, when people's spiritual eyes, i.e., when their attitudes, motives and desires are directed toward God's will, then the light of his Word enters their hearts to produce blessings, fruit and salvation (Gal 5:22–23). But if their desires are not focused on the things of God, then God's revelation and truth will have no effect.

(2) We must examine our lives to make sure that our spiritual eyes are such that the gospel can really sanctify us and renew our inward lives. Do we respond to the teaching or reading of Scripture with a spirit that loves God, Christ and the Word more and more — or, in spite of all the gospel messages and Bible teaching we have received, is there deadness in our souls and are we in bondage to sin? If the latter is the case, then our spiritual eyes are still evil and our bodies full of darkness. We must then confess our sins, repent and separate ourselves from all compromise that leads to darkness.

JESUS AND THE HOLY SPIRIT

***Lk 11:13** "If you then, though you are evil, know how to give good gifts to your children, how much more will your Father in heaven give the Holy Spirit to those who ask him?"*

Jesus had a special relationship with the Holy Spirit, a relationship that is important for our own personal lives. This article explores that relationship and its practical implications.

OLD TESTAMENT PROPHECY. In the OT prophecies about the coming Messiah, several predicted specifically that he would be empowered by the Holy Spirit (see Isa 11:2, note; 61:1–3, note). When Jesus read from Isa 61:1–2 in the synagogue at Nazareth, he stated "Today this scripture is fulfilled in your hearing" (Lk 4:18–21).

JESUS' BIRTH. Both Matthew and Luke state explicitly and unmistakably that Jesus came into this world as a result of a miraculous deed of God. He was conceived by the Holy Spirit and born of the virgin Mary (Mt 1:18,23; Lk 1:27). Because of the miraculous conception, Jesus was "holy" (Lk 1:35), that is, free from all taint of sin. This made him worthy to take the guilt of our sin on himself and to make atonement (see Mt 1:23, note). Without a perfect, sinless Savior, we could not experience redemption.

JESUS' BAPTISM. When he was baptized by John the Baptist, Jesus, who would later baptize his disciples in the Spirit at Pentecost and throughout the church age (see Lk 3:16; Ac 1:4–5; 2:33,38–39), was himself personally anointed by the Spirit (Mt 3:16–17; Lk 3:21–22). The Spirit came upon him in the form of a dove, equipping him with great power to perform his ministry, including his work of redemption. When our Lord departed into the desert after his water baptism, he was "full of the Holy Spirit" (Lk 4:1). Just as with our Lord, all who have experienced a supernatural rebirth by the Holy Spirit ought to experience the baptism in the Spirit to give them power in their lives and for their ministry (see Ac 1:8, notes).

JESUS' TEMPTATION BY SATAN. Immediately after his baptism, Jesus was led by the Spirit into the desert, where he was tempted by the devil for forty days (Lk 4:1–2). It was only because he was full of the Holy Spirit that he was able to face Satan squarely and resist the temptations that came his way. Likewise, it is God's intention that we never face the spiritual forces of evil and sin without the power of the Spirit. We must be equipped with his fullness and follow his leading in order to be victorious against Satan. In God's sight we are not "normal" children of his unless we are filled with the Spirit and live by his power.

JESUS' MINISTRY. In Jesus' reference to the fulfillment of Isaiah's prophecy about the Spirit coming on him, he used the same passage to outline the nature of his ministry as a preaching, healing and liberating one (Isa 61:1–2; Lk 4:16–19). (1) The Spirit anointed Jesus and empowered him for his mission. Jesus was God (Jn 1:1), but he was also human (1Ti 2:5). As a human being he had to rely on the Spirit's help and power to fulfill his responsibilities before God (cf. Mt 12:28; Lk 4:1,14; Ro 8:11; Heb 9:14). (2) It was only as a Spirit-anointed man that Jesus could live, serve and proclaim the gospel (Ac 10:38). In this he is a perfect example for the Christian; each believer should receive the fullness of the Holy Spirit (see Ac 1:8, notes; 2:4, notes).

JESUS' PROMISE REGARDING THE HOLY SPIRIT. John the Baptist had prophesied that Jesus would baptize his followers in the Holy Spirit (Mt 3:11; Mk 1:8; Lk 3:16, see note; Jn 1:33), a prophecy that Jesus himself reiterated (Ac 1:5; 11:16). In Lk 11:13, Jesus promised to give the Holy Spirit to *all* who asked (see note on that verse). All of these verses refer to the fullness of the Spirit that Christ promises to give to those who are already children of the heavenly Father—a promise that was first fulfilled at Pentecost (see Ac 2:4, note), and remains a promise for all who have become his disciples and ask for the baptism in the Spirit (see Ac 1:5; 2:39, note).

JESUS' RESURRECTION. Through the power of the Holy Spirit, Jesus was raised from the grave and thereby vindicated as the true Messiah and Son of God. In Ro 1:3–4 we read that through the Spirit of holiness (i.e., the Holy Spirit) Jesus "was declared with power to be the Son of God," and in Ro 8:11, that "the Spirit . . . raised Jesus from the dead." As Jesus depended on the Holy Spirit for his resurrection, so believers depend on the Spirit for spiritual life now and bodily resurrection in the future (Ro 8:10–11).

JESUS' ASCENSION INTO HEAVEN. After Jesus' resurrection he ascended into heaven and sat down at the right hand of his Father as co-ruler of God's kingdom (Mk 16:19; Lk 24:51; Ac 1:9–11; Eph 4:8–10). In this exalted position he received the Holy Spirit from his Father and poured out the Spirit on his people at Pentecost (Ac 2:33; cf. Jn 16:5–14), thereby affirming his lordship as prophet, priest and king. This outpouring of the Holy Spirit at Pentecost and throughout this present age testifies to the exalted Savior's continual presence and authority.

JESUS' NEARNESS TO HIS PEOPLE. As one of his present tasks, the Holy Spirit takes that which is Christ's and reveals it to believers (Jn 16:14–15). That is, the redemptive benefits of salvation in Christ are mediated to us through the Spirit (cf. Ro 8:14–16; Gal 4:6). Most important is Jesus' nearness to us (Jn 14:18). The Spirit makes us aware of the personal presence of Jesus, his love, blessing, help, forgiveness, healing and all that is ours through faith. Likewise, the Spirit draws our hearts to seek the Lord in love, prayer and worship (see Jn 4:23–24; 16:14, note).

JESUS' RETURN FOR HIS PEOPLE. Jesus has promised to return and take his faithful people to be with him always (see Jn 14:3, note; 1Th 4:13–18). This is the blessed hope of all believers (Tit 2:13), the event that we pray and long for (2Ti 4:8). Scripture reveals that the Holy Spirit directs our hearts to cry out to God for our Lord's return. It is the Spirit who testifies that our redemption remains incomplete until Christ returns (cf. Ro 8:23). At the very close of the Bible, the Holy Spirit inspired the words, "come, Lord Jesus" (Rev 22:20).

full of greed and wickedness.[f] 40 You
foolish people![g] Did not the one who
made the outside make the inside also?
41 But give what is inside ⌊the dish⌋[c] to
the poor,[h] and everything will be
clean for you.[i]
42 "Woe to you Pharisees, because
you give God a tenth[j] of your mint,
rue and all other kinds of garden herbs,
but you neglect justice and the love of
God.[k] You should have practiced the
latter without leaving the former undone.[l]
43 "Woe to you Pharisees, because
you love the most important seats in
the synagogues and greetings in the
marketplaces.[m]
44 "Woe to you, because you are like
unmarked graves,[n] which men walk
over without knowing it."
45 One of the experts in the law[o] answered him, "Teacher, when you say
these things, you insult us also."
46 Jesus replied, "And you experts in
the law, woe to you, because you load
people down with burdens they can
hardly carry, and you yourselves will
not lift one finger to help them.[p]
47 "Woe to you, because you build
tombs for the prophets, and it was your
forefathers who killed them. 48 So you
testify that you approve of what your
forefathers did; they killed the prophets, and you build their tombs.[q] 49 Because of this, God in his wisdom[r] said,
'I will send them prophets and apostles, some of whom they will kill and
others they will persecute.'[s] 50 Therefore this generation will be held responsible for the blood of all the prophets that has been shed since the
beginning of the world, 51 from the
blood of Abel[t] to the blood of Zechariah,[u] who was killed between the altar
and the sanctuary. Yes, I tell you, this
generation will be held responsible for
it all.[v]
52 "Woe to you experts in the law, because you have taken away the key to
knowledge. You yourselves have not
entered, and you have hindered those
who were entering."[w]
53 When Jesus left there, the Pharisees and the teachers of the law began
to oppose him fiercely and to besiege
him with questions, 54 waiting to catch
him in something he might say.[x]

Warnings and Encouragements

12:2–9pp — Mt 10:26–33

12 Meanwhile, when a crowd of
many thousands had gathered,
so that they were trampling on one another, Jesus began to speak first to his
disciples, saying: "Be on your guard
against the yeast of the Pharisees,
which is hypocrisy.[y] 2 There is nothing
concealed that will not be disclosed, or
hidden that will not be made known.[z]
3 What you have said in the dark will be
heard in the daylight, and what you
have whispered in the ear in the inner
rooms will be proclaimed from the
roofs.
4 "I tell you, my friends,[a] do not be
afraid of those who kill the body and
after that can do no more. 5 But I will
show you whom you should fear: Fear
him who, after the killing of the body,
has power to throw you into hell. Yes,
I tell you, fear him.[b] 6 Are not five
sparrows sold for two pennies[d]? Yet
not one of them is forgotten by God.
7 Indeed, the very hairs of your head
are all numbered.[c] Don't be afraid;
you are worth more than many sparrows.[d]

11:39 [f]Mt 23:25,26; Mk 7:20-23
11:40 [g]Lk 12:20; 1Co 15:36
11:41 [h]Lk 12:33 [i]S Ac 10:15
11:42 [j]Lk 18:12 [k]Dt 6:5; Mic 6:8 [l]Mt 23:23
11:43 [m]Mt 23:6,7; Lk 14:7; 20:46
11:44 [n]Mt 23:27
11:45 [o]S Mt 22:35
11:46 [p]S Mt 23:4
11:48 [q]Mt 23:29-32; Ac 7:51-53
11:49 [r]1Co 1:24,30; Col 2:3 [s]Mt 23:34
11:51 [t]Ge 4:8 [u]2Ch 24:20,21 [v]Mt 23:35,36
11:52 [w]Mt 23:13
11:54 [x]S Mt 12:10
12:1 [y]Mt 16:6,11,12
12:2 [z]S Mk 4:22
12:4 [a]Jn 15:14,15
12:5 [b]Heb 10:31
12:7 [c]S Mt 10:30 [d]Mt 12:12

[c]41 Or *what you have* [d]6 Greek *two assaria*

11:42 WOE TO YOU. See Mt 23:13, note on Christ's denunciation of the sins of the Pharisees.

12:1 HYPOCRISY. Jesus condemns the hypocrisy of the Pharisees, warning his disciples to be careful that this sin does not enter their own lives and ministry. (1) Hypocrisy means acting as if you are what you are not—for example, acting publicly as a godly and faithful believer, when in reality you harbor hidden sin, immorality, greed, lust or other unrighteousness. The hypocrite is a deceiver in the area of observable righteousness (see article on FALSE TEACHERS, p. 1506).

(2) Since hypocrisy involves living a lie, it makes one a co-worker and ally with Satan, the father of lies (Jn 8:44).

(3) Jesus warns his disciples that all hypocrisy and hidden sin will be exposed, if not in this life, certainly on the day of judgment (see Ro 2:16; 1Co 3:13; 4:5; Rev 20:12). What is done secretly behind closed doors will be at some point openly revealed (vv. 2–3).

(4) Hypocrisy is a sign that one does not fear God (v. 5) and does not possess the Holy Spirit with his regenerating grace (see Ro 8:5–14; 1Co 6:9–10; Gal 5:19–21; Eph 5:5). While remaining in this condition, one cannot "escape being condemned to hell" (Mt 23:33).

12:5 FEAR HIM. The disciples of Jesus must stand in awe of God's majesty and holiness and his wrath against sin (cf. Isa 6:1–5).

8"I tell you, whoever acknowledges
me before men, the Son of Man will
also acknowledge him before the angels of God.[e] 9But he who disowns me
before men will be disowned[f] before
the angels of God. 10And everyone who
speaks a word against the Son of
Man[g] will be forgiven, but anyone who
blasphemes against the Holy Spirit will
not be forgiven.[h]
11"When you are brought before synagogues, rulers and authorities, do not
worry about how you will defend yourselves or what you will say,[i] 12for the
Holy Spirit will teach you at that time
what you should say."[j]

The Parable of the Rich Fool

13Someone in the crowd said to him,
"Teacher, tell my brother to divide the
inheritance with me."
14Jesus replied, "Man, who appointed me a judge or an arbiter between
you?" 15Then he said to them, "Watch
out! Be on your guard against all kinds
of greed; a man's life does not consist
in the abundance of his possessions."[k]
16And he told them this parable:
"The ground of a certain rich man produced a good crop. 17He thought to
himself, 'What shall I do? I have no
place to store my crops.'
18"Then he said, 'This is what I'll do.
I will tear down my barns and build bigger ones, and there I will store all my
grain and my goods. 19And I'll say to
myself, "You have plenty of good
things laid up for many years. Take life
easy; eat, drink and be merry." '
20"But God said to him, 'You fool![l]
This very night your life will be demanded from you.[m] Then who will get
what you have prepared for yourself?'[n]
21"This is how it will be with anyone
who stores up things for himself but is
not rich toward God."[o]

Do Not Worry

12:22–31pp — Mt 6:25–33

22Then Jesus said to his disciples:
"Therefore I tell you, do not worry
about your life, what you will eat; or
about your body, what you will wear.
23Life is more than food, and the body
more than clothes. 24Consider the ravens: They do not sow or reap, they
have no storeroom or barn; yet God
feeds them.[p] And how much more
valuable you are than birds! 25Who of
you by worrying can add a single hour
to his life[e]? 26Since you cannot do this
very little thing, why do you worry
about the rest?
27"Consider how the lilies grow.
They do not labor or spin. Yet I tell you,
not even Solomon in all his splendor[q]
was dressed like one of these. 28If that
is how God clothes the grass of the
field, which is here today, and tomorrow is thrown into the fire, how much
more will he clothe you, O you of little
faith![r] 29And do not set your heart on
what you will eat or drink; do not worry
about it. 30For the pagan world runs
after all such things, and your Father[s]
knows that you need them.[t] 31But
seek his kingdom,[u] and these things
will be given to you as well.[v]
32"Do not be afraid,[w] little flock, for
your Father has been pleased to give
you the kingdom.[x] 33Sell your posses-

Lk 17:5-6

12:8 [e]Lk 15:10
12:9 [f]Mk 8:38; 2Ti 2:12
12:10 [g]S Mt 8:20 [h]Mt 12:31,32; S 1Jn 5:16
12:11 [i]Mt 10:17, 19; Lk 21:12,14
12:12 [j]Ex 4:12; Mt 10:20; Mk 13:11; Lk 21:15
12:15 [k]Job 20:20; 31:24; Ps 62:10
12:20 [l]Jer 17:11; Lk 11:40 [m]Job 27:8 [n]Ps 39:6; 49:10
12:21 [o]ver 33
12:24 [p]Job 38:41; Ps 147:9
12:27 [q]1Ki 10:4-7
12:28 [r]S Mt 6:30
12:30 [s]S Lk 6:36 [t]Mt 6:8
12:31 [u]S Mt 3:2 [v]Mt 19:29
12:32 [w]S Mt 14:27 [x]S Mt 25:34

[e]25 Or *single cubit to his height*

12:8 ACKNOWLEDGES ME BEFORE MEN. See Mt 10:32, note.

12:9 HE WHO DISOWNS ME. To disown Christ is (1) to fail to acknowledge before the ungodly that we are followers of Jesus, and (2) to refuse to stand with the gospel and Christ's principles of righteousness in the face of society's non-Christian values.

12:10 BLASPHEMES AGAINST THE HOLY SPIRIT. See Mt 12:31, note.

12:15 GUARD AGAINST ... GREED. To make earthly gain or riches the desire of one's life is a fatal error that leads to eternal loss (vv. 20–21). (1) The Greek word for greed (*pleonexia*) literally signifies the thirst for having more. (2) Covetousness does not refer to providing for one's own needs and those of one's family (cf. Pr 6:6). While we work for our needs, however, we must be rich toward God by seeking first his kingdom and his righteousness (v. 31; cf. Mt 6:33, note). (3) Each of us should heed Jesus' warning and examine whether selfishness and greed exist in our own hearts. For more on this subject, see article on RICHES AND POVERTY, p. 1562.

12:22 DO NOT WORRY ABOUT YOUR LIFE. See Mt 6:25, note.

12:24 HOW MUCH MORE VALUABLE. See Mt 6:25,30, notes.

12:31 SEEK HIS KINGDOM. See Mt 6:33, note.

12:33 SELL YOUR POSSESSIONS. See Mt 19:21, note; 1Co 16:2; 2Co 8:1–5 for the meaning of what Jesus says here.

sions and give to the poor.[y] Provide
purses for yourselves that will not
wear out, a treasure in heaven[z] that
will not be exhausted, where no thief
comes near and no moth destroys.[a]
34For where your treasure is, there
your heart will be also.[b]

Watchfulness

12:35,36pp — Mt 25:1-13; Mk 13:33-37
12:39,40; 42-46pp — Mt 24:43-51

35"Be dressed ready for service and
keep your lamps burning, 36like men
waiting for their master to return from
a wedding banquet, so that when he
comes and knocks they can immediately open the door for him. 37It will be
good for those servants whose master
finds them watching when he comes.[c]
I tell you the truth, he will dress himself to serve, will have them recline at
the table and will come and wait on
them.[d] 38It will be good for those servants whose master finds them ready,
even if he comes in the second or third
watch of the night. 39But understand
this: If the owner of the house had
known at what hour the thief[e] was
coming, he would not have let his
house be broken into. 40You also must
be ready,[f] because the Son of Man
will come at an hour when you do not
expect him."

41Peter asked, "Lord, are you telling
this parable to us, or to everyone?"
42The Lord[g] answered, "Who then
is the faithful and wise manager, whom
the master puts in charge of his servants to give them their food allowance
at the proper time? 43It will be good for
that servant whom the master finds doing so when he returns. 44I tell you the
truth, he will put him in charge of all
his possessions. 45But suppose the
servant says to himself, 'My master is
taking a long time in coming,' and he
then begins to beat the menservants
and maidservants and to eat and drink
and get drunk. 46The master of that
servant will come on a day when he
does not expect him and at an hour he
is not aware of.[h] He will cut him to

12:33 [y] S Ac 2:45 [z] S Mt 6:20 [a] S Jas 5:2
12:34 [b] Mt 6:21
12:37 [c] Mt 24:42, 46; 25:13 [d] S Mt 20:28
12:39 [e] Mt 6:19; 1Th 5:2; 2Pe 3:10; Rev 3:3; 16:15
12:40 [f] Mk 13:33; Lk 21:36
12:42 [g] S Lk 7:13
12:46 [h] ver 40

12:34 YOUR TREASURE . . . YOUR HEART. A person's heart (i.e., feelings, thinking, desires, values, will and decisions; see article on THE HEART, p. 906) is attracted to the things that are most important to him or her. (1) If you treasure earthly things, then your heart will be enslaved to such things. (2) If God's kingdom, heavenly things, his Word, his presence, his holiness and your relationship to him are your treasure, then your heart will be drawn to the things of his kingdom and your life will be directed toward heaven, waiting for the return of your Lord (vv. 35–40).

12:35–40 DRESSED READY FOR SERVICE. Concerning the Lord's coming for his people, the NT church knew no other attitude than that it was near and could happen at any time (see Mk 13:35, note; see article on THE RAPTURE, p. 1864). Every believer was called on to be spiritually ready at all times and to wait for the return of the Lord. This NT norm is enjoined on all true believers in Christ. (1) Believers must be so bound to the Lord as their greatest treasure (v. 34) that their hope and longing is the return of Jesus (vv. 35–37). (2) Believers must be dressed and ready, waiting for the uncertain time of Christ's coming (vv. 38,40, notes). (3) Christ's coming is imminent, i.e., he could come at any time (v. 38). The believer must be waiting and looking for Christ himself, not for a complex of events that might begin at any time (see Mt 24:42,44, notes; Jn 14:3, note; 1Co 15:51, notes).

12:36 WAITING FOR THEIR MASTER. See Mt 25:1,4, notes.

12:38 IT WILL BE GOOD FOR THOSE SERVANTS. A special blessing of Christ's presence and care is reserved for those who in full readiness and faithfulness "wait" (v. 36) and "watch" (v. 37) for their Lord's return during the interval between his ascension and second coming.

12:40 WHEN YOU DO NOT EXPECT HIM. God's servants must always be spiritually ready and obedient (v. 35) because the Lord will come at an uncertain time. Passages stressing the same truth are Mt 24:36,42–44; Lk 21:34; 1Th 5:2–4.

12:42–48 FAITHFUL AND UNFAITHFUL SERVANT. Jesus uses this parable to illustrate the two possible ways of living open to all disciples in the light of his absence and promised return. (1) They can be faithful and obedient, ever watchful and spiritually ready for the Lord's return at any time, and they will receive their Master's blessing (see v. 35, note; Mk 13:35, note; Jn 14:3, note). (2) They can grow careless and worldly-minded, believe that the Lord will delay his coming, cease to resist sin and depart from the path of faithfulness; they will then receive God's condemnation and inherit everlasting shame and ruin at his coming (vv. 45–46; see Mt 24:44, note; Jn 5:24, note; 15:6, note).

12:45 MY MASTER IS TAKING A LONG TIME. Denying that Christ may return at any time to judge the careless, indifferent disciple takes away the force of Christ's exhortation to persevere in faith in light of his unexpected coming (vv. 35, 37–38,40). It is precisely because there is no more opportunity for spiritual repentance when he returns that his coming is so perilous for apostate believers. In other words, Christ's coming is like death: it is final and can happen at any time (see Mt 24:42,44, notes; Mk 13:35, note; 2Th 2:11, note).

pieces and assign him a place with the unbelievers.

47"That servant who knows his master's will and does not get ready or does not do what his master wants will be beaten with many blows.[i] **48**But the one who does not know and does things deserving punishment will be beaten with few blows.[j] From everyone who has been given much, much will be demanded; and from the one who has been entrusted with much,
1 much more will be asked.

Not Peace but Division

12:51–53pp — Mt 10:34–36

49"I have come to bring fire on the earth, and how I wish it were already kindled! **50**But I have a baptism[k] to undergo, and how distressed I am until it is completed![l] **51**Do you think I came to bring peace on earth? No, I tell you, but division. **52**From now on there will be five in one family divided against each other, three against two and two against three. **53**They will be divided, father against son and son against father, mother against daughter and daughter against mother, mother-in-law against daughter-in-law and daughter-in-law against mother-in-law."[m]

Interpreting the Times

54He said to the crowd: "When you see a cloud rising in the west, immediately you say, 'It's going to rain,' and it does.[n] **55**And when the south wind blows, you say, 'It's going to be hot,' and it is. **56**Hypocrites! You know how to interpret the appearance of the earth and the sky. How is it that you don't know how to interpret this present time?[o]

57"Why don't you judge for yourselves what is right? **58**As you are going with your adversary to the magistrate, try hard to be reconciled to him on the way, or he may drag you off to the judge, and the judge turn you over to the officer, and the officer throw you into prison.[p] **59**I tell you, you will not get out until you have paid the last penny.[f]"[q]

Repent or Perish

13 Now there were some present at that time who told Jesus about the Galileans whose blood Pilate[r] had mixed with their sacrifices. **2**Jesus answered, "Do you think that these Galileans were worse sinners than all the other Galileans because they suffered this way?[s] **3**I tell you, no! But unless you repent, you too will all perish. **4**Or those eighteen who died when the tower in Siloam[t] fell on them—do you think they were more guilty than all the others living in Jerusalem? **5**I tell you, no! But unless you repent,[u] you too will all perish."

6Then he told this parable: "A man had a fig tree, planted in his vineyard, and he went to look for fruit on it, but did not find any.[v] **7**So he said to the man who took care of the vineyard, 'For three years now I've been coming to look for fruit on this fig tree and haven't found any. Cut it down![w] Why should it use up the soil?'

8" 'Sir,' the man replied, 'leave it alone for one more year, and I'll dig around it and fertilize it. **9**If it bears fruit next year, fine! If not, then cut it down.' "

A Crippled Woman Healed on the Sabbath

10On a Sabbath Jesus was teaching in one of the synagogues,[x] **11**and a woman was there who had been crip-

12:47 [i] Dt 25:2
12:48 [j] Lev 5:17; Nu 15:27-30
12:50 [k] Mk 10:38 [l] S Jn 19:30
12:53 [m] Mic 7:6; Mt 10:21
12:54 [n] Mt 16:2
12:56 [o] Mt 16:3
12:58 [p] Mt 5:25
12:59 [q] Mt 5:26; Mk 12:42
13:1 [r] S Mt 27:2
13:2 [s] Jn 9:2,3
13:4 [t] Jn 9:7,11
13:5 [u] Mt 3:2; Ac 2:38
13:6 [v] Isa 5:2; Jer 8:13; Mt 21:19
13:7 [w] S Mt 3:10
13:10 [x] S Mt 4:23

[f] 59 Greek *lepton*

12:47–48 BEATEN WITH FEW BLOWS. Just as there will be degrees of reward in heaven (1Co 15:41–42), so there will also be degrees of punishment in hell. Those who are eternally lost will undergo different grades of punishment according to their privileges and responsibility (cf. Mt 23:14; Heb 10:29).

12:51 I CAME TO BRING . . . DIVISION. See Mt 10:34, note.

13:6–9 FIG TREE . . . CUT IT DOWN. The parable of the fig tree refers primarily to Israel (cf. 3:9; Hos 9:10; Joel 1:7). However, its truth applies also to all individuals who profess to believe in Jesus, yet fail to turn from sin. While God gives everyone sufficient opportunity to repent, he will not tolerate sin forever. A time will come when God's grace will be withdrawn and the unrepentant punished without mercy (cf. 20:16; 21:20–24).

13:11 CRIPPLED BY A SPIRIT. Jesus sees some physical sickness as the direct result of demonic activity or oppression. This crippled woman was afflicted by "a spirit" (i.e., a representative of Satan; see v. 16; cf. Mt 9:32–33; 12:22; Mk 5:1–5; 9:17–18; Ac 10:38).

pled by a spirit for eighteen years.[y]
She was bent over and could not
straighten up at all. 12When Jesus saw
her, he called her forward and said to
her, "Woman, you are set free from
your infirmity." 13Then he put his
hands on her,[z] and immediately she
straightened up and praised God.

14Indignant because Jesus had
healed on the Sabbath,[a] the synagogue ruler[b] said to the people,
"There are six days for work.[c] So
come and be healed on those days, not
on the Sabbath."

15The Lord answered him, "You hypocrites! Doesn't each of you on the
Sabbath untie his ox or donkey from
the stall and lead it out to give it water?[d] 16Then should not this woman,
a daughter of Abraham,[e] whom Satan[f] has kept bound for eighteen long
years, be set free on the Sabbath day
from what bound her?"

17When he said this, all his opponents were humiliated,[g] but the people were delighted with all the wonderful things he was doing. Lk 17:19

The Parables of the Mustard Seed and the Yeast

13:18,19pp — Mk 4:30–32
13:18–21pp — Mt 13:31–33

18Then Jesus asked, "What is the
kingdom of God[h] like?[i] What shall I
compare it to? 19It is like a mustard
seed, which a man took and planted in
his garden. It grew and became a
tree,[j] and the birds of the air perched
in its branches."[k]

20Again he asked, "What shall I
compare the kingdom of God to? 21It is
like yeast that a woman took and

13:11 [y] ver 16
13:13 [z] S Mk 5:23
13:14 [a] S Mt 12:2 [b] S Mk 5:22 [c] Ex 20:9
13:15 [d] Lk 14:5
13:16 [e] S Lk 3:8 [f] S Mt 4:10
13:17 [g] Isa 66:5
13:18 [h] S Mt 3:2 [i] S Mt 13:24
13:19 [j] Lk 17:6 [k] S Mt 13:32

13:16 THIS WOMAN . . . SATAN HAS KEPT BOUND. It is a detestable sin in Christ's eyes when a person no longer hears the sighs of suffering humanity (vv. 11–14). Jesus teaches that people are imprisoned by sin, sickness and death, and are in distress and great need (vv. 11,16; Mt 4:23; Ac 26:18). Today we are in great danger of becoming insensitive to the world's misery and suffering because of the entertainment media that revel in showing immorality and violence for the sake of pleasure. True disciples will be like their Master, able to see the distresses of life and hear the groaning of creation (10:33–37; Ro 8:22; see article on THE CARE OF THE POOR AND NEEDY, p. 1316).

13:19 MUSTARD SEED. The parables of the mustard seed and the yeast form a pair. They speak of the growth of evil within the visible kingdom. The parable of the mustard seed illustrates the small beginning of the kingdom and its development through the ages. It began only with Jesus and a group of committed disciples (see Jn 20:22; Ac 2:4). However, the visible manifestation of the kingdom grows until it becomes large, organized and powerful. It will then accept in its "branches" (fellowship) "the birds of the air," i.e., evil imposters who take away the seed of truth. Note that in Mt 13:4,19, birds are agents of evil in Christ's parable, and in Rev 18:2, Babylon the Great (representing the apostate church) becomes a home for demons and "a haunt for every unclean and detestable bird" (see Rev 2–3 for Christ's description of how spiritual decay had permeated the majority of the seven churches; Rev 18:4, note on the false church).

13:21 THE YEAST. Yeast is normally regarded in the OT as a symbol of the presence of evil or impurity; it ferments, disintegrates or corrupts (see Ex 12:19; 13:6–8; Lev 2:11; 6:17; Dt 16:3–4; Am 4:4–5; see Ex 13:7, note). In the NT, yeast represents the false teaching and evil doctrines of the Pharisees, Sadducees (16:12) and Herodians (see Mk 8:15, note). In 1Co 5:6–8 yeast is regarded by Paul as representing "malice and wickedness," while the absence of yeast represents "sincerity and truth" (cf. Gal 5:9). Therefore, many understand this parable to indicate evil, false doctrine and unrighteousness existing and spreading within the visible kingdom of God.

(1) This yeast of evil will spread throughout all parts of God's work. It is found in: (a) modernism, liberalism and liberation theology, which exalt human ideas over the authority of Scripture (cf. Mt 22:23,29); (b) worldliness and immorality within the churches (cf. 1Co 5:1–2; Rev 2–3); (c) the seeking of position or power within the church by those who are concerned more for their own ambition than for God's honor (cf. Mt 23); (d) false doctrines (cf. Gal 1:9); (e) false teachers (cf. Mt 24:11,24); (f) professing Christians who appear righteous, but are not really born again (cf. Mt 23; Jude 12–19). Toward the end of this present age these evils will infiltrate God's work in Christian churches, denominations, colleges and seminaries until the NT apostolic gospel and righteous living are diluted and corrupted on a grand scale (see 18:8; Mt 24:10–12; Gal 1:9, note; 2Th 2:3; 1Ti 4:1, note; Rev 2–3; see articles on THE GREAT TRIBULATION, p. 1456, and OVERSEERS AND THEIR DUTIES, p. 1690).

(2) Every Christian must be careful that the yeast of evil does not affect his or her own life. The secret of victory lies in keeping our eyes fixed on Jesus in faith (Tit 2:13; Heb 12:2,15), despising the things of the world (Jas 1:27; 1Jn 2:15–17), remaining in God's Word (Jn 15:7; Jas 1:21), looking forward to Christ's return (12:35–40), continually listening to the voice of the Holy Spirit (Ro 8:12–14; Gal 5:16–18), being willing to suffer (1Pe 4:1–2), fighting against evil (1Co 10:6; 1Th 5:15; 1Pe 3:11), defending the gospel (Php 1:17) and putting on the full armor of God (Eph 6:11–18).

mixed into a large amount[g] of flour until it worked all through the dough."[l]

The Narrow Door

22Then Jesus went through the towns and villages, teaching as he made his way to Jerusalem.[m] 23Someone asked him, "Lord, are only a few people going to be saved?"

He said to them, 24"Make every effort to enter through the narrow door,[n] because many, I tell you, will try to enter and will not be able to. 25Once the owner of the house gets up and closes the door, you will stand outside knocking and pleading, 'Sir, open the door for us.'

"But he will answer, 'I don't know you or where you come from.'[o]

26"Then you will say, 'We ate and drank with you, and you taught in our streets.'

27"But he will reply, 'I don't know you or where you come from. Away from me, all you evildoers!'[p]

28"There will be weeping there, and gnashing of teeth,[q] when you see Abraham, Isaac and Jacob and all the prophets in the kingdom of God, but you yourselves thrown out. 29People will come from east and west[r] and north and south, and will take their places at the feast in the kingdom of God. 30Indeed there are those who are last who will be first, and first who will be last."[s]

Jesus' Sorrow for Jerusalem

13:34,35pp — Mt 23:37–39
13:34,35Ref — Lk 19:41

31At that time some Pharisees came to Jesus and said to him, "Leave this place and go somewhere else. Herod[t] wants to kill you."

32He replied, "Go tell that fox, 'I will drive out demons and heal people today and tomorrow, and on the third day I will reach my goal.'[u] 33In any case, I must keep going today and tomorrow and the next day—for surely no prophet[v] can die outside Jerusalem!

34"O Jerusalem, Jerusalem, you who kill the prophets and stone those sent to you, how often I have longed to gather your children together, as a hen gathers her chicks under her wings,[w] but you were not willing! 35Look, your house is left to you desolate.[x] I tell you, you will not see me again until you say, 'Blessed is he who comes in the name of the Lord.'[h]"[y]

Jesus at a Pharisee's House

14:8–10Ref — Pr 25:6,7

14 One Sabbath, when Jesus went to eat in the house of a prominent Pharisee,[z] he was being carefully watched.[a] 2There in front of him was a man suffering from dropsy. 3Jesus asked the Pharisees and experts in the law,[b] "Is it lawful to heal on the Sabbath or not?"[c] 4But they remained silent. So taking hold of the man, he healed him and sent him away.

5Then he asked them, "If one of you has a son[i] or an ox that falls into a well on the Sabbath day, will you not immediately pull him out?"[d] 6And they had nothing to say.

7When he noticed how the guests picked the places of honor at the table,[e] he told them this parable: 8"When someone invites you to a wedding feast, do not take the place of honor, for a person more distinguished than you may have been invited. 9If so, the host who invited both of you will come and say to you, 'Give this man your seat.' Then, humiliated, you will have to take the least important place. 10But when you are invited, take the lowest place, so that when your host comes, he will say to you, 'Friend, move up to a better place.' Then you will be honored in the presence of all your fellow guests. 11For everyone who exalts himself will be humbled, and he who humbles himself will be exalted."[f]

13:21 [l]1Co 5:6
13:22 [m]S Lk 9:51
13:24 [n]Mt 7:13
13:25 [o]Mt 7:23; 25:10-12
13:27 [p]S Mt 7:23
13:28 [q]S Mt 8:12
13:29 [r]S Mt 8:11
13:30 [s]S Mt 19:30
13:31 [t]S Mt 14:1
13:32 [u]S Heb 2:10
13:33 [v]S Mt 21:11
13:34 [w]S Mt 23:37
13:35 [x]Jer 12:17; 22:5 [y]Ps 118:26; Lk 19:38
14:1 [z]Lk 7:36; 11:37 [a]S Mt 12:10
14:3 [b]S Mt 22:35 [c]S Mt 12:2
14:5 [d]Lk 13:15
14:7 [e]S Lk 11:43
14:11 [f]S Mt 23:12

[g]*21* Greek *three satas* (probably about 1/2 bushel or 22 liters) [h]*35* Psalm 118:26
[i]*5* Some manuscripts *donkey*

13:24 THE NARROW DOOR. See Mt 7:14, note.

13:30 LAST ... WILL BE FIRST. See Mt 19:30, note.

13:34 THE LORD'S GREAT SORROW. Our Lord's tears (cf. 19:41) over Jerusalem's stubbornness bear witness to the freedom of the human will to resist the grace and will of God (see 19:41, note; Ac 7:51; Ro 1:18–32; 2:5).

14:11 EXALTS HIMSELF ... HUMBLED. The Savior warns that those who exalt themselves in this life will be put to shame in the future kingdom of heaven. Much more important than earthly honor is our place of honor before God. Such honor cannot be secured by self-assertiveness, for it comes only through humility and servanthood (vv.

12Then Jesus said to his host, "When you give a luncheon or dinner, do not invite your friends, your brothers or relatives, or your rich neighbors; if you do, they may invite you back and so you will be repaid. 13But when you give a banquet, invite the poor, the crippled, the lame, the blind,[g] 14and you will be blessed. Although they cannot repay you, you will be repaid at the resurrection of the righteous."[h]

The Parable of the Great Banquet

14:16–24Ref — Mt 22:2–14

15When one of those at the table with him heard this, he said to Jesus, "Blessed is the man who will eat at the feast[i] in the kingdom of God."[j]

16Jesus replied: "A certain man was preparing a great banquet and invited many guests. 17At the time of the banquet he sent his servant to tell those who had been invited, 'Come, for everything is now ready.'

18"But they all alike began to make excuses. The first said, 'I have just bought a field, and I must go and see it. Please excuse me.'

19"Another said, 'I have just bought five yoke of oxen, and I'm on my way to try them out. Please excuse me.'

20"Still another said, 'I just got married, so I can't come.'

21"The servant came back and reported this to his master. Then the owner of the house became angry and ordered his servant, 'Go out quickly into the streets and alleys of the town and bring in the poor, the crippled, the blind and the lame.'[k]

22" 'Sir,' the servant said, 'what you ordered has been done, but there is still room.'

23"Then the master told his servant, 'Go out to the roads and country lanes and make them come in, so that my house will be full. 24I tell you, not one of those men who were invited will get a taste of my banquet.' "[l]

The Cost of Being a Disciple

25Large crowds were traveling with Jesus, and turning to them he said: 26"If anyone comes to me and does not hate his father and mother, his wife and children, his brothers and sisters—yes, even his own life—he cannot be my disciple.[m] 27And anyone who does not carry his cross and follow me cannot be my disciple.[n]

28"Suppose one of you wants to build a tower. Will he not first sit down and estimate the cost to see if he has enough money to complete it? 29For if he lays the foundation and is not able to finish it, everyone who sees it will ridicule him, 30saying, 'This fellow began to build and was not able to finish.'

31"Or suppose a king is about to go to war against another king. Will he not first sit down and consider whether he is able with ten thousand men to

14:13 [g] ver 21
14:14 [h] Ac 24:15
14:15 [i] Isa 25:6; Mt 26:29; Lk 13:29; Rev 19:9 [j] S Mt 3:2
14:21 [k] ver 13
14:24 [l] Mt 21:43; Ac 13:46
14:26 [m] Mt 10:37; S Jn 12:25
14:27 [n] Mt 10:38; Lk 9:23

12–14), and by seeking "the praise that comes from the only God" (Jn 5:44).

14:15–24 THE PARABLE OF THE GREAT BANQUET. Although this parable originally applied to Israel and its rejection of the gospel, it also applies to the churches and every believer today. (1) The subject of this parable is the day of resurrection in its future heavenly glory (vv. 14–15; cf. 22:18), i.e., the return of Christ to bring his people into the heavenly kingdom.

(2) Those who initially accepted the invitation but then refused to come represent those who have accepted or have appeared to accept the invitation of Jesus to salvation, yet their love for him and the heavenly kingdom has grown cold (vv. 17–20).

(3) Such people have ceased to set their goals by heavenly standards (vv. 18–20). They have rejected the Biblical admonition to set their "minds on things above, not on earthly things," while waiting for the appearing of Christ (Col 3:1–4). Their hope and life are centered on the things of this world, and they no longer long for "a better country—a heavenly one" (Heb 11:16).

(4) Vv. 21–23 indicate that there will also be those whose hearts are with Christ in heaven and not fixed on their prospects in this world. They pray with the Spirit and the bride: "Amen. Come, Lord Jesus" (Rev 22:20).

14:26 DOES NOT HATE HIS FATHER. The word "hate" in this passage means "love less" (compare this text with Mt 10:37; see Ge 29:31, note; Mal 1:3, note). Jesus demands that our loyalty to and love for him be greater than every other attachment, even to our own families.

14:27 CARRY HIS CROSS. See 9:23, note; Mk 8:34, note.

14:28–33 THE COST OF DISCIPLESHIP. Jesus teaches that whoever desires to follow him and be his disciple should first decide whether he or she is prepared to pay the cost. The cost of real discipleship is to give up all relationships and possessions, i.e., all that we have: material things, family, our own lives, desires, plans and interests (v. 33). This does not mean that we must reject all we have, but that all that we have must be placed at Christ's service and under his guidance (see 13:24; Mt 7:14; cf. Jn 16:33; 2Ti 3:12).

oppose the one coming against him with twenty thousand? 32If he is not able, he will send a delegation while the other is still a long way off and will ask for terms of peace. 33In the same way, any of you who does not give up everything he has cannot be my disciple.[o]

34"Salt is good, but if it loses its saltiness, how can it be made salty again?[p] 35It is fit neither for the soil nor for the manure pile; it is thrown out.[q]

"He who has ears to hear, let him hear."[r]

The Parable of the Lost Sheep

15:4–7pp — Mt 18:12–14

15 Now the tax collectors[s] and "sinners" were all gathering around to hear him. 2But the Pharisees and the teachers of the law muttered, "This man welcomes sinners and eats with them."[t]

3Then Jesus told them this parable:[u] 4"Suppose one of you has a hundred sheep and loses one of them. Does he not leave the ninety-nine in the open country and go after the lost sheep until he finds it?[v] 5And when he finds it, he joyfully puts it on his shoulders 6and goes home. Then he calls his friends and neighbors together and says, 'Rejoice with me; I have found my lost sheep.'[w] 7I tell you that in the same way there will be more rejoicing in heaven over one sinner who repents than over ninety-nine righteous persons who do not need to repent.[x]

14:33 [o]Php 3:7,8
14:34 [p]Mk 9:50
14:35 [q]Mt 5:13 [r]S Mt 11:15
15:1 [s]Lk 5:29
15:2 [t]S Mt 9:11
15:3 [u]Mt 13:3
15:4 [v]Ps 23; 119:176; Jer 31:10; Eze 34:11-16; Lk 5:32; 19:10
15:6 [w]ver 9
15:7 [x]ver 10

The Parable of the Lost Coin

8"Or suppose a woman has ten silver coins[j] and loses one. Does she not light a lamp, sweep the house and search carefully until she finds it? 9And when she finds it, she calls her friends and neighbors together and says, 'Rejoice with me; I have found my lost coin.'[y] 10In the same way, I tell you, there is rejoicing in the presence of the angels of God over one sinner who repents."[z]

The Parable of the Lost Son

11Jesus continued: "There was a man who had two sons.[a] 12The younger one said to his father, 'Father, give me my share of the estate.'[b] So he divided his property[c] between them.

13"Not long after that, the younger son got together all he had, set off for a distant country and there squandered his wealth[d] in wild living. 14After he had spent everything, there was a severe famine in that whole country, and he began to be in need. 15So he went and hired himself out to a citizen of that country, who sent him to his fields to feed pigs.[e] 16He longed to fill his stomach with the pods that the pigs were eating, but no one gave him anything.

17"When he came to his senses, he said, 'How many of my father's hired men have food to spare, and here I am

15:9 [y]ver 6
15:10 [z]ver 7
15:11 [a]Mt 21:28
15:12 [b]Dt 21:17 [c]ver 30
15:13 [d]ver 30; Lk 16:1
15:15 [e]Lev 11:7

j 8 Greek *ten drachmas,* each worth about a day's wages

15:4 THE LOST SHEEP. The key verse in Luke's Gospel states that "the Son of Man came to seek and to save what was lost" (19:10). The three parables in ch. 15 illustrate this purpose of Jesus' earthly mission and reveal God's desire to save the lost for time and eternity. We learn that (1) seeking lost sinners to bring them to redemption is of utmost importance to the heart of God (vv. 4,8,20,24); (2) both God and heaven rejoice when even one sinner repents (vv. 7,10); and (3) no amount of sacrifice or suffering is too great in seeking the lost and bringing them to Jesus (vv. 4,8).

15:7 REJOICING IN HEAVEN. God and the angels in heaven have such love, compassion and grief for those who have fallen into sin and spiritual death that when one sinner repents, they openly rejoice. On God's love for sinners, see Isa 62:5; Jer 32:41; Eze 18:23,32; Hos 11:8; Jn 3:16; Ro 5:6–11; 2Pe 3:9.

15:8 SEARCH CAREFULLY UNTIL SHE FINDS. We should pray that the Holy Spirit may fill our hearts with an earnest desire to bring sinners to salvation.

15:13 SET OFF FOR A DISTANT COUNTRY. In this parable the Lord teaches that a life of sin and selfishness, in its deepest sense, is a separation from God's love, fellowship and authority. The sinner or backslider is like the young son who, pursuing the pleasures of sin, wastes the physical, intellectual and spiritual gifts given by God. Such waste results in disillusionment and sorrow, sometimes degrading personal conditions, and always the lack of a true and real life that can be found only in a right relationship with God.

15:17 HE CAME TO HIS SENSES. Before the lost can come to God, they must see their true state of slavery to sin and separation from God (vv. 14–17). They must humbly return to the Father, confess their sin and be willing to do whatever the Father requires (vv. 17–19). To bring the lost to this realization is the work of the Holy Spirit (Jn 16:7–11).

starving to death! 18I will set out and
go back to my father and say to him:
Father, I have sinned[f] against heaven
and against you. 19I am no longer worthy to be called your son; make me like
one of your hired men.' 20So he got up
and went to his father.
"But while he was still a long way
off, his father saw him and was filled
with compassion for him; he ran to his
son, threw his arms around him and
kissed him.[g]
21"The son said to him, 'Father, I
have sinned against heaven and
against you.[h] I am no longer worthy to
be called your son.[k]'
22"But the father said to his servants, 'Quick! Bring the best robe[i]
and put it on him. Put a ring on his
finger[j] and sandals on his feet.
23Bring the fattened calf and kill it.
Let's have a feast and celebrate. 24For
this son of mine was dead and is alive
again;[k] he was lost and is found.' So
they began to celebrate.[l]
25"Meanwhile, the older son was in
the field. When he came near the
house, he heard music and dancing.
26So he called one of the servants and
asked him what was going on. 27'Your
brother has come,' he replied, 'and
your father has killed the fattened calf
because he has him back safe and
sound.'
28"The older brother became an-
gry[m] and refused to go in. So his father
went out and pleaded with him. 29But
he answered his father, 'Look! All
these years I've been slaving for you
and never disobeyed your orders. Yet
you never gave me even a young goat
so I could celebrate with my friends.
30But when this son of yours who has
squandered your property[n] with prostitutes[o] comes home, you kill the fattened calf for him!'
31" 'My son,' the father said, 'you
are always with me, and everything I
have is yours. 32But we had to celebrate and be glad, because this brother
of yours was dead and is alive again; he
was lost and is found.' "[p]

The Parable of the Shrewd Manager

16 Jesus told his disciples: "There
was a rich man whose manager
was accused of wasting his possessions.[q] 2So he called him in and asked
him, 'What is this I hear about you?
Give an account of your management,
because you cannot be manager any
longer.'
3"The manager said to himself,
'What shall I do now? My master is
taking away my job. I'm not strong
enough to dig, and I'm ashamed to
beg— 4I know what I'll do so that,
when I lose my job here, people will
welcome me into their houses.'
5"So he called in each one of his
master's debtors. He asked the first,
'How much do you owe my master?'
6" 'Eight hundred gallons[1] of olive
oil,' he replied.
"The manager told him, 'Take your
bill, sit down quickly, and make it four
hundred.'
7"Then he asked the second, 'And
how much do you owe?'
" 'A thousand bushels[m] of wheat,'
he replied.

15:18 [f]Lev 26:40; Mt 3:2 **15:20** [g]Ge 45:14, 15; 46:29; Ac 20:37 **15:21** [h]Ps 51:4 **15:22** [i]Zec 3:4; Rev 6:11 [j]Ge 41:42 **15:24** [k]Eph 2:1, 5; 5:14; 1Ti 5:6 [l]ver 32 **15:28** [m]Jnh 4:1 **15:30** [n]ver 12,13 [o]Pr 29:3 **15:32** [p]ver 24; Mal 3:17 **16:1** [q]Lk 15:13, 30

k *21* Some early manuscripts *son. Make me like one of your hired men.* **l** *6* Greek *one hundred batous* (probably about 3 kiloliters) **m** *7* Greek *one hundred korous* (probably about 35 kiloliters)

15:20 WHILE HE WAS STILL A LONG WAY OFF. Every Christian father and mother must understand that God loves their wandering child and desires his or her salvation as much as they do. Pray and trust God to seek that child until he or she returns to the heavenly Father.

15:20 HIS FATHER SAW HIM AND WAS FILLED WITH COMPASSION. Jesus' description of the father's response to the son's return teaches several important truths: (1) God has compassion for the lost because of their sorrowful condition. (2) God's love for them is so great that he never ceases to grieve over them and to wait for their return. (3) When sinners sincerely turn to God, God is more than ready to receive them with forgiveness, love, compassion, grace and the full rights of children (cf. Jn 1:12). The benefits of Christ's death, the Holy Spirit's influence and God's rich grace are all made available to those who seek God. (4) God's joy over the return of sinners is immeasurable (vv. 6–7,10,22–24).

15:24 THIS SON OF MINE ... WAS LOST. "Lost" is used in the sense of being lost to God, like "sheep going astray" (1Pe 2:25; cf. Isa 53:6). Life away from God's fellowship is spiritual death (Eph 2:1; 1Jn 3:14). Returning to God brings true life (Jn 11:26).

15:28 BECAME ANGRY. The "older son" represents those who have a form of religion and outwardly keep God's commands, but inwardly they are separated from him and his purposes for the kingdom (vv. 28–30).

“He told him, ‘Take your bill and
make it eight hundred.’
8“The master commended the dishonest manager because he had acted
shrewdly. For the people of this
world[r] are more shrewd[s] in dealing
with their own kind than are the people
of the light.[t] 9I tell you, use worldly
wealth[u] to gain friends for yourselves,
so that when it is gone, you will be welcomed into eternal dwellings.[v]
10“Whoever can be trusted with very
little can also be trusted with much,[w]
and whoever is dishonest with very little will also be dishonest with much.
11So if you have not been trustworthy
in handling worldly wealth,[x] who will
trust you with true riches? 12And if you
have not been trustworthy with someone else’s property, who will give you
property of your own?
13“No servant can serve two masters. Either he will hate the one and
love the other, or he will be devoted to
the one and despise the other. You cannot serve both God and Money.”[y]
14The Pharisees, who loved money,[z] heard all this and were sneering
at Jesus.[a] 15He said to them, “You are
the ones who justify yourselves[b] in
the eyes of men, but God knows your
hearts.[c] What is highly valued among
men is detestable in God’s sight.

Additional Teachings

16“The Law and the Prophets were
proclaimed until John.[d] Since that
time, the good news of the kingdom of
God is being preached,[e] and everyone
is forcing his way into it. 17It is easier
for heaven and earth to disappear than
for the least stroke of a pen to drop out
of the Law.[f]
18“Anyone who divorces his wife and
marries another woman commits adultery, and the man who marries a divorced woman commits adultery.[g]

The Rich Man and Lazarus

19“There was a rich man who was
dressed in purple and fine linen and
lived in luxury every day.[h] 20At his
gate was laid a beggar[i] named Lazarus, covered with sores 21and longing
to eat what fell from the rich man’s ta-

16:8 [r] Ps 17:14 [s] Ps 18:26 [t] Jn 12:36; Eph 5:8; 1Th 5:5 **16:9** [u] ver 11,13 [v] Mt 19:21; Lk 12:33 **16:10** [w] Mt 25:21,23; Lk 19:17 **16:11** [x] ver 9,13 **16:13** [y] ver 9,11; Mt 6:24 **16:14** [z] S 1Ti 3:3

[a] Lk 23:35 **16:15** [b] Lk 10:29 [c] S Rev 2:23 **16:16** [d] Mt 5:17; 11:12,13 [e] S Mt 4:23 **16:17** [f] S Mt 5:18 **16:18** [g] Mt 5:31, 32; 19:9; Mk 10:11; Ro 7:2, 3; 1Co 7:10,11 **16:19** [h] Eze 16:49 **16:20** [i] Ac 3:2

16:8 COMMENDED THE DISHONEST MANAGER. The point of Jesus’ illustration is that the worldly are earthly-minded enough to promote their own interest and welfare. In contrast, believers often are not heavenly-minded enough to use their earthly possessions to promote their spiritual and heavenly interest.

16:9 WORLDLY WEALTH. Injustice, greed and power are often involved in the accumulation and use of “worldly wealth” (see article on RICHES AND POVERTY, p. 1562). We must use possessions and money in a way that promotes God’s interests and the salvation of others.

16:11 IF YOU HAVE NOT BEEN TRUSTWORTHY. Those who are not trustworthy in their acquisition and use of worldly goods will be the same with spiritual things. This is why believers, and especially church leaders, must be free from the love of money (1Ti 3:1–3).

16:13 YOU CANNOT SERVE BOTH GOD AND MONEY. The world’s riches make it very difficult to keep God at the center of our lives. For more on this subject, see article on RICHES AND POVERTY, p. 1562.

16:14 PHARISEES . . . LOVED MONEY. The Pharisees regarded riches as a blessing from God for their faithful observance of the law. They “sneered at” Jesus, who was poor, for they regarded his poverty as a sign that God had not honored him (see article on RICHES AND POVERTY, p. 1562).

16:18 COMMITS ADULTERY. Anyone who divorces (or deserts) his or her marriage partner for unscriptural reasons (see Mt 19:9, note), and then remarries, “commits adultery.” “Commits adultery” in Greek is a present active indicative, denoting continuing action; i.e., as long as the innocent and divorced spouse desires and seeks reconciliation, the guilty party who enters into another marriage relationship is living in an adulterous union. Since God does not regard the former marriage as annulled, any other union is sexual adultery. (1) The primary moral issue in this case is whether the remarriage of the guilty partner involves disregarding the covenant obligations and parental responsibilities of the first marriage, which are still capable of fulfillment. If the innocent partner desires reconciliation, the issue is decisive. The guilty party is living in adultery if he or she marries another (cf. Mk 10:11–12). (2) However, if the offending party (a) does not have the possibility of returning to the first marriage, (b) has already entered into the adulterous type of marriage relationship described by Jesus, and (c) sincerely repents before God and makes the commitment to build the present relationship on godly principles, then the present marriage relationship may become legitimate (i.e., accepted by God).

16:19–31 THE RICH MAN AND LAZARUS. The rich man’s life was consumed in self-centered living. He made the wrong choice and suffered eternally (vv. 22–23). Lazarus lived all his life in poverty, but his heart was right with God. His name means “God is my help,” and he never gave up his faith in God. He died and was immediately taken to paradise with Abraham (v. 22; see 23:43; Ac 7:59; 2Co 5:8; Php 1:23). The destinies of both men were irreversible at death (vv. 24–26).

ble.[j] Even the dogs came and licked his sores.

22 "The time came when the beggar died and the angels carried him to Abraham's side. The rich man also died and was buried. 23 In hell,[n] where he was in torment, he looked up and saw Abraham far away, with Lazarus by his side. 24 So he called to him, 'Father Abraham,[k] have pity on me and send Lazarus to dip the tip of his finger in water and cool my tongue, because I am in agony in this fire.'[l]

25 "But Abraham replied, 'Son, remember that in your lifetime you received your good things, while Lazarus received bad things,[m] but now he is comforted here and you are in agony.[n] 26 And besides all this, between us and you a great chasm has been fixed, so that those who want to go from here to you cannot, nor can anyone cross over from there to us.'

27 "He answered, 'Then I beg you, father, send Lazarus to my father's house, 28 for I have five brothers. Let him warn them,[o] so that they will not also come to this place of torment.'

29 "Abraham replied, 'They have Moses[p] and the Prophets;[q] let them listen to them.'

30 " 'No, father Abraham,'[r] he said, 'but if someone from the dead goes to them, they will repent.'

31 "He said to him, 'If they do not listen to Moses and the Prophets, they will not be convinced even if someone rises from the dead.' "

Sin, Faith, Duty

17 Jesus said to his disciples: "Things that cause people to sin[s] are bound to come, but woe to that person through whom they come.[t] 2 It would be better for him to be thrown into the sea with a millstone tied around his neck than for him to cause one of these little ones[u] to sin.[v] 3 So watch yourselves.

"If your brother sins, rebuke him,[w] and if he repents, forgive him.[x] 4 If he sins against you seven times in a day, and seven times comes back to you and says, 'I repent,' forgive him."[y]

5 The apostles[z] said to the Lord,[a] "Increase our faith!"

6 He replied, "If you have faith as small as a mustard seed,[b] you can say to this mulberry tree, 'Be uprooted and planted in the sea,' and it will obey you.[c]

7 "Suppose one of you had a servant plowing or looking after the sheep. Would he say to the servant when he comes in from the field, 'Come along now and sit down to eat'? 8 Would he not rather say, 'Prepare my supper, get yourself ready and wait on me[d] while I eat and drink; after that you may eat and drink'? 9 Would he thank the servant because he did what he was told to do? 10 So you also, when you have done everything you were told to do, should say, 'We are unworthy servants; we have only done our duty.' "[e]

Ten Healed of Leprosy

11 Now on his way to Jerusalem,[f] Jesus traveled along the border between Samaria and Galilee.[g] 12 As he was going into a village, ten men who had leprosy[o][h] met him. They stood at a distance[i] 13 and called out in a loud voice, "Jesus, Master,[j] have pity on us!"

14 When he saw them, he said, "Go, show yourselves to the priests."[k] And as they went, they were cleansed.

15 One of them, when he saw he was healed, came back, praising God[l] in a loud voice. 16 He threw himself at

Jn 14

16:21 [j] Mt 15:27; Lk 15:16
16:24 [k] ver 30; S Lk 3:8 [l] S Mt 5:22
16:25 [m] Ps 17:14 [n] Lk 6:21,24,25
16:28 [o] Ac 2:40; 20:23; 1Th 4:6
16:29 [p] S Lk 24:27,44; Jn 1:45; 5:45-47; Ac 15:21 [q] Lk 4:17; 24:27,44; Jn 1:45
16:30 [r] ver 24; S Lk 3:8
17:1 [s] S Mt 5:29 [t] Mt 18:7
17:2 [u] Mk 10:24; Lk 10:21 [v] S Mt 5:29
17:3 [w] S Mt 18:15 [x] Eph 4:32; Col 3:13
17:4 [y] Mt 18:21,22
17:5 [z] S Mk 6:30 [a] S Lk 7:13
17:6 [b] Mt 13:31; 17:20; Lk 13:19 [c] S Mt 21:21; Mk 9:23
17:8 [d] Lk 12:37
17:10 [e] 1Co 9:16
17:11 [f] S Lk 9:51 [g] Lk 9:51,52; Jn 4:3,4
17:12 [h] S Mt 8:2 [i] Lev 13:45,46
17:13 [j] S Lk 5:5
17:14 [k] Lev 14:2; Mt 8:4
17:15 [l] S Mt 9:8

[n] *23* Greek *Hades*
[o] *12* The Greek word was used for various diseases affecting the skin—not necessarily leprosy.

17:2 MILLSTONE TIED AROUND HIS NECK. Causing someone to sin because of our example, attitude or neglect will bring such severe punishment that death before committing this sin would be preferable (see Mt 18:6, note).

17:3 IF HE REPENTS, FORGIVE. Concerning Jesus' statement about forgiving, observe the following: (1) Jesus is concerned that we possess an attitude that desires to forgive and help those who offend us, rather than a spirit of revenge or hatred. (2) Forgiveness and reconciliation cannot truly occur until the offending person acknowledges his or her wrong action and sincerely repents. Furthermore, Jesus was not referring to the same offense constantly repeated. (3) We should be willing to persevere in forgiveness if the offender sincerely repents. Jesus' statement concerning forgiving "seven times in a day" is not meant to condone habitual sin. Nor is he saying that the believer must allow someone to severely mistreat or abuse him or her indefinitely. Instead, he teaches that we must maintain an attitude that is always ready to help and forgive the offender.

17:6 FAITH. See Mt 17:20, note; 21:21, note; Mk 11:24, note; see article on FAITH AND GRACE, p. 1720.

Jesus' feet and thanked him — and he
was a Samaritan.[m]
17Jesus asked, "Were not all ten
cleansed? Where are the other nine?
18Was no one found to return and give
praise to God except this foreigner?"
19Then he said to him, "Rise and go;
your faith has made you well."[n]

The Coming of the Kingdom of God

17:26,27pp — Mt 24:37–39

20Once, having been asked by the
Pharisees when the kingdom of God
would come,[o] Jesus replied, "The
kingdom of God does not come with
your careful observation, **21**nor will
people say, 'Here it is,' or 'There it
is,'[p] because the kingdom of God is
within[p] you."
22Then he said to his disciples, "The
time is coming when you will long to
see one of the days of the Son of
Man,[q] but you will not see it.[r] **23**Men
will tell you, 'There he is!' or 'Here he
is!' Do not go running off after them.[s]
24For the Son of Man in his day[q] will
be like the lightning,[t] which flashes
and lights up the sky from one end to
the other. **25**But first he must suffer
many things[u] and be rejected[v] by
this generation.[w]
26"Just as it was in the days of
Noah,[x] so also will it be in the days of
the Son of Man. **27**People were eating,
drinking, marrying and being given in
marriage up to the day Noah entered
the ark. Then the flood came and destroyed them all.
28"It was the same in the days of
Lot.[y] People were eating and drinking, buying and selling, planting and
building. **29**But the day Lot left Sodom,
fire and sulfur rained down from heav-
en and destroyed them all.
30"It will be just like this on the day
the Son of Man is revealed.[z] **31**On that
day no one who is on the roof of his
house, with his goods inside, should go
down to get them. Likewise, no one in
the field should go back for anything.[a]
32Remember Lot's wife![b] **33**Whoever
tries to keep his life will lose it, and
whoever loses his life will preserve
it.[c] **34**I tell you, on that night two people will be in one bed; one will be taken
and the other left. **35**Two women will
be grinding grain together; one will be
taken and the other left.[r]"[d]
37"Where, Lord?" they asked.
He replied, "Where there is a dead
body, there the vultures will gather."[e] Jn 14:3

The Parable of the Persistent Widow

18 Then Jesus told his disciples a
parable to show them that they
should always pray and not give up.[f]

17:16 [m]S Mt 10:5
17:19 [n]S Mt 9:22
17:20 [o]S Mt 3:2
17:21 [p]ver 23
17:22 [q]S Mt 8:20 [r]S Lk 5:35
17:23 [s]Mt 24:23; Lk 21:8
17:24 [t]Mt 24:27
17:25 [u]S Mt 16:21 [v]Lk 9:22; 18:32 [w]Mk 13:30; Lk 21:32
17:26 [x]Ge 6:5-8; 7:6-24
17:28 [y]Ge 19:1-28
17:30 [z]Mt 10:23; S 16:27; 24:3,27, 37,39; 25:31; S 1Co 1:7; S 1Th 2:19; 2Th 1:7; 2:8; 2Pe 3:4; S Rev 1:7
17:31 [a]Mt 24:17, 18
17:32 [b]Ge 19:26
17:33 [c]S Jn 12:25
17:35 [d]Mt 24:41
17:37 [e]Mt 24:28
18:1 [f]Isa 40:31; Lk 11:5-8; S Ac 1:14; S Ro 1:10; 12:12; Eph 6:18; Col 4:2; 1Th 5:17

[p]21 Or *among* [q]24 Some manuscripts do not have *in his day.* [r]35 Some manuscripts *left.* [36]*Two men will be in the field; one will be taken and the other left.*

17:16 THANKED HIM. We who have received from God love, grace, salvation and all his spiritual blessings must not forget to thank him. What he has done for us should cause us to come to him with grateful hearts. "We love because he first loved us" (1Jn 4:19).

17:21 THE KINGDOM OF GOD IS WITHIN YOU. According to Jesus, the present nature of the kingdom is spiritual, not material or political. The "kingdom of God does not come with your careful observation" (v. 20), i.e., it does not come as an earthly political power. Instead it is within the hearts and in the midst of God's people, consisting of "righteousness, peace and joy in the Holy Spirit" (Ro 14:17). We demonstrate it by conquering, through the power of the Spirit, the forces of sin, sickness and Satan, not by conquering kings and nations (see article on THE KINGDOM OF GOD, p. 1430). When Jesus comes to earth the second time, then the kingdom will be seen in its full power and glory (v. 24; cf. Mt 24:30) as it triumphs over kings and nations (Rev 11:15–18; 19:11–21).

17:26 THE DAYS OF NOAH. See Mt 24:37, note.

17:31 ON THAT DAY. See Mk 13:14, note on the abomination that causes desolation; see article on THE GREAT TRIBULATION, p. 1456.

17:32 REMEMBER LOT'S WIFE! The tragic error of Lot's wife was to place her affections on an earthly society rather than on a heavenly one (cf. Heb 11:10). She turned back because her heart was still in Sodom (Ge 19:17,26; see 19:26, note). Every believer should ask: Is my heart more attached to earthly things than to Jesus and the hope of his return?

17:37 A DEAD BODY . . . THE VULTURES. This verse suggests the certainty of judgment on those who are spiritually dead (cf. Mt 24:28; Rev 19:17–18). Just as surely as vultures come to the corpse, so judgment will come on the wicked when Christ returns.

18:1 THEY SHOULD ALWAYS PRAY. Jesus was concerned that his followers pray continually in order to accomplish God's will for their lives (see article on EFFECTIVE PRAYING, p. 496). From this parable of the persistent widow we learn several things: (1) We must persevere in prayer with regard to all matters until Jesus returns (vv. 7–8; Ro 12:12; Eph 6:18; Col 4:2; 1Th 5:17). (2) In this life we have an adversary (v. 3), Satan (1Pe

2He said: "In a certain town there was
a judge who neither feared God nor
cared about men. 3And there was a
widow in that town who kept coming to
him with the plea, 'Grant me justice[g]
against my adversary.'
4"For some time he refused. But finally he said to himself, 'Even though
I don't fear God or care about men, 5yet
because this widow keeps bothering
me, I will see that she gets justice, so
that she won't eventually wear me out
with her coming!' "[h]
6And the Lord[i] said, "Listen to
what the unjust judge says. 7And will
not God bring about justice for his chosen ones, who cry out[j] to him day and
night? Will he keep putting them off? 8I
tell you, he will see that they get justice, and quickly. However, when the
Son of Man[k] comes,[l] will he find
faith on the earth?"

The Parable of the Pharisee and the Tax Collector

9To some who were confident of
their own righteousness[m] and looked
down on everybody else,[n] Jesus told
this parable: 10"Two men went up to
the temple to pray,[o] one a Pharisee
and the other a tax collector. 11The
Pharisee stood up[p] and prayed
about[s] himself: 'God, I thank you that
I am not like other men—robbers, evildoers, adulterers—or even like this
tax collector. 12I fast[q] twice a week
and give a tenth[r] of all I get.'
13"But the tax collector stood at
a distance. He would not even look up
to heaven, but beat his breast[s] and
said, 'God, have mercy on me, a sinner.'[t]
14"I tell you that this man, rather
than the other, went home justified before God. For everyone who exalts himself will be humbled, and he who humbles himself will be exalted."[u]

The Little Children and Jesus

18:15–17pp — Mt 19:13–15; Mk 10:13–16

15People were also bringing babies
to Jesus to have him touch them. When
the disciples saw this, they rebuked
them. 16But Jesus called the children
to him and said, "Let the little children
come to me, and do not hinder them,
for the kingdom of God belongs to such
as these. 17I tell you the truth, anyone
who will not receive the kingdom of
God like a little child[v] will never enter
it."

18:3 [g]Isa 1:17
18:5 [h]Lk 11:8
18:6 [i]S Lk 7:13
18:7 [j]Ex 22:23; Ps 88:1; Rev 6:10
18:8 [k]S Mt 8:20 [l]S Mt 16:27
18:9 [m]Lk 16:15 [n]Isa 65:5
18:10 [o]Ac 3:1
18:11 [p]Mt 6:5; Mk 11:25
18:12 [q]Isa 58:3; Mt 9:14 [r]Mal 3:8; Lk 11:42
18:13 [s]Isa 66:2; Jer 31:19; Lk 23:48 [t]Lk 5:32; 1Ti 1:15
18:14 [u]S Mt 23:12
18:17 [v]Mt 11:25; 18:3

[s] *11* Or *to*

5:8). Prayer can protect us from the evil one (Mt 6:13). (3) In our prayers, we should cry out against sin and for justice (v. 7). (4) Persistent prayer is counted as faith (v. 8). (5) In the final days before Christ's return, there will be increased diabolic opposition to the prayers of the faithful (1Ti 4:1). Because of Satan and the pleasures of the world, many will cease having a persistent prayer life (8:14; Mt 13:22; Mk 4:19).

18:7 CHOSEN ONES, WHO CRY OUT . . . DAY AND NIGHT. God's true chosen ones (i.e., those persevering in faith and holiness) will never cease crying out to God for Christ's return to destroy Satan's power and the present evil world system. They will persevere in prayer to "see that they get justice, and quickly" (v. 8), and for Christ to reign in righteousness, knowing that Christ's coming is the only real hope for this world (cf. Jn 14:2; 1Th 5:2–3; 2Th 2:8; Rev 19:11–21).

18:8 HE WILL SEE THAT THEY GET JUSTICE. When Jesus returns for those who cry out to him day and night (v. 7), he will put an end to the distress and suffering received at the hands of a hostile and evil world, and he will take them to himself (Jn 14:2–3, notes). At his coming, the faithful of his churches will be "caught up together with them in the clouds to meet the Lord in the air" (1Th 4:17). Then God will administer his justice and wrath on the wicked (1Th 5:2–3,9).

18:8 WILL HE FIND FAITH ON THE EARTH? Jesus' question probably indicates that as the time for his return draws near, evil will become so dominant that many in the church will fall away from genuine faith (Mt 24:11–13,24; 1Ti 4:1; see articles on THE GREAT TRIBULATION, p. 1456, THE AGE OF THE ANTICHRIST, p. 1872, and PERSONAL APOSTASY, p. 1918). As we approach history's end, the question for each believer is: Am I persevering in faith, continuing steadfast in prayer and calling on God that justice may be done and his righteous cause may triumph completely and forever? Or am I so preoccupied with this life that I am not looking forward to Christ's return and his eternal kingdom (Rev 19–22)?

18:9–14 THE PHARISEE AND THE TAX COLLECTOR. (1) The Pharisee was self-righteous. Self-righteous people think they are righteous because of their own efforts; they are not conscious of their sinful nature, their own unworthiness and their constant need for God's help, mercy and grace. Because of their exceptional acts of piety and outward goodness, they think that they do not need God's grace. (2) The tax collector, on the other hand, was deeply conscious of his sin and guilt, and in true repentance turned from sin to God for forgiveness and mercy. He typifies the true child of God.

The Rich Ruler

18:18–30pp — Mt 19:16–29; Mk 10:17–30

18A certain ruler asked him, "Good teacher, what must I do to inherit eternal life?"[w]

19"Why do you call me good?" Jesus answered. "No one is good—except God alone. 20You know the commandments: 'Do not commit adultery, do not murder, do not steal, do not give false testimony, honor your father and mother.'[t]"[x]

21"All these I have kept since I was a boy," he said.

22When Jesus heard this, he said to him, "You still lack one thing. Sell everything you have and give to the poor,[y] and you will have treasure in heaven.[z] Then come, follow me."

23When he heard this, he became very sad, because he was a man of great wealth. 24Jesus looked at him and said, "How hard it is for the rich to enter the kingdom of God![a] 25Indeed, it is easier for a camel to go through the eye of a needle than for a rich man to enter the kingdom of God."

26Those who heard this asked, "Who then can be saved?"

27Jesus replied, "What is impossible with men is possible with God."[b]

28Peter said to him, "We have left all we had to follow you!"[c]

29"I tell you the truth," Jesus said to them, "no one who has left home or wife or brothers or parents or children for the sake of the kingdom of God 30will fail to receive many times as much in this age and, in the age to come,[d] eternal life."[e]

Jesus Again Predicts His Death

18:31–33pp — Mt 20:17–19; Mk 10:32–34

31Jesus took the Twelve aside and told them, "We are going up to Jerusalem,[f] and everything that is written by the prophets[g] about the Son of Man[h] will be fulfilled. 32He will be handed over to the Gentiles.[i] They will mock him, insult him, spit on him, flog him[j] and kill him.[k] 33On the third day[l] he will rise again."[m]

34The disciples did not understand any of this. Its meaning was hidden from them, and they did not know what he was talking about.[n]

A Blind Beggar Receives His Sight

18:35–43pp — Mt 20:29–34; Mk 10:46–52

35As Jesus approached Jericho,[o] a blind man was sitting by the roadside begging. 36When he heard the crowd going by, he asked what was happening. 37They told him, "Jesus of Nazareth is passing by."[p]

38He called out, "Jesus, Son of David,[q] have mercy[r] on me!"

39Those who led the way rebuked him and told him to be quiet, but he shouted all the more, "Son of David, have mercy on me!"[s]

40Jesus stopped and ordered the man to be brought to him. When he came near, Jesus asked him, 41"What do you want me to do for you?"

"Lord, I want to see," he replied.

42Jesus said to him, "Receive your sight; your faith has healed you."[t] 43Immediately he received his sight and followed Jesus, praising God. When all the people saw it, they also praised God.[u] Lk 19:36-40

Zacchaeus the Tax Collector

19 Jesus entered Jericho[v] and was passing through. 2A man was there by the name of Zacchaeus; he was a chief tax collector and was wealthy. 3He wanted to see who Jesus was, but being a short man he could not, because of the crowd. 4So he ran ahead and climbed a sycamore-fig[w] tree to see him, since Jesus was coming that way.[x]

5When Jesus reached the spot, he looked up and said to him, "Zacchaeus,

18:18 [w]Lk 10:25 **18:20** [x]Ex 20:12-16; Dt 5:16-20; Ro 13:9 **18:22** [y]S Ac 2:45 [z]S Mt 6:20 **18:24** [a]Pr 11:28 **18:27** [b]S Mt 19:26 **18:28** [c]S Mt 4:19 **18:30** [d]S Mt 12:32 [e]S Mt 25:46 **18:31** [f]S Lk 9:51 [g]Ps 22; Isa 53 [h]S Mt 8:20 **18:32** [i]Lk 23:1 [j]S Mt 16:21 [k]S Ac 2:23 **18:33** [l]S Mt 16:21 [m]S Mt 16:21 **18:34** [n]S Mk 9:32 **18:35** [o]Lk 19:1 **18:37** [p]Lk 19:4 **18:38** [q]ver 39; S Mt 9:27 [r]Mt 17:15; Lk 18:13 **18:39** [s]ver 38 **18:42** [t]S Mt 9:22 **18:43** [u]S Mt 9:8; Lk 13:17 **19:1** [v]Lk 18:35 **19:4** [w]1Ki 10:27; 1Ch 27:28; Isa 9:10 [x]Lk 18:37

[t]*20* Exodus 20:12-16; Deut. 5:16-20

18:22 SELL EVERYTHING YOU HAVE. See Mt 19:21, note.

18:25 A RICH MAN . . . THE KINGDOM. The disciples, holding the view generally held by the Jews, were amazed at these declarations of Jesus about the rich (vv. 24–26). For more on this topic, see RICHES AND POVERTY, p. 1562.

18:30 RECEIVE MANY TIMES AS MUCH. See Mk 10:30, note.

19:1–10 CONVERSION OF ZACCHAEUS. Jesus was still seeking to save the lost (v. 10) only a few days before his crucifixion; this was the purpose of his coming (cf. 15:3–7; Eze 34:16). Zacchaeus, a tax collector, earned his living by collecting more than he should have from the people. For this reason, tax collectors were despised by the people. Jesus' concern for Zacchaeus admonishes us to bring the gospel to the undesirables of society, for all people are lost and in need of salvation.

RICHES AND POVERTY

***Lk 18:24–25** "Jesus looked at him and said, 'How hard it is for the rich to enter the kingdom of God! Indeed, it is easier for a camel to go through the eye of a needle than for a rich man to enter the kingdom of God.'"*

One of the Lord's most shocking statements is that it is virtually impossible for a rich person to enter God's kingdom. Yet this is but one of many statements he made about riches and poverty, giving a perspective repeated by the apostles in several NT letters.

RICHES. (1) The prevailing view among NT Jews was that to be wealthy was a sign of God's special favor and that to be poor was a sign of faithlessness and God's displeasure (see Pr 10:15, note). The Pharisees, for example, thought this way and derided Jesus for his poverty (Lk 16:14). Although this false idea recurs at times in the history of the Christian church, it is soundly rejected by Christ (see Lk 6:20; 16:13; 18:24–25).

(2) The Bible identifies greed and the pursuit of wealth with idolatry, which is demonic (cf. 1Co 10:19–20; Col 3:5); (see article on THE NATURE OF IDOLATRY, p. 394). Because of the demonic power associated with possessions, the desire for wealth and the pursuit of it often bring enslavement (cf. Mt 6:24).

(3) Riches are, in Jesus' perspective, an obstacle both to salvation and to discipleship (Mt 19:24; 13:22). They give a false sense of security (Lk 12:15ff), they deceive (Mt 13:22) and they demand the total loyalty of one's heart (Mt 6:21). The rich often live as if they have no need of God. By searching for riches, their spiritual lives are choked (Lk 8:14), and they are led into temptation and harmful desires (1Ti 6:9), resulting in the abandonment of saving faith (1Ti 6:10). All too often those who are rich take advantage of the poor (Jas 2:5–6). Therefore, no Christian ought to desire to get rich (1Ti 6:9–11).

(4) Selfish amassing of material possessions is an indication that life is no longer seen from eternity's vantage point (Col 3:1). Selfish, greedy people no longer find their goals and fulfillment centered in God, but rather in themselves and their possessions. The tragedy of Lot's wife, for example, was her placing all her affections on an earthly city rather than a heavenly one (Ge 19:16,26; Lk 17:28–33; Heb 11:8–10). In other words, striving after wealth has in it the seed of total alienation from God (1Ti 6:10).

(5) True riches for a Christian consist in faith and love that express themselves in self-denial and following Jesus (1Co 13:4–7; Php 2:3–5). The truly rich are those who have gained freedom from the things of the world through confidence that God is their Father and that he will not forsake them (2Co 9:8; Php 4:19; Heb 13:5–6).

(6) With regard to the proper attitude toward, and use of, our possessions, the righteous are obligated to be faithful (Lk 16:11). Christians must not hold tightly to possessions as personal wealth or security, but they must relinquish their wealth and place their resources in the Lord's hands for use in his kingdom, for the furtherance of Christ's cause on earth, and for the salvation and need of others (see article on TITHES AND OFFERINGS, p. 1392). Thus, believers who possess wealth and material goods must see themselves as no longer rich, but merely as stewards of that which is God's (Lk 12:31–48), and they must be generous, ready to share and rich in good deeds (Eph 4:28; 1Ti 6:17–19).

(7) Every Christian should examine his or her own heart and desires: Am I a greedy person? Am I a selfish person? Do I yearn for abundance? Do I have a great desire for the honor, prestige and power that often come from gaining great wealth?

POVERTY. One of the tasks that Jesus saw as his Spirit-directed mission was "to preach good news to the poor" (Lk 4:18; cf. Isa 61:1). In other words, the gospel of Christ can be defined as a gospel of the poor (Mt 5:3; 11:5; Lk 7:22; Jas 2:5).

(1) The "poor" (Gk *ptōchos*) are the humble and afflicted within the world who turn to God in great need and seek his help. At the same time they are faithful to God and look forward to God's redemption of his people from the sin, suffering, hunger and hatred that are in the world. They do not seek their wealth and life in earthly things (see Ps 18:27; 22:26; 25:9; 37:11; 72:2,12–13; 74:19; 147:6; Isa 11:4; 29:19; Lk 6:20; 16:25; Jn 14:3, note).

(2) Deliverance from suffering, oppression, injustice and poverty will most certainly come to God's poor (Lk 6:20–23; 18:1–8). Their relief, at least in part, must come from benevolent offerings given by those among God's people who have been blessed with material possessions (see article on THE CARE OF THE POOR AND NEEDY, p. 1316).

(3) God sees his people in poverty and declares that they "are rich" (Rev 2:9). In no way can they be seen as spiritually or morally inferior (see Rev 2:9, note).

JESUS IN GALILEE

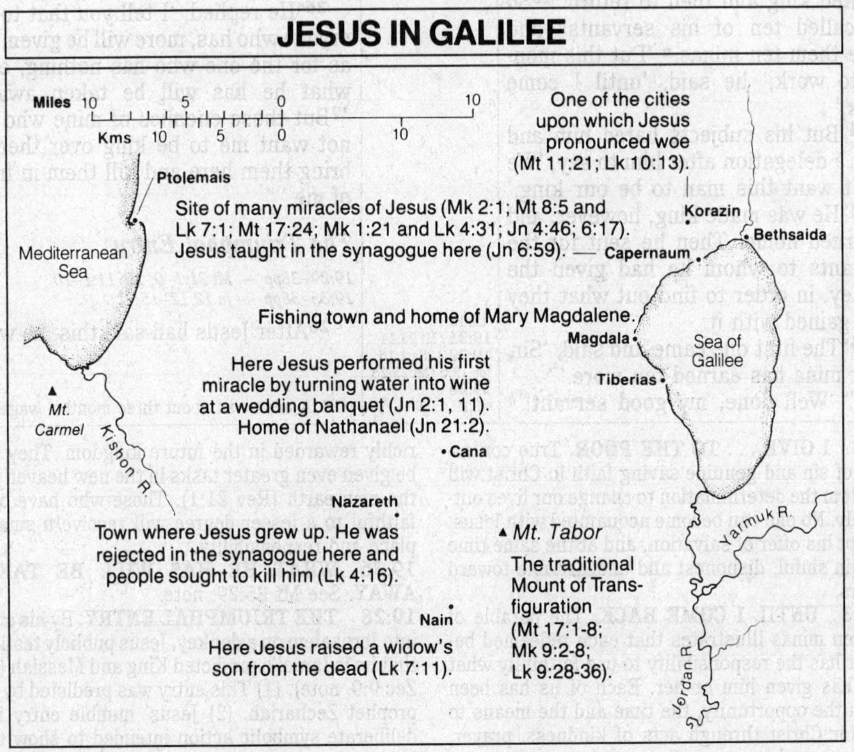
Miles 10 5 0 10
Kms 10 5 0 10
One of the cities upon which Jesus pronounced woe (Mt 11:21; Lk 10:13).
Ptolemais
Site of many miracles of Jesus (Mk 2:1; Mt 8:5 and Lk 7:1; Mt 17:24; Mk 1:21 and Lk 4:31; Jn 4:46; 6:17). Jesus taught in the synagogue here (Jn 6:59). — Capernaum
Korazin
Bethsaida
Mediterranean Sea
Fishing town and home of Mary Magdalene.
Magdala
Sea of Galilee
Tiberias
Here Jesus performed his first miracle by turning water into wine at a wedding banquet (Jn 2:1, 11). Home of Nathanael (Jn 21:2).
Mt. Carmel
Kishon R.
Cana
Nazareth
Town where Jesus grew up. He was rejected in the synagogue here and people sought to kill him (Lk 4:16).
Mt. Tabor
The traditional Mount of Transfiguration (Mt 17:1-8; Mk 9:2-8; Lk 9:28-36).
Yarmuk R.
Nain
Here Jesus raised a widow's son from the dead (Lk 7:11).
Jordan R.

come down immediately. I must stay at
your house today." **6**So he came down
at once and welcomed him gladly.
7All the people saw this and began
to mutter, "He has gone to be the guest
of a 'sinner.' "[y]
8But Zacchaeus stood up and said to
the Lord,[z] "Look, Lord! Here and now
I give half of my possessions to the
poor, and if I have cheated anybody out
of anything,[a] I will pay back four
times the amount."[b]
9Jesus said to him, "Today salvation
has come to this house, because this
man, too, is a son of Abraham.[c] **10**For
the Son of Man came to seek and to
save what was lost."[d]

✝ Jn 1:12

The Parable of the Ten Minas

19:12–27Ref — Mt 25:14–30

11While they were listening to this,
he went on to tell them a parable, because he was near Jerusalem and the
people thought that the kingdom of
God[e] was going to appear at once.[f]
12He said: "A man of noble birth went
to a distant country to have himself appointed king and then to return. **13**So
he called ten of his servants[g] and
gave them ten minas.[u] 'Put this money to work,' he said, 'until I come
back.'
14"But his subjects hated him and
sent a delegation after him to say, 'We
don't want this man to be our king.'
15"He was made king, however, and
returned home. Then he sent for the
servants to whom he had given the
money, in order to find out what they
had gained with it.
16"The first one came and said, 'Sir,
your mina has earned ten more.'
17" 'Well done, my good servant!'[h]
his master replied. 'Because you have
been trustworthy in a very small matter, take charge of ten cities.'[i]
18"The second came and said, 'Sir,
your mina has earned five more.'
19"His master answered, 'You take
charge of five cities.'
20"Then another servant came and
said, 'Sir, here is your mina; I have
kept it laid away in a piece of cloth. **21**I
was afraid of you, because you are a
hard man. You take out what you did
not put in and reap what you did not
sow.'[j]
22"His master replied, 'I will judge
you by your own words,[k] you wicked
servant! You knew, did you, that I am
a hard man, taking out what I did not
put in, and reaping what I did not
sow?[l] **23**Why then didn't you put my
money on deposit, so that when I came
back, I could have collected it with interest?'
24"Then he said to those standing
by, 'Take his mina away from him and
give it to the one who has ten minas.'
25" 'Sir,' they said, 'he already has
ten!'
26"He replied, 'I tell you that to everyone who has, more will be given, but
as for the one who has nothing, even
what he has will be taken away.[m]
27But those enemies of mine who did
not want me to be king over them—
bring them here and kill them in front
of me.' "

The Triumphal Entry

19:29–38pp — Mt 21:1–9; Mk 11:1–10
19:35–38pp — Jn 12:12–15

28After Jesus had said this, he went

19:7 [y] S Mt 9:11
19:8 [z] S Lk 7:13 [a] Lk 3:12,13 [b] Ex 22:1; Lev 6:4,5; Nu 5:7; 2Sa 12:6; Eze 33:14,15
19:9 [c] S Lk 3:8
19:10 [d] Eze 34:12,16; S Jn 3:17
19:11 [e] S Mt 3:2 [f] Lk 17:20; Ac 1:6
19:13 [g] Mk 13:34
19:17 [h] Pr 27:18 [i] Lk 16:10
19:21 [j] Mt 25:24
19:22 [k] 2Sa 1:16; Job 15:6 [l] Mt 25:26
19:26 [m] S Mt 25:29

[u] *13* A mina was about three months' wages.

19:8 I GIVE . . . TO THE POOR. True confession of sin and genuine saving faith in Christ will result in the determination to change our lives outwardly. No one can become acquainted with Jesus, accept his offer of salvation, and at the same time remain sinful, dishonest and uncharitable toward others.

19:13 UNTIL I COME BACK. The parable of the ten minas illustrates that each redeemed believer has the responsibility to use faithfully what God has given him or her. Each of us has been given the opportunity, the time and the means to live for Christ through acts of kindness, prayer, offerings and in many other ways.

19:17 YOU HAVE BEEN TRUSTWORTHY. Whoever has been faithful in service for the Lord and has shared his burden here on earth will be richly rewarded in the future kingdom. They will be given even greater tasks in the new heaven and the new earth (Rev 21:1). Those who have been faithful to a lesser degree will receive a smaller place and responsibility.

19:26 WHAT HE HAS WILL BE TAKEN AWAY. See Mt 25:29, note.

19:28 THE TRIUMPHAL ENTRY. By his entry into Jerusalem on a donkey, Jesus publicly testifies that he is Israel's predicted King and Messiah (see Zec 9:9, note). (1) This entry was predicted by the prophet Zechariah. (2) Jesus' humble entry is a deliberate symbolic action intended to show that his kingdom is not of this world and that he did not come to rule the world with force or violence. His refusal to take action as a military conqueror demonstrates that his kingdom is spiritual.

on ahead, going up to Jerusalem.[n]
29 As he approached Bethphage and
Bethany[o] at the hill called the Mount
of Olives,[p] he sent two of his disciples, saying to them, 30 "Go to the village ahead of you, and as you enter it,
you will find a colt tied there, which no
one has ever ridden. Untie it and bring
it here. 31 If anyone asks you, 'Why are
you untying it?' tell him, 'The Lord
needs it.' "
32 Those who were sent ahead went
and found it just as he had told them.[q]
33 As they were untying the colt, its
owners asked them, "Why are you untying the colt?"
34 They replied, "The Lord needs it."
35 They brought it to Jesus, threw
their cloaks on the colt and put Jesus
on it. 36 As he went along, people
spread their cloaks[r] on the road.
37 When he came near the place
where the road goes down the Mount
of Olives,[s] the whole crowd of disciples began joyfully to praise God in
loud voices for all the miracles they
had seen:

38 "Blessed is the king who comes in
the name of the Lord!"[v][t]

"Peace in heaven and glory in the
highest!"[u]

39 Some of the Pharisees in the
crowd said to Jesus, "Teacher, rebuke
your disciples!"[v]
40 "I tell you," he replied, "if they
keep quiet, the stones will cry out."[w]

19:28 [n]Mk 10:32; S Lk 9:51
19:29 [o]S Mt 21:17 [p]S Mt 21:1
19:32 [q]Lk 22:13
19:36 [r]2Ki 9:13
19:37 [s]S Mt 21:1
19:38 [t]Ps 118:26; Lk 13:35 [u]S Lk 2:14
19:39 [v]Mt 21:15, 16
19:40 [w]Hab 2:11
19:41 [x]Isa 22:4; Lk 13:34,35
19:43 [y]Isa 29:3; Jer 6:6; Eze 4:2; 26:8; Lk 21:20
19:44 [z]Ps 137:9 [a]Lk 21:6 [b]1Pe 2:12
19:46 [c]Isa 56:7 [d]Jer 7:11

Ac 2:46-47

Jesus Weeps Over Jerusalem

41 As he approached Jerusalem and
saw the city, he wept over it[x] 42 and
said, "If you, even you, had only known
on this day what would bring you
peace — but now it is hidden from your
eyes. 43 The days will come upon you
when your enemies will build an em-
bankment against you and encircle you
and hem you in on every side.[y] 44 They
will dash you to the ground, you and
the children within your walls.[z] They
will not leave one stone on another,[a]
because you did not recognize the time
of God's coming[b] to you."

Jesus at the Temple

19:45,46pp — Mt 21:12–16; Mk 11:15–18; Jn 2:13–16

45 Then he entered the temple area
and began driving out those who were
selling. 46 "It is written," he said to
them, " 'My house will be a house of
prayer'[w];[c] but you have made it 'a
den of robbers.'[x]"[d]
47 Every day he was teaching at the

[v] *38* Psalm 118:26 [w] *46* Isaiah 56:7
[x] *46* Jer. 7:11

19:41 SAW THE CITY, HE WEPT. Jesus, knowing that the people and their leaders expect a political Messiah and will ultimately reject him as God's promised Messiah, weeps in pity for the people who will soon suffer terrible judgment. The word "wept" in Greek means more than shedding tears. It suggests a lamentation, a wailing, a heaving of the bosom — the sob and the cry of a soul in agony. Jesus, as God, reveals not only his own feelings, but also God's broken heart over the lostness of the human race and their refusal to repent and accept salvation (see Mk 11:9, note).

19:43 YOUR ENEMIES . . . ENCIRCLE YOU. Jesus' prediction was fulfilled forty years later (A.D. 70) when Jerusalem was destroyed by the Roman army and hundreds of thousands of Jews were killed.

19:45 DRIVING OUT THOSE WHO WERE SELLING. The cleansing of the temple was the first great public act of Jesus' ministry (Jn 2:13–22) and the last great public act of his ministry (cf. Mt 21:12–17; Mk 11:15–17). In blazing anger, he drove from God's house the ungodly, the greedy and those who were destroying its true spiritual purpose. Jesus' double cleansing of the temple during his three-year ministry indicates how important the spiritual lessons are:

(1) Christ's greatest concern is for holiness and godly sincerity within his church (cf. Jn 17:17,19). He died to "make her holy, cleansing her . . . and to present her . . . holy and blameless" (Eph 5:25–27).

(2) Worship in the church must be in spirit and in truth (Jn 4:24). The church must be a place of prayer and communion with God (cf. Mt 21:13).

(3) Christ will condemn all who use the church, the gospel or his kingdom for personal gain, glory, or self-promotion.

(4) Sincere love for God and for his redemptive purposes will result in a consuming "zeal" for the righteousness of God's house and kingdom (Jn 2:17). True Christlikeness includes intolerance toward unrighteousness within the church (cf. Rev 2–3).

(5) Essential to all true Christian ministry is protest against those who profane and degrade the kingdom of God (cf. 1Co 6:9–11; Gal 1:6–10; Rev 2–3).

(6) Either we will allow Christ into our assemblies to purge out deceit, immorality, secularization and desecration (see Rev 2–3) or at his second coming, he, in divine judgment, will cleanse his churches with finality (see Mal 3:2).

19:46 HOUSE OF PRAYER. See Mk 11:17, note.

temple.[e] But the chief priests, the teachers of the law and the leaders among the people were trying to kill him.[f] 48Yet they could not find any way to do it, because all the people hung on his words.

The Authority of Jesus Questioned

20:1–8pp — Mt 21:23–27; Mk 11:27–33

20 One day as he was teaching the people in the temple courts[g] and preaching the gospel,[h] the chief priests and the teachers of the law, together with the elders, came up to him. 2"Tell us by what authority you are doing these things," they said. "Who gave you this authority?"[i]

3He replied, "I will also ask you a question. Tell me, 4John's baptism[j]—was it from heaven, or from men?"

5They discussed it among themselves and said, "If we say, 'From heaven,' he will ask, 'Why didn't you believe him?' 6But if we say, 'From men,' all the people[k] will stone us, because they are persuaded that John was a prophet."[l]

7So they answered, "We don't know where it was from."

8Jesus said, "Neither will I tell you by what authority I am doing these things."

The Parable of the Tenants

20:9–19pp — Mt 21:33–46; Mk 12:1–12

9He went on to tell the people this parable: "A man planted a vineyard,[m] rented it to some farmers and went away for a long time.[n] 10At harvest time he sent a servant to the tenants so they would give him some of the fruit of the vineyard. But the tenants beat him and sent him away empty-handed. 11He sent another servant, but that one also they beat and treated shamefully and sent away empty-handed. 12He sent still a third, and they wounded him and threw him out.

13"Then the owner of the vineyard said, 'What shall I do? I will send my son, whom I love;[o] perhaps they will respect him.'

14"But when the tenants saw him, they talked the matter over. 'This is the heir,' they said. 'Let's kill him, and the inheritance will be ours.' 15So they threw him out of the vineyard and killed him.

"What then will the owner of the vineyard do to them? 16He will come and kill those tenants[p] and give the vineyard to others."

When the people heard this, they said, "May this never be!"

17Jesus looked directly at them and asked, "Then what is the meaning of that which is written:

" 'The stone the builders rejected
has become the capstone[y]'[z]?[q]

18Everyone who falls on that stone will be broken to pieces, but he on whom it falls will be crushed."[r]

19The teachers of the law and the chief priests looked for a way to arrest him[s] immediately, because they knew he had spoken this parable against them. But they were afraid of the people.[t]

Paying Taxes to Caesar

20:20–26pp — Mt 22:15–22; Mk 12:13–17

20Keeping a close watch on him, they sent spies, who pretended to be honest. They hoped to catch Jesus in something he said[u] so that they might hand him over to the power and authority of the governor.[v] 21So the spies questioned him: "Teacher, we know that you speak and teach what is right, and that you do not show partiality but teach the way of God in accordance

19:47 [e] S Mt 26:55 [f] S Mt 12:14; Mk 11:18
20:1 [g] S Mt 26:55 [h] Lk 8:1
20:2 [i] Jn 2:18; Ac 4:7; 7:27
20:4 [j] S Mk 1:4
20:6 [k] Lk 7:29 [l] S Mt 11:9
20:9 [m] Isa 5:1-7 [n] Mt 25:14
20:13 [o] S Mt 3:17
20:16 [p] Lk 19:27
20:17 [q] Ps 118:22; S Ac 4:11
20:18 [r] Isa 8:14, 15
20:19 [s] Lk 19:47 [t] S Mk 11:18
20:20 [u] S Mt 12:10 [v] Mt 27:2

[y] 17 Or *cornerstone*   [z] 17 Psalm 118:22

20:2 BY WHAT AUTHORITY? The religious leaders questioned Jesus' authority to cleanse the temple or to teach the people (19:45–48). They were offended and angered because Jesus condemned the evil practices within God's house, while they themselves tolerated and participated in those practices. Such actions demonstrate how unfit they were to be spiritual leaders. Jesus, as a true spiritual leader, used his authority for the sake of truth and righteousness, even though it cost him his life.

20:9–16 THE PARABLE OF THE TENANTS. See Mt 21:33, note.

20:16 GIVE THE VINEYARD TO OTHERS. See Mt 21:43, note on the kingdom of God taken from Israel.

20:18 THAT STONE. Those who do not accept Jesus will be broken, and those who fall under his judgment will be completely pulverized. See Isa 8:14 and Lk 2:34, where Christ is presented as a stone that causes stumbling and a rock that makes people fall; also Da 2:34–35,44–45, where the Messiah is a rock that crushes the kingdoms of the world.

with the truth.[w] **22**Is it right for us to
pay taxes to Caesar or not?"
23He saw through their duplicity and
said to them, **24**"Show me a denarius.
Whose portrait and inscription are on
it?"
25"Caesar's," they replied.
He said to them, "Then give to Caesar what is Caesar's,[x] and to God
what is God's."
26They were unable to trap him in
what he had said there in public. And
astonished by his answer, they became
silent.

The Resurrection and Marriage

20:27–40pp — Mt 22:23–33; Mk 12:18–27

27Some of the Sadducees,[y] who say
there is no resurrection,[z] came to
Jesus with a question. **28**"Teacher,"
they said, "Moses wrote for us that if
a man's brother dies and leaves a wife
but no children, the man must marry
the widow and have children for his
brother.[a] **29**Now there were seven
brothers. The first one married a woman and died childless. **30**The second
31and then the third married her, and
in the same way the seven died, leaving
no children. **32**Finally, the woman died
too. **33**Now then, at the resurrection
whose wife will she be, since the seven
were married to her?"
34Jesus replied, "The people of this
age marry and are given in marriage.
35But those who are considered worthy
of taking part in that age[b] and in the
resurrection from the dead will neither
marry nor be given in marriage, **36**and
they can no longer die; for they are like
the angels. They are God's children,[c]
since they are children of the resurrection. **37**But in the account of the bush,
even Moses showed that the dead rise,
for he calls the Lord 'the God of Abraham, and the God of Isaac, and the God
of Jacob.'[a][d] **38**He is not the God of the
dead, but of the living, for to him all are
alive."
39Some of the teachers of the law
responded, "Well said, teacher!" **40**And
no one dared to ask him any more
questions.[e]

Whose Son Is the Christ?

20:41–47pp — Mt 22:41–23:7; Mk 12:35–40

41Then Jesus said to them, "How is
it that they say the Christ[b] is the Son
of David?[f] **42**David himself declares
in the Book of Psalms:

" 'The Lord said to my Lord:
"Sit at my right hand
43until I make your enemies
a footstool for your feet." '[c][g]

44David calls him 'Lord.' How then can
he be his son?"
45While all the people were listening, Jesus said to his disciples, **46**"Beware of the teachers of the law. They
like to walk around in flowing robes
and love to be greeted in the marketplaces and have the most important
seats in the synagogues and the places
of honor at banquets.[h] **47**They devour
widows' houses and for a show make
lengthy prayers. Such men will be punished most severely."

The Widow's Offering

21:1–4pp — Mk 12:41–44

21 As he looked up, Jesus saw the
rich putting their gifts into the

20:21 [w] Jn 3:2
20:25 [x] Lk 23:2; Ro 13:7
20:27 [y] S Ac 4:1 [z] Ac 23:8; 1Co 15:12
20:28 [a] Dt 25:5
20:35 [b] S Mt 12:32
20:36 [c] S Jn 1:12
20:37 [d] Ex 3:6
20:40 [e] Mt 22:46; Mk 12:34
20:41 [f] S Mt 1:1
20:43 [g] Ps 110:1; S Mt 22:44
20:46 [h] S Lk 11:43

[a] *37* Exodus 3:6 [b] *41* Or *Messiah*
[c] *43* Psalm 110:1

20:25 THEN GIVE TO CAESAR. Believers under normal circumstances must pay taxes and submit to governmental authority (see Ro 13:1–7), even though our highest loyalty is to God. We must obey secular government except when it conflicts with the law of God; we must *never* disobey Jesus' command to "give to Caesar what is Caesar's."

20:36 LIKE THE ANGELS. About the believer's life in the next age, Jesus reveals that it begins with a resurrection from the dead, involves having a glorified body that can never die, but no longer includes earthly relationships such as marriage. The fact that earthly relationships will be different does not mean we will not recognize each other. Jesus, after his resurrection, was recognized by his disciples (24:31,39; Mt 28:9).

20:44 DAVID CALLS HIM 'LORD'. The Jews thought that the Messiah would be a descendant of David and therefore only a human ruler. Jesus shows that David's statement in Ps 110:1, where he refers to his son as "Lord," indicates that the Messiah is more than a human ruler; he is also the divine Son of God (see Ps 110:1–7, note).

20:46 BEWARE OF THE TEACHERS OF THE LAW. See Mt 23:13, note; see article on FALSE TEACHERS, p. 1506.

21:1–4 THE WIDOW'S OFFERING. Jesus gives a lesson on how God evaluates giving. (1) A person's gift is determined not by the amount he or she gives, but by the amount of sacrifice involved in the giving. The rich at times give only out of their wealth—it involves no sacrifice. The gift of the widow cost her everything. She gave as much as she possibly could. (2) This principle can

PASSION WEEK

1. ARRIVAL IN BETHANY — FRIDAY — Jn 12:1

Jesus arrived in Bethany six days before the Passover to spend some time with his friends, Mary, Martha and Lazarus. While here, Mary anointed his feet with costly perfume as an act of humility. This tender expression indicated Mary's devotion to Jesus and her willingness to serve him.

2. SABBATH — DAY OF REST — SATURDAY — Not mentioned in the Gospels

Since this day was the Sabbath, the Lord spent the day in traditional fashion with his friends.

3. THE TRIUMPHAL ENTRY — SUNDAY — Mt 21:1-11; Mk 11:1-11; Lk 19:28-44; Jn 12:12-19

On the first day of the week Jesus rode into Jerusalem on a donkey, fulfilling an ancient prophecy (Zec 9:9). The crowd welcomed him with "Hosanna" and the words of Ps 118:25-26, thus ascribing to him a Messianic title as the agent of the Lord, the coming King of Israel.

4. CLEARING OF THE TEMPLE — MONDAY — Mt 21:10-17; Mk 11:15-18; Lk 19:45-48

On this day he returned to the temple and found the court of the Gentiles full of traders and money changers making a large profit as they gave out Jewish coins in exchange for "pagan" money. Jesus drove them out and overturned their tables.

5. DAY OF CONTROVERSY AND PARABLES — TUESDAY — Mt 21:23–24:51; Mk 11:27–13:37; Lk 20:1–21:36

In Jerusalem - Jesus evaded the traps set by the priests.
On the Mount of Olives Overlooking Jerusalem - He taught in parables and warned the people against the Pharisees. He predicted the destruction of Herod's great temple and told his disciples about future events, including his own return.

6. DAY OF REST — WEDNESDAY — Not mentioned in the Gospels

The Scriptures do not mention this day, but the counting of the days (Mk 14:1; Jn 12:1) seems to indicate that there was another day concerning which the Gospels record nothing.

7. PASSOVER LAST SUPPER — THURSDAY — Mt 26:17-30; Mk 14:12-26; Lk 22:7-23; Jn 13:1-30

In an upper room Jesus prepared both himself and his disciples for his death. He gave the Passover meal a new meaning. The loaf of bread and cup of wine represented his body soon to be sacrificed and his blood soon to be shed. And so he instituted the "Lord's Supper." After singing a hymn they went to the Garden of Gethsemane, where Jesus prayed in agony, knowing what lay ahead for him.

8. CRUCIFIXION — FRIDAY — Mt 27:1-66; Mk 15:1-47; Lk 22:66–23:56; Jn 18:28–19:37

Following betrayal, arrest, desertion, false trials, denial, condemnation, beatings and mockery, Jesus was required to carry his cross to "The Place of the Skull," where he was crucified with two other prisoners.

9. IN THE TOMB — FRIDAY — Mt 27:57-61; Mk 15:42-47; Lk 23:50-56; Jn 19:38-42

Jesus' body was placed in the tomb before 6:00 P.M. Friday night, when the Sabbath began and all work stopped, and it lay in the tomb throughout the Sabbath.

10. RESURRECTION — SUNDAY — Mt 28:1-13; Mk 16:1-20; Lk 24:1-49; Jn 20:1-31

Early in the morning, women went to the tomb and found that the stone closing the tomb's entrance had been rolled back. An angel told them Jesus was alive and gave them a message. Jesus appeared to Mary Magdalene in the garden, to Peter, to two disciples on the road to Emmaus, and later that day to all the disciples but Thomas. His resurrection was established as a fact.

temple treasury.[i] 2He also saw a poor
widow put in two very small copper
coins.[d] 3"I tell you the truth," he said,
"this poor widow has put in more than
all the others. 4All these people gave
their gifts out of their wealth; but she
out of her poverty put in all she had to
live on."[j]

Signs of the End of the Age

21:5–36pp — Mt 24; Mk 13
21:12–17pp — Mt 10:17–22

5Some of his disciples were remark-
ing about how the temple was adorned
with beautiful stones and with gifts
dedicated to God. But Jesus said, 6"As
for what you see here, the time will
come when not one stone will be left on
another;[k] every one of them will be
thrown down."

7"Teacher," they asked, "when will
these things happen? And what will be
the sign that they are about to take
place?"

8He replied: "Watch out that you are
not deceived. For many will come in my
name, claiming, 'I am he,' and, 'The
time is near.' Do not follow them.[l]
9When you hear of wars and revolutions, do not be frightened. These
things must happen first, but the end
will not come right away."

10Then he said to them: "Nation will
rise against nation, and kingdom
against kingdom.[m] 11There will be
great earthquakes, famines and pestilences in various places, and fearful
events and great signs from heaven.[n]

12"But before all this, they will lay
hands on you and persecute you. They
will deliver you to synagogues and
prisons, and you will be brought before
kings and governors, and all on account of my name. 13This will result in
your being witnesses to them.[o] 14But
make up your mind not to worry beforehand how you will defend yourselves.[p] 15For I will give you[q] words
and wisdom that none of your adversaries will be able to resist or contradict. 16You will be betrayed even by
parents, brothers, relatives and
friends,[r] and they will put some of you
to death. 17All men will hate you because of me.[s] 18But not a hair of your
head will perish.[t] 19By standing firm
you will gain life.[u]

20"When you see Jerusalem being
surrounded by armies,[v] you will know
that its desolation is near. 21Then let
those who are in Judea flee to the
mountains, let those in the city get out,
and let those in the country not enter
the city.[w] 22For this is the time of punishment[x] in fulfillment[y] of all that
has been written. 23How dreadful it
will be in those days for pregnant wom-

21:1 [i] Mt 27:6; Jn 8:20
21:4 [j] 2Co 8:12
21:6 [k] Lk 19:44
21:8 [l] Lk 17:23
21:10 [m] 2Ch 15:6; Isa 19:2
21:11 [n] Isa 29:6; Joel 2:30
21:13 [o] Php 1:12
21:14 [p] Lk 12:11
21:15 [q] S Lk 12:12
21:16 [r] Lk 12:52, 53
21:17 [s] S Jn 15:21
21:18 [t] S Mt 10:30
21:19 [u] S Mt 10:22
21:20 [v] S Lk 19:43
21:21 [w] Lk 17:31
21:22 [x] Isa 63:4; Da 9:24-27; Hos 9:7 [y] S Mt 1:22

[d] 2 Greek *two lepta*

be applied to all our service for Jesus. He judges our work and ministry not by its size or influence or success, but by the amount of sincere dedication, sacrifice, faith and love involved (see 22:24–30, note; Mt 20:26, note).

21:6 NOT ONE STONE WILL BE LEFT ON ANOTHER. The fulfillment of this prediction occurred in A.D. 70, when the Roman general Titus and his army destroyed Jerusalem and burned the temple after a siege of 134 days. The temple was destroyed as a judgment on Israel for their rejection of God's Son and his redemption.

21:7–19 WHEN WILL THESE THINGS HAPPEN? Jesus' response to the disciples' question links the destruction of Jerusalem so closely with his return to earth after the tribulation that it is difficult to distinguish between the portions referring only to Jerusalem and those referring to his second coming. Jesus probably meant the destruction of Jerusalem as a type of his coming to judge the world.

21:8 WATCH OUT THAT YOU ARE NOT DECEIVED. See Mt 24:5, note.

21:9 WARS AND REVOLUTIONS. See Mt 24:4, note.

21:16 THEY WILL PUT SOME OF YOU TO DEATH. Ancient writers state that all the apostles (except John) died as martyrs at the hands of persecutors. Many believers were tortured and killed in the early days of Christianity (see Mt 24:9, note).

21:18 NOT A HAIR . . . WILL PERISH. This promise guarantees spiritual security, not physical preservation (cf. death referred to in v. 16). If believers remain faithful, in all things God works for their good (cf. Ro 8:28); nothing can separate them from his love (Ro 8:35–39).

21:19 STANDING FIRM. We must engage in the most intense devotion to Christ through the means of grace, i.e., prayer, witness, study of the Word, worship, Christian fellowship and daily resistance to sin (see Jn 15:6, note). By persevering in true faith, believers gain eternal life and are victorious in all circumstances.

21:20 JERUSALEM BEING SURROUNDED WITH ARMIES. Once again Jesus refers to the events of A.D. 70 (see note on v. 6). Those events fulfilled Jesus' prophecy that divine justice would "come upon this generation" (Mt 23:36; cf. Lk 23:27–30) for their rejection of the Messiah and refusal to turn from their sins. Jesus warns his followers to flee the city when they first see the armies (v. 21).

en and nursing mothers! There will be great distress in the land and wrath against this people. **24**They will fall by the sword and will be taken as prisoners to all the nations. Jerusalem will be trampled[z] on by the Gentiles until the times of the Gentiles are fulfilled.

25"There will be signs in the sun, moon and stars. On the earth, nations will be in anguish and perplexity at the roaring and tossing of the sea.[a] **26**Men will faint from terror, apprehensive of what is coming on the world, for the heavenly bodies will be shaken.[b] **27**At that time they will see the Son of Man[c] coming in a cloud[d] with power and great glory. **28**When these things begin to take place, stand up and lift up your heads, because your redemption is drawing near."[e]

29He told them this parable: "Look at the fig tree and all the trees. **30**When they sprout leaves, you can see for yourselves and know that summer is near. **31**Even so, when you see these things happening, you know that the kingdom of God[f] is near.

32"I tell you the truth, this generation[e][g] will certainly not pass away until all these things have happened. **33**Heaven and earth will pass away, but my words will never pass away.[h]

34"Be careful, or your hearts will be weighed down with dissipation, drunkenness and the anxieties of life,[i] and that day will close on you unexpectedly[j] like a trap. **35**For it will come upon all those who live on the face of the whole earth. **36**Be always on the watch, and pray[k] that you may be able to escape all that is about to happen, and that you may be able to stand before the Son of Man."

37Each day Jesus was teaching at the temple,[l] and each evening he went out[m] to spend the night on the hill called the Mount of Olives,[n] **38**and all the people came early in the morning to hear him at the temple.[o]

Judas Agrees to Betray Jesus

22:1,2pp — Mt 26:2–5; Mk 14:1,2,10,11

22 Now the Feast of Unleavened Bread, called the Passover, was approaching,[p] **2**and the chief priests and the teachers of the law

21:24 [z] Isa 5:5; 63:18; Da 8:13; Rev 11:2
21:25 [a] 2Pe 3:10, 12
21:26 [b] S Mt 24:29
21:27 [c] S Mt 8:20 [d] S Rev 1:7
21:28 [e] Lk 18:7
21:31 [f] S Mt 3:2
21:32 [g] Lk 11:50; 17:25
21:33 [h] S Mt 5:18
21:34 [i] Mk 4:19 [j] Lk 12:40,46; 1Th 5:2-7
21:36 [k] Mt 26:41
21:37 [l] S Mt 26:55 [m] Mk 11:19 [n] S Mt 21:1
21:38 [o] Jn 8:2
22:1 [p] S Jn 11:55

[e] *32* Or *race*

21:24 THE TIMES OF THE GENTILES. "The times of the Gentiles" refers to the time Israel would be under the domination or oppression of non-Jews. It began when a part of Israel was taken to Babylon in 586 B.C. (2Ch 36:1–21; Da 1:1–2). It will not end until the times are fulfilled, which probably means when Christ comes in glory and power to establish his rule over all the nations (1:32–33; Jer 23:5–6; Zec 6:13; 9:10; Ro 11:25–26; Rev 20:4).

21:25 SIGNS IN THE SUN, MOON AND STARS. Cosmic signs will precede Jesus' coming, and the world will be in utmost distress because of the great tribulation (see Mt 24:29, note; article on THE GREAT TRIBULATION, p. 1456). The impenitent will be in great terror and despair.

21:27 THE SON OF MAN COMING. "Son of Man" is the term Jesus often used to refer to himself (see Mt 24:30, note on Christ's coming after the tribulation).

21:31 WHEN YOU SEE THESE THINGS HAPPENING. One can tell that the time of Jesus' glorious appearing to establish his kingdom is near by watching the signs (see Mt 24:33, note). On the other hand, Christ's return for the faithful believers of his churches at an unknown and unexpected time (i.e., the rapture or catching away of all true believers, cf. Jn 14:1–4; 1Th 4:13–18) is probably referred to in vv. 34–36 (see Mt 24:44, note).

21:31 KINGDOM OF GOD IS NEAR. See Mt 24:33, note.

21:32 THIS GENERATION. See Mt 24:34, note.

21:34 DAY WILL CLOSE ON YOU UNEXPECTEDLY. Jesus concludes his prophetic message by warning his followers not to be so preoccupied with the pleasures and cares of the world that they fail to be prepared for his coming. (1) These words are meant for all God's people of all ages, not just those living during the final days of tribulation. The demand for spiritual faithfulness is critical in the light of Jesus' teaching that he will return for the faithful believers at an unexpected time. Since the time of his coming for the church cannot be determined, believers must always be ready (see Mt 24:40,42, notes; Jn 14:3, note). (2) Christ's rapture of the faithful (1Th 4:16–17) "rescues us from the coming wrath" (1Th 1:10), in order that we "may be able to escape all that is about to happen" on earth (vv. 35–36; cf. vv. 25–26; see next note; Rev 3:10, note).

21:36 ESCAPE ALL THAT IS ABOUT TO HAPPEN. Followers of Christ must be on the watch against sin and pray that their love for Christ will not diminish, in order that they might receive strength to persevere in faith and righteousness in Jesus Christ. Only by such perseverance will they be able to "escape" all the terrible things coming on the world in the last days (see 1Th 1:10, note; Rev 3:10, note; see article on THE GREAT TRIBULATION, p. 1456). Many believe that the means of "escape" for those who faithfully keep on praying is the rapture (see Jn 14:3, note; see article on THE RAPTURE, p. 1864).

22:1 PASSOVER. See Mt 26:2, note.

were looking for some way to get rid of
Jesus,[q] for they were afraid of the people. **3**Then Satan[r] entered Judas,
called Iscariot,[s] one of the Twelve.
4And Judas went to the chief priests
and the officers of the temple guard[t]
and discussed with them how he might
betray Jesus. **5**They were delighted and
agreed to give him money.[u] **6**He consented, and watched for an opportunity
to hand Jesus over to them when no
crowd was present.

The Last Supper

22:7–13pp — Mt 26:17–19; Mk 14:12–16
22:17–20pp — Mt 26:26–29; Mk 14:22–25; 1Co 11:23–25
22:21–23pp — Mt 26:21–24; Mk 14:18–21; Jn 13:21–30
22:25–27pp — Mt 20:25–28; Mk 10:42–45
22:33,34pp — Mt 26:33–35; Mk 14:29–31; Jn 13:37,38

7Then came the day of Unleavened
Bread on which the Passover lamb had
to be sacrificed.[v] **8**Jesus sent Peter
and John,[w] saying, "Go and make
preparations for us to eat the Passover."
9"Where do you want us to prepare
for it?" they asked.
10He replied, "As you enter the city,
a man carrying a jar of water will meet
you. Follow him to the house that he
enters, **11**and say to the owner of the
house, 'The Teacher asks: Where is
the guest room, where I may eat the
Passover with my disciples?' **12**He will
show you a large upper room, all furnished. Make preparations there."
13They left and found things just as
Jesus had told them.[x] So they prepared the Passover.
14When the hour came, Jesus and
his apostles[y] reclined at the table.[z]
15And he said to them, "I have eagerly
desired to eat this Passover with you
before I suffer.[a] **16**For I tell you, I will
not eat it again until it finds fulfillment
in the kingdom of God."[b]
17After taking the cup, he gave
thanks and said, "Take this and divide
it among you. **18**For I tell you I will not
drink again of the fruit of the vine until
the kingdom of God comes."
19And he took bread, gave thanks
and broke it,[c] and gave it to them,
saying, "This is my body given for you;
do this in remembrance of me."
20In the same way, after the supper
he took the cup, saying, "This cup is
the new covenant[d] in my blood, which
is poured out for you. **21**But the hand
of him who is going to betray me is with
mine on the table.[e] **22**The Son of
Man[f] will go as it has been decreed,[g]
but woe to that man who betrays him."
23They began to question among themselves which of them it might be who
would do this.
24Also a dispute arose among them

22:2 [q] S Mt 12:14 **22:3** [r] S Mt 4:10 [s] S Mt 10:4 **22:4** [t] ver 52; Ac 4:1; 5:24 **22:5** [u] Zec 11:12 **22:7** [v] Ex 12:18-20; Dt 16:5-8; S Mk 14:12 **22:8** [w] Ac 3:1,11; 4:13,19; 8:14
22:13 [x] Lk 19:32 **22:14** [y] S Mk 6:30 [z] Mt 26:20; Mk 14:17,18 **22:15** [a] S Mt 16:21 **22:16** [b] S Lk 14:15 **22:19** [c] S Mt 14:19 **22:20** [d] Ex 24:8; Isa 42:6; Jer 31:31-34; Zec 9:11; 2Co 3:6; Heb 8:6; 9:15 **22:21** [e] Ps 41:9 **22:22** [f] S Mt 8:20 [g] Ac 2:23; 4:28

22:3 SATAN ENTERED JUDAS. The tragic story of Judas, who at one time was in intimate fellowship with Jesus (Ps 41:9; cf. Jn 13:18) but then forsook his Lord by betraying him (see Jn 6:64, note), serves as a warning to all who follow Christ. In this life there is always the possibility that we might grow cold toward Christ, allow Satan little by little to lead us into compromise with the world, and then in the end betray the Lord and his cause.

22:18 THE LORD'S SUPPER. See 1Co 11:24–25, note.

22:18 THE FRUIT OF THE VINE. What Jesus and the disciples drank at the Passover supper is called "the cup" or "the cup of thanksgiving" (22:17; Mt 26:27; Mk 14:23; 1Co 10:16; 11:25), and "the fruit of the vine" (22:18; Mt 26:29; Mk 14:25). Scriptural evidence supports the view that the juice of the vine was unfermented at the Lord's Supper (see article on WINE IN NEW TESTAMENT TIMES (1), p. 1534).

22:20 THE NEW COVENANT IN MY BLOOD. Jesus announces the inauguration of the new covenant based on his sacrificial death (cf. Mt 26:28; 1Co 11:25; see Jer 31:31, note). Scripture teaches that the new covenant could only become valid by the death of Christ (Heb 9:15–18). The disciples entered into this new covenant when they were regenerated and indwelt by the Holy Spirit on the evening of Jesus' resurrection (see article on THE REGENERATION OF THE DISCIPLES, p. 1627). They later were baptized in the Holy Spirit on the day of Pentecost (see Ac 2:4, note; see article on BAPTISM IN THE HOLY SPIRIT, p. 1642).

22:20 MY BLOOD, WHICH IS POURED OUT FOR YOU. See Mt 26:28, note.

22:24–30 TRUE GREATNESS. True greatness is a matter of inward spirit and heart. It is seen in the person who expresses his or her love for Christ in sincere humility (Php 2:3), in a desire to serve both God and fellow humans, and in a willingness to be seen as the least important in God's kingdom.

(1) We must understand that greatness is not position, office, leadership, power, influence, academic degrees, fame, ability, great accomplishments or success. It is not so much what we *do* for God as what we *are* in spirit before him (vv. 25–27; Mt 18:3–4; 20:25–28).

(2) True greatness requires that we become great in the right areas. We need to learn to be great in faith, humility, godly character, wisdom, self-control, patience and love (Gal 5:22–23). It is

as to which of them was considered to
be greatest.[h] 25Jesus said to them,
"The kings of the Gentiles lord it over
them; and those who exercise authority over them call themselves Benefac-
tors. 26But you are not to be like that.
Instead, the greatest among you
should be like the youngest,[i] and the
one who rules like the one who
serves.[j] 27For who is greater, the one
who is at the table or the one who
serves? Is it not the one who is at the
table? But I am among you as one who
serves.[k] 28You are those who have
stood by me in my trials. 29And I confer
on you a kingdom,[l] just as my Father
conferred one on me, 30so that you may
eat and drink at my table in my kingdom[m] and sit on thrones, judging the
twelve tribes of Israel.[n]
31"Simon, Simon, Satan has asked[o]
to sift you[f] as wheat.[p] 32But I have
prayed for you,[q] Simon, that your
faith may not fail. And when you have
turned back, strengthen your brothers."[r]
33But he replied, "Lord, I am ready
to go with you to prison and to
death."[s]
34Jesus answered, "I tell you, Peter,
before the rooster crows today, you
will deny three times that you know
me."

35Then Jesus asked them, "When I
sent you without purse, bag or sandals,[t] did you lack anything?"
"Nothing," they answered.
36He said to them, "But now if you
have a purse, take it, and also a bag;
and if you don't have a sword, sell your
cloak and buy one. 37It is written: 'And
he was numbered with the transgressors'[g];[u] and I tell you that this must
be fulfilled in me. Yes, what is written
about me is reaching its fulfillment."
38The disciples said, "See, Lord,
here are two swords."
"That is enough," he replied.

Jesus Prays on the Mount of Olives

22:40–46pp — Mt 26:36–46; Mk 14:32–42

39Jesus went out as usual[v] to the
Mount of Olives,[w] and his disciples
followed him. 40On reaching the place,
he said to them, "Pray that you will not
fall into temptation."[x] 41He withdrew
about a stone's throw beyond them,
knelt down[y] and prayed, 42"Father, if
you are willing, take this cup[z] from
me; yet not my will, but yours be
done."[a] 43An angel from heaven appeared to him and strengthened him.[b]
44And being in anguish, he prayed

22:24 [h]Mk 9:34; Lk 9:46 **22:26** [i]1Pe 5:5 [j]S Mk 9:35 **22:27** [k]S Mt 20:28 **22:29** [l]S Mt 25:34; 2Ti 2:12 **22:30** [m]S Lk 14:15 [n]S Mt 19:28 **22:31** [o]Job 1:6-12 [p]Am 9:9 **22:32** [q]Jn 17:9, 15; S Ro 8:34 [r]Jn 21:15-17 **22:33** [s]Jn 11:16 **22:35** [t]Mt 10:9, 10; Lk 9:3; 10:4 **22:37** [u]Isa 53:12 **22:39** [v]Lk 21:37 [w]S Mt 21:1 **22:40** [x]Mt 6:13 **22:41** [y]Lk 18:11 **22:42** [z]S Mt 20:22 [a]S Mt 26:39 **22:43** [b]Mt 4:11; Mk 1:13

[f]31 The Greek is plural. [g]37 Isaiah 53:12

to have the greatness of Christ, who "loved righteousness and hated wickedness" (Heb 1:9).

(3) True greatness is a matter of heartfelt love for and commitment to God. It requires being consecrated and faithful wherever God chooses to place us. Therefore, in God's sight, the greatest in his kingdom are those with the greatest love for him and commitment to his revealed Word (21:3; Ro 12:1–2).

(4) Consecration will improve your results in God's work, but only in that area in which God has placed you and in the context of the gifts he has given you (Ro 12:3–8; 1Co 12).

22:27 THE ONE WHO SERVES. Concerning those who are chosen to lead in the church (1Ti 3:1–7), Christ says that they must lead as servants, helping others to fulfill God's will for their lives. They must never misuse or betray their position by seeking fame, power, wealth or special privilege.

22:28 STOOD BY ME. Jesus acknowledges that he is grateful for the disciples' faithfulness to him during his life and the trying circumstances that surrounded it. Our greatest concern should also be to stand by him in a world that is hostile to his cause and to his righteous standards.

22:29 CONFER ON YOU A KINGDOM. Jesus provides "a kingdom" for his faithful followers, one he has established (v. 30). The disciples must not expect earthly glory and worldly power in this age.

22:31–32 SATAN . . . SIFT YOU AS WHEAT. Jesus' statement concerning Peter reveals two important truths. (1) God allows Satan to tempt us only within certain limits and by God's permission (see Job 1:10,12, notes). The devil is not free to do what he wants with God's people. (2) Jesus prays that the faith of his people may not fail. As our heavenly intercessor, he prays for all who "come to God through him, because he always lives to intercede for them" (Heb 7:25). God is faithful in all our temptations to provide a way of escape (1Co 10:13). However, the fulfillment of Jesus' prayers are conditional. If a person rejects the grace of God, Christ's intercession is then of no effect (see 19:41, note).

22:36 SWORD . . . BUY ONE. Jesus may be using irony here in his statement that his disciples ought to buy a sword. After all, up to this point he has been challenging them to live the life of the cross rather than choose the way of the world. Jesus then goes on to state (v. 37) his commitment to God's way of suffering and to the cross. V. 38 indicates that the disciples did not understand what Jesus meant.

22:42 THIS CUP. See Mt 26:39, note.

22:44 SWEAT WAS LIKE DROPS OF BLOOD. For the ten stages of Christ's redemptive suffering, see notes on Mt 26:37ff.

more earnestly, and his sweat was like
drops of blood falling to the ground.[h]
45When he rose from prayer and
went back to the disciples, he found
them asleep, exhausted from sorrow.
46"Why are you sleeping?" he asked
them. "Get up and pray so that you will
not fall into temptation."[c]

Jesus Arrested

22:47–53pp — Mt 26:47–56; Mk 14:43–50; Jn 18:3–11

47While he was still speaking a
crowd came up, and the man who was
called Judas, one of the Twelve, was
leading them. He approached Jesus to
kiss him, 48but Jesus asked him, "Judas, are you betraying the Son of Man
with a kiss?"
49When Jesus' followers saw what
was going to happen, they said, "Lord,
should we strike with our swords?"[d]
50And one of them struck the servant
of the high priest, cutting off his right
ear.
51But Jesus answered, "No more of
this!" And he touched the man's ear
and healed him.
52Then Jesus said to the chief
priests, the officers of the temple
guard,[e] and the elders, who had come
for him, "Am I leading a rebellion, that
you have come with swords and clubs?
53Every day I was with you in the temple courts,[f] and you did not lay a hand
on me. But this is your hour[g]—when
darkness reigns."[h]

Peter Disowns Jesus

22:55–62pp — Mt 26:69–75; Mk 14:66–72; Jn 18:16–18,25–27

54Then seizing him, they led him
away and took him into the house of
the high priest.[i] Peter followed at a
distance.[j] 55But when they had kindled a fire in the middle of the courtyard and had sat down together, Peter
sat down with them. 56A servant girl
saw him seated there in the firelight.
She looked closely at him and said,
"This man was with him."

22:46 [c]ver 40
22:49 [d]ver 38
22:52 [e]ver 4
22:53 [f]S Mt 26:55 [g]Jn 12:27 [h]Mt 8:12; Jn 1:5; 3:20
22:54 [i]Mt 26:57; Mk 14:53 [j]Mt 26:58; Mk 14:54; Jn 18:15

57But he denied it. "Woman, I don't
know him," he said.
58A little later someone else saw
him and said, "You also are one of
them."
"Man, I am not!" Peter replied.
59About an hour later another asserted, "Certainly this fellow was with
him, for he is a Galilean."[k]
60Peter replied, "Man, I don't know
what you're talking about!" Just as he
was speaking, the rooster crowed.
61The Lord[l] turned and looked
straight at Peter. Then Peter remembered the word the Lord had spoken to
him: "Before the rooster crows today,
you will disown me three times."[m]
62And he went outside and wept bitterly.

The Guards Mock Jesus

22:63–65pp — Mt 26:67,68; Mk 14:65; Jn 18:22,23

63The men who were guarding Jesus
began mocking and beating him.
64They blindfolded him and demanded,
"Prophesy! Who hit you?" 65And they
said many other insulting things to
him.[n]

Jesus Before Pilate and Herod

22:67–71pp — Mt 26:63–66; Mk 14:61–63; Jn 18:19–21
23:2,3pp — Mt 27:11–14; Mk 15:2–5; Jn 18:29–37
23:18–25pp — Mt 27:15–26; Mk 15:6–15; Jn 18:39–19:16

66At daybreak the council[o] of the
elders of the people, both the chief
priests and teachers of the law, met together,[p] and Jesus was led before
them. 67"If you are the Christ,[i]" they
said, "tell us."
Jesus answered, "If I tell you, you
will not believe me, 68and if I asked
you, you would not answer.[q] 69But
from now on, the Son of Man will be
seated at the right hand of the mighty
God."[r]

22:59 [k]Lk 23:6
22:61 [l]S Lk 7:13 [m]ver 34
22:65 [n]S Mt 16:21
22:66 [o]S Mt 5:22 [p]Mt 27:1; Mk 15:1
22:68 [q]Lk 20:3-8
22:69 [r]S Mk 16:19

h *44* Some early manuscripts do not have verses 43 and 44. i *67* Or *Messiah*

22:54 THEN SEIZING HIM. For the order of events from Christ's arrest to his crucifixion, see Mt 26:57, note.

22:62 WEPT BITTERLY. Peter denied the Lord out of weakness, not out of wickedness, for he never ceased to love his Master and to believe in him. Peter was spiritually weak and incapable of resisting great temptation since he had not yet, along with the other disciples, received the Holy Spirit and his regenerating grace in the full new covenant sense. They received the Holy Spirit's indwelling presence only on the resurrection day (see Mk 14:50, note; see article on THE REGENERATION OF THE DISCIPLES, p. 1627).

22:63 MOCKING AND BEATING HIM. See Mt 26:67, note.

70 They all asked, "Are you then the
Son of God?"[s]
He replied, "You are right in saying
I am."[t]
71 Then they said, "Why do we need
any more testimony? We have heard it
from his own lips."

23 Then the whole assembly rose
and led him off to Pilate.[u]
2 And they began to accuse him, saying,
"We have found this man subverting
our nation.[v] He opposes payment of
taxes to Caesar[w] and claims to be
Christ,[j] a king."[x]
3 So Pilate asked Jesus, "Are you the
king of the Jews?"
"Yes, it is as you say," Jesus replied.
4 Then Pilate announced to the chief
priests and the crowd, "I find no basis
for a charge against this man."[y]
5 But they insisted, "He stirs up the
people all over Judea[k] by his teaching.
He started in Galilee[z] and has come
all the way here."
6 On hearing this, Pilate asked if the
man was a Galilean.[a] 7 When he
learned that Jesus was under Herod's
jurisdiction, he sent him to Herod,[b]
who was also in Jerusalem at that time.
8 When Herod saw Jesus, he was
greatly pleased, because for a long
time he had been wanting to see him.[c]
From what he had heard about him, he
hoped to see him perform some miracle. 9 He plied him with many questions, but Jesus gave him no answer.[d]
10 The chief priests and the teachers of
the law were standing there, vehe-
mently accusing him. 11 Then Herod
and his soldiers ridiculed and mocked
him. Dressing him in an elegant
robe,[e] they sent him back to Pilate.
12 That day Herod and Pilate became
friends[f]—before this they had been
enemies.
13 Pilate called together the chief
priests, the rulers and the people,
14 and said to them, "You brought me
this man as one who was inciting the
people to rebellion. I have examined
him in your presence and have found
no basis for your charges against
him.[g] 15 Neither has Herod, for he sent
him back to us; as you can see, he has
done nothing to deserve death.
16 Therefore, I will punish him[h] and
then release him.[l]"
18 With one voice they cried out,
"Away with this man! Release Barabbas to us!"[i] 19 (Barabbas had been
thrown into prison for an insurrection
in the city, and for murder.)
20 Wanting to release Jesus, Pilate
appealed to them again. 21 But they
kept shouting, "Crucify him! Crucify
him!"
22 For the third time he spoke to
them: "Why? What crime has this man
committed? I have found in him no
grounds for the death penalty. Therefore I will have him punished and then
release him."[j]
23 But with loud shouts they insistently demanded that he be crucified,
and their shouts prevailed. 24 So Pilate
decided to grant their demand. 25 He released the man who had been thrown
into prison for insurrection and murder, the one they asked for, and surrendered Jesus to their will.

22:70 [s] S Mt 4:3 [t] Mt 27:11; Lk 23:3
23:1 [u] S Mt 27:2
23:2 [v] ver 14 [w] Lk 20:22 [x] Jn 19:12
23:4 [y] ver 14,22, 41; Mt 27:23; Jn 18:38; 1Ti 6:13; S 2Co 5:21
23:5 [z] Mk 1:14
23:6 [a] Lk 22:59
23:7 [b] S Mt 14:1
23:8 [c] Lk 9:9
23:9 [d] S Mk 14:61
23:11 [e] Mk 15:17-19; Jn 19:2,3
23:12 [f] Ac 4:27
23:14 [g] S ver 4
23:16 [h] ver 22; Mt 27:26; Jn 19:1; Ac 16:37; 2Co 11:23,24
23:18 [i] Ac 3:13, 14
23:22 [j] ver 16

[j] 2 Or *Messiah*; also in verses 35 and 39
[k] 5 Or *over the land of the Jews*
[l] 16 Some manuscripts *him.*" [17] *Now he was obliged to release one man to them at the Feast.*

23:1 PILATE. Pilate was the Roman governor in Jerusalem at the time of the Passover. Jesus was brought to him because under Roman law the Jews could not legally carry out the death penalty. Pilate has become a symbol of those who make religious decisions based on political expediency rather than truth and justice. Believers must not compromise the Word of God; they must stand for what is right, and not for those things that would only serve their own selfish ambitions.

23:3 ARE YOU THE KING OF THE JEWS? See Mt 27:2, note.

23:8–11 JESUS BEFORE KING HEROD. This is the same Herod who had John the Baptist beheaded. Because Herod's heart is so hardened, Jesus refuses to speak to him. In anger Herod and his men mock Jesus' claim to be the king of the Jews.

23:11 MOCKED HIM ... ELEGANT ROBE. See Mt 27:28–29, note.

23:14 NO BASIS FOR YOUR CHARGES. Jesus was accused of treason against Rome. Pilate comes to the conclusion that Jesus is innocent of any rebellion against the Roman government. Jesus declares that his kingdom is not a political kingdom of this world, but a spiritual kingdom (see Jn 18:36).

23:22 HAVE HIM PUNISHED. See Mt 27:26, note.

23:25 SURRENDERED JESUS TO THEIR WILL. It is because of political expediency that Pilate hands Jesus over to the Jewish authorities (see v. 1, note).

The Crucifixion

23:33–43pp — Mt 27:33–44; Mk 15:22–32; Jn 19:17–24

26As they led him away, they seized
Simon from Cyrene,[k] who was on his
way in from the country, and put the
cross on him and made him carry it behind Jesus.[l] **27**A large number of people followed him, including women
who mourned and wailed[m] for him.
28Jesus turned and said to them,
"Daughters of Jerusalem, do not weep
for me; weep for yourselves and for
your children.[n] **29**For the time will
come when you will say, 'Blessed are
the barren women, the wombs that
never bore and the breasts that never
nursed!'[o] **30**Then

" 'they will say to the mountains,
"Fall on us!"
and to the hills, "Cover us!" '[m][p]

31For if men do these things when the
tree is green, what will happen when it
is dry?"[q]
32Two other men, both criminals,
were also led out with him to be executed.[r] **33**When they came to the
place called the Skull, there they crucified him, along with the criminals—
one on his right, the other on his left.
34Jesus said, "Father,[s] forgive them,
for they do not know what they are doing."[n][t] And they divided up his
clothes by casting lots.[u]
35The people stood watching, and
the rulers even sneered at him.[v] They
said, "He saved others; let him save
himself if he is the Christ of God, the
Chosen One."[w]
36The soldiers also came up and
mocked him.[x] They offered him wine
vinegar[y] **37**and said, "If you are the
king of the Jews,[z] save yourself."
38There was a written notice above
him, which read: THIS IS THE KING OF THE
JEWS.[a]
39One of the criminals who hung
there hurled insults at him: "Aren't you
the Christ? Save yourself and us!"[b]
40But the other criminal rebuked
him. "Don't you fear God," he said,
"since you are under the same sentence? **41**We are punished justly, for we
are getting what our deeds deserve.
But this man has done nothing
wrong."[c]
42Then he said, "Jesus, remember

23:26 [k] S Mt 27:32 [l] Mk 15:21; Jn 19:17
23:27 [m] Lk 8:52
23:28 [n] Lk 19:41-44; 21:23,24
23:29 [o] Mt 24:19
23:30 [p] Hos 10:8; Isa 2:19; Rev 6:16
23:31 [q] Eze 20:47
23:32 [r] Isa 53:12; Mt 27:38; Mk 15:27; Jn 19:18
23:34 [s] S Mt 11:25 [t] S Mt 5:44 [u] Ps 22:18
23:35 [v] Ps 22:17 [w] Isa 42:1
23:36 [x] Ps 22:7 [y] Ps 69:21; Mt 27:48
23:37 [z] Lk 4:3,9
23:38 [a] S Mt 2:2
23:39 [b] ver 35,37
23:41 [c] S ver 4

[m] *30* Hosea 10:8 [n] *34* Some early manuscripts do not have this sentence.

23:31 TREE IS GREEN . . . DRY. If the innocent Jesus meets with such a fate, what will be the fate of guilty Jerusalem?

23:33 SKULL. Jesus was crucified in a place outside the city (cf. Heb 13:12). It was called "the Skull" for reasons that are still debated. The Greek word for skull was translated in the Latin version as *calvaria*, from which we get the word "Calvary."

23:33 THEY CRUCIFIED HIM. The crucifixion and death of Jesus are the core and foundation of God's plan of redemption (1Co 1:23–24). Jesus, who had never sinned, died in the place of sinful humanity. Through his crucifixion the penalty for our sin was paid and the work of Satan undone (cf. Ro 3:25, note). Now all people may turn to God in repentance and faith and receive forgiveness and eternal life.

23:34 SEVEN LAST SAYINGS OF CHRIST. In all probability, v. 34 is the first of the seven last sayings of Christ on the cross. The seven sayings were spoken in the following order:

(1) From 9 o'clock until noon: (a) The word of forgiveness: "Father, forgive them" (v. 34). (b) The word of salvation: "Today you will be with me in paradise" (v. 43). (c) The word of love: "Dear woman, here is your son, . . . Here is your mother!" (Jn 19:26–27).

(2) The three hours of darkness: from noon until 3 o'clock, no words reported.

(3) About 3 o'clock: (a) The word of spiritual suffering: "My God, my God, why have you forsaken me?" (Mk 15:34). (b) The word of physical suffering: "I am thirsty" (Jn 19:28). (c) The word of triumph: "It is finished" (Jn 19:30). (d) The word of committal: "Father, into your hands I commit my spirit" (v. 46).

23:35 THE PEOPLE STOOD WATCHING. One of the surest proofs of the depravity of the human heart is the fact that people take pleasure in violence, blood and death. (1) We see it in the Roman and Greek arenas, where spectators cheered as people fought and killed each other. We see it in the onlookers who watched Jesus die a horrible death (vv. 35–37). We see it in the history of the persecution of believers. (2) We see it in modern society as well, as millions of adults and children find pleasure and entertainment in television and other media that depict human suffering, blood, violence and death (see Ro 1:32, note). (3) Jesus died to change this attitude and to bring love and care. He wants us to see the impact of sin on human life with eyes of compassion and to hear the groaning of suffering humanity (see 13:16, note). (4) It is the responsibility of parents to guard themselves and their families against all influences that would desensitize them to human pain and tragedy (see Mt 18:6, note).

23:35 SNEERED AT HIM. See Mt 27:39, note.

me when you come into your kingdom.[o]"[d]
43Jesus answered him, "I tell you the
truth, today you will be with me in paradise."[e]

Jesus' Death

23:44–49pp — Mt 27:45–56; Mk 15:33–41

44It was now about the sixth hour,
and darkness came over the whole
land until the ninth hour,[f] 45for the
sun stopped shining. And the curtain of
the temple[g] was torn in two.[h]
46Jesus called out with a loud voice,[i]
"Father, into your hands I commit my
spirit."[j] When he had said this, he
breathed his last.[k]
47The centurion, seeing what had
happened, praised God[l] and said,
"Surely this was a righteous man."
48When all the people who had gathered to witness this sight saw what
took place, they beat their breasts[m]
and went away. 49But all those who
knew him, including the women who
had followed him from Galilee,[n] stood
at a distance,[o] watching these things.

Jesus' Burial

23:50–56pp — Mt 27:57–61; Mk 15:42–47; Jn 19:38–42

50Now there was a man named Joseph, a member of the Council, a good
and upright man, 51who had not consented to their decision and action. He
came from the Judean town of Arimathea and he was waiting for the kingdom of God.[p] 52Going to Pilate, he
asked for Jesus' body. 53Then he took
it down, wrapped it in linen cloth and
placed it in a tomb cut in the rock, one
in which no one had yet been laid. 54It
was Preparation Day,[q] and the Sabbath was about to begin.
55The women who had come with
Jesus from Galilee[r] followed Joseph
and saw the tomb and how his body
was laid in it. 56Then they went home
and prepared spices and perfumes.[s]
But they rested on the Sabbath in obedience to the commandment.[t]

The Resurrection

24:1–10pp — Mt 28:1–8; Mk 16:1–8; Jn 20:1–8

24 On the first day of the week,
very early in the morning, the
women took the spices they had prepared[u] and went to the tomb. 2They
found the stone rolled away from the
tomb, 3but when they entered, they did
not find the body of the Lord Jesus.[v]
4While they were wondering about
this, suddenly two men in clothes that
gleamed like lightning[w] stood beside
them. 5In their fright the women
bowed down with their faces to the
ground, but the men said to them,
"Why do you look for the living among
the dead? 6He is not here; he has risen!
Remember how he told you, while he
was still with you in Galilee:[x] 7'The
Son of Man[y] must be delivered into
the hands of sinful men, be crucified

23:42 [d]S Mt 16:27
23:43 [e]2Co 12:3, 4; Rev 2:7
23:44 [f]Am 8:9
23:45 [g]Ex 26:31-33; Heb 9:3,8 [h]Heb 10:19,20
23:46 [i]Mt 27:50 [j]Ps 31:5; 1Pe 2:23 [k]Jn 19:30
23:47 [l]S Mt 9:8
23:48 [m]Lk 18:13
23:49 [n]Lk 8:2 [o]Ps 38:11
23:51 [p]Lk 2:25, 38
23:54 [q]Mt 27:62
23:55 [r]ver 49
23:56 [s]Mk 16:1; Lk 24:1 [t]Ex 12:16; 20:10
24:1 [u]Lk 23:56
24:3 [v]ver 23,24
24:4 [w]S Jn 20:12
24:6 [x]Mt 17:22, 23; Lk 9:22; 24:44
24:7 [y]S Mt 8:20

[o] 42 Some manuscripts *come with your kingly power*

23:43 PARADISE. The term "paradise" is used to indicate heaven or the presence of God (that "heaven" and "paradise" indicate the same place is clear from 2Co 12:2,4). Jesus' words clearly teach that after death the saved go immediately into Jesus' presence in heaven.

23:45 CURTAIN OF THE TEMPLE WAS TORN. See Mt 27:51, note.

23:46 FATHER, INTO YOUR HANDS. Jesus voluntarily gave his life over to death. At that moment he went in spirit to his Father in heaven (see Ps 31:5, note).

23:46 I COMMIT MY SPIRIT. See Mt 27:50, note.

24:6 HE HAS RISEN! Jesus' resurrection (see Mt 28:6, note) is confirmed by the following facts. (1) The empty tomb. If the enemies of Jesus had taken his body, they surely would have displayed it to prove he had not risen. If the disciples had taken his body, they would have never sacrificed their lives and possessions for what they knew to be a lie. The empty tomb reveals that Jesus did arise and truly was the Son of God.

(2) The existence, power, joy and devotion of the early church. If Jesus had not risen and appeared to them, they would have never changed from despondency to unheard-of joy, courage and hope (vv. 52–53).

(3) The writing of the NT. The NT was written by men giving their lives for the truth and righteousness taught by Jesus. They would never have taken the trouble to write about a Messiah and his teaching if his ministry had ended in death and disillusionment (see 1Co 15:12–19).

(4) The baptism in the Holy Spirit and his accompanying manifestations within the church. That the Holy Spirit was poured out at Pentecost as an experiential reality is proof that Jesus had risen and was exalted at God's right hand (cf. Ac 1:3–5; 2:33). If Christ had not risen, there would have been no experiential baptism in the Holy Spirit (cf. Jn 16:7).

(5) The millions of people throughout the last 2,000 years who have experienced in their own hearts and lives the presence of Jesus and the witness of the Holy Spirit.

and on the third day be raised again.' "[z] **8**Then they remembered his words.[a]

9When they came back from the tomb, they told all these things to the Eleven and to all the others. **10**It was Mary Magdalene, Joanna, Mary the mother of James, and the others with them[b] who told this to the apostles.[c] **11**But they did not believe[d] the women, because their words seemed to them like nonsense. **12**Peter, however, got up and ran to the tomb. Bending over, he saw the strips of linen lying by themselves,[e] and he went away,[f] wondering to himself what had happened.

On the Road to Emmaus

13Now that same day two of them were going to a village called Emmaus, about seven miles[p] from Jerusalem.[g] **14**They were talking with each other about everything that had happened. **15**As they talked and discussed these things with each other, Jesus himself came up and walked along with them;[h] **16**but they were kept from recognizing him.[i]

17He asked them, "What are you discussing together as you walk along?"

They stood still, their faces downcast. **18**One of them, named Cleopas,[j] asked him, "Are you only a visitor to Jerusalem and do not know the things that have happened there in these days?"

19"What things?" he asked.

"About Jesus of Nazareth,"[k] they replied. "He was a prophet,[l] powerful in word and deed before God and all the people. **20**The chief priests and our rulers[m] handed him over to be sentenced to death, and they crucified him; **21**but we had hoped that he was the one who was going to redeem Israel.[n] And what is more, it is the third day[o] since all this took place. **22**In addition, some of our women amazed us.[p] They went to the tomb early this morning **23**but didn't find his body. They came and told us that they had seen a vision of angels, who said he was alive. **24**Then some of our companions went to the tomb and found it just as the women had said, but him they did not see."[q]

25He said to them, "How foolish you are, and how slow of heart to believe all that the prophets have spoken! **26**Did not the Christ[q] have to suffer these things and then enter his glory?"[r] **27**And beginning with Moses[s] and all the Prophets,[t] he explained to them what was said in all the Scriptures concerning himself.[u]

28As they approached the village to which they were going, Jesus acted as if he were going farther. **29**But they urged him strongly, "Stay with us, for it is nearly evening; the day is almost over." So he went in to stay with them.

30When he was at the table with them, he took bread, gave thanks, broke it[v] and began to give it to them. **31**Then their eyes were opened and they recognized him,[w] and he disappeared from their sight. **32**They asked each other, "Were not our hearts burning within us[x] while he talked with us on the road and opened the Scriptures[y] to us?"

33They got up and returned at once to Jerusalem. There they found the Eleven and those with them, assembled together **34**and saying, "It is true! The Lord[z] has risen and has appeared to Simon."[a] **35**Then the two told what had happened on the way, and how Jesus was recognized by them when he broke the bread.[b]

Jesus Appears to the Disciples

36While they were still talking about this, Jesus himself stood among them and said to them, "Peace be with you."[c]

37They were startled and frightened, thinking they saw a ghost.[d] **38**He said to them, "Why are you troubled, and why do doubts rise in your minds? **39**Look at my hands and my feet. It is

24:7 z S Mt 16:21 **24:8** a Jn 2:22 **24:10** b Lk 8:1-3 c S Mk 6:30 **24:11** d Mk 16:11 **24:12** e Jn 20:3-7 f Jn 20:10 **24:13** g Mk 16:12 **24:15** h ver 36 **24:16** i Jn 20:14; 21:4 **24:18** j Jn 19:25 **24:19** k S Mk 1:24 l S Mt 21:11 **24:20** m Lk 23:13 **24:21** n Lk 1:68; 2:38; 21:28 o S Mt 16:21 **24:22** p ver 1-10 **24:24** q ver 12 **24:26** r Heb 2:10; 1Pe 1:11 **24:27** s Ge 3:15; Nu 21:9; Dt 18:15 t Isa 7:14; 9:6; 40:10,11; 53; Eze 34:23; Da 9:24; Mic 7:20; Mal 3:1 u Jn 1:45 **24:30** v S Mt 14:19 **24:31** w ver 16 **24:32** x Ps 39:3 y ver 27,45 **24:34** z S Lk 7:13 a 1Co 15:5 **24:35** b ver 30,31 **24:36** c Jn 20:19, 21,26; S 14:27 **24:37** d Mk 6:49

p *13* Greek *sixty stadia* (about 11 kilometers)
q *26* Or *Messiah*; also in verse 46

24:15 JESUS HIMSELF CAME UP. For the post-resurrection appearances of Christ, see Mt 28:9, note.

24:19 JESUS . . . A PROPHET. The Gospel writers understood Jesus as "the prophet" sent from God (cf. Dt 18:15–16,19; Mk 6:4; Ac 3:22; see Lk 6:23, note).

24:27 HE EXPLAINED . . . THE SCRIPTURES. The Messiah and his redemptive work through suffering is a central OT theme. Christ may have cited such passages as Ge 3:15; 22:18; 49:10; Nu 24:17; Ps 22:1,18; 110:1; Isa 25:8; 52:14; 53; Jer 23:5; Da 2:24,35,44; Mic 5:2; Zec 3:8; 9:9; 13:7; Mal 3:1 (see article on CHRIST IN THE OLD TESTAMENT, p. 518).

24:39 A GHOST DOES NOT HAVE FLESH.

I myself! Touch me and see;[e] a ghost
does not have flesh and bones, as you
see I have."
40When he had said this, he showed
them his hands and feet. **41**And while
they still did not believe it because of
joy and amazement, he asked them,
"Do you have anything here to eat?"
42They gave him a piece of broiled fish,
43and he took it and ate it in their presence.[f]
44He said to them, "This is what
I told you while I was still with
you:[g] Everything must be fulfilled[h]
that is written about me in the Law
of Moses,[i] the Prophets[j] and the
Psalms."[k]
45Then he opened their minds so
they could understand the Scriptures.
46He told them, "This is what is written: The Christ will suffer[l] and rise
from the dead on the third day,[m] **47**and
repentance and forgiveness of sins will
be preached in his name[n] to all
nations,[o] beginning at Jerusalem.[p]
48You are witnesses[q] of these things. Jn 1:7
49I am going to send you what my Father has promised;[r] but stay in the
city until you have been clothed with
power from on high." Jn 1:33

24:39 [e] Jn 20:27; 1Jn 1:1 **24:43** [f] Ac 10:41 **24:44** [g] Lk 9:45; 18:34 [h] S Mt 1:22; 16:21; Lk 9:22,44; 18:31-33; 22:37 [i] S ver 27 [j] S ver 27 [k] Ps 2; 16; 22; 69; 72; 110; 118 **24:46** [l] S Mt 16:21 [m] S Mt 16:21 **24:47** [n] Ac 5:31; 10:43; 13:38 [o] Mt 28:19; Mk 13:10 [p] Isa 2:3 **24:48** [q] S Jn 15:27; Ac 1:8; 2:32; 4:20; 5:32; 13:31; 1Pe 5:1 **24:49** [r] S Jn 14:16; Ac 1:4 **24:50** [s] S Mt 21:17 **24:51** [t] 2Ki 2:11 **24:53** [u] S Ac 2:46

The Ascension

50When he had led them out to the
vicinity of Bethany,[s] he lifted up his
hands and blessed them. **51**While he
was blessing them, he left them and
was taken up into heaven.[t] **52**Then
they worshiped him and returned to Jerusalem with great joy. **53**And they
stayed continually at the temple,[u]
praising God.

Jesus has a glorified, spiritual body (Php 3:20–21), as do the saints in heaven (1Co 15:40).

24:46 THE IMPORTANCE OF THE RESURRECTION. See Mt 28:6, note.

24:47 REPENTANCE AND FORGIVENESS OF SINS. The disciples were not to preach forgiveness of sins without the demand of repentance. The preacher who offers salvation on the basis of an easy faith or by a mere acceptance of salvation without a commitment to obey Christ and his Word preaches a false gospel. Repentance involves forsaking sin; this has always been an essential element in the true gospel of the NT (see Mt 3:2, note on repentance).

24:47 WILL BE PREACHED. For comments on the Great Commission, see Mt 28:19, note.

24:47 TO ALL NATIONS. Christ himself institutes Christian missions as a holy and mandatory task of the church. Missions is a main theme in both the OT (Ge 22:18; 1Ki 8:41–43; Ps 72:8–11; Isa 2:3; 45:22–25) and the NT (Mt 28:19; Ac 1:8; 28:28; Eph 2:14–18).

24:49 WHAT MY FATHER HAS PROMISED. "What my Father has promised" that will bring "power from on high" refers to the outpouring of the Holy Spirit that began at Pentecost (see Ac 1:4, note; 2:4, note; see article on BAPTISM IN THE HOLY SPIRIT, p. 1642); we find this promise recorded in the OT (Isa 32:15; 44:3; Eze 39:29; Joel 2:28) and in the NT (Jn 14:16–17,26; 15:26; 16:7; Ac 1:4–8; 2:33,38–39). The disciples devoted themselves to prayer as they waited for the fulfillment of the promise (see Ac 1:14, note). The believer today seeking the baptism in the Holy Spirit should do the same.

24:50 HE ... BLESSED THEM. God's blessing on the lives of his followers is essential. Concerning God's blessing, Scripture teaches several things:

(1) The word "blessing" (Gk *eulogia*) has the meaning of: (a) a divine gift causing our work to succeed (Dt 28:12); (b) God's presence with us (Ge 26:3); (c) God giving us strength, power and help (Eph 3:16; Col 1:11); and (d) God working in and through us to produce good (Php 2:13).

(2) In the OT, words related to "blessing" occur more than 400 times. The first thing God did in relation to humanity was to bless them (Ge 1:28). God also sustains his work by blessing (Eze 34:26). The life and history of God's people are under the operation of blessing and cursing (Dt 11:26ff).

(3) In the NT the whole work of Christ can be summed up by the statement that God has "sent him first to you to bless you" (Ac 3:26). We see his blessing given to children (Mk 10:13–16) and to his followers during his departure from earth (vv. 50–51). Blessing likewise plays an integral part in the ministry of the apostles (Ro 15:29).

(4) The blessing of God is conditional. God's people must make a choice: either blessing through obedience or cursing through disobedience (Dt 30:15–18; Jer 17:5,7).

(5) How do we receive the Lord's blessing? Three things are required: (a) We must always look to Jesus for his blessing on our ministry, work and family (Heb 12:2). (b) We must believe in, love and obey him (cf. Mt 5:3–11; 24:45–46; Rev 1:3; 16:15; 22:7). (c) We must remove everything from our lives that would hinder the blessing (Ro 13:12; Eph 4:22; Heb 12:1).

(6) God's "blessing" may not be equated with personal material gain or the absence of suffering in our lives (see Heb 11:37–39; Rev 2:8–10).

JOHN

Outline

The Logos Prologue (1:1–18)

I. Introduction of the Christ to Israel (1:19–51)
   A. By John the Baptist (1:19–36)
   B. To the First Disciples (1:37–51)

II. Christ's Signs and Discourses to Israel and His Rejection (2:1—12:50)
   A. Christ's Revelation to Israel (2:1—11:46)
      1. First Sign: Water into Wine (2:1–11)
         Interlude (2:12)
      2. Initial Witness to the Jews in Jerusalem (2:13–25)
         Feast in Jerusalem (Passover) (2:23–25)
      3. First Discourse: New Birth and New Life (3:1–21)
         Interlude: About John the Baptist and Jesus (3:22—4:3)
      4. Second Discourse: The Water of Life (4:4–42)
         Interlude in Galilee (4:43–45)
      5. Second Sign: Healing the Official's Son (4:46–54)
         Feast in Jerusalem (5:1)
      6. Third Sign: Healing the Paralytic at Bethesda on the Sabbath (5:2–18)
      7. Third Discourse: The Divine Sonship of Christ (5:19–47)
      8. Fourth Sign: Feeding the Five Thousand (6:1–15)
      9. Fifth Sign: Walking on the Water (6:16–21)
      10. Fourth Discourse: The Bread of Life (6:22–59)
      11. Sifting of the Disciples (6:60–71)
          Interlude (7:1)
      12. Feast in Jerusalem (Tabernacles) (7:2–36)
      13. Fifth Discourse: The Life-Giving Spirit (7:37–52)
          [Woman Caught in Adultery (7:53—8:11)]
      14. Sixth Discourse: The Light of the World (8:12–30)
      15. Debate with the Jews (8:31–59)
      16. Sixth Sign: Healing the Man Born Blind (9:1–41)
      17. Seventh Discourse: The Good Shepherd (10:1–21)
          Feast in Jerusalem (Dedication) 10:22–42
      18. Seventh Sign: The Raising of Lazarus (11:1–46)
   B. Christ's Rejection by Israel (11:47—12:50)

III. Christ and the Inception of the New Covenant People (13:1—20:29)
   A. The Last Supper (13:1—14:31)
      1. Washing the Disciples' Feet and Subsequent Conversation (13:1–38)
      2. Jesus, the Way to the Father (14:1–31)
   B. Discourse on the True Vine and the Consequences of Union with Christ (15:1—16:33)
   C. Prayer of Consecration for Himself and the New Covenant People (17:1–26)
   D. The Suffering Servant (18:1—19:42)
      1. Arrest (18:1–12)
      2. Jewish Trial (18:13–27)
      3. Roman Trial (18:28—19:16)

4. Crucifixion (19:17–37)
5. Burial (19:38–42)
E. The Risen Lord (20:1–29)
The Author's Statement of Purpose (20:30–31)
The Epilogue (21:1–25)

Author: John

Theme: Jesus, the Son of God

Date of Writing: A.D. 80–95

Background

John's Gospel is unique among the four Gospels. It records much about Jesus' ministry in Judea and Jerusalem that the other three Gospels omit, and reveals more fully the mystery of Jesus' personhood. The author is identified indirectly as "the disciple whom Jesus loved" (13:23; 19:26; 20:2; 21:7,20). The testimony of ancient Christianity and the internal evidence of the Gospel itself point to authorship by John the son of Zebedee, one of the twelve original disciples and a member of Jesus' inner circle (Peter, James and John).

According to several ancient sources, the elderly apostle John, while residing at Ephesus, was requested by the elders of Asia to write this "spiritual Gospel" in order to counteract and refute a dangerous heresy about the nature, person and deity of Jesus led by a persuasive Jew named Cerinthus. John's Gospel continues to serve the church as a profound theological statement about "the truth" as it is incarnate in Jesus Christ.

Purpose

John states his purpose for writing in 20:31, namely, "that you may believe that Jesus is the Christ, the Son of God, and that by believing you may have life in his name." Ancient Greek manuscripts of John have one of two tenses for the word translated "believe" (20:31): the aorist subjunctive ("that you may begin believing") and the present subjunctive ("that you may go on believing"). If John intended the former, he wrote to convince unbelievers to believe in the Lord Jesus Christ and be saved. If the latter, John wrote to strengthen the foundations of faith so that believers might go on believing in spite of false teaching, and so enter fully into fellowship with the Father and the Son (cf. 17:3). While both of these purposes find support in John, the content of the Gospel as a whole favors the latter emphasis as the overriding purpose.

Survey

The fourth Gospel presents carefully selected evidence that Jesus was Israel's Messiah and God's incarnate (not adopted) Son. The supporting evidence includes (1) seven signs (2:1–11; 4:46–54; 5:2–18; 6:1–15; 6:16–21; 9:1–41; 11:1–46) and seven discourses (3:1–21; 4:4–42; 5:19–47; 6:22–59; 7:37–44; 8:12–30; 10:1–21) by which Jesus disclosed clearly his true identity; (2) seven "I am" statements (6:35; 8:12; 10:7; 10:11; 11:25; 14:6; 15:1) by which Jesus revealed figuratively what he is redemptively for the human race; and (3) the bodily resurrection of Jesus as the ultimate sign and the climactic proof that he is "the Christ, the Son of God" (20:31).

John has two major divisions. (1) Chs. 1–12 present the incarnation and public ministry of Jesus. In spite of Jesus' seven convincing signs, seven profound discourses and seven astounding "I am" claims, the Jews rejected him as their Messiah. (2) Having been rejected by the old covenant Israel, Jesus then (chs. 13–21) focused on his disciples as the nucleus of the new covenant people (i.e., the church he founded). These chapters include Jesus' last supper (ch. 13), his last discourses (chs. 14–16) and his final prayer (ch. 17) for his disciples and for all believers. The new covenant was then initiated and established by his death (chs. 18–19) and resurrection (chs. 20–21).

Special Features

Eight major emphases characterize John's Gospel. (1) It emphasizes the deity of Jesus as "the Son of God." From John's prologue with its grand declaration, "we have seen his glory" (1:14), to the conclusion with Thomas's confession, "my Lord and my God" (20:28), Jesus is God the Son come in the flesh. (2) The word "believe" occurs 98 times, is the equivalent of receiving Christ (1:12), and involves a heart (not just a mental) response that results in an ongoing commitment of one's whole life to him. (3) "Eternal life" is a key Johannine concept, referring not so much to endless existence as to a changed quality of life that comes through a saving union with Christ and results in freedom from both slavery to sin and demons and in a growing knowledge of and fellowship with God. (4) Personal encounters with Jesus are featured throughout the Gospel (no less than 27 of them). (5) The ministry of the Holy Spirit enables believers to experience Jesus' life and power in an ongoing way after Jesus' death and resurrection. (6) It emphasizes "truth"—Jesus is the truth, the Holy Spirit is the Spirit of truth, and God's Word is truth. Truth sets people free (8:32), makes them clean (15:3), and is the antithesis of Satan's nature and activity (8:44–47,51). (7) The number seven is prominent: seven signs, seven discourses and seven "I am" claims testify to who Jesus is (cf. the prominence of the number "seven" in John's book of Revelation). (8) Other prominent Johannine words and concepts are: "light," "word," "flesh," "love," "witness," "know," "darkness" and "world."

Reading John

In order to read the entire New Testament in one year, the book of John should be read in 37 days, according to the following schedule:
☐ 1:1–18 ☐ 1:19–51 ☐ 2 ☐ 3:1–21 ☐ 3:22–36 ☐ 4:1–26 ☐ 4:27–54 ☐ 5:1–30 ☐ 5:31–47 ☐ 6:1–24 ☐ 6:25–59 ☐ 6:60–71 ☐ 7:1–24 ☐ 7:25—8:11 ☐ 8:12–30 ☐ 8:31–47 ☐ 8:48–59 ☐ 9 ☐ 10:1–21 ☐ 10:22–42 ☐ 11:1–16 ☐ 11:17–57 ☐ 12:1–19 ☐ 12:20–50 ☐ 13:1–30 ☐ 13:31—14:14 ☐ 14:15–31 ☐ 15:1–17 ☐ 15:18—16:16 ☐ 16:17–33 ☐ 17 ☐ 18:1–27 ☐ 18:28—19:16 ☐ 19:17–42 ☐ 20:1–18 ☐ 20:19–31 ☐ 21

NOTES

The Word Became Flesh

1 In the beginning was the Word,[a]
and the Word was with God,[b] and
the Word was God.[c] **2**He was with God
in the beginning.[d]
3Through him all things were made;
without him nothing was made that
has been made.[e] **4**In him was life,[f]
and that life was the light[g] of men.
5The light shines in the darkness,[h]
but the darkness has not understood**a**
it.[i]
6There came a man who was sent
Jn 4:7-30 from God; his name was John.[j] **7**He
came as a witness to testify[k] concerning that light, so that through him all
men might believe.[l] **8**He himself was
not the light; he came only as a witness
to the light. **9**The true light[m] that gives
light to every man[n] was coming into
the world.**b**
10He was in the world, and though
the world was made through him,[o] the
world did not recognize him. **11**He
came to that which was his own, but
his own did not receive him.[p] **12**Yet to
all who received him, to those who believed[q] in his name,[r] he gave the
right to become children of God[s]—
13children born not of natural de-

1:1 [a]Isa 55:11; Rev 19:13 [b]Jn 17:5; 1Jn 1:2 [c]Php 2:6
1:2 [d]Ge 1:1; Jn 8:58; 17:5,24; 1Jn 1:1; Rev 1:8
1:3 [e]ver 10; 1Co 8:6; Col 1:16; Heb 1:2
1:4 [f]S Jn 5:26; 6:57; 11:25; 14:6; Ac 3:15; Heb 7:16; 1Jn 1:1,2; 5:20; Rev 1:18 [g]Ps 36:9; Jn 3:19; 8:12; 9:5; 12:46
1:5 [h]Ps 18:28 [i]Jn 3:19
1:6 [j]S Mt 3:1
1:7 [k]ver 15,19, 32; Jn 3:26; 5:33 [l]ver 12; S Jn 3:15
1:9 [m]1Jn 2:8 [n]Isa 49:6
1:10 [o]S ver 3
1:11 [p]Isa 53:3
1:12 [q]ver 7; S Jn 3:15 [r]S 1Jn 3:23 [s]Dt 14:1; S Ro 8:14; 8:16,21; Eph 5:1; 1Jn 3:1,2

a5 Or *darkness, and the darkness has not overcome* **b**9 Or *This was the true light that gives light to every man who comes into the world*

1:1 THE WORD. John begins his Gospel by calling Jesus "the Word" (Gk *logos*). In using this designation for Christ, John presents him as the personal Word of God and indicates that in these last days God has spoken to us in his Son (cf. Heb 1:1–3). Scripture declares that Jesus Christ is the manifold wisdom of God (1Co 1:30; Eph 3:10–11; Col 2:2–3) and the perfect revelation of the nature and person of God (Jn 1:3–5,14,18; Col 2:9). Just as a person's words reveal his or her heart and mind, Christ as "the Word" reveals the heart and mind of God (14:9; see article on THE WORD OF GOD, p. 1062). John gives us three main characteristics of Jesus Christ as "the Word."

(1) The Word's relation to the Father. (a) Christ was preexistent "with God" before the creation of the world (cf. Col 1:15). He was a person existing from eternity, distinct from but in eternal fellowship with God the Father. (b) Christ was divine ("the Word was God"), having the same nature and essence as the Father (Col 2:9; see Mk 1:11, note).

(2) The Word's relation to the world. It was through Christ that God the Father created and now sustains the world (v. 3; Col 1:16; Heb 1:2).

(3) The Word's relation to humanity. "The Word became flesh" (v. 14). In Jesus, God became a human being, having the same nature as humanity but without sin. This is the basic statement of the incarnation: Christ left heaven and entered the condition of human life through the gateway of human birth (see Mt 1:23, note).

1:2 WITH GOD IN THE BEGINNING. Christ was not created; he is eternal, and he has always been in loving fellowship with the Father and the Holy Spirit (see Mk 1:11, note on the Trinity).

1:4 LIFE WAS THE LIGHT OF MEN. True, genuine life is embodied in Christ (cf. 14:6; 17:3). His life was the light for everyone, i.e., God's truth, nature and power are made available to all people through him (8:12; 12:35–36,46).

1:5 LIGHT SHINES IN THE DARKNESS. The light of Christ shines in an evil and sinful world controlled by Satan. The majority of the world has not accepted his life or light, but the darkness has not "understood it" (i.e., mastered it, won over it).

1:9 GIVES LIGHT TO EVERY MAN. Christ illumines all who hear his gospel by imparting a measure of grace and understanding in order that they may freely choose to accept or reject that message. Apart from this light of Christ, there is no other light by which we may see the truth and be saved.

1:10 THE WORLD DID NOT RECOGNIZE HIM. The "world" refers to the whole of society organized and operating independently of God, his Word and his rule. The world will never recognize Christ; it will remain indifferent to or an enemy of Christ and his gospel until the end of the age (see Jas 4:4). For John the world is the great opponent of the Savior in salvation history (cf. Jas 4:4; 1Jn 2:15–17; 4:5).

1:12 RECEIVED . . . BELIEVED. This verse depicts clearly how saving faith is both the act of a single instant and an ongoing attitude of a lifetime. (1) To become a child of God, one must "receive" (Gk *elabon*, from *lambanō*) Christ. The aorist (past) tense here denotes a definite act of faith. (2) Following the act of faith, there must be a continual action of believing. The word "believed" (Gk *pisteuousin*, from *pisteuō*) is a present participle, describing continued action and indicating the need for perseverance in believing. In order for one to be finally saved, true faith must continue after the initial act of accepting Christ (Mt 10:22; 24:12–13; Col 1:21–23; Heb 3:6,12–15).

1:12 BELIEVED. It is important to note that John never uses the noun "belief" (Gk *pistis*). Yet he uses the verb "believe" (*pisteuō*) 98 times. For John, saving faith is an activity, something that people do. True faith is not a static belief and trust in Jesus and his redeeming work, but a loving, self-abandoning commitment that constantly draws one near to him as Lord and Savior (cf. Heb 7:25).

1:12 CHILDREN OF GOD. People have the right to become the adopted children of God only if they are believing in the name of Christ. When they receive him, they are born again and become God's children (3:1–21). Not all people are "children of God."

1:13 BORN NOT OF . . . HUMAN DECISION.

scent,[c] nor of human decision or a husband's will, but born of God.[t]

14The Word became flesh[u] and made his dwelling among us. We have seen his glory,[v] the glory of the One and Only,[d] who came from the Father, full of grace[w] and truth.[x]

15John testifies[y] concerning him. He cries out, saying, "This was he of whom I said, 'He who comes after me has surpassed me because he was before me.' "[z] **16**From the fullness[a] of his grace[b] we have all received one blessing after another. **17**For the law was given through Moses;[c] grace and truth came through Jesus Christ.[d] **18**No one has ever seen God,[e] but God the One and Only,[d,e][f] who is at the Father's side, has made him known.

John the Baptist Denies Being the Christ

19Now this was John's[g] testimony when the Jews[h] of Jerusalem sent priests and Levites to ask him who he was. **20**He did not fail to confess, but confessed freely, "I am not the Christ.[f]"[i]

21They asked him, "Then who are you? Are you Elijah?"[j]

He said, "I am not."

"Are you the Prophet?"[k]

He answered, "No."

22Finally they said, "Who are you? Give us an answer to take back to those who sent us. What do you say about yourself?"

23John replied in the words of Isaiah the prophet, "I am the voice of one calling in the desert,[l] 'Make straight the way for the Lord.' "[g][m]

24Now some Pharisees who had been sent **25**questioned him, "Why then do you baptize if you are not the Christ, nor Elijah, nor the Prophet?"

26"I baptize with[h] water,"[n] John replied, "but among you stands one you do not know. **27**He is the one who comes after me,[o] the thongs of whose sandals I am not worthy to untie."[p]

28This all happened at Bethany on the other side of the Jordan,[q] where John was baptizing.

Jesus the Lamb of God

29The next day John saw Jesus coming toward him and said, "Look, the Lamb of God,[r] who takes away the sin of the world![s] **30**This is the one I meant when I said, 'A man who comes after me has surpassed me because he was before me.'[t] **31**I myself did not know him, but the reason I came baptizing with water was that he might be revealed to Israel."

Jesus Will Baptize in the Spirit

32Then John gave this testimony: "I saw the Spirit come down from heaven as a dove and remain on him.[u] **33**I would not have known him, except that

1:13 [t]Jn 3:6; Tit 3:5; Jas 1:18; 1Pe 1:23; 1Jn 3:9; 4:7; 5:1,4
1:14 [u]Gal 4:4; Php 2:7,8; 1Ti 3:16; Heb 2:14; 1Jn 1:1, 2; 4:2 [v]Ex 33:18; 40:34 [w]S Ro 3:24 [x]Jn 14:6
1:15 [y]ver 7 [z]ver 30; Mt 3:11
1:16 [a]Eph 1:23; Col 1:19; 2:9 [b]S Ro 3:24
1:17 [c]Dt 32:46; Jn 7:19 [d]ver 14
1:18 [e]Ex 33:20; Jn 6:46; Col 1:15; 1Ti 6:16; 1Jn 4:12 [f]Jn 3:16,18; 1Jn 4:9
1:19 [g]S Mt 3:1 [h]Jn 2:18; 5:10,16; 6:41,52; 7:1; 10:24
1:20 [i]Jn 3:28; Lk 3:15,16
1:21 [j]S Mt 11:14 [k]Dt 18:15
1:23 [l]Mt 3:1 [m]Isa 40:3
1:26 [n]S Mk 1:4
1:27 [o]ver 15,30 [p]Mk 1:7
1:28 [q]Jn 3:26; 10:40
1:29 [r]ver 36; Ge 22:8; Isa 53:7; 1Pe 1:19; Rev 5:6; 13:8 [s]S Jn 3:17
1:30 [t]ver 15,27
1:32 [u]Mt 3:16

[c] *13* Greek *of bloods* [d] *14* Or *the Only Begotten* [e] *18* Some manuscripts *but the only* (or *only begotten*) *Son* [f] *20* Or *Messiah.* "The Christ" (Greek) and "the Messiah" (Hebrew) both mean "the Anointed One"; also in verse 25. [g] *23* Isaiah 40:3 [h] *26* Or *in;* also in verses 31 and 33

God was under no constraint to offer us salvation through Christ's death other than the constraint of his own love and compassion. The initiative to bring salvation is with God.

1:14 THE WORD BECAME FLESH. Christ, the eternal God, became a human being (Php 2:5–9). Humanity and deity were united together in him. In a humble way he entered human life with all the limitations of human experiences (cf. 3:17; 6:38–42; 7:29; 9:5; 10:36).

1:17 GRACE AND TRUTH. For those under OT law there was a measure of grace as seen in the faith of the few (Ge 5:24; 7:1; 15:6) and in the promises of forgiveness (Ex 34:6–7; Lev 5:17–18). Now through Christ, grace and truth are available to the fullest extent (Ro 5:17–21). Truth is no longer veiled through the types (such as the sacrifices). "One blessing after another" (v. 16) means that a constant impartation of grace and power is given to believers who respond to the grace given them. Grace is the power, presence and blessing of God experienced by those who receive Christ (see article on FAITH AND GRACE, p. 1720). Salvation does not come by our efforts to keep the law, but by the Holy Spirit and Christ's grace coming into our lives to regenerate our spirits and to re-create us in Christ's image.

1:29 LAMB OF GOD. Jesus is the Lamb provided by God to be sacrificed in the place of sinners (cf. Ex 12:3–17; Isa 53:7; see article on THE PASSOVER, p. 104). By his death, Jesus provided for the removal of the guilt and power of sin and opened the way to God for all in the world.

1:33 WILL BAPTIZE WITH THE HOLY SPIRIT. The word "with" is a translation of the Greek preposition *en* and can be rendered "by," "with" or "in." An alternate translation would be "he who will baptize in the Holy Spirit," just as "baptize with water" may be rendered "baptize in water."

All the Gospels emphasize that Jesus is "he who will baptize with [in] the Holy Spirit" (Mt 3:11; Mk 1:8; Lk 3:16; Jn 1:33). This baptism was to be the sign and dynamic mark of the followers of Jesus.

the one who sent me to baptize with
water[v] told me, 'The man on whom
you see the Spirit come down and re-
Jn 7:38-39 main is he who will baptize with the
Holy Spirit.'[w] **34**I have seen and I testify that this is the Son of God."[x]

Jesus' First Disciples

1:40–42pp — Mt 4:18–22; Mk 1:16–20; Lk 5:2–11

35The next day John[y] was there
again with two of his disciples. **36**When
he saw Jesus passing by, he said,
"Look, the Lamb of God!"[z]
37When the two disciples heard him
say this, they followed Jesus. **38**Turning around, Jesus saw them following
and asked, "What do you want?"
They said, "Rabbi"[a] (which means
Teacher), "where are you staying?"
39"Come," he replied, "and you will
see."
So they went and saw where he was
staying, and spent that day with him.
It was about the tenth hour.
40Andrew, Simon Peter's brother,
was one of the two who heard what
John had said and who had followed
Jesus. **41**The first thing Andrew did
was to find his brother Simon and tell
him, "We have found the Messiah"
(that is, the Christ).[b] **42**And he
brought him to Jesus.
Jesus looked at him and said, "You
are Simon son of John. You will be
called[c] Cephas" (which, when translated, is Peter[i]).[d]

Jesus Calls Philip and Nathanael

43The next day Jesus decided to
leave for Galilee. Finding Philip,[e] he
said to him, "Follow me."[f]
44Philip, like Andrew and Peter, was
from the town of Bethsaida.[g] **45**Philip
found Nathanael[h] and told him, "We
have found the one Moses wrote about
in the Law,[i] and about whom the
prophets also wrote[j]—Jesus of Nazareth,[k] the son of Joseph."[l]
46"Nazareth! Can anything good
come from there?"[m] Nathanael asked.
"Come and see," said Philip.
47When Jesus saw Nathanael approaching, he said of him, "Here is a
true Israelite,[n] in whom there is nothing false."[o]
48"How do you know me?" Nathanael asked.
Jesus answered, "I saw you while
you were still under the fig tree before
Philip called you."
49Then Nathanael declared, "Rabbi,[p] you are the Son of God;[q] you are
the King of Israel."[r]
50Jesus said, "You believe[j] because
I told you I saw you under the fig tree.
You shall see greater things than that."
51He then added, "I tell you[k] the
truth, you[k] shall see heaven open,[s]
and the angels of God ascending and
descending[t] on the Son of Man."[u]

Jesus Changes Water to Wine

2 On the third day a wedding took
place at Cana in Galilee.[v] Jesus'
mother[w] was there, **2**and Jesus and his
disciples had also been invited to the
wedding. **3**When the wine was gone,

1:33 [v] S Mk 1:4 [w] S Mk 1:8 **1:34** [x] ver 49; S Mt 4:3 **1:35** [y] S Mt 3:1 **1:36** [z] S ver 29 **1:38** [a] ver 49; S Mt 23:7 **1:41** [b] Jn 4:25 **1:42** [c] Ge 17:5,15; 32:28; 35:10 [d] Mt 16:18 **1:43** [e] Mt 10:3; Jn 6:5-7; 12:21,22; 14:8,9 [f] S Mt 4:19 **1:44** [g] S Mt 11:21 **1:45** [h] Jn 21:2 [i] S Lk 24:27 [j] S Lk 24:27 [k] S Mk 1:24 [l] Lk 3:23 **1:46** [m] Jn 7:41,42, 52 **1:47** [n] Ro 9:4,6 [o] Ps 32:2 **1:49** [p] ver 38; S Mt 23:7 [q] ver 34; S Mt 4:3 [r] S Mt 2:2; 27:42; Jn 12:13 **1:51** [s] S Mt 3:16 [t] Ge 28:12 [u] S Mt 8:20 **2:1** [v] Jn 4:46; 21:2 [w] S Mt 12:46

[i] *42* Both *Cephas* (Aramaic) and *Peter* (Greek) mean *rock*. [j] *50* Or *Do you believe . . . ?* [k] *51* The Greek is plural.

The Holy Spirit would be poured out on them so that they might carry on his saving work in all the world (cf. Ac 1:8). Jesus' task of baptizing in the Spirit is his ongoing purpose throughout this age (see Mt 3:11, note; Ac 2:39, note).

1:51 YOU SHALL SEE HEAVEN OPEN. Jesus represents himself as the ladder by which God's revelation comes to the world (cf. Ge 28:12; see also Lk 5:24, note on the term "Son of Man").

2:3 WINE. The word "wine" (Gk *oinos*) in the NT is a generic term and can refer to either fermented wine or unfermented wine (see articles on WINE IN NEW TESTAMENT TIMES (1) and (2), p. 1534 and p. 1586). The nature of *oinos* must be determined by context and moral likelihood.

2:3 THEY HAVE NO MORE WINE. In contrast to the position taken in this study Bible, some believe that both the wine initially provided at the wedding and the wine made by Jesus were intoxicants consumed in great quantity. If this thesis is accepted, then the following implications must be acknowledged and reckoned with: (1) The guests at the wedding would likely be drunk. (2) Mary, the mother of Jesus, would be regretting that the intoxicating drink had run out and would be asking Jesus to furnish the already drunken festivity with more fermented wine. (3) In order to oblige his mother's wishes, Jesus would be making 120–180 gallons of intoxicating wine (vv. 6–9), more than enough to keep the guests totally drunk. (4) Jesus would be making this intoxicating wine as his very first "miraculous sign" in order to "reveal his glory" (v. 11) and to persuade people to believe in him as the holy and righteous Son of God.

The above implications of the thesis in question cannot be avoided. To allege that Jesus made and used alcoholic wine is not only beyond the warrant of exegetical requirement, but leads us into con-

Jesus' mother said to him, "They have
no more wine."
4"Dear woman,[x] why do you involve
me?"[y] Jesus replied. "My time[z] has
not yet come."
5His mother said to the servants,
"Do whatever he tells you."[a]
6Nearby stood six stone water jars,
the kind used by the Jews for ceremonial washing,[b] each holding from twenty to thirty gallons.[1]
7Jesus said to the servants, "Fill the
jars with water"; so they filled them to
the brim.
8Then he told them, "Now draw
some out and take it to the master of
the banquet."
They did so, **9**and the master of the
banquet tasted the water that had been
turned into wine.[c] He did not realize
where it had come from, though the
servants who had drawn the water
knew. Then he called the bridegroom
aside **10**and said, "Everyone brings out
the choice wine first and then the
cheaper wine after the guests have had
too much to drink; but you have saved
the best till now."
11This, the first of his miraculous
signs,[d] Jesus performed at Cana in
Galilee. He thus revealed his glory,[e]
and his disciples put their faith in
him.[f]

Jesus Cleanses the Temple

2:14–16pp — Mt 21:12,13; Mk 11:15–17; Lk 19:45,46

12After this he went down to Capernaum[g] with his mother[h] and brothers[i] and his disciples. There they
stayed for a few days.
13When it was almost time for the
Jewish Passover,[j] Jesus went up to Jerusalem.[k] **14**In the temple courts he
found men selling cattle, sheep and
doves,[l] and others sitting at tables
exchanging money.[m] **15**So he made a
whip out of cords, and drove all from
the temple area, both sheep and cattle;
he scattered the coins of the money
changers and overturned their tables.
16To those who sold doves he said,
"Get these out of here! How dare you
turn my Father's house[n] into a market!"
17His disciples remembered that it
is written: "Zeal for your house will
consume me."[m][o]
18Then the Jews[p] demanded of him,
"What miraculous sign[q] can you show
us to prove your authority to do all
this?"[r]
19Jesus answered them, "Destroy

2:4 [x]Jn 19:26 [y]S Mt 8:29 [z]S Mt 26:18 **2:5** [a]Ge 41:55 **2:6** [b]Mk 7:3,4; Jn 3:25 **2:9** [c]Jn 4:46 **2:11** [d]ver 23; Mt 12:38; Jn 3:2; S 4:48; 6:2,14,26, 30; 12:37; 20:30 [e]Jn 1:14 [f]Ex 14:31

2:12 [g]S Mt 4:13 [h]S Mt 12:46 [i]S Mt 12:46 **2:13** [j]S Jn 11:55 [k]Dt 16:1-6; Lk 2:41 **2:14** [l]Lev 1:14; Dt 14:26 [m]Dt 14:25 **2:16** [n]Lk 2:49 **2:17** [o]Ps 69:9 **2:18** [p]S Jn 1:19 [q]S ver 11 [r]S Mt 12:38

[1]6 Greek *two to three metretes* (probably about 75 to 115 liters) [m]17 Psalm 69:9

flict with moral principles embedded in the total witness of Scripture. Clearly, in light of God's nature, Christ's righteousness, his loving concern for humanity, and Mary's good character, the above implications of the view that the wine at Cana was fermented are blasphemous. An interpretation that involves such assertions and contradictions cannot be adopted. The only plausible explanation is that the wine made by Jesus to reveal his glory was the nonintoxicating pure juice of the grape. Furthermore, the initial inferior wine furnished by the one in charge of the wedding was most likely nonintoxicating as well. For further discussion of this issue, see article on WINE IN NEW TESTAMENT TIMES (2), p. 1586.

2:10 CHOICE WINE. According to various ancient writers, the "choice" (or best) wine was the sweetest wine—one that could be drunk freely and in large quantities without harm (i.e., wine that had not had its sugar content destroyed through fermentation). The "cheaper" wine was that which had been diluted with too much water. (1) The Roman writer Pliny affirms this. He expressly states that "good wine," called *sapa*, was not fermented. *Sapa* was grape juice boiled down to one-third of its bulk to increase its sweet flavor (IV.13). He writes elsewhere that "wines are most beneficial when all their potency has been removed by the strainer" (Pliny, *Natural History*, XIV.23–24). Pliny, Plutarch and Horace all suggest that the best wine was the type that was "harmless and innocent." (2) Rabbinical witnesses affirm that some rabbis recommended boiled wine. The Mishna says: "Rabbi Yehuda permits it [boiled wine as heave-offering], because it improves it." (3) It is significant that the Greek adjective translated "choice" is not *agathos* but *kalos*, meaning "morally excellent or befitting."

2:10 HAD TOO MUCH TO DRINK. The phrase "had too much to drink" is from the Greek word *methuskō*, a word that has two meanings: (1) to be or become drunk, and (2) to be filled or satisfied (without reference to intoxication). *Methuskō* should be understood here in the second of these two meanings. (1) Regardless of how one translates this text, it cannot be used to defend the thesis that fermented wine was consumed at this wedding. The master of ceremonies is merely stating here a general policy, a policy that covers any wedding celebration regardless of the type of drink served. (2) In no way may we imply that Jesus participated in and contributed to a drunken party (see v. 3, note; also see article on WINE IN NEW TESTAMENT TIMES (2), p. 1586).

2:15 DROVE ALL FROM THE TEMPLE AREA. See Lk 19:45, note.

2:19 TEMPLE. See article on THE TEMPLE, p. 608.

WINE IN NEW TESTAMENT TIMES (2)

Jn 2:11 "This, the first of his miraculous signs, Jesus performed at Cana in Galilee. He thus revealed his glory, and his disciples put their faith in him."

In conjunction with this article, be sure to read WINE IN NEW TESTAMENT TIMES (1), p. 1534.

WINE: MIXED OR FULL STRENGTH? Historical data concerning the making and use of wine by the Jews and other nations in the Biblical world indicate that it was (a) often unfermented and (b) normally mixed with water. The previous article on WINE IN NEW TESTAMENT TIMES (p. 1534) discusses one of the processes used in keeping freshly squeezed grape juice in a sweet and unfermented state. This article discusses two other processes of dealing with grapes, preparatory to mixing them with water.

(1) One method was to dehydrate the grapes, sprinkle them with olive oil to keep them moist and store them in earthenware jars (*The Zondervan Pictorial Encyclopedia of the Bible*, V.882; see also Columella, *On Agriculture*, 12.44.1–8). A very sweet grape beverage could be made from these stored grapes at any time by adding water and steeping or boiling them. Polybius indicated that the Roman women were allowed to drink this kind of grape beverage, but were forbidden to drink fermented wine (see Polybius, *Fragments*, 6.4; Pliny, *Natural History*, 14.11.81).

(2) Another method was to boil freshly squeezed grape juice until it became a thick paste or syrup (grape honey); this process made the juice storable, removed any intoxicating quality because of the high concentration of sugar, and preserved its sweetness (see Columella, 12.19.1–6 and 20.1–8; Pliny, 14.11.80). This paste was then stored in large jars or skins. The paste could be used as a jam for bread or dissolved in water to make grape juice once again (*The Zondervan Pictorial Encyclopedia of the Bible*, V.882–884). "It is probable that the grape was largely cultivated as a source of sugar: the juice expressed in the 'wine press' was reduced by boiling to a liquid . . . known as 'grape honey'" (*The International Standard Bible Encyclopedia*, V.3050). References to honey in the Bible frequently speak of grape honey (called *debash* by the Jews) rather than the honey of the bee.

(3) Water, then, could be mixed with dehydrated grapes and with grape syrup, as well as with fermented wine. Greek and Roman authors gave various ratios that were used. Homer (*Odyssey* IX.208ff) mentions a ratio of twenty parts water to one part wine. Plutarch (*Sumposiacs*, III.ix) states, "We call a mixture 'wine,' although the larger of the component parts is water." Pliny (14.6.54) mentions a ratio of eight parts water to one part wine.

(4) Among Jewish people in Bible times, social and religious customs mandated never serving unmixed wine, especially if it was fermented. The Talmud (a Jewish work that describes the traditions of Judaism from about 200 B.C. to A.D. 200) discusses in several tractates the mixture of water and wine (e.g., Shabbath 77a; Pesahim 1086). Some Jewish rabbis insisted that unless fermented wine was mixed with three parts water, it could not be blessed and would defile the drinker. Others demanded that ten parts of water must be mixed with one part of fermented wine before it would be acceptable.

(5) An interesting passage emerges in the book of Revelation: when speaking of "the wine of God's fury," an angel declares that it will be "full strength" (Rev 14:10; see Jer 25:15, note). It was so stated because the readers normally would expect all grape beverages to be mixed with water (see Jn 2:3, notes).

In summary, the normal uses of wine by the Jews in Biblical days differed from today's uses. The wine of old was (a) freshly squeezed grape juice, (b) preserved grape juice, (c) juice from dried grapes, (d) grape wine made from grape syrup and water, and (e) unfermented or fermented stored wine diluted with water at a ratio as high as 20 to 1.

If the wine was fermented and served unmixed, it was considered barbaric, defiling and incapable of being blessed by the rabbis. In the light of these facts, it is impossible to defend the modern-day practice of drinking alcoholic beverages on the basis of the Jews' use of "wine" in Biblical times. Furthermore, Christians of Biblical days were even more cautious about the various kinds of wines than the Jews (see Ro 14:21, note; 1Th 5:6, note; 1Ti 3:3, note; Tit 2:2, note).

JESUS' GLORY REVEALED THROUGH WINE. In his second chapter, John records that Jesus made "wine" out of water at a wedding at Cana. The question is, "What kind of wine?" As we have seen, it could be fermented or unfermented, full strength or diluted. We must determine our answer to this question by contextual implication and moral likelihood. The position of this study Bible is that Jesus made wine (*oinos*) that was pure unfermented grape juice. The following data supply strong rationale for rejecting the opinion that Jesus made intoxicating wine.

(1) The primary object of this miracle was to reveal his glory (Jn 2:11) in such a way as to induce personal faith in him as God's holy and righteous Son who came to save people from their sin (2:11; cf. Mt 1:21). To suggest that Christ showed his divinity as the One and Only Son of the Father (Jn 1:14) by miraculously creating gallons of intoxicating wine for a drunken party (note 2:10, which implies that the people had already drunk freely), and that this was immensely important to his Messianic mission, requires an irreverence few are willing to display. It would testify more to God's honor, and the honor and glory of Christ, to believe that Christ supernaturally created the same juice of the grape that God makes annually through the process of his natural created order (see Jn 2:3, note). This miracle, therefore, points to Christ's sovereignty over the natural world and becomes a symbol of his power to transform sinful people spiritually into God's children (Jn 3:1–15). Because of this miracle "we have seen his glory, the glory of the One and Only, who came from the Father, full of grace and truth" (Jn 1:14; cf. 2:11).

(2) It is contrary to Scriptural revelation concerning Christ's perfect obedience to his heavenly Father (cf. 2Co 5:21; Heb 4:15; 1Pe 2:22) to suppose that he disobeyed the Father's moral command, "do not gaze at wine when it is red, when it sparkles in the cup, when it goes down smoothly" i.e., when it is fermented (see Pr 23:31, note). Indeed, Christ came to fulfill the law (Mt 5:17) and would have supported the Biblical passages that condemn intoxicating wine as "a mocker" and beer as "a brawler" (see Pr 20:1, note) and the words of Hab 2:15, "woe to him who gives drink to his neighbors, pouring it . . . till they are drunk" (cf. Lev 10:8–11; Nu 6:1–5; Dt 21:20; Pr 31:4–7; Isa 28:7; Am 2:8,12; 4:1; 6:6; Ro 14:13,21).

(3) Furthermore, note the following modern medical evidence. (a) Leading medical experts have found unmistakable evidence that moderate alcoholic consumption is damaging to the reproductive systems of women of childbearing age, causing miscarriages and births of babies with incurable mental and physical defects. World authorities on early embryology maintain that women who drink even moderate amounts of alcohol around the time of conception (about a 48-hour time period) risk damaging the chromosomes of an egg preparing to leave the ovary and thus causing disastrous results to the mental and physical development of the infant. (b) It would be theologically absurd to maintain that Jesus encouraged the use of alcoholic beverages at a wedding that included many women as well as a young bride with the possibility of immediate conception. To maintain that he did not know of the potential terrible effects of intoxicating drink on unborn children is to call into question his deity, his wisdom, and his discernment of good and evil. To maintain that he knew of the potential harm and disfiguring results of alcohol, and yet promoted and encouraged its use, is to call into question his goodness, compassion and love.

The only sound conclusion rationally, theologically and Biblically is that the wine Christ made at the wedding to reveal his glory was pure, sweet, unfermented fruit of the vine.

this temple, and I will raise it again in three days."[s]

20The Jews replied, "It has taken forty-six years to build this temple, and you are going to raise it in three days?" **21**But the temple he had spoken of was his body.[t] **22**After he was raised from the dead, his disciples recalled what he had said.[u] Then they believed the Scripture[v] and the words that Jesus had spoken.

23Now while he was in Jerusalem at the Passover Feast,[w] many people saw the miraculous signs[x] he was doing and believed[y] in his name.[n] **24**But Jesus would not entrust himself to them, for he knew all men. **25**He did not need man's testimony about man,[z] for he knew what was in a man.[a]

Jesus Teaches Nicodemus

3 Now there was a man of the Pharisees named Nicodemus,[b] a member of the Jewish ruling council.[c] **2**He came to Jesus at night and said, "Rabbi,[d] we know[e] you are a teacher who has come from God. For no one could perform the miraculous signs[f] you are doing if God were not with him."[g]

3In reply Jesus declared, "I tell you the truth, no one can see the kingdom of God unless he is born again.[o]"[h i]

4"How can a man be born when he is old?" Nicodemus asked. "Surely he cannot enter a second time into his mother's womb to be born!"

5Jesus answered, "I tell you the truth, no one can enter the kingdom of God unless he is born of water and the Spirit.[j k] **6**Flesh gives birth to flesh, but the Spirit[p] gives birth to spirit.[l] **7**You should not be surprised at my saying, 'You[q] must be born again.' **8**The wind blows wherever it pleases. You hear its sound, but you cannot tell where it comes from or where it is going. So it is with everyone born of the Spirit."[m]

9"How can this be?"[n] Nicodemus asked.

10"You are Israel's teacher,"[o] said Jesus, "and do you not understand these things? **11**I tell you the truth, we speak of what we know,[p] and we testify to what we have seen, but still you people do not accept our testimony.[q] **12**I have spoken to you of earthly things and you do not believe; how then will you believe if I speak of heavenly things? **13**No one has ever gone into heaven[r] except the one who came from heaven[s]—the Son of Man.[r t] **14**Just as Moses lifted up the snake in the desert,[u] so the Son of Man must be lifted up,[v] **15**that everyone who believes[w] in him may have eternal life.[s x]

16"For God so loved[y] the world that he gave[z] his one and only Son,[t a] that whoever believes[b] in him shall not perish but have eternal life.[c] **17**For God did not send his Son into the world[d] to condemn the world, but to save the world through him.[e] **18**Whoever believes in him is not con-

2:19 [s]S Mt 16:21; 26:61; 27:40; Mk 14:58; 15:29; Ac 6:14
2:21 [t]1Co 6:19
2:22 [u]Lk 24:5-8; Jn 12:16; 14:26 [v]Ps 16:10; S Lk 24:27
2:23 [w]ver 13 [x]S ver 11 [y]S Jn 3:15
2:25 [z]Isa 11:3 [a]Dt 31:21; 1Ki 8:39; S Mt 9:4; Jn 6:61, 64; 13:11
3:1 [b]Jn 7:50; 19:39 [c]Lk 23:13
3:2 [d]S Mt 23:7 [e]ver 11 [f]S Jn 2:11 [g]Jn 10:38; 14:10, 11; Ac 2:22; 10:38
3:3 [h]S Jn 1:13 [i]S Mt 3:2
3:5 [j]S Ac 22:16 [k]Tit 3:5
3:6 [l]S Jn 1:13; 1Co 15:50
3:8 [m]1Co 2:14-16
3:9 [n]Jn 6:52,60
3:10 [o]Lk 2:46
3:11 [p]Jn 1:18; 7:16,17 [q]ver 32
3:13 [r]Pr 30:4; Ac 2:34; Eph 4:8-10 [s]ver 31; Jn 6:38, 42; Heb 4:14; 9:24 [t]S Mt 8:20
3:14 [u]Nu 21:8,9 [v]S Jn 12:32
3:15 [w]ver 16,36; Ge 15:6; Nu 14:11; Mt 27:42; Mk 1:15; Jn 1:7, 12; 2:23; 5:24; 7:38; 20:29; Ac 13:39; 16:31; Ro 3:22; 10:9,10; 1Jn 5:1,5,10 [x]ver 16,36; S Mt 25:46; Jn 20:31
3:16 [y]Ro 5:8; Eph 2:4; 1Jn 4:9, 10 [z]Isa 9:6; Ro 8:32 [a]Ge 22:12; Jn 1:18 [b]S ver 15 [c]ver 36; Jn 6:29,40; 11:25, 26
3:17 [d]Jn 6:29,57; 10:36; 11:42; 17:8,21; 20:21 [e]Isa 53:11; S Mt 1:21; S Lk 2:11; 19:10; Jn 1:29; 12:47; S Ro 11:14; 1Ti 1:15; 2:5,6; 1Jn 2:2; 3:5

[n] 23 Or *and believed in him* [o] 3 Or *born from above*; also in verse 7 [p] 6 Or *but spirit* [q] 7 The Greek is plural. [r] 13 Some manuscripts *Man, who is in heaven* [s] 15 Or *believes may have eternal life in him* [t] 16 Or *his only begotten Son*

3:3 BORN AGAIN. For a discussion of the Biblical doctrine of regeneration (being born again), see article on REGENERATION, p. 1589.

3:5 BORN OF WATER. Jesus was probably referring to the cleansing work of the Holy Spirit in the new birth. In Tit 3:5 Paul speaks of "the washing of rebirth and renewal by the Holy Spirit."

3:8 THE WIND . . . THE SPIRIT. As the wind, though unseen, is identified by its activity and sound, so also the Holy Spirit is observed by his activity in and effect on those who are born again.

3:16 GOD SO LOVED THE WORLD. This verse reveals the heart and purpose of God. (1) God's love is wide enough to embrace all persons, i.e., "the world" (cf. 1Ti 2:4).

(2) God "gave" his Son as an offering for sin on the cross. The atonement proceeds from the loving heart of God. It was not something forced on him (Ro 8:32; 1Jn 4:10).

(3) To believe (Gk *pisteuō*) includes three main elements: (a) a sure conviction that Jesus Christ is God's Son and the only Savior for lost humanity; (b) a self-surrendering fellowship with and obedience to Christ (cf. 15:1–10; see 14:21, note; 15:4, note); (c) a fully assured trust in Christ that he is both able and willing to bring you to final salvation and to fellowship with God in heaven (see article on FAITH AND GRACE, p. 1720).

(4) "Perish" is often the forgotten word of v. 16. It points not to physical death but to the dreadful reality of eternal punishment (Mt 10:28, note).

(5) "Eternal life" is the gift God bestows on us when we are born again (see article on REGENERATION, p. 1589). "Eternal" not only expresses perpetuity but also quality of life—a divine type of life, a life that frees us from the power of sin and Satan and removes us from what is merely earthly in order to know God (cf. 8:34–36; see 17:3, note).

REGENERATION

Jn 3:3 "In reply Jesus declared, 'I tell you the truth, no one can see the kingdom of God unless he is born again.'"

In Jn 3:1–8, Jesus discusses one of the fundamental doctrines of the Christian faith: regeneration (Tit 3:5), or spiritual birth. Without the new birth one cannot see the kingdom of God, i.e., receive eternal life and salvation through Jesus Christ. The following are important facts concerning the new birth.

(1) Regeneration is a re-creating and transformation of the person (Ro 12:2; Eph 4:23–24) by God the Holy Spirit (Jn 3:6; Tit 3:5; see article on THE REGENERATION OF THE DISCIPLES, p. 1627). Through this process eternal life from God himself is imparted to the believer's heart (Jn 3:16; 2Pe 1:4; 1 Jn 5:11), and he or she becomes a child of God (Jn 1:12; Ro 8:16–17; Gal 3:26) and a new person (2Co 5:17; Col 3:9–10). He or she no longer conforms to this world (Ro 12:2) but is now "created to be like God in true righteousness and holiness" (Eph 4:24).

(2) Regeneration is necessary because apart from Christ, all people, in their inherent natures, are sinners, incapable of obeying and pleasing God (Ps 51:5; Jer 17:9; Ro 8:7–8; 1Co 2:14; Eph 2:3).

(3) Regeneration comes to those who repent of sin, turn to God (Mt 3:2), and put their faith in Jesus Christ as Lord and Savior (see Jn 1:12, note).

(4) Regeneration involves a transition from an old life of sin to a new life of obedience to Jesus Christ (2Co 5:17; Gal 6:15; Eph 4:23–24; Col 3:10). Those who are truly born again are set free from sin's bondage (see Jn 8:36, note; Ro 6:14–23) and receive a spiritual desire and disposition to obey God and follow the leading of the Spirit (Ro 8:13–14). They live righteous lives (1Jn 2:29), love other believers (1Jn 4:7), avoid a life of sin (1Jn 3:9; 5:18) and do not love the world (1Jn 2:15–16).

(5) Those born of God cannot make sin a habitual practice in their lives (see 1Jn 3:9, note). They cannot remain born again without a sincere desire and victorious endeavor to please God and to avoid evil (1Jn 1:5–7). This is accomplished only through the grace given to believers by Christ (1Jn 2:3–11,15–17,24–29; 3:6–24; 4:7–8,20; 5:1), through a sustained relationship with Christ (see Jn 15:4, note) and through a dependence on the Holy Spirit (Ro 8:2–14).

(6) Those who live in immorality and follow the world's ways, no matter what they profess with their lips, demonstrate that they are still unregenerated children of Satan (1Jn 3:6–10).

(7) Just as one can be born of the Spirit by receiving the life of God, he or she can also extinguish that life by ungodly choices and unrighteous living, and therefore die spiritually. Scripture affirms, "if you live according to the sinful nature, you will die" (Ro 8:13). Thus, sin and the refusal to follow the Holy Spirit extinguish the life of God in the believer's soul and cause spiritual death and exclusion from God's kingdom (cf. Mt 12:31–32; 1Co 6:9–10; Gal 5:19–21; Heb 6:4–6; 1Jn 5:16).

(8) The new birth cannot be equated with physical birth, for God's relationship with the believer is a matter of spirit rather than flesh (Jn 3:6). Therefore, while the physical tie of a father and child can never be annulled, the father and child relationship that God desires with us is voluntary and not indissoluble during our probationary time on earth (see Ro 8:13, note). That relationship remains conditional on our faith in Christ throughout our earthly existence, a faith demonstrated by lives of sincere obedience and love (Ro 8:12–14; 2Ti 2:12).

demned,[f] but whoever does not believe stands condemned already because he has not believed in the name of God's one and only Son.[u][g] **19**This is the verdict: Light[h] has come into the world, but men loved darkness instead of light because their deeds were evil.[i] **20**Everyone who does evil hates the light, and will not come into the light for fear that his deeds will be exposed.[j] **21**But whoever lives by the truth comes into the light, so that it may be seen plainly that what he has done has been done through God."[v]

John the Baptist's Testimony About Jesus

22After this, Jesus and his disciples went out into the Judean countryside, where he spent some time with them, and baptized.[k] **23**Now John[l] also was baptizing at Aenon near Salim, because there was plenty of water, and people were constantly coming to be baptized. **24**(This was before John was put in prison.)[m] **25**An argument developed between some of John's disciples and a certain Jew[w] over the matter of ceremonial washing.[n] **26**They came to John and said to him, "Rabbi,[o] that man who was with you on the other side of the Jordan—the one you testified[p] about—well, he is baptizing, and everyone is going to him."

27To this John replied, "A man can receive only what is given him from heaven. **28**You yourselves can testify that I said, 'I am not the Christ[x] but am sent ahead of him.'[q] **29**The bride belongs to the bridegroom.[r] The friend who attends the bridegroom waits and listens for him, and is full of joy when he hears the bridegroom's voice. That joy is mine, and it is now complete.[s] **30**He must become greater; I must become less.

31"The one who comes from above[t] is above all; the one who is from the earth belongs to the earth, and speaks as one from the earth.[u] The one who comes from heaven is above all. **32**He testifies to what he has seen and heard,[v] but no one accepts his testimony.[w] **33**The man who has accepted it has certified that God is truthful. **34**For the one whom God has sent[x] speaks the words of God, for God[y] gives the Spirit[y] without limit. **35**The Father loves the Son and has placed everything in his hands.[z] **36**Whoever believes in the Son has eternal life,[a] but whoever rejects the Son will not see life, for God's wrath remains on him."[z]

Jesus Talks With a Samaritan Woman

4 The Pharisees heard that Jesus was gaining and baptizing more disciples than John,[b] **2**although in fact it was not Jesus who baptized, but his disciples. **3**When the Lord[c] learned of this, he left Judea[d] and went back once more to Galilee.

4Now he had to go through Samaria.[e] **5**So he came to a town in Samaria called Sychar, near the plot of ground Jacob had given to his son Joseph.[f] **6**Jacob's well was there, and Jesus, tired as he was from the journey, sat down by the well. It was about the sixth hour.

3:18 [f] Jn 5:24 [g] Jn 1:18; 1Jn 4:9
3:19 [h] S Jn 1:4 [i] Ps 52:3; Jn 7:7
3:20 [j] Eph 5:11, 13
3:22 [k] Jn 4:2
3:23 [l] S Mt 3:1
3:24 [m] Mt 4:12; 14:3
3:25 [n] Jn 2:6
3:26 [o] S Mt 23:7 [p] Jn 1:7
3:28 [q] Jn 1:20,23
3:29 [r] Mt 9:15 [s] Jn 16:24; 17:13; Php 2:2; 1Jn 1:4; 2Jn 12
3:31 [t] ver 13 [u] Jn 8:23; 1Jn 4:5
3:32 [v] Jn 8:26; 15:15 [w] ver 11
3:34 [x] S ver 17 [y] Isa 42:1; Mt 12:18; Lk 4:18; Ac 10:38
3:35 [z] S Mt 28:18
3:36 [a] S ver 15; Jn 5:24; 6:47
4:1 [b] Jn 3:22,26
4:3 [c] S Lk 7:13 [d] Jn 3:22
4:4 [e] S Mt 10:5
4:5 [f] Ge 33:19; Jos 24:32

[u] *18* Or *God's only begotten Son* [v] *21* Some interpreters end the quotation after verse 15.
[w] *25* Some manuscripts *and certain Jews*
[x] *28* Or *Messiah* [y] *34* Greek *he*
[z] *36* Some interpreters end the quotation after verse 30.

3:19 LOVED DARKNESS INSTEAD OF LIGHT. A fundamental characteristic of the wicked is that they love darkness, i.e., they find their pleasure in sin and immorality (Ro 1:18–32; Php 3:19; 2Ti 3:2–5; 2Pe 2:12–15). On the other hand, truly born-again persons love righteousness and hate wickedness (see Heb 1:9, note), and are grieved when they see the unrighteous deeds of depraved people (1Co 13:6). They take no pleasure in the sensual entertainment or the expression of sinful conduct shown so openly in contemporary society (Ps 97:10; Pr 8:13; Ro 12:9; see 2Pe 2:8, note; Rev 2:6 note).

3:34 GIVES THE SPIRIT WITHOUT LIMIT. See Mt 3:16 and Lk 3:22, notes on Jesus' anointing with the Holy Spirit; see article on JESUS AND THE HOLY SPIRIT, p. 1546.

3:36 WHOEVER REJECTS. The Greek word translated "rejects" is *apeitheō* and means to "disobey" or "not be subject to"; it is contrasted to "whoever believes" (Gk *pisteuō*) at the beginning of the verse. For John unbelief means to "reject the Son," or to disobey him. Faith and obedience can often be used interchangeably (compare Ro 1:8 with 16:19; 1Th 1:8; also see Ro 15:18). The gospel comes as a free gift (Ro 5:15–16; 6:23), but once accepted it does not leave us free to do as we please. It requires that we enter into the way of salvation ordained by God and subject ourselves to the righteousness of God (Ro 10:3; see 1:5, note; see article on FAITH AND GRACE, p. 1720).

7When a Samaritan woman came to
draw water, Jesus said to her, "Will you
give me a drink?"[g] **8**(His disciples had
gone into the town[h] to buy food.)
9The Samaritan woman said to him,
"You are a Jew and I am a Samaritan[i]
woman. How can you ask me for a
drink?" (For Jews do not associate with
Samaritans.[a])
10Jesus answered her, "If you knew
the gift of God and who it is that asks
you for a drink, you would have asked
him and he would have given you living
water."[j]
11"Sir," the woman said, "you have
nothing to draw with and the well is
deep. Where can you get this living water? **12**Are you greater than our father
Jacob, who gave us the well[k] and
drank from it himself, as did also his
sons and his flocks and herds?"
13Jesus answered, "Everyone who
drinks this water will be thirsty again,
14but whoever drinks the water I give
him will never thirst.[l] Indeed, the water I give him will become in him a
spring of water[m] welling up to eternal
life."[n]
15The woman said to him, "Sir, give
me this water so that I won't get
thirsty[o] and have to keep coming here
to draw water."
16He told her, "Go, call your husband and come back."
17"I have no husband," she replied.
Jesus said to her, "You are right
when you say you have no husband.
18The fact is, you have had five husbands, and the man you now have is
not your husband. What you have just
said is quite true."
19"Sir," the woman said, "I can see
that you are a prophet.[p] **20**Our fathers
worshiped on this mountain,[q] but you
Jews claim that the place where we
must worship is in Jerusalem."[r]
21Jesus declared, "Believe me, woman, a time is coming[s] when you will
worship the Father neither on this
mountain nor in Jerusalem.[t] **22**You
Samaritans worship what you do not
know;[u] we worship what we do know,
for salvation is from the Jews.[v] **23**Yet
a time is coming and has now come[w]
when the true worshipers will worship
the Father in spirit[x] and truth, for
they are the kind of worshipers the Father seeks. **24**God is spirit,[y] and his
worshipers must worship in spirit and
in truth."
25The woman said, "I know that
Messiah" (called Christ)[z] "is coming.
When he comes, he will explain everything to us."
26Then Jesus declared, "I who speak
to you am he."[a]

4:7 [g] Ge 24:17; 1Ki 17:10
4:8 [h] ver 5,39
4:9 [i] S Mt 10:5
4:10 [j] Isa 44:3; 55:1; Jer 2:13; 17:13; Zec 14:8; Jn 7:37,38; Rev 7:17; 21:6; 22:1,17
4:12 [k] ver 6
4:14 [l] Jn 6:35 [m] Isa 12:3; 58:11; Jn 7:38 [n] S Mt 25:46
4:15 [o] Jn 6:34
4:19 [p] S Mt 21:11
4:20 [q] Dt 11:29; Jos 8:33 [r] Lk 9:53
4:21 [s] Jn 5:28; 16:2 [t] Mal 1:11; 1Ti 2:8
4:22 [u] 2Ki 17:28-41 [v] Isa 2:3; Ro 3:1,2; 9:4,5; 15:8,9
4:23 [w] Jn 5:25; 16:32 [x] Php 3:3
4:24 [y] Php 3:3
4:25 [z] Mt 1:16; Jn 1:41
4:26 [a] Jn 8:24; 9:35-37

[a] 9 Or *do not use dishes Samaritans have used*

4:7 SAMARITAN WOMAN. Jesus' conversation with the Samaritan woman reveals his commitment to his heavenly Father's purpose and his own inner desire to bring this person to eternal life. Jesus' consuming passion was to save the lost (see Lk 15; cf. Pr 11:30; Da 12:3; Jas 5:20), a goal infinitely more important to him than food and drink (v. 34). We must follow Jesus' example. All around us people are ready to hear God's Word; we must speak to them about their spiritual need and about Jesus, who can meet that need.

4:13–14 DRINKS THIS WATER . . . ETERNAL LIFE. The "water" given by Jesus means spiritual life (cf. Isa 12:3). To partake of this living water, one must "drink" (see 7:37). This act of drinking is not a momentary, single act, but rather a progressive or repeated drinking. Drinking the water of life requires regular communion with the source of the living water, Jesus Christ himself. No one can continue to drink the water of life if he or she becomes severed from its source. Such people will become, as Peter describes it, "springs without water" (2Pe 2:17).

4:23 WORSHIP . . . IN SPIRIT AND TRUTH. Jesus teaches several things here: (1) "In spirit" points to the level at which true worship occurs. One must come to God in complete sincerity and with a spirit that is directed by the life and activity of the Holy Spirit. (2) "Truth" (Gk *alētheia*) is characteristic of God (Ps 31:5; Ro 1:25; 3:7; 15:8), incarnate in Christ (14:6; 2Co 11:10; Eph 4:21), intrinsic to the Holy Spirit (14:17; 15:26; 16:13) and at the heart of the gospel (8:32; Gal 2:5; Eph 1:13). Therefore, worship must take place according to the truth of the Father that is revealed in the Son and received through the Spirit. Those who advocate a worship that sets aside the truth and doctrines of the Word of God have in reality set aside the only foundation for true worship (see article on WORSHIP, p. 680).

4:24 TRUTH. Because Jesus Christ is the truth (1:14; 5:31; 14:6; Lk 4:25; 9:27; 12:44), to live in union with Christ requires speaking the truth (1Co 5:8; Eph 4:25). To claim to have fellowship with Christ and to possess salvation, yet not to live and speak according to the truth, is to be deceived (1Jn 1:6). Those who have no truth in them show the real condition of their hearts (8:44; Ac 5:3) — that they are in fundamental opposition to God and are outside the kingdom of heaven (Rev 21:8,27; 22:15; cf. Rev 14:5). A liar is of "the synagogue of Satan" (Rev 3:9).

The Disciples Rejoin Jesus

27Just then his disciples returned[b] and were surprised to find him talking with a woman. But no one asked, "What do you want?" or "Why are you talking with her?"

28Then, leaving her water jar, the woman went back to the town and said to the people, 29"Come, see a man who told me everything I ever did.[c] Could this be the Christ[b]?"[d] 30They came out of the town and made their way toward him.

Jn 15:26-27

31Meanwhile his disciples urged him, "Rabbi,[e] eat something."

32But he said to them, "I have food to eat[f] that you know nothing about."

33Then his disciples said to each other, "Could someone have brought him food?"

34"My food," said Jesus, "is to do the will[g] of him who sent me and to finish his work.[h] 35Do you not say, 'Four months more and then the harvest'? I tell you, open your eyes and look at the fields! They are ripe for harvest.[i] 36Even now the reaper draws his wages, even now he harvests[j] the crop for eternal life,[k] so that the sower and the reaper may be glad together. 37Thus the saying 'One sows and another reaps'[l] is true. 38I sent you to reap what you have not worked for. Others have done the hard work, and you have reaped the benefits of their labor."

Many Samaritans Believe

39Many of the Samaritans from that town[m] believed in him because of the woman's testimony, "He told me everything I ever did."[n] 40So when the Samaritans came to him, they urged him to stay with them, and he stayed two days. 41And because of his words many more became believers.

42They said to the woman, "We no longer believe just because of what you said; now we have heard for ourselves, and we know that this man really is the Savior of the world."[o]

Jesus Heals the Official's Son

43After the two days[p] he left for Galilee. 44(Now Jesus himself had pointed out that a prophet has no honor in his own country.)[q] 45When he arrived in Galilee, the Galileans welcomed him. They had seen all that he had done in Jerusalem at the Passover Feast,[r] for they also had been there.

46Once more he visited Cana in Galilee, where he had turned the water into wine.[s] And there was a certain royal official whose son lay sick at Capernaum. 47When this man heard that Jesus had arrived in Galilee from Judea,[t] he went to him and begged him to come and heal his son, who was close to death.

48"Unless you people see miraculous signs and wonders,"[u] Jesus told him, "you will never believe."

49The royal official said, "Sir, come down before my child dies."

50Jesus replied, "You may go. Your son will live."

The man took Jesus at his word and departed. 51While he was still on the way, his servants met him with the news that his boy was living. 52When he inquired as to the time when his son got better, they said to him, "The fever left him yesterday at the seventh hour."

53Then the father realized that this was the exact time at which Jesus had said to him, "Your son will live." So he and all his household[v] believed.

54This was the second miraculous sign[w] that Jesus performed, having come from Judea to Galilee.

4:27 [b] ver 8
4:29 [c] ver 17,18 [d] Mt 12:23; Jn 7:26,31
4:31 [e] S Mt 23:7
4:32 [f] Job 23:12; Mt 4:4; Jn 6:27
4:34 [g] S Mt 26:39 [h] S Jn 19:30
4:35 [i] Mt 9:37; Lk 10:2
4:36 [j] Ro 1:13 [k] S Mt 25:46
4:37 [l] Job 31:8; Mic 6:15
4:39 [m] ver 5 [n] ver 29
4:42 [o] S Lk 2:11
4:43 [p] ver 40
4:44 [q] Mt 13:57; Lk 4:24
4:45 [r] Jn 2:23
4:46 [s] Jn 2:1-11
4:47 [t] ver 3,54
4:48 [u] Da 4:2,3; S Jn 2:11; Ac 2:43; 14:3; Ro 15:19; 2Co 12:12; Heb 2:4
4:53 [v] S Ac 11:14
4:54 [w] S ver 48; S Jn 2:11

[b] 29 Or *Messiah*

4:35 LOOK AT THE FIELDS. See Mt 9:37, note.

4:36 CROP FOR ETERNAL LIFE. Those who bring others to saving faith in Jesus Christ are doing something of eternal consequence. They will one day rejoice in heaven over those who were saved because of their prayers and their witness. At the same time, they must understand that their work is often a reaping of the labors of others (v. 38). All that we do for God is in large part the result of the sacrificial labor of Christ and others.

4:48 SIGNS AND WONDERS. Signs and wonders are an authentic work of God's kingdom. However, our faith must not be centered on them but on Jesus Christ, to whom they bear witness (see article on THE KINGDOM OF GOD, p. 1430). We must believe in Jesus Christ because of who he is, God's Son, our Lord and Savior. Jesus must be worshiped and esteemed because of his love, mercy and righteous character, not just for what he can do for us in a physical or material way. Signs, wonders and miracles must lead to a deep attachment to the Lord and to a greater faith in him, as this miracle did for the official (vv. 50–53).

The Healing at the Pool

5 Some time later, Jesus went up to Jerusalem for a feast of the Jews. **2**Now there is in Jerusalem near the Sheep Gate[x] a pool, which in Aramaic[y] is called Bethesda[c] and which is surrounded by five covered colonnades. **3**Here a great number of disabled people used to lie—the blind, the lame, the paralyzed.[d] **5**One who was there had been an invalid for thirty-eight years. **6**When Jesus saw him lying there and learned that he had been in this condition for a long time, he asked him, "Do you want to get well?"

7"Sir," the invalid replied, "I have no one to help me into the pool when the water is stirred. While I am trying to get in, someone else goes down ahead of me."

8Then Jesus said to him, "Get up! Pick up your mat and walk."[z] **9**At once the man was cured; he picked up his mat and walked.

The day on which this took place was a Sabbath,[a] **10**and so the Jews[b] said to the man who had been healed, "It is the Sabbath; the law forbids you to carry your mat."[c]

11But he replied, "The man who made me well said to me, 'Pick up your mat and walk.'"

12So they asked him, "Who is this fellow who told you to pick it up and walk?"

13The man who was healed had no idea who it was, for Jesus had slipped away into the crowd that was there.

14Later Jesus found him at the temple and said to him, "See, you are well again. Stop sinning[d] or something worse may happen to you." **15**The man went away and told the Jews[e] that it was Jesus who had made him well.

Jn 9:1-12

Life Through the Son

16So, because Jesus was doing these things on the Sabbath, the Jews persecuted him. **17**Jesus said to them, "My Father[f] is always at his work[g] to this very day, and I, too, am working." **18**For this reason the Jews tried all the harder to kill him;[h] not only was he breaking the Sabbath, but he was even calling God his own Father, making himself equal with God.[i]

19Jesus gave them this answer: "I tell you the truth, the Son can do nothing by himself;[j] he can do only what he sees his Father doing, because whatever the Father does the Son also does. **20**For the Father loves the Son[k] and shows him all he does. Yes, to your amazement he will show him even greater things than these.[l] **21**For just as the Father raises the dead and gives them life,[m] even so the Son gives life[n] to whom he is pleased to give it. **22**Moreover, the Father judges no one,

5:2 [x]Ne 3:1; 12:39 [y]Jn 19:13, 17,20; 20:16; Ac 21:40; 22:2; 26:14
5:8 [z]Mt 9:5,6
5:9 [a]Mt 12:1-14; Jn 9:14
5:10 [b]ver 16 [c]Ne 13:15-22; Jer 17:21; S Mt 12:2
5:14 [d]Mk 2:5; Jn 8:11
5:15 [e]S Jn 1:19
5:17 [f]Lk 2:49 [g]Jn 9:4; 14:10
5:18 [h]S Mt 12:14 [i]Jn 10:30,33; 19:7
5:19 [j]ver 30; S Jn 14:24
5:20 [k]Jn 3:35 [l]Jn 14:12
5:21 [m]Ro 4:17; 8:11; 2Co 1:9; Heb 11:19 [n]Jn 11:25

[c] *2* Some manuscripts *Bethzatha*; other manuscripts *Bethsaida* [d] *3* Some less important manuscripts *paralyzed—and they waited for the moving of the waters.* [4]*From time to time an angel of the Lord would come down and stir up the waters. The first one into the pool after each such disturbance would be cured of whatever disease he had.*

5:5 THIRTY-EIGHT YEARS. Having suffered for thirty-eight years, this man had experienced prolonged disappointment at not being healed, while repeatedly looking to God in expectation. Yet healing finally came. It was largely because of the length of this man's suffering that Jesus, in compassion, chose to help him. We must never give up hope that God's time to move directly on our behalf may come soon.

5:9 THE MAN WAS CURED. Jesus often healed as a response to the faith of individuals. Here, however, he required no faith at all; the man was cured merely at the word of Jesus. Even today people may be healed according to God's purpose even though they do not demonstrate faith in Christ. The Bible teaches that there are three contacts for healing faith: (1) the faith of the one being healed (Mt 9:27–29); (2) the faith of others on behalf of the afflicted (Mt 8:5–10; cf. 17:15–20; Jas 5:14–16); (3) the faith of one who is anointed to heal (1Co 12:9).

5:14 STOP SINNING. Jesus demands from all who profess faith in his name to stop sinning; the truly saved will stop. Although not perfect or above occasional transgression, true believers will commit their lives to Christ so that, through the power of the Holy Spirit, sin will no longer be the characteristic of their lives (1Pe 1:5; 1Jn 3:6,9). Jesus' expectation for the born-again life contrasts sharply with those who emphasize that believers will continue to sin daily in thought, word and deed.

5:16 PERSECUTED HIM. At this point in his Gospel, John begins to show that in spite of Jesus' miracles, and even because of them, the religious leaders intensely opposed him.

5:18–24 MAKING HIMSELF EQUAL WITH GOD. Jesus makes several astounding claims here: (1) God is his Father in a unique way; (2) he maintains unity, communion and authority with God (vv. 19–20); (3) he has the power to give life and raise the dead (v. 21); (4) he has the right to judge all people (v. 22); (5) he has the right to divine honor (v. 23); and (6) he has the power to give eternal life (v. 24).

but has entrusted all judgment to the
Son,[o] **23**that all may honor the Son
just as they honor the Father. He who
does not honor the Son does not honor
the Father, who sent him.[p]
24"I tell you the truth, whoever
hears my word and believes him who
sent me[q] has eternal life[r] and will
not be condemned;[s] he has crossed
over from death to life.[t] **25**I tell you
the truth, a time is coming and has now
come[u] when the dead will hear[v] the
voice of the Son of God and those who
hear will live. **26**For as the Father has
life in himself, so he has granted the
Son to have life[w] in himself. **27**And he
has given him authority to judge[x] because he is the Son of Man.
28"Do not be amazed at this, for a
time is coming[y] when all who are in
their graves will hear his voice **29**and
come out—those who have done good
will rise to live, and those who have
done evil will rise to be condemned.[z]
30By myself I can do nothing;[a] I judge
only as I hear, and my judgment is
just,[b] for I seek not to please myself
but him who sent me.[c]

5:22 [o] ver 27; Ge 18:25; Jdg 11:27; Jn 9:39; S Ac 10:42
5:23 [p] Lk 10:16; S 1Jn 2:23
5:24 [q] S Mt 10:40; S Jn 3:15; S 3:17 [r] S Mt 25:46 [s] Jn 3:18 [t] 1Jn 3:14
5:25 [u] Jn 4:23; 16:32 [v] Jn 8:43,47
5:26 [w] Dt 30:20; Job 10:12; 33:4; Ps 36:9; S Jn 1:4
5:27 [x] S ver 22
5:28 [y] Jn 4:21; 16:2
5:29 [z] S Mt 25:46
5:30 [a] ver 19 [b] Isa 28:6; Jn 8:16 [c] S Mt 26:39
5:31 [d] Jn 8:14
5:32 [e] ver 37; Jn 8:18
5:33 [f] S Jn 1:7
5:34 [g] 1Jn 5:9 [h] Ac 16:30,31; Eph 2:8; Tit 3:5
5:35 [i] Da 12:3; 2Pe 1:19
5:36 [j] 1Jn 5:9 [k] Jn 14:11; 15:24 [l] S Jn 3:17
5:37 [m] Jn 8:18 [n] Dt 4:12; 1Ti 1:17; S Jn 1:18
5:38 [o] 1Jn 1:10; 2:14 [p] Isa 26:10 [q] S Jn 3:17
5:39 [r] Ro 2:17,18 [s] S Mt 25:46

Testimonies About Jesus

31"If I testify about myself, my testimony is not valid.[d] **32**There is another
who testifies in my favor,[e] and I know
that his testimony about me is valid.
33"You have sent to John and he has
testified[f] to the truth. **34**Not that I accept human testimony;[g] but I mention
it that you may be saved.[h] **35**John was
a lamp that burned and gave light,[i]
and you chose for a time to enjoy his
light.
36"I have testimony weightier than
that of John.[j] For the very work that
the Father has given me to finish, and
which I am doing,[k] testifies that the
Father has sent me.[l] **37**And the Father who sent me has himself testified
concerning me.[m] You have never
heard his voice nor seen his form,[n]
38nor does his word dwell in you,[o] for
you do not believe[p] the one he sent.[q]
39You diligently study[e] the Scriptures[r] because you think that by them
you possess eternal life.[s] These are

e *39* Or *Study diligently* (the imperative)

5:24 HEARS . . . BELIEVES. Jesus describes those who have eternal life and will not be condemned as "whoever hears . . . and believes." The verbs "hears" (Gk *akouōn*, from *akouō*) and "believes" (Gk *pisteuōn*, from *pisteuō*) are present participles, emphasizing ongoing action (i.e., "whoever is hearing and believing"). Thus, the "hearing" and "believing" are not acts of a single moment, but actions that must continue. Christ affirms that our present possession of eternal life is conditional on a present living faith rather than on a momentary decision of faith sometime in the past (see 1:12, note; 4:14, note).

5:24 WILL NOT BE CONDEMNED. "Condemned" (Gk *krisis*) is used in the sense of condemnation to eternal death. Believers will not be condemned with the world (1Co 11:32). This does not refer to their future accountability and judgment concerning their faithfulness to God's grace given to them while on earth (see article on THE JUDGMENT OF BELIEVERS, p. 1791).

5:26 HAS GRANTED THE SON TO HAVE LIFE IN HIMSELF. Jesus Christ's own nature is a source of eternal life; it is inherent within him. God, however, has not given believers the power to have eternal life inherent in themselves. We have life only as we have fellowship with Christ, i.e., Christ living in us through a living faith relationship (see 15:4,6, notes; Gal 2:20).

5:29 THOSE WHO HAVE DONE GOOD. According to Scripture, judgment is always on the basis of deeds, because one's deeds are a manifestation of his or her faith and inner condition. This means that we will be judged not by our profession of faith in Christ, but by the life we have lived (Mt 12:36–37; 16:27; Ro 2:6–10; 14:12; 1Co 3:13–15; 2Co 5:10; Eph 6:8; Col 3:25; Rev 2:23; 20:12; 22:12).

5:29 RISE TO LIVE. The NT does not teach a single general simultaneous resurrection for all the dead. (1) It speaks of a resurrection of many "holy people" occurring immediately after Jesus' resurrection (Mt 27:52–53), of a resurrection occurring at the time of the rapture or catching up of the church by Christ (1Co 15:51–52; see article on THE RAPTURE, p. 1864), of a "first resurrection" (see Rev 20:6, note), and of a resurrection occurring one thousand years after the "first resurrection" of Rev 20:6 (i.e., after the millennial reign of Christ on earth, Rev 20:4). (2) It is possible that "the first resurrection" includes the resurrection of *all* believers before the thousand-year reign of Christ (Rev 20:4–6). Therefore, the resurrection of Rev 20:4–6 would complete the first resurrection.

5:29 THOSE WHO HAVE DONE EVIL. Immorality, impurity, lust, evil desires, and the like have no place in the lives of believers (see Col 3:5). Those who teach, contrary to the teaching of Christ and the apostles, that a person can have eternal life while living outside of fellowship with Christ are teaching the ultimate deception. It leads them and their followers to trust in a false doctrine of eternal security (see 1Co 6:9–10; Gal 5:19–21; Eph 5:5–6). The words of Jesus must be heeded: "those who have done evil will rise to be condemned."

the Scriptures that testify about me,[t]
40yet you refuse to come to me[u] to
have life.
41"I do not accept praise from
men,[v] 42but I know you. I know that
you do not have the love of God in your
hearts. 43I have come in my Father's
name, and you do not accept me; but if
someone else comes in his own name,
you will accept him. 44How can you believe if you accept praise from one another, yet make no effort to obtain the
praise that comes from the only
God[f]?[w]
45"But do not think I will accuse you
before the Father. Your accuser is Moses,[x] on whom your hopes are set.[y]
46If you believed Moses, you would believe me, for he wrote about me.[z]
47But since you do not believe what he
wrote, how are you going to believe
what I say?"[a]

5:39 [t]S Lk 24:27, 44; Ac 13:27
5:40 [u]Jn 6:44
5:41 [v]ver 44
5:44 [w]S Ro 2:29
5:45 [x]Jn 9:28 [y]Ro 2:17
5:46 [z]Ge 3:15; S Lk 24:27,44; Ac 26:22
5:47 [a]Lk 16:29, 31

Jesus Feeds the Five Thousand

6:1–13pp — Mt 14:13–21; Mk 6:32–44; Lk 9:10–17

6 Some time after this, Jesus
crossed to the far shore of the Sea
of Galilee (that is, the Sea of Tiberias),
2and a great crowd of people followed
him because they saw the miraculous
signs[b] he had performed on the sick.
3Then Jesus went up on a mountainside[c] and sat down with his disciples.
4The Jewish Passover Feast[d] was
near.
5When Jesus looked up and saw a
great crowd coming toward him, he
said to Philip,[e] "Where shall we buy
bread for these people to eat?" 6He
asked this only to test him, for he already had in mind what he was going
to do.
7Philip answered him, "Eight
months' wages[g] would not buy
enough bread for each one to have a
bite!"
8Another of his disciples, Andrew,
Simon Peter's brother,[f] spoke up,
9"Here is a boy with five small barley
loaves and two small fish, but how far
will they go among so many?"[g]
10Jesus said, "Have the people sit
down." There was plenty of grass in
that place, and the men sat down,

6:2 [b]S Jn 2:11
6:3 [c]ver 15
6:4 [d]S Jn 11:55
6:5 [e]S Jn 1:43
6:8 [f]Jn 1:40
6:9 [g]2Ki 4:43

[f] 44 Some early manuscripts *the Only One*
[g] 7 Greek *two hundred denarii*

5:44 ACCEPT PRAISE FROM ONE ANOTHER. Those who have true saving faith will not be motivated by the love of praise or esteem from other people. They will have as their goal to please the Father. Those who establish a habit of receiving glory from others make idols of themselves and place themselves outside God's kingdom. To love the praise of other humans more than the praise of God is to disbelieve the gospel of Christ and make genuine faith impossible (cf. Ro 2:29).

5:47 DO NOT BELIEVE WHAT HE WROTE. This passage is important in establishing Jesus' view of the OT. He indeed believed that Moses wrote the Pentateuch. The lesson the Jews needed, and one we need today, is this: if one does not believe in the inspiration and truthfulness of the OT writings, he or she will not believe or submit to the authority of Jesus' words and the NT writings that bear witness to him (see Ac 24:14, note on Paul's view of the OT; see article on THE INSPIRATION AND AUTHORITY OF SCRIPTURE, p. 1898).

6:2 MIRACLES. (1) What are miracles? (a) They are works of a supernatural origin and power (Gk *dunamis*; see Ac 8:13; 19:11). (b) They function as a sign or mark (Gk *semeion*) of divine authority (Lk 23:8; Ac 4:16,30,33). The central and greatest miracle of the NT faith is the resurrection of Christ (1Co 15).

(2) Miracles serve at least three purposes in the kingdom of God. (a) They witness to Jesus Christ, authenticating the truth of his message and proving his identity as the Christ of God (2:23; 5:1–21; 10:25; 11:42). (b) They express Christ's compassionate love (Mk 8:2; Lk 7:12–15; Ac 10:38). (c) They signify the age of salvation (Mt 11:2ff), the coming of the kingdom of God (see article on THE KINGDOM OF GOD, p. 1430) and God's invasion into the realm of Satan (see article on POWER OVER SATAN AND DEMONS, p. 1484).

(3) The Scriptures maintain that miracles are to operate throughout the entire church age. (a) Jesus sent out his followers to preach and perform miracles (Mt 10:7–8; Mk 3:14–15; see Lk 9:2, note). (b) Jesus declared that those who believed in him through the preaching of the gospel were to do the works that he did, and would do even greater things (14:12; Mk 16:15–20). (c) The book of Acts speaks of the performing of miracles in the lives of the believers (Ac 3:1ff; 5:12; 6:8; 8:6ff; 9:32ff; 15:12; 20:7ff); elsewhere in the NT these are called "signs" by which the proclamation of the gospel was confirmed (Ac 4:29–30; 14:3; Ro 15:18–19; 2Co 12:12; Heb 2:3–4). (d) The Spirit wants to give these signs to the church throughout this present age (1Co 12:8–12,28; Jas 5:14–15; see article on SIGNS OF BELIEVERS, p. 1513).

(4) The NT also teaches that signs and wonders will be performed by the power of Satan through false teachers and preachers, especially by the antichrist and his false prophet (see articles on THE GREAT TRIBULATION, p. 1456, and FALSE TEACHERS, p. 1506).

6:5 THE FEEDING OF THE FIVE THOUSAND. See Mt 14:19, note.

about five thousand of them. **11**Jesus then took the loaves, gave thanks,[h] and distributed to those who were seated as much as they wanted. He did the same with the fish.

12When they had all had enough to eat, he said to his disciples, "Gather the pieces that are left over. Let nothing be wasted." **13**So they gathered them and filled twelve baskets with the pieces of the five barley loaves left over by those who had eaten.

14After the people saw the miraculous sign[i] that Jesus did, they began to say, "Surely this is the Prophet who is to come into the world."[j] **15**Jesus, knowing that they intended to come and make him king[k] by force, withdrew again to a mountain by himself.[l]

Jesus Walks on the Water

6:16–21pp — Mt 14:22–33; Mk 6:47–51

16When evening came, his disciples went down to the lake, **17**where they got into a boat and set off across the lake for Capernaum. By now it was dark, and Jesus had not yet joined them. **18**A strong wind was blowing and the waters grew rough. **19**When they had rowed three or three and a half miles,**h** they saw Jesus approaching the boat, walking on the water;[m] and they were terrified. **20**But he said to them, "It is I; don't be afraid."[n] **21**Then they were willing to take him into the boat, and immediately the boat reached the shore where they were heading.

22The next day the crowd that had stayed on the opposite shore of the lake[o] realized that only one boat had been there, and that Jesus had not entered it with his disciples, but that they had gone away alone.[p] **23**Then some boats from Tiberias[q] landed near the place where the people had eaten the bread after the Lord had given thanks.[r] **24**Once the crowd realized that neither Jesus nor his disciples were there, they got into the boats and went to Capernaum in search of Jesus.

Jesus the Bread of Life

25When they found him on the other side of the lake, they asked him, "Rabbi,[s] when did you get here?"

26Jesus answered, "I tell you the truth, you are looking for me,[t] not because you saw miraculous signs[u] but because you ate the loaves and had your fill. **27**Do not work for food that spoils, but for food that endures[v] to eternal life,[w] which the Son of Man[x] will give you. On him God the Father has placed his seal[y] of approval."

28Then they asked him, "What must we do to do the works God requires?"

29Jesus answered, "The work of God is this: to believe[z] in the one he has sent."[a]

30So they asked him, "What miraculous sign[b] then will you give that we may see it and believe you?[c] What will you do? **31**Our forefathers ate the manna[d] in the desert; as it is written: 'He gave them bread from heaven to eat.'**i**"[e]

32Jesus said to them, "I tell you the truth, it is not Moses who has given you the bread from heaven, but it is my Father who gives you the true bread from heaven. **33**For the bread of God is he who comes down from heaven[f] and gives life to the world."

34"Sir," they said, "from now on give us this bread."[g]

35Then Jesus declared, "I am[h] the bread of life.[i] He who comes to me will never go hungry, and he who believes[j] in me will never be thirsty.[k] **36**But as I told you, you have seen me and still you do not believe. **37**All that the Father gives me[l] will come to me, and whoever comes to me I will never drive away. **38**For I have come down from heaven[m] not to do my will but to

6:11 [h]ver 23; S Mt 14:19
6:14 [i]S Jn 2:11 [j]Dt 18:15,18; Mt 11:3; S 21:11
6:15 [k]Jn 18:36 [l]Mt 14:23; Mk 6:46
6:19 [m]Job 9:8
6:20 [n]S Mt 14:27
6:22 [o]ver 2 [p]ver 15-21
6:23 [q]ver 1 [r]ver 11
6:25 [s]S Mt 23:7
6:26 [t]ver 24 [u]ver 30; S Jn 2:11
6:27 [v]Isa 55:2 [w]ver 54; S Mt 25:46 [x]S Mt 8:20 [y]Ro 4:11; 1Co 9:2; 2Co 1:22; Eph 1:13; 4:30; 2Ti 2:19; Rev 7:3
6:29 [z]1Jn 3:23 [a]S Jn 3:17
6:30 [b]S Jn 2:11 [c]S Mt 12:38
6:31 [d]Nu 11:7-9 [e]Ex 16:4,15; Ne 9:15; Ps 78:24; 105:40
6:33 [f]ver 50; Jn 3:13,31
6:34 [g]Jn 4:15
6:35 [h]Ex 3:14; Jn 8:12; 10:7,11; 11:25; 14:6; 15:1 [i]ver 48,51 [j]S Jn 3:15 [k]Jn 4:14
6:37 [l]ver 39; Jn 17:2,6,9,24
6:38 [m]Jn 3:13,31

h *19* Greek *rowed twenty-five or thirty stadia* (about 5 or 6 kilometers) **i** *31* Exodus 16:4; Neh. 9:15; Psalm 78:24,25

6:15 JESUS PRAYS ALONE. See Mt 14:23, note.

6:20 DON'T BE AFRAID. See Mt 14:27, note.

6:35 I AM THE BREAD OF LIFE. "I am the bread of life" is the first of the seven "I am" statements recorded in John's Gospel, each one emphasizing an important aspect of the personal ministry of Jesus. This statement tells us that Christ is the sustenance that nourishes spiritual life (see v. 53). The other "I am" statements are: "the light of the world" (8:12), "the gate" (10:9), "the good shepherd" (10:11,14), "the resurrection and the life" (11:25), "the way and the truth and the life" (14:6), and "the true vine" (15:1,5).

6:37 I WILL NEVER DRIVE AWAY. Jesus promises to welcome all who come to him in repentance and faith. Those who come to Jesus come in response to the grace given them by God (see article on FAITH AND GRACE, p. 1720).

do the will[n] of him who sent me.[o]
39And this is the will of him who sent
me, that I shall lose none of all that he
has given me,[p] but raise them up at
the last day.[q] **40**For my Father's will
is that everyone who looks to the Son[r]
and believes in him shall have eternal
life,[s] and I will raise him up at the last
day."

41At this the Jews began to grumble
about him because he said, "I am the
bread that came down from heaven."
42They said, "Is this not Jesus, the son
of Joseph,[t] whose father and mother
we know?[u] How can he now say, 'I
came down from heaven'?"[v]

43"Stop grumbling among yourselves," Jesus answered. **44**"No one can
come to me unless the Father who sent
me draws him,[w] and I will raise him up
at the last day. **45**It is written in the
Prophets: 'They will all be taught by
God.'[j][x] Everyone who listens to the
Father and learns from him comes to
me. **46**No one has seen the Father except the one who is from God;[y] only he
has seen the Father. **47**I tell you the
truth, he who believes has everlasting
life.[z] **48**I am the bread of life.[a] **49**Your
forefathers ate the manna in the
desert, yet they died.[b] **50**But here is
the bread that comes down from heav-
en,[c] which a man may eat and not die.
51I am the living bread[d] that came

6:38 [n]S Mt 26:39 [o]S Jn 3:17
6:39 [p]Isa 27:3; Jer 23:4; Jn 10:28; 17:12; 18:9 [q]ver 40,44,54
6:40 [r]Jn 12:45 [s]S Mt 25:46
6:42 [t]Lk 4:22 [u]Jn 7:27,28 [v]ver 38,62
6:44 [w]ver 65; Jer 31:3; Jn 12:32
6:45 [x]Isa 54:13; Jer 31:33,34; 1Co 2:13; 1Th 4:9; Heb 8:10,11; 10:16; 1Jn 2:27
6:46 [y]S Jn 1:18; 5:37; 7:29
6:47 [z]S Mt 25:46
6:48 [a]ver 35,51
6:49 [b]ver 31,58
6:50 [c]ver 33
6:51 [d]ver 35,48 [e]ver 41,58 [f]Heb 10:10
6:52 [g]S Jn 1:19 [h]Jn 7:43; 9:16; 10:19
6:53 [i]Mt 26:26 [j]S Mt 8:20 [k]Mt 26:28
6:54 [l]ver 39
6:56 [m]Jn 15:4-7; 1Jn 2:24; 3:24; 4:15
6:57 [n]S Jn 3:17
6:58 [o]ver 49-51; Jn 3:36; 5:24
6:60 [p]ver 66 [q]ver 52

down from heaven.[e] If anyone eats of
this bread, he will live forever. This
bread is my flesh, which I will give for
the life of the world."[f]

52Then the Jews[g] began to argue
sharply among themselves,[h] "How
can this man give us his flesh to eat?"

53Jesus said to them, "I tell you the
truth, unless you eat the flesh[i] of the
Son of Man[j] and drink his blood,[k]
you have no life in you. **54**Whoever eats
my flesh and drinks my blood has eternal life, and I will raise him up at the
last day.[l] **55**For my flesh is real food
and my blood is real drink. **56**Whoever
eats my flesh and drinks my blood remains in me, and I in him.[m] **57**Just as
the living Father sent me[n] and I live
because of the Father, so the one who
feeds on me will live because of me.
58This is the bread that came down
from heaven. Your forefathers ate manna and died, but he who feeds on this
bread will live forever."[o] **59**He said
this while teaching in the synagogue in
Capernaum.

Many Disciples Desert Jesus

60On hearing it, many of his disciples[p] said, "This is a hard teaching.
Who can accept it?"[q]

61Aware that his disciples were

[j] *45* Isaiah 54:13

6:40 MY FATHER'S WILL. It is important to understand the relationship of the Father's will to human responsibility. (1) It is not God's will that any believer should fall from grace (cf. Gal 5:4) and subsequently be separated from God; neither is it his will that any individual should perish (2Pe 3:9) or fail to come to the truth and be saved (1Ti 2:4). (2) However, there is a great difference between God's perfect will and his permissive will (see article on THE WILL OF GOD, p. 1056). He does not abrogate the human responsibility to repent and believe, even if it means his perfect will is not done (see Lk 19:41, note on Jesus weeping over Jerusalem). (3) God's desire that believers be raised up at the last day does not relieve them of the responsibility of obeying his voice and following him (10:27; 14:21). Jesus acknowledged on the night of his betrayal that he protected his disciples and "kept them safe by that name you gave me. None has been lost except the one doomed to destruction" (17:12).

6:44 THE FATHER . . . DRAWS HIM. The Father draws people to Jesus through the Holy Spirit. God's work of drawing covers all people, as Jesus says: "I . . . will draw all men" (12:32). But this drawing is not irresistible, for it can be rejected (see Mt 23:37, "but you were not willing").

6:54 EATS MY FLESH AND DRINKS MY BLOOD. We receive spiritual life by believing in Christ and sharing in the redemptive benefits of his death on the cross (Ro 3:24–25; 1Jn 1:7). We continue to have spiritual life as we remain in fellowship with Christ and his Word. Compare v. 53 with v. 63, where he says, "The words I have spoken to you are spirit and they are life." Thus, we partake of Christ as we continue to have faith in him and prayerfully receive his Word.

(1) Jesus is the living Word (1:1–5); the Bible is the written Word (2Ti 3:16; 2Pe 1:21). Jesus calls himself here the "bread of life" (v. 35), and elsewhere he relates this bread to the Word of God: "Man does not live on bread alone, but on every word that comes from the mouth of God" (Mt 4:4). Therefore, we eat his flesh by remaining in him and by receiving and obeying the Word of God (v. 63).

(2) We are saved by God's grace and the Spirit's regenerating power when we first hear and receive the Word (1:12; Ac 2:41). We continue to be saved and receive grace by remaining in union with Christ and partaking of the Word of God continually through reading, obeying and absorbing its truths into our hearts (1Ti 4:13–16; Jas 1:21). It is fatal to withdraw from fellowship with Christ or to depart from his Word.

grumbling about this, Jesus said to them, "Does this offend you?[r] 62What if you see the Son of Man[s] ascend to where he was before![t] 63The Spirit gives life;[u] the flesh counts for nothing. The words I have spoken to you are spirit[k] and they are life. 64Yet there are some of you who do not believe." For Jesus had known[v] from the beginning which of them did not believe and who would betray him.[w] 65He went on to say, "This is why I told you that no one can come to me unless the Father has enabled him."[x]

66From this time many of his disciples[y] turned back and no longer followed him.

67"You do not want to leave too, do you?" Jesus asked the Twelve.[z]

68Simon Peter answered him,[a] "Lord, to whom shall we go? You have the words of eternal life.[b] 69We believe and know that you are the Holy One of God."[c]

70Then Jesus replied, "Have I not chosen you,[d] the Twelve? Yet one of you is a devil!"[e] 71(He meant Judas, the son of Simon Iscariot,[f] who, though one of the Twelve, was later to betray him.)[g]

Jesus Goes to the Feast of Tabernacles

7 After this, Jesus went around in Galilee, purposely staying away from Judea because the Jews[h] there were waiting to take his life.[i] 2But when the Jewish Feast of Tabernacles[j] was near, 3Jesus' brothers[k] said to him, "You ought to leave here and go to Judea, so that your disciples may see the miracles you do. 4No one who wants to become a public figure acts in secret. Since you are doing these things, show yourself to the world." 5For even his own brothers did not believe in him.[l]

6Therefore Jesus told them, "The right time[m] for me has not yet come; for you any time is right. 7The world cannot hate you, but it hates me[n] because I testify that what it does is evil.[o] 8You go to the Feast. I am not yet[l] going up to this Feast, because for me the right time[p] has not yet come." 9Having said this, he stayed in Galilee.

10However, after his brothers had left for the Feast, he went also, not publicly, but in secret. 11Now at the Feast the Jews were watching for him[q] and asking, "Where is that man?"

12Among the crowds there was widespread whispering about him. Some said, "He is a good man."

Others replied, "No, he deceives the people."[r] 13But no one would say anything publicly about him for fear of the Jews.[s]

Jesus Teaches at the Feast

14Not until halfway through the Feast did Jesus go up to the temple courts and begin to teach.[t] 15The Jews[u] were amazed and asked, "How did this man get such learning[v] without having studied?"[w]

16Jesus answered, "My teaching is not my own. It comes from him who sent me.[x] 17If anyone chooses to do God's will, he will find out[y] whether

6:61 [r]Mt 13:57
6:62 [s]S Mt 8:20 [t]S Mk 16:19; S Jn 3:13; 17:5
6:63 [u]2Co 3:6
6:64 [v]S Jn 2:25 [w]S Mt 10:4
6:65 [x]ver 37,44; S Mt 13:11
6:66 [y]ver 60
6:67 [z]Mt 10:2
6:68 [a]Mt 16:16 [b]ver 63; S Mt 25:46
6:69 [c]S Mk 1:24; 8:29; Lk 9:20
6:70 [d]Jn 15:16,19 [e]Jn 13:27; 17:12
6:71 [f]S Mt 26:14 [g]S Mt 10:4
7:1 [h]S Jn 1:19 [i]ver 19,25; S Mt 12:14
7:2 [j]Lev 23:34; Dt 16:16
7:3 [k]S Mt 12:46
7:5 [l]Ps 69:8; Mk 3:21
7:6 [m]S Mt 26:18
7:7 [n]Jn 15:18,19 [o]Jn 3:19,20
7:8 [p]ver 6; S Mt 26:18
7:11 [q]Jn 11:56
7:12 [r]ver 40,43
7:13 [s]Jn 9:22; 12:42; 19:38; 20:19
7:14 [t]ver 28; S Mt 26:55
7:15 [u]S Jn 1:19 [v]Ac 26:24 [w]Mt 13:54
7:16 [x]S Jn 14:24
7:17 [y]Ps 25:14

[k] *63* Or *Spirit* [l] *8* Some early manuscripts do not have *yet.*

6:64 JESUS HAD KNOWN FROM THE BEGINNING. This may mean that Jesus knew when Judas began to drift from his original faith and formed plans to betray him. Judas had the same choice as the other eleven disciples. He was a believer and a trusted familiar friend of Jesus (Ps 41:9; Jn 13:18), as shown by Christ's commitment to Judas (2:23–24; Mt 10:1–15). Judas later turned away by his own choice (Ac 1:25); he did not have to betray Jesus. In other words, the betrayal of Jesus was prophesied only as to its occurrence, and not to its perpetrator. The specific person to betray Christ was not predestined from all eternity. Judas's defection to the enemy and consequent tragedy should warn every follower of Christ not to reject the Spirit's warning about friendship with the world and turning away from Christ (Heb 10:29; 12:25; Jas 4:4).

7:2 FEAST OF TABERNACLES. The "Feast of Tabernacles" commemorated the post-exodus journeys of Israel and the time when they wandered in the desert, living in tabernacles (or tents) under God's care (see Lev 23:34–43, note; Zec 14:16–19).

7:7 IT HATES ME. Jesus was hated by the world because he proclaimed that all people separated from God are depraved, sinful and inherently selfish (cf. 2:14–16; 3:19–20; 5:30–47). Throughout his ministry Jesus faithfully denounced injustice, cruelty and immorality. This unfailing, forthright testimony to human sinfulness contradicts those ministers who self-righteously claim to preach a "positive gospel," i.e., one stripped of the prophetic demand for repentance and righteousness.

7:17 IF ANYONE CHOOSES TO DO GOD'S

my teaching comes from God or whether I speak on my own. **18**He who
speaks on his own does so to gain hon-
or for himself,[z] but he who works for
the honor of the one who sent him is a
man of truth; there is nothing false
about him. **19**Has not Moses given you
the law?[a] Yet not one of you keeps the
law. Why are you trying to kill me?"[b]
20"You are demon-possessed,"[c] the
crowd answered. "Who is trying to kill
you?"
21Jesus said to them, "I did one miracle,[d] and you are all astonished.
22Yet, because Moses gave you circumcision[e] (though actually it did not
come from Moses, but from the patriarchs),[f] you circumcise a child on the
Sabbath. **23**Now if a child can be circumcised on the Sabbath so that the
law of Moses may not be broken, why
are you angry with me for healing the
whole man on the Sabbath? **24**Stop
judging by mere appearances, and
make a right judgment."[g]

Is Jesus the Christ?

25At that point some of the people of
Jerusalem began to ask, "Isn't this the
man they are trying to kill?[h] **26**Here
he is, speaking publicly, and they are
not saying a word to him. Have the authorities[i] really concluded that he is
the Christ[m]?[j] **27**But we know where
this man is from;[k] when the Christ
comes, no one will know where he is
from."
28Then Jesus, still teaching in the
temple courts,[l] cried out, "Yes, you
know me, and you know where I am
from.[m] I am not here on my own, but
he who sent me is true.[n] You do not
know him, **29**but I know him[o] because
I am from him and he sent me."[p]
30At this they tried to seize him, but
no one laid a hand on him,[q] because
his time had not yet come.[r] **31**Still,
many in the crowd put their faith in
him.[s] They said, "When the Christ
comes, will he do more miraculous
signs[t] than this man?"
32The Pharisees heard the crowd
whispering such things about him.
Then the chief priests and the Pharisees sent temple guards to arrest him.
33Jesus said, "I am with you for only
a short time,[u] and then I go to the one
who sent me.[v] **34**You will look for me,
but you will not find me; and where I
am, you cannot come."[w]
35The Jews said to one another,
"Where does this man intend to go that
we cannot find him? Will he go where
our people live scattered[x] among the
Greeks,[y] and teach the Greeks?
36What did he mean when he said, 'You
will look for me, but you will not find
me,' and 'Where I am, you cannot
come'?"[z]
37On the last and greatest day of the
Feast,[a] Jesus stood and said in a loud
voice, "If anyone is thirsty, let him
come to me and drink.[b] **38**Whoever believes[c] in me, as[n] the Scripture has

7:18 [z]Jn 5:41; 8:50,54
7:19 [a]Dt 32:46; Jn 1:17 [b]ver 1; S Mt 12:14
7:20 [c]S Mk 3:22
7:21 [d]ver 23; Jn 5:2-9
7:22 [e]Lev 12:3 [f]Ge 17:10-14
7:24 [g]1Sa 16:7; Isa 11:3,4; Jn 8:15; 2Co 10:7
7:25 [h]ver 1; S Mt 12:14
7:26 [i]ver 48 [j]Jn 4:29
7:27 [k]Mt 13:55; Lk 4:22; Jn 6:42
7:28 [l]ver 14 [m]Jn 8:14 [n]Jn 8:26, 42
7:29 [o]S Mt 11:27 [p]S Jn 3:17
7:30 [q]ver 32,44; Jn 10:39 [r]S Mt 26:18
7:31 [s]Jn 8:30; 10:42; 11:45; 12:11,42 [t]S Jn 2:11
7:33 [u]Jn 12:35; 13:33; 16:16 [v]Jn 16:5,10,17,28
7:34 [w]ver 36; Jn 8:21; 13:33
7:35 [x]S Jas 1:1 [y]Jn 12:20; Ac 17:4; 18:4
7:36 [z]ver 34
7:37 [a]Lev 23:36 [b]Isa 55:1; Rev 22:17
7:38 [c]S Jn 3:15

[m] *26* Or *Messiah*; also in verses 27, 31, 41 and 42 [n] *37,38* Or / *If anyone is thirsty, let him come to me. / And let him drink, [38]who believes in me. / As*

WILL. True saving faith and an experiential knowledge of his teachings require a sincere desire to do the will of God. To believe is to make a commitment to obey (see article on FAITH AND GRACE, p. 1720).

7:18 GAIN HONOR FOR HIMSELF. Jesus emphasizes an all-important criterion for testing whether religious speakers are from God: Do they seek their own glory or advancement? In evaluating ministers, ask whether their preaching magnifies themselves or the Lord Jesus.

7:38 AS THE SCRIPTURE HAS SAID. Jesus referred to the "Scripture" because it was the very Word of his Father and therefore the supreme authority for his life and teaching. Scripture is also the supreme authority for Christians, for God alone has the right to determine our standards of conduct. He has chosen to exercise this authority by making his truth known in Scripture. The Bible, as God's revelation, carries the same authority as if God himself were speaking to us directly (see article on THE INSPIRATION AND AUTHORITY OF SCRIPTURE, p. 1898).

(1) The inspired Scriptures are the believer's ultimate authority. Ecclesiastical traditions, prophecies, supposed new revelations, doctrines and human ideas must be tested against Scripture and should never be elevated to a place of equal authority with the Bible (cf. Mk 7:13; Col 2:8; 1Pe 1:18–19).

(2) To profess equal or greater allegiance to any other authority than to God and his inspired Word is to remove oneself from the Biblical faith and the lordship of Christ. To say that any person, institution, creed or church possesses equal or higher authority than God's inspired revelation is tantamount to idolatry. Thus, all those who are not willing to submit their beliefs to the authority of the NT place themselves outside of Biblical Christianity and salvation in Christ.

7:38 STREAMS OF LIVING WATER. When the gift of the Spirit is given to believers, they will experience his overflowing life. Then this "living water" will "flow" out to others with the healing

said,[d] streams of living water[e] will flow from within him."[f] 39By this he meant the Spirit,[g] whom those who believed in him were later to receive.[h] Up to that time the Spirit had not been given, since Jesus had not yet been glorified.[i]

Ac 1:4-5

40On hearing his words, some of the people said, "Surely this man is the Prophet."[j]

41Others said, "He is the Christ."

Still others asked, "How can the Christ come from Galilee?[k] 42Does not the Scripture say that the Christ will come from David's family[o][l] and from Bethlehem,[m] the town where David lived?" 43Thus the people were divided[n] because of Jesus. 44Some wanted to seize him, but no one laid a hand on him.[o]

Unbelief of the Jewish Leaders

45Finally the temple guards went back to the chief priests and Pharisees, who asked them, "Why didn't you bring him in?"

46"No one ever spoke the way this man does,"[p] the guards declared.

47"You mean he has deceived you also?"[q] the Pharisees retorted. 48"Has any of the rulers or of the Pharisees believed in him?[r] 49No! But this mob that knows nothing of the law—there is a curse on them."

50Nicodemus,[s] who had gone to Jesus earlier and who was one of their own number, asked, 51"Does our law condemn anyone without first hearing him to find out what he is doing?"

52They replied, "Are you from Galilee, too? Look into it, and you will find that a prophet[p] does not come out of Galilee."[t]

7:38 [d]Isa 58:11 [e]S Jn 4:10 [f]S Jn 4:14
7:39 [g]Joel 2:28; Jn 1:33; Ac 2:17, 33 [h]S Jn 20:22 [i]Jn 12:23; 13:31, 32
7:40 [j]S Mt 21:11
7:41 [k]ver 52; Jn 1:46
7:42 [l]S Mt 1:1 [m]Mic 5:2; Mt 2:5, 6; Lk 2:4
7:43 [n]Jn 6:52; 9:16; 10:19
7:44 [o]ver 30
7:46 [p]S Mt 7:28
7:47 [q]ver 12
7:48 [r]Jn 12:42
7:50 [s]Jn 3:1; 19:39
7:52 [t]ver 41

8:1 [u]S Mt 21:1
8:2 [v]ver 20; S Mt 26:55
8:5 [w]Lev 20:10; Dt 22:22; Job 31:11
8:6 [x]Mt 22:15,18 [y]S Mt 12:10
8:7 [z]Dt 17:7; Eze 16:40 [a]Ro 2:1,22
8:11 [b]Jn 3:17

[The earliest manuscripts and many other ancient witnesses do not have John 7:53–8:11.]

53Then each went to his own home.

8 But Jesus went to the Mount of Olives.[u] 2At dawn he appeared again in the temple courts, where all the people gathered around him, and he sat down to teach them.[v] 3The teachers of the law and the Pharisees brought in a woman caught in adultery. They made her stand before the group 4and said to Jesus, "Teacher, this woman was caught in the act of adultery. 5In the Law Moses commanded us to stone such women.[w] Now what do you say?" 6They were using this question as a trap,[x] in order to have a basis for accusing him.[y]

But Jesus bent down and started to write on the ground with his finger. 7When they kept on questioning him, he straightened up and said to them, "If any one of you is without sin, let him be the first to throw a stone[z] at her."[a] 8Again he stooped down and wrote on the ground.

9At this, those who heard began to go away one at a time, the older ones first, until only Jesus was left, with the woman still standing there. 10Jesus straightened up and asked her, "Woman, where are they? Has no one condemned you?"

11"No one, sir," she said.

"Then neither do I condemn you,"[b]

[o] 42 Greek *seed* [p] 52 Two early manuscripts *the Prophet*

message of Jesus Christ (10:10; 14:12; 15:5; see also Ps 1:3; 46:4; Isa 32:15; 44:3; 58:11; Jer 31:12; Eze 47:1–12; Joel 3:18; Zec 14:8).

7:39 JESUS HAD NOT YET BEEN GLORIFIED. This refers to Jesus' glory on the cross (see 12:23–24). The Spirit cannot be fully given until sin is dealt with. "The Spirit" refers to all the work of the Holy Spirit in the believer, both regeneration (20:22) and the baptism in the Spirit (Ac 2:4).

8:7 IF ANY ONE OF YOU IS WITHOUT SIN. These words must not be taken as justification for refusing to condemn sin within the church, or for treating lightly the moral failure of professed Christians. To do so distorts the Bible's attitude toward sin among God's people. (1) The church's conduct toward sinners outside the church who have had little chance to respond to God's grace in Christ, and its conduct towards those within the church who sin and do not obey Christ, are two different situations. (2) Scripture teaches that sins committed by those within the church must not be tolerated (Rev 2:20), but ought to be sharply rebuked and exposed (Lk 17:3; 1Co 5:1–13; 2Co 2:6–8; Eph 5:11; 2Ti 4:2; Tit 1:13; 2:15; Rev 3:19; see Mt 13:30, note on church discipline).

8:11 NEITHER DO I CONDEMN YOU. Jesus' attitude reflects his redemptive purpose for the human race (Jn 3:16). He does not condemn the woman as unfit for forgiveness, but treats her with kindness and patience in order to lead her to repentance. For her there is salvation if she leaves her "life of sin," i.e., stops living in adultery and returns to her own husband (cf. Lk 7:47). (1) However, it would be blasphemous to use these words of Jesus to suggest that he looks casually at the sin of adultery and the untold heartbreak it causes

Jesus declared. "Go now and leave your
life of sin."[c]

The Validity of Jesus' Testimony

12When Jesus spoke again to the
people, he said, "I am[d] the light of the
world.[e] Whoever follows me will never walk in darkness, but will have the
light of life."[f]
13The Pharisees challenged him,
"Here you are, appearing as your own
witness; your testimony is not valid."[g]
14Jesus answered, "Even if I testify
on my own behalf, my testimony is valid, for I know where I came from and
where I am going.[h] But you have no
idea where I come from[i] or where I
am going. 15You judge by human standards;[j] I pass judgment on no one.[k]
16But if I do judge, my decisions are
right, because I am not alone. I stand
with the Father, who sent me.[l] 17In
your own Law it is written that the testimony of two men is valid.[m] 18I am
one who testifies for myself; my
other witness is the Father, who sent
me."[n]
19Then they asked him, "Where is
your father?"
"You do not know me or my Fa-
ther,"[o] Jesus replied. "If you knew me,
you would know my Father also."[p]
20He spoke these words while teaching[q] in the temple area near the place
where the offerings were put.[r] Yet no
one seized him, because his time had
not yet come.[s]
21Once more Jesus said to them, "I
am going away, and you will look for
me, and you will die[t] in your sin.
Where I go, you cannot come."[u]
22This made the Jews ask, "Will he
kill himself? Is that why he says,
'Where I go, you cannot come'?"
23But he continued, "You are from
below; I am from above. You are of this
world; I am not of this world.[v] 24I told
you that you would die in your sins; if
you do not believe that I am ⌞the one I
claim to be⌟,[q][w] you will indeed die in
your sins."
25"Who are you?" they asked.
"Just what I have been claiming all
along," Jesus replied. 26"I have much
to say in judgment of you. But he who
sent me is reliable,[x] and what I have
heard from him I tell the world."[y]
27They did not understand that he
was telling them about his Father.
28So Jesus said, "When you have lifted
up the Son of Man,[z] then you will
know that I am ⌞the one I claim to be⌟
and that I do nothing on my own but
speak just what the Father has taught
me.[a] 29The one who sent me is with
me; he has not left me alone,[b] for I
always do what pleases him."[c] 30Even
as he spoke, many put their faith in
him.[d]

The Children of Abraham

31To the Jews who had believed him,
Jesus said, "If you hold to my teaching,[e] you are really my disciples.
32Then you will know the truth, and
the truth will set you free."[f]
33They answered him, "We are Abraham's descendants[r][g] and have never

Jn 14:21-24

8:11 [c]Jn 5:14
8:12 [d]S Jn 6:35 [e]S Jn 1:4 [f]Pr 4:18; Mt 5:14
8:13 [g]Jn 5:31
8:14 [h]Jn 13:3; 16:28 [i]Jn 7:28; 9:29
8:15 [j]S Jn 7:24 [k]Jn 3:17
8:16 [l]Jn 5:30
8:17 [m]S Mt 18:16
8:18 [n]Jn 5:37
8:19 [o]Jn 16:3 [p]S 1Jn 2:23
8:20 [q]S Mt 26:55 [r]Mk 12:41 [s]S Mt 26:18
8:21 [t]Eze 3:18 [u]Jn 7:34; 13:33
8:23 [v]Jn 3:31; 17:14
8:24 [w]Jn 4:26; 13:19
8:26 [x]Jn 7:28 [y]Jn 3:32; 15:15
8:28 [z]S Jn 12:32 [a]S Jn 14:24
8:29 [b]ver 16; Jn 16:32 [c]Isa 50:5; Jn 4:34; 5:30; 6:38
8:30 [d]S Jn 7:31
8:31 [e]Jn 15:7; 2Jn 9
8:32 [f]ver 36; Ro 8:2; 2Co 3:17; Gal 5:1,13
8:33 [g]ver 37,39; S Lk 3:8

[q]*24* Or *I am he*; also in verse 28
[r]*33* Greek *seed*; also in verse 37

for both adults and children. (2) What Jesus offers this woman is salvation and a way out of her life of sin. His condemnation awaits her if she refuses to repent and enter the kingdom of God (Ro 2:1–10).

8:12 I AM THE LIGHT OF THE WORLD. Jesus is the true light (1:9); he removes darkness and deception by illuminating the right way to God and salvation. (1) All those who follow Jesus are delivered from the darkness of sin, the world and Satan. Those who still walk in darkness do not follow him (cf. 1Jn 1:6–7). (2) "Whoever follows me" is a present participle, picturing a continuing action — "whoever keeps on following." Jesus recognized only a persevering discipleship (see next note).

8:31 IF YOU HOLD TO MY TEACHING. Jesus never encouraged his disciples to place confidence in past faith or past experience. It is only "if you hold to my teaching" that confidence of salvation is warranted. Genuine disciples of Christ continue to obey the words of Christ (see 15:6, note; Lk 21:19).

8:32 THE TRUTH WILL SET YOU FREE. In the context of human knowledge, many things are true. Yet there is only one truth that will set people free from sin, destruction and Satan's dominion — the truth of Jesus Christ found in God's Word. Some observations about truth are as follows: (1) Scripture, especially the original revelation of Christ and the NT apostles, testifies to the truth that frees one from sin, the world and the demonic (see Eph 2:20, note). (2) Further revelation of "truth" is not needed to complete or make more adequate the gospel of Christ. (3) Saving truth is revealed only from God "by his Spirit" (1Co 2:10) and does not originate from any person or from human wisdom (1Co 2:12–13).

been slaves of anyone. How can you say that we shall be set free?"

34Jesus replied, "I tell you the truth, everyone who sins is a slave to sin.[h] **35**Now a slave has no permanent place in the family, but a son belongs to it forever.[i] **36**So if the Son sets you free,[j] you will be free indeed. **37**I know you are Abraham's descendants. Yet you are ready to kill me,[k] because you have no room for my word. **38**I am telling you what I have seen in the Father's presence,[l] and you do what you have heard from your father.[s]"[m]

39"Abraham is our father," they answered.

"If you were Abraham's children,"[n] said Jesus, "then you would[t] do the things Abraham did. **40**As it is, you are determined to kill me,[o] a man who has told you the truth that I heard from God.[p] Abraham did not do such things. **41**You are doing the things your own father does."[q]

"We are not illegitimate children," they protested. "The only Father we have is God himself."[r]

The Children of the Devil

42Jesus said to them, "If God were your Father, you would love me,[s] for I came from God[t] and now am here. I have not come on my own;[u] but he sent me.[v] **43**Why is my language not clear to you? Because you are unable to hear what I say. **44**You belong to your father, the devil,[w] and you want to carry out your father's desire.[x] He was a murderer from the beginning, not holding to the truth, for there is no truth in him. When he lies, he speaks his native language, for he is a liar and the father of lies.[y] **45**Yet because I tell the truth,[z] you do not believe me! **46**Can any of you prove me guilty of sin? If I am telling the truth, why don't you believe me? **47**He who belongs to God hears what God says.[a] The reason you do not hear is that you do not belong to God."

The Claims of Jesus About Himself

48The Jews answered him, "Aren't we right in saying that you are a Samaritan[b] and demon-possessed?"[c]

8:34 [h] S Ro 6:16 **8:35** [i] Gal 4:30 **8:36** [j] ver 32 **8:37** [k] ver 39,40 **8:38** [l] Jn 5:19,30; 14:10,24 [m] ver 41, 44 **8:39** [n] ver 37; S Lk 3:8 **8:40** [o] S Mt 12:14 [p] ver 26 **8:41** [q] ver 38,44 [r] Isa 63:16; 64:8 **8:42** [s] 1Jn 5:1 [t] S Jn 13:3 [u] Jn 7:28 [v] S Jn 3:17 **8:44** [w] 1Jn 3:8 [x] ver 38,41 [y] Ge 3:4; 4:9; 2Ch 18:21; Ps 5:6; 12:2 **8:45** [z] Jn 18:37 **8:47** [a] Jn 18:37; 1Jn 4:6 **8:48** [b] S Mt 10:5 [c] ver 52; S Mk 3:22

[s] *38* Or *presence. Therefore do what you have heard from the Father.* [t] *39* Some early manuscripts *"If you are Abraham's children,"* said Jesus, *"then*

8:34 EVERYONE WHO SINS. The NT clearly teaches that the Lord Jesus Christ himself breaks the power and dominion of sin in the lives of those who are his true followers (vv. 31–32,36). Individuals who habitually sin are still slaves to sin and unrighteousness and therefore the property of Satan (cf. 1Jn 3:6–10). The union of sincere believers with Christ in his death and resurrection will result in freedom from sin (cf. Ro 6; see next note).

8:36 YOU WILL BE FREE INDEED. Unsaved persons are slaves to sin, impurity and Satan (v. 34; Ro 6:17–20). They live according to the cravings of the sinful nature and the ways of Satan (Eph 2:1–3). (1) True believers, who possess salvation in Christ with the accompanying grace of the indwelling Holy Spirit, are set free from the power of sin and immorality (Ro 6:17–22; 8:1–17). When they face temptation to sin, they now have the power to act according to God's will. They are free to be enslaved to God and righteousness (Ro 6:18,22).

(2) Freedom from sin's bondage is one sure criterion by which all professing believers may test whether they have eternal life with its regenerating and sanctifying grace living in them. Anyone presently in bondage to immorality either has never experienced spiritual rebirth by the Holy Spirit or, having experienced spiritual regeneration, has yielded to sin and once more entered into the spiritual death that brings slavery to sin (Ro 6:16,21, 23; 8:12–13; see 1Jn 3:15, note).

(3) This is not to say, however, that believers are free from spiritual warfare against sin. Throughout our lives, we will have to constantly fight against the pressures of the world, the sinful nature and the devil (see Gal 5:17, note; Eph 6:11–12, notes). Full freedom from temptation and the pull of sin will come only with complete redemption at death or at Christ's return for his faithful. What Christ offers us now is the sanctifying power of his life, whereby those who follow the Spirit are set free from the desires of the sinful nature (Gal 5:16–24) and enabled to live holy and blameless lives before him in love (Eph 1:4).

8:42 IF GOD WERE YOUR FATHER. Here Jesus states a fundamental principle of salvation, namely, that the evidence of being a true child of God (i.e., born again of God) lies in one's attitude of love for Jesus. For this reason, one must demonstrate an attitude of sincere faith and obedience. Otherwise, the claim to be a child of God is illegitimate (cf. v. 31; 10:2–5,14,27–28; 14:15,21).

8:44 HE IS A LIAR AND THE FATHER OF LIES. Lying is specifically mentioned as a characteristic of the devil; he is the source of all falsehood (Ge 3:1–6; Ac 5:3; 2Th 2:9–11; Rev 12:9). It is a sin wholly opposed to the mind of God, who is truth (Rev 19:11). An indifference to the sin of lying is one of the most unmistakable symptoms of an ungodly condition, an indication that one is not born of the Spirit (3:6) but is under the influence of Satan as his or her spiritual father (see 4:24, note; Rev 22:15, note).

49"I am not possessed by a demon,"
said Jesus, "but I honor my Father and
you dishonor me. **50**I am not seeking
glory for myself;[d] but there is one who
seeks it, and he is the judge. **51**I tell
you the truth, if anyone keeps my
word, he will never see death."[e]

52At this the Jews exclaimed, "Now
we know that you are demon-possessed![f] Abraham died and so did the
prophets, yet you say that if anyone
keeps your word, he will never taste
death. **53**Are you greater than our father Abraham?[g] He died, and so did
the prophets. Who do you think you
are?"

54Jesus replied, "If I glorify myself,[h] my glory means nothing. My Father, whom you claim as your God, is
the one who glorifies me.[i] **55**Though
you do not know him,[j] I know him.[k]
If I said I did not, I would be a liar like
you, but I do know him and keep his
word.[l] **56**Your father Abraham[m] rejoiced at the thought of seeing my day;
he saw it[n] and was glad."

57"You are not yet fifty years old,"
the Jews said to him, "and you have
seen Abraham!"

58"I tell you the truth," Jesus answered, "before Abraham was born,[o]
I am!"[p] **59**At this, they picked up
stones to stone him,[q] but Jesus hid
himself,[r] slipping away from the temple grounds.

Jesus Heals a Man Born Blind

9 As he went along, he saw a man
blind from birth. **2**His disciples
asked him, "Rabbi,[s] who sinned,[t]
this man[u] or his parents,[v] that he
was born blind?"

3"Neither this man nor his parents
sinned," said Jesus, "but this happened
so that the work of God might be displayed in his life.[w] **4**As long as it is
day,[x] we must do the work of him who
sent me. Night is coming, when no one
can work. **5**While I am in the world, I
am the light of the world."[y]

6Having said this, he spit[z] on the
ground, made some mud with the saliva, and put it on the man's eyes. **7**"Go,"
he told him, "wash in the Pool of Siloam"[a] (this word means Sent). So the
man went and washed, and came home
seeing.[b]

8His neighbors and those who had
formerly seen him begging asked,
"Isn't this the same man who used to
sit and beg?"[c] **9**Some claimed that he
was.

Others said, "No, he only looks like
him."

But he himself insisted, "I am the
man."

10"How then were your eyes
opened?" they demanded.

11He replied, "The man they call
Jesus made some mud and put it on my
eyes. He told me to go to Siloam and
wash. So I went and washed, and then
I could see."[d]

12"Where is this man?" they asked
him.

"I don't know," he said.

Ac 3:1-10

The Pharisees Investigate the Healing

13They brought to the Pharisees the
man who had been blind. **14**Now the
day on which Jesus had made the mud
and opened the man's eyes was a Sabbath.[e] **15**Therefore the Pharisees also
asked him how he had received his
sight.[f] "He put mud on my eyes," the
man replied, "and I washed, and now I
see."

16Some of the Pharisees said, "This
man is not from God, for he does not
keep the Sabbath."[g]

But others asked, "How can a sinner
do such miraculous signs?"[h] So they
were divided.[i]

17Finally they turned again to the
blind man, "What have you to say about
him? It was your eyes he opened."

The man replied, "He is a prophet."[j]

18The Jews[k] still did not believe
that he had been blind and had received his sight until they sent for the
man's parents. **19**"Is this your son?"
they asked. "Is this the one you say
was born blind? How is it that now he
can see?"

20"We know he is our son," the parents answered, "and we know he was

8:50 [d]ver 54; Jn 5:41
8:51 [e]Jn 11:26
8:52 [f]ver 48; S Mk 3:22
8:53 [g]ver 39; Jn 4:12
8:54 [h]ver 50 [i]Jn 16:14; 17:1,5
8:55 [j]ver 19 [k]Jn 7:28,29 [l]Jn 15:10
8:56 [m]ver 37,39; Ge 18:18 [n]S Mt 13:17
8:58 [o]S Jn 1:2 [p]Ex 3:14; 6:3
8:59 [q]Ex 17:4; Lev 24:16; 1Sa 30:6; Jn 10:31; 11:8 [r]Jn 12:36
9:2 [s]S Mt 23:7 [t]ver 34; Lk 13:2; Ac 28:4 [u]Eze 18:20 [v]Ex 20:5; Job 21:19
9:3 [w]Jn 11:4
9:4 [x]Jn 11:9; 12:35
9:5 [y]S Jn 1:4
9:6 [z]Mk 7:33; 8:23
9:7 [a]ver 11; 2Ki 5:10; Lk 13:4 [b]Isa 35:5; Jn 11:37
9:8 [c]Ac 3:2,10
9:11 [d]ver 7
9:14 [e]Mt 12:1-14; Jn 5:9
9:15 [f]ver 10
9:16 [g]S Mt 12:2 [h]S Jn 2:11 [i]S Jn 6:52
9:17 [j]S Mt 21:11
9:18 [k]S Jn 1:19

9:3 WORK OF GOD MIGHT BE DISPLAYED. Jesus corrects the disciples' erroneous belief that every serious affliction is the result of some sin. At times sickness does result from a serious sin (5:14), but not always. Sometimes suffering is permitted because of a divine purpose, i.e., to display God's mercy, love and power. Often in the world the innocent suffer when the wicked do not (cf. Ps 73:1–14; see article on THE SUFFERING OF THE RIGHTEOUS, p. 710).

born blind. **21**But how he can see now, or who opened his eyes, we don't know. Ask him. He is of age; he will speak for himself." **22**His parents said this because they were afraid of the Jews,[l] for already the Jews had decided that anyone who acknowledged that Jesus was the Christ[u] would be put out[m] of the synagogue.[n] **23**That was why his parents said, "He is of age; ask him."[o]

24A second time they summoned the man who had been blind. "Give glory to God,[v]"[p] they said. "We know this man is a sinner."[q]

25He replied, "Whether he is a sinner or not, I don't know. One thing I do know. I was blind but now I see!"

26Then they asked him, "What did he do to you? How did he open your eyes?"

27He answered, "I have told you already[r] and you did not listen. Why do you want to hear it again? Do you want to become his disciples, too?"

28Then they hurled insults at him and said, "You are this fellow's disciple! We are disciples of Moses![s] **29**We know that God spoke to Moses, but as for this fellow, we don't even know where he comes from."[t]

30The man answered, "Now that is remarkable! You don't know where he comes from, yet he opened my eyes. **31**We know that God does not listen to sinners. He listens to the godly man who does his will.[u] **32**Nobody has ever heard of opening the eyes of a man born blind. **33**If this man were not from God,[v] he could do nothing."

34To this they replied, "You were steeped in sin at birth;[w] how dare you lecture us!" And they threw him out.[x]

Spiritual Blindness

35Jesus heard that they had thrown him out, and when he found him, he said, "Do you believe[y] in the Son of Man?"[z]

36"Who is he, sir?" the man asked. "Tell me so that I may believe in him."[a]

37Jesus said, "You have now seen him; in fact, he is the one speaking with you."[b]

38Then the man said, "Lord, I believe," and he worshiped him.[c]

39Jesus said, "For judgment[d] I have come into this world,[e] so that the blind will see[f] and those who see will become blind."[g]

40Some Pharisees who were with him heard him say this and asked, "What? Are we blind too?"[h]

41Jesus said, "If you were blind, you would not be guilty of sin; but now that you claim you can see, your guilt remains.[i]

The Shepherd and His Flock

10 "I tell you the truth, the man who does not enter the sheep pen by the gate, but climbs in by some other way, is a thief and a robber.[j] **2**The man who enters by the gate is the shepherd of his sheep.[k] **3**The watchman opens the gate for him, and the sheep listen to his voice.[l] He calls his own sheep by name and leads them out.[m] **4**When he has brought out all his own, he goes on ahead of them, and his sheep follow him because they know his voice.[n] **5**But they will never follow a stranger; in fact, they will run away from him because they do not recognize a stranger's voice." **6**Jesus used this figure of speech,[o] but they did not understand what he was telling them.[p]

7Therefore Jesus said again, "I tell you the truth, I am[q] the gate[r] for the sheep. **8**All who ever came before me[s]

9:22 [l] S Jn 7:13 [m] ver 34; Lk 6:22 [n] Jn 12:42; 16:2
9:23 [o] ver 21
9:24 [p] Jos 7:19 [q] ver 16
9:27 [r] ver 15
9:28 [s] Jn 5:45
9:29 [t] Jn 8:14
9:31 [u] Ge 18:23-32; Ps 34:15,16; 66:18; 145:19,20; Pr 15:29; Isa 1:15; 59:1,2; Jn 15:7; Jas 5:16-18; 1Jn 5:14,15
9:33 [v] ver 16; Jn 3:2
9:34 [w] ver 2 [x] ver 22,35; Isa 66:5
9:35 [y] S Jn 3:15 [z] S Mt 8:20
9:36 [a] Ro 10:14
9:37 [b] Jn 4:26
9:38 [c] Mt 28:9
9:39 [d] S Jn 5:22 [e] Jn 3:19; 12:47 [f] Lk 4:18 [g] Mt 13:13
9:40 [h] Ro 2:19
9:41 [i] Jn 15:22,24
10:1 [j] ver 8,10
10:2 [k] ver 11,14; Mk 6:34
10:3 [l] ver 4,5,14, 16,27 [m] ver 4,5,14, 16,27
10:4 [n] S ver 3
10:6 [o] S Jn 16:25 [p] S Mk 9:32
10:7 [q] S Jn 6:35 [r] ver 9
10:8 [s] Jer 23:1,2; Eze 34:2

[u] *22* Or *Messiah* [v] *24* A solemn charge to tell the truth (see Joshua 7:19)

9:34 THEY THREW HIM OUT. One of the best things that happened to the man born blind was excommunication from his former religion. If he had been allowed to stay in the synagogue, he would have been in danger of drifting back to the traditional ways of Judaism and becoming alienated from Christ and the gospel. Today the same thing can happen to those who are in lukewarm churches or unbiblical religious organizations. If they remain in that church or system, they may lose their hunger for true Biblical Christianity and return to embrace the ways of their former religion. The best thing is to be separated from what is not of God, so that Christ may come near to us in the fullest sense (vv. 35–38).

10:1 JESUS THE GOOD SHEPHERD. The discourse about the good shepherd (vv. 1–30) displays Jesus as the true shepherd and ruler of his people in contrast to all false shepherds. (To better understand this chapter, OT passages condemning false shepherds should be read: Isa 56:9–12; Jer 23:1–4; Eze 34; Zec 11.) In vv. 7–18, Jesus applies vv. 1–5 to himself.

were thieves and robbers,[t] but the sheep did not listen to them. **9**I am the gate; whoever enters through me will be saved.[w] He will come in and go out, and find pasture. **10**The thief comes only to steal and kill and destroy; I have come that they may have life,[u] and have it to the full.[v]

11"I am[w] the good shepherd.[x] The good shepherd lays down his life for the sheep.[y] **12**The hired hand is not the shepherd who owns the sheep. So when he sees the wolf coming, he abandons the sheep and runs away.[z] Then the wolf attacks the flock and scatters it. **13**The man runs away because he is a hired hand and cares nothing for the sheep.

14"I am the good shepherd;[a] I know my sheep[b] and my sheep know me— **15**just as the Father knows me and I know the Father[c]—and I lay down my life for the sheep.[d] **16**I have other sheep[e] that are not of this sheep pen. I must bring them also. They too will listen to my voice, and there shall be one flock[f] and one shepherd.[g] **17**The reason my Father loves me is that I lay down my life[h]—only to take it up again. **18**No one takes it from me, but I lay it down of my own accord.[i] I have authority to lay it down and authority to take it up again. This command I received from my Father."[j]

19At these words the Jews were again divided.[k] **20**Many of them said, "He is demon-possessed[l] and raving mad.[m] Why listen to him?"

21But others said, "These are not the sayings of a man possessed by a demon.[n] Can a demon open the eyes of the blind?"[o]

The Unbelief of the Jews

22Then came the Feast of Dedication[x] at Jerusalem. It was winter, **23**and Jesus was in the temple area walking in Solomon's Colonnade.[p] **24**The Jews[q] gathered around him, saying, "How long will you keep us in suspense? If you are the Christ,[y] tell us plainly."[r]

25Jesus answered, "I did tell you,[s] but you do not believe. The miracles I do in my Father's name speak for me,[t] **26**but you do not believe because you are not my sheep.[u] **27**My sheep listen to my voice; I know them,[v] and they follow me.[w] **28**I give them eternal life,[x] and they shall never perish;[y] no one can snatch them out of my hand.[z] **29**My Father, who has given them to me,[a] is greater than all[z];[b] no one

10:8 [t] ver 1 **10:10** [u] S Jn 1:4; 3:15,16; 5:40; 20:31 [v] Ps 65:11; Ro 5:17 **10:11** [w] S Jn 6:35 [x] ver 14; Ps 23:1; Isa 40:11; Eze 34:11-16,23; Mt 2:6; Lk 12:32; Heb 13:20; 1Pe 2:25; 5:4; Rev 7:17 [y] ver 15, 17,18; Jn 15:13; 1Jn 3:16 **10:12** [z] Zec 11:16,17 **10:14** [a] S ver 11 [b] ver 27; Ex 33:12 **10:15** [c] Mt 11:27 [d] ver 11,17,18 **10:16** [e] Isa 56:8; Ac 10:34,35 [f] Jn 11:52; 17:20, 21; Eph 2:11-19 [g] Eze 34:23; 37:24 **10:17** [h] ver 11,15, 18 **10:18** [i] Mt 26:53 [j] Jn 15:10; Php 2:8; Heb 5:8

10:19 [k] S Jn 6:52 **10:20** [l] S Mk 3:22 [m] 2Ki 9:11; Jer 29:26; Mk 3:21 **10:21** [n] S Mt 4:24 [o] Ex 4:11; Jn 9:32, 33 **10:23** [p] Ac 3:11; 5:12 **10:24** [q] S Jn 1:19 [r] Lk 22:67; Jn 16:25,29 **10:25** [s] Jn 4:26; 8:58 [t] Jn 5:36; 14:11 **10:26** [u] Jn 8:47 **10:27** [v] ver 14 [w] ver 4 **10:28** [x] S Mt 25:46 [y] Isa 66:22 [z] S Jn 6:39 **10:29** [a] Jn 17:2,6,24 [b] Jn 14:28

[w] 9 Or *kept safe* [x] 22 That is, Hanukkah [y] 24 Or *Messiah* [z] 29 Many early manuscripts *What my Father has given me is greater than all*

10:9 I AM THE GATE. Those who enter through Jesus will be "saved," i.e., will have abundant eternal life (v. 10); they will have all they need to be delivered from sin, guilt and condemnation. Jesus is the *only* gate for salvation; none other exists (Ac 4:12).

10:11 I AM THE GOOD SHEPHERD. Jesus declares himself to be the promised good shepherd (see Ps 23:1, note; Isa 40:11, note; Eze 34:23, note; 37:24). (1) This metaphor illustrates Jesus' tender and devoted care for his people. It is as if he is saying, "I am toward all who believe in me, as a good shepherd is toward his sheep—caring, watchful and loving."

(2) The distinguishing mark of Christ as the good shepherd is his willingness to die for his sheep. This emphasizes the uniqueness of Christ the shepherd: his death on the cross saves his sheep (Isa 53:12; Mt 20:28; Mk 10:45). Christ is called the "good shepherd" here, the "great Shepherd" in Heb 13:20 and the "Chief Shepherd" in 1Pe 5:4.

(3) Be sure to note that the minister who serves merely to earn a living or to gain honor is the "hired hand" of vv. 12–13. True pastors care for their sheep, while false pastors think first of all of themselves and their position.

10:14 I KNOW MY SHEEP. God's knowledge of and love for his children involves personal affection, faithfulness and constant providential care. We are engraved on the palms of his hands (see Isa 49:14–17, note). We are never out of God's mind, for God's eye continually watches over us for our good (cf. Ex 33:17; Jer 1:5; see Mt 10:31, note; Ro 8:28, note; see article on THE PROVIDENCE OF GOD, p. 78).

10:27 MY SHEEP LISTEN TO MY VOICE. Those who are true sheep of Christ obey his voice and follow him; they are in constant fellowship with the shepherd. "Listen to" and "follow" are in the present tense, denoting repeated or habitual activity. To those who are following, the shepherd gives eternal life. Those sheep who stray from the shepherd and refuse to listen prove that they are not his sheep (15:1–6).

10:28 THEY SHALL NEVER PERISH. Here is a precious promise given to all who are Christ's sheep. They will never be banished from God's love or presence, nor will any power or circumstance on earth take them from the shepherd (cf. Ro 8:35–39). There is indeed safety and security for even the weakest sheep who follow and listen to the good shepherd (see previous note).

can snatch them out of my Father's
hand. **30**I and the Father are one."[c]
31Again the Jews picked up stones
to stone him,[d] **32**but Jesus said to
them, "I have shown you many great
miracles from the Father. For which of
these do you stone me?"
33"We are not stoning you for any of
these," replied the Jews, "but for blasphemy, because you, a mere man,
claim to be God."[e]
34Jesus answered them, "Is it not
written in your Law,[f] 'I have said you
are gods'[a]?[g] **35**If he called them
'gods,' to whom the word of God[h]
came—and the Scripture cannot be
broken[i]— **36**what about the one
whom the Father set apart[j] as his
very own[k] and sent into the world?[l]
Why then do you accuse me of blasphemy because I said, 'I am God's Son'?[m]
37Do not believe me unless I do what
my Father does.[n] **38**But if I do it, even
though you do not believe me, believe
the miracles, that you may know and
understand that the Father is in me,
and I in the Father."[o] **39**Again they
tried to seize him,[p] but he escaped
their grasp.[q]
40Then Jesus went back across the
Jordan[r] to the place where John had
been baptizing in the early days. Here
he stayed **41**and many people came to
him. They said, "Though John never
performed a miraculous sign,[s] all that
John said about this man was true."[t]
42And in that place many believed in
Jesus.[u]

The Death of Lazarus

11 Now a man named Lazarus was
sick. He was from Bethany,[v]
the village of Mary and her sister Martha.[w] **2**This Mary, whose brother Lazarus now lay sick, was the same one
who poured perfume on the Lord and
wiped his feet with her hair.[x] **3**So the
sisters sent word to Jesus, "Lord, the
one you love[y] is sick."
4When he heard this, Jesus said,
"This sickness will not end in death.
No, it is for God's glory[z] so that God's
Son may be glorified through it."
5Jesus loved Martha and her sister and
Lazarus. **6**Yet when he heard that Lazarus was sick, he stayed where he was
two more days.
7Then he said to his disciples, "Let
us go back to Judea."[a]
8"But Rabbi,"[b] they said, "a short
while ago the Jews tried to stone you,[c]
and yet you are going back there?"
9Jesus answered, "Are there not
twelve hours of daylight? A man who
walks by day will not stumble, for he
sees by this world's light.[d] **10**It is
when he walks by night that he stumbles, for he has no light."
11After he had said this, he went on
to tell them, "Our friend[e] Lazarus has

10:30 [c] Dt 6:4; Jn 17:21-23
10:31 [d] S Jn 8:59
10:33 [e] Lev 24:16; Mt 26:63-66; Jn 5:18
10:34 [f] Jn 8:17; 12:34; 15:25; Ro 3:19; 1Co 14:21 [g] Ps 82:6
10:35 [h] S Heb 4:12 [i] S Mt 5:18
10:36 [j] Jer 1:5 [k] Jn 6:69 [l] S Jn 3:17 [m] Jn 5:17,18
10:37 [n] ver 25
10:38 [o] Jn 14:10, 11,20; 17:21
10:39 [p] Jn 7:30 [q] Lk 4:30; Jn 8:59
10:40 [r] Jn 1:28
10:41 [s] S Jn 2:11 [t] Jn 1:26,27,30,34
10:42 [u] S Jn 7:31
11:1 [v] S Mt 21:17 [w] Lk 10:38
11:2 [x] Mk 14:3; Lk 7:38; Jn 12:3
11:3 [y] ver 5,36
11:4 [z] ver 40
11:7 [a] Jn 10:40
11:8 [b] S Mt 23:7 [c] Jn 8:59; 10:31
11:9 [d] Jn 9:4; 12:35
11:11 [e] ver 3

[a] *34* Psalm 82:6

10:34 YOU ARE GODS? In no way does this statement of Jesus teach that believers are to consider themselves gods. On the contrary, those who declare themselves to be gods will fall under God's condemnation (Jer 10:11). (1) The term "you are 'gods' " was spoken to corrupt rulers of Israel who were partial to the wicked and were cruel to children (Ps 82:1–4). These rulers, who thought they were gods, were to suffer judgment and die (Ps 82:7; see 82:6, note). (2) To declare oneself a god is the sin of the antichrist (2Th 2:4,11; see article on THE AGE OF THE ANTICHRIST, p. 1872).

11:4 SICKNESS . . . FOR GOD'S GLORY. Sickness among God's people will never result in death as the final outcome. Death ultimately will be destroyed by the resurrection (vv. 25–26). The final truth is that those who believe in Christ "will never die" (v. 26; see article on DEATH, p. 732).

11:5 JESUS LOVED MARTHA AND HER SISTER AND LAZARUS. Here is a family that had a genuine and strong devotion to Jesus (v. 2), enjoyed intimate fellowship with him (Lk 10:38–42) and was especially loved by him (vv. 3–5). Nevertheless, they experienced sorrow, sickness and death. Today these troubles can and will happen to God's faithful and chosen believers (see article on THE SUFFERING OF THE RIGHTEOUS, p. 710. Churches will have people like Mary persevering in loving devotion to the Lord, Martha faithful in good deeds, and Lazarus suffering and dying. Families like this may cry out, "How long, O Lord? Will you forget me forever?" (Ps 13:1; cf. Mt 27:46; Rev 6:10). Jesus says that his delay is not for lack of love, mercy or compassion, but for the glory of God (v. 4) and his kingdom and for the ultimate eternal good of the sufferers (vv. 15,23–26, 40–44).

11:6 STAYED WHERE HE WAS TWO MORE DAYS. Jesus delayed going to the family he loved (v. 5) in order to strengthen the faith of that family and the disciples, and to perform for them a greater good. Initially, Jesus' actions appeared to indicate that he was unconcerned by their suffering. However, John repeatedly emphasizes that Jesus loved the family and shared their sorrow (vv. 3,5, 35). Jesus' timing and purpose was different from what they wanted. God's timing and will, in the midst of our trials, may be different from what we want. God answers us according to his wisdom and love.

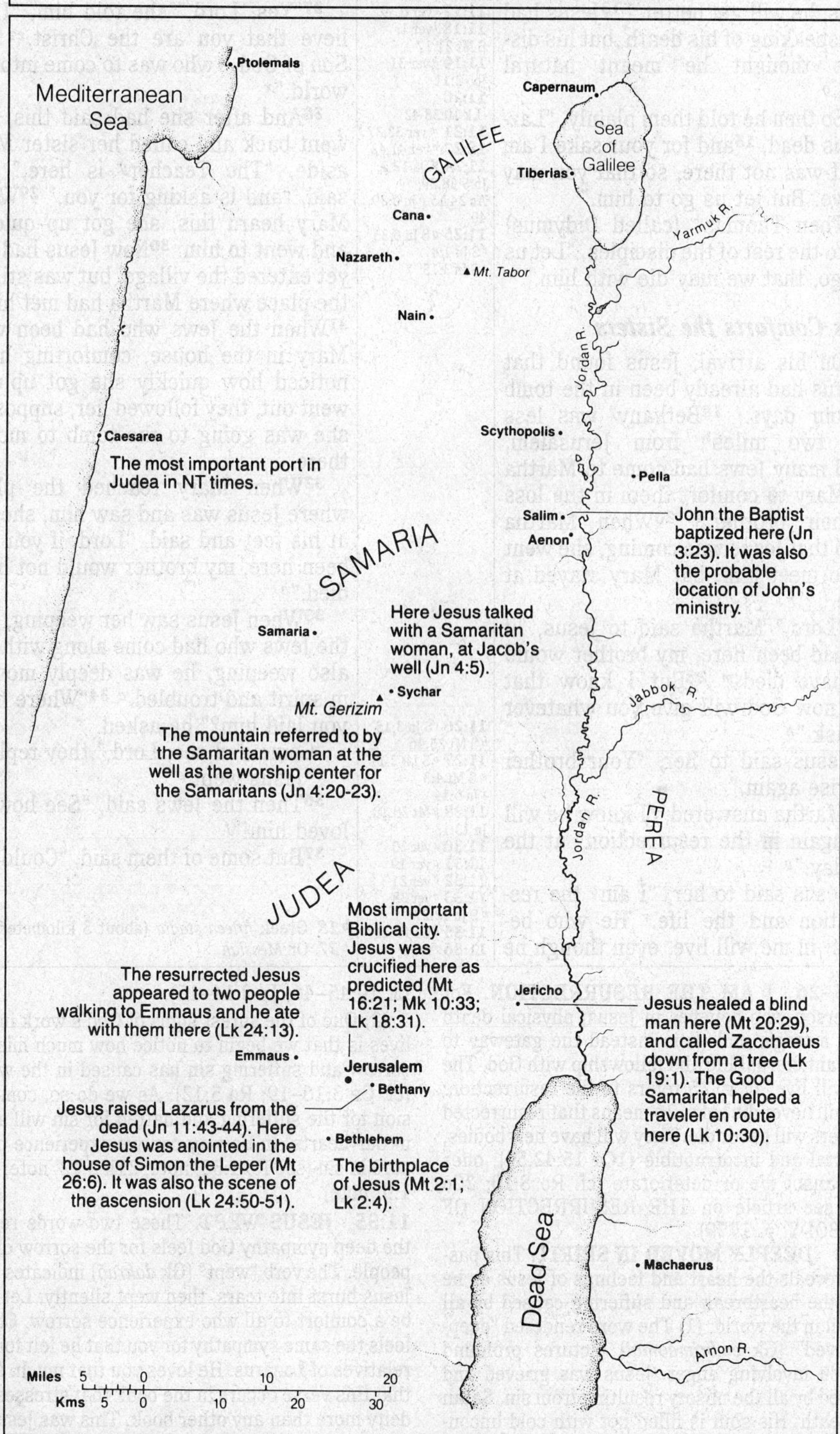

JESUS IN JUDEA AND SAMARIA
Ptolemais
Mediterranean Sea
Capernaum
Sea of Galilee
GALILEE
Tiberias
Cana
Yarmuk R.
Nazareth
Mt. Tabor
Nain
Jordan R.
Scythopolis
Caesarea
The most important port in Judea in NT times.
Pella
Salim
Aenon
John the Baptist baptized here (Jn 3:23). It was also the probable location of John's ministry.
SAMARIA
Here Jesus talked with a Samaritan woman, at Jacob's well (Jn 4:5).
Samaria
Sychar
Mt. Gerizim
Jabbok R.
The mountain referred to by the Samaritan woman at the well as the worship center for the Samaritans (Jn 4:20-23).
Jordan R.
PEREA
JUDEA
Most important Biblical city. Jesus was crucified here as predicted (Mt 16:21; Mk 10:33; Lk 18:31).
The resurrected Jesus appeared to two people walking to Emmaus and he ate with them there (Lk 24:13).
Jericho
Jesus healed a blind man here (Mt 20:29), and called Zacchaeus down from a tree (Lk 19:1). The Good Samaritan helped a traveler en route here (Lk 10:30).
Emmaus
Jerusalem
Bethany
Jesus raised Lazarus from the dead (Jn 11:43-44). Here Jesus was anointed in the house of Simon the Leper (Mt 26:6). It was also the scene of the ascension (Lk 24:50-51).
Bethlehem
The birthplace of Jesus (Mt 2:1; Lk 2:4).
Dead Sea
Machaerus
Arnon R.
Miles 5 0 10 20
Kms 5 0 10 20 30

fallen asleep;[f] but I am going there to
wake him up."
12His disciples replied, "Lord, if he
sleeps, he will get better." 13Jesus had
been speaking of his death, but his disciples thought he meant natural
sleep.[g]
14So then he told them plainly, "Lazarus is dead, 15and for your sake I am
glad I was not there, so that you may
believe. But let us go to him."
16Then Thomas[h] (called Didymus)
said to the rest of the disciples, "Let us
also go, that we may die with him."

Jesus Comforts the Sisters

17On his arrival, Jesus found that
Lazarus had already been in the tomb
for four days.[i] 18Bethany[j] was less
than two miles[b] from Jerusalem,
19and many Jews had come to Martha
and Mary to comfort them in the loss
of their brother.[k] 20When Martha
heard that Jesus was coming, she went
out to meet him, but Mary stayed at
home.[l]
21"Lord," Martha said to Jesus, "if
you had been here, my brother would
not have died.[m] 22But I know that
even now God will give you whatever
you ask."[n]
23Jesus said to her, "Your brother
will rise again."
24Martha answered, "I know he will
rise again in the resurrection[o] at the
last day."[p]
25Jesus said to her, "I am[q] the resurrection and the life.[r] He who believes[s] in me will live, even though he
dies; 26and whoever lives and believes[t] in me will never die.[u] Do you
believe this?"
27"Yes, Lord," she told him, "I believe that you are the Christ,[c][v] the
Son of God,[w] who was to come into the
world."[x]
28And after she had said this, she
went back and called her sister Mary
aside. "The Teacher[y] is here," she
said, "and is asking for you." 29When
Mary heard this, she got up quickly
and went to him. 30Now Jesus had not
yet entered the village, but was still at
the place where Martha had met him.[z]
31When the Jews who had been with
Mary in the house, comforting her,[a]
noticed how quickly she got up and
went out, they followed her, supposing
she was going to the tomb to mourn
there.
32When Mary reached the place
where Jesus was and saw him, she fell
at his feet and said, "Lord, if you had
been here, my brother would not have
died."[b]
33When Jesus saw her weeping, and
the Jews who had come along with her
also weeping, he was deeply moved[c]
in spirit and troubled.[d] 34"Where have
you laid him?" he asked.
"Come and see, Lord," they replied.
35Jesus wept.[e]
36Then the Jews said, "See how he
loved him!"[f]
37But some of them said, "Could not

11:11 [f] S Mt 9:24 **11:13** [g] Mt 9:24 **11:16** [h] Mt 10:3; Jn 14:5; 20:24-28; 21:2; Ac 1:13 **11:17** [i] ver 6,39 **11:18** [j] ver 1; S Mt 21:17 **11:19** [k] ver 31; Job 2:11 **11:20** [l] Lk 10:38-42 **11:21** [m] ver 32,37 **11:22** [n] ver 41,42 **11:24** [o] Da 12:2; Jn 5:28,29; Ac 24:15 [p] Jn 6:39, 40 **11:25** [q] S Jn 6:35 [r] S Jn 1:4 [s] S Jn 3:15 **11:26** [t] S Jn 3:15 [u] S Mt 25:46 **11:27** [v] S Lk 2:11 [w] S Mt 4:3 [x] Jn 6:14 **11:28** [y] Mt 26:18; Jn 13:13 **11:30** [z] ver 20 **11:31** [a] ver 19 **11:32** [b] ver 21 **11:33** [c] ver 38 [d] S Jn 12:27 **11:35** [e] Lk 19:41 **11:36** [f] ver 3

[b] *18* Greek *fifteen stadia* (about 3 kilometers)
[c] *27* Or *Messiah*

11:25–26 I AM THE RESURRECTION. For the person who believes in Jesus, physical death is not a tragic end. It is instead the gateway to abundant eternal life and fellowship with God. The "... will live" of v. 25 refers to the resurrection; the "will never die" of v. 26 means that resurrected believers will never die. They will have new bodies, immortal and incorruptible (1Co 15:42,54), ones that cannot die or deteriorate (cf. Ro 8:10; 2Co 4:16; see article on THE RESURRECTION OF THE BODY, p. 1779).

11:33 DEEPLY MOVED IN SPIRIT. This passage reveals the heart and feelings of Jesus as he faces the heartbreak and suffering caused by all the evil in the world. (1) The word rendered "deeply moved" (Gk *embrimaomai*) pictures profound emotion involving anger. Jesus was grieved and angered by all the misery resulting from sin, Satan and death. His soul is filled not with cold unconcern, but with rage against evil, as he fights for the salvation of the human race (see 11:35, note; Mt 23:13, note; also Mt 21:12–13; Mk 11:15,17; Lk 19:45–46; Jn 2:14–16).

(2) One of the surest signs of God's work in our lives is that we begin to notice how much misery, sorrow and suffering sin has caused in the world (cf. Ge 3:16–19; Ro 5:12). As we do so, compassion for the suffering and hatred for sin will arise in our hearts. In no way can we experience pleasure in sin (see Ro 1:32, note; 2Th 2:12, note; Heb 1:9, note).

11:35 JESUS WEPT. These two words reveal the deep sympathy God feels for the sorrow of his people. The verb "wept" (Gk *dakruō*) indicates that Jesus burst into tears, then wept silently. Let this be a comfort to all who experience sorrow. Christ feels the same sympathy for you that he felt for the relatives of Lazarus. He loves you that much. Note that this verse occurs in the book that stresses his deity more than any other book. This was Jesus — the God/man, deity himself — weeping. God does have a deep, emotional and sympathetic love for you and others (Lk 19:41).

he who opened the eyes of the blind
man[g] have kept this man from dying?"[h]

Jesus Raises Lazarus From the Dead

38Jesus, once more deeply moved,[i]
came to the tomb. It was a cave with
a stone laid across the entrance.[j]
39"Take away the stone," he said.
"But, Lord," said Martha, the sister
of the dead man, "by this time there is
a bad odor, for he has been there four
days."[k]
40Then Jesus said, "Did I not tell you
that if you believed,[l] you would see
the glory of God?"[m]
41So they took away the stone. Then
Jesus looked up[n] and said, "Father,[o]
I thank you that you have heard me. **42**I
knew that you always hear me, but I
said this for the benefit of the people
standing here,[p] that they may believe
that you sent me."[q]
43When he had said this, Jesus
called in a loud voice, "Lazarus, come
out!"[r] **44**The dead man came out, his
hands and feet wrapped with strips of
linen,[s] and a cloth around his face.[t]
Jesus said to them, "Take off the
grave clothes and let him go."

The Plot to Kill Jesus

45Therefore many of the Jews who
had come to visit Mary,[u] and had seen
what Jesus did,[v] put their faith in
him.[w] **46**But some of them went to the
Pharisees and told them what Jesus
had done. **47**Then the chief priests and
the Pharisees[x] called a meeting[y] of
the Sanhedrin.[z]
"What are we accomplishing?" they
asked. "Here is this man performing
many miraculous signs.[a] **48**If we let
him go on like this, everyone will believe in him, and then the Romans will
come and take away both our place[d]
and our nation."
49Then one of them, named Caiaphas,[b] who was high priest that
year,[c] spoke up, "You know nothing
at all! **50**You do not realize that it is
better for you that one man die for the
people than that the whole nation perish."[d]
51He did not say this on his own, but
as high priest that year he prophesied
that Jesus would die for the Jewish nation, **52**and not only for that nation but
also for the scattered children of God,
to bring them together and make them
one.[e] **53**So from that day on they plotted to take his life.[f]
54Therefore Jesus no longer moved
about publicly among the Jews.[g] Instead he withdrew to a region near the
desert, to a village called Ephraim,
where he stayed with his disciples.
55When it was almost time for the
Jewish Passover,[h] many went up from
the country to Jerusalem for their ceremonial cleansing[i] before the Passover. **56**They kept looking for Jesus,[j]
and as they stood in the temple area
they asked one another, "What do you
think? Isn't he coming to the Feast at
all?" **57**But the chief priests and Pharisees had given orders that if anyone
found out where Jesus was, he should
report it so that they might arrest him.

Jesus Anointed at Bethany

12:1–8Ref — Mt 26:6–13; Mk 14:3–9; Lk 7:37–39

12 Six days before the Passover,[k]
Jesus arrived at Bethany,[l]
where Lazarus lived, whom Jesus had
raised from the dead. **2**Here a dinner
was given in Jesus' honor. Martha
served,[m] while Lazarus was among
those reclining at the table with him.
3Then Mary took about a pint[e] of pure
nard, an expensive perfume;[n] she
poured it on Jesus' feet and wiped his
feet with her hair.[o] And the house was
filled with the fragrance of the perfume.
4But one of his disciples, Judas Is-

11:37 [g] Jn 9:6,7 [h] ver 21,32
11:38 [i] ver 33 [j] Mt 27:60; Lk 24:2; Jn 20:1
11:39 [k] ver 17
11:40 [l] ver 23-25 [m] ver 4
11:41 [n] Jn 17:1 [o] S Mt 11:25
11:42 [p] Jn 12:30 [q] S Jn 3:17
11:43 [r] S Lk 7:14
11:44 [s] Jn 19:40 [t] Jn 20:7
11:45 [u] ver 19 [v] Jn 2:23 [w] Ex 14:31; S Jn 7:31
11:47 [x] ver 57 [y] Mt 26:3 [z] S Mt 5:22 [a] S Jn 2:11
11:49 [b] S Mt 26:3 [c] ver 51; Jn 18:13, 14
11:50 [d] Jn 18:14
11:52 [e] Isa 49:6; Jn 10:16
11:53 [f] S Mt 12:14
11:54 [g] Jn 7:1
11:55 [h] Ex 12:13, 23,27; Mt 26:1,2; Mk 14:1; Jn 13:1 [i] 2Ch 30:17,18
11:56 [j] Jn 7:11
12:1 [k] S Jn 11:55 [l] S Mt 21:17
12:2 [m] Lk 10:38-42
12:3 [n] Mk 14:3 [o] Jn 11:2

[d] *48* Or *temple* [e] *3* Greek *a litra* (probably about 0.5 liter)

11:44 THE DEAD MAN CAME OUT. The miracle of Lazarus's resurrection was a sign pointing to Jesus as the resurrection and the life. It was a demonstration of what God will do for all believers who have died, for they too will be raised from the dead (14:3; 1Th 4:13–18). This miracle was also the final issue that caused the Jewish leaders to resolve that Jesus must be put to death (vv. 45–53).

12:3 MARY ... POURED IT ON JESUS' FEET. Because the perfume was very expensive, Mary's anointing of Jesus was an act of great sacrifice and loving devotion. She knew that her opportunity to express devotion to Jesus would soon be over, so she took the opportunity she had. Her faith in and devotion to the Lord is the highest example of what God desires in believers. For this reason Jesus stated that her act of love would be told wherever the gospel is preached (see Mt 26:13, note).

cariot, who was later to betray him,[p]
objected, **5**"Why wasn't this perfume
sold and the money given to the poor?
It was worth a year's wages.[f]" **6**He
did not say this because he cared about
the poor but because he was a thief; as
keeper of the money bag,[q] he used to
help himself to what was put into it.
7"Leave her alone," Jesus replied.
"⌊It was intended⌋ that she should save
this perfume for the day of my burial.[r]
8You will always have the poor among
you,[s] but you will not always have
me."

9Meanwhile a large crowd of Jews
found out that Jesus was there and
came, not only because of him but also
to see Lazarus, whom he had raised
from the dead.[t] **10**So the chief priests
made plans to kill Lazarus as well,
11for on account of him[u] many of the
Jews were going over to Jesus and putting their faith in him.[v]

The Triumphal Entry

12:12–15pp — Mt 21:4–9; Mk 11:7–10; Lk 19:35–38

12The next day the great crowd that
had come for the Feast heard that
Jesus was on his way to Jerusalem.
13They took palm branches[w] and went
out to meet him, shouting,

"Hosanna![g]"

"Blessed is he who comes in the
name of the Lord!"[h][x]

"Blessed is the King of Israel!"[y]

14Jesus found a young donkey and sat
upon it, as it is written,

15"Do not be afraid, O Daughter of
Zion;
see, your king is coming,
seated on a donkey's colt."[i][z]

16At first his disciples did not understand all this.[a] Only after Jesus was
glorified[b] did they realize that these
things had been written about him and
that they had done these things to him.
17Now the crowd that was with
him[c] when he called Lazarus from the
tomb and raised him from the dead
continued to spread the word. **18**Many
people, because they had heard that he
had given this miraculous sign,[d] went
out to meet him. **19**So the Pharisees
said to one another, "See, this is getting us nowhere. Look how the whole
world has gone after him!"[e]

Jesus Predicts His Death

20Now there were some Greeks[f]
among those who went up to worship
at the Feast. **21**They came to Philip,
who was from Bethsaida[g] in Galilee,
with a request. "Sir," they said, "we
would like to see Jesus." **22**Philip went
to tell Andrew; Andrew and Philip in
turn told Jesus.

23Jesus replied, "The hour[h] has
come for the Son of Man to be glorified.[i] **24**I tell you the truth, unless a
kernel of wheat falls to the ground and
dies,[j] it remains only a single seed.
But if it dies, it produces many seeds.
25The man who loves his life will lose
it, while the man who hates his life in
this world will keep it[k] for eternal
life.[l] **26**Whoever serves me must follow me; and where I am, my servant
also will be.[m] My Father will honor the
one who serves me.

27"Now my heart is troubled,[n] and
what shall I say? 'Father,[o] save me
from this hour'?[p] No, it was for this
very reason I came to this hour. **28**Father, glorify your name!"

Then a voice came from heaven,[q] "I
have glorified it, and will glorify it
again." **29**The crowd that was there
and heard it said it had thundered; others said an angel had spoken to him.
30Jesus said, "This voice was for

12:4 [p] S Mt 10:4 **12:6** [q] Jn 13:29 **12:7** [r] Jn 19:40 **12:8** [s] Dt 15:11 **12:9** [t] Jn 11:43,44 **12:11** [u] ver 17, 18; Jn 11:45 [v] S Jn 7:31 **12:13** [w] Lev 23:40 [x] Ps 118:25,26 [y] S Jn 1:49 **12:15** [z] Zec 9:9 **12:16** [a] S Mk 9:32 [b] ver 23; Jn 2:22; 7:39

12:17 [c] Jn 11:42 **12:18** [d] ver 11; Lk 19:37 **12:19** [e] Jn 11:47, 48 **12:20** [f] Jn 7:35; Ac 11:20 **12:21** [g] S Mt 11:21 **12:23** [h] S Mt 26:18 [i] Jn 13:32; 17:1 **12:24** [j] 1Co 15:36 **12:25** [k] Mt 10:39; Mk 8:35; Lk 14:26; 17:33 [l] S Mt 25:46 **12:26** [m] Jn 14:3; 17:24; 2Co 5:8; Php 1:23; 1Th 4:17 **12:27** [n] Mt 26:38, 39; Jn 11:33,38; 13:21 [o] S Mt 11:25 [p] ver 23 **12:28** [q] S Mt 3:17

[f] *5* Greek *three hundred denarii* [g] *13* A Hebrew expression meaning "Save!" which became an exclamation of praise [h] *13* Psalm 118:25, 26 [i] *15* Zech. 9:9

12:12 THE TRIUMPHAL ENTRY. See Mk 11:9, note; Lk 19:28, note.

12:23 SON OF MAN . . . GLORIFIED. Jesus speaks of his death as a glorification rather than a tragedy. He tells his disciples that the way to fruitfulness is through suffering and death (v. 24).

12:25 HATES HIS LIFE IN THIS WORLD. Hating one's own life points to the attitude that values heavenly interests far above those of this earth. Those who follow Christ place little importance in the pleasures, philosophies, successes, values, goals or ways of the world. These will gain "eternal life," for they count nothing in this world so dear that they will not give it up for the sake of the Lord (Mt 16:24–25; Mk 8:34–35).

12:26 WHOEVER SERVES ME. Faith in Jesus involves a personal commitment to follow him, keep his teaching and be where he is. Following Jesus includes self-denial and taking up one's cross (see Mk 8:34, note on the meaning of taking up one's cross).

your benefit,[r] not mine. 31Now is the
time for judgment on this world;[s] now
the prince of this world[t] will be driven
out. 32But I, when I am lifted up from
the earth,[u] will draw all men to myself."[v] 33He said this to show the kind
of death he was going to die.[w]
34The crowd spoke up, "We have
heard from the Law[x] that the Christ[j]
will remain forever,[y] so how can you
say, 'The Son of Man[z] must be lifted
up'?[a] Who is this 'Son of Man'?"
35Then Jesus told them, "You are going to have the light[b] just a little while
longer. Walk while you have the
light,[c] before darkness overtakes
you.[d] The man who walks in the dark
does not know where he is going. 36Put
your trust in the light while you have
it, so that you may become sons of
light."[e] When he had finished speaking, Jesus left and hid himself from
them.[f]

The Jews Continue in Their Unbelief

37Even after Jesus had done all
these miraculous signs[g] in their presence, they still would not believe in
him. 38This was to fulfill the word of
Isaiah the prophet:

"Lord, who has believed our
message
and to whom has the arm of the
Lord been revealed?"[k][h]

39For this reason they could not believe, because, as Isaiah says elsewhere:

40"He has blinded their eyes
and deadened their hearts,
so they can neither see with their
eyes,
nor understand with their
hearts,
nor turn—and I would heal
them."[l][i]

41Isaiah said this because he saw
Jesus' glory[j] and spoke about him.[k]
42Yet at the same time many even
among the leaders believed in him.[l]
But because of the Pharisees[m] they
would not confess their faith for fear
they would be put out of the synagogue;[n] 43for they loved praise from
men[o] more than praise from God.[p]
44Then Jesus cried out, "When a
man believes in me, he does not believe
in me only, but in the one who sent
me.[q] 45When he looks at me, he sees
the one who sent me.[r] 46I have come
into the world as a light,[s] so that no
one who believes in me should stay in
darkness.
47"As for the person who hears my
words but does not keep them, I do not
judge him. For I did not come to judge
the world, but to save it.[t] 48There is
a judge for the one who rejects me and
does not accept my words; that very
word which I spoke will condemn
him[u] at the last day. 49For I did not
speak of my own accord, but the Father
who sent me commanded me[v] what to
say and how to say it. 50I know that his
command leads to eternal life.[w] So

12:30 [r]Ex 19:9; Jn 11:42
12:31 [s]Jn 16:11 [t]Jn 14:30; 16:11; 2Co 4:4; Eph 2:2; 1Jn 4:4; 5:19
12:32 [u]ver 34; Isa 11:10; Jn 3:14; 8:28 [v]Jn 6:44
12:33 [w]Jn 18:32; 21:19
12:34 [x]S Jn 10:34 [y]Ps 110:4; Isa 9:7; Eze 37:25; Da 7:14 [z]S Mt 8:20 [a]Jn 3:14
12:35 [b]ver 46 [c]Eph 5:8 [d]1Jn 1:6; 2:11
12:36 [e]ver 46; S Lk 16:8 [f]Jn 8:59
12:37 [g]S Jn 2:11
12:38 [h]Isa 53:1; Ro 10:16
12:40 [i]Isa 6:10; S Mt 13:13,15
12:41 [j]Isa 6:1-4 [k]Lk 24:27
12:42 [l]ver 11; Jn 7:48 [m]S Jn 7:13 [n]Jn 9:22
12:43 [o]1Sa 15:30 [p]S Ro 2:29
12:44 [q]S Mt 10:40; Jn 5:24
12:45 [r]S Jn 14:9
12:46 [s]S Jn 1:4
12:47 [t]S Jn 3:17
12:48 [u]Jn 5:45
12:49 [v]Jn 14:31
12:50 [w]S Mt 25:46

[j] *34* Or *Messiah* [k] *38* Isaiah 53:1
[l] *40* Isaiah 6:10

12:31 PRINCE OF THIS WORLD WILL BE DRIVEN OUT. Through the cross and resurrection of Christ the defeat of Satan and all he stands for has begun. His final defeat will occur when he is thrown into the lake of burning sulfur (Rev 20:10). At this present time, however, Satan is still active as the ruler or "prince of this world" (14:30; 16:11; 2Co 4:4; cf. Eph 2:2). Satan has power and authority in the world and uses the things of the world against Christ and the church. This is why "friendship with the world is hatred toward God" (Jas 4:4; see also 1Jn 2:15–16).

12:32 DRAW ALL MEN TO MYSELF. The grace of God is not exclusive, i.e., for some people, but not for others. However, some, because of their love for sin, nullify God's grace by their decisions and actions (see Mt 23:37).

12:39 THEY COULD NOT BELIEVE. The people could not believe because their decisions about Jesus brought God's action of hardening. The gospel never leaves unchanged the person who refuses to listen, repent and believe. The apostle Paul says that the people of Israel were broken off because of their unbelief (Ro 11:20; cf. Ps 95:8; Heb 3:8). Yet the hardening was not permanent for every individual in that nation. Anyone who believed would receive eternal life (vv. 44–50). In fact, many in Israel did believe after Pentecost (Ac 2:41).

12:43 LOVED PRAISE FROM MEN. Because they love the approval of their fellow human beings, many sacrifice their convictions and act contrary to their consciences. They are ready to join the majority (cf. Da 11:32,34) and seek the favorable opinion of the powerful or the crowd. What is the secret of gaining victory over the fear of others and the desire for their praise? It is our faith (1Jn 5:4)—the faith that sees God, Christ, heaven, hell, the judgment and eternity as ultimate realities (Ro 1:20; Eph 3:16–19; Heb 11). Professing to follow Christ while loving human glory above God's glory is blatant hypocrisy.

whatever I say is just what the Father
has told me to say."[x]

Jesus Washes His Disciples' Feet

13 It was just before the Passover
Feast.[y] Jesus knew that the
time had come[z] for him to leave this
world and go to the Father.[a] Having
loved his own who were in the world,
he now showed them the full extent of
his love.[m]
2The evening meal was being
served, and the devil had already
prompted Judas Iscariot, son of Simon,
to betray Jesus.[b] **3**Jesus knew that the
Father had put all things under his
power,[c] and that he had come from
God[d] and was returning to God; **4**so he
got up from the meal, took off his outer
clothing, and wrapped a towel around
his waist.[e] **5**After that, he poured water into a basin and began to wash his
disciples' feet,[f] drying them with the
towel that was wrapped around him.
6He came to Simon Peter, who said
to him, "Lord, are you going to wash
my feet?"
7Jesus replied, "You do not realize
now what I am doing, but later you will
understand."[g]
8"No," said Peter, "you shall never
wash my feet."
Jesus answered, "Unless I wash you,
you have no part with me."
9"Then, Lord," Simon Peter replied,
"not just my feet but my hands and my
head as well!"
10Jesus answered, "A person who
has had a bath needs only to wash his
feet; his whole body is clean. And you
are clean,[h] though not every one of
you."[i] **11**For he knew who was going
to betray him,[j] and that was why he
said not every one was clean.
12When he had finished washing
their feet, he put on his clothes and returned to his place. "Do you understand what I have done for you?" he
asked them. **13**"You call me 'Teacher'[k] and 'Lord,'[l] and rightly so, for
that is what I am. **14**Now that I, your
Lord and Teacher, have washed your
feet, you also should wash one another's feet.[m] **15**I have set you an example
that you should do as I have done for
you.[n] **16**I tell you the truth, no servant
is greater than his master,[o] nor is a
messenger greater than the one who
sent him. **17**Now that you know these
things, you will be blessed if you do
them.[p]

Jesus Predicts His Betrayal

18"I am not referring to all of you;[q]
I know those I have chosen.[r] But this
is to fulfill the scripture:[s] 'He who
shares my bread[t] has lifted up his
heel[u] against me.'[n][v]
19"I am telling you now before it
happens, so that when it does happen
you will believe[w] that I am He.[x] **20**I
tell you the truth, whoever accepts
anyone I send accepts me; and whoever accepts me accepts the one who
sent me."[y]
21After he had said this, Jesus was
troubled in spirit[z] and testified, "I tell
you the truth, one of you is going to
betray me."[a]
22His disciples stared at one another, at a loss to know which of them he
meant. **23**One of them, the disciple

12:50 [x]S Jn 14:24
13:1 [y]S Jn 11:55 [z]S Mt 26:18 [a]Jn 16:28
13:2 [b]S Mt 10:4
13:3 [c]S Mt 28:18 [d]Jn 8:42; 16:27, 28,30; 17:8
13:4 [e]S Mt 20:28
13:5 [f]S Lk 7:44
13:7 [g]ver 12
13:10 [h]Jn 15:3 [i]ver 18
13:11 [j]S Mt 10:4
13:13 [k]Mt 26:18; Jn 11:28 [l]S Mt 28:18; Lk 1:43; 2:11; 6:46; 11:1; Ac 10:36; Ro 10:9, 12; 14:9; 1Co 12:3; Php 2:11; Col 2:6
13:14 [m]1Pe 5:5
13:15 [n]S Mt 11:29; S 1Ti 4:12
13:16 [o]Mt 10:24; Lk 6:40; Jn 15:20
13:17 [p]Mt 7:24, 25; Lk 11:28; Jas 1:25
13:18 [q]ver 10 [r]Jn 15:16,19 [s]S Mt 1:22 [t]Mt 26:23 [u]Jn 6:70 [v]Ps 41:9
13:19 [w]Jn 14:29; 16:4 [x]Jn 4:26; 8:24
13:20 [y]S Mt 10:40
13:21 [z]S Jn 12:27 [a]Mt 26:21

[m] *1* Or *he loved them to the last* [n] *18* Psalm 41:9

12:50 ETERNAL LIFE. See 17:3, note.

13:5 WASH HIS DISCIPLES' FEET. This dramatic act of foot washing occurred on the last night of Jesus' life on earth. Jesus did it (1) to demonstrate to his disciples how much he loved them; (2) to foreshadow his self-sacrifice on the cross; and (3) to convey the truth that he was calling his disciples to serve one another in humility. The passion to be great had continually plagued the disciples (Mt 18:1–4; 20:20–27; Mk 9:33–37; Lk 9:46–48). Christ wanted them to see that the desire to be first—to be superior and honored above fellow Christians—is contrary to the spirit of their Lord (see Lk 22:24–30, note; Jn 13:12–17; 1Pe 5:5).

13:8 UNLESS I WASH YOU. These words point to a spiritual washing from sin through the cross. Apart from this washing no one can belong to Christ (1Jn 1:7).

13:14 WASH ONE ANOTHER'S FEET. The early church appears to have followed Jesus' example and literally obeyed his admonition to humbly wash one another's feet in love. For example, in 1Ti 5:10 Paul states that widows should not be cared for by the church if they failed to qualify according to certain standards. One of those qualifications was "washing the feet of the saints."

13:22 AT A LOSS TO KNOW WHICH OF THEM HE MEANT. It is important to note that at no time did the disciples discern Judas's duplicity. He had covered his hypocrisy very well. Even today there will be those in the church who outwardly appear righteous, yet inwardly have no real faith in and devotion to Christ (see article on FALSE TEACHERS, p. 1506).

whom Jesus loved,[b] was reclining
next to him. **24**Simon Peter motioned
to this disciple and said, "Ask him
which one he means."
25Leaning back against Jesus, he
asked him, "Lord, who is it?"[c]
26Jesus answered, "It is the one to
whom I will give this piece of bread
when I have dipped it in the dish."
Then, dipping the piece of bread, he
gave it to Judas Iscariot,[d] son of Simon. **27**As soon as Judas took the
bread, Satan entered into him.[e]
"What you are about to do, do quickly," Jesus told him, **28**but no one at the
meal understood why Jesus said this to
him. **29**Since Judas had charge of the
money,[f] some thought Jesus was telling him to buy what was needed for the
Feast,[g] or to give something to the
poor.[h] **30**As soon as Judas had taken
the bread, he went out. And it was
night.[i]

Jesus Predicts Peter's Denial

13:37,38pp — Mt 26:33–35; Mk 14:29–31; Lk 22:33,34

31When he was gone, Jesus said,
"Now is the Son of Man[j] glorified[k]
and God is glorified in him.[l] **32**If God
is glorified in him,[o] God will glorify
the Son in himself,[m] and will glorify
him at once.
33"My children, I will be with you
only a little longer. You will look for
me, and just as I told the Jews, so I tell
you now: Where I am going, you cannot
come.[n]
34"A new command[o] I give you:
Love one another.[p] As I have loved
you, so you must love one another.[q]
35By this all men will know that you
are my disciples, if you love one another."[r]
36Simon Peter asked him, "Lord,
where are you going?"[s]
Jesus replied, "Where I am going,
you cannot follow now,[t] but you will
follow later."[u]
37Peter asked, "Lord, why can't I
follow you now? I will lay down my life
for you."
38Then Jesus answered, "Will you
really lay down your life for me? I tell
you the truth, before the rooster crows,
you will disown me three times![v]

Jesus Promises to Return

14 "Do not let your hearts be
troubled.[w] Trust[x] in God[p];[y]
trust also in me. **2**In my Father's house
are many rooms; if it were not so, I
would have told you. I am going
there[z] to prepare a place for you.
3And if I go and prepare a place for

13:23 [b]Jn 19:26; 20:2; 21:7,20 **13:25** [c]Mt 26:22; Jn 21:20 **13:26** [d]S Mt 10:4 **13:27** [e]Lk 22:3 **13:29** [f]Jn 12:6 [g]ver 1 [h]Jn 12:5 **13:30** [i]Lk 22:53 **13:31** [j]S Mt 8:20 [k]Jn 7:39; 12:23 [l]Jn 14:13; 17:4; 1Pe 4:11 **13:32** [m]Jn 17:1 **13:33** [n]S Jn 7:33, 34 **13:34** [o]Jn 15:12; 1Jn 2:7-11; 3:11 [p]Lev 19:18; 1Th 4:9; 1Pe 1:22 [q]Jn 15:12; Eph 5:2; 1Jn 4:10, 11 **13:35** [r]1Jn 3:14; 4:20 **13:36** [s]Jn 16:5 [t]ver 33; Jn 14:2 [u]Jn 21:18,19; 2Pe 1:14 **13:38** [v]Jn 18:27 **14:1** [w]ver 27 [x]S Jn 3:15 [y]Ps 4:5 **14:2** [z]Jn 13:33, 36; 16:5

[o] *32* Many early manuscripts do not have *If God is glorified in him.* [p] *1* Or *You trust in God*

13:26 PIECE OF BREAD. Jesus' giving the piece of bread to Judas was probably a final appeal to persuade him to turn from his sin. Judas, however, refused to change his mind, and Satan took control (v. 27; see Lk 22:3, note).

13:34 LOVE ONE ANOTHER. The Christian is commanded to love, in a greater and special way, all true Christians, whether or not they are members of one's own church or followers of one's particular theological persuasion. (1) Believers must distinguish true Christians from those whose profession is false by examining their love for and obedience to Jesus Christ and their loyalty to God's holy Word (5:24; 8:31; 10:27; Mt 7:21; Gal 1:9, note).

(2) Any person who possesses a living faith in Jesus Christ and remains loyal to God's inspired and inerrant Word as he or she sincerely understands it, while standing against the prevailing popular spirit of our day, is my brother or sister in Christ and one who deserves my special love and support.

(3) Loving all true Christians, including those who are not of our church, does not mean that we must compromise or accommodate our particular Biblical beliefs or doctrinal differences. Nor does it mean we must necessarily seek organizational unity.

(4) Christians must never compromise God's holiness. Love for God and his will as revealed in his Word must control and direct our love for others. Love for God must always be first (see next note; Mt 22:37,39, notes).

13:35 KNOW THAT YOU ARE MY DISCIPLES. Love (Gk *agapē*) must be the distinguishing mark of Christ's followers (1Jn 3:23; 4:7–21). This agape love is basically a self-giving and sacrificial love that seeks the good of another (1Jn 4:9–10). Thus, the relationship among all believers must be characterized by a devoted concern that sacrificially seeks to promote the highest good of our brothers and sisters in Christ. Christians must befriend each other in trials, be careful of each other's feelings and reputation, and deny themselves to promote each other's welfare (cf. 1Co 13; Gal 6:2; 1Th 4:9; 2Th 1:3; 1Pe 1:22; 2Pe 1:7; 1Jn 3:23).

14:2 MY FATHER'S HOUSE. This phrase clearly refers to heaven, for Jesus must "go" there to prepare a place for us (Mt 6:9; cf. Ps 33:13–14; Isa 63:15). God has a home where there are many rooms and to which "God's household" now on earth (Eph 2:19) will be transferred; "here we do not have an enduring city" (Heb 13:14).

you, I will come back[a] and take you to
be with me that you also may be where
Ac 1:11 I am.[b] 4You know the way to the place
where I am going."

Jesus the Way to the Father

5Thomas[c] said to him, "Lord, we
don't know where you are going, so
how can we know the way?"
6Jesus answered, "I am[d] the way[e]
and the truth[f] and the life.[g] No one
comes to the Father except through
me.[h] 7If you really knew me, you
would know[q] my Father as well.[i]
From now on, you do know him and
have seen him."
8Philip[j] said, "Lord, show us the
Father and that will be enough for us."
9Jesus answered: "Don't you know
me, Philip, even after I have been
among you such a long time? Anyone
who has seen me has seen the Father.[k] How can you say, 'Show us the
Father'? 10Don't you believe that I am
in the Father, and that the Father is in
me?[l] The words I say to you are not
just my own.[m] Rather, it is the Father,
living in me, who is doing his work.
11Believe me when I say that I am in
the Father and the Father is in me; or
at least believe on the evidence of the
miracles themselves.[n] 12I tell you the
truth, anyone who has faith[o] in me
will do what I have been doing.[p] He
will do even greater things than these,
because I am going to the Father. Ac 3:1
13And I will do whatever you ask[q] in
my name, so that the Son may bring
glory to the Father. 14You may ask me
for anything in my name, and I will
do it.

Jesus Promises the Holy Spirit

15"If you love me, you will obey what
I command.[r] 16And I will ask the Fa-
ther, and he will give you another
Counselor[s] to be with you forever—

14:3 [a] ver 18,28; S Mt 16:27 [b] S Jn 12:26 **14:5** [c] S Jn 11:16 **14:6** [d] S Jn 6:35 [e] Jn 10:9; Eph 2:18; Heb 10:20 [f] Jn 1:14 [g] S Jn 1:4 [h] Ac 4:12 **14:7** [i] Jn 1:18; S 1Jn 2:23 **14:8** [j] S Jn 1:43 **14:9** [k] Isa 9:6; Jn 1:14; 12:45; 2Co 4:4; Php 2:6; Col 1:15; Heb 1:3
14:10 [l] ver 11,20; Jn 10:38; 17:21 [m] S ver 24 **14:11** [n] Jn 5:36; 10:38 **14:12** [o] Mt 21:21 [p] Lk 10:17 **14:13** [q] S Mt 7:7 **14:15** [r] ver 21,23; Ps 103:18; Jn 15:10; 1Jn 2:3-5; 3:22,24; 5:3; 2Jn 6; Rev 12:17; 14:12 **14:16** [s] ver 26; Jn 15:26; 16:7

[q] 7 Some early manuscripts *If you really have known me, you will know*

14:3 I WILL COME BACK. (1) As surely as Christ went to heaven, so he will return from his Father's presence and take his followers to be with him in heaven (see previous note; cf. 17:24), to the place prepared for them. This was the hope of NT Christians, and is the hope of all believers today. The ultimate purpose of the Lord's return is that believers may be with him forever (see articles on THE RESURRECTION OF THE BODY, p. 1779, and THE RAPTURE, p. 1864).

(2) The words "take you to be with me" refer to the rapture, when all living believers "will be caught up together . . . in the clouds to meet the Lord in the air. And so we will be with the Lord forever" (1Th 4:17).

(3) Christ's coming for his faithful will enable them to escape the future "hour of trial" that will come upon the world (see Lk 21:36, note; 1Th 1:10, note; 5:9; Rev 3:10, note).

(4) This glorious and eternal reunion is a comforting doctrine for all followers of Jesus who desire to "be with the Lord forever. Therefore encourage each other with these words" (1Th 4:17–18).

14:12 GREATER THINGS. It is Jesus' desire that his followers do the works that he did. (1) The "greater things" include both the work of converting people to Christ and the performing of miracles. This is shown in the narratives of Acts (Ac 2:41,43; 4:33; 5:12) and in Jesus' declaration in Mk 16:17–18 (see article on SIGNS OF BELIEVERS, p. 1513). (2) The reason for the "greater things" done by the disciples is that Jesus will go to his Father, send forth the power of the Holy Spirit (see v. 16; 16:7; Ac 1:8; 2:4) and answer prayer in his name (v. 14). The disciples' works will be "greater" in number and scope.

14:13 ASK IN MY NAME. Prayer in Jesus' name involves at least two things: (1) praying in harmony with his person, character and will; (2) praying with faith in him and his authority, and with the desire to glorify both the Father and the Son (Ac 3:16). Praying in the name of Jesus, therefore, means that Jesus will answer any prayer that he would have prayed himself. There is no limit to the power of prayer when addressed to Jesus or the Father in holy faith according to his desire (see Mt 17:20, note; see article on EFFECTIVE PRAYING, p. 496).

14:16 I WILL ASK THE FATHER. Jesus will ask the Father to give the Counselor only to those who are serious about their love for him and their devotion to his Word. Jesus uses the present tense in v. 15 ("If you love me"), thus emphasizing a continuing attitude of love and obedience.

14:16 COUNSELOR. Jesus calls the Holy Spirit "another Counselor." "Counselor" translates the Greek *paraklētos*, meaning literally "one called alongside to help." This is a rich word, meaning Counselor, Strengthener, Comforter, Helper, Adviser, Advocate, Intercessor, Ally and Friend. The Greek word for "another" is *allon*, meaning "another of the same kind," rather than *heteros*, meaning "another of a different kind." In other words, the Holy Spirit continues what Christ himself did while on earth.

(1) The Spirit will be by the disciples' side to help and strengthen them (cf. Mt 14:30–31), to teach the true course for their lives (v. 26), to comfort in difficult situations (v. 18), to intercede in prayer for them (Ro 8:26–27; cf. 8:34), to be a friend to further their best interest (v. 17) and to remain with them forever.

(2) The word *paraklētos* is applied to the Lord Jesus in 1Jn 2:1. Therefore Jesus is our helper and intercessor in heaven (cf. Heb 7:25), while the Holy Spirit is our indwelling helper and interces-

17the Spirit of truth.[t] The world cannot accept him,[u] because it neither
sees him nor knows him. But you know
him, for he lives with you and will be[r]
in you. 18I will not leave you as orphans;[v] I will come to you.[w] 19Before
long, the world will not see me anymore, but you will see me.[x] Because
I live, you also will live.[y] 20On that
day[z] you will realize that I am in my
Father,[a] and you are in me, and I am
in you.[b] 21Whoever has my commands
and obeys them, he is the one who
loves me.[c] He who loves me will be
loved by my Father,[d] and I too will
love him and show myself to him."

22Then Judas[e] (not Judas Iscariot)
said, "But, Lord, why do you intend to
show yourself to us and not to the
world?"[f]

23Jesus replied, "If anyone loves me,
he will obey my teaching.[g] My Father
will love him, and we will come to him
and make our home with him.[h] 24He
who does not love me will not obey my
teaching. These words you hear are
not my own; they belong to the Father
who sent me.[i]

25"All this I have spoken while still
with you. 26But the Counselor,[j] the
Holy Spirit, whom the Father will send
in my name,[k] will teach you all
things[l] and will remind you of everything I have said to you.[m] 27Peace I
leave with you; my peace I give you.[n]
I do not give to you as the world gives.
Do not let your hearts be troubled[o]
and do not be afraid.

28"You heard me say, 'I am going
away and I am coming back to you.'[p]
If you loved me, you would be glad that
I am going to the Father,[q] for the Father is greater than I.[r] 29I have told
you now before it happens, so that
when it does happen you will believe.[s]
30I will not speak with you much long-

Ac 10:34-35

14:17 [t] Jn 15:26; 16:13; 1Jn 4:6; 5:6 [u] 1Co 2:14
14:18 [v] 1Ki 6:13 [w] ver 3,28; S Mt 16:27
14:19 [x] Jn 7:33, 34; 16:16 [y] Jn 6:57
14:20 [z] Jn 16:23, 26 [a] ver 10,11; Jn 10:38; 17:21 [b] S Ro 8:10
14:21 [c] S ver 15 [d] Dt 7:13; Jn 16:27; 1Jn 2:5
14:22 [e] Lk 6:16; Ac 1:13 [f] Ac 10:41
14:23 [g] S ver 15 [h] S Ro 8:10
14:24 [i] ver 10; Dt 18:18; Jn 5:19; 7:16; 8:28; 12:49, 50
14:26 [j] ver 16; Jn 15:26; 16:7 [k] Ac 2:33 [l] Jn 16:13; 1Jn 2:20,27 [m] Jn 2:22
14:27 [n] Nu 6:26; Ps 85:8; Mal 2:6; S Lk 2:14; 24:36; Jn 16:33; Php 4:7; Col 3:15 [o] ver 1
14:28 [p] ver 2-4, 18; S Mt 16:27 [q] Jn 5:18 [r] Jn 10:29
14:29 [s] Jn 13:19; 16:4

[r] 17 Some early manuscripts *and is*

---

sor on earth (Ro 8:9,26; 1Co 3:16; 6:19; 2Co 6:16; 2Ti 1:14).

14:17 THE SPIRIT OF TRUTH. The Holy Spirit is called "the Spirit of truth" (15:26; 16:13; cf. 1Jn 4:6; 5:6), because he is the Spirit of Jesus, who is the truth. As such, he testifies to the truth (18:37), enlightens concerning the truth, exposes untruth (16:8) and guides the believer into all truth (16:13). Those who are willing to sacrifice truth for the sake of unity, love or any other reason deny the Spirit of truth, whom they claim lives in them. The church that abandons the truth abandons its Lord. The Holy Spirit will not be the Counselor of those who are indifferent to the faith or halfhearted in their commitment to the truth. He comes only to those who worship the Lord "in spirit and in truth" (4:24).

14:17 WITH YOU AND WILL BE IN YOU. The Holy Spirit now lives with the disciples, and Christ promises them that in the future he will "be in you." This promise of the indwelling of the Holy Spirit was fulfilled after Christ's resurrection when he breathed on them and said to them, "Receive the Holy Spirit" (20:22). For a discussion of the role of the Spirit in regeneration, see article on THE REGENERATION OF THE DISCIPLES, p. 1627.

14:18 I WILL COME TO YOU. Jesus reveals himself to the obedient believer through the Holy Spirit, who makes known the personal presence of Jesus in and with the one who loves him (v. 21). The Spirit makes us aware of the nearness of Jesus and the reality of his love, his blessing and his help. This is one of the Spirit's primary tasks. The fact that Christ comes to us through the Spirit should cause us to respond in love, worship and devotion.

14:21 WHOEVER HAS MY COMMANDS. Obeying the commands of Christ is not optional for those who would have eternal life (3:36; 14:21,23; 15:8–10,13–14; Lk 6:46–49; Jas 1:22; 2Pe 1:5–11, 1Jn 2:3–6). (1) Obedience to Christ, though never perfect, must nevertheless be genuine. It is an essential aspect of saving faith, springing from our love for him (vv. 15,21,23–24; see Mt 7:21, note). Without love for Christ, trying to obey his commands becomes legalism. (2) To the person who loves Christ and strives to obey his commands consistently, Christ promises a special love, grace and his deepest inward presence (cf. v. 23).

14:23 WE WILL . . . MAKE OUR HOME WITH HIM. Those who truly love Jesus and obey his words will experience the immediate presence and love of the Father and the Son. The Father and the Son come to believers by means of the Holy Spirit (see v. 18, note). It should be noted that the Father's love is conditioned on our loving Jesus and being loyal to his Word.

14:24 HE WHO DOES NOT LOVE ME. Those who do not obey Christ's teachings do not have a personal love for him, and without love for Jesus true saving faith does not exist (1Jn 2:3–4). To say that people remain saved even though they cease to love Christ and begin to live lives of immorality, blasphemy, cruelty, murder, drunkenness, etc., directly contradicts these and other words of Jesus concerning love, obedience and the indwelling of the Holy Spirit.

14:26 HOLY SPIRIT. The Counselor is identified here as the "Holy Spirit." For the NT Christian the most important thing about the Spirit is not his power (Ac 1:8), but that he is "Holy." His holy character, along with the manifestation of that holy character in the lives of believers, is what matters most (cf. Ro 1:4; Gal 5:22–26).

er, for the prince of this world[t] is coming. He has no hold on me, **31**but the
world must learn that I love the Father
and that I do exactly what my Father
has commanded me.[u]
"Come now; let us leave.

The Vine and the Branches

15 "I am[v] the true vine,[w] and my
Father is the gardener. **2**He
cuts off every branch in me that bears
no fruit,[x] while every branch that does
bear fruit[y] he prunes[s] so that it will
be even more fruitful. **3**You are already
clean because of the word I have spoken to you.[z] **4**Remain in me, and I will
remain in you.[a] No branch can bear
fruit by itself; it must remain in the
vine. Neither can you bear fruit unless
you remain in me.

14:30 [t]S Jn 12:31
14:31 [u]Jn 10:18; 12:49
15:1 [v]S Jn 6:35 [w]Ps 80:8-11; Isa 5:1-7
15:2 [x]ver 6; S Mt 3:10 [y]Ps 92:14; Mt 3:8; 7:20; Gal 5:22; Eph 5:9; Php 1:11
15:3 [z]Jn 13:10; 17:17; Eph 5:26
15:4 [a]S Jn 6:56
15:5 [b]ver 16
15:6 [c]ver 2; Eze 15:4; S Mt 3:10
15:7 [d]ver 4; S Jn 6:56 [e]S Mt 7:7
15:8 [f]S Mt 9:8 [g]Jn 8:31
15:9 [h]Jn 17:23, 24,26

5"I am the vine; you are the
branches. If a man remains in me and
I in him, he will bear much fruit;[b]
apart from me you can do nothing. **6**If
anyone does not remain in me, he is
like a branch that is thrown away and
withers; such branches are picked up,
thrown into the fire and burned.[c] **7**If
you remain in me[d] and my words remain in you, ask whatever you wish,
and it will be given you.[e] **8**This is to
my Father's glory,[f] that you bear
much fruit, showing yourselves to be
my disciples.[g]

Love Each Other

9"As the Father has loved me,[h] so
have I loved you. Now remain in my

[s] *2* The Greek for *prunes* also means *cleans.*

15:1 I AM THE TRUE VINE. In this parable or allegory, Jesus describes himself as "the true vine" and those who have become his disciples as "the branches." By remaining attached to him as the Source of life, they produce fruit. God is the gardener who takes care of the branches in order that they may bear fruit (vv. 2,8). God expects all of us to bear fruit (see next note).

15:2 EVERY BRANCH. Jesus speaks of two categories of branches: fruitless and fruitful. (1) The branches that cease to bear fruit are those who no longer have the life in them that comes from enduring faith in and love for Christ. These "branches" the Father cuts off, i.e., he separates them from vital union with Christ (cf. Mt 3:10). When they stop remaining in Christ, God then judges and rejects them (v. 6). (2) The branches that bear fruit are those who have life in them because of their enduring faith in and love for Christ (see article on THE ACTS OF THE SINFUL NATURE AND THE FRUIT OF THE SPIRIT, p. 1818). These "branches" the Father prunes so that they will become more fruitful. That is, he removes from their lives anything that diverts or hinders the vital life-flow of Christ into them. The fruit is the quality of Christian character that brings glory to God through life and witness (see Mt 3:8; 7:20; Ro 6:22; Gal 5:22–23; Eph 5:9; Php 1:11).

15:4 REMAIN IN ME. After a person believes in Christ and is forgiven, he or she receives eternal life and the power to remain in Christ. Given that power, the believer must then accept that responsibility in salvation and remain in Christ. The Greek word *menō* means to remain, continue, abide or live. Just as the branch has life only as long as the life of the vine flows into it, so believers have Christ's life only as long as Christ's life flows into them through their remaining in Christ. The conditions by which we remain in Christ are: (1) keeping God's Word continually in our hearts and minds and making it the guide for our actions (v. 7); (2) maintaining the habit of constant intimate communion with Christ in order to draw strength from him (v. 7); (3) obeying his commands, remaining in his love (v. 10) and loving each other (vv. 12, 17); (4) keeping our lives clean through the Word, resisting all sin and yielding to the Spirit's direction (v. 3; 17:17; Ro 8:14; Gal 5:16–25; Eph 5:26; 1Pe 1:22).

15:6 LIKE A BRANCH THAT IS THROWN AWAY. The parable of the vine and branches makes it unmistakably clear that Christ did not believe "once in the vine, always in the vine." Rather, in this parable Jesus gave his disciples a solemn but loving warning that it is indeed possible for true believers to ultimately abandon faith, turn their backs on Jesus, fail to remain in him, and thus to be thrown into the everlasting fire of hell.

(1) We have here the foundational principle governing the saving relationship of Christ and the believer, namely, that it is never a static relationship based solely on a past decision or experience. Rather, it is a progressive relationship as Christ lives in the believer and shares with him or her his divine life (see 17:3, note; Col 3:4; 1Jn 5:11–13).

(2) Three important truths are taught in this parable: (a) The responsibility of remaining in Christ is placed upon the disciples (see v. 4, note). This is our response to God's prior gift of divine life and power given at conversion. (b) Remaining in Christ results in Jesus' continued indwelling (v. 4a), the fruitfulness of the disciple (v. 5), success in prayer (v. 7) and fullness of joy (v. 11). (c) The consequences of failure to remain in Christ are fruitlessness (vv. 4–5), removal from Christ and destruction (vv. 2a,6).

15:7 ASK WHATEVER YOU WISH. The secret of answered prayer is remaining in Christ. The closer we live to Christ through meditation on and study of Scripture, the more our prayers will be in line with the nature and words of Christ, and thus the more effectual our prayers will be (see 14:13, note; 15:4, note; Ps 66:18, note; see article on EFFECTIVE PRAYING, p. 496).

15:9–10 REMAIN IN MY LOVE. The believer must live in the atmosphere of the love of Christ.

love. 10If you obey my commands,[i]
you will remain in my love, just as I
have obeyed my Father's commands
and remain in his love. 11I have told
you this so that my joy may be in you
and that your joy may be complete.[j]
12My command is this: Love each other
as I have loved you.[k] 13Greater love
has no one than this, that he lay down
his life for his friends.[l] 14You are my
friends[m] if you do what I command.[n]
15I no longer call you servants, because a servant does not know his
master's business. Instead, I have
called you friends, for everything that
I learned from my Father I have made
known to you.[o] 16You did not choose
me, but I chose you and appointed
you[p] to go and bear fruit[q]—fruit that
will last. Then the Father will give you
whatever you ask in my name.[r]
17This is my command: Love each other.[s]

The World Hates the Disciples

18"If the world hates you,[t] keep in
mind that it hated me first. 19If you belonged to the world, it would love you
as its own. As it is, you do not belong
to the world, but I have chosen you[u]
out of the world. That is why the world
hates you.[v] 20Remember the words I
spoke to you: 'No servant is greater
than his master.'[tw] If they persecuted me, they will persecute you also.[x]
If they obeyed my teaching, they will
obey yours also. 21They will treat you
this way because of my name,[y] for
they do not know the One who sent

15:10 [i]S Jn 14:15 **15:11** [j]S Jn 3:29 **15:12** [k]ver 17; S Jn 13:34 **15:13** [l]Ge 44:33; Jn 10:11; Ro 5:7,8 **15:14** [m]Job 16:20; Pr 18:24; Lk 12:4 [n]Mt 12:50 **15:15** [o]Jn 8:26 **15:16** [p]ver 19; Jn 13:18 [q]ver 5 [r]S Mt 7:7 **15:17** [s]ver 12 **15:18** [t]Isa 66:5; Jn 7:7; 1Jn 3:13 **15:19** [u]ver 16 [v]Jn 17:14 **15:20** [w]S Jn 13:16 [x]2Ti 3:12 **15:21** [y]Isa 66:5; Mt 5:10,11; 10:22; Lk 6:22; Ac 5:41; 1Pe 4:14; Rev 2:3

[z]Jn 16:3 **15:22** [a]Eze 2:5; 3:7 [b]Jn 9:41; Ro 1:20; 2:1 **15:24** [c]Jn 5:36 [d]Jn 9:41 **15:25** [e]S Jn 10:34 [f]Ps 35:19; 69:4; 109:3 **15:26** [g]Jn 14:16 [h]Jn 14:26; 16:7 [i]S Jn 14:17 [j]1Jn 5:7 **15:27** [k]S Lk 24:48; Jn 21:24; 1Jn 1:2; 4:14 [l]S Lk 1:2 **16:1** [m]Jn 15:18-27 [n]Mt 11:6 **16:2** [o]Jn 9:22; 12:42 [p]Isa 66:5; Ac 26:9,10; Rev 6:9 **16:3** [q]Jn 15:21; 17:25; 1Jn 3:1 **16:4** [r]Jn 13:19; 14:29 [s]Jn 15:27 **16:5** [t]ver 10,17, 28; Jn 7:33 [u]Jn 13:36; 14:5

me.[z] 22If I had not come and spoken
to them,[a] they would not be guilty of
sin. Now, however, they have no excuse for their sin.[b] 23He who hates me
hates my Father as well. 24If I had not
done among them what no one else
did,[c] they would not be guilty of sin.[d]
But now they have seen these miracles, and yet they have hated both me
and my Father. 25But this is to fulfill
what is written in their Law:[e] 'They
hated me without reason.'[uf]
26"When the Counselor[g] comes,
whom I will send to you from the Father,[h] the Spirit of truth[i] who goes
out from the Father, he will testify
about me.[j] 27And you also must testify,[k] for you have been with me from
the beginning.[l] Ac 1:8

16 "All this[m] I have told you so
that you will not go astray.[n]
2They will put you out of the synagogue;[o] in fact, a time is coming when
anyone who kills you will think he is
offering a service to God.[p] 3They will
do such things because they have not
known the Father or me.[q] 4I have told
you this, so that when the time comes
you will remember[r] that I warned
you. I did not tell you this at first because I was with you.[s]

The Work of the Holy Spirit

5"Now I am going to him who sent
me,[t] yet none of you asks me, 'Where
are you going?'[u] 6Because I have said
these things, you are filled with

[t]*20* John 13:16 [u]*25* Psalms 35:19; 69:4

Jesus goes on to state that this is done by obeying his commands.

15:16 GO AND BEAR FRUIT. All Christians are chosen "out of the world" (v. 19) to "bear fruit" (vv. 2,4–5,8). This fruit-bearing refers to (1) spiritual virtues, such as the fruit of the Spirit mentioned in Gal 5:22–23—love, joy, peace, patience, kindness, goodness, faithfulness, gentleness, self-control (cf. Eph 5:9; Col 1:6; Heb 12:11; Jas 3:18); and (2) working for the conversion of others to Christ (4:36; 12:24).

15:20 THEY WILL PERSECUTE YOU ALSO. While Christ's followers are in this world they will be hated, persecuted and rejected for his sake. The world is the great opponent of Christ and his people throughout history. (1) True believers must understand that the world—including false religious organizations and churches—will always oppose God and the principles of his kingdom; thus the world will remain an enemy and persecutor of faithful believers until the end (Jas 4:4; see Mt 5:10, note). (2) The reason believers suffer at the hands of the world is because they are fundamentally different; they do not "belong to the world" and have come "out of the world" (v. 19). The values, standards and direction of the faithful are in conflict with the unrighteous ways of their corrupt society. They refuse to compromise with its ungodly standards, and instead set their "minds on things above, not on earthly things" (Col 3:2).

16:2 PUT YOU OUT OF THE SYNAGOGUE. Jesus does not speak here of persecution from pagans, but of opposition and hostility from religious authorities and congregations. His reference earlier to the world hating believers (15:18–19) must include these religious people. (1) All professed believers or churches that do not adhere to Jesus' teaching and apostolic revelation, or that do not seek to remain separated from the corrupt systems of society, belong to the world (cf. 1Jn 4:5–6). (2) These so-called professed believers have values so different from the true NT gospel that when they persecute or kill true followers of Christ, they think they are serving God.

grief.[v] 7But I tell you the truth: It is
for your good that I am going away.
Unless I go away, the Counselor[w] will
not come to you; but if I go, I will send
him to you.[x] 8When he comes, he will
convict the world of guilt[v] in regard to
sin and righteousness and judgment:
9in regard to sin,[y] because men do not
believe in me; 10in regard to righteousness,[z] because I am going to the Father,[a] where you can see me no longer; 11and in regard to judgment,
because the prince of this world[b] now
stands condemned.
12"I have much more to say to you,
more than you can now bear.[c] 13But
when he, the Spirit of truth,[d] comes,
he will guide you into all truth.[e] He
will not speak on his own; he will
speak only what he hears, and he will
tell you what is yet to come. 14He
will bring glory to me by taking from
what is mine and making it known to
you. 15All that belongs to the Father
is mine.[f] That is why I said the Spirit
will take from what is mine and make
it known to you.
16"In a little while[g] you will see me
no more, and then after a little while
you will see me."[h]

16:6 [v]ver 22 **16:7** [w]Jn 14:16, 26; 15:26 [x]Jn 7:39; 14:26 **16:9** [y]Jn 15:22 **16:10** [z]Ac 3:14; 7:52; Ro 1:17; 3:21,22; 1Pe 3:18 [a]S ver 5 **16:11** [b]S Jn 12:31 **16:12** [c]Mk 4:33; 1Co 3:2 **16:13** [d]S Jn 14:17 [e]Ps 25:5; Jn 14:26 **16:15** [f]Jn 17:10 **16:16** [g]S Jn 7:33 [h]ver 22; Jn 14:18-24

[v]8 Or *will expose the guilt of the world*

16:7 IF I GO, I WILL SEND HIM. The Pentecostal outpouring of the Holy Spirit will occur only after Christ goes away (cf. Ac 2:33; see article on THE REGENERATION OF THE DISCIPLES, p. 1627). This outpouring at Pentecost fully ushered in the age of the Spirit.

16:8 CONVICT THE WORLD. When the Holy Spirit comes at Pentecost (see previous note; Ac 2:4), his principal work with respect to proclaiming the gospel will be that of convicting. The term "convict" (Gk *elenchō*) means to expose, refute and convince.

(1) The Spirit's ministry of convicting operates in three areas. (a) Sin. The Holy Spirit will expose sin and unbelief in order to awaken a consciousness of guilt and need for forgiveness. Conviction also makes clear the fearful results if the guilty persist in their wrongdoing. After conviction, a choice must be made. This will often lead to true repentance and a turning to Jesus as Lord and Savior (Ac 2:37–38). (b) Righteousness. The Spirit convinces people that Jesus is the righteous Son of God, resurrected, vindicated and now the Lord of all. He makes them aware of God's standard of righteousness in Christ, shows them what sin is and gives them power to overcome the world (Ac 3:12–16; 7:51–60; 17:31; 1Pe 3:18). (c) Judgment. The Spirit convinces people of Satan's defeat at the cross (12:31; 16:11), God's present judgment of the world (Ro 1:18–32) and the future judgment of the entire human race (Mt 16:27; Ac 17:31; 24:25; Ro 14:10; 1Co 6:2; 2Co 5:10; Jude 14).

(2) The Spirit's work of convicting people of sin, righteousness and judgment will be manifested in all who are baptized in the Holy Spirit and are truly Spirit-filled believers. Christ, filled with the Spirit (Lk 4:1), testified to the world that "what it does is evil" (see 7:7; 15:18) and called people to repent (Mt 4:17). John the Baptist, "filled with the Holy Spirit" from birth (see Lk 1:15, note), exposed the sin of the Jewish people and commanded them to change their ways (see Mt 11:7, note; Lk 3:1–20); Peter, "filled with the Holy Spirit" (Ac 2:4), convicted the hearts of 3,000 sinners and called them to repent and receive forgiveness (Ac 2:37–41).

(3) Clearly, any preacher or church that does not publicly expose sin and call for repentance and Biblical righteousness is not directed by the Holy Spirit. 1Co 14:24–25 explicitly states that God's presence in the congregation is recognized by the exposure of the sin of unbelievers (i.e., secrets of their hearts), and their consequent conviction and salvation.

16:13 HE WILL GUIDE YOU INTO ALL TRUTH. The convicting work of the Holy Spirit is not only directed toward the unsaved (vv. 7–8), but also operates in believers and the church in order to teach, correct and guide them into truth (Mt 18:15; 1Ti 5:20; Rev 3:19).

(1) The Holy Spirit will speak to believers concerning sin, the righteousness of Christ and the judgment of evil in order to (a) conform them to Christ and his standard of righteousness (cf. 2Co 3:18), (b) guide them into all truth, and (c) glorify Christ (v. 14). Thus, the Holy Spirit works within believers to reproduce Christ's holy life in their lives.

(2) If Spirit-filled believers reject the Spirit's guidance and convicting work, and if they do not "by the Spirit . . . put to death the misdeeds of the body" (Ro 8:13), then they will enter into condemnation. Only those who receive the truth and are "led by the Spirit of God" are "sons of God" (Ro 8:14) and are therefore able to continue in the Spirit's fullness (see Eph 5:18, note). Sin destroys both the life and fullness of the Holy Spirit within the believer (Ro 6:23; 8:13; Gal 5:17; cf. Eph 5:18; 1Th 5:19).

16:14 TAKING FROM WHAT IS MINE. The Spirit takes that which is Christ's and reveals it to the believer. He takes the presence, love, forgiveness, redemption, sanctification, power, spiritual gifts, healing and all that is ours through our faith relationship with Christ, and makes it experientially real in our lives. Through the Spirit Jesus returns to us to disclose his love, grace and personal fellowship (cf. 14:16–23). The Spirit works within us to do what is necessary to awaken and deepen our awareness of Jesus' presence in our lives, drawing our hearts toward him in faith, love, obedience, communion, worship and praise (see article on JESUS AND THE HOLY SPIRIT, p. 1546).

The Disciples' Grief Will Turn to Joy

17Some of his disciples said to one
another, "What does he mean by saying, 'In a little while you will see me no
more, and then after a little while you
will see me,'[i] and 'Because I am going to the Father'?"[j] 18They kept asking, "What does he mean by 'a little
while'? We don't understand what he is
saying."

19Jesus saw that they wanted to ask
him about this, so he said to them, "Are
you asking one another what I meant
when I said, 'In a little while you will
see me no more, and then after a little
while you will see me'? 20I tell you the
truth, you will weep and mourn[k] while
the world rejoices. You will grieve, but
your grief will turn to joy.[l] 21A woman giving birth to a child has pain[m] because her time has come; but when her
baby is born she forgets the anguish
because of her joy that a child is born
into the world. 22So with you: Now is
your time of grief,[n] but I will see you
again[o] and you will rejoice, and no
one will take away your joy.[p] 23In that
day[q] you will no longer ask me anything. I tell you the truth, my Father
will give you whatever you ask in my
name.[r] 24Until now you have not
asked for anything in my name. Ask
and you will receive,[s] and your joy
will be complete.[t]

25"Though I have been speaking figuratively,[u] a time is coming[v] when I
will no longer use this kind of language
but will tell you plainly about my Father. 26In that day you will ask in my
name.[w] I am not saying that I will ask
the Father on your behalf. 27No, the Father himself loves you because you
have loved me[x] and have believed that
I came from God.[y] 28I came from the
Father and entered the world; now I
am leaving the world and going back to
the Father."[z]

29Then Jesus' disciples said, "Now
you are speaking clearly and without
figures of speech.[a] 30Now we can see
that you know all things and that you
do not even need to have anyone ask
you questions. This makes us believe[b]
that you came from God."[c]

31"You believe at last!"[w] Jesus answered. 32"But a time is coming,[d] and
has come, when you will be scattered,[e] each to his own home. You will
leave me all alone.[f] Yet I am not
alone, for my Father is with me.[g]

33"I have told you these things, so
that in me you may have peace.[h] In
this world you will have trouble.[i] But
take heart! I have overcome[j] the
world." Jn 17:14-18

Jesus Prays for Himself

17 After Jesus said this, he looked
toward heaven[k] and prayed:

"Father, the time has come.[l]
Glorify your Son, that your Son
may glorify you.[m] 2For you granted him authority over all people[n]
that he might give eternal life[o] to
all those you have given him.[p]
3Now this is eternal life: that they

16:17 [i]ver 16 [j]ver 5 **16:20** [k]Mk 16:10; Lk 23:27 [l]Jn 20:20 **16:21** [m]Isa 13:8; 21:3; 26:17; Mic 4:9; 1Th 5:3 **16:22** [n]ver 6 [o]ver 16 [p]ver 20; Jer 31:12 **16:23** [q]ver 26; Jn 14:20 [r]S Mt 7:7 **16:24** [s]S Mt 7:7 [t]S Jn 3:29 **16:25** [u]ver 29; Ps 78:2; Eze 20:49; Mt 13:34; Mk 4:33,34; Jn 10:6 [v]ver 2 **16:26** [w]ver 23,24 **16:27** [x]Jn 14:21, 23 [y]ver 30; S Jn 13:3 **16:28** [z]ver 5,10, 17; Jn 13:3 **16:29** [a]S ver 25 **16:30** [b]1Ki 17:24 [c]ver 27; S Jn 13:3 **16:32** [d]ver 2,25 [e]Mt 26:31 [f]Mt 26:56 [g]Jn 8:16,29 **16:33** [h]S Jn 14:27 [i]Jn 15:18-21 [j]Ro 8:37; 1Jn 4:4; 5:4; Rev 2:7,11, 17,26; 3:5,12,21; 21:7 **17:1** [k]Jn 11:41 [l]S Mt 26:18 [m]Jn 12:23; 13:31, 32 **17:2** [n]S Mt 28:18 [o]S Mt 25:46 [p]ver 6,9,24; Da 7:14; Jn 6:37, 39

[w] *31* Or *"Do you now believe?"*

16:27 THE FATHER HIMSELF LOVES YOU. The Father loves all people (3:16). But it is also true that he has a special family love for those who through Jesus are reconciled to him, love him and remain loyal to him even while enduring trouble in this world (v. 33). Our affection for Jesus brings forth the Father's affection for us. Love responds to love.

17:1 CHRIST'S PRAYER FOR ALL BELIEVERS. Jesus' final prayer for his disciples shows our Lord's deepest longings for his followers, both then and now. It is also a Spirit-inspired example of how all pastors should pray for their people, and how Christian parents should pray for their children. In praying for those under our care, our greatest concerns should be: (1) that they may know Jesus Christ and his Word intimately (vv. 2–3,17,19; see v. 3, note); (2) that God may keep them from the world, from falling away, from Satan and from false teaching (vv. 6,11,14–17); (3) that they may constantly possess the full joy of Christ (v. 13); (4) that they may be holy in thought, deed and character (see v. 17, note); (5) that they may be one in purpose and fellowship, as demonstrated by Jesus and the Father (vv. 11,21–22; see v. 21, note); (6) that they may lead others to Christ (vv. 21,23); (7) that they may persevere in the faith and finally be with Christ in heaven (v. 24); and (8) that they may constantly live in God's love and presence (v. 26).

17:3 ETERNAL LIFE. Eternal life is more than endless existence. It is a special quality of life that we as believers receive when we partake of the essential life of God through Christ; this allows us to know God in an ever-growing knowledge and fellowship with the Father, Son and Holy Spirit. In the NT eternal life is described as:

(1) A present reality (5:24; 10:27–28). The present possession of eternal life requires a living faith. Eternal life is not secured and maintained merely by an act of repentance and faith occurring in the past (see 5:24, note). It involves also a

may know you,[q] the only true
God, and Jesus Christ, whom you
have sent.[r] **4**I have brought you
glory[s] on earth by completing
the work you gave me to do.[t]
5And now, Father, glorify me[u] in
your presence with the glory I had
with you[v] before the world began.[w]

Jesus Prays for His Disciples

6"I have revealed you[x][x] to
those whom you gave me[y] out of
the world. They were yours; you
gave them to me and they have
obeyed your word. **7**Now they
know that everything you have
given me comes from you. **8**For I
gave them the words you gave
me[z] and they accepted them.
They knew with certainty that I
came from you,[a] and they believed that you sent me.[b] **9**I pray
for them.[c] I am not praying for
the world, but for those you have
given me,[d] for they are yours.
10All I have is yours, and all you
have is mine.[e] And glory has
come to me through them. **11**I will
remain in the world no longer, but
they are still in the world,[f] and
I am coming to you.[g] Holy Father, protect them by the power of
your name—the name you gave
me—so that they may be one[h] as
we are one.[i] **12**While I was with
them, I protected them and kept
them safe by that name you gave
me. None has been lost[j] except
the one doomed to destruction[k]
so that Scripture would be fulfilled.[l]
13"I am coming to you now,[m]
but I say these things while I am
still in the world, so that they may
have the full measure of my joy[n]
within them. **14**I have given them
your word and the world has hated them,[o] for they are not of the
world any more than I am of the
world.[p] **15**My prayer is not that
you take them out of the world but
that you protect them from the
evil one.[q] **16**They are not of the
world, even as I am not of it.[r]
17Sanctify[y] them by the truth;
your word is truth.[s] **18**As you
sent me into the world,[t] I have
sent them into the world.[u] **19**For
them I sanctify myself, that they
too may be truly sanctified.[v]

Jesus Prays for All Believers

20"My prayer is not for them
alone. I pray also for those who
will believe in me through their
message, **21**that all of them may
be one,[w] Father, just as you are
in me and I am in you.[x] May they

17:3 [q] S Php 3:8 [r] ver 8,18,21,23, 25; S Jn 3:17 **17:4** [s] Jn 13:31 [t] S Jn 19:30 **17:5** [u] ver 1 [v] Php 2:6 [w] S Jn 1:2 **17:6** [x] ver 26; Jn 1:18 [y] S ver 2 **17:8** [z] ver 14,26; S Jn 14:24 [a] S Jn 13:3 [b] ver 3, 18,21,23,25; S Jn 3:17 **17:9** [c] Lk 22:32 [d] S ver 2 **17:10** [e] Jn 16:15 **17:11** [f] Jn 13:1 [g] ver 13; Jn 7:33 [h] ver 21-23; Ps 133:1 [i] Jn 10:30

17:12 [j] S Jn 6:39 [k] Jn 6:70 [l] S Mt 1:22 **17:13** [m] ver 11 [n] S Jn 3:29 **17:14** [o] Jn 15:19 [p] ver 16; Jn 8:23 **17:15** [q] S Mt 5:37 **17:16** [r] ver 14 **17:17** [s] S Jn 15:3; 2Sa 7:28; 1Ki 17:24 **17:18** [t] ver 3,8, 21,23,25; S Jn 3:17 [u] Jn 20:21 **17:19** [v] ver 17 **17:21** [w] Jer 32:39 [x] ver 11; Jn 10:38

[x] 6 Greek *your name*; also in verse 26
[y] 17 Greek *hagiazo (set apart for sacred use* or *make holy)*; also in verse 19

present living union and fellowship with Christ (1Jn 5:12); there is no eternal life apart from him (10:27f; 11:25f; 1Jn 5:11–13).

(2) A future hope. Eternal life is associated with the coming of Christ for his faithful (see 14:3, note; cf. Mk 10:30; 2Ti 1:1,10; Tit 1:2; 3:7) and is contingent on living by the Spirit (Ro 8:12–17; Gal 6:8).

17:6 THEY HAVE OBEYED YOUR WORD. Christ's prayer for protection, joy, sanctification, love and unity applies only to a particular people, i.e., to those who belong to God, believe in Christ (v. 8), are separated from the world (vv. 14–16), and obey the Word of Christ and accept his teachings (vv. 6,8).

17:17 SANCTIFY THEM BY THE TRUTH. "Sanctify" means to make holy, to separate or set apart. The evening before his crucifixion Jesus prays that his disciples will be a holy people, separated from the world and sin for the purpose of worshiping and serving God. They must be set apart in order to be near God, to live for him and to be like him. This sanctification is accomplished by their devotion to the truth revealed to them by the Spirit of truth (cf. 14:17; 16:13). The truth is both the living Word of God (see 1:1) and the revelation of God's written Word (see article on SANCTIFICATION, p. 1956).

17:19 I SANCTIFY MYSELF. Jesus sanctifies himself by setting himself apart to do the will of God, i.e., to die on the cross. Jesus suffered on the cross in order that his followers might be separated from the world and set apart for God (see Heb 13:12).

17:21 THAT ALL OF THEM MAY BE ONE. The unity that Jesus prayed for was not organizational unity but spiritual unity based on: living in Christ (v. 23); knowing and experiencing the love of the Father and the fellowship of Christ (v. 26); separation from the world (vv. 14–16); sanctification in truth (vv. 17,19); receiving and believing the truth of the Word (vv. 6,8,17); obedience to the Word (v. 6); and the desire to bring salvation to the lost (vv. 21,23). When any one of these factors is missing, the true unity that Jesus prayed for cannot exist.

(1) Jesus does not pray for his followers to "become one," but rather that they may "be one." The present subjunctive used here designates ongoing action: "continually be one," a oneness based on

also be in us so that the world may believe that you have sent me.[y] **22**I have given them the glory that you gave me,[z] that they may be one as we are one:[a] **23**I in them and you in me. May they be brought to complete unity to let the world know that you sent me[b] and have loved them[c] even as you have loved me.

24"Father, I want those you have given me[d] to be with me where I am,[e] and to see my glory,[f] the glory you have given me because you loved me before the creation of the world.[g]

25"Righteous Father, though the world does not know you,[h] I know you, and they know that you have sent me.[i] **26**I have made you known to them,[j] and will continue to make you known in order that the love you have for me may be in them[k] and that I myself may be in them."

Jesus Arrested

18:3–11pp — Mt 26:47–56; Mk 14:43–50; Lk 22:47–53

18 When he had finished praying, Jesus left with his disciples and crossed the Kidron Valley.[l] On the other side there was an olive grove,[m] and he and his disciples went into it.[n]

2Now Judas, who betrayed him, knew the place, because Jesus had often met there with his disciples.[o] **3**So Judas came to the grove, guiding[p] a detachment of soldiers and some officials from the chief priests and Pharisees.[q] They were carrying torches, lanterns and weapons.

4Jesus, knowing all that was going to happen to him,[r] went out and asked them, "Who is it you want?"[s]

5"Jesus of Nazareth,"[t] they replied.

"I am he," Jesus said. (And Judas the traitor was standing there with them.) **6**When Jesus said, "I am he," they drew back and fell to the ground.

7Again he asked them, "Who is it you want?"[u]

And they said, "Jesus of Nazareth."

8"I told you that I am he," Jesus answered. "If you are looking for me, then let these men go." **9**This happened so that the words he had spoken would be fulfilled: "I have not lost one of those you gave me."[z][v]

10Then Simon Peter, who had a sword, drew it and struck the high priest's servant, cutting off his right ear. (The servant's name was Malchus.)

11Jesus commanded Peter, "Put your sword away! Shall I not drink the cup[w] the Father has given me?"

Jesus Taken to Annas

18:12,13pp — Mt 26:57

12Then the detachment of soldiers with its commander and the Jewish officials[x] arrested Jesus. They bound him **13**and brought him first to Annas, who was the father-in-law of Caiaphas,[y] the high priest that year. **14**Caiaphas was the one who had advised the Jews that it would be good if one man died for the people.[z]

Peter's First Denial

18:16–18pp — Mt 26:69,70; Mk 14:66–68; Lk 22:55–57

15Simon Peter and another disciple were following Jesus. Because this disciple was known to the high priest,[a] he went with Jesus into the high priest's courtyard,[b] **16**but Peter had

17:21 [y]ver 3,8,18,23,25; S Jn 3:17
17:22 [z]Jn 1:14 [a]S Jn 14:20
17:23 [b]ver 3,8,18,21,25; S Jn 3:17 [c]Jn 16:27
17:24 [d]S ver 2 [e]S Jn 12:26 [f]Jn 1:14 [g]ver 5; S Mt 25:34; S Jn 1:2
17:25 [h]Jn 15:21; 16:3 [i]ver 3,8,18,21,23; S Jn 3:17; 16:27
17:26 [j]ver 6 [k]Jn 15:9
18:1 [l]2Sa 15:23 [m]ver 26; S Mt 21:1 [n]Mt 26:36
18:2 [o]Lk 21:37; 22:39
18:3 [p]Ac 1:16 [q]ver 12
18:4 [r]Jn 6:64; 13:1,11 [s]ver 7
18:5 [t]S Mk 1:24
18:7 [u]ver 4
18:9 [v]S Jn 6:39
18:11 [w]S Mt 20:22
18:12 [x]ver 3
18:13 [y]ver 24; S Mt 26:3
18:14 [z]Jn 11:49-51
18:15 [a]S Mt 26:3 [b]Mt 26:58; Mk 14:54; Lk 22:54

[z]9 John 6:39

their common relationship to the Father and the Son, and on having the same basic attitude toward the world, the Word and the need to reach out to the lost (cf. 1Jn 1:7).

(2) To attempt to create an artificial unity by meetings, conferences or complex organization can result in a betrayal of the very unity for which Jesus prayed. What Jesus had in mind is much more than cosmetic "unity meetings." It is a spiritual unity of heart, purpose, mind and will in those who are fully devoted to Christ, the Word and holiness (see Eph 4:3, note).

17:22 THE GLORY THAT YOU GAVE ME. The "glory" of Christ was his life of self-denying service and his dying on the cross in order to redeem the human race. Likewise, the "glory" of the believer is the path of humble service and bearing his or her cross (cf. Lk 9:23, note). Humility, self-denial and the willingness to suffer for Christ will ensure the true unity of believers and will lead to true glory (see article on THE GLORY OF GOD, p. 1192).

18:11 THE CUP. See Mt 26:39, note on Christ's cup of sorrow.

18:12 ARRESTED JESUS. See Mt 26:57, note on the order of the events from Christ's arrest to his crucifixion.

18:15 PETER'S DENIAL. See notes on Mk 14:50; 14:71; Lk 22:62.

to wait outside at the door. The other
disciple, who was known to the high
priest, came back, spoke to the girl on
duty there and brought Peter in.
17"You are not one of his disciples,
are you?" the girl at the door asked Peter.

He replied, "I am not."[c]
18It was cold, and the servants and
officials stood around a fire[d] they had
made to keep warm. Peter also was
standing with them, warming himself.[e]

The High Priest Questions Jesus

18:19–24pp — Mt 26:59–68; Mk 14:55–65; Lk 22:63–71

19Meanwhile, the high priest questioned Jesus about his disciples and his
teaching.
20"I have spoken openly to the
world," Jesus replied. "I always taught
in synagogues[f] or at the temple,[g]
where all the Jews come together. I
said nothing in secret.[h]
21Why question me? Ask those who heard me.
Surely they know what I said."
22When Jesus said this, one of the
officials[i] nearby struck him in the
face.[j] "Is this the way you answer
the high priest?" he demanded.
23"If I said something wrong," Jesus
replied, "testify as to what is wrong.
But if I spoke the truth, why did you
strike me?"[k]
24Then Annas sent him,
still bound, to Caiaphas[l] the high
priest.[a]

Peter's Second and Third Denials

18:25–27pp — Mt 26:71–75; Mk 14:69–72; Lk 22:58–62

25As Simon Peter stood warming
himself,[m] he was asked, "You are not
one of his disciples, are you?"

He denied it, saying, "I am not."[n]
26One of the high priest's servants,
a relative of the man whose ear Peter
had cut off,[o] challenged him, "Didn't
I see you with him in the olive
grove?"[p]
27Again Peter denied it, and
at that moment a rooster began to
crow.[q]

Jesus Before Pilate

18:29–40pp — Mt 27:11–18,20–23; Mk 15:2–15; Lk 23:2,3,18–25

28Then the Jews led Jesus from Caiaphas to the palace of the Roman governor.[r] By now it was early morning,
and to avoid ceremonial uncleanness
the Jews did not enter the palace;[s]
they wanted to be able to eat the Passover.[t]
29So Pilate came out to them
and asked, "What charges are you
bringing against this man?"
30"If he were not a criminal," they
replied, "we would not have handed
him over to you."
31Pilate said, "Take him yourselves
and judge him by your own law."

"But we have no right to execute
anyone," the Jews objected.
32This
happened so that the words Jesus had
spoken indicating the kind of death he
was going to die[u] would be fulfilled.
33Pilate then went back inside the
palace,[v] summoned Jesus and asked
him, "Are you the king of the Jews?"[w]
34"Is that your own idea," Jesus
asked, "or did others talk to you about
me?"
35"Am I a Jew?" Pilate replied. "It
was your people and your chief priests
who handed you over to me. What is it
you have done?"
36Jesus said, "My kingdom[x] is not

[a] 24 Or *(Now Annas had sent him, still bound, to Caiaphas the high priest.)*

18:17 [c] ver 25 **18:18** [d] Jn 21:9 [e] Mk 14:54,67 **18:20** [f] S Mt 4:23 [g] Mt 26:55 [h] Jn 7:26 **18:22** [i] ver 3 [j] Mt 16:21; Jn 19:3 **18:23** [k] Mt 5:39; Ac 23:2-5 **18:24** [l] ver 13; S Mt 26:3 **18:25** [m] ver 18
[n] ver 17 **18:26** [o] ver 10 [p] ver 1 **18:27** [q] Jn 13:38 **18:28** [r] S Mt 27:2 [s] ver 33; Jn 19:9 [t] Jn 11:55 **18:32** [u] Mt 20:19; 26:2; Jn 3:14; 8:28; 12:32,33 **18:33** [v] ver 28,29; Jn 19:9 [w] Lk 23:3; S Mt 2:2 **18:36** [x] S Mt 3:2

18:28 JESUS BEFORE PILATE. See Mt 27:2, note; Lk 23:1, note.

18:36 MY KINGDOM IS NOT OF THIS WORLD. Concerning the true nature of Christ's kingdom and its redemptive purpose, three points should be noted:

(1) What Jesus' kingdom is not. It is "not of this world." It did not originate in this world, nor does it seek to take over the world's system. Jesus did not come to establish a religio-political theocracy or aspire to world dominion. Jesus states that if he had come to establish a political kingdom on earth, then "my servants would fight." Since this is not the nature of the kingdom, they do not resort to war or revolution to promote Christ's purpose on earth (cf. Mt 26:51–52). They do not ally themselves with political parties, social pressure groups or any secular organizations in order to establish God's kingdom. They refuse to turn the cross into a boastful attempt to rule society. Rather than using worldly weapons (2Co 10:4), Jesus' followers are armed only with spiritual weapons (Eph 6:10–18). This does not mean, however, that Jesus' disciples are indifferent to God's demand for just government, justice, peace or curtailing lawlessness. Christians must bring a "prophetic word" to the state concerning its moral responsibilities under God.

(2) What Jesus' kingdom is. Christ's kingdom, i.e., the kingdom of God, involves his rule, lordship, power and spiritual activity in the lives of all who receive him and obey his word of truth (v. 37).

of this world. If it were, my servants would fight to prevent my arrest by the Jews.[y] But now my kingdom is from another place."[z]

37"You are a king, then!" said Pilate.

Jesus answered, "You are right in saying I am a king. In fact, for this reason I was born, and for this I came into the world, to testify to the truth.[a] Everyone on the side of truth listens to me."[b]

38"What is truth?" Pilate asked. With this he went out again to the Jews and said, "I find no basis for a charge against him.[c] 39But it is your custom for me to release to you one prisoner at the time of the Passover. Do you want me to release 'the king of the Jews'?"

40They shouted back, "No, not him! Give us Barabbas!" Now Barabbas had taken part in a rebellion.[d]

Jesus Sentenced to be Crucified

19:1-16pp — Mt 27:27-31; Mk 15:16-20

19 Then Pilate took Jesus and had him flogged.[e] 2The soldiers twisted together a crown of thorns and put it on his head. They clothed him in a purple robe 3and went up to him again and again, saying, "Hail, king of the Jews!"[f] And they struck him in the face.[g]

4Once more Pilate came out and said to the Jews, "Look, I am bringing him out[h] to you to let you know that I find no basis for a charge against him."[i] 5When Jesus came out wearing the crown of thorns and the purple robe,[j] Pilate said to them, "Here is the man!"

6As soon as the chief priests and their officials saw him, they shouted, "Crucify! Crucify!"

But Pilate answered, "You take him and crucify him.[k] As for me, I find no basis for a charge against him."[l]

7The Jews insisted, "We have a law, and according to that law he must die,[m] because he claimed to be the Son of God."[n]

8When Pilate heard this, he was even more afraid, 9and he went back inside the palace.[o] "Where do you come from?" he asked Jesus, but Jesus gave him no answer.[p] 10"Do you refuse to speak to me?" Pilate said. "Don't you realize I have power either to free you or to crucify you?"

11Jesus answered, "You would have no power over me if it were not given to you from above.[q] Therefore the one who handed me over to you[r] is guilty of a greater sin."

12From then on, Pilate tried to set Jesus free, but the Jews kept shouting, "If you let this man go, you are no friend of Caesar. Anyone who claims to be a king[s] opposes Caesar."

13When Pilate heard this, he brought Jesus out and sat down on the judge's seat[t] at a place known as the Stone Pavement (which in Aramaic[u] is Gabbatha). 14It was the day of Preparation[v] of Passover Week, about the sixth hour.[w]

18:36 [y] Mt 26:53 [z] Lk 17:21; Jn 6:15 **18:37** [a] Jn 3:32 [b] Jn 8:47; 1Jn 4:6 **18:38** [c] S Lk 23:4 **18:40** [d] Ac 3:14 **19:1** [e] Dt 25:3; Isa 50:6; 53:5; Mt 27:26 **19:3** [f] Mt 27:29 [g] Jn 18:22 **19:4** [h] Jn 18:38 [i] ver 6; S Lk 23:4

19:5 [j] ver 2 **19:6** [k] Ac 3:13 [l] ver 4; S Lk 23:4 **19:7** [m] Lev 24:16 [n] Mt 26:63-66; Jn 5:18; 10:33 **19:9** [o] Jn 18:33 [p] S Mk 14:61 **19:11** [q] S Ro 13:1 [r] Jn 18:28-30; Ac 3:13 **19:12** [s] Lk 23:2 **19:13** [t] Mt 27:19 [u] S Jn 5:2 **19:14** [v] Mt 27:62 [w] Mk 15:25

The kingdom of God is "righteousness, peace and joy in the Holy Spirit" (Ro 14:17). It confronts the spiritual forces of Satan with spiritual weapons (see Mt 12:28; Lk 11:20; Ac 26:18; Eph 6:12). The church's role is that of a servant of Jesus Christ, not that of a ruler of this present world. Her strength is not in worldly power but in the cross; her suffering and rejection at the hands of the world is her glory (2Co 3:7–18). Only in renouncing worldly power did the NT church find God's power. The church today faces this same choice: only by losing her life in the world will she find herself in God (see article on THE KINGDOM OF GOD, p. 1430).

(3) What Jesus' kingdom will be. In the future, Christ's kingdom and rule will be the new heaven and earth; this will occur after he comes to earth to judge the nations, destroy the antichrist, rule on earth for a thousand years and then bring Satan to a final end in the lake of fire (Rev 19:11—20:15).

18:37 TESTIFY TO THE TRUTH. An essential part of Jesus' mission was to testify to the truth and point people to it, i.e., his incarnate witness to the Father and to the revealed truth of his gospel now recorded in Scripture. How strange that some ministers today compromise truth and sound doctrine, obscure the clear meaning of Scripture and promote unity at the cost of Biblical faith. Such ministers err in tolerating false doctrine and refusing to draw distinctions between right and wrong, truth and error. In the name of love and broad-mindedness, they reject this purpose of Christ's coming. Truth is one thing churches must never sacrifice (cf. 17:8,17; 2Th 2:10).

19:1 HAD HIM FLOGGED. For details concerning the method of Roman floggings, see Mt 27:26, note.

19:4 I FIND NO BASIS FOR A CHARGE. See Lk 23:14, note.

19:11 POWER ... GIVEN TO YOU FROM ABOVE. Jesus says that all earthly power exists only as God permits it (cf. Da 4:34–35; Ro 13:1). Pilate's sin was yielding to the crowd because of political expediency. Israel's sin was greater—they were rejecting their Messiah.

19:14 THE SIXTH HOUR. John states that Jesus' trial neared completion "about the sixth hour." Mark, however, says that Jesus was cruci-

"Here is your king,"[x] Pilate said to
the Jews.
15 But they shouted, "Take him
away! Take him away! Crucify him!"
"Shall I crucify your king?" Pilate
asked.
"We have no king but Caesar," the
chief priests answered.
16 Finally Pilate handed him over to
them to be crucified.[y]

The Crucifixion

19:17–24pp — Mt 27:33–44; Mk 15:22–32; Lk 23:33–43

So the soldiers took charge of Jesus.
17 Carrying his own cross,[z] he went
out to the place of the Skull[a] (which
in Aramaic[b] is called Golgotha).
18 Here they crucified him, and with
him two others[c]—one on each side
and Jesus in the middle.
19 Pilate had a notice prepared and
fastened to the cross. It read: JESUS OF
NAZARETH,[d] THE KING OF THE JEWS.[e]
20 Many of the Jews read this sign, for
the place where Jesus was crucified
was near the city,[f] and the sign was
written in Aramaic, Latin and Greek.
21 The chief priests of the Jews protested to Pilate, "Do not write 'The King of
the Jews,' but that this man claimed to
be king of the Jews."[g]
22 Pilate answered, "What I have
written, I have written."
23 When the soldiers crucified Jesus,
they took his clothes, dividing them
into four shares, one for each of them,
with the undergarment remaining.
This garment was seamless, woven in
one piece from top to bottom.
24 "Let's not tear it," they said to one
another. "Let's decide by lot who will
get it."

This happened that the scripture
might be fulfilled[h] which said,

> "They divided my garments among
> them
> and cast lots for my
> clothing."[b][i]

So this is what the soldiers did.
25 Near the cross[j] of Jesus stood his
mother,[k] his mother's sister, Mary
the wife of Clopas, and Mary Magdalene.[l] 26 When Jesus saw his mother[m]
there, and the disciple whom he
loved[n] standing nearby, he said to his
mother, "Dear woman, here is your
son," 27 and to the disciple, "Here is
your mother." From that time on, this
disciple took her into his home.

The Death of Jesus

19:29,30pp — Mt 27:48,50; Mk 15:36,37; Lk 23:36

28 Later, knowing that all was now
completed,[o] and so that the Scripture
would be fulfilled,[p] Jesus said, "I am
thirsty." 29 A jar of wine vinegar[q] was
there, so they soaked a sponge in it,
put the sponge on a stalk of the hyssop
plant, and lifted it to Jesus' lips.
30 When he had received the drink,
Jesus said, "It is finished."[r] With that,
he bowed his head and gave up his spirit.
31 Now it was the day of Preparation,[s] and the next day was to be a
special Sabbath. Because the Jews did
not want the bodies left on the
crosses[t] during the Sabbath, they
asked Pilate to have the legs broken
and the bodies taken down. 32 The soldiers therefore came and broke the

19:14 [x] ver 19,21
19:16 [y] Mt 27:26; Mk 15:15; Lk 23:25
19:17 [z] Ge 22:6; Lk 14:27; 23:26 [a] Lk 23:33 [b] S Jn 5:2
19:18 [c] Lk 23:32
19:19 [d] S Mk 1:24 [e] ver 14,21
19:20 [f] Heb 13:12
19:21 [g] ver 14
19:24 [h] ver 28,36, 37; S Mt 1:22 [i] Ps 22:18
19:25 [j] Mt 27:55, 56 [k] S Mt 12:46 [l] Lk 24:18
19:26 [m] S Mt 12:46 [n] S Jn 13:23
19:28 [o] S ver 30; Jn 13:1 [p] ver 24, 36,37; S Mt 1:22
19:29 [q] Ps 69:21
19:30 [r] Lk 12:50; Jn 4:34; 17:4
19:31 [s] ver 14,42 [t] Dt 21:23; Jos 8:29; 10:26,27

[b] *24* Psalm 22:18

---

fied at "the third hour" (Mk 15:25). This apparent contradiction is resolved if we understand that John used the Roman method of computing time, while Mark used the Palestinian method. The Roman day began at midnight, and the Palestinian day began at sunrise.

19:16 HANDED HIM OVER . . . TO BE CRUCIFIED. See Lk 23:25, note.

19:17 CARRYING HIS OWN CROSS. See Mt 27:31, note.

19:18 THEY CRUCIFIED HIM. For comments on the crucifixion, see Mt 27:35, note.

19:26 DEAR WOMAN, HERE IS YOUR SON. Even in the agony of dying, Jesus is concerned about the welfare of his mother. He appoints "the disciple whom he loved" (probably John) to take care of her. To assist needy family members is a responsibility we have until death. The emphasis here is on the responsibility of children for their dependent parents.

19:29 WINE VINEGAR. The Greek word translated "wine vinegar" is *oxos*, a sour wine or vinegar. The English word "vinegar" is from the French *vin* (wine) and *aigre* (sour), thus, sour wine. Vinegar, or sour wine, is made when alcohol changes into vinegar by the formation of acetic acid. Christ's tasting of the vinegar was a fulfillment of the prophecy of Ps 69:21, "they . . . gave me vinegar for my thirst."

19:30 IT IS FINISHED. Jesus' sufferings in providing redemption for fallen humanity were over and his work of redemption completed. He had borne the punishment for our sins and opened the way of salvation for all (see Mt 27:50, note; Lk 23:46, note).

legs of the first man who had been crucified with Jesus, and then those of the
other.[u] 33But when they came to
Jesus and found that he was already
dead, they did not break his legs. 34In-
stead, one of the soldiers pierced[v]
Jesus' side with a spear, bringing a
sudden flow of blood and water.[w]
35The man who saw it[x] has given testimony, and his testimony is true.[y] He
knows that he tells the truth, and he
testifies so that you also may believe.
36These things happened so that the
scripture would be fulfilled:[z] "Not one
of his bones will be broken,"[c][a] 37and,
as another scripture says, "They will
look on the one they have pierced."[d][b]

The Burial of Jesus

19:38–42pp — Mt 27:57–61; Mk 15:42–47; Lk 23:50–56

38Later, Joseph of Arimathea asked
Pilate for the body of Jesus. Now Joseph was a disciple of Jesus, but secretly because he feared the Jews.[c]
With Pilate's permission, he came and
took the body away. 39He was accompanied by Nicodemus,[d] the man who
earlier had visited Jesus at night. Nicodemus brought a mixture of myrrh and
aloes, about seventy-five pounds.[e]
40Taking Jesus' body, the two of them
wrapped it, with the spices, in strips of
linen.[e] This was in accordance with
Jewish burial customs.[f] 41At the
place where Jesus was crucified, there
was a garden, and in the garden a new
tomb, in which no one had ever been
laid. 42Because it was the Jewish day
of Preparation[g] and since the tomb
was nearby,[h] they laid Jesus there.

The Empty Tomb

20:1–8pp — Mt 28:1–8; Mk 16:1–8; Lk 24:1–10

20 Early on the first day of the
week, while it was still dark,
Mary Magdalene[i] went to the tomb
and saw that the stone had been removed from the entrance.[j] 2So she
came running to Simon Peter and the
other disciple, the one Jesus loved,[k]
and said, "They have taken the Lord
out of the tomb, and we don't know
where they have put him!"[l]
3So Peter and the other disciple
started for the tomb.[m] 4Both were running, but the other disciple outran Peter and reached the tomb first. 5He
bent over and looked in[n] at the strips
of linen[o] lying there but did not go in.
6Then Simon Peter, who was behind
him, arrived and went into the tomb.
He saw the strips of linen lying there,
7as well as the burial cloth that had
been around Jesus' head.[p] The cloth
was folded up by itself, separate from
the linen. 8Finally the other disciple,
who had reached the tomb first,[q] also
went inside. He saw and believed.
9(They still did not understand from
Scripture[r] that Jesus had to rise from
the dead.)[s]

Jesus Appears to Mary Magdalene

10Then the disciples went back to
their homes, 11but Mary stood outside
the tomb crying. As she wept, she bent
over to look into the tomb[t] 12and saw
two angels in white,[u] seated where
Jesus' body had been, one at the head
and the other at the foot.
13They asked her, "Woman, why are
you crying?"[v]
"They have taken my Lord away,"
she said, "and I don't know where they
have put him."[w] 14At this, she turned
around and saw Jesus standing
there,[x] but she did not realize that it
was Jesus.[y]
15"Woman," he said, "why are you
crying?[z] Who is it you are looking
for?"
Thinking he was the gardener, she
said, "Sir, if you have carried him
away, tell me where you have put him,
and I will get him."
16Jesus said to her, "Mary."

19:32 [u] ver 18 **19:34** [v] Zec 12:10; Rev 1:7 [w] 1Jn 5:6, 8 **19:35** [x] S Lk 24:48 [y] Jn 15:27; 21:24 **19:36** [z] ver 24,28, 37; S Mt 1:22 [a] Ex 12:46; Nu 9:12; Ps 34:20 **19:37** [b] Zec 12:10; Rev 1:7 **19:38** [c] S Jn 7:13 **19:39** [d] Jn 3:1; 7:50 **19:40** [e] Lk 24:12; Jn 11:44; 20:5,7 [f] Mt 26:12 **19:42** [g] ver 14,31 [h] ver 20,41 **20:1** [i] ver 18; Lk 8:2; Jn 19:25 [j] Mt 27:60,66 **20:2** [k] S Jn 13:23 [l] ver 13 **20:3** [m] Lk 24:12 **20:5** [n] ver 11 [o] S Jn 19:40 **20:7** [p] Jn 11:44 **20:8** [q] ver 4 **20:9** [r] Mt 22:29; Jn 2:22 [s] Lk 24:26, 46; Ac 2:24 **20:11** [t] ver 5 **20:12** [u] Mt 28:2, 3; Mk 16:5; Lk 24:4; Ac 1:10; S 5:19; 10:30 **20:13** [v] ver 15 [w] ver 2 **20:14** [x] Mk 16:9 [y] Lk 24:16; Jn 21:4 **20:15** [z] ver 13

[c] *36* Exodus 12:46; Num. 9:12; Psalm 34:20
[d] *37* Zech. 12:10
[e] *39* Greek *a hundred litrai* (about 34 kilograms)

19:41 A NEW TOMB. The tomb had been hewn out of solid rock (Mk 15:46). It was probably large enough to walk into, but with a low entrance (20:11). After placing the body of Jesus in the tomb, Joseph rolled a big stone in front of its entrance (Mt 27:60).

20:9 HE HAD TO RISE. See Mt 28:6, note on the importance of Christ's resurrection, and Lk 24:6, note on the confirmation of Christ's resurrection.

20:16 JESUS APPEARS TO MARY. The first person to whom Jesus appears after his resurrection is Mary. She is not a particularly prominent person in the Gospels, yet Jesus appears first to her rather than to any of the outstanding leaders among the disciples. Throughout the ages, Jesus

She turned toward him and cried out
in Aramaic,[a] "Rabboni!"[b] (which
means Teacher).
17Jesus said, "Do not hold on to me,
for I have not yet returned to the Father. Go instead to my brothers[c] and
tell them, 'I am returning to my Father[d] and your Father, to my God and
your God.' "
18Mary Magdalene[e] went to the
disciples[f] with the news: "I have seen
the Lord!" And she told them that he
had said these things to her.

Jesus Appears to His Disciples

19On the evening of that first day of
the week, when the disciples were together, with the doors locked for fear
of the Jews,[g] Jesus came and stood
among them and said, "Peace[h] be
with you!"[i] 20After he said this, he
showed them his hands and side.[j]
The disciples were overjoyed[k] when
they saw the Lord.

The Disciples Receive the Holy Spirit

21Again Jesus said, "Peace be with
you![l] As the Father has sent me,[m] I
am sending you."[n] 22And with that he
breathed on them and said, "Receive
the Holy Spirit.[o] 23If you forgive anyone his sins, they are forgiven; if you
do not forgive them, they are not forgiven."[p]

Jesus Appears to Thomas

24Now Thomas[q] (called Didymus),
one of the Twelve, was not with the
disciples when Jesus came. 25So the
other disciples told him, "We have seen
the Lord!"

But he said to them, "Unless I see
the nail marks in his hands and put my
finger where the nails were, and put
my hand into his side,[r] I will not believe it."[s]
26A week later his disciples were in
the house again, and Thomas was with
them. Though the doors were locked,
Jesus came and stood among them and
said, "Peace[t] be with you!"[u] 27Then
he said to Thomas, "Put your finger
here; see my hands. Reach out your
hand and put it into my side. Stop
doubting and believe."[v]
28Thomas said to him, "My Lord and
my God!"
29Then Jesus told him, "Because you
have seen me, you have believed;[w]

20:16 [a] S Jn 5:2 [b] S Mt 23:7
20:17 [c] S Mt 28:10 [d] Jn 7:33
20:18 [e] S ver 1 [f] Lk 24:10,22,23
20:19 [g] S Jn 7:13 [h] S Jn 14:27 [i] ver 21,26; Lk 24:36-39
20:20 [j] Lk 24:39, 40; Jn 19:34 [k] Jn 16:20,22
20:21 [l] ver 19 [m] S Jn 3:17 [n] Mt 28:19; Jn 17:18
20:22 [o] Jn 7:39; Ac 2:38; 8:15-17; 19:2; Gal 3:2
20:23 [p] Mt 16:19; 18:18
20:24 [q] S Jn 11:16
20:25 [r] ver 20 [s] Mk 16:11
20:26 [t] S Jn 14:27 [u] ver 21
20:27 [v] ver 25; Lk 24:40
20:29 [w] S Jn 3:15

---

reveals his presence and love especially to those who are "least." God's special people are the unknown — those who, like Mary in her grief, maintain a steadfast love for their Lord.

20:17 DO NOT HOLD ON TO ME. This verse probably means, "Don't continue clinging to me; I am not yet going to ascend to my Father. You will still have opportunity to see me again." In the meantime he has a task for her.

20:22 RECEIVE THE HOLY SPIRIT. For an extensive discussion of this important verse and how it relates to our regeneration and baptism in the Holy Spirit, see article on THE REGENERATION OF THE DISCIPLES, p. 1627.

20:23 IF YOU FORGIVE ANYONE. See Mt 16:19, note.

20:28 MY LORD AND MY GOD. The Scriptures declare that Jesus is God. This is the foundation of the Christian faith and is of utmost importance for our salvation. Without Christ being divine, he could not have made atonement for the sins of the world. The deity of Jesus Christ is shown by the following:

(1) Divine names are given to him in Scripture: (a) God (20:28; Isa 9:6; Ro 9:5; Tit 2:13; Heb 1:8); (b) the Son of God (5:25; Mt 16:16–17; 8:29; 27:40,43; Mk 14:61–62; Lk 22:70); (c) the First and the Last (Rev 1:17; 2:8; 22:13); (d) the Alpha and the Omega (Rev 1:8; 22:13); (e) the Beginning and the End (Rev 22:13); (f) the Holy One (Hos 11:9; Ac 3:14); (g) the Lord (Lk 2:11; Ac 4:33; 9:17; 16:31); (h) Lord of all and Lord of glory (Ps 24:8–10; Ac 10:36; 1Co 2:8).

(2) Divine worship is given to Christ (5:23; 13:13; 20:28; Mt 14:33; Lk 5:8), and prayers are addressed to him (Ac 7:59; 1Co 1:2; 2Co 12:8–9).

(3) Divine offices are assigned to Christ: (a) creator of the universe (1:3; Col 1:16; Heb 1:8,10; Rev 3:14); (b) sustainer of all things (Col 1:17; Heb 1:3); (c) forgiver of sins (Mk 2:5,10; Lk 7:48–50); (d) bestower of resurrection life (5:28–29; 6:39–44); (e) judge of all people (5:21–23; Mt 25:31–46; Ac 17:31; 2Ti 4:1); (f) giver of salvation (5:24–26; 6:47; 10:28; 17:2).

(4) The NT sees Christ in OT statements about the Lord. Compare Ps 23:1 with Jn 10:11; Ps 102:24–27 with Heb 1:10–12; Isa 8:13–14 with 1Pe 2:7–8; Jer 17:10 with Rev 2:23; Eze 34:11–12 with Lk 19:10.

(5) The name of Jesus Christ is associated with that of God the Father (14:1,23; Mt 28:19; Ro 1:7; 2Co 13:14; Col 2:2; 1Th 3:11; Jas 1:1; Rev 5:13; 7:10).

(6) Christ's sinlessness and holiness testify to his deity (Lk 1:35; 2Co 5:21; Heb 4:15).

(7) Christ was declared to be the Son of God by his resurrection (Ro 1:4).

These conclusive proofs of Christ's deity mean that believers must act toward Christ in exactly the same manner as they act toward God the Father. They must believe in him, worship him, pray to him, serve him and love him (see also 1:1, note; Mk 1:11, note on the Trinity).

THE REGENERATION OF THE DISCIPLES

Jn 20:22 "And with that he breathed on them and said, 'Receive the Holy Spirit.'"

The impartation of the Holy Spirit by Jesus to his disciples on resurrection day was not the baptism in the Spirit as experienced at Pentecost (Ac 1:5; 2:4). It was rather an infusing of the disciples for the first time with the regenerating presence of the Holy Spirit and with new life from the risen Christ.

(1) During Jesus' last discourse with his disciples before his trial and crucifixion, he promised them that they would receive the Holy Spirit as the One who would regenerate them: "he lives with you and will be in you" (Jn 14:17, see note). Jesus now fulfills that promise.

(2) That Jn 20:22 refers to regeneration can be inferred from the phrase, "he breathed on them." The Greek word for "breathed" (*emphusaō*) is the same verb used in the Septuagint (the Greek translation of the OT) at Ge 2:7, where God "breathed into his [Adam's] nostrils the breath of life, and the man became a living being." It is the same verb found in Eze 37:9, "Breathe into these slain, that they may live." John's use of this verb indicates that Jesus was giving the Spirit in order to bring forth life and a new creation. That is, just as God breathed into physical man the breath of life and he became a new creation (Ge 2:7), so Jesus now breathed on the disciples spiritually and they became a new creation (see article on REGENERATION, p. 1589). Through his resurrection, Jesus became a "life-giving spirit" (1Co 15:45).

(3) The phrase "receive the Holy Spirit" establishes that the Spirit, *at that historical moment*, entered and began to live in the disciples. The verb form for "receive" is aorist imperative (Gk *labete*, from the word *lambanō*), denoting a single act of reception. The Holy Spirit was given to regenerate them, to make them new creatures in Christ (cf. 2Co 5:17). This "receiving" of life from the Spirit preceded both their receiving the authority of Jesus (Jn 20:23) and their baptism in the Holy Spirit on the day of Pentecost (Ac 2:4).

(4) Prior to this time, the disciples were technically true believers and followers of Jesus and were saved according to the old covenant provisions. Yet they were not regenerated in the full new covenant sense. Not until this point did the disciples enter into the new covenant provisions based on Jesus' death and resurrection (see Mt 26:28; Lk 22:20; 1Co 11:25; Eph 2:15–16; Heb 9:15–17; see article on REGENERATION, p. 1589). It was also technically at this time and not at Pentecost that the church was born. The spiritual birth of the first disciples and the birth of the church are one and the same.

(5) This passage is crucial in understanding the Holy Spirit's ministry to God's people. These two statements are true: (a) the disciples received the Holy Spirit (i.e., were indwelt and regenerated by the Holy Spirit) before the day of Pentecost, and (b) the outpouring of the Spirit in Ac 2:4 was an experience occurring after their regeneration by the Spirit. Their baptism in the Spirit at Pentecost was, therefore, a second and distinct work of the Spirit in them.

(6) These two separate and distinct works of the Holy Spirit in the lives of Jesus' disciples are normative for all Christians. That is, all believers receive the Holy Spirit at the time of their regeneration, and afterwards must experience the baptism in the Spirit for power to be his witnesses (Ac 1:5,8; 2:4; see 2:39, note).

(7) There is no Scriptural foundation to suggest that Jesus' bestowal of the Holy Spirit in Jn 20:22 was simply symbolical prophecy of the coming of the Holy Spirit at Pentecost. The use of the aorist imperative for "receive" (see above) denotes reception at that moment and in that place. What occurred was a historical reality in space and time, and John records it as such.

blessed are those who have not seen and yet have believed."[x]

30Jesus did many other miraculous signs[y] in the presence of his disciples, which are not recorded in this book.[z] **31**But these are written that you may[f] believe[a] that Jesus is the Christ, the Son of God,[b] and that by believing you may have life in his name.[c]

Ac 4:12

Jesus and the Miraculous Catch of Fish

21 Afterward Jesus appeared again to his disciples,[d] by the Sea of Tiberias.[g][e] It happened this way: **2**Simon Peter, Thomas[f] (called Didymus), Nathanael[g] from Cana in Galilee,[h] the sons of Zebedee,[i] and two other disciples were together. **3**"I'm going out to fish," Simon Peter told them, and they said, "We'll go with you." So they went out and got into the boat, but that night they caught nothing.[j]

4Early in the morning, Jesus stood on the shore, but the disciples did not realize that it was Jesus.[k]

5He called out to them, "Friends, haven't you any fish?"

"No," they answered.

6He said, "Throw your net on the right side of the boat and you will find some." When they did, they were unable to haul the net in because of the large number of fish.[l]

7Then the disciple whom Jesus loved[m] said to Peter, "It is the Lord!" As soon as Simon Peter heard him say, "It is the Lord," he wrapped his outer garment around him (for he had taken it off) and jumped into the water. **8**The other disciples followed in the boat, towing the net full of fish, for they were not far from shore, about a hundred yards.[h] **9**When they landed, they saw a fire[n] of burning coals there with fish on it,[o] and some bread.

10Jesus said to them, "Bring some of the fish you have just caught."

11Simon Peter climbed aboard and dragged the net ashore. It was full of large fish, 153, but even with so many the net was not torn. **12**Jesus said to them, "Come and have breakfast." None of the disciples dared ask him, "Who are you?" They knew it was the Lord. **13**Jesus came, took the bread and gave it to them, and did the same with the fish.[p] **14**This was now the third time Jesus appeared to his disciples[q] after he was raised from the dead.

Jesus Reinstates Peter

15When they had finished eating, Jesus said to Simon Peter, "Simon son of John, do you truly love me more than these?"

"Yes, Lord," he said, "you know that I love you."[r]

Jesus said, "Feed my lambs."[s]

16Again Jesus said, "Simon son of John, do you truly love me?"

He answered, "Yes, Lord, you know that I love you."

Jesus said, "Take care of my sheep."[t]

20:29 [x] 1Pe 1:8 **20:30** [y] S Jn 2:11 [z] Jn 21:25 **20:31** [a] S Jn 3:15; 19:35 [b] S Mt 4:3 [c] S Mt 25:46 **21:1** [d] ver 14; Jn 20:19,26 [e] Jn 6:1 **21:2** [f] S Jn 11:16 [g] Jn 1:45 [h] Jn 2:1 [i] S Mt 4:21 **21:3** [j] Lk 5:5 **21:4** [k] Lk 24:16; Jn 20:14 **21:6** [l] Lk 5:4-7 **21:7** [m] S Jn 13:23 **21:9** [n] Jn 18:18 [o] ver 10,13 **21:13** [p] ver 9 **21:14** [q] Jn 20:19, 26 **21:15** [r] Mt 26:33, 35; Jn 13:37 [s] Lk 12:32 **21:16** [t] 2Sa 5:2; Eze 34:2; Mt 2:6; S Jn 10:11; Ac 20:28; 1Pe 5:2, 3

[f] *31* Some manuscripts *may continue to* [g] *1* That is, Sea of Galilee [h] *8* Greek *about two hundred cubits* (about 90 meters)

21:1 JESUS APPEARED AGAIN. See Mt 28:9, note on Christ's resurrection appearances.

21:3 I'M GOING OUT TO FISH. The disciples' plan to go fishing does not mean they were forsaking their commitment to Christ and their calling to preach the gospel. They knew that Jesus had risen from the grave, yet they did not know what to do next. They had not yet received the instruction to wait in Jerusalem until the Holy Spirit came on them in power (Ac 1:4–5). To go fishing was a necessity, for these men still had to provide for themselves and their families.

21:6 THROW YOUR NET ON THE RIGHT SIDE. It is crucial to receive guidance from the Lord in all our work. If we live without Christ's presence and guiding hand, then much of what we do becomes empty failure and wasted effort.

21:15 DO YOU TRULY LOVE ME. The most important question that Peter ever faced was whether he possessed a devoted love for his Lord. (1) Two Greek words for "love" are used here. The first, *agapaō*, means an intelligent and purposeful love, primarily of mind and will. The second, *phileō*, involves warm natural affection of the emotions, thus a more personal and feeling love. Through these two words, Jesus indicates that Peter's love must be not only of the will, but also of the heart, a love springing from both purpose and personal attachment. (2) Jesus' question to Peter is the great question for all believers. We must all have a personal heartfelt love for and devotion to Jesus (14:15; 16:27; Mt 10:37; Lk 7:47; 1Co 16:22; 2Co 5:14; Gal 5:6; Eph 6:24; Jas 1:12; 1Pe 1:8; Rev 2:4).

21:16 TAKE CARE OF MY SHEEP. Jesus' description of believers as lambs (v. 15) and sheep (v. 16) implies three things. (1) We need pastoral care. (2) We need to feed constantly on the Word. (3) Since sheep are prone to wander into danger, we need repeated guidance, protection and correction.

17The third time he said to him, "Simon son of John, do you love me?"
Peter was hurt because Jesus asked
him the third time, "Do you love me?"[u]
He said, "Lord, you know all things;[v]
you know that I love you."
Jesus said, "Feed my sheep.[w] **18**I
tell you the truth, when you were younger you dressed yourself and went
where you wanted; but when you are
old you will stretch out your hands,
and someone else will dress you and
lead you where you do not want to go."
19Jesus said this to indicate the kind of
death[x] by which Peter would glorify
God.[y] Then he said to him, "Follow
me!"[z]
20Peter turned and saw that the disciple whom Jesus loved[a] was following them. (This was the one who had
leaned back against Jesus at the supper and had said, "Lord, who is going
to betray you?")[b] **21**When Peter saw
him, he asked, "Lord, what about
him?"
22Jesus answered, "If I want him to
remain alive until I return,[c] what is
that to you? You must follow me."[d]
23Because of this, the rumor spread
among the brothers[e] that this disciple
would not die. But Jesus did not say
that he would not die; he only said, "If
I want him to remain alive until I return, what is that to you?"
24This is the disciple who testifies to
these things[f] and who wrote them
down. We know that his testimony is
true.[g]
25Jesus did many other things as
well.[h] If every one of them were
written down, I suppose that even
the whole world would not have
room for the books that would be written.

21:17 [u]Jn 13:38 [v]Jn 16:30 [w]S ver 16
21:19 [x]Jn 12:33; 18:32 [y]Jn 13:36; 2Pe 1:14 [z]S Mt 4:19
21:20 [a]ver 7; S Jn 13:23
[b]Jn 13:25
21:22 [c]S Mt 16:27 [d]ver 19; S Mt 4:19
21:23 [e]S Ac 1:16
21:24 [f]S Jn 15:27 [g]Jn 19:35
21:25 [h]Jn 20:30

21:17 DO YOU LOVE ME? ... FEED MY SHEEP. Jesus sees love as the basic qualification for Christian service. Other qualifications are needed (1Ti 3:1–13), but love for Christ and for others is indispensable (cf. 1Co 13:1–3).

21:18 YOU WILL STRETCH OUT YOUR HANDS. These words refer to the kind of death by which Peter would glorify God. Tradition records that Peter was crucified in Rome under Nero at about the same time that Paul was martyred (c. A.D. 67/68), and that at his own request he was crucified upside down because he considered himself unworthy to be crucified in the same manner as his Lord.

THE YEAR OF INAUGURATION

Event	Place	Matthew	Mark	Luke	John
Jesus baptized	Jordan River	3:13–17	1:9–11	3:21–23	1:29–39
Jesus tempted by Satan	Desert	4:1–11	1:12–13	4:1–13	
Jesus' first miracle	Cana				2:1–11
Jesus and Nicodemus	Judea				3:1–21
Jesus talks to a Samaritan woman	Samaria				4:5–42
Jesus heals an official's son	Cana				4:46–54
The people of Nazareth try to kill Jesus	Nazareth			4:16–31	

THE YEAR OF POPULARITY

Event	Place	Matthew	Mark	Luke	John
Jesus calls four fishermen	Sea of Galilee	4:18–22	1:16–20	5:1–11	
Jesus heals Peter's mother-in-law	Capernaum	8:14–17	1:29–34	4:38–41	
Jesus begins preaching in Galilee	Galilee	4:23–25	1:35–39	4:42–4	
Matthew decides to follow Jesus	Capernaum	9:9–13	2:13–17	5:27–32	
Jesus chooses twelve disciples	Galilee	10:2–4	3:13–19	6:12–15	
Jesus preaches the Sermon on the Mount	Galilee	5:1–7:29		6:20–49	
A sinful woman anoints Jesus	Capernaum			7:36–50	
Jesus travels again through Galilee	Galilee			8:1–3	
Jesus tells kingdom parables	Galilee	13:1–52	4:1–34	8:4–18	
Jesus quiets the storm	Sea of Galilee	8:23–27	4:35–41	8:22–25	
Jairus's daughter raised to life	Capernaum	9:18–26	5:21–43	8:40–56	
Jesus sends out the twelve	Galilee	9:35—11:1	6:6–13	9:1–6	

THE YEAR OF OPPOSITION

Event	Place	Matthew	Mark	Luke	John
John the Baptist killed by Herod	Machaerus in Judea	14:1–12	6:14–29	9:7–9	
Jesus feeds the 5000	Bethsaida	14:13–21	6:30–44	9:10–17	6:1–14
Jesus walks on water	Sea of Galilee	14:22–23	6:45–52		6:16–21
Jesus feeds the 4000	Sea of Galilee	15:32–39	8:1–9		
Peter confesses Jesus as the Son of God	Caesarea Philippi	16:13–20	8:27–30	9:18–21	
Jesus predicts his death	Caesarea Philippi	16:21–26	8:31–37	9:22–25	
Jesus is transfigured	Mount Hermon	17:1–13	9:2–13	9:28–36	

THE YEAR OF OPPOSITION (cont.)

Event	Place	Matthew	Mark	Luke	John
Jesus pays his temple taxes	Capernaum	17:24–27			
Jesus attends the Feast of Tabernacles	Jerusalem				7:11–52
Jesus heals a man born blind	Jerusalem				9:1–41
Jesus visits Mary and Martha	Bethany			10:38–42	
Jesus raises Lazarus from the dead	Bethany				11:1–44
Jesus begins his last trip to Jerusalem	Border road			17:11	
Jesus blesses the little children	Transjordan	19:13–15	10:13–16	18:15–17	
Jesus talks to the rich young man	Transjordan	19:16–30	10:17–31	18:18–30	
Jesus again predicts his death	Near the Jordan	20:17–19	10:32–34	18:31–34	
Jesus heals blind Bartimaeus	Jericho	20:29–34	10:46–52	18:35–43	
Jesus talks to Zacchaeus	Jericho			19:1–10	
Jesus visits Mary and Martha again	Bethany				11:55–12:1

THE LAST WEEK

Event	Place	Day of Week	Matthew	Mark	Luke	John
The triumphal entry	Jerusalem	Sunday	21:1–11	11:1–10	19:29–44	12:12–19
Jesus curses the fig tree	Jerusalem	Monday	21:18–19	11:12–14		
Jesus clears the temple	Jerusalem	Monday	21:12–13	11:15–18	19:45–48	
The authority of Jesus questioned	Jerusalem	Tuesday	21:23–27	11:27–33	20:1–8	
Jesus teaches in the temple	Jerusalem	Tuesday	21:28–23:29	12:1–44	20:9–21:4	
Jesus' feet anointed	Bethany	Tuesday	26:6–13	14:3–9		12:2–11
The plot against Jesus	Jerusalem	Wednesday	26:14–16	14:10–11	22:3–6	
The Last Supper	Jerusalem	Thursday	26:17–29	14:12–25	22:7–20	13:1–38
Jesus comforts his disciples	Jerusalem	Thursday				14:1–16:33
Jesus' high priestly prayer	Jerusalem	Thursday				17:1–26
Gethsemane	Jerusalem	Thursday	26:36–46	14:32–42	22:40–46	
Jesus' arrest and trial	Jerusalem	Friday	26:47–27:26	14:43–15:15	22:47–23:25	18:2–19:16
Jesus' crucifixion and death	Golgotha	Friday	27:27–56	15:16–41	23:26–49	19:17–30
The burial of Jesus	Garden tomb	Friday	27:57–66	15:42–47	23:50–56	19:31–42

Event	Place	Day of week	Matthew	Mark	Luke	John	Acts	1 Corinthians
The empty tomb	Jerusalem	Resurrection Sunday	28:1–8	16:1–8	24:1–12	20:1–10		
To Mary Magdalene in the garden	Jerusalem	Resurrection Sunday		16:9–11		20:11–18		
To other women	Jerusalem	Resurrection Sunday	28:9–10					
To two people going to Emmaus	Road to Emmaus	Resurrection Sunday		16:12–13	24:13–32			
To Peter	Jerusalem	Resurrection Sunday			24:34			15:5
To the ten disciples in the upper room	Jerusalem	Resurrection Sunday			24:36–43	20:19–25		
To the eleven disciples in the upper room	Jerusalem	Following Sunday		16:14		20:26–31		15:5
To seven disciples fishing	Sea of Galilee	Some time later				21:1–25		
To the eleven disciples on a mountain	Galilee	Some time later	28:16–20	16:15–18				
To more than five hundred	Unknown	Some time later						15:6
To James	Unknown	Some time later						15:7
To his disciples at his ascension	Mount of Olives	Forty days after Jesus' Resurrection			24:44–51		1:3–9	15:7
To Paul	Damascus	Several years later					9:1–19; 22:3–16; 26:9–18	9:1; 15:8

Parable	Matthew	Mark	Luke
Lamp under a bowl	5:14–15	4:21–22	8:16; 11:33
Wise and foolish builders	7:24–27		6:47–49
New cloth on an old garment	9:16	2:21	5:36
New wine in old wineskins	9:17	2:22	5:37–38
Sower and the soils	13:3–8, 18–23	4:3–8, 14–20	8:5–8, 11–15
Weeds	13:24–30, 36–43		
Mustard seed	13:31–32	4:30–32	13:18–19
Yeast	13:33		13:20–21
Hidden treasure	13:44		
Valuable pearl	13:45–46		
Net	13:47–50		
Owner of a house	13:52		
Lost sheep	18:12–14		15:4–7
Unmerciful servant	18:23–34		
Workers in the vineyard	20:1–16		
Two sons	21:28–32		
Tenants	21:33–44	12:1–11	20:9–18
Wedding banquet	22:2–14		
Fig tree	24:32–35	13:28–29	21:29–31
Faithful and wise servant	24:45–51		12:42–48
Ten virgins	25:1–13		
Talents (minas)	25:14–30		19:12–27
Sheep and goats	25:31–46		
Growing seed		4:26–29	
Watchful servants		13:35–37	12:35–40
Moneylender			7:41–43
Good Samaritan			10:30–37
Friend in need			11:5–8
Rich fool			12:16–21
Unfruitful fig tree			13:6–9
Lowest seat at the feast			14:7–14
Great banquet			14:16–24
Cost of discipleship			14:28–33
Lost coin			15:8–10
Lost (prodigal) son			15:11–32
Shrewd manager			16:1–8
Rich man and Lazarus			16:19–31

THE PARABLES OF JESUS (cont.)

Parable	Matthew	Mark	Luke
Master and his servant			17:7–10
Persistent widow			18:2–8

THE MIRACLES OF JESUS

	Matthew	Mark	Luke	John
Healing Miracles				
Man with leprosy	8:2–4	1:40–42	5:12–13	
Roman centurion's servant	8:5–13		7:1–10	
Peter's mother-in-law	8:14–15	1:30–31	4:38–39	
Two men from Gadara	8:28–34	5:1–15	8:27–35	
Paralyzed man	9:2–7	2:3–12	5:18–25	
Woman with bleeding	9:20–22	5:25–29	8:43–48	
Two blind men	9:27–31			
Mute, demon-possessed man	9:32–33			
Man with a shriveled hand	12:10–13	3:1–5	6:6–10	
Blind, mute, demon-possessed man	12:22		11:14	
Canaanite woman's daughter	15:21–28	7:24–30		
Boy with a demon	17:14–18	9:17–29	9:38–43	
Two blind men (including Bartimaeus)	20:29–34	10:46–52	18:35–43	
Deaf mute		7:31–37		
Possessed man in synagogue		1:23–26	4:33–35	
Blind man at Bethsaida		8:22–26		
Crippled woman			13:11–13	
Man with dropsy			14:1–4	
Ten men with leprosy			17:11–19	
The high priest's servant			22:50–51	
Official's son at Capernaum				4:46–54
Sick man at pool of Bethesda				5:1–9
Man born blind				9:1–7
Miracles showing power over nature				
Calming the storm	8:23–27	4:37–41	8:22–25	
Walking on water	14:25	6:48–51		6:19–21
Feeding of the 5000	14:15–21	6:35–44	9:12–17	6:5–13
Feeding of the 4000	15:32–38	8:1–9		
Coin in fish	17:24–27			
Fig tree withered	21:18–22	11:12–14, 20–25		

THE MIRACLES OF JESUS (cont.)

	Matthew	Mark	Luke	John
Miracles showing power over nature				
Large catch of fish			5:4–11	
Water turned into wine				2:1– 11
Another large catch of fish				21:1–11
Miracles of raising the dead				
Jairus's daughter	9:18–19, 23–25	5:22–24, 38–42	8:41–42, 49–56	
Widow's son at Nain			7:11–15	
Lazarus				11:1–44

THE MIRACLES OF THE APOSTLES

Miracle	Acts
Lame man cured (by Peter)	3:6–9
Death of Ananias and Sapphira	5:1–10
Saul's sight restored	9:17–18
Healing of Aeneas	9:33–35
Raising of Dorcas	9:36–41
Elymas blinded	13:8–11
Lame man cured (by Paul)	14:8–10
Demon cast out of a girl	16:16–18
Raising of Eutychus	20:9–10
Paul unharmed by viper	28:3–5
Healing of Publius's father	28:7–9

ACTS

Outline

Introduction (1:1–11)
- I. The Outpouring of the Holy Spirit (1:12—2:41)
  - A. Preparing for the Promise (1:12–26)
  - B. The Day of Pentecost (2:1–41)
- II. Early Days of the Church in Jerusalem (2:42—8:1a)
  - A. Characteristics of the Apostolic Church After the Outpouring of the Spirit (2:42–47)
  - B. A Remarkable Miracle and its Effects (3:1—4:31)
  - C. The Continuing Experiment in Community Sharing (4:32—5:11)
  - D. Further Healings and Resistance from the Religious Establishment (5:12–42)
  - E. The Selection of Seven Deacons (6:1–7)
  - F. Stephen: The First-Known Christian Martyr (6:8—8:1a)
- III. Persecution Leads to Expansion (8:1b—9:31)
  - A. Christians Scattered Throughout Judea and Samaria (8:1b-4)
  - B. Philip: The Ministry of an Evangelist (8:5–40)
  - C. Saul of Tarsus: The Conversion of a Persecutor (9:1–31)
- IV. Christianity Began Spreading to the Gentiles (9:32—12:25)
  - A. Peter's Ministry at Lydda and Joppa (9:32–43)
  - B. Peter's Mission to the Gentiles at Caesarea (10:1–48)
  - C. Peter's Report to the Jerusalem Church and His Action Approved (11:1–18)
  - D. Antioch: The First Gentile Church (11:19–30)
  - E. Persecution Under Herod Agrippa I (12:1–23)
  - F. Summary of the Church's Progress (12:24–25)
- V. Paul's First Missionary Journey (13:1—14:28)
  - A. Paul and Barnabas Commissioned by the Local Church at Antioch (13:1–3)
  - B. The Territory Evangelized (13:4—14:28)
- VI. The Jerusalem Conference (15:1–35)
- VII. Paul's Second Missionary Journey (15:36—18:22)
  - A. Disagreement Between Paul and Barnabas (15:36–40)
  - B. Old Territory Revisited (15:41—16:5)
  - C. New Territory Evangelized (16:6—18:21)
  - D. Return to Syrian Antioch (18:22)
- VIII. Paul's Third Missionary Journey (18:23—21:16)
  - A. En Route to Ephesus (18:23)
    Parenthesis: The Ministry of Apollos (18:24–28)
  - B. A Lengthy Ministry at Ephesus (19:1–41)
  - C. To Macedonia, Greece, and Back to Macedonia (20:1–5)
  - D. Return Trip to Jerusalem (20:6—21:16)
- IX. Paul's Arrest and Ministry During Imprisonment (21:17—28:31)
  - A. In Jerusalem (21:17—23:35)
  - B. In Caesarea (24:1—26:32)
  - C. En Route to Rome (27:1—28:15)
  - D. In Rome (28:16–31)

Author: Luke

Theme: The Triumphant Spread of the Gospel through the Power of the Holy Spirit

Date of Writing: c. A.D. 63

Background

The book of Acts, like the Gospel of Luke, is addressed to a man named "Theophilus" (1:1). Although the author is not identified by name in either book, the unanimous testimony of early Christianity and the corroborating internal evidence of the two books point to common authorship by Luke, "our dear friend . . . the doctor" (Col 4:14).

The Holy Spirit prompted Luke to write to Theophilus in order to fill a need in the Gentile church for a full account of the beginnings of Christianity—(1) the "former book" being his Gospel about Jesus' life, and (2) the latter book being his account in Acts about the outpouring of the Spirit at Jerusalem and the subsequent development of the early church. It is apparent that Luke was a skilled writer, a careful historian and an inspired theologian.

Acts selectively covers the first thirty years of the church's history. As a church historian, Luke traces the spread of the gospel from Jerusalem to Rome, mentioning no fewer than 32 countries, 54 cities, 9 Mediterranean islands, 95 different persons by name, and a variety of governmental officials and administrators by their precise titles. Archaeology continues to confirm Luke's amazing accuracy in all his details. As a theologian, Luke astutely describes the significance of various experiences and events in the church's early years.

In its first stages, the NT Scriptures comprised two collections: (1) the four Gospels and (2) the letters of Paul. Acts played an indispensable role as the connecting link between the two collections and rightly belongs in its present canonical order. Chs. 13–28 provide the historical background necessary for understanding more fully Paul's ministry and letters. Luke's "we" passages in Acts (16:10–17; 20:5—21:18; 27:1—28:16) reveal his personal participation in Paul's travels.

Purpose

Luke has at least two purposes in recounting the church's beginnings. (1) He shows that the gospel moved triumphantly from the narrow borders of Judaism into the Gentile world in spite of opposition and persecution. (2) He reveals the role of the Holy Spirit in the church's life and mission, emphasizing the baptism in the Holy Spirit as God's provision for empowering the church to proclaim the gospel and to continue Jesus' ministry. Luke explicitly records three times that the baptism in the Spirit was accompanied by speaking in tongues (2:4ff; 10:45–46; 19:1–7). The context of these passages indicates that this was normative in early Christianity and is God's enduring pattern for the church.

Survey

Whereas Luke's Gospel records "all that Jesus began to do and to teach" (Ac 1:1), Acts describes what Jesus continued to do and teach after his ascension, by the power of the Holy Spirit working in and through his disciples and the early church. When Jesus ascended into heaven (1:9–11), his last instruction to his disciples was to wait in Jerusalem until they were baptized in the Holy Spirit (1:4–5). The key verse of Acts (1:8) contains a theological and geographical capsule summary of the book: Jesus promises the disciples they will receive power when the Holy Spirit comes on them—power to be his witnesses (1) "in Jerusalem" (chs. 1–7), (2) "in all Judea and Samaria" (chs. 8–12), and (3) "to the ends of the earth" (chs. 13–28).

Acts contains an intermingling of divine and human action. The entire church, not just the apostles, "preached the word wherever they went" (8:4). Deacons like Stephen and Philip (6:1–6) became mighty in the Holy Spirit and faith, performing "great wonders and miraculous signs" (6:8) and even shaking entire cities with the gospel (8:5–13). Godly men prayed fervently, saw angels, had visions, witnessed mighty signs and wonders, drove out demons, healed the sick and proclaimed the gospel with great boldness and authority. In spite of problems within the church, such as the Jewish-Gentile tension (ch. 15), and in spite of persistent persecution from outside the church by religious and civil authorities, the name of the Lord Jesus was magnified in word and deed from one city to the next.

In chs. 1–12 the main center of the church's outreach is Jerusalem; here Peter is the foremost human vessel God used to spread the gospel. In chs. 13–28 the main center of the church's outreach is Antioch in Syria; here Paul is the foremost human vessel God used to spread the gospel to the Gentiles. Acts ends abruptly with Paul in Rome, still awaiting his trial before Caesar. Though the outcome of the trial is left hanging, the book ends on a triumphant note with Paul, still a prisoner, boldly and without hindrance preaching and teaching about the kingdom and about Jesus (28:31).

Special Features

Nine major emphases characterize Acts: (1) The church: Acts reveals the church's source of power and the true nature of its mission, along with principles that should govern the church in every generation. (2) The Holy Spirit: the third person of the Trinity is mentioned specifically 50 times; the baptism in and ministry of the Spirit imparts power (1:8), boldness (4:31), holy fear of God (5:3,5,11), wisdom (6:3,10), guidance (16:6–10) and spiritual gifts (19:6). (3) Early church messages: Luke skillfully recounts inspired sermons by Peter, Stephen, Paul, James and others, providing insight into the early church not found elsewhere in the NT. (4) Prayer: the early Christians devoted themselves to regular and fervent prayer, sometimes lasting all night and producing great results. (5) Signs, wonders and miracles: these manifestations accompanied the proclamation of the gospel in the power of the Holy Spirit. (6) Persecution: proclaiming the gospel with power consistently stirred up religious and/or secular opposition and persecution. (7) Jew/Gentile sequence: throughout Acts the gospel goes first to the Jews and then to the Gentiles. (8) Women: special mention is made of women involved in the ongoing work of the church. (9) Triumph: no barriers (national, religious, cultural or racial) and no opposition or persecution could thwart the advance of the gospel.

Hermeneutical Principle

Some interpreters view the book of Acts as if it were under another NT covenant instead of seeing it as God's standard for the church and its witness during the entire period of time the NT calls "the last days" (cf. 2:17, note). Acts is not just a history book of the early church; it is a handbook for the Christian life and for a Spirit-filled church. Believers ought to desire and expect, as the norm for today's church, all elements in the NT church's ministry and experience (except the writing of NT Scripture); these are attainable when the church moves in the full power of the Spirit. Nothing in Acts or the NT indicates that signs, wonders, miracles, spiritual gifts, or the apostolic standard for the church's life and ministry generally were to cease suddenly or permanently at the end of the apostolic age. Acts records what the church must be and do in any generation as it continues Jesus' ministry in the Pentecostal power of the Holy Spirit (see Ac 7:44, notes).

Reading Acts

In order to read the entire New Testament in one year, the book of Acts should be read in 46 days, according to the following schedule:
□ 1 □ 2:1–36 □ 2:37–47 □ 3 □ 4:1–31 □ 4:32—5:11 □ 5:12–42 □ 6 □ 7:1–53 □ 7:54—8:8 □ 8:9–40 □ 9:1–31 □ 9:32–43 □ 10:1–23 □ 10:24–48 □ 11:1–18 □ 11:19–30 □ 12 □ 13:1–12 □ 13:13–52 □ 14 □ 15:1–21 □ 15:22–35 □ 15:36—16:15 □ 16:16–40 □ 17:1–15 □ 17:16–34 □ 18:1–23 □ 18:24—19:7 □ 19:8–41 □ 20:1–26 □ 20:27–38 □ 21:1–16 □ 21:17–36 □ 21:37—22:21 □ 22:22—23:11 □ 23:12–35 □ 24 □ 25:1–12 □ 25:13—26:1 □ 26:2–18 □ 26:19–32 □ 27:1–26 □ 27:27–44 □ 28:1–16 □ 28:17–31

NOTES

COUNTRIES OF PEOPLE MENTIONED AT PENTECOST

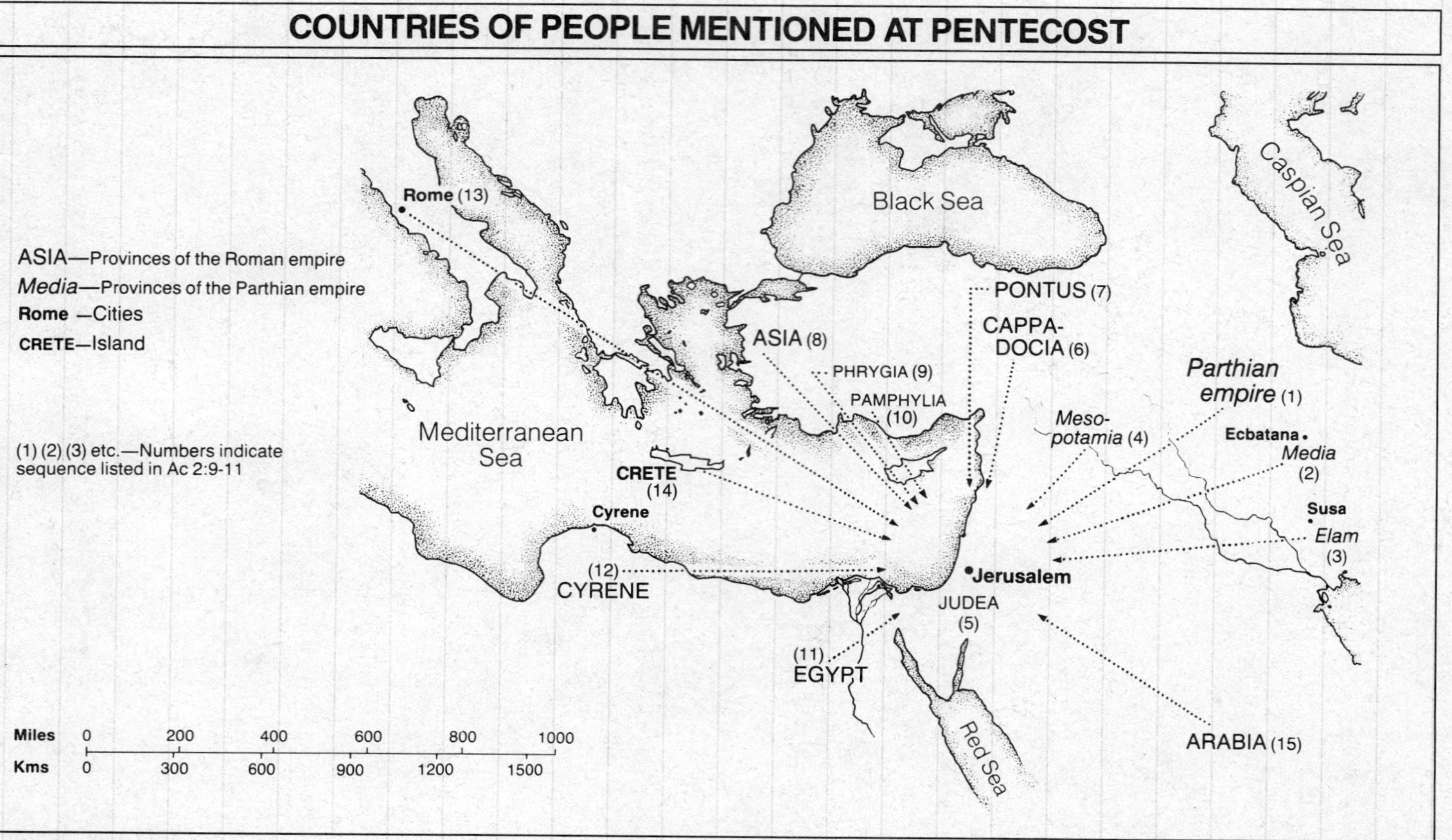
ASIA—Provinces of the Roman empire
Media—Provinces of the Parthian empire
Rome —Cities
CRETE—Island
(1) (2) (3) etc.—Numbers indicate sequence listed in Ac 2:9-11
Rome (13)
Black Sea
Caspian Sea
PONTUS (7)
CAPPA-DOCIA (6)
ASIA (8)
PHRYGIA (9)
PAMPHYLIA (10)
Parthian empire (1)
Ecbatana
Media (2)
Susa
Elam (3)
Meso-potamia (4)
Mediterranean Sea
CRETE (14)
Cyrene
(12) CYRENE
Jerusalem
JUDEA (5)
(11) EGYPT
Red Sea
ARABIA (15)
Miles 0 200 400 600 800 1000
Kms 0 300 600 900 1200 1500

The Promised Baptism in the Spirit

1 In my former book,[a] Theophilus,
I wrote about all that Jesus began
to do and to teach[b] **2**until the day he
was taken up to heaven,[c] after giving
instructions[d] through the Holy Spirit
to the apostles[e] he had chosen.[f] **3**After his suffering, he showed himself to
these men and gave many convincing
proofs that he was alive. He appeared
to them[g] over a period of forty days
and spoke about the kingdom of God.[h]
4On one occasion, while he was eating
with them, he gave them this command: "Do not leave Jerusalem, but
wait[i] for the gift my Father promised,
which you have heard me speak
about.[j] **5**For John baptized with[a] water,[k] but in a few days you will be bap- Ac 2:4-13
tized with the Holy Spirit."[l]
6So when they met together, they
asked him, "Lord, are you at this time
going to restore[m] the kingdom to Israel?"
7He said to them: "It is not for you
to know the times or dates the Father
has set by his own authority.[n] **8**But
you will receive power when the Holy

1:1 [a]Lk 1:1-4 [b]Lk 3:23 **1:2** [c]ver 9,11; S Mk 16:19 [d]Mt 28:19,20 [e]S Mk 6:30 [f]Jn 13:18; 15:16, 19 **1:3** [g]Mt 28:17; Lk 24:34,36; Jn 20:19,26; 21:1, 14; 1Co 15:5-7 [h]S Mt 3:2 **1:4** [i]Ps 27:14 [j]Lk 24:49; Jn 14:16; Ac 2:33 **1:5** [k]S Mk 1:4 [l]S Mk 1:8 **1:6** [m]Mt 17:11; Ac 3:21 **1:7** [n]Dt 29:29; Ps 102:13; Mt 24:36

[a]*5* Or *in*

1:1 MY FORMER BOOK. In Luke's Gospel we have the account of all Jesus began to do and to teach in the power of the Holy Spirit (Lk 4:1,18). In the book of Acts we have the continuing story of how Jesus' followers, in the same power of the Spirit, proclaimed the same gospel, worked the same kind of miracles and lived the same kind of life. The Holy Spirit reproducing the life and ministry of Jesus through the church is the theological keynote of Acts. The book could well be called "The Acts of the Holy Spirit." Observe the following concerning the Holy Spirit's inspired record in the book of Acts:

(1) All Scripture, including the historical narratives in Acts, has didactic (i.e., teaching) and theological significance. This is confirmed by two facts: (a) the Biblical declaration that "all Scripture is God-breathed and is useful for teaching, rebuking, correcting and training in righteousness" (2Ti 3:16); (b) Paul's statement that the OT historical narratives have a teaching and instructional purpose (1Co 10:11). He maintains that these stories are examples with practical and theological relevance for the believer (Ro 15:4). What is true for historical narrative in the OT is also true for Acts.

(2) Luke's inspired record of the history of the early church provides: (a) a definitive pattern of the Holy Spirit's activity to be followed during the entire church age, (b) data for developing a doctrine of the Holy Spirit and (c) revelation about how the Spirit's ministry must relate to the lives of believers in Christ. Note specifically two elements in this book that are theologically and practically normative: (i) the baptism in or filling with the Holy Spirit, God's promise for all believers (see 2:39, note; cf. 1:5,8; 2:4; 4:8,31; 8:15–17; 9:17; 10:44–46; 13:9,52; 15:8; 19:1–6); (ii) the Spirit's numerous activities that provided the church with the standards of righteousness, witness and power that God desires for his people in the last days (i.e., the church age).

1:3 SHOWED HIMSELF. See Mt 28:9, note on Christ's resurrection appearances.

1:4 GIFT MY FATHER PROMISED. The gift the Father promised (Joel 2:28–29; Mt 3:11) is the baptism in the Holy Spirit (see v. 5, note). The fulfillment of that promise is described as being "filled with the Holy Spirit" (2:4). Thus, "baptized in the Spirit" and "filled with the Spirit" are at times used interchangeably in Acts.

This baptism in the Holy Spirit should not be identified with receiving the Holy Spirit at regeneration (see article on REGENERATION, p. 1589). These are two distinct works of the Spirit, often separated by a period of time (see article on THE REGENERATION OF THE DISCIPLES, p. 1627).

1:5 WITH [IN] THE HOLY SPIRIT. The preposition "with" is the translation of the Greek word *en* and is often translated as "in." Many prefer the rendering, "you will be baptized in the Holy Spirit." Likewise, "baptized with water" may be translated "baptized in water." Jesus himself is the one who baptizes his believers in the Holy Spirit (see Jn 1:33, note).

1:8 YOU WILL RECEIVE POWER. This is the key verse in the book of Acts. The primary purpose of the baptism in the Spirit is the receiving of power to witness for Christ so that the lost will be won over to him and taught to obey all that Christ commanded. The end result is that Christ may be known, loved, praised and made Lord of God's chosen people (cf. Mt 28:18–20; Lk 24:49; Jn 5:23; 15:26–27).

(1) "Power" (Gk *dunamis*) means more than strength or ability; it designates especially power in operation, in action. Luke (in his Gospel and in Acts) emphasizes that the Holy Spirit's power included the authority to drive out evil spirits and the anointing to heal the sick as the two essential signs accompanying the proclamation of God's kingdom (e.g., Lk 4:14,18,36; 5:17; 6:19; 9:1–2; Ac 6:8; 8:4–8,12–13; 10:38; 14:3; 19:8–12). The baptism in the Holy Spirit is God's provision for releasing the power of the Holy Spirit into the believer's life (see article on BAPTISM IN THE HOLY SPIRIT, p. 1642).

(2) Luke here does not relate the baptism in the Spirit to personal salvation and regeneration, but to the power within the believer to witness with great effect (see article on THE REGENERATION OF THE DISCIPLES, p. 1627).

(3) The Holy Spirit's principal work in witnessing and proclamation concerns his coming upon believers for power and his testimony to Christ's saving work and resurrection (cf. 2:14–42). See

BAPTISM IN THE HOLY SPIRIT

Ac 1:5 "For John baptized with water, but in a few days you will be baptized with the Holy Spirit."

One of the cardinal doctrines of Scripture is the baptism in the Holy Spirit (see Ac 1:4, note on reading "baptism *in*" rather than "baptism with" the Holy Spirit). Concerning the baptism in the Holy Spirit, the Word of God teaches the following.

(1) The baptism in the Spirit is intended for all who profess faith in Christ, have been born again and have received the indwelling of the Spirit.

(2) One of Christ's key goals in his earthly mission was to baptize his followers in the Holy Spirit (Mt 3:11; Mk 1:8; Lk 3:16; Jn 1:33). He instructed his disciples not to begin witnessing until they were baptized in the Holy Spirit and "clothed with power from on high" (Lk 24:49; Ac 1:4–5,8). Jesus Christ himself did not enter his ministry until he had been "anointed . . . with the Holy Spirit and power" (Ac 10:38; cf. Lk 4:1,18).

(3) The baptism in the Holy Spirit is an operation of the Spirit distinct and separate from his work of regeneration. Just as the Spirit's sanctifying work is a distinct work complementing his regenerating work, so the baptism in the Spirit complements the regenerating and sanctifying work of the Spirit. On the day of Christ's resurrection he breathed on his disciples and said, "Receive the Holy Spirit" (Jn 20:22), indicating that regeneration and new life were being given to them (see article on THE REGENERATION OF THE DISCIPLES, p. 1627). Then later he told them they must also be "clothed with power" by the Holy Spirit (Lk 24:49; cf. Ac 1:5,8). For the disciples it was clearly a post-regeneration experience (see Ac 11:17, note). One can be regenerated and indwelt by the Holy Spirit, but still not be baptized in the Holy Spirit (see Ac 19:6, note).

(4) To be baptized in the Spirit means to be filled with the Spirit (compare Ac 1:5; 2:4). However, this baptism occurred only at and after Pentecost. Concerning those filled with the Spirit before Pentecost (e.g. Lk 1:15,67), Luke does not use the term baptized in the Holy Spirit. This would occur only after Christ's ascension (Lk 24:49–51; Jn 16:7–14; Ac 1:4).

(5) In the book of Acts, speaking in tongues as the Spirit gives utterance is the initial outward sign accompanying the baptism in the Holy Spirit (Ac 2:4; 10:45–46; 19:6). Baptism in the Holy Spirit is linked so closely with the external manifestation of speaking in tongues that this should be considered the norm when receiving that baptism (see article on SPEAKING IN TONGUES, p. 1646).

(6) The baptism in the Holy Spirit will bring the personal boldness and power of the Spirit into the believer's life in order to accomplish mighty works in Christ's name and to make his or her witness and proclamation effective (cf. Ac 1:8; 2:14–41; 4:31; 6:8; Ro 15:18–19; 1Co 2:4). This power is not some impersonal force, but is a manifestation of the Holy Spirit by which Jesus and his glory and works are present with his people (Jn 14:16–18; 16:14; 1Co 12:7).

(7) Other results of a genuine baptism in the Holy Spirit are: (a) prophetic utterances and declarations of praise (Ac 2:4,17; 10:46; 1Co 14:2); (b) enhanced sensitivity to sin that grieves the Holy Spirit, a greater seeking after righteousness and a deeper awareness of God's judgment against ungodliness (see Jn 16:8, note; Ac 1:8, note); (c) a life that brings glory to Jesus Christ (Jn 16:13–14; Ac 4:33); (d) new visions (Ac 2:17); (e) a manifestation of the various gifts of the Spirit (1Co 12:4–10); (f) a greater desire

to pray (Ac 2:41–42; 3:1; 4:23–31; 6:4; 10:9; Ro 8:26); (g) a deeper love and understanding of God's Word (Jn 16:13; Ac 2:42); and (h) an increasing awareness of God as one's Father (Ac 1:4; Ro 8:15; Gal 4:6).

(8) God's Word cites several conditions by which the baptism in the Holy Spirit is given. (a) We must accept by faith Jesus Christ as Lord and Savior and turn from sin and the world (Ac 2:38–40; 8:12–17). This involves surrendering our wills to God ("to those who obey him," Ac 5:32). We must turn from that which offends God before we can be "an instrument for noble purposes, made holy, useful to the Master" (2Ti 2:21). (b) We must desire to be filled. Christians should have a deep hunger for the baptism in the Spirit (Jn 7:37–39; cf. Isa 44:3; Mt 5:6; 6:33). (c) We often receive this baptism in answer to prayer (Lk 11:13; Ac 1:14; 2:1–4; 4:31; 8:15,17). (d) We should expect that God will baptize us in the Holy Spirit (Mk 11:24; Ac 1:4–5).

(9) The baptism in the Holy Spirit is sustained in the believer's life by prayer (Ac 4:31), witness (4:31,33), worship in the Spirit (Eph 5:18–19) and a sanctified life (see Eph 5:18, notes). However powerful the initial coming of the Holy Spirit on the believer may be, if this does not find expression in a life of prayer, witness and holiness, the experience will soon become a fading glory.

(10) The baptism in the Spirit occurs only once in a believer's life and points to the consecrating of the believer to God's work of witnessing in power and righteousness. The Bible teaches that there may be new fillings with the Holy Spirit after the believer has been baptized in the Spirit (see Ac 4:31, note; cf. 2:4; 4:8,31; 13:9; Eph 5:18). Thus, the baptism in the Spirit brings the believer into a relationship with the Spirit that is to be renewed (Ac 4:31) and maintained (Eph 5:18).

Spirit comes on you;[o] and you will be
my witnesses[p] in Jerusalem, and in all
Ac Judea and Samaria,[q] and to the ends
2:32 of the earth."[r]

Jesus Taken Up Into Heaven

9After he said this, he was taken
up[s] before their very eyes, and a cloud
hid him from their sight.
10They were looking intently up into
the sky as he was going, when suddenly two men dressed in white[t] stood
beside them. 11"Men of Galilee,"[u]
they said, "why do you stand here looking into the sky? This same Jesus, who
has been taken from you into heaven,
1Co will come back[v] in the same way you
4:5 have seen him go into heaven."

Matthias Chosen to Replace Judas

12Then they returned to Jerusalem[w]
from the hill called the Mount of Olives,[x] a Sabbath day's walk[b] from
the city. 13When they arrived, they
went upstairs to the room[y] where
they were staying. Those present were
Peter, John, James and Andrew; Philip
and Thomas, Bartholomew and Matthew; James son of Alphaeus and Simon the Zealot, and Judas son of
James.[z] 14They all joined together
constantly in prayer,[a] along with the
women[b] and Mary the mother of
Jesus, and with his brothers.[c]
15In those days Peter stood up
among the believers[c] (a group numbering about a hundred and twenty)
16and said, "Brothers,[d] the Scripture
had to be fulfilled[e] which the Holy
Spirit spoke long ago through the
mouth of David concerning Judas,[f]
who served as guide for those who arrested Jesus— 17he was one of our
number[g] and shared in this ministry."[h]

1:8 [o] Ac 2:1-4 [p] S Lk 24:48 [q] Ac 8:1-25 [r] S Mt 28:19 **1:9** [s] ver 2; S Mk 16:19 **1:10** [t] S Jn 20:12 **1:11** [u] Ac 2:7 [v] S Mt 16:27 **1:12** [w] Lk 24:52 [x] S Mt 21:1 **1:13** [y] Ac 9:37; 20:8 [z] Mt 10:2-4; Mk 3:16-19; Lk 6:14-16 **1:14** [a] Ac 2:42; 4:24; 6:4; S Lk 18:1; S Ro 1:10 [b] Lk 23:49,55 [c] S Mt 12:46 **1:16** [d] Ac 6:3; 11:1,12,29; 14:2; 18:18,27; 21:7; S 22:5; S Ro 7:1 [e] ver 20; S Mt 1:22 [f] S Mt 10:4 **1:17** [g] Jn 6:70,71 [h] ver 25

[b] *12* That is, about 3/4 mile (about 1,100 meters) [c] *15* Greek *brothers*

next note for comments on how the Spirit witnesses and what that means in our personal lives.

1:8 YOU WILL BE MY WITNESSES. The baptism in the Holy Spirit not only imparts power to preach Jesus as Lord and Savior (see previous note), but also increases the effectiveness of that witness because of a strengthening and deepening relationship with the Father, Son and Holy Spirit that comes from being filled with the Spirit (cf. Jn 14:26; 15:26–27).

(1) The Holy Spirit discloses and makes more real to us the personal presence of Jesus (Jn 14:16–18). Any witness to an intimate fellowship with Jesus Christ himself will result in an ever-growing desire on our part to love, honor and please our Savior (see article on THE DOCTRINE OF THE HOLY SPIRIT, p. 1654).

(2) The Holy Spirit witnesses to "righteousness" (Jn 16:8,10) and "truth" (Jn 16:13), which "bring glory to" Christ (Jn 16:14), not only with words, but also in deeds. Thus, we who have received the witness of the Spirit to Christ's redemptive work will necessarily manifest Christlikeness, love, truth and righteousness in our lives (cf. 1Co 13).

(3) The baptism in the Holy Spirit is the initiation point whereby Spirit-filled believers receive the power to witness for Christ and to bring conviction of sin, righteousness and judgment on the lost (see Jn 16:8, note). The effects of such conviction will become evident both in those who sincerely proclaim the message and in those who receive it (2:39–40).

(4) The baptism in the Holy Spirit can be given only to those whose hearts are turned toward God in repentance from their wicked ways (2:38; 3:26). It is maintained by the same sincere commitment to Christ (see 5:32, note).

(5) The baptism in the Holy Spirit is a baptism into the Spirit who is holy (cf. "Spirit of holiness," Ro 1:4). Thus, if the Spirit is truly at work in us in all his fullness, we will live in greater conformity to Christ's holiness.

In light of these Scriptural truths, we who have been baptized in the Holy Spirit will have an intense desire to please Christ in whatever way we can; i.e., the fullness of the Spirit complements (i.e., completes, fills up) the saving and sanctifying work of the Holy Spirit in our lives. Those who claim the fullness of the Spirit, yet live a life contrary to the Spirit of holiness, are deceived and untruthful. Those who display spiritual gifts, miracles, spectacular signs or inspiring oratory, yet lack true faith, love and righteousness, are operating not by the Holy Spirit but by an unholy spirit not from God (Mt 7:21–23; cf. Mt 24:24; 2Co 11:13–15; see also article on TESTING FOR GENUINE BAPTISM IN THE SPIRIT, p. 1668). For further comments on witnessing for Christ, see 13:31, note.

1:14 JOINED TOGETHER CONSTANTLY IN PRAYER. The experience of Pentecost always involves human responsibility. Those needing the Spirit's outpouring for power to do God's work should make themselves available to the Holy Spirit through commitment to God's will and through prayer (v. 4; 2:38; 9:11–17; cf. Isa 40:29–31; Lk 11:5–13; 24:49). Notice the parallels between the Spirit coming on Jesus and the Spirit coming on the disciples. (1) The Spirit descended on them after they had prayed (Lk 3:21–22; Ac 1:14; 2:4). (2) There were observable manifestations of the Spirit (Lk 3:22; Ac 2:2–4). (3) The ministries of both Jesus and the disciples began after the Spirit came on them (compare Mt 3:16 with 4:17; Lk 3:21–23 with 4:14–19; cf. Ac 2:14–47).

18(With the reward[i] he got for his
wickedness, Judas bought a field;[j]
there he fell headlong, his body burst
open and all his intestines spilled out.
19Everyone in Jerusalem heard about
this, so they called that field in their
language[k] Akeldama, that is, Field of
Blood.)
20"For," said Peter, "it is written in
the book of Psalms,

" 'May his place be deserted;
let there be no one to dwell in
it,'[d][l]

and,

" 'May another take his place of
leadership.'[e][m]

21Therefore it is necessary to choose
one of the men who have been with us
the whole time the Lord Jesus went in
and out among us, 22beginning from
John's baptism[n] to the time when
Jesus was taken up from us. For one of
these must become a witness[o] with us
of his resurrection."
23So they proposed two men: Joseph
called Barsabbas (also known as Justus) and Matthias. 24Then they
prayed,[p] "Lord, you know everyone's
heart.[q] Show us[r] which of these two
you have chosen 25to take over this apostolic ministry, which Judas left to go
where he belongs." 26Then they cast
lots, and the lot fell to Matthias; so he
was added to the eleven apostles.[s]

The Holy Spirit Comes at Pentecost

2 When the day of Pentecost[t]
came, they were all together[u] in
one place. 2Suddenly a sound like the
blowing of a violent wind came from
heaven and filled the whole house
where they were sitting.[v] 3They saw
what seemed to be tongues of fire that
separated and came to rest on each of
them. 4All of them were filled with the
Holy Spirit[w] and began to speak in
other tongues[f][x] as the Spirit enabled
them.
5Now there were staying in Jerusalem God-fearing[y] Jews from every nation under heaven. 6When they heard
this sound, a crowd came together in
bewilderment, because each one heard
them speaking in his own language.

1:18 [i] Mt 26:14,15 [j] Mt 27:3-10
1:19 [k] S Jn 5:2
1:20 [l] Ps 69:25 [m] Ps 109:8
1:22 [n] S Mk 1:4 [o] ver 8; S Lk 24:48
1:24 [p] Ac 6:6; 13:3; 14:23
[q] S Rev 2:23 [r] 1Sa 14:41
1:26 [s] Ac 2:14
2:1 [t] Lev 23:15,16; Ac 20:16; 1Co 16:8 [u] Ac 1:14
2:2 [v] Ac 4:31
2:4 [w] S Lk 1:15 [x] S Mk 16:17
2:5 [y] Lk 2:25; Ac 8:2

[d] *20* Psalm 69:25 [e] *20* Psalm 109:8
[f] *4* Or *languages*; also in verse 11

2:1 PENTECOST. Pentecost was the second great festival of the Jewish year. It was a harvest festival when the firstfruits of the grain harvest were presented to God (cf. Lev 23:17). In like manner Pentecost symbolizes for the church the beginning of God's harvest for souls in the world.

2:2–3 A VIOLENT WIND . . . AND . . . TONGUES OF FIRE. These external manifestations demonstrated that God was present and active in a powerful way (cf. Ex 3:1–6; 1Ki 18:38–39). The "fire" may symbolize consecrating and separating believers to God for the work of bringing glory to Christ (Jn 16:13–14) and of witnessing for him (1:8). These two manifestations preceded the baptism in the Holy Spirit and were not repeated elsewhere in Acts.

2:4 FILLED WITH THE HOLY SPIRIT. What is the significance of the filling with the Holy Spirit at Pentecost? (1) It meant the beginning of the fulfillment of God's promise in Joel 2:28–29 to pour out his Spirit on all his people in the end times (cf. 1:4–5; Mt 3:11; Lk 24:49; Jn 1:33; see Joel 2:28–29, notes).

(2) Since the last days of this age had begun (v. 17; cf. Heb 1:2; 1Pe 1:20), everyone was now confronted with the decision to repent and believe in Christ (3:19; Mt 3:2; Lk 13:3; see Ac 2:17, notes).

(3) The disciples were "clothed with power from on high" (Lk 24:49; cf. Ac 1:8), enabling them to witness for Christ and to be people through whom the Holy Spirit could bring great conviction on the lost in relation to sin, righteousness and God's judgment, and turn the lost from sin to salvation in Christ (cf. 1:8, notes; 4:13,33; 6:8; Ro 15:19; see Jn 16:8, note).

(4) The Holy Spirit revealed his nature as a Spirit who longs and strives for the salvation of people of every nation. Those who received the baptism in the Holy Spirit were filled with the same longing for the salvation of the human race (vv. 38–40; 4:12,33; Ro 9:1–3; 10:1). Thus, Pentecost is the beginning of world missions (vv. 6–11,39; 1:8).

(5) The disciples became ministers of the Spirit. They not only preached Jesus crucified and resurrected, leading others to repentance and faith in Christ, but they also influenced converts to receive the "gift of the Holy Spirit" (vv. 38–39), whom they themselves had received at Pentecost. This leading others into the baptism in the Holy Spirit is the key to the apostolic work in the NT (see 8:17; 9:17–18; 10:44–46; 19:6).

(6) Through this baptism in the Spirit Christ's followers became successors to his earthly ministry. They continued to do and to teach, in the power of the Holy Spirit, the same things that Jesus "began both to do and to teach" (1:1; see Jn 14:12, note; see article on SIGNS OF BELIEVERS, p. 1513).

2:4 BEGAN TO SPEAK IN OTHER TONGUES. For a discussion on the meaning of speaking in tongues at Pentecost and elsewhere in the NT church, and on the possibility of false tongues, see article on SPEAKING IN TONGUES, p. 1646.

SPEAKING IN TONGUES

Ac 2:4 "All of them were filled with the Holy Spirit and began to speak in other tongues as the Spirit enabled them."

Speaking in tongues, or glossalalia (from Gk *glōssais lalō*), was considered by NT Christians as a God-given sign accompanying the baptism in the Holy Spirit (see Ac 2:4; 10:45–47; 19:6). This Biblical pattern for the Spirit-filled life is still valid for us today.

TRUE SPEAKING IN TONGUES. (1) *Tongues as a manifestation of the Spirit*. Speaking in tongues is a supernatural manifestation of the Holy Spirit, i.e., a Spirit-inspired utterance whereby believers speak in a language (Gk *glōssa*) they have never learned (Ac 2:4; 1Co 14:14–15). It may be in existing spoken human languages (Ac 2:6) or in languages unknown on earth (cf. 1Co 13:1). It is not "ecstatic speech," as rendered in some translations, for the Bible never uses the term "ecstatic utterance" to refer to speaking in tongues.

(2) *Tongues as the initial outward sign of the baptism in the Holy Spirit*. Speaking in tongues is an inspired utterance whereby the believer's spirit and the Holy Spirit join in verbal praise and/or prophecy. God linked speaking in tongues with the baptism in the Spirit from the very beginning (Ac 2:4), so that the 120 believers at Pentecost, and believers thereafter, would have an experiential confirmation that they have indeed received the baptism in the Holy Spirit (cf. Ac 10:45–46). Thus this experience could be objectively validated as to place and time of reception. Throughout the history of the church, whenever tongues as a confirming sign has been denied or lost from view, the truth and experience of Pentecost has been distorted or ignored entirely.

(3) *Tongues as a gift*. Speaking in tongues is also described as a gift of the Holy Spirit to the believer (1Co 12:4–10). This gift has two main purposes: (a) Speaking in tongues accompanied by interpretation is used in public worship to communicate the content of the utterance to the congregation, so that all may enter into Spirit-directed worship, praise or prophecy (1Co 14:5–6,13–17). (b) Speaking in tongues is used by the believer to speak to God in his or her personal devotions and thus to build up one's spiritual life (1Co 14:4). It means speaking at the level of the spirit (14:2,14) for the purpose of praying (14:2,14,15,28), giving thanks (14:16–17) or singing (14:15; see 1Co 14, notes; see article on SPIRITUAL GIFTS FOR BELIEVERS, p. 1770).

FALSE SPEAKING IN TONGUES. The mere occurrence of speaking in "other tongues," or any other supernatural manifestation, is not uncontestable evidence of the work and presence of the Spirit. Speaking in tongues can be counterfeited by human initiative or demonic activity. The Bible cautions us not to believe every spirit, but to examine whether our spiritual experiences really do come from God (see 1 Jn 4:1, note).

(1) In order to be valid, speaking in tongues must be "as the Spirit enabled" (Ac 2:4). To follow the norm in the book of Acts, speaking in tongues must be the *spontaneous* result of the initial filling of the Holy Spirit. It is not a learned phenomenon, nor can it be taught by instructing believers to speak incoherent syllables.

(2) The Holy Spirit explicitly warns that in the last days there will be within the church hypocrisy (1Ti 4:1–2), signs and wonders from satanic powers (Mt 7:22–23; cf. 2Th 2:9), and deceitful workers disguising themselves as God's servants (2Co 11:13–15). We must heed these warnings about counterfeit spiritual manifestations and signs (Mt 7:22–23; 2Th 2:8–10).

(3) In order to discern whether our speaking in tongues is genuine, i.e., truly from the Holy Spirit, we must look for the Biblically defined results of the baptism in the Spirit (see article on TESTING FOR GENUINE BAPTISM IN THE SPIRIT, p. 1668). If someone claiming to speak in tongues is not committed to Christ and the authority of Scripture, and is not attempting to obey God's Word, whatever manifestations he or she may have are not from the Spirit (1Jn 3:6–10; 4:1–3; cf. Mt 24:11,24; Jn 8:31; Gal 1:9, note).

7Utterly amazed,[z] they asked: "Are
not all these men who are speaking
Galileans?[a] 8Then how is it that each
of us hears them in his own native language? 9Parthians, Medes and Elamites; residents of Mesopotamia, Judea
and Cappadocia,[b] Pontus[c] and
Asia,[d] 10Phrygia[e] and Pamphylia,[f]
Egypt and the parts of Libya near Cyrene;[g] visitors from Rome 11(both Jews
and converts to Judaism); Cretans and
Arabs—we hear them declaring the
wonders of God in our own tongues!"
12Amazed and perplexed, they asked
one another, "What does this mean?"
13Some, however, made fun of them
and said, "They have had too much
wine.[g]"[h]

2:7 [z]ver 12 [a]Ac 1:11
2:9 [b]1Pe 1:1 [c]Ac 18:2; 1Pe 1:1 [d]Ac 16:6; 19:10; Ro 16:5; 1Co 16:19; 2Co 1:8; Rev 1:4
2:10 [e]Ac 16:6; 18:23 [f]Ac 13:13; 14:24; 15:38 [g]S Mt 27:32
2:13 [h]1Co 14:23; Eph 5:18
2:15 [i]1Th 5:7
2:17 [j]Nu 11:25; Isa 44:3; Eze 39:29; Jn 7:37-39; Ac 10:45

Peter Explains the Coming of the Spirit

14Then Peter stood up with the Elev-
en, raised his voice and addressed the
crowd: "Fellow Jews and all of you who
live in Jerusalem, let me explain this to
you; listen carefully to what I say.
15These men are not drunk, as you
suppose. It's only nine in the morning![i] 16No, this is what was spoken by
the prophet Joel:

17" 'In the last days, God says,
I will pour out my Spirit on all
people.[j]

[g] 13 Or *sweet wine*

2:13 WINE. "Sweet wine" (Gk *gleukos*; see NIV footnote) normally refers to unfermented grape juice. Those mocking the disciples may have used this term rather than the common NT word for wine (*oinos*) because they believed that Jesus' disciples used only this type of wine. In this case, their mockery would have been spoken in sarcasm.

2:14–40 PETER'S PENTECOST SERMON. Peter's sermon at Pentecost, along with his message in 3:11–26, contains a pattern for the proclamation of the gospel.

(1) Jesus is both Lord and Christ—crucified, resurrected and exalted (vv. 22–36; 3:13–15).

(2) Now at the right hand of his Father, Jesus Christ has received the authority to pour out the Holy Spirit on all believers (vv. 16–18,32–33; 3:19).

(3) Everyone must place his or her faith in Jesus as Lord, repent of sin and be baptized in connection with forgiveness of sins (vv. 36–38; 3:19).

(4) Believers must expect the promised gift of or baptism in the Holy Spirit after faith and repentance (vv. 38–39).

(5) Those who hear in faith must separate themselves from the world and be saved from this corrupt generation (v. 40; 3:26).

(6) Jesus Christ will return to restore God's kingdom completely (3:20–21).

2:16 SPOKEN BY THE PROPHET JOEL. The baptism in the Holy Spirit and the accompanying spiritual manifestations are a fulfillment of Joel 2:28–29 (see notes on that passage).

2:17 THE LAST DAYS. (1) In the OT "the last days" were considered the time when the Lord would act in a mighty way to judge evil and bring salvation to his people (cf. Isa 2:2–21; 3:18—4:6; 10:20–23; Hos 1–2; Joel 1–3; Am 8:9–11; 9:9–12). (2) The NT reveals that "the last days" began with the first coming of Christ and the initial outpouring of the Spirit on God's people, and that the last days will end with the Lord's second coming (Mk 1:15; Lk 4:18–21; Heb 1:1–2). This specific time is characterized as the age of judgment against evil, authority over demons, salvation for the human race and the presence of the kingdom of God.

(a) These "last days" will be carried on by the power of the Spirit (Mt 12:28).

(b) "The last days" involve the invasion of God's power through Christ into the realm of Satan and sin. Yet the warfare has only begun; it is not yet consummated, for evil and satanic activity are still present in a mighty way (Eph 6:10–18). Only the second coming of Jesus will bring to an end the activity of evil forces and complete "the last days" (cf. 1Pe 1:3–5; Rev 19).

(c) "The last days" constitute a time of prophetic witness calling everyone to repent, believe in Christ and experience the outpouring of the Holy Spirit (1:8; 2:4,38–40; Joel 2:28–32). We must proclaim the saving work of Christ through the power of the Spirit, even as we anticipate the final day of wrath (Ro 2:5), i.e., "the great and glorious day of the Lord" (2:20b). We must live every day alertly, waiting for the day of redemption and the return of Christ for his people (Jn 14:3; 1Th 4:15–17).

(d) "The last days" inaugurate the kingdom of God, which now comes with all power (see Lk 11:20, note; see article on THE KINGDOM OF GOD, p. 1430). We must experience the fullness of that power as we face spiritual warfare (2Co 10:3–5; Eph 6:11–12) and suffering because of righteousness (Mt 5:10–12; 1Pe 1:6–7).

2:17 SONS AND DAUGHTERS WILL PROPHESY. Peter associates the speaking in other tongues (vv. 4,11) with prophecy (vv. 17–18). Thus, speaking in other tongues is considered one form of prophesying. The essential meaning of prophecy is using one's voice for the service and glory of God under the direct initiation of the Holy Spirit. In the book of Acts: (1) the 120 "were filled with the Holy Spirit and began to speak in other tongues as the Spirit enabled them" (2:4); (2) the Holy Spirit came on Cornelius and his household, and Peter "heard them speaking in tongues and praising God" (10:44–47); and (3) the disciples at Ephesus, when "the Holy Spirit came on them, . . . spoke in tongues and prophesied" (19:6).

Your sons and daughters will
prophesy,[k]
your young men will see visions,
your old men will dream dreams.
18Even on my servants, both men
and women,
I will pour out my Spirit in
those days,
and they will prophesy.[l]
19I will show wonders in the heaven
above
and signs on the earth below,[m]
blood and fire and billows of
smoke.
20The sun will be turned to darkness
and the moon to blood[n]
before the coming of the great
and glorious day of the
Lord.
21And everyone who calls
on the name of the Lord[o] will
be saved.'[h][p]

22"Men of Israel, listen to this: Jesus
of Nazareth[q] was a man accredited by
God to you by miracles, wonders and
signs,[r] which God did among you
through him,[s] as you yourselves
know. 23This man was handed over to
you by God's set purpose and foreknowledge;[t] and you, with the help of
wicked men,[i] put him to death by nailing him to the cross.[u] 24But God
raised him from the dead,[v] freeing
him from the agony of death, because
it was impossible for death to keep
its hold on him.[w] 25David said about
him:

" 'I saw the Lord always before
me.
Because he is at my right hand,
I will not be shaken.
26Therefore my heart is glad and my
tongue rejoices;
my body also will live in hope,
27because you will not abandon me
to the grave,
nor will you let your Holy One
see decay.[x]
28You have made known to me the
paths of life;
you will fill me with joy in your
presence.'[j][y]

29"Brothers,[z] I can tell you confidently that the patriarch[a] David died
and was buried,[b] and his tomb is
here[c] to this day. 30But he was a
prophet and knew that God had promised him on oath that he would place
one of his descendants on his throne.[d]
31Seeing what was ahead, he spoke of
the resurrection of the Christ,[k] that he
was not abandoned to the grave, nor
did his body see decay.[e] 32God has
raised this Jesus to life,[f] and we are
all witnesses[g] of the fact. 33Exalted[h]
to the right hand of God,[i] he has received from the Father[j] the promised
Holy Spirit[k] and has poured out[l]
what you now see and hear. 34For David did not ascend to heaven, and yet
he said,

" 'The Lord said to my Lord:
"Sit at my right hand
35until I make your enemies
a footstool for your feet." '[l][m]

36"Therefore let all Israel be assured of this: God has made this Jesus,
whom you crucified, both Lord[n] and
Christ."[o]

The Spirit Is for All Believers

37When the people heard this, they

2:17 [k]S Ac 21:9
2:18 [l]Ac 21:9-12
2:19 [m]Lk 21:11
2:20 [n]S Mt 24:29
2:21 [o]Ge 4:26; 26:25; Ps 105:1; Ac 9:14; 1Co 1:2; 2Ti 2:22 [p]Joel 2:28-32; Ro 10:13
2:22 [q]S Mk 1:24 [r]S Jn 4:48 [s]S Jn 3:2
2:23 [t]Isa 53:10; Ac 3:18; 4:28 [u]Mt 16:21; Lk 24:20; Ac 3:13
2:24 [v]ver 32; Ac 13:30,33,34, 37; 17:31; Ro 6:4; 8:11; 10:9; 1Co 6:14; 15:15; Eph 1:20; Col 2:12; Heb 13:20; 1Pe 1:21 [w]Jn 20:9
2:27 [x]ver 31; Ac 13:35
2:28 [y]Ps 16:8-11
2:29 [z]S Ac 22:5 [a]Ac 7:8,9 [b]Ac 13:36; 1Ki 2:10 [c]Ne 3:16
2:30 [d]S Mt 1:1
2:31 [e]Ps 16:10
2:32 [f]S ver 24 [g]S Lk 24:48
2:33 [h]S Php 2:9 [i]S Mk 16:19 [j]Ac 1:4 [k]Jn 7:39; 14:26; 15:26 [l]Ac 10:45
2:35 [m]Ps 110:1; S Mt 22:44
2:36 [n]S Mt 28:18 [o]S Lk 2:11

h *21* Joel 2:28-32 i *23* Or *of those not having the law* (that is, Gentiles) j *28* Psalm 16:8-11 k *31* Or *Messiah.* "The Christ" (Greek) and "the Messiah" (Hebrew) both mean "the Anointed One"; also in verse 36. l *35* Psalm 110:1

2:18 MY SERVANTS, BOTH MEN AND WOMEN. According to Joel's prophecy, applied by Peter, the baptism in the Holy Spirit is for those already in God's kingdom—i.e., believers, or God's servants, both men and women, who are saved and regenerated and who belong to God.

2:18 IN THOSE DAYS. Peter, quoting Joel, says that God will pour out his Spirit *in those days*. The outpouring of the Holy Spirit and the accompanying supernatural signs cannot be limited to just the one "day" of Pentecost. The power and blessing of the Spirit is for every Christian to have and experience throughout the church age, i.e., the entire period of time between Christ's first and second coming (Rev 19–20; see Ac 2:39, note).

2:33 THE RIGHT HAND OF GOD. The pouring out of the Holy Spirit by Jesus proves that he is indeed the exalted Messiah, now sitting at the right hand of God and interceding for his representatives on earth (Heb 7:25). (1) From Jesus' baptism onward the Spirit was fully on him as the Christ (i.e., the one anointed by the Spirit; cf. Lk 3:21–22; 4:1,14,18–19). Now at the right hand of God, he lives to pour out the same Spirit on those who believe in him (see article on JESUS AND THE HOLY SPIRIT, p. 1546). (2) In pouring out the Spirit, Jesus intends that the Spirit will mediate Jesus' presence to believers and empower them to continue to do all that he did while on earth.

were cut to the heart and said to Peter
and the other apostles, "Brothers,
what shall we do?"[p]
38Peter replied, "Repent and be baptized,[q] every one of you, in the name
of Jesus Christ for the forgiveness of
your sins.[r] And you will receive the
gift of the Holy Spirit.[s] 39The promise
is for you and your children[t] and for
all who are far off[u]—for all whom the
Lord our God will call."
40With many other words he warned
them; and he pleaded with them, "Save
yourselves from this corrupt generation."[v] 41Those who accepted his
message were baptized, and about
three thousand were added to their
number[w] that day.

The Fellowship of the Believers

42They devoted themselves to the
apostles' teaching[x] and to the fellowship, to the breaking of bread[y] and to
prayer.[z] 43Everyone was filled with
awe, and many wonders and miraculous signs were done by the apostles.[a]
44All the believers were together and
had everything in common.[b] 45Selling
their possessions and goods, they gave
to anyone as he had need.[c] 46Every
day they continued to meet together in
the temple courts.[d] They broke
bread[e] in their homes and ate together with glad and sincere hearts,
47praising God and enjoying the favor
of all the people.[f] And the Lord added
to their number[g] daily those who were
being saved. Ro 15:5-11

Peter Heals the Crippled Beggar

3 One day Peter and John[h] were going up to the temple[i] at the time
of prayer—at three in the afternoon.[j]
2Now a man crippled from birth[k] was
being carried to the temple gate[l]
called Beautiful, where he was put every day to beg[m] from those going into
the temple courts. 3When he saw Peter
and John about to enter, he asked them
for money. 4Peter looked straight at
him, as did John. Then Peter said,
"Look at us!" 5So the man gave them
his attention, expecting to get something from them.
6Then Peter said, "Silver or gold I do
not have, but what I have I give you. In

2:37 [p] Lk 3:10,12, 14; Ac 16:30
2:38 [q] ver 41; Ac 8:12,16,36,38; 9:18; 10:48; 16:15,33; 19:5; 22:16; Col 2:12 [r] Jer 36:3; Mk 1:4; S Lk 24:47; Ac 3:19 [s] S Jn 20:22
2:39 [t] Isa 44:3; 65:23 [u] Isa 57:19; Ac 10:45; Eph 2:13
2:40 [v] Dt 32:5; Php 2:15
2:41 [w] ver 47; Ac 4:4; 5:14; 6:1, 7; 9:31,35,42; 11:21,24; 14:1,21; 16:5; 17:12
2:42 [x] Mt 28:20 [y] S Mt 14:19 [z] S Ac 1:14
2:43 [a] Ac 5:12
2:44 [b] Ac 4:32
2:45 [c] Mt 19:21; Lk 12:33; 18:22; Ac 4:34,35; 6:1
2:46 [d] Lk 24:53; Ac 3:1; 5:21,42 [e] ver 42; S Mt 14:19
2:47 [f] S Ro 14:18 [g] S ver 41
3:1 [h] S Lk 22:8 [i] Ac 2:46 [j] Ps 55:17; Ac 10:30
3:2 [k] Ac 14:8 [l] Lk 16:20 [m] Jn 9:8

2:38 REPENT AND BE BAPTIZED. Repentance, forgiveness of sins and baptism are the prior conditions for receiving the gift of the Holy Spirit. However, Peter's demand that his hearers be baptized in water before receiving the promise of the Father (cf. 1:4,8) must not be taken as an absolute requirement for the infilling with the Spirit, nor is baptism in the Spirit an automatic consequence of water baptism.

(1) In this situation, Peter required water baptism prior to receiving the promise because in the minds of his Jewish listeners, the rite of baptism was taken for granted as being involved in any conversion decision. Water baptism did not precede the baptism in the Spirit, however, in the instances recorded in 9:17–18 (the apostle Paul) and 10:44–48 (those in Cornelius's house).

(2) Each believer, after repenting of his or her sins and accepting Jesus Christ by faith, must "receive" (cf. Gal 3:14) a personal baptism in the Spirit. The gift of the Spirit in the book of Acts was consciously desired, sought and appropriated (1:4, 14; 4:31; 8:14–17; 19:2–6); the only possible exception to the rule in the NT was the case of Cornelius (10:44–48). Consequently, the baptism in the Spirit should not be considered as a gift automatically provided to the believer in Christ.

2:39 FOR YOU AND YOUR CHILDREN AND FOR ALL. The promise of the baptism in the Holy Spirit was not just for those present on the day of Pentecost (v. 4), but for all who would believe in Christ throughout this age: "for you"—Peter's audience; "your children"—the next generation; "for all who are far off"—the third and subsequent generations. (1) The baptism in the Spirit with its accompanying power was not a once-for-all occurrence in the church's history. It did not cease with Pentecost (cf. v. 38; 8:15; 9:17; 10:44–46; 19:6), nor with the close of the apostolic age. (2) It is the birthright of every Christian to seek, expect and experience the same baptism in the Spirit that was promised and given to the NT Christians (1:4,8; Joel 2:28; Mt 3:11; Lk 24:49).

2:40 THIS CORRUPT GENERATION. No one can be saved who does not turn away from the corruption of present society (cf. Lk 9:41; 11:29; 17:25; Php 2:15). New Christians should be taught to break off from all evil companions, forsake the ungodly world, unite themselves to Christ and his people, and give themselves to God's work (2Co 6:14,17).

2:42 APOSTLES' TEACHING . . . FELLOWSHIP . . . BREAKING OF BREAD . . . PRAYER. See 12:5, note on the 16 characteristics of a NT church.

3:6 IN THE NAME OF JESUS . . . WALK. The healing of the crippled beggar was done by the power of Christ working through his apostles. Jesus said to his followers concerning those who would believe in him: "In my name . . . they will place their hands on sick people, and they will get well" (Mk 16:17–18). The church continued Jesus' healing ministry in obedience to his will. The miracle was accomplished through faith "in the name of Jesus Christ" and "gifts of healing" operating through Peter (see 1Co 12:1,9).

Peter stated that he had no silver or gold, but would give the crippled beggar something much

the name of Jesus Christ of Nazareth,[n] walk." **7**Taking him by the right hand, he helped him up, and instantly the man's feet and ankles became strong. **8**He jumped to his feet and began to walk. Then he went with them into the temple courts, walking and jumping,[o] and praising God. **9**When all the people[p] saw him walking and praising God, **10**they recognized him as the same man who used to sit begging at the temple gate called Beautiful,[q] and they were filled with wonder and
Ac 5:15-16 amazement at what had happened to him.

Peter Speaks to the Onlookers

11While the beggar held on to Peter and John,[r] all the people were astonished and came running to them in the place called Solomon's Colonnade.[s] **12**When Peter saw this, he said to them: "Men of Israel, why does this surprise you? Why do you stare at us as if by our own power or godliness we had made this man walk? **13**The God of Abraham, Isaac and Jacob,[t] the God of our fathers,[u] has glorified his servant Jesus. You handed him over[v] to be killed, and you disowned him before Pilate,[w] though he had decided to let him go.[x] **14**You disowned the Holy[y] and Righteous One[z] and asked that a murderer be released to you.[a] **15**You killed the author of life, but God raised him from the dead.[b] We are witnesses[c] of this. **16**By faith in the name of Jesus,[d] this man whom you see and know was made strong. It is Jesus' name and the faith that comes through him that has given this complete healing to him, as you can all see.

17"Now, brothers,[e] I know that you acted in ignorance,[f] as did your leaders.[g] **18**But this is how God fulfilled[h] what he had foretold[i] through all the prophets,[j] saying that his Christ[m] would suffer.[k] **19**Repent, then, and turn to God, so that your sins may be wiped out,[l] that times of refreshing may come from the Lord, **20**and that he may send the Christ,[m] who has been appointed for you—even Jesus. **21**He must remain in heaven[n] until the time comes for God to restore everything,[o] as he promised long ago through his holy prophets.[p] **22**For Moses said, 'The Lord your God will raise up for you a prophet like me from among your own people; you must listen to every-

3:6 [n] ver 16; S Mk 1:24 **3:8** [o] Isa 35:6; Ac 14:10 **3:9** [p] Ac 4:16,21 **3:10** [q] ver 2 **3:11** [r] S Lk 22:8 [s] Jn 10:23; Ac 5:12 **3:13** [t] Ex 3:6 [u] Ac 5:30; 7:32; 22:14 [v] Ac 2:23 [w] S Mt 27:2
[x] S Lk 23:4 **3:14** [y] S Mk 1:24; Ac 4:27 [z] Ac 7:52 [a] Mk 15:11; Lk 23:18-25 **3:15** [b] S Ac 2:24 [c] S Lk 24:48 **3:16** [d] ver 6 **3:17** [e] S Ac 22:5 [f] Lk 23:34 [g] Ac 13:27 **3:18** [h] S Mt 1:22 [i] Ac 2:23 [j] S Lk 24:27 [k] Ac 17:2,3; 26:22, 23 **3:19** [l] Ps 51:1; Isa 43:25; 44:22; S Ac 2:38 **3:20** [m] S Lk 2:11 **3:21** [n] Ac 1:11 [o] Mt 17:11; Ac 1:6 [p] Lk 1:70

[m] *18* Or *Messiah*; also in verse 20

more valuable. Churches that possess a fair degree of material prosperity should ponder these words of Peter. Many churches today can no longer say "Silver and gold I do not have," nor do they seem capable of saying, "In the name of Jesus Christ of Nazareth, walk."

3:19 REPENT . . . AND TURN TO GOD. God has chosen to bless his people with the outpouring of the Holy Spirit only on the conditions of repentance, i.e., turning from sin and the unrighteous ways of their surrounding corrupt generation, and conversion, i.e., turning to God, listening to everything that Christ, the prophet, tells them (vv. 22–23), and always moving toward sincere obedience to Christ (cf. 2:38–41; 5:29–32).

3:19 TIMES OF REFRESHING. Throughout this present age and until Christ's return, God will send "times of refreshing" (i.e., the outpouring of the Holy Spirit) to all who repent and are converted. Although perilous times will come toward the end of this age and a great falling away from the faith will occur (2Th 2:3; 2Ti 3:1), God still promises to send revival and times of refreshing on the faithful. Christ's presence, spiritual blessings, miracles and outpourings of the Spirit will come on the remnant who faithfully seek him and overcome the world, the sinful nature and Satan's dominion (cf. 26:18).

3:21 TIME COMES FOR GOD TO RESTORE EVERYTHING. Christ will return from heaven to put down evil and establish the kingdom of God on earth free from all sin. Ultimately all things prophesied in the OT to be restored (cf. Zec 12–14; Lk 1:32–33) will be restored. Christ will redeem or renovate all nature (Ro 8:18–23) and reign personally on the earth (see Rev 20–21). Note that not people on earth but Christ and the armies from heaven will bring in the triumph of God and his kingdom (Rev 19:11—20:9).

3:22 A PROPHET. Moses' prediction in Dt 18:18–19 that "the Lord your God will raise up for you a prophet like me" was a prophecy concerning Jesus Christ. In what way was Jesus like Moses? (1) Moses was anointed by the Spirit (Nu 11:17); the Spirit of the Lord was on Jesus to preach the gospel (Lk 4:18–19). (2) God used Moses to initiate the old covenant; Jesus brought in the new covenant. (3) Moses led Israel out of Egypt to Sinai and established the covenant relationship with God; Christ redeemed his people from sin and satanic bondage and established a new, living relationship with God whereby his people might enter the very presence of God. (4) Moses in the OT laws referred to the sacrifice of a lamb to bring redemption; Christ himself became the Lamb of God to give salvation to all who accept him. (5) Moses faithfully pointed to the law and the obligation of God's people to obey its commands in order to receive God's blessing; Christ pointed to himself and the Holy Spirit as God's way of fulfilling his will and receiving God's blessing and eternal life.

thing he tells you.[q] 23Anyone who does not listen to him will be completely cut off from among his people.'[n][r]

24"Indeed, all the prophets[s] from Samuel on, as many as have spoken, have foretold these days. 25And you are heirs[t] of the prophets and of the covenant[u] God made with your fathers. He said to Abraham, 'Through your offspring all peoples on earth will be blessed.'[o][v] 26When God raised up[w] his servant, he sent him first[x] to you to bless you by turning each of you from your wicked ways."

Peter and John Before the Sanhedrin

4 The priests and the captain of the temple guard[y] and the Sadducees[z] came up to Peter and John while they were speaking to the people. 2They were greatly disturbed because the apostles were teaching the people and proclaiming in Jesus the resurrection of the dead.[a] 3They seized Peter and John, and because it was evening, they put them in jail[b] until the next day. 4But many who heard the message believed, and the number of men grew[c] to about five thousand.

5The next day the rulers,[d] elders and teachers of the law met in Jerusalem. 6Annas the high priest was there, and so were Caiaphas,[e] John, Alexander and the other men of the high priest's family. 7They had Peter and John brought before them and began to question them: "By what power or what name did you do this?"

8Then Peter, filled with the Holy Spirit,[f] said to them: "Rulers and elders of the people![g] 9If we are being called to account today for an act of kindness shown to a cripple[h] and are asked how he was healed, 10then know this, you and all the people of Israel: It is by the name of Jesus Christ of Nazareth,[i] whom you crucified but whom God raised from the dead,[j] that this man stands before you healed. 11He is

" 'the stone you builders rejected,
which has become the
capstone.[p]'[q][k]

12Salvation is found in no one else, for there is no other name under heaven given to men by which we must be saved."[l] (Ac 13:38-39)

13When they saw the courage of Peter and John[m] and realized that they were unschooled, ordinary men,[n] they were astonished and they took note that these men had been with Jesus.[o] 14But since they could see the man who had been healed standing there with them, there was nothing they could say. 15So they ordered them to withdraw from the Sanhedrin[p] and then conferred together. 16"What are we going to do with these men?"[q] they asked. "Everybody living in Jerusalem knows they have done an outstanding miracle,[r] and we cannot deny it. 17But to stop this thing from spreading any further among the people, we must warn these men to speak no longer to anyone in this name."

18Then they called them in again and commanded them not to speak or teach at all in the name of Jesus.[s] 19But Peter and John replied, "Judge for yourselves whether it is right in God's sight to obey you rather than God.[t] 20For we cannot help speaking[u] about what we have seen and heard."[v] (Ac 4:33)

21After further threats they let them

3:22 [q]Dt 18:15,18; Ac 7:37
3:23 [r]Dt 18:19
3:24 [s]S Lk 24:27
3:25 [t]Ac 2:39 [u]Ro 9:4,5 [v]Ge 12:3; 22:18; 26:4; 28:14
3:26 [w]ver 22; S Ac 2:24 [x]Ac 13:46; Ro 1:16
4:1 [y]Lk 22:4 [z]Mt 3:7; 16:1,6; 22:23,34; Ac 5:17; 23:6-8
4:2 [a]Ac 17:18
4:3 [b]Ac 5:18
4:4 [c]S Ac 2:41
4:5 [d]Lk 23:13
4:6 [e]S Mt 26:3
4:8 [f]S Lk 1:15 [g]ver 5; Lk 23:13
4:9 [h]Ac 3:6
4:10 [i]S Mk 1:24 [j]S Ac 2:24
4:11 [k]Ps 118:22; Isa 28:16; Zec 10:4; Mt 21:42; Eph 2:20; 1Pe 2:7
4:12 [l]S Mt 1:21; Jn 14:6; Ac 10:43; S Ro 11:14; 1Ti 2:5
4:13 [m]S Lk 22:8 [n]Mt 11:25 [o]Mk 3:14
4:15 [p]S Mt 5:22
4:16 [q]Jn 11:47 [r]Ac 3:6-10
4:18 [s]Am 7:13; Ac 5:40
4:19 [t]Ac 5:29
4:20 [u]Job 32:18; Jer 20:9; Am 3:8 [v]S Lk 24:48

[n] *23* Deut. 18:15,18,19 [o] *25* Gen. 22:18; 26:4 [p] *11* Or *cornerstone* [q] *11* Psalm 118:22

3:26 TURNING ... FROM YOUR WICKED WAYS. Peter once again emphasizes that believing in Christ and receiving the baptism in the Holy Spirit are conditioned on turning from sin and being separated from evil (see 2:38,40, notes; 3:19, note; 8:21, note). In the original apostolic message, there was no promised blessing without holiness.

4:8 PETER, FILLED WITH THE HOLY SPIRIT. Peter received a fresh filling with the Holy Spirit that brought a sudden inspiration, wisdom and boldness by which to proclaim the truth of God. It is theologically significant that the filling with the Spirit was not a one-time experience, but a repetitive one. This episode is a fulfillment of Jesus' promise in Lk 12:11–12; other instances of renewed fillings can be found in Ac 7:55 and 13:9.

4:12 SALVATION ... IN NO ONE ELSE. The disciples were convinced that the greatest need of every individual was salvation from sin and the wrath of God, and they preached that this need could be met by no one other than the person of Jesus Christ. This truth reveals the exclusive nature of the gospel and the church's heavy responsibility of preaching the gospel to every person. If there were other ways of salvation, the church could be at ease. But according to Christ himself (Jn 14:6), there is no hope for anyone apart from salvation through Christ (cf. 10:43; 1Ti 2:5–6). This is the basis for the missionary imperative.

go. They could not decide how to punish them, because all the people[w]
were praising God[x] for what had happened. 22For the man who was miraculously healed was over forty years old.

The Believers' Prayer

23On their release, Peter and John
went back to their own people and reported all that the chief priests and elders had said to them. 24When they
heard this, they raised their voices together in prayer to God.[y] "Sovereign
Lord," they said, "you made the heaven
and the earth and the sea, and everything in them.[z] 25You spoke by the
Holy Spirit through the mouth of your
servant, our father David:[a]

" 'Why do the nations rage
and the peoples plot in vain?
26The kings of the earth take their
stand
and the rulers gather together
against the Lord
and against his Anointed
One.[r][s][b]

27Indeed Herod[c] and Pontius Pilate[d]
met together with the Gentiles and the
people[t] of Israel in this city to conspire against your holy servant
Jesus,[e] whom you anointed. 28They
did what your power and will had decided beforehand should happen.[f]
29Now, Lord, consider their threats
and enable your servants to speak your
word with great boldness.[g] 30Stretch
out your hand to heal and perform miraculous signs and wonders[h] through
the name of your holy servant Jesus."[i]
31After they prayed, the place where
they were meeting was shaken.[j] And
they were all filled with the Holy Spirit[k] and spoke the word of God[l] boldly.[m]

The Believers Share Their Possessions

32All the believers were one in heart
and mind. No one claimed that any of

4:21 [w]Ac 5:26 [x]S Mt 9:8 **4:24** [y]S Ac 1:14 [z]Ne 9:6; Job 41:11; Isa 37:16 **4:25** [a]Ac 1:16 **4:26** [b]Ps 2:1,2; Da 9:25; Lk 4:18; Ac 10:38; Heb 1:9
4:27 [c]S Mt 14:1 [d]S Mt 27:2; Lk 23:12 [e]ver 30; Ac 3:13,14 **4:28** [f]Ac 2:23 **4:29** [g]ver 13,31; Ps 138:3; Ac 9:27; 13:46; 14:3; 28:31; Eph 6:19; Php 1:14 **4:30** [h]S Jn 4:48 [i]ver 27 **4:31** [j]Ac 2:2 [k]S Lk 1:15 [l]S Heb 4:12 [m]S ver 29

[r]*26* That is, Christ or Messiah [s]*26* Psalm 2:1,2 [t]*27* The Greek is plural.

4:20 WE CANNOT HELP SPEAKING. The Holy Spirit created in the apostles an overwhelming desire to proclaim the gospel. Throughout the book of Acts the Spirit impelled believers to carry the gospel to others (1:8; 2:14–41; 3:12–26; 8:25, 35; 9:15; 10:44–48; 13:1–4).

4:29 SERVANTS TO SPEAK ... WITH GREAT BOLDNESS. The disciples needed renewed courage to witness and speak for Christ. Throughout our Christian life, we too need to pray in order to overcome our fear of embarrassment, rejection, criticism or persecution. God's grace, through fillings of the Holy Spirit, will help us speak about Jesus with boldness (cf. Mt 10:32).

4:30 HEAL AND PERFORM MIRACULOUS SIGNS AND WONDERS. Preaching and miracles belong together (3:1–10; 4:8–22,29–33; 5:12–16; 6:7–8; 8:6ff; 15:12; 20:7ff). Miracles are accompanying signs by which Christ confirms the word of witnesses (14:3; cf. Mk 16:20). (1) "Miraculous signs" generally refer to deeds performed in order to certify the existence of a divine power, to give warning or to encourage faith. (2) "Wonders" refer to unusual events that cause the observer to marvel. Note that the church is *praying* that healings, miraculous signs and wonders will take place. As it faces the challenge of the last days, the church today needs to pray earnestly that God will confirm the gospel with great power, miracles and abundant grace (v. 33). Only when we proclaim the gospel in the power of the NT witness will we be able to reach this lost generation for Christ.

4:31 THEY WERE ALL FILLED WITH THE HOLY SPIRIT. Several important truths stand out here. (1) The term "baptized with [or in] the Holy Spirit" (see 1:5, note) describes the consecrating work of the Holy Spirit in initiating the believer into divine power for witness. The terms "filled," "clothed" and "empowered" describe his actual equipping them for ministry (2:4; 4:8,31; 9:17; 13:9,52). As need arises, the "filling" may be repeated.

(2) The terms "pouring out the Spirit" (2:17–18; 10:45), "receiving the gift of the Holy Spirit" (2:38; 8:15), "coming of the Spirit on" (8:16; 10:44; 11:15; 19:6) are different expressions for the occasion when believers are "filled with the Holy Spirit" (2:4; 4:31; 9:17).

(3) All the believers, including the apostles who had been previously filled (2:4), are freshly filled to meet the continuing opposition of the Jews (v. 29). Fresh fillings with the Holy Spirit are part of God's will and provision for all who have received the baptism in the Holy Spirit (cf. v. 8, note; 13:52). We should expect and seek those fillings.

(4) The Spirit here visits a whole congregation. Therefore, to fulfill God's will for the church, not only must individuals be filled with the Spirit (v. 8; 9:17; 13:9), but entire congregations (2:4; 4:31; 13:53) should experience repeated visitations of the Holy Spirit when special needs and challenges are present.

(5) God's moving upon the entire congregation with a renewed filling of the Holy Spirit results in boldness and power in witness, love for one another and abundant grace for all.

4:31 SPOKE THE WORD OF GOD BOLDLY. The inner power of the Spirit and the reality of God's presence brought about by the filling of the Spirit frees the believer from fear of others and greatly increases the courage to speak out for God.

his possessions was his own, but they
shared everything they had.[n] 33With
great power the apostles continued to
testify[o] to the resurrection[p] of the
Lord Jesus, and much grace[q] was
upon them all. 34There were no needy
persons among them. For from time to
time those who owned lands or houses
sold them,[r] brought the money from
the sales 35and put it at the apostles'
feet,[s] and it was distributed to anyone
as he had need.[t]

36Joseph, a Levite from Cyprus,
whom the apostles called Barnabas[u]
(which means Son of Encouragement),
37sold a field he owned and brought the
money and put it at the apostles'
feet.[v]

Ananias and Sapphira

5 Now a man named Ananias, together with his wife Sapphira, also
sold a piece of property. 2With his
wife's full knowledge he kept back part
of the money for himself,[w] but brought
the rest and put it at the apostles'
feet.[x]

3Then Peter said, "Ananias, how is
it that Satan[y] has so filled your
heart[z] that you have lied to the Holy
Spirit[a] and have kept for yourself
some of the money you received for the
land?[b] 4Didn't it belong to you before
it was sold? And after it was sold,
wasn't the money at your disposal?[c]
What made you think of doing such a
thing? You have not lied to men but to
God."[d]

5When Ananias heard this, he fell
down and died.[e] And great fear[f]
seized all who heard what had hap- Ac 16:16-18
pened. 6Then the young men came forward, wrapped up his body,[g] and carried him out and buried him.

7About three hours later his wife
came in, not knowing what had happened. 8Peter asked her, "Tell me, is
this the price you and Ananias got for
the land?"

"Yes," she said, "that is the price."[h]

9Peter said to her, "How could you
agree to test the Spirit of the Lord?[i]
Look! The feet of the men who buried
your husband are at the door, and they
will carry you out also."

10At that moment she fell down at
his feet and died.[j] Then the young
men came in and, finding her dead, carried her out and buried her beside her
husband.[k] 11Great fear[l] seized the
whole church and all who heard about
these events.

4:32 [n] Ac 2:44
4:33 [o] S Lk 24:48 [p] Ac 1:22 [q] S Ro 3:24
4:34 [r] Mt 19:21; Ac 2:45
4:35 [s] ver 37; Ac 5:2 [t] Ac 2:45; 6:1
4:36 [u] Ac 9:27; 11:22,30; 13:2; 1Co 9:6; Gal 2:1,9, 13
4:37 [v] ver 35; Ac 5:2
5:2 [w] Jos 7:11 [x] Ac 4:35,37
5:3 [y] S Mt 4:10 [z] Jn 13:2,27 [a] ver 9
[b] Dt 23:21
5:4 [c] Dt 23:22 [d] Lev 6:2
5:5 [e] ver 10; Ps 5:6 [f] ver 11
5:6 [g] Jn 19:40
5:8 [h] ver 2
5:9 [i] ver 3
5:10 [j] ver 5 [k] ver 6
5:11 [l] ver 5; Ac 19:17

4:33 WITH GREAT POWER. "Great power" is the distinguishing characteristic of apostolic preaching and witness (cf. 1:8) for three reasons: (1) Apostolic witness was based on God's Word (v. 29) and the conviction that it was given by the inspiration of the Holy Spirit (see article on THE INSPIRATION AND AUTHORITY OF SCRIPTURE, p. 1898). (2) The disciples were conscious that they had been sent and commissioned by Jesus Christ himself, the resurrected Lord. (3) The Holy Spirit, through the disciples (v. 31), brought great conviction on those who heard the gospel concerning personal sin, Christ's righteousness and God's judgment (see Jn 16:8, note).

5:3 LIED TO THE HOLY SPIRIT. In order to gain glory and recognition, Ananias and Sapphira lied to the church about their giving. God considered this lie against the Holy Spirit a serious offense. The deaths of Ananias and Sapphira are intended to be standing examples of God's attitude toward any deceitful heart among those who profess to be born-again, Spirit-filled believers. Notice too that lying to the Holy Spirit is the same as lying to God (vv. 3–4; see Rev 22:15, note; see article on THE DOCTRINE OF THE HOLY SPIRIT, p. 1654).

5:4 WHAT MADE YOU THINK OF DOING SUCH A THING? The root of the sin of Ananias and Sapphira was their love for money and the praise of others. This set them against the Holy Spirit (v. 9). Once the love of money and human praise takes possession of a person, his or her spirit becomes open to all kinds of satanic evil (1Ti 6:10). A person cannot love money and at the same time love and serve God (Mt 6:24; Jn 5:41–44).

5:5 ANANIAS . . . FELL DOWN AND DIED. God harshly struck down Ananias and Sapphira (vv. 5,10) in order to reveal his hatred of all deceit and dishonesty in the kingdom of God. One of the most abominable sins in the church is to deceive God's people about your relationship with Christ, your work for him and the extent of your ministry. To engage in this hypocrisy means using Christ's shed blood to glorify your own self before other people. This sin disregards the very purpose for which Christ suffered and died (Eph 1:4; Heb 13:12), indicating an absence of the fear of the Lord (vv. 5,11) and of respect and honor for the Holy Spirit (v. 3); it merits God's righteous judgment.

5:11 GREAT FEAR SEIZED THE WHOLE CHURCH. God's judgment on the sin of Ananias and Sapphira caused an increase in humility, awe and fear. Without a proper fear of the holy God and his wrath against sin, God's people will soon return to the ungodly ways of the world, cease to experience the outpouring of the Spirit and God's miraculous presence, and be cut off from the flow of God's grace. The fear of the Lord is an essential element in the NT faith and in Biblical Christianity today (see article on THE FEAR OF THE LORD, p. 260).

THE DOCTRINE OF THE HOLY SPIRIT

Ac 5:3–4 "Then Peter said, 'Ananias, how is it that Satan has so filled your heart that you have lied to the Holy Spirit and have kept for yourself some of the money you received for the land? Didn't it belong to you before it was sold? And after it was sold, wasn't the money at your disposal? What made you think of doing such a thing? You have not lied to men but to God.'"

It is essential that believers recognize the importance of the Holy Spirit in God's redemptive purpose. Many Christians have no idea what difference it would make if there were no Holy Spirit in this world. Without the Holy Spirit there would be no creation, no universe, no human race (Ge 1:2; Job 33:4). Without the Holy Spirit there would be no Bible (2Pe 1:21), no New Testament (Jn 14:26; 15:26–27; 1Co 2:10–14), no power to proclaim the gospel (Ac 1:8). Without the Holy Spirit there would be no faith, no new birth, no holiness, no Christians at all in the world. This article explores some of the basic teachings about the Holy Spirit.

THE PERSON OF THE HOLY SPIRIT. Throughout Scripture the Spirit is revealed as a person with an individuality all his own (2Co 3:17–18; Heb 9:14; 1Pe 1:2). He is a divine person like the Father and the Son. Thus we may never think of the Holy Spirit as a mere influence or power. He has personal characteristics, for he thinks (Ro 8:27), feels (Ro 15:30), wills (1Co 12:11), and has the capacity to love and to enjoy fellowship. He was sent by the Father to bring believers into the intimate presence and fellowship of Jesus (Jn 14:16–18,26; see article on JESUS AND THE HOLY SPIRIT, p. 1546). In the light of these truths we should treat him as a person and regard him as the infinite living God within our hearts, worthy of our worship, love and surrender (see Mk 1:11, note on the Trinity).

THE WORK OF THE HOLY SPIRIT. (1) Revelation about the Holy Spirit in the OT. For a description of the work of the Spirit of God in the OT, see article on THE SPIRIT IN THE OLD TESTAMENT, p. 1302.

(2) Revelation about the Holy Spirit in the NT. (a) The Holy Spirit is the agent of salvation, convicting us of guilt (Jn 16:7–8), revealing to us the truth about Jesus (Jn 14:16,26), giving us new birth (Jn 3:3–6) and incorporating us into the body of Christ (1Co 12:13). At conversion we receive the Spirit (Jn 3:3–6; 20:22) and become participants in the divine nature (2Pe 1:4; see article on THE REGENERATION OF THE DISCIPLES, p. 1627).

(b) The Holy Spirit is the agent of sanctification. At conversion believers are indwelt by the Holy Spirit and come under his sanctifying influence (Ro 8:9; 1Co 6:19). Notice some of the things the Spirit does as he lives in us. He sanctifies us, i.e., cleanses, leads and motivates us into holy lives, delivering us from sin's bondage (Ro 8:2–4; Gal 5:16–17; 2Th 2:13). He tells us that we are children of God (Ro 8:16), helps us in our worship of God (Ac 10:46) and in our prayer lives, and intercedes for us as we cry out to God (Ro 8:26–27). He produces Christlike graces of character that glorify Christ (Gal 5:22–23; 1Pe 1:2). He is our divine teacher, guiding us into all truth (Jn 16:13; 14:26; 1Co 2:9–16), disclosing Jesus to us and guiding us into close fellowship and oneness with Jesus (Jn 14:16–18; 16:14). He continually imparts God's love to us (Ro 5:5) and gives us joy, comfort and help (Jn 14:16; 1Th 1:6).

(c) The Holy Spirit is the agent of service, empowering believers for service and witness. This work of the Holy Spirit is related to the baptism in the Spirit or the fullness of the Spirit (see article on BAPTISM IN THE HOLY SPIRIT, p. 1642). When we are baptized in the Spirit, we receive power to witness for Christ and work effectively within the church and before the world (Ac 1:8). We receive the same divine anointing that descended on Christ (Jn 1:32–33) and on the disciples (Ac 2:4; see 1:5), enabling us to proclaim God's Word (Ac 1:8; 4:31) and work miracles (Ac 2:43; 3:2–8; 5:15; 6:8; 10:38). It is God's intended purpose that all Christians experience the baptism in the Holy Spirit throughout this age (Ac 2:39). In the area of service, the Holy Spirit gives spiritual gifts to individual members of the church to edify or strengthen the church (1Co 12–14). These gifts are a manifestation of the Spirit through individuals by which Christ's presence, love, truth and righteous standards are made real to the fellowship of believers for the common good (1Co 12:7–11).

(d) The Holy Spirit is the agent who incorporates believers into the one body of Christ (1Co 12:13), lives in the church (1Co 3:16), builds the church (Eph 2:22), inspires her worship (Php 3:3), directs her mission (Ac 13:2,4), appoints her workers (Ac 20:28), gives gifts to the church (1Co 12:1–11), anoints her preachers (Ac 2:4; 1 Cor 2:4), guards the gospel (2Ti 1:14) and promotes her righteousness (Jn 16:8; 1Co 3:16; 6:18–20).

(3) The various activities of the Spirit are complementary and not contradictory. At the same time, these facets of the Holy Spirit's work are interlocked and cannot be fully separated. We cannot experience (a) the fullness of new life in Christ, (b) righteousness as a way of living, (c) the power to witness for our Lord or (d) fellowship in his body without becoming involved in all four. For example, baptism in the Holy Spirit cannot be maintained independently of the Spirit's work of producing righteousness within us and leading us into the knowledge of and commitment to Biblical truth.

The Apostles Heal Many

12The apostles performed many miraculous signs and wonders[m] among the people. And all the believers used to meet together[n] in Solomon's Colonnade.[o] 13No one else dared join them, even though they were highly regarded by the people.[p] 14Nevertheless, more and more men and women believed in the Lord and were added to their number.[q] 15As a result, people brought the sick into the streets and laid them on beds and mats so that at least Peter's shadow might fall on some of them as he passed by.[r] 16Crowds gathered also from the towns around Jerusalem, bringing their sick and those tormented by evil[u] spirits, and all of them were healed.[s]

Ac 8:6-7

The Apostles Persecuted

17Then the high priest and all his associates, who were members of the party[t] of the Sadducees,[u] were filled with jealousy. 18They arrested the apostles and put them in the public jail.[v] 19But during the night an angel[w] of the Lord opened the doors of the jail[x] and brought them out.[y] 20"Go, stand in the temple courts," he said, "and tell the people the full message of this new life."[z]

21At daybreak they entered the temple courts, as they had been told, and began to teach the people.

When the high priest and his associates[a] arrived, they called together the Sanhedrin[b]—the full assembly of the elders of Israel—and sent to the jail for the apostles. 22But on arriving at the jail, the officers did not find them there.[c] So they went back and reported, 23"We found the jail securely locked, with the guards standing at the doors; but when we opened them, we found no one inside." 24On hearing this report, the captain of the temple guard and the chief priests[d] were puzzled, wondering what would come of this.

25Then someone came and said, "Look! The men you put in jail are standing in the temple courts teaching the people." 26At that, the captain went with his officers and brought the apostles. They did not use force, because they feared that the people[e] would stone them.

27Having brought the apostles, they made them appear before the Sanhedrin[f] to be questioned by the high priest. 28"We gave you strict orders not to teach in this name,"[g] he said. "Yet you have filled Jerusalem with your teaching and are determined to make us guilty of this man's blood."[h]

29Peter and the other apostles replied: "We must obey God rather than men![i] 30The God of our fathers[j] raised Jesus from the dead[k]—whom you had killed by hanging him on a tree.[l] 31God exalted him to his own right hand[m] as Prince and Savior[n] that he might give repentance and forgiveness of sins to Israel.[o] 32We are witnesses of these things,[p] and so is the Holy Spirit,[q] whom God has given to those who obey him."

33When they heard this, they were furious[r] and wanted to put them to death. 34But a Pharisee named Gamaliel,[s] a teacher of the law,[t] who was honored by all the people, stood up in the Sanhedrin and ordered that the men be put outside for a little while. 35Then he addressed them: "Men of Israel, consider carefully what you intend to do to these men. 36Some time ago Theudas appeared, claiming to be somebody, and about four hundred

5:12 [m]S Jn 4:48; Ac 2:43 [n]Ac 4:32 [o]Jn 10:23; Ac 3:11
5:13 [p]Ac 2:47; 4:21
5:14 [q]S Ac 2:41
5:15 [r]Ac 19:12
5:16 [s]Mt 8:16; S Mk 16:17
5:17 [t]Ac 15:5 [u]S Ac 4:1
5:18 [v]Ac 4:3
5:19 [w]Ge 16:7; Ex 3:2; Mt 1:20; 2:13,19; 28:2; Lk 1:11; 2:9; S Jn 20:12; Ac 8:26; 10:3; 12:7,23; 27:23 [x]Ac 16:26 [y]Ps 34:7
5:20 [z]Jn 6:63,68
5:21 [a]Ac 4:5,6 [b]ver 27,34,41; S Mt 5:22
5:22 [c]Ac 12:18, 19
5:24 [d]Ac 4:1
5:26 [e]Ac 4:21
5:27 [f]S Mt 5:22
5:28 [g]Ac 4:18 [h]Mt 23:35; 27:25; Ac 2:23,36; 3:14, 15; 7:52
5:29 [i]Ex 1:17; Ac 4:19
5:30 [j]S Ac 3:13 [k]S Ac 2:24 [l]Ac 10:39; 13:29; Gal 3:13
5:31 [m]S Mk 16:19 [n]S Lk 2:11 [o]S Mt 1:21; Mk 1:4; Lk 24:47; Ac 2:38; 3:19; 10:43
5:32 [p]S Lk 24:48 [q]Jn 15:26
5:33 [r]Ac 2:37; 7:54
5:34 [s]Ac 22:3 [t]Lk 2:46; 5:17

[u]16 Greek *unclean*

5:16 ALL OF THEM WERE HEALED. The apostles did as their Lord had done: they healed those tormented with evil spirits (see Mk 1:34). This was a paramount sign that the kingdom of God had come among the people with great power (see article on POWER OVER SATAN AND DEMONS, p. 1484). It is never wrong to pray that through the Holy Spirit we might do good and heal those oppressed by sickness and Satan (4:30; see article on DIVINE HEALING, p. 1420).

5:29 OBEY GOD RATHER THAN MEN. The great question before every believer is not, "Is it expedient, safe, pleasurable or popular among other humans?" but, "What is right in the sight of God?" (cf. Gal 1:10).

5:32 HOLY SPIRIT ... TO THOSE WHO OBEY HIM. If there is no real obedience to Christ or a sincere seeking the righteousness of his kingdom (Mt 6:33; Ro 14:17), then any claim to possess the fullness of the Holy Spirit is invalid. Pentecost without the lordship of Christ is impossible (cf. 2:38–42), for the Spirit in all his power is given only to those living in "obedience that comes from faith" (Ro 1:5; see article on TESTING FOR GENUINE BAPTISM IN THE SPIRIT, p. 1668).

men rallied to him. He was killed, all
his followers were dispersed, and it all
came to nothing. **37**After him, Judas
the Galilean appeared in the days of
the census[u] and led a band of people
in revolt. He too was killed, and all his
followers were scattered. **38**Therefore,
in the present case I advise you: Leave
these men alone! Let them go! For if
their purpose or activity is of human
origin, it will fail.[v] **39**But if it is from
God, you will not be able to stop these
men; you will only find yourselves
fighting against God."[w]
40His speech persuaded them. They
called the apostles in and had them
flogged.[x] Then they ordered them not
to speak in the name of Jesus, and let
them go.
41The apostles left the Sanhedrin,
rejoicing[y] because they had been
counted worthy of suffering disgrace
for the Name.[z] **42**Day after day, in the
temple courts[a] and from house to
house, they never stopped teaching
and proclaiming the good news[b] that
Jesus is the Christ.[v][c]

5:37 [u] Lk 2:1,2
5:38 [v] Mt 15:13
5:39 [w] 2Ch 13:12; Pr 21:30; Isa 46:10; Ac 7:51; 11:17
5:40 [x] S Mt 10:17
5:41 [y] S Mt 5:12 [z] S Jn 15:21
5:42 [a] S Ac 2:46 [b] S Ac 13:32 [c] S Ac 9:22
6:1 [d] S Ac 2:41 [e] Ac 9:29 [f] Ac 9:39, 41; 1Ti 5:3 [g] Ac 4:35
6:2 [h] S Ac 11:26 [i] S Heb 4:12
6:3 [j] S Ac 1:16 [k] S Lk 1:15 [l] Ex 18:21; Ne 13:13
6:4 [m] S Ac 1:14
6:5 [n] ver 8; Ac 7:55-60; 11:19; 22:20 [o] S Lk 1:15 [p] Ac 8:5-40; 21:8

The Choosing of the Seven

6 In those days when the number of
disciples was increasing,[d] the
Grecian Jews[e] among them complained against the Hebraic Jews because their widows[f] were being overlooked in the daily distribution of
food.[g] **2**So the Twelve gathered all the
disciples[h] together and said, "It
would not be right for us to neglect the
ministry of the word of God[i] in order
to wait on tables. **3**Brothers,[j] choose
seven men from among you who are
known to be full of the Spirit[k] and wisdom. We will turn this responsibility
over to them[l] **4**and will give our atten- Ac 7:55
tion to prayer[m] and the ministry of the
word."
5This proposal pleased the whole
group. They chose Stephen,[n] a man
full of faith and of the Holy Spirit;[o]
also Philip,[p] Procorus, Nicanor, Ti-
mon, Parmenas, and Nicolas from An- Ac 14:9-10
tioch, a convert to Judaism. **6**They pre-

v 42 Or *Messiah*

6:3 FULL OF THE SPIRIT AND WISDOM. The apostles stipulated that the seven men had to give evidence of having continued faithfully under the influence of the Holy Spirit. Apparently the apostles assumed that not all believers continued to be full of the Spirit. In other words, those who fail to live faithfully by the Spirit (Gal 5:16–25) will cease to be full of the Spirit. Concerning the terms "full of the Holy Spirit" and "filled with the Holy Spirit," the following should be noted:

(1) The phrase "full of the Spirit" (cf. 6:5; 11:24) expresses a continuing character, quality or condition within believers that results from experiencing the Spirit's fullness and that enables them to minister in the power of the Holy Spirit and to speak under prophetic inspiration as the Spirit gives utterance.

(2) The term "filled with the Holy Spirit" is used in three ways: (a) to indicate the reception of the baptism in the Holy Spirit (1:5; 2:4; 9:17; 11:16); (b) to indicate the empowering of a believer or believers on a specific occasion to speak under the impulse of the Holy Spirit (4:8; 13:9; Lk 1:41–45,67–79); and (c) to indicate a general prophetic ministry under the inspiration or anointing of the Holy Spirit without specifying the duration of that ministry (4:31–33; 13:52; Lk 1:15).

(3) After the initial reception of the baptism in the Spirit, individuals who faithfully walk in the Spirit, putting to death the misdeeds of the body (Ro 8:13–14), may be described as "full of the Holy Spirit," i.e., maintaining the abiding fullness of the Holy Spirit (e.g., the seven men, especially Stephen, vv. 3,5; 7:55; or Barnabas, 11:24). Also, those who maintain the fullness of the Spirit may receive a fresh filling with the Spirit for a particular purpose or task, especially a divine enabling to speak under the impulse of the Holy Spirit.

6:4 GIVE OUR ATTENTION TO PRAYER. Baptism in the Holy Spirit alone is insufficient for effective Christian leadership. Church leaders must constantly devote themselves to prayer and to the preaching of the Word. The verb translated "give our attention to" (Gk *proskartereō*) denotes a steadfast and single-minded fidelity and a giving of much time to a certain course of action. The apostles felt that prayer and the ministry of the Word were the highest work of Christian leaders. Note the frequent references to prayer in Acts (see 1:14, 24; 2:42; 4:24–31; 6:4,6; 9:40; 10:2,4,9,31; 11:5; 12:5; 13:3; 14:23; 16:25; 22:17; 28:8).

6:6 LAID THEIR HANDS ON THEM. In the NT the laying on of hands was used in five ways: (1) in connection with miracles of healing (28:8; Mt 9:18; Mk 5:23; 6:5); (2) in blessing others (Mt 19:13,15); (3) in connection with the baptism in the Spirit (8:17,19; 19:6); (4) in commissioning for a specific work (v. 6; 13:3); and (5) in imparting spiritual gifts by the elders (1Ti 4:14). As one of the means by which God mediates gifts and blessings to others, laying on of hands became a foundational doctrine in the early church (Heb 6:2). It must not be disassociated from prayer, for prayer indicates that the gifts of grace, healing or baptism in the Holy Spirit are from God and not from the persons who are ministering.

Consecrating or ordaining the seven men here meant primarily two things. (1) It was a public witness by the church that these seven men had a history of perseverance in godliness and faithful-

sented these men to the apostles, who
prayed[q] and laid their hands on
them.[r]
7So the word of God spread.[s] The
number of disciples in Jerusalem increased rapidly,[t] and a large number
of priests became obedient to the
faith.

Stephen, Full of Grace and Power

Ac 11:27-28
8Now Stephen, a man full of God's
grace and power, did great wonders
and miraculous signs[u] among the
people. 9Opposition arose, however,
from members of the Synagogue of
the Freedmen (as it was called)—
Jews of Cyrene[v] and Alexandria as
well as the provinces of Cilicia[w]
and Asia.[x] These men began to argue with Stephen, 10but they
could not stand up against his wisdom or the Spirit by whom he
spoke.[y]
11Then they secretly[z] persuaded
some men to say, "We have heard Stephen speak words of blasphemy
against Moses and against God."[a]

Stephen Seized

12So they stirred up the people
and the elders and the teachers of
the law. They seized Stephen and
brought him before the Sanhedrin.[b]
13They produced false witnesses,[c]
who testified, "This fellow never
stops speaking against this holy
place[d] and against the law. 14For we
have heard him say that this Jesus of
Nazareth will destroy this place[e] and
change the customs Moses handed
down to us."[f]
15All who were sitting in the Sanhedrin[g] looked intently at Stephen, and
they saw that his face was like the face
of an angel.

6:6 [q] S Ac 1:24 [r] Nu 8:10; 27:18; Ac 9:17; 19:6; 28:8; 1Ti 4:14; S Mk 5:23 **6:7** [s] Ac 12:24; 19:20 [t] S Ac 2:41 **6:8** [u] S Jn 4:48 **6:9** [v] S Mt 27:32 [w] Ac 15:23,41; 22:3; 23:34 [x] S Ac 2:9 **6:10** [y] Lk 21:15 **6:11** [z] 1Ki 21:10 [a] Mt 26:59-61 **6:12** [b] S Mt 5:22 **6:13** [c] Ex 23:1; Ps 27:12 [d] Mt 24:15; Ac 7:48; 21:28 **6:14** [e] S Jn 2:19 [f] Ac 15:1; 21:21; 26:3; 28:17 **6:15** [g] S Mt 5:22

7:2 [h] Ac 22:1 [i] Ps 29:3 [j] Ge 11:31; 15:7 **7:3** [k] Ge 12:1 **7:4** [l] Ge 12:5 **7:5** [m] Heb 11:13 [n] Ge 12:7; 17:8; 26:3 **7:6** [o] Ex 1:8-11; 12:40 **7:7** [p] Ge 15:13,14; Ex 3:12 **7:8** [q] Ge 17:9-14 [r] Ge 21:2-4 [s] Ge 25:26 [t] Ge 29:31-35; 30:5-13,17-24; 35:16-18,22-26 **7:9** [u] Ge 37:4,11 [v] Ge 37:28; Ps 105:17 [w] Ge 39:2,21,23; Hag 2:4

Stephen's Speech to the Sanhedrin

7 Then the high priest asked him,
"Are these charges true?"
2To this he replied: "Brothers and
fathers,[h] listen to me! The God of glory[i] appeared to our father Abraham
while he was still in Mesopotamia, before he lived in Haran.[j] 3'Leave your
country and your people,' God said,
'and go to the land I will show you.'[w][k]
4"So he left the land of the Chaldeans and settled in Haran. After the
death of his father, God sent him to
this land where you are now living.[l]
5He gave him no inheritance here,[m]
not even a foot of ground. But God
promised him that he and his descendants after him would possess the
land,[n] even though at that time Abraham had no child. 6God spoke to him
in this way: 'Your descendants will be
strangers in a country not their own,
and they will be enslaved and mistreated four hundred years.[o] 7But I will
punish the nation they serve as slaves,'
God said, 'and afterward they will
come out of that country and worship
me in this place.'[x][p] 8Then he gave
Abraham the covenant of circumcision.[q] And Abraham became the father of Isaac and circumcised him
eight days after his birth.[r] Later Isaac
became the father of Jacob,[s] and Jacob became the father of the twelve patriarchs.[t]
9"Because the patriarchs were jealous of Joseph,[u] they sold him as a
slave into Egypt.[v] But God was with
him[w] 10and rescued him from all his
troubles. He gave Joseph wisdom and
enabled him to gain the goodwill of
Pharaoh king of Egypt; so he made him

[w] 3 Gen. 12:1 [x] 7 Gen. 15:13,14

ness to the Spirit's leading (cf. 1Ti 3:1–10). (2) It was an act consecrating the men to the work of God and a testimony of their willingness to accept the responsibility of God's call.

6:8 STEPHEN . . . GOD'S GRACE AND POWER. The Holy Spirit empowered Stephen to perform "great wonders and miraculous signs among the people" and gave him great wisdom to preach the gospel in such a way that his opponents could not refute his arguments (v. 10; cf. Ex 4:15; Lk 21:15).

7:2–53 BROTHERS AND FATHERS, LISTEN. Stephen's speech before the Sanhedrin is a defense of the faith as preached by Christ and the apostles. He is the forerunner of all who defend the Biblical faith against those who oppose or distort its teaching, and he is the first to die for that reason. Jesus vindicates Stephen's action by standing in honor of him before his Father in heaven (v. 55, note). Stephen's love of the truth and his willingness to give his life to safeguard that truth contrast sharply with those who show little concern to "contend for the faith that was once for all entrusted to the saints" (Jude 3) and who, in the name of love, peace and tolerance, feel no need to oppose false teachers and distorters of the pure gospel for which Christ died (see Gal 1:9, note; see article on OVERSEERS AND THEIR DUTIES, p. 1690).

ruler over Egypt and all his palace.[x]
11“Then a famine struck all Egypt
and Canaan, bringing great suffering,
and our fathers could not find food.[y]
12When Jacob heard that there was
grain in Egypt, he sent our fathers on
their first visit.[z] 13On their second
visit, Joseph told his brothers who he
was,[a] and Pharaoh learned about Joseph's family.[b] 14After this, Joseph
sent for his father Jacob and his whole
family,[c] seventy-five in all.[d] 15Then
Jacob went down to Egypt, where he
and our fathers died.[e] 16Their bodies
were brought back to Shechem and
placed in the tomb that Abraham had
bought from the sons of Hamor at Shechem for a certain sum of money.[f]
17“As the time drew near for God to
fulfill his promise to Abraham, the
number of our people in Egypt greatly
increased.[g] 18Then another king, who
knew nothing about Joseph, became
ruler of Egypt.[h] 19He dealt treacherously with our people and oppressed
our forefathers by forcing them to
throw out their newborn babies so that
they would die.[i]
20“At that time Moses was born, and
he was no ordinary child.[y] For three
months he was cared for in his father's
house.[j] 21When he was placed outside, Pharaoh's daughter took him and
brought him up as her own son.[k]
22Moses was educated in all the wisdom of the Egyptians[l] and was powerful in speech and action.
23“When Moses was forty years old,
he decided to visit his fellow Israelites.
24He saw one of them being mistreated
by an Egyptian, so he went to his defense and avenged him by killing the
Egyptian. 25Moses thought that his
own people would realize that God was
using him to rescue them, but they did
not. 26The next day Moses came upon
two Israelites who were fighting. He
tried to reconcile them by saying,
‘Men, you are brothers; why do you
want to hurt each other?’
27“But the man who was mistreating
the other pushed Moses aside and said,
‘Who made you ruler and judge over
us?[m] 28Do you want to kill me as you
killed the Egyptian yesterday?’[z]
29When Moses heard this, he fled to
Midian, where he settled as a foreigner
and had two sons.[n]
30“After forty years had passed, an
angel appeared to Moses in the flames
of a burning bush in the desert near
Mount Sinai. 31When he saw this, he
was amazed at the sight. As he went
over to look more closely, he heard the
Lord's voice:[o] 32‘I am the God of your
fathers,[p] the God of Abraham, Isaac
and Jacob.’[a] Moses trembled with fear
and did not dare to look.[q]
33“Then the Lord said to him, ‘Take
off your sandals; the place where you
are standing is holy ground.[r] 34I have
indeed seen the oppression of my people in Egypt. I have heard their groaning and have come down to set them
free. Now come, I will send you back to
Egypt.’[b][s]
35“This is the same Moses whom
they had rejected with the words, ‘Who
made you ruler and judge?’[t] He was
sent to be their ruler and deliverer by
God himself, through the angel who appeared to him in the bush. 36He led
them out of Egypt[u] and did wonders
and miraculous signs[v] in Egypt, at the
Red Sea[c][w] and for forty years in the
desert.[x]
37“This is that Moses who told the
Israelites, ‘God will send you a prophet
like me from your own people.’[d][y]
38He was in the assembly in the desert,
with the angel[z] who spoke to him on
Mount Sinai, and with our fathers;[a]
and he received living words[b] to pass
on to us.[c]
39“But our fathers refused to obey
him. Instead, they rejected him and in
their hearts turned back to Egypt.[d]
40They told Aaron, ‘Make us gods who
will go before us. As for this fellow Mo-

7:10 [x] Ge 41:37-43; Ps 105:20-22
7:11 [y] Ge 41:54
7:12 [z] Ge 42:1,2
7:13 [a] Ge 45:1-4 [b] Ge 45:16
7:14 [c] Ge 45:9,10 [d] Ge 46:26,27; Ex 1:5; Dt 10:22
7:15 [e] Ge 46:5-7; 49:33; Ex 1:6
7:16 [f] Ge 23:16-20; 33:18,19; 50:13; Jos 24:32
7:17 [g] Ex 1:7; Ps 105:24
7:18 [h] Ex 1:8
7:19 [i] Ex 1:10-22
7:20 [j] Ex 2:2; Heb 11:23
7:21 [k] Ex 2:3-10
7:22 [l] 1Ki 4:30; Isa 19:11

7:27 [m] Ge 19:9; Nu 16:13
7:29 [n] Ex 2:11-15
7:31 [o] Ex 3:1-4
7:32 [p] S Ac 3:13 [q] Ex 3:6
7:33 [r] Ex 3:5; Jos 5:15
7:34 [s] Ex 3:7-10
7:35 [t] ver 27
7:36 [u] Ex 12:41; 33:1 [v] Ex 11:10; S Jn 4:48 [w] Ex 14:21 [x] Ex 15:25; 17:5,6
7:37 [y] Dt 18:15,18; Ac 3:22
7:38 [z] ver 53 [a] Ex 19:17; Lev 27:34 [b] Dt 32:45-47; Heb 4:12 [c] Ro 3:2
7:39 [d] Nu 14:3,4

[y] 20 Or *was fair in the sight of God*
[z] 28 Exodus 2:14 [a] 32 Exodus 3:6
[b] 34 Exodus 3:5,7,8,10 [c] 36 That is, Sea of Reeds [d] 37 Deut. 18:15

7:38 THE ASSEMBLY IN THE DESERT. "The assembly in the desert" refers to Israel as the people of God. In Hebrew the word translated "church" is *qahal* and is rendered in the Septuagint (Greek translation of the OT) as *ekklēsia* (i.e., "assembly" or "church"). (1) Just as Moses led the church of the OT, Christ leads the church of the NT. The NT church, designated "Abraham's seed" (Gal 3:29; cf. Ro 4:11–18) and the "Israel of God" (Gal 6:16), stands in continuity with the church of the OT. (2) Like the OT church, the church of the NT is "in the desert," i.e., it is a pilgrim church, far from the promised land (Heb 11:6–16). For this reason we must never become too comfortable with life here on this earth.

ses who led us out of Egypt—we don't
know what has happened to him!'[e][e]
41That was the time they made an idol
in the form of a calf. They brought sacrifices to it and held a celebration in
honor of what their hands had made.[f]
42But God turned away[g] and gave
them over to the worship of the heavenly bodies.[h] This agrees with what is
written in the book of the prophets:

" 'Did you bring me sacrifices and
offerings
forty years in the desert,
O house of Israel?
43You have lifted up the shrine of
Molech
and the star of your god
Rephan,
the idols you made to worship.
Therefore I will send you into
exile'[f][i] beyond Babylon.

44"Our forefathers had the tabernacle of the Testimony[j] with them in the
desert. It had been made as God directed Moses, according to the pattern he
had seen.[k] 45Having received the tabernacle, our fathers under Joshua
brought it with them when they took
the land from the nations God drove
out before them.[l] It remained in the
land until the time of David,[m] 46who
enjoyed God's favor and asked that he
might provide a dwelling place for the
God of Jacob.[g][n] 47But it was Solomon
who built the house for him.[o]

48"However, the Most High[p] does
not live in houses made by men.[q] As
the prophet says:

49" 'Heaven is my throne,
and the earth is my footstool.[r]
What kind of house will you build
for me?
says the Lord.
Or where will my resting place
be?
50Has not my hand made all these
things?'[h][s]

51"You stiff-necked people,[t] with
uncircumcised hearts[u] and ears! You
are just like your fathers: You always
resist the Holy Spirit! 52Was there ever

7:40 [e] Ex 32:1,23
7:41 [f] Ex 32:4-6; Ps 106:19,20; Rev 9:20
7:42 [g] Jos 24:20; Isa 63:10 [h] Jer 19:13
7:43 [i] Am 5:25-27
7:44 [j] Ex 38:21; Nu 1:50; 17:7 [k] Ex 25:8,9,40
7:45 [l] Jos 3:14-17; 18:1; 23:9; 24:18; Ps 44:2 [m] 2Sa 7:2,6
7:46 [n] 2Sa 7:8-16; 1Ki 8:17; Ps 132:1-5
7:47 [o] 1Ki 6:1-38
7:48 [p] S Mk 5:7 [q] 1Ki 8:27; 2Ch 2:6
7:49 [r] Mt 5:34,35
7:50 [s] Isa 66:1,2
7:51 [t] Ex 32:9; 33:3,5 [u] Lev 26:41; Dt 10:16; Jer 4:4; 9:26

[e] 40 Exodus 32:1 [f] 43 Amos 5:25-27
[g] 46 Some early manuscripts *the house of Jacob*
[h] 50 Isaiah 66:1,2

7:42 GOD . . . GAVE THEM OVER. Stephen's words reflect a principle well established in Scripture and redemptive history. Those who persist in repudiating God are given over to the influence of evil, Satan and immorality (cf. Ro 1:24,28). Contrary to popular teaching, God does not continue to show love and forgiveness without any condition on our part. He forgives and communicates his love only to those who turn their hearts to him in sincere repentance and true obedience. For those who harden their hearts, resist the Spirit and refuse to accept God's salvation, there remains only his wrath (Ro 2:4–6,8).

7:44 ACCORDING TO THE PATTERN. God has always had a divine pattern to be followed by his people. (1) God had a pattern for Moses that served as the standard under the old covenant. (a) In Ex 12, God gave Moses specific instructions for the original Passover in Egypt, which became a pattern for all subsequent generations of Israelites to follow. (b) In Ex 20, God gave Moses the Ten Commandments as the pattern and moral standard for all subsequent generations. (c) In Ex 25, God instructed Moses to erect a tabernacle as a copy and shadow of heavenly things and the redemption that God planned to accomplish in the Lord Jesus Christ on earth. Moses carefully made the tabernacle and all its furnishings "exactly like the pattern" that God had fashioned in wisdom (Ex 25:9,40; cf. Heb 8:1–5).

(2) Just as surely as God had a pattern for the tabernacle under the old covenant, he has a pattern for his church under the new. The NT apostles did not arbitrarily decide how the church was to be fashioned. It was the Father and the Son, through what the Holy Spirit recorded in the Gospels, Acts, the letters and the letters to the seven churches (Rev 2–3), who established the apostolic pattern for the church.

(3) Tragically, after the apostolic age the church began to depart from divine revelation and modify God's heavenly pattern by accommodating itself culturally and organizationally according to human, earthly ideas. This has resulted in a proliferation of man-made patterns for the church.

(4) If the church of Jesus Christ is to experience again the full plan, power and presence of God, she must turn from her own ways and embrace the NT apostolic pattern as God's timeless standard for his church.

7:51 ALWAYS RESIST THE HOLY SPIRIT. The history of Israel is the story of a people who repeatedly refused to obey their God and his revealed Word. Instead of submitting to the restraints of his law, their hearts turned toward the ways and lifestyle of the ungodly nations around them. They killed the prophets who called them to repentance and who prophesied about the coming of Christ (vv. 52–53). This is what resisting the Holy Spirit means.

Likewise, the Israel of Christ under the new covenant must be aware of its tendency to live as did the Israel of God under the old. Christ's churches can turn from him and his Word and refuse to heed the voice of the Holy Spirit. When this happens, they too will incur judgment from God: the kingdom will be taken from them (see Ro 11:20–22; Rev 2–3).

a prophet your fathers did not persecute?[v] They even killed those who
predicted the coming of the Righteous
One. And now you have betrayed and
murdered him[w]— **53**you who have received the law that was put into effect
through angels[x] but have not obeyed
it."

The Stoning of Stephen

54When they heard this, they were
furious[y] and gnashed their teeth at
him. **55**But Stephen, full of the Holy
Spirit,[z] looked up to heaven and saw
the glory of God, and Jesus standing at
the right hand of God.[a] **56**"Look," he
said, "I see heaven open[b] and the Son
of Man[c] standing at the right hand of
God."

57At this they covered their ears
and, yelling at the top of their voices,
they all rushed at him, **58**dragged him
out of the city[d] and began to stone
him.[e] Meanwhile, the witnesses[f]
laid their clothes[g] at the feet of a
young man named Saul.[h]

59While they were stoning him, Stephen prayed, "Lord Jesus, receive my
spirit."[i] **60**Then he fell on his knees[j]
and cried out, "Lord, do not hold this
sin against them."[k] When he had said
this, he fell asleep.[l]

7:52 [v] S Mt 5:12 [w] Ac 3:14; 1Th 2:15 **7:53** [x] ver 38; Gal 3:19; Heb 2:2 **7:54** [y] Ac 5:33 **7:55** [z] S Lk 1:15 [a] S Mk 16:19 **7:56** [b] S Mt 3:16 [c] S Mt 8:20 **7:58** [d] Lk 4:29 [e] Lev 24:14,16 [f] Dt 17:7 [g] Ac 22:20 [h] Ac 8:1 **7:59** [i] Ps 31:5; Lk 23:46 **7:60** [j] Lk 22:41; Ac 9:40 [k] S Mt 5:44 [l] S Mt 9:24

8:1 [m] Ac 7:58 [n] ver 4; Ac 11:19 [o] Ac 9:31 **8:3** [p] Ac 7:58 [q] Ac 9:1,13,21; 22:4,19; 26:10,11; 1Co 15:9; Gal 1:13,23; Php 3:6; 1Ti 1:13 **8:4** [r] ver 1 [s] Ac 15:35 **8:5** [t] Ac 6:5; 21:8 **8:7** [u] S Mk 16:17 [v] S Mt 4:24

8 And Saul[m] was there, giving approval to his death.

The Church Persecuted and Scattered

On that day a great persecution
broke out against the church at Jerusalem, and all except the apostles were
scattered[n] throughout Judea and Samaria.[o] **2**Godly men buried Stephen
and mourned deeply for him. **3**But
Saul[p] began to destroy the church.[q]
Going from house to house, he dragged
off men and women and put them in
prison.

Philip in Samaria

4Those who had been scattered[r]
preached the word wherever they
went.[s] **5**Philip[t] went down to a city
in Samaria and proclaimed the Christ[i]
there. **6**When the crowds heard Philip
and saw the miraculous signs he did,
they all paid close attention to what he
said. **7**With shrieks, evil[j] spirits came
out of many,[u] and many paralytics
and cripples were healed.[v] **8**So there
was great joy in that city.

Ac 8:26-40

Ac 19:11-12

[i] 5 Or *Messiah* [j] 7 Greek *unclean*

7:55 SAW ... JESUS STANDING. The Bible normally speaks of Jesus as seated at the right hand of God (2:34; Mk 14:62; Lk 22:69; Col 3:1). But here Jesus stood in order to welcome his first martyr to himself. Stephen had confessed Christ before fellow humans and defended the faith. Now Christ, in honor of his servant, confesses him before his heavenly Father. For all faithful believers near death, the Savior stands ready to receive you as your intercessor and advocate (cf. Mk 8:38; Lk 12:8; Ro 8:34; 1Jn 2:1).

8:1 A GREAT PERSECUTION. Saul seems to have been the leader (vv. 1–3; 9:1) of the church's first widespread persecution; it was intense and severe. Men and women were put in prison (v. 3) and beaten (22:19), and many were put to death (22:20; 26:10–11). Yet God used this persecution to start the great missionary work of the church (v. 4).

8:5–24 PHILIP WENT DOWN TO ... SAMARIA. Notice the sequence of events in this record of the outpouring of the Spirit on the Samaritan believers. (1) Philip preached the gospel of the kingdom and God confirmed the Word with miraculous signs (vv. 5–7).

(2) Many Samaritans received the Word of God (v. 14), believed in Jesus (v. 12), were healed and delivered from evil spirits (v. 7), and were baptized in water (vv. 12–13). Thus, they experienced salvation, the regenerative work of the Holy Spirit and the power of the kingdom of God (see v. 12, note).

(3) The Holy Spirit, however, "had not yet come upon any of them" after their conversion to Christ and their water baptism (v. 16).

(4) After some days following the Samaritans' conversion, Peter and John came to Samaria and prayed that the Samaritans might receive the Spirit (vv. 14–15). There was a definite interval between their conversion to Christ and their receiving the baptism in the Holy Spirit (vv. 16–17; cf. 2:4). The Samaritans' reception of the Spirit, in other words, follows the pattern of the disciples' experience at Pentecost (see articles on THE REGENERATION OF THE DISCIPLES, p. 1627, and BAPTISM IN THE HOLY SPIRIT, p. 1642).

(5) Some external manifestation must have accompanied receiving the Holy Spirit, undoubtedly speaking in other tongues and prophesying (see v. 18, note).

8:6 THE MIRACULOUS SIGNS HE DID. Christ's promise to use miraculous signs to confirm the preaching of the Word was not limited to the apostles (Mk 16:15–18; see article on SIGNS OF BELIEVERS, p. 1513). He promises that the disciples' converts ("whoever believes") will perform signs in the name of Jesus, such as driving out demons (Mk 16:17) and healing the sick (Mk 16:18). This is exactly what Philip did.

Simon the Sorcerer

9Now for some time a man named
Simon had practiced sorcery[w] in the
city and amazed all the people of Samaria. He boasted that he was someone great,[x] **10**and all the people, both
high and low, gave him their attention
and exclaimed, "This man is the divine
power known as the Great Power."[y]
11They followed him because he had
amazed them for a long time with his
magic. **12**But when they believed Philip
as he preached the good news of the
kingdom of God[z] and the name of
Jesus Christ, they were baptized,[a]
both men and women. **13**Simon himself
believed and was baptized. And he followed Philip everywhere, astonished
by the great signs and miracles[b] he
saw.

Samaritans Receive the Spirit

14When the apostles in Jerusalem
heard that Samaria[c] had accepted the
word of God,[d] they sent Peter and
John[e] to them. **15**When they arrived,
they prayed for them that they might
receive the Holy Spirit,[f] **16**because
the Holy Spirit had not yet come upon
any of them;[g] they had simply been
baptized into[k] the name of the Lord
Jesus.[h] **17**Then Peter and John placed
their hands on them,[i] and they received the Holy Spirit.[j]

Peter Rebukes Simon

18When Simon saw that the Spirit
was given at the laying on of the apostles' hands, he offered them money
19and said, "Give me also this ability so
that everyone on whom I lay my hands
may receive the Holy Spirit."
20Peter answered: "May your money
perish with you, because you thought
you could buy the gift of God with money![k] **21**You have no part or share[l] in
this ministry, because your heart is not

8:9 [w] Ac 13:6 [x] Ac 5:36
8:10 [y] Ac 14:11; 28:6
8:12 [z] S Mt 3:2 [a] S Ac 2:38
8:13 [b] ver 6; Ac 19:11
8:14 [c] ver 1 [d] S Heb 4:12 [e] S Lk 22:8
8:15 [f] S Jn 20:22
8:16 [g] S Ac 10:44; 19:2 [h] Mt 28:19; S Ac 2:38
8:17 [i] S Ac 6:6 [j] S Jn 20:22
8:20 [k] 2Ki 5:16; Da 5:17; Mt 10:8; Ac 2:38
8:21 [l] Ne 2:20

[k] *16* Or *in*

8:12 THEY BELIEVED ... THE NAME OF JESUS CHRIST. The Samaritans fully met the conditions for salvation and were Christians before the Spirit came upon them. (1) They "believed" and were "baptized." Two facts make it clear that the faith of the Samaritans was genuine saving faith. (a) Both Philip (v. 12) and the apostles (v. 14) considered the Samaritans' faith to be valid. (b) The Samaritans publicly committed themselves to Christ by water baptism. Scripture affirms that "whoever believes and is baptized will be saved" (Mk 16:16). Thus, they were regenerated and indwelt by the Holy Spirit (Ro 8:9).

(2) Their receiving the Holy Spirit several days later (v. 17) was not for salvation. It was rather a receiving of the Spirit as the disciples did at Pentecost, i.e., to equip them with power for service and witness (1:8; 2:4). Luke uses the term "receive the Spirit" primarily in an empowering sense (1:8; 2:38; 8:17; 10:47; 19:2), not in the sense of new birth or regeneration (see articles on REGENERATION, p. 1589, THE REGENERATION OF THE DISCIPLES, p. 1627, and BAPTISM IN THE HOLY SPIRIT, p. 1642).

(3) Some have taught that the faith of the Samaritans was not a saving and regenerating faith. However, it is unreasonable to believe that Philip, a man full of the Holy Spirit and wisdom (6:3–5), would baptize, heal and drive demons out of people whose faith he thought was not genuine.

8:16 HAD NOT YET COME UPON ANY OF THEM. The Spirit had not yet come upon any of them in the same way he descended on the believers on the day of Pentecost (2:4). He had not yet come upon them as the Father had promised (1:4) and as Christ had foretold when he said, "You will be baptized with the Holy Spirit" (1:5). Evidently they had not demonstrated the expected spiritual manifestations, especially divinely inspired utterances (see vv. 5–24, note; v. 18, note).

8:17 THEY RECEIVED THE HOLY SPIRIT. Through the laying on of hands, the Samaritans received the Holy Spirit in the same sense as the baptism in the Spirit that occurred at Pentecost (1:8; 2:4).

The Samaritans' "two-stage" experience—i.e., first believing, and then being filled with the Spirit—shows that the "two-stage" experience of the believers at Pentecost was not abnormal. The experiences of both Paul in 9:5–17 and the Ephesian disciples in 19:1–6 were the same as the Samaritans. They accepted Christ as Lord and afterwards were filled with the Spirit. There need not be a long time lapse, however, between saving faith and baptism in the Spirit, as demonstrated by the Gentiles at Caesarea (ch. 10).

8:18 WHEN SIMON SAW. The Spirit's coming upon the Samaritans was accompanied by observable external manifestations apparent even to Simon the sorcerer. It is reasonable to conclude that the observable manifestations were like those that occurred after the Spirit's coming upon the earliest disciples at Pentecost, i.e., speaking in other tongues (see 2:4; 10:45–46; 11:15, note; 19:6; see article on SPEAKING IN TONGUES, p. 1646). This manifestation gave both the Samaritans and the apostles a verifiable sign that the Holy Spirit had come upon the new believers.

8:21 YOUR HEART IS NOT RIGHT. The baptism in the Holy Spirit throughout the book of Acts occurs only in the context of committed discipleship to Jesus Christ. (1) Simon, who sought the power and gift of the Holy Spirit as well as the authority to impart the gift (v. 19), was rejected by God because his heart was not right with God, and he was still wicked and "captive to sin" (vv.

right[m] before God. 22Repent[n] of this
wickedness and pray to the Lord. Perhaps he will forgive you for having
such a thought in your heart. 23For I
see that you are full of bitterness and
captive to sin."
24Then Simon answered, "Pray to
the Lord for me[o] so that nothing you
have said may happen to me."
25When they had testified and proclaimed the word of the Lord,[p] Peter
and John returned to Jerusalem,
preaching the gospel in many Samaritan villages.[q]

Philip and the Ethiopian

26Now an angel[r] of the Lord said to
Philip,[s] "Go south to the road—the
desert road—that goes down from Jerusalem to Gaza." 27So he started out,
and on his way he met an Ethiopian[1t] eunuch,[u] an important official
in charge of all the treasury of Canda-
ce, queen of the Ethiopians. This man
had gone to Jerusalem to worship,[v]
28and on his way home was sitting in
his chariot reading the book of Isaiah
the prophet. 29The Spirit told[w] Philip,
"Go to that chariot and stay near it."
30Then Philip ran up to the chariot
and heard the man reading Isaiah the
prophet. "Do you understand what you
are reading?" Philip asked.
31"How can I," he said, "unless
someone explains it to me?" So he invited Philip to come up and sit with
him.
32The eunuch was reading this passage of Scripture:

"He was led like a sheep to the
slaughter,
and as a lamb before the shearer
is silent,
so he did not open his mouth.
33In his humiliation he was deprived
of justice.
Who can speak of his
descendants?
For his life was taken from the
earth."[mx]

34The eunuch asked Philip, "Tell
me, please, who is the prophet talking
about, himself or someone else?"
35Then Philip began[y] with that very
passage of Scripture[z] and told him
the good news[a] about Jesus.
36As they traveled along the road,
they came to some water and the eunuch said, "Look, here is water. Why
shouldn't I be baptized?"[nb] 38And he
gave orders to stop the chariot. Then
both Philip and the eunuch went down
into the water and Philip baptized him.
39When they came up out of the water,
the Spirit of the Lord suddenly took
Philip away,[c] and the eunuch did not
see him again, but went on his way rejoicing. 40Philip, however, appeared at
Azotus and traveled about, preaching
the gospel in all the towns[d] until he
reached Caesarea.[e] Ac 16:29-32

Saul's Conversion

9:1–19pp — Ac 22:3–16; 26:9–18

9 Meanwhile, Saul was still breathing out murderous threats against
the Lord's disciples.[f] He went to the
high priest 2and asked him for letters
to the synagogues in Damascus,[g] so
that if he found any there who belonged to the Way,[h] whether men or
women, he might take them as prisoners to Jerusalem. 3As he neared Damascus on his journey, suddenly a
light from heaven flashed around
him.[i] 4He fell to the ground and heard

8:21 [m]Ps 78:37 **8:22** [n]Ac 2:38 **8:24** [o]Ex 8:8; Nu 21:7; 1Ki 13:6; Jer 42:2 **8:25** [p]S Ac 13:48 [q]ver 40 **8:26** [r]S Ac 5:19 [s]Ac 6:5 **8:27** [t]Ps 68:31; 87:4; Zep 3:10 [u]Isa 56:3-5 [v]1Ki 8:41-43; Jn 12:20 **8:29** [w]Ac 10:19; 11:12; 13:2; 20:23; 21:11 **8:33** [x]Isa 53:7,8 **8:35** [y]Mt 5:2 [z]Lk 24:27; Ac 17:2; 18:28; 28:23 [a]S Ac 13:32 **8:36** [b]S Ac 2:38; 10:47 **8:39** [c]1Ki 18:12; 2Ki 2:16; Eze 3:12,14; 8:3; 11:1,24; 43:5; 2Co 12:2; 1Th 4:17; Rev 12:5 **8:40** [d]ver 25 [e]Ac 10:1,24; 12:19; 21:8,16; 23:23,33; 25:1,4, 6,13 **9:1** [f]S Ac 8:3 **9:2** [g]Isa 17:1; Jer 49:23 [h]Ac 19:9,23; 22:4; 24:14,22 **9:3** [i]1Co 15:8

[1]*27* That is, from the upper Nile region [m]*33* Isaiah 53:7,8 [n]*36* Some late manuscripts *baptized?" 37Philip said, "If you believe with all your heart, you may." The eunuch answered, "I believe that Jesus Christ is the Son of God."*

22–23). The genuine gift of the Holy Spirit will be poured out only on those "who fear him and do what is right" (10:35, cf. 10:44–48; see also 5:32).

(2) Before and after the day of Pentecost, the followers of Christ were devoted to the risen Lord (1:2–14; 2:32) and engaged in continual prayer (1:14; 6:4). They lived lives of separation from sin and the world (2:38–40) and obeyed the apostles' teaching (2:42; 6:4). Repeated or new outpourings of the Spirit were given only to believers who had turned from their sins and wicked ways to lives of obedience to Christ (cf. 2:42; 3:1,19,22–26; 4:8, 19–35; 5:29–32; 6:4; 8:14–21; 9:1–19; 10:34–47; 19:1–6; 24:16). Walking by the Spirit and being led by him are always conditions of being filled with the Spirit (see Gal 5:16–25; Eph 5:18).

(3) Any supernatural experience thought to be the baptism in the Spirit occurring in one who continues in the ways of the sinful nature is not from Christ (cf. 1Jn 4:1–6). It is rather a "counterfeit" baptism in the Spirit and may be accompanied by demonic gifts and powers (Mt 7:21–23; 2Th 2:7–10; see article on TESTING FOR GENUINE BAPTISM IN THE SPIRIT, p. 1668).

9:3–19 THE CONVERSION OF PAUL. Vv. 3–9 record Paul's conversion outside the city of Damascus (cf. 22:3–16; 26:9–18). That his conversion occurs here rather than later at the house

a voice[j] say to him, "Saul, Saul, why
do you persecute me?"
5"Who are you, Lord?" Saul asked.
"I am Jesus, whom you are persecuting," he replied. **6**"Now get up and go
into the city, and you will be told what
you must do."[k]
7The men traveling with Saul stood
there speechless; they heard the
sound[l] but did not see anyone.[m]
8Saul got up from the ground, but when
he opened his eyes he could see nothing.[n] So they led him by the hand into
Damascus. **9**For three days he was
blind, and did not eat or drink anything.
10In Damascus there was a disciple
named Ananias. The Lord called to him
in a vision,[o] "Ananias!"
"Yes, Lord," he answered.
11The Lord told him, "Go to the
house of Judas on Straight Street and
ask for a man from Tarsus[p] named
Saul, for he is praying. **12**In a vision he
has seen a man named Ananias come
and place his hands on[q] him to restore
his sight."
13"Lord," Ananias answered, "I have
heard many reports about this man and
all the harm he has done to your
saints[r] in Jerusalem.[s] **14**And he has
come here with authority from the
chief priests[t] to arrest all who call on
your name."[u]
15But the Lord said to Ananias, "Go!
This man is my chosen instrument[v] to
carry my name before the Gentiles[w]
and their kings[x] and before the people
of Israel. **16**I will show him how much
he must suffer for my name."[y]
17Then Ananias went to the house
and entered it. Placing his hands on[z]
Saul, he said, "Brother Saul, the
Lord—Jesus, who appeared to you on
the road as you were coming here—
has sent me so that you may see again
and be filled with the Holy Spirit."[a]
18Immediately, something like scales

9:4 [j] Isa 6:8 **9:6** [k] ver 16; Eze 3:22 **9:7** [l] Jn 12:29 [m] Da 10:7 **9:8** [n] ver 18 **9:10** [o] Ac 10:3,17, 19; 12:9; 16:9,10; 18:9 **9:11** [p] ver 30; Ac 11:25; 21:39; 22:3
9:12 [q] S Mk 5:23 **9:13** [r] ver 32; Ac 26:10; Ro 1:7; 15:25,26,31; 16:2, 15; Eph 1:1; Php 1:1 [s] S Ac 8:3 **9:14** [t] ver 2,21 [u] S Ac 2:21 **9:15** [v] Ac 13:2; Ro 1:1; Gal 1:15; 1Ti 1:12 [w] Ro 11:13; 15:15, 16; Gal 1:16; 2:7, 8 [x] Ac 25:22,23; 26:1 **9:16** [y] Ac 20:23; 21:11; 2Co 6:4-10; 11:23-27; 2Ti 1:8; 2:3,9 **9:17** [z] S Ac 6:6 [a] S Lk 1:15

---

of Judas (v. 11) is clear from the following: (1) Paul obeys Christ's instruction (v. 6; 22:10; 26:15–19), commits himself to be a "servant and . . . witness" of the gospel (26:16) and a missionary to the Gentiles (26:17–19), and gives himself to prayer (v. 11). (2) Paul is called "brother Saul" by Ananias (v. 17). Ananias already assumes Paul is a believer who has experienced the new birth (see Jn 3:3–6), is committed to Christ and to God's mission, and needs no more than to be baptized, have his sight restored and be filled with the Holy Spirit (vv. 17–18; see 9:17, note).

9:11 FOR HE IS PRAYING. After Paul encounters Jesus and accepts him as Lord and Messiah, he fasts and prays for guidance with an attitude of deep commitment to God. Saving faith and the consequent new birth will always result in believers seeking communion with their new Lord and Savior.

9:13 SAINTS. The believers in the NT are called "saints" (cf. 26:10; Ro 1:7; 1Co 1:2; Rev 13:7; 19:8). (1) The basic idea of the term "saint" (Gk *hagios*) is separation from sin and to God. Saints, in other words, are "God's separated ones" or "God's holy ones." This implies being led and sanctified by the Holy Spirit (Ro 8:14; 1Co 6:11; 2Th 2:13; 1Pe 1:2), and turning one's back on the world to follow Jesus (Jn 17:15–17; see article on SANCTIFICATION, p. 1956). However, the term "saint" does not mean that the believer is already perfect or incapable of sin (cf. 1Jn 2:1). (2) Calling believers "saved sinners" is not a NT practice. As the common Biblical term for all believers, "saint" emphasizes (a) the Scriptural expectation that all believers conform to God's way of righteousness (Eph 5:3), and (b) the necessity that holiness be an internal reality for all who belong to Christ (1Co 1:30).

9:16 SUFFER FOR MY NAME. Paul's conversion and salvation meant not only a commission to preach the gospel but also a call to suffer for Christ. Paul is told from the beginning that he must undergo much suffering for the cause of Christ. In Christ's kingdom, suffering for his sake is a sign of God's highest favor (14:22; Mt 5:11–12; Ro 8:17; 2Ti 2:12) and the means to a fruitful ministry (Jn 12:24; 2Co 1:3–6); it results in abundant reward in heaven (Mt 5:12; 2Ti 2:12). Death must work in believers in order that God's life might flow from them to others (Ro 8:17–18, 36–37; 2Co 4:10–12). For additional passages on the sufferings of Paul, see 20:23; 2Co 4:8–18; 6:3–10; 11:23–27; Gal 6:17; 2Ti 1:11–12; see also 2Co 1:4, note; 11:23, note.

9:17 BROTHER SAUL. See note on vv. 3–19.

9:17 FILLED WITH THE HOLY SPIRIT. Three days after Paul's conversion he is filled with the Holy Spirit. Paul's experience parallels that of the disciples' at Pentecost (see article on BAPTISM IN THE HOLY SPIRIT, p. 1642). First, he experiences the new birth and is saved (see vv. 3–19, note); then he is "filled with the Holy Spirit."

Although Luke does not specifically say that Paul spoke in tongues when he received the Pentecostal gift of the Holy Spirit, it is reasonable to assume that he did. (1) The NT norm indicates that one filled with the Spirit begins to speak in tongues (2:4; 10:45–46; 19:6; see 11:15, note). (2) Paul himself testifies that he frequently spoke in tongues: "I thank God that I speak in tongues more than all of you" (1Co 14:18).

9:18 HE . . . WAS BAPTIZED. Luke's primary concern is the actual baptism in the Spirit (v. 17), rather than whether Paul spoke in tongues. Seeking the Spirit's fullness should be centered on the Holy Spirit himself and not on any external manifestation. On the other hand, all believers who de-

fell from Saul's eyes, and he could see again. He got up and was baptized,[b] **19**and after taking some food, he regained his strength.

Saul in Damascus and Jerusalem

Saul spent several days with the disciples[c] in Damascus.[d] **20**At once he began to preach in the synagogues[e] that Jesus is the Son of God.[f] **21**All those who heard him were astonished and asked, "Isn't he the man who raised havoc in Jerusalem among those who call on this name?[g] And hasn't he come here to take them as prisoners to the chief priests?"[h] **22**Yet Saul grew more and more powerful and baffled the Jews living in Damascus by proving that Jesus is the Christ.[o][i]

23After many days had gone by, the Jews conspired to kill him,[j] **24**but Saul learned of their plan.[k] Day and night they kept close watch on the city gates in order to kill him. **25**But his followers took him by night and lowered him in a basket through an opening in the wall.[l]

26When he came to Jerusalem,[m] he tried to join the disciples, but they were all afraid of him, not believing that he really was a disciple. **27**But Barnabas[n] took him and brought him to the apostles. He told them how Saul on his journey had seen the Lord and that the Lord had spoken to him,[o] and how in Damascus he had preached fearlessly in the name of Jesus.[p] **28**So Saul stayed with them and moved about freely in Jerusalem, speaking boldly in the name of the Lord. **29**He talked and debated with the Grecian Jews,[q] but they tried to kill him.[r] **30**When the brothers[s] learned of this, they took him down to Caesarea[t] and sent him off to Tarsus.[u]

31Then the church throughout Judea, Galilee and Samaria[v] enjoyed a time of peace. It was strengthened; and encouraged by the Holy Spirit, it grew in numbers,[w] living in the fear of the Lord.

9:18 [b] S Ac 2:38 **9:19** [c] S Ac 11:26 [d] Ac 26:20 **9:20** [e] Ac 13:5,14; 14:1; 17:2,10,17; 18:4,19; 19:8 [f] S Mt 4:3 **9:21** [g] S Ac 8:3 [h] ver 14 **9:22** [i] S Lk 2:11; Ac 5:42; 17:3; 18:5,28 **9:23** [j] S Ac 20:3 **9:24** [k] Ac 20:3,19; 23:16,30 **9:25** [l] 1Sa 19:12; 2Co 11:32,33 **9:26** [m] Ac 22:17; 26:20; Gal 1:17,18 **9:27** [n] S Ac 4:36 [o] ver 3-6 [p] ver 20, 22 **9:29** [q] Ac 6:1 [r] 2Co 11:26 **9:30** [s] S Ac 1:16 [t] S Ac 8:40 [u] S ver 11 **9:31** [v] Ac 8:1

[w] S Ac 2:41 **9:32** [x] S ver 13 **9:34** [y] Ac 3:6,16; 4:10 **9:35** [z] 1Ch 5:16; 27:29; SS 2:1; Isa 33:9; 35:2; 65:10 [a] S Ac 2:41 **9:36** [b] Jos 19:46; 2Ch 2:16; Ezr 3:7; Jnh 1:3; Ac 10:5 [c] 1Ti 2:10; Tit 3:8 **9:37** [d] Ac 1:13; 20:8 **9:38** [e] S Ac 11:26 **9:39** [f] Ac 6:1; 1Ti 5:3 **9:40** [g] Mt 9:25 [h] Lk 22:41; Ac 7:60 [i] S Lk 7:14 **9:42** [j] S Ac 2:41 **9:43** [k] Ac 10:6

Aeneas and Dorcas

32As Peter traveled about the country, he went to visit the saints[x] in Lydda. **33**There he found a man named Aeneas, a paralytic who had been bedridden for eight years. **34**"Aeneas," Peter said to him, "Jesus Christ heals you.[y] Get up and take care of your mat." Immediately Aeneas got up. **35**All those who lived in Lydda and Sharon[z] saw him and turned to the Lord.[a]

36In Joppa[b] there was a disciple named Tabitha (which, when translated, is Dorcas[p]), who was always doing good[c] and helping the poor. **37**About that time she became sick and died, and her body was washed and placed in an upstairs room.[d] **38**Lydda was near Joppa; so when the disciples[e] heard that Peter was in Lydda, they sent two men to him and urged him, "Please come at once!"

39Peter went with them, and when he arrived he was taken upstairs to the room. All the widows[f] stood around him, crying and showing him the robes and other clothing that Dorcas had made while she was still with them.

40Peter sent them all out of the room;[g] then he got down on his knees[h] and prayed. Turning toward the dead woman, he said, "Tabitha, get up."[i] She opened her eyes, and seeing Peter she sat up. **41**He took her by the hand and helped her to her feet. Then he called the believers and the widows and presented her to them alive. **42**This became known all over Joppa, and many people believed in the Lord.[j] **43**Peter stayed in Joppa for some time with a tanner named Simon.[k]

[o] *22* Or *Messiah* [p] *36* Both *Tabitha* (Aramaic) and *Dorcas* (Greek) mean *gazelle.*

---

sire the fullness of the Holy Spirit should expect the spiritual manifestations of his coming (2:4,17).

9:31 THE FEAR OF THE LORD. Luke emphasizes the formula "to fear God," both in his Gospel (see Lk 1:50; 18:2; 23:40) and in Acts. It is the God-fearers (i.e., Gentile adherents to the Jewish faith) who form the starting point for the Gentile mission in ch. 10 (10:2,22,35; 13:16,26). The fear of the Lord produces trust and obedience, as well as the avoidance of evil (Job 28:28; Ps 111:10; Pr 1:7); this response in turn results in the encouragement of the Holy Spirit. For more on this subject, see article on THE FEAR OF THE LORD, p. 260.

9:36 DORCAS . . . ALWAYS DOING GOOD. As God worked through Peter to heal (vv. 33–35) and to raise the dead (v. 40), he also worked through Dorcas with her deeds of kindness and love. Acts of love that help those in need are as much a manifestation of the Holy Spirit as are miracles, signs and wonders. Paul emphasized this truth in 1Co 13 (cf. 1Pe 4:10–11).

Cornelius Calls for Peter

10 At Caesarea[l] there was a man
named Cornelius, a centurion
in what was known as the Italian Regiment. 2He and all his family were devout and God-fearing;[m] he gave generously to those in need and prayed to
God regularly. 3One day at about three
in the afternoon[n] he had a vision.[o]
He distinctly saw an angel[p] of God,
who came to him and said, "Cornelius!"
4Cornelius stared at him in fear.
"What is it, Lord?" he asked.
The angel answered, "Your prayers
and gifts to the poor have come up as
a memorial offering[q] before God.[r]
5Now send men to Joppa[s] to bring
back a man named Simon who is called
Peter. 6He is staying with Simon the
tanner,[t] whose house is by the sea."
7When the angel who spoke to him
had gone, Cornelius called two of his
servants and a devout soldier who was
one of his attendants. 8He told them
everything that had happened and sent
them to Joppa.[u]

Peter's Vision

10:9–32Ref — Ac 11:5–14

9About noon the following day as
they were on their journey and approaching the city, Peter went up on
the roof[v] to pray. 10He became hungry
and wanted something to eat, and
while the meal was being prepared, he
fell into a trance.[w] 11He saw heaven
opened[x] and something like a large
sheet being let down to earth by its
four corners. 12It contained all kinds of
four-footed animals, as well as reptiles
of the earth and birds of the air. 13Then
a voice told him, "Get up, Peter. Kill
and eat."
14"Surely not, Lord!"[y] Peter replied. "I have never eaten anything impure or unclean."[z]
15The voice spoke to him a second
time, "Do not call anything impure that
God has made clean."[a]
16This happened three times, and
immediately the sheet was taken back
to heaven.
17While Peter was wondering about
the meaning of the vision,[b] the men
sent by Cornelius[c] found out where
Simon's house was and stopped at the
gate. 18They called out, asking if Simon who was known as Peter was
staying there.
19While Peter was still thinking
about the vision,[d] the Spirit said[e] to

10:1 [l] S Ac 8:40 **10:2** [m] ver 22,35; Ac 13:16,26 **10:3** [n] Ps 55:17; Ac 3:1 [o] S Ac 9:10 [p] S Ac 5:19 **10:4** [q] Ps 20:3; S Mt 10:42; 26:13 [r] Rev 8:4 **10:5** [s] S Ac 9:36 **10:6** [t] Ac 9:43 **10:8** [u] S Ac 9:36 **10:9** [v] S Mt 24:17 **10:10** [w] Ac 22:17 **10:11** [x] S Mt 3:16 **10:14** [y] Ac 9:5 [z] Lev 11:4-8,13-20; 20:25; Dt 14:3-20; Eze 4:14 **10:15** [a] ver 28; Ge 9:3; Mt 15:11; Lk 11:41; Ac 11:9; Ro 14:14,17,20; 1Co 10:25; 1Ti 4:3,4; Tit 1:15 **10:17** [b] S Ac 9:10 [c] ver 7,8 **10:19** [d] S Ac 9:10 [e] S Ac 8:29

10:4 YOUR PRAYERS . . . A MEMORIAL OFFERING BEFORE GOD. God considers our prayers a sacrifice ascending to him, reminding him of our perseverance in calling on him in faith and devotion (see Ps 141:2; Heb 13:15–16).

10:9 PETER WENT UP ON THE ROOF TO PRAY. The Holy Spirit, the author of the Scriptures, has revealed that the NT Christians were a people devoted to much prayer. They understood that God's kingdom could not be manifested in its full power with only a few minutes of prayer a day (1:14; 2:42; 3:1; 6:4; Eph 6:18; Col 4:2). (1) The pious Jew prayed two or three times a day (cf. Ps 55:17; Da 6:10). It was the custom of Christ's followers, especially the apostles (6:4), to pray with the same devotion. Peter and John went up to the temple "at the time of prayer" (3:1), while Luke and Paul did the same (16:16). Peter prayed regularly at noon; God rewarded Cornelius for his faithfulness in keeping his hours of prayer (vv. 30ff).

(2) The Scriptures urge believers to continue faithfully in prayer (Ro 12:12), pray always (Lk 18:1), pray continually (1Th 5:17), pray everywhere (1Ti 2:8), pray on all occasions with all kinds of prayers (Eph 6:18), persevere in prayer (Col 4:2) and pray powerfully (Jas 5:16). These exhortations indicate there can be no real kingdom power in our battle against sin, Satan and the world, or victory in our attempt to win the lost, without much daily prayer (see article on EFFECTIVE PRAYING, p. 496).

(3) Would it not be pleasing to God in the light of the Lord's plea that his disciples watch and pray at least "one hour" (Mt 26:38–41), and in the light of the urgency of the end times in which we live, for every believer to commit at least one hour a day to prayer and the study of God's Word for the advancement of his kingdom on earth and all that this involves for us (Mt 6:10,33)?

(4) One hour of prayer might include the following: (a) praise, (b) singing to the Lord, (c) thanksgiving, (d) waiting on God, (e) reading the Word, (f) listening to the Holy Spirit, (g) praying the very words of Scripture, (h) confessing failings, (i) interceding for others, (j) petition for one's own needs and (k) praying in tongues.

10:19 THE SPIRIT SAID TO HIM. The Holy Spirit desires the salvation of all people (Mt 28:19; 2Pe 3:9). Since the apostles received the Spirit, they too wanted all people to be saved. Intellectually, however, they did not understand that salvation was no longer restricted to Israel, but was now for all nations (vv. 34–35). It was the Holy Spirit that brought the church to a broader vision. In Acts he is the power of the mission enterprise, directing the church into new areas of witness (8:29,39; 11:11–12; 13:2,4; 16:6; 19:21). The outpouring of the Spirit and the compulsion to mission always belong together (cf. 1:8). Even today, many believers desire the salvation of those in their own community, yet have not understood fully the Holy Spirit's purpose for world missions

him, "Simon, three[q] men are looking
for you. **20**So get up and go downstairs.
Do not hesitate to go with them, for I
have sent them."[f]
21Peter went down and said to the
men, "I'm the one you're looking for.
Why have you come?"
22The men replied, "We have come
from Cornelius the centurion. He is a
righteous and God-fearing man,[g] who
is respected by all the Jewish people. A
holy angel told him to have you come
to his house so that he could hear what
you have to say."[h] **23**Then Peter invited the men into the house to be his
guests.

Peter at Cornelius' House

The next day Peter started out with
them, and some of the brothers[i] from
Joppa went along.[j] **24**The following
day he arrived in Caesarea.[k] Correli-
us was expecting them and had called
together his relatives and close
friends. **25**As Peter entered the house,
Cornelius met him and fell at his feet
in reverence. **26**But Peter made him get
up. "Stand up," he said, "I am only a
man myself."[l]
27Talking with him, Peter went inside and found a large gathering of
people.[m] **28**He said to them: "You are
well aware that it is against our law for
a Jew to associate with a Gentile or visit him.[n] But God has shown me that I
should not call any man impure or unclean.[o] **29**So when I was sent for, I
came without raising any objection.
May I ask why you sent for me?"
30Cornelius answered: "Four days
ago I was in my house praying at this
hour, at three in the afternoon. Suddenly a man in shining clothes[p] stood
before me **31**and said, 'Cornelius, God
has heard your prayer and remembered
your gifts to the poor. **32**Send to Joppa
for Simon who is called Peter. He is a
guest in the home of Simon the tanner,
who lives by the sea.' **33**So I sent for
you immediately, and it was good of
you to come. Now we are all here in the
presence of God to listen to everything
the Lord has commanded you to tell
us."
34Then Peter began to speak: "I now
realize how true it is that God does not
show favoritism[q] **35**but accepts men
from every nation who fear him and do
what is right.[r] **36**You know the mes- Ro 6:1-14
sage[s] God sent to the people of Israel,
telling the good news[t] of peace[u]
through Jesus Christ, who is Lord of
all.[v] **37**You know what has happened
throughout Judea, beginning in Galilee
after the baptism that John preached—
38how God anointed[w] Jesus of Nazareth with the Holy Spirit and power,
and how he went around doing good
and healing[x] all who were under the
power of the devil, because God was
with him.[y]
39"We are witnesses[z] of everything
he did in the country of the Jews and
in Jerusalem. They killed him by hanging him on a tree,[a] **40**but God raised
him from the dead[b] on the third day
and caused him to be seen. **41**He was
not seen by all the people,[c] but by witnesses whom God had already chosen—by us who ate[d] and drank with
him after he rose from the dead. **42**He
commanded us to preach to the people[e] and to testify that he is the one
whom God appointed as judge of the
living and the dead.[f] **43**All the prophets testify about him[g] that everyone[h]
who believes[i] in him receives forgiveness of sins through his name."[j]

Gentiles Receive the Spirit

44While Peter was still speaking

10:20 [f]Ac 15:7-9 **10:22** [g]ver 2 [h]Ac 11:14 **10:23** [i]S Ac 1:16 [j]ver 45; Ac 11:12 **10:24** [k]S Ac 8:40 **10:26** [l]Ac 14:15; Rev 19:10; 22:8,9 **10:27** [m]ver 24 **10:28** [n]Jn 4:9; 18:28; Ac 11:3 [o]S ver 14,15; Ac 15:8,9 **10:30** [p]S Jn 20:12

10:34 [q]Dt 10:17; 2Ch 19:7; Job 34:19; Mk 12:14; Ro 2:11; Gal 2:6; Eph 6:9; Col 3:25; Jas 2:1; 1Pe 1:17 **10:35** [r]Ac 15:9 **10:36** [s]1Jn 1:5 [t]S Ac 13:32 [u]S Lk 2:14 [v]S Mt 28:18 **10:38** [w]S Ac 4:26 [x]S Mt 4:23 [y]S Jn 3:2 **10:39** [z]ver 41; S Lk 24:48 [a]S Ac 5:30 **10:40** [b]S Ac 2:24 **10:41** [c]Jn 14:17, 22 [d]Lk 24:43; Jn 21:13; Ac 1:4 **10:42** [e]Mt 28:19, 20 [f]S Jn 5:22; Ac 17:31; Ro 14:9; 2Co 5:10; 2Ti 4:1; 1Pe 4:5 **10:43** [g]Isa 53:11; Ac 26:22 [h]Ac 15:9 [i]S Jn 3:15 [j]S Lk 24:27

[q]*19* One early manuscript *two*; other manuscripts do not have the number.

(see Mt 28:19, note; Lk 24:47, note).

10:34 GOD DOES NOT SHOW FAVORITISM. God has no favorite nation or race, nor does he favor any individual because of nationality, birth or position in life (cf. Jas 2:1). God favors and accepts those from every nation who turn from sin, believe in Christ, fear God and live righteously (v. 35; cf. Ro 2:6–11). All who continue in this manner of life will remain in God's love and favor (Jn 15:10).

10:38 HEALING ALL WHO WERE UNDER THE POWER OF THE DEVIL. See article on POWER OVER SATAN AND DEMONS, p. 1484.

10:44 THE HOLY SPIRIT CAME ON ALL. The Gentile household of Cornelius listened and received the Word with saving faith (vv. 34–48; 11:14). (1) Because of their acceptance of Christ, God at once pours out the Holy Spirit on them as his witness that they have believed and received the regenerating life of Christ (cf. 11:17; 15:8–9).

(2) The coming of the Holy Spirit on Cornelius's household has the same purpose as the gift of the Spirit had for the disciples on the day of Pentecost (cf. 1:8; 2:4). This outpouring does not describe God's work of regeneration, but his coming on them for power. Note Peter's words later on, stressing the similarity of this experience with

TESTING FOR GENUINE BAPTISM IN THE SPIRIT

***Ac 10:44–45** "While Peter was still speaking these words, the Holy Spirit came on all who heard the message. The circumcised believers who had come with Peter were astonished that the gift of the Holy Spirit had been poured out even on the Gentiles."*

Scripture declares that believers must test and weigh all things alleging to be from the Holy Spirit (1Th 5:19–21; cf. 1Co 14:29). "Do not believe every spirit, but test the spirits to see whether they are from God" (1Jn 4:1). The following are Biblical principles by which to test whether a professed baptism in the Holy Spirit is from God.

(1) A genuine baptism in the Holy Spirit will cause us to love, magnify and glorify God the Father and the Lord Jesus Christ more than before (see Jn 16:13–14; Ac 2:11,36; 4:12; 7:55–56; 10:44–46). It is the Holy Spirit who causes love for God to grow in our hearts (Ro 5:5). Conversely, any assumed baptism in the Spirit that draws our prayers, worship and adoration toward anything or anyone other than God and the Lord Jesus is not from God.

(2) A genuine baptism in the Holy Spirit will increase the consciousness of our relationship with the heavenly Father (Ac 1:4; Ro 8:15–16), will lead to a greater awareness of Christ's presence in our daily lives (Jn 14:16,23; 15:26) and will increase the heartfelt cry of "*Abba*, Father" (Ro 8:15; Gal 4:6). Conversely, any assumed baptism in the Spirit that does not result in a greater fellowship with Christ and more intense communion with God as our Father is not from God.

(3) A genuine baptism in the Holy Spirit will cause a greater love for and appreciation of Scripture. The Spirit of truth (Jn 14:17), who inspired the Scriptures (2Ti 3:16; 2Pe 1:20–21), will deepen our love for the truth of God's Word (Jn 16:13; Ac 2:42; 3:22; 1Jn 4:6). Conversely, any assumed baptism in the Spirit that diminishes our hunger to read God's Word is not from God (cf. Jn 8:31; 15:4–7).

(4) A genuine baptism in the Holy Spirit will deepen our love and concern for other followers of Christ (Ac 2:42–47; 4:31–37). Christian fellowship and communion can take place only in the Spirit (2Co 13:14). Conversely, any assumed baptism in the Spirit that decreases our love for all who seek to sincerely follow Jesus Christ as Lord and Savior is not from God (compare Ro 5:5 with 1Jn 4:21).

(5) A genuine baptism in the Holy Spirit must be preceded by our turning from sin and faithfully obeying Christ (Ac 2:38; 8:15–24); it will be sustained only as long as we continue to be sanctified by the Spirit (Ac 2:40; 3:26; 5:29–32; 8:21; 26:18; Gal 5:16–25), to "put to death the misdeeds of the body," and to be "led by the Spirit of God" (Ro 8:13–14; cf. Gal 5:24–25). Conversely, any assumed baptism in the Spirit that rests on one who is not set free from sin and who lives according to the sinful nature cannot be ascribed to the Holy Spirit as its source (Ac 2:38–40; 8:18–23; Ro 6:22–23; 8:2–15); any power on that person is from another source, the deceptive activity of Satan (cf. Ps 5:4–5; 2Co 11:13–15; 2Th 2:9–10).

(6) A genuine baptism in the Holy Spirit will intensify our displeasure with the sinful enjoyments and godless pleasures of the world and will diminish the selfish pursuit of earthly riches and reputation (Ac 4:32–37; 8:14–24; 20:33; 1Jn 2:15–17). Conversely, any assumed baptism in the Spirit that increases one's acceptance of the world's ways and philosophies is not from God, for "we have not received the spirit of the world but the Spirit who is from God" (1Co 2:12).

(7) A genuine baptism in the Holy Spirit will give us a greater desire and power to witness concerning the saving work of the Lord Jesus Christ (cf. Lk 4:18; Ac 1:4–8; 2:1–4,37–42; 4:8–33; Ro 9:1–3; 10:1). Conversely, any assumed baptism in the Spirit that does not result in a more intense desire to see others enter into a saving relationship with Christ is not from God (see Ac 4:20, note).

(8) A genuine baptism in the Holy Spirit will cause us to be more receptive to the Spirit's operation within God's kingdom and his gifts within our personal lives, particularly the gift of speaking in tongues, which is presented in Acts as the initial outward sign of the baptism in the Holy Spirit (Ac 2:4,16–18,43; 4:29–30; 5:12–16; 6:8; 8:5–7; 10:38,44–46; 1Co 12–14; Gal 3:5; see article on SPEAKING IN TONGUES, p. 1646). Conversely, any assumed baptism in the Spirit that does not result in the manifestations of the Spirit in our lives is an obvious departure from the experience of NT believers and the norm presented in the book of Acts (Ac 2:4,18; 10:45–46; 19:6).

(9) A genuine baptism in the Holy Spirit will cause us to be more conscious of the work, guidance and presence of the Spirit in our daily lives. After receiving the fullness of the Spirit, NT believers were continually conscious of the Spirit's presence, power and guidance (Ac 2:4,16–18; 4:31; 6:5; 9:31; 10:19; 13:2,4,52; 15:28; 16:6–7; 20:23). Conversely, any assumed baptism in the Spirit that does not increase our awareness of the Spirit's presence, strengthen our desire to obey his leadings, and reinforce our goal to live before him in such a way as not to grieve him or put out his fire (Eph 4:30; 1Th 5:19) is not from God.

PHILIP'S AND PETER'S MISSIONARY JOURNEYS

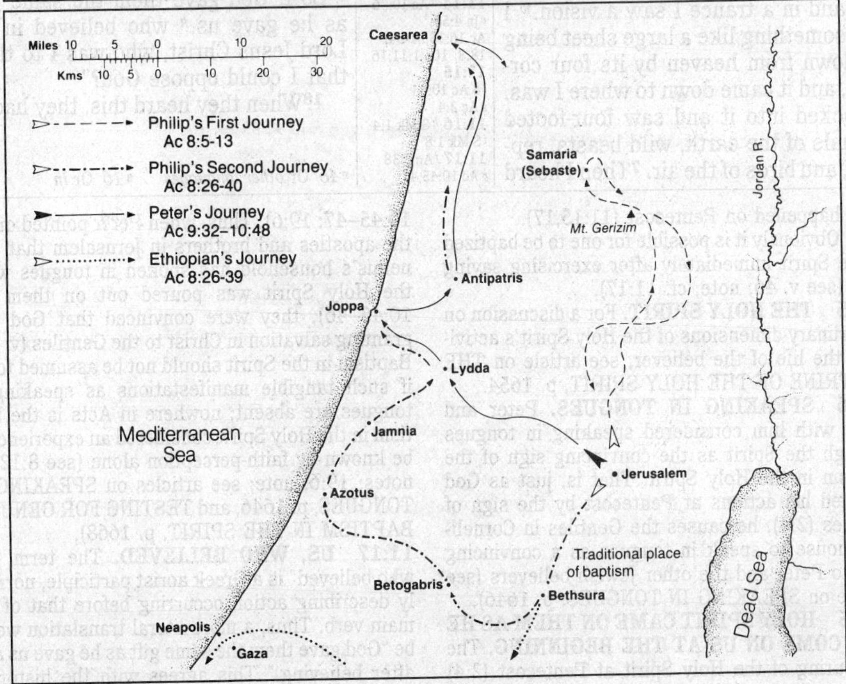

these words, the Holy Spirit came on[k] all who heard the message. **45**The circumcised believers who had come with Peter[l] were astonished that the gift of the Holy Spirit had been poured out[m] even on the Gentiles.[n] **46**For they heard them speaking in tongues[r][o] and praising God.

Then Peter said, **47**"Can anyone keep these people from being baptized with water?[p] They have received the Holy Spirit just as we have."[q] **48**So he ordered that they be baptized in the name of Jesus Christ.[r] Then they asked Peter to stay with them for a few days.

Ac 11:15-17

Peter Explains His Actions

11 The apostles and the brothers[s] throughout Judea heard that the Gentiles also had received the word of God.[t] **2**So when Peter went up to Jerusalem, the circumcised believers[u] criticized him **3**and said, "You went into the house of uncircumcised men and ate with them."[v]

4Peter began and explained everything to them precisely as it had happened: **5**"I was in the city of Joppa praying, and in a trance I saw a vision.[w] I saw something like a large sheet being let down from heaven by its four corners, and it came down to where I was. **6**I looked into it and saw four-footed animals of the earth, wild beasts, reptiles, and birds of the air. **7**Then I heard a voice telling me, 'Get up, Peter. Kill and eat.'

8"I replied, 'Surely not, Lord! Nothing impure or unclean has ever entered my mouth.'

9"The voice spoke from heaven a second time, 'Do not call anything impure that God has made clean.'[x] **10**This happened three times, and then it was all pulled up to heaven again.

11"Right then three men who had been sent to me from Caesarea[y] stopped at the house where I was staying. **12**The Spirit told[z] me to have no hesitation about going with them.[a] These six brothers[b] also went with me, and we entered the man's house. **13**He told us how he had seen an angel[c] appear in his house and say, 'Send to Joppa for Simon who is called Peter. **14**He will bring you a message[d] through which you and all your household[e] will be saved.'

15"As I began to speak, the Holy Spirit came on[f] them as he had come on us at the beginning.[g] **16**Then I remembered what the Lord had said: 'John baptized with[s] water,[h] but you will be baptized with the Holy Spirit.'[i] **17**So if God gave them the same gift[j] as he gave us,[k] who believed in the Lord Jesus Christ, who was I to think that I could oppose God?"

18When they heard this, they had no

10:44 [k] Ac 8:15,16; 11:15; 15:8; 19:6; S Lk 1:15
10:45 [l] ver 23 [m] Ac 2:33,38 [n] Ac 11:18; 15:8
10:46 [o] S Mk 16:17
10:47 [p] Ac 8:36 [q] S Jn 20:22; Ac 11:17
10:48 [r] S Ac 2:38
11:1 [s] S Ac 1:16 [t] S Heb 4:12
11:2 [u] Ac 10:45
11:3 [v] Ac 10:25,28; Gal 2:12
11:5 [w] Ac 10:9-32; S 9:10
11:9 [x] S Ac 10:15
11:11 [y] S Ac 8:40
11:12 [z] S Ac 8:29 [a] Ac 15:9; Ro 3:22 [b] ver 1,29; S Ac 1:16
11:13 [c] S Ac 5:19
11:14 [d] Ac 10:36 [e] Jn 4:53; Ac 16:15,31-34; 18:8; 1Co 1:11,16
11:15 [f] S Ac 10:44 [g] Ac 2:4
11:16 [h] S Mk 1:4 [i] S Mk 1:8
11:17 [j] Ac 2:38 [k] Ac 10:45,47

[r] 46 Or *other languages* [s] 16 Or *in*

what happened on Pentecost (11:15,17).

(3) Obviously it is possible for one to be baptized in the Spirit immediately after exercising saving faith (see v. 46, note; cf. 11:17).

10:45 THE HOLY SPIRIT. For a discussion on the primary dimensions of the Holy Spirit's activity in the life of the believer, see article on THE DOCTRINE OF THE HOLY SPIRIT, p. 1654.

10:46 SPEAKING IN TONGUES. Peter and those with him considered speaking in tongues through the Spirit as the convincing sign of the baptism in the Holy Spirit. That is, just as God attested his actions at Pentecost by the sign of tongues (2:4), he causes the Gentiles in Cornelius's house to speak in tongues as a convincing sign to Peter and the other Jewish believers (see article on SPEAKING IN TONGUES, p. 1646).

11:15 HOLY SPIRIT CAME ON THEM AS HE HAD COME ON US AT THE BEGINNING. The outpouring of the Holy Spirit at Pentecost (2:4) had set a pattern for the reception of the Spirit thereafter. The baptism in the Spirit would be determined by the visible transformation of the individual, the infusion of joy, Spirit-inspired utterances and boldness in witness (2:4; 4:31; 8:15–19; 10:45–47; 19:6). Thus, when Peter pointed out to the apostles and brothers in Jerusalem that Cornelius's household had spoken in tongues when the Holy Spirit was poured out on them (cf. 10:45–46), they were convinced that God was granting salvation in Christ to the Gentiles (v. 18). Baptism in the Spirit should not be assumed today if such tangible manifestations as speaking in tongues are absent; nowhere in Acts is the baptism in the Holy Spirit considered an experience to be known by faith-perception alone (see 8:12,16, notes; 19:6, note; see articles on SPEAKING IN TONGUES, p. 1646, and TESTING FOR GENUINE BAPTISM IN THE SPIRIT, p. 1668).

11:17 US, WHO BELIEVED. The term "us, who believed" is a Greek aorist participle, normally describing action occurring before that of the main verb. Thus, a more literal translation would be "God gave them the same gift as he gave us also after believing." This agrees with the historical facts that the disciples had believed in Jesus and were regenerated by the Spirit before Pentecost (see article on THE REGENERATION OF THE DISCIPLES, p. 1627).

11:18 WHEN THEY HEARD THIS. Peter's

further objections and praised God,
saying, "So then, God has granted even
the Gentiles repentance unto life."[l]

The Church in Antioch

19Now those who had been scattered
by the persecution in connection with
Stephen[m] traveled as far as Phoenicia,
Cyprus and Antioch,[n] telling the message only to Jews. 20Some of them,
however, men from Cyprus[o] and Cyrene,[p] went to Antioch[q] and began to
speak to Greeks also, telling them the
good news[r] about the Lord Jesus.
21The Lord's hand was with them,[s]
and a great number of people believed
and turned to the Lord.[t]
22News of this reached the ears of
the church at Jerusalem, and they sent
Barnabas[u] to Antioch. 23When he arrived and saw the evidence of the grace
of God,[v] he was glad and encouraged
them all to remain true to the Lord
with all their hearts.[w] 24He was a
good man, full of the Holy Spirit[x] and
faith, and a great number of people
were brought to the Lord.[y]
25Then Barnabas went to Tarsus[z]
to look for Saul, 26and when he found
him, he brought him to Antioch. So for
a whole year Barnabas and Saul met
with the church and taught great numbers of people. The disciples[a] were
called Christians first[b] at Antioch.
27During this time some prophets[c]
came down from Jerusalem to Antioch.
28One of them, named Agabus,[d] stood
up and through the Spirit predicted
that a severe famine would spread over
the entire Roman world.[e] (This happened during the reign of Claudius.)[f] Ac 14:3
29The disciples,[g] each according to
his ability, decided to provide help[h]
for the brothers[i] living in Judea.
30This they did, sending their gift to
the elders[j] by Barnabas[k] and Saul.[l]

James Put to Death; Peter Imprisoned

12 It was about this time that King
Herod[m] arrested some who belonged to the church, intending to persecute them. 2He had James, the brother of John,[n] put to death with the
sword.[o] 3When he saw that this
pleased the Jews,[p] he proceeded to
seize Peter also. This happened during
the Feast of Unleavened Bread.[q] 4Af-
ter arresting him, he put him in prison,
handing him over to be guarded by four
squads of four soldiers each. Herod intended to bring him out for public trial
after the Passover.[r]
5So Peter was kept in prison, but the

11:18 [l] Ro 10:12, 13; 2Co 7:10 **11:19** [m] Ac 8:1,4 [n] ver 26,27; Ac 13:1; 14:26; 18:22; Gal 2:11 **11:20** [o] Ac 4:36 [p] S Mt 27:32 [q] S ver 19 [r] S Ac 13:32 **11:21** [s] Lk 1:66 [t] S Ac 2:41 **11:22** [u] S Ac 4:36 **11:23** [v] Ac 13:43; 14:26; 15:40; 20:24 [w] Ac 14:22 **11:24** [x] S Lk 1:15 [y] S Ac 2:41 **11:25** [z] S Ac 9:11
11:26 [a] ver 29; Ac 6:1,2; 9:19,26, 38; 13:52 [b] Ac 26:28; 1Pe 4:16 **11:27** [c] Ac 13:1; 15:32; 1Co 11:4; 12:28,29; 14:29, 32,37; S Eph 4:11 **11:28** [d] Ac 21:10 [e] S Mt 24:14 [f] Ac 18:2 **11:29** [g] S ver 26 [h] Ro 15:26; 2Co 8:1-4; 9:2 [i] ver 1,12; S Ac 1:16 **11:30** [j] Ac 14:23; 15:2,22; 20:17; 1Ti 5:17; Tit 1:5; Jas 5:14; 1Pe 5:1; 2Jn 1 [k] S Ac 4:36 [l] Ac 12:25 **12:1** [m] S Mt 14:1 **12:2** [n] S Mt 4:21 [o] Mk 10:39 **12:3** [p] Ac 24:27; 25:9 [q] Ex 12:15; 23:15; Ac 20:6 **12:4** [r] S Jn 11:55

---

speech silenced all objections (vv. 4–18). God had baptized the Gentiles with the Holy Spirit (10:45), and accompanying this was the convincing evidence that they had spoken in other tongues (10:46). This was the only sign that was needed, and it was accepted without doubt.

11:23 REMAIN TRUE TO THE LORD. The NT disciples did not assume that those who received God's grace would automatically remain true to the Lord, for sin, the world and Satan's temptations could persuade a new believer to turn from the way of salvation in Christ. Barnabas gives us an example of how new converts ought to be treated: our main interest should be to help and encourage them to continue in faith, love and fellowship with Christ and his church (cf. 13:43; 14:22).

11:26 THE DISCIPLES WERE CALLED CHRISTIANS. The word "Christian" (Gk *christianos*) occurs only three times in the NT (11:26; 26:28; 1Pe 4:16). It originally was a term denoting a servant and follower of Christ. Today it has become a general term emptied of the original NT meaning. It should suggest the name of our Redeemer (Ro 3:24), the idea of our intimate relation to Christ (Ro 8:38–39), and the thought that we receive him as our Lord (Ro 5:1) and the source of eternal salvation (Heb 5:9). To claim the name "Christian" means that Christ and his Word revealed in Scripture have become our supreme authority and our only source of future hope (Col 1:5, 27).

11:27 PROPHETS. The place of prophets in the church is recognized in the Pauline letters (see article on THE MINISTRY GIFTS OF THE CHURCH, p. 1830).

12:2 JAMES . . . PUT TO DEATH. God allowed James, the brother of John (cf. Mt 4:21), to die, yet he sent an angel to rescue Peter (vv. 3–17). That James should die while Peter lived for further ministry is the mysterious way of God with his people. James had the honor of being the first of the apostles to meet a martyr's death. He died as his Lord had done—for the cause of God (cf. Mk 10:36–39).

12:5 THE CHURCH. From the book of Acts as well as other passages in the NT, we gain insight into the norms or authoritative standards for a NT church. (1) First and foremost, a church will consist of people formed into local congregations and united by the Holy Spirit, diligently seeking a faithful personal relationship with God and Jesus Christ (13:2; 16:5; 20:7; Ro 16:3–4; 1Co 16:19; 2Co 11:28; Heb 11:6, note).

(2) Through its powerful witness, sinners will be saved, born again, baptized in water and added to the church; they will partake of the Lord's Supper and wait for Christ's return (2:41–42; 4:33; 5:14; 11:24; 1Co 11:26).

church was earnestly praying to God
for him.[s]
6The night before Herod was to
bring him to trial, Peter was sleeping
between two soldiers, bound with two
chains,[t] and sentries stood guard at
the entrance. 7Suddenly an angel[u] of
the Lord appeared and a light shone
in the cell. He struck Peter on the side
and woke him up. "Quick, get up!" he
said, and the chains fell off Peter's
wrists.[v]
8Then the angel said to him, "Put on
your clothes and sandals." And Peter
did so. "Wrap your cloak around you
and follow me," the angel told him.
9Peter followed him out of the prison,
but he had no idea that what the angel
was doing was really happening; he
thought he was seeing a vision.[w]
10They passed the first and second
guards and came to the iron gate leading to the city. It opened for them by
itself,[x] and they went through it.
When they had walked the length of
one street, suddenly the angel left him.
11Then Peter came to himself[y] and
said, "Now I know without a doubt that
the Lord sent his angel and rescued
me[z] from Herod's clutches and from
everything the Jewish people were anticipating."

12:5 [s] S Ac 1:14; Ro 15:30,31; Eph 6:18
12:6 [t] Ac 21:33
12:7 [u] S Ac 5:19 [v] Ps 107:14; Ac 16:26
12:9 [w] S Ac 9:10
12:10 [x] Ac 5:19; 16:26
12:11 [y] Lk 15:17 [z] Ps 34:7; Da 3:28; 6:22; 2Co 1:10; 2Pe 2:9

(3) The baptism in the Holy Spirit will be preached and communicated to new believers (see 2:39, note), and the Spirit's presence and power manifested.

(4) The Holy Spirit's gifts will be in operation (Ro 12:6–8; 1Co 12:4–11; Eph 4:11–12), including wonders, miraculous signs and healings (2:18, 43; 4:30; 5:12; 6:8; 14:10; 19:11; 28:8; Mk 16:18).

(5) God gives a fivefold leadership to the church in order to equip the saints for the work of ministry (Eph 4:11–12; see article on THE MINISTRY GIFTS OF THE CHURCH, p. 1830).

(6) Believers will drive out demons (5:16; 8:7; 16:18; 19:12; Mk 16:17).

(7) There will be absolute loyalty to the gospel, i.e., the original teachings of Christ and the apostles (2:42; see Eph 2:20, note). The people will devote themselves to studying and obeying the Word of God (6:4; 18:11; Ro 15:18; Col 3:16; 2Ti 2:15).

(8) On the first day of the week (20:7; 1Co 16:2), the local congregation will meet together for worship and mutual edification through the written Word of God and the manifestations of the Spirit (1Co 12:7–11; 14:26; 1Ti 5:17).

(9) The church will stand in humility, awe and fear before the presence of a holy God (5:11). The people will be vitally concerned for the purity of the church, disciplining sinning members and teachers not loyal to the Biblical faith (20:28; 1Co 5:1–13; see Mt 18:15, note).

(10) Those who have persevered in godly character and the righteous standards set forth by the apostles will be ordained as elders to oversee local churches and maintain their spiritual life (Mt 18:15, note; 1Co 5:1–5; 1Ti 3:1–7; Tit 1:5–9; see article on OVERSEERS AND THEIR DUTIES, p. 1690).

(11) Likewise, the church will have deacons responsible for the temporal and material affairs of the church (see 1Ti 3:8, note).

(12) There will be observable love and fellowship in the Spirit among the members (2:42, 44–46; see Jn 13:34, note), not only within the local congregation but also between other Bible-believing congregations (15:1–31; 2Co 8:1–8).

(13) The church will be a praying and fasting church (1:14; 6:4; 12:5; 13:2; Ro 12:12; Col 4:2; Eph 6:18).

(14) Believers will separate themselves from the prevailing world view and the spirit of their surrounding culture (2:40; Ro 12:2; 2Co 6:17; Gal 1:4; 1Jn 2:15–16).

(15) There will be suffering and affliction because of the world and its ways (4:1–3; 5:40; 9:16; 14:22).

(16) The church will actively help send missionaries to other lands (2:39; 13:2–4).

No local church has the right to call itself a church after NT norms unless these 16 characteristics are in operation among its people. See article on THE CHURCH, p. 1439, for further discussion on the Biblical doctrine of the church.

12:5 EARNESTLY PRAYING. The NT believers faced persecution with fervent prayer. The situation looked impossible: James had already died, and Herod had Peter in the custody of sixteen soldiers. Yet the early church lived by the conviction that "the prayer of a righteous man is powerful and effective" (Jas 5:16), and they prayed intensely and steadily over Peter's situation. Their prayer was soon answered (vv. 6–17).

The NT churches often engaged in prolonged corporate prayer (1:14; 2:42; 4:24–31; 12:5,12; 13:2). God intends his people to gather together for meaningful, enduring prayer; note Jesus' words, "My house will be called a house of prayer" (Mt 21:13). Churches claiming to base their theology, practice and mission on the divine pattern set forth in the book of Acts and other NT writings should practice fervent corporate prayer as a vital element of their worship—and not just one or two minutes a service. In the early church God's power and presence and prayer meetings went together. No amount of preaching, teaching, singing, music or activity will bring forth the genuine power and presence of the Holy Spirit without NT prayer where believers "joined together constantly in prayer" (1:14).

12:7 AN ANGEL. Angels are "ministering spirits sent to serve those who will inherit salvation" (Heb 1:14; see article on ANGELS AND THE ANGEL OF THE LORD, p. 340).

12When this had dawned on him, he went to the house of Mary the mother of John, also called Mark,[a] where many people had gathered and were praying.[b] 13Peter knocked at the outer entrance, and a servant girl named Rhoda came to answer the door.[c] 14When she recognized Peter's voice, she was so overjoyed[d] she ran back without opening it and exclaimed, "Peter is at the door!"

15"You're out of your mind," they told her. When she kept insisting that it was so, they said, "It must be his angel."[e]

16But Peter kept on knocking, and when they opened the door and saw him, they were astonished. 17Peter motioned with his hand[f] for them to be quiet and described how the Lord had brought him out of prison. "Tell James[g] and the brothers[h] about this," he said, and then he left for another place.

18In the morning, there was no small commotion among the soldiers as to what had become of Peter. 19After Herod had a thorough search made for him and did not find him, he cross-examined the guards and ordered that they be executed.[i]

Herod's Death

Then Herod went from Judea to Caesarea[j] and stayed there a while. 20He had been quarreling with the people of Tyre and Sidon;[k] they now joined together and sought an audience with him. Having secured the support of Blastus, a trusted personal servant of the king, they asked for peace, because they depended on the king's country for their food supply.[l]

21On the appointed day Herod, wearing his royal robes, sat on his throne and delivered a public address to the people. 22They shouted, "This is the voice of a god, not of a man." 23Immediately, because Herod did not give praise to God, an angel[m] of the Lord struck him down,[n] and he was eaten by worms and died.

24But the word of God[o] continued to increase and spread.[p]

25When Barnabas[q] and Saul had finished their mission,[r] they returned from[t] Jerusalem, taking with them John, also called Mark.[s]

Barnabas and Saul Sent Off

13 In the church at Antioch[t] there were prophets[u] and teachers:[v] Barnabas,[w] Simeon called Niger, Lucius of Cyrene,[x] Manaen (who had been brought up with Herod[y] the tetrarch) and Saul. 2While they were worshiping the Lord and fasting, the Holy Spirit said,[z] "Set apart for me Barnabas and Saul for the work[a] to which I have called them."[b] 3So after they had fasted and prayed,

12:12 [a]ver 25; Ac 13:5,13; 15:37, 39; Col 4:10; 2Ti 4:11; Phm 24; 1Pe 5:13 [b]ver 5
12:13 [c]Jn 18:16, 17
12:14 [d]Lk 24:41
12:15 [e]S Mt 18:10
12:17 [f]Ac 13:16; 19:33; 21:40 [g]S Ac 15:13 [h]S Ac 1:16
12:19 [i]Ac 16:27 [j]S Ac 8:40
12:20 [k]S Mt 11:21 [l]1Ki 5:9,11; Eze 27:17
12:23 [m]S Ac 5:19 [n]1Sa 25:38; 2Sa 24:16,17; 2Ki 19:35
12:24 [o]S Heb 4:12 [p]Ac 6:7; 19:20
12:25 [q]S Ac 4:36 [r]Ac 11:30 [s]S ver 12
13:1 [t]S Ac 11:19 [u]S Ac 11:27 [v]S Eph 4:11 [w]S Ac 4:36 [x]S Mt 27:32 [y]S Mt 14:1
13:2 [z]S Ac 8:29 [a]Ac 14:26 [b]Ac 9:15; 22:21

[t]*25* Some manuscripts *to*

13:2 WORSHIPING . . . AND FASTING. Spirit-filled Christians are especially sensitive to the communication of the Holy Spirit during prayer and fasting (see Mt 6:16, note). The communication from the Holy Spirit probably came through a prophetic utterance (cf. v. 1).

13:2 FOR THE WORK TO WHICH I HAVE CALLED THEM. Paul and Barnabas were called into missionary service and were commissioned by the church at Antioch. The nature of this work is described in 9:15; 13:5; 22:14–15,21; and 26:16–18. (1) Paul and Barnabas were called to preach the gospel, bringing men and women into a saving relationship with Christ. Scripture nowhere indicates that the NT missionaries were sent out into the world to do social or political work, i.e., to propagate the gospel and establish churches by embarking on all sorts of organized social or political activities for the benefit of the people of the Roman empire. Their goal was to bring people to Christ (16:31; 20:21), deliver them from Satan's power (26:18), cause the Holy Spirit to come on them (19:6) and establish them in churches. In these new Christians the Spirit came to live and reveal himself through love; he gave spiritual gifts (1Co 12–13) and transformed them from within so that their lives would bring glory to their living Savior.

(2) Missionaries of the gospel today must be devoted to the same kind of activity: to be ministers of and witnesses to the gospel, bringing others to Christ by delivering them from Satan's dominion (26:18), making them disciples, encouraging them to receive the Holy Spirit and his gifts (2:38; 8:17), and teaching them to obey all that Christ commanded (Mt 28:19–20). Accompanying this should be signs and wonders, the healing of the sick and deliverance for those oppressed by demons (2:43; 4:30; 8:7; 10:38; Mk 16:17–18). The supreme task of preaching the gospel, however, should also include personal acts of love and kindness to those in need (cf. Gal 2:10). In this way, all those called to bear witness to the gospel will model their ministry after Jesus (see Lk 9:2, note).

13:3 SENT THEM OFF. With this passage begins the great missionary movement "to the ends of the earth" (1:8). The missionary principles described in ch. 13 are a model for all

they placed their hands on them[c] and
sent them off.[d]

On Cyprus

4The two of them, sent on their way
by the Holy Spirit,[e] went down to Seleucia and sailed from there to Cyprus.[f] 5When they arrived at Salamis,
they proclaimed the word of God[g] in
the Jewish synagogues.[h] John[i] was
with them as their helper.
6They traveled through the whole island until they came to Paphos. There
they met a Jewish sorcerer[j] and false
prophet[k] named Bar-Jesus, 7who was
an attendant of the proconsul,[l] Sergi-
us Paulus. The proconsul, an intelligent man, sent for Barnabas and Saul
because he wanted to hear the word of
God. 8But Elymas the sorcerer[m] (for
that is what his name means) opposed
them and tried to turn the proconsul[n]
from the faith.[o] 9Then Saul, who was
also called Paul, filled with the Holy
Spirit,[p] looked straight at Elymas and
said, 10"You are a child of the devil[q]

13:3 [c] S Ac 6:6 [d] Ac 14:26
13:4 [e] ver 2,3 [f] Ac 4:36
13:5 [g] S Heb 4:12 [h] S Ac 9:20 [i] S Ac 12:12
13:6 [j] Ac 8:9 [k] S Mt 7:15
13:7 [l] ver 8,12; Ac 18:12; 19:38
13:8 [m] Ac 8:9 [n] S ver 7 [o] Isa 30:11; Ac 6:7
13:9 [p] S Lk 1:15
13:10 [q] Mt 13:38; Jn 8:44

missionary-sending churches.

(1) Missionary activity is initiated by the Holy Spirit through spiritual leaders who are deeply devoted to the Lord and his kingdom, seeking him with prayer and fasting (v. 2).

(2) The church must be sensitive to the guidance and prophetic ministry and activity of the Holy Spirit (v. 2).

(3) Missionaries who go out must do so under the specific call and will of the Holy Spirit (v. 2b).

(4) By prayer and fasting, constantly seeking to be aligned with the Spirit's will (vv. 3–4), the church confirms that God has called certain individuals to missionary work. The goal is that the church send out only those whom the Spirit desires.

(5) Through the laying on of hands and the sending out of missionaries, the church indicates her commitment to the support and encouragement of those who go out. The responsibility of the sending church includes sending the missionaries on their way with love and in a manner worthy of God (3Jn 6), praying for them (13:3; Eph 6:18–19) and giving them financial support (Lk 10:7; 3Jn 6–8), including offerings of love for their needs (Php 4:10, 14–18). Missionaries are considered an extension of the purpose, concern and mission of the sending church; the church thus becomes those who "work together for the truth" (3Jn 8; cf. Php 1:5).

(6) Those who go out as missionaries must be willing to risk their lives for the name of Jesus Christ (15:26).

PAUL'S FIRST MISSIONARY JOURNEY

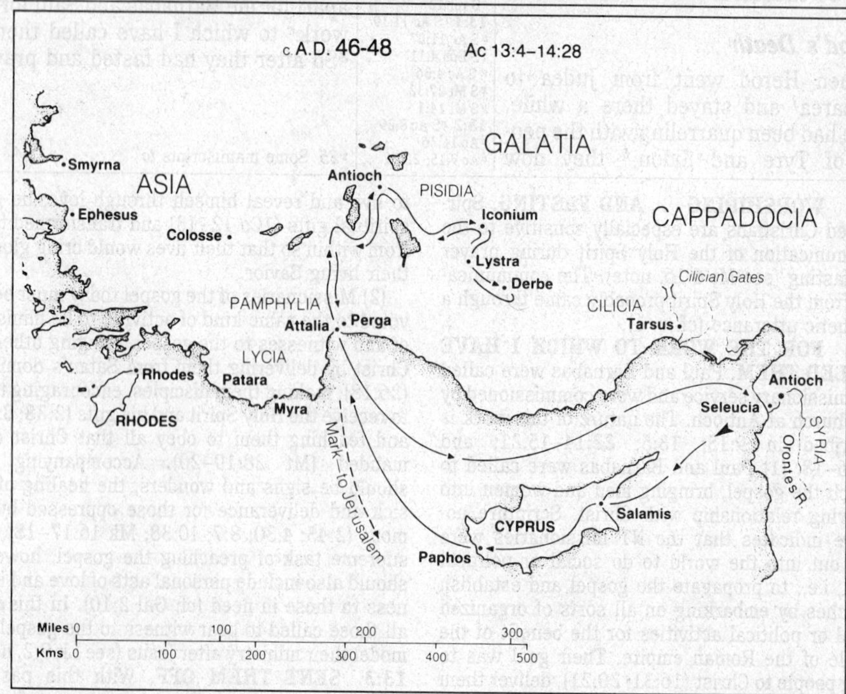

and an enemy of everything that is
right! You are full of all kinds of deceit
and trickery. Will you never stop perverting the right ways of the Lord?[r]
11Now the hand of the Lord is against
you.[s] You are going to be blind, and
for a time you will be unable to see the
light of the sun."[t]

Immediately mist and darkness
came over him, and he groped about,
seeking someone to lead him by the
hand. 12When the proconsul[u] saw
what had happened, he believed, for he
was amazed at the teaching about the
Lord.

In Pisidian Antioch

13From Paphos,[v] Paul and his companions sailed to Perga in Pamphylia,[w] where John[x] left them to return
to Jerusalem. 14From Perga they went
on to Pisidian Antioch.[y] On the Sabbath[z] they entered the synagogue[a]
and sat down. 15After the reading from
the Law[b] and the Prophets, the synagogue rulers sent word to them, saying, "Brothers, if you have a message
of encouragement for the people,
please speak."

16Standing up, Paul motioned with
his hand[c] and said: "Men of Israel and
you Gentiles who worship God, listen
to me! 17The God of the people of Israel chose our fathers; he made the people prosper during their stay in Egypt,
with mighty power he led them out of
that country,[d] 18he endured their conduct[u][e] for about forty years in the
desert,[f] 19he overthrew seven nations
in Canaan[g] and gave their land to his
people[h] as their inheritance.[i] 20All
this took about 450 years.

"After this, God gave them judges[j]
until the time of Samuel the prophet.[k]
21Then the people asked for a king,[l]
and he gave them Saul[m] son of Kish,
of the tribe of Benjamin,[n] who ruled
forty years. 22After removing Saul,[o]
he made David their king.[p] He testified concerning him: 'I have found David son of Jesse a man after my own
heart;[q] he will do everything I want
him to do.'[r]

23"From this man's descendants[s]
God has brought to Israel the Savior[t]
Jesus,[u] as he promised.[v] 24Before
the coming of Jesus, John preached repentance and baptism to all the people
of Israel.[w] 25As John was completing
his work,[x] he said: 'Who do you think
I am? I am not that one.[y] No, but he
is coming after me, whose sandals I am
not worthy to untie.'[z]

26"Brothers,[a] children of Abraham,[b] and you God-fearing Gentiles,
it is to us that this message of salvation[c] has been sent. 27The people of
Jerusalem and their rulers did not recognize Jesus,[d] yet in condemning him
they fulfilled the words of the prophets[e] that are read every Sabbath.
28Though they found no proper ground
for a death sentence, they asked Pilate
to have him executed.[f] 29When they
had carried out all that was written
about him,[g] they took him down from
the tree[h] and laid him in a tomb.[i]
30But God raised him from the dead,[j]
31and for many days he was seen by
those who had traveled with him from

13:10 [r]Hos 14:9 **13:11** [s]Ex 9:3; 1Sa 5:6,7; Ps 32:4 [t]Ge 19:10,11; 2Ki 6:18 **13:12** [u]S ver 7 **13:13** [v]ver 6 [w]S Ac 2:10 [x]S Ac 12:12 **13:14** [y]Ac 14:19, 21 [z]ver 27,42,44; Ac 16:13; 18:4 [a]S Ac 9:20 **13:15** [b]Ac 15:21 **13:16** [c]S Ac 12:17 **13:17** [d]Ex 6:6,7; Dt 7:6-8 **13:18** [e]Dt 1:31 [f]Nu 14:33; Ps 95:10; Ac 7:36 **13:19** [g]Dt 7:1 [h]Jos 19:51; Ac 7:45 [i]Ps 78:55 **13:20** [j]Jdg 2:16 [k]1Sa 3:19,20; Ac 3:24 **13:21** [l]1Sa 8:5, 19 [m]1Sa 10:1 [n]1Sa 9:1,2 **13:22** [o]1Sa 15:23,26 [p]1Sa 16:13; Ps 89:20 [q]1Sa 13:14; Jer 3:15 [r]Isa 44:28 **13:23** [s]S Mt 1:1 [t]S Lk 2:11 [u]Mt 1:21 [v]ver 32; 2Sa 7:11; 22:51; Jer 30:9 **13:24** [w]S Mk 1:4 **13:25** [x]Ac 20:24 [y]Jn 1:20 [z]Mt 3:11; Jn 1:27 **13:26** [a]S Ac 22:5 [b]S Lk 3:8 [c]Ac 4:12; 28:28 **13:27** [d]Ac 3:17 [e]S Lk 24:27; S Mt 1:22 **13:28** [f]Mt 27:20-25; Ac 3:14 **13:29** [g]S Mt 1:22; Lk 18:31 [h]S Ac 5:30 [i]Lk 23:53 **13:30** [j]S Mt 16:21; 28:6; S Ac 2:24

[u] *18* Some manuscripts *and cared for them*

13:8 THE SORCERER. The sorcerer was probably a Jewish astrologer. Astrologers taught that the destiny of the individual was determined by celestial bodies. They believed they could foretell the future by examining the position of the stars and planets. All sorcery or astrology stands in opposition to the gospel of Christ because it involves Satan and the demonic (v. 10; see Dt 18:9–11, notes).

13:9 SAUL ... FILLED WITH THE HOLY SPIRIT. One may be baptized in the Spirit as was Paul (9:17), yet in times of special need receive fresh fillings with the Spirit. Such repeated fillings are necessary (1) in confronting opposition to the gospel (4:8–12), (2) in advancing the gospel (4:8, 31) and (3) in directly challenging satanic activity (13:9,50–52). Repeated fillings with the Spirit should be the norm for all believers who are baptized in the Holy Spirit.

13:11 YOU ARE GOING TO BE BLIND. Miracles in the NT were not always healings; some, such as God's anger against Elymas (vv. 8–11) and Herod (12:20–23), involved judgment on ungodly individuals. God's anger against Ananias and Sapphira (5:1–11) is an example of a miraculous judgment against sin within the church.

13:31 HIS WITNESSES TO OUR PEOPLE. A witness (Gk *martus*) is "one who testifies by act or word to the truth." Christian witnesses are those who confirm and testify to the saving work of Jesus Christ by word, deed, life and, if necessary, even death. It involves seven principles:

(1) Christian witnessing is the obligation of all believers (1:8; Mt 4:19; 28:19–20).

(2) Christian witnesses must be missionary-minded, going to all the nations and bearing God's salvation to the ends of the earth (11:18; 13:2–4; 26:16–18; Mt 28:19–20; Lk 24:47).

Galilee to Jerusalem.[k] They are now
his witnesses[l] to our people.
32 "We tell you the good news:[m]
What God promised our fathers[n] 33 he
has fulfilled for us, their children, by
raising up Jesus.[o] As it is written in
the second Psalm:

" 'You are my Son;
today I have become your
Father.'[v][w][p]

34 The fact that God raised him from
the dead, never to decay, is stated in
these words:

" 'I will give you the holy and sure
blessings promised to
David.'[x][q]

35 So it is stated elsewhere:

" 'You will not let your Holy One
see decay.'[y][r]

36 "For when David had served God's
purpose in his own generation, he fell
asleep;[s] he was buried with his fathers[t] and his body decayed. 37 But
the one whom God raised from the
dead[u] did not see decay.
38 "Therefore, my brothers, I want
you to know that through Jesus the forgiveness of sins is proclaimed to you.[v]
39 Through him everyone who believes[w] is justified from everything
you could not be justified from by the
Ro 1:16 law of Moses.[x] 40 Take care that what
the prophets have said does not happen to you:
41 " 'Look, you scoffers,
wonder and perish,
for I am going to do something in
your days
that you would never believe,
even if someone told you.'[z]"[y]

42 As Paul and Barnabas were leaving the synagogue,[z] the people invited
them to speak further about these
things on the next Sabbath. 43 When
the congregation was dismissed, many
of the Jews and devout converts to Judaism followed Paul and Barnabas,
who talked with them and urged them
to continue in the grace of God.[a]
44 On the next Sabbath almost the
whole city gathered to hear the word of
the Lord. 45 When the Jews saw the
crowds, they were filled with jealousy
and talked abusively[b] against what
Paul was saying.[c]
46 Then Paul and Barnabas answered them boldly: "We had to speak
the word of God to you first.[d] Since
you reject it and do not consider yourselves worthy of eternal life, we now
turn to the Gentiles.[e] 47 For this is
what the Lord has commanded us:

" 'I have made you[a] a light for the
Gentiles,[f]
that you[a] may bring salvation
to the ends of the
earth.'[b]"[g]

48 When the Gentiles heard this, they
were glad and honored the word of the
Lord;[h] and all who were appointed for
eternal life believed.
49 The word of the Lord[i] spread
through the whole region. 50 But the
Jews incited the God-fearing women of

13:31 [k] Mt 28:16 [l] S Lk 24:48
13:32 [m] Isa 40:9; 52:7; Ac 5:42; 8:35; 10:36; 14:7, 15,21; 17:18 [n] Ac 26:6; Ro 1:2; 4:13; 9:4
13:33 [o] S Ac 2:24 [p] Ps 2:7; S Mt 3:17
13:34 [q] Isa 55:3
13:35 [r] Ps 16:10; Ac 2:27
13:36 [s] S Mt 9:24 [t] 2Sa 7:12; 1Ki 2:10; 2Ch 29:28; Ac 2:29
13:37 [u] S Ac 2:24
13:38 [v] S Lk 24:47; Ac 2:38
13:39 [w] S Jn 3:15 [x] S Ro 3:28
13:41 [y] Hab 1:5
13:42 [z] ver 14
13:43 [a] S Ac 11:23; 14:22; S Ro 3:24
13:45 [b] Ac 18:6; 1Pe 4:4; Jude 10 [c] S 1Th 2:16
13:46 [d] ver 26; Ac 3:26 [e] Mt 21:41; Ac 18:6; 22:21; 26:20; 28:28; Ro 11:11
13:47 [f] S Lk 2:32 [g] Isa 49:6
13:48 [h] ver 49; Ac 8:25; 15:35,36; 19:10,20
13:49 [i] S ver 48

[v] *33* Or *have begotten you* [w] *33* Psalm 2:7
[x] *34* Isaiah 55:3 [y] *35* Psalm 16:10
[z] *41* Hab. 1:5 [a] *47* The Greek is singular.
[b] *47* Isaiah 49:6

(3) Christian witnesses speak primarily about the meaning of Christ's life, death, resurrection, saving power and promised Holy Spirit (2:32, 38–39; 3:15; 10:39–41,43; 18:5; 26:16; 1Co 15:1–8).

(4) Christian witnesses must bring conviction concerning sin, righteousness and judgment (2:37–40; 7:51–54; 24:24–25; see Jn 16:8, note). Through such witness people are brought to saving faith (2:41; 4:33; 6:7; 11:21).

(5) Christian witnesses at times will suffer (7:57–60; 22:20; 2Co 11:23–29). The word "martyr" is derived from the Greek word for witness. Discipleship involves commitment, no matter what the cost.

(6) Christian witnessing must be accompanied by separation from the world (2:40), a life of righteousness (Ro 14:17), and an utter reliance on the Holy Spirit (4:29–33) that results in the manifestation of God's Spirit and power (1Co 2:4).

(7) Christian witnessing is prophetic (2:17), and empowered (1:8) and inspired by the Spirit (2:4; 4:8).

13:48 APPOINTED FOR ETERNAL LIFE. Some have understood this verse as teaching arbitrary predestination. However, neither the context nor the word translated "appointed" (Gk *tetagmenoi*, from *tassō*) warrant this interpretation. (1) V. 46 explicitly emphasizes human responsibility in accepting or rejecting eternal life. The best rendering of *tetagmenoi*, therefore, is "were disposed": "and all who were disposed to eternal life believed." This rendering agrees completely with the affirmations of 1Ti 2:4; Tit 2:11; 2Pe 3:9 (see article on ELECTION AND PREDESTINATION, p. 1824). (2) Furthermore, according to Paul, no person is unconditionally appointed for eternal life (see Ro 11:20–22).

high standing and the leading men of the city. They stirred up persecution against Paul and Barnabas, and expelled them from their region.[j] **51**So they shook the dust from their feet[k] in protest against them and went to Iconium.[l] **52**And the disciples[m] were filled with joy and with the Holy Spirit.[n]

In Iconium

14 At Iconium[o] Paul and Barnabas went as usual into the Jewish synagogue.[p] There they spoke so effectively that a great number[q] of Jews and Gentiles believed. **2**But the Jews who refused to believe stirred up the Gentiles and poisoned their minds against the brothers.[r] **3**So Paul and Barnabas spent considerable time there, speaking boldly[s] for the Lord, who confirmed the message of his grace by enabling them to do miracu-
32 lous signs and wonders.[t] **4**The people of the city were divided; some sided with the Jews, others with the apostles.[u] **5**There was a plot afoot among the Gentiles and Jews,[v] together with their leaders, to mistreat them and stone them.[w] **6**But they found out about it and fled[x] to the Lycaonian cities of Lystra and Derbe and to the surrounding country, **7**where they continued to preach[y] the good news.[z]

In Lystra and Derbe

8In Lystra there sat a man crippled in his feet, who was lame from birth[a] and had never walked. **9**He listened to Paul as he was speaking. Paul looked directly at him, saw that he had faith to be healed[b] **10**and called out, "Stand up on your feet!"[c] At that, the man jumped up and began to walk.[d] Ac 27:25

11When the crowd saw what Paul had done, they shouted in the Lycaonian language, "The gods have come down to us in human form!"[e] **12**Barnabas they called Zeus, and Paul they called Hermes because he was the chief speaker.[f] **13**The priest of Zeus, whose temple was just outside the city, brought bulls and wreaths to the city gates because he and the crowd wanted to offer sacrifices to them.

14But when the apostles Barnabas and Paul heard of this, they tore their clothes[g] and rushed out into the crowd, shouting: **15**"Men, why are you doing this? We too are only men,[h] human like you. We are bringing you good news,[i] telling you to turn from these worthless things[j] to the living God,[k] who made heaven and earth[l] and sea and everything in them.[m] **16**In the past, he let[n] all nations go their own way.[o] **17**Yet he has not left himself without testimony:[p] He has shown kindness by giving you rain from heaven and crops in their seasons;[q] he provides you with plenty of food and fills your hearts with joy."[r] **18**Even with these words, they had difficulty keeping the crowd from sacrificing to them.

19Then some Jews[s] came from Antioch and Iconium[t] and won the crowd over. They stoned Paul[u] and dragged him outside the city, thinking he was dead. **20**But after the disci-

13:50 [j]S 1Th 2:16
13:51 [k]S Mt 10:14 [l]Ac 14:1,19,21; 16:2; 2Ti 3:11
13:52 [m]S Ac 11:26 [n]S Lk 1:15
14:1 [o]S Ac 13:51 [p]S Ac 9:20 [q]S Ac 2:41
14:2 [r]S Ac 1:16
14:3 [s]S Ac 4:29 [t]S Jn 4:48
14:4 [u]Ac 17:4,5; 28:24
14:5 [v]S Ac 20:3 [w]ver 19
14:6 [x]Mt 10:23
14:7 [y]Ac 16:10 [z]ver 15,21; S Ac 13:32
14:8 [a]Ac 3:2
14:9 [b]Mt 9:28, 29; 13:58
14:10 [c]Eze 2:1 [d]Ac 3:8
14:11 [e]Ac 8:10; 28:6
14:12 [f]Ex 7:1
14:14 [g]S Mk 14:63
14:15 [h]S Ac 10:26 [i]ver 7,21; S Ac 13:32 [j]1Sa 12:21; 1Th 1:9 [k]S Mt 16:16 [l]Ge 1:1 [m]Ps 146:6; Rev 14:7
14:16 [n]Ac 17:30 [o]Ps 81:12; Mic 4:5
14:17 [p]Ro 1:20 [q]Dt 11:14; Job 5:10; Ps 65:10 [r]Ps 4:7
14:19 [s]Ac 13:45 [t]S Ac 13:51 [u]2Co 11:25; 2Ti 3:11

13:52 FILLED . . . WITH THE HOLY SPIRIT. The Greek verb translated "filled" is in the imperfect tense, expressing continued action in past time. The disciples were being continually filled and empowered day by day. The Spirit's fullness is not merely a one-time initial experience, but a life of renewed fillings for God-given needs and tasks (cf. Eph 5:18).

14:3 MIRACULOUS SIGNS AND WONDERS. God intended that the preaching of the gospel be accompanied by miraculous signs to confirm the truth of the gospel (cf. Mk 16:20; see article on SIGNS OF BELIEVERS, p. 1513). In this way the Lord worked with his people and bore witness to the truth of the message. Such confirmation of God's grace with signs and wonders is no less needed today as we face "terrible times in the last days" (1Ti 4:1; see 2Ti 3:1–13).

14:4 APOSTLES. Both Paul and Barnabas are called apostles. As a more general term, "apostle" was applied to the first Christian missionaries who were sent out by the church to preach the NT message (vv. 4,14). "Apostle" in a more specialized sense is applied only to those who received a direct commission by Christ to establish his original message and revelation (see Eph 2:20, note). Paul was an apostle in this special sense.

14:9 SAW THAT HE HAD FAITH. Discerning the faith of the crippled man most likely came through the Holy Spirit. Paul encouraged this man's faith by commanding him to stand up. Believers should pray for spiritual insight to recognize the faith of individuals needing God's grace and healing.

14:19 STONED PAUL. In NT times God did not always protect his servants from harm. This truth is inherent in the gospel and valid today as well: the kingdom of God advances at great cost to God's servants. Paul later described this incident of suffering by saying, "once I was stoned" (2Co 11:25; see Ac 9:16, note); he probably had this same episode in mind when he wrote to the Galatians, "I bear on my body the marks of Jesus" (Gal 6:17; see 2Co 11:23, note on Paul's suffering).

ples[v] had gathered around him, he got
up and went back into the city. The
next day he and Barnabas left for Derbe.

The Return to Antioch in Syria

21They preached the good news[w] in
that city and won a large number[x]
of disciples. Then they returned
to Lystra, Iconium[y] and Antioch,
22strengthening the disciples and encouraging them to remain true to the
faith.[z] "We must go through many
hardships[a] to enter the kingdom of
God," they said. **23**Paul and Barnabas
appointed elders[c][b] for them in each
church and, with prayer and fasting,[c]
committed them to the Lord,[d] in
whom they had put their trust. **24**After
going through Pisidia, they came into
Pamphylia,[e] **25**and when they had
preached the word in Perga, they went
down to Attalia.

26From Attalia they sailed back to
Antioch,[f] where they had been committed to the grace of God[g] for the
work they had now completed.[h] **27**On
arriving there, they gathered the
church together and reported all that
God had done through them[i] and how
he had opened the door[j] of faith to the
Gentiles. **28**And they stayed there a
long time with the disciples.[k]

The Council at Jerusalem

15 Some men[l] came down from
Judea to Antioch and were
teaching the brothers:[m] "Unless you
are circumcised,[n] according to the
custom taught by Moses,[o] you cannot
be saved." **2**This brought Paul and Barnabas into sharp dispute and debate
with them. So Paul and Barnabas were
appointed, along with some other believers, to go up to Jerusalem[p] to see
the apostles and elders[q] about this
question. **3**The church sent them on
their way, and as they traveled through
Phoenicia[r] and Samaria, they told
how the Gentiles had been converted.[s] This news made all the brothers
very glad. **4**When they came to Jerusalem, they were welcomed by the church
and the apostles and elders, to whom
they reported everything God had done
through them.[t]

5Then some of the believers who belonged to the party[u] of the Pharisees[v] stood up and said, "The Gentiles must be circumcised and required
to obey the law of Moses."[w]

6The apostles and elders met to consider this question. **7**After much discussion, Peter got up and addressed
them: "Brothers, you know that some
time ago God made a choice among you
that the Gentiles might hear from my
lips the message of the gospel and believe.[x] **8**God, who knows the heart,[y]
showed that he accepted them by giving the Holy Spirit to them,[z] just as he
did to us. **9**He made no distinction between us and them,[a] for he purified
their hearts by faith.[b] **10**Now then,
why do you try to test God[c] by putting
on the necks of the disciples a yoke[d]
that neither we nor our fathers have
been able to bear? **11**No! We believe it
is through the grace[e] of our Lord

14:20 [v] ver 22,28; S Ac 11:26
14:21 [w] S Ac 13:32 [x] S Ac 2:41 [y] S Ac 13:51
14:22 [z] Ac 11:23; 13:43 [a] Jn 16:33; 1Th 3:3; 2Ti 3:12
14:23 [b] S Ac 11:30 [c] Ac 13:3 [d] Ac 20:32
14:24 [e] S Ac 2:10
14:26 [f] S Ac 11:19 [g] S Ac 11:23 [h] Ac 13:1,3
14:27 [i] Ac 15:4, 12; 21:19 [j] 1Co 16:9; 2Co 2:12; Col 4:3; Rev 3:8
14:28 [k] S Ac 11:26
15:1 [l] ver 24; Gal 2:12 [m] S Ac 1:16 [n] ver 5; Gal 5:2,3 [o] S Ac 6:14
15:2 [p] Gal 2:2 [q] S Ac 11:30
15:3 [r] Ac 11:19 [s] Ac 14:27
15:4 [t] ver 12; Ac 14:27; 21:19
15:5 [u] Ac 5:17 [v] Mt 3:7 [w] ver 1
15:7 [x] Ac 10:1-48
15:8 [y] S Rev 2:23 [z] S Ac 10:44,47
15:9 [a] Ac 10:28, 34; 11:12 [b] Ac 10:43
15:10 [c] Ac 5:9 [d] S Mt 23:4; Gal 5:1
15:11 [e] S Ro 3:24; Gal 2:16; Eph 2:5-8

[c] 23 Or *Barnabas ordained elders*; or *Barnabas had elders elected*

14:22 THROUGH MANY HARDSHIPS. Those who commit themselves to Christ's lordship and who will finally enter the kingdom of God must suffer "many hardships" along the way. Living in a hostile world, they must engage in spiritual warfare against sin and Satan's power (Eph 6:12; cf. Ro 8:17; 2Th 1:4–7; 2Ti 2:12). (1) Those who are faithful to Christ, his Word and his righteous ways can expect trouble in this world (Jn 16:33). Only the lukewarm or compromising "believer" will find peace and comfort from the world (cf. Rev 3:14–17). (2) The present evil world and false believers will remain adversaries to the gospel of Christ until the Lord overthrows the world's evil system at his coming (Rev 19–20). Meanwhile the hope of believers is "stored up . . . in heaven" (Col 1:5) and will be "revealed in the last time" (1Pe 1:5). Their hope is not in this life nor in this world, but in the appearance of their Savior to take them to himself (Jn 14:1–3; 1Jn 3:2–3; see article on BIBLICAL HOPE, p. 792).

14:23 APPOINTED ELDERS. The appointing of elders (overseers or pastors) was done not only by seeking the Spirit's will through prayer and fasting, but also by examining the character, spiritual gifts, reputation and evidence of the Spirit's fruit in the men under consideration (1Ti 3:1–10). If they were found to be above reproach, they were appointed to serve (see article on MORAL QUALIFICATIONS FOR OVERSEERS, p. 1882).

15:8 GOD, WHO KNOWS THE HEART. God's knowledge of the hearts of the Gentiles (i.e., Cornelius and his household) refers to his seeing saving faith within them. God testified to the genuineness of their faith (1) by cleansing their hearts with the inward work of regeneration by the Holy Spirit (v. 9), and (2) by baptizing them in the Spirit immediately afterwards, with the accompanying sign of speaking in tongues (10:44–46; 11:15–18).

Jesus that we are saved, just as they
are."
12The whole assembly became silent
as they listened to Barnabas and Paul
telling about the miraculous signs and
wonders[f] God had done among the
Gentiles through them.[g] 13When they
finished, James[h] spoke up: "Brothers,
listen to me. 14Simon[d] has described
to us how God at first showed his concern by taking from the Gentiles a people for himself.[i] 15The words of the
prophets are in agreement with this, as
it is written:

16" 'After this I will return
and rebuild David's fallen tent.
Its ruins I will rebuild,
and I will restore it,
17that the remnant of men may seek
the Lord,
and all the Gentiles who bear
my name,
says the Lord, who does these
things'[e][j]
18 that have been known for
ages.[f][k]

19"It is my judgment, therefore, that
we should not make it difficult for the
Gentiles who are turning to God. 20In-
stead we should write to them, telling
them to abstain from food polluted by
idols,[l] from sexual immorality,[m]
from the meat of strangled animals and
from blood.[n] 21For Moses has been
preached in every city from the earliest
times and is read in the synagogues on
every Sabbath."[o]

15:12 [f]S Jn 4:48 [g]ver 4; Ac 14:27; 21:19
15:13 [h]Ac 12:17; 21:18; 1Co 15:7; Gal 1:19; 2:9,12
15:14 [i]2Pe 1:1
15:17 [j]Am 9:11, 12
15:18 [k]Isa 45:21
15:20 [l]1Co 8:7-13; 10:14-28; Rev 2:14,20 [m]1Co 10:7,8; Rev 2:14,20 [n]ver 29; Ge 9:4; Lev 3:17; 7:26; 17:10-13; 19:26; Dt 12:16,23
15:21 [o]Ac 13:15; 2Co 3:14,15
15:22 [p]S Ac 11:30 [q]S Ac 11:19 [r]ver 27,32,40; Ac 16:19,25,29; 2Co 1:19; 1Th 1:1; 2Th 1:1; 1Pe 5:12
15:23 [s]ver 1; S Ac 11:19 [t]S Lk 2:2 [u]ver 41; S Ac 6:9 [v]Ac 23:25,26; Jas 1:1
15:24 [w]ver 1; Gal 1:7; 5:10
15:26 [x]Ac 9:23-25; 14:19; 1Co 15:30
15:27 [y]S ver 22
15:28 [z]Ac 5:32

The Council's Letter to Gentile Believers

22Then the apostles and elders,[p]
with the whole church, decided to
choose some of their own men and
send them to Antioch[q] with Paul and
Barnabas. They chose Judas (called
Barsabbas) and Silas,[r] two men who
were leaders among the brothers.
23With them they sent the following
letter:

The apostles and elders, your brothers,

To the Gentile believers in Antioch,[s] Syria[t] and Cilicia:[u]

Greetings.[v]

24We have heard that some
went out from us without our authorization and disturbed you,
troubling your minds by what they
said.[w] 25So we all agreed to
choose some men and send them
to you with our dear friends Barnabas and Paul— 26men who
have risked their lives[x] for the
name of our Lord Jesus Christ.
27Therefore we are sending Judas
and Silas[y] to confirm by word of
mouth what we are writing. 28It
seemed good to the Holy Spirit[z]

[d] *14* Greek *Simeon,* a variant of *Simon;* that is, Peter [e] *17* Amos 9:11,12 [f] *17,18* Some manuscripts *things'— / [18]known to the Lord for ages is his work*

15:11 THROUGH THE GRACE OF OUR LORD JESUS. The crucial question at the Jerusalem council was whether circumcision and obedience to the law of Moses were required for salvation. The delegates concluded that Gentiles were saved through the grace of the Lord Jesus, who forgave them and made them a new creation (see article on FAITH AND GRACE, p. 1720). Grace comes to a person when he or she repents and believes in Christ as Lord and Savior (2:38–39). This response to God's grace enables him or her to receive power to become a child of God (Jn 1:12).

15:14 TAKING FROM THE GENTILES A PEOPLE. God's program for this age is to take from among all the nations a people, separated to him for his name. This body of Christ, gathered out of the present world system, prepares herself as the bride of Christ (Rev 19:7–8).

15:16 DAVID'S FALLEN TENT. James indicates that Christ's redemptive mission includes both Jew and Gentile. "David's fallen tent" (see Am 9:11–15, note) refers to a remnant of Israel that survives God's judgment. (1) Amos's prophecy states the following: (a) God will judge sinful Israel, yet not totally. (b) He will destroy all the sinners in the house of Jacob (Am 9:10). (c) After the destruction of the ungodly Jews, God will "restore David's fallen tent" (Am 9:11). (2) The salvation of this purified Jewish remnant will result in the nations seeking the Lord (v. 17). Elsewhere Paul says the same thing when he refers to a blessing for the Gentiles that will come from the Jewish remnant's reconciliation to God (see Ro 11:11–15,25–26).

15:28 IT SEEMED GOOD TO THE HOLY SPIRIT. The Jerusalem council was directed by the Holy Spirit. Jesus promised that the Spirit would guide them into all truth (Jn 16:13). Decisions of the church must not be made by humans alone; they must seek the Spirit's guidance through prayer, fasting and commitment to God's Word until his will is clearly discerned (cf. 13:2–4). The church, if it is to be the church of Christ, must hear what the Spirit says to the churches (cf. Rev 2:7).

and to us not to burden you with
anything beyond the following requirements: **29**You are to abstain
from food sacrificed to idols, from
blood, from the meat of strangled
animals and from sexual immorality.[a] You will do well to avoid
these things.

Farewell.

30The men were sent off and went
down to Antioch, where they gathered
the church together and delivered the
letter. **31**The people read it and were
glad for its encouraging message. **32**Ju-
Ac 21:9-12 das and Silas,[b] who themselves were
prophets,[c] said much to encourage
and strengthen the brothers. **33**After
spending some time there, they were
sent off by the brothers with the blessing of peace[d] to return to those who
had sent them.[g] **35**But Paul and Barnabas remained in Antioch, where they
and many others taught and
preached[e] the word of the Lord.[f]

Disagreement Between Paul and Barnabas

36Some time later Paul said to Barnabas, "Let us go back and visit the
brothers in all the towns[g] where we
preached the word of the Lord[h] and
see how they are doing." **37**Barnabas
wanted to take John, also called
Mark,[i] with them, **38**but Paul did not
think it wise to take him, because he
had deserted them[j] in Pamphylia and
had not continued with them in the
work. **39**They had such a sharp disagreement that they parted company.
Barnabas took Mark and sailed for Cyprus, **40**but Paul chose Silas[k] and left,
commended by the brothers to the
grace of the Lord.[l] **41**He went through
Syria[m] and Cilicia,[n] strengthening
the churches.[o]

Timothy Joins Paul and Silas

16 He came to Derbe and then to
Lystra,[p] where a disciple
named Timothy[q] lived, whose mother
was a Jewess and a believer,[r] but
whose father was a Greek. **2**The brothers[s] at Lystra and Iconium[t] spoke
well of him. **3**Paul wanted to take him
along on the journey, so he circumcised him because of the Jews who
lived in that area, for they all knew that
his father was a Greek.[u] **4**As they
traveled from town to town, they delivered the decisions reached by the apostles and elders[v] in Jerusalem[w] for the
people to obey.[x] **5**So the churches
were strengthened[y] in the faith and
grew daily in numbers.[z]

Paul's Vision of the Man of Macedonia

6Paul and his companions traveled
throughout the region of Phrygia[a] and
Galatia,[b] having been kept by the
Holy Spirit from preaching the word in
the province of Asia.[c] **7**When they
came to the border of Mysia, they tried
to enter Bithynia, but the Spirit of
Jesus[d] would not allow them to. **8**So
they passed by Mysia and went down
to Troas.[e] **9**During the night Paul had
a vision[f] of a man of Macedonia[g]
standing and begging him, "Come over
to Macedonia and help us." **10**After

15:29 [a] ver 20; Ac 21:25 **15:32** [b] S ver 22 [c] S Ac 11:27 **15:33** [d] 1Sa 1:17; Mk 5:34; Lk 7:50; Ac 16:36; 1Co 16:11 **15:35** [e] Ac 8:4 [f] S Ac 13:48 **15:36** [g] Ac 13:4, 13,14,51; 14:1,6, 24,25 [h] S Ac 13:48 **15:37** [i] S Ac 12:12 **15:38** [j] Ac 13:13 **15:40** [k] S ver 22 [l] S Ac 11:23 **15:41** [m] ver 23; S Lk 2:2 [n] S Ac 6:9 [o] Ac 16:5 **16:1** [p] Ac 14:6 [q] Ac 17:14; 18:5; 19:22; 20:4; Ro 16:21; 1Co 4:17; 16:10; 2Co 1:1,19; Php 1:1; 2:19; Col 1:1; 1Th 1:1; 3:2,6; 2Th 1:1; 1Ti 1:2,18; 2Ti 1:2,5,6; Phm 1 [r] 2Ti 1:5 **16:2** [s] ver 40; S Ac 1:16 [t] S Ac 13:51 **16:3** [u] Gal 2:3 **16:4** [v] S Ac 11:30 [w] Ac 15:2 [x] Ac 15:28,29 **16:5** [y] Ac 9:31; 15:41 [z] S Ac 2:41 **16:6** [a] Ac 2:10; 18:23 [b] Ac 18:23; Gal 1:2; 3:1 [c] S Ac 2:9 **16:7** [d] Ro 8:9; Gal 4:6; Php 1:19; 1Pe 1:11 **16:8** [e] ver 11; Ac 20:5; 2Co 2:12; 2Ti 4:13 **16:9** [f] S Ac 9:10 [g] Ac 19:21,29; 20:1,3; Ro 15:26; 1Co 16:5; 1Th 1:7,8

[g] 33 Some manuscripts *them,* [34]*but Silas decided to remain there*

15:29 YOU ARE TO ABSTAIN FROM. The Holy Spirit (v. 28) suggested certain restrictions for Gentiles that would enable Jewish Christians to live in harmony with their Gentile brothers and sisters. The Gentiles would be expected to abstain from activities that were offensive to Jews. One measure of Christian maturity is the willingness to refrain from activities that some Christians think are right and others believe are wrong (see Paul's discussion in 1Co 8:1–11).

15:39 A SHARP DISAGREEMENT. At times disagreements will occur among believers who love the Lord and one another. When these cannot be resolved, it is best to agree to disagree and let God work his will in the lives of all concerned. Differences in opinions that lead to a separation, as in the case of Paul and Barnabas, must never be accompanied by bitterness and hostility. Both Paul and Barnabas continued their work for God with his blessing and grace.

16:5 THE CHURCHES WERE STRENGTHENED. For comments on the form that churches in the NT took, see note on 12:5.

16:6 KEPT BY THE HOLY SPIRIT FROM PREACHING. Every initiative in evangelism and missionary activity, especially in the missionary journeys recorded in Acts, is the result of the leading of the Holy Spirit (1:8; 2:14–41; 4:8–12,31; 8:26–29,39–40; 10:19–20; 13:2; 16:6–10; 20:22). The guidance may have taken the form of a prophetic revelation, inward prompting, external circumstances or visions (vv. 6–9). Under the impulse of the Spirit believers moved forward to take the gospel to the unsaved. When checked by the Spirit from going in one direction, they would go in another, trusting in the Holy Spirit to either approve or disapprove of their traveling plans.

Paul had seen the vision, we[h] got
ready at once to leave for Macedonia,
concluding that God had called us to
preach the gospel[i] to them.

Lydia's Conversion in Philippi

11From Troas[j] we put out to sea
and sailed straight for Samothrace,
and the next day on to Neapolis.
12From there we traveled to Philippi,[k]
a Roman colony and the leading city of
that district of Macedonia.[l] And we
stayed there several days.
13On the Sabbath[m] we went outside
the city gate to the river, where we expected to find a place of prayer. We sat
down and began to speak to the women
who had gathered there. **14**One of
those listening was a woman named
Lydia, a dealer in purple cloth from the
city of Thyatira,[n] who was a worshiper of God. The Lord opened her heart[o]
to respond to Paul's message. **15**When
she and the members of her household[p] were baptized,[q] she invited us
to her home. "If you consider me a believer in the Lord," she said, "come and
stay at my house." And she persuaded
us.

Paul and Silas in Prison

16Once when we were going to the
place of prayer,[r] we were met by a
slave girl who had a spirit[s] by which
she predicted the future. She earned a
great deal of money for her owners by
fortune-telling. **17**This girl followed
Paul and the rest of us, shouting,
"These men are servants of the Most
High God,[t] who are telling you the
way to be saved." **18**She kept this up
for many days. Finally Paul became so

16:10 [h]ver 10-17; Ac 20:5-15; 21:1-18; 27:1-28:16 [i]Ac 14:7
16:11 [j]S ver 8
16:12 [k]Ac 20:6; Php 1:1; 1Th 2:2 [l]S ver 9
16:13 [m]S Ac 13:14
16:14 [n]Rev 1:11; 2:18,24 [o]Lk 24:45
16:15 [p]S Ac 11:14 [q]S Ac 2:38
16:16 [r]ver 13 [s]Dt 18:11; 1Sa 28:3,7
16:17 [t]S Mk 5:7

16:16 A SPIRIT BY WHICH SHE PREDICTED THE FUTURE. The slave girl's demonic utterances were regarded as a voice of a god; therefore, her services as a fortune-teller were much in demand. Through Paul, Christ showed his power over the world of evil (see article on POWER OVER SATAN AND DEMONS, p. 1484).

PAUL'S SECOND MISSIONARY JOURNEY

c. A.D. 49-52

Ac 15:39–18:22

SAMOTHRACE—Islands
Rhodes—Cities, Ports

troubled that he turned around and said to the spirit, "In the name of Jesus Christ I command you to come out of
Ac 19:13-20 her!" At that moment the spirit left her.[u]

[19]When the owners of the slave girl realized that their hope of making money[v] was gone, they seized Paul and Silas[w] and dragged[x] them into the marketplace to face the authorities. [20]They brought them before the magistrates and said, "These men are Jews, and are throwing our city into an uproar[y] [21]by advocating customs unlawful for us Romans[z] to accept or practice."[a]

[22]The crowd joined in the attack against Paul and Silas, and the magistrates ordered them to be stripped and beaten.[b] [23]After they had been severely flogged, they were thrown into prison, and the jailer[c] was commanded to guard them carefully. [24]Upon receiving such orders, he put them in the inner cell and fastened their feet in the stocks.[d]

[25]About midnight[e] Paul and Silas[f] were praying and singing hymns[g] to God, and the other prisoners were listening to them. [26]Suddenly there was such a violent earthquake that the foundations of the prison were shaken.[h] At once all the prison doors flew open,[i] and everybody's chains came loose.[j] [27]The jailer woke up, and when he saw the prison doors open, he drew his sword and was about to kill himself because he thought the prisoners had escaped.[k] [28]But Paul shouted, "Don't harm yourself! We are all here!"

[29]The jailer called for lights, rushed in and fell trembling before Paul and Silas.[l] [30]He then brought them out and asked, "Sirs, what must I do to be saved?"[m]

[31]They replied, "Believe[n] in the Lord Jesus, and you will be saved[o]—you and your household."[p] [32]Then they spoke the word of the Lord to him
and to all the others in his house. [33]At that hour of the night[q] the jailer took them and washed their wounds; then immediately he and all his family were baptized.[r] [34]The jailer brought them into his house and set a meal before them; he[s] was filled with joy because he had come to believe in God—he and his whole family.

[35]When it was daylight, the magistrates sent their officers to the jailer with the order: "Release those men." [36]The jailer[t] told Paul, "The magistrates have ordered that you and Silas be released. Now you can leave. Go in peace."[u]

[37]But Paul said to the officers: "They beat us publicly without a trial, even though we are Roman citizens,[v] and threw us into prison. And now do

16:18 [u]S Mk 16:17
16:19 [v]ver 16; Ac 19:25,26 [w]S Ac 15:22 [x]Ac 8:3; 17:6; 21:30; Jas 2:6
16:20 [y]Ac 17:6
16:21 [z]ver 12 [a]Est 3:8
16:22 [b]2Co 11:25; 1Th 2:2
16:23 [c]ver 27,36
16:24 [d]Job 13:27; 33:11; Jer 20:2,3; 29:26
16:25 [e]Ps 119:55,62 [f]S Ac 15:22 [g]S Eph 5:19
16:26 [h]Ac 4:31 [i]Ac 5:19; 12:10 [j]Ac 12:7
16:27 [k]Ac 12:19
16:29 [l]S Ac 15:22
16:30 [m]Ac 2:37
16:31 [n]S Jn 3:15 [o]S Ro 11:14 [p]S Ac 11:14
16:33 [q]ver 25 [r]S Ac 2:38
16:34 [s]S Ac 11:14
16:36 [t]ver 23,27 [u]S Ac 15:33
16:37 [v]Ac 22:25-29

16:23 SEVERELY FLOGGED. The Jewish law concerning whippings was "forty lashes minus one" (2Co 11:24). The Roman custom depended on the judge and could be terribly cruel. The beating was normally inflicted on the naked body.

16:25 PRAYING AND SINGING HYMNS. Paul and Silas had suffered the humiliation of imprisonment, their feet fastened in stocks and their backs lacerated. Yet in the middle of this suffering, they prayed and sang hymns of praise to God (cf. Mt 5:10–12). From their missionary experience we learn: (1) that the believer's joy is within, not conditioned by outward circumstances; persecution cannot destroy our peace and joy (Jas 1:2–4); (2) that Christ's enemies cannot destroy the believer's faith in and love for God (Ro 8:35–39); (3) that in the worst of circumstances God will provide sufficient grace for those who are in his will and suffer for his name's sake (Mt 5:10–12; 2Co 12:9–10); (4) that "the Spirit of glory and of God rests on" those who suffer for the name of Christ (1Pe 4:14).

16:26 EVERYBODY'S CHAINS CAME LOOSE. Throughout the book of Acts, Luke emphasizes that nothing can stop the gospel of Christ carried by faithful believers. At Philippi God intervened, and Paul and Silas were delivered by an earthquake. This resulted in further progress for the gospel, notably, the salvation of the jailer and his household.

16:30 WHAT MUST I DO TO BE SAVED? This is the most important question one can ask. The apostles' response is, "Believe in the Lord Jesus" (v. 31). (1) To believe in the Lord Jesus is to focus our faith and commitment on the person of Christ. It means turning to him as a living person who is our Redeemer from sin, our Savior from damnation and the Lord of our lives. It means believing that he is the Son of God sent by the Father and that all he said is true and authoritative for our lives. It means believing that he forgives our sins, makes us his children, gives us the Holy Spirit, and is present with us always to help, guide, comfort and lead us to heaven.

(2) Saving faith is much more than believing truths about Christ. It causes us to draw near to him, remain in him, and commit our troubled lives to him with assurance that he, his Word and the Spirit will lead us through this life to the Father's eternal presence (see article on FAITH AND GRACE, p. 1720).

they want to get rid of us quietly? No! Let them come themselves and escort us out."

38The officers reported this to the magistrates, and when they heard that Paul and Silas were Roman citizens, they were alarmed.[w] 39They came to appease them and escorted them from the prison, requesting them to leave the city.[x] 40After Paul and Silas came out of the prison, they went to Lydia's house,[y] where they met with the brothers[z] and encouraged them. Then they left.

In Thessalonica

17 When they had passed through Amphipolis and Apollonia, they came to Thessalonica,[a] where there was a Jewish synagogue. 2As his custom was, Paul went into the synagogue,[b] and on three Sabbath[c] days he reasoned with them from the Scriptures,[d] 3explaining and proving that the Christ[h] had to suffer[e] and rise from the dead.[f] "This Jesus I am proclaiming to you is the Christ,[h]"[g] he said. 4Some of the Jews were persuaded and joined Paul and Silas,[h] as did a large number of God-fearing Greeks and not a few prominent women.

5But the Jews were jealous; so they rounded up some bad characters from the marketplace, formed a mob and started a riot in the city.[i] They rushed to Jason's[j] house in search of Paul and Silas in order to bring them out to the crowd.[i] 6But when they did not find them, they dragged[k] Jason and some other brothers[l] before the city officials, shouting: "These men who have caused trouble all over the world[m] have now come here,[n] 7and Jason has welcomed them into his house. They are all defying Caesar's decrees, saying that there is another king, one called Jesus."[o] 8When they heard this, the crowd and the city officials were thrown into turmoil. 9Then they made Jason[p] and the others post bond and let them go.

In Berea

10As soon as it was night, the brothers sent Paul and Silas[q] away to Berea.[r] On arriving there, they went to the Jewish synagogue.[s] 11Now the Bereans were of more noble character than the Thessalonians,[t] for they received the message with great eagerness and examined the Scriptures[u] every day to see if what Paul said was true.[v] 12Many of the Jews believed, as did also a number of prominent Greek women and many Greek men.[w]

13When the Jews in Thessalonica learned that Paul was preaching the word of God at Berea,[x] they went there too, agitating the crowds and stirring them up. 14The brothers[y] immediately sent Paul to the coast, but Silas[z] and Timothy[a] stayed at Berea. 15The men who escorted Paul brought him to Athens[b] and then left with instructions for Silas and Timothy to join him as soon as possible.[c]

In Athens

16While Paul was waiting for them in Athens, he was greatly distressed to see that the city was full of idols. 17So he reasoned in the synagogue[d] with the Jews and the God-fearing Greeks, as well as in the marketplace day by day with those who happened to be there. 18A group of Epicurean and Stoic philosophers began to dispute with him. Some of them asked, "What is this babbler trying to say?" Others remarked, "He seems to be advocating foreign gods." They said this because

16:38 [w] Ac 22:29
16:39 [x] Mt 8:34; Lk 8:37
16:40 [y] ver 14 [z] ver 2; S Ac 1:16
17:1 [a] ver 11,13; Php 4:16; 1Th 1:1; 2Th 1:1; 2Ti 4:10
17:2 [b] S Ac 9:20 [c] S Ac 13:14 [d] Ac 8:35; 18:28
17:3 [e] Lk 24:26; Ac 3:18 [f] Lk 24:46; S Ac 2:24 [g] S Ac 9:22
17:4 [h] S Ac 15:22
17:5 [i] ver 13; S 1Th 2:16 [j] Ro 16:21
17:6 [k] S Ac 16:19 [l] S Ac 1:16 [m] S Mt 24:14 [n] Ac 16:20
17:7 [o] Lk 23:2; Jn 19:12
17:9 [p] ver 5
17:10 [q] S Ac 15:22 [r] ver 13; Ac 20:4 [s] S Ac 9:20
17:11 [t] S ver 1 [u] Lk 16:29; Jn 5:39 [v] Dt 29:29
17:12 [w] S Ac 2:41
17:13 [x] S Heb 4:12
17:14 [y] S Ac 9:30 [z] S Ac 15:22 [a] S Ac 16:1
17:15 [b] ver 16,21,22; Ac 18:1; 1Th 3:1 [c] Ac 18:5
17:17 [d] S Ac 9:20

[h] 3 Or *Messiah* [i] 5 Or *the assembly of the people*

17:11 EXAMINED THE SCRIPTURES EVERY DAY. The action of those in Berea is a model for all who listen to preachers and teachers expound the Scriptures. No interpretation or doctrine ought to be accepted passively. Rather, it must be examined carefully by personal study of the Scriptures. The word translated "examine" (Gk *anakrinō*) means "to sift up and down, make careful and exact research." Bible preaching should make Bible students out of the hearers. The truth of every doctrine should be examined according to the Word of God (see Eph 2:20, note).

17:16 HE WAS GREATLY DISTRESSED. At the sight of idolatry and moral corruption, Paul became indignant and grief-stricken (see Heb 1:9, note); his spirit stirred over people who were lost and in need of salvation. Paul expressed the same attitude as Jesus did toward sin and its destructive work (see Jn 11:33, note). An attitude of holy anger toward sin and immorality should characterize all those who have the spirit of Christ. For the cause of Christ and the salvation of the lost, our spirits should rebel against sin denounced in Scripture, offensive to God and destructive to the human race (cf. 1Co 6:17).

Paul was preaching the good news[e]
about Jesus and the resurrection.[f]
19Then they took him and brought him
to a meeting of the Areopagus,[g]
where they said to him, "May we know
what this new teaching[h] is that you
are presenting? **20**You are bringing
some strange ideas to our ears, and we
want to know what they mean." **21**(All
the Athenians[i] and the foreigners
who lived there spent their time doing
nothing but talking about and listening
to the latest ideas.)

22Paul then stood up in the meeting
of the Areopagus[j] and said: "Men of
Athens! I see that in every way you are
very religious.[k] **23**For as I walked
around and looked carefully at your objects of worship, I even found an altar
with this inscription: TO AN UNKNOWN GOD.
Now what you worship as something
unknown[l] I am going to proclaim to
you.

24"The God who made the world and
everything in it[m] is the Lord of heaven
and earth[n] and does not live in temples built by hands.[o] **25**And he is not
served by human hands, as if he needed anything, because he himself gives
all men life and breath and everything
else.[p] **26**From one man he made every
nation of men, that they should inhabit
the whole earth; and he determined the
times set for them and the exact places
where they should live.[q] **27**God did
this so that men would seek him and
perhaps reach out for him and find him,
though he is not far from each one of
us.[r] **28**'For in him we live and move
and have our being.'[s] As some of your
own poets have said, 'We are his offspring.'

29"Therefore since we are God's offspring, we should not think that the divine being is like gold or silver or
stone—an image made by man's design and skill.[t] **30**In the past God
overlooked[u] such ignorance,[v] but
now he commands all people everywhere to repent.[w] **31**For he has set a
day when he will judge[x] the world
with justice[y] by the man he has appointed.[z] He has given proof of this to
all men by raising him from the
dead."[a]

32When they heard about the resurrection of the dead,[b] some of them
sneered, but others said, "We want to
hear you again on this subject." **33**At
that, Paul left the Council. **34**A few
men became followers of Paul and believed. Among them was Dionysius, a
member of the Areopagus,[c] also a
woman named Damaris, and a number
of others.

In Corinth

18 After this, Paul left Athens[d]
and went to Corinth.[e] **2**There
he met a Jew named Aquila, a native of
Pontus, who had recently come from
Italy with his wife Priscilla,[f] because
Claudius[g] had ordered all the Jews to
leave Rome. Paul went to see them,
3and because he was a tentmaker as
they were, he stayed and worked with
them.[h] **4**Every Sabbath[i] he reasoned
in the synagogue,[j] trying to persuade
Jews and Greeks.

5When Silas[k] and Timothy[l] came
from Macedonia,[m] Paul devoted himself exclusively to preaching, testifying to the Jews that Jesus was the
Christ.[j][n] **6**But when the Jews opposed Paul and became abusive,[o] he
shook out his clothes in protest[p] and
said to them, "Your blood be on your
own heads![q] I am clear of my responsibility.[r] From now on I will go to the
Gentiles."[s]

7Then Paul left the synagogue and
went next door to the house of Titius
Justus, a worshiper of God.[t] **8**Crispus,[u] the synagogue ruler,[v] and his

17:18 [e] S Ac 13:32 [f] ver 31,32; Ac 4:2
17:19 [g] ver 22 [h] Mk 1:27
17:21 [i] S ver 15
17:22 [j] ver 19 [k] ver 16
17:23 [l] Jn 4:22
17:24 [m] Isa 42:5; Ac 14:15 [n] Dt 10:14; Isa 66:1,2; Mt 11:25 [o] 1Ki 8:27; Ac 7:48
17:25 [p] Ps 50:10-12; Isa 42:5
17:26 [q] Dt 32:8; Job 12:23
17:27 [r] Dt 4:7; Isa 55:6; Jer 23:23,24
17:28 [s] Dt 30:20; Job 12:10; Da 5:23
17:29 [t] Isa 40:18-20; Ro 1:23
17:30 [u] Ac 14:16; Ro 3:25 [v] ver 23; 1Pe 1:14
[w] Lk 24:47; Tit 2:11,12
17:31 [x] S Mt 10:15 [y] Ps 9:8; 96:13; 98:9 [z] S Ac 10:42 [a] S Ac 2:24
17:32 [b] ver 18,31
17:34 [c] ver 19,22
18:1 [d] S Ac 17:15 [e] Ac 19:1; 1Co 1:2; 2Co 1:1,23; 2Ti 4:20
18:2 [f] ver 19,26; Ro 16:3; 1Co 16:19; 2Ti 4:19 [g] Ac 11:28
18:3 [h] Ac 20:34; 1Co 4:12; 1Th 2:9; 2Th 3:8
18:4 [i] S Ac 13:14 [j] S Ac 9:20
18:5 [k] S Ac 15:22 [l] S Ac 16:1 [m] S Ac 16:9; 17:14,15 [n] S Ac 9:22
18:6 [o] S Ac 13:45 [p] S Mt 10:14 [q] 2Sa 1:16; Eze 33:4 [r] Eze 3:17-19; Ac 20:26 [s] S Ac 13:46
18:7 [t] Ac 16:14
18:8 [u] 1Co 1:14 [v] S Mk 5:22

[j] 5 Or *Messiah;* also in verse 28

17:30 COMMANDS ALL . . . TO REPENT. In times past, before full knowledge of God came through Jesus Christ, God overlooked much of human sin and ignorance of himself (cf. Ro 3:25). Now that his full and perfect revelation has come with Christ's appearing, all are commanded to repent and believe in Jesus as Lord and Savior. There are no exceptions, for God will not overlook anyone's sins. All must turn from sin or be condemned. Repentance, in other words, is essential for salvation (see Mt 3:2, note).

17:31 JUDGE THE WORLD WITH JUSTICE. For other Pauline references to the appointed day of judgment, see Ro 2:5,16; 1Co 1:8; Php 1:6,10; 1Th 5:2,4; 2Th 1:7–10; 2:2.

18:3 A TENTMAKER AS THEY WERE. Paul practiced a trade as well as preached the gospel; he was a tentmaker, earning his living in this way while traveling or staying in residence (20:34; 1Th 2:9; 2Th 3:8). From Paul's example it is clear that ministers who must work in order to help support themselves and their families are not engaged in a second-class ministry. A dual-vocational ministry has Biblical and apostolic precedence.

entire household[w] believed in the
Lord; and many of the Corinthians who
heard him believed and were baptized.
9One night the Lord spoke to Paul in
a vision:[x] "Do not be afraid;[y] keep on
speaking, do not be silent. **10**For I am
with you,[z] and no one is going to attack and harm you, because I have
many people in this city." **11**So Paul
stayed for a year and a half, teaching
them the word of God.[a]
12While Gallio was proconsul[b] of
Achaia,[c] the Jews made a united attack on Paul and brought him into
court. **13**"This man," they charged, "is
persuading the people to worship God
in ways contrary to the law."
14Just as Paul was about to speak,
Gallio said to the Jews, "If you Jews
were making a complaint about some
misdemeanor or serious crime, it
would be reasonable for me to listen to
you. **15**But since it involves questions
about words and names and your own
law[d]—settle the matter yourselves. I
will not be a judge of such things." **16**So
he had them ejected from the court.
17Then they all turned on Sosthenes[e]
the synagogue ruler[f] and beat him in
front of the court. But Gallio showed
no concern whatever.

Priscilla, Aquila and Apollos

18Paul stayed on in Corinth for some
time. Then he left the brothers[g] and
sailed for Syria,[h] accompanied by
Priscilla and Aquila.[i] Before he
sailed, he had his hair cut off at Cenchrea[j] because of a vow he had tak-
en.[k] **19**They arrived at Ephesus,[l]
where Paul left Priscilla and Aquila.
He himself went into the synagogue
and reasoned with the Jews. **20**When
they asked him to spend more time
with them, he declined. **21**But as he
left, he promised, "I will come back if
it is God's will."[m] Then he set sail from
Ephesus. **22**When he landed at Caesarea,[n] he went up and greeted the
church and then went down to Antioch.[o]
23After spending some time in Antioch, Paul set out from there and traveled from place to place throughout the
region of Galatia[p] and Phrygia,[q]
strengthening all the disciples.[r]
24Meanwhile a Jew named Apollos,[s] a native of Alexandria, came to
Ephesus.[t] He was a learned man,
with a thorough knowledge of the
Scriptures. **25**He had been instructed
in the way of the Lord, and he spoke

18:8 [w] S Ac 11:14
18:9 [x] S Ac 9:10 [y] S Mt 14:27
18:10 [z] S Mt 28:20
18:11 [a] S Heb 4:12
18:12 [b] Ac 13:7, 8,12; 19:38 [c] ver 27; Ro 15:26; 1Co 16:15; 2Co 9:2; 1Th 1:7,8
18:15 [d] Ac 23:29; 25:11,19
18:17 [e] 1Co 1:1 [f] ver 8
18:18 [g] ver 27; S Ac 1:16 [h] S Lk 2:2 [i] S ver 2 [j] Ro 16:1 [k] Nu 6:2, 5,18; Ac 21:24
18:19 [l] ver 21,24; Ac 19:1,17,26; 1Co 15:32; 16:8; Eph 1:1; 1Ti 1:3; Rev 1:11; 2:1
18:21 [m] Ro 1:10; 15:32; 1Co 4:19; Jas 4:15
18:22 [n] S Ac 8:40 [o] S Ac 11:19
18:23 [p] S Ac 16:6 [q] Ac 2:10; 16:6 [r] Ac 14:22; 15:32, 41
18:24 [s] Ac 19:1; 1Co 1:12; 3:5,6, 22; 4:6; 16:12; Tit 3:13 [t] S ver 19

18:9 DO NOT BE AFRAID. This passage reveals the inner, human feelings of the apostle. Evidently opposition and hatred against Paul and the gospel were increasing, and Paul was becoming afraid and having doubts whether he should leave Corinth or become silent for a while (cf. 1Co 2:3). These same feelings will occur at times in the hearts of all God's faithful, as is evident even in such men as Elijah (1Ki 19:4) and Jeremiah (Jer 15:15). In such circumstances God will minister to his saints and encourage their hearts. The promise of his presence (v. 10) is sufficient to deliver them from fear and to give the assurance and peace necessary to accomplish God's will for their lives (vv. 10–11).

18:10 FOR I AM WITH YOU. These words to Paul do not refer to Christ's general presence everywhere, i.e., his omnipresence (cf. 17:26–28; Ps 139; Jer 23:23–24; Am 9:2–4). Rather they refer to his special nearness to his faithful children. Christ's nearness means that he is personally here to communicate his will, love and fellowship to us. He is present to act in every situation of our lives to bless, help, protect and guide.

(1) We may learn something of the truth of "Christ with us" in the OT passages where God stated that he was with his faithful. When Moses was afraid to return to Egypt, God said: "I will be with you" (Ex 3:12). When Joshua assumed the leadership of Israel after Moses' death, God promised: "I will be with you; I will never leave you nor forsake you" (Jos 1:5). And God encouraged Israel with these words: "When you pass through the waters, I will be with you . . . . Do not be afraid, for I am with you" (Isa 43:2,5).

(2) In the NT Matthew states that the purpose of Jesus' coming to earth was to achieve the nearness of God to his people. His name is "Immanuel," meaning "God with us" (Mt 1:23). Again, at the end of his Gospel Matthew records Jesus' promise to his disciples: "And surely I am with you always" (Mt 28:20). Mark ends his Gospel with the words: "Then the disciples went out and preached everywhere, and the Lord worked with them" (Mk 16:20).

18:23 STRENGTHENING ALL THE DISCIPLES. This begins Paul's third missionary journey (18:23—21:15). He leaves to visit the churches established on his first (chs. 13–14) and second (15:36—18:22) journeys. Paul never won converts and then forgot them; he was just as concerned with following up on new believers and strengthening them in the way of Christ. All new believers should be contacted immediately by established Christians, prayed with, instructed in the Christian way, and encouraged to meet with other believers for worship, prayer, the ministry of the Word and the manifestations of the Holy Spirit for the common good (2:42; Mt 28:19–20; 1Co 12:7–11; 14).

18:25 KNEW ONLY THE BAPTISM OF JOHN. At this time Apollos's understanding of the gospel

with great fervor[k][u] and taught about
Jesus accurately, though he knew only
the baptism of John.[v] **26**He began to
speak boldly in the synagogue. When
Priscilla and Aquila[w] heard him, they
invited him to their home and explained to him the way of God more adequately.
27When Apollos wanted to go to
Achaia,[x] the brothers[y] encouraged
him and wrote to the disciples there to
welcome him. On arriving, he was a
great help to those who by grace had
believed. **28**For he vigorously refuted
the Jews in public debate, proving from
the Scriptures[z] that Jesus was the
Christ.[a]

Ephesian Disciples Receive the Spirit

19 While Apollos[b] was at Corinth,[c] Paul took the road
through the interior and arrived at
Ephesus.[d] There he found some disciples **2**and asked them, "Did you receive
the Holy Spirit[e] when[l] you believed?"
They answered, "No, we have not
even heard that there is a Holy Spirit."
3So Paul asked, "Then what baptism
did you receive?"
"John's baptism," they replied.
4Paul said, "John's baptism[f] was a
baptism of repentance. He told the people to believe in the one coming after
him, that is, in Jesus."[g] **5**On hearing
this, they were baptized into[m] the
name of the Lord Jesus.[h] **6**When Paul
placed his hands on them,[i] the Holy
Spirit came on them,[j] and they spoke

18:25 [u]Ro 12:11 [v]S Mk 1:4 **18:26** [w]S ver 2 **18:27** [x]S ver 12 [y]ver 18; S Ac 1:16 **18:28** [z]Ac 8:35; 17:2 [a]ver 5; S Ac 9:22 **19:1** [b]S Ac 18:24 [c]S Ac 18:1 [d]S Ac 18:19 **19:2** [e]S Jn 20:22 **19:4** [f]S Mk 1:4 [g]Jn 1:7 **19:5** [h]S Ac 2:38 **19:6** [i]S Ac 6:6 [j]S Ac 10:44

[k]*25* Or *with fervor in the Spirit* [l]*2* Or *after* [m]*5* Or *in*

was limited. He had accepted John's baptism and believed in Jesus as the crucified and resurrected Messiah. What he had not learned was that Jesus himself was now baptizing all believers in the Holy Spirit. The Ephesian disciples were in much the same situation (19:2,6).

19:1 EPHESUS . . . SOME DISCIPLES. Were these twelve disciples at Ephesus Christians or disciples of John the Baptist? Either is a possibility. (1) Some believe they were Christians. (a) Luke calls them "disciples," a word he commonly uses for Christians. Had Luke meant to indicate that they were disciples of only John the Baptist, not Christ, he most likely would have said so explicitly. (b) Paul speaks of them as already believing (v. 2). The verb "believe" is used about twenty times in Acts with no direct object. In every other case, the context indicates that believing in Christ for salvation is meant (see next note).

(2) Others maintain that the Ephesian disciples were disciples of John the Baptist who were still waiting for the Messiah. After they heard about Jesus from Paul, they believed in him as the predicted Christ and were born again by the Spirit (vv. 4–5).

(3) Whatever the case might be, it is clear that their being filled with the Holy Spirit came after their faith, their baptism and the laying on of hands (vv. 5–6).

19:2 DID YOU RECEIVE THE HOLY SPIRIT? Observe the following facts concerning Paul's question: (1) Paul's question strongly suggests that he regarded the Ephesian disciples as true converted Christians who had not yet been filled with the Holy Spirit.

(2) Paul's question here refers to the baptism in the Holy Spirit for power and ministry, the same as that which happened at Pentecost (cf. 1:8; 2:4). It cannot refer to the Spirit's indwelling presence in the believer, for Paul clearly knew that all believers have the Spirit living in them from the very moment of their belief, conversion and regeneration (Ro 8:9).

(3) The literal translation of Paul's question is, "Having believed, did you receive the Holy Spirit?" "Having believed" (Gk *pisteusantes*, from *pisteuō*) is an aorist participle, which normally indicates action prior to the action of the main verb (in this case, "receive"). Thus we may render this: "Did you receive the Holy Spirit after you believed?" This translation agrees fully with the context of the passage, for this is exactly what did happen to the Ephesian believers. (a) They had already believed in Christ before Paul met them (vv. 1–2). (b) They then listened to Paul and further believed all he told them about Christ and the Holy Spirit (v. 4). (c) Paul considered the Ephesians' belief in Christ to be genuine and adequate, for he baptized them in the name of the Lord Jesus (v. 5). (d) It was only then, after their belief and their water baptism, that Paul laid his hands on them and "the Holy Spirit came on them" (v. 6). Thus, there was an interval of time between their belief in Christ and the coming of the Spirit in all his power.

Paul's question here indicates that he thought it quite possible to "believe" in Christ without experiencing the baptism in the Holy Spirit. This passage is decisive in showing that one may be a Christian without possessing the fullness of the Holy Spirit (see article on BAPTISM IN THE HOLY SPIRIT, p. 1642).

19:2 WE HAVE NOT EVEN HEARD. The response of the Ephesian believers does not mean they had never heard of the Holy Spirit. They certainly were acquainted with the OT teaching about the Spirit, and they most assuredly had heard John's message concerning the baptism in the Holy Spirit that the Christ was to bring (Lk 3:16). They had not yet heard that the Spirit was being poured out on believers (1:5,8).

19:5 THEY WERE BAPTIZED. Water baptism into "the name of the Lord Jesus" of these twelve

in tongues[n][k] and prophesied. 7There were about twelve men in all.

Paul in Ephesus

8Paul entered the synagogue[l] and spoke boldly there for three months, arguing persuasively about the kingdom of God.[m] 9But some of them[n] became obstinate; they refused to believe and publicly maligned the Way.[o] So Paul left them. He took the disciples[p] with him and had discussions daily in the lecture hall of Tyrannus. 10This went on for two years,[q] so that all the Jews and Greeks who lived in the province of Asia[r] heard the word of the Lord.[s]

11God did extraordinary miracles[t] through Paul, 12so that even handkerchiefs and aprons that had touched him were taken to the sick, and their illnesses were cured[u] and the evil spirits left them.

13Some Jews who went around driving out evil spirits[v] tried to invoke the name of the Lord Jesus over those who were demon-possessed. They would say, "In the name of Jesus,[w] whom Paul preaches, I command you to come out." 14Seven sons of Sceva, a Jewish chief priest, were doing this. 15⌊One day,⌋ the evil spirit answered them, "Jesus I know, and I know about Paul, but who are you?" 16Then the man who had the evil spirit jumped on them and overpowered them all. He gave them such a beating that they ran out of the house naked and bleeding.

17When this became known to the Jews and Greeks living in Ephesus,[x] they were all seized with fear,[y] and the name of the Lord Jesus was held in high honor. 18Many of those who believed now came and openly confessed their evil deeds. 19A number who had practiced sorcery brought their scrolls together and burned them publicly. When they calculated the value of the scrolls, the total came to fifty thousand drachmas.[o] 20In this way the word of the Lord[z] spread widely and grew in power.[a] Ro 8:38-39

21After all this had happened, Paul decided to go to Jerusalem,[b] passing through Macedonia[c] and Achaia.[d] "After I have been there," he said, "I must visit Rome also."[e] 22He sent two of his helpers,[f] Timothy[g] and Erastus,[h] to Macedonia, while he stayed in the province of Asia[i] a little longer.

The Riot in Ephesus

23About that time there arose a great disturbance about the Way.[j] 24A silversmith named Demetrius,

19:6 [k] S Mk 16:17 **19:8** [l] S Ac 9:20 [m] S Mt 3:2; Ac 28:23 **19:9** [n] Ac 14:4 [o] ver 23; S Ac 9:2 [p] ver 30; S Ac 11:26 **19:10** [q] Ac 20:31 [r] ver 22,26,27; S Ac 2:9 [s] S Ac 13:48 **19:11** [t] Ac 8:13 **19:12** [u] Ac 5:15 **19:13** [v] Mt 12:27 [w] Mk 9:38 **19:17** [x] S Ac 18:19 [y] Ac 5:5,11 **19:20** [z] S Ac 13:48 [a] Ac 6:7; 12:24 **19:21** [b] Ac 20:16, 22; 21:4,12,15; Ro 15:25 [c] S Ac 16:9 [d] S Ac 18:12 [e] Ro 15:24,28 **19:22** [f] Ac 13:5 [g] S Ac 16:1 [h] Ro 16:23; 2Ti 4:20 [i] ver 10, 26,27; S Ac 2:9 **19:23** [j] S Ac 9:2

[n] *6* Or *other languages* [o] *19* A drachma was a silver coin worth about a day's wages.

people at Ephesus (v. 7) testifies that they had saving faith and were born again by the Spirit. This precedes their being filled with the Holy Spirit (v. 6).

19:6 THE HOLY SPIRIT CAME ON THEM. This event occurs some 25 years after the first Pentecost (2:4); yet, the pattern of these twelve people receiving the fullness of the Holy Spirit is consistent with the normal pattern already presented by Luke (see 8:5–24, note).

(1) They had believed in Jesus and were born again by the Spirit (see previous note).

(2) After they were baptized in water (v. 5), Paul laid his hands on them and they were baptized in the Holy Spirit.

(3) As the Holy Spirit came on them, they began speaking in tongues and prophesying. Luke never presents the outpouring of the Spirit as something one could only perceive by faith. Rather, he shows it to be a knowable and identifiable experience capable of being verified objectively; speaking in tongues was external and visible proof that the Holy Spirit had come on these followers of Jesus (see article on SPEAKING IN TONGUES, p. 1646).

19:12 HANDKERCHIEFS AND APRONS. Paul's ministry at Ephesus was marked by extraordinary miracles of healing and deliverance from demons, accomplished directly or through handkerchiefs and aprons that had been in contact with his body (i.e., sweat cloths and aprons used in his leatherworking). Diseases disappeared and evil spirits left when the afflicted touched the cloth (cf. 5:15; Mk 5:27). Any minister today who attempts to gain financial support by advertising handkerchiefs for healing is not acting according to Paul's motive and spirit, for Paul did not use these items to gain money. He simply multiplied the empowering that was on him through these tangible means, healing and delivering more people than he could personally touch with his hands.

19:19 PRACTICED SORCERY. The public burning of magical books shows that new believers were taught immediately to turn away from occult practices. Witchcraft, black magic, sorcery, spiritism and other occult practices are satanic activities completely incompatible with the Christian faith. One cannot be a true believer in Christ and at the same time deal with spirits or attempt to gain contact with the dead. God comdemns all such activity as detestable (see Dt 18:9–13, notes). Dabbling in the occult and spiritism will leave one open to powerful satanic influence and demonic possession.

who made silver shrines of Artemis, brought in no little business for the craftsmen. **25**He called them together, along with the workmen in related trades, and said: "Men, you know we receive a good income from this business.[k] **26**And you see and hear how this fellow Paul has convinced and led astray large numbers of people here in Ephesus[l] and in practically the whole province of Asia.[m] He says that man-made gods are no gods at all.[n] **27**There is danger not only that our trade will lose its good name, but also that the temple of the great goddess Artemis will be discredited, and the goddess herself, who is worshiped throughout the province of Asia and the world, will be robbed of her divine majesty."

28When they heard this, they were furious and began shouting: "Great is Artemis of the Ephesians!"[o] **29**Soon the whole city was in an uproar. The people seized Gaius[p] and Aristarchus,[q] Paul's traveling companions from Macedonia,[r] and rushed as one man into the theater. **30**Paul wanted to appear before the crowd, but the disciples[s] would not let him. **31**Even some of the officials of the province, friends of Paul, sent him a message begging him not to venture into the theater.

32The assembly was in confusion: Some were shouting one thing, some another.[t] Most of the people did not even know why they were there. **33**The Jews pushed Alexander to the front, and some of the crowd shouted instructions to him. He motioned[u] for silence in order to make a defense before the people. **34**But when they realized he was a Jew, they all shouted in unison for about two hours: "Great is Artemis of the Ephesians!"[v]

35The city clerk quieted the crowd and said: "Men of Ephesus,[w] doesn't all the world know that the city of Ephesus is the guardian of the temple of the great Artemis and of her image, which fell from heaven? **36**Therefore, since these facts are undeniable, you ought to be quiet and not do anything rash. **37**You have brought these men here, though they have neither robbed temples[x] nor blasphemed our goddess. **38**If, then, Demetrius and his fellow craftsmen[y] have a grievance against anybody, the courts are open and there are proconsuls.[z] They can press charges. **39**If there is anything further you want to bring up, it must be settled in a legal assembly. **40**As it is, we are in danger of being charged with rioting because of today's events. In that case we would not be able to account for this commotion, since there is no reason for it." **41**After he had said this, he dismissed the assembly.

Through Macedonia and Greece

20 When the uproar had ended, Paul sent for the disciples[a] and, after encouraging them, said good-by and set out for Macedonia.[b] **2**He traveled through that area, speaking many words of encouragement to the people, and finally arrived in Greece, **3**where he stayed three months. Because the Jews made a plot against him[c] just as he was about to sail for Syria,[d] he decided to go back through Macedonia.[e] **4**He was accompanied by Sopater son of Pyrrhus from Berea, Aristarchus[f] and Secundus from Thessalonica,[g] Gaius[h] from Derbe, Timothy[i] also, and Tychicus[j] and Trophimus[k] from the province of Asia.[l] **5**These men went on ahead and waited for us[m] at Troas.[n] **6**But we sailed from Philippi[o] after the Feast of Unleavened Bread, and five days later joined the others at Troas,[p] where we stayed seven days.

Eutychus Raised From the Dead at Troas

7On the first day of the week[q] we came together to break bread.[r] Paul spoke to the people and, because he intended to leave the next day, kept on talking until midnight. **8**There were many lamps in the upstairs room[s] where we were meeting. **9**Seated in a window was a young man named Eutychus, who was sinking into a deep sleep as Paul talked on and on. When he was sound asleep, he fell to the ground from the third story and was picked up dead. **10**Paul went down, threw himself on the young man[t] and put his arms around him. "Don't be alarmed," he said. "He's alive!"[u] **11**Then he went upstairs again and broke bread[v] and ate. After talking until daylight, he left. **12**The people took the young man home alive and were greatly comforted.

19:25 [k] Ac 16:16, 19,20
19:26 [l] S Ac 18:19 [m] S Ac 2:9 [n] Dt 4:28; Ps 115:4; Isa 44:10-20; Jer 10:3-5; Ac 17:29; 1Co 8:4; Rev 9:20
19:28 [o] S Ac 18:19
19:29 [p] Ac 20:4; Ro 16:23; 1Co 1:14 [q] Ac 20:4; 27:2; Col 4:10; Phm 24 [r] S Ac 16:9
19:30 [s] S Ac 11:26
19:32 [t] Ac 21:34
19:33 [u] S Ac 12:17
19:34 [v] ver 28
19:35 [w] S Ac 18:19
19:37 [x] Ro 2:22
19:38 [y] ver 24

[z] Ac 13:7,8,12; 18:12
20:1 [a] S Ac 11:26 [b] S Ac 16:9
20:3 [c] ver 19; Ac 9:23,24; 14:5; 23:12,15,30; 25:3; 2Co 11:26; S 1Th 2:16 [d] S Lk 2:2 [e] S Ac 16:9
20:4 [f] S Ac 19:29 [g] S Ac 17:1 [h] S Ac 19:29 [i] S Ac 16:1 [j] Eph 6:21; Col 4:7; Tit 3:12 [k] Ac 21:29; 2Ti 4:20 [l] S Ac 2:9
20:5 [m] S Ac 16:10 [n] S Ac 16:8
20:6 [o] S Ac 16:12 [p] S Ac 16:8
20:7 [q] 1Co 16:2; Rev 1:10 [r] S Mt 14:19
20:8 [s] Ac 1:13; 9:37
20:10 [t] 1Ki 17:21; 2Ki 4:34 [u] Mt 9:23,24
20:11 [v] ver 7; S Mt 14:19

Paul's Farewell to the Ephesian Elders

13We went on ahead to the ship and
sailed for Assos, where we were going
to take Paul aboard. He had made this
arrangement because he was going
there on foot. 14When he met us at Assos, we took him aboard and went on
to Mitylene. 15The next day we set sail
from there and arrived off Kios. The
day after that we crossed over to Samos, and on the following day arrived
at Miletus.[w] 16Paul had decided to sail
past Ephesus[x] to avoid spending time
in the province of Asia,[y] for he was in
a hurry to reach Jerusalem,[z] if possible, by the day of Pentecost.[a]

17From Miletus,[b] Paul sent to Ephesus for the elders[c] of the church.
18When they arrived, he said to them:
"You know how I lived the whole time
I was with you,[d] from the first day I
came into the province of Asia.[e] 19I
served the Lord with great humility
and with tears,[f] although I was severely tested by the plots of the Jews.[g]
20You know that I have not hesitated
to preach anything[h] that would be
helpful to you but have taught you publicly and from house to house. 21I have
declared to both Jews[i] and Greeks
that they must turn to God in repentance[j] and have faith in our Lord Ac 26:16-27
Jesus.[k]

22"And now, compelled by the Spirit,
I am going to Jerusalem,[l] not knowing what will happen to me there. 23I
only know that in every city the Holy
Spirit warns me[m] that prison and
hardships are facing me.[n] 24However,
I consider my life worth nothing to
me,[o] if only I may finish the race[p]
and complete the task[q] the Lord Jesus
has given me[r]—the task of testifying
to the gospel of God's grace.[s]

25"Now I know that none of you
among whom I have gone about
preaching the kingdom[t] will ever see
me again.[u] 26Therefore, I declare to
you today that I am innocent of the
blood of all men.[v] 27For I have not
hesitated to proclaim to you the whole
will of God.[w] 28Keep watch over yourselves and all the flock[x] of which the
Holy Spirit has made you overseers.[p][y] Be shepherds of the church
of God,[q][z] which he bought[a] with his
own blood.[b] 29I know that after I
leave, savage wolves[c] will come in
among you and will not spare the

20:15 [w]ver 17; 2Ti 4:20 **20:16** [x]S Ac 18:19 [y]S Ac 2:9 [z]S Ac 19:21 [a]S Ac 2:1 **20:17** [b]ver 15 [c]S Ac 11:30 **20:18** [d]Ac 18:19-21; 19:1-41 [e]S Ac 2:9 **20:19** [f]Ps 6:6 [g]S ver 3 **20:20** [h]ver 27; Ps 40:10; Jer 26:2; 42:4 **20:21** [i]Ac 18:5 [j]S Ac 2:38 [k]Ac 24:24; 26:18; Eph 1:15; Col 2:5; Phm 5 **20:22** [l]ver 16 **20:23** [m]S Ac 8:29; 21:4 [n]S Ac 9:16 **20:24** [o]Ac 21:13 [p]2Ti 4:7 [q]2Co 4:1 [r]Gal 1:1; Tit 1:3 [s]S Ac 11:23 **20:25** [t]S Mt 4:23 [u]ver 38 **20:26** [v]Eze 3:17-19; Ac 18:6 **20:27** [w]S ver 20 **20:28** [x]ver 29; S Jn 21:16 [y]S 1Ti 3:1 [z]S 1Co 10:32 [a]S 1Co 6:20 [b]S Ro 3:25 **20:29** [c]Eze 34:5; Mt 7:15

[p]28 Traditionally *bishops* [q]28 Many manuscripts *of the Lord*

20:19 WITH TEARS. Paul on several occasions mentions his serving the Lord with "tears" (v. 31; 2Co 2:4; Php 3:18). In this address to the Ephesian elders (vv. 17–38), he speaks of daily warning them with tears for a period of three years (v. 31). The tears were not the result of weakness; rather, Paul saw the lost condition of the human race, the evil of sin, the distortion of the gospel and the peril of rejecting the Lord as such grave realities that his preaching was often accompanied by tears (cf. Mk 9:24; Lk 19:41).

20:20 I HAVE NOT HESITATED TO PREACH ANYTHING. Paul preached whatever he believed was useful or needful for the salvation of his hearers. Ministers of the gospel must be faithful to declare the whole truth of God. They must not seek to satisfy the people's desires or gratify their tastes, nor should they seek to promote their own popularity. Even if they must speak words of rebuke, teach doctrines that challenge natural prejudices or preach Biblical standards that oppose the desires of the sinful nature, faithful preachers will deliver the whole truth for the sake of the flock (e.g., Gal 1:6–10; 2Ti 4:1–5).

20:22 COMPELLED BY THE SPIRIT. Paul knew that hardships and suffering awaited him (v. 23); yet he committed his way to God, not knowing whether it would mean life or death (see 21:4, note).

20:23 THE HOLY SPIRIT WARNS ME. The Holy Spirit's testimony that hardships and imprisonment awaited Paul was probably communicated through prophets or prophecy (cf. 1Co 12:10) in the churches.

20:24 I CONSIDER MY LIFE WORTH NOTHING. Paul's main concern was not preserving his own life; what counted most was that he might finish the ministry to which God had called him. Wherever it ended, even if in the sacrifice of his life, he would finish his course with joy and the prayer that "Christ will be exalted in my body, whether by life or by death" (Php 1:20). For Paul, life and service for Christ is represented as a race that one must run with absolute faithfulness to his or her Lord (cf. 13:25; 1Co 9:24; 2Ti 4:7; Heb 12:1).

20:26 I AM INNOCENT OF THE BLOOD OF ALL MEN. The word "blood" is used normally in the sense of bloodshed, i.e., the crime of causing someone's death (cf. 5:28; Mt 23:35; 27:25). (1) Here it means that if any should die spiritually and be lost forever, Paul would not be blamed. (2) If overseers do not want to be held responsible for the perishing of those under their ministry, they must declare to them the whole will of God.

20:28 KEEP WATCH OVER ... ALL THE FLOCK. For a discussion of this classic passage on overseers in the church, see article on OVERSEERS AND THEIR DUTIES, p. 1690.

20:29 SAVAGE WOLVES WILL COME IN. In-

OVERSEERS AND THEIR DUTIES

Ac 20:28 Keep watch over yourselves and all the flock of which the Holy Spirit has made you overseers. Be shepherds of the church of God, which he bought with his own blood."

No church can function without designated leaders. Thus, as Ac 14:23 indicates, certain individuals were appointed to the office of elder or overseer by Spirit-filled believers who sought God's will through prayer and fasting, in accordance with the spiritual qualifications set down by the Holy Spirit in 1Ti 3:1–7 and Tit 1:5–9 (see article on MORAL QUALIFICATIONS FOR OVERSEERS, p. 1882). Ultimately, therefore, it is the Spirit who makes someone an overseer of the church. Paul's final address to the Ephesian elders (Ac 20:18–35) is a classic passage giving Scriptural principles on how to function as an overseer within the visible church. Their task is not unlike that of the OT prophets (see article on THE PROPHET IN THE OLD TESTAMENT, p. 986).

PROMOTING THE FAITH. (1) One of the major duties of overseers is to feed the sheep by teaching God's Word. They must always keep in mind that the flock given to them is no other than the people that God has purchased for himself with his Son's precious blood (cf. Ac 20:28; 1Co 6:20; 1Pe 1:19; 2:9; Rev 5:9). (2) In Ac 20:19–27, Paul describes how he served as a shepherd of the church in Ephesus; he has declared the whole will of God by faithfully warning and teaching the Ephesian Christians (Ac 20:27). Consequently he is able to say, "I am innocent of the blood of all men" (20:26; see note). Overseers today must likewise declare to their churches God's whole will. They must "preach the word . . . correct, rebuke and encourage— with great patience and careful instruction" (2Ti 4:2), and refuse to be preachers who seek to please people and say only what they want to hear (2Ti 4:3).

GUARDING THE FAITH. The true pastor must diligently protect the sheep from their enemies. Paul knows that in the church's future, Satan will raise up false teachers from within the church and infiltrate God's flock from the outside with imposters who adhere to unbiblical doctrine, worldly thought, and pagan and humanistic ideas; both will destroy the Biblical faith of God's people (see article on FALSE TEACHERS, p. 1506). Paul calls them "savage wolves," meaning that they are strong, difficult to handle, ravenous and dangerous (see Ac 20:29, note; cf. Mt 10:16). Such individuals will draw people away from Christ's teachings and toward themselves and their distorted gospel. Paul's urgent plea (Ac 20:25–31) places a solemn obligation on all leaders to guard the church and oppose all who would distort the fundamental revelation of NT faith.

(1) The true church consists of only those who by Christ's grace and the fellowship of the Holy Spirit are faithful to the Lord Jesus Christ and the Word of God (see article on THE INSPIRATION AND AUTHORITY OF SCRIPTURE, p. 1898). Therefore, as a major aspect of guarding God's church, church leaders must discipline, correct in love (Eph 4:15) and firmly refute (2Ti 4:1–4; Tit 1:9–11) all within the church who "distort the truth" (Ac 20:30) by teaching things contrary to God's Word and apostolic witness.

(2) Church leaders, pastors of local congregations and administrative officials do well to remember that the Lord Jesus has made them responsible for the lives of all persons under their care (Ac 20:26–27; cf. Eze 3:20–21). If leaders fail to declare and perform God's whole purpose for the church (Ac 20:27), especially in the area of keeping watch over the flock (20:28), they will not be "innocent of the blood of all men" (20:26, see note; cf. Eze 34:1–10). Instead God will hold them guilty of the blood of all those who are lost because of the leaders' refusal to protect the flock from those who weaken and distort the Word (see 2Ti 1:14, note; Rev 2:2, note).

(3) Exercising discipline with regard to theological, doctrinal and moral matters by and upon those who are responsible for the church's direction is especially important. Purity of doctrine and life and adherence to the inerrancy of Scripture must be carefully guarded in colleges, Bible schools, seminaries, publishing institutions and all organizational structures of the church (2Ti 1:13–14).

(4) The main issue here is one's attitude toward divinely inspired Scripture, which Paul calls the "word of his grace" (Ac 20:32). False teachers, pastors and leaders will attempt to weaken the authority of the Bible by their subversive teachings and unbiblical principles. By rejecting the full authority of God's Word, they deny that the Bible is true and trustworthy in all that it teaches (Ac 20:28–31; see Gal 1:6, note; 1Ti 4:1; 2Ti 3:8). These people, for the sake of the church, must be disciplined and removed from the fellowship (2Jn 9–11, see Gal 1:9, note).

(5) The church that fails to share the Holy Spirit's burning concern for church purity (Ac 20:18–35), refuses to maintain a firm stand for the truth, and refrains from disciplining those who undermine the authority of God's Word will soon cease to exist as a church according to NT norms (see Ac 12:5, note; see article on THE CHURCH, p. 1439). It will become guilty of apostasy from the original revelation of Christ and the apostles, sliding further and further from the NT purpose, power and life.

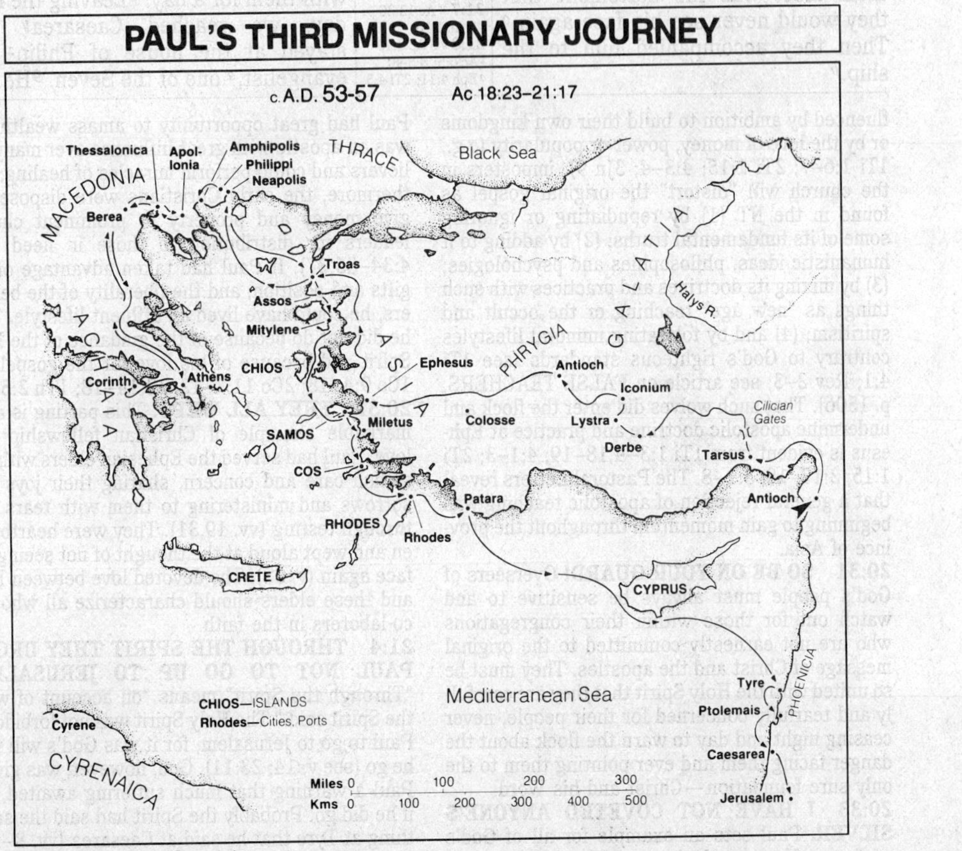

PAUL'S THIRD MISSIONARY JOURNEY

c. A.D. 53-57 Ac 18:23–21:17

flock.[d] **30**Even from your own number
men will arise and distort the truth in
order to draw away disciples[e] after
them. **31**So be on your guard! Remember that for three years[f] I never
stopped warning each of you night and
day with tears.[g]

32"Now I commit you to God[h] and to
the word of his grace, which can build
you up and give you an inheritance[i]
among all those who are sanctified.[j]
33I have not coveted anyone's silver or
gold or clothing.[k] **34**You yourselves
know that these hands of mine have
supplied my own needs and the needs
of my companions.[l] **35**In everything I
did, I showed you that by this kind of
hard work we must help the weak, remembering the words the Lord Jesus
himself said: 'It is more blessed to give
than to receive.' "

36When he had said this, he knelt
down with all of them and prayed.[m]
37They all wept as they embraced him
and kissed him.[n] **38**What grieved
them most was his statement that
they would never see his face again.[o]
Then they accompanied him to the
ship.[p]

20:29 [d]ver 28
20:30 [e]S Ac 11:26
20:31 [f]Ac 19:10 [g]ver 19
20:32 [h]Ac 14:23 [i]S Eph 1:14; S Mt 25:34; Col 1:12; 3:24; Heb 9:15; 1Pe 1:4 [j]Ac 26:18
20:33 [k]1Sa 12:3; 1Co 9:12; 2Co 2:17; 7:2; 11:9; 12:14-17; 1Th 2:5
20:34 [l]S Ac 18:3
20:36 [m]Lk 22:41; Ac 9:40; 21:5
20:37 [n]S Lk 15:20
20:38 [o]ver 25 [p]Ac 21:5

21:1 [q]S Ac 16:10
21:2 [r]Ac 11:19
21:3 [s]S Lk 2:2
21:4 [t]S Ac 11:26 [u]ver 11; Ac 20:23
21:5 [v]Lk 22:41; Ac 9:40; 20:36
21:7 [w]Ac 12:20 [x]S Ac 1:16
21:8 [y]S Ac 8:40 [z]Ac 6:5; 8:5-40 [a]Eph 4:11; 2Ti 4:5

On to Jerusalem

21 After we[q] had torn ourselves
away from them, we put out to
sea and sailed straight to Cos. The
next day we went to Rhodes and from
there to Patara. **2**We found a ship
crossing over to Phoenicia,[r] went on
board and set sail. **3**After sighting Cyprus and passing to the south of it, we
sailed on to Syria.[s] We landed at Tyre,
where our ship was to unload its cargo.
4Finding the disciples[t] there, we
stayed with them seven days. Through
the Spirit[u] they urged Paul not to go
on to Jerusalem. **5**But when our time
was up, we left and continued on our
way. All the disciples and their wives
and children accompanied us out of the
city, and there on the beach we knelt
to pray.[v] **6**After saying good-by to
each other, we went aboard the ship,
and they returned home.

7We continued our voyage from
Tyre[w] and landed at Ptolemais, where
we greeted the brothers[x] and stayed
with them for a day. **8**Leaving the next
day, we reached Caesarea[y] and
stayed at the house of Philip[z] the
evangelist,[a] one of the Seven. **9**He had

---

fluenced by ambition to build their own kingdoms or by the love of money, power or popularity (e.g., 1Ti 1:6–7; 2Ti 1:15; 4:3–4; 3Jn 9), imposters in the church will "distort" the original gospel as found in the NT (1) by repudiating or ignoring some of its fundamental truths; (2) by adding to it humanistic ideas, philosophies and psychologies; (3) by mixing its doctrines and practices with such things as "new age" teaching or the occult and spiritism; (4) and by tolerating immoral lifestyles contrary to God's righteous standards (see 1Ti 4:1; Rev 2–3; see article on FALSE TEACHERS, p. 1506). That such wolves did enter the flock and undermine apostolic doctrine and practice at Ephesus is evident from 1Ti 1:3–4,18–19; 4:1–3; 2Ti 1:15; 2:17–18; 3:1–8. The Pastoral Letters reveal that a general rejection of apostolic teaching was beginning to gain momentum throughout the province of Asia.

20:31 SO BE ON YOUR GUARD! Overseers of God's people must always be sensitive to and watch out for those within their congregations who are not earnestly committed to the original message of Christ and the apostles. They must be so united with the Holy Spirit that they are carefully and tearfully concerned for their people, never ceasing night and day to warn the flock about the danger facing them and ever pointing them to the only sure foundation — Christ and his Word.

20:33 I HAVE NOT COVETED ANYONE'S SILVER. Paul sets an example for all of God's ministers. He never desires wealth or seeks to get rich from his work in the gospel (cf. 2Co 12:14). Paul had great opportunity to amass wealth. He was an apostle with great influence over many believers and could perform miracles of healing; furthermore, the early Christians were disposed to give money and property to prominent church leaders for distribution to those in need (see 4:34–35,37). If Paul had taken advantage of his gifts and position, and the liberality of the believers, he could have lived an affluent lifestyle. This he did not do because of the guidance of the Holy Spirit and because of his love for the gospel (cf. 1Co 9:4–18; 2Co 11:7–12; 12:14–18; 1Th 2:5–6).

20:37 THEY ALL WEPT. This parting is a remarkable example of Christian fellowship and love. Paul had served the Ephesian elders with unselfish care and concern, sharing their joys and sorrows and ministering to them with tears and through testing (vv. 19,31). They were heartbroken and wept aloud at the thought of not seeing his face again (v. 38). The devoted love between Paul and these elders should characterize all who are co-laborers in the faith.

21:4 THROUGH THE SPIRIT THEY URGED PAUL NOT TO GO UP TO JERUSALEM. "Through the Spirit" means "on account of what the Spirit said." The Holy Spirit was not forbidding Paul to go to Jerusalem, for it was God's will that he go (see v. 14; 23:11). God, however, was giving Paul a warning that much suffering awaited him if he did go. Probably the Spirit had said the same thing at Tyre that he said at Caesarea (vv. 8–14). But Paul counted the cost and was willing even to die for the sake of the gospel (vv. 10–14).

four unmarried daughters who prophesied.[b]
10After we had been there a number
of days, a prophet named Agabus[c]
came down from Judea. **11**Coming over
to us, he took Paul's belt, tied his own
hands and feet with it and said, "The
Holy Spirit says,[d] 'In this way the
Jews of Jerusalem will bind[e] the owner of this belt and will hand him over
to the Gentiles.' "[f]
12When we heard this, we and the
people there pleaded with Paul not to
go up to Jerusalem. **13**Then Paul answered, "Why are you weeping and
breaking my heart? I am ready not only
to be bound, but also to die[g] in Jerusalem for the name of the Lord Jesus."[h]
14When he would not be dissuaded, we
gave up[i] and said, "The Lord's will be
done."[j]
15After this, we got ready and went
up to Jerusalem.[k] **16**Some of the disciples from Caesarea[l] accompanied us
and brought us to the home of Mnason,
where we were to stay. He was a man
from Cyprus[m] and one of the early disciples.

Paul's Arrival at Jerusalem

17When we arrived at Jerusalem, the
brothers[n] received us warmly.[o]
18The next day Paul and the rest of us
went to see James,[p] and all the elders[q] were present. **19**Paul greeted
them and reported in detail what God
had done among the Gentiles[r]
through his ministry.[s]
20When they heard this, they
praised God. Then they said to Paul:
"You see, brother, how many thousands of Jews have believed, and all of
them are zealous[t] for the law.[u]
21They have been informed that you
teach all the Jews who live among the
Gentiles to turn away from Moses,[v]
telling them not to circumcise their
children[w] or live according to our customs.[x] **22**What shall we do? They will
certainly hear that you have come, **23**so
do what we tell you. There are four
men with us who have made a vow.[y]
24Take these men, join in their purification rites[z] and pay their expenses,
so that they can have their heads
shaved.[a] Then everybody will know
there is no truth in these reports about
you, but that you yourself are living in
obedience to the law. **25**As for the Gentile believers, we have written to them
our decision that they should abstain
from food sacrificed to idols, from
blood, from the meat of strangled animals and from sexual immorality."[b]
26The next day Paul took the men
and purified himself along with them.
Then he went to the temple to give notice of the date when the days of purifi-

21:9 [b]Ex 15:20; Jdg 4:4; Ne 6:14; Lk 2:36; Ac 2:17; 1Co 11:5
21:10 [c]Ac 11:28
21:11 [d]S Ac 8:29 [e]ver 33 [f]1Ki 22:11; Isa 20:2-4; Jer 13:1-11; Mt 20:19
21:13 [g]Ac 20:24 [h]S Jn 15:21; S Ac 9:16
21:14 [i]Ru 1:18 [j]S Mt 26:39
21:15 [k]S Ac 19:21
21:16 [l]S Ac 8:40 [m]ver 3,4
21:17 [n]S Ac 9:30 [o]Ac 15:4
21:18 [p]S Ac 15:13 [q]S Ac 11:30
21:19 [r]Ac 14:27; 15:4,12 [s]Ac 1:17
21:20 [t]Ac 22:3; Ro 10:2; Gal 1:14; Php 3:6 [u]Ac 15:1, 5
21:21 [v]ver 28 [w]Ac 15:19-21; 1Co 7:18,19 [x]S Ac 6:14
21:23 [y]Nu 6:2,5, 18; Ac 18:18
21:24 [z]ver 26; Ac 24:18 [a]Ac 18:18
21:25 [b]Ac 15:20, 29

21:10 A PROPHET NAMED AGABUS. Agabus, one of the prophets who foretold the famine of A.D. 46 (11:27–28), now predicts Paul's arrest and imprisonment. The closer Paul got to Jerusalem, the clearer and more definite were the revelations (v. 11). Agabus's prophecy did not say Paul should not go to Jerusalem, but what awaited him if he did go.

Note that in no recorded incident in the NT was the gift of prophecy ever used to give personal guidance to individuals in matters that could be decided according to Scriptural principles. Decisions related to morality, buying or selling, marriage, home and family must be made by applying and obeying the principles of God's Word and not on the mere basis of a "prophecy." The NT prophetic utterances involved primarily strengthening, encouragement, comfort (1Co 14:3) and, frequently, guidance in mission (see 16:6, note).

21:13 THEN PAUL ANSWERED. The will of the majority or even the unanimous wish of genuine caring believers is not necessarily God's will. Paul was not indifferent to the pleas and tears of his friends; still, he could not change his resolute purpose to be willing to suffer imprisonment and even to die for the name of the Lord Jesus.

21:14 THE LORD'S WILL BE DONE. Many disciples (v. 4), as well as the prophet Agabus (v. 11), prophesied of the suffering that would come to Paul if he went to Jerusalem. These Christians interpreted the prophetic word as a personal directive to Paul that he should not go to Jerusalem (vv. 4,12). Paul, although recognizing the truth of the revelation (v. 11), did not accept the disciples' sincere interpretation of the revealed prophecy (v. 13). He relied on the personal guidance of the Holy Spirit and God's Word to him personally for such an important decision (23:11; see 21:4, note). In regard to future ministry, one ought to wait on a personal word from God, not just on the word of others.

21:20 BELIEVED, AND ALL OF THEM ARE ZEALOUS FOR THE LAW. James and Paul both knew that Jewish ceremonies could not bring salvation (cf. 15:13–21; Gal 2:15–21). But they did recognize that some parts of the law and Jewish custom could be followed as an expression of the believer's faith in and love for Christ. The Jewish believers had genuinely accepted Christ and been regenerated by and filled with the Spirit. Their zeal for the law and customs came not from an attitude of legalism, but from hearts dedicated to Christ and loyal to God's ways (see Mt 7:6).

cation would end and the offering would be made for each of them.[c]

Paul Arrested

27When the seven days were nearly over, some Jews from the province of Asia saw Paul at the temple. They stirred up the whole crowd and seized him,[d] 28shouting, "Men of Israel, help us! This is the man who teaches all men everywhere against our people and our law and this place. And besides, he has brought Greeks into the temple area and defiled this holy place."[e] 29(They had previously seen Trophimus[f] the Ephesian[g] in the city with Paul and assumed that Paul had brought him into the temple area.)

30The whole city was aroused, and the people came running from all directions. Seizing Paul,[h] they dragged him[i] from the temple, and immediately the gates were shut. 31While they were trying to kill him, news reached the commander of the Roman troops that the whole city of Jerusalem was in an uproar. 32He at once took some officers and soldiers and ran down to the crowd. When the rioters saw the commander and his soldiers, they stopped beating Paul.[j]

33The commander came up and arrested him and ordered him to be bound[k] with two[l] chains.[m] Then he asked who he was and what he had done. 34Some in the crowd shouted one thing and some another,[n] and since the commander could not get at the truth because of the uproar, he ordered that Paul be taken into the barracks.[o] 35When Paul reached the steps,[p] the violence of the mob was so great he had to be carried by the soldiers. 36The crowd that followed kept shouting, "Away with him!"[q]

Paul Speaks to the Crowd

22:3–16pp — Ac 9:1–22; 26:9–18

37As the soldiers were about to take Paul into the barracks,[r] he asked the commander, "May I say something to you?"

"Do you speak Greek?" he replied. 38"Aren't you the Egyptian who started a revolt and led four thousand terrorists out into the desert[s] some time ago?"[t]

39Paul answered, "I am a Jew, from Tarsus[u] in Cilicia,[v] a citizen of no ordinary city. Please let me speak to the people."

40Having received the commander's permission, Paul stood on the steps and motioned[w] to the crowd. When they were all silent, he said to them in Aramaic[r]:[x]

22

1"Brothers and fathers,[y] listen now to my defense."

2When they heard him speak to them in Aramaic,[z] they became very quiet.

Then Paul said: 3"I am a Jew,[a] born in Tarsus[b] of Cilicia,[c] but brought up in this city. Under[d] Gamaliel[e] I was thoroughly trained in the law of our fathers[f] and was just as zealous[g] for God as any of you are today. 4I persecuted[h] the followers of this Way[i] to their death, arresting both men and women and throwing them into prison,[j] 5as also the high priest and all the Council[k] can testify. I even obtained letters from them to their brothers[l] in Damascus,[m] and went there to bring these people as prisoners to Jerusalem to be punished.

6"About noon as I came near Damascus, suddenly a bright light from heaven flashed around me.[n] 7I fell to the ground and heard a voice say to me, 'Saul! Saul! Why do you persecute me?'

8" 'Who are you, Lord?' I asked.

" 'I am Jesus of Nazareth,[o] whom you are persecuting,' he replied. 9My companions saw the light,[p] but they did not understand the voice[q] of him who was speaking to me.

10" 'What shall I do, Lord?' I asked.

" 'Get up,' the Lord said, 'and go into Damascus. There you will be told all that you have been assigned to do.'[r] 11My companions led me by the hand into Damascus, because the brilliance of the light had blinded me.[s]

12"A man named Ananias came to see me.[t] He was a devout observer of the law and highly respected by all the Jews living there.[u] 13He stood beside me and said, 'Brother Saul, receive your sight!' And at that very moment I was able to see him.

14"Then he said: 'The God of our fathers[v] has chosen you to know his will and to see[w] the Righteous One[x] and to hear words from his mouth. 15You will be his witness[y] to all men of what you have seen[z] and heard.

21:26 [c]Nu 6:13-20; Ac 24:18
21:27 [d]Jer 26:8; Ac 24:18; 26:21; S 1Th 2:16
21:28 [e]Mt 24:15; Ac 6:13; 24:5,6
21:29 [f]Ac 20:4; 2Ti 4:20 [g]S Ac 18:19
21:30 [h]Ac 26:21 [i]S Ac 16:19
21:32 [j]Ac 23:27
21:33 [k]ver 11 [l]Ac 12:6 [m]Ac 20:23; 22:29; Eph 6:20; 2Ti 2:9
21:34 [n]Ac 19:32 [o]ver 37; Ac 22:24; 23:10,16,32
21:35 [p]ver 40
21:36 [q]Lk 23:18; Jn 19:15; Ac 22:22
21:37 [r]S ver 34
21:38 [s]Mt 24:26 [t]Ac 5:36
21:39 [u]S Ac 9:11 [v]S Ac 6:9

21:40 [w]S Ac 12:17 [x]S Jn 5:2
22:1 [y]Ac 7:2
22:2 [z]Ac 21:40; S Jn 5:2
22:3 [a]Ac 21:39 [b]S Ac 9:11 [c]S Ac 6:9 [d]Lk 10:39 [e]Ac 5:34 [f]Ac 26:5 [g]1Ki 19:10; S Ac 21:20
22:4 [h]S Ac 8:3 [i]S Ac 9:2 [j]ver 19, 20
22:5 [k]Lk 22:66 [l]S Ac 1:16; 2:29; 13:26; 23:1; 28:17,21; S Ro 7:1; 9:3 [m]Ac 9:2
22:6 [n]Ac 9:3
22:8 [o]S Mk 1:24
22:9 [p]Ac 26:13 [q]Ac 9:7
22:10 [r]Ac 16:30
22:11 [s]Ac 9:8
22:12 [t]Ac 9:17 [u]Ac 10:22
22:14 [v]S Ac 3:13 [w]S 1Co 15:8 [x]Ac 7:52
22:15 [y]Ac 23:11; 26:16 [z]ver 14

[r]*40* Or possibly *Hebrew*; also in 22:2

16And now what are you waiting for?
Get up, be baptized[a] and wash your
sins away,[b] calling on his name.'[c]
17"When I returned to Jerusalem[d]
and was praying at the temple, I fell
into a trance[e] **18**and saw the Lord
speaking. 'Quick!' he said to me.
'Leave Jerusalem immediately, because they will not accept your testimony about me.'
19" 'Lord,' I replied, 'these men
know that I went from one synagogue
to another to imprison[f] and beat[g]
those who believe in you. **20**And when
the blood of your martyr[s] Stephen
was shed, I stood there giving my approval and guarding the clothes of
those who were killing him.'[h]
21"Then the Lord said to me, 'Go; I
will send you far away to the Gentiles.' "[i]

Paul the Roman Citizen

22The crowd listened to Paul until
he said this. Then they raised their
voices and shouted, "Rid the earth of
him![j] He's not fit to live!"[k]
23As they were shouting and throwing off their cloaks[l] and flinging dust
into the air,[m] **24**the commander ordered Paul to be taken into the barracks.[n] He directed[o] that he be
flogged and questioned in order to find
out why the people were shouting at
him like this. **25**As they stretched him
out to flog him, Paul said to the centurion standing there, "Is it legal for you
to flog a Roman citizen who hasn't
even been found guilty?"[p]
26When the centurion heard this, he
went to the commander and reported
it. "What are you going to do?" he
asked. "This man is a Roman citizen."
27The commander went to Paul and
asked, "Tell me, are you a Roman citizen?"
"Yes, I am," he answered.
28Then the commander said, "I had
to pay a big price for my citizenship."
"But I was born a citizen," Paul replied.
29Those who were about to question
him[q] withdrew immediately. The commander himself was alarmed when he
realized that he had put Paul, a Roman
citizen,[r] in chains.[s]

Before the Sanhedrin

30The next day, since the commander wanted to find out exactly why Paul
was being accused by the Jews,[t] he
released him[u] and ordered the chief
priests and all the Sanhedrin[v] to assemble. Then he brought Paul and had
him stand before them.
23 Paul looked straight at the Sanhedrin[w] and said, "My broth-

[s] 20 Or *witness*

22:16 [a] S Ac 2:38 [b] Lev 8:6; Ps 51:2; Eze 36:25; Jn 3:5; 1Co 6:11; Eph 5:26; Tit 3:5; Heb 10:22; 1Pe 3:21 [c] Ro 10:13
22:17 [d] Ac 9:26 [e] Ac 10:10
22:19 [f] ver 4; S Ac 8:3 [g] S Mt 10:17
22:20 [h] Ac 7:57-60; 8:1
22:21 [i] S Ac 9:15; S 13:46
22:22 [j] Ac 21:36 [k] Ac 25:24
22:23 [l] Ac 7:58 [m] 2Sa 16:13
22:24 [n] S Ac 21:34 [o] ver 29
22:25 [p] Ac 16:37
22:29 [q] ver 24 [r] ver 24,25; Ac 16:38 [s] S Ac 21:33
22:30 [t] Ac 23:28 [u] Ac 21:33 [v] S Mt 5:22
23:1 [w] Ac 22:30

22:16 BE BAPTIZED. Water baptism accompanied the proclamation of the gospel from the beginning of the church's mission (2:38,41). It was a rite of Christian initiation used in the NT to indicate that a person was committing himself or herself fully to Jesus Christ. By going into the baptismal water in the name of the Trinity (Mt 28:19) or of Christ (19:5), believers visibly demonstrated their faith before the Christian community.

(1) Water baptism "into Christ" (Gal 3:27) or "in the name of Jesus Christ" (2:38; cf. Mt 28:19) signifies that one now is the property of Christ and has a share in his life, his Spirit and his inheritance with God (Ro 8:14–17; Gal 3:26—4:7).

(2) Water baptism is a response to what Christ has done for the believer. To be valid, it must be preceded by repentance (2:38) and a personal faith in Christ (Col 2:12).

(3) Water baptism, when undertaken with a sincere heart of faith and commitment to Jesus as Lord and Savior, is a means of receiving grace from Christ (cf. 1Pe 3:21; see article on FAITH AND GRACE, p. 1720).

(4) Water baptism is an outward sign and testimony of our receiving Christ as Lord and Savior and of the washing away of our sins (cf. 2:38; Tit 3:5; 1Pe 3:21).

(5) Water baptism portrays the union of the believer with Christ in his death, burial and resurrection (Ro 6:1–11; Col 2:11–12). This signifies an end (i.e., "death") to a life of sin (Ro 6:3–4,7,10,12; Col 3:3–14) and the beginning of a new life in Christ (Ro 6:4–5,11; Col 2:12–13). Therefore, water baptism involves a commitment to a lifelong practice of turning one's back on the world and all that is evil (Ro 6:6,11–13) and living a new life in the Spirit that reflects God's standards of righteousness (Col 2:1–17).

22:16 WASH YOUR SINS AWAY. Paul was converted and saved on the Damascus road (see 9:5, note). His baptism was his public testimony of forgiveness and commitment to forsake all sin and identify himself with the cause of Christ.

22:17 I FELL INTO A TRANCE. The term "trance" here denotes a state of mind where one's attention is primarily aware of the realm of the Spirit rather than that of the natural. At such times one is especially receptive to revelation from God. It means being brought by the Spirit into a deeper and more intense communion with God (see Peter's trance in 10:10 and 11:5; cf. 2Co 12:3–4).

23:1 IN ALL GOOD CONSCIENCE. The conscience is an inner awareness that witnesses to

ers,[x] I have fulfilled my duty to God in
all good conscience[y] to this day." 2At
this the high priest Ananias[z] ordered
those standing near Paul to strike him
on the mouth.[a] 3Then Paul said to
him, "God will strike you, you whitewashed wall![b] You sit there to judge
me according to the law, yet you yourself violate the law by commanding
that I be struck!"[c]

4Those who were standing near Paul
said, "You dare to insult God's high
priest?"

5Paul replied, "Brothers, I did not
realize that he was the high priest; for
it is written: 'Do not speak evil about
the ruler of your people.'[t]"[d]

6Then Paul, knowing that some of
them were Sadducees[e] and the others
Pharisees, called out in the Sanhedrin,
"My brothers,[f] I am a Pharisee,[g] the
son of a Pharisee. I stand on trial because of my hope in the resurrection of
the dead."[h] 7When he said this, a dispute broke out between the Pharisees
and the Sadducees, and the assembly
was divided. 8(The Sadducees say that
there is no resurrection,[i] and that
there are neither angels nor spirits,
but the Pharisees acknowledge them
all.)

9There was a great uproar, and
some of the teachers of the law who
were Pharisees[j] stood up and argued
vigorously. "We find nothing wrong
with this man,"[k] they said. "What if a
spirit or an angel has spoken to
him?"[l] 10The dispute became so violent that the commander was afraid
Paul would be torn to pieces by them.
He ordered the troops to go down and
take him away from them by force and
bring him into the barracks.[m]

11The following night the Lord stood
near Paul and said, "Take courage![n]
As you have testified about me in Jerusalem, so you must also testify in
Rome."[o]

The Plot to Kill Paul

12The next morning the Jews formed
a conspiracy[p] and bound themselves
with an oath not to eat or drink until
they had killed Paul.[q] 13More than
forty men were involved in this plot.
14They went to the chief priests and
elders and said, "We have taken a solemn oath not to eat anything until we
have killed Paul.[r] 15Now then, you
and the Sanhedrin[s] petition the commander to bring him before you on the
pretext of wanting more accurate information about his case. We are ready to
kill him before he gets here."

16But when the son of Paul's sister
heard of this plot, he went into the barracks[t] and told Paul.

17Then Paul called one of the centurions and said, "Take this young man
to the commander; he has something
to tell him." 18So he took him to the
commander.

The centurion said, "Paul, the prisoner,[u] sent for me and asked me to
bring this young man to you because he
has something to tell you."

19The commander took the young
man by the hand, drew him aside and
asked, "What is it you want to tell me?"

20He said: "The Jews have agreed to
ask you to bring Paul before the Sanhedrin[v] tomorrow on the pretext of
wanting more accurate information
about him.[w] 21Don't give in to them,
because more than forty[x] of them are
waiting in ambush for him. They have
taken an oath not to eat or drink until
they have killed him.[y] They are ready

23:1 [x] S Ac 22:5 [y] Ac 24:16; 1Co 4:4; 2Co 1:12; 1Ti 1:5,19; 3:9; 2Ti 1:3; Heb 9:14; 10:22; 13:18; 1Pe 3:16,21 **23:2** [z] Ac 24:1 [a] Jn 18:22 **23:3** [b] Mt 23:27 [c] Lev 19:15; Dt 25:1,2; Jn 7:51 **23:5** [d] Ex 22:28 **23:6** [e] ver 7,8; S Ac 4:1 [f] S Ac 22:5 [g] Ac 26:5; Php 3:5 [h] Ac 24:15,21; 26:8 **23:8** [i] Mt 22:23; 1Co 15:12 **23:9** [j] Mk 2:16 [k] ver 29; Jer 26:16; S Lk 23:4; Ac 25:25; 26:31; 28:18 [l] Ac 22:7,17, 18 **23:10** [m] S Ac 21:34 **23:11** [n] S Mt 14:27 [o] Ac 19:21; 28:23 **23:12** [p] S Ac 20:3 [q] ver 14,21,30; Ac 25:3 **23:14** [r] ver 12 **23:15** [s] ver 1; Ac 22:30 **23:16** [t] ver 10; S Ac 21:34 **23:18** [u] S Eph 3:1 **23:20** [v] ver 1 [w] ver 14,15 **23:21** [x] ver 13 [y] ver 12,14

[t] 5 Exodus 22:28

our personality concerning the rightness or wrongness of our actions. A "good conscience" gives the verdict that we have not offended God or his will. Paul's claim (probably referring to his public life before other humans) is sincere; note Php 3:6, where he states, "as for legalistic righteousness, faultless." Before his conversion he even believed he was doing God's will in persecuting believers (26:9).

Paul's commitment to God, his intense resolve to please him, and his "faultless" life even before his conversion to Christ shame and condemn professed believers who excuse their unfaithfulness to Christ by claiming that everyone sins and that it is impossible to live before God with a good conscience.

23:11 THE LORD STOOD NEAR PAUL. Paul is anxious and apprehensive about what will happen to him. It appears that he might be killed in Jerusalem and that his plans to carry the gospel to Rome and further west might never be realized. God appears to him at this critical time, encourages his heart and assures him that he will witness for God's cause in Rome. Scripture records that the Lord appeared to Paul three times in order to reassure him (18:9–10; 22:17–18; 23:11; cf. 27:23–24; see 18:10, note).

now, waiting for your consent to their request."

22 The commander dismissed the young man and cautioned him, "Don't tell anyone that you have reported this to me."

Paul Transferred to Caesarea

23 Then he called two of his centurions and ordered them, "Get ready a detachment of two hundred soldiers, seventy horsemen and two hundred spearmen[u] to go to Caesarea[z] at nine tonight.[a] 24 Provide mounts for Paul so that he may be taken safely to Governor Felix."[b]

25 He wrote a letter as follows:

26 Claudius Lysias,

To His Excellency,[c] Governor Felix:

Greetings.[d]

27 This man was seized by the Jews and they were about to kill him,[e] but I came with my troops and rescued him,[f] for I had learned that he is a Roman citizen.[g] 28 I wanted to know why they were accusing him, so I brought him to their Sanhedrin.[h] 29 I found that the accusation had to do with questions about their law,[i] but there was no charge against him[j] that deserved death or imprisonment. 30 When I was informed[k] of a plot[l] to be carried out against the man, I sent him to you at once. I also ordered his accusers[m] to present to you their case against him.

31 So the soldiers, carrying out their orders, took Paul with them during the night and brought him as far as Antipatris. 32 The next day they let the cavalry[n] go on with him, while they returned to the barracks.[o] 33 When the cavalry[p] arrived in Caesarea,[q] they delivered the letter to the governor[r] and handed Paul over to him. 34 The governor read the letter and asked what province he was from. Learning that he was from Cilicia,[s] 35 he said, "I will hear your case when your accusers[t] get here." Then he ordered that Paul be kept under guard[u] in Herod's palace.

The Trial Before Felix

24 Five days later the high priest Ananias[v] went down to Caesarea with some of the elders and a lawyer named Tertullus, and they brought their charges[w] against Paul before the governor.[x] 2 When Paul was called in, Tertullus presented his case before Felix: "We have enjoyed a long period of peace under you, and your foresight has brought about reforms in this nation. 3 Everywhere and in every way, most excellent[y] Felix, we acknowledge this with profound gratitude. 4 But in order not to weary you further, I would request that you be kind enough to hear us briefly.

5 "We have found this man to be a troublemaker, stirring up riots[z] among the Jews[a] all over the world. He is a ringleader of the Nazarene[b] sect[c] 6 and even tried to desecrate the temple;[d] so we seized him. 8 By[v] examining him yourself you will be able to learn the truth about all these charges we are bringing against him."

9 The Jews joined in the accusation,[e] asserting that these things were true.

10 When the governor[f] motioned for him to speak, Paul replied: "I know that for a number of years you have been a judge over this nation; so I gladly make my defense. 11 You can easily verify that no more than twelve days[g] ago I went up to Jerusalem to worship. 12 My accusers did not find me arguing with anyone at the temple,[h] or stirring up a crowd[i] in the synagogues or anywhere else in the city. 13 And they cannot prove to you the charges they are now making against me.[j] 14 However, I admit that I worship the God of our fathers[k] as a follower of the Way,[l]

23:23 [z]S Ac 8:40 [a]ver 33
23:24 [b]ver 26,33; Ac 24:1-3,10; 25:14
23:26 [c]Lk 1:3; Ac 24:3; 26:25 [d]Ac 15:23
23:27 [e]Ac 21:32 [f]Ac 21:33 [g]Ac 22:25-29
23:28 [h]Ac 22:30
23:29 [i]Ac 18:15; 25:19 [j]S ver 9
23:30 [k]ver 20,21 [l]S Ac 20:3 [m]ver 35; Ac 24:19; 25:16
23:32 [n]ver 23 [o]S Ac 21:34
23:33 [p]ver 23,24 [q]S Ac 8:40 [r]ver 26
23:34 [s]S Ac 6:9; 21:39
23:35 [t]ver 30; Ac 24:19; 25:16 [u]Ac 24:27
24:1 [v]Ac 23:2 [w]Ac 23:30,35 [x]S Ac 23:24
24:3 [y]Lk 1:3; Ac 23:26; 26:25
24:5 [z]Ac 16:20; 17:6 [a]Ac 21:28 [b]S Mk 1:24 [c]ver 14; Ac 26:5; 28:22
24:6 [d]Ac 21:28
24:9 [e]S 1Th 2:16
24:10 [f]S Ac 23:24
24:11 [g]Ac 21:27; ver 1
24:12 [h]Ac 25:8; 28:17 [i]ver 18
24:13 [j]Ac 25:7
24:14 [k]S Ac 3:13 [l]S Ac 9:2

[u] *23* The meaning of the Greek for this word is uncertain. [v] *6-8* Some manuscripts *him and wanted to judge him according to our law. 7But the commander, Lysias, came and with the use of much force snatched him from our hands 8and ordered his accusers to come before you. By*

24:14 THE WAY. The salvation provided by Christ is called "the Way" (cf. 9:2; 16:17; 19:9,23; 24:14,22). The Greek word used here (*hodos*) denotes a path or road. The NT believer saw salvation in Christ not only as an experience to receive but also as a road to walk in faith and fellowship with Jesus. We must walk that road to the end in order to enter the final salvation of the age to come

which they call a sect.[m] I believe everything that agrees with the Law and
that is written in the Prophets,[n] 15and
I have the same hope in God as these
men, that there will be a resurrection[o]
of both the righteous and the wicked.[p]
16So I strive always to keep my conscience clear[q] before God and man.
17"After an absence of several years,
I came to Jerusalem to bring my people
gifts for the poor[r] and to present offerings. 18I was ceremonially clean[s]
when they found me in the temple
courts doing this. There was no crowd
with me, nor was I involved in any disturbance.[t] 19But there are some Jews
from the province of Asia,[u] who ought
to be here before you and bring charges
if they have anything against me.[v]
20Or these who are here should state
what crime they found in me when I
stood before the Sanhedrin— 21unless
it was this one thing I shouted as I
stood in their presence: 'It is concerning the resurrection of the dead that I
am on trial before you today.' "[w]
22Then Felix, who was well acquainted with the Way,[x] adjourned
the proceedings. "When Lysias the
commander comes," he said, "I will decide your case." 23He ordered the centurion to keep Paul under guard[y] but
to give him some freedom[z] and permit
his friends to take care of his needs.[a]
24Several days later Felix came with
his wife Drusilla, who was a Jewess.
He sent for Paul and listened to him as
he spoke about faith in Christ Jesus.[b]
25As Paul discoursed on righteousness, self-control[c] and the judgment[d] to come, Felix was afraid[e] and
said, "That's enough for now! You may
leave. When I find it convenient, I will
send for you." 26At the same time he
was hoping that Paul would offer him
a bribe, so he sent for him frequently
and talked with him.
27When two years had passed, Felix
was succeeded by Porcius Festus,[f]
but because Felix wanted to grant a favor to the Jews,[g] he left Paul in prison.[h]

The Trial Before Festus

25 Three days after arriving in the
province, Festus[i] went up
from Caesarea[j] to Jerusalem, 2where
the chief priests and Jewish leaders appeared before him and presented the
charges against Paul.[k] 3They urgently requested Festus, as a favor to them,
to have Paul transferred to Jerusalem,
for they were preparing an ambush to
kill him along the way.[l] 4Festus answered, "Paul is being held[m] at Caesarea,[n] and I myself am going there
soon. 5Let some of your leaders come
with me and press charges against the
man there, if he has done anything
wrong."

24:14 [m] S ver 5 [n] Ac 26:6,22; 28:23
24:15 [o] Ac 23:6; 28:20 [p] S Mt 25:46
24:16 [q] S Ac 23:1
24:17 [r] Ac 11:29, 30; Ro 15:25-28, 31; 1Co 16:1-4,15; 2Co 8:1-4; Gal 2:10
24:18 [s] Ac 21:26 [t] ver 12
24:19 [u] S Ac 2:9 [v] Ac 23:30
24:21 [w] Ac 23:6
24:22 [x] S Ac 9:2
24:23 [y] Ac 23:35 [z] Ac 28:16 [a] Ac 23:16; 27:3
24:24 [b] S Ac 20:21
24:25 [c] Gal 5:23; 1Th 5:6; 1Pe 4:7; 5:8; 2Pe 1:6 [d] Ac 10:42 [e] Jer 36:16
24:27 [f] Ac 25:1,4, 9,14 [g] Ac 12:3; 25:9 [h] Ac 23:35; 25:14
25:1 [i] S Ac 24:27 [j] S Ac 8:40
25:2 [k] ver 15; Ac 24:1
25:3 [l] S Ac 20:3
25:4 [m] Ac 24:23 [n] S Ac 8:40

(see article on BIBLICAL WORDS FOR SALVATION, p. 1710).

24:14 I BELIEVE EVERYTHING . . . WRITTEN. Paul's faith in the holy Scriptures as inerrant, infallible and trustworthy in all things lies in sharp contrast to many religious teachers of these last days who claim to believe only "some things" written in the Law and the Prophets (see article on THE INSPIRATION AND AUTHORITY OF SCRIPTURE, p. 1898). Those who are of the spirit and mind of Christ (Mt 5:18) and of the apostles (2Ti 3:16; 1Pe 1:11) will believe and defend "everything" written in the Word of God. Those who are not of this mind will disagree with the words of the great apostle.

24:15 RESURRECTION OF BOTH THE RIGHTEOUS AND THE WICKED. The Bible teaches a resurrection of both the unrighteous and the righteous dead. The righteous will be resurrected to live forever in their redeemed bodies with the Lord (1Th 4:13–18), while the unrighteous will rise to be judged by God (for the two resurrections, see Da 12:2, note; Jn 5:29, notes; Rev 20:6–14, notes). The fact that both resurrections are mentioned in the same verse does not necessarily mean that both occur simultaneously (see Jn 5:29, note).

24:16 KEEP MY CONSCIENCE CLEAR. A clear conscience is listed in Scripture as one of our essential weapons for a successful spiritual life and ministry (2Co 1:12; 1Ti 1:19). (1) A good conscience involves an inner freedom of spirit that comes when we know that God is not offended by our thoughts and actions (see 23:1, note; Ps 32:1; 1Ti 1:5; 1Pe 3:16; 1Jn 3:21–22). (2) When a good conscience is corrupted, one's faith, prayer life, communion with God and life of good deeds are seriously damaged (Tit 1:15–16); if people reject a good conscience, that will result in the shipwreck of their faith (1Ti 1:19).

24:25 RIGHTEOUSNESS, SELF-CONTROL AND THE JUDGMENT TO COME. As Paul speaks before Felix about faith in Jesus Christ, preaching about "righteousness, self-control and the judgment to come," Felix becomes frightened. This corresponds to Jesus' words that when the Holy Spirit comes, he "will convict the world of guilt in regard to sin and righteousness and judgment" (Jn 16:8). The salvation of all people depends on the faithful proclamation of those solemn truths by which the Spirit produces conviction in the sinner (see Jn 16:8, note).

6After spending eight or ten days
with them, he went down to Caesarea,
and the next day he convened the
court[o] and ordered that Paul be
brought before him.[p] 7When Paul appeared, the Jews who had come down
from Jerusalem stood around him,
bringing many serious charges against
him,[q] which they could not prove.[r]
8Then Paul made his defense: "I
have done nothing wrong against the
law of the Jews or against the temple[s]
or against Caesar."
9Festus, wishing to do the Jews a favor,[t] said to Paul, "Are you willing to
go up to Jerusalem and stand trial before me there on these charges?"[u]
10Paul answered: "I am now standing before Caesar's court, where I
ought to be tried. I have not done any
wrong to the Jews,[v] as you yourself
know very well. 11If, however, I am
guilty of doing anything deserving
death, I do not refuse to die. But if the
charges brought against me by these
Jews are not true, no one has the right
to hand me over to them. I appeal to
Caesar!"[w]
12After Festus had conferred with
his council, he declared: "You have appealed to Caesar. To Caesar you will
go!"

Festus Consults King Agrippa

13A few days later King Agrippa and
Bernice arrived at Caesarea[x] to pay
their respects to Festus. 14Since they
were spending many days there, Festus discussed Paul's case with the
king. He said: "There is a man here
whom Felix left as a prisoner.[y]
15When I went to Jerusalem, the chief
priests and elders of the Jews brought
charges against him[z] and asked that
he be condemned.
16"I told them that it is not the Roman custom to hand over any man before he has faced his accusers and has
had an opportunity to defend himself
against their charges.[a] 17When they
came here with me, I did not delay the
case, but convened the court the next
day and ordered the man to be brought
in.[b] 18When his accusers got up to
speak, they did not charge him with
any of the crimes I had expected. 19In-
stead, they had some points of dispute[c] with him about their own religion[d] and about a dead man named
Jesus who Paul claimed was alive. 20I
was at a loss how to investigate such
matters; so I asked if he would be willing to go to Jerusalem and stand trial
there on these charges.[e] 21When Paul
made his appeal to be held over for the
Emperor's decision, I ordered him held
until I could send him to Caesar."[f]
22Then Agrippa said to Festus, "I
would like to hear this man myself."
He replied, "Tomorrow you will hear
him."[g]

Paul Before Agrippa

26:12–18pp — Ac 9:3–8; 22:6–11

23The next day Agrippa and Bernice[h] came with great pomp and entered the audience room with the high
ranking officers and the leading men of
the city. At the command of Festus,
Paul was brought in. 24Festus said:
"King Agrippa, and all who are present
with us, you see this man! The whole
Jewish community[i] has petitioned me
about him in Jerusalem and here in
Caesarea, shouting that he ought not
to live any longer.[j] 25I found he had
done nothing deserving of death,[k] but
because he made his appeal to the Emperor[l] I decided to send him to Rome.
26But I have nothing definite to write
to His Majesty about him. Therefore I
have brought him before all of you, and
especially before you, King Agrippa, so
that as a result of this investigation I
may have something to write. 27For
I think it is unreasonable to send on
a prisoner without specifying the
charges against him."

26 Then Agrippa said to Paul,
"You have permission to speak
for yourself."[m]

25:6 [o]ver 17 [p]ver 10
25:7 [q]Mk 15:3; Lk 23:2,10; Ac 24:5,6 [r]Ac 24:13
25:8 [s]Ac 6:13; 24:12; 28:17
25:9 [t]Ac 24:27; 12:3 [u]ver 20
25:10 [v]ver 8
25:11 [w]ver 21, 25; Ac 26:32; 28:19
25:13 [x]S Ac 8:40
25:14 [y]Ac 24:27
25:15 [z]ver 2; Ac 24:1
25:16 [a]ver 4,5; Ac 23:30
25:17 [b]ver 6,10
25:19 [c]Ac 18:15; 23:29 [d]Ac 17:22
25:20 [e]ver 9
25:21 [f]ver 11,12
25:22 [g]Ac 9:15
25:23 [h]ver 13; Ac 26:30
25:24 [i]ver 2,3,7 [j]Ac 22:22
25:25 [k]S Ac 23:9 [l]S ver 11
26:1 [m]Ac 9:15; 25:22

25:8 AGAINST THE LAW OF THE JEWS. Paul knows of no offense that he has committed against the Jews or the law. Paul indeed kept the moral law of the OT (cf. 21:24). He knew that the law's moral standards never change, any more than God himself does. To him, the law is holy, good and spiritual (Ro 7:12,14), expressing God's character and requirement for a righteous life (cf. Mt 5:18–19). Yet Paul did not keep the law as a set of codes or standards by which to make himself righteous. A righteous life requires the work of the Holy Spirit; only after we are regenerated through the grace of Christ can we successfully obey God's law as an expression of our desire to please God. We are never without God's law when we are under Christ's law (1Co 9:21; see Mt 5:17, note; Ro 3:21; 8:4).

So Paul motioned with his hand[n]
and began his defense: **2**"King Agrippa,
I consider myself fortunate to stand before you[o] today as I make my defense
against all the accusations of the
Jews,[p] **3**and especially so because you
are well acquainted with all the Jewish
customs[q] and controversies.[r] Therefore, I beg you to listen to me patiently.
4"The Jews all know the way I have
lived ever since I was a child,[s] from
the beginning of my life in my own
country, and also in Jerusalem. **5**They
have known me for a long time[t] and
can testify, if they are willing, that according to the strictest sect[u] of our
religion, I lived as a Pharisee.[v] **6**And
now it is because of my hope[w] in what
God has promised our fathers[x] that I
am on trial today. **7**This is the promise
our twelve tribes[y] are hoping to see
fulfilled as they earnestly serve God
day and night.[z] O king, it is because
of this hope that the Jews are accusing
me.[a] **8**Why should any of you consider
it incredible that God raises the
dead?[b]
9"I too was convinced[c] that I ought
to do all that was possible to oppose[d]
the name of Jesus of Nazareth.[e] **10**And
that is just what I did in Jerusalem. On
the authority of the chief priests I put
many of the saints[f] in prison,[g] and
when they were put to death, I cast my
vote against them.[h] **11**Many a time I
went from one synagogue to another to
have them punished,[i] and I tried to
force them to blaspheme. In my obsession against them, I even went to foreign cities to persecute them.

26:1 [n]S Ac 12:17 **26:2** [o]Ps 119:46 [p]Ac 24:1,5; 25:2, 7,11 **26:3** [q]ver 7; S Ac 6:14 [r]Ac 25:19 **26:4** [s]Gal 1:13, 14; Php 3:5 **26:5** [t]Ac 22:3 [u]S Ac 24:5 [v]Ac 23:6; Php 3:5 **26:6** [w]Ac 23:6; 24:15; 28:20 [x]S Ac 13:32; Ro 15:8 **26:7** [y]Jas 1:1 [z]1Th 3:10; 1Ti 5:5 [a]ver 2 **26:8** [b]Ac 23:6 **26:9** [c]1Ti 1:13 [d]Jn 16:2 [e]S Jn 15:21 **26:10** [f]S Ac 9:13 [g]S Ac 8:3; 9:2,14, 21 [h]Ac 22:20 **26:11** [i]S Mt 10:17

26:14 [j]Ac 9:7 [k]S Jn 5:2 **26:16** [l]Eze 2:1; Da 10:11 [m]Ac 22:14,15 **26:17** [n]Jer 1:8,19 [o]S Ac 9:15; S 13:46 **26:18** [p]Isa 35:5 [q]Ps 18:28; Isa 42:7,16; Eph 5:8; Col 1:13; 1Pe 2:9 [r]Lk 24:47; Ac 2:38 [s]S Ac 20:21,32 **26:19** [t]Isa 50:5 **26:20** [u]Ac 9:19-25 [v]Ac 9:26-29; 22:17-20 [w]S Ac 9:15; S 13:46 [x]Ac 3:19 [y]Jer 18:11; 35:15; Mt 3:8; Lk 3:8 **26:21** [z]Ac 21:27, 30 [a]Ac 21:31

12"On one of these journeys I was
going to Damascus with the authority
and commission of the chief priests.
13About noon, O king, as I was on the
road, I saw a light from heaven, brighter than the sun, blazing around me and
my companions. **14**We all fell to the
ground, and I heard a voice[j] saying to
me in Aramaic,[w][k] 'Saul, Saul, why do
you persecute me? It is hard for you to
kick against the goads.'
15"Then I asked, 'Who are you,
Lord?'
" 'I am Jesus, whom you are persecuting,' the Lord replied. **16**'Now get up
and stand on your feet.[l] I have appeared to you to appoint you as a servant and as a witness of what you have
seen of me and what I will show you.[m]
17I will rescue you[n] from your own
people and from the Gentiles.[o] I am
sending you to them **18**to open their
eyes[p] and turn them from darkness to
light,[q] and from the power of Satan to
God, so that they may receive forgiveness of sins[r] and a place among those
who are sanctified by faith in me.'[s]
19"So then, King Agrippa, I was not
disobedient[t] to the vision from heav-
en. **20**First to those in Damascus,[u]
then to those in Jerusalem[v] and in all
Judea, and to the Gentiles[w] also, I
preached that they should repent[x]
and turn to God and prove their repentance by their deeds.[y] **21**That is why
the Jews seized me[z] in the temple
courts and tried to kill me.[a] **22**But I
have had God's help to this very day,

[w] *14* Or *Hebrew*

26:18 PAUL'S DIVINE COMMISSION. This verse is a classic statement of what the Lord Jesus desires from the preaching of the gospel to the lost.

(1) "Open their eyes." The lost are blinded by Satan to the reality of their lost and perishing condition and to the truth of the gospel (2Co 4:4). Only preaching Jesus Christ in the power of the Holy Spirit will open their understanding (cf. 2Co 4:5; Eph 1:18).

(2) "Turn them from . . . the power of Satan to God." Satan is the ruler of the world, and all those without Christ are under his control and enslaved to his power. Satan's spirit works in all sinners, i.e., "in those who are disobedient" (Eph 2:2). The proclamation of the gospel in the power of the Spirit will rescue men and women from the power of Satan and bring them into the kingdom of Christ (see Col 1:13; 1Pe 2:9).

(3) "That they may receive forgiveness of sins." Forgiveness comes through faith in Christ that is based on his sacrificial death on the cross.

(4) "A place among those who are sanctified by faith in me." The one who is forgiven, delivered from the dominion of sin and Satan, and indwelt by and baptized in the Holy Spirit is set apart from the world and now lives unto God in fellowship with all those saved by faith in Christ.

26:19 I WAS NOT DISOBEDIENT. Paul's conversion to Christ occurred on his journey to Damascus. From that moment on he recognized Jesus as Lord and Savior and dedicated his life to obeying him (cf. Ro 1:5).

26:20 PROVE THEIR REPENTANCE BY THEIR DEEDS. Paul did not preach, as some do, that salvation required "only trusting in Christ and his atoning death." The NT apostles declare that no individuals will be saved in Christ unless they "repent and turn to God and prove their repentance by their deeds" (see article on FAITH AND GRACE, p. 1720).

and so I stand here and testify to small
and great alike. I am saying nothing
beyond what the prophets and Moses
said would happen[b]— 23that the
Christ[x] would suffer[c] and, as the
first to rise from the dead,[d] would proclaim light to his own people and to the
Gentiles."[e]
24At this point Festus interrupted
Paul's defense. "You are out of your
mind,[f] Paul!" he shouted. "Your great
learning[g] is driving you insane."
25"I am not insane, most excellent[h]
Festus," Paul replied. "What I am saying is true and reasonable. 26The king
is familiar with these things,[i] and I
can speak freely to him. I am convinced that none of this has escaped
his notice, because it was not done in
a corner. 27King Agrippa, do you believe the prophets? I know you do."
28Then Agrippa said to Paul, "Do
you think that in such a short time you
can persuade me to be a Christian?"[j]
29Paul replied, "Short time or
long—I pray God that not only you but
all who are listening to me today may
become what I am, except for these
chains."[k]
30The king rose, and with him the
governor and Bernice[l] and those sitting with them. 31They left the room,
and while talking with one another,
they said, "This man is not doing anything that deserves death or imprisonment."[m]
32Agrippa said to Festus, "This man
could have been set free[n] if he had not
appealed to Caesar."[o]

Paul Sails for Rome

27 When it was decided that we[p]
would sail for Italy,[q] Paul and
some other prisoners were handed
over to a centurion named Julius, who
belonged to the Imperial Regiment.[r]
2We boarded a ship from Adramyttium
about to sail for ports along the coast
of the province of Asia,[s] and we put
out to sea. Aristarchus,[t] a Macedonian[u] from Thessalonica,[v] was with
us.
3The next day we landed at Sidon;[w]
and Julius, in kindness to Paul,[x] allowed him to go to his friends so they
might provide for his needs.[y] 4From
there we put out to sea again and
passed to the lee of Cyprus because the
winds were against us.[z] 5When we
had sailed across the open sea off the

26:22 [b] S Lk 24:27,44; Ac 10:43; 24:14
26:23 [c] S Mt 16:21 [d] 1Co 15:20,23; Col 1:18; Rev 1:5 [e] S Lk 2:32
26:24 [f] S Jn 10:20; S 1Co 4:10 [g] Jn 7:15
26:25 [h] S Ac 23:26
26:26 [i] ver 3
26:28 [j] Ac 11:26
26:29 [k] S Ac 21:33
26:30 [l] Ac 25:23
26:31 [m] S Ac 23:9
26:32 [n] Ac 28:18 [o] S Ac 25:11
27:1 [p] S Ac 16:10 [q] Ac 18:2; 25:12, 25 [r] Ac 10:1
27:2 [s] S Ac 2:9 [t] S Ac 19:29 [u] S Ac 16:9 [v] S Ac 17:1
27:3 [w] Mt 11:21 [x] ver 43 [y] Ac 24:23; 28:16
27:4 [z] ver 7
27:5 [a] S Ac 6:9 [b] S Ac 2:10
27:6 [c] Ac 28:11 [d] ver 1; Ac 18:2; 25:12,25
27:7 [e] ver 4 [f] ver 12,13,21; Tit 1:5
27:9 [g] Lev 16:29-31; 23:27-29; Nu 29:7
27:10 [h] ver 21
27:12 [i] S ver 7
27:14 [j] Mk 4:37
27:16 [k] ver 30
27:17 [l] ver 26,39
27:18 [m] ver 19, 38; Jnh 1:5

coast of Cilicia[a] and Pamphylia,[b] we
landed at Myra in Lycia. 6There the
centurion found an Alexandrian ship[c]
sailing for Italy[d] and put us on board.
7We made slow headway for many days
and had difficulty arriving off Cnidus.
When the wind did not allow us to hold
our course,[e] we sailed to the lee of
Crete,[f] opposite Salmone. 8We moved
along the coast with difficulty and
came to a place called Fair Havens,
near the town of Lasea.
9Much time had been lost, and sailing had already become dangerous because by now it was after the Fast.[y][g]
So Paul warned them, 10"Men, I can
see that our voyage is going to be disastrous and bring great loss to ship
and cargo, and to our own lives also."[h]
11But the centurion, instead of listening to what Paul said, followed the advice of the pilot and of the owner of the
ship. 12Since the harbor was unsuit-
able to winter in, the majority decided
that we should sail on, hoping to reach
Phoenix and winter there. This was a
harbor in Crete,[i] facing both southwest and northwest.

The Storm

13When a gentle south wind began
to blow, they thought they had obtained what they wanted; so they
weighed anchor and sailed along the
shore of Crete. 14Before very long, a
wind of hurricane force,[j] called the
"northeaster," swept down from the island. 15The ship was caught by the
storm and could not head into the
wind; so we gave way to it and were
driven along. 16As we passed to the lee
of a small island called Cauda, we were
hardly able to make the lifeboat[k] secure. 17When the men had hoisted it
aboard, they passed ropes under the
ship itself to hold it together. Fearing
that they would run aground[l] on the
sandbars of Syrtis, they lowered the
sea anchor and let the ship be driven
along. 18We took such a violent battering from the storm that the next day
they began to throw the cargo overboard.[m] 19On the third day, they threw
the ship's tackle overboard with their
own hands. 20When neither sun nor
stars appeared for many days and the

[x] 23 Or *Messiah* [y] 9 That is, the Day of Atonement (Yom Kippur)

storm continued raging, we finally gave up all hope of being saved.

21After the men had gone a long time without food, Paul stood up before them and said: "Men, you should have taken my advice[n] not to sail from Crete;[o] then you would have spared yourselves this damage and loss. **22**But now I urge you to keep up your courage,[p] because not one of you will be lost; only the ship will be destroyed. **23**Last night an angel[q] of the God whose I am and whom I serve[r] stood beside me[s] **24**and said, 'Do not be afraid, Paul. You must stand trial before Caesar;[t] and God has graciously given you the lives of all who sail with you.'[u] **25**So keep up your courage,[v] men, for I have faith in God that it will happen just as he told me.[w] **26**Nevertheless, we must run aground[x] on some island."[y]

Ro 4:19-21

The Shipwreck

27On the fourteenth night we were still being driven across the Adriatic[z] Sea, when about midnight the sailors sensed they were approaching land. **28**They took soundings and found that the water was a hundred and twenty feet[a] deep. A short time later they took soundings again and found it was ninety feet[b] deep. **29**Fearing that we would be dashed against the rocks, they dropped four anchors from the stern and prayed for daylight. **30**In an attempt to escape from the ship, the sailors let the lifeboat[z] down into the sea, pretending they were going to lower some anchors from the bow. **31**Then Paul said to the centurion and the soldiers, "Unless these men stay with the ship, you cannot be saved."[a] **32**So the soldiers cut the ropes that held the lifeboat and let it fall away.

27:21 [n]ver 10 [o]S ver 7
27:22 [p]ver 25,36
27:23 [q]S Ac 5:19 [r]Ro 1:9 [s]Ac 18:9; 23:11; 2Ti 4:17
27:24 [t]Ac 23:11 [u]ver 44
27:25 [v]ver 22,36 [w]Ro 4:20,21
27:26 [x]ver 17,39 [y]Ac 28:1
27:30 [z]ver 16
27:31 [a]ver 24

33Just before dawn Paul urged them all to eat. "For the last fourteen days," he said, "you have been in constant suspense and have gone without food—you haven't eaten anything. **34**Now I urge you to take some food. You need it to survive. Not one of you will lose a single hair from his head."[b] **35**After he said this, he took some bread and gave thanks to God in front of them all. Then he broke it[c] and began to eat. **36**They were all encouraged[d] and ate some food themselves. **37**Altogether there were 276 of us on board. **38**When they had eaten as much as they wanted, they lightened the ship by throwing the grain into the sea.[e]

39When daylight came, they did not recognize the land, but they saw a bay with a sandy beach,[f] where they decided to run the ship aground if they could. **40**Cutting loose the anchors,[g] they left them in the sea and at the same time untied the ropes that held the rudders. Then they hoisted the foresail to the wind and made for the beach. **41**But the ship struck a sandbar and ran aground. The bow stuck fast and would not move, and the stern was broken to pieces by the pounding of the surf.[h]

42The soldiers planned to kill the prisoners to prevent any of them from swimming away and escaping. **43**But the centurion wanted to spare Paul's life[i] and kept them from carrying out their plan. He ordered those who could swim to jump overboard first and get to land. **44**The rest were to get there on

27:34 [b]S Mt 10:30
27:35 [c]S Mt 14:19
27:36 [d]ver 22,25
27:38 [e]ver 18; Jnh 1:5
27:39 [f]Ac 28:1
27:40 [g]ver 29
27:41 [h]2Co 11:25
27:43 [i]ver 3

[z]*27* In ancient times the name referred to an area extending well south of Italy.
[a]*28* Greek *twenty orguias* (about 37 meters)
[b]*28* Greek *fifteen orguias* (about 27 meters)

27:24 DO NOT BE AFRAID, PAUL. As long as God has a place and purpose for one's life on earth and that person is seeking God and following the guidance of the Holy Spirit (cf. 23:11; 24:16), the Lord will protect him or her from death. All of God's faithful have the right to pray, "O Lord, I am yours; I serve you; be my protector" (cf. Ps 16:1–2).

27:25 KEEP UP YOUR COURAGE. Paul is a prisoner in the ship; nevertheless, he is a free man in Christ, living free from fear in God's presence, while those who sail with him are paralyzed with terror because of this danger at sea. In this life, only the sincere and faithful believer experiencing God's nearness can face life's dangers with courage and assurance in Christ.

27:31 UNLESS THESE MEN STAY WITH THE SHIP. Paul's statement here appears inconsistent with vv. 22,24. If God promises Paul that he will spare the lives of all those sailing with him (v. 24), and Paul reports the promise without qualification that "not one of you will be lost" (v. 22), how could the desertion of the sailors cause anyone's death among the passengers? The answer is in the Biblical truth that God's promises to his people are normally conditioned on their obedience to his will (see Ge 1:26–31 and 6:5–7; Ex 3:7–8 and Nu 14:28–34; 2Sa 7:12–16 and 1Ki 11:11–13; 12:16).

planks or on pieces of the ship. In this
way everyone reached land in safety.[j]

Ashore on Malta

28 Once safely on shore, we[k]
found out that the island[l] was
called Malta. **2**The islanders showed
us unusual kindness. They built a fire
and welcomed us all because it was
raining and cold. **3**Paul gathered a pile
of brushwood and, as he put it on the
fire, a viper, driven out by the heat, fastened itself on his hand. **4**When the islanders saw the snake hanging from
his hand,[m] they said to each other,
"This man must be a murderer; for
though he escaped from the sea, Justice has not allowed him to live."[n]
5But Paul shook the snake off into the
fire and suffered no ill effects.[o] **6**The
people expected him to swell up or suddenly fall dead, but after waiting a long
time and seeing nothing unusual happen to him, they changed their minds
and said he was a god.[p]

7There was an estate nearby that belonged to Publius, the chief official of
the island. He welcomed us to his
home and for three days entertained us
hospitably. **8**His father was sick in bed,
suffering from fever and dysentery.
Paul went in to see him and, after
prayer,[q] placed his hands on him[r]
and healed him.[s] **9**When this had happened, the rest of the sick on the island
came and were cured. **10**They honored
us[t] in many ways and when we were
ready to sail, they furnished us with
the supplies we needed.

Arrival at Rome

11After three months we put out to
sea in a ship that had wintered in the
island. It was an Alexandrian ship[u]
with the figurehead of the twin gods
Castor and Pollux. **12**We put in at Syra-
cuse and stayed there three days.
13From there we set sail and arrived at
Rhegium. The next day the south wind
came up, and on the following day we
reached Puteoli. **14**There we found
some brothers[v] who invited us to
spend a week with them. And so we
came to Rome. **15**The brothers[w] there
had heard that we were coming, and
they traveled as far as the Forum of
Appius and the Three Taverns to meet
us. At the sight of these men Paul
thanked God and was encouraged.
16When we got to Rome, Paul was allowed to live by himself, with a soldier
to guard him.[x]

Paul Preaches at Rome Under Guard

17Three days later he called together the leaders of the Jews.[y] When they
had assembled, Paul said to them: "My
brothers,[z] although I have done nothing against our people[a] or against the
customs of our ancestors,[b] I was arrested in Jerusalem and handed over to
the Romans. **18**They examined me[c]
and wanted to release me,[d] because I
was not guilty of any crime deserving
death.[e] **19**But when the Jews objected,
I was compelled to appeal to Caesar[f]—not that I had any charge to
bring against my own people. **20**For
this reason I have asked to see you and
talk with you. It is because of the hope
of Israel[g] that I am bound with this
chain."[h]

21They replied, "We have not received any letters from Judea concerning you, and none of the brothers[i]
who have come from there has reported or said anything bad about you.
22But we want to hear what your views
are, for we know that people everywhere are talking against this sect."[j]

23They arranged to meet Paul on a
certain day, and came in even larger
numbers to the place where he was
staying. From morning till evening he
explained and declared to them the
kingdom of God[k] and tried to convince
them about Jesus[l] from the Law of
Moses and from the Prophets.[m]
24Some were convinced by what he
said, but others would not believe.[n]
25They disagreed among themselves
and began to leave after Paul had made

27:44 [j] ver 22,31
28:1 [k] S Ac 16:10 [l] Ac 27:26,39
28:4 [m] Mk 16:18 [n] Lk 13:2,4
28:5 [o] Lk 10:19
28:6 [p] Ac 14:11
28:8 [q] Jas 5:14,15 [r] S Ac 6:6 [s] Ac 9:40
28:10 [t] Ps 15:4
28:11 [u] Ac 27:6
28:14 [v] S Ac 1:16
28:15 [w] S Ac 1:16
28:16 [x] Ac 24:23; 27:3
28:17 [y] Ac 25:2 [z] S Ac 22:5 [a] S Ac 25:8 [b] S Ac 6:14
28:18 [c] Ac 22:24 [d] Ac 26:31,32 [e] S Ac 23:9
28:19 [f] S Ac 25:11
28:20 [g] Ac 26:6,7 [h] S Ac 21:33
28:21 [i] S Ac 22:5
28:22 [j] S Ac 24:5,14
28:23 [k] S Mt 3:2; Ac 19:8 [l] Ac 17:3 [m] S Ac 8:35
28:24 [n] Ac 14:4; 17:4,5

28:5 PAUL ... SUFFERED NO ILL EFFECTS. Paul's experience remarkably illustrates Jesus' promise in Mk 16:18 (see note on that verse).

28:16 WHEN WE GOT TO ROME. It had been Paul's desire to preach the gospel in Rome (Ro 15:22–29), and it was also God's will that he do so (23:11). Yet Paul arrived in Rome in chains and only after setbacks, storms, shipwreck and many trials. Though Paul remained faithful, God did not make his way easy and trouble free. Likewise, we may be in God's will and entirely faithful to him; nevertheless, he may direct us in unpleasant paths involving troubles. Yet we can know that "in all things God works for the good of those who love him" (Ro 8:28).

this final statement: "The Holy Spirit spoke the truth to your forefathers when he said[o] through Isaiah the prophet:

26" 'Go to this people and say,
"You will be ever hearing but never understanding;
you will be ever seeing but never perceiving."
27For this people's heart has become calloused;[p]
they hardly hear with their ears,
and they have closed their eyes.
Otherwise they might see with their eyes,
hear with their ears,
understand with their hearts
and turn, and I would heal them.'[c][q]

28"Therefore I want you to know that God's salvation[r] has been sent to the Gentiles,[s] and they will listen!"[d]
30For two whole years Paul stayed there in his own rented house and welcomed all who came to see him.
31Boldly[t] and without hindrance he preached the kingdom of God[u] and taught about the Lord Jesus Christ.

28:25 [o] S Heb 3:7 **28:27** [p] Ps 119:70 [q] Isa 6:9,10; S Mt 13:15 **28:28** [r] Lk 2:30 [s] S Ac 13:46 **28:31** [t] S Ac 4:29 [u] ver 23; S Mt 4:23

[c] *27* Isaiah 6:9,10 [d] *28* Some manuscripts *listen!"* [29]*After he said this, the Jews left, arguing vigorously among themselves.*

28:30 FOR TWO WHOLE YEARS PAUL STAYED THERE. Luke's history of the early church is brought to an end here. What happened to Paul afterwards is generally thought to be the following. Paul remained in confinement for two years. He was able to receive visitors and preach the gospel to them. During this time he wrote the letters to the Ephesians, Philippians, Colossians and to Philemon. In approximately A.D. 63, Paul was acquitted and released. For the next few years he continued his missionary endeavors, perhaps going to Spain as he had planned (Ro 15:28). During this period he wrote 1 Timothy and Titus. Paul was again arrested, about A.D. 67, and was taken back to Rome. He wrote 2 Timothy during this second imprisonment at Rome. Paul's imprisonment ended with his martyrdom (tradition says by beheading) under the Roman emperor Nero.

28:31 PREACHED THE KINGDOM OF GOD. The book of Acts breaks off suddenly, with no formal conclusion to what God did through the Holy Spirit and the NT apostles. God intends that the acts of the Holy Spirit and the preaching of the gospel continue in the lives of Christ's people until the end of the age (2:17–21; Mt 28:18–20). Luke, under the inspiration of the Spirit, has revealed God's pattern of what the church should be and do. He has given us examples of the faithfulness of believers, the triumph of the gospel against the opposition of the enemy and the power of the Holy Spirit operating in the church and among people. This is God's pattern for present and future churches, and we must faithfully proclaim it and live it (2Ti 1:14). All churches must measure themselves by what the Spirit said and did among the earliest believers. If the power, righteousness, joy and faith found in our churches are not the same as what we read about in Acts, then we must ask God once more for a renewed faith in the resurrected Christ and for a fresh, new outpouring of his Spirit.

ROMANS

Outline

Introduction (1:1–17)

- I. Man's Desperate Need of Righteousness (1:18—3:20)
  - A. The Gentiles' Need (1:18–32)
  - B. The Jews' Need (2:1—3:8)
  - C. The Universal Need (3:9–20)
- II. God's Glorious Provision of Righteousness (3:21—5:21)
  - A. Justification by Faith Summarized (3:21–31)
  - B. Justification by Faith Illustrated in Abraham (4:1–25)
  - C. The Blessings and Assurance Accompanying Justification (5:1–11)
  - D. Adam and Christ Contrasted (5:12–21)
    1. Adam/Sin/Condemnation/Death
    2. Christ/Grace/Justification/Life
- III. The Outworking of Righteousness Through Faith (6:1—8:39)
  - A. Freedom From Slavery to Sin (6:1–23)
    1. Dying With Christ to Sin (6:1–14)
    2. Living With Christ as Servants of Righteousness (6:15–23)
  - B. Freedom From the Conflict Under the Law (7:1–25)
  - C. Freedom Through the Law of the Spirit of Life (8:1–39)
- IV. Righteousness Through Faith As It Relates to Israel (9:1—11:36)
  - A. The Problem of Israel's Rejection (9:1—10:21)
  - B. The Triumph of God's Plan (11:1–36)
- V. Practical Applications of Righteousness Through Faith (12:1—15:13)
  - A. The Believer and Consecration (12:1–2)
  - B. The Believer and Community (12:3–21)
  - C. The Believer and the State (13:1–7)
  - D. The Believer and the Law of Love (13:8—15:13)

Conclusion (15:14—16:27)

Author: Paul

Theme: The Righteousness of God is Revealed

Date of Writing: c. A.D. 57

Background

Romans is Paul's longest, most theological and most influential letter. Probably for these reasons it is placed first among his thirteen NT books. Paul wrote Romans in connection with his apostolic mission to the Gentile world. Contrary to some ecclesiastical traditions, the church in Rome was not founded by Peter or any other apostle. The Roman church may have been established by Paul's converts from Macedonia and Asia, as well as by Jews and proselytes converted on the day of Pentecost (Ac 2:10). Paul did not regard Rome as the specific territory of another apostle (Ro 15:20).

In the book of Romans Paul assures the believers at Rome that he has often planned to preach the gospel to them but so far has been hindered from coming (1:13–15; 15:22). He affirms his earnest desire to come to them, and he communicates his plans for coming soon (15:23–32).

At the time of writing, toward the end of his third missionary journey (cf. 15:25–26; Ac 20:2–3; 1Co 16:5–6), Paul was at Corinth as a guest in the home of Gaius (Ro 16:23; 1Co 1:14). As he penned Romans through his assistant Tertius (16:22), he was planning to return to Jerusalem for the day of Pentecost (Ac 20:16; probably spring A.D. 57 or 58) and to deliver personally a relief offering from the Gentile churches for the poverty-stricken saints in Jerusalem (15:25–27). Immediately afterwards, Paul hoped to go to Spain with the gospel, visiting the church in Rome on his way and receiving assistance from them as he headed further west (15:24,28).

Purpose

Paul wrote this letter to prepare the way for his anticipated ministry at Rome and his planned mission to Spain. His purpose was twofold. (1) Since the Romans apparently received distorted rumors about Paul's message and theology (e.g., 3:8; 6:1–2,15), he felt it necessary to put into writing the gospel he had been preaching for twenty-five years. (2) He sought to correct certain problems in the church occurring because of wrong attitudes of Jews toward Gentiles (e.g., 2:1–29; 3:1,9) and Gentiles toward Jews (e.g., 11:11–32).

Survey

The theme of Romans is presented in 1:16–17, namely, that in the Lord Jesus a righteousness from God is revealed as the answer to his wrath against sin. Then Paul sets forth the gospel's foundational truths. First, he emphasizes that the problem of sin and humanity's need of righteousness are universal (1:18—3:20). Since both Jews and Gentiles are under sin and thus under God's wrath, no person can be justified before God apart from the gift of righteousness through faith in Jesus Christ (3:21—4:25).

Having been justified freely by grace through faith and having been given assurance of our salvation (ch. 5), God's gift of righteousness is demonstrated in our death with Christ to sin (ch. 6), our deliverance from the struggle of law-righteousness (ch. 7), and our adoption as God's children and our new life "through the Spirit," leading to glorification (ch. 8). God is working out his plan of redemption in spite of Israel's unbelief (chs. 9–11).

Finally, Paul declares that a transformed life in Christ results in the application of righteousness and love to all areas of behavior—social, civil and moral (chs. 12–14). Paul concludes Romans with an explanation of his personal plans (ch. 15) and a long list of personal greetings, a final admonition and a doxology (ch. 16).

Special Features

Seven major emphases characterize Romans. (1) Romans is Paul's most systematic letter, the theological letter *par excellence* in the NT. (2) Paul writes in a question and answer, or debating, style (e.g., 3:1,4–6,9,31). (3) Paul uses the OT extensively as Scriptural authority for his presentation of the true nature of the gospel. (4) Paul presents "a righteousness from God" as the core revelation of the gospel (1:16–17): God set things right in and through Jesus Christ. (5) Paul focuses on the twofold nature of sin, along with God's provision in Christ for each aspect: (a) sin as personal transgression (1:1—5:11), and the "sin" (Gk *hē hamartia*) principle, i.e., the inherent natural tendency to sin that lives within every person's heart since Adam's fall (5:12—8:39). (6) Ro 8 is the most extensive chapter in the Bible on the role of the Holy Spirit in the life of the believer. (7) Romans contains the Bible's most powerful discussion about the Jews' rejection of Christ (except for a remnant) and about God's plan for a full-circle redemption that ultimately comes back to Israel (chs. 9–11).

Reading Romans

In order to read the entire New Testament in one year, the book of Romans should be read in 21 days, according to the following schedule:
☐ 1:1–17 ☐ 1:18–32 ☐ 2 ☐ 3 ☐ 4 ☐ 5:1–11 ☐ 5:12–21 ☐ 6:1–14 ☐ 6:15—7:6 ☐ 7:7–25 ☐ 8:1–17 ☐ 8:18–39 ☐ 9:1–29 ☐ 9:30—10:21 ☐ 11:1–24 ☐ 11:25–36 ☐ 12:1–16 ☐ 12:17—13:14 ☐ 14:1—15:4 ☐ 15:5–33 ☐ 16

NOTES

1 Paul, a servant of Christ Jesus, called to be an apostle[a] and set apart[b] for the gospel of God[c]— **2**the gospel he promised beforehand[d] through his prophets[e] in the Holy Scriptures[f] **3**regarding his Son, who as to his human nature[g] was a descendant of David,[h] **4**and who through the Spirit[a] of holiness was declared with power to be the Son of God[b][i] by his resurrection from the dead:[j] Jesus Christ our Lord.[k] **5**Through him and for his name's sake, we received grace[l] and apostleship to call people from among all the Gentiles[m] to the obedience that comes from faith.[n] **6**And you also are among those who are called to belong to Jesus Christ.[o]

7To all in Rome who are loved by God[p] and called to be saints:[q]

Grace and peace to you from God our Father and from the Lord Jesus Christ.[r]

Paul's Longing to Visit Rome

8First, I thank my God through Jesus Christ for all of you,[s] because your faith is being reported all over the world.[t] **9**God, whom I serve[u] with my whole heart in preaching the gospel of his Son, is my witness[v] how constantly I remember you **10**in my prayers at all times;[w] and I pray that now at last by God's will[x] the way may be opened for me to come to you.[y]

11I long to see you[z] so that I may impart to you some spiritual gift[a] to make you strong— **12**that is, that you and I may be mutually encouraged by each other's faith. **13**I do not want you to be unaware,[b] brothers,[c] that I planned many times to come to you (but have been prevented from doing so until now)[d] in order that I might have a harvest among you, just as I have had among the other Gentiles.

14I am obligated[e] both to Greeks and non-Greeks, both to the wise and the foolish. **15**That is why I am so eager to preach the gospel also to you who are at Rome.[f]

16I am not ashamed of the gospel,[g] because it is the power of God[h] for the salvation of everyone who believes:[i] first for the Jew,[j] then for the Gentile.[k] **17**For in the gospel a righteousness from God is revealed,[l] a righteousness that is by faith[m] from first to last,[c] just as it is written: "The righteous will live by faith."[d][n]

God's Wrath Against Mankind

18The wrath of God[o] is being revealed from heaven against all the godlessness and wickedness of men who

1:1 [a]S 1Co 1:1 [b]S Ac 9:15 [c]Ro 15:16; S 2Co 2:12; 11:7; 1Th 2:8,9; 1Pe 4:17 **1:2** [d]S Ac 13:32; Tit 1:2 [e]Lk 1:70; Ro 3:21 [f]Gal 3:8 **1:3** [g]S Jn 1:14; Ro 9:5 [h]S Mt 1:1 **1:4** [i]S Mt 4:3 [j]S Ac 2:24 [k]1Co 1:2 **1:5** [l]1Ti 1:14 [m]S Ac 9:15 [n]Ac 6:7; Ro 16:26 **1:6** [o]Jude 1; Rev 17:14 **1:7** [p]Ro 8:39; 1Th 1:4 [q]S Ac 9:13 [r]1Co 1:3; Eph 1:2; 1Ti 1:2; Tit 1:4; 1Pe 1:2 **1:8** [s]1Co 1:4; Eph 1:16; 1Th 2:13; 2Th 1:3; 2Ti 1:3 [t]S Ro 10:18; 16:19 **1:9** [u]2Ti 1:3 [v]Job 16:19; Jer 42:5; 2Co 1:23; Gal 1:20; Php 1:8; 1Th 2:5,10 **1:10** [w]1Sa 12:23; S Lk 18:1; S Ac 1:14; Eph 1:16; Php 1:4; Col 1:9; 2Th 1:11; 2Ti 1:3; Phm 4 [x]S Ac 18:21 [y]ver 13; Ro 15:32

1:11 [z]Ro 15:23 [a]1Co 1:7; 12:1-31 **1:13** [b]S Ro 11:25 [c]S Ro 7:1 [d]Ro 15:22,23 **1:14** [e]1Co 9:16 **1:15** [f]Ro 15:20 **1:16** [g]2Ti 1:8 [h]1Co 1:18 [i]S Jn 3:15 [j]Ac 3:26; 13:46 [k]S Ac 13:46; Ro 2:9,10 **1:17** [l]Ro 3:21; Php 3:9 [m]S Ro 9:30 [n]Hab 2:4; Gal 3:11; Heb 10:38 **1:18** [o]Jn 3:36; Ro 5:9; Eph 5:6; Col 3:6; 1Th 1:10; Rev 19:15

[a]4 Or *who as to his spirit* [b]4 Or *was appointed to be the Son of God with power* [c]17 Or *is from faith to faith* [d]17 Hab. 2:4

1:4 THE SPIRIT OF HOLINESS. The "Spirit of holiness" refers to the Holy Spirit, the third person in the divine Trinity. His holiness separates him distinctly from the spirit of humanity, sin and the world, and describes both his preeminent characteristic and his work (cf. Gal 5:16–24).

1:5 OBEDIENCE THAT COMES FROM FAITH. Note that Paul, both at the beginning of the letter to the Romans and at the end (16:26), defines faith in terms of "obedience." For Paul the nature of saving faith must be determined by its initial intention, namely, a joining of one's life to God through Jesus Christ in love, devotion, gratitude and obedience (see Jas 2:17, note; cf. Jn 15:10,14; Heb 5:8–9; see article on FAITH AND GRACE, p. 1720).

1:7 CALLED TO BE SAINTS. Believers have been set apart (cf. v. 1) from sin and the world, brought near to God and consecrated for service (see Ex 19:6, note; Lev 11:44, note). With this action of consecration, the Spirit renews the characters of believers in true holiness (see Ac 9:13, note; cf. Eph 4:23–24; see article on SANCTIFICATION, p. 1956).

1:16 SALVATION. For a discussion of the meaning of the word "salvation," as well as two other words the Bible uses for salvation, see article on BIBLICAL WORDS FOR SALVATION, p. 1710.

1:17 BY FAITH FROM FIRST TO LAST. The righteous person continues to live by faith, and in so doing grows from one level of maturity to another. In this way, the believer progresses along the path of righteousness to live a rich spiritual life (see 8:12–13; 14:13–23; Heb 10:38, note; see article on FAITH AND GRACE, p. 1720).

1:18 THE WRATH OF GOD. The wrath (Gk *orgē*) of God is an expression of his righteousness and love (see article on THE ATTRIBUTES OF GOD, p. 882). It is God's personal anger and unchanging reaction to all sin (Eze 7:8–9; Eph 5:6; Rev 19:15), provoked by the wicked behavior of individuals (Ex 4:14; Nu 12:1–9; 2Sa 6:6–7) and nations (Isa 10:5; 13:3; Jer 50:13; Eze 30:15) and by the unfaithfulness of God's people (Nu 25:3; 32:10–13; Dt 29:24–28).

(1) In the past God's anger and hatred toward sin was revealed in the flood (Ge 6–8), famine and plague (Eze 6:11ff), annihilation (Dt 29:22–23),

suppress the truth by their wickedness, **19**since what may be known
about God is plain to them, because
God has made it plain to them.[p] **20**For
since the creation of the world God's
invisible qualities—his eternal power
and divine nature—have been clearly
seen, being understood from what has
been made,[q] so that men are without
excuse.[r]
21For although they knew God, they
neither glorified him as God nor gave
thanks to him, but their thinking became futile and their foolish hearts
were darkened.[s] **22**Although they
claimed to be wise, they became
fools[t] **23**and exchanged the glory of
the immortal God for images[u] made to
look like mortal man and birds and animals and reptiles.
24Therefore God gave them over[v] in
the sinful desires of their hearts to sexual impurity for the degrading of their
bodies with one another.[w] **25**They exchanged the truth of God for a lie,[x]
and worshiped and served created
things[y] rather than the Creator—who
is forever praised.[z] Amen.[a]
26Because of this, God gave them
over[b] to shameful lusts.[c] Even their
women exchanged natural relations
for unnatural ones.[d] **27**In the same
way the men also abandoned natural
relations with women and were in-

1:19 [p] Ac 14:17
1:20 [q] Ps 19:1-6 [r] Ro 2:1
1:21 [s] Ge 8:21; Jer 2:5; 17:9; Eph 4:17,18
1:22 [t] 1Co 1:20, 27; 3:18,19
1:23 [u] Dt 4:16,17; Ps 106:20; Jer 2:11; Ac 17:29
1:24 [v] ver 26,28; Ps 81:12; Eph 4:19 [w] 1Pe 4:3
1:25 [x] Isa 44:20 [y] Jer 10:14; 13:25; 16:19,20 [z] Ro 9:5; 2Co 11:31 [a] S Ro 11:36
1:26 [b] ver 24,28 [c] Eph 4:19; 1Th 4:5 [d] Lev 18:22,23

scattering (La 4:16) and burning of the land (Isa 9:18–19).

(2) In the present God's anger is seen in his giving the wicked over to uncleanness and vile passions (see v. 24, note) and in bringing ruin and death to all who disobey God (1:18—3:20; 6:23; Eze 18:4; Eph 2:3).

(3) In the future the wrath of God will include great distress for the ungodly of this world (Mt 24:21; Rev 5–19) and a coming day of judgment for all people and nations (Eze 7:19; Da 8:19)—"a day of trouble and ruin, a day of darkness and gloom" (Zep 1:15), a day of reckoning for the unrighteous (2:5; Mt 3:7; Lk 3:17; Eph 5:6; Col 3:6; Rev 11:18; 14:8–10; 19:15). Ultimately God's wrath results in eternal punishment for the unrepentant (see Mt 10:28, note).

(4) God's wrath is not his final word to humans, for he has provided a way of escape. A person may repent of sin and turn in faith to Jesus Christ (5:8; Jn 3:36; 1Th 1:10; 5:9; see article on BIBLICAL WORDS FOR SALVATION, p. 1710).

(5) Believers united to Christ must participate in God's anger against sin, not in the sense of vengeance, but in a sincere love of righteousness and hatred of wickedness (see Heb 1:9, note). The NT recognizes a holy anger that hates what God hates, an anger evident above all in Jesus himself (Mk 3:5; Jn 2:12–17; Heb 1:9; see Lk 19:45, note), in Paul (Ac 17:16) and in righteous people (2Pe 2:7–8; Rev 2:6, note).

1:21 THEY NEITHER GLORIFIED HIM. Although vv. 21–28 primarily address the downward course of depravity among the unregenerate, they also contain principles indicating why one of the major sins of fallen Christian leaders is immorality (see next note).

(1) When leaders in the church become proud (v. 22), they seek honor for themselves (v. 21) and exalt themselves (the creature) rather than the Creator (v. 25). A door is then opened within their lives to sexual impurity and shameful lusts (vv. 24,26; see 2Pe 2:2,15, notes). If they do not turn and repent, they will ultimately be given over to a depraved mind (v. 28).

(2) Such people may continue in shameful lust and sin while justifying their actions as common human weakness, persuading themselves that they are still in fellowship with the Holy Spirit and in possession of salvation. They blind themselves to the warning of Scripture that "no immoral, impure or greedy person . . . has any inheritance in the kingdom of Christ" (Eph 5:5).

1:24 GOD GAVE THEM OVER. A primary sign of God's abandonment of any society or people is that they become obsessed with sexual immorality and perversion. (1) The term "God gave them over" means that God abandoned these persons to intensified lusts. The term "sinful desires" (Gk *epithumia*) denotes a passionate lust for forbidden sexual pleasure (cf. 2Co 12:21; Gal 5:19; Eph 5:3).

(2) The three stages of abandonment to impurity are: (a) God giving them over to sinful sexual pleasures that degrade the body (v. 24); (b) God giving them over to shameful homosexual or lesbian passions (vv. 26–27); after this, (c) God giving them over to a depraved mind, i.e., their minds justify their unrighteous actions and they become continually preoccupied with evil and the pleasures of sexual sin (v. 28). These three stages occur among all people who reject the truth of God's revelation and seek pleasure in ungodliness (v. 18; see v. 27, note).

(3) God has two purposes in abandoning the unrighteous to sin: (a) to allow sin and its consequences to accelerate as part of his judgment on them (2:2), and (b) to make them realize their need for salvation (2:4).

1:25 A LIE. The "lie" is the word of Satan, the father of lies (Jn 8:44): "you will be like God" (Ge 3:5). (1) To believe the lie is to reject "the truth of God" and participate in idolatry (Ge 3:5; Col 3:5; 2Th 2:11, note). (2) Humanity's propensity to believe the lie and worship self is the reason the Bible incessantly warns against pride. "In the pride of your heart you say, 'I am a god' " (Eze 28:2; cf. Pr 6:17; 8:13; 16:18; 1Ti 3:6; Jas 4:6; 1Jn 2:16).

1:27 MEN . . . WITH OTHER MEN. The apostle likely regarded the homosexual/lesbian abomination as the greatest evidence of human degeneracy resulting from immorality and God's abandonment (see Ge 19:4–5; Lev 18:22). Any nation that justifies homosexuality or lesbianism as

BIBLICAL WORDS FOR SALVATION

Ro 1:16 "I am not ashamed of the gospel, because it is the power of God for the salvation of everyone who believes: first for the Jew, then for the Gentile."

God freely offers us eternal life in Jesus Christ. But understanding the exact process by which that life becomes available to us is sometimes difficult. Therefore, God paints various pictures in the Bible to help us grasp the concept, each one with its own unique emphasis. This article examines three of those pictures: Salvation, Redemption and Justification.

SALVATION. Salvation (Gk *sōtēria*) means "deliverance," "bringing safely through," "keeping from harm"; already in the OT God revealed himself as the One who saves his people (Ps 27:1, 88:1; see Dt 26:8, note; Ps 62:1, note; Isa 25:6, note; 53:5, note). It is described in the NT as "the way" or road that leads through life to eternal fellowship with God in heaven (Mt 7:14; Mk 12:14; Jn 14:16; Ac 16:17; 2Pe 2:2,21; cf. Ac 9:2; 22:4; Heb 10:20). This road of salvation must be walked to the very end. We can describe salvation as *one* way with *two* sides and *three* stages:

(1) The one way of salvation. Christ is the way to the Father (Jn 14:6; Ac 4:12). Salvation is provided for us by God's grace, which he gives in Christ Jesus (Ro 3:24), based on his death (3:25; 5:8), resurrection (5:10) and continued intercession for believers (Heb 7:25).

(2) The two sides of salvation. Salvation is received by grace through faith in Christ (Ro 3:22,24–25,28). That is, it comes as a result of God's grace (Jn 1:16) and the human response of faith (Ac 16:31; Ro 1:17; Eph 1:15; 2:8; see article on FAITH AND GRACE, p. 1720).

(3) The three stages of salvation.

(a) The past stage of salvation includes the personal experience by which we as believers receive forgiveness of sins (Ac 10:43; Ro 4:6–8) and pass from spiritual death to spiritual life (1Jn 3:14; see article on REGENERATION, p. 1589), from the power of sin to the power of the Lord (Ro 6:17–23), from Satan's dominion to God's dominion (Ac 26:18). It brings us into a new personal relationship with God (Jn 1:12) and rescues us from the penalty of sin (Ro 1:16; 6:23; 1Co 1:18).

(b) The present stage of salvation saves us from the practice and dominion of sin, filling us with the Holy Spirit. It includes: (i) the privilege of a person-to-person relationship with God as our Father and Jesus as our Lord and Savior (Mt 6:9; Jn 14:18–23; see Gal 4:6, note); (ii) the call to count ourselves dead to sin (Ro 6:1–14) and to submit to the leading of the Spirit (Ro 8:1–17) and God's Word (Jn 8:31; 14:21; 2Ti 3:15–16); (iii) the invitation to be filled with the Holy Spirit and the command to keep being filled (see Ac 2:33–39; Eph 5:18; see article on BAPTISM IN THE HOLY SPIRIT, p. 1642); (iv) the demand to separate ourselves from sin (Ro 6:1–14) and the present corrupt generation (Ac 2:40; 2Co 6:17); and (v) the call to fight for God's kingdom against Satan and his demonic host (2Co 10:4–5; Eph 6:11,16; 1Pe 5:8).

(c) The future stage of salvation (Ro 13:11–12; 1Th 5:8–9; 1Pe 1:5) includes: (i) our deliverance from God's coming wrath (Ro 5:9; 1Co 3:15; 5:5; 1Th 1:10; 5:9); (ii) our sharing the divine glory (Ro 8:29; 1Co 15:49) and receiving a resurrected or transformed body (1Co 15:52); and (iii) our receiving rewards as faithful overcomers (see Rev 2:7, note). This future salvation is the goal toward which all Christians strive (1Co 9:24–27; Php 3:8–14). All present warnings, discipline and punishment have as their purpose that believers should not forfeit this future salvation (1Co 5:1–13; 9:24–27; Php 2:12,16; 2Pe 1:5–11; see Heb 12:1, note).

REDEMPTION. The root meaning of "redemption" (Gk *apolutrōsis*) is ransom by the payment of a price. The expression denotes the means by which salvation is procured, namely, by the payment of a ransom. The doctrine of redemption can be summarized as follows:

(1) The state of sin out of which we must be redeemed: The NT represents humans as alienated from God (Ro 3:10–18), under the dominion of satanic powers (Ac 10:38; 26:18), slaves to sin (Ro 6:6; 7:14), and in need of deliverance from sin's guilt, punishment and power (Ac 26:18; Ro 1:18; 6:1–18,23; Eph 5:8; Col 1:13; 1Pe 2:9).

(2) The price paid to free us from this bondage: Christ secured the ransom by shedding his blood and giving his life (Mt 20:28; Mk 10:45; 1Co 6:20; Eph 1:7; Tit 2:14; Heb 9:12; 1Pe 1:18–19).

(3) The resultant state of the redeemed: Believers redeemed by Christ are now free from Satan's dominion and from the guilt and power of sin (Ac 26:18; Ro 6:7,12,14,18; Col 1:13). This freedom from sin, however, does not leave us free to do as we wish, for we become God's property. Freedom from sin makes us willing slaves of God (Ac 26:18; Ro 6:18,22; 1Co 6:19–20; 7:22–23).

(4) The NT teaching of redemption foreshadowed by redemption in the OT: The great OT redemptive event was the exodus from Egypt (see Ex 6:7, note; 12:26, note); furthermore, through the sacrificial system, the blood of animals was the price paid for the atonement for sin (see Lev 9:8, note; see article on THE DAY OF ATONEMENT, p. 174).

JUSTIFICATION. The word "justify" (Gk *dikaioō*) means to be "righteous in God's sight" (Ro 2:13), to be "made righteous" (Ro 5:18–19), to "establish as right," or to "set or put right." It denotes being in a right relationship with God rather than receiving a mere legal, judicial declaration. God forgives repentant sinners, whom he had pronounced guilty through the law and condemned to eternal death, restores them to divine favor, and sets them in a right relationship (fellowship) with himself and his will. The apostle Paul reveals several truths about justification and how it is accomplished:

(1) Being put right with God is a gift (Ro 3:24; Eph 2:8). No one can put himself or herself right with God by keeping the law perfectly or by performing good works (Ro 4:2–6) , "for all have sinned and fall short of the glory of God" (Ro 3:23).

(2) Being put right with God happens "through the redemption that came by Christ Jesus" (Ro 3:24). No one is justified who has not been redeemed by Christ from sin and its power.

(3) Being put right with God comes "by his grace" and is appropriated "through faith in Jesus Christ" as Lord and Savior (Ro 3:22–24; cf. 4:3–5; see article on FAITH AND GRACE, p. 1720).

(4) Being put right with God is related to the forgiveness of our sins (Ro 4:7). Sinners are declared guilty (Ro 3:9–18,23) but are forgiven because of Christ's atoning death and resurrection (see Ro 3:25, note; 4:5, note; 4:25; 5:6–11).

(5) When we are put right with God through faith in Christ, we are crucified with Christ and Christ comes to live in us (Gal 2:16–21). Through this experience, we actually *become* righteous and begin living for God (2:19–21). This transforming work of Christ in us through the Spirit (cf. 2Th 2:13; 1Pe 1:2) cannot be separated from Christ's redemptive work for us. The work of Christ and the Spirit are interdependent.

flamed with lust for one another. Men
committed indecent acts with other
men, and received in themselves the
due penalty for their perversion.[e]
28Furthermore, since they did not
think it worthwhile to retain the
knowledge of God, he gave them over[f]
to a depraved mind, to do what ought
not to be done. **29**They have become
filled with every kind of wickedness,
evil, greed and depravity. They are full
of envy, murder, strife, deceit and malice. They are gossips,[g] **30**slanderers,
God-haters, insolent, arrogant and
boastful; they invent ways of doing
evil; they disobey their parents;[h]
31they are senseless, faithless, heartless,[i] ruthless. **32**Although they know
God's righteous decree that those who
do such things deserve death,[j] they
not only continue to do these very
things but also approve[k] of those who
practice them.

God's Righteous Judgment

2 You, therefore, have no excuse,[l]
you who pass judgment on someone else, for at whatever point you
judge the other, you are condemning
yourself, because you who pass judgment do the same things.[m] **2**Now we
know that God's judgment against
those who do such things is based on
truth. **3**So when you, a mere man, pass
judgment on them and yet do the same
things, do you think you will escape
God's judgment? **4**Or do you show contempt for the riches[n] of his kindness,[o] tolerance[p] and patience,[q] not
realizing that God's kindness leads
you toward repentance?[r]
5But because of your stubbornness
and your unrepentant heart, you are
storing up wrath against yourself for
the day of God's wrath[s], when his
righteous judgment[t] will be revealed.
6God "will give to each person according to what he has done."[e][u] **7**To
those who by persistence in doing good
seek glory, honor[v] and immortality,[w]
he will give eternal life.[x] **8**But for
those who are self-seeking and who re-

1:27 [e]Lev 18:22; 20:13; 1Co 6:18 **1:28** [f]ver 24,26 **1:29** [g]2Co 12:20; 1Ti 5:13; Jas 3:2; 3Jn 10 **1:30** [h]2Ti 3:2 **1:31** [i]2Ti 3:3 **1:32** [j]S Ro 6:23 [k]Ps 50:18; Lk 11:48; Ac 8:1; 22:20 **2:1** [l]Ro 1:20 [m]2Sa 12:5-7; S Mt 7:1,2 **2:4** [n]Ro 9:23; 11:33; Eph 1:7,18; 2:7; 3:8,16; Col 2:2 [o]Ro 11:22 [p]Ro 3:25 [q]Ex 34:6; Ro 9:22; 1Ti 1:16; 1Pe 3:20; 2Pe 3:15 [r]2Pe 3:9 **2:5** [s]Ps 110:5; Rev 6:17 [t]Jude 6 **2:6** [u]Ps 62:12; S Mt 16:27 **2:7** [v]ver 10 [w]1Co 15:53,54; 2Ti 1:10 [x]S Mt 25:46

[e]*6* Psalm 62:12; Prov. 24:12

an acceptable lifestyle is in its final stages of moral corruption (see v. 24, note). For other Scriptures about this horrible act see Ge 19:4–9; Lev 20:13; Dt 23:17; 1Ki 14:24; 15:12; 22:46; Isa 3:9; 1Co 6:9–10; 1Ti 1:10; 2Pe 2:6; Jude 7.

1:32 APPROVE OF THOSE WHO PRACTICE THEM. Paul's last word on human sinfulness is God's condemnation of a condition even more damning than the practice itself, i.e., supporting and encouraging evil by taking pleasure in the immoral actions of others. This disposition is the ultimate in depravity—vicarious enjoyment of lust and evil. Sin becomes entertainment. (1) The word "approve" (Gk *suneudokeō*), meaning "agree with," "consent to" or "sympathize with," points to the casual enjoyment of the sins of others that prevails in human society.

(2) Today we know what great harm is produced by the portrayal of immorality that dominates the entertainment media; yet many approve of it and derive pleasure from it. Being entertained by watching other people sin and engage in ungodly actions, even while you yourself abstain, brings you under the same divine condemnation as those engaging in such evil practices. Sin is intensified in any society wherever it meets with no inhibition from the disapproval of others.

(3) Those (and especially those who profess faith in Christ) who use the immoral actions of others for entertainment and enjoyment are directly contributing to public opinion favorable to immorality and therefore to the corruption and eternal damnation of an indefinite number of other people. This sin is worthy of death and will be exposed and judged at the final day of judgment (2Th 2:12).

2:1 YOU . . . DO THE SAME THINGS. In ch. 1 Paul explained that the Gentiles were given over to sin. Now in ch. 2, he shows that the Jews practice the same things and also need salvation through Christ.

2:3 YET DO THE SAME THINGS. No one should attempt to direct others to do what is right while failing to correct his or her own evil conduct. Some churches attempt to persuade pagan society to follow Biblical law, while at the same time they are blind to the worldliness and immorality within their own membership (cf. Lk 6:42). Before the church seeks to influence the world to a better way of living, it must place its own life under the divine searchlight and reform itself accordingly.

2:7 GLORY, HONOR AND IMMORTALITY. In the very beginning of his treatise on salvation, Paul clarifies a fundamental truth concerning God's dealing with the entire human race: God punishes evildoers and rewards the righteous (see Jn 5:29, notes; Gal 6:7–8). (1) The righteous are those who have been justified by faith (1:16–17; 3:24) and persevere in doing what is right according to God's standard (vv. 7,10; cf. Mt 24:13; Col 1:23; Heb 3:14; Rev 2:10). They value highly the glory that comes from God (1:23; 2:7; 5:2; 8:18), and they seek eternal life (8:23; 1Co 15:51–57; 1Pe 1:4; Rev 21:1—22:5). (2) Those seeking immortality do so by grace through faith (3:24–25; Eph 1:4–7; 2:8–10; 2Ti 2:1; see Php 2:12–13, notes). The faithful enter into "glory, honor and immortality" by "persistence in doing good" (cf. Mt 24:12–13), through the enabling grace given to them by Christ (see Mt 7:21, note; see article on FAITH AND GRACE, p. 1720). (3) Those who do

ject the truth and follow evil,[y] there
will be wrath and anger.[z] **9**There will
be trouble and distress for every human being who does evil:[a] first for the
Jew, then for the Gentile;[b] **10**but glory,
honor and peace for everyone who does
good: first for the Jew, then for the
Gentile.[c] **11**For God does not show favoritism.[d]

12All who sin apart from the law will
also perish apart from the law, and all
who sin under the law[e] will be judged
by the law. **13**For it is not those who
hear the law who are righteous in
God's sight, but it is those who obey[f]
the law who will be declared righteous.
14(Indeed, when Gentiles, who do not
have the law, do by nature things required by the law,[g] they are a law for
themselves, even though they do not
have the law, **15**since they show that
the requirements of the law are written
on their hearts, their consciences also
bearing witness, and their thoughts
now accusing, now even defending
them.) **16**This will take place on the
day when God will judge men's secrets[h] through Jesus Christ,[i] as my
gospel[j] declares.

The Jews and the Law

17Now you, if you call yourself a Jew;
if you rely on the law and brag about
your relationship to God;[k] **18**if you
know his will and approve of what is
superior because you are instructed by
the law; **19**if you are convinced that you
are a guide for the blind, a light for
those who are in the dark, **20**an instructor of the foolish, a teacher of infants,
because you have in the law the embodiment of knowledge and truth—
21you, then, who teach others, do you
not teach yourself? You who preach
against stealing, do you steal?[l] **22**You
who say that people should not commit
adultery, do you commit adultery? You
who abhor idols, do you rob temples?[m]
23You who brag about the law,[n] do
you dishonor God by breaking the law?
24As it is written: "God's name is blasphemed among the Gentiles because of
you."[f][o]

25Circumcision has value if you observe the law,[p] but if you break the
law, you have become as though you
had not been circumcised.[q] **26**If those
who are not circumcised keep the law's
requirements,[r] will they not be regarded as though they were circumcised?[s] **27**The one who is not circumcised physically and yet obeys the law
will condemn you[t] who, even though
you have the[g] written code and circumcision, are a lawbreaker.

28A man is not a Jew if he is only one
outwardly,[u] nor is circumcision merely outward and physical.[v] **29**No, a man
is a Jew if he is one inwardly; and circumcision is circumcision of the
heart,[w] by the Spirit,[x] not by the written code.[y] Such a man's praise is not
from men, but from God.[z]

God's Faithfulness

3 What advantage, then, is there in
being a Jew, or what value is there
in circumcision? **2**Much in every
way![a] First of all, they have been en-

2:8 [y]2Th 2:12 [z]Eze 22:31
2:9 [a]Ps 32:10 [b]ver 10; Ro 1:16
2:10 [c]ver 9; Ro 1:16
2:11 [d]S Ac 10:34
2:12 [e]Ro 3:19; 6:14; 1Co 9:20,21; Gal 4:21; 5:18; S Ro 7:4
2:13 [f]Jas 1:22,23,25
2:14 [g]Ac 10:35
2:16 [h]Ecc 12:14; 1Co 4:5 [i]Ac 10:42 [j]Ro 16:25; 2Ti 2:8
2:17 [k]ver 23; Jer 8:8; Mic 3:11; Jn 5:45; Ro 9:4
2:21 [l]Mt 23:3,4
2:22 [m]Ac 19:37
2:23 [n]S ver 17
2:24 [o]Isa 52:5; Eze 36:22; 2Pe 2:2
2:25 [p]ver 13,27; Gal 5:3 [q]Jer 4:4; 9:25,26
2:26 [r]Ro 8:4 [s]S 1Co 7:19
2:27 [t]Mt 12:41,42
2:28 [u]Mt 3:9; Jn 8:39; Ro 9:6,7 [v]Gal 6:15
2:29 [w]Dt 30:6 [x]Php 3:3; Col 2:11 [y]Ro 7:6; 2Co 3:6 [z]Jn 5:44; 12:43; 1Co 4:5; 2Co 10:18; Gal 1:10; 1Th 2:4; 1Pe 3:4
3:2 [a]Ro 9:4,5

[f]*24* Isaiah 52:5; Ezek. 36:22 [g]*27* Or *who, by means of a*

---

evil are selfish, disobey the truth and take pleasure in unrighteousness. They receive anger and trouble (1:28–32; 2:8–9).

2:12–15 WILL ALSO PERISH. All who continue in sin, even though they have no knowledge of God's law, will perish because they have a measure of knowledge of right and wrong (vv. 14–15). God will not automatically save those who do not hear the gospel, nor will he give them a second chance after death. The eternal consequence facing those who have not had an adequate chance to understand the gospel should cause us to make an unfailing effort to take the gospel to every person in every nation (see Mt 4:19, note; 9:37, note).

2:13 THOSE WHO OBEY THE LAW . . . DECLARED RIGHTEOUS. Paul does not use the term "law" in the sense of a system of statutes that we may obey and earn our salvation without grace. "Law" here stands for God's will made known to the human race. Merely hearing God's Word avails nothing apart from faith, submission and obedience. There must be "obedience that comes from faith" (1:5; cf. 16:26), expressing itself through love (Gal 5:6).

2:16 GOD WILL JUDGE MEN'S SECRETS. See article on THE JUDGMENT OF BELIEVERS, p. 1791.

2:24 GOD'S NAME IS BLASPHEMED. The sins of the Jews gave occasion for the Gentiles to blaspheme God's name. Likewise today, the sins of permissive churches or professed believers enable the ungodly to blaspheme Christ's name.

2:29 CIRCUMCISION OF THE HEART, BY THE SPIRIT. This is God's work of grace in the hearts of believers whereby they participate in the divine nature and become capable of living a pure life separated from sin for God's glory (cf. Dt 10:16; Jer 4:4; 2Pe 1:4). Thus, holy living becomes the outward sign that we are under the new covenant.

trusted with the very words of God.[b]
3What if some did not have faith?[c]
Will their lack of faith nullify God's
faithfulness?[d] 4Not at all! Let God be
true,[e] and every man a liar.[f] As it is
written:

"So that you may be proved right
when you speak
and prevail when you judge."[h][g]

5But if our unrighteousness brings
out God's righteousness more clearly,[h] what shall we say? That God is
unjust in bringing his wrath on us? (I
am using a human argument.)[i] 6Cer-
tainly not! If that were so, how could
God judge the world?[j] 7Someone
might argue, "If my falsehood enhances God's truthfulness and so increases his glory,[k] why am I still condemned as a sinner?"[l] 8Why not
say—as we are being slanderously reported as saying and as some claim
that we say—"Let us do evil that good
may result"?[m] Their condemnation is
deserved.

No One Is Righteous

9What shall we conclude then? Are
we any better[i]?[n] Not at all! We have
already made the charge that Jews and
Gentiles alike are all under sin.[o] 10As
it is written:

"There is no one righteous, not
even one;
11 there is no one who
understands,
no one who seeks God.
12All have turned away,
they have together become
worthless;
there is no one who does good,
not even one."[j][p]
13"Their throats are open graves;
their tongues practice
deceit."[k][q]
"The poison of vipers is on their
lips."[l][r]
14 "Their mouths are full of cursing
and bitterness."[m][s]
15"Their feet are swift to shed blood;
16 ruin and misery mark their
ways,
17and the way of peace they do not
know."[n][t]
18 "There is no fear of God before
their eyes."[o][u]

19Now we know that whatever the
law says,[v] it says to those who are
under the law,[w] so that every mouth
may be silenced[x] and the whole world
held accountable to God.[y] 20There-
fore no one will be declared righteous
in his sight by observing the law;[z]
rather, through the law we become
conscious of sin.[a]

Righteousness Through Faith

21But now a righteousness from
God,[b] apart from law, has been made
known, to which the Law and the

3:2 [b]Dt 4:8; Ps 147:19; Ac 7:38
3:3 [c]Ro 10:16; Heb 4:2 [d]2Ti 2:13
3:4 [e]Jn 3:33 [f]Ps 116:11 [g]Ps 51:4
3:5 [h]Ro 5:8 [i]Ro 6:19; Gal 3:15
3:6 [j]Ge 18:25; Ro 2:16
3:7 [k]ver 4 [l]Ro 9:19
3:8 [m]Ro 6:1
3:9 [n]ver 1 [o]ver 19,23; 1Ki 8:46; 2Ch 6:36; Ps 106:6; Ro 5:12; 11:32; Gal 3:22
3:12 [p]Ps 14:1-3; 53:1-3; Ecc 7:20
3:13 [q]Ps 5:9 [r]Ps 140:3
3:14 [s]Ps 10:7
3:17 [t]Isa 59:7,8
3:18 [u]Ps 36:1
3:19 [v]S Jn 10:34 [w]S Ro 2:12 [x]Ps 63:11; 107:42; Eze 16:63 [y]ver 9
3:20 [z]Ac 13:39; Gal 2:16 [a]S Ro 4:15
3:21 [b]Isa 46:13; Jer 23:6; Ro 1:17; 9:30

h *4* Psalm 51:4 **i** *9* Or *worse* **j** *12* Psalms 14:1-3; 53:1-3; Eccles. 7:20 **k** *13* Psalm 5:9 **l** *13* Psalm 140:3 **m** *14* Psalm 10:7 **n** *17* Isaiah 59:7,8 **o** *18* Psalm 36:1

3:9 ARE ALL UNDER SIN. In chs. 1–2, Paul has shown that all people, both Gentiles and Jews, are in bondage to sin. In 3:9–18 he explains why and teaches that all people possess a sinful nature that draws them toward sin and evil (see next note). The result is that all are guilty and stand under God's condemnation (v. 23). God's response to this tragic situation is to offer forgiveness, help, grace, righteousness and salvation to all through the redemption that is in Christ Jesus (vv. 21–26).

3:10–18 NO ONE RIGHTEOUS. These verses portray a correct understanding of human nature. All people in their natural state are sinners. Their entire being is adversely affected by sin and inclines toward conformity to the world (see article on THE CHRISTIAN'S RELATIONSHIP TO THE WORLD, p. 1976), the devil (see Mt 4:10, note) and the sinful nature (see article on THE ACTS OF THE SINFUL NATURE AND THE FRUIT OF THE SPIRIT, p. 1818). All are guilty of turning aside from the way of godliness to the way of selfishness.

3:18 NO FEAR OF GOD. Why does the deplorable condition of humanity continue? Because "there is no fear of God before their eyes." If there had been the fear of God, they would have sought reconciliation and peace. "Through the fear of the Lord a man avoids evil" (Pr 16:6; cf. Pr 3:7; 8:13; 9:10; see Ac 5:11, note; see article on THE FEAR OF THE LORD, p. 260).

3:21 A RIGHTEOUSNESS FROM GOD. This phrase refers to God's redemptive activity in the sphere of human sin by which he, in a just way (v. 26), puts us in a right relationship with himself and liberates us from the power of evil (note the OT, where the working of salvation and the manifestation of righteousness are essentially the same thing—see Ps 98:1–2; Isa 46:13; 51:5–8; 56:1; 62:1; see Ps 32:2, note; Isa 56:1–2, note). (1) This revelation of God's righteousness in the gospel is not something that has ended. As the power of God for salvation that accompanies the believer, it is constantly fresh and relevant (see article on BIBLICAL WORDS FOR SALVATION, p. 1710). (2) This righteousness from God comes to us through faith in Jesus Christ (v. 22).

Prophets testify.[c] 22This righteousness from God[d] comes through faith[e]
in Jesus Christ[f] to all who believe.[g]
There is no difference,[h] 23for all have
sinned[i] and fall short of the glory of
God, 24and are justified[j] freely by his
grace[k] through the redemption[l] that
came by Christ Jesus. 25God presented
him as a sacrifice of atonement,[p][m]
through faith in his blood.[n] He did this
to demonstrate his justice, because in
his forbearance he had left the sins
committed beforehand unpunished[o]— 26he did it to demonstrate
his justice at the present time, so as to
be just and the one who justifies those
who have faith in Jesus.

27Where, then, is boasting?[p] It is
excluded. On what principle? On that
of observing the law? No, but on that of
faith. 28For we maintain that a man is
justified by faith apart from observing
the law.[q] 29Is God the God of Jews
only? Is he not the God of Gentiles too?
Yes, of Gentiles too,[r] 30since there is
only one God, who will justify the circumcised by faith and the uncircumcised through that same faith.[s] 31Do
we, then, nullify the law by this faith?
Not at all! Rather, we uphold the law.

Abraham Justified Apart From Works

4 What then shall we say[t] that
Abraham, our forefather,[u] discovered in this matter? 2If, in fact, Abraham was justified by works, he had
something to boast about—but not before God.[v] 3What does the Scripture
say? "Abraham believed God, and it

3:21 [c]Ac 10:43; Ro 1:2 **3:22** [d]Ro 1:17 [e]S Ro 9:30 [f]Gal 2:16; 3:22 [g]S Jn 3:15; Ro 4:11; 10:4 [h]Ro 10:12; Gal 3:28; Col 3:11 **3:23** [i]S ver 9 **3:24** [j]S Ro 4:25 [k]Jn 1:14,16,17; Ro 4:16; 5:21; 6:14; 11:5; 2Co 12:9; Eph 2:8; 4:7; Tit 2:11; Heb 4:16 [l]Ps 130:7; 1Co 1:30; Gal 4:5; Eph 1:7,14; Col 1:14; Heb 9:12 **3:25** [m]Ex 25:17; Lev 16:10; Ps 65:3; Heb 2:17; 9:28; 1Jn 4:10 [n]Ac 20:28; Ro 5:9; Eph 1:7; Heb 9:12, 14; 13:12; 1Pe 1:19; Rev 1:5 [o]Ac 14:16; 17:30 **3:27** [p]Ro 2:17, 23; 4:2; 1Co 1:29-31; Eph 2:9 **3:28** [q]ver 20,21; Ac 13:39; Gal 2:16; 3:11; Eph 2:9; Jas 2:20,24,26 **3:29** [r]Ac 10:34,35; Ro 9:24; 10:12; 15:9; Gal 3:28 **3:30** [s]Ro 4:11,12; Gal 3:8 **4:1** [t]S Ro 8:31 [u]S Lk 3:8 **4:2** [v]1Co 1:31

[p] 25 Or *as the one who would turn aside his wrath, taking away sin*

3:22 FAITH. Faith in Jesus Christ as Lord and Savior is the only condition God requires for salvation. For a discussion of what saving faith is, see article on FAITH AND GRACE, p. 1720.

3:24 JUSTIFIED FREELY BY HIS GRACE THROUGH THE REDEMPTION. This verse contains two of the most common words used by Paul to express salvation: "justified" and "redemption." For a discussion of these two concepts, see article on BIBLICAL WORDS FOR SALVATION, p. 1710.

3:25 HIS BLOOD. The NT emphasizes several truths concerning Christ's death.

(1) It was a sacrifice, i.e., an offering of his blood, his life (cf. 1Co 5:7; Eph 5:2).

(2) It was vicarious, i.e., he died not for his own sake, but for the sake of others (5:8; 8:32; Mk 10:45; Eph 5:2).

(3) It was substitutionary, i.e., Christ suffered death as the penalty for our sin, as our substitute (6:23; see article on THE DAY OF ATONEMENT, p. 174).

(4) It was propitiatory, i.e., Christ's death for sinners satisfied God's righteous nature and his moral order, thereby removing his wrath against the repentant sinner. God's integrity required that sin be punished and propitiation be made for our sake. Through propitiation by Christ's blood, God's holiness remained uncompromised and he was able to justly reveal his grace and love in salvation. It must be emphasized that God himself set forth Christ as a propitiation. God did not need to be persuaded to show mercy and love, for already "God was reconciling the world to himself in Christ" (2Co 5:19; cf. Jn 3:16; Ro 5:8; 8:3,32; 1Co 8:6; Eph 4:4–6).

(5) It was expiatory, i.e., a sacrifice to atone or make reparation for sin. As expiation, the sacrifice is directed toward annulling guilt. By Christ's death the guilt and power of sin that separated God and the believer were annulled.

(6) It was efficacious, i.e., his atoning death has within itself the power to produce the full desired effect of redemption when appropriated by faith.

(7) It was victorious, i.e., on the cross Christ fought against and was triumphant over the power of sin, of Satan and of his demonic host that held people captive. His death was the initial victory over the spiritual enemies of both God and humanity (8:3; Jn 12:31–32; Col 2:15). Thus, Christ's death is redemptive. By the ransom of his own life (1Pe 1:18–19), he liberated us from the enemies that hold the human race in bondage, i.e., sin (6:6), death (2Ti 1:10; 1Co 15:54–57) and Satan (Ac 10:38), making us free to serve God (6:18; see article on BIBLICAL WORDS FOR SALVATION, p. 1710).

All the above results of Christ's sacrificial death occur potentially for all people but only actually for individuals who through faith accept Jesus Christ and his death for them.

3:31 WE UPHOLD THE LAW. Salvation in Christ does not mean that the law has no value. In fact justification by faith upholds the law according to its right purpose and function. Through reconciliation with God and through the regenerating work of the Holy Spirit, the believer becomes capable of honoring and obeying God's moral law (see 8:2–4).

4:3 ABRAHAM BELIEVED GOD. Salvation by faith, not by deeds (i.e., keeping the law), is not an exclusively NT doctrine; it is also characteristic of the OT. Paul bypasses Moses and turns to Abraham as the example of faith. Abraham had faith in God, i.e., he maintained a loyal attachment to his God, believed in his promises (vv. 20–21; Ge 12:1–3; 15:5–6) and responded in obedience (Ge 12:1–4; 22:1–19; Heb 11:8–19; Jas 2:21–22; see article on THE CALL OF ABRAHAM, p. 25).

was credited to him as righteousness."[q][w]
4Now when a man works, his wages
are not credited to him as a gift,[x] but
as an obligation. **5**However, to the man
who does not work but trusts God who
justifies the wicked, his faith is credited as righteousness.[y] **6**David says the
same thing when he speaks of the
blessedness of the man to whom God
credits righteousness apart from
works:

7"Blessed are they
whose transgressions are
forgiven,
whose sins are covered.
8Blessed is the man
whose sin the Lord will never
count against him."[r][z]

9Is this blessedness only for the circumcised, or also for the uncircumcised?[a] We have been saying that
Abraham's faith was credited to him as
righteousness.[b] **10**Under what circumstances was it credited? Was it after he was circumcised, or before? It
was not after, but before! **11**And he received the sign of circumcision, a seal
of the righteousness that he had by
faith while he was still uncircumcised.[c] So then, he is the father[d] of
all who believe[e] but have not been circumcised, in order that righteousness
might be credited to them. **12**And he is
also the father of the circumcised who
not only are circumcised but who also
walk in the footsteps of the faith that
our father Abraham had before he was
circumcised.
13It was not through law that Abraham and his offspring received the
promise[f] that he would be heir of the
world,[g] but through the righteousness that comes by faith.[h] **14**For if
those who live by law are heirs, faith
has no value and the promise is worthless,[i] **15**because law brings wrath.[j]
And where there is no law there is no
transgression.[k]

Abraham Justified by Faith

16Therefore, the promise comes by
faith, so that it may be by grace[l] and

4:3 [w] ver 5,9,22; Ge 15:6; Gal 3:6; Jas 2:23
4:4 [x] Ro 11:6
4:5 [y] ver 3,9,22; S Ro 9:30
4:8 [z] Ps 32:1,2; 103:12; 2Co 5:19
4:9 [a] Ro 3:30 [b] S ver 3
4:11 [c] Ge 17:10, 11 [d] ver 16,17; S Lk 3:8 [e] S Ro 3:22
4:13 [f] S Ac 13:32; Gal 3:16,29 [g] Ge 17:4-6 [h] S Ro 9:30
4:14 [i] Gal 3:18
4:15 [j] Ro 7:7-25; 1Co 15:56; 2Co 3:7; Gal 3:10; S Ro 7:12 [k] Ro 3:20; 5:13; 7:7
4:16 [l] S Ro 3:24

[q] *3* Gen. 15:6; also in verse 22
[r] *8* Psalm 32:1,2

4:5 FAITH IS CREDITED AS RIGHTEOUSNESS. Abraham's *faith* was credited as righteousness. The saving faith of the Christian is treated as equivalent to righteousness in regard to its effect.

(1) Paul speaks of "crediting as righteousness" or "crediting righteousness" six times in ch. 4, and in all cases Paul associates faith or belief with the crediting; it is the believer's "faith" that is credited as "righteousness" (vv. 3,5–6,9,11,22,24; see Ge 15:6, note).

(2) The crediting of the believer's faith as righteousness, however, is not solely the result of faith or commitment to Christ; it is above all an act of divine grace and mercy (v. 16).

(3) When God sees the hearts of believers turn toward Christ in faith, he freely forgives their sins, credits their faith as righteousness and accepts them as his children (vv. 5–8; see article on BIBLICAL WORDS FOR SALVATION, p. 1710). Along with this crediting of faith as righteousness, God also gives grace for sanctification (see v. 16; 5:2; Php 3:9; Tit 3:5–7).

(4) The faith that is credited as righteousness and brings forgiveness is faith in Christ and his atoning death (3:24–26). Absolutely nothing else but Christ's sacrificial death on the cross is the ground for reconciliation with God (see 5:10, note).

4:7 TRANSGRESSIONS ARE FORGIVEN. This quotation from Ps 32:1–2 shows that both David (see Ps 32:2, note) and Paul understood that one's faith credited as righteousness includes forgiveness of sin and reconciliation with God. It is a gift based on God's mercy, made possible through Christ's death on the cross (see v. 5, note; cf. 2Co 5:19,21).

4:12 FAITH THAT OUR FATHER ABRAHAM HAD. The faith of Abraham was a true faith that endured, believed, trusted, obeyed, grew strong and gave glory to God (vv. 16–21). This is the type of faith that makes us children of God.

4:16 THE PROMISE COMES BY FAITH. Believers are saved through faith alone by grace. But two Biblical truths about the nature of saving faith should be noted. (1) While one is saved through faith alone, the faith that saves is not alone. James states "faith without deeds is dead" (Jas 2:14–26); Paul says it is "faith expressing itself through love" (Gal 5:6). Saving faith is a faith so vital that it cannot avoid the expressions of love for and obedience to the Savior and of service to others. Faith that merely trusts God to forgive our sins but does not include sincere repentance and an active commitment to Christ as Lord falls short of NT saving faith (see article on FAITH AND GRACE, p. 1720).

(2) It is unbiblical to emphasize "faith" and ignore the broader picture of salvation. Salvation by faith includes not only being saved from condemnation but also being saved for fellowship with God, for holiness and for good works (Eph 2:10).

4:16 SO THAT IT MAY BE BY GRACE. If the salvation, justification and righteousness that God provides came by perfect obedience to the law, no one would be saved because no one has obeyed it perfectly. But since it comes through faith by grace, then *all* may be saved who turn to God. God

may be guaranteed[m] to all Abraham's
offspring—not only to those who are of
the law but also to those who are of the
faith of Abraham. He is the father of us
all.[n] **17**As it is written: "I have made
you a father of many nations."[s][o] He
is our father in the sight of God, in
whom he believed—the God who gives
life[p] to the dead and calls[q] things
that are not[r] as though they were.

18Against all hope, Abraham in hope
believed and so became the father of
many nations,[s] just as it had been
said to him, "So shall your offspring
be."[t][t] **19**Without weakening in his
faith, he faced the fact that his body
was as good as dead[u]—since he was
about a hundred years old[v]—and that
Sarah's womb was also dead.[w] **20**Yet
he did not waver through unbelief regarding the promise of God, but was
strengthened[x] in his faith and gave
glory to God,[y] **21**being fully persuaded
that God had power to do what he had
promised.[z] **22**This is why "it was credited to him as righteousness."[a] **23**The
words "it was credited to him" were
written not for him alone, **24**but also for
us,[b] to whom God will credit righteousness—for us who believe in
him[c] who raised Jesus our Lord from
the dead.[d] **25**He was delivered over to
death for our sins[e] and was raised to
life for our justification.[f]

Peace and Joy

5 Therefore, since we have been justified[g] through faith,[h] we[u] have
peace[i] with God through our Lord
Jesus Christ,[j] **2**through whom we
have gained access[k] by faith into this
grace in which we now stand.[l] And
we[u] rejoice in the hope[m] of the glory
of God. **3**Not only so, but we[u] also rejoice in our sufferings,[n] because we
know that suffering produces perseverance;[o] **4**perseverance, character;
and character, hope. **5**And hope[p] does
not disappoint us, because God has
poured out his love[q] into our hearts by

4:16 [m]Ro 15:8 [n]ver 11; S Lk 3:8; S Gal 3:16
4:17 [o]Ge 17:5 [p]S Jn 5:21 [q]Isa 48:13 [r]1Co 1:28
4:18 [s]ver 17 [t]Ge 15:5
4:19 [u]Heb 11:11, 12 [v]Ge 17:17 [w]Ge 18:11
4:20 [x]1Sa 30:6 [y]S Mt 9:8
4:21 [z]Ge 18:14; S Mt 19:26
4:22 [a]S ver 3
4:24 [b]Ps 102:18; Hab 2:2; Ro 15:4; 1Co 9:10; 10:11; 2Ti 3:16,17 [c]Ro 10:9; 1Pe 1:21 [d]S Ac 2:24
4:25 [e]Isa 53:5,6; Ro 5:6,8; 8:32; 2Co 5:21 [f]Isa 53:11; Ro 3:24; 5:1,9,16, 18; 8:30; 1Co 6:11; 2Co 5:15
5:1 [g] S Ro 4:25 [h]S Ro 3:28 [i]S Lk 2:14 [j]ver 10
5:2 [k]Eph 2:18; 3:12 [l]1Co 15:1 [m]S Heb 3:6
5:3 [n]S Mt 5:12 [o]S Heb 10:36
5:5 [p]Php 1:20; S Heb 3:6; 1Jn 3:2,3 [q]ver 8; Jn 3:16; Ro 8:39

[s]*17* Gen. 17:5 [t]*18* Gen. 15:5
[u]*1* Or *let us*

mercifully forgives our sins and imparts divine grace (i.e., his Spirit and power) to regenerate our lives and make us God's children (see article on FAITH AND GRACE, p. 1720).

4:22 CREDITED TO HIM AS RIGHTEOUSNESS. In Paul's illustration of justification in ch. 4, nowhere does he state that the righteousness of God or of Christ is actually credited or transferred to the believer. We must be careful not to describe justification by stating that it comes by Christ's OT law-keeping transferred to the believer. If it did come by a transferred keeping of the law, then it is not the same kind of faith as Abraham that is credited as righteousness (v. 12), and that in turn nullifies the promise (v. 14) and makes salvation a result of merit rather than of grace (v. 16). Paul emphatically declares justification and righteousness come "not through law" (v. 13), but by God's mercy, grace, love and forgiveness (vv. 6–9), and that Abraham's *faith* (i.e., his believing, his attachment to God, his strong confidence and unwavering assurance in God and his promises) is credited as righteousness, by the mercy and grace of God (vv. 16–22).

4:25 RAISED TO LIFE FOR OUR JUSTIFICATION. Justification does not exist without the life, presence and grace of Jesus Christ operating in our lives. Justification is not a single judicial act in the past, but a lifelong justification in fellowship with Jesus Christ our Lord.

5:1 THEREFORE, SINCE WE HAVE BEEN JUSTIFIED. Justification through faith brings the believer various results: peace with God (see article on THE PEACE OF GOD, p. 1134), grace, hope, assurance, sufferings, the love of God, the Holy Spirit, salvation from wrath, reconciliation to God, salvation by the life and presence of Jesus, and joy in God (vv. 1–11).

5:3 WE ALSO REJOICE IN OUR SUFFERINGS. Paul lists "sufferings" as one of the blessings of our salvation in Christ. (1) The word "sufferings" refers to all kinds of trials that may press in on us. This includes such things as the pressures of financial or physical need, trying circumstances, sorrow, sickness, persecution, mistreatment or loneliness (see article on THE SUFFERING OF THE RIGHTEOUS, p. 710).

(2) In the middle of these troubles God's grace enables us to seek his face more diligently and produces in us a persevering spirit and character that overcome the trials of life. Instead of driving us to despair, suffering produces perseverance (v. 3), perseverance produces proven character (v. 4), and proven character results in a mature hope that will not disappoint (v. 5).

(3) God's grace lets us look beyond our present problems to a fervent hope in God and a certain hope for the return of our Lord to establish righteousness and godliness in the new heaven and earth (1Th 4:13; Rev 19–22). In the meantime, God has poured out his love into our hearts by the Holy Spirit to comfort us in our trials and bring Christ's presence near (Jn 14:16–23).

5:5 GOD HAS POURED OUT HIS LOVE INTO OUR HEARTS. Christians experience the love of God (i.e., God's love for believers) in their hearts through the Holy Spirit, especially in times of trouble. The verb "poured out" is a present perfect tense in the indicative mood, expressing an existing condition from a prior action, i.e., the Spirit

Ro 8:6 the Holy Spirit,[r] whom he has given
us.
6You see, at just the right time,[s]
when we were still powerless,[t] Christ
died for the ungodly.[u] 7Very rarely
will anyone die for a righteous man,
though for a good man someone might
possibly dare to die. 8But God demonstrates his own love for us in this:
While we were still sinners, Christ died
for us.[v]
9Since we have now been justified[w]
by his blood,[x] how much more shall
we be saved from God's wrath[y]
through him! 10For if, when we were
God's enemies,[z] we were reconciled[a]
to him through the death of his Son,
how much more, having been reconciled, shall we be saved through his
life![b] 11Not only is this so, but we also
rejoice in God through our Lord Jesus
Christ, through whom we have now received reconciliation.[c]

Death Through Adam, Life Through Christ

12Therefore, just as sin entered the
world through one man,[d] and death
through sin,[e] and in this way death
came to all men, because all
sinned[f]— 13for before the law was
given, sin was in the world. But sin is
not taken into account when there
is no law.[g] 14Nevertheless, death
reigned from the time of Adam to the
time of Moses, even over those who did
not sin by breaking a command, as did
Adam,[h] who was a pattern of the one
to come.[i]
15But the gift is not like the trespass. For if the many died by the trespass of the one man,[j] how much more
did God's grace and the gift that came
by the grace of the one man, Jesus
Christ,[k] overflow to the many!
16Again, the gift of God is not like the
result of the one man's sin: The judgment followed one sin and brought condemnation, but the gift followed many
trespasses and brought justification.
17For if, by the trespass of the one
man, death[l] reigned through that one
man, how much more will those who
receive God's abundant provision of
grace and of the gift of righteousness
reign in life[m] through the one man,
Jesus Christ.
18Consequently, just as the result of

5:5 [r] Ac 2:33; 10:45; Tit 3:5,6 **5:6** [s] Mk 1:15; Gal 4:4; Eph 1:10 [t] ver 8,10 [u] Ro 4:25 **5:8** [v] Jn 3:16; 15:13; 1Pe 3:18; 1Jn 3:16; 4:10 **5:9** [w] S Ro 4:25 [x] S Ro 3:25 [y] S Ro 1:18 **5:10** [z] Ro 11:28; Col 1:21 [a] ver 11; Ro 11:15; 2Co 5:18,19; Col 1:20,22 [b] Ro 8:34; Heb 7:25 **5:11** [c] S ver 10 **5:12** [d] ver 15,16, 17; Ge 3:1-7; 1Co 15:21,22 [e] ver 14,18; Ge 2:17; 3:19; S Ro 6:23 [f] S Ro 3:9 **5:13** [g] S Ro 4:15 **5:14** [h] Ge 3:11,12 [i] 1Co 15:22,45 **5:15** [j] ver 12,18, 19 [k] Ac 15:11 **5:17** [l] S ver 12 [m] Jn 10:10

continues to flood our hearts with love. It is this ever-present experience of God's love that sustains us in sufferings (v. 3) and assures us that our hope for future glory is not illusory (vv. 4–5). Christ's return for us is sure (cf. 8:17; Ps 22:4–5; Jn 14:3; see article on THE RAPTURE, p. 1864).

5:10 SAVED THROUGH HIS LIFE. The believer's salvation lies in Christ's blood and his resurrection life, whereby the believer is forgiven and reconciled to God. This experience is initial salvation (3:21–26; 4:5–9). The believer continues to be saved by a living faith and union with the living Christ (see article on BIBLICAL WORDS FOR SALVATION, p. 1710). If God loved us enough to send his Son to die for us while we were enemies, how much more, now that we are his children, will he make every provision to save us from the wrath to come through our present faith in his Son (4:22—5:2; 5:9–10; 1Co 1:30; Php 2:12–16; Col 3:3–4; 1Th 1:10; 2Ti 2:12; Jas 1:12; see Rev 2:7, note).

5:12 SIN ENTERED THE WORLD THROUGH ONE MAN. In the fall of Adam, sin as an active principle or power gained entrance into the human race (vv. 17,19; Ge 3; 1Co 15:21–22). (1) Two results followed: (a) Sin and corruption entered into Adam's heart and life. (b) Adam transmitted sin into the life-stream of the human race, corrupting all people thereafter. All humans are now born into the world with an impulse toward sin and evil (v. 19; 1:21; 7:24; Ge 6:5,12; 8:21; Ps 14:1–3; Jer 17:9; Mk 7:21–22; 1Co 2:14; Gal 5:19–21; Eph 2:1–3; Col 1:21; 1Jn 5:19).

(2) Paul does not explain how Adam's sin is transmitted to his descendants. Nor does he say that all people were present in Adam and participated in his sin, and therefore inherit Adam's guilt. Nowhere does Paul say that Adam was the federal head of his descendants and that his sin was imputed to them. All are guilty before God because of their own personal sin, "because all sinned." The only doctrine that finds Biblical support is that men and women inherit a moral corruption and an impulse toward sin and evil (see 6:1, note).

(3) Death entered the world through sin, and now all people are subject to death, "because all sinned" (vv. 12,14; cf. 3:23; Ge 2:17; 3:19; see article on DEATH, p. 732).

5:14 DEATH REIGNED FROM THE TIME OF ADAM TO THE TIME OF MOSES. The human race experienced death, not because they transgressed the spoken law of God with its death penalty as did Adam (vv. 13–14), but because they were in fact sinners by action as well by nature and transgressors of the law of conscience written in their hearts (2:14–15).

5:15 HOW MUCH MORE DID GOD'S GRACE. In vv. 12–21 Paul stresses the supreme adequacy of the redemption provided by Jesus Christ to undo the effects of the fall. This is the real point of the passage: Adam brought sin and death; Christ brought grace and life (v. 17).

5:18 JUSTIFICATION THAT BRINGS LIFE FOR ALL MEN. The condemnation for all people becomes actual for each person as he or she re-

one trespass was condemnation for all
men,[n] so also the result of one act of
righteousness was justification[o] that
brings life[p] for all men. 19For just as
through the disobedience of the one
man[q] the many were made sinners,[r]
so also through the obedience[s] of the
one man the many will be made righteous.

20The law was added so that the
trespass might increase.[t] But where
sin increased, grace increased all the
more,[u] 21so that, just as sin reigned in
death,[v] so also grace[w] might reign
through righteousness to bring eternal
life[x] through Jesus Christ our Lord.

Dead to Sin, Alive in Christ

6 What shall we say, then?[y] Shall
we go on sinning so that grace may
increase?[z] 2By no means! We died to
sin;[a] how can we live in it any longer?
3Or don't you know that all of us who
were baptized[b] into Christ Jesus were
baptized into his death? 4We were
therefore buried with him through baptism into death[c] in order that, just as
Christ was raised from the dead[d]
through the glory of the Father, we too
may live a new life.[e]

5If we have been united with him
like this in his death, we will certainly
also be united with him in his resurrection.[f] 6For we know that our old
self[g] was crucified with him[h] so that
the body of sin[i] might be done away

5:18 [n]S ver 12 [o]S Ro 4:25 [p]Isa 53:11 **5:19** [q]ver 12 [r]S Ro 3:9 [s]S Php 2:8 **5:20** [t]Ro 3:20; 7:7,8; Gal 3:19 [u]Ro 6:1; 1Ti 1:13, 14 **5:21** [v]ver 12,14; S Ro 6:16 [w]S Ro 3:24 [x]S Mt 25:46 **6:1** [y]S Ro 8:31 [z]ver 15; Ro 3:5,8 **6:2** [a]S ver 6; ver 10,11; S ver 18; Ro 8:13; Col 3:3,5; 1Pe 2:24 **6:3** [b]S Mt 28:19 **6:4** [c]S ver 6 [d]S Ac 2:24 [e]Ro 7:6; S 2Co 5:17; Eph 4:22-24; Col 3:10 **6:5** [f]ver 4,8; Ro 8:11; 2Co 4:10; Eph 2:6; Php 3:10,11; Col 2:12; 3:1; 2Ti 2:11 **6:6** [g]S Gal 5:24; Eph 4:22; Col 3:9 [h]S ver 2; ver 3-8; 2Co 4:10; Gal 2:20; 5:24; 6:14; Php 3:10; Col 2:12,20; 3:3 [i]Ro 7:24

jects God and his revelation written in their hearts or revealed in his written Word (cf. 2:12–16). The "justification that brings life" for all people is potential as well; it becomes actualized in individuals as they believe in Christ and receive grace, life and the gift of righteousness through Jesus Christ (v. 17).

5:21 GRACE. For a discussion of the meaning of the word "grace" in the Bible, see article on FAITH AND GRACE, p. 1720.

6:1 SHALL WE GO ON SINNING? In ch. 6 Paul challenges the erroneous idea that believers may continue in sin and yet remain secure from condemnation because of God's grace through Christ. Paul answers this antinomian distortion of the doctrine of grace by emphasizing one fundamental truth: true believers are identified as being "in Christ" by virtue of baptism into Christ and their death to sin. They have been translated from sin's realm into another realm of life—with Christ (vv. 2–12). Since true believers have made a definitive separation from sin, they will not continue to live in sin. Conversely, if people keep living in sin, they are not true believers (cf. 1Jn 3:4–10). Throughout this chapter Paul emphasizes that individuals cannot be slaves to sin and slaves to Christ at the same time (vv. 11–13,16–18). If they offer themselves to sin, the result will be condemnation and eternal death (vv. 16,23).

6:1 SIN. (1) The NT uses several Greek words to describe sin in its various aspects. The most important are: (a) *Hamartia*, which means "transgression," "wrongdoing" or "sin against God" (Jn 9:41). (b) *Adikia*, which stands for "wrongdoing," "wickedness" or "injustice" (1:18; 1Jn 5:17). It can be described as a lack of love, since all wrongdoing stems from a failure to love (Mt 22:37–40; Lk 10:27–37). *Adikia* is also a personal power that can enslave and deceive (5:12; Heb 3:13). (c) *Anomia*, which denotes "wickedness," "lawlessness" and "defiance of God's law" (v. 19; 1Jn 3:4). (d) *Apistia*, which indicates "unbelief" or "unfaithfulness" (3:3; Heb 3:12).

(2) From these definitions we can conclude that the essence of sin is selfishness, i.e., a grasping of things or pleasures for ourselves, regardless of the welfare of others and the commands of God, which leads to cruelty to others and to rebellion against God and his law. Ultimately sin becomes the refusal to be subject to God and his Word (1:18–25; 8:7). It is enmity against God (5:10; 8:7; Col 1:21) and disobedience to him (11:32; Eph 2:2; 5:6).

(3) Sin is also a moral corruption in humans that opposes all better human intentions. It causes us both to commit unrighteousness with delight and to take pleasure in the evil actions of others (1:21–32; cf. Ge 6:5). It is likewise a power that enslaves and corrupts (3:9; 6:12ff; 7:14; Gal. 3:22). Sin is rooted in human desire (Jas 1:14; 4:1–2; see 1Pe 2:11, note).

(4) Sin was brought into the human race through Adam (5:12), affects everyone (5:12), results in divine judgment (1:18), brings physical and spiritual death (v. 23; Ge 2:17), and can be eliminated as a power only by faith in Christ and his redemptive work (5:8–11; Gal 3:13; Eph 4:20–24; 1Jn 1:9; Rev 1:5).

6:2 DIED TO SIN. See v. 11, note.

6:4 BURIED WITH HIM THROUGH BAPTISM. Baptism for the Christian is a symbol of the believer's burial and resurrection with Christ, but it is more. When accompanied by true faith, baptism is part of our rejection of sin and our commitment to Christ, resulting in a continual flow of grace and divine life to us (see Ac 22:16, note on baptism). Baptism means identifying with Christ in his death and burial in order that we may live in union with his resurrected life (vv. 4–5). As surely as Christ rose from the dead, so surely we who exercise true saving faith in him will walk in newness of life (v. 5).

6:6 OLD SELF ... BODY OF SIN. Paul uses two terms here: (1) The "old self": this refers to the believer's unregenerate self, the person he or she once was, the life once lived in sin. This old self has been crucified (i.e., put to death) with Christ

FAITH AND GRACE

Ro 5:21 "So that, just as sin reigned in death, so also grace might reign through righteousness to bring eternal life through Jesus Christ our Lord."

Our salvation comes as a gift of God's *grace*, but it can only be appropriated by the human response of *faith*. To understand the process of salvation, we must understand these two words.

SAVING FAITH. Faith in Jesus Christ is the only condition God requires for salvation. Faith is not only a profession about Christ, but also an activity coming from the heart of the believer who seeks to follow Christ as Lord and Savior (cf. Mt 4:19; 16:24; Lk 9:23–25; Jn 10:4,27; 12:26; Rev 14:4). (1) The NT conception of faith includes four main elements:

(a) Faith means firmly believing and trusting in the crucified and risen Christ as our personal Lord and Savior (see Ro 1:17, note). It involves believing with all our hearts (Ro 6:17; Eph 6:6; Heb 10:22), yielding up our wills and committing our total selves to Jesus Christ as he is revealed in the NT.

(b) Faith involves repentance, i.e., in true sorrow turning from sin (Ac 17:30; 2Co 7:10) and turning to God through Christ. Saving faith is always a repentant faith (Ac 2:37–38; see Mt 3:2, note on repentance).

(c) Faith includes obedience to Jesus Christ and his Word as a way of life inspired by our faith, by our gratitude to God and by the regenerating work of the Spirit (Jn 3:3–6; 14:15,21–24; Heb 5:8–9). It is an "obedience that comes from faith" (Ro 1:5). Therefore, faith and obedience belong inseparably together (cf. Ro 16:26). Saving faith without the commitment to sanctification is illegitimate and impossible.

(d) Faith includes a heartfelt personal devotion and attachment to Jesus Christ that expresses itself in trust, love, gratitude and loyalty. Faith in an ultimate sense cannot properly be distinguished from love. It is a personal activity of sacrifice and self-giving directed toward Christ (cf. Mt 22:37; Jn 21:15–17; Ac 8:37; Ro 6:17; Gal 2:20; Eph 6:6; 1Pe 1:8).

(2) Faith in Jesus as Lord and Savior is both the act of a single moment and a continuing attitude that must grow and be strengthened (see Jn 1:12, note). Because we have faith in a definite person who died for us (Ro 4:25; 8:32; 1Th 5:9–10), our faith should become greater (Ro 4:20; 2Th 1:3; 1Pe 1:3–9). Trust and obedience develop into loyalty and devotion (Ro 14:8; 2Co 5:15); loyalty and devotion develop into an intense feeling of personal attachment to and love for the Lord Jesus Christ (Php 1:21; 3:8–10; see Jn 15:4, note; Gal 2:20, note). This faith in Christ brings us into a new relationship with God and exempts us from his wrath (Ro 1:18; 8:1); through that new relationship we become dead to sin (Ro 6:1–18) and indwelt by the Holy Spirit (Gal 3:5; 4:6).

GRACE. In the OT, God revealed himself as a God of grace and mercy who showed love to his people not because they deserved it but because of his own desire to be faithful to the promises made to Abraham, Isaac and Jacob (see Ex 6:9, note; see articles on THE PASSOVER, p. 104, and THE DAY OF ATONEMENT, p. 174). The NT authors continue this theme; grace is God's presence and love through Christ Jesus, given to believers by the Holy Spirit, imparting mercy, forgiveness, and the desire and power to do God's will (Jn 3:16; 1Co 15:10; Php 2:13; 1Ti 1:15–16). The whole movement of the Christian life from beginning to end is dependent on this grace.

(1) God gives a measure of grace as a gift (1Co 1:4) to unbelievers so that they may be able to believe in the Lord Jesus Christ (Eph 2:8–9; Tit 2:11; 3:4).

(2) God gives grace to believers to be "set free from sin" (Ro 6:20,22), "to will and to act according to his good purpose" (Php 2:13; cf. Tit 2:11–12; see Mt 7:21, note on obedience as a gift of God's grace), to pray (Zec 12:10), to grow in Christ (2Pe 3:18) and to witness for Christ (Ac 4:33; 11:23).

(3) God's grace must be diligently desired and sought (Heb 4:16). Some of the ways (i.e., means of grace) by which God's grace is received are: studying and obeying Scripture (Jn 15:1–11; 20:31; 2Ti 3:15); hearing the proclamation of the gospel (Lk 24:47; Ac 1:8; Ro 1:16; 1Co 1:17–18); praying (Heb 4:16; Jude 20); fasting (Mt 4:2; 6:16); worshiping Christ (Col 3:16); being continually filled with the Holy Spirit (Eph 5:18); and participating in the Lord's Supper (Ac 2:42; see Eph 2:9, note on how grace works).

(4) God's grace can be resisted (Heb 12:15), received in vain (2Co 6:1), put out (1Th 5:19), set aside (Gal 2:21) and abandoned by the believer (Gal 5:4).

with,[v] that we should no longer be
slaves to sin[j]— **7**because anyone who
has died has been freed from sin.[k]
8Now if we died with Christ, we believe that we will also live with him.[l]
9For we know that since Christ was
raised from the dead,[m] he cannot die
again; death no longer has mastery
over him.[n] **10**The death he died, he
died to sin[o] once for all;[p] but the life
he lives, he lives to God.
11In the same way, count yourselves
dead to sin[q] but alive to God in Christ
Jesus. **12**Therefore do not let sin
reign[r] in your mortal body so that you
obey its evil desires. **13**Do not offer the
parts of your body to sin, as instruments of wickedness,[s] but rather offer yourselves to God, as those who
have been brought from death to life;
and offer the parts of your body to him
as instruments of righteousness.[t]
14For sin shall not be your master,[u]
because you are not under law,[v] but
under grace.[w]

Slaves to Righteousness

15What then? Shall we sin because
we are not under law but under
grace?[x] By no means! **16**Don't you
know that when you offer yourselves to
someone to obey him as slaves, you are
slaves to the one whom you obey[y]—
whether you are slaves to sin,[z] which
leads to death,[a] or to obedience,
which leads to righteousness? **17**But
thanks be to God[b] that, though you
used to be slaves to sin,[c] you whole-

6:6 [j]S ver 16 **6:7** [k]S ver 18 **6:8** [l]S ver 5 **6:9** [m]ver 4; S Ac 2:24 [n]Rev 1:18 **6:10** [o]S ver 2 [p]S Heb 7:27 **6:11** [q]S ver 2 **6:12** [r]ver 16 **6:13** [s]ver 16,19; Ro 7:5 [t]Ro 12:1; 2Co 5:14,15; 1Pe 2:24 **6:14** [u]S ver 16 [v]S Ro 2:12 [w]S Ro 3:24 **6:15** [x]ver 1,14 **6:16** [y]2Pe 2:19 [z]ver 6,12,14,17, 20; Ge 4:7; Ps 51:5; 119:133; Jn 8:34; Ro 5:21; 7:14,23,25; 8:2; 2Pe 2:19 [a]S ver 23 **6:17** [b]Ro 1:8; S 2Co 2:14 [c]S ver 16

[v]6 Or *be rendered powerless*

on the cross in order that the believer might receive a new life in Christ and become a new person (cf. Gal 2:20). (2) "Body of sin": this refers to the human body as controlled by sinful desires. Its slavery to sin has now been broken (cf. 2Co 5:17; Eph 4:22; Col 3:9–10). From this point on, believers must not allow their old mode of existence again to dominate their lives and bodies (2Co 5:17; Eph 4:22; Col 3:9–10).

6:7 FREED FROM SIN. See Jn 8:36, note.

6:10 HE DIED TO SIN. Although Christ was sinless, he suffered from and was humiliated by the power of sin for our sake (5:21; cf. 2Co 5:21). In his death, he died to sin's influence; in his resurrection, he triumphed over its power. Likewise, those who are united with him in his death are freed from sin's power (vv. 2,11) to walk in newness of life (vv. 4–5,10).

6:11 COUNT YOURSELVES DEAD TO SIN. The fundamental premise in ch. 6 is the believer's union with Christ in both his death and life. Therefore, if you are a true believer, you have died to sin—and you need to reckon with this fact. (1) You died to sin in God's sight. You are considered by God to have died with Christ on the cross and to have been raised up in his resurrection (vv. 5–10). (2) You died to sin when you were born again by the Spirit (see article on REGENERATION, p. 1589). You have been given Christ's power to resist sin (vv. 14–18), to die to it daily by putting to death the misdeeds of the body (8:13), and to live a new life in obedience to God (vv. 5–14,18,22). (3) You died to sin in water baptism as you proclaimed your death to sin and committed yourself to reject sin and to live for Christ (vv. 3–5; see 6:4, note).

6:12 DO NOT LET SIN REIGN. Because sin has been dethroned, you must continually resist its effort to regain control. Since sin attempts to reign primarily through the desires of the body, these desires must be resisted by those with faith in Christ (see next note). We can do so by denying the evil desires of the body (v. 12), refusing to place any part of our body at the disposal of sin (v. 13), and presenting our bodies and our whole personalities as slaves to God and righteousness (vv. 13–19).

6:15 SHALL WE SIN? Some within the church in Paul's day thought that since grace pardons sin, the Christian does not need to be careful to resist sin. In answer to this, the apostle explains that every believer must continually reaffirm and implement his or her decision to resist sin and follow Christ (v. 19). (1) After accepting Christ, believers must continue to choose whom they will serve (v. 16). (a) They may return to sin, cease to oppose its dominion in their personal lives and become its slave once more, with death (spiritual and eternal) as the result (vv. 16,21,23); or (b) they may be freed from sin (v. 17) and may continue to present themselves as slaves of God and righteousness, with sanctification and eternal life as the result (vv. 19,22). (2) In the light of vv. 15–23, those not committed to Christ's lordship and not opposed to sin's dominion in their personal lives have no right to speak of Christ as their Savior: "No one can serve two masters" (Mt 6:24; see also Lk 6:46; 2Co 6:14—7:1; Jas 4:4; 1Jn 2:15–17).

6:16 SIN, WHICH LEADS TO DEATH. Paul solemnly warns believers who think they may securely sin because they are under grace. If believers give themselves to sin, they will in fact become slaves to sin (cf. Lk 16:13; Jn 8:34), resulting in "death" (cf. v. 23). "Death" here means "everlasting destruction and shut out from the presence of the Lord" (2Th 1:9), the opposite of "eternal life" (cf. v. 23).

6:17 OBEYED THE FORM OF TEACHING. In the early church new believers were committed to certain defined standards of teaching and conduct, based on apostolic principles and the believer's relation and commitment to Christ (cf. Mt 5–7; Ac 2:42). (1) These standards were most likely a summary of Christian doctrine and ethics to which converts subscribed when they accepted Christ as their new Master. It is the "sound doctrine" or "sound teaching" referred to in the Pastoral Let-

heartedly obeyed the form of teaching[d] to which you were entrusted.
18You have been set free from sin[e]
and have become slaves to righteousness.[f]
19I put this in human terms[g] because you are weak in your natural
selves. Just as you used to offer the
parts of your body in slavery to impurity and to ever-increasing wickedness,
so now offer them in slavery to righteousness[h] leading to holiness.
20When you were slaves to sin,[i] you
were free from the control of righteousness.[j] 21What benefit did you reap at
that time from the things you are now
ashamed of? Those things result in
death![k] 22But now that you have been
set free from sin[l] and have become
slaves to God,[m] the benefit you reap
leads to holiness, and the result is eternal life.[n] 23For the wages of sin is
death,[o] but the gift of God is eternal
life[p] in[w] Christ Jesus our Lord.

Believers Die to the Law

7 Do you not know, brothers[q]—for
I am speaking to men who know
the law—that the law has authority
over a man only as long as he lives?
2For example, by law a married woman
is bound to her husband as long as he
is alive, but if her husband dies, she is
released from the law of marriage.[r]
3So then, if she marries another man
while her husband is still alive, she is
called an adulteress.[s] But if her husband dies, she is released from that
law and is not an adulteress, even
though she marries another man.
4So, my brothers, you also died to
the law[t] through the body of Christ,[u]
that you might belong to another,[v] to
him who was raised from the dead, in
order that we might bear fruit to God.
5For when we were controlled by the
sinful nature,[x][w] the sinful passions
aroused by the law[x] were at work in
our bodies,[y] so that we bore fruit for
death.[z] 6But now, by dying to what
once bound us, we have been released
from the law[a] so that we serve in the
new way of the Spirit, and not in the old
way of the written code.[b]

Struggling With Sin

7What shall we say, then?[c] Is the
law sin? Certainly not![d] Indeed I
would not have known what sin was
except through the law.[e] For I would
not have known what coveting really
was if the law had not said, "Do not
covet."[y][f] 8But sin, seizing the opportunity afforded by the commandment,[g] produced in me every kind of
covetous desire. For apart from law,
sin is dead.[h] 9Once I was alive apart
from law; but when the commandment
came, sin sprang to life and I died. 10I
found that the very commandment that
was intended to bring life[i] actually
brought death. 11For sin, seizing the

6:17 [d]2Ti 1:13
6:18 [e]S ver 2; ver 7,22; Ro 8:2; 1Pe 4:1; S ver 16 [f]S ver 22
6:19 [g]Ro 3:5; Gal 3:15 [h]S ver 13; S ver 22
6:20 [i]S ver 16 [j]ver 16
6:21 [k]S ver 23
6:22 [l]S ver 18 [m]ver 18,19; Ro 7:25; 1Co 7:22; Eph 6:6; 1Pe 2:16 [n]S Mt 25:46
6:23 [o]ver 16,21; Ge 2:17; Pr 10:16; Eze 18:4; Ro 1:32; S 5:12; 7:5,13; 8:6,13; Gal 6:7,8; Jas 1:15 [p]S Mt 25:46
7:1 [q]S Ac 1:16; S 22:5; Ro 1:13; 1Co 1:10; 5:11; 6:6; 14:20,26; Gal 3:15; 6:18
7:2 [r]1Co 7:39
7:3 [s]S Lk 16:18
7:4 [t]ver 6; S Ro 6:6; 8:2; Gal 2:19; 3:23-25; 4:31; 5:1 [u]Col 1:22 [v]Gal 2:19,20
7:5 [w]S Gal 5:24 [x]Ro 7:7-11 [y]Ro 6:13 [z]S Ro 6:23
7:6 [a]S ver 4 [b]Ro 2:29; 2Co 3:6
7:7 [c]S Ro 8:31 [d]S ver 12 [e]S Ro 4:15 [f]Ex 20:17; Dt 5:21
7:8 [g]ver 11 [h]S Ro 4:15
7:10 [i]Lev 18:5; Lk 10:26-28; S Ro 10:5; Gal 3:12

[w]23 Or *through* [x]5 Or *the flesh*; also in verse 25 [y]7 Exodus 20:17; Deut. 5:21

ters (see 1Ti 1:10; 2Ti 1:13; 4:3; Tit 1:9; 2:1). (2) The supposition that Christianity has no pattern of teaching that regulates thought and practice, or that it is "legalism" to have rules of conduct, is alien to Paul's concept of the Christian faith. Christianity demands obedience from the heart to godly standards (see Mk 7:6, note on legalism).

7:4 DIED TO THE LAW. We no longer look to the OT law and sacrifices for salvation and acceptance from God (cf. Gal 3:23–25; 4:4–5; see article on THE OLD TESTAMENT LAW, p. 118). We have been separated from the old covenant of the law and united with Christ, and we now look to Christ for salvation. We must believe in Jesus (1Jn 5:13), receive his Spirit and grace (see article on FAITH AND GRACE, p. 1720), and thereby receive forgiveness, be regenerated, and become able to "bear fruit to God" (6:22–23; 8:3–4; Mt 5:17, note; Eph 2:10; Gal 5:22–23; Col 1:5–6).

7:7–25 KNOWN WHAT SIN WAS EXCEPT THROUGH THE LAW. This section describes the pre-conversion experience of Paul or anyone else who attempts to please God without depending on his grace, mercy and strength (see 8:5; see article on FAITH AND GRACE, p. 1720). (1) In vv. 7–12, Paul describes the stage of innocence until people reach an "age of accountability." They are "alive" (v. 9), i.e., without guilt and spiritual accountability, until they volitionally sin against God's law written externally or in their hearts (cf. 2:14–15; 7:7,9,11).

(2) In vv. 13–20, Paul depicts a state of slavery to sin because the law, when it becomes known, brings unconscious sin into consciousness and makes persons actual transgressors. Sin becomes their master, even though they try to resist it.

(3) In vv. 21–25, Paul discloses the utter despair that grips people as the knowledge and power of sin reduces them to wretchedness.

7:9–11 ONCE I WAS ALIVE. Paul's statements that "I was alive" and that "sin . . . put me to death" (v. 11) support the view that a child is innocent until he or she willfully sins against God's law from the heart (2:14–15; see previous note). The teaching that little infants come into the world guilty and worthy of eternal damnation is not found in Scripture.

opportunity afforded by the commandment,[j] deceived me,[k] and through
the commandment put me to death.
12So then, the law is holy, and the commandment is holy, righteous and
good.[l]
13Did that which is good, then, become death to me? By no means! But
in order that sin might be recognized
as sin, it produced death in me[m]
through what was good,[n] so that
through the commandment sin might
become utterly sinful.
14We know that the law is spiritual;
but I am unspiritual,[o] sold[p] as a
slave to sin.[q] **15**I do not understand
what I do. For what I want to do I do
not do, but what I hate I do.[r] **16**And
if I do what I do not want to do, I agree
that the law is good.[s] **17**As it is, it is
no longer I myself who do it, but it is
sin living in me.[t] **18**I know that nothing good lives in me, that is, in my sinful nature.[z][u] For I have the desire to
do what is good, but I cannot carry it
out. **19**For what I do is not the good I
want to do; no, the evil I do not want
to do—this I keep on doing.[v] **20**Now
if I do what I do not want to do, it is
no longer I who do it, but it is sin living
in me that does it.[w]
21So I find this law at work:[x] When
I want to do good, evil is right there
with me. **22**For in my inner being[y] I
delight in God's law;[z] **23**but I see another law at work in the members of
my body, waging war[a] against the law
of my mind and making me a prisoner
of the law of sin[b] at work within my
members. **24**What a wretched man I
am! Who will rescue me from this body

7:11 [j] ver 8 [k] Ge 3:13
7:12 [l] ver 7,13,14, 16; Ro 8:4; Gal 3:21; 1Ti 1:8; S Ro 4:15
7:13 [m] S Ro 6:23 [n] S ver 12
7:14 [o] 1Co 3:1 [p] 1Ki 21:20,25; 2Ki 17:17 [q] S Ro 6:16
7:15 [r] ver 19; Gal 5:17
7:16 [s] S ver 12
7:17 [t] ver 20
7:18 [u] ver 25; S Gal 5:24
7:19 [v] ver 15
7:20 [w] ver 17
7:21 [x] ver 23,25
7:22 [y] Eph 3:16 [z] Ps 1:2; 40:8
7:23 [a] Gal 5:17; Jas 4:1; 1Pe 2:11 [b] S Ro 6:16

[z] *18* Or *my flesh*

7:12 THE LAW IS HOLY. See Mt 5:17, note; Gal 3:19, note.

7:14 THE LAW. Remember that Paul in ch. 7 is analyzing the state of an unregenerate person who is under OT law and accepts its truth, yet is conscious of his or her inability to live a life that pleases God (cf. v. 1). He is describing a conflict between a person who struggles on his or her own against the power of sin, demonstrating that we cannot attain justification, goodness and sanctification by our own attempts to resist sin and obey God's law. The conflict of the Christian, on the other hand, is quite different: it is the conflict of a person in union with Christ and the Holy Spirit against the power of sin (cf. Gal 5:16–18). In ch. 8 Paul describes the way to victory over sin through life in the Spirit.

7:14 I AM UNSPIRITUAL, SOLD AS A SLAVE TO SIN. More than any other words in ch. 7, these clearly point to a pre-conversion period under the law. This is so for the following reasons: (1) In ch. 7 Paul is demonstrating the insufficiency of the law to redeem us apart from grace, not the insufficiency of the gospel of grace (cf. Gal 3:24).

(2) In v. 5 Paul states that those who are "controlled by the sinful nature" (i.e., unspiritual, sensual) are bearing "fruit for death" (i.e., eternal death). And in 8:13 he maintains that "if you live according to the sinful nature, you will die" (cf. Gal 5:19–21). Thus the person referred to in ch. 7 is spiritually dead.

(3) The expression "sold as a slave to sin" means bondage to sin's power (cf. 1Ki 21:20,25; 2Ki 17:17). This cannot apply to a believer in Christ, since Christ, by the ransom of his blood (see Mt 20:28, note), has redeemed us from the power of sin and declares that sin no longer has dominion over us (6:14). Christ himself affirmed: "So if the Son sets you free, you will be free indeed" (Jn 8:36, note; cf. Ro 8:2). In fact, the name Jesus means "he will save his people from their sins" (Mt 1:21).

(4) Nor does the indwelling presence of the Holy Spirit (ch. 8) leave believers "sold as a slave to sin." Paul goes on to declare that "through Christ Jesus the law of the Spirit of life set me free from the law of sin" (8:2), and he includes himself with those "who do not live according to the sinful nature but according to the Spirit" (8:4), because "we have an obligation—but it is not to the sinful nature" (8:12).

7:15 WHAT I WANT TO DO I DO NOT DO. Those who attempt to obey God's commandments *without the saving grace of Christ* find themselves unable to accomplish the good intentions of their heart. They are not their own master; evil and sin rule within them. They are slaves to them (vv. 15–21) and are "prisoners of the law of sin" (v. 23). Only in Christ will God "provide a way out" of temptation, "so that you can stand up under it" (1Co 10:13).

7:22 I DELIGHT IN GOD'S LAW. Many under the OT law found that within the inward being (soul, reason) they delighted in God's law and commandments (cf. Ps 119; Isa 58:2). At the same time, however, as long as help was sought only from the law, sinful passions remained in control (v. 23). Likewise, there may be those in the church today who acknowledge the righteousness, purity and excellence of the gospel of Christ, yet because they have not experienced Christ's regenerating grace, find themselves in bondage to sin. As we attempt to live a life free from the bondage of sin and immorality, all our efforts will be useless if we are not truly born again, reconciled to God, redeemed from Satan's power and made new creatures in Christ, living a renewed life in the Spirit (Jn 3:3; Ro 8; 2Co 5:17).

7:24 WHAT A WRETCHED MAN I AM! The unregenerate person, after maintaining a losing conflict against sin, is at last taken prisoner (v. 23). Sin finally triumphs and the person is sold as

of death?[c] **25**Thanks be to God—
through Jesus Christ our Lord![d]
So then, I myself in my mind am a
slave to God's law,[e] but in the sinful
nature a slave to the law of sin.[f]

Life Through the Spirit

8 Therefore, there is now no condemnation[g] for those who are in
Christ Jesus,[a h] **2**because through
Christ Jesus[i] the law of the Spirit of
life[j] set me free[k] from the law of
sin[l] and death. **3**For what the law was
powerless[m] to do in that it was weakened by the sinful nature,[b n] God did
by sending his own Son in the likeness
of sinful man[o] to be a sin offering.[c p]
And so he condemned sin in sinful
man,[d] **4**in order that the righteous requirements[q] of the law might be fully
met in us, who do not live according to
the sinful nature but according to the
Spirit.[r]
5Those who live according to the
sinful nature have their minds set on
what that nature desires;[s] but those
who live in accordance with the Spirit Ro 13:12-14
have their minds set on what the Spirit
desires.[t] **6**The mind of sinful man[e] is
death,[u] but the mind controlled by the
Spirit is life[v] and peace; **7**the sinful Ro 14:17
mind[f] is hostile to God.[w] It does not
submit to God's law, nor can it do so.
8Those controlled by the sinful nature[x] cannot please God.
9You, however, are controlled not by
the sinful nature[y] but by the Spirit, if
the Spirit of God lives in you.[z] And if
anyone does not have the Spirit of
Christ,[a] he does not belong to Christ.
10But if Christ is in you,[b] your body is
dead because of sin, yet your spirit is
alive because of righteousness. **11**And
if the Spirit of him who raised Jesus

7:24 [c]Ro 6:6; 8:2 **7:25** [d]S 2Co 2:14 [e]S Ro 6:22 [f]S Ro 6:16 **8:1** [g]ver 34 [h]ver 39; S Ro 16:3 **8:2** [i]Ro 7:25 [j]1Co 15:45 [k]Jn 8:32,36; S Ro 6:18 [l]S Ro 6:16; S 7:4 **8:3** [m]Heb 7:18; 10:1-4 [n]Ro 7:18, 19; S Gal 5:24 [o]S Php 2:7 [p]Heb 2:14,17 **8:4** [q]Ro 2:26 [r]S Gal 5:16 **8:5** [s]Gal 5:19-21 [t]Gal 5:22-25 **8:6** [u]S Ro 6:23 [v]ver 13; Gal 6:8 **8:7** [w]Jas 4:4 **8:8** [x]S Gal 5:24 **8:9** [y]S Gal 5:24 [z]ver 11; 1Co 6:19; 2Ti 1:14 [a]Jn 14:17; S Ac 16:7; 1Jn 4:13 **8:10** [b]ver 9; Ex 29:45; Jn 14:20,23; 2Co 13:5; Gal 2:20; Eph 3:17; Col 1:27; Rev 3:20

[a] *1* Some later manuscripts *Jesus, who do not live according to the sinful nature but according to the Spirit,* [b] *3* Or *the flesh*; also in verses 4, 5, 8, 9, 12 and 13 [c] *3* Or *man, for sin* [d] *3* Or *in the flesh* [e] *6* Or *mind set on the flesh* [f] *7* Or *the mind set on the flesh*

a slave to sin (v. 14). His state is miserable; who can rescue him? The answer is "through Jesus Christ our Lord" (v. 25). It is he alone who will set us free "from the law of sin and death" (8:2).

8:1 THOSE WHO ARE IN CHRIST JESUS. Paul has just shown that life without the grace of Christ is defeat, misery and bondage to sin. Now in ch. 8, Paul tells us that spiritual life, freedom from condemnation, victory over sin and fellowship with God come through union with Christ by the indwelling Holy Spirit. By receiving and following the Spirit, we are delivered from sin's power and are led onward to final glorification in Christ. This experience is the normal Christian life under the full provision of the gospel.

8:2 THE LAW OF THE SPIRIT. This "law of the Spirit of life" is the regulating and activating power and life of the Holy Spirit operating in the hearts of believers. The Holy Spirit comes into sinners and frees them from the power of sin (cf. 7:23). The law of the Spirit comes into full operation as believers commit themselves to obey the Spirit (vv. 4–5,13–14). They find a new power operating within, a power that allows them to overcome sin. "The law of sin and death" is the controlling power of sin, which places people in bondage (7:14) and reduces them to wretchedness (7:24).

8:4 THE LAW MIGHT BE FULLY MET IN US. The Holy Spirit working within believers allows them to live lives of righteousness, which is seen as the fulfillment of God's moral law. Thus, the operation of grace and obedience to God's law are not in conflict (cf. 2:13; 3:31; 6:15; 7:12,14). They both point to righteousness and holiness.

8:5–14 ACCORDING TO THE SINFUL NATURE ... THE SPIRIT. Paul describes two classes of people: those who live according to the sinful nature and those who live according to the Spirit. (1) To live "according to the sinful nature" is to desire, take pleasure in, be occupied with and gratify the corrupt desires of sinful human nature. Such living includes not only sexual immorality, adultery, hatred, selfish ambition, outbursts of anger, and so forth (see Gal 5:19–21), but also obscenity, pornographic addiction, drug addiction, mental and emotional pleasure from sex scenes in plays, books, TV or movies, and the like (see article on THE ACTS OF THE SINFUL NATURE AND THE FRUIT OF THE SPIRIT, p. 1818).

(2) To live "in accordance with the Spirit" is to seek and submit to the Holy Spirit's direction and enablement, and to concentrate one's attention on the things of God (see article on THE ACTS OF THE SINFUL NATURE AND THE FRUIT OF THE SPIRIT, p. 1818). It is to live consciously at all times in God's presence, trusting him to give us the help and grace we need to accomplish his will in and through us.

(3) It is impossible to follow the sinful nature and the Spirit at the same time (vv. 7–8; Gal 5:17–18). If anyone fails to resist by the Spirit his or her sinful desires and instead lives according to the sinful nature (v. 13), he or she becomes God's enemy (v. 7; Jas 4:4) and can expect spiritual and eternal death (v. 13). Those who make the things of God their chief love and concern can expect eternal life and communion with God (vv. 10–11,15–16).

8:9 IF THE SPIRIT OF GOD LIVES IN YOU. All believers from the moment they accept Jesus Christ as Lord and Savior have the Holy Spirit living in them (cf. 1Co 3:16; 6:19–20; Eph 1:13–14; see article on THE DOCTRINE OF THE HOLY SPIRIT, p. 1654).

8:10 YOUR BODY IS DEAD BECAUSE OF SIN. Because sin has invaded the physical aspect

from the dead[c] is living in you, he who
raised Christ from the dead will also
give life to your mortal bodies[d]
through his Spirit, who lives in you.
12Therefore, brothers, we have an
obligation—but it is not to the sinful
nature, to live according to it.[e] **13**For
if you live according to the sinful nature, you will die;[f] but if by the Spirit
you put to death the misdeeds of the
body,[g] you will live,[h] **14**because
those who are led by the Spirit of God[i]
are sons of God.[j] **15**For you did not
receive a spirit[k] that makes you a
slave again to fear,[l] but you received
the Spirit of sonship.[g] And by him we
cry, *"Abba,*[h] Father."[m] **16**The Spirit
himself testifies with our spirit[n] that
we are God's children.[o] **17**Now if we
are children, then we are heirs[p]—
heirs of God and co-heirs with Christ,
if indeed we share in his sufferings[q] in
order that we may also share in his glory.[r]

Future Glory

18I consider that our present sufferings are not worth comparing with the
glory that will be revealed in us.[s]
19The creation waits in eager expectation for the sons of God[t] to be revealed. **20**For the creation was subjected to frustration, not by its own choice,

8:11 [c]S Ac 2:24 [d]Jn 5:21; S Ro 6:5 **8:12** [e]ver 4; S Gal 5:24 **8:13** [f]S Ro 6:23 [g]S Ro 6:2 [h]ver 6; Gal 6:8 **8:14** [i]S Gal 5:18 [j]ver 19; Hos 1:10; Mal 3:17; Mt 5:9; S Jn 1:12; Gal 3:26; 4:5; Eph 1:5; Rev 21:7 **8:15** [k]S Jn 20:22 [l]S 2Ti 1:7 [m]Mk 14:36; Gal 4:5,6 **8:16** [n]2Co 1:22; Eph 1:13 [o]S ver 14; S Jn 1:12 **8:17** [p]S Ac 20:32; Gal 3:29; 4:7; Eph 3:6; Tit 3:7 [q]S 2Co 1:5 [r]2Ti 2:12; 1Pe 4:13

8:18 [s]2Co 4:17; 1Pe 4:13; 5:1 **8:19** [t]S ver 14

[g] *15* Or *adoption* [h] *15* Aramaic for *Father*

of our being, our bodies must die or be transformed (cf. 1Co 15:50–54; 1Th 4:13–17). Yet because Christ is in us, we now experience the life of the Spirit.

8:13 PUT TO DEATH THE MISDEEDS OF THE BODY. Paul emphasizes the necessity for continual warfare against all that would limit God's work in our lives (cf. 6:11–19), for sin is always striving to regain control over us. (1) This spiritual conflict, although directed against Satan and evil spiritual forces (Eph 6:12), is primarily against the passions and desires of the "sinful nature" (Gal 5:16–21; Jas 4:1; 1Pe 2:11). We as believers must continually decide whether we will surrender to sinful desires or to the demands of the divine nature in which we participate (Gal 5:16,18; 2Pe 1:4).

(2) The result of failing to put to death the misdeeds of the body is spiritual death (vv. 6,13) and the loss of inheritance in God's kingdom (Gal 5:19–21). The words "you will die" mean that a Christian can pass from spiritual life back into spiritual death. Thus, the life of God that we receive at our new birth (Jn 3:3–6) can be extinguished in the soul of a believer who refuses to put to death by the Spirit the misdeeds of the body.

8:13–14 THOSE . . . ARE SONS OF GOD. Paul gives the basis for the assurance of salvation here. If one is consistently putting to death the misdeeds of the body, then we are being led by the Spirit. Those led by the Spirit are God's children.

8:14 LED BY THE SPIRIT OF GOD. The Holy Spirit lives within the child of God in order to lead him or her to think, speak and act according to God's Word. (1) He leads primarily by promptings that (a) are inward urgings to do God's will and to put to death the misdeeds of the body (v. 13; Php 2:13; Tit 2:11–12); (b) are always in harmony with Scripture (1Co 2:12–13; cf. 2Pe 1:20–21); (c) are intended to give direction in life (Lk 4:1; Ac 10:19–20; 16:6–7); (d) are opposed to sinful desires (Gal 5:17–18; 1Pe 2:11); (e) are concerned with the guilt of sin, Christ's standard of righteousness and God's judgment against evil (Jn 16:8–11); (f) exhort believers to persevere in the faith and warn them concerning falling away from personal faith in Christ (v. 13; Heb 3:7–14); (g) become weaker the longer believers resist obeying the Spirit's prompting (1:28; Eph 4:17–19,30–31; 1Th 5:19); (h) result in spiritual death when rejected (vv. 6,13); (i) result in spiritual life and peace when obeyed (vv. 6,10–11,13; Gal 5:22–23).

(2) The Spirit's prompting comes by (a) reading God's Word (Jn 14:26; 15:7,26; 16:13; 2Ti 3:16–17); (b) praying fervently (v. 26; Ac 13:2–3); (c) listening to godly preaching and teaching (2Ti 4:1–2; Heb 13:7,17); (d) exercising the manifestations of the Spirit (see 1Co 12:7–10; 14:6); and (e) heeding the counsel of Christian parents and trustworthy spiritual leaders (Eph 6:1; Col 3:20).

8:15 *ABBA*, FATHER. See Gal 4:6, note.

8:16 THE SPIRIT HIMSELF TESTIFIES. The Holy Spirit imparts to us a confidence that through Christ and with Christ, we are now God's children (v. 15). He makes real the truth that Christ loved us, still loves us and lives for us in heaven as Mediator (cf. Heb 7:25). The Spirit also shows us that the Father loves us as his adopted children, no less than he loves his one and only Son (Jn 14:21,23; 17:23). Finally, the Spirit creates in us the love and confidence by which we cry to him, "*Abba*, Father" (v. 15).

8:17 IF . . . WE SHARE IN HIS SUFFERINGS. Paul reminds us that a victorious life in the Spirit is no easy path. Jesus suffered, and we who follow him will also suffer. This suffering is considered a suffering with him (cf. 2Co 1:5; Php 3:10; Col 1:24; 2Ti 2:11–12), and it is the consequence of our relationship to God as his children, our identification with Christ, our witness for him and our refusal to conform to the world (cf. 12:1–2).

8:18 OUR PRESENT SUFFERINGS. All the sufferings of this present age—sickness, pain, misery, disappointments, poverty, mistreatment, sorrow, persecution and trouble of any kind—must be considered insignificant when compared with the blessing, privileges and glory that will be given to the faithful believer in the age to come (cf. 2Co 4:17).

but by the will of the one who subjected
it,[u] in hope 21that[i] the creation itself
will be liberated from its bondage to
decay[v] and brought into the glorious
freedom of the children of God.[w]

22We know that the whole creation
has been groaning[x] as in the pains of
childbirth right up to the present time.
23Not only so, but we ourselves, who
have the firstfruits of the Spirit,[y]
groan[z] inwardly as we wait eagerly[a]
for our adoption as sons, the redemption of our bodies.[b] 24For in this hope
we were saved.[c] But hope that is seen
is no hope at all.[d] Who hopes for what
he already has? 25But if we hope for
what we do not yet have, we wait for
it patiently.[e]

26In the same way, the Spirit helps
us in our weakness. We do not know
what we ought to pray for, but the Spirit[f] himself intercedes for us[g] with
groans that words cannot express.
27And he who searches our hearts[h]
knows the mind of the Spirit, because
the Spirit intercedes[i] for the saints in
accordance with God's will.

More Than Conquerors

28And we know that in all things
God works for the good[j] of those who
love him,[j] who[k] have been called[k]
according to his purpose.[l] 29For
those God foreknew[m] he also predestined[n] to be conformed to the likeness
of his Son,[o] that he might be the first-

8:20 [u]Ge 3:17-19; 5:29 **8:21** [v]Ac 3:21; 2Pe 3:13; Rev 21:1 [w]S Jn 1:12 **8:22** [x]Jer 12:4 **8:23** [y]S 2Co 5:5 [z]2Co 5:2,4 [a]ver 19; Gal 5:5 [b]ver 11; Php 3:21 **8:24** [c]1Th 5:8; Tit 3:7 [d]S 2Co 4:18 **8:25** [e]Ps 37:7 **8:26** [f]ver 15,16 [g]Eph 6:18 **8:27** [h]S Rev 2:23 [i]S ver 34 **8:28** [j]Ge 50:20; Isa 38:17; Jer 29:11 [k]ver 30; Ro 11:29; 1Co 1:9; Gal 1:6,15; Eph 4:1,4; 1Th 2:12; 2Ti 1:9; Heb 9:15; 1Pe 2:9; 2Pe 1:10 [l]Eph 1:11; 3:11; Heb 6:17 **8:29** [m]Ro 11:2; 1Pe 1:2 [n]Eph 1:5, 11 [o]1Co 15:49; 2Co 3:18; Php 3:21; 1Jn 3:2

[i] *20,21* Or *subjected it in hope.* [21]*For*
[j] *28* Some manuscripts *And we know that all things work together for good to those who love God*
[k] *28* Or *works together with those who love him to bring about what is good—with those who*

8:22 THE WHOLE CREATION HAS BEEN GROANING. In vv. 22–27 Paul speaks of a threefold groaning: of creation (v. 22), of believers (v. 23) and of the Holy Spirit (v. 26). The "creation" (i.e., animate and inanimate nature) has been subjected to suffering and physical catastrophies because of human sin (v. 20). Thus, God has purposed that nature itself will be redeemed and re-created. There will be a new heaven and a new earth, a restoration of all things according to God's will (cf. 2Co 5:17; Gal 6:15; Rev 21:1,5), when God's faithful children receive their full inheritance (vv. 14,23).

8:23 WE OURSELVES ... GROAN. Although believers possess the Spirit and his blessings, they still groan inwardly, desiring their full redemption. This groaning is for two reasons. (1) Believers, living in a sinful world that grieves them, still experience imperfection, pain and sorrow. The groaning expresses the deep sorrow felt at these circumstances (cf. 2Co 5:2–4). (2) They groan for complete redemption and the fullness of the Holy Spirit that will be given at the resurrection. They groan for the glory to be revealed and for the privileges of their full rights as children (cf. 2Co 5:4).

8:26 SPIRIT HIMSELF INTERCEDES FOR US. Concerning the Holy Spirit's activity in helping the believer in prayer, three observations are important: (1) The child of God has two divine intercessors. Christ intercedes for the believer in heaven (v. 34; see Heb 7:25, note; 1Jn 2:1) and the Holy Spirit intercedes within the believer on earth (see article on INTERCESSION, p. 1268). (2) "With groans" probably indicates that the Spirit intercedes with the groans uttered by the believer. These groanings occur in the believer's heart. (3) The spiritual desires and yearnings of believers find their source in the Holy Spirit, who dwells within our hearts. The Spirit himself sighs, groans and suffers within us, longing for the final day of redemption (vv. 23–25). He appeals to the Father on behalf of our needs "in accordance with God's will" (v. 27).

8:28 IN ALL THINGS GOD WORKS FOR THE GOOD. This passage greatly encourages God's children when we must endure suffering in this life. (1) God will bring good out of all affliction, trials, persecution and suffering; the good that God works is conforming us to the image of Christ and ultimately bringing about our glorification (v. 29; see articles on THE PROVIDENCE OF GOD, p. 78, and THE SUFFERING OF THE RIGHTEOUS, p. 710). (2) This promise is limited to those who love God and have submitted to him through faith in Christ (cf. Ex 20:6; Dt 7:9; Ps 37:17; Isa 56:4–7; 1Co 2:9). (3) The "all things" do not include our sins and negligence (vv. 6,13; 6:16,21,23; Gal 6:8); no one can excuse sin by maintaining that God will work it out for good.

8:29 THOSE GOD FOREKNEW. "Foreknew" in this verse is equivalent to "foreloved" and is used in the sense of "to set loving regard on," "to choose to bestow love on from eternity" (cf. Ex 2:25; Ps 1:6; Hos 13:5; Mt 7:23; 1Co 8:3; Gal 4:9; 1Jn 3:1).

(1) Foreknowledge means that God purposed from eternity to love and redeem the human race through Christ (5:8; Jn 3:16). The recipient of God's foreknowledge or forelove is stated in the plural and refers to the church. That is, God's forelove is primarily for the corporate body of Christ (Eph 1:4; 2:4; 1Jn 4:19) and includes individuals only as they identify themselves with this corporate body through abiding faith in and union with Christ (Jn 15:1–6; see article on ELECTION AND PREDESTINATION, p. 1824).

(2) The corporate body of Christ will attain to glorification (v. 30). Individual believers will fall short of such glorification if they separate themselves from that foreloved body and fail to maintain their faith in Christ (vv. 12–14,17; Col 1:21–23).

born[p] among many brothers. [30]And those he predestined,[q] he also called;[r] those he called, he also justified;[s] those he justified, he also glorified.[t]

[31]What, then, shall we say in response to this?[u] If God is for us,[v] who can be against us?[w] [32]He who did not spare his own Son,[x] but gave him up for us all—how will he not also, along with him, graciously give us all things? [33]Who will bring any charge[y] against those whom God has chosen? It is God who justifies. [34]Who is he that condemns?[z] Christ Jesus, who died[a]—more than that, who was raised to life[b]—is at the right hand of God[c] and is also interceding for us.[d] [35]Who shall separate us from the love of Christ?[e] Shall trouble or hardship or persecution or famine or nakedness or danger or sword?[f] [36]As it is written:

> "For your sake we face death all day long;
> we are considered as sheep to be slaughtered."[l][g]

[37]No, in all these things we are more than conquerors[h] through him who loved us.[i] [38]For I am convinced that neither death nor life, neither angels nor demons,[m] neither the present nor the future,[j] nor any powers,[k] [39]neither height nor depth, nor anything else in all creation, will be able to separate us from the love of God[l] that is in Christ Jesus our Lord.[m]

God's Sovereign Choice

9 I speak the truth in Christ—I am not lying,[n] my conscience confirms[o] it in the Holy Spirit— [2]I have great sorrow and unceasing anguish in my heart. [3]For I could wish that I myself[p] were cursed[q] and cut off from Christ for the sake of my brothers,[r] those of my own race,[s] [4]the people of Israel.[t] Theirs is the adoption as sons;[u] theirs the divine glory,[v] the covenants,[w] the receiving of the law,[x] the temple worship[y] and the promises.[z] [5]Theirs are the patriarchs,[a] and from them is traced the human ancestry of Christ,[b] who is God over all,[c] forever praised![n][d] Amen.

[6]It is not as though God's word[e] had failed. For not all who are descended from Israel are Israel.[f] [7]Nor be-

8:29 [p]S Col 1:18 8:30 [q]Eph 1:5,11 [r]S ver 28 [s]S Ro 4:25 [t]Ro 9:23 8:31 [u]Ro 4:1; 6:1; 7:7; 9:14,30 [v]Ex 3:12; Isa 41:10; Hag 1:13 [w]Ps 56:9; 118:6; Isa 8:10; Jer 20:11; Heb 13:6 8:32 [x]Ge 22:13; Mal 3:17; Jn 3:16; Ro 5:8 8:33 [y]Isa 50:8,9 8:34 [z]ver 1 [a]Ro 5:6-8 [b]S Ac 2:24 [c]S Mk 16:19 [d]ver 27; Job 16:20; Isa 53:12; Heb 7:25; 9:24; 1Jn 2:1 8:35 [e]ver 37-39 [f]1Co 4:11; 2Co 11:26,27 8:36 [g]Ps 44:22; 1Co 4:9; 15:30,31; 2Co 4:11; 6:9; 11:23 8:37 [h]1Co 15:57 [i]Ro 5:8; Gal 2:20; Eph 5:2; Rev 1:5; 3:9 8:38 [j]1Co 3:22 [k]Eph 1:21; Col 1:16; 1Pe 3:22 8:39 [l]S Ro 5:8 [m]ver 1; S Ro 16:3 9:1 [n]Ps 15:2; 2Co 11:10; Gal 1:20; 1Ti 2:7 [o]S Ro 1:9 9:3 [p]Ex 32:32 [q]1Co 12:3; 16:22 [r]S Ac 22:5 [s]Ro 11:14 9:4 [t]ver 6 [u]Ex 4:22; 6:7; Dt 7:6 [v]Heb 9:5 [w]Ge 17:2; Dt 4:13; Ac 3:25; Eph 2:12 [x]Ps 147:19 [y]Heb 9:1 [z]S Ac 13:32; S Gal 3:16 9:5 [a]Ro 11:28 [b]Mt 1:1-16; Ro 1:3 [c]Jn 1:1; Col 2:9 [d]Ro 1:25; 2Co 11:31 9:6 [e]S Heb 4:12 [f]Ro 2:28,29; Gal 6:16

[l]36 Psalm 44:22 [m]38 Or *nor heavenly rulers* [n]5 Or *Christ, who is over all. God be forever praised!* Or *Christ. God who is over all be forever praised!*

8:30 PREDESTINED. For an explanation of predestination, see article on ELECTION AND PREDESTINATION, p. 1824.

8:34 IS ALSO INTERCEDING FOR US. See Heb 7:25, note on Christ's heavenly intercession for believers; see article on INTERCESSION, p. 1268.

8:36 SHEEP TO BE SLAUGHTERED. The adversities listed by the apostle in vv. 35–36 have been the experience of God's people in all generations (Ac 14:22; 2Co 11:23–29; Heb 11:35–38). Believers should not think it strange if they experience trouble, persecution, hunger, poverty or danger. Trouble and calamity do not necessarily mean that God has deserted us, nor that he has stopped loving us (v. 35). On the contrary, our suffering as believers will open up the means by which we experience more of God's love and comfort (2Co 1:4–5). Paul assures us that in all these adversities we will overcome and be more than conquerors through Christ (vv. 37–39; cf. Mt 5:10–12; Php 1:29).

8:39 THE LOVE OF GOD THAT IS IN CHRIST JESUS OUR LORD. If anyone fails in his or her spiritual life, it will neither be from a lack of divine grace and love (vv. 31–34), nor from external force or overwhelming adversity (vv. 35–39), but from their own neglect to remain in Christ Jesus (see Jn 15:6, note). Only "in Christ Jesus" is God's love revealed, and only in him do we experience it. Only as we remain in Christ Jesus as "our Lord" can we have the certainty that we will never be separated from God's love.

9:1 ISRAEL'S UNBELIEF. In chs. 9–11 Paul addresses the problem of Israel's past election (9:6–29), present rejection of the gospel (9:30—10:21), and future salvation (11:1–36). For an examination of his argument, see article on ISRAEL IN GOD'S PLAN OF SALVATION, p. 1730.

9:2 I HAVE GREAT SORROW ... IN MY HEART. Paul's ceaseless concern and sorrow over those without Christ (10:1; 11:14; 1Co 9:22) should be every Christian's attitude. This same attitude of grief and willingness to suffer for the salvation of others existed in Moses (Ex 32:32) and Jesus (Mt 23:37; Ro 3:24–25).

9:6 GOD'S WORD HAD FAILED. With this verse, Paul begins an extended discussion of God's dealings with the nation of Israel and the reason for their present unbelief (see article on ISRAEL IN GOD'S PLAN OF SALVATION, p. 1730).

cause they are his descendants are
they all Abraham's children. On the
contrary, "It is through Isaac that your
offspring will be reckoned."[o][g] **8**In
other words, it is not the natural children who are God's children,[h] but it is
the children of the promise who are regarded as Abraham's offspring.[i] **9**For
this was how the promise was stated:
"At the appointed time I will return,
and Sarah will have a son."[p][j]
10Not only that, but Rebekah's children had one and the same father, our
father Isaac.[k] **11**Yet, before the twins
were born or had done anything good
or bad[l]—in order that God's purpose[m] in election might stand: **12**not
by works but by him who calls—she
was told, "The older will serve
the younger."[q][n] **13**Just as it is written: "Jacob I loved, but Esau I
hated."[r][o]
14What then shall we say?[p] Is God
unjust? Not at all![q] **15**For he says to
Moses,

> "I will have mercy on whom I have mercy,
> and I will have compassion on whom I have compassion."[s][r]

16It does not, therefore, depend on
man's desire or effort, but on God's
mercy.[s] **17**For the Scripture says to
Pharaoh: "I raised you up for this very
purpose, that I might display my power
in you and that my name might be proclaimed in all the earth."[t][t] **18**Therefore God has mercy on whom he wants
to have mercy, and he hardens whom
he wants to harden.[u]
19One of you will say to me:[v] "Then
why does God still blame us?[w] For
who resists his will?"[x] **20**But who are
you, O man, to talk back to God?[y]
"Shall what is formed say to him who
formed it,[z] 'Why did you make me like
this?' "[u][a] **21**Does not the potter have
the right to make out of the same lump
of clay some pottery for noble purposes
and some for common use?[b]
22What if God, choosing to show his
wrath and make his power known, bore
with great patience[c] the objects of his
wrath—prepared for destruction?[d]
23What if he did this to make the riches

9:7 g Ge 21:12; Heb 11:18
9:8 h S Ro 8:14 i S Gal 3:16
9:9 j Ge 18:10,14
9:10 k Ge 25:21
9:11 l ver 16 m Ro 8:28
9:12 n Ge 25:23
9:13 o Mal 1:2,3
9:14 p S Ro 8:31 q 2Ch 19:7
9:15 r Ex 33:19
9:16 s Eph 2:8; Tit 3:5
9:17 t Ex 9:16; 14:4; Ps 76:10
9:18 u Ex 4:21; 7:3; 14:4,17; Dt 2:30; Jos 11:20; Ro 11:25
9:19 v Ro 11:19; 1Co 15:35; Jas 2:18 w Ro 3:7 x 2Sa 16:10; 2Ch 20:6; Da 4:35
9:20 y Job 1:22; 9:12; 40:2 z Isa 64:8; Jer 18:6 a Isa 29:16; 45:9; 10:15
9:21 b 2Ti 2:20
9:22 c S Ro 2:4 d Pr 16:4

o *7* Gen. 21:12 p *9* Gen. 18:10,14
q *12* Gen. 25:23 r *13* Mal. 1:2,3
s *15* Exodus 33:19 t *17* Exodus 9:16
u *20* Isaiah 29:16; 45:9

9:11 GOD'S PURPOSE. For comments on God's purpose fulfilled in Esau and Jacob, see articles on GOD'S COVENANT WITH ABRAHAM, ISAAC AND JACOB, p. 46, and ISRAEL IN GOD'S PLAN OF SALVATION, p. 1730.

9:13 JACOB I LOVED, BUT ESAU I HATED. This verse does not mean that Jacob and his descendants were elected to eternal salvation while Esau and his descendants were elected to eternal damnation. Rather, it was an election of Jacob's descendants to be the channel of God's revelation and blessing to the world (see Mal 1:3, note). Observe that according to chs. 9–11, the majority of Jacob's descendants failed to carry out their calling and thus were finally rejected by God (vv. 27,30–33; 10:3; 11:20). Furthermore, those who were not "loved" (i.e., the Gentiles) obeyed God through faith and became "sons of the living God" (vv. 25–26).

9:15 I WILL HAVE MERCY. This verse emphasizes the freedom of God's mercy. His overflowing active compassion cannot be earned or controlled by humans (v. 16). He has willed to have mercy on all (11:32).

9:18 ON WHOM HE WANTS TO HAVE MERCY. God intends to show mercy to those who repent and believe in Jesus as Lord and Savior, while he hardens all those who refuse to repent and choose to continue in their sins and thereby reject salvation in Christ. This divine purpose does not change for any person or nation (cf. 2:4–11).

9:18 WHOM HE WANTS TO HARDEN. The hardening of Pharaoh's heart is at times attributed to God (Ex 4:21; 7:3,13; 9:12; 10:1; 11:10; 14:17) and at other times to Pharaoh himself (Ex 7:22–23; 8:15,32). Pharaoh, whose heart was already in opposition to God, received God's appropriate judgment. When he resisted God's will, God responded by hardening him even more (see Ex 7:3, note). Thus, God's hardening of Pharaoh's heart was not arbitrary; God acted according to his righteous principle of hardening all who reject him (cf. 1:21–32).

9:21 DOES NOT THE POTTER HAVE THE RIGHT? Paul argues for God's right to use certain people to accomplish his redemptive purpose without having to answer to anyone. (1) We must not interpret this to mean that God has no moral principles inherent in his own holy character as he deals with individuals and nations. God is governed in his nature not by the human will but by his love (Jn 3:16), mercy (Ps 25:6), and moral integrity and compassion (Ps 116:5). (2) Those who interpret vv. 6–29 to mean that God arbitrarily chooses some people for salvation and others for destruction have misconstrued the passage (see article on ELECTION AND PREDESTINATION, p. 1824).

9:22–23 OBJECTS OF HIS WRATH . . . OBJECTS OF HIS MERCY. The phrase "objects of his wrath" refers to those being prepared for eternal destruction. People become objects of wrath by their own sinful acts and rebellion, as Paul stated earlier: "but because of your stubbornness and your unrepentant heart, you are storing up wrath" (2:5). However, objects of wrath may still repent,

ISRAEL IN GOD'S PLAN OF SALVATION

Ro 9:6 "It is not as though God's word had failed. For not all who are descended from Israel are Israel."

INTRODUCTION. In Ro 9–11, Paul addresses the problem of Israel's past election, present rejection of the gospel and future salvation. These three chapters were written to answer the question Jewish believers were asking: how could God's promises to Abraham and the nation of Israel remain valid while the nation of Israel as a whole seems to have no part in the gospel? This article summarizes Paul's argument.

OVERVIEW. There are three elements to Paul's discussion of Israel in God's plan of salvation.

(1) The first (Ro 9:6–29) is an examination of Israel's past election. (a) In 9:6–13, Paul maintains that God's promise to Israel has not failed, for the promise never included any except the faithful in the nation. It was meant only for true Israel, those who were faithful to the promise (see Ge 12:1–3; 17:19). There is always an Israel within Israel who have received the promise. (b) In 9:14–29, Paul points out that God has the right to do as he pleases with individuals and nations. He has a right to reject Israel if they disobey and the right to show mercy to the Gentiles and offer them salvation if he chooses.

(2) The second major section (Ro 9:30—10:21) analyzes Israel's present rejection of the gospel. Their failure to respond to Christ is not due to an unconditional divine decree, but to their own unbelief and disobedience (see Ro 10:3, note).

(3) Finally, Paul explains (Ro 11) that the rejection of Israel is only partial and temporary. Israel will eventually accept God's salvation in Christ. There are several steps in his argument. (a) God has not rejected the true Israel, for he has remained faithful to the "remnant" that has remained faithful to him by accepting Christ (11:1–6). (b) God's present hardening of the majority of Israel has come because they refused to believe in Christ (11:7–10; cf. 9:31—10:21). (c) God has turned Israel's transgression (i.e., the crucifixion of Christ) into an opportunity to proclaim salvation to all the world (11:11–12,15). (d) During this present time of Israel's national unbelief, the salvation of individuals, both Jew and Gentile (cf. 10:12–13), depends on faith in Jesus Christ (11:13–24). (e) Belief in Jesus Christ by a portion of national Israel will take place in the future (11:25–29). (f) God's sincere purpose is to have mercy on all, both Jew and Gentile, and to include in his kingdom all people who believe in Christ (11:30–36; cf. 10:12–13; 11:20–24).

PERSPECTIVE. Several things stand out in these three chapters of the book of Romans.

(1) This discussion about Israel does not refer primarily to the eternal life and death of individuals after physical death. Rather, Paul is discussing God's dealing with nations and people historically, i.e., his right to use certain nations and people as he chooses. For example, the choice of the person Jacob over his brother Esau (Ro 9:11) was a choice for the purpose of founding and using the nations of Israel and Edom that came from them. It had nothing to do with their individual eternal destiny to salvation or condemnation. The point is that God has the right to call and place responsibility on those individuals and nations that he chooses.

(2) Paul expresses ceaseless concern for and intense sorrow over the Jewish nation (Ro 9:1–3). The very fact that Paul prays for his countrymen to be saved indicates that he did not believe the form of predestination theology that teaches that all people are foreordained either to heaven or hell before they are born. Rather, Paul's heartfelt desire and prayer is a reflection of God's desire for the Jewish people (cf. Ro 10:21; see Lk 19:41, note on Jesus weeping over Israel's rejection of God's way of salvation). The NT nowhere teaches that some people have been predestined to hell before they come into the world (see article on ELECTION AND PREDESTINATION, p. 1824).

(3) The most significant element in this entire discussion is the issue of faith. The lost spiritual condition of the majority of Israel was not determined or fixed by an arbitrary decree of God, but came as a result of their own unwillingness to submit to God's plan of salvation through faith in Christ (Ro 9:33; 10:3; 11:20). Many Gentiles, however, accepted God's way of faith and attained the righteousness that is by faith. They obeyed God through faith and became "sons of the living God" (9:25–26). This underscores the importance of the obedience that comes through faith (1:5; 16:26) with respect to God's call and election.

(4) Hope is still offered to the nation of Israel if it ceases to continue in its unbelief (Ro 11:23). Similarly, the Gentile believers who now are a part of God's church are warned that they too face the same possibility of being cut off from salvation. Therefore, like the Israelites, they must be diligent to continue in the faith with fear (11:20–23). That warning is as valid today as it was when Paul wrote it.

(5) The Scriptures are full of promises of the eventual restoration of Israel through their acceptance of the Messiah; this restoration will occur at the end of the great tribulation, just before Christ's return (see Isa 11:10–16, note; 24:17–24, note; 49:22–26, note; Jer 31:31–34, note; Eze 37:12–14, note; Ro 11:26, note; Rev 12:6, note).

of his glory[e] known to the objects of
his mercy, whom he prepared in advance for glory[f]— 24even us, whom
he also called,[g] not only from the Jews
but also from the Gentiles?[h] 25As he
says in Hosea:

"I will call them 'my people' who
are not my people;
and I will call her 'my loved
one' who is not my loved
one,"[v][i]

26and,

"It will happen that in the very
place where it was said to
them,
'You are not my people,'
they will be called 'sons of the
living God.'"[w][j]

27Isaiah cries out concerning Israel:

"Though the number of the
Israelites be like the sand
by the sea,[k]
only the remnant will be
saved.[l]
28For the Lord will carry out
his sentence on earth with speed
and finality."[x][m]

29It is just as Isaiah said previously:

"Unless the Lord Almighty[n]
had left us descendants,
we would have become like Sodom,
we would have been like
Gomorrah."[y][o]

Israel's Unbelief

30What then shall we say?[p] That
the Gentiles, who did not pursue righteousness, have obtained it, a righteousness that is by faith;[q] 31but
Israel, who pursued a law of righteousness,[r] has not attained it.[s]
32Why not? Because they pursued it
not by faith but as if it were by works.
They stumbled over the "stumbling
stone."[t] 33As it is written:

"See, I lay in Zion a stone that
causes men to stumble
and a rock that makes them fall,
and the one who trusts in him will
never be put to shame."[z][u]

10 Brothers, my heart's desire[v]
and prayer to God for the Israelites is that they may be saved. 2For
I can testify about them that they are
zealous[w] for God, but their zeal is not
based on knowledge. 3Since they did
not know the righteousness that
comes from God and sought to establish their own, they did not submit to
God's righteousness.[x] 4Christ is the
end of the law[y] so that there may be
righteousness for everyone who believes.[z]

5Moses describes in this way the
righteousness that is by the law: "The
man who does these things will live by
them."[a][a] 6But the righteousness that
is by faith[b] says: "Do not say in your
heart, 'Who will ascend into heav-
en?'[b]"[c] (that is, to bring Christ
down) 7"or 'Who will descend into the
deep?'[c]"[d] (that is, to bring Christ up
from the dead).[e] 8But what does it
say? "The word is near you; it is in your
mouth and in your heart,"[d][f] that is,
the word of faith we are proclaiming:
9That if you confess[g] with your

9:23 [e] S Ro 2:4 [f] Ro 8:30 **9:24** [g] S Ro 8:28 [h] S Ro 3:29 **9:25** [i] Hos 2:23; 1Pe 2:10 **9:26** [j] Hos 1:10; S Mt 16:16; S Ro 8:14 **9:27** [k] Ge 22:17; Hos 1:10 [l] 2Ki 19:4; Jer 44:14; 50:20; Joel 2:32; Ro 11:5 **9:28** [m] Isa 10:22, 23 **9:29** [n] Jas 5:4 [o] Isa 1:9; Ge 19:24-29; Dt 29:23; Isa 13:19; Jer 50:40 **9:30** [p] S Ro 8:31 [q] Ro 1:17; 3:22; 4:5,13; 10:6; Gal 2:16; Php 3:9; Heb 11:7 **9:31** [r] Dt 6:25; Isa 51:1; Ro 10:2, 3; 11:7 [s] Gal 5:4 **9:32** [t] 1Pe 2:8 **9:33** [u] Isa 8:14; 28:16; Ro 10:11; 1Pe 2:6,8 **10:1** [v] Ps 20:4 **10:2** [w] S Ac 21:20 **10:3** [x] Ro 1:17; S 9:31 **10:4** [y] Gal 3:24; Ro 7:1-4 [z] S Ro 3:22 **10:5** [a] Lev 18:5; Dt 4:1; 6:24; Ne 9:29; Pr 19:16; Isa 55:3; Eze 20:11,13,21; S Ro 7:10 **10:6** [b] S Ro 9:30 [c] Dt 30:12 **10:7** [d] Dt 30:13 [e] S Ac 2:24 **10:8** [f] Dt 30:14 **10:9** [g] Mt 10:32

[v] 25 Hosea 2:23 [w] 26 Hosea 1:10 [x] 28 Isaiah 10:22,23 [y] 29 Isaiah 1:9 [z] 33 Isaiah 8:14; 28:16 [a] 5 Lev. 18:5 [b] 6 Deut. 30:12 [c] 7 Deut. 30:13 [d] 8 Deut. 30:14

---

turn to God and receive his mercy. The phrase "objects of his mercy" refers to those, both Jew and Gentile, who believe and follow Jesus Christ (vv. 24–33).

9:32 THEY PURSUED IT NOT BY FAITH. The spiritual condition of the majority of Israel was due to their unwillingness to submit to God's plan of salvation through faith in Christ (v. 33). Many Gentiles, however, accepted God's way of salvation and attained the righteousness that is by faith (v. 30).

10:1 MY HEART'S DESIRE AND PRAYER TO GOD. For comments on how Paul's concern demonstrates that he did not adhere to the doctrine of individuals being predestined or foreordained to heaven or hell, see article on ISRAEL IN GOD'S PLAN OF SALVATION, p. 1730.

10:3 THEY DID NOT SUBMIT. For comments on how ch. 10 fits into Paul's argument in chs. 9–11, see article on ISRAEL IN GOD'S PLAN OF SALVATION, p. 1730.

10:9–10 CONFESS ... BELIEVE IN YOUR HEART. The essentials of salvation are summarized here. They center on belief in the lordship of Christ and his bodily resurrection. Faith must be in the heart, which includes the emotions, intellect and will, and it takes hold of the whole person. Faith must also involve committing oneself publicly to Jesus as Lord, both in word and deed (see article on FAITH AND GRACE, p. 1720).

10:9 CONFESS . . . 'JESUS IS LORD'. The earliest creed or confession of the NT church was not "Jesus is Savior," but "Jesus is Lord" (cf. Ac 8:16; 19:5; 1Co 12:3). Jesus Christ is specifically called

mouth, "Jesus is Lord,"[h] and believe[i]
in your heart that God raised him
from the dead,[j] you will be saved.[k]
10For it is with your heart that you
believe and are justified, and it is
with your mouth that you confess
and are saved. 11As the Scripture
says, "Anyone who trusts in him will
never be put to shame."[e][l] 12For
there is no difference between Jew
and Gentile[m]—the same Lord is
Lord of all[n] and richly blesses all
who call on him, 13for, "Everyone
who calls on the name of the Lord[o]
8 will be saved."[f][p]

14How, then, can they call on the
one they have not believed in? And
how can they believe in the one
of whom they have not heard? And
how can they hear without someone
preaching to them? 15And how can
they preach unless they are sent?
As it is written, "How beautiful
are the feet of those who bring good
news!"[g][q]

16But not all the Israelites accepted
the good news.[r] For Isaiah says,
"Lord, who has believed our message?"[h][s] 17Consequently, faith comes
from hearing the message,[t] and the
message is heard through the word
of Christ.[u] 18But I ask: Did they
not hear? Of course they did:

"Their voice has gone out into all
the earth,
their words to the ends of the
world."[i][v]

19Again I ask: Did Israel not understand? First, Moses says,

"I will make you envious[w] by
those who are not a nation;
I will make you angry by a
nation that has no
understanding."[j][x]

20And Isaiah boldly says,

"I was found by those who did not
seek me;
I revealed myself to those who
did not ask for me."[k][y]

21But concerning Israel he says,

"All day long I have held out my
hands
to a disobedient and obstinate
people."[l][z]

A Remnant Chosen by Grace

11 I ask then: Did God reject his
people? By no means![a] I am an
Israelite myself, a descendant of Abraham,[b] from the tribe of Benjamin.[c]
2God did not reject his people,[d] whom
he foreknew.[e] Don't you know what
the Scripture says in the passage about
Elijah—how he appealed to God
against Israel: 3"Lord, they have killed
your prophets and torn down your altars; I am the only one left, and they
are trying to kill me"[m]?[f] 4And what
was God's answer to him? "I have reserved for myself seven thousand who
have not bowed the knee to Baal."[n][g]
5So too, at the present time there is a

10:9 [h] S Jn 13:13 [i] S Jn 3:15 [j] S Ac 2:24 [k] S Ro 11:14
10:11 [l] Isa 28:16; Ro 9:33
10:12 [m] S Ro 3:22,29 [n] S Mt 28:18
10:13 [o] S Ac 2:21 [p] Joel 2:32
10:15 [q] Isa 52:7; Na 1:15
10:16 [r] Heb 4:2 [s] Isa 53:1; Jn 12:38
10:17 [t] Gal 3:2,5 [u] Col 3:16
10:18 [v] Ps 19:4; S Mt 24:14; Ro 1:8; Col 1:6,23; 1Th 1:8
10:19 [w] Ro 11:11,14 [x] Dt 32:21
10:20 [y] Isa 65:1; Ro 9:30
10:21 [z] Isa 65:2; Jer 35:17
11:1 [a] Lev 26:44; 1Sa 12:22; Ps 94:14; Jer 31:37; 33:24-26 [b] 2Co 11:22 [c] Php 3:5
11:2 [d] S ver 1 [e] S Ro 8:29
11:3 [f] 1Ki 19:10, 14
11:4 [g] 1Ki 19:18

[e] *11* Isaiah 28:16 [f] *13* Joel 2:32 [g] *15* Isaiah 52:7 [h] *16* Isaiah 53:1 [i] *18* Psalm 19:4 [j] *19* Deut. 32:21 [k] *20* Isaiah 65:1 [l] *21* Isaiah 65:2 [m] *3* 1 Kings 19:10,14 [n] *4* 1 Kings 19:18

Savior 16 times in the NT and Lord more than 450 times. (1) The current teaching in some evangelical circles that Jesus can be one's Savior without necessarily being one's Lord is found nowhere in the NT. No one can receive Jesus as Savior without receiving him as Lord. This is an essential ingredient in apostolic preaching (Ac 2:36–40).

(2) "Lord" (Gk *kyrios*) means having power, dominion, authority and the right to master. To confess "Jesus is Lord" is to declare him to be equal with God (v. 13; Jn 20:28; Ac 2:36; Heb 1:10) and worthy of power (Rev 5:12), worship (Php 2:10–11), trust (Jn 14:1; Heb 2:13), obedience (Heb 5:9) and prayer (Ac 7:59–60; 2Co 12:8).

(3) When NT Christians called Jesus "Lord," this was not just an outward profession but an inward sincere attitude of the heart (cf. 1Pe 3:15) by which they made Christ and his Word Lord over all of life (Lk 6:46–49; Jn 15:14). Jesus must be Lord of spiritual matters at home and in the church, as well as Lord in intellectual, financial, educational, recreational and vocational spheres, in fact, in *all* areas of life (12:1–2; 1Co 10:31).

10:9 GOD RAISED HIM FROM THE DEAD. Anyone denying Christ's bodily resurrection cannot legitimately claim to be a Christian. He or she is still an unbeliever, for the death and resurrection of Christ is the central event in salvation (1:4; 4:25; 5:10,17; 6:4–10; 8:11,34).

11:1 DID GOD REJECT HIS PEOPLE? Paul now explains that God's rejection of Israel is only partial and temporary; Israel will eventually accept God's salvation in Christ. For comments on how ch. 11 fits into Paul's argument in chs. 9–11, see article on ISRAEL IN GOD'S PLAN OF SALVATION, p. 1730.

11:5 CHOSEN BY GRACE. This phrase refers to God's gracious design in sending his Son into the world to save all who believe in him. Election proceeds from God's saving purpose "before the creation of the world" (Eph 1:4). Since the coming of the Savior and his death and resurrection, this

remnant[h] chosen by grace.[i] 6And if
by grace, then it is no longer by
works;[j] if it were, grace would no
longer be grace.[o]
7What then? What Israel sought so
earnestly it did not obtain,[k] but the
elect did. The others were hardened,[l]
8as it is written:

"God gave them a spirit of stupor,
eyes so that they could not see
and ears so that they could not
hear,[m]
to this very day."[p][n]

9And David says:

"May their table become a snare
and a trap,
a stumbling block and a
retribution for them.
10May their eyes be darkened so
they cannot see,[o]
and their backs be bent
forever."[q][p]

Ingrafted Branches

11Again I ask: Did they stumble so
as to fall beyond recovery? Not at all![q]
Rather, because of their transgression,
salvation has come to the Gentiles[r] to
make Israel envious.[s] 12But if their
transgression means riches for the
world, and their loss means riches for
the Gentiles,[t] how much greater
riches will their fullness bring!
13I am talking to you Gentiles. Inas-

11:5 [h] S Ro 9:27
[i] S Ro 3:24
11:6 [j] Ro 4:4
11:7 [k] Ro 9:31
[l] ver 25; S Ro 9:18
11:8
[m] S Mt 13:13-15
[n] Dt 29:4;
Isa 29:10
11:10 [o] ver 8
[p] Ps 69:22,23
11:11 [q] ver 1
[r] S Ac 13:46
[s] ver 14; Ro 10:19
11:12 [t] ver 25
11:13 [u] S Ac 9:15
11:14 [v] ver 11;
Ro 10:19;
1Co 10:33;
1Th 2:16
[w] S Mt 1:21;
S Lk 2:11;
S Jn 3:17; Ac 4:12;
16:31; 1Co 1:21;
1Ti 2:4; Tit 3:5
11:15 [x] S Ro 5:10
[y] Lk 15:24,32
11:16
[z] Lev 23:10,17;
Nu 15:18-21
11:17 [a] Jer 11:16;
Jn 15:2 [b] Ac 2:39;
Eph 2:11-13
11:18 [c] Jn 4:22
11:20
[d] 1Co 10:12;
2Co 1:24
[e] 1Ti 6:17
[f] 1Pe 1:17
11:22 [g] Ro 2:4
[h] 1Co 15:2;
Col 1:23; Heb 3:6

much as I am the apostle to the Gentiles,[u] I make much of my ministry
14in the hope that I may somehow
arouse my own people to envy[v] and
save[w] some of them. 15For if their rejection is the reconciliation[x] of the
world, what will their acceptance be
but life from the dead?[y] 16If the part
of the dough offered as firstfruits[z] is
holy, then the whole batch is holy; if
the root is holy, so are the branches.
17If some of the branches have been
broken off,[a] and you, though a wild
olive shoot, have been grafted in
among the others[b] and now share in
the nourishing sap from the olive root,
18do not boast over those branches. If
you do, consider this: You do not support the root, but the root supports
you.[c] 19You will say then, "Branches
were broken off so that I could be grafted in." 20Granted. But they were broken off because of unbelief, and you
stand by faith.[d] Do not be arrogant,[e]
but be afraid.[f] 21For if God did not
spare the natural branches, he will not
spare you either.
22Consider therefore the kindness[g]
and sternness of God: sternness to
those who fell, but kindness to you,
provided that you continue[h] in his

[o] *6* Some manuscripts *by grace. But if by works, then it is no longer grace; if it were, work would no longer be work.* [p] *8* Deut. 29:4; Isaiah 29:10 [q] *10* Psalm 69:22,23

choosing includes all who believe and obey Christ and the gospel. Thus, both God and humans are active in election. The goal of this choosing by grace is "to be holy and blameless" in God's sight (Eph 1:4; cf. Ro 3:22; 4:1–5,16; 11:11–24; 2Co 5:19–20; Eph 2:8–10; see article on ELECTION AND PREDESTINATION, p. 1824).

11:7 THE OTHERS WERE HARDENED. See 9:18, note on the hardening of hearts.

11:11 SALVATION HAS COME TO THE GENTILES. Israel's transgression, i.e., their rejection and crucifixion of Jesus, has resulted in salvation coming to the whole world (see Isa 49:5–6, notes).

11:12 THEIR FULLNESS. The "fullness" of Israel may refer to a time when many in Israel will believe in Jesus Christ as God's divine Son and Messiah (see v. 15), bringing even greater blessing to the world (see Isa 11:10–16, note; 29:17–24, note).

11:14 AROUSE . . . TO ENVY. It should be the desire and prayer of all churches that God's power and blessing will rest on them to such a degree that some in Israel will be moved to jealousy and turn to the Lord. Christ's salvation and the privileges of his kingdom worked out in our lives will create in Israel a desire for the same blessings.

11:20 BECAUSE OF UNBELIEF. The key to Israel's destiny is not an arbitrary decree of God, but her own unbelief and rejection of God's grace in Christ (see article on ISRAEL IN GOD'S PLAN OF SALVATION, p. 1730).

11:22 YOU ALSO WILL BE CUT OFF. Paul directs a grave warning to all Gentile believers, i.e., to all Christian churches, denominations or fellowships. (1) The terrible possibility exists that God will "cut off" any individual, ministry, church or group of churches if they do not "continue in his kindness" and in the NT apostolic faith and standards of righteousness (v. 22).

(2) If God did not spare Israel, neither will he spare any particular church or fellowship (v. 21) if it rejects God's ways and conforms to the ways of this world (see 12:2, note). Therefore, all Christian churches are to "be afraid" (v. 20), keeping in mind both "the kindness and sternness of God" (v. 22) and making every effort to continue in the apostolic faith and practice of the NT. No Christian church or ministry may presume with confidence that it will never fall under God's judgment. With churches, as with individuals, "God does not show favoritism" (2:11; see also Rev 2–3, notes).

kindness. Otherwise, you also will be
cut off.[i] 23 And if they do not persist
in unbelief, they will be grafted in, for
God is able to graft them in again.[j]
24 After all, if you were cut out of an
olive tree that is wild by nature, and
contrary to nature were grafted into a
cultivated olive tree,[k] how much more
readily will these, the natural
branches, be grafted into their own olive tree!

All Israel Will Be Saved

25 I do not want you to be ignorant[l]
of this mystery,[m] brothers, so that you
may not be conceited:[n] Israel has experienced a hardening[o] in part until
the full number of the Gentiles has
come in.[p] 26 And so all Israel will be
saved,[q] as it is written:

"The deliverer will come from Zion;
he will turn godlessness away
from Jacob.
27 And this is[r] my covenant with
them
when I take away their
sins."[s r]

28 As far as the gospel is concerned,
they are enemies[s] on your account;
but as far as election is concerned,
they are loved on account of the patriarchs,[t] 29 for God's gifts and his call[u]
are irrevocable.[v] 30 Just as you who
were at one time disobedient[w] to God

11:22 [i] Jn 15:2
11:23 [j] 2Co 3:16
11:24 [k] Jer 11:16
11:25 [l] Ro 1:13; 1Co 10:1; 12:1; 2Co 1:8; 1Th 4:13
[m] S Ro 16:25
[n] Ro 12:16 [o] ver 7; S Ro 9:18
[p] Lk 21:24
11:26 [q] Isa 45:17; Jer 31:34
11:27 [r] Isa 59:20, 21; 27:9; Heb 8:10,12
11:28 [s] Ro 5:10
[t] Dt 7:8; 10:15; Ro 9:5
11:29 [u] S Ro 8:28
[v] S Heb 7:21
11:30 [w] S Eph 2:2
11:32 [x] S Ro 3:9
11:33 [y] S Ro 2:4
[z] Ps 92:5; Eph 3:10; Col 2:3
[a] Job 5:9; 11:7; Ps 139:6; Ecc 8:17; Isa 40:28
11:34 [b] Isa 40:13, 14; Job 15:8; 36:22; Jer 23:18; 1Co 2:16
11:35 [c] Job 41:11; 35:7
11:36 [d] 1Co 8:6; 11:12; Col 1:16; Heb 2:10
[e] Ro 16:27; Eph 3:21; 1Ti 1:17; 1Pe 5:11; Jude 25; Rev 5:13; 7:12
12:1 [f] Eph 4:1; 1Pe 2:11

have now received mercy as a result of
their disobedience, 31 so they too have
now become disobedient in order that
they too may now[t] receive mercy as a
result of God's mercy to you. 32 For God
has bound all men over to disobedience[x] so that he may have mercy on
them all.

Doxology

33 Oh, the depth of the riches[y] of
the wisdom and[u]
knowledge of God![z]
How unsearchable his
judgments,
and his paths beyond tracing
out![a]
34 "Who has known the mind of the
Lord?
Or who has been his
counselor?"[v b]
35 "Who has ever given to God,
that God should repay him?"[w c]
36 For from him and through him and
to him are all things.[d]
To him be the glory forever!
Amen.[e]

Living Sacrifices

12 Therefore, I urge you,[f] brothers, in view of God's mercy, to

[r] *27* Or *will be* [s] *27* Isaiah 59:20,21; 27:9; Jer. 31:33,34 [t] *31* Some manuscripts do not have *now.* [u] *33* Or *riches and the wisdom and the* [v] *34* Isaiah 40:13 [w] *35* Job 41:11

11:25 FULL NUMBER OF THE GENTILES. The "full number of the Gentiles" signifies the completion of God's purpose in calling out a people from among the Gentiles (Ac 15:14). It may also be related to a time when their wickedness is full, i.e., when sin in the world reaches a full level of rebellion against God (cf. Ge 15:16). At that time Christ will come to judge the world (Lk 21:24,27; cf. Ge 6:5–7,11–13; 18:20–33; 19:24–25; Lk 17:26–30).

11:26 ALL ISRAEL. The expression "all Israel" should be understood as the believers in Israel as a whole. (1) The number of Jews who believe in Christ will greatly increase during the dark days of the tribulation (Dt 4:30–31; Hos 5:14—6:3; Rev 7:1–8). The tribulation will end when Christ brings deliverance to the believers in Israel and destroys the remaining unbelieving Jews (see Isa 10:20, note; Zec 13:8–9, note). All rebels (i.e., ungodly Jews) will be rooted out (see Eze 20:34–44, note). (2) The believing remnant of Israel (i.e., the survivors at the end of the age) and the faithful in Israel of past generations constitute "all Israel" (see Eze 37:12–14, note).

11:29 GOD'S GIFTS AND HIS CALL. These words refer to the privileges of Israel mentioned in 9:4–5 and 11:26. The context clearly refers to Israel and God's purposes for her, and not to the spiritual gifts or ministerial calling associated with the Holy Spirit's work within the church (cf. 12:6–8; 1Co 12). The calling, placing and maintaining of someone in the office of pastor or overseer must be according to the personal character qualifications and spiritual history of the individual (see article on MORAL QUALIFICATIONS FOR OVERSEERS, p. 1882).

12:1 YOUR BODIES AS LIVING SACRIFICES. Believers must possess a single-minded passion to please God in love, devotion, praise and holiness, and to offer their bodies for his service. (1) Our greatest desire should be to live lives of holiness and to be accepted by God. This requires separating ourselves from the world and drawing ever nearer to God (v. 2). We must live for God, worship him, obey him, take his side against sin and for righteousness, resist and hate evil, perform works of kindness for others, imitate Christ, follow him, serve him, live by the Spirit and be filled with the Spirit. (2) We must offer our bodies to God as dead to sin and as the temple of the Holy Spirit (see next note; cf. 1Co 6:15,19).

offer your bodies as living sacrifices,[g]
holy and pleasing to God—this is your
spiritual[x] act of worship. **2**Do not conform[h] any longer to the pattern of this
world,[i] but be transformed by the renewing of your mind.[j] Then you will
be able to test and approve what God's
will is[k]—his good, pleasing[l] and
1Co 2:6-16 perfect will.
3For by the grace given me[m] I say
to every one of you: Do not think of
yourself more highly than you ought,
but rather think of yourself with sober
judgment, in accordance with the measure of faith God has given you. **4**Just
as each of us has one body with many
members, and these members do not
all have the same function,[n] **5**so in
Christ we who are many form one
body,[o] and each member belongs to
all the others. **6**We have different
gifts,[p] according to the grace given
us. If a man's gift is prophesying,[q] let
him use it in proportion to his[y] faith.[r]
7If it is serving, let him serve; if it is
teaching, let him teach;[s] **8**if it is encouraging, let him encourage;[t] if it is
contributing to the needs of others, let
him give generously;[u] if it is leadership, let him govern diligently; if it is
showing mercy, let him do it cheerful-
ly. Ro 15

Love

9Love must be sincere.[v] Hate what
is evil; cling to what is good.[w] **10**Be
devoted to one another in brotherly

12:1 [g] Ro 6:13,16,19; 1Co 6:20; 1Pe 2:5 **12:2** [h] 1Pe 1:14 [i] 1Co 1:20; 2Co 10:2; 1Jn 2:15 [j] Eph 4:23 [k] S Eph 5:17 [l] S 1Ti 5:4 **12:3** [m] Ro 15:15; 1Co 15:10; Gal 2:9; Eph 3:7; 4:7; 1Pe 4:10,11 **12:4** [n] 1Co 12:12-14; Eph 4:16 **12:5** [o] 1Co 6:15; 10:17; 12:12,20, 27; Eph 2:16; 4:4, 25; 5:30; Col 3:15 **12:6** [p] 1Co 7:7; 12:4,8-10 [q] S Eph 4:11 [r] 1Pe 4:10,11 **12:7** [s] S Eph 4:11 **12:8** [t] Ac 11:23; 13:15; 15:32 [u] 2Co 8:2; 9:5-13 **12:9** [v] 2Co 6:6; 1Ti 1:5 [w] Ps 97:10; Am 5:15; 1Th 5:21,22

[x] *1* Or *reasonable* [y] *6* Or *in agreement with the*

12:2 DO NOT CONFORM . . . BUT BE TRANSFORMED. Paul implies several things here: (1) We must realize that the present world system is evil (Ac 2:40; Gal 1:4) and under Satan's rule (Jn 12:31; 1Jn 5:19; see article on THE CHRISTIAN'S RELATIONSHIP TO THE WORLD, p. 1976).

(2) We must stand against the prevailing and popular forms of the spirit of this world, proclaiming instead the eternal truths and righteous standards of God's Word for Christ's sake (1Co 1:17–24).

(3) We must despise what is evil, love what is righteous (v. 9; 1Jn 2:15–17; see Heb 1:9, note) and refuse to yield to the various types of worldliness surrounding the church, such as greed, selfishness, expediency, humanistic thinking, political maneuvering for power, envy, hatred, revenge, impurity, filthy language, ungodly entertainment, tempting and immodest attire, immorality, drugs, alcohol and worldly companions.

(4) We must have our minds conformed to God's way of thinking (1Co 2:16; Php 2:5) by reading and meditating on his Word (Ps 119:11,148; Jn 8:31–32; 15:7). We must have our plans and ambitions determined by heavenly and eternal truths, not by this evil, temporal and transient age.

12:6 DIFFERENT GIFTS, ACCORDING TO THE GRACE. Paul lists what can be called the gifts of grace (Gk *charismata*). They are inward desires or dispositions as well as enablements or abilities (Php 2:13) given by the Holy Spirit to individuals in the congregation to build up God's people and express God's love to others (see 1Co 12:1, note; 14:12,26; 1Pe 4:10). Every believer has at least one such gift (1Co 12:11; 1Pe 4:10). However, one's primary gift does not exclude the exercise of any other of the gifts as need may arise. Paul's list of seven grace gifts should be taken as representative rather than exhaustive (see 1Co 12–14 for further explanation of spiritual gifts).

12:6 PROPHESYING. For comments on the gift of prophecy, see articles on SPIRITUAL GIFTS FOR BELIEVERS, p. 1770, and THE MINISTRY GIFTS OF THE CHURCH, p. 1830.

12:7 SERVING . . . TEACHING. (1) "Serving" is the God-given desire, ability and power to give practical assistance to members and leaders of the church to help them fulfill their responsibilities to God (cf. Ac 6:2–3). (2) "Teaching" is the God-given desire, ability and power to examine and study God's Word, and to clarify, defend and proclaim its truth in such a way that others grow in grace and godliness (1Co 2:10–16; 1Ti 4:16; 6:3; 2Ti 4:1–2; see 2Ti 2:2, note; see articles on THE MINISTRY GIFTS OF THE CHURCH, p. 1830, and BIBLE TRAINING FOR CHRISTIANS, p. 1894).

12:8 ENCOURAGING . . . CONTRIBUTING . . . LEADERSHIP . . . SHOWING MERCY. (1) "Encouraging" is the God-given desire, ability and power to proclaim God's Word in such a way that it touches the heart, conscience and will of the hearers, stimulates faith, and produces a deeper commitment to Christ and a more thorough separation from the world (see Ac 11:23; 14:22; 15:30–32; 16:40; 1Co 14:3; 1Th 5:14–22; Heb 10:24–25).

(2) "Contributing" is the God-given desire, ability and power, because one has resources above life's basic needs, to give freely of one's personal possessions to the needs of God's work or people (2Co 8:1–8; Eph 4:28).

(3) "Leadership" is the God-given desire, ability and power to guide and oversee the various activities of the church for the spiritual good of all (Eph 4:11–12; 1Ti 3:1–7; Heb 13:7,17,24; see article on THE MINISTRY GIFTS OF THE CHURCH, p. 1830).

(4) "Showing mercy" is the God-given desire, ability and power to help and comfort those in need or distress (cf. Eph 2:4).

12:9 HATE WHAT IS EVIL. See Heb 1:9, note.

12:10 BE DEVOTED TO ONE ANOTHER. All those devoted in faith to Jesus Christ must be devoted to one another as brothers and sisters in

love.[x] Honor one another above yourselves.[y] 11Never be lacking in zeal, but keep your spiritual fervor,[z] serving the Lord. 12Be joyful in hope,[a] patient in affliction,[b] faithful in prayer.[c] 13Share with God's people who are in need.[d] Practice hospitality.[e]

14Bless those who persecute you;[f] bless and do not curse. 15Rejoice with those who rejoice; mourn with those who mourn.[g] 16Live in harmony with one another.[h] Do not be proud, but be willing to associate with people of low position.[z] Do not be conceited.[i]

17Do not repay anyone evil for evil.[j] Be careful to do what is right in the eyes of everybody.[k] 18If it is possible, as far as it depends on you, live at peace with everyone.[l] 19Do not take revenge,[m] my friends, but leave room for God's wrath, for it is written: "It is mine to avenge; I will repay,"[a][n] says the Lord. 20On the contrary:

"If your enemy is hungry, feed
    him;
  if he is thirsty, give him
    something to drink.
In doing this, you will heap
    burning coals on his
    head."[b][o]

21Do not be overcome by evil, but overcome evil with good.

Submission to the Authorities

13 Everyone must submit himself to the governing authorities,[p] for there is no authority except that which God has established.[q] The authorities that exist have been established by God. 2Consequently, he who rebels against the authority is rebelling against what God has instituted,[r] and those who do so will bring judgment on themselves. 3For rulers hold no terror for those who do right, but for those who do wrong. Do you want to be free from fear of the one in authority? Then do what is right and he will commend you.[s] 4For he is God's servant to do you good. But if you do wrong, be afraid, for he does not bear the sword for nothing. He is God's servant, an agent of wrath to bring punishment on the wrongdoer.[t] 5Therefore, it is necessary to submit to the authorities, not only because of possible punishment but also because of conscience.[u]

6This is also why you pay taxes,[v] for the authorities are God's servants, who give their full time to governing. 7Give everyone what you owe him: If you owe taxes, pay taxes;[w] if revenue, then revenue; if respect, then respect; if honor, then honor.

Responsibility Toward Others

8Let no debt remain outstanding, except the continuing debt to love one another, for he who loves his fellowman has fulfilled the law.[x] 9The commandments, "Do not commit adultery," "Do not murder," "Do not steal," "Do not covet,"[c][y] and whatever other commandment there may be, are summed

12:10 [x]Ps 133:1; 1Th 4:9; Heb 13:1; 1Pe 1:22 [y]Php 2:3 **12:11** [z]Ac 18:25 **12:12** [a]Ro 5:2 [b]Heb 10:32,36 [c]S Lk 18:1 **12:13** [d]S Ac 24:17 [e]2Ki 4:10; Job 31:32; 1Ti 3:2; 5:10; Heb 13:2; 1Pe 4:9 **12:14** [f]S Mt 5:44 **12:15** [g]Job 30:25 **12:16** [h]S Ro 15:5 [i]ver 3; Ps 131:1; Isa 5:21; Jer 45:5; Ro 11:25 **12:17** [j]ver 19; Pr 20:22; 24:29 [k]2Co 8:21 **12:18** [l]S Mk 9:50; S Ro 14:19 **12:19** [m]ver 17; Lev 19:18; Pr 20:22; 24:29 [n]Dt 32:35; Ge 50:19; 1Sa 26:10; Ps 94:1; Jer 51:36 **12:20** [o]Pr 25:21, 22; Ex 23:4; Mt 5:44; Lk 6:27 **13:1** [p]Tit 3:1; 1Pe 2:13,14 [q]Da 2:21; 4:17; Jn 19:11

13:2 [r]Ex 16:8 **13:3** [s]1Pe 2:14 **13:4** [t]1Th 4:6 **13:5** [u]Pr 24:21, 22 **13:6** [v]Mt 22:17 **13:7** [w]Mt 17:25; 22:17,21; Lk 23:2 **13:8** [x]ver 10; S Mt 5:43; Jn 13:34; Col 3:14 **13:9** [y]Ex 20:13-15,17; Dt 5:17-19,21

[z] *16* Or *willing to do menial work*
[a] *19* Deut. 32:35 [b] *20* Prov. 25:21,22
[c] *9* Exodus 20:13-15,17; Deut. 5:17-19,21

Christ (1Th 4:9–10), with a sincere, kind and tender affection. We must be concerned for our brothers' and sisters' welfare, needs and spiritual condition, sympathizing with them and helping them in their sorrows and troubles. We must honor one another, eagerly respecting the good qualities in other believers (see Jn 13:34–35, notes).

13:1 SUBMIT ... TO THE GOVERNING AUTHORITIES. God commands Christians to obey the state, for the state as an institution is ordained and established by God. God has instituted government because in this fallen world we need certain restraints to protect us from the chaos and lawlessness that is a natural result of sin. (1) The civil government, as does all of life, stands under God's law. (2) God has ordained the state to be an agent of justice, to restrain evil by punishing the wrongdoer and to protect the good in society (vv. 3–4; 1Pe 2:13–17). (3) Paul describes government as it should be. When it abandons its proper function, it is no longer from God nor operating according to his purpose. For example, when the state requires something contrary to God's Word, Christians must obey God rather than other humans (Ac 5:29; cf. Da 3:16–18; 6:6–10). (4) It is the duty of all believers to pray for those in authority (1Ti 2:1–2).

13:4 THE SWORD. The sword is frequently associated with death as an instrument of execution (Mt 26:52; Lk 21:24; Ac 12:2; 16:27; Heb 11:34; Rev 13:10). God has clearly commanded the execution of dangerous criminals who have committed vicious crimes (Ge 9:6; Nu 35:31,33).

13:8 LET NO DEBT REMAIN OUTSTANDING. Believers should have no unpaid debts. This does not mean that we are prohibited from borrowing from others in case of serious need (cf. Ex 22:25; Ps 37:26; Mt 5:42; Lk 6:35). But it does speak against both going into debt for unnecessary things and showing an attitude of indifference in repaying debts (cf. Ps 37:21). The only debt from which there is no release is love for one another.

up[z] in this one rule: "Love your neighbor as yourself."[d][a] **10**Love does no
harm to its neighbor. Therefore love is
the fulfillment of the law.[b]
11And do this, understanding the
present time. The hour has come[c] for
you to wake up from your slumber,[d]
because our salvation is nearer now
than when we first believed. **12**The
night is nearly over; the day is almost
here.[e] So let us put aside the deeds of
darkness[f] and put on the armor[g] of
light. **13**Let us behave decently, as in
the daytime, not in orgies and drunkenness,[h] not in sexual immorality and
debauchery, not in dissension and jealousy.[i] **14**Rather, clothe yourselves
with the Lord Jesus Christ,[j] and do
Gal 5:13-18 not think about how to gratify the desires of the sinful nature.[e][k]

The Weak and the Strong

14 Accept him whose faith is
weak,[l] without passing judgment on disputable matters. **2**One
man's faith allows him to eat everything, but another man, whose faith is
weak, eats only vegetables.[m] **3**The
man who eats everything must not
look down on[n] him who does not, and
the man who does not eat everything
must not condemn[o] the man who
does, for God has accepted him. **4**Who
are you to judge someone else's servant?[p] To his own master he stands or
falls. And he will stand, for the Lord is
able to make him stand.
5One man considers one day more
sacred than another;[q] another man
considers every day alike. Each one
should be fully convinced in his own
mind. **6**He who regards one day as special, does so to the Lord. He who eats
meat, eats to the Lord, for he gives
thanks to God;[r] and he who abstains,
does so to the Lord and gives thanks
to God. **7**For none of us lives to himself
alone[s] and none of us dies to himself
alone. **8**If we live, we live to the Lord;
and if we die, we die to the Lord. So,
whether we live or die, we belong to the
Lord.[t]
9For this very reason, Christ died
and returned to life[u] so that he might
be the Lord of both the dead and the
living.[v] **10**You, then, why do you judge
your brother? Or why do you look down
on[w] your brother? For we will all stand
before God's judgment seat.[x] **11**It is
written:

> " 'As surely as I live,'[y] says the
> Lord,
> 'every knee will bow before me;

13:9 [z] Mt 7:12 [a] Lev 19:18; S Mt 5:43 **13:10** [b] S ver 8; ver 9 **13:11** [c] 1Co 7:29-31; 10:11; Jas 5:8; 1Pe 4:7; 1Jn 2:18; Rev 22:10 [d] Eph 5:14; 1Th 5:5,6 **13:12** [e] Heb 10:25; 1Jn 2:8 [f] Eph 5:11 [g] Eph 6:11,13; 1Th 5:8 **13:13** [h] S Eph 5:18 [i] Lk 21:34; Gal 5:20,21; Eph 5:18; 1Pe 4:3 **13:14** [j] Gal 3:27; Eph 4:24; Col 3:10,12 [k] S Gal 5:24 **14:1** [l] Ro 15:1; 1Co 8:9-12; 9:22 **14:2** [m] ver 14 **14:3** [n] ver 10; Lk 18:9 [o] ver 10, 13; Col 2:16 **14:4** [p] S Mt 7:1 **14:5** [q] Gal 4:10; Col 2:16 **14:6** [r] S Mt 14:19; 1Co 10:30,31; 1Ti 4:3,4 **14:7** [s] 2Co 5:15; Gal 2:20 **14:8** [t] Php 1:20 **14:9** [u] Rev 1:18; 2:8 [v] S Ac 10:42; 2Co 5:15 **14:10** [w] ver 3; S Mt 7:1 [x] S 2Co 5:10 **14:11** [y] Isa 49:18

[d] 9 Lev. 19:18 [e] 14 Or *the flesh*

13:10 LOVE DOES NO HARM TO ITS NEIGHBOR. "Love" is fulfilled not only by positive commands (12:9–21; 1Co 13:4,6–7), but also by negative ones. All of the commandments mentioned here are negative in form (v. 9; cf. 1Co 13:4–6). (1) Love is positive; yet it is also negative in that it accounts for the human propensity toward sin, selfishness and cruelty. Eight of the Ten Commandments are negative because sin comes naturally, while goodness does not. The first evidence of Christian love is a turning from sin and all that brings harm and sorrow to others. (2) The idea that Christian ethics must be only positive is a fallacy based on the ideas of a society that seeks to free itself from prohibitions that curb the sinful nature's unrestrained desires (Gal 5:19–21).

13:12 THE NIGHT IS NEARLY OVER. Paul believed in the Lord's imminent return to transfer the faithful of his churches to heaven (see Jn 14:3, note; see article on THE RAPTURE, p. 1864), an event that Paul believed could happen even in his generation. Christ warned that he would return at a time when the faithful were sure that he would not come (see Mt 24:42,44 notes). For this reason, God's children must always be spiritually ready and must "put aside the deeds of darkness" (see Lk 12:35, note).

13:14 CLOTHE YOURSELVES WITH THE LORD JESUS CHRIST. We must be so united and identified with Christ that we imitate his life as our pattern for living, adopt his principles, obey his commands and become like him. This calls for a complete rejection of immorality and the acts of the sinful nature (cf. Gal 5:19–21).

14:2 EAT EVERYTHING . . . EATS ONLY VEGETABLES. A number of believers in Rome were divided over a disputable issue: some were committed to eating only vegetables, while others were eating vegetables and all other foods, including meat. Paul states that eating in and of itself is not a moral matter, but that one's personal attitude about what to eat could lead to unjustly condemning one another.

14:5 CONSIDERS ONE DAY MORE SACRED THAN ANOTHER. This probably refers to the special feast days of the OT ceremonial law. Some Christians apparently still regarded the holy days as having abiding usefulness, whereas many others were ignoring them. In his answer, Paul does not attempt to abrogate God's principle of setting aside one day in seven as a special day of rest and worship (see Mt 12:1, note). God himself set aside one day in seven to rest from daily work (Ge 2:2–3; cf. Ex 20:11; 31:17; Isa 58:13–14). In the NT the first day of the week is recognized as having a special significance because of Jesus' resurrection (Ac 20:7; 1Co 16:2; Rev 1:10).

every tongue will confess to
God.' "[fz]

12So then, each of us will give an account of himself to God.[a]

13Therefore let us stop passing judgment[b] on one another. Instead, make
up your mind not to put any stumbling
block or obstacle in your brother's
way.[c] **14**As one who is in the Lord
Jesus, I am fully convinced that no
food[g] is unclean in itself.[d] But if anyone regards something as unclean,
then for him it is unclean.[e] **15**If your
brother is distressed because of what
you eat, you are no longer acting in
love.[f] Do not by your eating destroy
your brother for whom Christ died.[g]
16Do not allow what you consider good
to be spoken of as evil.[h] **17**For the
kingdom of God is not a matter of eating and drinking,[i] but of righteousness, peace[j] and joy in the Holy Spirit,[k] **18**because anyone who serves
Christ in this way is pleasing to God
and approved by men.[l]

19Let us therefore make every effort
to do what leads to peace[m] and to mutual edification.[n] **20**Do not destroy the
work of God for the sake of food.[o] All
food is clean,[p] but it is wrong for a
man to eat anything that causes someone else to stumble.[q] **21**It is better not
to eat meat or drink wine or to do anything else that will cause your brother
to fall.[r]

22So whatever you believe about
these things keep between yourself
and God. Blessed is the man who does
not condemn[s] himself by what he approves. **23**But the man who has
doubts[t] is condemned if he eats, because his eating is not from faith; and
everything that does not come from
faith is sin.

15 We who are strong ought to
bear with the failings of the
weak[u] and not to please ourselves.
2Each of us should please his neighbor
for his good,[v] to build him up.[w] **3**For
even Christ did not please himself[x]
but, as it is written: "The insults of
those who insult you have fallen on
me."[hy] **4**For everything that was
written in the past was written to teach
us,[z] so that through endurance and
the encouragement of the Scriptures
we might have hope.

5May the God who gives endurance
and encouragement give you a spirit of
unity[a] among yourselves as you follow Christ Jesus, **6**so that with one
heart and mouth you may glorify[b] the
God and Father[c] of our Lord Jesus
Christ.

7Accept one another,[d] then, just as
Christ accepted you, in order to bring
praise to God. **8**For I tell you that
Christ has become a servant of the
Jews[ie] on behalf of God's truth, to
confirm the promises[f] made to the pa-

14:11 [z]Isa 45:23; Php 2:10,11
14:12 [a]Mt 12:36; 1Pe 4:5
14:13 [b]ver 1; S Mt 7:1 [c]S 2Co 6:3
14:14 [d]ver 20; S Ac 10:15 [e]1Co 8:7
14:15 [f]Eph 5:2 [g]ver 20; 1Co 8:11
14:16 [h]1Co 10:30
14:17 [i]1Co 8:8 [j]Isa 32:17 [k]Ro 15:13; Gal 5:22
14:18 [l]Lk 2:52; Ac 24:16; 2Co 8:21
14:19 [m]Ps 34:14; Ro 12:18; 1Co 7:15; 2Ti 2:22; Heb 12:14 [n]Ro 15:2; 1Co 14:3-5,12,17,26; 2Co 12:19; Eph 4:12,29
14:20 [o]ver 15 [p]ver 14; S Ac 10:15 [q]ver 13; 1Co 8:9-12
14:21 [r]S Mt 5:29
14:22 [s]1Jn 3:21
14:23 [t]ver 5
15:1 [u]Ro 14:1; 1Th 5:14
15:2 [v]S 1Co 10:24 [w]S Ro 14:19
15:3 [x]2Co 8:9 [y]Ps 69:9
15:4 [z]S Ro 4:23,24
15:5 [a]Ro 12:16; 1Co 1:10; 2Co 13:11; Eph 4:3; Php 2:2; Col 3:14; 1Pe 3:8
15:6 [b]Ps 34:3 [c]Rev 1:6
15:7 [d]Ro 14:1
15:8 [e]Mt 15:24; Ac 3:25,26 [f]2Co 1:20

f *11* Isaiah 45:23 g *14* Or *that nothing*
h *3* Psalm 69:9 i *8* Greek *circumcision*

14:13 STOP PASSING JUDGMENT. Though we must refrain from judging each other in trivial matters, believers should consider how to encourage each other to true Christlikeness and holiness when it concerns faith, doctrine and morals (Heb 10:24). This involves sincerely evaluating (1Th 5:21; 1Jn 4:1), correcting and rebuking one another in love and humility (Lk 17:3), and, when necessary, exercising church discipline (cf. 1Co 5:12–13; 2Th 3:6,14; 1Ti 5:20–21; 2Ti 2:24–26; 4:2).

14:21 NOT TO ... DRINK WINE. The Bible gave the NT Christian two major laws regarding wine (Gk *oinos*), which included both unfermented and fermented fruit of the vine (see article on WINE IN NEW TESTAMENT TIMES (1), p. 1534): (1) the law of abstinence from wine when it is fermented and intoxicating (see Pr 23:31, note; 1Th 5:6, note; Tit 2:2, note); (2) the law of Christian love, which causes a person to abstain from what might lead others into harm (cf. 1Co 8:13; 10:27–32). Paul affirms that, in a pagan society (i.e., in a non-Jewish environment) where intoxicating beverages and drunkenness are prevalent, it is better to refuse to drink even the unfermented wines than to drink something that might cause another Christian to be led into sin. The use of nonintoxicating wines were technically safe for some believers, but they might influence weaker believers to drink fermented wine and thereby expose them to harm and drunkenness. Timothy carefully followed this law of Christian love (see 1Ti 5:23, note).

15:3 CHRIST DID NOT PLEASE HIMSELF. Disregarding the convictions of others in order to please ourselves destroys God's work (14:15,20); living sacrificially so as to help others will strengthen God's kingdom. Paul points to Christ's example, who did not live for his own interest but for the interests of others.

15:4 EVERYTHING THAT WAS WRITTEN IN THE PAST. The OT Scriptures are of utmost importance to the Christian's spiritual life. The wisdom and moral laws of God concerning every aspect of life, as well as his revelation concerning himself, salvation and Christ's coming, have permanent value (2Ti 3:16; see Mt 5:17, note; see article on THE OLD TESTAMENT LAW, p. 118).

triarchs [9]so that the Gentiles[g] may glorify God[h] for his mercy, as it is written:

"Therefore I will praise you among
the Gentiles;
I will sing hymns to your
name."[j][i]

[10]Again, it says,

"Rejoice, O Gentiles, with his
people."[k][j]

[11]And again,

"Praise the Lord, all you Gentiles,
and sing praises to him, all you
Eph 1:3-6 peoples."[l][k]

[12]And again, Isaiah says,

"The Root of Jesse[l] will spring
up,
one who will arise to rule over
the nations;
the Gentiles will hope in him."[m][m]

[13]May the God of hope fill you with all joy and peace[n] as you trust in him, so that you may overflow with hope by the power of the Holy Spirit.[o]

Paul the Minister to the Gentiles

[14]I myself am convinced, my brothers, that you yourselves are full of goodness,[p] complete in knowledge[q] and competent to instruct one another. [15]I have written you quite boldly on some points, as if to remind you of them again, because of the grace God gave me[r] [16]to be a minister of Christ Jesus to the Gentiles[s] with the priestly duty of proclaiming the gospel of God,[t] so that the Gentiles might become an offering[u] acceptable to God, sanctified by the Holy Spirit.

[17]Therefore I glory in Christ Jesus[v] in my service to God.[w] [18]I will not venture to speak of anything except what Christ has accomplished through me in leading the Gentiles[x] to obey God[y] by what I have said and done— [19]by the power of signs and miracles,[z] through the power of the Spirit.[a] So from Jerusalem[b] all the way around to Illyricum, I have fully proclaimed the gospel of Christ.[c] [20]It has always been my ambition to preach the gospel[d] where Christ was not known, so that I would not be building on someone else's foundation.[e] [21]Rather, as it is written:

"Those who were not told about
him will see,
and those who have not heard
will understand."[n][f]

[22]This is why I have often been hindered from coming to you.[g]

Paul's Plan to Visit Rome

[23]But now that there is no more place for me to work in these regions, and since I have been longing for many years to see you,[h] [24]I plan to do so when I go to Spain.[i] I hope to visit you while passing through and to have you assist[j] me on my journey there, after I have enjoyed your company for a while. [25]Now, however, I am on my way to Jerusalem[k] in the service[l] of the saints[m] there. [26]For Macedonia[n] and Achaia[o] were pleased to make a contribution for the poor among the saints in Jerusalem.[p] [27]They were pleased to do it, and indeed they owe it to them. For if the Gentiles have shared in the Jews' spiritual blessings, they owe it to the Jews to share with them their material blessings.[q] [28]So after I have completed this task and have made sure that they have received this fruit, I will go to Spain[r] and visit you on the way. [29]I know that when I come to you,[s] I will come in the full measure of the blessing of Christ.

1C 1:7

15:9 [g]S Ro 3:29 [h]S Mt 9:8 [i]2Sa 22:50; Ps 18:49
15:10 [j]Dt 32:43; Isa 66:10
15:11 [k]Ps 117:1
15:12 [l]S Rev 5:5 [m]Isa 11:10; Mt 12:21
15:13 [n]Ro 14:17 [o]ver 19; 1Co 2:4; 4:20; 1Th 1:5
15:14 [p]Eph 5:9 [q]S 2Co 8:7; 2Pe 1:12
15:15 [r]S Ro 12:3
15:16 [s]S Ac 9:15 [t]ver 19; S Ro 1:1 [u]Isa 66:20
15:17 [v]Php 3:3 [w]Heb 2:17
15:18 [x]Ac 15:12; 21:19; Ro 1:5 [y]Ro 16:26
15:19 [z]S Jn 4:48; Ac 19:11 [a]S ver 13 [b]Ac 22:17-21 [c]S 2Co 2:12
15:20 [d]Ro 1:15 [e]2Co 10:15,16
15:21 [f]Isa 52:15
15:22 [g]Ro 1:13
15:23 [h]Ac 19:21; Ro 1:10,11
15:24 [i]ver 28 [j]1Co 16:6; Tit 3:13
15:25 [k]S Ac 19:21 [l]S Ac 24:17 [m]S Ac 9:13
15:26 [n]S Ac 16:9 [o]S Ac 18:12 [p]S Ac 24:17
15:27 [q]1Co 9:11
15:28 [r]ver 24
15:29 [s]Ro 1:10, 11

j 9 2 Samuel 22:50; Psalm 18:49
k 10 Deut. 32:43
l 11 Psalm 117:1
m 12 Isaiah 11:10
n 21 Isaiah 52:15

15:17 I GLORY. It is not wrong to speak excitedly and joyfully about what God is doing through us if it is done in a spirit of humility and thankfulness to God. Glorying should not be in mere numbers, but in a ministry that produces the obedience of faith in word and deed and that issues from a genuine work and manifestation of the Spirit in power (vv. 18–19).

15:20 WHERE CHRIST WAS NOT KNOWN. Paul's policy of ministry was missionary-centered. He chose to direct his labors in areas where the gospel had not been preached sufficiently, thereby enabling those who had not heard to have opportunity to accept Christ (v. 21).

15:29 FULL MEASURE OF THE BLESSING OF CHRIST. Paul's ministry was accompanied by the fullness of Christ's blessing, power, grace and presence. Whenever he ministered, this blessing would be imparted to other believers. We who serve the Lord and his churches should seek the same fullness in our ministries.

[30]I urge you, brothers, by our Lord Jesus Christ and by the love of the Spirit,[t] to join me in my struggle by praying to God for me.[u] [31]Pray that I may be rescued[v] from the unbelievers in Judea and that my service[w] in Jerusalem may be acceptable to the saints[x] there, [32]so that by God's will[y] I may come to you[z] with joy and together with you be refreshed.[a] [33]The God of peace[b] be with you all. Amen.

Personal Greetings

16 I commend[c] to you our sister Phoebe, a servant[o] of the church in Cenchrea.[d] [2]I ask you to receive her in the Lord[e] in a way worthy of the saints[f] and to give her any help she may need from you, for she has been a great help to many people, including me.

[3]Greet Priscilla[p] and Aquila,[g] my fellow workers[h] in Christ Jesus.[i] [4]They risked their lives for me. Not only I but all the churches of the Gentiles are grateful to them.

[5]Greet also the church that meets at their house.[j]

Greet my dear friend Epenetus, who was the first convert[k] to Christ in the province of Asia.[l]

[6]Greet Mary, who worked very hard for you.

[7]Greet Andronicus and Junias, my relatives[m] who have been in prison with me.[n] They are outstanding among the apostles, and they were in Christ[o] before I was.

[8]Greet Ampliatus, whom I love in the Lord.

[9]Greet Urbanus, our fellow worker in Christ,[p] and my dear friend Stachys.

[10]Greet Apelles, tested and approved in Christ.[q]

Greet those who belong to the household[r] of Aristobulus.

[11]Greet Herodion, my relative.[s]

Greet those in the household[t] of Narcissus who are in the Lord.

[12]Greet Tryphena and Tryphosa, those women who work hard in the Lord.

Greet my dear friend Persis, another woman who has worked very hard in the Lord.

[13]Greet Rufus,[u] chosen[v] in the Lord, and his mother, who has been a mother to me, too.

[14]Greet Asyncritus, Phlegon, Hermes, Patrobas, Hermas and the brothers with them.

[15]Greet Philologus, Julia, Nereus and his sister, and Olympas and all the saints[w] with them.[x]

[16]Greet one another with a holy kiss.[y]

All the churches of Christ send greetings.

[17]I urge you, brothers, to watch out for those who cause divisions and put obstacles in your way that are contrary to the teaching you have learned.[z] Keep away from them.[a] [18]For such people are not serving our Lord Christ,[b] but their own appetites.[c] By smooth talk and flattery they deceive[d] the minds of naive people. [19]Everyone has heard[e] about your obedience, so I am full of joy over you; but I want you

15:30 [t]Gal 5:22; Col 1:8 [u]2Co 1:11; Col 4:12 **15:31** [v]2Co 1:10; 2Th 3:2; 2Ti 3:11; 2Pe 2:9 [w]ver 25; S Ac 24:17 [x]S Ac 9:13 **15:32** [y]S Ac 18:21 [z]Ro 1:10,13 [a]1Co 16:18; Phm 7 **15:33** [b]Ro 16:20; 2Co 13:11; Php 4:9; 1Th 5:23; 2Th 3:16; Heb 13:20 **16:1** [c]S 2Co 3:1 [d]Ac 18:18 **16:2** [e]Php 2:29 [f]S Ac 9:13 **16:3** [g]S Ac 18:2 [h]S Php 2:25 [i]ver 7,9,10; Ro 8:1,39; 1Co 1:30; 2Co 5:17; Gal 1:22; 5:6; Eph 1:13 **16:5** [j]1Co 16:19; Col 4:15; Phm 2 [k]1Co 16:15 [l]S Ac 2:9 **16:7** [m]ver 11,21 [n]Col 4:10; Phm 23 [o]S ver 3 **16:9** [p]S ver 3 **16:10** [q]S ver 3 [r]S Ac 11:14 **16:11** [s]ver 7,21 [t]S Ac 11:14 **16:13** [u]Mk 15:21 [v]S 2Jn 1 **16:15** [w]ver 2; S Ac 9:13 [x]ver 14 **16:16** [y]1Co 16:20; 2Co 13:12; 1Th 5:26; 1Pe 5:14 **16:17** [z]Gal 1:8,9; 1Ti 1:3; 6:3 [a]Mt 18:15-17; 1Co 5:11; 2Th 3:6, 14; 2Ti 3:5; Tit 3:10; 2Jn 10 **16:18** [b]Ro 14:18 [c]Php 3:19 [d]2Sa 15:6; Ps 12:2; Isa 30:10; Col 2:4 **16:19** [e]Ro 1:8

[o] *1* Or *deaconess* [p] *3* Greek *Prisca*, a variant of *Priscilla*

16:1 PHOEBE. Phoebe was probably the one who delivered this letter to the Romans. She was a servant (or woman deacon) in the church at Cenchrea who ministered to the poor, the sick and the needy, as well as assisted missionaries such as Paul. Paul's greetings to no less than eight women in this chapter indicate that women performed distinguished service in the churches.

16:7 OUTSTANDING AMONG THE APOSTLES. Andronicus and Junias are called apostles. The word "apostles" here is used in the general sense to refer to traveling messengers or missionaries rather than in the special sense of the word "apostle" (1Co 9:1–2; 2Co 8:23; 12:2; Php 2:25; cf. Ac 14:4, note; see article on THE MINISTRY GIFTS OF THE CHURCH, p. 1830).

16:17–18 WATCH OUT FOR THOSE. At the end of his letter, Paul gives a strong warning to the church in Rome to be alert to all those who do damage to the church by corrupting the "teaching" of Paul and the other apostles. They are to "watch out for" the proponents of false doctrine and "keep away from them" and their ministry. These may have been antinomians (i.e., against the law), who taught that because salvation is by grace, saving faith does not necessarily include obedience to Christ (cf. 6:1–2; 2Co 4:2; 11:3; Eph 4:14; Rev 2:4–5; see article on FALSE TEACHERS, p. 1506). They believed that a person could live in sin and reject God's moral law, and yet possess eternal salvation. These false teachers were eloquent orators, speaking with comforting words and flattering speeches (cf. Jude 16), but in reality they were deceivers.

16:19 INNOCENT ABOUT WHAT IS EVIL. The word "innocent" (Gk *akeraios*) means "un-

to be wise about what is good, and innocent about what is evil.[f]
20The God of peace[g] will soon
crush[h] Satan[i] under your feet.

The grace of our Lord Jesus be with
you.[j]
21Timothy,[k] my fellow worker,
sends his greetings to you, as do Lucius,[l] Jason[m] and Sosipater, my relatives.[n]
22I, Tertius, who wrote down this
letter, greet you in the Lord.
23Gaius,[o] whose hospitality I and
the whole church here enjoy, sends you
his greetings.

Erastus,[p] who is the city's director
of public works, and our brother Quar-
tus send you their greetings.[q]

25Now to him who is able[q] to establish you by my gospel[r] and the proclamation of Jesus Christ, according to
the revelation of the mystery[s] hidden
for long ages past, 26but now revealed
and made known through the prophetic writings[t] by the command of the
eternal God, so that all nations might
believe and obey[u] him— 27to the only
wise God be glory forever through
Jesus Christ! Amen.[v]

16:19 [f]S 1Co 14:20 **16:20** [g]S Ro 15:33 [h]Ge 3:15 [i]S Mt 4:10 [j]2Co 13:14; S Gal 6:18; 1Th 5:28; Rev 22:21 **16:21** [k]S Ac 16:1 [l]Ac 13:1 [m]Ac 17:5 [n]ver 7,11 **16:23** [o]S Ac 19:29 [p]Ac 19:22; 2Ti 4:20 **16:25** [q]2Co 9:8; Eph 3:20; Jude 24 [r]Ro 2:16; 2Ti 2:8 [s]Isa 48:6; Eph 1:9; 3:3-6,9; Col 1:26,27; 2:2; 1Ti 3:16 **16:26** [t]Ro 1:2 [u]Ro 1:5 **16:27** [v]S Ro 11:36

[q]*23* Some manuscripts *their greetings. 24May the grace of our Lord Jesus Christ be with all of you. Amen.*

mixed" or "pure," i.e., innocent like a child whose mind has not yet been exposed to evil or mixed with the values of the world (cf. 1Co 14:20). (1) This Biblical principle is in direct opposition to the idea advocated by some that children of Christians should be exposed to sin, immorality, ungodliness and the things of Satan in order to learn to confront temptation. Some suggest that children need not be guarded from ungodliness. However, according to Biblical revelation, this philosophy is not only against God's will, but is compatible with Satan's own desire that everyone be exposed to the knowledge of good and evil (Ge 3:5).

(2) Knowledge of evil, along with continual exposure to Satan's ways, will lead many from the path of faith and obedience. Lot found this out to his deep sorrow when he lost his entire family (Ge 13:12–13; 19:1–38). Scripture warns that "bad company corrupts good character" (1Co 15:33), and that "Jesus Christ . . . gave himself . . . to rescue us from the present evil age" (Gal 1:3–4). Those who advocate exposing innocent children to an ungodly environment and/or influence are in danger of violating Jesus' warning in Mt 18:6.

(3) Believers should do all in their power to keep their children from being exposed to sin's deceitfulness and the perverseness of this generation. To refuse to protect our children disregards the Holy Spirit's desire that they be innocent about what is evil.

THE GIFTS OF THE HOLY SPIRIT

A. The Ministry Gifts of the Church

Gift	Definition	General References	Specific Examples
Apostle (Specific)	Those specifically commissioned by the resurrected Lord to establish the church and the original message of the gospel	Ac 4:33–37; 5:12,18–42; 6:6; 8:14,18; 9:27; 11:1; 15:1–6,22–23; 16:4; 1Co 9:5; 12:28–29; Gal 1:17; Eph 2:20; 4:11; Jude 17	12 apostles: Mt 10:2; Mk 3:14; Lk 6:13; Ac 1:15–26; Rev 21:14 Paul: Ro 1:1; 11:13; 1Co 1:1; 9:1–2; 15:9–10; 2Co 1:1; Gal 1:1; 1Ti 2:7 Peter: 1Pe 1:1; 2Pe 1:1
Apostle (General)	Any messenger commissioned as a missionary or for other special responsibilities	Ac 13:1–3; 1Co 12:28–29; Eph 4:11	Barnabas: Ac 14:4,14 Andronicus and Junias: Ro 16:7 Titus and others: 2Co 8:23 Epaphroditus: Php 2:25 James, Jesus' brother: Gal 1:19
Prophet	Those who spoke under the inspiration of the Holy Spirit, bringing a message from God to the church, and whose main motivation and concern were with the spiritual life and purity of the church	Ro 12:6; 1Co 12:10; 14:1–33; Eph 4:11; 1Th 5:20–21; 1Ti 1:18; 1Pe 4:11; 1Jn 4:1–3	Peter: Ac 2:14–40; 3:12–26; 4:8–12; 10:34–44 Paul: Ac 13:1,16–41 Barnabas: Ac 13:1 Simeon: Ac 13:1 Lucius: Ac 13:1 Manaen: Ac 13:1 Agabus: Ac 11:27–28; 21:10 Judas and Silas: Ac 15:32 John: Rev 1:1,3; 10:8–11; 11:18
Evangelist	Those gifted by God to proclaim the gospel to the unsaved	Eph 4:11	Philip: Ac 8:5–8,26–40; 21:8 Paul: Ac 26:16–18
Pastor (Elder or Overseer)	Those chosen and gifted to oversee the church and care for its spiritual needs	Ac 14:23; 15:1–6,22–23; 16:4; 20:17–38; Ro 12:8; Eph 4:11–12; Php 1:1; 1Ti 3:1–7; 5:17–20; Tit 1:5–9; Heb 13:17; 1Pe 5:1–5	Timothy: 1Ti 1:1–4; 4:12–16; 2Ti 1:1–6; 4:2,5 Titus: Tit 1:4–5 Peter: 1Pe 5:1 John: 1Jn 2:1,12–14 Gaius: 3Jn 1–7

Gift	Definition	General References	Specific Examples
Teacher	Those gifted to clarify and explain God's Word in order to build up the church	Ro 12:7; Eph 4:11–12; Col 3:16; 1Ti 3:2; 5:17; 2Ti 2:2,24	Paul: Ac 15:35; 20:20; 28:31; Ro 12:19–21; 13:8–10; 1Co 4:17; 1Ti 1:5; 4:16; 2Ti 1:11 Barnabas: Ac 15:35 Apollos: Ac 18:25–28 Timothy: 1Co 4:17; 1Ti 1:3–5; 4:11–13; 6:2; 2Ti 4:2 Titus: Tit 2:1–3,9–10
Deacon	Those chosen and gifted to render practical assistance to members of the church	Ac 6:1–6; Ro 12:7; Php 1:1; 1Ti 3:8–13; 1Pe 4:11	Seven deacons: Ac 6:5 Phoebe: Ro 16:1–2
Helper	Those gifted for a variety of helpful deeds	1Co 12:28	Paul: Ac 20:35 Lydia: Ac 16:14–15 Gaius: 3Jn 5–8
Administrator	Those gifted to guide and oversee the various activities of the church	1Co 12:7; Eph 4:11–12; 1Ti 3:1–7; Heb 13:7–17,24	Peter: Ac 6:3–4; 11:1–18 Paul: Ac 20:17–35; 1Co 11:23–24; 14; 16:1–9
Encourager	Those gifted to motivate other Christians to a deeper faith and dedication to Christ, a fuller manifestation of the fruit of the Holy Spirit, and a more complete separation from the world	Ro 12:8; 1Co 14:3; 1Th 5:11,14–22; Heb 10:24–25	Barnabas: Ac 11:23–24; 14:22 Paul: Ac 14:22; 16:40; 20:1; Ro 8:26–39; 12:1–2; 2Co 6:14—7:1; Gal 5:16–26 Judas and Silas: Ac 15:32; 16:40 Timothy: 1Th 3:2; 2Ti 4:2 Titus: Tit 2:6,13 Peter: 1Pe 5:1–2 John: 1Jn 2:15–17; 3:1–3
Giver	Those gifted to give freely of their resources to the needs of God's people	Ac 2:44–45; 4:34–35; 11:29–30; 1Co 16:1–4; 2Co 8—9; Eph 4:28; 1Ti 6:17–19; Heb 13:16; 1Jn 3:16–18	Barnabas: Ac 4:36–37 Christians in Macedonia: Ro 15:26–27; 2Co 8:1–5 Christians in Achaia: Ro 15:26–27; 2Co 9:2

Gift	Definition	General References	Specific Examples
Comforter	Those gifted to give comfort by acts of mercy to people in distress	Ro 12:8; 2Co 1:3–7	Paul: 2Co 1:4 Hebrew Christians: Heb 10:34 Various Christians: Col 4:10–11 Dorcas: Ac 9:36–39

B. Manifestations of the Holy Spirit through Individual Believers

Gift	Definition	General References	Specific Examples
Message of wisdom	An utterance from the Holy Spirit applying God's Word or wisdom to a specific situation	Ac 6:3; 1Co 12:8; 13:2,9,12	Stephen: Ac 6:10 James: Ac 15:13–21
Message of knowledge	An utterance from the Holy Spirit revealing knowledge about people, circumstances or Biblical truth	Ac 10:47–48; 13:2; 15:7–11; 1Co 12:8; 13:2,9,12; 14:25	Peter: Ac 5:9–10
Faith	Supernatural faith imparted by the Holy Spirit, enabling a Christian to believe God for the miraculous	Mt 21:21–22; Mk 9:23–24; 11:22–24; Lk 17:6; Ac 3:1–8; 6:5–8; 1Co 12:9; 13:2; Jas 5:14–15	A centurion: Mt 8:5–10 A sick woman: Mt 9:20–22 Two blind men: Mt 9:27–29 A Canaanite woman: Mt 15:22–28 A sinful woman: Lk 9:36–50 A leper: Lk 17:11–19
Healing	Restoring someone to physical health by divinely supernatural means	Mt 4:23–24; 8:16; 9:35; 10:1,8; Mk 1:32–34; 6:13; 16:18; Lk 4:40–41; 9:1–2; Jn 6:2; 14:12; Ac 4:30; 5:15–16; 19:11–12; 1Co 12:9,28,30	Jesus: see chart on THE MIRACLES OF JESUS, p. 1634 Apostles: see chart on THE MIRACLES OF THE APOSTLES, p. 1635
Miraculous powers	Divine supernatural power to alter the course of nature, including driving out demons	Mt 4:23–24; 8:16; 10:1,8; 13:54; Mk 1:32–33,39; 3:15; 6:13; 16:17; Lk 4:40–41; 9:1; 10:17; Jn 7:3; 10:25,32; 14:11; 15:24; Ac 2:22,43; 4:30; 5:15–16; 6:8; 8:6–7; 14:3; 15:12; 19:11–12; Ro 15:19; 1Co 12;10,29; 2Co 12:12; Gal 3:5	Jesus: see chart on THE MIRACLES OF JESUS, p. 1634 Apostles: see chart on THE MIRACLES OF THE APOSTLES, p. 1635

Gift	Definition	General References	Specific Examples
Prophecy	A special temporary ability to bring a word, warning, exhortation or revelation from God under the impulse of the Holy Spirit	Lk 12:12; Ac 2:17–18; 1Co 12:10; 13:9; 14:1–33; Eph 4:11; 1Th 5:20–21; 2Pe 1:20–21; 1Jn 4:1–3	Elizabeth: Lk 1:40–45 Mary: Lk 1:46–55 Zechariah: Lk 1:67–79 Peter: Ac 2:14–40; 4:8–12 Twelve men from Ephesus: Ac 19:6 Four daughters of Philip: Ac 21:9 Agabus: Ac 21:10–11
Distinguishing between spirits	Special ability to judge whether prophecies and utterances are from the Holy Spirit	1Co 12:10; 14:29	Peter: Ac 8:18–24 Paul: Ac 13:8–12; 16:16–18
Speaking in tongues	Expressing oneself at the level of one's spirit under the direct influence of the Holy Spirit in a language he or she has not learned and does not know	1Co 12:10,28,30; 13:1; 14:1–40	Disciples: Ac 2:4–11 Cornelius and his family: Ac 10:44–45; 11:17 Ephesian believers: Ac 19:2–7 Paul: 1Co 14:6,15,18
Interpretation of tongues	Special ability to interpret what is spoken in tongues	1Co 12:10,30; 14:5,13,26–28	

1 CORINTHIANS

Outline

Introduction (1:1–9)

I. Discussion of Problems About Which Paul Had Been Informed (1:10—6:20)

A. Divisions in the Church (1:10—4:21)

1. Four Factions (1:10–17)
2. Causes of the Divisions (1:18—4:5)
   a. A Wrong Conception of Wisdom (1:18—3:4)
   b. A Wrong Conception of Christian Ministry (3:5—4:5)
3. An Appeal for Reconciliation (4:6–21)

Principle: The church as the one body of Christ (cf. 12:12ff) should not be split into separate parts (1:10,13)

B. Moral Problems in the Church (5:1—6:20)

1. A Problem of Incest and Church Discipline (5:1–13)
2. The Problem of Secular Lawsuits Between Christians (6:1–11)
3. The Problem of Sexual Immorality (6:12–20)

Principle: You who are united with the Lord conduct yourself so as to bring honor to him (6:17,20)

II. Answers to Questions About Which the Corinthians Had Written (7:1—16:9)

A. Questions Concerning Marriage (7:1–40)

1. Marriage and Celibacy (7:1–9)
2. Christian Obligations in Marriage (7:10–16)
3. Principle of Contentment (7:17–24)
4. Counsel to the Unmarried (7:25–38)
5. Instruction About Remarriage (7:39–40)

Principle: God gives some the gift of a husband or wife; others he gives the gift of remaining single for the sake of the kingdom (7:7,32)

B. Questions Concerning the Use of Christian Freedom (8:1—11:1)

1. The Problem of Food Offered to Idols (8:1–13)
2. Paul's Disciplined Use of Freedom (9:1–27)
3. A Warning Against Presumptuous Overconfidence (10:1–13)
4. The Incompatibility of Idol Feasts and the Lord's Table (10:14–23)
5. Some General Principles and Practical Advice (10:24—11:1)

Principle: Do everything to bring glory to God; do nothing that might make others stumble (10:31–32) or might disqualify you from the race (9:24–27)

C. Questions Concerning Public Worship (11:2—14:40)

1. Women's Head Covering in Church (11:2–16)
2. Behavior at the Lord's Supper (11:17–34)
3. Spiritual Gifts (12:1—14:40)

Principle: Let all things be done in a fitting and orderly manner (14:40)

D. Questions Concerning the Resurrection (15:1–58)

1. Q. How Can Some Say There Is No Resurrection of the Dead? (15:12)
   A. The Certainty of the Resurrection (15:1–34)
2. Q. How Are the Dead Raised? With What Kind of Body Will They Come? (15:35)
   A. The Nature of the Resurrection Body (15:35–57)

3. Conclusion to the Question (15:58)

Principle: Christ's resurrection from the dead guarantees the resurrection of those who belong to Christ when he comes back (15:22–23)

E. Questions Concerning the Collection for God's people (16:1–9)

Final Instructions (16:10–24)

Author: Paul

Theme: Church Problems and Solutions

Date of Writing: A.D. 55/56

Background

Corinth, an ancient city of Greece, was in many ways the most prominent Greek metropolis of Paul's time. Like many of today's prosperous cities, Corinth was intellectually arrogant, materially affluent and morally corrupt. Sin of every kind flourished in this notoriously sensual city.

In conjunction with Priscilla and Aquila (16:19) and his own apostolic team (Ac 18:5), Paul founded the Corinthian church during his eighteen-month ministry at Corinth during his second missionary journey (Ac 18:1–17). The church was made up of some Jews but mostly of ex-pagan Gentiles. After Paul left Corinth, a variety of problems arose in the young church, requiring his apostolic authority and teaching by written correspondence and visits in person.

The first letter to the Corinthians was written during his three-year ministry at Ephesus (Ac 20:31) on his third missionary journey (Ac 18:23—21:16). Reports reached Paul at Ephesus about the problems at Corinth (1Co 1:11); afterwards a delegation from the Corinthian congregation (16:17) delivered a letter to Paul, requesting his instruction on a variety of issues (7:1; cf. 8:1; 12:1; 16:1). In response to the reports and the letter from Corinth, Paul wrote this letter.

Purpose

Paul had two primary reasons in mind as he penned this letter: (1) To correct the serious problems in the Corinthian church that had been reported to him. These were disorders that the Corinthians viewed lightly, but that Paul regarded as serious sin. (2) To provide counsel and instruction on a variety of questions about which the Corinthians had written. These included both issues of doctrine and personal and corporate conduct and purity.

Survey

This letter addresses the kinds of problems that churches experience when members remain "worldly" (3:1–3) and do not decisively separate themselves from the pagan society around them (2Co 6:17)—problems such as divisiveness (1:10–13; 11:17–22), tolerance of a sin like incest (5:1–13), sexual immorality in general (6:12–20), secular lawsuits between Christians (6:1–11), humanistic thinking about apostolic truth (ch. 15) and conflicts over "Christian freedom" (chs. 8; 10). Paul also instructs the Corinthians about matters related to celibacy and marriage (ch. 7), public worship, including the Lord's Supper (chs. 11—14), and the collection for the Jerusalem saints (16:1–4).

Among the most important contributions of 1 Corinthians is Paul's teaching on the manifestations and gifts of the Holy Spirit in the context of corporate worship (chs. 12—14). More than anywhere else in the NT, these chapters provide insight into the character and components of worship in the early church (cf. 14:26–33). Paul indicates that God's purpose for the church includes a wide variety of the Spirit's manifestations occurring through faithful believers (12:4–10) and individuals called to certain ministries (12:28–30)—a diversity within unity analogous to the many functions of a human body (12:12–27). In providing guidelines for the corporate function of spiritual gifts, Paul makes an essential distinction between individual and corporate edification (14:2–6,12,16–19,26), insisting that all public manifestations or gifts must flow out of love (ch. 13) and exist for the edification of the gathered believers (12:7; 14:4–6,26).

Special Features

Five major features characterize 1 Corinthians. (1) It is the most problem-centered letter in the NT. In addressing the various problems and issues at Corinth, Paul gives clear and enduring spiritual principles (see the outline), each of which is applicable universally for the church (e.g. 1:10; 6:17,20; 7:7; 9:24–27; 10:31–32; 14:1–10; 15:22–23). (2) There is an overall emphasis on the oneness of the local church as the body of Christ, a focus that occurs in discussions about divisions, the Lord's Supper and spiritual gifts. (3) This letter contains the most extensive NT teaching on such important subjects as celibacy, marriage and remarriage (ch. 7); the Lord's Supper (10:16–21; 11:17–34); tongues, prophecy and spiritual gifts in corporate gatherings (chs. 12; 14); agape love (ch. 13); and the resurrection of the body (ch. 15). (4) It provides invaluable wisdom for pastoral oversight in relation to church discipline (ch. 5). (5) It emphasizes the real possibility of falling away from the faith by those who persist in unrighteous behavior and do not hold firmly to Christ (6:9–10; 9:24–27; 10:5–12,20–21; 15:1–2).

Reading 1 Corinthians

In order to read the entire New Testament in one year, the book of 1 Corinthians should be read in 19 days, according to the following schedule:
☐ 1 ☐ 2 ☐ 3 ☐ 4 ☐ 5 ☐ 6 ☐ 7 ☐ 8 ☐ 9 ☐ 10:1–13 ☐ 10:14—11:1 ☐ 11:2–34 ☐ 12 ☐ 13 ☐ 14:1–25 ☐ 14:26–40 ☐ 15:1–34 ☐ 15:35–58 ☐ 16

NOTES

1 Paul, called to be an apostle[a] of
Christ Jesus by the will of God,[b]
and our brother Sosthenes,[c]

2To the church of God[d] in Corinth,[e] to those sanctified in Christ
Jesus and called[f] to be holy, together
with all those everywhere who call on
the name[g] of our Lord Jesus Christ—
their Lord and ours:

3Grace and peace to you from God
our Father and the Lord Jesus
Christ.[h]

Thanksgiving

4I always thank God for you[i] because of his grace given you in Christ
Jesus. **5**For in him you have been enriched[j] in every way—in all your
speaking and in all your knowledge[k]— **6**because our testimony[l]
about Christ was confirmed in you.
1Co 12:1-31 **7**Therefore you do not lack any spiritual gift[m] as you eagerly wait for our
Lord Jesus Christ to be revealed.[n] **8**He
will keep you strong to the end, so that
you will be blameless[o] on the day of
our Lord Jesus Christ.[p] **9**God, who has
called you[q] into fellowship with his
Son Jesus Christ our Lord,[r] is faithful.[s]

Divisions in the Church

10I appeal to you, brothers,[t] in the
name of our Lord Jesus Christ, that all
of you agree with one another so that
there may be no divisions among you[u]
and that you may be perfectly united[v]
in mind and thought. **11**My brothers,
some from Chloe's household[w] have
informed me that there are quarrels
among you. **12**What I mean is this: One
of you says, "I follow Paul";[x] another,
"I follow Apollos";[y] another, "I follow
Cephas[a]";[z] still another, "I follow
Christ."

13Is Christ divided? Was Paul crucified for you? Were you baptized into[b]
the name of Paul?[a] **14**I am thankful
that I did not baptize any of you except
Crispus[b] and Gaius,[c] **15**so no one can
say that you were baptized into my
name. **16**(Yes, I also baptized the
household[d] of Stephanas;[e] beyond
that, I don't remember if I baptized
anyone else.) **17**For Christ did not send
me to baptize,[f] but to preach the gospel—not with words of human wis-

1:1 [a]Ro 1:1; Eph 1:1; 2Ti 1:1 [b]S 2Co 1:1 [c]Ac 18:17 **1:2** [d]S 1Co 10:32 [e]S Ac 18:1 [f]Ro 1:7 [g]S Ac 2:21 **1:3** [h]S Ro 1:7 **1:4** [i]S Ro 1:8 **1:5** [j]2Co 9:11 [k]S 2Co 8:7 **1:6** [l]2Th 1:10; 1Ti 2:6; Rev 1:2 **1:7** [m]Ro 1:11; 1Co 12:1-31 [n]S Mt 16:27; S Lk 17:30; 1Th 1:10; S 2:19; Tit 2:13; Jas 5:7,8; 1Pe 1:13; 2Pe 3:12; S Rev 1:7 **1:8** [o]S 1Th 3:13 [p]Am 5:18; 1Co 5:5; Php 1:6, 10; 2:16; 1Th 5:2 **1:9** [q]S Ro 8:28 [r]1Jn 1:3 [s]Dt 7:9; Isa 49:7; 1Co 10:13; 1Th 5:24; 2Th 3:3; 2Ti 2:13; Heb 10:23; 11:11 **1:10** [t]S Ro 7:1 [u]1Co 11:18 [v]S Ro 15:5 **1:11** [w]S Ac 11:14 **1:12** [x]1Co 3:4,22 [y]S Ac 18:24 [z]Jn 1:42; 1Co 3:22; 9:5 **1:13** [a]S Mt 28:19 **1:14** [b]Ac 18:8 [c]S Ac 19:29 **1:16** [d]S Ac 11:14 [e]1Co 16:15 **1:17** [f]Jn 4:2; S Ac 2:38

[a] *12* That is, Peter [b] *13* Or *in*; also in verse 15

1:2 CALLED TO BE HOLY. See Ac 9:13, note on the meaning of the term "saints."

1:7 YOU DO NOT LACK ANY SPIRITUAL GIFT. Paul commends the Corinthians because God in his grace (v. 4) has given them specific spiritual gifts. Such gifts are a valuable and indispensable accompaniment of the Holy Spirit's ministry in the church; without them believers fail to strengthen and help one another as God desires. Nowhere in this letter does Paul seek to eliminate these gifts. Rather he seeks to change the attitude of the Corinthians toward spiritual gifts so that they may use their gifts according to God's intention.

1:7 WAIT FOR OUR LORD JESUS CHRIST TO BE REVEALED. The early Christians lived in expectation of Christ's imminent return (see Mt 24:42, note; Jn 14:3, note). They fixed their faith firmly on the fact of the Lord's coming, living every day in anticipation of that great hope. Note that the Christian's hope is for the personal return of the Lord Jesus Christ, not for the general complex of events that comprises the last days (cf. 1Th 1:9–10; 4:13–17; Tit 2:13; Heb 9:28; see article on BIBLICAL HOPE, p. 792).

1:12 I FOLLOW PAUL . . . APOLLOS . . . CEPHAS. Division over leaders in the church was beginning to develop; some church members were becoming more attached to certain ministers of the gospel than to the gospel itself. Paul condemns this attitude, reminding them that neither he nor any other person was crucified for them. This same error is present today. Some believers become more attached to a pastor or evangelist than to Christ and his Word. This disposition can cause them to betray Christian principles, and can even divide the church. We must always be careful to center our love and loyalty on God and his Word, not on any minister or person.

1:12 I FOLLOW CHRIST. The "Christ party" probably consisted of false teachers who were enemies of the apostle (4:18–19) and claimed to have a superior spirituality and "wisdom." They believed that their knowledge (8:1) brought freedom from the restraints of the law (6:12; 10:23) and from the demands of morality (5:2). They were attempting to win the church over to their own distorted gospel (2Co 11:4,20–21). It is against them and their converts at Corinth that Paul mainly contends.

1:17 CHRIST DID NOT SEND ME TO BAPTIZE. Paul is not minimizing Jesus' teaching concerning baptism (Mt 28:19). Rather, he makes it clear that he delegated the performing of baptism to his associates, as did Christ (Jn 4:1–2) and Peter (Ac 10:47–48). The apostle does not want to provide an opportunity for his converts to presume that they were "baptized into the name of Paul" (v. 13). Paul himself focused on preaching the gospel.

dom,[g] lest the cross of Christ be emptied of its power.

Christ the Wisdom and Power of God

18For the message of the cross is
foolishness[h] to those who are perishing,[i] but to us who are being saved[j]
it is the power of God.[k] 19For it is written:

> "I will destroy the wisdom of the
> wise;
> the intelligence of the intelligent
> I will frustrate."[c][l]

20Where is the wise man?[m] Where
is the scholar? Where is the philosopher of this age?[n] Has not God made
foolish[o] the wisdom of the world?
21For since in the wisdom of God the
world[p] through its wisdom did not
know him, God was pleased through
the foolishness of what was preached
to save[q] those who believe.[r] 22Jews
demand miraculous signs[s] and
Greeks look for wisdom, 23but we
preach Christ crucified:[t] a stumbling
block[u] to Jews and foolishness[v] to
Gentiles, 24but to those whom God has
called,[w] both Jews and Greeks, Christ
the power of God[x] and the wisdom of
God.[y] 25For the foolishness[z] of God
is wiser than man's wisdom, and the
weakness[a] of God is stronger than
man's strength.

26Brothers, think of what you were
when you were called.[b] Not many of
you were wise[c] by human standards;
not many were influential; not many
were of noble birth. 27But God chose[d]
the foolish[e] things of the world to
shame the wise; God chose the weak
things of the world to shame the
strong. 28He chose the lowly things of
this world and the despised things—
and the things that are not[f]—to nullify the things that are, 29so that no one
may boast before him.[g] 30It is because
of him that you are in Christ Jesus,[h]
who has become for us wisdom from
God—that is, our righteousness,[i] holiness[j] and redemption.[k] 31There-
fore, as it is written: "Let him who
boasts boast in the Lord."[d][l]

2 When I came to you, brothers, I did
not come with eloquence or superi-
or wisdom[m] as I proclaimed to you the
testimony about God.[e] 2For I resolved
to know nothing while I was with you
except Jesus Christ and him cruci-

1:17 [g] 1Co 2:1,4,13
1:18 [h] ver 21,23,25; 1Co 2:14 [i] 2Co 2:15; 4:3; 2Th 2:10 [j] Ac 2:47 [k] ver 24; Ro 1:16
1:19 [l] Isa 29:14
1:20 [m] Isa 19:11,12 [n] 1Co 2:6,8; 3:18; 2Co 4:4; Gal 1:4 [o] ver 27; Job 12:17; Isa 44:25; Jer 8:9; Ro 1:22; 1Co 3:18,19
1:21 [p] ver 27,28; 1Co 6:2; 11:32 [q] S Ro 11:14 [r] S Ro 3:22
1:22 [s] S Mt 12:38; S Jn 2:11; S 4:48
1:23 [t] 1Co 2:2; Gal 3:1 [u] S Lk 2:34 [v] S ver 18
1:24 [w] S Ro 8:28 [x] ver 18; Ro 1:16 [y] ver 30; S Col 2:3
1:25 [z] S ver 18
[a] 2Co 13:4
1:26 [b] S Ro 8:28 [c] ver 20
1:27 [d] Jas 2:5 [e] ver 20; Ro 1:22; 1Co 3:18,19
1:28 [f] Ro 4:17
1:29 [g] Eph 2:9
1:30 [h] S Ro 16:3 [i] Jer 23:5,6; 33:16; 2Co 5:21; Php 3:9 [j] 1Co 1:2 [k] S Ro 3:24
1:31 [l] Jer 9:23,24; Ps 34:2; 44:8; 2Co 10:17
2:1 [m] ver 4,13; 1Co 1:17

c *19* Isaiah 29:14 **d** *31* Jer. 9:24
e *1* Some manuscripts *as I proclaimed to you God's mystery*

1:18 IT IS THE POWER OF GOD. The message of the cross not only involves wisdom and truth, but the active power of God coming down to save, heal, drive out demons and redeem from sin's power (see article on THE KINGDOM OF GOD, p. 1430).

1:20 THE WISDOM OF THE WORLD. The wisdom of the world is a wisdom that excludes God, emphasizes human self-sufficiency, makes humanity the highest authority and refuses to recognize God's revelation in Jesus Christ. (1) This wisdom God calls foolishness (3:19–20), for through it humans have failed to find the truth or come to know their Creator (v. 21). (2) The believer must develop a godly contempt for both human wisdom and a secular world view (see vv. 18–31; 2:1–16; Ac 17:18; Ro 1:20–32; Col 2:8, note; 2Th 2:10–12; 2Ti 3:1–9; 2Pe 2:1–3,7; Jude 4–19). The gospel and the message of the cross must never be accommodated to philosophy, science or any other so-called human wisdom (2:4–5; Gal 6:14).

1:21 THE FOOLISHNESS OF WHAT WAS PREACHED. It is not the method of preaching that is considered foolish, but the message of the lordship of the crucified and resurrected Christ.

1:27 GOD CHOSE THE FOOLISH THINGS. In vv. 25–29, Paul emphasizes that God's standards and values are different from those accepted by the world; God is now in the process of overthrowing the world's false standards and wisdom.

1:28 NULLIFY THE THINGS THAT ARE. Through Jesus' crucifixion and resurrection (vv. 18,23) and through choosing the lowly things of this world (vv. 26–27), God nullifies the esteemed things of this present age. God is now in the process of bringing humanistic philosophies, psychologies and all other worldly systems to an end.

1:30 CHRIST JESUS . . . HAS BECOME FOR US WISDOM. It is through Christ, in Christ and with Christ that the believer receives wisdom from God and experiences righteousness (cf. Ro 4), sanctification (2Th 2:13–15) and redemption (Ro 3:24; Eph 4:30). As long as one is joined to Christ, Christ is the source of all these blessings (see Jn 15:1–6, notes on remaining in Christ).

2:1 I DID NOT COME WITH . . . WISDOM. The content of Paul's preaching was not according to the latest human "wisdom," either in the world or the church. Instead he concentrated on the central truth of the gospel (redemption through Christ) and on the power of the Holy Spirit (see next note). He was well aware of his human limitations, his personal inadequacy, and his inner fear and trembling. Consequently, he relied not on himself but on his message and on the Spirit (v. 4). This resulted in a greater demonstration of the Spirit's work and power.

fied.[n] **3**I came to you[o] in weakness[p]
and fear, and with much trembling.[q]
4My message and my preaching were
not with wise and persuasive words,[r]
but with a demonstration of the Spirit's
power,[s] **5**so that your faith might not
rest on men's wisdom, but on God's
power.[t]

Wisdom From the Spirit

6We do, however, speak a message
of wisdom among the mature,[u] but not
the wisdom of this age[v] or of the rulers of this age, who are coming to nothing.[w] **7**No, we speak of God's secret
wisdom, a wisdom[x] that has been hidden[y] and that God destined for our
glory before time began. **8**None of the
rulers of this age[z] understood it, for if
they had, they would not have crucified
the Lord of glory.[a] **9**However, as it is
written:

"No eye has seen,
no ear has heard,
no mind has conceived
what God has prepared for those
who love him"[f][b] —

10but God has revealed[c] it to us by his
Spirit.[d]

The Spirit searches all things, even
the deep things of God. **11**For who
among men knows the thoughts of a
man[e] except the man's spirit[f] within
him? In the same way no one knows
the thoughts of God except the Spirit of
God. **12**We have not received the spirit[g] of the world[h] but the Spirit who is
from God, that we may understand
what God has freely given us. **13**This is
what we speak, not in words taught us
by human wisdom[i] but in words
taught by the Spirit, expressing spiritual truths in spiritual words.[g] **14**The
man without the Spirit does not accept
the things that come from the Spirit of
God,[j] for they are foolishness[k] to

2:2 [n] Gal 6:14; 1Co 1:23
2:3 [o] Ac 18:1-18 [p] 1Co 4:10; 9:22; 2Co 11:29,30; 12:5,9,10; 13:9 [q] S 2Co 7:15
2:4 [r] ver 1 [s] S Ro 15:13
2:5 [t] 2Co 4:7; 6:7
2:6 [u] Eph 4:13; Php 3:15; Col 4:12; Heb 5:14; 6:1; Jas 1:4 [v] ver 8; S 1Co 1:20 [w] Ps 146:4
2:7 [x] ver 1 [y] Ro 16:25
2:8 [z] ver 6; S 1Co 1:20 [a] Ps 24:7; Ac 7:2; Jas 2:1
2:9 [b] Isa 64:4; 65:17
2:10 [c] S Mt 13:11; 2Co 12:1,7; Gal 1:12; 2:2; Eph 3:3,5 [d] Jn 14:26
2:11 [e] Jer 17:9 [f] Pr 20:27
2:12 [g] Ro 8:15 [h] 1Co 1:20,27; Jas 2:5
2:13 [i] ver 1,4; 1Co 1:17
2:14 [j] Jn 14:17 [k] S 1Co 1:18

[f] 9 Isaiah 64:4 [g] 13 Or *Spirit, interpreting spiritual truths to spiritual men*

2:4 A DEMONSTRATION OF THE SPIRIT'S POWER. (1) As a demonstration of the Holy Spirit's power (1:18,24), Paul's preaching included (a) the Spirit's convicting people of sin, righteousness and judgment, and bearing witness to the saving power of the risen Christ (cf. chs. 5–6; see Jn 16:8, note; Ac 2:36–41); (b) the power to transform lives (1:26–27; cf. Ac 4:13); (c) the power to effect holiness in the believer (5:3–5); and (d) God's power manifested by signs and wonders (Ac 2:29–33; 4:29–30; 5:12; 14:3; 2Co 12:12).

(2) Several other NT passages emphasize that the preaching of the gospel was accompanied by a special power of the Holy Spirit: Mk 16:17–18; Lk 10:19; Ac 28:3–6; Ro 15:19; 1Co 4:20; 1Th 1:5; Heb 2:4.

(3) All ministers of the gospel should pray that through their ministry (a) persons will be saved (Ac 2:41; 11:21,24; 14:1), (b) new believers will be filled with the Holy Spirit (Ac 2:4; 4:31; 8:17; 19:6), (c) evil spirits will be driven out (Ac 5:16; 8:7; 16:18), (d) the sick will be healed (Ac 3:6; 4:29–30; 14:10), and (e) disciples will learn to obey Christ's righteous standards and teachings (Mt 28:18–20; Ac 11:23,26; see article on SIGNS OF BELIEVERS, p. 1513).

2:12 THAT WE MAY UNDERSTAND. The things that God has prepared for those who love him (v. 9) can be understood by believers through the Spirit's revelation and illumination (vv. 10–16). As believers read and study the Bible, the Spirit illuminates their understanding of the truth. The Spirit also gives to faithful believers a strong assurance of the divine origin of Scripture (Jn 16:13; Eph 1:17).

2:13 WORDS TAUGHT BY THE SPIRIT. Though Paul is writing about the divine origin of his preaching, vv. 9–13 suggest the steps by which the Holy Spirit also inspired the writing of Scripture.

Step 1: God desired to communicate his wisdom to humanity (vv. 7–9). This wisdom concerned our salvation, centering in Christ as the wisdom of God (cf. 1:30; 2:2,5).

Step 2: It is only through the Holy Spirit that God's truth and wisdom were revealed to humanity (v. 10). The Spirit knows fully the thoughts of God (v. 11).

Step 3: God's revelation was given to chosen believers through the indwelling presence of the Spirit (v. 12; cf. Ro 8:11,15).

Step 4: The writers of Scripture wrote with words taught by the Holy Spirit (v. 13); the Spirit directed the writers in the choice of the words they used (cf. Ex 24:4; Isa 51:16; Jer 1:9; 36:28,32; Eze 2:7; Mt 4:4). At the same time, the Spirit's guidance in the expression of divine truth was not mechanical; rather the Spirit used each writer's vocabulary and personal style.

Step 5: Divinely inspired Scripture is understood by spiritual believers as they examine its content through the illumination of the Holy Spirit (vv. 14–16).

Thus, both the thoughts and language of Scripture were inspired by the Spirit of God. Not a single writer uttered a false word or phrase. God's Word was protected from error and falsehood by the Holy Spirit (see articles on THE WORD OF GOD, p. 1062, and THE INSPIRATION AND AUTHORITY OF SCRIPTURE, p. 1898).

2:14 THE MAN WITHOUT THE SPIRIT. For comments on this verse, see article on THREE KINDS OF PEOPLE, p. 1754.

him, and he cannot understand them,
because they are spiritually discerned.
15The spiritual[l] man makes judgments about all things, but he himself
is not subject to any man's judgment:

16"For who has known the mind of
the Lord
that he may instruct him?"[h][m]

But we have the mind of Christ.[n]

On Divisions in the Church

3 Brothers, I could not address you
as spiritual[o] but as worldly[p]—
mere infants[q] in Christ. 2I gave you
milk, not solid food,[r] for you were not
yet ready for it.[s] Indeed, you are still
not ready. 3You are still worldly. For
since there is jealousy and quarreling[t] among you, are you not worldly?
Are you not acting like mere men? 4For
when one says, "I follow Paul," and another, "I follow Apollos,"[u] are you not
mere men?
5What, after all, is Apollos?[v] And
what is Paul? Only servants,[w] through
whom you came to believe—as the
Lord has assigned to each his task. 6I
planted the seed,[x] Apollos watered it,
but God made it grow. 7So neither he
who plants nor he who waters is anything, but only God, who makes things
grow. 8The man who plants and the
man who waters have one purpose, and
each will be rewarded according to his
own labor.[y] 9For we are God's fellow
workers;[z] you are God's field,[a] God's
building.[b]
10By the grace God has given me,[c]
I laid a foundation[d] as an expert builder, and someone else is building on it.
But each one should be careful how he
builds. 11For no one can lay any foundation other than the one already laid,
which is Jesus Christ.[e] 12If any man
builds on this foundation using gold,
silver, costly stones, wood, hay or
straw, 13his work will be shown for
what it is,[f] because the Day[g] will
bring it to light. It will be revealed with
fire, and the fire will test the quality of
each man's work.[h] 14If what he has
built survives, he will receive his reward.[i] 15If it is burned up, he will suffer loss; he himself will be saved, but

2:15 [l] 1Co 3:1; Gal 6:1
2:16 [m] Isa 40:13; S Ro 11:34 [n] Jn 15:15
3:1 [o] 1Co 2:15 [p] Ro 7:14; 1Co 2:14 [q] 1Co 14:20
3:2 [r] Heb 5:12-14; 1Pe 2:2 [s] Jn 16:12
3:3 [t] Ro 13:13; 1Co 1:11; Gal 5:20
3:4 [u] 1Co 1:12
3:5 [v] S Ac 18:24 [w] 1Co 4:1; 2Co 6:4; Eph 3:7; Col 1:23,25
3:6 [x] Ac 18:4-11; 1Co 4:15; 9:1; 15:1
3:8 [y] ver 14; Ps 18:20; 62:12; Mt 25:21; 1Co 9:17
3:9 [z] Mk 16:20; 2Co 6:1; 1Th 3:2 [a] Isa 61:3 [b] Eph 2:20-22; 1Pe 2:5
3:10 [c] S Ro 12:3 [d] Ro 15:20; S Eph 2:20
3:11 [e] Isa 28:16; Eph 2:20
3:13 [f] 1Co 4:5 [g] S 1Co 1:8; 2Th 1:7-10; 2Ti 1:12,18; 4:8 [h] Nu 31:22,23; Jer 23:28,29; Mal 3:3; S 2Th 1:7
3:14 [i] S ver 8

[h] *16* Isaiah 40:13

2:16 WE HAVE THE MIND OF CHRIST. To have the mind of Christ means knowing his will and his redemptive plan and purpose (vv. 9–10). It means appraising and seeing things the way God sees them, valuing things the way he values them, loving what he loves and hating what he hates (v. 15; Heb 1:9). It means understanding God's holiness and sin's awfulness. Thus, receiving the Spirit and following the Spirit (v. 12) cause the believer's values and world view to become radically different from the ways and wisdom of this age (cf. Php 2:5–8).

3:1 NOT ADDRESS YOU AS SPIRITUAL. One of the Corinthian church's major problems was its attempt to experience God's blessings while refusing to separate itself from the world's evil ways (see article on THE CHRISTIAN'S RELATIONSHIP TO THE WORLD, p. 1976). (1) The pastors and leaders of the Corinthian church were allowing professed converts to come into the congregations without forsaking their evil practices. The Corinthians were tolerating within their fellowship: selfish divisions (11:18), the world's philosophy (1:18–25; 3:19), jealousy and quarreling (3:3), pride (3:21; 4:7), immorality (5:1), trivial lawsuits (6:1–8), attendance at idolatrous festivals (chs. 8; 10) and the rejection of apostolic teaching (14:36–37). Because the Corinthians failed to see the absolute necessity of apostolic truth, love and godly standards (6:9–10; 13), they abused the gifts of the Spirit (chs. 12; 14) and the "Lord's Supper" (11:20–34), and distorted the message of the gospel (1:18–31).

(2) Jesus himself warns that any church that tolerates within its fellowship the world's unrighteous practices or the distortion of Biblical truth (see Rev 2:20, note) will be rejected by him and lose its place in God's kingdom (cf. Rev 2:5,16; 3:15–16). The Spirit calls such a church to true repentance (5:2), to separation from the world (2Co 6:16–18), and to "perfecting holiness out of reverence for God" (2Co 7:1).

3:3 YOU ARE STILL WORLDLY. For comments on the difference between worldly and spiritual Christians, see article on THREE KINDS OF PEOPLE, p. 1754.

3:15 HE WILL SUFFER LOSS. The Bible asserts that all the redeemed are free from God's judgment of condemnation (Jn 5:24; Ro 8:1; Heb 10:14–17). However, there is a future judgment for believers (1Jn 4:17) as to the degree of their faithfulness to God and the grace given to them during this life on earth (v. 10; 4:2–5; 2Co 5:10). In that judgment there is the possibility that a believer, although receiving salvation, may experience great loss (Gk *zēmioō*, meaning "to suffer loss or damage").

The careless believer is in danger of suffering loss or damage in the following ways: (1) a feeling of shame at Christ's coming (2Ti 2:15; 1Jn 2:28); (2) loss of his or her life's work for God (vv. 12–15); (3) loss of glory and honor before God (cf. Ro 2:7); (4) loss of opportunity for service and authority in heaven (Mt 25:14–30); (5) a low position in heaven (Mt 5:19; 19:30); (6) loss of rewards (cf. v. 14–15); and (7) repayment for the wrong done

THREE KINDS OF PEOPLE

***1Co 2:14–15** "The man without the Spirit does not accept the things that come from the Spirit of God, for they are foolishness to him, and he cannot understand them, because they are spiritually discerned. The spiritual man makes judgments about all things, but he himself is not subject to any man's judgment."*

BASIC DIVISION. Scripture typically divides all humans into two classes.

(1) The natural, or unspiritual, man/woman (Gk *psuchikos*, 1Co 2:14) identifies the unregenerated person, i.e., one governed by mere natural instincts (2Pe 2:12). This kind of person does not have the Holy Spirit (Ro 8:9), is under Satan's dominion (Ac 26:18), and is enslaved to the body and its passions (Eph 2:3). He or she belongs to the world, is in sympathy with it (Jas 4:4) and rejects the righteous ways of the Spirit (1Co 2:14). The unspiritual person is not able to understand God and his ways, but instead relies on human reasoning or emotions.

(2) The spiritual man/woman (Gk *pneumatikos*, 1Co 2:15; 3:1) identifies the regenerated person, i.e., one who has the Holy Spirit. This person is spiritually minded, thinks the thoughts of God (1Co 2:11–13) and lives by the Spirit of God (Ro 8:4–17; Gal 5:16–26). Such an individual believes in Jesus Christ, strives to follow the leading of the indwelling Spirit, and resists sensual desires and sin's dominion (Ro 8:13–14).

How does one become a spiritual man/woman? When a person accepts by faith the salvation provided through Christ, he or she is regenerated; the Holy Spirit imparts to him or her a new nature by an infusion of divine life (2Pe 1:4; see article on REGENERATION, p. 1589). He or she is born again (Jn 3:3,5,7), renewed (Ro 12:2), and made a new creation (2Co 5:17) and recipient of God's righteousness through faith in Christ (Php 3:9).

FURTHER DISTINCTION AMONG CHRISTIANS. Although born-again believers receive the new life of the Spirit, they retain the sinful nature with its evil inclinations (Gal 5:16–21). The sinful nature that remains in them cannot be made good; it must be put to death and overcome through the Spirit's power and grace (Ro 8:13). Believers overcome by denying themselves daily (Mt 16:24; Ro 8:12–13; Tit 2:12), removing every hindrance or sin (Heb 12:1), and resisting all sinful temptations (Ro 13:14; Gal 5:16; 1Pe 2:11). By the power of the Spirit believers themselves wage war against the sinful nature. (Ro 8:13–14; Gal 5:16–18), crucify it (Gal 5:24) and put it to death daily (Col 3:5). By this process of self-denial and yielding to the Holy Spirit's sanctifying work, they will be set free from the power of their sinful nature and live as spiritual Christians (Ro 6:13; Gal 5:16).

Not all Christians make the required effort to fully overcome this sinful nature. In addressing the Corinthians, Paul notes (1Co 3:1,3) that some of them are behaving in a worldly or unspiritual (Gk *sarkikos*) manner; instead of consistently resisting the inclinations of their sinful nature, they often yielded to at least some of them. Although they were not living in persistent disobedience, they were in the process of compromising with the world, the sinful nature and the devil in some areas of their lives, while still wanting to remain a part of God's people (10:21; 2Co 6:14–18; 11:3; 13:5).

(1) *The condition of worldly Christians*. Although sin and rebellion were not the rule in their lives, nor had they entered into the serious immorality and unrighteousness that would separate them from God's kingdom (see 1Co 6:9–11; cf. Gal 5:21; Eph 5:5), these

worldly Christians were behaving in such a way that they were no longer growing in grace, acting as if they were new converts who did not yet understand the full implication of salvation in Christ (1Co 3:1–2). Their worldliness was expressed in "jealousy and quarreling" (3:3). They were indifferent to and tolerant of immorality within the church (5:1–13; 6:13–20). They did not take God's Word or his apostle with utmost seriousness (4:18–19). They were going to law courts over trivial matters (6:6). Note that Paul considers the Corinthians who had entered into sexual immorality or other gross sins to be excluded altogether from salvation in Christ (1Co 5:1,9–11; 6:9–10).

(2) *The perils of worldly Christians.* These worldly Corinthian Christians were in danger of being led astray from sincere devotion to Christ (2Co 11:3) and being more and more conformed to the world (2Co 6:14–18). Because of this, they would be chastened and judged by the Lord, and if they continued to conform to the world, they would ultimately be excluded from God's kingdom (1Co 6:9–10; 11:31–32). In fact, spiritual death had already occurred for some of them who had committed flagrant sin leading to spiritual death (see 1Jn 3:15, note; 5:17, note; cf. Ro 8:13; 1Co 5:5; 2Co 12:21; 13:5).

(3) *The warnings to worldly Christians.* (a) Worldly Christians must know they are in danger of departing from the faith if they are unwilling to purify themselves from all that displeases God (Ro 6:14–16; 1Co 6:9–10; 2Co 11:3; Gal 6:7–9; Jas 1:12–16). (b) They must learn from the tragic example of the Israelites whom God destroyed because of sin (1Co 10:5–12). (c) They must understand that it is impossible to participate in the things of the Lord and the things of Satan at the same time (Mt 6:24; 1Co 10:21). (d) They must separate themselves completely from the world (2Co 6:14–18) and purify themselves "from everything that contaminates body and spirit, perfecting holiness out of reverence for God" (2Co 7:1).

only as one escaping through the flames.[j]

16Don't you know that you yourselves are God's temple[k] and that God's Spirit lives in you?[l] **17**If anyone destroys God's temple, God will destroy him; for God's temple is sacred, and you are that temple.

18Do not deceive yourselves. If any one of you thinks he is wise[m] by the standards of this age,[n] he should become a "fool" so that he may become wise. **19**For the wisdom of this world is foolishness[o] in God's sight. As it is written: "He catches the wise in their craftiness"[i];[p] **20**and again, "The Lord knows that the thoughts of the wise are futile."[j][q] **21**So then, no more boasting about men![r] All things are yours,[s] **22**whether Paul or Apollos[t] or Cephas[k][u] or the world or life or death or the present or the future[v]—all are yours, **23**and you are of Christ,[w] and Christ is of God.

Apostles of Christ

4 So then, men ought to regard us as servants[x] of Christ and as those entrusted[y] with the secret things[z] of God. **2**Now it is required that those who have been given a trust must prove faithful. **3**I care very little if I am judged by you or by any human court; indeed, I do not even judge myself. **4**My conscience[a] is clear, but that does not make me innocent.[b] It is the Lord who judges me.[c] **5**Therefore judge nothing[d] before the appointed time; wait till the Lord comes.[e] He will bring to light[f] what is hidden in darkness and will expose the motives of men's hearts. At that time each will receive his praise from God.[g]

6Now, brothers, I have applied these things to myself and Apollos for your benefit, so that you may learn from us the meaning of the saying, "Do not go beyond what is written."[h] Then you will not take pride in one man over against another.[i] **7**For who makes you different from anyone else? What do you have that you did not receive?[j] And if you did receive it, why do you boast as though you did not?

8Already you have all you want! Al-

3:15 [j]Jude 23
3:16 [k]1Co 6:19; 2Co 6:16; Eph 2:21,22; Heb 3:6 [l]S Ro 8:9
3:18 [m]Isa 5:21; 1Co 8:2; Gal 6:3 [n]S 1Co 1:20
3:19 [o]ver 18; Ro 1:22; 1Co 1:20, 27 [p]Job 5:13
3:20 [q]Ps 94:11
3:21 [r]1Co 4:6 [s]Ro 8:32
3:22 [t]ver 5,6 [u]S 1Co 1:12 [v]Ro 8:38
3:23 [w]1Co 15:23; 2Co 10:7; Gal 3:29
4:1 [x]S 1Co 3:5 [y]1Co 9:17; Tit 1:7 [z]S Ro 16:25
4:4 [a]S Ac 23:1 [b]Ro 2:13 [c]2Co 10:18
4:5 [d]S Mt 7:1,2 [e]S 1Th 2:19 [f]Job 12:22; Ps 90:8; 1Co 3:13 [g]S Ro 2:29
4:6 [h]1Co 1:19,31; 3:19,20 [i]1Co 1:12; 3:4
4:7 [j]Jn 3:27; Ro 12:3,6

[i]*19* Job 5:13 [j]*20* Psalm 94:11 [k]*22* That is, Peter

to others (Col 3:24–25). These passages should impress on us the necessity of complete dedication, including faithful, self-sacrificing service to our Lord (cf. Ro 12:1–2; Php 2:12; 4:3; see article on THE JUDGMENT OF BELIEVERS, p. 1791).

3:15 BUT ONLY AS ONE ESCAPING THROUGH THE FLAMES. "Escaping through the flames" is probably an expression meaning "barely saved." God will evaluate the quality of life, influence, teaching and work in the church of each person, and especially here, of each minister. If his work is judged unworthy, he will lose his reward, yet he himself may be saved. Note that this passage does not teach a doctrine of purgatory; it addresses a judgment of works, not the cleansing of a person from mortal sins.

3:16 YOU YOURSELVES ARE GOD'S TEMPLE. The emphasis here is on the entire congregation of believers as God's temple and the dwelling place of the Spirit (cf. v. 9; 2Co 6:16; Eph 2:21). As the temple of God in the midst of a corrupt society, God's people in Corinth were not to participate in the evils prevalent in that society, but were to reject all forms of immorality. God's temple must be holy (v. 17) because God is holy (cf. 1Pe 1:14–16; see article on THE TEMPLE, p. 608).

3:17 GOD WILL DESTROY HIM. Paul presents one of the strongest warnings in the NT to anyone responsible for building Christ's church. This passage has special relevance for all those in teaching/leadership positions. If anyone defiles or corrupts God's temple (i.e., a local congregation or a group of congregations), God himself will punish that individual with terrible ruin and eternal death. People corrupt and destroy Christ's church by: (1) engaging in immorality (5:1); (2) fostering lies, deceptions and selfish ambition (v. 3; Ac 5:1–11); (3) promoting false doctrine, rejecting apostolic revelation and showing indifference to Scriptural truth (1Ti 4:1; Jude 4); (4) accepting sin and worldliness within the congregation (5:1–2,5–7; Rev 3:17); (5) attempting to build the church by worldly wisdom or a distorted gospel (1:18—2:5; Php 1:15–16).

4:5 EXPOSE THE MOTIVES OF MEN'S HEARTS. God will bring to light the secret acts of all persons and expose their true thoughts and motives, good as well as bad (Mt 6:3–4,6; 1Ti 5:24–25; see article on THE JUDGMENT OF BELIEVERS, p. 1791). In other words, the inner lives of everyone will be revealed exactly as they were; nothing will be left hidden (Mk 4:22; Lk 12:2–3; Ro 2:16).

4:7 WHY DO YOU BOAST. The basis for Christian humility is to realize that the native endowments or spiritual gifts we possess are from God and thus provide no basis for superiority, status or pride. All that we have and all that we become are made possible by God and others. Consequently, there is no place for pride, but only gratefulness to God and others.

4:8 HAVE ALL YOU WANT ... HAVE BECOME RICH. Some at Corinth boasted of their wisdom, superior knowledge and spiritual gifts. Paul shows them that the true life of a faithful

ready you have become rich![k] You
have become kings—and that without
us! How I wish that you really had become kings so that we might be kings
with you! **9**For it seems to me that God
has put us apostles on display at the
end of the procession, like men condemned to die[l] in the arena. We have
been made a spectacle[m] to the whole
universe, to angels as well as to men.
10We are fools for Christ,[n] but you are
so wise in Christ![o] We are weak, but
you are strong![p] You are honored, we
are dishonored! **11**To this very hour we
go hungry and thirsty, we are in rags,
we are brutally treated, we are homeless.[q] **12**We work hard with our own
hands.[r] When we are cursed, we
bless;[s] when we are persecuted,[t] we
endure it; **13**when we are slandered,
we answer kindly. Up to this moment we have become the scum of the
earth, the refuse[u] of the world.

14I am not writing this to shame
you,[v] but to warn you, as my dear children.[w] **15**Even though you have ten
thousand guardians in Christ, you do
not have many fathers, for in Christ
Jesus I became your father[x] through
the gospel.[y] **16**Therefore I urge you to
imitate me.[z] **17**For this reason I am
sending to you[a] Timothy,[b] my son[c]
whom I love, who is faithful in the
Lord. He will remind you of my way of
life in Christ Jesus, which agrees with
what I teach everywhere in every
church.[d]

18Some of you have become arrogant,[e] as if I were not coming to
you.[f] **19**But I will come to you very
soon,[g] if the Lord is willing,[h] and
then I will find out not only how these
arrogant people are talking, but what
power they have. **20**For the kingdom of
God is not a matter of[i] talk but of
power.[j] **21**What do you prefer? Shall
I come to you with a whip,[k] or in love
and with a gentle spirit?

Expel the Immoral Brother!

5 It is actually reported that there is
sexual immorality among you, and

4:8 [k] Rev 3:17,18
4:9 [l] S Ro 8:36 [m] Ps 71:7; Heb 10:33
4:10 [n] S 1Co 1:18; Ac 17:18; 26:24 [o] 1Co 3:18; 2Co 11:19 [p] S 1Co 2:3
4:11 [q] Ro 8:35; 2Co 11:23-27
4:12 [r] S Ac 18:3 [s] Ro 12:14; 1Pe 3:9 [t] S Mt 5:44
4:13 [u] Jer 20:18; La 3:45
4:14 [v] 1Co 6:5; 15:34; 2Th 3:14 [w] S 1Th 2:11
4:15 [x] S ver 14 [y] 1Co 9:12,14,18, 23; 15:1
4:16 [z] 1Co 11:1; Php 3:17; 4:9; 1Th 1:6; 2Th 3:7,9
4:17 [a] 1Co 16:10 [b] S Ac 16:1 [c] S 1Ti 1:2 [d] S 1Co 7:17
4:18 [e] Jer 43:2 [f] ver 21
4:19 [g] 1Co 16:5,6; 2Co 1:15,16 [h] S Ac 18:21
4:20 [i] Ro 14:17 [j] S Ro 15:13
4:21 [k] 2Co 1:23; 2:1; 13:2,10

believer is the way of the cross and that suffering must precede glory (cf. Ro 8:17).

4:9–13 APOSTLES ... CONDEMNED TO DIE. Here Paul lists the trials endured by the apostles. The verb "put on display" suggests that God has appointed the apostles to a life of suffering, to be seen by the world, by angels and by the church. (1) Paul lacks (even at that present time) such things as food, drink and proper clothing. He is despised, roughly treated and homeless. He works hard night and day, and is cursed, persecuted, slandered, and considered the "scum of the earth, the refuse of the world" (cf. 2Co 4:8–9; 6:4–5,8–10; 11:23–29; 12:10). (2) Although suffering was in one sense a special appointment of the apostolic ministry (cf. Ac 9:16), it is also the common lot of all believers who, united with Christ, are opposed to sin, immorality, Satan, worldly evils and injustice. Their suffering is seen as a fellowship of sharing in Christ's suffering (Ro 8:17; Php 1:29; 3:10; 1Th 3:3).

4:20 KINGDOM OF GOD ... POWER. The "kingdom of God" reveals itself in power. Thus, members of that kingdom must have more than talk and message; they must manifest the power of the Spirit as well (2:4; Ac 1:8). In the NT this consisted of a power to convict people of sin, righteousness and judgment (Jn 16:8), to bring them into salvation (v. 15; Ac 26:16–18), to perform miracles (see 2:4, note; see article on THE KINGDOM OF GOD, p. 1430) and to live a righteous life (Ro 14:17).

5:1 SEXUAL IMMORALITY AMONG YOU. Paul writes about a report of immorality in the Corinthian church and the refusal of the leaders to deal with the offender (vv. 1–8). He declares that the church, as a holy people, must not permit or tolerate immorality among its members. He gives three reasons why the church should discipline offending members:

(1) For the good of the offenders (v. 5). Excommunication might awaken them to the tragedy of their sin and their need for forgiveness and restoration.

(2) For the sake of the church's purity (vv. 6–8). Tolerating evil within a church will gradually lower the moral standard of all.

(3) For the good of the world (cf. v. 1). The church cannot win men and women to Christ if it is like the world (cf. Mt 5:13). For other NT passages on church discipline, see Mt 5:22; 18:15–17; 2Th 3:6; and Rev 2:19–23.

5:1 HAS HIS FATHER'S WIFE. The exact sin is not clear. Paul's reference to "his father's wife" probably means the offender was sexually involved with his stepmother. (1) Paul was dismayed and appalled that the church would tolerate such immorality. He sees this as much more serious than the actual sin of the individual.

(2) The permissiveness of the Corinthians speaks to our situation today. Many churches today are tolerant of and silent about immorality among their members, including adultery and all forms of sexual immorality. Premarital sexual intimacy, especially among church youth, is not only tolerated but at times justified on the pretense of love and commitment. More than a few leaders in the church fail to challenge in Christ's name the immoral dating habits of today's youth. Like the Corinthian leaders, they refuse to mourn over the defilement of God's people as the people become more and more like the society in which

of a kind that does not occur even
among pagans: A man has his father's
wife.[l] 2 And you are proud! Shouldn't
you rather have been filled with grief[m]
and have put out of your fellowship[n]
the man who did this? 3 Even though I
am not physically present, I am with
you in spirit.[o] And I have already
passed judgment on the one who did
this, just as if I were present. 4 When
you are assembled in the name of our
Lord Jesus[p] and I am with you in spirit, and the power of our Lord Jesus is
present, 5 hand this man over[q] to Satan,[r] so that the sinful nature[1] may
be destroyed and his spirit saved on
the day of the Lord.[s]

6 Your boasting is not good.[t] Don't
you know that a little yeast[u] works
through the whole batch of dough?[v]
7 Get rid of the old yeast that you may
be a new batch without yeast—as you
really are. For Christ, our Passover
lamb, has been sacrificed.[w] 8 Therefore let us keep the Festival, not with
the old yeast, the yeast of malice and
wickedness, but with bread without
yeast,[x] the bread of sincerity and
truth.

9 I have written you in my letter not
to associate[y] with sexually immoral
people— 10 not at all meaning the people of this world[z] who are immoral, or
the greedy and swindlers, or idolaters.
In that case you would have to leave
this world. 11 But now I am writing you
that you must not associate with anyone who calls himself a brother[a] but
is sexually immoral or greedy, an idolater[b] or a slanderer, a drunkard or a
swindler. With such a man do not even
eat.[c]

12 What business is it of mine to
judge those outside[d] the church? Are
you not to judge those inside?[e] 13 God
will judge those outside. "Expel the
wicked man from among you."[m][f]

5:1 [l] Lev 18:8; Dt 22:30; 27:20 **5:2** [m] 2Co 7:7-11 [n] ver 13 **5:3** [o] Col 2:5; 1Th 2:17 **5:4** [p] 2Th 3:6 **5:5** [q] 1Ti 1:20 [r] S Mt 4:10 [s] S 1Co 1:8 **5:6** [t] Jas 4:16 [u] Mt 16:6,12 [v] Gal 5:9 **5:7** [w] Ex 12:3-6, 21; Mk 14:12; 1Pe 1:19 **5:8** [x] Ex 12:14,15; Dt 16:3 **5:9** [y] Eph 5:11; 2Th 3:6,14 **5:10** [z] 1Co 10:27 **5:11** [a] S Ro 7:1 [b] 1Co 10:7,14 [c] S Ro 16:17 **5:12** [d] S Mk 4:11 [e] ver 3-5; 1Co 6:1-4 **5:13** [f] Dt 13:5; 17:7; 19:19; 22:21,24; 24:7; Jdg 20:13

Lawsuits Among Believers

6 If any of you has a dispute with
another, dare he take it before the
ungodly for judgment instead of before

[1] 5 Or *that his body*; or *that the flesh*
[m] *13* Deut. 17:7; 19:19; 21:21; 22:21,24; 24:7

they live. In self-complacency these leaders permit sin because, so they claim, "we live in the modern day and must not be judgmental."

5:2 BEEN FILLED WITH GRIEF. Paul expresses what should be the normal reaction of a Spirit-filled church to the immorality found among its professing members. Those who embrace the Biblical view of God's holiness and his revulsion to sin will be moved to sorrow and regret (cf. Isa 6). They will remove wickedness from among them (vv. 2,4–5,7,13).

5:5 HAND THIS MAN OVER TO SATAN. To hand over to Satan means that the church must remove the immoral person from its fellowship and return him or her to Satan's domain. This will, in turn, expose him or her to the destructive influences of evil and the demonic (vv. 7,13). (1) This discipline has two purposes: (a) that the offender, by experiencing problems and physical suffering, may repent and ultimately be saved (cf. Lk 15:11–24); (b) that the church may "get rid of the old yeast" (v. 7; i.e., sinful influences), so that God's people may become a new bread of "sincerity and truth" (v. 8). (2) The same action can be taken by the church today in seeking the salvation of one who has forsaken the Christian life and returned to the world (cf. 1Ti 1:20).

5:6 LITTLE YEAST WORKS THROUGH THE WHOLE BATCH. In the Bible, "yeast" (which produces fermentation) is a symbol of that which permeates the whole and corrupts truth, righteousness and spiritual life (Gal 5:7–9; see Ex 13:7, note; Mk 8:15, note). Paul in this passage compares yeast with the process by which sin and wickedness slowly spread in a Christian community until many are corrupted by it. Any church that does not take radical action against sexual immorality among its members will find the influence of evil spreading throughout the fellowship and infecting many. Sin must be expelled rigorously, or in time the entire Christian fellowship will be corrupted and the Holy Spirit banished from the church (see Rev 2–3, notes).

5:12 JUDGE THOSE INSIDE. Believers must not be involved in superficial or unjust criticism of another believer (cf. Mt 7:1–5). However, Paul here does indicate that the church must judge its members according to God's Word and standards when serious sin, immorality or persistent ungodly conduct is involved. Such wicked actions demand judgment and discipline for the sake of the person involved, the purity of the church and the witness of Christ in the world (see v. 1, note).

6:1 BEFORE THE UNGODLY. When trivial disputes (v. 2) between Christians occur, they should be settled within the church and not in courts of law. The church must judge the right or wrong involved, render a verdict and exercise discipline if needed (see Mt 18:15, note). (1) This teaching does not mean that a believer may not use courts in serious cases with unbelievers. Paul himself appealed to the judicial system more than once (see Ac 16:37–39; 25:10–12).

(2) Nor is Paul saying the church must allow its members to unlawfully abuse or mistreat the innocent, such as widows, children or the weak. Rather, Paul was speaking of issues where there was no clear right or wrong. Blatant sinful actions must not be tolerated, but handled according to Christ's instruction in Mt 18:15–17.

the saints?[g] 2Do you not know that
the saints will judge the world?[h] And
if you are to judge the world, are you
not competent to judge trivial cases?
3Do you not know that we will judge
angels? How much more the things of
this life! 4Therefore, if you have disputes about such matters, appoint as
judges even men of little account in the
church![n] 5I say this to shame you.[i]
Is it possible that there is nobody
among you wise enough to judge a dispute between believers?[j] 6But instead, one brother[k] goes to law
against another—and this in front of
unbelievers![l]

7The very fact that you have lawsuits among you means you have been
completely defeated already. Why not
rather be wronged? Why not rather be
cheated?[m] 8Instead, you yourselves
cheat and do wrong, and you do this to
your brothers.[n]

The Wicked Will Not Inherit the Kingdom

9Do you not know that the wicked
will not inherit the kingdom of God?[o]
Do not be deceived:[p] Neither the sexually immoral nor idolaters nor adulterers[q] nor male prostitutes nor homosexual offenders[r] 10nor thieves nor
the greedy nor drunkards nor slanderers nor swindlers[s] will inherit the
kingdom of God. 11And that is what
some of you were.[t] But you were
washed,[u] you were sanctified,[v] you
were justified[w] in the name of the Lord
Jesus Christ and by the Spirit of our
God.

Sexual Immorality

12"Everything is permissible for
me"—but not everything is beneficial.[x] "Everything is permissible for
me"—but I will not be mastered by
anything. 13"Food for the stomach and
the stomach for food"—but God will
destroy them both.[y] The body is not
meant for sexual immorality, but for
the Lord,[z] and the Lord for the body.
14By his power God raised the Lord
from the dead,[a] and he will raise us
also.[b] 15Do you not know that your
bodies are members of Christ himself?[c] Shall I then take the members
of Christ and unite them with a prostitute? Never! 16Do you not know that he
who unites himself with a prostitute is
one with her in body? For it is said,
"The two will become one flesh."[o][d]
17But he who unites himself with the
Lord is one with him in spirit.[e]

18Flee from sexual immorality.[f] All

6:1 [g] Mt 18:17 **6:2** [h] Mt 19:28; Lk 22:30; 1Co 5:12 **6:5** [i] S 1Co 4:14 [j] Ac 1:15 **6:6** [k] S Ro 7:1 [l] 2Co 6:14,15; 1Ti 5:8 **6:7** [m] Mt 5:39,40 **6:8** [n] 1Th 4:6 **6:9** [o] S Mt 25:34 [p] Job 13:9; 1Co 15:33; Gal 6:7; Jas 1:16 [q] Lev 18:20; Dt 22:22 [r] Lev 18:22 **6:10** [s] 1Ti 1:10; Rev 21:8; 22:15 **6:11** [t] S Eph 2:2 [u] S Ac 22:16 [v] 1Co 1:2 [w] S Ro 4:25 **6:12** [x] 1Co 10:23 **6:13** [y] Col 2:22 [z] ver 15,19; Ro 12:1 **6:14** [a] S Ac 2:24 [b] S Ro 6:5; Eph 1:19,20; 1Th 4:16 **6:15** [c] S Ro 12:5 **6:16** [d] Ge 2:24; Mt 19:5; Eph 5:31 **6:17** [e] Jn 17:21-23; Ro 8:9-11; Gal 2:20 **6:18** [f] ver 9; 1Co 5:1; 2Co 12:21; Gal 5:19; Eph 5:3; 1Th 4:3,4; Heb 13:4

[n] 4 Or *matters, do you appoint as judges men of little account in the church?* [o] 16 Gen. 2:24

(3) Furthermore, in cases where a so-called "brother" has divorced or deserted his family and refuses to support his wife and children with alimony, a mother with the right motives and concern for her children may take recourse in the courts. Paul is not advocating that those who break the law be allowed to defraud and threaten the life or well-being of another. His statement in v. 8 indicates he is speaking of minor disputes where the wrong could be accepted and tolerated.

6:9 THE WICKED WILL NOT INHERIT THE KINGDOM. Some in Corinth were deceived into believing that even if they broke fellowship with Christ, disowned him, and lived in immorality and injustice, their salvation and inheritance in God's kingdom were still secure. (1) However, Paul declares that spiritual death is the inevitable consequence of habitual sinning, even for the Christian (cf. Ro 8:13). No one can live for immoral gratification and still inherit the kingdom of God (cf. Ro 6:16; Jas 1:15; see 1Jn 2:4, note; 3:9, note). The apostle Paul repeats this cardinal teaching often (e.g., Gal 5:21 and Eph 5:5–6). Note that this principle was frequently proclaimed by the OT prophets (see Jer 8:7, note; 23:17, note; Eze 13:10, note).

(2) Paul's warning is directed to the whole Christian community. We must not be deceived, for all who are "wicked will not inherit the kingdom of God." Salvation without the regenerating and sanctifying work of the Holy Spirit has no place in Paul's theology.

6:11 JUSTIFIED . . . BY THE SPIRIT. Justification involves not only the redeeming work of the Lord Jesus, but also the work of the Spirit of God in the believer's life (see article on BIBLICAL WORDS FOR SALVATION, p. 1710).

6:12 EVERYTHING IS PERMISSIBLE FOR ME. This statement is clearly a quotation of the theological position of Paul's opponents. They thought they had the right to do anything they wished.

6:15 MEMBERS OF CHRIST. The apostle, warning against moral laxity, shows the terrible consequences of sexual immorality for the believer. When he joins his body to an immoral woman, it causes him to become one with her, to come under her domination (v. 16; cf. Ge 2:24), to desecrate what the cross has made holy (v. 15) and to sever himself from the kingdom of God (v. 9). In sexual immorality people virtually remove themselves from union with Christ by making their bodies members of immoral and ungodly persons.

6:18 FLEE FROM SEXUAL IMMORALITY. Sexual immorality is particularly abhorrent to God. More than any other sinful act, it desecrates

other sins a man commits are outside
his body, but he who sins sexually sins
against his own body.[g] **19**Do you not
know that your body is a temple[h] of
the Holy Spirit, who is in you, whom
you have received from God? You are
not your own;[i] **20**you were bought at
a price.[j] Therefore honor God with
your body.[k]

Marriage

7 Now for the matters you wrote
about: It is good for a man not to
marry.[p] [l] **2**But since there is so much
immorality, each man should have his
own wife, and each woman her own
husband. **3**The husband should fulfill
his marital duty to his wife,[m] and likewise the wife to her husband. **4**The
wife's body does not belong to her
alone but also to her husband. In the
same way, the husband's body does not
belong to him alone but also to his
wife. **5**Do not deprive each other except
by mutual consent and for a time,[n] so
that you may devote yourselves to
prayer. Then come together again so
that Satan[o] will not tempt you[p] because of your lack of self-control. **6**I
say this as a concession, not as a command.[q] **7**I wish that all men were as
I am.[r] But each man has his own gift
from God; one has this gift, another
has that.[s]
8Now to the unmarried and the widows I say: It is good for them to stay
unmarried, as I am.[t] **9**But if they cannot control themselves, they should
marry,[u] for it is better to marry than
to burn with passion.
10To the married I give this command (not I, but the Lord): A wife must
not separate from her husband.[v]
11But if she does, she must remain unmarried or else be reconciled to her
husband.[w] And a husband must not divorce his wife.
12To the rest I say this (I, not the
Lord):[x] If any brother has a wife who
is not a believer and she is willing to
live with him, he must not divorce her.
13And if a woman has a husband who
is not a believer and he is willing to live
with her, she must not divorce him.
14For the unbelieving husband has

6:18 [g]Ro 6:12 **6:19** [h]Jn 2:21 [i]Ro 14:7,8 **6:20** [j]Ps 74:2; S Mt 20:28; Ac 20:28; 1Co 7:23; Rev 5:9; 14:4 [k]Php 1:20 **7:1** [l]ver 8,26 **7:3** [m]Ex 21:10; 1Pe 3:7 **7:5** [n]Ex 19:15; 1Sa 21:4,5 [o]S Mt 4:10 [p]1Th 3:5

7:6 [q]2Co 8:8 **7:7** [r]ver 8; 1Co 9:5 [s]Mt 19:11,12; Ro 12:6; 1Co 12:4, 11 **7:8** [t]ver 1,26 **7:9** [u]1Ti 5:14 **7:10** [v]Mal 2:14-16; S Lk 16:18 **7:11** [w]ver 39; Ro 7:2,3 **7:12** [x]ver 6,10; 2Co 11:17

p1 Or *"It is good for a man not to have sexual relations with a woman."*

---

the body, which is the temple of the Spirit (vv. 15–20). Therefore, Paul gives the admonition to flee from sexual immorality. The use of the present tense here indicates that the Christian must repeatedly flee sexual immorality (cf. Ge 39:12; see article on STANDARDS OF SEXUAL MORALITY, p. 1936).

6:19 YOUR BODY IS A TEMPLE OF THE HOLY SPIRIT. As a Christian, your body is the personal dwelling place of the Holy Spirit (see also Ro 8:11, where the Spirit is God's mark on you that you belong to him). Because the Spirit lives in you and you belong to God, your body must never be defiled by any impurity or evil, whether by immoral thoughts, desires, deeds, films, books or magazines. Rather, you must live in such a way as to honor and please God with your body (v. 20).

7:1 GOOD FOR A MAN NOT TO MARRY. The entire seventh chapter is Paul's response to questions asked by the church in Corinth concerning marriage relationships. His instructions must be read in light of v. 26, "Because of the present crisis, I think that it is good." A time of crisis and persecution was coming for the early Christians, and in this situation maintaining a marriage relationship would have been difficult.

7:3 THE HUSBAND SHOULD FULFILL. The commitment of marriage means that each partner relinquishes the exclusive right to his or her own body and gives the other a claim to it. That is, neither marriage partner may fail to submit to the normal sexual desires of the other. Such desires within marriage are natural and God-given, and to refuse to carry out one's responsibility in fulfilling the other's needs is to open up the marriage to Satan's temptation of adultery (v. 5).

7:11 SHE MUST REMAIN UNMARRIED. In v. 10 Paul recognizes that God wants marriage to be permanent. He also acknowledges, however, that sometimes a marriage relationship may become so unbearable that separation from the partner is necessary. Paul, therefore, is not talking here about divorce permitted by God because of adultery (see Mt 19:9, note) or abandonment of a marriage partner (see v. 15, note). Rather, Paul is speaking of separation without legal divorce. He may be referring to situations where a marriage partner is acting in such a way as to endanger the physical or spiritual life of the spouse and children. In such conditions, it may be best that one of the partners leave the home and not remarry. It is inconceivable that Paul would advocate that a partner remain with a spouse who repeatedly brought physical harm and abuse on her and the children.

7:12 I SAY THIS (I, NOT THE LORD). Paul is not merely giving his own opinion here; rather he says that he does not have a saying of Jesus to confirm what he is about to write. However, he writes as one who has apostolic authority and is under divine inspiration (cf. vv. 25,40; 14:37).

7:14 HUSBAND ... WIFE ... CHILDREN. When a believer is involved in a marriage with an unbeliever, the marriage as well as the children born to that union are legitimate before God.

been sanctified through his wife,
and the unbelieving wife has been
sanctified through her believing
husband. Otherwise your children
would be unclean, but as it is, they
are holy.[y]
15But if the unbeliever leaves, let
him do so. A believing man or woman
is not bound in such circumstances;
God has called us to live in peace.[z]
16How do you know, wife, whether you
will save[a] your husband?[b] Or, how
do you know, husband, whether you
will save your wife?
17Nevertheless, each one should retain the place in life that the Lord assigned to him and to which God has
called him.[c] This is the rule I lay down
in all the churches.[d] **18**Was a man already circumcised when he was called?
He should not become uncircumcised.
Was a man uncircumcised when he
was called? He should not be circumcised.[e] **19**Circumcision is nothing and
uncircumcision is nothing.[f] Keeping
God's commands is what counts.
20Each one should remain in the situation which he was in when God called
him.[g] **21**Were you a slave when you
were called? Don't let it trouble you—
although if you can gain your freedom,
do so. **22**For he who was a slave when
he was called by the Lord is the Lord's
freedman;[h] similarly, he who was a
free man when he was called is Christ's
slave.[i] **23**You were bought at a
price;[j] do not become slaves of men.
24Brothers, each man, as responsible

7:14 [y]Mal 2:15
7:15 [z]S Ro 14:19; 1Co 14:33
7:16 [a]S Ro 11:14 [b]1Pe 3:1
7:17 [c]Ro 12:3 [d]1Co 4:17; 14:33; 2Co 8:18; 11:28
7:18 [e]Ac 15:1,2
7:19 [f]Ro 2:25-27; Gal 5:6; 6:15; Col 3:11
7:20 [g]ver 24
7:22 [h]Jn 8:32,36 [i]S Ro 6:22
7:23 [j]S 1Co 6:20
7:24 [k]ver 20
7:25 [l]ver 6; 2Co 8:8 [m]2Co 4:1; 1Ti 1:13,16
7:26 [n]ver 1,8
7:27 [o]ver 20,21
7:28 [p]ver 36
7:29 [q]ver 31; S Ro 13:11,12
7:31 [r]ver 29; S Heb 12:27
7:32 [s]1Ti 5:5
7:34 [t]Lk 2:37

to God, should remain in the situation
God called him to.[k]
25Now about virgins: I have no command from the Lord,[l] but I give a
judgment as one who by the Lord's
mercy[m] is trustworthy. **26**Because of
the present crisis, I think that it is
good for you to remain as you are.[n]
27Are you married? Do not seek a divorce. Are you unmarried? Do not look
for a wife.[o] **28**But if you do marry, you
have not sinned;[p] and if a virgin marries, she has not sinned. But those who
marry will face many troubles in this
life, and I want to spare you this.
29What I mean, brothers, is that the
time is short.[q] From now on those
who have wives should live as if they
had none; **30**those who mourn, as if
they did not; those who are happy, as
if they were not; those who buy something, as if it were not theirs to keep;
31those who use the things of the
world, as if not engrossed in them. For
this world in its present form is passing away.[r]
32I would like you to be free from
concern. An unmarried man is concerned about the Lord's affairs[s]—
how he can please the Lord. **33**But a
married man is concerned about the affairs of this world—how he can please
his wife— **34**and his interests are divided. An unmarried woman or virgin
is concerned about the Lord's affairs:
Her aim is to be devoted to the Lord in
both body and spirit.[t] But a married
woman is concerned about the affairs

Therefore, the believer should live with the unbeliever and not seek to divide the marriage or the home. Furthermore, because the husband or wife is a believer, he/she may have a special influence so that the spouse is led to accept Christ (cf. 1Pe 3:1–2).

7:15 IS NOT BOUND. In the event that an unbelieving partner abandons or divorces a believer, the marriage relation is dissolved and the believer is freed from his or her marital obligation. "Not bound in such circumstances" means that the believer is released from the marital contract. The word "bound" (Gk *douloō*) literally means "to enslave"; the faithful believer is no longer enslaved to his or her marriage vows. In this case, the abandoned believer is free to remarry, provided he or she marries a Christian (v. 39; see Mt 19:9, note on divorce).

7:19 KEEPING GOD'S COMMANDS. How can Paul, who emphasized so strongly salvation by faith (Ro 3–4), say that what really matters is "keeping God's commands"? Because salvation by faith must lead to obeying, loving and serving God. Anything less than such obedience falls short of NT saving faith (cf. Gal 5:6; 6:15).

7:31 THOSE WHO USE THE THINGS OF THE WORLD. We live in the period when all worldly things are hastening toward an end. For this reason life in this world should not be our utmost concern; we should direct our greatest attention toward our heavenly home (Heb 11:13–16).

7:34 AN UNMARRIED WOMAN. Scripture maintains that the unmarried state is in no way inferior to the married. In fact, it is better in the most important way of all—the possibility of offering undistracted service to God. The unmarried man (vv. 32–33) or woman (v. 34) can concentrate on the things that belong to the Lord in a greater way than the married. To be "devoted to the Lord both in body and spirit" does not refer to ethical achievement, but to the possibility of a greater commitment to God unencumbered by family responsibilities, problems and concerns. The unmarried can devote themselves with all their gifts to the Lord, free from care, totally occupied with the Lord and his Word.

of this world—how she can please her
husband. **35**I am saying this for your
own good, not to restrict you, but that
you may live in a right way in undivided[u] devotion to the Lord.
36If anyone thinks he is acting im-
properly toward the virgin he is engaged to, and if she is getting along in
years and he feels he ought to marry,
he should do as he wants. He is not
sinning.[v] They should get married.
37But the man who has settled the
matter in his own mind, who is under
no compulsion but has control over his
own will, and who has made up his
mind not to marry the virgin—this
man also does the right thing. **38**So
then, he who marries the virgin does
right,[w] but he who does not marry her
does even better.[q]
39A woman is bound to her husband
as long as he lives.[x] But if her husband dies, she is free to marry anyone
she wishes, but he must belong to the
Lord.[y] **40**In my judgment,[z] she is
happier if she stays as she is—and I
think that I too have the Spirit of God.

Food Sacrificed to Idols

8 Now about food sacrificed to
idols:[a] We know that we all possess knowledge.[r][b] Knowledge puffs
up, but love builds up. **2**The man who
thinks he knows something[c] does not
yet know as he ought to know.[d] **3**But
the man who loves God is known by
God.[e]
4So then, about eating food sacrificed to idols:[f] We know that an idol
is nothing at all in the world[g] and that
there is no God but one.[h] **5**For even if
there are so-called gods,[i] whether in
heaven or on earth (as indeed there are
many "gods" and many "lords"), **6**yet
for us there is but one God,[j] the Father,[k] from whom all things came[l]
and for whom we live; and there is but
one Lord,[m] Jesus Christ, through
whom all things came[n] and through
whom we live.
7But not everyone knows this.[o]
Some people are still so accustomed to
idols that when they eat such food they
think of it as having been sacrificed to
an idol, and since their conscience is
weak,[p] it is defiled. **8**But food does not
bring us near to God;[q] we are no
worse if we do not eat, and no better if
we do.
9Be careful, however, that the exercise of your freedom does not become
a stumbling block[r] to the weak.[s]
10For if anyone with a weak conscience
sees you who have this knowledge eating in an idol's temple, won't he be em-
boldened to eat what has been sacrificed to idols?[t] **11**So this weak
brother, for whom Christ died, is destroyed[u] by your knowledge. **12**When
you sin against your brothers[v] in this

7:35 [u] Ps 86:11
7:36 [v] ver 28
7:38 [w] Heb 13:4
7:39 [x] Ro 7:2,3 [y] 2Co 6:14
7:40 [z] ver 25
8:1 [a] ver 4,7,10; Ac 15:20 [b] Ro 15:14
8:2 [c] 1Co 3:18 [d] 1Co 13:8,9,12; 1Ti 6:4
8:3 [e] Jer 1:5; Ro 8:29; Gal 4:9
8:4 [f] ver 1,7,10; Ex 34:15 [g] Ac 14:15; 1Co 10:19; Gal 4:8 [h] ver 6; Dt 6:4; Ps 86:10; Eph 4:6; 1Ti 2:5
8:5 [i] 2Th 2:4
8:6 [j] S ver 4 [k] Mal 2:10 [l] S Ro 11:36 [m] Eph 4:5 [n] S Jn 1:3
8:7 [o] ver 1 [p] Ro 14:14; 1Co 10:28
8:8 [q] Ro 14:17
8:9 [r] S 2Co 6:3; Gal 5:13 [s] Ro 14:1
8:10 [t] ver 1,4,7
8:11 [u] Ro 14:15, 20
8:12 [v] Mt 18:6

[q] *36-38* Or *36If anyone thinks he is not treating his daughter properly, and if she is getting along in years, and he feels she ought to marry, he should do as he wants. He is not sinning. He should let her get married. 37But the man who has settled the matter in his own mind, who is under no compulsion but has control over his own will, and who has made up his mind to keep the virgin unmarried—this man also does the right thing. 38So then, he who gives his virgin in marriage does right, but he who does not give her in marriage does even better.* [r] *1* Or *"We all possess knowledge," as you say*

8:1 FOOD SACRIFICED TO IDOLS. In chs. 8–10 Paul deals with the question of the Corinthians about meat offered to idols and whether it is right to buy and eat this meat and to participate in festivals at idol temples (v. 10). (1) In treating this subject he reveals an important principle by which Christians of all ages should live. This principle applies to questionable activities that might tempt some believers to sin and lead them to spiritual ruin (v. 11). The Holy Spirit through Paul has directed Christians to always act with a love for other believers that may in fact require self-denial.

(2) Self-denial means limiting one's freedom and setting aside all questionable activities in order not to offend or weaken the sincere convictions of other Christians, which they believe to be based on Biblical principles. The opposite of self-denial is defending one's own right to engage in a questionable activity, one that may entice others to follow—to their own hurt (cf. Ro 14:1—15:3; Ac 15:29, note; 1Co 9:19, note).

8:2 DOES NOT YET KNOW. Those who base their right to do certain questionable things on their "knowledge" and "mature understanding" show that in reality they do not know as they ought. Our knowledge in this life is always incomplete and imperfect. Thus, our actions must first be based on love for God and others. If love is our determining consideration, we will refuse to engage in or encourage any activity that might lead even one believer to stumble and head toward eternal ruin. Those who live by the rule of love are those who are "known by God " (v. 3).

8:12 YOU SIN AGAINST CHRIST. Those who by their example lead another believer into sin and spiritual ruin (v. 11) sin not only against that person, but also against Christ himself. A great sin has been committed; the purpose for which Christ died is considered of little value in comparison to

way and wound their weak conscience,
you sin against Christ.[w] **13**Therefore,
if what I eat causes my brother to fall
into sin, I will never eat meat again, so
that I will not cause him to fall.[x]

The Rights of an Apostle

9 Am I not free?[y] Am I not an apostle?[z] Have I not seen Jesus our
Lord?[a] Are you not the result of my
work in the Lord?[b] **2**Even though I
may not be an apostle to others, surely
I am to you! For you are the seal[c] of
my apostleship in the Lord.
3This is my defense to those who sit
in judgment on me. **4**Don't we have the
right to food and drink?[d] **5**Don't we
have the right to take a believing
wife[e] along with us, as do the other
apostles and the Lord's brothers[f] and
Cephas[s]?[g] **6**Or is it only I and Barnabas[h] who must work for a living?
7Who serves as a soldier[i] at his
own expense? Who plants a vineyard[j]
and does not eat of its grapes? Who
tends a flock and does not drink of the
milk? **8**Do I say this merely from a human point of view? Doesn't the Law
say the same thing? **9**For it is written
in the Law of Moses: "Do not muzzle an
ox while it is treading out the
grain."[t][k] Is it about oxen that God is
concerned?[l] **10**Surely he says this for
us, doesn't he? Yes, this was written
for us,[m] because when the plowman
plows and the thresher threshes, they
ought to do so in the hope of sharing
in the harvest.[n] **11**If we have sown
spiritual seed among you, is it too
much if we reap a material harvest
from you?[o] **12**If others have this right
of support from you, shouldn't we have
it all the more?
But we did not use this right.[p] On
the contrary, we put up with anything
rather than hinder[q] the gospel of
Christ. **13**Don't you know that those
who work in the temple get their food
from the temple, and those who serve
at the altar share in what is offered on
the altar?[r] **14**In the same way, the
Lord has commanded that those who
preach the gospel should receive their
living from the gospel.[s]
15But I have not used any of these
rights.[t] And I am not writing this in
the hope that you will do such things
for me. I would rather die than have
anyone deprive me of this boast.[u]
16Yet when I preach the gospel, I cannot boast, for I am compelled to
preach.[v] Woe to me if I do not preach
the gospel! **17**If I preach voluntarily, I
have a reward;[w] if not voluntarily, I
am simply discharging the trust committed to me.[x] **18**What then is my reward? Just this: that in preaching the
gospel I may offer it free of charge,[y]
and so not make use of my rights[z] in
preaching it.
19Though I am free[a] and belong to
no man, I make myself a slave to everyone,[b] to win as many as possible.[c]
20To the Jews I became like a Jew, to
win the Jews.[d] To those under the law
I became like one under the law
(though I myself am not under the
law),[e] so as to win those under the
law. **21**To those not having the law I
became like one not having the law[f]
(though I am not free from God's law
but am under Christ's law),[g] so as to
win those not having the law. **22**To the
weak I became weak, to win the
weak.[h] I have become all things to all
men[i] so that by all possible means I
might save some.[j] **23**I do all this for

8:12 [w]Mt 25:40, 45
8:13 [x]S Mt 5:29
9:1 [y]ver 19 [z]S 1Co 1:1; 2Co 12:12 [a]S 1Co 15:8 [b]1Co 3:6; 4:15
9:2 [c]2Co 3:2,3
9:4 [d]ver 14; S Ac 18:3
9:5 [e]1Co 7:7,8 [f]S Mt 12:46 [g]S 1Co 1:12
9:6 [h]S Ac 4:36
9:7 [i]2Ti 2:3,4 [j]Dt 20:6; Pr 27:18; 1Co 3:6, 8
9:9 [k]Dt 25:4; 1Ti 5:18 [l]Dt 22:1-4; Pr 12:10
9:10 [m]S Ro 4:23, 24 [n]Pr 11:25; 2Ti 2:6
9:11 [o]ver 14; Ro 15:27; Gal 6:6
9:12 [p]ver 15,18; S Ac 18:3 [q]2Co 6:3; 11:7-12
9:13 [r]Lev 6:16, 26; Dt 18:1
9:14 [s]S 1Ti 5:18
9:15 [t]ver 12,18; S Ac 18:3 [u]2Co 11:9,10
9:16 [v]Ro 1:14; Ac 9:15; 26:16-18
9:17 [w]1Co 3:8,14 [x]1Co 4:1; Gal 2:7; Col 1:25
9:18 [y]2Co 11:7; 12:13 [z]ver 12,15
9:19 [a]ver 1 [b]2Co 4:5; Gal 5:13 [c]Mt 18:15; 1Pe 3:1
9:20 [d]Ac 16:3; 21:20-26; Ro 11:14 [e]S Ro 2:12
9:21 [f]Ro 2:12,14 [g]Gal 6:2
9:22 [h]S Ro 14:1; S 1Co 2:3 [i]1Co 10:33 [j]S Ro 11:14

[s]*5* That is, Peter [t]*9* Deut. 25:4

one's own self-centered desires (see Mt 18:7, note).

9:1 AM I NOT AN APOSTLE? Paul personally illustrates the principle set forth in 8:13 (see 8:1, note) by willingly setting aside his own personal rights as an apostle in order not to hinder the gospel of Christ (v. 12; see 9:19, note).

9:14 RECEIVE THEIR LIVING FROM THE GOSPEL. Both the OT (Dt 25:4; cf. Lev 6:16,26; 7:6) and the NT (Mt 10:10; Lk 10:7) teach that those who are engaged in proclaiming God's Word should be supported by those who receive spiritual blessing from it (see Gal 6:6–10, note; 1Ti 5:18).

9:19 I MAKE MYSELF A SLAVE TO EVERYONE. Paul uses himself as an example of the principle of self-denial for the sake of others (see 8:1, note). He renounces his rights out of sympathetic consideration for the convictions of others (Ro 14:15–21), in order not to limit his ministry or hinder the gospel (v. 12). This practice does not mean that Paul compromises Christian principles or seeks to please others for the purpose of winning their esteem (Gal 1:8–10). What he affirms is that he is prepared to conform to the convictions of those whom he is trying to help, provided Christian principles are not violated. He understands that if he offends others by disregarding the conviction of their conscience, his ministry to them for Christ's sake could be seriously hindered (vv. 12,19–23; see 8:1, note).

the sake of the gospel, that I may share
in its blessings.
24Do you not know that in a race all
the runners run, but only one gets the
prize?[k] Run[l] in such a way as to get
the prize. **25**Everyone who competes in
the games goes into strict training.
They do it to get a crown[m] that will not
last; but we do it to get a crown that
will last forever.[n] **26**Therefore I do not
run like a man running aimlessly;[o] I
do not fight like a man beating the
air.[p] **27**No, I beat my body[q] and make
it my slave so that after I have
preached to others, I myself will not be
disqualified for the prize.[r]

Warnings From Israel's History

10 For I do not want you to be ignorant[s] of the fact, brothers,
that our forefathers were all under the
cloud[t] and that they all passed
through the sea.[u] **2**They were all baptized into[v] Moses in the cloud and in
the sea. **3**They all ate the same spiritual food[w] **4**and drank the same spiritual
drink; for they drank from the spiritual
rock[x] that accompanied them, and
that rock was Christ. **5**Nevertheless,
God was not pleased with most of
them; their bodies were scattered over
the desert.[y]
6Now these things occurred as examples[u][z] to keep us from setting our
hearts on evil things as they did. **7**Do
not be idolaters,[a] as some of them
were; as it is written: "The people sat
down to eat and drink and got up to
indulge in pagan revelry."[v][b] **8**We
should not commit sexual immorality,
as some of them did—and in one day
twenty-three thousand of them died.[c]
9We should not test the Lord,[d] as
some of them did—and were killed by
snakes.[e] **10**And do not grumble, as
some of them did[f]—and were killed[g]
by the destroying angel.[h]
11These things happened to them as
examples[i] and were written down as
warnings for us,[j] on whom the fulfillment of the ages has come.[k] **12**So, if
you think you are standing firm,[l] be
careful that you don't fall! **13**No temptation has seized you except what is

[u]6 Or *types*; also in verse 11 [v]7 Exodus 32:6

9:24 [k]Php 3:14; Col 2:18 [l]ver 25, 26; Gal 2:2; 5:7; Php 2:16; 2Ti 4:7; Heb 12:1
9:25 [m]2Ti 2:5 [n]2Ti 4:8; Jas 1:12; 1Pe 5:4; Rev 2:10; 3:11
9:26 [o]S ver 24 [p]1Ti 6:12
9:27 [q]Ro 8:13 [r]ver 24
10:1 [s]S Ro 11:25 [t]Ex 13:21; Ps 105:39 [u]Ex 14:22,29; Ps 66:6
10:2 [v]Ro 6:3
10:3 [w]S Jn 6:31
10:4 [x]Ex 17:6; Nu 20:11; Ps 78:15; 105:41
10:5 [y]Nu 14:29; Heb 3:17; Jude 5
10:6 [z]ver 11
10:7 [a]ver 14 [b]Ex 32:4,6,19
10:8 [c]Nu 25:1-9
10:9 [d]Ex 17:2; Ps 78:18; 95:9; 106:14 [e]Nu 21:5,6
10:10 [f]Nu 16:41; 17:5,10 [g]Nu 16:49 [h]Ex 12:23; 1Ch 21:15; Heb 11:28
10:11 [i]ver 6 [j]S Ro 4:24 [k]S Ro 13:11
10:12 [l]Ro 11:20; 2Co 1:24

9:24 THE PRIZE. The "prize," the "crown that will last forever" (v. 25), refers to the victory of eternal salvation, the precious goal of the Christian life (cf. 1:8; 4:5; 6:2,9–10; 15:12–19). This goal can only be achieved by giving up some of our rights for the sake of others (8:7–13) and by renouncing those things that would take us out of the race altogether (10:5–22).

9:24 RUN IN SUCH A WAY AS TO GET THE PRIZE. Paul illustrates the principle that if we fail to exercise self-control, self-denial and love in our relationships with others, we ourselves will be rejected by God (see next note).

9:27 I MYSELF WILL NOT BE DISQUALIFIED. "Be disqualified" (Gk *adokimos*) conveys the idea of "failing the test" or "being rejected." Paul uses this same term in 2Co 13:5, where he states that Christ does not live in any who "fail the test" (Gk *adokimoi*). Paul is not referring merely to the loss of a ministerial reward. What he recognizes is the possibility that he may fail to get the prize (i.e., the inheritance) of final salvation (vv. 24–25) if he should stop living a holy life, exercising self-control and enduring hardships for Christ (vv. 25–27).

10:1 I DO NOT WANT YOU TO BE IGNORANT. The fact that one may be redeemed, partake of divine grace, and yet later be rejected by God because of evil conduct (see 9:27, note) is now verified by examples from Israel's experience (vv. 1–12).

10:5 BODIES WERE SCATTERED OVER THE DESERT. The Israelites had experienced God's grace in the exodus. They had been delivered from bondage (v. 1), baptized (v. 2) and divinely sustained in the desert, experiencing close fellowship with Christ (vv. 3–4). Yet in spite of these spiritual blessings, they failed to please God, and were destroyed by him in the desert. They forfeited their election, and thus failed to reach the promised land (cf. Nu 14:30; see article on GOD'S COVENANT WITH THE ISRAELITES, p. 290). Paul's point is this: just as God did not tolerate Israel's idolatry, sin and immorality, so he will not tolerate the sin of believers under the new covenant.

10:6 THESE THINGS OCCURRED AS EXAMPLES. God's terrible judgment on the disobedient Israelites serves as an example and a warning for those under the new covenant not to desire evil things. Paul warns the Corinthians that if they repeat Israel's unfaithfulness (vv. 7–10), they too will receive God's judgment and fail to enter the promised heavenly country.

10:11 WRITTEN DOWN AS WARNINGS. The history of God's judgment of his people was written down in Scripture to provide those in the NT with ample warnings against sinning and falling from grace (v. 12; see Nu 14:29, note).

10:12 BE CAREFUL THAT YOU DON'T FALL! The Israelites, as God's elect, thought they could safely dabble in sin, idolatry and immorality; yet they met with condemnation. So also those who believe they can securely live in worldly gratification must realize that condemnation also awaits them.

common to man. And God is faithful;[m]
he will not let you be tempted beyond
what you can bear.[n] But when you are
tempted, he will also provide a way out
so that you can stand up under it.

Idol Feasts and the Lord's Supper

14Therefore, my dear friends,[o] flee
from idolatry.[p] **15**I speak to sensible
people; judge for yourselves what I
say. **16**Is not the cup of thanksgiving
for which we give thanks a participation in the blood of Christ? And is not
the bread that we break[q] a participation in the body of Christ?[r] **17**Because
there is one loaf, we, who are many,
are one body,[s] for we all partake of
the one loaf.
18Consider the people of Israel: Do
not those who eat the sacrifices[t] participate in the altar? **19**Do I mean then
that a sacrifice offered to an idol is anything, or that an idol is anything?[u]
20No, but the sacrifices of pagans are
offered to demons,[v] not to God, and I
do not want you to be participants with
demons. **21**You cannot drink the cup of
the Lord and the cup of demons too;
you cannot have a part in both the
Lord's table and the table of demons.[w]
22Are we trying to arouse the Lord's
jealousy?[x] Are we stronger than
he?[y]

The Believer's Freedom

23"Everything is permissible"—but
not everything is beneficial.[z] "Everything is permissible"—but not everything is constructive. **24**Nobody should
seek his own good, but the good of others.[a]
25Eat anything sold in the meat market without raising questions of conscience,[b] **26**for, "The earth is the
Lord's, and everything in it."[w][c]
27If some unbeliever invites you to a
meal and you want to go, eat whatever
is put before you[d] without raising
questions of conscience. **28**But if anyone says to you, "This has been offered
in sacrifice," then do not eat it, both for

10:13 [m] S 1Co 1:9 [n] 2Pe 2:9 **10:14** [o] Heb 6:9; 1Pe 2:11; 1Jn 2:7; Jude 3 [p] ver 7; 1Jn 5:21 **10:16** [q] S Mt 14:19 [r] Mt 26:26-28; 1Co 11:23-25 **10:17** [s] S Ro 12:5 **10:18** [t] Lev 7:6, 14,15 **10:19** [u] S 1Co 8:4 **10:20** [v] Lev 17:7; Dt 32:17; Ps 106:37; Rev 9:20
10:21 [w] 2Co 6:15, 16 **10:22** [x] Dt 32:16, 21; 1Ki 14:22; Ps 78:58; Jer 44:8 [y] Ecc 6:10; Isa 45:9 **10:23** [z] 1Co 6:12 **10:24** [a] ver 33; S Ro 15:1,2; 1Co 13:5; Php 2:4, 21 **10:25** [b] S Ac 10:15; 1Co 8:7 **10:26** [c] Ps 24:1; Ex 9:29; 19:5; Job 41:11; Ps 50:12; 1Ti 4:4 **10:27** [d] Lk 10:7

[w] *26* Psalm 24:1

10:13 GOD IS FAITHFUL. Professing believers may not justify sinning with excuses that they are simply human and thus imperfect, or that in this life all born-again believers continue sinning in word, thought and deed (cf. Ro 6:1). At the same time, Paul assures the Corinthians that no true believer need fall from God's grace.

(1) The Holy Spirit explicitly affirms that God provides his children with adequate grace to overcome every temptation and thus to resist sinning (cf. Rev 2:7,17,26). God's faithfulness expresses itself in two ways: (a) he will not allow us to be tempted above that which we can bear, and (b) he will with each temptation provide a way by which we can endure the temptation and overcome sin (cf. 2Th 3:3).

(2) God's grace (Eph 2:8–10; Tit 2:11–14), the blood of Jesus Christ (Eph 2:13; 1Pe 2:24), the Word of God (Eph 6:17; 2Ti 3:16–17), the Spirit's indwelling power (Tit 3:5–6; 1Pe 1:5) and Christ's heavenly intercession bring sufficient power for the believer's warfare against sin and the spiritual forces of wickedness (Eph 6:10–18; Heb 7:25).

(3) If Christians yield to sin, it is not because Christ's provision of grace is inadequate, but because believers fail to resist their own sinful desires by the power of the Spirit (Ro 8:13–14; Gal 5:16,24; Jas 1:13–15). God's "divine power has given us everything we need for life and godliness" (2Pe 1:3), and through the salvation provided by Christ we can "live a life worthy of the Lord and may please him in every way: bearing fruit in every good work, . . . being strengthened with all power according to his glorious might so that you may have great endurance and patience" (Col 1:10–11; see Mt 4:1, note on how to conquer temptation). We can bear every temptation and find a way out if we sincerely desire to and if we depend on God's power and faithfulness.

10:16 THE CUP OF THANKSGIVING. The cup we take at the Lord's Supper typifies Christ's death and his sacrificial suffering for sinful men and women. "Participation in the blood of Christ" refers to the believer sharing in the salvation provided by Christ's death (cf. 11:25). Scripture does not teach that the bread and the fruit of the vine actually become Christ's body and blood (see 11:24–25, note on the Lord's Supper).

10:20 OFFERED TO DEMONS. Idolatry involves the worship of demons (cf. Dt 32:17; Ps 106:35–38; see article on THE NATURE OF IDOLATRY, p. 394) and is associated with greed or covetousness (see Col 3:5, note). Therefore, demonic powers stand behind love for worldly possessions, honor or position.

10:21 THE CUP OF THE LORD AND THE CUP OF DEMONS. As participating in the Lord's Supper is a sharing in Christ's redemption, so participating in idolatrous feasts is a sharing with demons (v. 20). The error of some at Corinth was failing to distinguish between righteousness and unrighteousness, between that which is holy and that which is defiled, between that which is of Christ and that which is of the devil. They did not understand God's holy jealousy (v. 22; cf. Ex 20:5; Dt 4:24; Jos 24:19) and the seriousness of compromising with the world. Christ himself spoke of this fatal error: "No one can serve two masters" (Mt 6:24).

the sake of the man who told you and
for conscience' sake[x][e]— **29**the other
man's conscience, I mean, not yours.
For why should my freedom[f] be
judged by another's conscience? **30**If I
take part in the meal with thankfulness, why am I denounced because of
something I thank God for?[g]
31So whether you eat or drink or
whatever you do, do it all for the glory
of God.[h] **32**Do not cause anyone to
stumble,[i] whether Jews, Greeks or
the church of God[j]— **33**even as I try
to please everybody in every way.[k]
For I am not seeking my own good but
the good of many,[l] so that they may

11 be saved.[m] **1**Follow my example,[n] as I follow the example of
Christ.[o]

Propriety in Worship

2I praise you[p] for remembering me
in everything[q] and for holding to the
teachings,[y] just as I passed them on
to you.[r]
3Now I want you to realize that the

10:28 [e] 1Co 8:7, 10-12 **10:29** [f] 1Co 9:1, 19 **10:30** [g] S Ro 14:6 **10:31** [h] Zec 14:21; Col 3:17; 1Pe 4:11 **10:32** [i] S Mt 5:29; Ac 24:16; S 2Co 6:3 [j] Ac 20:28; 1Co 1:2; 11:16,22; 15:9; 1Ti 3:5,15 **10:33** [k] Ro 15:2; 1Co 9:22 [l] S ver 24
[m] S Ro 11:14 **11:1** [n] S 1Co 4:16 [o] Ro 15:3; 1Pe 2:21 **11:2** [p] ver 17,22 [q] 1Co 4:17 [r] ver 23; 1Co 15:2,3; 2Th 2:15; 3:6

[x] *28* Some manuscripts *conscience' sake, for "the earth is the Lord's and everything in it"*
[y] *2* Or *traditions*

10:31 DO IT ALL FOR THE GLORY OF GOD. The main object of the believer's life is to please God and promote his glory (see article on THE GLORY OF GOD, p. 1192). Thus what cannot be done for God's glory (i.e., in honor and thanksgiving to him as our Lord, Creator and Redeemer) should not be done at all. We honor him by obedience, thankfulness, reliance, prayer, faith and loyalty. This rule ("do it all for the glory of God") must be a primary direction of our lives, a guide for our conduct and a test of our actions.

11:1 FOLLOW THE EXAMPLE OF CHRIST. The believer, like Paul, is called to follow Christ's example and become a Christlike person (cf. Ro 13:14; Gal 3:27). What is Christlikeness?

(1) Christlikeness is, first and foremost, love for God and for others (Mt 22:37–39; Lk 10:27). The believer's love for God motivates and directs his or her love for others (1Jn 4:20–21), just as Christ's love for God was always first and his love for others subordinate to and based on that love for the Father (cf. Mt 22:37–39; Jn 17:23–24).

(2) Christ's love for his Father was revealed in his concern for God's glory (Mt 6:9; Jn 12:28; 17:4), for his will (Mt 26:42; Jn 4:34; Heb 10:7–12), for his Word (Mt 26:54; Jn 8:28; 17:14, 17) and for the nearness of his presence (Lk 5:16; Jn 17:21). We see this love in his faithfulness to God (Heb 3:2) and his willingness to carry out God's will by sacrificing his life for our redemption (Mt 26:42; Jn 3:16–17; Heb 10:4–9). Christ's love for his Father is further revealed in his love for righteousness and hatred of sin (see Heb 1:9, note).

(3) Christ's love for humans was seen in his compassion (Mt 9:36; 14:14; 15:32; 20:34; cf. Lk 15:11–24), kindness (Mt 8:3,16–17; 9:22), tears (Jn 11:35), humility (Mt 11:29), good deeds (Ac 10:38), gentleness (Mt 11:29), forgiveness (Lk 23:34), patience (Lk 13:34) and mercy (Mt 15:22–28; Jude 21). He also demonstrated love when he rebuked sin (Mt 16:23; Mk 9:19; 10:13–14), expressed anger at those who were cruel, heartless or insensitive to the suffering and needs of others (see Mk 3:5, note), warned us of hell (Mt 5:29–30; Lk 12:5) and offered himself as a sacrifice (Mt 26:38; Jn 10:11,17–18; 13:1).

11:2 TEACHINGS. "Teachings" were instructions relating to doctrine, moral standards and codes of conduct that Paul delivered to the churches by Christ's authority. Note that the instruction of ch. 11 outlines God's will for his people in such matters as outward dress, modesty, appearance and proper conduct. To teach that God is concerned only with inner attitudes and not with "externals" departs from God's clear revelation in Scripture. To dress properly and modestly is a Biblical principle of lasting validity (see 1Ti 2:9, note).

11:3 HEAD OF EVERY MAN. Paul is concerned about the proper relationship between men and women, and he seeks to uphold that relationship as ordained by God. (1) He maintains that in Christ a perfect spiritual equality exists among men and women as heirs of God's grace, yet it is an equality involving order and subordination with respect to authority (see Gal 3:28, note). As God is the head of Christ, Christ is the head of man, and man the head of woman. The word "head" seems to express both authority and divine order (cf. 3:23; 11:8,10; 15:28; Jdg 10:18; Eph 1:21–22; 5:23–24; Col 1:18; 2:10).

(2) Paul bases the husband's headship not on cultural considerations but on God's creative activity and purpose in creating the woman to help the man (vv. 8–9; see Ge 2:18, note; 1Ti 2:13, note).

(3) Subordination is not demeaning to one's person, for it does not imply suppression or oppression. Rather it states that the husband must recognize the worth God places on the woman and that his responsibility involves protecting and leading her in such a way as to fulfill God's will for her in the home and the church.

(4) Just as Christ is not inferior or second-class because the Father is his head, so the woman is not a second-class person because man is her head. Furthermore, in God's kingdom leadership never implies being "greater." Servanthood and obedience are the keys to greatness in the kingdom (Mt 20:25–28; Php 2:5–9). Paul's treatment of the relationship of men and women should be studied in conjunction with his treatment of the wife's and husband's responsibilities in marriage (see Eph 5:21–23, notes).

head of every man is Christ,[s] and
the head of the woman is man,[t]
and the head of Christ is God.[u] **4**Every
man who prays or prophesies[v] with
his head covered dishonors his head.
5And every woman who prays or prophesies[w] with her head uncovered dishonors her head—it is just as though her
head were shaved.[x] **6**If a woman does
not cover her head, she should have
her hair cut off; and if it is a disgrace
for a woman to have her hair cut or
shaved off, she should cover her head.
7A man ought not to cover his head,[z]
since he is the image[y] and glory of
God; but the woman is the glory of
man. **8**For man did not come from woman, but woman from man;[z] **9**neither
was man created for woman, but woman for man.[a] **10**For this reason, and
because of the angels, the woman
ought to have a sign of authority on her
head.

11In the Lord, however, woman is
not independent of man, nor is man independent of woman. **12**For as woman
came from man, so also man is born of
woman. But everything comes from
God.[b] **13**Judge for yourselves: Is it
proper for a woman to pray to God with
her head uncovered? **14**Does not the
very nature of things teach you that if
a man has long hair, it is a disgrace to
him, **15**but that if a woman has long
hair, it is her glory? For long hair is
given to her as a covering. **16**If anyone
wants to be contentious about this, we
have no other practice—nor do the
churches of God.[c]

11:3 [s] S Eph 1:22 [t] Ge 3:16; Eph 5:23 [u] 1Co 3:23
11:4 [v] S Ac 11:27
11:5 [w] S Ac 21:9 [x] Dt 21:12
11:7 [y] Ge 1:26; 5:1; 9:6; Jas 3:9
11:8 [z] Ge 2:21-23; 1Ti 2:13
11:9 [a] Ge 2:18
11:12 [b] S Ro 11:36
11:16 [c] S 1Co 7:17; S 10:32
11:17 [d] ver 2,22
11:18 [e] 1Co 1:10-12; 3:3
11:19 [f] 1Jn 2:19

The Lord's Supper

11:23–25pp — Mt 26:26–28; Mk 14:22–24; Lk 22:17–20

17In the following directives I have
no praise for you,[d] for your meetings
do more harm than good. **18**In the first
place, I hear that when you come together as a church, there are divisions[e] among you, and to some extent
I believe it. **19**No doubt there have to be
differences among you to show which
of you have God's approval.[f] **20**When
you come together, it is not the Lord's
Supper you eat, **21**for as you eat, each

z 4-7 Or *4Every man who prays or prophesies with long hair dishonors his head. 5And every woman who prays or prophesies with no covering ⌊of hair⌋ on her head dishonors her head—she is just like one of the "shorn women." 6If a woman has no covering, let her be for now with short hair, but since it is a disgrace for a woman to have her hair shorn or shaved, she should grow it again. 7A man ought not to have long hair*

11:6 SHE SHOULD COVER HER HEAD. The woman covered her head in Paul's day in order to show modesty and subordination to her husband and to demonstrate her dignity. The veil meant that she was to be respected and honored as a woman. Without a veil she had no dignity; men did not respect women without veils because they were in effect flaunting themselves publicly and shamefully. Thus, the veil served as a sign of the value and glory of womanhood as God created her.

The principle behind the wearing of veils is still needed today. A Christian woman should dress in a modest and careful way, with honorable and dignified attire that allows her to go anywhere with security and profound respect. When dressing modestly and properly for the glory of God, a woman enhances her own God-given place of dignity and worth.

11:10 SIGN OF AUTHORITY ON HER HEAD. Once again Paul emphasizes that a woman should be veiled in public, i.e., have a symbol of "authority" on her head (see vv. 3,6, notes). The phrase "because of the angels" may refer to the fact that angels are concerned with proper order and are shocked at conduct that is not in tune with God's will (cf. 4:9).

11:14 IF A MAN HAS LONG HAIR. God desires that the physical differences between men and women be observed. (1) Paul uses hair as an example, stating that the length of the hair of men and women should be such as to distinguish between one and the other. A woman's hair should be long in comparison to the man's, symbolizing her acceptance of the dignity and worth of her womanhood as God created her (see v. 6, note). A man's hair, in contrast to the woman's, should be short.

(2) In NT times, long hair was disgraceful and shunned by Jewish men as well as by those of first-century Corinth. Pictures portraying Jesus as having long hair are based wholly on the imagination of the artists from the Middle Ages, not on Biblical or historical evidence (thousands of paintings and sculptures from NT times prove this). The apostle would not have written, "if a man has long hair, it is a disgrace to him," if Christ had worn his hair long as did women. Therefore, Paul's statement is in conflict, not with Jesus' custom, but with the invention of artists (cf. Ex 20:4).

11:20 THE LORD'S SUPPER. The Lord's Supper is described in four passages: Mt 26:26–29; Mk 14:22–25; Lk 22:15–20; 1Co 11:23–25. Its significance relates to the past, the present and the future.

(1) The past significance. (a) It is a remembrance (Gk *anamnēsis*; vv. 24–26; Lk 22:19) of Christ's death for the believer's redemption from sin and condemnation. Through the Lord's Supper we are once again confronted with the saving death of Christ and its redemptive significance for our lives. Christ's death is our ultimate motivation against falling into sin and for abstaining from all

of you goes ahead without waiting for
anybody else.[g] One remains hungry,
another gets drunk. **22**Don't you have
homes to eat and drink in? Or do you
despise the church of God[h] and humiliate those who have nothing?[i] What
shall I say to you? Shall I praise you[j]
for this? Certainly not!
23For I received from the Lord[k]
what I also passed on to you:[l] The
Lord Jesus, on the night he was betrayed, took bread, **24**and when he had
given thanks, he broke it and said,
"This is my body,[m] which is for you; do
this in remembrance of me." **25**In the
same way, after supper he took the
cup, saying, "This cup is the new covenant[n] in my blood;[o] do this, whenever you drink it, in remembrance of
me." **26**For whenever you eat this bread
and drink this cup, you proclaim the
Lord's death until he comes.[p]

27Therefore, whoever eats the bread
or drinks the cup of the Lord in an unworthy manner will be guilty of sinning
against the body and blood of the
Lord.[q] **28**A man ought to examine
himself[r] before he eats of the bread
and drinks of the cup. **29**For anyone
who eats and drinks without recognizing the body of the Lord eats and
drinks judgment on himself. **30**That is
why many among you are weak and
sick, and a number of you have fallen
asleep.[s] **31**But if we judged ourselves,
we would not come under judgment.[t]
32When we are judged by the Lord, we
are being disciplined[u] so that we will
not be condemned with the world.[v]
33So then, my brothers, when you
come together to eat, wait for each other. **34**If anyone is hungry,[w] he should
eat at home,[x] so that when you meet
together it may not result in judgment.

11:21 [g] 2Pe 2:13; Jude 12
11:22 [h] S 1Co 10:32 [i] Jas 2:6 [j] ver 2,17
11:23 [k] Gal 1:12 [l] S ver 2
11:24 [m] 1Co 10:16
11:25 [n] S Lk 22:20 [o] 1Co 10:16
11:26 [p] S 1Co 1:7
11:27 [q] Heb 10:29
11:28 [r] 2Co 13:5
11:30 [s] S Mt 9:24
11:31 [t] Ps 32:5; 1Jn 1:9
11:32 [u] Ps 94:12; 118:18; Pr 3:11, 12; Heb 12:7-10; Rev 3:19 [v] Jn 15:18,19
11:34 [w] ver 21 [x] ver 22

appearance of evil (1Th 5:22). (b) It is a thanksgiving (Gk *eucharistia*) for the blessings and salvation of God made available by Christ's sacrifice on the cross (v. 24; Mt 26:27; Mk 14:23; Lk 22:19).

(2) The present significance. (a) The Lord's Supper is a fellowship (Gk *koinōnia*) with Christ and a participation in the benefits of his sacrificial death, as well as a fellowship with the other members of the body of Christ (10:16–17). In this supper with the risen Lord, he as the host becomes present in a special way (cf. Mt 18:20; Lk 24:35). (b) It is a recognition and proclamation of the new covenant (Gk *kainē diathēkē*) by which believers reaffirm the lordship of Christ and our commitment to do his will, to remain loyal, to resist sin and to identify ourselves with his mission (v. 25; Mt 26:28; Mk 14:24; Lk 22:20; see article on THE OLD COVENANT AND THE NEW COVENANT, p. 1926).

(3) The future significance. (a) The Lord's Supper is a foretaste of the future kingdom of God and the future Messianic banquet when all believers will be with the Lord (Mt 8:11; 22:1–14; Mk 14:25; Lk 13:29; 22:17–18,30). (b) It looks forward to Christ's imminent return for his people (v. 26) and dramatizes the prayer, "Your kingdom come" (Mt 6:10; cf. Rev 22:20).

At the Lord's Supper all the above significances are made meaningful only if we come before the Lord in true faith, sincere prayer and with commitment to God's Word and will.

11:21 ANOTHER GETS DRUNK. "One remains hungry, another gets drunk" can be translated, "One remains hungry, another is filled to the full." This is a preferred translation for the following reasons. (1) The word "drunk" (Gk *methuō*) carries two meanings. It can refer (a) to being drunk or (b) to being filled or satisfied without reference to intoxication (see Jn 2:10, note on the use of this word in relation to the wedding at Cana).

(2) The context of this verse clearly relates to the meal in general. When the Corinthians gathered together for their fellowship meals before eating the Lord's Supper (cf. 2Pe 2:13; Jude 12), some gathered in small groups and ate their meals separately (vv. 18–19). The poor who could not contribute to the meal were ignored and left hungry. Paul was not referring to an issue of intoxication here; if he had been, he surely would have severely condemned it as he did elsewhere in the letter (cf. 6:10). He regarded drunkenness not merely as an issue of disregard for others, but also a condition so serious that it excludes one from God's kingdom (6:10; Gal 5:21).

11:24–25 MY BODY ... MY BLOOD. These words refer to Christ's body given in death and his blood shed sacrificially on the cross. When Christ said of the bread, "This is my body," he meant that it represented his body. The "cup" represented the blood of Christ shed for ratification of the "new covenant." To eat the bread and drink the cup means to proclaim and accept the benefits of Christ's sacrificial death (v. 26).

11:27 EATS ... DRINKS ... UNWORTHY MANNER. To eat in an unworthy manner is to participate at the Lord's table with an indifferent, self-centered and irreverent spirit, without any intention or desire of departing from known sins and of accepting the covenant of grace with all its promises and obligations. Those who participate in such an unworthy manner sin terribly against the Lord. They are guilty of recrucifying Christ and immediately come under special judgment and retribution (vv. 29–32). To "be guilty of sinning against the body and blood of the Lord" means being held responsible for his death.

11:32 BEING DISCIPLINED. The purpose of the Lord's judgment (cf. v. 30) is that we might not be condemned eternally with the world. This merciful purpose avails for all who repent and judge themselves rightly (v. 31).

And when I come[y] I will give further directions.

Spiritual Gifts

12 Now about spiritual gifts,[z]
brothers, I do not want you to
be ignorant.[a] **2**You know that when
you were pagans,[b] somehow or other
you were influenced and led astray to
mute idols.[c] **3**Therefore I tell you that
no one who is speaking by the Spirit of
God says, "Jesus be cursed,"[d] and no
one can say, "Jesus is Lord,"[e] except
by the Holy Spirit.[f]
4There are different kinds of gifts,
but the same Spirit.[g] **5**There are different kinds of service, but the same
Lord. **6**There are different kinds of
working, but the same God[h] works all
of them in all men.[i]
7Now to each one the manifestation
of the Spirit is given for the common
good.[j] **8**To one there is given through
the Spirit the message of wisdom,[k] to
another the message of knowledge[l]
by means of the same Spirit, **9**to another faith[m] by the same Spirit, to another
gifts of healing[n] by that one Spirit,
10to another miraculous powers,[o] to
another prophecy,[p] to another distinguishing between spirits,[q] to another
speaking in different kinds of
tongues,[a][r] and to still another the interpretation of tongues.[a] **11**All these
are the work of one and the same Spirit,[s] and he gives them to each one,
just as he determines.

One Body, Many Parts

12The body is a unit, though it is
made up of many parts; and though all
its parts are many, they form one
body.[t] So it is with Christ.[u] **13**For we

11:34 [y]S 1Co 4:19
12:1 [z]Ro 1:11; 1Co 1:7; 14:1,37 [a]S Ro 11:25
12:2 [b]S Eph 2:2 [c]Ps 115:5; Jer 10:5; Hab 2:18,19
12:3 [d]Ro 9:3; 1Co 16:22 [e]S Jn 13:13 [f]1Jn 4:2,3
12:4 [g]ver 8-11; Ro 12:4-8; Eph 4:11; Heb 2:4
12:6 [h]Eph 4:6 [i]S Php 2:13
12:7 [j]1Co 14:12; Eph 4:12
12:8 [k]1Co 2:6 [l]S 2Co 8:7
12:9 [m]Mt 17:19,20; 1Co 13:2 [n]ver 28,30; Mt 10:1
12:10 [o]ver 28-30; Gal 3:5 [p]S Eph 4:11 [q]1Jn 4:1 [r]S Mk 16:17
12:11 [s]S ver 4
12:12 [t]S Ro 12:5 [u]ver 27

[a] *10* Or *languages*; also in verse 28

12:1 ABOUT SPIRITUAL GIFTS. In chs. 12–14 Paul deals with the gifts of the Holy Spirit given to the body of Christ. These gifts were an indispensable part of the early church's life and ministry. God intends that these gifts continue in operation until Christ returns (see 1:7, note). His purposes for the spiritual gifts are as follows:

(1) To manifest the grace, power and love of the Spirit among his people in their public gatherings, homes, families and individual lives (vv. 4–7; 14:25; Ro 15:18–19; Eph 4:8);

(2) To help make the preaching of the gospel effective by giving supernatural confirmation to the message (Mk 16:15–20; Ac 14:8–18; 16:16–18; 19:11–20; 28:1–10);

(3) To meet human needs and to strengthen and build up spiritually both the church (vv. 7,14–30; 14:3,12,26) and individual believers (14:4), i.e., to perfect believers in "love, which comes from a pure heart and a good conscience and a sincere faith" (1Ti 1:5; cf. 1Co 13);

(4) To wage effective spiritual war against Satan and the forces of evil (Isa 61:1; Ac 8:5–7; 26:18; Eph 6:11–12). Passages dealing with spiritual gifts include Ro 12:3–8; 1Co 1:7; 12–14; Eph 4:4–16; 1Pe 4:10–11.

12:1–6 SPIRITUAL GIFTS. The terms that the Bible uses for spiritual gifts specify their nature. (1) "Spiritual gifts" (Gk *pneumatika*, derived from *pneuma*, "Spirit") refers to supernatural manifestations that come as gifts from the Holy Spirit operating through believers for the common good (vv. 1,7; 14:1).

(2) "Gifts" or "grace gifts" (Gk *charismata*, derived from *charis*, "grace") indicates that spiritual gifts involve both an inward motivation and the power to perform ministry (i.e., actualized enablement), received from the Spirit; such gifts strengthen spiritually the body of Christ and those in need of spiritual help (v. 4; see Ro 12:6, note; Eph 4:11; 1Pe 4:10; see article on THE MINISTRY GIFTS OF THE CHURCH, p. 1830).

(3) "Service" or "ministries" (Gk *diakoniai*, derived from *diakonia*, "service") emphasizes that there are different ways of service and that certain gifts involve receiving the ability and power to help others (vv. 4–5,27–31; Eph 4:7,11–13). Paul indicates that the ministry aspect of the gifts reflect the "servant" ministry of the Lord Jesus. Thus the operation of the gifts are defined in terms of Christ's presence and operation among us (cf. v. 3; 1:4).

(4) "Working" or "effects" (Gk *energēmata*, from *energēs*, "active, energetic") signifies that spiritual gifts are direct operations of the power of God the Father and produce certain results (vv. 6,10).

(5) "The manifestation of the Spirit" (Gk *phanerōsis*, from *phaneros*, "manifest") emphasizes that spiritual gifts are direct manifestations of the working and presence of the Holy Spirit in the congregation (vv. 7–11).

12:3 JESUS IS LORD. Paul begins the discussion on spiritual gifts with the truth that the gifts and manifestations of the Holy Spirit will exalt Jesus as Lord of the church. The ultimate criterion of the Spirit's activity is an ever-growing expression of the person, presence, power, love and righteousness of the Lord Jesus Christ. In the manifestation of spiritual gifts Christ himself ministers by the Spirit through his people to his people (see vv. 12–27; Mt 25:40).

12:7 MANIFESTATION OF THE SPIRIT. For comments on spiritual gifts as manifestations of the Spirit, as well as a description of the various gifts listed here, see article on SPIRITUAL GIFTS FOR BELIEVERS, p. 1770.

12:12 SO IT IS WITH CHRIST. See v. 1, note on spiritual gifts and the body of Christ.

SPIRITUAL GIFTS FOR BELIEVERS

1Co 12:7 "Now to each one the manifestation of the Spirit is given for the common good."

GENERAL PERSPECTIVE. The Holy Spirit is manifested through a variety of spiritual gifts given to believers (1Co 12:7). These manifestations of the Spirit are intended for the upbuilding and sanctification of the church (1Co 12:7; see 14:26, note). These spiritual gifts are not the same as the gifts and ministries mentioned in Ro 12:6–8 and Eph 4:11, whereby a believer receives the power and ability to minister in a more permanent manner in the church. The list in 1Co 12:8–10 is not necessarily exhaustive, and the gifts may occur in various combinations.

(1) The manifestations of the Spirit are given according to the Spirit's will (1Co 12:11) when need arises and according to the believer's eager desire (12:31; 14:1).

(2) Some gifts may be manifested through an individual on a regular basis, and a believer may have more than one gift to minister to particular needs. The believer ought to desire "gifts," not just one gift (1Co 12:31; 14:1).

(3) It is unscriptural and unwise to assume that because someone exercises a spectacular gift, that person is more spiritual than one who has less spectacular gifts. Furthermore, possessing a gift does not mean that God approves of all a person does or teaches. Spiritual gifts must not be confused with the fruit of the Spirit, which relates more directly to Christian character and sanctification (Gal 5:22–23).

(4) The Spirit's manifestation through gifts may be counterfeited by Satan or false workers disguising themselves as servants of Christ (Mt 7:21–23; 24:11,24; 2Co 11:13–15; 2Th 2:8–10). The believer must not believe every spiritual manifestation, but ought to "test the spirits to see whether they are from God, because many false prophets have gone out into the world" (1Jn 4:1; cf. 1Th 5:20–21; see article on TESTING FOR GENUINE BAPTISM IN THE SPIRIT, p. 1668).

INDIVIDUAL GIFTS. In 1Co 12:8–10, Paul lists a variety of gifts that the Holy Spirit gives to believers. Though he does not define their characteristics here, we can glean from other passages of Scripture what they might be.

(1) *Message of wisdom*. This is a wise utterance spoken through the operation of the Holy Spirit. It applies the revelation of God's Word or the Holy Spirit's wisdom to a specific situation or problem (Ac 6:10; 15:13–22). It is not, however, the same as having the wisdom of God for daily living. The latter is obtained by diligent study and meditation on God's ways and Word, and by prayer (Jas 1:5–6).

(2) *Message of knowledge*. This is an utterance inspired by the Holy Spirit that reveals knowledge about people, circumstances or Biblical truth. It is often connected closely with prophecy (Ac 5:1–10; 10:47–48; 15:7–11; 1Co 14:24–25).

(3) *Faith*. This is not saving faith, but a special supernatural faith imparted by the Holy Spirit that enables the Christian to believe God for the extraordinary and miraculous. It is a faith that moves mountains (1Co 13:2) and is often found in combination with other manifestations such as healings and miracles (see Mt 17:20, note on true faith; Mk 11:22–24; Lk 17:6).

(4) *Gifts of healing*. These gifts are given to the church to restore physical health by supernatural means (Mt 4:23–25; 10:1; Ac 3:6–8; 4:30). The plural ("gifts") indicates healing of various illnesses and suggests that every act of healing is a special gift of God. Although gifts of healing are not given to every member of the body in a special way (cf. 1Co 12:11,30), all members may pray for the sick. When faith is present, the sick will be healed (see article on DIVINE HEALING, p. 1420.) Healing may also come as a result of obedience to the instructions of Jas 5:14–16 (see Jas 5:15, notes).

(5) *Miraculous powers*. These are deeds of supernatural power that alter the normal course of nature. They include divine acts in which God's kingdom is manifested against

Satan and evil spirits (see Jn 6:2, note; see article on THE KINGDOM OF GOD, p. 1430).

(6) *Prophecy*. We must distinguish between prophecy as a temporary manifestation of the Spirit (1Co 12:10) and prophecy as a ministry gift of the church (Eph 4:11). As a ministry gift, prophecy is given only to some believers, who must then function as prophets within the church (see article on THE MINISTRY GIFTS OF THE CHURCH, p. 1830). As a spiritual manifestation, prophecy is potentially available to every Spirit-filled Christian (Ac 2:17–18).

Concerning prophecy as a spiritual manifestation: (a) Prophecy is a special gift that enables a believer to bring a word or revelation directly from God under the impulse of the Holy Spirit (1Co 14:24–25,29–31). It is not the delivery of a previously prepared sermon. (b) In both the OT and the NT, prophecy is not primarily foretelling the future, but proclaiming God's will and exhorting and encouraging God's people to righteousness, faithfulness and endurance (14:3; see article on THE PROPHET IN THE OLD TESTAMENT, p. 986). (c) The message may expose the condition of a person's heart (14:25) or offer strengthening, encouragement, comfort, warning and judgment (14:3,25–26,31). (d) The church may not receive such prophecy as an infallible message, for many false prophets will enter the church (1Jn 4:1). Therefore, all prophecy must be tested for genuineness and truth (1Co 14:29,32; 1Th 5:20–21) by asking whether it conforms to God's Word (1Jn 4:1), whether it promotes godly living (1Ti 6:3), and whether it is uttered by one who is sincerely living under Christ's lordship (1Co 12:3). (e) Prophecy operates under God's will and not the will of humans. The NT never indicates that the church actively sought revelation or direction from those claiming to be prophets. Prophecy was given to the church only when God initiated the message (1Co 12:11; 2Pe 1:21).

(7) *Distinguishing between spirits*. This gift is a special Spirit-given ability to properly discern and judge prophecies and to distinguish whether or not an utterance is from the Holy Spirit (see 1Co 14:29, note; 1Jn 4:1). Toward the end of the age when false teachers (see Mt 24:5, note) and distortion of Biblical Christianity will greatly increase (see 1Ti 4:1, note), this gift will be extremely important for the church.

(8) *Speaking in different kinds of tongues*. Concerning "tongues" (Gk *glōssa*, meaning language) as a supernatural manifestation of the Spirit, the following must be noted:

(a) Tongues may be an existing spoken language (Ac 2:4–6) or a language unknown on earth, e.g., "tongues . . . of angels" (1Co 13:1; see ch. 14, notes; see article on SPEAKING IN TONGUES, p. 1646). Such speech has not been learned and is often unintelligible both to the speaker (14:14) and to the hearers (14:16).

(b) Speaking in tongues involves the human spirit and the Spirit of God intermingling so that the believer communicates directly to God (i.e., in prayer, praise, blessing or thanksgiving), giving expression or utterance at the level of one's spirit rather than the mind (1Co 14:2,14) and praying for oneself or others under the direct influence of the Holy Spirit apart from the activity of the mind (cf. 1Co 14:2,4,15,28; Jude 20).

(c) Tongues in the congregation must be accompanied by a Spirit-given interpretation that communicates the content and meaning of the utterance to the community of believers (1Co 14:3,27–28). It may contain a revelation, knowledge, prophecy or teaching for the assembly (cf. 1Co 14:6).

(d) Speaking in tongues within the congregation must be regulated. The speaker may never be "in ecstasy" or "out of control" (1Co 14:27–28; see article on SPEAKING IN TONGUES, p. 1646).

(9) *Interpretation of tongues*. This is the Spirit-given ability to understand and communicate the meaning of an utterance spoken in tongues. When interpreted for the congregation, tongues function either as a directive to worship and prayer or as prophecy. The body of believers can then participate in this Spirit-inspired revelation. Interpreted tongues can thus be a means of edification as the whole congregation responds to the utterance (cf. 14:6,13). The gift may be given to the one who speaks in tongues or to someone else. Those who speak in tongues should pray also for the gift of interpretation (1Co 14:13).

were all baptized[v] by[b] one Spirit[w]
into one body—whether Jews or
Greeks, slave or free[x]—and we were
all given the one Spirit to drink.[y]
14Now the body is not made up of
one part but of many.[z] **15**If the foot
should say, "Because I am not a hand,
I do not belong to the body," it would
not for that reason cease to be part of
the body. **16**And if the ear should say,
"Because I am not an eye, I do not belong to the body," it would not for that
reason cease to be part of the body. **17**If
the whole body were an eye, where
would the sense of hearing be? If the
whole body were an ear, where would
the sense of smell be? **18**But in fact God
has arranged[a] the parts in the body,
every one of them, just as he wanted
them to be.[b] **19**If they were all one
part, where would the body be? **20**As it
is, there are many parts, but one
body.[c]
21The eye cannot say to the hand, "I
don't need you!" And the head cannot
say to the feet, "I don't need you!" **22**On
the contrary, those parts of the body
that seem to be weaker are indispensable, **23**and the parts that we think are
less honorable we treat with special
honor. And the parts that are unpre-
sentable are treated with special modesty, **24**while our presentable parts
need no special treatment. But God
has combined the members of the body
and has given greater honor to the
parts that lacked it, **25**so that there
should be no division in the body, but
that its parts should have equal concern for each other. **26**If one part suffers, every part suffers with it; if one
part is honored, every part rejoices
with it.
27Now you are the body of Christ,[d]
and each one of you is a part of it.[e]
28And in the church[f] God has appointed first of all apostles,[g] second
prophets,[h] third teachers, then workers of miracles, also those having gifts
of healing,[i] those able to help others,
those with gifts of administration,[j]
and those speaking in different kinds
of tongues.[k] **29**Are all apostles? Are
all prophets? Are all teachers? Do all
work miracles? **30**Do all have gifts of
healing? Do all speak in tongues[c]?[l]
Do all interpret? **31**But eagerly desire[d][m] the greater gifts.

Love

And now I will show you the most
excellent way.

13 If I speak in the tongues[e][n] of
men and of angels, but have not

12:13 [v] S Mk 1:8 [w] Eph 2:18 [x] Gal 3:28; Col 3:11 [y] Jn 7:37-39 **12:14** [z] ver 12,20 **12:18** [a] ver 28 [b] ver 11 **12:20** [c] ver 12,14; S Ro 12:5 **12:27** [d] Eph 1:23; 4:12; Col 1:18,24 [e] S Ro 12:5 **12:28** [f] S 1Co 10:32 [g] S Eph 4:11 [h] S Eph 4:11 [i] ver 9 [j] Ro 12:6-8 [k] ver 10; S Mk 16:17 **12:30** [l] ver 10 **12:31** [m] 1Co 14:1, 39 **13:1** [n] ver 8; S Mk 16:17

[b] *13* Or *with;* or *in* [c] *30* Or *other languages* [d] *31* Or *But you are eagerly desiring* [e] *1* Or *languages*

12:13 WE WERE ALL BAPTIZED BY ONE SPIRIT. The baptism "by one Spirit" refers neither to water baptism nor to Christ's baptism of the believer in the Holy Spirit, such as occurred on the day of Pentecost (see Mk 1:8; Ac 2:4, note). Rather, it refers to the Spirit's baptizing believers into Christ's body, uniting them in the body and making them spiritually one with other believers. It is a spiritual transformation (i.e., regeneration) that occurs at conversion and puts the believer "in Christ" (see article on REGENERATION, p. 1589).

12:25 PARTS SHOULD HAVE EQUAL CONCERN FOR EACH OTHER. Spiritual gifts should not be the basis for honoring a person or considering one believer as more important than another (vv. 22–24). Rather each person is placed in Christ's body according to God's will (v. 18), and all members are important for the spiritual wellbeing and proper functioning of the body. Spiritual gifts must be used, not in pride or for personal exaltation, but with the sincere desire to help others and with a heart that genuinely cares for each other (see ch. 13).

12:28 IN THE CHURCH GOD HAS APPOINTED. Paul gives here a partial list of the ministry gifts (see Ro 12:6–8 and Eph 4:11–13 for other lists of ministry gifts). See article on THE MINISTRY GIFTS OF THE CHURCH, p. 1830, for the definition of apostles, prophets, evangelists, pastors and teachers; see also Jn 6:2, note, for definition of "miracles"; Ro 12:7–8, for notes on the gift of "helping others" ("showing mercy") and the gift of "administration" ("leadership").

12:30 DO ALL SPEAK IN TONGUES? Paul's rhetorical question here implies a negative answer. The context in ch. 12 shows that Paul is referring to the use of the gift of tongues and its companion gift of interpretation in public worship services. He is not attempting to limit the use of tongues in prayer and praise privately addressed to God (cf. 14:5). Most believers baptized in the Holy Spirit find it easy to pray in tongues as they yield themselves to the Spirit. On the day of Pentecost (Ac 2:4), at Caesarea (Ac 10:44–46) and at Ephesus (Ac 19:2–6), all who were filled with the Spirit spoke in tongues as a sign that they had received the fullness of the Spirit (see article on SPEAKING IN TONGUES, p. 1646).

13:1 BUT HAVE NOT LOVE. Ch. 13 is a continuation of Paul's discussion on the question of spiritual gifts. Here he emphasizes that to possess spiritual gifts without having love amounts to nothing (vv. 1–3). The "most excellent way" (12:31) is the exercise of spiritual gifts in love (vv. 4–8). As the only context in which spiritual gifts can fulfill God's will, love must be the governing

love, I am only a resounding gong or a
clanging cymbal. **2**If I have the gift of
prophecy[o] and can fathom all mysteries[p] and all knowledge,[q] and if I have
a faith[r] that can move mountains,[s]
but have not love, I am nothing. **3**If I
give all I possess to the poor[t] and surrender my body to the flames,[f][u] but
have not love, I gain nothing.

4Love is patient,[v] love is kind. It
does not envy, it does not boast, it is
not proud.[w] **5**It is not rude, it is not
self-seeking,[x] it is not easily angered,[y] it keeps no record of
wrongs.[z] **6**Love does not delight in
evil[a] but rejoices with the truth.[b] **7**It
always protects, always trusts, always
hopes, always perseveres.[c]

8Love never fails. But where there
are prophecies,[d] they will cease;
where there are tongues,[e] they will be
stilled; where there is knowledge, it
will pass away. **9**For we know in part[f]
and we prophesy in part, **10**but when
perfection comes,[g] the imperfect disappears. **11**When I was a child, I talked
like a child, I thought like a child, I
reasoned like a child. When I became
a man, I put childish ways[h] behind
me. **12**Now we see but a poor reflection
as in a mirror;[i] then we shall see face
to face.[j] Now I know in part; then I
shall know fully, even as I am fully
known.[k]

13And now these three remain: faith,
hope and love.[l] But the greatest of
these is love.[m]

Gifts of Prophecy and Tongues

14 Follow the way of love[n] and
eagerly desire[o] spiritual
gifts,[p] especially the gift of prophecy.[q] **2**For anyone who speaks in a
tongue[g][r] does not speak to men but

13:2 [o] ver 8; S Eph 4:11; S Ac 11:27 [p] 1Co 14:2 [q] S 2Co 8:7 [r] 1Co 12:9 [s] Mt 17:20; 21:21 **13:3** [t] Lk 19:8; S Ac 2:45 [u] Da 3:28 **13:4** [v] 1Th 5:14 [w] 1Co 5:2 **13:5** [x] S 1Co 10:24 [y] S Mt 5:22 [z] Job 14:16,17; Pr 10:12; 17:9; 1Pe 4:8 **13:6** [a] 2Th 2:12 [b] 2Jn 4; 3Jn 3,4 **13:7** [c] ver 8,13 **13:8** [d] ver 2 [e] ver 1 **13:9** [f] ver 12; S 1Co 8:2 **13:10** [g] Php 3:12 **13:11** [h] Ps 131:2 **13:12** [i] Job 26:14; 36:26 [j] Ge 32:30; Job 19:26; 1Jn 3:2 [k] 1Co 8:3; Gal 4:9 **13:13** [l] Ro 5:2-5; Gal 5:5,6; Eph 4:2-5; Col 1:4, 5; 1Th 1:3; 5:8; Heb 6:10-12 [m] Mt 22:37-40; 1Co 16:14; Gal 5:6; 1Jn 4:7-12,16 **14:1** [n] 1Co 16:14 [o] ver 39; 1Co 12:31 [p] S 1Co 12:1 [q] ver 39; S Eph 4:11 **14:2** [r] S Mk 16:17

[f] *3* Some early manuscripts *body that I may boast* [g] *2* Or *another language*; also in verses 4, 13, 14, 19, 26 and 27

principle of all spiritual manifestations. Paul therefore exhorts the Corinthians to "follow the way of love and eagerly desire spiritual gifts" (14:1). They must earnestly desire the things of the Spirit because they sincerely want to help, comfort and bless others in this life.

13:2 I AM NOTHING. Those whose lives are filled with "religious activities" are not necessarily approved by God; in fact, they may not be believers at all. For example, those who speak in tongues, prophesy, have knowledge or achieve great works of faith, yet at the same time lack Christlike love and righteousness, are "nothing" in God's sight. In God's judgment their spirituality and profession of faith are empty (v. 1), and they have no real place in his kingdom (cf. 6:9–10). They are not only lacking in the Spirit's fullness, but are also empty of his indwelling presence. The spiritual manifestations through them are not from God but from another spirit, i.e., an evil spirit (see Ac 8:21, note; 1Jn 4:1, note; see article on TESTING FOR GENUINE BAPTISM IN THE SPIRIT, p. 1668). What is essential to true Christian faith is love expressed through an ethic that does no harm to others and perseveres in loyalty to Christ and his Word (see also v. 13, note).

13:4–7 LOVE IS PATIENT. This section describes love as an activity and a behavior, not just as an inner feeling or motivation. The various aspects of love included here characterize God the Father, Son and Holy Spirit. Every believer must seek to grow in this kind of love.

13:8 TONGUES, THEY WILL BE STILLED. Spiritual gifts such as prophecy, tongues and knowledge will cease at the end of this age. That time is described as "when perfection comes" (v. 10)—i.e., at the end of history, when the believer's knowledge and character become perfect in eternity after Christ's second coming (v. 12; 1:7). Until then, we need the Holy Spirit and his gifts in our churches. There is no indication here or elsewhere in Scripture that the manifestation of the Spirit through his gifts would cease at the end of the first century era.

13:13 THE GREATEST ... IS LOVE. It is clear from this chapter that God exalts Christlike character more than ministry, faith or the possession of spiritual gifts. (1) God values and emphasizes character that acts in love, patience (v. 4), kindness (v. 4), unselfishness (v. 5), hatred for evil and love for the truth (v. 6), honesty (v. 6) and endurance in righteousness (v. 7) much more than faith to move mountains or to perform great achievements in the church (vv. 1–2,8,13).

(2) The greatest in God's kingdom will be those who are great in inward godliness and love for God, not necessarily those who are greatest in outward accomplishments (see Lk 22:24–30, note). God's love poured out within the believer's heart through the Holy Spirit is always greater than faith, hope or anything else (Ro 5:5).

14:1 DESIRE SPIRITUAL GIFTS. Believers who possess genuine love for others in the body of Christ must desire spiritual gifts in order to be able to help, comfort, encourage and strengthen those in need (cf. 12:17). They may not wait passively for God to give the gifts of the Spirit (12:7–10). Instead, they must earnestly desire, seek and pray for those gifts, especially those that serve to exhort, comfort and strengthen (vv. 3,13,19,26).

14:2 SPEAKS IN A TONGUE. The Corinthians had overestimated the importance of the gift of tongues in public worship (see article on SPIRITUAL GIFTS FOR BELIEVERS, p. 1770) and were

to God. Indeed, no one understands
him;[s] he utters mysteries[t] with his
spirit.[h] **3**But everyone who prophesies
speaks to men for their strengthening,[u] encouragement[v] and comfort.
4He who speaks in a tongue[w] edifies[x]
himself, but he who prophesies[y] edifies the church. **5**I would like every one
of you to speak in tongues,[i] but I
would rather have you prophesy.[z] He
who prophesies is greater than one
who speaks in tongues,[i] unless he interprets, so that the church may be edified.[a]

6Now, brothers, if I come to you and
speak in tongues, what good will I be
to you, unless I bring you some revelation[b] or knowledge[c] or prophecy or
word of instruction?[d] **7**Even in the
case of lifeless things that make
sounds, such as the flute or harp, how
will anyone know what tune is being
played unless there is a distinction in
the notes? **8**Again, if the trumpet does
not sound a clear call, who will get

14:2 [s] ver 6-11,16 [t] 1Co 13:2
14:3 [u] ver 4,5,12, 17,26; S Ro 14:19 [v] ver 31
14:4 [w] S Mk 16:17 [x] S ver 3 [y] S 1Co 13:2
14:5 [z] Nu 11:29 [a] S ver 3
14:6 [b] ver 26; Eph 1:17 [c] S 2Co 8:7 [d] Ro 6:17

[h] 2 Or *by the Spirit* [i] 5 Or *other languages;* also in verses 6, 18, 22, 23 and 39

emphasizing it at the expense of the other gifts. Furthermore, they were exercising this gift without interpretation. Paul seeks to correct this abuse by pointing out the unprofitableness of tongues without interpretation in public services. An outline of this chapter is as follows:

(1) Prophecy edifies the church more than uninterpreted tongues (vv. 1–4).

(2) Prophecy and tongues with interpretation are equally important to the church (v. 5).

(3) Speaking in tongues in public worship services without interpretation is of no benefit to others (vv. 6–12).

(4) Those who speak or pray in tongues in the church should seek to edify the church by praying for the gift of interpretation (v. 13).

(5) In Paul's personal life speaking in tongues to God is an important means of worship and spiritual growth (vv. 14–19).

(6) Prophecy is more useful than uninterpreted tongues because prophecy brings conviction of sin and the knowledge of God's presence (vv. 20–25).

(7) Speaking in tongues and prophesying must be regulated so that order is maintained in the church (vv. 26–40).

14:2 DOES NOT SPEAK TO MEN BUT TO GOD. There are basically two ways to understand this verse. (1) Some believe that this verse indicates that the principal use of tongues, whether in the church or in private, is to speak primarily to God and not to humans. When tongues are directed to God, the speaker communes with God by the Holy Spirit in the form of prayer, praise, singing, blessing and thanksgiving. What is spoken are "mysteries," i.e., things not understandable to the speaker or hearers (cf. vv. 2,13–17). Interpretation of the utterance (vv. 5,13) in tongues allows the congregation to enter into this manifestation of the Spirit-directed worship and thus to say "Amen" (v. 16) to the Spirit-inspired prayer or praise (v. 16; see also v. 6, note).

(2) On the other hand Paul's statement may mean that only God understands a tongue unless it is interpreted (v. 5). The implication would be that tongues, when interpreted, are directed to humans. This view is supported by Paul's statement that the reason why tongue-speaking is not spoken to humans is because "no one understands" it (see v. 6, note).

14:3 PROPHESIES . . . STRENGTHENING. The gift of prophecy in the church is motivated by the Holy Spirit, not primarily to foretell the future, but to strengthen the believer's faith, spiritual life and moral resolve to remain faithful to Christ and his teachings. Prophecy is not, however, preaching a prepared sermon, but giving a spontaneous word under the impulse of the Spirit for the edification of the individual or the congregation (see article on SPIRITUAL GIFTS FOR BELIEVERS, p. 1770).

14:4 EDIFIES HIMSELF. Tongues without interpretation edifies (i.e., builds up one's faith and spiritual life; see v. 26, note) the speaker because it puts him or her in direct communion with God by the Spirit (cf. Eph 3:16; Jude 20), bypassing the mind. Paul states that he prays and communes with God in this way as well as with the mind (vv. 14–15).

14:5 I WOULD LIKE EVERY ONE OF YOU TO SPEAK IN TONGUES. Paul's wish here refers to tongue-speaking in private devotion to God. Clearly such tongues have value for the individual Christian's personal worship and prayer (vv. 2,4). Paul adds that authentic tongues accompanied with interpretation in the assembly bring edification to the church, just as prophecy does. Tongues without interpretation does nothing for the church (vv. 7–9).

14:6 SPEAK IN TONGUES, WHAT GOOD WILL I BE TO YOU, UNLESS. Speaking in tongues can at times be directed toward the Christian community. Paul describes the hypothetical situation of coming to the Corinthians and speaking in tongues in the worship service. Such speaking would be of no benefit to them "unless" he brings some revelation or word of instruction. The construction of this verse suggests that his speaking in tongues, when interpreted, would consist of a message containing revelation, knowledge, prophecy or instruction to the congregation. This interpretation finds support in v. 8, where Paul gives the analogy of a trumpet that brings a message and warns to prepare for battle. In other words, speaking in tongues with interpretation can bring a message to God's people, such as a message to prepare for spiritual warfare with Satan, sin and the world's ungodly elements, or it can challenge us to be ready for Christ's imminent return.

14:8 TRUMPET . . . READY FOR BATTLE. Those who speak in tongues should produce

ready for battle?[e] 9So it is with you.
Unless you speak intelligible words
with your tongue, how will anyone
know what you are saying? You will
just be speaking into the air. 10Un-
doubtedly there are all sorts of languages in the world, yet none of them
is without meaning. 11If then I do not
grasp the meaning of what someone is
saying, I am a foreigner to the speaker,
and he is a foreigner to me.[f] 12So it
is with you. Since you are eager to have
spiritual gifts,[g] try to excel in gifts
that build up[h] the church.

13For this reason anyone who
speaks in a tongue should pray that he
may interpret what he says.[i] 14For if
I pray in a tongue, my spirit prays,[j]
but my mind is unfruitful. 15So what
shall I do? I will pray with my spirit,[k]
but I will also pray with my mind; I will
sing[l] with my spirit, but I will also
sing with my mind. 16If you are praising God with your spirit, how can one
who finds himself among those who do
not understand[j] say "Amen"[m] to your
thanksgiving,[n] since he does not
know what you are saying? 17You may
be giving thanks well enough, but the
other man is not edified.[o]

18I thank God that I speak in
tongues more than all of you. 19But in
the church I would rather speak five
intelligible words to instruct others
than ten thousand words in a tongue.[p]

20Brothers, stop thinking like children.[q] In regard to evil be infants,[r]
but in your thinking be adults. 21In the
Law[s] it is written:

"Through men of strange tongues
and through the lips of
foreigners
I will speak to this people,
but even then they will not
listen to me,"[k][t]
says the Lord.

22Tongues, then, are a sign, not for
believers but for unbelievers; prophecy,[u] however, is for believers, not for
unbelievers. 23So if the whole church
comes together and everyone speaks
in tongues, and some who do not understand[l] or some unbelievers come
in, will they not say that you are out of
your mind?[v] 24But if an unbeliever or
someone who does not understand[m]

14:8 [e] Nu 10:9; Jer 4:19 **14:11** [f] Ge 11:7 **14:12** [g] S 1Co 12:1 [h] S ver 3 **14:13** [i] ver 5 **14:14** [j] ver 2 **14:15** [k] ver 2,14 [l] S Eph 5:19 **14:16** [m] Dt 27:15-26; 1Ch 16:36; Ne 8:6; Ps 106:48; Rev 5:14; 7:12 [n] S Mt 14:19; 1Co 11:24 **14:17** [o] S ver 3

14:19 [p] ver 6 **14:20** [q] 1Co 3:11; Eph 4:14; Heb 5:12,13; 1Pe 2:2 [r] Jer 4:22; Mt 10:16; Ro 16:19 **14:21** [s] ver 34; S Jn 10:34 [t] Dt 28:49; Isa 28:11,12 **14:22** [u] ver 1 **14:23** [v] Ac 2:13

[j] *16* Or *among the inquirers*
[k] *21* Isaiah 28:11,12
[l] *23* Or *some inquirers*
[m] *24* Or *or some inquirer*

sounds easy to be identified (v. 7). Like trumpets, they must convey a clear message. Thus, those speaking in a tongue must pray that they may interpret what they say for the edification of others (v. 12).

14:15 PRAY WITH MY SPIRIT . . . PRAY WITH MY MIND. Paul refers to his own experience, to his own private use of tongues. "I pray with my spirit" means to pray in tongues with one's own spirit under the impulse of the Holy Spirit. The believer's spirit prays as the Holy Spirit gives the utterance (cf. 12:7,11; Ac 2:4). Paul is speaking here of the private use of tongues directed to God. Paul used tongues not only for praying, but also for singing, praising and giving thanks to God (vv. 14–16). To "pray with my mind" means to pray and praise with one's own mind in a learned language, also under the impulse of the Spirit.

14:18 I SPEAK IN TONGUES. Paul considered the gift of tongues an important part of his spiritual life, which was frequently given to praying, singing, praising and giving thanks in tongues. He speaks with reverence and gratitude for this manifestation of the Spirit. Some have interpreted this verse to mean that Paul spoke more learned languages than the Corinthians. However, this interpretation is incorrect, for the word "more" (Gk *mallon*) is not an adjective modifying the noun "tongues," but a comparative adverb, modifying the verb "speak." Thus, Paul did not say "I speak in more languages," but rather, "I speak in tongues more (i.e., more often) than all of you."

14:19 BUT IN THE CHURCH. In the church Paul preferred to utter a few words that people could understand than to speak ten thousand words in tongues without an interpretation. Vv. 18–19 imply that Paul spoke in tongues more in private devotions than in public worship.

14:22 TONGUES, THEN, ARE A SIGN. Tongues within the congregation become a negative sign to unbelievers in that they signify that the unbeliever is separated from God and cannot understand what is occurring (vv. 21,23). Prophecy, however, is a sign to believers, for they recognize that it is a supernatural work of the Holy Spirit and a proof that God is at work in the church (vv. 24–25). Tongues also may be a sign to believers indicating that the Spirit is being poured out (cf. Ac 10:44–46; 11:15–17) and manifested among God's people (cf. 12:7,10).

14:24 UNBELIEVER . . . JUDGED BY ALL. One of the surest signs that the Holy Spirit is present and at work in any congregation is his conviction of sin, righteousness and judgment (see Jn 16:8, note). (1) Through the manifestation of the Spirit among God's people, sin will be exposed, repentance called for, and sinners convicted. Where there is no exposing of unrighteousness, no conviction of sin or no plea for repentance, the Holy Spirit is clearly not at work according to the Biblical pattern. (2) The exposing of sin within a person's heart (v. 25) does not require a special gift of revelation or "mind reading." The word of

comes in while everybody is prophesying, he will be convinced by all that he
is a sinner and will be judged by all,
25and the secrets[w] of his heart will be
laid bare. So he will fall down and worship God, exclaiming, "God is really
among you!"[x]

Orderly Worship

26What then shall we say, brothers?[y] When you come together, everyone[z] has a hymn,[a] or a word of instruction,[b] a revelation, a tongue[c] or
an interpretation.[d] All of these must
be done for the strengthening[e] of the
church. 27If anyone speaks in a
tongue, two—or at the most three—
should speak, one at a time, and someone must interpret. 28If there is no interpreter, the speaker should keep
quiet in the church and speak to himself and God.
29Two or three prophets[f] should
speak, and the others should weigh
carefully what is said.[g] 30And if a revelation comes to someone who is sitting down, the first speaker should
stop. 31For you can all prophesy in turn
so that everyone may be instructed and
encouraged. 32The spirits of prophets
are subject to the control of prophets.[h] 33For God is not a God of disorder[i] but of peace.[j]
As in all the congregations[k] of the
saints,[l] 34women should remain silent in the churches. They are not al-

14:25 [w] Ro 2:16 [x] Isa 45:14; Zec 8:23 **14:26** [y] S Ro 7:1 [z] 1Co 12:7-10 [a] S Eph 5:19 [b] ver 6 [c] ver 2 [d] 1Co 12:10 [e] S Ro 14:19
14:29 [f] ver 32,37; S 1Co 13:2 [g] 1Co 12:10 **14:32** [h] 1Jn 4:1 **14:33** [i] ver 40 [j] S Ro 15:33 [k] S 1Co 7:17; S 10:32 [l] S Ac 9:13

prophecy and its moral truth when proclaimed under the impulse of the Spirit is sufficient to convict the sinner's heart (Heb 4:12).

14:26 ALL OF THESE . . . FOR THE STRENGTHENING. The principal purpose of all spiritual gifts is to strengthen the church and the individual (vv. 3–4,12,17,26). "Strengthening" (Gk *oikodomeō*) means to promote spiritual life, maturity and godly character in believers. It is a work of the Holy Spirit through spiritual gifts by which believers are increasingly spiritually transformed in order that they may not be conformed to this world (Ro 12:2–8), but may be built up in sanctification, love for God, concern for others, purity of heart, a good conscience and a sincere faith (see ch. 13; Ro 8:13; 14:1–4,26; Gal 5:16–26; Eph 2:19–22; 4:11–16; Col 3:16; 1Th 5:11; Jude 20; see 1Ti 1:5, note).

14:27 SOMEONE MUST INTERPRET. In the use of spiritual gifts there must be order and balance. The Biblical guidelines for speaking in tongues within the church are: (1) In any one meeting there must not be more than two or three who speak, pray or praise in tongues, and this must be done with interpretation (vv. 27–28). (2) Speaking in tongues must be done by one person at a time (v. 27). (3) All speaking in tongues must be judged by the church as to its authenticity (vv. 29,32). (4) If there is no interpreter present, a believer may speak in tongues privately in prayer to God (v. 28).

14:29 THE OTHERS SHOULD WEIGH CAREFULLY. All prophecy must be evaluated as to what is said. This shows that NT prophecy was less than infallible and might need to be corrected. (1) At times prophecy and speaking in tongues might not be a word from God (cf. 1Jn 4:1). Even evil spirits, through the presence of false teachers or prophets, can work in the congregation. Prophesying, speaking in tongues or possessing any supernatural gift is no guarantee that one is a true prophet or a true believer (see article on FALSE TEACHERS, p. 1506), for spiritual gifts may be counterfeited by Satan (Mt 24:24; 2Th 2:9–12; Rev 13:13–14).

(2) If the church has not set up proper and orderly ways (cf. v. 40) to judge prophecies, it has failed to follow Biblical guidelines. Note too that prophecy was not considered an irresistible impulse of the Spirit, for only one prophet could speak at a time (vv. 30–32).

(3) What should be the church's attitude toward prophetic messages? (a) All prophecy must be tested according to the standard of Biblical truth (cf. Dt 13:1–3). Believers should look for its fulfillment (cf. Dt 18:22), preparing themselves for the possibility that the prophecy may or may not be fulfilled. (b) If the word of prophecy is an exhortation, the congregation needs to ask, "What must we do to obey the will of the Spirit?"

14:31 YOU CAN ALL PROPHESY IN TURN. The distinction between prophecy as a spiritual gift and prophecy as part of Scripture must be clearly maintained, even though in both cases a message is received from God. (1) The writers of Scripture received their message by direct inspiration of the Holy Spirit and communicated it without error. The result was an infallible message (see article on THE INSPIRATION AND AUTHORITY OF SCRIPTURE, p. 1898).

(2) However, prophecy as described in chs. 12 and 14 may not be assigned the same authority or infallibility as the inspired Word of God (2Ti 3:16). Although coming from the impulse of the Spirit, this kind of prophecy must never be considered inerrant. Its message is always subject to human error. This is why prophecy today may never be equated with Scripture. Furthermore, present-day prophecy may not be accepted by the local church until other believers judge the utterance's content in order to determine its validity (see v. 29, note; 12:10). The primary basis for judging is the written Word of God: does it conform to apostolic teaching? God's written Word must always stand in judgment over all experiences and utterances.

14:34 WOMEN SHOULD REMAIN SILENT. This verse may be interpreted by v. 35 in the sense of forbidding women to interrupt the service by asking questions that could be asked at home. In 11:5 Paul assumes that women pray and prophesy

lowed to speak,[m] but must be in submission,[n] as the Law[o] says. **35**If they
want to inquire about something, they
should ask their own husbands at
home; for it is disgraceful for a woman
to speak in the church.

36Did the word of God[p] originate
with you? Or are you the only people it
has reached? **37**If anybody thinks he is
a prophet[q] or spiritually gifted,[r] let
him acknowledge that what I am writing to you is the Lord's command.[s]
38If he ignores this, he himself will be
ignored.**n**

39Therefore, my brothers, be eager[t] to prophesy,[u] and do not forbid
speaking in tongues. **40**But everything
should be done in a fitting and orderly[v] way.

The Resurrection of Christ

15 Now, brothers, I want to remind
you of the gospel[w] I preached
to you,[x] which you received and on
which you have taken your stand. **2**By
this gospel you are saved,[y] if you hold
firmly[z] to the word I preached to you.
Otherwise, you have believed in vain.

3For what I received[a] I passed on to
you[b] as of first importance**o**: that
Christ died for our sins[c] according to
the Scriptures,[d] **4**that he was buried,[e] that he was raised[f] on the third
day[g] according to the Scriptures,[h]
5and that he appeared to Peter,**p**[i]
and then to the Twelve.[j] **6**After that,
he appeared to more than five hundred
of the brothers at the same time, most
of whom are still living, though some
have fallen asleep.[k] **7**Then he appeared to James,[l] then to all the apostles,[m] **8**and last of all he appeared to
me also,[n] as to one abnormally born.

2Co 5:17–6:1

9For I am the least of the apostles[o]
and do not even deserve to be called an
apostle, because I persecuted[p] the
church of God.[q] **10**But by the grace[r]
of God I am what I am, and his grace
to me[s] was not without effect. No, I
worked harder than all of them[t]—yet
not I, but the grace of God that was
with me.[u] **11**Whether, then, it was I or
they,[v] this is what we preach, and this
is what you believed.

The Resurrection of the Dead

12But if it is preached that Christ
has been raised from the dead,[w] how
can some of you say that there is no
resurrection[x] of the dead?[y] **13**If there
is no resurrection of the dead, then not
even Christ has been raised. **14**And if
Christ has not been raised,[z] our
preaching is useless and so is your

14:34 [m] 1Co 11:5,13 [n] S Eph 5:22; 1Ti 2:11,12 [o] ver 21; Ge 3:16 **14:36** [p] S Heb 4:12 **14:37** [q] S Ac 11:27; 1Co 13:2; 2Co 10:7 [r] 1Co 2:15; S 12:1 [s] 1Jn 4:6 **14:39** [t] ver 1; 1Co 12:31 [u] ver 1; S Eph 4:11 **14:40** [v] ver 33; Col 2:5 **15:1** [w] Isa 40:9; Ro 2:16 [x] S 1Co 3:6; S Gal 1:8 **15:2** [y] Ro 1:16 [z] S Ro 11:22 **15:3** [a] Gal 1:12 [b] S 1Co 11:2 [c] Isa 53:5; Jn 1:29; S Gal 1:4; 1Pe 2:24 [d] S Mt 26:24; S Lk 24:27; S 24:44; Ac 17:2; 26:22,23 **15:4** [e] Mt 27:59,60 [f] S Ac 2:24 [g] S Mt 16:21 [h] Jn 2:21,22; Ac 2:25,30,31 **15:5** [i] Lk 24:34 [j] Mk 16:14; Lk 24:36-43 **15:6** [k] ver 18,20; S Mt 9:24 **15:7** [l] S Ac 15:13 [m] Lk 24:33,36,37; Ac 1:3,4 **15:8** [n] Ac 9:3-6,17; 1Co 9:1; Gal 1:16 **15:9** [o] 2Co 12:11; Eph 3:8; 1Ti 1:15 [p] S Ac 8:3 [q] S 1Co 10:32 **15:10** [r] S Ro 3:24 [s] S Ro 12:3 [t] 2Co 11:23; Col 1:29 [u] S Php 2:13 **15:11** [v] Gal 2:6 **15:12** [w] ver 4 [x] S Jn 11:24 [y] Ac 17:32; 23:8; 2Ti 2:18 **15:14** [z] 1Th 4:14

n *38* Some manuscripts *If he is ignorant of this, let him be ignorant* **o** *3* Or *you at the first* **p** *5* Greek *Cephas*

---

in public assemblies (cf. the "everyone" of 14:23–24,31).

14:39 PROPHESY, AND DO NOT FORBID . . . TONGUES. This double injunction concludes Paul's discussion of prophecy and tongues. If the Corinthians refuse to recognize that his instructions are "the Lord's commands," then they prove they are neither prophets nor the people of the Spirit (vv. 37–38). Churches today that claim to follow God's Word, yet forbid speaking in tongues and do not earnestly desire that their people prophesy, should ask themselves how vv. 37–38 might apply to them.

15:2 IF YOU HOLD FIRMLY TO THE WORD I PREACHED. Believers are not those who merely have faith in Jesus Christ. Rather believers are those who have faith in Christ as he is revealed in the full message of the gospel (vv. 1–4). Their faith in Christ is always bound to God's Word and the doctrine of the apostles (vv. 1,3; 11:2,23; Ro 6:17; Gal 1:12). For this reason, believers can be described as people who submit to the Christ of the Bible as Lord and Savior and who live under the Word of God. They submit without reservation to its authority, hold firmly to its teaching, trust its promises, heed its warnings and follow its commands. They are a people captive to God's Word, using Scripture to test all human ideas and accepting nothing that is contrary to the Bible.

15:8 AND LAST OF ALL. Paul's statement "last of all" must be taken absolutely. Paul was the last of the apostles defined in the sense of receiving a special commission through a personal meeting with the risen Lord in order to join in forming the original and fundamental testimony of Christ (cf. Ac 9:3–8; 22:6–11; 26:12–18). The original 12 apostles were the beginning and the foundation stones of the church (see Eph 2:20, note; cf. Mt 16:18; Rev 21:14). For this reason their apostolic office is unique and unrepeatable. As direct witnesses and messengers of the risen Lord, they built the foundation of the church of Jesus Christ, a foundation that can never be altered or added to. Thus, the original 12 apostles plus Paul can have no successors.

15:10 THE GRACE OF GOD. Grace is God's presence and love through Jesus Christ given to believers by the Holy Spirit, imparting to them God's mercy, forgiveness and the power to do God's will (Jn 3:16; Php 2:13; 1Ti 1:15–16; see article on FAITH AND GRACE, p. 1720).

faith. 15More than that, we are then
found to be false witnesses about God,
for we have testified about God that he
raised Christ from the dead.[a] But he
did not raise him if in fact the dead are
not raised. 16For if the dead are not
raised, then Christ has not been raised
either. 17And if Christ has not been
raised, your faith is futile; you are still
in your sins.[b] 18Then those also who
have fallen asleep[c] in Christ are lost.
19If only for this life we have hope in
Christ, we are to be pitied more than all
men.[d]

20But Christ has indeed been raised
from the dead,[e] the firstfruits[f] of
those who have fallen asleep.[g] 21For
since death came through a man,[h] the
resurrection of the dead[i] comes also
through a man. 22For as in Adam all
die, so in Christ all will be made
alive.[j] 23But each in his own turn:
Christ, the firstfruits;[k] then, when he
comes,[l] those who belong to him.[m]
24Then the end will come, when he
hands over the kingdom[n] to God the
Father after he has destroyed all dominion, authority and power.[o] 25For
he must reign[p] until he has put all his
enemies under his feet.[q] 26The last
enemy to be destroyed is death.[r]
27For he "has put everything under his
feet."[q][s] Now when it says that "everything" has been put under him, it is
clear that this does not include God
himself, who put everything under
Christ.[t] 28When he has done this,
then the Son himself will be made subject to him who put everything under
him,[u] so that God may be all in all.[v]

Php 3:20-21

29Now if there is no resurrection,
what will those do who are baptized for
the dead? If the dead are not raised at
all, why are people baptized for them?
30And as for us, why do we endanger
ourselves every hour?[w] 31I die every
day[x]—I mean that, brothers—just as
surely as I glory over you in Christ
Jesus our Lord. 32If I fought wild
beasts[y] in Ephesus[z] for merely human reasons, what have I gained? If
the dead are not raised,

> "Let us eat and drink,
> for tomorrow we die."[r][a]

33Do not be misled:[b] "Bad company
corrupts good character."[c] 34Come
back to your senses as you ought, and
stop sinning; for there are some who
are ignorant of God[d]—I say this to
your shame.[e]

The Resurrection Body

35But someone may ask,[f] "How are
the dead raised? With what kind of
body will they come?"[g] 36How foolish![h] What you sow does not come to
life unless it dies.[i] 37When you sow,
you do not plant the body that will be,
but just a seed, perhaps of wheat or of
something else. 38But God gives it a
body as he has determined, and to each
kind of seed he gives its own body.[j]
39All flesh is not the same: Men have
one kind of flesh, animals have another, birds another and fish another.
40There are also heavenly bodies and
there are earthly bodies; but the splendor of the heavenly bodies is one kind,
and the splendor of the earthly bodies
is another. 41The sun has one kind of
splendor,[k] the moon another and the
stars another;[l] and star differs from
star in splendor.

42So will it be[m] with the resurrection of the dead.[n] The body that is
sown is perishable, it is raised imperishable;[o] 43it is sown in dishonor, it is
raised in glory;[p] it is sown in weakness, it is raised in power; 44it is sown
a natural body, it is raised a spiritual
body.[q]

If there is a natural body, there is
also a spiritual body. 45So it is written:

[q]27 Psalm 8:6 [r]32 Isaiah 22:13

15:15 [a]S Ac 2:24
15:17 [b]S Ro 4:25
15:18 [c]ver 6,20; S Mt 9:24
15:19 [d]S 1Co 4:9
15:20 [e]1Pe 1:3 [f]ver 23; S Ac 26:23 [g]ver 6, 18; S Mt 9:24
15:21 [h]S Ro 5:12 [i]ver 12
15:22 [j]Ro 5:14-18; S 1Co 6:14
15:23 [k]ver 20 [l]ver 52; S 1Th 2:19 [m]S 1Co 3:23
15:24 [n]Da 2:44; 7:14,27; 2Pe 1:11 [o]Ro 8:38
15:25 [p]Isa 9:7; 52:7 [q]ver 27; S Mt 22:44
15:26 [r]2Ti 1:10; Rev 20:14; 21:4
15:27 [s]ver 25; Ps 8:6; S Mt 22:44 [t]S Mt 28:18
15:28 [u]Php 3:21 [v]1Co 3:23
15:30 [w]2Co 11:26
15:31 [x]S Ro 8:36
15:32 [y]2Co 1:8 [z]S Ac 18:19 [a]Isa 22:13; Lk 12:19
15:33 [b]S 1Co 6:9 [c]Pr 22:24,25
15:34 [d]S Gal 4:8 [e]S 1Co 4:14
15:35 [f]Ro 9:19 [g]Eze 37:3
15:36 [h]Lk 11:40; 12:20 [i]Jn 12:24
15:38 [j]Ge 1:11
15:41 [k]Ps 19:4-6 [l]Ps 8:1,3
15:42 [m]Da 12:3; Mt 13:43 [n]ver 12 [o]ver 50,53,54
15:43 [p]Php 3:21; Col 3:4
15:44 [q]ver 50

15:17 IF CHRIST HAS NOT BEEN RAISED. Some were denying Christ's bodily resurrection (v. 12). In response, Paul states that if Christ has not been raised, then there is no deliverance from sin. Clearly those who deny the objective reality of the resurrection of Christ are denying the Christian faith altogether. They are false witnesses who speak against God and his Word. Their faith is worthless; they are not, therefore, authentic Christians.

15:29 BAPTIZED FOR THE DEAD. These words (meaning "baptized because of the dead") may refer to those who became Christians and were baptized because they wanted to be reunited with their departed Christian friends or family members in the life to come. Doing so would be useless "if the dead are not raised" at all (vv. 16–17).

15:35–54 HOW ARE THE DEAD RAISED? Paul begins here a discussion of the doctrine of what the resurrection of the dead involves. For comments on these verses, see article on THE RESURRECTION OF THE BODY, p. 1779.

THE RESURRECTION OF THE BODY

***1Co 15:35** "But someone may ask, 'How are the dead raised? With what kind of body will they come?'"*

The resurrection of the body is an essential doctrine in Scripture. It refers to God's raising of a body from the dead and reuniting it with the person's soul and spirit, from which it was separated during the intermediate state.

(1) The Bible reveals at least three reasons why the resurrection of the body is necessary. (a) The body is essential to the total human personality; humans are incomplete without a body. Thus, the redemption Christ offers applies to the whole person, including the body (Ro 8:18–25; see article on HUMAN PERSONHOOD, p. 960). (b) The body is the temple of the Holy Spirit (1Co 6:19); it will become once more a temple of the Spirit at the resurrection. (c) To undo the result of sin at all levels, humanity's final enemy (death of the body) must be conquered through the resurrection (1Co 15:26).

(2) Both the OT (compare Ge 22:1–14 with Heb 11:17–19; Ps 16:10 with Ac 2:24ff; cf. Job 19:25–27; Isa 26:19; Da 12:2; Hos 13:14) and the NT (Lk 14:13–14; 20:35–36; Jn 5:21,28–29; 6:39–40,44,54; 1Co 15:22–23; Php 3:11; 1Th 4:14–16; Rev 20:4–6,13) teach the future bodily resurrection.

(3) Our bodily resurrection is guaranteed by the fact of Christ's resurrection (see Mt 28:6, note; Ac 17:31; 1Co 15:12,20–23).

(4) In general terms, the believer's resurrected body will be like the Lord's own resurrected body (Ro 8:29; 1Co 15:20,42–44,49; Php 3:20–21; 1Jn 3:2). More specifically, the resurrected body will be: (a) a body possessing continuity and identity with the body of this life and therefore recognizable (Lk 16:19–31); (b) a body changed into a heavenly body adapted for the new heaven and new earth (1Co 15:42–44,47–48; Rev 21:1); (c) an imperishable body, free from decay and death (1Co 15:42); (d) a glorified body, like Christ's (1Co 15:43; Php 3:20–21); (e) a powerful body not subject to disease or weakness (1Co 15:43); (f) a spiritual (i.e., not natural, but supernatural) body, not bound by the laws of nature (Lk 24:31; Jn 20:19; 1Co 15:44); (g) a body capable of eating and drinking (Lk 14:15; 22:14–18,30; 24:43).

(5) When believers receive their new bodies, they put on immortality (1Co 15:53). Scripture indicates at least three purposes for this: (a) so that believers may become all that God intended for humans at creation (cf. 1Co 2:9); (b) so that believers may come to know God in the full way he wants them to know him (Jn 17:3); (c) so that God may express his love to his children as he desires (Jn 3:16; Eph 2:7; 1Jn 4:8–16).

(6) The faithful who are still alive at Christ's return for his followers will experience the same bodily transformation as those who have died in Christ prior to the day of resurrection (1Co 15:51–53). They will be given new bodies identical to the bodies given to those raised from the dead at that time. They will never experience physical death (see article on THE RAPTURE, p. 1864).

(7) Jesus speaks of a resurrection of life for the believer and a resurrection of judgment for the wicked (Jn 5:28–29).

"The first man Adam became a living
being"[s];[r] the last Adam,[s] a life-giving spirit.[t] **46**The spiritual did not
come first, but the natural, and after
that the spiritual.[u] **47**The first man
was of the dust of the earth,[v] the second man from heaven.[w] **48**As was the
earthly man, so are those who are of
the earth; and as is the man from heav-
en, so also are those who are of heav-
en.[x] **49**And just as we have borne the
likeness of the earthly man,[y] so shall
we[t] bear the likeness of the man from
heaven.[z]

50I declare to you, brothers, that
flesh and blood[a] cannot inherit the
kingdom of God,[b] nor does the perishable inherit the imperishable.[c] **51**Listen, I tell you a mystery:[d] We will not
all sleep,[e] but we will all be
changed[f]— **52**in a flash, in the twinkling of an eye, at the last trumpet. For
the trumpet will sound,[g] the dead[h]
will be raised imperishable, and we will
be changed. **53**For the perishable[i]
must clothe itself with the imperishable,[j] and the mortal with immortality. **54**When the perishable has been
clothed with the imperishable, and the
mortal with immortality, then the saying that is written will come true:
"Death has been swallowed up in victory."[u][k]

55"Where, O death, is your victory?
Where, O death, is your
sting?"[v][l]

56The sting of death is sin,[m] and the
power of sin is the law.[n] **57**But thanks
be to God![o] He gives us the victory
through our Lord Jesus Christ.[p]

58Therefore, my dear brothers,
stand firm. Let nothing move you. Always give yourselves fully to the work
of the Lord,[q] because you know that
your labor in the Lord is not in vain.[r]

15:45 [r]Ge 2:7 [s]Ro 5:14 [t]Jn 5:21; 6:57,58; Ro 8:2
15:46 [u]ver 44
15:47 [v]Ge 2:7; 3:19; Ps 90:3 [w]Jn 3:13,31
15:48 [x]Php 3:20, 21
15:49 [y]Ge 5:3 [z]S Ro 8:29
15:50 [a]Eph 6:12; Heb 2:14 [b]S Mt 25:34 [c]ver 42,53,54
15:51 [d]1Co 13:2; 14:2 [e]S Mt 9:24 [f]2Co 5:4; Php 3:21
15:52 [g]S Mt 24:31 [h]Jn 5:25
15:53 [i]ver 42,50, 54 [j]2Co 5:2,4
15:54 [k]Isa 25:8; Heb 2:14; Rev 20:14
15:55 [l]Hos 13:14
15:56 [m]S Ro 5:12 [n]S Ro 4:15
15:57 [o]S 2Co 2:14 [p]Ro 8:37; Heb 2:14,15
15:58 [q]1Co 16:10 [r]Isa 65:23
16:1 [s]S Ac 24:17 [t]S Ac 9:13 [u]S Ac 16:6
16:2 [v]Ac 20:7 [w]2Co 9:4,5
16:3 [x]2Co 3:1; 8:18,19
16:5 [y]S 1Co 4:19 [z]S Ac 16:9
16:6 [a]Ro 15:24; Tit 3:13
16:7 [b]S Ac 18:21
16:8 [c]S Ac 18:19 [d]S Ac 2:1
16:9 [e]S Ac 14:27
16:10 [f]S Ac 16:1 [g]1Co 15:58
16:11 [h]1Ti 4:12 [i]2Co 1:16; 3Jn 6 [j]S Ac 15:33
16:12 [k]S Ac 18:24

The Collection for God's People

16 Now about the collection[s] for
God's people:[t] Do what I told
the Galatian[u] churches to do. **2**On the
first day of every week,[v] each one of
you should set aside a sum of money in
keeping with his income, saving it up,
so that when I come no collections will
have to be made.[w] **3**Then, when I arrive, I will give letters of introduction
to the men you approve[x] and send
them with your gift to Jerusalem. **4**If it
seems advisable for me to go also, they
will accompany me.

Personal Requests

5After I go through Macedonia, I will
come to you[y]—for I will be going
through Macedonia.[z] **6**Perhaps I will
stay with you awhile, or even spend the
winter, so that you can help me on my
journey,[a] wherever I go. **7**I do not
want to see you now and make only a
passing visit; I hope to spend some
time with you, if the Lord permits.[b]
8But I will stay on at Ephesus[c] until
Pentecost,[d] **9**because a great door for
effective work has opened to me,[e] and
there are many who oppose me.

10If Timothy[f] comes, see to it that
he has nothing to fear while he is with
you, for he is carrying on the work of
the Lord,[g] just as I am. **11**No one,
then, should refuse to accept him.[h]
Send him on his way[i] in peace[j] so
that he may return to me. I am expecting him along with the brothers.

12Now about our brother Apollos:[k]
I strongly urged him to go to you with

[s]*45* Gen. 2:7 [t]*49* Some early manuscripts *so let us* [u]*54* Isaiah 25:8 [v]*55* Hosea 13:14

15:51 A MYSTERY. The mystery Paul declares is the truth that when Jesus returns from heaven for his church, those believers who are alive will have their bodies immediately transformed and made imperishable and immortal (see Jn 14:3, note; see article on THE RAPTURE, p. 1864).

15:51 WE WILL NOT ALL SLEEP. Paul's use of "we" indicates he held to the NT perspective that Christ could come for the faithful of his churches in Paul's own generation. Although Christ did not return in Paul's lifetime, Paul did not err in believing as he did, for he knew that Christ could come at any time. All who look for Christ to return during their lifetime share the NT viewpoint. The words of Jesus and the entire NT urge every believer to believe it is the last hour and to live in the hope that Christ might return in his or her lifetime (cf. 1:7–8; Ro 13:12; Php 3:20; 1Th 1:10; 4:15–17; Tit 2:13; Jas 5:8–9; 1Jn 2:18,28; Rev 22:7,12,20; see Mt 24:42,44, notes; Lk 12:35, note). Thus, those who do not look for him in their lifetime are not living according to the apostolic pattern.

15:52 WE WILL BE CHANGED. See article on THE RESURRECTION OF THE BODY, p. 1779.

16:1 NOW ABOUT THE COLLECTION. In ch. 16 Paul gives direction for the collection for the poor believers at Jerusalem, describes his future plans and speaks about his fellow workers in the Lord.

the brothers. He was quite unwilling to
go now, but he will go when he has the
opportunity.
13 Be on your guard; stand firm[l] in
the faith; be men of courage; be
strong.[m] **14** Do everything in love.[n]
15 You know that the household of
Stephanas[o] were the first converts[p]
in Achaia,[q] and they have devoted
themselves to the service[r] of the
saints.[s] I urge you, brothers, **16** to submit[t] to such as these and to everyone
who joins in the work, and labors at it.
17 I was glad when Stephanas, Fortunatus and Achaicus arrived, because they
have supplied what was lacking from
you.[u] **18** For they refreshed[v] my spirit
and yours also. Such men deserve recognition.[w]

Final Greetings

19 The churches in the province of
Asia[x] send you greetings. Aquila and
Priscilla[w][y] greet you warmly in the
Lord, and so does the church that
meets at their house.[z] **20** All the brothers here send you greetings. Greet one
another with a holy kiss.[a]
21 I, Paul, write this greeting in my
own hand.[b]
22 If anyone does not love the
Lord[c]—a curse[d] be on him. Come,
O Lord[x]![e]
23 The grace of the Lord Jesus be
with you.[f]
24 My love to all of you in Christ
Jesus. Amen.[y]

16:13 [l] 1Co 1:8; 2Co 1:21; Gal 5:1; Php 1:27; 1Th 3:8; S Tit 1:9 [m] S Eph 6:10
16:14 [n] 1Co 14:1
16:15 [o] 1Co 1:16 [p] Ro 16:5 [q] S Ac 18:12 [r] S Ac 24:17 [s] S Ac 9:13
16:16 [t] 1Th 5:12; Heb 13:17
16:17 [u] 2Co 11:9; Php 2:30
16:18 [v] Ro 15:32; Phm 7 [w] Php 2:29
16:19 [x] S Ac 2:9 [y] S Ac 18:2 [z] S Ro 16:5
16:20 [a] S Ro 16:16
16:21 [b] Gal 6:11; Col 4:18; 2Th 3:17; Phm 19
16:22 [c] Eph 6:24 [d] Ro 9:3 [e] Rev 22:20
16:23 [f] S Ro 16:20

w *19* Greek *Prisca,* a variant of *Priscilla*
x *22* In Aramaic the expression *Come, O Lord* is *Marana tha.* y *24* Some manuscripts do not have *Amen.*

16:22 A CURSE. Paul ends this letter by reminding all professing believers that to claim to be believers, yet not to love the Lord, is to be accursed or doomed. To "not love the Lord" means to fail to have a heartfelt love for him, to disobey him (Jn 14:21) and to distort the apostolic gospel of NT revelation (see Gal 1:9, note). To be accursed means being excluded from the true spiritual church on earth and finally from the heavenly kingdom of the age to come. Paul wants his readers to understand that the ultimate test of Christian discipleship is a personal, heartfelt loyalty to the Lord Jesus Christ (cf. Ro 10:9).

16:22 COME, O LORD! The Aramaic expression *marana tha* was probably used as a prayer or greeting among Christians. The early church was constantly praying that Christ might return soon. Christians are those who long for his appearing (see 2Ti 4:8) and express this longing in word and deed (1Th 1:10; Rev 22:20).

2 CORINTHIANS

Outline

Introduction (1:1–11)

I. Paul's Defense for the Sake of the Loyal Majority (1:12—7:16)
   A. Denial That He Has Been Fickle (1:12–22)
   B. Explanation of His Change in Travel Plans (1:23—2:17)
   C. Clarification Concerning the Character of His Ministry (3:1—6:10)
      1. It Is in the Service of a New Covenant (3:1–18)
      2. It Is in Openness and Truth (4:1–6)
      3. It Is in Personal Suffering (4:7—5:10)
      4. It Is in Compassionate Dedication (5:11—6:10)
   D. Personal Appeal to and Affectionate Regard for the Corinthians (6:11—7:16)

II. The Collection for Needy Christians in Jerusalem (8:1—9:15)
   A. The Grace of Christian Generosity (8:1–15)
   B. Titus to Head Up Arrangements for the Collection (8:16–24)
   C. An Appeal for a Ready Response (9:1–5)
   D. An Appeal for a Generous Response (9:6–15)

III. Paul's Reply to the Rebellious Minority (10:1—13:10)
   A. An Answer to Charges of Cowardice and Weakness (10:1–18)
   B. A Reluctant Self-Defense of His Apostleship (11:1—12:18)
      1. Apology for Boastful Tone (11:1–15)
      2. Affirms He Is Not Inferior to the Judaizers (11:16—12:10)
      3. Legitimate Claims to Apostleship (12:11–18)
   C. An Upcoming Third Visit Mentioned as a Warning (12:19—13:10)
      1. Apprehensiveness Concerning the Corinthians (12:19–21)
      2. Determination to Be Firm (13:1–10)

Conclusion (13:11–14)

Author: Paul

Theme: Glory Through Suffering

Date of Writing: A.D. 55/56

Background

Paul wrote this letter to the church at Corinth and to believers throughout Achaia (1:1), identifying himself twice by name (1:1; 10:1). Having founded the Corinthian church during his second missionary journey, Paul and the Corinthians had frequent contacts thereafter because of problems in the church (see the introduction to 1 Corinthians).

The sequence of these contacts and the setting for writing 2 Corinthians are as follows. (1) After some initial contacts and correspondence between Paul and the church (e.g., 1Co 1:11; 5:9; 7:1), Paul wrote 1 Corinthians from Ephesus (spring A.D. 55 or 56). (2) Next, Paul made a trip across the Aegean Sea to Corinth to deal with further problems in the church. This visit between 1 and 2 Corinthians (cf. 13:1–2) was a painful one for Paul and the congregation (2:1–2). (3) After this painful visit, reports reached Paul at Ephesus that antagonists were still attacking him and his apostolic authority at Corinth, in hopes of persuading a portion of the church to reject Paul. (4) In response to this report, Paul wrote 2 Corinthians from Macedonia (fall A.D. 55 or 56). (5) Shortly thereafter Paul traveled to Corinth again (13:1), where he remained for about three months (cf. Ac 20:1–3a), and from there he wrote Romans.

Purpose

Paul wrote this letter to address three categories of people at Corinth. (1) First, he wrote to encourage the majority at Corinth who remained faithful to him as their spiritual father. (2) He wrote to challenge and expose the false apostles who continued to speak against him personally, hoping to undermine his authority and apostleship and to distort his message. (3) He also wrote to reprimand the minority in the church who were being influenced by Paul's opponents and who were resisting his authority and correction. Paul reaffirmed his integrity and apostolic authority, clarified his motives and warned them against further rebellion. 2 Corinthians served to prepare the church as a whole for his impending visit.

Survey

2 Corinthians has three main divisions. (1) In the first (chs. 1—7), Paul begins by thanking God for his comfort in the midst of suffering for the gospel, commends the Corinthians for disciplining a serious offender and defends his integrity in changing his travel plans. In 3:1—6:10 Paul shares the most extensive insight in the NT on the true character of Christian ministry. He stresses the importance of separation from the world (6:11—7:1) and expresses joy in learning from Titus of the repentance of many in the Corinthian church who had previously rebelled against his authority (ch. 7).

(2) In chs. 8 and 9, Paul exhorts the Corinthians to match the wholehearted Christian generosity of the Macedonians in contributing to the offering he was raising for the distressed Christians at Jerusalem.

(3) The letter's tone changes in chs. 10—13. Here Paul defends his apostleship by setting forth his calling, qualifications and sufferings as a true apostle. By this Paul hopes the Corinthians will discern the false apostles among them and thereby be spared further discipline when he arrives again in person. Paul concludes 2 Corinthians with the only trinitarian benediction in the NT (13:14).

Special Features

Four major features characterize this letter. (1) It is the most autobiographical of all Paul's letters. His many personal references are made with transparent humility, apology, and even embarrassment, but out of necessity because of the situation at Corinth. (2) It surpasses all other Pauline letters in revealing the intensity and depth of Paul's love and concern for his spiritual children. (3) It contains the NT's most developed theology about Christian suffering (1:3–11; 4:7–18; 6:3–10; 11:23–30; 12:1–10) and about Christian giving (chs. 8—9). (4) Key terms, such as weakness, grief, tears, danger, distress, suffering, comfort, boasting, truth, ministry and glory, underscore the unique character of this letter.

Reading 2 Corinthians

In order to read the entire New Testament in one year, the book of 2 Corinthians should be read in 12 days, according to the following schedule:
☐ 1:1—2:4 ☐ 2:5—3:6 ☐ 3:7—4:18 ☐ 5:1—6:2 ☐ 6:3—7:1 ☐ 7:2–16 ☐ 8–9 ☐ 10 ☐ 11:1–15 ☐ 11:16–33 ☐ 12 ☐ 13

NOTES

1 Paul, an apostle[a] of Christ Jesus
by the will of God,[b] and Timothy[c] our brother,

To the church of God[d] in Corinth,[e]
together with all the saints throughout
Achaia:[f]

2 Grace and peace to you from God
our Father and the Lord Jesus Christ.[g]

The God of All Comfort

3 Praise be to the God and Father of
our Lord Jesus Christ,[h] the Father of
compassion and the God of all comfort,
4 who comforts us[i] in all our troubles,
so that we can comfort those in any
trouble with the comfort we ourselves
have received from God. 5 For just as
the sufferings of Christ flow over into
our lives,[j] so also through Christ our
comfort overflows. 6 If we are distressed, it is for your comfort and salvation;[k] if we are comforted, it is for
your comfort, which produces in you
patient endurance of the same sufferings we suffer. 7 And our hope for you
is firm, because we know that just as
you share in our sufferings,[l] so also
you share in our comfort.
8 We do not want you to be unin-
formed,[m] brothers, about the hardships we suffered[n] in the province of
Asia.[o] We were under great pressure,
far beyond our ability to endure, so that
we despaired even of life. 9 Indeed, in
our hearts we felt the sentence of
death. But this happened that we
might not rely on ourselves but on
God,[p] who raises the dead.[q] 10 He has
delivered us from such a deadly peril,[r] and he will deliver us. On him we
have set our hope[s] that he will continue to deliver us, 11 as you help us by
your prayers.[t] Then many will give
thanks[u] on our[a] behalf for the gracious favor granted us in answer to the
prayers of many.

Paul's Change of Plans

12 Now this is our boast: Our conscience[v] testifies that we have conducted ourselves in the world, and especially in our relations with you, in
the holiness[w] and sincerity[x] that are
from God. We have done so not according to worldly wisdom[y] but according
to God's grace. 13 For we do not write
you anything you cannot read or understand. And I hope that, 14 as you have
understood us in part, you will come to
understand fully that you can boast of
us just as we will boast of you in the
day of the Lord Jesus.[z]
15 Because I was confident of this, I
planned to visit you[a] first so that you

1:1 [a] S 1Co 1:1 [b] 1Co 1:1; Eph 1:1; Col 1:1; 2Ti 1:1 [c] S Ac 16:1 [d] S 1Co 10:32 [e] S Ac 18:1 [f] S Ac 18:12 **1:2** [g] S Ro 1:7 **1:3** [h] Eph 1:3; 1Pe 1:3 **1:4** [i] Isa 49:13; 51:12; 66:13; 2Co 7:6,7,13 **1:5** [j] Ro 8:17; 2Co 4:10; Gal 6:17; Php 3:10; Col 1:24; 1Pe 4:13 **1:6** [k] 2Co 4:15 **1:7** [l] S ver 5 **1:8** [m] S Ro 11:25 [n] 1Co 15:32 [o] S Ac 2:9 **1:9** [p] Jer 17:5,7 [q] S Jn 5:21 **1:10** [r] S Ro 15:31 [s] 1Ti 4:10 **1:11** [t] Ro 15:30; Php 1:19 [u] 2Co 4:15; 9:11 **1:12** [v] S Ac 23:1 [w] 1Th 2:10 [x] 2Co 2:17 [y] 1Co 1:17; 2:1,4, 13 **1:14** [z] S 1Co 1:8 **1:15** [a] S 1Co 4:19

[a] *11* Many manuscripts *your*

1:4 COMFORTS US IN ALL OUR TROUBLES. The word "comfort" (Gk *paraklēsis*) means to stand beside a person, encouraging and helping him or her in a time of trouble. God supremely fulfills this role, for he sends to his children the Holy Spirit to comfort them (see Jn 14:16, note). Paul has learned in his many troubles that no suffering, however severe, can separate believers from the care and compassion of their heavenly Father (Ro 8:35–39). God occasionally permits troubles in our lives in order that we, having experienced his comfort, may comfort others in their troubles (see article on THE SUFFERING OF THE RIGHTEOUS, p. 710).

1:5 SUFFERINGS . . . COMFORT. Throughout this letter, Paul emphasizes that the Christian life includes both suffering (a sharing or partnership with Christ in suffering) and the comfort of Christ. That is, in this age Christ suffers with and for his people because of the tragedy of sin (cf. Mt 25:42–45; Ro 8:22–26). Our suffering is not necessarily a suffering because of disobedience, but is often a suffering at the hands of Satan, the world and false believers as we share in the cause of Christ.

1:8–10 WE DESPAIRED EVEN OF LIFE. A faithful believer, living in obedient fellowship with Christ and loved by him, may yet undergo experiences that involve danger, fear and despair, and may encounter circumstances that weigh one down beyond the human power of endurance. (1) When severe troubles occur in our lives, we need not feel that God has forsaken us or has stopped loving us. Rather, we must remind ourselves that these very things happened to God's faithful servants of NT times. (2) God allows these desperate trials so that Christ might come near and, as we look to him in faith, give us the grace to bring us to victory (2:14; 12:7–10; 13:4).

1:11 AS YOU HELP US BY YOUR PRAYERS. An indisputable Biblical principle is that our prayers for others will release God's power and activity in others' lives. Because of this, we should be encouraged to intercede for those in need (cf. Ro 1:9; Eph 1:16; Php 1:3; Col 1:3; 1Th 1:2).

1:12 THIS IS OUR BOAST. Paul's basis for rejoicing and boasting was the sincerity and integrity of his behavior. He had determined that for his entire Christian life he would remain faithful to his Lord, refuse to conform to the world that crucified his Savior, and persevere in holiness until God called him home (Ro 12:1–2). In the eternal age to come, one of our greatest joys will be the consciousness that we have lived our lives in "holiness and sincerity" for Christ our Savior.

might benefit twice.[b] **16**I planned to
visit you on my way[c] to Macedonia[d]
and to come back to you from Macedonia, and then to have you send me on
my way[e] to Judea.[f] **17**When I planned
this, did I do it lightly? Or do I make
my plans in a worldly manner[g] so that
in the same breath I say, "Yes, yes" and
"No, no"?
18But as surely as God is faithful,[h]
our message to you is not "Yes" and
"No." **19**For the Son of God,[i] Jesus
Christ, who was preached among you
by me and Silas[b][j] and Timothy,[k]
was not "Yes" and "No," but in him it
has always[l] been "Yes." **20**For no matter how many promises[m] God has
made, they are "Yes" in Christ. And so
through him the "Amen"[n] is spoken
by us to the glory of God.[o] **21**Now it is
God who makes both us and you stand
firm[p] in Christ. He anointed[q] us,
22set his seal[r] of ownership on us,
and put his Spirit in our hearts as a
deposit, guaranteeing what is to
come.[s]
23I call God as my witness[t] that it
was in order to spare you[u] that I did
not return to Corinth. **24**Not that we
lord it over[v] your faith, but we work
with you for your joy, because it is by
2 faith you stand firm.[w] **1**So I made
up my mind that I would not make
another painful visit to you.[x] **2**For if I
grieve you,[y] who is left to make me
glad but you whom I have grieved? **3**I
wrote as I did[z] so that when I came
I should not be distressed[a] by those
who ought to make me rejoice. I had
confidence[b] in all of you, that you
would all share my joy. **4**For I wrote
you[c] out of great distress and anguish
of heart and with many tears, not to
grieve you but to let you know the
depth of my love for you.

Forgiveness for the Sinner

5If anyone has caused grief,[d] he
has not so much grieved me as he has
grieved all of you, to some extent—not
to put it too severely. **6**The punishment[e] inflicted on him by the majority
is sufficient for him. **7**Now instead, you
ought to forgive and comfort him,[f] so
that he will not be overwhelmed by excessive sorrow. **8**I urge you, therefore,
to reaffirm your love for him. **9**The reason I wrote you[g] was to see if you
would stand the test and be obedient in
everything.[h] **10**If you forgive anyone,

1:15 [b] Ro 1:11,13; 15:29
1:16 [c] 1Co 16:5-7 [d] S Ac 16:9 [e] 1Co 16:11; 3Jn 6 [f] Ac 19:21
1:17 [g] 2Co 10:2,3; 11:18
1:18 [h] S 1Co 1:9
1:19 [i] S Mt 4:3 [j] S Ac 15:22 [k] S Ac 16:1 [l] Heb 13:8
1:20 [m] Ro 15:8 [n] S 1Co 14:16 [o] Ro 15:9
1:21 [p] S 1Co 16:13 [q] 1Jn 2:20,27
1:22 [r] Ge 38:18; Eze 9:4; Hag 2:23 [s] S 2Co 5:5
1:23 [t] S Ro 1:9 [u] 1Co 4:21; 2Co 2:1,3; 13:2,10
1:24 [v] 1Pe 5:3 [w] Ro 11:20; 1Co 15:1
2:1 [x] S 2Co 1:23
2:2 [y] 2Co 7:8
2:3 [z] ver 4,9; 2Co 7:8,12 [a] 2Co 12:21 [b] 2Co 7:16; 8:22; Gal 5:10; 2Th 3:4; Phm 21
2:4 [c] ver 3,9; 2Co 7:8,12
2:5 [d] 1Co 5:1,2
2:6 [e] 1Co 5:4,5; 2Co 7:11
2:7 [f] Gal 6:1; Eph 4:32; Col 3:13
2:9 [g] ver 3,4; 2Co 7:8,12 [h] 2Co 7:15; 10:6

[b] 19 Greek *Silvanus*, a variant of *Silas*

1:20 AMEN. The concluding "Amen" of the Christian's prayer and proclamation expresses confidence in God's love and faithfulness and the certainty of his promises. It is the voice of faith, reaffirming and identifying with the truth of Christ's unshakable gospel. In Rev 3:14 the Lord Jesus is called the "Amen."

1:22 SPIRIT IN OUR HEARTS AS A DEPOSIT. Paul outlines four aspects of God's work in believers through the Spirit. (1) The Holy Spirit establishes believers and helps them persevere in their life of faith (see 1Pe 1:5, note).

(2) The Spirit anoints believers in order to give them power to witness (see Ac 1:8, notes), to perform the works of Christ (Isa 61:1; Mt 10:19–20; Jn 14:12; Ac 10:38) and to know the truth (1Jn 2:20).

(3) The Spirit is the official seal of God's ownership, marking believers as his own property and producing godly character within their human personalities (cf. 3:18; Gal 5:22; Eph 1:13).

(4) The Spirit is an indwelling "deposit," i.e., a guarantee and a first installment to believers that a greater life with Christ will come in the future (5:5; Ro 8:23; see Eph 1:13–14, note).

2:4 OUT OF GREAT DISTRESS AND ANGUISH OF HEART. One of the essential qualifications of the Christian minister is a loving and sensitive heart, one that breaks into tears when it sees God's people drifting from the path of righteousness into sin and error (cf. Ps 126:5–6; Mk 9:24, note; see Lk 19:41, note; Jn 11:35, note; Ac 20:19, note).

2:6 THE PUNISHMENT ... IS SUFFICIENT. From this passage we gain insight into the NT pattern of discipline toward a member of the church who commits a serious offense (e.g., immorality, adultery, etc.; see 1Co 5). (1) In order to defend the integrity of Christ's church (cf. 1Co 5:1–2), the church must punish the offender with a punishment sufficient to produce spiritual reformation, yet not so harsh as to deny hope of divine mercy and reentry into the fellowship (v. 7). Note that forgiveness and love were not given unconditionally to the offender.

(2) After sufficient punishment, if the offender is repentant and sorrowful, he or she must be forgiven and comforted in a spirit of love (vv. 7–8).

(3) The offender's punishment and restoration must be done in a spirit of gentleness (Gal 6:1), sorrow, earnestness, indignation, fear of God and his Word, zeal for God's reputation, and readiness to see justice done by bringing the guilty to accountability (see 7:11; cf. 1Co 5:5,13).

Many churches today have abandoned NT church discipline. They advocate tolerance of sin, call for unconditional forgiveness, offer cheap grace and refuse to hear what the Spirit says to the churches (see Rev 2–3). As a result, sin is taken lightly and the fear of God is absent from among them (see Mt 18:15, note on church discipline).

I also forgive him. And what I have forgiven—if there was anything to forgive—I have forgiven in the sight of
Christ for your sake, **11**in order that Satan[i] might not outwit us. For we are
not unaware of his schemes.[j]

Ministers of the New Covenant

12Now when I went to Troas[k] to
preach the gospel of Christ[l] and
found that the Lord had opened a
door[m] for me, **13**I still had no peace of
mind,[n] because I did not find my
brother Titus[o] there. So I said good-by
to them and went on to Macedonia.[p]
14But thanks be to God,[q] who always leads us in triumphal procession
in Christ and through us spreads everywhere the fragrance[r] of the knowledge[s] of him. **15**For we are to God the
aroma[t] of Christ among those who are
being saved and those who are perishing.[u] **16**To the one we are the smell of
death;[v] to the other, the fragrance of
life. And who is equal to such a task?[w]
17Unlike so many, we do not peddle the
word of God for profit.[x] On the contrary, in Christ we speak before God
with sincerity,[y] like men sent from
God.[z]

3 Are we beginning to commend ourselves[a] again? Or do we need, like
some people, letters of recommenda-
tion[b] to you or from you? **2**You yourselves are our letter, written on our
hearts, known and read by every-
body.[c] **3**You show that you are a letter
from Christ, the result of our ministry,
written not with ink but with the Spirit
of the living God,[d] not on tablets of
stone[e] but on tablets of human
hearts.[f]
4Such confidence[g] as this is ours
through Christ before God. **5**Not that
we are competent in ourselves[h] to
claim anything for ourselves, but our
competence comes from God.[i] **6**He
has made us competent as ministers of
a new covenant[j]—not of the letter[k]
but of the Spirit; for the letter kills, but
the Spirit gives life.[l]

The Glory of the New Covenant

7Now if the ministry that brought
death,[m] which was engraved in letters
on stone, came with glory, so that the
Israelites could not look steadily at the
face of Moses because of its glory,[n]
fading though it was, **8**will not the ministry of the Spirit be even more glorious? **9**If the ministry that condemns
men[o] is glorious, how much more glorious is the ministry that brings righteousness![p] **10**For what was glorious
has no glory now in comparison with
the surpassing glory. **11**And if what
was fading away came with glory, how
much greater is the glory of that which
lasts!

2:11 [i]S Mt 4:10 [j]Lk 22:31; 2Co 4:4; 1Pe 5:8,9 **2:12** [k]S Ac 16:8 [l]S Ro 1:1; 2Co 4:3,4; 8:18; 9:13; 1Th 3:2 [m]S Ac 14:27 **2:13** [n]2Co 7:5 [o]2Co 7:6,13; 8:6, 16,23; 12:18; Gal 2:1,3; Tit 1:4 [p]S Ac 16:9 **2:14** [q]Ro 6:17; 7:25; 1Co 15:57; 2Co 9:15 [r]Eze 20:41; Eph 5:2; Php 4:18 [s]S 2Co 8:7 **2:15** [t]S ver 14; Ge 8:21; Ex 29:18; Nu 15:3 [u]S 1Co 1:18 **2:16** [v]S Lk 2:34; Jn 3:36 [w]2Co 3:5, 6 **2:17** [x]S Ac 20:33; 2Co 4:2; 1Th 2:5 [y]1Co 5:8 [z]2Co 1:12; 12:19 **3:1** [a]Ro 16:1; 2Co 5:12; 10:12, 18; 12:11 [b]Ac 18:27; Ro 16:1; 1Co 16:3
3:2 [c]1Co 9:2 **3:3** [d]S Mt 16:16 [e]ver 7; Ex 24:12; 31:18; 32:15,16 [f]Pr 3:3; 7:3; Jer 31:33; Eze 36:26 **3:4** [g]S Eph 3:12 **3:5** [h]2Co 2:16 [i]1Co 15:10 **3:6** [j]S Lk 22:20 [k]Ro 2:29; 7:6 [l]Jn 6:63 **3:7** [m]ver 9; S Ro 4:15 [n]ver 13; Ex 34:29-35; Isa 42:21
3:9 [o]ver 7; Dt 27:26 [p]Ro 1:17; 3:21,22

2:11 SATAN MIGHT NOT OUTWIT US. One of our key defenses against Satan's attack is awareness of the enemy's continual effort to gain an advantage over us and lead us away from devotion to Christ (see Eph 6:11, note).

2:14 TRIUMPHAL PROCESSION. Paul describes believers as being displayed by God to the world as a triumph and trophy of Christ's redeeming grace. Through this triumphal procession, the knowledge of Christ and the redeemed lives of believers are manifested as a sweet aroma before God and humans. To God it is pleasing; to humans it results in life or death (vv. 15–16).

2:17 PEDDLE THE WORD OF GOD. Paul here describes preachers who were watering down the demands of the gospel to gain money, acceptance and success (cf. 11:4,12–15). They were talented and persuasive, yet secretly insincere. They were greedy for money and prominence (cf. Jn 10:12–13; Php 1:15,17; 1Pe 5:2; 2Pe 2:1–3, 14–16).

3:3 WRITTEN . . . ON TABLETS OF HUMAN HEARTS. Under the new covenant established by Christ's blood (Mt 26:28), the Holy Spirit writes the law of God, not on tablets of stone as at Sinai (Ex 31:18), but on "tablets of human hearts" (see article on THE OLD COVENANT AND THE NEW COVENANT, p. 1926). Believers have God's law in their hearts, and through the power of the Spirit they are able to obey it (see Jer 31:33, note; Eze 11:19, note). This internal law consists of love for God and other people (cf. Mt 22:34–40; Ro 13:8–10).

3:6 THE LETTER KILLS. It is not the law or written Word of God itself that destroys. Rather, it is the demands of the law without the Spirit's life and power that brings condemnation (vv. 7,9; cf. Jer 31:33; Ro 3:31; see article on FAITH AND GRACE, p. 1720). Through salvation in Christ the Spirit gives to the believer spiritual life and power in order to fulfill God's will. With the Holy Spirit the letter no longer kills.

3:8 THE MINISTRY OF THE SPIRIT. Paul calls the new covenant "the ministry of the Spirit." Through faith in Christ one receives the Holy Spirit, is born again (see article on REGENERATION, p. 1589) and is promised the baptism in the Spirit (Ac 1:8; 2:4). All the redemptive benefits in Christ come by way of the Spirit. It is he who mediates Christ's presence and all his blessings (v. 9; see article on THE DOCTRINE OF THE HOLY SPIRIT, p. 1654).

12Therefore, since we have such a
hope,[q] we are very bold.[r] **13**We are
not like Moses, who would put a veil
over his face[s] to keep the Israelites
from gazing at it while the radiance
was fading away. **14**But their minds
were made dull,[t] for to this day the
same veil remains when the old covenant[u] is read.[v] It has not been removed, because only in Christ is it tak-
en away. **15**Even to this day when
Moses is read, a veil covers their
hearts. **16**But whenever anyone turns
to the Lord,[w] the veil is taken away.[x]
17Now the Lord is the Spirit,[y] and
where the Spirit of the Lord is, there is
freedom.[z] **18**And we, who with unveiled faces all reflect[c a] the Lord's
glory,[b] are being transformed into his
likeness[c] with ever-increasing glory,
which comes from the Lord, who is the
Spirit.

Treasures in Jars of Clay

4 Therefore, since through God's
mercy[d] we have this ministry, we
do not lose heart.[e] **2**Rather, we have
renounced secret and shameful
ways;[f] we do not use deception, nor
do we distort the word of God.[g] On the
contrary, by setting forth the truth
plainly we commend ourselves to every
man's conscience[h] in the sight of God.
3And even if our gospel[i] is veiled,[j] it
is veiled to those who are perishing.[k]
4The god[l] of this age[m] has blinded[n]
the minds of unbelievers, so that they
cannot see the light of the gospel of the
glory of Christ,[o] who is the image of
God.[p] **5**For we do not preach ourselves,[q] but Jesus Christ as Lord,[r]
and ourselves as your servants[s] for
Jesus' sake. **6**For God, who said, "Let
light shine out of darkness,"[d t] made
his light shine in our hearts[u] to give
us the light of the knowledge of the
glory of God in the face of Christ.[v]
7But we have this treasure in jars of
clay[w] to show that this all-surpassing
power is from God[x] and not from us.
8We are hard pressed on every side,[y]
but not crushed; perplexed,[z] but not

3:12 [q] Ro 5:4,5; 8:24,25 [r] S Ac 4:29
3:13 [s] ver 7; Ex 34:33
3:14 [t] Ro 11:7,8; 2Co 4:4 [u] Ac 13:15; 15:21 [v] ver 6
3:16 [w] Ro 11:23 [x] Ex 34:34; Isa 25:7
3:17 [y] Isa 61:1,2; Gal 4:6,7 [z] S Jn 8:32
3:18 [a] 1Co 13:12 [b] Jn 17:22,24; 2Co 4:4,6 [c] S Ro 8:29
4:1 [d] 1Co 7:25; 1Ti 1:13,16 [e] ver 16; Ps 18:45; Isa 40:31
4:2 [f] Ro 6:21; S 1Co 4:5 [g] 2Co 2:17; S Heb 4:12 [h] 2Co 5:11
4:3 [i] S 2Co 2:12 [j] 2Co 3:14 [k] S 1Co 1:18
4:4 [l] S Jn 12:31 [m] S 1Co 1:20 [n] 2Co 3:14 [o] ver 6 [p] S Jn 14:9
4:5 [q] 1Co 1:13 [r] 1Co 1:23 [s] 1Co 9:19
4:6 [t] Ge 1:3; Ps 18:28 [u] 2Pe 1:19 [v] ver 4
4:7 [w] Job 4:19; Isa 64:8; 2Ti 2:20 [x] Jdg 7:2; 1Co 2:5; 2Co 6:7
4:8 [y] 2Co 7:5 [z] Gal 4:20

[c] *18* Or *contemplate* [d] *6* Gen. 1:3

3:17 THE SPIRIT . . . THERE IS FREEDOM. The freedom that comes through Christ (Gal 5:1) is, first and foremost, liberation from the condemnation and slavery of sin (vv. 7–9; Ro 6:6,14; 8:2; Eph 4:22–24; Col 3:9–10) and the whole dominion of Satan (Ac 26:18; Col 1:13; 1Pe 5:8). (1) True liberation begins with the believer's union with Christ (Ac 4:12; Eph 1:7) and his or her receiving the Holy Spirit (see article on REGENERATION, p. 1589). Liberation from spiritual bondage is maintained through the Spirit's continued indwelling and through obedience to his direction (Ro 8:1ff; Gal 5:18; cf. Jn 15:1–11).

(2) Freedom provided by Christ is not a freedom for believers to do what they want (1Co 10:23–24) but to do what they should (Ro 6:18–23). Spiritual freedom must never be used as a cover-up for evil or as a justification for conflict (Jas 4:1–2; 1Pe 2:16–23). Christian liberation frees believers for service to God (1Th 1:9) and other people (1Co 9:19) in the way of righteousness (Ro 6:18ff). We are now Christ's slaves (Ro 1:1; 1Co 7:22; Php 1:1), living to God by grace (Ro 5:21; 6:10–13).

3:18 REFLECT THE LORD'S GLORY. As we experience Christ's nearness, love, righteousness and power through prayer and the Holy Spirit, it results in our being transformed into his likeness (4:6; cf. Col 1:15; Heb 1:3). In this age the transformation is progressive and partial. But when Christ returns, we will see him face to face, and our transformation will be complete (1Jn 3:2; Rev 22:4).

4:4 GOD OF THIS AGE. The "god of this age" refers to Satan (cf. Jn 12:31; 14:30; 16:11; Eph 2:2; 1Jn 5:19), who holds power over much of the activity of this present age. His rule is, however, temporary and conditional. He continues only by God's permissive will until the end of history (Rev 19:11—20:10). Those who do not submit themselves to Jesus Christ remain under Satan's sway. He blinds their eyes to the truth and glory of the gospel in order that they might not be saved. The solution to this fatal situation is to bind his activity through intercession and to preach the gospel in the power of the Spirit (Ac 1:8) in order that people may hear, understand and choose to believe or disbelieve (vv. 5–6; see Mt 4:10, note on Satan).

4:7 THIS TREASURE IN JARS OF CLAY. Christians are "jars of clay" who at times experience sadness, tears, troubles, perplexities, weakness and fears (cf. 1:4,8–9; 7:5). Yet because of the heavenly "treasure" within them, they are not defeated. Christianity is not the removal of weakness, nor is it merely the manifestation of divine power. Rather, it is the manifestation of divine power through human weakness (12:9). This means (1) that in every affliction we may be more than conquerors by God's power and love (Ro 8:37), and (2) that our weakness, troubles and suffering open us up to Christ's abundant grace and allow his life to be revealed in our bodies (vv. 8–11; cf. 12:7–10).

4:8 HARD PRESSED . . . NOT CRUSHED. If you experience Christ's presence and power in your life, absolutely no trouble, sickness or tragedy will cause your spiritual defeat. When outward circumstances become unbearable and your human resources are exhausted, God's resources are

in despair; 9persecuted,[a] but not
abandoned;[b] struck down, but not destroyed.[c] 10We always carry around
in our body the death of Jesus,[d] so
that the life of Jesus may also be revealed in our body.[e] 11For we who are
alive are always being given over to
death for Jesus' sake,[f] so that his life
may be revealed in our mortal body.
12So then, death is at work in us, but
life is at work in you.[g]
13It is written: "I believed; therefore
I have spoken."[e][h] With that same
spirit of faith[i] we also believe and
therefore speak, 14because we know
that the one who raised the Lord Jesus
from the dead[j] will also raise us with
Jesus[k] and present us with you in his
presence.[l] 15All this is for your benefit, so that the grace that is reaching
more and more people may cause
thanksgiving[m] to overflow to the glory
of God.
16Therefore we do not lose heart.[n]
Though outwardly we are wasting
away, yet inwardly[o] we are being renewed[p] day by day. 17For our light
and momentary troubles are achieving
for us an eternal glory that far outweighs them all.[q] 18So we fix our eyes
not on what is seen, but on what is unseen.[r] For what is seen is temporary,
but what is unseen is eternal.

Our Heavenly Dwelling

5 Now we know that if the earthly[s]
tent[t] we live in is destroyed, we
have a building from God, an eternal
house in heaven, not built by human
hands. 2Meanwhile we groan,[u] longing to be clothed with our heavenly
dwelling,[v] 3because when we are
clothed, we will not be found naked.
4For while we are in this tent, we
groan[w] and are burdened, because we
do not wish to be unclothed but to be
clothed with our heavenly dwelling,[x]
so that what is mortal may be swallowed up by life. 5Now it is God who
has made us for this very purpose and
has given us the Spirit as a deposit,
guaranteeing what is to come.[y]
6Therefore we are always confident
and know that as long as we are at
home in the body we are away from the
Lord. 7We live by faith, not by sight.[z]
8We are confident, I say, and would
prefer to be away from the body and at

4:9 [a]Jn 15:20; Ro 8:35 [b]Heb 13:5 [c]Ps 37:24; Pr 24:16
4:10 [d]S Ro 6:6; S 2Co 1:5 [e]S Ro 6:5
4:11 [f]Ro 8:36
4:12 [g]2Co 13:9
4:13 [h]Ps 116:10 [i]1Co 12:9
4:14 [j]S Ac 2:24 [k]1Th 4:14 [l]Eph 5:27; Col 1:22; Jude 24
4:15 [m]2Co 1:11; 9:11
4:16 [n]ver 1; Ps 18:45 [o]Ro 7:22 [p]Ps 103:5; Isa 40:31; Col 3:10
4:17 [q]Ps 30:5; Ro 8:18; 1Pe 1:6,7
4:18 [r]2Co 5:7; Ro 8:24; Heb 11:1
5:1 [s]1Co 15:47 [t]Isa 38:12; 2Pe 1:13,14
5:2 [u]ver 4; Ro 8:23 [v]ver 4; 1Co 15:53,54
5:4 [w]ver 2; Ro 8:23 [x]ver 2; 1Co 15:53,54
5:5 [y]Ro 8:23; 2Co 1:22; Eph 1:13,14
5:7 [z]1Co 13:12; S 2Co 4:18

[e] *13* Psalm 116:10

given to expand your faith, hope and strength. Under no circumstances will God forsake his faithful children (Ro 8:35–39; Heb 13:5).

4:11–12 GIVEN OVER TO DEATH. To minister life to another person, we must share Christ's sufferings and experience the working of death in our own lives (v. 12). Self-denial, trouble, disappointment and suffering for Christ's sake will allow our lives to minister grace to others (cf. 11:23–29; Ro 8:36–37; Php 1:29; 1Pe 4:14). Jesus taught this same great principle of brokenness in Jn 12:24–25.

4:16 OUTWARDLY ... INWARDLY. "Outwardly" refers to the physical body, subject to decay and moving toward death because of mortality and the troubles of life (v. 17). "Inwardly" refers to the human spirit that has the spiritual life of Christ. Although our bodies age and decay, we experience ongoing renewal through the constant impartation of Christ's life and power; his influence enables our minds, emotions and wills to be conformed to his likeness and eternal purpose.

4:17 MOMENTARY TROUBLE ... ETERNAL GLORY. The hardships endured in the lives of those who remain faithful to Christ are light in comparison to the abundance of glory we have through Christ. This glory is already present in part, but will be fully experienced in the future (cf. Ro 8:18). When we reach our heavenly inheritance, we will say that the severest tribulations were nothing compared with the glory of the eternal state. Therefore, we must not lose hope or give up our faith as we face our problems.

5:1 IF THE EARTHLY TENT. Paul uses the conditional clause, "if the earthly tent we live in is destroyed," because he knows that Christ could return soon, in which case he would not experience death; rather, his body would be immediately transformed (see article on THE RAPTURE, p. 1864). This same double possibility (death or transformation) exists for believers today. Christ has stated we do not know the day or the hour of his return (Mt 24:36,42,44); since this event is imminent, we have a powerful motivation for holy living (see Mt 24:42, notes; 1Jn 3:2–3).

5:1 EARTHLY TENT ... A BUILDING. (1) The term "earthly tent" refers either to the believer's earthly body or to the believer's earthly life. (2) The "building from God, an eternal house in heaven, not built by human hands" likely refers either to a temporary body prepared for believers in heaven while they await their resurrection body, or to the environment of the heavenly existence.

Some have used this difficult passage to teach that after death and while awaiting resurrection, believers exist as disembodied spirits, vague shadows or naked souls without form. However, note that both Moses and Elijah on the Mount of Transfiguration appeared clothed with a heavenly body, even though they were awaiting their resurrection bodies (see article on THE RESURRECTION OF THE BODY, p. 1779). Furthermore, in Rev 6:9–11 souls in heaven wear white robes and are described as being visible; they are not naked souls.

home with the Lord.[a] 9So we make it
our goal to please him,[b] whether we
are at home in the body or away from
it. 10For we must all appear before the
judgment seat of Christ, that each one
may receive what is due him[c] for the
things done while in the body, whether
good or bad.

The Ministry of Reconciliation

11Since, then, we know what it is to
fear the Lord,[d] we try to persuade
men. What we are is plain to God, and
I hope it is also plain to your conscience.[e] 12We are not trying to commend ourselves to you again,[f] but are
giving you an opportunity to take pride
in us,[g] so that you can answer those
who take pride in what is seen rather
than in what is in the heart. 13If we are
out of our mind,[h] it is for the sake of
God; if we are in our right mind, it is
for you. 14For Christ's love compels us,
because we are convinced that one
died for all, and therefore all died.[i]
15And he died for all, that those who
live should no longer live for themselves[j] but for him who died for
them[k] and was raised again.
16So from now on we regard no one
from a worldly[l] point of view. Though
we once regarded Christ in this way,
we do so no longer. 17Therefore, if anyone is in Christ,[m] he is a new creation;[n] the old has gone, the new has
come![o] 18All this is from God,[p] who
reconciled us to himself through
Christ[q] and gave us the ministry of
reconciliation: 19that God was reconciling the world to himself in Christ,
not counting men's sins against
them.[r] And he has committed to us
the message of reconciliation. 20We
are therefore Christ's ambassadors,[s]
as though God were making his appeal
through us.[t] We implore you on
Christ's behalf: Be reconciled to God.[u]
21God made him who had no sin[v] to be

5:8 [a]S Jn 12:26
5:9 [b]Ro 14:18; Eph 5:10; Col 1:10; 1Th 4:1
5:10 [c]S Mt 16:27; Ac 10:42; Ro 2:16; 14:10; Eph 6:8
5:11 [d]Job 23:15; Heb 10:31; 12:29; Jude 23 [e]2Co 4:2
5:12 [f]S 2Co 3:1 [g]2Co 1:14
5:13 [h]2Co 11:1, 16,17; 12:11
5:14 [i]Ro 6:6,7; Gal 2:20; Col 3:3
5:15 [j]Ro 14:7-9 [k]Ro 4:25
5:16 [l]2Co 10:4; 11:18
5:17 [m]S Ro 16:3 [n]S Jn 1:13; S Ro 6:4; Gal 6:15 [o]Isa 65:17; Rev 21:4,5
5:18 [p]S Ro 11:36 [q]S Ro 5:10
5:19 [r]S Ro 4:8
5:20 [s]2Co 6:1; Eph 6:20 [t]ver 18 [u]Isa 27:5
5:21 [v]Heb 4:15; 7:26; 1Pe 2:22,24; 1Jn 3:5

5:8 AT HOME WITH THE LORD. This verse and others (e.g., Lk 23:42–43; Php 1:23) clearly teach that there is no lapse of time between death and the life to come (see article on DEATH, p. 732). The believer's death brings him or her immediately into Christ's presence (1Co 13:12). Thus, "to die is gain" (Php 1:21). This does not mean that Christ is not present with believers now, for the Holy Spirit's work is to mediate Christ's presence to the believer (see article on THE DOCTRINE OF THE HOLY SPIRIT, p. 1654). But it does indicate that we are now with the Lord by faith and not by sight (Heb 11:1).

5:10 THE JUDGMENT SEAT OF CHRIST. For comments on what happens to believers on the day of judgment, see article on THE JUDGMENT OF BELIEVERS, p. 1791.

5:17 HE IS A NEW CREATION. Through the creative command of God (4:6), those who accept Jesus Christ by faith are made a new creation that belongs to God's totally new world in which the Spirit rules (Ro 8:14; Gal 5:25; Eph 2:10). The believer becomes a new person (Gal 6:15; Eph 2:10,15; 4:24; Col 3:10) renewed after God's image (4:16; 1Co 15:49; Eph 4:24; Col 3:10), sharing his glory (3:18) with a renewed knowledge (Col 3:10) and understanding (Ro 12:2), and living a life of holiness (Eph 4:24).

5:18 RECONCILED US TO HIMSELF. Reconciliation (Gk *katallagē*) is one aspect of Christ's work of redemption—the restoration of the sinner to fellowship with God. (1) The sin and rebellion of the human race have resulted in hostility toward and alienation from God (Eph 2:3; Col 1:21). This rebellion elicits God's wrath and judgment (Ro 1:18,24–32; 1Co 15:25–26; Eph 5:6).

(2) Through Christ's atoning death, God has removed the barrier of sin and opened a way for the sinner to return to God (v. 19; Ro 3:25; 5:10; Eph 2:15–16).

(3) Reconciliation becomes effective for each person through his or her personal repentance and faith in Christ (Mt 3:2; Ro 3:22).

(4) The church has been given the ministry of reconciliation, calling all people to be reconciled to God (v. 20; see Ro 3:25, note).

5:21 MADE HIM WHO HAD NO SIN TO BE SIN. Scripture nowhere states that Christ actually became a "sinner," for he remained the spotless Lamb of God. But Christ did take our sin upon himself (see article on THE DAY OF ATONEMENT, p. 174), and God the Father made him the object of his judgment when Christ became an offering for our sins on the cross (Isa 53:10). In taking our punishment, Jesus made it possible for God to justly forgive sinners (see Isa 53:5, note; Ro 3:24–25, notes).

5:21 WE MIGHT BECOME THE RIGHTEOUSNESS OF GOD. (1) Righteousness here does not refer to a legal righteousness, but to the experiential righteousness of the children of God as a new creation, i.e., to their character and moral state founded on and flowing from their faith in Christ (Php 3:9; see Ro 3:21, note; 4:22, note). The whole context of the passage (vv. 14–21) is concerned with believers living for Christ (v. 15), being controlled by "Christ's love" (v. 14), becoming a "new creation" (v. 17), and fulfilling the ministry of reconciliation as representatives of God and his righteousness in the world (vv. 18–20; see 1Co 1:30, note on Jesus Christ as the righteousness of the believer).

(2) God's righteousness is manifested and experienced by the believer in this world by remaining in Christ. Only to the extent that we live in union and fellowship with Christ do we become the righteousness of God (see Jn 15:4–5; Gal 2:20, note; 1Jn 1:9).

THE JUDGMENT OF BELIEVERS

2Co 5:10 "For we must all appear before the judgment seat of Christ, that each one may receive what is due him for the things done while in the body, whether good or bad."

The Bible teaches that believers will someday have to give an account at "the judgment seat of Christ." Concerning the judgment of believers, the following facts should be kept in mind:

(1) All Christians will be subject to judgment; there will be no exceptions (Ro 14:12; 1Co 3:12–15; 2Co 5:10; see Ecc 12:14, note).

(2) This judgment will occur when Christ returns for his church (see Jn 14:3, note; 1Th 4:14–17).

(3) The judge is Christ (Jn 5:22; 2Ti 4:8).

(4) The Bible speaks of the believer's judgment as something solemn and serious, especially since it includes the possibility of damage or "loss" (1Co 3:15; 2Jn 8), of being ashamed before him "at his coming" (1Jn 2:28) and of burning up one's whole life's work (1Co 3:13–15). The believer's judgment, however, will not involve a declaration of condemnation by God.

(5) Everything will be made manifest. The word "appear" (Gk *phaneroō*, 2Co 5:10) means "to be revealed openly or publicly." God will examine and openly reveal, in its true reality, (a) our secret acts (Mk 4:22; Ro 2:16), (b) our character (Ro 2:5–11), (c) our words (Mt 12:36–37), (d) our good deeds (Eph 6:8), (e) our attitudes (Mt 5:22), (f) our motives (1Co 4:5), (g) our lack of love (Col 3:18—4:1), and (h) our work and ministry (1Co 3:13).

(6) In sum, believers will have to give an account of their faithfulness or unfaithfulness to God (Mt 25:21,23; 1Co 4:2–5) and of their deeds in light of the grace, opportunity and understanding made available to them (Lk 12:48; Jn 5:24; Ro 8:1).

(7) The believer's bad deeds, when repented of, are forgiven with respect to eternal punishment (Ro 8:1), but they are still taken into account when being judged for repayment: "Anyone who does wrong will be repaid for his wrong" (Col 3:25; cf. Ecc 12:14; 1Co 3:15; 2Co 5:10). The believer's good deeds and love are remembered by God and rewarded (Heb 6:10): "The Lord will reward everyone for whatever good he does" (Eph 6:8).

(8) The specific results of the believer's judgment will be varied. There will be either the gain or loss of joy (1Jn 2:28), divine approval (Mt 25:21), tasks and authority (Mt 25:14–30), position (Mt 5:19; 19:30), rewards (1Co 3:12–14; Php 3:14; 2Ti 4:8) and honor (Ro 2:10; cf. 1Pe 1:7).

(9) The impending judgment of Christians should perfect in them the fear of the Lord (2Co 5:11; Php 2:12; 1Pe 1:17) and cause them to be clear minded and self-controlled, to watch and pray (1Pe 4:5,7), to live holy and godly lives (2Pe 3:11), and to show mercy and kindness to all (Mt 5:7; cf. 2Ti 1:16–18).

sin[f] for us, so that in him we might
become the righteousness of God.[w]

6

As God's fellow workers[x] we urge
Gal 2:16 you not to receive God's grace in
vain.[y] 2 For he says,

"In the time of my favor I heard
you,
and in the day of salvation I
helped you."[g][z]

I tell you, now is the time of God's favor, now is the day of salvation.

Paul's Hardships

3 We put no stumbling block in anyone's path,[a] so that our ministry will
not be discredited. 4 Rather, as servants of God we commend ourselves in
every way: in great endurance; in troubles, hardships and distresses; 5 in
beatings, imprisonments[b] and riots;
in hard work, sleepless nights and hunger;[c] 6 in purity, understanding, patience and kindness; in the Holy Spirit[d] and in sincere love;[e] 7 in truthful
speech[f] and in the power of God;[g]
with weapons of righteousness[h] in the
right hand and in the left; 8 through glory and dishonor,[i] bad report[j] and
good report; genuine, yet regarded as
impostors;[k] 9 known, yet regarded as
unknown; dying,[l] and yet we live
on;[m] beaten, and yet not killed; 10 sorrowful, yet always rejoicing;[n] poor,
yet making many rich;[o] having nothing,[p] and yet possessing everything.[q]
11 We have spoken freely to you, Corinthians, and opened wide our hearts
to you.[r] 12 We are not withholding our
affection from you, but you are withholding yours from us. 13 As a fair exchange—I speak as to my children[s]—open wide your hearts[t] also.

Do Not Be Yoked With Unbelievers

14 Do not be yoked together[u] with
unbelievers.[v] For what do righteousness and wickedness have in common?
Or what fellowship can light have with
darkness?[w] 15 What harmony is there
between Christ and Belial[h]?[x] What
does a believer[y] have in common with
an unbeliever?[z] 16 What agreement is
there between the temple of God and
idols?[a] For we are the temple[b] of the
living God.[c] As God has said: "I will
live with them and walk among them,

5:21 [w] S Ro 1:17; S 1Co 1:30
6:1 [x] S 1Co 3:9; 2Co 5:20 [y] 1Co 15:2
6:2 [z] Isa 49:8; Ps 69:13; Isa 55:6
6:3 [a] S Mt 5:29; Ro 14:13,20; 1Co 8:9,13; 9:12; 10:32
6:5 [b] Ac 16:23; 2Co 11:23-25 [c] 1Co 4:11
6:6 [d] 1Co 2:4; 1Th 1:5 [e] Ro 12:9; 1Ti 1:5
6:7 [f] 2Co 4:2 [g] 2Co 4:7 [h] Ro 13:12; 2Co 10:4; Eph 6:10-18
6:8 [i] 1Co 4:10 [j] 1Co 4:13 [k] Mt 27:63
6:9 [l] S Ro 8:36 [m] 2Co 1:8-10; 4:10,11
6:10 [n] S Mt 5:12; 2Co 7:4; Php 2:17; 4:4; Col 1:24; 1Th 1:6 [o] 2Co 8:9 [p] Ac 3:6 [q] Ro 8:32; 1Co 3:21
6:11 [r] 2Co 7:3
6:13 [s] S 1Th 2:11 [t] 2Co 7:2
6:14 [u] Ge 24:3; Dt 22:10; 1Co 5:9,10 [v] 1Co 6:6 [w] Eph 5:7,11; 1Jn 1:6
6:15 [x] 1Co 10:21 [y] Ac 5:14 [z] 1Co 6:6
6:16 [a] 1Co 10:21 [b] S 1Co 3:16 [c] S Mt 16:16

[f] *21* Or *be a sin offering* [g] *2* Isaiah 49:8
[h] *15* Greek *Beliar,* a variant of *Belial*

6:1 NOT TO RECEIVE GOD'S GRACE IN VAIN. Paul unquestionably believed that a believer could receive God's grace and experience salvation (v. 2), and afterwards, through spiritual carelessness or deliberate sin, abandon the faith and life of the gospel and again be lost. All people must be urged to be reconciled to God and to receive his grace (5:20). Those who receive God's grace must be urged not to receive it in vain (cf. vv. 14–18).

6:4 IN TROUBLES ... DISTRESSES. See 11:23, note on Paul's suffering.

6:10 POOR. It is not contradictory to the gospel for a truly dedicated Christian to be financially poor. Paul affirms he possessed little of this world's goods, yet as God's servant he made others spiritually rich (cf. 8:9; Ac 3:1ff; Eph 3:8).

6:14 YOKED TOGETHER WITH UNBELIEVERS. In God's eyes people ultimately are divided into two categories: those who are in Christ and those who are not (vv. 14–16; see article on THREE KINDS OF PEOPLE, p. 1754). Therefore, believers must not be in voluntary partnership or in intimate association with unbelievers, for such relationships can corrupt their relationship with Christ. This includes partnership in business, secret orders (lodges), dating, marriage and close friendships. A Christian's association with unbelievers should be only such as is necessary for social or economic existence, or to show unbelievers the way of salvation (see article on SPIRITUAL SEPARATION FOR BELIEVERS, p. 1794).

6:16 THE TEMPLE OF GOD AND IDOLS. Paul presents a strong argument that a born-again believer, as the temple of God and the Holy Spirit (Jn 14:23; 1Co 6:19; see article on THE TEMPLE, p. 608), cannot be indwelt by a demon. (1) Idols both in the OT and NT represented demons (Dt 32:17; 1Co 10:20–21; see article on THE NATURE OF IDOLATRY, p. 394). Therefore, the worst form of desecration in the OT was to erect idols in God's own temple (2Ki 21:7,11–14). Likewise, we must never desecrate our bodies as the Spirit's dwelling place by allowing demons access (cf. v. 15, where "Belial" refers to Satan; see also Lk 10:19, note; 2Ti 2:25–26; 1Jn 4:4; 5:18).

(2) Although an evil spirit cannot live alongside the Holy Spirit within the true believer, there may be circumstances in which an evil spirit lives in an individual who is actively in the process of conversion, but has not yet been fully regenerated by the Spirit (see article on REGENERATION, p. 1589). Conversion may at times require the driving out of demons from a person who sincerely desires to follow Christ, yet is undergoing problems with certain sins. Until the demonic power or stronghold is broken (see article on POWER OVER SATAN AND DEMONS, p. 1484), that person cannot experience a full salvation and so become "the temple of the living God" (cf. Mt 12:28–29).

and I will be their God, and they will be
my people."[i][d]

17"Therefore come out from them[e]
and be separate,
says the Lord.
Touch no unclean thing,
and I will receive you."[j][f]
18"I will be a Father to you,
and you will be my sons and
daughters,[g]
says the Lord
Almighty."[k][h]

7 Since we have these promises,[i]
dear friends,[j] let us purify ourselves from everything that contaminates body and spirit, perfecting holiness[k] out of reverence for God.

Paul's Joy

2Make room for us in your hearts.[l]
We have wronged no one, we have corrupted no one, we have exploited no
one. 3I do not say this to condemn you;
I have said before that you have such
a place in our hearts[m] that we would
live or die with you. 4I have great confidence in you; I take great pride in
you.[n] I am greatly encouraged;[o] in
all our troubles my joy knows no
bounds.[p]
5For when we came into Macedo-
nia,[q] this body of ours had no rest, but
we were harassed at every turn[r]—
conflicts on the outside, fears within.[s]
6But God, who comforts the downcast,[t] comforted us by the coming of
Titus,[u] 7and not only by his coming
but also by the comfort you had given
him. He told us about your longing for
me, your deep sorrow, your ardent concern for me, so that my joy was greater
than ever.
8Even if I caused you sorrow by my
letter,[v] I do not regret it. Though I did
regret it—I see that my letter hurt you,
but only for a little while— 9yet now I
am happy, not because you were made
sorry, but because your sorrow led you
to repentance. For you became sorrowful as God intended and so were not
harmed in any way by us. 10Godly sorrow brings repentance that leads to
salvation[w] and leaves no regret, but
worldly sorrow brings death. 11See
what this godly sorrow has produced in
you: what earnestness, what eagerness to clear yourselves, what indignation, what alarm, what longing, what
concern,[x] what readiness to see justice done. At every point you have
proved yourselves to be innocent in
this matter. 12So even though I wrote
to you,[y] it was not on account of the
one who did the wrong[z] or of the injured party, but rather that before God
you could see for yourselves how devoted to us you are. 13By all this we are
encouraged.
In addition to our own encouragement, we were especially delighted to
see how happy Titus[a] was, because
his spirit has been refreshed by all of

6:16 [d]Lev 26:12; Jer 32:38; Eze 37:27; Rev 21:3
6:17 [e]Rev 18:4 [f]Isa 52:11; Eze 20:34,41
6:18 [g]Ex 4:22; 2Sa 7:14; 1Ch 17:13; Isa 43:6; S Ro 8:14 [h]2Sa 7:8
7:1 [i]2Co 6:17,18 [j]S 1Co 10:14 [k]1Th 4:7; 1Pe 1:15,16
7:2 [l]2Co 6:12,13
7:3 [m]2Co 6:11,12; Php 1:7
7:4 [n]ver 14; 2Co 8:24 [o]ver 13 [p]S 2Co 6:10
7:5 [q]2Co 2:13; S Ac 16:9 [r]2Co 4:8 [s]Dt 32:25
7:6 [t]2Co 1:3,4 [u]ver 13; S 2Co 2:13
7:8 [v]2Co 2:2,4
7:10 [w]Ac 11:18
7:11 [x]ver 7
7:12 [y]ver 8; 2Co 2:3,9 [z]1Co 5:1,2
7:13 [a]ver 6; S 2Co 2:13

[i] *16* Lev. 26:12; Jer. 32:38; Ezek. 37:27
[j] *17* Isaiah 52:11; Ezek. 20:34,41
[k] *18* 2 Samuel 7:14; 7:8

6:17 AND BE SEPARATE. See article on SPIRITUAL SEPARATION FOR BELIEVERS, p. 1794.

7:1 SINCE WE HAVE THESE PROMISES. Paul makes it unmistakably clear that one cannot claim God's gracious promises listed in 6:16–18 without a life of separation and holiness (see article on SPIRITUAL SEPARATION FOR BELIEVERS, p. 1794). This explains why some have lost their Christian joy (Jn 15:11), divine protection (Jn 17:12,14–15), answer to prayers (Jn 15:7,16) and the sense of God's fatherly presence (Jn 14:21,23). To compromise with the world is to lose God's presence and promises.

7:1 LET US PURIFY OURSELVES. Believers must make a clean break with every form of ungodly compromise and continually resist the sinful desires of the body. We must put to death our sinful deeds, hate them more and more, and run away from them (vv. 9–11; Ro 8:12–13; Gal 5:16).

7:5 HARASSED . . . FEARS. Once again Paul's words and experiences remind us that outward problems and inward fears can be the experience of truly dedicated, born-again believers.

7:6 COMFORTS THE DOWNCAST. As a God of mercy and comfort (1:3), it is God's nature to comfort those who are depressed and downcast. In fact, the more we are afflicted, the greater will be the comfort and nearness of Christ in our life. Note that it was through the agency of Titus that God comforted Paul. We should always be sensitive to the Holy Spirit's leading us to comfort a person in need.

7:10 GODLY SORROW . . . WORLDLY SORROW. Paul identifies two kinds of sorrow here. (1) There is a genuine sorrow for sin that leads to repentance, i.e., a change of heart that causes us to turn from sin to God. This type of repentance leads to salvation. For Paul, repentance from sin and faith in Christ are human responsibilities in salvation (see Mt 3:2, note). (2) In contrast, the unrepentant often become sorry only for the consequences of their sin; such sorrow results in eternal death and judgment (Mt 13:42,50; 25:30; Ro 6:23).

SPIRITUAL SEPARATION FOR BELIEVERS

***2Co 6:17–18** "Therefore come out from them and be separate, says the Lord. Touch no unclean thing, and I will receive you. I will be a Father to you, and you will be my sons and daughters, says the Lord Almighty."*

The concept of separation from evil is fundamental to God's relationship with his people. According to the Bible, separation involves two dimensions—one negative and the other positive: (a) separating yourself morally and spiritually from sin and from everything that is contrary to Jesus Christ, righteousness and God's Word; (b) drawing near to God in a close and intimate fellowship through dedication, worship and service. Separation in this twofold sense results in a relationship where God is our heavenly Father who lives with us and is our God, and we in turn are his sons and daughters (2Co 6:16–18).

(1) In the OT separation was an ongoing requirement for God's people (see Ex 23:24, note; Lev 11:44, note; Dt 7:3, note; Ezr 9:2, note; see article on THE DESTRUCTION OF THE CANAANITES, p. 310). They were expected to be holy, different and separated from all other peoples in order to belong to God as his very own. One key reason God punished his people with exile into Assyria and Babylon was their persistent desire to accommodate themselves to the idolatry and wicked lifestyles of the nations around them (see 2Ki 17:7–8, notes; 24:3, note; 2Ch 36:14, note; Jer 2:5,13, notes; Eze 23:2, note; Hos 7:8, note).

(2) In the NT God commanded separation of the believer (a) from the corrupt world system and from unholy compromise (Jn 17:15–16; 2Ti 3:1–5; Jas 1:27; 4:4; see article on THE CHRISTIAN'S RELATIONSHIP TO THE WORLD, p. 1976), (b) from those in the church who sin and refuse to repent (Mt 18:15–17; 1Co 5:9–11; 2Th 3:6–15), and (c) from false teachers, churches or cults who teach theological error and deny Biblical truths (see Mt 7:15; Ro 16:17; Gal 1:9, note; Tit 3:9–11; 2Pe 2:17–22; 1Jn 4:1; 2Jn 10–11; Jude 12–13).

(3) Our attitude in separation must be one of (a) hatred toward sin, unrighteousness and the corrupt world system (Ro 12:9; Heb 1:9; 1Jn 2:15), (b) opposition to false doctrine (Gal 1:9), (c) genuine love for those from whom we must separate (Jn 3:16; 1Co 5:5; Gal 6:1; cf. Ro 9:1–3; 2Co 2:1–8; 11:28–29; Jude 22), and (d) fear of God as we perfect holiness (2Co 7:1).

(4) The purpose of separation is that we as God's people might (a) persevere in salvation (1Ti 4:16; Rev 2:14–17), faith (1Ti 1:19; 6:10,20–21) and holiness (Jn 17:14–21; 2Co 7:1); (b) live wholly for God as our Lord and Father (Mt 22:37; 2Co 6:16–18); and (c) convince the unbelieving world of the truth and blessings of the gospel (Jn 17:21; Php 2:15).

(5) If we separate ourselves properly, God himself rewards us by drawing near with his protection, blessing and fatherly care. He promises to be everything that a good Father should be. He will be our counselor and guide; he will love and cherish us as his own children (2Co 6:16–18).

(6) The refusal of believers to separate themselves from evil will inevitably result in the loss of fellowship with God (2Co 6:16), of acceptance by the Father (6:17) and of our rights as children (6:18; cf. Ro 8:15–16).

you. **14**I had boasted to him about
you,[b] and you have not embarrassed
me. But just as everything we said to
you was true, so our boasting about
you to Titus[c] has proved to be true as
well. **15**And his affection for you is all
the greater when he remembers that
you were all obedient,[d] receiving him
with fear and trembling.[e] **16**I am glad
I can have complete confidence in
you.[f]

Generosity Encouraged

8 And now, brothers, we want you to
know about the grace that God has
given the Macedonian[g] churches.
2Out of the most severe trial, their
overflowing joy and their extreme poverty welled up in rich generosity.[h]
3For I testify that they gave as much as
they were able,[i] and even beyond
their ability. Entirely on their own,
4they urgently pleaded with us for the
privilege of sharing[j] in this service[k]
to the saints.[l] **5**And they did not do as
we expected, but they gave themselves
first to the Lord and then to us in keeping with God's will. **6**So we urged[m] Titus,[n] since he had earlier made a beginning, to bring also to completion[o]
this act of grace on your part. **7**But just
as you excel in everything[p]—in faith,
in speech, in knowledge,[q] in complete
earnestness and in your love for
us[1]—see that you also excel in this
grace of giving.
8I am not commanding you,[r] but I
want to test the sincerity of your love
by comparing it with the earnestness
of others. **9**For you know the grace[s] of
our Lord Jesus Christ,[t] that though he
was rich, yet for your sakes he became
poor,[u] so that you through his poverty
might become rich.[v]
10And here is my advice[w] about
what is best for you in this matter: Last
year you were the first not only to give
but also to have the desire to do so.[x]
11Now finish the work, so that your eager willingness[y] to do it may be
matched by your completion of it, according to your means. **12**For if the
willingness is there, the gift is acceptable according to what one has,[z] not
according to what he does not have.
13Our desire is not that others might
be relieved while you are hard pressed,
but that there might be equality. **14**At
the present time your plenty will supply what they need,[a] so that in turn
their plenty will supply what you need.
Then there will be equality, **15**as it is
written: "He who gathered much did
not have too much, and he who gathered little did not have too little."[m][b]

Titus Sent to Corinth

16I thank God,[c] who put into the
heart[d] of Titus[e] the same concern I
have for you. **17**For Titus not only welcomed our appeal, but he is coming to
you with much enthusiasm and on his
own initiative.[f] **18**And we are sending
along with him the brother[g] who is
praised by all the churches[h] for his

[1] 7 Some manuscripts *in our love for you*
[m] 15 Exodus 16:18

7:14 [b]ver 4 [c]ver 6 **7:15** [d]2Co 2:9; 10:6 [e]Ps 55:5; 1Co 2:3; Php 2:12 **7:16** [f]S 2Co 2:3 **8:1** [g]S Ac 16:9 **8:2** [h]Ex 36:5; 2Co 9:11 **8:3** [i]1Co 16:2 **8:4** [j]ver 1 [k]S Ac 24:17 [l]S Ac 9:13 **8:6** [m]ver 17; 2Co 12:18 [n]ver 16,23; S 2Co 2:13 [o]ver 10,11 **8:7** [p]2Co 9:8 [q]Ro 15:14; 1Co 1:5; 12:8; 13:1,2; 14:6 **8:8** [r]1Co 7:6 **8:9** [s]S Ro 3:24 [t]2Co 13:14 [u]Mt 20:28; Php 2:6-8 [v]2Co 6:10 **8:10** [w]1Co 7:25, 40 [x]1Co 16:2,3; 2Co 9:2 **8:11** [y]ver 12,19; Ex 25:2; 2Co 9:2 **8:12** [z]Mk 12:43, 44; 2Co 9:7 **8:14** [a]Ac 4:34; 2Co 9:12 **8:15** [b]Ex 16:18 **8:16** [c]S 2Co 2:14 [d]Rev 17:17 [e]S 2Co 2:13 **8:17** [f]ver 6 **8:18** [g]2Co 12:18 [h]S 1Co 7:17

8:1—9:15 THE MACEDONIAN CHURCHES. These two chapters deal with instruction about the offering for the poor believers in Jerusalem. Paul's words contain the most extensive teaching about Christian giving found in the NT. The principles given here are a guide for believers and churches for all time (see next note).

8:2 RICH GENEROSITY. These two chapters reveal important principles and promises of Christian giving: (1) We belong to God; what we have is held as a trust for our Lord (v. 5). (2) We must make the basic decision in our hearts to serve God and not money (v. 5; Mt 6:24). (3) We give in order to help those in need (v. 14; 9:12; Pr 19:17; Gal 2:10; see article on THE CARE OF THE POOR AND NEEDY, p. 1316), to advance God's kingdom (1Co 9:14; Php 4:15–18), to store up treasures in heaven (Mt 6:20; Lk 6:32–35) and to learn to fear the Lord (Dt 14:22–23). (4) Giving should be in proportion to our income (vv. 3,12; 1Co 16:2). (5) Giving is seen as a proof of our love (v. 24) and should be done sacrificially (v. 3) and voluntarily (9:7). (6) By giving to God we sow not only money but also faith, time and service, thus reaping greater faith and blessing (v. 5; 9:6,10–12). (7) When God supplies an abundance, it is so that we may multiply our good works (9:8; Eph 4:28). (8) Giving increases our dedication to God (Mt 6:21) and activates the work of God in our financial affairs (Lk 6:38). For more on this subject, see article on TITHES AND OFFERINGS, p. 1392.

8:9 HE BECAME POOR. Sacrificial giving was an essential part of Christ's nature and character. By his becoming poor, we now partake of his eternal riches. God wants the same attitude among believers as evidence of his grace working within us. All the gifts of grace and salvation, the kingdom of heaven, and even disgrace for the sake of Christ are the everlasting riches we have received in exchange for the rags of sin (Lk 12:15; Eph 1:3; Php 4:11–13,18–19; Heb 11:26; Rev 3:17).

service to the gospel.[i] 19What is
more, he was chosen by the churches
to accompany us[j] as we carry the offering, which we administer in order to
honor the Lord himself and to show our
eagerness to help.[k] 20We want to
avoid any criticism of the way we administer this liberal gift. 21For we are
taking pains to do what is right, not
only in the eyes of the Lord but also in
the eyes of men.[l]
22In addition, we are sending with
them our brother who has often proved
to us in many ways that he is zealous,
and now even more so because of his
great confidence in you. 23As for Titus,[m] he is my partner[n] and fellow
worker[o] among you; as for our brothers,[p] they are representatives of the
churches and an honor to Christ.
24Therefore show these men the proof
of your love and the reason for our
pride in you,[q] so that the churches
can see it.

9 There is no need[r] for me to write
to you about this service[s] to the
saints.[t] 2For I know your eagerness
to help,[u] and I have been boasting[v]
about it to the Macedonians, telling
them that since last year[w] you in
Achaia[x] were ready to give; and your
enthusiasm has stirred most of them to
action. 3But I am sending the brothers[y] in order that our boasting about
you in this matter should not prove hollow, but that you may be ready, as I
said you would be.[z] 4For if any Macedonians[a] come with me and find you
unprepared, we—not to say anything
about you—would be ashamed of having been so confident. 5So I thought it
necessary to urge the brothers[b] to visit you in advance and finish the arrangements for the generous gift you
had promised. Then it will be ready as
a generous gift,[c] not as one grudging-
ly given.[d]

8:18 [i]S 2Co 2:12
8:19 [j]Ac 14:23; 1Co 16:3,4 [k]ver 11,12
8:21 [l]Ro 12:17; S 14:18; S Tit 2:14
8:23 [m]S 2Co 2:13 [n]Phm 17 [o]S Php 2:25 [p]ver 18,22
8:24 [q]2Co 7:4,14; 9:2
9:1 [r]1Th 4:9 [s]S Ac 24:17 [t]S Ac 9:13
9:2 [u]2Co 8:11,12, 19 [v]2Co 7:4,14; 8:24 [w]2Co 8:10 [x]S Ac 18:12
9:3 [y]2Co 8:23 [z]1Co 16:2
9:4 [a]Ro 15:26
9:5 [b]ver 3 [c]Php 4:17 [d]2Co 12:17,18

9:6 [e]Pr 11:24,25; 22:9; Gal 6:7,9
9:7 [f]Ex 25:2; 2Co 8:12 [g]Dt 15:10 [h]Ro 12:8
9:8 [i]Eph 3:20 [j]Php 4:19
9:9 [k]Mal 3:10 [l]Ps 112:9
9:10 [m]Isa 55:10 [n]Hos 10:12
9:11 [o]1Co 1:5 [p]ver 5 [q]2Co 1:11; 4:15
9:12 [r]2Co 8:14 [s]S 2Co 1:11
9:13 [t]S 2Co 8:4 [u]S Mt 9:8 [v]S Heb 3:1 [w]S 2Co 2:12 [x]ver 5
9:15 [y]S 2Co 2:14 [z]Ro 5:15,16

Sowing Generously

6Remember this: Whoever sows
sparingly will also reap sparingly, and
whoever sows generously will also
reap generously.[e] 7Each man should
give what he has decided in his heart
to give,[f] not reluctantly or under compulsion,[g] for God loves a cheerful giver.[h] 8And God is able[i] to make all
grace abound to you, so that in all
things at all times, having all that you
need,[j] you will abound in every good
work. 9As it is written:

"He has scattered abroad his
gifts[k] to the poor;
his righteousness endures
forever."[n][l]

10Now he who supplies seed to the
sower and bread for food[m] will also
supply and increase your store of seed
and will enlarge the harvest of your
righteousness.[n] 11You will be made
rich[o] in every way so that you can be
generous[p] on every occasion, and
through us your generosity will result
in thanksgiving to God.[q]
12This service that you perform is
not only supplying the needs[r] of
God's people but is also overflowing in
many expressions of thanks to God.[s]
13Because of the service[t] by which
you have proved yourselves, men will
praise God[u] for the obedience that accompanies your confession[v] of the
gospel of Christ,[w] and for your generosity[x] in sharing with them and with
everyone else. 14And in their prayers
for you their hearts will go out to you,
because of the surpassing grace God
has given you. 15Thanks be to God[y]
for his indescribable gift![z]

[n]9 Psalm 112:9

9:6 WILL ALSO REAP SPARINGLY. Christians can give either generously or sparingly; God will reward them accordingly (see Mt 7:1–2). To Paul, giving is not a loss, but a form of saving; it results in substantial benefits for those who give (see 8:2, note; 9:11, note). He is not speaking primarily of the quantity given, but of the quality of our hearts' desires and motives. The poor widow gave little, but God considered it much because of the proportion she gave and her complete dedication (see Lk 21:1–4, note; cf. Pr 11:24–25; 19:17; Mt 10:41–42; Lk 6:38).

9:8 GRACE ABOUND TO YOU. Believers who give what they can to help those in need will find that God's grace provides a sufficiency for their own needs, and even more, that they abound in every good work (cf. Eph 4:28).

9:11 MADE RICH IN EVERY WAY. In order for generosity to be outwardly expressed, the heart must be made rich in sincere love and compassion for others. Giving of ourselves and our possessions results in (1) supplying the needs of poorer brothers and sisters, (2) praise and thanksgiving to God (v. 12) and (3) reciprocal love from those who receive our help (v. 14).

Paul's Defense of His Ministry

10 By the meekness and gentleness[a] of Christ, I appeal to
you—I, Paul,[b] who am "timid" when
face to face with you, but "bold" when
away! **2**I beg you that when I come I
may not have to be as bold[c] as I expect to be toward some people who
think that we live by the standards of
this world.[d] **3**For though we live in the
world, we do not wage war as the world
does.[e] **4**The weapons we fight with[f]
are not the weapons of the world. On
the contrary, they have divine power[g]
to demolish strongholds.[h] **5**We demolish arguments and every pretension
that sets itself up against the knowledge of God,[i] and we take captive every thought to make it obedient[j] to
Christ. **6**And we will be ready to punish
every act of disobedience, once your
obedience is complete.[k]
7You are looking only on the surface
of things.[o][l] If anyone is confident
that he belongs to Christ,[m] he should
consider again that we belong to Christ
just as much as he.[n] **8**For even if I
boast somewhat freely about the authority the Lord gave us[o] for building
you up rather than pulling you down,[p]
I will not be ashamed of it. **9**I do not
want to seem to be trying to frighten
you with my letters. **10**For some say,
"His letters are weighty and forceful,
but in person he is unimpressive[q] and
his speaking amounts to nothing."[r]
11Such people should realize that what
we are in our letters when we are ab-

10:1 [a]Mt 11:29 [b]Gal 5:2; Eph 3:1
10:2 [c]S 1Co 4:21 [d]Ro 12:2
10:3 [e]ver 2
10:4 [f]S 2Co 6:7 [g]1Co 2:5 [h]ver 8; Jer 1:10; 23:29; 2Co 13:10
10:5 [i]Isa 2:11,12; 1Co 1:19 [j]2Co 9:13
10:6 [k]2Co 2:9; 7:15
10:7 [l]S Jn 7:24; 2Co 5:12 [m]1Co 1:12; S 3:23; 14:37 [n]2Co 11:23
10:8 [o]ver 13,15 [p]ver 4; Jer 1:10; 2Co 13:10
10:10 [q]ver 1; 1Co 2:3; Gal 4:13, 14 [r]1Co 1:17; 2Co 11:6

o 7 Or *Look at the obvious facts*

10:1 I APPEAL TO YOU—I, PAUL. The majority of Corinthian believers had accepted Paul's authority and submitted to his teachings and apostleship (7:8–16). Yet there was a minority, led by false ministers undermining the gospel and doing Satan's work (11:13), who continued to resist him and to slander his person and character. In chs. 10–13 Paul addresses these false believers.

10:4 WEAPONS WE FIGHT WITH. Our warfare is against spiritual forces of evil (Eph 6:12). Therefore, worldly weapons such as human ingenuity, talents, wealth, organizational skills, eloquence, propaganda, charisma and personality are in themselves inadequate to pull down Satan's strongholds. The only weapons adequate to destroy the fortresses of Satan, unrighteousness and false teaching are those God gives.

(1) These weapons are powerful because they are spiritual and come from God. Elsewhere Paul lists some of these weapons—commitment to truth, righteous living, gospel proclamation, faith, love, hope of salvation, the Word of God, and persevering prayer (Eph 6:11–19; 1Th 5:8). By using these weapons against the enemy, the church will emerge victorious. God's presence and kingdom will be powerfully revealed in order to save sinners, drive out demons, sanctify believers, baptize in the Holy Spirit and heal the sick (see article on SIGNS OF BELIEVERS, p. 1513).

(2) The church today is often tempted to meet the world's challenge through the world's weapons, i.e., through humanistic wisdom, philosophy, psychology, exciting attractions, entertainment-based church performances, etc. These often serve as a substitute for the basic NT practices of intense prayer, uncompromising commitment to God's Word, and proclamation of the gospel in power. Worldly weapons cannot bring about a Holy Spirit revival, for such weapons cannot possibly destroy sin's strongholds, deliver us from Satan's power or overthrow the evil passions running rampant in the world today. If we use the world's weapons, we will only secularize the church and separate it from the weapons of faith, righteousness and the power of the Spirit. Tragically, the church itself will then be overshadowed by the power of darkness and its families thrown down and taken captive by the world's forces.

10:5 TAKE CAPTIVE EVERY THOUGHT. Christian warfare involves bringing all our thoughts into alignment with Christ's will; failure to do so will lead to immorality and spiritual death (Ro 6:16,23; 8:13). Use the following four steps to bring your thought life under Christ's lordship. (1) Be aware that God knows every thought and that nothing is hidden from him (Ps 94:11; 139:2,4, 23–24). We will have to give account to God for our thoughts as well as for our words and deeds (5:10; Ecc 12:14; Mt 12:35–37; Ro 14:12).

(2) Be aware that the mind is a battleground. Some thoughts originate with us, while others come directly from the enemy. To take captive every thought requires warfare against both our sinful nature and satanic forces (Eph 6:12–13; cf. Mt 4:3–11). Steadfastly resist and reject evil and unwholesome thoughts in the name of the Lord Jesus Christ (Php 4:8). Remember that we as believers overcome our adversary by the blood of the Lamb, by the word of our testimony, and by persistently saying "No!" to the devil, temptation and sin (Tit 2:11–12; Jas 4:7; Rev 12:11; cf. Mt 4:3–11).

(3) Be resolute in focusing your mind on Christ and heavenly things rather than on earthly things (Php 3:19; Col 3:2), for the mind controlled by the Spirit is life and peace (Ro 8:6–7). Fill your mind with God's Word (Ps 1:1–3; 19:7–14; 119) and with those things that are noble, excellent and praiseworthy (Php 4:8).

(4) Always be careful what your eyes see and your ears hear. Resolutely refuse (a) to let your eyes be an instrument for lust (Job 31:1; 1Jn 2:16), or (b) to set any worthless or evil thing before your eyes, whether in books, magazines, pictures, television programs, or in real life (Ps 101:3; Isa 33:14–15; Ro 13:14).

sent, we will be in our actions when we are present.

12We do not dare to classify or compare ourselves with some who commend themselves.[s] When they measure themselves by themselves and compare themselves with themselves, they are not wise. 13We, however, will not boast beyond proper limits, but will confine our boasting to the field God has assigned to us,[t] a field that reaches even to you. 14We are not going too far in our boasting, as would be the case if we had not come to you, for we did get as far as you[u] with the gospel of Christ.[v] 15Neither do we go beyond our limits[w] by boasting of work done by others.[p x] Our hope is that, as your faith continues to grow,[y] our area of activity among you will greatly expand, 16so that we can preach the gospel[z] in the regions beyond you.[a] For we do not want to boast about work already done in another man's territory. 17But, "Let him who boasts boast in the Lord."[q b] 18For it is not the one who commends himself[c] who is approved, but the one whom the Lord commends.[d]

Paul and the False Apostles

11 I hope you will put up with[e] a little of my foolishness;[f] but you are already doing that. 2I am jealous for you with a godly jealousy. I promised you to one husband,[g] to Christ, so that I might present you[h] as a pure virgin to him. 3But I am afraid that just as Eve was deceived by the serpent's cunning,[i] your minds may somehow be led astray from your sincere and pure devotion to Christ. 4For if someone comes to you and preaches a Jesus other than the Jesus we preached,[j] or if you receive a different spirit[k] from the one you received, or a different gospel[l] from the one you accepted, you put up with it[m] easily enough. 5But I do not think I am in the least inferior to those "super-apostles."[n] 6I may not be a trained speaker,[o] but I do have knowledge.[p] We have made this perfectly clear to you in every way.

7Was it a sin[q] for me to lower myself in order to elevate you by preaching the gospel of God[r] to you free of charge?[s] 8I robbed other churches by receiving support from them[t] so as to serve you. 9And when I was with you and needed something, I was not a burden to anyone, for the brothers who came from Macedonia supplied what I needed.[u] I have kept myself from being a burden to you[v] in any way, and will continue to do so. 10As surely as the truth of Christ is in me,[w] nobody in the regions of Achaia[x] will stop this boasting[y] of mine. 11Why? Because I do not love you? God knows[z] I do![a] 12And I will keep on doing what I am doing in order to cut the ground from under those who want an opportunity to be considered equal with us in the things they boast about.

13For such men are false apostles,[b]

10:12 [s] ver 18; S 2Co 3:1
10:13 [t] ver 15,16; S Ro 12:3
10:14 [u] S 1Co 3:6 [v] S 2Co 2:12
10:15 [w] ver 13 [x] Ro 15:20 [y] 2Th 1:3
10:16 [z] S Ro 1:1; S 2Co 2:12 [a] S Ac 19:21
10:17 [b] Jer 9:24; Ps 34:2; 44:8; 1Co 1:31
10:18 [c] ver 12 [d] S Ro 2:29
11:1 [e] ver 4,19, 20; Mt 17:17 [f] ver 16,17,21; 2Co 5:13
11:2 [g] Hos 2:19; Eph 5:26,27 [h] S 2Co 4:14
11:3 [i] Ge 3:1-6, 13; 1Ti 2:14; Rev 12:9
11:4 [j] 1Co 3:11 [k] Ro 8:15 [l] Gal 1:6-9 [m] S ver 1
11:5 [n] 2Co 12:11; Gal 2:6
11:6 [o] S 1Co 1:17 [p] S 2Co 8:7; Eph 3:4
11:7 [q] 2Co 12:13 [r] S Ro 1:1 [s] 1Co 9:18
11:8 [t] Php 4:15, 18
11:9 [u] Php 4:15, 18 [v] 2Co 12:13,14, 16
11:10 [w] S Ro 9:1 [x] S Ac 18:12 [y] 1Co 9:15
11:11 [z] ver 31; S Ro 1:9 [a] 2Co 12:15
11:13 [b] S Mt 7:15

[p] 13-15 Or *13We, however, will not boast about things that cannot be measured, but we will boast according to the standard of measurement that the God of measure has assigned us—a measurement that relates even to you. 14 . . . 15Neither do we boast about things that cannot be measured in regard to the work done by others.* [q] 17 Jer. 9:24

10:12 MEASURE THEMSELVES BY THEMSELVES. To compare ourselves with contemporary standards and the lives of believers around us shows that we are yet without proper understanding of God's will. The standard by which we must measure ourselves is revealed by Christ and the apostles in the NT.

11:3 YOUR MINDS . . . LED ASTRAY. Some at Corinth were in grave danger of being deceived by false preachers and accepting a distorted gospel (v. 4). By accepting the teachings of these "deceitful workmen" (v. 13), they were being led astray from wholehearted devotion to Christ. In the churches today there are those who appear as ministers of righteousness, yet whose teachings contradict God's Word and lead their followers to spiritual disaster (see next two notes; Mt 23:13, note). We must be on our guard against them (see articles on FALSE TEACHERS, p. 1506, and OVERSEERS AND THEIR DUTIES, p. 1690).

11:4 PREACHES . . . A DIFFERENT GOSPEL. False teachers may state that Biblical revelation is true, but at the same time allege that they possess extrabiblical revelations or knowledge equal in authority to Scripture and valid for the church as a whole. Such false teaching usually draws the Christian faith into a syncretism with other religions or philosophies. This results in the following errors: (1) The supposed new revelation is put on the same level of authority as the original apostolic Biblical revelation in Christ. (2) Scripture becomes less important and Christ takes second place to "saints" or to founders of a movement or church. (3) The false teachers claim to have deeper or exclusive understanding of so-called "hidden revelations" in Scripture.

11:13 DECEITFUL WORKMEN, MASQUERADING AS APOSTLES. The great deceiver Satan

deceitful[c] workmen, masquerading
as apostles of Christ.[d] **14**And no wonder, for Satan[e] himself masquerades
as an angel of light. **15**It is not surprising, then, if his servants masquerade as servants of righteousness.
Their end will be what their actions
deserve.[f]

Paul Boasts About His Sufferings

16I repeat: Let no one take me for a
fool.[g] But if you do, then receive me
just as you would a fool, so that I may
do a little boasting. **17**In this self-confi-
dent boasting I am not talking as the
Lord would,[h] but as a fool.[i] **18**Since
many are boasting in the way the world
does,[j] I too will boast.[k] **19**You gladly
put up with[l] fools since you are so
wise![m] **20**In fact, you even put up
with[n] anyone who enslaves you[o] or
exploits you or takes advantage of you
or pushes himself forward or slaps you
in the face. **21**To my shame I admit that
we were too weak[p] for that!

What anyone else dares to boast
about—I am speaking as a fool—I
also dare to boast about.[q] **22**Are they
Hebrews? So am I.[r] Are they Israelites? So am I.[s] Are they Abraham's
descendants? So am I.[t] **23**Are they
servants of Christ?[u] (I am out of my
mind to talk like this.) I am more. I
have worked much harder,[v] been in

11:13 [c]Tit 1:10 [d]Rev 2:2 **11:14** [e]S Mt 4:10 **11:15** [f]S Mt 16:27; Php 3:19 **11:16** [g]ver 1 **11:17** [h]1Co 7:12, 25 [i]ver 21 **11:18** [j]2Co 5:16; 10:4 [k]ver 21; Php 3:3,4 **11:19** [l]S ver 1 [m]1Co 4:10 **11:20** [n]S ver 1 [o]Gal 2:4; 4:9; 5:1 **11:21** [p]2Co 10:1, 10 [q]ver 17,18; Php 3:4 **11:22** [r]Php 3:5 [s]Ro 9:4; 11:1 [t]S Lk 3:8; Ro 11:1 **11:23** [u]S 1Co 3:5 [v]S 1Co 15:10

(v. 3; Jn 8:44) uses evil people as his agents, transforming them into "false apostles, deceitful workmen." (1) The Bible speaks of these deceitful leaders as people who, energized by Satan, (a) appear to accomplish great things for God (v. 15; Rev 13:2), (b) preach attractive gospel messages (v. 4; see 1Ti 4:1, note), and (c) appear to be righteous but in reality reject godliness and deny its power (2Ti 3:5).

(2) These people disguise themselves as "apostles of Christ" and "servants of righteousness" (v. 15). Thus, they imitate genuine ministers of Christ, putting into their message every available "form of godliness" (2Ti 3:5). They may be sincerely caring and loving, and they may preach forgiveness, peace, fulfillment, love and many other helpful things—but they live under Satan's influence. Their gospel is often one of human reason and not a true interpretation of God's revelation found in Scripture (cf. Gal 1:6–7; 1Pe 2:1–3). Their message deviates from NT apostolic doctrine (see 1Jn 4:1, note).

(3) All believers must beware of these misleading ministers and leaders (vv. 3–4; Mt 7:15; 16:6) and not be deceived by their charisma, eloquent oration, education, miracles, numerical success or popular message.

(4) All religious leaders must be judged according to their attitude and loyalty to the blood redemption of Jesus Christ and to the gospel as presented by Christ and the NT writers (see Gal 1:9, note; see article on FALSE TEACHERS, p. 1506).

11:23 PAUL'S SUFFERINGS. The Holy Spirit, through Paul's words, reveals the anguish and suffering of someone fully committed to Christ, his Word and the cause for which Christ died (see article on THE SUFFERING OF THE RIGHTEOUS, p. 710). Paul was in fellowship with God's feelings and in sympathy with the heart and pathos of Christ. Here are twenty ways Paul shared Christ's sufferings:

(1) "many hardships" encountered in serving God (Ac 14:22);

(2) great distress at the overwhelming sin in society (Ac 17:16);

(3) serving the Lord with "many tears" (2:4);

(4) warning the church "night and day with tears" for three years because of the destruction brought about by the distortion of the gospel through teachers not faithful to Biblical apostolic faith (Ac 20:31; see article on OVERSEERS AND THEIR DUTIES, p. 1690);

(5) grief in departing from beloved believers (Ac 20:17–38), and his broken heart at their sorrow (21:13);

(6) "great sorrow and unceasing anguish" in his heart because of the refusal of his "brothers" to accept the gospel of Christ (Ro 9:2–3; 10:1);

(7) many trials and troubles that came to him in his work for Christ (4:8–12; 11:23–29; 1Co 4:11–13);

(8) grief over sin tolerated in the church (2:1–3; 12:21; 1Co 5:1–2; 6:8–10);

(9) "great distress and anguish of heart" as he wrote to those who were forsaking Christ and the true gospel (2:4);

(10) his groaning with the desire to be with Christ and free from the sin and concern of this world (5:1–4; cf. Php 1:23);

(11) his being "harassed at every turn" because of his commitment to the church's moral and doctrinal purity (7:5; 11:3–4);

(12) his daily "concern for all the churches" (11:28);

(13) his inward burning for Christians led into sin (11:29);

(14) his having to declare eternal condemnation for those who preached a gospel other than that of the revealed NT faith (Gal 1:6–9);

(15) his experience of "pains of childbirth" for those fallen from grace (Gal 4:19; 5:4);

(16) his "tears" over enemies of Christ's cross (Php 3:18);

(17) his "distress" in wondering whether some might fall from the faith (1Th 3:5–8);

(18) persecution because of his passion for righteousness and godliness (2Ti 3:12);

(19) sorrow at the defections of Asian believers (2Ti 1:15); and

(20) his anguished plea to Timothy to guard the true faith in light of the coming apostasy (1Ti 4:1; 6:20; 2Ti 1:14).

prison more frequently,[w] been flogged
more severely,[x] and been exposed to
death again and again.[y] **24**Five times
I received from the Jews the forty
lashes[z] minus one. **25**Three times I
was beaten with rods,[a] once I was
stoned,[b] three times I was shipwrecked,[c] I spent a night and a day in
the open sea, **26**I have been constantly
on the move. I have been in danger
from rivers, in danger from bandits, in
danger from my own countrymen,[d] in
danger from Gentiles; in danger in the
city,[e] in danger in the country, in danger at sea; and in danger from false
brothers.[f] **27**I have labored and
toiled[g] and have often gone without
sleep; I have known hunger and thirst
and have often gone without food;[h] I
have been cold and naked. **28**Besides
everything else, I face daily the pressure of my concern for all the
churches.[i] **29**Who is weak, and I do
not feel weak?[j] Who is led into sin,[k]
and I do not inwardly burn?

30If I must boast, I will boast[l] of
the things that show my weakness.[m]
31The God and Father of the Lord
Jesus, who is to be praised forever,[n]
knows[o] that I am not lying. **32**In Damascus the governor under King Are-
tas had the city of the Damascenes
guarded in order to arrest me.[p] **33**But
I was lowered in a basket from a window in the wall and slipped through his
hands.[q]

11:23 [w]Ac 16:23; 2Co 6:4,5 [x]Ac 16:23; 2Co 6:4,5 [y]S Ro 8:36
11:24 [z]Dt 25:3
11:25 [a]Ac 16:22 [b]Ac 14:19 [c]Ac 27:1-44
11:26 [d]S Ac 20:3 [e]Ac 21:31 [f]Gal 2:4
11:27 [g]S Ac 18:3; Col 1:29 [h]1Co 4:11,12; 2Co 6:5
11:28 [i]S 1Co 7:17
11:29 [j]S Ro 14:1; S 1Co 2:3 [k]S Mt 5:29
11:30 [l]ver 16; Gal 6:14; 2Co 12:5,9 [m]S 1Co 2:3
11:31 [n]Ro 1:25; 9:5 [o]ver 11; S Ro 1:9
11:32 [p]Ac 9:24
11:33 [q]Ac 9:25
12:1 [r]ver 5,9; 2Co 11:16,30 [s]ver 7; S 1Co 2:10
12:2 [t]S Ro 16:3 [u]ver 4; S Ac 8:39 [v]Eph 4:10 [w]2Co 11:11
12:4 [x]ver 2 [y]Lk 23:43; Rev 2:7
12:5 [z]ver 9,10; S 1Co 2:3
12:6 [a]2Co 10:8 [b]ver 11; 2Co 11:16
12:7 [c]ver 1; S 1Co 2:10 [d]Nu 33:55 [e]S Mt 4:10
12:8 [f]Mt 26:39, 44

Paul's Vision and His Thorn

12 I must go on boasting.[r] Although there is nothing to be
gained, I will go on to visions and revelations[s] from the Lord. **2**I know a man
in Christ[t] who fourteen years ago was
caught up[u] to the third heaven.[v]
Whether it was in the body or out of the
body I do not know—God knows.[w]
3And I know that this man—whether
in the body or apart from the body I do
not know, but God knows— **4**was
caught up[x] to paradise.[y] He heard inexpressible things, things that man is
not permitted to tell. **5**I will boast
about a man like that, but I will not
boast about myself, except about my
weaknesses.[z] **6**Even if I should
choose to boast,[a] I would not be a
fool,[b] because I would be speaking
the truth. But I refrain, so no one will
think more of me than is warranted by
what I do or say.

7To keep me from becoming conceited because of these surpassingly great
revelations,[c] there was given me a
thorn in my flesh,[d] a messenger of Satan,[e] to torment me. **8**Three times I
pleaded with the Lord to take it away
from me.[f] **9**But he said to me, "My

12:2 A MAN IN CHRIST. Paul refers to himself as "a man in Christ" who was taken up to heaven to receive revelations, probably concerning Christ's gospel and the unspeakable glories of heaven reserved for believers (v. 7; cf. Ro 8:18; 2Ti 4:8). This great privilege and revelation given to Paul strengthened him, enabling him to endure the long and severe sufferings during his apostolic ministry.

12:2 THIRD HEAVEN. Scripture indicates that there are three heavens. (1) The first heaven is the atmosphere that surrounds the earth (Hos 2:18; Da 7:13). (2) The second heaven is that of the stars (Ge 1:14–18). (3) The third heaven, also called paradise (vv. 3–4; Lk 23:43; Rev 2:7), is God's abode and the home of all departed believers (5:8; Php 1:23). Its location is not revealed.

12:7 A THORN IN MY FLESH. The word "thorn" communicates the idea of pain, trouble, sufferings, humiliation or physical infirmities, but not temptation to sin (cf. Gal 4:13–14). (1) Paul's thorn remains undefined, so that all those with a "thorn" can readily apply the spiritual lesson of this passage to themselves. (2) Paul's thorn is attributed to demonic activity or origin, permitted yet limited by God (cf. Job 2:1ff). (3) At the same time, Paul's thorn was given to keep him from becoming proud over revelations that he had received. (4) Paul's thorn kept him dependent in greater measure on divine grace (v. 9, note; Heb 12:10).

12:8 THREE TIMES I PLEADED. Many times when God answers a sincere prayer with a refusal, something much better is given (see next note; Eph 3:20).

12:9 MY GRACE IS SUFFICIENT FOR YOU. Grace is God's presence, favor and power. It is a force, a heavenly strength given those who call on God. This grace will rest on faithful believers who accept their weaknesses and difficulties for the gospel's sake (Php 4:13; see article on FAITH AND GRACE, p. 1720). (1) The greater our weakness and trials for Christ, the more grace God will give to accomplish his will. What he gives is always sufficient for us to live our daily lives, to work for him, and to endure our suffering and "thorns" in the flesh (cf. 1Co 10:13). As long as we draw near to Christ, Christ will give us his heavenly strength and comfort. (2) We should boast and see eternal value in our weaknesses, for they cause Christ's power to rest on us and live within us as we walk through life toward our heavenly home.

grace[g] is sufficient for you, for my
power[h] is made perfect in weakness.[i][n][j] Therefore I will boast all the
more gladly about my weaknesses, so
that Christ's power may rest on me.
10That is why, for Christ's sake, I delight[k] in weaknesses, in insults, in
hardships,[l] in persecutions,[m] in difficulties. For when I am weak, then I am
strong.[n]

Paul's Concern for the Corinthians

11I have made a fool of myself,[o] but
you drove me to it. I ought to have been
commended by you, for I am not in the
least inferior to the "super-apostles,"[p]
even though I am nothing.[q] **12**The
things that mark an apostle—signs,
wonders and miracles[r]—were done
among you with great perseverance.
13How were you inferior to the other
churches, except that I was never a
burden to you?[s] Forgive me this
wrong![t]

14Now I am ready to visit you for the
third time,[u] and I will not be a burden
to you, because what I want is not your
possessions but you. After all, children
should not have to save up for their
parents,[v] but parents for their children.[w] **15**So I will very gladly spend
for you everything I have and expend
myself as well.[x] If I love you more,[y]
will you love me less? **16**Be that as it
may, I have not been a burden to you.[z]
Yet, crafty fellow that I am, I caught
you by trickery! **17**Did I exploit you
through any of the men I sent you? **18**I
urged[a] Titus[b] to go to you and I sent
our brother[c] with him. Titus did not
exploit you, did he? Did we not act in
the same spirit and follow the same
course?

19Have you been thinking all along
that we have been defending ourselves
to you? We have been speaking in the
sight of God[d] as those in Christ; and
everything we do, dear friends,[e] is for
your strengthening.[f] **20**For I am
afraid that when I come[g] I may not
find you as I want you to be, and you
may not find me as you want me to
be.[h] I fear that there may be quarreling,[i] jealousy, outbursts of anger, factions,[j] slander,[k] gossip,[l] arrogance[m] and disorder.[n] **21**I am afraid
that when I come again my God will
humble me before you, and I will be
grieved[o] over many who have sinned
earlier[p] and have not repented of the
impurity, sexual sin and debauchery[q]
in which they have indulged.

Final Warnings

13 This will be my third visit to
you.[r] "Every matter must be
established by the testimony of two or
three witnesses."[r][s] **2**I already gave
you a warning when I was with you the
second time. I now repeat it while absent:[t] On my return I will not spare[u]
those who sinned earlier[v] or any of
the others, **3**since you are demanding
proof that Christ is speaking through
me.[w] He is not weak in dealing with
you, but is powerful among you. **4**For to
be sure, he was crucified in weakness,[x] yet he lives by God's power.[y]
Likewise, we are weak[z] in him, yet by
God's power we will live with him[a] to
serve you.

5Examine yourselves[b] to see

12:9 [g] S Ro 3:24 [h] S Php 4:13 [i] S 1Co 2:3 [j] 1Ki 19:12 **12:10** [k] S Mt 5:12 [l] 2Co 6:4 [m] 2Th 1:4 [n] 2Co 13:4 **12:11** [o] 2Co 11:1 [p] 2Co 11:5 [q] 1Co 15:9,10 **12:12** [r] S Jn 4:48 **12:13** [s] ver 14; 1Co 9:12,18 [t] 2Co 11:7 **12:14** [u] 2Co 13:1 [v] 1Co 4:14,15 [w] Pr 19:14 **12:15** [x] Php 2:17; 1Th 2:8 [y] 2Co 11:11 **12:16** [z] 2Co 11:9 **12:18** [a] 2Co 8:6, 16 [b] S 2Co 2:13 [c] 2Co 8:18 **12:19** [d] Ro 9:1 [e] S 1Co 10:14 [f] S Ro 14:19; 2Co 10:8 **12:20** [g] 2Co 2:1-4 [h] 1Co 4:21 [i] 1Co 1:11; 3:3 [j] Gal 5:20 [k] Ro 1:30 [l] S Ro 1:29 [m] 1Co 4:18 [n] 1Co 14:33 **12:21** [o] 2Co 2:1,4 [p] 2Co 13:2 [q] S 1Co 6:18 **13:1** [r] 2Co 12:14 [s] Dt 19:15; S Mt 18:16 **13:2** [t] ver 10 [u] 2Co 1:23 [v] 2Co 12:21 **13:3** [w] Mt 10:20; 1Co 5:4 **13:4** [x] 1Co 1:25; Php 2:7,8; 1Pe 3:18 [y] Ro 1:4; 6:4; 1Co 6:14 [z] ver 9; S 1Co 2:3 [a] S Ro 6:5 **13:5** [b] 1Co 11:28

[r] *1* Deut. 19:15

12:15 SPEND . . . AND EXPEND MYSELF AS WELL. Paul's spirit of dedicated love for those he is trying to help is an example for all pastors, teachers and missionaries. It reveals a committed love (cf. 6:11–13; 7:1–4) like that of a father for his children. It is a love ready to be spent to the utmost for the sake of the other, a love that does not think of itself but shows genuine concern for those under its care. Paul seeks nothing in return but the response of their hearts turned toward Christ. Every faithful minister of the gospel should have this type of love.

12:20 SLANDER, GOSSIP. The Bible condemns sins of speech that harm other people as grave offenses against the Christian law of love. Any kind of disparaging speech that defames the character of another person must be resisted. The discussion or exposing of another's misdeeds should be done only with a sincere motive to help that person or to protect others and God's kingdom (Ro 1:29; Eph 4:31; 2Ti 4:10,14–15; 1Pe 2:1).

12:21 I WILL BE GRIEVED OVER MANY WHO HAVE SINNED. Christian ministers must mourn over those in the church who refuse to repent of and forsake their sin, for they are spiritually dead. The tragic message for them is Paul's word to the Corinthians (1Co 6:9), the Galatians (Gal 5:21) and the Ephesians (Eph 5:5–6), a word pronouncing exclusion from God's kingdom.

13:2 I WILL NOT SPARE. A minister's love for his people (see 12:15, note) demands sternness as well as affection. There comes a time when patience runs its course, and when, for the good of the church, offenders should no longer be spared. A holy righteousness, not indulgence, is required.

13:5 EXAMINE . . . WHETHER YOU ARE IN

whether you are in the faith; test yourselves.[c] Do you not realize that Christ
Jesus is in you[d]—unless, of course,
you fail the test? 6And I trust that you
will discover that we have not failed
the test. 7Now we pray to God that you
will not do anything wrong. Not that
people will see that we have stood the
test but that you will do what is right
even though we may seem to have
failed. 8For we cannot do anything
against the truth, but only for the
truth. 9We are glad whenever we are
weak[e] but you are strong;[f] and our
prayer is for your perfection.[g] 10This
is why I write these things when I am
absent, that when I come I may not
have to be harsh[h] in my use of authority—the authority the Lord gave me for
building you up, not for tearing you
down.[i]

Final Greetings

11Finally, brothers,[j] good-by. Aim
for perfection, listen to my appeal, be
of one mind, live in peace.[k] And the
God of love[l] and peace[m] will be with
you.

12Greet one another with a holy
kiss.[n] 13All the saints send their
greetings.[o]

14May the grace of the Lord Jesus
Christ,[p] and the love of God,[q] and the
fellowship of the Holy Spirit[r] be with
you all.

13:5 [c] La 3:40; Jn 6:6 [d] S Ro 8:10
13:9 [e] S 1Co 2:3 [f] 2Co 4:12 [g] ver 11; Eph 4:13
13:10 [h] S 2Co 1:23 [i] 2Co 10:8
13:11 [j] 1Th 4:1; 2Th 3:1 [k] S Mk 9:50 [l] 1Jn 4:16 [m] S Ro 15:33; Eph 6:23
13:12 [n] S Ro 16:16
13:13 [o] Php 4:22
13:14 [p] S Ro 16:20; 2Co 8:9 [q] Ro 5:5; Jude 21 [r] Php 2:1

THE FAITH. No knowledge is as important to believers as the certainty that they have eternal life (cf. 1Jn 5:13; see Jn 17:3, note). All professing Christians should examine themselves to determine that their salvation is a present reality (see article on ASSURANCE OF SALVATION, p. 1982).

13:14 GRACE . . . LOVE . . . FELLOWSHIP. Paul's benediction witnesses to the NT church's belief in the Trinity. Paul prays that the Corinthians may continually experience (1) the grace of Christ, i.e., his nearness, power, mercy and comfort; (2) the fatherly love of God with all his blessings; and (3) a deepening fellowship with the Holy Spirit. If this threefold reality is our abiding blessing, then our everlasting salvation will be assured.

A. The Holy Spirit in Relation to Creation and Revelation

Task	References
1. Active in creation	Ge 1:2; Job 33:4
2. Imparts life to God's creatures	Ge 2:7; Job 33:4; Ps 104:30
3. Inspired the prophets and apostles	Nu 11:29; Isa 59:21; Mic 3:8; Zec 7:12; 2Ti 3:16; 2Pe 1:21
4. Speaks through the Word	2Sa 23:1–2; Ac 1:16–20; Eph 6:17; Heb 3:7–11; 9:8; 10:15

B. The Holy Spirit in Relation to Jesus Christ

Task	References
1. Jesus was conceived in Mary by the Spirit	Mt 1:18,20–23; Lk 1:34–35
2. Was filled with the Spirit	Mt 3:16–17; Mk 1:12–13; Lk 3:21–22; Lk 4:1
3. Preached in the Spirit	Isa 11:2–4; 61:1–2; Lk 4:16–27
4. Performed miracles by the power of the Spirit	Isa 61:1; Mt 12:28; Lk 11:20; Ac 10:38
5. Will baptize believers in the Holy Spirit	Mt 3:11; Mk 1:8; Lk 3:16; Jn 1:33; Ac 1:4–5; 11:16
6. Promises the Holy Spirit as the Counselor	Jn 14:16–18,25–26; 15:26–27; 16:7–15
7. Promises the ministry of the Holy Spirit to flow through believers	Jn 7:37–39
8. Is revealed to believers by the Spirit	Jn 16:13–15
9. Offered himself on the cross through the Spirit	Heb 9:14
10. Was raised from the dead by the Spirit	Ro 1:3–4; 8:11
11. Received the Spirit from the Father	Jn 16:5–14; Ac 2:33
12. Poured out the Spirit upon believers	Ac 2:33,38–39
13. Is glorified by the Spirit	Jn 16:13–14
14. Spirit prays for his return	Rev 22:17

C. The Holy Spirit in Relation to the Church

Task	References
1. Dwells in the church as his temple	1Co 3:16; Eph 2:22; cf. Hag 2:5
2. Is poured out like rain upon the church	Ac 1:5; 2:1–4,16–21; cf. Isa 32:15; 44:3; Hos 6:3; Joel 2:23–32
3. Speaks to the church	Rev 2:7,11,17,27; 3:6,13,22
4. Creates fellowship in the church	2Co 13:14; Php 2:1
5. Unites the church	1Co 12:13; Eph 4:4
6. Gives gifts to the church	Ro 12:6–8; Eph 4:11; see chart on THE GIFTS OF THE HOLY SPIRIT, p. 1743
7. Strengthens the church through supernatural manifestations	Ac 4:30–33; 1Co 12:7–13; 14:1–33

C. The Holy Spirit in Relation to the Church (cont.)

Task	References
8. Appoints leaders for the church	Ac 20:28; Eph 4:11; see chart on THE GIFTS OF THE HOLY SPIRIT, p. 1743
9. Works through Spirit-filled people	Ac 6:3,5,8; 8:6–12; 15:28,32; cf. Nu 27:18; Jdg 6:34; 1Sa 16:13; Zec 4:6
10. Empowers preachers	1Co 2:4
11. Commissions people of God	Ac 13:2–4
12. Directs the missionary enterprise	Ac 8:29,39; 16:6–7; 20:23
13. Guards the church against error	2Ti 1:14
14. Warns the church of apostasy	1Ti 4:1; cf. Ne 9:30
15. Equips the church for spiritual warfare	Eph 6:10–18
16. Glorifies Christ	Jn 16:13–15
17. Promotes righteousness	Ro 14:17; Eph 2:21–22; 3:16–21; 1Th 4:7–8

D. The Holy Spirit in Relation to Individual Believers

Task	References
1. Lives in every believer	Ro 8:11; 1Co 6:15–20; 2Co 3:3; Eph 1:13; Heb 6:4; 1Jn 3:24; 4:13
2. Convicts us of sin	Jn 16:7–11; Ac 2:37
3. Regenerates us	Jn 3:5–6; 14:17; 20:22; Ro 8:9; 2Co 3:6; Tit 3:5
4. Imparts God's love to us	Ro 5:5
5. Makes us realize God is our Father	Ro 8:14–16; Gal 4:6
6. Enables us to say "Jesus is Lord"	1Co 12:3
7. Reveals Christ to us	Jn 15:26; 16:14–15; 1Co 2:10–11
8. Reveals God's truth to us	Ne 9:20; Jn 14:16–17,26; 16:13–14; 1Co 2:9–16
9. Enables us to distinguish truth from error	1Jn 4:1–3
10. Incorporates us into the church	1Co 12:13
11. Is given to all who ask	Lk 11:13
12. Baptizes us into the body of Christ	1Co 12:13
13. Is the One into whom we are baptized by Christ	Mt 3:11; Mk 1:8; Lk 3:16; Jn 1:33; Ac 1:4–5; 11:16
14. Fills us	Lk 1:15,41,67; Ac 2:4; 4:8,31; 6:3–5; 7:55; 11:24; 13:9,52; Eph 5:18; cf. Ex 31:3; Jdg 14:19; 1Sa 10:10
15. Gives us power and boldness to witness	Lk 1:15–17; 24:47–49; Ac 1:8; 4:31; 6:9–10; 19:6; Ro 9:1–3
16. Gives us special gifts	Mk 16:17–18; 1Co 1:7; 12:7–11; 1Pe 4:10–11; see chart on THE GIFTS OF THE HOLY SPIRIT, p. 1743

D. The Holy Spirit in Relation to Individual Believers (cont.)

Task	References
17. Gives visions and prophecy	Joel 2:28–29; Ac 2:17–18; 10:9–22; 1Co 14:1–5,21–25
18. Develops his fruit in us	Ro 14:17; 1Co 13; Gal 5:22–23; 1Th 1:6
19. Enables us to live a holy life	Ps 51:10–12; 143:10; Eze 11:19–20; 37:26; Ro 8:4–10; 15:16; Gal 5:16–18,25; Php 2:12–13; 2Th 2:13; 1Pe 1:2
20. Frees us from the power of sin	Ro 8:2; Eph 3:16
21. Enables us to fight Satan with the Word	Eph 6:17
22. Enables us to speak in difficult moments	Mt 10:17–20; Mk 13:11; Lk 12:11–12
23. Gives us comfort and encouragement	Jn 14:17–18,26–27; Ac 9:31
24. Helps us to pray	Ac 4:23–24; Ro 8:26; Eph 6:18; Jude 20
25. Enables us to worship	Jn 4:23–24; Ac 10:46; Eph 5:18–19; Php 3:3
26. Is grieved by our sin	Ge 6:3; Eph 4:30; cf. Mt 12:31–32
27. Is our pledge of final redemption	2Co 1:22; 5:5; Eph 1:13–14
28. Makes us yearn for Christ's return	Ro 8:23; Rev 22:20
29. Gives life to our mortal bodies	Ro 8:11

E. The Holy Spirit in Relation to Sinners

Task	References
1. Convicts of sin, righteousness and judgment	Jn 16:7–11
2. Commissions believers to proclaim the gospel to sinners	Ac 1:8; 2:17,21; 4:31; 11:12–18; 13:1–4
3. Reveals the saving truth of the gospel	Lk 4:18–19; Jn 15:26–27; Ac 4:8; 11:15,18; 14:3; 1Co 2:4,12; 1Th 1:5

GALATIANS

Outline

Introduction (1:1–10)
- A. Greetings (1:1–5)
- B. Astonishment at Their Lapse from the Gospel of Grace (1:6–10)

I. Paul Defends the Authority of His Gospel and Calling (Personal) (1:11—2:21)
- A. It Was Revealed to Him By Christ (1:11–24)
- B. It Was Recognized and Ratified by James, Peter and John (2:1–10)
- C. It Was Vindicated in Conflict With Peter (2:11–21)

II. Paul Defends the Message of His Gospel (Doctrinal) (3:1—4:31)
- A. Receiving the Spirit and New Life Is by Faith Rather Than by Works (3:1–14)
- B. Salvation Is Through Promise Rather Than Through Law (3:15–24)
- C. Those Who Trust in Christ Are Children Rather Than Slaves (3:25—4:7)
- D. An Appeal for the Galatians to Reconsider Their Action (4:8–20)
- E. Those Who Trust in the Law Are Slaves Rather Than Children (4:21–31)

III. Paul Defends the Freedom of His Gospel (Practical) (5:1—6:10)
- A. Christian Freedom Relates to Salvation by Grace (5:1–12)
  1. Preserve Christian Freedom (5:1)
  2. The Consequence of Submitting to Circumcision in the Law (5:2–12)
- B. Christian Freedom Must Not Become an Excuse for Indulging the Sinful Nature (5:13–26)
  1. The Command of Love (5:13–15)
  2. Live by the Spirit, Not by the Sinful Nature (5:16–26)
- C. Christian Freedom Must Be Expressed Through the Law of Christ (6:1–10)
  1. Carry Each Other's Burdens (6:1–5)
  2. Assist Ministers of the Word (6:6)
  3. Do Not Become Weary in Doing Good (6:7–10)

Conclusion (6:11–18)

Author: Paul

Theme: Salvation by Grace Through Faith

Date of Writing: c. A.D. 49

Background

Paul wrote this letter (1:1; 5:2; 6:11) "to the churches in Galatia" (1:2). Some believe the Galatians were the Gauls in northern Galatia. It is far more likely that Paul wrote this letter to cities in the southern region of the province of Galatia (Pisidian Antioch, Iconium, Lystra, Derbe) where he and Barnabas evangelized and established churches during their first missionary journey (Ac 13–14). The most satisfactory date for writing is shortly after Paul returned to his sending church in Antioch of Syria and just prior to the Jerusalem council (Ac 15).

The main issue in Galatians is the same one debated and resolved at Jerusalem (c. A.D. 49; cf. Ac 15). The main issue involves a twofold question: Is faith in Jesus Christ as Lord and Savior the only prerequisite for salvation? (2) Or is obedience to certain OT Jewish practices and laws required in order to gain salvation in Christ? It appears that Paul wrote Galatians before the law controversy was formally debated at Jerusalem and the official church position was pronounced. This would mean that Galatians was the first letter that Paul wrote.

Purpose

Paul learned that certain Jewish teachers were unsettling his new converts in Galatia by imposing on them circumcision and the yoke of the Mosaic law as necessary requirements for salvation and inclusion in the church. On hearing this, Paul wrote (1) to deny emphatically that legal requirements such as circumcision under the old covenant have anything to do with the operation of God's grace in Christ for salvation under the new covenant; and (2) to reaffirm clearly that we receive the Holy Spirit and spiritual life through faith in the Lord Jesus Christ, and not through attachment to OT law.

Survey

From the contents of this letter, it appears that Paul's Jewish opponents in Galatia were attacking him personally in order to undermine his influence in the churches. Paul's opponents charged that (1) he was not among the original apostles and therefore was without authentic authority (cf. 1:1,7,12; 2:8–9); (2) his message departed from the gospel preached at Jerusalem (cf. 1:9; 2:2–10); and (3) his message of grace would result in lawless living (cf. 5:1,13,16,19–21).

Paul responded directly to all three charges. (1) He vigorously defended his own authority as an apostle of Jesus Christ, authority received directly from God and endorsed by James, Peter and John (chs. 1–2). (2) He passionately defended the gospel of salvation as being by grace through faith in Christ (chs. 3–4). (3) Finally, Paul earnestly maintained that the true gospel of Christ involves a freedom from the slavery of Jewish legalism on the one hand, and a freedom from sin and the acts of the sinful nature on the other. True Christian freedom involves living by the Spirit and fulfilling the law of Christ (chs. 5–6).

Galatians contains a character sketch of the Jewish believers who opposed Paul in Galatia, Antioch and Jerusalem (Ac 15:1–2,5), and throughout most of the places in which he ministered. Paul characterized them as disturbers, perverters (1:7), hinderers (5:7), and individuals seeking to make a good impression outwardly and to avoid persecution because of the offense of Christ's cross (6:12). Indirectly Paul described them as people-pleasers (1:10), false brothers (2:4), the circumcision group (2:12) and manipulators (3:1).

Special Features

Four unique features characterize this letter. (1) It is the most vigorous NT defense of the essential nature of the gospel. Its tone is sharp, intense and urgent, as Paul deals with erring opponents (e.g., 1:8–9; 5:12) and rebukes the Galatians for their gullibility (1:6; 3:1; 4:19–20). (2) It is second only to 2 Corinthians in containing autobiographical references. (3) This is Paul's only letter explicitly addressed to a plurality of churches (see, however, the introduction to Ephesians). (4) It contains a list of the fruit of the Spirit (5:22–23) and the most extensive NT catalogue of the acts of the sinful nature (5:19–21).

Reading Galatians

In order to read the entire New Testament in one year, the book of Galatians should be read in 8 days, according to the following schedule:
☐ 1 ☐ 2 ☐ 3:1–14 ☐ 3:15–25 ☐ 3:26—4:20 ☐ 4:21—5:15 ☐ 5:16–26 ☐ 6

NOTES

1 Paul, an apostle[a]—sent not from
men nor by man,[b] but by Jesus
Christ[c] and God the Father,[d] who
raised him from the dead[e]— **2**and all
the brothers with me,[f]

To the churches in Galatia:[g]

3Grace and peace to you from God
our Father and the Lord Jesus Christ,[h]
4who gave himself for our sins[i] to rescue us from the present evil age,[j] according to the will of our God and Father,[k] **5**to whom be glory for ever and
ever. Amen.[l]

No Other Gospel

6I am astonished that you are so
quickly deserting the one who called[m]
you by the grace of Christ and are turning to a different gospel[n]— **7**which is
really no gospel at all. Evidently some
people are throwing you into confusion[o] and are trying to pervert[p] the
gospel of Christ. **8**But even if we or an
angel from heaven should preach a
gospel other than the one we preached
to you,[q] let him be eternally condemned![r] **9**As we have already said,
so now I say again: If anybody is

1:1 [a]S 1Co 1:1 [b]ver 11,12 [c]ver 15,16; S Ac 9:15; 20:24 [d]ver 15,16; S Ac 9:15; 20:24 [e]S Ac 2:24 **1:2** [f]Php 4:21 [g]S Ac 16:6 **1:3** [h]S Ro 1:7 **1:4** [i]S Mt 20:28; S Ro 4:25; S 1Co 15:3; Gal 2:20 [j]S 1Co 1:20 [k]S Php 4:20 **1:5** [l]S Ro 11:36 **1:6** [m]ver 15; S Ro 8:28 [n]2Co 11:4 **1:7** [o]Ac 15:24; Gal 5:10 [p]Jer 23:16,36 **1:8** [q]ver 11,16; 1Co 15:1; 2Co 11:4; Gal 2:2 [r]Ro 9:3

1:4 RESCUE US FROM THE PRESENT EVIL AGE. This verse is probably an early confession of faith that was well known throughout the NT churches. It connects Christ's death with the forgiveness of sins and deliverance from "the present evil age." Essential to Christ's saving purpose is the deliverance of believers from the evil that dominates this world's societies. The first gospel message preached after the Pentecostal outpouring of the Holy Spirit contained the words: "Save yourselves from this corrupt generation" (Ac 2:40). Believers must live for God and refuse to be governed by the prevailing values, wisdom, opinions, corrupt desires and selfish pleasures of the people of the world (cf. Ro 12:2, note; Tit 2:14; see article on THE CHRISTIAN'S RELATIONSHIP TO THE WORLD, p. 1976).

1:6 A DIFFERENT GOSPEL. False teachers had come to the Galatians, trying to persuade them to reject Paul's teaching and accept "a different gospel." Their gospel taught that salvation involved not only believing in Christ, but also being incorporated into the Jewish faith by being circumcised (5:2), observing the law (3:5) and keeping Jewish holy days (4:10). (1) The Bible clearly affirms that there is only one gospel, "the gospel of Christ" (v. 7). It has come to us through the "revelation from Jesus Christ" (v. 12) and the inspiration of the Holy Spirit (see article on THE INSPIRATION AND AUTHORITY OF SCRIPTURE, p. 1898). This gospel is defined and revealed in the Bible, the Word of God. (2) Any teachings, doctrines or ideas originating from persons, churches or traditions and not expressed or implied in God's Word may not be included in the gospel of Christ (v. 11). To mix them with the original content of the gospel is to "pervert the gospel of Christ" (v. 7).

1:9 LET HIM BE ETERNALLY CONDEMNED! The words "eternally condemned" (Gk *anathema*) mean that one lies under God's curse, is doomed to destruction, and will receive God's wrath and damnation. (1) The apostle Paul reveals the Holy Spirit's inspired attitude of judgment and indignation toward those who try to distort the original gospel of Christ (v. 7) and change the truth of apostolic witness. This same attitude was evident in Jesus Christ (see Mt 23:13, note), Peter (2Pe 2), John (2Jn 7–11) and Jude (Jude 3–4,12–19), and will be found in the heart of every follower of Christ who loves Christ's gospel as revealed in God's Word and who believes that it is the indispensable Good News of salvation for a world lost in sin (Ro 10:14–15).

(2) Condemned are all those who preach a gospel contrary to the message Paul preached, as revealed to him by Christ (vv. 11–12; see v. 6, note). Anyone adding to or taking away from the original and fundamental gospel of Christ and the apostles stands under God's curse; "God will take away from him his share in the tree of life" (Rev 22:18–19).

(3) God commands believers to defend the faith (Jude 3, note), to correct in love (2Ti 2:25–26), and to separate themselves from teachers, ministers and others in the church who deny fundamental Bible truths taught by Jesus and the apostles (vv. 8–9; Ro 16:17–18; 2Co 6:17). These truths include:

(a) The deity of Christ and his virgin birth (Mt 1:23; see Jn 20:28, note);

(b) The full inspiration and authority of God's Word in all it teaches (see article on THE INSPIRATION AND AUTHORITY OF SCRIPTURE, p. 1898);

(c) The historicity of the fall of Adam (Ro 5:12–19);

(d) The inherent corruption of human nature (Ge 6:5; 8:21; Ro 1:21–32; 3:10–18; 7:14,21);

(e) Humanity's lostness without Christ (see Ac 4:12, note; Ro 1:16–32; 10:13–15);

(f) Salvation by grace through faith in Christ as Lord and Savior, accomplished by his death and blood atonement (Ro 3:24–25; 5:10; see article on FAITH AND GRACE, p. 1720);

(g) Christ's bodily resurrection (see Mt 28:6, note; 1Co 15:3–4);

(h) The historical reality of miracles in both the OT and NT (1Co 10:1);

(i) The reality of Satan and demons as spiritual beings (Mt 4:1; 8:28; 2Co 4:4; Eph 2:2; 6:11–18; 1Pe 5:8);

(j) The Biblical teaching about hell (see Mt 10:28, note);

preaching to you a gospel other than what you accepted,[s] let him be eternally condemned!

10Am I now trying to win the approval of men, or of God? Or am I trying to please men?[t] If I were still trying to please men, I would not be a servant of Christ.

Paul Called by God

11I want you to know, brothers,[u] that the gospel I preached[v] is not something that man made up. 12I did not receive it from any man,[w] nor was I taught it; rather, I received it by revelation[x] from Jesus Christ.[y]

13For you have heard of my previous way of life in Judaism,[z] how intensely I persecuted the church of God[a] and tried to destroy it.[b] 14I was advancing in Judaism beyond many Jews of my own age and was extremely zealous[c] for the traditions of my fathers.[d] 15But when God, who set me apart from birth[a][e] and called me[f] by his grace, was pleased 16to reveal his Son in me so that I might preach him among the Gentiles,[g] I did not consult any man,[h] 17nor did I go up to Jerusalem to see those who were apostles before I was, but I went immediately into Arabia and later returned to Damascus.[i]

18Then after three years,[j] I went up to Jerusalem[k] to get acquainted with Peter[b] and stayed with him fifteen days. 19I saw none of the other apostles—only James,[l] the Lord's brother. 20I assure you before God[m] that what I am writing you is no lie.[n] 21Later I went to Syria[o] and Cilicia.[p] 22I was personally unknown to the churches of Judea[q] that are in Christ.[r] 23They only heard the report: "The man who formerly persecuted us is now preaching the faith[s] he once tried to destroy."[t] 24And they praised God[u] because of me.

Paul Accepted by the Apostles

2 Fourteen years later I went up again to Jerusalem,[v] this time with Barnabas.[w] I took Titus[x] along also. 2I went in response to a revelation[y] and set before them the gospel that I preach among the Gentiles.[z] But I did this privately to those who seemed to be leaders, for fear that I was running or had run my race[a] in vain. 3Yet not even Titus,[b] who was with me, was compelled to be circumcised, even though he was a Greek.[c] 4⌊This matter arose⌋ because some false brothers[d] had infiltrated our ranks to spy on[e] the freedom[f] we have in Christ Jesus and to make us slaves. 5We did not give in to them for a moment, so that the truth of the gospel[g] might remain with you.

6As for those who seemed to be im-

[a] *15* Or *from my mother's womb* [b] *18* Greek *Cephas*

1:9 [s]Ro 16:17
1:10 [t]S Ro 2:29
1:11 [u]1Co 15:1 [v]S ver 8
1:12 [w]ver 1 [x]ver 16; S 1Co 2:10 [y]1Co 11:23; 15:3
1:13 [z]Ac 26:4,5 [a]S 1Co 10:32 [b]S Ac 8:3
1:14 [c]S Ac 21:20 [d]Mt 15:2
1:15 [e]Isa 49:1,5; Jer 1:5 [f]S Ac 9:15; S Ro 8:28
1:16 [g]S Ac 9:15; Gal 2:9 [h]Mt 16:17
1:17 [i]Ac 9:2, 19-22
1:18 [j]Ac 9:22,23 [k]Ac 9:26,27
1:19 [l]Mt 13:55; S Ac 15:13
1:20 [m]S Ro 1:9 [n]S Ro 9:1
1:21 [o]S Lk 2:2 [p]S Ac 6:9
1:22 [q]1Th 2:14 [r]S Ro 16:3
1:23 [s]Ac 6:7 [t]S Ac 8:3
1:24 [u]S Mt 9:8
2:1 [v]Ac 15:2 [w]S Ac 4:36 [x]S 2Co 2:13
2:2 [y]S 1Co 2:10 [z]Ac 15:4,12 [a]S 1Co 9:24
2:3 [b]ver 1; S 2Co 2:13 [c]Ac 16:3; 1Co 9:21
2:4 [d]S Ac 1:16; 2Co 11:26 [e]Jude 4 [f]Gal 5:1,13
2:5 [g]ver 14

(k) Christ's literal return to earth (Jn 14:3, note; Ac 1:11; 1Co 1:7, note; Rev 19:11, note).

(4) Similar passages containing warnings against false teachers are found in Ro 16:17; 2Pe 2:17–22; 2Jn 9–11; Jude 12–13; see 2Co 11:13, note; see article on FALSE TEACHERS, p. 1506.

1:10 OR AM I TRYING TO PLEASE MEN? One cannot be a genuine minister of the gospel and try to please people by compromising the truths of the gospel (cf. 1Co 4:3–6). Paul regarded it his duty to speak "not trying to please men but God, who tests our hearts" (1Th 2:4, note). All followers of the gospel of Christ must make it their aim to please God, even if it means displeasing some people (cf. Ac 5:29; Eph 6:6; Col 3:22).

1:15 GOD, WHO SET ME APART. Although Paul was primarily referring to his apostolic ministry, there is a sense in which each believer has been set apart by grace so that God may reveal his Son in him or her. We have been separated from sin and the present evil age (see v. 4, note), that we might live in fellowship with God and witness to Jesus Christ before the world. To be set apart means to be with God, for God and near God—living in faith and obedience for his glory and the revealing of his Son (see article on SPIRITUAL SEPARATION FOR BELIEVERS, p. 1794).

2:5 NOT GIVE IN TO THEM FOR A MOMENT. Paul was tolerant of and patient toward many things (cf. 1Co 13:4–7), but unyielding when it came to the "truth of the gospel." The revelation that he received from Christ (1:12) is the one and only gospel that possesses the power for the salvation of all who believe (Ro 1:16). Paul understood that this gospel may never be compromised for the sake of peace, unity or current opinion. Both the glory of Jesus Christ and the salvation of the lost were at stake. Today if we relinquish any part of the gospel according to NT revelation, we begin to tear down the only message that saves us from eternal destruction (cf. Mt 18:6).

2:6 GOD DOES NOT JUDGE BY EXTERNAL APPEARANCE. God does not show favoritism to any person because of his or her heritage, reputation, position or accomplishment (cf. Lev 19:15; Dt 10:17; Job 34:19; Ac 10:34; Eph 6:9). (1) God sees and evaluates the heart, i.e., the inner person, and his favor rests on those whose hearts are sincerely turned toward him in love, faith and purity (cf. 1Sa 16:7; Mt 23:28; Lk 16:15; Jn 7:24; 2Co 10:7; see

portant[h]—whatever they were makes
no difference to me; God does not judge
by external appearance[i]—those men
added nothing to my message.[j] **7**On
the contrary, they saw that I had been
entrusted with the task[k] of preaching
the gospel to the Gentiles,[c][l] just as
Peter[m] had been to the Jews.[d] **8**For
God, who was at work in the ministry
of Peter as an apostle[n] to the Jews,
was also at work in my ministry as an
apostle[o] to the Gentiles. **9**James,[p]
Peter[e][q] and John, those reputed to be
pillars,[r] gave me and Barnabas[s] the
right hand of fellowship when they recognized the grace given to me.[t] They
agreed that we should go to the Gentiles,[u] and they to the Jews. **10**All they
asked was that we should continue to
remember the poor,[v] the very thing I
was eager to do.

Paul Opposes Peter

11When Peter[w] came to Antioch,[x]
I opposed him to his face, because he
was clearly in the wrong. **12**Before certain men came from James,[y] he used
to eat with the Gentiles.[z] But when
they arrived, he began to draw back
and separate himself from the Gentiles
because he was afraid of those who belonged to the circumcision group.[a]
13The other Jews joined him in his hypocrisy, so that by their hypocrisy even
Barnabas[b] was led astray.
14When I saw that they were not acting in line with the truth of the gospel,[c] I said to Peter[d] in front of them
all, "You are a Jew, yet you live like a
Gentile and not like a Jew.[e] How is it,
then, that you force Gentiles to follow
Jewish customs?[f]
15"We who are Jews by birth[g] and
not 'Gentile sinners'[h] **16**know that a
man is not justified by observing the
law,[i] but by faith in Jesus Christ.[j] So
we, too, have put our faith in Christ
Jesus that we may be justified by faith
in Christ and not by observing the law,
because by observing the law no one
will be justified.[k] (Eph 2:4-9)
17"If, while we seek to be justified in
Christ, it becomes evident that we ourselves are sinners,[l] does that mean
that Christ promotes sin? Absolutely
not![m] **18**If I rebuild what I destroyed,
I prove that I am a lawbreaker. **19**For
through the law I died to the law[n] so
that I might live for God.[o] **20**I have
been crucified with Christ[p] and I no

2:6 [h] ver 2 [i] S Ac 10:34; S Rev 2:23 [j] 1Co 15:11 **2:7** [k] 1Th 2:4; 1Ti 1:11 [l] S Ac 9:15 [m] ver 9, 11,14 **2:8** [n] Ac 1:25 [o] S 1Co 1:1 **2:9** [p] S Ac 15:13 [q] ver 7,11,14 [r] 1Ti 3:15; Rev 3:12 [s] ver 1; S Ac 4:36 [t] S Ro 12:3 [u] S Ac 9:15 **2:10** [v] S Ac 24:17 **2:11** [w] ver 7,9,14 [x] S Ac 11:19 **2:12** [y] S Ac 15:13 [z] Ac 11:3 [a] Ac 10:45; 11:2 **2:13** [b] ver 1; S Ac 4:36 **2:14** [c] ver 5 [d] ver 7,9,11 [e] Ac 10:28 [f] ver 12 **2:15** [g] Php 3:4,5 [h] 1Sa 15:18; Lk 24:7 **2:16** [i] S Ro 3:28 [j] S Ro 9:30 [k] S Ro 3:28; S 4:25 **2:17** [l] ver 15 [m] Gal 3:21 **2:19** [n] S Ro 7:4 [o] Ro 6:10,11,14; 2Co 5:15 **2:20** [p] S Ro 6:6

[c] 7 Greek *uncircumcised* [d] 7 Greek *circumcised*; also in verses 8 and 9
[e] 9 Greek *Cephas*; also in verses 11 and 14

1Co 13:1, note). (2) Thus God does not prefer the love, fellowship and prayers of the educated more than the uneducated, the rich more than the poor, or the powerful more than the weak; God's eternal principle is that he "accepts men from every nation who fear him and do what is right" (Ac 10:35).

2:10 REMEMBER THE POOR. A repeated theme in Scripture is the special importance of helping the poor (Ex 23:10–11; Dt 15:7–11; Jer 22:16; Am 2:6–7; Mt 6:2–4; Jn 13:29). There will always be those around us who need help. The poor, especially "those who belong to the family of believers" (6:10), require both our material assistance and our prayers (see article on THE CARE OF THE POOR AND NEEDY, p. 1316).

2:11 I OPPOSED HIM TO HIS FACE. Any minister or spiritual leader who is guilty of error and hypocrisy (v. 13) must be opposed and rebuked (cf. 1Ti 5:20). This must be applied without respect of persons; even a prominent person like the apostle Peter, who was used mightily by God, needed corrective rebuke (vv. 11–17; cf. 1Ti 5:20–21). Scripture indicates that Peter recognized his error and accepted Paul's rebuke in a humble and repentant manner. He later refers to Paul as "our dear brother Paul" (2Pe 3:15).

2:12 AFRAID OF ... CIRCUMCISION GROUP. Those "who belonged to the circumcision group" were Jewish Christians, especially in the Jerusalem church, who believed that the OT sign of circumcision was necessary for all new covenant believers. They also taught that Jewish believers should not eat with any uncircumcised Gentile believers who did not follow Jewish customs and dietary restrictions. Peter, although knowing that God accepted Gentile believers without partiality (Ac 10:34–35), denied his own conviction out of fear of criticism and the possible loss of authority in the Jerusalem church. His separation from table fellowship with Gentile believers encouraged the error that there were two bodies of Christ—Jewish and Gentile.

2:16 JUSTIFIED BY ... FAITH. Paul deals here with the question of how sinners can be justified, i.e., forgiven of their sins, accepted by God and put in a right relationship with him. This will happen not by "observing the law," but by a living faith in Christ Jesus (see article on BIBLICAL WORDS FOR SALVATION, p. 1710).

2:19 I DIED TO THE LAW. See Ro 7:4, note on the meaning of dying to the law; Mt 5:17, note on the believer's relation to the law; see article on THE OLD TESTAMENT LAW, p. 118.

2:20 I HAVE BEEN CRUCIFIED WITH CHRIST. Paul describes his relationship to Christ in terms of a profound personal attachment to and reliance on his Lord. Those who have faith in Christ live their lives in intimate union with their Lord, both in his death and resurrection. (1) All believers have been crucified with Christ on the

longer live, but Christ lives in me.[q]
The life I live in the body, I live by faith
in the Son of God,[r] who loved me[s]
and gave himself for me.[t] **21**I do not
set aside the grace of God, for if righteousness could be gained through the
law,[u] Christ died for nothing!"[f]

Faith or Observance of the Law

3 You foolish[v] Galatians![w] Who
has bewitched you?[x] Before your
very eyes Jesus Christ was clearly portrayed as crucified.[y] **2**I would like to
learn just one thing from you: Did you
receive the Spirit[z] by observing the
law,[a] or by believing what you
heard?[b] **3**Are you so foolish? After beginning with the Spirit, are you now
trying to attain your goal by human effort? **4**Have you suffered so much for
nothing—if it really was for nothing?
5Does God give you his Spirit and work
miracles[c] among you because you observe the law, or because you believe
what you heard?[d]
6Consider Abraham: "He believed
God, and it was credited to him as righteousness."[g][e] **7**Understand, then,
that those who believe[f] are children
of Abraham.[g] **8**The Scripture foresaw
that God would justify the Gentiles by
faith, and announced the gospel in advance to Abraham: "All nations will be
blessed through you."[h][h] **9**So those
who have faith[i] are blessed along
with Abraham, the man of faith.[j]
10All who rely on observing the
law[k] are under a curse,[l] for it is written: "Cursed is everyone who does not
continue to do everything written in
the Book of the Law."[i][m] **11**Clearly no
one is justified before God by the law,[n]

2:20 [q]S Ro 8:10; 1Pe 4:2 [r]S Mt 4:3 [s]S Ro 8:37 [t]S Gal 1:4 **2:21** [u]Gal 3:21 **3:1** [v]Lk 24:25 [w]S Ac 16:6 [x]Gal 5:7 [y]1Co 1:23 **3:2** [z]S Jn 20:22 [a]ver 5,10; Gal 2:16 [b]Ro 10:17; Heb 4:2 **3:5** [c]1Co 12:10 [d]ver 2,10; Gal 2:16 **3:6** [e]Ge 15:6; S Ro 4:3 **3:7** [f]ver 9 [g]S Lk 3:8 **3:8** [h]Ge 12:3; 18:18; 22:18; 26:4; Ac 3:25 **3:9** [i]ver 7; Ro 4:16 [j]Ro 4:18-22 **3:10** [k]ver 2,5; Gal 2:16 [l]ver 13; S Ro 4:15 [m]Dt 27:26; Jer 11:3 **3:11** [n]S Ro 3:28

[f] *21* Some interpreters end the quotation after verse 14. [g] *6* Gen. 15:6 [h] *8* Gen. 12:3; 18:18; 22:18 [i] *10* Deut. 27:26

cross. They have died to the law as a means of salvation and now live through Christ for God (v. 19). Because of salvation in Christ, sin no longer has control over them (see Ro 6:11, note; cf. Ro 6:4,8,14; Gal 5:24; 6:14; Col 2:12,20).

(2)We who have been crucified with Christ now live with him in his resurrection life. Christ and his strength live within us, becoming the source of all of life and the center of all our thoughts, words and deeds (Jn 15:1–6; Eph 3:17). It is through the Holy Spirit that Christ's risen life is continually communicated to us (Jn 16:13–14; Ro 8:10–11).

(3) Our sharing in Christ's death and resurrection is appropriated through faith, i.e., the confident belief, love, devotion and loyalty we have in the Son of God, who loved us and gave himself for us (cf. Jn 3:16; see article on FAITH AND GRACE, p. 1720). This living by faith can be seen as living by the Spirit (3:3; 5:25; cf. Ro 8:9–11).

2:21 RIGHTEOUSNESS. Paul's understanding of justification (vv. 16–17) and righteousness includes more than a mere legal declaration by God. The righteousness that comes through faith involves a moral change (v. 19), the grace of God (v. 21) and a relationship with Christ whereby we share his resurrected life (v. 20). This is confirmed in 3:21, where Paul makes it clear that the righteousness that comes through faith in Christ imparts life, a life that is seen as receiving the Spirit (3:2–3,14; see article on BIBLICAL WORDS FOR SALVATION, p. 1710).

3:2 DID YOU RECEIVE THE SPIRIT BY . . . BELIEVING? Paul demonstrates the superiority of salvation by grace through faith in Christ over the attempt to gain salvation through obedience to the law. Through faith in Christ we receive the Holy Spirit and all his blessings, including the gift of eternal life (vv. 2–3,5,14,21; 4:6). However, the person who relies on the law to gain salvation does not receive the Spirit and life, for mere law cannot impart life (v. 21).

3:5 HIS SPIRIT. Paul's references to the Spirit (vv. 2,5,14; 4:6) include both the baptism in the Spirit and the Spirit's subsequent special operations (cf. Ac 1:4–5; 2:4; 8:14–17; 10:44–47; 11:16–17; 19:1–6; 1Co 12:4–11). This is indicated by (1) the use of the term "miracles" (Gk *dunamis*), which implies that the apostle is thinking of the charismatic manifestations of the Spirit and his coming with "power" (Gk *dunamis*) at Pentecost (Ac 1:8; cf. 2:1–4); (2) the use of the present participles ("give" and "work"), which indicate the continuous manifestation of the Spirit's gifts; (3) the use of the expression "the promise of the Spirit" (v. 14), which is nearly identical to Peter's words in Ac 2:33 (cf. Lk 24:49; Ac 1:4); and (4) the affirmation in 4:6 that adoption as God's children occurred prior to and is the basis for sending the Spirit into the believer's heart.

3:5 HIS SPIRIT . . . WORK MIRACLES. The ongoing work of the Spirit in the Galatian churches involved miracles. For Paul, receiving the Holy Spirit was not just an invisible inward work, but an experience that revealed itself in divine power among believers. The gifts of the Spirit were a determinative norm for the Spirit's presence and authority (cf. 1Co 12–14). Conversion and the baptism in the Holy Spirit should continually result in the working of miracles and the other manifestations of the Spirit.

3:6 IT WAS CREDITED TO HIM AS RIGHTEOUSNESS. See Ro 4:3,5,22, notes.

3:11 THE RIGHTEOUS WILL LIVE BY FAITH. Paul quotes Hab 2:4 to illustrate justification by faith (cf. Ro 1:17). Habakkuk emphasizes that one who is justified by faith possesses actual inward righteousness, for he contrasts the righteous person with the unrighteous person whose "desires are not upright" (see Hab 2:4, note). Thus, Paul believed justification involved an actu-

because, "The righteous will live by
faith."[j][o] 12The law is not based on
faith; on the contrary, "The man who
does these things will live by
them."[k][p] 13Christ redeemed us from
the curse of the law[q] by becoming a
curse for us, for it is written: "Cursed
is everyone who is hung on a tree."[l][r]
14He redeemed us in order that the
blessing given to Abraham might come
to the Gentiles through Christ Jesus,[s]
so that by faith we might receive the
promise of the Spirit.[t]

The Law and the Promise

15Brothers,[u] let me take an example from everyday life. Just as no one
can set aside or add to a human covenant that has been duly established,
so it is in this case. 16The promises
were spoken to Abraham and to his
seed.[v] The Scripture does not say
"and to seeds," meaning many people,
but "and to your seed,"[m][w] meaning
one person, who is Christ. 17What I
mean is this: The law, introduced 430
years[x] later, does not set aside the
covenant previously established by
God and thus do away with the promise. 18For if the inheritance depends on
the law, then it no longer depends on
a promise;[y] but God in his grace gave
it to Abraham through a promise.

19What, then, was the purpose of the
law? It was added because of transgressions[z] until the Seed[a] to whom
the promise referred had come. The
law was put into effect through angels[b] by a mediator.[c] 20A mediator,[d] however, does not represent just
one party; but God is one.

21Is the law, therefore, opposed to
the promises of God? Absolutely not![e]
For if a law had been given that could
impart life, then righteousness would
certainly have come by the law.[f]
22But the Scripture declares that the
whole world is a prisoner of sin,[g] so
that what was promised, being given
through faith in Jesus Christ, might be
given to those who believe.

23Before this faith came, we were
held prisoners[h] by the law, locked up
until faith should be revealed.[i] 24So
the law was put in charge to lead us to
Christ[n][j] that we might be justified by
faith.[k] 25Now that faith has come, we
are no longer under the supervision of
the law.[l]

Sons of God

26You are all sons of God[m] through
faith in Christ Jesus, 27for all of you
who were baptized into Christ[n] have
clothed yourselves with Christ.[o]
28There is neither Jew nor Greek, slave
nor free,[p] male nor female,[q] for you

3:11 [o]Hab 2:4; S Ro 9:30; Heb 10:38
3:12 [p]Lev 18:5; S Ro 10:5
3:13 [q]Gal 4:5 [r]Dt 21:23; S Ac 5:30
3:14 [s]Ro 4:9,16 [t]ver 2; Joel 2:28; S Jn 20:22; S Ac 2:33
3:15 [u]S Ro 7:1
3:16 [v]Ge 17:19; Ps 132:11; Mic 7:20; Lk 1:55; Ro 4:13,16; 9:4,8; Gal 3:29; 4:28 [w]Ge 12:7; 13:15; 17:7,8,10; 24:7
3:17 [x]Ge 15:13, 14; Ex 12:40; Ac 7:6
3:18 [y]Ro 4:14
3:19 [z]Ro 5:20 [a]ver 16 [b]Dt 33:2; Ac 7:53 [c]Ex 20:19; Dt 5:5
3:20 [d]1Ti 2:5; Heb 8:6; 9:15; 12:24
3:21 [e]Gal 2:17; S Ro 7:12 [f]Gal 2:21
3:22 [g]Ro 3:9-19; 11:32
3:23 [h]Ro 11:32 [i]ver 25
3:24 [j]ver 19; Ro 10:4; S 4:15 [k]Gal 2:16
3:25 [l]S Ro 7:4
3:26 [m]S Ro 8:14
3:27 [n]S Mt 28:19 [o]S Ro 13:14
3:28 [p]1Co 12:13; Col 3:11 [q]Ge 1:27; 5:2; Joel 2:29

[j]*11* Hab. 2:4 [k]*12* Lev. 18:5 [l]*13* Deut. 21:23 [m]*16* Gen. 12:7; 13:15; 24:7
[n]*24* Or *charge until Christ came*

---

al inner righteousness through the indwelling Holy Spirit (see article on BIBLICAL WORDS FOR SALVATION, p. 1710).

3:14 BLESSING GIVEN TO ABRAHAM. The content of God's promise to Abraham (v. 8) is defined as "the promise of the Spirit" (cf. Lk 24:49; Ac 1:4–5). To receive the Spirit is to have righteousness, life and all the other spiritual blessings (see v. 5, note; 4:6, note).

3:19 WHAT, THEN, WAS THE PURPOSE OF THE LAW? The word for "law" (Gk *nomos*; Heb *torah*) means "teaching" or "direction." The law can refer to the Ten Commandments, the Pentateuch or any commandment in the OT; Paul's use of law here would include the sacrificial system of the Mosaic covenant. Concerning the law Paul states several things: (1) It was given by God "because of transgressions," i.e., in order to show sin as the violation of God's will and to awaken humanity's sense of need for God's mercy, grace and salvation in Christ (v. 24; cf. Ro 5:20; 8:2).

(2) Although the OT law was holy, good and righteous (Ro 7:12), it was inadequate in that it could not impart spiritual life or moral strength (v. 21; Ro 8:3; Heb 7:18–19).

(3) The law acted as a temporary tutor for God's people until salvation through faith in Christ came (vv. 22–26). As such, the law revealed God's will for his people's behavior (Ex 19:4–6; 20:1–17; 21:1—24:8), provided for blood sacrifices to cover the people's sins (see Lev 1:5; 16:33) and pointed to Christ's atoning death (Heb 9:14; 10:12–14).

(4) The law was given "to lead us to Christ that we might be justified by faith" (v. 24). But now that Christ has come, the supervisory function of the law has ended (v. 25). Therefore we no longer seek salvation through the old covenant provisions, including obedience to its laws and the sacrificial system. Salvation now comes according to new covenant provisions, especially Jesus' atoning death and glorious resurrection, and the subsequent privilege of belonging to Christ (vv. 27–29; see Mt 5:17, note on the Christian's relation to law; see article on THE OLD TESTAMENT LAW, p. 118).

3:28 MALE NOR FEMALE. Paul removes all ethnic, racial, national, social and sexual distinctions with regard to one's spiritual relationship with Jesus Christ. All in Christ are equal heirs of "the gracious gift of life" (1Pe 3:7), the promised Spirit (v. 14; 4:6) and renewal in God's image (Col 3:10–11). On the other hand, within the context of

are all one in Christ Jesus.[r] **29**If you
belong to Christ,[s] then you are Abraham's seed,[t] and heirs[u] according to
the promise.[v]
4 What I am saying is that as long as
the heir is a child, he is no different
from a slave, although he owns the
whole estate. **2**He is subject to guardians and trustees until the time set by
his father. **3**So also, when we were children, we were in slavery[w] under the
basic principles of the world.[x] **4**But
when the time had fully come,[y] God
sent his Son,[z] born of a woman,[a]
born under law,[b] **5**to redeem[c] those
under law, that we might receive the
full rights[d] of sons.[e] **6**Because you
are sons, God sent the Spirit of his
Son[f] into our hearts,[g] the Spirit who
calls out, *"Abba,*[o] Father."[h] **7**So you
are no longer a slave, but a son; and
since you are a son, God has made you
also an heir.[i]

Paul's Concern for the Galatians

8Formerly, when you did not know
God,[j] you were slaves[k] to those who
by nature are not gods.[l] **9**But now
that you know God—or rather are
known by God[m]—how is it that you
are turning back to those weak and
miserable principles? Do you wish to
be enslaved[n] by them all over
again?[o] **10**You are observing special
days and months and seasons and
years![p] **11**I fear for you, that somehow
I have wasted my efforts on you.[q]
12I plead with you, brothers,[r] become like me, for I became like you.
You have done me no wrong. **13**As you
know, it was because of an illness[s]
that I first preached the gospel to you.
14Even though my illness was a trial to
you, you did not treat me with contempt or scorn. Instead, you welcomed
me as if I were an angel of God, as if
I were Christ Jesus himself.[t] **15**What
has happened to all your joy? I can testify that, if you could have done so, you
would have torn out your eyes and giv-
en them to me. **16**Have I now become
your enemy by telling you the truth?[u]
17Those people are zealous to win
you over, but for no good. What they
want is to alienate you ⌊from us⌋, so that
you may be zealous for them.[v] **18**It is
fine to be zealous, provided the purpose is good, and to be so always and
not just when I am with you.[w] **19**My
dear children,[x] for whom I am again
in the pains of childbirth until Christ is
formed in you,[y] **20**how I wish I could

3:28 [r] Jn 10:16; 17:11; Eph 2:14, 15
3:29 [s] S 1Co 3:23 [t] ver 16; S Lk 3:8 [u] S Ro 8:17 [v] ver 16
4:3 [w] ver 8,9,24, 25; Gal 2:4 [x] Col 2:8,20
4:4 [y] Mk 1:15; Ro 5:6; Eph 1:10 [z] S Jn 3:17 [a] S Jn 1:14 [b] Lk 2:27
4:5 [c] S Ro 3:24 [d] Jn 1:12 [e] S Ro 8:14
4:6 [f] S Ac 16:7 [g] Ro 5:5 [h] Ro 8:15, 16
4:7 [i] S Ro 8:17
4:8 [j] Ro 1:28; 1Co 1:21; 15:34; 1Th 4:5; 2Th 1:8 [k] S ver 3 [l] 2Ch 13:9; Isa 37:19; Jer 2:11; 5:7; 16:20; 1Co 8:4,5
4:9 [m] 1Co 8:3 [n] S ver 3 [o] Col 2:20
4:10 [p] Ro 14:5; Col 2:16
4:11 [q] 1Th 3:5
4:12 [r] S Ro 7:1; Gal 6:18
4:13 [s] 1Co 2:3
4:14 [t] Mt 10:40
4:16 [u] Am 5:10
4:17 [v] Gal 2:4,12
4:18 [w] ver 13,14
4:19 [x] S 1Th 2:11 [y] Ro 8:29; Eph 4:13

[o] 6 Aramaic for *Father*

spiritual equality men remain men and women remain women (Ge 1:27). Their God-assigned roles in marriage and society remain unchanged (1Pe 3:1–4; see Eph 5:22–23, notes; 1Ti 2:13,15, notes).

4:2 TRUSTEES UNTIL THE TIME SET BY HIS FATHER. Paul's statement here, although primarily used to illustrate the situation of a believer under the OT covenant, indicates that godly parents normally oversaw the instruction of their children (see Dt 6:7, note). Such supervision would have been done through education in the home or by placing the children under godly teachers. Scripture clearly teaches that parents should do all they can to ensure that their children receive a holy and Christlike education and are guarded from the world's ungodly philosophies and unbiblical principles (see Lk 1:17, note; see article on PARENTS AND CHILDREN, p. 1854).

4:6 THE SPIRIT WHO CALLS OUT, *"ABBA,* FATHER." One of the Holy Spirit's tasks is to create in God's children a feeling of filial love that causes them to know God as their Father. (1) The term *"Abba"* is Aramaic, meaning "Father." It was the word Jesus used when referring to the heavenly Father. The combining of the Aramaic term *"Abba"* with the Greek term for father (*patēr*) expresses the depth of intimacy, deep emotion, earnestness, warmth and confidence by which the Spirit causes us to cry out to God (cf. Mk 14:36; Ro 8:15,26–27). Two sure signs of the Spirit's work within us are the spontaneous cry to God as "Father" and the spontaneous obedience to Jesus as "Lord" (see 1Co 12:3, note).

(2) In this passage Paul may have in mind primarily the baptism in the Holy Spirit and his continual filling (cf. Ac 1:5; 2:4; Eph 5:18), since God makes our relationship to him as children the cause for sending the Spirit. Because we are already "sons" through faith in Christ, God pours forth the Spirit into our hearts. The receiving of "the full rights of sons" (v. 5) precedes the sending of the Spirit of God's Son (see 3:5, notes).

4:13 AN ILLNESS. This illness may have been eye trouble (v. 15), malaria, Paul's thorn in the flesh (2Co 12:7) or a physical disability due to stoning. Whatever it was, it seems to have involved some kind of physical problem. Faithful believers who do the Lord's will and are active in Christian service are not immune from times of ill health, bodily pain or weakness.

4:19 THE PAINS OF CHILDBIRTH. "The pains of childbirth" (Gk *ōdinō*) pictures the heartache, pain and yearning by which Paul desires the salvation of those Galatians who have become alienated from Christ and have "fallen away from grace" (5:4). He represents them as needing a second spiritual birth and himself as a mother suffering once more with birth pangs in order that Christ might be formed in them.

be with you now and change my tone, because I am perplexed about you!

Hagar and Sarah

[21]Tell me, you who want to be under the law,[z] are you not aware of what the law says? [22]For it is written that Abraham had two sons, one by the slave woman[a] and the other by the free woman.[b] [23]His son by the slave woman was born in the ordinary way;[c] but his son by the free woman was born as the result of a promise.[d]

[24]These things may be taken figuratively, for the women represent two covenants. One covenant is from Mount Sinai and bears children who are to be slaves: This is Hagar. [25]Now Hagar stands for Mount Sinai in Arabia and corresponds to the present city of Jerusalem, because she is in slavery with her children. [26]But the Jerusalem that is above[e] is free, and she is our mother. [27]For it is written:

"Be glad, O barren woman,
 who bears no children;
break forth and cry aloud,
 you who have no labor pains;
because more are the children of
 the desolate woman
 than of her who has a
 husband."[p][f]

[28]Now you, brothers, like Isaac, are children of promise.[g] [29]At that time the son born in the ordinary way[h] persecuted the son born by the power of the Spirit.[i] It is the same now. [30]But what does the Scripture say? "Get rid of the slave woman and her son, for the slave woman's son will never share in the inheritance with the free woman's son."[q][j] [31]Therefore, brothers, we are not children of the slave woman,[k] but of the free woman.[l]

Freedom in Christ

5 It is for freedom that Christ has set us free.[m] Stand firm,[n] then, and do not let yourselves be burdened again by a yoke of slavery.[o]

[2]Mark my words! I, Paul, tell you that if you let yourselves be circumcised,[p] Christ will be of no value to you at all. [3]Again I declare to every man who lets himself be circumcised that he is obligated to obey the whole law.[q] [4]You who are trying to be justified by law[r] have been alienated from Christ; you have fallen away from grace.[s] [5]But by faith we eagerly await through the Spirit the righteousness for which we hope.[t] [6]For in Christ Jesus[u] neither circumcision nor uncircumcision has any value.[v] The only thing that counts is faith expressing itself through love.[w]

[7]You were running a good race.[x] Who cut in on you[y] and kept you from

4:21 [z]S Ro 2:12 **4:22** [a]Ge 16:15 [b]Ge 21:2 **4:23** [c]ver 28,29; Ro 9:7,8 [d]Ge 17:16-21; 18:10-14; 21:1; Heb 11:11 **4:26** [e]Heb 12:22; Rev 3:12; 21:2,10 **4:27** [f]Isa 54:1 **4:28** [g]ver 23; S Gal 3:16 **4:29** [h]ver 23 [i]Ge 21:9 **4:30** [j]Ge 21:10 **4:31** [k]S Ro 7:4 [l]ver 22 **5:1** [m]ver 13; Jn 8:32; Gal 2:4; S Ro 7:4 [n]S 1Co 16:13 [o]S Mt 23:4; Gal 2:4 **5:2** [p]ver 3,6,11, 12; Ac 15:1 **5:3** [q]Ro 2:25; Gal 3:10; Jas 2:10 **5:4** [r]S Ro 3:28 [s]Heb 12:15; 2Pe 3:17 **5:5** [t]Ro 8:23,24 **5:6** [u]S Ro 16:3 [v]S 1Co 7:19 [w]1Th 1:3; Jas 2:22 **5:7** [x]S 1Co 9:24 [y]Gal 3:1

[p] *27* Isaiah 54:1 [q] *30* Gen. 21:10

4:22 ABRAHAM HAD TWO SONS. Paul uses an illustration to show the difference between the old and new covenants. Hagar represents the old covenant established at Mount Sinai (v. 25); her children now live under this covenant and are "born in the ordinary way" (v. 23), i.e., they do not have the Holy Spirit. Sarah, Abraham's other wife, represents the new covenant; her children, i.e., believers in Christ, possess the Spirit and are true children of God who are "born by the power of the Spirit" (v. 29; see articles on GOD'S COVENANT WITH THE ISRAELITES, p. 290, and THE OLD COVENANT AND THE NEW COVENANT, p. 1926).

5:4 FALLEN AWAY FROM GRACE. Some Galatians had transferred their faith in Christ to faith in legalistic observances of the law (1:6–7; 5:3). Paul states that they have fallen away from grace. To fall away from grace is to be alienated from Christ (cf. Jn 15:4–6) and to abandon the principle of God's grace that brings life and salvation. It is to have one's association with Christ nullified and to no longer remain "in Christ" (see Jn 15:6, note; 2Pe 2:15,20–22; see article on FAITH AND GRACE, p. 1720).

5:6 FAITH EXPRESSING ITSELF THROUGH LOVE. The Bible maintains that a person is saved through faith (2:15–16; Ro 3:22; Eph 2:8–9). (1) In this passage Paul defines the exact nature of that faith. Saving faith is a living faith in a living Savior, a faith so vital that it cannot avoid expression in love-motivated deeds. (2) Faith that does not sincerely love and obey Christ (cf. 1Jn 2:3; 5:3), show a real concern for the work of God's kingdom (cf. Mt 12:28), and actively resist sin and the world (vv. 16–17) does not qualify as saving faith (cf. Jas 2:14–16; see article on FAITH AND GRACE, p. 1720).

5:7 KEPT YOU FROM OBEYING THE TRUTH. False teaching either takes the form of denying the cardinal truths of the Christian faith (see 1:9, note), or it states that something else besides what is found in the NT is required for a believer to be a complete Christian (cf. 1:6; 2:16; 5:2,6). (1) All Christian teaching must undergo the test of apostolic truth, i.e., does the teaching conform to the original message of Christ and the apostles found in the NT? (cf. 1:11–12; 2:1–2,7–9; see Eph 2:20, note). We must ask: Does a teaching contain less than the apostolic message? Does it add something unbiblical to the truth while acknowledging the apostolic message? (2) We must

obeying the truth? **8**That kind of persuasion does not come from the one
who calls you.[z] **9**"A little yeast works
through the whole batch of dough."[a]
10I am confident[b] in the Lord that you
will take no other view.[c] The one who
is throwing you into confusion[d] will
pay the penalty, whoever he may be.
11Brothers, if I am still preaching circumcision, why am I still being persecuted?[e] In that case the offense[f] of
the cross has been abolished. **12**As for
those agitators,[g] I wish they would go
the whole way and emasculate themselves!

13You, my brothers, were called to
be free.[h] But do not use your freedom
to indulge the sinful nature[r];[i] rather, serve one another[j] in love. **14**The
entire law is summed up in a single
command: "Love your neighbor as
yourself."[s][k] **15**If you keep on biting
and devouring each other, watch out or
you will be destroyed by each other.

Life by the Spirit

16So I say, live by the Spirit,[l] and
you will not gratify the desires of the
sinful nature.[m] **17**For the sinful nature
desires what is contrary to the Spirit,
and the Spirit what is contrary to the
sinful nature.[n] They are in conflict
with each other, so that you do not do
what you want.[o] **18**But if you are led
by the Spirit,[p] you are not under
law.[q]

19The acts of the sinful nature are
obvious: sexual immorality,[r] impurity
and debauchery; **20**idolatry and witchcraft; hatred, discord, jealousy, fits of
rage, selfish ambition, dissensions,
factions **21**and envy; drunkenness, orgies, and the like.[s] I warn you, as I did
before, that those who live like this will
not inherit the kingdom of God.[t]

22But the fruit[u] of the Spirit is
love,[v] joy, peace,[w] patience, kindness, goodness, faithfulness, **23**gentleness and self-control.[x] Against such
things there is no law.[y] **24**Those who
belong to Christ Jesus have crucified
the sinful nature[z] with its passions
and desires.[a] **25**Since we live by the
Spirit,[b] let us keep in step with the
Spirit. **26**Let us not become conceited,[c] provoking and envying each other.

Doing Good to All

6 Brothers, if someone is caught
in a sin, you who are spiritual[d]

5:8 [z]S Ro 8:28 **5:9** [a]1Co 5:6 **5:10** [b]S 2Co 2:3 [c]Php 3:15 [d]ver 12; Gal 1:7 **5:11** [e]Gal 4:29; 6:12 [f]S Lk 2:34 **5:12** [g]ver 10 **5:13** [h]S ver 1 [i]S ver 24; 1Co 8:9; 1Pe 2:16 [j]1Co 9:19; 2Co 4:5; Eph 5:21 **5:14** [k]Lev 19:18; S Mt 5:43; Gal 6:2 **5:16** [l]ver 18,25; Ro 8:2,4-6,9,14; S 2Co 5:17 [m]S ver 24 **5:17** [n]Ro 8:5-8 [o]Ro 7:15-23 **5:18** [p]S ver 16 [q]S Ro 2:12; 1Ti 1:9 **5:19** [r]S 1Co 6:18 **5:21** [s]Mt 15:19; Ro 13:13 [t]S Mt 25:34 **5:22** [u]Mt 7:16-20; Eph 5:9 [v]Col 3:12-15 [w]Mal 2:6 **5:23** [x]S Ac 24:25 [y]ver 18 **5:24** [z]ver 13, 16-21; S Ro 6:6; 7:5,18; 8:3-5,8,9, 12,13; 13:14; Gal 6:8; Col 2:11 [a]ver 16,17 **5:25** [b]S ver 16 **5:26** [c]Php 2:3 **6:1** [d]1Co 2:15; 3:1

[r] *13* Or *the flesh*; also in verses 16, 17, 19 and 24 [s] *14* Lev. 19:18

never test teaching solely by feelings, experience, results, miracles or by what other people are saying. The NT is the ultimate standard for truth. (3) We must beware of any teaching that says God's Word is no longer sufficient and that the church needs modern scholarship, science, philosophy, psychology or new revelations in order to reach maturity in Christ.

5:13 CALLED TO BE FREE. See 2Co 3:17, note on Christian freedom.

5:17 THE SPIRIT . . . THE SINFUL NATURE. The spiritual conflict within believers involves the whole person; the struggle is whether they will surrender to the sinful nature's inclinations and again submit to sin's control, or whether they will yield to the Spirit's demands and continue under Christ's dominion (v. 16; Ro 8:4–14). The battlefield is within Christians themselves, and the conflict must continue throughout their earthly lives if they are to eventually reign with Christ (Ro 7:7–25; 2Ti 2:12; Rev 12:11; see Eph 6:11, note).

5:19 ACTS OF THE SINFUL NATURE. For comments on the individual acts, see article on THE ACTS OF THE SINFUL NATURE AND THE FRUIT OF THE SPIRIT, p. 1818.

5:21 NOT INHERIT THE KINGDOM OF GOD. Although Paul maintains that it is impossible to inherit the kingdom of God by observing the law (2:16; 5:4), he does teach it is possible to shut oneself out of the kingdom by engaging in evil practices (see 1Co 6:9, note; cf. Mt 25:41–46; Eph 5:7–11).

5:22–23 THE FRUIT OF THE SPIRIT. For comments on the various aspects of the fruit of the Spirit, see article on THE ACTS OF THE SINFUL NATURE AND THE FRUIT OF THE SPIRIT, p. 1818.

6:1 RESTORE HIM GENTLY. The word "restore" (Gk *katartizō*) is used in the NT for mending fishing nets (Mt 4:21) or for perfecting human character (2Co 13:11). Thus, to restore a person means to lead him or her back to true repentance and to a full commitment to Jesus Christ and his ways. This may involve disciplinary action (see Mt 13:30, note), undertaken "gently."

(1) Paul here is not thinking of the serious sins that bring public disgrace to the congregation (cf. 1Co 5:5). Such sins may require temporary expulsion from the fellowship before restoration is granted (1Co 5:11).

(2) The restoration Paul mentions does not refer to restoration to leadership positions or teaching roles within the church. Qualifications and standards for those desiring to serve in ministerial positions involve more than a person's present spiritual condition. They require a history of persevering faithfulness to God's principles for righteousness in order that they may set an example for believers (1Ti 4:12; see article on MORAL

should restore[e] him gently. But watch
yourself, or you also may be tempted.
2Carry each other's burdens, and in
this way you will fulfill the law of
Christ.[f] 3If anyone thinks he is something[g] when he is nothing, he deceives himself.[h] 4Each one should
test his own actions. Then he can
take pride in himself,[i] without comparing himself to somebody else,[j]
5for each one should carry his own
load.[k]

6Anyone who receives instruction in
the word must share all good things
with his instructor.[l]

7Do not be deceived:[m] God cannot
be mocked. A man reaps what he
sows.[n] 8The one who sows to please
his sinful nature,[o] from that nature[t]
will reap destruction;[p] the one who
sows to please the Spirit, from the
Spirit will reap eternal life.[q] 9Let us
not become weary in doing good,[r] for
at the proper time we will reap a harvest if we do not give up.[s] 10There-
fore, as we have opportunity, let us do
good[t] to all people, especially to
those who belong to the family[u] of believers.

6:1 [e] S Mt 18:15; S 2Co 2:7
6:2 [f] 1Co 9:21; Jas 2:8
6:3 [g] Ro 12:3; 1Co 8:2 [h] 1Co 3:18
6:4 [i] 2Co 13:5 [j] 2Co 10:12
6:5 [k] ver 2; Jer 31:30
6:6 [l] 1Co 9:11,14; 1Ti 5:17,18
6:7 [m] S 1Co 6:9 [n] Pr 22:8; Jer 34:17; Hos 10:12,13; 2Co 9:6
6:8 [o] S Gal 5:24 [p] Job 4:8; Hos 8:7; S Ro 6:23 [q] Jas 3:18
6:9 [r] 1Co 15:58; 2Co 4:1 [s] Job 42:12; Ps 126:5; Heb 12:3; Rev 2:10
6:10 [t] Pr 3:27; S Tit 2:14 [u] Eph 2:19; 1Pe 4:17
6:11 [v] S 1Co 16:21
6:12 [w] Mt 23:25,26 [x] Ac 15:1 [y] Gal 5:11
6:13 [z] Ro 2:25 [a] Php 3:3
6:14 [b] 1Co 2:2 [c] S Ro 6:2,6
6:15 [d] S 1Co 7:19 [e] S 2Co 5:17
6:17 [f] Isa 44:5; S 2Co 1:5; 11:23
6:18 [g] S Ro 16:20 [h] Php 4:23; 2Ti 4:22; Phm 25

Not Circumcision but a New Creation

11See what large letters I use as I
write to you with my own hand![v]

12Those who want to make a good
impression outwardly[w] are trying to
compel you to be circumcised.[x] The
only reason they do this is to avoid being persecuted[y] for the cross of
Christ. 13Not even those who are circumcised obey the law,[z] yet they want
you to be circumcised that they may
boast about your flesh.[a] 14May I never boast except in the cross of our Lord
Jesus Christ,[b] through which[u] the
world has been crucified to me, and I
to the world.[c] 15Neither circumcision 2Ti 3:1-5
nor uncircumcision means anything;[d]
what counts is a new creation.[e]
16Peace and mercy to all who follow
this rule, even to the Israel of God.

17Finally, let no one cause me trouble, for I bear on my body the marks[f]
of Jesus.

18The grace of our Lord Jesus
Christ[g] be with your spirit,[h] brothers. Amen.

[t] *8* Or *his flesh, from the flesh* [u] *14* Or *whom*

QUALIFICATIONS FOR OVERSEERS, p.1882).

6:2 CARRY EACH OTHER'S BURDENS. To carry each other's burdens includes helping needy people in times of sickness, sorrow and financial stress. Paul may have in mind the support of missionaries and teachers (see v. 6, note; cf. Ro 15:1; 1Co 9:14). To carry another's burden is a divine quality (Ps 55:22; 1Pe 5:7).

6:6–10 SHARE ALL GOOD THINGS. It is the duty of all who are taught God's Word to help provide material support for those who instruct (1Co 9:14; 1Ti 5:18). Those who are worthy of support include faithful pastors, workers, teachers, evangelists or missionaries (1Co 9:14; 3Jn 6–8). To refuse to give support, if means are available, is to sow selfishness and reap destruction (vv. 7–9). To give to those who minister in the Word is a part of doing good to those who belong to the family of believers (v. 10); "at the proper time we will reap" (v. 9) both reward (Mt 10:41–42) and eternal life (v. 8).

6:7 GOD CANNOT BE MOCKED. Those who claim to be born-again, Spirit-filled followers of Christ (v. 3), while at the same time consciously sowing to please the sinful nature (5:19–21), are guilty of mocking and despising God. Let there be no deception: such persons will not reap "eternal life" but "destruction" (v. 8) and "death" (Ro 6:20–23; see 1Co 6:9, note).

6:14 THE WORLD HAS BEEN CRUCIFIED TO ME. The cross of Christ, representing the horrible death that the Savior suffered for our eternal salvation, is now the barrier by which the world is fenced off from us and us from the world. "The world" means everything that is opposed to God, his kingdom and his righteousness (cf. 4:3; 1Co 2:12; 3:19; 1Jn 2:15–17). (1) For those who make the cross their life and their boast, the world with all its accepted standards, values, opinions, honors and lifestyles is no longer cherished or loved. (2) For us to be "crucified with Christ" (2:20) includes our being crucified to the world. There is no sharing in the salvation and glory of Christ's cross without turning our backs on all the earthly pleasures that draw our hearts away from Christ and his nearness.

6:16 ISRAEL OF GOD. This term refers to all God's people under the new covenant, i.e., both believing Jews and believing Gentiles. All who through "the cross of our Lord Jesus Christ" are crucified to the world (v. 14) and become a "new creation" (v. 15) constitute the true "Israel of God" (cf. Ro 2:28–29; 9:7–8; Eph 2:14–22; Php 3:3; 1Pe 2:9).

THE ACTS OF THE SINFUL NATURE AND THE FRUIT OF THE SPIRIT

Gal 5:22–23 "But the fruit of the Spirit is love, joy, peace, patience, kindness, goodness, faithfulness, gentleness and self-control. Against such things there is no law."

No passage in the Bible draws a clearer contrast between the lifestyle of the Spirit-filled believer and that of the person controlled by the sinful human nature than Gal 5:16–26. Paul not only discusses general lifestyle differences by emphasizing that the Spirit and the sinful nature are at war with each other, but he also includes a specific list of both the acts of the sinful nature and the fruit of the Spirit.

THE ACTS OF THE SINFUL NATURE. "Sinful nature" (Gk *sarx*) pictures the human nature with its corrupt desires. The sinful nature remains within Christians after their conversion and is their deadly enemy (Ro 8:6–8,13; Gal 5:17,21). Those who practice the acts of the sinful nature cannot inherit God's kingdom (Gal 5:21). Therefore, this sinful nature must be resisted and put to death in a continual warfare that the believer wages through the power of the Holy Spirit (Ro 8:4–14; see Gal 5:17, note). The acts of the sinful nature (Gal 5:19–21) include:

(1) "Sexual immorality" (Gk *porneia*), i.e., immoral sexual conduct and intercourse; it includes taking pleasure in pornographic pictures, films or writings (cf. Ex 20:14; Mt 5:31–32; 19:9; Ac 15:20,29; 21:25; 1Co 5:1);

(2) "Impurity" (Gk *akatharsia*), i.e., sexual sins, evil deeds and vices, including thoughts and desires of the heart (Eph 5:3; Col 3:5);

(3) "Debauchery" (Gk *aselgeia*), i.e., sensuality; following one's passions and desires to the point of having no shame or public decency (2Co 12:21);

(4) "Idolatry" (Gk *eidōlolatria*), i.e., worship of spirits, persons or graven images; trust in any person, institution or thing as having equal or greater authority than God and his Word (Col 3:5);

(5) "Witchcraft" (Gk *pharmakeia*), i.e., sorcery, spiritism, black magic, worship of demons and use of drugs to produce "spiritual" experiences (Ex 7:11,22; 8:18; Rev 9:21; 18:23);

(6) "Hatred" (Gk *echthra*), i.e., intense, hostile intentions and acts; extreme dislike or enmity;

(7) "Discord" (Gk *eris*), i.e., quarreling, antagonism; a struggle for superiority (Ro 1:29; 1Co 1:11; 3:3);

(8) "Jealousy" (Gk *zēlos*), i.e., resentfulness, envy of another's success (Ro 13:13; 1Co 3:3);

(9) "Fits of rage" (Gk *thumos*), i.e., explosive anger that flames into violent words or deeds (Col 3:8);

(10) "Selfish ambition" (Gk *eritheia*), i.e., seeking of power (2Co 12:20; Php 1:16–17);

(11) "Dissensions" (Gk *dichostasia*), i.e., introducing divisive teachings not supported by God's Word (Ro 16:17);

(12) "Factions" (Gk *hairesis*), i.e., division within the congregation into selfish groups or cliques that destroy the unity of the church (1Co 11:19);

(13) "Envy" (Gk *phthonos*), i.e., resentful dislike of another person who has something that one desires;

(14) "Drunkenness" (Gk *methē*), i.e., impairing one's mental or physical control by alcoholic drink;

(15) "Orgies" (Gk *kōmos*), i.e., excessive feasting and revelry; a party spirit involving alcohol, drugs, sex, or the like.

Paul's final comment on the acts of the sinful nature is stern and forceful: any so-called Christians who engage in these types of activities shut themselves out of the kingdom of God, i.e., they do not possess eternal salvation (Gal 5:21; see 1Co 6:9, note).

THE FRUIT OF THE SPIRIT. Contrasted to the acts of the sinful nature is a single-minded lifestyle called "the fruit of the Spirit." This is produced in God's children as they allow the Spirit to so direct and influence their lives that they destroy sin's power, especially the acts of the sinful nature, and walk in fellowship with God (see Ro 8:5–14, note; 8:14, note; cf. 2Co 6:6; Eph 4:2–3; 5:9; Col 3:12–15; 2Pe 1:4–9). The fruit of the Spirit includes:

(1) "Love" (Gk *agapē*), i.e., a caring for and seeking the highest good of another person without motive of personal gain (Ro 5:5; 1Co 13; Eph 5:2; Col 3:14);

(2) "Joy" (Gk *chara*), i.e., the feeling of gladness based on the love, grace, blessings, promises and nearness of God that belong to those who believe in Christ (Ps 119:16; 2Co 6:10; 12:9; 1Pe 1:8; see Php 1:14, note);

(3) "Peace" (Gk *eirēnē*), i.e., the quietness of heart and mind based on the knowledge that all is well between the believer and his or her heavenly Father (Ro 15:33; Php 4:7; 1Th 5:23; Heb 13:20);

(4) "Patience" (Gk *makrothumia*), i.e., endurance, long-suffering; being slow to anger or despair (Eph 4:2; 2Ti 3:10; Heb 12:1);

(5) "Kindness" (Gk *chrēstotēs*), i.e., not wanting to hurt anyone or cause them pain (Eph 4:32; Col 3:12; 1Pe 2:3);

(6) "Goodness" (Gk *agathōsunē*), i.e., zeal for truth and righteousness and a hatred of evil; it can be expressed in acts of kindness (Lk 7:37–50) or in rebuking and correcting evil (Mt 21:12–13);

(7) "Faithfulness" (Gk *pistis*), i.e., firm and unswerving loyalty to a person to whom one is united by promise, commitment, trustworthiness and honesty (Mt 23:23; Ro 3:3; 1Ti 6:12; 2Ti 2:2; 4:7; Tit 2:10);

(8) "Gentleness" (Gk *prautēs*), i.e., restraint coupled with strength and courage; it describes a person who can be angry when anger is needed and humbly submissive when submission is needed (2Ti 2:25; 1Pe 3:15; for gentleness in Jesus, compare Mt 11:29 with Mt 23 and Mk 3:5; in Paul, compare 2Co 10:1 with 10:4–6 and Gal 1:9; in Moses, compare Nu 12:3 with Ex 32:19–20);

(9) "Self-control" (Gk *egkrateia*), i.e., mastering one's own desires and passions, including faithfulness to one's marriage vows; also purity (1Co 7:9; 9:25; Tit 1:8; 2:5).

Paul's final comment on the fruit of the Spirit indicates that there are no restrictions to the lifestyle indicated here. Christians can—in fact, must—practice these virtues over and over again; they will never discover a law prohibiting them from living according to these principles.

EPHESIANS

Outline

Christian Greetings (1:1–2)
- I. Powerful Doctrine—The Believer's Redemption (1:3—3:21)
  - A. The Preeminence of Christ in Redemption (1:3–14)
    1. His Preeminence in the Father's Plan (1:3–6)
    2. His Preeminence in the Believer's Participation (1:7–12)
    3. His Preeminence in the Spirit's Application (1:13–14)

    Prayer: For the Believer's Spiritual Enlightenment (1:15–23)
  - B. The Results of Redemption in Christ (2:1—3:21)
    1. Releases Us From Sin and Death to New Life in Christ (2:1–10)
    2. Reconciles Us to Others Who Are Being Saved (2:11–15)
    3. Unites Us in Christ in One Household (2:16–22)
    4. Reveals God's Wisdom Through the Church (3:1–13)

    Prayer: For the Believer's Spiritual Fulfillment (3:14–21)
- II. Practical Instruction—The Believer's Life (4:1—6:20)
  - A. The Believer's New Life (4:1—5:21)
    1. In Harmony with God's Purpose for the Church (4:1–16)
    2. A New Life of Purity (4:17—5:7)
    3. Living as Children of Light (5:8–14)
    4. Careful and Spirit-filled (5:15–21)
  - B. The Believer's Domestic Relationships (5:22—6:9)
    1. Wives and Husbands (5:22–33)
    2. Children and Parents (6:1–4)
    3. Slaves and Masters (6:5–9)
  - C. The Believer's Spiritual Warfare (6:10–20)
    1. Our Ally—God (6:10–11a)
    2. Our Enemy—Satan and His Forces (6:11a–12)
    3. Our Equipment—Full Armor of God (6:13–20)

Conclusion (6:21–24)

Author: Paul

Theme: Christ and the Church

Date of Writing: C. A.D. 62

Background

Ephesians is one of the mountain peaks of Biblical revelation and has a unique place among Paul's letters. Rather than being hammered out on the anvil of doctrinal controversy or pastoral problems as many of Paul's other letters were, Ephesians conveys the impression of a rich overflow of revelation growing out of Paul's personal prayer life. Paul wrote this letter while a prisoner on behalf of Christ (3:1; 4:1; 6:20), most likely at Rome. Ephesians has numerous affinities with Colossians and probably was penned shortly after Colossians. Both letters may have been carried simultaneously to their destination by a co-worker of Paul named Tychicus (6:21; cf. Col 4:7).

It is commonly believed that Paul wrote Ephesians with a wider readership in mind than just the church in Ephesus—perhaps intending it to serve as a circular letter for churches throughout the province of Asia. Originally each church in Asia Minor may have inserted its own name in 1:1, testifying to the relevance of its profound message for all true churches of Jesus Christ. Many think Ephesians is the so-called letter to the Laodiceans, mentioned by Paul in Col 4:16.

Purpose

Paul's immediate purpose for writing Ephesians is implied in 1:15–17. He prayerfully longs for his readers to advance in faith, love, wisdom and revelation of the Father of glory. He earnestly desires that they live lives worthy of the Lord Jesus Christ (e.g., 4:1–3; 5:1–2). Paul, therefore, seeks to strengthen their faith and spiritual foundations by revealing the fullness of God's eternal purpose of redemption "in Christ" (1:3–14; 3:10–12) for the church (1:22–23; 2:11–22; 3:21; 4:11–16; 5:25–27) and for each individual (1:15–21; 2:1–10; 3:16–20; 4:1–3,17–32; 5:1—6:20).

Survey

In the simplest possible terms there are two basic themes in the NT: (1) how we are redeemed by God, and (2) how we as the redeemed must live. Chs. 1–3 of Ephesians address largely the former theme, while chs. 4–6 focus on the latter.

(1) Chs. 1–3 are introduced by an opening paragraph that is one of the most profound passages in the Bible (1:3–14). This magnificent hymn of redemption offers praise for the Father's election, predestination and adoption of us as his children (1:3–6), for the Son redeeming us through his blood (1:7–12), and for the Spirit as our seal and first installment of our inheritance (1:13–14). In these chapters Paul stresses that in redemption by grace through faith God is reconciling us to himself (2:1–10) and to others who are being saved (2:11–15), and is uniting us in Christ in one body, the church (2:16–22). The goal of redemption is "to bring all things in heaven and on earth together under one head, even Christ" (1:10).

(2) Chs. 4–6 consist largely of practical instructions for the church about the demands that redemption in Christ makes on our lives individually and corporately. Among the 35 directives given in Ephesians on how the redeemed ought to live, three broad categories are emphasized. (1) Believers are called to a new life of purity and separation from the world. They are called to "be holy and blameless in his sight" (1:4), "become a holy temple" (2:21), "live a life worthy of [their] calling" (4:1), "become mature" (4:13), live "in true righteousness and holiness" (4:24), "live a life of love" (5:2; cf. 3:17–19), and be holy "through the word" (5:26) in order that Christ may have a "church, without stain or wrinkle . . . holy and blameless" (5:27). (2) Believers are called to a new way of life in family and vocational relationships (5:22—6:9). These relationships are to be governed by principles that mark believers as distinctly different from the secular society in which they live. (3) Finally, believers are called to stand firm against all the devil's schemes and against the formidable "spiritual forces of evil in the heavenly realms" (6:10–20).

Special Features

Five major features characterize this letter. (1) The unfolding of great theological truth in chs. 1–3 is interrupted by two of the most powerful apostolic prayers of the NT: one asks for wisdom and revelation in a knowledge of God (1:15–23); the other focuses on knowing the love, power and glory of God (3:14–21). (2) "In Christ," a weighty Pauline expression (160 times in Paul's letters), is especially prominent in Ephesians (c. 36 times). "Every spiritual blessing" and every practical issue of life relate to being "in Christ." (3) God's eternal purpose and goal for the church is emphasized in Ephesians. (4) There is a multifaceted emphasis on the role of the Holy Spirit in the Christian life (1:13–14,17; 2:18; 3:5,16,20; 4:3–4,30; 5:18; 6:17–18). (5) Ephesians is sometimes regarded as a "twin letter" with Colossians, because the two have certain resemblances in content and were written about the same time (cf. the outlines to the two letters).

Reading Ephesians

In order to read the entire New Testament in one year, the book of Ephesians should be read in 9 days, according to the following schedule:
☐ 1:1–14 ☐ 1:15–2:10 ☐ 2:11–22 ☐ 3 ☐ 4:1–16 ☐ 4:17–5:2 ☐ 5:3–21 ☐ 5:22–6:9 ☐ 6:10–24

NOTES

1

Paul, an apostle[a] of Christ Jesus
by the will of God,[b]

To the saints[c] in Ephesus,[a][d] the
faithful[b][e] in Christ Jesus:

2Grace and peace to you from God
our Father and the Lord Jesus Christ.[f]

Spiritual Blessings in Christ

3Praise be to the God and Father of
our Lord Jesus Christ,[g] who has
blessed us in the heavenly realms[h]
with every spiritual blessing in Christ.
4For he chose us[i] in him before the
creation of the world[j] to be holy and
blameless[k] in his sight. In love[l]
5he[c] predestined[m] us to be adopted
as his sons[n] through Jesus Christ, in
accordance with his pleasure[o] and
will— 6to the praise of his glorious
grace,[p] which he has freely given us
in the One he loves.[q] 7In him we have
redemption[r] through his blood,[s] the
forgiveness of sins, in accordance with
the riches[t] of God's grace 8that he
lavished on us with all wisdom and understanding. 9And he[d] made known to
us the mystery[u] of his will according
to his good pleasure, which he purposed[v] in Christ, 10to be put into effect when the times will have reached
their fulfillment[w]—to bring all things
in heaven and on earth together under
one head, even Christ.[x]

11In him we were also chosen,[e]
having been predestined[y] according
to the plan of him who works out everything in conformity with the purpose[z]
of his will, 12in order that we, who were
the first to hope in Christ, might be for
the praise of his glory.[a] 13And you
also were included in Christ[b] when
you heard the word of truth,[c] the gospel of your salvation. Having believed,
you were marked in him with a seal,[d]
the promised Holy Spirit,[e] 14who is a
deposit guaranteeing our inheritance[f]
until the redemption[g] of those who
are God's possession—to the praise of
his glory.[h]

1:1 [a] S 1Co 1:1 [b] S 2Co 1:1 [c] S Ac 9:13 [d] S Ac 18:19 [e] Col 1:2
1:2 [f] S Ro 1:7
1:3 [g] 2Co 1:3; 1Pe 1:3 [h] ver 20; Eph 2:6; 3:10; 6:12
1:4 [i] 2Th 2:13 [j] S Mt 25:34 [k] Lev 11:44; 20:7; 2Sa 22:24; Ps 15:2; Eph 5:27; Col 1:22 [l] Eph 4:2, 15,16
1:5 [m] ver 11; Ro 8:29,30 [n] S Ro 8:14,15 [o] Lk 12:32; 1Co 1:21; Col 1:19
1:6 [p] ver 12,14 [q] Mt 3:17
1:7 [r] ver 14; S Ro 3:24 [s] S Ro 3:25 [t] S Ro 2:4
1:9 [u] S Ro 16:25 [v] S ver 11
1:10 [w] Mk 1:15; Ro 5:6; Gal 4:4 [x] Col 1:20
1:11 [y] ver 5; Ro 8:29,30 [z] ver 9; Ro 8:28; Eph 3:11; Heb 6:17
1:12 [a] ver 6,14
1:13 [b] S Ro 16:3 [c] Eph 4:21; Col 1:5 [d] Eph 4:30 [e] Jn 14:16,17
1:14 [f] S Ac 20:32; S 2Co 5:5 [g] ver 7; S Ro 3:24 [h] ver 6,12

[a] *1* Some early manuscripts do not have *in Ephesus.* [b] *1* Or *believers who are* [c] *4,5* Or *sight in love. 5He* [d] *8,9* Or *us. With all wisdom and understanding, 9he* [e] *11* Or *were made heirs*

1:1 IN CHRIST JESUS. Every "faithful" believer has life only "in Christ Jesus." (1) The terms "in Christ Jesus," "in the Lord," "in him," etc., occur 160 times in Paul's writings (36 times in Ephesians). "In Christ" means that the believer now lives and acts in the sphere of Christ Jesus. Union with Christ is the redeemed Christian's new environment. "In Christ" believers have conscious communion with their Lord, and in this relationship their very lives are seen as the life of Christ living in them (see Gal 2:20, note). This personal fellowship with Christ is the most important thing in Christian experience. Union with Christ comes as a gift of God through faith.

(2) The Bible contrasts our new life "in Christ" with our old unregenerated life "in Adam." Whereas the old life is characterized by disobedience, sin, condemnation and death, our new life "in Christ" is characterized by salvation, life in the Spirit, abundant grace, righteousness and eternal life (see Ro 5:12–21; 6; 8; 14:17–19; 1Co 15:21–22,45–49; Php 2:1–5; 4:6–9; see article on FAITH AND GRACE, p. 1720).

1:4 CHOSE. See article on ELECTION AND PREDESTINATION, p. 1824.

1:5 PREDESTINED. See article on ELECTION AND PREDESTINATION, p. 1824.

1:5 ADOPTED. See 1Jn 3:1, note.

1:13 SEAL . . . HOLY SPIRIT. As a seal, the Holy Spirit is given to believers as God's mark of ownership. By bestowing the Spirit, God marks us as his own (see 2Co 1:22). Therefore, we have the evidence that we are God's adopted children and that our redemption is real when the Holy Spirit is present in our lives (v. 5). We can know that we really belong to God when the Spirit regenerates and renews us (Jn 1:12–13; 3:3–6), delivers us from the power of sin (Ro 8:1–17; Gal 5:16–25), gives us a consciousness of God as our Father (v. 5; Ro 8:15; Gal 4:6) and fills us with power to witness for him (Ac 1:8; 2:4).

1:13 HOLY SPIRIT. The Holy Spirit and his place in the believer's redemption is a central emphasis in the book of Ephesians. The Holy Spirit (1) is the mark or seal of God's ownership (v. 13); (2) is the first installment of the believer's inheritance (v. 14); (3) is the Spirit of wisdom and revelation (v. 17); (4) helps the believer when he or she draws near to God (2:18); (5) builds the body of believers into a holy temple (2:21–22); (6) reveals the mystery of Christ (3:4–5); (7) strengthens the believer with power in the inner being (3:16); (8) motivates unity in the Christian faith in full Christlikeness (4:3,13–14); (9) grieves when there is sin in the life of the believer (4:30); (10) desires to repeatedly fill and empower the believer (5:18); and (11) helps in prayer and spiritual warfare (6:18).

1:13–14 HOLY SPIRIT . . . A DEPOSIT. The Holy Spirit is a "deposit," i.e., a first installment or down payment, guaranteeing our inheritance. In this age the Holy Spirit is given to believers as a down payment of what we are going to have in greater fullness in the future. His presence and work in our lives is a pledge of our future inheritance (cf. Ro 8:23; 2Co 1:22; 5:5).

ELECTION AND PREDESTINATION

Eph 1:4–5 "For he chose us in him before the creation of the world to be holy and blameless in his sight. In love he predestined us to be adopted as his sons through Jesus Christ, in accordance with his pleasure and will."

ELECTION. God's choice of those who believe in Christ is an important doctrine to the apostle Paul (see Ro 8:29–33; 9:6–26; 11:5,7,28; Col 3:12; 1Th 1:4; 2Th 2:13; Tit 1:1). Election (Gk *eklegō*) refers to God's choice in Christ of a people in order that they should be holy and blameless in his sight (cf. 2Th 2:13). Paul sees this election as expressing God's love as God receives as his own all who receive his Son, Jesus (Jn 1:12). The doctrine of election involves the following truths:

(1) Election is Christocentric, i.e., election of humans occurs only in union with Jesus Christ. "He chose us in him" (Eph 1:4; see 1:1, note). Jesus himself is first of all the elect of God. Concerning Jesus, God states, "Here is my servant whom I have chosen" (Mt 12:18; cf. Isa 42:1,6; 1Pe 2:4). Christ, as the elect, is the foundation of our election. Only in union with Christ do we become members of the elect (Eph 1:4,6–7,9–10,12–13). No one is elect apart from union with Christ through faith.

(2) Election is "in him . . . through his blood" (Eph 1:7). God purposed before creation (Eph 1:4) to form a people through Christ's redemptive death on the cross. Thus election is grounded in Christ's sacrificial death to save us from our sins (Ac 20:28; Ro 3:24–26).

(3) Election in Christ is primarily corporate, i.e., an election of a people (Eph 1:4–5,7,9). The elect are called "the body of Christ" (4:12), "my church" (Mt 16:18), "a people belonging to God" (1Pe 2:9), and the "bride" of Christ (Rev 19:7). Therefore, election is corporate and embraces individual persons only as they identify and associate themselves with the body of Christ, the true church (Eph 1:22–23; see Robert Shank, *Elect in the Son*, [Minneapolis: Bethany House Publishers], pp. 45–55). This was true already of Israel in the OT (see Dt 29:18–21, note; 2Ki 21:14, note; see article on GOD'S COVENANT WITH THE ISRAELITES, p. 290).

(4) The election to salvation and holiness of the body of Christ is always certain. But the certainty of election for individuals remains conditional on their personal living faith in Jesus Christ and perseverance in union with him. Paul demonstrates this as follows. (a) God's eternal purpose for the church is that we should "be holy and blameless in his sight" (Eph 1:4). This refers both to forgiveness of sins (1:7) and to the church's sanctification and holiness. God's elect people are being led by the Holy Spirit toward sanctification and holiness (see Ro 8:14; Gal 5:16–25). The apostle repeatedly emphasizes this paramount purpose of God (see Eph 2:10; 3:14–19; 4:1–3,13–24; 5:1–18). (b) Fulfillment of this purpose for the corporate church is certain: Christ will "present her to himself as a radiant church . . . holy and blameless" (Eph 5:27). (c) Fulfillment of this purpose for individuals in the church is conditional. Christ will present us "holy and blameless in his sight" (Eph 1:4) only if we continue in the faith. Paul states this clearly: Christ will "present you holy in his sight without blemish . . . if you continue in your faith, established and firm, not moved from the hope held out in the gospel" (Col 1:22–23).

(5) Election to salvation in Christ is offered to all (Jn 3:16–17; 1Ti 2:4–6; Tit 2:11; Heb 2:9) and becomes actual for particular persons contingent on their repentance and faith as they accept God's gift of salvation in Christ (Eph 2:8; 3:17; cf. Ac 20:21; Ro 1:16; 4:16). At the point of faith, the believer is incorporated into Christ's elect body (the church) by the Holy Spirit (1Co 12:13), thereby becoming one of the elect. Thus, both God and humans have a decision in election (see Ro 8:29, note; 2Pe 1:1–11).

PREDESTINATION. Predestination (Gk *proorizō*) means "to decide beforehand" and applies to God's purposes comprehended in election. Election is God's choice "in Christ" of a people (the true church) for himself. Predestination comprehends what will happen to God's people (all genuine believers in Christ).

(1) God predestines his elect to be: (a) called (Ro 8:30); (b) justified (Ro 3:24; 8:30); (c) glorified (Ro 8:30); (d) conformed to the likeness of his Son (Ro 8:29); (e) holy and blameless (Eph 1:4); (f) adopted as God's children (1:5); (g) redeemed (1:7); (h) recipients of an inheritance (1:14); (i) for the praise of his glory (Eph 1:12; 1Pe 2:9); (j) recipients of the Holy Spirit (Eph 1:13; Gal 3:14); and (k) created to do good works (Eph 2:10).

(2) Predestination, like election, refers to the corporate body of Christ (i.e., the true spiritual church), and comprehends individuals only in association with that body through a living faith in Jesus Christ (Eph 1:5,7,13; cf. Ac 2:38–41; 16:31).

SUMMARY. Concerning election and predestination, we might use the analogy of a great ship on its way to heaven. The ship (the church) is chosen by God to be his very own vessel. Christ is the Captain and Pilot of this ship. All who desire to be a part of this elect ship and its Captain can do so through a living faith in Christ, by which they come on board the ship. As long as they are on the ship, in company with the ship's Captain, they are among the elect. If they choose to abandon the ship and Captain, they cease to be part of the elect. Election is always only in union with the Captain and his ship. Predestination tells us about the ship's destination and what God has prepared for those remaining on it. God invites everyone to come aboard the elect ship through faith in Jesus Christ.

Thanksgiving and Prayer

15For this reason, ever since I heard
about your faith in the Lord Jesus[i]
and your love for all the saints,[j] 16I
have not stopped giving thanks for
you,[k] remembering you in my
prayers.[l] 17I keep asking that the
God of our Lord Jesus Christ, the glorious Father,[m] may give you the Spirit[f]
of wisdom[n] and revelation, so that you
may know him better. 18I pray also
that the eyes of your heart may be enlightened[o] in order that you may
know the hope to which he has called[p]
you, the riches[q] of his glorious inheritance[r] in the saints,[s] 19and his incomparably great power for us who believe. That power[t] is like the working
of his mighty strength,[u] 20which he
exerted in Christ when he raised him
from the dead[v] and seated him at his
right hand[w] in the heavenly realms,[x]
21far above all rule and authority, power and dominion,[y] and every title[z]
that can be given, not only in the
present age but also in the one to
come.[a] 22And God placed all things
under his feet[b] and appointed him to
be head[c] over everything for the
church, 23which is his body,[d] the fullness of him[e] who fills everything in
every way.[f]

1:15 [i]S Ac 20:21 [j]S Col 1:4
1:16 [k]S Ro 1:8 [l]S Ro 1:10
1:17 [m]Jn 20:17; Ro 15:6; Rev 1:6 [n]Ex 28:3; Isa 11:2; Php 1:9; Col 1:9
1:18 [o]Job 42:5; 2Co 4:6; Heb 6:4 [p]S Ro 8:28 [q]ver 7; S Ro 2:4 [r]ver 11 [s]Col 1:12
1:19 [t]Eph 3:7; Col 1:29 [u]Isa 40:26; Eph 6:10
1:20 [v]S Ac 2:24 [w]S Mk 16:19 [x]S ver 3
1:21 [y]Eph 3:10; Col 1:16 [z]Php 2:9,10 [a]S Mt 12:32
1:22 [b]S Mt 22:44; S 28:18 [c]1Co 11:3; Eph 4:15; 5:23; Col 1:18; 2:19
1:23 [d]S 1Co 12:27 [e]S Jn 1:16; Eph 3:19 [f]Eph 4:10
2:1 [g]ver 5; Col 2:13
2:2 [h]ver 3,11-13; Ro 11:30; 1Co 6:11; 5:8; Col 3:7; Tit 3:3; 1Pe 4:3 [i]Ro 12:2 [j]S Jn 12:31 [k]Eph 5:6
2:3 [l]S ver 2 [m]S Gal 5:24
2:4 [n]S Jn 3:16
2:5 [o]ver 1; Ps 103:12 [p]ver 8; Jn 5:24;

Made Alive in Christ

2 As for you, you were dead in your
transgressions and sins,[g] 2in
which you used to live[h] when you followed the ways of this world[i] and of
the ruler of the kingdom of the air,[j]
the spirit who is now at work in those
who are disobedient.[k] 3All of us also
lived among them at one time,[l] gratifying the cravings of our sinful nature[g][m] and following its desires and
thoughts. Like the rest, we were by nature objects of wrath. 4But because of
his great love for us,[n] God, who is rich
in mercy, 5made us alive with Christ
even when we were dead in transgressions[o]—it is by grace you have been
saved.[p] 6And God raised us up with
Christ[q] and seated us with him[r] in
the heavenly realms[s] in Christ Jesus,
7in order that in the coming ages he
might show the incomparable riches of
his grace,[t] expressed in his kindness[u] to us in Christ Jesus. 8For it is
by grace[v] you have been saved,[w]
through faith[x]—and this not from
yourselves, it is the gift of God— 9not
by works,[y] so that no one can boast.[z]

S Ac 15:11 2:6 [q]S Ro 6:5 [r]Eph 1:20 [s]S Eph 1:3
2:7 [t]S Ro 2:4 [u]Tit 3:4 2:8 [v]S Ro 3:24 [w]ver 5 [x]S Ro 9:30
2:9 [y]Dt 9:5; Ro 4:2; 2Ti 1:9; Tit 3:5 [z]1Co 1:29

[f]17 Or *a spirit* [g]3 Or *our flesh*

1:16–20 IN MY PRAYERS. Paul's prayer for the Ephesians reflects God's highest desire for every believer in Christ. He prays that the Spirit might work in them in greater measure (cf. 3:16). The reason for this increased measure of the Spirit's impartation is that believers may receive more wisdom, revelation and knowledge concerning God's redemptive purposes for present and future salvation (vv. 17–18), and experience a more abundant "power" of the Holy Spirit in their lives (vv. 19–20).

1:19 HIS . . . POWER. In order for believers to advance in grace, achieve victory over Satan and sin, witness effectively for Christ and gain final salvation, they must have God's power moving toward them (cf. 1Pe 1:5). This power is an activity, manifestation and strength of the Holy Spirit working within faithful believers. It is the same power and Spirit that raised Christ from the dead and seated him at God's right hand (v. 20; Ro 8:11–16,26–27; Gal 5:22–25).

2:2 THOSE . . . DISOBEDIENT. Vv. 1–4 reveal a major reason why Christians should have great compassion and mercy for those still living in transgressions and sins. (1) All who are without Christ are controlled by "the ruler of the kingdom of the air," i.e., Satan (v. 2). Their minds are blinded by Satan to the truth of God (v. 2; 2Co 4:3–4). They are enslaved to sin and the cravings of the sinful nature (v. 3; Lk 4:18). (2) Because of the spiritual condition of unregenerate people, they cannot understand or accept the truth apart from God's grace (vv. 5,8; 1Co 1:18; Tit 2:11–14). (3) Christians must see everyone from the Biblical perspective. Those involved in immorality and pride are to be pitied because of their slavery to sin and Satan (vv. 1–3; cf. Jn 3:16). (4) Those who are without Christ are still responsible for their sins, for God gives every human being a measure of light and grace by which to seek God and escape sin's bondage through faith in Christ (Jn 1:9; Ro 1:18–32; 2:1–16).

2:8 BY GRACE . . . THROUGH FAITH. See article on FAITH AND GRACE, p. 1720.

2:9 NOT BY WORKS. One cannot be saved by works, good deeds of love or strenuous efforts to keep God's commandments. One must be saved by the grace of God. The reasons for this are the following: (1) All the unsaved are spiritually dead (v. 1), under Satan's dominion (v. 2), enslaved to sin (v. 3) and under God's condemnation (v. 3).

(2) In order to be saved one must receive God's provision of salvation (vv. 4–5), be forgiven of sin (Ro 4:7–8), be made spiritually alive (Col 1:13), be delivered from the power of Satan and sin (Col 1:13), be made a new creation (v. 10; 2Co 5:17) and receive the Holy Spirit (Jn 7:37–39; 20:22). No amount of self-effort can accomplish the above.

10For we are God's workmanship,[a]
created[b] in Christ Jesus to do good
works,[c] which God prepared in ad-
15 vance for us to do.

One in Christ

11Therefore, remember that formerly[d] you who are Gentiles by birth and
called "uncircumcised" by those who
call themselves "the circumcision"
(that done in the body by the hands of
men)[e]— **12**remember that at that
time you were separate from Christ,
excluded from citizenship in Israel and
foreigners[f] to the covenants of the
promise,[g] without hope[h] and without
God in the world. **13**But now in Christ
Jesus you who once[i] were far away
have been brought near[j] through the
blood of Christ.[k]
14For he himself is our peace,[l] who
has made the two one[m] and has destroyed the barrier, the dividing wall of
hostility, **15**by abolishing in his flesh[n]
the law with its commandments and
regulations.[o] His purpose was to create in himself one[p] new man out of the
two, thus making peace, **16**and in this
one body to reconcile both of them to
God through the cross,[q] by which he
put to death their hostility. **17**He came
and preached peace[r] to you who were
far away and peace to those who were
near.[s] **18**For through him we both
have access[t] to the Father[u] by one
Spirit.[v]
19Consequently, you are no longer
foreigners and aliens,[w] but fellow citizens[x] with God's people and members
of God's household,[y] **20**built[z] on the
foundation[a] of the apostles and
prophets,[b] with Christ Jesus himself[c] as the chief cornerstone.[d] **21**In
him the whole building is joined together and rises to become a holy temple[e] in the Lord. **22**And in him you too
are being built together to become
a dwelling in which God lives by his
Spirit.[f]

2:10 [a]Isa 29:23; 43:7; 60:21 [b]Eph 4:24 [c]S Tit 2:14 **2:11** [d]S ver 2 [e]Col 2:11 **2:12** [f]Isa 14:1; 65:1 [g]Gal 3:17 [h]1Th 4:13 **2:13** [i]S ver 2 [j]ver 17 [k]Col 1:20 **2:14** [l]ver 15; S Jn 14:27 [m]1Co 12:13; Eph 3:6 **2:15** [n]Col 1:21,22 [o]Col 2:14 [p]Gal 3:28 **2:16** [q]2Co 5:18; Col 1:20,22 **2:17** [r]S Lk 2:14 [s]ver 13; Ps 148:14; Isa 57:19 **2:18** [t]Eph 3:12 [u]Col 1:12 [v]1Co 12:13; Eph 4:4 **2:19** [w]ver 12 [x]Php 3:20 [y]Gal 6:10 **2:20** [z]1Co 3:9 [a]Mt 16:18; 1Co 3:10; Rev 21:14 [b]S Eph 4:11 [c]1Co 3:11 [d]S Ac 4:11; 1Pe 2:4-8 **2:21** [e]1Co 3:16,17 **2:22** [f]1Co 3:16

(3) What brings salvation is God's grace through faith (vv. 5,8). God's gift of grace includes the following: (a) First comes the call to repentance and faith (Ac 2:38). With this call comes the work of the Holy Spirit within a person, giving him or her the power and ability to respond to God. (b) Those who respond in faith and repentance and accept Christ as Lord and Savior receive additional grace to be regenerated or born again by the Spirit (see article on REGENERATION, p. 1589) and to be filled with the Spirit (Ac 1:8; 2:38; Eph 5:18). (c) Those who become new creatures in Christ receive continuing grace to live the Christian life, resist sin and serve God (Ro 8:13–14; 2Co 9:8). Believers strive to live for God by his grace that works within them (1Co 15:10). God's grace operates within committed believers both to will and to act according to God's good purpose (Php 2:12–13). From beginning to end, salvation is by the grace of God (see article on FAITH AND GRACE, p. 1720).

2:18 ACCESS TO THE FATHER. Access to God the Father is through Jesus Christ by the Holy Spirit. "Access" means that we who have faith in Christ have the freedom and right to approach our heavenly Father with confidence that we will be accepted, loved and welcomed. (1) This access is gained through Christ—his shed blood on the cross (v. 13; Ro 5:1–2) and his heavenly intercession for all who come to him (Heb 7:25; cf. 4:14–16). (2) Access to God requires the Holy Spirit's help. The Spirit's indwelling power makes it possible to pray and call on God according to his will and purpose (Jn 14:16–17; 16:13–14; Ro 8:15–16,26–27).

2:20 FOUNDATION . . . APOSTLES. The church can only be a true church if it is founded on the Christ-inspired infallible revelation to the first apostles. (1) The NT apostles were the original messengers, witnesses and authorized representatives of the crucified and risen Lord. They were the foundation stones of the church, and their message is preserved in the writings of the NT as the original, fundamental testimony to the gospel of Christ, valid for all times.

(2) All believers and churches are dependent on the words, message and faith of the first apostles as recorded in Acts and in the apostles' inspired writings. Their authority is retained in the NT, and later generations of the church have the task of obeying the apostolic revelation and of witnessing to its truth. The gospel given to the NT apostles through the Holy Spirit is the enduring source of life, truth and direction for the church.

(3) All believers and churches are true believers and true churches only so long as they do the following: (a) They must agree with and sincerely strive to follow the apostles' original teaching and revelation concerning the gospel as found in the NT (Ac 2:42). To reject the apostles' teachings is to reject the Lord himself (Jn 16:13–15; 1Co 14:36–38; Gal 1:9–11). (b) They must continue the apostolic mission by communicating anew the apostolic message to the world and the church through faithful proclamation and teaching in the power of the Spirit (Ac 1:8; 2Ti 1:8–14; Tit 1:7–9). (c) They must not only believe the apostolic message but also defend and guard it against all distortion or alteration. The apostles' original revelation as found in the NT can never be replaced or nullified by later revelation, testimony or prophecy (Ac 20:27–31; 1Ti 6:20).

Paul the Preacher to the Gentiles

3 For this reason I, Paul, the prisoner[g] of Christ Jesus for the sake of you Gentiles—

2Surely you have heard about the administration of God's grace that was given to me[h] for you, **3**that is, the mystery[i] made known to me by revelation,[j] as I have already written briefly. **4**In reading this, then, you will be able to understand my insight[k] into the mystery of Christ, **5**which was not made known to men in other generations as it has now been revealed by the Spirit to God's holy apostles and prophets.[l] **6**This mystery is that through the gospel the Gentiles are heirs[m] together with Israel, members together of one body,[n] and sharers together in the promise in Christ Jesus.[o]

7I became a servant of this gospel[p] by the gift of God's grace given me[q] through the working of his power.[r] **8**Although I am less than the least of all God's people,[s] this grace was given me: to preach to the Gentiles[t] the unsearchable riches of Christ,[u] **9**and to make plain to everyone the administration of this mystery,[v] which for ages past was kept hidden in God, who created all things. **10**His intent was that now, through the church, the manifold wisdom of God[w] should be made known[x] to the rulers and authorities[y] in the heavenly realms,[z] **11**according to his eternal purpose[a] which he accomplished in Christ Jesus our Lord. **12**In him and through faith in him we may approach God[b] with freedom and confidence.[c] **13**I ask you, therefore, not to be discouraged because of my sufferings for you, which are your glory.

A Prayer for the Ephesians

14For this reason I kneel[d] before the Father, **15**from whom his whole family[h] in heaven and on earth derives its name. **16**I pray that out of his glorious riches[e] he may strengthen you with power[f] through his Spirit in your inner being,[g] **17**so that Christ may dwell in your hearts[h] through faith. And I pray that you, being rooted[i] and established in love, **18**may have power, together with all the saints,[j] to grasp how wide and long and high and deep[k] is the love of Christ, **19**and to know this love that surpasses knowledge[l]—that you may be filled[m] to the measure of all the fullness of God.[n]

20Now to him who is able[o] to do immeasurably more than all we ask[p] or

3:1 g Ac 23:18; Eph 4:1; 2Ti 1:8; Phm 1,9
3:2 h Col 1:25
3:3 i S Ro 16:25 j S 1Co 2:10
3:4 k 2Co 11:6
3:5 l Ro 16:26; S Eph 4:11
3:6 m S Ro 8:17 n Eph 2:15,16 o Eze 47:22
3:7 p S 1Co 3:5 q S Ro 12:3 r Eph 1:19; Col 1:29
3:8 s S 1Co 15:9 t S Ac 9:15 u S Ro 2:4
3:9 v S Ro 16:25
3:10 w S Ro 11:33; 1Co 2:7 x 1Pe 1:12 y Eph 1:21; 6:12; Col 2:10,15 z S Eph 1:3
3:11 a S Eph 1:11
3:12 b Eph 2:18 c 2Co 3:4; Heb 3:14; 4:16; 10:19,35; 1Jn 2:28; 3:21; 4:17
3:14 d Php 2:10
3:16 e ver 8; S Ro 2:4 f S Php 4:13 g Ro 7:22
3:17 h S Ro 8:10 i Col 2:7
3:18 j Eph 1:15 k Job 11:8,9; Ps 103:11
3:19 l Php 4:7 m Col 2:10 n Eph 1:23
3:20 o Ro 16:25; 2Co 9:8 p 1Ki 3:13

h *15* Or *whom all fatherhood*

3:4 MYSTERY OF CHRIST. Paul speaks of the "mystery of Christ," hidden for ages past in God (v. 9) and now made known by revelation (v. 3) through the Spirit to the apostles and prophets (v. 5). The mystery is God's purpose to "bring all things in heaven and on earth together under one head, even Christ" (1:10), and to include people of all nations in the promise of life and salvation (v. 6; Ro 16:25–26; 2Ti 1:1). From the Jews and the Gentile nations God created "in Christ Jesus" (v. 6) a new people for himself (1:4–6; 2:16; 4:4,16; Mt 16:18; Col 1:24–28; 1Pe 2:9–10).

3:7 GOD'S GRACE. The grace of God, given to each believer to accomplish God's will, is an energizing strength that flows from the risen Christ and operates through the Holy Spirit indwelling the believer (1:19; 4:7; Ac 6:8; 11:23; 14:26; 1Co 15:10; 2Co 12:9; Php 2:13; Col 1:29; Tit 2:11–13; see article on FAITH AND GRACE, p. 1720).

3:10 RULERS AND AUTHORITIES. There are two possible interpretations of this verse. (1) The "rulers and authorities in the heavenly realms" may refer to good angels (cf. Col 1:16). They see God's astonishing wisdom as he demonstrates that wisdom through the church (1Pe 1:10–12). (2) The "rulers and authorities in the heavenly realms" may refer to the ruling powers of darkness in the spiritual realm (cf. 6:12; Da 10:13,20–21) to whom God's "eternal purpose" (v. 11) is being made known through the church's proclamation of salvation and through spiritual warfare against Satan and his forces (cf. 6:12–18; Da 9:2–23; 10:12–13; 2Co 10:4–5).

3:16–19 STRENGTHEN ... INNER BEING. To have the "inner being" strengthened by the Spirit is to have our feelings, thoughts and purposes placed more and more under his influence and direction so that the Spirit can manifest his power through us in greater measure. The purpose of this strengthening is fourfold: (1) that Christ may establish his presence in our hearts (vv. 16–17; cf. Ro 8:9–10); (2) that we may be grounded in sincere love for God, Christ and others; (3) that we may comprehend with our minds and experience in our lives Christ's love for us (vv. 18–19); (4) that we may be filled with "all the fullness of God" (v. 19), i.e., that God's presence may so fill us that we reflect from our innermost being the character and stature that belong to the Lord Jesus Christ (cf. 4:13,15,22–24).

3:20 IMMEASURABLY MORE. God will do for us not only more than we ask and desire in prayer, but also even more than our imagination can perceive. This promise is conditioned and dependent on the degree of the Holy Spirit's presence, power and grace operating in our lives (1:19; 3:16–19; Isa 65:24; Jn 15:7; Php 2:13).

imagine, according to his power[q] that
is at work within us, **21**to him be glory
in the church and in Christ Jesus
throughout all generations, for ever
and ever! Amen.[r]

Unity in the Body of Christ

4 As a prisoner[s] for the Lord, then,
I urge you to live a life worthy[t] of
the calling[u] you have received. **2**Be
completely humble and gentle; be patient, bearing with one another[v] in
love.[w] **3**Make every effort to keep the
unity[x] of the Spirit through the bond
of peace.[y] **4**There is one body[z] and
one Spirit[a]— just as you were called
to one hope when you were called[b]—
5one Lord,[c] one faith, one baptism;
6one God and Father of all,[d] who is
over all and through all and in all.[e]
7But to each one of us[f] grace[g] has
been given[h] as Christ apportioned it.
8This is why it[i] says:

"When he ascended on high,
he led captives[i] in his train
and gave gifts to men."[j][j]

9(What does "he ascended" mean except that he also descended to the lower, earthly regions[k]? **10**He who descended is the very one who
ascended[k] higher than all the heavens, in order to fill the whole universe.)[l] **11**It was he who gave[m] some
to be apostles,[n] some to be prophets,[o] some to be evangelists,[p] and
some to be pastors and teachers,[q]
12to prepare God's people for works of
service, so that the body of Christ[r]
may be built up[s] **13**until we all reach
unity[t] in the faith and in the knowledge of the Son of God[u] and become
mature,[v] attaining to the whole measure of the fullness of Christ.[w]
14Then we will no longer be infants,[x] tossed back and forth by the
waves,[y] and blown here and there by
every wind of teaching and by the cunning and craftiness of men in their deceitful scheming.[z] **15**Instead, speaking the truth in love,[a] we will in all

3:20 [q] ver 7
3:21 [r] S Ro 11:36
4:1 [s] S Eph 3:1 [t] Php 1:27; Col 1:10; 1Th 2:12 [u] S Ro 8:28
4:2 [v] Col 3:12,13 [w] ver 15,16; Eph 1:4
4:3 [x] S Ro 15:5 [y] Col 3:15
4:4 [z] S Ro 12:5 [a] 1Co 12:13; Eph 2:18 [b] S Ro 8:28
4:5 [c] 1Co 8:6
4:6 [d] Dt 6:4; Zec 14:9 [e] S Ro 11:36
4:7 [f] 1Co 12:7,11 [g] S Ro 3:24 [h] S Ro 12:3
4:8 [i] Col 2:15 [j] Ps 68:18
4:10 [k] Pr 30:1-4 [l] Eph 1:23
4:11 [m] ver 8 [n] 1Co 12:28; Eph 2:20; 3:5; 2Pe 3:2; Jude 17 [o] S Ac 11:27; Ro 12:6; 1Co 12:10,28; 13:2,8; 14:1,39; Eph 2:20; 3:5; 2Pe 3:2 [p] Ac 21:8; 2Ti 4:5 [q] Ac 13:1; Ro 2:21; 12:7; 1Co 12:28; 14:26; 1Ti 1:7; Jas 3:1
4:12 [r] S 1Co 12:27 [s] S Ro 14:19
4:13 [t] ver 3,5 [u] S Php 3:8 [v] S 1Co 2:6; Col 1:28 [w] Jn 1:16; Eph 1:23; 3:19
4:14 [x] S 1Co 14:20 [y] Isa 57:20; Jas 1:6 [z] Eph 6:11
4:15 [a] ver 2,16; Eph 1:4

i8 Or *God* j8 Psalm 68:18 k9 Or *the depths of the earth*

4:3 KEEP THE UNITY. "The unity of the Spirit" cannot be created by any human being. It already exists for those who have believed the truth and received Christ as the apostle proclaimed in chs. 1–3. The Ephesians are now to keep that unity, not through human efforts or organizations, but by living "a life worthy of the calling [they] have received" (v. 1). Spiritual unity is maintained by being loyal to the truth and by keeping in step with the Spirit (vv. 1–3,14–15; Gal 5:22–26). It cannot be attained "by human effort" (Gal 3:3).

4:5 ONE LORD. Essential to Christian faith and unity is the confession that there is only "one Lord." (1) That there is only "one Lord" means that Jesus Christ's work of redemption is perfect and sufficient, and no other redeemer or mediator is needed to give the believer complete salvation (1Ti 2:5–6; Heb 9:15). The believer is to draw near to God through Christ alone (Heb 7:25).

(2) "One Lord" also means that to profess equal or greater allegiance to any authority (secular or religious) other than God revealed in Christ and the inspired Word is the same as withdrawing oneself from Christ's lordship and thus from the life that is in him alone. There can be no lordship of Christ or "unity of the Spirit" (v. 3) apart from the affirmation that the Lord Jesus is the ultimate authority for the believer and that Christ's authority is communicated in God's written Word.

4:11 IT WAS HE WHO GAVE. See article on THE MINISTRY GIFTS OF THE CHURCH, p. 1830.

4:13 UNITY IN THE FAITH. In ch. 4 Paul teaches that the "unity of the Spirit" (v. 3) and the "unity in the faith" are maintained and perfected by: (1) accepting only the faith and message of the NT apostles, prophets, evangelists, pastors and teachers (vv. 11–12); (2) growing in grace, advancing toward spiritual maturity and growing up in all aspects into Christ (v. 15), and being filled with all the fullness of Christ and God (v. 13; cf. 3:19); (3) no longer being children who accept "every wind of teaching" but who instead have a knowledge of the truth by which to reject false teachers (vv. 14–15); (4) holding and speaking the revealed truth of Scripture in love (v. 15); and (5) living in "true righteousness and holiness" (v. 24; cf. vv. 17–32).

4:14 NO LONGER BE INFANTS. In vv. 13–15 Paul defines spiritually "mature" persons who possess the fullness of Christ. (1) To be spiritually mature means not being infants who are unstable, easily deceived by the false doctrines of others and susceptible to crafty showmanship. People remain infants if their understanding of and commitment to Biblical truth are inadequate (vv. 14–15). (2) To be spiritually mature involves "speaking the truth in love" (v. 15). The truth of the gospel as presented in the NT is to be held in love, presented in love and contended for in a spirit of love. The love is first directed to "Christ" (v. 15), and then to the church (v. 16) and to one another (v. 32; cf. 1Co 16:14).

4:15 TRUTH IN LOVE. Maintaining the unity in the faith (v. 13) must be based on an active love that seeks to resolve problems and reconcile differences by mutual loyalty and obedience to Christ and his Word. This means that holding and speak-

THE MINISTRY GIFTS OF THE CHURCH

***Eph 4:11** "It was he who gave some to be apostles, some to be prophets, some to be evangelists, and some to be pastors and teachers."*

THE GIVER. Eph 4:11 lists the ministry gifts (i.e., gifted spiritual leaders) Christ gave to the church. Paul states that Christ gave these gifts (1) for preparing God's people for works of service (4:12) and (2) for the spiritual growth of the body of Christ as God intended (4:13–16; see article on SPIRITUAL GIFTS FOR BELIEVERS, p. 1770).

APOSTLES. The title "apostle" is applied to certain NT leaders. The verb *apostellō* means to send someone on a special mission as a messenger and personal representative of the one who sends him. The title is used of Christ (Heb 3:1), the 12 disciples (Mt 10:2), Paul (Ro 1:1; 2Co 1:1; Gal 1:1) and others (Ac 14:4,14; Ro 16:7; Gal 1:19; 2:8–9; 1Th 2:6–7).

(1) The term "apostle" was used in the NT in a general sense for a commissioned representative of a church, such as the first Christian missionaries. Therefore, in the NT "apostle" referred to any messenger appointed and sent as a missionary or for some other special responsibility (see Ac 14:4,14; Ro 16:7; 2Co 8:23; Php 2:25). They were men who manifested extraordinary spiritual leadership, were anointed with power to confront directly the powers of darkness and to confirm the gospel with miracles, and were dedicated to establishing churches according to apostolic truth and purity. These itinerant servants risked their lives for the name of the Lord Jesus Christ and the advancement of the gospel (Ac 11:21–26; 13:50; 14:19–22; 15:25–26). They were Spirit-filled men of faith and prayer (see Ac 11:23–25; 13:2–5; 46–52; 14:1–7,21–23).

(2) Apostles in this general sense remain essential to God's purpose in the church. If churches cease to send out Spirit-filled persons, then the spread of the gospel into all the world will be hindered. On the other hand, as long as the church produces and sends such people, it will fulfill its missionary task and remain faithful to the Lord's Great Commission (Mt 28:18–20).

(3) The term "apostle" is also used in a special sense to refer to those who saw Jesus after his resurrection and were personally commissioned by the resurrected Lord to preach the gospel and establish the church (e.g., the twelve disciples and Paul). They possessed a unique authority within the church that related to divine revelation and the original gospel message that can no longer exist in anyone today (see Eph 2:20, note). Thus, the office of apostle in this specialized sense is unique and unrepeatable. The original apostles can have no successors (see 1Co 15:8, note).

(4) A primary task of the NT apostles was to establish churches and to ensure that they were founded on, or restored to, sincere devotion to Christ and the NT faith (cf. Jn 21:15–17; 1Co 12:28; 2Co 11:2–3; Eph 4:11–13; Php 1:17). This task involved two main burdens: (a) an urgent God-given desire to maintain the church's purity and its separation from sin and the world (1Co 5:1–5; 2Co 6:14–18; Jas 2:14–26; 1Pe 2:11; 4:1–5; 1Jn 2:1,15–17; 3:3–10) and (b) a continuing burden to proclaim the NT gospel and to defend it against heresy, new theological trends and false teachers (Ro 16:17; 1Co 11:2; 2Co 11:3–4,14, notes; Gal 1:9, note; 2Pe 2:1–3; 1Jn 4:1–6; 2Jn 7–11; Jude 3–4,12–13; see article on OVERSEERS AND THEIR DUTIES, p. 1690).

(5) Although the first apostles who laid the church's foundation have no successors, the church today is still dependent on their words, message and faith. The church must obey and remain faithful to their original writings. To reject the inspired revelation of the apostles is to cease being a church according to the Biblical pattern and to reject the Lord himself (Jn 16:13–15; 1Co 14:36–38; Gal 1:9–11). On the other hand, to believe the apostolic message, obey it and guard it against all distortion is to remain true to the Holy Spirit (Ac 20:28, 2Ti 1:14) and to guarantee God's continued life, blessing and presence within the church (see Eph 2:20, note).

PROPHETS. Prophets were believers who spoke under the direct impulse of the Holy Spirit in the name of God and whose main concern was the spiritual life and purity of the church. Under the new covenant they were raised up and empowered by the Holy Spirit to bring a message from God to his people (Ac 2:17; 4:8; 21:4).

(1) OT prophets are foundational for understanding the prophetic ministry in the early church. Their primary task was to speak a word of God by the Spirit in order to encourage God's people to remain faithful to their covenant relationship. They also, at times, predicted the future as the Spirit revealed it to them (see article on THE PROPHET IN THE OLD TESTAMENT, p. 986). Christ and the apostles serve as examples of the OT ideal (Ac 3:22–23; 13:1–2).

(2) Prophets functioned within the NT church in the following ways: (a) They were Spirit-filled proclaimers and interpreters of the Word of God, called by God to warn, exhort, comfort and edify (Ac 2:14–36; 3:12–26; 1Co 12:10; 14:3). (b) They were to exercise the gift of prophecy (see article on SPIRITUAL GIFTS FOR BELIEVERS, p. 1770). (c) They were at times seers (cf. 1Ch 29:29) who foretold the future (Ac 11:28; 21:10–11). (d) Like the OT prophets, the NT prophets were called to expose sin, proclaim righteousness, warn of judgment to come, and combat worldliness and lukewarmness among God's people (Lk 1:14–17). Because of their message of righteousness, prophets and their ministry can expect rejection by many in the churches during times of lukewarmness and apostasy.

(3) The prophet's character, burden, desire and ability include: (a) a zeal for church purity (Jn 17:15–17; 1Co 6:9–11; Gal 5:22–25); (b) a deep sensitivity to evil and the capacity to identify and hate unrighteousness (Ro 12:9; Heb 1:9); (c) a keen understanding of the danger of false teachings (Mt 7:15; 24:11,24; Gal 1:9; 2Co 11:12–15); (d) an inherent dependence on God's Word to validate the prophet's message (Lk 4:17–19; 1Co 15:3–4; 2Ti 3:16); (e) a concern for the spiritual success of God's kingdom and a sharing in God's feelings (Mt 21:11–13; 23:37; Lk 13:34; Jn 2:14–17; Ac 20:27–31).

(4) The prophets' messages are not to be regarded as infallible. Their messages are subject to the evaluation of the church, other prophets and God's Word. The congregation is required to discern and test whether their witness is from God (1Co 14:29–33; 1Jn 4:1).

(5) Prophets continue to be essential to God's purpose for the church. A church that rejects God's prophets will be a declining church, drifting toward worldliness and the compromise of Biblical truth (1Co 14:3; cf. Mt 23:31–38; Lk 11:49; Ac 7:51–52). If prophets are not allowed to bring words of rebuke and warning, words prompted by the Spirit, words exposing sin and unrighteousness (Jn 16:8–11), then the church will become a place where the voice of the Spirit can no longer be heard. Ecclesiastical politics and worldly power will replace the Spirit (2Ti 3:1–9; 4:3–5; 2Pe 2:1–3,12–22). On the other hand, if the church, with its leaders, hears the voice of the prophets, it will be moved to renewed life and fellowship with Christ, sin will be forsaken, and the Spirit's presence will be evident among the faithful (1Co 14:3; 1Th 5:19–21; Rev 3:20–22).

EVANGELISTS. In the NT, evangelists were men of God who were gifted and commissioned by God to proclaim the gospel (i.e., good news) of salvation to the unsaved and to help establish a new work in a city. When proclaimed the gospel always carries with it the offer and power of salvation (Ro 1:16–17).

(1) The ministry of Philip "the evangelist" (Ac 21:8) gives a clear picture of the work of an evangelist according to the NT pattern. (a) Philip preached the gospel of Christ (Ac 8:4–5,35). (b) Many were saved and baptized with water (Ac 8:6,12). (c) Signs, miracles, healings and deliverance from evil spirits accompanied his preaching (Ac 8:6–7,13). (d) He wanted new converts to be filled with the Holy Spirit (Ac 8:12–17; cf. 2:38; 19:1–6).

(2) The evangelist is essential to God's purpose for the church. The church that fails to support the ministry of the evangelist will cease to gain converts as God desires. It will become a static church, devoid of growth and missionary outreach. The church that

values the spiritual gift of the evangelist and maintains an earnest love for the lost will proclaim the message of salvation with convicting and saving power (Ac 2:14–41).

PASTORS. Pastors are those who oversee and care for the spiritual needs of a local congregation. They are also called "elders" (Ac 20:17; Tit 1:5) and "overseers" (1Ti 3:1; Tit 1:7).

(1) The task of pastors is to proclaim sound doctrine, refute heresy (Tit 1:9–11), teach God's Word and exercise leadership in the local church (1Th 5:12; 1Ti 3:1–5); be an example of purity and sound doctrine (Tit 2:7–8); and see to it that all believers remain in divine grace (Heb 12:15; 13:17; 1Pe 5:2). Their task is described in Ac 20:28–31 as safeguarding apostolic truth and God's flock by watching out for false doctrine and false teachers within the church (see article on OVERSEERS AND THEIR DUTIES, p. 1690). Pastors function as shepherds of which Jesus as the good Shepherd is a model (Jn 10:11–16; 1Pe 2:25; 5:2–4).

(2) The NT pattern shows a plurality of pastors directing the spiritual life of a local church (Ac 20:28; Php 1:1). Pastors were chosen, not through politics, but through the Spirit's wisdom given to the body as it examined the candidate's spiritual qualifications (see article on MORAL QUALIFICATIONS FOR OVERSEERS, p. 1882).

(3) Pastors are essential to God's purpose for his church. The church that fails to select godly and faithful pastors will cease to be governed according to the mind of the Spirit (see 1Ti 3:1–7). It will be a church left open to the destructive forces of Satan and the world (see Ac 20:28–31). The preaching of the Word will be distorted and the standards of the gospel lost (2Ti 1:13–14). Members and families of the church will not be cared for according to God's purpose (1Ti 4:6,12–16; 6:20–21). Many will turn away from the truth and turn aside to myths (2Ti 4:4). On the other hand, if godly pastors are appointed, believers will be nourished on the words of faith and sound doctrine and disciplined for the purpose of godliness (1Ti 4:6–7). The church will be taught to persevere in the teaching of Christ and the apostles and thus ensure salvation for itself and those who hear (1Ti 4:16; 2Ti 2:2).

TEACHERS. Teachers are those who have a special, God-given gift to clarify, expound and proclaim God's Word in order to build up the body of Christ (Eph 4:12).

(1) The special task of teachers is to guard, by the Holy Spirit's help, the gospel entrusted to them (2Ti 1:11–14). They are faithfully to point the church to Biblical revelation and to the original message of Christ and the apostles, and to persevere in this task.

(2) The principal purpose of Biblical teaching is to preserve truth and to produce holiness by leading Christ's body into an uncompromising commitment to the godly lifestyle set forth in God's Word. Scripture states that the goal of Christian instruction is "love, which comes from a pure heart and a good conscience and a sincere faith" (1Ti 1:5). Thus, the evidence of Christian learning is not just in what one knows, but how one lives—i.e., the manifestation of love, purity, faith and godliness.

(3) Teachers are essential to God's purpose for his church. The church that rejects or refuses to hear those teachers and theologians who remain faithful to Scriptural revelation will stop being concerned about the genuineness of the Biblical message and the correct interpretation of the original teaching of Christ and the apostles. The church in which such teachers and theologians remain silent will not continue steadfast in the truth. New winds of doctrine will be uncritically accepted, and religious experience and human ideas, rather than revealed truth, will be the ultimate guide to the church's doctrine, standards and practices. On the other hand, the church that listens to godly teachers and theologians will have its teachings and practices measured by the fundamental testimony of the gospel, its false ideas exposed and the purity of Christ's original message handed down to its children. God's inspired Word will become the test of all teaching, and the church will be reminded that the Spirit's inspired Word is ultimate truth and authority, and as such, stands over the churches and their institutions.

things grow up into him who is the Head,[b] that is, Christ. **16**From him the whole body, joined and held together by every supporting ligament, grows[c] and builds itself up[d] in love,[e] as each part does its work.

Living as Children of Light

17So I tell you this, and insist on it in the Lord, that you must no longer[f] live as the Gentiles do, in the futility of their thinking.[g] **18**They are darkened in their understanding[h] and separated from the life of God[i] because of the ignorance that is in them due to the hardening of their hearts.[j] **19**Having lost all sensitivity,[k] they have given themselves over[l] to sensuality[m] so as to indulge in every kind of impurity, with a continual lust for more.

20You, however, did not come to know Christ that way. **21**Surely you heard of him and were taught in him in accordance with the truth that is in Jesus. **22**You were taught, with regard to your former way of life, to put off[n] your old self,[o] which is being corrupted by its deceitful desires;[p] **23**to be made new in the attitude of your minds;[q] **24**and to put on[r] the new self,[s] created to be like God in true righteousness and holiness.[t]

25Therefore each of you must put off falsehood and speak truthfully[u] to his neighbor, for we are all members of one body.[v] **26**"In your anger do not sin"[l].[w] Do not let the sun go down while you are still angry, **27**and do not give the devil a foothold.[x] **28**He who has been stealing must steal no longer, but must work,[y] doing something useful with his own hands,[z] that he may have something to share with those in need.[a]

29Do not let any unwholesome talk come out of your mouths,[b] but only what is helpful for building others up[c] according to their needs, that it may benefit those who listen. **30**And do not grieve the Holy Spirit of God,[d] with whom you were sealed[e] for the day of redemption.[f] **31**Get rid of[g] all bitterness, rage and anger, brawling and slander, along with every form of malice.[h] **32**Be kind and compassionate to one another,[i] forgiving each other, just as in Christ God forgave you.[j]

5 Be imitators of God,[k] therefore, as dearly loved children[l] **2**and live a life of love, just as Christ loved us[m] and gave himself up for us[n] as a fragrant offering and sacrifice to God.[o]

3But among you there must not be even a hint of sexual immorality,[p] or of any kind of impurity, or of greed,[q] because these are improper for God's holy people. **4**Nor should there be obscenity, foolish talk[r] or coarse joking, which are out of place, but rather thanksgiving.[s] **5**For of this you can be sure: No immoral, impure or greedy person—such a man is an idolater[t]—has any inheritance[u] in the kingdom of Christ and of God.[m][v] **6**Let no one deceive you[w] with empty words, for because of such things God's wrath[x]

4:15 [b] S Eph 1:22 **4:16** [c] Col 2:19 [d] 1Co 12:7 [e] ver 2, 15; Eph 1:4 **4:17** [f] Eph 2:2 [g] Ro 1:21 **4:18** [h] Dt 29:4; Ro 1:21 [i] Eph 2:12 [j] 2Co 3:14 **4:19** [k] 1Ti 4:2 [l] Ro 1:24 [m] Col 3:5; 1Pe 4:3 **4:22** [n] ver 25,31; Col 3:5,8,9; Jas 1:21; 1Pe 2:1 [o] S Ro 6:6 [p] Jer 17:9; Heb 3:13 **4:23** [q] Ro 12:2; Col 3:10 **4:24** [r] S Ro 13:14 [s] S Ro 6:4 [t] Eph 2:10 **4:25** [u] Ps 15:2; Lev 19:11; Zec 8:16; Col 3:9 [v] S Ro 12:5 **4:26** [w] Ps 4:4; S Mt 5:22 **4:27** [x] 2Co 2:10, 11 **4:28** [y] Ac 20:35 [z] 1Th 4:11 [a] Gal 6:10 **4:29** [b] Mt 12:36; Eph 5:4; Col 3:8 [c] S Ro 14:19 **4:30** [d] Isa 63:10; 1Th 5:19 [e] 2Co 1:22; 5:5; Eph 1:13 [f] Ro 8:23 **4:31** [g] S ver 22 [h] Col 3:8; 1Pe 2:1 **4:32** [i] 1Pe 3:8 [j] Mt 6:14,15; Col 3:12,13 **5:1** [k] Mt 5:48; Lk 6:36 [l] S Jn 1:12 **5:2** [m] S Jn 13:34 [n] ver 25; S Gal 1:4; 2:20 [o] Heb 7:27 **5:3** [p] S 1Co 6:18 [q] Col 3:5 **5:4** [r] Eph 4:29 [s] S ver 20 **5:5** [t] Col 3:5 [u] S Ac 20:32 [v] S Mt 25:34 **5:6** [w] S Mk 13:5 [x] S Ro 1:18

[l]26 Psalm 4:4 [m]5 Or *kingdom of the Christ and God*

ing NT truth in love have priority over loyalty to Christian institutions, tradition, individual people or the visible church. Any attempt to maintain fellowship or unity must never invalidate God's Word or be based on the compromise of Biblical truth (v. 14). Faithfulness to Scripture may involve separation from a part of the visible church that has become unfaithful to Christ and apostolic doctrine (see 2:20, note). Subsequently the Holy Spirit will initiate the formation of a new visible church loyal to Christ and the original NT truth.

4:30 GRIEVE ... HOLY SPIRIT. The Holy Spirit, who lives within the believer (Ro 8:9; 1Co 6:19), is a Person who can experience intense grief or sorrow as Jesus himself did when he wept over Jerusalem or grieved on other occasions (Mt 23:37; Mk 3:5; Lk 19:41; Jn 11:35). (1) Believers cause the Holy Spirit grief or pain when they ignore his presence, voice or leading (Ro 8:5–17; Gal 5:16–25; 6:7–9). (2) Grieving the Spirit leads to resisting the Holy Spirit (Ac 7:51); this, in turn, leads to putting out the Spirit's fire (1Th 5:19), and finally to insulting the Spirit of grace (Heb 10:29). This last activity may be identified with blasphemy against the Spirit, for which there is no forgiveness (see Mt 12:31, note).

5:5 BE SURE. The apostle Paul, as well as the Ephesians, knew with unqualified certainty that all individuals (whether within or outside of the church) who were immoral, impure or greedy (i.e., loved things more than God) were excluded from Christ's kingdom. This was taught with strong conviction by the OT prophets (see Jer 8:7, note; 23:17, note; Eze 13:10, note) and by the apostles and the NT church (see 1Co 6:9, note; Gal 5:21, note). People who committed such sins gave clear evidence of not being saved, of being devoid of the life of God and of being separated from eternal life (see Jn 8:42, note; 1Jn 3:15, note).

5:6 DECEIVE. Paul knew that some teachers would tell the Ephesians that they need not fear God's wrath against their immorality. Thus he ad-

comes on those who are disobedient.[y]
7Therefore do not be partners with
them.

8For you were once[z] darkness, but
now you are light in the Lord. Live as
children of light[a] **9**(for the fruit[b] of
the light consists in all goodness,[c]
righteousness and truth) **10**and find
out what pleases the Lord.[d] **11**Have
nothing to do with the fruitless deeds
of darkness,[e] but rather expose them.
12For it is shameful even to mention
what the disobedient do in secret.
13But everything exposed by the
light[f] becomes visible, **14**for it is light
that makes everything visible. This is
why it is said:

> "Wake up, O sleeper,[g]
> rise from the dead,[h]
> and Christ will shine on you."[i]

Php 2:12-16 **15**Be very careful, then, how you
live[j]—not as unwise but as wise,
16making the most of every opportunity,[k] because the days are evil.[l]
17Therefore do not be foolish, but understand what the Lord's will is.[m]
18Do not get drunk on wine,[n] which
leads to debauchery. Instead, be filled
with the Spirit.[o] **19**Speak to one another with psalms, hymns and spiritual
songs.[p] Sing and make music in your
heart to the Lord, **20**always giving
thanks[q] to God the Father for everything, in the name of our Lord Jesus
Christ.

21Submit to one another[r] out of
reverence for Christ.

Wives and Husbands

5:22–6:9pp — Col 3:18–4:1

22Wives, submit to your husbands[s]
as to the Lord.[t] **23**For the husband is

5:6 [y]Eph 2:2 **5:8** [z]S Eph 2:2 [a]Jn 8:12; S Lk 16:8; S Ac 26:18 **5:9** [b]Mt 7:16-20; Gal 5:22 [c]Ro 15:14 **5:10** [d]S 1Ti 5:4 **5:11** [e]Ro 13:12; 2Co 6:14 **5:13** [f]Jn 3:20,21 **5:14** [g]Ro 13:11 [h]Isa 26:19; Jn 5:25 [i]Isa 60:1; Mal 4:2 **5:15** [j]ver 2 **5:16** [k]Col 4:5 [l]Eph 6:13 **5:17** [m]Ro 12:2; Col 1:9; 1Th 4:3 **5:18** [n]Lev 10:9; Pr 20:1; Isa 28:7; Ro 13:13 [o]S Lk 1:15 **5:19** [p]Ps 27:6; 95:2; Ac 16:25; 1Co 14:15,26; Col 3:16 **5:20** [q]ver 4; Job 1:21; Ps 34:1; Col 3:17; Heb 13:15 **5:21** [r]Gal 5:13; 1Pe 5:5 **5:22** [s]Ge 3:16; 1Co 14:34; Col 3:18; 1Ti 2:12; Tit 2:5; 1Pe 3:1,5,6 [t]Eph 6:5

Co 3: 17

---

monishes, "Let no one deceive you." It is apparent here that one may be deceived into believing that some immoral and impure persons do have an inheritance in the kingdom of Christ (see article on FALSE TEACHERS, p. 1506).

5:11 DEEDS OF DARKNESS. Those whose allegiance belongs to Christ cannot be neutral or silent with respect to the "deeds of darkness" and immorality (vv. 3–6). They must be ever ready to expose, rebuke and speak against wickedness in all forms. To cry out sincerely against unrighteousness is to hate sin (Heb 1:9), to stand beside God against evil (Ps 94:16) and to remain faithful to Christ, who also exposed deeds of evil (Jn 7:7; 15:18–20; cf. Lk 22:28).

5:18 WINE. The fullness of the Holy Spirit is contingent on the response of believers to the grace given them to attain and maintain sanctification. That is, a person cannot be "drunk on wine" and at the same time "filled with the Spirit." Paul warns all believers about the acts of the sinful nature—that those who practice such things "will not inherit the kingdom of God" (Gal 5:19–21; cf. Eph 5:3–7). Furthermore, those who "live like this" (Gal 5:21) will have no part in the abiding presence and fullness of the Holy Spirit. In other words, to lack "the fruit of the Spirit" (Gal 5:22–23) is to lose the fullness of the Spirit (see Ac 8:21, note).

5:18 FILLED WITH THE SPIRIT. "Be filled" (present passive imperative) carries the meaning in Greek of "repeatedly being filled." God's children must experience constant renewal (3:14–19; 4:22–24; Ro 12:2) by repeatedly being filled with the Holy Spirit. (1) Christians are to be baptized in the Holy Spirit after conversion (see Ac 1:5; 2:4), yet they are to be filled with the Spirit repeatedly for worship, service and witness (see Ac 4:31–33, note; 6:3, note). (2) Believers experience repeated fillings with the Spirit by maintaining a living faith in Jesus Christ (Gal 3:5), being filled with God's Word (Col 3:16), praying, giving thanks and singing to the Lord (vv. 19–20; 1Co 14:15), serving others (v. 21) and doing what the Holy Spirit desires (4:30; Ro 8:1–14; Gal 5:16ff; 1Th 5:19). (3) Several results of being filled with the Spirit are noted here: (a) speaking with joy to God in psalms, hymns and spiritual songs (v. 19), (b) giving thanks (v. 20) and (c) submitting to one another (v. 21).

5:19 SING . . . TO THE LORD. All our spiritual songs, both in the church and in private, should be first and foremost directed to God as prayers of praise or petition (cf. Ps 40:3; 77:6). (1) Songs of praise or any spiritual song can be a manifestation of the Holy Spirit (v. 18ff; 1Co 14:14ff). (2) Singing spiritual songs is a means of edification, teaching, giving thanks and praying (Col 3:16). (3) Christian singing is an expression of joy (v. 19). (4) The goal of singing hymns or spiritual songs is not entertainment or individual aggrandizement, but worship and praise of God (Ro 15:9–11; Rev 5:9–10).

5:21 SUBMIT TO ONE ANOTHER. Mutual submission in Christ is a general spiritual principle. This principle is to be applied first of all to the Christian family. Submission, humility, gentleness, patience and tolerance must be characteristic of each member. The wife must submit (i.e., yield in love) to the husband's responsibility of leadership in the family (see next note). The husband must submit to the needs of the wife in an attitude of love and self-giving (see v. 23, note). Children must submit to the authority of the parents in obedience (see 6:1, note). And parents must submit to the needs of their children and bring them up in the instruction of the Lord (see 6:4, note).

5:22 WIVES, SUBMIT. The wife is given the God-appointed task of helping and submitting to her husband (vv. 22–24). Her duty to her husband

the head of the wife as Christ is the
head of the church,[u] his body, of
which he is the Savior. **24**Now as the
church submits to Christ, so also wives
should submit to their husbands[v] in
everything.
25Husbands, love your wives,[w] just
as Christ loved the church and gave
himself up for her[x] **26**to make her
holy,[y] cleansing[n] her by the washing[z] with water through the word,
27and to present her to himself[a] as a
radiant church, without stain or wrinkle or any other blemish, but holy and
blameless.[b] **28**In this same way, husbands ought to love their wives[c] as
their own bodies. He who loves his wife
loves himself. **29**After all, no one ever
hated his own body, but he feeds and
cares for it, just as Christ does the
church— **30**for we are members of his
body.[d] **31**"For this reason a man will
leave his father and mother and be
united to his wife, and the two will become one flesh."[o][e] **32**This is a profound mystery—but I am talking about
Christ and the church. **33**However,
each one of you also must love his
wife[f] as he loves himself, and the wife
must respect her husband.

Children and Parents

6 Children, obey your parents in the
Lord, for this is right.[g] **2**"Honor
your father and mother"—which is the
first commandment with a promise—
3"that it may go well with you and that
you may enjoy long life on the
earth."[p][h]
4Fathers, do not exasperate your
children;[i] instead, bring them up in
the training and instruction of the
Lord.[j]

Slaves and Masters

5Slaves, obey your earthly masters
with respect[k] and fear, and with sincerity of heart,[l] just as you would
obey Christ.[m] **6**Obey them not only to
win their favor when their eye is on
you, but like slaves of Christ,[n] doing
the will of God from your heart. **7**Serve
wholeheartedly, as if you were serving
the Lord, not men,[o] **8**because you
know that the Lord will reward everyone for whatever good he does,[p]
whether he is slave or free.
9And masters, treat your slaves in
the same way. Do not threaten them,
since you know that he who is both
their Master and yours[q] is in heaven,
and there is no favoritism[r] with him.

The Armor of God

10Finally, be strong in the Lord[s]
and in his mighty power.[t] **11**Put on
the full armor of God[u] so that you can
take your stand against the devil's

5:23 [u] S Eph 1:22
5:24 [v] S ver 22
5:25 [w] ver 28,33; Col 3:19 [x] S ver 2
5:26 [y] Jn 17:19; Heb 2:11; 10:10, 14; 13:12 [z] S Ac 22:16
5:27 [a] S 2Co 4:14 [b] Eph 1:4
5:28 [c] ver 25
5:30 [d] S Ro 12:5; S 1Co 12:27
5:31 [e] Ge 2:24; Mt 19:5; 1Co 6:16
5:33 [f] ver 25
6:1 [g] Pr 6:20; Col 3:20
6:3 [h] Ex 20:12; Dt 5:16
6:4 [i] Col 3:21 [j] Ge 18:19; Dt 6:7; Pr 13:24; 22:6
6:5 [k] 1Ti 6:1; Tit 2:9; 1Pe 2:18 [l] Col 3:22 [m] Eph 5:22
6:6 [n] S Ro 6:22
6:7 [o] Col 3:23
6:8 [p] S Mt 16:27; Col 3:24
6:9 [q] Job 31:13,14 [r] S Ac 10:34
6:10 [s] 2Sa 10:12; Ps 27:14; Hag 2:4; 1Co 16:13; 2Ti 2:1 [t] Eph 1:19
6:11 [u] ver 13; Ro 13:12; 1Th 5:8

[n] *26* Or *having cleansed* [o] *31* Gen. 2:24
[p] *3* Deut. 5:16

includes love (Tit 2:4), respect (v. 33; 1Pe 3:1–2), assistance (Ge 2:18), purity (Tit 2:5; 1Pe 3:2), submissiveness (v. 22; 1Pe 3:5), development of a gentle and quiet spirit (1Pe 3:4), and being a good mother (Tit 2:4) and homemaker (1Ti 2:15; 5:14; Tit 2:5). A wife's submissiveness to her husband is seen by God as an actual part of her obedience to Jesus, "as to the Lord" (see also Gal 3:28, note; 1Ti 2:13,15, notes; Tit 2:4, note).

5:23 HUSBAND ... HEAD. God has established the family as the basic unit in society. Every family must have a leader. Therefore, God has assigned to the husband the responsibility of being the head of the wife and family (vv. 23–33; 6:4). His headship must be exercised in love, gentleness and consideration for his wife and family (vv. 25–30; 6:4). The husband's God-given responsibility as "head of the wife" includes: (1) provision for the family's spiritual and domestic needs (vv. 23–24; Ge 3:16–19; 1Ti 5:8); (2) love, protection and interest in her welfare in the same way that Christ loves the church (vv. 25–33); (3) honor, understanding, appreciation and thoughtfulness (Col 3:19; 1Pe 3:7); (4) absolute faithfulness to the marriage relationship (v. 31; Mt 5:27–28).

6:1 CHILDREN, OBEY. Normally children of believers must remain under parental guidance until they become part of another family unit through marriage. (1) Small children must be taught to obey and honor their parents by being brought up in the training and instruction of the Lord (see Pr 13:24, note; 22:6, note; see next note). (2) Older children, even after marriage, must show respect for the counsel of their parents (v. 2) and honor them in old age through care and financial support if needed (Mt 15:1–6). (3) Children who honor their parents will be blessed by God, here on earth and in eternity (v. 3).

6:4 FATHERS, ... YOUR CHILDREN. For an extended discussion of the parents' role in bringing up their children, see article on PARENTS AND CHILDREN, p. 1854.

6:11 AGAINST THE DEVIL'S SCHEMES. Christians are engaged in a spiritual conflict with evil. This spiritual conflict is described as a warfare of faith (2Co 10:4; 1Ti 1:18–19; 6:12) that continues until they enter the life to come (2Ti 4:7–8; see Gal 5:17, note). (1) The believer's victory has been secured by Christ himself through Christ's death on the cross. Jesus waged a triumphant battle against Satan, disarmed the evil powers and authorities (Col 2:15; cf. Mt 12:29; Lk

schemes. **12**For our struggle is not
against flesh and blood,[v] but against
the rulers, against the authorities,[w]
against the powers[x] of this dark world
and against the spiritual forces of evil
in the heavenly realms.[y] **13**Therefore
put on the full armor of God,[z] so that
when the day of evil comes, you may be
able to stand your ground, and after
you have done everything, to stand.
14Stand firm then, with the belt of
truth buckled around your waist,[a]
with the breastplate of righteousness
in place,[b] **15**and with your feet fitted
with the readiness that comes from the
gospel of peace.[c] **16**In addition to all
this, take up the shield of faith,[d] with
which you can extinguish all the flaming arrows of the evil one.[e] **17**Take the
helmet of salvation[f] and the sword of
the Spirit,[g] which is the word of
God.[h] **18**And pray in the Spirit[i] on all
occasions[j] with all kinds of prayers
and requests.[k] With this in mind, be
alert and always keep on praying[l] for
all the saints.
19Pray also for me,[m] that whenever
I open my mouth, words may be given
me so that I will fearlessly[n] make
known the mystery[o] of the gospel,
20for which I am an ambassador[p] in
chains.[q] Pray that I may declare it
fearlessly, as I should.

Final Greetings

21Tychicus,[r] the dear brother and
faithful servant in the Lord, will tell
you everything, so that you also may
know how I am and what I am doing.
22I am sending him to you for this very
purpose, that you may know how we
are,[s] and that he may encourage
you.[t]
23Peace[u] to the brothers, and love
with faith from God the Father and the
Lord Jesus Christ. **24**Grace to all who
love our Lord Jesus Christ with an undying love.

6:12 [v] 1Co 15:50; Heb 2:14 [w] Eph 1:21; 3:10 [x] Ro 8:38 [y] S Eph 1:3
6:13 [z] ver 11; S 2Co 6:7
6:14 [a] Isa 11:5 [b] Ps 132:9; Isa 59:17; 1Th 5:8
6:15 [c] Isa 52:7; Ro 10:15
6:16 [d] 1Jn 5:4 [e] S Mt 5:37
6:17 [f] Isa 59:17 [g] Isa 49:2 [h] S Heb 4:12
6:18 [i] Ro 8:26,27 [j] S Lk 18:1 [k] Mt 26:41; Php 1:4; 4:6 [l] S Ac 1:14; Col 1:3
6:19 [m] S 1Th 5:25 [n] S Ac 4:29 [o] S Ro 16:25
6:20 [p] 2Co 5:20 [q] S Ac 21:33
6:21 [r] S Ac 20:4
6:22 [s] Col 4:7-9 [t] Col 2:2; 4:8
6:23 [u] Gal 6:16; 2Th 3:16; 1Pe 5:14

10:18; Jn 12:31), led captives in his train (4:8) and redeemed the believer from Satan's power (1:7; Ac 26:18; Ro 3:24; Col 1:13–14).

(2) At the present time Christians are involved in a spiritual warfare that they wage by the power of the Holy Spirit (Ro 8:13): (a) against the sinful desires within themselves (1Pe 2:11; see Gal 5:17, note), (b) against the ungodly pleasures of the world and temptations of every sort (Mt 13:22; Gal 1:4; Jas 1:14–15; 1Jn 2:16), and (c) against Satan and his forces (see next note). Believers are called on to separate themselves from the present world system (see article on SPIRITUAL SEPARATION FOR BELIEVERS, p. 1794), hating its evil (Heb 1:9; see article on THE CHRISTIAN'S RELATIONSHIP TO THE WORLD, p. 1976), overcoming and dying to its temptations (Gal 6:14; 1Jn 5:4), and condemning openly its sin (Jn 7:7).

(3) Christian soldiers must wage war against all evil, not in their own power (2Co 10:3) but with spiritual weapons (vv. 10–18; cf. 2Co 10:4–5).

(4) In their warfare of faith Christians are called on to endure hardships like good soldiers of Christ (2Ti 2:3), suffer for the gospel (Mt 5:10–12; Ro 8:17; 2Co 11:23; 2Ti 1:8), fight the good fight of the faith (1Ti 6:12; 2Ti 4:7), wage war (2Co 10:3), persevere (v. 18), conquer (Ro 8:37), be victorious (1Co 15:57), triumph (2Co 2:14), defend the gospel (Php 1:16), contend for the faith (Php 1:27; Jude 3), not be frightened by opponents (Php 1:28), put on the full armor of God, stand firm (v. 14), destroy Satan's strongholds (2Co 10:4), take captive every thought (2Co 10:5) and become powerful in battle (Heb 11:34).

6:12 FORCES OF EVIL. Christians face a spiritual conflict with Satan and a host of evil spirits (see Mt 4:10, note on Satan; see article on POWER OVER SATAN AND DEMONS, p. 1484). (1) These powers of darkness are the spiritual forces of evil (Jn 12:31; 14:30; 16:11; 2Co 4:4; 1Jn 5:19) who energize the ungodly (2:2), oppose God's will (Ge 3:1–7; Da 10:12–13; Mt 13:38–39) and frequently attack the believers of this age (1Pe 5:8). (2) They constitute a great multitude (Rev 12:4,7) and are organized into a highly systematized empire of evil with rank and order (2:2; Jn 14:30).

6:17 THE SWORD OF THE SPIRIT. The "sword of the Spirit" is the believer's offensive weapon to be used in the war against evil's power. Satan will make every effort to undermine or destroy the Christian's confidence in that sword, "which is the word of God." The church must defend the inspired Scriptures against allegations that Scripture is not God's Word in everything it teaches. To abandon the attitude of Christ and the apostles toward God's inspired Word is to destroy its power to rebuke or correct, to redeem, to heal, to drive out demons and to overcome all evil. To deny Scripture's absolute trustworthiness in all it teaches is to deliver ourselves into Satan's hand (cf. 2Pe 1:21, note; Mt 4:1–11; see article on THE INSPIRATION AND AUTHORITY OF SCRIPTURE, p. 1898).

6:18 PRAY IN THE SPIRIT. The Christian's warfare against Satan's spiritual forces calls for an intensity in prayer, i.e., praying "in the Spirit," "on all occasions," "with all kinds of prayers," "for all the saints," "and always keep on praying." Prayer is not to be seen just as another weapon, but as part of the actual conflict itself, where the victory is won for ourselves and others by working together with God himself. To fail to pray diligently, with all kinds of prayer in all situations, is to surrender to the enemy (Lk 18:1; Ro 12:12; Php 4:6; Col 4:2; 1Th 5:17).

PHILIPPIANS

Outline

Introduction (1:1–11)
A. Christian Greetings (1:1–2)
B. Thanksgiving and Prayer for the Philippians (1:3–11)

I. Paul's Present Circumstances (1:12–26)
A. The Gospel Has Advanced Because of His Imprisonment (1:12–14)
B. In Every Way Christ Is Proclaimed (1:15–18)
C. His Readiness for Life or Death (1:19–26)

II. Matters of Concern to the Church (1:27—4:9)
A. Paul's Exhortation to the Philippians (1:27—2:18)
1. To Steadfastness (1:27–30)
2. To Unity (2:1–2)
3. To Humility and Servanthood (2:3–11)
4. To Obedience and Blameless Conduct (2:12–18)
B. Paul's Messengers to the Church (2:19–30)
1. Timothy (2:19–24)
2. Epaphroditus (2:25–30)
C. Paul's Warning Concerning Erroneous Teaching (3:1–21)
1. The False Circumcision Versus the True (3:1–16)
2. The Earthly-minded Versus the Spiritual (3:17–21)
D. Paul's Concluding Counsel (4:1–9)
1. Stability and Harmony (4:1–3)
2. Joy and Gentleness (4:4–5)
3. Freedom From Anxiety (4:6–7)
4. Control of the Mind and the Will (4:8–9)

Conclusion (4:10–23)
A. Grateful Acknowledgment of Gifts Received (4:10–20)
B. Final Greetings and Benediction (4:21–23)

Author: Paul

Theme: Joy in Living for Christ

Date of Writing: c. A.D. 62/63

Background

The city of Philippi in eastern Macedonia, ten miles inland from the Aegean Sea, was named after King Philip II of Macedon, father of Alexander the Great. In Paul's day, it was an honored Roman city and military post.

The church in Philippi was founded by Paul and his team of co-laborers (Silas, Timothy, Luke) on his second missionary journey in response to a God-given vision at Troas (Ac 16:9–40). A strong bond of friendship developed between the apostle and the Philippian church. Several times the church sent Paul financial help (2Co 11:9; Php 4:15–16) and contributed generously to his offering for the distressed Christians in Jerusalem (cf. 2Co 8—9). It appears that Paul visited the church twice on his third missionary journey (Ac 20:1,3,6).

Purpose

From prison (1:7,13–14), most likely in Rome (Ac 28:16–31), Paul wrote this letter to the Philippian believers to thank them for their recent generous gift carried to him by Epaphroditus (4:14–19) and to update them on his present circumstances. In addition, he wrote to assure the congregation of the triumph of God's purpose in his imprisonment (1:12–30), to reassure the church that their messenger (Epaphroditus) had fulfilled his charge faithfully and was not returning to them prematurely (2:25–30), and to encourage them to press on to know the Lord in unity, humility, fellowship and peace.

Survey

Unlike many of Paul's letters, Philippians was not written primarily because of church problems or conflicts. Its basic tone is one of cordial affection and appreciation for the congregation. From salutation (1:1) to benediction (4:23), the letter focuses on Christ Jesus as the purpose for living and the believer's hope for eternal life.

Within this letter, Paul does address three minor problems at Philippi: (1) their *discouragement* over his prolonged imprisonment (1:12–26); (2) small seeds of *disunity* between two women in the church (4:2; cf. 2:2–4); and (3) the ever-present threat in the church of *disloyalty* because of Judaizers and the earthly-minded (ch. 3). In connection with these three potential problems, we have Paul's richest teaching about (1) joy in the midst of all life's circumstances (e.g., 1:4,12; 2:17–18; 4:4,11–13), (2) Christian humility and service (2:1–18), and (3) the surpassing value of knowing Christ (ch. 3).

Special Features

Five major features characterize this letter. (1) It is highly personal and affectionate, reflecting Paul's close relationship to the Philippian believers. (2) It is highly Christocentric, reflecting Paul's close relationship with Christ (e.g. 1:21; 3:7–14). (3) It contains one of the most profound Christological statements in the Bible (2:5–11). (4) It is preeminently the NT "letter of joy." (5) It presents an especially vigorous standard of the Christian life, including living in humility and as a servant (2:1–8), pressing earnestly toward the goal (3:13–14), rejoicing in the Lord always (4:4), experiencing freedom from anxiety (4:6), being content in all circumstances (4:11) and doing all things through Christ's enabling grace (4:13).

Reading Philippians

In order to read the entire New Testament in one year, the book of Philippians should be read in 5 days, according to the following schedule:
☐ 1 ☐ 2:1–18 ☐ 2:19—3:11 ☐ 3:12—4:3 ☐ 4:4–23

NOTES

1 Paul and Timothy,[a] servants of Christ Jesus,

To all the saints[b] in Christ Jesus at Philippi,[c] together with the overseers[a][d] and deacons:[e]

2Grace and peace to you from God our Father and the Lord Jesus Christ.[f]

Thanksgiving and Prayer

3I thank my God every time I remember you.[g] **4**In all my prayers for all of you, I always pray[h] with joy **5**because of your partnership[i] in the gospel from the first day[j] until now, **6**being confident of this, that he who began a good work in you will carry it on to completion[k] until the day of Christ Jesus.[l]

7It is right[m] for me to feel this way about all of you, since I have you in my heart;[n] for whether I am in chains[o] or defending[p] and confirming the gospel, all of you share in God's grace with me. **8**God can testify[q] how I long for all of you with the affection of Christ Jesus.

9And this is my prayer: that your love[r] may abound more and more in knowledge and depth of insight,[s] **10**so that you may be able to discern what is best and may be pure and blameless until the day of Christ,[t] **11**filled with the fruit of righteousness[u] that comes through Jesus Christ—to the glory and praise of God.

Paul's Chains Advance the Gospel

12Now I want you to know, brothers, that what has happened to me has really served to advance the gospel. **13**As a result, it has become clear throughout the whole palace guard[b] and to everyone else that I am in chains[v] for Christ. **14**Because of my chains,[w] most of the brothers in the Lord have been encouraged to speak the word of God more courageously and fearlessly.[x]

15It is true that some preach Christ out of envy and rivalry, but others out of goodwill. **16**The latter do so in love, knowing that I am put here for the defense of the gospel.[y] **17**The former

1:1 [a] S Ac 16:1; 2Co 1:1
[b] S Ac 9:13
[c] S Ac 16:12
[d] S 1Ti 3:1
[e] 1Ti 3:8
1:2 [f] S Ro 1:7
1:3 [g] S Ro 1:8
1:4 [h] S Ro 1:10
1:5 [i] Ac 2:42; Php 4:15
[j] Ac 16:12-40
1:6 [k] Ps 138:8
[l] ver 10; S 1Co 1:8
1:7 [m] 2Pe 1:13
[n] 2Co 7:3 [o] ver 13, 14,17; S Ac 21:33
[p] ver 16
1:8 [q] S Ro 1:9
1:9 [r] 1Th 3:12
[s] S Eph 1:17
1:10 [t] ver 6; S 1Co 1:8
1:11 [u] S Jas 3:18
1:13 [v] ver 7,14, 17; S Ac 21:33
1:14 [w] ver 7,13, 17; S Ac 21:33
[x] S Ac 4:29
1:16 [y] ver 7,12

[a] *1* Traditionally *bishops* [b] *13* Or *whole palace*

1:4 JOY. Joy is an integral part of our salvation in Christ. It is an inner peace and delight in God the Father, Son and Holy Spirit, and in the blessing that flows from our relationship with them (cf. 2Co 13:14). Scriptural teaching about joy includes the following: (1) Joy is associated with the salvation God provides in Christ (1Pe 1:3–6; cf. Ps 5:11; 9:2; Isa 35:10) and with God's Word (Jer 15:16; cf. Ps 119:14).

(2) Joy flows from God as one aspect of the Spirit's fruit (Ps 16:11; Ro 15:13; Gal 5:22). It does not come automatically, but is experienced only as we maintain an abiding relationship with Christ (Jn 15:1–11). Our joy becomes greater when the Spirit mediates a deep sense of God's presence and nearness in our lives (cf. Jn 14:15–21; see 16:14, note). Jesus taught that the fullness of joy is inseparably connected to our remaining in his Word, loving others, obeying his commands (Jn 15:7,10–11) and being separated from the world (Jn 17:13–17).

(3) Joy as a delight in God's nearness and his redemptive gifts cannot be destroyed by pain, suffering, weakness or difficult circumstances (Mt 5:12; Ac 16:23–25; 2Co 12:9).

1:6 BEING CONFIDENT OF THIS. Paul's confidence in the Philippians is based not only on God's good work in them, but also on their zeal and sacrifice for the faith (vv. 5,7; 4:15–18). God's faithfulness always avails for faithful believers, but his faithfulness can do nothing for those who resist his grace (see 2:13, note; 2Ti 2:13, note).

1:9 LOVE MAY ABOUND ... IN KNOWLEDGE. Love, if it is to be Christian, must be based on Biblical revelation and knowledge. (1) In the NT "knowledge" (Gk *epignōsis*) is not merely head knowledge, but is a spiritual knowing in the heart. It refers to God's revelation as experientially known and involves a personal relationship with God rather than intellectually knowing facts about God (vv. 10–11; Eph 3:16–19; see article on BIBLE TRAINING FOR CHRISTIANS, p. 1894).

(2) Thus, to know God's Word (cf. Ro 7:1) or to know God's will (Ac 22:14; Ro 2:18) implies a knowledge that expresses itself in fellowship, obedience, life and nearness to God (Jn 17:3; 1Jn 4:8). Knowing theological truth (1Ti 6:3; Tit 1:9; see Gal 1:9, note) has as its goal love for God and freedom from sin (Ro 6:6; see article on BIBLE TRAINING FOR CHRISTIANS, p. 1894). "Depth of insight" means that the believer, through love and knowledge, discerns what is good and evil.

1:10 PURE AND BLAMELESS. "Pure" means "without any mixture of evil"; "blameless" means "not causing offense" to God or another person. Such holiness must be the ultimate aim of all believers in the light of Christ's imminent return. Only by an abounding love poured out within our hearts by the Holy Spirit (Ro 5:5; cf. Tit 3:5–6) and a full commitment to God's Word will we be "pure and blameless until the day of Christ."

1:16 THE DEFENSE OF THE GOSPEL. God gave Paul the important task of defending the content of the gospel as defined in Scripture. Likewise, all believers are called to defend Biblical truth and to resist those who would distort the faith (v. 27; see Gal 1:9, note; Jude 3, note; see

preach Christ out of selfish ambition,[z]
not sincerely, supposing that they can
stir up trouble for me while I am in
chains.[c][a] **18**But what does it matter?
The important thing is that in every
way, whether from false motives or
true, Christ is preached. And because
of this I rejoice.
Yes, and I will continue to rejoice,
19for I know that through your
prayers[b] and the help given by the
Spirit of Jesus Christ,[c] what has happened to me will turn out for my deliverance.[d][d] **20**I eagerly expect[e] and
hope that I will in no way be ashamed,
but will have sufficient courage[f] so
that now as always Christ will be exalted in my body,[g] whether by life or by
death.[h] **21**For to me, to live is Christ[i]
and to die is gain. **22**If I am to go on
living in the body, this will mean fruitful labor for me. Yet what shall I
choose? I do not know! **23**I am torn between the two: I desire to depart[j] and
be with Christ,[k] which is better by far;
24but it is more necessary for you that
I remain in the body. **25**Convinced of
this, I know that I will remain, and I
will continue with all of you for your
progress and joy in the faith, **26**so that
through my being with you again your
joy in Christ Jesus will overflow on account of me.

1:17 [z]Php 2:3 [a]ver 7,13,14; S Ac 21:33
1:19 [b]2Co 1:11 [c]S Ac 16:7 [d]Phm 22
1:20 [e]Ro 8:19 [f]ver 14 [g]1Co 6:20 [h]Ro 14:8
1:21 [i]Gal 2:20
1:23 [j]2Ti 4:6 [k]S Jn 12:26
1:27 [l]S Eph 4:1 [m]S 1Co 16:13 [n]Jude 3
1:29 [o]Mt 5:11, 12; Ac 5:41 [p]S Ac 14:22
1:30 [q]1Th 2:2; Heb 10:32 [r]Ac 16:19-40 [s]ver 13
2:1 [t]2Co 13:14 [u]Col 3:12
2:2 [v]S Jn 3:29 [w]Php 4:2 [x]S Ro 15:5
2:3 [y]Gal 5:26

The Privilege of Suffering

27Whatever happens, conduct yourselves in a manner worthy[l] of the gospel of Christ. Then, whether I come and
see you or only hear about you in my
absence, I will know that you stand
firm[m] in one spirit, contending[n] as
one man for the faith of the gospel
28without being frightened in any way
by those who oppose you. This is a sign
to them that they will be destroyed, but
that you will be saved—and that by
God. **29**For it has been granted to you[o]
on behalf of Christ not only to believe
on him, but also to suffer[p] for him,
30since you are going through the
same struggle[q] you saw[r] I had, and
now hear[s] that I still have.

Imitating Christ's Humility

2 If you have any encouragement
from being united with Christ, if
any comfort from his love, if any fellowship with the Spirit,[t] if any tenderness and compassion,[u] **2**then make
my joy complete[v] by being like-minded,[w] having the same love, being
one[x] in spirit and purpose. **3**Do nothing out of selfish ambition or vain conceit,[y] but in humility consider others

c *16,17* Some late manuscripts have verses 16 and 17 in reverse order. **d** *19* Or *salvation*

article on THE MINISTRY GIFTS OF THE CHURCH, p. 1830). Paul's words seem foreign to those ministers today who feel no need to "contend for the faith that was once for all entrusted to the saints" (Jude 3).

1:19 THE SPIRIT OF JESUS CHRIST. The Holy Spirit, who dwells in the believer, is called the "Spirit of Jesus Christ" (cf. Ac 16:7; Ro 8:9; Gal 4:6) because it is Christ who imparts the Spirit to the believer at conversion (see article on THE REGENERATION OF THE DISCIPLES, p. 1627) and subsequently baptizes the believer in the Spirit (see Ac 1:8, note; see article on BAPTISM IN THE HOLY SPIRIT, p. 1642). This Spirit is the same Spirit who anointed Jesus to bring redemption to the world (see Lk 4:18; see article on JESUS AND THE HOLY SPIRIT, p. 1546).

1:21 TO DIE IS GAIN. True believers, living in the center of God's will, need not fear death. They know that God has a purpose for their living and that death, when it comes, is simply the end of their earthly mission and the beginning of a greater life with Christ (vv. 20–25; see Ro 8:28, note; see article on DEATH, p. 732).

1:27 STAND FIRM IN ONE SPIRIT. The true essence of the unity of the Spirit consists of living in a worthy manner (cf. Eph 4:1–3), standing firm in one spirit and purpose (cf. Eph 4:3), striving side by side like warriors for the defense of the gospel according to apostolic revelation (v. 16; cf. Eph 4:13–15) and defending gospel truth against those who are "enemies of the cross of Christ" (3:18, note).

2:3 IN HUMILITY. Due to fallen humanity's innate self-centeredness the world does not highly regard humility. Yet the Bible's God-centered view of humanity and salvation places the utmost importance on humility. (1) To be humble means we will be conscious of our weaknesses and quick to give credit to God and others for what we accomplish (Jn 3:27; 5:19; 14:10; Jas 4:6).

(2) We must be humble because we are lowly creatures (Ge 18:27) who are sinful apart from Christ (Lk 18:9–14) and can boast in nothing (Ro 7:18; Gal 6:3) except in the Lord (2Co 10:17). We are dependent on God for our worth and fruitfulness and can accomplish nothing of lasting good without God's help and the help of others (Ps 8:4–5; Jn 15:1–16).

(3) God lives with those who walk humbly (Isa 57:15; Mic 6:8). God gives more grace to the humble, but opposes the proud (Jas 4:6; 1Pe 5:5). His most zealous children serve "the Lord with great humility" (Ac 20:19).

(4) As believers we must live in humility toward others, considering them more important than ourselves (cf. Ro 12:3).

(5) The opposite of humility is pride, an exag-

better than yourselves.[z] **4**Each of you
should look not only to your own interests, but also to the interests of others.[a]

5Your attitude should be the same as
that of Christ Jesus:[b]

6Who, being in very nature[e] God,[c]
did not consider equality with
God[d] something to be
grasped,
7but made himself nothing,[e]
taking the very nature[f] of a
servant,[f]
being made in human likeness.[g]
8And being found in appearance as
a man,
he humbled himself
and became obedient to
death[h]—
even death on a cross![i]

2:3 [z] Ro 12:10; 1Pe 5:5
2:4 [a] S 1Co 10:24
2:5 [b] S Mt 11:29
2:6 [c] Jn 1:1; S 14:9 [d] Jn 5:18
2:7 [e] 2Co 8:9 [f] S Mt 20:28 [g] S Jn 1:14; Ro 8:3; Heb 2:17
2:8 [h] S Mt 26:39; Jn 10:18; Ro 5:19; Heb 5:8 [i] S 1Co 1:23
2:9 [j] Isa 52:13; 53:12; Da 7:14; Ac 2:33; Heb 2:9 [k] Eph 1:20,21
2:10 [l] Ps 95:6; Isa 45:23; Ro 14:11 [m] Mt 28:18; Eph 1:10; Col 1:20
2:11 [n] S Jn 13:13
2:12 [o] S 2Co 7:15
2:13 [p] Ezr 1:5; 1Co 12:6; 15:10; Gal 2:8; Heb 13:21

9Therefore God exalted him[j] to the
highest place
and gave him the name that is
above every name,[k]
10that at the name of Jesus every
knee should bow,[l]
in heaven and on earth and
under the earth,[m]
11and every tongue confess that
Jesus Christ is Lord,[n]
to the glory of God the Father.

Shining as Stars

12Therefore, my dear friends, as you
have always obeyed—not only in my
presence, but now much more in my
absence—continue to work out your
salvation with fear and trembling,[o]
13for it is God who works in you[p] to

[e] 6 Or *in the form of* [f] 7 Or *the form*

---

gerated feeling of self-importance and self-esteem in a person who believes in his or her own merit, superiority and accomplishments. The inevitable tendency of human nature and the world is toward pride, not humility (1Jn 2:16; cf. Isa 14:13–14; Eze 28:17; 1Ti 6:17).

2:5 YOUR ATTITUDE SHOULD BE THE SAME. Paul emphasizes how Jesus left incomparable glory in heaven and took the humiliating position of a servant, becoming obedient to death to benefit others (vv. 5–8). Christ's humility of heart and mind must be found in his followers, who are called to live sacrificially and unselfishly, caring about others and doing good to them.

2:6 BEING IN VERY NATURE GOD. Jesus Christ has always been God by nature, equal with the Father before, during and after his time on earth (see Jn 1:1; 8:58; 17:24; 20:28, note; Col 1:15,17; see Mk 1:11, note; Jn 20:28, note). That Christ "did not consider equality with God something to be grasped" means he let go of his privileges and glory in heaven in order that we on earth might be saved.

2:7 MADE HIMSELF NOTHING. The Greek literally says he "emptied himself," i.e., laid aside his heavenly glory (Jn 17:4), position (Jn 5:30; Heb 5:8), riches (2Co 8:9), rights (Lk 22:27; Mt 20:28) and the use of his divine attributes (Jn 5:19; 8:28; 14:10). This "emptying himself" meant not only a voluntary restraint on his divine capacities and privileges, but also an acceptance of suffering, misunderstanding, ill-treatment, hatred and a cursed death on the cross.

2:7 NATURE OF A SERVANT . . . HUMAN LIKENESS. For passages in the Bible dealing with Christ taking the nature of a servant, see Mk 13:32; Lk 2:40–52; Ro 8:3; 2Co 8:9; Heb 2:7,14. Although he remained fully divine, Christ took on a human nature with its temptations, humiliations and weaknesses, yet was without sin (vv. 7–8; Heb 4:15).

2:12 WORK OUT YOUR SALVATION. As believers saved by grace, we must work out our salvation to the end. If we fail to do this, we will lose the salvation given us. (1) We do not work out our salvation by mere human effort, but by means of God's grace and the Spirit's power given to us (see article on FAITH AND GRACE, p. 1720).

(2) In order to work out our salvation we must resist sin and follow the desires of the Holy Spirit within us. This involves a sustained effort to use every God-appointed means for defeating evil and revealing Christ's life. Thus, working out our salvation focuses on the importance of sanctification (see Gal 5:17, note; see article on THE ACTS OF THE SINFUL NATURE AND THE FRUIT OF THE SPIRIT, p. 1818).

(3) We work out our salvation by ever drawing near to Christ (see Heb 7:25, note) and receiving his power to will and to act according to God's good pleasure (see v. 13, note). Thus we are "God's fellow workers" (1Co 3:9) in bringing our salvation to completion in heaven.

(4) Working out our salvation is so vital that it must be performed "with fear and trembling" (see next note).

2:12 FEAR AND TREMBLING. In the salvation accomplished through Christ, Paul finds room for "fear and trembling." All of God's children should possess a holy fear that trembles at God's Word (Isa 66:2) and causes them to turn away from all evil (Pr 3:7; 8:13). The fear (Gk *phobos*) of the Lord is not, as is often defined, merely "reverential trust," but includes an awe of God's power, holiness and righteous retribution, and a dread of sinning against him and facing the consequences (cf. Ex 3:6; Ps 119:120; Lk 12:4–5). It is not a destructive fear, but a controlling and redeeming fear that leads to God's nearness and blessing, to moral purity, and to life and salvation (cf. Ps 5:7; 85:9; Pr 14:27; 16:6; see article on THE FEAR OF THE LORD, p. 260).

2:13 GOD WHO WORKS IN YOU. God's grace is at work in his children to produce in them both

will and to act according to his good
purpose.[q]
14Do everything without complaining[r] or arguing, **15**so that you may become blameless[s] and pure, children of
God[t] without fault in a crooked and
depraved generation,[u] in which you
shine like stars in the universe **16**as
you hold out[g] the word of life—in order that I may boast on the day of
Christ[v] that I did not run[w] or labor for
Col 3:5-14 nothing.[x] **17**But even if I am being
poured out like a drink offering[y] on
the sacrifice[z] and service coming
from your faith, I am glad and rejoice
with all of you.[a] **18**So you too should
be glad and rejoice with me.

Timothy and Epaphroditus

19I hope in the Lord Jesus to send
Timothy[b] to you soon,[c] that I also
may be cheered when I receive news
about you. **20**I have no one else like
him,[d] who takes a genuine interest in
your welfare. **21**For everyone looks out
for his own interests,[e] not those of
Jesus Christ. **22**But you know that Timothy has proved himself, because as a
son with his father[f] he has served
with me in the work of the gospel. **23**I
hope, therefore, to send him as soon as
I see how things go with me.[g] **24**And
I am confident[h] in the Lord that I myself will come soon.
25But I think it is necessary to send
back to you Epaphroditus, my brother,
fellow worker[i] and fellow soldier,[j]
who is also your messenger, whom you
sent to take care of my needs.[k] **26**For
he longs for all of you[l] and is distressed because you heard he was ill.
27Indeed he was ill, and almost died.
But God had mercy on him, and not on
him only but also on me, to spare me
sorrow upon sorrow. **28**Therefore I am
all the more eager to send him,[m] so
that when you see him again you may
be glad and I may have less anxiety.
29Welcome him in the Lord with great
joy, and honor men like him,[n] **30**because he almost died for the work of
Christ, risking his life to make up for
the help you could not give me.[o]

No Confidence in the Flesh

3 Finally, my brothers, rejoice in the
Lord! It is no trouble for me to
write the same things to you again,[p]
and it is a safeguard for you.
2Watch out for those dogs,[q] those

2:13 [q]Eph 1:5
2:14 [r]1Co 10:10; 1Pe 4:9
2:15 [s]S 1Th 3:13 [t]Mt 5:45,48; Eph 5:1 [u]Ac 2:40
2:16 [v]S 1Co 1:8 [w]S 1Co 9:24 [x]1Th 2:19
2:17 [y]2Co 12:15; 2Ti 4:6 [z]Ro 15:16 [a]S 2Co 6:10
2:19 [b]S Ac 16:1 [c]ver 23
2:20 [d]1Co 16:10
2:21 [e]S 1Co 10:24
2:22 [f]1Co 4:17; 1Ti 1:2
2:23 [g]ver 19
2:24 [h]Php 1:25
2:25 [i]Ro 16:3,9, 21; 2Co 8:23; Php 4:3; Col 4:11; Phm 1 [j]Phm 2 [k]Php 4:18
2:26 [l]Php 1:8
2:28 [m]ver 25
2:29 [n]1Co 16:18; 1Ti 5:17
2:30 [o]1Co 16:17
3:1 [p]Php 2:18
3:2 [q]Ps 22:16,20; Rev 22:15

[g]16 Or *hold on to*

the desire and power to do his will (see article on FAITH AND GRACE, p. 1720). However, God's work is not one of compulsion or irresistible grace. The work of grace within us (1:6; 1Th 5:24; 2Ti 4:18; Tit 3:5–7) is always dependent on our faithfulness and cooperation (vv. 12,14–16).

2:15 CROOKED AND DEPRAVED GENERATION. Jesus and the apostles emphasized that the world we live in is an "unbelieving and perverse generation" (Mt 17:17; cf. 12:39; Ac 2:40). The people of the world hold wrong views, have warped values, follow immoral ways of life and reject the norms of God's Word. God's children must separate themselves from the world and be blameless, pure and without fault in order to proclaim Christ's glorious redemption to the lost world (cf. 1Jn 2:15).

2:17 POURED OUT LIKE A DRINK OFFERING. Paul's love and concern for the Philippians was such that he was willing to give his life for them as if it were an offering to God. (1) Paul would not regret but rather rejoice in being the victim of sacrifice, if only it would deepen their faith in and love for Christ (cf. 2Ti 4:6). (2) If Paul had such sacrificial love for his spiritual children, what sacrifice and suffering should we be willing to undergo for the faith of our own children? If, in order to make our children as complete as possible in the Lord, it became necessary for us to pour out our lives, and even our blood, as an offering to the Lord, then we ought to be prepared to make such a sacrifice (see article on PARENTS AND CHILDREN, p. 1854, outlining fifteen steps parents should take to lead their children to godly living).

2:19 TIMOTHY. Timothy was a good example of what a minister and missionary of God should be. He was an eager and obedient student of God's Word (2Ti 3:15), a worthy servant of Christ (1Th 3:2), a man of good reputation (Ac 16:2), beloved and faithful (1Co 4:17), genuinely concerned for others (v. 20), dependable (2Ti 4:9,21), and devoted to Paul and the gospel (v. 22; Ro 16:21).

2:21 FOR EVERYONE LOOKS OUT FOR HIS OWN INTERESTS. There are ministers who preach, teach, pastor or write, not out of genuine concern for the furtherance of the gospel, but for their own interests, glory, prestige and selfish ambition. Rather than seeking to please the Lord Jesus, they seek instead to please people and gain their favor (vv. 20–21; 1:15; 2Ti 4:10,16). Such ministers are not true servants of the Lord.

3:2 DOGS . . . MEN WHO DO EVIL . . . MUTILATORS. Paul's greatest trial was the grief he experienced because of those who distorted the gospel of Christ. His love for Christ, the church and redemptive truth was so strong that it drove him to oppose fervently those who perverted pure doctrine, describing them as "dogs" and "men who do evil" (see 1:17, note; Gal 1:9, note; cf. Mt 23). "Mutilators of the flesh" is Paul's expression for the rite of circumcision as taught by the Judaizers, who claimed that the OT sign of circumcision was

men who do evil, those mutilators
of the flesh. **3**For it is we who are
the circumcision,[r] we who worship
by the Spirit of God, who glory in
Christ Jesus,[s] and who put no confidence in the flesh— **4**though I myself have reasons for such confidence.[t]

If anyone else thinks he has reasons
to put confidence in the flesh, I have
more: **5**circumcised[u] on the eighth
day, of the people of Israel,[v] of the
tribe of Benjamin,[w] a Hebrew of Hebrews; in regard to the law, a Pharisee;[x] **6**as for zeal,[y] persecuting the
church;[z] as for legalistic righteousness,[a] faultless.

Paul's Desire to Gain Christ

7But whatever was to my profit I
now consider loss[b] for the sake of
Christ. **8**What is more, I consider everything a loss compared to the surpassing greatness of knowing[c] Christ
Jesus my Lord, for whose sake I have
lost all things. I consider them rubbish,
that I may gain Christ[d] **9**and be found
in him, not having a righteousness of
my own that comes from the law,[e] but
that which is through faith in Christ—
the righteousness[f] that comes from
God and is by faith.[g] **10**I want to
know[h] Christ and the power of his resurrection and the fellowship of sharing
in his sufferings,[i] becoming like him
in his death,[j] **11**and so, somehow, to
attain to the resurrection[k] from the
dead.

Pressing on Toward the Goal

12Not that I have already obtained
all this, or have already been made perfect,[l] but I press on to take hold[m] of
that for which Christ Jesus took hold of
me.[n] **13**Brothers, I do not consider
myself yet to have taken hold of it. But
one thing I do: Forgetting what is behind[o] and straining toward what is

3:3 [r]Ro 2:28,29; Gal 6:15; Col 2:11 [s]Ro 15:17; Gal 6:14 **3:4** [t]2Co 11:21 **3:5** [u]S Lk 1:59 [v]2Co 11:22 [w]Ro 11:1 [x]Ac 23:6 **3:6** [y]S Ac 21:20 [z]S Ac 8:3 [a]ver 9; Ro 10:5 **3:7** [b]Mt 13:44; Lk 14:33 **3:8** [c]ver 10; Jer 9:23,24; Jn 17:3; Eph 4:13; S 2Pe 1:2 [d]Ps 73:25 **3:9** [e]ver 6; Ro 10:5 [f]Jer 33:16 [g]S Ro 9:30 **3:10** [h]S ver 8 [i]S 2Co 1:5 [j]S Ro 6:3-5 **3:11** [k]S Jn 11:24; S Ro 6:5; Rev 20:5,6 **3:12** [l]1Co 13:10 [m]1Ti 6:12 [n]Ac 9:5,6 **3:13** [o]Lk 9:62

necessary for salvation. Paul states that true circumcision is the Spirit's work in the heart of a person when sin and evil are cut away (v. 3; Ro 2:25–29; Col 2:11).

3:8–11 THAT I MAY GAIN CHRIST. These verses show the apostle's heart and the essence of Christianity. Paul's greatest longing was to know Christ and to experience his personal fellowship and nearness in a more intimate way. His pursuit involved the following:

(1) To know Christ personally as well as to know his ways, nature and character as revealed in God's Word. True knowledge of Christ involves listening to his Word, following his Spirit, responding to his dealings with us in faith, truth and obedience, and identifying with his concerns and purposes.

(2) To be found in Christ (v. 9), i.e., to have a union and fellowship with Christ that produces a righteousness experienced only as a gift from God (1:10–11; 1Co 1:30, note; see article on BIBLICAL WORDS FOR SALVATION, p. 1710).

(3) To know the power of his resurrection (v. 10), i.e., to experience renewal of life, deliverance from sin (Ro 6:4; Eph 2:5–6), and the Spirit's power to bring about effective witness, healing, miracles and finally one's own resurrection from the dead (v. 11; Eph 1:18–20).

(4) To share in Christ's sufferings by self-denial, crucifixion of the old self, and suffering for the sake of Christ and his cause (cf. 1:29; Ac 9:16; Ro 6:5–6; 1Co 15:31; 2Co 4:10; Gal 2:20; Col 1:24; 1Pe 4:13).

3:9 RIGHTEOUSNESS THAT COMES FROM GOD. The righteousness of believers consists first of all in being forgiven, justified and accepted by God through faith (see Ro 4:5, note).

(1) However, our righteousness is more than this. God's Word states that our righteousness is Christ Jesus himself, living within our hearts (cf. 1:20–21; Ro 8:10; 1Co 1:30; Gal 2:20; Eph 3:17; Col 3:4); in the OT the Messiah is referred to as the "righteous Branch" and "The Lord Our Righteousness" (see Jer 23:5–6, note). Thus the righteousness we have is not of ourselves but of Jesus, in whom we put our faith (1Co 1:30, note; Gal 2:20, note). Through this indwelling, we become in him "the righteousness of God" (see 2Co 5:21, note).

(2) The ground for our salvation and our only hope of righteousness is the sacrificial death and shed blood of Christ (Ro 3:24; 4:25; 5:9; 8:3–4; 1Co 15:3; Gal 1:4; 2:20; Eph 1:7; Heb 9:14; 1Pe 1:18–19; 1Jn 4:10) and his resurrection life within our hearts (Ro 4:25; 5:9–10; 8:10–11; Gal 2:20; Col 3:1–3; see Ro 4:22, note).

3:13 BUT ONE THING I DO. Paul sees himself as a runner in a race (cf. Heb 12:1, note), exerting all his strength and pressing on with intense concentration in order not to fall short of the goal that Christ has set for his life—Paul's perfect oneness with Christ (vv. 8–10), his final salvation and his resurrection from the dead (v. 11). (1) This was the motive of Paul's life. He had received a glimpse of the glory of heaven (2Co 12:4) and had resolved that his whole life, by God's grace, would be centered around his determination to press on and someday get to heaven and see Christ face to face (cf. 2Ti 4:8; Rev 2:10; 22:4).

(2) Such determination is necessary for all of us. Throughout our lives all kinds of distractions and temptations, such as life's worries, riches and evil desires, threaten to choke off our commitment to the Lord (cf. Mk 4:19; Lk 8:14). What is needed is a "forgetting what is behind," i.e., the corrupt world and our old life of sin (cf. Ge 19:17,26; Lk 17:32), and a "straining" for final salvation in Christ.

ahead, **14**I press on[p] toward the goal to win the prize[q] for which God has called[r] me heavenward in Christ Jesus.

15All of us who are mature[s] should take such a view of things.[t] And if on some point you think differently, that too God will make clear to you.[u] **16**Only let us live up to what we have already attained.

17Join with others in following my example,[v] brothers, and take note of those who live according to the pattern we gave you.[w] **18**For, as I have often told you before and now say again even with tears,[x] many live as enemies of the cross of Christ.[y] **19**Their destiny[z] is destruction, their god is their stomach,[a] and their glory is in their shame.[b] Their mind is on earthly things.[c] **20**But our citizenship[d] is in heaven.[e] And we eagerly await a Savior from there, the Lord Jesus Christ,[f] **21**who, by the power[g] that enables him to bring everything under his control, will transform our lowly bodies[h] so that they will be like his glorious body.[i]

4 Therefore, my brothers, you whom I love and long for,[j] my joy and crown, that is how you should stand firm[k] in the Lord, dear friends!

Exhortations

2I plead with Euodia and I plead with Syntyche to agree with each other[l] in the Lord. **3**Yes, and I ask you, loyal yokefellow,[h] help these women who have contended at my side in the cause of the gospel, along with Clement and the rest of my fellow workers,[m] whose names are in the book of life.[n]

4Rejoice in the Lord always. I will say it again: Rejoice![o] **5**Let your gentleness be evident to all. The Lord is near.[p] **6**Do not be anxious about anything,[q] but in everything, by prayer and petition, with thanksgiving, present your requests to God.[r] **7**And the peace of God,[s] which transcends

3:14 [p]Heb 6:1 [q]1Co 9:24 [r]S Ro 8:28
3:15 [s]S 1Co 2:6 [t]Gal 5:10 [u]Eph 1:17; 1Th 4:9
3:17 [v]S 1Co 4:16 [w]S 1Ti 4:12
3:18 [x]Ac 20:31 [y]Gal 6:12
3:19 [z]Ps 73:17 [a]Ro 16:18 [b]Ro 6:21; Jude 13 [c]Ro 8:5,6; Col 3:2
3:20 [d]Eph 2:19 [e]Col 3:1; Heb 12:22 [f]S 1Co 1:7
3:21 [g]Eph 1:19 [h]1Co 15:43-53 [i]Ro 8:29; Col 3:4
4:1 [j]Php 1:8 [k]S 1Co 16:13
4:2 [l]Php 2:2
4:3 [m]S Php 2:25 [n]S Rev 20:12
4:4 [o]Ps 85:6; 97:12; Hab 3:18; S Mt 5:12; Ro 12:12; Php 3:1
4:5 [p]Ps 119:151; 145:18; Heb 10:37; Jas 5:8,9
4:6 [q]Mt 6:25-34 [r]Eph 6:18; 1Ti 2:1
4:7 [s]Isa 26:3; S Jn 14:27

[h]3 Or *loyal Syzygus*

3:18 ENEMIES OF THE CROSS OF CHRIST. These enemies can best be understood as professed believers who were corrupting the gospel by immoral lives and false teachings. One key to Paul's greatness was that he was a man of intense feeling whose heart was stirred to the core when the gospel was distorted or when those whom he served were in danger (see v. 2, note; Gal 1:9, note; see article OVERSEERS AND THEIR DUTIES, p. 1690).

3:20 OUR CITIZENSHIP IS IN HEAVEN. Christians are no longer citizens of this world; they have become strangers and aliens on the earth (Ro 8:22–24; Gal 4:26; Heb 11:13; 12:22–23; 13:14; 1Pe 1:17; 2:11; see article on THE CALL OF ABRAHAM, p. 25). (1) In regard to our life's walk, values and direction, heaven is now our fatherland. We have been born from above (Jn 3:3), our names are written on heaven's register (4:3), our lives are guided by heavenly standards, and our rights and inheritance are reserved in heaven.

(2) It is to heaven that our prayers ascend (cf. 2Ch 6:21; 30:27) and our hope is directed. Many of our friends and family members are already there, and we will be there soon. Jesus is there also, preparing a place for us, and he has promised to return and take us to himself (see Jn 14:2–3, notes; cf. Jn 3:3; 14:1–4; Ro 8:17; Eph 2:6; Col 3:1–3; Heb 6:19–20; 12:22–24; 1Pe 1:4–5; Rev 7:9–17). For these reasons we long for a better country, i.e., a heavenly one. Therefore, God is not ashamed to be called our God, and he has prepared for us an eternal city (Heb 11:16).

4:4 REJOICE IN THE LORD. The believer must rejoice and gain strength by recalling the Lord's grace, nearness and promises (see 1:4, note).

4:5 THE LORD IS NEAR. We must believe the Lord may come at any time. The NT depicts Christ's return as imminent (see Lk 12:35–40, note); therefore, we must be ready, working and watching at all times (Mt 24:36; 25:1–13; Ro 13:12–14).

4:6 DO NOT BE ANXIOUS ABOUT ANYTHING. The one essential cure for worry is prayer, for the following reasons: (1) Through prayer we renew our trust in the Lord's faithfulness by casting all our anxieties and problems on him who cares for us (Mt 6:25–34; 1Pe 5:7). (2) God's peace comes to guard our hearts and minds as a result of our communion with Christ Jesus (vv. 6–7; Isa 26:3; Col 3:15). (3) God strengthens us to do all the things he desires of us (v. 13; 3:20, note; Eph 3:16). (4) We receive mercy, grace and help in time of need (Heb 4:16). (5) We are assured that in all things God works for our good (see v. 11, note; Ro 8:28, note).

4:7 PEACE OF GOD . . . WILL GUARD YOUR HEARTS. When we call on God from hearts that remain in Christ and his Word (Jn 15:7), then God's peace will flood our troubled souls. (1) This peace is an inner tranquility mediated by the Holy Spirit (Ro 8:15–16). It involves a firm conviction that Jesus is near and that God's love will be active in our lives for good (Ro 8:28,32; cf. Isa 26:3). (2) When we lay our troubles before God in prayer, this peace will stand guard at the door of our hearts and minds, preventing the cares and heartaches of life from upsetting our lives and undermining our hope in Christ (v. 6; Isa 26:3–4,12; 37:1–7; Ro 8:35–39; 1Pe 5:7). (3) If fear and anxiety return, prayer, petition and thanksgiving will

all understanding,[t] will guard your
hearts and your minds in Christ Jesus.
8Finally, brothers, whatever is true,
whatever is noble, whatever is right,
whatever is pure, whatever is lovely, whatever is admirable—if anything
is excellent or praiseworthy—think
about such things. 9Whatever you have
learned or received or heard from me,
or seen in me—put it into practice.[u]
And the God of peace[v] will be with
you.

Thanks for Their Gifts

10I rejoice greatly in the Lord that at
last you have renewed your concern for
me.[w] Indeed, you have been concerned, but you had no opportunity to
show it. 11I am not saying this because
I am in need, for I have learned to be
content[x] whatever the circumstances.
12I know what it is to be in need, and
I know what it is to have plenty. I have
learned the secret of being content in
any and every situation, whether well
fed or hungry,[y] whether living in plenty or in want.[z] 13I can do everything
through him who gives me strength.[a]
14Yet it was good of you to share[b]
in my troubles. 15Moreover, as you
Philippians know, in the early days[c]
of your acquaintance with the gospel,
when I set out from Macedonia,[d] not
one church shared with me in the matter of giving and receiving, except you
only;[e] 16for even when I was in Thessalonica,[f] you sent me aid again and
again when I was in need.[g] 17Not that
I am looking for a gift, but I am looking
for what may be credited to your account.[h] 18I have received full payment
and even more; I am amply supplied,
now that I have received from Epaphroditus[i] the gifts you sent. They are
a fragrant[j] offering, an acceptable
sacrifice, pleasing to God. 19And my
God will meet all your needs[k] according to his glorious riches[l] in Christ
Jesus.
20To our God and Father[m] be glory
for ever and ever. Amen.[n]

Final Greetings

21Greet all the saints in Christ
Jesus. The brothers who are with me[o]
send greetings. 22All the saints[p] send
you greetings, especially those who belong to Caesar's household.
23The grace of the Lord Jesus
Christ[q] be with your spirit.[r] Amen.[i]

4:7 [t]Eph 3:19 **4:9** [u]S 1Co 4:16 [v]S Ro 15:33 **4:10** [w]2Co 11:9 **4:11** [x]1Ti 6:6,8; Heb 13:5 **4:12** [y]S 1Co 4:11 [z]2Co 11:9 **4:13** [a]2Co 12:9; Eph 3:16; Col 1:11; 1Ti 1:12; 2Ti 4:17 **4:14** [b]Php 1:7 **4:15** [c]Php 1:5 [d]S Ac 16:9 [e]2Co 11:8,9 **4:16** [f]S Ac 17:1 [g]1Th 2:9 **4:17** [h]1Co 9:11, 12 **4:18** [i]Php 2:25 [j]S 2Co 2:14 **4:19** [k]Ps 23:1; 2Co 9:8 [l]S Ro 2:4 **4:20** [m]Gal 1:4; 1Th 1:3; 3:11,13 [n]S Ro 11:36 **4:21** [o]Gal 1:2 **4:22** [p]S Ac 9:13 **4:23** [q]S Ro 16:20 [r]S Gal 6:18

[i]23 Some manuscripts do not have *Amen*.

---

once again place us under the peace of God that guards our hearts. Once more we will feel safe and rejoice in the Lord (v. 4; see article on THE PEACE OF GOD, p. 1134).

4:8 WHATEVER IS PURE. To experience God's peace and freedom from anxiety, believers must fix their minds on those things that are true, noble, right, pure, etc. If you do these things, says Paul, "the God of peace will be with you " (v. 9). The consequence of fixing our minds on the unholy things of the world is that the joy, nearness and peace of God are lost and our hearts are no longer guarded.

4:11 I HAVE LEARNED TO BE CONTENT. The key to contentment is realizing that God has given you in your present circumstances everything you need to remain victorious in Christ (1Co 15:57; 2Co 2:14; 1Jn 5:4). The ability to live triumphantly above changing circumstances comes from Christ's power flowing in and through you (v. 13; see 1Ti 6:8, note). This ability does not come naturally, however; it must be learned through dependence on Christ.

4:13 I CAN DO EVERYTHING THROUGH HIM. Christ's power and grace rest on believers to enable them to do all that he has asked them to do (see article on FAITH AND GRACE, p. 1720).

4:16 YOU SENT ME AID AGAIN AND AGAIN. The Philippian church was a missionary church that ministered to Paul's needs during his travels (vv. 15–17; 1:4–5). Missionary support is honored and accepted by God as "a fragrant offering, an acceptable sacrifice, pleasing to God" (v. 18). Thus, what we give to the support of a faithful missionary is regarded as an offering brought to God. What is done for one of the least of our brothers or sisters is done for the Lord himself (Mt 25:40).

4:19 WILL MEET ALL YOUR NEEDS. Paul emphasizes the loving care of God the Father for his children. He will meet all your needs (material and spiritual) as you present them to him. He will meet them "in Christ Jesus." Only in union with Christ and in his fellowship can we experience God's provision. Among the many Scriptural promises that give hope and encouragement to God's people concerning his care and help are: Ge 28:15; 50:20; Ex 33:14; Dt 2:7; 32:7–14; 33:27; Jos 1:9; 1Sa 7:12; 1Ki 17:6,16; 2Ch 20:17; Ps 18:35; 23; 121; Isa 25:4; 32:2; 40:11; 41:10; 43:1–2; 46:3–4; Joel 2:21–27; Mal 3:10; Mt 6:25–34; 14:20; 23:37; Lk 6:38; 12:7; 22:35; Jn 10:27–28; 17:11; Ro 8:28, 31–39; 2Ti 1:12; 4:18; 1Pe 5:7; see article on THE PROVIDENCE OF GOD, p. 78.

COLOSSIANS

Outline

Introduction (1:1–12)
- A. Christian Greetings (1:1–2)
- B. Thanksgiving for Their Faith, Love and Hope (1:3–8)
- C. Prayer for Their Spiritual Advancement (1:9–12)

I. Powerful Doctrine—The Believer's Redemption (1:13—2:23)
- A. The Absolute Preeminence of Christ (1:13–23)
  1. As Vicarious Redeemer (1:13–14; cf. 1:20,22)
  2. As Lord of Creation (1:15–17)
  3. As Head of the Church (1:18)
  4. As Reconciler of All Things (1:19–20)
  5. As Reconciler of the Colossians to God (1:21–23)
- B. Paul's Ministry of God's Mystery in Christ (1:24—2:7)
  1. Filling Up the Afflictions of Christ (1:24–25)
  2. Perfecting Believers in Christ (1:26—2:7)
- C. Warnings Against Erroneous Teaching (2:8–23)
  1. Problem: Teaching Not According to Christ (2:8)
     Solution: Made Complete in Christ (2:9–15)
  2. Problem: Religious Practices Not According to Christ (2:16–23)
     Solution: Crucified with Christ (2:20)

II. Practical Instructions—The Believer's Life (3:1—4:6)
- A. The Believer's Personal Conduct (3:1–17)
  1. When Christ Is Our Life (3:1–4)
  2. Laying Aside the Old Life of Sin (3:5–9)
  3. Putting on the New Self in Christ (3:10–17)
- B. The Believer's Domestic Relationships (3:18—4:1)
  1. Wives and Husbands (3:18–19)
  2. Children and Parents (3:20–21)
  3. Slaves and Masters (3:22—4:1)
- C. The Believer's Spiritual Influence (4:2–6)
  1. A Life Devoted to Prayer (4:2–4)
  2. Wise Conduct Toward Outsiders (4:5)
  3. Speech Seasoned with Grace (4:6)

Conclusion (4:7–18)

Author: Paul

Theme: Supremacy of Christ

Date of Writing: c. A.D. 62

Background

The city of Colosse was located near Laodicea (cf. 4:16) in southwest Asia Minor, about 100 miles directly east of Ephesus. The Colossian church appears to have been founded as a result of Paul's exceptional three-year ministry at Ephesus (Ac 20:31), the effects of which were so powerful and far-reaching that "all the Jews and Greeks who lived in the province of Asia heard the word of the Lord" (Ac 19:10). Although Paul may never have visited Colosse in person (2:1), he had maintained contact with the church through Epaphras, one of his converts and associates from Colosse (1:7; 4:12).

The occasion for this letter was the appearance of false teaching that threatened the spiritual future of the Colossian church (2:8). When Epaphras, a leader in the Colossian church and perhaps its founder, traveled to visit Paul and to inform him about the situation at Colosse (1:8; 4:12), Paul responded by writing this letter. He was a prisoner at the time (4:3,10,18), most likely at Rome (Ac 28:16–31) awaiting his appeal before Caesar (Ac 25:11–12). Paul's co-worker, Tychicus, delivered the letter in person to Colosse on Paul's behalf (4:7).

The exact nature of the Colossian heresy is not described explicitly in the letter, for the original readers knew it well. From Paul's statements made in opposition to the false teachings, however, it is apparent that the heresy undermining and replacing the centrality of Jesus Christ was a strange mixture of Christian teaching, certain extrabiblical Jewish traditions and pagan philosophy (similar to the mixture of cults today).

Purpose

Paul wrote (1) to combat the dangerous false teaching at Colosse that was supplanting Christ's centrality and supremacy in creation, revelation, redemption and the church; and (2) to stress the true nature of new life in Christ and its demands on the believer.

Survey

After greeting the church and expressing gratitude for their faith, love and hope, and for their continued progress as believers, Paul focuses on two key issues: correct doctrine (1:13—2:23) and practical exhortations (3:1—4:6).

Theologically, Paul emphasizes the true character and glory of the Lord Jesus Christ. He is the image of the invisible God (1:15), the fullness of deity in bodily form (2:9), the Creator of all things (1:16–17), the head of the church (1:18) and the all-sufficient source of our salvation (1:14,20–22). Whereas Christ is completely adequate, the Colossian heresy is utterly inadequate—hollow, deceitful and humanistic (2:8); superficially spiritual and arrogant (2:18); and without power against the sinful desires of the body (2:23).

In his practical exhortations, Paul appeals for a life grounded in the complete sufficiency of Christ as the only way to progress in Christian living. The reality of the indwelling Christ (1:27) must be evident in Christian behavior (3:1–17), domestic relationships (3:18—4:1) and spiritual discipline (4:2–6).

Special Features

Three major features characterize this letter. (1) More than any other NT book, Colossians focuses on the twofold truth of Christ's preeminence and the believer's completeness in him. (2) It strongly affirms Christ's full deity (2:9) and contains one of the most exalted passages in the NT about his glory (1:15–23). (3) It is sometimes regarded as a "twin letter" with Ephesians, because the two have certain resemblances in content and were written about the same time (cf. the outlines to the two letters).

Reading Colossians

In order to read the entire New Testament in one year, the book of Colossians should be read in 5 days, according to the following schedule:
☐ 1:1–23 ☐ 1:24—2:5 ☐ 2:6–23 ☐ 3:1—4:1 ☐ 4:2–18

NOTES

1 Paul, an apostle[a] of Christ Jesus
by the will of God,[b] and Timothy[c] our brother,

2To the holy and faithful[a] brothers
in Christ at Colosse:

Grace[d] and peace to you from God
our Father.[b][e]

Thanksgiving and Prayer

3We always thank God,[f] the Father
of our Lord Jesus Christ, when we pray
for you, **4**because we have heard of
your faith in Christ Jesus and of the
love[g] you have for all the saints[h]—
5the faith and love that spring from the
hope[i] that is stored up for you in
heaven[j] and that you have already
heard about in the word of truth,[k] the
gospel **6**that has come to you. All over
the world[l] this gospel is bearing
fruit[m] and growing, just as it has been
doing among you since the day you
heard it and understood God's grace in
all its truth. **7**You learned it from Epaphras,[n] our dear fellow servant, who
is a faithful minister[o] of Christ on
our[c] behalf, **8**and who also told us of
your love in the Spirit.[p] 1Th 1:6

9For this reason, since the day we
heard about you,[q] we have not
stopped praying for you[r] and asking
God to fill you with the knowledge of
his will[s] through all spiritual wisdom
and understanding.[t] **10**And we pray
this in order that you may live a life
worthy[u] of the Lord and may please
him[v] in every way: bearing fruit in every good work, growing in the knowledge of God,[w] **11**being strengthened
with all power[x] according to his glorious might so that you may have great
endurance and patience,[y] and joyfully
12giving thanks to the Father,[z] who
has qualified you[d] to share in the inheritance[a] of the saints in the kingdom of light.[b] **13**For he has rescued
us from the dominion of darkness[c]
and brought us into the kingdom[d]
of the Son he loves,[e] **14**in whom we

1:1 [a]S 1Co 1:1 [b]S 2Co 1:1 [c]S Ac 16:1 **1:2** [d]Col 4:18 [e]S Ro 1:7 **1:3** [f]S Ro 1:8 **1:4** [g]Gal 5:6 [h]S Ac 9:13; Eph 1:15; Phm 5 **1:5** [i]ver 23; 1Th 5:8; Tit 1:2 [j]1Pe 1:4 [k]S 2Ti 2:15 **1:6** [l]ver 23; S Ro 10:18 [m]Jn 15:16 **1:7** [n]Col 4:12; Phm 23 [o]Col 4:7 **1:8** [p]Ro 15:30 **1:9** [q]ver 4; Eph 1:15 [r]S Ro 1:10 [s]S Eph 5:17 [t]S Eph 1:17 **1:10** [u]S Eph 4:1 [v]S 2Co 5:9 [w]ver 6 **1:11** [x]S Php 4:13 [y]Eph 4:2 **1:12** [z]Eph 5:20 [a]S Ac 20:32 [b]S Ac 26:18 **1:13** [c]S Ac 26:18 [d]2Pe 1:11 [e]Mt 3:17

[a] 2 Or *believing* [b] 2 Some manuscripts *Father and the Lord Jesus Christ* [c] 7 Some manuscripts *your* [d] 12 Some manuscripts *us*

1:2 FAITHFUL BROTHERS . . . AT COLOSSE. Paul wrote to the Colossians because the church there was being infiltrated by false teachers who taught that commitment to Jesus Christ and adherence to apostolic doctrine were inadequate for full redemption. This false teaching mixed human "philosophy" and "tradition" with the gospel (2:8) and called for the worship of angels as intermediaries between God and humans (2:18). The false teachers demanded observance to certain Jewish religious requirements (2:16, 21–23) and justified their error by claiming revelation through visions (2:18). (1) The underlying philosophy behind these errors appears today in the teaching that Jesus Christ and the original gospel of the NT are not adequate to meet our spiritual needs (see 2Pe 1:3, note).

(2) Paul refutes this heresy by showing that Christ is not only our personal Savior, but the head of the church and Lord of the universe and creation. Therefore, Jesus Christ and his power in our lives, not human philosophy or wisdom, redeems us and saves us eternally; intermediaries are unnecessary, and we must approach him directly.

(3) Being a believer means believing in Christ and his gospel, trusting him, loving him and living in his presence. We must not add anything to the gospel or promote modern, humanistic wisdom or philosophy.

1:9 KNOWLEDGE OF HIS WILL. The knowledge of God's will results from praying and remaining in his Word and in fellowship with him. Only this kind of knowledge results in spiritual wisdom and understanding and transforms our hearts and lives (vv. 9–11; see Php 1:9, note).

1:9–12 WE HAVE NOT STOPPED PRAYING FOR YOU. This is one of Paul's four great NT apostolic prayers, spoken under the inspiration of the Spirit (the other three are Eph 1:16–19; 3:14–19; Php 1:9–11). From these prayers we learn how to pray for others, such as our children, friends, fellow believers, missionaries, pastors, etc. We must pray that they may (1) understand God's will, (2) gain spiritual wisdom, (3) live holy lives pleasing to the Lord, (4) bear fruit for Christ, (5) be strengthened spiritually by the Holy Spirit, (6) persevere in faith and righteousness, (7) give thanks to the Father, (8) continue in the hope of heaven, (9) experience Christ's nearness, (10) know Christ's love, (11) be filled with God's fullness, (12) show love and kindness to others, (13) discern evil, (14) be sincere and blameless, and (15) eagerly await the Lord's return.

1:11 STRENGTHENED . . . ACCORDING TO HIS GLORIOUS MIGHT. In order to live in a manner worthy of the Lord (v. 10), we must be strengthened by his power. This impartation of power is an ongoing experience of receiving from God his own life. Nothing else can enable us to overcome sin, Satan and the world (cf. Php 4:13; see article on FAITH AND GRACE, p. 1720).

1:13 FROM THE DOMINION OF DARKNESS. Central to redemption is deliverance from the dominion and power of darkness, i.e., from Satan (Mt 4:8–11; Lk 22:52–53; Eph 2:2; 6:12). We are now in Christ's kingdom and under his rule (Ro 6:17–22; see Ac 26:18, note).

have redemption,[e][f] the forgiveness of
sins.[g]

The Supremacy of Christ

[15]He is the image[h] of the invisible
God,[i] the firstborn[j] over all creation. [16]For by him all things were created:[k] things in heaven and on earth,
visible and invisible, whether thrones
or powers or rulers or authorities;[l] all
things were created by him and for
him.[m] [17]He is before all things,[n] and
in him all things hold together. [18]And
he is the head[o] of the body, the
church;[p] he is the beginning and the
firstborn[q] from among the dead,[r] so
that in everything he might have the
supremacy. [19]For God was pleased[s]
to have all his fullness[t] dwell in him,
[20]and through him to reconcile[u] to
himself all things, whether things on
earth or things in heaven,[v] by making
peace[w] through his blood,[x] shed on
the cross.

[21]Once you were alienated from God
and were enemies[y] in your minds[z]
because of[f] your evil behavior. [22]But
now he has reconciled[a] you by
Christ's physical body[b] through death
to present you[c] holy in his sight, without blemish and free from accusation[d]— [23]if you continue[e] in your
faith, established[f] and firm, not
moved from the hope[g] held out in the
gospel. This is the gospel that you
heard and that has been proclaimed to
every creature under heaven,[h] and of
which I, Paul, have become a servant.[i]

Paul's Labor for the Church

[24]Now I rejoice[j] in what was suffered for you, and I fill up in my flesh
what is still lacking in regard to
Christ's afflictions,[k] for the sake of
his body, which is the church.[l] [25]I
have become its servant[m] by the commission God gave me[n] to present to
you the word of God[o] in its fullness—
[26]the mystery[p] that has been kept
hidden for ages and generations, but is
now disclosed to the saints. [27]To them

1:14 [f]S Ro 3:24 [g]Eph 1:7
1:15 [h]S Jn 14:9 [i]S Jn 1:18; 1Ti 1:17; Heb 11:27 [j]S ver 18
1:16 [k]S Jn 1:3 [l]Eph 1:20,21 [m]S Ro 11:36
1:17 [n]S Jn 1:2
1:18 [o]S Eph 1:22 [p]ver 24; S 1Co 12:27 [q]ver 15; Ps 89:27; Ro 8:29; Heb 1:6 [r]Ac 26:23; Rev 1:5
1:19 [s]S Eph 1:5 [t]S Jn 1:16
1:20 [u]S Ro 5:10 [v]Eph 1:10 [w]S Lk 2:14 [x]Eph 2:13
1:21 [y]Ro 5:10 [z]Eph 2:3
1:22 [a]ver 20; S Ro 5:10 [b]Ro 7:4 [c]S 2Co 4:14 [d]Eph 1:4; 5:27
1:23 [e]S Ro 11:22 [f]Eph 3:17 [g]ver 5 [h]ver 6; S Ro 10:18 [i]ver 25; S 1Co 3:5
1:24 [j]S 2Co 6:10 [k]S 2Co 1:5 [l]S 1Co 12:27
1:25 [m]ver 23; S 1Co 3:5 [n]Eph 3:2 [o]S Heb 4:12
1:26 [p]S Ro 16:25

[e]14 A few late manuscripts *redemption through his blood* [f]21 Or *minds, as shown by*

1:15 THE FIRSTBORN OVER ALL CREATION. This phrase does not mean Christ was a created being. Rather, "firstborn" has the OT meaning: "first in position," "heir" or "supreme" (e.g., Ex 4:22; Jer 31:9; note Ps 89:27, where "firstborn" is used of David's rulership, although he was not a firstborn son). Christ is heir and ruler of all creation as the eternal Son (cf. v. 18; Heb 1:1–2).

1:16 BY HIM ALL THINGS WERE CREATED. Paul affirms the creative activity of Christ. (1) All things, both material and spiritual, owe their existence to Christ's work as the active agent in creation (Jn 1:3; Heb 1:2). (2) All things hold together and are sustained in him (v. 17; Heb 1:3; see article on CREATION, p. 6).

1:18 FIRSTBORN FROM AMONG THE DEAD. Jesus Christ was the first to rise from the dead with a spiritual and immortal body (1Co 15:20). On his resurrection day Jesus became head of the church. The NT church began on the day of Jesus' resurrection when the disciples received the Holy Spirit (see article on THE REGENERATION OF THE DISCIPLES, p. 1627). The fact that Christ is the "firstborn from among the dead" implies the subsequent resurrection of all those for whom he died.

1:19 ALL HIS FULLNESS DWELL IN HIM. Paul states the deity of Christ in the plainest of terms. The full and complete Godhead with all its powers and nature resides with Christ (2:9; cf. Heb 1:8).

1:20 RECONCILE TO HIMSELF ALL THINGS. Humanity and everything in the universe are brought in unity and harmony under Christ (cf. vv. 16–18). It does not mean, however, that all people are reconciled irrespective of their wills. The person who rejects Christ's offer of reconciliation remains God's enemy (Ro 2:4–10).

1:23 IF YOU CONTINUE IN YOUR FAITH. Notice the human responsibility and activity that Paul states are essential for Christians to appear finally before Christ "holy in his sight, without blemish and free from accusation" (v. 22). We must (1) "continue in [our] faith," i.e., maintain a persevering faith in Jesus as Lord and Savior (see article on FAITH AND GRACE, p. 1720); (2) be "established and firm" in the teaching of Jesus and the apostles; and (3) be "not moved from the hope held out in the gospel," i.e., we must not return to our former state of hopelessness with its soul-destroying vices (3:5–11; see Heb 10:38, note).

1:24 SUFFERED FOR YOU. Paul sees Christ still suffering, not for our redemption, but in fellowship with his people as they carry the gospel to the lost (cf. Ac 9:4). Paul rejoices because he is allowed to share in Christ's sufferings (Php 3:10; cf. 2Co 1:4–5, notes; 4:7, note; 11:23, note on Paul's sufferings).

1:27 CHRIST IN YOU, THE HOPE OF GLORY. Christ's living in us is our assurance of future glory and eternal life. Only his indwelling and our continual intimate communion with him can dispel any doubt about obtaining heaven. To have him is to have life (cf. Ro 8:11; Eph 1:13–14; 1Jn 5:11–12).

God has chosen to make known[q]
among the Gentiles the glorious
riches[r] of this mystery, which is
Christ in you,[s] the hope of glory.
28We proclaim him, admonishing[t]
and teaching everyone with all wisdom,[u] so that we may present everyone perfect[v] in Christ. 29To this end
I labor,[w] struggling[x] with all his
energy, which so powerfully works
in me.[y]
2 I want you to know how much
I am struggling[z] for you and
for those at Laodicea,[a] and for all
who have not met me personally.
2My purpose is that they may be encouraged in heart[b] and united in
love, so that they may have the full
riches of complete understanding,
in order that they may know the
mystery[c] of God, namely, Christ, 3in
whom are hidden all the treasures of
wisdom and knowledge.[d] 4I tell you
this so that no one may deceive you
by fine-sounding arguments.[e] 5For
though I am absent from you in
body, I am present with you in spirit[f]
and delight to see how orderly[g] you
are and how firm[h] your faith in
Christ[i] is.

1:27 [q] S Mt 13:11
[r] S Ro 2:4
[s] S Ro 8:10
1:28 [t] Col 3:16
[u] 1Co 2:6,7
[v] Mt 5:48;
Eph 5:27
1:29 [w] 1Co 15:10;
2Co 11:23
[x] Col 2:1
[y] Eph 1:19; 3:7
2:1 [z] Col 1:29;
4:12 [a] Col 4:13,15,
16; Rev 1:11; 3:14
2:2 [b] Eph 6:22;
Col 4:8
[c] S Ro 16:25
2:3 [d] Isa 11:2;
Jer 23:5;
Ro 11:33;
1Co 1:24,30
2:4 [e] S Ro 16:18
2:5 [f] 1Co 5:4;
1Th 2:17
[g] 1Co 14:40
[h] 1Pe 5:9
[i] S Ac 20:21

2:6 [j] S Jn 13:13;
Col 1:10
2:7 [k] Eph 3:17
[l] Eph 4:21
2:8 [m] 1Ti 6:20
[n] ver 20; Gal 4:3
2:9 [o] S Jn 1:16
2:10 [p] S Eph 1:22
[q] S Mt 28:18
2:11 [r] Ro 2:29;
Php 3:3
[s] S Gal 5:24
2:12 [t] S Mt 28:19
[u] S Ro 6:5
[v] S Ac 2:24
2:13 [w] Eph 2:1,5

Freedom From Human Regulations Through Life With Christ

6So then, just as you received Christ
Jesus as Lord,[j] continue to live in
him, 7rooted[k] and built up in him,
strengthened in the faith as you were
taught,[l] and overflowing with thankfulness.
8See to it that no one takes you captive through hollow and deceptive philosophy,[m] which depends on human
tradition and the basic principles of
this world[n] rather than on Christ.
9For in Christ all the fullness[o] of
the Deity lives in bodily form, 10and
you have been given fullness in Christ,
who is the head[p] over every power
and authority.[q] 11In him you were
also circumcised,[r] in the putting off of
the sinful nature,[g][s] not with a circumcision done by the hands of men
but with the circumcision done by
Christ, 12having been buried with him
in baptism[t] and raised with him[u]
through your faith in the power of God,
who raised him from the dead.[v]
13When you were dead in your sins[w]

[g] 11 Or *the flesh*

2:8 DECEPTIVE PHILOSOPHY ... RATHER THAN ON CHRIST. Paul warns us to be on guard against all philosophies, religions and traditions that emphasize humans functioning independently from God and his written revelation. Today one of the greatest philosophical threats to Biblically based Christianity is "secular humanism." This has become the underlying philosophy and accepted religion in most of secular education, government and society in general, and is the established viewpoint of most of the news and entertainment media throughout the world.

(1) What does the philosophy of humanism teach? (a) It teaches that humanity, the universe and all that exists consist only of matter and energy shaped into their present form by impersonal chance. (b) It teaches that humans have not been created by a personal God, but are the product of a chance process of evolution. (c) It rejects belief in a personal, infinite God and denies that the Bible is God's inspired revelation to the human race. (d) It asserts that knowledge does not exist apart from human discovery and that human reason determines the appropriate ethics of society, thus making human beings the ultimate authority. (e) It seeks to modify or improve human behavior through education, economic redistribution, modern psychology or human wisdom. (f) It teaches that moral standards are not absolute but relative, determined by what makes people happy, brings them pleasure, or seems good for society according to the goals set by its leaders; Biblical values and morality are rejected. (g) It considers human self-fulfillment, satisfaction and pleasure to be the highest good in life. (h) It maintains that people should learn to cope with death and the difficulties in life without belief in or dependence on God.

(2) The philosophy of humanism began with Satan and is an expression of Satan's lie that humans can be like God (Ge 3:5). Scripture identifies humanists as those who have "exchanged the truth of God for a lie, and worshiped and served created things rather than the Creator" (Ro 1:25).

(3) All Christian leaders, pastors and parents must do their utmost to protect their sons and daughters from humanistic indoctrination by exposing its error and instilling in them a godly contempt for its destructive influence (Ro 1:20–32; 2Co 10:4–5; 2Ti 3:1–10; Jude 4–20; see 1Co 1:20, note; 2Pe 2:19, note).

2:11 CIRCUMCISION DONE BY CHRIST. In the OT circumcision was the sign that the individual Israelite stood in a covenant relationship with God (see Ge 17:11, note). It symbolized a cutting away or separation from sin and all that was unholy in the world. The believer under the NT covenant has undergone a spiritual circumcision, namely, the "putting off of the sinful nature." Such circumcision is a spiritual act whereby Christ cuts away our old unregenerate nature of rebellion against God and imparts to us the spiritual or resurrection life of Christ (vv. 12–13); it is a circumcision of the heart (Dt 10:16; 30:6; Jer 4:4; 9:26; Ro 2:29).

and in the uncircumcision of your sinful nature,[h] God made you[i] alive[x]
with Christ. He forgave us all our
sins,[y] 14having canceled the written
code, with its regulations,[z] that was
against us and that stood opposed to
us; he took it away, nailing it to the
cross.[a] 15And having disarmed the
powers and authorities,[b] he made a
public spectacle of them, triumphing
over them[c] by the cross.[j]

16Therefore do not let anyone judge
you[d] by what you eat or drink,[e] or
with regard to a religious festival,[f] a
New Moon celebration[g] or a Sabbath
day.[h] 17These are a shadow of the
things that were to come;[i] the reality,
however, is found in Christ. 18Do not
let anyone who delights in false humility[j] and the worship of angels disqualify you for the prize.[k] Such a person
goes into great detail about what he
has seen, and his unspiritual mind
puffs him up with idle notions. 19He
has lost connection with the Head,[l]
from whom the whole body,[m] supported and held together by its ligaments
and sinews, grows as God causes it to
grow.[n]

2:13 [x]Eph 2:5 [y]Eph 4:32
2:14 [z]Eph 2:15 [a]1Pe 2:24
2:15 [b]ver 10; Eph 6:12 [c]Mt 12:29; Lk 10:18; Jn 12:31
2:16 [d]Ro 14:3,4 [e]Mk 7:19; Ro 14:17 [f]Lev 23:2; Ro 14:5 [g]1Ch 23:31 [h]Mk 2:27,28; Gal 4:10
2:17 [i]Heb 8:5; 10:1
2:18 [j]ver 23 [k]1Co 9:24; Php 3:14
2:19 [l]S Eph 1:22 [m]S 1Co 12:27 [n]Eph 4:16
2:20 [o]S Ro 6:6 [p]ver 8; Gal 4:3,9 [q]ver 14,16
2:22 [r]1Co 6:13 [s]Isa 29:13; Mt 15:9; Tit 1:14
2:23 [t]ver 18
3:1 [u]S Ro 6:5 [v]S Mk 16:19
3:2 [w]Php 3:19,20
3:3 [x]S Ro 6:2; 2Co 5:14
3:4 [y]Gal 2:20 [z]1Co 1:7 [a]1Pe 1:13; 1Jn 3:2

20Since you died with Christ[o] to the
basic principles of this world,[p] why,
as though you still belonged to it, do
you submit to its rules:[q] 21"Do not
handle! Do not taste! Do not touch!"?
22These are all destined to perish[r]
with use, because they are based on
human commands and teachings.[s]
23Such regulations indeed have an appearance of wisdom, with their self-im-
posed worship, their false humility[t]
and their harsh treatment of the body,
but they lack any value in restraining
sensual indulgence.

Rules for Holy Living

3 Since, then, you have been raised
with Christ,[u] set your hearts on
things above, where Christ is seated at
the right hand of God.[v] 2Set your
minds on things above, not on earthly
things.[w] 3For you died,[x] and your life
is now hidden with Christ in God.
4When Christ, who is your[k] life,[y] appears,[z] then you also will appear with
him in glory.[a]

[h] *13* Or *your flesh* [i] *13* Some manuscripts *us* [j] *15* Or *them in him* [k] *4* Some manuscripts *our*

2:14 WRITTEN CODE, WITH ITS REGULATIONS. This refers to the Law of Moses, i.e., to commandments that pointed to right conduct but could not give life and the power to obey God (Gal 3:21). The old covenant as a way to salvation has been nailed to the cross (i.e., abolished), and God established a better covenant through Christ and by his Spirit (2Co 3:6–9; Heb 8:6–13; 10:16–17,29; 12:24; see article on THE OLD COVENANT AND THE NEW COVENANT, p. 1926).

2:15 DISARMED THE POWERS AND AUTHORITIES. Christ triumphed over all the demonic forces and satanic powers of the world through his death on the cross (cf. Eph 6:12). He stripped them of their power to hold men and women captive to evil's dominion against their will (cf. 1:13; Mt 12:29; Lk 10:18; 11:20–22; Heb 2:14; see article on POWER OVER SATAN AND DEMONS, p. 1484). The child of God shares in this triumph. We not only gain victory over the world and temptation (1Jn 4:4), but we also possess the power to wage war against the spiritual forces of evil (see Eph 6:12, note; see article on SIGNS OF BELIEVERS, p. 1513).

2:16 EAT ... DRINK ... SABBATH DAY. "What you eat or drink" probably refers to Jewish ascetic dietary rules urged on the Colossians as necessary for salvation (cf. v. 17). "A religious festival, a New Moon celebration or a Sabbath day" probably refers to certain required holy days of the Jewish calendar. Paul teaches that a Christian is freed from legal and ceremonial obligations of this kind (Gal 4:4–11; 5:1; see Mt 12:1, note on the Sabbath; Mk 7:6, note on legalism).

2:18 WORSHIP OF ANGELS. False teachers were saying that angels should be called on and worshiped as mediators in order for people to make contact with God. To Paul, calling on angels would be displacing Jesus Christ as the supreme and sufficient Head of the church (v. 19); consequently, he warns against this. Today the belief that Jesus Christ is not the only intermediary between God and humans is promoted in the practice of worshiping and praying to dead saints, who act as patrons and mediators. This practice robs Christ of his supremacy and centrality in God's redemptive plan. Worship and prayer to anyone other than God the Father, the Son and the Holy Spirit are unbiblical and must be rejected (see 1:2, note; see article on WORSHIP, p. 680).

3:2 SET YOUR MINDS ON THINGS ABOVE. Because our lives are with Christ in heaven (v. 3), we must set our minds on and let our attitudes be determined by things above. We must value, judge and consider everything from an eternal and heavenly perspective. Our goals and pursuits should be to seek spiritual things (vv. 1–4), resist sin (vv. 5–11) and put on Christ's character (vv. 12–17). Spiritual graces, power, experiences and blessings are all with Christ in heaven. He bestows those things on all who sincerely ask, diligently seek and persistently knock (Lk 11:1–13; 1Co 12:11; Eph 1:3; 4:7–8).

3:4 CHRIST, WHO IS YOUR LIFE. Although right doctrine (2Ti 1:13–14) and holy lives (3:5–17; Jn 14:15,21) are an essential part of re-

5Put to death,[b] therefore, whatever
belongs to your earthly nature:[c] sexual immorality,[d] impurity, lust, evil desires and greed,[e] which is idolatry.[f]
6Because of these, the wrath of God[g]
is coming.[1] **7**You used to walk in these
ways, in the life you once lived.[h] **8**But
now you must rid yourselves[i] of all
such things as these: anger, rage, malice, slander,[j] and filthy language
from your lips.[k] **9**Do not lie to each
other,[l] since you have taken off your
old self[m] with its practices **10**and have
put on the new self,[n] which is being
renewed[o] in knowledge in the image
of its Creator.[p] **11**Here there is no
Greek or Jew,[q] circumcised or uncircumcised,[r] barbarian, Scythian, slave
or free,[s] but Christ is all,[t] and is in
all.

12Therefore, as God's chosen people, holy and dearly loved, clothe yourselves[u] with compassion, kindness,
humility,[v] gentleness and patience.[w]
13Bear with each other[x] and forgive
whatever grievances you may have
against one another. Forgive as the
Lord forgave you.[y] **14**And over all these
virtues put on love,[z] which binds
them all together in perfect unity.[a]

3:5 [b] S Ro 6:2; S Eph 4:22 [c] S Gal 5:24 [d] S 1Co 6:18 [e] Eph 5:3 [f] Gal 5:19-21; Eph 5:5 **3:6** [g] S Ro 1:18 **3:7** [h] S Eph 2:2 **3:8** [i] S Eph 4:22 [j] Eph 4:31 [k] Eph 4:29 **3:9** [l] S Eph 4:22, 25 [m] S Ro 6:6 **3:10** [n] S Ro 6:4; S 13:14 [o] Ro 12:2; S 2Co 4:16; Eph 4:23 [p] Eph 2:10 **3:11** [q] Ro 10:12; 1Co 12:13 [r] S 1Co 7:19 [s] Gal 3:28 [t] Eph 1:23 **3:12** [u] ver 10 [v] Php 2:3 [w] 2Co 6:6; Gal 5:22,23; Eph 4:2 **3:13** [x] Eph 4:2 [y] Eph 4:32 **3:14** [z] 1Co 13:1-13 [a] S Ro 15:5 **3:15** [b] S Jn 14:27 [c] S Ro 12:5 [d] S Ro 14:19 **3:16** [e] Ro 10:17 [f] Col 1:28 [g] Ps 47:7 [h] S Eph 5:19 **3:17** [i] 1Co 10:31 [j] S Eph 5:20 **3:18** [k] S Eph 5:22

15Let the peace of Christ[b] rule in
your hearts, since as members of one
body[c] you were called to peace.[d] And
be thankful. **16**Let the word of Christ[e]
dwell in you richly as you teach and
admonish one another with all wisdom,[f] and as you sing psalms,[g]
hymns and spiritual songs with gratitude in your hearts to God.[h] **17**And
whatever you do,[i] whether in word or
deed, do it all in the name of the Lord
Jesus, giving thanks[j] to God the Father through him. Heb 13:15

Rules for Christian Households

3:18–4:1pp — Eph 5:22–6:9

18Wives, submit to your husbands,[k]
as is fitting in the Lord.
19Husbands, love your wives and do
not be harsh with them.
20Children, obey your parents in everything, for this pleases the Lord.
21Fathers, do not embitter your children, or they will become discouraged.
22Slaves, obey your earthly masters

[1] 6 Some early manuscripts *coming on those who are disobedient*

---

demption in Christ, it is fellowship with and love for Christ as a person that must always be kept central (cf. Ro 3:22). Notice the emphasis on the believer's personal communion with Christ in this letter (1:27; 2:6–7,10,20; 3:1,3–4).

3:5 GREED, WHICH IS IDOLATRY. What is idolatry? (1) It is allowing things to become the focus of a person's desires, values and dependence, displacing reliance on and faith in God himself (cf. Ex 20:3–6; Dt 7:25–26; Isa 40:18–23; see article on THE NATURE OF IDOLATRY, p. 394). For this reason greed is called idolatry. (2) Idolatry can involve professing allegiance to God and his Word while at the same time giving equal or greater allegiance to persons, institutions, traditions or authorities on earth. Nothing may be placed higher than one's faithful relationship to God and his Word as revealed in the Bible (Ro 1:22–23; Eph 5:5).

3:16 WORD OF CHRIST DWELL IN YOU. The word of Christ (i.e., Scripture) must be continually read, studied, meditated on and prayed over until it richly dwells in us. When this is our experience, our thoughts, words, deeds and motivations will be influenced and controlled by Christ (Ps 119:11; Jn 15:7; see 1Co 15:2, note). Psalms, hymns and spiritual songs should be used to teach the Word and admonish believers to live lives of obedience to Christ (see Eph 5:19, note on spiritual singing).

3:17 WHATEVER YOU DO, WHETHER IN WORD OR DEED. The Bible presents general principles that permit Spirit-led believers to determine the rightness or wrongness of actions not expressly mentioned in God's Word. In everything that we say, do, think or enjoy, we must ask the following questions: (1) Can it be done to God's glory (1Co 10:31)? (2) Can it be done "in the name of the Lord Jesus," asking his blessing on the activity (see Jn 14:13, note)? (3) Can it be done while sincerely giving thanks to God? (4) Is it a Christlike action (1Jn 2:6)? (5) Will it weaken the sincere convictions of other Christians (see 1Co 8:1, note)? (6) Will it weaken my desire for spiritual things, God's Word and prayer (Lk 8:14; see Mt 5:6, note)? (7) Will it weaken or hinder my witness for Christ (Mt 5:13–16)?

3:18–19 WIVES, SUBMIT TO YOUR HUSBANDS. See Eph 5:21–23, notes; 1Ti 2:13–15, notes on the responsibility of wives and husbands in the family relationship.

3:20 CHILDREN, OBEY YOUR PARENTS. See Eph 6:1, note on the responsibility of children in the family relationship.

3:21 FATHERS, DO NOT EMBITTER YOUR CHILDREN. For a discussion of this passage, including fifteen steps on how parents can lead their children to Christ, see article on PARENTS AND CHILDREN, p. 1854.

3:22 SLAVES, OBEY YOUR EARTHLY MASTERS. Paul instructs slaves how to live in a Christian way within their tragic situation. He never indicates that the slave-master relationship is ordained by God or should be perpetuated. Rather he sows the seeds for its abolition in Phm 10,12,

PARENTS AND CHILDREN

***Col 3:21** "Fathers, do not embitter your children, or they will become discouraged."*

It is the solemn obligation of parents (Gk *patēr*; plural, *pateres*, can mean "fathers" or "father and mother") to give their children the instruction and correction that belong to a Christian upbringing. Parents should be examples of Christian life and conduct, caring more for their children's salvation than for their jobs, professions, ministry in the church or social standing (cf. Ps 127:3).

(1) According to Paul's word in Eph 6:4 and Col 3:21, as well as God's instruction in many OT passages (see Ge 18:19, note; Dt 6:7, note; Ps 78:5, note; Pr 4:1–4, note; 6:20, note), it is the responsibility of parents to give their children the upbringing that prepares them for lives pleasing to God. It is the family, not the church or church school, that is primarily responsible for the Biblical and spiritual training of the children. Church and church school only assist parental training.

(2) The very core of Christian nurture is this: The heart of the father must be turned to the heart of the child in order to bring the heart of the child to the heart of the Savior (see Lk 1:17, note).

(3) In bringing up their children, parents should show no favoritism, encourage as well as correct, punish only intentional wrongdoing, and dedicate their lives in love to their children with hearts of compassion, kindness, humility, gentleness and patience (Col 3:12–14,21).

(4) Here are fifteen steps that you as parents should take to lead your children to lives of godliness in Christ:

(a) Dedicate your children to God at the beginning of their lives (1Sa 1:28; Lk 2:22).

(b) Teach your children to fear the Lord and turn away from evil, to love righteousness and to hate sin. Instill in them an awareness of God's attitude and judgment toward sin (see Heb 1:9, note).

(c) Teach your children to obey you through Biblical discipline (Dt 8:5; Pr 3:11–12; 13:24; 23:13–14; 29:15,17; Heb 12:7).

(d) Protect your children from ungodly influences by being aware of Satan's attempts to destroy them spiritually through attraction to the world or through immoral companions (Pr 13:20; 28:7; 1Jn 2:15–17).

(e) Make your children aware that God is always observing and evaluating what they do, think and say (Ps 139:1–12).

(f) Bring your children early in life to personal faith, repentance and water baptism in Christ (Mt 19:14).

(g) Establish your children in a spiritual church where God's Word is proclaimed, his righteous standards honored and the Holy Spirit manifested. Teach them the motto: "I am a friend to all who fear you" (Ps 119:63; see Ac 12:5, note).

(h) Encourage your children to remain separated from the world and to witness and work for God (2Co 6:14—7:1; Jas 4:4). Teach them that they are strangers and aliens on this earth (Heb 11:13–16), that their real home and citizenship is in heaven with Christ (Php 3:20; Col 3:1–3).

(i) Instruct your children in the importance of the baptism in the Holy Spirit (Ac 1:4–5,8; 2:4,39).

(j) Teach your children that God loves them and has a specific purpose for their lives (Lk 1:13–17; Ro 8:30; 1Pe 1:3–9).

(k) Instruct your children daily in God's Word, both in conversation and family devotions (Dt 4:9; 6:5–7; 1Ti 4:6; 2Ti 3:15).

(l) Through example and exhortation, encourage your children to live lives devoted to prayer (Ac 6:4; Ro 12:12; Eph 6:18; Jas 5:16).

(m) Prepare your children to suffer and endure persecution because of righteousness (Mt 5:10–12). They must know that "everyone who wants to live a godly life in Christ Jesus will be persecuted" (2Ti 3:12).

(n) Lift your children up to God by constant and earnest intercession (Eph 6:18; Jas 5:16–18; see Jn 17:1, note on Jesus' prayer for his disciples as a model of parents' prayers for their children).

(o) Have such love and concern for your children that you would be willing to pour out your life as if it were a sacrifice to the Lord, in order to deepen their faith and make their lives what they should be in the Lord (see Php 2:17, note).

in everything; and do it, not only when
their eye is on you and to win their favor, but with sincerity of heart and reverence for the Lord. **23**Whatever you
do, work at it with all your heart, as
working for the Lord, not for men,
24since you know that you will receive
an inheritance[l] from the Lord as a reward.[m] It is the Lord Christ you are
serving. **25**Anyone who does wrong will
be repaid for his wrong, and there is no
favoritism.[n]

4 Masters, provide your slaves with
what is right and fair,[o] because
you know that you also have a Master
in heaven.

Further Instructions

2Devote yourselves to prayer,[p] being watchful and thankful. **3**And pray
for us, too, that God may open a door[q]
for our message, so that we may proclaim the mystery[r] of Christ, for
which I am in chains.[s] **4**Pray that I
may proclaim it clearly, as I should.
5Be wise[t] in the way you act toward
outsiders;[u] make the most of every
opportunity.[v] **6**Let your conversation
be always full of grace,[w] seasoned
with salt,[x] so that you may know how
to answer everyone.[y]

Final Greetings

7Tychicus[z] will tell you all the
news about me. He is a dear brother, a
faithful minister and fellow servant[a]
in the Lord. **8**I am sending him to you
for the express purpose that you may
know about our[m] circumstances and
that he may encourage your hearts.[b]
9He is coming with Onesimus,[c] our
faithful and dear brother, who is one of
you.[d] They will tell you everything
that is happening here.

10My fellow prisoner Aristarchus[e]
sends you his greetings, as does
Mark,[f] the cousin of Barnabas.[g]
(You have received instructions about
him; if he comes to you, welcome him.)
11Jesus, who is called Justus, also
sends greetings. These are the only
Jews among my fellow workers[h] for

3:24 [l]S Ac 20:32 [m]S Mt 16:27
3:25 [n]S Ac 10:34
4:1 [o]Lev 25:43,53
4:2 [p]S Lk 18:1
4:3 [q]S Ac 14:27 [r]S Ro 16:25 [s]S Ac 21:33
4:5 [t]Eph 5:15 [u]S Mk 4:11 [v]Eph 5:16
4:6 [w]Eph 4:29 [x]Mk 9:50 [y]1Pe 3:15
4:7 [z]S Ac 20:4 [a]Eph 6:21,22; Col 1:7
4:8 [b]Eph 6:21,22; Col 2:2
4:9 [c]Phm 10 [d]ver 12
4:10 [e]S Ac 19:29 [f]S Ac 12:12 [g]S Ac 4:36
4:11 [h]S Php 2:25

[m]8 Some manuscripts *that he may know about your*

14–17,21, and in the meantime seeks to regulate it to the benefit of both masters and slaves (Eph 6:5–9; 1Ti 6:1–2; Tit 2:9–10; cf. 1Pe 2:18–19).

3:23 AS WORKING FOR THE LORD. Paul exhorts Christians to regard all labor as a service rendered to the Lord. We must work as though Christ were our employer, knowing that all work performed "for the Lord" will someday be rewarded (v. 24; cf. Eph 6:6–8).

3:25 ANYONE WHO DOES WRONG. Within family, church and employment relationships (vv. 12–25), Paul is concerned about the demonstration of love, justice and fairness to one another. If taken seriously, these verses would eliminate much of the unloving and unjust treatment of others within our homes and churches. Specifically, we learn that: (1) Mistreatment of others by Christians is a serious matter affecting our future glory in heaven (cf. 2Co 5:10). (a) Those who treat others in love and goodness will receive reward from the Lord (v. 24; Eph 6:8). (b) Anyone who mistreats and does wrong to another believer "will be repaid for his wrong." The guilty will carry that wrong to judgment and bear the consequences without partiality (Dt 10:17; 2Ch 19:7; Ac 10:34; Ro 2:11).

(2) The principle of future accountability to God should help motivate our love, kindness and mercy toward all human beings. Let all believers keep in mind that God will hold his children responsible for the way they have treated one another (Gal 6:7; see Mt 22:37,39 notes; Jn 13:34, note; see article on THE JUDGMENT OF BELIEVERS, p. 1791).

4:2 DEVOTE YOURSELVES TO PRAYER, BEING WATCHFUL. "Devote yourselves" (Gk *proskartereō*) means "continue steadfast" or "persevere," implying strong persistence and fervor, a holding fast to prayer. "Being watchful" (Gk *grēgoreō*) means "being spiritually awake or alert." (1) In order to devote ourselves intensely to prayer, we must be alert to the many things that would detour us from this purpose. Satan and the weakness of our human nature will try to cause us to neglect prayer itself or to become distracted while praying. We must discipline ourselves to achieve the prayer required for Christian victory. (2) This was an essential practice of those in the NT church who were baptized in the Spirit: "They devoted themselves . . . to prayer" (Ac 2:42). This devotion to prayer must be undergirded by thanksgiving to Christ for what he has done for us.

4:3 GOD MAY OPEN A DOOR. Paul was confident that God was working by opening and shutting doors in order to direct his life and ministry. The fruitfulness of our lives and our witness depends both on his providence and on his direct intervention. We should pray for God to open doors for us and to indicate where we ought to work (cf. Ac 16:6–10).

4:6 CONVERSATION . . . FULL OF GRACE. A believer's speech must be pleasant, winsome, kind and gracious. It must be language that results from the operation of God's grace in our hearts and speaks the truth in love (Eph 4:15). "Seasoned with salt" may mean conversation that is appropriate, and marked by purity and not corruption (cf. Eph 4:29). Graceful speech, however, does not rule out fervent and stern words, when necessary, to oppose those false believers who are enemies of the cross (see Mt 23; Ac 15:1–2; Gal 1:9).

the kingdom of God, and they have
proved a comfort to me. **12**Epaphras,[i]
who is one of you[j] and a servant of
Christ Jesus, sends greetings. He is always wrestling in prayer for you,[k]
that you may stand firm in all the will
of God, mature[l] and fully assured. **13**I
vouch for him that he is working hard
for you and for those at Laodicea[m] and
Hierapolis. **14**Our dear friend Luke,[n]
the doctor, and Demas[o] send greetings. **15**Give my greetings to the brothers at Laodicea,[p] and to Nympha and
the church in her house.[q]

16After this letter has been read to
you, see that it is also read[r] in the
church of the Laodiceans and that you
in turn read the letter from Laodicea.
17Tell Archippus:[s] "See to it that
you complete the work you have received in the Lord."[t]
18I, Paul, write this greeting in
my own hand.[u] Remember[v] my
chains.[w] Grace be with you.[x]

4:12 [i]Col 1:7; Phm 23 [j]ver 9 [k]S Ro 15:30 [l]S 1Co 2:6 **4:13** [m]S Col 2:1 **4:14** [n]2Ti 4:11; Phm 24 [o]2Ti 4:10; Phm 24 **4:15** [p]S Col 2:1 [q]S Ro 16:5 **4:16** [r]2Th 3:14; S 1Ti 4:13 **4:17** [s]Phm 2 [t]2Ti 4:5 **4:18** [u]S 1Co 16:21 [v]Heb 13:3 [w]S Ac 21:33 [x]1Ti 6:21; 2Ti 4:22; Tit 3:15; Heb 13:25

4:12 ALWAYS WRESTLING IN PRAYER. "Wrestling" (Gk *agōnizō*, from which we derive the English word "agonize") denotes an intense desire, an agonizing or a striving in prayer. Faithful NT believers not only were devoted to prayer (v. 2), but *agonized* with strong pleadings. The needs of our families, churches and the world are no less significant today. We must pray fervently, knowing that in our wrestling Christ's energy is working powerfully in us (cf. 1:29) and his purpose being realized on behalf of others.

4:16 AFTER THIS LETTER HAS BEEN READ. Paul's letters were read out loud to the congregation when they assembled for worship. The Colossian Christians, after receiving this letter, would most likely make a copy of it to keep for themselves and then send the letter on to the nearby Laodiceans. The "letter from Laodicea" was probably the letter we call Ephesians (see the introduction to Ephesians).

4:18 REMEMBER MY CHAINS. During Paul's first Roman imprisonment he wrote Colossians, Philemon, Ephesians and Philippians. In spite of being unjustly confined to prison for four or more years, note how these letters are filled with "thankfulness" (1:3,12; 2:7; 3:15; 4:2), "grace" (Eph 1:2,6–7; 2:5; 3:2; 4:7; 6:24), "joy" (Php 1:4,18; 2:2; 3:1; 4:1,4) and "love" (Phm 5,7,9).

1 THESSALONIANS

Outline

Christian Greetings (1:1)
- I. Paul's Personal Gratitude for the Thessalonians (1:2—3:13)
  - A. Rejoices About Their New Life in Christ (1:2–10)
    - 1. Their Faith, Love and Hope (1:2–3)
    - 2. Their Genuine Conversion (1:4–6)
    - 3. Their Good Example to Others (1:7–10)
  - B. Reminisces About His Role in Their Lives (2:1—3:8)
    - 1. Reviews His Labors (2:1–12)
    - 2. Recalls Their Response (2:13–16)
    - 3. Retains His Interest (2:17—3:8)
  - C. Prays for an Opportunity to Return, and for Their Spiritual Advancement and Establishment in Holiness (3:9–13)
- II. Paul's Practical Instruction to the Thessalonians (4:1—5:22)
  - A. Concerning Sexual Purity (4:1–8)
  - B. Concerning Brotherly Love (4:9–10)
  - C. Concerning Honest Labor (4:11–12)
  - D. Concerning the Coming of Christ (4:13—5:11)
    - 1. The State of the Dead in Christ (4:13–18)
    - 2. The Readiness of Those Living in Christ (5:1–11)
  - E. Concerning Esteem for Spiritual Leaders (5:12–13)
  - F. Concerning Christian Living (5:14–18)
  - G. Concerning Spiritual Discernment (5:19–22)

Conclusion (5:23–28)
- A. Prayer for Their Sanctification and Preservation (5:23–24)
- B. Final Requests and Benediction (5:25–28)

Author: Paul

Theme: The Return of Christ

Date of Writing: c. A.D. 51

Background

Thessalonica, located slightly less than a hundred miles southwest of Philippi, was the capital, foremost city and harbor of the Roman province of Macedonia. Among the city's population of 200,000 was a strong Jewish community. When Paul founded the Thessalonian church on his second missionary journey, his fruitful ministry there was prematurely terminated because of intense Jewish hostility (Ac 17:1–9).

Forced to leave Thessalonica, Paul went to Berea where another brief but successful ministry was cut short by persecution stirred up by hostile Jews who followed him from Thessalonica (Ac 17:10–13). Paul then traveled to Athens (Ac 17:15–34), where Timothy joined him afterwards. Paul sent Timothy back to Thessalonica to check on the infant church (3:1–5) while Paul went on to Corinth (Ac 18:1–17). Upon completing the assignment, Timothy traveled to Corinth with a report for Paul about the Thessalonian church

(3:6–8). In response to Timothy's report, Paul wrote this letter to the Thessalonians, perhaps three to six months after founding the church.

Purpose

Because Paul was forced by persecution to leave Thessalonica abruptly, his young converts received only minimal instruction about the Christian life. When Paul learned from Timothy about their present circumstances, he wrote this letter (1) to express his joy in their steadfast faith and perseverance in the midst of persecution, (2) to instruct them further in holiness and godly living, and (3) to clarify certain beliefs, especially concerning the status of believers who die before Christ's return.

Survey

After greeting the church (1:1), Paul joyfully commends the Thessalonians for their enduring zeal and faith in the face of great adversity (1:2–10; 2:13–16). Paul responds to criticism by reminding the church of the purity of his motives (2:1–6), the sincerity of his affection and concern for the flock (2:7–8,17–20; 3:1–10), and the integrity of his conduct among them (2:9–12).

Paul emphasizes the necessity and importance of holiness and power in the Christian life. The believer must be holy (3:13; 4:1–8; 5:23–24), and the gospel must be accompanied by the power and manifestation of the Holy Spirit (1:5). Paul urges the Thessalonians not to put out the Spirit's fire by despising his manifestations, especially prophecy (5:19–20).

A prominent theme is Christ's return to deliver his people from God's wrath on the earth (1:10; 4:13–18; 5:1–11). Apparently some Thessalonian believers had died already, raising concern about their participation in the final salvation to be revealed at the Lord's coming. Accordingly, Paul explains God's plan for departed saints when Christ returns for his church (4:13–18) and exhorts the living about the importance of being ready when Christ comes (5:1–11). Paul concludes by praying for the sanctification and preservation of the Thessalonians (5:23–24).

Special Features

Four major features characterize this letter. (1) It is among the very first books written in the NT. (2) It contains key passages about God raising the deceased saints when Christ returns to catch up his church (4:13–18) and about "the day of the Lord" (5:1–11). (3) All five chapters contain some reference to Christ's return and its significance for believers (1:10; 2:19; 3:13; 4:13–18; 5:1–11,23). (4) It provides unique insight (a) into the life of a zealous but immature church in the early 50s, and (b) into the quality of Paul's ministry as a pioneer of the gospel.

Reading 1 Thessalonians

In order to read the entire New Testament in one year, the book of 1 Thessalonians should be read in 4 days, according to the following schedule:
☐ 1:1—2:16 ☐ 2:17—3:13 ☐ 4 ☐ 5

NOTES

1

Paul, Silas[a][a] and Timothy,[b]
To the church of the Thessaloni-
ans[c] in God the Father and the Lord
Jesus Christ:

Grace and peace to you.[b][d]

Thanksgiving for the Thessalonians' Faith

2We always thank God for all of
you,[e] mentioning you in our
prayers.[f] **3**We continually remember
before our God and Father[g] your work
produced by faith,[h] your labor prompted by love,[i] and your endurance inspired by hope[j] in our Lord Jesus
Christ.
4For we know, brothers loved by
God,[k] that he has chosen you, **5**because our gospel[l] came to you not
simply with words, but also with power,[m] with the Holy Spirit and with deep
2Ti 1:8 conviction. You know[n] how we lived
among you for your sake. **6**You became
imitators of us[o] and of the Lord; in
spite of severe suffering,[p] you welcomed the message with the joy[q] giv-
Heb 12:11 en by the Holy Spirit.[r] **7**And so you
became a model[s] to all the believers
in Macedonia[t] and Achaia.[u] **8**The
Lord's message[v] rang out from you
not only in Macedonia and Achaia—
your faith in God has become known
everywhere.[w] Therefore we do not
need to say anything about it, **9**for they
themselves report what kind of reception you gave us. They tell how you
turned[x] to God from idols[y] to serve
the living and true God,[z] **10**and to
wait for his Son from heaven,[a] whom
he raised from the dead[b]—Jesus,
who rescues us from the coming 1T
4:
wrath.[c] 5:

1:1 [a]S Ac 15:22 [b]S Ac 16:1; 2Th 1:1 [c]S Ac 17:1 [d]S Ro 1:7
1:2 [e]S Ro 1:8; Eph 5:20 [f]S Ro 1:10
1:3 [g]S Php 4:20 [h]Gal 5:6; 2Th 1:11; Jas 2:14-26 [i]1Th 3:6; 2Th 1:3; S 1Co 13:13 [j]Ro 8:25
1:4 [k]Col 3:12; 2Th 2:13
1:5 [l]S 2Co 2:12; 2Th 2:14 [m]Ro 1:16; S Ro 15:13 [n]1Th 2:10
1:6 [o]S 1Co 4:16 [p]Ac 17:5-10 [q]S 2Co 6:10 [r]Ac 13:52
1:7 [s]S 1Ti 4:12 [t]S Ac 16:9 [u]S Ac 18:12
1:8 [v]2Th 3:1 [w]Ro 1:8
1:9 [x]Ac 14:15 [y]1Co 12:2; Gal 4:8 [z]S Mt 16:16
1:10 [a]S 1Co 1:7 [b]S Ac 2:24 [c]S Ro 1:18
2:1 [d]1Th 1:5,9 [e]2Th 1:10
2:2 [f]Ac 14:19; 16:22; Php 1:30 [g]S Ac 16:12 [h]Ac 17:1-9
2:3 [i]2Co 2:17 [j]2Co 4:2

Paul's Ministry in Thessalonica

2

You know, brothers, that our visit
to you[d] was not a failure.[e] **2**We
had previously suffered[f] and been insulted in Philippi,[g] as you know, but
with the help of our God we dared to
tell you his gospel in spite of strong
opposition.[h] **3**For the appeal we make
does not spring from error or impure
motives,[i] nor are we trying to trick
you.[j] **4**On the contrary, we speak as
men approved by God to be entrusted

[a] *1* Greek *Silvanus,* a variant of *Silas*
[b] *1* Some early manuscripts *you from God our Father and the Lord Jesus Christ*

1:4 HE HAS CHOSEN YOU. Paul's description of those who belong to the elect is found in vv. 6–10. They are those who imitate Christ, endure suffering with the joy given by the Holy Spirit, and model faith and righteousness. They have turned from sin, now serve God, and are waiting for God's Son to return from heaven. The doctrine some teach that people who profess Christ as Savior will be saved regardless of how they live (e.g., whether or not they repent, accept Christ as Lord, persevere in the faith or possess the fruit of the Spirit) is not found anywhere in God's Word and is a flagrant corruption of the original doctrine of salvation preached by Christ and the apostles (see articles on ELECTION AND PREDESTINATION, p. 1824, and FAITH AND GRACE, p. 1720).

1:5 WITH POWER, WITH THE HOLY SPIRIT. The apostolic preaching of the gospel consisted of four essential elements: (1) The apostles proclaimed the gospel of God (2:8) and Christ (3:2) to others.

(2) They preached God's Word in the power of the Holy Spirit (Mt 3:11; Ac 1:5–8; 2:4). This power resulted in conviction of sin, deliverance from satanic bondage, and the performing of miracles and healings (see Ac 4:30, note; 1Co 2:4, note).

(3) The message was proclaimed "with deep conviction." Because of their faith in Christ, and through the work of the Spirit in them, they possessed in their hearts a full assurance of the truth and power of the message (cf. Ro 1:16).

(4) Those who believed the message obeyed God's Word and lived it out in their lives; they were models of holiness and righteousness.

Without these four elements accompanying the proclamation of the gospel, Christ's full redemption will not be experienced in the churches.

1:10 TO WAIT FOR HIS SON FROM HEAVEN. The great hope of the Thessalonian believers was Christ's return and his delivering them from "the coming wrath." (1) A true NT conversion to Christ involves (a) turning from sin and (b) turning to God to wait for his Son to return (v. 9). Waiting for Christ implies a sustained expectation of Christ's return and a readiness for that time.

(2) "The coming wrath" refers to the future judgment that occurs during the tribulation period. However, believers need not fear, for God is sending Jesus back to deliver us from that time of wrath. Clearly Christ's return for his faithful precedes this coming wrath (see Rev 3:10, note; see article on THE GREAT TRIBULATION, p. 1456).

(3) This is the first reference in 1 Thessalonians to Christ's return, when he comes to catch up his saints and take them to his Father's house (see Jn 14:3, note); the other passages are 2:19; 3:13; 4:17, 5:1–11,23.

2:1 OUR VISIT TO YOU. In ch. 2 Paul vindicates his conduct while he was with the Thessalonians. Paul had been slandered by his opponents and accused of insincerity in his preaching of the gospel.

2:4 WE SPEAK . . . NOT TRYING TO PLEASE MEN. Every preacher of the gospel faces the

with the gospel.[k] We are not trying to
please men[l] but God, who tests our
hearts.[m] **5**You know we never used
flattery, nor did we put on a mask to
cover up greed[n]—God is our witness.[o] **6**We were not looking for
praise from men,[p] not from you or
anyone else.
As apostles[q] of Christ we could
have been a burden to you,[r] **7**but we
were gentle among you, like a mother
caring for her little children.[s] **8**We
loved you so much that we were delighted to share with you not only the
gospel of God[t] but our lives as well,[u]
because you had become so dear to us.
9Surely you remember, brothers, our
toil and hardship; we worked[v] night
and day in order not to be a burden to
anyone[w] while we preached the gospel
of God to you.
10You are witnesses,[x] and so is
God,[y] of how holy,[z] righteous and
blameless we were among you who believed. **11**For you know that we dealt
with each of you as a father deals with
his own children,[a] **12**encouraging,
comforting and urging you to live lives
worthy[b] of God, who calls[c] you into
his kingdom and glory.
13And we also thank God continually[d] because, when you received the
word of God,[e] which you heard from
us, you accepted it not as the word of
men, but as it actually is, the word of
God, which is at work in you who believe. **14**For you, brothers, became imitators[f] of God's churches in Judea,[g]
which are in Christ Jesus: You suffered
from your own countrymen[h] the same
things those churches suffered from
the Jews, **15**who killed the Lord Jesus[i]
and the prophets[j] and also drove us
out. They displease God and are hostile to all men **16**in their effort to keep
us from speaking to the Gentiles[k] so
that they may be saved. In this way
they always heap up their sins to the
limit.[l] The wrath of God has come
upon them at last.[c]

Paul's Longing to See the Thessalonians

17But, brothers, when we were torn
away from you for a short time (in person, not in thought),[m] out of our intense longing we made every effort to
see you.[n] **18**For we wanted to come
to you—certainly I, Paul, did, again
and again—but Satan[o] stopped us.[p]

2:4 [k] Gal 2:7; 1Ti 1:11 [l] S Ro 2:29 [m] S Rev 2:23 **2:5** [n] S Ac 20:33 [o] ver 10; S Ro 1:9 **2:6** [p] Jn 5:41,44 [q] 1Co 9:1,2 [r] 2Co 11:7-11 **2:7** [s] S ver 11 **2:8** [t] S Ro 1:1 [u] 2Co 12:15; 1Jn 3:16 **2:9** [v] S Ac 18:3 [w] S 2Co 11:9; 2Th 3:8 **2:10** [x] 1Th 1:5 [y] ver 5; S Ro 1:9 [z] 2Co 1:12 **2:11** [a] ver 7; 1Co 4:14; Gal 4:19; S 1Ti 1:2; Phm 10; S 1Jn 2:1 **2:12** [b] S Eph 4:1 [c] S Ro 8:28 **2:13** [d] 1Th 1:2; S Ro 1:8 [e] S Heb 4:12 **2:14** [f] 1Th 1:6 [g] Gal 1:22 [h] Ac 17:5; 2Th 1:4 **2:15** [i] Lk 24:20; Ac 2:23 [j] S Mt 5:12 **2:16** [k] Ac 13:45, 50; 17:5; S 20:3; 21:27; 24:9 [l] Mt 23:32 **2:17** [m] 1Co 5:3; Col 2:5 [n] 1Th 3:10 **2:18** [o] S Mt 4:10 [p] Ro 1:13; 15:22

[c] *16* Or *them fully*

---

temptation to please other people, i.e., seek acceptance, approval and glory from others (v. 6) by preaching only what will not offend. (1) Yielding to this temptation may take the form of tolerating sin and lukewarmness in the congregation (cf. Rev 2:20; 3:15–16). It may also involve the use of flattering speech in order to gain financial offerings, numerical gain, political office or praise from others (vv. 4–6). (2) If this occurs, irreparable damage is done to the righteousness and integrity of Christ's church. For this reason it is essential that our motive in preaching should always be to seek God's approval and not other people's (1Co 4:5; Gal 1:9–10; see Lk 1:17, note; 2Ti 4:3–4, note).

2:7 LIKE A MOTHER CARING FOR HER LITTLE CHILDREN. Paul and his helpers offer an example of the spiritual attitude that all missionaries, evangelists and pastors should have as they preach the gospel. (1) As missionaries, they had a mother's gentle and caring attitude; under great sacrifice, they made a special effort to nurture, protect and meet the spiritual needs of the new converts.

(2) Their gentleness implies they did not act like important or superior persons.

(3) The missionaries possessed such a yearning and love for the Thessalonians that they were willing to share their very lives with the people (v. 8).

(4) They devoted long hours, even to the point of weariness, in order to bring them the gospel (v. 9).

(5) They lived holy and blameless lives before the people, encouraging and urging them as any good father would (vv. 10–12).

2:10 HOW HOLY, RIGHTEOUS AND BLAMELESS WE WERE. Paul does not accept the erroneous view of "sinning Christianity," which says that the salvation provided by Christ and his atoning blood is not adequate to save us from sin's bondage and power. This unbiblical doctrine maintains that all Christians must expect to sin against God daily in word, thought and deed throughout their earthly lives. Contrary to the above doctrine, (1) Paul affirms, with regard to his own conduct among the Thessalonians, that he was "holy, righteous and blameless." (2) Paul called both the church and God himself as witnesses that God's sufficient grace through Christ had enabled him, as he affirmed elsewhere, to purify himself "from everything that contaminates body and spirit, perfecting holiness out of reverence for God" (2Co 7:1; cf. 2Co 1:12; 2:17; 6:3–10; 1Th 1:5; 2Ti 1:3).

2:16 THE WRATH OF GOD HAS COME UPON THEM. Paul denounces the Jews who oppose the gospel (vv. 14–16) and speaks of God's wrath already being upon them. This wrath includes both God's turning the already hardened Jews of Israel over to blindness and futile thinking (cf. Ro 1:21), and the future outpouring of his wrath foretold by Christ (Mt 21:43; 23:38; 24:15–28; Lk 21:5–24; 23:27–31).

2:18 BUT SATAN STOPPED US. Paul's mis-

19For what is our hope, our joy, or the
crown[q] in which we will glory[r] in the
presence of our Lord Jesus when he
comes?[s] Is it not you? **20**Indeed, you
are our glory[t] and joy.

3 So when we could stand it no longer,[u] we thought it best to be left
by ourselves in Athens.[v] **2**We sent
Timothy,[w] who is our brother and
God's fellow worker[d][x] in spreading
the gospel of Christ,[y] to strengthen
and encourage you in your faith, **3**so
that no one would be unsettled by
these trials.[z] You know quite well
that we were destined for them.[a] **4**In
fact, when we were with you, we kept
telling you that we would be persecuted. And it turned out that way, as you
well know.[b] **5**For this reason, when I
could stand it no longer,[c] I sent to find
out about your faith.[d] I was afraid that
in some way the tempter[e] might have
tempted you and our efforts might have
been useless.[f]

Timothy's Encouraging Report

6But Timothy[g] has just now come
to us from you[h] and has brought good
news about your faith and love.[i] He
has told us that you always have pleasant memories of us and that you long
to see us, just as we also long to see
you.[j] **7**Therefore, brothers, in all our
distress and persecution we were encouraged about you because of your 2T
faith. **8**For now we really live, since you 1:3
are standing firm[k] in the Lord. **9**How
can we thank God enough for you[l] in
return for all the joy we have in the
presence of our God because of you?[m]
10Night and day we pray[n] most earnestly that we may see you again[o]
and supply what is lacking in your
faith.

Paul's Prayer for the Church

11Now may our God and Father[p]
himself and our Lord Jesus clear the
way for us to come to you. **12**May the
Lord make your love increase and
overflow for each other[q] and for everyone else, just as ours does for you.
13May he strengthen your hearts so
that you will be blameless[r] and holy
in the presence of our God and Father[s] when our Lord Jesus comes[t]
with all his holy ones.[u]

2:19 [q] Isa 62:3; Php 4:1 [r] 2Co 1:14 [s] S Mt 16:27; S Lk 17:30; S 1Co 1:7; 4:5; 1Th 3:13; 2Th 1:8-10; 1Pe 1:7; 1Jn 2:28; S Rev 1:7
2:20 [t] 2Co 1:14
3:1 [u] ver 5 [v] S Ac 17:15
3:2 [w] S Ac 16:1 [x] S 1Co 3:9 [y] S 2Co 2:12
3:3 [z] Mk 4:17; Jn 16:33; Ro 5:3; 2Co 1:4; 4:17; 2Ti 3:12 [a] S Ac 9:16; 14:22
3:4 [b] 1Th 2:14
3:5 [c] ver 1 [d] ver 2 [e] Mt 4:3 [f] Gal 2:2; Php 2:16
3:6 [g] S Ac 16:1 [h] Ac 18:5 [i] 1Th 1:3
[j] 1Th 2:17,18
3:8 [k] S 1Co 16:13
3:9 [l] 1Th 1:2 [m] 1Th 2:19,20
3:10 [n] 2Ti 1:3 [o] 1Th 2:17
3:11 [p] ver 13; S Php 4:20
3:12 [q] Php 1:9; 1Th 4:9,10; 2Th 1:3
3:13 [r] Ps 15:2; 1Co 1:8; Php 2:15; 1Th 5:23; 1Ti 6:14; 2Pe 3:14 [s] ver 11; S Php 4:20 [t] S 1Th 2:19 [u] Mt 25:31; 2Th 1:7

[d] 2 Some manuscripts *brother and fellow worker*; other manuscripts *brother and God's servant*

sionary endeavors had at times been frustrated by Satan. Scriptural truths concerning Satan's opposition to faithful believers include the following: (1) Satan is permitted by God to war against believers and hinder them from doing what they sincerely desire to do for Christ (Eph 6:11–12; cf. Da 10:13,20–21; Zec 3:1; Mt 4:1–10).

(2) Satan's power is, however, subject to God's overruling (Job 1:9–12; 2:6; see 1:12, note); God can overrule Satan's activities and turn them into good for his kingdom (2Co 12:7–9).

(3) Satan's opposition can be overcome by the prayers of saints, by the blood of the Lamb, by the word of our testimony and by our committed love for God (cf. Rev 12:11); therefore, Satan's opposition need not be permanent (cf. 3:11). To this end, we must pray daily for deliverance from his schemes and power (see 3:5, note; Mt 4:10, note on Satan; 6:13; Eph 6:12, note; see article on POWER OVER SATAN AND DEMONS, p. 1484).

3:3 TRIALS. The followers of Christ must not regard trouble and persecution as alien to the Christian life. (1) True believers who refuse to conform to the prevailing characteristics of their world will "be persecuted" (v. 4; cf. Ac 14:22; Ro 8:18; 2Ti 3:12; see Mt 5:10, note). (2) These trials must not be identified with the outpouring of God's wrath on the ungodly at the end of time (5:9; Mt 24:21; 2Th 1:6; Rev 3:10, note).

3:5 THE TEMPTER MIGHT HAVE TEMPTED YOU. This is the second time Paul has referred to Satan's activity in this letter (cf. 2:18). Paul firmly believed in Satan and the realm of evil spirits (Eph 2:2; 2Th 2:9), as did Jesus Christ (Mt 13:39; Mk 3:14–15; 4:15; Lk 4:1–13,33–41). Today many no longer believe in a personal Satan; he is seldom mentioned, exposed or confronted directly in or by the church. The devil has tempted us to believe that he is no longer a real enemy who takes people captive, and that we need no longer drive out evil spirits as Jesus and the early NT believers did. Many churches feel no need to challenge Satan directly with the power of Christ's kingdom (see Mt 4:10, note on Satan; see article on POWER OVER SATAN AND DEMONS, p. 1484).

3:13 BLAMELESS AND HOLY ... WHEN OUR LORD JESUS COMES. Paul often prayed with Christ's return in mind (cf. Php 1:10). He considered it a tragedy if at the Lord's return some within the church were caught living in sin or lukewarmness. Jesus emphasized this same concern (Mt 24:42–51; 25:1–13). In light of Christ's return, the Biblical standard is to be "blameless and holy." We must be wholeheartedly committed to the Lord and separated from all that offends him. The phrase "with all his holy ones" refers to departed saints who are already with the Lord in heaven (see article on THE RAPTURE, p. 1864).

Living to Please God

4 Finally, brothers,[v] we instructed
you how to live[w] in order to please
God,[x] as in fact you are living. Now we
ask you and urge you in the Lord Jesus
to do this more and more. **2**For you
know what instructions we gave you by
the authority of the Lord Jesus.
3It is God's will[y] that you should be
sanctified: that you should avoid sexual immorality;[z] **4**that each of you
should learn to control his own
body[e][a] in a way that is holy and honorable, **5**not in passionate lust[b] like
the heathen,[c] who do not know
God;[d] **6**and that in this matter no one
should wrong his brother or take advantage of him.[e] The Lord will punish
men[f] for all such sins,[g] as we have
already told you and warned you. **7**For
God did not call us to be impure, but to
3- live a holy life.[h] **8**Therefore, he who
rejects this instruction does not reject
man but God, who gives you his Holy
Spirit.[i]
9Now about brotherly love[j] we do
not need to write to you,[k] for you yourselves have been taught by God[l] to
love each other.[m] **10**And in fact, you do
love all the brothers throughout Macedonia.[n] Yet we urge you, brothers, to
do so more and more.[o]
11Make it your ambition to lead a
quiet life, to mind your own business
and to work with your hands,[p] just as
we told you, **12**so that your daily life
may win the respect of outsiders[q] and
so that you will not be dependent on
anybody.

The Coming of the Lord

13Brothers, we do not want you to be
ignorant[r] about those who fall
asleep,[s] or to grieve like the rest of
men, who have no hope.[t] **14**We believe
that Jesus died and rose again[u] and so
we believe that God will bring with
Jesus those who have fallen asleep in
him.[v] **15**According to the Lord's own
word, we tell you that we who are still
alive, who are left till the coming of the
Lord,[w] will certainly not precede
those who have fallen asleep.[x] **16**For
the Lord himself will come down from

4:1 [v] 2Co 13:11; 2Th 3:1 [w] S Eph 4:1 [x] S 2Co 5:9 **4:3** [y] S Eph 5:17 [z] S 1Co 6:18 **4:4** [a] 1Co 7:2,9 **4:5** [b] Ro 1:26 [c] Eph 4:17 [d] S Gal 4:8 **4:6** [e] Lev 25:17; 1Co 6:8 [f] Dt 32:35; Ps 94:1; Ro 2:5-11; 12:19; Heb 10:30,31 [g] Heb 13:4 **4:7** [h] Lev 11:44; 1Pe 1:15 **4:8** [i] Eze 36:27; Ro 5:5; 2Co 1:22; Gal 4:6; 1Jn 3:24 **4:9** [j] S Ro 12:10 [k] 1Th 5:1 [l] S Jn 6:45 [m] S Jn 13:34 **4:10** [n] S Ac 16:9 [o] S 1Th 3:12 **4:11** [p] Eph 4:28; 2Th 3:10-12 **4:12** [q] S Mk 4:11 **4:13** [r] S Ro 11:25 [s] S Mt 9:24 [t] Eph 2:12 **4:14** [u] Ro 14:9; 1Co 15:3,4; 2Co 5:15 [v] 1Co 15:18 **4:15** [w] S 1Co 1:7 [x] 1Co 15:52

[e] 4 Or *learn to live with his own wife*; or *learn to acquire a wife*

4:3 IT IS GOD'S WILL. Although they lived in a society where sexual immorality was commonplace and acceptable, the apostles did not compromise God's holiness and truth. They would not lower their standards to accommodate the ideas or trends of their society. Whenever they found low standards in some of the churches (cf. Rev 2:14–15,20), they rebuked and sought to correct them. In the light of today's prevalent low morals, apostolic-type leaders are still needed to call the church to God's standards of righteousness.

4:3–7 AVOID SEXUAL IMMORALITY. God imposes on all believers high standards of purity and sanctification with regard to sexual matters. For a discussion of what these standards are, see article on STANDARDS OF SEXUAL MORALITY, p. 1936.

4:6 WRONG HIS BROTHER. Sexual immorality wrongs another person, whether a believer or not. To wrong (Gk *pleonokteō*) means "to go beyond what is right," "to transgress," "to overreach." All sexual activity or play outside of marriage is an act of terrible injustice against another individual. Adultery violates the rights of another married person. Sexual looseness before marriage defiles and robs another person of the holiness and chastity that God desires for him or her. It destroys the purity and virginity that must be brought into a marriage.

4:8 DOES NOT REJECT MAN BUT GOD. Those who reject the instructions of the apostle on sanctification and purity are rejecting God. (1) To disregard Paul's admonition is to stand squarely against the Holy Spirit, and the purity that the Spirit desires. God will judge and punish church members who disregard moral purity for the satisfaction of their own lusts (v. 6; cf. Heb 13:4).

(2) All those in the world and within the visible church who reject the truth and have "delighted in wickedness" (see 2Th 2:12, note) will be abandoned by Christ when faithful believers are caught up "to meet the Lord in the air" (v. 17; see article on THE RAPTURE, p. 1864). They will suffer destruction (5:3), wrath (5:9), punishment (2Th 1:8) and condemnation (2Th 1:9; 2:12) at the final coming of Christ from heaven in blazing fire to punish all who "do not obey the gospel of our Lord Jesus" (2Th 1:7–8).

4:13 ABOUT THOSE WHO FALL ASLEEP. This phrase refers to believers who had died and whose souls were in heaven; it does not mean that the dead are unconscious in a sort of soul-sleep (cf. Php 1:21, note). The Thessalonians did not understand how the resurrection of Christians who had already died related to the catching up of living Christians at Christ's coming (see Jn 14:3, note). They apparently thought that those who died before Christ returns for the church (vv. 16–17) would not be resurrected until a much later time. Paul tells them that the dead in Christ will rise at the same time the Lord returns for the faithful of his churches (see article on THE RAPTURE, p. 1864).

4:14–18 THE COMING OF THE LORD. The event described by Paul in these verses is often referred to as "the rapture of the church." For a discussion of this future event, see article on THE RAPTURE, p. 1864.

THE RAPTURE

***1Th 4:16–17** "For the Lord himself will come down from heaven with a loud command, with the voice of the archangel and with the trumpet call of God, and the dead in Christ will rise first. After that we who are still alive and are left will be caught up together with them in the clouds to meet the Lord in the air. And so we will be with the Lord forever."*

The word "rapture" is derived from the Latin word *raptu*, which means "caught away or caught up." This Latin word is equivalent to the Greek *harpazō*, translated as "caught up" in 1Th 4:17. This event, described here and in 1Co 15, refers to the catching up of the church from the earth to meet the Lord in the air. It involves only the faithful of Christ's churches.

(1) Just prior to the rapture, as Christ is descending from heaven for his church, the resurrection of the "dead in Christ" will occur (1Th 4:16). This is not the same resurrection described in Rev 20:4, for the latter is an event occurring after Christ returns to earth, destroys the wicked and binds Satan (Rev 19:11—20:3). The resurrection in Rev 20:4 relates to the martyred dead of the tribulation and possibly to OT saints (see Rev 20:6, note).

(2) At the same time as the dead in Christ rise, living believers will be transfigured; their bodies will be clothed with immortality (1Co 15:51,53). This will happen in a very short time, "in the twinkling of an eye" (1Co 15:52).

(3) Both the resurrected believers and the transfigured believers will be caught up together to meet Christ in the air, i.e., in the atmosphere between earth and heaven.

(4) They will be visibly united with Christ (1Th 4:16–17), taken to his Father's house in heaven (see Jn 14:2–3, notes) and united with loved ones who have died (1Th 4:13–18).

(5) They will be removed from all distress (2Co 5:2,4; Php 3:21), from all persecution and oppression (see Rev 3:10, note), from the entire realm of sin and from death (1Co 15:51–56); the rapture delivers them from "the coming wrath" (see 1Th 1:10, note; 5:9), i.e., from the great tribulation.

(6) The hope that our Savior will soon return to take us out of the world to "be with the Lord forever" (1Th 4:17) is the blessed hope of all the redeemed (Tit 2:13). It is a major source of comfort for suffering believers (1Th 4:17–18; 5:10).

(7) Paul uses "we" in 1Th 4:17 because he knows the Lord's return could have happened in his own lifetime, and he communicates this same anticipation to the Thessalonians. The Bible insists on a continual waiting with eagerness for the return of our Lord. Believers today must be ever watchful and hopeful for Christ's return to take them to himself (cf. Ro 13:11; 1Co 7:29; 10:11; 15:51–52; Php 4:5).

(8) The portion of the professing church that fails to abstain from evil and is unfaithful to Christ will be left behind (see Mt 25:1, note; Lk 12:45, note). They will remain as part of the apostate church (see Rev 17:1, note; see article on THE AGE OF THE ANTICHRIST, p. 1872), subject to God's wrath.

(9) Following the rapture is the day of the Lord, a time that brings distress and wrath to the ungodly (1Th 5:2–10; see 5:2, note). That will be followed by the second stage of Christ's coming, when he comes to destroy the ungodly and to reign on earth (see Mt 24:42,44 notes).

heaven,[y] with a loud command, with
the voice of the archangel[z] and with
the trumpet call of God,[a] and the dead
in Christ will rise first.[b] 17After that,
we who are still alive and are left[c] will
be caught up together with them in the
clouds[d] to meet the Lord in the air.
And so we will be with the Lord[e] forever. 18Therefore encourage each other[f] with these words.

5 Now, brothers, about times and
dates[g] we do not need to write to
you,[h] 2for you know very well that the
day of the Lord[i] will come like a thief
in the night.[j] 3While people are saying, "Peace and safety,"[k] destruction
will come on them suddenly,[l] as labor
pains on a pregnant woman, and they
will not escape.[m]

4But you, brothers, are not in darkness[n] so that this day should surprise
you like a thief.[o] 5You are all sons of
the light[p] and sons of the day. We do
not belong to the night or to the darkness. 6So then, let us not be like others, who are asleep,[q] but let us be
alert[r] and self-controlled.[s] 7For

2Th 1:7–2:8

4:16 [y]S Mt 16:27 [z]Jude 9 [a]S Mt 24:31 [b]1Co 15:23; 2Th 2:1; Rev 14:13 **4:17** [c]1Co 15:52 [d]Ac 1:9; S Ac 8:39; S Rev 1:7; 11:12 [e]S Jn 12:26 **4:18** [f]1Th 5:11 **5:1** [g]Ac 1:7 [h]1Th 4:9 **5:2** [i]S 1Co 1:8 [j]S Lk 12:39 **5:3** [k]Jer 4:10; 6:14; Eze 13:10 [l]Job 15:21; Ps 35:8; 55:15; Isa 29:5; 47:9,11 [m]2Th 1:9 **5:4** [n]S Ac 26:18; 1Jn 2:8 [o]ver 2 **5:5** [p]S Lk 16:8 **5:6** [q]Ro 13:11 [r]S Mt 25:13 [s]S Ac 24:25

4:18 ENCOURAGE EACH OTHER. Paul inspires hope in the Thessalonians, not by telling them to prepare for martyrdom during the period of "the day of the Lord" (5:2–10), i.e., the tribulation (Rev 6–19), but by informing them of the rapture (see vv. 14–17; Jn 14:3, note; 1Co 15:51–58; see article on THE RAPTURE, p. 1864). Knowing this doctrine, they will be able to encourage each other.

5:1 TIMES AND DATES. Having spoken about Christ's return to catch up his followers from the earth (4:13–18), Paul now turns to the subject of God's final judgment on all those who reject salvation in Christ in the final days, that terrible time called "the day of the Lord" (v. 2). The believers' rapture (4:17) must be simultaneous with the beginning of "the day of the Lord" in order for Christ's return to be imminent and unexpected, as Christ himself taught (see Mt 24:42,44, notes).

5:2 THE DAY OF THE LORD. The "day of the Lord" normally refers not to a 24-hour day but to an extended period of time when God's enemies are overthrown (Isa 2:12–21; 13:9–16; 34:1–4; Jer 46:10; Joel 1:15—2:11,28; 3:9,12–17; Am 5:18–20; Zec 14:1–3), followed by Christ's earthly reign (Zep 3:14–17; Rev 20:4–7). (1) This "day" begins when direct divine judgment falls upon the world toward the end of this age (v. 3). The tribulation period is included within the day of the Lord (Rev 6–19; see 6:1, note). This wrath of God culminates with Christ's coming to destroy all the wicked (see Joel 1:14, note; 2:30–31, note; Zep 1:7, note; Rev 16:16, note; 19:11–21).

(2) The day of the Lord apparently begins at a time when people are hoping for peace and safety (v. 3).

(3) The "day" will not overtake faithful believers like a thief, for they are appointed to receive salvation, not wrath, and they are alert and self-controlled, living in faith, love and righteousness (vv. 4–9).

(4) Believers are delivered from this "coming wrath" (1:10, note) through the Lord Jesus Christ (v. 9) when he comes to catch up the faithful of his churches and take them to heaven (cf. 4:17; see Jn 14:3, note; Rev. 3:10, note; see article on THE RAPTURE, p. 1864).

(5) The day of the Lord will end after the millennial kingdom (Rev 20:4–10) at the creation of the new heaven and new earth (cf. 2Pe 3:13; Rev 21:1).

5:2 LIKE A THIEF IN THE NIGHT. This metaphor means that the time when the day of the Lord begins is uncertain and unexpected. There is no way one can date it (see Mt 24:42–44, notes on the Lord's teaching on the unexpected time of his coming for the church).

5:3 PEACE AND SAFETY. It is the unbeliever who will be saying, "Peace and safety." This could mean that the world will be expecting and hoping for peace. The day of the Lord and its worldwide distress will come on them suddenly, destroying any hope for peace and security.

5:4 YOU, BROTHERS, ARE NOT IN DARKNESS. Believers do not live in sin and rebellion. They belong to the day that precedes the night and will not experience God's appointed night of wrath (vv. 8–9; see article on THE RAPTURE, p. 1864).

5:6 LET US BE ALERT. "Be alert" (Gk *grēgoreō*) means to "stay awake and keep watch." The context (vv. 4–9) indicates that Paul is not exhorting his readers to "be alert" for the "day of the Lord" (v. 2), but rather to be spiritually prepared in order to escape the wrath of that day (cf. 2:11–12; Lk 21:34–36). (1) If we wish to escape God's wrath (v. 3), we must remain spiritually awake and morally alert, and continue in faith, love and the hope of salvation (vv. 8–9; see Lk 21:36, note; Eph 6:11, note). (2) Since the faithful will be protected from God's wrath (see v. 2, note; see article on THE RAPTURE, p. 1864), they must not fear the day of the Lord, but must "wait for his Son from heaven . . . Jesus, who rescues us from the coming wrath" (1:10).

5:6 SELF-CONTROLLED. The word "self-controlled" (Gk *nēphō*) had two meanings in NT times. (1) The literal meaning, as given by various Greek lexicons, is "a state of abstinence from wine," "to drink no wine," "to abstain from wine," "to be completely unaffected by wine" or "to be sober." It carries a figurative or metaphorical meaning of alertness, self-restraint or self-control, i.e., to be alert spiritually and self-controlled, just as someone who does not drink alcoholic wine.

(2) The context here supports the view that Paul was not excluding the literal meaning. The words "let us be alert and self-controlled" are contrasted with the words of the following verse, "those who

those who sleep, sleep at night, and
those who get drunk, get drunk at
night.[t] **8**But since we belong to the
day,[u] let us be self-controlled, putting
on faith and love as a breastplate,[v]
and the hope of salvation[w] as a helmet.[x] **9**For God did not appoint us to
suffer wrath[y] but to receive salvation
through our Lord Jesus Christ.[z] **10**He
died for us so that, whether we are
awake or asleep, we may live together
2Th 2:13 with him.[a] **11**Therefore encourage one
another[b] and build each other up,[c]
just as in fact you are doing.

Final Instructions

12Now we ask you, brothers, to respect those who work hard[d] among
you, who are over you in the Lord[e]
and who admonish you. **13**Hold them in
the highest regard in love because of
their work. Live in peace with each other.[f] **14**And we urge you, brothers,
warn those who are idle,[g] encourage
the timid, help the weak,[h] be patient
with everyone. **15**Make sure that nobody pays back wrong for wrong,[i] but
always try to be kind to each other[j]
and to everyone else.

16Be joyful always;[k] **17**pray continually;[l] **18**give thanks in all circumstances,[m] for this is God's will for you
in Christ Jesus.

19Do not put out the Spirit's fire;[n]
20do not treat prophecies[o] with contempt. **21**Test everything.[p] Hold on to
the good.[q] **22**Avoid every kind of evil.

23May God himself, the God of
peace,[r] sanctify you through and
through. May your whole spirit, soul[s]
and body be kept blameless[t] at the
coming of our Lord Jesus Christ.[u]
24The one who calls[v] you is faithful[w]
and he will do it.[x]

25Brothers, pray for us.[y] **26**Greet
all the brothers with a holy kiss.[z] **27**I
charge you before the Lord to have this
letter read to all the brothers.[a]

28The grace of our Lord Jesus Christ
be with you.[b]

5:7 [t]Ac 2:15; Ro 13:13; 2Pe 2:13 **5:8** [u]ver 5 [v]S Eph 6:14 [w]Ro 8:24 [x]Isa 59:17; Eph 6:17 **5:9** [y]1Th 1:10 [z]2Th 2:13,14 **5:10** [a]Ro 14:9; 2Co 5:15 **5:11** [b]1Th 4:18 [c]Eph 4:29 **5:12** [d]Ro 16:6, 12; 1Co 15:10 [e]1Ti 5:17; Heb 13:17 **5:13** [f]S Mk 9:50 **5:14** [g]2Th 3:6,7, 11 [h]Ro 14:1; 1Co 8:7-12 **5:15** [i]Ro 12:17; 1Pe 3:9 [j]Eph 4:32 **5:16** [k]Php 4:4 **5:17** [l]S Lk 18:1 **5:18** [m]S Eph 5:20 **5:19** [n]Eph 4:30 **5:20** [o]1Co 14:1-40 **5:21** [p]1Co 14:29; 1Jn 4:1 [q]Ro 12:9 **5:23** [r]S Ro 15:33 [s]Heb 4:12 [t]S 1Th 3:13 [u]S 1Th 2:19 **5:24** [v]S Ro 8:28 [w]S 1Co 1:9 [x]Nu 23:19; Php 1:6

5:25 [y]Eph 6:19; Col 4:3; 2Th 3:1; Heb 13:18 **5:26** [z]S Ro 16:16 **5:27** [a]2Th 3:14; S 1Ti 4:13 **5:28** [b]S Ro 16:20

---

get drunk, get drunk at night" (v. 7). Thus, Paul's contrast of *nēphō* with physical drunkenness would indicate that he was including the literal meaning of "abstinence from wine." Compare Jesus' statement about those who eat and drink with drunkards and are thus caught unaware by his return (Mt 24:48–51).

5:9 NOT APPOINT US TO SUFFER WRATH. One reason why the hope of Christ's return is such a comfort to believers (4:17–18) is that he delivers us from God's terrible wrath, i.e., the judgments of the day of the Lord (v. 2–3; cf. Rev 6:16–17; 11:18; 14:10,19; 15:1,7; 16:1,19; 19:15).

5:10 LIVE TOGETHER WITH HIM. Paul identifies our hope of salvation and our deliverance from the day of God's wrath with Christ's sacrificial death and his return to take us to live together with him.

5:17 PRAY CONTINUALLY. To pray is to abide in the presence of the Father, continually crying out for his grace and blessing. "Continually" does not mean to be constantly uttering formal prayers. Rather, it implies recurrent prayer of all kinds and on all occasions throughout the day (Lk 18:1; Ro 12:12; Eph 6:18; Col 4:2).

5:19–20 DO NOT PUT OUT THE SPIRIT'S FIRE. (1) Paul equates putting out the Spirit's fire with the depreciation and rejection of the Holy Spirit's supernatural manifestations such as prophesying. To repress or reject the right and orderly use of prophecy or other spiritual gifts will result in the loss of any manifestation of the Spirit among believers (1Co 12:7–10,28–30). The Spirit's ministry is described in Jn 14:26; 15:26–27; 16:13–14; Ac 1:8; 13:2; Ro 8:4,11,16,26; 1Co 2:9–14; 12:1–11; Gal 5:22–25.

(2) These two verses clearly indicate that churches other than the one in Corinth experienced spiritual gifts in public worship. Note carefully that although prophetic utterances were not to be treated with contempt, they also were not to be accepted until they had been examined carefully (v. 21; see 1Co 14:29, note).

5:23 SANCTIFY YOU THROUGH AND THROUGH. Paul's final prayer for the Thessalonian believers is that they be sanctified. For a discussion of what the Bible means by sanctification, see article on SANCTIFICATION, p. 1956.

2 THESSALONIANS

Outline

Christian Greetings (1:1–2)
- I. Paul Encourages the Thessalonians in Persecution (1:3–12)
  - A. His Gratitude for Their Spiritual Growth (1:3)
  - B. His Praise to Other Churches for Their Endurance (1:4)
  - C. His Assurance Concerning the Final Outcome (1:5–10)
  - D. His Prayers for Them (1:11–12)
- II. Paul Corrects the Thessalonians in Profession (2:1–17)
  - A. The Day of the Lord Has Not Come (2:1–2)
  - B. The Man of Lawlessness Will First Be Revealed (2:3–12)
  - C. Stand Firm in the Assurance of Truth and Grace (2:13–17)
- III. Paul Admonishes the Thessalonians in Practice (3:1–15)
  - A. To Pray for Him (3:1–2)
  - B. To Remain Steadfast in the Lord (3:3–5)
  - C. To Keep Aloof from the Unruly and to Live a Disciplined Life (3:6–15)

Final Greeting and Benediction (3:16–18)

Author: Paul

Theme: The Return of Christ

Date of Writing: c. A.D. 51 or 52

Background

When this letter was written, the situation in the Thessalonian church was much the same as when Paul wrote his first letter (see the introduction to 1 Thessalonians). It is likely, therefore, that this letter was written only a few months after 1 Thessalonians while Paul was still working in Corinth with Silas and Timothy (1:1; cf. Ac 18:5). Apparently when Paul was informed about the reception of his first letter and about new developments in the Thessalonian church, he was prompted to write this second letter.

Purpose

Paul's purpose is similar to that of 1 Thessalonians: (1) to encourage his young, persecuted converts; (2) to exhort them to live disciplined lives and to work for a living; and (3) to correct some erroneous beliefs about end-time events related to "the day of the Lord" (2:2).

Survey

Whereas the tone of Paul's relationship to the Thessalonians in his first letter is that of a tender nurse caring for little ones (1Th 2:7), in this letter it is more that of a father disciplining some unruly children and correcting their course (3:7–12; cf. 1Th 2:11). He does commend them for their steadfast faith and again encourages them to remain faithful through the persecution they are encountering (1:3–7).

The main section of the letter deals with the eschatological day of the Lord (2:1–12; cf. 1:6–10). It appears from 2:2 that some at Thessalonica were claiming, either by a "prophecy" (a revelation), a "report" (verbal message) or a "letter" (supposedly from Paul), that the time of great tribulation and the day of the Lord had begun. Paul corrects this misunderstanding by stating that three significant events will signal that the day of the Lord has arrived (2:2): (1) a major apostasy and rebellion will occur (2:3), (2) God's appointed restraint against evil will be lifted (2:6–7), and (3) "the man of lawlessness" will be revealed (2:3–4,8–12). Paul rebukes those in the church who are using the expectation of Christ's imminent return as an excuse for not working daily. He exhorts all believers to live diligent and disciplined lives (3:6–12).

Special Features

Three major features characterize this letter. (1) It contains one of the NT's most developed passages about unrestrained lawlessness and deception at the end of history (2:3–12). (2) God's righteous judgment that will accompany Christ's second coming is described here in apocalyptic terms, similar to the book of Revelation (1:6–10; 2:8). (3) It uses terms for the eschatological antichrist not found elsewhere in the Bible (2:3,8).

Reading 2 Thessalonians

In order to read the entire New Testament in one year, the book of 2 Thessalonians should be read in 3 days, according to the following schedule:
☐ 1 ☐ 2 ☐ 3

NOTES

1 Paul, Silas[a][a] and Timothy,[b]
To the church of the Thessaloni-
ans[c] in God our Father and the Lord
Jesus Christ:

2Grace and peace to you from God
the Father and the Lord Jesus Christ.[d]

Thanksgiving and Prayer

3We ought always to thank God for
you,[e] brothers, and rightly so, because your faith is growing more and
more, and the love every one of you has
for each other is increasing.[f] **4**Therefore, among God's churches we
boast[g] about your perseverance and
faith[h] in all the persecutions and trials you are enduring.[i]

5All this is evidence[j] that God's
judgment is right, and as a result you
will be counted worthy[k] of the kingdom of God, for which you are suffering. **6**God is just:[l] He will pay back
trouble to those who trouble you[m]
7and give relief to you who are troubled, and to us as well. This will happen when the Lord Jesus is revealed
from heaven[n] in blazing fire[o] with his
powerful angels.[p] **8**He will punish[q]
those who do not know God[r] and do
not obey the gospel of our Lord
Jesus.[s] **9**They will be punished with
everlasting destruction[t] and shut out
from the presence of the Lord[u] and
from the majesty of his power[v] **10**on
the day[w] he comes to be glorified[x] in
his holy people and to be marveled at
among all those who have believed.
This includes you, because you believed our testimony to you.[y]

11With this in mind, we constantly
pray for you,[z] that our God may count
you worthy[a] of his calling,[b] and that
by his power he may fulfill every good
purpose[c] of yours and every act
prompted by your faith.[d] **12**We pray
this so that the name of our Lord Jesus
may be glorified in you,[e] and you in
him, according to the grace of our God
and the Lord Jesus Christ.[b]

Concerning the Lord's Coming

2 Concerning the coming of our Lord
Jesus Christ[f] and our being gathered to him,[g] we ask you, brothers,
2not to become easily unsettled or

1:1 [a]S Ac 15:22 [b]S Ac 16:1; 1Th 1:1 [c]S Ac 17:1
1:2 [d]S Ro 1:7
1:3 [e]S Ro 1:8; Eph 5:20 [f]S 1Th 3:12
1:4 [g]2Co 7:14 [h]1Th 1:3 [i]1Th 1:6; 2:14; S 3:3
1:5 [j]Php 1:28 [k]Lk 20:35
1:6 [l]Lk 18:7,8 [m]Ro 12:19; Col 3:25; S Rev 6:10
1:7 [n]S Lk 17:30 [o]Heb 10:27; S 12:29; 2Pe 3:7; S Rev 1:14 [p]Jude 14
1:8 [q]Ps 79:6; Isa 66:15; Jer 10:25 [r]S Gal 4:8 [s]Ro 2:8; S 2Co 2:12
1:9 [t]Php 3:19; 1Th 5:3; 2Pe 3:7 [u]2Ki 17:18 [v]Isa 2:10,19; 2Th 2:8
1:10 [w]1Co 3:13 [x]Jn 17:10 [y]1Co 1:6
1:11 [z]S Ro 1:10 [a]ver 5 [b]S Ro 8:28 [c]Ro 15:14 [d]1Th 1:3
1:12 [e]Isa 24:15; Php 2:9-11
2:1 [f]S 1Th 2:19 [g]Mk 13:27; 1Th 4:15-17

[a] *1* Greek *Silvanus,* a variant of *Silas*
[b] *12* Or *God and Lord, Jesus Christ*

1:5 GOD'S JUDGMENT IS RIGHT. The Thessalonians were persevering in faith amid persecution and trials (v. 4). Their attitude was "evidence" of God's righteous judgment, meaning that God judged the Thessalonians to be worthy of his grace and the kingdom for which they were suffering. Their unjust suffering was also a sign that the persecutors opposed God's own people and would thus experience God's justice and retribution (vv. 5–9).

1:7 GIVE RELIEF TO YOU. Although God will begin to pay back the wicked (v. 6) at the beginning of the tribulation (Rev 6; see article on THE GREAT TRIBULATION, p. 1456), complete retribution (vv. 6–9) will occur only at the end of the age when the Lord Jesus returns to earth in final judgment (vv. 7–10; Rev 19:11–21). Similarly, partial relief will come to God's people when he removes them from earth to be with him always (see article on THE RAPTURE, p. 1864), but full relief will occur only when the Lord Jesus returns to earth with his saints to judge evil and govern the human race. Full relief means seeing Christ "glorified in you, and you in him" at the final day (v. 12). The result is the total victory, when righteousness reigns, sin is defeated and Christ's faithful followers are vindicated (Rev 6:9–11; 19:14–15).

1:9 EVERLASTING DESTRUCTION. This is the clearest statement in Paul's letters concerning the eternal future punishment of the wicked (see Mt 10:28, note on hell).

1:10 HE COMES TO BE GLORIFIED. This passage is not speaking of the time when believers will be taken from earth to meet Christ in the air (Jn 14:2–3; 1Th 4:17). Rather, it speaks of the revelation of Jesus Christ in power and great glory to destroy the present world system and inaugurate his thousand-year reign on earth (Rev 19:11—20:4).

2:1 THE COMING OF OUR LORD JESUS CHRIST. In his first letter to the Thessalonians, Paul assured all true believers that they would be caught up to meet the Lord in the air, and thus would be with their Lord forever (1Th 4:13–18). This event would deliver them from God's coming wrath (1Th 1:10; 5:9–10). Now, however, false teachers were teaching that the day of the Lord had already begun and that God's final wrath was being poured out on the earth (see next note).

2:2 EASILY UNSETTLED OR ALARMED. The Thessalonians were alarmed because of what the false teachers were saying about the day of the Lord (see previous note). He tells them not to worry, for the day of God's wrath has not yet arrived. Two things will signal its arrival: (1) There must come a specific "rebellion," and (2) the "man of lawlessness" will be revealed (v. 3). Paul goes on to state that these two events will not be fulfilled until the one who holds it back "is taken out of the way" (v. 7).

Paul's words "by some prophecy, report or letter" may indicate that the false teaching was being passed on through tongues and interpretation or

alarmed by some prophecy, report or
letter[h] supposed to have come from
us, saying that the day of the Lord[i]
has already come.[j] **3**Don't let anyone
deceive you[k] in any way, for ⌊that day
will not come⌋ until the rebellion[l] occurs and the man of lawlessness[c] is
revealed,[m] the man doomed to destruction. **4**He will oppose and will exalt himself over everything that is
called God[n] or is worshiped, so that
he sets himself up in God's temple,
proclaiming himself to be God.[o]

The Man of Lawlessness

5Don't you remember that when I
was with you I used to tell you these
things?[p] **6**And now you know what is
holding him back,[q] so that he may be
revealed at the proper time. **7**For the
secret power of lawlessness is already
at work; but the one who now holds it
back[r] will continue to do so till he is
taken out of the way. **8**And then the
lawless one will be revealed,[s] whom
the Lord Jesus will overthrow with the
breath of his mouth[t] and destroy by
the splendor of his coming.[u] **9**The
coming of the lawless one will be in
accordance with the work of Satan[v]
displayed in all kinds of counterfeit
miracles, signs and wonders,[w] **10**and
in every sort of evil that deceives those
who are perishing.[x] They perish because they refused to love the truth
and so be saved.[y] **11**For this reason
God sends them[z] a powerful delu-

2:2 [h] ver 15; 2Th 3:17 [i] S 1Co 1:8 [j] 2Ti 2:18
2:3 [k] S Mk 13:5 [l] Mt 24:10-12 [m] ver 8; Da 7:25; 8:25; 11:36; Rev 13:5,6
2:4 [n] 1Co 8:5 [o] Isa 14:13,14; Eze 28:2
2:5 [p] 1Th 3:4
2:6 [q] ver 7
2:7 [r] ver 6
2:8 [s] S ver 3 [t] Isa 11:4; Rev 2:16; 19:15 [u] S Lk 17:30
2:9 [v] S Mt 4:10 [w] Mt 24:24; Rev 13:13; S Jn 4:48
2:10 [x] S 1Co 1:18 [y] Pr 4:6; Jn 3:17-19
2:11 [z] Ro 1:28

c 3 Some manuscripts *sin*

through prophecy (see 1Co 14:29, note on judging tongues and prophecy).

2:3 THAT DAY WILL NOT COME UNTIL. Paul explains the events that will signal the beginning of the day of the Lord and discusses the destruction of the man of lawlessness and the unrighteous at the end of the age. The sequence of events is as follows: (1) Throughout the entire church age, a "secret power of lawlessness" (v. 7) is at work, reminding us that the end is coming; evil will become progressively unrestrained as history draws to a close. (2) As that power becomes stronger, apostasy in the church will reach major proportions (v. 3; cf. Mt 24:12; 2Ti 4:3–4). (3) The restrainer (i.e., "the one who now holds it back") of the "secret power" is then taken out of the way (vv. 6–7). (4) Next, the man of lawlessness is revealed (vv. 3–4,7,9–10). (5) The apostasy reaches its climax in total rebellion against God and his Word; God sends a deluding influence on those who did not love the truth (vv. 9–11). (6) Sometime afterward the man of lawlessness is destroyed along with all who delighted in wickedness (v. 12); this occurs at Christ's coming after the tribulation, i.e., at the end of the age (v. 8; Rev 19:20–21).

2:3 REBELLION OCCURS AND THE MAN OF LAWLESSNESS IS REVEALED. For a discussion of the "rebellion" and "the man of lawlessness," see article on THE AGE OF THE ANTICHRIST, p. 1872.

2:6 WHAT IS HOLDING HIM BACK. Something or someone is holding back the man of lawlessness. When the one who holds him back is taken out of the way, then the day of the Lord will begin (v. 7; see article on THE AGE OF THE ANTICHRIST, p. 1872).

2:7 SECRET POWER OF LAWLESSNESS IS ALREADY AT WORK. The "secret power of lawlessness" is a behind-the-scenes activity of evil powers throughout the course of human history, preparing the way for the rebellion and the man of lawlessness. (1) It is an insidious process that entraps unbelievers and prepares many within the church to turn from true faith and to accept the lie embodied in the apostate church. It involves a spirit or movement against true Biblical faith and divine law; it seeks freedom from moral restraint and it takes pleasure in sin (vv. 10–12; see v. 12, note). (2) Though this spirit existed already in Paul's day, it will be especially prevalent in the world and in Christianity toward the end of the age (see Mt 24:11, note; 2Ti 4:3–4, note; see article on THE AGE OF THE ANTICHRIST, p. 1872).

2:8 WHOM THE LORD JESUS WILL OVERTHROW. After Satan and the man of lawlessness have done their work of deceit and evil (vv. 9–10), they will be overthrown by Christ's coming to earth at the end of the tribulation (see Rev 19:20, note).

2:9 IN ALL KINDS OF COUNTERFEIT MIRACLES, SIGNS AND WONDERS. For a discussion of the activities of the lawless one, see article on THE AGE OF THE ANTICHRIST, p. 1872.

2:10 LOVE THE TRUTH. From the very beginning of creation the central issue in humanity's relationship with God has been either our disregard of the Word and the truth of God or our love for them. That response is also a pivotal issue in the last days of this age. Salvation will be experienced only by those who through faith in Christ fervently and sincerely "love the truth," who believe with unwavering conviction what God has said, and who reject all new revelation or teaching that conflicts with that truth (see Mt 24:5,11, notes; see article on THE GREAT TRIBULATION, p. 1456).

2:11 SENDS THEM A POWERFUL DELUSION. After the removal of the restrainer (see article on THE AGE OF THE ANTICHRIST, p. 1872) and the revelation of the lawless one, there will be no more opportunity for salvation for a particular group of people: (1) This group consists of all those inside or outside the church who, after adequately hearing the truth of God's Word, have willingly and intentionally refused to love that truth

sion[a] so that they will believe the lie[b]
12and so that all will be condemned
who have not believed the truth but
have delighted in wickedness.[c]

Stand Firm

13But we ought always to thank God
for you,[d] brothers loved by the Lord,
because from the beginning God chose
you[d][e] to be saved[f] through the
sanctifying work of the Spirit[g] and
through belief in the truth. **14**He called
you[h] to this through our gospel,[i]
that you might share in the glory of
our Lord Jesus Christ. **15**So then,
brothers, stand firm[j] and hold to the
teachings[e] we passed on to you,[k]
whether by word of mouth or by
letter.

16May our Lord Jesus Christ himself
and God our Father,[l] who loved us[m]
and by his grace gave us eternal encouragement and good hope, **17**encourage[n] your hearts and strengthen[o]
you in every good deed and word.

2:11 [a] Mt 24:5; S Mk 13:5 [b] Ro 1:25
2:12 [c] Ro 1:32; 2:8
2:13 [d] S Ro 1:8 [e] Eph 1:4 [f] 1Th 5:9 [g] 1Pe 1:2
2:14 [h] S Ro 8:28; S 11:29 [i] 1Th 1:5
2:15 [j] S 1Co 16:13 [k] S 1Co 11:2
2:16 [l] S Php 4:20 [m] S Jn 3:16
2:17 [n] 1Th 3:2 [o] 2Th 3:3

3:1 [p] 1Th 4:1 [q] S 1Th 5:25 [r] 1Th 1:8 [s] 1Th 2:13
3:2 [t] S Ro 15:31
3:3 [u] S 1Co 1:9 [v] S Mt 5:37
3:4 [w] S 2Co 2:3
3:5 [x] 1Ch 29:18
3:6 [y] 1Co 5:4 [z] ver 14; S Ro 16:17 [a] ver 7,11

Request for Prayer

3 Finally, brothers,[p] pray for us[q]
that the message of the Lord[r]
may spread rapidly and be honored,
just as it was with you.[s] **2**And pray
that we may be delivered from wicked
and evil men,[t] for not everyone has
faith. **3**But the Lord is faithful,[u] and
he will strengthen and protect you
from the evil one.[v] **4**We have confidence[w] in the Lord that you are doing
and will continue to do the things we
command. **5**May the Lord direct your
hearts[x] into God's love and Christ's
perseverance.

Warning Against Idleness

6In the name of the Lord Jesus
Christ,[y] we command you, brothers,
to keep away from[z] every brother who
is idle[a] and does not live according to

[d] *13* Some manuscripts *because God chose you as his firstfruits* [e] *15* Or *traditions*

---

and have chosen instead to delight in the wickedness of the world (see vv. 10,12, notes).

(2) God will send those individuals a powerful delusion so that they may never again have an opportunity to believe the truth they refused to love (v. 12). They are forever doomed to believe "the lie" (i.e., the claims of the lawless one).

(3) God's purpose in sending the "powerful delusion" is that they "will be condemned" (v. 12). Therefore, for those who have heard and understood God's Word, yet have not loved its truth but have chosen instead the pleasure of sin, "no sacrifice for sins is left, but only a fearful expectation of judgment" (Heb 10:26–27; see article on PERSONAL APOSTASY, p. 1918).

(4) Salvation during the days of the tribulation will be offered only to those who never had an adequate opportunity to receive the knowledge of the truth or to hear and understand the gospel (cf. Rev 7:14; 11:3; 14:6–7). Those who proclaim the gospel during those days may include the 144,000 from the tribes of Israel (see Rev 7:4, note), the two witnesses (see Rev 11:3, note) and the angels (see Rev 14:6, note).

2:12 DELIGHTED IN WICKEDNESS. Delighting in wickedness while refusing to love the truth (v. 10) will be the deciding factor in God's judgment in the last days. (1) Those destined to experience God's wrath will be those who did not love the truth and therefore participated in, and entertained themselves with, evil and immorality (see 2Ti 3:1, note). They will be abandoned to divine justice, demonic deception and the power of darkness (see Lk 23:35, note; Ro 1:32, note; 1Ti 4:1, note).

(2) Those experiencing condemnation during the "day of the Lord" (see v. 2, note) will include not only unbelievers, but also those guilty of apostasy from the true faith. They chose to enjoy sin instead of enjoying God and refused to take a stand against the immorality of the last days (see vv. 3,7, notes; 2Ti 4:3–4, note).

3:1 PRAY FOR US. Paul was able to accomplish what he did for Christ partly because of the prayers of God's people. Therefore he often sought the prayers of those to whom he ministered, aware that God's will for his life and ministry would not be fully realized without the intercession of fellow believers (cf. Ro 15:30–32; 2Co 1:11; Php 1:19; Col 4:2; 1Th 5:25). This spiritual principle of God's kingdom is valid today. We need the prayers of other believers and they need our prayers. With faithful intercession in the churches, God's desires will be accomplished, Satan's purposes frustrated (v. 3) and the Spirit's full power revealed (Ac 4:24–33).

3:3 PROTECT YOU FROM THE EVIL ONE. When believers earnestly pray, they can be assured that God will protect them from Satan. God will strengthen them to face any temptation that may assail them (1Co 10:13; Heb 2:18) and will protect them from the powerful forces of the demonic (see Eph 6:12, note).

3:6 WHO IS IDLE. Those who were idle were people who were loafing and unwilling to work. They were taking advantage of the church's generosity (cf. 1Th 4:9–10) and receiving support from brothers who made a living by ordinary occupations (vv. 6–15). (1) Paul says that such people must be disciplined by keeping away from them and not associating with them (vv. 6,14). (2) Although Paul advocates that help must be given to those in real need, he nowhere teaches that believers ought to give food or money to able-bodied people who refuse to work steadily for a living (cf. v. 10).

THE AGE OF THE ANTICHRIST

2Th 2:3–4 "Don't let anyone deceive you in any way, for that day will not come until the rebellion occurs and the man of lawlessness is revealed, the man doomed to destruction. He will oppose and will exalt himself over everything that is called God or is worshiped, so that he sets himself up in God's temple, proclaiming himself to be God."

According to the Bible, the antichrist (cf. 1Jn 2:18) is coming, the one who engineers Satan's final onslaught against Christ and the saints just before Christ establishes his kingdom on earth. Paul's terms for the antichrist are "the man of lawlessness" and "the man doomed to destruction" (2Th 2:3). Other terms used in the Bible are the "beast coming out of the sea" (Rev 13:1–10), "a scarlet beast" (Rev 17:3) and "the beast" (Rev 17:8,16; 19:19–20; 20:10).

SIGNS OF THE ANTICHRIST'S COMING. Unlike the rapture (see article on THE RAPTURE, p. 1864), the coming of the antichrist will not be without warning. Several signs point to his coming and his appearance. At least three events must occur before he appears on earth: (1) the "secret power of lawlessness" already at work in the world must intensify (2Th 2:7); (2) the "rebellion" must come (2:3); (3) "the one who now holds it back" must be removed (2:7).

(1) The "secret power of lawlessness," that behind-the-scenes activity of evil powers evident throughout the world (see 2Th 2:7, note), will increase until it reaches its climax in the complete ridicule of and disregard for any standards and commands held sacred in the Bible. Because of a prevailing spirit of lawlessness, the love of many will grow cold (Mt 24:10–12; Lk 18:8). Yet a faithful remnant will remain loyal to the apostolic faith as revealed in the NT (Mt 24:13; 25:10; Lk 18:7; see Rev 2:7, note). Through these faithful people, the church will remain a warrior church, wielding the sword of the Spirit (see Eph 6:11, note).

(2) The "rebellion" (Gk *apostasia*), literally meaning "departure," "falling away" or "abandonment," will occur. In the last days, many within the professing church will depart from Biblical truth.

(a) Both Jesus and Paul paint a dismal picture of the condition of much of the visible church—morally, spiritually and doctrinally—as the present age closes (cf. Mt 24:5,10–13,24; 1Ti 4:1; 2Ti 4:3–4). Paul in particular stresses that the churches will be invaded by godless elements in the last days.

(b) This "rebellion" within the church will have two dimensions. (i) *Theological apostasy* is the departure from and rejection of a part or all of the original teachings of Christ and the apostles (1Ti 4:1; 2Ti 4:3). False leaders will offer "salvation" and cheap grace and ignore Christ's demand for repentance, separation from immorality, and loyalty to God and his standards (2Pe 2:1–3,12–19). False gospels centering on human desires and goals of self-interest will become popular (see 2Ti 4:3–4, note). (ii) *Moral apostasy* is the severing of one's saving relationship with Christ and returning to sin and immorality. Apostates may proclaim right doctrine and NT teaching, yet abandon God's moral standards (Isa 29:13; Mt 23:25–28; see article on PERSONAL APOSTASY, p. 1918). Many churches will tolerate almost anything for the sake of numbers, money, success and honor (see 1Ti 4:1, note). The gospel of the cross with its call to suffer (Php 1:29), to radically renounce sin (Ro 8:13), to sacrifice for God's kingdom and to deny oneself will become rare (Mt 24:12; 2Ti 3:1–5; 4:3).

(c) Both the history of the church and the predicted apostasy of the last days warn all believers not to take for granted a continual progress of God's kingdom through all ages until the end. At some point in time in the history of the church, rebellion against God and his Word will reach astounding proportions. The day of the Lord will bring God's wrath on those who reject his truth (1Th 5:2–9).

(d) The ultimate triumph of God's kingdom and his righteousness in the world, therefore, depends not on the gradual increase of the professing church's success, but on the final intervention of God when he breaks into the world with righteous judgment (Rev 19–22; see 2Th 2:7–8; 1Ti 4:1, note; 2Pe 3:10–13; and the book of Jude).

(3) A decisive event must occur before the "man of lawlessness" can be revealed and the day of the Lord can begin (2Th 2:2–3), namely, the taking "out of the way" of someone (2:7) or something that "holds back" the secret power of lawlessness and the man of lawlessness (2:3–6). When the restrainer is taken out of the way, the day of the Lord can begin (2:6–7).

(a) "The one who now holds it back" may best be understood as referring to the Holy Spirit, who alone has the power to hold back evil, the man of lawlessness, and Satan (2Th 2:9). The restrainer is referred to by both the masculine article ("the one who now holds it back," 2:7) and by the neuter article ("what is holding him back," 2:6). Likewise, the word for "Spirit" in the Greek can be referred to by a masculine or neuter pronoun (see Ge 6:3; Jn 16:8, note; Ro 8:13; see Gal 5:17 on the Spirit's work of restraining sin).

(b) At the beginning of the final seven years of tribulation, the Holy Spirit will be "taken out of the way." This does not mean he is taken out of the world, but only that his restraining influence against lawlessness and the antichrist's entrance will cease. All restraints against sin will be removed and the satanically inspired rebellion will begin. However, the Spirit will still remain on earth during the tribulation to convict people of their sins, convert them to Christ and empower them (Rev 7:9,14; 11:1–11; 14:6–7).

(c) The Holy Spirit's being taken out of the way enables the man of lawlessness to come on the scene (2Th 2:3–4). God will send a deluding influence on all those who refused to love the truth (see 2:11, note); they will accept the claims of the man of lawlessness, and human society will degenerate to a depth of depravity never before seen.

(d) The Holy Spirit's sin-restraining ministry is carried on largely through the church, which is the temple of the Holy Spirit (1Co 3:16; 6:19). Therefore, many interpreters believe the Spirit's removal is a strong indication that the rapture of the faithful will occur at the same time (1Th 4:17); i.e., Christ's return to gather his churches to himself and to deliver them from the coming wrath (1Th 1:10) will occur before the beginning of the day of the Lord and the revelation of the man of lawlessness (see article on THE RAPTURE, p. 1864).

(e) Some scholars believe that the restrainer of 2Th 2:6 (neuter gender) refers to the Holy Spirit and his restraining ministry, while in 2:7 the "one who now holds it back" (masculine gender) refers to the believers who are gathered together to Christ and taken out of the way, i.e., caught up to meet Christ in the air to be with the Lord (1Th 4:17).

THE ANTICHRIST'S ACTIVITIES. As the day of the Lord begins, the "man of lawlessness" is revealed. He will be a world ruler who will make a covenant with Israel seven years before the end of the age (see Da 9:27). (1) His true identification will be confirmed three and one-half years later as he breaks his covenant with Israel, becomes the world ruler, declares himself to be God, desecrates the temple in Jerusalem (see article on THE GREAT TRIBULATION, p. 1456), forbids the worship of the Lord (see 2Th 2:4, 8–9) and devastates the land of Palestine (see Da 9:27, note; 11:36–45, note).

(2) The antichrist will declare himself to be God and will severely persecute those who remain loyal to Christ (Rev 11:6–7; 13:7,15–18; see Da 7:8,24–25, notes). He will demand worship, evidently from a great temple that he uses as the center of his

pronouncements (cf. Da 7:8,25; 8:4; 11:31,36). Humans have sought this divine status since the beginning of creation (see 2Th 2:8, note; Rev 13:8,12, notes; see article on THE GREAT TRIBULATION, p. 1456).

(3) The "man of lawlessness" will demonstrate through Satan's power great signs, wonders and miracles in order to propagate error (2Th 2:9). "Counterfeit miracles" refers to genuine supernatural miracles that deceive people into accepting a lie. (a) It is possible these demonstrations of the supernatural will be seen on television around the world. Millions will be impressed, deceived and persuaded by this apparent charismatic leader because they have no deep commitment to or love for the truth of God's Word (2:9–12). (b) The words of both Paul (2Th 2:9) and Jesus (Mt 24:24) should caution believers against assuming that everything miraculous comes from God. Apparent manifestations of the Spirit (1Co 12:7–10) and alleged experiences from God or the Spirit must be tested by the person's loyalty to Christ and Scripture.

THE DEFEAT OF THE ANTICHRIST. At the end of the tribulation, Satan will gather many nations at Armageddon under the direction of the antichrist and make war against God and his people in a battle that will involve the entire world (see Da 11:45, note; Rev 16:16, note). When that time comes, Christ will return and supernaturally intervene to destroy the antichrist, his armies and all who disobey the gospel (see 19:15–21, notes). Thereupon Christ will bind Satan and establish his kingdom on earth (20:1–6).

the teaching[f] you received from us.[b]
7For you yourselves know how you
ought to follow our example.[c] We
were not idle when we were with you,
8nor did we eat anyone's food without
paying for it. On the contrary, we
worked[d] night and day, laboring and
toiling so that we would not be a burden to any of you. 9We did this, not because we do not have the right to such
help,[e] but in order to make ourselves
a model for you to follow.[f] 10For even
when we were with you,[g] we gave you
this rule: "If a man will not work,[h] he
shall not eat."

11We hear that some among you are
idle. They are not busy; they are busybodies.[i] 12Such people we command
and urge in the Lord Jesus Christ[j] to
settle down and earn the bread they
eat.[k] 13And as for you, brothers, never tire of doing what is right.[l]

3:6 [b]S 1Co 11:2
3:7 [c]ver 9; S 1Co 4:16
3:8 [d]S Ac 18:3; Eph 4:28
3:9 [e]1Co 9:4-14 [f]ver 7; S 1Co 4:16
3:10 [g]1Th 3:4 [h]1Th 4:11
3:11 [i]ver 6,7; 1Ti 5:13
3:12 [j]1Th 4:1 [k]1Th 4:11; Eph 4:28
3:13 [l]Gal 6:9
3:14 [m]ver 6; S Ro 16:17 [n]S 1Co 4:14
3:15 [o]Gal 6:1; 1Th 5:14; Phm 16
3:16 [p]S Ro 15:33 [q]Ru 2:4
3:17 [r]S 1Co 16:21
3:18 [s]S Ro 16:20

14If anyone does not obey our instruction in this letter, take special
note of him. Do not associate with
him,[m] in order that he may feel
ashamed.[n] 15Yet do not regard him as
an enemy, but warn him as a brother.[o]

Final Greetings

16Now may the Lord of peace[p] himself give you peace at all times and in
every way. The Lord be with all of
you.[q]

17I, Paul, write this greeting in my
own hand,[r] which is the distinguishing mark in all my letters. This is how
I write.

18The grace of our Lord Jesus Christ
be with you all.[s]

[f] 6 Or *tradition*

3:12 SETTLE DOWN AND EARN. Christians must not be loafers, but must work hard in order to provide for themselves and their families and to have enough to help others in need (1Co 16:1; 2Co 8:1–15; Eph 4:28).

1 TIMOTHY

Outline

Introduction (1:1–20)

I. Directions Concerning the Church's Ministry (2:1—4:5)
   - A. The Prominence of Prayer (2:1–8)
   - B. The Appropriate Conduct of Women (2:9–15)
   - C. Qualifications for Overseers (Elders) (3:1–7)
     1. Personal
        - a. Above Reproach (3:2)
        - b. Temperate (3:2)
        - c. Self-controlled (3:2)
        - d. Respectable (3:2)
        - e. Hospitable (3:2)
        - f. Able to Teach (3:2)
        - g. Not Given to Drunkenness (3:3)
        - h. Not Violent (3:3)
        - i. Gentle (3:3)
        - j. Not Quarrelsome (3:3)
        - k. Not a Lover of Money (3:3)
        - l. Not a Recent Convert (3:6)
        - m. Good Reputation With Outsiders (3:7)
     2. Family
        - a. Husband of One Wife (3:2)
        - b. Manages His Own Family Well (3:4–5)
        - c. Has Obedient and Respectful Children (3:4)
   - D. Qualifications for Deacons (3:8–12)
     1. Personal
        - a. Worthy of Respect (3:8)
        - b. Sincere (3:8)
        - c. Not Indulging in Much Wine (3:8)
        - d. Not Pursuing Dishonest Gain (3:8)
        - e. Holds to the Faith With a Clear Conscience (3:9)
        - f. Tested and Above Reproach (3:10)
     2. Family
        - a. Husband of One Wife (3:12)
        - b. A Godly and Trustworthy Wife (3:11)
        - c. Manages His Children and Household Well (3:12)
   - E. Reasons the Church Must Require High Qualifications for Leaders (3:13—4:5)

II. Directions Concerning Timothy's Ministry (4:6—6:19)
   - A. His Personal Life (4:6–16)
   - B. His Relationship to Persons in the Church (5:1—6:19)
     1. Older and Younger Men (5:1)
     2. Older and Younger Women (5:2)
     3. Widows (5:3–16)
     4. Elders and Prospective Elders (5:17–25)
     5. Servants (6:1–2)
     6. False Teachers (6:3–10)
        Parenthesis: Exhortation to Timothy Himself (6:11–16)
     7. The Rich (6:17–19)

Conclusion (6:20–21)

Author: Paul

Theme: Sound Doctrine and Godliness

Date of Writing: C. A.D. 65

Background

1 and 2 Timothy and Titus—commonly referred to as "The Pastoral Letters"—are letters from Paul (1Ti 1:1; 2Ti 1:1; Tit 1:1) to Timothy (at Ephesus) and Titus (at Crete) concerning pastoral care of the churches. Some critics have questioned Paul's authorship of these letters, but the early church emphatically placed them among Paul's authentic letters. Although differences in style and vocabulary do exist in the Pastoral Letters when compared with Paul's other letters, these differences may be adequately and convincingly accounted for within the context of Paul's advanced years and his personal concerns for the ministries of Timothy and Titus.

Paul wrote 1 Timothy after the events recorded at the end of Acts. Paul's first Roman imprisonment (Ac 28) apparently ended in his freedom (2Ti 4:16–17). Afterwards, according to Clement of Rome (c. A.D. 96) and the Muratorian Canon (c. A.D. 170), Paul went from Rome westward to Spain and fulfilled a long-desired ministry there (cf. Ro 15:23–24,28). Based on data in the Pastoral Letters, Paul then returned to the Aegean Sea region (especially Crete, Macedonia and Greece) for further ministry. During this time (c. A.D. 64–65), Paul commissioned Timothy as his apostolic representative to minister in Ephesus, and Titus to do the same at Crete. From Macedonia Paul wrote his first letter to Timothy, and a short time later he wrote to Titus. Afterwards, Paul again became a prisoner in Rome, during which time he wrote a second letter to Timothy, shortly before his martyrdom in A.D. 67/68 (see 2Ti 4:6–8; see also the introduction to 2 Timothy).

Purpose

Paul had a threefold purpose in writing 1 Timothy: (1) to exhort Timothy himself about his ministry and personal life; (2) to urge Timothy to defend the purity of the gospel and its holy standards from corruption by false teachers; and (3) to give Timothy instructions concerning various church matters and problems at Ephesus.

Survey

One of Paul's chief concerns communicated to his younger assistant is that Timothy earnestly contend for the faith and refute the false teachings that were diluting the saving power of the gospel (1:3–7; 4:1–8; 6:3–5,20–21). Paul also instructs Timothy about the spiritual and character qualifications for church leadership; he provides a composite picture of the kind of persons who are permitted to become spiritual leaders of the churches (see the detailed list of qualifications in the above outline).

Among other things, Paul instructs Timothy how to relate to various groups within the church, such as women (2:9–15; 5:2), widows (5:3–16), older and younger men (5:1), elders (5:17–25), slaves (6:1–2), false teachers (6:3–10) and the rich (6:17–19). Paul gives Timothy five clear instructions to fulfill (1:18–20; 3:14–16; 4:11–16; 5:21–25; 6:20–21). In this letter Paul conveys affection for Timothy as his convert and son in the faith and sets forth a high standard of godliness for Timothy's life and for the church.

Special Features

Four major features characterize this letter. (1) Addressed directly to Timothy as Paul's representative to the church at Ephesus, the letter is very personal and written with deep emotion and feeling. (2) Along with 2 Timothy, it stresses more than any other NT letter the pastoral responsibility to keep the gospel pure and free from false teachings that would weaken its saving power. (3) It emphasizes the supreme value of the gospel, the demonic influence behind its corruption, the church's holy calling and the high qualifications God requires for its leaders. (4) It provides the most specific direction in the NT about how a pastor is to relate properly to both sexes and to all age and social groups in the church.

Reading 1 Timothy

In order to read the entire New Testament in one year, the book of 1 Timothy should be read in 6 days, according to the following schedule:
☐ 1 ☐ 2 ☐ 3 ☐ 4 ☐ 5 ☐ 6

NOTES

1

Paul, an apostle of Christ Jesus by the command of God[a] our Savior[b] and of Christ Jesus our hope,[c]

2To Timothy[d] my true son[e] in the faith:

Grace, mercy and peace from God the Father and Christ Jesus our Lord.[f]

Warning Against False Teachers

3As I urged you when I went into Macedonia,[g] stay there in Ephesus[h] so that you may command certain men not to teach false doctrines[i] any longer 4nor to devote themselves to myths[j] and endless genealogies.[k] These promote controversies[l] rather than God's work—which is by faith. 5The goal of this command is love, which comes from a pure heart[m] and a good conscience[n] and a sincere faith.[o] 6Some have wandered away from these and turned to meaningless talk. 7They want to be teachers[p] of the law, but they do not know what they are talking about or what they so confidently affirm.[q]

8We know that the law is good[r] if one uses it properly. 9We also know that law[a] is made not for the righteous[s] but for lawbreakers and rebels,[t] the ungodly and sinful, the unholy and irreligious; for those who kill their fathers or mothers, for murderers, 10for adulterers and perverts, for slave traders and liars and perjurers—and for whatever else is contrary to the sound doctrine[u] 11that conforms to the glorious gospel of the blessed God, which he entrusted to me.[v]

The Lord's Grace to Paul

12I thank Christ Jesus our Lord, who has given me strength,[w] that he considered me faithful, appointing me to his service.[x] 13Even though I was once a blasphemer and a persecutor[y] and a violent man, I was shown mercy[z] because I acted in ignorance and unbelief.[a] 14The grace of our Lord was poured out on me abundantly,[b] along with the faith and love that are in Christ Jesus.[c]

15Here is a trustworthy saying[d] that deserves full acceptance: Christ Jesus came into the world to save sinners[e]—of whom I am the worst. 16But for that very reason I was shown mercy[f] so that in me, the worst of sinners, Christ Jesus might display his unlimited patience[g] as an example for those who would believe[h] on him and receive eternal life.[i] 17Now to the King[j] eternal, immortal,[k] invisible,[l] the only God,[m] be honor and glory for ever and ever. Amen.[n]

1Ti 2:3-6

Charge to Timothy

18Timothy, my son,[o] I give you this

1:1 [a] S 2Co 1:1; Tit 1:3 [b] S Lk 1:47 [c] Col 1:27
1:2 [d] S Ac 16:1 [e] ver 18; 1Co 4:17; S 1Th 2:11; 2Ti 1:2; Tit 1:4 [f] S Ro 1:7
1:3 [g] S Ac 16:9 [h] S Ac 18:19 [i] Gal 1:6,7; 1Ti 6:3
1:4 [j] 1Ti 4:7; 2Ti 4:4; Tit 1:14 [k] Tit 3:9 [l] S 2Ti 2:14
1:5 [m] 2Ti 2:22 [n] S Ac 23:1; 1Ti 4:2 [o] Gal 5:6; 2Ti 1:5
1:7 [p] S Eph 4:11 [q] Job 38:2
1:8 [r] Ro 7:12
1:9 [s] Gal 5:23 [t] Gal 3:19
1:10 [u] 1Ti 6:3; 2Ti 1:13; 4:3; Tit 1:9; 2:1
1:11 [v] Gal 2:7; 1Th 2:4; Tit 1:3
1:12 [w] S Php 4:13 [x] S Ac 9:15
1:13 [y] S Ac 8:3 [z] ver 16 [a] Ac 26:9
1:14 [b] 2Co 4:15 [c] 2Ti 1:13; S 1Th 1:3
1:15 [d] 1Ti 3:1; 4:9; 2Ti 2:11; Tit 3:8 [e] Mk 2:17; S Jn 3:17
1:16 [f] ver 13 [g] S Ro 2:4 [h] S Jn 3:15 [i] S Mt 25:46
1:17 [j] Rev 15:3 [k] 1Ti 6:16 [l] S Col 1:15 [m] Jude 25 [n] S Ro 11:36
1:18 [o] S ver 2

[a] 9 Or *that the law*

1:3 NOT TO TEACH FALSE DOCTRINES. Seven years before Paul wrote this letter he warned the Ephesian elders that false teachers would try to distort the true message of Christ (see Ac 20:29, note). Now that this was happening, Paul exhorted Timothy to confront them boldly. This young pastor must not compromise with the false teachings that were corrupting both the law and the gospel. He must faithfully fight a good fight against them (v. 18) by proclaiming the original faith as taught by Christ and the apostles (2Ti 1:13–14).

1:5 THE GOAL OF THIS COMMAND. The supreme goal of all instruction from God's Word is not Bible knowledge in itself, but an inward moral transformation that expresses itself in love, purity of heart, a clear conscience, and faith without hypocrisy (see Ac 24:16, note on a good conscience; see article on BIBLE TRAINING FOR CHRISTIANS, p. 1894). Concerning this truth two important facts must be kept in mind. (1) The Biblical concept of teaching and learning is not primarily to impart knowledge or to prepare oneself academically. It is to produce holiness and a righteous lifestyle, conforming to God's ways (cf. 2Ti 1:13). (2) The teacher of God's Word must be someone whose life illustrates perseverance in truth, faith and holiness (3:1–13).

1:8 THE LAW IS GOOD. See Mt 5:17, note on the law and the Christian; cf. Ro 7:12; see article on THE OLD TESTAMENT LAW, p. 118.

1:13 A BLASPHEMER AND A PERSECUTOR. Before his conversion, Paul was a violent persecutor of believers (cf. Ac 8:3; 9:1–2,4–5; 22:4–5; 26:9–11; Gal 1:13). His terrible crimes against God's people were sufficient reason for ranking himself as the worst of sinners (vv. 14–15; cf. 1Co 15:9; Eph 3:8). Yet, because he sincerely believed he was serving God (Ac 23:1; 26:9), he was shown mercy and great patience, and was given the opportunity to repent and accept Christ as Lord (Ac 9:1–19). God's mercy toward Paul should encourage us to present the gospel to sinners, confident that God's power and grace can redeem and change their lives.

1:18 IN KEEPING WITH THE PROPHECIES. Evidently prophecies had been made regarding God's will for Timothy's ministry in the church (see 1Co 14:29, note; see article on SPIRITUAL GIFTS FOR BELIEVERS, p. 1770). Paul exhorts Timothy to remain faithful to that revealed will for his life. As a pastor and overseer of the church, he

instruction in keeping with the prophecies once made about you,[p] so that by
following them you may fight the good
fight,[q] **19**holding on to faith and a
good conscience.[r] Some have rejected
these and so have shipwrecked their
faith.[s] **20**Among them are Hymenaeus[t] and Alexander,[u] whom I have
handed over to Satan[v] to be taught
not to blaspheme.

Instructions on Worship

2 I urge, then, first of all, that requests, prayers,[w] intercession
and thanksgiving be made for everyone— **2**for kings and all those in authority,[x] that we may live peaceful
and quiet lives in all godliness[y] and
holiness. **3**This is good, and pleases[z]
God our Savior,[a] **4**who wants[b] all
men[c] to be saved[d] and to come to a
knowledge of the truth.[e] **5**For there is
one God[f] and one mediator[g] between
God and men, the man Christ Jesus,[h]
6who gave himself as a ransom[i] for
all men—the testimony[j] given in its
proper time.[k] **7**And for this purpose I
was appointed a herald and an apostle—I am telling the truth, I am not
lying[l]—and a teacher[m] of the true
faith to the Gentiles.[n]
8I want men everywhere to lift up
holy hands[o] in prayer, without anger
or disputing.
9I also want women to dress modestly, with decency and propriety, not
with braided hair or gold or pearls or
expensive clothes,[p] **10**but with good
deeds,[q] appropriate for women who
profess to worship God.
11A woman should learn in quietness and full submission.[r] **12**I do not
permit a woman to teach or to have authority over a man; she must be silent.[s] **13**For Adam was formed first,
then Eve.[t] **14**And Adam was not the
one deceived; it was the woman who

1:18 [p] 1Ti 4:14 [q] 1Ti 6:12; 2Ti 2:3; 4:7 **1:19** [r] ver 5; S Ac 23:1 [s] 1Ti 6:21; 2Ti 2:18 **1:20** [t] 2Ti 2:17 [u] 2Ti 4:14 [v] 1Co 5:5 **2:1** [w] Eph 6:18 **2:2** [x] Ezr 6:10; Ro 13:1 [y] 1Ti 3:16; 4:7,8; 6:3,5,6,11; 2Ti 3:5; Tit 1:1 **2:3** [z] S 1Ti 5:4 [a] S Lk 1:47 **2:4** [b] Eze 18:23, 32; 33:11 [c] 1Ti 4:10; Tit 2:11; 2Pe 3:9 [d] S Jn 3:17; S Ro 11:14 [e] 2Ti 2:25; Tit 1:1; Heb 10:26 **2:5** [f] Dt 6:4; Ro 3:29,30; 10:12 [g] S Gal 3:20 [h] Ro 1:3 **2:6** [i] S Mt 20:28 [j] S 1Co 1:6 [k] 1Ti 6:15; Tit 1:3 **2:7** [l] S Ro 9:1 [m] 2Ti 1:11 [n] S Ac 9:15 **2:8** [o] Ps 24:4; 63:4; 134:2; 141:2; Lk 24:50 **2:9** [p] 1Pe 3:3 **2:10** [q] Pr 31:13 **2:11** [r] 1Pe 3:3,4 **2:12** [s] S Eph 5:22 **2:13** [t] Ge 2:7,22; 1Co 11:8

must remain loyal to the true apostolic faith and fight against the false doctrines creeping into the church.

1:19 SHIPWRECKED THEIR FAITH. Paul warns Timothy several times of the terrible possibility of apostasy (4:1; 5:11–15; 6:9–10; see article on PERSONAL APOSTASY, p. 1918).

1:20 HAVE HANDED OVER TO SATAN. Paul's action probably means that these two men were excommunicated from the church. Salvation and union with the body of Christ (the church) protect us from Satan's power. To be expelled from the church, on the other hand, exposes one's life to destructive, satanic attacks (cf. Job 2:6–7; 1Co 5:5; Rev 2:22). Church discipline serves to bring the individual back to repentance, true faith and salvation in Christ (see 1Co 5:5, note).

2:4 WHO WANTS ALL MEN TO BE SAVED. The Bible reveals two aspects of God's will for humankind with regard to salvation: his perfect will, which says that he wants everyone to be saved, and his permissive will, which acknowledges that God permits many to refuse to come to Christ and receive his salvation (see Mt 7:21; Lk 7:30; 13:34; Jn 7:17; Ac 7:51; see article on THE WILL OF GOD, p. 1056).

2:5 ONE MEDIATOR . . . CHRIST JESUS. We must draw near to God only through Christ Jesus (Heb 7:25), relying on his sacrificial death to cover our sins and praying in faith for strength and mercy to help us with all of our needs (Heb 4:14–16). We must not allow any other created being to take Christ's place by praying to him or her (see Heb 8:6; 9:15; 12:24).

2:6 A RANSOM FOR ALL. See Mt 20:28, note.

2:8 MEN EVERYWHERE TO LIFT UP HOLY HANDS. In the NT church's public worship, it was apparently customary for worshipers to offer prayers aloud (see Ac 4:24–31; cf. Ezr 3:12–13). To be acceptable, prayer had to be offered by those who were living holy and righteous lives, i.e., with "holy hands."

2:9 WOMEN TO DRESS MODESTLY, WITH DECENCY. It is God's will that Christian women dress modestly and discreetly. (1) The word "decency" (Gk *aidos*) implies a certain shame in exposing the body. It involves a refusal to dress in such a way as to draw attention to the body and to pass the boundaries of proper reserve. The source of modesty is in a person's heart or inner character. In other words, modesty is the outward manifestation of an inward purity.

(2) Dressing immodestly, which may excite impure desires in others, is as wrong as the immoral desire it provokes. No activity or condition justifies the wearing of immodest attire that would expose the body in such a way as to stimulate lust in someone else (cf. Gal 5:13; Eph 4:27; Tit 2:11–12; see Mt 5:28, note).

(3) It is a sad commentary on any church when the Biblical standard for modest dress is ignored and the world's customs are passively adopted. In a day of sexual permissiveness, the church should act and dress differently from a corrupt society that throws aside and ridicules the Spirit's desire for modesty, purity and godly restraint (cf. Ro 12:1–2).

2:9 BRAIDED HAIR OR GOLD. This possibly means the braiding of hair with gold or other articles of luxury.

2:13 ADAM WAS FORMED FIRST. Paul's argument for man's responsibility as head and spiritual leader in the home and church (see Eph 5:23, note; see article on PARENTS AND CHILDREN, p. 1854) has two bases. (1) It is based on God's purpose in creation. God created man first, thus re-

was deceived and became a sinner.[u]
15But women[b] will be saved[c]
through childbearing—if they continue in faith, love[v] and holiness with
propriety.

Overseers and Deacons

3 Here is a trustworthy saying:[w] If
anyone sets his heart on being an
overseer,[d][x] he desires a noble task.
2Now the overseer must be above reproach,[y] the husband of but one
wife,[z] temperate,[a] self-controlled,
respectable, hospitable,[b] able to
teach,[c] 3not given to drunkenness,[d]
not violent but gentle, not quarrelsome,[e] not a lover of money.[f] 4He
must manage his own family well and
see that his children obey him with
proper respect.[g] 5(If anyone does not
know how to manage his own family,
how can he take care of God's
church?)[h] 6He must not be a recent
convert, or he may become conceited[i]
and fall under the same judgment[j] as
the devil. 7He must also have a good
reputation with outsiders,[k] so that he

2:14 [u] Ge 3:1-6, 13; 2Co 11:3
2:15 [v] 1Ti 1:14
3:1 [w] S 1Ti 1:15 [x] Ac 20:28; Php 1:1; Tit 1:7
3:2 [y] Tit 1:6-8 [z] ver 12 [a] ver 11; Tit 2:2 [b] S Ro 12:13 [c] 2Ti 2:24
3:3 [d] Tit 1:7 [e] 2Ti 2:24 [f] Lk 16:14; 1Ti 6:10; 2Ti 3:2; Heb 13:5; 1Pe 5:2
3:4 [g] ver 12; Tit 1:6
3:5 [h] S 1Co 10:32
3:6 [i] 1Ti 6:4; 2Ti 3:4 [j] S 2Pe 2:4
3:7 [k] S Mk 4:11

[b] *15* Greek *she* [c] *15* Or *restored*
[d] *1* Traditionally *bishop*; also in verse 2

vealing God's intention that man was to direct and give leadership to the woman and family. The woman, created after man, was designed to be his companion and helper in fulfilling God's desire for their lives (Ge 2:18; 1Co 11:8–9; 14:34). (2) It is also based on the disastrous consequences when man and woman abandoned their God-given roles in the Garden of Eden. Eve, by acting independently of her husband as head, ate the forbidden fruit. Adam, by neglecting his responsibility of leadership under God, consented to Eve's disobedience. As a result he too fell and brought sin and death into the human race (v. 14; Ge 3:6,12; Ro 5:12).

2:15 WOMEN WILL BE SAVED THROUGH CHILDBEARING. Paul says that women in general will be saved by faith in God and by accepting the sphere of activity assigned to them by their Creator. (1) Woman's highest position and true dignity are in the home as a godly wife and mother. No greater joy, inner delight, blessing or honor can come to her than when, as a Christian wife and mother, she bears children (5:14), loves them (Tit 2:4), brings them up to live Christlike lives for God's glory (cf. 2Ti 1:5; 3:14–15; see article on PARENTS AND CHILDREN, p. 1854), and continues ever faithful to her Savior (v. 15b).

(2) The honor and dignity of childbearing must not be depreciated by the Christian. It was the childbearing of Mary that became the channel of salvation to the world (Ge 3:15; Mt 1:18–25).

(3) Those societies, cultures and churches that compromise or reject God's purpose for women and thereby depreciate the Christian family, home and motherhood will increasingly experience disintegration in their marriages, families and societies (see 2Ti 3:3, note).

(4) Paul's address to Christian women is not intended to demean women who are not married or who are unable to have children. The faith, love and sanctity of such women can be as great as those with a family (see 1Co 7:34, note).

3:1–7 IF ANYONE SETS HIS HEART ON BEING AN OVERSEER. For comments on the important qualifications for being an overseer or pastor, see article on MORAL QUALIFICATIONS FOR OVERSEERS, p. 1882.

3:2 MUST BE ABOVE REPROACH. The prospective overseer *must* be "above reproach" (Gk *anepilēmptos*, literally meaning "not to be laid hold of"). This has to do with proven observable conduct that is blameless in marital life, family life, social life and business life. No overseer should have a justifiable charge of immorality or misdoing alleged against him. Rather, he must have a blameless reputation with those inside and outside the church (see v. 7, note), because he has not marred his Christian life with serious sin or immorality by habit or incident. He therefore can set an example for all to follow (see 4:12, note).

3:3 NOT GIVEN TO DRUNKENNESS. This phrase (Gk *mē paroinon*, from *mē*, meaning "not," and *paroinos*, a compound meaning "at, by, near, next to or with wine") is literally translated "not by, near or with wine," "not being beside wine." The Bible here requires that no overseer may "sit beside wine" or "be with wine." In other words, he should not drink intoxicating wine, be tempted or enticed by it, or "eat and drink with drunkards" (Mt 24:49).

(1) Total abstinence from fermented wine was the standard for kings and judges in the OT (Pr 31:4–7). It was also the standard for all who sought the highest level of consecration to God (Lev 10:8–11; Nu 6:1–5; Jdg 13:4–7; 1Sa 1:14–15; Jer 35:2–6; see Pr 23:31, note; see article on WINE IN THE OLD TESTAMENT, p. 204).

(2) Those who rule in Christ's church certainly should not have a lower standard. Furthermore, all believers in the church are called priests and kings (1Pe 2:9; Rev 1:6) and as such should live by God's highest standard (Jn 2:3, note; Eph 5:18, note; 1Th 5:6, note; Tit 2:2, note; see articles on WINE IN NEW TESTAMENT TIMES (1) and (2), p. 1534 and p. 1586).

3:4 MANAGE HIS OWN FAMILY WELL. A key qualification for the candidate desiring the office of overseer is faithfulness in marriage and family relationships. For more on this, see MORAL QUALIFICATIONS FOR OVERSEERS, p. 1882.

3:7 HE MUST ALSO HAVE A GOOD REPUTATION. The overseer or prospective overseer must "have a good reputation" with two groups: (a) insiders, i.e., church members (vv. 1–6), and (b) outsiders, i.e., those outside of the church (v. 7). He must have a past and an ongoing reputation of a righteous lifestyle that accords with the gospel of Christ.

MORAL QUALIFICATIONS FOR OVERSEERS

***1Ti 3:1–2** "Here is a trustworthy saying: If anyone sets his heart on being an overseer, he desires a noble task. Now the overseer must be above reproach, the husband of but one wife, temperate, self-controlled, respectable, hospitable, able to teach."*

If a man wants to be an "overseer" (Gk *episkopos*, i.e., one who has pastoral oversight; a pastor), he desires an important work (1Ti 3:1). However, such people must have that desire confirmed by God's Word (3:1–10; 4:12) and the church (3:10), for God has established for the church certain specific qualifications. Any professed call of God to do the work of a pastor must be tested by the members of the church according to the Biblical standards of 1Ti 3:1–13; 4:12; Tit 1:5–9 (see article on THE MINISTRY GIFTS OF THE CHURCH, p. 1830). The church must not endorse any person for ministerial work based solely on his desire, education, burden, or alleged vision or call. The church today has no right to diminish the requirements that God has set forth by the Holy Spirit. They stand as absolutes and must be followed for the sake of God's name, his kingdom and the credibility of the high office of overseer.

(1) The standards listed for overseers are primarily moral and spiritual. The proven character of those who seek leadership in the church is more important than personality, preaching gifts, administrative abilities or academic accomplishments. The focal point of the qualifications falls on behavior that has persevered in godly wisdom, right choices and personal holiness. The spiritual history of the person who desires the office of overseer has to "first be tested" (cf. 1Ti 3:10). Thus, the Holy Spirit sets forth the high standard that the candidate must be a believer who has steadfastly adhered to Jesus Christ and his principles of righteousness, and who can therefore serve as a role model of faithfulness, truth, honesty and purity. In other words, his character must reflect Christ's teaching in Mt 25:21, that being "faithful with a few things" leads to a position of being "in charge of many things."

(2) Above all, Christian leaders must "set an example for the believers" (1Ti 4:12; cf. 1Pe 5:3), i.e., their Christian life and steadfast faith can be set before the congregation as preeminently worthy of imitation. (a) Overseers must demonstrate the highest example of perseverance in godliness, faithfulness, purity in the face of temptation, and loyalty to and love for Christ and the gospel (1Ti 4:12,15). (b) God's people must learn Christian ethics and true godliness not only from the Word of God but also from the example of pastors who live according to apostolic standards. Pastors whose quality of life is an illustration of the faith are absolutely essential in God's plan for Christian leadership. To throw aside the principle of having godly leadership that has set an unblemished pattern for those of the church to follow is to ignore Scripture's clear teaching. Pastors must be people whose faithfulness to Christ can be set forth as a pattern or example (cf. 1Co 11:1; Php 3:17; 1Th 1:6; 2Th 3:7,9; 2Ti 1:13).

(3) The Holy Spirit regards the believer's leadership in home, marriage and family relationships as of the highest importance (1Ti 3:2,4–5; Tit 1:6). The overseer must be an example to the family of God *especially* in his faithfulness to his wife and children. After all, if he has failed in this realm, "how can he take care of God's church?" (1Ti 3:5). He must be "the husband of but one wife" (1Ti 3:2). The phrase defends the position that a candidate for the office of an overseer should be a believer who has remained morally faithful to his wife. The literal translation of the Greek (*mias gunaikos*, an attributive genitive) is "a one-woman man," i.e., the faithful husband of his wife. This means that the candidate must be a person who gives evidence of being faithful in this all-important area. Persevering moral faithfulness to one's wife and family is required for anyone desiring to be a leader and an example in the church.

(4) Consequently, persons within the church who become guilty of serious sin or moral transgressions have disqualified themselves from the office of pastor and from any position of high leadership in the local church (cf. 1Ti 3:8–12). Such people may be abundantly pardoned by God's grace, but they have lost the capacity to serve as models of unfailing perseverance in faith, love, purity and sound doctrine (4:11–16; Tit 1:9). Already in the OT God had made it clear that the leaders among God's people were expected to maintain high moral and spiritual standards; if they did not, others would replace them (see Ge 49:4, note; Lev 10:2, note; 21:7,17, notes; Nu 20:12, note; 1Sa 2:23, note; Jer 23:14, note; 29:23, note).

(5) Furthermore, 1Ti 3:2,7 sets forth the principle that an overseer who throws aside his loyalty to God and his Word, and his fidelity to his wife and family must be removed from the office of an overseer. He cannot thereafter be regarded as "above reproach". Concerning one among God's people who commits adultery, God's Word states that "his shame will never be wiped away" (Pr 6:33; see Pr 6:32–33, note).

(6) This does not mean that God or the church will not forgive. God will indeed forgive any sin listed in 1Ti 3:1–13 if there is godly sorrow and repentance for that sin. Let it be clear that such a person may be mercifully forgiven and restored in his relationship to God and the church. However, what the Holy Spirit is stating is that there are some sins so grave that the disgrace and shame (i.e., reproach) of that sin will remain with an individual even after forgiveness and for the rest of their lives (cf. 2Sa 12:9–14).

(7) But what about King David? His continuation as Israel's king in spite of his sins of adultery and murder (2Sa 11:1–21; 12:9–15) is sometimes viewed as Biblical justification for one's continuance as an overseer even though he has violated the above-mentioned standards. This comparison, however, is faulty on several counts. (a) The office of the king of Israel under the old covenant and that of spiritual overseer of the church of Jesus Christ under the new covenant are two entirely different things. God allowed not only David but also many kings who were exceptionally wicked to remain as kings of Israel. Leadership of the NT church that was purchased with the blood of Jesus Christ requires much higher spiritual standards. (b) According to God's revelation and requirements in the NT, David would not have qualified for the office of an overseer in a NT church. He had multiple wives, was guilty of marital unfaithfulness, failed miserably to manage his own household, and was a murderer and a violent man of bloodshed. Note too that because of his sin, David remained under God's punishment for the rest of his life (see 2Sa 12:9–12, notes).

(8) Today's churches must not turn from the righteous requirements for an overseer set forth by God in the original revelation of the apostles. Instead the church must require from its leaders the highest standard of holiness, perseverance in faithfulness to God and his Word, and godly living. They are to be earnestly prayed for, encouraged and supported, while they "set an example for the believers in speech, in life, in love, in faith and in purity" (1Ti 4:12).

will not fall into disgrace and into the
devil's trap.[l]
8Deacons,[m] likewise, are to be men
worthy of respect, sincere, not indulging in much wine,[n] and not pursuing
dishonest gain. **9**They must keep hold
of the deep truths of the faith with a
clear conscience.[o] **10**They must first
be tested;[p] and then if there is nothing
against them, let them serve as deacons.
11In the same way, their wives[e] are
to be women worthy of respect, not malicious talkers[q] but temperate[r] and
trustworthy in everything.
12A deacon must be the husband of
but one wife[s] and must manage his
children and his household well.[t]
13Those who have served well gain an
excellent standing and great assurance in their faith in Christ Jesus.
14Although I hope to come to you
soon, I am writing you these instructions so that, **15**if I am delayed, you will
know how people ought to conduct
themselves in God's household, which
is the church[u] of the living God,[v] the
pillar and foundation of the truth.
16Beyond all question, the mystery[w]
of godliness[x] is great:

He[f] appeared in a body,[g y]
  was vindicated by the Spirit,
was seen by angels,
  was preached among the
    nations,[z]
was believed on in the world,
  was taken up in glory.[a]

Instructions to Timothy

4 The Spirit[b] clearly says that in
later times[c] some will abandon

3:7 [l] 2Ti 2:26 **3:8** [m] Php 1:1 [n] 1Ti 5:23; Tit 1:7; 2:3 **3:9** [o] S Ac 23:1 **3:10** [p] 1Ti 5:22 **3:11** [q] 2Ti 3:3; Tit 2:3 [r] ver 2 **3:12** [s] ver 2 [t] ver 4 **3:15** [u] ver 5; S 1Co 10:32 [v] S Mt 16:16 **3:16** [w] S Ro 16:25 [x] S 1Ti 2:2 [y] S Jn 1:14 [z] Ps 9:11; Col 1:23 [a] S Mk 16:19 **4:1** [b] Jn 16:13; S Ac 8:29; 1Co 2:10 [c] 2Ti 3:1; 2Pe 3:3

[e] 11 Or *way, deaconesses* [f] 16 Some manuscripts *God* [g] 16 Or *in the flesh*

3:8 DEACONS. Deacon (Gk *diakonos*) means "servant." One of their functions in the NT church is suggested in Ac 6:1–6. They were to assist pastors by administrating the temporal and material affairs of the church so that pastors might give themselves to prayer and the ministry of the Word (Ac 6:2). The spiritual qualifications for deacons are essentially the same as for pastors (compare vv. 1–7 with vv. 8–13; see Ac 6:3).

3:8 NOT INDULGING IN MUCH WINE. Concerning this qualification, the following should be noted (see also v. 3, note). (1) It is morally unthinkable that the apostle was approving the moderate use of all the kinds of wine available in his day. Many wines were mixed and dangerous (cf. Pr 23:29–35).

(2) Some interpret Paul as saying that deacons must not be habitual drunkards, thereby implicitly condoning moderate alcoholic drinking. However, Paul states that drunkenness is such a terrible sin that it excludes one from God's kingdom (1Co 6:10). It is absurd, therefore, that Paul would actually require, as one of his high standards for deacons (cf. v. 2), that the deacon not be a habitual drunkard (i.e., someone who is unsaved). Paul must have a different meaning in mind for "wine" than intoxicating wine.

(3) Rather than condoning moderate alcoholic drinking, Paul was most likely warning against the excessive desire and use, within a pagan society, of legitimate unfermented types of wines (see article on WINE IN NEW TESTAMENT TIMES (1), p. 1534). Addiction even to nonintoxicating wine was a vice prevalent in pagan societies, and corresponded to gluttony (see Pliny, *Natural History*, 14.28.139). Paul was emphasizing self-control in all areas of life, even in something good; note Pr 25:27, which states that "it is not good to eat too much honey."

(4) The apostle Paul was not alone in this kind of admonition. Rabbinic literature contains warnings about the excessive use of the sweet unfermented juice of the grape. This literature states concerning *tirosh*, a grape drink that included "all kinds of sweet juices and must, and does not include fermented wine" (Tosef., Ned. IV.3), that "if drunk in moderation it gives leadership; . . . if drunk in excess it leads to poverty" (Yoma 76b). "One that drinks it habitually is certain to become poor" (*The Jewish Encyclopedia*, 12.533; see article on WINE IN NEW TESTAMENT TIMES (1), p. 1534).

3:15 CHURCH . . . PILLAR AND FOUNDATION OF THE TRUTH. The church must be the foundation of the truth of the gospel. It upholds and preserves the truth revealed by Christ and the apostles by receiving and obeying it (Mt 13:23), hiding it in the heart (Ps 119:11), proclaiming it as the word of life (Php 2:16), defending it (Php 1:16) and demonstrating its power in the Holy Spirit (Mk 16:15–20; Ac 1:8; 4:29–33; 6:8).

4:1 SOME WILL ABANDON THE FAITH. The Holy Spirit has explicitly revealed that in later times there will be a falling away both from a personal faith in Jesus Christ (see article on PERSONAL APOSTASY, p. 1918) and from Scriptural truth (cf. 2Th 2:3; Jude 3–4). (1) There will appear within the church ministers who are highly gifted and mightily anointed by God. Some will accomplish great things for God and preach gospel truth effectively, but they will depart from the faith and gradually turn to seducing spirits and false doctrines. Because of their former anointing and zeal for God, they will mislead many (see article on THE GREAT TRIBULATION, p. 1456).

(2) Many believers will fall away from the faith because they will fail to love the truth (2Th 2:10) and resist the sinful trends of the last days (cf. Mt 24:5,10–12; see 2Ti 3:2–3, notes). Thus, the distorted gospel of compromising ministers and educators will find little resistance in many churches (4:1; 2Ti 3:5; 4:3; see 2Co 11:13, note).

the faith and follow deceiving spirits[d] and things taught by demons. 2Such teachings come through hypocritical liars, whose consciences have been seared as with a hot iron.[e] 3They forbid people to marry[f] and order them to abstain from certain foods,[g] which God created[h] to be received with thanksgiving[i] by those who believe and who know the truth. 4For everything God created is good,[j] and nothing is to be rejected[k] if it is received with thanksgiving, 5because it is consecrated by the word of God[l] and prayer.

6If you point these things out to the brothers, you will be a good minister of Christ Jesus, brought up in the truths of the faith[m] and of the good teaching that you have followed.[n] 7Have nothing to do with godless myths and old wives' tales;[o] rather, train yourself to be godly.[p] 8For physical training is of some value, but godliness has value for all things,[q] holding promise for both the present life[r] and the life to come.[s]

9This is a trustworthy saying[t] that deserves full acceptance 10(and for this we labor and strive), that we have put our hope in the living God,[u] who is the Savior of all men,[v] and especially of those who believe.

11Command and teach these things.[w] 12Don't let anyone look down on you[x] because you are young, but set an example[y] for the believers in speech, in life, in love, in faith[z] and in purity. 13Until I come,[a] devote yourself to the public reading of Scripture,[b] to preaching and to teaching. 14Do not neglect your gift, which was given you through a prophetic message[c] when the body of elders[d] laid their hands on you.[e] 2Ti 1:6

15Be diligent in these matters; give yourself wholly to them, so that everyone may see your progress. 16Watch your life and doctrine closely. Persevere in them, because if you do, you will save[f] both yourself and your hearers.

Advice About Widows, Elders and Slaves

5 Do not rebuke an older man[g] harshly,[h] but exhort him as if he were your father. Treat younger men[i] as brothers, 2older women as mothers, and younger women as sisters, with absolute purity.

3Give proper recognition to those widows who are really in need.[j] 4But if a widow has children or grandchildren, these should learn first of all to put their religion into practice by caring for their own family and so repaying their parents and grandparents,[k] for this is pleasing to God.[l] 5The widow who is really in need[m] and left all

4:1 [d]S Mk 13:5 **4:2** [e]Eph 4:19 **4:3** [f]Heb 13:4 [g]Col 2:16 [h]Ge 1:29; 9:3 [i]ver 4; Ro 14:6; 1Co 10:30 **4:4** [j]Ge 1:10,12, 18,21,25,31; Mk 7:18,19; Ro 14:14-18 [k]S Ac 10:15 **4:5** [l]S Heb 4:12 **4:6** [m]1Ti 1:10 [n]2Ti 3:15 **4:7** [o]1Ti 1:4; 2Ti 2:16 [p]S 1Ti 2:2 **4:8** [q]1Ti 6:6 [r]Ps 37:9,11; Pr 22:4; Mt 6:33; Mk 10:29,30 [s]Mk 10:29,30 **4:9** [t]S 1Ti 1:15 **4:10** [u]S Mt 16:16 [v]S Lk 1:47; S 2:11 **4:11** [w]1Ti 5:7; 6:2

4:12 [x]S 2Ti 1:7; Tit 2:15 [y]Php 3:17; 1Th 1:7; 2Th 3:9; Tit 2:7; 1Pe 5:3 [z]1Ti 1:14 **4:13** [a]1Ti 3:14 [b]Lk 4:16; Ac 13:14-16; Col 4:16; 1Th 5:27 **4:14** [c] 1Ti 1:18 [d]S Ac 11:30 [e]S Ac 6:6; 2Ti 1:6 **4:16** [f]S Ro 11:14 **5:1** [g]Tit 2:2 [h]Lev 19:32 [i]Tit 2:6 **5:3** [j]ver 5,16 **5:4** [k]ver 8; Eph 6:1,2 [l]Ro 12:2; Eph 5:10; 1Ti 2:3 **5:5** [m]ver 3,16

---

(3) The popularity of unbiblical teaching will be primarily the result of Satan's directing his demonic hosts in a more intensified opposition to God's work. Christ's second coming will be preceded by a greater intensity of satanism, spiritism, the occult, demon-possession and demonic deception in the world and in the church (Eph 6:11–12; see articles on POWER OVER SATAN AND DEMONS, p. 1484, and THE AGE OF THE ANTICHRIST, p. 1872).

(4) The believer's protection against such deception involves utter loyalty to God and his inspired Word, and the knowledge that persons of great charisma and anointing can be deceived and then deceive others with their mixture of truth and error. This awareness must be accompanied by a true desire within the believer's heart to do God's will (Jn 7:17) and to walk in righteousness and the fear of God (Ps 25:4–5,12–15).

(5) Faithful believers must not think that because apostasy is prevalent within Christianity during the last days that authentic revival cannot occur or evangelism according to the NT pattern cannot be successful. God has promised that during the "last days" he will save all who call on his name and separate themselves from this corrupt generation (Ac 2:16–21,33,38–40; 3:19), and he will pour out his Spirit on them.

4:12 SET AN EXAMPLE. This is one of the most important qualifications for a church leader. The Greek word translated "example" is *tupos*, meaning "model," "image," "ideal" or "pattern." A pastor, above all else, must be a model of faithfulness, purity and perseverance in godly living. The office of overseer may be occupied only by those of whom the church can say, "This leader has lived a godly life worthy of emulation." For more on this, see MORAL QUALIFICATIONS FOR OVERSEERS, p. 1882.

4:16 IF YOU DO, YOU WILL SAVE BOTH YOURSELF AND YOUR HEARERS. Living a holy life (v. 12), remaining sensitive to the Spirit's operation and gifts (v. 14), teaching sound doctrine (vv. 13,15–16), guarding the faith (6:20; 2Ti 1:13–14; see article on OVERSEERS AND THEIR DUTIES, p. 1690) and watching over one's spiritual life (v. 16) are more than a ministerial obligation for Timothy. These things are essential for his own salvation (present and future: see article on BIBLICAL WORDS FOR SALVATION, p. 1710) and for those to whom he ministers (cf. 2Ti 3:13–15).

5:5 THE WIDOW . . . NIGHT AND DAY TO

alone puts her hope in God[n] and continues night and day to pray[o] and to
ask God for help. **6**But the widow who
lives for pleasure is dead even while
she lives.[p] **7**Give the people these instructions,[q] too, so that no one may
be open to blame. **8**If anyone does not
provide for his relatives, and especially
for his immediate family, he has denied[r] the faith and is worse than an
unbeliever.
9No widow may be put on the list of
widows unless she is over sixty, has
been faithful to her husband,[h] **10**and is
well known for her good deeds,[s] such
as bringing up children, showing hospitality,[t] washing the feet[u] of the
saints, helping those in trouble[v] and
devoting herself to all kinds of good
deeds.
11As for younger widows, do not put
them on such a list. For when their sensual desires overcome their dedication
to Christ, they want to marry. **12**Thus
they bring judgment on themselves,
because they have broken their first
pledge. **13**Besides, they get into the
habit of being idle and going about
from house to house. And not only do
they become idlers, but also gossips[w]
and busybodies,[x] saying things they
ought not to. **14**So I counsel younger
widows to marry,[y] to have children, to
manage their homes and to give the enemy no opportunity for slander.[z]
15Some have in fact already turned
away to follow Satan.[a]
16If any woman who is a believer has
widows in her family, she should help
them and not let the church be burdened with them, so that the church
can help those widows who are really
in need.[b]
17The elders[c] who direct the affairs
of the church well are worthy of double
honor,[d] especially those whose work
is preaching and teaching. **18**For the
Scripture says, "Do not muzzle the ox
while it is treading out the grain,"[i][e]
and "The worker deserves his
wages."[j][f] **19**Do not entertain an accusation against an elder[g] unless it is
brought by two or three witnesses.[h]
20Those who sin are to be rebuked[i]
publicly, so that the others may take
warning.[j]
21I charge you, in the sight of God
and Christ Jesus[k] and the elect angels, to keep these instructions without partiality, and to do nothing out of
favoritism.
22Do not be hasty in the laying on of

5:5 [n] 1Co 7:34; 1Pe 3:5 [o] Lk 2:37; S Ro 1:10 **5:6** [p] S Lk 15:24 **5:7** [q] 1Ti 4:11; 6:2 **5:8** [r] 2Pe 2:1; Jude 4 **5:10** [s] Ac 9:36; 1Ti 6:18; 1Pe 2:12 [t] S Ro 12:13 [u] S Lk 7:44 [v] ver 16 **5:13** [w] S Ro 1:29 [x] 2Th 3:11 **5:14** [y] 1Co 7:9 [z] 1Ti 6:1 **5:15** [a] S Mt 4:10 **5:16** [b] ver 3-5 **5:17** [c] S Ac 11:30 [d] Php 2:29; 1Th 5:12 **5:18** [e] Dt 25:4; 1Co 9:7-9 [f] Lk 10:7; Lev 19:13; Dt 24:14,15; Mt 10:10; 1Co 9:14 **5:19** [g] S Ac 11:30 [h] S Mt 18:16 **5:20** [i] 2Ti 4:2; Tit 1:13; 2:15 [j] Dt 13:11 **5:21** [k] 1Ti 6:13; 2Ti 4:1

[h] *9* Or *has had but one husband* [i] *18* Deut. 25:4 [j] *18* Luke 10:7

PRAY. Widows who have given themselves to the supreme work of prayer should receive recognition and help (if need be) from the church (v. 3). One is reminded of the widow Anna, who "never left the temple but worshiped night and day, fasting and praying" (Lk 2:37). Early Christianity called such a widow "the intercessor of the church," "the keeper of the door" and "the altar of God."

5:9 MAY BE PUT ON THE LIST. The church in Ephesus apparently had an official list of widows who were entitled to material support from the church (see Dt 24:17, note). The church gave such assistance because in NT times there was no government help or pensions for widows who had no family or children to help them. The widows were required to demonstrate certain spiritual qualifications (vv. 9–10), including perseverance in good works (v. 10) and prayer (v. 5).

5:17–19 ELDERS WHO DIRECT THE AFFAIRS OF THE CHURCH WELL. These verses concern the proper honor of elders (i.e., overseers) who rule well in the local church and watch over the souls of believers (see article on OVERSEERS AND THEIR DUTIES, p. 1690). Those who sincerely work hard at preaching and teaching (cf. 1Co 15:10; 1Th 5:12–13) must receive double honor. This refers to (1) helping them with financial support (cf. 1Co 9:7–14) and (2) submitting to them with regard to matters of Christian conduct (Heb 13:7; 1Pe 5:5).

5:20 REBUKED PUBLICLY. God's Word gives principles and guidelines with regard to the discipline of elders or pastors (vv. 20–22). Because godly leaders are essential to the church, the following actions must be taken when a pastor or church worker sins and that sin is confirmed (v. 19). (1) Elders must not cover up or remain silent about the sins of other elders. The offending elder must "be rebuked" and disciplined. His sin must be exposed "publicly," in order that the rest of the elders may "take warning" and have a godly fear of sinning. (2) Paul warns that the above discipline must be carried out without partiality or favoritism because all will one day stand in the presence of God, Jesus Christ and the elect angels (v. 21).

5:22 DO NOT BE HASTY IN THE LAYING ON OF HANDS. Regarding the ordination of an elder (cf. 4:14; Ac 6:6), Paul maintains several things: (1) No one is to be ordained to this position hastily. That is, proper caution and Scriptural guidelines must be obeyed and followed (see Tit 1:5, note; see article on MORAL QUALIFICATIONS FOR OVERSEERS, p. 1882). (2) Ordaining a man as an elder is a public declaration to the church that the person's life has met God's standard of perseverance in godliness as found in 3:1–7. In other words, those to be ordained to a position of leadership must have a history of faithfulness to the Lord dur-

hands,[l] and do not share in the sins
of others.[m] Keep yourself pure.[n]
23Stop drinking only water, and use
a little wine[o] because of your stomach
and your frequent illnesses.
24The sins of some men are obvious,
reaching the place of judgment ahead
of them; the sins of others trail behind
them. 25In the same way, good deeds
are obvious, and even those that are
not cannot be hidden.

6 All who are under the yoke of slavery should consider their masters
worthy of full respect,[p] so that God's
name and our teaching may not be
slandered.[q] 2Those who have believing masters are not to show less respect for them because they are brothers.[r] Instead, they are to serve them
even better, because those who benefit
from their service are believers, and
dear to them. These are the things you
are to teach and urge on them.[s]

Love of Money

3If anyone teaches false doctrines[t]
and does not agree to the sound instruction[u] of our Lord Jesus Christ
and to godly teaching, 4he is conceited[v] and understands nothing. He has
an unhealthy interest in controversies
and quarrels about words[w] that result
in envy, strife, malicious talk, evil suspicions 5and constant friction between
men of corrupt mind, who have been
robbed of the truth[x] and who think
that godliness is a means to financial
gain.
6But godliness with contentment[y]
is great gain.[z] 7For we brought nothing into the world, and we can take
nothing out of it.[a] 8But if we have food
and clothing, we will be content with
that.[b] 9People who want to get rich[c]
fall into temptation and a trap[d] and
into many foolish and harmful desires
that plunge men into ruin and destruction. 10For the love of money[e] is a root
of all kinds of evil. Some people, eager
for money, have wandered from the
faith[f] and pierced themselves with
many griefs.[g]

Paul's Charge to Timothy

11But you, man of God,[h] flee from
all this, and pursue righteousness,
godliness,[i] faith, love,[j] endurance
and gentleness. 12Fight the good

5:22 [l]S Ac 6:6 [m]Eph 5:11 [n]Ps 18:26 **5:23** [o]1Ti 3:8 **6:1** [p]S Eph 6:5 [q]1Ti 5:14; Tit 2:5, 8 **6:2** [r]Phm 16 [s]1Ti 4:11 **6:3** [t]1Ti 1:3 [u]S 1Ti 1:10 **6:4** [v]1Ti 3:6; 2Ti 3:4 [w]S 2Ti 2:14 **6:5** [x]2Ti 3:8; Tit 1:15 **6:6** [y]Php 4:11; Heb 13:5 [z]1Ti 4:8 **6:7** [a]Job 1:21; Ps 49:17; Ecc 5:15 **6:8** [b]Pr 30:8; Heb 13:5 **6:9** [c]Pr 15:27; 28:20 [d]1Ti 3:7 **6:10** [e]S 1Ti 3:3 [f]ver 21; Jas 5:19 [g]Jos 7:21 **6:11** [h]2Ti 3:17 [i]ver 3,5,6; S 1Ti 2:2 [j]1Ti 1:14; 2Ti 2:22; 3:10

ing the time of their Christian profession. (3) For a church to ordain or appoint anyone to a position of leadership within the church hastily, i.e., in disregard to God's guidelines, causes it to "share in" that person's sins. Paul's admonition to "keep yourself pure" means to refuse to become involved in the choosing or ordaining of anyone unworthy for the office of pastor.

5:23 USE A LITTLE WINE. (1) This text clearly implies that Timothy did not normally drink any of the types of wine used by the Jews of NT times (see article on WINE IN NEW TESTAMENT TIMES (1), p. 1534). If it had been Timothy's habit to drink wine, Paul would not have had to advise him to use a little wine for medicinal purposes (see 3:3, note).

(2) Timothy had developed stomach trouble, probably due to the alkali in the water at Ephesus. Paul therefore recommends that Timothy use a little wine with that water to neutralize the harmful effect of the alkali. Wine used for the stomach, according to ancient Greek writings on medicine, was often unintoxicating. Athenaeus states, "Let him take sweet wine, either mixed with water or warmed, especially that kind called *protropos* [juice coming from the grapes before they are pressed], as being good for the stomach, for sweet wine [*oinos*] does not make the head heavy" (Athenaeus, *Banquet*, 2.24; see also Pliny, *Natural History* 14.18).

(3) Timothy, out of respect for the apostle Paul, would use a "little wine" when needed, and *only* for medicinal purposes. He would use it as an exception to his rule of abstinence. To quote the advice of Paul to Timothy in order to justify the drinking of intoxicating wine for personal gratification is to distort the intent of this passage.

6:1 UNDER THE YOKE OF SLAVERY. See Col 3:22, note.

6:3 GODLY TEACHING. Any message that does not come from the Lord Jesus and does not carry with it a fervent call for godliness and holiness is a different gospel than that presented in the NT.

6:5 MEN OF CORRUPT MIND. Paul returns to the discussion of false teachers (cf. ch. 1), informing Timothy what his judgment on such people must be. Modern indifference to extrabiblical doctrine is unapostolic and ignores the clear admonitions in this and other NT letters (cf. Gal 1:9).

6:6 GODLINESS ... IS GREAT GAIN. The false teachers at Ephesus outwardly practiced "godliness" in order to gain an abundance of riches. They were driven by an underlying motivation of greed and taught that their wealth was a sign of God's approval on their teachings.

6:8 WE WILL BE CONTENT WITH THAT. Believers should be content with the basics of food, clothing and shelter. If special financial needs arise, we must look to God to provide (Ps 50:15), while we continue to work (2Th 3:7–8), help those in need (2Co 8:2–3) and serve God with generous giving (2Co 8:3; 9:6–7). We must not want to get rich (vv. 9–11).

6:9 RICH FALL INTO TEMPTATION. See article on RICHES AND POVERTY, p. 1562.

fight[k] of the faith. Take hold of[l] the
eternal life[m] to which you were called
when you made your good confession[n]
in the presence of many witnesses.
13In the sight of God, who gives life to
everything, and of Christ Jesus, who
while testifying before Pontius Pilate[o] made the good confession,[p] I
charge you[q] **14**to keep this command
without spot or blame[r] until the appearing of our Lord Jesus Christ,[s]
15which God will bring about in his
own time[t]—God, the blessed[u] and
2Ti 4:8 only Ruler,[v] the King of kings and
Lord of lords,[w] **16**who alone is immortal[x] and who lives in unapproachable
light,[y] whom no one has seen or can
see.[z] To him be honor and might forever. Amen.[a]

17Command those who are rich[b] in
this present world not to be arrogant
nor to put their hope in wealth,[c]
which is so uncertain, but to put their
hope in God,[d] who richly provides us
with everything for our enjoyment.[e]
18Command them to do good, to be rich
in good deeds,[f] and to be generous
and willing to share.[g] **19**In this way
they will lay up treasure for themselves[h] as a firm foundation for the
coming age, so that they may take hold
of[i] the life that is truly life.

20Timothy, guard what has been entrusted[j] to your care. Turn away from
godless chatter[k] and the opposing
ideas of what is falsely called knowledge, **21**which some have professed
and in so doing have wandered from
the faith.[l]

Grace be with you.[m]

6:12 [k]1Co 9:25, 26; S 1Ti 1:18 [l]ver 19; Php 3:12 [m]S Mt 25:46 [n]S Heb 3:1 **6:13** [o]Jn 18:33-37 [p]ver 12 [q]1Ti 5:21; 2Ti 4:1 **6:14** [r]S 1Th 3:13 [s]S 1Co 1:7; 2Ti 1:10; 4:1,8 **6:15** [t]1Ti 2:6; Tit 1:3 [u]1Ti 1:11 [v]1Ti 1:17 [w]Dt 10:17; Ps 136:3; Da 2:47; Rev 1:5; 17:14; 19:16 **6:16** [x]1Ti 1:17 [y]Ps 104:2; 1Jn 1:7 [z]S Jn 1:18 [a]S Ro 11:36 **6:17** [b]ver 9 [c]Ps 62:10; Jer 49:4; Lk 12:20, 21 [d]1Ti 4:10 [e]Ac 14:17 **6:18** [f]S 1Ti 5:10 [g]Ro 12:8,13; Eph 4:28 **6:19** [h]S Mt 6:20 [i]ver 12; Php 3:12 **6:20** [j]2Ti 1:12,14 [k]2Ti 2:16 **6:21** [l]ver 10; 2Ti 2:18 [m]S Col 4:18

6:12 FIGHT THE GOOD FIGHT OF THE FAITH. The word "fight" is from the Greek word meaning "agonize." Paul sees the Christian life as a fight, an intense struggle that requires persevering in loyalty to Christ and contending with adversaries of the gospel. All of us are called to defend the gospel in whatever occupation God has placed us (see Eph 6:11–12, notes).

6:14 UNTIL THE APPEARING. Paul's admonition to Timothy clearly reveals that he believes that Christ's appearing could occur within his lifetime. The NT apostles repeatedly encouraged believers in their generation to expect and hope for the Lord's return in their lifetimes (Php 3:20; 1Th 1:9–10; Tit 2:13; Heb 9:28). Loving the Lord and longing for his return and immediate presence must be a basic motivation in our lives (see Rev 21:1—22:15).

6:16 WHO ALONE IS IMMORTAL. This term expresses God's transcendence. God is different and independent from his creation—whether humans, angels, spirits, or physical or material things (Ex 24:9–18; Isa 6:1–3; 40:12–26; 55:8–9; Eze 1). (1) God must not be placed on the same level with humans or any other beings he has created. His being and existence are in a totally different realm. He dwells in perfect and pure existence, far above his creation. He is not part of his creation nor is his creation a part of him. Furthermore, believers are not God and will never be "gods." We will always be limited and dependent beings, even in the age to come.

(2) Although a radical division exists between God and all creation, God is also present and active throughout the world. He lives and manifests himself in his people who repent of their sins and live by faith in Christ (Ex 33:17–23; Isa 57:15; see Mt 10:31, note; Ro 8:28, note; Gal 2:20, note; see article on THE ATTRIBUTES OF GOD, p. 882).

6:20 GUARD WHAT HAS BEEN ENTRUSTED. For the fourth time, Paul charges Timothy to guard the faith that has been entrusted to him (1:18–19; 4:6–11; 6:13–16; 6:20). The Greek literally means "keep the deposit" and refers to the sacred obligation of keeping safe a treasured possession committed to one's care. The gospel of Christ has been committed to us by the Holy Spirit (2Ti 1:14; 3:16). We must proclaim the pure and full gospel in the Pentecostal power of the Spirit (Ac 2:4), ever ready to defend the precious truths when they are attacked, distorted or denied.

2 TIMOTHY

Outline

Introduction (1:1–4)

I. Paul's Charge to Timothy (1:5–18)
   A. Fan Into Flame the Gift of God (1:5–7)
   B. Be Willing to Suffer for the Gospel (1:8–10)
   C. Paul's Example (1:11–12)
   D. Keep and Guard the Truth (1:13–14)
   E. Disloyal and Loyal Friends of Paul in Rome (1:15–18)

II. Requirements for a Faithful Minister (2:1–26)
   A. Be Strong in Grace (2:1)
   B. Entrust the Message to Reliable Men (2:2)
   C. Endure Hardship (2:3–7)
      1. Like a Good Soldier (2:3–4)
      2. Like a Disciplined Athlete (2:5)
      3. Like a Hardworking Farmer (2:6–7)
   D. Die With and Suffer for Jesus Christ (2:8–13)
   E. Avoid Foolish Arguments and Defend the Gospel in an Irreproachable Manner (2:14–26)

III. The Approaching Final Upsurge of Evil (3:1–9)

IV. Endurance in the Truth (3:10–17)
   A. As Learned From Paul (3:10–14)
   B. As Learned From the Scriptures (3:15–17)

V. Preach the Word (4:1–5)

VI. Paul's Testimony and Instructions (4:6–18)
   A. Paul's Farewell Testimony (4:6–8)
   B. Personal Instruction to Timothy (4:9–13)
   C. A Word of Caution (4:14–15)
   D. The Assurance of God's Faithfulness (4:16–18)

Conclusion (4:19–22)

Author: Paul

Theme: Steadfast Endurance

Date of Writing: c. A.D. 67

Background

This is Paul's last letter. At the time of writing, the emperor Nero was attempting to stop the spread of the Christian faith in Rome by severely persecuting believers; Paul was again the emperor's prisoner in Rome (1:16). He was suffering deprivation as a common criminal (2:9), deserted by most of his friends (1:15), and aware that his ministry was over and his death near (4:6–8,18; see the introduction to 1 Timothy for a fuller discussion of authorship and background).

Paul writes to Timothy as a "dear son" (1:2) and faithful co-worker (cf. Ro 16:21). His closeness to and reliance on Timothy is seen in naming him a co-sender of six letters, in

Timothy's presence with Paul during his first imprisonment (Php 1:1; Col 1:1; Phm 1) and in Paul's two personal letters to him. As Paul faces the imminent prospect of execution, he twice requests Timothy to join him in Rome again (4:9,21). Timothy was still at Ephesus (1:18; 4:19) when Paul wrote him this second letter.

Purpose

Knowing that Timothy was timid and facing hardship, and realizing the prospect of severe persecution from outside the church and false teachers from within, Paul exhorts Timothy to guard the gospel, preach the Word, endure hardship and fulfill his charge.

Survey

In ch. 1 Paul assures Timothy of his continuing love and prayers and urges him to remain uncompromisingly faithful to the gospel, to guard the truth diligently and to follow Paul's example.

In ch. 2 Paul charges his spiritual son to preserve the faith by passing on its truths to reliable men who will teach it to others also (2:2). He admonishes the young pastor to endure hardship like a good soldier (2:3), to serve God diligently and handle the word of truth accurately (2:15), to separate himself from those who depart from apostolic truth (2:18–21), to keep himself pure (2:22) and to labor patiently as a teacher (2:23–26).

In the next chapter Paul informs Timothy that evil and apostasy will increase (3:1–9), but that he must be unwaveringly faithful to his heritage and to the Scriptures (3:10–17).

In the final chapter Paul charges Timothy to preach the Word and discharge all the duties of his ministry (4:1–5). He concludes by updating Timothy on his present circumstances as he faces the end, urging Timothy to come soon (4:6–22).

Special Features

Five major features characterize this letter. (1) It contains Paul's last recorded words before his execution by Nero in Rome almost 35 years after his Damascus road conversion to Christ. (2) It contains one of the clearest statements in the Bible about the divine inspiration and purpose of Scripture (3:16–17): Paul emphasizes that Scripture must be accurately interpreted by ministers of the Word (2:15) and urges the commitment of God's Word to reliable men who can then teach others (2:2). (3) Terse exhortations occur throughout the letter; e.g., "fan into flame the gift of God" (1:6), "do not be ashamed" (1:8), suffer for the gospel (1:8), "keep . . . the pattern of sound teaching" (1:13), "guard the good deposit" (1:14), "be strong in the grace" (2:1), pass on the message (2:2), "endure hardship" (2:3), be diligent in the Word (2:15), "avoid" (2:16), "flee . . . pursue" (2:22), beware of approaching apostasy (3:1–9), "continue" in the truth (3:14), "preach the word" (4:2), "do the work of an evangelist" (4:5) and "discharge all the duties of your ministry" (4:5). (4) The recurring themes of its many exhortations are to hold fast to the faith (Jesus Christ and the original apostolic gospel), guard it from distortion and corruption, oppose false teachers, and preach the true gospel with unswerving perseverance. (5) Paul's farewell testimony is a moving example of courage and hope in the face of certain martyrdom (4:6–8).

Reading 2 Timothy

In order to read the entire New Testament in one year, the book of 2 Timothy should be read in 4 days, according to the following schedule:
□ 1 □ 2 □ 3 □ 4

NOTES

1 Paul, an apostle[a] of Christ Jesus
by the will of God,[b] according to
the promise of life that is in Christ
Jesus,[c]

2To Timothy,[d] my dear son:[e]

Grace, mercy and peace from God
the Father and Christ Jesus our Lord.[f]

Encouragement to Be Faithful

3I thank God,[g] whom I serve, as my
forefathers did, with a clear conscience,[h] as night and day I constantly remember you in my prayers.[i] **4**Recalling your tears,[j] I long to see
you,[k] so that I may be filled with joy.
5I have been reminded of your sincere
faith,[l] which first lived in your grandmother Lois and in your mother Eunice[m] and, I am persuaded, now lives in
you also. **6**For this reason I remind you
to fan into flame the gift of God, which
Heb 2:4 is in you through the laying on of my
hands.[n] **7**For God did not give us a
spirit of timidity,[o] but a spirit of power,[p] of love and of self-discipline.
8So do not be ashamed[q] to testify
about our Lord, or ashamed of me his
prisoner.[r] But join with me in suffering for the gospel,[s] by the power of
God, **9**who has saved[t] us and called[u]
us to a holy life—not because of anything we have done[v] but because of
his own purpose and grace. This grace
was given us in Christ Jesus before the
beginning of time, **10**but it has now
been revealed[w] through the appearing
of our Savior, Christ Jesus,[x] who has
destroyed death[y] and has brought life
and immortality to light through the
gospel. **11**And of this gospel[z] I was
appointed[a] a herald and an apostle
and a teacher.[b] **12**That is why I am
suffering as I am. Yet I am not
ashamed,[c] because I know whom I
have believed, and am convinced that
he is able to guard[d] what I have entrusted to him for that day.[e]
13What you heard from me,[f] keep[g]
as the pattern[h] of sound teaching,[i]
with faith and love in Christ Jesus.[j]
14Guard[k] the good deposit that was
entrusted to you—guard it with the
help of the Holy Spirit who lives in
us.[l]
15You know that everyone in the

1:1 [a]S 1Co 1:1 [b]S 2Co 1:1 [c]Eph 3:6; Tit 1:2; 1Ti 6:19 **1:2** [d]S Ac 16:1 [e]S 1Ti 1:2 [f]S Ro 1:7 **1:3** [g]S Ro 1:8 [h]S Ac 23:1 [i]S Ro 1:10 **1:4** [j]Ac 20:37 [k]2Ti 4:9 **1:5** [l]1Ti 1:5 [m]Ac 16:1; 2Ti 3:15 **1:6** [n]S Ac 6:6; 1Ti 4:14 **1:7** [o]Jer 42:11; Ro 8:15; 1Co 16:10,11; 1Ti 4:12; Heb 2:15 [p]Isa 11:2 **1:8** [q]ver 12,16; Mk 8:38 [r]S Eph 3:1 [s]2Ti 2:3,9; 4:5 **1:9** [t]S Ro 11:14 [u]S Ro 8:28 [v]S Eph 2:9 **1:10** [w]Eph 1:9 [x]S 1Ti 6:14 [y]1Co 15:26,54 **1:11** [z]ver 8 [a]S Ac 9:15 [b]1Ti 2:7 **1:12** [c]ver 8,16; Mk 8:38 [d]ver 14; 1Ti 6:20 [e]ver 18; S 1Co 1:8; 2Ti 4:8 **1:13** [f]2Ti 2:2 [g]S Tit 1:9 [h]Ro 6:17 [i]S 1Ti 1:10 [j]S 1Th 1:3; 1Ti 1:14 **1:14** [k]ver 12 [l]S Ro 8:9

1:4 I LONG TO SEE YOU. Paul is now a prisoner in Rome awaiting death, forsaken by many of his friends (v. 15; 4:16), and longing to see Timothy once more. He begs his co-worker to remain faithful to the truth of the gospel and to hurry to come to him during his last days on earth (4:21).

1:6 FAN INTO FLAME THE GIFT OF GOD. The "gift" (Gk *charisma*) given to Timothy is compared to a fire (cf. 1Th 5:19) that he must fan into flame. The gift was probably a special gift and power from the Holy Spirit to fulfill his ministry. Note that the gifts and power bestowed on us by the Spirit do not automatically remain strong and vital. They must be fueled by God's grace through our prayer, faith, obedience and diligence.

1:12 GUARD WHAT I HAVE ENTRUSTED. Paul does not define what he has entrusted to God. It may refer to his apostolic work, teaching, or even his life.

1:13 KEEP AS THE PATTERN OF SOUND TEACHING. The "sound teaching" is the original and fundamental revelation of Christ and the apostles, the doctrines taught to Timothy by Paul. Timothy must hold these truths fast in faith and love for Jesus Christ, and never depart from them or compromise them even if it means suffering, rejection and disgrace. Today it is popular in some churches to emphasize that experience, not doctrine, is the most important thing. This is firmly contradicted in Paul's Pastoral Letters (cf. 4:3; 1Ti 1:10; 6:3; Tit 1:9,13; 2:1–2,8).

1:14 GUARD IT WITH THE HELP OF THE HOLY SPIRIT. Pastoral leaders must guard and defend the gospel committed to them even in a day when many depart from the NT faith (3:13–15; 4:2–5; 1Ti 4:1). (1) They must defend it against attack, and challenge the church if it is tempted to lay aside the truth. This duty is essential to ensure salvation for themselves and for those under their charge (see 3:14–15; 1Ti 4:16, note; see article on OVERSEERS AND THEIR DUTIES, p. 1690). (2) Guarding the deposit of faith must be done with the help of the Holy Spirit. It is he who inspired the infallible truths of Scripture (see 3:16; 2Pe 1:21) and it is he who is the great guide and defender of the truth (Jn 16:13). Defending the ancient faith once for all entrusted to the saints (Jude 3) means standing faithfully alongside the Spirit (Jn 14:17; 15:26–27; 16:13).

1:15 EVERYONE ... HAS DESERTED ME. This is one of the saddest times in Paul's life. He is in prison in Rome with no hope of freedom. He is undergoing persecution for the sake of the gospel that he loved and for which he was soon to give his life (4:6–7). He is also experiencing such a staggering defection from him and his gospel in the east that he states, "everyone in the province of Asia has deserted me."

(1) Yet even through this terrible trial, Paul maintains his faith in God. He is assured that Christ will guard the true gospel and his ministry (v. 12), that there will always be people like Timothy who will guard and proclaim it (v. 14; 2:2), and that at his death the Lord will bring him safely to his heavenly kingdom (4:6,8,18).

(2) Paul's sorrowful plight will be the experi-

province of Asia[m] has deserted me,[n]
including Phygelus and Hermogenes.
16May the Lord show mercy to the
household of Onesiphorus,[o] because
he often refreshed me and was not
ashamed[p] of my chains.[q] 17On the
contrary, when he was in Rome, he
searched hard for me until he found
me. 18May the Lord grant that he will
find mercy from the Lord on that day![r]
You know very well in how many ways
he helped me[s] in Ephesus.[t]

2 You then, my son,[u] be strong[v] in
the grace that is in Christ Jesus.
2And the things you have heard me
say[w] in the presence of many witnesses[x] entrust to reliable men who
will also be qualified to teach others.
3Endure hardship with us[y] like a good
soldier[z] of Christ Jesus. 4No one serving as a soldier gets involved in civilian
affairs—he wants to please his commanding officer. 5Similarly, if anyone
competes as an athlete, he does not receive the victor's crown[a] unless he
competes according to the rules. 6The
hardworking farmer should be the first
to receive a share of the crops.[b] 7Re-
flect on what I am saying, for the Lord
will give you insight into all this.
8Remember Jesus Christ, raised
from the dead,[c] descended from David.[d] This is my gospel,[e] 9for which
I am suffering[f] even to the point of
being chained[g] like a criminal. But
God's word[h] is not chained. 10There-
fore I endure everything[i] for the sake
of the elect,[j] that they too may obtain
the salvation[k] that is in Christ Jesus,
with eternal glory.[l]
11Here is a trustworthy saying:[m]

If we died with him,
we will also live with him;[n]
12if we endure,
we will also reign with him.[o]
If we disown him,
he will also disown us;[p]
13if we are faithless,
he will remain faithful,[q]
for he cannot disown himself.

A Workman Approved by God

14Keep reminding them of these
things. Warn them before God against
quarreling about words;[r] it is of no
value, and only ruins those who listen.
15Do your best to present yourself to
God as one approved, a workman who
does not need to be ashamed and who
correctly handles the word of truth.[s]
16Avoid godless chatter,[t] because
those who indulge in it will become
more and more ungodly. 17Their teaching will spread like gangrene. Among
them are Hymenaeus[u] and Philetus,
18who have wandered away from the
truth. They say that the resurrection
has already taken place,[v] and they destroy the faith of some.[w] 19Neverthe-
less, God's solid foundation stands

1:15 [m] S Ac 2:9 [n] 2Ti 4:10,11,16
1:16 [o] 2Ti 4:19 [p] ver 8,12; Mk 8:38 [q] S Ac 21:33
1:18 [r] S ver 12 [s] Heb 6:10 [t] S Ac 18:19
2:1 [u] S 1Ti 1:2 [v] S Eph 6:10
2:2 [w] 2Ti 1:13 [x] 1Ti 6:12
2:3 [y] ver 9; 2Ti 1:8; 4:5 [z] S 1Ti 1:18
2:5 [a] S 1Co 9:25
2:6 [b] 1Co 9:10
2:8 [c] S Ac 2:24 [d] S Mt 1:1 [e] Ro 2:16; 16:25
2:9 [f] S Ac 9:16 [g] S Ac 21:33 [h] S Heb 4:12
2:10 [i] Col 1:24 [j] Tit 1:1 [k] 2Co 1:6 [l] 2Co 4:17; 1Pe 5:10
2:11 [m] S 1Ti 1:15 [n] Ro 6:2-11
2:12 [o] Ro 8:17; 1Pe 4:13 [p] Mt 10:33
2:13 [q] Ro 3:3; S 1Co 1:9
2:14 [r] ver 23; 1Ti 1:4; 6:4; Tit 3:9
2:15 [s] Eph 1:13; Col 1:5; Jas 1:18
2:16 [t] Tit 3:9; 1Ti 6:20
2:17 [u] 1Ti 1:20
2:18 [v] 2Th 2:2 [w] 1Ti 1:19; 6:21

ence of many of the faithful in the last days. Those loyal to the NT gospel will suffer similar grief as they see many abandon the true Biblical faith (Mt 24:10; see 1Ti 4:1, note) and as they find their ministry rejected by those who want to be in harmony with the prevailing spirit of this evil age (see 4:3–4, note). As Paul painfully discovered, many will desert the true child of God who remains loyal to the NT gospel.

2:2 ENTRUST TO RELIABLE MEN. For comments on the church's responsibility in instructing Christians in the faith, see article on BIBLE TRAINING FOR CHRISTIANS, p. 1894.

2:3 ENDURE HARDSHIP. Ministers of the gospel who remain loyal to Christ and the gospel will be called on to endure hardship (cf. 1:8; 2:9; 2Co 11:23–29). Like soldiers, they must be willing to undergo difficulties and suffering and to wage spiritual warfare in wholehearted devotion to their Lord (Eph 6:10–18); like athletes, they must be willing to sacrifice and live lives of strict discipline (v. 5); like farmers, they must be committed to hard work and long hours (v. 6).

2:12 IF WE ENDURE. Those who "endure" (Gk *hupomenō*) and remain steadfast in the faith to the end will live (cf. v. 11; Mt 10:22; 24:13) and reign with Christ (4:18; Rev 20:4). Christ will disown on the day of judgment those who do not endure and who disown him either in word or deed (cf. Mt 10:33; 25:1–12; see article on PERSONAL APOSTASY, p. 1918).

2:13 HE WILL REMAIN FAITHFUL. Christ will most certainly carry out both his promises to us (cf. Mt 10:32) and his warnings (cf. Mt 10:33). Divine faithfulness is a comfort for those who remain loyal (1Th 5:24; 2Th 3:3; Heb 10:23) and a solemn warning for those who depart from the faith. God must remain faithful to his Word (2Sa 7:28; Jer 10:10; Tit 1:2; Rev 3:7).

2:19 FOUNDATION STANDS FIRM. Despite the fact that many may stray from the truth (Mt 24:11) and false teachers may make inroads into the church (vv. 14–18), God's purpose for his faithful followers cannot be thwarted. "God's solid foundation," i.e., the true church, cannot be destroyed. On this foundation two truths are inscribed, referring to those who belong to Christ's church. (1) God unerringly knows those who remain true to his original gospel and those who compromise its truths (cf. Ge 18:19; Ex 33:12,17; Nu 16:5; 1Co 8:1–3), and (2) those who really belong to God turn away from wickedness and false

BIBLE TRAINING FOR CHRISTIANS

2Ti 2:2 "And the things you have heard me say in the presence of many witnesses entrust to reliable men who will also be qualified to teach others."

The church has the responsibility to safeguard the true and original apostolic doctrine found in Scripture and commit it to others without compromise or corruption. This implies the necessity of Biblical instruction within the church.

(1) The Bible gives the following reasons for Biblical or theological training, whether in home, church or school:

(a) to entrust the gospel of Christ to faithful believers in order that they may know (2Ti 3:15; see Jer 2:8, note), guard (2Ti 1:14, note), and teach the true Biblical faith (1Ti 4:6,11; 2Ti 2:2) and righteous standards (see Ro 6:17, note; 1Ti 6:3);

(b) to show students the vital necessity to "contend for the faith that was once for all entrusted to the saints" (see Jude 3, note), and to give them the means by which to defend it against all false theologies (see Ac 20:31, note; Gal 1:9, note; 1Ti 4:1, note; 6:3–4; Tit 1:9; see article on FALSE TEACHERS, p. 1506);

(c) to lead students into continual growth in character through "godly teaching" (1Ti 6:3; cf. Jos 1:8; Ps 1:2–3; 119:97–100; Mt 28:20; Jn 17:14–18; 1Th 4:1; 1Ti 1:5, note; 4:7,16; 2Ti 3:16);

(d) to equip students to strengthen and bring to maturity other believers, so that together they may reflect Christ's image in the home, the local church and the body of Christ (Eph 4:11–16);

(e) to bring students to a deeper understanding and experience of God's kingdom on earth and its conflict against Satan's power (Eph 6:10–18; see article on THE KINGDOM OF GOD, p. 1430);

(f) to motivate students, through the eternal truths of the gospel, to be wholeheartedly committed to evangelizing the lost and preaching the gospel to all nations in the power of the Holy Spirit (Mt 28:18–20; Mk 16:15–20);

(g) to deepen students' experience of Christ's love, personal fellowship and gift of the Spirit (Jn 17:3,21,26; Eph 3:18–19) by urging them to follow the leading of the indwelling Holy Spirit (Ro 8:14), by bringing them into the baptism in the Holy Spirit (cf. Ac 2:4; see article on BAPTISM IN THE HOLY SPIRIT, p. 1642), and by teaching them to pray (Mt 6:9, note), fast (Mt 6:16, note) and worship, as they long for the glorious appearing of Jesus Christ with the spiritual intensity of NT saints (2Ti 4:8; Tit 2:13).

(2) It is obvious from these purposes of Biblical training that instruction must be done only by those who are fervently loyal to Scripture as God's fully inspired Word (2Ti 1:13–14; see Ezr 7:10, note; see article on THE INSPIRATION AND AUTHORITY OF SCRIPTURE, p. 1898) and to the Holy Spirit and his ministry of truth, righteousness and power (1:14).

(3) Note that true Biblical training emphasizes true righteousness (i.e., knowing, being *and* doing) rather than mere apprehension of Biblical facts or truths. The great doctrines revealed in Scripture are redemptive truths, not academic ones. As issues involving life or death, they demand a personal response and decision from both teacher and student (Jas 2:17; see Php 1:9, note).

firm,[x] sealed with this inscription:
"The Lord knows those who are
his,"[a][y] and, "Everyone who confesses the name of the Lord[z] must
turn away from wickedness."
20 In a large house there are articles
not only of gold and silver, but also of
wood and clay; some are for noble purposes and some for ignoble.[a] 21 If a
man cleanses himself from the latter,
he will be an instrument for noble purposes, made holy, useful to the Master
and prepared to do any good work.[b]
22 Flee the evil desires of youth, and
pursue righteousness, faith, love[c] and
peace, along with those who call on the
Lord[d] out of a pure heart.[e] 23 Don't
have anything to do with foolish and
stupid arguments, because you know
they produce quarrels.[f] 24 And the
Lord's servant must not quarrel; instead, he must be kind to everyone,
able to teach, not resentful.[g] 25 Those
who oppose him he must gently instruct, in the hope that God will grant
them repentance leading them to a
knowledge of the truth,[h] 26 and that
they will come to their senses and escape from the trap of the devil,[i] who
has taken them captive to do his will.

Godlessness in the Last Days

3 But mark this: There will be terrible times in the last days.[j] 2 People will be lovers of themselves, lovers
of money,[k] boastful, proud,[l] abusive,[m] disobedient to their parents,[n]
ungrateful, unholy, 3 without love, unforgiving, slanderous, without self-
control, brutal, not lovers of the good,
4 treacherous,[o] rash, conceited,[p] lovers of pleasure rather than lovers of
God— 5 having a form of godliness[q]
but denying its power. Have nothing to
do with them.[r] Tit 2:11-12

2:19 [x] Isa 28:16 [y] Ex 33:12; Nu 16:5; Jn 10:14; 1Co 8:3; Gal 4:9 [z] 1Co 1:2 **2:20** [a] Ro 9:21 **2:21** [b] 2Co 9:8; Eph 2:10; 2Ti 3:17 **2:22** [c] 1Ti 1:14; 6:11 [d] S Ac 2:21 [e] 1Ti 1:5 **2:23** [f] S ver 14 **2:24** [g] 1Ti 3:2,3 **2:25** [h] S 1Ti 2:4 **2:26** [i] 1Ti 3:7 **3:1** [j] 1Ti 4:1; 2Pe 3:3 **3:2** [k] S 1Ti 3:3 [l] Ro 1:30 [m] 2Pe 2:10-12 [n] Ro 1:30 **3:4** [o] Ps 25:3 [p] 1Ti 3:6; 6:4 **3:5** [q] S 1Ti 2:2 [r] S Ro 16:17

[a] *19* Num. 16:5 (see Septuagint)

teaching (cf. 1Ti 6:3–5,11).

2:21 CLEANSES HIMSELF. In God's external or visible church on earth there are many "articles." There are articles "for noble purposes," i.e., faithful believers who separate from evil and hold firmly to the true gospel according to Biblical revelation, and articles for "ignoble" purposes, i.e., false believers who stray from the truth (vv. 14–19). Those among the faithful who desire to be useful to the Master must keep themselves separate from all religions and professed believers advocating doctrines contrary to Scripture (v. 19). Any contact with those who teach unbiblical doctrine may be made only for the purpose of correction in love, in order that they might repent and turn to the truth (v. 25).

3:1 TERRIBLE TIMES IN THE LAST DAYS. The last days include the entire Christian era. Yet Paul prophesies through the Holy Spirit (cf. 1Ti 4:1) that things will become worse as the end approaches (cf. 2Pe 3:3; 1Jn 2:18; Jude 17–18). (1) The last days will be marked by ever-increasing wickedness in the world, a collapse of moral standards, and the multiplying of false believers and churches within God's kingdom (Mt 24:11–12; see 1Ti 4:1, note; see article on THE AGE OF THE ANTICHRIST, p. 1872). These times will be especially grievous and trying for God's true servants.

(2) Paul issues this warning in order to fortify those ministers and their churches who remain loyal to Christ and his revelation. The full blessing of salvation in Christ and the mighty outpouring of the Holy Spirit will still be available for those who remain true to NT faith and practice. The church in apostasy only means greater grace and power for those who hold fast to the original faith entrusted to the saints (Ac 4:33; Ro 5:20; Jude 3).

3:2 LOVERS OF THEMSELVES. Paul gives a list of sins that all have their root in self-love (vv. 2–4). Today some teach that a lack of love for oneself is the root of sin. Apostolic revelation teaches the opposite.

3:3 WITHOUT LOVE. In the last days believers must be prepared to face an overwhelming deluge of ungodliness. (1) The apostle prophesies that Satan will bring great destruction on the family. Children will be "disobedient to their parents" (v. 2), and men and women will be "without love" (Gk *astorgoi*). This can be translated "without family affection" and refers to a lack of the feelings of natural tenderness and love, as demonstrated by a mother who rejects her children or kills her baby, a father who abandons his family, or children who neglect to care for their aging parents (see Lk 1:17, note).

(2) Men and women will become lovers of money and pleasure and will pursue their own selfish desires (v. 2). Parenthood, with its demands for sacrificial love and nurture, will no longer be considered a worthy or dignified task (vv. 2–4). Loving parents will be replaced more and more by those who are selfish and brutal and who abandon their children (cf. Ps 113:9; 127:3–5; Pr 17:6; Tit 2:4–5; see 2Ti 4:3–4, note).

(3) If Christian parents are to save their families in the difficult times of the last days, they must shield them against the corrupt values of the society in which they live (Jn 21:15–17; Ac 20:28–30), separate them from the world's ways and refuse to let the ungodly influence their children (Ac 2:40; Ro 12:1–2; see article on SPIRITUAL SEPARATION FOR BELIEVERS, p. 1794). They must accept God's plan for the family (see Eph 5:21–25, notes; see article on PARENTS AND CHILDREN, p. 1854) and not live as the ungodly do (Lev 18:3–5; Eph 4:17). They and their families must indeed become strangers and aliens on earth (Heb 11:13–16).

6They are the kind who worm their
way[s] into homes and gain control over
weak-willed women, who are loaded
down with sins and are swayed by all
kinds of evil desires, **7**always learning
but never able to acknowledge the
truth.[t] **8**Just as Jannes and Jambres
opposed Moses,[u] so also these men
oppose[v] the truth—men of depraved
minds,[w] who, as far as the faith is concerned, are rejected. **9**But they will not
get very far because, as in the case of
those men,[x] their folly will be clear to
everyone.

Paul's Charge to Timothy

10You, however, know all about my
teaching,[y] my way of life, my purpose,
faith, patience, love, endurance, **11**persecutions, sufferings—what kinds of
things happened to me in Antioch,[z]
Iconium[a] and Lystra,[b] the persecutions I endured.[c] Yet the Lord rescued[d] me from all of them.[e] **12**In fact,
everyone who wants to live a godly life
in Christ Jesus will be persecuted,[f]

3:6 [s]Jude 4
3:7 [t]S 1Ti 2:4
3:8 [u]Ex 7:11
[v]Ac 13:8 [w]1Ti 6:5
3:9 [x]Ex 7:12; 8:18; 9:11
3:10 [y]1Ti 4:6
3:11 [z]Ac 13:14, 50 [a]S Ac 13:51
[b]Ac 14:6
[c]2Co 11:23-27
[d]S Ro 15:31
[e]Ps 34:19
3:12 [f]Jn 15:20; S Ac 14:22

3:13 [g]2Ti 2:16
[h]S Mk 13:5
3:14 [i]2Ti 1:13
3:15 [j]2Ti 1:5
[k]Jn 5:39 [l]Dt 4:6; Ps 119:98,99
3:16 [m]2Pe 1:20, 21 [n]S Ro 4:23,24
[o]Dt 29:29
3:17 [p]1Ti 6:11
[q]2Ti 2:21
4:1 [r]S Ac 10:42
[s]ver 8; S 1Ti 6:14
[t]1Ti 5:21; 6:13
4:2 [u]1Ti 4:13
[v]Gal 6:6
[w]1Ti 5:20; Tit 1:13; 2:15
[x]Tit 2:15

13while evil men and impostors will go
from bad to worse,[g] deceiving and being deceived.[h] **14**But as for you, continue in what you have learned and
have become convinced of, because
you know those from whom you
learned it,[i] **15**and how from infancy[j]
you have known the holy Scriptures,[k]
which are able to make you wise[l] for
salvation through faith in Christ Jesus.
16All Scripture is God-breathed[m] and
is useful for teaching,[n] rebuking, correcting and training in righteousness,[o] **17**so that the man of God[p] may
be thoroughly equipped for every good
work.[q]

4 In the presence of God and of
Christ Jesus, who will judge the
living and the dead,[r] and in view of his
appearing[s] and his kingdom, I give
you this charge:[t] **2**Preach[u] the
Word;[v] be prepared in season and out
of season; correct, rebuke[w] and encourage[x]—with great patience and
careful instruction. **3**For the time will
come when men will not put up with

3:5 HAVING A FORM OF GODLINESS. Paul refers to those who profess to be Christians and appear to be religious, but who do not manifest God's power that can save them from sin, selfishness and immorality. Such people tolerate immorality within their churches and teach that a person may practice the sins listed in vv. 2–4 and yet inherit salvation and God's kingdom (cf. vv. 5–9; 4:3–4; 2Pe 2:12–19; see 1Co 6:9, note).

3:8 OPPOSE THE TRUTH. False teachers in the church can often be identified by their opposition or indifference to the essential truths of the gospel (see 1Ti 4:1, note).

3:12 LIVE A GODLY LIFE . . . BE PERSECUTED. Persecution in one form or another is inevitable for those who want to live a godly life in Christ Jesus (Mt 5:10–12; 10:22; Ac 14:22; Php 1:29; 1Pe 4:12; see Mt 5:10, note). Loyalty to Christ, his truth and his righteous standards involves a constant determination not to compromise our faith or give in to the deluge of voices calling us to conform to the world and to lay aside Scriptural truth. Because of their godly standards, the faithful will be deprived of privilege and will be ridiculed; they will experience grief at seeing godliness rejected by the majority. We should all ask ourselves: have I suffered persecution because of my commitment to live in a godly manner? Or is my lack of suffering a sign that I have not stood firmly for the righteousness for which Christ died?

3:16–17 SCRIPTURE IS GOD-BREATHED. A discussion of the inspiration and authority of Scripture can be found in the article THE INSPIRATION AND AUTHORITY OF SCRIPTURE, p. 1898.

4:3–4 WILL NOT PUT UP WITH SOUND DOCTRINE. Throughout the history of the church some have always refused to love sound doctrine; yet as the end draws near, the situation will grow worse (cf. 3:1–5; 1Ti 4:1). (1) "Men will not put up with sound doctrine" (v. 3). Many will profess to be Christians, gather at churches, appear to revere God, but will not tolerate the original NT apostolic faith or the Biblical demand to separate from unrighteousness (3:5; cf. Ro 1:16; see article on SPIRITUAL SEPARATION FOR BELIEVERS, p. 1794).

(2) "They will turn their ears away from the truth" (v. 4). Sound Biblical preaching from a man of God will no longer be tolerated by many within the churches. Those who turn from the truth will want preaching that demands less than the true gospel (cf. 2:18; 3:7–8; 1Ti 6:5; Tit 1:14). They will not accept God's Word when it speaks of repentance, sin, damnation, and the necessity of holiness and separation from the world (cf. 3:15–17; Jer 5:31; Eze 33:32).

(3) "They will gather around them a great number of teachers to say what their itching ears want to hear" (v. 3). These professing believers will not seek pastors according to the standards of God's Word (cf. 1:13–14; 1Ti 3:1–10) but will seek those who conform to their own self-seeking and worldly desires. They will choose preachers with gifts of oratory, the ability to entertain, and messages that reassure them that they can remain a Christian while living according to the sinful nature (cf. Ro 8:4–13; 2Pe 2).

(4) The Holy Spirit warns all who remain faithful to God and submit to his Word to expect persecution and suffering because of righteousness (3:10–12; Mt 5:10–12). Furthermore, they must

sound doctrine.[y] Instead, to suit their
own desires, they will gather around
them a great number of teachers to say
what their itching ears want to hear.[z]
4They will turn their ears away from
the truth and turn aside to myths.[a]
5But you, keep your head in all situations, endure hardship,[b] do the work
of an evangelist,[c] discharge all the
duties of your ministry.

6For I am already being poured out
like a drink offering,[d] and the time
has come for my departure.[e] 7I have
fought the good fight,[f] I have finished
the race,[g] I have kept the faith. 8Now
there is in store for me[h] the crown of
righteousness,[i] which the Lord, the
righteous Judge, will award to me on
that day[j]—and not only to me, but
also to all who have longed for his appearing.[k]

Personal Remarks

9Do your best to come to me quickly,[l] 10for Demas,[m] because he loved
this world,[n] has deserted me and has
gone to Thessalonica.[o] Crescens has
gone to Galatia,[p] and Titus[q] to Dalmatia. 11Only Luke[r] is with me.[s] Get
Mark[t] and bring him with you, because he is helpful to me in my ministry. 12I sent Tychicus[u] to Ephesus.[v]
13When you come, bring the cloak that
I left with Carpus at Troas,[w] and my
scrolls, especially the parchments.

14Alexander[x] the metalworker did
me a great deal of harm. The Lord will
repay him for what he has done.[y]
15You too should be on your guard
against him, because he strongly opposed our message.

16At my first defense, no one came
to my support, but everyone deserted
me. May it not be held against them.[z]
17But the Lord stood at my side[a] and
gave me strength,[b] so that through
me the message might be fully proclaimed and all the Gentiles might hear
it.[c] And I was delivered from the
lion's mouth.[d] 18The Lord will rescue
me from every evil attack[e] and will
bring me safely to his heavenly kingdom.[f] To him be glory for ever and
ever. Amen.[g]

4:3 [y] S 1Ti 1:10 [z] Isa 30:10
4:4 [a] S 1Ti 1:4
4:5 [b] 2Ti 1:8; 2:3, 9 [c] Ac 21:8; Eph 4:11
4:6 [d] Nu 15:1-12; 28:7,24; Php 2:17 [e] Php 1:23
4:7 [f] S 1Ti 1:18 [g] S 1Co 9:24; Ac 20:24
4:8 [h] Col 1:5; 1Pe 1:4 [i] S 1Co 9:25 [j] S 2Ti 1:12 [k] S 1Ti 6:14
4:9 [l] ver 21; Tit 3:12
4:10 [m] Col 4:14; Phm 24 [n] 1Jn 2:15 [o] S Ac 17:1 [p] S Ac 16:6 [q] S 2Co 2:13
4:11 [r] Col 4:14; Phm 24 [s] 2Ti 1:15 [t] S Ac 12:12
4:12 [u] S Ac 20:4 [v] S Ac 18:19
4:13 [w] S Ac 16:8
4:14 [x] Ac 19:33; 1Ti 1:20 [y] Ps 28:4; 109:20; Ro 2:6; 12:19
4:16 [z] Ac 7:60
4:17 [a] Ac 23:11 [b] S Php 4:13 [c] S Ac 9:15 [d] 1Sa 17:37; Ps 22:21; Da 6:22; 1Co 15:32
4:18 [e] Ps 121:7; 2Pe 2:9 [f] ver 1 [g] S Ro 11:36

---

separate from people, churches and institutions who deny God's power in salvation and who preach a compromising gospel (3:5; see Gal 1:9, note; 1Ti 4:1–2; 2Pe 2:1; Jude 3; Rev 2:24). We must ever be loyal to the NT gospel and to God's faithful ministers who proclaim it. Doing this, we can be assured of intimate fellowship with Christ (Rev 3:20–22) and times of refreshing from the Lord (Ac 3:19–20).

4:4 THE TRUTH. God's written Word must be our ultimate guide to truth and practice. (1) We must use God's Word, given by the Holy Spirit, as our full and sufficient guide by which to judge what we believe and do. (2) The tendency within some churches to base doctrine, practice or new truth on subjective experiences, miracles, success, man-centered goals or man-made theories without solid Scriptural authentication will be one of Satan's chief means of deception in the apostasy of the last days (see Mt 24:5,11, notes; 2Th 2:11, note; see article on THE GREAT TRIBULATION, p. 1456).

4:7 FOUGHT THE GOOD FIGHT. In reviewing his life for God, Paul knows death is imminent (v. 6) and describes his Christian life in the following terms. (1) He considers the Christian life as a "good fight," the only fight worth fighting. He fought against Satan (Eph 6:12), Jewish and pagan vices (3:1–5; Ro 1:21–32; Gal 5:19–21), Judaism (Ac 14:19; 20:19; Gal 5:1–6), antinomianism and immorality in the church (3:5; 4:3; Ro 6; 1Co 5:1; 6:9–10; 2Co 12:20–21), false teachers (vv. 3–5; Ac 20:28–31; Ro 16:17–18), the distortion of the gospel (Gal 1:6–12), worldliness (Ro 12:2) and sin (Ro 6; 8:13; 1Co 9:24–27). (2) He has finished his race amid trials and temptations and has remained faithful to his Lord and Savior throughout his life (cf. 2:12; Heb 10:23; 11; 12:1–2). (3) He has kept the faith in times of severe testing, great discouragement and much trouble, both when forsaken by friends and opposed by false teachers. He never compromised the original truth of the gospel (1:13–14; 2:2; 3:14–16; 1Ti 6:12).

4:8 CROWN OF RIGHTEOUSNESS. Because Paul remained faithful to his Lord and the gospel entrusted to him, the Spirit witnessed to him that God's loving approval and the "crown of righteousness" was awaiting him in heaven. God has reserved in heaven rewards for all who keep the faith in righteousness (cf. Mt 19:27–29; 2Co 5:10).

4:8 ALL WHO HAVE LONGED FOR HIS APPEARING. The NT Christians possessed an intense longing for the Lord's return to take them from earth to be with him forever (see 1Th 4:13–18; cf. Php 3:20–21; Tit 2:13; see article on THE RAPTURE, p. 1864). A distinctive mark of God's people is that they do not feel at home in this world and are looking forward to their heavenly home (Heb 11:13–16).

4:17 THE LORD STOOD AT MY SIDE. Because of the severe persecution against Christians in Rome, no one dared identify himself or herself with the faithful and outspoken apostle (v. 16). Paul was deeply disappointed and felt deserted. But in such times he experienced the Lord's special nearness as he stood by him and strengthened him (cf. Ac 23:11; 27:23; Ro 4:20; 2Co 1:3–5; Eph 6:10; Php 4:13).

THE INSPIRATION AND AUTHORITY OF SCRIPTURE

***2Ti 3:16–17** "All Scripture is God-breathed and is useful for teaching, rebuking, correcting and training in righteousness, so that the man of God may be thoroughly equipped for every good work."*

"Scripture" as used in 2Ti 3:16 refers primarily to the OT writings (3:15). There is indication, however, that at about the time Paul wrote 2 Timothy some NT writings were already viewed as inspired and authoritative Scripture (1Ti 5:18, which quotes Lk 10:7; 2Pe 3:15–16). For us today, Scripture refers to the authoritative writings of both the OT and NT, i.e., "the Bible." They are God's original message to humanity and the only infallible witness to God's saving activity for all people.

(1) Paul affirms that all Scripture is "God-breathed" (Gk *theopneustos*, from two Greek words: *theos*, meaning "God," and *pneō*, meaning "to breathe"). Scripture is the very life and Word of God. Down to the very words of the original manuscripts, the Bible is without error, absolutely true, trustworthy and infallible. This is true not only when it speaks of salvation, ethical values and morality, but it is also without error on all subjects about which it speaks, including history and the cosmos (cf. 2Pe 1:20–21; note also the attitude of the psalmist toward Scripture in Ps 119).

(2) The OT writers were conscious of the fact that what they said to the people and what they wrote down was God's word to them (see Dt 18:18; 2Sa 23:2; see articles on THE PROPHET IN THE OLD TESTAMENT, p. 986, and THE WORD OF GOD, p. 1062). Over and over the prophets prefaced their comments with, "This is what the LORD says."

(3) Jesus Christ himself taught that Scripture is God's inspired Word to even the smallest detail (Mt 5:18). He also affirmed that all he said he received from the Father and is true (Jn 5:19,30–31; 7:16; 8:26). He further spoke of revelation yet to come (i.e., the truth revealed in the NT) from the Holy Spirit through the apostles (Jn 16:13; cf. 14:16–17; 15:26–27).

(4) To deny the full inspiration of holy Scripture, therefore, is to set aside the fundamental witness of Jesus Christ (Mt 5:18; 15:3–6; Lk 16:7; 24:25–27,44–45; Jn 10:35), the Holy Spirit (Jn 15:26; 16:13; 1Co 2:12–13; 1Ti 4:1) and the apostles (2Ti 3:16; 2Pe 1:20–21). Furthermore, to limit or disregard its inerrancy is to impair its divine authority.

(5) In his work of inspiration by his Spirit, God, while not violating the personality of the writers, moved on them in such a way that they wrote without error (2Ti 3:16; 2Pe 1:20–21; see 1Co 2:12–13, notes).

(6) The inspired Word of God is the expression of God's wisdom and character and is therefore able to give wisdom and spiritual life through faith in Christ (Mt 4:4; Jn 6:63; 2Ti 3:15; 1Pe 2:2).

(7) The Bible is God's infallible, true witness to his saving activity for humanity in Christ Jesus. For this reason Scripture is incomparable, forever finished and uniquely binding. No human words or declarations of religious institutions are equal to its authority.

(8) All doctrines, commentaries, interpretations, explanations and traditions must be judged and legitimized by the words and message in Scripture (see Dt 13:3, note; see article on FALSE TEACHERS, p. 1506).

(9) God's Word must be received, believed and obeyed as the final authority in all things pertaining to life and godliness (Mt 5:17–19; Jn 14:21; 15:10; 2Ti 3:15–16; see Ex 20:3, note). It must be used in the church as the final authority in all matters for teaching, rebuking, correcting and training in righteous living (2Ti 3:16–17). One cannot submit to Christ's lordship without submitting to God and his Word as the ultimate authority (Jn 8:31–32,37).

(10) The Bible can only be understood when we are in a right relation to the Holy Spirit. It is he who opens our minds to understand its meaning and gives us the inward witness of its authority (see 1Co 2:12, note; see article on THREE KINDS OF PEOPLE, p. 1754).

(11) We must use the inspired Word to conquer the power of sin, Satan and the world in our lives (Mt 4:4; Eph 6:12,17; Jas 1:21).

(12) Scripture must be loved, treasured and guarded by all church members who see it as God's only truth for a lost and dying world. We must safeguard its doctrines by faithfully adhering to its teaching, proclaiming its saving message, entrusting it to reliable people, and defending it against all those who would distort or destroy its eternal truths (see Php 1:16; 2Ti 1:13–14, notes; 2:2; Jude 3). No one may add anything to or take anything away from Scripture (see Dt 4:2, note; Rev 22:19, note).

(13) Finally, we should note that inerrant inspiration applies only to the original writing of the Biblical books. Thus, whenever one finds in Scripture something that appears to be in error, rather than assuming that the writer made a mistake, one should remember that three possibilities exist with regard to any apparent problem: (a) the existing copies of the original manuscript may not be totally accurate; (b) the present-day translation of the Hebrew or Greek Biblical text may be faulty; or (c) one's understanding or interpretation of the Biblical text may be inadequate or incorrect.

Final Greetings

[19]Greet Priscilla[b] and Aquila[h] and
the household of Onesiphorus.[i]
[20]Erastus[j] stayed in Corinth, and I
left Trophimus[k] sick in Miletus.[l]
[21]Do your best to get here before winter.[m] Eubulus greets you, and so do Pudens, Linus, Claudia and all the brothers.
[22]The Lord be with your spirit.[n]
Grace be with you.[o]

4:19 [h]S Ac 18:2 [i]2Ti 1:16
4:20 [j]Ac 19:22 [k]Ac 20:4; 21:29 [l]Ac 20:15,17
4:21 [m]ver 9; Tit 3:12
4:22 [n]S Gal 6:18 [o]S Col 4:18

[b]*19* Greek *Prisca,* a variant of *Priscilla*

4:22 GRACE BE WITH YOU. These are the last words of Paul recorded in Scripture, written while awaiting martyrdom in a Roman prison. From the world's perspective, Paul's life was about to end in tragic failure. (1) For thirty years he had given up everything for Christ; he had gained little but persecution and hatred from his own countrymen. His preaching had resulted in the establishment of a good number of churches, yet many of these churches were falling away from loyalty to him and from the apostolic faith (1:15). And now in prison, with all his loyal friends gone except for Luke (vv. 11,16), he awaits death. These circumstances point to apparent failure with regard to his Gentile mission. Yet, the battle-scarred apostle of the cross shows no regrets as he lays down his life for his Lord.

(2) Now, nearly 2,000 years later, Paul's influence surpasses that of all God's servants in the kingdom. His writings are a crucial part of Scripture and have led countless numbers to faith in Christ. Let no one who has remained faithful to Jesus Christ, though he or she seems to have accomplished little for God, think that death terminates the results. God takes our faithful efforts and multiplies them far beyond what we would have imagined or ever hoped for. Even our apparent failure may be seed whose harvest will be reaped bountifully by others (Jn 4:37–38).

TITUS

Outline

Introduction (1:1–4)

I. Instruction About Appointing Elders (1:5–9)
   A. Appoint Elders in Every Town (1:5)
   B. Various Qualifications for Elders (1:6–9)
      1. Personal
         a. Blameless (1:6)
         b. A Trustworthy Steward (1:7)
         c. Not Overbearing (1:7)
         d. Not Quick-tempered (1:7)
         e. Not Given to Drunkenness (1:7)
         f. Not Violent (1:7)
         g. Not Pursuing Dishonest Gain (1:7)
         h. Hospitable (1:8)
         i. Loves What Is Good (1:8)
         j. Self-Controlled (1:8)
         k. Upright (1:8)
         l. Devout/Holy (1:18)
         m. Holding Firmly to the Trustworthy Message (1:9)
         n. Able to Encourage From the Word (1:9)
         o. Able to Refute Those Who Oppose the Word (1:9)
      2. Family
         a. Husband of One Wife (1:6)
         b. Has Believing Children (1:6)
         c. His Children Are Not Wild or Disobedient (1:6)

II. Instruction Concerning False Teachers (1:10–16)
   A. Their Character (1:10)
   B. Their Conduct (1:11–12)
   C. Their Correction (1:13–16)

III. Instruction Concerning Various Groups in the Churches (2:1–15)
   A. The Scope of the Instruction (2:1–10)
   B. The Foundation for the Instruction (2:11–14)
   C. The Responsibility of Titus (2:15)

IV. Exhortations Concerning Good Works (3:1–11)
   A. Our Conduct Toward Others (3:1–2)
   B. God's Mercy Toward Us (3:3–7)
   C. Discerning What Is Profitable and Unprofitable (3:8–11)

Conclusion (3:12–15)

Author: Paul

Theme: Sound Doctrine and Good Works

Date of Writing: c. A.D. 65/66

Background

Like 1 and 2 Timothy, Titus is a personal letter from Paul to one of his younger assistants. It is called a "Pastoral Letter" because it deals with matters relating to church order and ministry. Titus, a Gentile convert (Gal 2:3), became a close companion of Paul in the apostolic ministry. Although not mentioned by name in Acts (perhaps because he was Luke's brother), Titus's closeness to the apostle Paul is indicated by (1) the thirteen references to Titus in Paul's letters, (2) his being one of Paul's converts and sons (1:4) in the ministry (like Timothy) and a trustworthy co-worker (2Co 8:23), (3) his serving as Paul's representative on at least one important mission to Corinth during Paul's third missionary journey (2Co 2:12–13; 7:6–15; 8:6,16–24), and (4) his working as a co-laborer with Paul at Crete (1:5).

Paul and Titus worked together briefly on the island of Crete (southwest of Asia Minor in the Mediterranean Sea) between Paul's first and second Roman imprisonments (see the introduction to 1 Timothy). Paul commissioned Titus to continue working with the Cretans (1:5) while he traveled on to Macedonia (cf. 1Ti 1:3). Sometime thereafter Paul wrote this letter to Titus, instructing him to complete the task that the two of them had begun. It is probable that Paul sent the letter with Zenas and Apollos who were traveling through Crete (3:13).

In this letter Paul conveys his plans to send either Artemas or Tychicus soon to replace Titus, at which time Titus was to join Paul at Nicopolis (Greece), where the apostle planned to remain during the winter (3:12). We know that this did occur, since Paul later reassigned Titus to Dalmatia (modern Yugoslavia) (2Ti 4:10).

Purpose

Paul wrote primarily to instruct Titus in his task of (1) setting in order what Paul had left unfinished in the churches of Crete, including the appointment of elders (1:5); (2) helping the churches grow in faith, in knowledge of the truth and in godly living (1:1); (3) silencing false teachers (1:11); and (4) coming to Paul after Titus is relieved by Artemas or Tychicus (3:12).

Survey

Paul discusses four main issues in this letter. (1) He instructs Titus about the character and spiritual qualifications necessary for all those who are to be selected as elders (or overseers) in the church. Elders must be godly men of proven character who have succeeded as leaders in their own homes (1:5–9). (2) Paul directs Titus to teach sound doctrine and to rebuke and silence false teachers (1:10—2:1). In the course of the letter, Paul gives two succinct summaries of sound doctrine (2:11–14; 3:4–7). (3) Paul delineates for Titus (cf. 1Ti 5:1—6:2) the proper role of older men (2:1–2), older women (2:3–4), young women (2:4–5), young men (2:6–8) and slaves (2:9–10). (4) Finally, Paul emphasizes that good works and a righteous life are the necessary fruit of genuine faith (1:16; 2:7,14; 3:1,8,14; cf. Jas 2:14–26).

Special Features

Three major features characterize this letter. (1) It contains two short classic summaries of the true nature of salvation in Christ Jesus (2:11–14; 3:4–7). (2) It emphasizes that the church and its ministry must be built on strong spiritual, theological and ethical foundations. (3) It contains one of two NT lists enumerating the required qualifications for leadership in the church's ministry (1:5–9; cf. 1Ti 3:1–13).

Reading Titus

In order to read the entire New Testament in one year, the book of Titus should be read in 2 days, according to the following schedule:
☐ 1–2 ☐ 3

NOTES

1 Paul, a servant of God[a] and an
apostle[b] of Jesus Christ for the
faith of God's elect and the knowledge
of the truth[c] that leads to godliness[d]— **2**a faith and knowledge resting on the hope of eternal life,[e] which
God, who does not lie,[f] promised before the beginning of time,[g] **3**and at
his appointed season[h] he brought his
word to light[i] through the preaching
entrusted to me[j] by the command of
God[k] our Savior,[l]

4To Titus,[m] my true son[n] in our
common faith:

Grace and peace from God the Father and Christ Jesus our Savior.[o]

Titus' Task on Crete

1:6–8Ref — 1Ti 3:2–4

5The reason I left you in Crete[p] was
that you might straighten out what
was left unfinished and appoint[a] elders[q] in every town, as I directed you.
6An elder must be blameless,[r] the
husband of but one wife, a man whose
children believe and are not open to the
charge of being wild and disobedient.
7Since an overseer[b][s] is entrusted
with God's work,[t] he must be blameless—not overbearing, not quick-tempered, not given to drunkenness, not
violent, not pursuing dishonest gain.[u]
8Rather he must be hospitable,[v] one
who loves what is good,[w] who is self-
controlled,[x] upright, holy and disciplined. **9**He must hold firmly[y] to the
trustworthy message as it has been
taught, so that he can encourage others by sound doctrine[z] and refute
those who oppose it.

10For there are many rebellious people, mere talkers[a] and deceivers, especially those of the circumcision
group.[b] **11**They must be silenced, because they are ruining whole households[c] by teaching things they ought
not to teach—and that for the sake of
dishonest gain. **12**Even one of their
own prophets[d] has said, "Cretans[e]
are always liars, evil brutes, lazy gluttons." **13**This testimony is true. Therefore, rebuke[f] them sharply, so that
they will be sound in the faith[g] **14**and
will pay no attention to Jewish myths[h]
or to the commands[i] of those who reject the truth.[j] **15**To the pure, all
things are pure,[k] but to those who are

1:1 [a] Ro 1:1; Jas 1:1 [b] S 1Co 1:1 [c] S 1Ti 2:4 [d] S 1Ti 2:2 **1:2** [e] Tit 3:7; 2Ti 1:1 [f] Nu 23:19; Heb 6:18 [g] 2Ti 1:9 **1:3** [h] 1Ti 2:6; 6:15 [i] 2Ti 1:10 [j] S 1Ti 1:11 [k] S 2Co 1:1; 1Ti 1:1 [l] S Lk 1:47 **1:4** [m] S 2Co 2:13 [n] S 1Ti 1:2 [o] S Ro 1:7 **1:5** [p] Ac 27:7 [q] S Ac 11:30 **1:6** [r] S 1Th 3:13; 1Ti 3:2 **1:7** [s] S 1Ti 3:1 [t] 1Co 4:1 [u] S 1Ti 3:3,8 **1:8** [v] S Ro 12:13 [w] 2Ti 3:3 [x] Tit 2:2, 5,6,12 **1:9** [y] S 1Co 16:13; 1Ti 1:19; 2Ti 1:13; 3:14 [z] S 1Ti 1:10 **1:10** [a] 1Ti 1:6 [b] Ac 10:45; 11:2 **1:11** [c] 1Ti 5:13 **1:12** [d] Ac 17:28 [e] Ac 2:11 **1:13** [f] S 1Ti 5:20 [g] Tit 2:2 **1:14** [h] S 1Ti 1:4 [i] S Col 2:22 [j] 2Ti 4:4 **1:15** [k] Ps 18:26; Mt 15:10,11; Mk 7:14-19; Ac 10:9-16,28; Col 2:20-22

[a] *5* Or *ordain* [b] *7* Traditionally *bishop*

1:1 TRUTH THAT LEADS TO GODLINESS. Those who say they proclaim the true gospel must be ready to have their message judged by whether it produces godliness in the lives of those who accept it. No church or denomination has the right to claim that its message or doctrine agrees with the "sound doctrine" of the apostles (v. 9; 2Ti 1:11–14; 2:2; 3:10–12) and "the sound instruction of our Lord Jesus Christ" (1Ti 6:3) if that message or doctrine does not lead its adherents to lives of godliness (v. 16, note; 1Ti 6:3; Heb 1:9; see 1Co 13:1, note).

1:2 GOD, WHO DOES NOT LIE. See Heb 6:18, note.

1:5 APPOINT ELDERS . . . AS I DIRECTED YOU. All pastoral ministries must refer back to and be based on the message of Jesus Christ as proclaimed by the apostles; i.e., they must be founded on the apostolic standard of vv. 5–9 and 1Ti 3:1–7. Such ministry is valid only as long as it holds firmly to the trustworthy Word in accordance with the teaching, the ministry and the writings of the NT (v. 9; Ac 14:23; see Eph 2:20, note).

1:6 BLAMELESS, THE HUSBAND OF BUT ONE WIFE. See article on MORAL QUALIFICATIONS FOR OVERSEERS, p. 1882.

1:7 OVERSEER. The terms "elder" (Gk *presbuteros*, v. 6) and "overseer" (Gk *episkopos*, v. 7) are interchangeable and refer to the same church office. The former points to the spiritual maturity and dignity required for the office; the latter refers to the task of overseeing the church as a steward of God's house.

1:7 HE MUST BE BLAMELESS. God insists on the highest moral standards for overseers in the church. If leaders are not above reproach, then the church will depart from righteousness because of the lack of godly role models. For more on this, see article on MORAL QUALIFICATIONS FOR OVERSEERS, p. 1882.

1:9 HOLD FIRMLY TO THE TRUSTWORTHY MESSAGE. Elders must not only meet the moral and spiritual standards listed in vv. 6–8, but they must also hold firmly to the original apostolic testimony about the saving work of Jesus Christ, love it, know it and give their lives for it. This kind of commitment is essential for two reasons. (1) They must be able to teach, encourage and exhort from God's Word in order to lead the hearts and minds of God's people to wholehearted devotion to Christ, truth and righteousness (cf. 2Ti 4:2). (2) They must be able to correct those who teach things contrary to Scripture in order to lead them to the truth (2Ti 2:24–26). If correction is refused, then they must convince other believers of the error of those teachings (see articles on THE MINISTRY GIFTS OF THE CHURCH, p. 1830, and OVERSEERS AND THEIR DUTIES, p. 1690).

1:15 ALL THINGS ARE PURE. Paul is probably speaking about the ritual purity of Jewish food laws (cf. Mt 15:10–11; Mk 7:15; 1Ti 4:3–5). Some teachers were obsessed with the distinction between pure and impure food, teaching that proper observance in these things was essential for true

corrupted and do not believe, nothing
is pure.[l] In fact, both their minds and
consciences are corrupted.[m] 16They
claim to know God, but by their actions
they deny him.[n] They are detestable,
disobedient and unfit for doing anything good.[o]

What Must Be Taught to Various Groups

2 You must teach what is in accord
with sound doctrine.[p] 2Teach the
older men[q] to be temperate,[r] worthy
of respect, self-controlled,[s] and sound
in faith,[t] in love and in endurance.
3Likewise, teach the older women to
be reverent in the way they live, not to
be slanderers[u] or addicted to much
wine,[v] but to teach what is good.
4Then they can train the younger wom-
en[w] to love their husbands and children, 5to be self-controlled[x] and pure,
to be busy at home,[y] to be kind, and
to be subject to their husbands,[z] so
that no one will malign the word of
God.[a]
6Similarly, encourage the young
men[b] to be self-controlled.[c] 7In everything set them an example[d] by doing what is good.[e] In your teaching
show integrity, seriousness 8and
soundness of speech that cannot be
condemned, so that those who oppose
you may be ashamed because they
have nothing bad to say about us.[f]
9Teach slaves to be subject to their
masters in everything,[g] to try to
please them, not to talk back to them,

1:15 [l] Ro 14:14, 23 [m] 1Ti 6:5
1:16 [n] Jer 5:2; 12:2; 1Jn 2:4 [o] Hos 8:2,3
2:1 [p] S 1Ti 1:10
2:2 [q] 1Ti 5:1 [r] 1Ti 3:2 [s] ver 5,6, 12; Tit 1:8 [t] Tit 1:13
2:3 [u] 1Ti 3:11 [v] 1Ti 3:8
2:4 [w] 1Ti 5:2
2:5 [x] ver 2,6,12; Tit 1:8 [y] 1Ti 5:14 [z] S Eph 5:22 [a] 1Ti 6:1; S Heb 4:12
2:6 [b] 1Ti 5:1 [c] ver 2,5,12; Tit 1:8
2:7 [d] S 1Ti 4:12 [e] S ver 14
2:8 [f] S 1Pe 2:12
2:9 [g] S Eph 6:5

righteousness. They ignored true moral character, inward purity and outward righteousness (v. 16). Paul emphasizes that if a person's moral condition is pure, then distinction between pure and impure foods has no moral meaning for him or her. Paul is not referring to things or actions that are morally wrong, but only to ceremonial purity.

1:16 THEY CLAIM . . . THEY DENY HIM. One of the greatest abominations in God's eyes is to profess faith in Christ and the hope of eternal life (v. 2), while at the same time to live in disobedience to him and his Word (cf. Lk 6:46; Jn 14:12; 15:10–14; 1Jn 2:4).

2:2 OLDER MEN TO BE TEMPERATE. The clear intent of this text is that older men must be an example to all believers of offering themselves to God as living sacrifices without the use of intoxicating wine (see 1Ti 3:2,11, where this word is used in reference to pastors and women). This is supported by the following facts:

(1) "Temperate" (Gk *nēphalios*) is defined in NT Greek lexicons with the primary meaning of abstaining from wine. Consider the following definitions: "The word originally connotes abstinence from alcohol" (Reinecher and Rogers); "one who does not drink wine" (*Greek Dictionary of Byzantius*, Athens, 1839); "not with wine, wineless" (Liddell and Scott); "free from all infusion of wine" (Moulton-Milligan); "holding no wine" (Kittel and Friedrich); "not mixed with wine" (Abbott-Smith); "literally, of a state of abstinence from wine" (Brown, *Dictionary of New Testament Theology*, Vol. 1). Brown adds: "*Nēphalios* occurs only in the Pastoral Letters and denotes the abstinence style of life required of bishops (1Ti 3:2), women (1Ti 3:11) and elders (Tit 2:2)." R. Laird Harris states that "it is used regularly in the classical authors meaning free from all wine" (*The Bible Today*, p. 139).

(2) Jewish writers, contemporaries of Paul and Peter, confirm the common use of the primary definition. Josephus states in reference to Jewish priests that "they are in all respects pure and abstinent (*nēphalioi*), being forbidden to drink wine while they wear the priestly robe" (*Antiquities*, 3.12.2). Philo states that the regenerate soul "abstains (*nēphein*) continually and during the whole of its life" (*Drunkedness*, 37).

(3) In the light of the foregoing, it cannot be reasonably supposed that Paul used this term without knowledge of its principal meaning (cf. 1Th 5:6, note).

2:3 NOT TO BE . . . ADDICTED TO MUCH WINE. See 1Ti 3:8, note.

2:4–5 WOMEN TO LOVE THEIR HUSBANDS AND CHILDREN. God has a distinct purpose for the woman in relation to family, home and motherhood. (1) God's desire for a wife and mother is that her attention and devotion be focused on her family. The home, husband and children must be the center of a Christian mother's world; this is her divinely appointed way of honoring the Word of God (cf. Dt 6:7; Pr 31:27; 1Ti 5:14).

(2) The woman's specific God-given tasks as they relate to the family include: (a) caring for the children God has entrusted to her (v. 4; 1Ti 5:14) as a service for the Lord (Ps 127:3; Mt 18:5; Lk 9:48); (b) being a helper and faithful companion to her husband (vv. 4–5; see Ge 2:18, note); (c) helping the father train the children in godly character and practical life skills (Dt 6:7; Pr 1:8–9; Col 3:20; 1Ti 5:10; see article on PARENTS AND CHILDREN, p. 1854); (d) providing hospitality (Isa 58:6–8; Lk 14:12–14; 1Ti 5:10); (e) using her skill to provide for the needs of the home (Pr 31:13, 15–16,18–19,22,24); (f) caring in her home for elderly parents (1Ti 5:8; Jas 1:27).

(3) Mothers who desire to fulfill God's plan for their lives and their families, but because of economic necessity must seek employment away from the children, should commit their circumstances to the Lord while praying to God to make a way for her to fulfill her God-given place and function in the home with her children (Pr 3:5–6; 1Ti 5:3; see also Eph 5:21–23, notes).

2:7 SET THEM AN EXAMPLE. See article on MORAL QUALIFICATIONS FOR OVERSEERS, p. 1882.

10and not to steal from them, but to
show that they can be fully trusted, so
that in every way they will make the
teaching about God our Savior[h] attractive.[i]
11For the grace[j] of God that brings
salvation has appeared[k] to all men.[l]
12It teaches us to say "No" to ungodli-
Heb 11:13-16 ness and worldly passions,[m] and to
live self-controlled,[n] upright and godly lives[o] in this present age, **13**while
we wait for the blessed hope—the glorious appearing[p] of our great God and
Heb 9:28 Savior, Jesus Christ,[q] **14**who gave
himself for us[r] to redeem us from all
wickedness[s] and to purify[t] for himself a people that are his very own,[u]
eager to do what is good.[v]
15These, then, are the things you
should teach. Encourage and rebuke
with all authority. Do not let anyone
despise you.

Doing What Is Good

3 Remind the people to be subject to
rulers and authorities,[w] to be obedient, to be ready to do whatever is
good,[x] **2**to slander no one,[y] to be
peaceable and considerate, and to
show true humility toward all men.

2:10 [h] S Lk 1:47 [i] Mt 5:16
2:11 [j] S Ro 3:24 [k] 2Ti 1:10 [l] S 1Ti 2:4
2:12 [m] Tit 3:3 [n] ver 2,5,6; Tit 1:8 [o] 2Ti 3:12
2:13 [p] S 1Co 1:7; S 1Ti 6:14 [q] 2Pe 1:1
2:14 [r] S Mt 20:28 [s] S Mt 1:21 [t] Heb 1:3; 1Jn 1:7 [u] Ex 19:5; Dt 4:20; 14:2; Ps 135:4; Mal 3:17; 1Pe 2:9 [v] ver 7; Pr 16:7; Mt 5:16; 2Co 8:21; Eph 2:10; Tit 3:1, 8,14; 1Pe 2:12,15; 3:13
3:1 [w] Ro 13:1; 1Pe 2:13,14 [x] S 2Ti 2:21; S Tit 2:14
3:2 [y] Eph 4:31
3:3 [z] S Eph 2:2
3:4 [a] Eph 2:7 [b] S Lk 1:47 [c] Tit 2:11
3:5 [d] S Ro 11:14 [e] S Eph 2:9 [f] 1Pe 1:3 [g] S Ac 22:16 [h] Ro 12:2
3:6 [i] S Ro 5:5
3:7 [j] S Ro 3:24 [k] S Ro 8:17 [l] Ro 8:24 [m] S Mt 25:46; Tit 1:2
3:8 [n] S 1Ti 1:15 [o] S Tit 2:14
3:9 [p] 2Ti 2:16

3At one time[z] we too were foolish,
disobedient, deceived and enslaved by
all kinds of passions and pleasures. We
lived in malice and envy, being hated
and hating one another. **4**But when the
kindness[a] and love of God our Savior[b] appeared,[c] **5**he saved us,[d] not
because of righteous things we had
done,[e] but because of his mercy.[f] He
saved us through the washing[g] of rebirth and renewal[h] by the Holy Spirit,
6whom he poured out on us[i] generously through Jesus Christ our Savior,
7so that, having been justified by his
grace,[j] we might become heirs[k] having the hope[l] of eternal life.[m] **8**This
is a trustworthy saying.[n] And I want
you to stress these things, so that
those who have trusted in God may be
careful to devote themselves to doing
what is good.[o] These things are excellent and profitable for everyone.
9But avoid[p] foolish controversies
and genealogies and arguments and
quarrels[q] about the law,[r] because
these are unprofitable and useless.[s]
10Warn a divisive person once, and
then warn him a second time. After

[q] S 2Ti 2:14 [r] Tit 1:10-16 [s] 2Ti 2:14

2:11 THE GRACE OF GOD. Vv. 11–14 describe the character and purpose of God's saving grace. According to Paul, saving grace (1) instructs believers to decisively reject the ungodly passions, pleasures and values of the present age and regard them as abominable (v. 12; cf. Ro 1:18–32; 2Ti 2:22; 1Jn 2:15–17), and (2) commands and empowers believers to live "upright and godly lives," while waiting expectantly for the blessed hope and appearing of Christ Jesus (v. 13; Gal 5:5; Col 1:5; 2Ti 4:8; see article on FAITH AND GRACE, p. 1720).

2:13 THE BLESSED HOPE. The "blessed hope" for which every Christian should long is "the glorious appearing of our great God and Savior, Jesus Christ" and our union with him for eternity (see Jn 14:3, note; see article on THE RAPTURE, p. 1864). This hope is capable of being realized at any time (cf. Mt 24:42; Lk 12:36–40; Jas 5:7–9). Thus, Christians should never surrender their prayerful hope that perhaps today the trumpet will sound and the Lord will return.

2:14 GAVE HIMSELF FOR US. Christ shed his blood on the cross (1Pe 1:18–19) in order (1) to redeem us from all wickedness and the desire to defy God's law and holy standards (cf. 1Jn 3:4), and (2) to make us a holy people, separated from sin and the world to be God's very own special possession. Those struggling with sin and Satan's power should know that if Christ died for their redemption, how much more will he now give adequate grace to live victoriously over the power of sin and evil (Ro 5:9–11).

3:1 SUBJECT TO RULERS. Since it is important for the ongoing witness and furtherance of the gospel, believers must be obedient to civil and governmental authorities, obey civil law, be good citizens and act as respectful neighbors (cf. Mt 17:24–27; 22:15–22; Ro 13:1–7; 1Pe 2:13–17). The only exception occurs when governmental law conflicts with Biblical teaching (cf. Ac 5:29).

3:5 WASHING OF REBIRTH. This refers to the new birth of believers, symbolically pictured in Christian baptism (see article on REGENERATION, p. 1589). "Renewal by the Holy Spirit" points to the constant imparting of divine life to believers as they surrender their lives to God (cf. Ro 12:2).

3:6 POURED OUT ON US GENEROUSLY. Paul's reference to the Holy Spirit's work points back to the outpouring of the Spirit on the day of Pentecost and afterward (cf. Ac 2:33; 11:15). God supplies an abundant and adequate supply of his grace and power as a result of the new birth and the Spirit's work in us.

3:10 DIVISIVE PERSON ... HAVE NOTHING TO DO WITH HIM. Divisive persons here are false teachers who teach opinions and doctrines that have no Biblical basis. After a second admonition proves ineffective in dealing with such persons, they must be rejected, i.e., expelled from church membership. Those who reject Biblical truth and substitute their own ideas and opinions are "warped and sinful" (v. 11).

that, have nothing to do with him.[t]
11You may be sure that such a man is
warped and sinful; he is self-con-
demned.

Final Remarks

12As soon as I send Artemas or
Tychicus[u] to you, do your best to
come to me at Nicopolis, because I
have decided to winter there.[v] 13Do
everything you can to help Zenas the
lawyer and Apollos[w] on their way and
see that they have everything they
need. 14Our people must learn to devote themselves to doing what is
good,[x] in order that they may provide
for daily necessities and not live unproductive lives.

15Everyone with me sends you
greetings. Greet those who love us in
the faith.[y]

Grace be with you all.[z]

3:10 [t] S Ro 16:17
3:12 [u] S Ac 20:4
[v] 2Ti 4:9,21
3:13 [w] S Ac 18:24
3:14 [x] S Tit 2:14
3:15 [y] 1Ti 1:2
[z] S Col 4:18

3:14 DOING WHAT IS GOOD. Paul emphasizes that "doing what is good" is the result of the believer's conversion and life in the Holy Spirit (vv. 4–8). Believers must "set an example by doing what is good" (2:7), and must be "eager to do what is good" (2:14), "ready to do whatever is good" (v. 1) and "careful to devote themselves to doing what is good" (v. 8).

PHILEMON

Outline

Christian Greetings (1–3)

I. Appreciation for Philemon (4–7)
  A. An Object of Thankful Prayer (4–6)
  B. An Occasion of Great Joy (7)

II. Appeal for Onesimus (8–21)
  A. An Entreaty Rather Than a Command (8–11)
  B. Motives for Sending Onesimus Back (12–16)
  C. A Substitutionary Appeal (17–19)
  D. A Positive Response Expected From Philemon (20–21)

Closing Matters (22–25)
  A. Hopes to Make a Visit Soon (22)
  B. Greetings from Paul's Companions (23–24)
  C. Benediction (25)

Author: Paul

Theme: Reconciliation

Date of Writing: c. A.D. 62

Background

Paul wrote this "prison letter" (vv. 1,9) as a personal letter to a man named Philemon, most likely during Paul's first imprisonment at Rome (Ac 28:16–31). The identical names mentioned in Philemon (vv. 1–2,10,23–24) and Colossians (Col 4:9–10,12,14,17) indicate that Philemon lived at Colosse, and that both letters were written and delivered at the same time.

Philemon was a slaveowner (v. 16) and church member at Colosse (compare vv. 1–2 with Col 4:17), perhaps a convert of Paul (v. 19). Onesimus was Philemon's slave who had run away to Rome; there he came into contact with Paul, who led him to Christ. A strong bond of friendship developed between the two of them (vv. 9–13). Paul now reluctantly sends Onesimus back to Philemon, accompanied by Paul's co-worker Tychicus and this letter (cf. Col 4:7–9).

Purpose

Paul wrote Philemon to deal with the specific problem of his runaway slave Onesimus. According to Roman law, a runaway slave could be punished by death. Paul intercedes on Onesimus's behalf with Philemon and petitions him to graciously receive Onesimus back as a fellow believer and as Paul's companion, with the same love with which he would receive Paul himself.

Survey

Paul's appeal to Philemon goes as follows: (1) He entreats Philemon as a Christian brother (vv. 8–9,20–21) to receive Onesimus back, not as a slave but as a brother in Christ (vv. 15–16). (2) In a wordplay Paul observes that Onesimus (whose name means "useful") was formerly "useless," but now is "useful" to both Paul and Philemon (vv. 10–12). (3) Paul wishes Onesimus could remain with him in Rome but sends him back instead to his lawful master (vv. 13–14). (4) Paul offers himself as a substitute for Onesimus's debt and reminds Philemon of his indebtedness to Paul (vv. 17–19). The letter concludes with greetings from some of Paul's co-workers in Rome (vv. 23–24) and with a benediction (v. 25).

Special Features

Three major features characterize this letter. (1) This is the shortest of all Paul's letters. (2) More than any other NT portion, it illustrates how Paul and the early church dealt with the problem of Roman slavery. Rather than attacking it directly or stirring up armed rebellion, Paul set forth Christian principles that removed the harshness of Roman slavery and eventually led to its banishment altogether within Christianity. (3) It provides unique insight into Paul's inner life, for he identifies himself with a slave so closely that he calls Onesimus "my very heart" (v. 12).

Reading Philemon

In order to read the entire New Testament in one year, the book of Philemon should be read in 1 day: □ Philemon

NOTES

1Paul, a prisoner[a] of Christ Jesus,
and Timothy[b] our brother,[c]

To Philemon our dear friend and fellow worker,[d] 2to Apphia our sister, to
Archippus[e] our fellow soldier[f] and to
the church that meets in your home:[g]

3Grace to you and peace from God
our Father and the Lord Jesus Christ.[h]

Thanksgiving and Prayer

4I always thank my God[i] as I remember you in my prayers,[j] 5because
I hear about your faith in the Lord
Jesus[k] and your love for all the
saints.[l] 6I pray that you may be active
in sharing your faith, so that you will
have a full understanding of every good
thing we have in Christ. 7Your love has
given me great joy and encouragement,[m] because you, brother, have refreshed[n] the hearts of the saints.

Paul's Plea for Onesimus

8Therefore, although in Christ I
could be bold and order you to do what
you ought to do, 9yet I appeal to you[o]
on the basis of love. I then, as Paul—
an old man and now also a prisoner[p]
of Christ Jesus— 10I appeal to you for
my son[q] Onesimus,[a][r] who became
my son while I was in chains.[s] 11For-
merly he was useless to you, but now
he has become useful both to you and
to me.

12I am sending him—who is my very
heart—back to you. 13I would have
liked to keep him with me so that he
could take your place in helping me
while I am in chains[t] for the gospel.
14But I did not want to do anything
without your consent, so that any favor
you do will be spontaneous and not
forced.[u] 15Perhaps the reason he was
separated from you for a little while
was that you might have him back for
good— 16no longer as a slave,[v] but
better than a slave, as a dear brother.[w] He is very dear to me but even
dearer to you, both as a man and as a
brother in the Lord.

17So if you consider me a partner,[x]
welcome him as you would welcome
me. 18If he has done you any wrong or
owes you anything, charge it to me.[y]
19I, Paul, am writing this with my own
hand.[z] I will pay it back—not to mention that you owe me your very self. 20I
do wish, brother, that I may have some
benefit from you in the Lord; refresh[a]
my heart in Christ. 21Confident[b] of
your obedience, I write to you, knowing
that you will do even more than I ask.

22And one thing more: Prepare a
guest room for me, because I hope to
be[c] restored to you in answer to your
prayers.[d]

23Epaphras,[e] my fellow prisoner[f]
in Christ Jesus, sends you greetings.
24And so do Mark,[g] Aristarchus,[h]
Demas[i] and Luke, my fellow workers.[j]

25The grace of the Lord Jesus Christ
be with your spirit.[k]

1:1 [a] ver 9,23; S Eph 3:1 [b] S Ac 16:1 [c] 2Co 1:1 [d] S Php 2:25 **1:2** [e] Col 4:17 [f] Php 2:25 [g] S Ro 16:5 **1:3** [h] S Ro 1:7 **1:4** [i] S Ro 1:8 [j] S Ro 1:10 **1:5** [k] S Ac 20:21 [l] S Col 1:4; 1Th 3:6 **1:7** [m] 2Co 7:4,13 [n] ver 20; Ro 15:32; 1Co 16:18 **1:9** [o] 1Co 1:10 [p] ver 1,23; S Eph 3:1 **1:10** [q] S 1Th 2:11 [r] Col 4:9 [s] S Ac 21:33 **1:13** [t] ver 10; S Ac 21:33 **1:14** [u] 2Co 9:7; 1Pe 5:2 **1:16** [v] 1Co 7:22 [w] Mt 23:8; S Ac 1:16; 1Ti 6:2 **1:17** [x] 2Co 8:23 **1:18** [y] Ge 43:9 **1:19** [z] S 1Co 16:21 **1:20** [a] ver 7; 1Co 16:18 **1:21** [b] S 2Co 2:3 **1:22** [c] Php 1:25; 2:24; Heb 13:19 [d] 2Co 1:11; Php 1:19 **1:23** [e] Col 1:7 [f] ver 1; Ro 16:7; Col 4:10 **1:24** [g] S Ac 12:12 [h] S Ac 19:29 [i] Col 4:14; 2Ti 4:10 [j] ver 1 **1:25** [k] S Gal 6:18

[a] *10 Onesimus* means *useful.*

---

1 A PRISONER OF CHRIST JESUS. Paul wrote this letter to Philemon during Paul's two-year imprisonment in Rome (vv. 1,9; cf. Ac 28:30).

2 THE CHURCH THAT MEETS IN YOUR HOME. Philemon evidently made his home available as a place of worship for the believers in Colosse. House churches were common in NT times (cf. Ro 16:5; 1Co 16:19; Col 4:15). It is not until the third century that separate church buildings are mentioned.

10 ONESIMUS. Onesimus, a slave belonging to Philemon, had run away, possibly taking with him some of his master's goods (vv. 15–16,18–19). Somehow he reached Rome, came into contact with Paul and was converted to Christ under Paul's ministry. Paul now writes this letter, asking Philemon to take Onesimus back with kindness, love and forgiveness.

12 SENDING HIM . . . BACK TO YOU. The NT did not advocate a direct movement to free the slaves, even Christian slaves. To have initiated such an effort in the socio-political conditions of NT times would have destroyed the church and the cause of Christ. Instead of direct confrontation, guidelines were laid down for both the Christian slave and master that would undermine slavery from within and eventually bring about its abolition (vv. 10,12,14–17,21; see v. 16, note).

14 SPONTANEOUS AND NOT FORCED. Onesimus should be set free if he so desires. The ethics and love demanded in the gospel of Christ all point to this fact. Yet, Paul does not state it directly. He wanted Philemon and all masters to do it voluntarily.

16 AS A DEAR BROTHER. Slavery cannot exist among believers who have seen the truth of Christian brotherhood. Onesimus must no longer be treated as a slave, but as a fellow believer and dear brother, one who in God's sight is equal with the apostle Paul and with Philemon (see Col 3:22, note).

HEBREWS

Outline

I. The Argument: Christ and the Christian Faith Superior to Judaism (1:1—10:18)
  A. In Revelation (1:1—4:13)
    Jesus Christ is the Full and Final Revelation of God to Humanity
    1. Superior to the Prophets (1:1–3)
    2. Superior to the Angels (1:4—2:18)
       Exhortation: Danger of Neglect (2:1–4)
    3. Superior to Moses (3:1–6)
       Exhortation: Danger of Unbelief (3:7–19)
    4. Superior to Joshua (4:1–13)
  B. In Mediation (4:14—10:18)
    As Our Great High Priest, Jesus Far Surpasses the OT Levitical Priesthood
    1. Superior in His Qualifications (4:14—7:25)
       Exhortation: Danger of Remaining Spiritually Immature (5:11—6:3)
       Exhortation: Danger of Falling Away (6:4–20)
    2. Superior in His Character (7:26–28)
    3. Superior in His Ministry (8:1—10:18)
       a. Located in a Better Sanctuary (8:1–5)
       b. Based on a Better Covenant (8:6–13)
       c. Performed Through a Better Service (9:1–22)
       d. Fulfilled by a Better Sacrifice (9:23—10:18)

II. The Application: Exhortation to Steadfastness (10:19—13:17)
  A. In the Realm of Salvation (10:19–38)
  B. In the Realm of Faith (10:39—11:40)
    1. The Nature of Faith (10:39—11:3)
    2. Examples of Faith From the Old Testament (11:4–38)
    3. The Vindication of Faith: Completed in Christ (11:39–40)
  C. In the Realm of Endurance (12:1–13)
  D. In the Realm of Holiness (12:14—13:17)
    1. The Priority of Holiness (12:14–29)
    2. The Practice of Holiness (13:1–17)

Conclusion (13:18–25)

Author: Undesignated

Theme: The Better Covenant

Date of Writing: A.D. 67–69 (uncertain)

Background

The destination of this letter is uncertain, though Rome is a likely possibility. The book's title in the oldest Greek manuscripts is simply "To the Hebrews." However, its content reveals that the letter was written to Jewish Christians. The author's use of the Septuagint (Greek translation of the OT) when quoting from the OT indicates that the readers were probably Greek-speaking Jews outside of Palestine. The phrase "those from Italy send you their greetings" (13:24) most likely means that the author was writing to Rome and was including greetings from Italian believers living away from their homeland. The recipients may have consisted of house churches within the larger church community at Rome, some of whom were on the verge of forsaking their faith in Jesus and turning back to their former Jewish faith because of persecution and discouragement.

The author of Hebrews is not identified in its original title nor in the book, though he was well known to his readers (13:18–24). For some reason, his identity was lost by the end of the first century. Subsequently in early church tradition (second to fourth centuries) many different opinions were expressed about who may have written Hebrews. The opinion that Paul wrote Hebrews did not prevail until the fifth century.

Many conservative Bible scholars today believe Paul's authorship is unlikely, since the author's polished and Alexandrian writing style, reliance on the Septuagint, manner of introducing OT quotations, method of argument and teaching, structure of the argumentation, and exclusion of personal identification are all distinctly different from that of Paul. Moreover, while Paul always appeals to his firsthand revelation from Christ (cf. Gal 1:11–12), this writer places himself among the second-generation Christians to whom the gospel was confirmed by eyewitnesses of Jesus' ministry (2:3). Among the men mentioned by name in the NT, Luke's description of Apollos in Ac 18:24–28 most perfectly fits the profile of the author of Hebrews.

Regardless of who wrote Hebrews, this much is certain: the author wrote with the apostolic fullness of the Spirit and with apostolic insight, revelation and authority. The absence of any reference in Hebrews to the destruction of the Jerusalem temple and its Levitical worship strongly suggests the author wrote before A.D. 70.

Purpose

Hebrews was written primarily to Jewish Christians who were undergoing persecution and discouragement. The writer strives to strengthen their faith in Christ by carefully explaining the superiority and finality of God's revelation and redemption in Jesus Christ. He shows that God's redemptive provisions under the old covenant have been fulfilled and made obsolete by Jesus' coming and the establishment of the new covenant through his atoning death. The writer challenges his readers (1) to hold on to their confession of Christ until the end, (2) to go on to spiritual maturity and (3) not to turn back to condemnation by abandoning faith in Jesus Christ.

Survey

Hebrews is more like a sermon than a letter. The author describes his work as a "word of exhortation" (13:22). It has three major divisions. (1) First, Jesus as the powerful Son of God (1:1–3) is declared to be God's full revelation to humanity—greater than the prophets (1:1–3), angels (1:4—2:18), Moses (3:1–6) and Joshua (4:1–11). A solemn warning occurs in this division about the consequences of spiritually drifting from the faith or hardening one's heart in unbelief (2:1–3; 3:7—4:2). (2) The second division presents Jesus as the high priest whose qualifications (4:14—5:10, 6:19—7:25), character (7:26–28) and ministry (8:1—10:18) are perfect and everlasting. A solemn warning is given about remaining spiritually immature or even "falling away" after becoming partakers of Christ (5:11—6:12). (3) The final division (10:19—13:17) strongly exhorts believers to persevere in salvation, faith, suffering and holiness.

Special Features

Eight major features characterize this letter. (1) It is unique among NT letters in its format: "it begins like a treatise, proceeds like a sermon, and concludes like a letter" (Origen). (2) It is the NT's most polished book, approaching classical Greek style more nearly than any other NT writer (except perhaps for Luke in Lk 1:1–4). (3) It is the only NT writing that develops the concept of Jesus' high priestly ministry. (4) Its Christology is richly varied, with more than twenty names and titles for Christ being used. (5) Its key word is "better"

(13 times). Jesus is better than the angels and all OT mediators. He offers a better rest, covenant, hope, priesthood, sacrifice/blood atonement, and better promises. (6) It contains the foremost chapter in the Bible on faith (ch. 11). (7) It is saturated with OT references and allusions that provide a rich insight into early Christian interpretation of OT history and worship, particularly in the realm of typology. (8) It warns about the dangers of spiritual apostasy more than any other NT writing.

Reading Hebrews

In order to read the entire New Testament in one year, the book of Hebrews should be read in 17 days, according to the following schedule:
□ 1 □ 2 □ 3 □ 4:1–13 □ 4:14—5:10 □ 5:11—6:20 □ 7 □ 8 □ 9:1–10 □ 9:11–28 □ 10:1–18 □ 10:19–39 □ 11:1–16 □ 11:17–40 □ 12:1–13 □ 12:14–29 □ 13

NOTES

The Son Superior to Angels

1 In the past God spoke[a] to our
forefathers through the prophets[b] at many times and in various
ways,[c] **2**but in these last days[d] he
has spoken to us by his Son,[e] whom
he appointed heir[f] of all things, and
through whom[g] he made the universe.[h] **3**The Son is the radiance of
God's glory[i] and the exact representation of his being,[j] sustaining all
things[k] by his powerful word. After he
had provided purification for sins,[l] he
sat down at the right hand of the Majesty in heaven.[m] **4**So he became as
much superior to the angels as the
name he has inherited is superior to
theirs.[n]

5For to which of the angels did God ever say,

"You are my Son;
today I have become your
Father[a]"[b]?[o]

Or again,

"I will be his Father,
and he will be my Son"[c]?[p]

6And again, when God brings his firstborn[q] into the world,[r] he says,

"Let all God's angels worship
him."[d][s]

7In speaking of the angels he says,

"He makes his angels winds,
his servants flames of fire."[e][t]

8But about the Son he says,

"Your throne, O God, will last for
ever and ever,[u]
and righteousness will be the
scepter of your kingdom.
9You have loved righteousness and
hated wickedness;
therefore God, your God, has set
you above your
companions[v]
by anointing you with the oil[w]
of joy."[f][x]

10He also says,

"In the beginning, O Lord, you laid
the foundations of the
earth,
and the heavens are the work of
your hands.[y]
11They will perish, but you remain;
they will all wear out like a
garment.[z]

1:1 [a]Jn 9:29; Heb 2:2,3; 4:8; 12:25 [b]Lk 1:70; Ac 2:30 [c]Nu 12:6, 8
1:2 [d]Dt 4:30; Heb 9:26; 1Pe 1:20 [e]ver 5; S Mt 3:17; Heb 3:6; 5:8; 7:28 [f]Ps 2:8; Mt 11:27; S 28:18 [g]S Jn 1:3 [h]Heb 11:3
1:3 [i]Jn 1:14 [j]S Jn 14:9 [k]Col 1:17 [l]Tit 2:14; Heb 7:27; 9:11-14 [m]S Mk 16:19
1:4 [n]Eph 1:21; Php 2:9,10; Heb 8:6
1:5 [o]Ps 2:7; S Mt 3:17 [p]2Sa 7:14
1:6 [q]Jn 3:16; S Col 1:18 [r]Heb 10:5 [s]Dt 32:43 (LXX and DSS) Ps 97:7
1:7 [t]Ps 104:4
1:8 [u]S Lk 1:33
1:9 [v]Php 2:9 [w]Isa 61:1,3 [x]Ps 45:6,7
1:10 [y]Ps 8:6; Zec 12:1
1:11 [z]Isa 34:4; 51:6; S Heb 12:27

[a]*5* Or *have begotten you* [b]*5* Psalm 2:7
[c]*5* 2 Samuel 7:14; 1 Chron. 17:13
[d]*6* Deut. 32:43 (see Dead Sea Scrolls and Septuagint) [e]*7* Psalm 104:4
[f]*9* Psalm 45:6,7

1:1–2 SPOKEN TO US BY HIS SON. These verses establish a major theme of this letter: in the past God used the prophets as his foremost instrument of revelation, but now he has spoken or revealed himself to us by his Son Jesus Christ, who is supreme over all things. God's Word through his Son is final; it fulfills and transcends all previous words by God (see article on THE WORD OF GOD, p. 1062). Absolutely nothing, neither prophets (v. 1) nor angels (v. 4), has greater authority than Christ. He is the only way to eternal salvation and the only mediator between God and humans. The author confirms Christ's supremacy by listing seven great revelations about Christ (vv. 2–3).

1:3 SAT DOWN AT THE RIGHT HAND. After Christ provided the forgiveness of our sins by his death on the cross, he took his place of authority at God's right hand. Christ's redeeming activity in heaven involves his ministry as divine mediator (8:6; 13:15; 1Jn 2:1–2), high priest (2:17–18; 4:14–16; 8:1–3), intercessor (7:25) and baptizer in the Spirit (Ac 2:33).

1:4 SUPERIOR TO THE ANGELS. Just as Jesus is superior to the prophets because he is the Son, so he is superior to angels because he is the Son (vv. 4–14). Angels had played an important part in the giving of the OT covenant (Dt 33:2; Ac 7:53; Gal 3:19). The author, writing to Jewish believers, establishes Christ's superiority to the angels by quoting from the OT. For more on angels, see article on ANGELS AND THE ANGEL OF THE LORD, p. 340.

1:5 TODAY I HAVE BECOME YOUR FATHER. See Jn 1:14, note.

1:8 ABOUT THE SON ... O GOD. The author is pointing out the deity of Christ (see Jn 1:1, note).

1:9 LOVED RIGHTEOUSNESS AND HATED WICKEDNESS. It is not enough for God's children to love righteousness; they must also hate evil. We see this clearly in Christ's devotion to righteousness (Isa 11:5) and his hatred of wickedness in his life, ministry and death (see Jn 3:19, note; 11:33, note). (1) Christ's faithfulness to his Father while on earth, as demonstrated by his love of righteousness and hatred of wickedness, is the basis for God's anointing of his Son. In the same way, our anointing will come only as we identify with our Master's attitude toward righteousness and evil (Ps 45:7).

(2) Our love of righteousness and hatred of evil will increase by two means: (a) by growing in heartfelt love and compassion for those whose lives are being destroyed by sin, and (b) by experiencing more and more oneness with our God and Savior, who "loved righteousness and hated wickedness" (see Ps 94:16; 97:10; Pr 8:13; Am 5:15; Ro 12:9; 1Jn 2:15; Rev 2:6).

12You will roll them up like a robe;
like a garment they will be
changed.
But you remain the same,[a]
and your years will never
end."[g][b]

13To which of the angels did God ever
say,

"Sit at my right hand[c]
until I make your enemies
a footstool[d] for your feet"[h]?[e]

14Are not all angels ministering spirits[f] sent to serve those who will inherit[g] salvation?[h]

Warning Against Drifting Away

2 We must pay more careful attention, therefore, to what we have
heard, so that we do not drift away.[i]
2For if the message spoken[j] by angels[k] was binding, and every violation
and disobedience received its just punishment,[l] 3how shall we escape if we
ignore such a great salvation?[m] This
salvation, which was first announced
by the Lord,[n] was confirmed to us by
those who heard him.[o] 4God also testified to it by signs, wonders and various miracles,[p] and gifts of the Holy
Spirit[q] distributed according to his
will.[r]

Jesus Made Like His Brothers

5It is not to angels that he has subjected the world to come, about which
we are speaking. 6But there is a place
where someone[s] has testified:

"What is man that you are mindful
of him,
the son of man that you care for
him?[t]
7You made him a little[i] lower than
the angels;
you crowned him with glory and
honor
8 and put everything under his
feet."[j][u]

In putting everything under him, God
left nothing that is not subject to him.
Yet at present we do not see everything
subject to him. 9But we see Jesus, who
was made a little lower than the angels, now crowned with glory and hon-
or[v] because he suffered death,[w] so

1:12 [a]Heb 13:8 [b]Ps 102:25-27 **1:13** [c]ver 3; S Mk 16:19 [d]Jos 10:24; Heb 10:13 [e]Ps 110:1; S Mt 22:44 **1:14** [f]Ps 91:11; 103:20; Da 7:10 [g]Mt 25:34; Mk 10:17; S Ac 20:32 [h]S Ro 11:14; Heb 2:3; 5:9; 9:28 **2:1** [i]S Ro 11:22 **2:2** [j]S Heb 1:1 [k]Dt 33:2; Ac 7:53; Gal 3:19 [l]Heb 10:28 **2:3** [m]Heb 10:29; 12:25 [n]Heb 1:2 [o]S Lk 1:2 **2:4** [p]Mk 16:20; S Jn 4:48 [q]S 1Co 12:4 [r]S Eph 1:5 **2:6** [s]Heb 4:4 [t]Job 7:17; Ps 144:3 **2:8** [u]Ps 8:4-6; S Mt 22:44 **2:9** [v]ver 7; Ac 3:13; S Php 2:9 [w]Php 2:7-9 1Pe 4:10-11

[g] *12* Psalm 102:25-27 [h] *13* Psalm 110:1
[i] *7* Or *him for a little while*; also in verse 9
[j] *8* Psalm 8:4-6

1:13 THE ANGELS. For a discussion of the role that angels play in our lives, see article on ANGELS AND THE ANGEL OF THE LORD, p. 340.

2:1–3 SO THAT WE DO NOT DRIFT AWAY. One reason the writer of Hebrews emphasizes the superiority of God's Son and his revelation is to stress to those who have experienced salvation that they must take with intense seriousness the original witness and doctrine of Christ and the apostles. Therefore, we must pay close attention to God's Word, our relation to Christ and the leading of the Holy Spirit (Gal 5:16–25). (1) Neglect, carelessness or apathy is fatal. A believer who, because of negligence, allows the truth and teachings of the gospel to slip, is in great danger of being swept along downstream past a fixed landing place and of failing to gain security.

(2) Like the recipients of this letter, all Christians are tempted to become indifferent to God's Word. Because of carelessness and indifference, we may easily begin to pay less attention to God's warnings (v. 2), stop persevering in our struggle against sin (12:4; 1Pe 2:11), and slowly drift away from God's Son, Jesus Christ (vv. 1–3; 6:4–8; 10:31–32; see Ro 8:13, note).

2:3 CONFIRMED TO US. The apostolic gospel was first announced by the Lord Jesus and then confirmed by (1) the firsthand testimony of those who had actually heard and known Jesus during his earthly life (cf. Ac 1:4; 1Jn 1:1), and (2) the testimony of God himself, who bore witness to the authenticity of the gospel proclamation of salvation by "signs, wonders and various miracles" (v. 4) and by spiritual gifts (cf. 1Co 12:4–11). Thus the early church proclaimed the gospel not only in word but also "with power, with the Holy Spirit and with deep conviction" (1Th 1:5).

2:4 GOD ALSO TESTIFIED TO IT. The Holy Spirit through the writer of Hebrews reaffirms that God confirmed and supported the gospel message with signs, wonders, miracles and gifts of the Spirit (Ac 2:22). After his resurrection Christ promised that miraculous confirmation of the gospel message would accompany all who believe (see article on SIGNS OF BELIEVERS, p. 1513). God desires that the believer's witness be more than simply words (Mk 16:20; Jn 10:25; Ac 2:22,43; 1Co 2:4–5; Gal 3:5; 1Th 1:5; 1Pe 1:12; see Ac 4:30, note).

2:8 WE DO NOT SEE EVERYTHING SUBJECT. In this fallen world dominated by Satan, all is not yet in subjection to Christ. Yet Jesus is already crowned with glory and honor in heaven (v. 9); all the evil powers in the world are doomed to defeat and judgment.

2:9 TASTE DEATH FOR EVERYONE. Christ experienced the humiliation and suffering of death for all people. His death was not, as some claim, a "limited atonement." Since he bore the punishment of the sins of all humanity, his death avails for all who accept him (see Ro 3:25, note).

that by the grace of God he might taste
death for everyone.[x]
10In bringing many sons to glory, it
was fitting that God, for whom and
through whom everything exists,[y]
should make the author of their salvation perfect through suffering.[z]
11Both the one who makes men holy[a]
and those who are made holy[b] are of
the same family. So Jesus is not
ashamed to call them brothers.[c] **12**He
says,

"I will declare your name to my
brothers;
in the presence of the
congregation I will sing
your praises."[k][d]

13And again,

"I will put my trust in him."[l][e]

And again he says,

"Here am I, and the children God
has given me."[m][f]

14Since the children have flesh and
blood,[g] he too shared in their humanity[h] so that by his death he might destroy[i] him who holds the power of
death—that is, the devil[j]— **15**and
free those who all their lives were held
in slavery by their fear[k] of death.
16For surely it is not angels he helps,
but Abraham's descendants.[l] **17**For
this reason he had to be made like his
brothers[m] in every way, in order that
he might become a merciful[n] and
faithful high priest[o] in service to
God,[p] and that he might make atonement for[n] the sins of the people.[q]
18Because he himself suffered when he
was tempted, he is able to help those
who are being tempted.[r]

Jesus Greater Than Moses

3 Therefore, holy brothers,[s] who
share in the heavenly calling,[t] fix
your thoughts on Jesus, the apostle
and high priest[u] whom we confess.[v]
2He was faithful to the one who appointed him, just as Moses was faithful
in all God's house.[w] **3**Jesus has been
found worthy of greater honor than
Moses,[x] just as the builder of a house
has greater honor than the house it-

2:9 [x]2Co 5:15
2:10 [y]S Ro 11:36
[z]Lk 24:26;
Heb 5:8,9; 7:28
2:11 [a]Heb 13:12
[b]S Eph 5:26
[c]S Mt 28:10
2:12 [d]Ps 22:22;
68:26
2:13 [e]Isa 8:17
[f]Isa 8:18; Jn 10:29
2:14 [g]1Co 15:50;
Eph 6:12
[h]S Jn 1:14
[i]Ge 3:15;
1Co 15:54-57;
2Ti 1:10
[j]1Jn 3:8
2:15 [k]S 2Ti 1:7
2:16 [l]S Lk 3:8
2:17 [m]ver 14;
S Php 2:7
[n]Heb 5:2
[o]Heb 3:1; 4:14,15;
5:5,10; 7:26,28;
8:1,3; 9:11
[p]Heb 5:1
[q]S Ro 3:25
2:18 [r]Heb 4:15
3:1 [s]Heb 2:11
[t]S Ro 8:28
[u]S Heb 2:17
[v]1Ti 6:12;
Heb 4:14; 10:23;
2Co 9:13
3:2 [w]ver 5;
Nu 12:7
3:3 [x]Dt 34:12

[k]*12* Psalm 22:22 [l]*13* Isaiah 8:17
[m]*13* Isaiah 8:18 [n]*17* Or *and that he might turn aside God's wrath, taking away*

2:10 PERFECT THROUGH SUFFERING. This does not mean that Christ needed to be made morally and spiritually perfect. What was perfected was his role as author or leader—one who goes before to make a way for others to follow. He could only be the perfect Savior of all those who believe if he first endured suffering and death as a human. His obedience and death qualified him to be the perfect representative of fallen humanity and to bear the penalty of sin on their behalf.

2:11 THE ONE WHO MAKES MEN HOLY. "The one who makes men holy" is Christ (cf. 10:10,14,29; 13:12) and "those who are made holy" are those who have been redeemed from sin's guilt and power and set apart as God's people. Christ's consecration of himself to die for us provides the way for our sanctification (see article on SANCTIFICATION, p. 1956).

2:14 SHARED IN THEIR HUMANITY. Because those whom Jesus came to redeem are flesh and blood (i.e., human), Jesus also had to take on human nature. For only as a true human being could he qualify to redeem the human race from Satan's power. Christ died to destroy Satan's power over those who believe (cf. 1Jn 3:8) and to deliver them from the fear of death (Rev 1:18) by promising eternal life with God (Jn 17:3; Rev 21–22).

2:17 MERCIFUL AND FAITHFUL HIGH PRIEST. Christ became one with humankind in order to become a high priest and so to represent believers before God. (1) In this ministry, the Son's death makes atonement by removing God's wrath against us because of our sins (cf. Ro 1:18; 5:10). As a result we can now approach God in confidence. (2) The Son mercifully sympathizes with us when we are tempted and comes to our aid because he, as a human, has experienced suffering, trials and temptations, yet did not sin (cf. 4:14–15; 2Co 6:2).

2:18 HE IS ABLE TO HELP. When we are tempted to be disloyal to God and give in to sin, we must pray to Christ, who triumphed over temptation and now, as our high priest, promises to give us the strength and grace to resist sin. Our responsibility is to draw near to him in time of trouble; his responsibility is to give help in every time of need (see 4:16, note).

3:1 HOLY BROTHERS. This letter was probably written to a group of Jewish Christians who, after their conversion to Christ, had been exposed to persecution and discouragement (10:32–39). That the readers were true born-again Christians is apparent from the following: (1) 2:1–4, which speaks of the danger of their drifting away from salvation; (2) 3:1, where the readers are called "holy brothers, who share in the heavenly calling"; (3) 3:6, where they are called God's house. For further evidence that the readers were saved by Christ, see 3:12–19; 4:14–16; 6:9–12,18–20; 10:19–25,32–36; 12:1–29; 13:1–6,10–14,20–21.

3:1 APOSTLE AND HIGH PRIEST. Under the old covenant Moses (vv. 2–5) was the apostle (i.e., one sent by God with his authority) and Aaron (5:1–5) the high priest of God's people. Now under the new covenant, these two offices are combined in the person of Jesus.

self. 4For every house is built by someone, but God is the builder of everything.[y] 5Moses was faithful as a
servant[z] in all God's house,[a] testifying to what would be said in the future.
6But Christ is faithful as a son[b] over
God's house. And we are his house,[c]
if we hold on[d] to our courage and the
hope[e] of which we boast.

Warning Against Unbelief

7So, as the Holy Spirit says:[f]

"Today, if you hear his voice,
8 do not harden your hearts[g]
as you did in the rebellion,
during the time of testing in the desert,
9where your fathers tested and tried me
and for forty years saw what I did.[h]
10That is why I was angry with that generation,
and I said, 'Their hearts are always going astray,
and they have not known my ways.'
11So I declared on oath in my anger,[i]
'They shall never enter my rest.' [j]"[o][k]

12See to it, brothers, that none of
you has a sinful, unbelieving heart that
turns away from the living God.[l]
13But encourage one another daily,[m]
as long as it is called Today, so that
none of you may be hardened by sin's
deceitfulness.[n] 14We have come to
share in Christ if we hold firmly[o] till
the end the confidence[p] we had at
first. 15As has just been said:

"Today, if you hear his voice,
do not harden your hearts
as you did in the rebellion."[p][q]

16Who were they who heard and rebelled? Were they not all those Moses
led out of Egypt?[r] 17And with whom
was he angry for forty years? Was it
not with those who sinned, whose bodies fell in the desert?[s] 18And to whom
did God swear that they would never

3:4 [y] Ge 1:1
3:5 [z] Ex 14:31 [a] ver 2; Nu 12:7
3:6 [b] S Heb 1:2 [c] S 1Co 3:16; 1Ti 3:15 [d] ver 14; S Ro 11:22; Heb 4:14 [e] Ro 5:2; Heb 6:11,18,19; 7:19; 11:1
3:7 [f] Ac 28:25; Heb 9:8; 10:15
3:8 [g] ver 15; Heb 4:7
3:9 [h] Nu 14:33; Dt 1:3; Ac 7:36
3:11 [i] Dt 1:34,35 [j] Heb 4:3,5 [k] Ps 95:7-11
3:12 [l] S Mt 16:16
3:13 [m] Heb 10:24,25 [n] Jer 17:9; Eph 4:22
3:14 [o] ver 6 [p] S Eph 3:12
3:15 [q] ver 7,8; Ps 95:7,8; Heb 4:7
3:16 [r] Nu 14:2
3:17 [s] Nu 14:29; Ps 106:26; 1Co 10:5

[o] *11* Psalm 95:7-11 [p] *15* Psalm 95:7,8

3:6 IF WE HOLD ON TO OUR COURAGE AND THE HOPE. The conditional statements in the book of Hebrews deserve special attention (see 2:3; 3:6,14; 10:26), for they warn that salvation is conditional. (1) The security of believers is maintained only as they cooperate with God's grace by persevering in faith and holiness to the end of their earthly existence. This truth was emphasized by Christ (Jn 8:31; Rev 2:7,11,17,25–26; 3:5, 11–12,21) and is a repeated admonition in the letter to the Hebrews (2:1; 3:6,14; 4:16; 7:25; 10:34–38; 12:1–4,14). (2) The reassurance of salvation for church members who willfully sin, so prevalent in some circles today, finds no place in the NT (Rev 3:14–16; see Lk 12:42–48, note; Jn 15:6, note).

3:7 THE HOLY SPIRIT SAYS. Along with other NT writers, the writer of Hebrews regards Scripture in the ultimate and truest sense as the words of the Holy Spirit rather than the mere words of humans (cf. 9:8; 10:15; 2Ti 3:16; 2Pe 1:21; see article on THE INSPIRATION AND AUTHORITY OF SCRIPTURE, p. 1898). When we read the Bible, we should not think that we are reading merely the opinions of Matthew, Paul, Peter, John, etc., but the very words of the Holy Spirit revealing God's will for the church and for our lives.

3:7–11 TODAY, IF YOU HEAR HIS VOICE. Quoting Ps 95:7–11, the writer refers to Israel's disobedience in the desert after their exodus from Egypt as a warning for believers under the new covenant. Because of the Israelites' failure to resist sin and remain loyal to God, they were barred from entering into the promised land (see Nu 14:29–43, notes; Ps 95:7–10, notes). Likewise, believers must realize that they too may fail to enter God's rest in heaven if they disobey and allow their hearts to grow hard.

3:8 DO NOT HARDEN YOUR HEARTS. The Holy Spirit speaks to us concerning sin, righteousness and judgment (Jn 16:8–11; Ro 8:11–14; Gal 5:16–25). If we ignore his voice, our hearts will increasingly grow hard and unyielding until they are no longer sensitive to God's Word or the desires of the Spirit (v. 7). Commitment to truth and to righteous living will no longer be a priority, but we will more and more seek pleasure in the ways of the world rather than God's ways (v. 10). The Holy Spirit warns us that God will not go on pleading with us indefinitely if we harden our hearts in rebellion (vv. 7–11; Ge 6:3). There is a point of no return (vv. 10–11; 6:6; 10:26).

3:12 TURNS AWAY FROM THE LIVING GOD. At regular intervals throughout this letter, the author warns his readers about the danger of falling away from the faith. For more on this subject, see article on PERSONAL APOSTASY, p. 1918.

3:13 ENCOURAGE ONE ANOTHER DAILY. Many ministers fail to "encourage" or admonish believers to continue in the faith. Such ministers do not preach the urgent warnings of the apostles (Col 1:21–23; 1Ti 4:1,16; Jas 5:19–20; 2Pe 1:8–11; 1Jn 2:23–25), the writer of Hebrews (2:3; 3:6–19) or Jesus himself (Mt 24:11–13; Jn 15:1–6).

3:18 THEY WOULD NEVER ENTER HIS REST. The possibility of the believer missing God's promised rest is illustrated by the Israelites who failed to enter the promised land after Moses

PERSONAL APOSTASY

***Heb 3:12** "See to it, brothers, that none of you has a sinful, unbelieving heart that turns away from the living God."*

Apostasy (Gk *apostasia*) appears twice in the NT as a noun (Ac 21:21; 2Th 2:3) and here in Heb 3:12 as a verb (Gk *aphistēmi*, translated "turn away"). The Greek term is defined as a falling away, defection, rebellion, abandonment, withdrawal or turning from what one has formerly turned to.

(1) To apostatize means to sever one's saving relationship with Christ or to withdraw from vital union with and true faith in him (see article on FAITH AND GRACE, p. 1720). Thus, individual apostasy is possible only for those who have first experienced salvation, regeneration and renewal through the Holy Spirit (cf. Lk 8:13; Heb 6:4–5); it is not a mere denial of NT doctrine by the unsaved within the visible church. Apostasy may involve two separate, though related, aspects: (a) theological apostasy, i.e., a rejection of all or some of the original teachings of Christ and the apostles (1Ti 4:1; 2Ti 4:3), and (b) moral apostasy, i.e., the former believer ceases to remain in Christ and instead becomes enslaved again to sin and immorality (Isa 29:13; Mt 23:25–28; Ro 6:15–23; 8:6–13).

(2) The Bible issues urgent warnings about apostasy, designed both to alert us to the deadly danger of abandoning our union with Christ and to motivate us to persevere in faith and obedience. The divine purpose of these warning passages must not be weakened by the view that states, "the warnings are real, but the possibility of actual apostasy is not." Rather, we must see these warnings as speaking to the reality of our probationary period, and we should regard them with alarm if we want to attain final salvation. A few of the many NT warning passages are: Mt 24:4–5,11–13; Jn 15:1–6; Ac 11:21–23; 14:21–22; 1Co 15:1–2; Col 1:21–23; 1Ti 4:1,16; 6:10–12; 2Ti 4:2–5; Heb 2:1–3; 3:6–8,12–14; 6:4–6; Jas 5:19–20; 2Pe 1:8–11; 1Jn 2:23–25.

(3) Examples of actual apostasy can be found in Ex 32; 2Ki 17:7–23; Ps 106; Isa 1:2–4; Jer 2:1–9; Ac 1:25; Gal 5:4; 1Ti 1:18–20; 2Pe 2:1,15,20–22; Jude 4,11–13; see article on THE AGE OF THE ANTICHRIST, p. 1872, for comments on apostasy predicted to occur within the professing church in the last days of this age.

(4) The steps that lead to apostasy are as follows:

(a) Believers, through unbelief, fail to take the truths, exhortations, warnings, promises and teachings of God's Word with utmost seriousness (Mk 1:15; Lk 8:13; Jn 5:44,47; 8:46).

(b) As the realities of the world become greater than the realities of God's heavenly kingdom, believers gradually cease to draw near to God through Christ (Heb 4:16; 7:19,25; 11:6).

(c) Through the deceitfulness of sin, they become increasingly tolerant of sin in their own lives (1Co 6:9–10; Eph 5:5; Heb 3:13). They no longer love righteousness and hate wickedness (see Heb 1:9, note).

(d) Through hardness of heart (Heb 3:8,13) and rejecting God's way (3:10), they ignore the repeated voice and rebuke of the Holy Spirit (Eph 4:30; 1Th 5:19–22).

(e) The Holy Spirit is grieved (Eph 4:30; cf. Heb 3:7–8) and his fire put out (1Th 5:19) and his temple violated (1Co 3:16). He eventually departs from the former believers (Jdg 16:20; Ps 51:11; Ro 8:13; 1Co 3:16–17; Heb 3:14).

(5) If apostasy continues on its course unchecked, individuals may eventually reach the point when no second beginning is possible. (a) Those who once had a saving experience with Christ but deliberately and continually harden their hearts to the Spirit's voice (Heb 3:7–19), continue to sin willfully (Heb 10:26), and refuse to repent and return to God may reach a point of no return where repentance and salvation are no longer possible (Heb 6:4–6; see Dt 29:18–21, note; 1Sa 2:25, note; Pr 29:1, note). There is a limit to God's patience (see 1Sa 3:11–14; Mt 12:31–32; 2Th 2:9–11; Heb 10:26–29,31; 1Jn 5:16). (b) This point of no return cannot be defined in advance. Therefore, the only safeguard against the danger of ultimate apostasy is found in the admonition: "Today, if you hear his voice, do not harden your hearts" (Heb 3:7–8,15; 4:7).

(6) It must be emphasized that while apostasy is a danger for all who drift from the faith (Heb 2:1–3) and fall away from God (6:6), it is not made complete without constant and willful sinning against the voice of the Holy Spirit (see Mt 12:31, note on sin against the Holy Spirit).

(7) Those who by unbelieving hearts depart from God (Heb 3:12) may think they are Christians but their indifference to the demands of Christ and the Spirit and the warnings of Scripture points otherwise. Because of this possibility of self-deception, Paul urges all those claiming salvation to "examine yourselves to see whether you are in the faith; test yourselves" (2Co 13:5, note).

(8) Those who genuinely become concerned about their spiritual condition and find in their hearts the desire to return to God in repentance have sure evidence they have not committed unpardonable apostasy. Scripture clearly affirms that God does not want anyone to perish (2Pe 3:9; cf. Isa 1:18–19; 55:6–7) and declares that God will receive all who were once under saving grace if they repent and return to him (compare Gal 5:4 with 4:19; 1Co 5:1–5 with 2Co 2:5–11; see also Lk 15:11–24; Ro 11:20–23; Jas 5:19–20; Rev 3:14–20; note the example of Peter, Mt 16:16; 26:74–75; Jn 21:15–22).

enter his rest[t] if not to those who disobeyed[q]?[u] **19**So we see that they
were not able to enter, because of their
unbelief.[v]

A Sabbath-Rest for the People of God

4 Therefore, since the promise of entering his rest still stands, let us
be careful that none of you be found to
have fallen short of it.[w] **2**For we also
have had the gospel preached to us,
just as they did; but the message they
heard was of no value to them, because
those who heard did not combine it
with faith.[r][x] **3**Now we who have believed enter that rest, just as God has
said,

"So I declared on oath in my
anger,
'They shall never enter my
rest.'"[s][y]

And yet his work has been finished
since the creation of the world. **4**For
somewhere he has spoken about the
seventh day in these words: "And on
the seventh day God rested from all his
work."[t][z] **5**And again in the passage
above he says, "They shall never enter
my rest."[a]
6It still remains that some will enter
that rest, and those who formerly had
the gospel preached to them did not go
in, because of their disobedience.[b]
7Therefore God again set a certain day,
calling it Today, when a long time later
he spoke through David, as was said
before:

"Today, if you hear his voice,
do not harden your hearts."[u][c]

8For if Joshua had given them rest,[d]
God would not have spoken[e] later
about another day. **9**There remains,
then, a Sabbath-rest for the people of
God; **10**for anyone who enters God's
rest also rests from his own work,[f]
just as God did from his.[g] **11**Let us,
therefore, make every effort to enter
that rest, so that no one will fall by following their example of disobedience.[h]
12For the word of God[i] is living[j]
and active.[k] Sharper than any double-
edged sword,[l] it penetrates even to
dividing soul and spirit, joints and marrow; it judges the thoughts and attitudes of the heart.[m] **13**Nothing in all
creation is hidden from God's sight.[n]

3:18 [t]Nu 14:20-23; Dt 1:34,35 [u]Heb 4:6
3:19 [v]Ps 78:22; 106:24; Jn 3:36
4:1 [w]Heb 12:15
4:2 [x]1Th 2:13
4:3 [y]Ps 95:11; Dt 1:34,35; Heb 3:11
4:4 [z]Ge 2:2,3; Ex 20:11
4:5 [a]Ps 95:11; S ver 3
4:6 [b]ver 11; Heb 3:18
4:7 [c]Ps 95:7,8; Heb 3:7,8,15
4:8 [d]Jos 22:4 [e]S Heb 1:1
4:10 [f]Lev 23:3; Rev 14:13 [g]ver 4
4:11 [h]ver 6; Heb 3:18
4:12 [i]S Mk 4:14; Lk 5:1; 11:28; Jn 10:35; Ac 12:24; 1Th 2:13; 2Ti 2:9; 1Pe 1:23; 1Jn 2:14; Rev 1:2, 9 [j]Ac 7:38; 1Pe 1:23 [k]Isa 55:11; Jer 23:29; 1Th 2:13 [l]Eph 6:17; S Rev 1:16 [m]1Co 14:24,25
4:13 [n]Ps 33:13-15; Pr 5:21; Jer 16:17; 23:24; Da 2:22

[q] *18* Or *disbelieved* [r] *2* Many manuscripts *because they did not share in the faith of those who obeyed* [s] *3* Psalm 95:11; also in verse 5 [t] *4* Gen. 2:2 [u] *7* Psalm 95:7,8

had led them out of Egypt (see Nu 14:29, note; Dt 1:26, note). The writer points out two things: (1) The Israelites had experienced God's redemptive power (v. 16), seen God's mighty works (v. 9), and yet were disobedient because they would not believe God's promises or heed his warnings (vv. 18–19). Therefore, they were destroyed in the desert (v. 17) and failed to enter the promised land. (2) The Israelites' initial experiences with God did not guarantee their safe arrival in Canaan. By failing to persevere, they threw aside their only source of security: the grace, mercy and presence of "the living God" (v. 12).

4:1 HIS REST . . . HAVE FALLEN SHORT OF IT. Ceasing to persevere in faith and in obedience to Jesus results in the failure to reach the eternal promised rest of heaven (cf. 11:16; 12:22–24). (1) The phrase "let us be careful" is spoken in the light of this terrible possibility and of God's judgment. (2) Perseverance in faith requires that we continue to draw near to God through Christ with sincere determination (v. 16; 7:25).

4:3 ENTER THAT REST. Only we who have believed the saving message of Christ enter God's spiritual rest. Christ takes our burdens and sins and gives us the "rest" of his forgiveness, salvation and Spirit (Mt 11:28). However, in this life our rest is only partial, for we are pilgrims plodding through a harsh world. One by one, as we die in the Lord, we enter his perfect rest in heaven (see next note).

4:9 REMAINS, THEN, A SABBATH-REST. God's promised rest is not only earthly, but heavenly as well (vv. 7–8; cf. 13:14). For believers, there remains an eternal rest in heaven (Jn 14:1–3; cf. Heb 11:10,16). Entering this final rest means ceasing from the labors, sufferings and persecutions common to our lives on this earth (cf. Rev 14:13), participating in God's own rest, and experiencing unending joy, delight, love and fellowship with God and other redeemed saints. It will be a seventh day without end (Rev 21–22).

4:11 MAKE EVERY EFFORT TO ENTER. In light of the glorious blessing of the eternal state and the terrible fate of those who fail to enter it, believers must diligently strive to arrive at the heavenly home of God's people. This requires pressing on toward the heavenly goal (Php 3:13–14) and clinging to the Word (v. 12) in devotion to prayer (v. 16).

4:12 THE WORD OF GOD. The Word of God determines who will enter into God's rest. It is a sharp sword that cuts into our innermost being in order to discern whether our thoughts and motives are spiritual or unspiritual. It has two edges, either cutting to save our lives or judging us to eternal death (cf. Jn 6:63; 12:48). Therefore, our response to God's Word should be to draw near to Jesus as our high priest (vv. 14–16; see article on THE WORD OF GOD, p. 1062).

Everything is uncovered and laid bare
before the eyes of him to whom we
must give account.

Jesus the Great High Priest

14Therefore, since we have a great
high priest[o] who has gone through the
heavens,[v][p] Jesus the Son of God,[q]
let us hold firmly to the faith we profess.[r] **15**For we do not have a high
priest[s] who is unable to sympathize
with our weaknesses, but we have one
who has been tempted in every way,
just as we are[t]—yet was without
sin.[u] **16**Let us then approach[v] the
throne of grace with confidence,[w] so
that we may receive mercy and find
grace to help us in our time of need.

5 Every high priest is selected from
among men and is appointed to
represent them in matters related to
God,[x] to offer gifts and sacrifices[y]
for sins.[z] **2**He is able to deal gently
with those who are ignorant and are
going astray,[a] since he himself is subject to weakness.[b] **3**This is why he has
to offer sacrifices for his own sins, as
well as for the sins of the people.[c]
4No one takes this honor upon himself; he must be called by God, just as
Aaron was.[d] **5**So Christ also did not
take upon himself the glory[e] of becoming a high priest.[f] But God said[g]
to him,

"You are my Son;
today I have become your
Father.[w]"[x][h]

6And he says in another place,

"You are a priest forever,
in the order of
Melchizedek.[i]"[y][j]

7During the days of Jesus' life on
earth, he offered up prayers and petitions[k] with loud cries and tears[l] to
the one who could save him from
death, and he was heard[m] because of
his reverent submission.[n] **8**Although
he was a son,[o] he learned obedience
from what he suffered[p] **9**and, once
made perfect,[q] he became the source
of eternal salvation for all who obey
him **10**and was designated by God to be Heb 7:25
high priest[r] in the order of Melchizedek.[s]

Warning Against Immaturity

6:4–6Ref — Heb 10:26–31

11We have much to say about this,
but it is hard to explain because you

v 14 Or *gone into heaven* w 5 Or *have begotten you* x 5 Psalm 2:7 y 6 Psalm 110:4

4:14 o S Heb 2:17 p Heb 6:20; 8:1; 9:24 q S Mt 4:3 r S Heb 3:1 **4:15** s S Heb 2:17 t Heb 2:18 u S 2Co 5:21 **4:16** v S Heb 7:19 w S Eph 3:12 **5:1** x Heb 2:17 y Heb 8:3; 9:9 z Heb 7:27 **5:2** a Isa 29:24; Heb 2:18; 4:15 b Heb 7:28 **5:3** c Lev 9:7; 16:6; Heb 7:27; 9:7 **5:4** d Ex 28:1; Nu 14:40; 18:7 **5:5** e Jn 8:54 f S Heb 2:17 g S Heb 1:1 h Ps 2:7; S Mt 3:17 **5:6** i ver 10; Ge 14:18; Heb 6:20; 7:1-22 j Ps 110:4; Heb 7:17,21 **5:7** k Lk 22:41-44 l Mt 27:46,50; Lk 23:46 m Ps 22:24 n Mk 14:36 **5:8** o S Heb 1:2 p S Php 2:8 **5:9** q S Heb 2:10 **5:10** r ver 5; S Heb 2:17 s S ver 6

4:14 WE HAVE A GREAT HIGH PRIEST. See 8:1, note on Jesus' ministry as high priest.

4:16 APPROACH THE THRONE OF GRACE WITH CONFIDENCE. Because Christ sympathizes with our weaknesses (v. 15), we can confidently approach the heavenly throne, knowing that our prayers and petitions are welcomed and desired by our heavenly Father (cf. 10:19–20). It is called the "throne of grace" because from it flow God's love, help, mercy, forgiveness, spiritual power, outpouring of the Holy Spirit, spiritual gifts, the fruit of the Spirit, and all that we need under any circumstances. One of the greatest blessings of salvation is that Christ is now our high priest, opening a way to his personal presence whereby we can always seek the help we need.

5:1 EVERY HIGH PRIEST. Two qualifications are necessary for a valid priesthood: (1) The priest must be sympathetic, gentle and patient with those who go astray through ignorance, unintentional sin or weakness (v. 2; 4:15; cf. Lev 4; Nu 15:27–29). (2) He must be appointed by God (vv. 4–6). Christ qualified in both ways (see Lev 8:2, note).

5:6 THE ORDER OF MELCHIZEDEK. Melchizedek is a mysterious OT figure who appears in Ge 14 as God's priest of Salem (perhaps Jerusalem, 7:1; Ge 14:18; Ps 110:1–4) before the time of the Levitical priesthood. Christ's priesthood is of the same kind as Melchizedek's (see 7:1–3, notes).

5:7 LOUD CRIES AND TEARS. This passage probably refers to the intensity of Jesus' prayer in the Garden of Gethsemane. Jesus' prayer was "heard" not in the sense that God removed all that was involved in death, but in the sense that he received God's aid to undergo his appointed suffering. There will be times when we too face trials and our fervent prayers seem to go unanswered. In such times, we must remember that Jesus was tested in the same way and that God will give us sufficient grace to undergo what he allows for our lives (see Mt 26:39, note).

5:8 HE LEARNED OBEDIENCE. Christ learned by experience the suffering and cost that often result from faithful obedience to God in a corrupt world (cf. 12:2; Isa 50:4–6; Php 2:8). He became a perfect Savior and high priest because his suffering and death were accomplished without sin. Therefore, he was qualified in every way (vv. 1–6) to bring us eternal salvation (v. 9; see 2:10, note).

5:9 SALVATION FOR ALL WHO OBEY HIM. The eternal salvation gained by Jesus' suffering (v. 8) is made available only to those who are obedient to him through faith. The faith that saves is an obedient faith (Jn 8:31; Ro 1:5; 16:26; Jas 2:17–26).

are slow to learn. **12**In fact, though by this time you ought to be teachers, you need someone to teach you the elementary truths[t] of God's word all over again. You need milk, not solid food![u] **13**Anyone who lives on milk, being still an infant,[v] is not acquainted with the teaching about righteousness. **14**But solid food is for the mature,[w] who by constant use have trained themselves to distinguish good from evil.[x]

6 Therefore let us leave[y] the elementary teachings[z] about Christ and go on to maturity, not laying again the foundation of repentance from acts that lead to death,[za] and of faith in God, **2**instruction about baptisms,[b] the laying on of hands,[c] the resurrection of the dead,[d] and eternal judgment. **3**And God permitting,[e] we will do so.

Warning Against Falling Away

4It is impossible for those who have once been enlightened,[f] who have tasted the heavenly gift,[g] who have shared in the Holy Spirit,[h] **5**who have tasted the goodness[i] of the word of God[j] and the powers of the coming age, **6**if they fall away, to be brought back to repentance,[k] because[a] to their loss they are crucifying the Son of God[l] all over again and subjecting him to public disgrace.

7Land that drinks in the rain often falling on it and that produces a crop useful to those for whom it is farmed receives the blessing of God. **8**But land that produces thorns and thistles is worthless and is in danger of being cursed.[m] In the end it will be burned.

9Even though we speak like this, dear friends,[n] we are confident of better things in your case—things that accompany salvation. **10**God is not unjust; he will not forget your work and the love you have shown him as you have helped his people and continue to help them.[o] **11**We want each of you to show this same diligence to the very end, in order to make your hope[p] sure. **12**We do not want you to become lazy, but to imitate[q] those who through faith and patience[r] inherit what has been promised.[s]

The Certainty of God's Promise

13When God made his promise to Abraham, since there was no one greater for him to swear by, he swore by himself,[t] **14**saying, "I will surely bless you and give you many descendants."[b][u] **15**And so after waiting patiently, Abraham received what was promised.[v]

16Men swear by someone greater than themselves, and the oath confirms what is said and puts an end to all argument.[w] **17**Because God wanted to make the unchanging[x] nature of his purpose very clear to the heirs of what was promised,[y] he confirmed it with an oath. **18**God did this so that, by two unchangeable things in which it is impossible for God to lie,[z] we who have

5:12 [t] Heb 6:1 [u] 1Co 3:2; 1Pe 2:2
5:13 [v] S 1Co 14:20
5:14 [w] S 1Co 2:6 [x] Isa 7:15
6:1 [y] Php 3:12-14 [z] Heb 5:12 [a] Heb 9:14
6:2 [b] Jn 3:25 [c] S Ac 6:6 [d] S Ac 2:24; Ac 17:18,32
6:3 [e] Ac 18:21
6:4 [f] Heb 10:32 [g] Eph 2:8 [h] Gal 3:2
6:5 [i] Ps 34:8 [j] S Heb 4:12
6:6 [k] 2Pe 2:21; 1Jn 5:16 [l] S Mt 4:3
6:8 [m] Ge 3:17,18; Isa 5:6; 27:4
6:9 [n] S 1Co 10:14
6:10 [o] S Mt 10:40,42; 1Th 1:3
6:11 [p] S Heb 3:6
6:12 [q] Heb 13:7 [r] 2Th 1:4; Jas 1:3; Rev 13:10; 14:12 [s] Heb 10:36
6:13 [t] Ge 22:16; Lk 1:73
6:14 [u] Ge 22:17
6:15 [v] Ge 21:5
6:16 [w] Ex 22:11
6:17 [x] ver 18; Ps 110:4 [y] Ro 4:16; Heb 11:9
6:18 [z] Nu 23:19; Tit 1:2

[z] 1 Or *from useless rituals* [a] 6 Or *repentance while* [b] 14 Gen. 22:17

5:12 MILK, NOT SOLID FOOD. See article on THREE KINDS OF PEOPLE, p. 1754.

5:14 DISTINGUISH GOOD FROM EVIL. Those who are weak and immature in the faith lack spiritual sensitivity and discernment with regard to what is good and what is evil in this life, and what honors God and what dishonors God. Mature believers, on the other hand, have trained their senses to carefully distinguish between good and evil through the continual practice of righteousness and obedience. Having learned to love righteousness and hate wickedness (see 1:9, note), having renewed their minds according to principles of righteousness (Ro 12:1–2), and being enabled by the Holy Spirit to see things from God's point of view, they are able to receive the solid food of God's Word and grow toward the full stature of Christ (cf. Eph 4:13).

6:4–6 IT IS IMPOSSIBLE ... TO BE BROUGHT BACK TO REPENTANCE. Here the author of Hebrews discusses the consequences of apostasy (falling away from the faith). For more on this, see article on PERSONAL APOSTASY, p. 1918.

6:6 IF THEY FALL AWAY. This phrase (Gk *parapesontas*, from *parapiptō*) is an aorist participle and should be rendered in the past tense—literally, "having fallen away." The word "if" does not appear in any Greek text. The writer of Hebrews presents "falling away" as a real possibility.

6:9–20 BETTER THINGS IN YOUR CASE. The writer is confident that his readers have not entered into the apostasy described in vv. 4–8. He assures them that for those who remain loyal to Christ in faith and love (vv. 10–12), their hope of eternal salvation is certain and unchangeable, because God cannot lie and his promises remain steadfast (vv. 13–20).

6:18 IMPOSSIBLE FOR GOD TO LIE. Because God cannot lie, his promises to Abraham are true (v. 14). God's truthfulness applies not only to his word to Abraham, but also to his Word in all Scripture. That is, because Scripture is the inspired Word of God, it is completely true and trust-

fled to take hold of the hope[a] offered to us may be greatly encouraged. 19 We have this hope as an anchor for the soul, firm and secure. It enters the inner sanctuary behind the curtain,[b] 20 where Jesus, who went before us, has entered on our behalf.[c] He has become a high priest[d] forever, in the order of Melchizedek.[e]

Melchizedek the Priest

7 This Melchizedek was king of Salem[f] and priest of God Most High.[g] He met Abraham returning from the defeat of the kings and blessed him,[h] 2 and Abraham gave him a tenth of everything. First, his name means "king of righteousness"; then also, "king of Salem" means "king of peace." 3 Without father or mother, without genealogy,[i] without beginning of days or end of life, like the Son of God[j] he remains a priest forever.

4 Just think how great he was: Even the patriarch[k] Abraham gave him a tenth of the plunder![l] 5 Now the law requires the descendants of Levi who become priests to collect a tenth from the people[m]—that is, their brothers—even though their brothers are descended from Abraham. 6 This man, however, did not trace his descent from Levi, yet he collected a tenth from Abraham and blessed[n] him who had the promises.[o] 7 And without doubt the lesser person is blessed by the greater. 8 In the one case, the tenth is collected by men who die; but in the other case, by him who is declared to be living.[p] 9 One might even say that Levi, who collects the tenth, paid the tenth through Abraham, 10 because when Melchizedek met Abraham, Levi was still in the body of his ancestor.

Jesus Like Melchizedek

11 If perfection could have been attained through the Levitical priesthood (for on the basis of it the law was given to the people),[q] why was there still need for another priest to come[r]—one in the order of Melchizedek,[s] not in the order of Aaron? 12 For when there is a change of the priesthood, there must also be a change of the law. 13 He of whom these things are said belonged to a different tribe,[t] and no one from that tribe has ever served at the altar.[u] 14 For it is clear that our Lord descended from Judah,[v] and in regard to that tribe Moses said nothing about priests. 15 And what we have said is even more clear if another priest like Melchizedek appears, 16 one who has become a priest not on the basis of a regulation as to his ancestry but on the basis of the power of an indestructible life. 17 For it is declared:

> "You are a priest forever,
> in the order of Melchizedek."[c][w]

18 The former regulation is set aside because it was weak and useless[x] 19 (for the law made nothing perfect),[y] and a better hope[z] is introduced, by which we draw near to God.[a]

6:18 [a]S Heb 3:6 **6:19** [b]Lev 16:2; Heb 9:2,3,7 **6:20** [c]S Heb 4:14 [d]S Heb 2:17 [e]S Heb 5:6 **7:1** [f]Ps 76:2 [g]S Mk 5:7 [h]ver 6; Ge 14:18-20 **7:3** [i]ver 6 [j]S Mt 4:3 **7:4** [k]Ac 2:29 [l]Ge 14:20 **7:5** [m]Nu 18:21,26 **7:6** [n]Ge 14:19,20 [o]Ro 4:13 **7:8** [p]Heb 5:6; 6:20 **7:11** [q]ver 18,19; Heb 8:7 [r]Heb 10:1 [s]ver 17; S Heb 5:6 **7:13** [t]ver 11 [u]ver 14 **7:14** [v]Isa 11:1; Mt 1:3; 2:6; Lk 3:33; Rev 5:5 **7:17** [w]Ps 110:4; ver 21; S Heb 5:6 **7:18** [x]Ro 8:3 **7:19** [y]ver 11; Ro 3:20; 7:7,8; Gal 3:21; Heb 9:9; 10:1 [z]S Heb 3:6 [a]ver 25; Heb 4:16; 10:1,22; Jas 4:8

[c] *17* Psalm 110:4

---

worthy. The truth of God's Word is inherent in the very words and sentences of Scripture. Its authors were guided by the Holy Spirit to write the original manuscripts in such a way that the transmission of God's message to humanity was communicated without error (see articles on THE WORD OF GOD, p. 1062, and THE INSPIRATION AND AUTHORITY OF SCRIPTURE, p. 1898).

7:1 MELCHIZEDEK. Melchizedek, a contemporary of Abraham, was a Canaanite king of Salem and a priest of God (Ge 14:18). Abraham paid tithes to him and was blessed by him (vv. 2–7). The author of Hebrews considered him a type of Jesus Christ, who was both priest and king (v. 3). Christ's priesthood is "in the order of Melchizedek" (6:20), meaning that Christ is both before and greater than Abraham, Levi and the Levitical priests.

7:3 WITHOUT FATHER OR MOTHER. This does not mean that Melchizedek literally had no parents or family or that he was an angel. It simply means that Scripture does not record his genealogy and says nothing about his beginning and end. Therefore, he serves as a type of the eternal Christ, whose priesthood will never end (vv. 24–25).

7:11 IF PERFECTION COULD HAVE BEEN ATTAINED. Because the Levitical priesthood was imperfect (cf. 10:4) and administered by sinful humans (vv. 27–28), it was replaced by the perfect priest, the Son of God. Christ is a perfect priest because he is wholly righteous, had to die only once as a sacrifice for our sins, serves as our eternal priest before God in heaven, and lives forever (vv. 24–28). Therefore, he is able to save completely and forever all who come to God through him (see v. 25, note).

7:19 THE LAW MADE NOTHING PERFECT. The OT law was imperfect because it could not impart divine life or the power to fulfill its demands, nor did it offer complete and perfect access to God (v. 25; see Gal 3:19, note; see article on THE OLD TESTAMENT LAW, p. 118).

20And it was not without an oath! Others became priests without any oath, 21but he became a priest with an oath when God said to him:

> "The Lord has sworn
> and will not change his mind:[b]
> 'You are a priest forever.' "[d][c]

22Because of this oath, Jesus has become the guarantee of a better covenant.[d]

7:21 [b]Nu 23:19; 1Sa 15:29; Mal 3:6; Ro 11:29 [c]Ps 110:4; S Heb 5:6 7:22 [d]S Lk 22:20 7:24 [e]ver 28 7:25 [f]S Ro 11:14 [g]S ver 19 [h]S Ro 8:34 7:26 [i]S Heb 2:17

Jesus Our Intercessor

23Now there have been many of those priests, since death prevented them from continuing in office; 24but because Jesus lives forever, he has a permanent priesthood.[e] 25Therefore he is able to save[f] completely[e] those who come to God[g] through him, because he always lives to intercede for
1Jn 5:11-12 them.[h]

26Such a high priest[i] meets our need—one who is holy, blameless, pure, set apart from sinners,[j] exalted above the heavens.[k] 27Unlike the other high priests, he does not need to offer sacrifices[l] day after day, first for his own sins,[m] and then for the sins of the people. He sacrificed for their sins once for all[n] when he offered himself.[o] 28For the law appoints as high priests men who are weak;[p] but the oath, which came after the law, appointed the Son,[q] who has been made perfect[r] forever.

[j]S 2Co 5:21 [k]S Heb 4:14 7:27 [l]Heb 5:1 [m]S Heb 5:3 [n]Ro 6:10; Heb 9:12,26,28; 10:10; 1Pe 3:18 [o]Eph 5:2; Heb 9:14,28 7:28 [p]Heb 5:2 [q]S Heb 1:2 [r]S Heb 2:10 8:1 [s]S Heb 2:17 [t]S Mk 16:19; S Heb 4:14 8:2 [u]Heb 9:11,24

The High Priest of a New Covenant

8 The point of what we are saying is this: We do have such a high priest,[s] who sat down at the right hand of the throne of the Majesty in heaven,[t] 2and who serves in the sanctuary, the true tabernacle[u] set up by the Lord, not by man.

[d] *21* Psalm 110:4 [e] *25* Or *forever*

7:25 ALWAYS LIVES TO INTERCEDE. Christ lives in heaven in his Father's presence (8:1), interceding for each and every one of his followers according to the Father's will (cf. Ro 8:33–34; 1Ti 2:5; 1Jn 2:1; see article on INTERCESSION, p. 1268). (1) Through Christ's ministry of intercession, we experience God's love and presence and find mercy and grace to help in any kind of need (4:16), temptation (Lk 22:32), weakness (4:15; 5:2), sin (1Jn 1:9; 2:1) and trial (Ro 8:31–39).

(2) Christ's high-priestly prayer for his people (Jn 17), as well as his desire to pour out the Spirit on all believers (Ac 2:33), help us understand the content of Christ's intercessory ministry (see Jn 17:1, note).

(3) Through Christ's intercession, the one who comes (i.e., continually comes, for the Greek participle is in the present tense, emphasizing continual activity) to God may receive grace to be saved completely. Christ's intercession as our high priest is essential to our salvation. Without that and without his grace, mercy and help mediated to us through that intercession, we would fall away from God, once again be enslaved to sin and Satan's dominion, and incur just condemnation. Our only hope is to come to God through Christ in faith (see 1Pe 1:5, note).

(4) Note that Christ does not remain an advocate and intercessor for those who refuse to confess and forsake sin and who depart from fellowship with God (cf. 1Jn 1:5–7,9; 3:10). His intercession to "save completely" is only for "those who come to God through him" (cf. 4:16). There is no safety and security for those who deliberately sin and refuse to seek God (10:21–31; see 3:6, note; see article on PERSONAL APOSTASY, p. 1918).

(5) Since Christ is our only mediator and intercessor in heaven, any attempt to treat angels or dead saints as mediators and to offer prayers to the Father through them is both futile and unbiblical (see Col 1:2, note; 2:18, note).

8:1 WE DO HAVE SUCH A HIGH PRIEST. After Christ took upon himself the punishment for our sins by giving his life as a sacrifice, he entered heaven, where he serves in God's presence on behalf of us who believe. Jesus' ministry as high priest (cf. 2:17) embraces six areas: (1) Jesus was both the priest and the sacrifice itself. He offered himself for all people as a perfect sacrifice for sin by shedding his blood and dying in the sinner's place (2:17–18; 4:15; 7:26–28; Mk 10:45; 1Co 15:3; 1Pe 1:18–19; 2:22–24; 3:18; see article on THE DAY OF ATONEMENT, p. 174).

(2) Jesus mediates the new and better covenant in order that all "who are called may receive the promised eternal inheritance" (9:15–22; see article on THE OLD COVENANT AND THE NEW COVENANT, p. 1926), and with confidence may have continual access to God (4:16; 6:19–20; 7:25; 10:19–22; see Jn 17:1, note on Jesus' high-priestly prayer).

(3) He is in heaven in God's presence to give God's grace to us who believe (4:14–16). By this grace mediated to us by him, Christ regenerates us (Jn 3:3) and pours out the Holy Spirit on us (Ac 1:4; 2:4,33).

(4) Jesus acts as a mediator between God and all who have broken God's law and seek forgiveness and reconciliation (1Jn 2:1–2).

(5) Jesus holds his priesthood permanently, sympathizing with believers' temptations and aiding them in their needs (2:18; 4:15–16).

(6) Jesus lives forever to intercede continually in heaven for all those who in faith "come to God through him" (7:25). He will eventually bring the believer's salvation to final fulfillment (see 7:25, note; 9:28, note).

3Every high priest[v] is appointed to
offer both gifts and sacrifices,[w] and so
it was necessary for this one also to
have something to offer.[x] **4**If he were
on earth, he would not be a priest, for
there are already men who offer the
gifts prescribed by the law.[y] **5**They
serve at a sanctuary that is a copy[z]
and shadow[a] of what is in heaven.
This is why Moses was warned[b] when
he was about to build the tabernacle:
"See to it that you make everything according to the pattern shown you on
the mountain."[f][c] **6**But the ministry
Jesus has received is as superior to
theirs as the covenant[d] of which he is
mediator[e] is superior to the old one,
and it is founded on better promises.
7For if there had been nothing wrong
with that first covenant, no place
would have been sought for another.[f]
8But God found fault with the people
and said[g]:

"The time is coming, declares the Lord,
when I will make a new covenant[g]
with the house of Israel
and with the house of Judah.
9It will not be like the covenant
I made with their forefathers[h]
when I took them by the hand
to lead them out of Egypt,
because they did not remain
faithful to my covenant,
and I turned away from them,
declares the Lord.
10This is the covenant[i] I will make
with the house of Israel
after that time, declares the Lord.
I will put my laws in their minds
and write them on their hearts.[j]
I will be their God,
and they will be my people.[k]
11No longer will a man teach his neighbor,
or a man his brother, saying,
'Know the Lord,'
because they will all know me,[l]
from the least of them to the greatest.
12For I will forgive their wickedness
and will remember their sins no more.[m]"[h][n]

13By calling this covenant "new,"[o]
he has made the first one obsolete;[p]
and what is obsolete and aging will
soon disappear.

Worship in the Earthly Tabernacle

9 Now the first covenant had regulations for worship and also an
earthly sanctuary.[q] **2**A tabernacle[r]
was set up. In its first room were the
lampstand,[s] the table[t] and the consecrated bread;[u] this was called the
Holy Place.[v] **3**Behind the second curtain was a room called the Most Holy
Place,[w] **4**which had the golden altar of
incense[x] and the gold-covered ark of
the covenant.[y] This ark contained the
gold jar of manna,[z] Aaron's staff that
had budded,[a] and the stone tablets of
the covenant.[b] **5**Above the ark were
the cherubim of the Glory,[c] overshadowing the atonement cover.[i][d] But

8:3 [v]S Heb 2:17 [w]Heb 5:1; 9:9 [x]Heb 9:14 **8:4** [y]Heb 5:1; 9:9 **8:5** [z]Heb 9:23 [a]Col 2:17; Heb 10:1 [b]Heb 11:7; 12:25 [c]Ex 25:40 **8:6** [d]ver 8,13; S Lk 22:20 [e]S Gal 3:20 **8:7** [f]Heb 7:11,18; 10:1 **8:8** [g]ver 6,13; S Lk 22:20 **8:9** [h]Ex 19:5,6; 20:1-17 **8:10** [i]Ro 11:27 [j]2Co 3:3; Heb 10:16 [k]Eze 11:20; Zec 8:8 **8:11** [l]Isa 54:13; S Jn 6:45 **8:12** [m]Heb 10:17 [n]Jer 31:31-34 **8:13** [o]ver 6,8; S Lk 22:20 [p]2Co 5:17 **9:1** [q]Ex 25:8 **9:2** [r]Ex 25:8,9 [s]Ex 25:31-39 [t]Ex 25:23-29 [u]Ex 25:30; Lev 24:5-8 [v]Ex 26:33,34 **9:3** [w]Ex 26:31-33 **9:4** [x]Ex 30:1-5 [y]Ex 25:10-22 [z]Ex 16:32,33 [a]Nu 17:10 [b]Ex 31:18; 32:15 **9:5** [c]Ex 25:17-19 [d]Ex 25:20-22; 26:34

[f]5 Exodus 25:40 [g]8 Some manuscripts may be translated *fault and said to the people.* [h]12 Jer. 31:31-34 [i]5 Traditionally *the mercy seat*

8:6–13 COVENANT . . . IS SUPERIOR. A significant theme of chs. 8–10 is the contrast between the old covenant that was centered around the Law of Moses and the new covenant that was instituted by Jesus Christ. See article on THE OLD COVENANT AND THE NEW COVENANT, p. 1926.

9:1–7 THE FIRST COVENANT. In his discussion on how the new covenant is so much superior to the old (or first) covenant, the writer to the Hebrews analyzes the major features of worship and sacrifice in Israel's religion. See article on THE OLD COVENANT AND THE NEW COVENANT, p. 1926.

9:4 ARK OF THE COVENANT. The ark of the covenant was a sacred box or chest containing a jar of manna (a reminder of God's provision), Aaron's staff (a reminder of God's mighty acts), and the two stone tablets on which were written the Ten Commandments (a reminder of the law's importance as God's standard of holiness for his people). The lid of the ark was a golden plate called the atonement cover, or mercy seat, which declared God's redeeming mercy through shed blood (see next note).

9:5 THE ATONEMENT COVER. On the Day of Atonement, both the bull's blood that made atonement for the high priest and his family and the goat's blood that served as a sin offering for the nation were sprinkled on the atonement cover before God (Lev 16:2,14; see article on THE DAY OF ATONEMENT, p. 174). The earthly atonement cover is a figure or type of the heavenly throne of grace, which believers approach because of Christ's blood in order to receive grace and help (4:16).

THE OLD COVENANT AND THE NEW COVENANT

Heb 8:6 "But the ministry Jesus has received is as superior to theirs as the covenant of which he is mediator is superior to the old one, and it is founded on better promises."

Heb 8–10 describes numerous aspects of the old covenant, such as the worship, regulations and sacrificial ritual in the tabernacle; it discusses the various rooms and furniture of this OT worship center. The author's purpose is twofold: (1) to contrast the high priest's service in the earthly sanctuary under the old covenant with Christ's ministry as high priest in the heavenly sanctuary under the new covenant; (2) to show how these various aspects in the old covenant foreshadow or serve as a type of the ministry of Christ, the one who inaugurated the new covenant. This article summarizes the relationship between these two covenants.

(1) Under the old covenant, salvation and a right relationship with God came through a faith expressed by obedience to his law and its sacrificial system (see article on GOD'S COVENANT WITH THE ISRAELITES, p. 290). Sacrifices in the OT had three main purposes: (a) They taught God's people the gravity of sin. Sin separated sinners from a holy God, and they could be reconciled to God and find forgiveness only through the shedding of blood (Ex 12:3–14; Lev 16; 17:11; Heb 9:22; see Lev 1:2–3, notes; 4:3, note; 9:8, note). (b) They provided a way for Israel to come to God through faith, obedience and love (cf. Heb 4:16; 7:25; 10:1). (c) They pointed forward to or foreshadowed (Heb 8:5; 10:1) Christ's perfect sacrifice for the sins of the human race (cf. Jn 1:29; 1Pe 1:18–19; see Ex 12:3–14; Lev 16; see Gal 3:19, note; see article on THE DAY OF ATONEMENT, p. 174).

(2) Jeremiah prophesied that at some time in the future God would make a new covenant, a better one, with his people (see Jer 31:31–34, notes; cf. Heb 8:8–12). It is a better covenant than the old (cf. Ro 7) because it completely forgives the sins of the repentant (Heb 8:12), makes them children of God (Ro 8:15–16), gives them a new heart and nature so that they can spontaneously love and obey God (Heb 8:10; cf. Eze 11:19–20), brings them into an intimate personal relationship with Jesus Christ and the Father (Heb 8:11), and provides a greater experience in the Holy Spirit (Joel 2:28; Ac 1:5,8; 2:16–17,33,38–39; Ro 8:14–15,26).

(3) Jesus is the one who instituted the new covenant or new testament (both ideas are present in the Greek word *diathēkē*), and his heavenly ministry is far superior to the ministry of OT earthly priests. The new covenant is an agreement, promise, last will and testament, and a statement of intention to bestow divine grace and blessing on those who respond to God in obedient faith. Specifically, it is a covenant of promise for those who through faith accept Christ as God's Son, receive his promises, and commit themselves personally to him and to the obligations of the new covenant.

(a) Jesus Christ's position as mediator of the new covenant (Heb 8:6; 9:15; 12:24) is based on his sacrificial death (Mt 26:28; Mk 14:24; Heb 9:14–15; 10:29; 12:24). The promises and obligations of this new covenant are embodied in the entire NT. Its purpose is (i) to save from guilt and condemnation all those who believe in Christ and commit their lives to the truths and obligations of his covenant (Heb 9:16–17; cf. Mk 14:24; 1Co 11:25), and (ii) to form them into a people who are God's very own (Heb 8:10; cf. Eze 11:19–20; 1Pe 2:9).

(b) Jesus' sacrifice is a better one than the sacrifices of the old covenant because it was a voluntary and obedient sacrifice of a righteous person (Jesus Christ) rather than the involuntary sacrifice of an animal. Jesus' sacrifice and fulfillment of God's will were perfect and thus opened the way for complete forgiveness, reconciliation and sanctification (Heb 10:10,15–17; see Lev 9:8, note).

(c) The new covenant can be called the new covenant of the Spirit, for it is the Holy Spirit who ministers life and power to those who accept God's covenant (2Co 3:1–6; see Jn 17:3, note; see articles on BIBLICAL WORDS FOR SALVATION, p. 1710, and FAITH AND GRACE, p. 1720).

(4) All who participate in the new covenant through Jesus Christ receive its blessings and salvation only as they persevere in faith and obedience (see Heb 3:6, note). The faithless are excluded from its blessings (see 3:18, note; see article on PERSONAL APOSTASY, p. 1918).

(5) With the coming of the new covenant through Christ, the old covenant became obsolete (Heb 8:13). In doing so, however, the new covenant does not render the entire body of OT Scripture obsolete, but only the Mosaic covenant whereby salvation was gained by obedience to the law and its sacrificial system. The OT is not obsolete; much of its revelation points toward Christ (see article on CHRIST IN THE OLD TESTAMENT, p. 518) and, as God's inspired Word, is useful for teaching, rebuking, correcting and training in righteousness (see article on THE INSPIRATION AND AUTHORITY OF SCRIPTURE, p. 1898).

we cannot discuss these things in detail now.
6When everything had been arranged like this, the priests entered
regularly[e] into the outer room to carry
on their ministry. **7**But only the high
priest entered[f] the inner room,[g] and
that only once a year,[h] and never
without blood,[i] which he offered for
himself[j] and for the sins the people
had committed in ignorance.[k] **8**The
Holy Spirit was showing[l] by this that
the way[m] into the Most Holy Place had
not yet been disclosed as long as the
first tabernacle was still standing.
9This is an illustration[n] for the
present time, indicating that the gifts
and sacrifices being offered[o] were not
able to clear the conscience[p] of the
worshiper. **10**They are only a matter of
food[q] and drink[r] and various ceremonial washings[s]—external regulations[t] applying until the time of the
new order.

The Blood of Christ

11When Christ came as high priest[u]
of the good things that are already
here,[j][v] he went through the greater
and more perfect tabernacle[w] that is
not man-made,[x] that is to say, not a
part of this creation. **12**He did not enter
by means of the blood of goats and
calves;[y] but he entered the Most Holy
Place[z] once for all[a] by his own
blood,[b] having obtained eternal redemption. **13**The blood of goats and
bulls[c] and the ashes of a heifer[d]
sprinkled on those who are ceremonially unclean sanctify them so that they
are outwardly clean. **14**How much
more, then, will the blood of Christ,
who through the eternal Spirit[e] offered himself[f] unblemished to God,
cleanse our consciences[g] from acts
that lead to death,[k][h] so that we may
serve the living God![i]
15For this reason Christ is the mediator[j] of a new covenant,[k] that those
who are called[l] may receive the promised[m] eternal inheritance[n]—now
that he has died as a ransom to set
them free from the sins committed under the first covenant.[o]
16In the case of a will,[l] it is necessary to prove the death of the one who
made it, **17**because a will is in force
only when somebody has died; it never
takes effect while the one who made it
is living. **18**This is why even the first
covenant was not put into effect without blood.[p] **19**When Moses had proclaimed[q] every commandment of the
law to all the people, he took the blood
of calves,[r] together with water, scarlet wool and branches of hyssop, and
sprinkled the scroll and all the people.[s] **20**He said, "This is the blood of
the covenant, which God has commanded you to keep."[m][t] **21**In the
same way, he sprinkled with the blood
both the tabernacle and everything
used in its ceremonies. **22**In fact, the
law requires that nearly everything be
cleansed with blood,[u] and without the

9:6 [e]Nu 28:3 **9:7** [f]Lev 16:11-19 [g]ver 2,3 [h]Lev 16:34 [i]Lev 16:11,14 [j]Lev 16:11; Heb 5:2,3 [k]Heb 5:2,3 **9:8** [l]S Heb 3:7 [m]Jn 14:6; Heb 10:19,20 **9:9** [n]Heb 10:1 [o]Heb 5:1; 8:3 [p]S Heb 7:19 **9:10** [q]Lev 11:2-23 [r]Nu 6:3; Col 2:16 [s]Lev 11:25,28,40 [t]Heb 7:16 **9:11** [u]S Heb 2:17 [v]Heb 10:1 [w]ver 24; Heb 8:2 [x]S Jn 2:19 **9:12** [y]ver 19; Lev 16:6,15; Heb 10:4 [z]ver 24 [a]ver 26,28; S Heb 7:27 [b]ver 14; S Ro 3:25 **9:13** [c]Heb 10:4 [d]Nu 19:9,17,18

9:14 [e]1Pe 3:18 [f]S Eph 5:2 [g]Ps 51:2; 65:3; Jer 33:8; Zec 13:1; S Tit 2:14; Heb 10:2,22 [h]Heb 6:1 [i]S Mt 16:16 **9:15** [j]S Gal 3:20 [k]S Lk 22:20 [l]S Ro 8:28; S 11:29 [m]Heb 6:15; 10:36 [n]S Ac 20:32 [o]Heb 7:22 **9:18** [p]Ex 24:6-8 **9:19** [q]Heb 1:1 [r]ver 12 [s]Ex 24:6-8 **9:20** [t]Ex 24:8; S Mt 26:28 **9:22** [u]Ex 29:21; Lev 8:15

j *11* Some early manuscripts *are to come*
k *14* Or *from useless rituals*
l *16* Same Greek word as *covenant*; also in verse 17
m *20* Exodus 24:8

9:7 THE INNER ROOM. The inner sanctuary, called the Most Holy Place, symbolized God's presence. The high priest was strictly forbidden to enter the Most Holy Place more than once a year. The Holy Spirit was teaching that under the old covenant, unimpeded access to God's presence was not yet possible because intimate communion with him could exist only when a person's inward conscience had been cleansed perfectly (vv. 8–9). This cleansing was provided for when Christ died as an eternal sacrifice for sin.

9:14 THE BLOOD OF CHRIST. The blood of Jesus Christ is central to the NT concept of redemption (1Co 10:16; 11:27; Eph 2:13; 1Pe 1:2; Rev 7:14; 12:11). On the cross Christ shed his innocent blood in order to remove our sins and to reconcile us with God (5:8; Ro 5:19; Php 2:8; cf. Lev 16).

By his blood Christ accomplished the following: (1) His blood forgives the sins of all who repent and believe (Mt 26:28). (2) His blood ransoms all believers from the power of Satan and evil powers (Ac 20:28; Eph 1:7; 1Pe 1:18–19; Rev 5:9; 12:11). (3) His blood justifies all who believe in him (Ro 3:24–25). (4) His blood cleanses believers' consciences that they might serve God without guilt in full assurance (9:14; 10:22; 13:18). (5) His blood sanctifies God's people (13:12; 1Jn 1:7–10). (6) His blood opens the way for believers to come directly before God through Christ in order to find grace, mercy, help and salvation (7:25; 10:19; Eph 2:13,18). (7) His blood is a guarantee of all the promises of the new covenant (10:29; 13:20; Mt 26:28; 1Co 11:25). (8) The saving, reconciling and purifying power of Christ's blood is continually appropriated to believers as they come to God through Christ (7:25; 10:22; 1Jn 1:7).

9:15 MEDIATOR OF A NEW COVENANT. For comments on Jesus' function as mediator of a new covenant, see article on THE OLD COVENANT AND THE NEW COVENANT, p. 1926.

shedding of blood there is no forgiveness.[v]
23It was necessary, then, for the
copies[w] of the heavenly things to be
purified with these sacrifices, but the
heavenly things themselves with better sacrifices than these. **24**For Christ
did not enter a man-made sanctuary
that was only a copy of the true one;[x]
he entered heaven itself,[y] now to appear for us in God's presence.[z] **25**Nor
did he enter heaven to offer himself
again and again, the way the high
priest enters the Most Holy Place[a] every year with blood that is not his
own.[b] **26**Then Christ would have had
to suffer many times since the creation
of the world.[c] But now he has appeared[d] once for all[e] at the end of the
ages to do away with sin by the sacrifice of himself.[f] **27**Just as man is destined to die once,[g] and after that to
face judgment,[h] **28**so Christ was sacrificed once[i] to take away the sins of
many people; and he will appear a second time,[j] not to bear sin,[k] but to
bring salvation[l] to those who are
waiting for him.[m]

Christ's Sacrifice Once for All

10 The law is only a shadow[n] of
the good things[o] that are coming—not the realities themselves.[p]
For this reason it can never, by the
same sacrifices repeated endlessly
year after year, make perfect[q] those
who draw near to worship.[r] **2**If it
could, would they not have stopped being offered? For the worshipers would
have been cleansed once for all, and
would no longer have felt guilty for
their sins.[s] **3**But those sacrifices are
an annual reminder of sins,[t] **4**because
it is impossible for the blood of bulls
and goats[u] to take away sins.[v]
5Therefore, when Christ came into
the world,[w] he said:

"Sacrifice and offering you did not
desire,
but a body you prepared for
me;[x]
6with burnt offerings and sin
offerings
you were not pleased.
7Then I said, 'Here I am—it is
written about me in the
scroll[y]—
I have come to do your will,
O God.' "[n][z]

8First he said, "Sacrifices and offerings, burnt offerings and sin offerings
you did not desire, nor were you
pleased with them"[a] (although the
law required them to be made). **9**Then
he said, "Here I am, I have come to do
your will."[b] He sets aside the first to
establish the second. **10**And by that
will, we have been made holy[c]
through the sacrifice of the body[d] of
Jesus Christ once for all.[e]
11Day after day every priest stands
and performs his religious duties;
again and again he offers the same sacrifices,[f] which can never take away
sins.[g] **12**But when this priest had offered for all time one sacrifice for
sins,[h] he sat down at the right hand of
God.[i] **13**Since that time he waits for
his enemies to be made his footstool,[j]
14because by one sacrifice he has made

9:22 [v] Lev 17:11
9:23 [w] Heb 8:5
9:24 [x] Heb 8:2 [y] ver 12; S Heb 4:14 [z] S Ro 8:34
9:25 [a] Heb 10:19 [b] ver 7,8
9:26 [c] Heb 4:3 [d] 1Jn 3:5 [e] ver 12, 28; S Heb 7:27 [f] ver 12
9:27 [g] Ge 3:19 [h] 2Co 5:10
9:28 [i] ver 12,26; S Heb 7:27 [j] S Mt 16:27 [k] 1Pe 2:24 [l] Heb 5:9 [m] S 1Co 1:7
10:1 [n] Col 2:17; Heb 8:5 [o] Heb 9:11 [p] Heb 9:23 [q] ver 4, 11; S Heb 7:19 [r] S Heb 7:19
10:2 [s] Heb 9:9
10:3 [t] Lev 16:34; Heb 9:7
10:4 [u] Heb 9:12, 13 [v] ver 1,11
10:5 [w] Heb 1:6 [x] Heb 2:14; 1Pe 2:24
10:7 [y] Ezr 6:2; Jer 36:2 [z] Ps 40:6-8; S Mt 26:39
10:8 [a] ver 5,6; S Mk 12:33
10:9 [b] ver 7
10:10 [c] ver 14; S Eph 5:26 [d] Heb 2:14; 1Pe 2:24 [e] S Heb 7:27
10:11 [f] Heb 5:1 [g] ver 1,4
10:12 [h] Heb 5:1 [i] S Mk 16:19
10:13 [j] Jos 10:24; Heb 1:13

[n] 7 Psalm 40:6-8 (see Septuagint)

9:28 WILL APPEAR A SECOND TIME. Under the old covenant, the Israelites watched intensely for the reappearance of their high priest after he had gone into the sanctuary to make atonement. Likewise believers, knowing that their high priest has entered the heavenly sanctuary as their advocate, wait with earnest hope for his reappearing to bring a complete salvation (see Jn 14:3, note; 2Ti 4:8; see article on THE RAPTURE, p. 1864).

10:1 THE SAME SACRIFICES REPEATED ENDLESSLY. For comments on the purposes of OT sacrifices, see article on THE OLD COVENANT AND THE NEW COVENANT, p. 1926.

10:4 THE BLOOD OF BULLS. The blood of animals was only a temporary provision or atonement for the sins of the people; ultimately, a human was needed to serve as a substitute for humanity (see article on THE DAY OF ATONEMENT, p. 174). Thus Christ came to earth and was born as a human so that he might offer himself in our place (2:9,14, notes). Furthermore, only a human who was free from sin could take our punishment for sin (2:14–18; 4:15) and thus adequately and perfectly satisfy the demands of God's holiness (cf. Ro 3:25–26).

10:5–10 SACRIFICE AND OFFERING. Ps 40:6–8 is cited to prove that the voluntary and obedient sacrifice of Jesus Christ is better than the involuntary animal sacrifices in the OT; see article on THE OLD COVENANT AND THE NEW COVENANT, p. 1926.

10:14 MADE PERFECT FOREVER THOSE WHO ARE BEING MADE HOLY. The one offering of Christ on the cross and its benefit (i.e., perfect salvation) are eternally efficacious. Perfect salvation in Christ is imparted to all who are being made holy as they draw near to God through Christ (v. 22; 7:25). Note that the Greek word "made

perfect[k] forever those who are being
made holy.[l]
15The Holy Spirit also testifies[m] to
us about this. First he says:

16"This is the covenant I will make
with them
after that time, says the Lord.
I will put my laws in their hearts,
and I will write them on their
minds."[o][n]

17Then he adds:

"Their sins and lawless acts
I will remember no more."[p][o]

18And where these have been forgiven,
there is no longer any sacrifice for sin.

A Call to Persevere

19Therefore, brothers, since we have
confidence[p] to enter the Most Holy
Place[q] by the blood of Jesus, 20by a
new and living way[r] opened for us
through the curtain,[s] that is, his body,
21and since we have a great priest[t]
over the house of God,[u] 22let us draw
near to God[v] with a sincere heart in
full assurance of faith,[w] having our
hearts sprinkled to cleanse us from a
guilty conscience[x] and having our
bodies washed with pure water.[y]
23Let us hold unswervingly to the
hope[z] we profess,[a] for he who promised is faithful.[b] 24And let us consider
how we may spur one another on toward love and good deeds.[c] 25Let us
not give up meeting together,[d] as
some are in the habit of doing, but let
us encourage one another[e]—and all
the more as you see the Day approaching.[f]
26If we deliberately keep on sinning[g] after we have received the
knowledge of the truth,[h] no sacrifice
for sins is left, 27but only a fearful expectation of judgment and of raging
fire[i] that will consume the enemies of
God. 28Anyone who rejected the law of
Moses died without mercy on the testimony of two or three witnesses.[j]
29How much more severely do you
think a man deserves to be punished
who has trampled the Son of God[k] under foot,[l] who has treated as an unholy thing the blood of the covenant[m]
that sanctified him,[n] and who has insulted the Spirit[o] of grace?[p] 30For we
know him who said, "It is mine to
avenge; I will repay,"[q][q] and again,
"The Lord will judge his people."[r][r]
31It is a dreadful thing[s] to fall into the
hands[t] of the living God.[u]
32Remember those earlier days after
you had received the light,[v] when you
stood your ground in a great contest in
the face of suffering.[w] 33Sometimes
you were publicly exposed to insult
and persecution;[x] at other times you
stood side by side with those who were
so treated.[y] 34You sympathized with
those in prison[z] and joyfully accepted
the confiscation of your property, be-

10:14 [k] ver 1 [l] ver 10; S Eph 5:26 **10:15** [m] S Heb 3:7 **10:16** [n] Jer 31:33; Heb 8:10 **10:17** [o] Jer 31:34; Heb 8:12 **10:19** [p] S Eph 3:12 [q] Lev 16:2; Eph 2:18; Heb 9:8, 12,25 **10:20** [r] Heb 9:8 [s] Heb 6:19; 9:3 **10:21** [t] S Heb 2:17 [u] S Heb 3:6 **10:22** [v] ver 1; S Heb 7:19 [w] Eph 3:12 [x] Eze 36:25; Heb 9:14; 12:24; 1Pe 1:2 [y] S Ac 22:16 **10:23** [z] S Heb 3:6 [a] S Heb 3:1 [b] S 1Co 1:9 **10:24** [c] S Tit 2:14 **10:25** [d] Ac 2:42 [e] Heb 3:13 [f] S 1Co 3:13 **10:26** [g] Ex 21:14; Nu 15:30; Heb 5:2; 6:4-8; 2Pe 2:20 [h] S 1Ti 2:4 **10:27** [i] Isa 26:11; 2Th 1:7; Heb 9:27; 12:29 **10:28** [j] Dt 17:6,7; S Mt 18:16; Heb 2:2 **10:29** [k] S Mt 4:3 [l] Heb 6:6 [m] S Mt 26:28 [n] 1Co 6:11; Rev 1:5 [o] Eph 4:30; Heb 6:4 [p] Heb 2:3; 12:25 **10:30** [q] Dt 32:35; Ro 12:19 [r] Dt 32:36; Ps 135:14 **10:31** [s] S 2Co 5:11 [t] Isa 19:16 [u] S Mt 16:16
10:32 [v] Heb 6:4 [w] Php 1:29,30 **10:33** [x] 1Co 4:9 [y] Php 4:14; 1Th 2:14 **10:34** [z] Heb 13:3

[o] *16* Jer. 31:33 [p] *17* Jer. 31:34 [q] *30* Deut. 32:35 [r] *30* Deut. 32:36; Psalm 135:14

holy" here and in v. 10 is a present participle, emphasizing continuous action in the present.

10:19 SINCE WE HAVE. In contrast to the limited access to God that the Israelites had, Christ, by giving his life as a perfect sacrifice, has opened a way into God's very presence and the throne of grace. Therefore, we as believers may in gratefulness constantly draw near to God in prayer.

10:22 LET US DRAW NEAR. Faith and drawing near to God through Jesus Christ are inseparable. (1) Faith is defined as sincerely coming to God and believing in his goodness (11:6). By coming to God through Christ, one finds mercy, grace, help (v. 1; 4:16; 7:19), salvation (7:25), sanctification (v. 14) and cleansing (v. 22). (2) Clearly this implies that where there is no drawing near to God in prayer and fellowship with Christ, there is no saving faith (cf. v. 38). Jesus himself equates faith with earnest prayer to God (Lk 18:8).

10:25 AS YOU SEE THE DAY APPROACHING. The day of Christ's return for his faithful is approaching (see article on THE RAPTURE, p. 1864). As it does, we will face many spiritual trials and persecutions, and much doctrinal deception. We must meet together regularly in order to encourage one another to hold firmly to Christ and the apostolic faith of the new covenant.

10:26 IF WE DELIBERATELY KEEP ON SINNING. The author of Hebrews here speaks of the falling away from Christ about which he warned his readers in 6:4–8 (see article on PERSONAL APOSTASY, p. 1918).

10:29 TRAMPLED THE SON OF GOD. To keep on sinning deliberately after we have received the knowledge of the truth (v. 26) is (1) to be guilty of trampling underfoot Jesus Christ, treating him with contempt, and despising his life and death; (2) to count the blood of Christ as unworthy of our loyalty; and (3) to insult and rebel against the Holy Spirit, who brings God's grace to our hearts (see article on PERSONAL APOSTASY, p. 1918).

cause you knew that you yourselves
had better and lasting possessions.[a]
35So do not throw away your confidence;[b] it will be richly rewarded.
36You need to persevere[c] so that
when you have done the will of God,
you will receive what he has promised.[d] 37For in just a very little while,

"He who is coming[e] will come and
will not delay.[f]
38 But my righteous one[s] will live
by faith.[g]
And if he shrinks back,
I will not be pleased with
him."[t][h]

39But we are not of those who shrink
back and are destroyed, but of those
who believe and are saved.

By Faith

11 Now faith is being sure of what
we hope for[i] and certain of
what we do not see.[j] 2This is what the
ancients were commended for.[k]
3By faith we understand that the
universe was formed at God's command,[l] so that what is seen was not
made out of what was visible.

The Faith of the Patriarchs

4By faith Abel offered God a better
sacrifice than Cain did. By faith he was
commended[m] as a righteous man,
when God spoke well of his offerings.[n]
And by faith he still speaks, even
though he is dead.[o]
5By faith Enoch was taken from this
life, so that he did not experience
death; he could not be found, because
God had taken him away.[p] For before
he was taken, he was commended as
one who pleased God. 6And without
faith it is impossible to please God, because anyone who comes to him[q]
must believe that he exists and that he
rewards those who earnestly seek him.
7By faith Noah, when warned about
things not yet seen,[r] in holy fear built
an ark[s] to save his family.[t] By his
faith he condemned the world and became heir of the righteousness that
comes by faith.[u]

The Faith of Abraham and Family

8By faith Abraham, when called to
go to a place he would later receive as
his inheritance,[v] obeyed and went,[w]
even though he did not know where he
was going. 9By faith he made his home
in the promised land[x] like a stranger
in a foreign country; he lived in tents,[y]
as did Isaac and Jacob, who were heirs
with him of the same promise.[z] 10For
he was looking forward to the city[a]

10:34 [a]Heb 11:16; 1Pe 1:4,5
10:35 [b]S Eph 3:12
10:36 [c]Ro 5:3; Heb 12:1; Jas 1:3, 4,12; 5:11; 2Pe 1:6 [d]Heb 6:15; 9:15
10:37 [e]Mt 11:3 [f]Rev 22:20
10:38 [g]Ro 1:17; Gal 3:11 [h]Hab 2:3, 4
11:1 [i]S Heb 3:6 [j]S 2Co 4:18
11:2 [k]ver 4,39
11:3 [l]Ge 1; Jn 1:3; Heb 1:2; 2Pe 3:5
11:4 [m]ver 2,39 [n]Ge 4:4; 1Jn 3:12 [o]Heb 12:24
11:5 [p]Ge 5:21-24
11:6 [q]Heb 7:19
11:7 [r]S ver 1 [s]Ge 6:13-22 [t]1Pe 3:20 [u]Ge 6:9; Eze 14:14,20; S Ro 9:30
11:8 [v]Ge 12:7 [w]Ge 12:1-4; Ac 7:2-4
11:9 [x]Ac 7:5 [y]Ge 12:8; 18:1,9 [z]Heb 6:17
11:10 [a]Heb 12:22; 13:14

[s] *38* One early manuscript *But the righteous*
[t] *38* Hab. 2:3,4

10:38 MY RIGHTEOUS ONE WILL LIVE BY FAITH. This fundamental principle, affirmed four times in Scripture (Hab 2:4; Ro 1:17; Gal 3:11; Heb 10:38), governs our relationship to God and our participation in the salvation provided through Jesus Christ. (1) This cardinal truth affirms that the righteous will possess eternal life by faithfully drawing near to God with a sincere believing heart (see v. 22, note). (2) For anyone who shrinks back from Christ and deliberately keeps on sinning, God "will not be pleased with him" and he will incur eternal damnation.

11:1 NOW FAITH IS. Ch. 11 demonstrates the nature of the only kind of faith acceptable before God, a faith triumphant in the worst of situations. It is a faith that believes in spiritual realities (v. 1), leads to righteousness (v. 4), seeks God (v. 6), believes in his goodness (v. 6), has confidence in his Word (vv. 7,11), obeys his commands (v. 8), regulates life on his promises (vv. 13,39), rejects the spirit of this present evil age (v. 13), seeks a heavenly home (vv. 14–16; cf. 13:13–14), perseveres in testing (vv. 17–19), blesses the next generation (v. 21), refuses sin's pleasures (v. 25), endures persecution (v. 27), performs mighty acts of righteousness (vv. 33–35), suffers for God (vv. 25, 35–38), and does not return to "the country they had left," i.e., the world (vv. 15–16; see article on FAITH AND GRACE, p. 1720).

11:3 UNIVERSE WAS FORMED AT GOD'S COMMAND. The faith by which we understand that God created the world is faith in the divinely inspired revelation found in Ge 1 and other passages (cf. Ps 33:6,9; Isa 55:11).

11:4 A BETTER SACRIFICE. God accepted Abel's sacrifice because Abel was righteous, devoted and obedient (cf. Pr 15:8; Mt 23:35; 1Jn 3:12).

11:6 BELIEVE THAT HE EXISTS. This verse describes the convictions that are a part of saving faith. (1) We must believe in the existence of a personal, infinite, holy God who cares for us. (2) We must believe that God will reward us when we earnestly seek him, knowing that our greatest reward is the joy and presence of God himself. He is our shield and our very great reward (Ge 15:1; cf. Dt 4:29; Mt 7:7–8, note; Jn 14:21, note). (3) We must diligently seek God and earnestly desire his presence and his grace.

11:8 BY FAITH ABRAHAM . . . OBEYED. Faith and obedience are inseparable, just as unbelief and disobedience are inseparable (3:18–19; see Jn 3:36, note).

11:10 LOOKING FORWARD TO THE CITY.

with foundations,[b] whose architect and builder is God.[c]

11By faith Abraham, even though he was past age—and Sarah herself was barren[d]—was enabled to become a father[e] because he[u] considered him faithful[f] who had made the promise. **12**And so from this one man, and he as good as dead,[g] came descendants as numerous as the stars in the sky and as countless as the sand on the seashore.[h]

13All these people were still living by faith when they died. They did not receive the things promised;[i] they only saw them and welcomed them from a distance.[j] And they admitted that they were aliens and strangers on earth.[k] **14**People who say such things show that they are looking for a country of their own. **15**If they had been thinking of the country they had left, they would have had opportunity to return.[l] **16**Instead, they were longing for a better country—a heavenly one.[m] Therefore God is not ashamed[n] to be called their God,[o] for he has prepared a city[p] for them.

Jas 1:27

17By faith Abraham, when God tested him, offered Isaac as a sacrifice.[q] He who had received the promises was about to sacrifice his one and only son, **18**even though God had said to him, "It is through Isaac that your offspring[v] will be reckoned."[w][r] **19**Abraham reasoned that God could raise the dead,[s] and figuratively speaking, he did receive Isaac back from death.

20By faith Isaac blessed Jacob and Esau in regard to their future.[t]

21By faith Jacob, when he was dying, blessed each of Joseph's sons,[u] and worshiped as he leaned on the top of his staff.

22By faith Joseph, when his end was near, spoke about the exodus of the Israelites from Egypt and gave instructions about his bones.[v]

The Faith of Moses

23By faith Moses' parents hid him for three months after he was born,[w] because they saw he was no ordinary child, and they were not afraid of the king's edict.[x]

24By faith Moses, when he had grown up, refused to be known as the son of Pharaoh's daughter.[y] **25**He chose to be mistreated[z] along with the people of God rather than to enjoy the pleasures of sin for a short time. **26**He regarded disgrace[a] for the sake of Christ[b] as of greater value than the treasures of Egypt, because he was looking ahead to his reward.[c] **27**By faith he left Egypt,[d] not fearing the king's anger; he persevered because he saw him who is invisible. **28**By faith he kept the Passover and the sprinkling of blood, so that the destroyer[e] of the firstborn would not touch the firstborn of Israel.[f]

The Faith of the Israelites and Rahab

29By faith the people passed through the Red Sea[x] as on dry land;

11:10 [b]Rev 21:2, 14 [c]ver 16
11:11 [d]Ge 17:17-19; 18:11-14 [e]Ge 21:2 [f]S 1Co 1:9
11:12 [g]Ro 4:19 [h]Ge 22:17
11:13 [i]ver 39 [j]S Mt 13:17 [k]Ge 23:4; Lev 25:23; Php 3:20; 1Pe 1:17; 2:11
11:15 [l]Ge 24:6-8
11:16 [m]2Ti 4:18 [n]Mk 8:38 [o]Ge 26:24; 28:13; Ex 3:6,15 [p]ver 10; Heb 13:14
11:17 [q]Ge 22:1-10; Jas 2:21
11:18 [r]Ge 21:12; Ro 9:7
11:19 [s]Ro 4:21; S Jn 5:21
11:20 [t]Ge 27:27-29,39, 40
11:21 [u]Ge 48:1, 8-22
11:22 [v]Ge 50:24, 25; Ex 13:19; Jos 24:32
11:23 [w]Ex 2:2 [x]Ex 1:16,22
11:24 [y]Ex 2:10, 11
11:25 [z]ver 37
11:26 [a]Heb 13:13 [b]Lk 14:33 [c]Heb 10:35
11:27 [d]Ex 12:50, 51
11:28 [e]1Co 10:10 [f]Ex 12:21-23

[u] *11* Or *By faith even Sarah, who was past age, was enabled to bear children because she*
[v] *18* Greek *seed* [w] *18* Gen. 21:12
[x] *29* That is, Sea of Reeds

Abraham knew that the earthly land of promise was not the end of his pilgrimage. Rather, it pointed beyond to the heavenly city that God had prepared for his faithful servants (see article on THE CALL OF ABRAHAM, p. 25). Abraham serves as an example for all God's people; we must realize that we are only traveling through this world on our way to our true home in heaven. In this life we must not seek ultimate security in or be fascinated with this present world (vv. 14,16; 13:14). We must see ourselves as strangers and exiles on the earth. This is not our homeland, but foreign territory; the end of our pilgrimage will be "a better country" (v. 16), "the heavenly Jerusalem" (12:22) and the "city that is to come" (13:14).

11:13 DID NOT RECEIVE THE THINGS PROMISED. These OT saints died with the faith that God had something better in store for them. In their lifetime they did not see the final promised blessing of the redeemed. Their basic hope was for eternal life with God in a heavenly homeland, and they fixed their eyes on their citizenship in the new heaven and the new earth (vv. 13–16; cf. Isa 65:17; 66:22; Php 3:20; Rev 21:1). Believers today must also persevere in faith and trust in God, even when they do not see all of God's promises fulfilled in their lives. The faith that God approves of is a faith that is able to surrender God's promises back to him for their fulfillment according to his will.

11:16 GOD IS NOT ASHAMED. Those who honor God by living as "aliens and strangers" (1Pe 2:11) and by desiring a better country God will honor by calling himself their God. He will not be ashamed to acknowledge them as his very own children (cf. Ex 3:6).

11:25 ENJOY THE PLEASURES OF SIN. Every believer faces the recurring choice either of enjoying the passing pleasures of sin or of suffering as he or she continues in obedience to God's will (see Gal 5:17, note).

but when the Egyptians tried to do so,
they were drowned.[g]
30By faith the walls of Jericho fell,
after the people had marched around
them for seven days.[h]
31By faith the prostitute Rahab, because she welcomed the spies, was not
killed with those who were disobedient.[y][i]

The Faith of the Judges and Prophets

32And what more shall I say? I do
not have time to tell about Gideon,[j]
Barak,[k] Samson,[l] Jephthah,[m] David,[n] Samuel[o] and the prophets,
33who through faith conquered kingdoms,[p] administered justice, and
gained what was promised; who shut
the mouths of lions,[q] 34quenched the
fury of the flames,[r] and escaped the
edge of the sword;[s] whose weakness
was turned to strength;[t] and who became powerful in battle and routed foreign armies.[u] 35Women received back
their dead, raised to life again.[v] Others were tortured and refused to be released, so that they might gain a better
resurrection. 36Some faced jeers and
flogging,[w] while still others were
chained and put in prison.[x] 37They
were stoned[z];[y] they were sawed in
two; they were put to death by the
sword.[z] They went about in sheepskins and goatskins,[a] destitute, persecuted and mistreated — 38the world
was not worthy of them. They wandered in deserts and mountains, and in
caves[b] and holes in the ground.
39These were all commended[c] for
their faith, yet none of them received
what had been promised.[d] 40God had
planned something better for us so
that only together with us[e] would
they be made perfect.[f]

God Disciplines His Sons

12 Therefore, since we are surrounded by such a great cloud
of witnesses, let us throw off everything that hinders and the sin that so
easily entangles, and let us run[g] with
perseverance[h] the race marked out
for us. 2Let us fix our eyes on Jesus,[i]
the author[j] and perfecter of our faith,

Jas 2:14-26

11:29 [g] Ex 14:21-31 **11:30** [h] Jos 6:12-20 **11:31** [i] Jos 2:1, 9-14; 6:22-25; Jas 2:25 **11:32** [j] Jdg 6-8 [k] Jdg 4-5 [l] Jdg 13-16 [m] Jdg 11-12 [n] 1Sa 16:1,13 [o] 1Sa 1:20 **11:33** [p] 2Sa 8:1-3 [q] Da 6:22 **11:34** [r] Da 3:19-27 [s] Ex 18:4 [t] 2Ki 20:7 [u] Jdg 15:8 **11:35** [v] 1Ki 17:22,23; 2Ki 4:36,37 **11:36** [w] Jer 20:2; 37:15 [x] Ge 39:20 **11:37** [y] 2Ch 24:21 [z] 1Ki 19:10; Jer 26:23 [a] 2Ki 1:8 **11:38** [b] 1Ki 18:4; 19:9 **11:39** [c] ver 2,4 [d] ver 13; Heb 10:36 **11:40** [e] Rev 6:11 [f] S Heb 2:10 **12:1** [g] S 1Co 9:24 [h] S Heb 10:36 **12:2** [i] Ps 25:15 [j] Heb 2:10

[y] 31 Or *unbelieving* [z] 37 Some early manuscripts *stoned; they were put to the test;*

11:35 OTHERS WERE TORTURED. God permitted some of his faithful children to experience great suffering and trouble (see article on THE SUFFERING OF THE RIGHTEOUS, p. 710). Though they enjoyed divine companionship, God did not deliver all of them from suffering and death (vv. 35–39). (1) Notice that through faith some "escaped the edge of the sword" (v. 34) and some "were put to death by the sword" (v. 37). Through faith one was delivered and another died (cf. 1Ki 19:10; Jer 26:23; Ac 12:2). Sincere faith will not only lead believers to do great things for God (vv. 33–35), but will also at times bring them into suffering, persecution, hardship and destitution (vv. 35–39; cf. Ps 44:22; Ro 8:36; see Mt 5:10, note).

(2) Faithfulness to God does not guarantee comfort or deliverance from persecution in this world. But it does assure us of God's grace, help and strength in times of persecution, trials or suffering (cf. 12:2; Jer 20:1,7–8; 37:13–15; 38:5; 2Co 6:9).

11:38 THEY WANDERED IN DESERTS AND MOUNTAINS. God's faithful saints refused to conform to the world's low standards or to enjoy its immoral pleasures, and in return they received scorn and affliction from the world. Because they rejected the world, they were rejected by the world. Even though blessings were promised for the faithful in the OT (Dt 29:9; Jos 1:8), they had to endure persecution and destitution (vv. 35–39). In the NT the faithful are taught to expect adversity (see 2Ti 3:12, note), be identified with the cross (see Mt 10:38, note; Gal 2:20, note) and follow the "man of sorrows" (Isa 53:3; cf. Heb 12:2).

11:40 SO THAT ONLY TOGETHER WITH US. All the OT saints died without receiving the full blessings and promises of God. But at Christ's death and resurrection, he procured perfect salvation for them, and they will receive their full inheritance with us in the new heaven and earth (Rev 20–22).

12:1 THE RACE MARKED OUT FOR US. This race is the lifelong test of faith in this world (10:23,38; 11; 12:25; 13:13). (1) The race must be run with "perseverance" (Gk *hupomonē*), i.e., with patience and endurance (cf. 10:36; Php 3:12–14). The way of victory is the same as that of the saints in ch. 11 — pressing on to the finish (cf. 6:11–12; 12:1–4; Lk 21:19; 1Co 9:24–25; Php 3:11–14; Rev 3:21). (2) The race must be run by throwing off the sins that impede or slow us down and by fixing our eyes, lives and hearts on Jesus and the example of persevering obedience he set on earth (vv. 1–4). (3) The race must be run with an awareness that the greatest danger confronting us is the temptation to yield to sin (vv. 1,4), to return to "the country [we] had left" (11:15; Jas 1:12), and to once again become citizens of the world (11:13; Jas 4:4; 1Jn 2:15; see Heb 11:10, note).

12:2 FIX OUR EYES ON JESUS. In our race of faith we look to Jesus as (1) our example of trust in God (2:13), of commitment to his will (10:7–10; Mk 14:36), of prayer (5:7; Mk 1:35; Jn 17), of overcoming temptation and suffering (2:10; 4:15), of endurance in loyalty to the Father (vv. 2–3), and of seeking the joy of completing the work to which God has called us (v. 2; cf. Lk 15:6,24,32; Jn

who for the joy set before him endured the cross,[k] scorning its shame,[l] and sat down at the right hand of the throne of God.[m] **3**Consider him who endured such opposition from sinful men, so that you will not grow weary[n] and lose heart.

4In your struggle against sin, you have not yet resisted to the point of shedding your blood.[o] **5**And you have forgotten that word of encouragement that addresses you as sons:

"My son, do not make light of the
  Lord's discipline,
 and do not lose heart[p] when he
  rebukes you,
6because the Lord disciplines those
  he loves,[q]
 and he punishes everyone he
  accepts as a son."[a][r]

7Endure hardship as discipline; God is treating you as sons.[s] For what son is not disciplined by his father? **8**If you are not disciplined (and everyone undergoes discipline),[t] then you are illegitimate children and not true sons. **9**Moreover, we have all had human fathers who disciplined us and we respected them for it. How much more should we submit to the Father of our spirits[u] and live![v] **10**Our fathers disciplined us for a little while as they thought best; but God disciplines us for our good, that we may share in his holiness.[w] **11**No discipline seems pleasant at the time, but painful. Later on, however, it produces a harvest of righteousness and peace[x] for those who have been trained by it.

12Therefore, strengthen your feeble arms and weak knees.[y] **13**"Make level paths for your feet,"[b][z] so that the lame may not be disabled, but rather healed.[a]

Warning Against Refusing God

14Make every effort to live in peace with all men[b] and to be holy;[c] without holiness no one will see the Lord.[d] **15**See to it that no one misses the grace

12:2 [k]Php 2:8,9; Heb 2:9 [l]Heb 13:13 [m]S Mk 16:19
12:3 [n]Gal 6:9; Rev 2:3
12:4 [o]Heb 10:32-34; 13:13
12:5 [p]ver 3
12:6 [q]Ps 94:12; 119:75; Rev 3:19 [r]Pr 3:11,12
12:7 [s]Dt 8:5; 2Sa 7:14; Pr 13:24
12:8 [t]1Pe 5:9
12:9 [u]Nu 16:22; 27:16; Rev 22:6 [v]Isa 38:16
12:10 [w]S 2Pe 1:4
12:11 [x]Isa 32:17; Jas 3:17,18
12:12 [y]Isa 35:3
12:13 [z]Pr 4:26 [a]Gal 6:1
12:14 [b]S Ro 14:19 [c]Ro 6:22 [d]S Mt 5:8

[a] *6* Prov. 3:11,12 [b] *13* Prov. 4:26

15:11); (2) our source of strength, love, grace, mercy and help (4:16; 7:25; 10:22; Rev 3:21).

12:5 THE LORD'S DISCIPLINE. Note several facts about God's discipline of believers and the hardships and troubles he allows us to suffer. (1) They are a sign that we are God's children (vv. 7–8).

(2) They are an assurance of God's love and concern for us (v. 6).

(3) The Lord's discipline has two purposes: (a) that we might not be finally condemned with the world (1Co 11:31–32), and (b) that we might share God's holiness and continue to live sanctified lives without which we will never see the Lord (vv. 10–11,14).

(4) There are two possible consequences of the Lord's discipline. (a) We may endure the hardships God leads us through, submit to God's will and continue to remain faithful (vv. 5–6). By doing this we will continue to live as God's spiritual children (vv. 7–9) and share his holiness (v. 10); it will yield the harvest of righteousness (v. 11). (b) We may "make light of" the discipline of our Father (v. 5), rebel against God because of suffering and hardship, and thereby fall away from God (v. 25; 3:12–14).

(5) Under God's will, trouble may come (a) as a result of our spiritual warfare with Satan (Eph 6:11–18), (b) as a test to strengthen our faith (1Pe 1:6–7) and our works (Mt 7:24–27; 1Co 3:13–15), or (c) as a preparation for us to comfort others (2Co 1:3–5) and to manifest the life of Christ (2Co 4:8–10,12,16).

(6) In all kinds of adversity we must seek God, examine our lives (2Ch 26:5; Ps 3:4; 9:12; 34:17) and forsake all that is contrary to his holiness (vv. 10,14; see Ps 60:1–12, note; 66:18, note; see article on THE SUFFERING OF THE RIGHTEOUS, p. 710).

12:14 MAKE EVERY EFFORT ... TO BE HOLY. To be holy is to be separated from sin and set apart for God; it is to be close to God, to be like him, and to seek his presence, righteousness and fellowship with all our hearts. Above all things, holiness is God's priority for his followers (Eph 4:21–24). (1) Holiness was God's purpose for his people when he planned their salvation in Christ (Eph 1:4).

(2) Holiness was Christ's purpose for his people when he came to this earth (Mt 1:21; 1Co 1:2,30).

(3) Holiness was Christ's purpose for his people when he gave himself for them on the cross (Eph 5:25–27).

(4) Holiness is God's purpose in making us a new creation and in giving us the Holy Spirit (Ro 8:2–15; Gal 5:16–25; Eph 2:10).

(5) Without holiness no one can be useful to God (2Ti 2:20–21).

(6) Without holiness there is no nearness to or fellowship with God (Ps 15:1–2).

(7) Without holiness no one will see the Lord (v. 14; Mt 5:8; see article on SANCTIFICATION, p. 1956).

12:15 BITTER ROOT. A "bitter root" refers to a spirit and attitude characterized by intense animosity and resentment. Here it may refer to an attitude of bitter resentment toward God's discipline instead of humble submission to his will for our lives. Bitterness can also be directed toward persons in the church. It results in defiling the person who is bitter, i.e., making him or her unfit to approach God in prayer. Bitterness in the com-

of God[e] and that no bitter root[f]
grows up to cause trouble and defile
many. **16**See that no one is sexually immoral,[g] or is godless like Esau, who
for a single meal sold his inheritance
rights as the oldest son.[h] **17**Afterward, as you know, when he wanted to
inherit this blessing, he was rejected.
He could bring about no change of
mind, though he sought the blessing
with tears.[i]

18You have not come to a mountain
that can be touched and that is burning
with fire; to darkness, gloom and
storm;[j] **19**to a trumpet blast[k] or to
such a voice speaking words[l] that
those who heard it begged that no further word be spoken to them,[m] **20**because they could not bear what was
commanded: "If even an animal
touches the mountain, it must be
stoned."[c][n] **21**The sight was so terrifying that Moses said, "I am trembling
with fear."[d][o]

22But you have come to Mount
Zion,[p] to the heavenly Jerusalem,[q]
the city[r] of the living God.[s] You have
come to thousands upon thousands of
angels in joyful assembly, **23**to the
church of the firstborn,[t] whose names
are written in heaven.[u] You have
come to God, the judge of all men,[v] to
the spirits of righteous men made perfect,[w] **24**to Jesus the mediator[x] of a
new covenant, and to the sprinkled
blood[y] that speaks a better word than
the blood of Abel.[z]

25See to it that you do not refuse[a]
him who speaks.[b] If they did not escape when they refused him who
warned[c] them on earth, how much
less will we, if we turn away from him
who warns us from heaven?[d] **26**At
that time his voice shook the earth,[e]
but now he has promised, "Once more
I will shake not only the earth but also
the heavens."[e][f] **27**The words "once
more" indicate the removing of what
can be shaken[g]—that is, created
things—so that what cannot be shak-
en may remain.

28Therefore, since we are receiving
a kingdom that cannot be shaken,[h]
let us be thankful, and so worship
God acceptably with reverence and
awe,[i] **29**for our "God is a consuming
fire."[f][j]

Concluding Exhortations

13 Keep on loving each other as
brothers.[k] **2**Do not forget to
entertain strangers,[l] for by so doing
some people have entertained angels
without knowing it.[m] **3**Remember
those in prison[n] as if you were their
fellow prisoners, and those who are
mistreated as if you yourselves were
suffering.

4Marriage should be honored by
all,[o] and the marriage bed kept pure,
for God will judge the adulterer and all
the sexually immoral.[p] **5**Keep your
lives free from the love of money[q] and
be content with what you have,[r] because God has said,

12:15 [e] Gal 5:4; Heb 3:12; 4:1 [f] Dt 29:18
12:16 [g] S 1Co 6:18 [h] Ge 25:29-34
12:17 [i] Ge 27:30-40
12:18 [j] Ex 19:12-22; 20:18; Dt 4:11
12:19 [k] Ex 20:18 [l] Dt 4:12 [m] Ex 20:19; Dt 5:5,25; 18:16
12:20 [n] Ex 19:12, 13
12:21 [o] Dt 9:19
12:22 [p] Isa 24:23; 60:14; Rev 14:1 [q] S Gal 4:26 [r] Heb 11:10; 13:14 [s] S Mt 16:16
12:23 [t] Ex 4:22 [u] S Rev 20:12 [v] Ge 18:25; Ps 94:2 [w] Php 3:12
12:24 [x] S Gal 3:20 [y] Heb 9:19; 10:22; 1Pe 1:2 [z] Ge 4:10; Heb 11:4
12:25 [a] Heb 3:12 [b] S Heb 1:1 [c] Heb 8:5; 11:7 [d] Dt 18:19; Heb 2:2,3; 10:29
12:26 [e] Ex 19:18 [f] Hag 2:6
12:27 [g] Isa 34:4; 54:10; 1Co 7:31; Heb 1:11,12; 2Pe 3:10; 1Jn 2:17
12:28 [h] Ps 15:5; Da 2:44 [i] Mal 2:5; 4:2; Heb 13:15
12:29 [j] Ex 24:17; Dt 4:24; 9:3; Ps 97:3; Isa 33:14; S 2Th 1:7
13:1 [k] S Ro 12:10
13:2 [l] Job 31:32; Mt 25:35; S Ro 12:13 [m] Ge 18:1-33; 19:1-3
13:3 [n] Mt 25:36; Col 4:18; Heb 10:34
13:4 [o] Mal 2:15; 1Co 7:38; 1Ti 4:3 [p] Dt 22:22; 1Co 6:9; Rev 22:15
13:5 [q] S 1Ti 3:3 [r] Php 4:11; 1Ti 6:6,8

[c] *20* Exodus 19:12,13 [d] *21* Deut. 9:19
[e] *26* Haggai 2:6 [f] *29* Deut. 4:24

munity of believers can spread and defile many, destroying the holiness without which "no one will see the Lord" (v. 14).

12:18–25 MOUNTAIN THAT CAN BE TOUCHED. The awesome circumstances of the giving of the law (cf. Ex 19:10–25; Dt 4:11–12; 5:22–26) and the features of the gospel are contrasted. The consequences of turning away from the gospel are far more dreadful than were the consequences of rejecting the law.

12:26–29 SHOOK THE EARTH. God will one day bring down the present world order and shake to pieces the whole material universe (see Hag 2:6–9,21, notes). The present form of the world is not eternal; it will be destroyed by fire and replaced by a new heaven and earth (Rev 20:11; 21:1; cf. 2Pe 3:10–13). The only thing that will survive in its present form will be God's kingdom and those who belong to it (v. 28).

13:1 LOVING EACH OTHER AS BROTHERS. In the NT church believers thought of and addressed each other as brothers and sisters in Christ (cf. 1Th 4:9–10; 1Pe 1:22; 2Pe 1:7). Christian brotherhood comes from our mutual relationship with the Father and his only Son (1:2). As we participate in the grace of Christ, we are all made sons and daughters with him and fellow heirs of the Father's blessings (1:2; Jn 1:12–13; Ro 8:14–17; Eph 1:5–7). Because of this brotherhood, we are taught by the Father to love each other (1Th 4:9; 1Jn 4:11; see Jn 13:34–35, notes).

13:4 MARRIAGE SHOULD BE HONORED. God has high standards for his people in marriage and sexuality. For a discussion of this important issue, see article on STANDARDS OF SEXUAL MORALITY, p. 1936.

13:5 FREE FROM THE LOVE OF MONEY. Notice that this exhortation follows the warning against immorality (v. 4). Greed and immorality are closely connected in the NT (1Co 5:11; 6:9–10; Eph 5:3; Col 3:5). All too often the love of abundance and luxury and the constant desire for

STANDARDS OF SEXUAL MORALITY

***Heb 13:4** "Marriage should be honored by all, and the marriage bed kept pure, for God will judge the adulterer and all the sexually immoral."*

Above all, believers must be morally and sexually pure (2Co 11:2; Tit 2:5; 1Pe 3:2). The word "pure" (Gk *hagnos* or *amiantos*) means to be free from all taint of that which is lewd. It suggests refraining from all acts and thoughts that incite desire not in accordance with one's virginity or one's marriage vows. It stresses restraint and avoidance of all sexual actions and excitements that would defile one's purity before God. It includes controlling one's own body "in a way that is holy and honorable" (1Th 4:4), and not in "passionate lust" (4:5). This Scriptural instruction is for both those who are single and those who are married. With regard to the Biblical teaching concerning sexual morality, note the following:

(1) Sexual intimacy is reserved for the marriage relationship and is approved and blessed by God only in that state (see Ge 2:24, note; SS 2:7, note; 4:12, note). Through marriage the husband and wife become one flesh according to God's will. The physical and emotional pleasures resulting from a faithful marriage relationship are ordained by God and held in honor by him.

(2) Adultery, sexual immorality, homosexuality, sensuality, impurity and degrading passions are considered grave sins in God's sight, since they are a transgression of God's law (see Ex 20:14, note) and a defiling of the marriage relationship. Such sins are severely condemned in Scripture (see Pr 5:3, note) and place one outside God's kingdom (Ro 1:24–32; 1Co 6:9–10; Gal 5:19–21).

(3) Sexual immorality and impurity include not only forbidden intercourse or consummated acts, but also involve any act of sexual gratification with another person other than one's marriage partner, achieved by uncovering or exploring the nakedness of that person. The contemporary teaching that says sexual intimacy among "committed" unmarried youth and adults is acceptable as long as it stops short of full sexual union is a teaching contrary to God's holiness and the Biblical standard of purity. God explicitly prohibits having any kind of "sexual relations with" (literally, "uncovering the nakedness of") anyone who is not a lawful wife or husband (Lev 18:6–30; 20:11,17,19–21; see 18:6, note).

(4) The believer must exercise self-control with reference to all sexual matters before marriage. To justify premarital intimacy in the name of Christ merely on the ground of a real or a felt commitment to another flagrantly compromises God's holy standards with the world's impure ways and, in effect, justifies immorality. After marriage, sexual intimacy must be confined to one's marriage partner. The Bible names self-control as one aspect of the Spirit's fruit, the positive and pure behavior that is in contrast to immoral sexual play, gratification, adultery and impurity. One's faith commitment to God's will with regard to purity will open the way to receiving this gift of self-control through the Spirit (Gal 5:22–24).

(5) Biblical terms used for sexual immorality, describing the breadth of its evil, are as follows: (a) Sexual immorality (Gk *porneia*) describes a wide variety of sexual activities before or outside of marriage; it is not limited to consummated sexual acts. Any intimate sexual activity or play outside the marriage relationship, including the touching of the intimate parts of the body or seeing another person's nakedness, is included in this term and is clearly a transgression of God's moral standards for his people (see Lev 18:6–30; 20:11–12,17,19–21; 1Co 6:18; 1Th 4:3). (b) Debauchery, or sensuality, (Gk *aselgeia*) denotes the absence of clear moral principles, especially disregard of sexual self-control that maintains pure behavior (see 1Ti 2:9, note on modesty). It includes the inclination toward indulging in or arousing sinful lust, and thus is a participation in Biblically unjustifiable conduct (Gal 5:19; Eph 4:19; 1Pe 4:3; 2Pe 2:2,18). (c) Exploiting or taking advantage of someone (Gk *pleonekteō*) means to deprive another of the moral purity that God desires for that person in order to satisfy one's own self-centered desires. To arouse in another person sexual desires that cannot be righteously fulfilled is to exploit or take advantage of that person (1Th 4:6; cf. Eph 4:19). (d) Lust (Gk *epithumia*) is having an immoral desire that one would fulfill if the opportunity arose (Eph 4:19,22; 1Pe 4:3; 2Pe 2:18; see Mt 5:28, note).

"Never will I leave you;
never will I forsake you."[g][s]

6So we say with confidence,

"The Lord is my helper; I will not
be afraid.
What can man do to me?"[h][t]

7Remember your leaders,[u] who
spoke the word of God[v] to you. Consider the outcome of their way of life
and imitate[w] their faith. **8**Jesus Christ
is the same yesterday and today and
forever.[x]
9Do not be carried away by all kinds
of strange teachings.[y] It is good for
our hearts to be strengthened[z] by
grace, not by ceremonial foods,[a]
which are of no value to those who eat
them.[b] **10**We have an altar from which
those who minister at the tabernacle[c]
have no right to eat.[d]
11The high priest carries the blood
of animals into the Most Holy Place as
a sin offering,[e] but the bodies are
burned outside the camp.[f] **12**And so
Jesus also suffered outside the city
gate[g] to make the people holy[h]
through his own blood.[i] **13**Let us,
then, go to him[j] outside the camp,
bearing the disgrace he bore.[k] **14**For
here we do not have an enduring city,[l]
but we are looking for the city that is
to come.[m]
15Through Jesus, therefore, let us
continually offer to God a sacrifice[n] of
praise—the fruit of lips[o] that confess
his name. **16**And do not forget to do
good and to share with others,[p] for
with such sacrifices[q] God is pleased.
17Obey your leaders[r] and submit to
their authority. They keep watch over
you[s] as men who must give an account. Obey them so that their work
will be a joy, not a burden, for that
would be of no advantage to you.
18Pray for us.[t] We are sure that we
have a clear conscience[u] and desire to
live honorably in every way. **19**I particularly urge you to pray so that I may
be restored to you soon.[v]
20May the God of peace,[w] who
through the blood of the eternal covenant[x] brought back from the dead[y]
our Lord Jesus, that great Shepherd of
the sheep,[z] **21**equip you with everything good for doing his will,[a] and
may he work in us[b] what is pleas-

13:5 [s]Dt 31:6,8; Jos 1:5
13:6 [t]Ps 118:6,7
13:7 [u]ver 17,24; 1Co 16:16 [v]S Heb 4:12 [w]Heb 6:12
13:8 [x]Ps 102:27; Heb 1:12
13:9 [y]Eph 4:14 [z]Col 2:7 [a]Col 2:16 [b]Heb 9:10
13:10 [c]Heb 8:5 [d]1Co 9:13; 10:18
13:11 [e]Lev 16:15 [f]Ex 29:14; Lev 4:12,21; 9:11; 16:27
13:12 [g]Jn 19:17 [h]S Eph 5:26 [i]S Ro 3:25
13:13 [j]Lk 9:23 [k]Heb 11:26
13:14 [l]Heb 12:27 [m]Php 3:20; Heb 11:10,27; 12:22
13:15 [n]1Pe 2:5 [o]Isa 57:19; Hos 14:2
13:16 [p]Ro 12:13 [q]Php 4:18
13:17 [r]ver 7,24 [s]Isa 62:6; Ac 20:28
13:18 [t]S 1Th 5:25 [u]S Ac 23:1
13:19 [v]Phm 22
13:20 [w]S Ro 15:33 [x]Ge 9:16; 17:7,13, 19; Isa 55:3; 61:8; Eze 37:26; S Mt 26:28 [y]S Ac 2:24 [z]S Jn 10:11
13:21 [a]2Co 9:8 [b]S Php 2:13

[g]5 Deut. 31:6 [h]6 Psalm 118:6,7

wealth open up a person to sexual sins (see 1Ti 6:6–10).

13:6 THE LORD IS MY HELPER. No matter how limited our earthly possessions may be or how trying our circumstances, we never need fear that God will desert or forsake us (see Jos 1:5, note). Scripture declares that the heavenly Father cares for us. Thus, we can say with the author of Hebrews, who echoes the psalmist, "The Lord is my helper; I will not be afraid." This can be affirmed with confidence in times of distress, trials or trouble (see Mt 6:30,33 notes).

13:8 JESUS CHRIST IS THE SAME. The truth that Jesus Christ does not change provides a sure anchor for our faith. It means that present-day believers must not be content until they experience the same salvation, communion with God, baptism in the Holy Spirit and kingdom power that the NT believers experienced in their service to God through Christ Jesus (see article on THE KINGDOM OF GOD, p. 1430).

13:12 MAKE THE PEOPLE HOLY. Jesus suffered outside the city gate of Jerusalem in order that we might be made holy, i.e., separated from the old sinful life and dedicated to God's service (see articles on SANCTIFICATION, p. 1956, and SPIRITUAL SEPARATION FOR BELIEVERS, p. 1794).

13:13 LET US, THEN, GO TO HIM. To be a follower of Christ involves going "outside the camp." For these Jewish Christians the camp represented Judaism. For us it represents the world with all its sinful pleasures, ungodly values and temporal goals. We must bear the disgrace Christ bore in order to follow him, sympathize with him, be his friend, identify with him, and announce to the world our commitment to his standards and purposes. In going outside the gate we find ourselves strangers and aliens on the earth (v. 14; 11:13). Yet we are not without a city, for we seek a city that is to come, a city with foundations, "whose architect and builder is God" (11:10,14,16; 13:14).

13:17 OBEY THEM. Obedience and faithfulness to Christian leaders, pastors and teachers must be based on a higher loyalty to God. The believer's loyalty on a descending scale is as follows: (1) first, to God in a person-to-person relationship (see Mt 22:37, note), including faithfulness to the truth and principles of his Word (see article on THE INSPIRATION AND AUTHORITY OF SCRIPTURE, p. 1898); (2) second, to the visible church as it remains faithful to God and his written Word (Jn 15:12; Gal 6:10); (3) third, to human leaders within the church, as long as they remain faithful and loyal to God, to his Word and to his purpose for the church.

ing to him,[c] through Jesus Christ, to
whom be glory for ever and ever.
Amen.[d]
22Brothers, I urge you to bear with
my word of exhortation, for I have written you only a short letter.[e]
23I want you to know that our brother Timothy[f] has been released. If he
arrives soon, I will come with him to
see you.
24Greet all your leaders[g] and all
God's people. Those from Italy[h] send
you their greetings.
25Grace be with you all.[i]

13:21 [c] 1Jn 3:22 [d] S Ro 11:36
13:22 [e] 1Pe 5:12
13:23 [f] S Ac 16:1
13:24 [g] ver 7,17 [h] Ac 18:2
13:25 [i] S Col 4:18

JAMES

Outline

Christian Greetings (1:1)

- I. Facing Trials and Benefiting From Them (1:2–18)
  - A. Accept Them as a Means of Growth (1:2–4)
  - B. Pray for Wisdom in Coping With Them (1:5–8)
  - C. Rejoice in Their Leveling Action (1:9–12)
  - D. Recognize the Difference Between Trials and Temptations (1:13–18)
- II. Hearing the Word and Doing It (1:19–27)
- III. Being Impartial and Showing It (2:1–13)
- IV. Professing Faith and Proving It (2:14–26)
- V. Recognizing Pitfalls and Avoiding Them (3:1—5:6)
  - A. The Unruly Tongue (3:1–12)
  - B. Unspiritual Wisdom (3:13–18)
  - C. Sinful Behavior (4:1–10)
  - D. Speaking Against a Brother (4:11–12)
  - E. Presumptuous Living (4:13–17)
  - F. Selfish Wealth (5:1–6)
- VI. Christian Virtues and Living by Them (5:7–20)
  - A. Patience and Endurance (5:7–11)
  - B. Simple Honesty (5:12)
  - C. Prevailing Prayers for the Sick (5:13–18)
  - D. Reclaiming the Wandering (5:19–20)

Author: James

Theme: Faith That Works

Date of Writing: A.D. 45–49

Background

James is classified as a "general letter" because it was originally addressed to a wider audience than a local church. The salutation, "to the twelve tribes scattered among the nations" (1:1), along with other references (2:19,21), indicate that the letter was written initially to Jewish Christians living outside Palestine. It is possible that the recipients of the letter were among the first converts in Jerusalem who, after Stephen's martyrdom, were scattered by persecution (Ac 8:1) as far as Phoenicia, Cyprus, Antioch and beyond (Ac 11:19). This would explain (1) the letter's opening emphasis on joyfully enduring trials that test faith and require perseverance (1:2–12), (2) James's personal knowledge of the "scattered" believers, and (3) the authoritative tone of the letter. As leader of the Jerusalem church, James was writing to his scattered sheep.

The author's prominence is indicated by the way he identifies himself simply as "James" (1:1). James, the half-brother of Jesus and the leader of the Jerusalem church, is generally regarded as the author. His speech at the Jerusalem council (Ac 15:13–21) as well as descriptions of him elsewhere in the NT (e.g., Ac 12:17; 21:18; Gal 1:19; 2:9,12; 1Co 15:7) correspond perfectly with what is known about the author of this letter. James most likely wrote his letter during the 40s. This early date for writing is indicated by several factors, such as the fact that James uses the Greek word *synagōgē* to refer to the Christians' place of meeting (2:2). According to the Jewish historian Josephus, James, the Lord's brother, was martyred at Jerusalem in A.D. 62.

Purpose

James wrote (1) to encourage Jewish believers who were suffering various trials that were testing their faith, (2) to correct erroneous ideas about the nature of saving faith, and (3) to exhort and instruct the readers about the practical outworkings of their faith in righteous living and good deeds.

Survey

This letter covers a wide variety of topics related to living a genuine Christian life. James urges believers to endure their trials joyfully and benefit from them (1:2–11); to resist temptations (1:12–18); to be doers of the Word, not just hearers (1:19–27); and to demonstrate an active faith, not an empty profession (2:14–26). He solemnly warns about the sinfulness of an unruly tongue (3:1–12; 4:11–12), worldly wisdom (3:13–16), sinful behavior (4:1–10), presumptuous living (4:13–17) and self-centered wealth (5:1–6). James concludes with an emphasis on patience, prayer and reclaiming the wandering (5:7–20).

Throughout its five chapters, the relationship between true faith and godly living is emphasized. Genuine faith is a tested faith (1:2–16), is an active faith (1:19–27), loves one's neighbor as oneself (2:1–13), manifests itself in good deeds (2:14–26), keeps a tight rein on the tongue (3:1–12), seeks God's wisdom (3:13–18), submits to God as the righteous judge (4:1–12), trusts God in daily living (4:13–17), is not self-centered or self-indulgent (5:1–6), is patient in suffering (5:7–12) and is diligent in prayer (5:13–20).

Special Features

Seven major features characterize this letter. (1) It is most likely the first book written in the NT. (2) Although it contains only two references to Christ by name, there are more reminiscences of Jesus' teaching in this letter, including at least fifteen allusions to the Sermon on the Mount, than in all the other NT letters combined. (3) More than half of its 108 verses are imperatives or commands. (4) In many ways it is the Proverbs of the NT, for (a) it is full of godly wisdom and practical instructions for living a genuine Christian life, and (b) it is written in terse style, with crisp commands and vivid analogies. (5) James is an astute observer of the operations of nature and of fallen human nature. He often draws lessons from the former to expose the latter (e.g., 3:1–12). (6) It emphasizes more than any other NT book the necessary relation between faith and deeds (esp. 2:14–26). (7) James is sometimes called the Amos of the NT, because he vigorously addresses issues of social injustice and inequality.

Reading James

In order to read the entire New Testament in one year, the book of James should be read in 4 days, according to the following schedule:
☐ 1 ☐ 2:1—3:13 ☐ 3:14—4:12 ☐ 4:13—5:20

NOTES

1 James,[a] a servant of God[b] and of
the Lord Jesus Christ,

To the twelve tribes[c] scattered[d]
among the nations:

Greetings.[e]

Trials and Temptations

2Consider it pure joy, my brothers,
whenever you face trials of many
kinds,[f] **3**because you know that the
testing of your faith[g] develops perseverance.[h] **4**Perseverance must finish
its work so that you may be mature[i]
and complete, not lacking anything. **5**If
any of you lacks wisdom, he should ask
God,[j] who gives generously to all
without finding fault, and it will be giv-
en to him.[k] **6**But when he asks, he
must believe and not doubt,[l] because
he who doubts is like a wave of the sea,
blown and tossed by the wind. **7**That
man should not think he will receive
anything from the Lord; **8**he is a double-minded man,[m] unstable[n] in all he
does.

9The brother in humble circumstances ought to take pride in his high
position.[o] **10**But the one who is rich
should take pride in his low position,
because he will pass away like a wild
flower.[p] **11**For the sun rises with
scorching heat[q] and withers[r] the
plant; its blossom falls and its beauty
is destroyed.[s] In the same way, the
rich man will fade away even while he
goes about his business.

12Blessed is the man who perseveres under trial,[t] because when he
has stood the test, he will receive the
crown of life[u] that God has promised
to those who love him.[v]

13When tempted, no one should say,
"God is tempting me." For God cannot
be tempted by evil, nor does he tempt
anyone; **14**but each one is tempted
when, by his own[w] evil desire, he is
dragged away and enticed. **15**Then, after desire has conceived, it gives birth
to sin;[x] and sin, when it is full-grown,
gives birth to death.[y]

16Don't be deceived,[z] my dear
brothers.[a] **17**Every good and perfect
gift is from above,[b] coming down from
the Father of the heavenly lights,[c]
who does not change[d] like shifting
shadows. **18**He chose to give us birth[e]
through the word of truth,[f] that we
might be a kind of firstfruits[g] of all he
created.

Listening and Doing

19My dear brothers,[h] take note of
this: Everyone should be quick to listen, slow to speak[i] and slow to become angry, **20**for man's anger[j] does
not bring about the righteous life that
God desires. **21**Therefore, get rid of[k]
all moral filth and the evil that is so
prevalent and humbly accept the word

1:1 [a]S Ac 15:13 [b]Ro 1:1; Tit 1:1 [c]Ac 26:7 [d]Dt 32:26; Jn 7:35; 1Pe 1:1 [e]Ac 15:23 **1:2** [f]ver 12; S Mt 5:12; Heb 10:34; 12:11 **1:3** [g]1Pe 1:7 [h]S Heb 10:36 **1:4** [i]S 1Co 2:6 **1:5** [j]1Ki 3:9,10; Pr 2:3-6 [k]Ps 51:6; Da 1:17; 2:21; S Mt 7:7 **1:6** [l]S Mt 21:21; Mk 11:24 **1:8** [m]Ps 119:113; Jas 4:8 [n]2Pe 2:14; 3:16 **1:9** [o]S Mt 23:12 **1:10** [p]Job 14:2; Ps 103:15,16; Isa 40:6,7; 1Co 7:31; 1Pe 1:24 **1:11** [q]Mt 20:12 [r]Ps 102:4,11 [s]Isa 40:6-8 **1:12** [t]ver 2; Ge 22:1; Jas 5:11; 1Pe 3:14 [u]S 1Co 9:25 [v]Ex 20:6; 1Co 2:9; 8:3; Jas 2:5 **1:14** [w]Pr 19:3 **1:15** [x]Ge 3:6; Job 15:35; Ps 7:14; Isa 59:4 [y]S Ro 6:23 **1:16** [z]S 1Co 6:9 [a]ver 19; Jas 2:5 **1:17** [b]Ps 85:12; Jn 3:27; Jas 3:15, 17 [c]Ge 1:16; Ps 136:7; Da 2:22; 1Jn 1:5 [d]Nu 23:19; Ps 102:27; Mal 3:6 **1:18** [e]S Jn 1:13 [f]S 2Ti 2:15 [g]Jer 2:3; Rev 14:4 **1:19** [h]ver 16; Jas 2:5 [i]Pr 10:19; Jas 3:3-12 **1:20** [j]S Mt 5:22 **1:21** [k]S Eph 4:22

1:2 TRIALS. The word "trials" (Gk *peirasmoi*) refers to persecution and troubles from the world or Satan. (1) The believer must meet these trials with joy (cf. Mt 5:11–12; Ro 5:3; 1Pe 1:6), for testing will develop persevering faith, proven character and mature hope (cf. Ro 5:3–5). Our faith can only reach full maturity when faced with difficulties and opposition (v. 3). (2) James calls these trials a "testing of your faith." Trials are sometimes brought into believers' lives so that God can test the sincerity of their faith. Scripture nowhere teaches that troubles in life are always an indication that God is displeased with us. They can be a sign that he recognizes our firm commitment to him (cf. Job 1–2).

1:4 YOU MAY BE MATURE. "Mature" (Gk *teleios*) reflects the Biblical idea of maturity, defined as a right relationship with God that bears fruit in a sincere endeavor to love him with all one's heart in undivided devotion, obedience and blamelessness (Dt 6:5; 18:13; Mt 22:37; see 1Th 2:10, note; see article on SANCTIFICATION, p. 1956).

1:5 IF ANY OF YOU LACKS WISDOM. Wisdom means the spiritual capacity to see and evaluate life and conduct from God's point of view (see Pr 1:2, note). It involves making right choices and doing right things according to both God's will revealed in his Word and the leading of the Spirit (Ro 8:4–17). We can receive wisdom by coming to God and asking for it in faith (vv. 6–8; cf. Pr 2:6; 1Co 1:30).

1:9–10 THE BROTHER IN HUMBLE CIRCUMSTANCES . . . THE ONE WHO IS RICH. See article on RICHES AND POVERTY, p. 1562.

1:13 TEMPTED. No person who sins can evade guilt by throwing the blame on God. God may test us in order to strengthen our faith, but never with the intent of leading us to sin. God's nature demonstrates that he cannot be a source of temptation to sin (see article on THE ATTRIBUTES OF GOD, p. 882).

1:14 BY HIS OWN EVIL DESIRE. Temptation essentially comes from our own inward desires or inclinations (cf. Mt 15:19). If evil desire is not resisted and purged by the Holy Spirit, it leads to sin and then to spiritual death (v. 15; Ro 6:23; 7:5,10, 13).

1:21 GET RID OF ALL MORAL FILTH. The Word of God, either preached or written, cannot

planted in you,[l] which can save you.
[22]Do not merely listen to the word,
and so deceive yourselves. Do what it
says.[m] [23]Anyone who listens to the
word but does not do what it says is
like a man who looks at his face in a
mirror [24]and, after looking at himself,
goes away and immediately forgets
what he looks like. [25]But the man who
looks intently into the perfect law that
gives freedom,[n] and continues to do
this, not forgetting what he has heard,
but doing it—he will be blessed in
what he does.[o]
[26]If anyone considers himself religious
and yet does not keep a tight rein
on his tongue,[p] he deceives himself
and his religion is worthless. [27]Reli-
gion that God our Father accepts as
pure and faultless is this: to look after[q] orphans and widows[r] in their
distress and to keep oneself from being
polluted by the world.[s]

1:21 [l]Eph 1:13
1:22 [m]S Mt 7:21; Jas 2:14-20
1:25 [n]Ps 19:7; Jn 8:32; Gal 2:4; Jas 2:12 [o]S Jn 13:17
1:26 [p]Ps 34:13; 39:1; 141:3; Jas 3:2-12; 1Pe 3:10
1:27 [q]Mt 25:36 [r]Dt 14:29; Job 31:16,17,21; Ps 146:9; Isa 1:17,23 [s]Ro 12:2; Jas 4:4; 2Pe 1:4; 2:20
2:1 [t]Ac 7:2; 1Co 2:8 [u]ver 9; Dt 1:17; Lev 19:15; Pr 24:23; S Ac 10:34
2:4 [v]S Jn 7:24
2:5 [w]Jas 1:16,19

Favoritism Forbidden

2 My brothers, as believers in our glorious[t] Lord Jesus Christ, don't
show favoritism.[u] [2]Suppose a man
comes into your meeting wearing a
gold ring and fine clothes, and a poor
man in shabby clothes also comes in.
[3]If you show special attention to the
man wearing fine clothes and say,
"Here's a good seat for you," but say to
the poor man, "You stand there" or "Sit
on the floor by my feet," [4]have you not
discriminated among yourselves and
become judges[v] with evil thoughts?
[5]Listen, my dear brothers:[w] Has not
God chosen those who are poor in the

effectively take hold of a person's life if he or she is not separated from moral filth and evil. (1) God commands believers to set aside all the ungodly filth that permeates a corrupt society and seeks to influence them and their families. This filth defiles people's souls and blights their lives (cf. Eph 4:22,25,31; Col 3:8; 1Pe 2:1).

(2) Scripture tells us what is improper for God's holy people. Accordingly, we must not engage in any kind of impurity or obscenity (Eph 5:3–4). We must be aware that allowing *any kind* of moral filth into our lives or homes, including filthy language or obscenity through videos or television, grieves the Spirit and violates God's holy standards for his people. God's Word warns us, "Let no one deceive you with empty words, for because of such things God's wrath comes . . . Therefore do not be partners with them" (Eph 5:6–7).

(3) We as believers must take righteousness and holiness seriously. Our houses must be swept clean and filled with God's Word and the holiness of Christ (cf. Mt 12:43–45; see article on SANCTIFICATION, p. 1956).

1:21 WORD PLANTED IN YOU. Christians begin their new life in Christ by being born again "through the word of truth" (v. 18; see article on REGENERATION, p. 1589). New life in Christ demands that we get rid of all moral filth that offends the Holy Spirit (see previous note), and that we be steadfast in accepting God's Word into our hearts. The term "planted" (Gk *emphutos*) implies that the Word must become a part of our very nature. The implanted Word brings us to our final salvation (cf. Mt 13:3–23; Ro 1:16; 1Co 15:2; Eph 1:13; see Jn 6:54, note).

1:25 LAW THAT GIVES FREEDOM. This law (cf. 2:12) is the will of God internalized in our hearts by the indwelling Holy Spirit (cf. Eze 11:19–20). Through faith in Christ we receive not only mercy and forgiveness (2:12–13), but also the power and freedom to obey God's law (Ro 3:31; see 8:4, note). It is called the "law that gives freedom" because the believer desires to do God's will: "I will walk about in freedom, for I have sought out your precepts" (Ps 119:45). It must never be viewed as a freedom to violate Christ's commands, but rather as the freedom and power to obey them.

1:27 RELIGION . . . PURE AND FAULTLESS. James gives two principles that define the content of true Christianity. (1) Genuine love for those in need. In NT days, orphans and widows had few ways to support themselves; they often had no guardian or helper. Believers were expected to show them the same care and love that God shows toward the fatherless and widows (see Dt 10:18; Ps 146:9; Mt 6:32; see Dt 24:17, note; Ps 68:5, note). Today among our brothers and sisters in Christ are those who need loving care. We should seek to alleviate their distress and thereby show them that God cares for them (see Lk 7:13, note; cf. Gal 6:10; see article on THE CARE OF THE POOR AND NEEDY, p. 1316).

(2) Keeping ourselves holy before God. James says that love for others must be accompanied by a love for God expressed in separation from the world's sinful ways. Love for others must be accompanied by holiness before God or it is not Christian love.

2:1 FAVORITISM. To show favoritism is to give special attention to people because of their wealth, clothing or position. To do so is wrong for several reasons. (1) It displeases God, who does not look at the outward appearance but at the heart (1Sa 16:7). (2) It is not motivated by genuine love for all (v. 8). The admiration of social status is a sin against the law of love. (3) It makes us "judges with evil thoughts" (v. 4); instead of honoring "our glorious Lord" and accepting persons on the basis of their faith in Christ, we unjustly favor the rich or influential from an evil motive for the advantage we might receive.

2:5 HAS NOT GOD CHOSEN THOSE WHO ARE POOR. The poor are special and precious to God (cf. Isa 61:1; Lk 4:18; 6:20; 7:22). Often it is the poor in this world who are the richest in faith and spiritual gifts and who, in their need, cry out

eyes of the world[x] to be rich in faith[y]
and to inherit the kingdom[z] he promised those who love him?[a] **6**But you
have insulted the poor.[b] Is it not the
rich who are exploiting you? Are they
not the ones who are dragging you into
court?[c] **7**Are they not the ones who
are slandering the noble name of him
to whom you belong?
8If you really keep the royal law
found in Scripture, "Love your neighbor as yourself,"[a][d] you are doing
right. **9**But if you show favoritism,[e]
you sin and are convicted by the law as
lawbreakers.[f] **10**For whoever keeps
the whole law and yet stumbles[g] at
just one point is guilty of breaking all
of it.[h] **11**For he who said, "Do not commit adultery,"[b][i] also said, "Do not
murder."[c][j] If you do not commit
adultery but do commit murder, you
have become a lawbreaker.
12Speak and act as those who are
going to be judged[k] by the law that
gives freedom,[l] **13**because judgment
without mercy will be shown to anyone
who has not been merciful.[m] Mercy triumphs over judgment!

Faith and Deeds

14What good is it, my brothers, if a
man claims to have faith but has no
deeds?[n] Can such faith save him?
15Suppose a brother or sister is without clothes and daily food.[o] **16**If one of
you says to him, "Go, I wish you well;
keep warm and well fed," but does
nothing about his physical needs, what
good is it?[p] **17**In the same way, faith
by itself, if it is not accompanied by action, is dead.[q]
18But someone will say, "You have
faith; I have deeds."
Show me your faith without deeds,[r]
and I will show you my faith[s] by what
I do.[t] **19**You believe that there is one
God.[u] Good! Even the demons believe
that[v]—and shudder.
20You foolish man, do you want evidence that faith without deeds is useless[d]?[w] **21**Was not our ancestor Abraham considered righteous for what he
did when he offered his son Isaac on

2:5 [x]Job 34:19; 1Co 1:26-28 [y]Lk 12:21; Rev 2:9 [z]S Mt 25:34 [a]S Jas 1:12 **2:6** [b]1Co 11:22 [c]Ac 8:3; 16:19 **2:8** [d]Lev 19:18; S Mt 5:43 **2:9** [e]ver 1 [f]Dt 1:17 **2:10** [g]Jas 3:2 [h]Mt 5:19; Gal 3:10; 5:3 **2:11** [i]Ex 20:14; Dt 5:18 [j]Ex 20:13; Dt 5:17 **2:12** [k]S Mt 16:27 [l]S Jas 1:25 **2:13** [m]Mt 5:7; 9:13; 12:7; 18:32-35; Lk 6:37
2:14 [n]Mt 7:26; Jas 1:22-25 **2:15** [o]Mt 25:35, 36 **2:16** [p]Lk 3:11; 1Jn 3:17,18 **2:17** [q]ver 20,26; Gal 5:6 **2:18** [r]Ro 3:28 [s]Heb 11 [t]Mt 7:16, 17; Jas 3:13 **2:19** [u]Dt 6:4; Mk 12:29; 1Co 8:4-6 [v]Mt 8:29; Lk 4:34 **2:20** [w]ver 17,26

[a] *8* Lev. 19:18 [b] *11* Exodus 20:14; Deut. 5:18 [c] *11* Exodus 20:13; Deut. 5:17
[d] *20* Some early manuscripts *dead*

---

most intensely to God in sincere hunger for his presence, mercy and help (Lk 6:20–21). The economically depressed around the world learn that they cannot put their trust in material possessions. Therefore, they respond more readily to Jesus' invitation to "come to me, all you who are weary and burdened, and I will give you rest" (Mt 11:28; see article on RICHES AND POVERTY, p. 1562).

2:12 SPEAK AND ACT. We must speak and act from the perspective of those who will be judged by God and the "law that gives freedom," i.e., the law and love of God poured into our hearts by God's Spirit. God will condemn all showing of favoritism, for it transgresses the law of love (see v. 1, note; see article on THE JUDGMENT OF BELIEVERS, p. 1791).

2:14 FAITH BUT HAS NO DEEDS. Vv. 14–26 treat the ever-present problem of those in the church who profess to have saving faith in the Lord Jesus Christ, yet at the same time show no evidence of sincere devotion to him and his Word. (1) Saving faith is always a living faith that does not stop with mere confession of Christ as Savior, but also prompts obedience to him as Lord. Thus, obedience is an essential aspect of faith. Only those who obey can believe, and only those who believe can obey (see v. 24, note; Ro 1:5, note on "obedience that comes from faith"; see article on FAITH AND GRACE, p. 1720).

(2) Note that there is no contradiction between Paul and James with regard to the matter of saving faith. Normally Paul emphasizes faith as the means by which we accept Christ as Savior (Ro 3:22). James calls attention to the fact that true faith must be an active and enduring faith that shapes our very existence.

2:17 NOT ACCOMPANIED BY ACTION, IS DEAD. (1) True saving faith is so vital that it cannot help but express itself in godly action and devotion to Jesus Christ. Deeds without faith are dead deeds. Faith without deeds is dead faith. True faith always manifests itself in obedience to God and compassionate deeds done for needy people (see v. 22, note; Ro 1:5, note; see articles on THE CARE OF THE POOR AND NEEDY, p. 1316, and FAITH AND GRACE, p. 1720).

(2) James is directing his teaching against those in the church who professed faith in Christ and his blood atonement and believed that such profession was all that was necessary for salvation. They believed that a personal, obedient relationship with Christ as Lord was not essential. James says that such faith is dead and will produce neither salvation nor anything good (vv. 14–16,20–24). The only kind of faith that saves is "faith expressing itself through love" (Gal 5:6).

(3) On the other hand, we must not think that we maintain a living faith solely by our own effort. The grace of God, the indwelling Holy Spirit and the intercession of Christ (see Heb 7:25, note) work in our lives to enable us to respond to God 'by faith from first to last" (Ro 1:17). If we ever stop being receptive to God's grace and the leading of the Spirit, then our faith will die.

2:21 CONSIDERED RIGHTEOUS FOR WHAT HE DID. Abraham's righteousness came not from "observing the law" (Ro 3:28), but through faith

the altar?[x] **22**You see that his faith and his actions were working together,[y] and his faith was made complete by what he did.[z] **23**And the scripture was fulfilled that says, "Abraham believed God, and it was credited to him as righteousness,"[e][a] and he was called God's friend.[b] **24**You see that a person is justified by what he does and not by faith alone.

25In the same way, was not even Rahab the prostitute considered righteous for what she did when she gave lodging to the spies and sent them off in a different direction?[c] **26**As the body without the spirit is dead, so faith without deeds is dead.[d]

1Pe 1:13-16

Taming the Tongue

3 Not many of you should presume to be teachers,[e] my brothers, because you know that we who teach will be judged[f] more strictly.[g] **2**We all stumble[h] in many ways. If anyone is never at fault in what he says,[i] he is a perfect man,[j] able to keep his whole body in check.[k]

3When we put bits into the mouths of horses to make them obey us, we can turn the whole animal.[l] **4**Or take ships as an example. Although they are so large and are driven by strong winds, they are steered by a very small rudder wherever the pilot wants to go.

2:21 [x] Ge 22:9,12
2:22 [y] Heb 11:17
[z] 1Th 1:3
2:23 [a] Ge 15:6; S Ro 4:3
[b] 2Ch 20:7; Isa 41:8
2:25
[c] S Heb 11:31
2:26 [d] ver 17,20
3:1 [e] S Eph 4:11
[f] S Mt 7:1
[g] Ro 2:21
3:2 [h] 1Ki 8:46; Ro 3:9-20; Jas 2:10; 1Jn 1:8
[i] Ps 39:1; Pr 10:19; 1Pe 3:10
[j] S Mt 12:37
[k] Jas 1:26
3:3 [l] Ps 32:9
3:5 [m] Ps 12:3,4; 73:8,9
3:6 [n] Pr 16:27
[o] Mt 15:11,18,19
[p] S Mt 5:22
3:8 [q] Ps 140:3; Ro 3:13
3:9 [r] Ge 1:26,27; 1Co 11:7
3:12 [s] Mt 7:16
3:13 [t] Jas 2:18
[u] S 1Pe 2:12

5Likewise the tongue is a small part of the body, but it makes great boasts.[m] Consider what a great forest is set on fire by a small spark. **6**The tongue also is a fire,[n] a world of evil among the parts of the body. It corrupts the whole person,[o] sets the whole course of his life on fire, and is itself set on fire by hell.[p]

7All kinds of animals, birds, reptiles and creatures of the sea are being tamed and have been tamed by man, **8**but no man can tame the tongue. It is a restless evil, full of deadly poison.[q]

9With the tongue we praise our Lord and Father, and with it we curse men, who have been made in God's likeness.[r] **10**Out of the same mouth come praise and cursing. My brothers, this should not be. **11**Can both fresh water and salt[f] water flow from the same spring? **12**My brothers, can a fig tree bear olives, or a grapevine bear figs?[s] Neither can a salt spring produce fresh water.

Two Kinds of Wisdom

13Who is wise and understanding among you? Let him show it[t] by his good life, by deeds[u] done in the humility that comes from wisdom. **14**But if you harbor bitter envy and selfish am-

[e] *23* Gen. 15:6 [f] *11* Greek *bitter* (see also verse 14)

and actions working together in love. His willingness to sacrifice Isaac was an expression of his faith in and commitment to God (see Ge 15:6, note; 22:1, note). James uses the example of Abraham to demolish the belief that faith can exist without commitment to and love for God. The apostle Paul uses the example of Abraham's faith to destroy the view that salvation rests on the merit of one's own deeds rather than on God's grace (Ro 4:3; Gal 3:6).

2:22 FAITH AND HIS ACTIONS WERE WORKING TOGETHER. James is not saying that faith *and* actions save us. This separates faith from deeds. James contends instead for faith at work. Thus, faith and deeds can never be separated; the latter flows naturally from the former (see Gal 5:6, note).

2:24 JUSTIFIED BY WHAT HE DOES. The Greek word *ergōn*, here translated "what he does," is used by James with a different meaning than the same word used by Paul in Eph 2:9, there translated "works." (1) For James, "what he does" refers to the obligations to God and fellow humans that are commanded in Scripture and that proceed from a sincere faith, a pure heart, the grace of God and the desire to please Christ. (2) For Paul, "works" refers to a desire to gain favor and salvation through obeying the law by one's own effort rather than through repentance and faith in Christ. (3) Note that both Paul and James state emphatically that true saving faith will inevitably produce deeds of love (1:27; 2:8; Gal 5:6; 1Co 13; cf. Jn 14:15).

3:1 TEACHERS. This includes pastors, church leaders, missionaries, preachers of the Word or anyone who gives instruction to a congregation. The teacher must understand that no one has a more solemn responsibility than those who teach the Word of God. In the future judgment, Christian teachers will be judged more strictly than other believers.

3:6 THE TONGUE ALSO IS A FIRE. James emphasizes our inclination to sin in our speaking. Sins of speech include harsh and unkind words, lying, exaggeration, teaching false doctrine, slander, gossiping and boasting. Mature believers keep their tongues under control by the guidance of the Holy Spirit, taking "captive every thought to make it obedient to Christ" (2Co 10:5). Because of the tendency to sin with the tongue, James exhorts every person to "be quick to listen, slow to speak and slow to become angry" (1:19).

3:14 SELFISH AMBITION. "Selfish ambition" refers to the vice that prompts us to promote our own interests. Selfish ambition in the church is (1) "earthly," i.e., it defiles that which is holy and of

bition[v] in your hearts, do not boast
about it or deny the truth.[w] **15**Such
"wisdom" does not come down from
heaven[x] but is earthly, unspiritual, of
the devil.[y] **16**For where you have envy
and selfish ambition,[z] there you find
disorder and every evil practice.
17But the wisdom that comes from
heaven[a] is first of all pure; then
peace-loving,[b] considerate, submissive, full of mercy[c] and good fruit, impartial and sincere.[d] **18**Peacemakers[e] who sow in peace raise a harvest
of righteousness.[f]

Submit Yourselves to God

4 What causes fights and quarrels[g]
among you? Don't they come from
your desires that battle[h] within you?
2You want something but don't get it.
You kill[i] and covet, but you cannot
have what you want. You quarrel and
fight. You do not have, because you do
not ask God. **3**When you ask, you do
not receive,[j] because you ask with
wrong motives,[k] that you may spend
what you get on your pleasures.

3:14 [v]ver 16; 2Co 12:20 [w]Jas 5:19
3:15 [x]ver 17; Jas 1:17 [y]1Ti 4:1
3:16 [z]ver 14; Gal 5:20,21
3:17 [a]1Co 2:6; Jas 1:17 [b]Heb 12:11 [c]Lk 6:36 [d]Ro 12:9
3:18 [e]Mt 5:9; S Ro 14:19 [f]Pr 11:18; Isa 32:17; Hos 10:12; Php 1:11
4:1 [g]Tit 3:9 [h]S Ro 7:23
4:2 [i]Mt 5:21,22; Jas 5:6; 1Jn 3:15
4:3 [j]Ps 18:41; S Mt 7:7 [k]Ps 66:18; 1Jn 3:22; 5:14
4:4 [l]Isa 54:5; Jer 3:20; Hos 2:2-5; 3:1; 9:1 [m]S Jas 1:27 [n]Ro 8:7; 1Jn 2:15 [o]Jn 15:19
4:5 [p]1Co 6:19
4:6 [q]Pr 3:34; S Mt 23:12
4:7 [r]Eph 4:27; 6:11; 1Pe 5:6-9
4:8 [s]Ps 73:28; Zec 1:3; Mal 3:7; Heb 7:19 [t]Isa 1:16

4You adulterous[l] people, don't you
know that friendship with the world[m]
is hatred toward God?[n] Anyone who
chooses to be a friend of the world becomes an enemy of God.[o] **5**Or do you
think Scripture says without reason
that the spirit he caused to live in us[p]
envies intensely?[g] **6**But he gives us
more grace. That is why Scripture
says:

> "God opposes the proud
> but gives grace to the
> humble."[h][q]

1Pe 2:11-12

7Submit yourselves, then, to God.
Resist the devil,[r] and he will flee from
you. **8**Come near to God and he will
come near to you.[s] Wash your
hands,[t] you sinners, and purify your
hearts,[u] you double-minded.[v] **9**Grieve,
mourn and wail. Change your

1Pe 5:8-9

[u]Ps 24:4; Jer 4:14 [v]Ps 119:113; Jas 1:8

g5 Or *that God jealously longs for the spirit that he made to live in us*; or *that the Spirit he caused to live in us longs jealously* h6 Prov. 3:34

the Spirit; (2) "unspiritual," i.e., without the Holy Spirit; and (3) "of the devil," i.e., it is inspired by demons (see 1Ti 4:1, note).

4:1 WHAT CAUSES FIGHTS AND QUARRELS AMONG YOU? The major source of quarrels and conflicts in the church centers in a desire for recognition, honor, power, pleasure, money and superiority. The satisfaction of selfish desires becomes more important than righteousness and God's will (cf. Mk 4:19; Lk 8:14; Gal 5:16–20). When this happens, self-centered conflicts are created in the fellowship. Those responsible show themselves to be without the Spirit and outside of God's kingdom (Gal 5:19–21; Jude 16–19).

4:2 YOU KILL. This phrase may be used figuratively in the sense of hate (cf. Mt 5:21–22).

4:3 WHEN YOU ASK, YOU DO NOT RECEIVE. God refuses to answer the prayers of those who are selfishly ambitious, love pleasure, and desire honor, power or riches (see v. 1, note). All of us should take note, for God will not listen to our prayers if we have hearts filled with selfish desires (see article on EFFECTIVE PRAYING, p. 496). Scripture tells us God hears only the prayers of the righteous (Ps 34:13–15; 66:18–19), of those who call on him in truth (145:18), of the genuinely repentant and humble (Lk 18:14), and of those who ask according to his will (1Jn 5:14).

4:4 FRIENDSHIP WITH THE WORLD IS HATRED TOWARD GOD. "Friendship with the world" is spiritual adultery, i.e., unfaithfulness to God and our pledge of commitment to him (1Jn 2:15–17; cf. Isa 54:5; Jer 3:20). It involves embracing the world's sin, values and evil pleasures (see article on THE CHRISTIAN'S RELATIONSHIP TO THE WORLD, p. 1976). God will not accept such friendship (Mt 6:24), for he is a jealous God (Ex 20:5; Dt 5:9).

One example of such friendship is participation in secret orders (e.g., lodge membership) that demand unscriptural religious oaths and yoking together with unbelievers, both of which are forbidden in God's Word (Mt 5:33–37; 2Co 6:14). Believers cannot belong to such groups without compromising Christian doctrine (cf. 2Pe 3:16), godly standards, separation from the world (2Co 6:17–18), and loyalty to Christ (Mt 6:24).

4:5 THE SPIRIT ... ENVIES INTENSELY. The construction of this verse in the Greek is unclear. It may mean that the human spirit naturally hates God and neighbor and desires the sinful pleasures of the world (v. 4). Yet this can be changed by God's grace, which comes to all who humbly accept salvation in Christ (v. 6).

4:6 GOD OPPOSES THE PROUD. It should be impressed on our hearts and minds how much God hates pride. Pride causes God to turn from our prayers and withhold his presence and grace. To be exalted in our own minds or to seek the honor and esteem of others in order to satisfy our pride is to shut out God's help. But for those who humbly submit to God and draw near to him, he gives abundant grace, mercy and help in every situation of life (see Php 2:3, note; Heb 4:16; 7:25).

4:8 COME NEAR TO GOD. God promises to come near to all who turn from sin, purify their hearts and call on him in true repentance. God's nearness will bring his presence, grace, blessings and love.

laughter to mourning and your joy to
gloom.[w] **10**Humble yourselves before
the Lord, and he will lift you up.[x]
11Brothers, do not slander one another.[y] Anyone who speaks against
his brother or judges him[z] speaks
against the law[a] and judges it. When
you judge the law, you are not keeping
it,[b] but sitting in judgment on it.
12There is only one Lawgiver and
Judge,[c] the one who is able to save
and destroy.[d] But you—who are you
to judge your neighbor?[e]

Boasting About Tomorrow

13Now listen,[f] you who say, "Today
or tomorrow we will go to this or that
city, spend a year there, carry on business and make money."[g] **14**Why, you
do not even know what will happen tomorrow. What is your life? You are a
mist that appears for a little while and
then vanishes.[h] **15**Instead, you ought
to say, "If it is the Lord's will,[i] we will
live and do this or that." **16**As it is, you
boast and brag. All such boasting is
evil.[j] **17**Anyone, then, who knows the
good he ought to do and doesn't do it,
sins.[k]

Warning to Rich Oppressors

5 Now listen,[l] you rich people,[m]
weep and wail[n] because of the
misery that is coming upon you. **2**Your
wealth has rotted, and moths have eat-
en your clothes.[o] **3**Your gold and silver are corroded. Their corrosion will
testify against you and eat your flesh
like fire. You have hoarded wealth in
the last days.[p] **4**Look! The wages you
failed to pay the workmen[q] who
mowed your fields are crying out
against you. The cries[r] of the harvesters have reached the ears of the Lord
Almighty.[s] **5**You have lived on earth
in luxury and self-indulgence. You
have fattened yourselves[t] in the day
of slaughter.[i][u] **6**You have condemned and murdered[v] innocent
men,[w] who were not opposing you.

Patience in Suffering

7Be patient, then, brothers, until the
Lord's coming.[x] See how the farmer
waits for the land to yield its valuable
crop and how patient he is[y] for the
autumn and spring rains.[z] **8**You too,
be patient and stand firm, because the
Lord's coming[a] is near.[b] **9**Don't
grumble against each other, brothers,[c] or you will be judged. The
Judge[d] is standing at the door![e]
10Brothers, as an example of patience in the face of suffering, take the
prophets[f] who spoke in the name of
the Lord. **11**As you know, we consider
blessed[g] those who have persevered.

[i]5 Or *yourselves as in a day of feasting*

4:9 [w]Lk 6:25
4:10 [x]ver 6; Job 5:11; 1Pe 5:6
4:11 [y]Ro 1:30; 2Co 12:20; 1Pe 2:1 [z]S Mt 7:1 [a]Jas 2:8 [b]Jas 1:22
4:12 [c]Isa 33:22; S Jas 5:9 [d]Mt 10:28 [e]S Mt 7:1
4:13 [f]Jas 5:1 [g]Pr 27:1; Lk 12:18-20
4:14 [h]Job 7:7; Ps 39:5; 102:3; 144:4; Isa 2:22
4:15 [i]S Ac 18:21
4:16 [j]1Co 5:6
4:17 [k]Lk 12:47; Jn 9:41
5:1 [l]Jas 4:13 [m]Lk 6:24; 1Ti 6:9; Jas 2:2-6 [n]Isa 13:6; Eze 30:2
5:2 [o]Job 13:28; Ps 39:11; Isa 50:9; Mt 6:19, 20
5:3 [p]ver 7,8
5:4 [q]Lev 19:13; Jer 22:13; Mal 3:5 [r]Dt 24:15 [s]Ro 9:29
5:5 [t]Eze 16:49; Am 6:1; Lk 16:19 [u]Jer 12:3; 25:34
5:6 [v]Jas 4:2 [w]Heb 10:38
5:7 [x]S 1Co 1:7 [y]Gal 6:9 [z]Dt 11:14; Jer 5:24; Joel 2:23
5:8 [a]S 1Co 1:7 [b]S Ro 13:11
5:9 [c]Jas 4:11 [d]Ps 94:2; 1Co 4:5; Jas 4:12; 1Pe 4:5 [e]Mt 24:33
5:10 [f]S Mt 5:12
5:11 [g]Mt 5:10

4:11 DO NOT SLANDER ONE ANOTHER. By neglecting to learn all the facts about a situation, by failing to speak to an accused person about a problem, and by slandering him or her, we set aside God's law of love.

4:15 IF IT IS THE LORD'S WILL. In making goals and plans for the future, believers must always consider God and his will. We must not act like the rich fool (Lk 12:16–21); rather we must recognize that true happiness and useful living are completely dependent on God. The principle by which we live must be, "If it is the Lord's will." If our prayer is truly, "May your will be done" (Mt 26:42), then we have the assurance that our present and future are in the protective care of our heavenly Father (cf. Ac 18:21; 1Co 4:19; 16:7; Heb 6:3; see article on THE WILL OF GOD, p. 1056).

4:16 BOASTING. For those who set goals and succeed in meeting them, the temptation is to boast. Boasting is based on the false assumption that whatever we accomplished, we did by ourselves and not with the help of God and others. The NT urges us to boast in our weaknesses and our dependence on God (2Co 11:30; 12:5,9).

5:1 YOU RICH PEOPLE, WEEP AND WAIL. The Bible does not teach that all rich people are ungodly. Nevertheless, what James is describing is characteristic of many people with wealth (vv. 1–6; 2:1–3). The exceptions are the rich people who are not possessed by their wealth and use it instead to advance the gospel and to help those in need (see article on RICHES AND POVERTY, p. 1562).

5:7 BE PATIENT ... UNTIL THE LORD'S COMING. James speaks of Christ's return as drawing near (v. 8). Christ will come as judge to punish the wicked and to reward the righteous and deliver them from wrongs they have suffered (v. 9). Patience is the virtue of enduring injustice, suffering, trouble and mistreatment, while committing our lives to God in the faith that he will make all things right at his coming (Dt 32:35; Ro 12:12; Heb 10:30; 12:1–2; see Job 2:3, note; Ps 73:17, note).

5:9 STANDING AT THE DOOR. The motive for patience and perseverance in the faith is the imminent coming of the Lord (v. 8). He is "standing at the door." The door may not open until tomorrow, or next week, or next year, but it could open at any time.

5:11 JOB'S PERSEVERANCE. The word "perseverance" (Gk *hupomonē*) indicates endurance in whatever trials we may face without losing our faith in God. It is born of a faith that triumphs to

You have heard of Job's perseverance[h] and have seen what the Lord
finally brought about.[i] The Lord is
full of compassion and mercy.[j]
12Above all, my brothers, do not
swear—not by heaven or by earth or by
anything else. Let your "Yes" be yes,
and your "No," no, or you will be condemned.[k]

The Prayer of Faith

13Is any one of you in trouble? He
should pray.[l] Is anyone happy? Let
him sing songs of praise.[m] **14**Is any
one of you sick? He should call the elders[n] of the church to pray over him
and anoint him with oil[o] in the name
of the Lord. **15**And the prayer offered in
faith[p] will make the sick person well;
the Lord will raise him up. If he has
sinned, he will be forgiven. **16**Therefore
confess your sins[q] to each other and
pray for each other so that you may be
healed.[r] The prayer of a righteous
man is powerful and effective.[s] 1Pe 2:24
17Elijah was a man just like us.[t] He
prayed earnestly that it would not
rain, and it did not rain on the land for
three and a half years.[u] **18**Again he
prayed, and the heavens gave rain,
and the earth produced its crops.[v]

5:11 [h]Job 1:21, 22; 2:10; S Heb 10:36 [i]Job 42:10,12-17 [j]Ex 34:6; Nu 14:18; Ps 103:8 **5:12** [k]Mt 5:34-37 **5:13** [l]Ps 50:15 [m]Col 3:16 **5:14** [n]S Ac 11:30 [o]Ps 23:5; Isa 1:6; Mk 6:13; 16:18; Lk 10:34 **5:15** [p]Jas 1:6 **5:16** [q]Mt 3:6; Ac 19:18 [r]Heb 12:13; 1Pe 2:24 [s]S Mt 7:7; S Jn 9:31 **5:17** [t]Ac 14:15 [u]1Ki 17:1; Lk 4:25 **5:18** [v]1Ki 18:41-45

the end in the midst of sufferings (Job 13:15). The outcome of the Lord's dealings with Job reveals that in all Job's troubles, God cared deeply about him and mercifully sustained him. James wants us to know that God is concerned about all his people and that, in their suffering, he will sustain them in love and mercy (see Job 6:4, note; 42:10, note).

5:13 IS ANY ONE OF YOU IN TROUBLE . . . HAPPY? When you are experiencing trouble, poverty or distress, Scripture invites you to seek strength from God through prayer. Draw near to your mediator, Jesus Christ. He will represent you before God, make intercession for you (Heb 7:25), and give mercy and grace to help in time of need (Heb 4:16). Take seriously God's Word: "Cast all your anxiety on him because he cares for you" (1Pe 5:7). If we are happy in the Lord, we must sing songs of praise to him (cf. Ps 33:2–3; 81:1–2; 92:1–3; 98:4–6; 144:9; 149:1–5; 150).

5:15 PRAYER OFFERED IN FAITH WILL MAKE THE SICK PERSON WELL. James is speaking of physical sickness. We may deal with illness by asking for the prayers of the elders or leaders of the church. (1) It is the duty of pastors and leaders of the church to pray for the sick and to anoint them with oil. Note that it is the elders' responsibility to pray the prayer of faith and not the responsibility of the sick person. The NT places the major burden for healing on the church and its leaders. (2) The oil probably represents the healing power of the Holy Spirit; it was used as an aid to faith (cf. Mk 6:13).

(3) It is prayer that James emphasizes as most important. Effective prayer must be offered in faith if the sick are to be healed. The Lord will give faith according to his will (see Mt 17:20, note; see article on DIVINE HEALING, p. 1420).

(4) People may not always be healed; nevertheless, the church must continue to seek the kingdom's healing power in compassion for the sick and to the glory of Christ (see article on DIVINE HEALING, p. 1420).

5:15 IF HE HAS SINNED. James recognizes that sickness may be due to sin (v. 16). Therefore, whenever sickness occurs, one should examine himself or herself before the Lord in prayer to determine if the sickness is due to personal sin. The word "if" makes it clear that sickness is not always the result of personal sin (see article on DIVINE HEALING, p. 1420).

5:16 CONFESS . . . PRAY . . . BE HEALED. This verse gives us an important reason why healing is often lacking in the Christian community. Sin must be confessed to others, and fervent prayer for one another be made to God. Sin in the church hinders the prayers of believers and blocks God's healing power from being manifested in the congregation.

5:16 PRAYER OF A RIGHTEOUS MAN IS POWERFUL. The prayers of the righteous (1) bring them near to God (Heb 7:25); (2) open the way to a Spirit-filled life (Lk 11:13; Ac 1:14); (3) bring them power for ministry (Ac 1:8; 4:31,33) and Christian devotion (Eph 1:19); (4) build them up spiritually (Jude 20); (5) give them insight into Christ's provision for them (Eph 1:16–19); (6) help them overcome Satan (Da 10:12–13; Eph 6:12–13,18); (7) clarify God's will for them (Ps 32:6–8; Pr 3:5–6; Mk 1:35–39); (8) enable them to receive spiritual gifts (1Co 14:1); (9) bring them into fellowship with God (Mt 6:9; Jn 7:37; 14:16); (10) bring them grace, mercy and peace (Php 4:6–7; Heb 4:16); (11) bring the lost to Christ (v. 20); (12) bring them the wisdom, revelation and knowledge of Christ (Eph 1:16–17); (13) bring them healing (v. 15); (14) bring them deliverance from trouble (Ps 34:4–7; Php 1:19); (15) glorify God with praise and thanksgiving (Ps 100:4); (16) make Christ's presence real to them (cf. Rev 3:20); and (17) ensure them of their final salvation and of Christ's intercession for them (Heb 7:25; see article on EFFECTIVE PRAYING, p. 496).

5:18 HE PRAYED, AND THE HEAVENS GAVE RAIN. Elijah was a man who had faith that his prayers to God would accomplish much, even to the point of God's intervention in the course of nature. He believed that prayer by a righteous person does change things (vv. 13–16; Ps 34:6; Isa 38:1–5; Mt 17:21; 26:41,53; Mk 11:24; 2Th 3:1; see 1Ki 17:22, note; 18:42, note).

(1) We must be careful not to accept any teaching that undermines our faith in the power of prayer to bring about God's intervention in our lives. One such teaching is the concept of "fate,"

[19]My brothers, if one of you should
wander from the truth[w] and someone
should bring him back,[x] [20]remember
this: Whoever turns a sinner from the
error of his way will save[y] him from
death and cover over a multitude of
sins.[z]

5:19 [w] Jas 3:14 [x] S Mt 18:15
5:20 [y] S Ro 11:14 [z] 1Pe 4:8

the pagan notion that everything we do and everything that happens to us is fixed unchangeably in advance, long before it occurs. Belief in fate is contrary to Scripture and causes one to assume that both good and bad are absolutely determined and unalterable, and that nothing is really changed by fervent, believing prayer.

(2) Scripture teaches that God deals with his children, not through absolute determinism, but by divine providence, whereby he interacts with and responds to the prayers of the righteous. Our prayers and faith in God do cause many good things to happen that would otherwise not occur (Ex 32:9–14).

5:19–20 IF ONE OF YOU SHOULD WANDER. Believers should do everything possible to turn back to God those who stray from the truth (e.g., Gal 4:19; 6:1; 2Ti 2:18,25–26; Jude 22–23). The salvation of a wandering brother or sister should always be a high priority in the Christian community. If the backslider returns to Christ, the one who converts him or her will have saved the sinner "from death," i.e., spiritual death and eternal separation from God (cf. Ro 6:23; Gal 6:8; Rev 20:14).

1 PETER

Outline

Christian Greetings (1:1–2)

- I. The Believer's Relationship to God (1:3—2:10)
  - A. Salvation Through Faith (1:3–12)
  - B. Holiness Through Obedience (1:13—2:10)
- II. The Believer's Relationship to Others (2:11—3:12)
  - A. Public Responsibilities (2:11–17)
  - B. Domestic Responsibilities (2:18—3:7)
    1. Slaves' Responsibility to Their Masters (2:18–25)
    2. Wives' Responsibility to Their Husbands (3:1–6)
    3. Husbands' Responsibility to Their Wives (3:7)
  - C. Summary of Principles Governing the Believer's Relationship to Others (3:8–12)
- III. The Believer's Relationship to Suffering (3:13—5:11)
  - A. Endurance in the Face of Suffering (3:13—4:11)
    1. Because of the Blessing of Suffering Unjustly (3:13–17)
    2. Because of the Powerful Example of Christ (3:18—4:6)
    3. Because of the Urgency of the End Time (4:7–11)
  - B. Rejoicing in the Face of Suffering (4:12–19)
    1. Because It Tests the Reality of Our Faith (4:12)
    2. Because It Is a Sharing in Christ's Sufferings (4:13a,14–16)
    3. Because It Prepares Us for the Glory of His Coming (4:13b,17–19)
  - C. Exhortations in the Face of Suffering (5:1–11)
    1. To Elders — Shepherd the Flock (5:1–4)
    2. To Younger Men (5:5–11)

Conclusion (5:12–14)

Author: Peter

Theme: Suffering for Christ

Date of Writing: A.D. 60–63

Background

This is the first of two NT letters written by the apostle Peter (1:1; 2Pe 1:1). Peter testifies that he wrote his first letter with the assistance of Silas (Gk *Silvanus*) as his scribe (5:12). Silas's fluent Greek and writing style are reflected here, while possibly Peter's own less polished Greek appears in his second letter. The tone and content of 1 Peter is consistent with what we know about Simon Peter. His years of close fellowship with the Lord Jesus underlie his recalling of Jesus' death (1:11,19; 2:21–24; 3:18; 5:1) and resurrection (1:3,21; 3:21); indirectly he seems to refer even to Jesus' post-resurrection appearance to him in Galilee (2:25; 5:2a; cf. Jn 21:15–23). In addition, many similarities occur between this letter and Peter's sermons recorded in Acts.

Peter addresses this letter to "strangers . . . scattered" throughout the Roman provinces of Asia Minor (1:1). Some of these may have been converts who had responded to

Peter's message on the day of Pentecost and had returned to their respective cities with their newfound faith (cf. Ac 2:9–11). These believers are called "aliens and strangers" (2:11) to remind them that their Christian pilgrimage is in a world that is hostile to Jesus Christ and from which they can expect persecution. Peter probably wrote this letter in response to reports from believers in Asia Minor of growing opposition (4:12–16) that did not yet have official governmental sanction (2:12–17).

Peter wrote from "Babylon" (5:13). This may be understood literally as the country of Babylon in Mesopotamia or as a figurative expression for Rome, the supreme center of organized godlessness in the first century. Although Peter may have once visited the large colony of orthodox Jews in Babylon, we can more readily account for Peter, Silas (5:12) and Mark (5:13) being together at Rome (Col 4:10; cf. Papias's comments about Peter and Mark at Rome) in the early 60s rather than at literal Babylon. Peter wrote most likely from Rome between A.D. 60–63, surely before the terrible bloodbath of Nero in Rome (A.D. 64).

Purpose

Peter wrote this letter of joyful hope to provide believers with a divine and eternal perspective on their earthly lives and to give practical guidance to those who were beginning to experience a fiery trial of suffering as Christians in a pagan environment. Peter was concerned that believers should not provoke governmental structures unnecessarily and that they should follow Jesus' example in suffering innocently, righteously and nobly.

Survey

1 Peter begins by reminding believers (1) that they have a glorious calling and heavenly inheritance in Jesus Christ (1:2–5); (2) that their faith and love in this life will be subjected to testing and refining and will result in praise, glory and honor at the Lord's appearing (1:6–9); (3) that this great salvation was foreseen by the OT prophets (1:10–12); and (4) that believers must live holy lives, clearly different from the unregenerate world around them (1:13–21). Believers, chosen and sanctified (1:2), are growing infants who need the pure milk of the Word (2:1–3), living stones who are being built into a spiritual house (2:4–10), and aliens who are passing through a foreign land (2:11–12); they must live honorably and humbly in their relations with all people during their journey (2:13—3:12).

The preeminent message of 1 Peter concerns submission and suffering righteously for Christ's sake and according to his own example (2:18–24; 3:9—5:11). Peter assures believers that for righteous suffering they will obtain God's favor and reward. In the context of this teaching concerning suffering for Christ, Peter stresses the interrelated themes of salvation, hope, love, joy, faith, holiness, humility, fear of God, obedience and submission.

Special Features

Five major features characterize this letter. (1) Along with Hebrews and Revelation, its message revolves around believers who are facing the prospect of severe persecution because of their identity with Jesus Christ. (2) More than any other NT letter, it provides instruction on how to respond as a Christian to unjust persecution and suffering (3:9—5:11). (3) Peter stresses the truth that believers are aliens and strangers on earth (1:1; 2:11). (4) Many OT titles for God's people are applied to NT believers (e.g., 2:5,9–10). (5) It contains one of the most difficult NT passages to interpret: when, where and how Jesus "went and preached to the spirits in prison who disobeyed . . . in the days of Noah" (3:19–20).

Reading 1 Peter

In order to read the entire New Testament in one year, the book of 1 Peter should be read in 5 days, according to the following schedule:
☐ 1:1–21 ☐ 1:22—2:25 ☐ 3 ☐ 4 ☐ 5

NOTES

1 Peter, an apostle of Jesus Christ,[a]
To God's elect,[b] strangers in the
world,[c] scattered[d] throughout Pontus,[e] Galatia,[f] Cappadocia, Asia and
Bithynia,[g] **2**who have been chosen according to the foreknowledge[h] of God
the Father, through the sanctifying
work of the Spirit,[i] for obedience[j] to
Jesus Christ and sprinkling by his
blood:[k]

Grace and peace be yours in abundance.[l]

Praise to God for a Living Hope

3Praise be to the God and Father of
our Lord Jesus Christ![m] In his great
mercy[n] he has given us new birth[o]
into a living hope[p] through the resurrection of Jesus Christ from the dead,[q]
4and into an inheritance[r] that can
never perish, spoil or fade[s]—kept in
heaven for you,[t] **5**who through faith
are shielded by God's power[u] until the
coming of the salvation[v] that is ready
to be revealed[w] in the last time. **6**In
this you greatly rejoice,[x] though now
for a little while[y] you may have had to
suffer grief in all kinds of trials.[z]
7These have come so that your faith—
of greater worth than gold, which perishes even though refined by fire[a]—
may be proved genuine[b] and may
result in praise, glory and honor[c]
when Jesus Christ is revealed.[d]
8Though you have not seen him, you
love him; and even though you do not
see him now, you believe in him[e] and
are filled with an inexpressible and glorious joy, **9**for you are receiving the
goal of your faith, the salvation of your
souls.[f]

10Concerning this salvation, the
prophets, who spoke[g] of the grace
that was to come to you,[h] searched
intently and with the greatest care,[i]
11trying to find out the time and circumstances to which the Spirit of

1:1 [a]2Pe 1:1 [b]Mt 24:22 [c]S Heb 11:13 [d]S Jas 1:1 [e]Ac 2:9; 18:2 [f]S Ac 16:6 [g]Ac 16:7 **1:2** [h]Ro 8:29 [i]2Th 2:13 [j]ver 14, 22 [k]Heb 10:22; 12:24 [l]S Ro 1:7 **1:3** [m]2Co 1:3; Eph 1:3 [n]Tit 3:5 [o]ver 23; S Jn 1:13 [p]ver 13,21; S Heb 3:6 [q]1Co 15:20; 1Pe 3:21 **1:4** [r]S Ac 20:32; S Ro 8:17 [s]1Pe 5:4 [t]Col 1:5; 2Ti 4:8 **1:5** [u]1Sa 2:9; Jn 10:28 [v]S Ro 11:14 [w]S Ro 8:18 **1:6** [x]Ro 5:2 [y]1Pe 5:10 [z]Jas 1:2; 1Pe 4:12 **1:7** [a]Job 23:10; Ps 66:10; Pr 17:3; Isa 48:10 [b]Jas 1:3 [c]2Co 4:17 [d]ver 13; S 1Th 2:19; 1Pe 4:13 **1:8** [e]Jn 20:29 **1:9** [f]Ro 6:22 **1:10** [g]S Mt 26:24 [h]ver 13 [i]S Mt 13:17

1:2 THE FOREKNOWLEDGE OF GOD. Divine foreknowledge must be understood as God's eternal love and intention for his people, the church (see Ro 8:29, note). The "chosen" are the company of true believers, chosen in harmony with God's determination to redeem the church by the blood of Jesus Christ through the Spirit's sanctifying work (see article on ELECTION AND PREDESTINATION, p. 1824). All believers must participate in their election by being eager to make their calling and election sure (see 2Pe 1:5,10, notes).

1:2 SANCTIFYING WORK OF THE SPIRIT. For a discussion of the Christian's life of sanctification, see article on SANCTIFICATION, p. 1956.

1:3 GIVEN US NEW BIRTH. See article on REGENERATION, p. 1589.

1:5 THROUGH FAITH ARE SHIELDED BY GOD'S POWER. This verse presents three truths concerning the security of believers, a particularly relevant message for Peter's audience since many of them were experiencing intense persecution. (1) Believers are "shielded by God's power" against all the forces of evil that would destroy their lives and salvation in Christ (2Ti 4:18; Jude 1,24) (cf. Ro 8:31–39).

(2) The essential condition required for God's protection is "faith" (see article on FAITH AND GRACE, p. 1720). God's shielding us by his grace does not work arbitrarily, for only "through faith" are believers protected by God's power, just as only "through faith" are believers saved (Eph 2:8). Thus, a living faith in Christ as Lord and Savior is our present responsibility in maintaining God's continued protection (v. 9; Jn 15:4,6; Col 1:23; 2Ti 3:14–15; 4:7; Rev 3:8,10).

(3) The ultimate goal of God's protection through the believer's faith is "salvation." Here salvation refers to the future dimension of salvation (cf. Ro 1:16), i.e., the obtaining of an inheritance in heaven (v. 4) and "the salvation of your souls" (v. 9).

1:7 YOUR FAITH ... PROVED GENUINE. The theme of suffering is emphasized throughout this letter (2:19–23; 3:14–17; 4:1–4,12–19; 5:10). We must rejoice in our trials (v. 6), because remaining faithful to Christ in the midst of them will purify our faith and result in praise, glory and honor both to us and to the Lord Jesus at his coming. The Lord considers our perseverance through trials and our faith in Christ precious to him throughout eternity.

1:8 HAVE NOT SEEN HIM, YOU LOVE. God considers the faith of believers today as greater than the faith of those who saw and heard Jesus personally, even after his resurrection. Believers now, although they have never seen him, love him and believe in him. According to Jesus, there is a special blessing for "those who have not seen and yet have believed" (Jn 20:29). As we live by faith we are given joy as God's gift to us (Ps 16:11; Jn 16:24; Ro 15:13; Gal 5:22).

1:11 SPIRIT OF CHRIST IN THEM. Our faith is based not only on the Word of God in the NT but also on God's Word in the OT. The Holy Spirit through the prophets predicted Christ's sufferings and the glories to follow (Ge 49:10; Ps 22; Isa 52:13—53:12; Da 2:44; Zec 9:9–10; 13:7; cf. Lk 24:26–27; see 2Pe 1:21, note; see article on CHRIST IN THE OLD TESTAMENT, p. 518). The Spirit is called "the Spirit of Christ" because he spoke about Christ through the prophets and he was sent from Christ (vv. 11–12; cf. Jn 16:7; 20:22; Ac 2:33).

Christ[j] in them was pointing when he
predicted[k] the sufferings of Christ
and the glories that would follow. **12**It
was revealed to them that they were
not serving themselves but you,[l]
when they spoke of the things that
have now been told you by those who
have preached the gospel to you[m] by
the Holy Spirit sent from heaven.[n]
Even angels long to look into these
things.

Be Holy

13Therefore, prepare your minds for
action; be self-controlled;[o] set your
hope[p] fully on the grace to be given
you[q] when Jesus Christ is revealed.[r]
14As obedient[s] children, do not conform[t] to the evil desires you had when
you lived in ignorance.[u] **15**But just as
he who called you is holy, so be holy in
all you do;[v] **16**for it is written: "Be
1 holy, because I am holy."[a w]
17Since you call on a Father[x] who
judges each man's work[y] impartially,[z] live your lives as strangers[a] here
in reverent fear.[b] **18**For you know that
it was not with perishable things such
as silver or gold that you were redeemed[c] from the empty way of life[d]
handed down to you from your forefathers, **19**but with the precious blood[e]
of Christ, a lamb[f] without blemish or
defect.[g] **20**He was chosen before the
creation of the world,[h] but was revealed in these last times[i] for your
sake. **21**Through him you believe in
God,[j] who raised him from the dead[k]
and glorified him,[l] and so your faith
and hope[m] are in God.
22Now that you have purified[n] yourselves by obeying[o] the truth so that
you have sincere love for your brothers, love one another deeply,[p] from
the heart.[b] **23**For you have been born
again,[q] not of perishable seed, but of
imperishable,[r] through the living and
enduring word of God.[s] **24**For,

"All men are like grass,
and all their glory is like the flowers of the field;
the grass withers and the flowers fall,
25 but the word of the Lord stands forever."[c t]

And this is the word that was preached
to you.

2 Therefore, rid yourselves[u] of all
malice and all deceit, hypocrisy,
envy, and slander[v] of every kind.
2Like newborn babies, crave pure spiri-

1:11 [j] S Ac 16:7; 2Pe 1:21 [k] S Mt 26:24
1:12 [l] S Ro 4:24 [m] ver 25 [n] S Lk 24:49
1:13 [o] S Ac 24:25 [p] ver 3,21; S Heb 3:6 [q] ver 10 [r] ver 7; S 1Co 1:7
1:14 [s] ver 2,22 [t] Ro 12:2 [u] Eph 4:18
1:15 [v] Isa 35:8; 1Th 4:7; 1Jn 3:3
1:16 [w] Lev 11:44, 45; 19:2; 20:7
1:17 [x] S Mt 6:9 [y] S Mt 16:27 [z] S Ac 10:34 [a] S Heb 11:13 [b] Heb 12:28
1:18 [c] S Mt 20:28; S 1Co 6:20 [d] Gal 4:3
1:19 [e] S Ro 3:25 [f] S Jn 1:29
[g] Ex 12:5
1:20 [h] Eph 1:4; S Mt 25:34 [i] Heb 9:26
1:21 [j] Ro 4:24; 10:9 [k] S Ac 2:24 [l] Php 2:7-9; Heb 2:9 [m] ver 3, 13; S Heb 3:6
1:22 [n] Jas 4:8 [o] ver 2,14 [p] S Jn 13:34; S Ro 12:10
1:23 [q] ver 3; S Jn 1:13 [r] Jn 1:13 [s] S Heb 4:12
1:25 [t] Isa 40:6-8; S Jas 1:10,11
2:1 [u] S Eph 4:22 [v] S Jas 4:11

[a] *16* Lev. 11:44,45; 19:2; 20:7 [b] *22* Some early manuscripts *from a pure heart* [c] *25* Isaiah 40:6-8

1:12 PREACHED . . . BY THE HOLY SPIRIT. The same Spirit who inspired the OT prophets (v. 11) has inspired the truth of the gospel; thus, the message originates from God, not from humans. On the day of Pentecost, the same Spirit who inspired the truth of the gospel began to give power to all believers to proclaim the message (Ac 1:8; 2:4).

1:14 DO NOT CONFORM. See Ro 12:2, note.

1:16 BE HOLY. God is holy, and what is true of God must be true of his people. Holiness carries the thought of being separated from the ungodly ways of the world and set apart for love, for service and for worship of God (see Lev 11:44, note). Holiness is the goal and purpose of our election in Christ (Eph 1:4); it means being like God and being dedicated to him, while living to please him (Ro 12:1; Eph 1:4; 2:10; 1Jn 3:2–3; see Heb 12:14, note). It is accomplished by the Spirit of God, who cleanses our souls from sin, renews us in the image of Christ, and enables us by an infusion of grace to obey God according to his Word (Gal 5:16, 22–23,25; Col 3:10; Tit 3:5; 2Pe 1:9). For more on holiness as a way of life, see article on SANCTIFICATION, p. 1956.

1:17 WHO JUDGES. See article on THE JUDGMENT OF BELIEVERS, p. 1791.

1:17 IN REVERENT FEAR. See Ac 5:11, note; 9:31, note; Ro 3:18, note; Php 2:12, note.

1:18 REDEEMED. See article on BIBLICAL WORDS FOR SALVATION, p. 1710.

1:19 THE PRECIOUS BLOOD OF CHRIST. Scripture plainly sets forth Christ's sacrificial death as that which procures the believer's redemption, i.e., release from bondage to sin (cf. Eph 1:7; see Heb 9:14, note).

1:22 LOVE ONE ANOTHER DEEPLY. See Jn 13:34–35, notes; Ro 12:10, note.

1:25 THE WORD OF THE LORD STANDS FOREVER. Peter's quotation of Isa 40:6–8 indicates that, like the earth itself, all human glory and attainments (such as culture, science and philosophy) come and go (cf. Ps 90:5–10; Jas 4:13–17). But God's Word abides forever. All human endeavors and the prevailing spirit of the world must be constantly judged by the Bible, rather than the Bible being judged by them. Those who bend God's Word to conform to the intellectual trends and diluted standards of their generation betray the "living and enduring word of God" (v. 23).

2:2 CRAVE PURE SPIRITUAL MILK. As born-again children of God (1Co 6:19; Gal 4:6), we should long for the pure milk of God's Word (1:23–25). A sure sign of our spiritual growth is a deep desire to feed on the living and enduring Word of God. Thus, we must be alert to a loss of

SANCTIFICATION

1Pe 1:2 "Who have been chosen according to the foreknowledge of God the Father, through the sanctifying work of the Spirit, for obedience to Jesus Christ and sprinkling by his blood: Grace and peace be yours in abundance."

Sanctification (Gk *hagiasmos*) means to make holy, to consecrate, to separate from the world, and to be set apart from sin so that we may have intimate fellowship with God and serve him gladly (see article on SPIRITUAL SEPARATION FOR BELIEVERS, p. 1794).

(1) In addition to the word "sanctify" (cf. 1Th 5:23), the Scriptural standard of sanctification is expressed in such terms as "love the Lord your God with all your heart . . . soul . . . mind" (Mt 22:37), "blameless and holy" (1Th 3:13), "perfecting holiness" (2Co 7:1), "love, which comes from a pure heart and a good conscience and a sincere faith" (1Ti 1:5), "pure and blameless" (Php 1:10), "set free from sin" (Ro 6:18), "died to sin" (Ro 6:2), "in slavery to righteousness leading to holiness" (Ro 6:19), "obey his commands" (1Jn 3:22), and "overcomes the world" (1Jn 5:4). Such terms describe the operation of the Holy Spirit through salvation in Christ by which he delivers us from sin's bondage and power (Ro 6:1–11), separates us from the sinful practices of this present world, renews our nature according to the image of Christ, produces in us the fruit of the Spirit, and enables us to live holy and victorious lives of dedication to God (Jn 17:15–19,23; Ro 6:5,13,16,19; 12:1; Gal 5:16,22–23; see 2Co 5:17, note).

(2) These terms do not imply an absolute perfection, but an ethical righteousness of unblemished character demonstrated in purity, obedience and blamelessness (Php 2:14–15; Col 1:22; 1Th 2:10; cf. Lk 1:6). Christians, by the grace of God given to them, have died with Christ and are set free from sin's power and dominion (Ro 6:18); therefore, they need not and ought not sin, but can find adequate victory in their Savior, Jesus Christ. Through the Holy Spirit we are able not to sin (1Jn 2:1; 3:6), even though we never come to the place where we are free from temptation and the possibility of sin.

(3) Sanctification was God's will for the Israelites in the OT; they were to live holy or sanctified lives, separated from the lifestyles of the nations around them (see Ex 19:6, note; Lev 11:44, note; 19:2, note; 2Ch 29:5, note). Likewise, sanctification is a requirement for believers in Christ. Scripture teaches that "without holiness no one will see the Lord" (Heb 12:14).

(4) God's children achieve sanctification by faith (Ac 26:18), by union with Christ in his death and resurrection (Jn 15:4–10; Ro 6:1–11; 1Co 1:30), by the blood of Christ (1Jn 1:7–9), by the Word (Jn 17:17), and by the regenerating and sanctifying work of the Holy Spirit in their hearts (Jer 31:31–34; Ro 8:13; 1Co 6:11; Php 2:12–13; 2Th 2:13).

(5) Sanctification is both a work of God and a work of his people (Php 2:12–13). In order to accomplish God's will in sanctification, believers must participate in the Spirit's sanctifying work by ceasing to do evil (Ro 6:1–2), purifying themselves "from everything that contaminates body and spirit" (2Co 7:1; cf. Ro 6:12; Gal 5:16–25), and keeping themselves from being polluted by the world (Jas 1:27; cf. Ro 6:13,19; 8:13; 12:1–2; 13:14; Eph 4:31; 5:18; Col 3:5,10; Heb 6:1; Jas 4:8).

(6) True sanctification requires that believers maintain intimate communion with Christ (see Jn 15:4, note), engage in fellowship with believers (Eph 4:15–16), devote themselves to prayer (Mt 6:5–13; Col 4:2) obey God's Word (Jn 17:17), be sensitive to God's presence and care (Mt 6:25–34), love righteousness and hate wickedness (Heb 1:9), put sin to death (Ro 6), submit to God's discipline (Heb 12:5–11), continue to obey, and be filled with the Holy Spirit (Ro 8:14; Eph 5:18).

(7) In the NT, sanctification is not pictured as a slow process of forsaking sin little by little. Rather, it is presented as a definitive act by which the believer by grace is set free from Satan's bondage and makes a clear break with sin in order to live for God (Ro 6:18; 2Co 5:17; Eph 2:4–6; Col 3:1–3). At the same time, however, sanctification is described as a lifelong process by which we continue to put to death the misdeeds of the body (Ro 8:1–17), are progressively transformed into Christ's likeness (2Co 3:18), grow in grace (2Pe 3:18), and exercise a greater love for God and others (Mt 22:37–39; 1Jn 4:7–8,11,20–21).

(8) Sanctification can involve a definite crisis experience after initial salvation. Believers may receive a clear revelation of God's holiness as well as a consciousness that God is calling them to separate themselves in a greater way from sin and the world and to walk closer to God (2Co 6:16–18). Through this awareness, believers present themselves to God as living sacrifices and receive from the Holy Spirit grace, purity, power and victory to live holy lives pleasing to God (Ro 6:19–22; 12:1–2).

tual milk,[w] so that by it you may grow
up[x] in your salvation, 3now that you
have tasted that the Lord is good.[y]

The Living Stone and a Chosen People

4As you come to him, the living
Stone[z]—rejected by men but chosen
by God[a] and precious to him— 5you
also, like living stones, are being
built[b] into a spiritual house[c] to be a
holy priesthood,[d] offering spiritual
sacrifices acceptable to God through
Jesus Christ.[e] 6For in Scripture it
says:

> "See, I lay a stone in Zion,
> a chosen and precious
> cornerstone,[f]
> and the one who trusts in him
> will never be put to shame."[d][g]

7Now to you who believe, this stone is
precious. But to those who do not believe,[h]

> "The stone the builders rejected[i]
> has become the capstone,[e]"[f][j]

8and,

> "A stone that causes men to
> stumble
> and a rock that makes them
> fall."[g][k]

They stumble because they disobey the
message—which is also what they
were destined for.[l]
9But you are a chosen people,[m] a
royal priesthood,[n] a holy nation,[o] a
people belonging to God,[p] that you
may declare the praises of him who
called you out of darkness into his
wonderful light.[q] 10Once you were not
a people, but now you are the people of
God;[r] once you had not received mercy, but now you have received mercy.
11Dear friends,[s] I urge you, as
aliens and strangers in the world,[t] to
abstain from sinful desires,[u] which
war against your soul.[v] 12Live such
good lives among the pagans that,
though they accuse you of doing
wrong, they may see your good deeds[w]
and glorify God[x] on the day he visits
us.

Submission to Rulers and Masters

13Submit yourselves for the Lord's
sake to every authority[y] instituted
among men: whether to the king, as
the supreme authority, 14or to governors, who are sent by him to punish
those who do wrong[z] and to commend
those who do right.[a] 15For it is God's
will[b] that by doing good you should
silence the ignorant talk of foolish

2:2 [w] 1Co 3:2; Heb 5:12,13 [x] Eph 4:15,16
2:3 [y] Ps 34:8; Heb 6:5
2:4 [z] ver 7 [a] Isa 42:1
2:5 [b] Pr 9:1; 1Co 3:9; Eph 2:20-22 [c] 1Ti 3:15 [d] ver 9; Ex 19:6; Isa 61:6; Rev 1:6; 5:10; 20:6 [e] Php 4:18; Heb 13:15
2:6 [f] Eph 2:20 [g] Isa 28:16; Ro 9:32,33; 10:11
2:7 [h] 2Co 2:16 [i] ver 4 [j] Ps 118:22; S Ac 4:11
2:8 [k] Isa 8:14; S Lk 2:34 [l] Ro 9:22
2:9 [m] Dt 10:15; 1Sa 12:22 [n] ver 5 [o] Ex 19:6; Dt 7:6; Isa 62:12 [p] S Tit 2:14 [q] S Ac 26:18
2:10 [r] Hos 1:9,10; 2:23; Ro 9:25,26
2:11 [s] S 1Co 10:14 [t] S Heb 11:13 [u] Ro 13:14; Gal 5:16 [v] Jas 4:1
2:12 [w] Php 2:15; Tit 2:8; S Tit 2:14; 1Pe 3:16 [x] S Mt 9:8
2:13 [y] Ro 13:1; Tit 3:1
2:14 [z] Ro 13:4 [a] Ro 13:3
2:15 [b] 1Pe 3:17; 4:19

[d] *6* Isaiah 28:16 [e] *7* Or *cornerstone* [f] *7* Psalm 118:22 [g] *8* Isaiah 8:14

---

hunger and thirst for God's Word, a yearning that we can destroy through wrong attitudes (v. 1) and through being "choked by life's worries, riches and pleasures" (Lk 8:14; see Mt 5:6, note; 1Co 15:2, note).

2:5 A HOLY PRIESTHOOD. In the OT the priesthood was restricted to a qualified minority. Their distinctive activity was to offer sacrifices to God on behalf of his people and to communicate directly with God (Ex 28:1; 2Ch 29:11). Now through Jesus Christ, every Christian has been made a priest before God (Rev 1:6; 5:10; 20:6). The priesthood of all believers means the following: (1) All believers have direct access to God through Christ (3:18; Jn 14:6; Eph 2:18).

(2) All believers are under obligation to live holy lives (vv. 5,9; 1:14–17).

(3) All believers must offer up "spiritual sacrifices" to God, including: (a) living in obedience to God and nonconformity to the world (Ro 12:1–2); (b) praying to and praising God (Ps 50:14; Heb 13:15; see article on PRAISE, p. 770); (c) serving with whole hearts and willing minds (1Ch 28:9; Eph 5:1–2; Php 2:17); (d) performing good deeds (Heb 13:16); (e) giving of our material possessions (Ro 12:13; Php 4:18); and (f) presenting our bodies to God as instruments of righteousness (Ro 6:13,19).

(4) All believers must intercede and pray for one another and for all people (Col 4:12; 1Ti 2:1; Rev 8:3; see article on INTERCESSION, p. 1268).

(5) All believers must declare the Word and pray for its success (v. 9; 3:15; Ac 4:31; 1Co 14:26; 2Th 3:1).

(6) All believers may administer baptism and the Lord's Supper (Mt 28:19; Lk 22:19).

2:9 A HOLY NATION. Believers are set apart from the world in order to belong completely to God (cf. Ac 20:28; Tit 2:14) and to proclaim the gospel of salvation to his glory and praise (see Ex 19:6, note; Isa 42:1, notes).

2:11 ALIENS AND STRANGERS. Our new position as God's own possession sets us apart from the people of this world to become aliens in this world. We now live in a country to which we do not belong, and our true citizenship is with Christ in heaven (cf. Php 3:20; Heb 11:9–16). Because we are foreigners on this earth, we must abstain from the world's evil pleasures, which seek to destroy our souls (see article on THE ACTS OF THE SINFUL NATURE AND THE FRUIT OF THE SPIRIT, p. 1818).

2:13 SUBMIT ... TO EVERY AUTHORITY. See Ro 13:1, note.

men.[c] [16]Live as free men,[d] but do not
use your freedom as a cover-up for
evil;[e] live as servants of God.[f]
[17]Show proper respect to everyone:
Love the brotherhood of believers,[g]
fear God, honor the king.[h]

[18]Slaves, submit yourselves to your
masters with all respect,[i] not only to
those who are good and considerate,[j]
but also to those who are harsh. [19]For
it is commendable if a man bears up
under the pain of unjust suffering because he is conscious of God.[k] [20]But
how is it to your credit if you receive a
beating for doing wrong and endure it?
But if you suffer for doing good and you
endure it, this is commendable before
God.[l] [21]To this[m] you were called,[n]
because Christ suffered for you,[o] leaving you an example,[p] that you should
follow in his steps.

[22]"He committed no sin,[q]
and no deceit was found in his
mouth."[h r]

[23]When they hurled their insults at
him,[s] he did not retaliate; when he
suffered, he made no threats.[t] Instead, he entrusted himself[u] to him
who judges justly.[v] [24]He himself bore
our sins[w] in his body on the tree,[x] so
that we might die to sins[y] and live for
righteousness; by his wounds you have
been healed.[z] [25]For you were like
sheep going astray,[a] but now you
have returned to the Shepherd[b] and
Overseer of your souls.[c]

End

Wives and Husbands

3 Wives, in the same way be submissive[d] to your husbands[e] so that,
if any of them do not believe the word,
they may be won over[f] without words
by the behavior of their wives, [2]when
they see the purity and reverence of
your lives. [3]Your beauty should not
come from outward adornment, such
as braided hair and the wearing of gold
jewelry and fine clothes.[g] [4]Instead, it
should be that of your inner self,[h] the
unfading beauty of a gentle and quiet

2:15 [c]S ver 12 **2:16** [d]S Jn 8:32 [e]Gal 5:13 [f]S Ro 6:22 **2:17** [g]S Ro 12:10 [h]Pr 24:21; Ro 13:7 **2:18** [i]S Eph 6:5 [j]Jas 3:17 **2:19** [k]1Pe 3:14, 17 **2:20** [l]1Pe 3:17 **2:21** [m]S Ac 14:22; Php 1:29; 1Pe 3:9 [n]S Ro 8:28 [o]1Pe 3:18; 4:1,13 [p]S Mt 11:29; 16:24 **2:22** [q]S 2Co 5:21 [r]Isa 53:9 **2:23** [s]Heb 12:3; 1Pe 3:9 [t]Isa 53:7 [u]Lk 23:46 [v]Ps 9:4 **2:24** [w]Isa 53:4, 11; Heb 9:28 [x]S Ac 5:30 [y]S Ro 6:2 [z]Dt 32:39; Ps 103:3; Isa 53:5; Heb 12:13; Jas 5:16 **2:25** [a]Isa 53:6 [b]S Jn 10:11 [c]Job 10:12 **3:1** [d]1Pe 2:18 [e]S Eph 5:22 [f]1Co 7:16; 9:19 **3:3** [g]Isa 3:18-23; 1Ti 2:9 **3:4** [h]Ro 7:22; Eph 3:16

[h] *22* Isaiah 53:9

2:21 CHRIST SUFFERED ... FOLLOW IN HIS STEPS. The highest glory and privilege of any believer is to suffer for Christ and the gospel (see Mt 5:10, note). In suffering, believers follow the example of Christ and the apostles (Isa 53; Mt 16:21; 20:28; Ac 9:16, note; Heb 5:8). (1) Christians must be willing to suffer (4:1; 2Co 11:23–29), i.e., to share in the sufferings of Christ (4:13; 2Co 1:5; Php 3:10), and expect suffering to be a part of their ministry (2Co 4:10–12; cf. 1Co 11:1).

(2) Suffering for Christ is called suffering "according to God's will" (4:19), for his "name" (Ac 9:16), "for the gospel" (2Ti 1:8), "for what is right" (3:14) and for "the kingdom of God" (2Th 1:5).

(3) Suffering for Christ is a way to arrive at spiritual maturity (Heb 2:10), to obtain God's blessing (4:14) and to minister life to others (2Co 4:10–12). Sharing in Christ's suffering is a prerequisite for being glorified with Christ (Ro 8:17) and attaining eternal glory (Ro 8:18). In this sense it may be regarded as a precious gift from God (v. 19; Php 1:29).

(4) In living for Christ and the gospel, suffering should not be sought, but believers must be willing to undergo it out of devotion to Christ.

2:24 BORE OUR SINS. Christ bore our sins on the cross (cf. Isa 53:4,11–12), becoming our substitute by taking on himself the penalty for our sins (Jn 1:29; Heb 9:28; 10:10; see article on THE DAY OF ATONEMENT, p. 174). The purpose of this substitutionary death was that we might be totally separated from sin's guilt, power and influence. By his death Christ removed our guilt and the punishment for our sins, opening a way whereby we might justly return to God (Ro 3:24–26) and receive grace to live righteously before him (Ro 6:2–3; 2Co 5:15; Gal 2:20). Peter uses the word "healed" in relation to salvation with all its benefits (cf. Isa 53:5; Mt 8:16–17).

3:1 HUSBANDS ... MAY BE WON OVER. Peter instructs a wife how to act in order to bring her unsaved husband to Christ. (1) She must be submissive to her husband and recognize his leadership in the family (see Eph 5:22, note). (2) She must conduct herself in a pure and reverent manner, with a gentle and quiet spirit (vv. 2–4; see 1Ti 2:13,15, notes). (3) She must attempt to win her husband more by her behavior than by her words.

3:3–4 BEAUTY ... OF YOUR INNER SELF. Gaudy or expensive adornment is contrary to the spirit of modesty that God desires for the Christian wife (see 1Ti 2:9, note). (1) What God highly values in a Christian wife is a gentle and quiet disposition (cf. Mt 11:29; 21:5) that seeks to honor him by giving herself to help her husband and family achieve God's will for their lives. (a) The adjective "gentle" describes an unassuming disposition that expresses itself in gracious submissiveness and a concern for others (cf. Mt 5:5; 2Co 10:1; Gal 5:23). (b) The adjective "quiet" refers to a disposition that is not boisterous and does not create disturbances. In other words, God declares that true beauty is a matter of character and not a matter of decoration.

(2) Christian wives must remain loyal to Christ and his Word in a world governed by materialism, manipulative fashions, self-assertion, obsession with sex, and contempt for the values of home and family.

spirit, which is of great worth in God's sight.[i] **5**For this is the way the holy women of the past who put their hope in God[j] used to make themselves beautiful.[k] They were submissive to their own husbands, **6**like Sarah, who obeyed Abraham and called him her master.[l] You are her daughters if you do what is right and do not give way to fear.

7Husbands,[m] in the same way be considerate as you live with your wives, and treat them with respect as the weaker partner and as heirs with you of the gracious gift of life, so that nothing will hinder your prayers.

Christian Conduct

8Finally, all of you, live in harmony with one another;[n] be sympathetic, love as brothers,[o] be compassionate and humble.[p] **9**Do not repay evil with evil[q] or insult with insult,[r] but with blessing,[s] because to this[t] you were called[u] so that you may inherit a blessing.[v] **10**For,

"Whoever would love life
 and see good days
must keep his tongue from evil
 and his lips from deceitful
 speech.
11He must turn from evil and do
 good;
 he must seek peace and pursue
 it.
12For the eyes of the Lord are on
 the righteous
 and his ears are attentive to
 their prayer,
 but the face of the Lord is against
 those who do evil."[i][w]

Suffering for Doing Good

13Who is going to harm you if you are eager to do good?[x] **14**But even if you should suffer for what is right, you are blessed.[y] "Do not fear what they fear[j]; do not be frightened."[k][z] **15**But in your hearts set apart Christ as Lord. Always be prepared to give an answer[a] to everyone who asks you to give the reason for the hope[b] that you have. But do this with gentleness and respect, **16**keeping a clear conscience,[c] so that those who speak maliciously against your good behavior in Christ may be ashamed of their slander.[d] **17**It is better, if it is God's will,[e] to suffer for doing good[f] than for doing evil. **18**For Christ died for sins[g] once for all,[h] the righteous for the unrighteous, to bring you to God.[i] He was put to death in the body[j] but made alive by the Spirit,[k] **19**through whom[1] also he went and preached to the spirits in prison[l] **20**who disobeyed long ago when God waited patiently[m]

i *12* Psalm 34:12-16 j *14* Or *not fear their threats* k *14* Isaiah 8:12 l *18,19* Or *alive in the spirit, 19through which*

3:4 [i]S Ro 2:29
3:5 [j]1Ti 5:5 [k]Est 2:15
3:6 [l]Ge 18:12
3:7 [m]Eph 5:25-33; Col 3:19
3:8 [n]S Ro 15:5 [o]S Ro 12:10 [p]Eph 4:2; 1Pe 5:5
3:9 [q]Ro 12:17; 1Th 5:15 [r]1Pe 2:23 [s]S Mt 5:44 [t]S 1Pe 2:21 [u]S Ro 8:28 [v]Heb 6:14
3:12 [w]Ps 34:12-16
3:13 [x]S Tit 2:14
3:14 [y]ver 17; 1Pe 2:19,20; 4:15,16 [z]Isa 8:12,13
3:15 [a]Col 4:6 [b]S Heb 3:6
3:16 [c]ver 21; S Ac 23:1 [d]1Pe 2:12,15
3:17 [e]1Pe 2:15; 4:19 [f]1Pe 2:20; 4:15,16
3:18 [g]1Pe 2:21; 4:1,13 [h]S Heb 7:27 [i]S Ro 5:2 [j]Col 1:22; 1Pe 4:1 [k]1Pe 4:6
3:19 [l]1Pe 4:6
3:20 [m]S Ro 2:4

3:7 HUSBANDS. Peter mentions three things that husbands must be concerned about with regard to their wives. (1) Husbands must be considerate and understanding, living with their wives in love and in harmony with God's Word (Eph 5:25–33; Col 3:19).

(2) They must treat them with respect as equal heirs of God's grace and salvation. Wives must be honored, provided for and protected according to their needs. "Weaker" probably refers to the woman's physical strength. A husband must praise and highly treasure his wife as she strives to love and help him according to God's will (vv. 1–6; see Eph 5:23, note).

(3) They must avoid any unjust and improper treatment of their wives. Peter indicates that a husband who fails to live with his wife in an understanding way and to give her honor as a fellow child of God will damage his relation with God by creating a barrier between his prayers and God (cf. Col 3:19).

3:10 LOVE LIFE AND SEE GOOD DAYS. Peter quotes Ps 34:12–16 to emphasize that those who turn away from evil in both word and deed and pursue peace will experience (1) lives full of God's blessing and favor, (2) God's close presence with his help and grace (v. 12), and (3) God's answer to their prayers (cf. Jas 5:16; 1Jn 3:21–22).

3:15 IN YOUR HEARTS SET APART CHRIST AS LORD. Peter calls for an inner reverence for and commitment to Christ as Lord that is always ready to speak for him and to explain the gospel to others (cf. Isa 8:13). Thus, we must know God's Word and truth in order to rightly witness for Christ and lead others to him (cf. Jn 4:4–26).

3:19 PREACHED TO THE SPIRITS. Vv. 18–20 have long been difficult for interpreters. (1) One view is that Christ, after his death and resurrection (v. 18), went to imprisoned angels who had sinned in Noah's day (v. 20; cf. 2Pe 2:4–5) and proclaimed to them his victory over death and Satan (v. 22). Another interpretation is that Christ by the Holy Spirit proclaimed through the mouth of Noah (cf. 2Pe 2:5) a message of warning to Noah's disobedient generation, who are now in Hades awaiting final judgment. This interpretation fits best with the context, which speaks of the disobedient and unsaved people of Noah's day. It would be in harmony with Peter's statement that the Spirit of Christ spoke in times past through the prophets (2Pe 1:20–21). (2) Neither this passage nor 4:6 teaches that unregenerate sinners will

in the days of Noah while the ark was
being built.[n] In it only a few people,
eight in all,[o] were saved[p] through
water, **21**and this water symbolizes
baptism that now saves you[q] also—
not the removal of dirt from the body
but the pledge[m] of a good conscience[r] toward God. It saves you by
the resurrection of Jesus Christ,[s]
22who has gone into heaven[t] and is at
God's right hand[u]—with angels, authorities and powers in submission to
him.[v]

Living for God

4 Therefore, since Christ suffered in
his body,[w] arm yourselves also
with the same attitude, because he
who has suffered in his body is done
with sin.[x] **2**As a result, he does not
live the rest of his earthly life for evil
human desires,[y] but rather for the will
of God. **3**For you have spent enough
time in the past[z] doing what pagans
choose to do—living in debauchery,
lust, drunkenness, orgies, carousing
and detestable idolatry.[a] **4**They think
it strange that you do not plunge with
them into the same flood of dissipation, and they heap abuse on you.[b]
5But they will have to give account to
him who is ready to judge the living
and the dead.[c] **6**For this is the reason
the gospel was preached even to those
who are now dead,[d] so that they might
be judged according to men in regard
to the body, but live according to God
in regard to the spirit.

7The end of all things is near.[e]
Therefore be clear minded and self-
controlled[f] so that you can pray.
8Above all, love each other deeply,[g]
because love covers over a multitude of
sins.[h] **9**Offer hospitality[i] to one another without grumbling.[j] **10**Each one
should use whatever gift he has received to serve others,[k] faithfully[l]
administering God's grace in its various forms. **11**If anyone speaks, he
should do it as one speaking the very
words of God.[m] If anyone serves, he
should do it with the strength God provides,[n] so that in all things God may
be praised[o] through Jesus Christ. To
him be the glory and the power for ever
and ever. Amen.[p] End

Suffering for Being a Christian

12Dear friends, do not be surprised
at the painful trial you are suffering,[q]

3:20 [n]Ge 6:3,5,13,14 [o]Ge 8:18 [p]Heb 11:7
3:21 [q]S Ac 22:16 [r]ver 16; S Ac 23:1 [s]1Pe 1:3
3:22 [t]S Heb 4:14 [u]S Mk 16:19 [v]S Mt 28:18; S Ro 8:38
4:1 [w]S 1Pe 2:21 [x]S Ro 6:18
4:2 [y]Ro 6:2; 1Pe 1:14
4:3 [z]S Eph 2:2 [a]S Ro 13:13
4:4 [b]1Pe 3:16
4:5 [c]S Ac 10:42
4:6 [d]1Pe 3:19
4:7 [e]S Ro 13:11 [f]S Ac 24:25
4:8 [g]S 1Pe 1:22 [h]Pr 10:12; Jas 5:20
4:9 [i]S Ro 12:13 [j]Php 2:14
4:10 [k]Ro 12:6,7 [l]1Co 4:2
4:11 [m]1Th 2:4 [n]Eph 6:10 [o]1Co 10:31 [p]S Ro 11:36
4:12 [q]1Pe 1:6,7

[m]*21* Or *response*

have a second chance to accept salvation after death. After death comes judgment (see Heb 9:27) and one's fixed destiny in eternity (Lk 16:26).

3:21 BAPTISM THAT NOW SAVES YOU ALSO. Water baptism saves us in the sense that it is an obedient expression of our repentance, our faith in Christ and our commitment to come out of the world. It is our confession and pledge that we belong to Christ and have died and risen with him (Ro 6:3–5; Gal 3:27; Col 2:12; cf. Ac 2:38–39). Note the comparison with the flood (v. 20): just as Noah's obedience to God's instructions regarding the flood was a testimony to his faith that preceded the flood, so going through the waters of baptism is a testimony to our faith that brought salvation through Christ before we were baptized.

4:1 HE WHO HAS SUFFERED. Those who willingly suffer for Christ's cause find it easier to resist sin and to follow God's will. They have united themselves with Christ and shared his cross. As a result the pull of sin is made insignificant and God's will paramount (v. 2). This spiritual principle will work in the lives of all believers. Obeying God even when it means suffering, ridicule or rejection will strengthen us morally and spiritually, and we will receive from God a greater grace (v. 14).

4:6 THOSE WHO ARE NOW DEAD. This term is best understood as referring to those to whom the gospel was preached while they were still living on earth, but who are now dead. They heard the gospel and believed, and although they have died (i.e., "judged according to men in regard to the body"), they now live with God. The verse could be paraphrased to read, "the gospel was preached to those who believed and later died, that they might have eternal life with God."

4:7 END OF ALL THINGS IS NEAR. We should view our lives in light of Christ's imminent coming and the end of the world (cf. Heb 10:25; Jas 5:8–9; 1Jn 2:18). To Peter, this calls for the following commitments: (1) to pray to God fervently and daily (see Ac 10:9, note; 12:5, note; Col 4:2,12, notes); (2) to love one another deeply, from the heart (v. 8; cf. 1:22; Mt 22:37–39; 1Th 4:9–10; 2Pe 1:7); (3) to be hospitable and kind to those in need (v. 9); (4) to serve other believers through the use of spiritual gifts given by the Spirit (v. 10; see article on SPIRITUAL GIFTS FOR BELIEVERS, p. 1770); (5) to witness for Christ and serve God in the power of the Spirit (v. 11; Ac 1:5–8); (6) to praise God (v. 11); and (7) to remain loyal to Christ in trials (vv. 12–19).

4:12 THE PAINFUL TRIAL. The NT emphasizes that trials are the inevitable experience of faithful believers in an ungodly world controlled by Satan and opposed to the gospel (see article on THE SUFFERING OF THE RIGHTEOUS, p. 710). Those who are committed to Jesus Christ with a devoted and loyal faith, who live by the Spirit and who love the truth of the gospel will experience trouble and sorrow. In fact, suffering because of

as though something strange were
happening to you. 13But rejoice[r] that
you participate in the sufferings of
Christ,[s] so that you may be overjoyed
when his glory is revealed.[t] 14If you
are insulted because of the name of
Christ,[u] you are blessed,[v] for the
Spirit of glory and of God rests on you.
15If you suffer, it should not be as a
murderer or thief or any other kind of
criminal, or even as a meddler. 16However,
if you suffer as a Christian, do not
be ashamed, but praise God that you
bear that name.[w] 17For it is time for
judgment to begin with the family of
God;[x] and if it begins with us, what
will the outcome be for those who do
not obey the gospel of God?[y] 18And,

> "If it is hard for the righteous to
> be saved,
> what will become of the ungodly
> and the sinner?"[n][z]

19So then, those who suffer according
to God's will[a] should commit
themselves to their faithful Creator
and continue to do good.

To Elders and Young Men

5 To the elders among you, I appeal
as a fellow elder,[b] a witness[c] of
Christ's sufferings and one who also
will share in the glory to be revealed:[d]
2Be shepherds of God's flock[e] that is
under your care, serving as overseers—not
because you must, but because
you are willing, as God wants
you to be;[f] not greedy for money,[g]
but eager to serve; 3not lording it
over[h] those entrusted to you, but being
examples[i] to the flock. 4And
when the Chief Shepherd[j] appears,
you will receive the crown of glory[k]
that will never fade away.[l]

5Young men, in the same way be
submissive[m] to those who are older.
All of you, clothe yourselves with humility[n]
toward one another, because,

4:13 [r]S Mt 5:12 [s]S 2Co 1:5 [t]Ro 8:17; 1Pe 1:7; 5:1
4:14 [u]S Jn 15:21 [v]Mt 5:11
4:16 [w]Ac 5:41
4:17 [x]Jer 25:29; Eze 9:6; Am 3:2; 1Ti 3:15 [y]2Th 1:8
4:18 [z]Pr 11:31; Lk 23:31
4:19 [a]1Pe 2:15; 3:17
5:1 [b]S Ac 11:30 [c]S Lk 24:48 [d]1Pe 1:5,7; 4:13; Rev 1:9
5:2 [e]S Jn 21:16 [f]2Co 9:7; Phm 14 [g]S 1Ti 3:3
5:3 [h]Eze 34:4; Mt 20:25-28 [i]S 1Ti 4:12
5:4 [j]S Jn 10:11 [k]S 1Co 9:25 [l]1Pe 1:4
5:5 [m]Eph 5:21 [n]1Pe 3:8

[n] *18* Prov. 11:31

righteousness is an evidence of the genuineness of your devotion to Christ (cf. Mt 5:10–12; Ac 14:22; Ro 8:17–18; 2Ti 2:12). For this reason problems in your life may be a sign that you are pleasing God and are faithful to him. They frequently accompany your warfare of faith against sin, the ungodly world and Satan (1:6–9; Eph 6:12). Through painful trials God allows you to share in his suffering and forms within you the quality of character he desires (Ro 5:3–5; 2Co 1:3–7; Jas 1:2–4). Yet when you suffer and remain faithful to Christ, you will be considered blessed, for "the Spirit of glory and of God rests on you" (v. 14, note; see 2:21, note).

4:13 REJOICE THAT YOU PARTICIPATE IN. It is a principle within God's kingdom that suffering for Christ's cause will increase the depth of the believer's joy in the Lord (see Mt 5:10–12; Ac 5:41; 16:25; Ro 5:3; Col 1:24; Heb 10:34; see next note). Therefore, those involved in little or no suffering for the Lord are not to be envied.

4:14 THE SPIRIT OF GLORY AND OF GOD. Those who suffer because of their loyalty to Christ are blessed (cf. v. 13; 3:14; Mt 5:11–12), for the Holy Spirit will rest on them in a special way. Their lives will be full of the presence of the Spirit to work in them, bless them, help them and provide them with a foretaste of heaven's glory (cf. Isa 11:1–2; Jn 1:29–34; Ac 6:9–15).

4:17 JUDGMENT TO BEGIN WITH THE FAMILY OF GOD. See article on THE JUDGMENT OF BELIEVERS, p. 1791.

5:2 BE SHEPHERDS. Elders (overseers or pastors) have the responsibility of caring for believers, discipling them, feeding them with the Word and protecting them (see articles on THE MINISTRY GIFTS OF THE CHURCH, p. 1830, and OVERSEERS AND THEIR DUTIES, p. 1690).

5:2 NOT GREEDY FOR MONEY. Pastors and church leaders must beware of two dangerous sins: (1) The desire for money (see 1Ti 3:3,8; Tit 1:7). The NT standard for those who oversee God's work is to receive adequate support from the church (Lk 10:7; 1Co 9:14; 1Ti 5:17) and to be content with basic and necessary provisions for themselves and their families. No minister ought to make himself rich from God's work. Those who fall victim to this temptation open themselves up to sins of greed, compromise and theft. For the sake of money, they compromise God's Word, righteous standards and kingdom principles.

(2) The desire for power. Those greedy for power will dominate those whom they are to serve by excessively using their authority. Instead, the pastor must lead the church by being an example to the flock in devotion to Christ, humble service, perseverance in righteousness, steadfastness in prayer, and love for the Word.

5:5 CLOTHE YOURSELVES WITH HUMILITY. Humility must be the mark of all God's people. It means an absence of pride, a consciousness of one's weaknesses, and the disposition to ascribe to God and others the credit for what one is achieving or has accomplished (cf. Mt 11:29; Php 2:3–4; Col 3:12). The word "clothe" (Gk *egkomboomai*) means to attach a piece of clothing to oneself. In NT times slaves fastened a white piece of cloth or apron over their clothing so that others would know that they were slaves. Peter exhorts us to tie the cloth of humility on ourselves in order (1) to be identified as believers in Christ as we act humbly toward others, and (2) to receive God's grace and help (vv. 5–7). Peter may have had in mind Jesus' action of tying on a towel and washing the disciples' feet (Jn 13:4–5).

"God opposes the proud
but gives grace to the humble."[o][o]

6Humble yourselves, therefore, under
God's mighty hand, that he may lift
you up in due time.[p] **7**Cast all your anxiety on him[q] because he cares for
you.[r]
8Be self-controlled[s] and alert. Your
enemy the devil prowls around[t] like a
roaring lion[u] looking for someone to
devour. **9**Resist him,[v] standing firm in
the faith,[w] because you know that
your brothers throughout the world are
undergoing the same kind of sufferings.[x]
10And the God of all grace, who
called you[y] to his eternal glory[z] in
Christ, after you have suffered a little
while,[a] will himself restore you and
make you strong,[b] firm and steadfast.
11To him be the power for ever and
ever. Amen.[c]

Final Greetings

12With the help of Silas,[p][d] whom I
regard as a faithful brother, I have
written to you briefly,[e] encouraging
you and testifying that this is the true
grace of God. Stand fast in it.[f]
13She who is in Babylon, chosen together with you, sends you her greetings, and so does my son Mark.[g]
14Greet one another with a kiss of
love.[h]
Peace[i] to all of you who are in
Christ.

5:5 [o] Pr 3:34; S Mt 23:12
5:6 [p] Job 5:11; Jas 4:10
5:7 [q] Ps 37:5; Mt 6:25
[r] Ps 55:22; Heb 13:5
5:8 [s] S Ac 24:25
[t] Job 1:7 [u] 2Ti 4:17
5:9 [v] S Jas 4:7
[w] Col 2:5
[x] S Ac 14:22
5:10 [y] S Ro 8:28
[z] 2Co 4:17; 2Ti 2:10 [a] 1Pe 1:6
[b] Ps 18:32; 2Th 2:17
5:11 [c] S Ro 11:36
5:12 [d] S Ac 15:22
[e] Heb 13:22
[f] S 1Co 16:13
5:13 [g] S Ac 12:12
5:14 [h] S Ro 16:16
[i] S Eph 6:23

[o] *5* Prov. 3:34 [p] *12* Greek *Silvanus,* a variant of *Silas*

5:7 HE CARES FOR YOU. God's care for the troubles of every one of his children is a truth emphasized throughout his Word (see Ps 27:10; 37:5; 40:17; 55:22; Mt 6:25–34; 10:29–31; 11:28–30; Php 4:6, note). All your fears, anxieties and concerns must be decisively cast on God (cf. Ps 55:22; Lk 12:11–12; see article on THE PROVIDENCE OF GOD, p. 78).

5:8 YOUR ENEMY THE DEVIL. When humanity fell into sin, Satan became the ruler of the world (Jn 12:31; 14:30; 16:11). He dominates the whole world (1Jn 5:19), patrols this earth, and is commander of a host of evil spirits through whom he enslaves and keeps captive those without Christ (Eph 2:2; see article on POWER OVER SATAN AND DEMONS, p. 1484). Only believers have been delivered from his power (see article on THE KINGDOM OF GOD, p. 1430). Yet, as a roaring lion, he remains a threat to believers (cf. Ps 22:13; Eze 22:25) and seeks to destroy them, especially through experiences of suffering (vv. 8–10). He will spiritually destroy anyone who abandons God's protection. Through our faith in Christ's blood (Rev 12:11), our spiritual warfare by the Spirit (Eph 6:11–18) and our prayers to God (Mt 6:13), we are fully equipped to defeat Satan's schemes (Eph 6:11), to resist him and to stand firm in the faith (v. 9). "The one who is in you is greater than the one who is in the world" (1Jn 4:4).

2 PETER

Outline

Christian Greetings (1:1–2)

I. The Commendation of True Knowledge (1:2b-21)
  A. The Transforming Power of a True Knowledge of God (1:2b-4)
  B. The Progressive Character of Christian Growth (1:5–11)
  C. The Apostle's Attestation of the Word of Truth (1:12–21)
    1. His Motive (1:12–15)
    2. His Method (1:16–21)
      a. Eyewitness of the Prophetic Word (1:16–19)
      b. Inspiration of Prophetic Scripture (1:20–21)

II. The Condemnation of False Teachers (2:1–22)
  A. What to Expect From False Teachers (2:1–3)
  B. What They May Expect From God (2:4–10a)
  C. Some Characteristics of False Teachers (2:10b-19)
  D. The Dangers of Relapse From the Truth (2:20–22)

III. The Certainty of the Lord's Coming (3:1–18a)
  A. Denial of His Coming (3:1–7)
  B. Assurance of His Coming (3:8–10)
  C. Living for His Coming (3:11–18a)

Benediction (3:18b)

Author: Peter

Theme: Faithful Truth Versus False Teachers

Date of Writing: c. A.D. 66–68

Background

In the salutation, Simon Peter identifies himself as author of this letter; he later remarks that this is his second letter to the readers (3:1), indicating that he is writing the same believers in Asia Minor who had received his first letter (1Pe 1:1). Since Peter, like Paul, was put to death by an edict of the wicked Nero (who himself died in June, A.D. 68), it is most likely that Peter wrote this letter between A.D. 66–68, shortly before his martyrdom in Rome (1:13–15).

Some scholars in ancient and modern times, ignoring certain remarkable similarities between 1 and 2 Peter and stressing instead the differences between them, have assumed that Peter was not the author of this letter. However, the differences in content, vocabulary, emphases and literary style between the two letters can be accounted for adequately by the different circumstances of both Peter and his readers in the two letters. (1) The original circumstances of the recipients had changed from serious persecution inflicted by their surrounding society to serious assault from within by false teachers that threatened the churches' foundations of truth and righteousness. (2) Peter's circumstances were also different. Whereas he had the skilled assistance of Silas when writing his first letter (1Pe 5:12), it appears that Silas was not available when writing this one. Peter may have used his own rough Galilean Greek or relied on a less capable scribe than Silas.

Purpose

Peter wrote (1) to exhort believers to diligently pursue godliness and a true knowledge of Christ, and (2) to expose and repudiate the insidious activity of false prophets and teachers among the churches in Asia Minor who were undermining apostolic truth. Peter summarizes his purpose in 3:17–18, where he exhorts true believers (1) to be on their guard so that they may not "be carried away by the error of lawless men" (3:17), and (2) to "grow in the grace and knowledge of our Lord and Savior Jesus Christ" (3:18).

Survey

This short letter earnestly instructs believers to take hold of life and godliness through a true knowledge of Christ. The first chapter emphasizes the importance of Christian growth. Having begun by faith, the believer must diligently pursue moral excellence, knowledge, self-control, perseverance, godliness, brotherly kindness and selfless love, resulting in a mature faith and true knowledge of the Lord Jesus (1:3–11).

The next chapter solemnly warns about false prophets and teachers who were arising among the churches. Peter denounces them as lawless men (2:1,3; 3:17) who indulge the corrupt desires of the sinful nature (2:2,7,10,13–14,18–19), who are greedy (2:3,14–15), arrogant (2:18) and self-willed (2:10), and who despise authority (2:10–12). Peter seeks to protect true believers against those destructive heresies (2:1) by exposing their evil motives and conduct.

In ch. 3, Peter refutes the skepticism of these teachers about the Lord's coming (3:3–4). As Noah's generation mistakenly scoffed at the idea of the judgment of a great flood from God, these scoffers are equally blind concerning the promises of Christ's return. But with the same decisive action as the judgment of the flood (3:5–6), Christ will return and dissolve the present earth by fire (3:7–12) and create a righteous new order (3:13). In view of this, believers must live holy and godly lives in this present age (3:11,14).

Special Features

Four major features characterize this letter. (1) It contains one of the Bible's strongest statements about the inspiration, reliability and authority of Scripture (1:19–21). (2) Ch. 2 and Jude's letter are remarkably similar in their denunciation of false teachers. Perhaps Jude, facing at a later date the same problem of false teachers, utilized portions of Peter's inspired teaching to make the same point (see the introduction to Jude). (3) Ch. 3 is one of the great NT chapters on Christ's second coming. (4) Peter indirectly refers to Paul's writings as Scripture by mentioning them in relation to "the other Scriptures" (3:15–16).

Reading 2 Peter

In order to read the entire New Testament in one year, the book of 2 Peter should be read in 3 days, according to the following schedule:
☐ 1 ☐ 2 ☐ 3

NOTES

1 Simon Peter, a servant[a] and
apostle of Jesus Christ,[b]

To those who through the righteousness[c] of our God and Savior Jesus Christ[d] have received a faith as precious as ours:

2Grace and peace be yours in abundance[e] through the knowledge of God and of Jesus our Lord.[f]

Making One's Calling and Election Sure

3His divine power[g] has given us everything we need for life and godliness
through our knowledge of him[h] who
called us[i] by his own glory and goodness. 4Through these he has given us
his very great and precious promises,[j] so that through them you may
participate in the divine nature[k] and
escape the corruption in the world
caused by evil desires.[l]
5For this very reason, make every effort to add to your faith goodness; and
to goodness, knowledge;[m] 6and to
knowledge, self-control;[n] and to self-
control, perseverance;[o] and to perseverance, godliness;[p] 7and to godliness, brotherly kindness; and to
brotherly kindness, love.[q] 8For if you
possess these qualities in increasing
measure, they will keep you from being
ineffective and unproductive[r] in your
knowledge of our Lord Jesus Christ.[s]
9But if anyone does not have them, he
is nearsighted and blind,[t] and has forgotten that he has been cleansed from
his past sins.[u]
10Therefore, my brothers, be all the
more eager to make your calling[v] and
election sure. For if you do these
things, you will never fall,[w] 11and you
will receive a rich welcome into the
eternal kingdom[x] of our Lord and Savior Jesus Christ.[y]

Eyewitnesses of Christ's Majesty

12So I will always remind you of
these things,[z] even though you know
them and are firmly established in the
truth[a] you now have. 13I think it is
right to refresh your memory[b] as long
as I live in the tent of this body,[c] 14be-
cause I know that I will soon put it
aside,[d] as our Lord Jesus Christ has
made clear to me.[e] 15And I will make
every effort to see that after my departure[f] you will always be able to remember these things.
16We did not follow cleverly invented stories when we told you about the
power and coming of our Lord Jesus
Christ,[g] but we were eyewitnesses of
his majesty.[h] 17For he received honor
and glory from God the Father when
the voice came to him from the Majes-

1:1 [a]Ro 1:1 [b]1Pe 1:1 [c]Ro 3:21-26 [d]Tit 2:13 **1:2** [e]S Ro 1:7 [f]ver 3,8; 2Pe 2:20; 3:18; S Php 3:8 **1:3** [g]1Pe 1:5 [h]S ver 2 [i]S Ro 8:28 **1:4** [j]2Co 7:1 [k]Eph 4:24; Heb 12:10; 1Jn 3:2 [l]Jas 1:27; 2Pe 2:18-20 **1:5** [m]S ver 2; Col 2:3 **1:6** [n]S Ac 24:25 [o]S Heb 10:36 [p]ver 3 **1:7** [q]S Ro 12:10; 1Th 3:12 **1:8** [r]Jn 15:2; Col 1:10; Tit 3:14 [s]S ver 2 **1:9** [t]1Jn 2:11 [u]Eph 5:26; S Mt 1:21 **1:10** [v]S Ro 8:28 [w]Ps 15:5; 2Pe 3:17; Jude 24 **1:11** [x]Ps 145:13; 2Ti 4:18 [y]2Pe 2:20; 3:18 **1:12** [z]Php 3:1; 1Jn 2:21; Jude 5 [a]2Jn 2 **1:13** [b]2Pe 3:1 [c]Isa 38:12; 2Co 5:1,4 **1:14** [d]2Ti 4:6 [e]Jn 13:36; 21:18,19 **1:15** [f]Lk 9:31 **1:16** [g]Mk 13:26; 14:62 [h]Mt 17:1-8

1:3 EVERYTHING WE NEED FOR LIFE AND GODLINESS. The love of our heavenly Father, salvation through Jesus Christ, Christ's intercession for us in heaven, the indwelling of and baptism in the Holy Spirit, the communion of the saints and God's inspired Word are sufficient to meet all that believers need for life and godliness (Mt 11:28–30; Heb 4:16; 7:25; 9:14).

(1) No additional human wisdom, technique or theory is needed to complete the sufficiency of God's Word that reveals our perfect salvation in Christ. The words of Jesus, the NT apostolic faith and God's grace were adequate in the early days of the church to meet the needs of the lost, and they are just as adequate today. Absolutely nothing can offer more height, depth, strength and help than what Jesus himself proclaimed and provided and what the apostles testified to in Biblical revelation. Jesus Christ alone is "the way and the truth and the life" (Jn 14:6).

(2) If the gospel we hold is found wanting in these days, it is because our gospel is something less than the gospel of Christ and the apostles.

1:4 PARTICIPATE IN THE DIVINE NATURE. Our participation in God's very nature is another description of the new birth by which we receive God's life (see article on REGENERATION, p. 1589). We share God's nature in order to conform to God and his holiness (cf. 1Co 6:19–20; Eph 4:24).

1:5 ADD TO YOUR FAITH. Peter lists the virtues a Christian must develop in order to be spiritually victorious and fruitful before God (v. 8). The phrase "make every effort" demonstrates that believers must be actively involved in their Christian growth (cf. Php 2:12–13). Those who become Christians must immediately strive to add to their faith these seven qualities (vv. 5–8). Note that godly characteristics do not automatically grow without our diligent effort to cultivate them (see article on THE ACTS OF THE SINFUL NATURE AND THE FRUIT OF THE SPIRIT, p. 1818).

1:10 MAKE YOUR CALLING AND ELECTION SURE. Our faith and salvation must not be taken for granted. We will continue faithful to the end only if we make every effort by God's grace to add to our faith the spiritual qualities listed in vv. 5–9 (see article on ELECTION AND PREDESTINATION, p. 1824).

1:11 RICH WELCOME INTO THE ETERNAL KINGDOM. Some believers, because of negligence, will barely make it into the kingdom (1Co 3:15), while others who remain steadfast in holiness will be welcomed richly with honor (Mt 25:21; Ac 7:55–56; 2Ti 4:7–8,18).

tic Glory, saying, "This is my Son,
whom I love; with him I am well
pleased."[a i] **18**We ourselves heard
this voice that came from heaven when
we were with him on the sacred mountain.[j]

Prophecy of Scripture

19And we have the word of the
prophets made more certain,[k] and you
will do well to pay attention to it, as to
a light[l] shining in a dark place, until
the day dawns[m] and the morning
star[n] rises in your hearts.[o] **20**Above
all, you must understand[p] that no
prophecy of Scripture came about by
the prophet's own interpretation.
21For prophecy never had its origin in
the will of man, but men spoke from
God[q] as they were carried along by
the Holy Spirit.[r]

False Teachers and Their Destruction

2 But there were also false prophets[s] among the people, just as
there will be false teachers among
you.[t] They will secretly introduce destructive heresies, even denying the
sovereign Lord[u] who bought
them[v]—bringing swift destruction on
themselves. **2**Many will follow their
shameful ways[w] and will bring the
way of truth into disrepute. **3**In their
greed[x] these teachers will exploit
you[y] with stories they have made up.

1:17 [i] S Mt 3:17 **1:18** [j] Mt 17:6 **1:19** [k] 1Pe 1:10, 11 [l] Ps 119:105 [m] Lk 1:78 [n] Rev 22:16 [o] 2Co 4:6 **1:20** [p] 2Pe 3:3 **1:21** [q] 2Ti 3:16 [r] 2Sa 23:2; Ac 1:16; 3:18; 1Pe 1:11 **2:1** [s] Dt 13:1-3; Jer 6:13; S Mt 7:15 [t] 1Ti 4:1 [u] Jude 4 [v] S 1Co 6:20 **2:2** [w] Jude 4 **2:3** [x] ver 14 [y] 2Co 2:17; 1Th 2:5

[a] *17* Matt. 17:5; Mark 9:7; Luke 9:35

1:19 WORD OF THE PROPHETS MADE MORE CERTAIN. Peter contrasts humanistic ideas with God's Word (v. 16). He goes on to attest to the divine origin of Scripture and affirms that all prophecy originated from God, not from humans (v. 21). This assures us that God's message is infallible (incapable of mistakes or errors) and inerrant (free from error, falsehood or deceit). Infallibility and inerrancy cannot be separated, for the inerrancy of Scripture is the result of the infallibility of God's own Word. Scripture in its entirety is true and reliable in all its teaching (cf. 2Sa 23:2; Jer 1:7–9; 1Co 14:37; see article on THE INSPIRATION AND AUTHORITY OF SCRIPTURE, p. 1898).

1:20 NO PROPHECY OF SCRIPTURE. No prophecy in Scripture came about by the writer's own ideas or reasoning, but it came from the Holy Spirit.

1:21 MEN SPOKE FROM GOD ... BY THE HOLY SPIRIT. Peter affirms the divine origin and authority of prophecy in Scripture (see article on THE PROPHET IN THE OLD TESTAMENT, p. 986). All believers must likewise maintain a strong uncompromising view of holy Scripture as inspired and authoritative. There are several reasons for this. (1) It is the only way to be true to what Jesus Christ, the apostles and the Bible itself teach about Scripture (see Ps 119; Jn 5:47, note; see article on THE INSPIRATION AND AUTHORITY OF SCRIPTURE, p. 1898).

(2) Without a strong view of holy Scripture, the church has no true and sure foundation for its faith, no certainty of salvation, no moral absolutes, no message to preach without doubt, no sure expectancy for the baptism in the Holy Spirit and the working of miracles, and no hope for Christ's imminent return.

(3) Without a strong view of holy Scripture, Bible-believing Christians have no absolute and objective truth based on the authority of God himself by which to judge and reject this world's ever-changing values, human philosophies and the culture's ungodly practices (Ps 119:160).

(4) Without a strong view of holy Scripture, Christians will not be ready to withstand the extreme difficulties of the last days (see 1Th 2:1–12; 1Ti 4:1, note; 2Ti 3:1, note).

(5) Without a strong view of holy Scripture, the full authority and teaching of the Bible are weakened; the Bible will subsequently be replaced by subjective religious experience or by independent and critical reasoning (2:1–3).

2:1 THERE WILL BE FALSE TEACHERS AMONG YOU. The Holy Spirit repeatedly warns that there will be many false teachers within the churches. The warnings concerning teachers and leaders who introduce destructive heresies among God's people began with Jesus (see Mt 24:11, note; 24:24–25) and were continued by the Spirit through Paul (see 2Th 2:7, note; 1Ti 4:1, note; 2Ti 3:1–5), Peter (vv. 1–22), John (1Jn 2:18; 4:1; 2Jn 7–11); Jude (Jude 3–4,12,18) and Christ's letters to the seven churches (see Rev 2:2,6, notes; see article on FALSE TEACHERS, p. 1506).

2:1 DENYING THE SOVEREIGN LORD WHO BOUGHT THEM. According to Peter, the false teachers within the church who were "denying [Gk *arneomai*, meaning to disown or renounce] the sovereign Lord" had left the straight way, wandered off (v. 15) and become "springs without water" (v. 17). At one time they had escaped the wickedness of the world through Jesus Christ, but now were again entangled in sin (v. 20).

2:2 WAY OF TRUTH INTO DISREPUTE. Many professed believers will follow these false preachers and their "shameful" (i.e., sexually immoral) ways. Because of the sinful lifestyles of the leaders and their followers, God and his gospel will be put to shame (see 2Ti 4:3–4, note).

2:3 IN THEIR GREED ... STORIES THEY HAVE MADE UP. The false teachers will commercialize the gospel, being experts in greed and in getting money from believers to enhance their ministries and affluent lifestyles. (1) Believers must be aware that one of the chief methods of false ministers is to use "stories they have made up," i.e., to tell impressive, but false, stories, or to

Their condemnation has long been
hanging over them, and their destruction has not been sleeping.
4For if God did not spare angels
when they sinned,[z] but sent them to
hell,[b] putting them into gloomy dungeons[c] to be held for judgment;[a] **5**if
he did not spare the ancient world[b]
when he brought the flood on its ungodly people,[c] but protected Noah, a
preacher of righteousness, and seven
others;[d] **6**if he condemned the cities of
Sodom and Gomorrah by burning them
to ashes,[e] and made them an example[f] of what is going to happen to the
ungodly;[g] **7**and if he rescued Lot,[h] a
righteous man, who was distressed by
the filthy lives of lawless men[i] **8**(for
that righteous man,[j] living among
them day after day, was tormented in
his righteous soul by the lawless deeds
he saw and heard) — **9**if this is so, then
the Lord knows how to rescue godly
men from trials[k] and to hold the unrighteous for the day of judgment,[l]
while continuing their punishment.[d]
10This is especially true of those who
follow the corrupt desire[m] of the sinful
nature[e] and despise authority.
Bold and arrogant, these men are
not afraid to slander celestial beings;[n]
11yet even angels, although they are
stronger and more powerful, do not
bring slanderous accusations against
such beings in the presence of the
Lord.[o] **12**But these men blaspheme in
matters they do not understand. They
are like brute beasts, creatures of instinct, born only to be caught and destroyed, and like beasts they too will
perish.[p]
13They will be paid back with harm
for the harm they have done. Their idea
of pleasure is to carouse in broad daylight.[q] They are blots and blemishes,
reveling in their pleasures while they
feast with you.[f] [r] **14**With eyes full of
adultery, they never stop sinning; they
seduce[s] the unstable;[t] they are experts in greed[u] — an accursed
brood![v] **15**They have left the straight
way and wandered off to follow the way
of Balaam[w] son of Beor, who loved the
wages of wickedness. **16**But he was rebuked for his wrongdoing by a donkey — a beast without speech — who

2:4 [z] Ge 6:1-4 [a] 1Ti 3:6; Jude 6; Rev 20:1,2
2:5 [b] 2Pe 3:6 [c] Ge 6:5-8:19 [d] Heb 11:7; 1Pe 3:20
2:6 [e] Ge 19:24,25 [f] Nu 26:10; Jude 7 [g] Mt 10:15; 11:23, 24; Ro 9:29
2:7 [h] Ge 19:16 [i] 2Pe 3:17
2:8 [j] Heb 11:4
2:9 [k] Ps 37:33; S Ro 15:31; Rev 3:10 [l] S Mt 10:15
2:10 [m] 2Pe 3:3; Jude 16,18 [n] Jude 8
2:11 [o] Jude 9
2:12 [p] Ps 49:12; Jude 10
2:13 [q] S Ro 13:13; 1Th 5:7 [r] 1Co 11:20,21; Jude 12
2:14 [s] ver 18 [t] Jas 1:8; 2Pe 3:16 [u] ver 3 [v] Eph 2:3
2:15 [w] Nu 22:4-20; 31:16; Dt 23:4; Jude 11; Rev 2:14

[b] *4* Greek *Tartarus* [c] *4* Some manuscripts *into chains of darkness* [d] *9* Or *unrighteous for punishment until the day of judgment* [e] *10* Or *the flesh* [f] *13* Some manuscripts *in their love feasts*

give exaggerated statistics in order to inspire God's people to give money. They glorify themselves and enhance their ministries with these fabricated stories (cf. 2Co 2:17). Thus, the unwary and sincere child of God becomes an object of exploitation. (2) Because these ministers defile God's truth and people with greed and deceit, they are assigned to condemnation and destruction.

2:4 ANGELS ... SENT THEM TO HELL. This probably refers to the angels who rebelled with Satan against God (see Eze 28:12, note), becoming the wicked spirits spoken of in the NT. Why some of the wicked spirits are in dungeons and some are free to work with Satan on earth is not explained in Scripture (cf. Jude 6; see article on POWER OVER SATAN AND DEMONS, p. 1484).

2:8 TORMENTED IN HIS RIGHTEOUS SOUL. An essential characteristic of truly righteous people is that they love righteousness and hate wickedness (see Heb 1:9, note). Their souls are distressed and tormented (vv. 7–8) by the sin, immorality and ungodliness in the world (see Eze 9:4, note; Jn 2:13–17; Ac 17:16).

2:9 RESCUE GODLY MEN. Lot's response to the evil and immorality around him (v. 8) became a test that determined both his own deliverance and his destiny in eternity. (1) God rescued Lot because he rejected evil and was repulsed at the "filthy lives of lawless men" (v. 7; see previous note).

(2) When Christ returns to receive his people (see Jn 14:3, note) and to pour out his wrath on the ungodly (3:10–12), he will gather to himself those in the visible church who, because of their faith in and love for him, are, like Lot, tormented by sensual conduct, filthy living and blatant sin within society (see article on THE RAPTURE, p. 1864).

(3) We can be sure that God knows how to deliver his faithful believers from immoral and corrupt people in every generation (cf. Mt 6:13; 2Ti 4:18; Rev 3:10).

2:10 DESPISE AUTHORITY ... CELESTIAL BEINGS. Peter speaks of unrighteous and immoral people who, like the homosexuals of Sodom (v. 8; cf. Ge 19:4–11), despise all manner of authority that restrains evil, including Christ and his Word.

2:15 WAY OF BALAAM. This phrase refers to a love for personal honor and material gain at the expense of God's people (cf. Nu 31:16; Rev 2:14; see Nu 25:2, note). Peter emphasizes that sexual immorality, love of honor and greed for money characterize false teachers and preachers.

2:16 SPOKE WITH A MAN'S VOICE. Peter clearly believes in the miracles recorded in the OT. Today self-appointed critics within the church arrogantly scoff at the miracles recorded in God's Word and regard those who believe in them as being unenlightened or naive. Genuine children of God, however, believe in God and accept all the Bible's miracles. They also believe that God performs miracles today in response to the prayers and faith of his people (see Jn 6:2, note).

spoke with a man's voice and restrained the prophet's madness.[x]
17These men are springs without
water[y] and mists driven by a storm.
Blackest darkness is reserved for
them.[z] 18For they mouth empty,
boastful words[a] and, by appealing to
the lustful desires of sinful human nature, they entice people who are just
escaping[b] from those who live in error. 19They promise them freedom,
while they themselves are slaves of depravity—for a man is a slave to whatever has mastered him.[c] 20If they
have escaped the corruption of the
world by knowing[d] our Lord and Savior Jesus Christ[e] and are again entangled in it and overcome, they are worse
off at the end than they were at the
beginning.[f] 21It would have been better for them not to have known the way
of righteousness, than to have known
it and then to turn their backs on the
sacred command that was passed on to
them.[g] 22Of them the proverbs are
true: "A dog returns to its vomit,"[g][h]
and, "A sow that is washed goes back
to her wallowing in the mud."

The Day of the Lord

3 Dear friends,[i] this is now my second letter to you. I have written
both of them as reminders[j] to stimulate you to wholesome thinking. 2I
want you to recall the words spoken in
the past by the holy prophets[k] and the
command given by our Lord and Savior
through your apostles.[l]
3First of all, you must understand
that in the last days[m] scoffers will
come, scoffing and following their own
evil desires.[n] 4They will say, "Where
is this 'coming' he promised?[o] Ever
since our fathers died, everything goes
on as it has since the beginning of creation."[p] 5But they deliberately forget
that long ago by God's word[q] the
heavens existed and the earth was
formed out of water and by water.[r]
6By these waters also the world of that
time[s] was deluged and destroyed.[t]
7By the same word the present heavens and earth are reserved for fire,[u]
being kept for the day of judgment[v]
and destruction of ungodly men.
8But do not forget this one thing,
dear friends: With the Lord a day is like
a thousand years, and a thousand
years are like a day.[w] 9The Lord is not
slow in keeping his promise,[x] as some
understand slowness. He is patient[y]
with you, not wanting anyone to perish, but everyone to come to repentance.[z]
10But the day of the Lord will come
like a thief.[a] The heavens will disappear with a roar;[b] the elements will be

2:16 [x] Nu 22:21-30
2:17 [y] Jude 12 [z] Jude 13
2:18 [a] Jude 16 [b] ver 20; 2Pe 1:4
2:19 [c] S Ro 6:16
2:20 [d] S 2Pe 1:2 [e] 2Pe 1:11; 3:18 [f] Mt 12:45
2:21 [g] Eze 18:24; Heb 6:4-6; 10:26, 27
2:22 [h] Pr 26:11
3:1 [i] S 1Co 10:14 [j] 2Pe 1:13
3:2 [k] Lk 1:70; Ac 3:21 [l] S Eph 4:11
3:3 [m] 1Ti 4:1; 2Ti 3:1 [n] 2Pe 2:10; Jude 18
3:4 [o] Isa 5:19; Eze 12:22; Mt 24:48; S Lk 17:30 [p] Mk 10:6
3:5 [q] Ge 1:6,9; Heb 11:3 [r] Ps 24:2
3:6 [s] 2Pe 2:5 [t] Ge 7:21,22
3:7 [u] ver 10,12; S 2Th 1:7 [v] S Mt 10:15
3:8 [w] Ps 90:4
3:9 [x] Hab 2:3; Heb 10:37 [y] S Ro 2:4 [z] S 1Ti 2:4; Rev 2:21
3:10 [a] S Lk 12:39 [b] Isa 34:4

[g] 22 Prov. 26:11

2:19 THEY PROMISE THEM FREEDOM. The spirit of lawlessness that promises freedom from godly restraint will be especially prevalent in society and in the church in the last days before Christ comes again (see 1Ti 4:1, note; 2Ti 3:1, note). God's moral absolutes will be considered outdated and mere legalistic restraint to one's personal autonomy, self-fulfillment and happiness. As people set themselves up as the ultimate authority, they become slaves of depravity (see Ro 1:24,27, notes).

2:20 ESCAPED ... ARE AGAIN ENTANGLED. Vv. 20–22 obviously mean that some of the false teachers were once redeemed from sin's power, and then forfeited salvation (cf. vv. 1,15).

3:4 WHERE IS THIS 'COMING' HE PROMISED? In the last days, the period between Christ's first and second coming, false teachers will deny that Christ will return to destroy the ungodly and the world (cf. Rev 19:11–21).

3:7 RESERVED FOR FIRE. Because sin has contaminated the heavens and earth, God has determined to completely destroy them by fire (vv. 7,10,12). This day will come as surely as the flood did in Noah's time. God's intervention to purify the earth by fire signifies that he will not allow sin to go unpunished forever.

3:8 A DAY IS LIKE A THOUSAND YEARS. God views time from the perspective of eternity (cf. Ps 90:4). "A thousand years" looks different to God than to humans. He can accomplish in one day what we might expect would take a thousand years, or he can take a thousand years to accomplish what we would like to see done in a day.

3:9 NOT WANTING ANYONE TO PERISH. The delay of Christ's return is related to the preaching of the gospel of the kingdom to the whole world (Mt 24:14). God wants everyone to hear the gospel and does not want anyone to perish eternally (1Ti 2:4; see Eze 33:11, note; Jnh 3:10, note). This truth does not mean that all will be saved, for if a person rejects God's grace and salvation, then he or she remains lost.

3:10 THE DAY OF THE LORD. The day of the Lord refers to the events that begin with Christ's return to catch up the faithful of his churches to meet him in the air (see article on THE RAPTURE, p. 1864) and culminates with the destruction of the present heaven and earth and the creation of the new heaven and the new earth (Rev 21—22; see Joel 1:14, note; Zep 1:7, note; 1Th 5:2, note). The beginning of the day of the Lord is unknown and will be marked by an unexpected suddenness (see Mt 24:42,44, notes).

destroyed by fire,[c] and the earth and everything in it will be laid bare.[h][d]

11Since everything will be destroyed in this way, what kind of people ought you to be? You ought to live holy and godly lives **12**as you look forward[e] to the day of God and speed its coming.[i][f] That day will bring about the destruction of the heavens by fire, and the elements will melt in the heat.[g] **13**But in keeping with his promise we are looking forward to a new heaven and a new earth,[h] the home of righteousness.

14So then, dear friends, since you are looking forward to this, make every effort to be found spotless, blame-
1Jn 3:2 less[i] and at peace with him. **15**Bear in mind that our Lord's patience[j] means salvation,[k] just as our dear brother Paul also wrote you with the wisdom that God gave him.[l] **16**He writes the same way in all his letters, speaking in them of these matters. His letters contain some things that are hard to understand, which ignorant and unstable[m] people distort,[n] as they do the other Scriptures,[o] to their own destruction.

17Therefore, dear friends, since you already know this, be on your guard[p] so that you may not be carried away by the error[q] of lawless men[r] and fall from your secure position.[s] **18**But grow in the grace[t] and knowledge[u] of our Lord and Savior Jesus Christ.[v] To him be glory both now and forever! Amen.[w]

3:10 [c]ver 7,12; S 2Th 1:7 [d]Mt 24:35; S Heb 12:27; Rev 21:1
3:12 [e]S 1Co 1:7 [f]Ps 50:3 [g]ver 10
3:13 [h]Isa 65:17; 66:22; Rev 21:1
3:14 [i]S 1Th 3:13
3:15 [j]S Ro 2:4 [k]ver 9
[l]Eph 3:3
3:16 [m]Jas 1:8; 2Pe 2:14 [n]Ps 56:5; Jer 23:36 [o]ver 2
3:17 [p]1Co 10:12 [q]2Pe 2:18 [r]2Pe 2:7 [s]Rev 2:5
3:18 [t]S Ro 3:24 [u]S 2Pe 1:2 [v]2Pe 1:11; 2:20 [w]S Ro 11:36

h *10* Some manuscripts *be burned up* **i** *12* Or *as you wait eagerly for the day of God to come*

3:11 HOLY AND GODLY LIVES. Because God will soon destroy the world and judge the unrighteous, we must not become attached to this world's system or things within it. Our values, goals and purposes in life must be centered around God and the hope of a new heaven and a new earth (v. 13; see articles on SPIRITUAL SEPARATION FOR BELIEVERS, p. 1794, and SANCTIFICATION, p. 1956).

3:12 SPEED ITS COMING. The church can help shorten the time before Christ's return by (1) committing themselves to evangelism and missionary work throughout the whole world (v. 9; Mt 24:14), and (2) eagerly desiring his return by praying, "Come, Lord Jesus" (Rev 22:20; cf. Mt 6:10).

3:13 LOOKING FORWARD TO A NEW HEAVEN. See Heb 11:10, note.

3:16 HIS LETTERS . . . OTHER SCRIPTURES. Peter speaks of Paul's letters as being on the same level as the other inspired and authoritative Scriptures, i.e., the OT. When we talk of "Scripture" today, we mean the writings of both the OT and NT, God's original message to humanity and his witness to his saving activity in Jesus Christ (see article on THE INSPIRATION AND AUTHORITY OF SCRIPTURE, p. 1898).

1 JOHN

Outline

Introduction (1:1–4)

I. Fellowship With God (1:5—2:28)
  A. The Principles of Fellowship With God (1:5—2:2)
    1. "No Darkness" in God (1:5)
    2. No Fellowship in the Darkness (1:6)
    3. Fellowship in the Light (1:7)
    4. Fellowship in the Cleansing of Sin (1:8—2:2)
  B. The Manifestations of Fellowship With God (2:3–28)
    1. Obedience (2:3–5)
    2. Christlikeness (2:6)
    3. Love (2:7–11)
    4. Separation From the World (2:12–17)
    5. Loyalty to the Truth (2:18–28)

II. Children of God (2:29—3:24)
  A. Characteristics of God's Children (2:29—3:18)
  B. Confidence of God's Children (3:19–24)

III. Spirit of Truth (4:1–6)
  A. Recognizing the Spirit of Error (4:1,3,5)
  B. Affirming the Spirit of Truth (4:2,4,6)

IV. Love of God (4:7—5:3)
  A. Divine Origin of Love (4:7–10)
  B. Proper Response to God's Love (4:11–13,19–21)
  C. Abiding in God's Love (4:14–16)
  D. Perfection of Love (4:17–18)
  E. Obedience of Love (5:1–3)

V. Assurances From God (5:4–20)
  A. About Overcoming the World (5:4–5)
  B. About the Trustworthiness of the Gospel (5:6–10)
  C. About Eternal Life in His Son (5:11–13)
  D. About Answers to Prayer (5:14–17)
  E. About Three Great Certainties (5:18–20)

Conclusion (5:21)

Author: John

Theme: Truth and Righteousness

Date of Writing: A.D. 85–95

Background

Five NT books are associated with the name John: a Gospel, three letters, and the book of Revelation. Although John does not identify himself by name in this letter, second-century witnesses (e.g., Papias, Irenaeus, Tertullian, Clement of Alexandria) affirm that it was written by the apostle John, one of Jesus' original twelve disciples. Strong similarities in style, vocabulary and themes between 1 John and the Gospel of John substantiate the reliable testimony of ancient Christianity that both books were written by the apostle John (see the introduction to John's Gospel).

The recipients of this letter are undesignated. There are no greetings or mention of persons, places or events in the letter. The most likely explanation for this uncommon format is that John wrote from his residence at Ephesus to a number of churches in the province of Asia over which he had apostolic responsibility (cf. Rev 1:11). Since the congregations shared a common problem and similar needs, John wrote this as a circular letter and dispatched it by a personal emissary along with his verbal greetings.

The foremost background issue in this letter is the problem of false teaching about salvation in Christ and its operation in the believer. Certain people, formerly associated with the readers, had left the congregations (2:19), but the results of their false teaching were still distorting the gospel as to how they might "know" that they had eternal life. Doctrinally, their heresy denied that Jesus is the Christ (2:22; cf. 5:1) or that Christ came in the flesh (4:2–3); ethically, they taught that obeying Christ's commands (2:3–4; 5:3) and living holy lives separated from sin (3:7–12) and the world (2:15–17) were not necessary for saving faith (cf. 1:6; 5:4–5).

Purpose

John's purpose in writing this letter was twofold: (1) to expose and repudiate the doctrinal and ethical errors of the false teachers, and (2) to exhort his spiritual children to pursue a life of holy fellowship with God in truth and righteousness, in the full joy (1:4) and assurance (5:13) of eternal life, through an obedient faith in Jesus as the Son of God (4:15; 5:3–5,12), and by the abiding presence of the Holy Spirit (2:20; 4:4,13). Some believe that it was also intended as a letter accompanying the Gospel of John.

Survey

Belief and behavior are inseparably woven together in this letter. The false teachers, whom John calls "antichrists" (2:18–22), were departing from the apostolic teaching about Christ and righteous living. Like 2 Peter and Jude, 1 John vigorously repudiates and condemns the false teachers (e.g., 2:18–19,22–23,26; 4:1,3,5) with their destructive beliefs and behavior.

On the positive side, 1 John sets forth the characteristics of true fellowship with God (e.g., 1:3—2:2) and reveals five specific tests by which believers may know with assurance that they have eternal life: (1) the test of apostolic truth about Christ (1:1–3; 2:21–23; 4:2–3,15; 5:1,5,10,20); (2) the test of an obedient faith that keeps Christ's commands (2:3–11; 5:3–4); (3) the test of holy living, i.e., turning from sin to fellowship with God (1:6–9; 2:3–6,15–17,29; 3:1–10; 5:2–3); (4) the test of love for God and other believers (2:9–11; 3:10–11,14,16–18; 4:7–12,18–21); and (5) the test of the Spirit's witness (2:20,27; 4:13; 5:7–12). John concludes that people may know with confidence that they have eternal life (5:13) when the fruit of these five areas is evident in their lives.

Special Features

Five major features characterize this letter. (1) It defines the Christian life by using contrasting terms and by seeming to allow no middle ground between light and darkness, truth and lies, righteousness and sin, love and hate, loving God and loving the world, and children of God and children of the devil. (2) Significantly, it is the only NT writing to speak of Jesus as our advocate (Gk *paraklētos*) with the Father when we sin as sincere believers (2:1–2; cf. Jn 14:16–17,26; 15:26; 16:7–8). (3) Its message is grounded almost entirely in the apostolic witness rather than in prior OT revelation; references to OT Scripture are noticeably absent. (4) Since it presents Christology in connection with refuting a particular kind of heresy, it focuses on the incarnation and blood (i.e., the cross) of Jesus without making specific mention of his resurrection. (5) Its style is simple and repetitive as John discusses certain terms such as "light," "truth," "believe," "remain," "know," "love," "righteousness," "witness," "born of God" and "eternal life."

Reading 1 John

In order to read the entire New Testament in one year, the book of 1 John should be read in 5 days, according to the following schedule:
☐ 1:1–2:14 ☐ 2:15–3:10 ☐ 3:11–24 ☐ 4 ☐ 5

NOTES

The Word of Life

1 That which was from the beginning,[a] which we have heard, which we have seen with our eyes,[b] which we have looked at and our hands have touched[c]—this we proclaim concerning the Word of life. **2**The life appeared;[d] we have seen it and testify to it,[e] and we proclaim to you the eternal life,[f] which was with the Father and has appeared to us. **3**We proclaim to you what we have seen and heard,[g] so that you also may have fellowship with us. And our fellowship is with the Father and with his Son, Jesus Christ.[h] **4**We write this[i] to make our**a** joy complete.[j]

Rev 1:9

Walking in the Light

5This is the message we have heard[k] from him and declare to you: God is light;[l] in him there is no darkness at all. **6**If we claim to have fellowship with him yet walk in the darkness,[m] we lie and do not live by the truth.[n] **7**But if we walk in the light,[o] as he is in the light, we have fellowship with one another, and the blood of Jesus, his Son, purifies us from all**b** sin.[p]

8If we claim to be without sin,[q] we deceive ourselves and the truth is not in us.[r] **9**If we confess our sins, he is faithful and just and will forgive us our sins[s] and purify us from all unrighteousness.[t] **10**If we claim we have not sinned,[u] we make him out to be a liar[v] and his word has no place in our lives.[w]

2 My dear children,[x] I write this to you so that you will not sin. But if anybody does sin, we have one who speaks to the Father in our defense[y]—Jesus Christ, the Righteous One. **2**He is the atoning sacrifice for our sins,[z] and not only for ours but

1:1 [a]S Jn 1:2 [b]S Lk 24:48; Jn 1:14; 19:35; Ac 4:20; 2Pe 1:16; 1Jn 4:14 [c]Jn 20:27 **1:2** [d]Jn 1:1-4; 11:25; 14:6; 1Ti 3:16; 1Pe 1:20; 1Jn 3:5, 8 [e]S Jn 15:27 [f]S Mt 25:46 **1:3** [g]S ver 1 [h]1Co 1:9 **1:4** [i]1Jn 2:1 [j]S Jn 3:29 **1:5** [k]1Jn 3:11 [l]1Ti 6:16 **1:6** [m]Jn 3:19-21; 8:12; 2Co 6:14; Eph 5:8; 1Jn 2:11 [n]Jn 3:19-21; 1Jn 2:4; 4:20 **1:7** [o]Isa 2:5 [p]Heb 9:14; Rev 1:5; 7:14 **1:8** [q]Pr 20:9; Jer 2:35; Ro 3:9-19; Jas 3:2 [r]Jn 8:44; 1Jn 2:4 **1:9** [s]Ps 32:5; 51:2; Pr 28:13 [t]ver 7; Mic 7:18-20; Heb 10:22 **1:10** [u]ver 8 [v]1Jn 5:10 [w]Jn 5:38; 1Jn 2:14 **2:1** [x]ver 12,13, 28; 1Jn 3:7,18; 4:4; 5:21; S 1Th 2:11 [y]S Ro 8:34; 1Ti 2:5 **2:2** [z]Ro 3:25; 1Jn 4:10

a *4* Some manuscripts *your* **b** *7* Or *every*

1:2 ETERNAL LIFE. John defines eternal life in terms of Christ. It can be found only through faith in and fellowship with Jesus Christ (vv. 2,6–7; 2:22–25; 5:20).

1:3 FELLOWSHIP WITH US. "Fellowship" (Gk *koinōnia*) literally means "having in common" and involves sharing and participation. Christians have fellowship because they have a common faith (Tit 1:4; Jude 3), common grace of God in Christ (1Co 1:9; Php 1:7), common indwelling of the Spirit (Jn 20:22; Ro 8:9,11), common gifts of the Spirit (Ro 15:27) and a common enemy (2:15–18; 1Pe 5:8). There can be no true fellowship with those who reject the teaching of NT faith (2Jn 7–11; see Gal 1:9, note).

1:6 FELLOWSHIP WITH HIM. To "walk in the darkness" means to live in sin and immoral pleasure. Such people do not "have fellowship with him," i.e., they are not born of God (cf. 3:7–9; Jn 3:19; 2Co 6:14). Those who have fellowship with God experience his grace and live lives of holiness in his presence (v. 7; 2:4; 3:10).

1:7 WALK IN THE LIGHT. This means to believe God's truth as revealed in his Word and to make a sincere and sustained effort by his grace to follow it in word and deed. "The blood of Jesus, his Son, purifies us from all sin" refers to the ongoing work of sanctification within the believer and the continual cleansing through Christ's blood for our inadvertent sins. John is probably not thinking here of deliberate sin against God, since he speaks of walking in the light. This continual purifying allows us to have intimate fellowship with God (see article on SANCTIFICATION, p. 1956).

1:8 IF WE CLAIM TO BE WITHOUT SIN. John uses the noun ("sin") rather than the verb to emphasize sin as a principle in human nature. (1) John is probably arguing against those who affirm that sin does not exist as a principle or power in human nature, or those who say their evil actions are not really sin. This heresy is with us today in those who deny the fact of sin and interpret evil in terms of deterministic, psychological or social causes (see Ro 6:1, note; 7:9–11, note). (2) Believers must be aware that the sinful nature is a constant threat in their lives and that they must ever be putting to death its misdeeds through the Holy Spirit who lives within (Ro 8:13; Gal 5:16–25).

1:9 CONFESS OUR SINS. We must admit our sins and seek forgiveness and purifying from God. The two results are (1) forgiveness and reconciliation with God, and (2) the purifying from (i.e., removal of) guilt and the destruction of sin's power in order to live lives of holiness (Ps 32:1–5; Pr 28:13; Jer 31:34; Lk 15:18; Ro 6:2–14).

1:10 CLAIM WE HAVE NOT SINNED. If we claim that we have never sinned and therefore do not need the saving efficacy of Christ's death, we are making God a liar (cf. Ro 3:23).

2:1 SO THAT YOU WILL NOT SIN. John believed that born-again Christians are still capable of some kinds of sin. However, he does not teach that the Christian *must* sin; instead he exhorts his readers to live without sin (cf. Ro 6:15, note; 1Th 2:10, note). For those who do fall into sin, the remedy is to confess and forsake that sin (see 1:9, note). The assurance of forgiveness lies in the blood of Jesus Christ (v. 2; 1:7) and his heavenly ministry as "one who speaks to the Father in our defense" (Gk *paraklētos*). Jesus intercedes before God on our behalf on the basis of his atoning death, our repentance and our faith in him (cf. Ro 8:34; Heb 7:25, note; see 1Jn 3:15, note; see article on INTERCESSION, p. 1268).

also for[c] the sins of the whole
world.[a]
3We know[b] that we have come to
know him[c] if we obey his commands.[d] 4The man who says, "I know
him,"[e] but does not do what he commands is a liar, and the truth is not in
him.[f] 5But if anyone obeys his
word,[g] God's love[d] is truly made
complete in him.[h] This is how we
know[i] we are in him: 6Whoever
claims to live in him must walk as
-18 Jesus did.[j]
7Dear friends,[k] I am not writing you
a new command but an old one, which
you have had since the beginning.[l]
This old command is the message you
have heard. 8Yet I am writing you a
new command;[m] its truth is seen in
him and you, because the darkness is
passing[n] and the true light[o] is already shining.[p]
9Anyone who claims to be in the
light but hates his brother[q] is still in
the darkness.[r] 10Whoever loves his
brother lives in the light,[s] and there is
nothing in him[e] to make him stumble.[t] 11But whoever hates his brother[u] is in the darkness and walks
around in the darkness;[v] he does not
know where he is going, because the
darkness has blinded him.[w]

12I write to you, dear children,[x]
because your sins have been
forgiven on account of his
name.[y]
13I write to you, fathers,
because you have known him
who is from the
beginning.[z]
I write to you, young men,
because you have overcome[a]
the evil one.[b]
I write to you, dear children,[c]
because you have known the
Father.
14I write to you, fathers,
because you have known him
who is from the
beginning.[d]
I write to you, young men,
because you are strong,[e]
and the word of God[f] lives in
you,[g]
and you have overcome the evil
one.[h]

Do Not Love the World

15Do not love the world or anything
in the world.[i] If anyone loves the
world, the love of the Father is not in
him.[j] 16For everything in the world—
the cravings of sinful man,[k] the lust of
his eyes[l] and the boasting of what he
has and does—comes not from the Father but from the world. 17The world
and its desires pass away,[m] but the
man who does the will of God[n] lives 1Jn
forever. 5:4-5

Warning Against Antichrists

18Dear children, this is the last
hour;[o] and as you have heard that the
antichrist is coming,[p] even now many
antichrists have come.[q] This is how
we know it is the last hour. 19They
went out from us,[r] but they did not

2:2 [a] S Mt 1:21; S Jn 3:17 **2:3** [b] ver 5; 1Jn 3:24; 4:13; 5:2 [c] S ver 4 [d] S Jn 14:15 **2:4** [e] ver 3; Tit 1:16; 1Jn 3:6; 4:7,8 [f] 1Jn 1:6,8 **2:5** [g] S Jn 14:15 [h] 1Jn 4:12 [i] S ver 3 **2:6** [j] S Mt 11:29 **2:7** [k] S 1Co 10:14 [l] ver 24; 1Jn 3:11, 23; 4:21; 2Jn 5,6 **2:8** [m] S Jn 13:34 [n] Ro 13:12; Heb 10:25 [o] Jn 1:9 [p] Eph 5:8; 1Th 5:5 **2:9** [q] ver 11; Lev 19:17; 1Jn 3:10,15,16; 4:20,21 [r] 1Jn 1:5 **2:10** [s] 1Jn 3:14 [t] ver 11; Ps 119:165 **2:11** [u] S ver 9 [v] S 1Jn 1:6 [w] Jn 11:9; 12:35 **2:12** [x] S ver 1 [y] S 1Jn 3:23 **2:13** [z] S Jn 1:1 [a] S Jn 16:33 [b] ver 14; S Mt 5:37 [c] S ver 1 **2:14** [d] S Jn 1:1 [e] Eph 6:10 [f] S Heb 4:12 [g] Jn 5:38; 1Jn 1:10 [h] S ver 13 **2:15** [i] Ro 12:2 [j] Jas 4:4 **2:16** [k] Ge 3:6; Ro 13:14; Eph 2:3 [l] Pr 27:20 **2:17** [m] S Heb 12:27 [n] Mt 12:50 **2:18** [o] S Ro 13:11 [p] ver 22; 1Jn 4:3; 2Jn 7 [q] 1Jn 4:1 **2:19** [r] Ac 20:30

[c] 2 Or *He is the one who turns aside God's wrath, taking away our sins, and not only ours but also* [d] 5 Or *word, love for God* [e] 10 Or *it*

2:2 ATONING SACRIFICE. As our "atoning sacrifice," Jesus took on himself the punishment for our sins and satisfied God's righteous judgment against sin. Forgiveness is now offered to everyone throughout the world and is received by those who turn to Christ in repentance and faith (4:9,14; Jn 1:29; 3:16; 5:24; see article on BIBLICAL WORDS FOR SALVATION, p. 1710).

2:4 DOES NOT DO WHAT HE COMMANDS. John was contending against a misunderstanding of the doctrine of grace and salvation. He opposed antinomian teachers, who taught that forsaking a sinful life was optional for the believer. (1) They declared that one can legitimately claim to "know" God in a saving relationship and at the same time be indifferent to God's will and his commands, and disobey them (see Jn 17:3, note). (2) Those who make such a claim, John states, are liars and do not have God's truth in them. The attempt to be justified through faith in Christ without a commitment to follow Christ is doomed to failure.

2:10 WHOEVER LOVES HIS BROTHER. See Jn 13:34–35, notes.

2:15–16 THE WORLD. See article on THE CHRISTIAN'S RELATIONSHIP TO THE WORLD, p. 1976.

2:18 MANY ANTICHRISTS. An antichrist or false Christ will come toward the end of the age to rule the world and to lead a great rebellion against Christ and the NT faith (see Rev 13:1,8,18, notes; 19:20; 20:10; see article on THE AGE OF THE ANTICHRIST, p. 1872). Yet John says that "many antichrists" have already entered into the church. These are professed believers who love the world and its sinful pleasures and distort the gospel and its message of the cross, thus placing themselves against Christ and his righteousness.

2:19 THEY WENT OUT FROM US. When the antichrists departed from fellowship with true believers, they were not in a saving relationship with

THE CHRISTIAN'S RELATIONSHIP TO THE WORLD

***1 Jn 2:15–16** "Do not love the world or anything in the world. If anyone loves the world, the love of the Father is not in him. For everything in the world—the cravings of sinful man, the lust of his eyes and the boasting of what he has and does—comes not from the Father but from the world."*

The term "world" (Gk *kosmos*) often refers to the vast system of this age that Satan promotes and that exists independent of God. It consists not only in the obviously evil, immoral and sinful pleasures of the world, but also refers to the spirit of rebellion against or indifference to God and his revelation that exists within all human enterprises not under Christ's lordship. In this age Satan uses the world's ideas, morality, philosophies, psychology, desires, governments, culture, education, science, art, medicine, music, economic systems, entertainment, mass media, religions, sports, agriculture, etc., to oppose God, his people, his Word and his righteous standards (Mt 16:26; 1Co 2:12; 3:19; Tit 2:12; 1Jn 2:15–16). For example, Satan will use the medical profession to promote the killing of unborn babies, agriculture to produce life-destroying drugs such as alcohol and narcotics, educational systems to promote ungodly and humanistic philosophy, and the entertainment media to destroy godly standards. Believers must be aware that behind all human enterprises there is a spirit or power that moves against God and his Word, some to a lesser degree, some to a greater degree. Finally, the "world" also includes all man-made religious systems and all unbiblical, worldly or lukewarm "Christian" organizations and churches.

(1) Satan (see Mt 4:10, note on Satan) is the god of the present world system (see Jn 12:31, note; 14:30; 16:11; 2Co 4:4; 1Jn 5:19). Along with a host of subordinate evil spirits, he controls it (Da 10:13; Lk 4:5–7; Eph 6:12–13; see article on POWER OVER SATAN AND DEMONS, p. 1484).

(2) Satan has organized the world into political, cultural, economic and religious systems that are innately hostile toward God and his people (Jn 7:7; 15:18; Jas 4:4; 1Jn 2:16,18) and that refuse to submit to his truth, which exposes its evil (Jn 7:7).

(3) The world and the true church are two distinct groups of people. The world is under Satan's dominion (see Jn 12:31, note); the church belongs exclusively to God (Eph 5:23–24; Rev 21:2; see article on THREE KINDS OF PEOPLE, p. 1754). Thus, believers must separate themselves from the world (see articles on SPIRITUAL SEPARATION FOR BELIEVERS, p. 1794, and SANCTIFICATION, p. 1956).

(4) In the world believers are aliens and strangers (Heb 11:13; 1Pe 2:11). (a) They must come out of the world (Jn 15:19), not be conformed to the world (see Ro 12:2, note), not love the world (1Jn 2:15), overcome the world (1Jn 5:4), hate the world's evil (see Heb 1:9, note), die to the world (Gal 6:14) and be delivered from the world (Col 1:13–14). (b) Loving the world (cf. 1Jn 2:15) defiles our fellowship with God and leads to spiritual destruction. It is impossible to love the world and the Father at the same time (Mt 6:24; Lk 16:13; see Jas 4:4, note). To love the world means to be in intimate fellowship with and devoted to its values, interest, ways and pleasures; it means taking pleasure in or enjoying what is offensive and opposed to God (see Lk 23:35, note). Note, of course, that the terms "world" and "earth" are not synonymous; God does not forbid a love for the created earth, i.e., nature, mountains, forests, and the like.

(5) According to 1Jn 2:16, three aspects of the sinful world create open hostility to God: (a) "The cravings of sinful man": this includes impure desires and running after sinful pleasures and sensual gratification (1Co 6:18; Php 3:19; Jas 1:14). (b) "The lust of his eyes": this refers to coveting or lusting after things that are attractive to the eye but forbidden by God, including the desire to watch that which gives sinful pleasure (Ex 20:17; Ro 7:7). In the present modern age this includes the desire to entertain oneself by viewing pornography, violence, ungodliness and immorality on stage and on television, or in movies or magazines (Ge 3:6; Jos 7:21; 2Sa 11:2; Mt 5:28). (c) "The boasting of what he has and does": this means the spirit of arrogance and self-sufficient independence that does not recognize God as Lord or his Word as final authority. It is the spirit that seeks to exalt, glorify and promote oneself as the center of life (Jas 4:16).

(6) Believers must not have close fellowship with those who participate in the world's evil system (see Mt 9:11, note; 2Co 6:14, note), must condemn openly their sin (Jn 7:7; Eph 5:11, note), must be light and salt to them (Mt 5:13–14), must love them (Jn 3:16) and must attempt to win them to Christ (Mk 16:15; Jude 22–23).

(7) From the world the true Christian will experience trouble (Jn 16:2–3), hatred (Jn 15:19), persecution (Mt 5:10–12) and suffering (Ro 8:22–23; 1Pe 2:19–21). Using the lures of the world, Satan makes an unceasing effort to destroy the life of God in the Christian (2Co 11:3; 1Pe 5:8).

(8) The world system is temporary and will be destroyed by God (Da 2:34–35,44; 1Co 7:31; 2Th 1:7–10; 2Pe 3:10, note; Rev 18:2). Even now it is passing away (1Jn 2:17).

really belong to us. For if they had belonged to us, they would have remained with us; but their going showed
that none of them belonged to us.[s]
20But you have an anointing[t] from
the Holy One,[u] and all of you know the
truth.[f][v] 21I do not write to you because you do not know the truth, but
because you do know it[w] and because
no lie comes from the truth. 22Who is
the liar? It is the man who denies that
Jesus is the Christ. Such a man is the
antichrist—he denies the Father and
the Son.[x] 23No one who denies the
Son has the Father; whoever acknowledges the Son has the Father also.[y]
24See that what you have heard from
the beginning[z] remains in you. If it
does, you also will remain in the Son
and in the Father.[a] 25And this is what
he promised us—even eternal life.[b]
26I am writing these things to you
about those who are trying to lead you
astray.[c] 27As for you, the anointing[d]
you received from him remains in you,
and you do not need anyone to teach
you. But as his anointing teaches you
about all things[e] and as that anointing is real, not counterfeit—just as it
has taught you, remain in him.[f]

Children of God

28And now, dear children,[g] continue in him, so that when he appears[h]
we may be confident[i] and unashamed
before him at his coming.[j]
29If you know that he is righteous,[k]
you know that everyone who does what
is right has been born of him.[l]

3 How great is the love[m] the Father
has lavished on us, that we should
be called children of God![n] And that is
what we are! The reason the world
does not know us is that it did not
know him.[o] 2Dear friends,[p] now we
are children of God,[q] and what we will
be has not yet been made known. But
we know that when he appears,[g][r] we
shall be like him,[s] for we shall see
him as he is.[t] 3Everyone who has this
hope in him purifies himself,[u] just as
he is pure.[v]
4Everyone who sins breaks the law;
in fact, sin is lawlessness.[w] 5But you
know that he appeared so that he
might take away our sins.[x] And in him
is no sin.[y] 6No one who lives in him
keeps on sinning.[z] No one who contin-

2:19 [s] 1Co 11:19 **2:20** [t] ver 27; 2Co 1:21 [u] S Mk 1:24 [v] Jer 31:34; Mt 13:11; Jn 14:26 **2:21** [w] 2Pe 1:12; Jude 5 **2:22** [x] 1Jn 4:3; 2Jn 7 **2:23** [y] Jn 8:19; 14:7; 1Jn 4:15; 5:1; 2Jn 9 **2:24** [z] S ver 7 [a] Jn 14:23; 15:4; 1Jn 1:3; 2Jn 9 **2:25** [b] S Mt 25:46 **2:26** [c] 1Jn 3:7 **2:27** [d] ver 20 [e] 1Co 2:12 [f] Jn 15:4 **2:28** [g] S ver 1 [h] Col 3:4; 1Jn 3:2 [i] S Eph 3:12 [j] S 1Th 2:19 **2:29** [k] 1Jn 3:7 [l] S Jn 1:13 **3:1** [m] S Jn 3:16 [n] ver 2,10; S Jn 1:12 [o] Jn 15:21; 16:3 **3:2** [p] S 1Co 10:14 [q] ver 1,10; S Jn 1:12 [r] Col 3:4; 1Jn 2:28 [s] Ro 8:29; 2Pe 1:4 [t] Ps 17:15; Jn 17:24; 2Co 3:18 **3:3** [u] 2Co 7:1; 2Pe 3:13,14 [v] Ps 18:26 **3:4** [w] 1Jn 5:17 **3:5** [x] ver 8; S Jn 3:17 [y] S 2Co 5:21 **3:6** [z] ver 9; 1Jn 5:18

[f] *20* Some manuscripts *and you know all things*
[g] *2* Or *when it is made known*

Christ. This allows for two possibilities: (1) They were never true believers to begin with, or (2) they had once been in a saving relationship with Christ but afterward abandoned their faith in Christ (see article on PERSONAL APOSTASY, p. 1918).

2:20 AN ANOINTING. Believers receive an anointing from Christ, namely, the Holy Spirit (cf. 2Co 1:21–22). Through the Spirit we "know the truth" (see v. 27, note).

2:24 HEARD FROM THE BEGINNING. Believers will remain in Christ and experience salvation only as long as they remain in the original teaching of Christ and the apostles (see Eph 2:20, note). This suggests two things: (1) To abandon the original gospel of NT faith is spiritually fatal and separates one from Jesus Christ (cf. Gal 1:6–8; 5:1–4). Believers must be Biblical in their theology in the sense of always adhering to the teachings of the NT. (2) It is dangerous to run after new teachings or teachers who preach new things not found in the Christian faith (cf. Jude 3). For this reason, it is important to study and hold firmly to God's Word; our very souls and our eternal destiny depend on it.

2:27 HIS ANOINTING TEACHES YOU. All children of God are given the "anointing" (i.e., the Holy Spirit) to help lead them into truth (Jn 14:26; 16:13). As believers remain in Christ and read the Word of God, the Spirit helps them understand its redemptive truths. (1) All believers may study and know God's truth and learn from each other through mutual teaching and exhorting (Mt 28:20; Eph 3:18; Col 3:16). (2) Thus, believers have two safeguards against doctrinal error—Biblical revelation (cf. v. 24) and the Holy Spirit. (3) Believers do not need those who teach extrabiblical doctrine. This is the meaning of John's words, "you do not need anyone to teach you."

3:1 CHILDREN OF GOD. The truth that God is our heavenly Father and we are his children is one of the greatest revelations in the NT. (1) Being a child of God is the highest privilege of our salvation (Jn 1:12; Gal 4:7). (2) Being a child of God is the basis for our faith and trust in God (Mt 6:25–34) and our hope of glory for the future. As God's children, we are heirs of God and co-heirs with Christ (Ro 8:16–17; Gal 4:7). (3) God wants us to be increasingly made aware through the Holy Spirit, the "Spirit of sonship" (Ro 8:15), that we are his children. The Spirit produces the cry "*Abba*, Father" in our hearts (see Gal 4:6, note) and gives us the desire to be "led by the Spirit" (Ro 8:14). (4) Being a child of God is the basis for our discipline by the Father (Heb 12:6–7,11) and the reason we live to please God (v. 9; 4:17–19). God's ultimate goal in making us his children is to save us forever (Jn 3:16) and to conform us to the likeness of his Son (Ro 8:29).

3:6 LIVES IN HIM. The words "lives in him" and "born of God" (v. 9) are equivalent expressions. Only those who continue to live in God continue to be born of God (see Jn 15:4, note; see article on REGENERATION, p. 1589).

3:6 SEEN HIM OR KNOWN HIM. The verbs

ues to sin has either seen him[a] or
known him.[b]
7Dear children,[c] do not let anyone
lead you astray.[d] He who does what is
right is righteous, just as he is righteous.[e] **8**He who does what is sinful is
of the devil,[f] because the devil has
been sinning from the beginning. The
reason the Son of God[g] appeared was
to destroy the devil's work.[h] **9**No one
who is born of God[i] will continue to
sin,[j] because God's seed[k] remains in
him; he cannot go on sinning, because
he has been born of God. **10**This is how
we know who the children of God[l] are
and who the children of the devil[m] are:
Anyone who does not do what is right
is not a child of God; nor is anyone who
does not love[n] his brother.[o]

3:6 [a] 3Jn 11 [b] S 1Jn 2:4 **3:7** [c] S 1Jn 2:1 [d] 1Jn 2:26 [e] 1Jn 2:29 **3:8** [f] ver 10; Jn 8:44 [g] S Mt 4:3 [h] Heb 2:14 **3:9** [i] S Jn 1:13 [j] ver 6; Ps 119:3; 1Jn 5:18 [k] 1Pe 1:23 **3:10** [l] ver 1,2; S Jn 1:12 [m] ver 8 [n] 1Jn 4:8 [o] S 1Jn 2:9

3:11 [p] 1Jn 1:5 [q] S 1Jn 2:7 [r] Jn 13:34,35; 15:12; 1Jn 4:7,11, 21; 2Jn 5 **3:12** [s] S Mt 5:37 [t] Ge 4:8 [u] Ps 38:20; Pr 29:10 **3:13** [v] Jn 15:18, 19; 17:14 **3:14** [w] Jn 5:24 [x] S 1Jn 2:9

Love One Another

11This is the message you heard[p]
from the beginning:[q] We should love
one another.[r] **12**Do not be like Cain,
who belonged to the evil one[s] and
murdered his brother.[t] And why did
he murder him? Because his own actions were evil and his brother's were
righteous.[u] **13**Do not be surprised, my
brothers, if the world hates you.[v]
14We know that we have passed from
death to life,[w] because we love our
brothers. Anyone who does not love remains in death.[x] **15**Anyone who hates
his brother[y] is a murderer,[z] and you

3:15 [y] S 1Jn 2:9 [z] Mt 5:21,22; Jn 8:44

"seen" and "known" are in the perfect tense (the Greek perfect tense refers to action that occurred in the past with its results continuing to the present moment). Therefore, John says that no one who is living in sin has seen (and continues to see) him, nor has he known (and continues to know) him. Thus, this can be applied either to those who have never had real faith in Christ or to apostates who knew God in the past but have not continued knowing him in the present.

3:9 HE CANNOT GO ON SINNING. The verb "to sin" (Gk *hamartanō*) is a present active infinitive, implying continued action. John emphasizes that those truly born of God cannot make sin their way of life, because God's life cannot exist in those who practice sin (cf. 1:5–7; 2:3–11,15–17,24–29; 3:6–24; 4:7–8,20).

(1) The new birth produces spiritual life that results in an ever-present relationship with God. In this letter, every time John speaks of the new birth of the believer, he uses the Greek perfect tense to emphasize the continued and sustained relationship that the new birth began (2:29; 3:9; 4:7; 5:1,4,18; see article on REGENERATION, p. 1589).

(2) For people to have God's life in them (i.e., be born of God) and to go on sinning is a spiritual impossibility. Believers may occasionally lapse from God's high standard, but they will not continue in sin (vv. 6,10).

(3) That which keeps the faithful from sinning is "God's seed" in them, i.e., God's very life, Spirit and nature living in them (5:11–12; Jn 15:4; 2Pe 1:4).

(4) By faith (5:4), the indwelling Christ, the Spirit's power and the written Word (see 1Th 2:10, note), all believers can live moment by moment free from offense and sin.

3:10 CHILDREN OF GOD . . . CHILDREN OF THE DEVIL. This is the heart and conclusion of John's teaching in 2:28—3:10. He has warned his readers not to be deceived about the nature of salvation (v. 7). Consequently, the believer must reject any theology or teaching that alleges that one can be out of fellowship with God (1:3), continue to sin, do the works of the devil (v. 8), love the world (2:15), do harm to others (vv. 14–18), and yet be a child of God who is saved and destined for heaven.

Contrary to this false teaching, John clearly believed that anyone who continues in sin (see v. 9, note) "is of the devil" (v. 8) and "is not a child of God." If those who habitually practice sin claim to possess eternal life and be God's children, they are deceived and are liars (cf. 2:4). Furthermore, what characterizes true children of God is a love for God shown by keeping his commands (5:2) and demonstrating genuine concern for the spiritual and physical needs of other believers (vv. 16–17).

3:15 NO MURDERER HAS ETERNAL LIFE. The Bible generally distinguishes between different kinds of sins: unintentional sins (Lev 4:2,13, 22; 5:4–6; see Lev 4:3, note; Nu 15:31, note), less serious sins (Mt 5:19), deliberate sins (cf. 1Jn 5:16–17) and sins bringing spiritual death (5:16). John emphasizes that there are certain sins that true born-again believers will not commit because of the eternal life of Christ abiding in them (cf. 2:11,15–16; 3:6–10,14–15; 4:20; 5:2; 2Jn 9). These sins, because of their gravity and their origin in the very center of one's spirit, indicate an intense rebellion against God, a severing from Christ, a falling from grace and a separation from the vital life of salvation (Gal 5:4).

(1) Examples of sins that give conclusive evidence that one is still in bondage to wickedness or has fallen from grace and eternal life are apostasy (2:19; 4:6; Heb 10:26–31), murder (v. 15; 2:11), sexual impurity or immorality (Ro 1:21–27; 1Co 5; Eph 5:5; Rev 21:8), abandonment of one's family (1Ti 5:8), leading others into sin (Mt 18:6–10), and cruelty (Mt 24:48–51). These abominable sins reveal utter rejection of honor toward God and loving care for others (cf. 2:9–10; 3:6–10; 1Co 6:9–11; Gal 5:19–21; 1Th 4:5; 2Ti 3:1–5; Heb 3:7–19). Thus, anyone who says, "I have fellowship with Jesus Christ, am indwelt by the Spirit, and am in a saving relationship with him," yet par-

know that no murderer has eternal life
in him.[a]
16This is how we know what love is:
Jesus Christ laid down his life for us.[b]
And we ought to lay down our lives for
our brothers.[c] **17**If anyone has material possessions and sees his brother in
need but has no pity on him,[d] how can
the love of God be in him?[e] **18**Dear
children,[f] let us not love with words
or tongue but with actions and in
Rev 3:1-4 truth.[g] **19**This then is how we know
that we belong to the truth, and how
we set our hearts at rest in his presence **20**whenever our hearts condemn
us. For God is greater than our hearts,
and he knows everything.
21Dear friends,[h] if our hearts do not
condemn us, we have confidence before God[i] **22**and receive from him anything we ask,[j] because we obey his
commands[k] and do what pleases
him.[l] **23**And this is his command: to
believe[m] in the name of his Son, Jesus
Christ,[n] and to love one another as he
commanded us.[o] **24**Those who obey
his commands[p] live in him,[q] and he
in them. And this is how we know that
he lives in us: We know it by the Spirit
he gave us.[r]

Test the Spirits

4 Dear friends,[s] do not believe every spirit,[t] but test the spirits to see whether they are from God, because many false prophets have gone out into the world.[u] **2**This is how you can recognize the Spirit of God: Every spirit that acknowledges that Jesus Christ has come in the flesh[v] is from God,[w] **3**but every spirit that does not acknowledge Jesus is not from God. This is the spirit of the antichrist,[x] which you have heard is coming and even now is already in the world.[y]
4You, dear children,[z] are from God

3:15 [a]Gal 5:20, 21; Rev 21:8 **3:16** [b]Jn 10:11 [c]Jn 15:13; Php 2:17; 1Th 2:8 **3:17** [d]Dt 15:7,8; Jas 2:15,16 [e]1Jn 4:20 **3:18** [f]S 1Jn 2:1 [g]Eze 33:31; Ro 12:9 **3:21** [h]S 1Co 10:14 [i]S Eph 3:12; 1Jn 5:14 **3:22** [j]S Mt 7:7 [k]S Jn 14:15 [l]Jn 8:29; Heb 13:21 **3:23** [m]Jn 6:29 [n]S Lk 24:47; Jn 1:12; 3:18; 20:31; 1Co 6:11; 1Jn 5:13 [o]S Jn 13:34 **3:24** [p]1Jn 2:3 [q]1Jn 2:6; 4:15 [r]1Th 4:8; 1Jn 4:13 **4:1** [s]S 1Co 10:14 [t]Jer 29:8; 1Co 12:10; 2Th 2:2 [u]S Mt 7:15; 1Jn 2:18 **4:2** [v]S Jn 1:14; 1Jn 2:23 [w]1Co 12:3 **4:3** [x]1Jn 2:22; 2Jn 7 [y]1Jn 2:18 **4:4** [z]S 1Jn 2:1

ticipates in the above-mentioned sins, is deceiving himself or herself and "is a liar, and the truth is not in him" (2:4; cf. 1:6; 3:7–8).

(2) Believers must keep in mind, however, that all sin, even the less serious ones, can lead to a weakening of spiritual life, to a rejection of the Holy Spirit's leading, and thus, to spiritual death (Ro 6:15–23; 8:5–13).

3:17 HIS BROTHER IN NEED. Love is expressed by sincerely helping persons in need, i.e., by sharing our earthly possessions with them (cf. Jas 2:14–17). To refuse to give of our food, clothing or money to help others in real need is to close our hearts to them (cf. Dt 15:7–11). This also includes giving our money to help bring the gospel to those who have not heard (4:9–10).

3:22 BECAUSE WE OBEY HIS COMMANDS. Why are some prayers answered and others not? John declares that an effective prayer life is related to our devotion to God. Obeying, loving and pleasing God (Jn 8:29; 2Co 5:9; Eph 5:10; Heb 13:21) are indispensable conditions in order to receive what we ask for in prayer (cf. Ps 50:14–15; Pr 15:29; Isa 59:1–2; Mt 6:15; Mk 11:25; Jas 5:16; see article on EFFECTIVE PRAYING, p. 496).

4:1 TEST THE SPIRITS. The reason for testing every spirit (i.e., a person moved or inspired by a spirit) is that "many false prophets" will enter the church (see article on FALSE TEACHERS, p. 1506). This will be especially true as tolerance for unbiblical doctrine increases toward the end of the age (see Mt 24:11, note; 1Ti 4:1, note; 2Ti 4:3–4, note; 2Pe 2:1–2). Christians are commanded to test all professed Christian teachers, writers, preachers and prophets, and in fact any individual who claims his or her work or message comes from the Holy Spirit. Believers may never assume that a ministry or spiritual experience is from God merely because one claims it is. Furthermore, no teaching or doctrine may be accepted as true solely on the basis of success, miracles or apparent anointing (Mt 7:22; 1Co 14:29; 2Th 2:8–10; 2Jn 7; Rev 13:4; 16:14; 19:20).

(1) All teaching must be tested against the revelation of God's truth in Scripture (see Gal 1:9, note).

(2) It is the spirit of the teaching that must be tested. Does the teaching bear the same kind of spirit and emphasis as NT apostolic teaching? Beware of any teaching that a person claims to have received from the Holy Spirit or an angel that cannot be supported by sound Biblical exegesis.

(3) Teachers' lives must be tested as to their relation to the ungodly world (see v. 5; see article on THE CHRISTIAN'S RELATIONSHIP TO THE WORLD, p. 1976) and to Christ's lordship (vv. 2,6; Ro 10:9, note; see article on TESTING FOR GENUINE BAPTISM IN THE SPIRIT, p. 1668).

4:2 JESUS CHRIST HAS COME IN THE FLESH. Theological liberalism and religious cults betray themselves as "antichrist" (v. 3) when they deny the full deity of Jesus Christ (see Jn 1:1, note), his virgin birth (see Mt 1:23, note), or his redemptive death and resurrection for our salvation (vv. 9–10; 2:2; see article on BIBLICAL WORDS FOR SALVATION, p. 1710). Every departure from Biblical revelation about Christ opens itself up to demonic "spirits" of deception (v. 1) because it sets aside the authority and complete trustworthiness of God's Word (see 2Pe 1:3, note; see article on THE INSPIRATION AND AUTHORITY OF SCRIPTURE, p. 1898).

4:4 THE ONE WHO IS IN YOU IS GREATER. Scripture emphasizes that the Holy Spirit lives in the believer (1Co 6:19). Through the Spirit, we can overcome the evil in the world, including sin, Satan, trials, temptations, sorrow, persecution and

and have overcome them,[a] because
the one who is in you[b] is greater than
the one who is in the world.[c] 5They
are from the world[d] and therefore
speak from the viewpoint of the world,
and the world listens to them. 6We are
from God, and whoever knows God listens to us; but whoever is not from God
does not listen to us.[e] This is how we
recognize the Spirit[h] of truth[f] and
the spirit of falsehood.[g]

God's Love and Ours

7Dear friends, let us love one another,[h] for love comes from God. Everyone who loves has been born of God[i]
and knows God.[j] 8Whoever does not
love does not know God, because God
is love.[k] 9This is how God showed his
love among us: He sent his one and
only Son[i][l] into the world that we
might live through him.[m] 10This is
love: not that we loved God, but that he
loved us[n] and sent his Son as an atoning sacrifice for[j] our sins.[o] 11Dear
friends,[p] since God so loved us,[q] we
also ought to love one another.[r]
12No one has ever seen God;[s] but if
we love one another, God lives in
us and his love is made complete
in us.[t]

13We know[u] that we live in him and
he in us, because he has given us of his
Spirit.[v] 14And we have seen and testify[w] that the Father has sent his Son to
be the Savior of the world.[x] 15If anyone acknowledges that Jesus is the
Son of God,[y] God lives in him and he
in God.[z] 16And so we know and rely
on the love God has for us.

God is love.[a] Whoever lives in love
lives in God, and God in him.[b] 17In
this way, love is made complete[c]
among us so that we will have confidence[d] on the day of judgment,[e] because in this world we are like him.
18There is no fear in love. But perfect
love drives out fear,[f] because fear has
to do with punishment. The one who
fears is not made perfect in love.

19We love because he first loved
us.[g] 20If anyone says, "I love God,"
yet hates his brother,[h] he is a liar.[i]
For anyone who does not love his
brother, whom he has seen,[j] cannot
love God, whom he has not seen.[k]
21And he has given us this command:[l] Whoever loves God must also
love his brother.[m]

Faith in the Son of God

5 Everyone who believes[n] that
Jesus is the Christ[o] is born of
God,[p] and everyone who loves the father loves his child as well.[q] 2This is
how we know[r] that we love the children of God:[s] by loving God and carrying out his commands. 3This is love for
God: to obey his commands.[t] And his
commands are not burdensome,[u] 4for
everyone born of God[v] overcomes[w] 

4:4 [a] S Jn 16:33 [b] Ro 8:31 [c] 2Ki 6:16; S Jn 12:31 **4:5** [d] Jn 15:19; 17:14,16 **4:6** [e] Jn 8:47 [f] S Jn 14:17 [g] S Mk 13:5 **4:7** [h] S 1Jn 3:11 [i] S Jn 1:13 [j] S 1Jn 2:4 **4:8** [k] ver 7,16 **4:9** [l] Jn 1:18 [m] Jn 3:16,17; 1Jn 5:11 **4:10** [n] Ro 5:8,10 [o] S Ro 3:25 **4:11** [p] S 1Co 10:14 [q] S Jn 3:16 [r] Jn 15:12; S 1Jn 3:11 **4:12** [s] S Jn 1:18 [t] ver 17; 1Jn 2:5 **4:13** [u] S 1Jn 2:3 [v] 1Jn 3:24 **4:14** [w] S Jn 15:27 [x] S Lk 2:11; S Jn 3:17 **4:15** [y] S 1Jn 2:23; 5:5 [z] 1Jn 3:24 **4:16** [a] ver 8 [b] ver 12,13; 1Jn 3:24 **4:17** [c] ver 12; 1Jn 2:5 [d] S Eph 3:12 [e] S Mt 10:15 **4:18** [f] Ro 8:15 **4:19** [g] ver 10 **4:20** [h] S 1Jn 2:9 [i] S 1Jn 1:6; 2:4 [j] 1Jn 3:17 [k] ver 12; S Jn 1:18 **4:21** [l] 1Jn 2:7 [m] S Mt 5:43; S 1Jn 2:9 **5:1** [n] S Jn 3:15 [o] 1Jn 2:22; 4:2,15 [p] S Jn 1:13; S 1Jn 2:23 [q] Jn 8:42 **5:2** [r] S 1Jn 2:3 [s] 1Jn 3:14 **5:3** [t] S Jn 14:15 [u] Mt 11:30; 23:4 **5:4** [v] S Jn 1:13 [w] S Jn 16:33

[h] 6 Or *spirit* [i] 9 Or *his only begotten Son* [j] 10 Or *as the one who would turn aside his wrath, taking away*

false teaching, and we can victoriously achieve God's will for our lives.

4:7 LET US LOVE ONE ANOTHER. Although love is an aspect of the Spirit's fruit (Gal 5:22–23) and an evidence of the new birth (2:29; 3:9–10; 5:1), it is also something that we are responsible to develop. For this reason John exhorts us to love others, to be concerned about them and to seek their welfare. John is not talking about a feeling of goodwill, but a decision and disposition to help people in their needs (3:16–18; cf. Lk 6:31). John urges us to demonstrate love for three reasons: (1) Love is the very nature of God (vv. 7–9), which he showed by giving his own Son for us (vv. 9–10). We share his nature because we are born of him (v. 7). (2) Because God loved us, we who have experienced his love, forgiveness and help are obligated to help others, even at great personal cost. (3) If we love one another, God continues to live in us and his love is made complete in us (v. 12).

4:17 CONFIDENCE ON THE DAY OF JUDGMENT. If we remain in Christ, have fellowship with the Father (1:3), strive to obey his commands (2:3), remain separate from the world (2:15–17), remain in the truth (2:24) and love others (vv. 7–12), then we can have confidence that we will not be condemned on the day of judgment (vv. 17–18; see article on ASSURANCE OF SALVATION, p. 1982).

5:1 BELIEVES . . . LOVES. Genuine faith will express itself in gratitude to and love for the Father and Jesus Christ his Son. Faith and love are inseparable, for when we are born of God, the Holy Spirit pours the love of God into our hearts (Ro 5:5).

5:2 THIS IS HOW WE KNOW. Love for others is genuine Christian love only if it is accompanied by love for God and obedience to his commands (cf. 2:3; 3:23; Jn 15:10; see Mt 22:37, note; Jn 14:21, note).

5:4 OVERCOME THE WORLD, EVEN OUR FAITH. The faith that overcomes the world is a faith that sees eternal realities, experiences God's power and loves Christ to such an extent that the world's sinful pleasures, secular values, ungodly ways and selfish materialism not only lose their

ASSURANCE OF SALVATION

1Jn 5:13 "I write these things to you who believe in the name of the Son of God so that you may know that you have eternal life."

Every Christian desires to have assurance of salvation, i.e., the certainty that when Christ returns or when death comes, he or she will go to be with the Lord Jesus in heaven (Php 1:23). John's purpose in writing his first letter is that God's people may have that assurance (1Jn 5:13). Note that nowhere in the letter does John state that a past experience of conversion constitutes an assurance or guarantee of salvation. To assume we possess eternal life based solely on a past experience or on a faith that is no longer vital is a grave error. This letter sets out nine ways for us to know that we are in a saving relationship with Jesus Christ.

(1) We have assurance of eternal life if we believe "in the name of the Son of God" (1Jn 5:13; cf. 4:15; 5:1,5). There is no eternal life or assurance of salvation without an earnest faith in Jesus Christ that confesses him as God's Son, sent to be our Lord and Savior (see article on FAITH AND GRACE, p. 1720).

(2) We have assurance of eternal life if we are honoring Christ as Lord of our lives and are sincerely trying to obey his commands. "We know that we have come to know him if we obey his commands. The man who says, 'I know him,' but does not do what he commands is a liar, and the truth is not in him. But if anyone obeys his word, God's love is truly made complete in him. This is how we know we are in him" (1Jn 2:3–5; cf. 3:24; 5:2; Jn 8:31,51; 14:21–24; 15:9–14; Heb 5:9).

(3) We have assurance of eternal life if we love the Father and the Son rather than the world, and if we overcome the influence of the world. "Do not love the world or anything in the world. If anyone loves the world, the love of the Father is not in him. For everything in the world—the cravings of sinful man, the lust of his eyes and the boasting of what he has and does—comes not from the Father but from the world" (1Jn 2:15–16; cf. 4:4–6; 5:4; see article on THE CHRISTIAN'S RELATIONSHIP TO THE WORLD, p. 1976).

(4) We have assurance of eternal life if we habitually and persistently practice righteousness rather than sin. "If you know that he is righteous, you know that everyone who does what is right has been born of him" (1Jn 2:29). On the other hand, "He who does what is sinful is of the devil" (3:7–10; see 3:9, note).

(5) We have assurance of eternal life if we love our brothers and sisters. "We know that we have passed from death to life, because we love our brothers . . . This then is how we know that we belong to the truth, and how we set our hearts at rest in his presence" (1Jn 3:14,19; cf. 2:9–11; 3:23; 4:8,11–12,16,20; 5:1; Jn 13:34–35).

(6) We have assurance of eternal life if we are conscious of the Holy Spirit dwelling within us. "And this is how we know that he [Jesus Christ] lives in us: We know it by the Spirit he gave us" (1Jn 3:24). Again, "We know that we live in him and he in us, because he has given us of his Spirit" (4:13).

(7) We have assurance of eternal life if we strive to follow Jesus' example and live as he lived. "Whoever claims to live in him must walk as Jesus did" (1Jn 2:6; cf. Jn 8:12).

(8) We have assurance of eternal life if we believe, accept and remain in the "Word of life," i.e., the living Christ (1Jn 1:1), and in the original message of Christ and the NT apostles. "See that what you have heard from the beginning remains in you. If it does, you also will remain in the Son and in the Father" (2:24; cf. 1:1–5; 4:6).

(9) We have assurance of eternal life if we have an earnest longing and an unbending hope for Christ's return to receive us to himself. "Dear friends, now we are children of God, and what we will be has not yet been made known. But we know that when he appears, we shall be like him, for we shall see him as he is. Everyone who has this hope in him purifies himself, just as he is pure" (1Jn 3:2–3; cf. Jn 14:1–3).

the world. This is the victory that has
overcome the world, even our faith.
5Who is it that overcomes the world?
Only he who believes that Jesus is the
Son of God.[x]
6This is the one who came by water
and blood[y]—Jesus Christ. He did not
come by water only, but by water and
blood. And it is the Spirit who testifies,
because the Spirit is the truth.[z] **7**For
there are three[a] that testify: **8**the[k]
Spirit, the water and the blood; and
the three are in agreement. **9**We accept man's testimony,[b] but God's
testimony is greater because it is
the testimony of God,[c] which he
has given about his Son. **10**Anyone
who believes in the Son of God has
this testimony in his heart.[d] Anyone who does not believe God has
made him out to be a liar,[e] because
he has not believed the testimony
God has given about his Son. **11**And
this is the testimony: God has
given us eternal life,[f] and this life is
in his Son.[g] **12**He who has the Son has
life; he who does not have the Son of
God does not have life.[h] Rev 3:20

The Certainties of Faith

13I write these things to you who believe in the name of the Son of God[i]
so that you may know that you have
eternal life.[j] **14**This is the confidence[k] we have in approaching God:
that if we ask anything according to his
will, he hears us.[l] **15**And if we know
that he hears us—whatever we ask—
we know[m] that we have what we
asked of him.[n]
16If anyone sees his brother commit
a sin that does not lead to death, he
should pray and God will give him
life.[o] I refer to those whose sin does
not lead to death. There is a sin that
leads to death.[p] I am not saying that
he should pray about that.[q] **17**All

5:5 [x] ver 1; S 1Jn 2:23 **5:6** [y] Jn 19:34 [z] S Jn 14:17 **5:7** [a] S Mt 18:16 **5:9** [b] Jn 5:34 [c] Mt 3:16,17; Jn 5:32,37; 8:17, 18 **5:10** [d] Ro 8:16; Gal 4:6 [e] Jn 3:33; 1Jn 1:10 **5:11** [f] S Mt 25:46 [g] S Jn 1:4 **5:12** [h] Jn 3:15,16, 36 **5:13** [i] S 1Jn 3:23 [j] ver 11; S Mt 25:46 **5:14** [k] S Eph 3:12; 1Jn 3:21 [l] S Mt 7:7 **5:15** [m] ver 18,19, 20 [n] 1Ki 3:12 **5:16** [o] Jas 5:15 [p] Ex 23:21; Heb 6:4-6; 10:26 [q] Jer 7:16; 14:11

[k] 7,8 Late manuscripts of the Vulgate *testify in heaven: the Father, the Word and the Holy Spirit, and these three are one. [8]And there are three that testify on earth: the* (not found in any Greek manuscript before the sixteenth century)

attraction for us, but also are looked on with disgust, aversion and grief (see Rev 2:7, note).

5:6 BY WATER AND BLOOD. This phrase probably refers to Jesus' baptism at the beginning of his ministry and to his death on the cross. John may have written this because some were teaching that the divine Christ did not experience death. He maintains that Jesus Christ died as the God-man and is thereby fully able to make atonement for our sins. The Spirit also bears witness to this truth (vv. 7–8).

5:12 HE WHO HAS THE SON HAS LIFE. All people should hear the gospel because eternal life is in God's Son and cannot be received or possessed in any other way. He is the only "way . . . and the life" (Jn 14:6). Eternal life is Christ's life in us. We have it as we maintain a vital faith relationship with him (Jn 15:4; see Jn 17:3, note; Col 3:4).

5:13 THAT YOU MAY KNOW THAT YOU HAVE ETERNAL LIFE. John declares his purpose in writing this letter: to provide God's people with the Biblical standard for assurance of salvation. For a discussion of this, see article on ASSURANCE OF SALVATION, p. 1982.

5:14 ASK ANYTHING ACCORDING TO HIS WILL. In our prayers we must submit to God and pray that his will may be done in our lives (Jn 14:13). We know God's will in many instances because it is revealed in Scripture. At other times it becomes clear only as we earnestly seek his will. Once we know his will about any given issue, then we can ask in confidence and faith. When we do this, we know that he hears us and that his purposes for us will be accomplished (see 3:22, note; see article on EFFECTIVE PRAYING, p. 496).

5:16 HE SHOULD PRAY AND GOD WILL GIVE HIM LIFE. John refers to a type of prayer according to God's will that we can have confidence that he will answer (cf. vv. 14–15), i.e., prayer for spiritually weak believers who need the prayers of God's people to minister life and grace to them. The conditions guiding such a prayer are the following: (1) The person needing prayer must be a brother or sister, i.e., a believer who has committed sin unintentionally or inadvertently, and whose sin did not involve a deliberate rebellion against God's will (see next note). Thus, they have not committed sin to the point of spiritual death (cf. Ro 8:13); they still have spiritual life, but are weak spiritually. They are repentant and desire to be free from all that displeases God, yet need help in conquering the power of Satan and sin.

(2) For such people the church must pray that God will give them "life." "Life" here means a restoration of spiritual strength and God's grace (see article on FAITH AND GRACE, p. 1720), which is being threatened by the sin (cf. Ro 8:6; 2Co 3:6; 1Pe 3:7). God promises to answer that prayer.

(3) For former believers who have committed a sin "that leads to death" (i.e., spiritual death), the church cannot pray with assurance that God will give more grace and life. This type of sin involves willful transgression that comes from a deliberate refusal to obey him (see article on THE ACTS OF THE SINFUL NATURE AND THE FRUIT OF THE SPIRIT, p. 1818). Such persons, having died spiritually, can only be given life if they repent and turn to God (see Ro 8:13, note). We must pray that God will so direct the circumstances of their lives that they may have an adequate opportunity to accept once more God's salvation in Christ.

wrongdoing is sin,[r] and there is sin
that does not lead to death.[s]
18We know that anyone born of
God[t] does not continue to sin; the one
who was born of God keeps him safe,
and the evil one[u] cannot harm him.[v]
19We know that we are children of
God,[w] and that the whole world is under the control of the evil one.[x]
20We know also that the Son of God
has come[y] and has given us understanding,[z] so that we may know him
who is true.[a] And we are in him
who is true—even in his Son Jesus
Christ. He is the true God and eternal
life.[b]
21Dear children,[c] keep yourselves
from idols.[d]

5:17 [r] 1Jn 3:4 [s] ver 16; 1Jn 2:1
5:18 [t] S Jn 1:13 [u] S Mt 5:37 [v] Jn 14:30
5:19 [w] 1Jn 4:6 [x] Jn 12:31; 14:30; 17:15
5:20 [y] ver 5 [z] Lk 24:45 [a] Jn 17:3 [b] ver 11; S Mt 25:46
5:21 [c] S 1Jn 2:1 [d] 1Co 10:14; 1Th 1:9

5:17 SIN THAT DOES NOT LEAD TO DEATH. John distinguishes between two types of sins: (1) Less serious sins that occur unconsciously or inadvertently and do not immediately lead to spiritual death; and (2) sins so terrible that they indicate a purposeful rebellion against God and his Word, resulting from or leading to spiritual death and separation from the life of God (see 3:15, note; Nu 15:31, note; Ro 8:13, note; Gal 5:4, note).

5:19 UNDER THE CONTROL OF THE EVIL ONE. We will never adequately understand the NT unless we recognize its underlying conviction that Satan is the god of this world. He is the evil one and his power controls the present evil age (cf. Lk 13:16; 2Co 4:4; Gal 1:4; Eph 6:12; Heb 2:14; see Mt 4:10, note; see article on THE KINGDOM OF GOD, p. 1430).

(1) Scripture does not teach that God is now in direct control of the ungodly world that involves sinful people, evil, cruelty and injustice. In no way does God desire or cause all the suffering in the world, nor is everything that happens his perfect will (see Mt 23:37; Lk 13:34; 19:41–44; see article on THE WILL OF GOD, p. 1056). The Bible indicates that at this present time the world is not under God's dominion, but is in rebellion against his rule and is enslaved to Satan. Because of this condition Christ came to die (Jn 3:16) and to reconcile the world to God (2Co 5:18–19). We should never use the statement "God is in control" in order to free ourselves from the responsibility of battling sin, evil or spiritual lukewarmness.

(2) However, there is a sense in which God *is* in control of the ungodly world. God is sovereign, and thus all things happen under his permissive will and oversight, or at times through his direct involvement according to his purpose. Nevertheless, at this time in history God has limited his supreme power and rule over the world. Yet this self-limitation is only temporary, for at the time determined by his wisdom he will destroy Satan and all evil (Rev 19–20). Only then will "the kingdom of the world . . . become the kingdom of our Lord and of his Christ, and he will reign for ever and ever" (Rev 11:15).

2 JOHN

Outline

Christian Greetings (1–3)
- A. To the Chosen Lady and Her Children (1)
- B. On Behalf of the Truth (2–3)

I. Commendation and Commandment (4–6)
- A. Past Loyalty to Truth Commended (4)
- B. Love and Obedience Commanded (5–6)

II. Counsel and Warning (7–11)
- A. Recognize False Teachers (7)
- B. Beware of Being Influenced by Them (8–9)
- C. Refuse Them the Use of Your Home (10–11)

Conclusion (12–13)

Author: John

Theme: Walking in Truth

Date of Writing: A.D. 85–95

Background

The author identifies himself as "the elder" (v. 1). This was probably a title of honor widely ascribed to the apostle John during the last two decades of the first century because of his advanced age and his venerated position of authority as the only surviving original apostle.

John addresses this letter to "the chosen lady and her children" (v. 1). Some interpret "the chosen lady" figuratively as a local church, "her children" as the members, and her "chosen sister" (v. 13) as a sister congregation. Others interpret the addressee literally as a prominent Christian widow of John's acquaintance in one of the nearby church communities in Asia Minor over which he had spiritual authority. Her family (v. 1) and her sister's children (v. 13) are persons of prominence among the churches in that region. As with John's other letters, 2 John was probably written from Ephesus in the late 80s or early 90s.

Purpose

John wrote this letter to caution "the chosen lady" about extending hospitality, greetings or support to traveling ministers (teachers, evangelists and prophets) who departed from the apostolic truth and propagated false teaching, lest she help spread their error and thereby share their guilt. It repudiates the same false teaching that is denounced in 1 John.

Survey

This letter underscores a warning also found in 1 John about the danger of false teachers who deny the incarnation of Jesus Christ and depart from the apostolic message (vv. 7–8). John commends "the chosen lady" and her children for "walking in the truth" (v. 4). True love involves obeying Christ's commands and loving each other (v. 6). Christian love must discern between truth and error and not provide an open door to false teachers (vv. 7–9). To cordially receive false teachers is to participate in their error (vv. 10–11). The letter is brief because John plans soon to visit the lady "face to face" (v. 12).

Special Features

Three major features characterize this letter. (1) It is the shortest book in the NT. (2) It is strikingly similar to 1 and 3 John in its message, vocabulary and simple writing style. (3) It provides an important balance to the message of 3 John by advising caution concerning the indiscriminate support of ministers not belonging to one's own congregation. It urges careful discernment in the light of the teachings of Christ and the apostles before supporting such ministers.

Reading 2 John

In order to read the entire New Testament in one year, the book of 2 John should be read in 1 day: □ 2 John

NOTES

1The elder,[a]

To the chosen[b] lady and her children, whom I love in the truth[c]—and
not I only, but also all who know the
truth[d]— 2because of the truth,[e]
which lives in us[f] and will be with us
forever:

3Grace, mercy and peace from God
the Father and from Jesus Christ,[g] the
Father's Son, will be with us in truth
and love.

4It has given me great joy to find
some of your children walking in the
truth,[h] just as the Father commanded
us. 5And now, dear lady, I am not writing you a new command but one we
have had from the beginning.[i] I ask
that we love one another. 6And this is
love:[j] that we walk in obedience to his
commands.[k] As you have heard from
the beginning,[l] his command is that
you walk in love.
7Many deceivers, who do not acknowledge Jesus Christ[m] as coming in
the flesh,[n] have gone out into the
world.[o] Any such person is the deceiver and the antichrist.[p] 8Watch out
that you do not lose what you have
worked for, but that you may be rewarded fully.[q] 9Anyone who runs
ahead and does not continue in the
teaching of Christ[r] does not have
God; whoever continues in the teaching has both the Father and the Son.[s]
10If anyone comes to you and does not
bring this teaching, do not take him
into your house or welcome him.[t]
11Anyone who welcomes him shares[u]
in his wicked work.
12I have much to write to you, but I
do not want to use paper and ink. Instead, I hope to visit you and talk with
you face to face,[v] so that our joy may
be complete.[w]

13The children of your chosen[x] sister send their greetings.

1:1 [a] S Ac 11:30; 3Jn 1 [b] ver 13; Ro 16:13; 1Pe 5:13 [c] ver 3 [d] Jn 8:32; 1Ti 2:4 **1:2** [e] 2Pe 1:12 [f] Jn 14:17; 1Jn 1:8 **1:3** [g] S Ro 1:7 **1:4** [h] 3Jn 3,4 **1:5** [i] S 1Jn 2:7 **1:6** [j] 1Jn 2:5 [k] S Jn 14:15 [l] S 1Jn 2:7
1:7 [m] 1Jn 2:22; 4:2,3 [n] S Jn 1:14 [o] 1Jn 4:1 [p] S 1Jn 2:18 **1:8** [q] S Mt 10:42; Mk 10:29,30; 1Co 3:8; Heb 10:35,36; 11:26 **1:9** [r] Jn 8:31 [s] S 1Jn 2:23 **1:10** [t] S Ro 16:17 **1:11** [u] 1Ti 5:22 **1:12** [v] 3Jn 13,14 [w] S Jn 3:29 **1:13** [x] ver 1

---

1 **CHOSEN LADY.** Some take this to mean John's letter was addressed to a godly woman named *Kyria* (Greek, meaning "lady") and her family. However, the term "chosen lady and her children" is most likely a figurative way of saying "the church and its members" (cf. 1Pe 5:13).

1 **I LOVE IN THE TRUTH.** John loves and cares for others in a way consistent with NT revelation about Christ. It is possible to love others, yet not be committed to the truth of God's Word. Such persons place love, acceptance, friendship and unity above the truth and commands of God (vv. 5–6). On the other hand, it is also possible for a person in the church to promote Biblical truth and defend its doctrines, yet not show love and concern for others. What God requires is that we demonstrate both love for his truth and love for others. We must speak the truth in love (Eph 4:15; cf. 1Co 13:6).

3 **GRACE, MERCY AND PEACE.** The conditions for receiving God's grace, mercy and peace are to guard the truth (vv. 7–11) and to love others (vv. 5–6). To fail to do either will cause the church to lose God's blessings.

5 **LOVE ONE ANOTHER.** See Jn 13:34–35, notes.

6 **HIS COMMANDS.** See Jn 14:21, note.

7 **MANY DECEIVERS.** John warns that many deceivers and false teachers are perverting God's Word and attempting to persuade Christians to accept their views. Their false teaching concerns the person of Jesus Christ. They deny that Jesus Christ was the eternal Son of God, born of the virgin (Mt 1:18; Lk 1:27), whose blood provides forgiveness for the sins of all who believe (1Jn 2:2; 4:9–10) and who is "the true God and eternal life" (1Jn 5:20).

9 **DOES NOT CONTINUE IN THE TEACHING OF CHRIST.** Those who reject the original revelation of Christ and the apostles do not have God. Although they may claim to know God (1Jn 2:4), they are deceived if they do not continue in the teaching of Christ; those who forsake Christ's doctrine forsake Christ. All theology that does not hold to the truth and righteousness revealed in the NT is not Christian theology and must be rejected (see Eph 2:20, note).

10 **DO NOT . . . WELCOME HIM.** The believer's love for and faithfulness to Christ and the Word of God must lead him or her to reject and count as an enemy of Christ's gospel any professed believer (minister or layperson) who is not committed to the "teaching of Christ" and the apostles (v. 9). Those who distort and oppose the NT faith must not be received into the fellowship of believers. (1) God warns true believers to guard against accepting false teaching (v. 8). They must be aware that "many deceivers . . . have gone out into the world" (v. 7).

(2) Believers must consider all supposed Christian teachers who do not continue in the teaching of Christ as teachers who do not have God (v. 9) and who are condemned by God (see Gal 1:9, note).

(3) God commands believers not to give encouragement or financial support to, or to remain under, the ministry of such teachers. To do so is to join them in opposing God and his Word and to come under the same condemnation as the compromising teachers (v. 11).

(4) These authoritative words of John, inspired by the Holy Spirit, are an offense to many in the church today. They feel John's admonition lacks a loving attitude or a spirit of unity. However, John's instruction will seem wrong only to those who have little concern for Christ's glory, for the authority of God's Word and for people whose eternal souls are destroyed by throwing aside God's truth.

3 JOHN

Outline

Christian Greetings (1)

I. Commendation of Gaius (2–8)
   A. For His Spiritual Health (2)
   B. For His Walking in the Truth (3–4)
   C. For His Hospitality to Traveling Brothers (5–8)

II. Counsel to Gaius (9–12)
   A. Concerning the Bad Example of Diotrephes (9–11)
   B. Concerning the Good Example of Demetrius (12)

Conclusion (13–14)

Author: John

Theme: Acting Faithfully

Date of Writing: A.D. 85–95

Background

John, the beloved apostle, again identifies himself by the title of "the elder" (v. 1; see the introduction to 2 John). This personal letter is addressed to a loyal believer named Gaius (v. 1), probably in one of the church communities in Asia Minor. As with John's other letters, 3 John was most likely written from Ephesus in the late 80s or early 90s.

Toward the end of the first century, itinerant ministers who traveled from city to city were commonly supported by believers who received them into their homes and helped them on their way (vv. 5–8; cf. 2Jn 10). Gaius was one of many faithful Christians who graciously hosted and supported trustworthy traveling ministers (vv. 1–8). However, a leader named Diotrephes arrogantly resisted John's authority and refused to receive traveling brothers whom John had sent.

Purpose

John wrote to commend Gaius for his faithful hospitality and support of trustworthy traveling ministers, to indirectly warn the rebellious leader Diotrephes and to prepare the way for his own personal visit.

Survey

Three men are mentioned by name in 3 John. (1) Gaius is warmly commended for his godly walk in the truth (vv. 3–4) and his exemplary hospitality to traveling brothers (vv. 5–8). (2) Diotrephes, a dictatorial leader, is denounced for his pride ("loves to be first," v. 9) and its manifestations: rejecting a previous letter from John (v. 9), slandering John, refusing to receive John's messengers and threatening to excommunicate those who do (v. 10). (3) Demetrius, perhaps the bearer of this letter or a pastor in a nearby community, is commended as a man of good reputation and loyalty to the truth (v. 12).

Special Features

Two major features characterize this letter. (1) Though brief, it provides insight into several important facets of early church history toward the end of the first century. (2) There are remarkable similarities between 3 John and 2 John. Nevertheless, the two letters differ in one important aspect: 3 John commends hospitality and support for trustworthy traveling ministers, while 2 John urges that hospitality and support not be given to untrustworthy ministers, so that believers might not be found promoting error or evil deeds.

Reading 3 John

In order to read the entire New Testament in one year, the book of 3 John should be read in 1 day: ☐ 3 John

NOTES

[1]The elder,[a]

To my dear friend Gaius, whom I
love in the truth.

[2]Dear friend, I pray that you may enjoy good health and that all may go
well with you, even as your soul is getting along well. [3]It gave me great joy
to have some brothers[b] come and tell
about your faithfulness to the truth
and how you continue to walk in the
truth.[c] [4]I have no greater joy than to
hear that my children[d] are walking in
the truth.[e]

[5]Dear friend, you are faithful in what
you are doing for the brothers,[f] even
though they are strangers to you.[g]
[6]They have told the church about your
love. You will do well to send them on
their way[h] in a manner worthy[i] of
God. [7]It was for the sake of the Name[j]

1:1 [a]S Ac 11:30; 2Jn 1 **1:3** [b]ver 5,10; S Ac 1:16 [c]2Jn 4 **1:4** [d]S 1Jn 2:1 [e]ver 3 **1:5** [f]S ver 3 [g]Ro 12:13; Heb 13:2 **1:6** [h]1Co 16:11; 2Co 1:16 [i]S Eph 4:1 **1:7** [j]S Jn 15:21

2 ALL MAY GO WELL. It is normally God's will that believers be healthy and that our lives be accompanied by his blessings. He wants all to go well with us, i.e., that our work, plans, purposes, ministry, families, etc., go according to God's will and direction. Thus, God's blessings through redemption in Christ are intended to meet both physical and spiritual needs.

Concerning prosperity, both physical and spiritual, Scripture teaches the following: (1) The word here translated "all may go well" (Gk *euodoō*) literally means "to have a good journey, to be led along a good road." According to that meaning, John's primary prayer was that as believers walk the road of salvation, they may continue in God's will and his truth and enjoy his blessing (cf. vv. 3–4).

(2) It is God's will that we earn enough to provide shelter, food and clothing for ourselves and our families, and have enough to help others and to further Christ's cause (Php 4:15–19). We know that God is able to give us enough for our needs (2Co 9:8–12) and that he promises to supply us "according to his glorious riches in Christ Jesus" (Php 4:19; see article on THE PROVIDENCE OF GOD, p. 78).

(3) Although we may pray that God will supply all our needs materially, we must recognize the Bible's teaching that God may allow his children to experience times of need. (a) We may be in want or experience need in order to be encouraged to trust him more and to develop our faith, spiritual endurance and ministry (Ro 8:35–39; 2Co 4:7–12; 6:4–10; 12:7–10; 1Pe 1:6–7). (b) We may undergo severe distress when our testimony about and service to Christ bring persecution and oppression from the world (Lk 6:20–23; Heb 10:32–34; 1Pe 2:19–21; Rev 2:9–10; see article on THE SUFFERING OF THE RIGHTEOUS, p. 710). (c) We may experience poverty due to national or natural circumstances, such as war, famine, drought, or poor economic or social conditions (Ac 11:28–30; 2Co 8:2,12–14).

(4) God's presence, help and blessing in our physical lives is related to the prosperity of our spiritual lives. We must seek God's will (Mt 6:10; 26:39; Heb 10:7–9), obey the Holy Spirit (Ro 8:14), remain separated from the world (Ro 12:1–2; 2Co 6:16–18), love God's Word (Jas 1:21; 1Pe 2:2), seek his help in prayer (Mt 6:9–13; Heb 4:16), work hard (2Th 3:6–12), trust him to supply our needs (Mt 6:25–34; 1Pe 5:7), and live by the principle of seeking first the kingdom of God and his righteousness (Mt 6:33; see Mt 6:11, note; Lk 11:3, note; Col 4:12, note; see article on DIVINE HEALING, p. 1420).

(5) Although our souls may be getting along well, we will not automatically be exempt from difficulties in other areas of our lives. Adversity, troubles and needs must be faced by prayer and trust in God.

5 YOU ARE FAITHFUL. John praises Gaius for one particular aspect of his walking in the truth (vv. 3–4), namely, that he has been faithful in helping traveling missionaries (vv. 5–8). He has supplied them with lodging, food, money and whatever other help they needed for their journey (cf. Tit 3:13). His commitment to Christ's missionary cause was so impressive that missionaries had specifically mentioned it to John (v. 6). Gaius's action toward these preachers of the gospel came from his love for them, for the gospel and for those without Christ.

7 FOR THE SAKE OF THE NAME. Vv. 5–8 refer to traveling messengers of the gospel of Christ. It is a duty and privilege of God's people to contribute to missionary needs and work. (1) Receiving, sending and supporting missionaries must be done in a manner worthy of God (v. 6; 1Co 9:14; Php 4:10–18). They must not be treated like beggars, but must be received as the Lord (Mt 10:40) and as his servants carrying the gospel to all the world (see Mt 28:19, note).

(2) The sending of missionaries in the early church consisted of providing for their journey and supplying them with food and with money to pay expenses and live adequately (see Gal 6:6–10, note; Php 4:16, note; Tit 3:13). By supporting missionaries God's people worked together in spreading the truth (v. 8).

7 RECEIVING NO HELP FROM THE PAGANS. Missionaries who leave their homes and go to other places to proclaim the name of the Lord Jesus Christ should refuse help from the unbelievers they are trying to win to Christ. To accept help from an unbeliever might hinder the gospel and expose the missionary to charges of preaching for financial gain (cf. 1Co 9:12). Therefore, missionaries should receive help from individual believers and from the church (Lk 10:7; 1Co 9:14; 1Ti 5:18). In contributing to the missionary work of our church, we must remember the words of Christ, "Anyone who receives a prophet because he is a prophet will receive a prophet's reward, and anyone who receives a righteous man because he is a righteous man will receive a righteous man's reward" (Mt 10:41, note).

that they went out, receiving no help
from the pagans.[k] **8**We ought therefore to show hospitality to such men so
that we may work together for the
truth.

9I wrote to the church, but Diotrephes, who loves to be first, will have
nothing to do with us. **10**So if I come,[l]
I will call attention to what he is doing,
gossiping maliciously about us. Not
satisfied with that, he refuses to welcome the brothers.[m] He also stops
those who want to do so and puts them
out of the church.[n]

11Dear friend, do not imitate what is
evil but what is good.[o] Anyone who
does what is good is from God.[p] Anyone who does what is evil has not seen
God.[q] **12**Demetrius is well spoken of
by everyone[r]—and even by the truth
itself. We also speak well of him, and
you know that our testimony is true.[s]

13I have much to write you, but I do
not want to do so with pen and ink. **14**I
hope to see you soon, and we will talk
face to face.[t]

Peace to you.[u] The friends here
send their greetings. Greet the friends
there by name.[v]

1:7 [k] Ac 20:33,35
1:10 [l] ver 14; 2Jn 12 [m] ver 5 [n] Jn 9:22,34
1:11 [o] Ps 34:14; 37:27 [p] 1Jn 2:29 [q] 1Jn 3:6,9,10
1:12 [r] 1Ti 3:7 [s] Jn 19:35; 21:24
1:14 [t] 2Jn 12 [u] S Ro 1:7; S Eph 6:23 [v] Jn 10:3

JUDE

Outline

Christian Greetings (1–2)
- I. An Explanation for Writing the Letter (3–4)
- II. Exposing the False Teachers (5–16)
  - A. Their Doom Illustrated From the Past (5–7)
    1. The Experience of Israel (5)
    2. The Experience of Unbelieving Rebellious Angels (6)
    3. The Experience of Sodom and Gomorrah (7)
  - B. Their Description in the Present (8–16)
    1. Abusive Speech (8–10)
    2. Unholy Character (11)
    3. Guilty Conduct (12–16)
- III. Exhorting the True Believers (17–23)
  - A. Remember the Predictions of the Apostles (17–19)
  - B. Keep Yourselves in God's Love (20–21)
  - C. Help Others in Mercy, Mixed With Fear (22–23)

Doxology (24–25)

Author: Jude

Theme: Contending for the Faith

Date of Writing: A.D. 70–80

Background

Jude identifies himself simply as the "brother of James" (v. 1). The only brothers in the NT by the names of Jude (Judas) and James are the half-brothers of Jesus (Mt 13:55; Mk 6:3). Perhaps Jude mentioned James because his brother's prominence as leader of the Jerusalem church would serve to clarify his own identity and authority.

This brief but hard-hitting letter was written against false teachers who were blatantly antinomian (i.e., they taught that salvation by grace allowed them to sin without condemnation) and who were contemptuously denying the original apostolic revelation about the person and nature of Jesus Christ (v. 4). Thus they were dividing the churches on what to believe (vv. 19a,22) and how to behave (vv. 4,8,16). Jude describes these unprincipled men as "ungodly" (v. 15) and as those who "do not have the Spirit" (v. 19).

The probable relationship between Jude and 2Pe 2:1—3:4 has a bearing on when Jude was written. Most likely Jude was familiar with 2 Peter (vv. 17–18) and therefore wrote after Peter, i.e., sometime between A.D. 70–80. The recipients are not identified specifically but may have been the same as those addressed in 2 Peter (see the introduction to 2 Peter).

Purpose

Jude wrote this letter (1) to urgently warn believers about the serious threat of false teachers and their subversive influence within the churches, and (2) to forcefully challenge all true believers to rise up and "contend for the faith that was once for all entrusted to the saints" (v. 3).

Survey

After his greetings (vv. 1–2), Jude reveals that his original intention was to write about the nature of salvation (v. 3a). However, he was constrained instead to write this letter because of the apostate teachers who were perverting God's grace and in so doing were undermining truth and righteousness in the churches (v. 4). Jude indicts them as sexually impure (vv. 4,8,16,18), compromising like Cain (v. 11), greedy like Balaam (v. 11), rebellious like Korah (v. 11), arrogant (vv. 8,16), deceptive (vv. 4a,12), sensual (v. 19) and divisive (v. 19). He declares the certainty of God's judgment on all who commit such sins and illustrates the same by six OT examples (vv. 5–11). A twelvefold description of their lives reveals their ripeness for God's wrath (vv. 12–16). Believers are exhorted to guard themselves and to have compassion mixed with fear for those who are wavering (vv. 20–23). Jude concludes with a crescendo of inspiration in his benediction (vv. 24–25).

Special Features

Four major features characterize this letter. (1) It contains the NT's most direct and vigorous denunciation of false teachers. It underscores for all generations the seriousness of the threat that false teaching always poses to genuine faith and holy living. (2) It demonstrates a fondness for illustrating in series of threes—e.g., three OT examples of judgment (vv. 5–7), a threefold description of the false teachers (v. 8) and three OT examples of unholy men (v. 11). (3) Under the full influence of the Holy Spirit, Jude freely refers to written sources: (a) OT Scriptures (vv. 5–7,11), (b) Jewish traditions (vv. 9,14–15) and (c) 2 Peter, quoting directly from 3:3, which he acknowledges as being from the apostles (vv. 17–18). (4) It contains the most majestic NT benediction.

Reading Jude

In order to read the entire New Testament in one year, the book of Jude should be read in 1 day: ☐ Jude

NOTES

1Jude,[a] a servant of Jesus Christ[b]
and a brother of James,

To those who have been called,[c]
who are loved by God the Father and
kept by[a] Jesus Christ:[d]

2Mercy, peace[e] and love be yours in
abundance.[f]

Contend for the Faith

3Dear friends,[g] although I was very
eager to write to you about the salvation we share,[h] I felt I had to write and
urge you to contend[i] for the faith[j]
that was once for all entrusted to the
saints.[k] **4**For certain men whose condemnation was written about[b] long
ago have secretly slipped in among
you.[l] They are godless men, who
change the grace of our God into a license for immorality and deny Jesus
Christ our only Sovereign and Lord.[m]

The Doom of False Teachers

5Though you already know all
this,[n] I want to remind you[o] that the
Lord[c] delivered his people out of
Egypt, but later destroyed those who
did not believe.[p] **6**And the angels who
did not keep their positions of authority but abandoned their own home—
these he has kept in darkness, bound
with everlasting chains for judgment
on the great Day.[q] **7**In a similar way,
Sodom and Gomorrah[r] and the surrounding towns[s] gave themselves up
to sexual immorality and perversion.
They serve as an example of those who
suffer the punishment of eternal fire.[t]
8In the very same way, these dreamers pollute their own bodies, reject authority and slander celestial beings.[u]
9But even the archangel[v] Michael,[w]
when he was disputing with the devil
about the body of Moses,[x] did not dare
to bring a slanderous accusation
against him, but said, "The Lord rebuke you!"[y] **10**Yet these men speak
abusively against whatever they do not
understand; and what things they do
understand by instinct, like unreason-

1:1 [a] Mt 13:55; Jn 14:22; Ac 1:13 [b] Ro 1:1 [c] Ro 1:6,7 [d] Jn 17:12
1:2 [e] Gal 6:16; 1Ti 1:2 [f] S Ro 1:7
1:3 [g] S 1Co 10:14 [h] Tit 1:4 [i] 1Ti 6:12 [j] ver 20; Ac 6:7 [k] S Ac 9:13
1:4 [l] Gal 2:4 [m] Tit 1:16; 2Pe 2:1; 1Jn 2:22
1:5 [n] S 1Jn 2:20 [o] 2Pe 1:12,13; 3:1,2 [p] Nu 14:29; Dt 1:32; 2:15; Ps 106:26; 1Co 10:1-5; Heb 3:16,17
1:6 [q] S 2Pe 2:4,9
1:7 [r] S Mt 10:15 [s] Dt 29:23 [t] S Mt 25:41; 2Pe 3:7
1:8 [u] 2Pe 2:10
1:9 [v] 1Th 4:16 [w] Da 10:13,21; 12:1; Rev 12:7 [x] Dt 34:6 [y] Zec 3:2

[a] *1* Or *for;* or *in* [b] *4* Or *men who were marked out for condemnation* [c] *5* Some early manuscripts *Jesus*

2 MERCY ... IN ABUNDANCE. The word "be in abundance" (Gk *plēthunō*) literally means "be multiplied." As we draw near to God, his mercy, peace and love can be doubled, tripled or even quadrupled to us.

3 THE FAITH ... ENTRUSTED TO THE SAINTS. Those faithful to Christ are placed under the solemn obligation to "contend for the faith" that God delivered to the apostles and saints (Php 1:27; cf. 1Ti 1:18–19; 6:12). (1) "The faith" consists of the gospel proclaimed by Christ and the apostles. It is the fixed and unalterable truth, given by the Holy Spirit and embodied in the NT. However, "the faith" is more than objective truth. It is also a way of life to be lived in love and purity (Col 1:9–11; 1Ti 1:5). It is a kingdom that comes in power to baptize all believers in the Holy Spirit (see articles on THE KINGDOM OF GOD, p. 1430, and BAPTISM IN THE HOLY SPIRIT, p. 1642), that they may proclaim the gospel to all nations (Mk 16:15–17; see 1Th 1:5, note) with signs and miracles and gifts of the Spirit (see Ac 2:22; 14:3; Ro 15:19; Heb 2:4, note; see article on SIGNS OF BELIEVERS, p. 1513).

(2) The word "contend" (Gk *epagonizomai*) describes the battle that the faithful believer must fight in the defense of the faith. It means literally to "struggle," "suffer," "be under great stress" or "fight a fight." We must exert ourselves to the utmost in the defense of God's Word and the NT faith, even though it may be costly and agonizing. We must deny ourselves and, if need be, accept martyrdom for the sake of the gospel (cf. 2Ti 4:7).

(3) Contending for the faith means (a) taking a direct stand against those within the visible church who deny the Bible's authority or distort the ancient faith as presented by Christ and the apostles, and (b) proclaiming it as redemptive truth to all people (see Jn 5:47, note; see article on THE INSPIRATION AND AUTHORITY OF SCRIPTURE, p. 1898). Those whose allegiance is to Christ and the full NT faith must never allow its message to be weakened by compromising its authority, distorting its truth, or explaining away its power and promises.

4 GRACE OF OUR GOD INTO A LICENSE FOR IMMORALITY. Jude denounces certain persons who teach that salvation by grace allows professed believers to indulge in serious sin and yet not be condemned by God. They may have taught that God will freely forgive those who continually engage in sexual lust, or that those who presently live in moral filth are eternally secure if they have trusted in Christ at some time in the past (cf. Ro 5:20; 6:1–2). They preached pardon for sin but not the imperative of holiness.

6 THE ANGELS. Jude refers to angels who did not remain in their initial position of authority, but who rebelled against God, broke his law, and are now in prison awaiting judgment. However, not all fallen angels are locked up, for Satan and many demons are on the earth right now (see 2 Pe 2:4, note; 1Jn 5:19, note).

8 REJECT AUTHORITY. See 2Pe 2:10, note.

9 MICHAEL ... DISPUTING WITH THE DEVIL. If the greatest archangel Michael refused to slander Satan but relied on God's power, how much more should we as humans refrain from bringing slanderous accusations against all things, including evil spirits (see 2Pe 2:11).

ing animals—these are the very things
that destroy them.[z]
11Woe to them! They have taken the
way of Cain;[a] they have rushed for
profit into Balaam's error;[b] they have
been destroyed in Korah's rebellion.[c]
12These men are blemishes at your
love feasts,[d] eating with you without
the slightest qualm—shepherds who
feed only themselves.[e] They are
clouds without rain,[f] blown along by
the wind;[g] autumn trees, without fruit
and uprooted[h]—twice dead. **13**They
are wild waves of the sea,[i] foaming up
their shame;[j] wandering stars, for
whom blackest darkness has been reserved forever.[k]
14Enoch,[l] the seventh from Adam,
prophesied about these men: "See, the
Lord is coming[m] with thousands upon
thousands of his holy ones[n] **15**to
judge[o] everyone, and to convict all the
ungodly of all the ungodly acts they
have done in the ungodly way, and of
all the harsh words ungodly sinners
have spoken against him."[p] **16**These
men are grumblers[q] and faultfinders;
they follow their own evil desires;[r]
they boast[s] about themselves and
flatter others for their own advantage.

1:10 [z]2Pe 2:12
1:11 [a]Ge 4:3-8; Heb 11:4; 1Jn 3:12 [b]S 2Pe 2:15 [c]Nu 16:1-3,31-35
1:12 [d]2Pe 2:13; 1Co 11:20-22 [e]Eze 34:2,8,10 [f]Pr 25:14; 2Pe 2:17 [g]Eph 4:14 [h]Mt 15:13
1:13 [i]Isa 57:20 [j]Php 3:19 [k]2Pe 2:17
1:14 [l]Ge 5:18, 21-24 [m]S Mt 16:27 [n]Dt 33:2; Da 7:10; Zec 14:5; Heb 12:22
1:15 [o]2Pe 2:6-9 [p]1Ti 1:9
1:16 [q]1Co 10:10 [r]ver 18; 2Pe 2:10 [s]2Pe 2:18
1:17 [t]S Eph 4:11 [u]Heb 2:3; 2Pe 3:2
1:18 [v]1Ti 4:1; 2Ti 3:1; 2Pe 3:3 [w]ver 16; 2Pe 2:1; 3:3
1:19 [x]1Co 2:14, 15
1:20 [y]Col 2:7; 1Th 5:11 [z]ver 3 [a]Eph 6:18
1:21 [b]Tit 2:13; Heb 9:28; 2Pe 3:12 [c]S Mt 25:46
1:23 [d]Am 4:11; Zec 3:2-5; 1Co 3:15 [e]Rev 3:4
1:24 [f]S Ro 16:25 [g]S 2Co 4:14 [h]Col 1:22
1:25 [i]Jn 5:44; 1Ti 1:17

A Call to Persevere

17But, dear friends, remember what
the apostles[t] of our Lord Jesus Christ
foretold.[u] **18**They said to you, "In the
last times[v] there will be scoffers who
will follow their own ungodly desires."[w] **19**These are the men who divide you, who follow mere natural instincts and do not have the Spirit.[x]
20But you, dear friends, build yourselves up[y] in your most holy faith[z]
and pray in the Holy Spirit.[a] **21**Keep
yourselves in God's love as you wait[b]
for the mercy of our Lord Jesus Christ
to bring you to eternal life.[c]
22Be merciful to those who doubt;
23snatch others from the fire and save
them;[d] to others show mercy, mixed
with fear—hating even the clothing
stained by corrupted flesh.[e]

Doxology

24To him who is able[f] to keep you
from falling and to present you before
his glorious presence[g] without fault[h]
and with great joy— **25**to the only
God[i] our Savior be glory, majesty,
power and authority, through Jesus
Christ our Lord, before all ages, now
and forevermore![j] Amen.[k]

[j]Heb 13:8 [k]S Ro 11:36

---

12 TWICE DEAD. The apostate teachers among Jude's readers are "twice dead" (literally, "twice having died"). The false teachers were once believers in Christ who had "crossed over from death to life" (Jn 5:24) but had sometime afterward severed their union with Christ and gone out of life back into death (cf. Eph 2:1; see Ro 8:13, note). The previous verse gives the reason for their spiritual death.

14 ENOCH ... PROPHESIED. Jude may be quoting from the book of Enoch, written prior to 110 B.C., or simply from Jewish tradition. Jude's use of this passage confirms only the truth of Enoch's prophecy; it does not mean that he endorses the entire book of Enoch.

18 IN THE LAST TIMES. See 1Ti 4:1, note; 2Ti 3:1, note.

20 BUILD YOURSELVES UP. Believers must defend and propagate the faith and resist false teaching in four ways. (1) By building ourselves up in our most holy faith. The holy faith is the NT revelation handed down by Christ and the apostles (v. 3). This requires study of God's Word and a determined effort to know the truth and teachings of Scripture (cf. Ac 2:42; 20:27; 2Ti 2:15; Heb 5:12).

(2) By praying in the Spirit. We must pray by the enabling power of the Holy Spirit, i.e., by looking to the Spirit to inspire, guide, energize, sustain and help us to do battle in our praying (see Ro 8:26, note; cf. Gal 4:6; Eph 6:18). Praying in the Spirit includes both praying with one's mind and praying with one's spirit (see 1Co 14:15, note).

(3) By remaining in the sphere of God's love for us. This involves faithful obedience to God and his Word (Jn 15:9–10).

(4) By longing and waiting for our Lord's return and the eternal glory that will accompany his return (see Jn 14:2, note).

Event	Description	References
Last Days of Preparation	Increase of false prophets and religious compromise within the church	Mt 24:4–5,10–11,24; Lk 18:8; 2Th 2:3; 1Ti 4:1; 2Ti 3:1,13; 4:3–4; 2Pe 2:1–3; 3:3–4
	Increase of crime and disregard of God's law	Mt 24:12,37–39; Lk 17:26–30; 18:8; 1Ti 4:1; 2Ti 3:1–8
	Increase of wars, famines and earthquakes	Mt 24:6–8; Mk 13:7–8; Lk 21:9
	Decrease in love and family affection	Mt 10:21; 24:12; Mk 13:12; 2Ti 3:1–3
	More severe persecution of God's people	Mt 10:22–23; 24:9–10; Mk 13:13; Jn 15:19–20; 16:33; Ac 14:22; Ro 5:3
	Those who stand firm will be saved	Mt 24:13; Mk 13:13
	Gospel will be preached to the whole world	Mt 24:14; Mk 13:10
	The Spirit will be poured out on God's people	Ac 2:17–21,38–39

Event	Description	References
The Rapture	Believers must be prepared and wait constantly for this imminent event	Mt 24:42,44; 25:1–13; Mk 13:33–37; Lk 12:35; 21:19,34–36; Ro 13:11; Php 4:5; 1Th 1:10; 4:16–18; 5:6–11; 2Ti 4:8; Tit 2:13
	Christ will come unexpectedly, since the time cannot be calculated	Mt 24:36,42,44; 25:5–7,13; Mk 13:32–37; Lk 12:35–46
	Christ will come to catch up believers living on earth at this time	Lk 21:36; Jn 14:3; 1Th 1:10; 4:15–17; 2Th 2:1; Rev 3:10–11
	Believers will be delivered from the coming wrath	Lk 21:36; 1Th 1:10; 5:2–9; Rev 3:10–11
	Believers living at this time will receive transformed bodies	Ro 8:23; 1Co 15:51–54; 1Th 4:16–17
	Believers who died before this event will rise and be caught up with Christ	1Co 15:50–55; 1Th 4:16–17
	All raptured saints will be judged by Christ	Jn 5:22; Ro 14:12; 1Co 3:12–15; 2Co 5:10; 2Ti 4:8
	Believers will be judged according to their deeds	Ecc 12:14; Mt 5:22; 12:36–37; Mk 4:22; Ro 2:5–11,16; 1Co 4:5; 2Co 5:10; Eph 6:8; Col 3:23–25

Event	Description	References
The Rapture (cont.)	Faithful believers will receive rewards	Mt 5:11–12; 25:14–23; Lk 19:12–19; 22:28–30; Gal 6:8–10; 1Co 3:12–14; 9:25–27; 13:3; Eph 6:8; 2Ti 4:8; Heb 6:10; 1Pe 5:4; Rev 2:7,11,17, 26–28; 3:4–5,12,21
	Less faithful believers will not be condemned, but will receive little or no reward	Ecc 12:14; Mt 5:19; 1Co 2:13–15; 2Co 5:10; Col 3:25; 1Jn 2:28

Event	Description	References
The Tribulation	The faithful in Christ's churches will be kept from this time of trial	Lk 21:36; Jn 14:1–3; 2Co 5:2,4; Php 3:20–21; 1Th 1:10; 4:16–18; 5:8–10; Rev 3:10
	Will begin after the restrainer is taken out of the way	2Th 2:6–8
	Will begin after the secret power of lawlessness intensifies	2Th 2:7–8
	Will begin after a great rebellion against the faith occurs	2Th 2:3
	The antichrist (the man of lawlessness) will appear	Da 9:26–27; 2Th 2:3–10; Rev 13:1–18; 16:2; 17:9–18; 19:19–20
	Will begin with the opening of the seven seals	Rev 6:1
	A time of worldwide distress	Mt 24:21–22; Rev 6–19
	Will last for seven years	Da 9:27
	False prophets will perform great signs and wonders	Mt 24:24; 2Th 2:8–10; Rev 13:13; 16:14; 19:20
	The gospel will be preached by angels and possibly Jews	Rev 7:1–4; 11:3–6; 14:6–7
	People will be saved during these days	Dt 4:30–31; Rev 7:9–17; 14:6–7; 11:13
	Many Jews will turn to Christ	Ro 11:25–26; Rev 7:1–8
	Those who had opportunity to believe in Jesus before the rapture will have no further opportunity to repent	Mt 25:1–12; Lk 12:45–46; 2Th 2:10–12
	Will be a time of persecution for all who are faithful to Jesus	Da 12:10; Mt 24:15–21; Rev 6:9–11; 7:9–17; 9:3–5; 12:12,17; 13:7,15–17; 14:6,13; 17:6; 18:24; 20:4

Event	Description	References
The Great Tribulation	Last three and one-half years of "The Tribulation"	Da 9:27; Rev 11:1–2; 12:6; 13:5–7
	Will begin with the abomination that causes desolation standing in the holy place (the temple)	Da 9:27; 12:11; Mt 24:15; Mk 13:14; 2Th 2:4; Rev 13:14–15
	Demonic activity will increase greatly	Rev 9:3–11,14–19; 16:12–14
	Sorcery and witchcraft will increase greatly	1Ti 4:1; Rev 9:21; 18:23; 22:15
	Cosmic events related to sun, moon and stars will occur	Isa 13:9–11; Mt 24:29; Mk 13:24–25; Lk 21:25; Rev 6:12–14; 8:10,12; 9:2
	Religious deceit will be widespread	Mt 24:24; Mk 13:6,21–22; 2Th 2:9–11
	Time of terrible suffering for Jews	Jer 30:5–7; Rev 11:2; 12:12–17
	The world's worst and most intense time of worldwide distress	Da 12:1; Mt 24:21; Mk 13:15–19; Rev 6:9–17; 9:1—9:21; 16:1–21
	God will extend his wrath on the ungodly	Isa 13:6–13; Jer 30:4–11; Da 12:1; Zec 14:1–4; Rev 3:10; 6:17; 9:1–6,18–21; 14:9–11; 19:15
	The apostate church will be destroyed	Rev 17:16–17
	Two witnesses who preached the gospel and were killed will be resurrected	Rev 11:11–12
	End of great tribulation can be known by definite signs	Mt 24:15–29,32–33; Mk 13:28–29; Lk 21:28
	Will end with the battle of Armageddon and God's full wrath on the ungodly	Jer 25:29–38; Eze 39:17–20; Joel 3:2,9–17; Zep 3:8; Zec 14:2–5; Rev 14:9–11, 14–20; 16:12–21; 19:17–18
	Christ will triumph over the antichrist and his armies	Mt 24:30–31; 2Pe 3:10–13; Rev 19:11–21

Event	Description	References
The Antichrist	Ruler during the tribulation who controls the entire world	Da 7:2–7,24–27; 8:4; 11:36; Rev 13:1–18; 17:11–17
	An incredibly wicked person, a "man of lawlessness" and sin	Da 9:27; 2Th 2:3; Rev 13:12
	Described as a beast	Rev 13:1–18; 17:3,8,16; 19:19–20; 20:10

Event	Description	References
The Antichrist (cont.)	Will set up an image of himself in the temple and will demand worship	Da 7:8,25; 11:31,36; Mt 24:15; Mk 13:14; 2Th 2:3–4; Rev 13:4,8,12,14–15; 14:9; 16:2
	Will exercise miracles through the power of Satan	Mt 24:24; 2Th 2:9–10; Rev 13:3,12–14; 16:14; 17:8
	Will have ability to deceive the nations	1Th 2:9–10; 1Jn 2:18; Rev 20:3
	Will be assisted by the false prophet (the beast of the earth)	Rev 13:11–17; 16:13; 19:20; 20:10
	Will kill the two witnesses who proclaimed the gospel	Rev 11:7–10
	Will attempt to kill all who do not have the mark of the beast	Rev 6:9; 13:15–17; 14:12–13
	Will eventually destroy the religious system with which he was aligned	Rev 17:16–17
	Will be defeated by Christ when Christ returns to earth to establish his kingdom	2Th 2:8; Rev 16:16; 19:15–21

Event	Description	References
Christ's glorious appearing from heaven to judge and to wage war	Christ will return with believers and his angels	2Th 1:7–10; Jude 14–15; Rev 19:14
	Christ will gather the tribulation saints	Mt 24:31; 25:31–40,46; Mk 13:27; Rev 20:4
	Unbelievers will be unprepared for this event	Mt 24:38–39,43
	Christ will separate peoples on earth	Mt 13:40–41,47–50; 25:31–46
	Nations will be enraged at this event	Rev 11:18
	Saints will rejoice at this event	Rev 19:1–8
	Christ will judge and destroy the ungodly, including the antichrist and Satan	Isa 13:6–12; Eze 20:34–38; Mt 13:41–50; 24:30; 25:41–46; Lk 19:11–27; 1Th 5:1–11; 2Th 2:7–10,12; Rev 6:16–17; 11:18; 17:14; 18:1–24; 19:11—20:3
	Tribulation saints will receive rewards	Mt 5:11–12; 1Co 3:12–14; 9:25–27; Gal 6:9–10; 2Ti 4:8; Rev 20:4
	Tribulation saints will share in Christ's glory and kingdom	Mt 25:31–40; Ro 8:29; 2Th 2:13–14; Rev 20:4

Event	Description	References
The Millennium	Satan will be bound	Rev 20:2–3
	Tribulation saints (and possibly OT saints) will rise from the dead	Rev 20:4
	The church and all martyred tribulation saints will reign with Christ	Rev 2:26–27; 3:21; 5:9–10; 11:15–18; 20:4–6
	Christ will reign on earth over the tribulation saints alive at his coming	Isa 9:6–7; Mic 4:1–8; Da 2:44; Zec 14:6–9; Rev 5:10; 11:15–18; 20:4–6
	Time span of reign will be a thousand years	Rev 20:4–7
	God's children will have rest	2Th 1:7
	Nature will be restored to its original order and perfection	Ps 96:11–13; 98:7–9; Isa 14:7–8; 35:1–2,6–7; 51:3; 55:12–13; Eze 34:25; Ro 8:18–23
	Satan will be released for a brief time at the end of the Millennium	Rev 20:7
	Will end with Christ turning over the kingdom to the Father	1Co 15:24

Event	Description	References
The Final Judgment	Final battle of Gog and Magog	Rev 20:7–9
	All the wicked will be raised from the dead to face judgment	Isa 26:19–21; Da 12:2; Jn 5:28–29; Rev 20:12–15
	The great white throne judgment	Rev 20:11–15
	All God's enemies will be put into the lake of fire	2Th 1:9; Rev 20:10,12–15; 21:8

Event	Description	References
The New Heavens and New Earth	God will destroy the present earth	Ps 102:25–26; Isa 34:4; 51:6; Hag 2:6; Heb 12:26–28; 2Pe 3:7,10,12
	God will create a new heaven and a new earth	Isa 51:6; 65:17; 66:22; Ro 8:19–21; 2Pe 3:10–13; Rev 21:1—22:6
	God will wipe away all effects of sin	2Pe 3:13; Rev 21:4; 22:3,15
	New earth will become the headquarters of God	Rev 21:1–3

REVELATION

Outline

The Prologue (1:1–8)

- I. The Exalted Lord and His Churches (1:9—3:22)
  - A. Vision of the Exalted Lord Among the Lampstands (1:9–20)
  - B. His Messages to the Seven Churches (2:1—3:22)
- II. The Worthy Lamb and His Role in the Outcome of History (4:1—11:19)
  - A. Vision of the Majestic Court of Heaven (4:1—5:14)
    - 1. The Creator-God on His Throne in Awesome Holiness (4:1–11)
    - 2. The Sealed Scroll and the Worthy Lamb (5:1–14)
  - B. Vision of the Lamb in Relation to the Seven Seals and Seven Trumpets (6:1—11:19)
    - 1. Opening the First Six Seals (6:1–17)
      FIRST INTERLUDE: The Two Multitudes (7:1–17)
    - 2. Opening the Seventh Seal: Seven Angels With Seven Trumpets (8:1–6)
    - 3. The First Six Trumpets (8:7—9:21)
      SECOND INTERLUDE: The Little Scroll (10:1–11)
      The Two Witnesses (11:1–14)
    - 4. The Seventh Trumpet (11:15–19)
- III. The Lord God and His Christ in the Great Conflict with Satan (12:1—22:5)
  - A. Perspective of the Conflict (12:1—15:8)
    - 1. From the Viewpoint of the Earth's Enemies (12:1—13:18)
      - a. The Dragon (12:1–17)
      - b. The Sea Beast (13:1–10)
      - c. The Earth Beast (13:11–18)
    - 2. From the Viewpoint of Heaven (14:1–20)
      THIRD INTERLUDE: Seven Angels With Seven Plagues (15:1–8)
  - B. Final Progression of the Conflict (16:1—19:10)
    - 1. The Seven Bowls of God's Wrath (16:1–21)
    - 2. Judgment of the Great Prostitute (17:1–18)
    - 3. The Fall of Babylon the Great (18:1–24)
    - 4. Rejoicing in Heaven (19:1–10)
  - C. Climax of the Conflict (19:11—20:10)
    - 1. The Return and Triumph of Christ (19:11–18)
    - 2. The Defeat of the Beast and His Allies (19:19–21)
    - 3. Binding, Releasing and Finally Defeating Satan (20:1–10)
  - D. Aftermath of the Conflict (20:11–22:5)
    - 1. Great White Throne Judgment (20:11–15)
    - 2. The Doom of the Unrighteous (20:14–15; 21:8)
    - 3. New Heaven and New Earth (21:1–22:5)

The Epilogue (22:6–21)

Author: John

Theme: Conflict and Consummation

Date of Writing: c. A.D. 90–96

Background

Revelation is the last NT book and the most unusual. It is at once an apocalypse (1:1–2,20), a prophecy (1:3; 22:7,10,18–19) and a composite of seven letters (1:4,11; 2:1—3:22). ("Apocalypse" is derived from the Greek word *apocalupsis*, translated "revelation" in 1:1.) The book is an apocalypse with regard to the nature of its content, a prophecy with respect to its message and a letter in relation to its addressees.

Five important facts about the book's background are revealed in ch. 1. (1) It is "the revelation of Jesus Christ" (1:1). (2) This revelation was communicated supernaturally to the author through the exalted Christ, angels and visions (1:1,10–18). (3) The communication was to God's servant John (1:1,4,9; 22:8). (4) John received the visions and apocalyptic message while exiled on the island of Patmos (50 miles southwest of Ephesus) because of God's Word and John's own testimony (1:9). (5) The original recipients were seven churches in the province of Asia (1:4,11).

Historical and internal evidence point to John the apostle as the author. Irenaeus verifies that Polycarp (Irenaeus knew Polycarp, and Polycarp knew the apostle John) spoke about John writing Revelation near the end of Domitian's reign as Roman emperor (A.D. 81–96).

The book's content reflects the historical circumstances of Domitian's reign when he demanded that all his subjects address him as "Lord and God." The emperor's decree undoubtedly created a confrontation between those willing to worship the emperor and faithful Christians who confessed that only Jesus was "Lord and God." Thus the book was written at a time when believers were undergoing a measure of serious persecution because of the word of their testimony, a situation that obviously forms the background to Revelation itself (1:19; 2:10,13; 6:9–11; 7:14–17; 11:7; 12:11,17; 17:6; 18:24; 19:2; 20:4).

Purpose

The purpose of the book is threefold. (1) The letters to the seven churches reveal that serious deviation from the NT apostolic standard of truth and righteousness was occurring among many churches in Asia. John writes on Christ's behalf to rebuke their compromise and sin, and to call them to repent and return to their first love. (2) In view of persecution resulting from Domitian's self-deification, Revelation was given to the churches to strengthen their faith, resolve and loyalty to Jesus Christ, and to inspire them to be overcomers and remain faithful even unto death. (3) Finally, it was written to provide believers of all generations with God's perspective on their fierce conflict with Satan's combined forces by revealing the future outcome of history. It particularly discloses the events during the last seven years preceding Christ's second coming— that God will prevail and vindicate the saints by pouring out his wrath on Satan's kingdom; this will be followed by the second coming of Christ.

Survey

The prophetic message of this book is communicated through dramatic apocalyptic images and symbolism, depicting the consummation of the whole Biblical message of redemption. It features Christ's role as the worthy Lamb who was slain (ch. 5) and the wrathful Lamb who is coming to judge the world and purge it of evil (chs. 6–19). The other major symbolic images in the book are the dragon (Satan), the sea beast (the antichrist), the earth beast (the false prophet) and Babylon the Great (the center of satanic deception and world power).

After the prologue (1:1–8), there are three main sections in the book. In the first section (1:9—3:22), John has an awesome vision of the exalted Christ in the midst of the lampstands (churches), who commissions John to write letters to seven churches in Asia Minor (1:11,19). Each letter (2:1—3:22) includes a symbolic description of the exalted Lord from the opening vision, an evaluation of the church, words of commendation or rebuke or both, words of warning to five churches, an exhortation to hear and repent, and a promise to all overcomers. Emphasis on the number seven in this section indicates that the letters represent a collective fullness of what the exalted Lord says to the church in every city and generation.

The book's second main section (4:1—11:19) contains visions of things in heaven and on earth concerning the Lamb and his role in the outcome of history. It begins with a vision of the majestic heavenly court where God sits enthroned in holiness and unapproachable light (ch. 4). Ch. 5 focuses on a sealed scroll of destiny in God's right hand and on the Lamb, who alone is worthy to break its seals and disclose its contents. The opening of the first six seals (ch. 6) continues the vision begun in chs. 4–5, except now the scene shifts to events on earth. The first five seals unveil God's judgments in the last days that lead up to the end. The sixth seal announces God's coming wrath. The book's "First Interlude" occurs in ch. 7, describing the sealing of the 144,000 on the threshold of the great tribulation (7:1–8) and the reward of the saints in heaven after the great tribulation (7:9–17). Chs. 8–9 reveal the opening of the seventh seal, unveiling another series of judgments, i.e., the seven trumpets. A "Second Interlude" occurs between the sixth and seventh trumpets, involving John and a little scroll (10:1–11), and two mighty prophetic witnesses in the great city (11:1–14). Finally, the seventh trumpet (11:15–19) serves as a preview of the consummation (v. 15) and a prelude to the final scenes of God's unfolding mystery (chs. 12–22).

The third main section (12:1—22:5) provides a detailed picture of the great end-time conflict between God and his adversary, Satan. Chs. 12–13 reveal that the saints on earth must face a terrible conspiracy and triad of evil, consisting of (1) the dragon (ch. 12), (2) the sea beast (13:1–10) and (3) the earth beast (13:11–18). Chs. 14–15 contain visions to reassure the tribulation saints that justice will prevail as God is about to pour out his final wrath on the civilization of the antichrist. A full disclosure of God's wrath then occurs in the series of seven bowl judgments (ch. 16), the judgment of the great prostitute (ch. 17), and the fall of Babylon the Great (ch. 18). At this point, great rejoicing bursts forth in heaven, and the marriage supper of the Lamb and his bride is announced (19:1–10).

However, the grand finale is yet to occur. John then sees heaven opened and Christ riding forth on the white horse as the King of kings and Lord of lords to defeat the beast and all his allies (19:11–21). Satan's final defeat is preceded by his being bound for a thousand years (20:1–6), during which Christ reigns with the saints (20:4) and after which Satan is released for a short time (20:7–9) and then thrown into "the lake of fire" forever (20:10). The apocalyptic prophecy concludes with the great white throne judgment scene (20:11–15), the just doom of the wicked (20:14–15; 21:8), and the new heaven and new earth as the destiny of the saints (21:1—22:5). The book ends with warnings about heeding its message and entering into eternal life (22:6–21).

Special Features

Eight major features characterize this book. (1) Revelation is the only NT book classified as prophecy and apocalyptic. (2) As an apocalyptic book, its message is conveyed in symbols that represent realities about future times and events while preserving a certain enigma or mystery. (3) Numbers are used prolifically, including 2; 3; 3 and 1/2; 4; 5; 6; 7; 10; 12; 24; 42; 144; 666; 1,000; 1,260; 7,000; 12,000; 144,000; 100,000,000; and 200,000,000. The book especially features the number seven, which occurs no less than 54 times and symbolizes perfect completeness or fullness. (4) Visions are prominent, with the scenes often shifting in locale from earth to heaven and back to earth. (5) Angels are prominently associated with the visions and the heavenly decrees. (6) It is a polemical book that (a) exposes the demonic character of any earthly ruler's claim to deity, and (b) reveals Jesus Christ as the exalted Lord and the ruler of the kings of the earth (1:5; 19:16). (7) It is a dramatic book that makes the truth of its message as vivid and forceful as possible. (8) It breathes the spirit of OT prophecy without any formal OT quotations.

Interpretation

This is the most difficult NT book to interpret. Although the original readers probably understood its message without excessive perplexity, in subsequent centuries varying opinions about the book have resulted in four major schools of interpretation. (1) The *preterist* interpretation views the book and its prophecies as having been fulfilled in the original historical setting of the Roman empire, except for chs. 19–22— which await future fulfillment. (2) The *historicist* interpretation views Revelation as a prophetic forecast of the entire sweep of church history from John's day to the end of the age. (3) The *idealist* interpretation regards the book's symbolism as conveying certain timeless spiritual principles about good and evil in history generally, without reference to actual historical events. (4) The *futurist* interpretation approaches chs. 4–22 as prophecy concerning events in history that will occur only at the end of this age. This study Bible interprets Revelation primarily from the futurist perspective.

Reading Revelation

In order to read the entire New Testament in one year, the book of Revelation should be read in 24 days, according to the following schedule:
☐ 1 ☐ 2:1–17 ☐ 2:18–3:6 ☐ 3:7–22 ☐ 4 ☐ 5 ☐ 6 ☐ 7 ☐ 8 ☐ 9 ☐ 10 ☐ 11 ☐ 12 ☐ 13:1–10 ☐ 13:11–14:20 ☐ 15 ☐ 16 ☐ 17 ☐ 18 ☐ 19:1–10 ☐ 19:11–21 ☐ 20 ☐ 21 ☐ 22

NOTES

Prologue

1 The revelation of Jesus Christ,
which God gave[a] him to show his
servants what must soon take place.[b]
He made it known by sending his angel[c] to his servant John,[d] 2who testifies to everything he saw—that is, the
word of God[e] and the testimony of
Jesus Christ.[f] 3Blessed is the one who
reads the words of this prophecy, and
blessed are those who hear it and take
to heart what is written in it,[g] because
the time is near.[h]

Greetings and Doxology

4John,

To the seven churches[i] in the province of Asia:

Grace and peace to you[j] from him
who is, and who was, and who is to
come,[k] and from the seven spirits[a][l]
before his throne, 5and from Jesus
Christ, who is the faithful witness,[m]
the firstborn from the dead,[n] and the
ruler of the kings of the earth.[o]

To him who loves us[p] and has freed
us from our sins by his blood,[q] 6and
has made us to be a kingdom and

1:1 [a]Jn 12:49; 17:8 [b]ver 19; Da 2:28,29; Rev 22:6 [c]Rev 22:16 [d]ver 4,9; Rev 22:8
1:2 [e]ver 9; S Heb 4:12 [f]ver 9; 1Co 1:6; Rev 6:9; 12:17; 19:10
1:3 [g]Lk 11:28; Rev 22:7 [h]S Ro 13:11
1:4 [i]ver 11,20 [j]S Ro 1:7 [k]ver 8; Rev 4:8; 11:17; 16:5 [l]Isa 11:2; Rev 3:1; 4:5; 5:6
1:5 [m]Isa 55:4; Jn 18:37; Rev 3:14 [n]Ps 89:27; Col 1:18 [o]S 1Ti 6:15 [p]S Ro 8:37 [q]S Ro 3:25
1:6 [r]S 1Pe 2:5; Rev 5:10; 20:6 [s]Ro 15:6 [t]S Ro 11:36
1:7 [u]Da 7:13; S Mt 16:27; 24:30; 26:64; S Lk 17:30; S 1Co 1:7; S 1Th 2:19; 4:16, 17 [v]Jn 19:34,37 [w]Zec 12:10; Mt 24:30
1:8 [x]S ver 17; Rev 21:6; 22:13 [y]S ver 4 [z]Rev 4:8; 15:3; 19:6
1:9 [a]ver 1 [b]S Ac 14:22; 2Co 1:7; Php 4:14 [c]ver 6 [d]2Ti 2:12 [e]ver 2; S Heb 4:12 [f]S ver 2

priests[r] to serve his God and Father[s]—to him be glory and power for
ever and ever! Amen.[t]

7Look, he is coming with the
clouds,[u]
and every eye will see him,
even those who pierced him;[v]
and all the peoples of the earth
will mourn[w] because of
him.
So shall it be! Amen. Rev 16:15

8"I am the Alpha and the Omega,"[x]
says the Lord God, "who is, and who
was, and who is to come,[y] the Almighty."[z]

One Like a Son of Man

9I, John,[a] your brother and companion in the suffering[b] and kingdom[c]
and patient endurance[d] that are ours
in Jesus, was on the island of Patmos
because of the word of God[e] and the
testimony of Jesus.[f] 10On the Lord's Rev 11:3
Day[g] I was in the Spirit,[h] and I heard
behind me a loud voice like a trumpet,[i] 11which said: "Write on a scroll

1:10 [g]Ac 20:7 [h]Rev 4:2; 17:3; 21:10 [i]Ex 20:18; Rev 4:1

[a]4 Or *the sevenfold Spirit*

1:1 REVELATION OF JESUS CHRIST. This book is a revelation from Jesus Christ about himself. This is extremely important, for (1) it reveals Jesus' evaluation of his churches 60 to 65 years after his resurrection and ascension, and (2) it discloses future events concerning the tribulation, God's triumph over evil, Christ's return to reign on earth and the blessedness of God's eternal kingdom.

1:3 BLESSED IS THE ONE WHO READS. This is the first of seven "beatitudes" or blessings found in Revelation, given to those who read, hear and obey the things written in the book. The other six blessings are found in 14:13; 16:15; 19:9; 20:6; 22:7; 22:14 (cf. Lk 11:28). That believers must keep the commands of Revelation indicates that this is a practical book with moral instructions and not merely a prophecy about the future. We should read the book not only to understand God's future program for the world and his people, but also to learn and apply great spiritual principles. Above all it should draw us nearer to Jesus Christ in faith, hope and love.

1:4 TO THE SEVEN CHURCHES. Revelation is addressed to seven churches in Asia (located in what is now part of western Turkey). Each particular church was comprised of various congregations. These churches were probably selected because they represented the totality of churches of that day, for the word "seven" stands for a complete whole. What was said to them is meant for the whole church. In other words, the "seven churches" represent all the churches throughout this church age. The "seven spirits" may represent the perfection and ministry of the Holy Spirit to the church (cf. 4:5; 5:6; Isa 11:2–3).

1:7 HE IS COMING. The primary purpose of the book of Revelation is to describe the triumph of God's kingdom when Christ returns to establish his kingdom on earth; the end-time events surrounding that coming are also set forth (cf. Da 7:13; Mt 24:29–30). It presents an eschatology of victory for the faithful, teaching that history will end in the judgment of Satan's system in this world (chs. 17–18) and in the eternal reign of Christ and his people (20:4; 21:1—22:5).

1:8 THE ALPHA AND THE OMEGA. Alpha is the first letter of the Greek alphabet and Omega is the last letter. God is eternal, and from creation to consummation he is Lord over all. To him belong the final victory over evil and the rulership over all things (cf. 22:13).

1:9 ISLAND OF PATMOS. Patmos is a small island in the Aegean Sea, about 50 miles southwest of Ephesus. John was a prisoner there because he faithfully proclaimed the gospel and remained loyal to Christ and his Word.

1:10 IN THE SPIRIT. This expression refers to a special intensity of spiritual awareness and receptivity to the communication of the Holy Spirit by which visions may be received (cf. Ac 10:10).

what you see[j] and send it to the seven
churches:[k] to Ephesus,[l] Smyrna,[m]
Pergamum,[n] Thyatira,[o] Sardis,[p]
Philadelphia[q] and Laodicea."[r]
12I turned around to see the voice
that was speaking to me. And when I
turned I saw seven golden lampstands,[s] 13and among the lampstands[t] was someone "like a son of
man,"[b][u] dressed in a robe reaching
down to his feet[v] and with a golden
sash around his chest.[w] 14His head
and hair were white like wool, as white
as snow, and his eyes were like blazing
fire.[x] 15His feet were like bronze
glowing in a furnace,[y] and his voice
was like the sound of rushing waters.[z] 16In his right hand he held sev-
en stars,[a] and out of his mouth came
a sharp double-edged sword.[b] His
face was like the sun[c] shining in all
its brilliance.
17When I saw him, I fell at his feet[d]
as though dead. Then he placed his
right hand on me[e] and said: "Do not
be afraid.[f] I am the First and the
Last.[g] 18I am the Living One; I was
dead,[h] and behold I am alive for ever
and ever![i] And I hold the keys of
death and Hades.[j]
19"Write, therefore, what you have
seen,[k] what is now and what will take
place later. 20The mystery of the seven
stars that you saw in my right hand[l]
and of the seven golden lampstands[m]
is this: The seven stars are the angels[c] of the seven churches,[n] and the
seven lampstands are the seven
churches.[o]

To the Church in Ephesus

2 "To the angel[d] of the church in
Ephesus[p] write:

These are the words of him who
holds the seven stars in his right
hand[q] and walks among the sev-
en golden lampstands:[r] 2I know
your deeds,[s] your hard work and
your perseverance. I know that
you cannot tolerate wicked men,
that you have tested[t] those who
claim to be apostles but are not,
and have found them false.[u]
3You have persevered and have
endured hardships for my
name,[v] and have not grown weary.
4Yet I hold this against you:
You have forsaken your first
love.[w] 5Remember the height
from which you have fallen! Re-

1:11 [j]ver 19 [k]ver 4,20 [l]S Ac 18:19 [m]Rev 2:8 [n]Rev 2:12 [o]Ac 16:14; Rev 2:18,24 [p]Rev 3:1 [q]Rev 3:7 [r]S Col 2:1; Rev 3:14 **1:12** [s]ver 20; Ex 25:31-40; Zec 4:2; Rev 2:1 **1:13** [t]Rev 2:1 [u]Eze 1:26; Da 7:13; 10:16; Rev 14:14 [v]Isa 6:1 [w]Da 10:5; Rev 15:6 **1:14** [x]Da 7:9; 10:6; Rev 2:18; 19:12 **1:15** [y]Eze 1:7; Da 10:6; Rev 2:18 [z]Eze 43:2; Rev 14:2; 19:6 **1:16** [a]ver 20; Rev 2:1; 3:1 [b]Isa 1:20; 49:2; Heb 4:12; Rev 2:12,16; 19:15,21 [c]Jdg 5:31; Mt 17:2 **1:17** [d]Eze 1:28; Da 8:17,18 [e]Da 8:18 [f]S Mt 14:27 [g]Isa 41:4; 44:6; 48:12; Rev 2:8; 22:13 **1:18** [h]Ro 6:9; Rev 2:8 [i]Dt 32:40; Da 4:34; 12:7; Rev 4:9,10; 10:6; 15:7 [j]Rev 9:1; 20:1 **1:19** [k]ver 11; Hab 2:2 **1:20** [l]S ver 16 [m]S ver 12 [n]ver 4, 11 [o]Mt 5:14,15 **2:1** [p]S Ac 18:19 [q]Rev 1:16 [r]Rev 1:12,13 **2:2** [s]ver 19; Rev 3:1,8,15 [t]1Jn 4:1 [u]2Co 11:13 **2:3** [v]S Jn 15:21 **2:4** [w]Jer 2:2; Mt 24:12

[b]*13* Daniel 7:13 [c]*20* Or *messengers*
[d]*1* Or *messenger*; also in verses 8, 12 and 18

1:12 SEVEN GOLDEN LAMPSTANDS. These stands hold oil lamps, not candles (see Zec 4:2, note); they represent the seven churches mentioned in v. 11 (cf. v. 20).

1:13 A SON OF MAN. This term refers to the exalted Christ, a term also used by the OT prophet Daniel (see Da 7:13, note; 10:16). In this vision, Christ is described as king, priest and judge of his churches (cf. vv. 13–16).

1:16 SEVEN STARS. The seven stars represent either angels who are assigned, each to a church, to assist it in its spiritual warfare (see v. 20; cf. Mt 18:10), or the pastors of these churches. The "double-edged sword" represents the Word of God, which either cuts away sin from the churches and brings God's grace, or in judgment cuts a church away from God's kingdom (3:14–22).

1:19 WHAT YOU HAVE SEEN, WHAT IS NOW AND WHAT WILL TAKE PLACE. Here we have an outline of the book of Revelation: (1) the things John saw (ch. 1); (2) the things that are now (chs. 2–3); (3) the things that will take place in the future (i.e., events preceding and following Christ's coming to earth, chs. 4–22).

1:20 THE SEVEN CHURCHES. See article on CHRIST'S MESSAGE TO THE SEVEN CHURCHES, p. 2008.

2:2 WHO CLAIM TO BE APOSTLES. One of the major concerns Christ expresses in his final message to the seven churches was that they not fall away by tolerating false teachers, prophets or apostles who were distorting his Word or weakening its power and authority. (1) Christ instructs the churches to test all who claim spiritual authority. (2) Note Christ's condemnation of the churches in Pergamum (vv. 14–16) and Thyatira (v. 20) for accepting rather than withstanding those disloyal to the truth and the standards of God's Word (see article on OVERSEERS AND THEIR DUTIES, p. 1690).

2:4 FORSAKEN YOUR FIRST LOVE. This refers to the Ephesians' first deep love for and devotion to Christ and his Word (Jn 14:15,21; 15:10). (1) This warning teaches us that knowing correct doctrine, obeying some of the commands, and worshiping in the church are not enough. The church must have above all a heartfelt love for Jesus Christ and all his Word (2Co 11:3; cf. Dt 10:12). (2) Sincere love for Christ results in single-hearted devotion to him, purity of life and a love of the truth (2Co 11:3; see 2Ch 30:6, note; Mt 22:37,39, notes; Jn 21:15, note).

2:5 REMOVE YOUR LAMPSTAND. Christ will reject any congregation or church and remove it from his kingdom if it does not repent of its declining love for and obedience to the Lord Jesus Christ.

pent[x] and do the things you did
at first. If you do not repent, I will
come to you and remove your
lampstand[y] from its place. 6But
you have this in your favor: You
hate the practices of the Nicolaitans,[z] which I also hate.
7He who has an ear, let him
hear[a] what the Spirit says to the
churches. To him who overcomes,[b] I will give the right to
eat from the tree of life,[c] which
is in the paradise[d] of God.

To the Church in Smyrna

8"To the angel of the church in Smyrna[e] write:

These are the words of him who
is the First and the Last,[f] who
died and came to life again.[g] 9I
know your afflictions and your
poverty—yet you are rich![h] I
know the slander of those who
say they are Jews and are not,[i]
but are a synagogue of Satan.[j]
10Do not be afraid of what you are
about to suffer. I tell you, the devil
will put some of you in prison to
test you,[k] and you will suffer persecution for ten days.[l] Be faithful,[m] even to the point of death,
and I will give you the crown of
life.[n]
11He who has an ear, let him
hear[o] what the Spirit says to the
churches. He who overcomes will
not be hurt at all by the second
death.[p]

To the Church in Pergamum

12"To the angel of the church in Pergamum[q] write: 

These are the words of him
who has the sharp, double-edged
sword.[r] 13I know where you
live—where Satan has his throne.
Yet you remain true to my name.
You did not renounce your faith in
me,[s] even in the days of Antipas,
my faithful witness,[t] who was
put to death in your city—where
Satan lives.[u]
14Nevertheless, I have a few
things against you:[v] You have

2:5 [x] ver 16,22; Rev 3:3,19 [y] Rev 1:20 **2:6** [z] ver 15 **2:7** [a] S Mt 11:15; ver 11,17,29; Rev 3:6,13,22; 13:9 [b] S Jn 16:33 [c] Ge 2:9; 3:22-24; Rev 22:2,14,19 [d] Lk 23:43 **2:8** [e] Rev 1:11 [f] S Rev 1:17 [g] Rev 1:18 **2:9** [h] 2Co 6:10; Jas 2:5 [i] Rev 3:9 [j] ver 13,24; S Mt 4:10 **2:10** [k] Rev 3:10 [l] Da 1:12,14 [m] ver 13; Rev 17:14 [n] S Mt 10:22; S 1Co 9:25 **2:11** [o] S ver 7 [p] Rev 20:6,14; 21:8 **2:12** [q] Rev 1:11 [r] ver 16; S Rev 1:16 **2:13** [s] Rev 14:12 [t] Rev 1:5; 11:3 [u] ver 9,24; S Mt 4:10 **2:14** [v] ver 20

2:6 YOU HATE THE PRACTICES OF THE NICOLAITANS, WHICH I ALSO HATE. The Nicolaitans (cf. v. 15) probably affirmed, as did the teaching of Balaam (see v. 14, note), that sexual immorality did not affect one's salvation in Christ. The NT clearly states the contrary; such persons will not inherit God's kingdom (1Co 6:9–10). God hates the heresy that teaches we can be saved and at the same time live immoral lives. To hate what God hates is an essential characteristic of those loyal to Christ (Ps 139:21; Pr 8:13; see Jn 3:19, note).

2:7 TO HIM WHO OVERCOMES. An overcomer (Gk *nikōn*) is one who, by God's grace received through faith in Christ, has experienced the new birth and remains constant in victory over sin, the world and Satan. (1) Surrounded by great opposition and rebellion, overcomers refuse to conform to the world and to any ungodliness within the visible church (v. 24). They hear and respond to what the Spirit says to the churches, remain faithful to Christ to the very end (v. 26) and accept only God's standard revealed in his holy Word (3:8).

(2) Overcomers in God's churches, and only the overcomers, will eat of the tree of life, will not be hurt by the second death (v. 11), will receive hidden manna and be given a new name in heaven (v. 17), will be given authority over the nations (v. 26), will not have their names removed from the book of life but will be honored by Christ before his Father and the angels (3:5), will remain with God in his temple and will bear the name of God, Christ and the new Jerusalem (3:12), will sit with Christ on his throne (3:21), and will be forever God's children (21:7).

(3) The secret of victory for overcomers is Christ's atoning death, their own faithful testimony about Jesus, and their perseverance in love for Christ even to death (12:11; cf. 1Jn 5:4). Note that we either overcome sin, the world and Satan, or we are overcome by them and are ultimately thrown into the lake of fire (v. 11; 3:5; 20:15; 21:8). There is no intermediate group.

2:9 POVERTY. Poverty (Gk *ptōcheia*) means "having nothing at all." The poverty of the Christians at Smyrna was extensive; they were economically destitute, yet Jesus says they were spiritually rich. Note the contrast to the Laodicean church, which had great material wealth, yet was considered spiritually "wretched, pitiful, poor" (3:17; cf. Mt 6:20; 2Co 6:10; Jas 2:5).

2:11 THE SECOND DEATH. This refers to eternal punishment, the lake of fire (cf. 20:6,14; 21:8), which only the faithful overcomer will escape (see v. 7, note).

2:13 WHERE SATAN HAS HIS THRONE. This may mean a place where the influence of Satan and evil was in great prominence, for Pergamum was a center of imperial worship.

2:14 THE TEACHING OF BALAAM. Balaam was a false prophet who sold his services to a heathen king and advised him to tempt Israel to compromise their faith by idolatry and immorality (Nu 22:5,7; 25:1–2; 31:16; see Nu 25:2, note; 2Pe 2:15, note). The teaching of Balaam therefore refers to corrupt teachers and preachers who were leading people into fatal compromise with immorality, worldliness and false ideologies, all for the sake of personal advancement or monetary gain. The church at Pergamum evidently had teachers

CHRIST'S MESSAGE TO THE SEVEN CHURCHES

***Rev 1:19–20** "Write, therefore, what you have seen, what is now and what will take place later. The mystery of the seven stars that you saw in my right hand and of the seven golden lampstands is this: The seven stars are the angels of the seven churches, and the seven lampstands are the seven churches."*

Christ's messages to seven local churches existing in western Asia Minor (see Rev 1:4, note) are intended for the exhortation, warning and edification of believers and churches throughout this entire age (cf. 2:7,11,17,29; 3:6,13,22). The value of these messages for churches today includes: (1) a revelation of what Jesus Christ himself loves and values in his churches as well as what he hates and condemns; (2) a clear statement from Christ regarding (a) the consequences of disobedience and spiritual neglect and (b) the rewards for spiritual vigilance and faithfulness to Christ; (3) a standard by which any church or individual may judge their true spiritual state before God; (4) an example of the methods of Satan's attack on the church or the individual Christian (see also Jdg 3:7, note). This article examines each of these aspects by using a question and answer format.

(1) What does Christ praise? Christ praises a church for not tolerating wicked persons (Rev 2:2); for testing the life, doctrine and claims of Christian leaders (2:2); for persevering in faith, love, witness, service and suffering for Christ (2:3,10,13,19,26); for hating what God hates (2:6); for overcoming sin, Satan and the ungodly world (2:7,11,17,26; 3:5,12,21); for refusing to conform to immorality in the world and worldliness in the church (2:24; 3:4); and for keeping God's Word (3:8,10).

(2) How does Christ reward churches that persevere and remain loyal to him and his Word? He rewards such churches (a) by delivering them from the time of trial that will come upon the whole world (3:10); (b) by giving them his love, presence and intimate fellowship (3:20); and (c) by blessing them with eternal life with God (Rev 2:11,17,26; 3:5,12; 21:7).

(3) What does Christ condemn? Christ condemns a church for diminishing an intimate personal devotion to himself and God (Rev 2:4); for departing from Biblical faith; for tolerating immoral church leaders, teachers or laypersons (2:14–15,20); for becoming spiritually dead (3:1) or lukewarm (3:15–16); and for substituting outward success and affluence (3:17) for real spirituality, i.e., purity, righteousness and spiritual wisdom (3:18).

(4) How does Christ punish churches that decline spiritually and tolerate immorality? He punishes such churches (a) by removing them from their place in God's kingdom (Rev 2:5; 3:16); (b) by causing them to lose God's presence, the genuine power of the Spirit, the true Biblical message of salvation and the protection of their members from Satan's destruction (Rev 2:5,16,22–23; 3:4,16; see Mt 13, notes concerning the good and the evil within the kingdom of heaven during this age); and (c) by placing their leaders under God's judgment (Rev 2:20–23).

(5) What does Christ's message reveal about the natural trend of churches toward spiritual stagnation, decline and apostasy? (a) The seven letters suggest that it is the inherent tendency of churches to err, to accept false teaching, and to adapt to the evil, anti-God elements of the world (see Gal 5:17, note). (b) In addition, we see that churches

are often affected by apostate, wicked and unfaithful people (Rev 2:2,14–15,20). For this reason a church's present spiritual state can never be taken as a valid test of God's will or as an ultimate justification for determining truth and sound doctrine. The gospel, i.e., the original message of Christ and the apostles, is the ultimate authority by which to measure truth and falsehood.

(6) How can churches avoid spiritual decline and the accompanying judgment by Christ? These letters reveal several ways. (a) First and foremost, all churches must be willing to "hear what the Spirit says to the churches" (Rev 2:5–7,16–17,21). The Word of Jesus Christ must always be the church's guide (1:1–5), for his Word, as revealed to the NT apostles through the Holy Spirit, is the guide by which churches must examine their beliefs and activities and renew their spiritual lives (2:7,11,17,29). (b) Churches must continually examine their spiritual condition before God and, if necessary, correct their degree of toleration of worldliness and immorality among their members (2:4,14–15,20; 3:1–2,14–17). (c) Spiritual decline can be halted in any church or group only if there is sincere repentance and a diligent return to the original love, truth, purity and power of Jesus Christ's Biblical revelation (2:5–7,16–17; 3:1–3,15–22).

THE SEVEN CHURCHES OF REVELATION

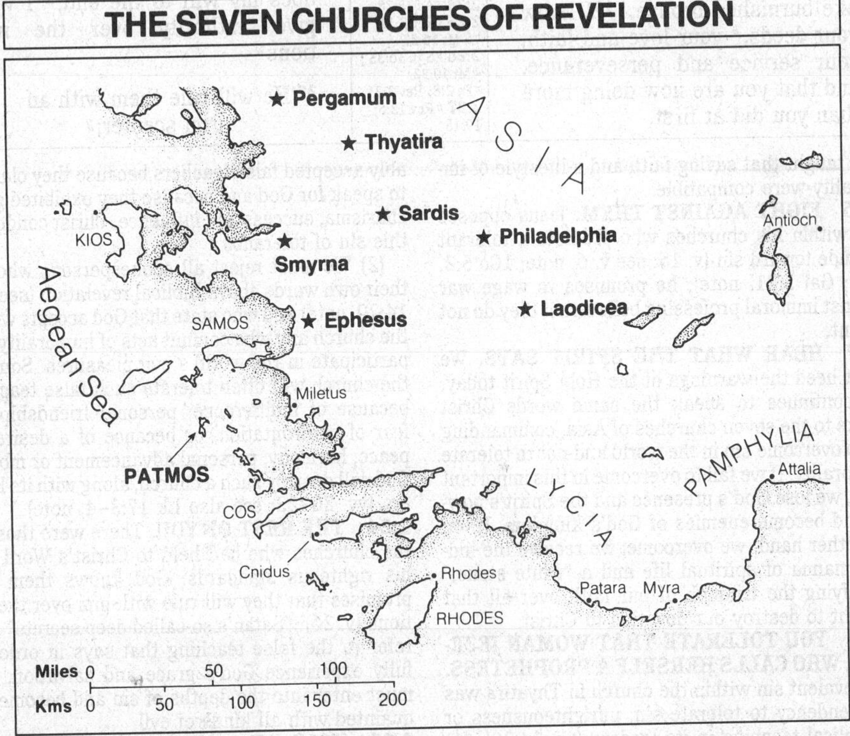

people there who hold to the
teaching of Balaam,[w] who taught
Balak to entice the Israelites to
sin by eating food sacrificed to
idols[x] and by committing sexual
immorality.[y] **15**Likewise you also
have those who hold to the teaching of the Nicolaitans.[z] **16**Repent[a] therefore! Otherwise, I will
soon come to you and will fight
against them with the sword of
my mouth.[b]
17He who has an ear, let him
hear[c] what the Spirit says to the
churches. To him who overcomes,[d] I will give some of the
hidden manna.[e] I will also give
him a white stone with a new
Rev 3:21-22 name[f] written on it, known only
to him who receives it.[g]

To the Church in Thyatira

18"To the angel of the church in Thyatira[h] write:

These are the words of the Son
of God,[i] whose eyes are like
blazing fire and whose feet are
like burnished bronze.[j] **19**I know
your deeds,[k] your love and faith,
your service and perseverance,
and that you are now doing more
than you did at first.
20Nevertheless, I have this
against you: You tolerate that
woman Jezebel,[l] who calls herself a prophetess. By her teaching
she misleads my servants into
sexual immorality and the eating
of food sacrificed to idols.[m] **21**I
have given her time[n] to repent of
her immorality, but she is unwilling.[o] **22**So I will cast her on a bed
of suffering, and I will make those
who commit adultery[p] with her
suffer intensely, unless they repent of her ways. **23**I will strike
her children dead. Then all the
churches will know that I am he
who searches hearts and minds,[q]
and I will repay each of you according to your deeds.[r] **24**Now I
say to the rest of you in Thyatira,
to you who do not hold to her
teaching and have not learned Satan's so-called deep secrets (I will
not impose any other burden on
you):[s] **25**Only hold on to what
you have[t] until I come.[u]
26To him who overcomes[v] and
does my will to the end,[w] I will
give authority over the nations[x]—
27'He will rule them with an
iron scepter;[y]

2:14 [w] S 2Pe 2:15 [x] S Ac 15:20 [y] 1Co 6:13
2:15 [z] ver 6
2:16 [a] S ver 5 [b] 2Th 2:8; S Rev 1:16
2:17 [c] S ver 7 [d] S Jn 16:33 [e] Jn 6:49,50 [f] Isa 56:5; 62:2; 65:15 [g] Rev 19:12
2:18 [h] ver 24; Ac 16:14; Rev 1:11 [i] S Mt 4:3 [j] S Rev 1:14,15
2:19 [k] S ver 2
2:20 [l] 1Ki 16:31; 21:25; 2Ki 9:7 [m] ver 14; S Ac 15:20
2:21 [n] Ro 2:4; 2Pe 3:9 [o] Ro 2:5; Rev 9:20; 16:9,11
2:22 [p] Rev 17:2; 18:9
2:23 [q] 1Sa 16:7; 1Ki 8:39; Ps 139:1,2,23; Pr 21:2; Jer 17:10; Lk 16:15; Ro 8:27; 1Th 2:4 [r] S Mt 16:27
2:24 [s] Ac 15:28
2:25 [t] Rev 3:11 [u] S Mt 16:27
2:26 [v] S Jn 16:33 [w] Mt 10:22 [x] Ps 2:8; Rev 3:21
2:27 [y] Rev 12:5; 19:15

---

who taught that saving faith and a lifestyle of immorality were compatible.

2:16 FIGHT AGAINST THEM. Jesus opposes any within his churches who promote a tolerant attitude toward sin (v. 15; see v. 6, note; 1Co 5:2, note; Gal 5:21, note); he promises to wage war against immoral professing believers if they do not repent.

2:17 HEAR WHAT THE SPIRIT SAYS. We must heed the warnings of the Holy Spirit today. He continues to speak the same words Christ spoke to the seven churches of Asia, commanding us to overcome sin in the world and not to tolerate immorality. If we fail to overcome in this important area, we lose God's presence and the Spirit's power and become enemies of God's kingdom. If, on the other hand, we overcome, we receive the hidden manna of spiritual life and a "white stone," signifying the triumph of our faith over all that sought to destroy our devotion to Christ.

2:20 YOU TOLERATE THAT WOMAN JEZEBEL, WHO CALLS HERSELF A PROPHETESS. A prevalent sin within the church in Thyatira was the tendency to tolerate sin, unrighteousness or unbiblical teaching in its leaders (vv. 14,20). (1) John calls one particular person Jezebel, a name derived from the OT Jezebel and synonymous with idolatry and persecution (1Ki 16:31; 19:1–3; 21:1–15; see 21:25, note). Some at Thyatira probably accepted false teachers because they claimed to speak for God and because they exhibited great charisma, success and influence. Christ condemns this sin of tolerance.

(2) We must reject all spokespersons who put their own words above Biblical revelation (see 1Co 14:29, note) and who state that God accepts within the church any who commit acts of immorality and participate in the world's evil pleasures. Some in the church will often tolerate such false teaching because of indifference, personal friendships or fear of confrontation, or because of a desire for peace, harmony, personal advancement or money. God will destroy such a church, along with its leaders (vv. 20–23; see also Lk 17:3–4, note).

2:24 THE REST OF YOU. There were those in the churches who had held to Christ's Word and his righteous standards. God knows them and promises that they will rule with him over the nations (v. 26). "Satan's so-called deep secrets" may refer to the false teaching that says in order to fully experience God's grace and salvation, one must enter into the depths of sin and become acquainted with all kinds of evil.

2:25 HOLD ON . . . UNTIL I COME. Christ's words "until I come" and "to the end" (v. 26) make it clear that his messages, warnings and promises to the seven churches apply also to all churches until the end.

he will dash them to
pieces like pottery'[e][z] —
just as I have received authority
from my Father. **28**I will also give
him the morning star.[a] **29**He who
has an ear, let him hear[b] what
the Spirit says to the churches.

To the Church in Sardis

3 "To the angel[f] of the church in
Sardis[c] write:

These are the words of him who
holds the seven spirits[g][d] of God
and the seven stars.[e] I know
your deeds;[f] you have a reputation of being alive, but you are
dead.[g] **2**Wake up! Strengthen
what remains and is about to die,
for I have not found your deeds
complete in the sight of my God.
3Remember, therefore, what you
have received and heard; obey it,
and repent.[h] But if you do not
wake up, I will come like a thief,[i]
and you will not know at what
time[j] I will come to you.
4Yet you have a few people in
Sardis who have not soiled their
clothes.[k] They will walk with me,
dressed in white,[l] for they are
worthy. **5**He who overcomes[m]
will, like them, be dressed in

2:27 [z]Ps 2:9; Isa 30:14; Jer 19:11
2:28 [a]Rev 22:16
2:29 [b]S ver 7
3:1 [c]Rev 1:11 [d]S Rev 1:4 [e]S Rev 1:16 [f]S Rev 2:2 [g]1Ti 5:6
3:3 [h]S Rev 2:5 [i]S Lk 12:39 [j]Lk 12:39
3:4 [k]Jude 23 [l]ver 5,18; Rev 4:4; 6:11; 7:9,13,14; 19:14
3:5 [m]S Jn 16:33 [n]S ver 4 [o]S Rev 20:12 [p]Mt 10:32
3:6 [q]S Rev 2:7
3:7 [r]Rev 1:11 [s]S Mk 1:24 [t]1Jn 5:20; Rev 6:10; 19:11 [u]Isa 22:22; Mt 16:19
3:8 [v]S Rev 2:2 [w]S Ac 14:27 [x]Rev 2:13
3:9 [y]Rev 2:9 [z]Rev 2:9 [a]Isa 49:23 [b]Isa 43:4; S Ro 8:37

white.[n] I will never blot out his
name from the book of life,[o] but
will acknowledge his name before
my Father[p] and his angels. **6**He
who has an ear, let him hear[q]
what the Spirit says to the
churches.

To the Church in Philadelphia

7"To the angel of the church in Philadelphia[r] write:

These are the words of him who
is holy[s] and true,[t] who holds
the key of David.[u] What he opens
no one can shut, and what he
shuts no one can open. **8**I know
your deeds.[v] See, I have placed
before you an open door[w] that no
one can shut. I know that you
have little strength, yet you have
kept my word and have not denied
my name.[x] **9**I will make those
who are of the synagogue of Satan,[y] who claim to be Jews
though they are not,[z] but are liars—I will make them come and
fall down at your feet[a] and acknowledge that I have loved
you.[b] **10**Since you have kept my
command to endure patiently, I

[e] *27* Psalm 2:9 [f] *1* Or *messenger*; also in verses 7 and 14 [g] *1* Or *the sevenfold Spirit*

3:1 YOU ARE DEAD. The church in Sardis was spiritually dead, with only a few of its members remaining faithful to the gospel. Outwardly it appeared alive and active and had a reputation of success and spirituality. It may have had an exciting form of worship, but not the true power and righteousness of the Holy Spirit. But Jesus saw the inner lives and hearts of the people.

3:4 A FEW PEOPLE IN SARDIS. Throughout church history, there have always been a few (i.e., a remnant) who have not "soiled their clothes" and who have sought to return to the simplicity and purity of devotion to Christ that the apostles and many others in the NT knew (2Co 11:3).

3:5 BLOT OUT HIS NAME. Clearly any person who experiences the new birth, but later refuses to persevere in faith and to overcome, will have his or her name taken out of the book of life (see 2:7, note). To have one's name blotted out of the book of life is to lose eternal life itself (2:7,10–11) and to be condemned to the lake of fire in the end (20:15). This is what the Spirit says to the churches (v. 6; 13:8; 17:8; 20:12; 21:27; cf. Ex 32:32).

3:7 PHILADELPHIA. Philadelphia was a faithful church that kept Christ's Word and did not deny him. They had endured opposition from the world and resisted conforming to the evil trends of other churches, yet had persevered in loyalty to Christ and the truth of the NT gospel (vv. 7–10). Because of their persevering faithfulness, God promises to deliver them from the hour of trial (see next note).

3:10 THE HOUR OF TRIAL. Christ's promise to keep the faithful in Philadelphia from the hour of trial is identical to Paul's promise to the Thessalonians that they would be rescued from the "coming wrath" (1Th 1:10); it extends to all of God's faithful throughout the ages (vv. 13,22). This hour includes the divinely appointed time of trial, wrath and distress that will come on "the whole world" in the last years of this age, just prior to the establishment of Christ's kingdom on earth (5:10; 6–19; 20:4). Concerning this time, the Bible reveals the following truths.

(1) This time of trial involves God's wrath on the ungodly (chs. 6—19; Isa 13:6–13; 17:4–11; Da 9:27; 12:1; Zec 14:1–4; Mt 24:9–31; see 1Th 5:2, note; see article on THE GREAT TRIBULATION, p. 1456).

(2) Also included in this time of trial, however, is Satan's wrath on the godly, i.e., on those accepting Christ during this terrible time. For them there will be hunger, thirst, exposure to elements (7:16), and great suffering and tears (7:9–17; Da 12:10; Mt 24:15–21). They will experience indirectly the

will also keep you[c] from the hour
of trial that is going to come upon
the whole world[d] to test[e] those
who live on the earth.[f]
11 I am coming soon.[g] Hold on
to what you have,[h] so that no one
will take your crown.[i] 12 Him
who overcomes[j] I will make a
pillar[k] in the temple of my God.
Never again will he leave it. I will
write on him the name of my
God[l] and the name of the city of
my God,[m] the new Jerusalem,[n]
which is coming down out of heav-
en from my God; and I will also
write on him my new name. 13 He
who has an ear, let him hear[o]
what the Spirit says to the
churches.

To the Church in Laodicea

14 "To the angel of the church in Laodicea[p] write:

These are the words of the
Amen, the faithful and true witness,[q] the ruler of God's creation.[r] 15 I know your deeds,[s]
that you are neither cold nor
hot.[t] I wish you were either one
or the other! 16 So, because you
are lukewarm—neither hot nor
cold—I am about to spit you out
of my mouth. 17 You say, 'I am
rich; I have acquired wealth and
do not need a thing.'[u] But you do
not realize that you are wretched,
pitiful, poor, blind and naked.[v]
18 I counsel you to buy from me
gold refined in the fire,[w] so you
can become rich; and white
clothes[x] to wear, so you can cover your shameful nakedness;[y]
and salve to put on your eyes, so
you can see.
19 Those whom I love I rebuke
and discipline.[z] So be earnest,
and repent.[a] 20 Here I am! I stand
at the door[b] and knock. If anyone
hears my voice and opens the
door,[c] I will come in[d] and eat
with him, and he with me.
21 To him who overcomes,[e] I
will give the right to sit with me
on my throne,[f] just as I overcame[g] and sat down with my Father on his throne. 22 He who has
an ear, let him hear[h] what the
Spirit says to the churches."

3:10 [c] 2Pe 2:9 [d] S Mt 24:14 [e] Rev 2:10 [f] Rev 6:10; 8:13; 11:10; 13:8,14; 17:8
3:11 [g] S Mt 16:27 [h] Rev 2:25 [i] S 1Co 9:25
3:12 [j] S Jn 16:33 [k] Gal 2:9 [l] Rev 14:1; 22:4 [m] Eze 48:35 [n] Gal 4:26; Rev 21:2,10
3:13 [o] S Rev 2:7
3:14 [p] S Col 2:1; Rev 1:11 [q] Jn 18:37; Rev 1:5 [r] Pr 8:22; Jn 1:3; Col 1:16,18
3:15 [s] S Rev 2:2 [t] Ro 12:11
3:17 [u] Hos 12:8; 1Co 4:8 [v] Pr 13:7
3:18 [w] S 1Pe 1:7 [x] S ver 4 [y] Rev 16:15
3:19 [z] Dt 8:5; Pr 3:12; 1Co 11:32; Heb 12:5,6 [a] S Rev 2:5
3:20 [b] Mt 24:33; Jas 5:9 [c] Lk 12:36 [d] S Ro 8:10
3:21 [e] S Jn 16:33 [f] S Mt 19:28 [g] Rev 5:5
3:22 [h] S Rev 2:7

natural catastrophes of war, famine and death. They will be persecuted, tortured, and many will suffer martyrdom (6:11; 13:7; 14:13). They will undergo the ravages of Satan and demonic forces (9:3–5; 12:12), evil and violence from wicked people, and persecution by the antichrist (6:9; 12:17; 13:15–17). They will suffer loss of home and will need to flee in fear (Mt 24:15–21). It will be an especially disastrous time for those with families and children (Mt 24:19), so terrible that the tribulation saints who die are counted blessed, for they rest from their labor and are free from persecution (14:13).

(3) For those who are overcomers before that day arrives (see 2:7, note; Lk 21:36, note), God will keep them from that hour of trial, most likely through the rapture, i.e., the catching up of the faithful to meet Christ in the air before God pours out his wrath (see Jn 14:3, note; see article on THE RAPTURE, p. 1864). This deliverance is a reward for those who persevere in keeping God's Word in true faith.

(4) Present-day believers who hope to escape all these things that are going to come on the world will do so only by faithfulness to Christ and his Word and by constant vigilance in prayer (see Lk 21:36, note), so that they will not be deceived (see Mt 24:5, note).

3:11 I AM COMING SOON. The close connection of this verse with v. 10 indicates (1) that Christ's coming to take up his church from the earth will be the means of their deliverance (cf. 1Th 1:10; 4:14–18), and (2) that rescue from the hour of trial and tribulation will come only to those faithful of the churches who hold on to Christ and his Word (v. 8).

3:15–16 NEITHER COLD NOR HOT . . . LUKEWARM. This describes the spiritual condition of the church in Laodicea. (1) A lukewarm church is one that compromises with the world and resembles its surrounding society; it professes Christianity, yet in reality is spiritually wretched and pitiful (vv. 17–18). (2) Christ severely warns the church about his judgment against spiritual lukewarmness (vv. 15–17). (3) Christ sincerely invites the church to repent and be restored to a place of faith, righteousness, revelation and fellowship (vv. 18–19). (4) In the midst of a lukewarm church age, Christ's promises to overcoming churches remain valid. He will come to them in blessing and in the power of the Spirit (vv. 20–22), opening a door that no one can shut, so that they may glorify his name and proclaim the everlasting gospel (v. 8).

3:20 IF ANYONE HEARS MY VOICE. In its self-sufficient prosperity and worldliness (vv. 15–18), the church in Laodicea had excluded the Lord Jesus Christ from its congregations. Christ's invitation, spoken from outside the door, is a request for fellowship with any individual who will repent of and overcome the spiritual lukewarmness of the church (v. 21).

3:22 THE SPIRIT . . . THE CHURCHES. The distinction between the churches and the Holy Spirit must be continually affirmed. Churches are subordinate to the Spirit of God and to his inspired

The Throne in Heaven

4 After this I looked, and there before me was a door standing
open[i] in heaven. And the voice I had
first heard speaking to me like a trumpet[j] said, "Come up here,[k] and I will
show you what must take place after
this."[l] **2** At once I was in the Spirit,[m]
and there before me was a throne in
heaven[n] with someone sitting on it.
3 And the one who sat there had the appearance of jasper[o] and carnelian.[p]
A rainbow,[q] resembling an emerald,[r]
encircled the throne. **4** Surrounding the
throne were twenty-four other thrones,
and seated on them were twenty-four
elders.[s] They were dressed in white[t]
and had crowns of gold on their heads.
5 From the throne came flashes of lightning, rumblings and peals of thunder.[u] Before the throne, seven
lamps[v] were blazing. These are the
seven spirits[h][w] of God. **6** Also before
the throne there was what looked like
a sea of glass,[x] clear as crystal.
In the center, around the throne,
were four living creatures,[y] and they
were covered with eyes, in front and in
back.[z] **7** The first living creature was
like a lion, the second was like an ox,
the third had a face like a man, the
fourth was like a flying eagle.[a]
8 Each of the four living creatures[b]
had six wings[c] and was covered with
eyes all around,[d] even under his
wings. Day and night[e] they never stop
saying:

"Holy, holy, holy
is the Lord God Almighty,[f]
who was, and is, and is to come."[g]

9 Whenever the living creatures give
glory, honor and thanks to him who
sits on the throne[h] and who lives for
ever and ever,[i] **10** the twenty-four elders[j] fall down before him[k] who sits
on the throne,[l] and worship him
who lives for ever and ever. They
lay their crowns before the throne
and say:

11 "You are worthy, our Lord and
God,

4:1 [i]S Mt 3:16 [j]Rev 1:10 [k]Rev 11:12 [l]Rev 1:19; 22:6 **4:2** [m]S Rev 1:10 [n]ver 9,10; 1Ki 22:19; Isa 6:1; Eze 1:26-28; Da 7:9; Rev 20:11 **4:3** [o]Rev 21:11 [p]Rev 21:20 [q]Eze 1:28; Rev 10:1 [r]Rev 21:19 **4:4** [s]ver 10; Rev 5:6,8,14; 11:16; 19:4 [t]S Rev 3:4,5 **4:5** [u]Ex 19:16; Rev 8:5; 11:19; 16:18 [v]Zec 4:2 [w]S Rev 1:4 **4:6** [x]Rev 15:2 [y]ver 8,9; Eze 1:5; Rev 5:6; 6:1; 7:11; 14:3; 15:7; 19:4 [z]Eze 1:18; 10:12 **4:7** [a]Eze 1:10; 10:14 **4:8** [b]S ver 6 [c]Isa 6:2 [d]Eze 1:18 [e]Rev 14:11 [f]Isa 6:3; S Rev 1:8 [g]S Rev 1:4 **4:9** [h]ver 2; Ps 47:8; S Rev 5:1 [i]S Rev 1:18 **4:10** [j]S ver 4 [k]Dt 33:3; Rev 5:8, 14; 7:11; 11:16 [l]S ver 2

[h]5 Or *the sevenfold Spirit*

Word (2Ti 3:15–16; 1Pe 1:24–25; 2Pe 1:20–21). This distinction between the Spirit and the churches can be expressed by the following Biblical truths. (1) The Spirit is not the possession of the churches or any human institution. He is the Spirit of God and of Christ, not the Spirit of the churches (v. 1). The Spirit remains free to come and leave according to God's righteous standards (cf. Jn 1:33; 7:39; 14:17).

(2) The Holy Spirit represents Christ's present lordship over the churches. The Spirit and his Word are the ultimate authority. Churches must constantly judge their beliefs and actions by the Spirit. They must never trust in, obey and listen to themselves alone. The Spirit and the inspired Word are greater than the churches of history.

(3) The Holy Spirit will remain with any church only as long as it remains faithful to Christ and his Word and hears what the Spirit says to the churches (2:5,16,22–23; 3:3,15–16).

4:1 AFTER THIS. Many Bible expositors believe that at this point in Revelation, Christ has already taken the faithful overcomers of his churches out of the world. Thus, the catching up of the true church (see Jn 14:3, note; see article on THE RAPTURE, p. 1864) precedes the tribulation period (chs. 6–18). This is believed for the following reasons: (1) Beginning with 4:1, the terms "church" or "churches" disappear until 22:16. (2) The bride of Christ (i.e., the church) appears in ch. 19 already with Christ in heaven before he returns to earth to judge the wicked and to reign in the millennial kingdom (see 20:4, note). (3) The promise given to the Philadelphia church to keep it from the hour of worldwide trial pertains to all believers who stand true to Christ before the tribulation (see 3:10, note).

4:4 TWENTY-FOUR ELDERS. Who are these elders? Some believe they represent the entire church in heaven (see Jn 14:3, note; 2Ti 4:8; 1Pe 5:4). Others believe they may be ruling angels; note, however, that angels stand around the elders (7:11; cf. 5:8–10). Still others believe they represent Israel and the church joined in worship to God and the Lamb, i.e., the combining of 12 (Israel) and 12 (the church) equals 24 (God's people of both ages).

4:5 SEVEN SPIRITS OF GOD. The seven spirits of God represent the presence of the Holy Spirit at God's throne. The language may come from the sevenfold expression of the Spirit in Isa 11:2. The Holy Spirit is like a burning fire filled with judgment against sin and with God's purity (cf. Isa 4:4; Jn 16:8).

4:6 FOUR LIVING CREATURES. These four creatures probably represent the entire living creation (v. 7). All of God's living creatures will bring glory and honor to him in heaven and be redeemed from the curse of sin (vv. 8–11).

4:8 HOLY, HOLY, HOLY. The entire creation emphasizes and praises God's holiness (see article on PRAISE, p. 770). To be holy means to be separated from sin, unrighteousness and evil, and to be dedicated to righteousness, goodness, justice and purity. Holiness is an eternal attribute of God; his holiness will never change (see Isa 6:1,3, notes; see article on THE ATTRIBUTES OF GOD, p. 882).

to receive glory and honor and
power,[m]
for you created all things,
and by your will they were
created
and have their being."[n]

The Scroll and the Lamb

5 Then I saw in the right hand of him
who sat on the throne[o] a scroll
with writing on both sides[p] and
sealed[q] with seven seals. **2**And I saw
a mighty angel[r] proclaiming in a loud
voice, "Who is worthy to break the
seals and open the scroll?" **3**But no one
in heaven or on earth or under the
earth could open the scroll or even
look inside it. **4**I wept and wept because no one was found who was worthy to open the scroll or look inside.
5Then one of the elders said to me, "Do
not weep! See, the Lion[s] of the tribe
of Judah,[t] the Root of David,[u] has triumphed. He is able to open the scroll
and its seven seals."

6Then I saw a Lamb,[v] looking as if
it had been slain, standing in the center of the throne, encircled by the four
living creatures[w] and the elders.[x] He
had seven horns and seven eyes,[y]
which are the seven spirits[i][z] of God
sent out into all the earth. **7**He came
and took the scroll from the right hand
of him who sat on the throne.[a] **8**And
when he had taken it, the four living
creatures[b] and the twenty-four elders[c] fell down before the Lamb. Each
one had a harp[d] and they were holding
golden bowls full of incense, which are
the prayers[e] of the saints. **9**And they
sang a new song:[f]

"You are worthy[g] to take the
scroll
and to open its seals,
because you were slain,
and with your blood[h] you
purchased[i] men for God
from every tribe and language
and people and nation.[j]
10You have made them to be a
kingdom and priests[k] to
serve our God,
and they will reign on the
earth."[l]

11Then I looked and heard the voice
of many angels, numbering thousands
upon thousands, and ten thousand
times ten thousand.[m] They encircled
the throne and the living creatures[n]
and the elders.[o] **12**In a loud voice they
sang:

"Worthy is the Lamb,[p] who was
slain,[q]
to receive power and wealth and
wisdom and strength
and honor and glory and praise!"[r]

13Then I heard every creature in
heaven and on earth and under the
earth[s] and on the sea, and all that is
in them, singing:

"To him who sits on the throne[t]
and to the Lamb[u]
be praise and honor and glory and
power,
for ever and ever!"[v]

14The four living creatures[w] said,
"Amen,"[x] and the elders[y] fell down
and worshiped.[z]

4:11 m Rev 1:6; 5:12 n Ac 14:15; Rev 10:6
5:1 o ver 7,13; Rev 4:2,9; 6:16 p Eze 2:9,10 q Isa 29:11; Da 12:4
5:2 r Rev 10:1
5:5 s Ge 49:9 t S Heb 7:14 u Isa 11:1,10; Ro 15:12; Rev 22:16
5:6 v ver 8,9,12, 13; S Jn 1:29 w S Rev 4:6 x S Rev 4:4 y Zec 4:10 z S Rev 1:4
5:7 a S ver 1
5:8 b S Rev 4:6 c S Rev 4:4 d Rev 14:2; 15:2 e Ps 141:2; Rev 8:3,4
5:9 f Ps 40:3; 98:1; 149:1; Isa 42:10; Rev 14:3,4
g Rev 4:11 h Heb 9:12 i S 1Co 6:20 j S Rev 13:7
5:10 k S 1Pe 2:5 l Rev 3:21; 20:4
5:11 m Da 7:10; Heb 12:22; Jude 14 n S Rev 4:6 o S Rev 4:4
5:12 p ver 13 q ver 9 r Rev 1:6; 4:11
5:13 s ver 3; Php 2:10 t S ver 1, 7 u ver 6; Rev 6:16; 7:10 v 1Ch 29:11; Mal 1:6; 2:2; S Ro 11:36
5:14 w S Rev 4:6 x Rev 4:9 y S Rev 4:4 z Rev 4:10

i 6 Or *the sevenfold Spirit*

5:1 A SCROLL. This scroll is of utmost importance, for it contains the revelation of what God has determined for the future course of the world and humanity. It describes how the world will be judged and portrays the final triumph of God and his people over all evil. When each seal is opened, a portion of the book's content is revealed in a vision (ch. 6; cf. Eze 2:9–10).

5:4 I WEPT AND WEPT. John weeps because he knows that if a worthy person is not found to open the book, God's purpose of judgment and blessing for the world will remain unfulfilled.

5:5 THE LION OF THE TRIBE OF JUDAH. Christ is pictured as a Lion, indicating he will rule all the earth. He is from the tribe of Judah and the family of David. These titles of Jesus as the conquering Messiah (Ge 49:9–10) and eternal king accord with the promises made to David (Isa 11:1,10).

5:6 AS IF IT HAD BEEN SLAIN. Christ, appearing as a Lamb that bears the marks of having been slain, represents his giving of himself on the cross for the sins of the human race. It signifies that Christ's worthiness, power, authority and victory come from his sacrificial death (vv. 9–14). "Lamb" is Revelation's foremost symbol for Christ (e.g., vv. 6–7; 12:11; 15:3; 17:14; 21:22; 22:1,3). Christ's judgment is on those who rejected his sacrifice as the Lamb of God (6:16–17). The "seven horns" represent the power and strength of a ruler (1Ki 22:11; Da 7:24); for "seven spirits," see 4:5, note.

5:8 THE PRAYERS OF SAINTS. This refers to the intercession of the saints for the coming of the kingdom when they will reign on earth (vv. 9–10). Their prayer is, "Your kingdom come, your will be done on earth as it is in heaven" (Mt 6:10; see 6:6, note; 2Pe 3:12, note; cf. Ps 141:2).

The Seals

6 I watched as the Lamb[a] opened
the first of the seven seals.[b] Then
I heard one of the four living creatures[c] say in a voice like thunder,[d]
"Come!" **2**I looked, and there before me
was a white horse![e] Its rider held a
bow, and he was given a crown,[f] and
he rode out as a conqueror bent on conquest.[g]
3When the Lamb opened the second
seal, I heard the second living creature[h] say, "Come!" **4**Then another
horse came out, a fiery red one.[i] Its
rider was given power to take peace
from the earth[j] and to make men slay
each other. To him was given a large
sword.
5When the Lamb opened the third
seal, I heard the third living creature[k]
say, "Come!" I looked, and there before
me was a black horse![l] Its rider was
holding a pair of scales in his hand.
6Then I heard what sounded like a
voice among the four living creatures,[m] saying, "A quart[j] of wheat for
a day's wages,[k] and three quarts of
barley for a day's wages,[k][n] and do
not damage[o] the oil and the wine!"
7When the Lamb opened the fourth
seal, I heard the voice of the fourth living creature[p] say, "Come!" **8**I looked,
and there before me was a pale
horse![q] Its rider was named Death,
and Hades[r] was following close behind him. They were given power over
a fourth of the earth to kill by sword,
famine and plague, and by the wild
beasts of the earth.[s]
9When he opened the fifth seal, I
saw under[t] the altar[u] the souls of
those who had been slain[v] because of
the word of God[w] and the testimony
they had maintained. **10**They called out
in a loud voice, "How long,[x] Sovereign
Lord,[y] holy and true,[z] until you judge

6:1 [a] S Rev 5:6 [b] Rev 5:1 [c] S Rev 4:6,7 [d] Rev 14:2; 19:6 **6:2** [e] Zec 1:8; 6:3; Rev 19:11 [f] Zec 6:11; Rev 14:14; 19:12 [g] Ps 45:4 **6:3** [h] Rev 4:7 **6:4** [i] Zec 1:8; 6:2 [j] Mt 10:34 **6:5** [k] Rev 4:7 [l] Zec 6:2 **6:6** [m] S Rev 4:6,7 [n] Eze 4:16 [o] Rev 7:1,3; 9:4 **6:7** [p] Rev 4:7 **6:8** [q] Zec 6:3 [r] Hos 13:14; Rev 1:18; 20:13,14 [s] Jer 15:2,3; 24:10; Eze 5:12,17 **6:9** [t] Ex 29:12; Lev 4:7 [u] Rev 14:18; 16:7 [v] Rev 20:4 [w] Ro 1:2; S Heb 4:12 **6:10** [x] Ps 119:84; Zec 1:12 [y] Lk 2:29; 2Pe 2:1 [z] S Rev 3:7

j 6 Greek *a choinix* (probably about a liter)
k 6 Greek *a denarius*

6:1 THE LAMB OPENED. Jesus Christ himself (i.e., the Lamb) opens all the seals, which disclose God's devastating judgments on the world (vv. 1, 3,5,7,9,12). The judgments are divine in origin, for they have been given into Christ's hands (5:1,7; cf. Jn 5:22). Throughout the book of Revelation, the plague judgments are called God's wrath (vv. 16–17; 11:18; 14:10,19; 15:1,7; 16:1,19; 19:15).

6:1 THE FIRST OF THE SEVEN SEALS. Some interpreters understand the opening of the first seal as the beginning of the seven-year tribulation, that future time of unprecedented suffering and judgment leading up to Christ's second coming (see Da 9:27; cf. Jer 30:7; Da 12:1; Rev 6:17; 7:14; see article on THE GREAT TRIBULATION, p. 1456). Others believe the seals describe the final three and one-half years of the seven-year tribulation, often called the great tribulation. Still others see them as the beginning of God's judgment toward the end of the age. God's judgments are revealed in successive series. The first series is the seven seals (ch. 6); the second, the seven trumpet judgments (chs. 8–9; 11:15–19); and the third, the "seven bowls of God's wrath" (ch. 16; see 8:1, note).

6:2 A WHITE HORSE. Four horsemen come out as the first four seals are opened (cf. Zec 1:8–17; 6:1–8), representing God's judgment on the corrupt and evil world system and the ungodly. The rider of the white horse is thought by many Bible interpreters to be the antichrist (1Jn 2:18), the future world ruler who is to begin his activity at the beginning of the last seven years (see article on THE AGE OF THE ANTICHRIST, p. 1872). He is allowed by God to deceive all who oppose Christ. His initial conquest will be accomplished without open warfare, for peace is taken from the earth beginning with the second horseman (v. 4; cf. Da 9:26–27; 1Th 5:3). On the other hand, all the other horsemen are personifications, so the rider on the white horse may simply represent conquest or a strong spirit of antichrist let loose in the end time.

6:4 HORSE . . . FIERY RED ONE. The red horse and its rider represent war and violent death, which God will allow in bringing his wrath on the world (cf. Zec 1:8; 6:2). The tribulation will be a time of violence, murder and war.

6:5 A BLACK HORSE. The black horse and its rider symbolize great famine (cf. Jer 4:26–28; La 4:8–9; 5:10). Basic necessities of life will be scarce and prices extremely high; hunger will spread throughout the world. The oil and wine refer to the olive tree and grapevine, which are not hurt as much by drought as the grain. Though famines have occurred throughout the church age (Mt 24:7), this passage is dealing with a specific famine during the tribulation.

6:8 A PALE HORSE. The pale horse and its rider named Death symbolize a terrible intensification of war, famine, death, plagues, disease and evil beasts. This judgment will be so terrible that one-fourth of the human race will be killed.

6:9 SLAIN BECAUSE OF THE WORD OF GOD. When the fifth seal is opened, John sees what is happening in heaven. Those "slain because of the word of God" are those who are martyred for their faith in Christ and the truth of his Word. (1) They are told to have patience, for many more will yet die for their faith (cf. 7:13–14; 13:15; 18:24; 20:4). (2) The period of tribulation will be a terrible time of persecution for those who accept the gospel and remain faithful to God and his Word (see 3:10, note; 7:9, note; 14:6, note). Perhaps all the martyrs of past ages are included among those under the altar.

6:10 JUDGE . . . AND AVENGE OUR BLOOD.

the inhabitants of the earth[a] and
avenge our blood?"[b] 11Then each of
them was given a white robe,[c] and
they were told to wait a little longer,
until the number of their fellow servants and brothers who were to be
killed as they had been was completed.[d]
12I watched as he opened the sixth
seal. There was a great earthquake.[e]
The sun turned black[f] like sackcloth[g] made of goat hair, the whole
moon turned blood red, 13and the stars
in the sky fell to earth,[h] as late figs
drop from a fig tree[i] when shaken by
a strong wind. 14The sky receded like
a scroll, rolling up,[j] and every mountain and island was removed from its
place.[k]
15Then the kings of the earth, the
princes, the generals, the rich, the
mighty, and every slave and every free
man[l] hid in caves and among the
rocks of the mountains.[m] 16They
called to the mountains and the rocks,
"Fall on us[n] and hide us from the face
of him who sits on the throne[o] and
from the wrath of the Lamb! 17For the
great day[p] of their wrath has come,
and who can stand?"[q]

144,000 Sealed

7 After this I saw four angels standing at the four corners[r] of the
earth, holding back the four winds[s] of
the earth to prevent[t] any wind from
blowing on the land or on the sea or on
any tree. 2Then I saw another angel
coming up from the east, having the
seal[u] of the living God.[v] He called
out in a loud voice to the four angels
who had been given power to harm the
land and the sea:[w] 3"Do not harm[x]
the land or the sea or the trees until we
put a seal on the foreheads[y] of the
servants of our God." 4Then I heard the
number[z] of those who were sealed:
144,000[a] from all the tribes of Israel.

5From the tribe of Judah 12,000
were sealed,
from the tribe of Reuben 12,000,
from the tribe of Gad 12,000,
6from the tribe of Asher 12,000,

6:10 [a]S Rev 3:10 [b]Dt 32:43; 2Ki 9:7; Ps 79:10; Rev 16:6; 18:20; 19:2 **6:11** [c]S Rev 3:4 [d]Heb 11:40 **6:12** [e]Ps 97:4; Isa 29:6; Eze 38:19; Rev 8:5; 11:13; 16:18 [f]S Mt 24:29 [g]Isa 50:3 **6:13** [h]S Mt 24:29; Rev 8:10; 9:1 [i]Isa 34:4 **6:14** [j]S 2Pe 3:10; Rev 20:11; 21:1 [k]Ps 46:2; Isa 54:10; Jer 4:24; Eze 38:20; Na 1:5; Rev 16:20; 21:1 **6:15** [l]Rev 19:18 [m]Isa 2:10,19,21 **6:16** [n]Hos 10:8; Lk 23:30 [o]S Rev 5:1 **6:17** [p]Joel 1:15; 2:1,2,11,31; Zep 1:14,15; Rev 16:14 [q]Ps 76:7; Na 1:6; Mal 3:2 **7:1** [r]Isa 11:12 [s]Jer 49:36; Eze 37:9; Da 7:2; Zec 6:5; Mt 24:31 [t]S Rev 6:6 **7:2** [u]Rev 9:4 [v]S Mt 16:16 [w]ver 1

7:3 [x]S Rev 6:6 [y]Eze 9:4; Rev 9:4; 14:1; 22:4 **7:4** [z]Rev 9:16 [a]Rev 14:1,3

Those in heaven pray that the wicked who have rejected God and killed his followers will receive divine justice. There are times when God leads his people to pray for justice to prevail, for evil to be destroyed, for righteousness to be established on earth, and for Christ to be exalted above all those who oppose him. The prayer is not for personal vengeance, for it comes out of a concern for God, righteousness and the suffering of his people.

6:11 BROTHERS WHO WERE TO BE KILLED. Some people will be given the opportunity to be saved during the tribulation, namely, those on earth who had never adequately heard or understood the gospel. But those who heard the gospel before the rapture of the church and yet continued to live in sin will be given no further opportunity for salvation after the church is taken out of the world (see article on THE RAPTURE, p. 1864). God will send them a powerful delusion, that they may never believe again (see 2Th 2:10–12, notes).

6:12 GREAT EARTHQUAKE. The catastrophic judgments of God portrayed here involve a physical shaking of the world, cosmic upheaval, and great darkness and terror for earth's inhabitants (vv. 15–17; cf. Isa 34:4; Joel 2:30–31; Hag 2:6; Mt 24:29). This is not the end of the tribulation. There is yet a seventh seal (ch. 8).

6:16 FALL ON US. The ungodly who are left behind after believers are caught up from the earth to meet the Lord in the air (1Th 4:17) will experience intense fear and despair as they attempt to run and hide.

6:16 THE WRATH OF THE LAMB. The Lamb's wrath portrayed in chs. 6–19 should alert all readers to see the extent that God hates sin, immorality and impenitent wickedness. It is identical with the wrath of God (cf. 15:7; see Ro 1:18, note; Heb 1:9, note). The faithful of Christ's churches are not appointed to suffer God's wrath (1Th 5:9), for Jesus has promised to rescue them from the coming wrath (see 3:10, note; 1Th 1:10, note; see article on THE RAPTURE, p. 1864).

7:1 I SAW FOUR ANGELS. Ch. 7 is an interlude between the sixth and seventh seals, revealing those who became faithful to Christ during the great tribulation. Those who take their stand for God (6:17) are both Jew (vv. 3–8) and non-Jew (vv. 9–10,13–15). They accept the everlasting gospel proclaimed by angels (14:6).

7:2 SEAL OF THE LIVING GOD. The seal was a tool or ring that stamped an owner's mark of identification on something. God's seal on a person identifies that person as belonging to God and under his care (cf. Eph 1:13).

7:4 144,000 FROM ALL THE TRIBES OF ISRAEL. The 144,000 are described as servants of God (v. 3) from the tribes of Israel (vv. 4–8). God will put a seal or mark on their foreheads to indicate consecration and ownership (cf. 9:4; Eze 9:1–6; 2Ti 2:19). (1) Some Bible interpreters believe these new believers from the tribes of Israel will be commissioned and empowered by the Spirit to preach the gospel during the tribulation days. (2) Their being sealed by God does not mean they are protected from physical death or from martyrdom resulting from Satan's persecution (v. 14). However, they are protected from God's direct judgment and from demonic affliction (9:4).

from the tribe of Naphtali 12,000,
from the tribe of Manasseh 12,000,
7from the tribe of Simeon 12,000,
from the tribe of Levi 12,000,
from the tribe of Issachar 12,000,
8from the tribe of Zebulun 12,000,
from the tribe of Joseph 12,000,
from the tribe of Benjamin 12,000.

The Great Multitude in White Robes

9After this I looked and there before
me was a great multitude that no one
could count, from every nation, tribe,
people and language,[b] standing before the throne[c] and in front of the
Lamb. They were wearing white
robes[d] and were holding palm
branches in their hands. 10And they
cried out in a loud voice:

"Salvation belongs to our God,[e]
who sits on the throne,[f]
and to the Lamb."

11All the angels were standing around
the throne and around the elders[g] and
the four living creatures.[h] They fell
down on their faces[i] before the throne
and worshiped God, 12saying:

"Amen!
Praise and glory
and wisdom and thanks and honor
and power and strength
be to our God for ever and ever.
Amen!"[j]

13Then one of the elders asked me,
"These in white robes[k]—who are
they, and where did they come from?"
14I answered, "Sir, you know."
And he said, "These are they who
have come out of the great tribulation;
they have washed their robes[l] and
made them white in the blood of the
Lamb.[m] 15Therefore,

"they are before the throne of God[n]
and serve him[o] day and night
in his temple;[p]
and he who sits on the throne[q]
will spread his tent over them.[r]
16Never again will they hunger;
never again will they thirst.[s]
The sun will not beat upon them,
nor any scorching heat.[t]
17For the Lamb at the center of the
throne will be their shepherd;[u]
he will lead them to springs of
living water.[v]
And God will wipe away every tear
from their eyes."[w]

The Seventh Seal and the Golden Censer

8 When he opened the seventh
seal,[x] there was silence in heaven
for about half an hour.
2And I saw the seven angels[y] who
stand before God, and to them were
given seven trumpets.[z]
3Another angel,[a] who had a golden

7:9 [b]S Rev 13:7 [c]ver 15 [d]S Rev 3:4 **7:10** [e]Ps 3:8; Rev 12:10; 19:1 [f]S Rev 5:1 **7:11** [g]S Rev 4:4 [h]S Rev 4:6 [i]S Rev 4:10 **7:12** [j]S Ro 11:36; Rev 5:12-14 **7:13** [k]S Rev 3:4 **7:14** [l]Rev 22:14 [m]Heb 9:14; 1Jn 1:7; Rev 12:11 **7:15** [n]ver 9 [o]Rev 22:3 [p]Rev 11:19 [q]S Rev 5:1 [r]Isa 4:5,6; Rev 21:3 **7:16** [s]Jn 6:35 [t]Isa 49:10 **7:17** [u]S Jn 10:11 [v]S Jn 4:10 [w]Isa 25:8; 35:10; 51:11; 65:19; Rev 21:4 **8:1** [x]Rev 6:1 **8:2** [y]ver 6-13; Rev 9:1,13; 11:15 [z]S Mt 24:31 **8:3** [a]Rev 7:2

7:9 A GREAT MULTITUDE. John describes a scene in heaven of a great multitude of people from all nations who come to salvation through faith in Christ. They will be with God (v. 15), free from pain and sorrow (vv. 16–17; see 6:9, note). Many believe that this multitude saved by the "blood of the Lamb" (v. 14) are tribulation saints, because John states that they "have come out of the great tribulation" (v. 14). Those who accept Christ are special objects of persecution from Satan and evil people (cf. 12:9–17).

7:14 THE GREAT TRIBULATION. The great tribulation is a time of divine judgment on an ungodly world that has rejected Christ, but it is also a time of satanic wrath and persecution against those who receive Christ and his Word during the tribulation (12:12). During this period, many saints will suffer terribly as objects of the wrath of Satan and the ungodly (vv. 9–17; 6:9–11; 20:4; cf. 14:13; see article on THE GREAT TRIBULATION, p. 1456). So intense is the conflict between righteousness and wickedness that it can only be called a "great tribulation." This phrase in the Greek literally reads "the tribulation, the great"; in the Greek language repeating the article "the" makes a statement emphatic.

7:17 GOD WILL WIPE AWAY EVERY TEAR. This promise may refer to the removal of any memory that might cause us suffering, regret or remorse. In heaven nothing that involves deprivation, suffering or sorrow remains (v. 16).

8:1 THE SEVENTH SEAL. The opening of the seventh seal initiates the seven trumpets of judgment; thus, the trumpet judgments are the seventh seal. The trumpet judgments are partial judgments (chs. 8–9; 11:15–19), while the judgments of the seven bowls (ch. 16) are more severe. The seventh trumpet judgment will announce the seven bowls of judgment (16:1–21). The silence in heaven is due to the horror of the coming judgments against sin.

8:3 PRAYERS OF ALL THE SAINTS. The repeated mentioning of the prayers of the saints (5:8; 8:3–4) indicates that the intercessory prayers of believers are extremely important in the destruction of evil and the establishment of righteousness on the earth (see 5:8, note). (1) John mentions the prayers of *all* the saints. Thus, the

censer, came and stood at the altar. He
was given much incense to offer, with
the prayers of all the saints,[b] on the
golden altar[c] before the throne. **4**The
smoke of the incense, together with
the prayers of the saints, went up before God[d] from the angel's hand.
5Then the angel took the censer, filled
it with fire from the altar,[e] and hurled
it on the earth; and there came peals of
thunder,[f] rumblings, flashes of lightning and an earthquake.[g]

The First Four Trumpets

6Then the seven angels who had the
seven trumpets[h] prepared to sound
them.
7The first angel[i] sounded his trumpet, and there came hail and fire[j]
mixed with blood, and it was hurled
down upon the earth. A third[k] of the
earth was burned up, a third of the
trees were burned up, and all the green
grass was burned up.[l]
8The second angel sounded his
trumpet, and something like a huge
mountain,[m] all ablaze, was thrown
into the sea. A third[n] of the sea turned
into blood,[o] **9**a third[p] of the living
creatures in the sea died, and a third of
the ships were destroyed.
10The third angel sounded his trumpet, and a great star, blazing like a
torch, fell from the sky[q] on a third of
the rivers and on the springs of water[r]— **11**the name of the star is
Wormwood.[1] A third[s] of the waters
turned bitter, and many people died
from the waters that had become bitter.[t]
12The fourth angel sounded his
trumpet, and a third of the sun was
struck, a third of the moon, and a third
of the stars, so that a third[u] of them
turned dark.[v] A third of the day was
without light, and also a third of the
night.[w]
13As I watched, I heard an eagle
that was flying in midair[x] call out in
a loud voice: "Woe! Woe! Woe[y] to the
inhabitants of the earth,[z] because of
the trumpet blasts about to be sounded
by the other three angels!"

The Fifth and Sixth Trumpets

9 The fifth angel sounded his trumpet, and I saw a star that had fall-
en from the sky to the earth.[a] The star
was given the key[b] to the shaft of the
Abyss.[c] **2**When he opened the Abyss,
smoke rose from it like the smoke from
a gigantic furnace.[d] The sun and sky
were darkened[e] by the smoke from
the Abyss.[f] **3**And out of the smoke locusts[g] came down upon the earth and
were given power like that of scorpions[h] of the earth. **4**They were told not
to harm[i] the grass of the earth or any
plant or tree,[j] but only those people
who did not have the seal of God on

8:3 [b] Rev 5:8 [c] ver 5; Ex 30:1-6; Heb 9:4; Rev 9:13
8:4 [d] Ps 141:2
8:5 [e] Lev 16:12,13 [f] S Rev 4:5 [g] S Rev 6:12
8:6 [h] S ver 2
8:7 [i] S ver 2 [j] Eze 38:22 [k] ver 7-12; Rev 9:15,18; 12:4 [l] Rev 9:4
8:8 [m] Jer 51:25 [n] S ver 7 [o] Rev 16:3
8:9 [p] S ver 7
8:10 [q] Isa 14:12; Rev 6:13; 9:1 [r] Rev 14:7; 16:4
8:11 [s] S ver 7 [t] Jer 9:15; 23:15
8:12 [u] S ver 7 [v] Ex 10:21-23; Rev 6:12,13 [w] Eze 32:7
8:13 [x] Rev 14:6; 19:17 [y] Rev 9:12; 11:14; 12:12 [z] S Rev 3:10
9:1 [a] Rev 8:10 [b] Rev 1:18 [c] ver 2, 11; S Lk 8:31
9:2 [d] Ge 19:28; Ex 19:18 [e] Joel 2:2,10 [f] ver 1,11; S Lk 8:31
9:3 [g] Ex 10:12-15 [h] ver 5,10
9:4 [i] S Rev 6:6 [j] Rev 8:7

[1] *11* That is, Bitterness

prayers of tribulation saints on earth are joined by the intercession of all the saints in heaven (cf. 6:9–11). The saints in heaven are vitally concerned about the events on earth. (2) Note that God in some sense stores up our prayers. Although the Lord may not answer all our prayers immediately, he does not throw them aside, but keeps them for the proper time of fulfillment.

8:7 HAIL AND FIRE MIXED WITH BLOOD. The first four trumpet judgments begin. (1) One-third of the earth's vegetation is destroyed by fire and hail; one-third of the sea and rivers is polluted; the heavens, sun, moon and stars are darkened for a third part of both day and night (vv. 7–13). (2) The judgments affect humans also, for many are killed (v. 11). The judgment is limited to one-third of the world, because the purpose of the judgment is partially to warn people and bring them to repentance (9:20–21).

8:8 HUGE MOUNTAIN, ALL ABLAZE. This may be a great burning meteor, which falls into the sea and kills one-third of the sea creatures and destroys many ships.

8:11 WORMWOOD. "Wormwood" is a bitter plant, representing God's judgment and human sorrow (see Dt 29:18; Pr 5:4; Jer 9:15; Am 5:7).

8:13 AN EAGLE THAT WAS FLYING. The eagle's threefold cry of woe is to warn that the next three trumpet judgments will be much more intense and devastating than those that preceded. The fifth and sixth judgments will involve horrible demonic forces (ch. 9).

9:1 THE STAR . . . THE ABYSS. The star falling from the sky is probably an angel who carries out God's judgment; it is referred to as "he" in v. 2. The Abyss is the place of imprisonment for demons (cf. 11:7; 17:8; 20:1,3; 2Pe 2:4; Jude 6). The beast, who is the antichrist, comes out of the Abyss (11:7), and Satan will be imprisoned there for one thousand years (20:3).

9:3 LOCUSTS CAME DOWN. These locusts represent an increased number of demons and demonic activity released on the earth toward the end of history (see previous note; see Mt 25:41, note on fallen angels). They have the power of scorpions to cause pain and misery (v. 10). Their assault is directed against the wicked on the earth for a time period of five months (vv. 5,10), though they are not permitted to torment believers (v. 4).

their foreheads.[k] **5**They were not giv-
en power to kill them, but only to torture them for five months.[l] And the
agony they suffered was like that of the
sting of a scorpion[m] when it strikes a
man. **6**During those days men will seek
death, but will not find it; they will long
to die, but death will elude them.[n]

7The locusts looked like horses prepared for battle.[o] On their heads they
wore something like crowns of gold,
and their faces resembled human
faces.[p] **8**Their hair was like women's
hair, and their teeth were like lions'
teeth.[q] **9**They had breastplates like
breastplates of iron, and the sound of
their wings was like the thundering of
many horses and chariots rushing into
battle.[r] **10**They had tails and stings
like scorpions, and in their tails they
had power to torment people for five
months.[s] **11**They had as king over
them the angel of the Abyss,[t] whose
name in Hebrew[u] is Abaddon,[v] and
in Greek, Apollyon.[m]

12The first woe is past; two other
woes are yet to come.[w]

13The sixth angel sounded his trumpet, and I heard a voice coming from
the horns[n][x] of the golden altar that
is before God.[y] **14**It said to the sixth
angel who had the trumpet, "Release
the four angels[z] who are bound at the
great river Euphrates."[a] **15**And the
four angels who had been kept ready
for this very hour and day and month
and year were released[b] to kill a
third[c] of mankind.[d] **16**The number of
the mounted troops was two hundred
million. I heard their number.[e]

17The horses and riders I saw in my
vision looked like this: Their breastplates were fiery red, dark blue, and
yellow as sulfur. The heads of the
horses resembled the heads of lions,
and out of their mouths[f] came fire,
smoke and sulfur.[g] **18**A third[h] of
mankind was killed[i] by the three
plagues of fire, smoke and sulfur[j]
that came out of their mouths. **19**The
power of the horses was in their
mouths and in their tails; for their tails
were like snakes, having heads with
which they inflict injury.

20The rest of mankind that were not
killed by these plagues still did not repent[k] of the work of their hands;[l]
they did not stop worshiping demons,[m] and idols of gold, silver,
bronze, stone and wood—idols that
cannot see or hear or walk.[n] **21**Nor did
they repent[o] of their murders, their

m *11 Abaddon* and *Apollyon* mean *Destroyer.*
n *13* That is, projections

9:4 [k] S Rev 7:2,3
9:5 [l] ver 10
[m] ver 3
9:6 [n] Job 3:21; 7:15; Jer 8:3; Rev 6:16
9:7 [o] Joel 2:4
[p] Da 7:8
9:8 [q] Joel 1:6
9:9 [r] Joel 2:5
9:10 [s] ver 3,5,19
9:11 [t] ver 1,2; S Lk 8:31
[u] Rev 16:16
[v] Job 26:6; 28:22; 31:12; Ps 88:11
9:12 [w] S Rev 8:13
9:13 [x] Ex 30:1-3
[y] Rev 8:3
9:14 [z] Rev 7:1
[a] Ge 15:18; Dt 1:7; Jos 1:4; Isa 11:15; Rev 16:12
9:15 [b] Rev 20:7
[c] S Rev 8:7
[d] ver 18
9:16 [e] Rev 5:11; 7:4
9:17 [f] Rev 11:5
[g] ver 18; Ps 11:6; Isa 30:33; Eze 38:22; Rev 14:10; 19:20; 20:10; 21:8
9:18 [h] S Rev 8:7
[i] ver 15 [j] S ver 17
9:20 [k] S Rev 2:21
[l] Dt 4:28; 31:29; Jer 1:16; Mic 5:13; Ac 7:41
[m] S 1Co 10:20
[n] Ps 115:4-7; 135:15-17; Da 5:23
9:21 [o] S Rev 2:21

9:6 SEEK DEATH, BUT WILL NOT FIND IT. The pain inflicted by the demonic locusts will be so severe that people will want to die, but will not be able to. This judgment reveals (1) that evil and impenitence will most certainly receive divine retribution (see Ro 1:18, note), and (2) that when people oppose God and his truth and seek evil, they become the prey of the demonic. Evil forces will possess their very nature, soul and life (see 1Ti 4:1, note; see article on POWER OVER SATAN AND DEMONS, p. 1484).

9:7 THE LOCUSTS LOOKED LIKE HORSES. The appearance and sound of the demons will be terrifying (vv. 7–9). Their "breastplates" (v. 9) may indicate that man-made weapons cannot destroy them.

9:11 AS KING OVER THEM. The leading angel of the demonic locusts is called "Abaddon," or "Apollyon," which means Destroyer, or Destruction (cf. Job 26:6; Pr 15:11).

9:14 RELEASE THE FOUR ANGELS. The sixth angel releases four angels; these must be evil angels or demons, since holy angels are not bound. They are let loose to kill one-third of the world's population (v. 15). They are released from the river Euphrates, because in OT history the Euphrates area symbolized a military invasion by which God brings judgment (cf. Isa 8:5–8; 10:5–7).

9:16 TWO HUNDRED MILLION. Bible interpreters differ widely as to the meaning of the two hundred million mounted troops. (1) Some say they represent demonlike evil spirits from the Abyss under the leadership of the four angels (v. 14; see v. 3, note). (2) Others see the mounted troops as representing many armies gathered for battle.

9:18 FIRE, SMOKE AND SULFUR. What John saw is a reminder of God's judgment on Sodom and Gomorrah (Ge 19:24,28; cf. Jude 7). These words are God's warning that those who indulge in the sinful ways of Sodom will most surely experience Sodom's judgment (Ge 19:14).

9:20 STILL DID NOT REPENT. Even God's judgment does not bring people to repentance. This demonstrates the depth of human depravity and its love for sinful pleasure (cf. Jer 17:9). The most prominent sins of the last days and the tribulation period are (vv. 20–21): (1) the worship of demons and participation in spiritism, the occult and magic (Dt 32:17; 1Co 10:20); (2) murder and violence; (3) magic arts (Gk *pharmekeia*), which involves drugs, occult worship and witchcraft (18:23; 21:8; 22:15; Gal 5:20; see next note); (4) sexual immorality, lust and pornography; (5) thefts and lawlessness (cf. Ro 1:24,28–31).

9:21 THEIR MAGIC ARTS. Magic arts will be greatly revived in the last days before and during

magic arts,[p] their sexual immorality[q] or their thefts.

The Angel and the Little Scroll

10 Then I saw another mighty angel[r] coming down from heav-
en.[s] He was robed in a cloud, with a
rainbow[t] above his head; his face was
like the sun,[u] and his legs were like
fiery pillars.[v] **2**He was holding a little
scroll,[w] which lay open in his hand. He
planted his right foot on the sea and his
left foot on the land,[x] **3**and he gave a
loud shout like the roar of a lion.[y]
When he shouted, the voices of the sev-
en thunders[z] spoke. **4**And when the
seven thunders spoke, I was about to
write;[a] but I heard a voice from heav-
en[b] say, "Seal up what the seven
thunders have said and do not write it
down."[c]

5Then the angel I had seen standing
on the sea and on the land[d] raised his
right hand to heaven.[e] **6**And he
swore[f] by him who lives for ever and
ever,[g] who created the heavens and
all that is in them, the earth and all
that is in it, and the sea and all that is
in it,[h] and said, "There will be no more
delay![i] **7**But in the days when the seventh angel is about to sound his trumpet,[j] the mystery[k] of God will be accomplished, just as he announced to
his servants the prophets."[l]

8Then the voice that I had heard
from heaven[m] spoke to me once more:
"Go, take the scroll[n] that lies open in
the hand of the angel who is standing
on the sea and on the land."

9So I went to the angel and asked
him to give me the little scroll. He said
to me, "Take it and eat it. It will turn
your stomach sour, but in your mouth
it will be as sweet as honey."[o] **10**I took
the little scroll from the angel's hand
and ate it. It tasted as sweet as honey
in my mouth,[p] but when I had eaten
it, my stomach turned sour. **11**Then I
was told, "You must prophesy[q] again
about many peoples, nations, languages and kings."[r]

The Two Witnesses

11 I was given a reed like a measuring rod[s] and was told, "Go
and measure the temple of God and the
altar, and count the worshipers there.
2But exclude the outer court;[t] do not
measure it, because it has been given
to the Gentiles.[u] They will trample on

9:21 [p] Isa 47:9, 12; Rev 18:23 [q] Rev 17:2,5
10:1 [r] Rev 5:2 [s] Rev 18:1; 20:1 [t] Eze 1:28; Rev 4:3 [u] Mt 17:2; Rev 1:16 [v] Rev 1:15
10:2 [w] ver 8-10; Rev 5:1 [x] ver 5,8
10:3 [y] Hos 11:10 [z] Rev 4:5
10:4 [a] Rev 1:11, 19 [b] ver 8 [c] Da 8:26; 12:4,9; Rev 22:10
10:5 [d] ver 1,2 [e] Dt 32:40; Da 12:7
10:6 [f] Ge 14:22; Ex 6:8; Nu 14:30 [g] S Rev 1:18 [h] Ps 115:15; 146:6; Rev 4:11; 14:7 [i] Rev 16:17
10:7 [j] S Mt 24:31 [k] S Ro 16:25 [l] Am 3:7
10:8 [m] ver 4 [n] ver 2
10:9 [o] Jer 15:16; Eze 2:8-3:3
10:10 [p] S ver 9
10:11 [q] Eze 37:4, 9 [r] Da 3:4; S Rev 13:7
11:1 [s] Eze 40:3; Rev 21:15
11:2 [t] Eze 40:17, 20 [u] Lk 21:24

---

the tribulation period (18:23; 21:8; 22:15; 1Ti 4:1). Magic arts is associated with the occult, which includes contact with the dead, supernatural powers, paranormal energies or demonic forces in order to gain power to manipulate or influence things or people. The use of drugs may be involved with magic arts.

10:1 ANOTHER MIGHTY ANGEL. Ch. 10 reveals the vision of the angel with the little scroll. It is an interlude between the sixth trumpet (blown in 9:13) and the seventh trumpet (blown in 11:15).

10:2 A LITTLE SCROLL. The angel planting his right foot on the sea and his left foot on the land signifies that this little scroll contains a message affecting the destiny of the whole world.

10:3 SEVEN THUNDERS. These signify certain aspects of God's coming wrath and judgment (cf. 8:5; 11:19; 16:18), though John is forbidden to disclose the message of the seven peals of thunder (v. 4). This indicates that during the tribulation period, judgments not revealed in the seals, trumpets and bowls will occur. Therefore, no one knows in advance everything that will happen. Thus we should not be dogmatic about the sequence of events in the book of Revelation.

10:7 MYSTERY OF GOD. Within the period following the sound of the seventh trumpet (11:15), all the prophecies that God revealed to his prophets about the final days will come to pass. This concerns the fulfillment of God's purpose in Christ's return to earth and the establishment of his kingdom (11:15).

10:9 TAKE IT AND EAT IT. The "little scroll," tasting as sweet as honey but turning sour in John's stomach, refers to the scroll's mixture of blessing and curse. God's word is sweet, both to hear and to obey for his servants (Ps 19:9–10; Jer 15:16; Eze 3:1–3), but it also pronounces the judgment on sin and evil that unbelievers must face (cf. Lk 19:41–44; Jer 20:8–9; Am 5:10).

11:1 MEASURE THE TEMPLE. Ch. 11 continues an interlude (begun in ch. 10) that discusses Israel and the temple and gives an appraisal of her spiritual life. The events recorded here occur in the city where the "Lord was crucified," i.e., Jerusalem (v. 8). Israel is basically still in unbelief during this part of the tribulation. The "temple of God" may imply the existence of a temple in Jerusalem at this time; it will be desecrated by the antichrist (see 13:14–15; Da 9:27; 12:11; 2Th 2:4; see article on THE GREAT TRIBULATION, p. 1456). The measuring of the temple signifies God's measuring of the spiritual condition of the Jewish people (cf. Eze 40; Zec 2).

11:2 TRAMPLE ON THE HOLY CITY. During the tribulation, Israel and the "holy city" will be oppressed by the Gentiles and suffer greatly for 42 months (see Lk 21:24, note). Israel will be severely judged because of her rejection of Christ and her immorality like that of Sodom (vv. 8,13). The "42 months" probably refers to the final three and one-half years of the tribulation (cf. Da 7:25; 12:7; see Da 9:27, note).

the holy city[v] for 42 months.[w] **3**And
I will give power to my two witnesses,[x] and they will prophesy
for 1,260 days,[y] clothed in sackcloth."[z] **4**These are the two olive
trees[a] and the two lampstands that
stand before the Lord of the earth.[b]
5If anyone tries to harm them, fire
comes from their mouths and devours
their enemies.[c] This is how anyone
who wants to harm them must die.[d]
6These men have power to shut up the
sky[e] so that it will not rain during the
time they are prophesying;[f] and they
have power to turn the waters into
blood[g] and to strike the earth with every kind of plague as often as they
want.
7Now when they have finished their
testimony, the beast[h] that comes up
from the Abyss[i] will attack them,[j]
and overpower and kill them. **8**Their
bodies will lie in the street of the great
city,[k] which is figuratively called Sodom[l] and Egypt, where also their Lord
was crucified.[m] **9**For three and a half
days men from every people, tribe, language and nation[n] will gaze on their
bodies and refuse them burial.[o] **10**The
inhabitants of the earth[p] will gloat
over them and will celebrate by sending each other gifts,[q] because these
two prophets had tormented those who
live on the earth.
11But after the three and a half
days[r] a breath of life from God entered them,[s] and they stood on their
feet, and terror struck those who saw
them. **12**Then they heard a loud voice
from heaven saying to them, "Come up
here."[t] And they went up to heaven in
a cloud,[u] while their enemies looked
on.
13At that very hour there was a severe earthquake[v] and a tenth of the
city collapsed. Seven thousand people
were killed in the earthquake, and the
survivors were terrified and gave glory[w] to the God of heaven.[x]
14The second woe has passed; the
third woe is coming soon.[y]

The Seventh Trumpet

15The seventh angel sounded his
trumpet,[z] and there were loud
voices[a] in heaven, which said:

"The kingdom of the world has
become the kingdom of our
Lord and of his Christ,[b]
and he will reign for ever and
ever."[c]

16And the twenty-four elders,[d] who
were seated on their thrones before
God, fell on their faces[e] and worshiped God, **17**saying:

"We give thanks[f] to you, Lord
God Almighty,[g]
the One who is and who was,[h]

11:2 [v]S Rev 21:2 [w]ver 3; Da 7:25; 12:7; Rev 12:6,14; 13:5 **11:3** [x]Rev 1:5; 2:13 [y]S ver 2 [z]Ge 37:34; 2Sa 3:31; Ne 9:1; Jnh 3:5 **11:4** [a]Ps 52:8; Jer 11:16; Zec 4:3, 11 [b]Zec 4:14 **11:5** [c]2Sa 22:9; 2Ki 1:10; Jer 5:14; Rev 9:17,18 [d]Nu 16:29,35 **11:6** [e]S Lk 4:25 [f]ver 3 [g]Ex 7:17, 19; Rev 8:8 **11:7** [h]Rev 13:1-4 [i]S Lk 8:31 [j]Da 7:21; Rev 13:7 **11:8** [k]Rev 16:19 [l]Isa 1:9; Jer 23:14; Eze 16:46 [m]Heb 13:12 **11:9** [n]S Rev 13:7 [o]Ps 79:2,3 **11:10** [p]S Rev 3:10 [q]Ne 8:10,12; Est 9:19,22 **11:11** [r]ver 9 [s]Eze 37:5,9,10,14 **11:12** [t]Rev 4:1 [u]2Ki 2:11; Ac 1:9 **11:13** [v]S Rev 6:12 [w]Rev 14:7; 16:9; 19:7 [x]Rev 16:11 **11:14** [y]S Rev 8:13 **11:15** [z]S Mt 24:31 [a]Rev 16:17; 19:1 [b]Rev 12:10 [c]Ps 145:13; Da 2:44; 7:14,27; Mic 4:7; Zec 14:9; Lk 1:33 **11:16** [d]S Rev 4:4 [e]S Rev 4:10 **11:17** [f]Ps 30:12 [g]S Rev 1:8 [h]S Rev 1:4

11:3 MY TWO WITNESSES. God will send two witnesses to preach the gospel and prophesy about the future; they will possess great supernatural power (vv. 5–6) and perform their ministry in the power of the Spirit. They will be a great threat to the antichrist and the entire wicked world for a period of 1,260 days and counteract the signs and wonders of the prophets of the antichrist (13:13–14). The two witnesses have the power of both Moses and Elijah (see Mal 4:5, note).

11:4 OLIVE TREES ... LAMPSTANDS. By using this language John says that the two witnesses will be empowered by the Holy Spirit in order to reveal the light or truth of God (see Zec 4:2–14, notes).

11:7 THE BEAST ... KILL THEM. The two witnesses are killed because they brought the truth of the gospel and faithfully cried out against the sins of the people. Jerusalem is called "Sodom" because of its immorality and "Egypt" because of its worldliness (v. 8). The beast is the antichrist (cf. 13:1; 14:9,11; 15:2; 16:2; 17:3,13; 19:20; 20:10) or the "man of lawlessness" (2Th 2:3–10). Note that the two witnesses could not be killed until they finished their work. This is true of all of God's servants who remain faithful to him.

11:11 TERROR STRUCK THOSE WHO SAW THEM. Because of the resurrection of the two witnesses (vv. 11–12) and God's judgment (v. 13), a remnant in Jerusalem will receive the message of the two witnesses and give glory to God (v. 13).

11:15 THE SEVENTH ANGEL SOUNDED. The sounding of the seventh trumpet brings an announcement that the world has become the kingdom of Christ, and he will reign forever (see 20:4, note; Eze 21:26–27; Da 2:44; 4:3; 6:26; Zec 14:9). In other words, the seventh trumpet involves events extending to Christ's return, including therefore the judgments of the seven bowls (beginning in ch. 16). The sound of the seventh trumpet is followed by a parenthetical passage that reveals some events related to the tribulation period (12:1—15:4).

11:16 TWENTY-FOUR ELDERS. The twenty-four elders prophesy what will happen at Christ's coming. The nations will be enraged (v. 18), the dead will be judged (v. 18), and God will destroy those who destroy the earth, i.e., those who are evil (cf. 19:20–21).

because you have taken your great
power
and have begun to reign.[i]
18The nations were angry;[j]
and your wrath has come.
The time has come for judging the
dead,[k]
and for rewarding your servants
the prophets[l]
and your saints and those who
reverence your name,
both small and great[m]—
and for destroying those who
destroy the earth."

19Then God's temple[n] in heaven
was opened, and within his temple was
seen the ark of his covenant.[o] And
there came flashes of lightning, rumblings, peals of thunder,[p] an earthquake and a great hailstorm.[q]

The Woman and the Dragon

12 A great and wondrous sign[r]
appeared in heaven:[s] a woman
clothed with the sun, with the moon
under her feet and a crown of twelve
stars[t] on her head. 2She was pregnant and cried out in pain[u] as she was
about to give birth. 3Then another sign
appeared in heaven:[v] an enormous
red dragon[w] with seven heads[x] and
ten horns[y] and seven crowns[z] on his
heads. 4His tail swept a third[a] of the
stars out of the sky and flung them to
the earth.[b] The dragon stood in front
of the woman who was about to give
birth, so that he might devour her
child[c] the moment it was born. 5She
gave birth to a son, a male child, who
will rule all the nations with an iron
scepter.[d] And her child was snatched
up[e] to God and to his throne. 6The
woman fled into the desert to a place
prepared for her by God, where she
might be taken care of for 1,260
days.[f]

7And there was war in heaven. Michael[g] and his angels fought against
the dragon,[h] and the dragon and his
angels[i] fought back. 8But he was not
strong enough, and they lost their
place in heaven. 9The great dragon
was hurled down—that ancient serpent[j] called the devil,[k] or Satan,[l]
who leads the whole world astray.[m]
He was hurled to the earth,[n] and his
angels with him.

10Then I heard a loud voice in heav-
en[o] say:

"Now have come the salvation[p]
and the power and the
kingdom of our God,

11:17 [i]Rev 19:6 11:18 [j]Ps 2:1 [k]Rev 20:12 [l]Rev 10:7 [m]S Rev 19:5 11:19 [n]Rev 15:5,8 [o]Ex 25:10-22; 2Ch 5:7; Heb 9:4 [p]S Rev 4:5 [q]Rev 16:21 12:1 [r]ver 3 [s]Rev 11:19 [t]Ge 37:9 12:2 [u]Isa 26:17; Gal 4:19 12:3 [v]ver 1; Rev 15:1 [w]ver 9, 13,16,17; Rev 13:1 [x]Rev 13:1; 17:3,7, 9 [y]Da 7:7,20; Rev 13:1; 17:3,7, 12,16 [z]Rev 19:12 12:4 [a]S Rev 8:7 [b]Da 8:10 [c]Mt 2:16 12:5 [d]Ps 2:9; Rev 2:27; 19:15 [e]S Ac 8:39 12:6 [f]S Rev 11:2 12:7 [g]S Jude 9 [h]ver 3 [i]Mt 25:41 12:9 [j]ver 15; Ge 3:1-7 [k]Mt 25:41; Rev 20:2 [l]S Mt 4:10 [m]Rev 20:3,8,10 [n]Lk 10:18; Jn 12:31 12:10 [o]Rev 11:15 [p]Rev 7:10

12:1 WONDROUS SIGN APPEARED. Ch. 12 presents four great conflicts between God and Satan: (1) Satan's conflict with Christ and his work of redemption (vv. 1–5), (2) Satan's conflict with the faithful of Israel (vv. 6,13–16), (3) Satan's conflict with heaven (vv. 7–9) and (4) Satan's conflict with believers (vv. 10–11,17).

12:1 A WOMAN. This woman refers to the faithful of Israel through whom the Messiah (i.e., the Christ child, vv. 2,4–5) came into the world (cf. Ro 9:5). This is indicated not only by the birth of the child, but also by the reference to the sun and the moon (see Ge 37:9–11) and the twelve stars, which would naturally refer to the twelve tribes of Israel.

12:3 AN ENORMOUS RED DRAGON. This dragon is Satan (see v. 9). The seven heads, horns and crowns may represent his great power.

12:4 A THIRD OF THE STARS. This may refer to Satan's original fall from heaven and the angels who fell with him (2Pe 2:4; Jude 6), or to the great power that Satan has in the universe over those who oppose his power. Satan attempts to destroy the Christ child.

12:5 A MALE CHILD. The male child is Jesus Christ (19:15) and the snatching up of the child refers to his ascension into heaven after his resurrection (Lk 24:51; Ac 1:9–11).

12:6 THE WOMAN FLED. Here the woman refers to the persecuted faithful ones of Israel during the last half of the tribulation (cf. the 1,260 days, exactly half of the length of the tribulation period). (1) During the tribulation, the faithful of Israel are God-fearing Jews who oppose the religion of the antichrist. Sincerely searching the Scriptures, they accept the truth about Jesus Christ as the Messiah (Dt 4:30–31; Zec 13:8–9). They receive divine help during the last three and a half years of the tribulation, and Satan will not be allowed to overcome them completely (see vv. 13–16). (2) Those from Israel who accept the religion of the antichrist and reject the Scriptural truth of the Messiah will be judged and destroyed in the days of the great tribulation (see Eze 11:17–21; 20:34–38; Zec 13:8–9).

12:7–9 WAR IN HEAVEN. The tribulation will involve not only great spiritual conflict on earth, but also war in heaven. Satan and his angels will put forth a supreme effort to defeat God and his angels in heaven. (1) Satan is defeated, hurled down to earth (cf. Lk 10:18) and allowed no further access to heaven. (2) Heaven rejoices (vv. 10–12), for Satan is no longer a spiritual force in heavenly places (see Eph 6:12, note). At the same time it causes "woe" to those on earth (vv. 12–13). This fall of Satan may begin the great tribulation.

12:10 ACCUSER OF OUR BROTHERS. Satan accuses believers before God of serving God for personal advantage (cf. Job 1:6–11; Zec 3:1).

and the authority of his Christ.
For the accuser of our brothers,[q]
who accuses them before our
God day and night,
has been hurled down.
11They overcame[r] him
by the blood of the Lamb[s]
and by the word of their
testimony;[t]
they did not love their lives so
much
3 as to shrink from death.[u]
12Therefore rejoice, you heavens[v]
and you who dwell in them!
But woe[w] to the earth and the
sea,[x]
because the devil has gone down
to you!
He is filled with fury,
because he knows that his time
is short."

13When the dragon[y] saw that he
had been hurled to the earth, he pursued the woman who had given birth to
the male child.[z] 14The woman was
given the two wings of a great eagle,[a]
so that she might fly to the place prepared for her in the desert, where she
would be taken care of for a time, times
and half a time,[b] out of the serpent's
reach. 15Then from his mouth the serpent[c] spewed water like a river, to
overtake the woman and sweep her
away with the torrent. 16But the earth
helped the woman by opening its
mouth and swallowing the river that
the dragon had spewed out of his
mouth. 17Then the dragon was enraged at the woman and went off to
make war[d] against the rest of her offspring[e]—those who obey God's commandments[f] and hold to the testimony of Jesus.[g]

13

1And the dragon° stood on the shore of
the sea.

The Beast out of the Sea

And I saw a beast coming out of the
sea.[h] He had ten horns and seven
heads,[i] with ten crowns on his horns,
and on each head a blasphemous
name.[j] 2The beast I saw resembled a
leopard,[k] but had feet like those of
a bear[l] and a mouth like that of a
lion.[m] The dragon gave the beast his
power and his throne and great authority.[n] 3One of the heads of the beast
seemed to have had a fatal wound, but
the fatal wound had been healed.[o]
The whole world was astonished[p] and
followed the beast. 4Men worshiped
the dragon because he had given authority to the beast, and they also wor-

12:10 [q]Job 1:9-11; Zec 3:1; 1Pe 5:8 **12:11** [r]S Jn 16:33; Rev 15:2 [s]S Rev 7:14 [t]Rev 6:9 [u]Lk 14:26; Rev 2:10 **12:12** [v]Ps 96:11; Isa 44:23; 49:13; Rev 18:20 [w]S Rev 8:13 [x]Rev 10:6 **12:13** [y]ver 3 [z]ver 5 **12:14** [a]Ex 19:4 [b]S Rev 11:2 **12:15** [c]ver 9 **12:17** [d]Rev 11:7; 13:7 [e]Ge 3:15 [f]S Jn 14:15 [g]S Rev 1:2 **13:1** [h]Da 7:1-6; Rev 15:2; 16:13 [i]S Rev 12:3 [j]Da 11:36; Rev 17:3 **13:2** [k]Da 7:6 [l]Da 7:5 [m]Da 7:4 [n]Rev 2:13; 16:10 **13:3** [o]ver 12,14 [p]Rev 17:8

° *1* Some late manuscripts *And I*

12:11 THEY OVERCAME HIM. Faithful believers on earth overcome Satan by being freed from his power by the blood of the Lamb, by determining to speak for Christ and by showing a willingness to serve Christ at any cost.

12:12 DEVIL . . . FILLED WITH FURY. Satan, knowing he is doomed and will shortly be defeated, has power only on the earth. The short time refers to the tribulation period. His great fury results in widespread suffering for the saints (v. 11).

12:13 PURSUED THE WOMAN. Satan attempts to destroy the woman (see v. 6, note). Those from Israel who accept Christ will be hunted and persecuted by Satan and the followers of the antichrist (cf. Mt 24:15–21). God will give supernatural protection for the saints of Israel during this time (vv. 14–16).

12:17 DRAGON . . . WENT OFF TO MAKE WAR. Satan, confined to earth, knows he has only a short time to persecute the woman (see v. 6, note) and the rest of her offspring. "The woman" may refer to the faithful of Israel in Judea and "the rest of her offspring" to believing Jews elsewhere in the world.

13:1 A BEAST COMING OUT OF THE SEA. Ch. 13 describes the conflict between the antichrist and God and his people during the tribulation. The beast coming out of the sea is history's final great world government, consisting of ten kingdoms under the control of the antichrist (see 17:12, note; Da 2:40–45, notes; 7:24–25, note; 11:36–45, note). The sea represents many nations (cf. 17:15). Satan gives his power to this government and uses it against God and his people (v. 2). See 17:8–11 for the angel's explanation of the beast.

13:2 BEAST . . . LEOPARD. The beast here, the same beast of v. 1, represents not only the end-time Gentile world kingdom, but also the king of that kingdom. The beast is a person, as cruel as a beast, who will gain the political and religious power of the world at that time (see 17:13; Da 7:4–6; 8:25; 9:27). He is called the "man of lawlessness" in 2Th 2:3–4 and the "antichrist" in 1Jn 2:18 ("anti" means "instead of"; thus the antichrist may claim he is the real Christ, the true Messiah, Mt 24:24–25; 2Th 2:3–4). He will make a covenant with the nation of Israel (see Da 9:27, note; see article on THE AGE OF THE ANTICHRIST, p. 1872).

13:3 A FATAL WOUND. It appears to the whole world that the antichrist has suffered a fatal wound, but is brought back to life again by Satan's supernatural power (vv. 2,14; cf. 2Th 2:9; see Rev 17:8, note). Evidently God will permit Satan to try to duplicate Christ's power. This may be Satan's chief means of deceiving the human race (cf. 2Th 2:9–10).

shiped the beast and asked, "Who is
like[q] the beast? Who can make war
against him?"
5The beast was given a mouth to utter proud words and blasphemies[r]
and to exercise his authority for forty-
two months.[s] 6He opened his mouth
to blaspheme God, and to slander his
name and his dwelling place and those
who live in heaven.[t] 7He was given
power to make war[u] against the
saints and to conquer them. And he
was given authority over every tribe,
people, language and nation.[v] 8All
inhabitants of the earth[w] will worship the beast—all whose names
have not been written in the book of
life[x] belonging to the Lamb[y] that
was slain from the creation of the
world.[p][z]
9He who has an ear, let him hear.[a]

10If anyone is to go into captivity,
into captivity he will go.
If anyone is to be killed[q] with the
sword,
with the sword he will be
killed.[b]

This calls for patient endurance and
faithfulness[c] on the part of the
saints.[d]

13:4 [q]Ex 15:11
13:5 [r]Da 7:8,11, 20,25; 11:36; 2Th 2:4
[s]S Rev 11:2
13:6 [t]Rev 12:12
13:7 [u]Da 7:21; Rev 11:7
[v]Rev 5:9; 7:9; 10:11; 17:15
13:8 [w]ver 12,14; S Rev 3:10
[x]S Rev 20:12
[y]S Jn 1:29
[z]S Mt 25:34
13:9 [a]S Rev 2:7
13:10 [b]Jer 15:2; 43:11 [c]S Heb 6:12
[d]Rev 14:12

13:11 [e]ver 1,2
[f]Rev 16:13
13:12 [g]ver 4
[h]ver 14; Rev 19:20 [i]ver 15; Rev 14:9,11; 16:2; 19:20; 20:4 [j]ver 3
13:13
[k]S Mt 24:24
[l]1Ki 18:38; 2Ki 1:10; Lk 9:54; Rev 20:9
13:14 [m]2Th 2:9, 10 [n]Rev 12:9
[o]S Rev 3:10
[p]ver 3,12
13:15 [q]S ver 12
[r]Da 3:3-6
13:16
[s]S Rev 19:5
[t]Rev 7:3; 14:9; 20:4

The Beast out of the Earth

11Then I saw another beast, coming
out of the earth.[e] He had two horns
like a lamb, but he spoke like a dragon.[f] 12He exercised all the authority[g] of the first beast on his behalf,[h]
and made the earth and its inhabitants
worship the first beast,[i] whose fatal
wound had been healed.[j] 13And he
performed great and miraculous
signs,[k] even causing fire to come
down from heaven[l] to earth in full
view of men. 14Because of the signs[m]
he was given power to do on behalf of
the first beast, he deceived[n] the inhabitants of the earth.[o] He ordered
them to set up an image in honor of the
beast who was wounded by the sword
and yet lived.[p] 15He was given power
to give breath to the image of the first
beast, so that it could speak and cause
all who refused to worship[q] the image
to be killed.[r] 16He also forced everyone, small and great,[s] rich and poor,
free and slave, to receive a mark on his
right hand or on his forehead,[t] 17so
that no one could buy or sell unless he

[p] 8 Or *written from the creation of the world in the book of life belonging to the Lamb that was slain* [q] 10 Some manuscripts *anyone kills*

13:7 MAKE WAR AGAINST THE SAINTS. During the tribulation, people will have to choose whether to follow the easy and popular way of the new religion or to believe in Christ and remain faithful. (1) Those who remain faithful to God and his Word will be persecuted and possibly killed (see 6:9, note; 7:9, note). (2) Satan will "conquer them," not in the sense that their faith is destroyed, but in the martyrdom of many (6:9–11). For "forty-two months" the antichrist will make war against the saints (v. 5).

13:8 ALL . . . WILL WORSHIP THE BEAST. The antichrist declares himself to be deity and possesses supernatural power of the demonic world (2Th 2:4,9). Accordingly, he will be worshiped (vv. 4,8,12; 14:9; 16:2). The religion of the antichrist, in other words, teaches the doctrine of the divinity of humanity (cf. Ge 3:5). Instead of the truth that in Christ God became flesh (Jn 1:14), he speaks the lie that in himself humanity has and can become God (2Th 2:4). New Age teaching today emphasizes this doctrine of the antichrist and may be preparing the masses for its ultimate acceptance.

13:8 LAMB THAT WAS SLAIN FROM THE CREATION. Christ's redemptive death for the salvation of humanity was decreed from the very beginning of the creation of the world (see 17:8, note; Ge 3:15; 1Pe 1:18–20).

13:11 ANOTHER BEAST. This other beast will assist the first beast (see v. 2, note), directing the world to worship the antichrist (v. 12) and misleading humanity by working great miracles (vv. 13–14; cf. Dt 13:1–3; 2Th 2:9–12). He is also referred to as "the false prophet" (19:20; 20:10). An image of the antichrist will probably be placed in God's temple (Da 9:27; Mt 24:15; 2Th 2:4). His "two horns like a lamb" signify his attempt to deceive by portraying himself as a loving, gentle and caring person. In reality, however, his character is not like that of a lamb but of a dragon (cf. Mt 7:15).

13:12 WORSHIP THE FIRST BEAST. The second beast will promote an ecumenical false church that will worship the antichrist. He will bring this about largely by performing great signs and wonders (vv. 13–14). His ministry will in some ways counterfeit the supernatural ministry of the Holy Spirit (cf. 2Th 2:9–10).

13:15 REFUSED TO WORSHIP THE IMAGE TO BE KILLED. A decree will be given to kill all who refuse to worship the world ruler and his images. In other words, many who resist the antichrist and remain faithful to Jesus will pay with their lives (see 6:9, note; 14:12–13).

13:16 A MARK. The antichrist will seek to gain total economic control of the world. All people must worship him and receive a mark on their hands or foreheads in order to buy or sell (vv. 16–17), identifying the followers of the world religion promoted by the antichrist. Those who refuse to take the mark will be hunted down in order to be killed (v. 15).

had the mark,[u] which is the name
of the beast or the number of his
name.[v]
18This calls for wisdom.[w] If anyone
has insight, let him calculate the number of the beast, for it is man's number.[x] His number is 666.

The Lamb and the 144,000

14 Then I looked, and there before
me was the Lamb,[y] standing
on Mount Zion,[z] and with him
144,000[a] who had his name and his
Father's name[b] written on their foreheads.[c] **2**And I heard a sound from
heaven like the roar of rushing waters[d] and like a loud peal of thunder.[e] The sound I heard was like that
of harpists playing their harps.[f] **3**And
they sang a new song[g] before the
throne and before the four living creatures[h] and the elders.[i] No one could
learn the song except the 144,000[j]
who had been redeemed from the
earth. **4**These are those who did not defile themselves with women, for they
kept themselves pure.[k] They follow
the Lamb wherever he goes.[l] They
were purchased from among men[m]
and offered as firstfruits[n] to God and
the Lamb. **5**No lie was found in their
mouths;[o] they are blameless.[p]

The Three Angels

6Then I saw another angel flying in
midair,[q] and he had the eternal gospel
to proclaim to those who live on the
earth[r]—to every nation, tribe, language and people.[s] **7**He said in a loud
voice, "Fear God[t] and give him glory,[u] because the hour of his judgment
has come. Worship him who made[v]
the heavens, the earth, the sea and the
springs of water."[w]
8A second angel followed and said,
"Fallen! Fallen is Babylon the Great,[x]
which made all the nations drink the
maddening wine of her adulteries."[y]
9A third angel followed them and
said in a loud voice: "If anyone worships the beast[z] and his image[a] and
receives his mark on the forehead[b] or
on the hand, **10**he, too, will drink of the
wine of God's fury,[c] which has been
poured full strength into the cup of his
wrath.[d] He will be tormented with
burning sulfur[e] in the presence of the
holy angels and of the Lamb. **11**And the
smoke of their torment rises for ever
and ever.[f] There is no rest day or
night[g] for those who worship the
beast and his image,[h] or for anyone

13:17 [u]Rev 14:9 [v]ver 18; Rev 14:11; 15:2 **13:18** [w]Rev 17:9 [x]Rev 15:2; 21:17 **14:1** [y]S Rev 5:6 [z]Ps 2:6; Heb 12:22 [a]ver 3; Rev 7:4 [b]Rev 3:12; 22:4 [c]S Rev 7:3 **14:2** [d]S Rev 1:15 [e]Rev 6:1 [f]Rev 5:8; 15:2 **14:3** [g]S Rev 5:9 [h]S Rev 4:6 [i]S Rev 4:4 [j]ver 1 **14:4** [k]2Co 11:2; Rev 3:4 [l]Rev 7:17 [m]Rev 5:9 [n]Jer 2:3; Jas 1:18 **14:5** [o]Ps 32:2; Zep 3:13; Jn 1:47; 1Pe 2:22 [p]Eph 5:27
14:6 [q]Rev 8:13; 19:17 [r]S Rev 3:10 [s]S Rev 13:7 **14:7** [t]Ps 34:9; Rev 15:4 [u]S Rev 11:13 [v]S Rev 10:6 [w]Rev 8:10; 16:4 **14:8** [x]Isa 21:9; Jer 51:8; Rev 16:19; 17:5; 18:2,10 [y]Rev 17:2,4; 18:3, 9 **14:9** [z]S Rev 13:12 [a]Rev 13:14 [b]S Rev 13:16 **14:10** [c]Isa 51:17; Jer 25:15 [d]Jer 51:7; Rev 18:6 [e]S Rev 9:17
14:11 [f]Isa 34:10; Rev 19:3 [g]Rev 4:8 [h]ver 9; S Rev 13:12

13:18 HIS NUMBER IS 666. Although the antichrist is called "the beast" throughout Revelation, his number is 666. Many commentators believe that six is the number for humanity in Scripture and three is the number for God. Therefore, the three sixes could very well refer to a man who makes himself god. Like the Roman emperors and many both before and after them, he believes he is a god (see v. 8, note; 2Th 2:4).

14:1 WITH HIM 144,000. Chs. 14 and 15 introduce the judgments of chs. 16–18, showing the reward awaiting those who persevere in their faith in Jesus (v. 12; 15:2–4). Ch. 14 begins by describing the scene of 144,000 outstanding believers appearing in heaven close to the Lamb. The 144,000 symbolically represent the most consecrated and faithful of God's people of all time, who enjoy a special position and favor in heaven (see next note). Thus the number 144,000 does not mean they are limited to that number. Any believer may be among this group by consecrated and devoted faith, love and service.

14:4 DID NOT DEFILE THEMSELVES WITH WOMEN. This phrase is best understood in a spiritual sense. The 144,000 overcomers remained pure by refusing to conform to the pagan world system (see article on THE CHRISTIAN'S RELATIONSHIP TO THE WORLD, p. 1976) or to become a part of the apostate church of the last days (see 17:1, notes). Note the character of those who will be close to Christ in heaven. (1) They are separated from the world and the apostate church (see article on SPIRITUAL SEPARATION FOR BELIEVERS, p. 1794). (2) They follow Christ (cf. Mk 8:34; Jn 14:21, note). (3) They give themselves to God and Christ (v. 4). (4) They do not speak lies (v. 5; cf. 21:27—22:15). (5) They are morally blameless (see article on SANCTIFICATION, p. 1956).

14:6 THE ETERNAL GOSPEL TO PROCLAIM. During the last half of the tribulation the gospel of Jesus will be proclaimed by an angel (or angels) to the entire world in clarity, power and warning. It is a call to fear God, give him glory, and worship him rather than the antichrist (vv. 7–10).

14:8 FALLEN IS BABYLON. Babylon represents the political, religious and commercial system of the whole world in the time of the end (see 17:1, note), and its fall is foretold here (see chs. 17–18 for more details).

14:9 IF ANYONE WORSHIPS THE BEAST. Those who worship the beast and receive his mark (see 13:16, note) will seal their doom, suffer severe divine judgments and be tormented for ever and ever (vv. 9–11; 9:4,13–21; 16:2; see Mt 10:28, note). The warning is directed to unbelievers (v. 6) and to saints who will be tempted to deny their faith in the face of the great danger of martyrdom (vv. 12–13).

who receives the mark of his name."[i]
12This calls for patient endurance[j] on
the part of the saints[k] who obey God's
commandments[l] and remain faithful
to Jesus.
13Then I heard a voice from heaven
say, "Write: Blessed are the dead who
die in the Lord[m] from now on."
"Yes," says the Spirit,[n] "they will
rest from their labor, for their deeds
will follow them."

The Harvest of the Earth

14I looked, and there before me was
a white cloud,[o] and seated on the
cloud was one "like a son of man"[r][p]
with a crown[q] of gold on his head and
a sharp sickle in his hand. 15Then another angel came out of the temple[r]
and called in a loud voice to him who
was sitting on the cloud, "Take your
sickle[s] and reap, because the time to
reap has come, for the harvest[t] of the
earth is ripe." 16So he who was seated
on the cloud swung his sickle over the
earth, and the earth was harvested.
17Another angel came out of the
temple in heaven, and he too had a
sharp sickle.[u] 18Still another angel,
who had charge of the fire, came from
the altar[v] and called in a loud voice to
him who had the sharp sickle, "Take
your sharp sickle[w] and gather the
clusters of grapes from the earth's
vine, because its grapes are ripe."
19The angel swung his sickle on the
earth, gathered its grapes and threw
them into the great winepress of God's
wrath.[x] 20They were trampled in the
winepress[y] outside the city,[z] and
blood[a] flowed out of the press, rising
as high as the horses' bridles for a distance of 1,600 stadia.[s]

Seven Angels With Seven Plagues

15 I saw in heaven another great
and marvelous sign:[b] seven
angels[c] with the seven last
plagues[d]—last, because with them
God's wrath is completed. 2And I saw
what looked like a sea of glass[e] mixed
with fire and, standing beside the sea,
those who had been victorious[f] over
the beast[g] and his image[h] and over
the number of his name.[i] They held
harps[j] given them by God 3and sang
the song of Moses[k] the servant of
God[l] and the song of the Lamb:[m]

"Great and marvelous are your
deeds,[n]
Lord God Almighty.[o]
Just and true are your ways,[p]
King of the ages.
4Who will not fear you, O Lord,[q]
and bring glory to your name?[r]
For you alone are holy.
All nations will come
and worship before you,[s]
for your righteous acts[t] have
been revealed."

5After this I looked and in heaven

14:11 [i]Rev 13:17
14:12 [j]S Heb 6:12 [k]Rev 13:10 [l]S Jn 14:15
14:13 [m]1Co 15:18; 1Th 4:16 [n]Rev 2:7; 22:17
14:14 [o]Mt 17:5 [p]Da 7:13; S Rev 1:13 [q]S Rev 6:2
14:15 [r]ver 17; Rev 11:19 [s]ver 18; Joel 3:13; Mk 4:29 [t]Jer 51:33
14:17 [u]S ver 15
14:18 [v]Rev 6:9; 8:5; 16:7 [w]S ver 15
14:19 [x]Rev 19:15
14:20 [y]ver 19; Isa 63:3; Joel 3:13; Rev 19:15 [z]Heb 13:12; Rev 11:8 [a]Ge 49:11; Dt 32:14
15:1 [b]Rev 12:1,3 [c]ver 6-8; Rev 16:1; 17:1; 21:9 [d]Lev 26:21; Rev 9:20
15:2 [e]Rev 4:6 [f]Rev 12:11 [g]Rev 13:1 [h]Rev 13:14 [i]Rev 13:17 [j]Rev 5:8; 14:2
15:3 [k]Ex 15:1 [l]Jos 1:1 [m]S Rev 5:9 [n]Ps 111:2 [o]S Rev 1:8 [p]Ps 145:17
15:4 [q]Jer 10:7 [r]Ps 86:9 [s]Isa 66:23 [t]Rev 19:8

[r]*14* Daniel 7:13 [s]*20* That is, about 180 miles (about 300 kilometers)

14:12 WHO OBEY GOD'S COMMANDMENTS. The fate of the followers of the beast is awful (vv. 9–11). Therefore, the saints must continue to "obey God's commandments and remain faithful to Jesus." For their allegiance to Christ they will probably die (see next note).

14:13 BLESSED ... DIE IN THE LORD. Those dying for their faith in Christ during the tribulation are especially blessed. They are released from persecution, torture and suffering and are taken to be with Christ.

14:14–16 LIKE A SON OF MAN. One like a son of man (i.e., Christ) is pictured as ready to wield the sickle of judgment on a world ripe with wickedness (vv. 14–20). Vv. 14–16 are a prediction or preview of the events of 16:12–16 and 19:11–21.

14:19 THE GREAT WINEPRESS. In Biblical days grapes were put in a trough and trampled by foot to remove the wine (i.e., the juice of the grape). The treading of grapes was used in the OT as a figure for the execution of divine wrath on the ungodly (see Isa 63:3, note; cf. Rev 19:15). At Christ's return at the end of the tribulation, all unbelievers in the world will be gathered and judged in the Valley of Jehoshaphat (see Ps 110:6, note; Joel 3:2, note; Mt 25:32, note) and then killed (see Mt 13:40; Lk 17:37, note; cf. Ps 97:3–5; Pr 2:22; Isa 63:1–6; 66:15–17; Jer 25:30–33; Rev 19:15).

14:20 BLOOD FLOWED OUT. A great slaughter occurs in the last days of the tribulation. This refers to the battle of Armageddon (Zec 14:1–4; see Rev 16:16, note; 19:17–19).

15:1 SEVEN LAST PLAGUES. These plagues contain God's final judgments on the earth during the tribulation. They are called judgments of the "seven golden bowls" (v. 7), and they begin in ch. 16. The seven bowls of judgment may be the unfolding of the seventh trumpet judgment (see 11:15, note).

15:2 VICTORIOUS OVER THE BEAST. Standing on a crystal surface (cf. 4:6) are those who did not abandon their faith in Christ when persecuted, threatened or killed by the antichrist (cf. 13:7–10).

15:5 THE TABERNACLE OF THE TESTIMONY. John saw a temple in heaven like the taberna-

the temple,[u] that is, the tabernacle of
the Testimony,[v] was opened.[w] **6**Out
of the temple[x] came the seven angels
with the seven plagues.[y] They were
dressed in clean, shining linen[z] and
wore golden sashes around their
chests.[a] **7**Then one of the four living
creatures[b] gave to the seven angels[c]
seven golden bowls filled with the
wrath of God, who lives for ever and
ever.[d] **8**And the temple was filled with
smoke[e] from the glory of God and
from his power, and no one could
enter the temple[f] until the seven
plagues of the seven angels were completed.

The Seven Bowls of God's Wrath

16 Then I heard a loud voice from
the temple[g] saying to the sev-
en angels,[h] "Go, pour out the seven
bowls of God's wrath on the earth."[i]
2The first angel went and poured out
his bowl on the land,[j] and ugly and
painful sores[k] broke out on the people
who had the mark of the beast and worshiped his image.[l]
3The second angel poured out his
bowl on the sea, and it turned into
blood like that of a dead man, and every living thing in the sea died.[m]
4The third angel poured out his bowl
on the rivers and springs of water,[n]
and they became blood.[o] **5**Then I
heard the angel in charge of the waters
say:

"You are just in these judgments,[p]
you who are and who were,[q]
the Holy One,[r]
because you have so judged;[s]
6for they have shed the blood of
your saints and prophets,[t]
and you have given them blood
to drink[u] as they deserve."

7And I heard the altar[v] respond:

"Yes, Lord God Almighty,[w]
true and just are your
judgments."[x]

8The fourth angel[y] poured out his
bowl on the sun,[z] and the sun was giv-
en power to scorch people with fire.[a]
9They were seared by the intense heat
and they cursed the name of God,[b]
who had control over these plagues,
but they refused to repent[c] and glorify
him.[d]
10The fifth angel poured out his bowl
on the throne of the beast,[e] and his
kingdom was plunged into darkness.[f]
Men gnawed their tongues in agony
11and cursed[g] the God of heaven[h] because of their pains and their sores,[i]
but they refused to repent of what they
had done.[j]
12The sixth angel poured out his

15:5 [u]Rev 11:19 [v]Ex 38:21; Nu 1:50 [w]S Mt 3:16
15:6 [x]Rev 14:15 [y]S ver 1 [z]Eze 9:2; Da 10:5 [a]Rev 1:13
15:7 [b]S Rev 4:6 [c]S ver 1 [d]S Rev 1:18
15:8 [e]Isa 6:4 [f]Ex 40:34,35; 1Ki 8:10,11; 2Ch 5:13,14
16:1 [g]Rev 11:19 [h]S Rev 15:1 [i]ver 2-21; Ps 79:6; Zep 3:8
16:2 [j]Rev 8:7 [k]ver 11; Ex 9:9-11; Dt 28:35 [l]Rev 13:15-17; 14:9
16:3 [m]Ex 7:17-21; Rev 8:8,9; Rev 11:6
16:4 [n]Rev 8:10 [o]Ex 7:17-21
16:5 [p]Rev 15:3 [q]S Rev 1:4 [r]Rev 15:4 [s]Rev 6:10
16:6 [t]Lk 11:49-51 [u]Isa 49:26; Rev 17:6; 18:24
16:7 [v]Rev 6:9; 14:18 [w]S Rev 1:8 [x]Rev 15:3; 19:2
16:8 [y]Rev 8:12 [z]Rev 6:12 [a]Rev 14:18
16:9 [b]ver 11,21 [c]S Rev 2:21 [d]S Rev 11:13
16:10 [e]Rev 13:2 [f]Ex 10:21-23; Isa 8:22; Rev 8:12; 9:2
16:11 [g]ver 9,21 [h]Rev 11:13 [i]ver 2 [j]S Rev 2:21

---

cle in the OT that contained the Ten Commandments (cf. Ex 32:15; 40:34–35). This signifies that the judgments are the result of God's opposition to sin and of human rejection of his law and Word.

15:7 FILLED WITH THE WRATH OF GOD. This will be the last of the divine judgments on a wicked world before Christ's reign. The fact that no one can enter the temple until the plagues are completed means that no one can intercede to stop the judgment (v. 8). God has declared the end; his judgment will be complete and without mercy.

16:1 GOD'S WRATH. Pouring out the seven bowls of God's wrath now begins, at a point just before Christ returns to earth. A great world war will occur toward the end of these judgments (v. 14; see v. 16, note; Da 11:36–45, note), judgments more intense and severe than the preceding ones.

16:3 IT TURNED INTO BLOOD. The sea becomes so corrupt that every living creature in it dies and its polluted color looks like blood (Ex 7:20–25). This also happens with the rivers and springs (v. 4).

16:7 JUST ARE YOUR JUDGMENTS. Those who question God's righteousness in his judgments do not understand sin's terrible evil or God's intense hatred of it. A holy and just God must of necessity oppose and punish evil (see Jn 3:19, note; Heb 1:9, note; cf. Ps 119:137).

16:9 INTENSE HEAT. A great heat wave will spread across the earth and become so unbearable that people will blaspheme God (cf. Mal 4:1). Their hearts will be so hardened that they will refuse to repent (see v. 11, note). Compare this with the condition of those in heaven, of whom it is said, "the sun will not beat upon them, nor any scorching heat" (7:16).

16:10 THE THRONE OF THE BEAST. The fifth bowl begins to throw the world dominion of the antichrist into confusion. This special judgment centers on his headquarters and followers.

16:11 REFUSED TO REPENT. Even in the middle of God's terrible judgment, men and women will choose to live in sin and to persist in their rebellion against righteousness. Repentance is the only act that will stop God's judgments (cf. 2:21; 9:21; 16:9), but that act they refuse to do.

16:12 KINGS FROM THE EAST. These are nations from the Orient that will participate in a great conflict, driven by satanic power to the war of Armageddon (see v. 16, note; 19:17–21). The sixth angel prepares the way for the final war of the age by a drying up of the river Euphrates, allowing armies from the east to approach the vicinity of Israel (Isa 11:15).

bowl on the great river Euphrates,[k]
and its water was dried up to prepare
the way[l] for the kings from the
East.[m] **13**Then I saw three evil[t] spirits[n] that looked like frogs;[o] they
came out of the mouth of the dragon,[p]
out of the mouth of the beast[q] and out
of the mouth of the false prophet.[r]
14They are spirits of demons[s] performing miraculous signs,[t] and they
go out to the kings of the whole
world,[u] to gather them for the battle[v]
on the great day[w] of God Almighty.

15"Behold, I come like a thief![x]
Blessed is he who stays awake[y] and
keeps his clothes with him, so that he
may not go naked and be shamefully
exposed."[z]

Rev 19:11-16

16Then they gathered the kings together[a] to the place that in Hebrew[b]
is called Armageddon.[c]

17The seventh angel poured out his
bowl into the air,[d] and out of the temple[e] came a loud voice[f] from the
throne, saying, "It is done!"[g] **18**Then
there came flashes of lightning, rumblings, peals of thunder[h] and a severe
earthquake.[i] No earthquake like it
has ever occurred since man has been
on earth,[j] so tremendous was the
quake. **19**The great city[k] split into
three parts, and the cities of the nations collapsed. God remembered[l]
Babylon the Great[m] and gave her the
cup filled with the wine of the fury of
his wrath.[n] **20**Every island fled away
and the mountains could not be
found.[o] **21**From the sky huge hailstones[p] of about a hundred pounds
each fell upon men. And they cursed
God[q] on account of the plague of
hail,[r] because the plague was so terrible.

The Woman on the Beast

17 One of the seven angels[s] who
had the seven bowls[t] came
and said to me, "Come, I will show you

16:12 [k]S Rev 9:14 [l]Isa 11:15,16 [m]Isa 41:2; 46:11 **16:13** [n]Rev 18:2 [o]Ex 8:6 [p]S Rev 12:3 [q]S Rev 13:1 [r]Rev 19:20; 20:10 **16:14** [s]1Ti 4:1 [t]S Mt 24:24 [u]S Mt 24:14 [v]Rev 17:14; 19:19; 20:8 [w]S Rev 6:17 **16:15** [x]S Lk 12:39 [y]Lk 12:37 [z]Rev 3:18 **16:16** [a]ver 14 [b]Rev 9:11 [c]Jdg 5:19; 2Ki 23:29,30; Zec 12:11 **16:17** [d]Eph 2:2 [e]Rev 14:15 [f]Rev 11:15 [g]Rev 21:6 **16:18** [h]S Rev 4:5 [i]S Rev 6:12 [j]Da 12:1; Mt 24:21 **16:19** [k]S Rev 17:18 [l]Rev 18:5 [m]S Rev 14:8 [n]Rev 14:10 **16:20** [o]S Rev 6:14 **16:21** [p]Eze 13:13; 38:22; Rev 8:7; 11:19 [q]ver 9,11 [r]Ex 9:23-25 **17:1** [s]S Rev 15:1 [t]Rev 15:7

t *13* Greek *unclean*

16:13 FROGS. These unclean spirits are demons who can work miracles and thus deceive the nations in order to support evil, sin and the antichrist. The "dragon" must be identified with Satan (12:9), and the "beast" with the antichrist (see ch. 13).

16:14 SPIRITS OF DEMONS PERFORMING MIRACULOUS SIGNS. During the tribulation rulers of the nations will be demonized. Deceived by Satan through miracles, they will enter into an insane scheme plunging the entire world into a great holocaust (see article on THE GREAT TRIBULATION, p. 1456, and THE AGE OF THE ANTICHRIST, p. 1872).

16:16 ARMAGEDDON. Armageddon (Gk *harmagedōn*), located in northcentral Palestine, means "the mountain of Megiddo"; it will be the center of "the battle on the great day of God Almighty" (v. 14). This war will occur toward the end of the tribulation and conclude when Christ returns to destroy the wicked (see 14:19, note), to deliver his people and to inaugurate his Messianic kingdom. Note the following concerning this event. (1) The prophets of the OT prophesied the event (Dt 32:43; Jer 25:31; Joel 3:2,9–17; Zep 3:8; Zec 14:2–5).

(2) Satan and demons will gather together many nations under the direction of the antichrist in order to make war against God, his armies and his people, and to destroy Jerusalem (vv. 13–14,16; 17:14; 19:14,19; see also Eze 38–39, Zec 14:2). Although the focal point will be in the land of Israel, the event of Armageddon will involve the whole world (Jer 25:29–38).

(3) Christ will return and supernaturally intervene to destroy the antichrist and his armies (19:19–21; Zec 14:1–5) and all who disobey the gospel (Ps 110:5; Isa 66:15–16; 2Th 1:7–10). God will also send destruction and earthquakes on the whole world at this time (vv. 18–19; Jer 25:29–33).

16:19 BABYLON THE GREAT. See next note.

17:1 SAID TO ME. Chs. 17–18 portray the fall of Babylon the Great. (1) Babylon (v. 5) is the symbol for the whole world system dominated by Satan and manifesting wickedness politically, religiously and commercially (see Jer 50:1, note; 51:1–64, note). (2) Babylon will be completely destroyed during the last three and a half years of this age. Religious Babylon (i.e., the prostitute) will be destroyed by the antichrist (vv. 16–17), while political Babylon will be destroyed by Christ at his coming (19:11–21).

17:1 THE GREAT PROSTITUTE. The prostitute represents religious Babylon and encompasses all false religions, including apostate Christianity. In the Bible prostitution and adultery, when used figuratively, normally denote religious apostasy and unfaithfulness to God (Isa 1:21; Jer 3:9; Eze 16:14–18,32; Jas 4:4), and signify a people who profess to serve God while actually worshiping and serving other gods. Note the sharp contrast between the great prostitute and the bride of the Lamb (see 19:7–8). The prostitute is subject to Satan; the bride is subject to Christ. Satan clothes the one (v. 4); God clothes the other (19:8). Eternal death is the portion of the prostitute; eternal glory the lot of the bride.

Concerning this false religion, (1) the prostitute will reject the gospel of Christ and the apostles, the power of godliness and the basic doctrines of Christianity (Mt 24:24; 2Ti 3:5; 4:3).

the punishment[u] of the great prostitute,[v] who sits on many waters.[w]
2With her the kings of the earth committed adultery and the inhabitants of
the earth were intoxicated with the
wine of her adulteries."[x]
3Then the angel carried me away in
the Spirit[y] into a desert.[z] There I
saw a woman sitting on a scarlet[a]
beast that was covered with blasphemous names[b] and had seven heads
and ten horns.[c] 4The woman was
dressed in purple and scarlet, and was
glittering with gold, precious stones
and pearls.[d] She held a golden cup[e]
in her hand, filled with abominable
things and the filth of her adulteries.[f]
5This title was written on her forehead:

MYSTERY[g]
BABYLON THE GREAT[h]
THE MOTHER OF PROSTITUTES[i]
AND OF THE ABOMINATIONS OF THE EARTH.

17:1 [u]Rev 16:19 [v]ver 5,15,16; Isa 23:17; Rev 19:2 [w]Jer 51:13
17:2 [x]S Rev 14:8
17:3 [y]S Rev 1:10 [z]Rev 12:6,14 [a]Rev 18:12,16 [b]Rev 13:1 [c]S Rev 12:3
17:4 [d]Eze 28:13; Rev 18:16 [e]Jer 51:7; Rev 18:6 [f]ver 2; S Rev 14:8
17:5 [g]ver 7 [h]S Rev 14:8 [i]ver 1,2
17:6 [j]Rev 16:6; 18:24
17:7 [k]ver 5 [l]ver 3; S Rev 12:3
17:8 [m]S Lk 8:31 [n]Rev 13:10 [o]S Rev 3:10 [p]S Rev 20:12 [q]Rev 13:3
17:9 [r]Rev 13:18 [s]ver 3

6I saw that the woman was drunk
with the blood of the saints,[j] the
blood of those who bore testimony to
Jesus.
When I saw her, I was greatly astonished. 7Then the angel said to me:
"Why are you astonished? I will explain to you the mystery[k] of the woman and of the beast she rides, which
has the seven heads and ten horns.[l]
8The beast, which you saw, once was,
now is not, and will come up out of the
Abyss[m] and go to his destruction.[n]
The inhabitants of the earth[o] whose
names have not been written in the
book of life[p] from the creation of the
world will be astonished[q] when they
see the beast, because he once was,
now is not, and yet will come.
9"This calls for a mind with wisdom.[r] The seven heads[s] are seven
hills on which the woman sits. 10They
are also seven kings. Five have fallen,
one is, the other has not yet come; but

(2) She will enter into partnership with the powers and philosophy of "Babylon," i.e., the world system with its immorality (3:16). Religious and political power will be combined to take spiritual control over the nations (v. 18).

(3) Her leaders will persecute Christ's true followers (v. 6). She will be a melting pot for many faiths and creeds, and doctrine will not be of primary importance. Her chief concern will be fellowship and unity with her religious system, values and goals. She will become a "home for demons and a haunt for every evil spirit" (18:2; cf. Isa 47:12–13).

(4) All true believers are commanded to come out of her or they will be condemned with her (18:4).

(5) God will cause the antichrist to destroy her (see v. 16, note).

17:2 INHABITANTS OF THE EARTH. The true kinship of the great prostitute (see previous note) is not with Christ but with the world. (1) Hypocrites and false prophets achieve worldly success as a result of her doctrine, for she encourages worldly people to join her. The false religious system allows her members to profess to be of God, yet at the same time to commit adultery. (2) Compromise with political power and toleration of unrighteousness are her trademarks. As a prostitute the apostate church sells her favor to the world at every opportunity (18:3).

17:3 A SCARLET BEAST. This beast is the world government or political Babylon, which supports the apostate spiritual power. For comments on the "seven heads," see v. 10, note; on the "ten horns," see v. 12, note.

17:4 A GOLDEN CUP. This cup, "filled with abominable things" but beautiful on the outside, reveals the spiritual condition of the apostate church of the last days (cf. Mt 23:27–28). The church that holds the golden cup will offer people both God and worldly satisfaction, i.e., a perverted Christianity that assures its members they can enjoy immorality and still be accepted by God.

17:5 BABYLON THE GREAT. The origin of the name "Babylon" is from "Babel," which symbolizes false religion, sorcery, astrology and rebellion against God (Ge 10:8–10; 11:4; Isa 47:13).

17:6 THE BLOOD OF THE SAINTS. The false religion in league with the world system will persecute everyone truly devoted to Christ and the Biblical faith.

17:8 THE BOOK OF LIFE FROM THE CREATION OF THE WORLD. These words cannot be used to prove a predetermined individual election to salvation or damnation, for according to John, a person's name may be erased from the book of life by disloyalty and a failure to overcome (3:5; see 13:8, note; cf. Ps 69:28).

17:8 BEAST . . . ONCE WAS . . . NOW IS NOT, AND YET WILL COME. Some interpret this verse to mean the antichrist is a person who once lived in history, but is now dead, and in the future will come up out of the Abyss, remain on earth for a period and then finally be destroyed (cf. vv. 8–11; 19:20). Others relate it to John's statement in 13:3 (see note there).

17:10 SEVEN KINGS. Some believe the seven kings represent seven secular kingdoms of the world (the five fallen kingdoms are most likely Egypt, Assyria, Babylonia, Medo-Persia and Greece). John informs his readers that the Roman empire is part of this sequence (i.e., the one that "is"). The one yet to come refers to the feet of iron and clay on the image pictured in Da 2 (see Da 2:41–43, notes). This kingdom represents the nationalistic states that have followed the fall of the Roman empire, up to and including the present

when he does come, he must remain for a little while. **11**The beast who once was, and now is not,[t] is an eighth king. He belongs to the seven and is going to his destruction.

12"The ten horns[u] you saw are ten kings who have not yet received a kingdom, but who for one hour[v] will receive authority as kings along with the beast. **13**They have one purpose and will give their power and authority to the beast.[w] **14**They will make war[x] against the Lamb, but the Lamb will overcome[y] them because he is Lord of lords and King of kings[z]—and with him will be his called, chosen[a] and faithful followers."

15Then the angel said to me, "The waters[b] you saw, where the prostitute sits, are peoples, multitudes, nations and languages.[c] **16**The beast and the ten horns[d] you saw will hate the prostitute.[e] They will bring her to ruin[f] and leave her naked;[g] they will eat her flesh[h] and burn her with fire.[i] **17**For God has put it into their hearts[j] to accomplish his purpose by agreeing to give the beast their power to rule,[k] until God's words are fulfilled.[l] **18**The woman you saw is the great city[m] that rules over the kings of the earth."

17:11 [t]ver 8
17:12 [u]S Rev 12:3 [v]Rev 18:10,17,19
17:13 [w]ver 17
17:14 [x]S Rev 16:14 [y]S Jn 16:33 [z]S 1Ti 6:15 [a]Mt 22:14
17:15 [b]ver 1; Isa 8:7; Jer 47:2 [c]S Rev 13:7
17:16 [d]S Rev 12:3 [e]ver 1 [f]Rev 18:17, 19 [g]Eze 16:37,39 [h]Rev 19:18 [i]Rev 18:8
17:17 [j]2Co 8:16 [k]ver 13 [l]Jer 39:16; Rev 10:7
17:18 [m]Rev 16:19; 18:10,18,19,21

The Fall of Babylon

18 After this I saw another angel[n] coming down from heaven.[o] He had great authority, and the earth was illuminated by his splendor.[p] **2**With a mighty voice he shouted:

"Fallen! Fallen is Babylon the
  Great![q]
She has become a home for
  demons
and a haunt for every evil[u]
  spirit,[r]
a haunt for every unclean and
  detestable bird.[s]
3For all the nations have drunk
  the maddening wine of her
  adulteries.[t]
The kings of the earth committed
  adultery with her,[u]
and the merchants of the earth
  grew rich[v] from her
  excessive luxuries."[w]

4Then I heard another voice from heaven say:

"Come out of her, my people,[x]
  so that you will not share in her
  sins,

18:1 [n]Rev 17:1 [o]Rev 10:1; 20:1 [p]Eze 43:2
18:2 [q]S Rev 14:8 [r]Rev 16:13 [s]Isa 13:21,22; 34:11,13-15; Jer 50:39; 51:37; Zep 2:14,15
18:3 [t]S Rev 14:8 [u]Rev 17:2 [v]ver 11,15,23; Eze 27:9-25 [w]ver 7,9
18:4 [x]Isa 48:20; Jer 50:8; 51:6,9, 45; 2Co 6:17

[u]2 Greek *unclean*

time. The next kingdom, the eighth (v. 11), will be that of the antichrist.

17:11 AN EIGHTH KING. The beast, i.e., the antichrist (ch. 13), will be the head of the final world empire. He "belongs to the seven" (see previous note), but is also "an eighth." He belongs to the same ungodly world system as did the first seven, yet he is not a part of them (see v. 8, note). The antichrist will be destroyed at the end of the tribulation.

17:12 TEN HORNS . . . TEN KINGS. These kings are ten nations that will have great political power and support the future world ruler (v. 13). They make up a world confederacy of nations that will oppose Christ and the true Biblical faith (cf. Da 7:23–25).

17:14 MAKE WAR AGAINST THE LAMB. At the final battle Christ will overthrow the antichrist and those who align themselves with him (see 16:14,16, notes).

17:15 WATERS. The prostitute sitting on the waters indicates that there will be one ecumenical, universal, apostate religious system in the first part of the tribulation. This system will be replaced by the religion of the antichrist when he gains great political power (Mt 24:15; 2Th 2:3–4).

17:16 WILL HATE THE PROSTITUTE. Sometime during the antichrist's rule, the prostitute (see v. 1, note) will be hated by the antichrist and his supporters, and they will utterly destroy her and her institutions. This is God's judgment against the world religious system that rejected God's truth in Christ, and it may occur at the midpoint of the seven-year tribulation, when the beast professes to be god and demands that all worship him (13:8,15; cf. Da 9:27; 11:36–38; see articles on THE GREAT TRIBULATION, p. 1456, and THE AGE OF THE ANTICHRIST, p. 1872).

18:2 FALLEN IS BABYLON THE GREAT! In ch. 18, Babylon the Great is portrayed primarily in its commercial and political aspect. (1) Some believe Babylon here represents a literal city or nation that embodies the ungodly aspects of the city described in the chapter. (2) Others believe it represents the whole ungodly world system brought under the antichrist's rule. Here her commercial system is destroyed; in ch. 19 her political system is judged by God at the end of the tribulation (cf. 19:17–21; Isa 13:1–11).

18:4 COME OUT OF HER, MY PEOPLE. This is God's prophetic call to the last generation of believers to come out of Babylon the Great (v. 2), because those among God's people who remain in the ungodly system will inevitably "share in her sins" and therefore "receive . . . her plagues." The call to be separate from the world and false religious institutions has been an essential aspect of salvation throughout redemptive history (cf. Isa 52:11; Jer 51:45; 1Co 11:32; see article on SPIRITUAL SEPARATION FOR BELIEVERS, p. 1794).

so that you will not receive any
of her plagues;[y]
5 for her sins are piled up to
heaven,[z]
and God has remembered[a] her
crimes.
6 Give back to her as she has given;
pay her back[b] double[c] for
what she has done.
Mix her a double portion from
her own cup.[d]
7 Give her as much torture and grief
as the glory and luxury she gave
herself.[e]
In her heart she boasts,
'I sit as queen; I am not a
widow,
and I will never mourn.'[f]
8 Therefore in one day[g] her plagues
will overtake her:
death, mourning and famine.
She will be consumed by fire,[h]
for mighty is the Lord God who
judges her.

9 "When the kings of the earth who
committed adultery with her[i] and
shared her luxury[j] see the smoke of
her burning,[k] they will weep and
mourn over her.[l] 10 Terrified at her
torment, they will stand far off[m] and
cry:

" 'Woe! Woe, O great city,[n]
O Babylon, city of power!
In one hour[o] your doom has
come!'

11 "The merchants[p] of the earth will
weep and mourn[q] over her because no
one buys their cargoes any more[r]—
12 cargoes of gold, silver, precious
stones and pearls; fine linen, purple,
silk and scarlet cloth; every sort of cit-
ron wood, and articles of every kind
made of ivory, costly wood, bronze,
iron and marble;[s] 13 cargoes of cinnamon and spice, of incense, myrrh and
frankincense, of wine and olive oil, of
fine flour and wheat; cattle and sheep;
horses and carriages; and bodies and
souls of men.[t]

14 "They will say, 'The fruit you
longed for is gone from you. All your
riches and splendor have vanished,
never to be recovered.' 15 The merchants who sold these things and
gained their wealth from her[u] will
stand far off,[v] terrified at her torment.
They will weep and mourn[w] 16 and cry
out:

" 'Woe! Woe, O great city,[x]
dressed in fine linen, purple and
scarlet,
and glittering with gold,
precious stones and
pearls![y]
17 In one hour[z] such great wealth
has been brought to ruin!'[a]

"Every sea captain, and all who travel by ship, the sailors, and all who earn
their living from the sea,[b] will stand
far off.[c] 18 When they see the smoke of
her burning,[d] they will exclaim, 'Was
there ever a city like this great
city[e]?'[f] 19 They will throw dust on
their heads,[g] and with weeping and
mourning[h] cry out:

" 'Woe! Woe, O great city,[i]
where all who had ships on the
sea
became rich through her wealth!
In one hour she has been brought
to ruin![j]
20 Rejoice over her, O heaven![k]
Rejoice, saints and apostles and
prophets!

18:4 [y] Ge 19:15 **18:5** [z] 2Ch 28:9; Ezr 9:6; Jer 51:9 [a] Rev 16:19 **18:6** [b] Ps 137:8; Jer 50:15,29 [c] Isa 40:2 [d] Rev 14:10; 16:19; 17:4 **18:7** [e] Eze 28:2-8 [f] Ps 10:6; Isa 47:7, 8; Zep 2:15 **18:8** [g] ver 10; Isa 9:14; 47:9; Jer 50:31,32 [h] Rev 17:16 **18:9** [i] ver 3; Rev 14:8; 17:2,4 [j] ver 3,7 [k] ver 18; Rev 14:11; 19:3 [l] Jer 51:8; Eze 26:17,18 **18:10** [m] ver 15,17 [n] ver 16,19 [o] ver 17; Rev 17:12 **18:11** [p] Eze 27:27 [q] ver 15,19; Eze 27:31 [r] S ver 3

18:12 [s] Eze 27:12-22; Rev 17:4 **18:13** [t] Eze 27:13; 1Ti 1:10 **18:15** [u] S ver 3 [v] ver 10,17 [w] ver 11,19; Eze 27:31 **18:16** [x] ver 10,19 [y] Rev 17:4 **18:17** [z] ver 10; Rev 17:12 [a] Rev 17:16 [b] Eze 27:28-30 [c] ver 10,15 **18:18** [d] ver 9; Rev 19:3 [e] S Rev 17:18 [f] Eze 27:32; Rev 13:4 **18:19** [g] Jos 7:6; La 2:10; Eze 27:30 [h] ver 11, 15; Eze 27:31 [i] ver 10,16; Rev 17:18 [j] Rev 17:16 **18:20** [k] Jer 51:48; S Rev 12:12

18:7 GLORY AND LUXURY SHE GAVE HERSELF. The suffering and misery to fall on commercial Babylon will be in proportion to the self-glorifying and luxurious lifestyle she lived. The rich, powerful and unscrupulous enterprisers who rejected God and piled up wealth to the injury of others will be stripped of their wealth in one day (v. 8; cf. Jas 5:1–6).

18:9 KINGS . . . WEEP AND MOURN OVER HER. All those whose main concern was money, luxury and gratification of pleasure will weep and mourn, for the god of their life is destroyed. They can no longer profit in merchandise, since their great riches are gone (cf. Jas 5:1–6). God clearly indicates here his hatred for businesses and governments founded on greed and oppressive power. He stands against individuals who seek riches, status and pleasure instead of the humble values of Jesus Christ. Those who live in selfish luxury and pleasure will be brought down by God's wrath.

18:20 REJOICE OVER HER. All the godly in heaven and earth rejoice at God's righteous judgment on the great satanic system of evil with all its wicked manifestations, sinful pleasures, self-centered luxury, humanistic government and godless commerce. The exuberant celebration of the saints in heaven, described in 19:1–10, is proportionate to their present grief at evil's triumph in this world. The mark of God's true children is their distress at the immoral conduct around them. They will be tormented day after day by the lawless deeds they see and about which they hear (2Pe 2:7–8).

God has judged her for the way
she treated you.' "[l]

21Then a mighty angel[m] picked up
a boulder the size of a large millstone
and threw it into the sea,[n] and said:

"With such violence
the great city[o] of Babylon will
be thrown down,
never to be found again.
22The music of harpists and
musicians, flute players and
trumpeters,
will never be heard in you
again.[p]
No workman of any trade
will ever be found in you again.
The sound of a millstone
will never be heard in you
again.[q]
23The light of a lamp
will never shine in you again.
The voice of bridegroom and bride
will never be heard in you
again.[r]
Your merchants were the world's
great men.[s]
By your magic spell[t] all the
nations were led astray.
24In her was found the blood of
prophets and of the
saints,[u]
and of all who have been killed
on the earth."[v]

Hallelujah!

19 After this I heard what sounded
like the roar of a great multitude[w] in heaven shouting:

"Hallelujah![x]
Salvation[y] and glory and power[z]
belong to our God,
2 for true and just are his
judgments.[a]
He has condemned the great
prostitute[b]
who corrupted the earth by her
adulteries.
He has avenged on her the blood
of his servants."[c]

3And again they shouted:

"Hallelujah![d]
The smoke from her goes up for
ever and ever."[e]

4The twenty-four elders[f] and the
four living creatures[g] fell down[h] and
worshiped God, who was seated on the
throne. And they cried:

"Amen, Hallelujah!"[i]

5Then a voice came from the throne,
saying:

"Praise our God,
all you his servants,[j]
you who fear him,
both small and great!"[k]

6Then I heard what sounded like a
great multitude,[l] like the roar of rushing waters[m] and like loud peals of
thunder, shouting:

"Hallelujah![n]
For our Lord God Almighty[o]
reigns.[p]
7Let us rejoice and be glad
and give him glory![q]
For the wedding of the Lamb[r] has
come,
and his bride[s] has made herself
ready.
8Fine linen,[t] bright and clean,
was given her to wear."

18:20 [l]Rev 19:2 **18:21** [m]Rev 5:2; 10:1 [n]Jer 51:63 [o]S Rev 17:18 **18:22** [p]Isa 24:8; Eze 26:13 [q]Jer 25:10 **18:23** [r]Jer 7:34; 16:9; 25:10 [s]ver 3; Isa 23:8 [t]Na 3:4 **18:24** [u]Rev 16:6; 17:6 [v]Jer 51:49; Mt 23:35 **19:1** [w]ver 6; Rev 11:15 [x]ver 3, 4,6 [y]Rev 7:10; 12:10 [z]Rev 4:11; 7:12

19:2 [a]Rev 16:7 [b]S Rev 17:1 [c]S Rev 6:10 **19:3** [d]ver 1,4,6 [e]Isa 34:10; Rev 14:11 **19:4** [f]S Rev 4:4 [g]S Rev 4:6 [h]S Rev 4:10 [i]ver 1,3,6 **19:5** [j]Ps 134:1 [k]ver 18; Ps 115:13; Rev 11:18; 13:16; 20:12 **19:6** [l]ver 1; Rev 11:15 [m]S Rev 1:15 [n]ver 1,3,4 [o]S Rev 1:8 [p]Rev 11:15 **19:7** [q]S Rev 11:13 [r]ver 9; Mt 22:2; 25:10; Eph 5:32 [s]Rev 21:2,9; 22:17 **19:8** [t]ver 14; Rev 15:6

18:21 NEVER TO BE FOUND AGAIN. An angel declares the final fall of political Babylon. The antichrist and his ungodly world system will be totally destroyed at "the battle on the great day of God Almighty," when Christ returns to earth (16:14; see 14:8; 16:14,16, notes; 19:11–21; cf. the record of Babylon's fall in Da 5).

19:1 AFTER THIS. Ch. 19 deals with the end of the tribulation and Christ's glorious second coming to earth to destroy the ungodly and reign with his people.

19:1 HALLELUJAH! This is the first of four times the word "Hallelujah" occurs in the NT (see vv. 1,3–4,6). It is derived from two Hebrew words: *halal*, meaning "praise," and *jah*, meaning "Yahweh" or "LORD"; thus, it means "Praise the Lord!" The people in heaven praise the Lord because God has judged the world and avenged those who suffered at its hand, and because Jesus Christ is returning to earth to reign (vv. 6,11; 20:4). This is heaven's "Hallelujah Chorus."

19:7 HIS BRIDE HAS MADE HERSELF READY. The chronology of ch. 19 places the bride (i.e., the church, 2Co 11:2) already in heaven before Christ's coming to earth. Many interpreters believe this indicates the church has already been caught up to heaven before Christ's coming pictured in vv. 11–21 (see article on THE RAPTURE, p. 1864). Two reasons are given: (1) The bride is entirely dressed and ready in heaven for the "wedding of the Lamb"; thus, the church must already be raptured and in heaven. (2) The bride who is already in heaven is fully clothed in "the righteous acts of the saints" (v. 8). For the righteous acts of the saints to be complete, they must be in heaven and delivered from all impurity.

(Fine linen stands for the righteous
acts[u] of the saints.)

9Then the angel said to me,[v]
"Write:[w] 'Blessed are those who are
invited to the wedding supper of the
Lamb!'"[x] And he added, "These are
the true words of God."[y]
10At this I fell at his feet to worship
him.[z] But he said to me, "Do not do it!
I am a fellow servant with you and with
your brothers who hold to the testimony of Jesus. Worship God![a] For the
testimony of Jesus[b] is the spirit of
prophecy."

The Rider on the White Horse

11I saw heaven standing open[c] and
there before me was a white horse,
whose rider[d] is called Faithful and
True.[e] With justice he judges and
makes war.[f] **12**His eyes are like blazing fire,[g] and on his head are many
crowns.[h] He has a name written on
him[i] that no one knows but he himself.[j] **13**He is dressed in a robe dipped
in blood,[k] and his name is the Word of
God.[l] **14**The armies of heaven were
following him, riding on white horses
and dressed in fine linen,[m] white[n]
and clean. **15**Out of his mouth comes a
sharp sword[o] with which to strike
down[p] the nations. "He will rule them
with an iron scepter."[v][q] He treads
the winepress[r] of the fury of the
wrath of God Almighty. **16**On his robe
and on his thigh he has this name written:[s]

KING OF KINGS AND LORD OF LORDS.[t] Rev 22:12

17And I saw an angel standing in the
sun, who cried in a loud voice to all the
birds[u] flying in midair,[v] "Come,[w]
gather together for the great supper of
God,[x] **18**so that you may eat the flesh
of kings, generals, and mighty men, of
horses and their riders, and the flesh of
all people,[y] free and slave,[z] small
and great."[a]
19Then I saw the beast[b] and the
kings of the earth[c] and their armies
gathered together to make war against
the rider on the horse[d] and his army.
20But the beast was captured, and with
him the false prophet[e] who had performed the miraculous signs[f] on his

19:8 [u] Isa 61:10; Eze 44:17; Zec 3:4; Rev 15:4
19:9 [v] ver 10 [w] Rev 1:19 [x] Lk 14:15 [y] Rev 21:5; 22:6
19:10 [z] Rev 22:8 [a] Ac 10:25,26; Rev 22:9 [b] S Rev 1:2
19:11 [c] S Mt 3:16 [d] ver 19,21; Rev 6:2 [e] Rev 3:14 [f] Ex 15:3; Ps 96:13; Isa 11:4
19:12 [g] S Rev 1:14 [h] Rev 6:2; 12:3 [i] ver 16 [j] S Rev 2:17
19:13 [k] Isa 63:2,3 [l] Jn 1:1
19:14 [m] ver 8 [n] S Rev 3:4
19:15 [o] ver 21; S Rev 1:16 [p] Isa 11:4; 2Th 2:8 [q] Ps 2:9; Rev 2:27; 12:5 [r] S Rev 14:20
19:16 [s] ver 12 [t] S 1Ti 6:15
19:17 [u] ver 21 [v] Rev 8:13; 14:6 [w] Jer 12:9; Eze 39:17 [x] Isa 34:6; Jer 46:10
19:18 [y] Eze 39:18-20 [z] Rev 6:15 [a] S ver 5
19:19 [b] S Rev 13:1 [c] Rev 16:14,16 [d] ver 11,21
19:20 [e] Rev 16:13 [f] S Mt 24:24

[v] *15* Psalm 2:9

19:10 OF JESUS IS THE SPIRIT OF PROPHECY. Ultimately, all prophecy is related to Jesus and his redemptive work and exalts him.

19:11 I SAW HEAVEN STANDING OPEN. This verse sets forth the beginning of Christ's second coming to earth as King of kings and Lord of lords (v. 16). He comes from heaven as the Warrior-Messiah (cf. 2Th 1:7–8) to establish truth and justice (Ps 96:13), to judge the nations and to wage war against evil (cf. Jn 5:30). This is the event for which the faithful of all generations have waited.

19:14 ARMIES. The armies who return with Christ include all the saints who are already in heaven (cf. 17:14). Their white clothing confirms this.

19:15 STRIKE DOWN THE NATIONS. When Christ returns to earth, he will punish the wicked nations. To "rule them with an iron scepter" means to destroy them (cf. Ps 2:9). "He treads the winepress" indicates the awfulness of his judgment (cf. Isa 64:1–2; Zec 14:3–4; Mt 24:29–30; cf. Rev 14:19, note).

19:15 FURY OF THE WRATH OF GOD ALMIGHTY. This is a stern reminder that God hates sin. The sentimental view that Christ tolerates sin and immorality because of his love finds no place in Christ's own revelation of himself in this book (see next note).

19:17 THE GREAT SUPPER OF GOD. This supper refers to the battle of Armageddon (see 16:16, note). (1) The destruction of God's enemies will be so great that it will require a multitude of birds to clean up the battlefield. It is called the "great supper of God," for God will provide food for the birds of prey. (2) The scene is one of judgment against this world's terrible cruelty and evil. Other prophecies that in all probability refer to this coming event are 14:14–20; 16:13–16; 17:14; Jer 51:27–44; Eze 39:17–20; Joel 3:9–16; Zep 3:8; Zec 14:2–5.

19:19 TO MAKE WAR. In preparation for the war, God through demonic agency will gather the nations together in the vicinity of Armageddon (see 16:16, note; Joel 3:2; Zep 3:8; Zec 14:2–3). (1) The war will end swiftly with the destruction of the antichrist and all the ungodly (vv. 19–21). (2) God's judgment not only includes the gathered armies but extends to the entire world (Jer 25:29–33).

19:20 FALSE PROPHET . . . THE MIRACULOUS SIGNS. John again describes the false prophet by one outstanding characteristic: he deceived many by performing miraculous signs (cf. 13:13–15; cf. 2Th 2:9–10). The conclusion is obvious: in the last days those who seek to persevere in faithfulness to Christ and his commandments (cf. 14:12) must not base their evaluation of truth solely on success or miracles. The Lord himself solemnly warns: "For false Christs and false prophets will appear and perform great signs and miracles to deceive even the elect—if that were possible" (Mt 24:24; see article on THE GREAT TRIBULATION, p. 1456).

behalf.[g] With these signs he had deluded[h] those who had received the
mark of the beast[i] and worshiped his
image.[j] The two of them were thrown
alive into the fiery lake[k] of burning
sulfur.[l] 21The rest of them were
killed with the sword[m] that came out
of the mouth of the rider on the
horse,[n] and all the birds[o] gorged
themselves on their flesh.

The Thousand Years

20 And I saw an angel coming
down out of heaven,[p] having
the key[q] to the Abyss[r] and holding in
his hand a great chain. 2He seized the
dragon, that ancient serpent, who is
the devil, or Satan,[s] and bound him
for a thousand years.[t] 3He threw him
into the Abyss,[u] and locked and
sealed[v] it over him, to keep him from
deceiving the nations[w] anymore until
the thousand years were ended. After
that, he must be set free for a short
time.

4I saw thrones[x] on which were
seated those who had been given authority to judge.[y] And I saw the souls
of those who had been beheaded[z] because of their testimony for Jesus[a]
and because of the word of God.[b] They
had not worshiped the beast[c] or his
image and had not received his mark
on their foreheads or their hands.[d]
They came to life and reigned[e] with

19:20 [g]Rev 13:12 [h]Rev 13:14 [i]Rev 13:16 [j]Rev 13:15 [k]Da 7:11; Rev 20:10,14,15; 21:8 [l]S Rev 9:17
19:21 [m]ver 15; S Rev 1:16 [n]ver 11,19 [o]ver 17
20:1 [p]Rev 10:1; 18:1 [q]Rev 1:18 [r]S Lk 8:31
20:2 [s]S Mt 4:10 [t]Isa 24:22; S 2Pe 2:4
20:3 [u]ver 1 [v]Da 6:17; Mt 27:66 [w]ver 8, 10; Rev 12:9
20:4 [x]Da 7:9 [y]Mt 19:28; Rev 3:21 [z]Rev 6:9 [a]S Rev 1:2 [b]S Heb 4:12 [c]S Rev 13:12 [d]S Rev 13:16 [e]ver 6; Rev 22:5

19:21 THE REST OF THEM WERE KILLED. God destroys the wicked throughout the whole earth (see Jer 25:29–33). Therefore no unsaved or unrighteous person will enter God's thousand-year kingdom (20:4). During the tribulation, the gospel was adequately presented by angels from the skies to everyone living on earth. Those who rejected the truth were given "a powerful delusion so that they will believe the lie and so that all will be condemned who have not believed the truth" (2Th 2:11–12). Note that the unrighteous "will not inherit the kingdom of God" (1Co 6:9–11; cf. Gal 5:19–21). They will be separated from the righteous after Christ returns in glory and will be assigned to eternal punishment (Mt 25:31–46).

20:2 DRAGON . . . BOUND HIM FOR A THOUSAND YEARS. After Christ's return and the events of ch. 19, Satan will be bound and imprisoned for a thousand years, in order that he may not deceive the nations. This implies a complete cessation of his influence during this time. After the thousand years, he will be released for a short time in order to deceive those who rebel against God's rule (vv. 3,7–9). Satan's most characteristic work is to deceive (see Ge 3:13; Mt 24:24; 2Th 2:9–10).

20:3 KEEP HIM FROM DECEIVING THE NATIONS ANYMORE. The nations that will exist during Christ's reign on earth are formed from those believers who are alive at the end of the tribulation (see 19:21, note; 20:4, note). Although at times the term "nations" is used specifically of the ungodly, John also uses it to represent the saved (21:24; 22:2).

20:4 THRONES ON WHICH WERE SEATED. Those who sit on the thrones are probably the overcomers from all churches of all time (cf. 2:7, note), possibly including the OT saints (see Eze 37:11–14; Eph 2:14–22; 3:6; Heb 11:39–40). Those who came to life after Christ's return are said to be the faithful who died during the tribulation (6:9; 12:17). John does not mention the resurrection of the church saints who have died, for this occurred when Christ removed his church from earth and took it to heaven (i.e., the rapture; see Jn 14:3, note; 1Co 15:51, note; see article on THE RAPTURE, p. 1864).

20:4 REIGNED WITH CHRIST A THOUSAND YEARS. This thousand-year reign of Christ is sometimes called "the millennium," meaning "a thousand years" (*mille* is a Latin word meaning "thousand," and *annus* a Latin word meaning "year"). The characteristics of this reign are the following:

(1) It was predicted in the OT (Isa 9:6; 65:19–25; Da 7:13–14; Mic 4:1–8; Zec 14:1–9; cf. Rev 2:25–28).

(2) Satan will be bound (see vv. 2,3, notes).

(3) Christ's reign will be shared by the faithful of his churches (2:26–27; 3:21; 5:10; 20:4), and possibly also by the resurrected OT saints (see Eze 37:11–14; Eph 2:14–22; 3:6; Heb 11:39–40) and martyred tribulation saints (see previous note).

(4) The people ruled by Christ will consist of those on earth who were faithful to Christ during the tribulation and who survived until the Lord's coming and those born during the millennium (14:12; 18:4; Isa 65:20–23; see Mt 25:1, note).

(5) No unsaved persons will enter the kingdom (see 19:21, note).

(6) Those reigning with Christ stand far above all the nations, for they will minister to and rule both Israel and the other nations (v. 6; 3:21; 5:10; Mt 19:28; see Zep 3:9–20, note).

(7) There will be peace, safety, prosperity and righteousness throughout the earth (Isa 2:2–4; Mic 4:4; Zec 9:10; see Zec 2:5, note; 9:8, note).

(8) Nature will be restored to its original order, perfection and beauty (Ps 96:11–13; 98:7–9; Isa 14:7–8; 35:1–2,6–7; 51:3; 55:12–13; 65:25; Eze 34:25; Ro 8:18–23; see Isa 65:17–25, note; Eze 36:8–15, note; Zec 14:8, note).

(9) The nations during this reign are obliged to continue in faith in Christ and obedience to his rule. However, some will choose the way of rebellion and disobedience and will be punished (vv. 7–10).

(10) At the end of the thousand years, the kingdom will be handed over by Jesus to the Father (1Co 15:24); then will begin the final and everlasting kingdom of God and the Lamb (21:1—22:5).

Christ a thousand years. **5**(The rest of
the dead did not come to life until the
thousand years were ended.) This is
the first resurrection.[f] **6**Blessed[g]
and holy are those who have part in the
first resurrection. The second death[h]
has no power over them, but they will
be priests[i] of God and of Christ and
will reign with him[j] for a thousand
years.

Satan's Doom

7When the thousand years are
over,[k] Satan will be released from his
prison **8**and will go out to deceive the
nations[l] in the four corners of the
earth[m]—Gog and Magog[n]—to gather them for battle.[o] In number they
are like the sand on the seashore.[p]
9They marched across the breadth of
the earth and surrounded[q] the camp
of God's people, the city he loves.[r]
But fire came down from heaven[s] and
devoured them. **10**And the devil, who
deceived them,[t] was thrown into the
lake of burning sulfur,[u] where the
beast[v] and the false prophet[w] had
been thrown. They will be tormented
day and night for ever and ever.[x]

20:5 [f] ver 6; Lk 14:14; Php 3:11; 1Th 4:16 **20:6** [g] Rev 14:13 [h] S Rev 2:11 [i] S 1Pe 2:5 [j] ver 4; Rev 22:5 **20:7** [k] ver 2 **20:8** [l] ver 3,10; Rev 12:9 [m] Isa 11:12; Eze 7:2; Rev 7:1 [n] Eze 38:2; 39:1 [o] S Rev 16:14 [p] Eze 38:9,15; Heb 11:12 **20:9** [q] Eze 38:9,16 [r] Ps 87:2 [s] Eze 38:22; 39:6; S Rev 13:13 **20:10** [t] ver 3,8; Rev 12:9; 19:20 [u] S Rev 9:17 [v] Rev 16:13 [w] Rev 16:13 [x] Rev 14:10,11

20:11 [y] S Rev 4:2 [z] S Rev 6:14 **20:12** [a] S Rev 19:5 [b] Da 7:10 [c] ver 15; Ex 32:32; Dt 29:20; Da 12:1; Mal 3:16; Lk 10:20; Rev 3:5; 21:27 [d] Rev 11:18 [e] Jer 17:10; S Mt 16:27 **20:13** [f] Rev 1:18; 6:8 [g] Isa 26:19 [h] S Mt 16:27 **20:14** [i] 1Co 15:26 [j] ver 13

The Dead Are Judged

11Then I saw a great white throne[y]
and him who was seated on it. Earth
and sky fled from his presence,[z] and
there was no place for them. **12**And I
saw the dead, great and small,[a] standing before the throne, and books were
opened.[b] Another book was opened,
which is the book of life.[c] The dead
were judged[d] according to what they
had done[e] as recorded in the books.
13The sea gave up the dead that were
in it, and death and Hades[f] gave up
the dead[g] that were in them, and each
person was judged according to what
he had done.[h] **14**Then death[i] and Hades[j] were thrown into the lake of
fire.[k] The lake of fire is the second
death.[l] **15**If anyone's name was not
found written in the book of life,[m] he
was thrown into the lake of fire.

The New Jerusalem

21 Then I saw a new heaven and a
new earth,[n] for the first heav-
en and the first earth had passed

[k] S Rev 19:20 [l] S Rev 2:11 **20:15** [m] S ver 12 **21:1** [n] S 2Pe 3:13

20:6 THE FIRST RESURRECTION. This term includes the resurrection of Christ and all God's people, in contrast to the resurrection of the wicked at the end of the millennium (vv. 12–13; Isa 26:19–21; Da 12:2,13; Mt 27:52–53; Jn 11:25–26; 14:19; 1Co 15:20,52; see article on THE RAPTURE, p. 1864).

20:7 SATAN WILL BE RELEASED. At the close of Christ's reign, Satan will be released. (1) Satan himself, deceived in believing he can yet defeat God, will be allowed to deceive those who desire to rebel against Christ's rule and will gather a multitude of such rebels together. (2) "Gog and Magog" (v. 8; derived from Eze 38–39) represent all the nations of the world and their spirit of rebellion against God and righteousness.

20:8 DECEIVE THE NATIONS. This is the last rebellion against God in history. Many of those born during the millennium evidently choose to reject Christ's visible lordship and choose instead Satan and his lie. God's judgment is total destruction (v. 9).

20:10 THE DEVIL . . . THE LAKE OF BURNING SULFUR. Satan's power will not last forever, for God will throw him into the lake of burning sulfur (see Isa 14:9–17). There he will not rule, but will be tormented day and night forever.

20:11–13 GREAT WHITE THRONE. The judgment described here is called the "Great White Throne Judgment" and includes the lost of all ages. Some believe that those saved during Christ's thousand-year reign on earth will be included in this judgment.

20:11 EARTH AND SKY FLED. This may refer to the destruction of the universe and the creation of a new heaven and earth (21:1; cf. Isa 51:6; 2Pe 3:7,10–12).

20:14 THE LAKE OF FIRE. The Bible portrays a terrible picture of the final destiny of the lost. (1) It speaks of "trouble and distress" (Ro 2:9), "weeping and gnashing of teeth" (Mt 22:13; 25:30), "everlasting destruction" (2Th 1:9), and a "fiery furnace" (Mt 13:42,50). It speaks of "gloomy dungeons" (2Pe 2:4), "eternal punishment" (Mt 25:46), a "hell, where the fire never goes out" (Mk 9:43), a "fiery lake of burning sulfur" (19:20), and "the smoke of their torment rises for ever and ever. There is no rest day or night" (14:11). Indeed, "It is a dreadful thing to fall into the hands of the living God" (Heb 10:31); "It would be better for him if he had not been born" (Mt 26:24; see also Mt 10:28, note).

(2) The believers of the NT church were keenly aware of the fate of those who lived in sin. It was for this reason they preached with tears (see Ac 20:19, note) and defended God's infallible Word and saving gospel against all distortion and false doctrine (see Php 1:17, note; 2Ti 1:14, note; see article on OVERSEERS AND THEIR DUTIES, p. 1690).

(3) The solemn fact of eternal punishment for the wicked is the greatest motivation for carrying the gospel to all the world and doing everything possible to persuade people to repent and receive Christ before it is too late (see Jn 3:16, note).

20:15 BOOK OF LIFE. See 3:5, note.

away,[o] and there was no longer any
sea. **2**I saw the Holy City,[p] the new
Jerusalem, coming down out of heaven
from God,[q] prepared as a bride[r]
beautifully dressed for her husband.
3And I heard a loud voice from the
throne saying, "Now the dwelling of
God is with men, and he will live with
them.[s] They will be his people, and
God himself will be with them and be
their God.[t] **4**He will wipe every tear
from their eyes.[u] There will be no
more death[v] or mourning or crying or
pain,[w] for the old order of things has
passed away."[x]

5He who was seated on the throne[y]
said, "I am making everything new!"[z]
Then he said, "Write this down, for
these words are trustworthy and
true."[a]

6He said to me: "It is done.[b] I am
the Alpha and the Omega,[c] the Beginning and the End. To him who is thirsty
I will give to drink without cost[d] from
the spring of the water of life.[e] **7**He
who overcomes[f] will inherit all this,
and I will be his God and he will be my
son.[g] **8**But the cowardly, the unbelieving, the vile, the murderers, the sexually immoral, those who practice magic
arts, the idolaters and all liars[h]—
their place will be in the fiery lake of
burning sulfur.[i] This is the second
death."[j]

9One of the seven angels who had
the seven bowls full of the seven last
plagues[k] came and said to me, "Come,
I will show you the bride,[l] the wife of
the Lamb." **10**And he carried me
away[m] in the Spirit[n] to a mountain
great and high, and showed me the
Holy City, Jerusalem, coming down out
of heaven from God.[o] **11**It shone with
the glory of God,[p] and its brilliance
was like that of a very precious jewel,
like a jasper,[q] clear as crystal.[r] **12**It
had a great, high wall with twelve

21:1 [o]S Rev 6:14 **21:2** [p]ver 10; Ne 11:18; Isa 52:1; Rev 11:2; 22:19 [q]ver 10; Heb 11:10; 12:22; Rev 3:12 [r]S Rev 19:7 **21:3** [s]Ex 25:8; 2Ch 6:18; Eze 48:35; Zec 2:10 [t]S 2Co 6:16 **21:4** [u]S Rev 7:17 [v]Isa 25:8; 1Co 15:26; Rev 20:14 [w]Isa 35:10; 65:19 [x]S 2Co 5:17 **21:5** [y]Rev 4:9; 20:11 [z]ver 4 [a]Rev 19:9; 22:6 **21:6** [b]Rev 16:17 [c]Rev 1:8; 22:13 [d]Isa 55:1 [e]S Jn 4:10 **21:7** [f]S Jn 16:33 [g]ver 3; 2Sa 7:14; 2Co 6:16; S Ro 8:14 **21:8** [h]ver 27; Ps 5:6; 1Co 6:9; Heb 12:14; Rev 22:15 [i]S Rev 9:17 [j]S Rev 2:11 **21:9** [k]S Rev 15:1,6,7 [l]S Rev 19:7 **21:10** [m]Eze 40:2; Rev 17:3 [n]S Rev 1:10 [o]S ver 2 **21:11** [p]ver 23; Isa 60:1,2; Eze 43:2; Rev 15:8; 22:5 [q]ver 18,19; Rev 4:3 [r]Rev 4:6

21:1 A NEW HEAVEN AND A NEW EARTH. The final goal and expectation of the NT faith is a new, transformed and redeemed world where Christ lives with his people and righteousness dwells in holy perfection (cf. Ps 102:25–26; Isa 65:17; 66:22; Ro 8:19–22; Heb 1:12; 12:27; 2Pe 3:13). To erase all traces of sin, there will be a destruction of the earth, stars and galaxies. Heaven and earth will be shaken (Hag 2:6; Heb 12:26–28) and will vanish like smoke (Isa 51:6); the stars will be dissolved and the elements destroyed (Isa 34:4; 2Pe 3:7,10,12). The renewed earth will become the dwelling place of both humans and God (vv. 2–3; 22:3–5). All the redeemed will possess bodies like Christ's resurrection body, ones that are real, visible and tangible, but incorruptible and immortal (Ro 8:23; 1Co 15:51–54).

21:2 NEW JERUSALEM. The new Jerusalem already exists in heaven (Gal 4:26); it will soon come to earth as the city of God for which Abraham and all of God's faithful waited, and of which God is architect and builder (Php 3:20; Heb 11:10, 13,16; see article on THE CITY OF JERUSALEM, p. 576). The new earth will become God's headquarters, and he will remain with his people forever (cf. Lev 26:11–12; Jer 31:33; Eze 37:27; Zec 8:8).

21:4 WIPE EVERY TEAR FROM THEIR EYES. The effects of sin, such as sorrow, pain, unhappiness and death (7:16–17; Ge 3; Isa 35:10; 65:19; Ro 5:12), are gone forever, for the evil things of the first heaven and earth have completely passed away. Believers, although remembering all things worth remembering, will evidently not remember that which would cause them sorrow (Isa 65:17).

21:7 HE WHO OVERCOMES. God himself declares who will inherit the blessings of the new heaven and the new earth—those who faithfully persevere as Christ's overcomers (see 2:7, note). Those who do not overcome sin and ungodliness will be thrown into the fiery lake (see next note).

21:8 BUT THE COWARDLY, THE UNBELIEVING. God mentions several classes of people whose place will be in the fiery lake of burning sulfur. (1) The "cowardly" are those who fear the disapproval and threat of people more than they value loyalty to Christ and the truth of his Word. Their personal safety and status among others mean more than faithfulness. Among "the cowardly" are the compromisers among God's people who give up the fight and do not conquer (cf. Mk 8:35; 1Th 2:4, note; 2Ti 2:12–13, notes).

(2) The "unbelieving" include former believers in Christ who were overcome by various sins, such as those listed here. To profess Christ and then practice such evil is an abomination to God.

(3) Many churches today proclaim that it is possible for a person to be simultaneously a true child of God and an immoral person, liar, adulterer, homosexual or murderer. Such people contradict God's clear words here (cf. 1Co 6:9–10; Gal 5:19–21; Eph 5:5–7).

21:9 THE BRIDE, THE WIFE OF THE LAMB. This metaphor for the new city means that God's people live within it. John uses symbolic language to describe the Holy City, whose glory cannot be totally comprehended by human understanding, (see 21:9—22:5).

21:12–14 TWELVE GATES. The wall of the city suggests the security that the saved have in the new city. The twelve gates represent Israel (v. 12) and the twelve foundations represent the church (v. 14). This emphasizes the unity of God's people of OT and NT times.

gates,[s] and with twelve angels at the
gates. On the gates were written the
names of the twelve tribes of Israel.[t]
13There were three gates on the east,
three on the north, three on the south
and three on the west. **14**The wall of
the city had twelve foundations,[u] and
on them were the names of the twelve
apostles[v] of the Lamb.
15The angel who talked with me had
a measuring rod[w] of gold to measure
the city, its gates[x] and its walls.
16The city was laid out like a square,
as long as it was wide. He measured
the city with the rod and found it to be
12,000 stadia[w] in length, and as wide
and high as it is long. **17**He measured
its wall and it was 144 cubits[x] thick,[y]
by man's[y] measurement, which the
angel was using. **18**The wall was made
of jasper,[z] and the city of pure gold,
as pure as glass.[a] **19**The foundations
of the city walls were decorated with
every kind of precious stone.[b] The
first foundation was jasper,[c] the second sapphire, the third chalcedony, the
fourth emerald, **20**the fifth sardonyx,
the sixth carnelian,[d] the seventh
chrysolite, the eighth beryl, the ninth
topaz, the tenth chrysoprase, the eleventh jacinth, and the twelfth amethyst.[z] **21**The twelve gates[e] were
twelve pearls,[f] each gate made of a
single pearl. The great street of the
city was of pure gold, like transparent
glass.[g]
22I did not see a temple[h] in the city,
because the Lord God Almighty[i] and
the Lamb[j] are its temple. **23**The city
does not need the sun or the moon to
shine on it, for the glory of God[k] gives
it light,[l] and the Lamb[m] is its lamp.
24The nations will walk by its light,
and the kings of the earth will bring
their splendor into it.[n] **25**On no day
will its gates[o] ever be shut,[p] for
there will be no night there.[q] **26**The
glory and honor of the nations will be
brought into it.[r] **27**Nothing impure
will ever enter it, nor will anyone who
does what is shameful or deceitful,[s]
but only those whose names are written in the Lamb's book of life.[t]

The River of Life

22 Then the angel showed me the
river[u] of the water of life,[v] as
clear as crystal,[w] flowing[x] from the
throne of God and of the Lamb **2**down
the middle of the great street of the
city. On each side of the river stood the
tree of life,[y] bearing twelve crops of
fruit, yielding its fruit every month.
And the leaves of the tree are for the
healing of the nations.[z] **3**No longer
will there be any curse.[a] The throne of
God and of the Lamb will be in the city,
and his servants will serve him.[b]
4They will see his face,[c] and his name
will be on their foreheads.[d] **5**There
will be no more night.[e] They will not
need the light of a lamp or the light of
the sun, for the Lord God will give
them light.[f] And they will reign for
ever and ever.[g]

21:12 [s] ver 15,21, 25; Rev 22:14 [t] Eze 48:30-34
21:14 [u] S Eph 2:20; Heb 11:10 [v] Ac 1:26; Eph 2:20
21:15 [w] Eze 40:3; Rev 11:1 [x] S ver 12
21:17 [y] Rev 13:18
21:18 [z] S ver 11 [a] ver 21
21:19 [b] Ex 28:17-20; Isa 54:11,12; Eze 28:13 [c] S ver 11
21:20 [d] Rev 4:3
21:21 [e] S ver 12 [f] Isa 54:12 [g] ver 18
21:22 [h] Jn 4:21, 23 [i] S Rev 1:8 [j] S Rev 5:6
21:23 [k] S ver 11 [l] Isa 24:23; 60:19, 20; Rev 22:5 [m] S Rev 5:6
21:24 [n] ver 26; Isa 60:3,5
21:25 [o] S ver 12 [p] Isa 60:11 [q] Zec 14:7; Rev 22:5
21:26 [r] ver 24
21:27 [s] Isa 52:1; Joel 3:17; Rev 22:14,15 [t] S Rev 20:12
22:1 [u] Ps 36:8; 46:4 [v] ver 17; S Jn 4:10 [w] Rev 4:6 [x] Eze 47:1; Zec 14:8
22:2 [y] S Rev 2:7 [z] Eze 47:12
22:3 [a] Zec 14:11 [b] Rev 7:15
22:4 [c] S Mt 5:8 [d] S Rev 7:3
22:5 [e] Rev 21:25; Zec 14:7 [f] Isa 60:19,20; Rev 21:23 [g] Da 7:27; Rev 20:4

[w] *16* That is, about 1,400 miles (about 2,200 kilometers) [x] *17* That is, about 200 feet (about 65 meters) [y] *17* Or *high* [z] *20* The precise identification of some of these precious stones is uncertain.

21:16 LAID OUT LIKE A SQUARE. The size of the city indicates that it will have sufficient space for the believers of all ages. "1,200 stadia" is approximately 1,400 miles. The city is portrayed as a square. In the OT the Most Holy Place where God met his people was a perfect square. The entire city will be filled with God's glory and holiness.

21:22 LORD . . . LAMB ARE ITS TEMPLE. God's presence and nearness will permeate the entire city, not just a temple.

21:24–26 THE NATIONS WILL WALK. The new Jerusalem does not include the whole new earth, for the city has gates through which the righteous may enter and leave. The new Jerusalem may be the capital of the new earth.

21:25 NO NIGHT THERE. This refers only to the Holy City, for John does not say there is no night on the new earth. Some believe that there will be night outside the city, for God has promised that day and night will never pass away (cf. Ps 148:3–6; Isa 66:22–23; Jer 33:20–21,25).

22:1 RIVER OF THE WATER OF LIFE. This could be a literal river symbolizing the Holy Spirit and the life, blessing and spiritual power that he gives (cf. 7:17; 21:6; 22:17; Isa 44:3; Jn 7:37–39).

22:2 THE TREE OF LIFE. This tree refers to the eternal life given to all who populate the new city (Ge 2:9; 3:22). The healing leaves picture the absence of anything that brings physical or spiritual harm (cf. Eze 47:12); note that even in our new bodies we will be dependent on the Lord for life, strength and health.

22:4 THEY WILL SEE HIS FACE. This is the final goal of redemptive history: God living among his faithful people on an earth purged from all evil. On this new earth the saints will see and live with Jesus, the Lamb of God, who through love redeemed them by his death on the cross. Their greatest happiness will be: "Blessed are the pure in heart, for they will see God" (Mt 5:8; cf. Ex 33:20,23; Isa 33:17; Jn 14:9; 1Jn 3:2).

[6]The angel said to me,[h] "These words are trustworthy and true.[i] The Lord, the God of the spirits of the prophets,[j] sent his angel[k] to show his servants the things that must soon take place."

Jesus Is Coming

[7]"Behold, I am coming soon![l] Blessed[m] is he who keeps the words of the prophecy in this book."[n]

[8]I, John, am the one who heard and saw these things.[o] And when I had heard and seen them, I fell down to worship at the feet[p] of the angel who had been showing them to me. [9]But he said to me, "Do not do it! I am a fellow servant with you and with your brothers the prophets and of all who keep the words of this book.[q] Worship God!"[r]

[10]Then he told me, "Do not seal up[s] the words of the prophecy of this book,[t] because the time is near.[u] [11]Let him who does wrong continue to do wrong; let him who is vile continue to be vile; let him who does right continue to do right; and let him who is holy continue to be holy."[v]

Rev 22:20

[12]"Behold, I am coming soon![w] My reward is with me,[x] and I will give to everyone according to what he has done.[y] [13]I am the Alpha and the Omega,[z] the First and the Last,[a] the Beginning and the End.[b]

[14]"Blessed are those who wash their robes,[c] that they may have the right to the tree of life[d] and may go through the gates[e] into the city.[f] [15]Outside[g] are the dogs,[h] those who practice magic arts, the sexually immoral, the murderers, the idolaters and everyone who loves and practices falsehood.

[16]"I, Jesus,[i] have sent my angel[j] to give you[a] this testimony for the churches.[k] I am the Root[l] and the Offspring of David,[m] and the bright Morning Star."[n]

[17]The Spirit[o] and the bride[p] say, "Come!" And let him who hears say, "Come!" Whoever is thirsty, let him come; and whoever wishes, let him take the free gift of the water of life.[q]

[18]I warn everyone who hears the words of the prophecy of this book:[r] If anyone adds anything to them,[s] God will add to him the plagues described in this book.[t] [19]And if anyone takes words away[u] from this book of prophecy,[v] God will take away from him his share in the tree of life[w] and

22:6 [h]Rev 1:1 [i]Rev 21:5 [j]1Co 14:32; Heb 12:9 [k]ver 16; Rev 1:1
22:7 [l]ver 12,20; S Mt 16:27 [m]Rev 1:3; 16:15 [n]ver 10,18,19
22:8 [o]S Rev 1:1 [p]Rev 19:10
22:9 [q]ver 10,18,19 [r]Rev 19:10
22:10 [s]Da 8:26; Rev 10:4 [t]ver 7,18,19 [u]S Ro 13:11
22:11 [v]Eze 3:27; Da 12:10
22:12 [w]ver 7,20; S Mt 16:27 [x]Isa 40:10; 62:11 [y]S Mt 16:27
22:13 [z]Rev 1:8 [a]S Rev 1:17 [b]Rev 21:6
22:14 [c]Rev 7:14 [d]S Rev 2:7 [e]S Rev 21:12 [f]S Rev 21:27
22:15 [g]Dt 23:18; 1Co 6:9,10; Gal 5:19-21; Col 3:5,6; Rev 21:8 [h]Php 3:2
22:16 [i]Rev 1:1 [j]ver 6 [k]Rev 1:4 [l]S Rev 5:5 [m]S Mt 1:1 [n]2Pe 1:19; Rev 2:28
22:17 [o]Rev 2:7; 14:13 [p]S Rev 19:7 [q]S Jn 4:10
22:18 [r]ver 7,10,19 [s]Dt 4:2; 12:32; Pr 30:6 [t]Rev 15:6-16:21
22:19 [u]Dt 4:2; 12:32; Pr 30:6 [v]ver 7,10,18 [w]S Rev 2:7

[a] *16* The Greek is plural.

22:7 I AM COMING SOON! See 1Co 15:51, note on the NT time perspective related to Christ's return (see also Ro 13:12, note).

22:10 DO NOT SEAL UP THE WORDS. The message and prophecy of the book must be proclaimed to all believers and all churches (cf. Da 12:4).

22:11 CONTINUE TO DO WRONG. This may mean that those who reject John's prophecy will continue in their sins. Believers, however, must persevere in righteousness and holiness until Christ's return.

22:12 ACCORDING TO WHAT HE HAS DONE. See 1Co 3:15, note; see article on THE JUDGMENT OF BELIEVERS, p. 1791.

22:15 EVERYONE WHO LOVES AND PRACTICES FALSEHOOD. Notice how the Bible's last two chapters focus on the issue of lying. Those who practice falsehood are mentioned three times: (1) All liars "will be in the fiery lake of burning sulfur" (21:8); (2) those who do what is "deceitful" will not enter God's eternal city (21:27); (3) those who love and practice falsehood will be outside God's eternal kingdom. Lying is the last sin condemned in the Bible, possibly because it was a lie that brought the fall of the human race (Ge 3:1–5; cf. Jn 8:44). These solemn words should be a warning for all in the churches who believe that God tolerates lying and deceit.

22:17 THE SPIRIT AND THE BRIDE SAY, COME! The last mention of the Holy Spirit in the Bible shows him inspiring the bride (i.e., the church) to invite all who want salvation to come to Christ. The church is now empowered by the Spirit to accomplish the evangelism of the world (Ac 1:5–8; 2:4).

22:19 GOD WILL TAKE AWAY. John ends this revelation of Jesus Christ by warning about the terrible possibility of losing one's share in the tree of life and the Holy City. We may not have a careless attitude toward this book or any part of God's holy Scripture. Such an attitude is manifested if we choose to believe only certain parts of God's revelation and reject other parts that we do not like, or if we teach our own ideas as if they were part of God's Word itself (v. 18). As at the beginning of the human pilgrimage on earth, failure to take God's Word with absolute seriousness is a matter of life and death (see Ge 3:3–4).

in the holy city, which are described in
this book.
20He who testifies to these things[x]
says, "Yes, I am coming soon."[y]
Amen. Come, Lord Jesus.[z]

22:20 [x] Rev 1:2 [y] ver 7,12; S Mt 16:27 [z] 1Co 16:22

21The grace of the Lord Jesus be
with God's people.[a] Amen.

22:21 [a] S Ro 16:20

22:20 COME, LORD JESUS. The Bible ends with Jesus' promise that he is coming soon, to which John responds, "Come, Lord Jesus." This longing is shared by all true Christians. (1) This prayer is a confession that until he comes, our redemption remains incomplete, evil and sin are not yet overthrown, and this world is not yet renewed.

(2) We have every reason to believe that the day is fast approaching when he who is called "the Word of God" (19:13) and "the bright Morning Star" (v. 16) will come down from heaven to take his faithful away from the earth to his Father's house (Jn 14:1–3; 1Th 4:16–18), after which he will triumphantly return in glory to reign forever as "KING OF KINGS AND LORD OF LORDS" (19:16). This is our unfailing hope and joyful expectation (2Pe 1:19).

Table of Weights and Measures

BIBLICAL UNIT		APPROXIMATE AMERICAN EQUIVALENT	APPROXIMATE METRIC EQUIVALENT
		WEIGHTS	
talent	*(60 minas)*	75 pounds	34 kilograms
mina	*(50 shekels)*	1 1/4 pounds	0.6 kilogram
shekel	*(2 bekas)*	2/5 ounce	11.5 grams
pim	*(2/3 shekel)*	1/3 ounce	7.6 grams
beka	*(10 gerahs)*	1/5 ounce	5.5 grams
gerah		1/50 ounce	0.6 gram
		LENGTH	
cubit		18 inches	0.5 meter
span		9 inches	23 centimeters
handbreadth		3 inches	8 centimeters
		CAPACITY	
		Dry Measure	
cor [homer]	*(10 ephahs)*	6 bushels	220 liters
lethek	*(5 ephahs)*	3 bushels	110 liters
ephah	*(10 omers)*	3/5 bushel	22 liters
seah	*(1/3 ephah)*	7 quarts	7.3 liters
omer	*(1/10 ephah)*	2 quarts	2 liters
cab	*(1/18 ephah)*	1 quart	1 liter
		Liquid Measure	
bath	*(1 ephah)*	6 gallons	22 liters
hin	*(1/6 bath)*	4 quarts	4 liters
log	*(1/72 bath)*	1/3 quart	0.3 liter

The figures of the table are calculated on the basis of a shekel equaling 11.5 grams, a cubit equaling 18 inches and an ephah equaling 22 liters. The quart referred to is either a dry quart (slightly larger than a liter) or a liquid quart (slightly smaller than a liter), whichever is applicable. The ton referred to in the footnotes is the American ton of 2,000 pounds.

This table is based upon the best available information, but it is not intended to be mathematically precise; like the measurement equivalents in the footnotes, it merely gives approximate amounts and distances. Weights and measures differed somewhat at various times and places in the ancient world. There is uncertainty particularly about the ephah and the bath; further discoveries may give more light on these units of capacity.

Subject Index

This subject index will enable you to locate where various topics are discussed in the study notes and articles. Page numbers are given in boldface type.

Themefinder™ Index

This Themefinder™ Index will provide an "at-a-glance" listing of the passages assigned to a particular theme of importance in the Pentecostal tradition. Themefinders link the most significant texts on crucial Bible topics.

Baptized in/Filled with the Holy Spirit

Exodus 31:1–6
Numbers 27:18
Judges 3:9–10
Judges 6:34
Judges 11:29
Judges 15:14–15
1 Samuel 11:6–7
1 Samuel 16:13
1 Chronicles 12:18
2 Chronicles 24:20–21
Psalm 51:10–12
Isaiah 11:1–3a
Isaiah 32:15
Isaiah 42:1
Isaiah 44:3
Isaiah 59:21
Ezekiel 2:1–2
Ezekiel 11:19–20
Ezekiel 36:26–27
Ezekiel 37:14
Ezekiel 39:29
Joel 2:28–29
Micah 3:8
Zechariah 4:6
Matthew 3:11
Mark 1:7–8
Luke 1:15
Luke 1:41
Luke 1:67
Luke 3:16
Luke 4:1
Luke 24:49
John 1:32–33
John 7:38–39
Acts 1:4–5
Acts 2:4–13
Acts 2:38–39
Acts 4:8
Acts 4:31
Acts 6:3
Acts 7:55
Acts 8:14–17
Acts 9:17
Acts 10:44–47
Acts 11:15–17
Acts 13:9
Acts 15:8
Acts 19:1–7
Ephesians 5:18

Gifts of the Holy Spirit

Exodus 35:30–35
Numbers 11:24–29
Judges 4:4
1 Samuel 10:5–11
2 Samuel 23:1–2
Nehemiah 9:30
Isaiah 61:1–3
Ezekiel 8:3–4
Zechariah 7:12
Mark 16:17–18
Acts 6:8
Acts 11:27–28
Acts 14:3
Acts 15:32
Acts 21:9–12
Romans 1:11
Romans 12:6–8
Romans 15:19
1 Corinthians 1:7
1 Corinthians 12:1–31
1 Corinthians 14:1–40
Galatians 3:5
Ephesians 4:7–12
1 Timothy 4:14
2 Timothy 1:6
Hebrews 2:4
1 Peter 4:10–11

Fruit of the Holy Spirit

Genesis 50:19–21
Numbers 6:24–26
Numbers 12:3–7
Ruth 3:10–11
2 Samuel 9:1–7
Psalm 1:3
Isaiah 3:10
Isaiah 27:6
Isaiah 32:16–18
Ezekiel 17:22–24
Hosea 6:1–3
Hosea 14:4–8
Matthew 7:16–20
Matthew 12:33
Luke 6:43–44
John 15:1–8
Acts 13:52
Romans 5:5
Romans 8:6
Romans 14:17
Romans 15:30
Galatians 5:22–23
Ephesians 3:17–21
Colossians 1:6–8
1 Thessalonians 1:6
Hebrews 12:11
James 3:17–18

Healing

Genesis 20:17–18
Exodus 15:26
Numbers 12:10–15
Numbers 21:7–9
Deuteronomy 7:15
Deuteronomy 32:39
1 Kings 13:6
1 Kings 17:17–24
2 Kings 5:9–14
2 Kings 20:1–7
2 Chronicles 7:14
2 Chronicles 30:18–20
Psalm 6:1–3
Psalm 41:1–3
Psalm 103:1–5
Isaiah 38:1–21
Isaiah 53:4–5
Isaiah 57:18–19
Jeremiah 17:14
Jeremiah 30:17
Ezekiel 47:12
Hosea 11:3–4
Matthew 4:23–24
Matthew 8:16–17
Matthew 10:1
Matthew 12:22
Matthew 15:22–31
Mark 2:3–12
Mark 5:25–34
Mark 6:13
Mark 7:32–37
Luke 6:17–19
Luke 9:1–6
Luke 10:9
Luke 13:10–17
Luke 17:12–19
John 4:46–53
John 5:5–15
John 9:1–12
Acts 3:1–10
Acts 5:15–16
Acts 8:6–7
Acts 19:11–12
Acts 28:8–9
James 5:14–16
1 Peter 2:24

Faith that moves mountains

Genesis 15:3–6
Genesis 22:1–14
Exodus 17:8–13
Joshua 3:9–17
Judges 7:9–23
1 Samuel 17:38–51
1 Kings 18:41–46
2 Kings 4:18–37
2 Kings 19:19–36
2 Chronicles 20:20–24
2 Chronicles 32:20–23
Nehemiah 6:15–16
Esther 4:14—5:2
Job 13:15
Psalm 46
Isaiah 28:16
Daniel 3:1–27
Daniel 6:1–23
Habakkuk 3:17–19
Matthew 8:10
Matthew 9:2
Matthew 9:29–30
Matthew 17:20
Matthew 21:21–22
Mark 4:40
Mark 9:23–24
Mark 10:52
Mark 11:22–24
Luke 7:50
Luke 8:48
Luke 12:28
Luke 17:5–6
John 14:12
Acts 3:16
Acts 6:5
Acts 14:9–10
Acts 27:25
Romans 4:19–21
1 Corinthians 13:2
1 Thessalonians 3:7
2 Thessalonians 1:3
Hebrews 11:29–35

Witnessing

Exodus 10:1–2
Numbers 10:29
Psalm 67
Psalm 96
Proverbs 11:30
Isaiah 6:8
Isaiah 42:6–7
Isaiah 43:9–10
Isaiah 45:22–23
Isaiah 49:5–6
Isaiah 52:7–10
Ezekiel 3:10–11
Ezekiel 33:7–11
Amos 7:14–15
Jonah 1:1–2
Jonah 3:1–5
Zechariah 8:20–23
Matthew 10:18–20
Matthew 24:14
Matthew 28:18–20
Mark 16:15–16
Luke 24:47–48
John 1:7
John 4:7–30
John 15:26–27
Acts 1:8
Acts 2:32
Acts 4:20
Acts 4:33
Acts 5:32
Acts 8:4
Acts 8:26–40
Acts 16:29–32
Acts 18:9–10
Acts 20:20–21
Acts 26:16–27
Ephesians 6:19
1 Thessalonians 1:5
2 Timothy 1:8
1 Peter 3:15
1 John 1:2
Revelation 1:9
Revelation 11:3

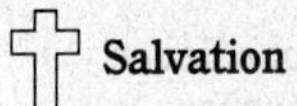

Salvation

Genesis 12:1–3
Exodus 12:29–42
Exodus 14:13–14
Leviticus 16:15–22
Deuteronomy 26:6–9
1 Samuel 2:1–2
Psalm 13:5–6
Psalm 18:1–3
Psalm 27:1
Psalm 37:39–40
Psalm 62:1–8
Psalm 85:4–7
Psalm 98:1–3
Psalm 116:1–13
Isaiah 12:1–3
Isaiah 25:9
Isaiah 43:11–13
Isaiah 51:4–6
Isaiah 53:6–12
Isaiah 55:6–7
Isaiah 59:15–17
Isaiah 61:10
Isaiah 63:1–6
Jeremiah 23:5–6
Ezekiel 3:16–21
Ezekiel 18:21–23
Ezekiel 33:14–16
Joel 2:32
Micah 7:7
Matthew 1:21
Luke 1:76–79
Luke 19:10
John 1:12
John 3:14–17
John 11:25–26
John 20:31
Acts 4:12
Acts 13:38–39
Romans 1:16
Romans 3:21–26
Romans 10:4–13
1 Corinthians 15:1–8
2 Corinthians 5:17—6:1
Galatians 2:16
Ephesians 2:4–9
1 Thessalonians 5:8–10
2 Thessalonians 2:13
1 Timothy 1:15–16
1 Timothy 2:3–6
2 Timothy 3:15
Titus 3:3–7
Hebrews 2:3
Hebrews 5:9
Hebrews 7:25
1 John 5:11–12
Revelation 3:20

Second Coming

Psalm 98:8–9
Isaiah 11:3b–4
Isaiah 35:3–5
Isaiah 40:10–11
Isaiah 62:11–12
Isaiah 66:15–16
Ezekiel 43:2
Joel 1:15
Zechariah 8:3–15
Zechariah 9:10
Zechariah 14:3–9
Malachi 4:2–3
Matthew 16:27–28
Matthew 24:15–51
Matthew 25:31–46
Matthew 26:64
Mark 13:1–37
Luke 17:22–37
John 14:3
Acts 1:11
1 Corinthians 4:5
1 Corinthians 15:23
Philippians 3:20–21
1 Thessalonians 1:10
1 Thessalonians 4:15—5:3
2 Thessalonians 1:7—2:8
1 Timothy 6:14–15
2 Timothy 4:8
Titus 2:13
Hebrews 9:28
1 Peter 5:4
2 Peter 3:8–14
1 John 3:2
Jude 14–15
Revelation 1:7
Revelation 16:15
Revelation 19:11–16
Revelation 22:12
Revelation 22:20

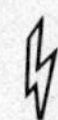

Victory over Satan and demons

Genesis 3:15
Exodus 7:10–12
Judges 6:25–32
Judges 16:23–30
1 Samuel 16:22–23
1 Kings 18:21–39
Job 1:6–22
Psalm 91:1–13
Isaiah 14:12–20
Isaiah 24:21–23
Daniel 10:11
Matthew 4:1–11
Matthew 8:28–33
Matthew 17:14–18
Mark 1:23–28
Mark 3:10–15
Mark 3:20–27
Mark 5:1–16
Luke 4:2–13
Luke 4:33–36
Luke 10:17–19
Luke 11:20–26
Acts 5:3–5
Acts 16:16–18
Acts 19:13–20
Romans 8:38–38
2 Corinthians 11:12–15
2 Corinthians 12:7–10
Ephesians 6:10–18
James 4:7
1 Peter 5:8–9
1 John 3:8
Jude 9
Revelation 12:7–11
Revelation 20:2–3
Revelation 20:7–10

Overcoming the world and worldliness

Genesis 19:15–26
Exodus 23:23–24
Leviticus 11:44–45
Leviticus 18:1–5
Deuteronomy 7:1–6
Joshua 23:11–13
1 Kings 19:18
2 Chronicles 30:6–9
Ezra 4:1–5
Nehemiah 2:18–20
Psalm 2
Psalm 18:37–40
Psalm 37:1–6
Psalm 49:13–15
Psalm 144
Proverbs 16:7
Isaiah 44:24–25
Jeremiah 1:18–19
Ezekiel 9:4
Daniel 1:8–20
Matthew 5:3–16
Matthew 6:19–24
John 15:18–20
John 16:33
John 17:14–18
John 18:36–37
Romans 12:1–2
1 Corinthians 2:6–16
2 Corinthians 6:14—7:1
Galatians 6:14
2 Timothy 3:1–5
Titus 2:11–12
Hebrews 11:13–16
James 1:27
James 4:4–6
1 Peter 2:11–12
1 John 2:15–17
1 John 5:4–5
Revelation 2:7
Revelation 2:12–17
Revelation 3:21–22
Revelation 21:7

Praise

Exodus 15:1–21
Deuteronomy 8:10
Judges 5:1–2
2 Samuel 22:47–50
1 Chronicles 16:7–43
1 Chronicles 29:20
Ezra 3:10–13
Psalm 9:1–2
Psalm 34:1–3
Psalm 92:1–4
Psalm 100
Psalm 113
Psalm 135:1–4
Psalm 146
Psalm 150
Isaiah 12:4–6
Isaiah 26:1–4
Isaiah 42:10–12
Jeremiah 20:13
Jeremiah 31:7
Daniel 2:20–23
Joel 2:23–27
Habakkuk 3:3
Zephaniah 3:19–20
Matthew 9:8
Matthew 21:15–16
Luke 1:42–47
Luke 2:13–14
Luke 2:20
Luke 18:43
Luke 19:36–40
Acts 2:46–47
Romans 15:5–11
Ephesians 1:3–6
Ephesians 5:19–20
Colossians 3:16–17
Hebrews 13:15
1 Peter 2:9
Revelation 5:9–14
Revelation 7:9–12
Revelation 19:1–6

Walking in obedience and righteousness

Genesis 5:22
Genesis 6:9–10
Genesis 17:1–2
Genesis 26:2–6
Exodus 19:3–6
Exodus 20:1–17
Leviticus 20:26
Deuteronomy 10:12–13
Deuteronomy 11:26–28
Joshua 1:7–8
Joshua 22:5
1 Samuel 12:14–15
1 Samuel 15:22–23
1 Kings 2:2–4
1 Kings 9:3–8
1 Chronicles 28:6–9
2 Chronicles 13:4–12
Ezra 7:10
Nehemiah 10:28–39
Job 1:1–5
Job 23:10–12
Psalm 1:1–2
Psalm 40:6–8
Psalm 78:1–8
Psalm 119:1–16
Proverbs 3:1–6
Ecclesiastes 12:13–14
Isaiah 2:3–5
Isaiah 35:8–9
Isaiah 58:1–8
Jeremiah 11:1–5
Ezekiel 20:39–44
Daniel 9:4–6
Micah 6:8
Malachi 2:5–6
Matthew 7:21–23
Matthew 19:16–26
Mark 9:42–48
Luke 6:46–49
Luke 10:25–37
Luke 12:42–48
John 8:31
John 14:21–24
Acts 10:34–35
Romans 6:1–14
Romans 8:1–5
Romans 13:12–14
Galatians 5:13–18
Ephesians 2:10
Ephesians 5:1–15
Philippians 2:12–16
Colossians 3:5–14
1 Thessalonians 4:1–7
Hebrews 10:23–26
Hebrews 12:1
James 2:14–26
1 Peter 1:13–16
2 Peter 1:3–11
1 John 2:3–6
1 John 3:9–18
Revelation 3:1–4
Revelation 21:8

The Entire Bible in a Year

This reading plan gives you a structured pattern for reading through the entire Bible in one year. There are two readings for each day, one in the Old Testament, the other in the New Testament. If you feel bogged down by so much reading each day, an alternative plan is to read the Old Testament passages the first year and the New Testament passages the second year, completing the entire Bible in two years rather than one.

JANUARY	A.M.	P.M.
1	Gen 1–2	Matt 1
2	Gen 3–5	Matt 2
3	Gen 6–8	Matt 3
4	Gen 9–11	Matt 4
5	Gen 12–14	Matt 5:1–20
6	Gen 15–17	Matt 5:21–48
7	Gen 18–19	Matt 6:1–18
8	Gen 20–22	Matt 6:19–7:6
9	Gen 23–24	Matt 7:7–29
10	Gen 25–26	Matt 8:1–27
11	Gen 27–28	Matt 8:28–9:17
12	Gen 29–30	Matt 9:18–38
13	Gen 31–33	Matt 10:1–23
14	Gen 34–35	Matt 10:24–42
15	Gen 36–37	Matt 11:1–30
16	Gen 38–39	Matt 12:1–21
17	Gen 40–41	Matt 12:22–50
18	Gen 42–43	Matt 13:1–23
19	Gen 44–45	Matt 13:24–43
20	Gen 46–48	Matt 13:44–14:12
21	Gen 49–50	Matt 14:13–36
22	Exod 1–2	Matt 15:1–28
23	Exod 3–5	Matt 15:29–16:12
24	Exod 6–7	Matt 16:13–17:13
25	Exod 8–9	Matt 17:14–18:14
26	Exod 10–12	Matt 18:15–35
27	Exod 13–14	Matt 19:1–15
28	Exod 15	Matt 19:16–20:16
29	Exod 16–17	Matt 20:17–34
30	Exod 18–19	Matt 21:1–32
31	Exod 20–21	Matt 21:33–22:14

FEBRUARY	A.M.	P.M.
1	Exod 22–23	Matt 22:15–46
2	Exod 24–25	Matt 23
3	Exod 26–27	Matt 24:1–35
4	Exod 28	Matt 24:36–51
5	Exod 29–30	Matt 25:1–30
6	Exod 31	Matt 25:31–46
7	Exod 32–33	Matt 26:1–30
8	Exod 34–35	Matt 26:31–56
9	Exod 36–37	Matt 26:57–75
10	Exod 38–39	Matt 27:1–26
11	Exod 40	Matt 27:27–44
12	Lev 1–3	Matt 27:45–66
13	Lev 4–5	Matt 28
14	Lev 6–7	Acts 1
15	Lev 8	Acts 2:1–21
16	Lev 9–10	Acts 2:22–47
17	Lev 11–12	Acts 3
18	Lev 13–14	Acts 4:1–31
19	Lev 15	Acts 4:32–5:11
20	Lev 16–18	Acts 5:12–42
21	Lev 19–21	Acts 6
22	Lev 22–23	Acts 7:1–53
23	Lev 24	Acts 7:54–8:8
24	Lev 25	Acts 8:9–40
25	Lev 26–27	Acts 9:1–31
26	Num 1–2	Acts 9:32–43
27	Num 3–4	Acts 10:1–23
28	Num 5–6	Acts 10:24–48
29	John 17	Heb 13

MARCH	A.M.	P.M.
1 ………	Num 7–8	Acts 11:1–18
2 ………	Num 9–10	Acts 11:19–30
3 ………	Num 11–13	Acts 12
4 ………	Num 14–15	Acts 13:1–12
5 ………	Num 16–17	Acts 13:13–52
6 ………	Num 18–19	Acts 14
7 ………	Num 20–21	Acts 15:1–21
8 ………	Num 22–23	Acts 15:22–35
9 ………	Num 24–26	Acts 15:36–16:15
10 ………	Num 27–28	Acts 16:16–40
11 ………	Num 29–31	Acts 17:1–15
12 ………	Num 32–33	Acts 17:16–34
13 ………	Num 34–36	Acts 18:1–23
14 ………	Deut 1–2	Acts 18:24–19:7
15 ………	Deut 3–4	Acts 19:8–41
16 ………	Deut 5–7	Acts 20:1–16
17 ………	Deut 8–10	Acts 20:17–38
18 ………	Deut 11–12	Acts 21:1–16
19 ………	Deut 13–15	Acts 21:17–36
20 ………	Deut 16–17	Acts 21:37–22:21
21 ………	Deut 18–21	Acts 22:22–23:11
22 ………	Deut 22–24	Acts 23:12–35
23 ………	Deut 25–27	Acts 24
24 ………	Deut 28	Acts 25:1–12
25 ………	Deut 29–30	Acts 25:13–26:1
26 ………	Deut 31–32	Acts 26:2–18
27 ………	Deut 33–34	Acts 26:19–32
28 ………	Josh 1–2	Acts 27:1–26
29 ………	Josh 3–4	Acts 27:27–44
30 ………	Josh 5–6	Acts 28:1–16
31 ………	Josh 7–9	Acts 28:17–31

APRIL	A.M.	P.M.
1 ………	Josh 10–12	Mark 1:1–20
2 ………	Josh 13–15	Mark 1:21–45
3 ………	Josh 16–19	Mark 2:1–22
4 ………	Josh 20–22	Mark 2:23–3:12
5 ………	Josh 23–24	Mark 3:13–35
6 ………	Judg 1–2	Mark 4:1–20
7 ………	Judg 3–4	Mark 4:21–41
8 ………	Judg 5–6	Mark 5:1–20
9 ………	Judg 7–8	Mark 5:21–43
10 ………	Judg 9	Mark 6:1–29
11 ………	Judg 10–11	Mark 6:30–56
12 ………	Judg 12–13	Mark 7:1–23
13 ………	Judg 14–16	Mark 7:24–8:13
14 ………	Judg 17–18	Mark 8:14–26
15 ………	Judg 19–21	Mark 8:27–9:13
16 ………	Ruth	Mark 9:14–32
17 ………	1 Sam 1–2	Mark 9:33–50
18 ………	1 Sam 3–7	Mark 10:1–31
19 ………	1 Sam 8–10	Mark 10:32–52
20 ………	1 Sam 11–13	Mark 11:1–26
21 ………	1 Sam 14–15	Mark 11:27–12:17
22 ………	1 Sam 16–17	Mark 12:18–44
23 ………	1 Sam 18–19	Mark 13
24 ………	1 Sam 20–22	Mark 14:1–26
25 ………	1 Sam 23–25	Mark 14:27–52
26 ………	1 Sam 26–28	Mark 14:53–72
27 ………	1 Sam 29–31	Mark 15:1–20
28 ………	2 Sam 1–3	Mark 15:21–47
29 ………	2 Sam 4–6	Mark 16
30 ………	2 Sam 7–8	Jude

MAY	A.M.	P.M.
1 ………	2 Sam 9–11	1 Pet 1:1–21
2 ………	2 Sam 12–14	1 Pet 1:22–2:25
3 ………	2 Sam 15–17	1 Pet 3
4 ………	2 Sam 18–19	1 Pet 4
5 ………	2 Sam 20–21	1 Pet 5
6 ………	2 Sam 22	2 Pet 1
7 ………	2 Sam 23–24	2 Pet 2
8 ………	1 Kings 1	2 Pet 3
9 ………	1 Kings 2–3	Jas 1
10 ………	1 Kings 4–6	Jas 2–3:13
11 ………	1 Kings 7–8	Jas 3:14–4:12
12 ………	1 Kings 9	Jas 4:13–5:20
13 ………	1 Kings 10–11	Luke 1:1–25
14 ………	1 Kings 12–14	Luke 1:26–56
15 ………	1 Kings 15–17	Luke 1:57–80
16 ………	1 Kings 18–19	Luke 2:1–20
17 ………	1 Kings 20–21	Luke 2:21–52
18 ………	1 Kings 22	Luke 3
19 ………	2 Kings 1–3	Luke 4:1–13
20 ………	2 Kings 4–5	Luke 4:14–44
21 ………	2 Kings 6–7	Luke 5:1–16
22 ………	2 Kings 8–9	Luke 5:17–39
23 ………	2 Kings 10–12	Luke 6:1–16
24 ………	2 Kings 13–15	Luke 6:17–49
25 ………	2 Kings 16–17	Luke 7:1–35
26 ………	2 Kings 18–19	Luke 7:36–50
27 ………	2 Kings 20–22	Luke 8:1–21
28 ………	2 Kings 23–25	Luke 8:22–39
29 ………	1 Chron 1–2	Luke 8:40–56
30 ………	1 Chron 3–4	Luke 9:1–17
31 ………	1 Chron 5–6	Luke 9:18–36

JUNE	A.M.	P.M.
1 ………	1 Chron 7–8	Luke 9:37–62
2 ………	1 Chron 9–10	Luke 10:1–24
3 ………	1 Chron 11–13	Luke 10:25–42
4 ………	1 Chron 14–16	Luke 11:1–13
5 ………	1 Chron 17–19	Luke 11:14–36
6 ………	1 Chron 20–22	Luke 11:37–54
7 ………	1 Chron 23–25	Luke 12:1–21
8 ………	1 Chron 26–29	Luke 12:22–48
9 ………	2 Chron 1–4	Luke 12:49–59
10 ………	2 Chron 5–7	Luke 13:1–21
11 ………	2 Chron 8–11	Luke 13:22–35
12 ………	2 Chron 12–15	Luke 14:1–24
13 ………	2 Chron 16–19	Luke 14:25–15:10
14 ………	2 Chron 20–22	Luke 15:11–32
15 ………	2 Chron 23–25	Luke 16
16 ………	2 Chron 26–28	Luke 17:1–19
17 ………	2 Chron 29–30	Luke 17:20–18:14
18 ………	2 Chron 31–32	Luke 18:15–43
19 ………	2 Chron 33–34	Luke 19:1–27
20 ………	2 Chron 35–36	Luke 19:28–48
21 ………	Ezra 1–3	Luke 20:1–19
22 ………	Ezra 4–6	Luke 20:20–21:4
23 ………	Ezra 7–8	Luke 21:5–38
24 ………	Ezra 9–10	Luke 22:1–38
25 ………	Neh 1–3	Luke 22:39–65
26 ………	Neh 4–6	Luke 22:66–23:25
27 ………	Neh 7–8	Luke 23:26–49
28 ………	Neh 9–10	Luke 23:50–24:12
29 ………	Neh 11–13	Luke 24:13–35
30 ………	Est 1–4	Luke 24:36–53

JULY	A.M.	P.M.
1	Est 5–7	1 Thess 1–2:16
2	Est 8–10	1 Thess 2:17–3:13
3	Job 1–2	1 Thess 4
4	Job 3–5	1 Thess 5
5	Job 6–8	2 Thess 1
6	Job 9–11	2 Thess 2
7	Job 12–14	2 Thess 3
8	Job 15–18	1 Cor 1
9	Job 19–21	1 Cor 2
10	Job 22–24	1 Cor 3
11	Job 25–28	1 Cor 4
12	Job 29–31	1 Cor 5
13	Job 32–35	1 Cor 6
14	Job 36–39	1 Cor 7
15	Job 40–42	1 Cor 8
16	Psa 1–6	1 Cor 9
17	Psa 7–10	1 Cor 10:1–13
18	Psa 11–16	1 Cor 10:14–11:1
19	Psa 17–18	1 Cor 11:2–34
20	Psa 19–20	1 Cor 12
21	Psa 21–22	1 Cor 13
22	Psa 23–25	1 Cor 14
23	Psa 26–29	1 Cor 15:1–34
24	Psa 30–31	1 Cor 15:35–58
25	Psa 32–34	1 Cor 16
26	Psa 35–37	2 Cor 1–2:4
27	Psa 38–41	2 Cor 2:5–3:6
28	Psa 42–44	2 Cor 3:7–4:18
29	Psa 45–48	2 Cor 5:1–6:2
30	Psa 49–51	2 Cor 6:3–7:1
31	Psa 52–55	2 Cor 7:2–16

AUGUST	A.M.	P.M.
1	Psa 56–59	2 Cor 8–9
2	Psa 60–63	2 Cor 10
3	Psa 64–67	2 Cor 11:1–15
4	Psa 68–69	2 Cor 11:16–33
5	Psa 70–73	2 Cor 12
6	Psa 74–77	2 Cor 13
7	Psa 78	Rom 1:1–17
8	Psa 79–81	Rom 1:18–32
9	Psa 82–84	Rom 2
10	Psa 85–88	Rom 3
11	Psa 89	Rom 4
12	Psa 90–93	Rom 5:1–11
13	Psa 94–98	Rom 5:12–21
14	Psa 99–101	Rom 6:1–14
15	Psa 102–103	Rom 6:15–7:6
16	Psa 104–106	Rom 7:7–25
17	Psa 107–108	Rom 8:1–17
18	Psa 109–112	Rom 8:18–39
19	Psa 113–116	Rom 9:1–29
20	Psa 117–118	Rom 9:30–10:21
21	Psa 119:1–112	Rom 11:1–24
22	Psa 119:113–176	Rom 11:25–36
23	Psa 120–127	Rom 12:1–16
24	Psa 128–134	Rom 12:17–13:14
25	Psa 135–138	Rom 14–15:4
26	Psa 139–141	Rom 15:5–13
27	Psa 142–145	Rom 15:14–33
28	Psa 146–150	Rom 16
29	Prov 1–2	Gal 1
30	Prov 3–4	Gal 2
31	Prov 5–7	Gal 3:1–14

SEPTEMBER	A.M.	P.M.
1	Prov 8–9	Gal 3:15–25
2	Prov 10–11	Gal 3:26–4:20
3	Prov 12–13	Gal 4:21–5:15
4	Prov 14–15	Gal 5:16–26
5	Prov 16–17	Gal 6
6	Prov 18–19	Eph 1:1–14
7	Prov 20–21	Eph 1:15–2:10
8	Prov 22–23	Eph 2:11–22
9	Prov 24–26	Eph 3
10	Prov 27–28	Eph 4:1–16
11	Prov 29–31	Eph 4:17–5:2
12	Ecc 1–2	Eph 5:3–21
13	Ecc 3–5	Eph 5:22–6:9
14	Ecc 6–8	Eph 6:10–24
15	Ecc 9–12	Php 1
16	S of S 1–2	Php 2:1–18
17	S of S 3–5	Php 2:19–3:11
18	S of S 6–8	Php 3:12–4:3
19	Obadiah	Php 4:4–23
20	Joel	Col 1:1–23
21	Jonah	Col 1:24–2:5
22	Amos 1–4	Col 2:6–23
23	Amos 5–9	Col 3:1–4:1
24	Hos 1–2	Col 4:2–18
25	Hos 3–6	Philemon
26	Hos 7–10	Heb 1
27	Hos 11–14	Heb 2
28	Isa 1–2	Heb 3
29	Isa 3–5	Heb 4:1–13
30	Isa 6–8	Heb 4:14–5:10

OCTOBER	A.M.	P.M.
1	Isa 9–10	Heb 5:11–6:20
2	Isa 11–12	Heb 7
3	Isa 13–14	Heb 8
4	Isa 15–18	Heb 9:1–10
5	Isa 19–22	Heb 9:11–28
6	Isa 23–24	Heb 10:1–18
7	Isa 25–26	Heb 10:19–39
8	Isa 27–28	Heb 11:1–16
9	Isa 29–30	Heb 11:17–40
10	Isa 31–32	Heb 12:1–13
11	Isa 33–34	Heb 12:14–29
12	Isa 35–37	Heb 13
13	Isa 38–39	Titus 1–2
14	Isa 40–41	Titus 3
15	Isa 42–43	1 Tim 1
16	Isa 44–45	1 Tim 2
17	Isa 46–47	1 Tim 3
18	Isa 48–49	1 Tim 4
19	Isa 50–51	1 Tim 5
20	Isa 52–53	1 Tim 6
21	Isa 54–56	2 Tim 1
22	Isa 57–58	2 Tim 2
23	Isa 59–60	2 Tim 3
24	Isa 61–63	2 Tim 4
25	Isa 64–66	John 1:1–18
26	Mic 1–3	John 1:19–51
27	Mic 4–5	John 2
28	Mic 6–7	John 3:1–21
29	Nahum	John 3:22–36
30	Habakkuk	John 4:1–26
31	Zephaniah	John 4:27–54

NOVEMBER	A.M.	P.M.
1	Jer 1–2	John 5:1–30
2	Jer 3–4	John 5:31–47
3	Jer 5–6	John 6:1–24
4	Jer 7–8	John 6:25–59
5	Jer 9–10	John 6:60–71
6	Jer 11–12	John 7:1–24
7	Jer 13–14	John 7:25–8:11
8	Jer 15–16	John 8:12–30
9	Jer 17–18	John 8:31–47
10	Jer 19–22	John 8:48–59
11	Jer 23–25	John 9
12	Jer 26–28	John 10:1–21
13	Jer 29–30	John 10:22–42
14	Jer 31–32	John 11:1–16
15	Jer 33	John 11:17–57
16	Jer 34–35	John 12:1–19
17	Jer 36–37	John 12:20–50
18	Jer 38–40	John 13:1–30
19	Jer 41–43	John 13:31–14:14
20	Jer 44–47	John 14:15–31
21	Jer 48–49	John 15:1–17
22	Jer 50–51	John 15:18–16:16
23	Jer 52	John 16:17–33
24	Lam 1–2	John 17
25	Lam 3–5	John 18:1–27
26	Ezek 1–2	John 18:28–19:16
27	Ezek 3–4	John 19:17–42
28	Ezek 5–7	John 20:1–18
29	Ezek 8–10	John 20:19–31
30	Ezek 11–12	John 21

DECEMBER	A.M.	P.M.
1	Ezek 13–15	1 John 1–2:14
2	Ezek 16	1 John 2:15–3:10
3	Ezek 17–19	1 John 3:11–24
4	Ezek 20–21	1 John 4
5	Ezek 22–23	1 John 5
6	Ezek 24–26	2 John
7	Ezek 27–28	3 John
8	Ezek 29–30	Rev 1
9	Ezek 31–32	Rev 2:1–17
10	Ezek 33–34	Rev 2:18–3:6
11	Ezek 35–36	Rev 3:7–22
12	Ezek 37–38	Rev 4
13	Ezek 39–40	Rev 5
14	Ezek 41–42	Rev 6
15	Ezek 43–44	Rev 7
16	Ezek 45–46	Rev 8
17	Ezek 47–48	Rev 9
18	Dan 1–2	Rev 10
19	Dan 3–4	Rev 11
20	Dan 5–6	Rev 12
21	Dan 7–8	Rev 13:1–10
22	Dan 9–10	Rev 13:11–14:20
23	Dan 11–12	Rev 15
24	Haggai	Rev 16
25	Zech 1–3	Rev 17
26	Zech 4–6	Rev 18
27	Zech 7–8	Rev 19:1–10
28	Zech 9–11	Rev 19:11–21
29	Zech 12–14	Rev 20
30	Mal 1–2	Rev 21
31	Mal 3–4	Rev 22

Concordance

Word or block entries marked with an asterisk (*) list every verse in the Bible in which the word appears. Words in parentheses after an entry remind the reader to check other forms of that word in locating a passage.

AARON

Genealogy of (Ex 6:16-20; Jos 21:4, 10; 1Ch 6:3-15).

Priesthood of (Ex 28:1; Nu 17; Heb 5:1-4; 7), garments (Ex 28; 39), consecration (Ex 29), ordination (Lev 8).

Spokesman for Moses (Ex 4:14-16, 27-31; 7:1-2). Supported Moses' hands in battle (Ex 17:8-13). Built golden calf (Ex 32; Dt 9:20). Talked against Moses (Nu 12). Priesthood opposed (Nu 16); staff budded (Nu 17). Forbidden to enter land (Nu 20:1-12). Death (Nu 20:22-29; 33:38-39).

ABADDON*

Rev 9:11 whose name in Hebrew is *A*,

ABANDON (ABANDONED)

Dt 4:31 he will not *a* or destroy you
1Ki 6:13 and will not *a* my people Israel."
Ne 9:19 compassion you did not *a* them
9:31 an end to them or *a* them,
Ps 16:10 you will not *a* me to the grave,
Ac 2:27 you will not *a* me to the grave,
1Ti 4: 1 in later times some will *a* the faith

ABANDONED (ABANDON)

Ge 24:27 who has not *a* his kindness
2Co 4: 9 persecuted, but not *a*; struck down,

ABBA*

Mk 14:36 "*A*, Father," he said, "everything is
Ro 8:15 And by him we cry, "*A*, Father."
Gal 4: 6 the Spirit who calls out, "*A*, Father

ABEDNEGO

Deported to Babylon with Daniel (Da 1:1-6). Name changed from Azariah (Da 1:7). Refused defilement by food (Da 1:8-20). Refused idol worship (Da 3:1-12); saved from furnace (Da 3:13-30).

ABEL

Second son of Adam (Ge 4:2). Offered proper sacrifice (Ge 4:4; Heb 11:4). Murdered by Cain (Ge 4:8; Mt 23:35; Lk 11:51; 1Jn 3:12).

ABHOR (ABHORS)

Lev 26:30 of your idols, and I will *a* you.
Dt 7:26 Utterly *a* and detest it,
Ps 26: 5 I *a* the assembly of evildoers
119:163 I hate and *a* falsehood
139: 21 and *a* those who rise up against you
Am 6: 8 "I *a* the pride of Jacob
Ro 2:22 You who *a* idols, do you rob

ABHORS (ABHOR)

Pr 11: 1 The LORD *a* dishonest scales,

ABIATHAR

High priest in days of Saul and David (1Sa 22; 2Sa 15; 1Ki 1-2; Mk 2:26). Escaped Saul's slaughter of priests (1Sa 22:18-23). Supported David in Absalom's revolt (2Sa 15:24-29). Supported Adonijah (1Ki 1:7-42); deposed by Solomon (1Ki 2:22-35; cf. 1Sa 2:31-35).

ABIGAIL

1. Sister of David (1Ch 2:16-17).
2. Wife of Nabal (1Sa 25:30); pled for his life with David (1Sa 25:14-35). Became David's wife after Nabal's death (1Sa 25:36-42); bore him Kileab (2Sa 3:3) also known as Daniel (1Ch 3:1).

ABIHU

Son of Aaron (Ex 6:23; 24:1, 9); killed for offering unauthorized fire (Lev 10; Nu 3:2-4; 1Ch 24:1-2).

ABIJAH

1. Second son of Samuel (1Ch 6:28); a corrupt judge (1Sa 8:1-5).
2. An Aaronic priest (1Ch 24:10; Lk 1:5).
3. Son of Jeroboam I of Israel; died as prophesied by Ahijah (1Ki 14:1-18).
4. Son of Rehoboam; king of Judah who fought Jeroboam I attempting to reunite the kingdom (1Ki 14:31-15:8; 2Ch 12:16-14:1; Mt 1:7).

ABILITY (ABLE)

Ex 35:34 tribe of Dan, the *a* to teach others.
Dt 8:18 for it is he who gives you the *a*
Ezr 2:69 According to their *a* they gave
Mt 25:15 one talent, each according to his *a*.
Ac 11:29 disciples, each according to his *a*,
2Co 1: 8 far beyond our *a* to endure,
8: 3 were able, and even beyond their *a*.

ABIMELECH

1. King of Gerar who took Abraham's wife Sarah, believing her to be his sister (Ge 20). Later made a covenant with Abraham (Ge 21:22-33).
2. King of Gerar who took Isaac's wife Rebekah, believing her to be his sister (Ge 26:1-11). Later made a covenant with Isaac (Ge 26:12-31).
3. Son of Gideon (Jdg 8:31). Attempted to make himself king (Jdg 9).

ABISHAG*

Shunammite virgin; attendant of David in his old age (1Ki 1:1-15; 2:17-22).

ABISHAI

Son of Zeruiah, David's sister (1Sa 26:6; 1Ch 2:16). One of David's chief warriors (1Ch 11:15-21): against Edom (1Ch 18:12-13), Ammon (2Sa 10), Absalom (2Sa 18), Sheba (2Sa 20). Wanted to kill Saul (1Sa 26), killed Abner (2Sa 2:18-27; 3:22-39), wanted to kill Shimei (2Sa 16:5-13; 19:16-23).

ABLE (ABILITY ENABLE ENABLED ENABLES ENABLING)

Nu 14:16 'The LORD was not *a*
1Ch 29:14 that we should be *a* to give
2Ch 2: 6 who is *a* to build a temple for him,
Eze 7:19 and gold will not be *a* to save them
Da 3:17 the God we serve is *a* to save us
4:37 walk in pride he is *a* to humble.
Mt 9:28 "Do you believe that I am *a*
Lk 13:24 will try to enter and will not be *a* to
14:30 to build and was not *a* to finish.'
21:15 none of your adversaries will be *a*
21:36 and that you may be *a* to stand
Ac 5:39 you will not be *a* to stop these men;
Ro 8:39 will be *a* to separate us
14: 4 for the Lord is *a* to make him stand
16:25 to him who is *a* to establish you
2Co 9: 8 God is *a* to make all grace abound
Eph 3:20 him who is *a* to do immeasurably
6:13 you may be *a* to stand your ground,
1Ti 3: 2 respectable, hospitable, *a* to teach,
2Ti 1:12 and am convinced that he is *a*
2:24 kind to everyone, *a* to teach,
3:15 which are *a* to make you wise
Heb 2:18 he is *a* to help those who are being
7:25 he is *a* to save completely
Jas 3: 2 *a* to keep his whole body in check.
Jude :24 To him who is *a* to keep you
Rev 5: 5 He is *a* to open the scroll

ABNER

Cousin of Saul and commander of his army (1Sa 14:50; 17:55-57; 26). Made Ish-Bosheth king after Saul (2Sa 2:8-10), but later defected to David (2Sa 3:6-21). Killed Asahel (2Sa 2:18-32), for which he was killed by Joab and Abishai (2Sa 3:22-39).

ABOLISH (ABOLISHED ABOLISHING)

Hos 2:18 I will *a* from the land,
Mt 5:17 that I have come to *a* the Law

ABOLISHED (ABOLISH)

Gal 5:11 the offense of the cross has been *a*.

ABOLISHING* (ABOLISH)

Eph 2:15 by *a* in his flesh the law

ABOMINATION*

Da 11:31 set up the *a* that causes desolation.
12:11 *a* that causes desolation is set up,
Mt 24:15 the holy place 'the *a* that causes
Mk 13:14 you see 'the *a* that causes

ABOUND (ABOUNDING)

2Co 9: 8 able to make all grace *a* to you,
9: 8 you will *a* in every good work.
Php 1: 9 that your love may *a* more

ABOUNDING (ABOUND)

Ex 34: 6 slow to anger, *a* in love
Nu 14:18 *a* in love and forgiving sin
Ne 9:17 slow to anger and *a* in love.
Ps 86: 5 *a* in love to all who call to you.
86:15 slow to anger, *a* in love
103: 8 slow to anger, *a* in love.
Joel 2:13 slow to anger and *a* in love,
Jnh 4: 2 slow to anger and *a* in love,

ABRAHAM

Abram, son of Terah (Ge 11:26-27), husband of Sarah (Ge 11:29).

Covenant relation with the LORD (Ge 12:1-3; 13:14-17; 15; 17; 22:15-18; Ex 2:24; Ne 9:8; Ps 105; Mic 7:20; Lk 1:68-75; Ro 4; Heb 6:13-15).

Called from Ur, via Haran, to Canaan (Ge 12:1; Ac 7:2-4; Heb 11:8-10). Moved to Egypt, nearly lost Sarah to Pharaoh (Ge 12:10-20). Divided the land with Lot; settled in Hebron (Ge 13). Saved Lot from four kings (Ge 14:1-16); blessed by Melchizedek (Ge 14:17-20; Heb 7:1-20). Declared righteous by faith (Ge 15:6; Ro 4:3; Gal 3:6-9). Fathered Ishmael by Hagar (Ge 16).

Name changed from Abram (Ge 17:5; Ne 9:7). Circumcised (Ge 17; Ro 4:9-12). Entertained three visitors (Ge 18); promised a son by Sarah (Ge 18:9-15; 17:16). Questioned destruction of Sodom and Gomorrah (Ge 18:16-33). Moved to Gerar; nearly lost Sarah to Abimelech (Ge 20). Fathered Isaac by Sarah (Ge 21:1-7; Ac 7:8; Heb 11:11-12); sent away Hagar and Ishmael (Ge 21:8-21; Gal 4:22-30). Covenant with Abimelech (Ge 21:22-32). Tested by offering Isaac (Ge 22; Heb 11:17-19; Jas 2:21-24). Sarah died; bought field of Ephron for burial (Ge 23). Secured wife for Isaac (Ge 24). Fathered children by Keturah (Ge 25:1-6; 1Ch 1:32-33). Death (Ge 25:7-11).

Called servant of God (Ge 26:24), friend of God (2Ch 20:7; Isa 41:8; Jas 2:23), prophet (Ge 20:7), father of Israel (Ex 3:15; Isa 51:2; Mt 3:9; Jn 8:39-58).

ABSALOM

Son of David by Maacah (2Sa 3:3; 1Ch 3:2). Killed Amnon for rape of his sister Tamar; banished by David (2Sa 13). Returned to Jerusalem; received by David (2Sa 14). Rebelled against David; seized kingdom (2Sa 15-17). Killed (2Sa 18).

ABSENT

Col 2: 5 though I am *a* from you in body,

ABSOLUTE*

1Ti 5: 2 women as sisters, with *a* purity.

ABSTAIN (ABSTAINS)

Ex 19:15 *A* from sexual relations."
Nu 6: 3 he must *a* from wine and other
Ac 15:20 them to *a* from food polluted
1Pe 2:11 to *a* from sinful desires,

ABSTAINS* (ABSTAIN)

Ro 14: 6 thanks to God; and he who *a*,

ABUNDANCE (ABUNDANT)

Ge 41:29 Seven years of great *a* are coming
Job 36:31 and provides food in *a*.
Ps 66:12 but you brought us to a place of *a*.
Ecc 5:12 but the *a* of a rich man
Isa 66:11 and delight in her overflowing *a*."
Jer 2:22 and use an *a* of soap,
Mt 13:12 given more, and he will have an *a*.
25:29 given more, and he will have an *a*.
Lk 12:15 consist in the *a* of his possessions."
1Pe 1: 2 Grace and peace be yours in *a*.
2Pe 1: 2 yours in *a* through the knowledge
Jude : 2 peace and love be yours in *a*.

ABUNDANT (ABUNDANCE)

Dt 28:11 will grant you *a* prosperity—
32: 2 like *a* rain on tender plants.
Job 36:28 and *a* showers fall on mankind.
Ps 68: 9 You gave *a* showers, O God;
78:15 gave them water as *a* as the seas;
132: 15 I will bless her with *a* provisions;
145: 7 will celebrate your *a* goodness
Pr 12:11 works his land will have *a* food,
28:19 works his land will have *a* food,
Jer 33: 9 and will tremble at the *a* prosperity
Ro 5:17 who receive God's *a* provision

ABUSIVE

2Ti 3: 2 *a*, disobedient to their parents,

ABYSS*

Lk 8:31 not to order them to go into the *A*.
Rev 9: 1 the key to the shaft of the *A*.
9: 2 When he opened the *A*, smoke rose
9: 2 darkened by the smoke from the *A*.
9:11 king over them the angel of the *A*,
11: 7 up from the *A* will attack them,

Rev 17: 8 and will come up out of the *A*
20: 1 having the key to the *A*
20: 3 He threw him into the *A*,

ACCEPT (ACCEPTABLE ACCEPTANCE ACCEPTED ACCEPTS)
Ex 23: 8 "Do not *a* a bribe,
Dt 16:19 Do not *a* a bribe, for a bribe blinds
Job 42: 8 and I will *a* his prayer and not deal
Pr 10: 8 The wise in heart *a* commands,
19:20 Listen to advice and *a* instruction,
Ro 15: 7 *A* one another, then, just
Jas 1:21 humbly *a* the word planted in you,

ACCEPTABLE (ACCEPT)
Pr 21: 3 is more *a* to the LORD

ACCEPTANCE* (ACCEPT)
Ro 11:15 what will their *a* be but life
1Ti 1:15 saying that deserves full *a*:
4: 9 saying that deserves full *a*

ACCEPTED (ACCEPT)
Ge 4: 7 will you not be *a*? But if you do not
Job 42: 9 and the LORD *a* Job's prayer.
Lk 4:24 "no prophet is *a* in his hometown.
Gal 1: 9 you a gospel other than what you *a*,

ACCEPTS (ACCEPT)
Ps 6: 9 the LORD *a* my prayer.
Jn 13:20 whoever *a* anyone I send *a* me;
13:20 whoever *a* me *a* the one who sent

ACCESS
Ro 5: 2 through whom we have gained *a*
Eph 2:18 For through him we both have *a*

ACCOMPANIED (ACCOMPANY)
1Co 10: 4 from the spiritual rock that *a* them,
Jas 2:17 if it is not *a* by action, is dead.

ACCOMPANIES (ACCOMPANY)
2Co 9:13 obedience that *a* your confession

ACCOMPANY (ACCOMPANIED ACCOMPANIES)
Dt 28: 2 *a* you if you obey the LORD your
Mk 16:17 these signs will *a* those who believe
Heb 6: 9 your case—things that *a* salvation.

ACCOMPLISH
Ecc 2: 2 And what does pleasure *a*?"
Isa 44:28 and will *a* all that I please;
55:11 but will *a* what I desire

ACCORD
Nu 24:13 not do anything of my own *a*,
Jn 10:18 but I lay it down of my own *a*.
12:49 For I did not speak of my own *a*,

ACCOUNT (ACCOUNTABLE)
Ge 2: 4 This is the *a* of the heavens
5: 1 This is the written *a* of Adam's line
6: 9 This is the *a* of Noah.
10: 1 This is the *a* of Shem, Ham
11:10 This is the *a* of Shem.
11:27 This is the *a* of Terah.
25:12 This is the *a* of Abraham's son
25:19 This is the *a* of Abraham's son
36: 1 This is the *a* of Esau (that is, Edom
36: 9 This is the *a* of Esau the father
37: 2 This is the *a* of Jacob.
Mt 12:36 to give *a* on the day of judgment
Lk 16: 2 Give an *a* of your management,
Ro 14:12 each of us will give an *a* of himself
Heb 4:13 of him to whom we must give *a*.

ACCOUNTABLE* (ACCOUNT)
Eze 3:18 and I will hold you *a* for his blood.
3:20 and I will hold you *a* for his blood.
33: 6 but I will hold the watchman *a*
33: 8 and I will hold you *a* for his blood.
34:10 and will hold them *a* for my flock.
Da 6: 2 The satraps were made *a* to them
Jnh 1:14 Do not hold us *a* for killing
Ro 3:19 and the whole world held *a* to God.

ACCURATE
Dt 25:15 You must have *a* and honest
Pr 11: 1 but *a* weights are his delight.

ACCURSED (CURSE)
2Pe 2:14 experts in greed—an *a* brood!

ACCUSATION (ACCUSE)
1Ti 5:19 Do not entertain an *a*

ACCUSATIONS (ACCUSE)
2Pe 2:11 do not bring slanderous *a*

ACCUSE (ACCUSATION ACCUSATIONS ACCUSER ACCUSES ACCUSING)
Pr 3:30 Do not *a* a man for no reason—
Lk 3:14 and don't *a* people falsely—

ACCUSER (ACCUSE)
Jn 5:45 Your *a* is Moses, on whom your
Rev 12:10 For the *a* of our brothers,

ACCUSES (ACCUSE)
Job 40: 2 Let him who *a* God answer him!"
Rev 12:10 who *a* them before our God day

ACCUSING (ACCUSE)
Ro 2:15 and their thoughts now *a*,

ACHAN*
Sin at Jericho caused defeat at Ai; stoned (Jos 7; 22:20; 1Ch 2:7).

ACHE*
Pr 14:13 Even in laughter the heart may *a*,

ACHIEVE
Isa 55:11 *a* the purpose for which I sent it.

ACHISH
King of Gath before whom David feigned insanity (1Sa 21:10-15). Later "ally" of David (2Sa 27-29).

ACKNOWLEDGE (ACKNOWLEDGED ACKNOWLEDGES)
Pr 3: 6 in all your ways *a* him,
Jer 3:13 Only *a* your guilt—
Hos 6: 3 let us press on to *a* him.
Mt 10:32 *a* him before my Father in heaven.
Lk 12: 8 *a* him before the angels of God.
1Jn 4: 3 spirit that does not *a* Jesus is not

ACKNOWLEDGED (ACKNOWLEDGE)
Lk 7:29 *a* that God's way was right,

ACKNOWLEDGES* (ACKNOWLEDGE)
Ps 91:14 for he *a* my name.
Mt 10:32 "Whoever *a* me before men,
Lk 12: 8 whoever *a* me before men,
1Jn 2:23 whoever *a* the Son has the Father
4: 2 Every spirit that *a* that Jesus Christ
4:15 If anyone *a* that Jesus is the Son

ACQUIRES (ACQUIRING)
Pr 18:15 of the discerning *a* knowledge;

ACQUIRING* (ACQUIRES)
Pr 1: 3 for *a* a disciplined and prudent life,

ACQUIT (ACQUITTING)
Ex 23: 7 to death, for I will not *a* the guilty.

ACQUITTING* (ACQUIT)
Dt 25: 1 *a* the innocent and condemning
Pr 17:15 *A* the guilty and condemning

ACT (ACTION ACTIONS ACTIVE ACTIVITY ACTS)
Ps 119:126 It is time for you to *a*, O LORD;

ACTION (ACT)
2Co 9: 2 has stirred most of them to *a*.
Jas 2:17 if it is not accompanied by *a*,
1Pe 1:13 minds for *a*; be self-controlled;

ACTIONS (ACT)
Mt 11:19 wisdom is proved right by her *a*."
Gal 6: 4 Each one should test his own *a*.
Tit 1:16 but by their *a* they deny him.

ACTIVE* (ACT)
Phm : 6 I pray that you may be *a*
Heb 4:12 For the word of God is living and *a*

ACTIVITY (ACT)
Ecc 3: 1 a season for every *a* under heaven:
3:17 for there will be a time for every *a*,

ACTS (ACT)
1Ch 16: 9 tell of all his wonderful *a*.
Ps 71:16 proclaim your mighty *a*,
71:24 tell of your righteous *a*
105: 2 tell of all his wonderful *a*.
106: 2 Who can proclaim the mighty *a*
145: 4 they will tell of your mighty *a*.
145: 12 all men may know of your mighty *a*
150: 2 Praise him for his *a* of power;
Isa 64: 6 all our righteous *a* are like filthy
Mt 6: 1 not to do your '*a* of righteousness'

ADAM
1. First man (Ge 1:26-2:25; Ro 5:14; 1Ti 2:13). Sin of (Ge 3; Hos 6:7; Ro 5:12-21). Children of (Ge 4:1-5:5). Death of (Ge 5:5; Ro 5:12-21; 1Co 15:22).
2. City (Jos 3:16).

ADD (ADDED)
Dt 4: 2 Do not *a* to what I command you
12:32 do not *a* to it or take away from it.
Pr 1: 5 let the wise listen and *a*
9: 9 he will *a* to his learning.
30: 6 Do not *a* to his words,
Mt 6:27 by worrying can *a* a single hour
Lk 12:25 by worrying can *a* a single hour
Rev 22:18 God will *a* to him the plagues

ADDED (ADD)
Ecc 3:14 nothing can be *a* to it and nothing
Ac 2:47 Lord *a* to their number daily those
Ro 5:20 The law was *a* so that the trespass
Gal 3:19 It was *a* because of transgressions

ADDICTED*
Tit 2: 3 to be slanderers or *a* to much wine,

ADMINISTRATION*
1Co 12:28 with gifts of *a*, and those speaking
Eph 3: 2 Surely you have heard about the *a*
3: 9 to everyone the *a* of this mystery,

ADMIRABLE*
Php 4: 8 whatever is lovely, whatever is *a*—

ADMIT
Hos 5:15 until they *a* their guilt.

ADMONISH* (ADMONISHING)
Col 3:16 and *a* one another with all wisdom,
1Th 5:12 you in the Lord and who *a* you.

ADMONISHING* (ADMONISH)
Col 1:28 *a* and teaching everyone

ADONIJAH
1. Son of David by Haggith (2Sa 3:4; 1Ch 3:2). Attempted to be king after David; killed by Solomon's order (1Ki 1-2).
2. Levite; teacher of the Law (2Ch 17:8).

ADOPTED (ADOPTION)
Eph 1: 5 In love he predestined us to be *a*

ADOPTION* (ADOPTED)
Ro 8:23 as we wait eagerly for our *a* as sons,
9: 4 Theirs is the *a* as sons; theirs

ADORE*
SS 1: 4 How right they are to *a* you!

ADORNMENT* (ADORNS)
1Pe 3: 3 should not come from outward *a*,

ADORNS* (ADORNMENT)
Ps 93: 5 holiness *a* your house
Isa 61:10 as a bride *a* herself with her jewels.
61:10 bridegroom *a* his head like a priest,

ADULTERER (ADULTERY)
Lev 20:10 both the *a* and the adulteress must
Heb 13: 4 for God will judge the *a*

ADULTERERS (ADULTERY)
1Co 6: 9 idolaters nor *a* nor male prostitutes
1Ti 1:10 for murderers, for *a* and perverts,

ADULTERESS (ADULTERY)
Hos 3: 1 she is loved by another and is an *a*.

ADULTERIES (ADULTERY)
Jer 3: 8 sent her away because of all her *a*.

ADULTEROUS (ADULTERY)
Mk 8:38 in this *a* and sinful generation,
Jas 4: 4 You *a* people, don't you know that

ADULTERY (ADULTERER ADULTERERS ADULTERESS ADULTERIES ADULTEROUS)
Ex 20:14 "You shall not commit *a*.
Dt 5:18 "You shall not commit *a*.
Mt 5:27 that it was said, 'Do not commit *a*.'
5:28 lustfully has already committed *a*
5:32 the divorced woman commits *a*.
15:19 murder, *a*, sexual immorality, theft
19: 9 marries another woman commits *a*
19:18 do not commit *a*, do not steal,
Mk 7:21 theft, murder, *a*, greed, malice,
10:11 marries another woman commits *a*
10:12 another man, she commits *a*."
10:19 do not commit *a*, do not steal,
Lk 16:18 a divorced woman commits *a*.
16:18 marries another woman commits *a*
18:20 'Do not commit *a*, do not murder,
Jn 8: 4 woman was caught in the act of *a*.
Rev 18: 3 of the earth committed *a* with her,

ADULTS*
1Co 14:20 but in your thinking be *a.*

ADVANCE (ADVANCED)
Ps 18:29 With your help I can *a*
Php 1:12 has really served to *a* the gospel.

ADVANCED (ADVANCE)
Job 32: 7 *a* years should teach wisdom.'

ADVANTAGE
Ex 22:22 "Do not take *a* of a widow
Dt 24:14 Do not take *a* of a hired man who is
Ro 3: 1 What *a,* then, is there
2Co 11:20 or exploits you or takes *a* of you
1Th 4: 6 should wrong his brother or take *a*

ADVERSITY*
Pr 17:17 and a brother is born for *a.*
Isa 30:20 the Lord gives you the bread of *a*

ADVICE (ADVISERS)
1Ki 12: 8 rejected the *a* the elders
12:14 he followed the *a* of the young men
2Ch 10: 8 rejected the *a* the elders
Pr 12: 5 but the *a* of the wicked is deceitful.
12:15 but a wise man listens to *a.*
19:20 Listen to *a* and accept instruction,
20:18 Make plans by seeking *a;*

ADVISERS (ADVICE)
Pr 11:14 but many *a* make victory sure.

ADVOCATE*
Job 16:19 my *a* is on high.

AFFLICTED (AFFLICTION)
Job 2: 7 and *a* Job with painful sores
36: 6 but gives the *a* their rights.
Ps 9:12 he does not ignore the cry of the *a.*
9:18 nor the hope of the *a* ever perish.
119: 67 Before I was *a* I went astray,
119: 71 It was good for me to be *a*
119: 75 and in faithfulness you have *a* me.
Isa 49:13 will have compassion on his *a* ones.
53: 4 smitten by him, and *a.*
53: 7 He was oppressed and *a,*
Na 1:12 Although I have *a* you, O Judah,

AFFLICTION (AFFLICTED AFFLICTIONS)
Dt 16: 3 bread of *a,* because you left Egypt
Ps 107: 41 he lifted the needy out of their *a*
Isa 30:20 of adversity and the water of *a,*
48:10 in the furnace of *a.*
La 3:33 For he does not willingly bring *a*
Ro 12:12 patient in *a,* faithful in prayer.

AFFLICTIONS (AFFLICTION)
Col 1:24 lacking in regard to Christ's *a,*

AFRAID (FEAR)
Ge 3:10 and I was *a* because I was naked;
26:24 Do not be *a,* for I am with you;
Ex 2:14 Then Moses was *a* and thought,
3: 6 because he was *a* to look at God.
Dt 1:21 Do not be *a;* do not be discouraged
1:29 "Do not be terrified; do not be *a*
20: 1 do not be *a* of them,
20: 3 Do not be fainthearted or *a;*
2Ki 25:24 "Do not be *a* of the Babylonian
1Ch 13:12 David was *a* of God that day
Ps 27: 1 of whom shall I be *a?*
56: 3 When I am *a,* / I will trust in you.
56: 4 in God I trust; I will not be *a.*
Pr 3:24 lie down, you will not be *a;*
Isa 10:24 do not be *a* of the Assyrians,
12: 2 I will trust and not be *a.*
44: 8 Do not tremble, do not be *a.*
Jer 1: 8 Do not be *a* of them, for I am
Mt 8:26 You of little faith, why are you so *a*
10:28 be *a* of the One who can destroy
10:31 So don't be *a;* you are worth more
Mk 5:36 "Don't be *a;* just believe."
Lk 9:34 and they were *a* as they entered
Jn 14:27 hearts be troubled and do not be *a.*
Ac 27:24 beside me and said, 'Do not be *a,*
Ro 11:20 Do not be arrogant, but be *a.*
Heb 13: 6 Lord is my helper; I will not be *a.*

AGAG (AGAGITE)
King of Amalekites not killed by Saul (1Sa 15).

AGAGITE (AGAG)
Est 8: 3 to the evil plan of Haman the *A,*

AGED (AGES)
Job 12:12 Is not wisdom found among the *a?*
Pr 17: 6 children are a crown to the *a,*

AGES (AGED)
Ro 16:25 the mystery hidden for long *a* past,
Eph 2: 7 that in the coming *a* he might show
3: 9 which for *a* past was kept hidden
Col 1:26 that has been kept hidden for *a*
Rev 15: 3 King of the *a.*

AGONY
Lk 16:24 because I am in *a* in this fire.'
Rev 16:10 Men gnawed their tongues in *a*

AGREE (AGREEMENT AGREES)
Mt 18:19 on earth *a* about anything you ask
Ro 7:16 want to do, I *a* that the law is good.
Php 4: 2 with Syntyche to *a* with each other

AGREEMENT (AGREE)
2Co 6:16 What *a* is there between the temple

AGREES* (AGREE)
Ac 7:42 This *a* with what is written
24:14 I believe everything that *a*
1Co 4:17 which *a* with what I teach

AGRIPPA*
Descendant of Herod; king before whom Paul pled his case in Caesarea (Ac 25:13-26:32).

AHAB
1. Son of Omri; king of Israel (1Ki 16:28-22:40), husband of Jezebel (1Ki 16:31). Promoted Baal worship (1Ki 16:31-33); opposed by Elijah (1Ki 17:1; 18; 21), a prophet (1Ki 20:35-43), Micaiah (1Ki 22:1-28). Defeated Ben-Hadad (1Ki 20). Killed for failing to kill Ben-Hadad and for murder of Naboth (1Ki 20:35-21:40).
2. A false prophet (Jer 29:21-22).

AHAZ
1. Son of Jotham; king of Judah, (2Ki 16; 2Ch 28). Idolatry of (2Ki 16:3-4, 10-18; 2Ch 28:1-4, 22-25). Defeated by Aram and Israel (2Ki 16:5-6; 2Ch 28:5-15). Sought help from Assyria rather than the LORD (2Ki 16:7-9; 2Ch 28:16-21; Isa 7).
2. Benjamite, descendant of Saul (1Ch 8:35-36).

AHAZIAH
1. Son of Ahab; king of Israel (1Ki 22:51-2Ki 1:18; 2Ch 20:35-37). Made an unsuccessful alliance with Jehoshaphat of Judah (2Ch 20:35-37). Died for seeking Baal rather than the LORD (2Ki 1).
2. Son of Jehoram; king of Judah (2Ki 8:25-29; 9:14-29), also called Jehoahaz (2Ch 21:17-22:9; 25:23). Killed by Jehu while visiting Joram (2Ki 9:14-29; 2Ch 22:1-9).

AHIJAH
1Sa 14:18 Saul said to *A,* "Bring the ark
1Ki 14: 2 *A* the prophet is there—the one

AHIMELECH
1. Priest who helped David in his flight from Saul (1Sa 21-22).
2. One of David's warriors (1Sa 26:6).

AHITHOPHEL
One of David's counselors who sided with Absalom (2Sa 15:12, 31-37; 1Ch 27:33-34); committed suicide when his advice was ignored (2Sa 16:15-17:23).

AI
Jos 7: 4 they were routed by the men of *A,*
8:28 So Joshua burned *A* and made it

AID
Isa 38:14 troubled; O Lord, come to my *a!*"
Php 4:16 you sent me *a* again and again

AIM
1Co 7:34 Her *a* is to be devoted to the Lord
2Co 13:11 *A* for perfection, listen

AIR
Mt 8:20 and birds of the *a* have nests,
Lk 9:58 and birds of the *a* have nests,
1Co 9:26 not fight like a man beating the *a.*
14: 9 You will just be speaking into the *a*
Eph 2: 2 of the ruler of the kingdom of the *a,*
1Th 4:17 clouds to meet the Lord in the *a.*

ALABASTER*
Mt 26: 7 came to him with an *a* jar
Mk 14: 3 a woman came with an *a* jar
Lk 7:37 she brought an *a* jar of perfume,

ALARM (ALARMED)
2Co 7:11 indignation, what *a,* what longing,

ALARMED (ALARM)
Mk 13: 7 and rumors of wars, do not be *a.*
2Th 2: 2 not to become easily unsettled or *a*

ALERT*
Jos 8: 4 All of you be on the *a.*
Ps 17:11 with eyes *a,* to throw me
Isa 21: 7 let him be *a,* / fully *a.*"
Mk 13:33 Be *a!* You do not know
Eph 6:18 be *a* and always keep on praying
1Th 5: 6 but let us be *a* and self-controlled.
1Pe 5: 8 Be self-controlled and *a.*

ALIEN (ALIENATED ALIENS)
Ex 22:21 "Do not mistreat an *a*
Lev 24:22 are to have the same law for the *a*
Ps 146: 9 The LORD watches over the *a*

ALIENATED (ALIEN)
Gal 5: 4 by law have been *a* from Christ;
Col 1:21 Once you were *a* from God

ALIENS (ALIEN)
Ex 23: 9 know how it feels to be *a,*
1Pe 2:11 as *a* and strangers in the world,

ALIVE (LIVE)
1Sa 2: 6 LORD brings death and makes *a;*
Lk 24:23 vision of angels, who said he was *a.*
Ac 1: 3 convincing proofs that he was *a.*
Ro 6:11 but *a* to God in Christ Jesus.
1Co 15:22 so in Christ all will be made *a.*
Eph 2: 5 made us *a* with Christ

ALMIGHTY (MIGHT)
Ge 17: 1 "I am God *A;* walk before me
Ex 6: 3 to Isaac and to Jacob as God *A,*
Ru 1:20 the *A* has made my life very bitter.
Job 11: 7 Can you probe the limits of the *A?*
33: 4 the breath of the *A* gives me life.
Ps 89: 8 O LORD God *A,* who is like you?
91: 1 will rest in the shadow of the *A.*
Isa 6: 3 "Holy, holy, holy is the LORD *A;*
45:13 says the LORD *A.*"
47: 4 the LORD *A* is his name—
48: 2 the LORD *A* is his name:
51:15 the LORD *A* is his name.
54: 5 the LORD *A* is his name—
Am 5:14 the LORD God *A* will be with you,
5:15 the LORD God *A* will have mercy
Rev 4: 8 holy is the Lord God *A,* who was,
19: 6 For our Lord God *A* reigns.

ALPHA*
Rev 1: 8 "I am the *A* and the Omega,"
21: 6 I am the *A* and the Omega,
22:13 I am the *A* and the Omega,

ALTAR
Ge 8:20 Then Noah built an *a* to the LORD
12: 7 So he built an *a* there to the LORD
13:18 where he built an *a* to the LORD.
22: 9 Abraham built an *a* there
22: 9 his son Isaac and laid him on the *a,*
26:25 Isaac built an *a* there and called
35: 1 and build an *a* there to God,
Ex 17:15 Moses built an *a* and called it
27: 1 "Build an *a* of acacia wood,
30: 1 "Make an *a* of acacia wood
37:25 They made the *a* of incense out
Dt 27: 5 an *a* to the LORD your God, an *a*
Jos 8:30 on Mount Ebal an *a* to the LORD,
22:10 built an imposing *a* there
Jdg 6:24 So Gideon built an *a* to the LORD
21: 4 the next day the people built an *a*
1Sa 7:17 he built an *a* there to the LORD.
14:35 Then Saul built an *a* to the LORD;
2Sa 24:25 David built an *a* to the LORD
1Ki 12:33 sacrifices on the *a* he had built
13: 2 "O *a, a!* This is what the LORD
16:32 He set up an *a* for Baal
18:30 and he repaired the *a* of the LORD
2Ki 16:11 So Uriah the priest built an *a*
1Ch 21:26 David built an *a* to the LORD
2Ch 4: 1 made a bronze *a* twenty cubits
4:19 the golden *a;* the tables
15: 8 He repaired the *a* of the LORD
32:12 'You must worship before one *a*
33:16 he restored the *a* of the LORD
Ezr 3: 2 to build the *a* of the God of Israel
Isa 6: 6 taken with tongs from the *a.*
Eze 40:47 the *a* was in front of the temple.
Mt 5:23 if you are offering your gift at the *a*
Ac 17:23 found an *a* with this inscription:
Heb 13:10 We have an *a* from which those
Rev 6: 9 I saw under the *a* the souls

ALTER*
Ps 89:34 or *a* what my lips have uttered.

ALWAYS
Dt 15:11 There will *a* be poor people
Ps 16: 8 I have set the LORD *a* before me.
51: 3 and my sin is *a* before me.

Pr 23: 7 who is *a* thinking about the cost.
Mt 26:11 The poor you will *a* have with you,
28:20 And surely I am with you *a*,
Mk 14: 7 The poor you will *a* have with you,
Jn 12: 8 You will *a* have the poor
1Co 13: 7 *a* protects, *a* trusts, *a* hopes, *a*
Php 4: 4 Rejoice in the Lord *a*.
1Pe 3:15 *A* be prepared to give an answer

AMALEKITES

Ex 17: 8 *A* came and attacked the Israelites
1Sa 15: 2 'I will punish the *A*

AMASA

Nephew of David (1Ch 2:17). Commander of Absalom's forces (2Sa 17:24-27). Returned to David (2Sa 19:13). Killed by Joab (2Sa 20:4-13).

AMASSES*

Pr 28: 8 *a* it for another, who will be kind

AMAZED

Mt 7:28 the crowds were *a* at his teaching,
Mk 6: 6 And he was *a* at their lack of faith.
10:24 The disciples were *a* at his words.
Ac 2: 7 Utterly *a*, they asked: "Are not all
13:12 for he was *a* at the teaching about

AMAZIAH

1. Son of Joash; king of Judah (2Ki 14; 2Ch 25). Defeated Edom (2Ki 14:7; 2Ch 25:5-13); defeated by Israel for worshiping Edom's gods (2Ki 14:8-14; 2Ch 25:14-24).

2. Idolatrous priest who opposed Amos (Am 7: 10-17).

AMBASSADOR* (AMBASSADORS)

Eph 6:20 for which I am an *a* in chains.

AMBASSADORS (AMBASSADOR)

2Co 5:20 We are therefore Christ's *a*,

AMBITION*

Ro 15:20 It has always been my *a*
Gal 5:20 fits of rage, selfish *a*, dissensions,
Php 1:17 preach Christ out of selfish *a*,
2: 3 Do nothing out of selfish *a*
1Th 4:11 Make it your *a* to lead a quiet life,
Jas 3:14 and selfish *a* in your hearts,
3:16 where you have envy and selfish *a*,

AMENDS

Pr 14: 9 Fools mock at making *a* for sin,

AMNON

Firstborn of David (2Sa 3:2; 1Ch 3:1). Killed by Absalom for raping his sister Tamar (2Sa 13).

AMON

1. Son of Manasseh; king of Judah (2Ki 21: 18-26; 1Ch 3:14; 2Ch 33:21-25).

2. Ruler of Samaria under Ahab (1Ki 22:26; 2Ch 18:25).

AMOS

1. Prophet from Tekoa (Am 1:1; 7:10-17).
2. Ancestor of Jesus (Lk 3:25).

ANAK (ANAKITES)

Nu 13:28 even saw descendants of *A* there.

ANAKITES (ANAK)

Dt 1:28 We even saw the *A* there.'"
2:10 and numerous, and as tall as the *A*.
9: 2 "Who can stand up against the *A*?"

ANANIAS

1. Husband of Sapphira; died for lying to God (Ac 5:1-11).
2. Disciple who baptized Saul (Ac 9:10-19).
3. High priest at Paul's arrest (Ac 22:30-24:1).

ANCESTORS (ANCESTRY)

1Ki 19: 4 I am no better than my *a*."

ANCESTRY (ANCESTORS)

Ro 9: 5 from them is traced the human *a*

ANCHOR

Heb 6:19 We have this hope as an *a*

ANCIENT

Da 7: 9 and the *A* of Days took his seat.
7:13 He approached the *A* of Days
7:22 until the *A* of Days came

ANDREW*

Apostle; brother of Simon Peter (Mt 4:18; 10:2; Mk 1:16-18, 29; 3:18; 13:3; Lk 6:14; Jn 1:35-44; 6: 8-9; 12:22; Ac 1:13).

ANGEL (ANGELS ARCHANGEL)

Ge 16: 7 The *a* of the LORD found Hagar
22:11 But the *a* of the LORD called out
Ex 23:20 I am sending an *a* ahead of you
Nu 22:23 When the donkey saw the *a*
Jdg 2: 1 The *a* of the LORD went up
6:22 Gideon realized that it was the *a*
13:15 Manoah said to the *a* of the LORD
2Sa 24:16 The *a* of the LORD was then
1Ki 19: 7 The *a* of the LORD came back
2Ki 19:35 That night the *a* of the LORD went
Ps 34: 7 The *a* of the LORD encamps
Hos 12: 4 He struggled with the *a*
Mt 2:13 an *a* of the Lord appeared
28: 2 for an *a* of the Lord came
Lk 1:26 God sent the *a* Gabriel
2: 9 An *a* of the Lord appeared to them,
22:43 An *a* from heaven appeared to him
Ac 6:15 his face was like the face of an *a*.
12: 7 Suddenly an *a* of the Lord
2Co 11:14 Satan himself masquerades as an *a*
Gal 1: 8 or an *a* from heaven should preach

ANGELS (ANGEL)

Ps 91:11 command his *a* concerning you
Mt 4: 6 command his *a* concerning you,
13:39 of the age, and the harvesters are *a*.
13:49 The *a* will come and separate
18:10 For I tell you that their *a*
25:41 prepared for the devil and his *a*.
Lk 4:10 command his *a* concerning you
20:36 for they are like the *a*.
1Co 6: 3 you not know that we will judge *a*?
13: 1 in the tongues of men and of *a*,
Col 2:18 and the worship of *a* disqualify you
Heb 1: 4 as much superior to the *a*
1: 6 "Let all God's *a* worship him."
1: 7 "He makes his *a* winds,
1:14 Are not all *a* ministering spirits
2: 7 made him a little lower than the *a*;
2: 9 was made a little lower than the *a*,
13: 2 some people have entertained *a*
1Pe 1:12 Even *a* long to look
2Pe 2: 4 For if God did not spare *a*
Jude : 6 *a* who did not keep their positions

ANGER (ANGERED ANGRY)

Ex 15: 7 You unleashed your burning *a*;
22:24 My *a* will be aroused, and I will kill
32:10 alone so that my *a* may burn
32:11 "why should your *a* burn
32:12 Turn from your fierce *a*; relent
32:19 his *a* burned and he threw
34: 6 slow to *a*, abounding in love
Lev 26:28 then in my *a* I will be hostile
Nu 14:18 slow to *a*, abounding in love
25:11 has turned my *a* away
32:10 LORD's *a* was aroused that day
32:13 The LORD's *a* burned
Dt 9:19 I feared the *a* and wrath
29:28 In furious *a* and in great wrath
Jdg 14:19 Burning with *a*, he went up
2Sa 12: 5 David burned with *a*
2Ki 22:13 Great is the LORD's *a* that burns
Ne 9:17 slow to *a* and abounding in love.
Ps 30: 5 For his *a* lasts only a moment,
78:38 Time after time he restrained his *a*
86:15 slow to *a*, abounding in love
90: 7 We are consumed by your *a*
103: 8 slow to *a*, abounding in love.
Pr 15: 1 but a harsh word stirs up *a*.
29:11 A fool gives full vent to his *a*,
30:33 so stirring up *a* produces strife."
Jnh 4: 2 slow to *a* and abounding in love,
Eph 4:26 "In your *a* do not sin": Do not let
Jas 1:20 for man's *a* does not bring about

ANGERED (ANGER)

Pr 22:24 do not associate with one easily *a*,
1Co 13: 5 it is not easily *a*, it keeps no record

ANGRY (ANGER)

Ps 2:12 Kiss the Son, lest he be *a*
95:10 For forty years I was *a*
Pr 29:22 An *a* man stirs up dissension,
Mt 5:22 But I tell you that anyone who is *a*
Jas 1:19 slow to speak and slow to become *a*

ANGUISH

Ps 118: 5 In my *a* I cried to the LORD,
Jer 4:19 Oh, my *a*, my *a*!
Zep 1:15 a day of distress and *a*,
Lk 21:25 nations will be in *a* and perplexity
22:44 in *a*, he prayed more earnestly,
Ro 9: 2 and unceasing *a* in my heart.

ANIMALS

Ge 1:24 wild *a*, each according to its kind."
7:16 The *a* going in were male

Dt 14: 4 These are the *a* you may eat: the ox
Job 12: 7 ask the *a*, and they will teach you,
Isa 43:20 The wild *a* honor me,

ANNOUNCE (ANNOUNCED)

Mt 6: 2 give to the needy, do not *a* it

ANNOUNCED (ANNOUNCE)

Isa 48: 5 before they happened I *a* them
Gal 3: 8 and *a* the gospel in advance

ANNOYANCE*

Pr 12:16 A fool shows his *a* at once,

ANNUAL*

Ex 30:10 This *a* atonement must be made
Jdg 21:19 there is the *a* festival of the LORD
1Sa 1:21 family to offer the *a* sacrifice
2:19 husband to offer the *a* sacrifice.
20: 6 an *a* sacrifice is being made there
2Ch 8:13 New Moons and the three *a* feasts
Heb 10: 3 those sacrifices are an *a* reminder

ANOINT (ANOINTED ANOINTING)

Ex 30:26 use it to *a* the Tent of Meeting,
30:30 "*A* Aaron and his sons
1Sa 9:16 *A* him leader over my people Israel
15: 1 to *a* you king over his people Israel;
2Ki 9: 3 what the LORD says: I *a* you king
Ps 23: 5 You *a* my head with oil;
Da 9:24 prophecy and to *a* the most holy.
Jas 5:14 and *a* him with oil in the name

ANOINTED (ANOINT)

1Ch 16:22 "Do not touch my *a* ones;
Ps 105: 15 "Do not touch my *a* ones;
Isa 61: 1 because the LORD has *a* me
Da 9:26 the *A* One will be cut off
Lk 4:18 because he has *a* me
Ac 10:38 how God *a* Jesus of Nazareth

ANOINTING (ANOINT)

Lev 8:12 some of the *a* oil on Aaron's head
1Ch 29:22 *a* him before the LORD to be ruler
Ps 45: 7 by *a* you with the oil of joy.
Heb 1: 9 by *a* you with the oil of joy."
1Jn 2:20 you have an *a* from the Holy One,
2:27 about all things and as that *a* is real,

ANT* (ANTS)

Pr 6: 6 Go to the *a*, you sluggard;

ANTICHRIST* (ANTICHRISTS)

1Jn 2:18 have heard that the *a* is coming,
2:22 a man is the *a*— he denies
4: 3 of the *a*, which you have heard is
2Jn : 7 person is the deceiver and the *a*.

ANTICHRISTS* (ANTICHRIST)

1Jn 2:18 even now many *a* have come.

ANTIOCH

Ac 11:26 were called Christians first at *A*.

ANTS* (ANT)

Pr 30:25 *A* are creatures of little strength,

ANXIETIES* (ANXIOUS)

Lk 21:34 drunkenness and the *a* of life,

ANXIETY (ANXIOUS)

1Pe 5: 7 Cast all your *a* on him

ANXIOUS (ANXIETIES ANXIETY)

Pr 12:25 An *a* heart weighs a man down,
Php 4: 6 Do not be *a* about anything,

APOLLOS*

Christian from Alexandria, learned in the Scriptures; instructed by Aquila and Priscilla (Ac 18: 24-28). Ministered at Corinth (Ac 19:1; 1Co 1:12; 3; Tit 3:13).

APOLLYON*

Rev 9:11 is Abaddon, and in Greek, *A*.

APOSTLE (APOSTLES APOSTLES')

Ro 11:13 as I am the *a* to the Gentiles,
1Co 9: 1 Am I not an *a*? Have I not seen
2Co 12:12 The things that mark an *a*— signs,
Gal 2: 8 of Peter as an *a* to the Jews,
1Ti 2: 7 was appointed a herald and an *a*—
2Ti 1:11 I was appointed a herald and an *a*
Heb 3: 1 *a* and high priest whom we confess.

APOSTLES (APOSTLE)

See also Andrew, Bartholomew, James, John, Judas, Matthew, Matthias, Nathanael, Paul, Peter, Philip, Simon, Thaddaeus, Thomas.
Mk 3:14 twelve—designating them *a*—
Lk 11:49 'I will send them prophets and *a*,
Ac 1:26 so he was added to the eleven *a*.

Ac 2:43 signs were done by the *a*.
1Co 12:28 God has appointed first of all *a*,
15: 9 For I am the least of the *a*
2Co 11:13 masquerading as *a* of Christ.
Eph 2:20 built on the foundation of the *a*
4:11 It was he who gave some to be *a*,
Rev 21:14 names of the twelve *a* of the Lamb.

APOSTLES' (APOSTLE)
Ac 5: 2 the rest and put it at the *a*' feet.
8:18 at the laying on of the *a*' hands,

APPEAL
Ac 25:11 I *a* to Caesar!" After Festus had
Phm : 9 yet I *a* to you on the basis of love.

APPEAR (APPEARANCE APPEARANCES APPEARED APPEARING APPEARS)
Ge 1: 9 to one place, and let dry ground *a*."
Lev 16: 2 I *a* in the cloud over the atonement
Mt 24:30 of the Son of Man will *a* in the sky,
Mk 13:22 false prophets will *a* and perform
Lk 19:11 of God was going to *a* at once.
2Co 5:10 we must all *a* before the judgment
Col 3: 4 also will *a* with him in glory.
Heb 9:24 now to *a* for us in God's presence.
9:28 and he will *a* a second time,

APPEARANCE (APPEAR)
1Sa 16: 7 Man looks at the outward *a*,
Isa 52:14 his *a* was so disfigured beyond that
53: 2 in his *a* that we should desire him.
Gal 2: 6 God does not judge by external *a*—

APPEARANCES* (APPEAR)
Jn 7:24 Stop judging by mere *a*,

APPEARED (APPEAR)
Nu 14:10 glory of the LORD *a* at the Tent
Mt 1:20 an angel of the Lord *a* to him
Lk 2: 9 An angel of the Lord *a* to them,
1Co 15: 5 and that he *a* to Peter,
Heb 9:26 now he has *a* once for all at the end

APPEARING (APPEAR)
1Ti 6:14 until the *a* of our Lord Jesus Christ,
2Ti 1:10 through the *a* of our Savior,
4: 8 to all who have longed for his *a*.
Tit 2:13 the glorious *a* of our great God

APPEARS (APPEAR)
Mal 3: 2 Who can stand when he *a*?
Col 3: 4 When Christ, who is your life, *a*,
1Pe 5: 4 And when the Chief Shepherd *a*,
1Jn 3: 2 But we know that when he *a*,

APPETITE
Pr 16:26 The laborer's *a* works for him;
Ecc 6: 7 yet his *a* is never satisfied.
Jer 50:19 his *a* will be satisfied

APPLES
Pr 25:11 is like *a* of gold in settings of silver.

APPLY (APPLYING)
Pr 22:17 *a* your heart to what I teach,
23:12 *A* your heart to instruction

APPLYING (APPLY)
Pr 2: 2 and *a* your heart to understanding,

APPOINT (APPOINTED)
Ps 61: 7 *a* your love and faithfulness
1Th 5: 9 For God did not *a* us
Tit 1: 5 and *a* elders in every town,

APPOINTED (APPOINT)
Dt 1:15 *a* them to have authority over you
Pr 8:23 I was *a* from eternity,
Da 11:27 an end will still come at the *a* time.
Hab 2: 3 For the revelation awaits an *a* time;
Jn 15:16 Chose you and *a* you to go
Ro 9: 9 "At the *a* time I will return,

APPROACH (APPROACHING)
Ex 24: 2 but Moses alone is to *a* the LORD;
Eph 3:12 in him we may *a* God with freedom
Heb 4:16 Let us then *a* the throne of grace

APPROACHING (APPROACH)
Heb 10:25 all the more as you see the Day *a*.
1Jn 5:14 is the confidence we have in *a* God:

APPROPRIATE
1Ti 2:10 *a* for women who profess

APPROVAL (APPROVE)
Jdg 18: 6 Your journey has the LORD's *a*."
Jn 6:27 the Father has placed his seal of *a*."
1Co 11:19 to show which of you have God's *a*
Gal 1:10 trying to win the *a* of men,

APPROVE (APPROVAL APPROVED APPROVES)
Ro 2:18 if you know his will and *a*
12: 2 and *a* what God's will is—

APPROVED* (APPROVE)
Ro 14:18 pleasing to God and *a* by men.
16:10 Greet Apelles, tested and *a*
2Co 10:18 who commends himself who is *a*,
1Th 2: 4 as men *a* by God to be entrusted
2Ti 2:15 to present yourself to God as one *a*,

APPROVES* (APPROVE)
Ro 14:22 not condemn himself by what he *a*.

APT*
Pr 15:23 A man finds joy in giving an *a* reply

AQUILA*
Husband of Priscilla; co-worker with Paul, instructor of Apollos (Ac 18; Ro 16:3; 1Co 16:19; 2Ti 4:19).

ARABIA
Gal 1:17 but I went immediately into *A*
4:25 Hagar stands for Mount Sinai in *A*

ARARAT
Ge 8: 4 came to rest on the mountains of *A*.

ARAUNAH
2Sa 24:16 threshing floor of *A* the Jebusite.

ARBITER* (ARBITRATE)
Lk 12:14 who appointed me a judge or an *a*

ARBITRATE* (ARBITER)
Job 9:33 If only there were someone to *a*

ARCHANGEL* (ANGEL)
1Th 4:16 with the voice of the *a*
Jude : 9 *a* Michael, when he was disputing

ARCHER
Pr 26:10 Like an *a* who wounds at random

ARCHIPPUS*
Col 4:17 Tell *A*: "See to it that you complete
Phm : 2 to *A* our fellow soldier

ARCHITECT*
Heb 11:10 whose *a* and builder is God.

AREOPAGUS*
Ac 17:19 brought him to a meeting of the *A*,
17:22 up in the meeting of the *A*
17:34 of the *A*, also a woman named

ARGUE (ARGUMENT ARGUMENTS)
Job 13: 3 and to *a* my case with God.
13: 8 Will you *a* the case for God?
Pr 25: 9 If you *a* your case with a neighbor,

ARGUMENT (ARGUE)
Heb 6:16 is said and puts an end to all *a*.

ARGUMENTS (ARGUE)
Isa 41:21 "Set forth your *a*," says Jacob's
Col 2: 4 you by fine-sounding *a*.
2Ti 2:23 to do with foolish and stupid *a*,
Tit 3: 9 and *a* and quarrels about the law,

ARK
Ge 6:14 So make yourself an *a*
Ex 25:21 and put in the *a* the Testimony,
Dt 10: 5 put the tablets in the *a* I had made,
1Sa 4:11 The *a* of God was captured,
7: 2 that the *a* remained at Kiriath
2Sa 6:17 They brought the *a* of the LORD
1Ki 8: 9 There was nothing in the *a*
1Ch 13: 9 out his hand to steady the *a*,
2Ch 35: 3 "Put the sacred *a* in the temple that
Heb 9: 4 This *a* contained the gold jar
11: 7 in holy fear built an *a*
Rev 11:19 within his temple was seen the *a*

ARM (ARMY)
Nu 11:23 "Is the LORD's *a* too short?
Dt 4:34 hand and an outstretched *a*,
7:19 mighty hand and outstretched *a*,
Ps 44: 3 it was your right hand, your *a*,
98: 1 his right hand and his holy *a*
Jer 27: 5 outstretched *a* I made the earth
1Pe 4: 1 *a* yourselves also with the same

ARMAGEDDON*
Rev 16:16 that in Hebrew is called *A*.

ARMIES (ARMY)
1Sa 17:26 Philistine that he should defy the *a*
Rev 19:14 *a* of heaven were following him,

ARMOR (ARMY)
1Ki 20:11 on his *a* should not boast like one
Jer 46: 4 put on your *a*!
Ro 13:12 deeds of darkness and put on the *a*
Eph 6:11 Put on the full *a* of God
6:13 Therefore put on the full *a* of God,

ARMS (ARMY)
Dt 33:27 underneath are the everlasting *a*.
Ps 18:32 It is God who *a* me with strength
Pr 31:17 her *a* are strong for her tasks.
31:20 She opens her *a* to the poor
Isa 40:11 He gathers the lambs in his *a*
Mk 10:16 And he took the children in his *a*,
Heb 12:12 strengthen your feeble *a*

ARMY (ARM ARMIES ARMOR ARMS)
Ps 33:16 No king is saved by the size of his *a*
Joel 2: 2 a large and mighty *a* comes,
2: 5 like a mighty *a* drawn up for battle.
2:11 thunders at the head of his *a*;
Rev 19:19 the rider on the horse and his *a*.

AROMA
Ge 8:21 The LORD smelled the pleasing *a*
Ex 29:18 a pleasing *a*, an offering made
Lev 3:16 made by fire, a pleasing *a*.
2Co 2:15 For we are to God the *a* of Christ

AROUSE (AROUSED)
Ro 11:14 I may somehow *a* my own people

AROUSED (AROUSE)
Ps 78:58 they *a* his jealousy with their idols.

ARRANGED
1Co 12:18 But in fact God has *a* the parts

ARRAYED*
Ps 110: 3 *A* in holy majesty,
Isa 61:10 and *a* me in a robe of righteousness

ARREST
Mt 10:19 But when they *a* you, do not worry

ARROGANCE (ARROGANT)
1Sa 2: 3 or let your mouth speak such *a*,
Pr 8:13 I hate pride and *a*,
Mk 7:22 lewdness, envy, slander, *a* and folly
2Co 12:20 slander, gossip, *a* and disorder.

ARROGANT (ARROGANCE)
Ps 5: 5 The *a* cannot stand
119: 78 May the *a* be put to shame
Pr 17: 7 *A* lips are unsuited to a fool—
21:24 a man—"Mocker" is his name;
Ro 1:30 God-haters, insolent, *a*
11:20 Do not be *a*, but be afraid.
1Ti 6:17 in this present world not to be *a*

ARROW (ARROWS)
Ps 91: 5 nor the *a* that flies by day,
Pr 25:18 Like a club or a sword or a sharp *a*

ARROWS (ARROW)
Ps 64: 3 and aim their words like deadly *a*.
64: 7 But God will shoot them with *a*;
127: 4 Like *a* in the hands of a warrior
Pr 26:18 firebrands or deadly *a*
Eph 6:16 you can extinguish all the flaming *a*

ARTAXERXES
King of Persia; allowed rebuilding of temple under Ezra (Ezr 4; 7), and of walls of Jerusalem under his cupbearer Nehemiah (Ne 2; 5:14; 13:6).

ARTEMIS
Ac 19:28 "Great is *A* of the Ephesians!"

ASA
King of Judah (1Ki 15:8-24; 1Ch 3:10; 2Ch 14-16). Godly reformer (2Ch 15); in later years defeated Israel with help of Aram, not the LORD (1Ki 15:16-22; 2Ch 16).

ASAHEL
1. Nephew of David, one of his warriors (2Sa 23:24; 1Ch 2:16; 11:26; 27:7). Killed by Abner (2Sa 2); avenged by Joab (2Sa 3:22-39).
2. Levite; teacher (2Ch 17:8).

ASAPH
1. Recorder to Hezekiah (2Ki 18:18, 37; Isa 36:3, 22).
2. Levitical musician (1Ch 6:39; 15:17-19; 16:4-7, 37). Sons of (1Ch 25; 2Ch 5:12; 20:14; 29:13; 35:15; Ezr 2:41; 3:10; Ne 7:44; 11:17; 12:27-47). Psalms of (2Ch 29:30; Ps 50; 73-83).

ASCEND* (ASCENDED ASCENDING)

Dt 30:12 "Who will *a* into heaven to get it
Ps 24: 3 Who may *a* the hill of the LORD?
Isa 14:13 "I will *a* to heaven;
14:14 I will *a* above the tops of the clouds
Jn 6:62 of Man *a* to where he was before!
Ac 2:34 For David did not *a* to heaven,
Ro 10: 6 'Who will *a* into heaven?'" (that is,

ASCENDED (ASCEND)

Ps 68:18 When you *a* on high,
Eph 4: 8 "When he *a* on high,

ASCENDING (ASCEND)

Ge 28:12 and the angels of God were *a*
Jn 1:51 and the angels of God *a*

ASCRIBE*

1Ch 16:28 *A* to the LORD, O families
16:28 *a* to the LORD glory and strength,
16:29 *a* to the LORD the glory due his
Job 36: 3 I will *a* justice to my Maker.
Ps 29: 1 *A* to the LORD, O mighty ones,
29: 1 *a* to the LORD glory and strength.
29: 2 *A* to the LORD the glory due his
96: 7 *A* to the LORD, O families
96: 7 *a* to the LORD glory and strength.
96: 8 *A* to the LORD the glory due his

ASHAMED (SHAME)

Mk 8:38 If anyone is *a* of me and my words
Lk 9:26 If anyone is *a* of me and my words,
Ro 1:16 I am not *a* of the gospel,
2Ti 1: 8 So do not be *a* to testify about our
2:15 who does not need to be *a*

ASHER

Son of Jacob by Zilpah (Ge 30:13; 35:26; 46:17; Ex 1:4; 1Ch 2:2). Tribe of blessed (Ge 49:20; Dt 33:24-25), numbered (Nu 1:40-41; 26:44-47), allotted land (Jos 10:24-31; Eze 48:2), failed to fully possess (Jdg 1:31-32), failed to support Deborah (Jdg 5:17), supported Gideon (Jdg 6:35; 7:23) and David (1Ch 12:36), 12,000 from (Rev 7:6).

ASHERAH (ASHERAHS)

Ex 34:13 and cut down their *A* poles.
1Ki 18:19 the four hundred prophets of *A*,

ASHERAHS* (ASHERAH)

Jdg 3: 7 and served the Baals and the *A*.

ASHES

Job 42: 6 and repent in dust and *a*."
Mt 11:21 ago in sackcloth and *a*.

ASHTORETHS

Jdg 2:13 and served Baal and the *A*.
1Sa 7: 4 put away their Baals and *A*,

ASLEEP (SLEEP)

1Co 15:18 who have fallen *a* in Christ are lost.
1Th 4:13 be ignorant about those who fall *a*,

ASSEMBLY

Ps 1: 5 nor sinners in the *a* of the righteous
35:18 I will give you thanks in the great *a*
82: 1 God presides in the great *a*;
149: 1 his praise in the *a* of the saints.

ASSIGNED

1Ki 7:14 and did all the work *a* to him.
Mk 13:34 with his *a* task, and tells the one
1Co 3: 5 as the Lord has *a* to each his task.
7:17 place in life that the Lord *a* to him
2Co 10:13 to the field God has *a* to us,

ASSOCIATE

Pr 22:24 do not *a* with one easily angered,
Jn 4: 9 (For Jews do not *a* with Samaritans
Ac 10:28 law for a Jew to *a* with a Gentile
Ro 12:16 but be willing to *a* with people
1Co 5: 9 to *a* with sexually immoral people
5:11 am writing you that you must not *a*
2Th 3:14 Do not *a* with him,

ASSURANCE (ASSURED)

Heb 10:22 with a sincere heart in full *a* of faith

ASSURED (ASSURANCE)

Col 4:12 the will of God, mature and fully *a*.

ASTRAY

Ps 119: 67 Before I was afflicted I went *a*,
Pr 10:17 ignores correction leads others *a*.
20: 1 whoever is led *a* by them is not
Isa 53: 6 We all, like sheep, have gone *a*,
Jer 50: 6 their shepherds have led them *a*
Jn 16: 1 you so that you will not go *a*.
1Pe 2:25 For you were like sheep going *a*,
1Jn 3: 7 do not let anyone lead you *a*.

ASTROLOGERS

Isa 47:13 Let your *a* come forward,
Da 2: 2 *a* to tell him what he had dreamed.

ATE (EAT)

Ge 3: 6 wisdom, she took some and *a* it.
27:25 Jacob brought it to him and he *a*;
2Sa 9:11 Mephibosheth *a* at David's table
Ps 78:25 Men *a* the bread of angels;
Jer 15:16 When your words came, I *a* them;
Eze 3: 3 So I *a* it, and it tasted as sweet
Mt 14:20 They all *a* and were satisfied,
15:37 They all *a* and were satisfied.
Mk 6:42 They all *a* and were satisfied,
Lk 9:17 They all *a* and were satisfied,

ATHALIAH

Granddaughter of Omri; wife of Jehoram and mother of Ahaziah; encouraged their evil ways (2Ki 8:18, 27; 2Ch 22:2). At death of Ahaziah she made herself queen, killing all his sons but Joash (2Ki 11:1-3; 2Ch 22:10-12); killed six years later when Joash was revealed (2Ki 11:4-16; 2Ch 23:1-15).

ATHLETE*

2Ti 2: 5 if anyone competes as an *a*,

ATONE* (ATONEMENT)

Ex 30:15 to the LORD to *a* for your lives.
2Ch 29:24 for a sin offering to *a* for all Israel,
Da 9:24 an end to sin, to *a* for wickedness,

ATONED* (ATONEMENT)

Dt 21: 8 And the bloodshed will be *a* for.
1Sa 3:14 guilt of Eli's house will never be *a*
Pr 16: 6 faithfulness sin is *a* for;
Isa 6: 7 guilt is taken away and your sin *a*
22:14 your dying day this sin will not be *a*
27: 9 then, will Jacob's guilt be *a* for,

ATONEMENT (ATONE ATONED)

Ex 25:17 "Make an *a* cover of pure gold—
30:10 Once a year Aaron shall make *a*
Lev 17:11 it is the blood that makes *a*
23:27 this seventh month is the Day of *A*.
Nu 25:13 and made *a* for the Israelites."
Ro 3:25 presented him as a sacrifice of *a*,
Heb 2:17 that he might make *a* for the sins

ATTACK

Ps 109: 3 they *a* me without cause.

ATTAINED

Php 3:16 up to what we have already *a*.
Heb 7:11 If perfection could have been *a*

ATTENTION (ATTENTIVE)

Pr 4: 1 pay *a* and gain understanding.
4:20 My son, pay *a* to what I say;
5: 1 My son, pay *a* to my wisdom,
7:24 pay *a* to what I say.
22:17 Pay *a* and listen to the sayings
Ecc 7:21 Do not pay *a* to every word people
Isa 42:20 many things, but have paid no *a*;
Tit 1:14 and will pay no *a* to Jewish myths
Heb 2: 1 We must pay more careful *a*,

ATTENTIVE (ATTENTION)

Ne 1:11 let your ear be *a* to the prayer
1Pe 3:12 and his ears are *a* to their prayer,

ATTITUDE (ATTITUDES)

Eph 4:23 new in the *a* of your minds;
Php 2: 5 Your *a* should be the same
1Pe 4: 1 yourselves also with the same *a*,

ATTITUDES (ATTITUDE)

Heb 4:12 it judges the thoughts and *a*

ATTRACTIVE

Tit 2:10 teaching about God our Savior *a*.

AUDIENCE

Pr 29:26 Many seek an *a* with a ruler,

AUTHORITIES (AUTHORITY)

Ro 13: 1 *a* that exist have been established
13: 5 it is necessary to submit to the *a*,
13: 6 for the *a* are God's servants,
Eph 3:10 and *a* in the heavenly realms,
6:12 but against the rulers, against the *a*,
Col 1:16 thrones or powers or rulers or *a*;
2:15 having disarmed the powers and *a*,
Tit 3: 1 people to be subject to rulers and *a*,
1Pe 3:22 *a* and powers in submission to him.

AUTHORITY (AUTHORITIES)

Mt 7:29 because he taught as one who had *a*
9: 6 the Son of Man has *a* on earth
28:18 "All *a* in heaven and on earth has
Mk 1:22 he taught them as one who had *a*,
2:10 the Son of Man has *a* on earth
Lk 4:32 because his message had *a*.
5:24 the Son of Man has *a* on earth
Jn 10:18 *a* to lay it down and *a*
Ac 1: 7 the Father has set by his own *a*.
Ro 7: 1 that the law has *a* over a man only
13: 1 for there is no *a* except that which
13: 2 rebels against the *a* is rebelling
1Co 11:10 to have a sign of *a* on her head.
15:24 he has destroyed all dominion, *a*
1Ti 2: 2 for kings and all those in *a*,
2:12 to teach or to have *a* over a man;
Tit 2:15 Encourage and rebuke with all *a*.
Heb 13:17 your leaders and submit to their *a*.

AUTUMN*

Dt 11:14 both *a* and spring rains,
Ps 84: 6 the *a* rains also cover it with pools.
Jer 5:24 who gives *a* and spring rains
Joel 2:23 both *a* and spring rains, as before.
Jas 5: 7 and how patient he is for the *a*
Jude :12 blown along by the wind; *a* trees,

AVENGE (VENGEANCE)

Lev 26:25 sword upon you to *a* the breaking
Dt 32:35 It is mine to *a*; I will repay.
32:43 for he will *a* the blood
Ro 12:19 "It is mine to *a*; I will repay,"
Heb 10:30 "It is mine to *a*; I will repay,"
Rev 6:10 of the earth and *a* our blood?"

AVENGER (VENGEANCE)

Nu 35:27 the *a* of blood may kill the accused
Jos 20: 3 find protection from the *a* of blood.
Ps 8: 2 to silence the foe and the *a*.

AVENGES (VENGEANCE)

Ps 94: 1 O LORD, the God who *a*,

AVENGING (VENGEANCE)

1Sa 25:26 and from *a* yourself with your own
Na 1: 2 The LORD is a jealous and *a* God;

AVOID (AVOIDS)

Pr 4:15 *A* it, do not travel on it;
20: 3 It is to a man's honor to *a* strife,
20:19 so *a* a man who talks too much.
Ecc 7:18 who fears God will *a* all ⌊extremes⌋.
1Th 4: 3 you should *a* sexual immorality;
5:22 *A* every kind of evil.
2Ti 2:16 *A* godless chatter, because those
Tit 3: 9 But *a* foolish controversies

AVOIDS* (AVOID)

Pr 16: 6 of the LORD a man *a* evil.
16:17 The highway of the upright *a* evil;

AWAITS (WAIT)

Pr 15:10 Stern discipline *a* him who leaves
28:22 and is unaware that poverty *a* him.

AWAKE (WAKE)

Ps 17:15 when I *a*, I will be satisfied
Pr 6:22 when you *a*, they will speak to you.

AWARD*

2Ti 4: 8 will *a* to me on that day—

AWARE

Ex 34:29 he was not *a* that his face was
Mt 24:50 and at an hour he is not *a* of.
Lk 12:46 and at an hour he is not *a* of.

AWE* (AWESOME OVERAWED)

1Sa 12:18 So all the people stood in *a*
1Ki 3:28 they held the king in *a*,
Job 25: 2 "Dominion and *a* belong to God;
Ps 119: 120 I stand in *a* of your laws.
Ecc 5: 7 Therefore stand in *a* of God.
Isa 29:23 will stand in *a* of the God of Israel.
Jer 2:19 and have no *a* of me,"
33: 9 they will be in *a* and will tremble
Hab 3: 2 I stand in *a* of your deeds,
Mal 2: 5 and stood in *a* of my name.
Mt 9: 8 they were filled with *a*;
Lk 1:65 The neighbors were all filled with *a*
5:26 They were filled with *a* and said,
7:16 They were all filled with *a*
Ac 2:43 Everyone was filled with *a*,
Heb 12:28 acceptably with reverence and *a*,

AWESOME* (AWE)

Ge 28:17 and said, "How *a* is this place!
Ex 15:11 *a* in glory,
34:10 among will see how *a* is the work
Dt 4:34 or by great and *a* deeds,
7:21 is among you, is a great and *a* God.
10:17 the great God, mighty and *a*,
10:21 and *a* wonders you saw
28:58 revere this glorious and *a* name—
34:12 performed the *a* deeds that Moses

Jdg 13: 6 like an angel of God, very *a*.
2Sa 7:23 *a* wonders by driving out nations
1Ch 17:21 *a* wonders by driving out nations
Ne 1: 5 of heaven, the great and *a* God,
4:14 and *a*, and fight for your brothers,
9:32 the great, mighty and *a* God,
Job 10:16 again display your *a* power
37:22 God comes in *a* majesty.
Ps 45: 4 let your right hand display *a* deeds.
47: 2 How *a* is the LORD Most High,
65: 5 us with *a* deeds of righteousness,
66: 3 to God, "How *a* are your deeds!
66: 5 how *a* his works in man's behalf!
68:35 You are *a*, O God,
89: 7 he is more *a* than all who surround
99: 3 praise your great and *a* name—
106: 22 and *a* deeds by the Red Sea.
111: 9 holy and *a* is his name.
145: 6 of the power of your *a* works,
Isa 64: 3 when you did *a* things that we did
Eze 1:18 Their rims were high and *a*,
1:22 expanse, sparkling like ice, and *a*.
Da 2:31 dazzling statue, *a* in appearance.
9: 4 "O Lord, the great and *a* God,
Zep 2:11 The LORD will be *a* to them

AX
Mt 3:10 The *a* is already at the root
Lk 3: 9 The *a* is already at the root

BAAL
Jdg 6:25 Tear down your father's altar to *B*
1Ki 16:32 *B* in the temple of *B* that he built
18:25 Elijah said to the prophets of *B*,
19:18 knees have not bowed down to *B*
2Ki 10:28 Jehu destroyed *B* worship in Israel.
Jer 19: 5 places of *B* to burn their sons
Ro 11: 4 have not bowed the knee to *B*."

BAASHA
King of Israel (1Ki 15:16-16:7; 2Ch 16:1-6).

BABBLER* (BABBLING)
Ac 17:18 "What is this *b* trying to say?"

BABBLING* (BABBLER)
Mt 6: 7 do not keep on *b* like pagans,

BABIES* (BABY)
Ge 25:22 The *b* jostled each other within her
Ex 2: 6 "This is one of the Hebrew *b*,"
Lk 18:15 also bringing *b* to Jesus
Ac 7:19 them to throw out their newborn *b*
1Pe 2: 2 Like newborn *b*, crave pure

BABY* (BABIES BABY'S)
Ex 2: 6 She opened it and saw the *b*.
2: 7 women to nurse the *b* for you?"
2: 9 So the woman took the *b*
2: 9 "Take this *b* and nurse him for me,
1Ki 3:17 I had a *b* while she was there
3:18 was born, this woman also had a *b*.
3:26 give her the living *b*! Don't kill him
3:27 Give the living *b* to the first woman
Isa 49:15 "Can a mother forget the *b*
Lk 1:41 the *b* leaped in her womb,
1:44 the *b* in my womb leaped for joy.
1:57 time for Elizabeth to have her *b*,
2: 6 the time came for the *b* to be born,
2:12 You will find a *b* wrapped in strips
2:16 the *b*, who was lying in the manger.
Jn 16:21 but when her *b* is born she forgets

BABY'S* (BABY)
Ex 2: 8 the girl went and got the *b* mother.

BABYLON
Ps 137: 1 By the rivers of *B* we sat and wept
Jer 29:10 seventy years are completed for *B*,
51:37 *B* will be a heap of ruins,
Rev 14: 8 "Fallen! Fallen is *B* the Great,
17: 5 MYSTERY *B* THE GREAT

BACKS
2Pe 2:21 and then to turn their *b*

BACKSLIDING* (BACKSLIDINGS)
Jer 2:19 your *b* will rebuke you.
3:22 I will cure you of *b*."
14: 7 For our *b* is great;
15: 6 "You keep on *b*.
Eze 37:23 them from all their sinful *b*,

BACKSLIDINGS* (BACKSLIDING)
Jer 5: 6 and their *b* many.

BALAAM
Prophet who attempted to curse Israel (Nu 22-24; Dt 23:4-5; 2Pe 2:15; Jude 11). Killed in Israel's vengeance on Midianites (Nu 31:8; Jos 13:22).

BALAK
Moabite king who hired Balaam to curse Israel (Nu 22-24; Jos 24:9).

BALDHEAD
2Ki 2:23 "Go on up, you *b*!" they said.

BALM
Jer 8:22 Is there no *b* in Gilead?

BANISH (BANISHED)
Jer 25:10 I will *b* from them the sounds of joy

BANISHED (BANISH)
Dt 30: 4 Even if you have been *b*

BANNER
Ex 17:15 and called it The LORD is my *B*.
SS 2: 4 and his *b* over me is love.
Isa 11:10 the Root of Jesse will stand as a *b*

BANQUET
SS 2: 4 He has taken me to the *b* hall,
Lk 14:13 when you give a *b*, invite the poor,

BAPTISM* (BAPTIZE)
Mt 21:25 John's *b*—where did it come from?
Mk 1: 4 and preaching a *b* of repentance
10:38 baptized with the *b* I am baptized
10:39 baptized with the *b* I am baptized
11:30 John's *b*—was it from heaven,
Lk 3: 3 preaching a *b* of repentance
12:50 But I have a *b* to undergo,
20: 4 John's *b*—was it from heaven,
Ac 1:22 beginning from John's *b*
10:37 after the *b* that John preached—
13:24 and *b* to all the people of Israel.
18:25 though he knew only the *b* of John.
19: 3 did you receive?" "John's *b*,"
19: 3 "Then what *b* did you receive?"
19: 4 "John's *b* was a *b* of repentance.
Ro 6: 4 with him through *b* into death
Eph 4: 5 one Lord, one faith, one *b*;
Col 2:12 having been buried with him in *b*
1Pe 3:21 this water symbolizes *b* that now

BAPTISMS* (BAPTIZE)
Heb 6: 2 instruction about *b*, the laying

BAPTIZE* (BAPTISM BAPTISMS BAPTIZED BAPTIZING)
Mt 3:11 He will *b* you with the Holy Spirit
3:11 "I *b* you with water for repentance.
Mk 1: 8 I *b* you with water, but he will
1: 8 he will *b* you with the Holy Spirit."
Lk 3:16 He will *b* you with the Holy Spirit
3:16 John answered them all, "I *b* you
Jn 1:25 "Why then do you *b*
1:26 nor the Prophet?" "I *b* with water,"
1:33 and remain is he who will *b*
1:33 me to *b* with water told me,
1Co 1:14 I am thankful that I did not *b* any
1:17 For Christ did not send me to *b*,

BAPTIZED* (BAPTIZE)
Mt 3: 6 they were *b* by him in the Jordan
3:13 to the Jordan to be *b* by John.
3:14 saying, "I need to be *b* by you,
3:16 as Jesus was *b*, he went up out
Mk 1: 5 they were *b* by him in the Jordan
1: 9 and was *b* by John in the Jordan.
10:38 or be *b* with the baptism I am
10:38 with the baptism I am *b* with?"
10:39 and be *b* with the baptism I am
10:39 with the baptism I am *b* with,
16:16 believes and is *b* will be saved,
Lk 3: 7 to the crowds coming out to be *b*
3:12 Tax collectors also came to be *b*.
3:21 were being *b*, Jesus was *b* too.
7:29 because they had been *b* by John.
7:30 they had not been *b* by John.)
Jn 3:22 spent some time with them, and *b*.
3:23 were constantly coming to be *b*.
4: 2 in fact it was not Jesus who *b*,
Ac 1: 5 For John *b* with water,
1: 5 but in a few days you will be *b*
2:38 Repent and be *b*, every one of you,
2:41 who accepted his message were *b*,
8:12 they were *b*, both men and women.
8:13 Simon himself believed and was *b*.
8:16 they had simply been *b*
8:36 Why shouldn't I be *b*?"
8:38 into the water and Philip *b* him.
9:18 was *b*, and after taking some food,
10:47 people from being *b* with water?
10:48 So he ordered that they be *b*
11:16 what the Lord had said, 'John *b*
11:16 you will be *b* with the Holy Spirit.'
16:15 members of her household were *b*,
16:33 he and all his family were *b*.
Ac 18: 8 heard him believed and were *b*.
19: 5 they were *b* into the name
22:16 be *b* and wash your sins away,
Ro 6: 3 *b* into Christ Jesus were *b*
1Co 1:13 Were you *b* into the name of Paul?
1:15 so no one can say that you were *b*
1:16 I also *b* the household of Stephanas
1:16 I don't remember if I *b* anyone else
10: 2 They were all *b* into Moses
12:13 For we were all *b* by one Spirit
15:29 what will those do who are *b*
15:29 why are people *b* for them?
Gal 3:27 all of you who were *b*

BAPTIZING* (BAPTIZE)
Mt 3: 7 coming to where he was *b*,
28:19 *b* them in the name of the Father
Mk 1: 4 *b* in the desert region
Jn 1:28 of the Jordan, where John was *b*.
1:31 but the reason I came *b*
3:23 also was *b* at Aenon near Salim,
3:26 he is *b*, and everyone is going
4: 1 and *b* more disciples than John,
10:40 to the place where John had been *b*

BAR-JESUS*
Ac 13: 6 and false prophet named *B*,

BARABBAS
Mt 27:26 Then he released *B* to them.

BARAK*
Judge who fought with Deborah against Canaanites (Jdg 4-5; 1Sa 12:11; Heb 11:32).

BARBARIAN*
Col 3:11 circumcised or uncircumcised, *b*,

BARBS*
Nu 33:55 allow to remain will become *b*

BARE
Hos 2: 3 as *b* as on the day she was born;
Heb 4:13 and laid *b* before the eyes of him

BARNABAS*
Disciple, originally Joseph (Ac 4:36), prophet (Ac 13:1), apostle (Ac 14:14). Brought Paul to apostles (Ac 9:27), Antioch (Ac 11:22-29; Gal 2:1-13), on the first missionary journey (Ac 13-14). Together at Jerusalem Council, they separated over John Mark (Ac 15). Later co-workers (1Co 9:6; Col 4:10).

BARREN
Ge 11:30 Sarai was *b*; she had no children.
29:31 her womb, but Rachel was *b*.
Ps 113: 9 He settles the *b* woman
Isa 54: 1 "Sing, O *b* woman,
Lk 1: 7 children, because Elizabeth was *b*;
Gal 4:27 "Be glad, O *b* woman,
Heb 11:11 and Sarah herself was *b*—

BARTHOLOMEW*
Apostle (Mt 10:3; Mk 3:18; Lk 6:14; Ac 1:13). Possibly also known as Nathanael (Jn 1:45-49; 21:2).

BARUCH
Jeremiah's secretary (Jer 32:12-16; 36; 43:1-6; 45:1-2).

BARZILLAI
1. Gileadite who aided David during Absalom's revolt (2Sa 17:27; 19:31-39).
2. Son-in-law of 1. (Ezr 2:61; Ne 7:63).

BASHAN
Jos 22: 7 Moses had given land in *B*,
Ps 22:12 strong bulls of *B* encircle me.

BASIN
Ex 30:18 "Make a bronze *b*,

BASKET
Ex 2: 3 she got a papyrus *b* for him
Ac 9:25 him in a *b* through an opening
2Co 11:33 I was lowered in a *b* from a window

BATCH*
Ro 11:16 then the whole *b* is holy;
1Co 5: 6 through the whole *b* of dough?
5: 7 old yeast that you may be a new *b*
Gal 5: 9 through the whole *b* of dough."

BATH (BATHING)
Jn 13:10 person who has had a *b* needs only

BATHING (BATH)
2Sa 11: 2 From the roof he saw a woman *b*.

BATHSHEBA*
Wife of Uriah who committed adultery with and became wife of David (2Sa 11), mother of Solomon (2Sa 12:24; 1Ki 1-2; 1Ch 3:5).

BATTLE (BATTLES)
1Sa 17:47 for the *b* is the LORD's,
2Ch 20:15 For the *b* is not yours, but God's.
Ps 24: 8 the LORD mighty in *b*.
Ecc 9:11 or the *b* to the strong,
Isa 31: 4 down to do *b* on Mount Zion
Eze 13: 5 in the *b* on the day of the LORD.
Rev 16:14 them for the *b* on the great day
20: 8 and Magog—to gather them for *b*.

BATTLES* (BATTLE)
1Sa 8:20 to go out before us and fight our *b*."
18:17 and fight the *b* of the LORD."
25:28 because he fights the LORD's *b*.
2Ch 32: 8 God to help us and to fight our *b*."

BEAR (BEARING BEARS BIRTH BIRTHRIGHT BORE BORN CHILDBEARING CHILDBIRTH FIRSTBORN NEWBORN REBIRTH)
Ge 4:13 punishment is more than I can *b*.
Ps 38: 4 like a burden too heavy to *b*.
Isa 11: 7 The cow will feed with the *b*,
53:11 and he will *b* their iniquities.
Da 7: 5 beast, which looked like a *b*.
Mt 7:18 A good tree cannot *b* bad fruit,
Jn 15: 2 branch that does *b* fruit he prunes
15: 8 glory, that you *b* much fruit,
15:16 appointed you to go and *b* fruit—
Ro 7: 4 in order that we might *b* fruit
15: 1 ought to *b* with the failings
1Co 10:13 tempted beyond what you can *b*.
Col 3:13 *B* with each other and forgive

BEARD
Lev 19:27 or clip off the edges of your *b*.
Isa 50: 6 to those who pulled out my *b*;

BEARING (BEAR)
Eph 4: 2 *b* with one another in love.
Col 1:10 *b* fruit in every good work,
Heb 13:13 outside the camp, *b* the disgrace he

BEARS (BEAR)
1Ki 8:43 house I have built *b* your Name.
Ps 68:19 who daily *b* our burdens.

BEAST (BEASTS)
Rev 13:18 him calculate the number of the *b*,
16: 2 people who had the mark of the *b*
19:20 who had received the mark of the *b*

BEASTS (BEAST)
Da 7: 3 Four great *b*, each different
1Co 15:32 If I fought wild *b* in Ephesus

BEAT (BEATEN BEATING BEATINGS)
Isa 2: 4 They will *b* their swords
Joel 3:10 *B* your plowshares into swords
Mic 4: 3 They will *b* their swords
1Co 9:27 I *b* my body and make it my slave

BEATEN (BEAT)
Lk 12:47 do what his master wants will be *b*
12:48 deserving punishment will be *b*
2Co 11:25 Three times I was *b* with rods,

BEATING (BEAT)
1Co 9:26 I do not fight like a man *b* the air.
1Pe 2:20 if you receive a *b* for doing wrong

BEATINGS (BEAT)
Pr 19:29 and *b* for the backs of fools.

BEAUTIFUL* (BEAUTY)
Ge 6: 2 that the daughters of men were *b*,
12:11 "I know what a *b* woman you are.
12:14 saw that she was a very *b* woman.
24:16 The girl was very *b*, a virgin;
26: 7 of Rebekah, because she is *b*."
29:17 Rachel was lovely in form, and *b*.
49:21 that bears *b* fawns.
Nu 24: 5 "How *b* are your tents, O Jacob,
Dt 21:11 among the captives a *b* woman
Jos 7:21 saw in the plunder a *b* robe
1Sa 25: 3 was an intelligent and *b* woman,
2Sa 11: 2 The woman was very *b*,
13: 1 the *b* sister of Absalom son
14:27 and she became a *b* woman.
1Ki 1: 3 throughout Israel for a *b* girl
1: 4 The girl was very *b*; she took care
Est 2: 2 for *b* young virgins for the king.
2: 3 realm to bring all these *b* girls
Job 38:31 "Can you bind the *b* Pleiades?
42:15 land were there found women as *b*
Ps 48: 2 It is *b* in its loftiness,
Pr 11:22 is a *b* woman who shows no
24: 4 filled with rare and *b* treasures.
Ecc 3:11 He has made everything *b*
SS 1: 8 *Lover* If you do not know, most *b*
1:10 Your cheeks are *b* with earrings,
1:15 Oh, how *b*!
1:15 *Lover* How *b* you are, my darling!
2:10 my *b* one, and come with me.
2:13 my *b* one, come with me."
4: 1 How *b* you are, my darling!
4: 1 Oh, how *b*!
4: 7 All *b* you are, my darling;
5: 9 most *b* of women?
6: 1 most *b* of women?
6: 4 *Lover* You are *b*, my darling,
7: 1 How *b* your sandaled feet,
7: 6 How *b* you are and how pleasing,
Isa 4: 2 of the LORD will be *b*
28: 5 a *b* wreath
52: 7 How *b* on the mountains
Jer 3:19 the most *b* inheritance
6: 2 so *b* and delicate.
11:16 with fruit *b* in form.
46:20 "Egypt is a *b* heifer,
Eze 7:20 They were proud of their *b* jewelry
16: 7 and became the most *b* of jewels.
16:12 and a *b* crown on your head.
16:13 You became very *b* and rose
20: 6 and honey, the most *b* of all lands.
20:15 and honey, most *b* of all lands—
23:42 and *b* crowns on their heads.
27:24 traded with you *b* garments,
31: 3 with *b* branches overshadowing
31: 9 I made it *b*
33:32 who sings love songs with a *b* voice
Da 4:12 Its leaves were *b*, its fruit abundant
4:21 with *b* leaves and abundant fruit,
8: 9 to the east and toward the *B* Land.
11:16 will establish himself in the *B* Land
11:41 He will also invade the *B* Land.
11:45 the seas at the *b* holy mountain.
Zec 9:17 How attractive and *b* they will be!
Mt 23:27 which look *b* on the outside
26:10 She has done a *b* thing to me.
Mk 14: 6 She has done a *b* thing to me.
Lk 21: 5 temple was adorned with *b* stones
Ac 3: 2 carried to the temple gate called *B*,
3:10 at the temple gate called *B*,
Ro 10:15 "How *b* are the feet
1Pe 3: 5 in God used to make themselves *b*.

BEAUTY* (BEAUTIFUL)
Est 1:11 order to display her *b* to the people
2: 3 let *b* treatments be given to them.
2: 9 her with her *b* treatments
2:12 months of *b* treatments prescribed
Ps 27: 4 to gaze upon the *b* of the LORD
37:20 LORD's enemies will be like the *b*
45:11 The king is enthralled by your *b*;
50: 2 From Zion, perfect in *b*,
Pr 6:25 lust in your heart after her *b*
31:30 is deceptive, and *b* is fleeting;
Isa 3:24 instead of *b*, branding.
28: 1 to the fading flower, his glorious *b*,
28: 4 That fading flower, his glorious *b*,
33:17 Your eyes will see the king in his *b*
53: 2 He had no *b* or majesty
61: 3 to bestow on them a crown of *b*
La 2:15 the perfection of *b*,
Eze 16:14 had given you made your *b* perfect,
16:14 the nations on account of your *b*,
16:15 passed by and your *b* became his.
16:15 "'But you trusted in your *b*
16:25 lofty shrines and degraded your *b*,
27: 3 "I am perfect in *b*."
27: 4 your builders brought your *b*
27:11 they brought your *b* to perfection.
28: 7 draw their swords against your *b*
28:12 full of wisdom and perfect in *b*.
28:17 proud on account of your *b*,
31: 7 It was majestic in *b*,
31: 8 could match its *b*.
Jas 1:11 blossom falls and its *b* is destroyed.
1Pe 3: 3 Your *b* should not come
3: 4 the unfading *b* of a gentle

BED (SICKBED)
Isa 28:20 The *b* is too short to stretch out on,
Lk 11: 7 and my children are with me in *b*.
17:34 night two people will be in one *b*;
Heb 13: 4 and the marriage *b* kept pure,

BEELZEBUB*
Mt 10:25 of the house has been called *B*,
12:24 "It is only by *B*, the prince
12:27 And if I drive out demons by *B*,
Mk 3:22 possessed by *B*! By the prince
Lk 11:15 "By *B*, the prince of demons,
Lk 11:18 claim that I drive out demons by *B*.
11:19 Now if I drive out demons by *B*,

BEER
Pr 20: 1 Wine is a mocker and *b* a brawler;

BEERSHEBA
Ge 21:14 and wandered in the desert of *B*.
Jdg 20: 1 all the Israelites from Dan to *B*
1Sa 3:20 to *B* recognized that Samuel was
2Sa 3:10 and Judah from Dan to *B*."
17:11 Let all Israel, from Dan to *B*—
24: 2 the tribes of Israel from Dan to *B*
24:15 of the people from Dan to *B* died.
1Ki 4:25 from Dan to *B*, lived in safety,
1Ch 21: 2 count the Israelites from *B* to Dan.
2Ch 30: 5 throughout Israel, from *B* to Dan,

BEFALLS*
Pr 12:21 No harm *b* the righteous,

BEGGING
Ps 37:25 or their children *b* bread.
Ac 16: 9 of Macedonia standing and *b* him,

BEGINNING
Ge 1: 1 In the *b* God created the heavens
Ps 102: 25 In the *b* you laid the foundations
111: 10 of the LORD is the *b* of wisdom;
Pr 1: 7 of the LORD is the *b* of knowledge
9:10 of the LORD is the *b* of wisdom,
Ecc 3:11 fathom what God has done from *b*
Isa 40:21 Has it not been told you from the *b*
46:10 I make known the end from the *b*,
Mt 24: 8 All these are the *b* of birth pains.
Lk 1: 3 investigated everything from the *b*,
Jn 1: 1 In the *b* was the Word,
1Jn 1: 1 That which was from the *b*,
Rev 21: 6 and the Omega, the *B* and the End.
22:13 and the Last, the *B* and the End.

BEHAVE (BEHAVIOR)
Ro 13:13 Let us *b* decently, as in the daytime

BEHAVIOR (BEHAVE)
1Pe 3: 1 without words by the *b* of their wives,
3:16 maliciously against your good *b*

BEHEMOTH*
Job 40:15 "Look at the *b*,

BELIEVE (BELIEVED BELIEVER BELIEVERS BELIEVES BELIEVING)
Ex 4: 1 "What if they do not *b* me
1Ki 10: 7 I did not *b* these things until I came
2Ch 9: 6 But I did not *b* what they said
Ps 78:32 of his wonders, they did not *b*.
Hab 1: 5 that you would not *b*,
Mt 18: 6 one of these little ones who *b* in me
21:22 If you *b*, you will receive whatever
27:42 from the cross, and we will *b* in him
Mk 1:15 Repent and *b* the good news!"
5:36 ruler, "Don't be afraid; just *b*."
9:24 "I do *b*; help me overcome my
9:42 one of these little ones who *b* in me
11:24 *b* that you have received it,
15:32 the cross, that we may see and *b*."
16:16 but whoever does not *b* will be
16:17 signs will accompany those who *b*:
Lk 8:12 so that they may not *b* and be saved.
8:13 They *b* for a while, but in the time
8:50 just *b*, and she will be healed."
22:67 you will not *b* me,
24:25 to *b* all that the prophets have
Jn 1: 7 that through him all men might *b*.
3:18 does not *b* stands condemned
4:42 "We no longer *b* just
5:38 for you do not *b* the one he sent.
5:46 believed Moses, you would *b* me,
6:29 to *b* in the one he has sent."
6:69 We *b* and know that you are
7: 5 his own brothers did not *b* in him.
8:24 if you do not *b* that I am the one I
9:35 "Do you *b* in the Son of Man?"
9:36 "Tell me so that I may *b* in him."
9:38 "Lord, I *b*," and he worshiped him.
10:26 you do not *b* because you are not
10:37 Do not *b* me unless I do what my
10:38 you do not *b* me, *b* the miracles,
11:27 "I *b* that you are the Christ,
12:37 they still would not *b* in him.
12:39 For this reason they could not *b*,
12:44 in me, he does not *b* in me only,
13:19 does happen you will *b* that I am
14:10 Don't you *b* that I am in the Father
14:11 *B* me when I say that I am
14:11 or at least *b* on the evidence
16:30 This makes us *b* that you came
16:31 "You *b* at last!" Jesus answered.
17:21 that the world may *b* that you have

Jn 19:35 he testifies so that you also may *b*.
20:27 Stop doubting and *b*."
20:31 written that you may *b* that Jesus is
Ac 16:31 They replied, "*B* in the Lord Jesus,
19: 4 the people to *b* in the one coming
24:14 I *b* everything that agrees
26:27 Agrippa, do you *b* the prophets?
Ro 3:22 faith in Jesus Christ to all who *b*.
4:11 he is the father of all who *b*
10: 9 *b* in your heart that God raised him
10:10 For it is with your heart that you *b*
10:14 And how can they *b* in the one
16:26 so that all nations might *b*
1Co 1:21 preached to save those who *b*.
Gal 3:22 might be given to those who *b*.
Php 1:29 of Christ not only to *b* on him,
1Th 4:14 We *b* that Jesus died and rose again
2Th 2:11 delusion so that they will *b* the lie
1Ti 4:10 and especially of those who *b*.
Tit 1: 6 a man whose children *b*
Heb 11: 6 comes to him must *b* that he exists
Jas 1: 6 But when he asks, he must *b*
2:19 Even the demons *b* that—
2:19 You *b* that there is one God.
1Pe 2: 7 to you who *b*, this stone is precious
1Jn 3:23 to *b* in the name of his Son,
4: 1 Dear friends, do not *b* every spirit,
5:13 things to you who *b* in the name

BELIEVED (BELIEVE)

Ge 15: 6 Abram *b* the LORD, and he
Ex 4:31 signs before the people, and they *b*.
Isa 53: 1 Who has *b* our message
Jnh 3: 5 The Ninevites *b* God.
Lk 1:45 is she who has *b* that what the Lord
Jn 1:12 to those who *b* in his name,
2:22 Then they *b* the Scripture
3:18 because he has not *b* in the name
5:46 If you *b* Moses, you would believe
7:39 whom those who *b*
11:40 "Did I not tell you that if you *b*,
12:38 "Lord, who has *b* our message
20: 8 He saw and *b*.
20:29 who have not seen and yet have *b*."
Ac 13:48 were appointed for eternal life *b*.
19: 2 the Holy Spirit when you *b*?"
Ro 4: 3 Scripture say? "Abraham *b* God,
10:14 call on the one they have not *b* in?
10:16 "Lord, who has *b* our message?"
1Co 15: 2 Otherwise, you have *b* in vain.
Gal 3: 6 Consider Abraham: "He *b* God,
2Th 2:12 who have not *b* the truth
1Ti 3:16 was *b* on in the world,
2Ti 1:12 because I know whom I have *b*,
Jas 2:23 that says, "Abraham *b* God,

BELIEVER* (BELIEVE)

1Ki 18: 3 (Obadiah was a devout *b*
Ac 16: 1 whose mother was a Jewess and a *b*
16:15 "If you consider me a *b* in the Lord
1Co 7:12 brother has a wife who is not a *b*
7:13 has a husband who is not a *b*
2Co 6:15 What does a *b* have in common
1Ti 5:16 any woman who is a *b* has widows

BELIEVERS* (BELIEVE)

Jn 4:41 of his words many more became *b*.
Ac 1:15 among the *b* (a group numbering
2:44 All the *b* were together
4:32 All the *b* were one in heart
5:12 And all the *b* used to meet together
9:41 he called the *b* and the widows
10:45 The circumcised *b* who had come
11: 2 the circumcised *b* criticized him
15: 2 along with some other *b*,
15: 5 Then some of the *b* who belonged
15:23 To the Gentile *b* in Antioch,
21:25 for the Gentile *b*, we have written
1Co 6: 5 to judge a dispute between *b*?
14:22 is for *b*, not for unbelievers.
14:22 not for *b* but for unbelievers;
Gal 6:10 who belong to the family of *b*.
1Th 1: 7 a model to all the *b* in Macedonia
1Ti 4:12 set an example for the *b* in speech,
6: 2 benefit from their service are *b*,
Jas 2: 1 *b* in our glorious Lord Jesus Christ,
1Pe 2:17 Love the brotherhood of *b*,

BELIEVES* (BELIEVE)

Pr 14:15 A simple man *b* anything,
Mk 9:23 is possible for him who *b*."
11:23 *b* that what he says will happen,
16:16 Whoever *b* and is baptized will be
Jn 3:15 that everyone who *b*
3:16 that whoever *b* in him shall not
3:18 Whoever *b* in him is not
3:36 Whoever *b* in the Son has eternal
5:24 *b* him who sent me has eternal life
6:35 and he who *b* in me will never be

Jn 6:40 and *b* in him shall have eternal life,
6:47 he who *b* has everlasting life.
7:38 Whoever *b* in me, as the Scripture
11:25 He who *b* in me will live, even
11:26 and *b* in me will never die.
12:44 Jesus cried out, "When a man *b*
12:46 so that no one who *b*
Ac 10:43 about him that everyone who *b*
13:39 him everyone who *b* is justified
Ro 1:16 for the salvation of everyone who *b*
10: 4 righteousness for everyone who *b*.
1Jn 5: 1 Everyone who *b* that Jesus is
5: 5 Only he who *b* that Jesus is the Son
5:10 Anyone who *b* in the Son

BELIEVING* (BELIEVE)

Jn 20:31 and that by *b* you may have life
Ac 9:26 not *b* that he really was a disciple.
1Co 7:14 sanctified through her *b* husband.
7:15 A *b* man or woman is not bound
9: 5 right to take a *b* wife along with us,
Gal 3: 2 or by *b* what you heard? Are you
1Ti 6: 2 Those who have *b* masters are not

BELLY

Ge 3:14 You will crawl on your *b*
Da 2:32 its *b* and thighs of bronze,
Mt 12:40 three nights in the *b* of a huge fish,

BELONG (BELONGING BELONGS)

Ge 40: 8 "Do not interpretations *b* to God?
Lev 25:55 for the Israelites *b* to me
Dt 10:14 LORD your God *b* the heavens,
29:29 The secret things *b*
Job 12:13 "To God *b* wisdom and power;
12:16 To him *b* strength and victory;
25: 2 "Dominion and awe *b* to God;
Ps 47: 9 for the kings of the earth *b* to God;
95: 4 and the mountain peaks *b* to him.
115: 16 The highest heavens *b*
Jer 5:10 for these people do not *b*
Jn 8:44 You *b* to your father, the devil,
15:19 As it is, you do not *b* to the world,
Ro 1: 6 called to *b* to Jesus Christ.
7: 4 that you might *b* to another,
8: 9 of Christ, he does not *b* to Christ.
14: 8 we live or die, we *b* to the Lord.
1Co 7:39 but he must *b* to the Lord.
15:23 when he comes, those who *b*
Gal 3:29 If you *b* to Christ, then you are
5:24 Those who *b* to Christ Jesus have
1Th 5: 5 We do not *b* to the night
5: 8 But since we *b* to the day, let us be
1Jn 3:19 then is how we know that we *b*

BELONGING (BELONG)

1Pe 2: 9 a holy nation, a people *b* to God,

BELONGS (BELONG)

Lev 27:30 *b* to the LORD; it is holy
Dt 1:17 of any man, for judgment *b* to God.
Job 41:11 Everything under heaven *b* to me.
Ps 22:28 for dominion *b* to the LORD
89:18 Indeed, our shield *b* to the LORD,
111: 10 To him *b* eternal praise.
Eze 18: 4 For every living soul *b* to me,
Jn 8:47 He who *b* to God hears what God
Ro 12: 5 each member *b* to all the others.
Rev 7:10 "Salvation *b* to our God,

BELOVED* (LOVE)

Dt 33:12 "Let the *b* of the LORD rest secure
SS 5: 9 How is your *b* better than others,
5: 9 *Friends* How is your *b* better
Jer 11:15 "What is my *b* doing in my temple

BELSHAZZAR

King of Babylon in days of Daniel (Da 5).

BELT

Ex 12:11 with your cloak tucked into your *b*,
1Ki 18:46 and, tucking his cloak into his *b*,
2Ki 4:29 "Tuck your cloak into your *b*,
9: 1 "Tuck your cloak into your *b*,
Isa 11: 5 Righteousness will be his *b*
Eph 6:14 with the *b* of truth buckled

BENEFICIAL* (BENEFIT)

1Co 6:12 for me"—but not everything is *b*.
10:23 but not everything is *b*.

BENEFIT (BENEFICIAL BENEFITS)

Job 22: 2 "Can a man be of *b* to God?
Isa 38:17 Surely it was for my *b*
Ro 6:22 the *b* you reap leads to holiness,
2Co 4:15 All this is for your *b*,

BENEFITS (BENEFIT)

Ps 103: 2 and forget not all his *b*.
Jn 4:38 you have reaped the *b* of their labor

BENJAMIN

Twelfth son of Jacob by Rachel (Ge 35:16-24; 46:19-21; 1Ch 2:2). Jacob refused to send him to Egypt, but relented (Ge 42-45). Tribe of blessed (Ge 49:27; Dt 33:12), numbered (Nu 1:37; 26:41), allotted land (Jos 18:11-28; Eze 48:23), failed to fully possess (Jdg 1:21), nearly obliterated (Jdg 20-21), sided with Ish-Bosheth (2Sa 2), but turned to David (1Ch 12:2, 29). 12,000 from (Rev 7:8).

BEREANS*

Ac 17:11 the *B* were of more noble character

BESTOWING* (BESTOWS)

Pr 8:21 *b* wealth on those who love me

BESTOWS (BESTOWING)

Ps 84:11 the LORD *b* favor and honor;

BETHANY

Mk 11: 1 and *B* at the Mount of Olives,

BETHEL

Ge 28:19 He called that place *B*,

BETHLEHEM

Ru 1:19 went on until they came to *B*.
1Sa 16: 1 I am sending you to Jesse of *B*.
2Sa 23:15 from the well near the gate of *B*!"
Mic 5: 2 "But you, *B* Ephrathah,
Mt 2: 1 After Jesus was born in *B* in Judea,
2: 6 " 'But you, *B*, in the land of Judah,

BETHPHAGE

Mt 21: 1 came to *B* on the Mount of Olives,

BETHSAIDA

Jn 12:21 who was from *B* in Galilee,

BETRAY (BETRAYED BETRAYS)

Ps 89:33 nor will I ever *b* my faithfulness.
Pr 25: 9 do not *b* another man's confidence,
Mt 10:21 "Brother will *b* brother to death,
26:21 the truth, one of you will *b* me."

BETRAYED (BETRAY)

Mt 27: 4 "for I have *b* innocent blood."

BETRAYS (BETRAY)

Pr 11:13 A gossip *b* a confidence,
20:19 A gossip *b* a confidence;

BEULAH*

Isa 62: 4 and your land *B*;

BEWITCHED*

Gal 3: 1 foolish Galatians! Who has *b* you?

BEZALEL

Judahite craftsman in charge of building the tabernacle (Ex 31:1-11; 35:30-39:31).

BIDDING*

Ps 103: 20 you mighty ones who do his *b*,
148: 8 stormy winds that do his *b*,

BILDAD

One of Job's friends (Job 8; 18; 25).

BILHAH

Servant of Rachel, mother of Jacob's sons Dan and Naphtali (Ge 30:1-7; 35:25; 46:23-25).

BIND (BINDS BOUND)

Dt 6: 8 and *b* them on your foreheads.
Pr 3: 3 *b* them around your neck,
6:21 *B* them upon your heart forever;
7: 3 *B* them on your fingers;
Isa 61: 1 me to *b* up the brokenhearted,
Mt 16:19 whatever you *b* on earth will be

BINDS (BIND)

Ps 147: 3 and *b* up their wounds.
Isa 30:26 when the LORD *b* up the bruises

BIRD (BIRDS)

Pr 27: 8 Like a *b* that strays from its nest
Ecc 10:20 a *b* of the air may carry your words,

BIRDS (BIRD)

Mt 8:20 and *b* of the air have nests,
Lk 9:58 and *b* of the air have nests,

BIRTH (BEAR)

Ps 51: 5 Surely I was sinful at *b*,
58: 3 Even from *b* the wicked go astray;
Isa 26:18 but we gave *b* to wind.
Mt 1:18 This is how the *b* of Jesus Christ
24: 8 these are the beginning of *b* pains.
Jn 3: 6 Flesh gives *b* to flesh, but the Spirit
1Pe 1: 3 great mercy he has given us new *b*

BIRTHRIGHT (BEAR)
Ge 25:34 So Esau despised his *b*.

BITTEN
Nu 21: 8 anyone who is *b* can look at it

BITTER (BITTERNESS EMBITTER)
Ex 12: 8 along with *b* herbs, and bread made
Pr 27: 7 what is *b* tastes sweet.

BITTERNESS (BITTER)
Pr 14:10 Each heart knows its own *b*,
17:25 and *b* to the one who bore him.
Ro 3:14 full of cursing and *b*."
Eph 4:31 Get rid of all *b*, rage and anger,

BLACK
Zec 6: 6 The one with the *b* horses is going
Rev 6: 5 and there before me was a *b* horse!

BLAMELESS* (BLAMELESSLY)
Ge 6: 9 *b* among the people of his time,
17: 1 walk before me and be *b*.
Dt 18:13 You must be *b* before the LORD
2Sa 22:24 I have been *b* before him
22:26 to the *b* you show yourself *b*,
Job 1: 1 This man was *b* and upright;
1: 8 one on earth like him; he is *b*
2: 3 one on earth like him; he is *b*
4: 6 and your *b* ways your hope?
8:20 God does not reject a *b* man
9:20 if I were *b*, it would pronounce me
9:21 "Although I am *b*,
9:22 'He destroys both the *b*
12: 4 though righteous and *b*!
22: 3 gain if your ways were *b*?
31: 6 and he will know that I am *b*—
Ps 15: 2 He whose walk is *b*
18:23 I have been *b* before him
18:25 to the *b* you show yourself *b*,
19:13 Then will I be *b*,
26: 1 for I have led a *b* life;
26:11 But I lead a *b* life;
37:18 The days of the *b* are known
37:37 Consider the *b*, observe the upright
84:11 from those whose walk is *b*.
101: 2 I will be careful to lead a *b* life—
101: 2 house with *b* heart.
101: 6 he whose walk is *b*
119: 1 Blessed are they whose ways are *b*,
119: 80 May my heart be *b*
Pr 2: 7 a shield to those whose walk is *b*,
2:21 and the *b* will remain in it;
11: 5 of the *b* makes a straight way
11:20 in those whose ways are *b*.
19: 1 Better a poor man whose walk is *b*
20: 7 The righteous man leads a *b* life;
28: 6 Better a poor man whose walk is *b*
28:10 *b* will receive a good inheritance.
28:18 He whose walk is *b* is kept safe,
Eze 28:15 You were *b* in your ways
1Co 1: 8 so that you will be *b* on the day
Eph 1: 4 world to be holy and *b* in his sight.
5:27 any other blemish, but holy and *b*.
Php 1:10 and *b* until the day of Christ,
2:15 so that you may become *b* and pure
1Th 2:10 and *b* we were among you who
3:13 hearts so that you will be *b*
5:23 and body be kept *b* at the coming
Tit 1: 6 An elder must be *b*, the husband of
1: 7 he must be *b*— not overbearing,
Heb 7:26 *b*, pure, set apart from sinners,
2Pe 3:14 effort to be found spotless, *b*
Rev 14: 5 found in their mouths; they are *b*.

BLAMELESSLY* (BLAMELESS)
Lk 1: 6 commandments and regulations *b*.

BLASPHEME* (BLASPHEMED BLASPHEMER BLASPHEMES BLASPHEMIES BLASPHEMING BLASPHEMOUS BLASPHEMY)
Ex 22:28 "Do not *b* God or curse the ruler
Ac 26:11 and I tried to force them to *b*.
1Ti 1:20 over to Satan to be taught not to *b*.
2Pe 2:12 these men *b* in matters they do not
Rev 13: 6 He opened his mouth to *b* God,

BLASPHEMED* (BLASPHEME)
Lev 24:11 of the Israelite woman *b* the Name
2Ki 19: 6 of the king of Assyria have *b* me.
19:22 Who is it you have insulted and *b*?
Isa 37: 6 of the king of Assyria have *b* me.
37:23 Who is it you have insulted and *b*?
52: 5 my name is constantly *b*.
Eze 20:27 your fathers *b* me by forsaking me:
Ac 19:37 robbed temples nor *b* our goddess.
Ro 2:24 name is *b* among the Gentiles

BLASPHEMER* (BLASPHEME)
Lev 24:14 "Take the *b* outside the camp.
24:23 they took the *b* outside the camp
1Ti 1:13 I was once a *b* and a persecutor

BLASPHEMES* (BLASPHEME)
Lev 24:16 anyone who *b* the name
24:16 native-born, when he *b* the Name,
Nu 15:30 native-born or alien, *b* the LORD,
Mk 3:29 whoever *b* against the Holy Spirit
Lk 12:10 but anyone who *b* against the Holy

BLASPHEMIES* (BLASPHEME)
Ne 9:18 or when they committed awful *b*.
9:26 to you; they committed awful *b*.
Mk 3:28 and *b* of men will be forgiven them.
Rev 13: 5 and *b* and to exercise his authority

BLASPHEMING* (BLASPHEME)
Mt 9: 3 "This fellow is *b*!" Knowing their
Mk 2: 7 He's *b*! Who can forgive sins

BLASPHEMOUS* (BLASPHEME)
Rev 13: 1 and on each head a *b* name.
17: 3 that was covered with *b* names

BLASPHEMY* (BLASPHEME)
Mt 12:31 and *b* will be forgiven men,
12:31 the *b* against the Spirit will not be
26:65 Look, now you have heard the *b*.
26:65 "He has spoken *b*! Why do we
Mk 14:64 "You have heard the *b*.
Lk 5:21 "Who is this fellow who speaks *b*?
Jn 10:33 replied the Jews, "but for *b*,
10:36 Why then do you accuse me of *b*
Ac 6:11 words of *b* against Moses

BLAST*
Ex 15: 8 By the *b* of your nostrils
19:13 horn sounds a long *b* may they go
19:16 and a very loud trumpet *b*.
Nu 10: 5 When a trumpet *b* is sounded,
10: 6 At the sounding of a second *b*,
10: 6 The *b* will be the signal
10: 9 sound a *b* on the trumpets.
Jos 6: 5 you hear them sound a long *b*
6:16 the priests sounded the trumpet *b*,
2Sa 22:16 at the *b* of breath from his nostrils.
Job 4: 9 at the *b* of his anger they perish.
39:25 At the *b* of the trumpet he snorts,
Ps 18:15 the *b* of breath from your nostrils.
98: 6 and the *b* of the ram's horn—
147: 17 Who can withstand his icy *b*?
Isa 27: 8 with his fierce *b* he drives her out,
Eze 22:20 a furnace to melt it with a fiery *b*,
Am 2: 2 tumult amid war cries and the *b*
Heb 12:19 to a trumpet *b* or to such a voice

BLEATING*
1Sa 15:14 "What then is this *b* of sheep

BLEMISH (BLEMISHES)
Lev 22:21 be without defect or *b*
Eph 5:27 or wrinkle or any other *b*,
Col 1:22 without *b* and free from accusation
1Pe 1:19 a lamb without *b* or defect.

BLEMISHES* (BLEMISH)
2Pe 2:13 and *b*, reveling in their pleasures
Jude :12 These men are *b* at your love feasts

BLESS (BLESSED BLESSES BLESSING BLESSINGS)
Ge 12: 3 I will *b* those who *b* you,
32:26 not let you go unless you *b* me."
Dt 7:13 He will love you and *b* you
33:11 *B* all his skills, O LORD,
Ps 72:15 and *b* him all day long.
Ro 12:14 Bless those who persecute you; *b*

BLESSED (BLESS)
Ge 1:22 God *b* them and said, "Be fruitful
2: 3 And God *b* the seventh day
22:18 nations on earth will be *b*,
Nu 24: 9 "May those who bless you be *b*
1Ch 17:27 have *b* it, and it will be *b* forever."
Ps 1: 1 *B* is the man
2:12 *B* are all who take refuge in him.
32: 2 *B* is the man
33:12 *B* is the nation whose God is
40: 4 *B* is the man
41: 1 *B* is he who has regard for the weak
84: 5 *B* are those whose strength is
89:15 *B* are those who have learned
94:12 *B* is the man you discipline,
106: 3 *B* are they who maintain justice,
112: 1 *B* is the man who fears the LORD,
118: 26 *B* is he who comes in the name
119: 1 *B* are they whose ways are
119: 2 *B* are they who keep his statutes
127: 5 *B* is the man
Pr 3:13 *B* is the man who finds wisdom,
8:34 *B* is the man who listens to me,
28:20 A faithful man will be richly *b*,
29:18 but *b* is he who keeps the law.
31:28 Her children arise and call her *b*;
Isa 30:18 *B* are all who wait for him!
Mal 3:12 Then all the nations will call you *b*,
3:15 But now we call the arrogant *b*.
Mt 5: 3 saying: "*B* are the poor in spirit,
5: 4 *B* are those who mourn,
5: 5 *B* are the meek,
5: 6 *B* are those who hunger
5: 7 *B* are the merciful,
5: 8 *B* are the pure in heart,
5: 9 *B* are the peacemakers,
5:10 *B* are those who are persecuted
5:11 "*B* are you when people insult you,
Lk 1:48 on all generations will call me *b*,
Jn 12:13 "*B* is he who comes in the name
Ac 20:35 'It is more *b* to give than to receive
Tit 2:13 while we wait for the *b* hope—
Jas 1:12 *B* is the man who perseveres
Rev 1: 3 *B* is the one who reads the words
22: 7 *B* is he who keeps the words
22:14 "*B* are those who wash their robes,

BLESSES (BLESS)
Ps 29:11 the LORD *b* his people with peace.
Ro 10:12 and richly *b* all who call on him,

BLESSING (BLESS)
Ge 27: 4 so that I may give you my *b*
Dt 23: 5 turned the curse into a *b* for you,
33: 1 This is the *b* that Moses the man
Pr 10:22 The *b* of the LORD brings wealth,
Eze 34:26 there will be showers of *b*.

BLESSINGS (BLESS)
Dt 11:29 proclaim on Mount Gerizim the *b*,
Jos 8:34 all the words of the law—the *b*
Pr 10: 6 *B* crown the head of the righteous,
Ro 15:27 shared in the Jews' spiritual *b*,

BLIND (BLINDED)
Mt 15:14 a *b* man leads a *b* man, both will fall
23:16 "Woe to you, *b* guides! You say,
Mk 10:46 a *b* man, Bartimaeus (that is,
Lk 6:39 "Can a *b* man lead a *b* man?
Jn 9:25 I was *b* but now I see!"

BLINDED (BLIND)
Jn 12:40 elsewhere: "He has *b* their eyes
2Co 4: 4 The god of this age has *b* the minds

BLOOD (BLOODSHED BLOODTHIRSTY)
Ge 4:10 Your brother's *b* cries out to me
9: 6 "Whoever sheds the *b* of man,
Ex 12:13 and when I see the *b*, I will pass
24: 8 "This is the *b* of the covenant that
Lev 16:15 and take its *b* behind the curtain
17:11 For the life of a creature is in the *b*,
Dt 12:23 eat the *b*, because the *b* is the life,
Ps 72:14 for precious is their *b* in his sight.
Pr 6:17 hands that shed innocent *b*,
Isa 1:11 pleasure in the *b* of bulls and lambs
Mt 26:28 This is my *b* of the covenant,
27:24 "I am innocent of this man's *b*,"
Mk 14:24 "This is my *b* of the covenant,
Lk 22:44 drops of *b* falling to the ground.
Jn 6:53 of the Son of Man and drink his *b*,
Ac 15:20 of strangled animals and from *b*.
20:26 innocent of the *b* of all men.
Ro 3:25 of atonement, through faith in his *b*
5: 9 have now been justified by his *b*,
1Co 11:25 cup is the new covenant in my *b*;
Eph 1: 7 we have redemption through his *b*,
2:13 near through the *b* of Christ.
Col 1:20 by making peace through his *b*,
Heb 9: 7 once a year, and never without *b*,
9:12 once for all by his own *b*,
9:20 "This is the *b* of the covenant,
9:22 of *b* there is no forgiveness.
12:24 word than the *b* of Abel.
1Pe 1:19 but with the precious *b* of Christ,
1Jn 1: 7 and the *b* of Jesus, his Son,
Rev 1: 5 has freed us from our sins by his *b*,
5: 9 with your *b* you purchased men
7:14 white in the *b* of the Lamb.
12:11 him by the *b* of the Lamb
19:13 He is dressed in a robe dipped in *b*,

BLOODSHED (BLOOD)
Jer 48:10 on him who keeps his sword from *b*
Eze 35: 6 did not hate *b*, *b* will pursue you.
Hab 2:12 to him who builds a city with *b*

BLOODTHIRSTY* (BLOOD)
Ps 5: 6 *b* and deceitful men
26: 9 my life with *b* men,

Ps 55:23 *b* and deceitful men
59: 2 and save me from *b* men.
139: 19 Away from me, you *b* men!
Pr 29:10 *B* men hate a man of integrity

BLOSSOM
Isa 35: 1 the wilderness will rejoice and *b*.

BLOT (BLOTS)
Ex 32:32 then *b* me out of the book you have
Ps 51: 1 *b* out my transgressions.
Rev 3: 5 I will never *b* out his name

BLOTS (BLOT)
Isa 43:25 "I, even I, am he who *b* out

BLOWN
Eph 4:14 and *b* here and there by every wind
Jas 1: 6 doubts is like a wave of the sea, *b*
Jude :12 without rain, *b* along by the wind;

BLUSH
Jer 6:15 they do not even know how to *b*.

BOAST (BOASTS)
1Ki 20:11 armor should not *b* like one who
Ps 34: 2 My soul will *b* in the LORD;
44: 8 In God we make our *b* all day long,
Pr 27: 1 Do not *b* about tomorrow,
Jer 9:23 or the rich man *b* of his riches,
1Co 1:31 Let him who boasts *b* in the Lord."
2Co 10:17 Let him who boasts *b* in the Lord."
11:30 I do not inwardly burn? If I must *b*,
Gal 6:14 May I never *b* except in the cross
Eph 2: 9 not by works, so that no one can *b*.

BOASTS (BOAST)
Jer 9:24 but let him who *b* boast about this:

BOAZ
Wealthy Bethlehemite who showed favor to Ruth (Ru 2), married her (Ru 4). Ancestor of David (Ru 4:18-22; 1Ch 2:12-15), Jesus (Mt 1:5-16; Lk 3:23-32).

BODIES (BODY)
Isa 26:19 their *b* will rise.
Ro 12: 1 to offer your *b* as living sacrifices,
1Co 6:15 not know that your *b* are members
Eph 5:28 to love their wives as their own *b*.

BODILY (BODY)
Col 2: 9 of the Deity lives in *b* form,

BODY (BODIES BODILY EMBODIMENT)
Zec 13: 6 What are these wounds on your *b*?'
Mt 10:28 afraid of those who kill the *b*
26:26 saying, "Take and eat; this is my *b*
26:41 spirit is willing, but the *b* is weak."
Mk 14:22 saying, "Take it; this is my *b*."
Lk 22:19 saying, "This is my *b* given for you;
Jn 13:10 wash his feet; his whole *b* is clean.
Ro 6:13 Do not offer the parts of your *b*
12: 4 us has one *b* with many members,
1Co 6:19 not know that your *b* is a temple
6:20 Therefore honor God with your *b*.
11:24 "This is my *b*, which is for you;
12:12 The *b* is a unit, though it is made up
12:13 baptized by one Spirit into one *b*—
15:44 a natural *b*, it is raised a spiritual *b*.
Eph 1:23 which is his *b*, the fullness
4:25 for we are all members of one *b*.
5:30 for we are members of his *b*.
Php 1:20 Christ will be exalted in my *b*,
Col 1:24 sake of his *b*, which is the church.

BOLD (BOLDNESS)
Ps 138: 3 you made me *b* and stouthearted.
Pr 21:29 A wicked man puts up a *b* front,
28: 1 but the righteous are as *b* as a lion.

BOLDNESS* (BOLD)
Lk 11: 8 of the man's *b* he will get up
Ac 4:29 to speak your word with great *b*.

BONDAGE
Ezr 9: 9 God has not deserted us in our *b*.

BONES
Ge 2:23 "This is now bone of my *b*
Ps 22:14 and all my *b* are out of joint.
22:17 I can count all my *b*;
Eze 37: 1 middle of a valley; it was full of *b*.
Jn 19:36 "Not one of his *b* will be broken,"

BOOK (BOOKS)
Ex 32:33 against me I will blot out of my *b*.
Jos 1: 8 Do not let this *B* of the Law depart
2Ki 22: 8 "I have found the *B* of the Law
2Ch 34:15 "I have found the *B* of the Law
Ne 8: 8 They read from the *B* of the Law
Ps 69:28 May they be blotted out of the *b*
Da 12: 1 name is found written in the *b*—
Jn 20:30 which are not recorded in this *b*.
Php 4: 3 whose names are in the *b* of life.
Rev 3: 5 never blot out his name from the *b*
20:12 *b* was opened, which is the *b*
20:15 was not found written in the *b*
21:27 written in the Lamb's *b* of life.
22:18 him the plagues described in this *b*.

BOOKS* (BOOK)
Ecc 12:12 Of making many *b* there is no end,
Da 7:10 and the *b* were opened.
Jn 21:25 for the *b* that would be written.
Rev 20:12 the throne, and *b* were opened.
20:12 they had done as recorded in the *b*.

BORE (BEAR)
Isa 53:12 For he *b* the sin of many,
1Pe 2:24 He himself *b* our sins in his body

BORN (BEAR)
Ecc 3: 2 a time to be *b* and a time to die,
Isa 9: 6 For to us a child is *b*,
66: 8 Can a country be *b* in a day
Lk 2:11 of David a Savior has been *b* to you
Jn 3: 3 see the kingdom of God unless he is *b* again.
3: 4 How can a man be *b* when he is old
3: 5 unless he is *b* of water
3: 7 at my saying, 'You must be *b* again
3: 8 it is with everyone *b* of the Spirit."
1Pe 1:23 For you have been *b* again,
1Jn 3: 9 because he has been *b* of God.
4: 7 Everyone who loves has been *b*
5: 1 believes that Jesus is the Christ is *b*
5: 4 for everyone *b* of God overcomes
5:18 We know that anyone *b*

BORROWER
Pr 22: 7 and the *b* is servant to the lender.

BOTHER (BOTHERING)
Lk 11: 7 one inside answers, 'Don't *b* me.

BOTHERING (BOTHER)
Lk 18: 5 yet because this widow keeps *b* me,

BOUGHT (BUY)
Ac 20:28 which he *b* with his own blood.
1Co 6:20 You are not your own; you were *b*
7:23 You were *b* at a price; do not
2Pe 2: 1 the sovereign Lord who *b* them—

BOUND (BIND)
Is 56: 3 Let no foreigner who has *b* himself
Mt 16:19 bind on earth will be *b* in heaven,
18:18 bind on earth will be *b* in heaven,
Ro 7: 2 by law a married woman is *b*
1Co 7:39 A woman is *b* to her husband
Jude : 6 *b* with everlasting chains
Rev 20: 2 and *b* him for a thousand years.

BOUNDARY (BOUNDS)
Nu 34: 3 your southern *b* will start
Pr 23:10 Do not move an ancient *b* stone
Hos 5:10 who move *b* stones.

BOUNDS (BOUNDARY)
2Co 7: 4 all our troubles my joy knows no *b*.

BOUNTY*
Ge 49:26 than the *b* of the age-old hills.
Dt 28:12 heavens, the storehouse of his *b*,
1Ki 10:13 he had given her out of his royal *b*.
Ps 65:11 You crown the year with your *b*,
68:10 from your *b*, O God, you provided
Jer 31:12 rejoice in the *b* of the LORD—
31:14 my people will be filled with my *b*

BOW (BOWED BOWS)
Dt 5: 9 You shall not *b* down to them
1Ki 22:34 But someone drew his *b* at random
Ps 5: 7 in reverence will I *b* down
44: 6 I do not trust in my *b*,
95: 6 Come, let us *b* down in worship,
138: 2 I will *b* down toward your holy
Isa 44:19 Shall I *b* down to a block of wood?"
45:23 Before me every knee will *b*;
Ro 14:11 'every knee will *b* before me;
Php 2:10 name of Jesus every knee should *b*,

BOWED (BOW)
Ps 145: 14 and lifts up all who are *b* down.
146: 8 the LORD lifts up those who are *b*

BOWS (BOW)
Isa 44:15 he makes an idol and *b* down to it.
44:17 he *b* down to it and worships.

BOY (BOY'S BOYS)
Ge 21:17 God heard the *b* crying,
22:12 not lay a hand on the *b*
Jdg 13: 5 *b* is to be a Nazirite,
1Sa 2:11 *b* ministered before the LORD.
3: 8 the LORD was calling the *b*.
Isa 7:16 before the *b* knows enough
Mt 17:18 demon, and it came out of the *b*
Lk 2:43 the *b* Jesus stayed behind

BOY'S (BOY)
1Ki 17:22 the *b* life returned to him
2Ki 4:34 the *b* body grew warm

BOYS (BOY)
Ge 25:24 twin *b* in her womb
Ex 1:18 they let the *b* live.

BRACE*
Job 38: 3 *B* yourself like a man;
40: 7 out of the storm: "*B* yourself like
Na 2: 1 *b* yourselves,

BRAG*
Am 4: 5 and *b* about your freewill offerings
Ro 2:17 *b* about your relationship to God;
2:23 temples? You who *b* about the law,
Jas 4:16 As it is, you boast and *b*.

BRAIDED
1Ti 2: 9 not with *b* hair or gold or pearls
1Pe 3: 3 as *b* hair and the wearing

BRANCH (BRANCHES)
Isa 4: 2 In that day the *B* of the LORD will
Jer 23: 5 up to David a righteous *B*,
33:15 I will make a righteous *B* sprout
Zec 3: 8 going to bring my servant, the *B*.
6:12 is the man whose name is the *B*,
Jn 15: 2 while every *b* that does bear fruit
15: 4 No *b* can bear fruit by itself;

BRANCHES (BRANCH)
Jn 15: 5 "I am the vine; you are the *b*.
Ro 11:21 if God did not spare the natural *b*,

BRAVE
2Sa 2: 7 Now then, be strong and *b*,
13:28 you this order? Be strong and *b*."

BREACH (BREAK)
Ps 106: 23 stood in the *b* before him

BREACHING (BREAK)
Pr 17:14 Starting a quarrel is like *b* a dam;

BREAD
Ex 12: 8 and *b* made without yeast.
23:15 the Feast of Unleavened *B*;
25:30 Put the *b* of the Presence
Dt 8: 3 that man does not live on *b* alone
Ps 78:25 Men ate the *b* of angels;
Pr 30: 8 but give me only my daily *b*.
Ecc 11: 1 Cast your *b* upon the waters,
Isa 55: 2 Why spend money on what is not *b*
Mt 4: 3 tell these stones to become *b*."
4: 4 'Man does not live on *b* alone,
6:11 Give us today our daily *b*.
26:26 Jesus took *b*, gave thanks
Mk 14:22 Jesus took *b*, gave thanks
Lk 4: 3 tell this stone to become *b*."
4: 4 'Man does not live on *b* alone.'"
9:13 "We have only five loaves of *b*
11: 3 Give us each day our daily *b*.
22:19 And he took *b*, gave thanks
Jn 6:33 For the *b* of God is he who comes
6:35 Jesus declared, "I am the *b* of life.
6:41 "I am the *b* that came
6:48 I am the *b* of life.
6:51 I am the living *b* that came
6:51 This *b* is my flesh, which I will give
21:13 took the *b* and gave it to them,
1Co 10:16 And is not the *b* that we break
11:23 took *b*, and when he had given
11:26 For whenever you eat this *b*

BREAK (BREACH BREACHING BREAKERS BREAKING BREAKS BROKE BROKEN BROKENNESS)
Nu 30: 2 he must not *b* his word
Jdg 2: 1 'I will never *b* my covenant
Pr 25:15 and a gentle tongue can *b* a bone.
Isa 42: 3 A bruised reed he will not *b*,
Mal 2:15 and do not *b* faith with the wife
Mt 12:20 A bruised reed he will not *b*,
Ac 20: 7 week we came together to *b* bread.
1Co 10:16 the bread that we *b* a participation
Rev 5: 2 "Who is worthy to *b* the seals

BREAKERS* (BREAK)
Ps 42: 7 all your waves and *b*
93: 4 mightier than the *b* of the sea—
Jnh 2: 3 all your waves and *b*

BREAKING (BREAK)
Jos 9:20 fall on us for *b* the oath we swore
Eze 16:59 oath by *b* the covenant.
17:18 the oath by *b* the covenant.
Ac 2:42 to the *b* of bread and to prayer.
Jas 2:10 at just one point is guilty of *b* all

BREAKS (BREAK)
Jer 23:29 "and like a hammer that *b* a rock
1Jn 3: 4 Everyone who sins *b* the law;

BREASTPIECE (BREASTPLATE)
Ex 28:15 Fashion a *b* for making decisions—

BREASTPLATE* (BREASTPIECE)
Isa 59:17 He put on righteousness as his *b*,
Eph 6:14 with the *b* of righteousness in place
1Th 5: 8 putting on faith and love as a *b*,

BREASTS
La 4: 3 Even jackals offer their *b*

BREATH (BREATHED GOD-BREATHED)
Ge 2: 7 into his nostrils the *b* of life,

BREATHED (BREATH)
Ge 2: 7 *b* into his nostrils the breath of life,
Mk 15:37 With a loud cry, Jesus *b* his last.
Jn 20:22 And with that he *b* on them

BREEDS*
Pr 13:10 Pride only *b* quarrels,

BRIBE
Ex 23: 8 "Do not accept a *b*,
Dt 16:19 for a *b* blinds the eyes of the wise
27:25 "Cursed is the man who accepts a *b*
Pr 6:35 will refuse the *b*, however great it

BRIDE
Isa 62: 5 as a bridegroom rejoices over his *b*,
Rev 19: 7 and his *b* has made herself ready.
21: 2 as a *b* beautifully dressed
21: 9 I will show you the *b*, the wife
22:17 The Spirit and the *b* say, "Come!"

BRIDEGROOM
Ps 19: 5 which is like a *b* coming forth
Mt 25: 1 and went out to meet the *b*.
25: 5 The *b* was a long time in coming,

BRIGHTENS* (BRIGHTNESS)
Pr 16:15 When a king's face *b*, it means life;
Ecc 8: 1 Wisdom *b* a man's face

BRIGHTER (BRIGHTNESS)
Pr 4:18 shining ever *b* till the full light

BRIGHTNESS* (BRIGHTENS BRIGHTER)
2Sa 22:13 Out of the *b* of his presence
23: 4 like the *b* after rain
Ps 18:12 of the *b* of his presence clouds
Isa 59: 9 for *b*, but we walk in deep shadows.
60: 3 and kings to the *b* of your dawn.
60:19 will the *b* of the moon shine on you
Da 12: 3 who are wise will shine like the *b*
Am 5:20 pitch-dark, without a ray of *b*?

BRILLIANCE* (BRILLIANT)
Ac 22:11 the *b* of the light had blinded me.
Rev 1:16 was like the sun shining in all its *b*.
21:11 its *b* was like that of a very precious

BRILLIANT* (BRILLIANCE)
Ecc 9:11 or wealth to the *b*
Eze 1: 4 and surrounded by *b* light.
1:27 and *b* light surrounded him.

BRINK*
Pr 5:14 I have come to the *b* of utter ruin

BRITTLE
Da 2:42 will be partly strong and partly *b*.

BROAD
Mt 7:13 and *b* is the road that leads

BROKE (BREAK)
Mt 26:26 took bread, gave thanks and *b* it,
Mk 14:22 took bread, gave thanks and *b* it,
Ac 2:46 They *b* bread in their homes
20:11 he went upstairs again and *b* bread
1Co 11:24 when he had given thanks, he *b* it

BROKEN (BREAK)
Ps 34:20 not one of them will be *b*.
51:17 The sacrifices of God are a *b* spirit;
Ecc 4:12 of three strands is not quickly *b*.
Lk 20:18 on that stone will be *b* to pieces,
Jn 7:23 the law of Moses may not be *b*,
10:35 and the Scripture cannot be *b*—
19:36 "Not one of his bones will be *b*,"
Ro 11:20 they were *b* off because of unbelief,

BROKENHEARTED* (HEART)
Ps 34:18 The LORD is close to the *b*
109: 16 and the needy and the *b*.
147: 3 He heals the *b*
Isa 61: 1 He has sent me to bind up the *b*,

BROKENNESS* (BREAK)
Isa 65:14 and wail in *b* of spirit.

BRONZE
Ex 27: 2 and overlay the altar with *b*.
30:18 "Make a *b* basin, with its *b* stand,
Nu 21: 9 So Moses made a *b* snake
Da 2:32 and thighs of *b*, its legs of iron,
10: 6 legs like the gleam of burnished *b*,
Rev 1:15 His feet were like *b* glowing
2:18 whose feet are like burnished *b*.

BROTHER (BROTHER'S BROTHERHOOD BROTHERLY BROTHERS)
Pr 17:17 and a *b* is born for adversity.
18:24 a friend who sticks closer than a *b*.
27:10 neighbor nearby than a *b* far away.
Mt 5:24 and be reconciled to your *b*;
18:15 "If your *b* sins against you,
Mk 3:35 Whoever does God's will is my *b*
Lk 17: 3 "If your *b* sins, rebuke him,
Ro 14:15 not by your eating destroy your *b*
14:21 anything else that will cause your *b*
1Co 8:13 if what I eat causes my *b* to fall
2Th 3: 6 away from every *b* who is idle
3:15 as an enemy, but warn him as a *b*.
Phm :16 but better than a slave, as a dear *b*.
Jas 2:15 Suppose a *b* or sister is
4:11 Anyone who speaks against his *b*
1Jn 2: 9 hates his *b* is still in the darkness.
2:10 Whoever loves his *b* lives
2:11 But whoever hates his *b* is
3:10 is anyone who does not love his *b*.
3:15 who hates his *b* is a murderer,
3:17 material possessions and sees his *b*
4:20 For anyone who does not love his *b*
4:20 yet hates his *b*, he is a liar.
4:21 loves God must also love his *b*.
5:16 If anyone sees his *b* commit a sin

BROTHER'S (BROTHER)
Ge 4: 9 "Am I my *b* keeper?" The LORD
Mt 7: 5 remove the speck from your *b* eye.
Ro 14:13 or obstacle in your *b* way.

BROTHERHOOD (BROTHER)
1Pe 2:17 Love the *b* of believers, fear God,

BROTHERLY* (BROTHER)
Ro 12:10 devoted to one another in *b* love.
1Th 4: 9 Now about *b* love we do not need
2Pe 1: 7 and to godliness, *b* kindness;
1: 7 kindness; and to *b* kindness,

BROTHERS (BROTHER)
Jos 1:14 You are to help your *b*
Ps 133: 1 is when *b* live together in unity!
Pr 6:19 who stirs up dissension among *b*.
Mt 12:49 "Here are my mother and my *b*.
19:29 everyone who has left houses or *b*
25:40 one of the least of these *b* of mine,
Mk 3:33 "Who are my mother and my *b*?"
10:29 or *b* or sisters or mother or father
Lk 21:16 will be betrayed even by parents, *b*,
22:32 turned back, strengthen your *b*."
Jn 7: 5 his own *b* did not believe in him.
Ac 15:32 to encourage and strengthen the *b*.
Ro 9: 3 off from Christ for the sake of my *b*
1Co 8:12 sin against your *b* in this way
2Co 11:26 and in danger from false *b*.
Gal 2: 4 some false *b* had infiltrated our
1Th 4:10 you do love all the *b*
5:26 Greet all the *b* with a holy kiss.
1Ti 6: 2 for them because they are *b*.
Heb 2:11 Jesus is not ashamed to call them *b*.
2:17 to be made like his *b* in every way,
13: 1 Keep on loving each other as *b*.
1Pe 1:22 you have sincere love for your *b*,
3: 8 be sympathetic, love as *b*,
1Jn 3:14 death to life, because we love our *b*.
3:16 to lay down our lives for our *b*.
3Jn :10 he refuses to welcome the *b*.
Rev 12:10 For the accuser of our *b*,

BROW
Ge 3:19 By the sweat of your *b*

BRUISED (BRUISES)
Isa 42: 3 A *b* reed he will not break,
Mt 12:20 A *b* reed he will not break,

BRUISES (BRUISED)
Isa 30:26 when the LORD binds up the *b*

BRUTAL (BRUTE)
2Ti 3: 3 slanderous, without self-control, *b*,

BRUTE* (BRUTAL)
Ps 73:22 I was a *b* beast before you.
2Pe 2:12 They are like *b* beasts, creatures

BUBBLING*
Pr 18: 4 the fountain of wisdom is a *b* brook
Isa 35: 7 the thirsty ground *b* springs.

BUCKET*
Isa 40:15 the nations are like a drop in a *b*;

BUCKLED* (BUCKLER)
Eph 6:14 belt of truth *b* around your waist,

BUCKLER* (BUCKLED)
Ps 35: 2 Take up shield and *b*;

BUD (BUDDED)
Isa 27: 6 Israel will *b* and blossom

BUDDED (BUD)
Heb 9: 4 Aaron's staff that had *b*,

BUILD (BUILDER BUILDERS BUILDING BUILDS BUILT REBUILD REBUILT)
2Sa 7: 5 Are you the one to *b* me a house
1Ki 6: 1 he began to *b* the temple
Ecc 3: 3 a time to tear down and a time to *b*,
Mt 16:18 and on this rock I will *b* my church,
Ac 20:32 which can *b* you up and give you
Ro 15: 2 neighbor for his good, to *b* him up.
1Co 14:12 excel in gifts that *b* up the church.
1Th 5:11 one another and *b* each other up,
Jude :20 *b* yourselves up in your most holy

BUILDER* (BUILD)
1Co 3:10 I laid a foundation as an expert *b*,
Heb 3: 3 the *b* of a house has greater honor
3: 4 but God is the *b* of everything.
11:10 whose architect and *b* is God.

BUILDERS (BUILD)
Ps 118: 22 The stone the *b* rejected
Mt 21:42 " 'The stone the *b* rejected
Mk 12:10 " 'The stone the *b* rejected
Lk 20:17 " 'The stone the *b* rejected
Ac 4:11 " 'the stone you *b* rejected,
1Pe 2: 7 "The stone the *b* rejected

BUILDING (BUILD)
Ezr 3: 8 to supervise the *b* of the house
Ne 4:17 of Judah who were *b* the wall.
Ro 15:20 so that I would not be *b*
1Co 3: 9 you are God's field, God's *b*.
2Co 5: 1 we have a *b* from God, an eternal
10: 8 us for *b* you up rather
13:10 the Lord gave me for *b* you up,
Eph 2:21 him the whole *b* is joined together
4:29 helpful for *b* others up according

BUILDS (BUILD)
Ps 127: 1 Unless the LORD *b* the house,
Pr 14: 1 The wise woman *b* her house,
1Co 3:10 one should be careful how he *b*.
3:12 If any man *b* on this foundation
8: 1 Knowledge puffs up, but love *b* up.
Eph 4:16 grows and *b* itself up in love,

BUILT (BUILD)
1Ki 6:14 So Solomon *b* the temple
Mt 7:24 is like a wise man who *b* his house
Lk 6:49 is like a man who *b* a house
Ac 17:24 does not live in temples *b* by hands.
1Co 3:14 If what he has *b* survives, he will
2Co 5: 1 in heaven, not *b* by human hands.
Eph 2:20 *b* on the foundation of the apostles
4:12 the body of Christ may be *b* up
Col 2: 7 live in him, rooted and *b* up in him,
1Pe 2: 5 are being *b* into a spiritual house

BULL (BULLS)
Lev 4: 3 bring to the LORD a young *b*

BULLS (BULL)
1Ki 7:25 The Sea stood on twelve *b*,
Heb 10: 4 it is impossible for the blood of *b*

BURDEN (BURDENED BURDENS BURDENSOME)
Ps 38: 4 like a *b* too heavy to bear.
Ecc 1:13 What a heavy *b* God has laid

Mt 11:30 my yoke is easy and my *b* is light."
Ac 15:28 to us not to *b* you with anything
2Co 11: 9 from being a *b* to you in any way,
12:14 and I will not be a *b* to you,
1Th 2: 9 day in order not to be a *b* to anyone
2Th 3: 8 so that we would not be a *b* to any
Heb 13:17 not a *b*, for that would be

BURDENED* (BURDEN)
Isa 43:23 have not *b* you with grain offerings
43:24 But you have *b* me with your sins
Mic 6: 3 How have I *b* you? Answer me.
Mt 11:28 all you who are weary and *b*,
2Co 5: 4 are in this tent, we groan and are *b*,
Gal 5: 1 do not let yourselves be *b* again
1Ti 5:16 not let the church be *b* with them,

BURDENS (BURDEN)
Ps 68:19 who daily bears our *b*.
Lk 11:46 down with *b* they can hardly carry,
Gal 6: 2 Carry each other's *b*,

BURDENSOME (BURDEN)
1Jn 5: 3 And his commands are not *b*,

BURIED (BURY)
Ru 1:17 die I will die, and there I will be *b*.
Ro 6: 4 *b* with him through baptism
1Co 15: 4 that he was *b*, that he was raised
Col 2:12 having been *b* with him in baptism

BURN (BURNING BURNT)
Dt 7: 5 and *b* their idols in the fire.
Ps 79: 5 long will your jealousy *b* like fire?
1Co 7: 9 to marry than to *b* with passion.

BURNING (BURN)
Ex 27:20 so that the lamps may be kept *b*.
Lev 6: 9 the fire must be kept *b* on the altar.
Ps 18:28 You, O LORD, keep my lamp *b*;
Pr 25:22 you will heap *b* coals on his head,
Ro 12:20 you will heap *b* coals on his head."
Rev 19:20 alive into the fiery lake of *b* sulfur.

BURNISHED*
1Ki 7:45 of the LORD were of *b* bronze.
Eze 1: 7 and gleamed like *b* bronze.
Da 10: 6 and legs like the gleam of *b* bronze,
Rev 2:18 and whose feet are like *b* bronze.

BURNT (BURN)
Ge 8:20 he sacrificed *b* offerings on it.
22: 2 as a *b* offering on one
Ex 10:25 and *b* offerings to present
18:12 brought a *b* offering and other
40: 6 Place the altar of *b* offering in front
Lev 1: 3 " 'If the offering is a *b* offering
Jos 8:31 offered to the LORD *b* offerings
Jdg 6:26 offer the second bull as a *b* offering
13:16 But if you prepare a *b* offering,
1Ki 3: 4 offered a thousand *b* offerings
9:25 year Solomon sacrificed *b* offerings
10: 5 and the *b* offerings he made
Ezr 3: 2 Israel to sacrifice *b* offerings on it,
Eze 43:18 for sacrificing *b* offerings

BURST
Ps 98: 4 *b* into jubilant song with music;
Isa 44:23 *B* into song, you mountains,
49:13 *b* into song, O mountains!
52: 9 *B* into songs of joy together,
54: 1 *b* into song, shout for joy,
55:12 will *b* into song before you,

BURY (BURIED)
Mt 8:22 and let the dead *b* their own dead."
Lk 9:60 "Let the dead *b* their own dead,

BUSH
Ex 3: 2 the *b* was on fire it did not burn up.
Mk 12:26 the account of the *b*, how God said
Lk 20:37 But in the account of the *b*,
Ac 7:35 who appeared to him in the *b*.

BUSINESS
Ecc 4: 8 a miserable *b*!
Da 8:27 and went about the king's *b*.
1Co 5:12 What *b* is it of mine to judge those
1Th 4:11 to mind your own *b* and to work
Jas 1:11 even while he goes about his *b*.

BUSY*
1Ki 18:27 Perhaps he is deep in thought, or *b*,
20:40 While your servant was *b* here
Isa 32: 6 his mind is *b* with evil:
Hag 1: 9 of you is *b* with his own house.
2Th 3:11 They are not *b*; they are
Tit 2: 5 to be *b* at home, to be kind,

BUSYBODIES*
2Th 3:11 They are not busy; they are *b*.

1Ti 5:13 *b*, saying things they ought not to.

BUY (BOUGHT BUYS)
Pr 23:23 *B* the truth and do not sell it;
Isa 55: 1 Come, *b* wine and milk
Rev 13:17 so that no one could *b* or sell

BUYS (BUY)
Pr 31:16 She considers a field and *b* it;

BYWORD (WORD)
1Ki 9: 7 Israel will then become a *b*
Ps 44:14 You have made us a *b*
Joel 2:17 a *b* among the nations.

CAESAR
Mt 22:21 "Give to *C* what is Caesar's,

CAIN
Firstborn of Adam (Ge 4:1), murdered brother Abel (Ge 4:1-16; 1Jn 3:12).

CAKE
Hos 7: 8 Ephraim is a flat *c* not turned over.

CALEB
Judahite who spied out Canaan (Nu 13:6); allowed to enter land because of faith (Nu 13:30-14:38; Dt 1:36). Possessed Hebron (Jos 14:6-15:19).

CALF
Ex 32: 4 into an idol cast in the shape of a *c*,
Pr 15:17 than a fattened *c* with hatred.
Lk 15:23 Bring the fattened *c* and kill it.
Ac 7:41 made an idol in the form of a *c*.

CALL (CALLED CALLING CALLS)
1Ki 18:24 I will *c* on the name of the LORD.
2Ki 5:11 *c* on the name of the LORD his
1Ch 16: 8 to the LORD, *c* on his name;
Ps 105: 1 to the LORD, *c* on his name;
116: 13 and *c* on the name of the LORD.
116: 17 and *c* on the name of the LORD.
145: 18 near to all who *c* on him,
Pr 31:28 children arise and *c* her blessed;
Isa 5:20 Woe to those who *c* evil good
12: 4 to the LORD, *c* on his name;
55: 6 *c* on him while he is near.
65:24 Before they *c* I will answer;
Jer 33: 3 '*C* to me and I will answer you
Zep 3: 9 that all of them may *c* on the name
Zec 13: 9 They will *c* on my name
Mt 9:13 come to *c* the righteous,
Mk 2:17 I have not come to *c* the righteous,
Lk 5:32 I have not come to *c* the righteous,
Ac 2:39 all whom the Lord our God will *c*."
9:14 to arrest all who *c* on your name."
9:21 among those who *c* on this name?
Ro 10:12 and richly blesses all who *c* on him,
11:29 gifts and his *c* are irrevocable.
1Co 1: 2 with all those everywhere who *c*
1Th 4: 7 For God did not *c* us to be impure,
2Ti 2:22 along with those who *c*

CALLED (CALL)
Ge 2:23 she shall be *c* 'woman,'
5: 2 he blessed them and *c* them "man
12: 8 and *c* on the name of the LORD.
21:33 and there he *c* upon the name
26:25 and *c* on the name of the LORD.
1Sa 3: 5 and said, "Here I am; you *c* me."
2Ch 7:14 if my people, who are *c*
Ps 34: 6 This poor man *c*, and the LORD
116: 4 Then I *c* on the name of the LORD
Isa 56: 7 for my house will be *c*
La 3:55 I *c* on your name, O LORD,
Hos 11: 1 and out of Egypt I *c* my son.
Mt 1:16 was born Jesus, who is *c* Christ.
2:15 "Out of Egypt I *c* my son."
21:13 " 'My house will be *c* a house
Mk 11:17 " 'My house will be *c*
Lk 1:32 will be *c* the Son of the Most High.
1:35 to be born will be *c* the Son of God.
Ro 1: 1 *c* to be an apostle and set apart
1: 6 among those who are *c* to belong
1: 7 loved by God and *c* to be saints:
8:28 who have been *c* according
8:30 And those he predestined, he also *c*
1Co 1: 1 *c* to be an apostle of Christ Jesus
1: 2 in Christ Jesus and *c* to be holy,
1:24 but to those whom God has *c*,
1:26 of what you were when you were *c*.
7:15 God has *c* us to live in peace.
7:17 and to which God has *c* him.
Gal 1: 6 deserting the one who *c* you
1:15 from birth and *c* me by his grace,
5:13 You, my brothers, were *c* to be free
Eph 1:18 the hope to which he has *c* you,
4: 4 as you were *c* to one hope
Col 3:15 of one body you were *c* to peace.

2Th 2:14 He *c* you to this through our gospel
1Ti 6:12 life to which you were *c*
2Ti 1: 9 who has saved us and *c* us
Heb 9:15 that those who are *c* may receive
1Pe 1:15 But just as he who *c* you is holy,
2: 9 of him who *c* you out of darkness
3: 9 to this you were *c* so that you may
5:10 who *c* you to his eternal glory
2Pe 1: 3 of him who *c* us by his own glory
Jude : 1 To those who have been *c*,

CALLING (CALL)
Isa 40: 3 A voice of one *c*:
Mt 3: 3 "A voice of one *c* in the desert,
Mk 1: 3 "a voice of one *c* in the desert,
10:49 Cheer up! On your feet! He's *c* you
Lk 3: 4 "A voice of one *c* in the desert,
Jn 1:23 I am the voice of one *c* in the desert
Ac 22:16 wash your sins away, *c* on his name
Eph 4: 1 worthy of the *c* you have received.
2Th 1:11 may count you worthy of his *c*,
2Pe 1:10 all the more eager to make your *c*

CALLOUS* (CALLOUSED)
Ps 17:10 They close up their *c* hearts,
73: 7 From their *c* hearts comes iniquity;
119: 70 Their hearts are *c* and unfeeling,

CALLOUSED* (CALLOUS)
Isa 6:10 Make the heart of this people *c*;
Mt 13:15 this people's heart has become *c*;
Ac 28:27 this people's heart has become *c*;

CALLS (CALL)
Ps 147: 4 and *c* them each by name.
Isa 40:26 and *c* them each by name.
Joel 2:32 And everyone who *c*
Mt 22:43 speaking by the Spirit, *c* him 'Lord
Jn 10: 3 He *c* his own sheep by name
Ac 2:21 And everyone who *c*
Ro 10:13 "Everyone who *c* on the name
1Th 2:12 who *c* you into his kingdom
5:24 The one who *c* you is faithful

CALM (CALMS)
Ps 107: 30 They were glad when it grew *c*,
Isa 7: 4 keep *c* and don't be afraid.
Eze 16:42 I will be *c* and no longer angry.

CALMS* (CALM)
Pr 15:18 but a patient man *c* a quarrel.

CAMEL
Mt 19:24 it is easier for a *c* to go
23:24 strain out a gnat but swallow a *c*.
Mk 10:25 It is easier for a *c* to go
Lk 18:25 it is easier for a *c* to go

CAMP (ENCAMPS)
Heb 13:13 outside the *c*, bearing the disgrace

CANAAN (CANAANITE CANAANITES)
Ge 10:15 *C* was the father of Sidon his
Lev 14:34 "When you enter the land of *C*,
25:38 of Egypt to give you the land of *C*
Nu 13: 2 men to explore the land of *C*,
33:51 'When you cross the Jordan into *C*,
Jdg 4: 2 a king of *C*, who reigned in Hazor.
1Ch 16:18 "To you I will give the land of *C*
Ps 105: 11 "To you I will give the land of *C*
Ac 13:19 he overthrew seven nations in *C*

CANAANITE (CANAAN)
Ge 10:18 Later the *C* clans scattered
28: 1 "Do not marry a *C* woman.
Jos 5: 1 all the *C* kings along the seacoast
Jdg 1:32 lived among the *C* inhabitants

CANAANITES (CANAAN)
Ex 33: 2 before you and drive out the *C*,

CANCEL (CANCELED)
Dt 15: 1 seven years you must *c* debts.

CANCELED (CANCEL)
Mt 18:27 pity on him, *c* the debt
Lk 7:42 so he *c* the debts of both.
Col 2:14 having *c* the written code,

CANDLESTICKS see LAMPSTANDS

CANOPY*
2Sa 22:12 He made darkness his *c*
2Ki 16:18 away the Sabbath *c* that had been
Ps 18:11 made darkness his covering, his *c*
Isa 4: 5 over all the glory will be a *c*.
40:22 stretches out the heavens like a *c*,
Jer 43:10 he will spread his royal *c*

CAPERNAUM
Mt 4:13 Nazareth, he went and lived in *C*,

Jn 6:59 teaching in the synagogue in *C*.

CAPITAL
Dt 21:22 guilty of a *c* offense is put to death

CAPSTONE* (STONE)
Ps 118: 22 has become the *c*;
Zec 4: 7 he will bring out the *c* to shouts
Mt 21:42 has become the *c*;
Mk 12:10 has become the *c*;
Lk 20:17 has become the *c*'?
Ac 4:11 which has become the *c*.'
1Pe 2: 7 has become the *c*,"

CAPTIVATE* (CAPTIVE)
Pr 6:25 or let her *c* you with her eyes,

CAPTIVATED* (CAPTIVE)
Pr 5:19 may you ever be *c* by her love.
5:20 Why be *c*, my son, by an adulteress

CAPTIVE (CAPTIVATE CAPTIVATED CAPTIVES CAPTIVITY CAPTURED)
Ac 8:23 full of bitterness and *c* to sin."
2Co 10: 5 and we take *c* every thought
Col 2: 8 See to it that no one takes you *c*
2Ti 2:26 who has taken them *c* to do his will.

CAPTIVES (CAPTIVE)
Ps 68:18 you led *c* in your train;
Isa 61: 1 to proclaim freedom for the *c*
Eph 4: 8 he led *c* in his train

CAPTIVITY (CAPTIVE)
Dt 28:41 because they will go into *c*.
2Ki 25:21 So Judah went into *c*, away
Jer 30: 3 Israel and Judah back from *c*
52:27 So Judah went into *c*, away
Eze 29:14 I will bring them back from *c*

CAPTURED (CAPTIVE)
1Sa 4:11 The ark of God was *c*,
2Sa 5: 7 David *c* the fortress of Zion,
2Ki 17: 6 the king of Assyria *c* Samaria

CARCASS
Jdg 14: 9 taken the honey from the lion's *c*.
Mt 24:28 there is a *c*, there the vultures

CARE (CAREFUL CARES CARING)
Ps 8: 4 the son of man that you *c* for him?
65: 9 You *c* for the land and water it;
144: 3 what is man that you *c* for him,
Pr 29: 7 The righteous *c* about justice
Mk 5:26 deal under the *c* of many doctors
Lk 10:34 him to an inn and took *c* of him.
18: 4 I don't fear God or *c* about men,
Jn 21:16 Jesus said, "Take *c* of my sheep."
1Ti 3: 5 how can he take *c* of God's church
6:20 what has been entrusted to your *c*.
Heb 2: 6 the son of man that you *c* for him?
1Pe 5: 2 of God's flock that is under your *c*,

CAREFUL* (CARE)
Ge 31:24 "Be *c* not to say anything to Jacob,
31:29 'Be *c* not to say anything to Jacob,
Ex 19:12 'Be *c* that you do not go up
23:13 "Be *c* to do everything I have said
34:12 Be *c* not to make a treaty
34:15 "Be *c* not to make a treaty
Lev 18: 4 and be *c* to follow my decrees.
25:18 " 'Follow my decrees and be *c*
26: 3 and are *c* to obey my commands,
Dt 2: 4 afraid of you, but be very *c*.
4: 9 before you today? Only be *c*,
4:23 Be *c* not to forget the covenant
5:32 So be *c* to do what the LORD your
6: 3 be *c* to obey so that it may go well
6:12 be *c* that you do not forget
6:25 And if we are *c* to obey all this law
7:12 attention to these laws and are *c*
8: 1 Be *c* to follow every command I am
8:11 Be *c* that you do not forget
11:16 Be *c*, or you will be enticed
12: 1 and laws you must be *c* to follow
12:13 Be *c* not to sacrifice your burnt
12:19 Be *c* not to neglect the Levites
12:28 Be *c* to obey all these regulations I
12:30 be *c* not to be ensnared
15: 5 are *c* to follow all these commands
15: 9 Be *c* not to harbor this wicked
17:10 Be *c* to do everything they direct
24: 8 cases of leprous diseases be very *c*
Jos 1: 7 Be *c* to obey all the law my servant
1: 8 so that you may be *c*
22: 5 But be very *c* to keep
23: 6 be *c* to obey all that is written
23:11 be very *c* to love the LORD your
1Ki 8:25 if only your sons are *c* in all they do
2Ki 10:31 Yet Jehu was not *c* to keep the law
2Ki 17:37 You must always be *c*
21: 8 if only they will be *c*
1Ch 22:13 if you are *c* to observe the decrees
28: 8 Be *c* to follow all the commands
2Ch 6:16 if only your sons are *c* in all they do
33: 8 if only they will be *c*
Ezr 4:22 Be *c* not to neglect this matter.
Job 36:18 Be *c* that no one entices you
Ps 101: 2 I will be *c* to lead a blameless life—
Pr 13:24 he who loves him is *c*
27:23 give *c* attention to your herds;
Isa 7: 4 Be *c*, keep calm and don't be afraid.
Jer 17:21 Be *c* not to carry a load
17:24 But if you are *c* to obey me,
22: 4 For if you are *c* to carry out these
Eze 11:20 will follow my decrees and be *c*
18:19 has been *c* to keep all my decrees,
20:19 follow my decrees and be *c*
20:21 they were not *c* to keep my laws—
36:27 you to follow my decrees and be *c*
37:24 and be *c* to keep my decrees.
Mic 7: 5 be *c* of your words.
Hag 1: 5 "Give *c* thought to your ways.
1: 7 "Give *c* thought to your ways.
2:15 give *c* thought to this from this day
2:18 Give *c* thought: Is there yet any
2:18 give *c* thought to the day
Mt 2: 8 and make a *c* search for the child.
6: 1 "Be *c* not to do your 'acts
16: 6 "Be *c*," Jesus said to them.
Mk 8:15 "Be *c*," Jesus warned them.
Lk 21:34 Be *c*, or your hearts will be weighed
Ro 12:17 Be *c* to do what is right in the eyes
1Co 3:10 each one should be *c* how he builds
8: 9 Be *c*, however, that the exercise
10:12 standing firm, be *c* that you don't
Eph 5:15 Be very *c*, then, how you live—
2Ti 4: 2 great patience and *c* instruction.
Tit 3: 8 may be *c* to devote themselves
Heb 2: 1 We must pay more *c* attention,
4: 1 let us be *c* that none

CARELESS*
Mt 12:36 for every *c* word they have spoken.

CARES* (CARE)
Dt 11:12 It is a land the LORD your God *c*
Job 39:16 she *c* not that her labor was in vain,
Ps 55:22 Cast your *c* on the LORD
142: 4 no one *c* for my life.
Pr 12:10 A righteous man *c* for the needs
Ecc 5: 3 when there are many *c*,
Jer 12:11 because there is no one who *c*.
30:17 Zion for whom no one *c*.'
Na 1: 7 He *c* for those who trust in him,
Jn 10:13 and *c* nothing for the sheep.
Eph 5:29 but he feeds and *c* for it, just
1Pe 5: 7 on him because he *c* for you.

CARING* (CARE)
1Th 2: 7 like a mother *c* for her little
1Ti 5: 4 practice by *c* for their own family

CARPENTER (CARPENTER'S)
Mk 6: 3 does miracles! Isn't this the *c*?

CARPENTER'S* (CARPENTER)
Mt 13:55 "Isn't this the *c* son? Isn't his

CARRIED (CARRY)
Ex 19: 4 and how I *c* you on eagles' wings
Dt 1:31 how the LORD your God *c* you,
Isa 53: 4 and *c* our sorrows,
63: 9 he lifted them up and *c* them
Mt 8:17 and *c* our diseases."
Heb 13: 9 Do not be *c* away by all kinds
2Pe 1:21 as they were *c* along by the Holy
3:17 so that you may not be *c* away

CARRIES (CARRY)
Dt 32:11 and *c* them on its pinions.
Isa 40:11 and *c* them close to his heart;

CARRY (CARRIED CARRIES CARRYING)
Lev 16:22 goat will *c* on itself all their sins
26:15 and fail to *c* out all my commands
Isa 46: 4 I have made you and I will *c* you;
Lk 14:27 anyone who does not *c* his cross
Gal 6: 2 *C* each other's burdens,
6: 5 for each one should *c* his own load.

CARRYING (CARRY)
Jn 19:17 *C* his own cross, he went out
1Jn 5: 2 loving God and *c* out his

CARVED (CARVES)
Nu 33:52 Destroy all their *c* images
Mic 5:13 I will destroy your *c* images

CARVES* (CARVED)
Dt 27:15 "Cursed is the man who *c* an image

CASE
Pr 18:17 to present his *c* seems right,
22:23 for the LORD will take up their *c*
23:11 he will take up their *c* against you.

CAST (CASTING)
Ex 34:17 "Do not make *c* idols.
Lev 16: 8 He is to *c* lots for the two goats—
Ps 22:18 and *c* lots for my clothing.
55:22 *C* your cares on the LORD
Pr 16:33 The lot is *c* into the lap,
Ecc 11: 1 *C* your bread upon the waters,
Jn 19:24 and *c* lots for my clothing."
1Pe 5: 7 *C* all your anxiety on him

CASTING (CAST)
Pr 18:18 *C* the lot settles disputes
Mt 27:35 divided up his clothes by *c* lots.

CATCH (CATCHES CAUGHT)
Lk 5: 4 and let down the nets for a *c*."
5:10 from now on you will *c* men."

CATCHES (CATCH)
Job 5:13 He *c* the wise in their craftiness,
1Co 3:19 "He *c* the wise in their craftiness";

CATTLE
Ps 50:10 and the *c* on a thousand hills.

CAUGHT (CATCH)
Ge 22:13 there in a thicket he saw a ram *c*
2Co 12: 2 who fourteen years ago was *c* up
1Th 4:17 and are left will be *c* up together with them

CAUSE (CAUSES)
Pr 24:28 against your neighbor without *c*,
Ecc 8: 3 Do not stand up for a bad *c*,
Mt 18: 7 of the things that *c* people to sin!
Ro 14:21 else that will *c* your brother
1Co 10:32 Do not *c* anyone to stumble,

CAUSES (CAUSE)
Ps 7:16 The trouble he *c* recoils on himself;
Isa 8:14 a stone that *c* men to stumble
Mt 5:29 If your right eye *c* you to sin,
5:30 And if your right hand *c* you to sin,
18: 6 if anyone *c* one of these little ones
18: 8 or your foot *c* you to sin,
Ro 14:20 to eat anything that *c* someone else
1Co 8:13 if what I eat *c* my brother to fall
1Pe 2: 8 "A stone that *c* men to stumble

CAUTIOUS*
Pr 12:26 A righteous man is *c* in friendship,

CEASE
Ps 46: 9 He makes wars *c* to the ends

CELEBRATE*
Ex 10: 9 we are to *c* a festival to the LORD
12:14 generations to come you shall *c* it
12:17 *C* this day as a lasting ordinance
12:17 "*C* the Feast of Unleavened Bread,
12:47 community of Israel must *c* it.
12:48 to *c* the LORD's Passover must
23:14 are to *c* a festival to me.
23:15 "*C* the Feast of Unleavened Bread;
23:16 "*C* the Feast of Harvest
23:16 "*C* the Feast of Ingathering
34:18 "*C* the Feast of Unleavened Bread.
34:22 "*C* the Feast of Weeks
Lev 23:39 *c* the festival to the LORD
23:41 *C* this as a festival to the LORD
23:41 for the generations to come; *c* it
Nu 9: 2 "Have the Israelites *c* the Passover
9: 3 *C* it at the appointed time,
9: 4 told the Israelites to *c* the Passover,
9: 6 of them could not *c* the Passover
9:10 they may still *c* the LORD's
9:11 are to *c* it on the fourteenth day
9:12 When they *c* the Passover,
9:13 on a journey fails to *c* the Passover,
9:14 to *c* the LORD's Passover must do
29:12 *C* a festival to the LORD
Dt 16: 1 *c* the Passover of the LORD your
16:10 Then *c* the Feast of Weeks
16:13 *C* the Feast of Tabernacles
16:15 For seven days *c* the Feast
Jdg 16:23 to Dagon their god and to *c*,
2Sa 6:21 the LORD's people Israel—I will *c*
2Ki 23:21 "*C* the Passover to the LORD your
2Ch 30: 1 and *c* the Passover to the LORD,
30: 2 decided to *c* the Passover
30: 3 able to *c* it at the regular time
30: 5 and *c* the Passover to the LORD,

2Ch 30:13 in Jerusalem to *c* the Feast
30:23 to *c* the festival seven more days;
Ne 8:12 of food and to *c* with great joy,
12:27 to *c* joyfully the dedication
Est 9:21 to have them *c* annually
Ps 145: 7 They will *c* your abundant
Isa 30:29 as on the night you *c* a holy festival
Na 1:15 *C* your festivals, O Judah,
Zec 14:16 and to *c* the Feast of Tabernacles.
14:18 up to *c* the Feast of Tabernacles.
14:19 up to *c* the Feast of Tabernacles.
Mt 26:18 I am going to *c* the Passover
Lk 15:23 Let's have a feast and *c*.
15:24 So they began to *c*.
15:29 goat so I could *c* with my friends.
15:32 But we had to *c* and be glad,
Rev 11:10 will *c* by sending each other gifts,

CELESTIAL*
2Pe 2:10 afraid to slander *c* beings;
Jude : 8 authority and slander *c* beings.

CENSER (CENSERS)
Lev 16:12 is to take a *c* full of burning coals
Rev 8: 3 Another angel, who had a golden *c*,

CENSERS (CENSER)
Nu 16: 6 Take *c* and tomorrow put fire

CENTURION
Mt 8: 5 had entered Capernaum, a *c* came
27:54 When the *c* and those
Mk 15:39 And when the *c*, who stood there
Lk 7: 3 The *c* heard of Jesus and sent some
23:47 The *c*, seeing what had happened,
Ac 10: 1 a *c* in what was known
27: 1 handed over to a *c* named Julius,

CEPHAS* (PETER)
Jn 1:42 You will be called *C*" (which,
1Co 1:12 another, "I follow *C*"; still another,
3:22 Paul or Apollos or *C* or the world
9: 5 and the Lord's brothers and *C*?

CEREMONIAL* (CEREMONY)
Lev 14: 2 at the time of his *c* cleansing,
15:13 off seven days for his *c* cleansing;
Mk 7: 3 they give their hands a *c* washing,
Jn 2: 6 used by the Jews for *c* washing,
3:25 Jew over the matter of *c* washing.
11:55 to Jerusalem for their *c* cleansing
18:28 to avoid *c* uncleanness the Jews did
Heb 9:10 drink and various *c* washings—
13: 9 not by *c* foods, which are

CEREMONIALLY* (CEREMONY)
Lev 4:12 outside the camp to a place *c* clean,
5: 2 touches anything *c* unclean—
6:11 the camp to a place that is *c* clean.
7:19 anyone *c* clean may eat it.
7:19 touches anything *c* unclean must
10:14 Eat them in a *c* clean place;
11: 4 not have a split hoof; it is *c* unclean
12: 2 birth to a son will be *c* unclean
12: 7 and then she will be *c* clean
13: 3 he shall pronounce him *c* unclean.
14: 8 with water; then he will be *c* clean.
15:28 and after that she will be *c* clean.
15:33 lies with a woman who is *c* unclean.
17:15 he will be *c* unclean till evening.
21: 1 must not make himself *c* unclean
22: 3 of your descendants is *c* unclean
27:11 he vowed is a *c* unclean animal—
Nu 5: 2 who is *c* unclean because of a dead
6: 7 must not make himself *c* unclean
8: 6 Israelites and make them *c* clean.
9: 6 they were *c* unclean on account
9:13 But if a man who is *c* clean
18:11 household who is *c* clean may eat
18:13 household who is *c* clean may eat
19: 7 but he will be *c* unclean till evening
19: 9 and put them in a *c* clean place
19:18 Then a man who is *c* clean is
Dt 12:15 Both the *c* unclean and the clean
12:22 Both the *c* unclean and the clean
14: 7 they are *c* unclean for you.
15:22 Both the *c* unclean and the clean
1Sa 20:26 to David to make him *c* unclean—
2Ch 13:11 the bread on the *c* clean table
30:17 for all those who were not *c* clean
Ezr 6:20 themselves and were all *c* clean.
Ne 12:30 Levites had purified themselves *c*,
Isa 66:20 of the LORD in *c* clean vessels.
Eze 22:10 period, when they are *c* unclean.
Ac 24:18 I was *c* clean when they found me
Heb 9:13 those who are *c* unclean sanctify

CEREMONY* (CEREMONIAL CEREMONIALLY)
Ge 50:11 Egyptians are holding a solemn *c*
Ex 12:25 as he promised, observe this *c*.
12:26 'What does this *c* mean to you?'
13: 5 are to observe this *c* in this month:

CERTAIN (CERTAINTY)
2Pe 1:19 word of the prophets made more *c*,

CERTAINTY* (CERTAIN)
Lk 1: 4 so that you may know the *c*
Jn 17: 8 They knew with *c* that I came

CERTIFICATE* (CERTIFIED)
Dt 24: 1 and he writes her a *c* of divorce,
24: 3 and writes her a *c* of divorce,
Isa 50: 1 "Where is your mother's *c*
Jer 3: 8 I gave faithless Israel her *c*
Mt 5:31 divorces his wife must give her a *c*
19: 7 that a man give his wife a *c*
Mk 10: 4 a man to write a *c* of divorce

CERTIFIED* (CERTIFICATE)
Jn 3:33 has accepted it has *c* that God is

CHAFF
Ps 1: 4 They are like *c*
35: 5 May they be like *c* before the wind,
Da 2:35 became like *c* on a threshing floor
Mt 3:12 up the *c* with unquenchable fire."

CHAINED (CHAINS)
2Ti 2: 9 But God's word is not *c*.

CHAINS (CHAINED)
Eph 6:20 for which I am an ambassador in *c*.
Col 4:18 Remember my *c*.
2Ti 1:16 and was not ashamed of my *c*.
Jude : 6 with everlasting *c* for judgment

CHAMPION
Ps 19: 5 like a *c* rejoicing to run his course.

CHANCE
Ecc 9:11 but time and *c* happen to them all.

CHANGE (CHANGED)
1Sa 15:29 of Israel does not lie or *c* his mind;
Ps 110: 4 and will not *c* his mind:
Jer 7: 5 If you really *c* your ways
Mal 3: 6 "I the LORD do not *c*.
Mt 18: 3 unless you *c* and become like little
Heb 7:21 and will not *c* his mind:
Jas 1:17 who does not *c* like shifting

CHANGED (CHANGE)
1Sa 10: 6 you will be *c* into a different person
Hos 11: 8 My heart is *c* within me;
1Co 15:51 but we will all be *c*—in a flash,

CHARACTER*
Ru 3:11 that you are a woman of noble *c*.
Pr 12: 4 of noble *c* is her husband's crown,
31:10 A wife of noble *c* who can find?
Ac 17:11 noble *c* than the Thessalonians,
Ro 5: 4 perseverance, *c*; and *c*, hope.
1Co 15:33 "Bad company corrupts good *c*."

CHARGE (CHARGES)
Job 34:13 him in *c* of the whole world?
Ro 8:33 Who will bring any *c*
1Co 9:18 the gospel I may offer it free of *c*,
2Co 11: 7 the gospel of God to you free of *c*?
2Ti 4: 1 I give you this *c*: Preach the Word;
Phm :18 or owes you anything, *c* it to me.

CHARGES (CHARGE)
Isa 50: 8 Who then will bring *c* against me?

CHARIOT (CHARIOTS)
2Ki 2:11 suddenly a *c* of fire and horses
Ps 104: 3 He makes the clouds his *c*
Ac 8:28 sitting in his *c* reading the book

CHARIOTS (CHARIOT)
2Ki 6:17 and *c* of fire all around Elisha.
Ps 20: 7 Some trust in *c* and some in horses,
68:17 The *c* of God are tens of thousands

CHARM* (CHARMING)
Pr 17: 8 bribe is a *c* to the one who gives it;
31:30 *C* is deceptive, and beauty is

CHARMING* (CHARM)
Pr 26:25 his speech is *c*, do not believe
SS 1:16 Oh, how *c*!

CHASE (CHASES)
Lev 26: 8 Five of you will *c* a hundred,

CHASES* (CHASE)
Pr 12:11 he who *c* fantasies lacks judgment.
28:19 one who *c* fantasies will have his

CHASM*
Lk 16:26 and you a great *c* has been fixed,

CHATTER* (CHATTERING)
1Ti 6:20 Turn away from godless *c*
2Ti 2:16 Avoid godless *c*, because those

CHATTERING* (CHATTER)
Pr 10: 8 but a *c* fool comes to ruin.
10:10 and a *c* fool comes to ruin.

CHEAT* (CHEATED CHEATING CHEATS)
Mal 1:14 "Cursed is the *c* who has
1Co 6: 8 you yourselves *c* and do wrong,

CHEATED* (CHEAT)
Ge 31: 7 yet your father has *c* me
1Sa 12: 3 Whom have I *c*? Whom have I
12: 4 "You have not *c* or oppressed us,"
Lk 19: 8 if I have *c* anybody out of anything,
1Co 6: 7 Why not rather be *c*? Instead,

CHEATING* (CHEAT)
Am 8: 5 and *c* with dishonest scales,

CHEATS* (CHEAT)
Lev 6: 2 or if he *c* him, or if he finds lost

CHEEK (CHEEKS)
Mt 5:39 someone strikes you on the right *c*,
Lk 6:29 If someone strikes you on one *c*,

CHEEKS (CHEEK)
Isa 50: 6 my *c* to those who pulled out my

CHEERFUL* (CHEERS)
Pr 15:13 A happy heart makes the face *c*,
15:15 but the *c* heart has a continual feast
15:30 A *c* look brings joy to the heart,
17:22 A *c* heart is good medicine,
2Co 9: 7 for God loves a *c* giver.

CHEERS (CHEERFUL)
Pr 12:25 but a kind word *c* him up.

CHEMOSH
2Ki 23:13 for *C* the vile god of Moab,

CHERISH (CHERISHED CHERISHES)
Ps 17:14 You still the hunger of those you *c*;

CHERISHED (CHERISH)
Ps 66:18 If I had *c* sin in my heart,

CHERISHES* (CHERISH)
Pr 19: 8 he who *c* understanding prospers.

CHERUB (CHERUBIM)
Ex 25:19 Make one *c* on one end
Eze 28:14 You were anointed as a guardian *c*,

CHERUBIM (CHERUB)
Ge 3:24 side of the Garden of Eden *c*
1Sa 4: 4 who is enthroned between the *c*.
2Sa 6: 2 enthroned between the *c* that are
22:11 He mounted the *c* and flew;
1Ki 6:23 a pair of *c* of olive wood,
2Ki 19:15 of Israel, enthroned between the *c*,
1Ch 13: 6 who is enthroned between the *c*—
Ps 18:10 He mounted the *c* and flew;
80: 1 who sit enthroned between the *c*,
99: 1 he sits enthroned between the *c*,
Isa 37:16 of Israel, enthroned between the *c*,
Eze 10: 1 was over the heads of the *c*.

CHEST
Ex 25:10 "Have them make a *c*
2Ki 12: 9 Jehoiada the priest took a *c*
Da 2:32 its *c* and arms of silver, its belly
Rev 1:13 with a golden sash around his *c*.

CHEWS
Lev 11: 3 divided and that *c* the cud.

CHIEF
1Pe 5: 4 And when the *C* Shepherd appears,

CHILD (CHILDISH CHILDREN CHILDREN'S GRANDCHILDREN)
Pr 20:11 Even a *c* is known by his actions,
22: 6 Train a *c* in the way he should go,
22:15 Folly is bound up in the heart of a *c*
23:13 not withhold discipline from a *c*;
29:15 *c* left to himself disgraces his mother.
Isa 7:14 The virgin will be with *c*
9: 6 For to us a *c* is born,
11: 6 and a little *c* will lead them.
66:13 As a mother comforts her *c*,

Mt 1:23 "The virgin will be with c
18: 2 He called a little c and had him
Lk 1:42 and blessed is the c you will bear!
1:80 And the c grew and became strong
1Co 13:11 When I was a c, I talked like a c,
1Jn 5: 1 who loves the father loves his c

CHILDBEARING (BEAR)
Ge 3:16 greatly increase your pains in c;

CHILDBIRTH (BEAR)
Gal 4:19 the pains of c until Christ is formed

CHILDISH* (CHILD)
1Co 13:11 When I became a man, I put c ways

CHILDREN (CHILD)
Ex 20: 5 punishing the c for the sin
Dt 4: 9 Teach them to your c
6: 7 Impress them on your c.
11:19 them to your c, talking about them
14: 1 You are the c of the LORD your
24:16 nor c put to death for their fathers;
30:19 so that you and your c may live
32:46 so that you may command your c
Job 1: 5 "Perhaps my c have sinned
Ps 8: 2 From the lips of c and infants
78: 5 forefathers to teach their c,
Pr 17: 6 Children's c are a crown
20: 7 blessed are his c after him.
31:28 Her c arise and call her blessed;
Joel 1: 3 Tell it to your c,
Mal 4: 6 the hearts of the fathers to their c,
Mt 7:11 how to give good gifts to your c,
11:25 and revealed them to little c.
18: 3 you change and become like little c
19:14 "Let the little c come to me,
21:16 " 'From the lips of c and infants
Mk 9:37 one of these little c in my name
10:14 "Let the little c come to me,
10:16 And he took the c in his arms,
13:12 C will rebel against their parents
Lk 10:21 and revealed them to little c.
18:16 "Let the little c come to me,
Jn 1:12 the right to become c of God—
Ac 2:39 The promise is for you and your c
Ro 8:16 with our spirit that we are God's c.
1Co 14:20 Brothers, stop thinking like c.
2Co 12:14 parents, but parents for their c.
Eph 6: 1 C, obey your parents in the Lord,
6: 4 do not exasperate your c; instead,
Col 3:20 C, obey your parents in everything,
3:21 Fathers, do not embitter your c,
1Ti 3: 4 and see that his c obey him
3:12 and must manage his c and his
5:10 bringing up c, showing hospitality,
Heb 2:13 and the c God has given me."
1Jn 3: 1 that we should be called c of God!

CHILDREN'S (CHILD)
Isa 54:13 and great will be your c peace.

CHOKE
Mk 4:19 come in and c the word,

CHOOSE (CHOOSES CHOSE CHOSEN)
Dt 30:19 Now c life, so that you
Jos 24:15 then c for yourselves this day
Pr 8:10 C my instruction instead of silver,
16:16 to c understanding rather
Jn 15:16 You did not c me, but I chose you

CHOOSES (CHOOSE)
Mt 11:27 to whom the Son c to reveal him.
Lk 10:22 to whom the Son c to reveal him."
Jn 7:17 If anyone c to do God's will,

CHOSE (CHOOSE)
Ge 13:11 So Lot c for himself the whole plain
Ps 33:12 the people he c for his inheritance.
Jn 15:16 but I c you and appointed you to go
1Co 1:27 But God c the foolish things
Eph 1: 4 he c us in him before the creation
2Th 2:13 from the beginning God c you

CHOSEN (CHOOSE)
Isa 41: 8 Jacob, whom I have c,
Mt 22:14 For many are invited, but few are c
Lk 10:42 Mary has c what is better,
23:35 the Christ of God, the C One."
Jn 15:19 but I have c you out of the world.
1Pe 1:20 He was c before the creation
2: 9 But you are a c people, a royal

CHRIST (CHRIST'S CHRISTIAN CHRISTIANS CHRISTS)
Mt 1:16 was born Jesus, who is called C.
16:16 Peter answered, "You are the C,
22:42 "What do you think about the C?
Mk 1: 1 of the gospel about Jesus C,
8:29 Peter answered, "You are the C."
14:61 "Are you the C, the Son
Lk 9:20 Peter answered, "The C of God."
Jn 1:41 found the Messiah" (that is, the C).
20:31 you may believe that Jesus is the C,
Ac 2:36 you crucified, both Lord and C."
5:42 the good news that Jesus is the C.
9:22 by proving that Jesus is the C.
9:34 said to him, "Jesus C heals you.
17: 3 proving that the C had to suffer
18:28 the Scriptures that Jesus was the C.
26:23 that the C would suffer and,
Ro 1: 4 from the dead: Jesus C our Lord.
3:22 comes through faith in Jesus C
5: 1 God through our Lord Jesus C,
5: 6 we were still powerless, C died
5: 8 While we were still sinners, C died
5:11 in God through our Lord Jesus C,
5:17 life through the one man, Jesus C.
6: 4 as C was raised from the dead
6: 9 that since C was raised
6:23 life in C Jesus our Lord.
7: 4 to the law through the body of C,
8: 1 for those who are in C Jesus,
8: 9 Spirit of C, he does not belong to C.
8:17 heirs of God and co-heirs with C,
8:34 Who is he that condemns? C Jesus,
8:35 us from the love of C?
9: 5 is traced the human ancestry of C,
10: 4 C is the end of the law
12: 5 so in C we who are many form one
13:14 yourselves with the Lord Jesus C,
14: 9 C died and returned to life
15: 3 For even C did not please himself
15: 5 yourselves as you follow C Jesus,
15: 7 then, just as C accepted you,
16:18 people are not serving our Lord C,
1Co 1: 2 to those sanctified in C Jesus
1: 7 for our Lord Jesus C to be revealed.
1:13 Is C divided? Was Paul crucified
1:17 For C did not send me to baptize,
1:23 but we preach C crucified:
1:30 of him that you are in C Jesus,
2: 2 except Jesus C and him crucified.
3:11 one already laid, which is Jesus C.
5: 7 For C, our Passover lamb,
6:15 bodies are members of C himself?
8: 6 and there is but one Lord, Jesus C,
8:12 conscience, you sin against C.
10: 4 them, and that rock was C.
11: 1 as I follow the example of C.
11: 3 the head of every man is C,
12:27 Now you are the body of C,
15: 3 that C died for our sins according
15:14 And if C has not been raised,
15:22 so in C all will be made alive.
15:57 victory through our Lord Jesus C.
2Co 1: 5 as the sufferings of C flow
2:14 us in triumphal procession in C
3: 3 show that you are a letter from C,
3:14 because only in C is it taken away.
4: 4 light of the gospel of the glory of C,
4: 5 not preach ourselves, but Jesus C
4: 6 of the glory of God in the face of C.
5:10 before the judgment seat of C,
5:17 Therefore, if anyone is in C,
6:15 What harmony is there between C
10: 1 the meekness and gentleness of C,
11: 2 you to one husband, to C,
Gal 1: 7 are trying to pervert the gospel of C
2: 4 on the freedom we have in C Jesus
2:16 but by faith in Jesus C.
2:17 does that mean that C promotes sin
2:20 I have been crucified with C
2:21 C died for nothing!" You foolish
3:13 C redeemed us from the curse
3:16 meaning one person, who is C.
3:26 of God through faith in C Jesus,
4:19 of childbirth until C is formed
5: 1 for freedom that C has set us free.
5: 4 by law have been alienated from C;
5:24 to C Jesus have crucified the sinful
6:14 in the cross of our Lord Jesus C,
Eph 1: 3 with every spiritual blessing in C.
1:10 together under one head, even C.
1:20 which he exerted in C
2: 5 made us alive with C
2:10 created in C Jesus
2:12 time you were separate from C,
2:20 with C Jesus himself as the chief
3: 8 the unsearchable riches of C,
3:17 so that C may dwell in your hearts
4: 7 has been given as C apportioned it.
4:13 measure of the fullness of C.
4:15 into him who is the Head, that is, C
4:32 just as in C God forgave you.
5: 2 as C loved us and gave himself up
5:21 out of reverence for C.
5:23 as C is the head of the church,
5:25 just as C loved the church
Php 1:18 motives or true, C is preached.
1:21 to live is C and to die is gain.
1:23 I desire to depart and be with C,
1:27 worthy of the gospel of C.
1:29 on behalf of C not only to believe
2: 5 be the same as that of C Jesus:
3: 7 now consider loss for the sake of C.
3:10 I want to know C and the power
3:18 as enemies of the cross of C.
4:19 to his glorious riches in C Jesus.
Col 1: 4 heard of your faith in C Jesus
1:27 which is C in you, the hope of glory
1:28 may present everyone perfect in C.
2: 2 the mystery of God, namely, C,
2: 6 as you received C Jesus as Lord,
2: 9 For in C all the fullness
2:13 God made you alive with C.
2:17 the reality, however, is found in C.
3: 1 then, you have been raised with C,
3: 3 and your life is now hidden with C
3:15 Let the peace of C rule
1Th 5: 9 through our Lord Jesus C.
2Th 2: 1 the coming of our Lord Jesus C
2:14 in the glory of our Lord Jesus C.
1Ti 1:12 I thank C Jesus our Lord, who has
1:15 C Jesus came into the world
1:16 C Jesus might display his unlimited
2: 5 the man C Jesus, who gave himself
2Ti 1: 9 us in C Jesus before the beginning
1:10 appearing of our Savior, C Jesus,
2: 1 in the grace that is in C Jesus.
2: 3 us like a good soldier of C Jesus.
2: 8 Remember Jesus C, raised
2:10 the salvation that is in C Jesus,
3:12 life in C Jesus will be persecuted,
3:15 salvation through faith in C Jesus.
4: 1 presence of God and of C Jesus,
Tit 2:13 our great God and Savior, Jesus C,
Heb 3: 6 But C is faithful as a son
3:14 to share in C if we hold firmly
5: 5 So C also did not take
6: 1 the elementary teachings about C
9:11 When C came as high priest
9:14 more, then, will the blood of C,
9:15 For this reason C is the mediator
9:24 For C did not enter a man-made
9:26 Then C would have had
9:28 so C was sacrificed once
10:10 of the body of Jesus C once for all.
13: 8 Jesus C is the same yesterday
1Pe 1: 2 for obedience to Jesus C
1: 3 of Jesus C from the dead,
1:11 he predicted the sufferings of C
1:19 but with the precious blood of C,
2:21 because C suffered for you,
3:15 in your hearts set apart C as Lord.
3:18 For C died for sins once for all,
3:21 you by the resurrection of Jesus C,
4:13 participate in the sufferings of C,
4:14 insulted because of the name of C,
2Pe 1: 1 and Savior Jesus C have received
1:16 and coming of our Lord Jesus C,
1Jn 2: 1 Jesus C, the Righteous One.
2:22 man who denies that Jesus is the C.
3:16 Jesus C laid down his life for us.
3:23 in the name of his Son, Jesus C,
4: 2 that Jesus C has come
5: 1 believes that Jesus is the C is born
5:20 even in his Son Jesus C.
2Jn : 9 teaching of C does not have God;
Jude : 4 deny Jesus C our only Sovereign
Rev 1: 1 The revelation of Jesus C,
1: 5 from Jesus C, who is the faithful
11:15 kingdom of our Lord and of his C,
20: 4 reigned with C a thousand years.
20: 6 they will be priests of God and of C

CHRIST'S (CHRIST)
1Co 9:21 from God's law but am under C law
2Co 5:14 For C love compels us,
5:20 We are therefore C ambassadors,
12: 9 so that C power may rest on me.
Col 1:22 by C physical body through death

CHRISTIAN* (CHRIST)
Ac 26:28 you can persuade me to be a C?"
1Pe 4:16 as a C, do not be ashamed,

CHRISTIANS* (CHRIST)
Ac 11:26 The disciples were called C first

CHRISTS* (CHRIST)
Mt 24:24 For false C and false prophets will
Mk 13:22 For false C and false prophets will

CHURCH
Mt 16:18 and on this rock I will build my c,
18:17 if he refuses to listen even to the c,

Ac 20:28 Be shepherds of the *c* of God,
1Co 5:12 of mine to judge those outside the *c*
14: 4 but he who prophesies edifies the *c*.
14:12 to excel in gifts that build up the *c*.
14:26 done for the strengthening of the *c*.
15: 9 because I persecuted the *c* of God.
Gal 1:13 how intensely I persecuted the *c*
Eph 5:23 as Christ is the head of the *c*,
Col 1:18 he is the head of the body, the *c*;
1:24 the sake of his body, which is the *c*.

CHURNING
Pr 30:33 For as *c* the milk produces butter,

CIRCLE
Isa 40:22 enthroned above the *c* of the earth,

CIRCUMCISE (CIRCUMCISED CIRCUMCISION)
Dt 10:16 *C* your hearts, therefore,

CIRCUMCISED (CIRCUMCISE)
Ge 17:10 Every male among you shall be *c*.
17:12 who is eight days old must be *c*,
Jos 5: 3 and *c* the Israelites at Gibeath
Gal 5: 2 that if you let yourselves be *c*,

CIRCUMCISION (CIRCUMCISE)
Ro 2:25 *C* has value if you observe the law,
2:29 and *c* is *c* of the heart, by the Spirit,
1Co 7:19 *C* is nothing and uncircumcision is

CIRCUMSTANCES
Php 4:11 to be content whatever the *c*.
1Th 5:18 continually; give thanks in all *c*,

CITIES (CITY)
Lk 19:17 small matter, take charge of ten *c*.'
19:19 'You take charge of five *c*.'

CITIZENS (CITIZENSHIP)
Eph 2:19 but fellow *c* with God's people

CITIZENSHIP* (CITIZENS)
Ac 22:28 "I had to pay a big price for my *c*."
Eph 2:12 excluded from *c* in Israel
Php 3:20 But our *c* is in heaven.

CITY (CITIES)
Mt 5:14 A *c* on a hill cannot be hidden.
Ac 18:10 I have many people in this *c*."
Heb 13:14 here we do not have an enduring *c*,
Rev 21: 2 saw the Holy *C*, the new

CIVILIAN*
2Ti 2: 4 a soldier gets involved in *c* affairs—

CLAIM (CLAIMS RECLAIM)
Pr 25: 6 do not *c* a place among great men;
1Jn 1: 6 If we *c* to have fellowship
1: 8 If we *c* to be without sin, we
1:10 If we *c* we have not sinned,

CLAIMS (CLAIM)
Jas 2:14 if a man *c* to have faith
1Jn 2: 6 Whoever *c* to live in him must walk
2: 9 Anyone who *c* to be in the light

CLANGING*
1Co 13: 1 a resounding gong or a *c* cymbal.

CLAP* (CLAPPED CLAPS)
Job 21: 5 *c* your hand over your mouth.
Ps 47: 1 *C* your hands, all you nations;
98: 8 Let the rivers *c* their hands,
Pr 30:32 *c* your hand over your mouth!
Isa 55:12 will *c* their hands.
La 2:15 *c* their hands at you;

CLAPPED* (CLAP)
2Ki 11:12 and the people *c* their hands
Eze 25: 6 Because you have *c* your hands

CLAPS* (CLAP)
Job 27:23 It *c* its hands in derision
34:37 scornfully he *c* his hands among us
Na 3:19 *c* his hands at your fall,

CLASSIFY*
2Co 10:12 dare to *c* or compare ourselves

CLAUDIUS
Ac 11:28 happened during the reign of *C*.)
18: 2 because *C* had ordered all the Jews

CLAY
Isa 45: 9 Does the *c* say to the potter,
64: 8 We are the *c*, you are the potter;
Jer 18: 6 "Like *c* in the hand of the potter,
La 4: 2 are now considered as pots of *c*,
Da 2:33 partly of iron and partly of baked *c*.
Ro 9:21 of the same lump of *c* some pottery
2Co 4: 7 we have this treasure in jars of *c*
2Ti 2:20 and *c*; some are for noble purposes

CLEAN (CLEANNESS CLEANSE CLEANSED CLEANSES CLEANSING)
Ge 7: 2 seven of every kind of *c* animal,
Lev 4:12 the camp to a place ceremonially *c*,
16:30 you will be *c* from all your sins.
Ps 24: 4 He who has *c* hands and a pure
51: 7 with hyssop, and I will be *c*;
Pr 20: 9 I am *c* and without sin"?
Eze 36:25 I will sprinkle *c* water on you,
Mt 8: 2 are willing, you can make me *c*."
12:44 the house unoccupied, swept *c*
23:25 You *c* the outside of the cup
Mk 7:19 Jesus declared all foods "*c*.")
Jn 13:10 to wash his feet; his whole body is *c*
15: 3 are already *c* because of the word
Ac 10:15 impure that God has made *c*."
Ro 14:20 All food is *c*, but it is wrong

CLEANNESS (CLEAN)
2Sa 22:25 according to my *c* in his sight.

CLEANSE (CLEAN)
Ps 51: 2 and *c* me from my sin.
51: 7 *C* me with hyssop, and I will be
Pr 20:30 Blows and wounds *c* away evil,
Heb 9:14 *c* our consciences from acts that
10:22 having our hearts sprinkled to *c* us

CLEANSED (CLEAN)
Heb 9:22 requires that nearly everything be *c*
2Pe 1: 9 has forgotten that he has been *c*

CLEANSES* (CLEAN)
2Ti 2:21 If a man *c* himself from the latter,

CLEANSING (CLEAN)
Eph 5:26 *c* her by the washing with water

CLEFT*
Ex 33:22 I will put you in a *c* in the rock

CLEVER
Isa 5:21 and *c* in their own sight.

CLING
Ro 12: 9 Hate what is evil; *c* to what is good.

CLINGS
Ps 63: 8 My soul *c* to you;

CLOAK
Ex 12:11 with your *c* tucked into your belt,
2Ki 4:29 "Tuck your *c* into your belt,
9: 1 "Tuck your *c* into your belt,
Mt 5:40 let him have your *c* as well.

CLOSE (CLOSER CLOSES)
2Ki 11: 8 Stay *c* to the king wherever he goes
2Ch 23: 7 Stay *c* to the king wherever he goes
Ps 34:18 LORD is *c* to the brokenhearted
148: 14 of Israel, the people *c* to his heart.
Isa 40:11 and carries them *c* to his heart;
Jer 30:21 himself to be *c* to me?'

CLOSER (CLOSE)
Ex 3: 5 "Do not come any *c*," God said.
Pr 18:24 there is a friend who sticks *c*

CLOSES (CLOSE)
Pr 28:27 he who *c* his eyes to them receives

CLOTHE (CLOTHED CLOTHES CLOTHING)
Ps 45: 3 *c* yourself with splendor
Isa 52: 1 *c* yourself with strength.
Ro 13:14 *c* yourselves with the Lord Jesus
Col 3:12 *c* yourselves with compassion,
1Pe 5: 5 *c* yourselves with humility

CLOTHED (CLOTHE)
Ps 30:11 removed my sackcloth and *c* me
104: 1 you are *c* with splendor
Pr 31:22 she is *c* in fine linen and purple.
31:25 She is *c* with strength and dignity;
Isa 61:10 For he has *c* me with garments
Lk 24:49 until you have been *c* with power
Gal 3:27 into Christ have *c* yourselves

CLOTHES (CLOTHE)
Dt 8: 4 Your *c* did not wear out
Mt 6:25 the body more important than *c*?
6:28 "And why do you worry about *c*?
27:35 they divided up his *c* by casting lots
Jn 11:44 Take off the grave *c* and let him go

CLOTHING (CLOTHE)
Dt 22: 5 A woman must not wear men's *c*,
Job 29:14 I put on righteousness as my *c*;
Ps 22:18 and cast lots for my *c*.
Mt 7:15 They come to you in sheep's *c*,
1Ti 6: 8 But if we have food and *c*,

CLOUD (CLOUDS)
Ex 13:21 them in a pillar of *c* to guide them
1Ki 18:44 *c* as small as a man's hand is rising
Pr 16:15 his favor is like a rain *c* in spring.
Isa 19: 1 See, the LORD rides on a swift *c*
Lk 21:27 of Man coming in a *c* with power
Heb 12: 1 by such a great *c* of witnesses,
Rev 14:14 seated on the *c* was one "like a son

CLOUDS (CLOUD)
Dt 33:26 and on the *c* in his majesty.
Ps 68: 4 extol him who rides on the *c*—
104: 3 He makes the *c* his chariot
Pr 25:14 Like *c* and wind without rain
Da 7:13 coming with the *c* of heaven.
Mt 24:30 of Man coming on the *c* of the sky,
26:64 and coming on the *c* of heaven."
Mk 13:26 coming in *c* with great power
1Th 4:17 with them in the *c* to meet the Lord
Rev 1: 7 Look, he is coming with the *c*,

CLUB
Pr 25:18 Like a *c* or a sword or a sharp arrow

CO-HEIRS* (INHERIT)
Ro 8:17 heirs of God and *c* with Christ,

COALS
Pr 25:22 you will heap burning *c* on his head
Ro 12:20 you will heap burning *c* on his head

COARSE*
Eph 5: 4 or *c* joking, which are out of place,

CODE*
Ro 2:27 even though you have the written *c*
2:29 by the Spirit, not by the written *c*.
7: 6 not in the old way of the written *c*.
Col 2:14 having canceled the written *c*,

COINS
Mt 26:15 out for him thirty silver *c*.
Lk 15: 8 suppose a woman has ten silver *c*

COLD
Pr 25:25 Like *c* water to a weary soul
Mt 10:42 if anyone gives even a cup of *c* water
24:12 the love of most will grow *c*,

COLLECTION
1Co 16: 1 Now about the *c* for God's people:

COLT
Zec 9: 9 on a *c*, the foal of a donkey.
Mt 21: 5 on a *c*, the foal of a donkey.'"

COMB
Ps 19:10 than honey from the *c*.

COMFORT* (COMFORTED COMFORTER COMFORTERS COMFORTING COMFORTS)
Ge 5:29 "He will *c* us in the labor
37:35 and daughters came to *c* him,
Ru 2:13 "You have given me *c*
1Ch 7:22 and his relatives came to *c* him.
Job 2:11 sympathize with him and *c* him.
7:13 When I think my bed will *c* me
16: 5 *c* from my lips would bring you
36:16 to the *c* of your table laden
Ps 23: 4 rod and your staff, they *c* me.
71:21 and *c* me once again.
119: 50 My *c* in my suffering is this:
119: 52 and I find *c* in them.
119: 76 May your unfailing love be my *c*,
119: 82 I say, "When will you *c* me?"
Isa 40: 1 *C*, *c* my people,
51: 3 The LORD will surely *c* Zion
51:19 who can *c* you?—
57:18 I will guide him and restore *c*
61: 2 to *c* all who mourn,
66:13 so will I *c* you;
Jer 16: 7 food to *c* those who mourn
31:13 I will give them *c* and joy instead
La 1: 2 there is none to *c* her.
1: 9 there was none to *c* her.
1:16 No one is near to *c* me,
1:17 but there is no one to *c* her.
1:21 but there is no one to *c* me.
2:13 that I may *c* you,
Eze 16:54 all you have done in giving them *c*.
Na 3: 7 Where can I find anyone to *c* you?"
Zec 1:17 and the LORD will again *c* Zion
10: 2 they give *c* in vain.
Lk 6:24 you have already received your *c*.
Jn 11:19 and Mary to *c* them in the loss
1Co 14: 3 encouragement and *c*.
2Co 1: 3 of compassion and the God of all *c*,
1: 4 so that we can *c* those

2Co 1: 4 with the *c* we ourselves have
1: 5 through Christ our *c* overflows.
1: 6 if we are comforted, it is for your *c*,
1: 6 it is for your *c* and salvation;
1: 7 so also you share in our *c*.
2: 7 you ought to forgive and *c* him,
7: 7 also by the *c* you had given him.
Php 2: 1 if any *c* from his love,
Col 4:11 and they have proved a *c* to me.

COMFORTED* (COMFORT)
Ge 24:67 Isaac was *c* after his mother's death
37:35 comfort him, but he refused to be *c*.
2Sa 12:24 Then David *c* his wife Bathsheba,
Job 42:11 They *c* and consoled him
Ps 77: 2 and my soul refused to be *c*.
86:17 have helped me and *c* me.
Isa 12: 1 and you have *c* me.
52: 9 for the LORD has *c* his people,
54:11 lashed by storms and not *c*,
66:13 and you will be *c* over Jerusalem."
Jer 31:15 and refusing to be *c*,
Mt 2:18 and refusing to be *c*,
5: 4 for they will be *c*.
Lk 16:25 but now he is *c* here and you are
Ac 20:12 man home alive and were greatly *c*.
2Co 1: 6 if we are *c*, it is for your comfort,
7: 6 *c* us by the coming of Titus,

COMFORTER* (COMFORT)
Ecc 4: 1 and they have no *c*;
4: 1 and they have no *c*.
Jer 8:18 O my *C* in sorrow,

COMFORTERS* (COMFORT)
Job 16: 2 miserable *c* are you all!
Ps 69:20 for *c*, but I found none.

COMFORTING* (COMFORT)
Isa 66:11 satisfied at her *c* breasts;
Zec 1:13 *c* words to the angel who talked
Jn 11:31 *c* her, noticed how quickly she got
1Th 2:12 *c* and urging you to live lives

COMFORTS* (COMFORT)
Job 29:25 I was like one who *c* mourners.
Isa 49:13 For the LORD *c* his people
51:12 "I, even I, am he who *c* you.
66:13 As a mother *c* her child,
2Co 1: 4 who *c* us in all our troubles,
7: 6 But God, who *c* the downcast,

COMMAND (COMMANDED COMMANDING COMMANDMENT COMMANDMENTS COMMANDS)
Ex 7: 2 You are to say everything I *c* you,
Nu 14:41 are you disobeying the LORD's *c*?
24:13 to go beyond the *c* of the LORD—
Dt 4: 2 Do not add to what I *c* you
8: 1 to follow every *c* I am giving you
12:32 See that you do all I *c* you;
15:11 I *c* you to be openhanded
30:16 For I *c* you today to love
32:46 so that you may *c* your children
Ps 91:11 For he will *c* his angels concerning
Pr 13:13 but he who respects a *c* is rewarded
Ecc 8: 2 Obey the king's *c*, I say,
Jer 1: 7 you to and say whatever I *c* you.
1:17 and say to them whatever I *c* you.
7:23 Walk in all the ways I *c* you,
11: 4 Obey me and do everything I *c* you
26: 2 Tell them everything I *c* you;
Joel 2:11 mighty are those who obey his *c*.
Mt 4: 6 He will *c* his angels concerning you
15: 3 why do you break the *c* of God
Lk 4:10 " 'He will *c* his angels concerning
Jn 14:15 love me, you will obey what I *c*.
15:12 My *c* is this: Love each other
15:14 friends if you do what I *c*.
15:17 This is my *c*: Love each other.
1Co 14:37 writing to you is the Lord's *c*.
Gal 5:14 law is summed up in a single *c*:
1Ti 1: 5 goal of this *c* is love, which comes
6:14 to you keep this *c* without spot
6:17 *C* those who are rich
Heb 11: 3 universe was formed at God's *c*,
2Pe 2:21 on the sacred *c* that was passed
3: 2 and the *c* given by our Lord
1Jn 2: 7 I am not writing you a new *c*
3:23 this is his *c*: to believe in the name
4:21 And he has given us this *c*:
2Jn : 6 his *c* is that you walk in love.

COMMANDED (COMMAND)
Ge 2:16 And the LORD God *c* the man,
7: 5 Noah did all that the LORD *c* him.
50:12 Jacob's sons did as he had *c* them:
Ex 7: 6 did just as the LORD *c* them.
19: 7 all the words the LORD had *c* him
Dt 4: 5 laws as the LORD my God *c* me,
6:24 The LORD *c* us to obey all these
Jos 1: 9 Have I not *c* you? Be strong
1:16 Whatever you have *c* us we will do,
2Sa 5:25 So David did as the LORD *c* him,
2Ki 17:13 the entire Law that I *c* your fathers
21: 8 careful to do everything I *c* them
2Ch 33: 8 do everything I *c* them concerning
Ps 33: 9 he *c*, and it stood firm.
78: 5 which he *c* our forefathers
148: 5 for he *c* and they were created.
Mt 28:20 to obey everything I have *c* you.
1Co 9:14 Lord has *c* that those who preach
1Jn 3:23 and to love one another as he *c* us.
2Jn : 4 in the truth, just as the Father *c* us.

COMMANDING (COMMAND)
2Ti 2: 4 he wants to please his *c* officer.

COMMANDMENT* (COMMAND)
Jos 22: 5 But be very careful to keep the *c*
Mt 22:36 which is the greatest *c* in the Law?"
22:38 This is the first and greatest *c*.
Mk 12:31 There is no *c* greater than these."
Lk 23:56 the Sabbath in obedience to the *c*.
Jn 13:34 "A new *c* I give you: Love one
Ro 7: 8 the opportunity afforded by the *c*,
7: 9 when the *c* came, sin sprang to life
7:10 that the very *c* that was intended
7:11 and through the *c* put me to death.
7:11 the opportunity afforded by the *c*,
7:12 and the *c* is holy, righteous
7:13 through the *c* sin might become
13: 9 and whatever other *c* there may be,
Eph 6: 2 which is the first *c* with a promise
Heb 9:19 Moses had proclaimed every *c*

COMMANDMENTS* (COMMAND)
Ex 20: 6 who love me and keep my *c*.
34:28 of the covenant—the Ten *C*.
Dt 4:13 to you his covenant, the Ten *C*,
5:10 who love me and keep my *c*.
5:22 These are the *c* the LORD
6: 6 These *c* that I give you today are
9:10 were all the *c* the LORD
10: 4 The Ten *C* he had proclaimed
Ecc 12:13 Fear God and keep his *c*,
Mt 5:19 one of the least of these *c*
19:17 If you want to enter life, obey the *c*."
22:40 the Prophets hang on these two *c*."
Mk 10:19 You know the *c*: 'Do not murder,
12:28 "Of all the *c*, which is the most
Lk 1: 6 observing all the Lord's *c*
18:20 You know the *c*: 'Do not commit
Ro 13: 9 The *c*, "Do not commit adultery,"
Eph 2:15 in his flesh the law with its *c*
Rev 12:17 those who obey God's *c*
14:12 part of the saints who obey God's *c*

COMMANDS (COMMAND)
Ex 24:12 and *c* I have written for their
25:22 give you all my *c* for the Israelites.
34:32 gave them all the *c* the LORD had
Lev 22:31 "Keep my *c* and follow them.
Nu 15:39 and so you will remember all the *c*
Dt 7: 9 those who love him and keep his *c*.
7:11 Therefore, take care to follow the *c*
11: 1 decrees, his laws and his *c* always.
11:27 the blessing if you obey the *c*
28: 1 carefully follow all his *c* I give you
30:10 LORD your God and keep his *c*
Jos 22: 5 to walk in all his ways, to obey his *c*
1Ki 2: 3 and keep his decrees and *c*,
8:58 in all his ways and to keep the *c*,
8:61 to live by his decrees and obey his *c*
1Ch 28: 7 unswerving in carrying out my *c*
29:19 devotion to keep your *c*,
2Ch 31:21 in obedience to the law and the *c*,
Ne 1: 5 those who love him and obey his *c*,
Ps 78: 7 but would keep his *c*.
112: 1 who finds great delight in his *c*.
119: 10 do not let me stray from your *c*.
119: 32 I run in the path of your *c*,
119: 35 Direct me in the path of your *c*,
119: 47 for I delight in your *c*
119: 48 I lift up my hands to your *c*,
119: 73 me understanding to learn your *c*.
119: 86 All your *c* are trustworthy;
119: 96 but your *c* are boundless.
119: 98 Your *c* make me wiser
119:115 that I may keep the *c* of my God!
119:127 Because I love your *c*
119:131 longing for your *c*.
119:143 but your *c* are my delight.
119:151 and all your *c* are true.
119:172 for all your *c* are righteous.
119:176 for I have not forgotten your *c*.
Pr 2: 1 and store up my *c* within you,
3: 1 but keep my *c* in your heart,
6:23 For these *c* are a lamp,
10: 8 The wise in heart accept *c*,
Isa 48:18 you had paid attention to my *c*,
Da 9: 4 all who love him and obey his *c*,
Mt 5:19 teaches these *c* will be called great
Mk 7: 8 You have let go of the *c* of God
7: 9 way of setting aside the *c* of God
Jn 14:21 Whoever has my *c* and obeys them,
15:10 If you obey my *c*, you will remain
Ac 17:30 but now he *c* all people everywhere
1Co 7:19 Keeping God's *c* is what counts.
1Jn 2: 3 come to know him if we obey his *c*.
2: 4 but does not do what he *c* is a liar,
3:22 we obey his *c* and do what pleases
3:24 Those who obey his *c* live in him,
5: 2 loving God and carrying out his *c*.
5: 3 And his *c* are not burdensome,
5: 3 This is love for God: to obey his *c*.
2Jn : 6 that we walk in obedience to his *c*.

COMMEMORATE
Ex 12:14 "This is a day you are to *c*;

COMMEND* (COMMENDABLE COMMENDED COMMENDS)
Ps 145: 4 One generation will *c* your works
Ecc 8:15 So I *c* the enjoyment of life,
Ro 13: 3 do what is right and he will *c* you.
16: 1 I *c* to you our sister Phoebe,
2Co 3: 1 beginning to *c* ourselves again?
4: 2 the truth plainly we *c* ourselves
5:12 trying to *c* ourselves to you again,
6: 4 as servants of God we *c* ourselves
10:12 with some who *c* themselves.
1Pe 2:14 and to *c* those who do right.

COMMENDABLE* (COMMEND)
1Pe 2:19 For it is *c* if a man bears up
2:20 you endure it, this is *c* before God.

COMMENDED* (COMMEND)
Ne 11: 2 The people *c* all the men who
Job 29:11 and those who saw me *c* me,
Lk 16: 8 master *c* the dishonest manager
Ac 15:40 *c* by the brothers to the grace
2Co 12:11 I ought to have been *c* by you,
Heb 11: 2 This is what the ancients were *c* for
11: 4 By faith he was *c* as a righteous
11: 5 he was *c* as one who pleased God.
11:39 These were all *c* for their faith,

COMMENDS* (COMMEND)
Pr 15: 2 of the wise *c* knowledge,
2Co 10:18 but the one whom the Lord *c*.
10:18 not the one who *c* himself who is

COMMIT (COMMITS COMMITTED)
Ex 20:14 "You shall not *c* adultery.
Dt 5:18 "You shall not *c* adultery.
1Sa 7: 3 and *c* yourselves to the LORD
Ps 31: 5 Into your hands I *c* my spirit;
37: 5 *C* your way to the LORD;
Pr 16: 3 *C* to the LORD whatever you do,
Mt 5:27 that it was said, 'Do not *c* adultery.'
5:32 causes her to *c* adultery,
19:18 do not *c* adultery, do not steal,
Mk 10:19 do not *c* adultery, do not steal,
Lk 18:20 'Do not *c* adultery, do not murder,
23:46 into your hands I *c* my spirit."
Ac 20:32 I *c* you to God and to the word
Ro 2:22 do you *c* adultery? You who abhor
2:22 that people should not *c* adultery,
13: 9 "Do not *c* adultery,"
1Co 10: 8 We should not *c* sexual immorality,
Jas 2:11 do not *c* adultery but do *c* murder,
1Pe 4:19 to God's will should *c* themselves
Rev 2:22 I will make those who *c* adultery

COMMITS (COMMIT)
Pr 6:32 man who *c* adultery lacks
29:22 a hot-tempered one *c* many sins.
Ecc 8:12 a wicked man *c* a hundred crimes
Eze 18:12 He *c* robbery.
18:14 who sees all the sins his father *c*,
18:24 from his righteousness and *c* sin
18:26 from his righteousness and *c* sin,
22:11 you one man *c* a detestable offense
Mt 5:32 the divorced woman *c* adultery.
19: 9 marries another woman *c* adultery
Mk 10:11 marries another woman *c* adultery
10:12 another man, she *c* adultery."
Lk 16:18 a divorced woman *c* adultery.
16:18 marries another woman *c* adultery,

COMMITTED (COMMIT)
Nu 5: 7 and must confess the sin he has *c*.
1Ki 8:61 But your hearts must be fully *c*
15:14 Asa's heart was fully *c*
2Ch 16: 9 those whose hearts are fully *c*
Mt 5:28 lustfully has already *c* adultery
11:27 "All things have been *c* to me

Lk 10:22 "All things have been *c* to me
Ac 14:23 *c* them to the Lord,
14:26 where they had been *c* to the grace
1Co 9:17 I am simply discharging the trust *c*
2Co 5:19 And he has *c* to us the message
1Pe 2:22 "He *c* no sin,
Rev 17: 2 the kings of the earth *c* adultery
18: 3 of the earth *c* adultery with her,
18: 9 kings of the earth who *c* adultery

COMMON
Ge 11: 1 had one language and a *c* speech.
Lev 10:10 between the holy and the *c*,
Pr 22: 2 Rich and poor have this in *c*:
29:13 the oppressor have this in *c*:
Ac 2:44 together and had everything in *c*.
1Co 10:13 has seized you except what is *c*
2Co 6:14 and wickedness have in *c*?

COMPANION (COMPANIONS)
Ps 55:13 my *c*, my close friend,
55:20 My *c* attacks his friends;
Pr 13:20 but a *c* of fools suffers harm.
28: 7 a *c* of gluttons disgraces his father.
29: 3 *c* of prostitutes squanders his
Rev 1: 9 your brother and *c* in the suffering

COMPANIONS (COMPANION)
Ps 45: 7 your God, has set you above your *c*
Pr 18:24 A man of many *c* may come to ruin
Heb 1: 9 your God, has set you above your *c*

COMPANY
Ps 14: 5 present in the *c* of the righteous.
Pr 21:16 comes to rest in the *c* of the dead.
24: 1 do not desire their *c*;
Jer 15:17 I never sat in the *c* of revelers,
1Co 15:33 "Bad *c* corrupts good character."

COMPARE* (COMPARED COMPARING COMPARISON)
Job 28:17 Neither gold nor crystal can *c*
28:19 The topaz of Cush cannot *c* with it;
39:13 but they cannot *c* with the pinions
Ps 86: 8 no deeds can *c* with yours.
89: 6 skies above can *c* with the LORD?
Pr 3:15 nothing you desire can *c* with her.
8:11 nothing you desire can *c* with her.
Isa 40:18 To whom, then, will you *c* God?
40:18 What image will you *c* him to?
40:25 "To whom will you *c* me?
46: 5 "To whom will you *c* me
La 2:13 With what can I *c* you,
Eze 31: 8 *c* with its branches—
Da 1:13 Then *c* our appearance with that
Mt 11:16 "To what can I *c* this generation?
Lk 7:31 I *c* the people of this generation?
13:18 What shall I *c* it to? It is like
13:20 What shall I *c* the kingdom of God
2Co 10:12 and *c* themselves with themselves,
10:12 or *c* ourselves with some who

COMPARED* (COMPARE)
Jdg 8: 2 What have I accomplished *c* to you
8: 3 What was I able to do *c* to you?"
Isa 46: 5 you liken me that we may be *c*?
Eze 31: 2 Who can be *c* with you in majesty?
31:18 the trees of Eden can be *c* with you
Php 3: 8 I consider everything a loss *c*

COMPARING* (COMPARE)
Ro 8:18 present sufferings are not worth *c*
2Co 8: 8 the sincerity of your love by *c* it
Gal 6: 4 without *c* himself to somebody else

COMPARISON* (COMPARE)
2Co 3:10 now in *c* with the surpassing glory.

COMPASSION* (COMPASSIONATE COMPASSIONS)
Ex 33:19 I will have *c* on whom I will have *c*.
Dt 13:17 he will show you mercy, have *c*
28:54 man among you will have no *c*
30: 3 restore your fortunes and have *c*
32:36 and have *c* on his servants
Jdg 2:18 for the LORD had *c* on them
1Ki 3:26 son was alive was filled with *c*
2Ki 13:23 and had *c* and showed concern
2Ch 30: 9 and your children will be shown *c*
Ne 9:19 of your great *c* you did not
9:27 and in your great *c* you gave them
9:28 in your *c* you delivered them time
Ps 51: 1 according to your great *c*
77: 9 Has he in anger withheld his *c*?"
90:13 Have *c* on your servants.
102: 13 You will arise and have *c* on Zion,
103: 4 and crowns you with love and *c*.
103: 13 As a father has *c* on his children,
103: 13 so the LORD has *c*
116: 5 our God is full of *c*.
Ps 119: 77 Let your *c* come to me that I may
119: 156 Your *c* is great, O LORD;
135: 14 and have *c* on his servants.
145: 9 he has *c* on all he has made.
Isa 13:18 will they look with *c* on children.
14: 1 The LORD will have *c* on Jacob;
27:11 so their Maker has no *c* on them,
30:18 he rises to show you *c*.
49:10 He who has *c* on them will guide
49:13 and will have *c* on his afflicted ones
49:15 and have no *c* on the child she has
51: 3 and will look with *c* on all her ruins
54: 7 with deep *c* I will bring you back.
54: 8 I will have *c* on you,"
54:10 says the LORD, who has *c* on you.
60:10 in favor I will show you *c*.
63: 7 to his *c* and many kindnesses.
63:15 and *c* are withheld from us.
Jer 12:15 I will again have *c* and will bring
13:14 *c* to keep me from destroying them
15: 6 I can no longer show *c*.
21: 7 show them no mercy or pity or *c*.'
30:18 and have *c* on his dwellings;
31:20 I have great *c* for him,"
33:26 restore their fortunes and have *c*
42:12 I will show you *c* so that he will
42:12 so that he will have *c* on you
La 3:32 he brings grief, he will show *c*,
Eze 9: 5 without showing pity or *c*.
16: 5 or had *c* enough to do any
39:25 and will have *c* on all the people
Hos 2:19 in love and *c*.
11: 8 all my *c* is aroused.
13:14 "I will have no *c*,
14: 3 for in you the fatherless find *c*."
Am 1:11 stifling all *c*,
Jnh 3: 9 with *c* turn from his fierce anger
3:10 he had *c* and did not bring
Mic 7:19 You will again have *c* on us;
Zec 7: 9 show mercy and *c* to one another.
10: 6 because I have *c* on them.
Mal 3:17 as in *c* a man spares his son who
Mt 9:36 When he saw the crowds, he had *c*
14:14 he had *c* on them and healed their
15:32 "I have *c* for these people;
20:34 Jesus had *c* on them and touched
Mk 1:41 with *c*, Jesus reached out his hand
6:34 and saw a large crowd, he had *c*
8: 2 "I have *c* for these people;
Lk 15:20 and was filled with *c* for him;
Ro 9:15 and I will have *c* on whom I have *c*
2Co 1: 3 the Father of *c* and the God
Php 2: 1 and *c*, then make my joy complete
Col 3:12 clothe yourselves with *c*, kindness,
Jas 5:11 The Lord is full of *c* and mercy.

COMPASSIONATE* (COMPASSION)
Ex 22:27 out to me, I will hear, for I am *c*.
34: 6 the LORD, the *c* and gracious God
2Ch 30: 9 LORD your God is gracious and *c*.
Ne 9:17 gracious and *c*, slow to anger
Ps 86:15 O Lord, are a *c* and gracious God,
103: 8 The LORD is *c* and gracious,
111: 4 the LORD is gracious and *c*.
112: 4 the gracious and *c* and righteous
145: 8 The LORD is gracious and *c*,
La 4:10 With their own hands *c* women
Joel 2:13 for he is gracious and *c*,
Jnh 4: 2 that you are a gracious and *c* God,
Eph 4:32 Be kind and *c* to one another,
1Pe 3: 8 love as brothers, be *c* and humble.

COMPASSIONS* (COMPASSION)
La 3:22 for his *c* never fail.

COMPELLED (COMPULSION)
Ac 20:22 "And now, *c* by the Spirit,
1Co 9:16 I cannot boast, for I am *c* to preach.

COMPELS (COMPULSION)
Job 32:18 and the spirit within me *c* me;
2Co 5:14 For Christ's love *c* us, because we

COMPETENCE* (COMPETENT)
2Co 3: 5 but our *c* comes from God.

COMPETENT* (COMPETENCE)
Ro 15:14 and *c* to instruct one another.
1Co 6: 2 are you not *c* to judge trivial cases?
2Co 3: 5 Not that we are *c* in ourselves to claim
3: 6 He has made us *c* as ministers

COMPETES*
1Co 9:25 Everyone who *c* in the games goes
2Ti 2: 5 Similarly, if anyone *c* as an athlete,
2: 5 unless he *c* according to the rules.

COMPLACENCY* (COMPLACENT)
Pr 1:32 and the *c* of fools will destroy them
Eze 30: 9 ships to frighten Cush out of her *c*.

COMPLACENT* (COMPLACENCY)
Isa 32: 9 You women who are so *c*,
32:11 Tremble, you *c* women;
Am 6: 1 Woe to you who are *c* in Zion,
Zep 1:12 and punish those who are *c*,

COMPLAINING*
Php 2:14 Do everything without *c* or arguing

COMPLETE
Dt 16:15 your hands, and your joy will be *c*.
Jn 3:29 That joy is mine, and it is now *c*.
15:11 and that your joy may be *c*.
16:24 will receive, and your joy will be *c*.
17:23 May they be brought to *c* unity
Ac 20:24 *c* the task the Lord Jesus has given
Php 2: 2 then make my joy *c*
Col 4:17 to it that you *c* the work you have
Jas 1: 4 so that you may be mature and *c*,
2:22 his faith was made *c* by what he did
1Jn 1: 4 We write this to make our joy *c*.
2: 5 God's love is truly made *c* in him.
4:12 and his love is made *c* in us.
4:17 love is made *c* among us
2Jn :12 to face, so that our joy may be *c*.

COMPLIMENTS*
Pr 23: 8 and will have wasted your *c*.

COMPREHEND* (COMPREHENDED)
Job 28:13 Man does not *c* its worth;
Ecc 8:17 No one can *c* what goes
8:17 he knows, he cannot really *c* it.

COMPREHENDED* (COMPREHEND)
Job 38:18 Have you *c* the vast expanses

COMPULSION (COMPELLED COMPELS)
2Co 9: 7 not reluctantly or under *c*,

CONCEAL (CONCEALED CONCEALS)
Ps 40:10 I do not *c* your love and your truth
Pr 25: 2 It is the glory of God to *c* a matter;

CONCEALED (CONCEAL)
Jer 16:17 nor is their sin *c* from my eyes.
Mt 10:26 There is nothing *c* that will not be
Mk 4:22 and whatever is *c* is meant
Lk 8:17 nothing *c* that will not be known
12: 2 There is nothing *c* that will not be

CONCEALS* (CONCEAL)
Pr 10:18 He who *c* his hatred has lying lips,
28:13 He who *c* his sins does not prosper,

CONCEIT* (CONCEITED CONCEITS)
Isa 16: 6 her overweening pride and *c*,
Jer 48:29 her overweening pride and *c*,
Php 2: 3 out of selfish ambition or vain *c*,

CONCEITED* (CONCEIT)
1Sa 17:28 I know how *c* you are and how
Ro 11:25 brothers, so that you may not be *c*:
12:16 Do not be *c*.
2Co 12: 7 To keep me from becoming *c*
Gal 5:26 Let us not become *c*, provoking
1Ti 3: 6 or he may become *c* and fall
6: 4 he is *c* and understands nothing.
2Ti 3: 4 of the good, treacherous, rash, *c*,

CONCEITS* (CONCEIT)
Ps 73: 7 evil *c* of their minds know no

CONCEIVED (CONCEIVES)
Ps 51: 5 from the time my mother *c* me.
Mt 1:20 what is *c* in her is from the Holy
1Co 2: 9 no mind has *c*
Jas 1:15 after desire has *c*, it gives birth

CONCEIVES* (CONCEIVED)
Ps 7:14 *c* trouble gives birth

CONCERN* (CONCERNED)
Ge 39: 6 he did not *c* himself with anything
39: 8 "my master does not *c* himself
1Sa 23:21 "The LORD bless you for your *c*
2Ki 13:23 and had compassion and showed *c*
Job 9:21 I have no *c* for myself;
19: 4 my error remains my *c* alone.
Ps 131: 1 I do not *c* myself with great matters
Pr 29: 7 but the wicked have no such *c*.
Eze 36:21 I had *c* for my holy name, which
Ac 15:14 God at first showed his *c* by taking
18:17 But Gallio showed no *c* whatever.
1Co 7:32 I would like you to be free from *c*.
12:25 that its parts should have equal *c*
2Co 7: 7 your deep sorrow, your ardent *c*
7:11 what alarm, what longing, what *c*,
8:16 of Titus the same *c* I have for you.
11:28 of my *c* for all the churches.
Php 4:10 at last you have renewed your *c*

CONCERNED (CONCERN)
Ex 2:25 Israelites and was *c* about them.
Ps 142: 4 no one is *c* for me.
Jnh 4:10 "You have been *c* about this vine,
4:11 Should I not be *c* about that great
1Co 7:32 An unmarried man is *c* about
9: 9 Is it about oxen that God is *c?*
Php 4:10 you have been *c,* but you had no

CONCESSION*
1Co 7: 6 I say this as a *c,* not as a command.

CONDEMN* (CONDEMNATION CONDEMNED CONDEMNING CONDEMNS)
Job 9:20 innocent, my mouth would *c* me;
10: 2 I will say to God: Do not *c* me,
34:17 Will you *c* the just and mighty One
34:29 if he remains silent, who can *c* him?
40: 8 Would you *c* me to justify yourself?
Ps 94:21 and *c* the innocent to death.
109: 7 and may his prayers *c* him.
109: 31 from those who *c* him.
Isa 50: 9 Who is he that will *c* me?
Mt 12:41 with this generation and *c* it;
12:42 with this generation and *c* it;
20:18 They will *c* him to death
Mk 10:33 They will *c* him to death
Lk 6:37 Do not *c,* and you will not be
11:31 men of this generation and *c* them;
11:32 with this generation and *c* it;
Jn 3:17 Son into the world to *c* the world,
7:51 "Does our law *c* anyone
8:11 "Then neither do I *c* you,"
12:48 very word which I spoke will *c* him
Ro 2:27 yet obeys the law will *c* you who,
14: 3 everything must not *c* the man who
14:22 is the man who does not *c* himself
2Co 7: 3 this to *c* you; I have said
1Jn 3:20 presence whenever our hearts *c* us.
3:21 if our hearts do not *c* us,

CONDEMNATION* (CONDEMN)
Jer 42:18 of *c* and reproach; you will never
44:12 and horror, of *c* and reproach.
Ro 3: 8 may result"? Their *c* is deserved.
5:16 followed one sin and brought *c,*
5:18 of one trespass was *c* for all men,
8: 1 there is now no *c* for those who are
2Pe 2: 3 Their *c* has long been hanging
Jude : 4 certain men whose *c* was written

CONDEMNED* (CONDEMN)
Dt 13:17 of those *c* things shall be found
Job 32: 3 to refute Job, and yet had *c* him.
Ps 34:21 the foes of the righteous will be *c.*
34:22 will be *c* who takes refuge in him.
37:33 let them be *c* when brought to trial.
79:11 preserve those *c* to die.
102: 20 and release those *c* to death."
Mt 12: 7 you would not have *c* the innocent.
12:37 and by your words you will be *c."*
23:33 How will you escape being *c* to hell
27: 3 betrayed him, saw that Jesus was *c,*
Mk 14:64 They all *c* him as worthy of death.
16:16 whoever does not believe will be *c.*
Lk 6:37 condemn, and you will not be *c.*
Jn 3:18 Whoever believes in him is not *c,*
3:18 does not believe stands *c* already
5:24 has eternal life and will not be *c;*
5:29 who have done evil will rise to be *c.*
8:10 Has no one *c* you?" "No one, sir,"
16:11 prince of this world now stands *c.*
Ac 25:15 against him and asked that he be *c.*
Ro 3: 7 why am I still *c* as a sinner?"
8: 3 And so he *c* sin in sinful man,
14:23 But the man who has doubts is *c*
1Co 4: 9 like men *c* to die in the arena.
11:32 disciplined so that we will not be *c*
Gal 1: 8 let him be eternally *c!* As we have
1: 9 let him be eternally *c!* Am I now
2Th 2:12 that all will be *c* who have not
Tit 2: 8 of speech that cannot be *c,*
Heb 11: 7 By his faith he *c* the world
Jas 5: 6 You have *c* and murdered innocent
5:12 and your "No," no, or you will be *c*
2Pe 2: 6 if he *c* the cities of Sodom
Rev 19: 2 He has *c* the great prostitute

CONDEMNING* (CONDEMN)
Dt 25: 1 the innocent and *c* the guilty.
1Ki 8:32 *c* the guilty and bringing
Pr 17:15 the guilty and *c* the innocent—
Ac 13:27 yet in *c* him they fulfilled the words
Ro 2: 1 judge the other, you are *c* yourself,

CONDEMNS* (CONDEMN)
Job 15: 6 Your own mouth *c* you, not mine;
Pr 12: 2 but the LORD *c* a crafty man.
Ro 8:34 Who is he that *c?* Christ Jesus,

2Co 3: 9 the ministry that *c* men is glorious,

CONDITION
Pr 27:23 Be sure you know the *c*

CONDUCT (CONDUCTED CONDUCTS)
Pr 10:23 A fool finds pleasure in evil *c,*
20:11 by whether his *c* is pure and right.
21: 8 but the *c* of the innocent is upright.
Ecc 6: 8 how to *c* himself before others?
Jer 4:18 "Your own *c* and actions
17:10 to reward a man according to his *c,*
Eze 7: 3 I will judge you according to your *c*
Php 1:27 *c* yourselves in a manner worthy
1Ti 3:15 to *c* themselves in God's household

CONDUCTED* (CONDUCT)
2Co 1:12 testifies that we have *c* ourselves

CONDUCTS* (CONDUCT)
Ps 112: 5 who *c* his affairs with justice.

CONFESS* (CONFESSED CONFESSES CONFESSING CONFESSION)
Lev 5: 5 he must *c* in what way he has
16:21 and *c* over it all the wickedness
26:40 " 'But if they will *c* their sins
Nu 5: 7 must *c* the sin he has committed.
1Ki 8:33 back to you and *c* your name,
8:35 toward this place and *c* your name
2Ch 6:24 they turn back and *c* your name,
6:26 toward this place and *c* your name
Ne 1: 6 I *c* the sins we Israelites, including
Ps 32: 5 I said, "I will *c*
38:18 I *c* my iniquity;
Jn 1:20 fail to *c,* but confessed freely,
12:42 they would not *c* their faith
Ro 10: 9 That if you *c* with your mouth,
10:10 it is with your mouth that you *c*
14:11 every tongue will *c* to God.' "
Php 2:11 every tongue *c* that Jesus Christ is
Heb 3: 1 and high priest whom we *c.*
13:15 the fruit of lips that *c* his name.
Jas 5:16 Therefore *c* your sins to each other
1Jn 1: 9 If we *c* our sins, he is faithful

CONFESSED* (CONFESS)
1Sa 7: 6 day they fasted and there they *c,*
Ne 9: 2 in their places and *c* their sins
Da 9: 4 to the LORD my God and *c:*
Jn 1:20 but *c* freely, "I am not the Christ."
Ac 19:18 and openly *c* their evil deeds.

CONFESSES* (CONFESS)
Pr 28:13 whoever *c* and renounces them
2Ti 2:19 and, "Everyone who *c* the name

CONFESSING* (CONFESS)
Ezr 10: 1 While Ezra was praying and *c,*
Da 9:20 *c* my sin and the sin
Mt 3: 6 *C* their sins, they were baptized
Mk 1: 5 *C* their sins, they were baptized

CONFESSION* (CONFESS)
Ezr 10:11 Now make *c* to the LORD,
Ne 9: 3 and spent another quarter in *c*
2Co 9:13 obedience that accompanies your *c*
1Ti 6:12 called when you made your good *c*
6:13 Pontius Pilate made the good *c,*

CONFIDENCE* (CONFIDENT)
Jdg 9:26 and its citizens put their *c* in him.
2Ki 18:19 On what are you basing this *c*
2Ch 32: 8 And the people gained *c*
32:10 On what are you basing your *c,*
Job 4: 6 Should not your piety be your *c*
Ps 71: 5 my *c* since my youth.
Pr 3:26 for the LORD will be your *c*
3:32 but takes the upright into his *c.*
11:13 A gossip betrays a *c,*
20:19 A gossip betrays a *c;*
25: 9 do not betray another man's *c,*
31:11 Her husband has full *c* in her
Isa 32:17 will be quietness and *c* forever.
36: 4 On what are you basing this *c*
Jer 17: 7 whose *c* is in him.
49:31 which lives in *c,"*
Eze 29:16 a source of *c* for the people of Israel
Mic 7: 5 put no *c* in a friend.
2Co 2: 3 I had *c* in all of you, that you would
3: 4 Such *c* as this is ours
7: 4 I have great *c* in you; I take great
7:16 I am glad I can have complete *c*
8:22 so because of his great *c* in you.
Eph 3:12 God with freedom and *c.*
Php 3: 3 and who put no *c* in the flesh—
3: 4 I myself have reasons for such *c.*
3: 4 reasons to put *c* in the flesh,
2Th 3: 4 We have *c* in the Lord that you are
Heb 3:14 till the end the *c* we had at first.

Heb 4:16 the throne of grace with *c,*
10:19 since we have *c* to enter the Most
10:35 So do not throw away your *c;*
13: 6 So we say with *c,*
1Jn 3:21 we have *c* before God and receive
4:17 us so that we will have *c* on the day
5:14 This is the *c* we have

CONFIDENT* (CONFIDENCE)
Job 6:20 because they had been *c;*
Ps 27: 3 even then will I be *c.*
27:13 I am still *c* of this:
Lk 18: 9 To some who were *c*
2Co 1:15 Because I was *c* of this, I planned
5: 6 Therefore we are always *c*
5: 8 We are *c,* I say, and would prefer
9: 4 ashamed of having been so *c.*
10: 7 If anyone is *c* that he belongs
Gal 5:10 I am *c* in the Lord that you will
Php 1: 6 day until now, being *c* of this,
2:24 I am *c* in the Lord that I myself will
Phm :21 *C* of your obedience, I write to you,
Heb 6: 9 we are *c* of better things
1Jn 2:28 that when he appears we may be *c*

CONFIDES*
Ps 25:14 The LORD *c* in those who fear him

CONFORM* (CONFORMED CONFORMITY CONFORMS)
Ro 12: 2 Do not *c* any longer to the pattern
1Pe 1:14 do not *c* to the evil desires you had

CONFORMED* (CONFORM)
Eze 5: 7 *c* to the standards of the nations
11:12 but have *c* to the standards
Ro 8:29 predestined to be *c* to the likeness

CONFORMITY* (CONFORM)
Eph 1:11 in *c* with the purpose of his will,

CONFORMS* (CONFORM)
1Ti 1:11 to the sound doctrine that *c*

CONQUEROR* (CONQUERORS)
Mic 1:15 I will bring a *c* against you
Rev 6: 2 he rode out as a *c* bent on conquest.

CONQUERORS (CONQUEROR)
Ro 8:37 than *c* through him who loved us.

CONSCIENCE* (CONSCIENCE-STRICKEN CONSCIENCES CONSCIENTIOUS)
Ge 20: 5 I have done this with a clear *c*
20: 6 I know you did this with a clear *c,*
1Sa 25:31 have on his *c* the staggering burden
Job 27: 6 my *c* will not reproach me as long
Ac 23: 1 to God in all good *c* to this day."
24:16 to keep my *c* clear before God
Ro 9: 1 my *c* confirms it in the Holy Spirit
13: 5 punishment but also because of *c.*
1Co 4: 4 My *c* is clear, but that does not
8: 7 since their *c* is weak, it is defiled.
8:10 with a weak *c* sees you who have
8:12 in this way and wound their weak *c*
10:25 without raising questions of *c,*
10:27 you without raising questions of *c.*
10:28 man who told you and for *c'* sake—
10:29 freedom be judged by another's *c?*
10:29 the other man's *c,* I mean,
2Co 1:12 Our *c* testifies that we have
4: 2 to every man's *c* in the sight of God
5:11 and I hope it is also plain to your *c.*
1Ti 1: 5 and a good *c* and a sincere faith.
1:19 holding on to faith and a good *c.*
3: 9 truths of the faith with a clear *c.*
2Ti 1: 3 as my forefathers did, with a clear *c*
Heb 9: 9 able to clear the *c* of the worshiper.
10:22 to cleanse us from a guilty *c*
13:18 We are sure that we have a clear *c*
1Pe 3:16 and respect, keeping a clear *c,*
3:21 the pledge of a good *c* toward God.

CONSCIENCE-STRICKEN* (CONSCIENCE)
1Sa 24: 5 David was *c* for having cut
2Sa 24:10 David was *c* after he had counted

CONSCIENCES* (CONSCIENCE)
Ro 2:15 their *c* also bearing witness,
1Ti 4: 2 whose *c* have been seared
Tit 1:15 their minds and *c* are corrupted.
Heb 9:14 cleanse our *c* from acts that lead

CONSCIENTIOUS* (CONSCIENCE)
2Ch 29:34 for the Levites had been more *c*

CONSCIOUS*
Ro 3:20 through the law we become *c* of sin
1Pe 2:19 of unjust suffering because he is *c*

CONSECRATE (CONSECRATED)
Ex 13: 2 "*C* to me every firstborn male.
40: 9 *c* it and all its furnishings,
Lev 20: 7 " '*C* yourselves and be holy,
25:10 *C* the fiftieth year and proclaim
1Ch 15:12 fellow Levites are to *c* yourselves

CONSECRATED (CONSECRATE)
Ex 29:43 and the place will be *c* by my glory.
Lev 8:30 So he *c* Aaron and his garments
2Ch 7:16 *c* this temple so that my Name may
Lk 2:23 is to be *c* to the Lord"),
1Ti 4: 5 because it is *c* by the word of God

CONSENT
1Co 7: 5 except by mutual *c* and for a time,

CONSIDER (CONSIDERATE CONSIDERED CONSIDERS)
1Sa 12:24 *c* what great things he has done
16: 7 "Do not *c* his appearance
2Ch 19: 6 "*C* carefully what you do,
Job 37:14 stop and *c* God's wonders.
Ps 8: 3 When I *c* your heavens,
77:12 and *c* all your mighty deeds.
107: 43 and *c* the great love of the LORD.
143: 5 and *c* what your hands have done.
Pr 6: 6 *c* its ways and be wise!
20:25 and only later to *c* his vows.
Ecc 7:13 *C* what God has done:
Lk 12:24 *C* the ravens: They do not sow
12:27 about the rest? "*C* how the lilies
Php 2: 3 but in humility *c* others better
3: 8 I *c* everything a loss compared
Heb 10:24 And let us *c* how we may spur one
Jas 1: 2 *C* it pure joy, my brothers,

CONSIDERATE* (CONSIDER)
Tit 3: 2 to be peaceable and *c*,
Jas 3:17 then peace-loving, *c*, submissive,
1Pe 2:18 only to those who are good and *c*,
3: 7 in the same way be *c* as you live

CONSIDERED (CONSIDER)
Job 1: 8 "Have you *c* my servant Job?
2: 3 "Have you *c* my servant Job?
Ps 44:22 we are *c* as sheep to be slaughtered.
Isa 53: 4 yet we *c* him stricken by God,
Ro 8:36 we are *c* as sheep to be slaughtered

CONSIDERS (CONSIDER)
Pr 31:16 She *c* a field and buys it;
Ro 14: 5 One man *c* one day more sacred
Jas 1:26 If anyone *c* himself religious

CONSIST (CONSISTS)
Lk 12:15 a man's life does not *c*

CONSISTS (CONSIST)
Eph 5: 9 fruit of the light *c* in all goodness,

CONSOLATION
Ps 94:19 your *c* brought joy to my soul.

CONSPIRE
Ps 2: 1 Why do the nations *c*

CONSTANT
Dt 28:66 You will live in *c* suspense,
Pr 19:13 wife is like a *c* dripping.
27:15 a *c* dripping on a rainy day;
Ac 27:33 "you have been in *c* suspense
Heb 5:14 by *c* use have trained themselves

CONSTRUCTIVE*
1Co 10:23 but not everything is *c*.

CONSULT
Pr 15:12 he will not *c* the wise.
Gal 1:16 I did not *c* any man, nor did I go up

CONSUME (CONSUMES CONSUMING)
Jn 2:17 "Zeal for your house will *c* me."

CONSUMES (CONSUME)
Ps 69: 9 for zeal for your house *c* me,

CONSUMING (CONSUME)
Dt 4:24 For the LORD your God is a *c* fire,
Heb 12:29 and awe, for our "God is a *c* fire."

CONTAIN* (CONTAINED CONTAINS)
1Ki 8:27 the highest heaven, cannot *c* you.
2Ch 2: 6 the highest heavens, cannot *c* him?
6:18 the highest heavens, cannot *c* you.
Ecc 8: 8 power over the wind to *c* it;
2Pe 3:16 His letters *c* some things that are

CONTAINED (CONTAIN)
Heb 9: 4 This ark *c* the gold jar of manna,

CONTAINS (CONTAIN)
Pr 15: 6 of the righteous *c* great treasure,

CONTAMINATES*
2Co 7: 1 from everything that *c* body

CONTEMPT
Pr 14:31 He who oppresses the poor shows *c*
17: 5 He who mocks the poor shows *c*
18: 3 When wickedness comes, so does *c*
Da 12: 2 others to shame and everlasting *c*.
Mal 1: 6 O priests, who show *c* for my name.
Ro 2: 4 Or do you show *c* for the riches
Gal 4:14 you did not treat me with *c*
1Th 5:20 do not treat prophecies with *c*.

CONTEND (CONTENDED CONTENDING CONTENTIOUS)
Ge 6: 3 "My Spirit will not *c*
Ps 35: 1 *C*, O LORD, with those who
Isa 49:25 I will *c* with those who *c* with you,
Jude :3 you to *c* for the faith that was once

CONTENDED (CONTEND)
Php 4: 3 help these women who have *c*

CONTENDING* (CONTEND)
Php 1:27 *c* as one man for the faith

CONTENT* (CONTENTMENT)
Jos 7: 7 If only we had been *c* to stay
Pr 13:25 The righteous eat to their hearts' *c*,
19:23 one rests *c*, untouched by trouble.
Ecc 4: 8 yet his eyes were not *c*
Lk 3:14 don't accuse people falsely—be *c*
Php 4:11 to be *c* whatever the circumstances
4:12 I have learned the secret of being *c*
1Ti 6: 8 and clothing, we will be *c* with that.
Heb 13: 5 and be *c* with what you have,

CONTENTIOUS* (CONTEND)
1Co 11:16 If anyone wants to be *c* about this,

CONTENTMENT* (CONTENT)
Job 36:11 and their years in *c*.
SS 8:10 like one bringing *c*.
1Ti 6: 6 But godliness with *c* is great gain.

CONTEST*
Heb 10:32 in a great *c* in the face of suffering.

CONTINUAL (CONTINUE)
Pr 15:15 but the cheerful heart has a *c* feast.
Eph 4:19 of impurity, with a *c* lust for more.

CONTINUE (CONTINUAL CONTINUES CONTINUING)
1Ki 8:23 servants who *c* wholeheartedly
2Ch 6:14 servants who *c* wholeheartedly
Ps 36:10 *C* your love to those who know you
Ac 13:43 urged them to *c* in the grace of God
Ro 11:22 provided that you *c* in his kindness.
Gal 3:10 Cursed is everyone who does not *c*
Php 2:12 *c* to work out your salvation
Col 1:23 if you *c* in your faith, established
2: 6 received Christ Jesus as Lord, *c*
1Ti 2:15 if they *c* in faith, love and holiness
2Ti 3:14 *c* in what you have learned
1Jn 2:28 And now, dear children, *c* in him,
3: 9 born of God will *c* to sin,
5:18 born of God does not *c* to sin;
2Jn :9 and does not *c* in the teaching
Rev 22:11 and let him who is holy *c* to be holy
22:11 let him who does right *c* to do right;

CONTINUES (CONTINUE)
Ps 100: 5 *c* through all generations.
119: 90 Your faithfulness *c*
2Co 10:15 Our hope is that, as your faith *c*
1Jn 3: 6 No one who *c* to sin has

CONTINUING (CONTINUE)
Ro 13: 8 the *c* debt to love one another,

CONTRIBUTION (CONTRIBUTIONS)
Ro 15:26 pleased to make a *c* for the poor

CONTRIBUTIONS (CONTRIBUTION)
2Ch 24:10 all the people brought their *c* gladly
31:12 they faithfully brought in the *c*,

CONTRITE*
Ps 51:17 a broken and *c* heart,
Isa 57:15 also with him who is *c* and lowly
57:15 and to revive the heart of the *c*.
66: 2 he who is humble and *c* in spirit,

CONTROL (CONTROLLED CONTROLS SELF-CONTROL SELF-CONTROLLED)
Pr 29:11 a wise man keeps himself under *c*.
1Co 7: 9 But if they cannot *c* themselves,
1Co 7:37 but has *c* over his own will,
1Th 4: 4 you should learn to *c* his own body

CONTROLLED (CONTROL)
Ps 32: 9 but must be *c* by bit and bridle
Ro 8: 6 but the mind *c* by the Spirit is life
8: 8 Those *c* by the sinful nature cannot

CONTROLS* (CONTROL)
Job 37:15 you know how God *c* the clouds
Pr 16:32 a man who *c* his temper

CONTROVERSIES*
Ac 26: 3 with all the Jewish customs and *c*.
1Ti 1: 4 These promote *c* rather
6: 4 He has an unhealthy interest in *c*
Tit 3: 9 But avoid foolish *c* and genealogies

CONVERSATION
Col 4: 6 Let your *c* be always full of grace,

CONVERT
1Ti 3: 6 He must not be a recent *c*,

CONVICT (CONVICTION)
Pr 24:25 with those who *c* the guilty,
Jn 16: 8 he will *c* the world of guilt in regard
Jude :15 and to *c* all the ungodly

CONVICTION* (CONVICT)
1Th 1: 5 the Holy Spirit and with deep *c*.

CONVINCE* (CONVINCED CONVINCING)
Ac 28:23 and tried to *c* them about Jesus

CONVINCED* (CONVINCE)
Ge 45:28 "I'm *c*! My son Joseph is still alive.
Lk 16:31 will not be *c* even if someone rises
Ac 19:26 and hear how this fellow Paul has *c*
26: 9 "I too was *c* that I ought
26:26 I am *c* that none of this has escaped
28:24 Some were *c* by what he said,
Ro 2:19 if you are *c* that you are a guide
8:38 For I am *c* that neither death
14: 5 Each one should be fully *c*
14:14 I am fully *c* that no food is unclean
15:14 I myself am *c*, my brothers,
1Co 14:24 he will be *c* by all that he is a sinner
2Co 5:14 we are *c* that one died for all,
Php 1:25 *C* of this, I know that I will remain,
2Ti 1:12 and am *c* that he is able
3:14 have learned and have become *c*

CONVINCING* (CONVINCE)
Ac 1: 3 and gave many *c* proofs that he was

COOLNESS*
Pr 25:13 Like the *c* of snow at harvest time

COPIES (COPY)
Heb 9:23 for the *c* of the heavenly things

COPY (COPIES)
Dt 17:18 for himself on a scroll a *c* of this law
Heb 8: 5 They serve at a sanctuary that is a *c*
9:24 sanctuary that was only a *c*

CORBAN*
Mk 7:11 received from me is *C*' (that is,

CORD (CORDS)
Jos 2:18 you have tied this scarlet *c*
Ecc 4:12 *c* of three strands is not quickly

CORDS (CORD)
Pr 5:22 the *c* of his sin hold him fast.
Isa 54: 2 lengthen your *c*,
Hos 11: 4 them with *c* of human kindness,

CORINTH
Ac 18: 1 Paul left Athens and went to *C*.
1Co 1: 2 To the church of God in *C*,
2Co 1: 1 To the church of God in *C*,

CORNELIUS*
Roman to whom Peter preached; first Gentile Christian (Ac 10).

CORNER (CORNERS)
Ru 3: 9 "Spread the *c* of your garment
Pr 21: 9 Better to live on a *c* of the roof
25:24 Better to live on a *c* of the roof
Ac 26:26 because it was not done in a *c*.

CORNERS (CORNER)
Mt 6: 5 on the street *c* to be seen by men.
22: 9 Go to the street *c* and invite

CORNERSTONE* (STONE)
Job 38: 6 or who laid its *c*—
Isa 28:16 a precious *c* for a sure foundation;
Jer 51:26 rock will be taken from you for a *c*,

Zec 10: 4 From Judah will come the *c*,
Eph 2:20 Christ Jesus himself as the chief *c*.
1Pe 2: 6 a chosen and precious *c*,

CORRECT* (CORRECTED CORRECTING CORRECTION CORRECTIONS CORRECTS)
Job 6:26 Do you mean to *c* what I say,
40: 2 contends with the Almighty *c* him?
Jer 10:24 *C* me, LORD, but only with justice
2Ti 4: 2 *c*, rebuke and encourage—

CORRECTED* (CORRECT)
Pr 29:19 A servant cannot be *c*

CORRECTING* (CORRECT)
2Ti 3:16 *c* and training in righteousness,

CORRECTION* (CORRECT)
Lev 26:23 things you do not accept my *c*
Job 36:10 He makes them listen to *c*
Pr 5:12 How my heart spurned *c*!
10:17 whoever ignores *c* leads others
12: 1 but he who hates *c* is stupid.
13:18 but whoever heeds *c* is honored.
15: 5 whoever heeds *c* shows prudence.
15:10 he who hates *c* will die.
15:12 A mocker resents *c*;
15:32 whoever heeds *c* gains
29:15 The rod of *c* imparts wisdom,
Jer 2:30 they did not respond to *c*.
5: 3 crushed them, but they refused *c*.
7:28 LORD its God or responded to *c*.
Zep 3: 2 she accepts no *c*.
3: 7 you will fear me / and accept *c*!'

CORRECTIONS* (CORRECT)
Pr 6:23 and the *c* of discipline

CORRECTS* (CORRECT)
Job 5:17 "Blessed is the man whom God *c*;
Pr 9: 7 Whoever *c* a mocker invites insult;

CORRUPT (CORRUPTED CORRUPTION CORRUPTS)
Ge 6:11 Now the earth was *c* in God's sight
Ps 14: 1 They are *c*, their deeds are vile;
14: 3 they have together become *c*;
Pr 4:24 keep *c* talk far from your lips.
6:12 who goes about with a *c* mouth,
19:28 A *c* witness mocks at justice,

CORRUPTED (CORRUPT)
2Co 7: 2 wronged no one, we have *c* no one,
Tit 1:15 but to those who are *c* and do not

CORRUPTION (CORRUPT)
2Pe 1: 4 escape the *c* in the world caused
2:20 If they have escaped the *c*

CORRUPTS* (CORRUPT)
Ecc 7: 7 and a bribe *c* the heart.
1Co 15:33 "Bad company *c* good character."
Jas 3: 6 It *c* the whole person, sets

COST (COSTS)
Nu 16:38 sinned at the *c* of their lives.
Pr 4: 7 Though it *c* all you have, get
7:23 little knowing it will *c* him his life.
Isa 55: 1 milk without money and without *c*.
Lk 14:28 and estimate the *c* to see
Rev 21: 6 to drink without *c* from the spring

COSTS (COST)
Pr 6:31 it *c* him all the wealth of his house.

COUNCIL
Ps 89: 7 In the *c* of the holy ones God is
107: 32 and praise him in the *c* of the elders

COUNSEL (COUNSELOR COUNSELS)
1Ki 22: 5 "First seek the *c* of the LORD."
2Ch 18: 4 "First seek the *c* of the LORD."
Job 38: 2 "Who is this that darkens my *c*
42: 3 'Who is this that obscures my *c*
Ps 1: 1 walk in the *c* of the wicked
73:24 You guide me with your *c*,
107: 11 despised the *c* of the Most High.
Pr 8:14 *C* and sound judgment are mine;
15:22 Plans fail for lack of *c*,
27: 9 from his earnest *c*.
Isa 28:29 wonderful in *c* and magnificent
1Ti 5:14 So I *c* younger widows to marry,
Rev 3:18 I *c* you to buy from me gold refined

COUNSELOR (COUNSEL)
Isa 9: 6 Wonderful *C*, Mighty God,
Jn 14:16 he will give you another *C* to be
14:26 But the *C*, the Holy Spirit,
15:26 "When the *C* comes, whom I will
16: 7 the *C* will not come to you;
Ro 11:34 Or who has been his *c*?"

COUNSELS (COUNSEL)
Ps 16: 7 I will praise the LORD, who *c* me;

COUNT (COUNTED COUNTING COUNTS)
Ps 22:17 I can *c* all my bones;
Ro 4: 8 whose sin the Lord will never *c*
6:11 *c* yourselves dead to sin
2Th 1:11 that our God may *c* you worthy

COUNTED (COUNT)
Ac 5:41 because they had been *c* worthy
2Th 1: 5 and as a result you will be *c* worthy

COUNTERFEIT*
2Th 2: 9 displayed in all kinds of *c* miracles,
1Jn 2:27 not *c*— just as it has taught you,

COUNTING (COUNT)
2Co 5:19 not *c* men's sins against them.

COUNTRY
Pr 28: 2 When a *c* is rebellious, it has many
29: 4 By justice a king gives a *c* stability,
Isa 66: 8 Can a *c* be born in a day
Lk 15:13 off for a distant *c* and there
Jn 4:44 prophet has no honor in his own *c*.)
2Co 11:26 in danger in the *c*, in danger at sea;
Heb 11:14 looking for a *c* of their own.

COUNTRYMEN
2Co 11:26 danger from my own *c*, in danger

COUNTS (COUNT)
Jn 6:63 The Spirit gives life; the flesh *c*
1Co 7:19 God's commands is what *c*.
Gal 5: 6 only thing that *c* is faith expressing

COURAGE* (COURAGEOUS)
Jos 2:11 everyone's *c* failed because of you,
5: 1 and they no longer had the *c*
2Sa 4: 1 he lost *c*, and all Israel became
7:27 So your servant has found *c*
1Ch 17:25 So your servant has found *c* to pray
2Ch 15: 8 son of Oded the prophet, he took *c*.
19:11 Act with *c*, and may the LORD be
Ezr 7:28 I took *c* and gathered leading men
10: 4 We will support you, so take *c*
Ps 107: 26 in their peril their *c* melted away.
Eze 22:14 Will your *c* endure or your hands
Da 11:25 and *c* against the king of the South.
Mt 14:27 said to them: "Take *c*!
Mk 6:50 spoke to them and said, "Take *c*!
Ac 4:13 When they saw the *c* of Peter
23:11 "Take *c*! As you have testified
27:22 now I urge you to keep up your *c*,
27:25 So keep up your *c*, men,
1Co 16:13 stand firm in the faith; be men of *c*;
Php 1:20 will have sufficient *c* so that now
Heb 3: 6 if we hold on to our *c* and the hope

COURAGEOUS* (COURAGE)
Dt 31: 6 Be strong and *c*.
31: 7 of all Israel, "Be strong and *c*,
31:23 son of Nun: "Be strong and *c*,
Jos 1: 6 and *c*, because you will lead these
1: 7 Be strong and very *c*.
1: 9 commanded you? Be strong and *c*.
1:18 Only be strong and *c*!"
10:25 Be strong and *c*.
1Ch 22:13 Be strong and *c*.
28:20 "Be strong and *c*, and do the work.
2Ch 26:17 priest with eighty other *c* priests
32: 7 with these words: "Be strong and *c*.

COURSE
Ps 19: 5 a champion rejoicing to run his *c*.
Pr 2: 8 for he guards the *c* of the just
15:21 of understanding keeps a straight *c*.
16: 9 In his heart a man plans his *c*,
17:23 to pervert the *c* of justice.
Jas 3: 6 sets the whole *c* of his life on fire,

COURT (COURTS)
Pr 22:22 and do not crush the needy in *c*,
25: 8 do not bring hastily to *c*,
Mt 5:25 adversary who is taking you to *c*.
1Co 4: 3 judged by you or by any human *c*;

COURTS (COURT)
Ps 84:10 Better is one day in your *c*
100: 4 and his *c* with praise;
Am 5:15 maintain justice in the *c*.
Zec 8:16 and sound judgment in your *c*;

COURTYARD
Ex 27: 9 "Make a *c* for the tabernacle.

COUSIN
Col 4:10 as does Mark, the *c* of Barnabas.

COVENANT (COVENANTS)
Ge 9: 9 "I now establish my *c* with you
17: 2 I will confirm my *c* between me
Ex 19: 5 if you obey me fully and keep my *c*,
24: 7 Then he took the Book of the *C*
Dt 4:13 declared to you his *c*, the Ten
29: 1 in addition to the *c* he had made
Jdg 2: 1 'I will never break my *c* with you,
1Sa 23:18 of them made a *c* before the LORD
1Ki 8:21 in which is the *c* of the LORD that
8:23 you who keep your *c* of love
2Ki 23: 2 the words of the Book of the *C*,
1Ch 16:15 He remembers his *c* forever,
2Ch 6:14 you who keep your *c* of love
34:30 the words of the Book of the *C*,
Ne 1: 5 who keeps his *c* of love
Job 31: 1 "I made a *c* with my eyes
Ps 105: 8 He remembers his *c* forever,
Pr 2:17 ignored the *c* she made before God
Isa 42: 6 you to be a *c* for the people
61: 8 make an everlasting *c* with them.
Jer 11: 2 "Listen to the terms of this *c*
31:31 "when I will make a new *c*
31:32 It will not be like the *c*
31:33 "This is the *c* I will make
Eze 37:26 I will make a *c* of peace with them;
Da 9:27 He will confirm a *c* with many
Hos 6: 7 Like Adam, they have broken the *c*
Mal 2:14 the wife of your marriage *c*.
3: 1 of the *c*, whom you desire,
Mt 26:28 blood of the *c*, which is poured out
Mk 14:24 "This is my blood of the *c*,
Lk 22:20 "This cup is the new *c* in my blood,
1Co 11:25 "This cup is the new *c* in my blood;
2Co 3: 6 as ministers of a new *c*—
Gal 4:24 One *c* is from Mount Sinai
Heb 8: 6 as the *c* of which he is mediator is
8: 8 when I will make a new *c*
9:15 Christ is the mediator of a new *c*,
12:24 to Jesus the mediator of a new *c*,

COVENANTS (COVENANT)
Ro 9: 4 theirs the divine glory, the *c*,
Gal 4:24 for the women represent two *c*.

COVER (COVER-UP COVERED COVERING COVERINGS COVERS)
Ex 25:17 "Make an atonement *c* of pure gold
25:21 Place the *c* on top of the ark
33:22 and *c* you with my hand
Lev 16: 2 in the cloud over the atonement *c*.
Ps 32: 5 and did not *c* up my iniquity.
91: 4 He will *c* you with his feathers,
Hos 10: 8 say to the mountains, "*C* us!"
Lk 23:30 and to the hills, "*C* us!"
1Co 11: 6 If a woman does not *c* her head,
11: 6 shaved off, she should *c* her head.
11: 7 A man ought not to *c* his head,
Jas 5:20 and *c* over a multitude of sins.

COVER-UP* (COVER)
1Pe 2:16 but do not use your freedom as a *c*

COVERED (COVER)
Ps 32: 1 whose sins are *c*.
85: 2 and *c* all their sins.
Isa 6: 2 With two wings they *c* their faces,
51:16 *c* you with the shadow of my hand
Ro 4: 7 whose sins are *c*.
1Co 11: 4 with his head *c* dishonors his head.

COVERING (COVER)
1Co 11:15 For long hair is given to her as a *c*.

COVERINGS (COVER)
Ge 3: 7 and made *c* for themselves.
Pr 31:22 She makes *c* for her bed;

COVERS (COVER)
Pr 10:12 but love *c* over all wrongs.
17: 9 He who *c* over an offense promotes
2Co 3:15 Moses is read, a veil *c* their hearts.
1Pe 4: 8 love *c* over a multitude of sins.

COVET* (COVETED COVETING COVETOUS)
Ex 20:17 You shall not *c* your neighbor's
20:17 "You shall not *c* your neighbor's
34:24 and no one will *c* your land
Dt 5:21 "You shall not *c* your neighbor's
7:25 Do not *c* the silver and gold
Mic 2: 2 They *c* fields and seize them,
Ro 7: 7 if the law had not said, "Do not *c*."
13: 9 "Do not steal," "Do not *c*,"
Jas 4: 2 *c*, but you cannot have what you

COVETED* (COVET)
Jos 7:21 weighing fifty shekels, I *c* them
Ac 20:33 I have not *c* anyone's silver or gold

COVETING
Ro 7: 7 what c really was if the law

COVETOUS* (COVET)
Ro 7: 8 in me every kind of c desire.

COWARDLY*
Rev 21: 8 But the c, the unbelieving, the vile,

COWS
Ge 41: 2 of the river there came up seven c,
Ex 25: 5 skins dyed red and hides of sea c;
Nu 4: 6 are to cover this with hides of sea c,
1Sa 6: 7 Hitch the c to the cart,

CRAFTINESS* (CRAFTY)
Job 5:13 He catches the wise in their c,
1Co 3:19 "He catches the wise in their c";
Eph 4:14 and c of men in their deceitful

CRAFTSMAN
Pr 8:30 Then I was the c at his side.

CRAFTY* (CRAFTINESS)
Ge 3: 1 the serpent was more c than any
1Sa 23:22 They tell me he is very c.
Job 5:12 He thwarts the plans of the c,
15: 5 you adopt the tongue of the c.
Pr 7:10 like a prostitute and with c intent.
12: 2 but the LORD condemns a c man.
14:17 and a c man is hated.
2Co 12:16 c fellow that I am, I caught you

CRAVE* (CRAVED CRAVES CRAVING CRAVINGS)
Nu 11: 4 with them began to c other food,
Dt 12:20 you c meat and say, "I would like
Pr 23: 3 Do not c his delicacies,
23: 6 do not c his delicacies;
31: 4 not for rulers to c beer,
Mic 7: 1 none of the early figs that I c.
1Pe 2: 2 newborn babies, c pure spiritual

CRAVED* (CRAVE)
Nu 11:34 the people who had c other food.
Ps 78:18 by demanding the food they c.
78:29 for he had given them what they c.
78:30 turned from the food they c,

CRAVES* (CRAVE)
Pr 13: 4 The sluggard c and gets nothing,
21:10 The wicked man c evil;
21:26 All day long he c for more,

CRAVING* (CRAVE)
Job 20:20 he will have no respite from his c;
Ps 106: 14 In the desert they gave in to their c;
Pr 10: 3 but he thwarts the c of the wicked.
13: 2 the unfaithful have a c for violence.
21:25 The sluggard's c will be the death
Jer 2:24 sniffing the wind in her c—

CRAVINGS* (CRAVE)
Ps 10: 3 He boasts of the c of his heart;
Eph 2: 3 gratifying the c of our sinful nature
1Jn 2:16 in the world—the c of sinful man,

CRAWL
Ge 3:14 You will c on your belly

CREATE* (CREATED CREATES CREATING CREATION CREATOR)
Ps 51:10 C in me a pure heart, O God,
Isa 4: 5 Then the LORD will c over all
45: 7 I bring prosperity and c disaster;
45: 7 I form the light and c darkness,
45:18 he did not c it to be empty,
65:17 "Behold, I will c / new heavens
65:18 for I will c Jerusalem to be a delight
65:18 forever in what I will c,
Jer 31:22 The LORD will c a new thing
Mal 2:10 one Father? Did not one God c us?
Eph 2:15 His purpose was to c

CREATED* (CREATE)
Ge 1: 1 In the beginning God c the heavens
1:21 God c the great creatures of the sea
1:27 So God c man in his own image,
1:27 in the image of God he c him;
1:27 male and female he c them.
2: 4 and the earth when they were c.
5: 1 When God c man, he made him
5: 2 He c them male and female
5: 2 when they were c, he called them
6: 7 whom I have c, from the face
Dt 4:32 from the day God c man
Ps 89:12 You c the north and the south;
89:47 what futility you have c all men!
102: 18 a people not yet c may praise
104: 30 you send your Spirit, / they are c,
Ps 139: 13 For you c my inmost being;
148: 5 for he commanded and they were c
Isa 40:26 Who c all these?
41:20 that the Holy One of Israel has c it.
42: 5 he who c the heavens and stretched
43: 1 he who c you, O Jacob,
43: 7 whom I c for my glory,
45: 8 I, the LORD, have c it.
45:12 and c mankind upon it.
45:18 he who c the heavens,
48: 7 They are c now, and not long ago;
54:16 And it is I who have c the destroyer
54:16 "See, it is I who c the blacksmith
57:16 the breath of man that I have c.
Eze 21:30 In the place where you were c,
28:13 the day you were c they were
28:15 ways from the day you were c
Mk 13:19 when God c the world, until now—
Ro 1:25 and served c things rather
1Co 11: 9 neither was man c for woman,
Eph 2:10 c in Christ Jesus to do good works,
3: 9 hidden in God, who c all things.
4:24 c to be like God in true
Col 1:16 For by him all things were c:
1:16 all things were c by him
1Ti 4: 3 which God c to be received
4: 4 For everything God c is good,
Heb 12:27 c things—so that what cannot be
Jas 1:18 a kind of firstfruits of all he c.
Rev 4:11 and by your will they were c
4:11 for you c all things,
10: 6 who c the heavens and all that is

CREATES* (CREATE)
Am 4:13 c the wind,

CREATING* (CREATE)
Ge 2: 3 the work of c that he had done.
Isa 57:19 c praise on the lips of the mourners

CREATION* (CREATE)
Hab 2:18 he who makes it trusts in his own c;
Mt 13:35 hidden since the c of the world."
25:34 for you since the c of the world.
Mk 10: 6 of c God 'made them male
16:15 and preach the good news to all c.
Jn 17:24 me before the c of the world.
Ro 1:20 For since the c of the world God's
8:19 The c waits in eager expectation
8:20 For the c was subjected
8:21 in hope that the c itself will be
8:22 that the whole c has been groaning
8:39 depth, nor anything else in all c,
2Co 5:17 he is a new c; the old has gone,
Gal 6:15 anything; what counts is a new c.
Eph 1: 4 us in him before the c of the world
Col 1:15 God, the firstborn over all c.
Heb 4: 3 finished since the c of the world.
4:13 Nothing in all c is hidden
9:11 that is to say, not a part of this c.
9:26 times since the c of the world.
1Pe 1:20 chosen before the c of the world,
2Pe 3: 4 as it has since the beginning of c."
Rev 3:14 true witness, the ruler of God's c.
13: 8 slain from the c of the world.
17: 8 life from the c of the world will be

CREATOR* (CREATE)
Ge 14:19 C of heaven and earth.
14:22 God Most High, C of heaven
Dt 32: 6 Is he not your Father, your C,
Ecc 12: 1 Remember your C
Isa 27:11 and their C shows them no favor.
40:28 the C of the ends of the earth.
43:15 Israel's C, your King."
Mt 19: 4 the beginning the C 'made them
Ro 1:25 created things rather than the C—
Col 3:10 in knowledge in the image of its C.
1Pe 4:19 themselves to their faithful C

CREATURE (CREATURES)
Lev 17:11 For the life of a c is in the blood,
17:14 the life of every c is its blood.
Ps 136: 25 and who gives food to every c.
Eze 1:15 beside each c with its four faces.
Rev 4: 7 The first living c was like a lion,

CREATURES (CREATURE)
Ge 6:19 bring into the ark two of all living c,
8:21 again will I destroy all living c,
Ps 104: 24 the earth is full of your c.
Eze 1: 5 was what looked like four living c.

CREDIT (CREDITED CREDITOR CREDITS)
Lk 6:33 what c is that to you? Even
Ro 4:24 to whom God will c righteousness
1Pe 2:20 it to your c if you receive a beating

CREDITED (CREDIT)
Ge 15: 6 and he c it to him as righteousness.
Ps 106: 31 This was c to him as righteousness
Eze 18:20 of the righteous man will be c
Ro 4: 3 and it was c to him as righteousness
4: 4 his wages are not c to him as a gift,
4: 5 his faith is c as righteousness.
4: 9 saying that Abraham's faith was c
4:23 The words "it was c
Gal 3: 6 and it was c to him as righteousness
Php 4:17 for what may be c to your account.
Jas 2:23 and it was c to him as righteousness

CREDITOR (CREDIT)
Dt 15: 2 Every c shall cancel the loan he has

CREDITS (CREDIT)
Ro 4: 6 whom God c righteousness apart

CRETANS (CRETE)
Tit 1:12 "C are always liars, evil brutes,

CRETE (CRETANS)
Ac 27:12 harbor in C, facing both southwest

CRIED (CRY)
Ex 2:23 groaned in their slavery and c out,
14:10 They were terrified and c out
Nu 20:16 but when we c out to the LORD,
Jos 24: 7 But they c to the LORD for help,
Jdg 3: 9 But when they c out to the LORD,
3:15 Again the Israelites c out
4: 3 they c to the LORD for help.
6: 6 the Israelites that they c out
10:12 Maonites oppressed you and you c
1Sa 7: 9 He c out to the LORD
12: 8 they c to the LORD for help,
12:10 They c out to the LORD and said,
Ps 18: 6 I c to my God for help.

CRIMINALS
Lk 23:32 both c, were also led out with him

CRIMSON
Isa 1:18 though they are red as c,
63: 1 with his garments stained c?

CRIPPLED
2Sa 9: 3 of Jonathan; he is c in both feet."
Mk 9:45 better for you to enter life c

CRISIS*
1Co 7:26 of the present c, I think that it is

CRITICISM*
2Co 8:20 We want to avoid any c

CROOKED*
Dt 32: 5 but a warped and c generation.
2Sa 22:27 to the c you show yourself shrewd.
Ps 18:26 to the c you show yourself shrewd.
125: 5 But those who turn to c ways
Pr 2:15 whose paths are c
5: 6 her paths are c, but she knows it
8: 8 none of them is c or perverse.
10: 9 he who takes c paths will be found
Ecc 7:13 what he has made c?
Isa 59: 8 have turned them into c roads;
La 3: 9 he has made my paths c.
Lk 3: 5 The c roads shall become straight,
Php 2:15 children of God without fault in a c

CROP (CROPS)
Mt 13: 8 where it produced a c—a hundred,
21:41 share of the c at harvest time."

CROPS (CROP)
Pr 3: 9 with the firstfruits of all your c;
10: 5 He who gathers c in summer is
28: 3 like a driving rain that leaves no c.
2Ti 2: 6 the first to receive a share of the c.

CROSS (CROSSED CROSSING)
Dt 4:21 swore that I would not c the Jordan
12:10 But you will c the Jordan
Mt 10:38 and anyone who does not take his c
16:24 and take up his c and follow me.
Mk 8:34 and take up his c and follow me.
Lk 9:23 take up his c daily and follow me.
14:27 anyone who does not carry his c
Jn 19:17 Carrying his own c, he went out
Ac 2:23 to death by nailing him to the c.
1Co 1:17 lest the c of Christ be emptied
1:18 the message of the c is foolishness
Gal 5:11 offense of the c has been abolished.
6:12 persecuted for the c of Christ.
6:14 in the c of our Lord Jesus Christ,
Eph 2:16 both of them to God through the c,
Php 2: 8 even death on a c!
3:18 as enemies of the c of Christ.
Col 1:20 through his blood, shed on the c.
2:14 he took it away, nailing it to the c.
2:15 triumphing over them by the c.

Heb 12: 2 set before him endured the *c,*

CROSSED (CROSS)
Jos 4: 7 When it *c* the Jordan, the waters
Jn 5:24 he has *c* over from death to life.

CROSSING (CROSS)
Ge 48:14 he was the younger, and *c* his arms,

CROSSROADS (ROAD)
Jer 6:16 "Stand at the *c* and look;

CROUCHING
Ge 4: 7 sin is *c* at your door; it desires

CROWD (CROWDS)
Ex 23: 2 Do not follow the *c* in doing wrong.

CROWDS (CROWD)
Mt 9:36 he saw the *c,* he had compassion

CROWED (CROWS)
Mt 26:74 the man!" Immediately a rooster *c.*

CROWN (CROWNED CROWNS)
Pr 4: 9 present you with a *c* of splendor."
10: 6 Blessings *c* the head
12: 4 noble character is her husband's *c,*
16:31 Gray hair is a *c* of splendor;
17: 6 Children's children are a *c*
Isa 35:10 everlasting joy will *c* their heads.
51:11 everlasting joy will *c* their heads.
61: 3 to bestow on them a *c* of beauty
62: 3 You will be a *c* of splendor
Eze 16:12 and a beautiful *c* on your head.
Zec 9:16 like jewels in a *c.*
Mt 27:29 and then twisted together a *c* of thorns
Mk 15:17 then twisted together a *c* of thorns
Jn 19: 2 The soldiers twisted together a *c*
19: 5 When Jesus came out wearing the *c*
1Co 9:25 it to get a *c* that will last forever.
9:25 it to get a *c* that will not last;
Php 4: 1 and long for, my joy and *c,*
1Th 2:19 or the *c* in which we will glory
2Ti 2: 5 he does not receive the victor's *c*
4: 8 store for me the *c* of righteousness,
Jas 1:12 he will receive the *c*
1Pe 5: 4 you will receive the *c*
Rev 2:10 and I will give you the *c* of life.
3:11 so that no one will take your *c.*
14:14 a son of man" with a *c* of gold

CROWNED* (CROWN)
Ps 8: 5 and *c* him with glory and honor.
Pr 14:18 the prudent are *c* with knowledge.
SS 3:11 crown with which his mother *c* him
Heb 2: 7 you *c* him with glory and honor
2: 9 now *c* with glory and honor

CROWNS (CROWN)
Ps 103: 4 and *c* me with love and compassion
149: 4 he *c* the humble with salvation.
Pr 11:26 blessing *c* him who is willing to sell.
Rev 4: 4 and had *c* of gold on their heads.
4:10 They lay their *c* before the throne
12: 3 ten horns and seven *c* on his heads.
19:12 and on his head are many *c.*

CROWS (CROWED)
Mt 26:34 this very night, before the rooster *c*

CRUCIFIED* (CRUCIFY)
Mt 20:19 to be mocked and flogged and *c.*
26: 2 of Man will be handed over to be *c*
27:26 and handed him over to be *c.*
27:35 When they had *c* him, they divided
27:38 Two robbers were *c* with him,
27:44 same way the robbers who were *c*
28: 5 looking for Jesus, who was *c.*
Mk 15:15 and handed him over to be *c.*
15:24 And they *c* him.
15:25 the third hour when they *c* him.
15:27 They *c* two robbers with him,
15:32 Those *c* with him also heaped
16: 6 for Jesus the Nazarene, who was *c.*
Lk 23:23 insistently demanded that he be *c,*
23:33 *c* him, along with the criminals—
24: 7 be *c* and on the third day be raised
24:20 sentenced to death, and they *c* him;
Jn 19:16 him over to them to be *c.*
19:18 Here they *c* him, and with him two
19:20 for the place where Jesus was *c* was
19:23 When the soldiers *c* Jesus,
19:32 of the first man who had been *c*
19:41 At the place where Jesus was *c,*
Ac 2:36 whom you *c,* both Lord and Christ
4:10 whom you *c* but whom God raised
Ro 6: 6 For we know that our old self was *c*
1Co 1:13 Is Christ divided? Was Paul *c*
1:23 but we preach Christ *c:* a stumbling
2: 2 except Jesus Christ and him *c.*
1Co 2: 8 they would not have *c* the Lord
2Co 13: 4 to be sure, he was *c* in weakness,
Gal 2:20 I have been *c* with Christ
3: 1 Christ was clearly portrayed as *c.*
5:24 Christ Jesus have *c* the sinful
6:14 which the world has been *c*
Rev 11: 8 where also their Lord was *c.*

CRUCIFY* (CRUCIFIED CRUCIFYING)
Mt 23:34 Some of them you will kill and *c;*
27:22 They all answered, "*C* him!" "Why
27:23 they shouted all the louder, "*C* him
27:31 Then they led him away to *c* him.
Mk 15:13 "*C* him!" they shouted.
15:14 they shouted all the louder, "*C* him
15:20 Then they led him out to *c* him.
Lk 23:21 they kept shouting, "*C* him! *C* him
Jn 19: 6 they shouted, "*C! C!*"
19: 6 "You take him and *c* him.
19:10 either to free you or to *c* you?"
19:15 Crucify him!" "Shall I *c* your king
19:15 away! Take him away! *C* him!"

CRUCIFYING* (CRUCIFY)
Heb 6: 6 to their loss they are *c* the Son

CRUSH (CRUSHED)
Ge 3:15 he will *c* your head,
Isa 53:10 it was the LORD's will to *c* him
Ro 16:20 The God of peace will soon *c* Satan

CRUSHED (CRUSH)
Ps 34:18 and saves those who are *c* in spirit.
Pr 17:22 but a *c* spirit dries up the bones.
18:14 but a *c* spirit who can bear?
Isa 53: 5 he was *c* for our iniquities;
2Co 4: 8 not *c;* perplexed, but not in despair;

CRY (CRIED)
Ex 2:23 *c* for help because of their slavery
Ps 5: 2 Listen to my *c* for help,
34:15 and his ears are attentive to their *c;*
40: 1 he turned to me and heard my *c.*
130: 1 Out of the depths I *c* to you,
Pr 21:13 to the *c* of the poor,
La 2:18 *c* out to the Lord.
Hab 2:11 The stones of the wall will *c* out,
Lk 19:40 keep quiet, the stones will *c* out."

CUNNING
2Co 11: 3 deceived by the serpent's *c,*
Eph 4:14 and by the *c* and craftiness of men

CUP
Ps 23: 5 my *c* overflows.
Isa 51:22 from that *c,* the goblet of my wrath,
51:22 the *c* that made you stagger;
Mt 10:42 if anyone gives even a *c* of cold water
20:22 "Can you drink the *c* I am going
23:25 You clean the outside of the *c*
23:26 First clean the inside of the *c*
26:27 Then he took the *c,* gave thanks
26:39 may this *c* be taken from me.
26:42 possible for this *c* to be taken away
Mk 9:41 anyone who gives you a *c* of water
10:38 "Can you drink the *c* I drink
10:39 "You will drink the *c* I drink
14:23 Then he took the *c,* gave thanks
14:36 Take this *c* from me.
Lk 11:39 Pharisees clean the outside of the *c*
22:17 After taking the *c,* he gave thanks
22:20 after the supper he took the *c,*
22:20 "This *c* is the new covenant
22:42 if you are willing, take this *c*
Jn 18:11 I not drink the *c* the Father has
1Co 10:16 Is not the *c* of thanksgiving
10:21 the *c* of the Lord and the *c*
11:25 after supper he took the *c,* saying,
11:25 "This *c* is the new covenant

CUPBEARER
Ge 40: 1 the *c* and the baker of the king
Ne 1:11 I was *c* to the king.

CURE (CURED)
Jer 17: 9 and beyond *c.*
30:15 your pain that has no *c?*
Hos 5:13 But he is not able to *c* you,
Lk 9: 1 out all demons and to *c* diseases,

CURED (CURE)
Mt 11: 5 those who have leprosy are *c,*
Lk 6:18 troubled by evil spirits were *c,*

CURSE (ACCURSED CURSED CURSES CURSING)
Ge 4:11 Now you are under a *c*
8:21 "Never again will I *c* the ground
12: 3 and whoever curses you I will *c;*
Dt 11:26 before you today a blessing and a *c*
Dt 11:28 the *c* if you disobey the commands
21:23 hung on a tree is under God's *c.*
23: 5 turned the *c* into a blessing for you,
Job 1:11 he will surely *c* you to your face."
2: 5 he will surely *c* you to your face."
2: 9 *C* God and die!" He replied,
Ps 109: 28 They may *c,* but you will bless;
Pr 3:33 The LORD's *c* is on the house
24:24 peoples will *c* him and nations
Mal 2: 2 and I will *c* your blessings.
Lk 6:28 bless those who *c* you, pray
Ro 12:14 persecute you; bless and do not *c.*
Gal 3:10 on observing the law are under a *c,*
3:13 of the law by becoming a *c* for us,
Jas 3: 9 with it we *c* men, who have been
Rev 22: 3 No longer will there be any *c.*

CURSED (CURSE)
Ge 3:17 "*C* is the ground because of you;
Dt 27:15 "*C* is the man who carves an image
27:16 "*C* is the man who dishonors his
27:17 "*C* is the man who moves his
27:18 "*C* is the man who leads the blind
27:19 *C* is the man who withholds justice
27:20 "*C* is the man who sleeps
27:21 "*C* is the man who has sexual
27:22 "*C* is the man who sleeps
27:23 "*C* is the man who sleeps
27:24 "*C* is the man who kills his
27:25 "*C* is the man who accepts a bribe
27:26 "*C* is the man who does not uphold
Jer 17: 5 "*C* is the one who trusts in man,
Mal 1:14 "*C* is the cheat who has
Ro 9: 3 I could wish that I myself were *c*
1Co 4:12 When we are *c,* we bless;
12: 3 "Jesus be *c,*" and no one can say,
Gal 3:10 "*C* is everyone who does not
3:13 *C* is everyone who is hung on a tree

CURSES (CURSE)
Ex 21:17 "Anyone who *c* his father
Lev 20: 9 " 'If anyone *c* his father or mother,
Nu 5:23 is to write these *c* on a scroll
Jos 8:34 the blessings and the *c*—just
Pr 20:20 If a man *c* his father or mother,
28:27 to them receives many *c.*
Mt 15: 4 and 'Anyone who *c* his father
Mk 7:10 and, 'Anyone who *c* his father

CURSING (CURSE)
Ps 109: 18 He wore *c* as his garment;
Ro 3:14 "Their mouths are full of *c*
Jas 3:10 the same mouth come praise and *c.*

CURTAIN
Ex 26:31 "Make a *c* of blue, purple
26:33 The *c* will separate the Holy Place
Mt 27:51 At that moment the *c*
Mk 15:38 The *c* of the temple was torn in two
Lk 23:45 the *c* of the temple was torn in two.
Heb 6:19 the inner sanctuary behind the *c,*
9: 3 Behind the second *c* was a room
10:20 opened for us through the *c,*

CUSTOM
Job 1: 5 This was Job's regular *c.*
Mk 10: 1 and as was his *c,* he taught them.
Lk 4:16 into the synagogue, as was his *c.*
Ac 17: 2 As his *c* was, Paul went

CUT
Lev 19:27 " 'Do not *c* the hair at the sides
21: 5 of their beards or *c* their bodies.
1Ki 3:25 "*C* the living child in two
Isa 51: 1 to the rock from which you were *c*
53: 8 For he was *c* off from the land
Da 2:45 of the rock *c* out of a mountain,
9:26 the Anointed One will be *c* off
Mt 3:10 not produce good fruit will be *c*
24:22 If those days had not been *c* short,
1Co 11: 6 for a woman to have her hair *c*

CYMBAL* (CYMBALS)
1Co 13: 1 a resounding gong or a clanging *c.*

CYMBALS (CYMBAL)
1Ch 15:16 instruments: lyres, harps and *c.*
2Ch 5:12 dressed in fine linen and playing *c,*
Ps 150: 5 praise him with resounding *c.*

CYRUS
Persian king who allowed exiles to return (2Ch 36:22-Ezr 1:8), to rebuild temple (Ezr 5:13-6:14), as appointed by the LORD (Isa 44:28-45:13).

DAGON
Jdg 16:23 offer a great sacrifice to *D* their god
1Sa 5: 2 Dagon's temple and set it beside *D.*

DAMASCUS
Ac 9: 3 As he neared *D* on his journey,

DAN
1. Son of Jacob by Bilhah (Ge 30:4-6; 35:25; 46:23). Tribe of blessed (Ge 49:16-17; Dt 33:22), numbered (Nu 1:39; 26:43), allotted land (Jos 19:40-48; Eze 48:1), failed to fully possess (Jdg 1:34-35), failed to support Deborah (Jdg 5:17), possessed Laish/Dan (Jdg 18).
2. Northernmost city in Israel (Ge 14:14; Jdg 18; 20:1).

DANCE (DANCED DANCING)
Ecc 3: 4 a time to mourn and a time to *d,*
Mt 11:17 and you did not *d;*

DANCED (DANCE)
2Sa 6:14 *d* before the LORD
Mk 6:22 of Herodias came in and *d,*

DANCING (DANCE)
Ps 30:11 You turned my wailing into *d;*
149: 3 Let them praise his name with *d*

DANGER
Pr 22: 3 A prudent man sees *d*
27:12 The prudent see *d* and take refuge,
Mt 5:22 will be in *d* of the fire of hell.
Ro 8:35 famine or nakedness or *d* or sword?
2Co 11:26 I have been in *d* from rivers,

DANIEL
1. Hebrew exile to Babylon, name changed to Belteshazzar (Da 1:6-7). Refused to eat unclean food (Da 1:8-21). Interpreted Nebuchadnezzar's dreams (Da 2; 4), writing on the wall (Da 5). Thrown into lion's den (Da 6). Visions of (Da 7-12).
2. Son of David (1Ch 3:1).

DARIUS
1. King of Persia (Ezr 4:5), allowed rebuilding of temple (Ezr 5-6).
2. Mede who conquered Babylon (Da 5:31).

DARK (DARKENED DARKENS DARKNESS)
Job 34:22 There is no *d* place, no deep
Ps 18: 9 *d* clouds were under his feet.
Pr 31:15 She gets up while it is still *d;*
SS 1: 6 Do not stare at me because I am *d,*
Jn 12:35 in the *d* does not know where he is
Ro 2:19 a light for those who are in the *d,*
2Pe 1:19 as to a light shining in a *d* place,

DARKENED (DARK)
Joel 2:10 the sun and moon are *d,*
Mt 24:29 " 'the sun will be *d,*
Ro 1:21 and their foolish hearts were *d.*
Eph 4:18 They are *d* in their understanding

DARKENS (DARK)
Job 38: 2 "Who is this that *d* my counsel

DARKNESS (DARK)
Ge 1: 2 *d* was over the surface of the deep,
1: 4 he separated the light from the *d.*
Ex 10:22 and total *d* covered all Egypt
20:21 approached the thick *d* where God
2Sa 22:29 the LORD turns my *d* into light.
Ps 18:28 my God turns my *d* into light.
91: 6 the pestilence that stalks in the *d,*
112: 4 Even in *d* light dawns
139: 12 even the *d* will not be dark to you;
Pr 4:19 the way of the wicked is like deep *d*
Isa 5:20 and light for *d,*
42:16 I will turn the *d* into light
45: 7 I form the light and create *d,*
58:10 then your light will rise in the *d,*
61: 1 and release from *d,*
Joel 2:31 The sun will be turned to *d*
Mt 4:16 the people living in *d*
6:23 how great is that *d!* "No one can
Lk 11:34 are bad, your body also is full of *d.*
23:44 and *d* came over the whole land
Jn 1: 5 The light shines in the *d,*
3:19 but men loved *d* instead of light
Ac 2:20 The sun will be turned to *d*
2Co 4: 6 who said, "Let light shine out of *d*
6:14 fellowship can light have with *d?*
Eph 5: 8 For you were once *d,* but now you
5:11 to do with the fruitless deeds of *d,*
1Pe 2: 9 out of *d* into his wonderful light.
2Pe 2:17 Blackest *d* is reserved for them.
1Jn 1: 5 in him there is no *d* at all.
2: 9 but hates his brother is still in the *d.*
Jude : 6 in *d,* bound with everlasting chains
:13 for whom blackest *d* has been

DASH
Ps 2: 9 you will *d* them to pieces like

DAUGHTER (DAUGHTERS)
Ex 1:10 she took him to Pharaoh's *d*
Jdg 11:34 to commemorate the *d* of Jephthah
Est 2: 7 Mordecai had taken her as his own *d*
Ps 9:14 praises in the gates of the *D* of Zion
137: 8 O *D* of Babylon, doomed
Isa 62:11 "Say to the *D* of Zion,
Zec 9: 9 Shout, *D* of Jerusalem!
Mk 5:34 *"D,* your faith has healed you.
7:29 the demon has left your *d.*

DAUGHTERS (DAUGHTER)
Ge 6: 2 the *d* of men were beautiful,
19:36 Lot's *d* became pregnant
Nu 36:10 Zelophehad's *d* did as the LORD
Joel 2:28 sons and *d* will prophesy,

DAVID
Son of Jesse (Ru 4:17-22; 1Ch 2:13-15), ancestor of Jesus (Mt 1:1-17; Lk 3:31). Wives and children (1Sa 18; 25:39-44; 2Sa 3:2-5; 5:13-16; 11:27; 1Ch 3:1-9).
Anointed king by Samuel (1Sa 16:1-13). Musician to Saul (1Sa 16:14-23; 18:10). Killed Goliath (1Sa 17). Relation with Jonathan (1Sa 18:1-4; 19-20; 23:16-18; 2Sa 1). Disfavor of Saul (1Sa 18:6-23:29). Spared Saul's life (1Sa 24; 26). Among Philistines (1Sa 21:10-14; 27-30). Lament for Saul and Jonathan (2Sa 1).
Anointed king of Judah (2Sa 2:1-11). Conflict with house of Saul (2Sa 2-4). Anointed king of Israel (2Sa 5:1-4; 1Ch 11:1-3). Conquered Jerusalem (2Sa 5:6-10; 1Ch 11:4-9). Brought ark to Jerusalem (2Sa 6; 1Ch 13; 15-16). The LORD promised eternal dynasty (2Sa 7; 1Ch 17; Ps 132). Showed kindness to Mephibosheth (2Sa 9). Adultery with Bathsheba, murder of Uriah (2Sa 11-12). Son Amnon raped daughter Tamar; killed by Absalom (2Sa 13). Absalom's revolt (2Sa 14-17); death (2Sa 18). Sheba's revolt (2Sa 20). Victories: Philistines (2Sa 5:17-25; 1Ch 14:8-17; 2Sa 21:15-22; 1Ch 20:4-8), Ammonites (2Sa 10; 1Ch 19), various (2Sa 8; 1Ch 18). Mighty men (2Sa 23:8-39; 1Ch 11-12). Punished for numbering army (2Sa 24; 1Ch 21). Appointed Solomon king (1Ki 1:28-2:9). Prepared for building of temple (1Ch 22-29). Last words (2Sa 23:1-7). Death (1Ki 2:10-12; 1Ch 29:28).
Psalmist (Mt 22:43-45), musician (Am 6:5), prophet (2Sa 23:2-7; Ac 1:16; 2:30).
Psalms of: 2 (Ac 4:25), 3-32, 34-41, 51-65, 68-70, 86, 95 (Heb 4:7), 101, 103, 108-110, 122, 124, 131, 133, 138-145.

DAWN (DAWNED DAWNS)
Ps 37: 6 your righteousness shine like the *d,*
Pr 4:18 is like the first gleam of *d,*
Isa 14:12 O morning star, son of the *d!*
Am 4:13 he who turns *d* to darkness,
5: 8 who turns blackness into *d*

DAWNED (DAWN)
Isa 9: 2 a light has *d.*
Mt 4:16 a light has *d."*

DAWNS* (DAWN)
Ps 65: 8 where morning *d* and evening
112: 4 in darkness light *d* for the upright,
Hos 10:15 When that day *d,*
2Pe 1:19 until the day *d* and the morning

DAY (DAYS)
Ge 1: 5 God called the light *"d,"*
1: 5 and there was morning—the first *d*
1: 8 there was morning—the second *d.*
1:13 there was morning—the third *d.*
1:19 there was morning—the fourth *d.*
1:23 there was morning—the fifth *d.*
1:31 there was morning—the sixth *d.*
2: 2 so on the seventh *d* he rested
8:22 *d* and night
Ex 16:30 the people rested on the seventh *d.*
20: 8 "Remember the Sabbath *d*
Lev 16:30 on this *d* atonement will be made
23:28 because it is the *D* of Atonement,
Nu 14:14 before them in a pillar of cloud by *d*
Jos 1: 8 meditate on it *d* and night,
2Ki 7: 9 This is a *d* of good news
25:30 *D* by *d* the king gave Jehoiachin
1Ch 16:23 proclaim his salvation *d* after *d.*
Ne 8:18 *D* after *d,* from the first *d*
Ps 84:10 Better is one *d* in your courts
96: 2 proclaim his salvation *d* after *d.*
118: 24 This is the *d* the LORD has made;
Pr 27: 1 not know what a *d* may bring forth.
Isa 13: 9 a cruel *d,* with wrath and fierce
Jer 46:10 But that *d* belongs to the Lord,
50:31 "for your *d* has come,
Eze 30: 2 "Alas for that *d!"*
Joel 1:15 "Alas for that *d!*
Joel 2:31 and dreadful *d* of the LORD.
Am 3:14 On the *d* I punish Israel for her sins
5:20 Will not the *d* of the LORD be
Ob :15 "The *d* of the LORD is near
Zep 1:14 The great *d* of the LORD is near—
Zec 2:11 joined with the LORD in that *d*
14: 1 A *d* of the LORD is coming
14: 7 It will be a unique *d,*
Mal 4: 5 dreadful *d* of the LORD comes.
Mt 24:38 up to the *d* Noah entered the ark;
Lk 11: 3 Give us each *d* our daily bread.
17:24 in his *d* will be like the lightning,
Ac 5:42 *D* after *d,* in the temple courts
17:11 examined the Scriptures every *d*
17:17 as in the marketplace *d* by *d*
Ro 14: 5 man considers every *d* alike.
1Co 5: 5 his spirit saved on the *d* of the Lord
2Co 4:16 we are being renewed *d* by *d.*
11:25 I spent a night and a *d*
1Th 5: 2 for you know very well that the *d*
5: 4 so that this *d* should surprise you
2Th 2: 2 saying that the *d* of the Lord has
Heb 7:27 need to offer sacrifices *d* after *d,*
2Pe 3: 8 With the Lord a *d* is like
3:10 *d* of the Lord will come like a thief.
Rev 6:17 For the great *d* of their wrath has
16:14 on the great *d* of God Almighty.

DAYS (DAY)
Dt 17:19 he is to read it all the *d* of his life
32: 7 Remember the *d* of old;
Ps 23: 6 all the *d* of my life,
34:12 and desires to see many good *d,*
39: 5 have made my *d* a mere
90:10 The length of our *d* is seventy years
90:12 Teach us to number our *d* aright,
103: 15 As for man, his *d* are like grass,
128: 5 all the *d* of your life;
Pr 31:12 all the *d* of her life.
Ecc 9: 9 all the *d* of this meaningless life
12: 1 Creator in the *d* of your youth,
Isa 38:20 all the *d* of our lives
Da 7: 9 and the Ancient of *D* took his seat.
7:13 He approached the Ancient of *D*
7:22 until the Ancient of *D* came
Hos 3: 5 and to his blessings in the last *d.*
Joel 2:29 I will pour out my Spirit in those *d.*
Mic 4: 1 In the last *d*
Lk 19:43 The *d* will come upon you
Ac 2:17 by the prophet Joel: " 'In the last *d,*
2Ti 3: 1 will be terrible times in the last *d.*
Heb 1: 2 in these last *d* he has spoken to us
2Pe 3: 3 that in the last *d* scoffers will come,

DAZZLING*
Da 2:31 *d* statue, awesome in appearance.
Mk 9: 3 His clothes became *d* white,

DEACON* (DEACONS)
1Ti 3:12 A *d* must be the husband of

DEACONS* (DEACON)
Php 1: 1 together with the overseers and *d:*
1Ti 3: 8 *D,* likewise, are to be men worthy
3:10 against them, let them serve as *d.*

DEAD (DIE)
Lev 17:15 who eats anything found *d*
Dt 18:11 or spiritist or who consults the *d.*
Isa 8:19 Why consult the *d* on behalf
Mt 8:22 and let the *d* bury their own *d."*
28: 7 'He has risen from the *d*
Lk 15:24 For this son of mine was *d*
24:46 rise from the *d* on the third day,
Ro 6:11 count yourselves *d* to sin
1Co 15:29 do who are baptized for the *d?*
Eph 2: 1 you were *d* in your transgressions
1Th 4:16 and the *d* in Christ will rise first.
Jas 2:17 is not accompanied by action, is *d.*
2:26 so faith without deeds is *d.*
Rev 14:13 Blessed are the *d* who die
20:12 And I saw the *d,* great and small,

DEADENED* (DIE)
Jn 12:40 and *d* their hearts,

DEAR* (DEARER)
2Sa 1:26 you were very *d* to me.
Ps 102: 14 For her stones are *d*
Jer 31:20 Is not Ephraim my *d* son,
Jn 2: 4 *"D* woman, why do you involve me
19:26 he said to his mother, *"D* woman,
Ac 15:25 to you with our *d* friends Barnabas
Ro 16: 5 Greet my *d* friend Epenetus,
16: 9 in Christ, and my *d* friend Stachys.
16:12 Greet my *d* friend Persis, another
1Co 4:14 but to warn you, as my *d* children.
10:14 my *d* friends, flee from idolatry.
15:58 Therefore, my *d* brothers,
2Co 7: 1 we have these promises, *d* friends,

2Co 12:19 and everything we do, *d* friends,
Gal 4:19 My *d* children, for whom I am
Eph 6:21 the *d* brother and faithful servant
Php 2:12 my *d* friends, as you have always
4: 1 firm in the Lord, *d* friends!
Col 1: 7 Epaphras, our *d* fellow servant,
4: 7 He is a *d* brother, a faithful
4: 9 our faithful and *d* brother,
4:14 Our *d* friend Luke, the doctor,
1Th 2: 8 because you had become so *d* to us.
1Ti 6: 2 their service are believers, and *d*
2Ti 1: 2 To Timothy, my *d* son: Grace,
Phm : 1 To Philemon our *d* friend
:16 He is very *d* to me but
:16 better than a slave, as a *d* brother.
Heb 6: 9 we speak like this, *d* friends,
Jas 1:16 Don't be deceived, my *d* brothers.
1:19 My *d* brothers, take note of this:
2: 5 thoughts? Listen, my *d* brothers:
1Pe 2:11 *D* friends, I urge you, as aliens
4:12 *D* friends, do not be surprised
2Pe 3: 1 *D* friends, this is now my second
3: 8 not forget this one thing, *d* friends:
3:14 *d* friends, since you are looking
3:15 just as our *d* brother Paul
3:17 *d* friends, since you already know
1Jn 2: 1 My *d* children, I write this to you
2: 7 *D* friends, I am not writing you
2:12 I write to you, *d* children,
2:13 I write to you, *d* children,
2:18 *D* children, this is the last hour;
2:28 *d* children, continue in him,
3: 2 *D* friends, now we are children
3: 7 *D* children, do not let anyone lead
3:18 love of God be in him? *D* children,
3:21 *D* friends, if our hearts do not
4: 1 *D* friends, do not believe every
4: 4 *d* children, are from God
4: 7 *D* friends, let us love one another,
4:11 *D* friends, since God so loved us,
5:21 *D* children, keep yourselves
2Jn : 5 *d* lady, I am not writing you a new
3Jn : 1 The elder, To my *d* friend Gaius,
: 2 *D* friend, I pray that you may enjoy
: 5 *D* friend, you are faithful
:11 *D* friend, do not imitate what is evil
Jude : 3 *D* friends, although I was very
:17 But, *d* friends, remember what
:20 *d* friends, build yourselves up

DEARER* (DEAR)
Phm :16 dear to me but even *d* to you,

DEATH (DIE)
Ex 21:12 kills him shall surely be put to *d.*
Nu 35:16 the murderer shall be put to *d.*
Dt 30:19 set before you life and *d,*
Ru 1:17 if anything but *d* separates you
2Ki 4:40 O man of God, there is *d* in the pot
Job 26: 6 *D* is naked before God;
Ps 23: 4 the valley of the shadow of *d,*
44:22 for your sake we face *d* all day long
89:48 What man can live and not see *d,*
116: 15 is the *d* of his saints.
Pr 8:36 all who hate me love *d.*"
11:19 he who pursues evil goes to his *d.*
14:12 but in the end it leads to *d.*
15:11 *D* and Destruction lie open
16:25 but in the end it leads to *d.*
18:21 tongue has the power of life and *d,*
19:18 do not be a willing party to his *d.*
23:14 and save his soul from *d.*
Ecc 7: 2 for *d* is the destiny of every man;
Isa 25: 8 he will swallow up *d* forever.
53:12 he poured out his life unto *d,*
Eze 18:23 pleasure in the *d* of the wicked?
18:32 pleasure in the *d* of anyone,
33:11 pleasure in the *d* of the wicked,
Hos 13:14 Where, O *d,* are your plagues?
Jn 5:24 he has crossed over from *d* to life.
Ro 4:25 delivered over to *d* for our sins
5:12 and in this way *d* came to all men,
5:14 *d* reigned from the time of Adam
6: 3 Jesus were baptized into his *d?*
6:23 For the wages of sin is *d,*
7:24 me from this body of *d?*
8:13 put to *d* the misdeeds of the body,
8:36 your sake we face *d* all day long;
1Co 15:21 For since *d* came through a man,
15:26 The last enemy to be destroyed is *d*
15:55 Where, O *d,* is your sting?"
2Ti 1:10 who has destroyed *d* and has
Heb 2:14 him who holds the power of *d*—
1Jn 5:16 There is a sin that leads to *d.*
Rev 1:18 And I hold the keys of *d* and Hades
2:11 hurt at all by the second *d.*
20: 6 The second *d* has no power
20:14 The lake of fire is the second *d.*
20:14 Then *d* and Hades were thrown

Rev 21: 4 There will be no more *d*
21: 8 This is the second *d.*"

DEBAUCHERY*
Ro 13:13 not in sexual immorality and *d,*
2Co 12:21 and *d* in which they have indulged.
Gal 5:19 impurity and *d;* idolatry
Eph 5:18 drunk on wine, which leads to *d.*
1Pe 4: 3 living in *d,* lust, drunkenness,

DEBORAH*
1. Prophetess who led Israel to victory over Canaanites (Jdg 4-5).
2. Rebekah's nurse (Ge 35:8).

DEBT* (DEBTOR DEBTORS DEBTS)
Dt 15: 3 must cancel any *d* your brother
24: 6 the upper one—as security for a *d,*
1Sa 22: 2 or in *d* or discontented gathered
Job 24: 9 of the poor is seized for a *d.*
Mt 18:25 that he had be sold to repay the *d.*
18:27 canceled the *d* and let him go.
18:30 into prison until he could pay the *d.*
18:32 'I canceled all that *d* of yours
Lk 7:43 who had the bigger *d* canceled."
Ro 13: 8 Let no *d* remain outstanding,
13: 8 continuing *d* to love one another,

DEBTOR* (DEBT)
Isa 24: 2 for *d* as for creditor.

DEBTORS* (DEBT)
Hab 2: 7 Will not your *d* suddenly arise?
Mt 6:12 as we also have forgiven our *d.*
Lk 16: 5 called in each one of his master's *d.*

DEBTS* (DEBT)
Dt 15: 1 seven years you must cancel *d.*
15: 2 time for canceling *d* has been
15: 9 the year for canceling *d,* is near,"
31:10 in the year for canceling *d,*
2Ki 4: 7 "Go, sell the oil and pay your *d.*
Ne 10:31 the land and will cancel all *d.*
Pr 22:26 or puts up security for *d;*
Mt 6:12 Forgive us our *d,*
Lk 7:42 so he canceled the *d* of both.

DECAY*
Ps 16:10 will you let your Holy One see *d.*
49: 9 and not see *d.*
49:14 their forms will *d* in the grave,
Pr 12: 4 a disgraceful wife is like *d*
Isa 5:24 so their roots will *d*
Hab 3:16 *d* crept into my bones,
Ac 2:27 will you let your Holy One see *d.*
2:31 to the grave, nor did his body see *d.*
13:34 never to *d,* is stated in these words:
13:35 will not let your Holy One see *d.*'
13:37 raised from the dead did not see *d.*
Ro 8:21 liberated from its bondage to *d*

DECEIT (DECEIVE)
Ps 5: 9 with their tongue they speak *d.*
Isa 53: 9 nor was any *d* in his mouth.
Da 8:25 He will cause *d* to prosper,
Zep 3:13 nor will *d* be found in their mouths.
Mk 7:22 greed, malice, *d,* lewdness, envy,
Ac 13:10 You are full of all kinds of *d*
Ro 1:29 murder, strife, *d* and malice.
3:13 their tongues practice *d.*"
1Pe 2: 1 yourselves of all malice and all *d,*
2:22 and no *d* was found in his mouth."

DECEITFUL (DECEIVE)
Jer 17: 9 The heart is *d* above all things
Hos 10: 2 Their heart is *d,*
2Co 11:13 men are false apostles, *d* workmen,
Eph 4:14 of men in their *d* scheming.
4:22 is being corrupted by its *d* desires;
1Pe 3:10 and his lips from *d* speech.
Rev 21:27 who does what is shameful or *d,*

DECEITFULNESS* (DECEIVE)
Ps 119:118 for their *d* is in vain.
Mt 13:22 and the *d* of wealth choke it,
Mk 4:19 the *d* of wealth and the desires
Heb 3:13 of you may be hardened by sin's *d.*

DECEIVE (DECEIT DECEITFUL DECEITFULNESS DECEIVED DECEIVER DECEIVERS DECEIVES DECEIVING DECEPTION DECEPTIVE)
Lev 19:11 " 'Do not *d* one another.
Pr 14: 5 A truthful witness does not *d,*
24:28 or use your lips to *d.*
Jer 37: 9 Do not *d* yourselves, thinking,
Zec 13: 4 garment of hair in order to *d.*
Mt 24: 5 'I am the Christ,' and will *d* many.
24:11 will appear and *d* many people.
24:24 and miracles to *d* even the elect—

Mk 13: 6 'I am he,' and will *d* many.
13:22 and miracles to *d* the elect—
Ro 16:18 and flattery they *d* the minds
1Co 3:18 Do not *d* yourselves.
Eph 5: 6 Let no one *d* you with empty words
Col 2: 4 this so that no one may *d* you
2Th 2: 3 Don't let anyone *d* you in any way,
Jas 1:22 to the word, and so *d* yourselves.
1Jn 1: 8 we *d* ourselves and the truth is not
Rev 20: 8 and will go out to *d* the nations

DECEIVED (DECEIVE)
Ge 3:13 "The serpent *d* me, and I ate."
Lk 21: 8 "Watch out that you are not *d.*
1Co 6: 9 the kingdom of God? Do not be *d:*
2Co 11: 3 Eve was *d* by the serpent's cunning
Gal 6: 7 Do not be *d:* God cannot be
1Ti 2:14 And Adam was not the one *d;*
2Ti 3:13 to worse, deceiving and being *d.*
Tit 3: 3 *d* and enslaved by all kinds
Jas 1:16 Don't be *d,* my dear brothers.
Rev 13:14 he *d* the inhabitants of the earth.
20:10 And the devil, who *d* them,

DECEIVER (DECEIVE)
Mt 27:63 while he was still alive that *d* said,
2Jn : 7 Any such person is the *d*

DECEIVERS* (DECEIVE)
Ps 49: 5 when wicked *d* surround me—
Tit 1:10 and *d,* especially those
2Jn : 7 Many *d,* who do not acknowledge

DECEIVES (DECEIVE)
Pr 26:19 is a man who *d* his neighbor
Mt 24: 4 "Watch out that no one *d* you.
Mk 13: 5 "Watch out that no one *d* you.
Gal 6: 3 when he is nothing, he *d* himself.
2Th 2:10 sort of evil that *d* those who are
Jas 1:26 he *d* himself and his religion is

DECEIVING* (DECEIVE)
Lev 6: 2 by *d* his neighbor about something
1Ti 4: 1 follow *d* spirits and things taught
2Ti 3:13 go from bad to worse, *d*
Rev 20: 3 him from *d* the nations anymore

DECENCY* (DECENTLY)
1Ti 2: 9 women to dress modestly, with *d*

DECENTLY* (DECENCY)
Ro 13:13 Let us behave *d,* as in the daytime,

DECEPTION (DECEIVE)
Pr 14: 8 but the folly of fools is *d.*
26:26 His malice may be concealed by *d,*
Mt 27:64 This last *d* will be worse
2Co 4: 2 we do not use *d,* nor do we distort

DECEPTIVE (DECEIVE)
Pr 11:18 The wicked man earns *d* wages,
31:30 Charm is *d,* and beauty is fleeting;
Jer 7: 4 Do not trust in *d* words and say,
Col 2: 8 through hollow and *d* philosophy,

DECIDED (DECISION)
2Co 9: 7 man should give what he has *d*

DECISION (DECIDED)
Ex 28:29 heart on the breastpiece of *d*
Joel 3:14 multitudes in the valley of *d!*

DECLARE (DECLARED DECLARING)
1Ch 16:24 *D* his glory among the nations,
Ps 19: 1 The heavens *d* the glory of God;
96: 3 *D* his glory among the nations,
Isa 42: 9 and new things I *d;*

DECLARED (DECLARE)
Mk 7:19 Jesus *d* all foods "clean.")
Ro 2:13 the law who will be *d* righteous.
3:20 no one will be *d* righteous

DECLARING (DECLARE)
Ps 71: 8 *d* your splendor all day long.
Ac 2:11 we hear them *d* the wonders

DECREE (DECREED DECREES)
Ex 15:25 There the LORD made a *d*
1Ch 16:17 He confirmed it to Jacob as a *d,*
Ps 2: 7 I will proclaim the *d* of the LORD:
7: 6 Awake, my God; *d* justice.
81: 4 this is a *d* for Israel,
148: 6 he gave a *d* that will never pass
Da 4:24 and this is the *d* the Most High has
Lk 2: 1 Augustus issued a *d* that a census
Ro 1:32 know God's righteous *d* that those

DECREED (DECREE)
Ps 78: 5 He *d* statutes for Jacob
Jer 40: 2 LORD your God *d* this disaster

La 3:37 happen if the Lord has not *d* it?
Da 9:24 "Seventy 'sevens' are *d*
9:26 and desolations have been *d*.
Lk 22:22 Son of Man will go as it has been *d*,

DECREES (DECREE)
Ge 26: 5 my commands, my *d* and my laws
Ex 15:26 to his commands and keep all his *d*,
18:16 inform them of God's *d* and laws."
18:20 Teach them the *d* and laws,
Lev 10:11 Israelites all the *d* the LORD has
18: 4 and be careful to follow my *d*.
18: 5 Keep my *d* and laws,
18:26 you must keep my *d* and my laws.
Ps 119: 12 teach me your *d*.
119: 16 I delight in your *d*;
119: 48 and I meditate on your *d*.
119: 112 My heart is set on keeping your *d*

DEDICATE (DEDICATED DEDICATION)
Nu 6:12 He must *d* himself to the LORD
Pr 20:25 for a man to *d* something rashly

DEDICATED (DEDICATE)
Lev 21:12 he has been *d* by the anointing oil
Nu 6: 9 thus defiling the hair he has *d*,
6:18 shave off the hair that he *d*.
18: 6 *d* to the LORD to do the work
1Ki 8:63 and all the Israelites *d* the temple
2Ch 29:31 "You have now *d* yourselves
Ne 3: 1 They *d* it and set its doors in place,

DEDICATION (DEDICATE)
Nu 6:19 shaved off the hair of his *d*,
Jn 10:22 came the Feast of *D* at Jerusalem.
1Ti 5:11 sensual desires overcome their *d*

DEED (DEEDS)
Jer 32:10 and sealed the *d*, had it witnessed,
32:16 After I had given the *d* of purchase
Col 3:17 you do, whether in word or *d*,
2Th 2:17 and strengthen you in every good *d*

DEEDS (DEED)
Dt 3:24 or on earth who can do the *d*
4:34 or by great and awesome *d*,
34:12 the awesome *d* that Moses
1Sa 2: 3 and by him *d* are weighed.
1Ch 16:24 his marvelous *d* among all peoples.
Job 34:25 Because he takes note of their *d*,
Ps 26: 7 and telling of all your wonderful *d*.
45: 4 right hand display awesome *d*.
65: 5 with awesome *d* of righteousness,
66: 3 "How awesome are your *d*!
71:17 day I declare your marvelous *d*.
72:18 who alone does marvelous *d*.
73:28 I will tell of all your *d*.
75: 1 men tell of your wonderful *d*.
77:11 I will remember the *d* of the LORD
77:12 and consider all your mighty *d*.
78: 4 the praiseworthy *d* of the LORD,
78: 7 and would not forget his *d*
86: 8 no *d* can compare with yours.
86:10 you are great and do marvelous *d*;
88:12 or your righteous *d* in the land
90:16 May your *d* be shown
92: 4 For you make me glad by your *d*,
96: 3 his marvelous *d* among all peoples.
107: 8 and his wonderful *d* for men,
107: 15 and his wonderful *d* for men,
107: 21 and his wonderful *d* for men.
107: 24 his wonderful *d* in the deep.
107: 31 and his wonderful *d* for men.
111: 3 Glorious and majestic are his *d*,
145: 6 and I will proclaim your great *d*.
Jer 32:19 purposes and mighty are your *d*.
Hab 3: 2 I stand in awe of your *d*, O LORD.
Mt 5:16 that they may see your good *d*
Lk 1:51 He has performed mighty *d*
23:41 we are getting what our *d* deserve.
Ac 26:20 prove their repentance by their *d*.
1Ti 6:18 rich in good *d*, and to be generous
Heb 10:24 on toward love and good *d*.
Jas 2:14 claims to have faith but has no *d*?
2:18 Show me your faith without *d*,
2:20 faith without *d* is useless?
2:26 so faith without *d* is dead.
1Pe 2:12 they may see your good *d*
Rev 2:19 I know your *d*, your love and faith,
2:23 each of you according to your *d*.
3: 1 I know your *d*; you have
3: 2 I have not found your *d* complete
3: 8 I know your *d*.
3:15 I know your *d*, that you are neither
14:13 for their *d* will follow them."
15: 3 "Great and marvelous are your *d*,

DEEP (DEPTH DEPTHS)
Ge 1: 2 was over the surface of the *d*,
8: 2 Now the springs of the *d*

Ps 42: 7 *D* calls to *d*
Lk 5: 4 to Simon, "Put out into *d* water,
1Co 2:10 all things, even the *d* things
1Ti 3: 9 hold of the *d* truths of the faith

DEER
Ps 42: 1 As the *d* pants for streams of water,

DEFAMED*
Isa 48:11 How can I let myself be *d*?

DEFEATED
1Co 6: 7 have been completely *d* already.

DEFEND (DEFENDED DEFENDER DEFENDING DEFENDS DEFENSE)
Ps 72: 4 He will *d* the afflicted
74:22 Rise up, O God, and *d* your cause;
82: 2 "How long will you *d* the unjust
82: 3 *D* the cause of the weak
119: 154 *D* my cause and redeem me;
Pr 31: 9 *d* the rights of the poor and needy
Isa 1:17 *D* the cause of the fatherless,
1:23 They do not *d* the cause
Jer 5:28 they do not *d* the rights of the poor.
50:34 He will vigorously *d* their cause

DEFENDED (DEFEND)
Jer 22:16 He *d* the cause of the poor

DEFENDER (DEFEND)
Ex 22: 2 the *d* is not guilty of bloodshed;
Ps 68: 5 to the fatherless, a *d* of widows,
Pr 23:11 for their *D* is strong;

DEFENDING (DEFEND)
Ps 10:18 *d* the fatherless and the oppressed,
Ro 2:15 now accusing, now even *d* them.)
Php 1: 7 or *d* and confirming the gospel,

DEFENDS* (DEFEND)
Dt 10:18 He *d* the cause of the fatherless
33: 7 With his own hands he *d* his cause.
Isa 51:22 your God, who *d* his people:

DEFENSE (DEFEND)
Ps 35:23 Awake, and rise to my *d*!
Php 1:16 here for the *d* of the gospel.
1Jn 2: 1 speaks to the Father in our *d*—

DEFERRED*
Pr 13:12 Hope *d* makes the heart sick,

DEFIED
1Sa 17:45 armies of Israel, whom you have *d*.
1Ki 13:26 the man of God who *d* the word

DEFILE (DEFILED)
Da 1: 8 Daniel resolved not to *d* himself
Rev 14: 4 are those who did not *d* themselves

DEFILED (DEFILE)
Isa 24: 5 The earth is *d* by its people;

DEFRAUD
Lev 19:13 Do not *d* your neighbor or rob him.
Mk 10:19 do not *d*, honor your father

DEITY*
Col 2: 9 of the *D* lives in bodily form,

DELAY
Ecc 5: 4 vow to God, do not *d* in fulfilling it.
Isa 48: 9 my own name's sake I *d* my wrath;
Heb 10:37 is coming will come and will not *d*.
Rev 10: 6 and said, "There will be no more *d*!

DELICACIES
Ps 141: 4 let me not eat of their *d*.
Pr 23: 3 Do not crave his *d*,
23: 6 do not crave his *d*;

DELICIOUS*
Pr 9:17 food eaten in secret is *d*!"

DELIGHT* (DELIGHTED DELIGHTFUL DELIGHTING DELIGHTS)
Lev 26:31 and I will take no *d* in the pleasing
Dt 30: 9 The LORD will again *d* in you
1Sa 2: 1 for I *d* in your deliverance.
15:22 "Does the LORD *d*
Ne 1:11 the prayer of your servants who *d*
Job 22:26 Surely then you will find *d*
27:10 Will he find *d* in the Almighty?
Ps 1: 2 But his *d* is in the law of the LORD
16: 3 in whom is all my *d*.
35: 9 and *d* in his salvation.
35:27 those who *d* in my vindication
37: 4 *D* yourself in the LORD
43: 4 to God, my joy and my *d*.
51:16 You do not *d* in sacrifice,
51:19 whole burnt offerings to *d* you;

Ps 62: 4 they take *d* in lies.
68:30 Scatter the nations who *d* in war.
111: 2 by all who *d* in them.
112: 1 who finds great *d* in his commands.
119: 16 I *d* in your decrees;
119: 24 Your statutes are my *d*;
119: 35 for there I find *d*.
119: 47 for I *d* in your commands
119: 70 but I *d* in your law.
119: 77 for your law is my *d*.
119: 92 If your law had not been my *d*,
119: 143 but your commands are my *d*.
119: 174 and your law is my *d*.
147: 10 nor his *d* in the legs of a man;
149: 4 For the LORD takes *d*
Pr 1:22 How long will mockers *d*
2:14 who *d* in doing wrong
8:30 I was filled with *d* day after day,
11: 1 but accurate weights are his *d*.
29:17 he will bring *d* to your soul.
Ecc 2:10 My heart took *d* in all my work,
SS 1: 4 We rejoice and *d* in you;
2: 3 I *d* to sit in his shade,
Isa 5: 7 are the garden of his *d*.
11: 3 he will *d* in the fear of the LORD.
13:17 and have no *d* in gold.
32:14 the *d* of donkeys, a pasture
42: 1 my chosen one in whom I *d*;
55: 2 and your soul will *d* in the richest
58:13 if you call the Sabbath a *d*
61:10 I *d* greatly in the LORD;
62: 4 for the LORD will take *d* in you,
65:18 for I will create Jerusalem to be a *d*
65:19 and take *d* in my people;
66: 3 their souls *d* in their abominations;
66:11 *d* in her overflowing abundance."
Jer 9:24 for in these I *d*,"
15:16 they were my joy and my heart's *d*,
31:20 the child in whom I *d*?
49:25 the town in which I *d*?
Eze 24:16 away from you the *d* of your eyes.
24:21 in which you take pride, the *d*
24:25 and glory, the *d* of their eyes,
Hos 7: 3 *d* the king with their wickedness,
Mic 1:16 for the children in whom you *d*;
7:18 but *d* to show mercy.
Zep 3:17 He will take great *d* in you,
Mt 12:18 the one I love, in whom I *d*;
Mk 12:37 large crowd listened to him with *d*.
Lk 1:14 He will be a joy and *d* to you,
Ro 7:22 in my inner being I *d* in God's law;
1Co 13: 6 Love does not *d* in evil
2Co 12:10 for Christ's sake, I *d* in weaknesses,
Col 2: 5 and *d* to see how orderly you are

DELIGHTED (DELIGHT)
2Sa 22:20 he rescued me because he *d* in me.
1Ki 10: 9 who has *d* in you and placed you
2Ch 9: 8 who has *d* in you and placed you
Ps 18:19 he rescued me because he *d* in me.
Lk 13:17 but the people were *d* with all

DELIGHTFUL* (DELIGHT)
Ps 16: 6 surely I have a *d* inheritance.
SS 1: 2 for your love is more *d* than wine.
4:10 How *d* is your love, my sister,
Mal 3:12 for yours will be a *d* land,"

DELIGHTING* (DELIGHT)
Pr 8:31 and *d* in mankind.

DELIGHTS (DELIGHT)
Est 6: 6 for the man the king *d* to honor?"
Ps 22: 8 since he *d* in him."
35:27 who *d* in the well-being
36: 8 from your river of *d*.
37:23 if the LORD *d* in a man's way
147: 11 the LORD *d* in those who fear him,
Pr 3:12 as a father the son he *d* in.
10:23 of understanding *d* in wisdom.
11:20 he *d* in those whose ways are
12:22 but he *d* in men who are truthful.
14:35 A king *d* in a wise servant,
18: 2 but *d* in airing his own opinions.
23:24 he who has a wise son *d* in him.
Col 2:18 Do not let anyone who *d*

DELILAH*
Woman who betrayed Samson (Jdg 16:4-22).

DELIVER (DELIVERANCE DELIVERED DELIVERER DELIVERS)
Dt 32:39 and no one can *d* out of my hand.
Ps 22: 8 Let him *d* him,
72:12 For he will *d* the needy who cry out
79: 9 *d* us and forgive our sins
109: 21 out of the goodness of your love, *d* me.
119: 170 *d* me according to your promise.
Mt 6:13 but *d* us from the evil one.'

2Co 1:10 hope that he will continue to *d* us,

DELIVERANCE (DELIVER)
1Sa 2: 1 for I delight in your *d*.
Ps 3: 8 From the LORD comes *d*.
32: 7 and surround me with songs of *d*.
33:17 A horse is a vain hope for *d*;
Ob :17 But on Mount Zion will be *d*;

DELIVERED (DELIVER)
Ps 34: 4 he *d* me from all my fears.
107: 6 and he *d* them from their distress.
116: 8 have *d* my soul from death,
Da 12: 1 written in the book—will be *d*.
Ro 4:25 He was *d* over to death for our sins

DELIVERER* (DELIVER)
Jdg 3: 9 for them a *d*, Othniel son of Kenaz,
3:15 and he gave them a *d*— Ehud,
2Sa 22: 2 is my rock, my fortress and my *d*;
2Ki 13: 5 The LORD provided a *d* for Israel,
Ps 18: 2 is my rock, my fortress and my *d*;
40:17 You are my help and my *d*;
70: 5 You are my help and my *d*;
140: 7 O Sovereign LORD, my strong *d*,
144: 2 my stronghold and my *d*,
Ac 7:35 sent to be their ruler and *d*
Ro 11:26 "The *d* will come from Zion;

DELIVERS (DELIVER)
Ps 34:17 he *d* them from all their troubles.
34:19 but the LORD *d* him from them all
37:40 The LORD helps them and *d* them
37:40 he *d* them from the wicked

DELUSION*
2Th 2:11 God sends them a powerful *d*

DEMAND (DEMANDED)
Lk 6:30 belongs to you, do not *d* it back.

DEMANDED (DEMAND)
Lk 12:20 This very night your life will be *d*
12:48 been given much, much will be *d*;

DEMETRIUS
Ac 19:24 A silversmith named *D*, who made

DEMON* (DEMONS)
Mt 9:33 And when the *d* was driven out,
11:18 and they say, 'He has a *d*.'
17:18 Jesus rebuked the *d*, and it came
Mk 7:26 to drive the *d* out of her daughter.
7:29 the *d* has left your daughter."
7:30 lying on the bed, and the *d* gone.
Lk 4:33 there was a man possessed by a *d*,
4:35 Then the *d* threw the man
7:33 wine, and you say, 'He has a *d*.'
8:29 driven by the *d* into solitary places.
9:42 the *d* threw him to the ground
11:14 When the *d* left, the man who had
11:14 was driving out a *d* that was mute.
Jn 8:49 "I am not possessed by a *d*,"
10:21 Can a *d* open the eyes of the blind
10:21 sayings of a man possessed by a *d*.

DEMON-POSSESSED* (DEMON-POSSESSION)
Mt 4:24 those suffering severe pain, the *d*,
8:16 many who were *d* were brought
8:28 two *d* men coming
8:33 what had happened to the *d* men.
9:32 man who was *d* and could not talk
12:22 they brought him a *d* man who was
Mk 1:32 brought to Jesus all the sick and *d*.
5:16 what had happened to the *d* man—
5:18 the man who had been *d* begged
Lk 8:27 met by a *d* man from the town.
8:36 the people how the *d* man had been
Jn 7:20 "You are *d*," the crowd answered.
8:48 that you are a Samaritan and *d*?"
8:52 "Now we know that you are *d*!
10:20 Many of them said, "He is *d*
Ac 19:13 Jesus over those who were *d*.

DEMON-POSSESSION* (DEMON-POSSESSED)
Mt 15:22 is suffering terribly from *d*."

DEMONS* (DEMON)
Dt 32:17 to *d*, which are not God—
Ps 106: 37 and their daughters to *d*.
Mt 7:22 and in your name drive out *d*
8:31 *d* begged Jesus, "If you drive us
9:34 prince of *d* that he drives out *d*."
10: 8 who have leprosy, drive out *d*.
12:24 of *d*, that this fellow drives out
12:24 that this fellow drives out *d*."
12:27 And if I drive out *d* by Beelzebub,
12:28 if I drive out *d* by the Spirit of God,
Mk 1:34 He also drove out many *d*,
1:34 but he would not let the *d* speak
1:39 their synagogues and driving out *d*.
3:15 to have authority to drive out *d*.
3:22 the prince of *d* he is driving out *d*."
5:12 The *d* begged Jesus, "Send us
5:15 possessed by the legion of *d*,
6:13 They drove out many *d*
9:38 "we saw a man driving out *d*
16: 9 out of whom he had driven seven *d*
16:17 In my name they will drive out *d*;
Lk 4:41 *d* came out of many people,
8: 2 from whom seven *d* had come out;
8:30 because many *d* had gone into him.
8:32 The *d* begged Jesus to let them go
8:33 When the *d* came out of the man,
8:35 from whom the *d* had gone out,
8:38 from whom the *d* had gone out
9: 1 and authority to drive out all *d*
9:49 "we saw a man driving out *d*
10:17 the *d* submit to us in your name."
11:15 the prince of *d*, he is driving out *d*."
11:18 you claim that I drive out *d*
11:19 Now if I drive out *d* by Beelzebub,
11:20 if I drive out *d* by the finger of God,
13:32 'I will drive out *d* and heal people
Ro 8:38 neither angels nor *d*, neither
1Co 10:20 of pagans are offered to *d*,
10:20 you to be participants with *d*.
10:21 of the Lord and the cup of *d* too;
10:21 the Lord's table and the table of *d*.
1Ti 4: 1 spirits and things taught by *d*.
Jas 2:19 Good! Even the *d* believe that—
Rev 9:20 they did not stop worshiping *d*,
16:14 of *d* performing miraculous signs,
18: 2 She has become a home for *d*

DEMONSTRATE* (DEMONSTRATES DEMONSTRATION)
Ro 3:25 He did this to *d* his justice,
3:26 he did it to *d* his justice

DEMONSTRATES* (DEMONSTRATE)
Ro 5: 8 God *d* his own love for us in this:

DEMONSTRATION* (DEMONSTRATE)
1Co 2: 4 but with a *d* of the Spirit's power,

DEN
Da 6:16 and threw him into the lions' *d*.
Mt 21:13 you are making it a '*d* of robbers.'"
Mk 11:17 you have made it 'a *d* of robbers.'"
Lk 19:46 but you have made it 'a *d* of robbers

DENARII* (DENARIUS)
Mt 18:28 who owed him a hundred *d*.
Lk 7:41 One owed him five hundred *d*,

DENARIUS (DENARII)
Mt 20: 2 agreed to pay them a *d* for the day
Mk 12:15 Bring me a *d* and let me look at it."

DENIED (DENY)
Mt 26:70 But he *d* it before them all.
Mk 14:68 But he *d* it.
Lk 22:57 But he *d* it.
Jn 18:25 He *d* it, saying, "I am not."
1Ti 5: 8 he has *d* the faith and is worse
Rev 3: 8 my word and have not *d* my name.

DENIES (DENY)
1Jn 2:22 It is the man who *d* that Jesus is
2:23 No one who *d* the Son has

DENY (DENIED DENIES DENYING)
Ex 23: 6 "Do not *d* justice to your poor
Job 27: 5 till I die, I will not *d* my integrity.
Isa 5:23 but *d* justice to the innocent.
La 3:35 to *d* a man his rights
Am 2: 7 and *d* justice to the oppressed.
Mt 16:24 he must *d* himself and take up his
Mk 8:34 he must *d* himself and take up his
Lk 9:23 he must *d* himself and take up his
22:34 you will *d* three times that you
Ac 4:16 miracle, and we cannot *d* it.
Tit 1:16 but by their actions they *d* him.
Jas 3:14 do not boast about it or *d* the truth.
Jude : 4 *d* Jesus Christ our only Sovereign

DENYING* (DENY)
Eze 22:29 mistreat the alien, *d* them justice.
2Ti 3: 5 a form of godliness but *d* its power.
2Pe 2: 1 *d* the sovereign Lord who bought

DEPART (DEPARTED DEPARTS DEPARTURE)
Ge 49:10 The scepter will not *d* from Judah,
Job 1:21 and naked I will *d*.
Mt 25:41 '*D* from me, you who are cursed,
Php 1:23 I desire to *d* and be with Christ,

DEPARTED (DEPART)
1Sa 4:21 "The glory has *d* from Israel"—
Ps 119: 102 I have not *d* from your laws,

DEPARTS (DEPART)
Ecc 5:15 and as he comes, so he *d*.

DEPARTURE (DEPART)
Lk 9:31 spoke about his *d*, which he was
2Ti 4: 6 and the time has come for my *d*.
2Pe 1:15 after my *d* you will always be able

DEPEND
Ps 62: 7 My salvation and my honor *d*

DEPOSES*
Da 2:21 he sets up kings and *d* them.

DEPOSIT
Mt 25:27 money on *d* with the bankers,
Lk 19:23 didn't you put my money on *d*,
2Co 1:22 put his Spirit in our hearts as a *d*,
5: 5 and has given us the Spirit as a *d*,
Eph 1:14 who is a *d* guaranteeing our
2Ti 1:14 Guard the good *d* that was

DEPRAVED* (DEPRAVITY)
Eze 16:47 ways you soon became more *d*
23:11 and prostitution she was more *d*
Ro 1:28 he gave them over to a *d* mind,
Php 2:15 fault in a crooked and *d* generation,
2Ti 3: 8 oppose the truth—men of *d* minds,

DEPRAVITY* (DEPRAVED)
Ro 1:29 of wickedness, evil, greed and *d*.
2Pe 2:19 they themselves are slaves of *d*—

DEPRIVE
Dt 24:17 Do not *d* the alien or the fatherless
Pr 18: 5 or to *d* the innocent of justice.
31: 5 *d* all the oppressed of their rights.
Isa 10: 2 to *d* the poor of their rights
29:21 with false testimony *d* the innocent
La 3:36 to *d* a man of justice—
1Co 7: 5 Do not *d* each other
9:15 die than have anyone *d* me

DEPTH (DEEP)
Ro 8:39 any powers, neither height nor *d*,
11:33 the *d* of the riches of the wisdom

DEPTHS (DEEP)
Ps 130: 1 Out of the *d* I cry to you, O LORD;

DERIDES*
Pr 11:12 who lacks judgment *d* his neighbor,

DERIVES*
Eph 3:15 in heaven and on earth *d* its name.

DESCEND (DESCENDED DESCENDING)
Ro 10: 7 "or 'Who will *d* into the deep?'"

DESCENDED (DESCEND)
Eph 4: 9 except that he also *d* to the lower,
Heb 7:14 For it is clear that our Lord *d*

DESCENDING (DESCEND)
Ge 28:12 of God were ascending and *d* on it.
Mt 3:16 the Spirit of God *d* like a dove
Mk 1:10 and the Spirit *d* on him like a dove.
Jn 1:51 and *d* on the Son of Man."

DESECRATING*
Ne 13:17 you are doing—*d* the Sabbath day?
13:18 against Israel by *d* the Sabbath."
Isa 56: 2 who keeps the Sabbath without *d* it
56: 6 who keep the Sabbath without *d* it
Eze 44: 7 *d* my temple while you offered me

DESERT
Nu 32:13 wander in the *d* forty years,
Dt 8:16 He gave you manna to eat in the *d*,
29: 5 years that I led you through the *d*,
Ne 9:19 you did not abandon them in the *d*.
Ps 78:19 "Can God spread a table in the *d*?
78:52 led them like sheep through the *d*.
Pr 21:19 Better to live in a *d*
Isa 32: 2 like streams of water in the *d*
32:15 and the *d* becomes a fertile field,
35: 6 and streams in the *d*.
43:20 because I provide water in the *d*
Mk 1: 3 "a voice of one calling in the *d*,
1:13 and he was in the *d* forty days,
Rev 12: 6 fled into the *d* to a place prepared

DESERTED (DESERTS)
Ezr 9: 9 our God has not *d* us
Mt 26:56 all the disciples *d* him and fled.
2Ti 1:15 in the province of Asia has *d* me,

DESERTING (DESERTS)
Gal 1: 6 are so quickly *d* the one who called

DESERTS (DESERTED DESERTING)
Zec 11:17 who *d* the flock!

DESERVE* (DESERVED DESERVES)
Ge 40:15 to *d* being put in a dungeon."
Lev 26:21 times over, as your sins *d*.
Jdg 20:10 it can give them what they *d*
1Sa 26:16 you and your men *d* to die,
1Ki 2:26 You *d* to die, but I will not put you
Ps 28: 4 bring back upon them what they *d*.
94: 2 pay back to the proud what they *d*.
103: 10 he does not treat us as our sins *d*
Pr 3:27 from those who *d* it,
Ecc 8:14 men who get what the righteous *d*,
8:14 men who get what the wicked *d*,
Isa 66: 6 repaying his enemies all they *d*.
Jer 14:16 out on them the calamity they *d*.
17:10 according to what his deeds *d*."
21:14 I will punish you as your deeds *d*,
32:19 to his conduct and as his deeds *d*.
49:12 "If those who do not *d*
La 3:64 Pay them back what they *d*,
Eze 16:59 I will deal with you as you *d*,
Zec 1: 6 to us what our ways and practices *d*
Mt 8: 8 I do not *d* to have you come
22: 8 those I invited did not *d* to come.
Lk 7: 6 for I do not *d* to have you come
23:15 he has done nothing to *d* death.
23:41 for we are getting what our deeds *d*
Ro 1:32 those who do such things *d* death,
1Co 15: 9 even *d* to be called an apostle,
16:18 Such men *d* recognition.
2Co 11:15 end will be what their actions *d*.
Rev 16: 6 blood to drink as they *d*."

DESERVED* (DESERVE)
2Sa 19:28 descendants *d* nothing
Ezr 9:13 less than our sins have *d*
Job 33:27 but I did not get what I *d*.
Ac 23:29 charge against him that *d* death
Ro 3: 8 Their condemnation is *d*.

DESERVES* (DESERVE)
Nu 35:31 the life of a murderer, who *d* to die.
Dt 25: 2 If the guilty man *d* to be beaten,
25: 2 the number of lashes his crime *d*,
Jdg 9:16 and if you have treated him as he *d*
2Sa 12: 5 the man who did this *d* to die!
Job 34:11 upon him what his conduct *d*.
Jer 51: 6 he will pay her what she *d*.
Lk 7: 4 "This man *d* to have you do this,
10: 7 for the worker *d* his wages.
Ac 26:31 is not doing anything that *d* death
1Ti 1:15 saying that *d* full acceptance:
4: 9 saying that *d* full acceptance
5:18 and "The worker *d* his wages."
Heb 10:29 severely do you think a man *d*

DESIGNATED
Lk 6:13 also *d* apostles: Simon (whom he
Heb 5:10 and was *d* by God to be high priest

DESIRABLE* (DESIRE)
Ge 3: 6 and also *d* for gaining wisdom,
Pr 22: 1 A good name is more *d*
Jer 3:19 and give you a *d* land,

DESIRE* (DESIRABLE DESIRED DESIRES)
Ge 3:16 Your *d* will be for your husband,
Dt 5:21 You shall not set your *d*
1Sa 9:20 to whom is all the *d* of Israel turned
2Sa 19:38 anything you *d* from me I will do
23: 5 and grant me my every *d*?
1Ch 29:18 keep this *d* in the hearts
2Ch 1:11 "Since this is your heart's *d*
9: 8 and his *d* to uphold them forever,
Job 13: 3 But I *d* to speak to the Almighty
21:14 We have no *d* to know your ways.
Ps 10:17 O LORD, the *d* of the afflicted;
20: 4 May he give you the *d*
21: 2 You have granted him the *d*
27:12 me over to the *d* of my foes,
40: 6 Sacrifice and offering you did not *d*
40: 8 I *d* to do your will, O my God;
40:14 may all who *d* my ruin
41: 2 him to the *d* of his foes.
51: 6 Surely you *d* truth
70: 2 may all who *d* my ruin
73:25 earth has nothing I *d* besides you
Pr 3:15 nothing you *d* can compare
8:11 and nothing you *d* can compare
10:24 what the righteous *d* will be
11:23 The *d* of the righteous ends only
12:12 The wicked *d* the plunder
17:16 since he has no *d* to get wisdom?
24: 1 do not *d* their company;
Ecc 12: 5 and *d* no longer is stirred.
SS 6:12 my *d* set me among the royal
7:10 and his *d* is for me.
Isa 26: 8 are the *d* of our hearts.
53: 2 appearance that we should *d* him.
55:11 but will accomplish what I *d*
Eze 24:25 delight of their eyes, their heart's *d*,
Hos 6: 6 For I *d* mercy, not sacrifice,
Mic 7: 3 the powerful dictate what they *d*—
Mal 3: 1 whom you *d*, will come," says
Mt 9:13 learn what this means: 'I *d* mercy,
12: 7 what these words mean, 'I *d* mercy,
Jn 8:44 want to carry out your father's *d*.
Ro 7: 8 in me every kind of covetous *d*.
7:18 For I have the *d* to do what is good,
9:16 depend on man's *d* or effort,
10: 1 my heart's *d* and prayer to God
1Co 12:31 But eagerly *d* the greater gifts.
14: 1 and eagerly *d* spiritual gifts,
2Co 8:10 but also to have the *d* to do so.
8:13 Our *d* is not that others might be
Php 1:23 I *d* to depart and be with Christ,
Heb 10: 5 Sacrifice and offering you did not *d*
10: 8 and sin offerings you did not *d*,
13:18 *d* to live honorably in every way.
Jas 1:14 by his own evil *d*, he is dragged
1:15 Then, after *d* has conceived,
2Pe 2:10 of those who follow the corrupt *d*

DESIRED (DESIRE)
Hag 2: 7 and the *d* of all nations will come,
Lk 22:15 "I have eagerly *d* to eat this

DESIRES* (DESIRE)
Ge 4: 7 at your door; it *d* to have you,
41:16 will give Pharaoh the answer he *d*."
2Sa 3:21 rule over all that your heart *d*."
1Ki 11:37 rule over all that your heart *d*;
Job 17:11 and so are the *d* of my heart.
31:16 "If I have denied the *d* of the poor
Ps 34:12 and *d* to see many good days,
37: 4 he will give you the *d* of your heart.
103: 5 who satisfies your *d* with good things,
140: 8 do not grant the wicked their *d*,
145: 16 satisfy the *d* of every living thing.
145: 19 He fulfills the *d* of those who fear
Pr 11: 6 the unfaithful are trapped by evil *d*.
13: 4 *d* of the diligent are fully satisfied.
19:22 What a man *d* is unfailing love;
Ecc 6: 2 so that he lacks nothing his heart *d*,
SS 2: 7 or awaken love / until it so *d*.
3: 5 or awaken love / until it so *d*.
8: 4 or awaken love / until it so *d*.
Hab 2: 4 his *d* are not upright—
Mk 4:19 and the *d* for other things come in
Ro 1:24 over in the sinful *d* of their hearts
6:12 body so that you obey its evil *d*.
8: 5 set on what that nature *d*;
8: 5 set on what the Spirit *d*.
13:14 to gratify the *d* of the sinful nature.
Gal 5:16 and you will not gratify the *d*
5:17 the sinful nature *d* what is contrary
5:24 nature with its passions and *d*.
Eph 2: 3 and following its *d* and thoughts.
4:22 being corrupted by its deceitful *d*;
Col 3: 5 impurity, lust, evil *d* and greed,
1Ti 3: 1 an overseer, he *d* a noble task.
5:11 their sensual *d* overcome their
6: 9 and harmful *d* that plunge men
2Ti 2:22 Flee the evil *d* of youth,
3: 6 are swayed by all kinds of evil *d*,
4: 3 Instead, to suit their own *d*,
Jas 1:20 about the righteous life that God *d*.
4: 1 from your *d* that battle within you?
1Pe 1:14 conform to the evil *d* you had
2:11 to abstain from sinful *d*, which war
4: 2 of his earthly life for evil human *d*,
2Pe 1: 4 in the world caused by evil *d*.
2:18 to the lustful *d* of sinful human
3: 3 and following their own evil *d*.
1Jn 2:17 The world and its *d* pass away,
Jude :16 they follow their own evil *d*;
:18 will follow their own ungodly *d*."

DESOLATE (DESOLATION)
Isa 54: 1 are the children of the *d* woman
Gal 4:27 are the children of the *d* woman

DESOLATION (DESOLATE)
Da 11:31 up the abomination that causes *d*.
12:11 abomination that causes *d* is set up,
Mt 24:15 'the abomination that causes *d*,'

DESPAIR (DESPAIRED)
Isa 61: 3 instead of a spirit of *d*.
2Co 4: 8 perplexed, but not in *d*; persecuted,

DESPAIRED* (DESPAIR)
2Co 1: 8 ability to endure, so that we *d*

DESPERATE*
2Sa 12:18 He may do something *d*."
Ps 60: 3 have shown your people *d* times;
79: 8 for we are in *d* need.
142: 6 for I am in *d* need;

DESPISE (DESPISED DESPISES)
2Sa 12: 9 Why did you *d* the word
Job 5:17 so do not *d* the discipline
36: 5 God is mighty, but does not *d* men;
42: 6 Therefore I *d* myself
Ps 51:17 O God, you will not *d*.
102: 17 he will not *d* their plea.
Pr 1: 7 but fools *d* wisdom and discipline.
3:11 do not *d* the LORD's discipline
6:30 Men do not *d* a thief if he steals
23:22 do not *d* your mother
Jer 14:21 of your name do not *d* us;
Am 5:10 and *d* him who tells the truth.
5:21 "I hate, I *d* your religious feasts;
Mt 6:24 devoted to the one and *d* the other.
Lk 16:13 devoted to the one and *d* the other.
1Co 11:22 Or do you *d* the church of God
Tit 2:15 Do not let anyone *d* you.
2Pe 2:10 of the sinful nature and *d* authority.

DESPISED (DESPISE)
Ge 25:34 So Esau *d* his birthright.
Ps 22: 6 by men and *d* by the people.
Pr 12: 8 but men with warped minds are *d*.
Isa 53: 3 He was *d* and rejected by men,
53: 3 he was *d*, and we esteemed him not
1Co 1:28 of this world and the *d* things—

DESPISES (DESPISE)
Pr 14:21 He who *d* his neighbor sins,
15:20 but a foolish man *d* his mother.
15:32 who ignores discipline *d* himself,
Zec 4:10 "Who *d* the day of small things?

DESTINED (DESTINY)
Lk 2:34 "This child is *d* to cause the falling
1Co 2: 7 and that God *d* for our glory
Col 2:22 These are all *d* to perish with use,
1Th 3: 3 know quite well that we were *d*
Heb 9:27 Just as man is *d* to die once,
1Pe 2: 8 which is also what they were *d* for.

DESTINY* (DESTINED PREDESTINED)
Job 8:13 Such is the *d* of all who forget God;
Ps 73:17 then I understood their final *d*.
Ecc 7: 2 for death is the *d* of every man;
9: 2 share a common *d*— the righteous
9: 3 the sun: The same *d* overtakes all.
Isa 65:11 and fill bowls of mixed wine for *D*,
Php 3:19 Their *d* is destruction, their god is

DESTITUTE
Ps 102: 17 to the prayer of the *d*;
Pr 31: 8 for the rights of all who are *d*.
Heb 11:37 *d*, persecuted and mistreated—

DESTROY (DESTROYED DESTROYING DESTROYS DESTRUCTION DESTRUCTIVE)
Ge 6:17 floodwaters on the earth to *d* all life
9:11 will there be a flood to *d* the earth."
Pr 1:32 complacency of fools will *d* them;
Mt 10:28 of the One who can *d* both soul
Mk 14:58 'I will *d* this man-made temple
Lk 4:34 to *d* us? I know who you are—
Jn 10:10 only to steal and kill and *d*;
Ac 8: 3 But Saul began to *d* the church.
Rev 11:18 destroying those who *d* the earth."

DESTROYED (DESTROY)
Dt 8:19 you today that you will surely be *d*.
Job 19:26 And after my skin has been *d*,
Pr 6:15 he will suddenly be *d*—
11: 3 the unfaithful are *d*
21:28 listens to him will be *d* forever.
29: 1 will suddenly be *d*—
Isa 55:13 which will not be *d*."
Da 2:44 up a kingdom that will never be *d*,
6:26 his kingdom will not be *d*,
1Co 5: 5 so that the sinful nature may be *d*
8:11 for whom Christ died, is *d*
15:24 Father after he has *d* all dominion,
15:26 The last enemy to be *d* is death.
2Co 4: 9 abandoned; struck down, but not *d*.
5: 1 if the earthly tent we live in is *d*,
Gal 5:15 or you will be *d* by each other.
Eph 2:14 the two one and has *d* the barrier,
2Ti 1:10 who has *d* death and has brought
Heb 10:39 of those who shrink back and are *d*,
2Pe 2:12 born only to be caught and *d*,
3:10 the elements will be *d* by fire,
3:11 Since everything will be *d*
Jude : 5 later *d* those who did not believe.
:11 have been *d* in Korah's rebellion.

DESTROYING (DESTROY)
Jer 23: 1 "Woe to the shepherds who are *d*

DESTROYS (DESTROY)
Pr 6:32 whoever does so *d* himself.
11: 9 mouth the godless *d* his neighbor,
18: 9 is brother to one who *d.*
28:24 he is partner to him who *d.*
Ecc 9:18 but one sinner *d* much good.
1Co 3:17 If anyone *d* God's temple,

DESTRUCTION (DESTROY)
Nu 32:15 and you will be the cause of their *d*
Pr 16:18 Pride goes before *d,*
17:19 he who builds a high gate invites *d.*
24:22 for those two will send sudden *d*
Hos 13:14 Where, O grave, is your *d?*
Mt 7:13 broad is the road that leads to *d,*
Lk 6:49 it collapsed and its *d* was complete
Jn 17:12 except the one doomed to *d*
Ro 9:22 of his wrath—prepared for *d?*
Gal 6: 8 from that nature will reap *d;*
Php 3:19 Their destiny is *d,* their god is their
1Th 5: 3 *d* will come on them suddenly,
2Th 1: 9 punished with everlasting *d*
2: 3 is revealed, the man doomed to *d.*
1Ti 6: 9 that plunge men into ruin and *d.*
2Pe 2: 1 bringing swift *d* on themselves.
2: 3 and their *d* has not been sleeping.
3: 7 of judgment and *d* of ungodly men.
3:12 That day will bring about the *d*
3:16 other Scriptures, to their own *d.*
Rev 17: 8 out of the Abyss and go to his *d.*
17:11 to the seven and is going to his *d.*

DESTRUCTIVE (DESTROY)
2Pe 2: 1 will secretly introduce *d* heresies,

DETERMINED (DETERMINES)
Job 14: 5 Man's days are *d;*
Isa 14:26 This is the plan *d* for the whole
Da 11:36 for what has been *d* must take place
Ac 17:26 and he *d* the times set for them

DETERMINES* (DETERMINED)
Ps 147: 4 He *d* the number of the stars
Pr 16: 9 but the LORD *d* his steps.
1Co 12:11 them to each one, just as he *d.*

DETEST (DETESTABLE DETESTED DETESTS)
Lev 11:10 in the water—you are to *d.*
Pr 8: 7 for my lips *d* wickedness.
13:19 but fools *d* turning from evil.
16:12 Kings *d* wrongdoing,
24: 9 and men *d* a mocker.
29:27 The righteous *d* the dishonest;
29:27 the wicked *d* the upright.

DETESTABLE (DETEST)
Pr 6:16 seven that are *d* to him:
21:27 The sacrifice of the wicked is *d*—
28: 9 even his prayers are *d.*
Isa 1:13 Your incense is *d* to me.
41:24 he who chooses you is *d.*
44:19 Shall I make a *d* thing
Jer 44: 4 'Do not do this *d* thing that I hate!'
Eze 8:13 doing things that are even more *d."*
Lk 16:15 among men is *d* in God's sight.
Tit 1:16 They are *d,* disobedient
1Pe 4: 3 orgies, carousing and *d* idolatry.

DETESTED* (DETEST)
Zec 11: 8 The flock *d* me, and I grew weary

DETESTS* (DETEST)
Dt 22: 5 LORD your God *d* anyone who
23:18 the LORD your God *d* them both.
25:16 LORD your God *d* anyone who
Pr 3:32 for the LORD *d* a perverse man
11:20 The LORD *d* men
12:22 The LORD *d* lying lips,
15: 8 The LORD *d* the sacrifice
15: 9 The LORD *d* the way
15:26 The LORD *d* the thoughts
16: 5 The LORD *d* all the proud of heart
17:15 the LORD *d* them both.
20:10 the LORD *d* them both.
20:23 The LORD *d* differing weights,

DEVIATE*
2Ch 8:15 They did not *d* from the king's

DEVICES*
Ps 81:12 to follow their own *d.*

DEVIL* (DEVIL'S)
Mt 4: 1 the desert to be tempted by the *d.*
4: 5 the *d* took him to the holy city
4: 8 *d* took him to a very high mountain
Mt 4:11 the *d* left him, and angels came
13:39 the enemy who sows them is the *d.*
25:41 the eternal fire prepared for the *d*
Lk 4: 2 forty days he was tempted by the *d.*
4: 3 *d* said to him, "If you are the Son
4: 5 The *d* led him up to a high place
4: 9 The *d* led him to Jerusalem
4:13 When the *d* had finished all this
8:12 then the *d* comes and takes away
Jn 6:70 of you is a *d!"* (He meant Judas,
8:44 You belong to your father, the *d,*
13: 2 the *d* had already prompted Judas
Ac 10:38 were under the power of the *d,*
13:10 "You are a child of the *d*
Eph 4:27 and do not give the *d* a foothold.
1Ti 3: 6 under the same judgment as the *d.*
2Ti 2:26 and escape from the trap of the *d,*
Heb 2:14 the *d*— and free those who all their
Jas 3:15 but is earthly, unspiritual, of the *d.*
4: 7 Resist the *d,* and he will flee
1Pe 5: 8 Your enemy the *d* prowls
1Jn 3: 8 because the *d* has been sinning
3: 8 who does what is sinful is of the *d,*
3:10 and who the children of the *d* are:
Jude : 9 with the *d* about the body of Moses
Rev 2:10 the *d* will put some of you in prison
12: 9 that ancient serpent called the *d*
12:12 the *d* has gone down to you!
20: 2 that ancient serpent, who is the *d,*
20:10 And the *d,* who deceived them,

DEVIL'S* (DEVIL)
Eph 6:11 stand against the *d* schemes.
1Ti 3: 7 into disgrace and into the *d* trap.
1Jn 3: 8 was to destroy the *d* work.

DEVIOUS*
Pr 2:15 and who are *d* in their ways.
14: 2 he whose ways are *d* despises him.
21: 8 The way of the guilty is *d,*

DEVOTE* (DEVOTED DEVOTING DEVOTION DEVOUT)
1Ch 22:19 Now *d* your heart and soul
2Ch 31: 4 Levites so they could *d* themselves
Job 11:13 "Yet if you *d* your heart to him
Jer 30:21 for who is he who will *d* himself
Mic 4:13 You will *d* their ill-gotten gains
1Co 7: 5 so that you may *d* yourselves
Col 4: 2 *D* yourselves to prayer, being
1Ti 1: 4 nor to *d* themselves to myths
4:13 *d* yourself to the public reading
Tit 3: 8 may be careful to *d* themselves
3:14 people must learn to *d* themselves

DEVOTED (DEVOTE)
1Ki 11: 4 and his heart was not fully *d*
Ezr 7:10 For Ezra had *d* himself to the study
Ps 86: 2 Guard my life, for I am *d* to you.
Mt 6:24 or he will be *d* to the one
Mk 7:11 from me is Corban' (that is, a gift *d*
Ac 2:42 They *d* themselves
18: 5 Paul *d* himself exclusively
Ro 12:10 Be *d* to one another
1Co 7:34 Her aim is to be *d* to the Lord
16:15 and they have *d* themselves
2Co 7:12 for yourselves how *d* to us you are.

DEVOTING* (DEVOTE)
1Ti 5:10 *d* herself to all kinds of good deeds.

DEVOTION* (DEVOTE)
2Ki 20: 3 and with wholehearted *d* and have
1Ch 28: 9 and serve him with wholehearted *d*
29: 3 in my *d* to the temple
29:19 son Solomon the wholehearted *d*
2Ch 32:32 and his acts of *d* are written
35:26 of Josiah's reign and his acts of *d,*
Job 6:14 despairing man should have the *d*
15: 4 and hinder *d* to God.
Isa 38: 3 and with wholehearted *d* and have
Jer 2: 2 " 'I remember the *d* of your youth,
Eze 33:31 With their mouths they express *d,*
1Co 7:35 way in undivided *d* to the Lord.
2Co 11: 3 from your sincere and pure *d*

DEVOUR (DEVOURED DEVOURING DEVOURS)
2Sa 2:26 "Must the sword *d* forever?
Mk 12:40 They *d* widows' houses
1Pe 5: 8 lion looking for someone to *d.*

DEVOURED (DEVOUR)
Jer 30:16 But all who devour you will be *d;*

DEVOURING (DEVOUR)
Gal 5:15 keep on biting and *d* each other,

DEVOURS (DEVOUR)
2Sa 11:25 the sword *d* one as well as another.
Pr 21:20 but a foolish man *d* all he has.

DEVOUT* (DEVOTE)
1Ki 18: 3 (Obadiah was a *d* believer
Isa 57: 1 *d* men are taken away,
Lk 2:25 Simeon, who was righteous and *d.*
Ac 10: 2 his family were *d* and God-fearing;
10: 7 a *d* soldier who was one of his attendants
13:43 and *d* converts to Judaism followed
22:12 He was a *d* observer of the law

DEW
Jdg 6:37 If there is *d* only on the fleece

DICTATED
Jer 36: 4 and while Jeremiah *d* all the words

DIE (DEAD DEADENED DEATH DIED DIES DYING)
Ge 2:17 when you eat of it you will surely *d*
3: 3 you must not touch it, or you will *d*
3: 4 will not surely *d,"* the serpent said
Ex 11: 5 Every firstborn son in Egypt will *d,*
Ru 1:17 Where you *d* I will *d,* and there I
2Ki 14: 6 each is to *d* for his own sins."
Job 2: 9 Curse God and *d!"* He replied,
Pr 5:23 He will *d* for lack of discipline,
10:21 but fools *d* for lack of judgment.
15:10 he who hates correction will *d.*
23:13 with the rod, he will not *d.*
Ecc 3: 2 a time to be born and a time to *d,*
Isa 22:13 "for tomorrow we *d!"*
66:24 their worm will not *d,* nor will their
Jer 31:30 everyone will *d* for his own sin;
Eze 3:18 that wicked man will *d* for his sin,
3:19 he will *d* for his sin; but you will
3:20 block before him, he will *d.*
18: 4 soul who sins is the one who will *d.*
18:20 soul who sins is the one who will *d.*
18:31 Why will you *d,* O house of Israel?
33: 8 'O wicked man, you will surely *d,'*
Mt 26:52 "for all who draw the sword will *d*
Mk 9:48 " 'their worm does not *d,*
Jn 8:21 and you will *d* in your sin.
11:26 and believes in me will never *d.*
Ro 5: 7 Very rarely will anyone *d*
14: 8 and if we *d,* we *d* to the Lord.
1Co 15:22 in Adam all *d,* so in Christ all will
15:31 I *d* every day—I mean that,
15:32 for tomorrow we *d."*
Php 1:21 to live is Christ and to *d* is gain.
Heb 9:27 Just as man is destined to *d* once,
1Pe 2:24 so that we might *d* to sins
Rev 14:13 Blessed are the dead who *d*

DIED (DIE)
1Ki 16:18 So he *d,* because of the sins he had
1Ch 1:51 Hadad also *d.*
10:13 Saul *d* because he was unfaithful
Lk 16:22 "The time came when the beggar *d*
Ro 5: 6 we were still powerless, Christ *d*
5: 8 we were still sinners, Christ *d*
6: 2 By no means! We *d* to sin;
6: 7 anyone who has *d* has been freed
6: 8 if we *d* with Christ, we believe that
6:10 The death he *d,* he *d* to sin once
14: 9 Christ *d* and returned to life
14:15 brother for whom Christ *d.*
1Co 8:11 for whom Christ *d,* is destroyed
15: 3 that Christ *d* for our sins according
2Co 5:14 *d* for all, and therefore all *d.*
5:15 he *d* for all, that those who live
Col 2:20 Since you *d* with Christ
3: 3 For you *d,* and your life is now
1Th 4:14 We believe that Jesus *d*
5:10 He *d* for us so that, whether we are
2Ti 2:11 If we *d* with him,
Heb 9:15 now that he has *d* as a ransom
9:17 in force only when somebody has *d*
1Pe 3:18 For Christ *d* for sins once for all,
Rev 2: 8 who *d* and came to life again.

DIES (DIE)
Job 14:14 If a man *d,* will he live again?
Pr 11: 7 a wicked man *d,* his hope perishes;
26:20 without gossip a quarrel *d* down.
Jn 11:25 in me will live, even though he *d;*
12:24 But if it *d,* it produces many seeds.
Ro 7: 2 but if her husband *d,* she is released
14: 7 and none of us *d* to himself alone.
1Co 7:39 But if her husband *d,* she is free
15:36 does not come to life unless it *d.*

DIFFERENCE* (DIFFERENT)
2Sa 19:35 Can I tell the *d* between what is
2Ch 12: 8 so that they may learn the *d*
Eze 22:26 they teach that there is no *d*
44:23 are to teach my people the *d*
Ro 3:22 There is no *d,* for all have sinned

Ro 10:12 For there is no *d* between Jew
Gal 2: 6 whatever they were makes no *d*

DIFFERENCES* (DIFFERENT)
1Co 11:19 to be *d* among you to show which

DIFFERENT* (DIFFERENCE DIFFERENCES DIFFERING DIFFERS)
Lev 19:19 " 'Do not mate *d* kinds of animals.
Nu 14:24 my servant Caleb has a *d* spirit
1Sa 10: 6 you will be changed into a *d* person
Est 1: 7 each one *d* from the other,
3: 8 whose customs are *d* from those
Da 7: 3 Four great beasts, each *d*
7: 7 It was *d* from all the former beasts,
7:19 which was *d* from all the others
7:23 It will be *d* from all the other
7:24 them another king will arise, *d*
11:29 but this time the outcome will be *d*
Mk 16:12 Jesus appeared in a *d* form
Ro 12: 6 We have *d* gifts, according
1Co 4: 7 For who makes you *d*
12: 4 There are *d* kinds of gifts,
12: 5 There are *d* kinds of service,
12: 6 There are *d* kinds of working,
12:10 speaking in *d* kinds of tongues,
12:28 and those speaking in *d* kinds
2Co 11: 4 or a *d* gospel from the one you
11: 4 or if you receive a *d* spirit
Gal 1: 6 and are turning to a *d* gospel—
4: 1 he is no *d* from a slave,
Heb 7:13 are said belonged to a *d* tribe,
Jas 2:25 and sent them off in a *d* direction?

DIFFERING* (DIFFERENT)
Dt 25:13 Do not have two *d* weights
25:14 Do not have two *d* measures
Pr 20:10 Differing weights and *d* measures
20:10 *D* weights and differing measures
20:23 The LORD detests *d* weights,

DIFFERS* (DIFFERENT)
1Co 15:41 and star *d* from star in splendor.

DIFFICULT (DIFFICULTIES)
Ex 18:22 but have them bring every *d* case
Dt 30:11 commanding you today is not too *d*
2Ki 2:10 "You have asked a *d* thing,"
Eze 3: 5 of obscure speech and *d* language,
Ac 15:19 that we should not make it *d*

DIFFICULTIES* (DIFFICULT)
Dt 31:17 and *d* will come upon them,
31:21 when many disasters and *d* come
2Co 12:10 in hardships, in persecutions, in *d.*

DIGNITY
Pr 31:25 She is clothed with strength and *d;*

DIGS
Pr 26:27 If a man *d* a pit, he will fall into it;

DILIGENCE (DILIGENT)
Ezr 5: 8 The work is being carried on with *d*
Heb 6:11 to show this same *d* to the very end

DILIGENT (DILIGENCE)
Pr 10: 4 but *d* hands bring wealth.
12:24 *D* hands will rule,
12:27 the *d* man prizes his possessions.
13: 4 of the *d* are fully satisfied.
21: 5 The plans of the *d* lead to profit
1Ti 4:15 Be *d* in these matters; give yourself

DINAH*
Only daughter of Jacob, by Leah (Ge 30:21; 46:15). Raped by Shechem; avenged by Simeon and Levi (Ge 34).

DINE
Pr 23: 1 When you sit to *d* with a ruler,

DIOTREPHES*
3Jn : 9 but *D,* who loves to be first,

DIRECT (DIRECTED DIRECTIVES DIRECTS)
Ge 18:19 so that he will *d* his children
Dt 17:10 to do everything they *d* you to do.
Ps 119: 35 *D* me in the path of your
119: 133 *D* my footsteps according
Jer 10:23 it is not for man to *d* his steps.
2Th 3: 5 May the Lord *d* your hearts
1Ti 5:17 The elders who *d* the affairs

DIRECTED (DIRECT)
Ge 24:51 master's son, as the LORD has *d.*"
Nu 16:40 as the LORD *d* him through Moses
Dt 2: 1 Sea, as the LORD had *d* me.
6: 1 laws the LORD your God *d* me
Jos 11: 9 did to them as the LORD had *d:*
11:23 just as the LORD had *d* Moses,
Pr 20:24 A man's steps are *d* by the LORD.
Jer 13: 2 as the LORD *d,* and put it
Ac 7:44 It had been made as God *d* Moses,
Tit 1: 5 elders in every town, as I *d* you.

DIRECTIVES* (DIRECT)
1Co 11:17 In the following *d* I have no praise

DIRECTS (DIRECT)
Ps 42: 8 By day the LORD *d* his love,
Isa 48:17 who *d* you in the way you should

DIRGE*
Mt 11:17 we sang a *d,*
Lk 7:32 we sang a *d,*

DISABLED*
Jn 5: 3 number of *d* people used to lie—
Heb 12:13 so that the lame may not be *d,*

DISAGREEMENT*
Ac 15:39 had such a sharp *d* that they parted

DISAPPEAR (DISAPPEARED DISAPPEARS)
Mt 5:18 will by any means *d* from the Law
Lk 16:17 earth to *d* than for the least stroke
Heb 8:13 is obsolete and aging will soon *d.*
2Pe 3:10 The heavens will *d* with a roar;

DISAPPEARED (DISAPPEAR)
1Ki 20:40 busy here and there, the man *d.*"

DISAPPEARS (DISAPPEAR)
1Co 13:10 perfection comes, the imperfect *d.*

DISAPPOINT* (DISAPPOINTED)
Ro 5: 5 And hope does not *d* us,

DISAPPOINTED (DISAPPOINT)
Ps 22: 5 in you they trusted and were not *d.*

DISAPPROVE*
Pr 24:18 or the LORD will see and *d*

DISARMED*
Col 2:15 And having *d* the powers

DISASTER
Ex 32:12 and do not bring *d* on your people.
Ps 57: 1 wings until the *d* has passed.
Pr 1:26 I in turn will laugh at your *d;*
3:25 Have no fear of sudden *d*
6:15 Therefore *d* will overtake him
16: 4 even the wicked for a day of *d.*
17: 5 over *d* will not go unpunished.
27:10 house when *d* strikes you—
Isa 45: 7 I bring prosperity and create *d;*
Jer 17:17 you are my refuge in the day of *d.*
Eze 7: 5 An unheard-of *d* is coming.

DISCERN (DISCERNED DISCERNING DISCERNMENT)
Ps 19:12 Who can *d* his errors?
139: 3 You *d* my going out and my lying
Php 1:10 you may be able to *d* what is best

DISCERNED (DISCERN)
1Co 2:14 because they are spiritually *d.*

DISCERNING (DISCERN)
1Ki 3: 9 So give your servant a *d* heart
3:12 I will give you a wise and *d* heart,
Pr 1: 5 and let the *d* get guidance—
8: 9 To the *d* all of them are right;
10:13 on the lips of the *d,*
14: 6 knowledge comes easily to the *d.*
14:33 in the heart of the *d*
15:14 The *d* heart seeks knowledge,
16:21 The wise in heart are called *d,*
17:24 A *d* man keeps wisdom in view,
17:28 and *d* if he holds his tongue.
18:15 heart of the *d* acquires knowledge;
19:25 rebuke a *d* man, and he will gain
28: 7 He who keeps the law is a *d* son,

DISCERNMENT (DISCERN)
Ps 119: 125 I am your servant; give me *d*
Pr 3:21 preserve sound judgment and *d,*
17:10 A rebuke impresses a man of *d*
28:11 a poor man who has *d* sees

DISCHARGED* (DISCHARGING)
Ecc 8: 8 As no one is *d* in time of war,

DISCHARGING* (DISCHARGED)
1Co 9:17 I am simply *d* the trust committed

DISCIPLE (DISCIPLES DISCIPLES')
Mt 10:42 these little ones because he is my *d,*
Lk 14:26 his own life—he cannot be my *d.*
14:27 and follow me cannot be my *d.*
14:33 everything he has cannot be my *d.*
Jn 13:23 of them, the *d* whom Jesus loved,
19:26 and the *d* whom he loved standing
21: 7 Then the *d* whom Jesus loved said
21:20 saw that the *d* whom Jesus loved

DISCIPLES (DISCIPLE)
Mt 10: 1 He called his twelve *d* to him
26:56 Then all the *d* deserted him
28:19 Therefore go and make *d*
Mk 3: 7 withdrew with his *d* to the lake,
16:20 Then the *d* went out and preached
Lk 6:13 he called his *d* to him and chose
Jn 2:11 and his *d* put their faith in him.
6:66 many of his *d* turned back
8:31 to my teaching, you are really my *d*
12:16 At first his *d* did not understand all
13:35 men will know that you are my *d*
15: 8 showing yourselves to be my *d.*
20:20 The *d* were overjoyed
Ac 6: 1 the number of *d* was increasing,
11:26 The *d* were called Christians first
14:22 strengthening the *d*
18:23 Phrygia, strengthening all the *d.*

DISCIPLES' (DISCIPLE)
Jn 13: 5 and began to wash his *d* feet,

DISCIPLINE* (DISCIPLINED DISCIPLINES SELF-DISCIPLINE)
Dt 4:36 made you hear his voice to *d* you.
11: 2 and experienced the *d*
21:18 listen to them when they *d* him,
Job 5:17 so do not despise the *d*
Ps 6: 1 or *d* me in your wrath.
38: 1 or *d* me in your wrath.
39:11 You rebuke and *d* men for their sin;
94:12 Blessed is the man you *d,* O LORD
Pr 1: 2 for attaining wisdom and *d;*
1: 7 but fools despise wisdom and *d.*
3:11 do not despise the LORD's *d*
5:12 You will say, "How I hated *d!*
5:23 He will die for lack of *d,*
6:23 and the corrections of *d*
10:17 He who heeds *d* shows the way
12: 1 Whoever loves *d* loves knowledge,
13:18 He who ignores *d* comes to poverty
13:24 who loves him is careful to *d* him.
15: 5 A fool spurns his father's *d,*
15:10 Stern *d* awaits him who leaves
15:32 He who ignores *d* despises himself,
19:18 *D* your son, for in that there is hope
22:15 the rod of *d* will drive it far
23:13 Do not withhold *d* from a child;
23:23 get wisdom, *d* and understanding.
29:17 *D* your son, and he will give you
Jer 17:23 would not listen or respond to *d.*
30:11 I will *d* you but only with justice;
32:33 would not listen or respond to *d.*
46:28 I will *d* you but only with justice;
Hos 5: 2 I will *d* all of them.
Heb 12: 5 do not make light of the Lord's *d,*
12: 7 as *d;* God is treating you
12: 8 (and everyone undergoes *d),*
12:11 No *d* seems pleasant at the time,
Rev 3:19 Those whom I love I rebuke and *d.*

DISCIPLINED* (DISCIPLINE)
Pr 1: 3 for acquiring a *d* and prudent life,
Isa 26:16 when you *d* them,
Jer 31:18 and I have been *d.*
31:18 'You *d* me like an unruly calf,
1Co 11:32 we are being *d* so that we will not
Tit 1: 8 upright, holy and *d.*
Heb 12: 7 For what son is not *d* by his father?
12: 8 you are not *d* (and everyone
12: 9 all had human fathers who *d* us
12:10 Our fathers *d* us for a little while

DISCIPLINES* (DISCIPLINE)
Dt 8: 5 so the LORD your God *d* you.
8: 5 your heart that as a man *d* his son,
Ps 94:10 Does he who *d* nations not punish?
Pr 3:12 the LORD *d* those he loves,
Heb 12: 6 because the Lord *d* those he loves,
12:10 but God *d* us for our good,

DISCLOSED
Lk 8:17 is nothing hidden that will not be *d,*
Col 1:26 and generations, but is now *d*
Heb 9: 8 Holy Place had not yet been *d*

DISCORD
Gal 5:20 idolatry and witchcraft; hatred, *d,*

DISCOURAGED* (DISCOURAGEMENT)
Nu 32: 9 they *d* the Israelites
Dt 1:21 Do not be afraid; do not be *d.*"
31: 8 Do not be afraid; do not be *d.*"
Jos 1: 9 Do not be terrified; do not be *d,*
8: 1 "Do not be afraid; do not be *d.*

Jos 10:25 "Do not be afraid; do not be *d.*
1Ch 22:13 Do not be afraid or *d.*
28:20 or *d,* for the LORD God,
2Ch 20:15 or *d* because of this vast army.
20:17 Do not be afraid; do not be *d.*
32: 7 or *d* because of the king of Assyria
Job 4: 5 to you, and you are *d;*
Isa 42: 4 he will not falter or be *d*
Eph 3:13 to be *d* because of my sufferings
Col 3:21 children, or they will become *d.*

DISCOURAGEMENT* (DISCOURAGED)
Ex 6: 9 of their *d* and cruel bondage.

DISCOVERED
2Ki 23:24 book that Hilkiah the priest had *d*

DISCREDIT* (DISCREDITED)
Ne 6:13 would give me a bad name to *d* me.
Job 40: 8 "Would you *d* my justice?

DISCREDITED (DISCREDIT)
2Co 6: 3 so that our ministry will not be *d.*

DISCRETION*
1Ch 22:12 May the LORD give you *d*
Pr 1: 4 knowledge and *d* to the young—
2:11 *D* will protect you,
5: 2 that you may maintain *d*
8:12 I possess knowledge and *d.*
11:22 a beautiful woman who shows no *d.*

DISCRIMINATED*
Jas 2: 4 have you not *d* among yourselves

DISEASE (DISEASES)
Mt 4:23 and healing every *d* and sickness
9:35 and healing every *d* and sickness.
10: 1 and to heal every *d* and sickness.

DISEASES (DISEASE)
Ps 103: 3 and heals all my *d;*
Mt 8:17 and carried our *d.*"
Mk 3:10 those with *d* were pushing forward
Lk 9: 1 drive out all demons and to cure *d,*

DISFIGURE* (DISFIGURED)
Mt 6:16 for they *d* their faces

DISFIGURED (DISFIGURE)
Isa 52:14 his appearance was so *d*

DISGRACE (DISGRACEFUL DISGRACES)
Ps 44:15 My *d* is before me all day long,
52: 1 you who are a *d* in the eyes of God?
74:21 not let the oppressed retreat in *d;*
Pr 6:33 Blows and *d* are his lot,
11: 2 When pride comes, then comes *d,*
14:34 but sin is a *d* to any people.
19:26 is a son who brings shame and *d.*
Mt 1:19 want to expose her to public *d,*
Ac 5:41 of suffering *d* for the Name.
1Co 11: 6 and if it is a *d* for a woman
11:14 it is a *d* to him, but that
1Ti 3: 7 so that he will not fall into *d*
Heb 6: 6 and subjecting him to public *d.*
11:26 He regarded *d* for the sake
13:13 the camp, bearing the *d* he bore.

DISGRACEFUL (DISGRACE)
Pr 10: 5 during harvest is a *d* son.
12: 4 a *d* wife is like decay in his bones.
17: 2 wise servant will rule over a *d* son,
1Co 14:35 for it is *d* for a woman to speak

DISGRACES (DISGRACE)
Pr 28: 7 of gluttons *d* his father.
29:15 but a child left to himself *d* his mother

DISGUISES*
Pr 26:24 A malicious man *d* himself

DISH
Pr 19:24 sluggard buries his hand in the *d;*
Mt 23:25 the outside of the cup and *d,*

DISHONEST*
Ex 18:21 trustworthy men who hate *d* gain
Lev 19:35 " 'Do not use *d* standards
1Sa 8: 3 They turned aside after *d* gain
Pr 11: 1 The LORD abhors *d* scales,
13:11 *D* money dwindles away,
20:23 and *d* scales do not please him.
29:27 The righteous detest the *d;*
Jer 22:17 are set only on *d* gain,
Eze 28:18 By your many sins and *d* trade
Hos 12: 7 The merchant uses *d* scales;
Am 8: 5 and cheating with *d* scales,
Mic 6:11 Shall I acquit a man with *d* scales,
Lk 16: 8 master commended the *d* manager
16:10 whoever is *d* with very little will
Lk 16:10 with very little will also be *d*
1Ti 3: 8 wine, and not pursuing *d* gain.
Tit 1: 7 not violent, not pursuing *d* gain.
1:11 and that for the sake of *d* gain.

DISHONOR* (DISHONORED DISHONORS)
Lev 18: 7 " 'Do not *d* your father
18: 8 wife; that would *d* your father.
18:10 daughter; that would *d* you.
18:14 " 'Do not *d* your father's brother
18:16 that would *d* your brother.
20:19 for that would *d* a close relative;
Dt 22:30 he must not *d* his father's bed.
Pr 30: 9 and so *d* the name of my God.
Jer 14:21 do not *d* your glorious throne.
20:11 their *d* will never be forgotten.
La 2: 2 princes down to the ground in *d.*
Eze 22:10 are those who *d* their fathers' bed;
Jn 8:49 I honor my Father and you *d* me.
Ro 2:23 do you *d* God by breaking the law?
1Co 15:43 it is sown in *d,* it is raised in glory;
2Co 6: 8 through glory and *d,* bad report

DISHONORED* (DISHONOR)
Lev 20:11 father's wife, he has *d* his father.
20:17 He has *d* his sister and will be held
20:20 with his aunt, he has *d* his uncle.
20:21 of impurity; he has *d* his brother.
Dt 21:14 as a slave, since you have *d* her.
Ezr 4:14 proper for us to see the king *d,*
1Co 4:10 You are honored, we are *d!*

DISHONORS* (DISHONOR)
Dt 27:16 Cursed is the man who *d* his father
27:20 for he *d* his father's bed."
Job 20: 3 I hear a rebuke that *d* me,
Mic 7: 6 For a son *d* his father,
1Co 11: 4 with his head covered *d* his head.
11: 5 her head uncovered *d* her head—

DISILLUSIONMENT*
Ps 7:14 conceives trouble gives birth to *d.*

DISMAYED
Isa 28:16 the one who trusts will never be *d.*
41:10 do not be *d,* for I am your God.

DISOBEDIENCE* (DISOBEY)
Jos 22:22 in rebellion or *d* to the LORD,
Jer 43: 7 So they entered Egypt in *d*
Ro 5:19 as through the *d* of the one man
11:30 mercy as a result of their *d,*
11:32 to *d* so that he may have mercy
2Co 10: 6 ready to punish every act of *d,*
Heb 2: 2 and *d* received its just punishment,
4: 6 go in, because of their *d.*
4:11 fall by following their example of *d.*

DISOBEDIENT* (DISOBEY)
Ne 9:26 "But they were *d* and rebelled
Lk 1:17 and the *d* to the wisdom
Ac 26:19 I was not *d* to the vision
Ro 10:21 hands to a *d* and obstinate people."
11:30 as you who were at one time *d*
11:31 so they too have now become *d*
Eph 2: 2 now at work in those who are *d.*
5: 6 comes on those who are *d.*
5:12 to mention what the *d* do in secret.
2Ti 3: 2 proud, abusive, *d* to their parents,
Tit 1: 6 to the charge of being wild and *d.*
1:16 *d* and unfit for doing anything
3: 3 At one time we too were foolish, *d,*
Heb 11:31 killed with those who were *d.*

DISOBEY* (DISOBEDIENCE DISOBEDIENT DISOBEYED DISOBEYING DISOBEYS)
Dt 11:28 the curse if you *d* the commands
2Ch 24:20 'Why do you *d* the LORD's
Est 3: 3 Why do you *d* the king's command
Jer 42:13 and so *d* the LORD your God,
Ro 1:30 they *d* their parents; they are
1Pe 2: 8 because they *d* the message—

DISOBEYED* (DISOBEY)
Nu 14:22 and in the desert but who *d* me
27:14 both of you *d* my command
Jdg 2: 2 Yet you have *d* me.
Ne 9:29 arrogant and *d* your commands.
Isa 24: 5 they have *d* the laws,
Jer 43: 4 and all the people *d* the LORD's
Lk 15:29 for you and never *d* your orders.
Heb 3:18 rest if not to those who *d?*
1Pe 3:20 the spirits in prison who *d* long ago

DISOBEYING* (DISOBEY)
Nu 14:41 "Why are you *d* the LORD's

DISOBEYS* (DISOBEY)
Eze 33:12 man will not save him when he *d,*

DISORDER
1Co 14:33 For God is not a God of *d*
2Co 12:20 slander, gossip, arrogance and *d.*
Jas 3:16 there you find *d* and every evil

DISOWN (DISOWNS)
Pr 30: 9 I may have too much and *d* you
Mt 10:33 I will *d* him before my Father
26:35 to die with you, I will never *d* you."
2Ti 2:12 If we *d* him,

DISOWNS (DISOWN)
Lk 12: 9 he who *d* me before men will be

DISPENSATION see ADMINISTRATION, TRUST

DISPLACES
Pr 30:23 a maidservant who *d* her mistress.

DISPLAY (DISPLAYED DISPLAYS)
Ps 45: 4 your right hand *d* awesome deeds.
Eze 39:21 I will *d* my glory among the nations
Ro 9:17 that I might *d* my power in you
1Co 4: 9 on *d* at the end of the procession,
1Ti 1:16 Christ Jesus might *d* his unlimited

DISPLAYED (DISPLAY)
Jn 9: 3 work of God might be *d* in his life.
2Th 2: 9 the work of Satan *d* in all kinds

DISPLAYS (DISPLAY)
Isa 44:23 he *d* his glory in Israel.

DISPLEASE (DISPLEASED)
1Th 2:15 They *d* God and are hostile

DISPLEASED (DISPLEASE)
2Sa 11:27 David had done *d* the LORD.

DISPUTABLE* (DISPUTE)
Ro 14: 1 passing judgment on *d* matters.

DISPUTE (DISPUTABLE DISPUTES DISPUTING)
Pr 17:14 before a *d* breaks out.
1Co 6: 1 If any of you has a *d* with another,

DISPUTES (DISPUTE)
Pr 18:18 Casting the lot settles *d*

DISPUTING (DISPUTE)
1Ti 2: 8 in prayer, without anger or *d.*

DISQUALIFIED*
1Co 9:27 I myself will not be *d* for the prize.

DISREPUTE*
2Pe 2: 2 will bring the way of truth into *d.*

DISSENSION* (DISSENSIONS)
Pr 6:14 he always stirs up *d.*
6:19 and a man who stirs up *d*
10:12 Hatred stirs up *d,*
15:18 A hot-tempered man stirs up *d,*
16:28 A perverse man stirs up *d,*
28:25 A greedy man stirs up *d,*
29:22 An angry man stirs up *d,*
Ro 13:13 debauchery, not in *d* and jealousy.

DISSENSIONS* (DISSENSION)
Gal 5:20 selfish ambition, *d,* factions

DISSIPATION*
Lk 21:34 will be weighed down with *d,*
1Pe 4: 4 with them into the same flood of *d,*

DISTINCTION
Ac 15: 9 He made no *d* between us

DISTINGUISH (DISTINGUISHING)
1Ki 3: 9 and to *d* between right and wrong.
Heb 5:14 themselves to *d* good from evil.

DISTINGUISHING
1Co 12:10 the *d* between spirits,

DISTORT
Ac 20:30 and *d* the truth in order
2Co 4: 2 nor do we *d* the word of God.
2Pe 3:16 ignorant and unstable people *d,*

DISTRACTED*
Lk 10:40 But Martha was *d* by all

DISTRESS (DISTRESSED)
2Ch 15: 4 in their *d* they turned to the LORD
Ps 18: 6 In my *d* I called to the LORD;
81: 7 In your *d* you called and I rescued
120: 1 I call on the LORD in my *d,*
Jnh 2: 2 "In my *d* I called to the LORD,
Mt 24:21 For then there will be great *d,*

Jas 1:27 after orphans and widows in their *d*

DISTRESSED (DISTRESS)
Lk 12:50 how *d* I am until it is completed!
Ro 14:15 If your brother is *d*

DIVIDE (DIVIDED DIVIDING DIVISION DIVISIONS DIVISIVE)
Ps 22:18 They *d* my garments among them

DIVIDED (DIVIDE)
Mt 12:25 household *d* against itself will not
Lk 23:34 they *d* up his clothes by casting lots
1Co 1:13 Is Christ *d*? Was Paul crucified

DIVIDING (DIVIDE)
Eph 2:14 destroyed the barrier, the *d* wall
Heb 4:12 it penetrates even to *d* soul

DIVINATION
Lev 19:26 " 'Do not practice *d* or sorcery.

DIVINE
Ro 1:20 his eternal power and *d* nature—
2Co 10: 4 they have *d* power
2Pe 1: 4 you may participate in the *d* nature

DIVISION (DIVIDE)
Lk 12:51 on earth? No, I tell you, but *d*.
1Co 12:25 so that there should be no *d*

DIVISIONS (DIVIDE)
Ro 16:17 to watch out for those who cause *d*
1Co 1:10 another so that there may be no *d*
11:18 there are *d* among you,

DIVISIVE* (DIVIDE)
Tit 3:10 Warn a *d* person once,

DIVORCE* (DIVORCED DIVORCES)
Dt 22:19 he must not *d* her as long as he lives
22:29 He can never *d* her as long
24: 1 and he writes her a certificate of *d*,
24: 3 and writes her a certificate of *d*,
Isa 50: 1 is your mother's certificate of *d*
Jer 3: 8 faithless Israel her certificate of *d*
Mal 2:16 "I hate *d*," says the LORD God
Mt 1:19 he had in mind to *d* her quietly.
5:31 must give her a certificate of *d*.'
19: 3 for a man to *d* his wife for any
19: 7 man give his wife a certificate of *d*
19: 8 permitted you to *d* your wives
Mk 10: 2 Is it lawful for a man to *d* his wife?"
10: 4 a man to write a certificate of *d*
1Co 7:11 And a husband must not *d* his wife.
7:12 to live with him, he must not *d* her.
7:13 to live with her, she must not *d* him
7:27 Are you married? Do not seek a *d*.

DIVORCED* (DIVORCE)
Lev 21: 7 or *d* from their husbands,
21:14 not marry a widow, a *d* woman,
22:13 daughter becomes a widow or is *d*,
Nu 30: 9 or *d* woman will be binding on her.
Dt 24: 4 then her first husband, who *d* her,
1Ch 8: 8 after he had *d* his wives Hushim
Eze 44:22 not marry widows or *d* women;
Mt 5:32 marries the *d* woman commits adultery.
Lk 16:18 who marries a *d* woman commits

DIVORCES* (DIVORCE)
Jer 3: 1 "If a man *d* his wife
Mt 5:31 'Anyone who *d* his wife must give
5:32 tell you that anyone who *d* his wife,
19: 9 tell you that anyone who *d* his wife,
Mk 10:11 "Anyone who *d* his wife
10:12 And if she *d* her husband
Lk 16:18 "Anyone who *d* his wife

DOCTOR
Mt 9:12 "It is not the healthy who need a *d*,

DOCTRINE* (DOCTRINES)
1Ti 1:10 to the sound *d* that conforms
4:16 Watch your life and *d* closely.
2Ti 4: 3 men will not put up with sound *d*.
Tit 1: 9 can encourage others by sound *d*
2: 1 is in accord with sound *d*.

DOCTRINES* (DOCTRINE)
1Ti 1: 3 not to teach false *d* any longer
6: 3 If anyone teaches false *d*

DOEG*
Edomite; Saul's head shepherd; responsible for murder of priests at Nob (1Sa 21:7; 22:6-23; Ps 52).

DOG (DOGS)
Pr 26:11 As a *d* returns to its vomit,
Ecc 9: 4 a live *d* is better off than a dead lion
2Pe 2:22 "A *d* returns to its vomit," and,

DOGS (DOG)
Mt 7: 6 "Do not give *d* what is sacred;
15:26 bread and toss it to their *d*."

DOMINION
Job 25: 2 "*D* and awe belong to God;
Ps 22:28 for *d* belongs to the LORD

DONKEY
Nu 22:30 *d* said to Balaam, "Am I not your
Zec 9: 9 gentle and riding on a *d*,
Mt 21: 5 gentle and riding on a *d*,
2Pe 2:16 for his wrongdoing by a *d*—

DOOR (DOORS)
Job 31:32 for my *d* was always open
Ps 141: 3 keep watch over the *d* of my lips.
Mt 6: 6 close the *d* and pray to your Father
7: 7 and the *d* will be opened to you.
Ac 14:27 how he had opened the *d* of faith
1Co 16: 9 a great *d* for effective work has
2Co 2:12 found that the Lord had opened a *d*
Rev 3:20 I stand at the *d* and knock.

DOORFRAMES
Dt 6: 9 Write them on the *d* of your houses

DOORKEEPER
Ps 84:10 I would rather be a *d* in the house

DOORS (DOOR)
Ps 24: 7 be lifted up, you ancient *d*,

DORCAS
Ac 9:36 is *D*), who was always doing good

DOUBLE
2Ki 2: 9 "Let me inherit a *d* portion
1Ti 5:17 church well are worthy of *d* honor,

DOUBLE-EDGED (EDGE)
Heb 4:12 Sharper than any *d* sword,
Rev 1:16 of his mouth came a sharp *d* sword.
2:12 of him who has the sharp, *d* sword.

DOUBLE-MINDED* (MIND)
Ps 119:113 I hate *d* men,
Jas 1: 8 he is a *d* man, unstable
4: 8 and purify your hearts, you *d*.

DOUBT (DOUBTING DOUBTS)
Mt 14:31 he said, "why did you *d*?"
21:21 if you have faith and do not *d*,
Mk 11:23 and does not *d* in his heart
Jas 1: 6 he must believe and not *d*,
Jude :22 Be merciful to those who *d*;

DOUBTING* (DOUBT)
Jn 20:27 Stop *d* and believe."

DOUBTS* (DOUBT)
Lk 24:38 and why do *d* rise in your minds?
Ro 14:23 the man who has *d* is condemned
Jas 1: 6 he who *d* is like a wave of the sea,

DOVE (DOVES)
Ge 8: 8 Then he sent out a *d* to see
Mt 3:16 Spirit of God descending like a *d*

DOVES (DOVE)
Lev 12: 8 is to bring two *d* or two young
Mt 10:16 as snakes and as innocent as *d*.
Lk 2:24 "a pair of *d* or two young pigeons."

DOWNCAST
Ps 42: 5 Why are you *d*, O my soul?
2Co 7: 6 But God, who comforts the *d*,

DOWNFALL
Hos 14: 1 Your sins have been your *d*!

DRAGON
Rev 12: 7 and his angels fought against the *d*,
13: 2 The *d* gave the beast his power
20: 2 He seized the *d*, that ancient

DRAW (DRAWING DRAWS)
Mt 26:52 "for all who *d* the sword will die
Jn 12:32 up from the earth, will *d* all men
Heb 10:22 let us *d* near to God

DRAWING (DRAW)
Lk 21:28 because your redemption is *d* near

DRAWS (DRAW)
Jn 6:44 the Father who sent me *d* him,

DREAD (DREADFUL)
Ps 53: 5 they were, overwhelmed with *d*,

DREADFUL (DREAD)
Mt 24:19 How *d* it will be in those days
Heb 10:31 It is a *d* thing to fall into the hands

DREAM
Joel 2:28 your old men will *d* dreams,
Ac 2:17 your old men will *d* dreams.

DRESS
1Ti 2: 9 I also want women to *d* modestly,

DRIFT*
Heb 2: 1 so that we do not *d* away.

DRINK (DRINKING DRINKS DRUNK DRUNKARD DRUNKARD'S DRUNKARDS DRUNKENNESS)
Ex 29:40 of a hin of wine as a *d* offering.
Nu 6: 3 He must not *d* grape juice
Jdg 7: 5 from those who kneel down to *d*."
2Sa 23:15 that someone would get me a *d*
Pr 5:15 *D* water from your own cistern,
Mt 20:22 "Can you *d* the cup I am going to *d*
26:27 saying, "*D* from it, all of you.
Mk 16:18 and when they *d* deadly poison,
Lk 12:19 Take life easy; eat, *d* and be merry
Jn 7:37 let him come to me and *d*.
18:11 Shall I not *d* the cup the Father has
1Co 10: 4 and drank the same spiritual *d*;
12:13 were all given the one Spirit to *d*.
Php 2:17 being poured out like a *d* offering
2Ti 4: 6 being poured out like a *d* offering,
Rev 14:10 too, will *d* of the wine of God's fury
21: 6 to *d* without cost from the spring

DRINKING (DRINK)
Ro 14:17 God is not a matter of eating and *d*,

DRINKS (DRINK)
Isa 5:22 and champions at mixing *d*,
Jn 4:13 "Everyone who *d* this water will be
6:54 and *d* my blood has eternal life,
1Co 11:27 or *d* the cup of the Lord

DRIPPING
Pr 19:13 wife is like a constant *d*.
27:15 a constant *d* on a rainy day;

DRIVE (DRIVES)
Ex 23:30 Little by little I will *d* them out
Nu 33:52 *d* out all the inhabitants of the land
Jos 13:13 Israelites did not *d* out the people
23:13 will no longer *d* out these nations
Pr 22:10 *D* out the mocker, and out goes
Mt 10: 1 authority to *d* out evil spirits
Jn 6:37 comes to me I will never *d* away.

DRIVES (DRIVE)
Mt 12:26 If Satan *d* out Satan, he is divided
1Jn 4:18 But perfect love *d* out fear,

DROP (DROPS)
Pr 17:14 so *d* the matter before a dispute
Isa 40:15 Surely the nations are like a *d*

DROPS (DROP)
Lk 22:44 his sweat was like *d* of blood falling

DROSS
Ps 119:119 of the earth you discard like *d*;
Pr 25: 4 Remove the *d* from the silver,

DROUGHT
Jer 17: 8 It has no worries in a year of *d*

DROWNED
Ex 15: 4 are *d* in the Red Sea.
Mt 18: 6 and to be *d* in the depths of the sea.
Heb 11:29 tried to do so, they were *d*.

DROWSINESS*
Pr 23:21 and *d* clothes them in rags.

DRUNK (DRINK)
1Sa 1:13 Eli thought she was *d* and said
Ac 2:15 men are not *d*, as you suppose.
Eph 5:18 Do not get *d* on wine, which leads

DRUNKARD (DRINK)
Mt 11:19 and a *d*, a friend of tax collectors
1Co 5:11 or a slanderer, a *d* or a swindler.

DRUNKARD'S* (DRINK)
Pr 26: 9 Like a thornbush in a *d* hand

DRUNKARDS (DRINK)
Pr 23:21 for *d* and gluttons become poor,
1Co 6:10 nor the greedy nor *d* nor slanderers

DRUNKENNESS (DRINK)
Lk 21:34 weighed down with dissipation, *d*

Ro 13:13 and *d,* not in sexual immorality
Gal 5:21 factions and envy; *d,* orgies,
1Ti 3: 3 not given to *d,* not violent
1Pe 4: 3 living in debauchery, lust, *d,* orgies,

DRY
Ge 1: 9 place, and let *d* ground appear."
Ex 14:16 go through the sea on *d* ground.
Jos 3:17 the crossing on *d* ground.
Isa 53: 2 and like a root out of *d* ground.
Eze 37: 4 '*D* bones, hear the word

DULL
Isa 6:10 make their ears *d*
2Co 3:14 But their minds were made *d,*

DUST
Ge 2: 7 man from the *d* of the ground
3:19 for *d* you are
Job 42: 6 and repent in *d* and ashes."
Ps 22:15 you lay me in the *d* of death.
103: 14 he remembers that we are *d.*
Ecc 3:20 all come from *d,* and to *d* all return.
Mt 10:14 shake the *d* off your feet
1Co 15:47 was of the *d* of the earth,

DUTIES (DUTY)
2Ti 4: 5 discharge all the *d* of your ministry

DUTY (DUTIES)
Ecc 12:13 for this is the whole *d* of man.
Ac 23: 1 I have fulfilled my *d* to God
1Co 7: 3 husband should fulfill his marital *d*

DWELL (DWELLING DWELLINGS DWELLS DWELT)
Ex 25: 8 for me, and I will *d* among them.
2Sa 7: 5 the one to build me a house to *d* in?
1Ki 8:27 "But will God really *d* on earth?
Ps 23: 6 I will *d* in the house of the LORD
37: 3 *d* in the land and enjoy safe pasture
61: 4 I long to *d* in your tent forever
Pr 8:12 wisdom, *d* together with prudence;
Isa 33:14 of us can *d* with the consuming fire
43:18 do not *d* on the past.
Jn 5:38 nor does his word *d* in you,
Eph 3:17 so that Christ may *d* in your hearts
Col 1:19 to have all his fullness *d* in him,
3:16 the word of Christ *d* in you richly

DWELLING (DWELL)
Lev 26:11 I will put my *d* place among you,
Dt 26:15 from heaven, your holy *d* place,
Ps 90: 1 Lord, you have been our *d* place
2Co 5: 2 to be clothed with our heavenly *d,*
Eph 2:22 to become a *d* in which God lives

DWELLINGS (DWELL)
Lk 16: 9 will be welcomed into eternal *d.*

DWELLS (DWELL)
Ps 46: 4 holy place where the Most High *d.*
91: 1 He who *d* in the shelter

DWELT (DWELL)
Dt 33:16 of him who *d* in the burning bush.

DYING (DIE)
Ro 7: 6 by *d* to what once bound us,
2Co 6: 9 yet regarded as unknown; *d,*

EAGER
Pr 31:13 and works with *e* hands.
Ro 8:19 The creation waits in *e* expectation
1Co 14:12 Since you are *e* to have spiritual
14:39 my brothers, be *e* to prophesy,
Tit 2:14 a people that are his very own, *e*
1Pe 5: 2 greedy for money, but *e* to serve;

EAGLE (EAGLE'S EAGLES)
Dt 32:11 like an *e* that stirs up its nest
Eze 1:10 each also had the face of an *e.*
Rev 4: 7 the fourth was like a flying *e.*
12:14 given the two wings of a great *e,*

EAGLE'S (EAGLE)
Ps 103: 5 your youth is renewed like the *e.*

EAGLES (EAGLE)
Isa 40:31 They will soar on wings like *e;*

EAR (EARS)
Ex 21: 6 and pierce his *e* with an awl.
Ps 5: 1 Give *e* to my words, O LORD,
Pr 2: 2 turning your *e* to wisdom
1Co 2: 9 no *e* has heard,
12:16 if the *e* should say, "Because I am
Rev 2: 7 He who has an *e,* let him hear what

EARN (EARNED EARNINGS)
2Th 3:12 down and *e* the bread they eat.

EARNED (EARN)
Pr 31:31 Give her the reward she has *e,*

EARNESTNESS
2Co 7:11 what *e,* what eagerness
8: 7 in complete *e* and in your love

EARNINGS (EARN)
Pr 31:16 out of her *e* she plants a vineyard.

EARRING (EARRINGS)
Pr 25:12 Like an *e* of gold or an ornament

EARRINGS (EARRING)
Ex 32: 2 Take off the gold *e* that your wives,

EARS (EAR)
Job 42: 5 My *e* had heard of you
Ps 34:15 and his *e* are attentive to their cry;
Pr 21:13 If a man shuts his *e* to the cry
26:17 Like one who seizes a dog by the *e*
Isa 6:10 hear with their *e,*
Mt 11:15 He who has *e,* let him hear.
2Ti 4: 3 to say what their itching *e* want
1Pe 3:12 his *e* are attentive to their prayer,

EARTH (EARTH'S EARTHLY)
Ge 1: 1 God created the heavens and the *e.*
1: 2 Now the *e* was formless and empty,
7:24 The waters flooded the *e*
14:19 Creator of heaven and *e.*
1Ki 8:27 "But will God really dwell on *e?*
Job 26: 7 he suspends the *e* over nothing.
Ps 24: 1 *e* is the LORD's, and everything
46: 6 he lifts his voice, the *e* melts.
90: 2 or you brought forth the *e*
97: 5 before the Lord of all the *e.*
102: 25 you laid the foundations of the *e,*
108: 5 and let your glory be over all the *e.*
Pr 8:26 before he made the *e* or its fields
Isa 6: 3 the whole *e* is full of his glory."
24:20 The *e* reels like a drunkard,
37:16 You have made heaven and *e.*
40:22 enthroned above the circle of the *e,*
51: 6 the *e* will wear out like a garment
54: 5 he is called the God of all the *e.*
55: 9 the heavens are higher than the *e,*
65:17 new heavens and a new *e.*
66: 1 and the *e* is my footstool.
Jer 10:10 When he is angry, the *e* trembles;
23:24 "Do not I fill heaven and *e?"*
33:25 and the fixed laws of heaven and *e,*
Hab 2:20 let all the *e* be silent before him."
Mt 5: 5 for they will inherit the *e.*
5:35 or by the *e,* for it is his footstool;
6:10 done on *e* as it is in heaven.
16:19 bind on *e* will be bound
24:35 Heaven and *e* will pass away,
28:18 and on *e* has been given to me.
Lk 2:14 on *e* peace to men
Jn 12:32 when I am lifted up from the *e,*
Ac 4:24 "you made the heaven and the *e*
7:49 and the *e* is my footstool.
1Co 10:26 The *e* is the Lord's, and everything
Eph 3:15 in heaven and on *e* derives its name
Php 2:10 in heaven and on *e* and under the *e,*
Heb 1:10 you laid the foundations of the *e,*
2Pe 3:13 to a new heaven and a new *e,*
Rev 8: 7 A third of the *e* was burned up,
12:12 But woe to the *e* and the sea,
20:11 *E* and sky fled from his presence,
21: 1 I saw a new heaven and a new *e,*
21: 1 and the first *e* had passed away,

EARTH'S (EARTH)
Job 38: 4 when I laid the *e* foundation?

EARTHENWARE
Pr 26:23 Like a coating of glaze over *e*

EARTHLY (EARTH)
Eph 4: 9 descended to the lower, *e* regions?
Php 3:19 Their mind is on *e* things.
Col 3: 2 on things above, not on *e* things.
3: 5 whatever belongs to your *e* nature:

EARTHQUAKE (EARTHQUAKES)
Eze 38:19 at that time there shall be a great *e*
Mt 28: 2 There was a violent *e,* for an angel
Rev 6:12 There was a great *e.*

EARTHQUAKES (EARTHQUAKE)
Mt 24: 7 There will be famines and *e*

EASE
Pr 1:33 and be at *e,* without fear of harm."

EASIER (EASY)
Lk 16:17 It is *e* for heaven and earth
18:25 it is *e* for a camel to go

EAST
Ge 2: 8 God had planted a garden in the *e,*
Ps 103: 12 as far as the *e* is from the west,
Eze 43: 2 God of Israel coming from the *e.*
Mt 2: 1 Magi from the *e* came to Jerusalem
2: 2 We saw his star in the *e*

EASY (EASIER)
Mt 11:30 For my yoke is *e* and my burden is

EAT (ATE EATEN EATER EATING EATS)
Ge 2:16 "You are free to *e* from any tree
2:17 but you must not *e* from the tree
3:19 you will *e* your food
Ex 12:11 *E* it in haste; it is the LORD's
Lev 11: 2 these are the ones you may *e:*
17:12 "None of you may *e* blood,
Dt 8:16 He gave you manna to *e*
14: 4 These are the animals you may *e:*
Jdg 14:14 "Out of the eater, something to *e;*
2Sa 9: 7 and you will always *e* at my table."
Pr 31:27 and does not *e* the bread of idleness
Isa 55: 1 come, buy and *e!*
65:25 and the lion will *e* straw like the ox,
Eze 3: 1 *e* what is before you, *e* this scroll;
Mt 14:16 You give them something to *e."*
15: 2 wash their hands before they *e!"*
26:26 "Take and *e;* this is my body."
Mk 14:14 where I may *e* the Passover
Lk 10: 8 and are welcomed, *e* what is set
12:19 Take life easy; *e,* drink
12:22 what you will *e;* or about your body
Jn 4:32 to *e* that you know nothing about."
6:31 bread from heaven to *e.'"*
6:52 can this man give us his flesh to *e?"*
Ac 10:13 Kill and *e."*
Ro 14: 2 faith allows him to *e* everything,
14:15 is distressed because of what you *e,*
14:20 to *e* anything that causes someone
14:21 It is better not to *e* meat
1Co 5:11 With such a man do not even *e.*
8:13 if what I *e* causes my brother to fall
10:25 *E* anything sold in the meat market
10:27 *e* whatever is put before you
10:31 So whether you *e* or drink
11:26 For whenever you *e* this bread
2Th 3:10 man will not work, he shall not *e."*
Rev 2: 7 the right to *e* from the tree of life,
3:20 I will come in and *e* with him,

EATEN (EAT)
Ge 3:11 Have you *e* from the tree that I
Ac 10:14 "I have never *e* anything impure
Rev 10:10 when I had *e* it, my stomach turned

EATER (EAT)
Isa 55:10 for the sower and bread for the *e,*

EATING (EAT)
Ex 34:28 and forty nights without *e* bread
Ro 14:15 not by your *e* destroy your brother
14:17 kingdom of God is not a matter of *e*
14:23 because his *e* is not from faith;
1Co 8: 4 about *e* food sacrificed to idols:
8:10 you who have this knowledge *e*
Jude :12 *e* with you without the slightest

EATS (EAT)
1Sa 14:24 "Cursed be any man who *e* food
Lk 15: 2 "This man welcomes sinners and *e*
Jn 6:51 If anyone *e* of this bread, he will live
6:54 Whoever *e* my flesh and drinks my
Ro 14: 2 faith is weak, *e* only vegetables.
14: 3 man who *e* everything must not
14: 6 He who *e* meat, *e* to the Lord,
14:23 has doubts is condemned if he *e,*
1Co 11:27 whoever *e* the bread or drinks

EBAL
Dt 11:29 and on Mount *E* the curses.
Jos 8:30 Joshua built on Mount *E* an altar

EBENEZER
1Sa 7:12 He named it *E,* saying, "Thus far

EDEN
Ge 2: 8 in *E;* and there he put the man
Eze 28:13 You were in *E,*

EDGE (DOUBLE-EDGED)
Mt 9:20 and touched the *e* of his cloak.

EDICT
Heb 11:23 they were not afraid of the king's *e.*

EDIFICATION (EDIFIED EDIFIES)
Ro 14:19 leads to peace and to mutual *e.*

EDIFIED* (EDIFICATION)
1Co 14: 5 so that the church may be *e.*
14:17 but the other man is not *e.*

EDIFIES* (EDIFICATION)
1Co 14: 4 but he who prophesies *e* the church
14: 4 speaks in a tongue *e* himself,

EDOM
Ge 36: 1 the account of Esau (that is, *E).*
36: 8 *E)* settled in the hill country of Seir
Isa 63: 1 Who is this coming from *E,*
Ob : 1 Sovereign LORD says about *E—*

EDUCATED*
Ac 7:22 Moses was *e* in all the wisdom

EFFECT* (EFFECTIVE)
Job 41:26 sword that reaches him has no *e,*
Isa 32:17 *e* of righteousness will be quietness
Ac 7:53 put into *e* through angels
1Co 15:10 his grace to me was not without *e.*
Gal 3:19 put into *e* through angels
Eph 1:10 put into *e* when the times will have
Heb 9:17 it never takes *e* while the one who
9:18 put into *e* without blood.

EFFECTIVE* (EFFECT)
1Co 16: 9 a great door for *e* work has opened
Jas 5:16 a righteous man is powerful and *e.*

EFFORT*
Ecc 2:19 into which I have poured my *e*
Da 6:14 and made every *e* until sundown
Lk 13:24 "Make every *e* to enter
Jn 5:44 yet make no *e* to obtain the praise
Ro 9:16 depend on man's desire or *e,*
14:19 make every *e* to do what leads
Gal 3: 3 to attain your goal by human *e?*
Eph 4: 3 Make every *e* to keep the unity
1Th 2:16 to all men in their *e* to keep us
2:17 intense longing we made every *e*
Heb 4:11 make every *e* to enter that rest,
12:14 Make every *e* to live in peace
2Pe 1: 5 make every *e* to add
1:15 And I will make every *e* to see that
3:14 make every *e* to be found spotless,

EGG
Lk 11:12 for an *e,* will give him a scorpion?

EGLON
1. Fat king of Moab killed by Ehud (Jdg 3:12-30).
2. City in Canaan (Jos 10).

EGYPT (EGYPTIANS)
Ge 12:10 went down to *E* to live there
37:28 Ishmaelites, who took him to *E.*
42: 3 went down to buy grain from *E.*
45:20 the best of all *E* will be yours.' "
46: 6 and all his offspring went to *E.*
47:27 Now the Israelites settled in *E*
Ex 3:11 and bring the Israelites out of *E?"*
12:40 lived in *E* was 430 years.
12:41 all the LORD's divisions left *E.*
32: 1 Moses who brought us up out of *E,*
Nu 11:18 We were better off in *E!"*
14: 4 choose a leader and go back to *E."*
24: 8 "God brought them out of *E;*
Dt 6:21 "We were slaves of Pharaoh in *E,*
1Ki 4:30 greater than all the wisdom of *E.*
10:28 horses were imported from *E*
11:40 but Jeroboam fled to *E,*
14:25 king of *E* attacked Jerusalem.
2Ch 35:20 Neco king of *E* went up to fight
36: 3 The king of *E* dethroned him
Isa 19:23 a highway from *E* to Assyria.
Hos 11: 1 and out of *E* I called my son.
Mt 2:15 "Out of *E* I called my son."
Heb 11:27 By faith he left *E,* not fearing
Rev 11: 8 is figuratively called Sodom and *E,*

EGYPTIANS (EGYPT)
Nu 14:13 "Then the *E* will hear about it!

EHUD
Left-handed judge who delivered Israel from Moabite king, Eglon (Jdg 3:12-30).

EKRON
1Sa 5:10 So they sent the ark of God to *E.*

ELAH
Son of Baasha; king of Israel (1Ki 16:6-14).

ELATION
Pr 28:12 righteous triumph, there is great *e;*

ELDER* (ELDERLY ELDERS)
Isa 3: 2 the soothsayer and *e,*
1Ti 5:19 an accusation against an *e*
Tit 1: 6 *e* must be blameless, the husband
1Pe 5: 1 among you, I appeal as a fellow *e,*
2Jn : 1 The *e,* To the chosen lady
3Jn : 1 The *e,* To my dear friend Gaius,

ELDERLY* (ELDER)
Lev 19:32 show respect for the *e*

ELDERS (ELDER)
1Ki 12: 8 rejected the advice the *e* gave him
Mt 15: 2 break the tradition of the *e?*
Mk 7: 3 holding to the tradition of the *e.*
7: 5 to the tradition of the *e* instead
Ac 11:30 gift to the *e* by Barnabas
14:23 and Barnabas appointed *e* for them
15: 2 the apostles and *e* about this
15: 4 the church and the apostles and *e,*
15: 6 and *e* met to consider this question.
15:22 and *e,* with the whole church,
15:23 The apostles and *e,* your brothers,
16: 4 and *e* in Jerusalem for the people
20:17 to Ephesus for the *e* of the church.
21:18 and all the *e* were present.
23:14 They went to the chief priests and *e*
24: 1 to Caesarea with some of the *e*
1Ti 4:14 when the body of *e* laid their hands
5:17 The *e* who direct the affairs
Tit 1: 5 and appoint *e* in every town,
Jas 5:14 He should call the *e* of the church
1Pe 5: 1 To the *e* among you, I appeal
Rev 4: 4 seated on them were twenty-four *e.*
4:10 the twenty-four *e* fall

ELEAZAR
Third son of Aaron (Ex 6:23-25). Succeeded Aaron as high priest (Nu 20:26; Dt 10:6). Allotted land to tribes (Jos 14:1). Death (Jos 24:33).

ELECT* (ELECTION)
Mt 24:22 the sake of the *e* those days will be
24:24 miracles to deceive even the *e—*
24:31 and they will gather his *e*
Mk 13:20 sake of the *e,* whom he has chosen,
13:22 and miracles to deceive the *e—*
13:27 gather his *e* from the four winds,
Ro 11: 7 it did not obtain, but the *e* did.
1Ti 5:21 and Christ Jesus and the *e* angels,
2Ti 2:10 everything for the sake of the *e,*
Tit 1: 1 Christ for the faith of God's *e*
1Pe 1: 1 To God's *e,* strangers in the world,

ELECTION* (ELECT)
Ro 9:11 God's purpose in *e* might stand:
11:28 but as far as *e* is concerned,
2Pe 1:10 to make your calling and *e* sure.

ELEMENTARY* (ELEMENTS)
Heb 5:12 someone to teach you the *e* truths
6: 1 us leave the *e* teachings about

ELEMENTS* (ELEMENTARY)
2Pe 3:10 the *e* will be destroyed by fire,
3:12 and the *e* will melt in the heat.

ELEVATE*
2Co 11: 7 to *e* you by preaching the gospel

ELI
High priest in youth of Samuel (1Sa 1-4). Blessed Hannah (1Sa 1:12-18); raised Samuel (1Sa 2:11-26). Prophesied against because of wicked sons (1Sa 2:27-36). Death of Eli and sons (1Sa 4: 11-22).

ELIHU
One of Job's friends (Job 32-37).

ELIJAH
Prophet; predicted famine in Israel (1Ki 17:1; Jas 5:17). Fed by ravens (1Ki 17:2-6). Raised Sidonian widow's son (1Ki 17:7-24). Defeated prophets of Baal at Carmel (1Ki 18:16-46). Ran from Jezebel (1Ki 19:1-9). Prophesied death of Azariah (2Ki 1). Succeeded by Elishah (1Ki 19:19-21; 2Ki 2:1-18). Taken to heaven in whirlwind (2Ki 2: 11-12).

Return prophesied (Mal 4:5-6); equated with John the Baptist (Mt 17:9-13; Mk 9:9-13; Lk 1:17). Appeared with Moses in transfiguration of Jesus (Mt 17:1-8; Mk 9:1-8).

ELIMELECH
Ru 1: 3 Now *E,* Naomi's husband, died,

ELIPHAZ
1. Firstborn of Esau (Ge 36).
2. One of Job's friends (Job 4-5; 15; 22).

ELISHA
Prophet; successor of Elijah (1Ki 19:16-21); inherited his cloak (2Ki 2:1-18). Purified bad water (2Ki 2:19-22). Cursed young men (2Ki 2:23-25). Aided Israel's defeat of Moab (2Ki 3). Provided widow with oil (2Ki 4:1-7). Raised Shunammite woman's son (2Ki 4:8-37). Purified food (2Ki 4: 38-41). Fed 100 men (2Ki 4:42-44). Healed Naaman's leprosy (2Ki 5). Made axhead float (2Ki 6: 1-7). Captured Arameans (2Ki 6:8-23). Political adviser to Israel (2Ki 6:24-8:6; 9:1-3; 13:14-19), Damascus (2Ki 8:7-15). Death (2Ki 13:20).

ELIZABETH*
Mother of John the Baptist, relative of Mary (Lk 1:5-58).

ELKANAH
Husband of Hannah, father of Samuel (1Sa 1-2).

ELOI*
Mt 27:46 *"E, E, lama sabachthani?"—*
Mk 15:34 *"E, E, lama sabachthani?"—*

ELOQUENCE* (ELOQUENT)
1Co 2: 1 come with *e* or superior wisdom

ELOQUENT* (ELOQUENCE)
Ex 4:10 "O Lord, I have never been *e,*

ELYMAS
Ac 13: 8 *E* the sorcerer (for that is what his

EMBEDDED*
Ecc 12:11 sayings like firmly *e* nails—

EMBERS
Pr 26:21 As charcoal to *e* and as wood to fire

EMBITTER* (BITTER)
Col 3:21 Fathers, do not *e* your children,

EMBODIMENT* (BODY)
Ro 2:20 have in the law the *e* of knowledge

EMPTIED (EMPTY)
1Co 1:17 the cross of Christ be *e* of its power.

EMPTY (EMPTIED)
Ge 1: 2 Now the earth was formless and *e,*
Job 26: 7 the northern skies over *e* space;
Isa 45:18 he did not create it to be *e,*
55:11 It will not return to me *e,*
Jer 4:23 and it was formless and *e;*
Lk 1:53 but has sent the rich away *e.*
Eph 5: 6 no one deceive you with *e* words,
1Pe 1:18 from the *e* way of life handed
2Pe 2:18 For they mouth *e,* boastful words

ENABLE (ABLE)
Lk 1:74 to *e* us to serve him without fear
Ac 4:29 *e* your servants to speak your word

ENABLED* (ABLE)
Lev 26:13 *e* you to walk with heads held high.
Ru 4:13 And the LORD *e* her to conceive,
Jn 6:65 unless the Father has *e* him."
Ac 2: 4 other tongues as the Spirit *e* them.
7:10 and *e* him to gain the goodwill
Heb 11:11 was *e* to become a father

ENABLES (ABLE)
Php 3:21 by the power that *e* him

ENABLING* (ABLE)
Ac 14: 3 the message of his grace by *e* them

ENCAMPS* (CAMP)
Ps 34: 7 The angel of the LORD *e*

ENCOURAGE* (ENCOURAGED ENCOURAGEMENT ENCOURAGES ENCOURAGING)
Dt 1:38 *E* him, because he will lead Israel
3:28 and *e* and strengthen him,
2Sa 11:25 Say this to *e* Joab."
19: 7 Now go out and *e* your men.
Job 16: 5 But my mouth would *e* you;
Ps 10:17 you *e* them, and you listen
64: 5 They *e* each other in evil plans,
Isa 1:17 *e* the oppressed.
Jer 29: 8 to the dreams you *e* them to have.
Ac 15:32 to *e* and strengthen the brothers.
Ro 12: 8 if it is encouraging, let him *e;*
Eph 6:22 how we are, and that he may *e* you.
Col 4: 8 and that he may *e* your hearts.
1Th 3: 2 to strengthen and *e* you
4:18 Therefore *e* each other
5:11 Therefore *e* one another
5:14 those who are idle, *e* the timid,
2Th 2:17 *e* your hearts and strengthen you

2Ti 4: 2 rebuke and *e*— with great patience
Tit 1: 9 so that he can *e* others
2: 6 *e* the young men to be
2:15 *E* and rebuke with all authority.
Heb 3:13 But *e* one another daily, as long
10:25 but let us *e* one another—

ENCOURAGED* (ENCOURAGE)
Jdg 7:11 you will be *e* to attack the camp."
20:22 But the men of Israel *e* one another
2Ch 22: 3 for his mother *e* him
32: 6 and *e* them with these words:
35: 2 and *e* them in the service
Eze 13:22 you *e* the wicked not to turn
Ac 9:31 It was strengthened; and *e*
11:23 and *e* them all to remain true
16:40 met with the brothers and *e* them.
18:27 the brothers *e* him and wrote
27:36 They were all *e* and ate some food
28:15 men Paul thanked God and was *e*.
Ro 1:12 and I may be mutually *e*
1Co 14:31 everyone may be instructed and *e*.
2Co 7: 4 I am greatly *e*; in all our troubles
7:13 By all this we are *e*.
Php 1:14 brothers in the Lord have been *e*
Col 2: 2 My purpose is that they may be *e*
1Th 3: 7 persecution we were *e* about you
Heb 6:18 offered to us may be greatly *e*.

ENCOURAGEMENT* (ENCOURAGE)
Ac 4:36 Barnabas (which means Son of *E*),
13:15 a message of *e* for the people,
20: 2 speaking many words of *e*
Ro 15: 4 *e* of the Scriptures we might have
15: 5 and *e* give you a spirit of unity
1Co 14: 3 to men for their strengthening, *e*
2Co 7:13 to our own *e*, we were especially
Php 2: 1 If you have any *e* from being united
2Th 2:16 and by his grace gave us eternal *e*
Phm : 7 love has given me great joy and *e*,
Heb 12: 5 word of *e* that addresses you

ENCOURAGES* (ENCOURAGE)
Isa 41: 7 The craftsman *e* the goldsmith,

ENCOURAGING* (ENCOURAGE)
Ac 14:22 *e* them to remain true to the faith.
15:31 and were glad for its *e* message.
20: 1 for the disciples and, after *e* them,
Ro 12: 8 if it is *e*, let him encourage;
1Th 2:12 *e*, comforting and urging you
1Pe 5:12 *e* you and testifying that this is

ENCROACH
Pr 23:10 or *e* on the fields of the fatherless,

END (ENDS)
Ps 119: 33 then I will keep them to the *e*.
119:112 to the very *e*.
Pr 1:19 Such is the *e* of all who go
5: 4 but in the *e* she is bitter as gall,
5:11 At the *e* of your life you will groan,
14:12 but in the *e* it leads to death.
14:13 and joy may *e* in grief.
16:25 but in the *e* it leads to death.
19:20 and in the *e* you will be wise.
20:21 will not be blessed at the *e*.
23:32 In the *e* it bites like a snake
25: 8 for what will you do in the *e*
28:23 in the *e* gain more favor
29:21 he will bring grief in the *e*.
Ecc 3:11 done from beginning to *e*.
7: 8 The *e* of a matter is better
12:12 making many books there is no *e*,
Eze 7: 2 The *e*! The *e* has come
Mt 10:22 firm to the *e* will be saved.
24:13 firm to the *e* will be saved.
24:14 nations, and then the *e* will come.
Lk 21: 9 but the *e* will not come right away
Ro 10: 4 Christ is the *e* of the law
1Co 15:24 the *e* will come, when he hands
Rev 21: 6 Omega, the Beginning and the *E*.
22:13 the Last, the Beginning and the *E*.

ENDS (END)
Ps 19: 4 their words to the *e* of the world.
Pr 20:17 he *e* up with a mouth full of gravel.
Isa 49: 6 salvation to the *e* of the earth."
62:11 proclamation to the *e* of the earth:
Ac 13:47 salvation to the *e* of the earth.' "
Ro 10:18 their words to the *e* of the world."

ENDURANCE* (ENDURE)
Ro 15: 4 through *e* and the encouragement
15: 5 May the God who gives *e*
2Co 1: 6 which produces in you patient *e*
6: 4 in great *e*; in troubles, hardships
Col 1:11 might so that you may have great *e*
1Th 1: 3 and your *e* inspired by hope
1Ti 6:11 faith, love, *e* and gentleness.
2Ti 3:10 patience, love, *e*, persecutions,
Tit 2: 2 and sound in faith, in love and in *e*.
Rev 1: 9 and patient *e* that are ours in Jesus,
13:10 This calls for patient *e*
14:12 This calls for patient *e* on the part

ENDURE (ENDURANCE ENDURED ENDURES ENDURING)
Ps 72:17 May his name *e* forever;
Pr 12:19 Truthful lips *e* forever,
27:24 for riches do not *e* forever,
Ecc 3:14 everything God does will *e* forever;
Da 2:44 to an end, but it will itself *e* forever.
Mal 3: 2 who can *e* the day of his coming?
1Co 4:12 when we are persecuted, we *e* it;
2Co 1: 8 far beyond our ability to *e*,
2Ti 2: 3 *E* hardship with us like a good
2:10 Therefore I *e* everything
2:12 if we *e*, / we will also reign
4: 5 head in all situations, *e* hardship,
Heb 12: 7 *E* hardship as discipline; God is
1Pe 2:20 a beating for doing wrong and *e* it?
2:20 suffer for doing good and you *e* it,
Rev 3:10 kept my command to *e* patiently,

ENDURED* (ENDURE)
Ps 123: 3 for we have *e* much contempt.
123: 4 We have *e* much ridicule
132: 1 and all the hardships he *e*.
Ac 13:18 and *e* their conduct forty years
2Ti 3:11 and Lystra, the persecutions I *e*.
Heb 12: 2 set before him *e* the cross,
12: 3 him who *e* such opposition
Rev 2: 3 and have *e* hardships for my name,

ENDURES (ENDURE)
Ps 102: 12 renown *e* through all generations.
112: 9 his righteousness *e* forever;
136: 1 *His love e forever.*
Da 9:15 made for yourself a name that *e*
2Co 9: 9 his righteousness *e* forever."

ENDURING (ENDURE)
2Th 1: 4 persecutions and trials you are *e*.
1Pe 1:23 through the living and *e* word

ENEMIES (ENEMY)
Ps 23: 5 in the presence of my *e*.
110: 1 hand until I make your *e*
Pr 16: 7 his *e* live at peace with him.
Isa 59:18 wrath to his *e*
Mic 7: 6 a man's *e* are the members
Mt 5:44 Love your *e* and pray
10:36 a man's *e* will be the members
Lk 6:27 Love your *e*, do good
6:35 But love your *e*, do good to them,
20:43 hand until I make your *e*
Ro 5:10 For if, when we were God's *e*,
1Co 15:25 reign until he has put all his *e*
Php 3:18 many live as *e* of the cross of Christ
Heb 1:13 hand until I make your *e*
10:13 for his *e* to be made his footstool,

ENEMY (ENEMIES ENMITY)
Pr 24:17 Do not gloat when your *e* falls;
25:21 If your *e* is hungry, give him food
27: 6 but an *e* multiplies kisses.
29:24 of a thief is his own *e*;
Lk 10:19 to overcome all the power of the *e*;
Ro 12:20 "If your *e* is hungry, feed him;
1Co 15:26 The last *e* to be destroyed is death.
1Ti 5:14 and to give the *e* no opportunity
1Pe 5: 8 Your *e* the devil prowls

ENERGY*
Col 1:29 struggling with all his *e*, which

ENGRAVED
Isa 49:16 I have *e* you on the palms
2Co 3: 7 which was *e* in letters on stone,

ENHANCES*
Ro 3: 7 my falsehood *e* God's truthfulness

ENJOY (JOY)
Dt 6: 2 and so that you may *e* long life.
Ps 37: 3 dwell in the land and *e* safe pasture.
Pr 28:16 ill-gotten gain will *e* a long life.
Ecc 3:22 better for a man than to *e* his work,
Eph 6: 3 and that you may *e* long life
Heb 11:25 rather than to *e* the pleasures of sin
3Jn : 2 I pray that you may *e* good health

ENJOYMENT (JOY)
Ecc 4: 8 and why am I depriving myself of *e*
1Ti 6:17 us with everything for our *e*.

ENLARGE (ENLARGES)
2Co 9:10 *e* the harvest of your righteousness.

ENLARGES (ENLARGE)
Dt 33:20 Blessed is he who *e* Gad's domain!

ENLIGHTENED* (LIGHT)
Eph 1:18 that the eyes of your heart may be *e*
Heb 6: 4 for those who have once been *e*,

ENMITY* (ENEMY)
Ge 3:15 And I will put *e*

ENOCH
1. Son of Cain (Ge 4:17-18).
2. Descendant of Seth; walked with God and taken by him (Ge 5:18-24; Heb 11:5). Prophet (Jude 14).

ENSLAVED (SLAVE)
Gal 4: 9 Do you wish to be *e* by them all
Tit 3: 3 and *e* by all kinds of passions

ENSNARE (SNARE)
Pr 5:22 of a wicked man *e* him;
Ecc 7:26 but the sinner she will *e*.

ENSNARED* (SNARE)
Dt 7:25 for yourselves, or you will be *e* by it
12:30 be careful not to be *e*
Ps 9:16 the wicked are *e* by the work
Pr 6: 2 *e* by the words of your mouth,
22:25 and get yourself *e*.

ENTANGLED (ENTANGLES)
2Pe 2:20 and are again *e* in it and overcome,

ENTANGLES* (ENTANGLED)
Heb 12: 1 and the sin that so easily *e*,

ENTER (ENTERED ENTERING ENTERS ENTRANCE)
Ps 95:11 "They shall never *e* my rest."
100: 4 *E* his gates with thanksgiving
Pr 2:10 For wisdom will *e* your heart,
Mt 5:20 will certainly not *e* the kingdom
7:13 "*E* through the narrow gate.
7:21 Lord,' will *e* the kingdom of heaven
18: 3 you will never *e* the kingdom
18: 8 It is better for you to *e* life maimed
19:17 to *e* life, obey the commandments
19:23 man to *e* the kingdom of heaven.
Mk 9:43 It is better for you to *e* life maimed
9:45 It is better for you to *e* life crippled
9:47 for you to *e* the kingdom of God
10:15 like a little child will never *e* it."
10:23 is for the rich to *e* the kingdom
Lk 13:24 will try to *e* and will not be able to.
13:24 "Make every effort to *e*
18:17 like a little child will never *e* it."
18:24 is for the rich to *e* the kingdom
Jn 3: 5 no one can *e* the kingdom of God.
Heb 3:11 'They shall never *e* my rest.' "
4:11 make every effort to *e* that rest,

ENTERED (ENTER)
Ps 73:17 me till I *e* the sanctuary of God;
Eze 4:14 meat has ever *e* my mouth."
Ac 11: 8 or unclean has ever *e* my mouth.'
Ro 5:12 as sin *e* the world through one man,
Heb 9:12 but he *e* the Most Holy Place once

ENTERING (ENTER)
Mt 21:31 the prostitutes are *e* the kingdom
Lk 11:52 have hindered those who were *e*."
Heb 4: 1 the promise of *e* his rest still stands,

ENTERS (ENTER)
Mk 7:18 you see that nothing that *e* a man
Jn 10: 2 The man who *e* by the gate is

ENTERTAIN* (ENTERTAINED ENTERTAINMENT)
Jdg 16:25 "Bring out Samson to *e* us."
Mt 9: 4 "Why do you *e* evil thoughts
1Ti 5:19 Do not *e* an accusation
Heb 13: 2 Do not forget to *e* strangers,

ENTERTAINED* (ENTERTAIN)
Ac 28: 7 and for three days *e* us hospitably.
Heb 13: 2 so doing some people have *e* angels

ENTERTAINMENT* (ENTERTAIN)
Da 6:18 without any *e* being brought to him

ENTHRALLED*
Ps 45:11 The king is *e* by your beauty;

ENTHRONED* (THRONE)
1Sa 4: 4 who is *e* between the cherubim.
2Sa 6: 2 who is *e* between the cherubim that
2Ki 19:15 of Israel, *e* between the cherubim,
1Ch 13: 6 who is *e* between the cherubim—
Ps 2: 4 The One *e* in heaven laughs;

Ps 9:11 to the LORD, *e* in Zion;
22: 3 Yet you are *e* as the Holy One;
29:10 The LORD sits *e* over the flood;
29:10 the LORD is *e* as King forever.
55:19 God, who is *e* forever,
61: 7 May he be *e* in God's presence
80: 1 who sit *e* between the cherubim,
99: 1 he sits *e* between the cherubim,
102: 12 But you, O LORD, sit *e* forever;
113: 5 the One who sits *e* on high,
132: 14 here I will sit *e*, for I have desired it
Isa 14:13 I will sit *e* on the mount
37:16 of Israel, *e* between the cherubim,
40:22 He sits *e* above the circle
52: 2 rise up, sit *e*, O Jerusalem.

ENTHRONES* (THRONE)
Job 36: 7 he *e* them with kings

ENTHUSIASM*
2Co 8:17 he is coming to you with much *e*
9: 2 and your *e* has stirred most of them

ENTICE* (ENTICED ENTICES)
Pr 1:10 My son, if sinners *e* you,
2Pe 2:18 they *e* people who are just escaping
Rev 2:14 who taught Balak to *e* the Israelites

ENTICED* (ENTICE)
Dt 4:19 do not be *e* into bowing
11:16 or you will be *e* to turn away
2Ki 17:21 Jeroboam *e* Israel away
Job 31: 9 If my heart has been *e* by a woman,
31:27 so that my heart was secretly *e*
Jas 1:14 desire, he is dragged away and *e*.

ENTICES* (ENTICE)
Dt 13: 6 your closest friend secretly *e* you,
Job 36:18 Be careful that no one *e* you
Pr 16:29 A violent man *e* his neighbor

ENTIRE
Gal 5:14 The *e* law is summed up

ENTRANCE (ENTER)
Mt 27:60 stone in front of the *e* to the tomb
Mk 15:46 a stone against the *e* of the tomb.
16: 3 away from the *e* of the tomb?"
Jn 11:38 cave with a stone laid across the *e*.
20: 1 had been removed from the *e*.

ENTRUST (TRUST)
Jn 2:24 Jesus would not *e* himself to them,
2Ti 2: 2 the presence of many witnesses *e*

ENTRUSTED (TRUST)
Jer 13:20 Where is the flock that was *e* to you
Jn 5:22 but has *e* all judgment to the Son,
Ro 3: 2 they have been *e* with the very
6:17 of teaching to which you were *e*.
1Co 4: 1 as those *e* with the secret things
1Th 2: 4 by God to be *e* with the gospel.
1Ti 1:11 of the blessed God, which he *e*
6:20 guard what has been *e* to your care.
2Ti 1:12 able to guard what I have *e* to him
1:14 Guard the good deposit that was *e*
Tit 1: 3 light through the preaching *e* to me
1: 7 Since an overseer is *e*
1Pe 2:23 he *e* himself to him who judges
5: 3 not lording it over those *e* to you,
Jude : 3 once for all *e* to the saints.

ENVIES
Jas 4: 5 spirit he caused to live in us *e*

ENVIOUS (ENVY)
Dt 32:21 I will make them *e*
Pr 24:19 or be *e* of the wicked,
Ro 10:19 "I will make you *e*

ENVOY
Pr 13:17 but a trustworthy *e* brings healing.

ENVY (ENVIOUS ENVYING)
Pr 3:31 Do not *e* a violent man
14:30 but *e* rots the bones.
23:17 Do not let your heart *e* sinners,
24: 1 Do not *e* wicked men,
Mk 7:22 malice, deceit, lewdness, *e*, slander
Ro 1:29 They are full of *e*, murder, strife,
11:14 arouse my own people to *e*
1Co 13: 4 It does not *e*, it does not boast,
Gal 5:21 factions and *e*; drunkenness, orgies
Php 1:15 that some preach Christ out of *e*
1Ti 6: 4 and quarrels about words that result in *e*,
Tit 3: 3 lived in malice and *e*, being hated
Jas 3:14 But if you harbor bitter *e*
3:16 where you have *e* and selfish
1Pe 2: 1 *e*, and slander of every kind.

ENVYING* (ENVY)
Gal 5:26 provoking and *e* each other.

EPHAH
Eze 45:11 The *e* and the bath are

EPHESUS
Ac 18:19 at *E*, where Paul left Priscilla
19: 1 the interior and arrived at *E*.
Eph 1: 1 To the saints in *E*, the faithful
Rev 2: 1 the angel of the church in *E* write:

EPHRAIM

1. Second son of Joseph (Ge 41:52; 46:20). Blessed as firstborn by Jacob (Ge 48). Tribe of numbered (Nu 1:33; 26:37), blessed (Dt 33:17), allotted land (Jos 16:4-9; Eze 48:5), failed to fully possess (Jos 16:10; Jdg 1:29).

2. Synonymous with Northern Kingdom (Isa 7: 17; Hos 5).

EQUAL (EQUALITY EQUITY)
Dt 33:25 and your strength will *e* your days.
1Sa 9: 2 without *e* among the Israelites—
Isa 40:25 who is my *e*?" says the Holy One.
46: 5 you compare me or count me *e*?
Da 1:19 and he found none *e* to Daniel,
Jn 5:18 making himself *e* with God.
1Co 12:25 that its parts should have *e* concern
2Co 2:16 And who is *e* to such a task?

EQUALITY* (EQUAL)
2Co 8:13 pressed, but that there might be *e*.
8:14 Then there will be *e*, as it is written:
Php 2: 6 did not consider *e*

EQUIP* (EQUIPPED)
Heb 13:21 *e* you with everything good

EQUIPPED (EQUIP)
2Ti 3:17 man of God may be thoroughly *e*

EQUITY* (EQUAL)
Ps 96:10 he will judge the peoples with *e*.
98: 9 and the peoples with *e*.
99: 4 you have established *e*;

ERODES*
Job 14:18 "But as a mountain *e* and crumbles

ERROR (ERRORS)
Jas 5:20 Whoever turns a sinner from the *e*
2Pe 2:18 escaping from those who live in *e*.

ERRORS* (ERROR)
Ps 19:12 Who can discern his *e*?
Ecc 10: 4 calmness can lay great *e* to rest.

ESAU

Firstborn of Isaac, twin of Jacob (Ge 25:21-26). Also called Edom (Ge 25:30). Sold Jacob his birthright (Ge 25:29-34); lost blessing (Gen 27). Married Hittites (Ge 26:34), Ishmaelites (Ge 28:6-9). Reconciled to Jacob (Gen 33). Genealogy (Ge 36). The LORD chose Jacob over Esau (Mal 1:2-3), but gave Esau land (Dt 2:2-12). Descendants eventually obliterated (Ob 1-21; Jer 49:7-22).

ESCAPE (ESCAPED ESCAPES ESCAPING)
Ps 68:20 from the Sovereign LORD comes *e*
Pr 11: 9 through knowledge the righteous *e*.
Ro 2: 3 think you will *e* God's judgment?
1Th 5: 3 woman, and they will not *e*.
2Ti 2:26 and *e* from the trap of the devil,
Heb 2: 3 how shall we *e* if we ignore such
12:25 If they did not *e* when they refused
2Pe 1: 4 and *e* the corruption in the world

ESCAPED (ESCAPE)
2Pe 2:20 If they have *e* the corruption

ESCAPES (ESCAPE)
Pr 12:13 but a righteous man *e* trouble.

ESCAPING (ESCAPE)
1Co 3:15 only as one *e* through the flames.
2Pe 2:18 they entice people who are just *e*

ESTABLISH (ESTABLISHED ESTABLISHES)
Ge 6:18 But I will *e* my covenant with you,
17:21 But my covenant I will *e* with Isaac
2Sa 7:11 the LORD himself will *e* a house
1Ki 9: 5 I will *e* your royal throne
1Ch 28: 7 I will *e* his kingdom forever
Ps 90:17 *e* the work of our hands for us—
Isa 26:12 LORD, you *e* peace for us;
Ro 10: 3 God and sought to *e* their own,
16:25 able to *e* you by my gospel
Heb 10: 9 sets aside the first to *e* the second.

ESTABLISHED (ESTABLISH)
Ge 9:17 the sign of the covenant I have *e*
Ex 6: 4 also *e* my covenant with them
Pr 16:12 a throne is *e* through righteousness.

ESTABLISHES (ESTABLISH)
Job 25: 2 he *e* order in the heights of heaven.
Isa 42: 4 till he *e* justice on earth.

ESTATE
Ps 136: 23 who remembered us in our low *e*

ESTEEMED
Pr 22: 1 to be *e* is better than silver or gold.
Isa 53: 3 he was despised, and we *e* him not.

ESTHER

Jewess, originally named Hadassah, who lived in Persia; cousin of Mordecai (Est 2:7). Chosen queen of Xerxes (Est 2:8-18). Persuaded by Mordecai to foil Haman's plan to exterminate the Jews (Est 3-4). Revealed Haman's plans to Xerxes, resulting in Haman's death (Est 7), the Jews' preservation (Est 8-9), Mordecai's exaltation (Est 8:15; 9:4; 10). Decreed celebration of Purim (Est 9:18-32).

ETERNAL* (ETERNALLY ETERNITY)
Ge 21:33 the name of the LORD, the *E* God.
Dt 33:27 The *e* God is your refuge,
1Ki 10: 9 of the LORD's *e* love for Israel,
Ps 16:11 with *e* pleasures at your right hand.
21: 6 you have granted him *e* blessings
111: 10 To him belongs *e* praise.
119: 89 Your word, O LORD, is *e*;
119: 160 all your righteous laws are *e*.
Ecc 12: 5 Then man goes to his *e* home
Isa 26: 4 LORD, the LORD, is the Rock *e*.
47: 7 the *e* queen!'
Jer 10:10 he is the living God, the *e* King.
Da 4: 3 His kingdom is an *e* kingdom;
4:34 His dominion is an *e* dominion;
Hab 3: 6 His ways are *e*.
Mt 18: 8 two feet and be thrown into *e* fire.
19:16 good thing must I do to get *e* life?"
19:29 as much and will inherit *e* life.
25:41 into the *e* fire prepared for the devil
25:46 but the righteous to *e* life."
25:46 they will go away to *e* punishment,
Mk 3:29 be forgiven; he is guilty of an *e* sin."
10:17 "what must I do to inherit *e* life?"
10:30 and in the age to come, *e* life.
Lk 10:25 "what must I do to inherit *e* life?"
16: 9 will be welcomed into *e* dwellings.
18:18 what must I do to inherit *e* life?"
18:30 and, in the age to come, *e* life."
Jn 3:15 believes in him may have *e* life.
3:16 him shall not perish but have *e* life.
3:36 believes in the Son has *e* life,
4:14 spring of water welling up to *e* life."
4:36 now he harvests the crop for *e* life,
5:24 believes him who sent me has *e* life
5:39 that by them you possess *e* life.
6:27 but for food that endures to *e* life,
6:40 believes in him shall have *e* life,
6:54 and drinks my blood has *e* life,
6:68 You have the words of *e* life.
10:28 I give them *e* life, and they shall
12:25 in this world will keep it for *e* life.
12:50 that his command leads to *e* life.
17: 2 all people that he might give *e* life
17: 3 this is *e* life: that they may know
Ac 13:46 yourselves worthy of *e* life,
13:48 were appointed for *e* life believed.
Ro 1:20 his *e* power and divine nature—
2: 7 and immortality, he will give *e* life.
5:21 righteousness to bring *e* life
6:22 to holiness, and the result is *e* life.
6:23 but the gift of God is *e* life
16:26 by the command of the *e* God,
2Co 4:17 for us an *e* glory that far outweighs
4:18 temporary, but what is unseen is *e*.
5: 1 from God, an *e* house in heaven,
Gal 6: 8 from the Spirit will reap *e* life.
Eph 3:11 to his *e* purpose which he
2Th 2:16 his grace gave us *e* encouragement
1Ti 1:16 believe on him and receive *e* life.
1:17 Now to the King *e*, immortal,
6:12 Take hold of the *e* life
2Ti 2:10 is in Christ Jesus, with *e* glory.
Tit 1: 2 resting on the hope of *e* life,
3: 7 heirs having the hope of *e* life.
Heb 5: 9 he became the source of *e* salvation
6: 2 of the dead, and *e* judgment.
9:12 having obtained *e* redemption.
9:14 through the *e* Spirit offered himself
9:15 the promised *e* inheritance—
13:20 of the *e* covenant brought back
1Pe 5:10 you to his *e* glory in Christ,

2Pe 1:11 into the *e* kingdom of our Lord
1Jn 1: 2 and we proclaim to you the *e* life,
2:25 what he promised us—even *e* life.
3:15 know that no murderer has *e* life
5:11 God has given us *e* life,
5:13 you may know that you have *e* life.
5:20 He is the true God and *e* life.
Jude : 7 who suffer the punishment of *e* fire.
:21 Christ to bring you to *e* life.
Rev 14: 6 and he had the *e* gospel to proclaim

ETERNALLY* (ETERNAL)

Gal 1: 8 let him be *e* condemned! As we
1: 9 let him be *e* condemned! Am I now

ETERNITY* (ETERNAL)

Ps 93: 2 you are from all *e*.
Pr 8:23 I was appointed from *e*,
Ecc 3:11 also set *e* in the hearts of men;

ETHIOPIAN*

Jer 13:23 Can the *E* change his skin
Ac 8:27 and on his way he met an *E* eunuch

EUNUCH (EUNUCHS)

Ac 8:27 on his way he met an Ethiopian *e*,

EUNUCHS (EUNUCH)

Isa 56: 4 "To the *e* who keep my Sabbaths,
Mt 19:12 For some are *e* because they were

EUTYCHUS*

Ac 20: 9 was a young man named *E*,

EVANGELIST* (EVANGELISTS)

Ac 21: 8 stayed at the house of Philip the *e*,
2Ti 4: 5 hardship, do the work of an *e*,

EVANGELISTS* (EVANGELIST)

Eph 4:11 some to be prophets, some to be *e*,

EVE*

Ge 3:20 Adam named his wife *E*,
4: 1 Adam lay with his wife *E*,
2Co 11: 3 as *E* was deceived by the serpent's
1Ti 2:13 For Adam was formed first, then *E*

EVEN-TEMPERED* (TEMPER)

Pr 17:27 and a man of understanding is *e*.

EVENING

Ge 1: 5 there was *e*, and there was morning

EVER (EVERLASTING FOREVER FOREVERMORE)

Ex 15:18 LORD will reign for *e* and *e*."
Dt 8:19 If you *e* forget the LORD your
1Ki 3:12 anyone like you, nor will there *e* be.
Job 4: 7 were the upright *e* destroyed?
Ps 5:11 let them *e* sing for joy.
10:16 The LORD is King for *e* and *e*;
21: 4 length of days, for *e* and *e*.
25: 3 will *e* be put to shame,
25:15 My eyes are *e* on the LORD,
26: 3 for your love is *e* before me,
45: 6 O God, will last for *e* and *e*;
45:17 nations will praise you for *e* and *e*.
48:14 For this God is our God for *e* and *e*;
52: 8 God's unfailing love for *e* and *e*.
61: 8 will I *e* sing praise to your name
71: 6 I will *e* praise you.
84: 4 they are *e* praising you.
89:33 nor will I *e* betray my faithfulness.
111: 8 They are steadfast for *e* and *e*,
119: 44 your law, for *e* and *e*.
119: 98 for they are *e* with me.
132: 12 sit on your throne for *e* and *e*."
145: 1 I will praise your name for *e* and *e*.
145: 2 and extol your name for *e* and *e*.
145: 21 his holy name for *e* and *e*.
Pr 4:18 shining *e* brighter till the full light
5:19 may you *e* be captivated
Isa 66: 8 Who has *e* heard of such a thing?
66: 8 Who has *e* seen such things?
Jer 7: 7 I gave your forefathers for *e* and *e*.
25: 5 and your fathers for *e* and *e*.
31:36 the descendants of Israel *e* cease
Da 2:20 be to the name of God for *e* and *e*;
7:18 it forever—yes, for *e* and *e*.'
12: 3 like the stars for *e* and *e*.
Mic 4: 5 our God for *e* and *e*.
Mt 13:14 you will be *e* seeing but never
13:14 " 'You will be *e* hearing
Mk 4:12 *e* hearing but never understanding;
Jn 1:18 No one has *e* seen God,
Gal 1: 5 to whom be glory for *e* and *e*.
Eph 3:21 all generations, for *e* and *e*!
Php 4:20 and Father be glory for *e* and *e*.
1Ti 1:17 be honor and glory for *e* and *e*.
2Ti 4:18 To him be glory for *e* and *e*.
Heb 1: 8 O God, will last for *e* and *e*,
13:21 to whom be glory for *e* and *e*.
1Pe 4:11 the glory and the power for *e* and *e*.
5:11 To him be the power for *e* and *e*.
1Jn 4:12 No one has *e* seen God;
Rev 1: 6 him be glory and power for *e* and *e*!
1:18 and behold I am alive for *e* and *e*!
21:27 Nothing impure will *e* enter it,
22: 5 And they will reign for *e* and *e*.

EVER-INCREASING* (INCREASE)

Ro 6:19 to impurity and to *e* wickedness,
2Co 3:18 into his likeness with *e* glory,

EVERLASTING* (EVER)

Ge 9:16 and remember the *e* covenant
17: 7 an *e* covenant between me and you
17: 8 I will give as an *e* possession to you
17:13 in your flesh is to be an *e* covenant.
17:19 an *e* covenant for his descendants
48: 4 *e* possession to your descendants
Nu 18:19 It is an *e* covenant of salt
Dt 33:15 and the fruitfulness of the *e* hills;
33:27 and underneath are the *e* arms.
2Sa 23: 5 made with me an *e* covenant,
1Ch 16:17 to Israel as an *e* covenant:
16:36 from *e* to *e*.
29:10 from *e* to *e*.
Ezr 9:12 to your children as an *e* inheritance
Ne 9: 5 your God, who is from *e* to *e*."
Ps 41:13 from *e* to *e*.
52: 5 God will bring you down to *e* ruin:
74: 3 toward these *e* ruins,
78:66 he put them to *e* shame.
90: 2 from *e* to *e* you are God.
103: 17 But from *e* to *e*
105: 10 to Israel as an *e* covenant:
106: 48 from *e* to *e*.
119:142 Your righteousness is *e*
139: 24 and lead me in the way *e*.
145: 13 Your kingdom is an *e* kingdom,
Isa 9: 6 *E* Father, Prince of Peace.
24: 5 and broken the *e* covenant.
30: 8 it may be an *e* witness.
33:14 Who of us can dwell with *e* burning
35:10 *e* joy will crown their heads.
40:28 The LORD is the *e* God,
45:17 the LORD with an *e* salvation;
45:17 to ages *e*.
51:11 *e* joy will crown their heads.
54: 8 but with *e* kindness
55: 3 I will make an *e* covenant with you,
55:13 for an *e* sign,
56: 5 I will give them an *e* name
60:15 I will make you the *e* pride
60:19 for the LORD will be your *e* light,
60:20 the LORD will be your *e* light,
61: 7 and *e* joy will be theirs.
61: 8 and make an *e* covenant with them.
63:12 to gain for himself *e* renown,
Jer 5:22 an *e* barrier it cannot cross.
23:40 I will bring upon you *e* disgrace—
23:40 *e* shame that will not be forgotten."
25: 9 of horror and scorn, and an *e* ruin.
31: 3 "I have loved you with an *e* love;
32:40 I will make an *e* covenant
50: 5 the LORD in an *e* covenant
Eze 16:60 and I will establish an *e* covenant
37:26 with them; it will be an *e* covenant.
Da 7:14 dominion is an *e* dominion that will
7:27 His kingdom will be an *e* kingdom,
9:24 to bring in *e* righteousness,
12: 2 others to shame and *e* contempt.
12: 2 some to *e* life, others to shame
Mic 6: 2 you *e* foundations of the earth.
Hab 1:12 O LORD, are you not from *e*?
Jn 6:47 the truth, he who believes has *e* life.
2Th 1: 9 punished with *e* destruction
Jude : 6 bound with *e* chains for judgment

EVER-PRESENT*

Ps 46: 1 an *e* help in trouble

EVIDENCE (EVIDENT)

Jn 14:11 on the *e* of the miracles themselves.
Ac 11:23 and saw the *e* of the grace of God,
2Th 1: 5 All this is *e* that God's judgment is
Jas 2:20 do you want *e* that faith

EVIDENT (EVIDENCE)

Php 4: 5 Let your gentleness be *e* to all.

EVIL (EVILDOER EVILDOERS EVILS)

Ge 2: 9 of the knowledge of good and *e*.
3: 5 be like God, knowing good and *e*."
6: 5 of his heart was only *e* all the time.
Ex 32:22 how prone these people are to *e*.
Jdg 2:11 Then the Israelites did *e* in the eyes
3: 7 The Israelites did *e* in the eyes
3:12 Once again the Israelites did *e*
Jdg 4: 1 the Israelites once again did *e*
6: 1 Again the Israelites did *e*
10: 6 Again the Israelites did *e*
13: 1 Again the Israelites did *e*
1Ki 11: 6 So Solomon did *e* in the eyes
16:25 But Omri did *e* in the eyes
2Ki 15:24 Pekahiah did *e* in the eyes
Job 1: 1 he feared God and shunned *e*.
1: 8 a man who fears God and shuns *e*."
34:10 Far be it from God to do *e*,
36:21 Beware of turning to *e*,
Ps 5: 4 not a God who takes pleasure in *e*;
23: 4 I will fear no *e*,
34:13 keep your tongue from *e*
34:14 Turn from *e* and do good;
34:16 is against those who do *e*,
37: 1 Do not fret because of *e* men
37: 8 do not fret—it leads only to *e*.
37:27 Turn from *e* and do good;
49: 5 fear when *e* days come,
51: 4 and done what is *e* in your sight,
97:10 those who love the LORD hate *e*,
101: 4 I will have nothing to do with *e*.
141: 4 not my heart be drawn to what is *e*,
Pr 4:27 keep your foot from *e*.
8:13 To fear the LORD is to hate *e*;
10:23 A fool finds pleasure in *e* conduct,
11:19 he who pursues *e* goes to his death.
11:27 *e* comes to him who searches for it.
14:16 man fears the LORD and shuns *e*,
17:13 If a man pays back *e* for good,
20:30 Blows and wounds cleanse away *e*,
24:19 Do not fret because of *e* men
24:20 for the *e* man has no future hope,
26:23 are fervent lips with an *e* heart.
28: 5 *E* men do not understand justice,
29: 6 An *e* man is snared by his own sin,
Ecc 12:14 whether it is good or *e*.
Isa 5:20 Woe to those who call *e* good
13:11 I will punish the world for its *e*,
55: 7 and the *e* man his thoughts.
Jer 4:14 wash the *e* from your heart
18: 8 nation I warned repents of its *e*,
18:11 So turn from your *e* ways,
Eze 33:11 Turn! Turn from your *e* ways!
33:13 he will die for the *e* he has done.
33:15 and does no *e*, he will surely live;
Am 5:13 for the times are *e*.
Hab 1:13 Your eyes are too pure to look on *e*;
Zec 8:17 do not plot *e* against your neighbor,
Mt 5:45 He causes his sun to rise on the *e*
6:13 but deliver us from the *e* one.'
7:11 If you, then, though you are *e*,
12:34 you who are *e* say anything good?
12:35 and the *e* man brings *e* things out
12:35 out of the *e* stored up in him.
12:43 "When an *e* spirit comes out
15:19 out of the heart come *e* thoughts,
Mk 7:21 come *e* thoughts, sexual
Lk 6:45 and the *e* man brings *e* things out
11:13 If you then, though you are *e*,
Jn 3:19 of light because their deeds were *e*.
3:20 Everyone who does *e* hates
17:15 you protect them from the *e* one.
Ro 1:30 they invent ways of doing *e*;
2: 8 who reject the truth and follow *e*,
2: 9 for every human being who does *e*:
3: 8 "Let us do *e* that good may result"?
6:12 body so that you obey its *e* desires.
7:19 no, the *e* I do not want to do—
7:21 to do good, *e* is right there with me.
12: 9 Hate what is *e*; cling
12:17 Do not repay anyone *e* for *e*.
12:21 Do not be overcome by *e*,
14:16 good to be spoken of as *e*.
16:19 and innocent about what is *e*.
1Co 13: 6 Love does not delight in *e*
14:20 In regard to *e* be infants,
Eph 5:16 because the days are *e*.
6:12 forces of *e* in the heavenly realms.
6:16 all the flaming arrows of the *e* one.
Col 3: 5 impurity, lust, *e* desires and greed,
1Th 5:22 Avoid every kind of *e*.
2Th 3: 3 and protect you from the *e* one.
1Ti 6:10 of money is a root of all kinds of *e*.
2Ti 2:22 Flee the *e* desires of youth,
3: 6 are swayed by all kinds of *e* desires,
3:13 while *e* men and impostors will go
Heb 5:14 to distinguish good from *e*.
Jas 1:13 For God cannot be tempted by *e*,
1:21 and the *e* that is so prevalent,
3: 6 a world of *e* among the parts
3: 8 It is a restless *e*, full
1Pe 2:16 your freedom as a cover-up for *e*;
3: 9 Do not repay *e* with *e* or insult
3:10 must keep his tongue from *e*
3:17 for doing good than for doing *e*.
1Jn 2:13 you have overcome the *e* one.
2:14 and you have overcome the *e* one.

1Jn 3:12 who belonged to the *e* one
5:18 and the *e* one cannot harm him.
5:19 is under the control of the *e* one.
3Jn :11 do not imitate what is *e*

EVILDOER* (EVIL)
2Sa 3:39 the LORD repay the *e* according
Ps 101: 8 I will cut off every *e*
Mal 4: 1 and every *e* will be stubble,

EVILDOERS* (EVIL)
1Sa 24:13 saying goes, 'From *e* come evil
Job 8:20 or strengthen the hands of *e*.
34: 8 He keeps company with *e*;
34:22 where *e* can hide.
Ps 14: 4 Will *e* never learn—
14: 6 You *e* frustrate the plans
26: 5 I abhor the assembly of *e*
36:12 See how the *e* lie fallen—
53: 4 Will the *e* never learn—
59: 2 Deliver me from *e*
64: 2 from that noisy crowd of *e*.
92: 7 and all *e* flourish,
92: 9 all *e* will be scattered.
94: 4 all the *e* are full of boasting.
94:16 will take a stand for me against *e*?
119:115 Away from me, you *e*,
125: 5 the LORD will banish with the *e*.
141: 4 deeds with men who are *e*;
141: 5 ever against the deeds of *e*;
141: 9 from the traps set by *e*.
Pr 21:15 but terror to *e*.
Isa 1: 4 a brood of *e*,
31: 2 against those who help *e*.
Jer 23:14 They strengthen the hands of *e*,
Hos 10: 9 the *e* in Gibeah?
Mal 3:15 Certainly the *e* prosper, and
Mt 7:23 you *e*!' "Therefore everyone who
Lk 13:27 Away from me, all you *e*!'
18:11 *e*, adulterers—or even like this tax

EVILS* (EVIL)
Mk 7:23 All these *e* come from inside

EWE
2Sa 12: 3 one little *e* lamb he had bought.

EXACT*
Ge 43:21 the *e* weight—in the mouth
Est 4: 7 including the *e* amount
Mt 2: 7 from them the *e* time the star had
Jn 4:53 realized that this was the *e* time
Ac 17:26 the *e* places where they should live.
Heb 1: 3 the *e* representation of his being,

EXALT* (EXALTED EXALTS)
Ex 15: 2 my father's God, and I will *e* him.
Jos 3: 7 begin to *e* you in the eyes
1Sa 2:10 and *e* the horn of his anointed."
1Ch 25: 5 the promises of God to *e* him.
29:12 power to *e* and give strength to all.
Job 19: 5 If indeed you would *e* yourselves
Ps 30: 1 I will *e* you, O LORD,
34: 3 let us *e* his name together.
35:26 may all who *e* themselves over me
37:34 He will *e* you to inherit the land;
38:16 *e* themselves over me
75: 6 or from the desert can *e* a man.
89:17 and by your favor you *e* our horn.
99: 5 *E* the LORD our God
99: 9 *E* the LORD our God
107: 32 Let them *e* him in the assembly
118: 28 you are my God, and I will *e* you.
145: 1 I will *e* you, my God the King;
Pr 4: 8 Esteem her, and she will *e* you;
25: 6 Do not *e* yourself in the king's
Isa 24:15 *e* the name of the LORD, the God
25: 1 I will *e* you and praise your name,
Eze 29:15 and will never again *e* itself
Da 4:37 *e* and glorify the King of heaven,
11:36 He will *e* and magnify himself
11:37 but will *e* himself above them all.
Hos 11: 7 he will by no means *e* them.
2Th 2: 4 will *e* himself over everything that is

EXALTED* (EXALT)
Ex 15: 1 for he is highly *e*.
15:21 for he is highly *e*.
Nu 24: 7 their kingdom will be *e*.
Jos 4:14 That day the LORD *e* Joshua
2Sa 5:12 and had *e* his kingdom for the sake
22:47 *E* be God, the Rock, my Savior!
22:49 You *e* me above my foes;
23: 1 of the man *e* by the Most High,
1Ch 14: 2 that his kingdom had been highly *e*
17:17 as though I were the most *e* of men,
29:11 you are *e* as head over all.
29:25 The LORD highly *e* Solomon
Ne 9: 5 and may it be *e* above all blessing
Job 24:24 For a little while they are *e*,
36:22 "God is *e* in his power.
37:23 beyond our reach and *e* in power;
Ps 18:46 *E* be God my Savior!
18:48 You *e* me above my foes;
21:13 Be *e*, O LORD, in your strength;
27: 6 Then my head will be *e*
35:27 they always say, "The LORD be *e*,
40:16 "The LORD be *e*!"
46:10 I will be *e* among the nations,
46:10 I will be *e* in the earth."
47: 9 he is greatly *e*.
57: 5 Be *e*, O God, above the heavens;
57:11 Be *e*, O God, above the heavens;
70: 4 "Let God be *e*!"
89:13 hand is strong, your right hand *e*.
89:19 I have *e* a young man
89:24 through my name his horn will be *e*
89:27 the most *e* of the kings of the earth.
89:42 You have *e* the right hand
92: 8 But you, O LORD, are *e* forever.
92:10 You have *e* my horn like that
97: 9 you are *e* far above all gods.
99: 2 he is *e* over all the nations.
108: 5 Be *e*, O God, above the heavens,
113: 4 The LORD is *e* over all the nations
138: 2 for you have *e* above all things
148: 13 for his name alone is *e*;
Pr 11:11 of the upright a city is *e*,
30:32 have played the fool and *e* yourself,
Isa 2:11 the LORD alone will be *e*
2:12 for all that is *e*
2:17 the LORD alone will be *e*
5:16 the LORD Almighty will be *e*
6: 1 *e*, and the train of his robe filled
12: 4 and proclaim that his name is *e*.
24: 4 the *e* of the earth languish.
33: 5 The LORD is *e*, for he dwells
33:10 "Now will I be *e*;
52:13 be raised and lifted up and highly *e*.
Jer 17:12 A glorious throne, *e*
La 2:17 he has *e* the horn of your foes.
Eze 21:26 The lowly will be *e* and the *e* will be
Hos 13: 1 he was *e* in Israel.
Mic 6: 6 and bow down before the *e* God?
Mt 23:12 whoever humbles himself will be *e*.
Lk 14:11 he who humbles himself will be *e*."
18:14 he who humbles himself will be *e*."
Ac 2:33 *E* to the right hand of God,
5:31 God *e* him to his own right hand
Php 1:20 always Christ will be *e* in my body,
2: 9 Therefore God *e* him
Heb 7:26 from sinners, *e* above the heavens.

EXALTS* (EXALT)
1Sa 2: 7 he humbles and he *e*.
Job 36: 7 and *e* them forever.
Ps 75: 7 He brings one down, he *e* another.
Pr 14:34 Righteousness *e* a nation,
Mt 23:12 For whoever *e* himself will be
Lk 14:11 For everyone who *e* himself will be
18:14 For everyone who *e* himself will be

EXAMINE (EXAMINED EXAMINES)
Ps 11: 4 his eyes *e* them.
17: 3 you probe my heart and *e* me
26: 2 *e* my heart and my mind;
Jer 17:10 and *e* the mind,
20:12 Almighty, you who *e* the righteous
La 3:40 Let us *e* our ways and test them,
1Co 11:28 A man ought to *e* himself
2Co 13: 5 *E* yourselves to see whether you

EXAMINED (EXAMINE)
Job 13: 9 Would it turn out well if he *e* you?
Ac 17:11 *e* the Scriptures every day to see

EXAMINES (EXAMINE)
Ps 11: 5 The LORD *e* the righteous,
Pr 5:21 and he *e* all his paths.

EXAMPLE* (EXAMPLES)
2Ki 14: 3 In everything he followed the *e*
Ecc 9:13 also saw under the sun this *e*
Eze 14: 8 and make him an *e* and a byword.
Jn 13:15 have set you an *e* that you should
Ro 7: 2 as long as he lives? For *e*,
1Co 11: 1 Follow my *e*, as I follow
11: 1 as I follow the *e* of Christ.
Gal 3:15 let me take an *e* from everyday life.
Php 3:17 Join with others in following my *e*,
2Th 3: 7 how you ought to follow our *e*.
1Ti 1:16 as an *e* for those who would believe
4:12 set an *e* for the believers in speech,
Tit 2: 7 In everything set them an *e*
Heb 4:11 fall by following their *e*
Jas 3: 4 Or take ships as an *e*.
5:10 as an *e* of patience in the face
1Pe 2:21 leaving you an *e*, that you should
2Pe 2: 6 made them an *e* of what is going
Jude : 7 as an *e* of those who suffer

EXAMPLES* (EXAMPLE)
1Co 10: 6 Now these things occurred as *e*
10:11 as *e* and were written down
1Pe 5: 3 to you, but being *e* to the flock.

EXASPERATE*
Eph 6: 4 Fathers, do not *e* your children;

EXCEL* (EXCELLENT)
Ge 49: 4 as the waters, you will no longer *e*,
1Co 14:12 to *e* in gifts that build up the church
2Co 8: 7 But just as you *e* in everything—
8: 7 also *e* in this grace of giving.

EXCELLENT (EXCEL)
1Co 12:31 now I will show you the most *e* way
Php 4: 8 if anything is *e* or praiseworthy—
1Ti 3:13 have served well gain an *e* standing
Tit 3: 8 These things are *e* and profitable

EXCESSIVE
Eze 18: 8 or take *e* interest.
2Co 2: 7 not be overwhelmed by *e* sorrow.

EXCHANGE (EXCHANGED)
Mt 16:26 Or what can a man give in *e*
Mk 8:37 Or what can a man give in *e*
2Co 6:13 As a fair *e*—I speak

EXCHANGED (EXCHANGE)
Ps 106: 20 They *e* their Glory
Jer 2:11 But my people have *e* their Glory
Hos 4: 7 they *e* their Glory
Ro 1:23 *e* the glory of the immortal God
1:25 They *e* the truth of God for a lie,
1:26 their women *e* natural relations

EXCLAIM
Ps 35:10 My whole being will *e*,

EXCUSE* (EXCUSES)
Ps 25: 3 who are treacherous without *e*.
Lk 14:18 Please *e* me.'
14:19 Please *e* me.'
Jn 15:22 they have no *e* for their sin.
Ro 1:20 so that men are without *e*.
2: 1 You, therefore, have no *e*,

EXCUSES* (EXCUSE)
Lk 14:18 "But they all alike began to make *e*.

EXERTED*
Eph 1:20 which he *e* in Christ

EXHORT*
1Ti 5: 1 but *e* him as if he were your father.

EXILE
2Ki 17:23 taken from their homeland into *e*
25:11 into *e* the people who remained

EXISTED* (EXISTS)
2Pe 3: 5 ago by God's word the heavens *e*

EXISTS (EXISTED)
Heb 2:10 and through whom everything *e*,
11: 6 to him must believe that he *e*

EXPANSE
Ge 1: 7 So God made the *e* and separated
1: 8 God called the *e* "sky."

EXPECT (EXPECTATION EXPECTED EXPECTING)
Mt 24:44 at an hour when you do not *e* him.
Lk 12:40 at an hour when you do not *e* him."
Php 1:20 I eagerly *e* and hope that I will

EXPECTATION (EXPECT)
Ro 8:19 waits in eager *e* for the sons
Heb 10:27 but only a fearful *e* of judgment

EXPECTED (EXPECT)
Pr 11: 7 all he *e* from his power comes
Hag 1: 9 "You *e* much, but see, it turned out

EXPECTING (EXPECT)
Lk 6:35 and lend to them without *e*

EXPEL* (EXPELLED)
1Co 5:13 *E* the wicked man from among you

EXPELLED (EXPEL)
Eze 28:16 and I *e* you, O guardian cherub,

EXPENSE (EXPENSIVE)
1Co 9: 7 Who serves as a soldier at his own *e*

EXPENSIVE* (EXPENSE)
Mt 26: 7 jar of very *e* perfume,

Mk 14: 3 jar of very *e* perfume,
Lk 7:25 those who wear *e* clothes
Jn 12: 3 a pint of pure nard, an *e* perfume;
1Ti 2: 9 or gold or pearls or *e* clothes,

EXPERT
1Co 3:10 I laid a foundation as an *e* builder,

EXPLAINING (EXPLAINS)
Ac 17: 3 *e* and proving that the Christ had

EXPLAINS* (EXPLAINING)
Ac 8:31 he said, "unless someone *e* it to me

EXPLOIT* (EXPLOITED EXPLOITING EXPLOITS)
Pr 22:22 Do not *e* the poor because they are
Isa 58: 3 and *e* all your workers.
2Co 12:17 Did I *e* you through any
12:18 Titus did not *e* you, did he?
2Pe 2: 3 greed these teachers will *e* you

EXPLOITED* (EXPLOIT)
2Co 7: 2 no one, we have *e* no one.

EXPLOITING* (EXPLOIT)
Jas 2: 6 Is it not the rich who are *e* you?

EXPLOITS (EXPLOIT)
2Co 11:20 or *e* you or takes advantage of you

EXPLORE
Nu 13: 2 "Send some men to *e* the land

EXPOSE (EXPOSED)
1Co 4: 5 will *e* the motives of men's hearts.
Eph 5:11 of darkness, but rather *e* them.

EXPOSED (EXPOSE)
Jn 3:20 for fear that his deeds will be *e*.
Eph 5:13 everything *e* by the light becomes

EXPRESS (EXPRESSING)
Ro 8:26 us with groans that words cannot *e*.

EXPRESSING* (EXPRESS)
1Co 2:13 *e* spiritual truths in spiritual words.
Gal 5: 6 thing that counts is faith *e* itself

EXTENDS (EXTENT)
Pr 31:20 and *e* her hands to the needy.
Lk 1:50 His mercy *e* to those who fear him,

EXTENT (EXTENDS)
Jn 13: 1 he now showed them the full *e*

EXTERNAL
Gal 2: 6 judge by *e* appearance—

EXTINGUISH (EXTINGUISHED)
Eph 6:16 which you can *e* all the flaming

EXTINGUISHED (EXTINGUISH)
2Sa 21:17 the lamp of Israel will not be *e*."

EXTOL*
Job 36:24 Remember to *e* his work,
Ps 34: 1 I will *e* the LORD at all times;
68: 4 *e* him who rides on the clouds—
95: 2 and *e* him with music and song.
109: 30 mouth I will greatly *e* the LORD;
111: 1 I will *e* the LORD with all my heart
115: 18 it is we who *e* the LORD,
117: 1 *e* him, all you peoples.
145: 2 and *e* your name for ever and ever.
145: 10 your saints will *e* you.
147: 12 *E* the LORD, O Jerusalem;

EXTORT*
Lk 3:14 "Don't *e* money and don't accuse

EXTRAORDINARY*
Ac 19:11 God did *e* miracles through Paul,

EXTREME (EXTREMES)
2Co 8: 2 and their *e* poverty welled up

EXTREMES* (EXTREME)
Ecc 7:18 who fears God will avoid all *e*.

EXULT
Ps 89:16 they *e* in your righteousness.
Isa 45:25 will be found righteous and will *e*.

EYE (EYES)
Ge 3: 6 good for food and pleasing to the *e*,
Ex 21:24 you are to take life for life, *e* for *e*,
Dt 19:21 life for life, *e* for *e*, tooth for tooth,
Ps 94: 9 Does he who formed the *e* not see?
Mt 5:29 If your right *e* causes you to sin,
5:38 '*E* for *e*, and tooth for tooth.'
6:22 "The *e* is the lamp of the body.
Mt 7: 3 of sawdust in your brother's *e*
1Co 2: 9 "No *e* has seen,
12:16 I am not an *e*, I do not belong
15:52 of an *e*, at the last trumpet.
Eph 6: 6 favor when their *e* is on you,
Col 3:22 not only when their *e* is on you
Rev 1: 7 and every *e* will see him,

EYES (EYE)
Nu 15:39 the lusts of your own hearts and *e*.
33:55 remain will become barbs in your *e*
Dt 11:12 the *e* of the LORD your God are
12:25 right in the *e* of the LORD.
16:19 for a bribe blinds the *e* of the wise
Jos 23:13 on your backs and thorns in your *e*,
1Sa 15:17 you were once small in your own *e*,
1Ki 10: 7 I came and saw with my own *e*.
2Ki 9:30 heard about it, she painted her *e*,
2Ch 16: 9 For the *e* of the LORD range
Job 31: 1 "I made a covenant with my *e*
36: 7 He does not take his *e*
Ps 25:15 My *e* are ever on the LORD,
36: 1 God before his *e*.
101: 6 My *e* will be on the faithful
118: 23 and it is marvelous in our *e*.
119: 18 Open my *e* that I may see
119: 37 my *e* away from worthless things;
121: 1 I lift up my *e* to the hills—
123: 1 I lift up my *e* to you,
139: 16 your *e* saw my unformed body.
141: 8 But my *e* are fixed on you,
Pr 3: 7 Do not be wise in your own *e*;
4:25 Let your *e* look straight ahead,
15: 3 The *e* of the LORD are everywhere
17:24 a fool's *e* wander to the ends
Isa 6: 5 and my *e* have seen the King,
33:17 Your *e* will see the king
42: 7 to open *e* that are blind,
Jer 24: 6 My *e* will watch over them
Hab 1:13 Your *e* are too pure to look on evil;
Mt 6:22 If your *e* are good, your whole
21:42 and it is marvelous in our *e*'?
Lk 16:15 ones who justify yourselves in the *e*
24:31 Then their *e* were opened
Jn 4:35 open your *e* and look at the fields!
Ac 1: 9 he was taken up before their very *e*,
2Co 4:18 So we fix our *e* not on what is seen,
8:21 not only in the *e* of the Lord but
Eph 1:18 also that the *e* of your heart may be
Heb 12: 2 Let us fix our *e* on Jesus, the author
Jas 2: 5 poor in the *e* of the world to be rich
1Pe 3:12 For the *e* of the Lord are
Rev 7:17 wipe away every tear from their *e*."
21: 4 He will wipe every tear from their *e*

EYEWITNESSES* (WITNESS)
Lk 1: 2 by those who from the first were *e*
2Pe 1:16 but we were *e* of his majesty.

EZEKIEL*
Priest called to be prophet to the exiles (Eze 1-3). Symbolically acted out destruction of Jerusalem (Eze 4-5; 12; 24).

EZRA*
Priest and teacher of the Law who led a return of exiles to Israel to reestablish temple and worship (Ezr 7-8). Corrected intermarriage of priests (Ezr 9-10). Read Law at celebration of Feast of Tabernacles (Ne 8). Participated in dedication of Jerusalem's walls (Ne 12).

FACE (FACES)
Ge 32:30 "It is because I saw God *f* to *f*,
Ex 3: 6 Moses hid his *f*, because he was
33:11 would speak to Moses *f* to *f*,
33:20 But," he said, "you cannot see my *f*
34:29 was not aware that his *f* was radiant
Nu 6:25 the LORD make his *f* shine
12: 8 With him I speak *f* to *f*,
14:14 O LORD, have been seen *f* to *f*,
Dt 5: 4 The LORD spoke to you *f* to *f* out
31:17 I will hide my *f* from them,
34:10 whom the LORD knew *f* to *f*,
Jdg 6:22 the angel of the LORD *f* to *f*!"
2Ki 14: 8 challenge: "Come, meet me *f* to *f*."
1Ch 16:11 seek his *f* always.
2Ch 7:14 and seek my *f* and turn
25:17 of Israel: "Come, meet me *f* to *f*."
Ezr 9: 6 and disgraced to lift up my *f* to you,
Ps 4: 6 Let the light of your *f* shine upon us
27: 8 Your *f*, LORD, I will seek.
31:16 Let your *f* shine on your servant;
44: 3 and the light of your *f*,
44:22 Yet for your sake we *f* death all day
51: 9 Hide your *f* from my sins
67: 1 and make his *f* shine upon us; *Selah*
80: 3 make your *f* shine upon us,
105: 4 seek his *f* always.
Ps 119:135 Make your *f* shine
SS 2:14 and your *f* is lovely.
Isa 50: 7 Therefore have I set my *f* like flint,
50: 8 Let us *f* each other!
54: 8 I hid my *f* from you for a moment,
Jer 32: 4 and will speak with him *f* to *f*
34: 3 and he will speak with you *f* to *f*.
Eze 1:10 Each of the four had the *f* of a man,
20:35 *f* to *f*, I will execute judgment
Mt 17: 2 His *f* shone like the sun,
18:10 angels in heaven always see the *f*
Lk 9:29 the appearance of his *f* changed,
Ro 8:36 "For your sake we *f* death all day
1Co 13:12 mirror; then we shall see *f* to *f*.
2Co 3: 7 could not look steadily at the *f*
4: 6 the glory of God in the *f* of Christ.
10: 1 who am "timid" when *f* to *f*
1Pe 3:12 but the *f* of the Lord is
2Jn :12 to visit you and talk with you *f* to *f*,
3Jn :14 see you soon, and we will talk *f* to *f*.
Rev 1:16 His *f* was like the sun shining
22: 4 They will see his *f*, and his name

FACES (FACE)
2Co 3:18 who with unveiled *f* all reflect

FACTIONS
2Co 12:20 outbursts of anger, *f*, slander,
Gal 5:20 selfish ambition, dissensions, *f*

FADE (FADING)
Jas 1:11 the rich man will *f* away
1Pe 5: 4 of glory that will never *f* away.

FADING (FADE)
2Co 3: 7 *f* though it was, will not
3:11 if what was *f* away came with glory,
3:13 at it while the radiance was *f* away.

FAIL (FAILED FAILING FAILINGS FAILS FAILURE)
Lev 26:15 and *f* to carry out all my commands
1Ki 2: 4 you will never *f* to have a man
1Ch 28:20 He will not *f* you or forsake you
2Ch 34:33 they did not *f* to follow the LORD,
Ps 89:28 my covenant with him will never *f*.
Pr 15:22 Plans *f* for lack of counsel,
Isa 51: 6 my righteousness will never *f*.
La 3:22 for his compassions never *f*.
Lk 22:32 Simon, that your faith may not *f*.
2Co 13: 5 unless, of course, you *f* the test?

FAILED (FAIL)
Jos 23:14 has been fulfilled; not one has *f*.
1Ki 8:56 Not one word has *f*
Ps 77: 8 Has his promise *f* for all time?
Ro 9: 6 as though God's word had *f*.
2Co 13: 6 discover that we have not *f* the test.

FAILING (FAIL)
1Sa 12:23 sin against the LORD by *f* to pray

FAILINGS (FAIL)
Ro 15: 1 ought to bear with the *f* of the weak

FAILS (FAIL)
Jer 14: 6 their eyesight *f*
Joel 1:10 the oil *f*.
1Co 13: 8 Love never *f*.

FAILURE* (FAIL)
1Th 2: 1 that our visit to you was not a *f*.

FAINT
Isa 40:31 they will walk and not be *f*.

FAINTHEARTED* (HEART)
Dt 20: 3 Do not be *f* or afraid; do not be
20: 8 shall add, "Is any man afraid or *f*?

FAIR (FAIRNESS)
Pr 1: 3 doing what is right and just and *f*;
Col 4: 1 slaves with what is right and *f*,

FAIRNESS* (FAIR)
Pr 29:14 If a king judges the poor with *f*,

FAITH* (FAITHFUL FAITHFULLY FAITHFULNESS FAITHLESS)
Ex 21: 8 because he has broken *f* with her.
Dt 32:51 both of you broke *f* with me
Jos 22:16 'How could you break *f*
Jdg 9:16 and in good *f* when you made
9:19 and in good *f* toward Jerub-Baal
1Sa 14:33 "You have broken *f*," he said.
2Ch 20:20 Have *f* in the LORD your God
20:20 have *f* in his prophets and you will
Isa 7: 9 If you do not stand firm in your *f*,
26: 2 the nation that keeps *f*.
Hab 2: 4 but the righteous will live by his *f*—
Mal 2:10 by breaking *f* with one another?

Mal 2:11 one another? Judah has broken *f*.
2:14 because you have broken *f* with her
2:15 and do not break *f* with the wife
2:16 in your spirit, and do not break *f*.
Mt 6:30 O you of little *f*? So do not worry,
8:10 anyone in Israel with such great *f*.
8:26 He replied, "You of little *f*,
9: 2 When Jesus saw their *f*, he said
9:22 he said, "your *f* has healed you."
9:29 According to your *f* will it be done
13:58 there because of their lack of *f*.
14:31 of little *f*," he said, "why did you
15:28 "Woman, you have great *f*!
16: 8 Jesus asked, "You of little *f*,
17:20 if you have *f* as small as a mustard
17:20 "Because you have so little *f*.
21:21 if you have *f* and do not doubt,
24:10 many will turn away from the *f*
Mk 2: 5 When Jesus saw their *f*, he said
4:40 still have no *f*?" They were
5:34 "Daughter, your *f* has healed you.
6: 6 he was amazed at their lack of *f*.
10:52 said Jesus, "your *f* has healed you."
11:22 "Have *f* in God," Jesus answered.
16:14 he rebuked them for their lack of *f*
Lk 5:20 When Jesus saw their *f*, he said,
7: 9 I have not found such great *f*
7:50 the woman, "Your *f* has saved you;
8:25 "Where is your *f*?" he asked his
8:48 "Daughter, your *f* has healed you.
12:28 will he clothe you, O you of little *f*!
17: 5 "Increase our *f*!" He replied,
17: 6 "If you have *f* as small
17:19 your *f* has made you well."
18: 8 will he find *f* on the earth?"
18:42 your sight; your *f* has healed you."
22:32 Simon, that your *f* may not fail.
Jn 2:11 and his disciples put their *f* in him.
7:31 in the crowd put their *f* in him.
8:30 he spoke, many put their *f* in him.
11:45 had seen what Jesus did, put their *f*
12:11 to Jesus and putting their *f* in him.
12:42 they would not confess their *f*
14:12 anyone who has *f* in me will do
Ac 3:16 By *f* in the name of Jesus, this man
3:16 *f* that comes through him that has
6: 5 full of *f* and of the Holy Spirit;
6: 7 of priests became obedient to the *f*.
11:24 full of the Holy Spirit and *f*,
13: 8 to turn the proconsul from the *f*.
14: 9 saw that he had *f* to be healed
14:22 them to remain true to the *f*.
14:27 the door of *f* to the Gentiles.
15: 9 for he purified their hearts by *f*.
16: 5 were strengthened in the *f*
20:21 and have *f* in our Lord Jesus.
24:24 as he spoke about *f* in Christ Jesus.
26:18 those who are sanctified by *f*
27:25 for I have *f* in God that it will
Ro 1: 5 to the obedience that comes from *f*.
1: 8 because your *f* is being reported all
1:12 encouraged by each other's *f*.
1:17 is by *f* from first to last,
1:17 "The righteous will live by *f*."
3: 3 What if some did not have *f*?
3: 3 lack of *f* nullify God's faithfulness?
3:22 comes through *f* in Jesus Christ
3:25 a sacrifice of atonement, through *f*
3:26 one who justifies those who have *f*
3:27 the law? No, but on that of *f*.
3:28 by *f* apart from observing the law.
3:30 through that same *f*.
3:30 will justify the circumcised by *f*
3:31 nullify the law by this *f*? Not at all!
4: 5 his *f* is credited as righteousness.
4: 9 that Abraham's *f* was credited
4:11 had by *f* while he was still
4:12 of the *f* that our father Abraham
4:13 the righteousness that comes by *f*.
4:14 *f* has no value and the promise is
4:16 Therefore, the promise comes by *f*,
4:16 are of the *f* of Abraham.
4:19 Without weakening in his *f*,
4:20 but was strengthened in his *f*
5: 1 we have been justified through *f*,
5: 2 access by *f* into this grace
9:30 a righteousness that is by *f*;
9:32 Because they pursued it not by *f*
10: 6 the righteousness that is by *f* says:
10: 8 the word of *f* we are proclaiming:
10:17 *f* comes from hearing the message,
11:20 of unbelief, and you stand by *f*.
12: 3 measure of *f* God has given you.
12: 6 let him use it in proportion to his *f*.
14: 1 Accept him whose *f* is weak,
14: 2 One man's *f* allows him
14: 2 but another man, whose *f* is weak,
14:23 because his eating is not from *f*;
14:23 that does not come from *f* is sin.
1Co 2: 5 so that your *f* might not rest
12: 9 to another *f* by the same Spirit,
13: 2 and if I have a *f* that can move
13:13 And now these three remain: *f*,
15:14 is useless and so is your *f*.
15:17 has not been raised, your *f* is futile;
16:13 stand firm in the *f*; be men
2Co 1:24 Not that we lord it over your *f*,
1:24 because it is by *f* you stand firm.
4:13 With that same spirit of *f* we
5: 7 We live by *f*, not by sight.
8: 7 in *f*, in speech, in knowledge,
10:15 as your *f* continues to grow,
13: 5 to see whether you are in the *f*;
Gal 1:23 now preaching the *f* he once tried
2:16 Jesus that we may be justified by *f*
2:16 but by *f* in Jesus Christ.
2:16 have put our *f* in Christ Jesus that
2:20 I live by *f* in the Son of God,
3: 8 would justify the Gentiles by *f*,
3: 9 So those who have *f* are blessed
3: 9 along with Abraham, the man of *f*.
3:11 "The righteous will live by *f*."
3:12 based on *f*; on the contrary,
3:14 by *f* we might receive the promise
3:22 being given through *f*
3:23 Before this *f* came, we were held
3:23 up until *f* should be revealed.
3:24 that we might be justified by *f*.
3:25 that *f* has come, we are no longer
3:26 of God through *f* in Christ Jesus,
5: 5 But by *f* we eagerly await
5: 6 that counts is *f* expressing itself
Eph 1:15 ever since I heard about your *f*
2: 8 through *f*— and this not
3:12 through *f* in him we may approach
3:17 dwell in your hearts through *f*.
4: 5 one Lord, one *f*, one baptism;
4:13 up until we all reach unity in the *f*
6:16 to all this, take up the shield of *f*,
6:23 love with *f* from God the Father
Php 1:25 for your progress and joy in the *f*,
1:27 as one man for the *f* of the gospel
2:17 and service coming from your *f*,
3: 9 comes from God and is by *f*.
3: 9 that which is through *f* in Christ—
Col 1: 4 heard of your *f* in Christ Jesus
1: 5 the *f* and love that spring
1:23 continue in your *f*, established
2: 5 and how firm your *f* in Christ is.
2: 7 in the *f* as you were taught,
2:12 him through your *f* in the power
1Th 1: 3 Father your work produced by *f*,
1: 8 your *f* in God has become known
3: 2 and encourage you in your *f*,
3: 5 I sent to find out about your *f*.
3: 6 brought good news about your *f*
3: 7 about you because of your *f*.
3:10 supply what is lacking in your *f*.
5: 8 on *f* and love as a breastplate,
2Th 1: 3 because your *f* is growing more
1: 4 and *f* in all the persecutions
1:11 and every act prompted by your *f*.
3: 2 evil men, for not everyone has *f*.
1Ti 1: 2 To Timothy my true son in the *f*:
1: 4 than God's work—which is by *f*.
1: 5 a good conscience and a sincere *f*.
1:14 along with the *f* and love that are
1:19 and so have shipwrecked their *f*.
1:19 on to *f* and a good conscience.
2: 7 of the true *f* to the Gentiles.
2:15 if they continue in *f*, love
3: 9 of the *f* with a clear conscience.
3:13 assurance in their *f* in Christ Jesus.
4: 1 later times some will abandon the *f*
4: 6 brought up in the truths of the *f*
4:12 in life, in love, in *f* and in purity.
5: 8 he has denied the *f* and is worse
6:10 have wandered from the *f*
6:11 pursue righteousness, godliness, *f*,
6:12 Fight the good fight of the *f*.
6:21 so doing have wandered from the *f*.
2Ti 1: 5 been reminded of your sincere *f*,
1:13 with *f* and love in Christ Jesus.
2:18 and they destroy the *f* of some.
2:22 and pursue righteousness, *f*,
3: 8 as far as the *f* is concerned,
3:10 my purpose, *f*, patience, love,
3:15 wise for salvation through *f*
4: 7 finished the race, I have kept the *f*.
Tit 1: 1 Christ for the *f* of God's elect
1: 2 a *f* and knowledge resting
1: 4 my true son in our common *f*:
1:13 so that they will be sound in the *f*
2: 2 self-controlled, and sound in *f*,
3:15 Greet those who love us in the *f*.
Phm : 5 because I hear about your *f*
: 6 may be active in sharing your *f*,
Heb 4: 2 heard did not combine it with *f*.
Heb 4:14 firmly to the *f* we profess.
6: 1 and of *f* in God, instruction about
6:12 but to imitate those who through *f*
10:22 heart in full assurance of *f*,
10:38 But my righteous one will live by *f*.
11: 1 *f* is being sure of what we hope for
11: 3 By *f* we understand that
11: 4 And by *f* he still speaks, even
11: 4 By *f* Abel offered God a better
11: 4 By *f* he was commended
11: 5 By *f* Enoch was taken from this life
11: 6 And without *f* it is impossible
11: 7 By his *f* he condemned the world
11: 7 By *f* Noah, when warned about
11: 7 the righteousness that comes by *f*.
11: 8 By *f* Abraham, when called to go
11: 9 By *f* he made his home
11:11 By *f* Abraham, even though he was
11:13 living by *f* when they died.
11:17 By *f* Abraham, when God tested
11:20 By *f* Isaac blessed Jacob
11:21 By *f* Jacob, when he was dying,
11:22 By *f* Joseph, when his end was near
11:23 By *f* Moses' parents hid him
11:24 By *f* Moses, when he had grown up
11:27 By *f* he left Egypt, not fearing
11:28 By *f* he kept the Passover
11:29 By *f* the people passed
11:30 By *f* the walls of Jericho fell,
11:31 By *f* the prostitute Rahab,
11:33 through *f* conquered kingdoms,
11:39 were all commended for their *f*,
12: 2 the author and perfecter of our *f*,
13: 7 way of life and imitate their *f*.
Jas 1: 3 of your *f* develops perseverance.
2: 5 the eyes of the world to be rich in *f*
2:14 has no deeds? Can such *f* save him?
2:14 if a man claims to have *f*
2:17 In the same way, *f* by itself,
2:18 I will show you my *f* by what I do.
2:18 Show me your *f* without deeds,
2:18 "You have *f*; I have deeds."
2:20 do you want evidence that *f*
2:22 You see that his *f* and his actions
2:22 and his *f* was made complete
2:24 by what he does and not by *f* alone.
2:26 so *f* without deeds is dead.
5:15 in *f* will make the sick person well;
1Pe 1: 5 who through *f* are shielded
1: 7 These have come so that your *f*—
1: 9 you are receiving the goal of your *f*,
1:21 and so your *f* and hope are in God.
5: 9 Resist him, standing firm in the *f*,
2Pe 1: 1 Jesus Christ have received a *f*
1: 5 effort to add to your *f* goodness;
1Jn 5: 4 overcome the world, even our *f*.
Jude : 3 to contend for the *f* that was once
:20 up in your most holy *f*
Rev 2:13 You did not renounce your *f* in me,
2:19 your love and *f*, your service

FAITHFUL* (FAITH)
Nu 12: 7 he is *f* in all my house.
Dt 7: 9 your God is God; he is the *f* God,
32: 4 A *f* God who does no wrong,
1Sa 2:35 I will raise up for myself a *f* priest,
2Sa 20:19 We are the peaceful and *f* in Israel.
22:26 "To the *f* you show yourself *f*,
1Ki 3: 6 because he was *f* to you
2Ch 31:18 were *f* in consecrating themselves.
31:20 and *f* before the LORD his God.
Ne 9: 8 You found his heart *f* to you,
Ps 12: 1 the *f* have vanished
18:25 To the *f* you show yourself *f*,
25:10 of the LORD are loving and *f*
31:23 The LORD preserves the *f*,
33: 4 he is *f* in all he does.
37:28 and will not forsake his *f* ones.
78: 8 whose spirits were not *f* to him.
78:37 they were not *f* to his covenant.
89:19 to your *f* people you said:
89:24 My *f* love will be with him,
89:37 the *f* witness in the sky."
97:10 for he guards the lives of his *f* ones
101: 6 My eyes will be on the *f* in the land,
111: 7 The works of his hands are *f*
145: 13 The LORD is *f* to all his promises
146: 6 the LORD, who remains *f* forever.
Pr 2: 8 and protects the way of his *f* ones.
20: 6 but a *f* man who can find?
28:20 A *f* man will be richly blessed,
31:26 and *f* instruction is on her tongue.
Isa 1:21 See how the *f* city has become
1:26 the *F* City."
49: 7 because of the LORD, who is *f*,
55: 3 my *f* love promised to David.
Jer 42: 5 *f* witness against us if we do not act
Eze 43:11 so that they may be *f* to its design
48:11 who were *f* in serving me

Hos 11:12 even against the *f* Holy One.
Zec 8: 8 I will be *f* and righteous to them
Mt 24:45 Who then is the *f* and wise servant,
25:21 'Well done, good and *f* servant!
25:21 You have been *f* with a few things;
25:23 You have been *f* with a few things;
25:23 'Well done, good and *f* servant!
Lk 12:42 then is the *f* and wise manager,
Ro 12:12 patient in affliction, *f* in prayer.
1Co 1: 9 his Son Jesus Christ our Lord, is *f*.
4: 2 been given a trust must prove *f*.
4:17 my son whom I love, who is *f*
10:13 And God is *f*; he will not let you be
2Co 1:18 no"? But as surely as God is *f*,
Eph 1: 1 in Ephesus, the *f* in Christ Jesus:
6:21 the dear brother and *f* servant
Col 1: 2 and *f* brothers in Christ at Colosse:
1: 7 who is a *f* minister of Christ
4: 7 a *f* minister and fellow servant
4: 9 He is coming with Onesimus, our *f*
1Th 5:24 The one who calls you is *f*
2Th 3: 3 the Lord is *f*, and he will strengthen
1Ti 1:12 he considered me *f*, appointing me
5: 9 has been *f* to her husband,
2Ti 2:13 he will remain *f*,
Heb 2:17 and *f* high priest in service to God,
3: 2 He was *f* to the one who appointed
3: 2 as Moses was *f* in all God's house.
3: 5 Moses was *f* as a servant
3: 6 But Christ is *f* as a son
8: 9 because they did not remain *f*
10:23 for he who promised is *f*.
11:11 he considered him *f* who had made
1Pe 4:19 themselves to their *f* Creator
5:12 whom I regard as a *f* brother,
1Jn 1: 9 he is *f* and just and will forgive us
3Jn : 5 you are *f* in what you are doing
Rev 1: 5 who is the *f* witness, the firstborn
2:10 Be *f*, even to the point of death,
2:13 the days of Antipas, my *f* witness,
3:14 the words of the Amen, the *f*
14:12 commandments and remain *f*
17:14 his called, chosen and *f* followers."
19:11 whose rider is called *F* and True.

FAITHFULLY* (FAITH)

Dt 11:13 if you *f* obey the commands I am
Jos 2:14 *f* when the LORD gives us the land
1Sa 12:24 and serve him *f* with all your heart;
1Ki 2: 4 and if they walk *f* before me
2Ki 20: 3 how I have walked before you *f*
22: 7 because they are acting *f*."
2Ch 19: 9 must serve *f* and wholeheartedly
31:12 they *f* brought in the contributions,
31:15 and Shecaniah assisted him *f*
32: 1 all that Hezekiah had so *f* done,
34:12 The men did the work *f*.
Ne 9:33 you have acted *f*, while we did
13:14 so *f* done for the house of my God
Isa 38: 3 how I have walked before you *f*
Jer 23:28 one who has my word speak it *f*.
Eze 18: 9 and *f* keeps my laws.
44:15 and who *f* carried out the duties
1Pe 4:10 *f* administering God's grace

FAITHFULNESS* (FAITH)

Ge 24:27 not abandoned his kindness and *f*
24:49 if you will show kindness and *f*
32:10 and *f* you have shown your servant.
47:29 you will show me kindness and *f*.
Ex 34: 6 *f*, maintaining love to thousands,
Jos 24:14 the LORD and serve him with all *f*.
1Sa 26:23 man for his righteousness and *f*.
2Sa 2: 6 now show you kindness and *f*,
15:20 May kindness and *f* be with you."
Ps 30: 9 Will it proclaim your *f*?
36: 5 your *f* to the skies.
40:10 I speak of your *f* and salvation.
54: 5 in your *f* destroy them.
57: 3 God sends his love and his *f*.
57:10 your *f* reaches to the skies.
61: 7 appoint your love and *f*
71:22 the harp for your *f*, O my God;
85:10 Love and *f* meet together;
85:11 *F* springs forth from the earth,
86:15 to anger, abounding in love and *f*.
88:11 your *f* in Destruction?
89: 1 mouth I will make your *f* known
89: 2 that you established your *f*
89: 5 your *f* too, in the assembly
89: 8 and your *f* surrounds you.
89:14 love and *f* go before you.
89:33 nor will I ever betray my *f*.
89:49 which in your *f* you swore to David
91: 4 his *f* will be your shield
92: 2 and your *f* at night,
98: 3 and his *f* to the house of Israel;
100: 5 *f* continues through all
108: 4 your *f* reaches to the skies.
Ps 111: 8 done in *f* and uprightness.
115: 1 because of your love and *f*.
117: 2 the *f* of the LORD endures forever.
119: 75 and in *f* you have afflicted me.
119: 90 *f* continues through all
138: 2 name for your love and your *f*,
143: 1 in your *f* and righteousness
Pr 3: 3 Let love and *f* never leave you;
14:22 plan what is good find love and *f*.
16: 6 Through love and *f* sin is atoned for
20:28 Love and *f* keep a king safe;
Isa 11: 5 and *f* the sash around his waist.
16: 5 in *f* a man will sit on it—
25: 1 for in perfect *f*
38:18 cannot hope for your *f*.
38:19 about your *f*.
42: 3 In *f* he will bring forth justice;
61: 8 In my *f* I will reward them
La 3:23 great is your *f*.
Hos 2:20 I will betroth you in *f*,
4: 1 "There is no *f*, no love,
Mt 23:23 of the law—justice, mercy and *f*.
Ro 3: 3 lack of faith nullify God's *f*?
Gal 5:22 patience, kindness, goodness, *f*,
3Jn : 3 and tell about your *f* to the truth
Rev 13:10 and *f* on the part of the saints.

FAITHLESS* (FAITH)

Ps 78:57 fathers they were disloyal and *f*,
101: 3 The deeds of *f* men I hate;
119:158 I look on the *f* with loathing,
Pr 14:14 The *f* will be fully repaid
Jer 3: 6 you seen what *f* Israel has done?
3: 8 I gave *f* Israel her certificate
3:11 "*F* Israel is more righteous
3:12 *f* Israel,' declares the LORD,
3:14 *f* people," declares the LORD,
3:22 "Return, *f* people;
12: 1 Why do all the *f* live at ease?
Ro 1:31 they are senseless, *f*, heartless,
2Ti 2:13 if we are *f*,

FALL (FALLEN FALLING FALLS)

Ps 37:24 though he stumble, he will not *f*,
55:22 he will never let the righteous *f*.
69: 9 of those who insult you *f* on me.
145: 14 The LORD upholds all those who *f*
Pr 11:28 Whoever trusts in his riches will *f*,
Isa 40: 7 The grass withers and the flowers *f*,
Mt 7:25 yet it did not *f*, because it had its
Lk 10:18 "I saw Satan *f* like lightning
11:17 a house divided against itself will *f*.
23:30 say to the mountains, "*F* on us!"
Ro 3:23 and *f* short of the glory of God,
Heb 6: 6 if they *f* away, to be brought back

FALLEN (FALL)

2Sa 1:19 How the mighty have *f*!
Isa 14:12 How you have *f* from heaven,
1Co 11:30 and a number of you have *f* asleep.
15: 6 though some have *f* asleep.
15:18 who have *f* asleep in Christ are lost.
15:20 of those who have *f* asleep.
Gal 5: 4 you have *f* away from grace.
1Th 4:15 precede those who have *f* asleep.

FALLING (FALL)

Jude :24 able to keep you from *f*

FALLS (FALL)

Pr 11:14 For lack of guidance a nation *f*,
24:17 Do not gloat when your enemy *f*;
28:14 he who hardens his heart *f*
Mt 13:21 of the word, he quickly *f* away.
21:44 He who *f* on this stone will be
Jn 12:24 a kernel of wheat *f* to the ground
Ro 14: 4 To his own master he stands or *f*.

FALSE (FALSEHOOD FALSELY)

Ex 20:16 "You shall not give *f* testimony
23: 1 "Do not spread *f* reports.
23: 7 Have nothing to do with a *f* charge
Dt 5:20 "You shall not give *f* testimony
Pr 12:17 but a *f* witness tells lies.
13: 5 The righteous hate what is *f*,
14: 5 but a *f* witness pours out lies.
14:25 but a *f* witness is deceitful.
19: 5 A *f* witness will not go unpunished,
19: 9 A *f* witness will not go unpunished,
21:28 A *f* witness will perish,
25:18 is the man who gives *f* testimony
Isa 44:25 who foils the signs of *f* prophets
Jer 23:16 they fill you with *f* hopes.
Mt 7:15 "Watch out for *f* prophets.
15:19 theft, *f* testimony, slander.
19:18 not steal, do not give *f* testimony,
24:11 and many *f* prophets will appear
24:24 For *f* Christs and *f* prophets will
Mk 10:19 do not give *f* testimony, do not
13:22 For *f* Christs and *f* prophets will
Lk 6:26 their fathers treated the *f* prophets.
18:20 not steal, do not give *f* testimony,
Jn 1:47 in whom there is nothing *f*."
1Co 15:15 found to be *f* witnesses about God,
2Co 11:13 For such men are *f* apostles,
11:26 and in danger from *f* brothers.
Gal 2: 4 some *f* brothers had infiltrated our
Php 1:18 whether from *f* motives or true,
Col 2:18 anyone who delights in *f* humility
2:23 their *f* humility and their harsh
1Ti 1: 3 not to teach *f* doctrines any longer
6: 3 If anyone teaches *f* doctrines
2Pe 2: 1 also *f* prophets among the people,
2: 1 there will be *f* teachers among you.
1Jn 4: 1 many *f* prophets have gone out
Rev 16:13 out of the mouth of the *f* prophet.
19:20 with him the *f* prophet who had
20:10 and the *f* prophet had been thrown.

FALSEHOOD* (FALSE)

Job 21:34 left of your answers but *f*!"
31: 5 "If I have walked in *f*
Ps 52: 3 *f* rather than speaking the truth.
119:163 I hate and abhor *f*
Pr 30: 8 Keep *f* and lies far from me;
Isa 28:15 and *f* our hiding place."
Ro 3: 7 "If my *f* enhances God's
Eph 4:25 each of you must put off *f*
1Jn 4: 6 Spirit of truth and the spirit of *f*.
Rev 22:15 everyone who loves and practices *f*

FALSELY (FALSE)

Lev 19:12 " 'Do not swear *f* by my name
Mt 5:11 *f* say all kinds of evil against you
Lk 3:14 and don't accuse people *f*—
1Ti 6:20 ideas of what is *f* called knowledge,

FALTER*

Pr 24:10 If you *f* in times of trouble,
Isa 42: 4 he will not *f* or be discouraged

FAME

Jos 9: 9 of the *f* of the LORD your God.
Isa 66:19 islands that have not heard of my *f*
Hab 3: 2 LORD, I have heard of your *f*;

FAMILIES (FAMILY)

Ps 68: 6 God sets the lonely in *f*,

FAMILY (FAMILIES)

Pr 15:27 greedy man brings trouble to his *f*,
31:15 she provides food for her *f*
Mk 5:19 to your *f* and tell them how much
Lk 9:61 go back and say good-by to my *f*."
12:52 in one *f* divided against each other,
Ac 10: 2 He and all his *f* were devout
16:33 and all his *f* were baptized.
16:34 he and his whole *f*.
1Ti 3: 4 He must manage his own *f* well
3: 5 how to manage his own *f*,
5: 4 practice by caring for their own *f*
5: 8 and especially for his immediate *f*,

FAMINE

Ge 12:10 Now there was a *f* in the land,
26: 1 Now there was a *f* in the land—
41:30 seven years of *f* will follow them.
Ru 1: 1 the judges ruled, there was a *f*
1Ki 18: 2 Now the *f* was severe in Samaria,
Am 8:11 but a *f* of hearing the words
Ro 8:35 or persecution or *f* or nakedness

FAN*

2Ti 1: 6 you to *f* into flame the gift of God,

FANTASIES*

Ps 73:20 you will despise them as *f*.
Pr 12:11 but he who chases *f* lacks judgment
28:19 one who chases *f* will have his fill

FAST (FASTING)

Dt 10:20 Hold *f* to him and take your oaths
11:22 in all his ways and to hold *f* to him
13: 4 serve him and hold *f* to him.
30:20 to his voice, and hold *f* to him.
Jos 22: 5 to hold *f* to him and to serve him
23: 8 to hold *f* to the LORD your God,
2Ki 18: 6 He held *f* to the LORD
Ps 119: 31 I hold *f* to your statutes, O LORD;
139: 10 your right hand will hold me *f*.
Mt 6:16 "When you *f*, do not look somber
1Pe 5:12 Stand *f* in it.

FASTING (FAST)

Ps 35:13 and humbled myself with *f*.
Ac 13: 2 were worshiping the Lord and *f*,
14:23 and *f*, committed them to the Lord

FATHER (FATHER'S FATHERED FATHERLESS FATHERS FOREFATHERS)
Ge 2:24 this reason a man will leave his *f*
17: 4 You will be the *f* of many nations.
Ex 20:12 "Honor your *f* and your mother,
21:15 "Anyone who attacks his *f*
21:17 "Anyone who curses his *f*
Lev 18: 7 " 'Do not dishonor your *f*
19: 3 you must respect his mother and *f*,
20: 9 " 'If anyone curses his *f* or mother,
Dt 1:31 carried you, as a *f* carries his son,
5:16 "Honor your *f* and your mother,
21:18 son who does not obey his *f*
32: 6 Is he not your *F*, your Creator,
2Sa 7:14 I will be his *f*, and he will be my son
1Ch 17:13 I will be his *f*, and he will be my son
22:10 will be my son, and I will be his *f*.
28: 6 to be my son, and I will be his *f*.
Job 38:28 Does the rain have a *f*?
Ps 2: 7 today I have become your *F*.
27:10 Though my *f* and mother forsake
68: 5 A *f* to the fatherless, a defender
89:26 to me, 'You are my *F*,
103: 13 As a *f* has compassion
Pr 3:12 as a *f* the son he delights in.
10: 1 A wise son brings joy to his *f*,
17:21 there is no joy for the *f* of a fool.
17:25 A foolish son brings grief to his *f*
23:22 Listen to your *f*, who gave you life,
23:24 *f* of a righteous man has great joy;
28: 7 of gluttons disgraces his *f*.
28:24 He who robs his *f* or mother
29: 3 loves wisdom brings joy to his *f*,
Isa 9: 6 Everlasting *F*, Prince of Peace.
45:10 Woe to him who says to his *f*,
63:16 But you are our *F*,
Jer 2:27 They say to wood, 'You are my *f*,'
3:19 I thought you would call me '*F*'
31: 9 because I am Israel's *f*,
Eze 18:19 the son not share the guilt of his *f*?'
Mic 7: 6 For a son dishonors his *f*,
Mal 1: 6 If I am a *f*, where is the honor due
2:10 we not all one *F*? Did not one God
Mt 3: 9 'We have Abraham as our *f*.'
5:16 and praise your *F* in heaven.
6: 9 " 'Our *F* in heaven,
6:26 yet your heavenly *F* feeds them.
10:37 "Anyone who loves his *f*
11:27 no one knows the *F* except the Son
15: 4 'Honor your *f* and mother'
18:10 the face of my *F* in heaven.
19: 5 this reason a man will leave his *f*
19:19 honor your *f* and mother,'
19:29 or brothers or sisters or *f* or mother
23: 9 And do not call anyone on earth '*f*,'
Mk 7:10 'Honor your *f* and your mother,' and,
Lk 9:59 "Lord, first let me go and bury my *f*
12:53 *f* against son and son against *f*,
14:26 and does not hate his *f* and mother,
18:20 honor your *f* and mother.' "
23:34 Jesus said, "*F*, forgive them,
Jn 3:35 The *F* loves the Son and has placed
4:21 you will worship the *F* neither
5:17 "My *F* is always at his work
5:18 he was even calling God his own *F*,
5:20 For the *F* loves the Son
6:44 the *F* who sent me draws him,
6:46 No one has seen the *F*
8:19 "You do not know me or my *F*,"
8:28 speak just what the *F* has taught me
8:41 The only *F* we have is God himself
8:42 God were your *F*, you would love
8:44 You belong to your *f*, the devil,
10:17 reason my *F* loves me is that I lay
10:30 I and the *F* are one."
10:38 and understand that the *F* is in me,
14: 6 No one comes to the *F*
14: 9 who has seen me has seen the *F*.
14:28 for the *F* is greater than I.
15: 9 "As the *F* has loved me,
15:23 He who hates me hates my *F*
20:17 'I am returning to my *F* and your *F*,
Ac 13:33 today I have become your *F*.'
Ro 4:11 he is the *f* of all who believe
4:16 He is the *f* of us all.
8:15 And by him we cry, "*Abba*, *F*."
1Co 4:15 for in Christ Jesus I became your *f*
2Co 6:18 "I will be a *F* to you,
Eph 5:31 this reason a man will leave his *f*
6: 2 "Honor your *f* and mother"—
Php 2:11 to the glory of God the *F*.
Heb 1: 5 today I have become your *F*"?
12: 7 what son is not disciplined by his *f*?
1Jn 1: 3 And our fellowship is with the *F*
2:15 the love of the *F* is not in him.
2:22 he denies the *F* and the Son.

FATHER'S (FATHER)
Pr 13: 1 A wise son heeds his *f* instruction,
15: 5 A fool spurns his *f* discipline,
19:13 A foolish son is his *f* ruin,
Mt 16:27 going to come in his *F* glory
Lk 2:49 had to be in my *F* house?"
Jn 2:16 How dare you turn my *F* house
10:29 can snatch them out of my *F* hand.
14: 2 In my *F* house are many rooms;
15: 8 to my *F* glory, that you bear much

FATHERED (FATHER)
Dt 32:18 You deserted the Rock, who *f* you;

FATHERLESS (FATHER)
Dt 10:18 He defends the cause of the *f*
14:29 the *f* and the widows who live
24:17 Do not deprive the alien or the *f*
24:19 Leave it for the alien, the *f*
26:12 the alien, the *f* and the widow,
Ps 68: 5 A father to the *f*, a defender
82: 3 Defend the cause of the weak and *f*
Pr 23:10 or encroach on the fields of the *f*,

FATHERS (FATHER)
Ex 20: 5 for the sin of the *f* to the third
Jer 31:29 'The *f* have eaten sour grapes,
Mal 4: 6 the hearts of the children to their *f*;
Lk 1:17 the hearts of the *f* to their children
11:11 "Which of you *f*, if your son asks
Jn 4:20 Our *f* worshiped on this mountain,
1Co 4:15 you do not have many *f*,
Eph 6: 4 *F*, do not exasperate your children;
Col 3:21 *F*, do not embitter your children,
Heb 12: 9 all had human *f* who disciplined us

FATHOM* (FATHOMED)
Job 11: 7 "Can you *f* the mysteries of God?
Ps 145: 3 his greatness no one can *f*.
Ecc 3:11 yet they cannot *f* what God has
Isa 40:28 and his understanding no one can *f*
1Co 13: 2 and can *f* all mysteries and all

FATHOMED* (FATHOM)
Job 5: 9 performs wonders that cannot be *f*,
9:10 performs wonders that cannot be *f*,

FATTENED
Pr 15:17 than a *f* calf with hatred.
Lk 15:23 Bring the *f* calf and kill it.

FAULT (FAULTS)
1Sa 29: 3 I have found no *f* in him."
Mt 18:15 and show him his *f*, just
Php 2:15 of God without *f* in a crooked
Jas 1: 5 generously to all without finding *f*,
Jude :24 his glorious presence without *f*

FAULTFINDERS*
Jude :16 These men are grumblers and *f*;

FAULTLESS*
Pr 8: 9 they are *f* to those who have
Php 3: 6 as for legalistic righteousness, *f*.
Jas 1:27 Father accepts as pure and *f* is this:

FAULTS* (FAULT)
Job 10: 6 that you must search out my *f*
Ps 19:12 Forgive my hidden *f*.

FAVOR (FAVORITISM)
Ge 4: 4 The LORD looked with *f* on Abel
6: 8 But Noah found *f* in the eyes
Ex 33:12 and you have found *f* with me.'
34: 9 if I have found *f* in your eyes,"
Lev 26: 9 " 'I will look on you with *f*
Nu 11:15 if I have found *f* in your eyes—
Jdg 6:17 "If now I have found *f* in your eyes,
1Sa 2:26 in *f* with the LORD and with men.
2Sa 2: 6 and I too will show you the same *f*
2Ki 13: 4 Jehoahaz sought the LORD's *f*,
2Ch 33:12 In his distress he sought the *f*
Est 7: 3 "If I have found *f* with you, O king,
Ps 90:17 May the *f* of the Lord our God rest
Pr 8:35 and receives *f* from the LORD.
18:22 and receives *f* from the LORD.
19: 6 Many curry *f* with a ruler,
Isa 61: 2 proclaim the year of the LORD's *f*
Zec 11: 7 called one *F* and the other Union,
Lk 1:30 Mary, you have found *f* with God.
2:14 to men on whom his *f* rests."
2:52 and in *f* with God and men.
4:19 to proclaim the year of the Lord's *f*
2Co 6: 2 now is the time of God's *f*,

FAVORITISM* (FAVOR)
Ex 23: 3 and do not show *f* to a poor man
Lev 19:15 to the poor or *f* to the great,
Ac 10:34 true it is that God does not show *f*
Ro 2:11 For God does not show *f*.
Eph 6: 9 and there is no *f* with him.
Col 3:25 for his wrong, and there is no *f*.
1Ti 5:21 and to do nothing out of *f*.
Jas 2: 1 Lord Jesus Christ, don't show *f*.
2: 9 But if you show *f*, you sin

FEAR (AFRAID FEARED FEARS FRIGHTENED GOD-FEARING)
Dt 6:13 *F* the LORD your God, serve him
10:12 but to *f* the LORD your God,
31:12 and learn to *f* the LORD your God
31:13 and learn to *f* the LORD your God
Jos 4:24 you might always *f* the LORD
24:14 "Now *f* the LORD and serve him
1Sa 12:14 If you *f* the LORD and serve
12:24 But be sure to *f* the LORD
2Sa 23: 3 when he rules in the *f* of God,
2Ch 19: 7 let the *f* of the LORD be upon you.
26: 5 who instructed him in the *f* of God.
Job 1: 9 "Does Job *f* God for nothing?"
Ps 2:11 Serve the LORD with *f*
19: 9 The *f* of the LORD is pure,
23: 4 I will *f* no evil,
27: 1 whom shall I *f*?
33: 8 Let all the earth *f* the LORD;
34: 7 around those who *f* him,
34: 9 *F* the LORD, you his saints,
46: 2 Therefore we will not *f*,
86:11 that I may *f* your name.
90:11 great as the *f* that is due you.
91: 5 You will not *f* the terror of night,
111: 10 *f* of the LORD is the beginning
118: 4 Let those who *f* the LORD say:
128: 1 Blessed are all who *f* the LORD,
145: 19 of those who *f* him;
147: 11 delights in those who *f* him,
Pr 1: 7 *f* of the LORD is the beginning
1:33 and be at ease, without *f* of harm."
8:13 To *f* the LORD is to hate evil;
9:10 *f* of the LORD is the beginning
10:27 The *f* of the LORD adds length
14:27 The *f* of the LORD is a fountain
15:33 *f* of the LORD teaches a man
16: 6 through the *f* of the LORD a man
19:23 The *f* of the LORD leads to life:
22: 4 Humility and the *f* of the LORD
29:25 *F* of man will prove to be a snare,
31:21 she has no *f* for her household;
Ecc 12:13 *F* God and keep his
Isa 11: 3 delight in the *f* of the LORD.
33: 6 the *f* of the LORD is the key
35: 4 "Be strong, do not *f*;
41:10 So do not *f*, for I am with you;
41:13 and says to you, Do not *f*;
43: 1 "*F* not, for I have redeemed you;
51: 7 Do not *f* the reproach of men
54:14 you will have nothing to *f*.
Jer 17: 8 It does not *f* when heat comes;
Lk 12: 5 I will show you whom you should *f*:
2Co 5:11 we know what it is to *f* the Lord,
Php 2:12 to work out your salvation with *f*
1Jn 4:18 But perfect love drives out *f*,
Jude :23 to others show mercy, mixed with *f*
Rev 14: 7 "*F* God and give him glory,

FEARED (FEAR)
Job 1: 1 he *f* God and shunned evil.
Ps 76: 7 You alone are to be *f*.
Mal 3:16 those who *f* the LORD talked

FEARS (FEAR)
Job 1: 8 a man who *f* God and shuns evil."
2: 3 a man who *f* God and shuns evil.
Ps 34: 4 he delivered me from all my *f*.
112: 1 is the man who *f* the LORD,
Pr 14:16 A wise man *f* the LORD
14:26 He who *f* the LORD has a secure
31:30 a woman who *f* the LORD is
2Co 7: 5 conflicts on the outside, *f* within.
1Jn 4:18 The one who *f* is not made perfect

FEAST (FEASTING FEASTS)
Pr 15:15 the cheerful heart has a continual *f*.
2Pe 2:13 pleasures while they *f* with you.

FEASTING (FEAST)
Pr 17: 1 than a house full of *f*, with strife.

FEASTS (FEAST)
Am 5:21 "I hate, I despise your religious *f*;
Jude :12 men are blemishes at your love *f*,

FEATHERS
Ps 91: 4 He will cover you with his *f*,

FEEBLE
Job 4: 3 you have strengthened *f* hands.
Isa 35: 3 Strengthen the *f* hands,
Heb 12:12 strengthen your *f* arms

FEED (FEEDS)
Jn 21:15 Jesus said, "*F* my lambs."
21:17 Jesus said, "*F* my sheep.
Ro 12:20 "If your enemy is hungry, *f* him;
Jude :12 shepherds who *f* only themselves.

FEEDS (FEED)
Pr 15:14 but the mouth of a fool *f* on folly.
Mt 6:26 yet your heavenly Father *f* them.
Jn 6:57 so the one who *f* on me will live

FEEL
Jdg 16:26 me where I can *f* the pillars that
Ps 115: 7 they have hands, but cannot *f*,

FEET (FOOT)
Ru 3: 8 discovered a woman lying at his *f*.
Ps 8: 6 you put everything under his *f*:
22:16 have pierced my hands and my *f*.
40: 2 he set my *f* on a rock
56:13 and my *f* from stumbling,
66: 9 and kept our *f* from slipping.
73: 2 as for me, my *f* had almost slipped;
110: 1 a footstool for your *f*."
119:105 Your word is a lamp to my *f*
Pr 4:26 Make level paths for your *f*
Isa 52: 7 are the *f* of those who bring good
Da 2:33 its *f* partly of iron and partly
Na 1:15 the *f* of one who brings good news,
Mt 10:14 shake the dust off your *f*
22:44 enemies under your *f*." '
Lk 1:79 to guide our *f* into the path of peace
20:43 a footstool for your *f*." '
24:39 Look at my hands and my *f*.
Jn 13: 5 and began to wash his disciples' *f*,
13:14 also should wash one another's *f*.
Ro 3:15 "Their *f* are swift to shed blood;
10:15 "How beautiful are the *f*
16:20 will soon crush Satan under your *f*.
1Co 12:21 And the head cannot say to the *f*,
15:25 has put all his enemies under his *f*.
Eph 1:22 God placed all things under his *f*
1Ti 5:10 washing the *f* of the saints,
Heb 1:13 a footstool for your *f*"?
2: 8 and put everything under his *f*."
12:13 "Make level paths for your *f*,"
Rev 1:15 His *f* were like bronze glowing

FELIX
Governor before whom Paul was tried (Ac 23:23-24:27).

FELLOWSHIP
Ex 20:24 burnt offerings and *f* offerings,
Lev 3: 1 If someone's offering is a *f* offering,
1Co 1: 9 who has called you into *f*
5: 2 out of your *f* the man who did this?
2Co 6:14 what *f* can light have with darkness
13:14 and the *f* of the Holy Spirit be
Gal 2: 9 and Barnabas the right hand of *f*
Php 2: 1 if any *f* with the Spirit,
3:10 the *f* of sharing in his sufferings,
1Jn 1: 3 And our *f* is with the Father
1: 3 so that you also may have *f* with us.
1: 6 claim to have *f* with him yet walk
1: 7 we have *f* with one another,

FEMALE
Ge 1:27 male and *f* he created them.
5: 2 He created them male and *f*
Mt 19: 4 Creator 'made them male and *f*,'
Mk 10: 6 God 'made them male and *f*.'
Gal 3:28 *f*, for you are all one in Christ Jesus

FEROCIOUS
Mt 7:15 but inwardly they are *f* wolves.

FERTILE (FERTILIZE)
Isa 32:15 and the desert becomes a *f* field,
Jer 2: 7 I brought you into a *f* land

FERTILIZE* (FERTILE)
Lk 13: 8 and I'll dig around it and *f* it.

FERVOR*
Ac 18:25 and he spoke with great *f*
Ro 12:11 but keep your spiritual *f*, serving

FESTIVAL
1Co 5: 8 Therefore let us keep the *F*,
Col 2:16 or with regard to a religious *f*,

FESTUS
Successor of Felix; sent Paul to Caesar (Ac 25-26).

FEVER
Job 30:30 my body burns with *f*.
Mt 8:14 mother-in-law lying in bed with a *f*.
Lk 4:38 was suffering from a high *f*,
Jn 4:52 "The *f* left him yesterday
Ac 28: 8 suffering from *f* and dysentery.

FIELD (FIELDS)
Ge 4: 8 Abel, "Let's go out to the *f*."
Lev 19: 9 reap to the very edges of your *f*
19:19 Do not plant your *f* with two kinds
Pr 31:16 She considers a *f* and buys it;
Isa 40: 6 glory is like the flowers of the *f*.
Mt 6:28 See how the lilies of the *f* grow.
6:30 how God clothes the grass of the *f*,
13:38 *f* is the world, and the good seed
13:44 is like treasure hidden in a *f*.
Lk 14:18 I have just bought a *f*, and I must go
1Co 3: 9 you are God's *f*, God's building.
1Pe 1:24 glory is like the flowers of the *f*;

FIELDS (FIELD)
Ru 2: 2 go to the *f* and pick up the leftover
Lk 2: 8 were shepherds living out in the *f*
Jn 4:35 open your eyes and look at the *f*!

FIG (FIGS SYCAMORE-FIG)
Ge 3: 7 so they sewed *f* leaves together
Jdg 9:10 "Next, the trees said to the *f* tree,
1Ki 4:25 man under his own vine and *f* tree.
Pr 27:18 He who tends a *f* tree will eat its
Mic 4: 4 and under his own *f* tree,
Zec 3:10 to sit under his vine and *f* tree,'
Mt 21:19 Seeing a *f* tree by the road,
Lk 13: 6 "A man had a *f* tree, planted
Jas 3:12 brothers, can a *f* tree bear olives,
Rev 6:13 drop from a *f* tree when shaken

FIGHT (FIGHTING FIGHTS FOUGHT)
Ex 14:14 The LORD will *f* for you; you need
Dt 1:30 going before you, will *f* for you,
3:22 the LORD your God himself will *f*
Ne 4:20 Our God will *f* for us!"
Ps 35: 1 *f* against those who *f* against me.
Jn 18:36 my servants would *f*
1Co 9:26 I do not *f* like a man beating the air.
2Co 10: 4 The weapons we *f*
1Ti 1:18 them you may *f* the good *f*,
6:12 Fight the good *f* of the faith.
2Ti 4: 7 fought the good *f*, I have finished

FIGHTING (FIGHT)
Jos 10:14 Surely the LORD was *f* for Israel!

FIGHTS (FIGHT)
Jos 23:10 the LORD your God *f* for you,
1Sa 25:28 because he *f* the LORD's battles.
Jas 4: 1 What causes *f* and quarrels

FIGS (FIG)
Lk 6:44 People do not pick *f*
Jas 3:12 grapevine bear *f*? Neither can a salt

FILL (FILLED FILLING FILLS FULL FULLNESS FULLY)
Ge 1:28 and increase in number; *f* the earth
Ps 16:11 you will *f* me with joy
81:10 wide your mouth and I will *f* it.
Pr 28:19 who chases fantasies will have his *f*
Hag 2: 7 and I will *f* this house with glory,'
Jn 6:26 you ate the loaves and had your *f*.
Ac 2:28 you will *f* me with joy
Ro 15:13 the God of hope *f* you with all joy

FILLED (FILL)
Ex 31: 3 I have *f* him with the Spirit of God,
35:31 he has *f* him with the Spirit of God,
Dt 34: 9 son of Nun was *f* with the spirit
1Ki 8:10 the cloud *f* the temple
8:11 glory of the LORD *f* his temple.
2Ch 5:14 of the LORD *f* the temple of God.
7: 1 the glory of the LORD *f* the temple
Ps 72:19 may the whole earth be *f*
119: 64 The earth is *f* with your love,
Isa 6: 4 and the temple was *f* with smoke.
Eze 10: 3 and a cloud *f* the inner court.
10: 4 The cloud *f* the temple,
43: 5 the glory of the LORD *f* the temple
Hab 2:14 For the earth will be *f*
3: 3 and his praise *f* the earth.
Mt 5: 6 for they will be *f*.
Lk 1:15 and he will be *f* with the Holy Spirit
1:41 and Elizabeth was *f* with the Holy
1:67 His father Zechariah was *f*
2:40 and became strong; he was *f*
Jn 12: 3 the house was *f* with the fragrance
Ac 2: 2 *f* the whole house where they were
2: 4 All of them were *f*
4: 8 Then Peter, *f* with the Holy Spirit,
4:31 they were all *f* with the Holy Spirit
9:17 and be *f* with the Holy Spirit."
13: 9 called Paul, *f* with the Holy Spirit,
Eph 5:18 Instead, be *f* with the Spirit.
Php 1:11 *f* with the fruit of righteousness
Rev 15: 8 And the temple was *f* with smoke

FILLING (FILL)
Eze 44: 4 the glory of the LORD *f* the temple

FILLS (FILL)
Nu 14:21 of the LORD *f* the whole earth,
Ps 107: 9 and *f* the hungry with good things.
Eph 1:23 fullness of him who *f* everything

FILTH (FILTHY)
Isa 4: 4 The Lord will wash away the *f*
Jas 1:21 rid of all moral *f* and the evil that is

FILTHY (FILTH)
Isa 64: 6 all our righteous acts are like *f* rags;
Col 3: 8 and *f* language from your lips.
2Pe 2: 7 by the *f* lives of lawless men

FINAL (FINALITY)
Ps 73:17 then I understood their *f* destiny.

FINALITY* (FINAL)
Ro 9:28 on earth with speed and *f*."

FINANCIAL*
1Ti 6: 5 that godliness is a means to *f* gain.

FIND (FINDS FOUND)
Nu 32:23 be sure that your sin will *f* you out.
Dt 4:29 you will *f* him if you look for him
1Sa 23:16 and helped him *f* strength in God.
Job 23: 3 If only I knew where to *f* him;
Ps 36: 7 *f* refuge in the shadow
62: 5 *F* rest, O my soul, in God alone;
91: 4 under his wings you will *f* refuge;
Pr 8:17 and those who seek me *f* me.
14:22 those who plan what is good *f* love
20: 6 but a faithful man who can *f*?
24:14 if you *f* it, there is a future hope
31:10 A wife of noble character who can *f*
Jer 6:16 and you will *f* rest for your souls.
29:13 and *f* me when you seek me
Mt 7: 7 seek and you will *f*; knock
11:29 and you will *f* rest for your souls.
16:25 loses his life for me will *f* it.
22: 9 invite to the banquet anyone you *f*.'
Lk 11: 9 seek and you will *f*; knock
18: 8 will he *f* faith on the earth?"
Jn 10: 9 come in and go out, and *f* pasture.

FINDS (FIND)
Ps 62: 1 My soul *f* rest in God alone;
112: 1 who *f* great delight
119:162 like one who *f* great spoil.
Pr 3:13 Blessed is the man who *f* wisdom,
8:35 For whoever *f* me *f* life
11:27 He who seeks good *f* good will,
18:22 He who *f* a wife *f* what is good
Mt 7: 8 he who seeks *f*; and to him who
10:39 Whoever *f* his life will lose it,
Lk 11:10 he who seeks *f*; and to him who
12:37 whose master *f* them watching
12:43 servant whom the master *f* doing
15: 4 go after the lost sheep until he *f* it?
15: 8 and search carefully until she *f* it?

FINE-SOUNDING* (SOUND)
Col 2: 4 may deceive you by *f* arguments.

FINGER
Ex 8:19 to Pharaoh, "This is the *f* of God."
31:18 of stone inscribed by the *f* of God.
Dt 9:10 two stone tablets inscribed by the *f*
Lk 11:20 But if I drive out demons by the *f*
16:24 to dip the tip of his *f* in water
Jn 8: 6 to write on the ground with his *f*.
20:25 and put my *f* where the nails were,

FINISH (FINISHED)
Jn 4:34 him who sent me and to *f* his work.
5:36 that the Father has given me to *f*,
Ac 20:24 if only I may *f* the race
2Co 8:11 Now *f* the work, so that your eager
Jas 1: 4 Perseverance must *f* its work

FINISHED (FINISH)
Ge 2: 2 seventh day God had *f* the work he
Jn 19:30 the drink, Jesus said, "It is *f*."
2Ti 4: 7 I have *f* the race, I have kept

FIRE
Ex 3: 2 in flames of *f* from within a bush.
13:21 in a pillar of *f* to give them light,
Lev 6:12 *f* on the altar must be kept burning;
9:24 *F* came out from the presence
1Ki 18:38 Then the *f* of the LORD fell
2Ki 2:11 suddenly a chariot of *f*
Isa 5:24 as tongues of *f* lick up straw
30:27 and his tongue is a consuming *f*.
Jer 23:29 my word like *f*," declares

Da 3:25 four men walking around in the *f*,
Zec 3: 2 stick snatched from the *f*?"
Mal 3: 2 For he will be like a refiner's *f*
Mt 3:11 you with the Holy Spirit and with *f*.
3:12 the chaff with unquenchable *f*."
5:22 will be in danger of the *f* of hell.
18: 8 and be thrown into eternal *f*.
25:41 into the eternal *f* prepared
Mk 9:43 where the *f* never goes out.
9:48 and the *f* is not quenched.'
9:49 Everyone will be salted with *f*.
Lk 3:16 you with the Holy Spirit and with *f*.
12:49 I have come to bring *f* on the earth,
Ac 2: 3 to be tongues of *f* that separated
1Co 3:13 It will be revealed with *f*,
1Th 5:19 Do not put out the Spirit's *f*;
Heb 12:29 for our "God is a consuming *f*."
Jas 3: 5 set on *f* by a small spark.
3: 6 also is a *f*, a world of evil
2Pe 3:10 the elements will be destroyed by *f*,
Jude : 7 suffer the punishment of eternal *f*.
:23 snatch others from the *f*
Rev 1:14 and his eyes were like blazing *f*.
20:14 The lake of *f* is the second death.

FIRM*
Ex 14:13 Stand *f* and you will see
15: 8 surging waters stood *f* like a wall;
Jos 3:17 the covenant of the LORD stood *f*
2Ch 20:17 stand *f* and see the deliverance
Ezr 9: 8 giving us a *f* place in his sanctuary,
Job 11:15 you will stand *f* and without fear.
36: 5 he is mighty, and *f* in his purpose.
41:23 they are *f* and immovable.
Ps 20: 8 but we rise up and stand *f*.
30: 7 you made my mountain stand *f*;
33: 9 he commanded, and it stood *f*.
33:11 of the LORD stand *f* forever,
37:23 he makes his steps *f*;
40: 2 and gave me a *f* place to stand.
75: 3 it is I who hold its pillars *f*.
78:13 made the water stand *f* like a wall.
89: 2 that your love stands *f* forever,
89: 4 and make your throne *f*
93: 5 Your statutes stand *f*;
119: 89 it stands *f* in the heavens.
Pr 4:26 and take only ways that are *f*.
10:25 but the righteous stand *f* forever.
12: 7 the house of the righteous stands *f*.
Isa 7: 9 If you do not stand *f* in your faith,
22:17 about to take *f* hold of you
22:23 drive him like a peg into a *f* place;
22:25 into the *f* place will give way;
Eze 13: 5 so that it will stand *f* in the battle
Zec 8:23 nations will take *f* hold of one Jew
Mt 10:22 he who stands *f* to the end will be
24:13 he who stands *f* to the end will be
Mk 13:13 he who stands *f* to the end will be
Lk 21:19 By standing *f* you will gain life.
1Co 10:12 So, if you think you are standing *f*,
15:58 my dear brothers, stand *f*.
16:13 on your guard; stand *f* in the faith;
2Co 1: 7 for you is *f*, because we know that
1:21 who makes both us and you stand *f*
1:24 because it is by faith you stand *f*.
Gal 5: 1 Stand *f*, then, and do not let
Eph 6:14 Stand *f* then, with the belt
Php 1:27 I will know that you stand *f*
4: 1 that is how you should stand *f*
Col 1:23 in your faith, established and *f*,
2: 5 and how *f* your faith in Christ is.
4:12 that you may stand *f* in all the will
1Th 3: 8 since you are standing *f* in the Lord
2Th 2:15 stand *f* and hold to the teachings
1Ti 6:19 a *f* foundation for the coming age,
2Ti 2:19 God's solid foundation stands *f*,
Heb 6:19 an anchor for the soul, *f* and secure
Jas 5: 8 You too, be patient and stand *f*,
1Pe 5: 9 Resist him, standing *f* in the faith,
5:10 make you strong, *f* and steadfast.

FIRST
Ge 1: 5 and there was morning—the *f* day.
13: 4 and where he had *f* built an altar.
Ex 34:19 *f* offspring of every womb belongs
1Ki 22: 5 "*F* seek the counsel of the LORD."
Pr 18:17 *f* to present his case seems right,
Isa 44: 6 I am the *f* and I am the last;
48:12 I am the *f* and I am the last.
Mt 5:24 *F* go and be reconciled
6:33 But seek *f* his kingdom
7: 5 *f* take the plank out
19:30 But many who are *f* will be last,
20:16 last will be *f*, and the *f* will be last."
20:27 wants to be *f* must be your slave—
22:38 This is the *f* and greatest
23:26 *F* clean the inside of the cup
Mk 9:35 to be *f*, he must be the very last,
10:31 are *f* will be last, and the last *f*."
10:44 wants to be *f* must be slave
13:10 And the gospel must *f* be preached
Lk 13:30 will be *f*, and *f* who will be last."
Jn 8: 7 let him be the *f* to throw a stone
Ac 11:26 disciples were called Christians *f*
Ro 1:16 *f* for the Jew, then for the Gentile.
1:17 is by faith from *f* to last,
2: 9 *f* for the Jew, then for the Gentile;
2:10 *f* for the Jew, then for the Gentile.
1Co 12:28 in the church God has appointed *f*
15:45 "The *f* man Adam became a living
2Co 8: 5 they gave themselves *f* to the Lord
Eph 6: 2 which is the *f* commandment
1Th 4:16 and the dead in Christ will rise *f*.
1Ti 2:13 For Adam was formed *f*, then Eve.
Heb 10: 9 He sets aside the *f*
Jas 3:17 comes from heaven is *f* of all pure;
1Jn 4:19 We love because he *f* loved us.
3Jn : 9 but Diotrephes, who loves to be *f*,
Rev 1:17 I am the *F* and the Last.
2: 4 You have forsaken your *f* love.
22:13 and the Omega, the *F* and the Last,

FIRSTBORN (BEAR)
Ex 11: 5 Every *f* son in Egypt will die,
34:20 Redeem all your *f* sons.
Ps 89:27 I will also appoint him my *f*,
Lk 2: 7 and she gave birth to her *f*, a son.
Ro 8:29 that he might be the *f*
Col 1:15 image of the invisible God, the *f*
1:18 and the *f* from among the dead,
Heb 1: 6 when God brings his *f*
12:23 of the *f*, whose names are written
Rev 1: 5 who is the faithful witness, the *f*

FIRSTFRUITS
Ex 23:16 the Feast of Harvest with the *f*
23:19 "Bring the best of the *f* of your soil
Ro 8:23 who have the *f* of the Spirit,
1Co 15:23 Christ, the *f*; then, when he comes,
Rev 14: 4 offered as *f* to God and the Lamb.

FISH (FISHERS)
Ge 1:26 let them rule over the *f* of the sea
Jnh 1:17 But the LORD provided a great *f*
Mt 7:10 asks for a *f*, will give him a snake?
12:40 three nights in the belly of a huge *f*,
14:17 loaves of bread and two *f*,"
Mk 6:38 they said, "Five—and two *f*."
Lk 5: 6 of *f* that their nets began to break.
9:13 loaves of bread and two *f*—
Jn 6: 9 small barley loaves and two small *f*,
21: 5 haven't you any *f*?" "No,"
21:11 It was full of large *f*, 153, but

FISHERMEN
Mk 1:16 a net into the lake, for they were *f*.

FISHERS (FISH)
Mt 4:19 "and I will make you *f* of men."
Mk 1:17 "and I will make you *f* of men."

FISHHOOK*
Job 41: 1 pull in the leviathan with a *f*

FISTS
Mt 26:67 and struck him with their *f*.

FIT (FITTING)
Jdg 17: 6 no king; everyone did as he saw *f*.
21:25 no king; everyone did as he saw *f*.

FITTING* (FIT)
Ps 33: 1 it is *f* for the upright to praise him.
147: 1 how pleasant and *f* to praise him!
Pr 10:32 of the righteous know what is *f*,
19:10 It is not *f* for a fool to live in luxury
26: 1 honor is not *f* for a fool.
1Co 14:40 everything should be done in a *f*
Col 3:18 to your husbands, as is *f* in the Lord
Heb 2:10 sons to glory, it was *f* that God,

FIX* (FIXED)
Dt 11:18 *F* these words of mine
Job 14: 3 Do you *f* your eye on such a one?
Pr 4:25 *f* your gaze directly before you.
Isa 46: 8 "Remember this, *f* it in mind,
Am 9: 4 I will *f* my eyes upon them
2Co 4:18 we *f* our eyes not on what is seen,
Heb 3: 1 heavenly calling, *f* your thoughts
12: 2 Let us *f* our eyes on Jesus,

FIXED* (FIX)
2Ki 8:11 stared at him with a *f* gaze
Job 38:10 when I *f* limits for it
Ps 141: 8 my eyes are *f* on you, O Sovereign
Pr 8:28 *f* securely the fountains of the deep
Jer 33:25 and night and the *f* laws of heaven
Lk 16:26 and you a great chasm has been *f*,

FLAME (FLAMES FLAMING)
2Ti 1: 6 you to fan into *f* the gift of God,

FLAMES (FLAME)
1Co 3:15 only as one escaping through the *f*.
13: 3 and surrender my body to the *f*,

FLAMING (FLAME)
Eph 6:16 you can extinguish all the *f* arrows

FLANK
Eze 34:21 Because you shove with *f*

FLASH
1Co 15:52 in a *f*, in the twinkling of an eye,

FLATTER* (FLATTERING FLATTERS FLATTERY)
Job 32:21 nor will I *f* any man;
Ps 78:36 But then they would *f* him
Jude :16 *f* others for their own advantage.

FLATTERING* (FLATTER)
Ps 12: 2 their *f* lips speak with deception.
12: 3 May the LORD cut off all *f* lips
Pr 26:28 and a *f* mouth works ruin.
28:23 than he who has a *f* tongue.
Eze 12:24 or *f* divinations among the people

FLATTERS* (FLATTER)
Ps 36: 2 For in his own eyes he *f* himself
Pr 29: 5 Whoever *f* his neighbor

FLATTERY* (FLATTER)
Job 32:22 for if I were skilled in *f*,
Da 11:32 With *f* he will corrupt those who
Ro 16:18 and *f* they deceive the minds
1Th 2: 5 You know we never used *f*,

FLAWLESS*
2Sa 22:31 the word of the LORD is *f*.
Job 11: 4 You say to God, 'My beliefs are *f*
Ps 12: 6 And the words of the LORD are *f*,
18:30 the word of the LORD is *f*.
Pr 30: 5 "Every word of God is *f*;
SS 5: 2 my dove, my *f* one.

FLEE (FLEES)
Ps 139: 7 Where can I *f* from your presence?
1Co 6:18 *F* from sexual immorality.
10:14 my dear friends, *f* from idolatry.
1Ti 6:11 But you, man of God, *f* from all this
2Ti 2:22 *F* the evil desires of youth,
Jas 4: 7 Resist the devil, and he will *f*

FLEECE
Jdg 6:37 I will place a wool *f*

FLEES (FLEE)
Pr 28: 1 The wicked man *f* though no one

FLEETING*
Job 14: 2 like a *f* shadow, he does not endure
Ps 39: 4 let me know how *f* is my life.
89:47 Remember how *f* is my life.
144: 4 his days are like a *f* shadow.
Pr 21: 6 is a *f* vapor and a deadly snare.
31:30 Charm is deceptive, and beauty is *f*

FLESH
Ge 2:23 and *f* of my *f*;
2:24 and they will become one *f*.
2Ch 32: 8 With him is only the arm of *f*,
Job 19:26 yet in my *f* I will see God;
Eze 11:19 of stone and give them a heart of *f*.
36:26 of stone and give you a heart of *f*.
Mt 19: 5 and the two will become one *f*'?
Mk 10: 8 and the two will become one *f*.'
Jn 1:14 The Word became *f* and made his
6:51 This bread is my *f*, which I will give
1Co 6:16 "The two will become one *f*."
15:39 All *f* is not the same: Men have one
Eph 5:31 and the two will become one *f*."
6:12 For our struggle is not against *f*
Php 3: 2 do evil, those mutilators of the *f*.
1Jn 4: 2 come in the *f* is from God,
Jude :23 the clothing stained by corrupted *f*.

FLIGHT
Dt 32:30 or two put ten thousand to *f*,

FLINT
Isa 50: 7 Therefore have I set my face like *f*,
Zec 7:12 They made their hearts as hard as *f*

FLIRTING*
Isa 3:16 *f* with their eyes,

FLOCK (FLOCKS)
Ps 77:20 You led your people like a *f*
78:52 he brought his people out like a *f*;

Ps 95: 7 the *f* under his care.
Isa 40:11 He tends his *f* like a shepherd:
Jer 10:21 and all their *f* is scattered.
23: 2 "Because you have scattered my *f*
31:10 watch over his *f* like a shepherd.'
Eze 34: 2 not shepherds take care of the *f*?
Zec 11:17 who deserts the *f*!
Mt 26:31 the sheep of the *f* will be scattered.'
Lk 12:32 little *f*, for your Father has been
Jn 10:16 shall be one *f* and one shepherd.
Ac 20:28 all the *f* of which the Holy Spirit
1Co 9: 7 Who tends a *f* and does not drink
1Pe 5: 2 Be shepherds of God's *f* that is
5: 3 but being examples to the *f*.

FLOCKS (FLOCK)
Lk 2: 8 keeping watch over their *f* at night.

FLOG (FLOGGED FLOGGING)
Pr 19:25 *F* a mocker, and the simple will
Ac 22:25 to *f* a Roman citizen who hasn't

FLOGGED (FLOG)
Jn 19: 1 Pilate took Jesus and had him *f*.
Ac 5:40 the apostles in and had them *f*.
16:23 After they had been severely *f*,
2Co 11:23 frequently, been *f* more severely,

FLOGGING (FLOG)
Heb 11:36 *f*, while still others were chained

FLOOD (FLOODGATES)
Ge 7: 7 ark to escape the waters of the *f*.
Mal 2:13 You *f* the LORD's altar with tears.
Mt 24:38 For in the days before the *f*,
2Pe 2: 5 world when he brought the *f*

FLOODGATES (FLOOD)
Ge 7:11 the *f* of the heavens were opened.
Mal 3:10 see if I will not throw open the *f*

FLOOR
Jas 2: 3 or "Sit on the *f* by my feet,"

FLOUR
Lev 2: 1 his offering is to be of fine *f*.
Nu 7:13 filled with fine *f* mixed with oil
28: 9 of an ephah of fine *f* mixed with oil.

FLOURISH (FLOURISHES FLOURISHING)
Ps 72: 7 In his days the righteous will *f*;
92: 7 and all evildoers *f*,
92:12 The righteous will *f* like a palm tree
Pr 14:11 but the tent of the upright will *f*.

FLOURISHES (FLOURISH)
Pr 12:12 but the root of the righteous *f*.

FLOURISHING (FLOURISH)
Ps 52: 8 *f* in the house of God;

FLOW (FLOWING)
Nu 13:27 and it does *f* with milk and honey!
Jn 7:38 streams of living water will *f*

FLOWER (FLOWERS)
Job 14: 2 up like a *f* and withers away;
Ps 103: 15 he flourishes like a *f* of the field;
Jas 1:10 he will pass away like a wild *f*.

FLOWERS (FLOWER)
Isa 40: 6 and all their glory is like the *f*
40: 7 The grass withers and the *f* fall,
1Pe 1:24 and all their glory is like the *f*

FLOWING (FLOW)
Ex 3: 8 a land *f* with milk and honey—
33: 3 Go up to the land *f* with milk
Nu 16:14 us into a land *f* with milk
Jos 5: 6 a land *f* with milk and honey.
Ps 107: 33 *f* springs into thirsty ground,
107: 35 the parched ground into *f* springs;
Jer 32:22 a land *f* with milk and honey.
Eze 20: 6 a land *f* with milk and honey,
Rev 22: 1 *f* from the throne of God

FLUTE
Ps 150: 4 praise him with the strings and *f*,
Mt 11:17 " 'We played the *f* for you,
1Co 14: 7 that make sounds, such as the *f*

FOAL*
Zec 9: 9 on a colt, the *f* of a donkey.
Mt 21: 5 on a colt, the *f* of a donkey.' "

FOILS*
Ps 33:10 The LORD *f* the plans
Isa 44:25 who *f* the signs of false prophets

FOLDING* (FOLDS)
Pr 6:10 a little *f* of the hands to rest—
24:33 a little *f* of the hands to rest—

FOLDS (FOLDING)
Ecc 4: 5 The fool *f* his hands

FOLLOW (FOLLOWED FOLLOWING FOLLOWS)
Ex 23: 2 Do not *f* the crowd in doing wrong.
Lev 18: 4 and be careful to *f* my decrees.
Dt 5: 1 Learn them and be sure to *f* them.
17:19 *f* carefully all the words of this law
1Ki 11: 6 he did not *f* the LORD completely,
2Ch 34:33 they did not fail to *f* the LORD,
Ps 23: 6 Surely goodness and love will *f* me
119:166 and I *f* your commands.
Mt 4:19 *f* me," Jesus said, "and I will make
8:19 I will *f* you wherever you go."
8:22 But Jesus told him, "*F* me,
16:24 and take up his cross and *f* me.
19:27 "We have left everything to *f* you!
Lk 9:23 take up his cross daily and *f* me.
9:61 Still another said, "I will *f* you,
Jn 10: 4 his sheep *f* him because they know
10: 5 But they will never *f* a stranger;
10:27 I know them, and they *f* me.
12:26 Whoever serves me must *f* me;
21:19 Then he said to him, "*F* me!"
1Co 1:12 One of you says, "I *f* Paul";
11: 1 *F* my example, as I follow
14: 1 *F* the way of love and eagerly
2Th 3: 9 ourselves a model for you to *f*.
1Pe 2:21 that you should *f* in his steps.
Rev 14: 4 They *f* the Lamb wherever he goes.

FOLLOWED (FOLLOW)
Nu 32:11 they have not *f* me wholeheartedly,
Dt 1:36 he *f* the LORD wholeheartedly."
Jos 14:14 he *f* the LORD, the God of Israel,
2Ch 10:14 he *f* the advice of the young men
Mt 4:20 once they left their nets and *f* him.
9: 9 and Matthew got up and *f* him.
26:58 But Peter *f* him at a distance,
Lk 18:43 he received his sight and *f* Jesus,

FOLLOWING (FOLLOW)
Ps 119: 14 I rejoice in *f* your statutes
Php 3:17 Join with others in *f* my example,
1Ti 1:18 by *f* them you may fight the good

FOLLOWS (FOLLOW)
Jn 8:12 Whoever *f* me will never walk

FOLLY (FOOL)
Pr 14:29 a quick-tempered man displays *f*.
19: 3 A man's own *f* ruins his life,
Ecc 10: 1 so a little *f* outweighs wisdom
Mk 7:22 envy, slander, arrogance and *f*.
2Ti 3: 9 their *f* will be clear to everyone.

FOOD (FOODS)
Ge 1:30 I give every green plant for *f*."
Pr 12: 9 to be somebody and have no *f*.
12:11 his land will have abundant *f*,
20:13 you will have *f* to spare.
20:17 *F* gained by fraud tastes sweet
21:20 of the wise are stores of choice *f*
22: 9 for he shares his *f* with the poor.
23: 3 for that *f* is deceptive.
23: 6 Do not eat the *f* of a stingy man,
25:21 If your enemy is hungry, give him *f*
31:14 bringing her *f* from afar.
31:15 she provides *f* for her family
Isa 58: 7 not to share your *f* with the hungry
Eze 18: 7 but gives his *f* to the hungry
Da 1: 8 to defile himself with the royal *f*
Mt 3: 4 His *f* was locusts and wild honey.
6:25 Is not life more important than *f*,
Jn 4:32 "I have *f* to eat that you know
4:34 have brought him *f*?" "My *f*,"
6:27 Do not work for *f* that spoils,
6:55 my flesh is real *f* and my blood is
Ac 15:20 to abstain from *f* polluted by idols,
Ro 14:14 fully convinced that no *f* is unclean
1Co 8: 1 Now about *f* sacrificed to idols:
8: 8 But *f* does not bring us near to God
2Co 11:27 and have often gone without *f*;
1Ti 6: 8 But if we have *f* and clothing,
Heb 5:14 But solid *f* is for the mature,
Jas 2:15 sister is without clothes and daily *f*.

FOODS (FOOD)
Mk 7:19 Jesus declared all *f* "clean.")

FOOL (FOLLY FOOL'S FOOLISH FOOLISHNESS FOOLS)
1Sa 25:25 his name is *F*, and folly goes
Ps 14: 1 The *f* says in his heart,
Pr 10:10 and a chattering *f* comes to ruin.
10:18 and whoever spreads slander is a *f*.
12:15 The way of a *f* seems right to him,
12:16 A *f* shows his annoyance at once,
14:16 but a *f* is hotheaded and reckless.
15: 5 A *f* spurns his father's discipline,
17:12 than a *f* in his folly.
17:16 use is money in the hand of a *f*,
17:21 To have a *f* for a son brings grief;
17:28 Even a *f* is thought wise
18: 2 A *f* finds no pleasure
20: 3 but every *f* is quick to quarrel.
23: 9 Do not speak to a *f*,
24: 7 Wisdom is too high for a *f*;
26: 4 Do not answer a *f* according
26: 5 Answer a *f* according to his folly,
26: 7 is a proverb in the mouth of a *f*.
26:11 so a *f* repeats his folly.
26:12 for a *f* than for him.
27:22 Though you grind a *f* in a mortar,
28:26 He who trusts in himself is a *f*,
29:11 A *f* gives full vent to his anger,
29:20 for a *f* than for him.
Mt 5:22 But anyone who says, 'You *f*!'
Lk 12:20 "But God said to him, 'You *f*!
1Co 3:18 he should become a "*f*"
2Co 11:21 I am speaking as a *f*—I

FOOL'S (FOOL)
Pr 14: 3 A *f* talk brings a rod to his back,
18: 7 A *f* mouth is his undoing,

FOOLISH (FOOL)
Pr 10: 1 but a *f* son grief to his mother.
14: 1 her own hands the *f* one tears hers
15:20 but a *f* man despises his mother.
17:25 A *f* son brings grief to his father
19:13 A *f* son is his father's ruin,
Mt 7:26 practice is like a *f* man who built
25: 2 of them were *f* and five were wise.
Lk 11:40 You *f* people! Did not the one who
24:25 He said to them, "How *f* you are,
1Co 1:20 Has not God made *f* the wisdom
1:27 God chose the *f* things of the world
Gal 3: 1 died for nothing!" You *f* Galatians!
Eph 5: 4 should there be obscenity, *f* talk
5:17 Therefore do not be *f*,
Tit 3: 9 But avoid *f* controversies

FOOLISHNESS (FOOL)
1Co 1:18 of the cross is *f* to those who are
1:21 through the *f* of what was preached
1:23 block to Jews and *f* to Gentiles,
1:25 For the *f* of God is wiser
2:14 for they are *f* to him, and he cannot
3:19 of this world is *f* in God's sight.

FOOLS (FOOL)
Pr 1: 7 but *f* despise wisdom and discipline
3:35 but *f* he holds up to shame.
12:23 but the heart of *f* blurts out folly.
13:19 but *f* detest turning from evil.
13:20 but a companion of *f* suffers harm.
14: 9 *F* mock at making amends for sin,
14:24 but the folly of *f* yields folly.
Ecc 7: 5 than to listen to the song of *f*.
7: 6 so is the laughter of *f*.
10: 6 *F* are put in many high positions,
Mt 23:17 You blind *f*! Which is greater:
Ro 1:22 they became *f* and exchanged
1Co 4:10 We are *f* for Christ, but you are

FOOT (FEET FOOTHOLD)
Jos 1: 3 every place where you set your *f*,
Ps 121: 3 He will not let your *f* slip—
Pr 3:23 and your *f* will not stumble;
4:27 keep your *f* from evil.
25:17 Seldom set *f* in your neighbor's
Isa 1: 6 From the sole of your *f* to the top
Mt 18: 8 or your *f* causes you to sin,
Lk 4:11 so that you will not strike your *f*
1Co 12:15 If the *f* should say, "Because I am
Rev 10: 2 He planted his right *f* on the sea

FOOTHOLD* (FOOT)
Ps 69: 2 where there is no *f*.
73: 2 I had nearly lost my *f*.
Eph 4:27 and do not give the devil a *f*.

FOOTSTEPS (STEP)
Ps 119: 133 Direct my *f* according

FOOTSTOOL
Ps 99: 5 and worship at his *f*;
110: 1 a *f* for your feet."
Isa 66: 1 and the earth is my *f*.
Mt 5:35 for it is his *f*; or by Jerusalem,
Ac 7:49 and the earth is my *f*.
Heb 1:13 a *f* for your feet"?
10:13 for his enemies to be made his *f*,

FORBEARANCE*
Ro 3:25 because in his *f* he had left the sins

FORBID
1Co 14:39 and do not *f* speaking in tongues.
1Ti 4: 3 They *f* people to marry

FORCE (FORCED FORCEFUL FORCES FORCING)
Jn 6:15 to come and make him king by *f*,
Ac 26:11 and I tried to *f* them to blaspheme.
Gal 2:14 that you *f* Gentiles

FORCED (FORCE)
Mt 27:32 and they *f* him to carry the cross.
Phm :14 do will be spontaneous and not *f*.

FORCEFUL* (FORCE)
Mt 11:12 forcefully advancing, and *f* men lay
2Co 10:10 "His letters are weighty and *f*,

FORCES (FORCE)
Mt 5:41 If someone *f* you to go one mile,
Eph 6:12 and against the spiritual *f* of evil

FORCING (FORCE)
Lk 16:16 and everyone is *f* his way into it.

FOREFATHERS (FATHER)
Heb 1: 1 spoke to our *f* through the prophets
1Pe 1:18 handed down to you from your *f*,

FOREHEAD (FOREHEADS)
Ex 13: 9 a reminder on your *f* that the law
13:16 on your *f* that the LORD brought
1Sa 17:49 and struck the Philistine on the *f*.
Rev 13:16 a mark on his right hand or on his *f*,

FOREHEADS (FOREHEAD)
Dt 6: 8 hands and bind them on your *f*.
Rev 9: 4 not have the seal of God on their *f*.
14: 1 his Father's name written on their *f*

FOREIGN (FOREIGNER FOREIGNERS)
Ge 35: 2 "Get rid of the *f* gods you have
2Ch 14: 3 He removed the *f* altars
33:15 He got rid of the *f* gods
Isa 28:11 with *f* lips and strange tongues

FOREIGNER (FOREIGN)
Lk 17:18 give praise to God except this *f*?"
1Co 14:11 I am a *f* to the speaker,

FOREIGNERS (FOREIGN)
Eph 2:12 *f* to the covenants of the promise,
2:19 you are no longer *f* and aliens,

FOREKNEW* (KNOW)
Ro 8:29 For those God *f* he
11: 2 not reject his people, whom he *f*.

FOREKNOWLEDGE* (KNOW)
Ac 2:23 to you by God's set purpose and *f*;
1Pe 1: 2 to the *f* of God the Father,

FORESAW*
Gal 3: 8 Scripture *f* that God would justify

FOREST
Jas 3: 5 Consider what a great *f* is set

FOREVER (EVER)
Ge 3:22 the tree of life and eat, and live *f*."
6: 3 Spirit will not contend with man *f*,
Ex 3:15 This is my name *f*, the name
2Sa 7:26 so that your name will be great *f*.
1Ki 2:33 may there be the LORD's peace *f*."
9: 3 by putting my Name there *f*.
1Ch 16:15 He remembers his covenant *f*,
16:34 his love endures *f*.
16:41 "for his love endures *f*."
17:24 and that your name will be great *f*.
2Ch 5:13 his love endures *f*."
20:21 for his love endures *f*."
Ps 9: 7 The LORD reigns *f*;
23: 6 dwell in the house of the LORD *f*.
28: 9 be their shepherd and carry them *f*.
29:10 the LORD is enthroned as King *f*.
33:11 the plans of the LORD stand firm *f*
37:28 They will be protected *f*,
44: 8 and we will praise your name *f*.
61: 4 I long to dwell in your tent *f*
72:19 Praise be to his glorious name *f*;
73:26 and my portion *f*.
77: 8 Has his unfailing love vanished *f*?
79:13 will praise you *f*;
81:15 and their punishment would last *f*.
86:12 I will glorify your name *f*.
89: 1 of the LORD's great love *f*;
92: 8 But you, O LORD, are exalted *f*.
100: 5 is good and his love endures *f*;
102: 12 But you, O LORD, sit enthroned *f*;
104: 31 of the LORD endure *f*;
107: 1 his love endures *f*.
Ps 110: 4 "You are a priest *f*,
111: 3 and his righteousness endures *f*.
112: 6 man will be remembered *f*.
117: 2 of the LORD endures *f*.
118: 1 his love endures *f*.
119: 111 Your statutes are my heritage *f*;
119: 152 that you established them to last *f*.
136: 1 *His love endures f.*
146: 6 the LORD, who remains faithful *f*.
Pr 10:25 but the righteous stand firm *f*.
27:24 for riches do not endure *f*,
Isa 25: 8 he will swallow up death *f*.
26: 4 Trust in the LORD *f*,
32:17 will be quietness and confidence *f*.
40: 8 but the word of our God stands *f*."
51: 6 But my salvation will last *f*,
51: 8 But my righteousness will last *f*,
57:15 he who lives *f*, whose name is holy:
59:21 from this time on and *f*,"
Jer 33:11 his love endures *f*."
Eze 37:26 put my sanctuary among them *f*.
Da 2:44 to an end, but it will itself endure *f*.
3: 9 live *f*! You have issued a decree,
Jn 6:51 eats of this bread, he will live *f*.
14:16 Counselor to be with you *f*—
Ro 9: 5 who is God over all, *f* praised!
16:27 to the only wise God be glory *f*
1Co 9:25 it to get a crown that will last *f*.
1Th 4:17 And so we will be with the Lord *f*.
Heb 5: 6 "You are a priest *f*,
7:17 "You are a priest *f*,
7:24 Jesus lives *f*, he has a permanent
13: 8 same yesterday and today and *f*.
1Pe 1:25 but the word of the Lord stands *f*."
1Jn 2:17 who does the will of God lives *f*.
2Jn : 2 lives in us and will be with us *f*:

FOREVERMORE (EVER)
Ps 113: 2 both now and *f*.

FORFEIT
Mk 8:36 the whole world, yet *f* his soul?
Lk 9:25 and yet lose or *f* his very self?

FORGAVE (FORGIVE)
Ps 32: 5 and you *f*
65: 3 you *f* our transgressions
78:38 you *f* their iniquities
Eph 4:32 just as in Christ God *f* you.
Col 2:13 He *f* us all our sins, having
3:13 Forgive as the Lord *f* you.

FORGET (FORGETS FORGETTING FORGOT FORGOTTEN)
Dt 4:23 Be careful not to *f* the covenant
6:12 that you do not *f* the LORD,
2Ki 17:38 Do not *f* the covenant I have made
Ps 9:17 all the nations that *f* God.
10:12 Do not *f* the helpless.
50:22 "Consider this, you who *f* God,
78: 7 and would not *f* his deeds
103: 2 and *f* not all his benefits.
119: 93 I will never *f* your precepts,
137: 5 may my right hand *f* its skill.
Pr 3: 1 My son, do not *f* my teaching,
4: 5 do not *f* my words or swerve
Isa 49:15 "Can a mother *f* the baby
51:13 that you *f* the LORD your Maker,
Jer 2:32 Does a maiden *f* her jewelry,
23:39 I will surely *f* you and cast you out
Heb 6:10 he will not *f* your work
13: 2 Do not *f* to entertain strangers,
13:16 And do not *f* to do good
2Pe 3: 8 But do not *f* this one thing,

FORGETS (FORGET)
Jn 16:21 her baby is born she *f* the anguish
Jas 1:24 immediately *f* what he looks like.

FORGETTING* (FORGET)
Php 3:13 *F* what is behind and straining
Jas 1:25 to do this, not *f* what he has heard,

FORGIVE* (FORGAVE FORGIVENESS FORGIVES FORGIVING)
Ge 50:17 I ask you to *f* your brothers the sins
50:17 please *f* the sins of the servants
Ex 10:17 Now *f* my sin once more
23:21 he will not *f* your rebellion,
32:32 But now, please *f* their sin—
34: 9 *f* our wickedness and our sin,
Nu 14:19 with your great love, *f* the sin
Dt 29:20 will never be willing to *f* him;
Jos 24:19 He will not *f* your rebellion
1Sa 15:25 *f* my sin and come back with me,
25:28 Please *f* your servant's offense,
1Ki 8:30 place, and when you hear, *f*.
8:34 and *f* the sin of your people Israel
8:36 and *f* the sin of your servants,
8:39 *F* and act; deal with each man
1Ki 8:50 *f* all the offenses they have
8:50 *f* your people, who have sinned
2Ki 5:18 But may the LORD *f* your servant
5:18 may the LORD *f* your servant
24: 4 and the LORD was not willing to *f*.
2Ch 6:21 place; and when you hear, *f*.
6:25 and *f* the sin of your people Israel
6:27 and *f* the sin of your servants,
6:30 *F*, and deal with each man
6:39 *f* your people, who have sinned
7:14 will *f* their sin and will heal their
Job 7:21 and *f* my sins?
Ps 19:12 *F* my hidden faults.
25:11 *f* my iniquity, though it is great.
79: 9 deliver us and *f* our sins
Isa 2: 9 do not *f* them.
Jer 5: 1 I will *f* this city.
5: 7 "Why should I *f* you?
18:23 Do not *f* their crimes
31:34 "For I will *f* their wickedness
33: 8 and will *f* all their sins of rebellion
36: 3 then I will *f* their wickedness
50:20 for I will *f* the remnant I spare.
Da 9:19 O Lord, listen! O Lord, *f*! O Lord,
Hos 1: 6 that I should at all *f* them.
14: 2 "*F* all our sins
Am 7: 2 *f*! How can Jacob survive?
Mt 6:12 *F* us our debts,
6:14 For if you *f* men when they sin
6:14 heavenly Father will also *f* you.
6:15 But if you do not *f* men their sins,
6:15 your Father will not *f* your sins.
9: 6 authority on earth to *f* sins..
18:21 many times shall I *f* my brother
18:35 you *f* your brother from your heart
Mk 2: 7 Who can *f* sins but God alone?"
2:10 authority on earth to *f* sins
11:25 anything against anyone, *f* him,
11:25 in heaven may *f* you your sins."
Lk 5:21 Who can *f* sins but God alone?"
5:24 authority on earth to *f* sins..
6:37 *F*, and you will be forgiven.
11: 4 *F* us our sins,
11: 4 *f* everyone who sins against us.
17: 3 rebuke him, and if he repents, *f* him
17: 4 and says, 'I repent,' *f* him."
23:34 Jesus said, "Father, *f* them,
Jn 20:23 If you *f* anyone his sins, they are
20:23 if you do not *f* them, they are not
Ac 8:22 Perhaps he will *f* you
2Co 2: 7 you ought to *f* and comfort him,
2:10 If you *f* anyone, I also *f* him.
2:10 if there was anything to *f*—
12:13 a burden to you? *F* me this wrong!
Col 3:13 and *f* whatever grievances you may
3:13 *F* as the Lord forgave you.
Heb 8:12 For I will *f* their wickedness
1Jn 1: 9 and just and will *f* us our sins

FORGIVENESS* (FORGIVE)
Ps 130: 4 But with you there is *f*;
Mt 26:28 out for many for the *f* of sins.
Mk 1: 4 of repentance for the *f* of sins.
Lk 1:77 salvation through the *f* of their sins,
3: 3 of repentance for the *f* of sins.
24:47 and *f* of sins will be preached
Ac 5:31 that he might give repentance and *f*
10:43 believes in him receives *f* of sins
13:38 that through Jesus the *f*
26:18 so that they may receive *f* of sins
Eph 1: 7 through his blood, the *f* of sins,
Col 1:14 in whom we have redemption, the *f*
Heb 9:22 the shedding of blood there is no *f*.

FORGIVES* (FORGIVE)
Ps 103: 3 He *f* all my sins
Mic 7:18 pardons sin and *f* the transgression
Lk 7:49 "Who is this who even *f* sins?"

FORGIVING* (FORGIVE)
Ex 34: 7 and *f* wickedness, rebellion and sin.
Nu 14:18 abounding in love and *f* sin
Ne 9:17 But you are a *f* God, gracious
Ps 86: 5 You are *f* and good, O Lord,
99: 8 you were to Israel a *f* God,
Da 9: 9 The Lord our God is merciful and *f*
Eph 4:32 to one another, *f* each other,

FORGOT (FORGET)
Dt 32:18 you *f* the God who gave you birth.
Ps 78:11 They *f* what he had done,
106: 13 But they soon *f* what he had done

FORGOTTEN (FORGET)
Job 11: 6 God has even *f* some of your sin.
Ps 44:20 If we had *f* the name of our God
Isa 17:10 You have *f* God your Savior;
Hos 8:14 Israel has *f* his Maker
Lk 12: 6 Yet not one of them is *f* by God.

2Pe 1: 9 and has *f* that he has been cleansed

FORM (FORMED)
Isa 52:14 *f* marred beyond human likeness—
2Ti 3: 5 having a *f* of godliness

FORMED (FORM)
Ge 2: 7 —the LORD God *f* the man
2:19 Now the LORD God had *f* out
Ps 103: 14 for he knows how we are *f*,
Ecc 11: 5 or how the body is *f* in a mother's
Isa 29:16 Shall what is *f* say to him who *f* it,
45:18 but *f* it to be inhabited—
49: 5 he who *f* me in the womb
Jer 1: 5 "Before I *f* you in the womb I knew
Ro 9:20 "Shall what is *f* say to him who *f* it,
Gal 4:19 of childbirth until Christ is *f* in you,
1Ti 2:13 For Adam was *f* first, then Eve.
Heb 11: 3 understand that the universe was *f*
2Pe 3: 5 and the earth was *f* out of water

FORMLESS*
Ge 1: 2 Now the earth was *f* and empty,
Jer 4:23 and it was *f* and empty;

FORSAKE (FORSAKEN)
Dt 31: 6 he will never leave you nor *f* you."
Jos 1: 5 I will never leave you nor *f* you.
24:16 "Far be it from us to *f* the LORD
2Ch 15: 2 but if you *f* him, he will *f* you.
Ps 27:10 Though my father and mother *f* me
94:14 he will never *f* his inheritance.
Isa 55: 7 Let the wicked *f* his way
Heb 13: 5 never will I *f* you."

FORSAKEN (FORSAKE)
Ps 22: 1 my God, why have you *f* me?
37:25 I have never seen the righteous *f*
Mt 27:46 my God, why have you *f* me?"
Rev 2: 4 You have *f* your first love.

FORTRESS
2Sa 22: 2 "The LORD is my rock, my *f*
Ps 18: 2 The LORD is my rock, my *f*
31: 2 a strong *f* to save me.
59:16 for you are my *f*,
71: 3 for you are my rock and my *f*.
Pr 14:26 who fears the LORD has a secure *f*,

FORTUNE-TELLING*
Ac 16:16 deal of money for her owners by *f*.

FORTY
Ge 7: 4 on the earth for *f* days and *f* nights,
18:29 "What if only *f* are found there?"
Ex 16:35 The Israelites ate manna *f* years,
24:18 on the mountain *f* days and *f* nights
Nu 14:34 For *f* years—one year for each
Jos 14: 7 I was *f* years old when Moses
1Sa 4:18 He had led Israel *f* years.
2Sa 5: 4 king, and he reigned *f* years.
1Ki 19: 8 he traveled *f* days and *f* nights
2Ki 12: 1 and he reigned in Jerusalem *f* years
2Ch 9:30 in Jerusalem over all Israel *f* years.
Eze 29:12 her cities will lie desolate *f* years
Jnh 3: 4 "*F* more days and Nineveh will be
Mt 4: 2 After fasting *f* days and *f* nights,

FOUGHT (FIGHT)
1Co 15:32 If I *f* wild beasts in Ephesus
2Ti 4: 7 I have *f* the good fight, I have

FOUND (FIND)
2Ki 22: 8 "I have *f* the Book of the Law
1Ch 28: 9 If you seek him, he will be *f* by you;
2Ch 15:15 sought God eagerly, and he was *f*
Isa 55: 6 Seek the LORD while he may be *f*;
65: 1 I was *f* by those who did not seek
Da 5:27 on the scales and *f* wanting.
Mt 1:18 she was *f* to be with child
Lk 15: 6 with me; I have *f* my lost sheep.'
15: 9 with me; I have *f* my lost coin.'
15:24 is alive again; he was lost and is *f*.'
Ac 4:12 Salvation is *f* in no one else,
Ro 10:20 "I was *f* by those who did not seek
Jas 2: 8 If you really keep the royal law *f*
Rev 5: 4 no one was *f* who was worthy

FOUNDATION (FOUNDATIONS FOUNDED)
Isa 28:16 a precious cornerstone for a sure *f*;
Mt 7:25 because it had its *f* on the rock.
Lk 14:29 For if he lays the *f* and is not able
Ro 15:20 building on someone else's *f*.
1Co 3:10 I laid a *f* as an expert builder,
3:11 For no one can lay any *f* other
Eph 2:20 built on the *f* of the apostles
1Ti 3:15 the pillar and *f* of the truth.
2Ti 2:19 God's solid *f* stands firm,
Heb 6: 1 not laying again the *f* of repentance

FOUNDATIONS (FOUNDATION)
Ps 102: 25 In the beginning you laid the *f*
Heb 1:10 O Lord, you laid the *f* of the earth,

FOUNDED (FOUNDATION)
Jer 10:12 he *f* the world by his wisdom
Heb 8: 6 and it is *f* on better promises.

FOUNTAIN
Ps 36: 9 For with you is the *f* of life;
Pr 14:27 The fear of the LORD is a *f* of life,
18: 4 the *f* of wisdom is a bubbling brook.
Zec 13: 1 "On that day a *f* will be opened

FOX (FOXES)
Lk 13:32 He replied, "Go tell that *f*,

FOXES (FOX)
SS 2:15 the little *f*
Mt 8:20 "*F* have holes and birds

FRAGRANCE (FRAGRANT)
Ex 30:38 it to enjoy its *f* must be cut
Jn 12: 3 filled with the *f* of the perfume.
2Co 2:14 us spreads everywhere the *f*
2:16 of death; to the other, the *f* of life.

FRAGRANT (FRAGRANCE)
Eph 5: 2 as a *f* offering and sacrifice to God.
Php 4:18 They are a *f* offering, an acceptable

FREE (FREED FREEDOM FREELY)
Ge 2:16 "You are *f* to eat from any tree
Ps 118: 5 and he answered by setting me *f*.
119: 32 for you have set my heart *f*.
146: 7 The LORD sets prisoners *f*,
Pr 6: 3 then do this, my son, to *f* yourself,
Jn 8:32 and the truth will set you *f*."
8:36 if the Son sets you *f*, you will be *f*
Ro 6:18 You have been set *f* from sin
8: 2 of life set me *f* from the law of sin
1Co 12:13 whether Jews or Greeks, slave or *f*
Gal 3:28 slave nor *f*, male nor female,
5: 1 for freedom that Christ has set us *f*.
1Pe 2:16 *f* men, but do not use your freedom

FREED (FREE)
Ps 116: 16 you have *f* me from my chains.
Ro 6: 7 anyone who has died has been *f*
Rev 1: 5 has *f* us from our sins by his blood,

FREEDOM (FREE)
Ps 119: 45 I will walk about in *f*,
Isa 61: 1 to proclaim *f* for the captives
Lk 4:18 me to proclaim *f* for the prisoners
Ro 8:21 into the glorious *f* of the children
1Co 7:21 although if you can gain your *f*,
2Co 3:17 the Spirit of the Lord is, there is *f*.
Gal 2: 4 ranks to spy on the *f* we have
5:13 But do not use your *f* to indulge
Jas 1:25 into the perfect law that gives *f*,
1Pe 2:16 but do not use your *f* as a cover-up

FREELY (FREE)
Isa 55: 7 and to our God, for he will *f* pardon
Mt 10: 8 Freely you have received, *f* give.
Ro 3:24 and are justified *f* by his grace
Eph 1: 6 which he has *f* given us

FRESH
Jas 3:11 Can both *f* water and salt water

FRET*
Ps 37: 1 Do not *f* because of evil men
37: 7 do not *f* when men succeed
37: 8 do not *f*— it leads only to evil.
Pr 24:19 Do not *f* because of evil men

FRICTION
1Ti 6: 5 and constant *f* between men

FRIEND (FRIENDS FRIENDSHIP)
Ex 33:11 as a man speaks with his *f*.
2Ch 20: 7 descendants of Abraham your *f*?
Pr 17:17 A *f* loves at all times,
18:24 there is a *f* who sticks closer
27: 6 Wounds from a *f* can be trusted
27:10 Do not forsake your *f* and the *f*
Isa 41: 8 you descendants of Abraham my *f*,
Mt 11:19 a *f* of tax collectors and "sinners." '
Lk 11: 8 him the bread because he is his *f*,
Jn 19:12 "If you let this man go, you are no *f*
Jas 2:23 and he was called God's *f*.
4: 4 Anyone who chooses to be a *f*

FRIENDS (FRIEND)
Pr 16:28 and a gossip separates close *f*.
17: 9 the matter separates close *f*.
Zec 13: 6 given at the house of my *f*.'
Jn 15:13 that he lay down his life for his *f*.
15:14 You are my *f* if you do what I

FRIENDSHIP (FRIEND)
Jas 4: 4 don't you know that *f*

FRIGHTENED (FEAR)
Php 1:28 gospel without being *f* in any way
1Pe 3:14 fear what they fear; do not be *f*."

FROGS
Ex 8: 2 plague your whole country with *f*.
Rev 16:13 three evil spirits that looked like *f*;

FRUIT (FRUITFUL)
Jdg 9:11 'Should I give up my *f*, so good
Ps 1: 3 which yields its *f* in season
Pr 11:30 The *f* of the righteous is a tree
12:14 From the *f* of his lips a man is filled
27:18 He who tends a fig tree will eat its *f*
Isa 11: 1 from his roots a Branch will bear *f*.
27: 6 and fill all the world with *f*.
32:17 The *f* of righteousness will be peace
Jer 17: 8 and never fails to bear *f*."
Hos 10:12 reap the *f* of unfailing love,
14: 2 that we may offer the *f* of our lips.
Am 8: 1 showed me: a basket of ripe *f*.
Mt 3: 8 Produce *f* in keeping
3:10 does not produce good *f* will be cut
7:16 By their *f* you will recognize them.
7:17 good *f*, but a bad tree bears bad *f*.
7:20 by their *f* you will recognize them.
12:33 a tree good and its *f* will be good,
Lk 3: 9 does not produce good *f* will be cut
6:43 nor does a bad tree bear good *f*.
13: 6 and he went to look for *f* on it,
Jn 15: 2 branch in me that bears no *f*,
15:16 and bear *f*—*f* that will last.
Ro 7: 4 in order that we might bear *f*
Gal 5:22 But the *f* of the Spirit is love, joy,
Php 1:11 with the *f* of righteousness that
Col 1:10 bearing *f* in every good work,
Heb 13:15 the *f* of lips that confess his name.
Jas 3:17 and good *f*, impartial and sincere.
Jude :12 autumn trees, without *f*
Rev 22: 2 of *f*, yielding its *f* every month.

FRUITFUL (FRUIT)
Ge 1:22 "Be *f* and increase in number
9: 1 "Be *f* and increase in number
35:11 be *f* and increase in number.
Ex 1: 7 the Israelites were *f* and multiplied
Ps 128: 3 Your wife will be like a *f* vine
Jn 15: 2 prunes so that it will be even more *f*.
Php 1:22 this will mean *f* labor for me.

FRUITLESS*
Eph 5:11 to do with the *f* deeds of darkness,

FRUSTRATION
Ro 8:20 For the creation was subjected to *f*,

FUEL
Isa 44:19 "Half of it I used for *f*;

FULFILL (FULFILLED FULFILLMENT FULFILLS)
Nu 23:19 Does he promise and not *f*?
Ps 61: 8 and *f* my vows day after day.
116: 14 I will *f* my vows to the LORD
138: 8 The LORD will *f* his purpose,
Ecc 5: 5 than to make a vow and not *f* it.
Isa 46:11 far-off land, a man to *f* my purpose.
Jer 33:14 'when I will *f* the gracious promise
Mt 1:22 place to *f* what the Lord had said
3:15 us to do this to *f* all righteousness."
4:14 *f* what was said
5:17 come to abolish them but to *f* them.
8:17 This was to *f* what was spoken
12:17 This was to *f* what was spoken
21: 4 place to *f* what was spoken
Jn 12:38 This was to *f* the word
13:18 But this is to *f* the scripture:
15:25 But this is to *f* what is written
1Co 7: 3 husband should *f* his marital duty

FULFILLED (FULFILL)
Jos 21:45 of Israel failed; every one was *f*.
23:14 Every promise has been *f*;
Pr 13:12 but a longing *f* is a tree of life.
13:19 A longing *f* is sweet to the soul,
Mt 2:15 so was *f* what the Lord had said
2:17 the prophet Jeremiah was *f*:
2:23 So was *f* what was said
13:14 In them is *f* the prophecy of Isaiah:
13:35 So was *f* what was spoken
26:54 would the Scriptures be *f* that say it
26:56 of the prophets might be *f*."
27: 9 by Jeremiah the prophet was *f*:
Mk 13: 4 that they are all about to be *f*?"
14:49 But the Scriptures must be *f*."
Lk 4:21 "Today this scripture is *f*
18:31 about the Son of Man will be *f*.

Lk 24:44 Everything must be *f* that is
Jn 18: 9 words he had spoken would be *f*:
19:24 the Scripture might be *f* which said,
19:28 and so that the Scripture would be *f*
19:36 so that the Scripture would be *f*:
Ac 1:16 to be *f* which the Holy Spirit spoke
Ro 13: 8 loves his fellowman has *f* the law.
Jas 2:23 And the scripture was *f* that says,

FULFILLMENT (FULFILL)
Ro 13:10 Therefore love is the *f* of the law.

FULFILLS (FULFILL)
Ps 57: 2 to God, who *f* his purpose, for me.
145: 19 He *f* the desires of those who fear

FULL (FILL)
2Ch 24:10 them into the chest until it was *f*.
Ps 127: 5 whose quiver is *f* of them.
Pr 27: 7 He who is *f* loathes honey,
31:11 Her husband has *f* confidence
Isa 6: 3 the whole earth is *f* of his glory."
11: 9 for the earth will be *f*
Lk 4: 1 Jesus, *f* of the Holy Spirit,
Jn 10:10 may have life, and have it to the *f*.
Ac 6: 3 known to be *f* of the Spirit
6: 5 a man *f* of faith and of the Holy
7:55 But Stephen, *f* of the Holy Spirit,
11:24 *f* of the Holy Spirit and faith,

FULL-GROWN* (GROW)
Jas 1:15 when it is *f*, gives birth to death.

FULLNESS* (FILL)
Dt 33:16 gifts of the earth and its *f*
Jn 1:16 From the *f* of his grace we have all
Ro 11:12 greater riches will their *f* bring!
Eph 1:23 the *f* of him who fills everything
3:19 to the measure of all the *f* of God.
4:13 to the whole measure of the *f*
Col 1:19 to have all his *f* dwell in him,
1:25 to you the word of God in its *f*—
2: 9 in Christ all the *f* of the Deity lives
2:10 and you have been given *f* in Christ

FULLY (FILL)
1Ki 8:61 your hearts must be *f* committed
2Ch 16: 9 whose hearts are *f* committed
Ps 119: 4 that are to be *f* obeyed.
119: 138 they are *f* trustworthy.
Pr 13: 4 of the diligent are *f* satisfied.
Lk 6:40 everyone who is *f* trained will be
Ro 4:21 being *f* persuaded that God had
14: 5 Each one should be *f* convinced
1Co 13:12 shall know *f*, even as I am *f* known.
15:58 Always give yourselves *f*
2Ti 4:17 the message might be *f* proclaimed

FURIOUS (FURY)
Dt 29:28 In *f* anger and in great wrath
Jer 32:37 where I banish them in my *f* anger

FURNACE
Isa 48:10 in the *f* of affliction.
Da 3: 6 be thrown into a blazing *f*."
Mt 13:42 will throw them into the fiery *f*,

FURY (FURIOUS)
Isa 14: 6 and in *f* subdued nations
Jer 21: 5 and a mighty arm in anger and *f*
Rev 14:10 will drink of the wine of God's *f*,
16:19 with the wine of the *f* of his wrath.
19:15 the winepress of the *f* of the wrath

FUTILE (FUTILITY)
Mal 3:14 You have said, 'It is *f* to serve God.
1Co 3:20 that the thoughts of the wise are *f*."

FUTILITY (FUTILE)
Eph 4:17 in the *f* of their thinking.

FUTURE
Ps 37:37 there is a *f* for the man of peace.
Pr 23:18 There is surely a *f* hope for you,
Ecc 7:14 anything about his *f*.
8: 7 Since no man knows the *f*,
Jer 29:11 plans to give you hope and a *f*.
31:17 So there is hope for your *f*,"
Ro 8:38 neither the present nor the *f*,
1Co 3:22 life or death or the present or the *f*

GABRIEL*
Angel who interpreted Daniel's visions (Da 8: 16-26; 9:20-27); announced births of John (Lk 1: 11-20), Jesus (Lk 1:26-38).

GAD
1. Son of Jacob by Zilpah (Ge 30:9-11; 35:26; 1Ch 2:2). Tribe of blessed (Ge 49:19; Dt 33:20-21), numbered (Nu 1:25; 26:18), allotted land east of the Jordan (Nu 32; 34:14; Jos 18:7; 22), west (Eze 48:27-28), 12,000 from (Rev 7:5).
2. Prophet; seer of David (1Sa 22:5; 2Sa 24: 11-19; 1Ch 29:29).

GAIN (GAINED GAINS)
Ex 14:17 And I will *g* glory through Pharaoh
Ps 60:12 With God we will *g* the victory,
Pr 4: 1 pay attention and *g* understanding.
8: 5 You who are simple, *g* prudence;
28:16 he who hates ill-gotten *g* will enjoy
28:23 in the end *g* more favor
Isa 63:12 to *g* for himself everlasting renown
Da 2: 8 that you are trying to *g* time,
Mk 8:36 it for a man to *g* the whole world,
Lk 9:25 it for a man to *g* the whole world,
21:19 standing firm you will *g* life.
1Co 13: 3 but have not love, I *g* nothing.
Php 1:21 to live is Christ and to die is *g*.
3: 8 that I may *g* Christ and be found
1Ti 3:13 have served well *g* an excellent
6: 5 godliness is a means to financial *g*.
6: 6 with contentment is great *g*.

GAINED (GAIN)
Jer 32:20 have *g* the renown that is still yours
Ro 5: 2 through whom we have *g* access

GAINS (GAIN)
Pr 3:13 the man who *g* understanding,
11:16 A kindhearted woman *g* respect,
15:32 heeds correction *g* understanding.
29:23 but a man of lowly spirit *g* honor.
Mt 16:26 for a man if he *g* the whole world,

GALILEE
Isa 9: 1 but in the future he will honor *G*
Mt 4:15 *G* of the Gentiles—
26:32 I will go ahead of you into *G*."
28:10 Go and tell my brothers to go to *G*;

GALL
Mt 27:34 mixed with *g*; but after tasting it,

GALLIO
Ac 18:12 While *G* was proconsul of Achaia,

GALLOWS
Est 7:10 Haman on the *g* he had prepared

GAMALIEL
Ac 5:34 But a Pharisee named *G*, a teacher

GAMES
1Co 9:25 in the *g* goes into strict training.

GAP
Eze 22:30 stand before me in the *g* on behalf

GAPE*
Ps 35:21 They *g* at me and say, "Aha! Aha!

GARDEN (GARDENER)
Ge 2: 8 the LORD God had planted a *g*
2:15 put him in the *G* of Eden to work it
SS 4:12 You are a *g* locked up, my sister,
Isa 58:11 You will be like a well-watered *g*,
Jer 31:12 They will be like a well-watered *g*,
Eze 28:13 the *g* of God;
31: 9 Eden in the *g* of God.

GARDENER (GARDEN)
Jn 15: 1 true vine, and my Father is the *g*.

GARLAND*
Pr 1: 9 They will be a *g* to grace your head
4: 9 She will set a *g* of grace

GARMENT (GARMENTS)
Ps 102: 26 they will all wear out like a *g*.
Isa 50: 9 They will all wear out like a *g*;
51: 6 the earth will wear out like a *g*
61: 3 and a *g* of praise
Mt 9:16 of unshrunk cloth on an old *g*,
Jn 19:23 This *g* was seamless, woven
Heb 1:11 they will all wear out like a *g*.

GARMENTS (GARMENT)
Ge 3:21 The LORD God made *g* of skin
Ex 28: 2 Make sacred *g* for your brother
Lev 16:23 and take off the linen *g* he put
16:24 holy place and put on his regular *g*.
Isa 61:10 me with *g* of salvation
63: 1 with his *g* stained crimson?
Joel 2:13 and not your *g*.
Zec 3: 4 and I will put rich *g* on you."
Jn 19:24 "They divided my *g* among them

GATE (GATES)
Ps 118: 20 This is the *g* of the LORD
Pr 31:23 husband is respected at the city *g*,
31:31 works bring her praise at the city *g*.
Mt 7:13 For wide is the *g* and broad is
7:13 "Enter through the narrow *g*.
Jn 10: 1 not enter the sheep pen by the *g*,
10: 2 enters by the *g* is the shepherd
10: 7 "I tell you the truth, I am the *g*
10: 9 I am the *g*; whoever enters
Heb 13:12 also suffered outside the city *g*
Rev 21:21 each *g* made of a single pearl.

GATES (GATE)
Ps 24: 7 Lift up your heads, O you *g*;
24: 9 Lift up your heads, O you *g*;
100: 4 Enter his *g* with thanksgiving
118: 19 Open for me the *g* of righteousness
Isa 60:11 Your *g* will always stand open,
60:18 and your *g* Praise.
62:10 Pass through, pass through the *g*!
Mt 16:18 the *g* of Hades will not overcome it
Rev 21:12 On the *g* were written the names
21:21 The twelve *g* were twelve pearls,
21:25 On no day will its *g* ever be shut,
22:14 may go through the *g* into the city.

GATH
1Sa 17:23 the Philistine champion from *G*,
2Sa 1:20 "Tell it not in *G*,
Mic 1:10 Tell it not in *G*;

GATHER (GATHERED GATHERS)
Ps 106: 47 and *g* us from the nations,
Isa 11:12 and *g* the exiles of Israel;
Jer 3:17 and all nations will *g* in Jerusalem
23: 3 "I myself will *g* the remnant
31:10 who scattered Israel will *g* them
Zep 2: 1 *G* together, *g* together,
3:20 At that time I will *g* you;
Zec 14: 2 I will *g* all the nations to Jerusalem
Mt 12:30 he who does not *g* with me scatters
13:30 then *g* the wheat and bring it
23:37 longed to *g* your children together,
24:31 and they will *g* his elect
25:26 *g* where I have not scattered seed?
Mk 13:27 and *g* his elect from the four winds,
Lk 3:17 and to *g* the wheat into his barn,
11:23 and he who does not *g* with me,
13:34 longed to *g* your children together,

GATHERED (GATHER)
Ex 16:18 and he who *g* little did not have too
Pr 30: 4 Who has *g* up the wind
Mt 25:32 All the nations will be *g* before him
2Co 8:15 and he who *g* little did not have too
2Th 2: 1 Lord Jesus Christ and our being *g*
Rev 16:16 Then they *g* the kings together

GATHERS (GATHER)
Ps 147: 2 he *g* the exiles of Israel.
Pr 10: 5 He who *g* crops in summer is a wise
Isa 40:11 He *g* the lambs in his arms
Mt 23:37 a hen *g* her chicks under her wings,

GAVE (GIVE)
Ge 2:20 man *g* names to all the livestock,
3: 6 She also *g* some to her husband,
14:20 Abram *g* him a tenth of everything.
28: 4 the land God *g* to Abraham."
35:12 The land I *g* to Abraham
39:23 *g* him success in whatever he did.
47:11 *g* them property in the best part
Ex 4:11 to him, "Who *g* man his mouth?
31:18 he *g* him the two tablets
Dt 2:12 did in the land the LORD *g* them
2:36 The LORD our God *g* us all
3:12 I *g* the Reubenites and the Gadites
3:13 I *g* to the half tribe of Manasseh.
3:15 And I *g* Gilead to Makir.
3:16 Gadites I *g* the territory extending
8:16 He *g* you manna to eat in the desert
26: 9 us to this place and *g* us this land,
32: 8 the Most High *g* the nations their
Jos 11:23 and he *g* it as an inheritance
13:14 tribe of Levi he *g* no inheritance,
14:13 *g* him Hebron as his inheritance.
21:44 The LORD *g* them rest
24:13 I *g* you a land on which you did not
1Sa 27: 6 So on that day Achish *g* him Ziklag
2Sa 12: 8 I *g* you the house of Israel
1Ki 4:29 God *g* Solomon wisdom
5:12 The LORD *g* Solomon wisdom,
Ezr 2:69 According to their ability they *g*
Ne 9:15 In their hunger you *g* them bread
9:20 You *g* your good Spirit
9:22 You *g* them kingdoms and nations,
9:27 compassion you *g* them deliverers,
Job 1:21 LORD *g* and the LORD has taken
42:10 prosperous again and *g* him twice
Ps 69:21 and *g* me vinegar for my thirst.
135: 12 he *g* their land as an inheritance,
Ecc 12: 7 the spirit returns to God who *g* it.
Eze 3: 2 and he *g* me the scroll to eat.

Mt 1:25 And he *g* him the name Jesus.
25:35 and you *g* me something to drink,
25:42 and you *g* me nothing to drink,
26:26 Jesus took bread, *g* thanks
27:50 in a loud voice, he *g* up his spirit.
Mk 6: 7 *g* them authority over evil spirits.
Jn 1:12 he *g* the right to become children
3:16 so loved the world that he *g* his one
17: 4 by completing the work you *g* me
17: 6 you *g* them to me and they have
19:30 bowed his head and *g* up his spirit.
Ac 1: 3 *g* many convincing proofs that he
2:45 they *g* to anyone as he had need.
11:17 *g* them the same gift as he *g* us,
Ro 1:24 Therefore God *g* them
1:26 God *g* them over to shameful lusts.
1:28 he *g* them over to a depraved mind,
8:32 not spare his own Son, but *g* him up
2Co 5:18 *g* us the ministry of reconciliation:
8: 3 For I testify that they *g* as much
8: 5 they *g* themselves first to the Lord
Gal 1: 4 who *g* himself for our sins
2:20 who loved me and *g* himself for me
Eph 4: 8 and *g* gifts to men."
5: 2 as Christ loved us and *g* himself up
5:25 and *g* himself up for her
2Th 2:16 and by his grace *g* us eternal
1Ti 2: 6 who *g* himself as a ransom
Tit 2:14 who *g* himself for us to redeem us
1Jn 3:24 We know it by the Spirit he *g* us.

GAZE
Ps 27: 4 to *g* upon the beauty of the LORD
Pr 4:25 fix your *g* directly before you.

GEDALIAH
Governor of Judah appointed by Nebuchadnezzar (2Ki 25:22-26; Jer 39-41).

GEHAZI*
Servant of Elisha (2Ki 4:12-5:27; 8:4-5).

GENEALOGIES
1Ti 1: 4 themselves to myths and endless *g*.
Tit 3: 9 avoid foolish controversies and *g*

GENERATION (GENERATIONS)
Ex 3:15 am to be remembered from *g* to *g*.
Nu 32:13 until the whole *g* of those who had
Dt 1:35 of this evil *g* shall see the good land
Jdg 2:10 After that whole *g* had been
Ps 24: 6 Such is the *g* of those who seek him
48:13 tell of them to the next *g*.
71:18 I declare your power to the next *g*,
78: 4 we will tell the next *g*
102: 18 Let this be written for a future *g*,
112: 2 the *g* of the upright will be blessed
145: 4 One *g* will commend your works
La 5:19 your throne endures from *g* to *g*.
Da 4: 3 his dominion endures from *g* to *g*.
4:34 his kingdom endures from *g* to *g*.
Joel 1: 3 and their children to the next *g*.
Mt 12:39 adulterous *g* asks for a miraculous
17:17 "O unbelieving and perverse *g*,"
23:36 all this will come upon this *g*.
24:34 this *g* will certainly not pass away
Mk 9:19 "O unbelieving *g*," Jesus replied,
13:30 this *g* will certainly not pass away
Lk 1:50 who fear him, from *g* to *g*.
11:29 Jesus said, "This is a wicked *g*.
11:30 will the Son of Man be to this *g*.
11:50 Therefore this *g* will be held
21:32 this *g* will certainly not pass away
Ac 2:40 Save yourselves from this corrupt *g*
Php 2:15 fault in a crooked and depraved *g*,

GENERATIONS (GENERATION)
Ge 9:12 a covenant for all *g* to come:
17: 7 after you for the *g* to come,
17: 9 after you for the *g* to come.
Ex 20: 6 a thousand *g* of those
31:13 and you for the *g* to come,
Dt 7: 9 covenant of love to a thousand *g*
32: 7 consider the *g* long past.
1Ch 16:15 he commanded, for a thousand *g*,
Job 8: 8 "Ask the former *g*
Ps 22:30 future *g* will be told about the Lord
33:11 of his heart through all *g*.
45:17 your memory through all *g*;
89: 1 faithfulness known through all *g*.
90: 1 throughout all *g*.
100: 5 continues through all *g*.
102: 12 your renown endures through all *g*.
105: 8 he commanded, for a thousand *g*,
119: 90 continues through all *g*;
135: 13 renown, O LORD, through all *g*.
145: 13 dominion endures through all *g*.
146: 10 your God, O Zion, for all *g*.
Pr 27:24 and a crown is not secure for all *g*.
Isa 41: 4 forth the *g* from the beginning?
Isa 51: 8 my salvation through all *g*."
Lk 1:48 now on all *g* will call me blessed,
Eph 3: 5 not made known to men in other *g*
3:21 in Christ Jesus throughout all *g*,
Col 1:26 been kept hidden for ages and *g*,

GENEROSITY* (GENEROUS)
2Co 8: 2 poverty welled up in rich *g*.
9:11 and through us your *g* will result
9:13 and for your *g* in sharing with them

GENEROUS* (GENEROSITY)
Ps 37:26 They are always *g* and lend freely;
112: 5 Good will come to him who is *g*
Pr 11:25 A *g* man will prosper;
22: 9 A *g* man will himself be blessed,
Mt 20:15 Or are you envious because I am *g*
2Co 9: 5 Then it will be ready as a *g* gift,
9: 5 for the *g* gift you had promised.
9:11 way so that you can be *g*
1Ti 6:18 and to be *g* and willing to share.

GENTILE (GENTILES)
Ac 21:25 As for the *G* believers, we have
Ro 1:16 first for the Jew, then for the *G*.
2: 9 first for the Jew, then for the *G*;
2:10 first for the Jew, then for the *G*.
10:12 difference between Jew and *G*—

GENTILES (GENTILE)
Isa 42: 6 and a light for the *G*,
49: 6 also make you a light for the *G*,
49:22 "See, I will beckon to the *G*,
Lk 2:32 a light for revelation to the *G*
21:24 on by the *G* until the times
Ac 9:15 to carry my name before the *G*
10:45 been poured out even on the *G*.
11:18 granted even the *G* repentance unto
13:16 and you *G* who worship God,
13:46 of eternal life, we now turn to the *G*
13:47 I have made you a light for the *G*,
14:27 opened the door of faith to the *G*.
15:14 by taking from the *G* a people
18: 6 From now on I will go to the *G*."
22:21 I will send you far away to the *G*.'"
26:20 and in all Judea, and to the *G* also,
28:28 salvation has been sent to the *G*,
Ro 2:14 when *G*, who do not have the law,
3: 9 and *G* alike are all under sin.
3:29 Is he not the God of *G* too? Yes,
9:24 from the Jews but also from the *G*?
11:11 to the *G* to make Israel envious.
11:12 their loss means riches for the *G*,
11:13 as I am the apostle to the *G*,
15: 9 I will praise you among the *G*;
15: 9 so that the *G* may glorify God
1Co 1:23 block to Jews and foolishness to *G*,
Gal 1:16 I might preach him among the *G*,
2: 2 gospel that I preach among the *G*.
2: 8 my ministry as an apostle to the *G*.
2: 9 agreed that we should go to the *G*,
3: 8 that God would justify the *G*
3:14 to the *G* through Christ Jesus,
Eph 3: 6 the gospel the *G* are heirs together
3: 8 to the *G* the unsearchable riches
Col 1:27 among the *G* the glorious riches
1Ti 2: 7 a teacher of the true faith to the *G*.
2Ti 4:17 and all the *G* might hear it.

GENTLE* (GENTLENESS)
Dt 28:54 Even the most *g* and sensitive man
28:56 The most *g* and sensitive woman
28:56 and *g* that she would not venture
2Sa 18: 5 Be *g* with the young man Absalom
1Ki 19:12 And after the fire came a *g* whisper
Job 41: 3 Will he speak to you with *g* words?
Pr 15: 1 A *g* answer turns away wrath,
25:15 and a *g* tongue can break a bone.
Jer 11:19 I had been like a *g* lamb led
Zec 9: 9 *g* and riding on a donkey,
Mt 11:29 for I am *g* and humble in heart,
21: 5 *g* and riding on a donkey,
Ac 27:13 When a *g* south wind began
1Co 4:21 or in love and with a *g* spirit?
Eph 4: 2 Be completely humble and *g*;
1Th 2: 7 but we were *g* among you,
1Ti 3: 3 not violent but *g*, not quarrelsome,
1Pe 3: 4 the unfading beauty of a *g*

GENTLENESS* (GENTLE)
2Co 10: 1 By the meekness and *g* of Christ,
Gal 5:23 faithfulness, *g* and self-control.
Php 4: 5 Let your *g* be evident to all.
Col 3:12 kindness, humility, *g* and patience.
1Ti 6:11 faith, love, endurance and *g*.
1Pe 3:15 But do this with *g* and respect,

GENUINE*
2Co 6: 8 *g*, yet regarded as impostors;
Php 2:20 who takes a *g* interest
1Pe 1: 7 may be proved *g* and may result

GERIZIM
Dt 27:12 on Mount *G* to bless the people:

GERSHOM
Ex 2:22 and Moses named him *G*, saying,

GETHSEMANE*
Mt 26:36 disciples to a place called *G*,
Mk 14:32 They went to a place called *G*,

GHOST see also SPIRIT
Lk 24:39 a *g* does not have flesh and bones,

GIBEON
Jos 10:12 "O sun, stand still over *G*,

GIDEON*
Judge, also called Jerub-Baal; freed Israel from Midianites (Jdg 6-8; Heb 11:32). Given sign of fleece (Jdg 8:36-40).

GIFT (GIFTED GIFTS)
Pr 18:16 A *g* opens the way for the giver
21:14 A *g* given in secret soothes anger,
Ecc 3:13 in all his toil—this is the *g* of God.
Mt 5:23 if you are offering your *g*
Jn 4:10 "If you knew the *g* of God
Ac 1: 4 wait for the *g* my Father promised,
2:38 And you will receive the *g*
11:17 So if God gave them the same *g*
Ro 6:23 but the *g* of God is eternal life
12: 6 If a man's *g* is prophesying,
1Co 7: 7 each man has his own *g* from God;
2Co 8:12 the *g* is acceptable according
9:15 be to God for his indescribable *g*!
Eph 2: 8 it is the *g* of God—not by works,
1Ti 4:14 not neglect your *g*, which was
2Ti 1: 6 you to fan into flame the *g* of God,
Heb 6: 4 who have tasted the heavenly *g*,
Jas 1:17 and perfect *g* is from above,
1Pe 3: 7 with you of the gracious *g* of life,
4:10 should use whatever *g* he has
Rev 22:17 let him take the free *g* of the water

GIFTED* (GIFT)
1Co 14:37 he is a prophet or spiritually *g*,

GIFTS (GIFT)
Ps 76:11 bring *g* to the One to be feared.
112: 9 He has scattered abroad his *g*
Pr 25:14 of *g* he does not give.
Mt 2:11 and presented him with *g* of gold
7:11 Father in heaven give good *g*
7:11 to give good *g* to your children,
Lk 11:13 to give good *g* to your children,
Ac 10: 4 and *g* to the poor have come up
Ro 11:29 for God's *g* and his call are
12: 6 We have different *g*, according
1Co 12: 1 Now about spiritual *g*, brothers,
12: 4 There are different kinds of *g*,
12:28 those with *g* of administration,
12:30 all work miracles? Do all have *g*
12:31 But eagerly desire the greater *g*.
14: 1 and eagerly desire spiritual *g*,
14:12 eager to have spiritual *g*,
14:12 excel in *g* that build up the church.
2Co 9: 9 "He has scattered abroad his *g*
Eph 4: 8 and gave *g* to men."
Heb 2: 4 and *g* of the Holy Spirit distributed
9: 9 indicating that the *g* and sacrifices

GILEAD
1Ch 27:21 the half-tribe of Manasseh in *G*:
Jer 8:22 Is there no balm in *G*?
46:11 "Go up to *G* and get balm,

GILGAL
Jos 5: 9 So the place has been called *G*

GIRD*
Ps 45: 3 *G* your sword upon your side,

GIRL
Ge 24:16 *g* was very beautiful, a virgin;
2Ki 5: 2 a young *g* from Israel.
Mk 5:41 Little *g*, I say to you, get up!

GIVE (GAVE GIVEN GIVER GIVES GIVING LIFE-GIVING)
Ge 28: 4 you and your descendants the blessing *g* to Abraham
28:22 that you *g* me I will *g* you a tenth."
Ex 20:16 "You shall not *g* false testimony
30:15 The rich are not to *g* more
Nu 6:26 and *g* you peace."'
Dt 5:20 "You shall not *g* false testimony
15:10 *G* generously to him and do
15:14 *G* to him as the LORD your God
1Sa 1:11 then I will *g* him to the LORD

1Sa 1:28 So now I *g* him to the LORD.
2Ch 15: 7 be strong and do not *g* up,
Pr 21:26 but the righteous *g* without sparing
23:26 My son, *g* me your heart
25:21 if he is thirsty, *g* him water to drink
30: 8 but *g* me only my daily bread.
31:31 *G* her the reward she has earned,
Ecc 3: 6 a time to search and a time to *g* up,
Isa 42: 8 I will not *g* my glory to another
Eze 36:26 I will *g* you a new heart
Mt 6:11 *G* us today our daily bread.
7:11 know how to *g* good gifts
10: 8 Freely you have received, freely *g*.
16:19 I will *g* you the keys
22:21 "*G* to Caesar what is Caesar's,
Mk 8:37 Or what can a man *g* in exchange
10:19 not steal, do not *g* false testimony,
Lk 6:38 *G*, and it will be given to you.
11: 3 *G* us each day our daily bread.
11:13 Father in heaven *g* the Holy Spirit
14:33 who does not *g* up everything he
Jn 10:28 I *g* them eternal life, and they shall
13:34 "A new commandment I *g* you:
14:16 he will *g* you another Counselor
14:27 I do not *g* to you as the world gives.
14:27 leave with you; my peace I *g* you.
17: 2 people that he might *g* eternal life
Ac 20:35 blessed to *g* than to receive.' "
Ro 2: 7 immortality, he will *g* eternal life.
8:32 with him, graciously *g* us all things
12: 8 let him *g* generously;
13: 7 *G* everyone what you owe him:
14:12 each of us will *g* an account
2Co 9: 7 Each man should *g* what he has
Gal 2: 5 We did not *g* in to them
6: 9 reap a harvest if we do not *g* up.
Heb 10:25 Let us not *g* up meeting together,
Rev 14: 7 "Fear God and *g* him glory,

GIVEN (GIVE)
Nu 8:16 are to be *g* wholly to me.
Dt 26:11 things the LORD your God has *g*
Job 3:23 Why is life *g* to a man
Ps 115: 16 but the earth he has *g* to man.
Isa 9: 6 to us a son is *g*,
Mt 6:33 and all these things will be *g* to you
7: 7 "Ask and it will be *g* to you;
13:12 Whoever has will be *g* more,
22:30 people will neither marry nor be *g*
25:29 everyone who has will be *g* more,
Lk 6:38 Give, and it will be *g* to you.
8:10 kingdom of God has been *g* to you,
11: 9 Ask and it will be *g* to you;
22:19 saying, "This is my body *g* for you;
Jn 3:27 man can receive only what is *g* him
15: 7 you wish, and it will be *g* you.
17:24 I want those you have *g* me to be
17:24 the glory you have *g* me
18:11 the cup the Father has *g* me?"
Ac 5:32 whom God has *g* to those who
20:24 the task the Lord Jesus has *g* me—
Ro 5: 5 the Holy Spirit, whom he has *g* us.
1Co 4: 2 those who have been *g* a trust must
11:24 and when he had *g* thanks,
12:13 we were all *g* the one Spirit to drink
2Co 5: 5 and has *g* us the Spirit as a deposit,
Eph 1: 6 which he has freely *g* us
4: 7 to each one of us grace has been *g*
1Ti 4:14 was *g* you through a prophetic
1Jn 4:13 because he has *g* us of his Spirit.

GIVER* (GIVE)
Pr 18:16 A gift opens the way for the *g*
2Co 9: 7 for God loves a cheerful *g*.

GIVES (GIVE)
Job 35:10 who *g* songs in the night,
Ps 119: 130 The unfolding of your words *g* light;
Pr 3:34 but *g* grace to the humble.
11:24 One man *g* freely, yet gains
14:30 A heart at peace *g* life to the body,
15:30 good news *g* health to the bones.
19: 6 of a man who *g* gifts.
25:26 is a righteous man who *g* way
28:27 He who *g* to the poor will lack
29: 4 justice a king *g* a country stability,
Isa 40:29 He *g* strength to the weary
Hab 2:15 "Woe to him who *g* drink
Mt 10:42 if anyone *g* even a cup of cold water
Jn 5:21 even so the Son *g* life to whom he is
6:63 The Spirit *g* life; the flesh counts
1Co 15:57 He *g* us the victory
2Co 3: 6 the letter kills, but the Spirit *g* life.
1Th 4: 8 who *g* you his Holy Spirit.
Jas 1:25 into the perfect law that *g* freedom,
4: 6 but *g* grace to the humble."
1Pe 5: 5 but *g* grace to the humble."

GIVING (GIVE)
Ne 8: 8 *g* the meaning so that the people
Est 9:19 a day for *g* presents to each other.
Ps 19: 8 *g* joy to the heart.
Pr 15:23 A man finds joy in *g* an apt reply—
Mt 6: 4 so that your *g* may be in secret.
24:38 marrying and *g* in marriage,
Ac 15: 8 them by *g* the Holy Spirit to them,
2Co 8: 7 also excel in this grace of *g*.
Php 4:15 shared with me in the matter of *g*.

GLAD* (GLADDENS GLADNESS)
Ex 4:14 his heart will be *g* when he sees you
Jos 22:33 They were *g* to hear the report
Jdg 8:25 "We'll be *g* to give them."
18:20 household?" Then the priest was *g*.
1Sa 19: 5 and you saw it and were *g*.
2Sa 1:20 daughters of the Philistines be *g*,
1Ki 8:66 *g* in heart for all the good things
1Ch 16:31 heavens rejoice, let the earth be *g*;
2Ch 7:10 and *g* in heart for the good things
Ps 5:11 let all who take refuge in you be *g*;
9: 2 I will be *g* and rejoice in you;
14: 7 let Jacob rejoice and Israel be *g*!
16: 9 Therefore my heart is *g*
21: 6 made him *g* with the joy
31: 7 I will be *g* and rejoice in your love,
32:11 Rejoice in the LORD and be *g*,
40:16 rejoice and be *g* in you;
45: 8 music of the strings makes you *g*.
46: 4 whose streams make *g* the city
48:11 the villages of Judah are *g*
53: 6 let Jacob rejoice and Israel be *g*!
58:10 The righteous will be *g*
67: 4 May the nations be *g* and sing
68: 3 But may the righteous be *g*
69:32 The poor will see and be *g*—
70: 4 rejoice and be *g* in you;
90:14 for joy and be *g* all our days.
90:15 Make us *g* for as many days
92: 4 For you make me *g* by your deeds,
96:11 heavens rejoice, let the earth be *g*;
97: 1 LORD reigns, let the earth be *g*;
97: 8 and the villages of Judah are *g*
105: 38 Egypt was *g* when they left,
107: 30 They were *g* when it grew calm,
118: 24 let us rejoice and be *g* in it.
149: 2 of Zion be *g* in their King.
Pr 23:15 then my heart will be *g*;
23:25 May your father and mother be *g*;
29: 6 a righteous one can sing and be *g*.
Ecc 8:15 sun than to eat and drink and be *g*.
Isa 25: 9 let us rejoice and be *g*
35: 1 and the parched land will be *g*;
65:18 But be *g* and rejoice forever
66:10 with Jerusalem and be *g* for her,
Jer 20:15 who made him very *g*, saying,
31:13 Then maidens will dance and be *g*,
41:13 were with him, they were *g*.
50:11 "Because you rejoice and are *g*,
La 4:21 be *g*, O Daughter of Edom,
Joel 2:21 be *g* and rejoice.
2:23 Be *g*, O people of Zion,
Hab 1:15 and so he rejoices and is *g*.
Zep 3:14 Be *g* and rejoice with all your heart
Zec 2:10 and be *g*, O Daughter of Zion.
8:19 will become joyful and *g* occasions
10: 7 their hearts will be *g* as with wine.
Mt 5:12 be *g*, because great is your reward
Lk 15:32 But we had to celebrate and be *g*,
Jn 4:36 and the reaper may be *g* together.
8:56 my day; he saw it and was *g*."
11:15 for your sake I am *g* I was not there
14:28 you would be *g* that I am going
Ac 2:26 Therefore my heart is *g*
2:46 together with *g* and sincere hearts,
11:23 he was *g* and encouraged them all
13:48 they were *g* and honored the word
15: 3 news made all the brothers very *g*.
15:31 were *g* for its encouraging message.
1Co 16:17 was *g* when Stephanas, Fortunatus
2Co 2: 2 who is left to make me *g*
7:16 I am *g* I can have complete
13: 9 We are *g* whenever we are weak
Gal 4:27 "Be *g*, O barren woman,
Php 2:17 I am *g* and rejoice with all of you.
2:18 So you too should be *g* and rejoice
2:28 you see him again you may be *g*
Rev 19: 7 Let us rejoice and be *g*

GLADDENS* (GLAD)
Ps 104: 15 wine that *g* the heart of man,

GLADNESS* (GLAD)
2Ch 29:30 So they sang praises with *g*
Est 8:16 a time of happiness and joy, *g*
8:17 there was joy and *g*
Job 3:22 who are filled with *g*
Ps 35:27 shout for joy and *g*;
45:15 They are led in with joy and *g*;
51: 8 Let me hear joy and *g*;
65:12 the hills are clothed with *g*.
100: 2 Worship the LORD with *g*;
Ecc 5:20 God keeps him occupied with *g*
9: 7 Go, eat your food with *g*,
Isa 16:10 *g* are taken away from the orchards
35:10 *G* and joy will overtake them,
51: 3 Joy and *g* will be found in her,
51:11 *G* and joy will overtake them,
61: 3 the oil of *g* / instead of mourning,
Jer 7:34 and *g* and to the voices of bride
16: 9 and *g* and to the voices of bride
25:10 from them the sounds of joy and *g*,
31:13 I will turn their mourning into *g*;
33:11 once more the sounds of joy and *g*,
48:33 Joy and *g* are gone
Joel 1:16 joy and *g*

GLAZE*
Pr 26:23 of *g* over earthenware

GLEAM*
Pr 4:18 of the righteous is like the first *g*
Da 10: 6 legs like the *g* of burnished bronze,

GLOAT (GLOATS)
Pr 24:17 Do not *g* when your enemy falls;

GLOATS* (GLOAT)
Pr 17: 5 whoever *g* over disaster will not go

GLORIES* (GLORY)
1Pe 1:11 and the *g* that would follow.

GLORIFIED* (GLORY)
Isa 66: 5 'Let the LORD be *g*,
Eze 39:13 day I am *g* will be a memorable day
Da 4:34 and *g* him who lives forever.
Jn 7:39 since Jesus had not yet been *g*.
11: 4 glory so that God's Son may be *g*
12:16 after Jesus was *g* did they realize
12:23 come for the Son of Man to be *g*.
12:28 "I have *g* it, and will glorify it again
13:31 Son of Man *g* and God is *g* in him.
13:32 If God is *g* in him, God will glorify
Ac 3:13 our fathers, has *g* his servant Jesus.
Ro 1:21 they neither *g* him as God
8:30 those he justified, he also *g*.
2Th 1:10 comes to be *g* in his holy people
1:12 of our Lord Jesus may be *g* in you,
1Pe 1:21 him from the dead and *g* him,

GLORIFIES* (GLORY)
Lk 1:46 My soul *g* the Lord
Jn 8:54 as your God, is the one who *g* me.

GLORIFY* (GLORY)
Ps 34: 3 *G* the LORD with me;
63: 3 my lips will *g* you.
69:30 and *g* him with thanksgiving.
86:12 I will *g* your name forever.
Isa 60:13 and I will *g* the place of my feet.
Da 4:37 and exalt and *g* the King of heaven,
Jn 8:54 Jesus replied, "If I *g* myself,
12:28 glorified it, and will *g* it again."
12:28 *g* your name!" Then a voice came
13:32 God will *g* the Son in himself,
13:32 in himself, and will *g* him at once.
17: 1 *G* your Son, that your Son may
17: 1 your Son, that your Son may *g* you.
17: 5 *g* me in your presence
21:19 death by which Peter would *g* God.
Ro 15: 6 and mouth you may *g* the God
15: 9 so that the Gentiles may *g* God
1Pe 2:12 and *g* God on the day he visits us.
Rev 16: 9 they refused to repent and *g* him.

GLORIFYING* (GLORY)
Lk 2:20 *g* and praising God

GLORIOUS* (GLORY)
Dt 28:58 not revere this *g* and awesome
33:29 and your *g* sword.
1Ch 29:13 and praise your *g* name.
Ne 9: 5 "Blessed be your *g* name,
Ps 16: 3 they are the *g* ones
45:13 All *g* is the princess
66: 2 make his praise *g*.
72:19 Praise be to his *g* name forever;
87: 3 *G* things are said of you,
111: 3 *G* and majestic are his deeds,
145: 5 of the *g* splendor of your majesty,
145: 12 the *g* splendor of your kingdom.
Isa 3: 8 defying his *g* presence.
4: 2 the LORD will be beautiful and *g*,
11:10 and his place of rest will be *g*.
12: 5 for he has done *g* things;
28: 1 to the fading flower, his *g* beauty,
28: 4 That fading flower, his *g* beauty,

Isa 28: 5 will be a *g* crown,
42:21 to make his law great and *g*.
60: 7 and I will adorn my *g* temple.
63:12 who sent his *g* arm of power
63:14 to make for yourself a *g* name.
63:15 from your lofty throne, holy and *g*.
64:11 *g* temple, where our fathers praised
Jer 13:18 for your *g* crowns
14:21 do not dishonor your *g* throne.
17:12 A *g* throne, exalted
48:17 how broken the *g* staff!'
Mt 19:28 the Son of Man sits on his *g* throne,
Lk 9:31 appeared in *g* splendor, talking
Ac 2:20 of the great and *g* day of the Lord.
Ro 8:21 and brought into the *g* freedom
2Co 3: 8 of the Spirit be even more *g?*
3: 9 how much more *g* is the ministry
3: 9 ministry that condemns men is *g*,
3:10 For what was *g* has no glory now
Eph 1: 6 to the praise of his *g* grace,
1:17 *g* Father, may give you the Spirit
1:18 the riches of his *g* inheritance
3:16 of his *g* riches he may strengthen
Php 3:21 so that they will be like his *g* body.
4:19 to his *g* riches in Christ Jesus.
Col 1:11 all power according to his *g* might
1:27 among the Gentiles the *g* riches
1Ti 1:11 to the *g* gospel of the blessed God,
Tit 2:13 the *g* appearing of our great God
Jas 2: 1 believers in our *g* Lord Jesus Christ
1Pe 1: 8 with an inexpressible and *g* joy,
Jude :24 before his *g* presence without fault

GLORIOUSLY* (GLORY)
Isa 24:23 and before its elders, *g*.

GLORY (GLORIES GLORIFIED GLORIFIES GLORIFY GLORIFYING GLORIOUS GLORIOUSLY)
Ex 14: 4 But I will gain *g* for myself
14:17 And I will gain *g* through Pharaoh
15:11 awesome in *g*,
16:10 and there was the *g* of the LORD
24:16 and the *g* of the LORD settled
33:18 Moses said, "Now show me your *g*
40:34 and the *g* of the LORD filled
Nu 14:21 the *g* of the LORD fills the whole
Dt 5:24 LORD our God has shown us his *g*
Jos 7:19 "My son, give *g* to the LORD,
1Sa 4:21 "The *g* has departed from Israel"—
1Ch 16:10 *G* in his holy name;
16:24 Declare his *g* among the nations,
16:28 ascribe to the LORD *g*
29:11 and the *g* and the majesty
Ps 8: 1 You have set your *g*
8: 5 and crowned him with *g* and honor
19: 1 The heavens declare the *g* of God;
24: 7 that the King of *g* may come in.
26: 8 the place where your *g* dwells.
29: 1 ascribe to the LORD *g*
29: 9 And in his temple all cry, "*G!*"
57: 5 let your *g* be over all the earth.
66: 2 Sing the *g* of his name;
72:19 the whole earth be filled with his *g*.
96: 3 Declare his *g* among the nations,
102: 15 of the earth will revere your *g*.
108: 5 and let your *g* be over all the earth.
149: 9 This is the *g* of all his saints.
Pr 19:11 it is to his *g* to overlook an offense.
25: 2 It is the *g* of God to conceal
Isa 4: 5 over all the *g* will be a canopy.
6: 3 the whole earth is full of his *g*."
24:16 "*G* to the Righteous One."
26:15 You have gained *g* for yourself;
35: 2 they will see the *g* of the LORD,
40: 5 the *g* of the LORD will be revealed
42: 8 I will not give my *g* to another
42:12 Let them give *g* to the LORD
43: 7 whom I created for my *g*,
44:23 he displays his *g* in Israel.
48:11 I will not yield my *g* to another.
66:18 and they will come and see my *g*.
66:19 They will proclaim my *g*
Eze 1:28 the likeness of the *g* of the LORD.
10: 4 the radiance of the *g* of the LORD.
43: 2 and the land was radiant with his *g*.
44: 4 and saw the *g* of the LORD filling
Hab 2:14 knowledge of the *g* of the LORD,
3: 3 His *g* covered the heavens
Zec 2: 5 'and I will be its *g* within.'
Mt 16:27 in his Father's *g* with his angels,
24:30 of the sky, with power and great *g*.
25:31 sit on his throne in heavenly *g*.
25:31 the Son of Man comes in his *g*,
Mk 8:38 in his Father's *g* with the holy
13:26 in clouds with great power and *g*.
Lk 2: 9 and the *g* of the Lord shone
2:14 saying, "*G* to God in the highest,
9:26 and in the *g* of the Father
Lk 9:26 of him when he comes in his *g*
9:32 they saw his *g* and the two men
19:38 in heaven and *g* in the highest!"
21:27 in a cloud with power and great *g*.
24:26 these things and then enter his *g?*"
Jn 1:14 We have seen his *g*, the *g* of the One
2:11 He thus revealed his *g*,
8:50 I am not seeking *g* for myself;
8:54 myself, my *g* means nothing.
11: 4 for God's *g* so that God's Son may
11:40 you would see the *g* of God?"
12:41 he saw Jesus' *g* and spoke about
14:13 so that the Son may bring *g*
15: 8 is to my Father's *g*, that you bear
16:14 He will bring *g* to me by taking
17: 4 I have brought you *g* on earth
17: 5 presence with the *g* I had with you
17:10 *g* has come to me through them.
17:22 given them the *g* that you gave
17:24 to see my *g*, the *g* you have given
Ac 7: 2 The God of *g* appeared
7:55 up to heaven and saw the *g* of God,
Ro 1:23 exchanged the *g* of the immortal
2: 7 by persistence in doing good seek *g*
2:10 then for the Gentile; but *g*,
3: 7 truthfulness and so increases his *g*,
3:23 and fall short of the *g* of God,
4:20 in his faith and gave *g* to God,
8:17 that we may also share in his *g*.
8:18 with the *g* that will be revealed
9: 4 theirs the divine *g*, the covenants,
9:23 riches of his *g* known to the objects
9:23 whom he prepared in advance for *g*
11:36 To him be the *g* forever! Amen.
15:17 Therefore I *g* in Christ Jesus
16:27 to the only wise God be *g* forever
1Co 2: 7 for our *g* before time began.
10:31 whatever you do, do it all for the *g*
11: 7 but the woman is the *g* of man.
11: 7 since he is the image and *g* of God;
11:15 it is her *g?* For long hair is given
15:43 it is raised in *g*; it is sown
2Co 1:20 spoken by us to the *g* of God.
3: 7 in letters on stone, came with *g*,
3: 7 the face of Moses because of its *g*,
3:10 comparison with the surpassing *g*.
3:10 what was glorious has no *g* now
3:11 how much greater is the *g*
3:11 what was fading away came with *g*,
3:18 faces all reflect the Lord's *g*,
3:18 likeness with ever-increasing *g*,
4: 4 of the gospel of the *g* of Christ,
4: 6 of the knowledge of the *g* of God
4:15 to overflow to the *g* of God.
4:17 us an eternal *g* that far outweighs
Gal 1: 5 to whom be *g* for ever and ever.
Eph 1:12 might be for the praise of his *g*.
1:14 to the praise of his *g*.
3:13 for you, which are your *g*.
3:21 to him be *g* in the church
Php 1:11 to the *g* and praise of God.
2:11 to the *g* of God the Father.
3: 3 of God, who *g* in Christ Jesus,
4:20 and Father be *g* for ever and ever.
Col 1:27 Christ in you, the hope of *g*.
3: 4 also will appear with him in *g*.
1Th 2:12 you into his kingdom and *g*.
2:19 in which we will *g* in the presence
2:20 Indeed, you are our *g* and joy.
2Th 2:14 in the *g* of our Lord Jesus Christ.
1Ti 1:17 be honor and *g* for ever and ever.
3:16 was taken up in *g*.
2Ti 2:10 is in Christ Jesus, with eternal *g*.
4:18 To him be *g* for ever and ever.
Heb 1: 3 The Son is the radiance of God's *g*
2: 7 you crowned him with *g* and honor
2: 9 now crowned with *g* and honor
2:10 In bringing many sons to *g*,
5: 5 take upon himself the *g*
9: 5 the ark were the cherubim of the *G*,
13:21 to whom be *g* for ever and ever.
1Pe 1: 7 *g* and honor when Jesus Christ is
1:24 and all their *g* is like the flowers
4:11 To him be the *g* and the power
4:13 overjoyed when his *g* is revealed.
4:14 for the Spirit of *g* and of God rests
5: 1 will share in the *g* to be revealed:
5: 4 of *g* that will never fade away.
5:10 you to his eternal *g* in Christ,
2Pe 1: 3 of him who called us by his own *g*
1:17 and *g* from God the Father
1:17 came to him from the Majestic *G*,
3:18 To him be *g* both now and forever!
Jude :25 to the only God our Savior be *g*,
Rev 1: 6 to him be *g* and power for ever
4: 9 the living creatures give *g*,
4:11 to receive *g* and honor and power,
5:12 and honor and *g* and praise!"
5:13 and honor and *g* and power,
Rev 7:12 Praise and *g*
11:13 and gave *g* to the God of heaven.
14: 7 "Fear God and give him *g*,
15: 4 and bring *g* to your name?
15: 8 with smoke from the *g* of God
19: 1 *g* and power belong to our God,
19: 7 and give him *g!*
21:11 It shone with the *g* of God,
21:23 for the *g* of God gives it light,
21:26 *g* and honor of the nations will be

GLOWING
Eze 8: 2 was as bright as *g* metal.
Rev 1:15 His feet were like bronze *g*

GLUTTONS* (GLUTTONY)
Pr 23:21 for drunkards and *g* become poor,
28: 7 of *g* disgraces his father.
Tit 1:12 always liars, evil brutes, lazy *g*."

GLUTTONY* (GLUTTONS)
Pr 23: 2 throat if you are given to *g*.

GNASHING
Mt 8:12 where there will be weeping and *g*

GNAT* (GNATS)
Mt 23:24 You strain out a *g* but swallow

GNATS (GNAT)
Ex 8:16 of Egypt the dust will become *g*."

GOADS
Ecc 12:11 The words of the wise are like *g*,
Ac 26:14 hard for you to kick against the *g*.'

GOAL*
Lk 13:32 on the third day I will reach my *g*.'
2Co 5: 9 So we make it our *g* to please him,
Gal 3: 3 to attain your *g* by human effort?
Php 3:14 on toward the *g* to win the prize
1Ti 1: 5 The *g* of this command is love,
1Pe 1: 9 for you are receiving the *g*

GOAT (GOATS SCAPEGOAT)
Ge 15: 9 "Bring me a heifer, a *g* and a ram,
30:32 and every spotted or speckled *g*.
37:31 slaughtered a *g* and dipped
Ex 26: 7 Make curtains of *g* hair for the tent
Lev 16: 9 shall bring the *g* whose lot falls
Nu 7:16 one male *g* for a sin offering;
Isa 11: 6 the leopard will lie down with the *g*
Da 8: 5 suddenly a *g* with a prominent

GOATS (GOAT)
Nu 7:17 five male *g* and five male lambs
Mt 25:32 separates the sheep from the *g*.
Heb 10: 4 of bulls and *g* to take away sins.

GOD (GOD'S GODLINESS GODLY GODS)
Ge 1: 1 In the beginning *G* created
1: 2 and the Spirit of *G* was hovering
1: 3 And *G* said, "Let there be light,"
1: 7 So *G* made the expanse
1: 9 And *G* said, "Let the water
1:11 Then *G* said, "Let the land produce
1:20 And *G* said, "Let the water teem
1:21 So *G* created the great creatures
1:25 *G* made the wild animals according
1:26 Then *G* said, "Let us make man
1:27 So *G* created man in his own image
1:31 *G* saw all that he had made,
2: 3 And *G* blessed the seventh day
2: 7 And the LORD *G* formed the man
2: 8 the LORD *G* had planted a garden
2:18 The LORD *G* said, "It is not good
2:22 Then the LORD *G* made a woman
3: 1 to the woman, "Did *G* really say,
3: 5 you will be like *G*, knowing good
3: 8 from the LORD *G* among the trees
3: 9 But the LORD *G* called to the man
3:21 The LORD *G* made garments
3:22 LORD *G* said, "The man has now
3:23 So the LORD *G* banished him
5: 1 When *G* created man, he made him
5:22 Enoch walked with *G* 300 years
5:24 because *G* took him away.
6: 2 sons of *G* saw that the daughters
6: 9 of his time, and he walked with *G*.
6:12 *G* saw how corrupt the earth had
8: 1 But *G* remembered Noah
9: 1 Then *G* blessed Noah and his sons,
9: 6 for in the image of *G*
9:16 everlasting covenant between *G*
14:18 He was priest of *G* Most High,
14:19 Blessed be Abram by *G* Most High,
16:13 "You are the *G* who sees me,"
17: 1 "I am *G* Almighty; walk before me
17: 7 to be your *G* and the *G*
21: 4 him, as *G* commanded him.

Ge 21: 6 "G has brought me laughter,
21:20 G was with the boy as he grew up.
21:22 G is with you in everything you do.
21:33 name of the LORD, the Eternal G.
22: 1 Some time later G tested Abraham.
22: 8 "G himself will provide the lamb
22:12 Now I know that you fear G,
25:11 Abraham's death, G blessed his
28:12 and the angels of G were ascending
28:17 other than the house of G;
31:42 But G has seen my hardship
31:50 remember that G is a witness
32: 1 and the angels of G met him.
32:28 because you have struggled with G
32:30 "It is because I saw G face to face,
33:11 for G has been gracious to me
35: 1 and build an altar there to G,
35: 5 and the terror of G fell
35:10 G said to him, "Your name is Jacob
35:11 G said to him, "I am G Almighty;
41:51 G has made me forget all my
41:52 G has made me fruitful in the land
50:20 but G intended it for good
50:24 But G will surely come to your aid
Ex 2:24 G heard their groaning
3: 5 "Do not come any closer," G said.
3: 6 because he was afraid to look at G.
3:12 And G said, "I will be with you.
3:14 what shall I tell them?" G said
4:27 he met Moses at the mountain of G
6: 7 own people, and I will be your G.
8:10 is no one like the LORD our G.
10:16 sinned against the LORD your G
13:18 So G led the people
15: 2 He is my G, and I will praise him,
16:12 that I am the LORD your G.' "
17: 9 with the staff of G in my hands."
18: 5 camped near the mountain of G.
19: 3 Then Moses went up to G,
20: 1 And G spoke all these words:
20: 2 the LORD your G, who brought
20: 5 the LORD your G, am a jealous G,
20: 7 the name of the LORD your G,
20:10 a Sabbath to the LORD your G.
20:12 the LORD your G is giving you.
20:19 But do not have G speak to us
20:20 the fear of G will be with you
22:20 "Whoever sacrifices to any g other
22:28 "Do not blaspheme G
23:19 to the house of the LORD your G.
31:18 inscribed by the finger of G.
34: 6 the compassionate and gracious G,
34:14 name is Jealous, is a jealous G.
Lev 2:13 salt of the covenant of your G out
11:44 the LORD your G; consecrate
18:21 not profane the name of your G.
19: 2 the LORD your G, am holy.
20: 7 because I am the LORD your G.
21: 6 They must be holy to their G
22:33 out of Egypt to be your G.
26:12 walk among you and be your G,
Nu 15:40 and will be consecrated to your G.
22:18 the command of the LORD my G.
22:38 I must speak only what G puts
23:19 G is not a man, that he should lie,
25:13 zealous for the honor of his G
Dt 1:17 for judgment belongs to G.
1:21 the LORD your G has given you
1:30 The LORD your G, who is going
3:22 LORD your G himself will fight
3:24 For what g is there in heaven
4:24 is a consuming fire, a jealous G.
4:29 there you seek the LORD your G,
4:31 the LORD your G is a merciful G;
4:39 heart this day that the LORD is G
5: 9 the LORD your G, am a jealous G,
5:11 the name of the LORD your G,
5:12 the LORD your G has commanded
5:14 a Sabbath to the LORD your G.
5:15 the LORD your G brought you out
5:16 the LORD your G has commanded
5:16 the LORD your G is giving you.
5:24 LORD our G has shown us his
5:26 of the living G speaking out of fire,
6: 2 them may fear the LORD your G
6: 4 LORD our G, the LORD is one.
6: 5 Love the LORD your G
6:13 the LORD your G, serve him only
6:16 Do not test the LORD your G
7: 6 holy to the LORD your G.
7: 9 your G is G; he is the faithful G,
7:12 the LORD your G will keep his
7:19 LORD your G will do the same
7:21 is a great and awesome G.
8: 5 the LORD your G disciplines you.
8:11 do not forget the LORD your G,
8:18 But remember the LORD your G,
9:10 inscribed by the finger of G.
10:12 but to fear the LORD your G,

Dt 10:14 the LORD your G belong
10:17 For the LORD your G is G of gods
10:21 He is your praise; he is your G,
11: 1 Love the LORD your G
11:13 to love the LORD your G
12:12 rejoice before the LORD your G,
12:28 in the eyes of the LORD your G.
13: 3 The LORD your G is testing you
13: 4 the LORD your G you must
15: 6 the LORD your G will bless you
15:19 the LORD your G every firstborn
16:11 rejoice before the LORD your G
16:17 the LORD your G has blessed you.
18:13 before the LORD your G.
18:15 The LORD your G will raise up
19: 9 to love the LORD your G
22: 5 the LORD your G detests anyone
23: 5 the LORD your G loves you.
23:14 the LORD your G moves about
23:21 a vow to the LORD your G,
25:16 the LORD your G detests anyone
26: 5 declare before the LORD your G:
29:13 that he may be your G
29:29 belong to the LORD our G,
30: 2 return to the LORD your G
30: 4 the LORD your G will gather you
30: 6 The LORD your G will circumcise
30:16 today to love the LORD your G,
30:20 you may love the LORD your G,
31: 6 for the LORD your G goes
32: 3 Oh, praise the greatness of our G!
32: 4 A faithful G who does no wrong,
33:27 The eternal G is your refuge,
Jos 1: 9 for the LORD your G will be
14: 8 the LORD my G wholeheartedly.
14: 9 the LORD my G wholeheartedly.'
14:14 the G of Israel, wholeheartedly.
22: 5 to love the LORD your G,
22:22 The Mighty One, G, the LORD!
22:34 Between Us that the LORD is G.
23: 8 to hold fast to the LORD your G,
23:11 careful to love the LORD your G.
23:14 the LORD your G gave you has
23:15 of the LORD your G has come true
24:19 He is a holy G; he is a jealous G.
24:23 to the LORD, the G of Israel."
Jdg 5: 3 to the LORD, the G of Israel.
16:28 O G, please strengthen me just
Ru 1:16 be my people and your G my G.
2:12 by the LORD, the G of Israel,
1Sa 2: 2 there is no Rock like our G.
2: 3 for the LORD is a G who knows,
2:25 another man, G may mediate
10:26 men whose hearts G had touched.
12:12 the LORD your G was your king.
16:15 spirit from G is tormenting you.
17:26 defy the armies of the living G?"
17:36 defied the armies of the living G.
17:45 the G of the armies of Israel,
17:46 world will know that there is a G
23:16 and helped him find strength in G.
28:15 and G has turned away from me.
30: 6 strength in the LORD his G.
2Sa 7:22 and there is no G but you,
7:23 on earth that G went out to redeem
14:14 But G does not take away life;
21:14 G answered prayer in behalf
22: 3 my G is my rock, in whom I take
22:31 "As for G, his way is perfect;
22:32 And who is the Rock except our G
22:33 It is G who arms me with strength
22:47 Exalted be G, the Rock, my Savior!
1Ki 2: 3 what the LORD your G requires:
4:29 G gave Solomon wisdom
5: 5 for the Name of the LORD my G,
8:23 there is no G like you in heaven
8:27 "But will G really dwell on earth?
8:60 may know that the LORD is G
8:61 committed to the LORD our G,
10:24 to hear the wisdom G had put
15:30 he provoked the LORD, the G
18:21 If the LORD is G, follow him;
18:36 it be known today that you are G
18:37 are G, and that you are turning
20:28 a g of the hills and not a g
2Ki 5:15 "Now I know that there is no G
18: 5 in the LORD, the G of Israel.
19:15 G of Israel, enthroned
19:19 Now, O LORD our G, deliver us
1Ch 12:18 for your G will help you."
13: 2 if it is the will of the LORD our G,
16:35 Cry out, "Save us, O G our Savior;
17:20 and there is no G but you,
17:24 the G over Israel, is Israel's G!"
21: 8 said to G, "I have sinned greatly
22: 1 house of the LORD G is to be here,
22:19 soul to seeking the LORD your G.
28: 2 for the footstool of our G,
28: 9 acknowledge the G of your father,

1Ch 28:20 for the LORD G, my G, is with you
29: 1 not for man but for the LORD G.
29: 2 provided for the temple of my G—
29: 3 of my G I now give my personal
29:10 G of our father Israel,
29:13 Now, our G, we give you thanks,
29:16 O LORD our G, as for all this
29:17 my G, that you test the heart
29:18 G of our fathers Abraham,
2Ch 2: 4 for the Name of the LORD my G
5:14 of the LORD filled the temple of G
6: 4 be to the LORD, the G of Israel,
6:14 there is no G like you in heaven
6:18 "But will G really dwell on earth
10:15 for this turn of events was from G,
13:12 G is with us; he is our leader.
15: 3 was without the true G,
15:12 the G of their fathers,
15:15 They sought G eagerly,
18:13 I can tell him only what my G says
19: 3 have set your heart on seeking G."
19: 7 with the LORD our G there is no
20: 6 are you not the G who is in heaven?
20:20 Have faith in the LORD your G
25: 8 for G has the power to help
26: 5 sought the LORD, G gave him
30: 9 for the LORD your G is gracious
30:19 who sets his heart on seeking G—
31:21 he sought his G and worked
32:31 G left him to test him
33:12 the favor of the LORD his G
34:33 fail to follow the LORD, the G
Ezr 6:21 to seek the LORD, the G of Israel.
7:18 accordance with the will of your G.
7:23 Whatever the G of heaven has
8:22 "The gracious hand of our G is
8:31 The hand of our G was on us,
9: 6 "O my G, I am too ashamed
9: 9 our G has not deserted us
9:13 our G, you have punished us less
9:15 G of Israel, you are righteous!
Ne 1: 5 the great and awesome G,
5: 9 fear of our G to avoid the reproach
5:15 for G I did not act like that.
7: 2 feared G more than most men do.
8: 8 from the Book of the Law of G,
8:18 from the Book of the Law of G.
9: 5 and praise the LORD your G,
9:17 But you are a forgiving G,
9:31 you are a gracious and merciful G.
9:32 the great, mighty and awesome G,
10:29 oath to follow the Law of G given
10:39 not neglect the house of our G."
12:43 G had given them great joy.
13:11 Why is the house of G neglected?"
13:26 He was loved by his G,
13:31 Remember me with favor, O my G.
Job 1: 1 he feared G and shunned evil.
1:22 by charging G with wrongdoing.
2:10 Shall we accept good from G,
4:17 a mortal be more righteous than G?
5:17 is the man whom G corrects;
8: 3 Does G pervert justice?
8:20 "Surely G does not reject
9: 2 a mortal be righteous before G?
11: 7 Can you fathom the mysteries of G
12:13 "To G belong wisdom and power;
16: 7 Surely, O G, you have worn me out
19:26 yet in my flesh I will see G;
21:19 'G stores up a man's punishment
21:22 Can anyone teach knowledge to G,
22:12 "Is not G in the heights of heaven?
22:13 Yet you say, 'What does G know?
22:21 "Submit to G and be at peace
25: 2 "Dominion and awe belong to G;
25: 4 can a man be righteous before G?
26: 6 Death is naked before G;
30:20 O G, but you do not answer;
31: 6 let G weigh me in honest scales
31:14 do when G confronts me?
32:13 let G refute him, not man.'
33: 6 I am just like you before G;
33:14 For G does speak—now one way,
33:26 He prays to G and finds favor
34:10 Far be it from G to do evil,
34:12 is unthinkable that G would do
34:23 G has no need to examine men
34:33 Should G then reward you
36: 5 "G is mighty, but does not despise
36:26 is G—beyond our understanding!
37:22 G comes in awesome majesty.
Ps 5: 4 You are not a G who takes pleasure
7:11 G is a righteous judge,
10:14 O G, do see trouble and grief;
14: 5 for G is present in the company
18: 2 my G is my rock, in whom I take
18:28 my G turns my darkness into light.
18:30 As for G, his way is perfect;
18:31 And who is the Rock except our G

Ps 18:32 It is G who arms me with strength
18:46 Exalted be G my Savior!
19: 1 The heavens declare the glory of G;
22: 1 G, my G, why have you forsaken
22:10 womb you have been my G.
27: 9 O G my Savior.
29: 3 the G of glory thunders,
31: 5 redeem me, O LORD, the G
31:14 I say, "You are my G."
33:12 the nation whose G is the LORD,
35:24 righteousness, O LORD my G;
37:31 The law of his G is in his heart;
40: 3 a hymn of praise to our G.
40: 8 I desire to do your will, O my G;
42: 1 so my soul pants for you, O G.
42: 2 thirsts for G, for the living G.
42: 5 Put your hope in G,
42: 8 a prayer to the G of my life.
42:11 Put your hope in G,
43: 4 to G, my joy and my delight.
44: 8 In G we make our boast all day
45: 6 O G, will last for ever and ever;
45: 7 therefore G, your G, has set you
46: 1 G is our refuge and strength,
46: 5 G will help her at break of day.
46:10 "Be still, and know that I am G;
47: 1 shout to G with cries of joy.
47: 6 Sing praises to G, sing praises;
47: 7 For G is the King of all the earth;
48: 9 Within your temple, O G,
49: 7 or give to G a ransom for him—
50: 2 G shines forth.
50: 3 Our G comes and will not be silent;
51: 1 Have mercy on me, O G,
51:10 Create in me a pure heart, O G,
51:17 O G, you will not despise.
53: 2 any who seek G.
54: 4 Surely G is my help;
55:19 G, who is enthroned forever,
56: 4 In G, whose word I praise,
56:10 In G, whose word I praise,
56:13 that I may walk before G
57: 3 G sends his love and his
57: 7 My heart is steadfast, O G,
59:17 are my fortress, my loving G.
62: 1 My soul finds rest in G alone;
62: 7 my honor depend on G;
62: 8 for G is our refuge.
62:11 One thing G has spoken,
63: 1 O G, you are my G,
65: 5 O G our Savior,
66: 1 Shout with joy to G, all the earth!
66: 3 Say to G, "How awesome are your
66: 5 Come and see what G has done,
66:16 listen, all you who fear G;
66:20 Praise be to G,
68: 4 Sing to G, sing praise to his name,
68: 6 G sets the lonely in families,
68:20 Our G is a G who saves;
68:24 has come into view, O G,
68:35 You are awesome, O G,
69: 5 You know my folly, O G;
70: 1 Hasten, O G, to save me;
70: 4 "Let G be exalted!"
70: 5 come quickly to me, O G.
71:17 my youth, O G, you have taught
71:18 do not forsake me, O G,
71:19 reaches to the skies, O G,
71:22 harp for your faithfulness, O my G;
73:17 me till I entered the sanctuary of G;
73:26 but G is the strength of my heart
76:11 Make vows to the LORD your G
77:13 What g is so great as our God?
77:14 You are the G who performs
78:19 Can G spread a table in the desert?
79: 9 Help us, O G our Savior,
81: 1 Sing for joy to G our strength;
82: 1 G presides in the great assembly;
84: 2 out for the living G.
84:10 a doorkeeper in the house of my G
84:11 For the LORD G is a sun
86:12 O Lord my G, with all my heart;
86:15 a compassionate and gracious G,
87: 3 O city of G: *Selah*
89: 7 of the holy ones G is greatly feared;
90: 2 to everlasting you are G.
91: 2 my G, in whom I trust."
94:22 my G the rock in whom I take
95: 7 for he is our G
99: 8 you were to Israel a forgiving G,
99: 9 Exalt the LORD our G
100: 3 Know that the LORD is G.
108: 1 My heart is steadfast, O G;
113: 5 Who is like the LORD our G,
115: 3 Our G is in heaven;
116: 5 our G is full of compassion.
123: 2 look to the LORD our G,
136: 2 Give thanks to the G of gods.
136: 26 Give thanks to the G of heaven.
Ps 139: 17 to me are your thoughts, O G!
139: 23 Search me, O G, and know my
143: 10 for you are my G;
144: 2 He is my loving G and my fortress,
147: 1 is to sing praises to our G,
Pr 3: 4 in the sight of G and man.
14:31 to the needy honors G.
25: 2 of G to conceal a matter;
30: 5 "Every word of G is flawless;
Ecc 2:26 G gives wisdom, knowledge
3:11 cannot fathom what G has done
3:13 in all his toil—this is the gift of G.
3:14 G does it so that men will revere him.
5: 4 When you make a vow to G,
5:19 in his work—this is a gift of G.
8:12 who are reverent before G.
11: 5 cannot understand the work of G,
12: 7 the spirit returns to G who gave it.
12:13 Fear G and keep his
Isa 5:16 the holy G will show himself holy
9: 6 Wonderful Counselor, Mighty G,
12: 2 Surely G is my salvation;
25: 9 "Surely this is our G;
28:11 G will speak to this people,
29:23 will stand in awe of the G of Israel.
30:18 For the LORD is a G of justice.
35: 4 your G will come,
37:16 you alone are G over all
40: 1 says your G.
40: 3 a highway for our G.
40: 8 the word of our G stands forever."
40:18 then, will you compare G?
40:28 The LORD is the everlasting G,
41:10 not be dismayed, for I am your G.
41:13 For I am the LORD, your G,
43:10 Before me no g was formed,
44: 6 apart from me there is no G.
44:15 he also fashions a g and worships it;
45:18 he is G;
48:17 "I am the LORD your G,
52: 7 "Your G reigns!"
52:12 G of Israel will be your rear guard.
55: 7 to our G, for he will freely pardon.
57:21 says my G, "for the wicked."
59: 2 you from your G;
60:19 and your G will be your glory.
61: 2 and the day of vengeance of our G,
61:10 my soul rejoices in my G.
62: 5 so will your G rejoice over you.
Jer 7:23 I will be your G and you will be my
10:10 But the LORD is the true G;
10:12 But G made the earth by his power;
23:23 "Am I only a G nearby,"
23:36 distort the words of the living G,
31:33 I will be their G,
32:27 "I am the LORD, the G
42: 6 for we will obey the LORD our G."
51:10 what the LORD our G has done.'
51:56 For the LORD is a G of retribution
Eze 28:13 the garden of G;
34:31 and I am your G, declares
Da 2:28 there is a G in heaven who reveals
3:17 the G we serve is able to save us
3:29 for no other g can save in this way
6:16 "May your G, whom you serve
9: 4 O Lord, the great and awesome G,
10:12 to humble yourself before your G,
11:36 things against the G of gods.
Hos 1: 9 my people, and I am not your G.
1:10 will be called 'sons of the living G.'
4: 6 you have ignored the law of your G
6: 6 acknowledgment of G rather
9: 8 The prophet, along with my G,
12: 6 and wait for your G always.
Joel 2:13 Return to the LORD your G,
2:23 rejoice in the LORD your G,
Am 4:12 prepare to meet your G, O Israel."
4:13 the LORD G Almighty is his name
Jnh 1: 6 Get up and call on your g!
4: 2 a gracious and compassionate G,
Mic 6: 8 and to walk humbly with your G.
7: 7 I wait for G my Savior;
7:18 Who is a G like you,
Na 1: 2 LORD is a jealous and avenging G;
Hab 3:18 I will be joyful in G my Savior.
Zep 3:17 The LORD your G is with you,
Zec 14: 5 Then the LORD my G will come,
Mal 2:10 Father? Did not one G create us?
2:16 says the LORD G of Israel,
3: 8 Will a man rob G? Yet you rob me.
Mt 1:23 which means, "G with us."
4: 4 comes from the mouth of G.'"
4: 7 'Do not put the Lord your G
4:10 'Worship the Lord your G,
5: 8 for they will see G.
6:24 You cannot serve both G
19: 6 Therefore what G has joined
19:26 but with G all things are possible."
22:21 and to G what is God's."
Mt 22:32 He is not the G of the dead
22:37 "'Love the Lord your G
27:46 which means, "My G, my G,
Mk 2: 7 Who can forgive sins but G alone?"
7:13 Thus you nullify the word of G
10: 6 of creation G 'made them male
10: 9 Therefore what G has joined
10:18 "No one is good—except G alone.
10:27 all things are possible with G."
11:22 "Have faith in G," Jesus answered.
12:17 and to G what is God's."
12:29 the Lord our G, the Lord is one.
12:30 Love the Lord your G
15:34 which means, "My G, my G,
16:19 and he sat at the right hand of G.
Lk 1:30 Mary, you have found favor with G
1:37 For nothing is impossible with G."
1:47 my spirit rejoices in G my Savior,
2:14 "Glory to G in the highest,
2:52 and in favor with G and men.
4: 8 'Worship the Lord your G
5:21 Who can forgive sins but G alone?"
8:39 tell how much G has done for you."
10: 9 'The kingdom of G is near you.'
10:27 "'Love the Lord your G
13:18 "What is the kingdom of G like?
18:19 "No one is good—except G alone.
18:27 with men is possible with G."
20:25 and to G what is God's."
20:38 He is not the G of the dead,
22:69 at the right hand of the mighty G."
Jn 1: 1 was with G, and the Word was G.
1:18 ever seen G, but G the One and Only,
1:29 Lamb of G, who takes away the sin
3:16 "For G so loved the world that he
3:34 the one whom G has sent speaks
4:24 G is spirit, and his worshipers must
5:44 praise that comes from the only G?
6:29 answered, "The work of G is this:
7:17 my teaching comes from G or
8:42 to them, "If G were your Father,
8:47 belongs to G hears what G says.
11:40 you would see the glory of G?"
13: 3 from G and was returning to G;
13:31 of Man glorified and G is glorified
14: 1 Trust in G; trust also in me.
17: 3 the only true G, and Jesus Christ,
20:17 your Father, to my G and your G
20:28 "My Lord and my G!"
20:31 the Son of G, and that
Ac 2:11 wonders of G in our own tongues!"
2:24 But G raised him from the dead,
2:33 Exalted to the right hand of G,
2:36 G has made this Jesus, whom you
3:15 but G raised him from the dead.
3:19 Repent, then, and turn to G,
4:31 and spoke the word of G boldly.
5: 4 You have not lied to men but to G
5:29 "We must obey G rather than men!
5:31 G exalted him to his own right
5:32 whom G has given
7:55 to heaven and saw the glory of G,
8:21 your heart is not right before G.
11: 9 anything impure that G has made
12:24 But the word of G continued
13:32 What G promised our fathers he
15:10 to test G by putting on the necks
17:23 TO AN UNKNOWN G.
17:30 In the past G overlooked such
20:27 to you the whole will of G.
20:32 "Now I commit you to G
24:16 keep my conscience clear before G
Ro 1:16 the power of G for the salvation
1:17 a righteousness from G is revealed,
1:18 The wrath of G is being revealed
1:24 Therefore G gave them
1:26 G gave them over to shameful lusts
2:11 For G does not show favoritism.
2:16 when G will judge men's secrets
3: 4 Let G be true, and every man a liar.
3:19 world held accountable to G.
3:23 and fall short of the glory of G,
3:29 Is G the G of Jews only? Is he not
4: 3 say? "Abraham believed G,
4: 6 to whom G credits righteousness
4:17 the G who gives life to the dead
4:24 to whom G will credit
5: 1 we have peace with G
5: 5 because G has poured out his love
5: 8 G demonstrates his own love for us
6:22 and have become slaves to G,
6:23 but the gift of G is eternal life
8: 7 the sinful mind is hostile to G.
8:17 heirs of G and co-heirs with Christ,
8:28 in all things G works for the good
9:14 What then shall we say? Is G unjust
9:18 Therefore G has mercy
10: 9 in your heart that G raised him
11: 2 G did not reject his people,

Ro 11:22 the kindness and sternness of *G*:
11:32 For *G* has bound all men
13: 1 exist have been established by *G*.
14:12 give an account of himself to *G*.
16:20 *G* of peace will soon crush Satan
1Co 1:18 are being saved it is the power of *G*.
1:20 Has not *G* made foolish
1:25 For the foolishness of *G* is wiser
1:27 But *G* chose the foolish things
2: 9 what *G* has prepared
2:11 of *G* except the Spirit of *G*.
3: 6 watered it, but *G* made it grow.
3:17 God's temple, *G* will destroy
6:20 Therefore honor *G* with your body.
7: 7 each man has his own gift from *G*;
7:15 *G* has called us to live in peace.
7:20 was in when *G* called him.
7:24 each man, as responsible to *G*,
8: 3 man who loves *G* is known by *G*.
8: 8 food does not bring us near to *G*;
10:13 *G* is faithful; he will not let you be
10:31 do it all for the glory of *G*.
12:24 But *G* has combined the members
14:33 For *G* is not a *G* of disorder
15:24 over the kingdom to *G* the Father
15:28 so that *G* may be all in all.
15:34 are some who are ignorant of *G*—
15:57 be to *G*! He gives us the victory
2Co 1: 9 rely on ourselves but on *G*,
2:14 be to *G*, who always leads us
2:15 For we are to *G* the aroma of Christ
2:17 we do not peddle the word of *G*
3: 5 but our competence comes from *G*.
4: 2 nor do we distort the word of *G*.
4: 7 this all-surpassing power is from *G*
5: 5 Now it is *G* who has made us
5:19 that *G* was reconciling the world
5:20 though *G* were making his appeal
5:21 *G* made him who had no sin
6:16 we are the temple of the living *G*.
9: 7 for *G* loves a cheerful giver.
9: 8 *G* is able to make all grace abound
10:13 to the field *G* has assigned to us,
Gal 2: 6 *G* does not judge by external
3: 5 Does *G* give you his Spirit
3: 6 Abraham: "He believed *G*,
3:11 justified before *G* by the law,
3:26 You are all sons of *G* through faith
6: 7 not be deceived: *G* cannot be
Eph 1:22 *G* placed all things under his feet
2: 8 it is the gift of *G*— not by works,
2:10 which *G* prepared in advance for us
2:22 in which *G* lives by his Spirit.
4: 6 one baptism; one *G* and Father
4:24 to be like *G* in true righteousness
5: 1 Be imitators of *G*, therefore,
6: 6 doing the will of *G* from your heart.
Php 2: 6 Who, being in very nature *G*,
2: 9 Therefore *G* exalted him
2:13 for it is *G* who works in you to will
4: 7 peace of *G*, which transcends all
4:19 And my *G* will meet all your needs
Col 1:19 For *G* was pleased
2:13 *G* made you alive with Christ.
1Th 2: 4 trying to please men but *G*,
2:13 but as it actually is, the word of *G*,
3: 9 How can we thank *G* enough
4: 7 For *G* did not call us to be impure,
4: 9 taught by *G* to love each other.
5: 9 For *G* did not appoint us
1Ti 2: 5 one mediator between *G* and men,
4: 4 For everything *G* created is good,
5: 4 for this is pleasing to *G*.
2Ti 1: 6 you to fan into flame the gift of *G*,
Tit 1: 2 which *G*, who does not lie,
2:13 glorious appearing of our great *G*
Heb 1: 1 In the past *G* spoke
3: 4 but *G* is the builder of everything.
4: 4 "And on the seventh day *G* rested
4:12 For the word of *G* is living
6:10 *G* is not unjust; he will not forget
6:18 in which it is impossible for *G* to lie
7:19 by which we draw near to *G*.
7:25 come to *G* through him,
10:22 draw near to *G* with a sincere heart
10:31 to fall into the hands of the living *G*
11: 5 commended as one who pleased *G*.
11: 6 faith it is impossible to please *G*,
12: 7 as discipline; *G* is treating you
12:10 but *G* disciplines us for our good,
12:29 for our "*G* is a consuming fire."
13:15 offer to *G* a sacrifice of praise—
Jas 1:12 crown of life that *G* has promised
1:13 For *G* cannot be tempted by evil,
1:27 Religion that *G* our Father accepts
2:19 You believe that there is one *G*.
2:23 "Abraham believed *G*,
4: 4 the world becomes an enemy of *G*.
4: 6 "*G* opposes the proud
Jas 4: 8 Come near to *G* and he will come
1Pe 1:23 the living and enduring word of *G*.
2:20 this is commendable before *G*.
3:18 the unrighteous, to bring you to *G*.
4:11 it with the strength *G* provides,
5: 5 because, "*G* opposes the proud
2Pe 1:21 but men spoke from *G*
2: 4 For if *G* did not spare angels
1Jn 1: 5 *G* is light; in him there is no
2:17 the will of *G* lives forever.
3: 1 we should be called children of *G*!
3: 9 born of *G* will continue to sin,
3:10 we know who the children of *G* are
3:20 For *G* is greater than our hearts,
4: 7 for love comes from *G*.
4: 8 not know *G*, because *G* is love.
4: 9 This is how *G* showed his love
4:11 Dear friends, since *G* so loved us,
4:12 No one has ever seen *G*;
4:15 *G* lives in him and he in *G*.
4:16 *G* is love.
4:20 "I love *G*," yet hates his brother,
4:21 Whoever loves *G* must
5: 2 that we love the children of *G*:
5: 3 love for *G*: to obey his commands.
5: 4 born of *G* overcomes the world.
5:10 does not believe *G* has made him
5:14 have in approaching *G*:
5:18 born of *G* does not continue to sin;
Rev 4: 8 holy is the Lord *G* Almighty,
7:12 be to our *G* for ever and ever.
7:17 *G* will wipe away every tear
11:16 fell on their faces and worshiped *G*,
15: 3 Lord *G* Almighty.
17:17 For *G* has put it into their hearts
19: 6 For our Lord *G* Almighty reigns.
21: 3 Now the dwelling of *G* is with men,
21:23 for the glory of *G* gives it light,

GOD-BREATHED* (BREATH)
2Ti 3:16 All Scripture is *G* and is useful

GOD-FEARING* (FEAR)
Ecc 8:12 that it will go better with *G* men,
Ac 2: 5 staying in Jerusalem *G* Jews
10: 2 all his family were devout and *G*;
10:22 He is a righteous and *G* man,
13:26 of Abraham, and you *G* Gentiles,
13:50 But the Jews incited the *G* women
17: 4 as did a large number of *G* Greeks
17:17 with the Jews and the *G* Greeks,

GOD-HATERS* (HATE)
Ro 1:30 They are gossips, slanderers, *G*,

GOD'S (GOD)
2Ch 20:15 For the battle is not yours, but *G*.
Job 37:14 stop and consider *G* wonders.
Ps 52: 8 I trust in *G* unfailing love
69:30 I will praise *G* name in song
Mk 3:35 Whoever does *G* will is my brother
Jn 7:17 If anyone chooses to do *G* will,
10:36 'I am *G* Son'? Do not believe me
Ro 2: 3 think you will escape *G* judgment?
2: 4 not realizing that *G* kindness leads
3: 3 lack of faith nullify *G* faithfulness?
7:22 in my inner being I delight in *G* law
9:16 or effort, but on *G* mercy.
11:29 for *G* gifts and his call are
12: 2 and approve what *G* will is—
12:13 Share with *G* people who are
13: 6 for the authorities are *G* servants,
1Co 7:19 Keeping *G* commands is what
2Co 6: 2 now is the time of *G* favor,
Eph 1: 7 riches of *G* grace that he lavished
1Th 4: 3 It is *G* will that you should be sanctified;
5:18 for this is *G* will for you
1Ti 6: 1 so that *G* name and our teaching
2Ti 2:19 *G* solid foundation stands firm,
Tit 1: 7 overseer is entrusted with *G* work,
Heb 1: 3 The Son is the radiance of *G* glory
9:24 now to appear for us in *G* presence.
11: 3 was formed at *G* command,
1Pe 2:15 For it is *G* will that
3: 4 which is of great worth in *G* sight.
1Jn 2: 5 *G* love is truly made complete

GODLESS
Job 20: 5 the joy of the *g* lasts but a moment.
1Ti 6:20 Turn away from *g* chatter

GODLINESS (GOD)
1Ti 2: 2 and quiet lives in all *g* and holiness.
4: 8 but *g* has value for all things,
6: 5 and who think that *g* is a means
6: 6 *g* with contentment is great gain.
6:11 and pursue righteousness, *g*, faith,
2Pe 1: 6 and to perseverance, *g*;

GODLY (GOD)
Ps 4: 3 that the LORD has set apart the *g*
2Co 7:10 *G* sorrow brings repentance that
11: 2 jealous for you with a *g* jealousy.
2Ti 3:12 everyone who wants to live a *g* life
2Pe 3:11 You ought to live holy and *g* lives

GODS (GOD)
Ex 20: 3 "You shall have no other *g*
Dt 5: 7 "You shall have no other *g*
1Ch 16:26 For all the *g* of the nations are idols
Ps 82: 6 "I said, 'You are "*g*";
Jn 10:34 have said you are *g*'? If he called
Ac 19:26 He says that man-made *g* are no *g*

GOG
Eze 38:18 When *G* attacks the land of Israel,
Rev 20: 8 *G* and Magog—to gather them

GOLD
1Ki 20: 3 'Your silver and *g* are mine,
Job 22:25 then the Almighty will be your *g*,
23:10 tested me, I will come forth as *g*.
28:15 cannot be bought with the finest *g*,
31:24 "If I have put my trust in *g*
Ps 19:10 They are more precious than *g*,
119:127 more than *g*, more than pure *g*,
Pr 3:14 and yields better returns than *g*.
22: 1 esteemed is better than silver or *g*.
Hag 2: 8 The silver is mine and the *g* is mine
Mt 2:11 and presented him with gifts of *g*
Rev 3:18 to buy from me *g* refined in the fire,

GOLGOTHA*
Mt 27:33 to a place called *G* (which means
Mk 15:22 to the place called *G* (which means
Jn 19:17 (which in Aramaic is called *G*).

GOLIATH
Philistine giant killed by David (1Sa 17; 21:9).

GOMORRAH
Ge 19:24 sulfur on Sodom and *G*—
Mt 10:15 and *G* on the day of judgment
2Pe 2: 6 and *G* by burning them to ashes,
Jude : 7 *G* and the surrounding towns gave

GOOD
Ge 1: 4 God saw that the light was *g*,
1:10 And God saw that it was *g*.
1:12 And God saw that it was *g*.
1:18 And God saw that it was *g*.
1:21 And God saw that it was *g*.
1:25 And God saw that it was *g*.
1:31 he had made, and it was very *g*.
2: 9 and the tree of the knowledge of *g*
2: 9 pleasing to the eye and *g* for food.
2:18 "It is not *g* for the man to be alone.
3:22 become like one of us, knowing *g*
50:20 but God intended it for *g*
2Ch 7: 3 "He is *g*; / his love endures
31:20 doing what was *g* and right
Job 2:10 Shall we accept *g* from God,
Ps 14: 1 there is no one who does *g*.
34: 8 Taste and see that the LORD is *g*;
34:14 Turn from evil and do *g*;
37: 3 Trust in the LORD and do *g*;
37:27 Turn from evil and do *g*;
52: 9 for your name is *g*.
53: 3 there is no one who does *g*,
84:11 no *g* thing does he withhold
86: 5 You are forgiving and *g*, O Lord
100: 5 For the LORD is *g* and his love
103: 5 satisfies your desires with *g* things,
112: 5 *G* will come to him who is
119: 68 You are *g*, and what you do is *g*;
133: 1 How *g* and pleasant it is
145: 9 The LORD is *g* to all;
147: 1 How *g* it is to sing praises
Pr 3: 4 you will win favor and a *g* name
3:27 Do not withhold *g*
11:27 He who seeks *g* finds *g* will,
13:22 A *g* man leaves an inheritance
14:22 those who plan what is *g* find love
15: 3 on the wicked and the *g*.
15:23 and how *g* is a timely word!
15:30 *g* news gives health to the bones.
17:22 A cheerful heart is *g* medicine,
18:22 He who finds a wife finds what is *g*
19: 2 It is not *g* to have zeal
22: 1 A *g* name is more desirable
31:12 She brings him *g*, not harm,
Ecc 12:14 whether it is *g* or evil.
Isa 5:20 Woe to those who call evil *g*
40: 9 You who bring *g* tidings
52: 7 the feet of those who bring *g* news,
61: 1 me to preach *g* news to the poor.
Jer 6:16 ask where the *g* way is,
13:23 Neither can you do *g*

Jer 32:39 the *g* of their children after them.
Eze 34:14 I will tend them in a *g* pasture,
Mic 6: 8 has showed you, O man, what is *g*.
Na 1:15 the feet of one who brings *g* news,
Mt 5:45 sun to rise on the evil and the *g*,
7:11 Father in heaven give *g* gifts
7:17 Likewise every *g* tree bears *g* fruit,
7:18 A *g* tree cannot bear bad fruit,
12:35 The *g* man brings *g* things out
13: 8 Still other seed fell on *g* soil,
13:24 is like a man who sowed *g* seed
13:48 and collected the *g* fish in baskets,
19:17 "There is only One who is *g*.
22:10 both *g* and bad, and the wedding
25:21 'Well done, *g* and faithful servant!
Mk 1:15 Repent and believe the *g* news!"
3: 4 lawful on the Sabbath: to do *g*
4: 8 Still other seed fell on *g* soil.
8:36 What *g* is it for a man
10:18 "No one is *g*— except God alone.
16:15 preach the *g* news to all creation.
Lk 2:10 I bring you *g* news
3: 9 does not produce *g* fruit will be
6:27 do *g* to those who hate you,
6:43 nor does a bad tree bear *g* fruit.
6:45 The *g* man brings *g* things out
8: 8 Still other seed fell on *g* soil.
9:25 What *g* is it for a man
14:34 "Salt is *g*, but if it loses its saltiness,
18:19 "No one is *g*— except God alone.
19:17 " 'Well done, my *g* servant!'
Jn 10:11 "I am the *g* shepherd.
Ro 3:12 there is no one who does *g*,
7:12 is holy, righteous and *g*.
7:16 want to do, I agree that the law is *g*.
7:18 I have the desire to do what is *g*,
8:28 for the *g* of those who love him,
10:15 feet of those who bring *g* news!"
12: 2 his *g*, pleasing and perfect will.
12: 9 Hate what is evil; cling to what is *g*.
13: 4 For he is God's servant to do you *g*
16:19 you to be wise about what is *g*,
1Co 7: 1 It is *g* for a man not to marry.
10:24 should seek his own *g*, but the *g*
15:33 Bad company corrupts *g* character
2Co 9: 8 you will abound in every *g* work.
Gal 4:18 provided the purpose is *g*,
6: 9 us not become weary in doing *g*,
6:10 as we have opportunity, let us do *g*
Eph 2:10 in Christ Jesus to do *g* works,
6: 8 everyone for whatever *g* he does,
Php 1: 6 that he who began a *g* work
Col 1:10 bearing fruit in every *g* work,
1Th 5:21 Hold on to the *g*.
1Ti 3: 7 have a *g* reputation with outsiders,
4: 4 For everything God created is *g*,
6:12 Fight the *g* fight of the faith.
6:18 them to do *g*, to be rich in *g* deeds,
2Ti 3:17 equipped for every *g* work.
4: 7 I have fought the *g* fight, I have
Tit 1: 8 loves what is *g*, who is
2: 7 an example by doing what is *g*.
2:14 his very own, eager to do what is *g*.
Heb 5:14 to distinguish *g* from evil.
10:24 on toward love and *g* deeds.
12:10 but God disciplines us for our *g*,
13:16 do not forget to do *g* and to share
Jas 4:17 who knows the *g* he ought to do
1Pe 2: 3 you have tasted that the Lord is *g*.
2:12 Live such *g* lives among the pagans
2:18 not only to those who are *g*
3:17 to suffer for doing *g*

GOODS
Ecc 5:11 As *g* increase,

GORGE
Pr 23:20 or *g* themselves on meat,

GOSHEN
Ge 45:10 You shall live in the region of *G*
Ex 8:22 differently with the land of *G*,

GOSPEL
Ro 1:16 I am not ashamed of the *g*,
15:16 duty of proclaiming the *g* of God,
15:20 to preach the *g* where Christ was
1Co 1:17 to preach the *g*— not with words
9:12 rather than hinder the *g* of Christ.
9:14 who preach the *g* should receive
9:16 Woe to me if I do not preach the *g*!
15: 1 you of the *g* I preached to you,
15: 2 By this *g* you are saved,
2Co 4: 4 light of the *g* of the glory of Christ,
9:13 your confession of the *g*
Gal 1: 7 a different *g*— which is really no *g*
Eph 6:15 comes from the *g* of peace.
Php 1:27 in a manner worthy of the *g*
Col 1:23 This is the *g* that you heard
1Th 2: 4 by God to be entrusted with the *g*.
2Th 1: 8 do not obey the *g* of our Lord Jesus
2Ti 1:10 immortality to light through the *g*.
Rev 14: 6 he had the eternal *g* to proclaim

GOSSIP*
Pr 11:13 A *g* betrays a confidence,
16:28 and a *g* separates close friends.
18: 8 of a *g* are like choice morsels;
20:19 A *g* betrays a confidence;
26:20 without *g* a quarrel dies down.
26:22 of a *g* are like choice morsels;
2Co 12:20 slander, *g*, arrogance and disorder.

GOVERN (GOVERNMENT)
Ge 1:16 the greater light to *g* the day
Job 34:17 Can he who hates justice *g*?
Ro 12: 8 it is leadership, let him *g* diligently;

GOVERNMENT (GOVERN)
Isa 9: 6 and the *g* will be on his shoulders.

GRACE* (GRACIOUS)
Ps 45: 2 lips have been anointed with *g*,
Pr 1: 9 will be a garland to *g* your head
3:22 an ornament to *g* your neck.
3:34 but gives *g* to the humble.
4: 9 She will set a garland of *g*
Isa 26:10 Though *g* is shown to the wicked,
Jnh 2: 8 forfeit the *g* that could be theirs.
Zec 12:10 of Jerusalem a spirit of *g*
Lk 2:40 and the *g* of God was upon him.
Jn 1:14 who came from the Father, full of *g*
1:16 of his *g* we have all received one
1:17 *g* and truth came through Jesus
Ac 4:33 and much *g* was upon them all.
6: 8 a man full of God's *g* and power,
11:23 saw the evidence of the *g* of God,
13:43 them to continue in the *g* of God.
14: 3 message of his *g* by enabling them
14:26 they had been committed to the *g*
15:11 We believe it is through the *g*
15:40 by the brothers to the *g* of the Lord
18:27 to those who by *g* had believed.
20:24 testifying to the gospel of God's *g*.
20:32 to God and to the word of his *g*,
Ro 1: 5 we received *g* and apostleship
1: 7 *G* and peace to you
3:24 and are justified freely by his *g*
4:16 be by *g* and may be guaranteed
5: 2 access by faith into this *g*
5:15 came by the *g* of the one man,
5:15 how much more did God's *g*
5:17 God's abundant provision of *g*
5:20 where sin increased, *g* increased all
5:21 also *g* might reign
6: 1 on sinning so that *g* may increase?
6:14 you are not under law, but under *g*.
6:15 we are not under law but under *g*?
11: 5 there is a remnant chosen by *g*.
11: 6 if by *g*, then it is no longer by works
11: 6 if it were, *g* would no longer be *g*.
12: 3 For by the *g* given me I say
12: 6 according to the *g* given us.
15:15 because of the *g* God gave me
16:20 The *g* of our Lord Jesus be
1Co 1: 3 *G* and peace to you
1: 4 of his *g* given you in Christ Jesus.
3:10 By the *g* God has given me,
15:10 But by the *g* of God I am what I am
15:10 but the *g* of God that was with me.
15:10 his *g* to me was not without effect.
16:23 The *g* of the Lord Jesus be with you
2Co 1: 2 *G* and peace to you
1:12 wisdom but according to God's *g*.
4:15 so that the *g* that is reaching more
6: 1 not to receive God's *g* in vain.
8: 1 to know about the *g* that God has
8: 6 also to completion this act of *g*
8: 7 also excel in this *g* of giving.
8: 9 For you know the *g*
9: 8 able to make all *g* abound to you,
9:14 of the surpassing *g* God has given
12: 9 "My *g* is sufficient for you,
13:14 May the *g* of the Lord Jesus Christ,
Gal 1: 3 *G* and peace to you
1: 6 the one who called you by the *g*
1:15 from birth and called me by his *g*,
2: 9 when they recognized the *g* given
2:21 I do not set aside the *g* of God,
3:18 God in his *g* gave it to Abraham
5: 4 you have fallen away from *g*.
6:18 The *g* of our Lord Jesus Christ be
Eph 1: 2 *G* and peace to you
1: 6 to the praise of his glorious *g*,
1: 7 riches of God's *g* that he lavished
2: 5 it is by *g* you have been saved.
2: 7 the incomparable riches of his *g*,
2: 8 For it is by *g* you have been saved,
Eph 3: 2 of God's *g* that was given to me
3: 7 by the gift of God's *g* given me
3: 8 God's people, this *g* was given me:
4: 7 to each one of us *g* has been given
6:24 *G* to all who love our Lord Jesus
Php 1: 2 *G* and peace to you
1: 7 all of you share in God's *g* with me.
4:23 The *g* of the Lord Jesus Christ be
Col 1: 2 *G* and peace to you
1: 6 understood God's *g* in all its truth.
4: 6 conversation be always full of *g*,
4:18 *G* be with you.
1Th 1: 1 and the Lord Jesus Christ: *G*
5:28 The *g* of our Lord Jesus Christ be
2Th 1: 2 *G* and peace to you
1:12 according to the *g* of our God
2:16 and by his *g* gave us eternal
3:18 The *g* of our Lord Jesus Christ be
1Ti 1: 2 my true son in the faith: *G*,
1:14 The *g* of our Lord was poured out
6:21 *G* be with you.
2Ti 1: 2 To Timothy, my dear son: *G*,
1: 9 This *g* was given us in Christ Jesus
1: 9 because of his own purpose and *g*.
2: 1 be strong in the *g* that is
4:22 *G* be with you.
Tit 1: 4 *G* and peace from God the Father
2:11 For the *g* of God that brings
3: 7 having been justified by his *g*,
3:15 *G* be with you all.
Phm : 3 *G* to you and peace
:25 The *g* of the Lord Jesus Christ be
Heb 2: 9 that by the *g* of God he might taste
4:16 find *g* to help us in our time of need
4:16 the throne of *g* with confidence,
10:29 and who has insulted the Spirit of *g*
12:15 See to it that no one misses the *g*
13: 9 hearts to be strengthened by *g*,
13:25 *G* be with you all.
Jas 4: 6 but gives *g* to the humble."
4: 6 But he gives us more *g*. That is why
1Pe 1: 2 *G* and peace be yours in abundance
1:10 who spoke of the *g* that was
1:13 fully on the *g* to be given you
4:10 faithfully administering God's *g*
5: 5 but gives *g* to the humble."
5:10 the God of all *g*, who called you
5:12 and testifying that this is the true *g*
2Pe 1: 2 *G* and peace be yours in abundance
3:18 But grow in the *g* and knowledge
2Jn : 3 and will be with us forever: *G*,
Jude : 4 who change the *g* of our God
Rev 1: 4 *G* and peace to you
22:21 The *g* of the Lord Jesus be

GRACIOUS (GRACE)
Ex 34: 6 the compassionate and *g* God,
Nu 6:25 and be *g* to you;
Ne 9:17 But you are a forgiving God, *g*
Ps 67: 1 May God be *g* to us and bless us
Pr 22:11 a pure heart and whose speech is *g*
Isa 30:18 Yet the LORD longs to be *g* to you

GRAIN
Lev 2: 1 When someone brings a *g* offering
Lk 17:35 women will be grinding *g* together;
1Co 9: 9 ox while it is treading out the *g*."

GRANDCHILDREN (CHILD)
1Ti 5: 4 But if a widow has children or *g*,

GRANDMOTHER (MOTHER)
2Ti 1: 5 which first lived in your *g* Lois

GRANT (GRANTED)
Ps 20: 5 May the LORD *g* all your requests
51:12 *g* me a willing spirit, to sustain me.

GRANTED (GRANT)
Pr 10:24 what the righteous desire will be *g*.
Mt 15:28 great faith! Your request is *g*."
Php 1:29 For it has been *g* to you on behalf

GRAPES
Nu 13:23 branch bearing a single cluster of *g*.
Jer 31:29 'The fathers have eaten sour *g*,
Eze 18: 2 " 'The fathers eat sour *g*,
Mt 7:16 Do people pick *g* from thornbushes
Rev 14:18 and gather the clusters of *g*

GRASPED
Php 2: 6 with God something to be *g*,

GRASS
Ps 103: 15 As for man, his days are like *g*,
Isa 40: 6 "All men are like *g*,
Mt 6:30 If that is how God clothes the *g*
1Pe 1:24 "All men are like *g*,

GRASSHOPPERS
Nu 13:33 We seemed like *g* in our own eyes,

GRATIFY* (GRATITUDE)
Ro 13:14 think about how to *g* the desires
Gal 5:16 and you will not *g* the desires

GRATITUDE (GRATIFY)
Col 3:16 and spiritual songs with *g*

GRAVE (GRAVES)
Nu 19:16 who touches a human bone or a *g*,
Dt 34: 6 day no one knows where his *g* is.
Ps 5: 9 Their throat is an open *g*;
49:15 will redeem my life from the *g*;
Pr 7:27 Her house is a highway to the *g*,
Hos 13:14 Where, O *g*, is your destruction?
Jn 11:44 "Take off the *g* clothes
Ac 2:27 you will not abandon me to the *g*,

GRAVES (GRAVE)
Eze 37:12 I am going to open your *g*
Jn 5:28 are in their *g* will hear his voice
Ro 3:13 "Their throats are open *g*;

GRAY
Pr 16:31 *G* hair is a crown of splendor;
20:29 *g* hair the splendor of the old.

GREAT (GREATER GREATEST GREATNESS)
Ge 12: 2 I will make your name *g*,
12: 2 "I will make you into a *g* nation
Ex 32:11 out of Egypt with *g* power
Nu 14:19 In accordance with your *g* love,
Dt 4:32 so *g* as this ever happened,
10:17 the *g* God, mighty and awesome,
29:28 in *g* wrath the LORD uprooted
Jos 7: 9 do for your own *g* name?"
Jdg 16: 5 you the secret of his *g* strength
2Sa 7:22 "How *g* you are, O Sovereign
22:36 you stoop down to make me *g*.
24:14 for his mercy is *g*; but do not let me
1Ch 17:19 made known all these *g* promises.
Ps 18:35 you stoop down to make me *g*.
19:11 in keeping them there is *g* reward.
47: 2 the *g* King over all the earth!
57:10 For *g* is your love, reaching
68:11 and *g* was the company
89: 1 of the LORD's *g* love forever;
103: 11 so *g* is his love for those who fear
107: 43 consider the *g* love of the LORD.
108: 4 For *g* is your love, higher
117: 2 For *g* is his love toward us,
119:165 *G* peace have they who love your
145: 3 *G* is the LORD and most worthy
Pr 22: 1 is more desirable than *g* riches;
23:24 of a righteous man has *g* joy;
Isa 42:21 to make his law *g* and glorious.
Jer 27: 5 With my *g* power and outstretched
32:19 *g* are your purposes and mighty are
La 3:23 *g* is your faithfulness.
Da 9: 4 "O Lord, the *g* and awesome God,
Joel 2:11 The day of the LORD is *g*;
2:20 Surely he has done *g* things.
Zep 1:14 "The *g* day of the LORD is near—
Mal 1:11 My name will be *g*
4: 5 the prophet Elijah before that *g*
Mt 20:26 whoever wants to become *g*
Mk 10:43 whoever wants to become *g*
Lk 6:23 because *g* is your reward in heaven.
6:35 Then your reward will be *g*,
21:27 in a cloud with power and *g* glory.
Eph 1:19 and his incomparably *g* power
2: 4 But because of his *g* love for us,
1Ti 6: 6 with contentment is *g* gain.
Tit 2:13 glorious appearing of our *g* God
Heb 2: 3 if we ignore such a *g* salvation?
1Jn 3: 1 How *g* is the love the Father has
Rev 6:17 For the *g* day of their wrath has
20:11 Then I saw a *g* white throne

GREATER (GREAT)
Mt 11:11 there has not risen anyone *g*
12: 6 I tell you that one *g*
12:41 and now one *g* than Jonah is here.
12:42 now one *g* than Solomon is here.
Mk 12:31 There is no commandment *g*
Jn 1:50 You shall see *g* things than that."
3:30 He must become *g*; I must become
14:12 He will do even *g* things than these
15:13 *G* love has no one than this,
1Co 12:31 But eagerly desire the *g* gifts.
2Co 3:11 how much *g* is the glory
Heb 3: 3 the builder of a house has *g* honor
3: 3 worthy of *g* honor than Moses,
7: 7 lesser person is blessed by the *g*.
11:26 as of *g* value than the treasures
1Jn 3:20 For God is *g* than our hearts,
4: 4 is in you is *g* than the one who is

GREATEST (GREAT)
Mt 22:38 is the first and *g* commandment.
23:11 *g* among you will be your servant.
Lk 9:48 least among you all—he is the *g*."
1Co 13:13 But the *g* of these is love.

GREATNESS* (GREAT)
Ex 15: 7 In the *g* of your majesty
Dt 3:24 to show to your servant your *g*
32: 3 Oh, praise the *g* of our God!
1Ch 29:11 O LORD, is the *g* and the power
2Ch 9: 6 half the *g* of your wisdom was told
Est 10: 2 account of the *g* of Mordecai
Ps 145: 3 his *g* no one can fathom.
150: 2 praise him for his surpassing *g*.
Isa 63: 1 forward in the *g* of his strength?
Eze 38:23 I will show my *g* and my holiness,
Da 4:22 your *g* has grown until it reaches
5:18 and *g* and glory and splendor.
7:27 and *g* of the kingdoms
Mic 5: 4 will live securely, for then his *g*
Lk 9:43 And they were all amazed at the *g*
Php 3: 8 compared to the surpassing *g*

GREED (GREEDY)
Lk 12:15 on your guard against all kinds of *g*
Ro 1:29 kind of wickedness, evil, *g*
Eph 5: 3 or of any kind of impurity, or of *g*,
Col 3: 5 evil desires and *g*, which is idolatry
2Pe 2:14 experts in *g*— an accursed brood!

GREEDY (GREED)
Pr 15:27 A *g* man brings trouble
1Co 6:10 nor thieves nor the *g* nor drunkards
Eph 5: 5 No immoral, impure or *g* person—
1Pe 5: 2 not *g* for money, but eager to serve;

GREEK (GREEKS)
Gal 3:28 There is neither Jew nor *G*,
Col 3:11 Here there is no *G* or Jew,

GREEKS (GREEK)
1Co 1:22 miraculous signs and *G* look

GREEN
Ps 23: 2 makes me lie down in *g* pastures,

GREW (GROW)
Lk 1:80 And the child *g* and became strong
2:52 And Jesus *g* in wisdom and stature,
Ac 9:31 by the Holy Spirit, it *g* in numbers,
16: 5 in the faith and *g* daily in numbers.

GRIEF (GRIEFS GRIEVANCES GRIEVE GRIEVED)
Ps 10:14 O God, do see trouble and *g*;
Pr 10: 1 but a foolish son *g* to his mother.
14:13 and joy may end in *g*.
17:21 To have a fool for a son brings *g*;
Ecc 1:18 the more knowledge, the more *g*.
La 3:32 Though he brings *g*, he will show
Jn 16:20 but your *g* will turn to joy.
1Pe 1: 6 had to suffer *g* in all kinds of trials.

GRIEFS* (GRIEF)
1Ti 6:10 pierced themselves with many *g*.

GRIEVANCES* (GRIEF)
Col 3:13 forgive whatever *g* you may have

GRIEVE (GRIEF)
Eph 4:30 do not *g* the Holy Spirit of God,
1Th 4:13 or to *g* like the rest of men,

GRIEVED (GRIEF)
Isa 63:10 and *g* his Holy Spirit.

GRINDING
Lk 17:35 women will be *g* grain together;

GROAN (GROANING GROANS)
Ro 8:23 *g* inwardly as we wait eagerly
2Co 5: 4 For while we are in this tent, we *g*

GROANING (GROAN)
Ex 2:24 God heard their *g* and he
Eze 21: 7 'Why are you *g*?' you shall say,
Ro 8:22 that the whole creation has been *g*

GROANS (GROAN)
Ro 8:26 with *g* that words cannot express.

GROUND
Ge 1:10 God called the dry *g* "land,"
3:17 "Cursed is the *g* because of you;
4:10 blood cries out to me from the *g*.
Ex 3: 5 where you are standing is holy *g*."
15:19 walked through the sea on dry *g*.
Isa 53: 2 and like a root out of dry *g*.
Mt 10:29 fall to the *g* apart from the will
25:25 and hid your talent in the *g*.
Jn 8: 6 to write on the *g* with his finger.
Eph 6:13 you may be able to stand your *g*,

GROW (FULL-GROWN GREW GROWING GROWS)
Pr 13:11 by little makes it *g*.
20:13 not love sleep or you will *g* poor;
Isa 40:31 they will run and not *g* weary,
Mt 6:28 See how the lilies of the field *g*.
1Co 3: 6 watered it, but God made it *g*.
2Pe 3:18 But *g* in the grace and knowledge

GROWING (GROW)
Col 1: 6 this gospel is bearing fruit and *g*,
1:10 *g* in the knowledge of God,
2Th 1: 3 your faith is *g* more and more,

GROWS (GROW)
Eph 4:16 *g* and builds itself up in love,
Col 2:19 *g* as God causes it to grow.

GRUMBLE (GRUMBLED GRUMBLERS GRUMBLING)
1Co 10:10 And do not *g*, as some of them did
Jas 5: 9 Don't *g* against each other,

GRUMBLED (GRUMBLE)
Ex 15:24 So the people *g* against Moses,
Nu 14:29 and who has *g* against me.

GRUMBLERS* (GRUMBLE)
Jude :16 These men are *g* and faultfinders;

GRUMBLING (GRUMBLE)
Jn 6:43 "Stop *g* among yourselves,"
1Pe 4: 9 to one another without *g*.

GUARANTEE (GUARANTEEING)
Heb 7:22 Jesus has become the *g*

GUARANTEEING* (GUARANTEE)
2Co 1:22 as a deposit, *g* what is to come.
5: 5 as a deposit, *g* what is to come.
Eph 1:14 who is a deposit *g* our inheritance

GUARD (GUARDS)
1Sa 2: 9 He will *g* the feet of his saints,
Ps 141: 3 Set a *g* over my mouth, O LORD;
Pr 2:11 and understanding will *g* you.
4:13 *g* it well, for it is your life.
4:23 Above all else, *g* your heart,
7: 2 *g* my teachings as the apple
Isa 52:12 the God of Israel will be your rear *g*
Mk 13:33 Be on *g*! Be alert! You do not know
Lk 12: 1 "Be on your *g* against the yeast
12:15 Be on your *g* against all kinds
Ac 20:31 So be on your *g*! Remember that
1Co 16:13 Be on your *g*; stand firm in the faith
Php 4: 7 will *g* your hearts and your minds
1Ti 6:20 *g* what has been entrusted
2Ti 1:14 *G* the good deposit that was

GUARDS (GUARD)
Pr 13: 3 He who *g* his lips *g* his life,
19:16 who obeys instructions *g* his life,
21:23 He who *g* his mouth and his tongue
22: 5 he who *g* his soul stays far

GUIDANCE (GUIDE)
Pr 1: 5 and let the discerning get *g*—
11:14 For lack of *g* a nation falls,
24: 6 for waging war you need *g*,

GUIDE (GUIDANCE GUIDED GUIDES)
Ex 13:21 of cloud to *g* them on their way
15:13 In your strength you will *g* them
Ne 9:19 cease to *g* them on their path,
Ps 25: 5 *g* me in your truth and teach me,
43: 3 let them *g* me;
48:14 he will be our *g* even to the end.
67: 4 and *g* the nations of the earth.
73:24 You *g* me with your counsel,
139: 10 even there your hand will *g* me,
Pr 4:11 I *g* you in the way of wisdom
6:22 When you walk, they will *g* you;
Isa 58:11 The LORD will *g* you always;
Jn 16:13 comes, he will *g* you into all truth.

GUIDED (GUIDE)
Ps 107: 30 he *g* them to their desired haven.

GUIDES (GUIDE)
Ps 23: 3 He *g* me in paths of righteousness
25: 9 He *g* the humble in what is right
Pr 11: 3 The integrity of the upright *g* them,
16:23 A wise man's heart *g* his mouth,
Mt 23:16 "Woe to you, blind *g*! You say,
23:24 You blind *g*! You strain out a gnat

GUILT (GUILTY)
Lev 5:15 It is a *g* offering.
Ps 32: 5 the *g* of my sin.
38: 4 My *g* has overwhelmed me
Isa 6: 7 your *g* is taken away and your sin
Jer 2:22 the stain of your *g* is still before me
Eze 18:19 'Why does the son not share the *g*

GUILTY (GUILT)
Ex 34: 7 does not leave the *g* unpunished;
Mk 3:29 Spirit will never be forgiven; he is *g*
Jn 8:46 Can any of you prove me *g* of sin?
1Co 11:27 in an unworthy manner will be *g*
Heb 10: 2 and would no longer have felt *g*
10:22 to cleanse us from a *g* conscience
Jas 2:10 at just one point is *g* of breaking all

HABAKKUK*
Prophet to Judah (Hab 1:1; 3:1).

HABIT
1Ti 5:13 they get into the *h* of being idle
Heb 10:25 as some are in the *h* of doing,

HADAD
Edomite adversary of Solomon (1Ki 11:14-25).

HADES*
Mt 16:18 the gates of *H* will not overcome it.
Rev 1:18 And I hold the keys of death and *H*
6: 8 *H* was following close behind him.
20:13 and *H* gave up the dead that were
20:14 *H* were thrown into the lake of fire.

HAGAR
Servant of Sarah, wife of Abraham, mother of Ishmael (Ge 16:1-6; 25:12). Driven away by Sarah while pregnant (Ge 16:5-16); after birth of Isaac (Ge 21:9-21; Gal 4:21-31).

HAGGAI*
Post-exilic prophet who encouraged rebuilding of the temple (Ezr 5:1; 6:14; Hag 1-2).

HAIL
Ex 9:19 the *h* will fall on every man
Rev 8: 7 and there came *h* and fire mixed

HAIR (HAIRS HAIRY)
Lev 19:27 " 'Do not cut the *h* at the sides
Nu 6: 5 he must let the *h* of his head grow
Pr 16:31 Gray *h* is a crown of splendor;
20:29 gray *h* the splendor of the old.
Lk 7:44 and wiped them with her *h*.
21:18 But not a *h* of your head will perish
Jn 11: 2 and wiped his feet with her *h*.
12: 3 and wiped his feet with her *h*.
1Co 11: 6 for a woman to have her *h* cut
11: 6 she should have her *h* cut off;
11:14 that if a man has long *h*,
11:15 For long *h* is given to her
11:15 but that if a woman has long *h*,
1Ti 2: 9 not with braided *h* or gold or pearls
1Pe 3: 3 as braided *h* and the wearing
Rev 1:14 and *h* were white like wool,

HAIRS (HAIR)
Mt 10:30 even the very *h* of your head are all
Lk 12: 7 the very *h* of your head are all

HAIRY (HAIR)
Ge 27:11 "But my brother Esau is a *h* man,

HALF
Ex 30:13 This *h* shekel is an offering
Jos 8:33 *H* of the people stood in front
1Ki 3:25 give *h* to one and *h* to the other."
10: 7 Indeed, not even *h* was told me;
Est 5: 3 Even up to *h* the kingdom,
Da 7:25 him for a time, times and *h* a time.
Mk 6:23 up to *h* my kingdom."

HALF-TRIBE (TRIBE)
Nu 32:33 and the *h* of Manasseh son

HALLELUJAH*
Rev 19: 1, 3, 4, 6.

HALLOWED* (HOLY)
Mt 6: 9 *h* be your name,
Lk 11: 2 *h* be your name,

HALT
Job 38:11 here is where your proud waves *h*'?

HALTER*
Pr 26: 3 for the horse, a *h* for the donkey,

HAM
Son of Noah (Ge 5:32; 1Ch 1:4), father of Canaan (Ge 9:18; 10:6-20; 1Ch 1:8-16). Saw Noah's nakedness (Ge 9:20-27).

HAMAN
Agagite nobleman honored by Xerxes (Est 3:1-2). Plotted to exterminate the Jews because of Mordecai (Est 3:3-15). Forced to honor Mordecai (Est 5-6). Plot exposed by Esther (Est 5:1-8; 7:1-8). Hanged (Est 7:9-10).

HAMPERED*
Pr 4:12 you walk, your steps will not be *h*;

HAND (HANDED HANDFUL HANDS OPENHANDED)
Ge 24: 2 "Put your *h* under my thigh.
47:29 put your *h* under my thigh
Ex 13: 3 out of it with a mighty *h*.
15: 6 Your right *h*, O LORD,
33:22 and cover you with my *h*
Dt 12: 7 in everything you have put your *h*
1Ki 8:42 and your mighty *h* and your
13: 4 But the *h* he stretched out
1Ch 29:14 you only what comes from your *h*.
29:16 it comes from your *h*, and all
2Ch 6:15 with your *h* you have fulfilled it—
Ne 4:17 materials did their work with one *h*
Job 40: 4 I put my *h* over my mouth.
Ps 16: 8 Because he is at my right *h*,
32: 4 your *h* was heavy upon me;
37:24 the LORD upholds him with his *h*.
44: 3 it was your right *h*, your arm,
45: 9 at your right *h* is the royal bride
63: 8 your right *h* upholds me.
75: 8 In the *h* of the LORD is a cup
91: 7 ten thousand at your right *h*,
98: 1 his right *h* and his holy arm
109: 31 at the right *h* of the needy one,
110: 1 "Sit at my right *h*
137: 5 may my right *h* forget ⌊its skill⌋.
139: 10 even there your *h* will guide me,
145: 16 You open your *h*
Pr 27:16 or grasping oil with the *h*.
Ecc 5:15 that he can carry in his *h*.
9:10 Whatever your *h* finds to do,
Isa 11: 8 the young child put his *h*
40:12 the waters in the hollow of his *h*,
41:13 who takes hold of your right *h*
44: 5 still another will write on his *h*,
48:13 My own *h* laid the foundations
64: 8 we are all the work of your *h*.
La 3: 3 he has turned his *h* against me
Da 10:10 *h* touched me and set me trembling
Jnh 4:11 people who cannot tell their right *h*
Hab 3: 4 rays flashed from his *h*,
Mt 5:30 if your right *h* causes you to sin,
6: 3 know what your right *h* is doing,
12:10 a man with a shriveled *h* was there.
18: 8 If your *h* or your foot causes you
22:44 "Sit at my right *h*
26:64 at the right *h* of the Mighty One
Mk 3: 1 a man with a shriveled *h* was there.
9:43 If your *h* causes you to sin, cut it off
12:36 "Sit at my right *h*
16:19 and he sat at the right *h* of God.
Lk 6: 6 there whose right *h* was shriveled.
20:42 "Sit at my right *h*
22:69 at the right *h* of the mighty God."
Jn 10:28 one can snatch them out of my *h*.
20:27 Reach out your *h* and put it
Ac 7:55 Jesus standing at the right *h* of God
1Co 12:15 I am not a *h*, I do not belong
Heb 1:13 "Sit at my right *h*
Rev 13:16 to receive a mark on his right *h*

HANDED (HAND)
Da 7:25 The saints will be *h* over to him
1Ti 1:20 whom I have *h* over to Satan

HANDFUL (HAND)
Ecc 4: 6 Better one *h* with tranquillity

HANDLE (HANDLES)
Col 2:21 "Do not *h*! Do not taste! Do not

HANDLES (HANDLE)
2Ti 2:15 who correctly *h* the word of truth.

HANDS (HAND)
Ge 27:22 but the *h* are the *h* of Esau."
Ex 17:11 As long as Moses held up his *h*,
29:10 his sons shall lay their *h* on its head
Dt 6: 8 Tie them as symbols on your *h*
Jdg 7: 6 lapped with their *h* to their mouths.
2Ki 11:12 and the people clapped their *h*
2Ch 6: 4 who with his *h* has fulfilled what he
Ps 22:16 they have pierced my *h*
24: 4 He who has clean *h* and a pure
31: 5 Into your *h* I commit my spirit;
31:15 My times are in your *h*;
47: 1 Clap your *h*, all you nations;
63: 4 and in your name I will lift up my *h*
Pr 10: 4 Lazy *h* make a man poor,
21:25 because his *h* refuse to work.
31:13 and works with eager *h*.
31:20 and extends her *h* to the needy.
Ecc 10:18 if his *h* are idle, the house leaks.
Isa 35: 3 Strengthen the feeble *h*,
49:16 you on the palms of my *h*;
55:12 will clap their *h*.
65: 2 All day long I have held out my *h*
La 3:41 Let us lift up our hearts and our *h*
Lk 23:46 into your *h* I commit my spirit."
Ac 6: 6 who prayed and laid their *h*
8:18 at the laying on of the apostles' *h*,
13: 3 they placed their *h* on them
19: 6 When Paul placed his *h* on them,
28: 8 placed his *h* on him and healed him
1Th 4:11 and to work with your *h*,
1Ti 2: 8 to lift up holy *h* in prayer,
4:14 body of elders laid their *h* on you.
5:22 hasty in the laying on of *h*,
2Ti 1: 6 you through the laying on of my *h*.
Heb 6: 2 the laying on of *h*, the resurrection

HANDSOME*
Ge 39: 6 Now Joseph was well-built and *h*,
1Sa 16:12 a fine appearance and *h* features.
17:42 ruddy and *h*, and he despised him.
2Sa 14:25 praised for his *h* appearance
1Ki 1: 6 also very *h* and was born next
SS 1:16 *Beloved* How *h* you are, my lover!
Eze 23: 6 all of them *h* young men,
23:12 horsemen, all *h* young men.
23:23 with them, *h* young men,
Da 1: 4 without any physical defect, *h*,
Zec 11:13 the *h* price at which they priced me

HANG (HANGED HANGING HUNG)
Mt 22:40 and the Prophets *h* on these two

HANGED (HANG)
Mt 27: 5 Then he went away and *h* himself.

HANGING (HANG)
Ac 10:39 They killed him by *h* him on a tree,

HANNAH*
Wife of Elkanah, mother of Samuel (1Sa 1). Prayer at dedication of Samuel (1Sa 2:1-10). Blessed (1Sa 2:18-21).

HAPPIER (HAPPY)
Mt 18:13 he is *h* about that one sheep
1Co 7:40 she is *h* if she stays as she is—

HAPPINESS* (HAPPY)
Dt 24: 5 bring *h* to the wife he has married.
Est 8:16 For the Jews it was a time of *h*
Job 7: 7 my eyes will never see *h* again.
Ecc 2:26 gives wisdom, knowledge and *h*,
Mt 25:21 Come and share your master's *h*!'
25:23 Come and share your master's *h*!'

HAPPY* (HAPPIER HAPPINESS)
Ge 30:13 The women will call me *h*."
30:13 Then Leah said, "How *h* I am!
1Ki 4:20 they drank and they were *h*.
10: 8 How *h* your men must be!
10: 8 men must be! How *h* your officials,
2Ch 9: 7 How *h* your men must be!
9: 7 men must be! How *h* your officials,
Est 5: 9 Haman went out that day *h*
5:14 the king to the dinner and be *h*."
Ps 10: 6 I'll always be *h* and never have
68: 3 may they be *h* and joyful.
113: 9 as a *h* mother of children.
137: 8 *h* is he who repays you
Pr 15:13 A *h* heart makes the face cheerful,
Ecc 3:12 better for men than to be *h*
5:19 to accept his lot and be *h*
7:14 When times are good, be *h*;
11: 9 Be *h*, young man, while you are
Jnh 4: 6 Jonah was very *h* about the vine.
Zec 8:19 and glad occasions and *h* festivals
1Co 7:30 those who are *h*, as if they were not
2Co 7: 9 yet now I am *h*, not because you
7:13 delighted to see how *h* Titus was,
Jas 5:13 Is anyone *h*? Let him sing songs

HARD (HARDEN HARDENED HARDENING HARDENS HARDER HARDSHIP HARDSHIPS)
Ge 18:14 Is anything too *h* for the LORD?
1Ki 10: 1 came to test him with *h* questions.
Pr 14:23 All *h* work brings a profit,
Jer 32:17 Nothing is too *h* for you.
Zec 7:12 They made their hearts as *h* as flint
Mt 19:23 it is *h* for a rich man
Mk 10: 5 your hearts were *h* that Moses
Jn 6:60 disciples said, "This is a *h* teaching.

Ac 20:35 of *h* work we must help the weak,
26:14 It is *h* for you to kick
Ro 16:12 woman who has worked very *h*
1Co 4:12 We work *h* with our own hands.
2Co 6: 5 imprisonments and riots; in *h* work
1Th 5:12 to respect those who work *h*
Rev 2: 2 your *h* work and your

HARDEN (HARD)
Ex 4:21 I will *h* his heart so that he will not
Ps 95: 8 do not *h* your hearts as you did
Ro 9:18 he hardens whom he wants to *h*.
Heb 3: 8 do not *h* your hearts

HARDENED (HARD)
Ex 10:20 But the LORD *h* Pharaoh's heart,

HARDENING* (HARD)
Ro 11:25 Israel has experienced a *h* in part
Eph 4:18 in them due to the *h* of their hearts.

HARDENS* (HARD)
Pr 28:14 he who *h* his heart falls into trouble
Ro 9:18 and he *h* whom he wants to harden.

HARDER (HARD)
1Co 15:10 No, I worked *h* than all of them—
2Co 11:23 I have worked much *h*, been

HARDHEARTED* (HEART)
Dt 15: 7 do not be *h* or tightfisted

HARDSHIP (HARD)
Ro 8:35 Shall trouble or *h* or persecution
2Ti 2: 3 Endure *h* with us like a good
4: 5 endure *h*, do the work
Heb 12: 7 Endure *h* as discipline; God is

HARDSHIPS (HARD)
Ac 14:22 go through many *h* to enter
2Co 6: 4 in troubles, *h* and distresses;
12:10 in insults, in *h*, in persecutions,
Rev 2: 3 and have endured *h* for my name,

HARM (HARMS)
1Ch 16:22 do my prophets no *h*."
Ps 105: 15 do my prophets no *h*."
121: 6 the sun will not *h* you by day,
Pr 3:29 not plot *h* against your neighbor,
12:21 No *h* befalls the righteous,
31:12 She brings him good, not *h*,
Jer 10: 5 they can do no *h*
29:11 to prosper you and not to *h* you,
Ro 13:10 Love does no *h* to its neighbor.
1Co 11:17 for your meetings do more *h*
1Jn 5:18 the evil one cannot *h* him.

HARMONY*
Zec 6:13 there will be *h* between the two.'
Ro 12:16 Live in *h* with one another.
2Co 6:15 What *h* is there between Christ
1Pe 3: 8 live in *h* with one another;

HARMS* (HARM)
Pr 8:36 whoever fails to find me *h* himself;

HARP (HARPS)
Ge 4:21 the father of all who play the *h*
1Sa 16:23 David would take his *h* and play.
Ps 33: 2 Praise the LORD with the *h*;
98: 5 with the *h* and the sound of singing
150: 3 praise him with the *h* and lyre,
Rev 5: 8 Each one had a *h* and they were

HARPS (HARP)
Ps 137: 2 we hung our *h*,

HARSH
Pr 15: 1 but a *h* word stirs up anger.
Col 2:23 and their *h* treatment of the body,
3:19 and do not be *h* with them.
1Pe 2:18 but also to those who are *h*.
Jude :15 of all the *h* words ungodly sinners

HARVEST (HARVESTERS)
Ge 8:22 seedtime and *h*,
Ex 23:16 the Feast of *H* with the firstfruits
Dt 16:15 God will bless you in all your *h*
Pr 10: 5 during *h* is a disgraceful son.
Jer 8:20 "The *h* is past,
Joel 3:13 for the *h* is ripe.
Mt 9:37 *h* is plentiful but the workers are
Lk 10: 2 He told them, "The *h* is plentiful,
Jn 4:35 at the fields! They are ripe for *h*.
1Co 9:11 if we reap a material *h* from you?
2Co 9:10 the *h* of your righteousness.
Gal 6: 9 at the proper time we will reap a *h*
Heb 12:11 it produces a *h* of righteousness
Jas 3:18 in peace raise a *h* of righteousness.
Rev 14:15 for the *h* of the earth is ripe."

HARVESTERS (HARVEST)
Ru 2: 3 to glean in the fields behind the *h*.

HASTE (HASTEN HASTY)
Ex 12:11 it in *h*; it is the LORD's Passover.
Pr 21: 5 as surely as *h* leads to poverty.
29:20 Do you see a man who speaks in *h*?

HASTEN (HASTE)
Ps 70: 1 *H*, O God, to save me;
119: 60 I will *h* and not delay

HASTY* (HASTE)
Pr 19: 2 nor to be *h* and miss the way.
Ecc 5: 2 do not be *h* in your heart
1Ti 5:22 Do not be *h* in the laying

HATE (GOD-HATERS HATED HATES HATING HATRED)
Lev 19:17 "'Do not *h* your brother
Ps 5: 5 you *h* all who do wrong.
36: 2 too much to detect or *h* his sin.
45: 7 righteousness and *h* wickedness;
97:10 those who love the LORD *h* evil,
119: 104 therefore I *h* every wrong path.
119: 163 I *h* and abhor falsehood
139: 21 Do I not *h* those who *h* you,
Pr 8:13 To fear the LORD is to *h* evil;
9: 8 rebuke a mocker or he will *h* you;
13: 5 The righteous *h* what is false,
25:17 too much of you, and he will *h* you.
29:10 Bloodthirsty men *h* a man
Ecc 3: 8 a time to love and a time to *h*,
Isa 61: 8 I *h* robbery and iniquity.
Eze 35: 6 Since you did not *h* bloodshed,
Am 5:15 *H* evil, love good;
Mal 2:16 "I *h* divorce," says the LORD God
Mt 5:43 your neighbor and *h* your enemy.'
10:22 All men will *h* you because of me,
Lk 6:22 Blessed are you when men *h* you,
6:27 do good to those who *h* you,
14:26 does not *h* his father and mother,
Ro 12: 9 *H* what is evil; cling to what is good

HATED (HATE)
Mal 1: 3 loved Jacob, but Esau I have *h*,
Jn 15:18 keep in mind that it *h* me first.
Ro 9:13 "Jacob I loved, but Esau I *h*."
Eph 5:29 no one ever *h* his own body,
Heb 1: 9 righteousness and *h* wickedness;

HATES (HATE)
Pr 6:16 There are six things the LORD *h*,
13:24 He who spares the rod *h* his son,
15:27 but he who *h* bribes will live.
26:28 A lying tongue *h* those it hurts,
Jn 3:20 Everyone who does evil *h* the light,
12:25 while the man who *h* his life
1Jn 2: 9 *h* his brother is still in the darkness.
4:20 "I love God," yet *h* his brother,

HATING (HATE)
Jude :23 *h* even the clothing stained

HATRED (HATE)
Pr 10:12 *H* stirs up dissension,
15:17 than a fattened calf with *h*.
Jas 4: 4 with the world is *h* toward God?

HAUGHTY
Pr 6:17 detestable to him: / *h* eyes,
16:18 a *h* spirit before a fall.

HAVEN
Ps 107: 30 he guided them to their desired *h*.

HAY
1Co 3:12 costly stones, wood, *h* or straw,

HEAD (HEADS HOTHEADED)
Ge 3:15 he will crush your *h*,
Nu 6: 5 no razor may be used on his *h*.
Jdg 16:17 If my *h* were shaved, my strength
1Sa 9: 2 a *h* taller than any of the others.
2Sa 18: 9 Absalom's *h* got caught in the tree.
Ps 23: 5 You anoint my *h* with oil;
133: 2 is like precious oil poured on the *h*,
Pr 10: 6 Blessings crown the *h*
25:22 will heap burning coals on his *h*,
Isa 59:17 and the helmet of salvation on his *h*
Eze 33: 4 his blood will be on his own *h*.
Mt 8:20 of Man has no place to lay his *h*."
Jn 19: 2 crown of thorns and put it on his *h*.
Ro 12:20 will heap burning coals on his *h*."
1Co 11: 3 and the *h* of Christ is God.
11: 5 her *h* uncovered dishonors her *h*—
12:21 And the *h* cannot say to the feet,
Eph 1:22 him to be *h* over everything
5:23 For the husband is the *h* of the wife
Col 1:18 And he is the *h* of the body,
2Ti 4: 5 keep your *h* in all situations,
Rev 14:14 with a crown of gold on his *h*
19:12 and on his *h* are many crowns.

HEADS (HEAD)
Lev 26:13 you to walk with *h* held high.
Ps 22: 7 they hurl insults, shaking their *h*:
24: 7 Lift up your *h*, O you gates;
Isa 35:10 everlasting joy will crown their *h*.
51:11 everlasting joy will crown their *h*.
Mt 27:39 shaking their *h* and saying,
Lk 21:28 stand up and lift up your *h*,
Ac 18: 6 "Your blood be on your own *h*!
Rev 4: 4 and had crowns of gold on their *h*.

HEAL* (HEALED HEALING HEALS)
Nu 12:13 please *h* her!" The LORD replied
Dt 32:39 I have wounded and I will *h*,
2Ki 20: 5 and seen your tears; I will *h* you.
20: 8 the sign that the LORD will *h* me
2Ch 7:14 their sin and will *h* their land.
Job 5:18 he injures, but his hands also *h*.
Ps 6: 2 *h* me, for my bones are in agony.
41: 4 *h* me, for I have sinned against you
Ecc 3: 3 a time to kill and a time to *h*,
Isa 19:22 he will strike them and *h* them.
19:22 respond to their pleas and *h* them.
57:18 seen his ways, but I will *h* him;
57:19 "And I will *h* them."
Jer 17:14 *H* me, O LORD, and I will be
30:17 and *h* your wounds,'
33: 6 I will *h* my people and will let them
La 2:13 Who can *h* you?
Hos 5:13 not able to *h* your sores.
6: 1 but he will *h* us;
7: 1 whenever I would *h* Israel,
14: 4 "I will *h* their waywardness
Na 3:19 Nothing can *h* your wound;
Zec 11:16 or seek the young, or *h* the injured,
Mt 8: 7 said to him, "I will go and *h* him."
10: 1 to *h* every disease and sickness.
10: 8 *H* the sick, raise the dead,
12:10 "Is it lawful to *h* on the Sabbath?"
13:15 and turn, and I would *h* them.'
17:16 but they could not *h* him."
Mk 3: 2 if he would *h* him on the Sabbath.
6: 5 on a few sick people and *h* them.
Lk 4:23 to me: 'Physician, *h* yourself!
5:17 present for him to *h* the sick.
6: 7 to see if he would *h* on the Sabbath.
7: 3 him to come and *h* his servant.
8:43 years, but no one could *h* her.
9: 2 kingdom of God and to *h* the sick.
10: 9 *H* the sick who are there
13:32 and *h* people today and tomorrow,
14: 3 "Is it lawful to *h* on the Sabbath
Jn 4:47 begged him to come and *h* his son,
12:40 nor turn—and I would *h* them."
Ac 4:30 Stretch out your hand to *h*
28:27 and turn, and I would *h* them.'

HEALED* (HEAL)
Ge 20:17 to God, and God *h* Abimelech,
Ex 21:19 and see that he is completely *h*.
Lev 13:37 hair has grown in it, the itch is *h*.
14: 3 If the person has been *h*
Jos 5: 8 were in camp until they were *h*.
1Sa 6: 3 you will be *h*, and you will know
2Ki 2:21 LORD says: 'I have *h* this water.
2Ch 30:20 heard Hezekiah and *h* the people.
Ps 30: 2 and you *h* me.
107: 20 He sent forth his word and *h* them;
Isa 6:10 and turn and be *h*."
53: 5 and by his wounds we are *h*.
Jer 14:19 us so that we cannot be *h*?
17:14 Heal me, O LORD, and I will be *h*;
51: 8 perhaps she can be *h*.
51: 9 but she cannot be *h*;
51: 9 "'We would have *h* Babylon,
Eze 34: 4 the weak or *h* the sick
Hos 11: 3 it was I who *h* them.
Mt 4:24 and the paralyzed, and he *h* them.
8: 8 the word, and my servant will be *h*.
8:13 his servant was *h* at that very hour.
8:16 with a word and *h* all the sick.
9:21 If I only touch his cloak, I will be *h*
9:22 he said, "your faith has *h* you."
9:22 woman was *h* from that moment.
12:15 him, and he *h* all their sick,
12:22 Jesus *h* him, so that he could both
14:14 on them and *h* their sick.
14:36 and all who touched him were *h*.
15:28 And her daughter was *h*
15:30 laid them at his feet; and he *h* them
17:18 and he was *h* from that moment.
19: 2 followed him, and he *h* them there.
21:14 to him at the temple, and he *h* them
Mk 1:34 and Jesus *h* many who had various
3:10 For he had *h* many, so that those

Mk 5:23 hands on her so that she will be *h*
5:28 If I just touch his clothes, I will be *h*
5:34 "Daughter, your faith has *h* you.
6:13 people with oil and *h* them.
6:56 and all who touched him were *h*.
10:52 said Jesus, "your faith has *h* you."
Lk 4:40 hands on each one, he *h* them.
5:15 and to be *h* of their sicknesses.
6:18 and to be *h* of their diseases.
7: 7 the word, and my servant will be *h*.
8:47 and how she had been instantly *h*.
8:48 "Daughter, your faith has *h* you.
8:50 just believe, and she will be *h*."
9:11 and *h* those who needed healing.
9:42 *h* the boy and gave him back
13:14 Jesus had *h* on the Sabbath,
13:14 So come and be *h* on those days,
14: 4 he *h* him and sent him away.
17:15 when he saw he was *h*, came back,
18:42 your sight; your faith has *h* you."
22:51 touched the man's ear and *h* him.
Jn 5:10 said to the man who had been *h*,
5:13 man who was *h* had no idea who it
Ac 4: 9 and are asked how he was *h*,
4:10 stands before you *h*.
4:14 who had been *h* standing there
4:22 man who was miraculously *h* was
5:16 evil spirits, and all of them were *h*.
8: 7 paralytics and cripples were *h*.
14: 9 saw that he had faith to be *h*
28: 8 placed his hands on him and *h* him.
Heb 12:13 may not be disabled, but rather *h*.
Jas 5:16 for each other so that you may be *h*
1Pe 2:24 by his wounds you have been *h*.
Rev 13: 3 but the fatal wound had been *h*.
13:12 whose fatal wound had been *h*.

HEALING* (HEAL)
2Ch 28:15 food and drink, and *h* balm.
Pr 12:18 but the tongue of the wise brings *h*.
13:17 but a trustworthy envoy brings *h*.
15: 4 The tongue that brings *h* is a tree
16:24 sweet to the soul and *h* to the bones
Isa 58: 8 and your *h* will quickly appear;
Jer 8:15 for a time of *h*
8:22 Why then is there no *h*
14:19 for a time of *h*
30:12 your injury beyond *h*.
30:13 no *h* for you.
33: 6 I will bring health and *h* to it;
46:11 there is no *h* for you.
Eze 30:21 It has not been bound up for *h*
47:12 for food and their leaves for *h*."
Mal 4: 2 rise with *h* in its wings.
Mt 4:23 and *h* every disease and sickness
9:35 and *h* every disease and sickness.
Lk 6:19 coming from him and *h* them all.
9: 6 gospel and *h* people everywhere.
9:11 and healed those who needed *h*.
Jn 7:23 angry with me for *h* the whole man
Ac 3:16 him that has given this complete *h*
10:38 *h* all who were under the power
1Co 12: 9 to another gifts of *h*
12:28 also those having gifts of *h*,
12:30 Do all have gifts of *h*? Do all speak
Rev 22: 2 are for the *h* of the nations.

HEALS* (HEAL)
Ex 15:26 for I am the LORD, who *h* you."
Lev 13:18 a boil on his skin and it *h*,
Ps 103: 3 and *h* all your diseases;
147: 3 He *h* the brokenhearted
Isa 30:26 and *h* the wounds he inflicted.
Ac 9:34 said to him, "Jesus Christ *h* you.

HEALTH* (HEALTHIER HEALTHY)
1Sa 25: 6 And good *h* to all that is yours!
25: 6 Good *h* to you and your household
Ps 38: 3 of your wrath there is no *h*
38: 7 there is no *h* in my body.
Pr 3: 8 This will bring *h* to your body
4:22 and *h* to a man's whole body.
15:30 and good news gives *h* to the bones
Isa 38:16 You restored me to *h*
Jer 30:17 But I will restore you to *h*
33: 6 I will bring *h* and healing to it;
3Jn : 2 I pray that you may enjoy good *h*

HEALTHIER* (HEALTH)
Da 1:15 end of the ten days they looked *h*

HEALTHY* (HEALTH)
Ge 41: 5 Seven heads of grain, *h* and good,
41: 7 of grain swallowed up the seven *h*,
Ps 73: 4 their bodies are *h* and strong.
Zec 11:16 or heal the injured, or feed the *h*,
Mt 9:12 "It is not the *h* who need a doctor,
Mk 2:17 "It is not the *h* who need a doctor,
Lk 5:31 "It is not the *h* who need a doctor,

HEAP
Pr 25:22 you will *h* burning coals
Ro 12:20 you will *h* burning coals

HEAR (HEARD HEARING HEARS)
Ex 15:14 The nations will *h* and tremble;
22:27 I will *h*, for I am compassionate.
Nu 14:13 Then the Egyptians will *h* about it!
Dt 1:16 *H* the disputes between your
4:36 heaven he made you *h* his voice
6: 4 *H*, O Israel: The LORD our God,
19:20 The rest of the people will *h* of this
31:13 must *h* it and learn
Jos 7: 9 of the country will *h* about this
1Ki 8:30 *H* the supplication of your servant
2Ki 19:16 O LORD, and *h*; open your eyes,
2Ch 7:14 then will I *h* from heaven
Job 31:35 ("Oh, that I had someone to *h* me!
Ps 94: 9 he who implanted the ear not *h*?
95: 7 Today, if you *h* his voice,
Ecc 7:21 or you may *h* your servant cursing
Isa 21: 3 I am staggered by what I *h*,
29:18 that day the deaf will *h* the words
30:21 your ears will *h* a voice behind you,
51: 7 *H* me, you who know what is right,
59: 1 nor his ear too dull to *h*.
65:24 while they are still speaking I will *h*
Jer 5:21 who have ears but do not *h*:
Eze 33: 7 so *h* the word I speak and give
37: 4 'Dry bones, *h* the word
Mt 11: 5 the deaf *h*, the dead are raised,
11:15 He who has ears, let him *h*.
13:17 and to *h* what you *h* but did not *h* it
Mk 12:29 answered Jesus, "is this: '*H*,
Lk 7:22 the deaf *h*, the dead are raised,
Jn 8:47 reason you do not *h* is that you do
Ac 13: 7 he wanted to *h* the word of God.
13:44 gathered to *h* the word of the Lord.
17:32 "We want to *h* you again
Ro 2:13 is not those who *h* the law who are
10:14 they *h* without someone preaching
2Ti 4: 3 what their itching ears want to *h*.
Heb 3: 7 "Today, if you *h* his voice,
Rev 1: 3 and blessed are those who *h* it

HEARD (HEAR)
Ex 2:24 God *h* their groaning and he
Dt 4:32 has anything like it ever been *h* of?
2Sa 7:22 as we have *h* with our own ears.
Job 42: 5 My ears had *h* of you
Isa 40:21 Have you not *h*?
40:28 Have you not *h*?
66: 8 Who has ever *h* of such a thing?
Jer 18:13 Who has ever *h* anything like this?
Da 10:12 your words were *h*, and I have
12: 8 I *h*, but I did not understand.
Hab 3:16 I *h* and my heart pounded,
Mt 5:21 "You have *h* that it was said
5:27 "You have *h* that it was said,
5:33 you have *h* that it was said
5:38 "You have *h* that it was said,
5:43 "You have *h* that it was said,
Lk 12: 3 in the dark will be *h* in the daylight,
Jn 8:26 and what I have *h* from him I tell
Ac 2: 6 because each one *h* them speaking
1Co 2: 9 no ear has *h*,
2Co 12: 4 He *h* inexpressible things,
1Th 2:13 word of God, which you *h* from us,
2Ti 1:13 What you *h* from me, keep
Jas 1:25 not forgetting what he has *h*,
Rev 22: 8 am the one who *h* and saw these

HEARING (HEAR)
Isa 6: 9 Be ever *h*, but never understanding
Mt 13:14 will be ever *h* but never
Mk 4:12 ever *h* but never understanding;
Ac 28:26 will be ever *h* but never
Ro 10:17 faith comes from *h* the message,
1Co 12:17 where would the sense of *h* be?

HEARS (HEAR)
Jn 5:24 whoever *h* my word and believes
1Jn 5:14 according to his will, he *h* us.
Rev 3:20 If anyone *h* my voice and opens

HEART (BROKENHEARTED FAINT-HEARTED HARDHEARTED HEART'S HEARTACHE HEARTS KINDHEARTED SIMPLEHEARTED STOUTHEARTED WHOLEHEARTED WHOLEHEARTEDLY)
Ge 6: 5 of his *h* was only evil all the time.
Ex 4:21 But I will harden his *h*
25: 2 each man whose *h* prompts him
35:21 and whose *h* moved him came
Lev 19:17 Do not hate your brother in your *h*.
Dt 4: 9 or let them slip from your *h* as long
4:29 if you look for him with all your *h*
6: 5 LORD your God with all your *h*
10:12 LORD your God with all your *h*
Dt 11:13 and to serve him with all your *h*
13: 3 you love him with all your *h*
15:10 and do so without a grudging *h*;
26:16 observe them with all your *h*
29:18 you today whose *h* turns away
30: 2 and obey him with all your *h*
30: 6 you may love him with all your *h*
30:10 LORD your God with all your *h*
Jos 22: 5 and to serve him with all your *h*
23:14 You know with all your *h*
1Sa 10: 9 God changed Saul's *h*,
12:20 serve the LORD with all your *h*.
12:24 serve him faithfully with all your *h*;
13:14 sought out a man after his own *h*
14: 7 I am with you *h* and soul."
16: 7 but the LORD looks at the *h*."
17:32 "Let no one lose *h* on account
1Ki 2: 4 faithfully before me with all their *h*
3: 9 So give your servant a discerning *h*
3:12 give you a wise and discerning *h*,
8:48 back to you with all their *h*
9: 3 and my *h* will always be there.
9: 4 walk before me in integrity of *h*
10:24 the wisdom God had put in his *h*.
11: 4 and his *h* was not fully devoted
14: 8 and followed me with all his *h*,
15:14 Asa's *h* was fully committed
2Ki 22:19 Because your *h* was responsive
23: 3 with all his *h* and all his soul,
1Ch 28: 9 for the LORD searches every *h*
2Ch 6:38 back to you with all their *h*
7:16 and my *h* will always be there.
15:12 of their fathers, with all their *h*
15:17 Asa's *h* was fully committed
17: 6 His *h* was devoted to the ways
22: 9 sought the LORD with all his *h*."
34:31 with all his *h* and all his soul,
36:13 stiff-necked and hardened his *h*
Ezr 1: 5 everyone whose *h* God had moved
Ne 4: 6 the people worked with all their *h*.
Job 19:27 How my *h* yearns within me!
22:22 and lay up his words in your *h*.
37: 1 "At this my *h* pounds
Ps 9: 1 you, O LORD, with all my *h*;
14: 1 The fool says in his *h*,
16: 9 Therefore my *h* is glad
19:14 and the meditation of my *h*
20: 4 he give you the desire of your *h*
24: 4 who has clean hands and a pure *h*,
26: 2 examine my *h* and my mind;
37: 4 will give you the desires of your *h*.
37:31 The law of his God is in his *h*;
44:21 since he knows the secrets of the *h*
45: 1 My *h* is stirred by a noble theme
51:10 Create in me a pure *h*, O God,
51:17 a broken and contrite *h*,
53: 1 The fool says in his *h*,
66:18 If I had cherished sin in my *h*,
73: 1 to those who are pure in *h*.
73:26 My flesh and my *h* may fail,
86:11 give me an undivided *h*,
90:12 that we may gain a *h* of wisdom.
97:11 and joy on the upright in *h*.
108: 1 My *h* is steadfast, O God;
109: 22 and my *h* is wounded within me.
111: 1 I will extol the LORD with all my *h*
112: 7 his *h* is steadfast, trusting
112: 8 His *h* is secure, he will have no fear
119: 2 and seek him with all their *h*.
119: 10 I seek you with all my *h*;
119: 11 I have hidden your word in my *h*
119: 30 I have set my *h* on your laws.
119: 32 for you have set my *h* free.
119: 34 and obey it with all my *h*.
119: 36 Turn my *h* toward your statutes
119: 58 sought your face with all my *h*;
119: 69 I keep your precepts with all my *h*.
119:111 they are the joy of my *h*.
119:112 My *h* is set on keeping your
119:145 I call with all my *h*; answer me,
125: 4 to those who are upright in *h*.
138: 1 you, O LORD, with all my *h*;
139: 23 Search me, O God, and know my *h*
Pr 2: 2 applying your *h* to understanding,
3: 1 but keep my commands in your *h*,
3: 3 write them on the tablet of your *h*.
3: 5 Trust in the LORD with all your *h*
4: 4 hold of my words with all your *h*;
4:21 keep them within your *h*;
4:23 Above all else, guard your *h*,
6:21 Bind them upon your *h* forever;
7: 3 write them on the tablet of your *h*.
10: 8 The wise in *h* accept commands,
13:12 Hope deferred makes the *h* sick,
14:13 Even in laughter the *h* may ache,
14:30 A *h* at peace gives life to the body,
15:13 A happy *h* makes the face cheerful,
15:15 the cheerful *h* has a continual feast.
15:28 *h* of the righteous weighs its

Pr 15:30 A cheerful look brings joy to the *h*,
16:23 A wise man's *h* guides his mouth,
17:22 A cheerful *h* is good medicine,
20: 9 can say, "I have kept my *h* pure;
22:11 He who loves a pure *h*
22:17 apply your *h* to what I teach,
22:18 when you keep them in your *h*
23:15 My son, if your *h* is wise,
23:19 and keep your *h* on the right path.
23:26 My son, give me your *h*
24:17 stumbles, do not let your *h* rejoice,
27:19 so a man's *h* reflects the man.
Ecc 5: 2 do not be hasty in your *h*
8: 5 wise *h* will know the proper time
11:10 banish anxiety from your *h*
SS 3: 1 I looked for the one my *h* loves;
4: 9 You have stolen my *h*, my sister,
5: 2 *Beloved* I slept but my *h* was awake
5: 4 my *h* began to pound for him.
8: 6 Place me like a seal over your *h*,
Isa 6:10 Make the *h* of this people calloused
40:11 and carries them close to his *h*;
57:15 and to revive the *h* of the contrite.
66:14 you see this, your *h* will rejoice
Jer 3:15 give you shepherds after my own *h*,
4:14 wash the evil from your *h*
9:26 of Israel is uncircumcised in *h*."
17: 9 The *h* is deceitful above all things
20: 9 is in my *h* like a fire,
24: 7 I will give them a *h* to know me,
29:13 when you seek me with all your *h*.
32:39 I will give them singleness of *h*
32:41 them in this land with all my *h*
51:46 Do not lose *h* or be afraid
Eze 11:19 I will give them an undivided *h*
18:31 and get a new *h* and a new spirit.
36:26 I will give you a new *h*
44: 7 foreigners uncircumcised in *h*
Da 7: 4 and the *h* of a man was given to it.
Joel 2:12 "return to me with all your *h*,
2:13 Rend your *h*
Zep 3:14 Be glad and rejoice with all your *h*,
Mt 5: 8 Blessed are the pure in *h*,
5:28 adultery with her in his *h*.
6:21 treasure is, there your *h* will be
11:29 for I am gentle and humble in *h*,
12:34 of the *h* the mouth speaks.
13:15 For this people's *h* has become
15:18 out of the mouth come from the *h*,
15:19 For out of the *h* come evil thoughts
18:35 forgive your brother from your *h*."
22:37 the Lord your God with all your *h*
Mk 11:23 and does not doubt in his *h*
12:30 the Lord your God with all your *h*
12:33 To love him with all your *h*,
Lk 2:19 and pondered them in her *h*.
2:51 treasured all these things in her *h*.
6:45 out of the good stored up in his *h*,
6:45 overflow of his *h* his mouth speaks.
8:15 for those with a noble and good *h*,
10:27 the Lord your God with all your *h*
12:34 treasure is, there your *h* will be
Jn 12:27 "Now my *h* is troubled,
Ac 1:24 "Lord, you know everyone's *h*.
2:37 they were cut to the *h*
4:32 All the believers were one in *h*
8:21 your *h* is not right before God.
15: 8 who knows the *h*, showed that he
16:14 The Lord opened her *h* to respond
28:27 For this people's *h* has become
Ro 1: 9 with my whole *h* in preaching
2:29 is circumcision of the *h*,
10: 9 in your *h* that God raised him
10:10 is with your *h* that you believe
15: 6 with one *h* and mouth you may
1Co 14:25 the secrets of his *h* will be laid bare.
2Co 2: 4 anguish of *h* and with many tears,
4: 1 this ministry, we do not lose *h*.
4:16 Therefore we do not lose *h*.
9: 7 give what he has decided in his *h*
Eph 1:18 eyes of your *h* may be enlightened
5:19 make music in your *h* to the Lord,
6: 5 and with sincerity of *h*, just
6: 6 doing the will of God from your *h*.
Php 1: 7 since I have you in my *h*; for
Col 2: 2 is that they may be encouraged in *h*
3:22 but with sincerity of *h*
3:23 work at it with all your *h*,
1Ti 1: 5 which comes from a pure *h*
3: 1 If anyone sets his *h*
2Ti 2:22 call on the Lord out of a pure *h*.
Phm :12 who is my very *h*— back to you.
:20 in the Lord; refresh my *h* in Christ.
Heb 4:12 the thoughts and attitudes of the *h*.
1Pe 1:22 one another deeply, from the *h*.

HEART'S* (HEART)
2Ch 1:11 "Since this is your *h* desire
Jer 15:16 they were my joy and my *h* delight,
Eze 24:25 delight of their eyes, their *h* desire,
Ro 10: 1 my *h* desire and prayer to God

HEARTACHE* (HEART)
Pr 15:13 but *h* crushes the spirit.

HEARTLESS*
La 4: 3 but my people have become *h*,
Ro 1:31 they are senseless, faithless, *h*,

HEARTS (HEART)
Lev 26:41 their uncircumcised *h* are humbled
Dt 6: 6 are to be upon your *h*.
10:16 Circumcise your *h*, therefore,
11:18 Fix these words of mine in your *h*
30: 6 your God will circumcise your *h*
Jos 11:20 himself who hardened their *h*
24:23 and yield your *h* to the LORD,
1Sa 7: 3 to the LORD with all your *h*,
10:26 valiant men whose *h* God had
2Sa 15: 6 and so he stole the *h* of the men
1Ki 8:39 for you alone know the *h* of all men
8:61 your *h* must be fully committed
18:37 are turning their *h* back again."
1Ch 29:18 and keep their *h* loyal to you.
2Ch 6:30 (for you alone know the *h* of men),
11:16 tribe of Israel who set their *h*
29:31 all whose *h* were willing brought
Ps 7: 9 who searches minds and *h*,
33:21 In him our *h* rejoice,
62: 8 pour out your *h* to him,
95: 8 do not harden your *h* as you did
Ecc 3:11 also set eternity in the *h* of men;
Isa 26: 8 are the desire of our *h*.
29:13 but their *h* are far from me.
35: 4 say to those with fearful *h*,
51: 7 people who have my law in your *h*:
63:17 harden our *h* so we do not revere
65:14 out of the joy of their *h*,
Jer 4: 4 circumcise your *h*,
12: 2 but far from their *h*.
17: 1 on the tablets of their *h*
31:33 and write it on their *h*.
Mal 4: 6 He will turn the *h* of the fathers
Mt 15: 8 but their *h* are far from me.
Mk 6:52 the loaves; their *h* were hardened.
7: 6 but their *h* are far from me.
7:21 out of men's *h*, come evil thoughts,
Lk 1:17 to turn the *h* of the fathers
16:15 of men, but God knows your *h*.
24:32 "Were not our *h* burning within us
Jn 5:42 not have the love of God in your *h*.
14: 1 "Do not let your *h* be troubled.
14:27 Do not let your *h* be troubled
Ac 7:51 with uncircumcised *h* and ears!
11:23 true to the Lord with all their *h*.
15: 9 for he purified their *h* by faith.
28:27 understand with their *h*
Ro 1:21 and their foolish *h* were darkened.
2:15 of the law are written on their *h*,
5: 5 love into our *h* by the Holy Spirit,
8:27 who searches our *h* knows
1Co 4: 5 will expose the motives of men's *h*.
2Co 1:22 put his Spirit in our *h* as a deposit,
3: 2 written on our *h*, known
3: 3 but on tablets of human *h*.
4: 6 shine in our *h* to give us the light
6:11 and opened wide our *h* to you.
6:13 to my children—open wide your *h*
7: 2 Make room for us in your *h*.
Gal 4: 6 the Spirit of his Son into our *h*,
Eph 3:17 dwell in your *h* through faith.
Php 4: 7 will guard your *h* and your minds
Col 3: 1 set your *h* on things above,
3:15 the peace of Christ rule in your *h*,
3:16 with gratitude in your *h* to God.
1Th 2: 4 men but God, who tests our *h*.
3:13 May he strengthen your *h*
2Th 2:17 encourage your *h* and strengthen
Phm :7 have refreshed the *h* of the saints.
Heb 3: 8 do not harden your *h*
8:10 and write them on their *h*.
10:16 I will put my laws in their *h*,
10:22 having our *h* sprinkled
Jas 4: 8 purify your *h*, you double-minded.
2Pe 1:19 the morning star rises in your *h*.
1Jn 3:20 For God is greater than our *h*,

HEAT
Ps 19: 6 nothing is hidden from its *h*.
2Pe 3:12 and the elements will melt in the *h*.

HEAVEN (HEAVENLY HEAVENS HEAVENWARD)
Ge 14:19 Creator of *h* and earth.
28:12 with its top reaching to *h*,
Ex 16: 4 rain down bread from *h* for you.
20:22 that I have spoken to you from *h*:
Dt 26:15 from *h*, your holy dwelling place,
Dt 30:12 "Who will ascend into *h* to get it
1Ki 8:27 the highest *h*, cannot contain you.
8:30 Hear from *h*, your dwelling place,
22:19 the host of *h* standing around him
2Ki 2: 1 up to *h* in a whirlwind,
19:15 You have made *h* and earth.
2Ch 7:14 then will I hear from *h*
Isa 14:12 How you have fallen from *h*,
66: 1 "*H* is my throne,
Da 7:13 coming with the clouds of *h*.
Mt 3: 2 for the kingdom of *h* is near."
3:16 At that moment *h* was opened,
4:17 for the kingdom of *h* is near."
5:12 because great is your reward in *h*,
5:19 great in the kingdom of *h*.
6: 9 " 'Our Father in *h*,
6:10 done on earth as it is in *h*.
6:20 up for yourselves treasures in *h*,
7:21 Lord,' will enter the kingdom of *h*,
16:19 bind on earth will be bound in *h*,
18: 3 will never enter the kingdom of *h*.
18:18 bind on earth will be bound in *h*,
19:14 the kingdom of *h* belongs to such
19:21 and you will have treasure in *h*.
19:23 man to enter the kingdom of *h*.
23:13 the kingdom of *h* in men's faces.
24:35 *H* and earth will pass away,
26:64 and coming on the clouds of *h*."
28:18 "All authority in *h*
Mk 1:10 he saw *h* being torn open
10:21 and you will have treasure in *h*.
13:31 *H* and earth will pass away,
14:62 and coming on the clouds of *h*."
16:19 he was taken up into *h*
Lk 3:21 *h* was opened and the Holy Spirit
10:18 saw Satan fall like lightning from *h*.
10:20 that your names are written in *h*."
12:33 in *h* that will not be exhausted,
15: 7 in *h* over one sinner who repents
18:22 and you will have treasure in *h*.
21:33 *H* and earth will pass away,
24:51 left them and was taken up into *h*.
Jn 3:13 No one has ever gone into *h*
6:38 down from *h* not to do my will
12:28 Then a voice came from *h*,
Ac 1:11 has been taken from you into *h*,
7:49 the prophet says: " '*H* is my
7:55 looked up to *h* and saw the glory
9: 3 a light from *h* flashed around him.
26:19 disobedient to the vision from *h*.
Ro 10: 6 'Who will ascend into *h*?' " (that is,
1Co 15:47 the earth, the second man from *h*.
2Co 5: 1 an eternal house in *h*, not built
12: 2 ago was caught up to the third *h*.
Eph 1:10 to bring all things in *h*
Php 2:10 *h* and on earth and under the earth,
3:20 But our citizenship is in *h*.
Col 1:16 things in *h* and on earth, visible
4: 1 that you also have a Master in *h*.
1Th 1:10 and to wait for his Son from *h*,
4:16 himself will come down from *h*,
Heb 1: 3 hand of the Majesty in *h*.
8: 5 and shadow of what is in *h*.
9:24 he entered *h* itself, now to appear
12:23 whose names are written in *h*.
1Pe 1: 4 spoil or fade—kept in *h* for you,
3:22 who has gone into *h* and is
2Pe 3:13 we are looking forward to a new *h*
Rev 5:13 Then I heard every creature in *h*
11:19 God's temple in *h* was opened,
12: 7 And there was war in *h*.
15: 5 this I looked and in *h* the temple,
19: 1 of a great multitude in *h* shouting:
19:11 I saw *h* standing open and there
21: 1 Then I saw a new *h* and a new earth
21:10 coming down out of *h* from God.

HEAVENLY (HEAVEN)
Ps 8: 5 him a little lower than the *h* beings
2Co 5: 2 to be clothed with our *h* dwelling,
Eph 1: 3 in the *h* realms with every spiritual
1:20 at his right hand in the *h* realms,
2Ti 4:18 bring me safely to his *h* kingdom.
Heb 12:22 to the *h* Jerusalem, the city

HEAVENS (HEAVEN)
Ge 1: 1 In the beginning God created the *h*
11: 4 with a tower that reaches to the *h*,
Dt 33:26 who rides on the *h* to help you
1Ki 8:27 The *h*, even the highest heaven,
2Ch 2: 6 since the *h*, even the highest
Ezr 9: 6 and our guilt has reached to the *h*.
Ne 9: 6 You made the *h*, even the highest
Job 11: 8 They are higher than the *h*—
38:33 Do you know the laws of the *h*?
Ps 8: 3 When I consider your *h*,
19: 1 The *h* declare the glory of God;
33: 6 of the LORD were the *h* made,
57: 5 Be exalted, O God, above the *h*;

Ps 102: 25 the *h* are the work of your hands.
103: 11 as high as the *h* are above the earth,
108: 4 is your love, higher than the *h*;
115: 16 The highest *h* belong to the LORD
119: 89 it stands firm in the *h*.
135: 6 in the *h* and on the earth,
139: 8 If I go up to the *h*, you are there;
148: 1 Praise the LORD from the *h*,
Isa 40:26 Lift your eyes and look to the *h*:
45: 8 "You *h* above, rain
51: 6 Lift up your eyes to the *h*,
55: 9 "As the *h* are higher than the earth,
65:17 new *h* and a new earth.
Jer 31:37 if the *h* above can be measured
32:17 you have made the *h* and the earth
Eze 1: 1 *h* were opened and I saw visions
Da 12: 3 shine like the brightness of the *h*,
Joel 2:30 I will show wonders in the *h*
Mt 24:31 from one end of the *h* to the other.
Mk 13:27 of the earth to the ends of the *h*.
Eph 4:10 who ascended higher than all the *h*,
Heb 4:14 priest who has gone through the *h*,
7:26 from sinners, exalted above the *h*.
2Pe 3: 5 ago by God's word the *h* existed
3:10 The *h* will disappear with a roar;

HEAVENWARD (HEAVEN)
Php 3:14 for which God has called me *h*

HEAVIER (HEAVY)
Pr 27: 3 provocation by a fool is *h* than both

HEAVY (HEAVIER)
1Ki 12: 4 and the *h* yoke he put on us,
Ecc 1:13 What a *h* burden God has laid
Isa 47: 6 you laid a very *h* yoke.
Mt 23: 4 They tie up *h* loads and put them

HEBREW (HEBREWS)
Ge 14:13 and reported this to Abram the *H*.
2Ki 18:26 speak to us in *H* in the hearing
Php 3: 5 tribe of Benjamin, a *H* of Hebrews;

HEBREWS (HEBREW)
Ex 9: 1 of the *H*, says: "Let my people go,
2Co 11:22 Are they *H*? So am I.

HEBRON
Ge 13:18 near the great trees of Mamre at *H*,
23: 2 died at Kiriath Arba (that is, *H*)
Jos 14:13 and gave him *H* as his inheritance.
20: 7 *H*) in the hill country of Judah.
21:13 the priest they gave *H* (a city
2Sa 2:11 king in *H* over the house

HEDGE
Job 1:10 "Have you not put a *h* around him

HEED (HEEDS)
Ecc 7: 5 It is better to *h* a wise man's rebuke

HEEDS (HEED)
Pr 13: 1 wise son *h* his father's instruction,
13:18 whoever *h* correction is honored.
15: 5 whoever *h* correction shows
15:32 whoever *h* correction gains

HEEL
Ge 3:15 and you will strike his *h*."

HEIR (INHERIT)
Gal 4: 7 God has made you also an *h*.
Heb 1: 2 whom he appointed *h* of all things,

HEIRS (INHERIT)
Ro 8:17 then we are *h*— *h* of God
Gal 3:29 and *h* according to the promise.
Eph 3: 6 gospel the Gentiles are *h* together
1Pe 3: 7 as *h* with you of the gracious gift

HELD (HOLD)
Ex 17:11 As long as Moses *h* up his hands,
Dt 4: 4 but all of you who *h* fast
2Ki 18: 6 He *h* fast to the LORD
SS 3: 4 I *h* him and would not let him go
Isa 65: 2 All day long I have *h* out my hands
Ro 10:21 day long I have *h* out my hands
Col 2:19 and *h* together by its ligaments

HELL*
Mt 5:22 will be in danger of the fire of *h*.
5:29 body to be thrown into *h*.
5:30 for your whole body to go into *h*.
10:28 destroy both soul and body in *h*.
18: 9 and be thrown into the fire of *h*.
23:15 as much a son of *h* as you are.
23:33 you escape being condemned to *h*?
Mk 9:43 than with two hands to go into *h*,
9:45 have two feet and be thrown into *h*.
9:47 two eyes and be thrown into *h*,
Lk 12: 5 has power to throw you into *h*.
Lk 16:23 In *h*, where he was in torment,
Jas 3: 6 and is itself set on fire by *h*.
2Pe 2: 4 but sent them to *h*, putting them

HELMET
Isa 59:17 and the *h* of salvation on his head;
Eph 6:17 Take the *h* of salvation
1Th 5: 8 and the hope of salvation as a *h*.

HELP (HELPED HELPER HELPFUL HELPING HELPLESS HELPS)
Ex 23: 5 leave it there; be sure you *h* him
Lev 25:35 *h* him as you would an alien
Dt 33:26 who rides on the heavens to *h* you
2Ch 16:12 even in his illness he did not seek *h*
Ps 18: 6 I cried to my God for *h*.
30: 2 my God, I called to you for *h*
33:20 he is our *h* and our shield.
46: 1 an ever-present *h* in trouble.
72:12 the afflicted who have no one to *h*.
79: 9 *H* us, O God our Savior,
108: 12 for the *h* of man is worthless.
115: 9 he is their *h* and shield.
121: 1 where does my *h* come from?
Ecc 4:10 his friend can *h* him up.
Isa 41:10 I will strengthen you and *h* you;
Jnh 2: 2 depths of the grave I called for *h*,
Mk 9:24 *h* me overcome my unbelief!"
Lk 11:46 will not lift one finger to *h* them.
Ac 16: 9 Come over to Macedonia and *h* us
18:27 he was a great *h* to those who
20:35 of hard work we must *h* the weak,
26:22 I have had God's *h* to this very day,
1Co 12:28 those able to *h* others, those
2Co 9: 2 For I know your eagerness to *h*,
1Ti 5:16 she should *h* them and not let

HELPED (HELP)
1Sa 7:12 "Thus far has the LORD *h* us."

HELPER (HELP)
Ge 2:18 I will make a *h* suitable for him."
Ps 10:14 you are the *h* of the fatherless.
Heb 13: 6 Lord is my *h*; I will not be afraid.

HELPFUL (HELP)
Eph 4:29 only what is *h* for building others

HELPING (HELP)
Ac 9:36 always doing good and *h* the poor.
1Ti 5:10 *h* those in trouble and devoting

HELPLESS (HELP)
Ps 10:12 Do not forget the *h*.
Mt 9:36 because they were harassed and *h*,

HELPS (HELP)
Ro 8:26 the Spirit *h* us in our weakness.

HEN
Mt 23:37 as a *h* gathers her chicks
Lk 13:34 as a *h* gathers her chicks

HERALD
1Ti 2: 7 for this purpose I was appointed a *h*
2Ti 1:11 of this gospel I was appointed a *h*

HERBS
Ex 12: 8 with bitter *h*, and bread made

HERITAGE (INHERIT)
Ps 61: 5 you have given me the *h*
119:111 Your statutes are my *h* forever;
127: 3 Sons are a *h* from the LORD,

HEROD
1. King of Judea who tried to kill Jesus (Mt 2; Lk 1:5).
2. Son of 1. Tetrarch of Galilee who arrested and beheaded John the Baptist (Mt 14:1-12; Mk 6:14-29; Lk 3:1, 19-20; 9:7-9); tried Jesus (Lk 23:6-15).
3. Grandson of 1. King of Judea who killed James (Ac 12:2); arrested Peter (Ac 12:3-19). Death (Ac 12:19-23).

HERODIAS
Wife of Herod the Tetrarch who persuaded her daughter to ask for John the Baptist's head (Mt 14:1-12; Mk 6:14-29).

HEWN
Isa 51: 1 the quarry from which you were *h*;

HEZEKIAH
King of Judah. Restored the temple and worship (2Ch 29-31). Sought the LORD for help against Assyria (2Ki 18-19; 2Ch 32:1-23; Isa 36-37). Illness healed (2Ki 20:1-11; 2Ch 32:24-26; Isa 38). Judged for showing Babylonians his treasures (2Ki 20:12-21; 2Ch 32:31; Isa 39).

HID (HIDE)
Ge 3: 8 and they *h* from the LORD God
Ex 2: 2 she *h* him for three months.
Jos 6:17 because she *h* the spies we sent.
1Ki 18:13 I *h* a hundred of the LORD's
2Ch 22:11 she *h* the child from Athaliah
Isa 54: 8 I *h* my face from you for a moment,
Mt 13:44 When a man found it, he *h* it again,
25:25 and *h* your talent in the ground.
Heb 11:23 By faith Moses' parents *h* him

HIDDEN (HIDE)
1Sa 10:22 has *h* himself among the baggage."
Job 28:11 and brings *h* things to light.
Ps 19:12 Forgive my *h* faults.
78: 2 I will utter *h* things, things from of old—
119: 11 I have *h* your word in my heart
Pr 2: 4 and search for it as for *h* treasure,
27: 5 rebuke than *h* love.
Isa 59: 2 your sins have *h* his face from you,
Da 2:22 He reveals deep and *h* things;
Mt 5:14 A city on a hill cannot be *h*.
10:26 or *h* that will not be made known.
11:25 because you have *h* these things
13:35 I will utter things *h*
13:44 of heaven is like treasure *h*
Mk 4:22 For whatever is *h* is meant
Ro 16:25 of the mystery *h* for long ages past,
1Co 2: 7 a wisdom that has been *h*
Eph 3: 9 for ages past was kept *h* in God,
Col 1:26 the mystery that has been kept *h*
2: 3 in whom are *h* all the treasures
3: 3 and your life is now *h* with Christ

HIDE (HID HIDDEN HIDING)
Dt 31:17 I will *h* my face from them,
Ps 17: 8 *h* me in the shadow of your wings
27: 5 he will *h* me in the shelter
143: 9 for I *h* myself in you.
Isa 53: 3 one from whom men *h* their faces

HIDING (HIDE)
Ps 32: 7 You are my *h* place;
Pr 28:12 to power, men go into *h*.

HIGH
Ge 14:18 He was priest of God Most *H*,
14:22 God Most *H*, Creator of heaven
Ps 21: 7 the unfailing love of the Most *H*
82: 6 you are all sons of the Most *H*.'
Isa 14:14 I will make myself like the Most *H*
Da 4:17 know that the Most *H* is sovereign
Mk 5: 7 Jesus, Son of the Most *H* God?
Heb 7: 1 and priest of God Most *H*.

HIGHWAY
Isa 40: 3 a *h* for our God.

HILL (HILLS)
Ps 24: 3 ascend the *h* of the LORD?
Isa 40: 4 every mountain and *h* made low;
Mt 5:14 A city on a *h* cannot be hidden.
Lk 3: 5 every mountain and *h* made low.

HILLS (HILL)
1Ki 20:23 "Their gods are gods of the *h*.
Ps 50:10 and the cattle on a thousand *h*.
121: 1 I lift up my eyes to the *h*—
Hos 10: 8 and to the *h*, "Fall on us!"
Lk 23:30 and to the *h*, "Cover us!"'
Rev 17: 9 The seven heads are seven *h*

HINDER (HINDERED HINDERS)
1Sa 14: 6 Nothing can *h* the LORD
Mt 19:14 come to me, and do not *h* them,
1Co 9:12 anything rather than *h* the gospel
1Pe 3: 7 so that nothing will *h* your prayers.

HINDERED (HINDER)
Lk 11:52 and you have *h* those who were

HINDERS (HINDER)
Heb 12: 1 let us throw off everything that *h*

HINT*
Eph 5: 3 even a *h* of sexual immorality,

HIP
Ge 32:32 socket of Jacob's *h* was touched

HIRAM
King of Tyre; helped David build his palace (2Sa 5:11-12; 1Ch 14:1); helped Solomon build the temple (1Ki 5; 2Ch 2) and his navy (1Ki 9:10-27; 2Ch 8).

HIRED
Lk 15:15 and *h* himself out to a citizen
Jn 10:12 *h* hand is not the shepherd who

HOARDED (HOARDS)
Ecc 5:13 wealth *h* to the harm of its owner,
Jas 5: 3 You have *h* wealth in the last days.

HOARDS (HOARDED)
Pr 11:26 People curse the man who *h* grain,

HOLD (HELD HOLDS)
Ex 20: 7 LORD will not *h* anyone guiltless
Lev 19:13 " 'Do not *h* back the wages
Dt 5:11 LORD will not *h* anyone guiltless
11:22 in all his ways and to *h* fast to him
13: 4 serve him and *h* fast to him.
30:20 listen to his voice, and *h* fast to him
Jos 22: 5 to *h* fast to him and to serve him
2Ki 4:16 "you will *h* a son in your arms."
Ps 18:16 from on high and took *h* of me;
73:23 you *h* me by my right hand.
Pr 4: 4 "Lay *h* of my words
Isa 41:13 who takes *h* of your right hand
54: 2 do not *h* back;
Eze 3:18 and I will *h* you accountable
3:20 and I will *h* you accountable
33: 6 I will *h* the watchman accountable
Zec 8:23 nations will take firm *h* of one Jew
Mk 11:25 if you *h* anything against anyone,
Jn 20:17 Jesus said, "Do not *h* on to me,
Php 2:16 as you *h* out the word of life—
3:12 but I press on to take *h* of that
Col 1:17 and in him all things *h* together.
1Th 5:21 *H* on to the good.
1Ti 6:12 Take *h* of the eternal life
Heb 10:23 Let us *h* unswervingly

HOLDS (HOLD)
Pr 10:19 but he who *h* his tongue is wise.
17:28 and discerning if he *h* his tongue.

HOLES
Hag 1: 6 to put them in a purse with *h* in it."
Mt 8:20 "Foxes have *h* and birds

HOLINESS* (HOLY)
Ex 15:11 majestic in *h*,
Dt 32:51 because you did not uphold my *h*
1Ch 16:29 the LORD in the splendor of his *h*.
2Ch 20:21 him for the splendor of his *h*
Ps 29: 2 in the splendor of his *h*.
89:35 Once for all, I have sworn by my *h*
93: 5 *h* adorns your house
96: 9 in the splendor of his *h*;
Isa 29:23 they will acknowledge the *h*
35: 8 it will be called the Way of *H*.
Eze 36:23 I will show the *h* of my great name,
38:23 I will show my greatness and my *h*,
Am 4: 2 LORD has sworn by his *h*:
Lk 1:75 fear in *h* and righteousness
Ro 1: 4 the Spirit of *h* was declared
6:19 to righteousness leading to *h*.
6:22 the benefit you reap leads to *h*,
1Co 1:30 our righteousness, *h*
2Co 1:12 in the *h* and sincerity that are
7: 1 perfecting *h* out of reverence
Eph 4:24 God in true righteousness and *h*.
1Ti 2: 2 quiet lives in all godliness and *h*.
2:15 love and *h* with propriety.
Heb 12:10 that we may share in his *h*.
12:14 without *h* no one will see the Lord.

HOLY (HALLOWED HOLINESS)
Ge 2: 3 the seventh day and made it *h*,
Ex 3: 5 you are standing is *h* ground."
16:23 a *h* Sabbath to the LORD.
19: 6 kingdom of priests and a *h* nation.'
20: 8 the Sabbath day by keeping it *h*.
26:33 Place from the Most *H* Place.
26:33 curtain will separate the *H* Place
28:36 seal: *H* TO THE LORD.
29:37 Then the altar will be most *h*,
30:10 It is most *h* to the LORD."
30:29 them so they will be most *h*,
31:13 I am the LORD, who makes you *h*.
40: 9 all its furnishings, and it will be *h*.
Lev 10: 3 I will show myself *h*;
10:10 must distinguish between the *h*
10:13 in a *h* place, because it is your share
11:44 and be *h*, because I am *h*.
11:45 therefore be *h*, because I am *h*.
19: 2 'Be *h* because I, the LORD your
19: 8 he has desecrated what is *h*
19:24 the fourth year all its fruit will be *h*,
20: 3 and profaned my *h* name.
20: 7 " 'Consecrate yourselves and be *h*,
20: 8 I am the LORD, who makes you *h*.
20:26 You are to be *h* to me because I,
21: 6 They must be *h* to their God
21: 8 Consider them *h*, because I
22: 9 am the LORD, who makes them *h*.
22:32 Do not profane my *h* name.
Lev 25:12 For it is a jubilee and is to be *h*
27: 9 given to the LORD becomes *h*.
Nu 4:15 they must not touch the *h* things
6: 5 He must be *h* until the period
20:12 as *h* in the sight of the Israelites,
20:13 and where he showed himself *h*
Dt 5:12 the Sabbath day by keeping it *h*,
23:14 Your camp must be *h*,
26:15 from heaven, your *h* dwelling place
33: 2 He came with myriads of *h* ones
Jos 5:15 place where you are standing is *h*."
24:19 He is a *h* God; he is a jealous God.
1Sa 2: 2 "There is no one *h* like the LORD;
6:20 of the LORD, this *h* God?
21: 5 even on missions that are not *h*.
2Ki 4: 9 often comes our way is a *h* man
1Ch 16:10 Glory in his *h* name;
16:35 may give thanks to your *h* name,
29: 3 I have provided for this *h* temple:
2Ch 30:27 heaven, his *h* dwelling place.
Ezr 9: 2 and have mingled the *h* race
Ne 11: 1 the *h* city, while the remaining nine
Job 6:10 not denied the words of the *H* One.
Ps 2: 6 King on Zion, my *h* hill."
11: 4 The LORD is in his *h* temple;
16:10 will you let your *H* One see decay.
22: 3 you are enthroned as the *H* One;
24: 3 Who may stand in his *h* place?
30: 4 praise his *h* name.
77:13 Your ways, O God, are *h*.
78:54 to the border of his *h* land,
99: 3 he is *h*.
99: 5 he is *h*.
99: 9 for the LORD our God is *h*.
105: 3 Glory in his *h* name;
111: 9 *h* and awesome is his name.
Pr 9:10 of the *H* One is understanding.
Isa 5:16 the *h* God will show himself *h*
6: 3 *H*, *h*, *h* is the LORD Almighty;
8:13 is the one you are to regard as *h*,
29:23 they will keep my name *h*;
40:25 who is my equal?" says the *H* One.
43: 3 the *H* One of Israel, your Savior;
54: 5 *H* One of Israel is your Redeemer;
57:15 who lives forever, whose name is *h*:
58:13 and the LORD's *h* day honorable,
Jer 17:22 but keep the Sabbath day *h*,
Eze 20:41 I will show myself *h* among you
22:26 to my law and profane my *h* things;
28:22 and show myself *h* within her.
28:25 I will show myself *h* among them
36:20 nations they profaned my *h* name,
38:16 when I show myself *h* through you
44:23 the difference between the *h*
Da 9:24 prophecy and to anoint the most *h*.
Hab 2:20 But the LORD is in his *h* temple;
Zec 14: 5 and all the *h* ones with him.
14:20 On that day *H* TO THE LORD
Mt 24:15 in the *h* place 'the abomination
Mk 1:24 the *H* One of God!" "Be quiet!"
Lk 1:35 the *h* one to be born will be called
1:49 *h* is his name.
4:34 the *H* One of God!" "Be quiet!"
Jn 6:69 and know that you are the *H* One
Ac 2:27 will you let your *H* One see decay.
13:35 will not let your *H* One see decay.
Ro 1: 2 prophets in the *H* Scriptures
7:12 and the commandment is *h*,
11:16 if the root is *h*, so are the branches.
12: 1 as living sacrifices, *h* and pleasing
1Co 1: 2 in Christ Jesus and called to be *h*,
7:14 be unclean, but as it is, they are *h*.
Eph 1: 4 the creation of the world to be *h*
2:21 and rises to become a *h* temple
3: 5 by the Spirit to God's *h* apostles
5: 3 improper for God's *h* people.
5:26 up for her to make her *h*,
Col 1:22 death to present you *h* in his sight,
1Th 2:10 and so is God, of how *h*,
3:13 and *h* in the presence of our God
3:13 comes with all his *h* ones.
4: 7 us to be impure, but to live a *h* life.
2Th 1:10 to be glorified in his *h* people
1Ti 2: 8 to lift up *h* hands in prayer,
2Ti 1: 9 saved us and called us to a *h* life—
2:21 for noble purposes, made *h*,
3:15 you have known the *h* Scriptures,
Tit 1: 8 upright, *h* and disciplined.
Heb 2:11 Both the one who makes men *h*
7:26 one who is *h*, blameless, pure,
10:10 we have been made *h*
10:14 those who are being made *h*.
10:19 to enter the Most *H* Place
12:14 in peace with all men and to be *h*;
13:12 gate to make the people *h*
1Pe 1:15 But just as he who called you is *h*,
1:16 is written: "Be *h*, because I am *h*."
2: 5 house to be a *h* priesthood,
2: 9 a royal priesthood, a *h* nation,
1Pe 3: 5 For this is the way the *h* women
2Pe 3:11 You ought to live *h* and godly lives
Jude :14 upon thousands of his *h* ones
Rev 3: 7 are the words of him who is *h*
4: 8 "*H*, *h*, *h* is the Lord God
15: 4 For you alone are *h*.
20: 6 and *h* are those who have part
22:11 let him who is *h* continue to be *h*."

HOME (HOMES)
Dt 6: 7 Talk about them when you sit at *h*
11:19 about them when you sit at *h*
20: 5 Let him go *h*, or he may die
24: 5 is to be free to stay at *h*
Ru 1:11 "Return *h*, my daughters.
2Sa 7:10 them so that they can have a *h*
1Ch 16:43 and David returned *h* to bless his
Ps 84: 3 Even the sparrow has found a *h*,
113: 9 settles the barren woman in her *h*
Pr 3:33 but he blesses the *h* of the righteous
27: 8 is a man who strays from his *h*.
Ecc 12: 5 Then man goes to his eternal *h*
Eze 36: 8 for they will soon come *h*.
Mic 2: 2 They defraud a man of his *h*,
Mt 1:24 and took Mary *h* as his wife.
Mk 10:29 "no one who has left *h* or brothers
Lk 10:38 named Martha opened her *h*
Jn 14:23 to him and make our *h* with him.
19:27 this disciple took her into his *h*.
Ac 16:15 baptized, she invited us to her *h*.
Tit 2: 5 to be busy at *h*, to be kind,

HOMELESS*
1Co 4:11 we are brutally treated, we are *h*.

HOMES (HOME)
Ne 4:14 daughters, your wives and your *h*."
Isa 32:18 in secure *h*,
Mk 10:30 as much in this present age (*h*,
1Ti 5:14 to manage their *h* and to give

HOMETOWN
Mt 13:57 "Only in his *h*
Lk 4:24 "no prophet is accepted in his *h*.

HOMOSEXUAL*
1Co 6: 9 male prostitutes nor *h* offenders

HONEST (HONESTY)
Lev 19:36 Use *h* scales and *h* weights,
Dt 25:15 and *h* weights and measures,
Job 31: 6 let God weigh me in *h* scales
Pr 12:17 truthful witness gives *h* testimony,

HONESTY (HONEST)
2Ki 12:15 they acted with complete *h*.

HONEY (HONEYCOMB)
Ex 3: 8 a land flowing with milk and *h*—
Jdg 14: 8 a swarm of bees and some *h*,
1Sa 14:26 they saw the *h* oozing out,
Ps 19:10 than *h* from the comb.
119:103 sweeter than *h* to my mouth!
Pr 25:16 If you find *h*, eat just enough—
SS 4:11 milk and *h* are under your tongue.
Isa 7:15 and *h* when he knows enough
Eze 3: 3 it tasted as sweet as *h* in my mouth.
Mt 3: 4 His food was locusts and wild *h*.
Rev 10: 9 mouth it will be as sweet as *h*."

HONEYCOMB (HONEY)
SS 4:11 Your lips drop sweetness as the *h*,
5: 1 I have eaten my *h* and my honey;

HONOR (HONORABLE HONORABLY HONORED HONORS)
Ex 20:12 "*H* your father and your mother,
Nu 20:12 trust in me enough to *h* me
25:13 he was zealous for the *h* of his God
Dt 5:16 "*H* your father and your mother,
Jdg 4: 9 going about this, the *h* will not be
1Sa 2: 8 and has them inherit a throne of *h*.
2:30 Those who *h* me I will *h*,
1Ch 29:12 Wealth and *h* come from you;
2Ch 1:11 or *h*, nor for the death
18: 1 had great wealth and *h*,
Est 6: 6 for the man the king delights to *h*
Ps 8: 5 and crowned him with glory and *h*.
45:11 *h* him, for he is your lord.
84:11 the LORD bestows favor and *h*;
Pr 3: 9 *H* the LORD with your wealth,
3:35 The wise inherit *h*,
15:33 and humility comes before *h*.
18:12 but humility comes before *h*.
20: 3 It is to a man's *h* to avoid strife,
25:27 is it honorable to seek one's own *h*.
Isa 29:13 and *h* me with their lips,
Jer 33: 9 and *h* before all nations
Mt 13:57 own house is a prophet without *h*."
15: 4 '*H* your father and mother'

Mt 15: 8 These people *h* me with their lips,
19:19 *h* your father and mother,'
23: 6 they love the place of *h* at banquets
Mk 6: 4 own house is a prophet without *h*."
Lk 14: 8 do not take the place of *h*,
Jn 5:23 that all may *h* the Son just
7:18 does so to gain *h* for himself,
12:26 My Father will *h* the one who
Ro 12:10 *H* one another above yourselves.
1Co 6:20 Therefore *h* God with your body.
Eph 6: 2 "*H* your father and mother"—
1Ti 5:17 well are worthy of double *h*,
Heb 2: 7 you crowned him with glory and *h*
Rev 4: 9 *h* and thanks to him who sits

HONORABLE (HONOR)
1Th 4: 4 body in a way that is holy and *h*,

HONORABLY (HONOR)
Heb 13:18 and desire to live *h* in every way.

HONORED (HONOR)
Ps 12: 8 when what is vile is *h* among men.
Pr 13:18 but whoever heeds correction is *h*.
Da 4:34 I *h* and glorified him who lives
1Co 12:26 if one part is *h*, every part rejoices
Heb 13: 4 Marriage should be *h* by all,

HONORS (HONOR)
Ps 15: 4 but *h* those who fear the LORD,
Pr 14:31 to the needy *h* God.

HOOF
Ex 10:26 not a *h* is to be left behind.

HOOKS
Isa 2: 4 and their spears into pruning *h*.
Joel 3:10 and your pruning *h* into spears.
Mic 4: 3 and their spears into pruning *h*.

HOPE (HOPES)
Job 13:15 Though he slay me, yet will I *h*
Ps 25: 3 No one whose *h* is in you
33:17 A horse is a vain *h* for deliverance;
33:18 on those whose *h* is
42: 5 Put your *h* in God,
62: 5 my *h* comes from him.
119: 74 for I have put my *h* in your word.
130: 5 and in his word I put my *h*.
130: 7 O Israel, put your *h* in the LORD,
146: 5 whose *h* is in the LORD his God,
147: 11 who put their *h* in his unfailing love
Pr 13:12 *H* deferred makes the heart sick,
23:18 There is surely a future *h* for you,
Isa 40:31 but those who *h* in the LORD
Jer 29:11 plans to give you *h* and a future.
La 3:21 and therefore I have *h*:
Zec 9:12 to your fortress, O prisoners of *h*;
Ro 5: 4 character; and character, *h*.
8:20 in *h* that the creation itself will be
8:24 But *h* that is seen is no *h* at all.
8:25 if we *h* for what we do not yet have,
12:12 Be joyful in *h*, patient in affliction,
15: 4 of the Scriptures we might have *h*.
15:13 May the God of *h* fill you
1Co 13:13 now these three remain: faith, *h*
15:19 for this life we have *h* in Christ,
Eph 2:12 without *h* and without God
Col 1:27 Christ in you, the *h* of glory.
1Th 1: 3 and your endurance inspired by *h*
5: 8 and the *h* of salvation as a helmet.
1Ti 4:10 that we have put our *h*
6:17 but to put their *h* in God,
Tit 1: 2 resting on the *h* of eternal life,
2:13 while we wait for the blessed *h*—
Heb 6:19 We have this *h* as an anchor
10:23 unswervingly to the *h* we profess,
11: 1 faith is being sure of what we *h* for
1Jn 3: 3 Everyone who has this *h*

HOPES (HOPE)
1Co 13: 7 always *h*, always perseveres.

HORN (HORNS)
Ex 19:13 when the ram's *h* sounds a long
27: 2 Make a *h* at each of the four
Da 7: 8 This *h* had eyes like the eyes

HORNS (HORN)
Da 7:24 ten *h* are ten kings who will come
Rev 5: 6 He had seven *h* and seven eyes,
12: 3 and ten *h* and seven crowns
13: 1 He had ten *h* and seven heads,
17: 3 and had seven heads and ten *h*.

HORRIBLE (HORROR)
Jer 5:30 "A *h* and shocking thing

HORROR (HORRIBLE)
Jer 2:12 and shudder with great *h*,"

HORSE
Ps 147: 10 not in the strength of the *h*,
Pr 26: 3 A whip for the *h*, a halter
Zec 1: 8 before me was a man riding a red *h*
Rev 6: 2 and there before me was a white *h*!
6: 4 Come!" Then another *h* came out,
6: 5 and there before me was a black *h*!
6: 8 and there before me was a pale *h*!
19:11 and there before me was a white *h*,

HOSANNA
Mt 21: 9 "*H* in the highest!"
Mk 11: 9 "*H*!"
Jn 12:13 "*H*!"

HOSEA
Prophet whose wife and family pictured the unfaithfulness of Israel (Hos 1-3).

HOSHEA (JOSHUA)
1. Original name of Joshua (Nu 13:16).
2. Last king of Israel (2Ki 15:30; 17:1-6).

HOSPITABLE* (HOSPITALITY)
1Ti 3: 2 self-controlled, respectable, *h*,
Tit 1: 8 Rather he must be *h*, one who loves

HOSPITABLY* (HOSPITALITY)
Ac 28: 7 and for three days entertained us *h*.

HOSPITALITY* (HOSPITABLE HOSPITABLY)
Ro 12:13 Practice *h*.
16:23 whose *h* I and the whole church
1Ti 5:10 as bringing up children, showing *h*,
1Pe 4: 9 Offer *h* to one another
3Jn : 8 therefore to show *h* to such men

HOSTILE (HOSTILITY)
Ro 8: 7 the sinful mind is *h* to God.

HOSTILITY (HOSTILE)
Eph 2:14 wall of *h*, by abolishing
2:16 by which he put to death their *h*.

HOT
1Ti 4: 2 have been seared as with a *h* iron.
Rev 3:15 that you are neither cold nor *h*.

HOT-TEMPERED (TEMPER)
Pr 15:18 A *h* man stirs up dissension,
19:19 A *h* man must pay the penalty;
22:24 Do not make friends with a *h* man,
29:22 and a *h* one commits many sins.

HOTHEADED (HEAD)
Pr 14:16 but a fool is *h* and reckless.

HOUR
Ecc 9:12 knows when his *h* will come:
Mt 6:27 you by worrying can add a single *h*
Lk 12:40 the Son of Man will come at an *h*
Jn 12:23 The *h* has come for the Son of Man
12:27 for this very reason I came to this *h*

HOUSE (HOUSEHOLD HOUSEHOLDS HOUSES STOREHOUSE)
Ex 12:22 the door of his *h* until morning.
20:17 shall not covet your neighbor's *h*.
Nu 12: 7 he is faithful in all my *h*.
Dt 5:21 desire on your neighbor's *h*
2Sa 7:11 LORD himself will establish a *h*
1Ch 17:23 and his *h* be established forever.
Ne 10:39 "We will not neglect the *h*
Ps 23: 6 I will dwell in the *h* of the LORD
27: 4 dwell in the *h* of the LORD
69: 9 for zeal for your *h* consumes me,
84:10 a doorkeeper in the *h* of my God
122: 1 "Let us go to the *h* of the LORD."
127: 1 Unless the LORD builds the *h*,
Pr 7:27 Her *h* is a highway to the grave,
21: 9 than share a *h* with a quarrelsome
Isa 56: 7 a *h* of prayer for all nations."
Jer 7:11 Has this *h*, which bears my Name,
18: 2 "Go down to the potter's *h*,
Eze 33: 7 made you a watchman for the *h*
Joel 3:18 will flow out of the LORD's *h*
Zec 13: 6 given at the *h* of my friends.'
Mt 7:24 is like a wise man who built his *h*
10:11 and stay at his *h* until you leave.
12:29 can anyone enter a strong man's *h*
21:13 My *h* will be called a *h* of prayer,'
Mk 3:25 If a *h* is divided against itself,
11:17 " 'My *h* will be called
Lk 6:48 He is like a man building a *h*,
10: 7 Do not move around from *h* to *h*.
11:17 a *h* divided against itself will fall.
11:24 'I will return to the *h* I left.'
15: 8 sweep the *h* and search carefully
19: 9 Today salvation has come to this *h*,
Jn 2:16 How dare you turn my Father's *h*
2:17 "Zeal for your *h* will consume me."
12: 3 the *h* was filled with the fragrance
14: 2 In my Father's *h* are many rooms;
Ac 20:20 you publicly and from *h* to *h*.
Ro 16: 5 the church that meets at their *h*.
Heb 3: 3 the builder of a *h* has greater honor
1Pe 2: 5 built into a spiritual *h* to be a holy

HOUSEHOLD (HOUSE)
Ex 12: 3 lamb for his family, one for each *h*.
Jos 24:15 my *h*, we will serve the LORD."
Pr 31:21 it snows, she has no fear for her *h*;
31:27 over the affairs of her *h*
Mic 7: 6 are the members of his own *h*.
Mt 10:36 will be the members of his own *h*.'
12:25 or *h* divided against itself will not
Ac 16:31 you will be saved—you and your *h*
Eph 2:19 people and members of God's *h*,
1Ti 3:12 manage his children and his *h* well.
3:15 to conduct themselves in God's *h*,

HOUSEHOLDS (HOUSE)
Tit 1:11 because they are ruining whole *h*

HOUSES (HOUSE)
Ex 12:27 passed over the *h* of the Israelites
Mt 19:29 everyone who has left *h* or brothers

HOVERING* (HOVERS)
Ge 1: 2 of God was *h* over the waters.
Isa 31: 5 Like birds *h* overhead,

HOVERS* (HOVERING)
Dt 32:11 and *h* over its young,

HULDAH*
Prophetess inquired by Hilkiah for Josiah (2Ki 22; 2Ch 34:14-28).

HUMAN (HUMANITY)
Lev 24:17 If anyone takes the life of a *h* being,
Isa 52:14 his form marred beyond *h* likeness
Jn 8:15 You judge by *h* standards;
Ro 1: 3 as to his *h* nature was a descendant
9: 5 from them is traced the *h* ancestry
1Co 1:17 not with words of *h* wisdom,
1:26 of you were wise by *h* standards;
2:13 not in words taught us by *h* wisdom
2Co 3: 3 of stone but on tablets of *h* hearts.
Gal 3: 3 to attain your goal by *h* effort?
2Pe 2:18 lustful desires of sinful *h* nature,

HUMANITY* (HUMAN)
Heb 2:14 he too shared in their *h* so that

HUMBLE (HUMBLED HUMBLES HUMILIATE HUMILIATED HUMILITY)
Nu 12: 3 (Now Moses was a very *h* man,
2Ch 7:14 will *h* themselves and pray
Ps 18:27 You save the *h*
25: 9 He guides the *h* in what is right
149: 4 he crowns the *h* with salvation.
Pr 3:34 but gives grace to the *h*.
Isa 66: 2 he who is *h* and contrite in spirit,
Mt 11:29 for I am gentle and *h* in heart,
Eph 4: 2 Be completely *h* and gentle;
Jas 4: 6 but gives grace to the *h*."
4:10 *H* yourselves before the Lord,
1Pe 5: 5 but gives grace to the *h*."
5: 6 *H* yourselves,

HUMBLED (HUMBLE)
Mt 23:12 whoever exalts himself will be *h*,
Lk 14:11 who exalts himself will be *h*,
Php 2: 8 he *h* himself

HUMBLES* (HUMBLE)
1Sa 2: 7 he *h* and he exalts.
Isa 26: 5 He *h* those who dwell on high,
Mt 18: 4 whoever *h* himself like this child is
23:12 whoever *h* himself will be exalted.
Lk 14:11 he who *h* himself will be exalted."
18:14 he who *h* himself will be exalted."

HUMILIATE* (HUMBLE)
Pr 25: 7 than for him to *h* you
1Co 11:22 and *h* those who have nothing?

HUMILIATED (HUMBLE)
Jer 31:19 I was ashamed and *h*
Lk 14: 9 *h*, you will have to take the least

HUMILITY* (HUMBLE)
Ps 45: 4 of truth, *h* and righteousness;
Pr 11: 2 but with *h* comes wisdom.
15:33 and *h* comes before honor.
18:12 but *h* comes before honor.
22: 4 *H* and the fear of the LORD
Zep 2: 3 Seek righteousness, seek *h*;
Ac 20:19 I served the Lord with great *h*

Php 2: 3 but in *h* consider others better
Col 2:18 let anyone who delights in false *h*
2:23 their false *h* and their harsh
3:12 *h*, gentleness and patience.
Tit 3: 2 and to show true *h* toward all men.
Jas 3:13 in the *h* that comes from wisdom.
1Pe 5: 5 clothe yourselves with *h*

HUNG (HANG)
Dt 21:23 anyone who is *h* on a tree is
Mt 18: 6 him to have a large millstone *h*
Lk 19:48 all the people *h* on his words.
Gal 3:13 "Cursed is everyone who is *h*

HUNGER (HUNGRY)
Ne 9:15 In their *h* you gave them bread
Pr 6:30 to satisfy his *h* when he is starving.
Mt 5: 6 Blessed are those who *h*
Lk 6:21 Blessed are you who *h* now,
2Co 6: 5 sleepless nights and *h*; in purity,
11:27 I have known *h* and thirst
Rev 7:16 Never again will they *h*;

HUNGRY (HUNGER)
Job 24:10 carry the sheaves, but still go *h*.
Ps 107: 9 and fills the *h* with good things.
146: 7 and gives food to the *h*.
Pr 19:15 and the shiftless man goes *h*.
25:21 If your enemy is *h*, give him food
27: 7 to the *h* even what is bitter tastes
Isa 58: 7 not to share your food with the *h*
58:10 spend yourselves in behalf of the *h*
Eze 18: 7 but gives his food to the *h*
18:16 but gives his food to the *h*
Mt 15:32 I do not want to send them away *h*,
25:35 For I was *h* and you gave me
25:42 For I was *h* and you gave me
Lk 1:53 He has filled the *h* with good things
Jn 6:35 comes to me will never go *h*,
Ro 12:20 "If your enemy is *h*, feed him;
1Co 4:11 To this very hour we go *h*
Php 4:12 whether well fed or *h*,

HUR
Ex 17:12 Aaron and *H* held his hands up—

HURL
Mic 7:19 *h* all our iniquities into the depths

HURT (HURTS)
Ecc 8: 9 it over others to his own *h*.
Mk 16:18 deadly poison, it will not *h* them
Rev 2:11 He who overcomes will not be *h*

HURTS* (HURT)
Ps 15: 4 even when it *h*,
Pr 26:28 A lying tongue hates those it *h*,

HUSBAND (HUSBAND'S HUSBANDS)
Pr 31:11 Her *h* has full confidence in her
31:23 Her *h* is respected at the city gate,
31:28 her *h* also, and he praises her:
Isa 54: 5 For your Maker is your *h*—
Jer 3:14 the LORD, "for I am your *h*.
3:20 like a woman unfaithful to her *h*,
Jn 4:17 "I have no *h*," she replied.
Ro 7: 2 a married woman is bound to her *h*
1Co 7: 2 and each woman her own *h*.
7: 3 The *h* should fulfill his marital duty
7:10 wife must not separate from her *h*.
7:11 And a *h* must not divorce his wife.
7:13 And if a woman has a *h* who is not
7:14 For the unbelieving *h* has been
7:39 A woman is bound to her *h* as long
7:39 But if her *h* dies, she is free
2Co 11: 2 I promised you to one *h*, to Christ,
Gal 4:27 woman than of her who has a *h*."
Eph 5:23 For the *h* is the head of the wife
5:33 and the wife must respect her *h*.
1Ti 3: 2 the *h* of but one wife, temperate,
3:12 A deacon must be the *h* of
5: 9 has been faithful to her *h*,
Tit 1: 6 An elder must be blameless, the *h*

HUSBANDMAN see GARDENER

HUSBAND'S (HUSBAND)
Dt 25: 5 Her *h* brother shall take her
Pr 12: 4 of noble character is her *h* crown,
1Co 7: 4 the *h* body does not belong

HUSBANDS (HUSBAND)
Eph 5:22 submit to your *h* as to the Lord.
5:25 *H*, love your wives, just
5:28 *h* ought to love their wives
Col 3:18 submit to your *h*, as is fitting
3:19 *H*, love your wives and do not be
Tit 2: 4 the younger women to love their *h*
2: 5 and to be subject to their *h*,
1Pe 3: 1 same way be submissive to your *h*
3: 7 *H*, in the same way be considerate

HUSHAI
Wise man of David who frustrated Ahithophel's advice and foiled Absalom's revolt (2Sa 15:32-37; 16:15-17:16; 1Ch 27:33).

HYMN* (HYMNS)
Ps 40: 3 a *h* of praise to our God.
Mt 26:30 they had sung a *h*, they went out
Mk 14:26 they had sung a *h*, they went out
1Co 14:26 everyone has a *h*, or a word

HYMNS* (HYMN)
Ac 16:25 Silas were praying and singing *h*
Ro 15: 9 I will sing *h* to your name."
Eph 5:19 to one another with psalms, *h*
Col 3:16 *h* and spiritual songs with gratitude

HYPOCRISY* (HYPOCRITE HYPOCRITES HYPOCRITICAL)
Mt 23:28 but on the inside you are full of *h*
Mk 12:15 we?" But Jesus knew their *h*.
Lk 12: 1 yeast of the Pharisees, which is *h*.
Gal 2:13 The other Jews joined him in his *h*,
2:13 by their *h* even Barnabas was led
1Pe 2: 1 *h*, envy, and slander of every kind.

HYPOCRITE* (HYPOCRISY)
Mt 7: 5 You *h*, first take the plank out
Lk 6:42 You *h*, first take the plank out

HYPOCRITES* (HYPOCRISY)
Ps 26: 4 nor do I consort with *h*;
Mt 6: 2 as the *h* do in the synagogues
6: 5 when you pray, do not be like the *h*
6:16 do not look somber as the *h* do,
15: 7 You *h*! Isaiah was right
22:18 their evil intent, said, "You *h*,
23:13 of the law and Pharisees, you *h*!
23:15 of the law and Pharisees, you *h*!
23:23 of the law and Pharisees, you *h*!
23:25 of the law and Pharisees, you *h*!
23:27 you *h*! You are like whitewashed
23:29 of the law and Pharisees, you *h*!
24:51 and assign him a place with the *h*,
Mk 7: 6 when he prophesied about you *h*;
Lk 12:56 *H*! You know how
13:15 The Lord answered him, "You *h*!

HYPOCRITICAL* (HYPOCRISY)
1Ti 4: 2 teachings come through *h* liars,

HYSSOP
Ex 12:22 Take a bunch of *h*, dip it
Ps 51: 7 with *h*, and I will be clean;
Jn 19:29 the sponge on a stalk of the *h* plant,

ICHABOD
1Sa 4:21 She named the boy *I*, saying,

IDLE* (IDLENESS IDLERS)
Dt 32:47 They are not just *i* words for you—
Job 11: 3 Will your *i* talk reduce men
Ecc 10:18 if his hands are *i*, the house leaks.
11: 6 at evening let not your hands be *i*,
Isa 58:13 as you please or speaking *i* words,
Col 2:18 mind puffs him up with *i* notions.
1Th 5:14 those who are *i*, encourage
2Th 3: 6 away from every brother who is *i*
3: 7 We were not *i* when we were
3:11 We hear that some among you are *i*
1Ti 5:13 they get into the habit of being *i*

IDLENESS* (IDLE)
Pr 31:27 and does not eat the bread of *i*.

IDLERS* (IDLE)
1Ti 5:13 And not only do they become *i*,

IDOL (IDOLATER IDOLATERS IDOLATRY IDOLS)
Ex 20: 4 make for yourself an *i* in the form
32: 4 made it into an *i* cast in the shape
Isa 40:19 As for an *i*, a craftsman casts it,
41: 7 He nails down the *i*
44:15 he makes an *i* and bows down to it.
44:17 From the rest he makes a god, his *i*;
Hab 2:18 "Of what value is an *i*,
1Co 8: 4 We know that an *i* is nothing at all

IDOLATER* (IDOL)
1Co 5:11 an *i* or a slanderer, a drunkard
Eph 5: 5 greedy person—such a man is an *i*

IDOLATERS (IDOL)
1Co 5:10 or the greedy and swindlers, or *i*.
6: 9 Neither the sexually immoral nor *i*

IDOLATRY (IDOL)
1Sa 15:23 and arrogance like the evil of *i*.
1Co 10:14 my dear friends, flee from *i*.
Gal 5:20 and debauchery; *i* and witchcraft;
Col 3: 5 evil desires and greed, which is *i*.
1Pe 4: 3 orgies, carousing and detestable *i*.

IDOLS (IDOL)
Dt 32:16 angered him with their detestable *i*.
Ps 78:58 aroused his jealousy with their *i*.
Isa 44: 9 All who make *i* are nothing,
Eze 23:39 sacrificed their children to their *i*,
Ac 15:20 to abstain from food polluted by *i*,
21:25 abstain from food sacrificed to *i*,
1Co 8: 1 Now about food sacrificed to *i*:
1Jn 5:21 children, keep yourselves from *i*.
Rev 2:14 to sin by eating food sacrificed to *i*

IGNORANT (IGNORE)
1Co 15:34 for there are some who are *i* of God
Heb 5: 2 to deal gently with those who are *i*
1Pe 2:15 good you should silence the *i* talk
2Pe 3:16 which *i* and unstable people distort

IGNORE (IGNORANT IGNORED IGNORES)
Dt 22: 1 do not *i* it but be sure
Ps 9:12 he does not *i* the cry of the afflicted
Heb 2: 3 if we *i* such a great salvation?

IGNORED (IGNORE)
Hos 4: 6 you have *i* the law of your God,
1Co 14:38 he ignores this, he himself will be *i*.

IGNORES* (IGNORE)
Pr 10:17 whoever *i* correction leads others
13:18 He who *i* discipline comes
15:32 He who *i* discipline despises
1Co 14:38 If he *i* this, he himself will be

ILL (ILLNESS)
Mt 4:24 brought to him all who were *i*

ILL-GOTTEN
Pr 1:19 the end of all who go after *i* gain;
10: 2 *I* treasures are of no value,

ILL-TEMPERED* (TEMPER)
Pr 21:19 than with a quarrelsome and *i* wife.

ILLEGITIMATE
Heb 12: 8 then you are *i* children

ILLNESS (ILL)
2Ki 8: 9 'Will I recover from this *i*?' "
2Ch 16:12 even in his *i* he did not seek help
Ps 41: 3 and restore him from his bed of *i*.
Isa 38: 9 king of Judah after his *i*

ILLUMINATED*
Rev 18: 1 and the earth was *i* by his splendor.

IMAGE (IMAGES)
Ge 1:26 "Let us make man in our *i*,
1:27 So God created man in his own *i*,
9: 6 for in the *i* of God
Dt 27:15 "Cursed is the man who carves an *i*
Isa 40:18 What *i* will you compare him to?
Da 3: 1 King Nebuchadnezzar made an *i*
1Co 11: 7 since he is the *i* and glory of God;
2Co 4: 4 glory of Christ, who is the *i* of God.
Col 1:15 He is the *i* of the invisible God,
3:10 in knowledge in the *i* of its Creator.
Rev 13:14 them to set up an *i* in honor

IMAGES (IMAGE)
Ps 97: 7 All who worship *i* are put to shame,
Jer 10:14 His *i* are a fraud;
Ro 1:23 of the immortal God for *i* made

IMAGINATION (IMAGINE)
Eze 13: 2 who prophesy out of their own *i*:

IMAGINE (IMAGINATION)
Eph 3:20 more than all we ask or *i*,

IMITATE (IMITATORS)
1Co 4:16 Therefore I urge you to *i* me.
Heb 6:12 but to *i* those who through faith
13: 7 of their way of life and *i* their faith.
3Jn :11 do not *i* what is evil but what is

IMITATORS* (IMITATE)
Eph 5: 1 Be *i* of God, therefore,
1Th 1: 6 You became *i* of us and of the Lord
2:14 became *i* of God's churches

IMMANUEL*
Isa 7:14 birth to a son, and will call him *I*.
8: 8 O *I*!"
Mt 1:23 and they will call him *I*"—

IMMORAL* (IMMORALITY)
Pr 6:24 keeping you from the *i* woman,
1Co 5: 9 to associate with sexually *i* people
5:10 the people of this world who are *i*,
5:11 but is sexually *i* or greedy,

1Co 6: 9 Neither the sexually *i* nor idolaters
Eph 5: 5 No *i*, impure or greedy person—
Heb 12:16 See that no one is sexually *i*,
13: 4 the adulterer and all the sexually *i*.
Rev 21: 8 the murderers, the sexually *i*,
22:15 the sexually *i*, the murderers,

IMMORALITY* (IMMORAL)
Nu 25: 1 in sexual *i* with Moabite women,
Jer 3: 9 Because Israel's *i* mattered so little
Mt 15:19 murder, adultery, sexual *i*, theft,
Mk 7:21 sexual *i*, theft, murder, adultery,
Ac 15:20 from sexual *i*, from the meat
15:29 animals and from sexual *i*.
21:25 animals and from sexual *i*."
Ro 13:13 not in sexual *i* and debauchery,
1Co 5: 1 reported that there is sexual *i*
6:13 The body is not meant for sexual *i*,
6:18 Flee from sexual *i*.
7: 2 But since there is so much *i*,
10: 8 We should not commit sexual *i*,
Gal 5:19 sexual *i*, impurity and debauchery;
Eph 5: 3 must not be even a hint of sexual *i*,
Col 3: 5 sexual *i*, impurity, lust, evil desires
1Th 4: 3 that you should avoid sexual *i*;
Jude : 4 grace of our God into a license for *i*
: 7 gave themselves up to sexual *i*
Rev 2:14 and by committing sexual *i*.
2:20 misleads my servants into sexual *i*
2:21 given her time to repent of her *i*,
9:21 their sexual *i* or their thefts.

IMMORTAL* (IMMORTALITY)
Ro 1:23 glory of the *i* God for images made
1Ti 1:17 Now to the King eternal, *i*,
6:16 who alone is *i* and who lives

IMMORTALITY* (IMMORTAL)
Pr 12:28 along that path is *i*.
Ro 2: 7 honor and *i*, he will give eternal life
1Co 15:53 and the mortal with *i*.
15:54 with *i*, then the saying that is
2Ti 1:10 and *i* to light through the gospel.

IMPARTIAL*
Jas 3:17 and good fruit, *i* and sincere.

IMPARTS*
Pr 29:15 The rod of correction *i* wisdom,

IMPERFECT*
1Co 13:10 perfection comes, the *i* disappears.

IMPERISHABLE
1Co 15:42 it is raised *i*; it is sown in dishonor,
15:50 nor does the perishable inherit the *i*
1Pe 1:23 not of perishable seed, but of *i*,

IMPLANTED*
Ps 94: 9 Does he who *i* the ear not hear?

IMPLORE*
Mal 1: 9 "Now *i* God to be gracious to us.
2Co 5:20 We *i* you on Christ's behalf:

IMPORTANCE* (IMPORTANT)
1Co 15: 3 passed on to you as of first *i*:

IMPORTANT (IMPORTANCE)
Mt 6:25 Is not life more *i* than food,
23:23 have neglected the more *i* matters
Mk 12:29 "The most *i* one," answered Jesus,
12:33 as yourself is more *i* than all burnt
Php 1:18 The *i* thing is that in every way,

IMPOSSIBLE
Mt 17:20 Nothing will be *i* for you."
19:26 "With man this is *i*,
Mk 10:27 "With man this is *i*, but not
Lk 1:37 For nothing is *i* with God."
18:27 "What is *i* with men is possible
Ac 2:24 it was *i* for death to keep its hold
Heb 6: 4 It is *i* for those who have once been
6:18 things in which it is *i* for God to lie,
10: 4 because it is *i* for the blood of bulls
11: 6 without faith it is *i* to please God,

IMPOSTORS
2Ti 3:13 and *i* will go from bad to worse,

IMPRESS* (IMPRESSES)
Dt 6: 7 *I* them on your children.

IMPRESSES* (IMPRESS)
Pr 17:10 A rebuke *i* a man of discernment

IMPROPER*
Eph 5: 3 these are *i* for God's holy people.

IMPURE (IMPURITY)
Ac 10:15 not call anything *i* that God has
Eph 5: 5 No immoral, *i* or greedy person—
1Th 2: 3 spring from error or *i* motives,
4: 7 For God did not call us to be *i*,
Rev 21:27 Nothing *i* will ever enter it,

IMPURITY (IMPURE)
Ro 1:24 hearts to sexual *i* for the degrading
Gal 5:19 sexual immorality, *i*
Eph 4:19 as to indulge in every kind of *i*,
5: 3 or of any kind of *i*, or of greed,
Col 3: 5 *i*, lust, evil desires and greed,

INCENSE
Ex 30: 1 altar of acacia wood for burning *i*.
40: 5 Place the gold altar of *i* in front
Ps 141: 2 my prayer be set before you like *i*;
Mt 2:11 him with gifts of gold and of *i*
Heb 9: 4 which had the golden altar of *i*
Rev 5: 8 were holding golden bowls full of *i*,
8: 4 The smoke of the *i*, together

INCLINATION (INCLINES)
Ge 6: 5 and that every *i* of the thoughts

INCLINES* (INCLINATION)
Ecc 10: 2 The heart of the wise *i* to the right,

INCOME
Ecc 5:10 wealth is never satisfied with his *i*.
1Co 16: 2 sum of money in keeping with his *i*,

INCOMPARABLE*
Eph 2: 7 ages he might show the *i* riches

INCREASE (EVER-INCREASING INCREASED INCREASES INCREASING)
Ge 1:22 "Be fruitful and *i* in number
3:16 "I will greatly *i* your pains
8:17 be fruitful and *i* in number upon it
Ps 62:10 though your riches *i*,
Pr 22:16 oppresses the poor to *i* his wealth
Isa 9: 7 Of the *i* of his government
Mt 24:12 Because of the *i* of wickedness,
Lk 17: 5 said to the Lord, "*I* our faith!"
Ac 12:24 But the word of God continued to *i*
Ro 5:20 added so that the trespass might *i*.
1Th 3:12 May the Lord make your love *i*

INCREASED (INCREASE)
Ac 6: 7 of disciples in Jerusalem *i* rapidly,
Ro 5:20 But where sin *i*, grace *i* all the more

INCREASES (INCREASE)
Pr 24: 5 and a man of knowledge *i* strength;

INCREASING (INCREASE)
Ac 6: 1 when the number of disciples was *i*,
2Th 1: 3 one of you has for each other is *i*.
2Pe 1: 8 these qualities in *i* measure,

INCREDIBLE*
Ac 26: 8 of you consider it *i* that God raises

INDECENT
Ro 1:27 Men committed *i* acts

INDEPENDENT*
1Co 11:11 however, woman is not *i* of man,
11:11 of man, nor is man *i* of woman.

INDESCRIBABLE*
2Co 9:15 Thanks be to God for his *i* gift!

INDESTRUCTIBLE*
Heb 7:16 on the basis of the power of an *i* life

INDIGNANT
Mk 10:14 When Jesus saw this, he was *i*.

INDISPENSABLE*
1Co 12:22 seem to be weaker are *i*,

INEFFECTIVE*
2Pe 1: 8 they will keep you from being *i*

INEXPRESSIBLE*
2Co 12: 4 He heard *i* things, things that man
1Pe 1: 8 are filled with an *i* and glorious joy,

INFANCY* (INFANTS)
2Ti 3:15 from *i* you have known the holy

INFANTS (INFANCY)
Ps 8: 2 From the lips of children and *i*
Mt 21:16 " 'From the lips of children and *i*
1Co 3: 1 but as worldly—mere *i* in Christ.
14:20 In regard to evil be *i*,
Eph 4:14 Then we will no longer be *i*,

INFIRMITIES*
Isa 53: 4 Surely he took up our *i*
Mt 8:17 "He took up our *i*

INFLAMED
Ro 1:27 were *i* with lust for one another.

INFLUENTIAL*
1Co 1:26 not many were *i*; not many were

INHABITANTS (INHABITED)
Nu 33:55 " 'But if you do not drive out the *i*
Rev 8:13 Woe! Woe to the *i* of the earth,

INHABITED (INHABITANTS)
Isa 45:18 but formed it to be *i*—

INHERIT (CO-HEIRS HEIR HEIRS HERITAGE INHERITANCE)
Dt 1:38 because he will lead Israel to *i* it.
Jos 1: 6 people to *i* the land I swore
Ps 37:11 But the meek will *i* the land
37:29 the righteous will *i* the land
Zec 2:12 The LORD will *i* Judah
Mt 5: 5 for they will *i* the earth.
19:29 as much and will *i* eternal life.
Mk 10:17 "what must I do to *i* eternal life?"
Lk 10:25 "what must I do to *i* eternal life?"
18:18 what must I do to *i* eternal life?"
1Co 6: 9 the wicked will not *i* the kingdom
15:50 blood cannot *i* the kingdom of God
Rev 21: 7 He who overcomes will *i* all this,

INHERITANCE (INHERIT)
Lev 20:24 I will give it to you as an *i*,
Dt 4:20 to be the people of his *i*,
10: 9 the LORD is their *i*, as the LORD
Jos 14: 3 two-and-a-half tribes their *i* east
Ps 16: 6 surely I have a delightful *i*.
33:12 the people he chose for his *i*.
136: 21 and gave their land as an *i*,
Pr 13:22 A good man leaves an *i*
Mt 25:34 blessed by my Father; take your *i*,
Eph 1:14 who is a deposit guaranteeing our *i*
5: 5 has any *i* in the kingdom of Christ
Col 1:12 you to share in the *i* of the saints
3:24 you know that you will receive an *i*
Heb 9:15 receive the promised eternal *i*—
1Pe 1: 4 and into an *i* that can never perish,

INIQUITIES (INIQUITY)
Ps 78:38 he forgave their *i*
103: 10 or repay us according to our *i*.
Isa 53: 5 he was crushed for our *i*;
53:11 and he will bear their *i*.
59: 2 But your *i* have separated
Mic 7:19 and hurl all our *i* into the depths

INIQUITY (INIQUITIES)
Ps 25:11 forgive my *i*, though it is great.
32: 5 and did not cover up my *i*.
51: 2 Wash away all my *i*
51: 9 and blot out all my *i*.
Isa 53: 6 the *i* of us all.

INJURED
Eze 34:16 will bind up the *i* and strengthen
Zec 11:16 or heal the *i*, or feed the healthy,

INJUSTICE
2Ch 19: 7 the LORD our God there is no *i*

INK
2Co 3: 3 not with *i* but with the Spirit

INN*
Lk 2: 7 there was no room for them in the *i*
10:34 took him to an *i* and took care

INNOCENT
Ex 23: 7 do not put an *i* or honest person
Dt 25: 1 acquitting the *i* and condemning
Pr 6:17 hands that shed *i* blood,
17:26 It is not good to punish an *i* man,
Mt 10:16 shrewd as snakes and as *i* as doves.
27: 4 "for I have betrayed *i* blood."
27:24 I am *i* of this man's blood," he said.
Ac 20:26 declare to you today that I am *i*
Ro 16:19 what is good, and *i* about what is
1Co 4: 4 but that does not make me *i*.

INQUIRE
Isa 8:19 should not a people *i* of their God?

INSCRIPTION
Mt 22:20 And whose *i*?" "Caesar's,"
2Ti 2:19 with this *i*: "The Lord knows those

INSIGHT
1Ki 4:29 Solomon wisdom and very great *i*,
Ps 119: 99 I have more *i* than all my teachers,
Pr 5: 1 listen well to my words of *i*,
21:30 There is no wisdom, no *i*, no plan
Php 1: 9 more in knowledge and depth of *i*,
2Ti 2: 7 for the Lord will give you *i*

INSOLENT
Ro 1:30 God-haters, *i*, arrogant

INSPIRED*
Hos 9: 7 the *i* man a maniac.
1Th 1: 3 and your endurance *i* by hope

INSTALLED
Ps 2: 6 "I have *i* my King

INSTINCT* (INSTINCTS)
2Pe 2:12 are like brute beasts, creatures of *i*,
Jude :10 things they do understand by *i*,

INSTINCTS* (INSTINCT)
Jude :19 who follow mere natural *i*

INSTITUTED
Ro 13: 2 rebelling against what God has *i*,
1Pe 2:13 to every authority *i* among men:

INSTRUCT (INSTRUCTED INSTRUCTION INSTRUCTIONS INSTRUCTOR)
Ps 32: 8 I will *i* you and teach you
105: 22 to *i* his princes as he pleased
Pr 9: 9 *I* a wise man and he will be wiser
Ro 15:14 and competent to *i* one another.
1Co 2:16 that he may *i* him?"
14:19 to *i* others than ten thousand words
2Ti 2:25 who oppose him he must gently *i*,

INSTRUCTED (INSTRUCT)
2Ch 26: 5 who *i* him in the fear of God.
Pr 21:11 a wise man is *i*, he gets knowledge.
Isa 50: 4 LORD has given me an *i* tongue,
Mt 13:52 who has been *i* about the kingdom
1Co 14:31 in turn so that everyone may be *i*

INSTRUCTION (INSTRUCT)
Pr 1: 8 Listen, my son, to your father's *i*
4: 1 Listen, my sons, to a father's *i*;
4:13 Hold on to *i*, do not let it go;
8:10 Choose my *i* instead of silver,
8:33 Listen to my *i* and be wise;
13: 1 A wise son heeds his father's *i*,
13:13 He who scorns *i* will pay for it,
16:20 Whoever gives heed to *i* prospers,
16:21 and pleasant words promote *i*.
19:20 Listen to advice and accept *i*,
23:12 Apply your heart to *i*
1Co 14: 6 or prophecy or word of *i*?
14:26 or a word of *i*, a revelation,
Eph 6: 4 up in the training and *i* of the Lord.
1Th 4: 8 he who rejects this *i* does not reject
2Th 3:14 If anyone does not obey our *i*
1Ti 1:18 I give you this *i* in keeping
6: 3 to the sound *i* of our Lord Jesus
2Ti 4: 2 with great patience and careful *i*.

INSTRUCTIONS (INSTRUCT)
1Ti 3:14 I am writing you these *i* so that,

INSTRUCTOR (INSTRUCT)
Gal 6: 6 share all good things with his *i*.

INSTRUMENT* (INSTRUMENTS)
Eze 33:32 beautiful voice and plays an *i* well,
Ac 9:15 This man is my chosen *i*
2Ti 2:21 he will be an *i* for noble purposes,

INSTRUMENTS (INSTRUMENT)
Ro 6:13 as *i* of wickedness, but rather offer

INSULT (INSULTED INSULTS)
Pr 9: 7 corrects a mocker invites *i*;
12:16 but a prudent man overlooks an *i*.
Mt 5:11 Blessed are you when people *i* you,
Lk 6:22 when they exclude you and *i* you
1Pe 3: 9 evil with evil or *i* with *i*,

INSULTED (INSULT)
Heb 10:29 and who has *i* the Spirit of grace?
Jas 2: 6 love him? But you have *i* the poor.
1Pe 4:14 If you are *i* because of the name

INSULTS (INSULT)
Ps 22: 7 they hurl *i*, shaking their heads:
69: 9 the *i* of those who insult you fall
Pr 22:10 quarrels and *i* are ended.
Mk 15:29 passed by hurled *i* at him,
Jn 9:28 Then they hurled *i* at him and said,
Ro 15: 3 "The *i* of those who insult you have
2Co 12:10 in *i*, in hardships, in persecutions,
1Pe 2:23 When they hurled their *i* at him,

INTEGRITY*
Dt 9: 5 or your *i* that you are going
1Ki 9: 4 if you walk before me in *i* of heart
1Ch 29:17 the heart and are pleased with *i*.
Ne 7: 2 because he was a man of *i*
Job 2: 3 And he still maintains his *i*,
Job 2: 9 "Are you still holding on to your *i*?
6:29 reconsider, for my *i* is at stake.
27: 5 till I die, I will not deny my *i*.
Ps 7: 8 according to my *i*, O Most High.
25:21 May *i* and uprightness protect me,
41:12 In my *i* you uphold me
78:72 David shepherded them with *i*
Pr 10: 9 The man of *i* walks securely,
11: 3 The *i* of the upright guides them,
13: 6 Righteousness guards the man of *i*,
17:26 or to flog officials for their *i*.
29:10 Bloodthirsty men hate a man of *i*
Isa 45:23 my mouth has uttered in all *i*
59: 4 no one pleads his case with *i*.
Mt 22:16 "we know you are a man of *i*
Mk 12:14 we know you are a man of *i*.
Tit 2: 7 your teaching show *i*, seriousness

INTELLIGENCE (INTELLIGENT)
Isa 29:14 the *i* of the intelligent will vanish."
1Co 1:19 *i* of the intelligent I will frustrate."

INTELLIGENT (INTELLIGENCE)
Isa 29:14 the intelligence of the *i* will vanish

INTELLIGIBLE
1Co 14:19 I would rather speak five *i* words

INTENDED
Ge 50:20 place of God? You *i* to harm me,

INTENSE
1Th 2:17 out of our *i* longing we made every
Rev 16: 9 They were seared by the *i* heat

INTERCEDE (INTERCEDES INTERCEDING INTERCESSION INTERCESSOR)
Heb 7:25 he always lives to *i* for them.

INTERCEDES* (INTERCEDE)
Ro 8:26 but the Spirit himself *i* for us
8:27 because the Spirit *i* for the saints

INTERCEDING* (INTERCEDE)
Ro 8:34 hand of God and is also *i* for us.

INTERCESSION* (INTERCEDE)
Isa 53:12 and made *i* for the transgressors.
1Ti 2: 1 *i* and thanksgiving be made

INTERCESSOR* (INTERCEDE)
Job 16:20 My *i* is my friend

INTEREST (INTERESTS)
Lev 25:36 Do not take *i* of any kind from him,
Dt 23:20 You may charge a foreigner *i*,
Mt 25:27 would have received it back with *i*.
Php 2:20 who takes a genuine *i*

INTERESTS (INTEREST)
1Co 7:34 his wife—and his *i* are divided.
Php 2: 4 only to your own *i*, but also to the *i*
2:21 everyone looks out for his own *i*,

INTERFERE*
Ezr 6: 7 Do not *i* with the work

INTERMARRY (MARRY)
Dt 7: 3 Do not *i* with them.
Ezr 9:14 and *i* with the peoples who commit

INTERPRET (INTERPRETATION INTERPRETER INTERPRETS)
Ge 41:15 "I had a dream, and no one can *i* it.
Mt 16: 3 you cannot *i* the signs of the times.
1Co 12:30 Do all *i*? But eagerly desire
14:13 pray that he may *i* what he says.
14:27 one at a time, and someone must *i*.

INTERPRETATION (INTERPRET)
1Co 12:10 and to still another the *i* of tongues.
14:26 a revelation, a tongue or an *i*.
2Pe 1:20 about by the prophet's own *i*.

INTERPRETER (INTERPRET)
1Co 14:28 If there is no *i*, the speaker should

INTERPRETS (INTERPRET)
1Co 14: 5 he *i*, so that the church may be

INVADED
2Ki 17: 5 king of Assyria *i* the entire land,
24: 1 king of Babylon *i* the land,

INVENT* (INVENTED)
Ro 1:30 boastful; they *i* ways of doing evil;

INVENTED* (INVENT)
2Pe 1:16 We did not follow cleverly *i* stories

INVESTIGATED
Lk 1: 3 I myself have carefully *i* everything

INVISIBLE*
Ro 1:20 of the world God's *i* qualities—
Col 1:15 He is the image of the *i* God,
1:16 and on earth, visible and *i*,
1Ti 1:17 immortal, *i*, the only God,
Heb 11:27 because he saw him who is *i*.

INVITE (INVITED INVITES)
Mt 22: 9 *i* to the banquet anyone you find.'
25:38 did we see you a stranger and *i* you
Lk 14:12 do not *i* your friends, your brothers
14:13 you give a banquet, *i* the poor,

INVITED (INVITE)
Zep 1: 7 he has consecrated those he has *i*.
Mt 22:14 For many are *i*, but few are chosen
25:35 I was a stranger and you *i* me in,
Lk 14:10 But when you are *i*, take the lowest
Rev 19: 9 'Blessed are those who are *i*

INVITES (INVITE)
Pr 18: 6 and his mouth *i* a beating.
1Co 10:27 If some unbeliever *i* you to a meal

INVOLVED
2Ti 2: 4 a soldier gets *i* in civilian affairs—

IRON
2Ki 6: 6 threw it there, and made the *i* float.
Ps 2: 9 will rule them with an *i* scepter;
Pr 27:17 As *i* sharpens *i*,
Da 2:33 and thighs of bronze, its legs of *i*,
1Ti 4: 2 have been seared as with a hot *i*.
Rev 2:27 He will rule them with an *i* scepter;
12: 5 all the nations with an *i* scepter.
19:15 He will rule them with an *i* scepter

IRRELIGIOUS*
1Ti 1: 9 and sinful, the unholy and *i*;

IRREVOCABLE*
Ro 11:29 for God's gifts and his call are *i*.

ISAAC
Son of Abraham by Sarah (Ge 17:19; 21:1-7; 1Ch 1:28). Abrahamic covenant perpetuated through (Ge 17:21; 26:2-5). Offered up by Abraham (Ge 22; Heb 11:17-19). Rebekah taken as wife (Ge 24). Inherited Abraham's estate (Ge 25:5). Fathered Esau and Jacob (Ge 25:19-26; 1Ch 1:34). Nearly lost Rebekah to Abimelech (Ge 26:1-11). Covenant with Abimelech (Ge 26:12-31). Tricked into blessing Jacob (Ge 27). Death (Ge 35:27-29). Father of Israel (Ex 3:6; Dt 29:13; Ro 9:10).

ISAIAH
Prophet to Judah (Isa 1:1). Called by the LORD (Isa 6). Announced judgment to Ahaz (Isa 7), deliverance from Assyria to Hezekiah (2Ki 19; Isa 36-37), deliverance from death to Hezekiah (2Ki 20:1-11; Isa 38). Chronicler of Judah's history (2Ch 26:22; 32:32).

ISH-BOSHETH*
Son of Saul who attempted to succeed him as king (2Sa 2:8-4:12; 1Ch 8:33).

ISHMAEL
Son of Abraham by Hagar (Ge 16; 1Ch 1:28). Blessed, but not son of covenant (Ge 17:18-21; Gal 4:21-31). Sent away by Sarah (Ge 21:8-21). Children (Ge 25:12-18; 1Ch 1:29-31). Death (Ge 25:17).

ISLAND
Rev 1: 9 was on the *i* of Patmos
16:20 Every *i* fled away

ISRAEL (ISRAEL'S ISRAELITE ISRAELITES)
1. Name given to Jacob (see JACOB).
2. Corporate name of Jacob's descendants; often specifically Northern Kingdom.
Ex 28:11 Engrave the names of the sons of *I*
28:29 of the sons of *I* over his heart
Nu 24:17 a scepter will rise out of *I*.
Dt 6: 4 Hear, O *I*: The LORD our God,
10:12 O *I*, what does the LORD your
Jos 4:22 *I* crossed the Jordan on dry ground
Jdg 17: 6 In those days *I* had no king;
Ru 2:12 of *I*, under whose wings you have
1Sa 3:20 *I* from Dan to Beersheba
4:21 "The glory has departed from *I*"—
14:23 So the LORD rescued *I* that day,
15:26 has rejected you as king over *I*!"
17:46 will know that there is a God in *I*.
18:16 But all *I* and Judah loved David,
2Sa 5: 2 'You will shepherd my people *I*,
5: 3 they anointed David king over *I*.
14:25 In all *I* there was not a man

1Ki 1:35 I have appointed him ruler over *I*
10: 9 of the LORD's eternal love for *I*,
18:17 "Is that you, you troubler of *I*?"
19:18 Yet I reserve seven thousand in *I*—
2Ki 5: 8 know that there is a prophet in *I*."
1Ch 17:22 made your people *I* your very own
21: 1 incited David to take a census of *I*.
29:25 Solomon in the sight of all *I*
2Ch 9: 8 of the love of your God for *I*
Ps 73: 1 Surely God is good to *I*,
81: 8 if you would but listen to me, O *I*!
98: 3 his faithfulness to the house of *I*;
99: 8 you were to *I* a forgiving God,
Isa 11:12 and gather the exiles of *I*;
27: 6 *I* will bud and blossom
44:21 O *I*, I will not forget you.
46:13 my splendor to *I*.
Jer 2: 3 *I* was holy to the LORD,
23: 6 and *I* will live in safety.
31: 2 I will come to give rest to *I*."
31:10 'He who scattered *I* will gather
31:31 covenant with the house of *I*
33:17 sit on the throne of the house of *I*,
Eze 3:17 you a watchman for the house of *I*;
33: 7 you a watchman for the house of *I*;
34: 2 prophesy against the shepherds of *I*
37:28 that I the LORD make *I* holy,
39:23 of *I* went into exile for their sin,
Da 9:20 my sin and the sin of my people *I*
Hos 11: 1 "When *I* was a child, I loved him,
Am 4:12 prepare to meet your God, O *I*."
7:11 and *I* will surely go into exile,
8: 2 "The time is ripe for my people *I*;
9:14 I will bring back my exiled people *I*
Mic 5: 2 one who will be ruler over *I*,
Zep 3:13 The remnant of *I* will do no wrong;
Zec 11:14 brotherhood between Judah and *I*.
Mal 1: 5 even beyond the borders of *I*!'
Mt 2: 6 be the shepherd of my people *I*.'"
10: 6 Go rather to the lost sheep of *I*.
15:24 only to the lost sheep of *I*."
Mk 12:29 'Hear, O *I*, the Lord our God,
Lk 22:30 judging the twelve tribes of *I*.
Ac 1: 6 going to restore the kingdom to *I*?"
9:15 and before the people of *I*.
Ro 9: 4 of my own race, the people of *I*.
9: 6 all who are descended from *I* are *I*.
9:31 but *I*, who pursued a law
11: 7 What *I* sought so earnestly it did
11:26 And so all *I* will be saved,
Gal 6:16 who follow this rule, even to the *I*
Eph 2:12 excluded from citizenship in *I*
3: 6 Gentiles are heirs together with *I*,
Heb 8: 8 covenant with the house of *I*
Rev 7: 4 144,000 from all the tribes of *I*.
21:12 the names of the twelve tribes of *I*.

ISRAEL'S (ISRAEL)

Jdg 10:16 he could bear *I* misery no longer.
2Sa 23: 1 *I* singer of songs:
Isa 44: 6 *I* King and Redeemer, the LORD
Jer 3: 9 Because *I* immorality mattered
31: 9 because I am *I* father,
Jn 3:10 "You are *I* teacher," said Jesus,

ISRAELITE (ISRAEL)

Ex 16: 1 The whole *I* community set out
35:29 All the *I* men and women who
Nu 8:16 offspring from every *I* woman.
20: 1 the whole *I* community arrived
20:22 The whole *I* community set out
Jn 1:47 "Here is a true *I*, in whom there is
Ro 11: 1 I am an *I* myself, a descendant

ISRAELITES (ISRAEL)

Ex 1: 7 the *I* were fruitful and multiplied
2:23 The *I* groaned in their slavery
3: 9 the cry of the *I* has reached me,
12:35 The *I* did as Moses instructed
12:37 The *I* journeyed from Rameses
14:22 and the *I* went through the sea
16:12 I have heard the grumbling of the *I*.
16:35 The *I* ate manna forty years,
24:17 To the *I* the glory of the LORD
28:30 decisions for the *I* over his heart
29:45 Then I will dwell among the *I*
31:16 The *I* are to observe the Sabbath,
33: 5 "Tell the *I*, 'You are a stiff-necked
39:42 The *I* had done all the work just
Lev 22:32 be acknowledged as holy by the *I*.
25:46 rule over your fellow *I* ruthlessly.
25:55 for the *I* belong to me as servants.
Nu 2:32 These are the *I*, counted according
6:23 'This is how you are to bless the *I*.
9: 2 "Have the *I* celebrate the Passover
9:17 the *I* set out; wherever the cloud
10:12 Then the *I* set out from the Desert
14: 2 All the *I* grumbled against Moses
20:12 as holy in the sight of the *I*,
Nu 21: 6 they bit the people and many *I* died
26:65 had told those *I* they would surely
27:12 and see the land I have given the *I*.
33: 3 The *I* set out from Rameses
35:10 "Speak to the *I* and say to them:
Dt 33: 1 on the *I* before his death.
Jos 1: 2 about to give to them—to the *I*.
5: 6 The *I* had moved about
7: 1 the *I* acted unfaithfully in regard
8:32 There in the presence of the *I*,
18: 1 of the *I* gathered at Shiloh
21: 3 the *I* gave the Levites the following
22: 9 of Manasseh left the *I* at Shiloh
Jdg 2:11 Then the *I* did evil in the eyes
3:12 Once again the *I* did evil
4: 1 the *I* once again did evil in the eyes
6: 1 Again the *I* did evil in the eyes
10: 6 Again the *I* did evil in the eyes
13: 1 Again the *I* did evil in the eyes
1Sa 17: 2 Saul and the *I* assembled
1Ki 8:63 and all the *I* dedicated the temple
9:22 did not make slaves of any of the *I*;
12: 1 for all the *I* had gone there
12:17 But as for the *I* who were living
2Ki 17:24 towns of Samaria to replace the *I*.
1Ch 9: 2 in their own towns were some *I*,
10: 1 fought against Israel; the *I* fled
11: 4 and all the *I* marched to Jerusalem,
2Ch 7: 6 and all the *I* were standing.
Ne 1: 6 the sins we *I*, including myself
Jer 16:14 who brought the *I* up out of Egypt,'
Hos 1:10 "Yet the *I* will be like the sand
3: 1 Love her as the LORD loves the *I*,
Am 4: 5 boast about them, you *I*,
Mic 5: 3 return to join the *I*.
Ro 9:27 the number of the *I* be like the sand
10: 1 for the *I* is that they may be saved.
10:16 But not all the *I* accepted the good
2Co 11:22 Are they *I*? So am I.

ISSACHAR

Son of Jacob by Leah (Ge 30:18; 35:23; 1Ch 2:1). Tribe of blessed (Ge 49:14-15; Dt 33:18-19), numbered (Nu 1:29; 26:25), allotted land (Jos 19:17-23; Eze 48:25), assisted Deborah (Jdg 5:15), 12,000 from (Rev 7:7).

ISSUING*

Da 9:25 From the *i* of the decree to restore

ITALY

Ac 27: 1 decided that we would sail for *I*,
Heb 13:24 from *I* send you their greetings.

ITCHING*

2Ti 4: 3 to say what their *i* ears want to hear

ITHAMAR

Son of Aaron (Ex 6:23; 1Ch 6:3). Duties at tabernacle (Ex 38:21; Nu 4:21-33; 7:8).

ITTAI

2Sa 15:19 The king said to *I* the Gittite,

IVORY

1Ki 10:22 silver and *i*, and apes and baboons.
22:39 the palace he built and inlaid with *i*

JABBOK

Ge 32:22 and crossed the ford of the *J*.
Dt 3:16 and out to the *J* River,

JABESH

1Sa 11: 1 And all the men of *J* said to him,
31:12 wall of Beth Shan and went to *J*,
1Ch 10:12 and his sons and brought them to *J*.

JABESH GILEAD

Jdg 21: 8 that no one from *J* had come to
2Sa 2: 4 the men of *J* who had buried Saul,
1Ch 10:11 the inhabitants of *J* heard

JACOB

Second son of Isaac, twin of Esau (Ge 26:21-26; 1Ch 1:34). Bought Esau's birthright (Ge 26:29-34); tricked Isaac into blessing him (Ge 27:1-37). Fled to Haran (Ge 28:1-5). Abrahamic covenant perpetuated through (Ge 28:13-15; Mal 1:2). Vision at Bethel (Ge 28:10-22). Served Laban for Rachel and Leah (Ge 29:1-30). Children (Ge 29:31-30:24; 35:16-26; 1Ch 2-9). Flocks increased (Ge 30:25-43). Returned to Canaan (Ge 31). Wrestled with God; name changed to Israel (Ge 32:22-32). Reconciled to Esau (Ge 33). Returned to Bethel (Ge 35:1-15). Favored Joseph (Ge 37:3). Sent sons to Egypt during famine (Ge 42-43). Settled in Egypt (Ge 46). Blessed Ephraim and Manasseh (Ge 48). Blessed sons (Ge 49:1-28; Heb 11:21). Death (Ge 49:29-33). Burial (Ge 50:1-14).

JAEL*

Woman who killed Canaanite general, Sisera (Jdg 4:17-22; 5:24-27).

JAIR

Judge from Gilead (Jdg 10:3-5).

JAIRUS*

Synagogue ruler whose daughter Jesus raised (Mk 5:22-43; Lk 8:41-56).

JAMES

1. Apostle; brother of John (Mt 4:21-22; 10:2; Mk 3:17; Lk 5:1-10). At transfiguration (Mt 17:1-13; Mk 9:1-13; Lk 9:28-36). Killed by Herod (Ac 12:2).

2. Apostle; son of Alphaeus (Mt 10:3; Mk 3:18; Lk 6:15).

3. Brother of Jesus (Mt 13:55; Mk 6:3; Lk 24:10; Gal 1:19) and Judas (Jude 1). With believers before Pentecost (Ac 1:13). Leader of church at Jerusalem (Ac 12:17; 15; 21:18; Gal 2:9, 12). Author of epistle (Jas 1:1).

JAPHETH

Son of Noah (Ge 5:32; 1Ch 1:4-5). Blessed (Ge 9:18-28). Sons of (Ge 10:2-5).

JAR (JARS)

Ge 24:14 let down your *j* that I may have
1Ki 17:14 'The *j* of flour will not be used up
Jer 19: 1 "Go and buy a clay *j* from a potter.
Lk 8:16 hides it in a *j* or puts it under a bed.

JARS (JAR)

Jn 2: 6 Nearby stood six stone water *j*,
2Co 4: 7 we have this treasure in *j* of clay

JASPER

Ex 28:20 row a chrysolite, an onyx and a *j*.
Eze 28:13 chrysolite, onyx and *j*,
Rev 4: 3 sat there had the appearance of *j*
21:19 The first foundation was *j*,

JAVELIN

1Sa 17:45 me with sword and spear and *j*,

JAWBONE

Jdg 15:15 Finding a fresh *j* of a donkey,

JEALOUS (JEALOUSY)

Ex 20: 5 the LORD your God, am a *j* God,
34:14 whose name is Jealous, is a *j* God.
Dt 4:24 God is a consuming fire, a *j* God.
6:15 is a *j* God and his anger will burn
32:21 They made me *j* by what is no god
Jos 24:19 He is a holy God; he is a *j* God.
Eze 16:38 of my wrath and *j* anger.
16:42 my *j* anger will turn away from you
23:25 I will direct my *j* anger against you,
36: 6 in my *j* wrath because you have
Joel 2:18 the LORD will be *j* for his land
Na 1: 2 LORD is a *j* and avenging God;
Zep 3: 8 consumed by the fire of my *j* anger.
Zec 1:14 I am very *j* for Jerusalem and Zion,
8: 2 "I am very *j* for Zion; I am burning
2Co 11: 2 I am *j* for you with a godly jealousy

JEALOUSY (JEALOUS)

Ps 79: 5 How long will your *j* burn like fire?
Pr 6:34 for *j* arouses a husband's fury,
27: 4 but who can stand before *j*?
SS 8: 6 its *j* unyielding as the grave.
Zep 1:18 In the fire of his *j*
Zec 8: 2 I am burning with *j* for her."
Ro 13:13 debauchery, not in dissension and *j*
1Co 3: 3 For since there is *j* and quarreling
10:22 trying to arouse the Lord's *j*?
2Co 11: 2 I am jealous for you with a godly *j*.
12:20 *j*, outbursts of anger, factions,
Gal 5:20 hatred, discord, *j*, fits of rage,

JEERS*

Heb 11:36 Some faced *j* and flogging,

JEHOAHAZ

1. Son of Jehu; king of Israel (2Ki 13:1-9).

2. Son of Josiah; king of Judah (2Ki 23:31-34; 2Ch 36:1-4).

JEHOASH

1. See JOASH.

2. Son of Jehoahaz; king of Israel. Defeat of Aram prophesied by Elisha (2Ki 13:10-25). Defeated Amaziah in Jerusalem (2Ki 14:1-16; 2Ch 25:17-24).

JEHOIACHIN

Son of Jehoiakim; king of Judah exiled by Nebuchadnezzar (2Ki 24:8-17; 2Ch 36:8-10; Jer 22:24-30; 24:1). Raised from prisoner status (2Ki 25:

JEHOIACHIN

Son of Jehoiakim; king of Judah exiled by Nebuchadnezzar (2Ki 24:8-17; 2Ch 36:8-10; Jer 22:24-30; 24:1). Raised from prisoner status (2Ki 25:27-30; Jer 52:31-34).

JEHOIADA

Priest who sheltered Joash from Athaliah (2Ki 11-12; 2Ch 22:11-24:16).

JEHOIAKIM

Son of Josiah; made king of Judah by Pharaoh Neco (2Ki 23:34-24:6; 2Ch 36:4-8; Jer 22:18-23). Burned scroll of Jeremiah's prophecies (Jer 36).

JEHORAM

1. Son of Jehoshaphat; king of Judah (2Ki 8:16-24). Prophesied against by Elijah; killed by the LORD (2Ch 21).
2. See JORAM.

JEHOSHAPHAT

Son of Asa; king of Judah. Strengthened his kingdom (2Ch 17). Joined with Ahab against Aram (2Ki 22; 2Ch 18). Established judges (2Ch 19). Joined with Joram against Moab (2Ki 3; 2Ch 20).

JEHU

1. Prophet against Baasha (2Ki 16:1-7).
2. King of Israel. Anointed by Elijah to obliterate house of Ahab (1Ki 19:16-17); anointed by servant of Elisha (2Ki 9:1-13). Killed Joram and Ahaziah (2Ki 9:14-29; 2Ch 22:7-9), Jezebel (2Ki 9:30-37), relatives of Ahab (2Ki 10:1-17), ministers of Baal (2Ki 10:18-29). Death (2Ki 10:30-36).

JEPHTHAH

Judge from Gilead who delivered Israel from Ammon (Jdg 10:6-12:7). Made rash vow concerning his daughter (Jdg 11:30-40).

JEREMIAH

Prophet to Judah (Jer 1:1-3). Called by the LORD (Jer 1). Put in stocks (Jer 20:1-3). Threatened for prophesying (Jer 11:18-23; 26). Opposed by Hananiah (Jer 28). Scroll burned (Jer 36). Imprisoned (Jer 37). Thrown into cistern (Jer 38). Forced to Egypt with those fleeing Babylonians (Jer 43).

JERICHO

Nu 22: 1 along the Jordan across from J.
Jos 3:16 the people crossed over opposite J.
5:10 camped at Gilgal on the plains of J,
Lk 10:30 going down from Jerusalem to J,
Heb 11:30 By faith the walls of J fell,

JEROBOAM

1. Official of Solomon; rebelled to become first king of Israel (1Ki 11:26-40; 12:1-20; 2Ch 10). Idolatry (1Ki 12:25-33); judgment for (1Ki 13-14; 2Ch 13).
2. Son of Jehoash; king of Israel (1Ki 14:23-29).

JERUSALEM

Jos 10: 1 of J heard that Joshua had taken Ai
15: 8 of the Jebusite city (that is, J).
Jdg 1: 8 The men of Judah attacked J also
1Sa 17:54 head and brought it to J,
2Sa 5: 5 and in J he reigned over all Israel
5: 6 and his men marched to J
9:13 And Mephibosheth lived in J,
11: 1 But David remained in J.
15:29 took the ark of God back to J
24:16 stretched out his hand to destroy J,
1Ki 3: 1 the LORD, and the wall around J.
9:15 the wall of J, and Hazor, Megiddo
9:19 whatever he desired to build in J,
10:26 cities and also with him in J.
10:27 as common in J as stones,
11: 7 of J, Solomon built a high place
11:13 my servant and for the sake of J,
11:36 always have a lamp before me in J,
11:42 Solomon reigned in J
12:27 at the temple of the LORD in J,
14:21 and he reigned seventeen years in J
14:25 Shishak king of Egypt attacked J.
15: 2 and he reigned in J three years.
15:10 and he reigned in J forty-one years.
22:42 he reigned in J twenty-five years.
2Ki 8:17 and he reigned in J eight years.
8:26 and he reigned in J one year.
12: 1 and he reigned in J forty years.
12:17 Then he turned to attack J.
14: 2 he reigned in J twenty-nine years.
14:13 Then Jehoash went to J
15: 2 and he reigned in J fifty-two years.
15:33 and he reigned in J sixteen years.
16: 2 and he reigned in J sixteen years.
16: 5 Israel marched up to fight against J
18: 2 he reigned in J twenty-nine years.
18:17 Lachish to King Hezekiah at J.
19:31 For out of J will come a remnant,
21: 1 and he reigned in J fifty-five years.
21:12 going to bring such disaster on J
21:19 and he reigned in J two years.
22: 1 he reigned in J thirty-one years.
23:27 and I will reject J, the city I chose,
23:31 and he reigned in J three months.
23:36 and he reigned in J eleven years.
24: 8 and he reigned in J three months.
24:10 king of Babylon advanced on J
24:14 He carried into exile all J:
24:18 and he reigned in J eleven years.
24:20 anger that all this happened to J
25: 1 king of Babylon marched against J
25: 9 royal palace and all the houses of J.
1Ch 11: 4 and all the Israelites marched to J,
21:16 sword in his hand extended over J.
2Ch 1: 4 he had pitched a tent for it in J.
3: 1 the LORD in J on Mount Moriah,
6: 6 now I have chosen J for my Name
9: 1 she came to J to test him
20:15 and all who live in Judah and J!
20:27 and J returned joyfully to J,
29: 8 LORD has fallen on Judah and J;
36:19 and broke down the wall of J;
Ezr 1: 2 a temple for him at J in Judah.
2: 1 to Babylon (they returned to J
3: 1 people assembled as one man in J.
4:12 up to us from you have gone to J
4:24 of God in J came to a standstill
6:12 or to destroy this temple in J.
7: 8 Ezra arrived in J in the fifth month
9: 9 a wall of protection in Judah and J.
10: 7 for all the exiles to assemble in J.
Ne 1: 2 the exile, and also about J.
1: 3 The wall of J is broken down,
2:11 to J, and after staying there three
2:17 Come, let us rebuild the wall of J,
2:20 you have no share in J or any claim
3: 8 They restored J as far as the Broad
4: 8 fight against J and stir up trouble
11: 1 leaders of the people settled in J,
12:27 At the dedication of the wall of J,
12:43 in J could be heard far away.
Ps 51:18 build up the walls of J.
79: 1 they have reduced J to rubble.
122: 2 in your gates, O J.
122: 3 J is built like a city
122: 6 Pray for the peace of J:
125: 2 As the mountains surround J,
128: 5 may you see the prosperity of J,
137: 5 If I forget you, O J,
147: 2 The LORD builds up J;
147: 12 Extol the LORD, O J;
SS 6: 4 lovely as J,
Isa 1: 1 and J that Isaiah son of Amoz saw
2: 1 saw concerning Judah and J:
3: 1 is about to take from J and Judah
3: 8 J staggers,
4: 3 recorded among the living in J.
8:14 And for the people of J he will be
27:13 LORD on the holy mountain in J.
31: 5 the LORD Almighty will shield J;
33:20 your eyes will see J,
40: 2 Speak tenderly to J,
40: 9 You who bring good tidings to J,
52: 1 O J, the holy city.
52: 2 rise up, sit enthroned, O J.
62: 6 on your walls, O J;
62: 7 give him no rest till he establishes J
65:18 for I will create J to be a delight
Jer 2: 2 and proclaim in the hearing of J:
3:17 time they will call J The Throne
4: 5 and proclaim in J and say:
4:14 O J, wash the evil from your heart
5: 1 "Go up and down the streets of J,
6: 6 and build siege ramps against J.
8: 5 Why does J always turn away?
9:11 "I will make J a heap of ruins,
13:27 Woe to you, O J!
23:14 And among the prophets of J
24: 1 into exile from J to Babylon
26:18 J will become a heap of rubble,
32: 2 of Babylon was then besieging J,
33:10 the streets of J that are deserted,
39: 1 This is how J was taken: In
51:50 and think on J."
52:14 broke down all the walls around J.
La 1: 7 J remembers all the treasures
Eze 14:21 send against J my four dreadful
16: 2 confront J with her detestable
Da 6:10 the windows opened toward J.
9: 2 of J would last seventy years.
9:12 done like what has been done to J.
9:25 and rebuild J until the Anointed
Joel 3: 1 restore the fortunes of Judah and J,
3:16 and thunder from J;
3:17 J will be holy;
Am 2: 5 will consume the fortresses of J."
Ob :11 and cast lots for J,
Mic 1: 5 Is it not J?
4: 2 the word of the LORD from J.
Zep 3:16 On that day they will say to J,
Zec 1:14 'I am very jealous for J and Zion,
1:17 comfort Zion and choose J.' "
2: 2 He answered me, "To measure J,
2: 4 'J will be a city without walls
8: 3 I will return to Zion and dwell in J.
8: 8 I will bring them back to live in J;
8:15 determined to do good again to J
8:22 powerful nations will come to J
9: 9 Shout, Daughter of J!
9:10 and the war-horses from J,
12: 3 I will make J an immovable rock
12:10 the inhabitants of J a spirit of grace
14: 2 the nations to J to fight against it;
14: 8 living water will flow out from J,
14:16 that have attacked J will go up
Mt 16:21 to his disciples that he must go to J
20:18 said to them, "We are going up to J
21:10 When Jesus entered J, the whole
23:37 "O J, J, you who kill the prophets
Mk 10:33 "We are going up to J," he said,
Lk 2:22 Mary took him to J to present him
2:41 Every year his parents went to J
2:43 the boy Jesus stayed behind in J,
4: 9 The devil led him to J
9:31 about to bring to fulfillment at J.
9:51 Jesus resolutely set out for J,
13:34 die outside J! "O J, J,
18:31 told them, "We are going up to J,
19:41 As he approached J and saw
21:20 "When you see J being surrounded
21:24 J will be trampled
24:47 name to all nations, beginning at J.
Jn 4:20 where we must worship is in J."
Ac 1: 4 this command: "Do not leave J,
1: 8 and you will be my witnesses in J,
6: 7 of disciples in J increased rapidly,
20:22 by the Spirit, I am going to J,
23:11 As you have testified about me in J
Ro 15:19 So from J all the way
Gal 4:25 corresponds to the present city of J
4:26 But the J that is above is free,
Heb 12:22 to the heavenly J, the city
Rev 3:12 the new J, which is coming
21: 2 I saw the Holy City, the new J,
21:10 and showed me the Holy City, J,

JESSE

Father of David (Ru 4:17-22; 1Sa 16; 1Ch 2:12-17).

JESUS

LIFE: Genealogy (Mt 1:1-17; Lk 3:21-37). Birth announced (Mt 1:18-25; Lk 1:26-45). Birth (Mt 2:1-12; Lk 2:1-40). Escape to Egypt (Mt 2:13-23). As a boy in the temple (Lk 2:41-52). Baptism (Mt 3:13-17; Mk 1:9-11; Lk 3:21-22; Jn 1:32-34). Temptation (Mt 4:1-11; Mk 1:12-13; Lk 4:1-13). Ministry in Galilee (Mt 4:12-18:35; Mk 1:14-9:50; Lk 4:14-13:9; Jn 1:35-2:11; 4; 6), Transfiguration (Mt 17:1-8; Mk 9:2-8; Lk 9:28-36), on the way to Jerusalem (Mt 19-20; Mk 10; Lk 13:10-19:27), in Jerusalem (Mt 21-25; Mk 11-13; Lk 19:28-21:38; Jn 2:12-3:36; 5; 7-12). Last supper (Mt 26:17-35; Mk 14:12-31; Lk 22:1-38; Jn 13-17). Arrest and trial (Mt 26:36-27:31; Mk 14:43-15:20; Lk 22:39-23:25; Jn 18:1-19:16). Crucifixion (Mt 27:32-66; Mk 15:21-47; Lk 23:26-55; Jn 19:28-42). Resurrection and appearances (Mt 28; Mk 16; Lk 24; Jn 20-21; Ac 1:1-11; 7:56; 9:3-6; 1Co 15:1-8; Rev 1:1-20).

MIRACLES. Healings: official's son (Jn 4:43-54), demoniac in Capernaum (Mk 1:23-26; Lk 4:33-35), Peter's mother-in-law (Mt 8:14-17; Mk 1:29-31; Lk 4:38-39), leper (Mt 8:2-4; Mk 1:40-45; Lk 5:12-16), paralytic (Mt 9:1-8; Mk 2:1-12; Lk 5:17-26), cripple (Jn 5:1-9), shriveled hand (Mt 12:10-13; Mk 3:1-5; Lk 6:6-11), centurion's servant (Mt 8:5-13; Lk 7:1-10), widow's son raised (Lk 7:11-17), demoniac (Mt 12:22-23; Lk 11:14), Gadarene demoniacs (Mt 8:28-34; Mk 5:1-20; Lk 8:26-39), woman's bleeding and Jairus' daughter (Mt 9:18-26; Mk 5:21-43; Lk 8:40-56), blind man (Mt 9:27-31), mute man (Mt 9:32-33), Canaanite woman's daughter (Mt 15:21-28; Mk 7:24-30), deaf man (Mk 7:31-37), blind man (Mk 8:22-26), demoniac boy (Mt 17:14-18; Mk 9:14-29; Lk 9:37-43), ten lepers (Lk 17:11-19), man born blind (Jn 9:1-7), Lazarus raised (Jn 11), crippled woman (Lk 13:11-17), man with dropsy (Lk 14:1-6), two blind men (Mt 20:29-34; Mk 10:46-52; Lk 18:35-43), Malchus' ear (Lk 22:50-51). Other Miracles: water to wine (Jn 2:1-11), catch of fish (Lk 5:1-11), storm stilled (Mt 8:23-27; Mk 4:37-41; Lk 8:22-25), 5,000 fed (Mt 14:15-21; Mk 6:35-44; Lk 9:10-17; Jn 6:1-14), walking on water (Mt 14:25-33; Mk 6:48-52; Jn 6:15-21), 4,000 fed (Mt 15:32-39; Mk 8:1-9), money from fish (Mt 17:24-27), fig tree cursed (Mt 21:18-22; Mk 11:12-14), catch of fish (Jn 21:1-14).

MAJOR TEACHING: Sermon on the Mount (Mt 5-7; Lk 6:17-49), to Nicodemus (Jn 3), to Samaritan woman (Jn 4), Bread of Life (Jn 6:22-59), at Feast of Tabernacles (Jn 7-8), woes to Pharisees (Mt 23; Lk 11:37-54), Good Shepherd (Jn 10:1-18), Olivet Discourse (Mt 24-25; Mk 13; Lk 21:5-36), Upper Room Discourse (Jn 13-16).

PARABLES: Sower (Mt 13:3-23; Mk 4:3-25; Lk 8:5-18), seed's growth (Mk 4:26-29), wheat and weeds (Mt 13:24-30, 36-43), mustard seed (Mt 13:31-32; Mk 4:30-32), yeast (Mt 13:33; Lk 13:20-21), hidden treasure (Mt 13:44), valuable pearl (Mt 13:45-46), net (Mt 13:47-51), house owner (Mt 13:52), good Samaritan (Lk 10:25-37), unmerciful servant (Mt 18:15-35), lost sheep (Mt 18:10-14; Lk 15:4-7), lost coin (Lk 15:8-10), lost son (Lk 15:11-32), dishonest manager (Lk 16:1-13), rich man and Lazarus (Lk 16:19-31), persistent widow (Lk 18:1-8), Pharisee and tax collector (Lk 18:9-14), payment of workers (Mt 20:1-16), tenants and the vineyard (Mt 21:28-46; Mk 12:1-12; Lk 20:9-19), wedding banquet (Mt 22:1-14), faithful servant (Mt 24:45-51), ten virgins (Mt 25:1-13), talents (Mt 25:1-30; Lk 19:12-27).

DISCIPLES see APOSTLES. Call of (Jn 1:35-51; Mt 4:18-22; 9:9; Mk 1:16-20; 2:13-14; Lk 5:1-11, 27-28). Named Apostles (Mk 3:13-19; Lk 6:12-16). Twelve sent out (Mt 10; Mk 6:7-11; Lk 9:1-5). Seventy sent out (Lk 10:1-24). Defection of (Jn 6:60-71; Mt 26:56; Mk 14:50-52). Final commission (Mt 28:16-20; Jn 21:15-23; Ac 1:3-8).

Ac 2:32 God has raised this J to life,
9: 5 "I am J, whom you are persecuting
9:34 said to him, "J Christ heals you.
15:11 of our Lord J that we are saved,
16:31 "Believe in the Lord J,
20:24 the task the Lord J has given me—
Ro 3:24 redemption that came by Christ J.
5:17 life through the one man, J Christ.
8: 1 for those who are in Christ J,
1Co 1: 7 for our Lord J Christ to be revealed
2: 2 except J Christ and him crucified.
6:11 in the name of the Lord J Christ
8: 6 and there is but one Lord, J Christ,
12: 3 and no one can say, "J is Lord,"
2Co 4: 5 not preach ourselves, but J Christ
13: 5 Do you not realize that Christ J is
Gal 2:16 but by faith in J Christ.
3:28 for you are all one in Christ J.
5: 6 in Christ J neither circumcision
6:17 bear on my body the marks of J.
Eph 1: 5 as his sons through J Christ,
2:10 created in Christ J
2:20 with Christ J himself as the chief
Php 1: 6 until the day of Christ J.
2: 5 be the same as that of Christ J:
2:10 name of J every knee should bow,
Col 3:17 do it all in the name of the Lord J,
1Th 1:10 whom he raised from the dead—J,
4:14 We believe that J died
5:23 at the coming of our Lord J Christ.
2Th 1: 7 when the Lord J is revealed
2: 1 the coming of our Lord J Christ
1Ti 1:15 Christ J came into the world
2Ti 1:10 appearing of our Savior, Christ J,
2: 3 us like a good soldier of Christ J.
3:12 life in Christ J will be persecuted,
Tit 2:13 our great God and Savior, J Christ,
Heb 2: 9 But we see J, who was made a little
2:11 So J is not ashamed to call them
3: 1 fix your thoughts on J, the apostle
3: 3 J has been found worthy
4:14 through the heavens, J the Son
6:20 where J, who went before us,
7:22 J has become the guarantee
7:24 but because J lives forever,
8: 6 But the ministry J has received is
12: 2 Let us fix our eyes on J, the author
12:24 to J the mediator of a new
1Pe 1: 3 the resurrection of J Christ
2Pe 1:16 and coming of our Lord J Christ,
1Jn 1: 7 and the blood of J, his Son,
2: 1 J Christ, the Righteous One.
2: 6 to live in him must walk as J did.
4:15 anyone acknowledges that J is
Rev 1: 1 The revelation of J Christ,
22:16 J, have sent my angel
22:20 Come, Lord J.

JETHRO

Father-in-law and adviser of Moses (Ex 3:1; 18). Also known as Reuel (Ex 2:18).

JEW (JEWS JEWS' JUDAISM)

Est 2: 5 of Susa a J of the tribe of Benjamin,
Zec 8:23 of one J by the hem of his robe
Ac 21:39 "I am a J, from Tarsus in Cilicia,
Ro 1:16 first for the J, then for the Gentile.
2:28 A man is not a J if he is only one
Ro 10:12 there is no difference between J
1Co 9:20 To the Jews I became like a J,
Gal 2:14 "You are a J, yet you live like
3:28 There is neither J nor Greek,
Col 3:11 Here there is no Greek or J,

JEWEL (JEWELRY JEWELS)

Pr 20:15 that speak knowledge are a rare j.
SS 4: 9 with one j of your necklace.
Rev 21:11 that of a very precious j,

JEWELRY (JEWEL)

Ex 35:22 and brought gold j of all kinds:
Jer 2:32 Does a maiden forget her j,
Eze 16:11 you with j: I put bracelets
1Pe 3: 3 wearing of gold j and fine clothes.

JEWELS (JEWEL)

Isa 54:12 your gates of sparkling j,
61:10 as a bride adorns herself with her j.
Zec 9:16 like j in a crown.

JEWS (JEW)

Ne 4: 1 He ridiculed the J,
Est 3:13 kill and annihilate all the J—
4:14 and deliverance for the J will arise
Mt 2: 2 who has been born king of the J?
27:11 "Are you the king of the J?" "Yes,
Jn 4: 9 (For J do not associate
4:22 for salvation is from the J.
19: 3 saying, "Hail, king of the J!"
Ac 20:21 I have declared to both J
Ro 3:29 Is God the God of J only?
9:24 not only from the J but
15:27 they owe it to the J to share
1Co 1:22 J demand miraculous signs
9:20 To the J I became like a Jew,
12:13 whether J or Greeks, slave or free
Gal 2: 8 of Peter as an apostle to the J,
Rev 2: 9 slander of those who say they are J
3: 9 claim to be J though they are not,

JEWS' (JEW)

Ro 15:27 shared in the J spiritual blessings,

JEZEBEL

Sidonian wife of Ahab (1Ki 16:31). Promoted Baal worship (1Ki 16:32-33). Killed prophets of the LORD (1Ki 18:4, 13). Opposed Elijah (1Ki 19:1-2). Had Naboth killed (1Ki 21). Death prophesied (1Ki 21:17-24). Killed by Jehu (2Ki 9:30-37).

JEZREEL

2Ki 9:36 at J dogs will devour Jezebel's flesh
10: 7 and sent them to Jehu in J.
Hos 1: 4 house of Jehu for the massacre at J,

JOAB

Nephew of David (1Ch 2:16). Commander of his army (2Sa 8:16). Victorious over Ammon (2Sa 10; 1Ch 19), Rabbah (2Sa 11; 1Ch 20), Jerusalem (1Ch 11:6), Absalom (2Sa 18), Sheba (2Sa 20). Killed Abner (2Sa 3:22-39), Amasa (2Sa 20:1-13). Numbered David's army (2Sa 24; 1Ch 21). Sided with Adonijah (1Ki 1:17, 19). Killed by Benaiah (1Ki 2:5-6, 28-35).

JOASH

Son of Ahaziah; king of Judah. Sheltered from Athaliah by Jehoiada (2Ki 11; 2Ch 22:10-23:21). Repaired temple (2Ki 12; 2Ch 24).

JOB

Wealthy man from Uz; feared God (Job 1:1-5). Righteousness tested by disaster (Job 1:6-22), personal affliction (Job 2). Maintained innocence in debate with three friends (Job 3-31), Elihu (Job 32-37). Rebuked by the LORD (Job 38-41). Vindicated and restored to greater stature by the LORD (Job 42). Example of righteousness (Eze 14:14, 20).

JOCHEBED*

Mother of Moses and Aaron (Ex 6:20; Nu 26:59).

JOEL

Prophet (Joel 1:1; Ac 2:16).

JOHN

1. Son of Zechariah and Elizabeth (Lk 1). Called the Baptist (Mt 3:1-12; Mk 1:2-8). Witness to Jesus (Mt 3:11-12; Mk 1:7-8; Lk 3:15-18; Jn 1:6-35; 3:27-30; 5:33-36). Doubts about Jesus (Mt 11:2-6; Lk 7:18-23). Arrest (Mt 4:12; Mk 1:14). Execution (Mt 14:1-12; Mk 6:14-29; Lk 9:7-9). Ministry compared to Elijah (Mt 11:7-19; Mk 9:11-13; Lk 7:24-35).

2. Apostle; brother of James (Mt 4:21-22; 10:2; Mk 3:17; Lk 5:1-10). At transfiguration (Mt 17:1-13; Mk 9:1-13; Lk 9:28-36). Desire to be greatest (Mk 10:35-45). Leader of church at Jerusalem (Ac 4:1-3; Gal 2:9). Elder who wrote epistles (2Jn 1; 3Jn 1). Prophet who wrote Revelation (Rev 1:1; 22:8).

3. Cousin of Barnabas, co-worker with Paul, (Ac 12:12-13:13; 15:37), see MARK.

JOIN (JOINED JOINS)

Ne 10:29 all these now j their brothers
Pr 23:20 Do not j those who drink too much
24:21 and do not j with the rebellious,
Jer 3:18 of Judah will j the house of Israel,
Eze 37:17 J them together into one stick
Da 11:34 who are not sincere will j them.
Ro 15:30 to j me in my struggle by praying
2Ti 1: 8 j with me in suffering for the gospel

JOINED (JOIN)

Zec 2:11 "Many nations will be j
Mt 19: 6 Therefore what God has j together,
Mk 10: 9 Therefore what God has j together,
Ac 1:14 They all j together constantly
Eph 2:21 him the whole building is j together
4:16 j and held together

JOINS (JOIN)

1Co 16:16 and to everyone who j in the work,

JOINT (JOINTS)

Ps 22:14 and all my bones are out of j.

JOINTS (JOINT)

Heb 4:12 even to dividing soul and spirit, j

JOKING*

Ge 19:14 his sons-in-law thought he was j.
Pr 26:19 and says, "I was only j!"
Eph 5: 4 or coarse j, which are out of place,

JONAH

Prophet in days of Jeroboam II (2Ki 14:25). Called to Nineveh; fled to Tarshish (Jnh 1:1-3). Cause of storm; thrown into sea (Jnh 1:4-16). Swallowed by fish (Jnh 1:17). Prayer (Jnh 2). Preached to Nineveh (Jnh 3). Attitude reproved by the LORD (Jnh 4). Sign of (Mt 12:39-41; Lk 11:29-32).

JONATHAN

Son of Saul (1Sa 13:16; 1Ch 8:33). Valiant warrior (1Sa 13-14). Relation to David (1Sa 18:1-4; 19-20; 23:16-18). Killed at Gilboa (1Sa 31). Mourned by David (2Sa 1).

JOPPA

Ezr 3: 7 logs by sea from Lebanon to J,
Jnh 1: 3 to J, where he found a ship bound
Ac 9:43 Peter stayed in J for some time

JORAM

1. Son of Ahab; king of Israel. Fought with Jehoshaphat against Moab (2Ki 3). Killed with Ahaziah by Jehu (2Ki 8:25-29; 9:14-26; 2Ch 22:5-9).

2. See JEHORAM.

JORDAN

Ge 13:10 plain of the J was well watered,
Nu 22: 1 and camped along the J
34:12 boundary will go down along the J
Dt 3:27 you are not going to cross this J.
Jos 1: 2 get ready to cross the J River
3:11 go into the J ahead of you.
3:17 ground in the middle of the J,
4:22 Israel crossed the J on dry ground.'
2Ki 2: 7 and Elisha had stopped at the J.
2:13 and stood on the bank of the J.
5:10 wash yourself seven times in the J,
6: 4 They went to the J and began
Ps 114: 3 the J turned back;
Isa 9: 1 along the J— The people walking
Jer 12: 5 manage in the thickets by the J?
Mt 3: 6 baptized by him in the J River.
4:15 the way to the sea, along the J,
Mk 1: 9 and was baptized by John in the J.

JOSEPH

1. Son of Jacob by Rachel (Ge 30:24; 1Ch 2:2). Favored by Jacob, hated by brothers (Ge 37:3-4). Dreams (Ge 37:5-11). Sold by brothers (Ge 37:12-36). Served Potiphar; imprisoned by false accusation (Ge 39). Interpreted dreams of Pharaoh's servants (Ge 40), of Pharaoh (Ge 41:4-40). Made greatest in Egypt (Ge 41:41-57). Sold grain to brothers (Ge 42-45). Brought Jacob and sons to Egypt (Ge 46-47). Sons Ephraim and Manasseh blessed (Ge 48). Blessed (Ge 49:22-26; Dt 33:13-17). Death (Ge 50:22-26; Ex 13:19; Heb 11:22). 12,000 from (Rev 7:8).

2. Husband of Mary, mother of Jesus (Mt 1:16-24; 2:13-19; Lk 1:27; 2; Jn 1:45).

3. Disciple from Arimathea, who gave his tomb for Jesus' burial (Mt 27:57-61; Mk 15:43-47; Lk 24:50-52).

4. Original name of Barnabas (Ac 4:36).

JOSHUA (HOSHEA)

1. Son of Nun; name changed from Hoshea (Nu 13:8, 16; 1Ch 7:27). Fought Amalekites under Moses (Ex 17:9-14). Servant of Moses on Sinai (Ex 24:13; 32:17). Spied Canaan (Nu 13). With Caleb, allowed to enter land (Nu 14:6, 30). Succeeded Moses (Dt 1:38; 31:1-8; 34:9).

Charged Israel to conquer Canaan (Jos 1). Crossed Jordan (Jos 3-4). Circumcised sons of wilderness wanderings (Jos 5). Conquered Jericho (Jos 6), Ai (Jos 7-8), five kings at Gibeon (Jos 10:1-28), southern Canaan (Jos 10:29-43), northern Canaan (Jos 11-12). Defeated at Ai (Jos 7). Deceived by Gibeonites (Jos 9). Renewed covenant (Jos 8:30-35; 24:1-27). Divided land among tribes (Jos 13-22). Last words (Jos 23). Death (Jos 24:28-31).

2. High priest during rebuilding of temple (Hag 1-2; Zec 3:1-9; 6:11).

JOSIAH

Son of Amon; king of Judah (2Ki 21:26; 1Ch 3:14). Prophesied (1Ki 13:2). Book of Law discovered during his reign (2Ki 22; 2Ch 34:14-31). Reforms (2Ki 23:1-25; 2Ch 34:1-13; 35:1-19). Killed by Pharaoh Neco (2Ki 23:29-30; 2Ch 35:20-27).

JOTHAM

1. Son of Gideon (Jdg 9).
2. Son of Azariah (Uzziah); king of Judah (2Ki 15:32-38; 2Ch 26:21-27:9).

JOURNEY

Dt 1:33 who went ahead of you on your j,
2: 7 over your j through this vast desert
Jdg 18: 6 Your j has the LORD's approval."
Ezr 8:21 and ask him for a safe j for us
Job 16:22 before I go on the j of no return.
Isa 35: 8 The unclean will not j on it;
Mt 25:14 it will be like a man going on a j,
Ro 15:24 to have you assist me on my j there

JOY* (ENJOY ENJOYMENT JOYFUL JOYOUS OVERJOYED REJOICE REJOICES REJOICING)

Ge 31:27 so I could send you away with j
Lev 9:24 shouted for j and fell facedown.
Dt 16:15 and your j will be complete.
Jdg 9:19 may Abimelech be your j,
1Ch 12:40 and sheep, for there was j in Israel.
16:27 strength and j in his dwelling place.
16:33 sing for j before the LORD,
29:17 with j how willingly your people
29:22 drank with great j in the presence
2Ch 30:26 There was great j in Jerusalem,
Ezr 3:12 while many others shouted for j.
3:13 of the shouts of j from the sound
6:16 of the house of God with j.
6:22 with j by changing the attitude
6:22 j the Feast of Unleavened Bread,
Ne 8:10 for the j of the LORD is your
8:12 and to celebrate with great j,
8:17 And their j was very great.
12:43 God had given them great j.
Est 8:16 a time of happiness and j,
8:17 there was j and gladness
9:17 and made it a day of feasting and j.
9:18 and made it a day of feasting and j.
9:19 as a day of j and feasting,
9:22 and j and giving presents of food
9:22 their sorrow was turned into j
Job 3: 7 may no shout of j be heard in it.
6:10 my j in unrelenting pain—
8:21 and your lips with shouts of j.
9:25 they fly away without a glimpse of j
10:20 from me so I can have a moment's j
20: 5 the j of the godless lasts
33:26 he sees God's face and shouts for j;
38: 7 and all the angels shouted for j?
Ps 4: 7 have filled my heart with greater j
5:11 let them ever sing for j.
16:11 me with j in your presence,
19: 8 giving j to the heart.
20: 5 We will shout for j
21: 1 How great is his j in the victories
21: 6 with the j of your presence.
27: 6 will I sacrifice with shouts of j;
28: 7 My heart leaps for j
30:11 sackcloth and clothed me with j,
33: 3 play skillfully, and shout for j.
35:27 shout for j and gladness;
42: 4 with shouts of j and thanksgiving
43: 4 to God, my j and my delight.
45: 7 by anointing you with the oil of j.
45:15 They are led in with j and gladness;
47: 1 shout to God with cries of j.
47: 5 God has ascended amid shouts of j,
48: 2 the j of the whole earth.
51: 8 Let me hear j and gladness;
51:12 to me the j of your salvation
65: 8 you call forth songs of j.
Ps 65:13 they shout for j and sing.
66: 1 Shout with j to God, all the earth!
67: 4 the nations be glad and sing for j,
71:23 My lips will shout for j
81: 1 Sing for j to God our strength;
86: 4 Bring j to your servant,
89:12 Hermon sing for j at your name.
90:14 for j and be glad all our days.
92: 4 I sing for j at the works
94:19 your consolation brought j
95: 1 let us sing for j to the LORD;
96:12 the trees of the forest will sing for j;
97:11 and j on the upright in heart.
98: 4 for j to the LORD, all the earth,
98: 6 shout for j before the LORD,
98: 8 the mountains sing together for j;
100: 1 for j to the LORD, all the earth.
105: 43 his chosen ones with shouts of j;
106: 5 share in the j of your nation
107: 22 and tell of his works with songs of j
118: 15 Shouts of j and victory
119:111 they are the j of my heart.
126: 2 our tongues with songs of j.
126: 3 and we are filled with j.
126: 5 will reap with songs of j.
126: 6 will return with songs of j,
132: 9 may your saints sing for j."
132: 16 and her saints will ever sing for j.
137: 3 tormentors demanded songs of j;
137: 6 my highest j.
149: 5 and sing for j on their beds.
Pr 10: 1 A wise son brings j to his father,
10:28 The prospect of the righteous is j,
11:10 wicked perish, there are shouts of j.
12:20 but j for those who promote peace.
14:10 and no one else can share its j.
14:13 and j may end in grief.
15:20 A wise son brings j to his father,
15:23 A man finds j in giving an apt reply
15:30 A cheerful look brings j
17:21 there is no j for the father of a fool.
21:15 it brings j to the righteous
23:24 of a righteous man has great j;
27: 9 incense bring j to the heart,
27:11 my son, and bring j to my heart;
29: 3 A man who loves wisdom brings j
Ecc 8:15 Then j will accompany him
11: 9 let your heart give you j in the days
Isa 9: 3 and increased their j;
12: 3 With j you will draw water
12: 6 Shout aloud and sing for j,
16: 9 shouts of j over your ripened fruit
16:10 J and gladness are taken away
22:13 But see, there is j and revelry,
24:11 all j turns to gloom,
24:14 raise their voices, they shout for j;
26:19 wake up and shout for j.
35: 2 will rejoice greatly and shout for j.
35: 6 the mute tongue shout for j.
35:10 Gladness and j will overtake them,
35:10 everlasting j will crown their heads
42:11 Let the people of Sela sing for j;
44:23 Sing for j, O heavens,
48:20 Announce this with shouts of j
49:13 Shout for j, O heavens;
51: 3 J and gladness will be found in her,
51:11 Gladness and j will overtake them,
51:11 everlasting j will crown their heads
52: 8 together they shout for j.
52: 9 Burst into songs of j together,
54: 1 burst into song, shout for j,
55:12 You will go out in j
56: 7 give them j in my house of prayer.
58:14 then you will find your j
60: 5 heart will throb and swell with j;
60:15 and the j of all generations.
61: 7 and everlasting j will be theirs.
65:14 out of the j of their hearts,
65:18 and its people a j.
66: 5 that we may see your j!'
Jer 7:34 will bring an end to the sounds of j
15:16 they were my j and my heart's
16: 9 will bring an end to the sounds of j
25:10 banish from them the sounds of j
31: 7 "Sing with j for Jacob;
31:12 shout for j on the heights of Zion;
31:13 give them comfort and j instead
33: 9 this city will bring me renown, j,
33:11 be heard once more the sounds of j
48:33 J and gladness are gone
48:33 no one treads them with shouts of j
48:33 they are not shouts of j.
51:48 will shout for j over Babylon,
La 2:15 the j of the whole earth?"
5:15 J is gone from our hearts;
Eze 7: 7 not j, upon the mountains.
24:25 their j and glory, the delight
Joel 1:12 Surely the j of mankind
1:16 j and gladness
Mt 13:20 and at once receives it with j.
13:44 in his j went and sold all he had
28: 8 afraid yet filled with j,
Mk 4:16 and at once receive it with j.
Lk 1:14 He will be a j and delight to you,
1:44 the baby in my womb leaped for j.
1:58 great mercy, and they shared her j.
2:10 news of great j that will be
6:23 "Rejoice in that day and leap for j,
8:13 the word with j when they hear it,
10:17 The seventy-two returned with j
10:21 full of j through the Holy Spirit,
24:41 still did not believe it because of j
24:52 returned to Jerusalem with great j.
Jn 3:29 That j is mine, and it is now
3:29 full of j when he hears
15:11 and that your j may be complete.
15:11 this so that my j may be in you
16:20 but your grief will turn to j.
16:21 because of her j that a child is born
16:22 and no one will take away your j.
16:24 and your j will be complete.
17:13 measure of my j within them.
Ac 2:28 with j in your presence.'
8: 8 So there was great j in that city.
13:52 And the disciples were filled with j
14:17 and fills your hearts with j."
16:34 he was filled with j because he had come
Ro 14:17 peace and j in the Holy Spirit,
15:13 the God of hope fill you with all j
15:32 will I may come to you with j
16:19 so I am full of j over you;
2Co 1:24 but we work with you for your j,
2: 3 that you would all share my j.
7: 4 our troubles my j knows no
7: 7 so that my j was greater than ever.
8: 2 their overflowing j and their
Gal 4:15 What has happened to all your j?
5:22 j, peace, patience, kindness,
Php 1: 4 I always pray with j
1:25 for your progress and j in the faith,
1:26 being with you again your j
2: 2 then make my j complete
2:29 him in the Lord with great j,
4: 1 and long for, my j and crown,
1Th 1: 6 with the j given by the Holy Spirit.
2:19 For what is our hope, our j,
2:20 Indeed, you are our glory and j.
3: 9 you in return for all the j we have
2Ti 1: 4 so that I may be filled with j.
Phm : 7 Your love has given me great j
Heb 1: 9 by anointing you with the oil of j."
12: 2 for the j set before him endured
13:17 them so that their work will be a j,
Jas 1: 2 Consider it pure j, my brothers,
4: 9 to mourning and your j to gloom.
1Pe 1: 8 with an inexpressible and glorious j
1Jn 1: 4 this to make our j complete.
2Jn : 4 It has given me great j to find some
:12 so that our j may be complete.
3Jn : 3 It gave me great j to have some
: 4 I have no greater j
Jude :24 without fault and with great j—

JOYFUL* (JOY)

Dt 16:14 Be j at your Feast—you, your sons
1Sa 18: 6 with j songs and with tambourines
1Ki 8:66 j and glad in heart
1Ch 15:16 as singers to sing j songs,
2Ch 7:10 j and glad in heart
Ps 68: 3 may they be happy and j.
100: 2 come before him with j songs.
Ecc 9: 7 and drink your wine with a j heart,
Isa 24: 8 the j harp is silent.
Jer 31: 4 and go out to dance with the j.
Hab 3:18 I will be j in God my Savior.
Zec 8:19 and tenth months will become j
10: 7 Their children will see it and be j;
Ro 12:12 Be j in hope, patient in affliction,
1Th 5:16 Be j always; pray continually;
Heb 12:22 thousands of angels in j assembly,

JOYOUS* (JOY)

Est 8:15 the city of Susa held a j celebration.

JUBILANT

Ps 96:12 let the fields be j, and everything
98: 4 burst into j song with music;

JUBILEE

Lev 25:11 The fiftieth year shall be a j for you;

JUDAH (JUDEA)

1. Son of Jacob by Leah (Ge 29:35; 35:23; 1Ch 2:1). Did not want to kill Joseph (Ge 37:26-27). Among Canaanites, fathered Perez by Tamar (Ge 38). Tribe of blessed as ruling tribe (Ge 49:8-12; Dt 33:7), numbered (Nu 1:27; 26:22), allotted land

(Jos 15; Eze 48:7), failed to fully possess (Jos 15: 63; Jdg 1:1-20).

2. Name used for people and land of Southern Kingdom.

Ru 1: 7 take them back to the land of *J*.
2Sa 2: 4 king over the house of *J*.
Isa 1: 1 The vision concerning *J*
3: 8 *J* is falling;
Jer 13:19 All *J* will be carried into exile,
30: 3 bring my people Israel and *J* back
Hos 1: 7 I will show love to the house of *J*;
Zec 10: 4 From *J* will come the cornerstone,
Mt 2: 6 least among the rulers of *J*;
Heb 7:14 that our Lord descended from *J*,
8: 8 and with the house of *J*.
Rev 5: 5 of the tribe of *J*, the Root of David,

JUDAISM (JEW)

Ac 13:43 devout converts to *J* followed Paul
Gal 1:13 of my previous way of life in *J*,
1:14 advancing in *J* beyond many Jews

JUDAS

1. Apostle; son of James (Lk 6:16; Jn 14:22; Ac 1:13). Probably also called Thaddaeus (Mt 10:3; Mk 3:18).

2. Brother of James and Jesus (Mt 13:55; Mk 6:3), also called Jude (Jude 1).

3. Christian prophet (Ac 15:22-32).

4. Apostle, also called Iscariot, who betrayed Jesus (Mt 10:4; 26:14-56; Mk 3:19; 14:10-50; Lk 6:16; 22:3-53; Jn 6:71; 12:4; 13:2-30; 18:2-11). Suicide of (Mt 27:3-5; Ac 1:16-25).

JUDEA (JUDAH)

Mt 2: 1 born in Bethlehem in *J*,
24:16 are in *J* flee to the mountains.
Lk 3: 1 Pontius Pilate was governor of *J*,
Ac 1: 8 and in all *J* and Samaria,
9:31 Then the church throughout *J*,
1Th 2:14 imitators of God's churches in *J*,

JUDGE (JUDGED JUDGES JUDGING JUDGMENT JUDGMENTS)

Ge 16: 5 May the LORD *j* between you
18:25 Will not the *J* of all the earth do
Lev 19:15 but *j* your neighbor fairly.
Dt 1:16 between your brothers and *j* fairly,
17:12 man who shows contempt for the *j*
32:36 The LORD will *j* his people
Jdg 2:18 Whenever the LORD raised up a *j*
1Sa 2:10 the LORD will *j* the ends
3:13 that I would *j* his family forever
7:15 *j* over Israel all the days of his life.
24:12 May the LORD *j* between you
1Ki 8:32 *J* between your servants,
1Ch 16:33 for he comes to *j* the earth.
2Ch 6:23 *J* between your servants, repaying
19: 7 *J* carefully, for with the LORD our
Job 9:15 plead with my *J* for mercy.
Ps 7: 8 *J* me, O LORD, according
7: 8 let the LORD *j* the peoples.
7:11 God is a righteous *j*,
9: 8 He will *j* the world in righteousness
50: 6 for God himself is *j*.
51: 4 and justified when you *j*.
75: 2 it is I who *j* uprightly.
76: 9 when you, O God, rose up to *j*,
82: 8 Rise up, O God, *j* the earth,
94: 2 Rise up, O *J* of the earth;
96:10 he will *j* the peoples with equity.
96:13 He will *j* the world in righteousness
98: 9 He will *j* the world in righteousness
110: 6 He will *j* the nations, heaping up
Pr 31: 9 Speak up and *j* fairly;
Isa 2: 4 He will *j* between the nations
3:13 he rises to *j* the people.
11: 3 He will not *j* by what he sees
33:22 For the LORD is our *j*,
Jer 11:20 Almighty, you who *j* righteously
Eze 7: 3 I will *j* you according
7:27 by their own standards I will *j* them
18:30 O house of Israel, I will *j* you,
20:36 so I will *j* you, declares
22: 2 "Son of man, will you *j* her?
34:17 I will *j* between one sheep
Joel 3:12 sit to *j* all the nations on every side.
Mic 3:11 Her leaders *j* for a bribe,
4: 3 He will *j* between many peoples
Mt 7: 1 Do not *j*, or you too will be judged.
Lk 6:37 "Do not *j*, and you will not be
18: 2 there was a *j* who neither feared
Jn 5:27 And he has given him authority to *j*
5:30 By myself I can do nothing; I *j* only
8:16 But if I do *j*, my decisions are right,
12:47 For I did not come to *j* the world,
12:48 There is a *j* for the one who rejects
Ac 10:42 as *j* of the living and the dead.
17:31 a day when he will *j* the world
Ro 2:16 day when God will *j* men's secrets
3: 6 how could God *j* the world?
14:10 then, why do you *j* your brother?
1Co 4: 3 indeed, I do not even *j* myself.
4: 5 Therefore *j* nothing
6: 2 And if you are to *j* the world,
6: 2 that the saints will *j* the world?
Gal 2: 6 not *j* by external appearance—
Col 2:16 Therefore do not let anyone *j* you
2Ti 4: 1 who will *j* the living and the dead,
4: 8 which the Lord, the righteous *J*,
Heb 10:30 "The Lord will *j* his people."
12:23 come to God, the *j* of all men,
13: 4 for God will *j* the adulterer
Jas 4:12 There is only one Lawgiver and *J*,
4:12 who are you to *j* your neighbor?
1Pe 4: 5 to him who is ready to *j* the living
Rev 20: 4 who had been given authority to *j*.

JUDGED (JUDGE)

Mt 7: 1 "Do not judge, or you too will be *j*.
1Co 4: 3 I care very little if I am *j* by you
10:29 For why should my freedom be *j*
11:31 But if we *j* ourselves, we would not
14:24 all that he is a sinner and will be *j*
Jas 3: 1 who teach will be *j* more strictly.
Rev 20:12 The dead were *j* according

JUDGES (JUDGE)

Jdg 2:16 Then the LORD raised up *j*,
Job 9:24 he blindfolds its *j*.
Ps 58:11 there is a God who *j* the earth."
75: 7 But it is God who *j*:
Pr 29:14 If a king *j* the poor with fairness,
Jn 5:22 Moreover, the Father *j* no one,
1Co 4: 4 It is the Lord who *j* me.
Heb 4:12 it *j* the thoughts and attitudes
1Pe 1:17 on a Father who *j* each man's work
2:23 himself to him who *j* justly.
Rev 19:11 With justice he *j* and makes war.

JUDGING (JUDGE)

Ps 9: 4 on your throne, *j* righteously.
Pr 24:23 To show partiality in *j* is not good:
Isa 16: 5 one who in *j* seeks justice
Mt 19:28 *j* the twelve tribes of Israel.
Jn 7:24 Stop *j* by mere appearances,

JUDGMENT (JUDGE)

Nu 33: 4 for the LORD had brought *j*
Dt 1:17 of any man, for *j* belongs to God.
32:41 and my hand grasps it in *j*,
1Sa 25:33 May you be blessed for your good *j*
Ps 1: 5 the wicked will not stand in the *j*,
9: 7 he has established his throne for *j*.
76: 8 From heaven you pronounced *j*,
82: 1 he gives *j* among the "gods":
119: 66 Teach me knowledge and good *j*,
143: 2 Do not bring your servant into *j*,
Pr 3:21 preserve sound *j* and discernment,
6:32 man who commits adultery lacks *j*;
8:14 Counsel and sound *j* are mine;
10:21 but fools die for lack of *j*.
11:12 man who lacks *j* derides his
12:11 but he who chases fantasies lacks *j*.
17:18 A man lacking in *j* strikes hands
18: 1 he defies all sound *j*.
28:16 A tyrannical ruler lacks *j*,
Ecc 12:14 God will bring every deed into *j*,
Isa 3:14 The LORD enters into *j*
28: 6 justice to him who sits in *j*,
53: 8 By oppression and *j* he was taken
66:16 the LORD will execute *j*
Jer 2:35 But I will pass *j* on you
25:31 he will bring *j* on all mankind
51:18 when their *j* comes, they will
Eze 11:10 and I will execute *j* on you
Da 7:22 pronounced *j* in favor of the saints
Am 7: 4 Sovereign LORD was calling for *j*
Zec 8:16 and sound *j* in your courts;
Mal 3: 5 "So I will come near to you for *j*.
Mt 5:21 who murders will be subject to *j*.'
5:22 with his brother will be subject to *j*.
10:15 on the day of *j* than for that town.
11:24 on the day of *j* than for you."
12:36 have to give account on the day of *j*
12:41 up at the *j* with this generation
Jn 5:22 but has entrusted all *j* to the Son,
5:30 as I hear, and my *j* is just,
7:24 appearances, and make a right *j*."
8:26 "I have much to say in *j* of you.
9:39 "For *j* I have come into this world,
12:31 Now is the time for *j* on this world;
16: 8 to sin and righteousness and *j*:
16:11 in regard to *j*, because the prince
Ac 24:25 self-control and the *j* to come,
Ro 2: 1 you who pass *j* on someone else,
2: 2 Now we know that God's *j*
5:16 The *j* followed one sin
Ro 12: 3 rather think of yourself with sober *j*
14:10 stand before God's *j* seat.
14:13 Therefore let us stop passing *j*
1Co 7:40 In my *j*, she is happier if she stays
11:29 body of the Lord eats and drinks *j*
2Co 5:10 appear before the *j* seat of Christ,
2Th 1: 5 is evidence that God's *j* is right,
1Ti 3: 6 fall under the same *j* as the devil.
5:12 Thus they bring *j* on themselves,
Heb 6: 2 of the dead, and eternal *j*.
9:27 to die once, and after that to face *j*,
10:27 but only a fearful expectation of *j*
Jas 2:13 *j* without mercy will be shown
4:11 are not keeping it, but sitting in *j*
1Pe 4:17 For it is time for *j* to begin
2Pe 2: 9 the unrighteous for the day of *j*,
3: 7 being kept for the day of *j*
1Jn 4:17 have confidence on the day of *j*,
Jude : 6 bound with everlasting chains for *j*
Rev 14: 7 because the hour of his *j* has come.

JUDGMENTS (JUDGE)

Jer 1:16 I will pronounce my *j* on my people
Da 9:11 and sworn *j* written in the Law
Hos 6: 5 my *j* flashed like lightning
Ro 11:33 How unsearchable his *j*,
1Co 2:15 spiritual man makes *j* about all
Rev 16: 7 true and just are your *j*."

JUG

1Sa 26:12 and water *j* near Saul's head,
1Ki 17:12 of flour in a jar and a little oil in a *j*.

JUST* (JUSTICE JUSTIFICATION JUSTIFIED JUSTIFIES JUSTIFY JUSTIFYING JUSTLY)

Ge 18:19 LORD by doing what is right and *j*,
Dt 2:12 *j* as Israel did in the land
6: 3 *j* as the LORD, the God
27: 3 and honey, *j* as the LORD,
30: 9 *j* as he delighted in your fathers,
32: 4 and all his ways are *j*.
32: 4 upright and *j* is he.
32:47 They are not *j* idle words for you—
32:50 *j* as your brother Aaron died
2Sa 8:15 doing what was *j* and right
1Ch 18:14 doing what was *j* and right
2Ch 12: 6 and said, "The LORD is *j*."
Ne 9:13 and laws that are *j* and right,
9:33 you have been *j*; you have acted
Job 34:17 Will you condemn the *j*
35: 2 Elihu said: "Do you think this is *j*?
Ps 37:28 For the LORD loves the *j*
37:30 and his tongue speaks what is *j*.
99: 4 what is *j* and right.
111: 7 of his hands are faithful and *j*;
119:121 I have done what is righteous and *j*;
Pr 1: 3 doing what is right and *j* and fair;
2: 8 for he guards the course of the *j*
2: 9 will understand what is right and *j*
8: 8 All the words of my mouth are *j*;
8:15 and rulers make laws that are *j*;
12: 5 The plans of the righteous are *j*,
21: 3 To do what is right and *j*
Isa 32: 7 even when the plea of the needy is *j*
58: 2 They ask me for *j* decisions
Jer 4: 2 if in a truthful, *j* and righteous way
22: 3 what the LORD says: Do what is *j*
22:15 He did what was right and *j*,
23: 5 do what is *j* and right in the land.
33:15 he will do what is *j* and right
Eze 18: 5 who does what is *j* and right.
18:19 Since the son has done what is *j*
18:21 and does what is *j* and right,
18:25 'The way of the Lord is not *j*.'
18:27 and does what is *j* and right,
18:29 'The way of the Lord is not *j*.'
33:14 and does what is *j* and right—
33:16 He has done what is *j* and right;
33:17 But it is their way that is not *j*.
33:17 'The way of the Lord is not *j*.'
33:19 and does what is *j* and right,
33:20 'The way of the Lord is not *j*.'
45: 9 and oppression and do what is *j*
Da 4:37 does is right and all his ways are *j*.
Jn 5:30 as I hear, and my judgment is *j*,
Ro 3:26 as to be *j* and the one who justifies
2Th 1: 6 God is *j*: He will pay back trouble
Heb 2: 2 received its *j* punishment,
1Jn 1: 9 and *j* and will forgive us our sins
Rev 15: 3 *J* and true are your ways,
16: 5 "You are *j* in these judgments,
16: 7 true and *j* are your judgments."
19: 2 for true and *j* are his judgments.

JUSTICE* (JUST)

Ge 49:16 "Dan will provide *j* for his people
Ex 23: 2 do not pervert *j* by siding
23: 6 "Do not deny *j* to your poor people
Lev 19:15 " 'Do not pervert *j*; do not show

Dt 16:19 Do not pervert j or show partiality.
16:20 Follow j and j alone,
24:17 the alien or the fatherless of j,
27:19 Cursed is the man who withholds j
1Sa 8: 3 accepted bribes and perverted j.
2Sa 15: 4 and I would see that he gets j."
15: 6 came to the king asking for j,
1Ki 3:11 for discernment in administering j,
3:28 wisdom from God to administer j.
7: 7 the Hall of J, where he was to judge
10: 9 to maintain j and righteousness."
2Ch 9: 8 to maintain j and righteousness."
Ezr 7:25 and judges to administer j
Est 1:13 experts in matters of law and j,
Job 8: 3 Does God pervert j?
9:19 matter of j, who will summon him?
19: 7 though I call for help, there is no j.
27: 2 as God lives, who has denied me j,
29:14 j was my robe and my turban.
31:13 "If I have denied j
34: 5 but God denies me j.
34:12 that the Almighty would pervert j.
34:17 Can he who hates j govern?
36: 3 I will ascribe j to my Maker.
36:17 j have taken hold of you.
37:23 in his j and great righteousness,
40: 8 "Would you discredit my j?
Ps 7: 6 Awake, my God; decree j.
9: 8 he will govern the peoples with j.
9:16 The LORD is known by his j;
11: 7 he loves j;
33: 5 LORD loves righteousness and j;
36: 6 your j like the great deep.
37: 6 j of your cause like the noonday
45: 6 a scepter of j will be the scepter
72: 1 Endow the king with your j, O God
72: 2 your afflicted ones with j.
89:14 j are the foundation of your throne;
97: 2 j are the foundation of his throne.
99: 4 The King is mighty, he loves j—
101: 1 I will sing of your love and j;
103: 6 and j for all the oppressed.
106: 3 Blessed are they who maintain j,
112: 5 who conducts his affairs with j.
140: 12 I know that the LORD secures j
Pr 8:20 along the paths of j,
16:10 and his mouth should not betray j.
17:23 to pervert the course of j.
18: 5 or to deprive the innocent of j.
19:28 A corrupt witness mocks at j,
21:15 When j is done, it brings joy
28: 5 Evil men do not understand j,
29: 4 By j a king gives a country stability
29: 7 The righteous care about j
29:26 from the LORD that man gets j.
Ecc 3:16 place of j— wickedness was there.
5: 8 poor oppressed in a district, and j
Isa 1:17 Seek j,
1:21 She once was full of j;
1:27 Zion will be redeemed with j,
5: 7 he looked for j, but saw bloodshed;
5:16 Almighty will be exalted by his j,
5:23 but deny j to the innocent.
9: 7 it with j and righteousness
10: 2 and withhold j from the oppressed of
11: 4 with j he will give decisions
16: 5 one who in judging seeks j
28: 6 He will be a spirit of j
28:17 I will make j the measuring line
29:21 deprive the innocent of j.
30:18 For the LORD is a God of j.
32: 1 and rulers will rule with j.
32:16 J will dwell in the desert
33: 5 with j and righteousness.
42: 1 and he will bring j to the nations.
42: 3 In faithfulness he will bring forth j;
42: 4 till he establishes j on earth.
51: 4 my j will become a light
51: 5 my arm will bring j to the nations.
56: 1 "Maintain j
59: 4 No one calls for j;
59: 8 there is no j in their paths.
59: 9 So j is far from us,
59:11 We look for j, but find none;
59:14 So j is driven back,
59:15 that there was no j.
61: 8 "For I, the LORD, love j;
Jer 9:24 j and righteousness on earth,
10:24 Correct me, LORD, but only with j
12: 1 speak with you about your j:
21:12 " 'Administer j every morning;
30:11 I will discipline you but only with j;
46:28 I will discipline you but only with j;
La 3:36 to deprive a man of j—
Eze 22:29 mistreat the alien, denying them j.
34:16 I will shepherd the flock with j.
Hos 2:19 you in righteousness and j,
12: 6 maintain love and j,
Am 2: 7 and deny j to the oppressed.
Am 5: 7 You who turn j into bitterness
5:12 and you deprive the poor of j
5:15 maintain j in the courts.
5:24 But let j roll on like a river,
6:12 But you have turned j into poison
Mic 3: 1 Should you not know j,
3: 8 and with j and might,
3: 9 who despise j
Hab 1: 4 and j never prevails.
1: 4 so that j is perverted.
Zep 3: 5 by morning he dispenses his j,
Zec 7: 9 'Administer true j; show mercy
Mal 2:17 or "Where is the God of j?"
3: 5 and deprive aliens of j,
Mt 12:18 he will proclaim j to the nations.
12:20 till he leads j to victory.
23:23 important matters of the law—j,
Lk 11:42 you neglect j and the love of God.
18: 3 'Grant me j against my adversary.'
18: 5 I will see that she gets j,
18: 7 And will not God bring about j
18: 8 he will see that they get j,
Ac 8:33 humiliation he was deprived of j.
17:31 with j by the man he has appointed.
28: 4 J has not allowed him to live."
Ro 3:25 He did this to demonstrate his j,
3:26 it to demonstrate his j
2Co 7:11 what readiness to see j done.
Heb 11:33 administered j, and gained what
Rev 19:11 With j he judges and makes war.

JUSTIFICATION* (JUST)
Eze 16:52 for you have furnished some j
Ro 4:25 and was raised to life for our j.
5:16 many trespasses and brought j.
5:18 of righteousness was j that brings

JUSTIFIED* (JUST)
Ps 51: 4 and j when you judge.
Lk 18:14 rather than the other, went home j
Ac 13:39 from everything you could not be j
13:39 him everyone who believes is j
Ro 3:24 and are j freely by his grace
3:28 For we maintain that a man is j
4: 2 If, in fact, Abraham was j by works,
5: 1 since we have been j through faith,
5: 9 Since we have now been j
8:30 those he called, he also j; those he j,
10:10 heart that you believe and are j,
1Co 6:11 you were j in the name
Gal 2:16 in Christ Jesus that we may be j
2:16 observing the law no one will be j.
2:16 sinners' know that a man is not j
2:17 "If, while we seek to be j in Christ,
3:11 Clearly no one is j before God
3:24 to Christ that we might be j by faith
5: 4 to be j by law have been alienated
Tit 3: 7 so that, having been j by his grace,
Jas 2:24 You see that a person is j

JUSTIFIES* (JUST)
Ro 3:26 one who j those who have faith
4: 5 but trusts God who j the wicked,
8:33 God has chosen? It is God who j.

JUSTIFY* (JUST)
Est 7: 4 such distress would j disturbing
Job 40: 8 you condemn me to j yourself?
Isa 53:11 my righteous servant will j many,
Lk 10:29 But he wanted to j himself,
16:15 "You are the ones who j yourselves
Ro 3:30 who will j the circumcised by faith
Gal 3: 8 that God would j the Gentiles

JUSTIFYING* (JUST)
Job 32: 2 angry with Job for j himself rather

JUSTLY* (JUST)
Ps 58: 1 Do you rulers indeed speak j?
67: 4 for you rule the peoples j
Jer 7: 5 and deal with each other j,
Mic 6: 8 To act j and to love mercy
Lk 23:41 We are punished j,
1Pe 2:23 himself to him who judges j.

KADESH
Nu 20: 1 of Zin, and they stayed at K.
Dt 1:46 And so you stayed in K many days

KADESH BARNEA
Nu 32: 8 I sent them from K to look over

KEBAR
Eze 1: 1 among the exiles by the K River,

KEDORLAOMER
Ge 14:17 Abram returned from defeating K

KEEP (KEEPER KEEPING KEEPS KEPT)
Ge 31:49 "May the LORD k watch
Ex 15:26 his commands and k all his
20: 6 and k my commandments.
Lev 15:31 You must k the Israelites separate
Nu 6:24 and k you;
Dt 4: 2 but k the commands of the LORD
6:17 Be sure to k the commands
7: 9 who love him and k his commands.
7:12 your God will k his covenant
11: 1 your God and k his requirements,
13: 4 K his commands and obey him;
30:10 your God and k his commands
30:16 and to k his commands, decrees
Jos 22: 5 careful to k the commandment
1Ki 8:58 and to k the commands,
2Ki 17:19 Judah did not k the commands
23: 3 the LORD and k his commands,
1Ch 29:18 and k their hearts loyal to you.
2Ch 6:14 you who k your covenant of love
34:31 the LORD and k his commands,
Job 14:16 but not k track of my sin.
Ps 18:28 You, O LORD, k my lamp burning
19:13 K your servant also from willful
78:10 they did not k God's covenant
119: 2 Blessed are they who k his statutes
119: 9 can a young man k his way pure?
121: 7 The LORD will k you
141: 3 k watch over the door of my lips.
Pr 4:21 k them within your heart;
4:24 k corrupt talk far from your lips.
30: 8 K falsehood and lies far from me;
Ecc 3: 6 a time to k and a time
12:13 and k his commandments,
Isa 26: 3 You will k in perfect peace
42: 6 I will k you and will make you
58:13 "If you k your feet
Jer 16:11 forsook me and did not k my law.
Eze 20:19 and be careful to k my laws.
Mt 10:10 for the worker is worth his k.
Lk 12:35 and k your lamps burning,
17:33 tries to k his life will lose it,
Jn 10:24 How long will you k us in suspense
12:25 in this world will k it for eternal life
Ac 2:24 for death to k its hold on him.
18: 9 "Do not be afraid; k on speaking,
Ro 7:19 want to do—this I k on doing.
12:11 but k your spiritual fervor,
14:22 you believe about these things k
16:17 K away from them.
1Co 1: 8 He will k you strong to the end,
2Co 12: 7 To k me from becoming conceited
Gal 5:25 let us k in step with the Spirit.
Eph 4: 3 Make every effort to k the unity
2Th 3: 6 to k away from every brother who
1Ti 5:22 K yourself pure.
2Ti 4: 5 k your head in all situations,
Heb 9:20 God has commanded you to k."
13: 5 K your lives free from the love
Jas 1:26 and yet does not k a tight rein
2: 8 If you really k the royal law found
3: 2 able to k his whole body in check.
2Pe 1: 8 will k you from being ineffective
Jude :21 K yourselves in God's love
:24 able to k you from falling
Rev 3:10 also k you from the hour
22: 9 of all who k the words of this book.

KEEPER (KEEP)
Ge 4: 9 I my brother's k?" The LORD

KEEPING (KEEP)
Ex 20: 8 the Sabbath day by k it holy.
Dt 5:12 the Sabbath day by k it holy,
13:18 k all his commands that I am
Ps 19:11 in k them there is great reward.
119:112 My heart is set on k your decrees
Pr 15: 3 k watch on the wicked
Mt 3: 8 Produce fruit in k with repentance.
Lk 2: 8 k watch over their flocks at night.
1Co 7:19 K God's commands is what counts.
2Co 8: 5 and then to us in k with God's will.
Jas 4:11 you are not k it, but sitting
1Pe 3:16 and respect, k a clear conscience,
2Pe 3: 9 Lord is not slow in k his promise,

KEEPS (KEEP)
Ne 1: 5 who k his covenant of love
Ps 15: 4 who k his oath
Pr 12:23 A prudent man k his knowledge
15:21 of understanding k a straight
17:28 a fool is thought wise if he k silent,
29:11 a wise man k himself under control
Isa 56: 2 who k the Sabbath
Da 9: 4 who k his covenant of love
Am 5:13 Therefore the prudent man k quiet
Jn 7:19 Yet not one of you k the law.
8:51 if anyone k my word, he will never
1Co 13: 5 is not easily angered, it k no record

Jas 2:10 For whoever *k* the whole law
Rev 22: 7 Blessed is he who *k* the words

KEILAH
1Sa 23:13 that David had escaped from *K*,

KEPT (KEEP)
Ex 12:42 Because the LORD *k* vigil that
Dt 7: 8 and *k* the oath he swore
2Ki 18: 6 he *k* the commands the LORD had
Ne 9: 8 You have *k* your promise
Ps 130: 3 If you, O LORD, *k* a record of sins,
Isa 38:17 In your love you *k* me
Mt 19:20 these I have *k*," the young man
2Co 11: 9 I have *k* myself from being
2Ti 4: 7 finished the race, I have *k* the faith.
1Pe 1: 4 spoil or fade—*k* in heaven for you,

KERNEL
Mk 4:28 then the full *k* in the head.
Jn 12:24 a *k* of wheat falls to the ground

KEY (KEYS)
Isa 33: 6 the fear of the LORD is the *k*
Rev 20: 1 having the *k* to the Abyss

KEYS* (KEY)
Mt 16:19 I will give you the *k* of the kingdom
Rev 1:18 And I hold the *k* of death

KICK*
Ac 26:14 for you to *k* against the goads.'

KILL (KILLED KILLS)
Ecc 3: 3 a time to *k* and a time to heal,
Mt 10:28 *k* the body but cannot *k* the soul.
17:23 They will *k* him, and on the third
Mk 9:31 will *k* him, and after three days
10:34 spit on him, flog him and *k* him.

KILLED (KILL)
Ge 4: 8 his brother Abel and *k* him.
Ex 2:12 he *k* the Egyptian and hid him
13:15 the LORD *k* every firstborn
Nu 35:11 who has *k* someone accidentally
1Sa 17:50 down the Philistine and *k* him.
Ne 9:26 They *k* your prophets, who had
Hos 6: 5 I *k* you with the words
Lk 11:48 they *k* the prophets, and you build
Ac 3:15 You *k* the author of life,

KILLS (KILL)
Ex 21:12 *k* him shall surely be put to death.
Lev 24:21 but whoever *k* a man must be put
2Co 3: 6 for the letter *k*, but the Spirit gives

KIND (KINDNESS KINDNESSES KINDS)
Ge 1:24 animals, each according to its *k*."
2Ch 10: 7 "If you will be *k* to these people
Pr 11:17 A *k* man benefits himself,
12:25 but a *k* word cheers him up.
14:21 blessed is he who is *k* to the needy.
14:31 whoever is *k* to the needy honors
19:17 He who is *k* to the poor lends
Da 4:27 by being *k* to the oppressed.
Lk 6:35 because he is *k* to the ungrateful
1Co 13: 4 Love is patient, love is *k*.
15:35 With what *k* of body will they
Eph 4:32 Be *k* and compassionate
1Th 5:15 but always try to be *k* to each other
2Ti 2:24 instead, he must be *k* to everyone,
Tit 2: 5 to be busy at home, to be *k*,

KINDHEARTED* (HEART)
Pr 11:16 A *k* woman gains respect,

KINDNESS (KIND)
Ge 24:12 and show *k* to my master Abraham
32:10 I am unworthy of all the *k*
39:21 he showed him *k* and granted him
Jdg 8:35 failed to show *k* to the family
Ru 2:20 has not stopped showing his *k*
2Sa 9: 3 to whom I can show God's *k*?"
22:51 he shows unfailing *k*
Ps 18:50 he shows unfailing *k*
141: 5 righteous man strike me—it is a *k*;
Isa 54: 8 but with everlasting *k*
Jer 9:24 I am the LORD, who exercises *k*,
Hos 11: 4 I led them with cords of human *k*,
Ac 14:17 He has shown *k* by giving you rain
Ro 11:22 Consider therefore the *k*
2Co 6: 6 understanding, patience and *k*;
Gal 5:22 peace, patience, *k*, goodness,
Eph 2: 7 expressed in his *k* to us
Col 3:12 yourselves with compassion, *k*,
Tit 3: 4 But when the *k* and love
2Pe 1: 7 brotherly *k*; and to brotherly *k*,

KINDNESSES* (KIND)
Ps 106: 7 did not remember your many *k*,
Isa 63: 7 I will tell of the *k* of the LORD,
Isa 63: 7 to his compassion and many *k*.

KINDS (KIND)
Ge 1:12 bearing seed according to their *k*
1Co 12: 4 There are different *k* of gifts,
1Ti 6:10 of money is a root of all *k* of evil.
1Pe 1: 6 had to suffer grief in all *k* of trials.

KING (KING'S KINGDOM KINGDOMS KINGS)
1. Kings of Judah and Israel: see Saul, David, Solomon.
2. Kings of Judah: see Rehoboam, Abijah, Asa, Jehoshaphat, Jehoram, Ahaziah, Athaliah (Queen), Joash, Amaziah, Azariah (Uzziah), Jotham, Ahaz, Hezekiah, Manasseh, Amon, Josiah, Jehoahaz, Jehoiakim, Jehoiachin, Zedekiah.
3. Kings of Israel: see Jeroboam I, Nadab, Baasha, Elah, Zimri, Tibni, Omri, Ahab, Ahaziah, Joram, Jehu, Jehoahaz, Jehoash, Jeroboam II, Zechariah, Shallum, Menahem, Pekah, Pekahiah, Hoshea.
Ex 1: 8 a new *k*, who did not know about
Dt 17:14 "Let us set a *k* over us like all
Jdg 17: 6 In those days Israel had no *k*;
1Sa 8: 5 now appoint a *k* to lead us,
11:15 as *k* in the presence of the LORD.
12:12 the LORD your God was your *k*.
2Sa 2: 4 and there they anointed David *k*
1Ki 1:30 Solomon your son shall be *k*,
Ps 2: 6 "I have installed my *K*
24: 7 that the *K* of glory may come in.
44: 4 You are my *K* and my God,
47: 7 For God is the *K* of all the earth;
Isa 32: 1 See, a *k* will reign in righteousness
Jer 30: 9 and David their *k*,
Hos 3: 5 their God and David their *k*.
Mic 2:13 *k* will pass through before them,
Zec 9: 9 See, your *k* comes to you,
Mt 2: 2 is the one who has been born *k*
27:11 "Are you the *k* of the Jews?" "Yes,
Lk 19:38 "Blessed is the *k* who comes
23: 3 "Are you the *k* of the Jews?" "Yes,
23:38 THE *K* OF THE JEWS.
Jn 1:49 of God; you are the *K* of Israel."
12:13 "Blessed is the *K* of Israel!"
Ac 17: 7 saying that there is another *k*,
1Ti 1:17 Now to the *K* eternal, immortal,
6:15 the *K* of kings and Lord of lords,
Heb 7: 1 This Melchizedek was *k* of Salem
1Pe 2:13 to the *k*, as the supreme authority,
2:17 of believers, fear God, honor the *k*.
Rev 15: 3 *K* of the ages.
17:14 he is Lord of lords and *K* of kings—
19:16 *K* OF KINGS AND LORD

KING'S (KING)
Pr 21: 1 The *k* heart is in the hand
Ecc 8: 3 in a hurry to leave the *k* presence.

KINGDOM (KING)
Ex 19: 6 you will be for me a *k* of priests
Dt 17:18 When he takes the throne of his *k*,
2Sa 7:12 body, and I will establish his *k*.
1Ki 11:31 to tear the *k* out of Solomon's hand
1Ch 17:11 own sons, and I will establish his *k*.
29:11 Yours, O LORD, is the *k*;
Ps 45: 6 justice will be the scepter of your *k*.
103: 19 and his *k* rules over all.
145: 11 They will tell of the glory of your *k*
Eze 29:14 There they will be a lowly *k*.
Da 2:39 "After you, another *k* will rise,
4: 3 His *k* is an eternal *k*;
7:27 His *k* will be an everlasting *k*,
Ob :21 And the *k* will be the LORD's.
Mt 3: 2 Repent, for the *k* of heaven is near
4:17 Repent, for the *k* of heaven is near
4:23 preaching the good news of the *k*,
5: 3 for theirs is the *k* of heaven.
5:10 for theirs is the *k* of heaven.
5:19 great in the *k* of heaven.
5:19 least in the *k* of heaven,
5:20 you will certainly not enter the *k*
6:10 your *k* come,
6:33 But seek first his *k* and his
7:21 Lord,' will enter the *k* of heaven,
8:11 Isaac and Jacob in the *k* of heaven.
8:12 the subjects of the *k* will be thrown
9:35 preaching the good news of the *k*
10: 7 preach this message: 'The *k*
11:11 least in the *k* of heaven is greater
11:12 the *k* of heaven has been forcefully
12:25 "Every *k* divided against itself will
12:26 How then can his *k* stand?
12:28 then the *k* of God has come
13:11 knowledge of the secrets of the *k*
13:19 hears the message about the *k*
13:24 "The *k* of heaven is like a man who
13:31 *k* of heaven is like a mustard seed,
13:33 "The *k* of heaven is like yeast that
Mt 13:38 stands for the sons of the *k*.
13:41 of his *k* everything that causes sin
13:43 the sun in the *k* of their Father.
13:44 *k* of heaven is like treasure hidden
13:45 the *k* of heaven is like a merchant
13:47 *k* of heaven is like a net that was let
13:52 has been instructed about the *k*
16:19 the keys of the *k* of heaven;
16:28 the Son of Man coming in his *k*."
18: 1 the greatest in the *k* of heaven?"
18: 3 you will never enter the *k*
18: 4 the greatest in the *k* of heaven.
18:23 the *k* of heaven is like a king who
19:12 because of the *k* of heaven.
19:14 for the *k* of heaven belongs to such
19:23 man to enter the *k* of heaven.
19:24 for a rich man to enter the *k* of God
20: 1 "For the *k* of heaven is like
20:21 the other at your left in your *k*."
21:31 the prostitutes are entering the *k*
21:43 "Therefore I tell you that the *k*
22: 2 "The *k* of heaven is like a king who
23:13 You shut the *k* of heaven
24: 7 rise against nation, and *k* against *k*.
24:14 gospel of the *k* will be preached
25: 1 "At that time the *k*
25:34 the *k* prepared for you
26:29 anew with you in my Father's *k*."
Mk 1:15 "The *k* of God is near.
3:24 If a *k* is divided against itself,
3:24 against itself, that *k* cannot stand.
4:11 "The secret of the *k*
4:26 "This is what the *k* of God is like.
4:30 "What shall we say the *k*
6:23 I will give you, up to half my *k*."
9: 1 before they see the *k* of God come
9:47 better for you to enter the *k* of God
10:14 for the *k* of God belongs to such
10:15 anyone who will not receive the *k*
10:23 for the rich to enter the *k* of God!"
10:24 how hard it is to enter the *k* of God
10:25 for a rich man to enter the *k* of God
11:10 "Blessed is the coming *k*
12:34 "You are not far from the *k* of God
13: 8 rise against nation, and *k* against *k*.
14:25 day when I drink it anew in the *k*
15:43 who was himself waiting for the *k*
Lk 1:33 Jacob forever; his *k* will never
4:43 of the *k* of God to the other towns
6:20 for yours is the *k* of God.
7:28 in the *k* of God is greater than he."
8: 1 proclaiming the good news of the *k*
8:10 knowledge of the secrets of the *k*
9: 2 out to preach the *k* of God
9:11 spoke to them about the *k* of God,
9:27 before they see the *k* of God."
9:60 you go and proclaim the *k* of God
9:62 fit for service in the *k* of God."
10: 9 'The *k* of God is near you.'
10:11 sure of this: The *k* of God is near.'
11: 2 your *k* come.
11:17 "Any *k* divided against itself will
11:18 himself, how can his *k* stand?
11:20 then the *k* of God has come to you.
12:31 seek his *k*, and these things will be
12:32 has been pleased to give you the *k*.
13:18 "What is the *k* of God like?
13:20 What shall I compare the *k* of God
13:28 all the prophets in the *k* of God,
13:29 places at the feast in the *k* of God.
14:15 eat at the feast in the *k* of God."
16:16 the good news of the *k*
17:20 when the *k* of God would come,
17:20 *k* of God does not come with careful
17:21 because the *k* of God is within you
18:16 for the *k* of God belongs to such
18:17 anyone who will not receive the *k*
18:24 for the rich to enter the *k* of God!
18:25 for a rich man to enter the *k* of God
18:29 for the sake of the *k* of God will fail
19:11 and the people thought that the *k*
21:10 rise against nation, and *k* against *k*.
21:31 you know that the *k* of God is near.
22:16 until it finds fulfillment in the *k*
22:18 the vine until the *k* of God comes."
22:29 And I confer on you a *k*, just
22:30 and drink at my table in my *k*
23:42 me when you come into your *k*."
23:51 he was waiting for the *k* of God.
Jn 3: 3 no one can see the *k* of God.
3: 5 no one can enter the *k* of God.
18:36 now my *k* is from another place."
18:36 "My *k* is not of this world.
Ac 1: 3 and spoke about the *k* of God.
1: 6 going to restore the *k* to Israel?"
8:12 he preached the good news of the *k*
14:22 hardships to enter the *k* of God,"
19: 8 arguing persuasively about the *k*
20:25 about preaching the *k* will ever see

Ac 28:23 and declared to them the *k* of God
28:31 hindrance he preached the *k*
Ro 14:17 For the *k* of God is not a matter
1Co 4:20 For the *k* of God is not a matter
6: 9 the wicked will not inherit the *k*
6:10 swindlers will inherit the *k* of God.
15:24 hands over the *k* to God the Father
15:50 blood cannot inherit the *k* of God,
Gal 5:21 live like this will not inherit the *k*
Eph 2: 2 and of the ruler of the *k* of the air,
5: 5 has any inheritance in the *k*
Col 1:12 of the saints in the *k* of light.
1:13 and brought us into the *k*
4:11 among my fellow workers for the *k*
1Th 2:12 who calls you into his *k* and glory.
2Th 1: 5 will be counted worthy of the *k*
2Ti 4: 1 in view of his appearing and his *k*,
4:18 bring me safely to his heavenly *k*.
Heb 1: 8 will be the scepter of your *k*.
12:28 we are receiving a *k* that cannot be
Jas 2: 5 to inherit the *k* he promised those
2Pe 1:11 into the eternal *k* of our Lord
Rev 1: 6 has made us to be a *k* and priests
1: 9 companion in the suffering and *k*
5:10 You have made them to be a *k*
11:15 of the world has become the *k*
11:15 "The *k* of the world has become
12:10 the power and the *k* of our God,
16:10 his *k* was plunged into darkness.
17:12 who have not yet received a *k*,

KINGDOMS (KING)
2Ki 19:15 God over all the *k* of the earth.
19:19 so that all *k* on earth may know
2Ch 20: 6 rule over all the *k* of the nations.
Ps 68:32 Sing to God, O *k* of the earth,
Isa 37:16 God over all the *k* of the earth.
37:20 so that all *k* on earth may know
Eze 29:15 It will be the lowliest of *k*
37:22 or be divided into two *k*.
Da 4:17 Most High is sovereign over the *k*
7:17 great beasts are four *k* that will rise
Zep 3: 8 to gather the *k*

KINGS (KING)
Ps 2: 2 The *k* of the earth take their stand
47: 9 for the *k* of the earth belong to God
68:29 *k* will bring you gifts.
72:11 All *k* will bow down to him
110: 5 he will crush *k* on the day
149: 8 to bind their *k* with fetters,
Pr 16:12 *K* detest wrongdoing,
Isa 24:21 and the *k* on the earth below.
52:15 and *k* will shut their mouths
60:11 their *k* led in triumphal procession.
Da 2:21 he sets up *k* and deposes them.
7:24 ten horns are ten *k* who will come
Lk 21:12 and you will be brought before *k*
1Co 4: 8 You have become *k*—
1Ti 2: 2 for *k* and all those in authority,
6:15 the King of *k* and Lord of lords,
Rev 1: 5 and the ruler of the *k* of the earth.
17:14 he is Lord of lords and King of *k*—
19:16 KING OF *K* AND LORD

KINSMAN-REDEEMER (REDEEM)
Ru 3: 9 over me, since you are a *k*."
4:14 day has not left you without a *k*.

KISS (KISSED KISSES)
Ps 2:12 *K* the Son, lest he be angry
Pr 24:26 is like a *k* on the lips.
SS 1: 2 *Beloved* Let him *k* me
8: 1 I would *k* you,
Lk 22:48 the Son of Man with a *k*?"
Ro 16:16 Greet one another with a holy *k*.
1Co 16:20 Greet one another with a holy *k*.
2Co 13:12 Greet one another with a holy *k*.
1Th 5:26 Greet all the brothers with a holy *k*
1Pe 5:14 Greet one another with a *k* of love.

KISSED (KISS)
Mk 14:45 Judas said, "Rabbi!" and *k* him.
Lk 7:38 *k* them and poured perfume

KISSES* (KISS)
Pr 27: 6 but an enemy multiplies *k*.
SS 1: 2 with the *k* of his mouth—

KNEE (KNEES)
Isa 45:23 Before me every *k* will bow;
Ro 14:11 'every *k* will bow before me;
Php 2:10 name of Jesus every *k* should bow,

KNEEL (KNELT)
Est 3: 2 But Mordecai would not *k* down
Ps 95: 6 let us *k* before the LORD our
Eph 3:14 For this reason I *k*

KNEES (KNEE)
1Ki 19:18 all whose *k* have not bowed
Isa 35: 3 steady the *k* that give way;
Da 6:10 times a day he got down on his *k*
Lk 5: 8 he fell at Jesus' *k* and said,
Heb 12:12 your feeble arms and weak *k*.

KNELT* (KNEEL)
1Ki 1:16 Bathsheba bowed low and *k*
2Ch 6:13 and then *k* down before the whole
7: 3 they *k* on the pavement
29:29 everyone present with him *k* down
Est 3: 2 officials at the king's gate *k* down
Mt 8: 2 and *k* before him and said,
9:18 a ruler came and *k* before him
15:25 The woman came and *k* before him
17:14 a man approached Jesus and *k*
27:29 *k* in front of him and mocked him.
Lk 22:41 *k* down and prayed, "Father,
Ac 20:36 he *k* down with all of them
21: 5 there on the beach we *k* to pray.

KNEW (KNOW)
2Ch 33:13 Manasseh *k* that the LORD is God
Job 23: 3 If only I *k* where to find him;
Pr 24:12 "But we *k* nothing about this,"
Jer 1: 5 you in the womb I *k* you,
Jnh 4: 2 I *k* that you are a gracious
Mt 7:23 tell them plainly, 'I never *k* you.
12:25 Jesus *k* their thoughts
Jn 2:24 himself to them, for he *k* all men.
14: 7 If you really *k* me, you would know

KNIFE
Ge 22:10 and took the *k* to slay his son.
Pr 23: 2 and put a *k* to your throat

KNOCK* (KNOCKS)
Mt 7: 7 *k* and the door will be opened
Lk 11: 9 *k* and the door will be opened
Rev 3:20 I am! I stand at the door and *k*.

KNOCKS (KNOCK)
Mt 7: 8 and to him who *k*, the door will be

KNOW (FOREKNEW FOREKNOWLEDGE KNEW KNOWING KNOWLEDGE KNOWN KNOWS)
Ge 22:12 Now I *k* that you fear God,
Ex 6: 7 you will *k* that I am the LORD
14: 4 and the Egyptians will *k* that I am
33:13 teach me your ways so I may *k* you
Dt 7: 9 *K* therefore that the LORD your
18:21 "How can we *k* when a message
Jos 4:24 of the earth might *k* that the hand
23:14 You *k* with all your heart
1Sa 17:46 the whole world will *k* that there is
1Ki 8:39 heart (for you alone *k* the hearts
Job 11: 6 *K* this: God has even forgotten
19:25 I *k* that my Redeemer lives,
42: 3 things too wonderful for me to *k*.
Ps 9:10 Those who *k* your name will trust
46:10 "Be still, and *k* that I am God;
100: 3 *K* that the LORD is God.
139: 1 and you *k* me.
139: 23 Search me, O God, and *k* my heart;
145: 12 so that all men may *k*
Pr 27: 1 for you do not *k* what a day may
30: 4 Tell me if you *k*!
Ecc 8: 5 wise heart will *k* the proper time
Isa 29:15 "Who sees us? Who will *k*?"
40:21 Do you not *k*?
Jer 6:15 they do not even *k* how to blush.
22:16 Is that not what it means to *k* me?"
24: 7 I will give them a heart to *k* me,
31:34 his brother, saying, '*K* the LORD,'
33: 3 unsearchable things you do not *k*.'
Eze 2: 5 they will *k* that a prophet has been
6:10 they will *k* that I am the LORD;
Da 11:32 people who *k* their God will firmly
Mt 6: 3 let your left hand *k* what your right
7:11 *k* how to give good gifts
9: 6 But so that you may *k* that the Son
22:29 you do not *k* the Scriptures
24:42 you do not *k* on what day your
26:74 "I don't *k* the man!" Immediately
Mk 12:24 you do not *k* the Scriptures
Lk 1: 4 so that you may *k* the certainty
11:13 *k* how to give good gifts
12:48 But the one who does not *k*
13:25 'I don't *k* you or where you come
21:31 you *k* that the kingdom of God is
23:34 for they do not *k* what they are
Jn 1:26 among you stands one you do not *k*
3:11 we speak of what we *k*,
4:22 we worship what we do *k*,
4:42 and we *k* that this man really is
6:69 and *k* that you are the Holy One
7:28 You do not *k* him, but I *k* him
8:14 for I *k* where I came from
8:19 "You do not *k* me or my Father,"
8:32 Then you will *k* the truth,
8:55 Though you do not *k* him, I *k* him.
9:25 One thing I do *k*.
10: 4 him because they *k* his voice.
10:14 I *k* my sheep and my sheep *k* me—
10:27 I *k* them, and they follow me.
12:35 the dark does not *k* where he is
13:17 Now that you *k* these things,
13:35 all men will *k* that you are my
14:17 you *k* him, for he lives with you
15:21 for they do not *k* the One who sent
16:30 we can see that you *k* all things
17: 3 that they may *k* you, the only true
17:23 to let the world *k* that you sent me
21:15 he said, "you *k* that I love you."
21:24 We *k* that his testimony is true.
Ac 1: 7 "It is not for you to *k* the times
1:24 "Lord, you *k* everyone's heart.
Ro 3:17 and the way of peace they do not *k*
6: 3 Or don't you *k* that all
6: 6 For we *k* that our old self was
6:16 Don't you *k* that when you offer
7:14 We *k* that the law is spiritual;
7:18 I *k* that nothing good lives in me,
8:22 We *k* that the whole creation has
8:26 We do not *k* what we ought to pray
8:28 we *k* that in all things God works
1Co 1:21 through its wisdom did not *k* him,
2: 2 For I resolved to *k* nothing
3:16 Don't you *k* that you yourselves
5: 6 Don't you *k* that a little yeast
6: 2 Do you not *k* that the saints will
6:15 Do you not *k* that your bodies are
6:16 Do you not *k* that he who unites
6:19 Do you not *k* that your body is
7:16 How do you *k*, wife, whether you
8: 2 does not yet *k* as he ought to *k*.
9:13 Don't you *k* that those who work
9:24 Do you not *k* that
13: 9 For we *k* in part and we prophesy
13:12 Now I *k* in part; then I shall *k* fully,
15:58 because you *k* that your labor
2Co 5: 1 we *k* that if the earthly tent we live
5:11 we *k* what it is to fear the Lord,
8: 9 For you *k* the grace
Gal 1:11 you to *k*, brothers, that the gospel I
2:16 not 'Gentile sinners' *k* that a man
Eph 1:17 so that you may *k* him better.
1:18 in order that you may *k* the hope
6: 8 you *k* that the Lord will reward
6: 9 since you *k* that he who is both
Php 3:10 I want to *k* Christ and the power
4:12 I *k* what it is to be in need,
Col 2: 2 order that they may *k* the mystery
4: 1 because you *k* that you
4: 6 so that you may *k* how
1Th 3: 3 You *k* quite well that we were
5: 2 for you *k* very well that the day
2Th 1: 8 punish those who do not *k* God
1Ti 1: 7 they do not *k* what they are talking
3: 5 (If anyone does not *k* how
3:15 you will *k* how people ought
2Ti 1:12 because I *k* whom I have believed,
2:23 you *k* they produce quarrels.
3:14 you *k* those from whom you
Heb 8:11 because they will all *k* me,
11: 8 he did not *k* where he was going.
Jas 1: 3 because you *k* that the testing
3: 1 you *k* that we who teach will be
4: 4 don't you *k* that friendship
4:14 *k* what will happen tomorrow.
1Pe 1:18 For you *k* that it was not
2Pe 1:12 even though you *k* them
1Jn 2: 3 We *k* that we have come
2: 4 The man who says, "I *k* him,"
2: 5 This is how we *k* we are in him:
2:11 he does not *k* where he is going,
2:20 and all of you *k* the truth.
2:29 you *k* that everyone who does
3: 1 not *k* us is that it did not *k* him.
3: 2 But we *k* that when he appears,
3:10 This is how we *k* who the children
3:14 We *k* that we have passed
3:16 This is how we *k* what love is:
3:19 then is how we *k* that we belong
3:24 We *k* it by the Spirit he gave us.
4: 8 does not love does not *k* God,
4:13 We *k* that we live in him
4:16 so we *k* and rely on the love God
5: 2 This is how we *k* that we love
5:13 so that you may *k* that you have
5:15 And if we *k* that he hears us—
5:18 We *k* that anyone born
5:20 We *k* also that the Son
Rev 2: 2 I *k* your deeds, your hard work
2: 9 I *k* your afflictions and your
2:19 I *k* your deeds, your love and faith,

Rev 3: 3 you will not *k* at what time I will
3:15 I *k* your deeds, that you are neither

KNOWING (KNOW)
Ge 3: 5 and you will be like God, *k* good
3:22 now become like one of us, *k* good
Jn 19:28 *k* that all was now completed,
Php 3: 8 of *k* Christ Jesus my Lord,
Phm :21 *k* that you will do even more
Heb 13: 2 entertained angels without *k* it.

KNOWLEDGE (KNOW)
Ge 2: 9 the tree of the *k* of good and evil.
2:17 eat from the tree of the *k* of good
2Ch 1:10 and *k*, that I may lead this people,
Job 21:22 "Can anyone teach *k* to God,
38: 2 counsel with words without *k*?
42: 3 obscures my counsel without *k*?'
Ps 19: 2 night after night they display *k*.
73:11 Does the Most High have *k*?"
94:10 Does he who teaches man lack *k*?
119: 66 Teach me *k* and good judgment,
139: 6 Such *k* is too wonderful for me,
Pr 1: 4 *k* and discretion to the young—
1: 7 of the LORD is the beginning of *k*,
2: 5 and find the *k* of God.
2: 6 from his mouth come *k*
2:10 and *k* will be pleasant to your soul.
3:20 by his *k* the deeps were divided,
8:10 *k* rather than choice gold,
8:12 I possess *k* and discretion.
9:10 *k* of the Holy One is understanding
10:14 Wise men store up *k*,
12: 1 Whoever loves discipline loves *k*,
12:23 A prudent man keeps his *k*
13:16 Every prudent man acts out of *k*,
14: 6 *k* comes easily to the discerning.
15: 7 The lips of the wise spread *k*;
15:14 The discerning heart seeks *k*,
17:27 A man of *k* uses words
18:15 heart of the discerning acquires *k*;
19: 2 to have zeal without *k*,
19:25 discerning man, and he will gain *k*.
20:15 lips that speak *k* are a rare jewel.
23:12 and your ears to words of *k*.
24: 4 through *k* its rooms are filled
Ecc 7:12 but the advantage of *k* is this:
Isa 11: 2 the Spirit of *k* and of the fear
11: 9 full of the *k* of the LORD
40:14 Who was it that taught him *k*
Jer 3:15 who will lead you with *k*
Hos 4: 6 are destroyed from lack of *k*.
Hab 2:14 filled with the *k* of the glory
Mal 2: 7 lips of a priest ought to preserve *k*,
Mt 13:11 The *k* of the secrets of the kingdom
Lk 8:10 The *k* of the secrets of the kingdom
11:52 you have taken away the key to *k*.
Ac 18:24 with a thorough *k* of the Scriptures
Ro 1:28 worthwhile to retain the *k* of God,
10: 2 but their zeal is not based on *k*.
11:33 riches of the wisdom and *k* of God!
1Co 8: 1 *K* puffs up, but love builds up.
8:11 Christ died, is destroyed by your *k*.
12: 8 to another the message of *k*
13: 2 can fathom all mysteries and all *k*,
13: 8 where there is *k*, it will pass away.
2Co 2:14 everywhere the fragrance of the *k*
4: 6 light of the *k* of the glory of God
8: 7 in *k*, in complete earnestness
11: 6 a trained speaker, but I do have *k*.
Eph 3:19 to know this love that surpasses *k*
4:13 and in the *k* of the Son of God
Php 1: 9 and more in *k* and depth of insight,
Col 1: 9 God to fill you with the *k* of his will
1:10 every good work, growing in the *k*
2: 3 all the treasures of wisdom and *k*.
3:10 which is being renewed in *k*
1Ti 2: 4 and to come to a *k* of the truth.
6:20 ideas of what is falsely called *k*,
Tit 1: 1 and the *k* of the truth that leads
Heb 10:26 after we have received the *k*
2Pe 1: 5 and to goodness, *k*; and to *k*,
3:18 grow in the grace and *k* of our Lord

KNOWN (KNOW)
Ex 6: 3 the LORD I did not make myself *k*
Ps 16:11 You have made *k* to me the path
89: 1 I will make your faithfulness *k*
98: 2 LORD has made his salvation *k*
105: 1 make *k* among the nations what he
119:168 for all my ways are *k* to you.
Pr 20:11 Even a child is *k* by his actions,
Isa 12: 4 make *k* among the nations what he
46:10 *k* the end from the beginning,
61: 9 Their descendants will be *k*
Eze 38:23 I will make myself *k* in the sight
39: 7 " 'I will make *k* my holy name
Mt 10:26 or hidden that will not be made *k*.
24:43 of the house had *k* at what time
Lk 19:42 had only *k* on this day what would
Jn 15:15 from my Father I have made *k*
16:14 from what is mine and making it *k*
17:26 I have made you *k* to them,
Ac 2:28 You have made *k* to me the paths
Ro 1:19 since what may be *k* about God is
3:21 apart from law, has been made *k*,
9:22 his wrath and make his power *k*,
11:34 "Who has *k* the mind of the Lord?
15:20 the gospel where Christ was not *k*,
16:26 and made *k* through the prophetic
1Co 2:16 "For who has *k* the mind
8: 3 But the man who loves God is *k*
13:12 know fully, even as I am fully *k*.
2Co 3: 2 written on our hearts, *k*
Gal 4: 9 or rather are *k* by God—
Eph 3: 5 which was not made *k* to men
6:19 will fearlessly make *k* the mystery
2Ti 3:15 infancy you have *k* the holy
2Pe 2:21 than to have *k* it and then

KNOWS (KNOW)
1Sa 2: 3 for the LORD is a God who *k*,
Est 4:14 And who *k* but that you have come
Job 23:10 But he *k* the way that I take;
Ps 44:21 since he *k* the secrets of the heart?
94:11 The LORD *k* the thoughts of man;
103: 14 for he *k* how we are formed,
Ecc 8: 7 Since no man *k* the future,
8:17 Even if a wise man claims he *k*,
9:12 no man *k* when his hour will come:
Isa 29:16 "He *k* nothing"?
Jer 9:24 that he understands and *k* me,
Mt 6: 8 for your Father *k* what you need
11:27 No one *k* the Son
24:36 "No one *k* about that day or hour,
Lk 12:47 "That servant who *k* his master's
16:15 of men, but God *k* your hearts.
Ac 15: 8 who *k* the heart, showed that he
Ro 8:27 who searches our hearts *k* the mind
1Co 2:11 who among men *k* the thoughts
8: 2 who thinks he *k* something does
2Ti 2:19 The Lord *k* those who are his," and
Jas 4:17 who *k* the good he ought to do
1Jn 4: 6 and whoever *k* God listens to us;
4: 7 born of God and *k* God.

KOHATHITE (KOHATHITES)
Nu 3:29 The *K* clans were to camp

KOHATHITES (KOHATHITE)
Nu 3:28 The *K* were responsible
4:15 *K* are to carry those things that are

KORAH

Levite who led rebellion against Moses and Aaron (Nu 16; Jude 11).

KORAZIN
Mt 11:21 "Woe to you, *K!* Woe to you,

LABAN

Brother of Rebekah (Ge 24:29), father of Rachel and Leah (Ge 29:16). Received Abraham's servant (Ge 24:29-51). Provided daughters as wives for Jacob in exchange for Jacob's service (Ge 29:1-30). Provided flocks for Jacob's service (Ge 30:25-43). After Jacob's departure, pursued and covenanted with him (Ge 31).

LABOR (LABORING)
Ex 1:11 to oppress them with forced *l*,
20: 9 Six days you shall *l* and do all your
Dt 5:13 Six days you shall *l* and do all your
Ps 127: 1 its builders *l* in vain.
128: 2 You will eat the fruit of your *l*;
Pr 12:24 but laziness ends in slave *l*.
Isa 54: 1 you who were never in *l*;
55: 2 and your *l* on what does not satisfy
Mt 6:28 They do not *l* or spin.
Jn 4:38 have reaped the benefits of their *l*."
1Co 3: 8 rewarded according to his own *l*.
15:58 because you know that your *l*
Gal 4:27 you who have no *l* pains;
Php 2:16 day of Christ that I did not run or *l*
Rev 14:13 "they will rest from their *l*,

LABORING* (LABOR)
2Th 3: 8 *l* and toiling so that we would not

LACK (LACKED LACKING LACKS)
Ps 34: 9 for those who fear him *l* nothing.
Pr 5:23 He will die for *l* of discipline,
10:21 but fools die for *l* of judgment.
11:14 For *l* of guidance a nation falls,
15:22 Plans fail for *l* of counsel,
28:27 to the poor will *l* nothing,
Mk 6: 6 he was amazed at their *l* of faith.
16:14 he rebuked them for their *l* of faith
Ro 3: 3 Will their *l* of faith nullify God's
1Co 1: 7 you do not *l* any spiritual gift
7: 5 because of your *l* of self-control.
Col 2:23 *l* any value in restraining sensual

LACKED (LACK)
Dt 2: 7 and you have not *l* anything.
Ne 9:21 them in the desert; they *l* nothing,
1Co 12:24 honor to the parts that *l* it,

LACKING (LACK)
Pr 17:18 A man *l* in judgment strikes hands
Ro 12:11 Never be *l* in zeal, but keep your
Jas 1: 4 and complete, not *l* anything.

LACKS (LACK)
Pr 6:32 who commits adultery *l* judgment;
11:12 man who *l* judgment derides his
12:11 he who chases fantasies *l* judgment
15:21 delights a man who *l* judgment,
24:30 of the man who *l* judgment;
25:28 is a man who *l* self-control.
28:16 A tyrannical ruler *l* judgment,
31:11 and *l* nothing of value.
Eze 34: 8 because my flock *l* a shepherd
Jas 1: 5 any of you *l* wisdom, he should ask

LAID (LAY)
Isa 53: 6 and the LORD has *l* on him
Mk 6:29 took his body and *l* it in a tomb.
Lk 6:48 and *l* the foundation on rock.
Ac 6: 6 and *l* their hands on them.
1Co 3:11 other than the one already *l*,
1Ti 4:14 body of elders *l* their hands on you.
1Jn 3:16 Jesus Christ *l* down his life for us.

LAKE
Mt 8:24 a furious storm came up on the *l*,
14:25 out to them, walking on the *l*.
Mk 4: 1 into a boat and sat in it out on the *l*,
Lk 8:33 down the steep bank into the *l*
Jn 6:25 him on the other side of the *l*,
Rev 19:20 into the fiery *l* of burning sulfur.
20:14 The *l* of fire is the second death.

LAMB (LAMB'S LAMBS)
Ge 22: 8 "God himself will provide the *l*
Ex 12:21 and slaughter the Passover *l*.
Nu 9:11 are to eat the *l*, together
2Sa 12: 4 he took the ewe *l* that belonged
Isa 11: 6 The wolf will live with the *l*,
53: 7 he was led like a *l* to the slaughter,
Mk 14:12 to sacrifice the Passover *l*,
Jn 1:29 *L* of God, who takes away the sin
Ac 8:32 as a *l* before the shearer is silent,
1Co 5: 7 our Passover *l*, has been sacrificed.
1Pe 1:19 a *l* without blemish or defect.
Rev 5: 6 Then I saw a *L*, looking
5:12 "Worthy is the *L*, who was slain,
7:14 white in the blood of the *L*.
14: 4 They follow the *L* wherever he
15: 3 of God and the song of the *L*:
17:14 but the *L* will overcome them
19: 9 to the wedding supper of the *L!*"
21:23 gives it light, and the *L* is its lamp.

LAMB'S (LAMB)
Rev 21:27 written in the *L* book of life.

LAMBS (LAMB)
Lk 10: 3 I am sending you out like *l*
Jn 21:15 Jesus said, "Feed my *l*."

LAME
Isa 33:23 even the *l* will carry off plunder.
35: 6 Then will the *l* leap like a deer,
Mt 11: 5 The blind receive sight, the *l* walk,
15:31 the *l* walking and the blind seeing.
Lk 14:21 the crippled, the blind and the *l*.'

LAMENT
2Sa 1:17 took up this *l* concerning Saul
Eze 19: 1 Take up a *l* concerning the princes

LAMP (LAMPS LAMPSTAND LAMPSTANDS)
2Sa 22:29 You are my *l*, O LORD;
Ps 18:28 You, O LORD, keep my *l* burning;
119:105 Your word is a *l* to my feet
132: 17 and set up a *l* for my anointed one.
Pr 6:23 For these commands are a *l*,
20:27 *l* of the LORD searches the spirit
31:18 and her *l* does not go out at night.
Mt 6:22 "The eye is the *l* of the body.
Lk 8:16 "No one lights a *l* and hides it
Rev 21:23 gives it light, and the Lamb is its *l*.
22: 5 They will not need the light of a *l*

LAMPS (LAMP)
Mt 25: 1 be like ten virgins who took their *l*
Lk 12:35 for service and keep your *l* burning,

Rev 4: 5 the throne, seven *l* were blazing.

LAMPSTAND (LAMP)
Ex 25:31 "Make a *l* of pure gold
Zec 4: 2 "I see a solid gold *l* with a bowl
4:11 on the right and the left of the *l*?"
Heb 9: 2 In its first room were the *l*,
Rev 2: 5 and remove your *l* from its place.

LAMPSTANDS (LAMP)
2Ch 4: 7 He made ten gold *l* according
Rev 1:12 when I turned I saw seven golden *l*,
1:20 and of the seven golden *l* is this:

LAND (LANDS)
Ge 1:10 God called the dry ground "*l*,"
1:11 "Let the *l* produce vegetation:
1:24 "Let the *l* produce living creatures
12: 1 and go to the *l* I will show you.
12: 7 To your offspring I will give this *l*."
13:15 All the *l* that you see I will give
15:18 "To your descendants I give this *l*,
50:24 out of this *l* to the *l* he promised
Ex 3: 8 a *l* flowing with milk and honey—
6: 8 to the *l* I swore with uplifted hand
33: 3 Go up to the *l* flowing with milk
Lev 25:23 *l* must not be sold permanently,
Nu 14: 8 us into that *l*, a *l* flowing with milk
35:33 Do not pollute the *l* where you are.
Dt 1: 8 See, I have given you this *l*.
8: 7 God is bringing you into a good *l*—
11:10 The *l* you are entering to take
28:21 you from the *l* you are entering
29:19 will bring disaster on the watered *l*
34: 1 LORD showed him the whole *l*—
Jos 13: 2 "This is the *l* that remains:
14: 4 Levites received no share of the *l*
14: 9 *l* on which your feet have walked
2Sa 21:14 answered prayer in behalf of the *l*.
2Ki 17: 5 of Assyria invaded the entire *l*,
24: 1 king of Babylon invaded the *l*,
25:21 into captivity, away from her *l*.
2Ch 7:14 their sin and will heal their *l*.
7:20 then I will uproot Israel from my *l*,
36:21 The *l* enjoyed its sabbath rests;
Ezr 9:11 entering to possess is a *l* polluted
Ne 9:36 in the *l* you gave our forefathers
Ps 37:11 But the meek will inherit the *l*
37:29 the righteous will inherit the *l*
136: 21 and gave their *l* as an inheritance,
142: 5 my portion in the *l* of the living."
Pr 2:21 For the upright will live in the *l*,
12:11 who works his *l* will have abundant
Isa 6:13 though a tenth remains in the *l*,
53: 8 cut off from the *l* of the living;
Jer 2: 7 But you came and defiled my *l*
Eze 36:24 and bring you back into your own *l*.

LANDS (LAND)
Ps 111: 6 giving them the *l* of other nations.
Eze 20: 6 honey, the most beautiful of all *l*.
Zec 10: 9 in distant *l* they will remember me.

LANGUAGE (LANGUAGES)
Ge 11: 1 Now the whole world had one *l*
11: 9 there the LORD confused the *l*
Ps 19: 3 There is no speech or *l*
Jn 8:44 When he lies, he speaks his native *l*
Ac 2: 6 heard them speaking in his own *l*.
Col 3: 8 slander, and filthy *l* from your lips.
Rev 5: 9 from every tribe and *l* and people
7: 9 every nation, tribe, people and *l*,
14: 6 to every nation, tribe, *l* and people.

LANGUAGES (LANGUAGE)
Zec 8:23 "In those days ten men from all *l*

LAODICEA
Rev 3:14 the angel of the church in *L* write:

LAP
Jdg 7: 5 "Separate those who *l* the water

LASHES
Pr 17:10 more than a hundred *l* a fool.
2Co 11:24 from the Jews the forty *l* minus one

LAST (LASTING LASTS LATTER)
Ex 14:24 During the *l* watch of the night
2Sa 23: 1 These are the *l* words of David:
Isa 2: 2 and Jerusalem: In the *l* days
41: 4 and with the *l*— I am he."
44: 6 I am the first and I am the *l*;
48:12 I am the first and I am the *l*.
Hos 3: 5 and to his blessings in the *l* days.
Mic 4: 1 In the *l* days
Mt 19:30 But many who are first will be *l*,
20: 8 beginning with the *l* ones hired
21:37 *L* of all, he sent his son to them.
Mk 9:35 must be the very *l*, and the servant
10:31 are first will be *l*, and the *l* first."
15:37 a loud cry, Jesus breathed his *l*.
Jn 6:40 and I will raise him up at the *l* day."
15:16 and bear fruit—fruit that will *l*.
Ac 2:17 " 'In the *l* days, God says,
Ro 1:17 is by faith from first to *l*,
1Co 15:26 *l* enemy to be destroyed is death.
15:52 of an eye, at the *l* trumpet.
2Ti 3: 1 will be terrible times in the *l* days.
2Pe 3: 3 in the *l* days scoffers will come,
Jude :18 "In the *l* times there will be
Rev 1:17 I am the First and the *L*.
22:13 the First and the *L*, the Beginning

LASTING (LAST)
Ex 12:14 to the LORD—a *l* ordinance.
Lev 24: 8 of the Israelites, as a *l* covenant.
Nu 25:13 have a covenant of a *l* priesthood,
Heb 10:34 had better and *l* possessions.

LASTS (LAST)
Ps 30: 5 For his anger *l* only a moment,
2Co 3:11 greater is the glory of that which *l*!

LATTER (LAST)
Job 42:12 The LORD blessed the *l* part
Mt 23:23 You should have practiced the *l*,
Php 1:16 *l* do so in love, knowing that I am

LAUGH (LAUGHED LAUGHS LAUGHTER)
Ps 59: 8 But you, O LORD, *l* at them;
Pr 31:25 she can *l* at the days to come.
Ecc 3: 4 a time to weep and a time to *l*,
Lk 6:21 for you will *l*.
6:25 Woe to you who *l* now,

LAUGHED (LAUGH)
Ge 17:17 Abraham fell facedown; he *l*
18:12 So Sarah *l* to herself as she thought,

LAUGHS (LAUGH)
Ps 2: 4 The One enthroned in heaven *l*;
37:13 but the Lord *l* at the wicked,

LAUGHTER (LAUGH)
Ge 21: 6 Sarah said, "God has brought me *l*,
Ps 126: 2 Our mouths were filled with *l*,
Pr 14:13 Even in *l* the heart may ache,
Jas 4: 9 Change your *l* to mourning

LAVISHED
Eph 1: 8 of God's grace that he *l* on us
1Jn 3: 1 great is the love the Father has *l*

LAW (LAWFUL LAWGIVER LAWS)
Lev 24:22 are to have the same *l* for the alien
Nu 6:13 " 'Now this is the *l* for the Nazirite
Dt 1: 5 Moses began to expound this *l*,
6:25 to obey all this *l* before the LORD
27:26 of this *l* by carrying them out."
31:11 you shall read this *l* before them
31:26 "Take this Book of the *L*
Jos 1: 7 to obey all the *l* my servant Moses
1: 8 of the *L* depart from your mouth;
22: 5 and the *l* that Moses the servant
2Ki 22: 8 of the *L* in the temple of the LORD
2Ch 6:16 walk before me according to my *l*,
17: 9 the Book of the *L* of the LORD;
34:14 of the *L* of the LORD that had
Ezr 7: 6 versed in the *L* of Moses,
Ne 8: 2 Ezra the priest brought the *L*
8: 8 from the Book of the *L* of God,
Ps 1: 2 and on his *l* he meditates day
19: 7 The *l* of the LORD is perfect,
37:31 The *l* of his God is in his heart;
40: 8 your *l* is within my heart."
119: 18 wonderful things in your *l*.
119: 70 but I delight in your *l*.
119: 72 *l* from your mouth is more precious
119: 77 for your *l* is my delight.
119: 97 Oh, how I love your *l*!
119:163 but I love your *l*.
119:165 peace have they who love your *l*,
Pr 28: 9 If anyone turns a deaf ear to the *l*,
29:18 but blessed is he who keeps the *l*.
Isa 2: 3 The *l* will go out from Zion,
8:20 To the *l* and to the testimony!
42:21 to make his *l* great and glorious.
Jer 2: 8 deal with the *l* did not know me;
8: 8 for we have the *l* of the LORD,"
31:33 "I will put my *l* in their minds
Mic 4: 2 The *l* will go out from Zion,
Hab 1: 7 they are a *l* to themselves
Zec 7:12 as flint and would not listen to the *l*
Mt 5:17 that I have come to abolish the *L*
7:12 sums up the *L* and the Prophets.
22:36 greatest commandment in the *L*?"
22:40 All the *L* and the Prophets hang
23:23 more important matters of the *l*—
Lk 11:52 "Woe to you experts in the *l*,
16:17 stroke of a pen to drop out of the *L*.
24:44 me in the *L* of Moses,
Jn 1:17 For the *l* was given through Moses;
Ac 13:39 justified from by the *l* of Moses.
Ro 2:12 All who sin apart from the *l* will
2:15 of the *l* are written on their hearts,
2:20 you have in the *l* the embodiment
2:25 value if you observe the *l*,
3:19 we know that whatever the *l* says,
3:20 in his sight by observing the *l*;
3:21 apart from *l*, has been made known
3:28 by faith apart from observing the *l*.
3:31 Not at all! Rather, we uphold the *l*.
4:13 It was not through *l* that Abraham
4:15 worthless, because *l* brings wrath.
4:16 not only to those who are of the *l*
5:13 for before the *l* was given,
5:20 *l* was added so that the trespass
6:14 because you are not under *l*,
6:15 we are not under *l* but under grace?
7: 1 that the *l* has authority
7: 4 also died to the *l* through the body
7: 5 aroused by the *l* were at work
7: 6 released from the *l* so that we serve
7: 7 then? Is the *l* sin? Certainly not!
7: 8 For apart from *l*, sin is dead.
7:12 *l* is holy, and the commandment is
7:14 We know that the *l* is spiritual;
7:22 my inner being I delight in God's *l*;
7:25 in my mind am a slave to God's *l*,
8: 2 because through Christ Jesus the *l*
8: 3 For what the *l* was powerless to do
8: 4 of the *l* might be fully met in us,
8: 7 It does not submit to God's *l*,
9: 4 covenants, the receiving of the *l*,
9:31 who pursued a *l* of righteousness,
10: 4 Christ is the end of the *l*
13: 8 his fellowman has fulfilled the *l*.
13:10 love is the fulfillment of the *l*.
1Co 6: 6 goes to *l* against another—
9: 9 For it is written in the *L* of Moses:
9:20 the *l* I became like one under the *l*
9:21 I became like one not having the *l*
15:56 and the power of sin is the *l*.
Gal 2:16 justified by observing the *l*,
2:19 For through the *l* I died to the *l*
3: 2 the Spirit by observing the *l*,
3: 5 you because you observe the *l*,
3:10 on observing the *l* are under a curse
3:11 justified before God by the *l*,
3:13 curse of the *l* by becoming a curse
3:17 The *l*, introduced 430 years later,
3:19 then, was the purpose of the *l*?
3:21 Is the *l*, therefore, opposed
3:23 we were held prisoners by the *l*,
3:24 So the *l* was put in charge to lead us
4:21 you who want to be under the *l*,
5: 3 obligated to obey the whole *l*.
5: 4 justified by *l* have been alienated
5:14 The entire *l* is summed up
5:18 by the Spirit, you are not under *l*.
6: 2 and in this way you will fulfill the *l*
Eph 2:15 flesh the *l* with its commandments
Php 3: 9 of my own that comes from the *l*,
1Ti 1: 8 We know that the *l* is good
Heb 7:12 there must also be a change of the *l*.
7:19 (for the *l* made nothing perfect),
10: 1 The *l* is only a shadow
Jas 1:25 intently into the perfect *l* that gives
2: 8 If you really keep the royal *l* found
2:10 For whoever keeps the whole *l*
4:11 or judges him speaks against the *l*
1Jn 3: 4 Everyone who sins breaks the *l*;

LAWFUL (LAW)
Mt 12:12 Therefore it is *l* to do good

LAWGIVER* (LAW)
Isa 33:22 the LORD is our *l*,
Jas 4:12 There is only one *L* and Judge,

LAWLESS (LAWLESSNESS)
2Th 2: 8 And then the *l* one will be revealed
Heb 10:17 "Their sins and *l* acts

LAWLESSNESS* (LAWLESS)
2Th 2: 3 and the man of *l* is revealed,
2: 7 power of *l* is already at work;
1Jn 3: 4 sins breaks the law; in fact, sin is *l*.

LAWS (LAW)
Ex 21: 1 "These are the *l* you are to set
Lev 25:18 and be careful to obey my *l*,
Dt 4: 1 and *l* I am about to teach you.
30:16 decrees and *l*; then you will live
Ps 119: 30 I have set my heart on your *l*.
119: 43 for I have put my hope in your *l*.
119:120 I stand in awe of your *l*.
119:164 for your righteous *l*.

Ps 119:175 and may your *l* sustain me.
Eze 36:27 and be careful to keep my *l.*
Heb 8:10 I will put my *l* in their minds
10:16 I will put my *l* in their hearts,

LAWSUITS
Hos 10: 4 therefore *l* spring up
1Co 6: 7 The very fact that you have *l*

LAY (LAID LAYING LAYS)
Ex 29:10 and his sons shall *l* their hands
Lev 1: 4 He is to *l* his hand on the head
4:15 the community are to *l* their hands
Nu 8:10 the Israelites are to *l* their hands
27:18 whom is the spirit, and *l* your hand
1Sa 26: 9 Who can *l* a hand on the LORD's
Job 1:12 on the man himself do not *l* a finger
22:22 and *l* up his words in your heart.
Ecc 10: 4 calmness can *l* great errors to rest.
Isa 28:16 "See, I *l* a stone in Zion,
Mt 8:20 of Man has no place to *l* his head."
28: 6 Come and see the place where he *l.*
Mk 6: 5 *l* his hands on a few sick people
Lk 9:58 of Man has no place to *l* his head."
Jn 10:15 and I *l* down my life for the sheep.
10:18 but I *l* it down of my own accord.
15:13 that he *l* down his life
Ac 8:19 on whom I *l* my hands may receive
Ro 9:33 I *l* in Zion a stone that causes men
1Co 3:11 no one can *l* any foundation other
1Pe 2: 6 "See, I *l* a stone in Zion,
1Jn 3:16 And we ought to *l* down our lives
Rev 4:10 They *l* their crowns

LAYING (LAY)
Lk 4:40 and *l* his hands on each one,
Ac 8:18 at the *l* on of the apostles' hands,
1Ti 5:22 Do not be hasty in the *l* on of hands
2Ti 1: 6 is in you through the *l*
Heb 6: 1 not *l* again the foundation
6: 2 instruction about baptisms, the *l*

LAYS (LAY)
Jn 10:11 The good shepherd *l* down his life

LAZARUS
1. Poor man in Jesus' parable (Lk 16:19-31).
2. Brother of Mary and Martha whom Jesus raised from the dead (Jn 11:1-12:19).

LAZINESS* (LAZY)
Pr 12:24 but *l* ends in slave labor.
19:15 *L* brings on deep sleep,

LAZY* (LAZINESS)
Ex 5: 8 They are *l;* that is why they are
5:17 Pharaoh said, "*L,* that's what you
5:17 "Lazy, that's what you are—*l!*
Pr 10: 4 *L* hands make a man poor,
12:27 The *l* man does not roast his game,
26:15 he is too *l* to bring it back
Ecc 10:18 If a man is *l,* the rafters sag;
Mt 25:26 replied, 'You wicked, *l* servant!
Tit 1:12 liars, evil brutes, *l* gluttons."
Heb 6:12 We do not want you to become *l,*

LEAD (LEADER LEADERS LEADERSHIP LEADS LED)
Ex 15:13 "In your unfailing love you will *l*
Nu 14: 8 with us, he will *l* us into that land,
Dt 31: 2 and I am no longer able to *l* you.
Jos 1: 6 because you will *l* these people
1Sa 8: 5 now appoint a king to *l* us,
2Ch 1:10 knowledge, that I may *l* this people
Ps 27:11 *l* me in a straight path
61: 2 *l* me to the rock that is higher
139: 24 and *l* me in the way everlasting.
143: 10 *l* me on level ground.
Pr 4:11 and *l* you along straight paths.
Ecc 5: 6 Do not let your mouth *l* you
Isa 11: 6 and a little child will *l* them.
49:10 and *l* them beside springs of water.
Da 12: 3 those who *l* many to righteousness,
Mt 6:13 And *l* us not into temptation,
Lk 11: 4 And *l* us not into temptation.' "
Gal 3:24 So the law was put in charge to *l* us
1Th 4:11 it your ambition to *l* a quiet life,
1Jn 3: 7 do not let anyone *l* you astray.
Rev 7:17 he will *l* them to springs

LEADER (LEAD)
1Sa 7: 6 Samuel was *l* of Israel at Mizpah.
10: 1 Has not the LORD anointed you *l*
12: 2 I have been your *l* from my youth
13:14 and appointed him *l* of his people,

LEADERS (LEAD)
Heb 13: 7 Remember your *l,* who spoke
13:17 Obey your *l* and submit

LEADERSHIP* (LEAD)
Nu 33: 1 by divisions under the *l* of Moses
Ps 109: 8 may another take his place of *l.*
Ac 1:20 " 'May another take his place of *l.*'
Ro 12: 8 if it is *l,* let him govern diligently;

LEADS (LEAD)
Dt 27:18 is the man who *l* the blind astray
Ps 23: 2 he *l* me beside quiet waters,
37: 8 do not fret—it *l* only to evil.
68: 6 he *l* forth the prisoners
Pr 2:18 For her house *l* down to death
10:17 ignores correction *l* others astray.
14:23 but mere talk *l* only to poverty.
16:25 but in the end it *l* to death.
19:23 The fear of the LORD *l* to life:
20: 7 righteous man *l* a blameless life;
21: 5 as surely as haste *l* to poverty.
Isa 40:11 he gently *l* those that have young.
Mt 7:13 and broad is the road that *l*
12:20 till he *l* justice to victory.
15:14 If a blind man *l* a blind man,
Jn 10: 3 sheep by name and *l* them out.
Ro 6:16 which *l* to death, or to obedience,
6:22 the benefit you reap *l* to holiness,
14:19 effort to do what *l* to peace
2Co 2:14 always *l* us in triumphal procession
7:10 sorrow brings repentance that *l*
Tit 1: 1 of the truth that *l* to godliness—

LEAH
Wife of Jacob (Ge 29:16-30); bore six sons and one daughter (Ge 29:31-30:21; 34:1; 35:23).

LEAN (LEANED)
Pr 3: 5 *l* not on your own understanding;

LEANED (LEAN)
Ge 47:31 as he *l* on the top of his staff.
Jn 21:20 (This was the one who had *l* back
Heb 11:21 as he *l* on the top of his staff.

LEAP (LEAPED LEAPS)
Isa 35: 6 Then will the lame *l* like a deer,
Mal 4: 2 *l* like calves released from the stall.
Lk 6:23 "Rejoice in that day and *l* for joy,

LEAPED (LEAP)
Lk 1:41 heard Mary's greeting, the baby *l*

LEAPS (LEAP)
Ps 28: 7 My heart *l* for joy

LEARN (LEARNED LEARNING LEARNS)
Dt 4:10 so that they may *l* to revere me
5: 1 *L* them and be sure to follow them.
31:12 and *l* to fear the LORD your God
Ps 119: 7 as I *l* your righteous laws.
Isa 1:17 *l* to do right!
26: 9 of the world *l* righteousness.
Mt 11:29 yoke upon you and *l* from me,
Jn 14:31 world must *l* that I love the Father
1Th 4: 4 that each of you should *l*
1Ti 2:11 A woman should *l* in quietness
5: 4 these should *l* first of all

LEARNED (LEARN)
Ps 119:152 Long ago I *l* from your statutes
Mt 11:25 things from the wise and *l,*
Php 4: 9 Whatever you have *l* or received
4:11 for I have *l* to be content whatever
2Ti 3:14 continue in what you have *l*
Heb 5: 8 he *l* obedience from what he

LEARNING (LEARN)
Pr 1: 5 let the wise listen and add to their *l,*
9: 9 man and he will add to his *l.*
Isa 44:25 who overthrows the *l* of the wise
Jn 7:15 "How did this man get such *l*
2Ti 3: 7 always *l* but never able

LEARNS (LEARN)
Jn 6:45 and *l* from him comes to me.

LEATHER
2Ki 1: 8 and with a *l* belt around his waist."
Mt 3: 4 and he had a *l* belt around his waist

LEAVES
Ge 3: 7 so they sewed fig *l* together
Eze 47:12 for food and their *l* for healing."
Rev 22: 2 the *l* of the tree are for the healing

LEBANON
Dt 11:24 from the desert to *L,*
1Ki 4:33 from the cedar of *L*

LED (LEAD)
Ex 3: 1 and he *l* the flock to the far side
Dt 8: 2 the LORD your God *l* you all
1Ki 11: 3 and his wives *l* him astray.
2Ch 26:16 his pride *l* to his downfall.
Ne 13:26 he was *l* into sin by foreign women.
Ps 68:18 you *l* captives in your train;
78:52 he *l* them like sheep
Pr 7:21 persuasive words she *l* him astray;
20: 1 whoever is *l* astray
Isa 53: 7 he was *l* like a lamb to the slaughter
Jer 11:19 I had been like a gentle lamb *l*
Am 2:10 and I *l* you forty years in the desert
Mt 4: 1 Then Jesus was *l* by the Spirit
27:31 they *l* him away to crucify him.
Lk 4: 1 was *l* by the Spirit in the desert,
Ac 8:32 "He was *l* like a sheep
Ro 8:14 those who are *l* by the Spirit
2Co 7: 9 your sorrow *l* you to repentance.
Gal 5:18 But if you are *l* by the Spirit,
Eph 4: 8 he *l* captives in his train

LEEKS*
Nu 11: 5 melons, *l,* onions and garlic.

LEFT
Dt 28:14 or to the *l,* following other gods
Jos 1: 7 turn from it to the right or to the *l,*
23: 6 aside to the right or to the *l.*
2Ki 22: 2 aside to the right or to the *l.*
Pr 4:27 Do not swerve to the right or the *l;*
Isa 30:21 turn to the right or to the *l,*
Mt 6: 3 do not let your *l* hand know what
25:33 on his right and the goats on his *l.*

LEGALISTIC*
Php 3: 6 as for *l* righteousness, faultless.

LEGION
Mk 5: 9 "My name is *L,*" he replied,

LEND (LENDER LENDS MONEYLENDER)
Lev 25:37 You must not *l* him money
Dt 15: 8 freely *l* him whatever he needs.
Ps 37:26 are always generous and *l* freely;
Eze 18: 8 He does not *l* at usury
Lk 6:34 if you *l* to those from whom you

LENDER (LEND)
Pr 22: 7 and the borrower is servant to the *l.*
Isa 24: 2 for borrower as for *l,*

LENDS (LEND)
Ps 15: 5 who *l* his money without usury
112: 5 to him who is generous and *l* freely,
Pr 19:17 to the poor *l* to the LORD,

LENGTH (LONG)
Ps 90:10 The *l* of our days is seventy years—
Pr 10:27 The fear of the LORD adds *l* to life

LENGTHY* (LONG)
Mk 12:40 and for a show make *l* prayers.
Lk 20:47 and for a show make *l* prayers.

LEOPARD
Isa 11: 6 the *l* will lie down with the goat,
Da 7: 6 beast, one that looked like a *l.*
Rev 13: 2 The beast I saw resembled a *l,*

LEPROSY (LEPROUS)
Nu 12:10 toward her and saw that she had *l;*
2Ki 5: 1 was a valiant soldier, but he had *l.*
7: 3 men with *l* at the entrance
2Ch 26:21 King Uzziah had *l*
Mt 11: 5 those who have *l* are cured,
Lk 17:12 ten men who had *l* met him.

LEPROUS (LEPROSY)
Ex 4: 6 and when he took it out, it was *l,*

LETTER (LETTERS)
Mt 5:18 not the smallest *l,* not the least
2Co 3: 2 You yourselves are our *l,* written
3: 6 for the *l* kills, but the Spirit gives
2Th 3:14 not obey our instruction in this *l,*

LETTERS (LETTER)
2Co 3: 7 which was engraved in *l* on stone,
10:10 "His *l* are weighty and forceful,
2Pe 3:16 His *l* contain some things that are

LEVEL
Ps 143: 10 lead me on *l* ground.
Pr 4:26 Make *l* paths for your feet
Isa 26: 7 The path of the righteous is *l;*
40: 4 the rough ground shall become *l,*
Jer 31: 9 on a *l* path where they will not
Heb 12:13 "Make *l* paths for your feet,"

LEVI (LEVITE LEVITES LEVITICAL)
1. Son of Jacob by Leah (Ge 29:34; 46:11; 1Ch 2:1). With Simeon avenged rape of Dinah (Ge 34). Tribe of blessed (Ge 49:5-7; Dt 33:8-11), chosen as priests (Nu 3-4), numbered (Nu 3:39; 26:62), allot-

ted cities, but not land (Nu 18; 35; Dt 10:9; Jos 13: 14; 21), land (Eze 48:8-22), 12,000 from (Rev 7:7).
2. See MATTHEW.

LEVIATHAN
Job 41: 1 pull in the *l* with a fishhook
Ps 74:14 you who crushed the heads of *L*
Isa 27: 1 *L* the gliding serpent,

LEVITE (LEVI)
Dt 26:12 you shall give it to the *L*, the alien,
Jdg 19: 1 a *L* who lived in a remote area

LEVITES (LEVI)
Nu 1:53 The *L* are to be responsible
3:12 "I have taken the *L*
8: 6 "Take the *L* from among the other
18:21 I give to the *L* all the tithes in Israel
35: 7 must give the *L* forty-eight towns,
2Ch 31: 2 assigned the priests and *L*
Mal 3: 3 he will purify the *L* and refine them

LEVITICAL (LEVI)
Heb 7:11 attained through the *L* priesthood

LEWDNESS
Mk 7:22 malice, deceit, *l*, envy, slander,

LIAR* (LIE)
Dt 19:18 and if the witness proves to be a *l*,
Job 34: 6 I am considered a *l*;
Pr 17: 4 *l* pays attention to a malicious
19:22 better to be poor than a *l*.
30: 6 will rebuke you and prove you a *l*.
Mic 2:11 If a *l* and deceiver comes and says,
Jn 8:44 for he is a *l* and the father of lies.
8:55 I did not, I would be a *l* like you,
Ro 3: 4 Let God be true, and every man a *l*.
1Jn 1:10 we make him out to be a *l*
2: 4 not do what he commands is a *l*,
2:22 Who is the *l*? It is the man who
4:20 yet hates his brother, he is a *l*.
5:10 God has made him out to be a *l*,

LIARS* (LIE)
Ps 63:11 the mouths of *l* will be silenced.
116: 11 "All men are *l*."
Isa 57: 4 the offspring of *l*?
Mic 6:12 her people are *l*
1Ti 1:10 for slave traders and *l* and perjurers
4: 2 come through hypocritical *l*,
Tit 1:12 "Cretans are always *l*, evil brutes,
Rev 3: 9 though they are not, but are *l*—
21: 8 magic arts, the idolaters and all *l*—

LIBERATED*
Ro 8:21 that the creation itself will be *l*

LICENSE
Jude : 4 of our God into a *l* for immorality

LICK
Ps 72: 9 and his enemies will *l* the dust.
Isa 49:23 they will *l* the dust at your feet.
Mic 7:17 They will *l* dust like a snake,

LIE (LIAR LIARS LIED LIES LYING)
Lev 18:22 " 'Do not *l* with a man
19:11 " 'Do not *l*.
Nu 23:19 God is not a man, that he should *l*,
Dt 6: 7 when you *l* down and when you get
25: 2 the judge shall make him *l* down
1Sa 15:29 the Glory of Israel does not *l*
Ps 4: 8 I will *l* down and sleep in peace,
23: 2 me *l* down in green pastures,
89:35 and I will not *l* to David—
Pr 3:24 when you *l* down, you will not be
Isa 11: 6 leopard will *l* down with the goat,
28:15 for we have made a *l* our refuge
Jer 9: 5 They have taught their tongues to *l*
23:14 They commit adultery and live a *l*.
Eze 13: 6 are false and their divinations a *l*.
34:14 they will *l* down in good grazing
Ro 1:25 exchanged the truth of God for a *l*,
Col 3: 9 Do not *l* to each other,
2Th 2:11 so that they will believe the *l*
Tit 1: 2 which God, who does not *l*,
Heb 6:18 which it is impossible for God to *l*,
1Jn 2:21 because no *l* comes from the truth.
Rev 14: 5 No *l* was found in their mouths;

LIED (LIE)
Ac 5: 4 You have not *l* to men but to God."

LIES (LIE)
Lev 6: 3 finds lost property and *l* about it,
Ps 5: 6 You destroy those who tell *l*;
10: 7 His mouth is full of curses and *l*
12: 2 Everyone *l* to his neighbor;
34:13 and your lips from speaking *l*.
58: 3 they are wayward and speak *l*.
Ps 144: 8 whose mouths are full of *l*,
Pr 6:19 a false witness who pours out *l*
12:17 but a false witness tells *l*.
19: 5 he who pours out *l* will not go free.
19: 9 and he who pours out *l* will perish.
29:12 If a ruler listens to *l*,
30: 8 Keep falsehood and *l* far from me;
Isa 59: 3 Your lips have spoken *l*,
Jer 5:31 The prophets prophesy *l*,
9: 3 like a bow, to shoot *l*;
14:14 "The prophets are prophesying *l*
Hos 11:12 Ephraim has surrounded me with *l*,
Jn 8:44 for he is a liar and the father of *l*.

LIFE (LIVE)
Ge 1:30 everything that has the breath of *l*
2: 7 into his nostrils the breath of *l*,
2: 9 of the garden were the tree of *l*
6:17 to destroy all *l* under the heavens,
9: 5 for the *l* of his fellow man.
9:11 Never again will all *l* be cut
Ex 21: 6 Then he will be his servant for *l*.
21:23 you are to take *l* for *l*, eye for eye,
23:26 I will give you a full *l* span.
Lev 17:14 the *l* of every creature is its blood.
24:17 " 'If anyone takes the *l*
24:18 must make restitution—*l* for *l*.
Nu 35:31 a ransom for the *l* of a murderer,
Dt 4:42 one of these cities and save his *l*.
12:23 because the blood is the *l*,
19:21 Show no pity: *l* for *l*, eye for eye,
30:15 I set before you today *l*
30:19 Now choose *l*, so that you
30:20 For the LORD is your *l*,
32:39 I put to death and I bring to *l*,
32:47 words for you—they are your *l*.
1Sa 19: 5 He took his *l* in his hands
Job 2: 6 hands; but you must spare his *l*."
33: 4 of the Almighty gives me *l*.
33:30 that the light of *l* may shine on him.
Ps 16:11 known to me the path of *l*;
17:14 this world whose reward is in this *l*.
23: 6 all the days of my *l*,
27: 1 LORD is the stronghold of my *l*—
34:12 Whoever of you loves *l*
36: 9 For with you is the fountain of *l*;
39: 4 let me know how fleeting is my *l*.
41: 2 will protect him and preserve his *l*;
49: 7 No man can redeem the *l*
49: 8 the ransom for a *l* is costly,
63: 3 Because your love is better than *l*,
69:28 they be blotted out of the book of *l*
91:16 With long *l* will I satisfy him
104: 33 I will sing to the LORD all my *l*;
119: 25 preserve my *l* according to your word
Pr 1: 3 a disciplined and prudent *l*,
3: 2 will prolong your *l* many years
3:18 of *l* to those who embrace her;
4:23 for it is the wellspring of *l*.
6:23 are the way to *l*,
6:26 adulteress preys upon your very *l*.
7:23 little knowing it will cost him his *l*.
8:35 For whoever finds me finds *l*
10:11 of the righteous is a fountain of *l*,
10:27 of the LORD adds length to *l*,
11:30 of the righteous is a tree of *l*,
13: 3 He who guards his lips guards his *l*,
13:12 but a longing fulfilled is a tree of *l*.
13:14 of the wise is a fountain of *l*,
14:27 of the LORD is a fountain of *l*,
15: 4 that brings healing is a tree of *l*,
16:22 Understanding is a fountain of *l*
19: 3 A man's own folly ruins his *l*,
19:23 The fear of the LORD leads to *l*:
21:21 finds *l*, prosperity and honor.
Isa 53:10 LORD makes his *l* a guilt offering,
53:11 he will see the light of *l*,
53:12 he poured out his *l* unto death,
Jer 10:23 that a man's *l* is not his own;
La 3:58 you redeemed my *l*.
Eze 18:27 and right, he will save his *l*.
37: 5 enter you, and you will come to *l*.
Da 12: 2 some to everlasting *l*, others
Jnh 2: 6 you brought my *l* up from the pit,
Mal 2: 5 a covenant of *l* and peace,
Mt 6:25 Is not *l* more important than food,
7:14 and narrow the road that leads to *l*,
10:39 Whoever finds his *l* will lose it,
16:21 and on the third day be raised to *l*.
16:25 wants to save his *l* will lose it,
18: 8 better for you to enter *l* maimed
19:16 thing must I do to get eternal *l*?"
19:29 as much and will inherit eternal *l*.
20:28 to give his *l* as a ransom for many."
25:46 but the righteous to eternal *l*."
Mk 8:35 but whoever loses his *l* for me
9:43 better for you to enter *l* maimed
10:17 "what must I do to inherit eternal *l*
10:30 and in the age to come, eternal *l*.
Mk 10:45 to give his *l* as a ransom for many."
Lk 6: 9 to save *l* or to destroy it?"
9:22 and on the third day be raised to *l*."
9:24 wants to save his *l* will lose it,
12:15 a man's *l* does not consist
12:22 do not worry about your *l*,
12:25 can add a single hour to his *l*?
14:26 even his own *l*— he cannot be my
17:33 tries to keep his *l* will lose it,
21:19 standing firm you will gain *l*.
Jn 1: 4 In him was *l*, and that *l* was
3:15 believes in him may have eternal *l*.
3:36 believes in the Son has eternal *l*,
4:14 of water welling up to eternal *l*."
5:21 raises the dead and gives them *l*,
5:24 him who sent me has eternal *l*
5:26 For as the Father has *l* in himself,
5:39 that by them you possess eternal *l*.
5:40 refuse to come to me to have *l*.
6:27 for food that endures to eternal *l*,
6:33 down from heaven and gives *l*
6:35 Jesus declared, "I am the bread of *l*
6:40 believes in him shall have eternal *l*,
6:47 he who believes has everlasting *l*.
6:48 I am the bread of *l*.
6:51 give for the *l* of the world."
6:53 and drink his blood, you have no *l*
6:63 The Spirit gives *l*; the flesh counts
6:68 You have the words of eternal *l*.
8:12 but will have the light of *l*."
10:10 I have come that they may have *l*,
10:15 and I lay down my *l* for the sheep.
10:17 loves me is that I lay down my *l*—
10:28 I give them eternal *l*, and they shall
11:25 "I am the resurrection and the *l*.
12:25 The man who loves his *l* will lose it,
12:50 his command leads to eternal *l*.
13:37 I will lay down my *l* for you."
14: 6 am the way and the truth and the *l*.
15:13 lay down his *l* for his friends.
17: 2 people that he might give eternal *l*
17: 3 Now this is eternal *l*: that they may
20:31 that by believing you may have *l*
Ac 2:32 God has raised this Jesus to *l*,
3:15 You killed the author of *l*,
11:18 the Gentiles repentance unto *l*."
13:48 appointed for eternal *l* believed.
Ro 2: 7 immortality, he will give eternal *l*.
4:25 was raised to *l* for our justification.
5:10 shall we be saved through his *l*!
5:18 was justification that brings *l*
5:21 righteousness to bring eternal *l*
6: 4 the Father, we too may live a new *l*.
6:13 have been brought from death to *l*;
6:22 holiness, and the result is eternal *l*.
6:23 but the gift of God is eternal *l*
8: 6 mind controlled by the Spirit is *l*
8:11 also give *l* to your mortal bodies
8:38 convinced that neither death nor *l*,
1Co 15:19 If only for this *l* we have hope
15:36 What you sow does not come to *l*
2Co 2:16 to the other, the fragrance of *l*.
3: 6 letter kills, but the Spirit gives *l*.
4:10 so that the *l* of Jesus may
5: 4 is mortal may be swallowed up by *l*.
Gal 2:20 The *l* I live in the body, I live
3:21 had been given that could impart *l*,
6: 8 from the Spirit will reap eternal *l*.
Eph 4: 1 I urge you to live a *l* worthy
Php 2:16 as you hold out the word of *l*—
4: 3 whose names are in the book of *l*.
Col 1:10 order that you may live a *l* worthy
3: 3 your *l* is now hidden with Christ
1Th 4:12 so that your daily *l* may win
1Ti 1:16 on him and receive eternal *l*.
4: 8 for both the present *l* and the *l*
4:12 in *l*, in love, in faith and in purity.
4:16 Watch your *l* and doctrine closely.
6:12 Take hold of the eternal *l*
6:19 hold of the *l* that is truly *l*.
2Ti 1: 9 saved us and called us to a holy *l*—
1:10 destroyed death and has brought *l*
3:12 to live a godly *l* in Christ Jesus will
Tit 1: 2 resting on the hope of eternal *l*,
3: 7 heirs having the hope of eternal *l*.
Heb 7:16 of the power of an indestructible *l*.
Jas 1:12 crown of *l* that God has promised
3:13 Let him show it by his good *l*,
1Pe 3: 7 with you of the gracious gift of *l*,
3:10 "Whoever would love *l*
4: 2 rest of his earthly *l* for evil human
2Pe 1: 3 given us everything we need for *l*
1Jn 1: 1 proclaim concerning the Word of *l*.
2:25 he promised us—even eternal *l*.
3:14 we have passed from death to *l*,
3:16 Jesus Christ laid down his *l* for us.
5:11 has given us eternal *l*, and this *l* is
5:20 He is the true God and eternal *l*.
Jude :21 Christ to bring you to eternal *l*.

Rev 2: 7 the right to eat from the tree of *l*,
2: 8 who died and came to *l* again.
2:10 and I will give you the crown of *l*.
3: 5 name from the book of *l*,
13: 8 written in the book of *l* belonging
17: 8 in the book of *l* from the creation
20:12 was opened, which is the book of *l*.
20:15 not found written in the book of *l*,
21: 6 from the spring of the water of *l*.
21:27 written in the Lamb's book of *l*.
22: 1 me the river of the water of *l*,
22: 2 side of the river stood the tree of *l*,
22:14 may have the right to the tree of *l*
22:17 take the free gift of the water of *l*.
22:19 from him his share in the tree of *l*

LIFE-GIVING (GIVE)
Pr 15:31 He who listens to a *l* rebuke
1Co 15:45 being"; the last Adam, a *l* spirit.

LIFETIME (LIVE)
Ps 30: 5 but his favor lasts a *l*;
Lk 16:25 in your *l* you received your good

LIFT (LIFTED LIFTING LIFTS)
Ps 3: 3 you bestow glory on me and *l*
28: 2 as I *l* up my hands
63: 4 in your name I will *l* up my hands.
91:12 they will *l* you up in their hands,
121: 1 I *l* up my eyes to the hills—
123: 1 I *l* up my eyes to you,
134: 2 *L* up your hands in the sanctuary
143: 8 for to you I *l* up my soul.
Isa 40: 9 *l* up your voice with a shout,
La 2:19 *L* up your hands to him
3:41 Let us *l* up our hearts and our
Mt 4: 6 they will *l* you up in their hands,
Lk 21:28 stand up and *l* up your heads,
1Ti 2: 8 everywhere to *l* up holy hands
Jas 4:10 the Lord, and he will *l* you up.
1Pe 5: 6 that he may *l* you up in due time.

LIFTED (LIFT)
Ne 8: 6 and all the people *l* their hands
Ps 24: 7 be *l* up, you ancient doors,
40: 2 He *l* me out of the slimy pit,
41: 9 has *l* up his heel against me.
Isa 52:13 *l* up and highly exalted.
63: 9 he *l* them up and carried them
Jn 3:14 Moses *l* up the snake in the desert,
8:28 "When you have *l* up the Son
12:32 when I am *l* up from the earth,
12:34 'The Son of Man must be *l* up'?
13:18 shares my bread has *l* up his heel

LIFTING (LIFT)
Ps 141: 2 may the *l* up of my hands be like

LIFTS (LIFT)
Ps 113: 7 and *l* the needy from the ash heap;

LIGAMENT* (LIGAMENTS)
Eph 4:16 held together by every supporting *l*

LIGAMENTS* (LIGAMENT)
Col 2:19 held together by its *l* and sinews,

LIGHT (ENLIGHTENED LIGHTS)
Ge 1: 3 "Let there be *l*," and there was *l*.
Ex 13:21 in a pillar of fire to give them *l*,
25:37 it so that they *l* the space in front
2Sa 22:29 LORD turns my darkness into *l*.
Job 38:19 "What is the way to the abode of *l*?
Ps 4: 6 Let the *l* of your face shine upon us
18:28 my God turns my darkness into *l*.
19: 8 giving *l* to the eyes.
27: 1 LORD is my *l* and my salvation—
36: 9 in your *l* we see *l*.
56:13 God in the *l* of life.
76: 4 You are resplendent with *l*,
89:15 who walk in the *l* of your presence,
104: 2 He wraps himself in *l*
119:105 and a *l* for my path.
119:130 The unfolding of your words gives *l*;
139: 12 for darkness is as *l* to you.
Pr 4:18 till the full *l* of day.
Isa 2: 5 let us walk in the *l* of the LORD.
9: 2 have seen a great *l*;
42: 6 and a *l* for the Gentiles,
45: 7 I form the *l* and create darkness,
49: 6 also make you a *l* for the Gentiles,
53:11 he will see the *l* of life,
60: 1 "Arise, shine, for your *l* has come,
60:19 LORD will be your everlasting *l*,
Eze 1:27 and brilliant *l* surrounded him.
Mic 7: 8 the LORD will be my *l*.
Mt 4:16 have seen a great *l*;
5:14 "You are the *l* of the world.
5:15 it gives *l* to everyone in the house.
5:16 let your *l* shine before men,
Mt 6:22 your whole body will be full of *l*.
11:30 yoke is easy and my burden is *l*."
17: 2 his clothes became as white as the *l*
24:29 and the moon will not give its *l*;
Mk 13:24 and the moon will not give its *l*;
Lk 2:32 a *l* for revelation to the Gentiles
8:16 those who come in can see the *l*.
11:33 those who come in may see the *l*.
Jn 1: 4 and that life was the *l* of men.
1: 5 The *l* shines in the darkness,
1: 7 witness to testify concerning that *l*,
1: 9 The true *l* that gives *l*
3:19 but men loved darkness instead of *l*
3:20 Everyone who does evil hates the *l*,
8:12 he said, "I am the *l* of the world.
9: 5 in the world, I am the *l* of the world
12:35 Walk while you have the *l*,
12:46 I have come into the world as a *l*,
Ac 13:47 " 'I have made you a *l*
Ro 13:12 darkness and put on the armor of *l*.
2Co 4: 6 made his *l* shine in our hearts
6:14 Or what fellowship can *l* have
11:14 masquerades as an angel of *l*.
Eph 5: 8 but now you are *l* in the Lord.
1Th 5: 5 You are all sons of the *l*
1Ti 6:16 and who lives in unapproachable *l*,
1Pe 2: 9 of darkness into his wonderful *l*.
2Pe 1:19 as to a *l* shining in a dark place,
1Jn 1: 5 God is *l*; in him there is no
1: 7 But if we walk in the *l*,
2: 9 Anyone who claims to be in the *l*
Rev 21:23 for the glory of God gives it *l*,
22: 5 for the Lord God will give them *l*.

LIGHTNING
Ex 9:23 and *l* flashed down to the ground.
20:18 and *l* and heard the trumpet
Ps 18:12 with hailstones and bolts of *l*.
Eze 1:13 it was bright, and *l* flashed out of it.
Da 10: 6 his face like *l*, his eyes like flaming
Mt 24:27 For as the *l* that comes from the east
28: 3 His appearance was like *l*,
Lk 10:18 "I saw Satan fall like *l* from heaven.
Rev 4: 5 From the throne came flashes of *l*,

LIGHTS (LIGHT)
Ge 1:14 "Let there be *l* in the expanse
Lk 8:16 No one *l* a lamp and hides it in a jar

LIKE-MINDED* (MIND)
Php 2: 2 make my joy complete by being *l*,

LIKENESS
Ge 1:26 man in our image, in our *l*,
Ps 17:15 I will be satisfied with seeing your *l*
Isa 52:14 his form marred beyond human *l*—
Ro 8: 3 Son in the *l* of sinful man
8:29 to be conformed to the *l* of his Son,
2Co 3:18 his *l* with ever-increasing glory,
Php 2: 7 being made in human *l*.
Jas 3: 9 who have been made in God's *l*.

LILIES (LILY)
Lk 12:27 "Consider how the *l* grow.

LILY (LILIES)
SS 2: 1 a *l* of the valleys.
2: 2 *Lover* Like a *l* among thorns

LIMIT
Ps 147: 5 his understanding has no *l*.
Jn 3:34 for God gives the Spirit without *l*.

LINEN
Lev 16: 4 He is to put on the sacred *l* tunic,
Pr 31:22 she is clothed in fine *l* and purple.
31:24 She makes *l* garments
Mk 15:46 So Joseph bought some *l* cloth,
Jn 20: 6 He saw the strips of *l* lying there,
Rev 15: 6 shining *l* and wore golden sashes
19: 8 Fine *l*, bright and clean,

LINGER
Hab 2: 3 Though it *l*, wait for it;

LION (LION'S LIONS')
Jdg 14: 6 power so that he tore the *l* apart
1Sa 17:34 When a *l* or a bear came
Isa 11: 7 and the *l* will eat straw like the ox.
65:25 and the *l* will eat straw like the ox,
Eze 1:10 right side each had the face of a *l*,
10:14 the third the face of a *l*,
Da 7: 4 "The first was like a *l*,
1Pe 5: 8 around like a roaring *l* looking
Rev 4: 7 The first living creature was like a *l*
5: 5 See, the *L* of the tribe of Judah,

LION'S (LION)
Ge 49: 9 You are a *l* cub, O Judah;

LIONS' (LION)
Da 6: 7 shall be thrown into the *l* den.

LIPS
Ps 8: 2 From the *l* of children and infants
34: 1 his praise will always be on my *l*.
40: 9 I do not seal my *l*,
63: 3 my *l* will glorify you.
119:171 May my *l* overflow with praise,
140: 3 the poison of vipers is on their *l*.
141: 3 keep watch over the door of my *l*.
Pr 10:13 on the *l* of the discerning,
10:18 who conceals his hatred has lying *l*,
10:32 *l* of the righteous know what is
12:22 The LORD detests lying *l*,
13: 3 He who guards his *l* guards his life,
14: 7 will not find knowledge on his *l*.
24:26 is like a kiss on the *l*.
26:23 are fervent *l* with an evil heart.
27: 2 someone else, and not your own *l*.
Isa 6: 5 For I am a man of unclean *l*,
28:11 with foreign *l* and strange tongues
29:13 and honor me with their *l*,
Mal 2: 7 "For the *l* of a priest ought
Mt 15: 8 These people honor me with their *l*
21:16 " 'From the *l* of children
Lk 4:22 words that came from his *l*.
Ro 3:13 "The poison of vipers is on their *l*."
Col 3: 8 and filthy language from your *l*.
Heb 13:15 the fruit of *l* that confess his name.
1Pe 3:10 and his *l* from deceitful speech.

LISTEN (LISTENED LISTENING LISTENS)
Dt 18:15 You must *l* to him.
30:20 *l* to his voice, and hold fast to him.
1Ki 4:34 came to *l* to Solomon's wisdom,
2Ki 21: 9 But the people did not *l*.
Pr 1: 5 let the wise *l* and add
Ecc 5: 1 Go near to *l* rather
Eze 2: 5 And whether they *l* or fail to *l*—
Mt 12:42 earth to *l* to Solomon's wisdom,
Mk 9: 7 *L* to him!" Suddenly,
Jn 10:27 My sheep *l* to my voice; I know
Ac 3:22 you must *l* to everything he tells
Jas 1:19 Everyone should be quick to *l*,
1:22 Do not merely *l* to the word,
1Jn 4: 6 not from God does not *l* to us.

LISTENED (LISTEN)
Ne 8: 3 And all the people *l* attentively
Isa 66: 4 when I spoke, no one *l*.
Da 9: 6 We have not *l* to your servants

LISTENING (LISTEN)
1Sa 3: 9 Speak, LORD, for your servant is *l*
Pr 18:13 He who answers before *l*—
Lk 10:39 at the Lord's feet *l* to what he said.

LISTENS (LISTEN)
Pr 12:15 but a wise man *l* to advice.
Lk 10:16 "He who *l* to you *l*
1Jn 4: 6 and whoever knows God *l* to us;

LIVE (ALIVE LIFE LIFETIME LIVES LIVING)
Ge 3:22 tree of life and eat, and *l* forever."
Ex 20:12 so that you may *l* long
33:20 for no one may see me and *l*."
Nu 21: 8 who is bitten can look at it and *l*."
Dt 5:24 we have seen that a man can *l*
6: 2 as you *l* by keeping all his decrees
8: 3 to teach you that man does not *l*
Job 14:14 If a man dies, will he *l* again?
Ps 15: 1 Who may *l* on your holy hill?
24: 1 the world, and all who *l* in it;
26: 8 I love the house where you *l*,
119:175 Let me *l* that I may praise you,
Pr 21: 9 Better to *l* on a corner of the roof
21:19 Better to *l* in a desert
Ecc 9: 4 a *l* dog is better off than a dead lion
Isa 26:19 But your dead will *l*;
55: 3 hear me, that your soul may *l*.
Eze 17:19 LORD says: As surely as I *l*,
20:11 for the man who obeys them will *l*
37: 3 can these bones *l*?" I said,
Am 5: 6 Seek the LORD and *l*,
Hab 2: 4 but the righteous will *l* by his faith
Zec 2:11 I will *l* among you and you will
Mt 4: 4 'Man does not *l* on bread alone,
Lk 4: 4 'Man does not *l* on bread alone.' "
Jn 14:19 Because I *l*, you also will *l*.
Ac 17:24 does not *l* in temples built by hands
17:28 'For in him we *l* and move
Ro 1:17 "The righteous will *l* by faith."
2Co 5: 7 We *l* by faith, not by sight.
6:16 "I will *l* with them and walk
Gal 2:20 The life I *l* in the body, I *l* by faith
3:11 "The righteous will *l* by faith."
5:25 Since we *l* by the Spirit, let us keep

Eph 4:17 that you must no longer *l*
Php 1:21 to *l* is Christ and to die is gain.
Col 1:10 order that you may *l* a life worthy
1Th 4: 1 we instructed you how to *l* in order
5:13 *L* in peace with each other.
1Ti 2: 2 that we may *l* peaceful
2Ti 3:12 who wants to *l* a godly life
Tit 2:12 and to *l* self-controlled, upright
Heb 10:38 But my righteous one will *l* by faith
12:14 Make every effort to *l* in peace
1Pe 1:17 *l* your lives as strangers here
3: 8 *l* in harmony with one another;

LIVES (LIVE)
Ge 45: 7 and to save your *l* by a great
Job 19:25 I know that my Redeemer *l*,
Pr 1:19 it takes away the *l*
Isa 57:15 he who *l* forever, whose name is
Da 3:28 to give up their *l* rather than serve
Jn 14:17 for he *l* with you and will be in you.
Ro 6:10 but the life he *l*, he *l* to God.
7:18 I know that nothing good *l* in me,
8: 9 if the Spirit of God *l* in you.
14: 7 For none of us *l* to himself alone
1Co 3:16 and that God's Spirit *l* in you?
Gal 2:20 I no longer live, but Christ *l* in me.
1Th 2: 8 only the gospel of God but our *l*
1Ti 2: 2 quiet *l* in all godliness and holiness.
Tit 2:12 and godly *l* in this present age,
Heb 7:24 but because Jesus *l* forever,
13: 5 Keep your *l* free from the love
1Pe 3: 2 the purity and reverence of your *l*.
2Pe 3:11 You ought to live holy and godly *l*
1Jn 3:16 to lay down our *l* for our brothers.
4:16 Whoever *l* in love *l* in God,

LIVING (LIVE)
Ge 2: 7 and the man became a *l* being.
1Sa 17:26 defy the armies of the *l* God?"
Isa 53: 8 cut off from the land of the *l*;
Jer 2:13 the spring of *l* water,
Eze 1: 5 what looked like four *l* creatures.
Zec 14: 8 On that day *l* water will flow out
Mt 22:32 the God of the dead but of the *l*."
Jn 4:10 he would have given you *l* water."
6:51 I am the *l* bread that came
7:38 streams of *l* water will flow
Ro 8:11 Jesus from the dead is *l* in you,
12: 1 to offer your bodies as *l* sacrifices,
1Co 9:14 the gospel should receive their *l*
Heb 4:12 For the word of God is *l* and active.
10:20 and *l* way opened for us
10:31 to fall into the hands of the *l* God.
1Pe 1:23 through the *l* and enduring word
Rev 1:18 I am the *L* One; I was dead,
4: 6 the throne, were four *l* creatures,
7:17 to springs of *l* water.

LOAD (LOADS)
Gal 6: 5 for each one should carry his own *l*.

LOADS (LOAD)
Mt 23: 4 They tie up heavy *l* and put them

LOAF (LOAVES)
1Co 10:17 for we all partake of the one *l*.

LOAVES (LOAF)
Mk 6:41 Taking the five *l* and the two fish
8: 6 When he had taken the seven *l*
Lk 11: 5 'Friend, lend me three *l* of bread,

LOCKED
Jn 20:26 the doors were *l*, Jesus came
Gal 3:23 *l* up until faith should be revealed.

LOCUSTS
Ex 10: 4 I will bring *l* into your country
Joel 2:25 you for the years the *l* have eaten—
Mt 3: 4 His food was *l* and wild honey.
Rev 9: 3 And out of the smoke *l* came

LOFTY
Ps 139: 6 too *l* for me to attain.
Isa 57:15 is what the high and *l* One says—

LONELY
Ps 68: 6 God sets the *l* in families,
Lk 5:16 Jesus often withdrew to *l* places

LONG (LENGTH LENGTHY LONGED LONGING LONGINGS LONGS)
Ex 17:11 As *l* as Moses held up his hands,
Nu 6: 5 the hair of his head grow *l*.
1Ki 18:21 "How *l* will you waver
Ps 119: 97 I meditate on it all day *l*.
119:174 I *l* for your salvation, O LORD,
Hos 7:13 I *l* to redeem them
Am 5:18 Why do you *l* for the day
Mt 25: 5 The bridegroom was a *l* time
Jn 9: 4 As *l* as it is day, we must do
1Co 11:14 that if a man has *l* hair,
Eph 3:18 to grasp how wide and *l* and high
Php 1: 8 God can testify how I *l* for all
1Pe 1:12 Even angels *l* to look

LONGED (LONG)
Mt 13:17 righteous men *l* to see what you see
23:37 how often I have *l*
Lk 13:34 how often I have *l*
2Ti 4: 8 to all who have *l* for his appearing.

LONGING* (LONG)
Dt 28:65 with *l*, and a despairing heart.
Job 7: 2 Like a slave *l* for the evening
Ps 119: 20 My soul is consumed with *l*
119: 81 with *l* for your salvation,
119:131 *l* for your commands.
143: 7 my spirit faints with *l*.
Pr 13:12 but a *l* fulfilled is a tree of life.
13:19 A *l* fulfilled is sweet to the soul,
Eze 23:27 look on these things with *l*
Lk 16:21 and *l* to eat what fell from the rich
Ro 15:23 since I have been *l* for many years
2Co 5: 2 *l* to be clothed with our heavenly
7: 7 He told us about your *l* for me,
7:11 what alarm, what *l*, what concern,
1Th 2:17 out of our intense *l* we made every
Heb 11:16 they were *l* for a better country—

LONGINGS* (LONG)
Ps 38: 9 All my *l* lie open before you,
112: 10 the *l* of the wicked will come

LONGS* (LONG)
Ps 63: 1 my body *l* for you,
Isa 26: 9 in the morning my spirit *l* for you.
30:18 Yet the LORD *l* to be gracious
Php 2:26 For he *l* for all of you and is

LOOK (LOOKED LOOKING LOOKS)
Ge 19:17 "Flee for your lives! Don't *l* back,
Ex 3: 6 because he was afraid to *l* at God.
Nu 21: 8 anyone who is bitten can *l* at it
32: 8 Kadesh Barnea to *l* over the land.
Dt 4:29 you will find him if you *l* for him
1Sa 16: 7 The LORD does not *l*
Job 31: 1 not to *l* lustfully at a girl.
Ps 34: 5 Those who *l* to him are radiant;
105: 4 *L* to the LORD and his strength;
113: 6 who stoops down to *l*
123: 2 As the eyes of slaves *l* to the hand
Pr 1:28 they will *l* for me but will not find
4:25 Let your eyes *l* straight ahead,
15:30 A cheerful *l* brings joy to the heart,
Isa 17: 7 In that day men will *l*
31: 1 do not *l* to the Holy One of Israel,
40:26 Lift your eyes and *l* to the heavens:
60: 5 Then you will *l* and be radiant,
Jer 3: 3 Yet you have the brazen *l*
6:16 "Stand at the crossroads and *l*;
Eze 34:11 for my sheep and *l* after them.
Hab 1:13 Your eyes are too pure to *l* on evil;
Zec 12:10 They will *l* on me, the one they
Mt 18:10 "See that you do not *l* down on one
18:12 go to *l* for the one that wandered
23:27 which *l* beautiful on the outside
Mk 13:21 '*L*, here is the Christ!' or, '*L*,
Lk 6:41 "Why do you *l* at the speck
24:39 *L* at my hands and my feet.
Jn 1:36 he said, "*L*, the Lamb of God!"
4:35 open your eyes and *l* at the fields!
19:37 "They will *l* on the one they have
Ro 14:10 why do you *l* down on your brother
Php 2: 4 Each of you should *l* not only
1Ti 4:12 Don't let anyone *l* down on you
Jas 1:27 to *l* after orphans and widows
1Pe 1:12 long to *l* into these things.
2Pe 3:12 as you *l* forward to the day of God

LOOKED (LOOK)
Ge 19:26 Lot's wife *l* back, and she became
Ex 2:25 So God *l* on the Israelites
1Sa 6:19 because they had *l* into the ark
SS 3: 1 I *l* for the one my heart loves;
Eze 22:30 "I *l* for a man among them who
34: 6 and no one searched or *l* for them.
44: 4 I *l* and saw the glory
Da 7: 9 "As I *l*,
10: 5 I *l* up and there before me was
Hab 3: 6 he *l*, and made the nations tremble.
Mt 25:36 I was sick and you *l* after me,
Lk 18: 9 and *l* down on everybody else,
22:61 The Lord turned and *l* straight
1Jn 1: 1 which we have *l* at and our hands

LOOKING (LOOK)
Ps 69: 3 *l* for my God.
119: 82 My eyes fail, *l* for your promise;
119:123 My eyes fail, *l* for your salvation,
Mk 16: 6 "You are *l* for Jesus the Nazarene,
2Co 10: 7 You are *l* only on the surface
Php 4:17 Not that I am *l* for a gift,
1Th 2: 6 We were not *l* for praise from men,
2Pe 3:13 with his promise we are *l* forward
Rev 5: 6 I saw a Lamb, *l* as if it had been

LOOKS (LOOK)
1Sa 16: 7 Man *l* at the outward appearance,
Ezr 8:22 is on everyone who *l* to him,
Ps 104: 32 who *l* at the earth, and it trembles;
138: 6 on high, he *l* upon the lowly,
Pr 27:18 he who *l* after his master will be
Eze 34:12 As a shepherd *l* after his scattered
Mt 5:28 But I tell you that anyone who *l*
16: 4 and adulterous generation *l*
Lk 9:62 and *l* back is fit for service
Jn 6:40 Father's will is that everyone who *l*
12:45 When he *l* at me, he sees the one
Php 2:21 For everyone *l* out
Jas 1:25 But the man who *l* intently

LOOSE
Isa 33:23 Your rigging hangs *l*:
Mt 16:19 and whatever you *l* on earth will be
18:18 and whatever you *l* on earth will be

LORD† (LORD'S† LORDED LORDING)
Ge 18:27 been so bold as to speak to the *L*,
Ex 15:17 O *L*, your hands established.
Nu 16:13 now you also want to *l* it over us?
Dt 10:17 God of gods and *L* of lords,
Jos 3:13 the *L* of all the earth—set foot
1Ki 3:10 *L* was pleased that Solomon had
Ne 4:14 Remember the *L*, who is great
Job 28:28 'The fear of the *L*— that is wisdom,
Ps 37:13 but the *L* laughs at the wicked,
38:22 O *L* my Savior.
54: 4 the *L* is the one who sustains me.
62:12 and that you, O *L*, are loving.
69: 6 O *L*, the LORD Almighty;
86: 5 You are forgiving and good, O *L*,
86: 8 gods there is none like you, O *L*;
89:49 O *L*, where is your former great
110: 1 The LORD says to my *L*:
110: 5 The *L* is at your right hand;
130: 3 O *L*, who could stand?
135: 5 that our *L* is greater than all gods.
136: 3 Give thanks to the *L* of lords:
147: 5 Great is our *L* and mighty in power
Isa 6: 1 I saw the *L* seated on a throne,
Da 2:47 and the *L* of kings and a revealer
9: 4 "O *L*, the great and awesome God,
9: 7 "*L*, you are righteous,
9: 9 The *L* our God is merciful
9:19 O *L*, listen! O *L*, forgive! O *L*,
Mt 3: 3 'Prepare the way for the *L*,
4: 7 'Do not put the *L* your God
4:10 'Worship the *L* your God,
7:21 "Not everyone who says to me, '*L*,
9:38 Ask the *L* of the harvest, therefore,
12: 8 Son of Man is *L* of the Sabbath."
20:25 of the Gentiles *l* it over them,
21: 9 comes in the name of the *L*!"
22:37 " 'Love the *L* your God
22:44 For he says, " 'The *L* said to my *L*:
23:39 comes in the name of the *L*.' "
Mk 1: 3 'Prepare the way for the *L*,
12:11 the *L* has done this,
12:29 the *L* our God, the *L* is one.
12:30 Love the *L* your God
Lk 2: 9 glory of the *L* shone around them,
6: 5 The Son of Man is *L* of the Sabbath
6:46 "Why do you call me, '*L*, *L*,'
10:27 " 'Love the *L* your God
11: 1 one of his disciples said to him, "*L*,
24:34 The *L* has risen and has appeared
Jn 1:23 'Make straight the way for the *L*.' "
Ac 2:21 on the name of the *L* will be saved.'
2:25 " 'I saw the *L* always before me.
2:34 " 'The *L* said to my *L*:
8:16 into the name of the *L* Jesus.
9: 5 "Who are you, *L*?" Saul asked.
10:36 through Jesus Christ, who is *L*
11:23 true to the *L* with all their hearts.
16:31 replied, "Believe in the *L* Jesus,
Ro 4:24 in him who raised Jesus our *L*
5:11 in God through our *L* Jesus Christ,
6:23 life in Christ Jesus our *L*.
8:39 of God that is in Christ Jesus our *L*.
10: 9 with your mouth, "Jesus is *L*,"
10:13 on the name of the *L* will be saved
10:16 *L*, who has believed our message?"
11:34 Who has known the mind of the *L*?
12:11 your spiritual fervor, serving the *L*.
13:14 yourselves with the *L* Jesus Christ,
14: 4 for the *L* is able to make him stand.
14: 8 we live to the *L*; and if we die,
1Co 1:31 Let him who boasts boast in the *L*."

1Co 3: 5 the *L* has assigned to each his task.
4: 5 time; wait till the *L* comes.
6:13 for the *L*, and the *L* for the body.
6:14 By his power God raised the *L*
7:32 affairs—how he can please the *L*.
7:34 to be devoted to the *L* in both body
7:35 in undivided devotion to the *L*.
7:39 but he must belong to the *L*.
8: 6 and there is but one *L*, Jesus Christ,
10: 9 We should not test the *L*,
11:23 For I received from the *L* what I
12: 3 "Jesus is *L*," except by the Holy
15:57 victory through our *L* Jesus Christ.
15:58 fully to the work of the *L*,
16:22 If anyone does not love the *L*—
2Co 1:24 Not that we *l* it over your faith,
2:12 found that the *L* had opened a door
3:17 Now the *L* is the Spirit,
4: 5 but Jesus Christ as *L*, and ourselves
5: 6 in the body we are away from the *L*
8: 5 they gave themselves first to the *L*,
8:21 not only in the eyes of the *L* but
10:17 Let him who boasts boast in the *L*."
10:18 but the one whom the *L* commends
13:10 the authority the *L* gave me
Gal 6:14 in the cross of our *L* Jesus Christ,
Eph 4: 5 one *L*, one faith, one baptism;
5: 8 but now you are light in the *L*.
5:10 and find out what pleases the *L*.
5:19 make music in your heart to the *L*,
5:22 submit to your husbands as to the *L*
6: 1 obey your parents in the *L*,
6: 7 as if you were serving the *L*,
6: 8 know that the *L* will reward
6:10 in the *L* and in his mighty power.
Php 2:11 confess that Jesus Christ is *L*,
3: 1 my brothers, rejoice in the *L*!
3: 8 of knowing Christ Jesus my *L*,
4: 1 you should stand firm in the *L*,
4: 4 Rejoice in the *L* always.
4: 5 The *L* is near.
Col 1:10 you may live a life worthy of the *L*
2: 6 as you received Christ Jesus as *L*,
3:13 Forgive as the *L* forgave you.
3:17 do it all in the name of the *L* Jesus,
3:18 your husbands, as is fitting in the *L*.
3:20 in everything, for this pleases the *L*
3:23 as working for the *L*, not for men,
3:24 It is the *L* Christ you are serving.
3:24 receive an inheritance from the *L*
4:17 work you have received in the *L*."
1Th 3: 8 since you are standing firm in the *L*
3:12 May the *L* make your love increase
4: 1 and urge you in the *L* Jesus
4: 6 The *L* will punish men
4:15 who are left till the coming of the *L*
5: 2 day of the *L* will come like a thief
5:23 at the coming of our *L* Jesus Christ.
2Th 1: 7 when the *L* Jesus is revealed
1:12 of our *L* Jesus may be glorified
2: 1 the coming of our *L* Jesus Christ
2: 8 whom the *L* Jesus will overthrow
3: 3 *L* is faithful, and he will strengthen
3: 5 May the *L* direct your hearts
1Ti 6:15 the King of kings and *L* of lords,
2Ti 1: 8 ashamed to testify about our *L*,
2:19 "The *L* knows those who are his,"
4: 8 which the *L*, the righteous Judge,
4:17 But the *L* stood at my side
Heb 1:10 O *L*, you laid the foundations
10:30 "The *L* will judge his people."
12:14 holiness no one will see the *L*.
13: 6 *L* is my helper; I will not be afraid.
Jas 3: 9 With the tongue we praise our *L*
4:10 Humble yourselves before the *L*,
5:11 The *L* is full of compassion
1Pe 1:25 the word of the *L* stands forever."
2: 3 you have tasted that the *L* is good.
3:12 eyes of the *L* are on the righteous
3:15 in your hearts set apart Christ as *L*.
2Pe 1:11 into the eternal kingdom of our *L*
1:16 and coming of our *L* Jesus Christ,
2: 1 the sovereign *L* who bought
2: 9 then the *L* knows how
3: 9 The *L* is not slow in keeping his
3:18 and knowledge of our *L* and Savior
Jude :14 the *L* is coming with thousands
Rev 4: 8 holy, holy is the *L* God Almighty,
4:11 "You are worthy, our *L* and God,
11:15 has become the kingdom of our *L*
17:14 he is *L* of lords and King of kings—
19:16 KINGS AND *L* OF LORDS.
22: 5 for the *L* God will give them light.
22:20 Come, *L* Jesus.

LORD'S† (LORD†)

Lk 1:38 "I am the *L* servant," Mary
Ac 11:21 The *L* hand was with them,
21:14 and said, "The *L* will be done."
1Co 7:32 is concerned about the *L* affairs—
10:26 "The earth is the *L*, and everything
11:26 you proclaim the *L* death
2Co 3:18 faces all reflect the *L* glory,
Eph 5:17 but understand what the *L* will is.
2Ti 2:24 And the *L* servant must not quarrel
Heb 12: 5 light of the *L* discipline,
Jas 4:15 you ought to say, "If it is the *L* will,
5: 8 because the *L* coming is near.
1Pe 2:13 Submit yourselves for the *L* sake

LORDED* (LORD†)

Ne 5:15 Their assistants also *l* it

LORDING* (LORD†)

1Pe 5: 3 not *l* it over those entrusted to you,

LORD‡ (LORD'S‡)

Ge 2: 4 When the *L* God made the earth
2: 7 the *L* God formed the man
2:22 Then the *L* God made a woman
3:21 The *L* God made garments of skin
3:23 So the *L* God banished him
4: 4 The *L* looked with favor on Abel
4:26 began to call on the name of the *L*.
6: 7 So the *L* said, "I will wipe mankind
7:16 Then the *L* shut him in.
9:26 Blessed be the *L*, the God of Shem!
11: 9 there the *L* confused the language
12: 1 *L* had said to Abram, "Leave your
15: 6 Abram believed the *L*,
15:18 On that day the *L* made a covenant
17: 1 the *L* appeared to him and said,
18: 1 The *L* appeared to Abraham
18:14 Is anything too hard for the *L*?
18:19 way of the *L* by doing what is right
21: 1 Now the *L* was gracious to Sarah
22:14 that place The *L* Will Provide.
24: 1 the *L* had blessed him in every way
26: 2 The *L* appeared to Isaac and said,
28:13 There above it stood the *L*,
31:49 "May the *L* keep watch
39: 2 The *L* was with Joseph
39:21 in the prison, the *L* was with him;
Ex 3: 2 the angel of the *L* appeared to him
4:11 Is it not I, the *L*? Now go;
4:31 heard that the *L* was concerned
6: 2 also said to Moses, "I am the *L*.
9:12 the *L* hardened Pharaoh's heart
12:27 'It is the Passover sacrifice to the *L*,
12:43 The *L* said to Moses and Aaron,
13: 9 For the *L* brought you out of Egypt
13:21 By day the *L* went ahead of them
14:13 the deliverance the *L* will bring
14:30 That day the *L* saved Israel
15: 3 The *L* is a warrior;
15:11 among the gods is like you, O *L*?
15:26 for I am the *L*, who heals you."
16:12 know that I am the *L* your God.'"
16:23 day of rest, a holy Sabbath to the *L*.
17:15 and called it The *L* is my Banner.
19: 8 will do everything the *L* has said."
19:20 The *L* descended to the top
20: 2 "I am the *L* your God, who
20: 5 the *L* your God, am a jealous God,
20: 7 for the *L* will not hold anyone
20:10 a Sabbath to the *L* your God.
20:11 in six days the *L* made the heavens
20:12 in the land the *L* your God is giving
23:25 Worship the *L* your God,
24: 3 "Everything the *L* has said we will
24:12 The *L* said to Moses, "Come up
24:16 and the glory of the *L* settled
25: 1 The *L* said to Moses, "Tell
28:36 HOLY TO THE *L*.
30:11 Then the *L* said to Moses,
31:13 so you may know that I am the *L*,
31:18 When the *L* finished speaking
33:11 The *L* would speak to Moses face
33:19 And the *L* said, "I will cause all my
34: 1 *L* said to Moses, "Chisel out two
34: 6 proclaiming, "The *L*, the *L*,
34:10 awesome is the work that I, the *L*,
34:29 because he had spoken with the *L*.
40:34 glory of the *L* filled the tabernacle.
40:38 So the cloud of the *L* was
Lev 8:36 did everything the *L* commanded
9:23 and the glory of the *L* appeared
10: 2 and they died before the *L*.
19: 2 'Be holy because I, the *L* your God,
20: 8 I am the *L*, who makes you holy.
20:26 to be holy to me because I, the *L*,
23:40 and rejoice before the *L* your God
Nu 6:24 Say to them: "'"The *L* bless you
8: 5 *L* said to Moses: "Take the Levites
11: 1 hardships in the hearing of the *L*,
14:14 O *L*, have been seen face to face,
14:18 you have declared: 'The *L* is slow
14:21 glory of the *L* fills the whole earth,
21: 6 Then the *L* sent venomous snakes
22:31 Then the *L* opened Balaam's eyes,
23:12 "Must I not speak what the *L* puts
30: 2 When a man makes a vow to the *L*
32:12 followed the *L* wholeheartedly.'
Dt 1:21 and take possession of it as the *L*,
2: 7 forty years the *L* your God has
4:29 there you seek the *L* your God,
5: 6 And he said: "I am the *L* your God,
5: 9 the *L* your God, am a jealous God,
6: 4 The *L* our God, the *L* is one.
6: 5 Love the *L* your God
6:16 Do not test the *L* your God
6:25 law before the *L* our God,
7: 1 When the *L* your God brings you
7: 6 holy to the *L* your God.
7: 8 But it was because the *L* loved you
7: 9 that the *L* your God is God;
7:12 then the *L* your God will keep his
8: 5 so the *L* your God disciplines you.
9:10 The *L* gave me two stone tablets
10:12 but to fear the *L* your God,
10:14 To the *L* your God belong
10:17 For the *L* your God is God of gods
10:20 Fear the *L* your God and serve him
10:22 now the *L* your God has made you
11: 1 Love the *L* your God and keep his
11:13 to love the *L* your God
16: 1 the Passover of the *L* your God,
17:15 the king the *L* your God chooses.
28: 1 If you fully obey the *L* your God
28:15 if you do not obey the *L* your God
29: 1 covenant the *L* commanded Moses
29:29 things belong to the *L* our God,
30: 4 from there the *L* your God will
30: 6 *L* your God will circumcise your
30:10 if you obey the *L* your God
30:16 today to love the *L* your God,
30:20 For the *L* is your life, and he will
31: 6 for the *L* your God goes with you;
34: 5 of the *L* died there in Moab,
Jos 10:14 a day when the *L* listened to a man.
22: 5 to love the *L* your God, to walk
23:11 careful to love the *L* your God.
24:15 my household, we will serve the *L*
24:18 We too will serve the *L*,
Jdg 2:12 They forsook the *L*, the God
Ru 1: 8 May the *L* show kindness to you,
4:13 And the *L* enabled her to conceive,
1Sa 1:11 him to the *L* for all the days
1:15 I was pouring out my soul to the *L*.
1:28 So now I give him to the *L*.
2: 2 "There is no one holy like the *L*;
2:25 but if a man sins against the *L*,
2:26 in favor with the *L* and with men.
3: 9 *L*, for your servant is listening.'"
3:19 The *L* was with Samuel
7:12 "Thus far has the *L* helped us."
9:17 sight of Saul, the *L* said to him,
11:15 as king in the presence of the *L*.
12:18 all the people stood in awe of the *L*
12:22 his great name the *L* will not reject
12:24 But be sure to fear the *L*
13:14 the *L* has sought out a man
14: 6 Nothing can hinder the *L*
15:22 "Does the *L* delight
16:13 Spirit of the *L* came upon David
17:45 you in the name of the *L* Almighty,
2Sa 6:14 danced before the *L*
7:22 How great you are, O Sovereign *L*!
8: 6 *L* gave David victory everywhere
12: 7 This is what the *L*, the God
22: 2 "The *L* is my rock, my fortress
22:29 You are my lamp, O *L*;
22:31 the word of the *L* is flawless.
1Ki 1:30 today what I swore to you by the *L*,
2: 3 and observe what the *L* your God
3: 7 O *L* my God, you have made your
5: 5 for the Name of the *L* my God,
5:12 The *L* gave Solomon wisdom,
8:11 the glory of the *L* filled his temple.
8:23 toward heaven and said: "O *L*,
8:61 fully committed to the *L* our God,
9: 3 The *L* said to him: "I have heard
10: 9 Praise be to the *L* your God,
15:14 committed to the *L* all his life.
18:21 If the *L* is God, follow him;
18:36 "O *L*, God of Abraham, Isaac
18:39 "The *L*— he is God! The *L*—
21:23 also concerning Jezebel the *L* says:

‡This entry represents the translation of the Hebrew name for God, *Yahweh*, always indicated in the NIV by LORD. For Lord, see the concordance entries **LORD†** and **LORD'S†**.

2Ki 13:23 But the L was gracious to them
17:18 So the L was very angry with Israel
18: 5 Hezekiah trusted in the L,
19: 1 and went into the temple of the L.
20:11 L made the shadow go back the ten
21:12 Therefore this is what the L,
22: 2 right in the eyes of the L
22: 8 of the Law in the temple of the L."
23: 3 to follow the L and keep his
23:21 the Passover to the L your God,
23:25 a king like him who turned to the L
24: 2 The L sent Babylonian, Aramean,
24: 4 and the L was not willing to forgive
1Ch 10:13 because he was unfaithful to the L;
11: 3 with them at Hebron before the L,
11: 9 the L Almighty was with him.
13: 6 from there the ark of God the L, who
16: 8 Give thanks to the L, call
16:11 Look to the L and his strength;
16:14 He is the L our God;
16:23 Sing to the L, all the earth;
17: 1 covenant of the L is under a tent."
21:24 take for the L what is yours,
22: 5 to be built for the L should be
22:11 build the house of the L your God,
22:13 and laws that the L gave Moses
22:16 Now begin the work, and the L be
22:19 soul to seeking the L your God.
25: 7 and skilled in music for the L—
28: 9 for the L searches every heart
28:20 for the L God, my God, is with you
29: 1 not for man but for the L God.
29:11 O L, is the greatness and the power
29:18 O L, God of our fathers Abraham,
29:25 The L highly exalted Solomon
2Ch 1: 1 for the L his God was with him
5:13 to give praise and thanks to the L.
5:14 the glory of the L filled the temple
6:16 "Now L, God of Israel, keep
6:41 O L God, and come
6:42 O L God, do not reject your
7: 1 the glory of the L filled the temple.
7:12 the L appeared to him at night
7:21 'Why has the L done such a thing
9: 8 as king to rule for the L your God.
13:12 do not fight against the L,
14: 2 right in the eyes of the L his God.
15:14 to the L with loud acclamation,
16: 9 of the L range throughout the earth
17: 9 the Book of the Law of the L;
18:13 said, "As surely as the L lives,
19: 6 judging for man but for the L,
19: 9 wholeheartedly in the fear of the L.
20:15 This is what the L says to you:
20:20 Have faith in the L your God
20:21 appointed men to sing to the L
26: 5 As long as he sought the L,
26:16 He was unfaithful to the L his God,
29:30 to praise the L with the words
30: 9 for the L your God is gracious
31:20 and faithful before the L his God.
32: 8 with us is the L our God to help us
34:14 Law of the L that had been given
34:31 to follow the L and keep his
Ezr 3:10 foundation of the temple of the L,
7: 6 for the hand of the L his God was
7:10 observance of the Law of the L,
9: 5 hands spread out to the L my God
9: 8 the L our God has been gracious
9:15 O L, God of Israel, you are
Ne 1: 5 Then I said: "O L, God of heaven,
8: 1 which the L had commanded
9: 6 You alone are the L.
Job 1: 6 to present themselves before the L,
1:21 L gave and the L has taken away;
38: 1 the L answered Job out
42: 9 and the L accepted Job's prayer.
42:12 The L blessed the latter part
Ps 1: 2 But his delight is in the law of the L
1: 6 For the L watches over the way
4: 6 of your face shine upon us, O L.
4: 8 for you alone, O L,
5: 3 In the morning, O L,
6: 1 O L, do not rebuke me
8: 1 O L, our Lord,
9: 9 The L is a refuge for the oppressed,
9:19 Arise, O L, let not man triumph;
10:16 The L is King for ever and ever;
12: 6 And the words of the L are flawless
16: 5 L, you have assigned me my
16: 8 I have set the L always before me.
18: 1 I love you, O L, my strength.
18: 6 In my distress I called to the L;
18:30 the word of the L is flawless.
19: 7 The law of the L is perfect,
19:14 O L, my Rock and my Redeemer.
20: 5 May the L grant all your requests.
20: 7 in the name of the L our God.
22: 8 let the L rescue him.

Ps 23: 1 The L is my shepherd, I shall
23: 6 I will dwell in the house of the L
24: 3 Who may ascend the hill of the L?
24: 8 The L strong and mighty,
25:10 All the ways of the L are loving
27: 1 The L is my light and my salvation
27: 4 to gaze upon the beauty of the L
27: 6 I will sing and make music to the L.
29: 1 Ascribe to the L, O mighty ones,
29: 4 The voice of the L is powerful;
30: 4 Sing to the L, you saints of his;
31: 5 redeem me, O L, the God of truth.
32: 2 whose sin the L does not count
33: 1 joyfully to the L, you righteous;
33: 6 of the L were the heavens made,
33:12 is the nation whose God is the L,
33:18 But the eyes of the L are
34: 1 I will extol the L at all times;
34: 3 Glorify the L with me;
34: 4 I sought the L, and he answered me
34: 7 The angel of the L encamps
34: 8 Taste and see that the L is good;
34: 9 Fear the L, you his saints,
34:15 The eyes of the L are
34:18 The L is close to the brokenhearted
37: 4 Delight yourself in the L
37: 5 Commit your way to the L;
39: 4 "Show me, O L, my life's end
40: 1 I waited patiently for the L;
40: 5 Many, O L my God,
46: 8 Come and see the works of the L,
47: 2 How awesome is the L Most High,
48: 1 Great is the L, and most worthy
50: 1 The Mighty One, God, the L,
55:22 Cast your cares on the L
59: 8 But you, O L, laugh at them;
68: 4 his name is the L—
68:18 O L God, might dwell there.
68:20 from the Sovereign L comes escape
69:31 This will please the L more
72:18 Praise be to the L God, the God
75: 8 In the hand of the L is a cup
78: 4 the praiseworthy deeds of the L,
84: 8 my prayer, O L God Almighty;
84:11 For the L God is a sun and shield;
85: 7 Show us your unfailing love, O L,
86:11 Teach me your way, O L,
87: 2 the L loves the gates of Zion
89: 5 heavens praise your wonders, O L,
89: 8 O L God Almighty, who is like you
91: 2 I will say of the L, "He is my refuge
92: 1 It is good to praise the L
92: 4 by your deeds, O L;
92:13 planted in the house of the L,
93: 1 The L reigns, he is robed in majesty
93: 5 house for endless days, O L.
94: 1 O L, the God who avenges,
94:12 is the man you discipline, O L,
94:18 your love, O L, supported me.
95: 1 Come, let us sing for joy to the L;
95: 3 For the L is the great God,
95: 6 let us kneel before the L our Maker
96: 1 Sing to the L a new song;
96: 5 but the L made the heavens.
96: 8 to the L the glory due his name;
96: 9 Worship the L in the splendor
96:13 they will sing before the L,
97: 1 The L reigns, let the earth be glad;
97: 9 O L, are the Most High
98: 1 Sing to the L a new song,
98: 2 L has made his salvation known
98: 4 Shout for joy to the L, all the earth,
99: 1 The L reigns,
99: 2 Great is the L in Zion;
99: 5 Exalt the L our God
99: 9 Exalt the L our God
100: 1 Shout for joy to the L, all the earth.
100: 2 Worship the L with gladness;
100: 3 Know that the L is God.
100: 5 For the L is good and his love
101: 1 to you, O L, I will sing praise.
102: 12 But you, O L, sit enthroned forever
103: 1 Praise the L, O my soul;
103: 8 The L is compassionate
103: 19 The L has established his throne
104: 1 O L my God, you are very great;
104: 24 How many are your works, O L!
104: 33 I will sing to the L all my life;
105: 4 Look to the L and his strength;
105: 7 He is the L our God;
106: 2 proclaim the mighty acts of the L
107: 1 Give thanks to the L, for he is good
107: 8 to the L for his unfailing love
107: 21 to the L for his unfailing love
107: 43 and consider the great love of the L
108: 3 I will praise you, O L,
109: 26 Help me, O L my God;
110: 1 The L says to my Lord:
110: 4 The L has sworn

Ps 111: 2 Great are the works of the L;
111: 4 L is gracious and compassionate.
111: 10 The fear of the L is the beginning
112: 1 Blessed is the man who fears the L,
113: 1 Praise, O servants of the L,
113: 2 Let the name of the L be praised,
113: 4 L is exalted over all the nations,
113: 5 Who is like the L our God,
115: 1 Not to us, O L, not to us
115: 18 it is we who extol the L,
116: 12 How can I repay the L
116: 15 Precious in the sight of the L
117: 1 Praise the L, all you nations;
118: 1 Give thanks to the L, for he is good
118: 5 In my anguish I cried to the L,
118: 8 It is better to take refuge in the L
118: 18 The L has chastened me severely,
118: 23 the L has done this,
118: 24 This is the day the L has made;
118: 26 comes in the name of the L.
119: 1 to the law of the L.
119: 64 with your love, O L;
119: 89 Your word, O L, is eternal;
119:126 It is time for you to act, O L;
119:159 O L, according to your love.
120: 1 I call on the L in my distress,
121: 2 My help comes from the L,
121: 5 The L watches over you—
121: 8 the L will watch over your coming
122: 1 "Let us go to the house of the L."
123: 2 so our eyes look to the L our God,
124: 1 If the L had not been on our side—
124: 8 Our help is in the name of the L,
125: 2 so the L surrounds his people
126: 3 The L has done great things for us,
126: 4 Restore our fortunes, O L,
127: 1 Unless the L builds the house,
127: 3 Sons are a heritage from the L,
128: 1 Blessed are all who fear the L,
130: 1 O L; O Lord, hear my voice.
130: 3 If you, O L, kept a record of sins,
130: 5 I wait for the L, my soul waits,
131: 3 O Israel, put your hope in the L
132: 1 O L, remember David
132: 13 For the L has chosen Zion,
133: 3 For there the L bestows his
134: 3 May the L, the Maker of heaven
135: 4 For the L has chosen Jacob
135: 6 The L does whatever pleases him,
136: 1 Give thanks to the L, for he is good
137: 4 How can we sing the songs of the L
138: 1 I will praise you, O L,
138: 8 The L will fulfill ⌊his purpose⌋
139: 1 O L, you have searched me
140: 1 Rescue me, O L, from evil men;
141: 1 O L, I call to you; come quickly
141: 3 Set a guard over my mouth, O L;
142: 5 I cry to you, O L;
143: 9 Rescue me from my enemies, O L,
144: 3 O L, what is man that you care
145: 3 Great is the L and most worthy
145: 8 L is gracious and compassionate,
145: 9 The L is good to all;
145: 17 The L is righteous in all his ways
145: 18 The L is near to all who call on him
146: 5 whose hope is in the L his God,
146: 7 The L sets prisoners free,
147: 2 The L builds up Jerusalem;
147: 7 Sing to the L with thanksgiving;
147: 11 L delights in those who fear him,
147: 12 Extol the L, O Jerusalem;
148: 1 Praise the L from the heavens,
148: 7 Praise the L from the earth,
149: 4 For the L takes delight
150: 1 Praise the L.
150: 6 that has breath praise the L.
Pr 1: 7 The fear of the L is the beginning
1:29 and did not choose to fear the L,
2: 5 will understand the fear of the L
2: 6 For the L gives wisdom,
3: 5 Trust in the L with all your heart
3: 7 fear the L and shun evil.
3: 9 Honor the L with your wealth,
3:12 the L disciplines those he loves,
3:19 By wisdom the L laid the earth's
5:21 are in full view of the L,
6:16 There are six things the L hates,
8:13 To fear the L is to hate evil;
9:10 "The fear of the L is the beginning
10:27 The fear of the L adds length to life
11: 1 The L abhors dishonest scales,
12:22 The L detests lying lips,
14: 2 whose walk is upright fears the L,
14:26 He who fears the L has a secure
14:27 The fear of the L is a fountain
15: 3 The eyes of the L are everywhere,
15:16 Better a little with the fear of the L
15:33 of the L teaches a man wisdom,
16: 2 but motives are weighed by the L.

Pr 16: 3 Commit to the *L* whatever you do,
16: 4 The *L* works out everything
16: 5 The *L* detests all the proud of heart
16: 9 but the *L* determines his steps.
16:33 but its every decision is from the *L*.
18:10 The name of the *L* is a strong tower
18:22 and receives favor from the *L*.
19:14 but a prudent wife is from the *L*.
19:17 to the poor lends to the *L*,
19:23 The fear of the *L* leads to life:
20:10 the *L* detests them both.
21: 2 but the *L* weighs the heart.
21: 3 to the *L* than sacrifice.
21:30 that can succeed against the *L*.
21:31 but victory rests with the *L*.
22: 2 The *L* is the Maker of them all.
22:23 for the *L* will take up their case
23:17 for the fear of the *L*.
24:18 or the *L* will see and disapprove
24:21 Fear the *L* and the king, my son,
25:22 and the *L* will reward you.
28:14 is the man who always fears the *L*,
29:26 from the *L* that man gets justice.
30: 7 "Two things I ask of you, O *L*;
31:30 a woman who fears the *L* is
Isa 2: 3 up to the mountain of the *L*,
2:10 the ground from dread of the *L*
3:17 the *L* will make their scalps bald."
4: 2 of the *L* will be beautiful
5:16 the *L* Almighty will be exalted
6: 3 holy, holy is the *L* Almighty;
9: 7 The zeal of the *L* Almighty
11: 2 The Spirit of the *L* will rest on him
11: 9 full of the knowledge of the *L*
12: 2 The *L*, the *L*, is my strength
18: 7 of the Name of the *L* Almighty.
24: 1 the *L* is going to lay waste the earth
25: 1 O *L*, you are my God;
25: 6 this mountain the *L* Almighty will
25: 8 The Sovereign *L* will wipe away
26: 4 Trust in the *L* forever,
26: 8 *L*, walking in the way of your laws,
26:13 O *L*, our God, other lords
26:21 the *L* is coming out of his dwelling
27: 1 the *L* will punish with his sword,
27:12 In that day the *L* will thresh
28: 5 In that day the *L* Almighty
29: 6 the *L* Almighty will come
29:15 to hide their plans from the *L*,
30:18 For the *L* is a God of justice.
30:26 when the *L* binds up the bruises
30:27 the Name of the *L* comes from afar
30:30 The *L* will cause men
33: 2 O *L*, be gracious to us;
33: 6 the fear of the *L* is the key
33:22 For the *L* is our judge,
34: 2 The *L* is angry with all nations;
35: 2 they will see the glory of the *L*,
35:10 the ransomed of the *L* will return.
38: 7 to you that the *L* will do what he
40: 3 the way for the *L*;
40: 5 the glory of the *L* will be revealed,
40: 7 the breath of the *L* blows on them.
40:10 the Sovereign *L* comes with power,
40:14 Whom did the *L* consult
40:28 The *L* is the everlasting God,
40:31 but those who hope in the *L*
41:14 will help you," declares the *L*,
41:20 that the hand of the *L* has done this
42: 6 the *L*, have called you
42: 8 "I am the *L*; that is my name!
42:13 The *L* will march out like a mighty
42:21 It pleased the *L*
43: 3 For I am the *L*, your God,
43:11 I, even I, am the *L*,
44: 6 "This is what the *L* says—
44:24 I am the *L*,
45: 5 I am the *L*, and there is no other;
45: 7 I, the *L*, do all these things.
45:21 Was it not I, the *L*?
48:17 "I am the *L* your God,
50: 4 Sovereign *L* has given me
50:10 Who among you fears the *L*
51: 1 and who seek the *L*:
51:11 The ransomed of the *L* will return.
51:15 the *L* Almighty is his name.
53: 1 the arm of the *L* been revealed?
53: 6 and the *L* has laid on him
53:10 and the will of the *L* will prosper
54: 5 the *L* Almighty is his name—
55: 6 Seek the *L* while he may be found;
55: 7 to the *L*, and he will have mercy
56: 6 who bind themselves to the *L*
58: 8 of the *L* will be your rear guard.
58:11 The *L* will guide you always;
59: 1 the arm of the *L* is not too short
60: 1 the glory of the *L* rises upon you.
60:16 Then you will know that I, the *L*,
60:20 the *L* will be your everlasting light,

Isa 61: 1 Spirit of the Sovereign *L* is on me,
61: 3 a planting of the *L*
61:10 I delight greatly in the *L*;
61:11 so the Sovereign *L* will make
62: 4 for the *L* will take delight in you,
63: 7 I will tell of the kindnesses of the *L*,
64: 8 Yet, O *L*, you are our Father.
66:15 See, the *L* is coming with fire,
Jer 1: 9 Then the *L* reached out his hand
2:19 when you forsake the *L* your God
3:25 sinned against the *L* our God,
4: 4 Circumcise yourselves to the *L*,
8: 7 the requirements of the *L*.
9:24 I am the *L*, who exercises kindness,
10: 6 No one is like you, O *L*;
10:10 But the *L* is the true God;
12: 1 You are always righteous, O *L*,
14: 7 O *L*, do something for the sake
14:20 O *L*, we acknowledge our
16:15 will say, 'As surely as the *L* lives,
16:19 O *L*, my strength and my fortress,
17: 7 is the man who trusts in the *L*,
17:10 "I the *L* search the heart
20:11 *L* is with me like a mighty warrior;
23: 6 The *L* Our Righteousness.
24: 7 heart to know me, that I am the *L*.
28: 9 as one truly sent by the *L* only
31:11 For the *L* will ransom Jacob
31:22 The *L* will create a new thing
31:34 his brother, saying, 'Know the *L*,'
32:27 I am the *L*, the God of all mankind.
33:16 The *L* Our Righteousness.'
36: 6 the words of the *L* that you wrote
40: 3 now the *L* has brought it about;
42: 3 Pray that the *L* your God will tell
42: 4 I will tell you everything the *L* says
42: 6 we will obey the *L* our God,
50: 4 go in tears to seek the *L* their God.
51:10 "'The *L* has vindicated us;
51:56 For the *L* is a God of retribution;
La 3:24 to myself, "The *L* is my portion;
3:25 *L* is good to those whose hope is
3:40 and let us return to the *L*.
Eze 1: 3 the word of the *L* came
1:28 of the likeness of the glory of the *L*.
4:14 Sovereign *L*! I have never defiled
10: 4 Then the glory of the *L* rose
15: 7 you will know that I am the *L*.
30: 3 the day of the *L* is near—
36:23 nations will know that I am the *L*,
37: 4 'Dry bones, hear the word of the *L*!
43: 4 glory of the *L* entered the temple
44: 4 LORD filling the temple of the *L*,
Da 9: 2 to the word of the *L* given
Hos 1: 7 horsemen, but by the *L* their God."
2:20 and you will acknowledge the *L*.
3: 1 as the *L* loves the Israelites,
3: 5 They will come trembling to the *L*
6: 1 "Come, let us return to the *L*.
6: 3 Let us acknowledge the *L*;
10:12 for it is time to seek the *L*,
12: 5 the *L* is his name of renown!
14: 1 O Israel, to the *L* your God.
Joel 1: 1 The word of the *L* that came
1:15 For the day of the *L* is near;
2: 1 for the day of the *L* is coming.
2:11 The day of the *L* is great;
2:13 Return to the *L* your God,
2:23 rejoice in the *L* your God,
2:31 the great and dreadful day of the *L*.
2:32 on the name of the *L* will be saved;
3:14 For the day of the *L* is near
3:16 the *L* will be a refuge for his people,
Am 4:13 the *L* God Almighty is his name.
5: 6 Seek the *L* and live,
5:15 Perhaps the *L* God Almighty will
5:18 long for the day of the *L*?
7:15 *L* took me from tending the flock
8:12 searching for the word of the *L*,
9: 5 The Lord, the *L* Almighty,
Ob :15 "The day of the *L* is near
Jnh 1: 3 But Jonah ran away from the *L*
1: 4 the *L* sent a great wind on the sea,
1:17 But the *L* provided a great fish
2: 9 Salvation comes from the *L*."
4: 2 He prayed to the *L*, "O *L*,
4: 6 Then the *L* God provided a vine
Mic 1: 1 The word of the *L* that came to Micah
4: 2 up to the mountain of the *L*,
5: 4 flock in the strength of the *L*,
6: 2 For the *L* has a case
6: 8 And what does the *L* require of you
7: 7 as for me, I watch in hope for the *L*,
Na 1: 2 The *L* takes vengeance on his foes
1: 3 The *L* is slow to anger
Hab 2:14 knowledge of the glory of the *L*,
2:20 But the *L* is in his holy temple;
3: 2 I stand in awe of your deeds, O *L*.
Zep 1: 1 The word of the *L* that came

Zep 1: 7 for the day of the *L* is near.
3:17 The *L* your God is with you,
Hag 1: 1 the word of the *L* came
1: 8 and be honored," says the *L*.
2:23 that day,' declares the *L* Almighty,
Zec 1: 1 the word of the *L* came
1:17 and the *L* will again comfort Zion
3: 1 standing before the angel of the *L*,
4: 6 by my Spirit,' says the *L* Almighty.
6:12 and build the temple of the *L*.
8:21 the *L* and seek the *L* Almighty.
9:16 The *L* their God will save them
14: 5 Then the *L* my God will come,
14: 9 The *L* will be king
14:16 the *L* Almighty, and to celebrate
Mal 1: 1 The word of the *L* to Israel
3: 6 "I the *L* do not change.
4: 5 and dreadful day of the *L* comes.

LORD'S‡ (LORD‡)

Ex 4:14 the *L* anger burned against Moses
12:11 Eat it in haste; it is the *L* Passover.
34:34 he entered the *L* presence
Lev 23: 4 " 'These are the *L* appointed feasts,
Nu 9:23 At the *L* command they encamped
14:41 you disobeying the *L* command?
32:13 The *L* anger burned against Israel
Dt 6:18 is right and good in the *L* sight,
10:13 and to observe the *L* commands
32: 9 For the *L* portion is his people,
Jos 21:45 Not one of all the *L* good promises
1Sa 24:10 because he is the *L* anointed.'
1Ki 10: 9 Because of the *L* eternal love
Ps 24: 1 The earth is the *L*, and everything
32:10 but the *L* unfailing love
89: 1 of the *L* great love forever;
103: 17 *L* love is with those who fear him,
118: 15 "The *L* right hand has done mighty
Pr 3:11 do not despise the *L* discipline
19:21 but it is the *L* purpose that prevails.
Isa 24:14 west they acclaim the *L* majesty.
30: 9 to listen to the *L* instruction.
49: 4 Yet what is due me is in the *L* hand
53:10 Yet it was the *L* will to crush him
55:13 This will be for the *L* renown,
61: 2 to proclaim the year of the *L* favor
62: 3 of splendor in the *L* hand,
Jer 25:17 So I took the cup from the *L* hand
48:10 lax in doing the *L* work!
51: 7 was a gold cup in the *L* hand;
La 3:22 of the *L* great love we are not
Eze 7:19 them in the day of the *L* wrath.
Joel 3:18 will flow out of the *L* house
Ob :21 And the kingdom will be the *L*.
Mic 4: 1 of the *L* temple will be established
6: 2 O mountains, the *L* accusation;
Hab 2:16 from the *L* right hand is coming
Zep 2: 3 sheltered on the day of the *L* anger.

LOSE (LOSES LOSS LOST)

Dt 1:28 Our brothers have made us *l* heart.
1Sa 17:32 "Let no one *l* heart on account
Isa 7: 4 Do not *l* heart because of these two
Mt 10:39 Whoever finds his life will *l* it,
Lk 9:25 and yet *l* or forfeit his very self?
Jn 6:39 that I shall *l* none of all that he has
2Co 4: 1 this ministry, we do not *l* heart.
4:16 Therefore we do not *l* heart.
Heb 12: 3 will not grow weary and *l* heart.
12: 5 do not *l* heart when he rebukes you
2Jn : 8 that you do not *l* what you have

LOSES (LOSE)

Mt 5:13 But if the salt *l* its saltiness,
Lk 15: 4 you has a hundred sheep and *l* one
15: 8 has ten silver coins and *l* one.

LOSS (LOSE)

Ro 11:12 and their *l* means riches
1Co 3:15 he will suffer *l*; he himself will be
Php 3: 8 I consider everything a *l* compared

LOST (LOSE)

Ps 73: 2 I had nearly *l* my foothold.
Jer 50: 6 "My people have been *l* sheep;
Eze 34: 4 the strays or searched for the *l*.
34:16 for the *l* and bring back the strays.
Mt 18:14 any of these little ones should be *l*.
Lk 15: 4 go after the *l* sheep until he finds it?
15: 6 with me; I have found my *l* sheep.'
15: 9 with me; I have found my *l* coin.'
15:24 is alive again; he was *l* and is found
19:10 to seek and to save what was *l*."
Php 3: 8 for whose sake I have *l* all things.

LOT (LOTS)

Nephew of Abraham (Ge 11:27; 12:5). Chose to live in Sodom (Ge 13). Rescued from four kings (Ge 14). Rescued from Sodom (Ge 19:1-29; 2Pe 2:7). Fathered Moab and Ammon by his daughters (Ge 19:30-38).

Est 3: 7 the l) in the presence of Haman
9:24 the l) for their ruin and destruction.
Pr 16:33 The l is cast into the lap,
18:18 Casting the l settles disputes
Ecc 3:22 his work, because that is his l.
Ac 1:26 Then they cast lots, and the l fell

LOTS (LOT)

Jos 18:10 Joshua then cast l for them
Ps 22:18 and cast l for my clothing.
Joel 3: 3 They cast l for my people
Ob :11 and cast l for Jerusalem,
Mt 27:35 divided up his clothes by casting l.
Ac 1:26 Then they cast l, and the lot fell

LOVE* (BELOVED LOVED LOVELY LOVER LOVER'S LOVERS LOVES LOVING LOVING-KINDNESS)

Ge 20:13 'This is how you can show your l
22: 2 your only son, Isaac, whom you l,
29:18 Jacob was in l with Rachel and said
29:20 days to him because of his l for her.
29:32 Surely my husband will l me now."
Ex 15:13 "In your unfailing l you will lead
20: 6 showing l to a thousand generations
20: 6 of those who l me
21: 5 'I l my master and my wife
34: 6 abounding in l and faithfulness,
34: 7 maintaining l to thousands,
Lev 19:18 but l your neighbor as yourself.
19:34 L him as yourself,
Nu 14:18 abounding in l and forgiving sin
14:19 In accordance with your great l,
Dt 5:10 showing l to a thousand generations
5:10 of those who l me
6: 5 L the LORD your God
7: 9 generations of those who l him
7: 9 keeping his covenant of l
7:12 God will keep his covenant of l
7:13 He will l you and bless you
10:12 to walk in all his ways, to l him,
10:19 you are to l those who are aliens,
11: 1 L the LORD your God
11:13 to l the LORD your God
11:22 to l the LORD your God,
13: 3 you l him with all your heart
13: 6 wife you l, or your closest friend
19: 9 to l the LORD your God
21:15 the son of the wife he does not l,
21:16 the son of the wife he does not l.
30: 6 so that you may l him
30:16 today to l the LORD your God,
30:20 and that you may l the LORD your
33: 3 Surely it is you who l the people;
Jos 22: 5 to l the LORD your God, to walk
23:11 careful to l the LORD your God.
Jdg 5:31 may they who l you be like the sun
14:16 You hate me! You don't really l me
16: 4 he fell in l with a woman
16:15 "How can you say, 'I l you,'
1Sa 18:20 Saul's daughter Michal was in l
20:17 had David reaffirm his oath out of l
2Sa 1:26 Your l for me was wonderful,
7:15 But my l will never be taken away
13: 1 son of David fell in l with Tamar,
13: 4 said to him, "I'm in l with Tamar,
16:17 "Is this the l you show your friend?
19: 6 You l those who hate you
19: 6 hate you and hate those who l you.
1Ki 3: 3 Solomon showed his l
8:23 you who keep your covenant of l
10: 9 of the LORD's eternal l for Israel,
11: 2 Solomon held fast to them in l.
1Ch 16:34 his l endures forever.
16:41 "for his l endures forever."
17:13 I will never take my l away
2Ch 5:13 his l endures forever."
6:14 you who keep your covenant of l
6:42 Remember the great l promised
7: 3 his l endures forever."
7: 6 saying, "His l endures forever."
7: 8 Because of the l of your God
19: 2 and l those who hate the LORD?
20:21 for his l endures forever."
Ezr 3:11 his l to Israel endures forever."
Ne 1: 5 covenant of l with those who l him
9:17 slow to anger and abounding in l.
9:32 who keeps his covenant of l,
13:22 to me according to your great l.
Job 15:34 of those who l bribes.
19:19 those I l have turned against me.
37:13 or to water his earth and show his l.
Ps 4: 2 How long will you l delusions
5:11 that those who l your name may
6: 4 save me because of your unfailing l.
11: 5 wicked and those who l violence
13: 5 But I trust in your unfailing l;
17: 7 Show the wonder of your great l,

Ps 18: 1 I l you, O LORD, my strength.
21: 7 through the unfailing l
23: 6 Surely goodness and l will follow
25: 6 O LORD, your great mercy and l,
25: 7 according to your l remember me,
26: 3 for your l is ever before me,
26: 8 I l the house where you live,
31: 7 I will be glad and rejoice in your l,
31:16 save me in your unfailing l.
31:21 for he showed his wonderful l
31:23 L the LORD, all his saints!
32:10 but the LORD's unfailing l
33: 5 the earth is full of his unfailing l.
33:18 whose hope is in his unfailing l,
33:22 May your unfailing l rest upon us,
36: 5 Your l, O LORD, reaches
36: 7 How priceless is your unfailing l!
36:10 Continue your l to those who know
40:10 I do not conceal your l
40:11 may your l and your truth always
40:16 may those who l your salvation
42: 8 By day the LORD directs his l,
44:26 of your unfailing l.
45: 7 You l righteousness and hate
48: 9 we meditate on your unfailing l.
51: 1 according to your unfailing l;
52: 3 You l evil rather than good,
52: 4 You l every harmful word,
52: 8 I trust in God's unfailing l
57: 3 God sends his l and his faithfulness
57:10 For great is your l, reaching
59:16 in the morning I will sing of your l;
60: 5 that those you l may be delivered.
61: 7 appoint your l and faithfulness
63: 3 Because your l is better than life,
66:20 or withheld his l from me!
69:13 in your great l, O God,
69:16 out of the goodness of your l;
69:36 and those who l his name will dwell
70: 4 may those who l your salvation
77: 8 Has his unfailing l vanished forever
85: 7 Show us your unfailing l, O LORD
85:10 L and faithfulness meet together;
86: 5 abounding in l to all who call
86:13 For great is your l toward me;
86:15 abounding in l and faithfulness.
88:11 Is your l declared in the grave,
89: 1 of the LORD's great l forever;
89: 2 declare that your l stands firm
89:14 l and faithfulness go before you.
89:24 My faithful l will be with him,
89:28 I will maintain my l to him forever,
89:33 but I will not take my l from him,
89:49 where is your former great l,
90:14 with your unfailing l,
92: 2 to proclaim your l in the morning
94:18 your l, O LORD, supported me.
97:10 Let those who l the LORD hate
98: 3 He has remembered his l
100: 5 is good and his l endures forever;
101: 1 I will sing of your l and justice;
103: 4 crowns you with l and compassion.
103: 8 slow to anger, abounding in l.
103: 11 so great is his l for those who fear
103: 17 LORD's l is with those who fear
106: 1 his l endures forever.
106: 45 and out of his great l he relented.
107: 1 his l endures forever.
107: 8 to the LORD for his unfailing l
107: 15 to the LORD for his unfailing l
107: 21 to the LORD for his unfailing l
107: 31 to the LORD for his unfailing l
107: 43 consider the great l of the LORD.
108: 4 For great is your l, higher
108: 6 that those you l may be delivered.
109: 21 out of the goodness of your l,
109: 26 save me in accordance with your l.
115: 1 because of your l and faithfulness.
116: 1 I l the LORD, for he heard my
117: 2 For great is his l toward us,
118: 1 his l endures forever.
118: 2 "His l endures forever."
118: 3 "His l endures forever."
118: 4 "His l endures forever."
118: 29 his l endures forever.
119: 41 May your unfailing l come to me,
119: 47 because I l them.
119: 48 to your commands, which I l,
119: 64 The earth is filled with your l,
119: 76 May your unfailing l be my
119: 88 my life according to your l,
119: 97 Oh, how I l your law!
119:113 but I l your law.
119:119 therefore I l your statutes.
119:124 your servant according to your l
119:127 Because I l your commands
119:132 to those who l your name.
119:149 in accordance with your l;
119:159 O LORD, according to your l.

Ps 119:159 See how I l your precepts;
119:163 but I l your law.
119:165 peace have they who l your law,
119:167 for I l them greatly.
122: 6 "May those who l you be secure.
130: 7 for with the LORD is unfailing l
136: 1 -26 His l endures forever.
138: 2 for your l and your faithfulness,
138: 8 your l, O LORD, endures forever
143: 8 of your unfailing l,
143: 12 In your unfailing l, silence my
145: 8 slow to anger and rich in l.
145: 20 over all who l him,
147: 11 who put their hope in his unfailing l
Pr 1:22 you simple ones l your simple
3: 3 Let l and faithfulness never leave
4: 6 l her, and she will watch over you.
5:19 you ever be captivated by her l.
7:18 let's drink deep of l till morning;
7:18 let's enjoy ourselves with l!
8:17 I l those who l me,
8:21 wealth on those who l me
8:36 all who hate me l death."
9: 8 rebuke a wise man and he will l you
10:12 but l covers over all wrongs.
14:22 those who plan what is good find l
15:17 of vegetables where there is l
16: 6 Through l and faithfulness sin is
17: 9 over an offense promotes l,
18:21 and those who l it will eat its fruit.
19:22 What a man desires is unfailing l;
20: 6 claims to have unfailing l,
20:13 Do not l sleep or you will grow
20:28 L and faithfulness keep a king safe;
20:28 through l his throne is made secure
21:21 who pursues righteousness and l
27: 5 rebuke than hidden l.
Ecc 3: 8 a time to l and a time to hate,
9: 1 but no man knows whether l
9: 6 Their l, their hate
9: 9 life with your wife, whom you l,
SS 1: 2 for your l is more delightful
1: 3 No wonder the maidens l you!
1: 4 we will praise your l more
1: 7 you whom I l, where you graze
2: 4 and his banner over me is l.
2: 5 for I am faint with l.
2: 7 Do not arouse or awaken l
3: 5 Do not arouse or awaken l
4:10 How delightful is your l, my sister,
4:10 How much more pleasing is your l
5: 8 Tell him I am faint with l.
7: 6 O l, with your delights!
7:12 there I will give you my l.
8: 4 Do not arouse or awaken l
8: 6 for l is as strong as death,
8: 7 Many waters cannot quench l;
8: 7 all the wealth of his house for l,
Isa 1:23 they all l bribes
5: 1 I will sing for the one I l
16: 5 In l a throne will be established;
38:17 In your l you kept me
43: 4 and because I l you,
54:10 yet my unfailing l for you will not
55: 3 my faithful l promised to David.
56: 6 to l the name of the LORD,
56:10 they l to sleep.
57: 8 a pact with those whose beds you l,
61: 8 "For I, the LORD, l justice;
63: 9 In his l and mercy he redeemed
66:10 all you who l her;
Jer 2:25 I l foreign gods,
2:33 How skilled you are at pursuing l!
5:31 and my people l it this way.
12: 7 I will give the one I l
14:10 "They greatly l to wander;
16: 5 my l and my pity from this people
31: 3 you with an everlasting l;
32:18 You show l to thousands
33:11 his l endures forever."
La 3:22 of the LORD's great l we are not
3:32 so great is his unfailing l.
Eze 16: 8 saw that you were old enough for l,
23:17 of l, and in their lust they defiled
33:32 more than one who sings l songs
Da 9: 4 covenant of l with all who l him
Hos 1: 6 for I will no longer show l
1: 7 Yet I will show l to the house
2: 4 I will not show my l to her children
2:19 in l and compassion.
2:23 I will show my l to the one I called
3: 1 Go, show your l to your wife again,
3: 1 and l the sacred raisin cakes."
3: 1 L her as the LORD loves
4: 1 "There is no faithfulness, no l,
4:18 their rulers dearly l shameful ways.
6: 4 Your l is like the morning mist,
9: 1 you l the wages of a prostitute
9:15 I will no longer l them;

Hos 10:12 reap the fruit of unfailing l,
11: 4 with ties of l;
12: 6 maintain l and justice,
14: 4 and l them freely,
Joel 2:13 slow to anger and abounding in l,
Am 4: 5 for this is what you l to do,"
5:15 Hate evil, l good;
Jnh 4: 2 slow to anger and abounding in l,
Mic 3: 2 you who hate good and l evil;
6: 8 To act justly and to l mercy
Zep 3:17 he will quiet you with his l,
Zec 8:17 and do not l to swear falsely.
8:19 Therefore l truth and peace."
Mt 3:17 "This is my Son, whom I l;
5:43 'L your neighbor and hate your
5:44 L your enemies and pray
5:46 you l those who l you, what reward
6: 5 for they l to pray standing
6:24 he will hate the one and l the other,
12:18 the one I l, in whom I delight;
17: 5 "This is my Son, whom I l;
19:19 and 'l your neighbor as yourself.' "
22:37 " 'L the Lord your God
22:39 'L your neighbor as yourself.'
23: 6 they l the place of honor
23: 7 they l to be greeted
24:12 the l of most will grow cold,
Mk 1:11 "You are my Son, whom I l;
9: 7 "This is my Son, whom I l.
12:30 L the Lord your God
12:31 'L your neighbor as yourself.'
12:33 To l him with all your heart,
12:33 and to l your neighbor
Lk 3:22 "You are my Son, whom I l;
6:27 you who hear me: L your enemies,
6:32 Even 'sinners' l those who l them.
6:32 you l those who l you, what credit
6:35 l your enemies, do good to them,
7:42 which of them will l him more?"
10:27 and, 'L your neighbor as yourself
10:27 " 'L the Lord your God
11:42 you neglect justice and the l of God
11:43 you l the most important seats
16:13 he will hate the one and l the other,
20:13 whom I l; perhaps they will respect
20:46 l to be greeted in the marketplaces
Jn 5:42 I know that you do not have the l
8:42 were your Father, you would l me,
11: 3 "Lord, the one you l is sick."
13: 1 them the full extent of his l.
13:34 I give you: L one another.
13:34 so you must l one another.
13:35 disciples, if you l one another."
14:15 "If you l me, you will obey what I
14:21 I too will l him and show myself
14:23 My Father will l him, and we will
14:24 He who does not l me will not obey
14:31 world must learn that I l the Father
15: 9 Now remain in my l.
15:10 commands and remain in his l.
15:10 you will remain in my l,
15:12 L each other as I have loved you.
15:13 Greater l has no one than this,
15:17 This is my command: L each other.
15:19 to the world, it would l you
17:26 known in order that the l you have
21:15 do you truly l me more than these
21:15 he said, "you know that I l you."
21:16 Yes, Lord, you know that I l you."
21:16 do you truly l me?" He answered,
21:17 all things; you know that I l you."
21:17 "Do you l me?" He said, "Lord,
21:17 "Simon son of John, do you l me?"
Ro 5: 5 because God has poured out his l
5: 8 God demonstrates his own l for us
8:28 for the good of those who l him,
8:35 us from the l of Christ?
8:39 us from the l of God that is
12: 9 L must be sincere.
12:10 to one another in brotherly l.
13: 8 continuing debt to l one another,
13: 9 "L your neighbor as yourself."
13:10 Therefore l is the fulfillment
13:10 L does no harm to its neighbor.
14:15 you are no longer acting in l.
15:30 and by the l of the Spirit,
16: 8 Greet Ampliatus, whom I l
1Co 2: 9 prepared for those who l him"—
4:17 my son whom I l, who is faithful
4:21 or in l and with a gentle spirit?
8: 1 Knowledge puffs up, but l builds up
13: 1 have not l, I am only a resounding
13: 2 but have not l, I am nothing.
13: 3 but have not l, I gain nothing.
13: 4 Love is patient, l is kind.
13: 4 L is patient, love is kind.
13: 6 L does not delight in evil
13: 8 L never fails.
13:13 But the greatest of these is l.
1Co 13:13 three remain: faith, hope and l.
14: 1 way of l and eagerly desire spiritual
16:14 Do everything in l.
16:22 If anyone does not l the Lord—
16:24 My l to all of you in Christ Jesus.
2Co 2: 4 to let you know the depth of my l
2: 8 therefore, to reaffirm your l for him
5:14 For Christ's l compels us,
6: 6 in the Holy Spirit and in sincere l;
8: 7 complete earnestness and in your l
8: 8 sincerity of your l by comparing it
8:24 show these men the proof of your l
11:11 Why? Because I do not l you?
12:15 If I l you more, will you l me less?
13:11 And the God of l and peace will be
13:14 of the Lord Jesus Christ, and the l
Gal 5: 6 is faith expressing itself through l.
5:13 rather, serve one another in l.
5:14 "L your neighbor as yourself."
5:22 But the fruit of the Spirit is l, joy,
Eph 1: 4 In l he predestined us
1:15 and your l for all the saints,
2: 4 But because of his great l for us,
3:17 being rooted and established in l,
3:18 and high and deep is the l of Christ,
3:19 and to know this l that surpasses
4: 2 bearing with one another in l.
4:15 Instead, speaking the truth in l,
4:16 grows and builds itself up in l,
5: 2 loved children and live a life of l,
5:25 l your wives, just as Christ loved
5:28 husbands ought to l their wives
5:33 each one of you also must l his wife
6:23 l with faith from God the Father
6:24 Christ with an undying l.
6:24 to all who l our Lord Jesus Christ
Php 1: 9 that your l may abound more
1:16 so in l, knowing that I am put here
2: 1 from his l, if any fellowship
2: 2 having the same l, being one
4: 1 you whom I l and long for,
Col 1: 4 of the l you have for all the saints—
1: 5 l that spring from the hope that is
1: 8 also told us of your l in the Spirit.
2: 2 in heart and united in l,
3:14 And over all these virtues put on l,
3:19 l your wives and do not be harsh
1Th 1: 3 your labor prompted by l,
3: 6 good news about your faith and l.
3:12 May the Lord make your l increase
4: 9 about brotherly l we do not need
4: 9 taught by God to l each other.
4:10 you do l all the brothers
5: 8 on faith and l as a breastplate,
5:13 them in the highest regard in l
2Th 1: 3 and the l every one of you has
2:10 because they refused to l the truth
3: 5 direct your hearts into God's l
1Ti 1: 5 The goal of this command is l,
1:14 and l that are in Christ Jesus.
2:15 l and holiness with propriety.
4:12 in life, in l, in faith and in purity.
6:10 For the l of money is a root
6:11 faith, l, endurance and gentleness.
2Ti 1: 7 of power, of l and of self-discipline.
1:13 with faith and l in Christ Jesus.
2:22 and pursue righteousness, faith, l
3: 3 unholy, without l, unforgiving,
3:10 faith, patience, l, endurance,
Tit 2: 2 in faith, in l and in endurance.
2: 4 women to l their husbands
3: 4 and l of God our Savior appeared,
3:15 Greet those who l us in the faith.
Phm : 5 and your l for all the saints.
: 7 Your l has given me great joy
: 9 yet I appeal to you on the basis of l.
Heb 6:10 and the l you have shown him
10:24 may spur one another on toward l
13: 5 free from the l of money
Jas 1:12 promised to those who l him.
2: 5 he promised those who l him?
2: 8 "L your neighbor as yourself,"
1Pe 1: 8 you have not seen him, you l him;
1:22 the truth so that you have sincere l
1:22 l one another deeply,
2:17 L the brotherhood of believers,
3: 8 be sympathetic, l as brothers,
3:10 "Whoever would l life
4: 8 Above all, l each other deeply,
4: 8 l covers over a multitude of sins.
5:14 Greet one another with a kiss of l.
2Pe 1: 7 and to brotherly kindness, l.
1:17 "This is my Son, whom I l;
1Jn 2: 5 God's l is truly made complete
2:15 Do not l the world or anything
2:15 the l of the Father is not in him.
3: 1 How great is the l the Father has
3:10 anyone who does not l his brother.
3:11 We should l one another.
1Jn 3:14 Anyone who does not l remains
3:14 because we l our brothers.
3:16 This is how we know what l is:
3:17 how can the l of God be in him?
3:18 let us not l with words or tongue
3:23 to l one another as he commanded
4: 7 Dear friends, let us l one another,
4: 7 for l comes from God.
4: 8 Whoever does not l does not know
4: 8 not know God, because God is l.
4: 9 This is how God showed his l
4:10 This is l: not that we loved God,
4:11 we also ought to l one another.
4:12 seen God; but if we l one another,
4:12 and his l is made complete in us.
4:16 God is l.
4:16 Whoever lives in l lives in God,
4:16 and rely on the l God has for us.
4:17 l is made complete among us
4:18 But perfect l drives out fear,
4:18 There is no fear in l.
4:18 who fears is not made perfect in l.
4:19 We l because he first loved us.
4:20 If anyone says, "I l God,"
4:20 anyone who does not l his brother,
4:20 whom he has seen, cannot l God,
4:21 loves God must also l his brother.
5: 2 we know that we l the children
5: 3 This is l for God: to obey his
2Jn : 1 whom I l in the truth—
: 3 will be with us in truth and l.
: 5 I ask that we l one another.
: 6 his command is that you walk in l.
: 6 this is l: that we walk in obedience
3Jn : 1 To my dear friend Gaius, whom I l
: 6 have told the church about your l.
Jude : 2 peace and l be yours in abundance.
:12 men are blemishes at your l feasts,
:21 Keep yourselves in God's l
Rev 2: 4 You have forsaken your first l.
2:19 I know your deeds, your l and faith
3:19 Those whom I l I rebuke
12:11 they did not l their lives so much

LOVED* (LOVE)

Ge 24:67 she became his wife, and he l her;
25:28 l Esau, but Rebekah l Jacob.
29:30 and he l Rachel more than Leah.
29:31 the LORD saw that Leah was not l,
29:33 the LORD heard that I am not l,
34: 3 and he l the girl and spoke tenderly
37: 3 Now Israel l Joseph more than any
37: 4 saw that their father l him more
Dt 4:37 Because he l your forefathers
7: 8 But it was because the LORD l you
10:15 on your forefathers and l them,
1Sa 1: 5 a double portion because he l her,
18: 1 in spirit with David, and he l him
18: 3 with David because he l him
18:16 But all Israel and Judah l David,
18:28 that his daughter Michal l David,
20:17 because he l him as he l himself.
2Sa 1:23 in life they were l and gracious,
12:24 The LORD l him; and
12:25 and because the LORD l him,
13:15 hated her more than he had l her.
1Ki 11: 1 l many foreign women
2Ch 11:21 Rehoboam l Maacah daughter
26:10 in the fertile lands, for he l the soil.
Ne 13:26 He was l by his God, and God
Ps 44: 3 light of your face, for you l them.
47: 4 the pride of Jacob, whom he l.
78:68 Mount Zion, which he l.
88:18 taken my companions and l ones
109: 17 He l to pronounce a curse—
Isa 5: 1 My l one had a vineyard
Jer 2: 2 how as a bride you l me
8: 2 which they have l and served
31: 3 "I have l you with an everlasting
Eze 16:37 those you l as well as those you
Hos 2: 1 and of your sisters, 'My l one.'
2:23 to the one I called 'Not my l one.'
3: 1 though she is l by another
9:10 became as vile as the thing they l.
11: 1 "When Israel was a child, I l him,
Mal 1: 2 "But you ask, 'How have you l us?'
1: 2 "I have l you," says the LORD.
1: 2 "Yet I have l Jacob, but Esau I
Mk 10:21 Jesus looked at him and l him.
12: 6 left to send, a son, whom he l.
Lk 7:47 been forgiven—for she l much.
16:14 The Pharisees, who l money,
Jn 3:16 so l the world that he gave his one
3:19 but men l darkness instead of light
11: 5 Jesus l Martha and her sister
11:36 "See how he l him!" But some
12:43 for they l praise from men more
13: 1 Having l his own who were
13:23 the disciple whom Jesus l,

Jn 13:34 As I have *l* you, so you must love
14:21 He who loves me will be *l*
14:28 If you *l* me, you would be glad that
15: 9 the Father has *l* me, so have I *l* you.
15:12 Love each other as I have *l* you.
16:27 loves you because you have *l* me
17:23 have *l* them even as you have *l* me.
17:24 you *l* me before the creation
19:26 the disciple whom he *l* standing
20: 2 one Jesus *l*, and said, "They have
21: 7 the disciple whom Jesus *l* said
21:20 whom Jesus *l* was following
Ro 1: 7 To all in Rome who are *l* by God
8:37 conquerors through him who *l* us.
9:13 "Jacob I *l*, but Esau I hated."
9:25 her 'my *l* one' who is not my *l* one,"
11:28 they are *l* on account
Gal 2:20 who *l* me and gave himself for me.
Eph 5: 1 as dearly *l* children and live a life
5: 2 as Christ *l* us and gave himself up
5:25 just as Christ *l* the church
Col 3:12 and dearly *l*, clothe yourselves
1Th 1: 4 For we know, brothers *l* by God,
2: 8 We *l* you so much that we were
2Th 2:13 for you, brothers *l* by the Lord,
2:16 who *l* us and by his grace gave us
2Ti 4:10 for Demas, because he *l* this world,
Heb 1: 9 You have *l* righteousness
2Pe 2:15 who *l* the wages of wickedness.
1Jn 4:10 This is love: not that we *l* God,
4:10 but that he *l* us and sent his Son
4:11 Dear friends, since God so *l* us,
4:19 We love because he first *l* us.
Jude : 1 who are *l* by God the Father
Rev 3: 9 and acknowledge that I have *l* you.

LOVELY* (LOVE)
Ge 29:17 but Rachel was *l* in form,
Est 1:11 and nobles, for she was *l* to look at.
2: 7 was *l* in form and features,
Ps 84: 1 How *l* is your dwelling place,
SS 1: 5 Dark am I, yet *l*,
2:14 and your face is *l*.
4: 3 your mouth is *l*.
5:16 he is altogether *l*.
6: 4 *l* as Jerusalem,
Am 8:13 *l* young women and strong young
Php 4: 8 whatever is *l*, whatever is

LOVER* (LOVE)
SS 1:13 My *l* is to me a sachet of myrrh
1:14 My *l* is to me a cluster
1:16 How handsome you are, my *l*!
2: 3 is my *l* among the young men.
2: 8 Listen! My *l*!
2: 9 My *l* is like a gazelle or a young
2:10 My *l* spoke and said to me,
2:16 *Beloved* My *l* is mine and I am his;
2:17 turn, my *l*,
4:16 Let my *l* come into his garden
5: 2 Listen! My *l* is knocking:
5: 4 My *l* thrust his hand
5: 5 I arose to open for my *l*,
5: 6 I opened for my *l*,
5: 6 but my *l* had left; he was gone.
5: 8 if you find my *l*,
5:10 *Beloved* My *l* is radiant and ruddy,
5:16 This is my *l*, this my friend,
6: 1 Where has your *l* gone,
6: 1 Which way did your *l* turn,
6: 2 *Beloved* My *l* has gone
6: 3 I am my lover's and my *l* is mine;
7: 9 May the wine go straight to my *l*,
7:10 I belong to my *l*,
7:11 my *l*, let us go to the countryside,
7:13 that I have stored up for you, my *l*.
8: 5 leaning on her *l*?
8:14 *Beloved* Come away, my *l*,
1Ti 3: 3 not quarrelsome, not a *l* of money.

LOVER'S* (LOVE)
SS 6: 3 I am my *l* and my lover is mine;

LOVERS* (LOVE)
SS 5: 1 drink your fill, O *l*.
Jer 3: 1 as a prostitute with many *l*—
3: 2 the roadside you sat waiting for *l*,
4:30 Your *l* despise you;
La 1: 2 Among all her *l*
Eze 16:33 but you give gifts to all your *l*,
16:36 in your promiscuity with your *l*,
16:37 I am going to gather all your *l*,
16:39 Then I will hand you over to your *l*,
16:41 and you will no longer pay your *l*.
23: 5 she lusted after her *l*, the Assyrians
23: 9 I handed her over to her *l*,
23:20 There she lusted after her *l*,
23:22 I will stir up your *l* against you,
Hos 2: 5 She said, 'I will go after my *l*,
2: 7 She will chase after her *l*
2:10 lewdness before the eyes of her *l*;
2:12 she said were her pay from her *l*;
2:13 and went after her *l*,
8: 9 Ephraim has sold herself to *l*.
2Ti 3: 2 People will be *l* of themselves,
3: 2 *l* of money, boastful, proud,
3: 3 without self-control, brutal, not *l*
3: 4 *l* of pleasure rather than *l* of God—

LOVES* (LOVE)
Ge 44:20 sons left, and his father *l* him.'
Dt 10:18 and *l* the alien, giving him food
15:16 because he *l* you and your family
21:15 and he *l* one but not the other,
21:16 son of the wife he *l* in preference
23: 5 because the LORD your God *l* you
28:54 wife he *l* or his surviving children,
28:56 will begrudge the husband she *l*
33:12 and the one the LORD *l* rests
Ru 4:15 who *l* you and who is better to you
2Ch 2:11 "Because the LORD *l* his people,
Ps 11: 7 he *l* justice;
33: 5 The LORD *l* righteousness
34:12 Whoever of you *l* life
37:28 For the LORD *l* the just
87: 2 the LORD *l* the gates of Zion
91:14 Because he *l* me," says the LORD,
99: 4 The King is mighty, he *l* justice—
119:140 and your servant *l* them.
127: 2 for he grants sleep to those he *l*.
146: 8 the LORD *l* the righteous.
Pr 3:12 the LORD disciplines those he *l*,
12: 1 Whoever *l* discipline *l* knowledge,
13:24 he who *l* him is careful
15: 9 he *l* those who pursue
17:17 A friend *l* at all times,
17:19 He who *l* a quarrel *l* sin;
19: 8 He who gets wisdom *l* his own soul
21:17 He who *l* pleasure will become
21:17 whoever *l* wine and oil will never
22:11 He who *l* a pure heart and whose
29: 3 A man who *l* wisdom brings joy
Ecc 5:10 Whoever *l* money never has
5:10 whoever *l* wealth is never satisfied
SS 3: 1 I looked for the one my heart *l*;
3: 2 I will search for the one my heart *l*.
3: 3 "Have you seen the one my heart *l*
3: 4 when I found the one my heart *l*.
Hos 3: 1 as the LORD *l* the Israelites,
10:11 that *l* to thresh;
12: 7 he *l* to defraud.
Mal 2:11 the sanctuary the LORD *l*,
Mt 10:37 anyone who *l* his son or daughter
10:37 "Anyone who *l* his father
Lk 7: 5 because he *l* our nation
7:47 has been forgiven little *l* little."
Jn 3:35 Father *l* the Son and has placed
5:20 For the Father *l* the Son
10:17 reason my Father *l* me is that I lay
12:25 The man who *l* his life will lose it,
14:21 He who *l* me will be loved
14:21 obeys them, he is the one who *l* me.
14:23 Jesus replied, "If anyone *l* me,
16:27 the Father himself *l* you
Ro 13: 8 for he who *l* his fellowman has
1Co 8: 3 But the man who *l* God is known
2Co 9: 7 for God *l* a cheerful giver.
Eph 1: 6 has freely given us in the One he *l*.
5:28 He who *l* his wife *l* himself.
5:33 must love his wife as he *l* himself,
Col 1:13 us into the kingdom of the Son he *l*,
Tit 1: 8 one who *l* what is good, who is
Heb 12: 6 the Lord disciplines those he *l*,
1Jn 2:10 Whoever *l* his brother lives
2:15 If anyone *l* the world, the love
4: 7 Everyone who *l* has been born
4:21 Whoever *l* God must also love his
5: 1 who *l* the father *l* his child
3Jn : 9 but Diotrephes, who *l* to be first,
Rev 1: 5 To him who *l* us and has freed us
20: 9 camp of God's people, the city he *l*.
22:15 and everyone who *l* and practices

LOVING* (LOVE)
Ps 25:10 All the ways of the LORD are *l*
59:10 my *l* God.
59:17 O God, are my fortress, my *l* God.
62:12 and that you, O Lord, are *l*.
144: 2 He is my *l* God and my fortress,
145: 13 and *l* toward all he has made.
145: 17 and *l* toward all he has made.
Pr 5:19 A *l* doe, a graceful deer—
Heb 13: 1 Keep on *l* each other as brothers.
1Jn 5: 2 by *l* God and carrying out his

LOVING-KINDNESS* (LOVE)
Jer 31: 3 I have drawn you with *l*.

LOWER
Ps 8: 5 You made him a little *l*
2Co 11: 7 a sin for me to *l* myself in order
Heb 2: 7 You made him a little *l*

LOWING
1Sa 15:14 What is this *l* of cattle that I hear?"

LOWLY
Job 5:11 The *l* he sets on high,
Ps 138: 6 on high, he looks upon the *l*,
Pr 29:23 but a man of *l* spirit gains honor.
Isa 57:15 also with him who is contrite and *l*
Eze 21:26 *l* will be exalted and the exalted
1Co 1:28 He chose the *l* things of this world

LOYAL
1Ch 29:18 and keep their hearts *l* to you.
Ps 78: 8 whose hearts were not *l* to God,

LUKE*
Co-worker with Paul (Col 4:14; 2Ti 4:11; Phm 24).

LUKEWARM*
Rev 3:16 So, because you are *l*— neither hot

LUST (LUSTED LUSTS)
Pr 6:25 Do not *l* in your heart
Eze 20:30 and *l* after their vile images?
Col 3: 5 sexual immorality, impurity, *l*,
1Th 4: 5 not in passionate *l* like the heathen,
1Pe 4: 3 in debauchery, *l*, drunkenness,
1Jn 2:16 the *l* of his eyes and the boasting

LUSTED (LUST)
Eze 23: 5 she *l* after her lovers, the Assyrians

LUSTS* (LUST)
Nu 15:39 yourselves by going after the *l*
Ro 1:26 God gave them over to shameful *l*.

LUXURY
Jas 5: 5 You have lived on earth in *l*

LYDIA'S*
Ac 16:40 went to *L* house, where they met

LYING (LIE)
Pr 6:17 a *l* tongue,
12:22 The LORD detests *l* lips,
21: 6 A fortune made by a *l* tongue
26:28 A *l* tongue hates those it hurts,

MACEDONIA
Ac 16: 9 "Come over to *M* and help us."

MAD
Dt 28:34 The sights you see will drive you *m*

MADE (MAKE)
Ge 1: 7 So God *m* the expanse
1:16 God *m* two great lights—
1:16 He also *m* the stars.
1:25 God *m* the wild animals according
1:31 God saw all that he had *m*,
2:22 Then the LORD God *m* a woman
6: 6 was grieved that he had *m* man
9: 6 has God *m* man.
15:18 that day the LORD *m* a covenant
Ex 20:11 six days the LORD *m* the heavens
20:11 the Sabbath day and *m* it holy.
24: 8 the covenant that the LORD has *m*
32: 4 *m* it into an idol cast in the shape
Lev 16:34 Atonement is to be *m* once a year
Dt 32: 6 who *m* you and formed you?
Jos 24:25 On that day Joshua *m* a covenant
2Ki 19:15 You have *m* heaven and earth.
2Ch 2:12 the God of Israel, who *m* heaven
Ne 9: 6 You *m* the heavens,
9:10 You *m* a name for yourself,
Ps 33: 6 of the LORD were the heavens *m*,
95: 5 The sea is his, for he *m* it,
96: 5 but the LORD *m* the heavens.
100: 3 It is he who *m* us, and we are his;
118: 24 This is the day the LORD has *m*;
136: 7 who *m* the great lights—
139: 14 I am fearfully and wonderfully *m*;
Ecc 3:11 He has *m* everything beautiful
Isa 43: 7 whom I formed and *m*."
45:12 It is I who *m* the earth
45:18 he who fashioned and *m* the earth,
66: 2 Has not my hand *m* all these things
Jer 10:12 But God *m* the earth by his power;
27: 5 and outstretched arm I *m* the earth
32:17 you have *m* the heavens
33: 2 LORD says, he who *m* the earth,
51:15 "He *m* the earth by his power;
Eze 3:17 I have *m* you a watchman
33: 7 I have *m* you a watchman
Am 5: 8 (he who *m* the Pleiades and Orion,

Jnh 1: 9 who *m* the sea and the land."
Mk 2:27 "The Sabbath was *m* for man,
Jn 1: 3 Through him all things were *m*;
Ac 17:24 "The God who *m* the world
1Co 3: 6 watered it, but God *m* it grow.
Heb 1: 2 through whom he *m* the universe.
Jas 3: 9 who have been *m* in God's likeness
Rev 14: 7 Worship him who *m* the heavens,

MAGDALENE
Lk 8: 2 Mary (called *M)* from whom seven

MAGI
Mt 2: 1 *M* from the east came to Jerusalem

MAGIC (MAGICIANS)
Eze 13:20 I am against your *m* charms
Rev 21: 8 those who practice *m* arts,
22:15 those who practice *m* arts,

MAGICIANS (MAGIC)
Ex 7:11 the Egyptian *m* also did the same
Da 2: 2 So the king summoned the *m*,

MAGNIFICENCE* (MAGNIFICENT)
1Ch 22: 5 for the LORD should be of great *m*

MAGNIFICENT (MAGNIFICENCE)
1Ki 8:13 I have indeed built a *m* temple
Isa 28:29 in counsel and *m* in wisdom.
Mk 13: 1 stones! What *m* buildings!"

MAGOG
Eze 38: 2 of the land of *M*, the chief prince
39: 6 I will send fire on *M*
Rev 20: 8 and *M*— to gather them for battle.

MAIDEN (MAIDENS)
Pr 30:19 and the way of a man with a *m*.
Isa 62: 5 As a young man marries a *m*,
Jer 2:32 Does a *m* forget her jewelry,

MAIDENS (MAIDEN)
SS 1: 3 No wonder the *m* love you!

MAIMED
Mt 18: 8 It is better for you to enter life *m*

MAINTAIN (MAINTAINING)
Ps 82: 3 *m* the rights of the poor
106: 3 Blessed are they who *m* justice,
Hos 12: 6 *m* love and justice,
Am 5:15 *m* justice in the courts.
Ro 3:28 For we *m* that a man is justified

MAINTAINING* (MAINTAIN)
Ex 34: 7 faithfulness, *m* love to thousands,

MAJESTIC* (MAJESTY)
Ex 15: 6 was *m* in power.
15:11 *m* in holiness,
Job 37: 4 he thunders with his *m* voice.
Ps 8: 1 how *m* is your name in all the earth
8: 9 how *m* is your name in all the earth
29: 4 the voice of the LORD is *m*.
68:15 of Bashan are *m* mountains;
76: 4 more *m* than mountains rich
111: 3 Glorious and *m* are his deeds,
SS 6: 4 *m* as troops with banners.
6:10 *m* as the stars in procession?
Isa 30:30 men to hear his *m* voice
Eze 31: 7 It was *m* in beauty,
2Pe 1:17 came to him from the *M* Glory,

MAJESTY* (MAJESTIC)
Ex 15: 7 In the greatness of your *m*
Dt 5:24 has shown us his glory and his *m*,
11: 2 his *m*, his mighty hand, his
33:17 In *m* he is like a firstborn bull;
33:26 and on the clouds in his *m*.
1Ch 16:27 Splendor and *m* are before him;
29:11 and the *m* and the splendor,
Est 1: 4 the splendor and glory of his *m*.
7: 3 if it pleases your *m*, grant me my
Job 37:22 God comes in awesome *m*.
40:10 and clothe yourself in honor and *m*
Ps 21: 5 on him splendor and *m*.
45: 3 with splendor and *m*.
45: 4 In your *m* ride forth victoriously
68:34 whose *m* is over Israel,
93: 1 The LORD reigns, he is robed in *m*
93: 1 the LORD is robed in *m*
96: 6 Splendor and *m* are before him;
104: 1 clothed with splendor and *m*.
110: 3 Arrayed in holy *m*,
145: 5 of the glorious splendor of your *m*,
Isa 2:10 and the splendor of his *m!*
2:19 and the splendor of his *m*,
2:21 and the splendor of his *m*,
24:14 west they acclaim the LORD's *m*.
26:10 and regard not the *m* of the LORD.

Isa 53: 2 or *m* to attract us to him,
Eze 31: 2 can be compared with you in *m?*
31:18 with you in splendor and *m?*
Da 4:30 and for the glory of my *m?"*
Mic 5: 4 in the *m* of the name
Zec 6:13 and he will be clothed with *m*
Ac 19:27 will be robbed of her divine *m*."
25:26 to write to His *M* about him.
2Th 1: 9 and from the *m* of his power
Heb 1: 3 hand of the *M* in heaven.
8: 1 of the throne of the *M* in heaven,
2Pe 1:16 but we were eyewitnesses of his *m*.
Jude :25 only God our Savior be glory, *m*,

MAKE (MADE MAKER MAKERS MAKES MAKING MAN-MADE)
Ge 1:26 "Let us *m* man in our image,
2:18 I will *m* a helper suitable for him."
6:14 *m* yourself an ark of cypress wood;
12: 2 "I will *m* you into a great nation
Ex 22: 3 thief must certainly *m* restitution,
25: 9 *M* this tabernacle and all its
25:40 See that you *m* them according
Nu 6:25 the LORD *m* his face shine
2Sa 7: 9 Now I will *m* your name great,
Job 7:17 "What is man that you *m* so much
Ps 4: 8 *m* me dwell in safety.
20: 4 and *m* all your plans succeed.
108: 1 *m* music with all my soul.
110: 1 hand until I *m* your enemies
119:165 and nothing can *m* them stumble.
Pr 3: 6 and he will *m* your paths straight.
4:26 *M* level paths for your feet
20:18 *M* plans by seeking advice;
Isa 14:14 I will *m* myself like the Most High
29:16 "He did not *m* me"?
55: 3 I will *m* an everlasting covenant
61: 8 and *m* an everlasting covenant
Jer 31:31 "when I will *m* a new covenant
Eze 37:26 I will *m* a covenant of peace
Mt 3: 3 *m* straight paths for him.'"
28:19 and *m* disciples of all nations,
Mk 1:17 "and I will *m* you fishers of men."
Lk 13:24 "*M* every effort to enter
14:23 country lanes and *m* them come in,
Ro 14:19 *m* every effort to do what leads
2Co 5: 9 So we *m* it our goal to please him,
Eph 4: 3 *M* every effort to keep the unity
Col 4: 5 *m* the most of every opportunity.
1Th 4:11 *M* it your ambition
Heb 4:11 *m* every effort to enter that rest,
8: 5 it that you *m* everything according
12:14 *M* every effort to live in peace
2Pe 1: 5 *m* every effort to add
3:14 *m* every effort to be found spotless,

MAKER* (MAKE)
Job 4:17 Can a man be more pure than his *M*
9: 9 He is the *M* of the Bear and Orion,
32:22 my *M* would soon take me away.
35:10 no one says, 'Where is God my *M*,
36: 3 I will ascribe justice to my *M*.
40:19 yet his *M* can approach him
Ps 95: 6 kneel before the LORD our *M*;
115: 15 the *M* of heaven and earth.
121: 2 the *M* of heaven and earth.
124: 8 the *M* of heaven and earth.
134: 3 the *M* of heaven and earth,
146: 6 the *M* of heaven and earth,
149: 2 Let Israel rejoice in their *M*;
Pr 14:31 poor shows contempt for their *M*,
17: 5 poor shows contempt for their *M*;
22: 2 The LORD is the *M* of them all.
Ecc 11: 5 the *M* of all things.
Isa 17: 7 that day men will look to their *M*
27:11 so their *M* has no compassion
45: 9 to him who quarrels with his *M*,
45:11 the Holy One of Israel, and its *M*:
51:13 that you forget the LORD your *M*,
54: 5 For your *M* is your husband—
Jer 10:16 for he is the *M* of all things,
51:19 for he is the *M* of all things,
Hos 8:14 Israel has forgotten his *M*

MAKERS* (MAKE)
Isa 45:16 All the *m* of idols will be put

MAKES (MAKE)
Ps 23: 2 *m* me lie down in green pastures,
Pr 13:12 Hope deferred *m* the heart sick,
1Co 3: 7 but only God, who *m* things grow.

MAKING (MAKE)
Ps 19: 7 *m* wise the simple.
Ecc 12:12 Of *m* many books there is no end,
Jn 5:18 *m* himself equal with God.
Eph 5:16 *m* the most of every opportunity,

MALACHI*
Mal 1: 1 of the LORD to Israel through *M*.

MALE
Ge 1:27 *m* and female he created them.
Ex 13: 2 to me every firstborn *m*.
Nu 8:16 the first *m* offspring
Mt 19: 4 the Creator 'made them *m*
Gal 3:28 slave nor free, *m* nor female,

MALICE (MALICIOUS)
Mk 7:22 adultery, greed, *m*, deceit,
Ro 1:29 murder, strife, deceit and *m*.
1Co 5: 8 the yeast of *m* and wickedness,
Eph 4:31 along with every form of *m*.
Col 3: 8 *m*, slander, and filthy language
1Pe 2: 1 rid yourselves of all *m*

MALICIOUS (MALICE)
Pr 26:24 A *m* man disguises himself
1Ti 3:11 not *m* talkers but temperate
6: 4 *m* talk, evil suspicions

MALIGN
Tit 2: 5 so that no one will *m* the word

MAN (MAN'S MANKIND MEN MEN'S WOMAN WOMEN)
Ge 1:26 "Let us make *m* in our image,
2: 7 God formed the *m* from the dust
2: 8 *m* became a living being
2:15 God took the *m* and put
2:18 for the *m* to be alone
2:20 *m* gave names to all the
2:23 she was taken out of *m*.
2:25 *m* and his wife were both
3: 9 God called to the *m*,
3:22 *m* has now become like
4: 1 I have brought forth a *m*.
6: 3 not contend with *m* forever,
6: 6 grieved that he had made *m*
9: 6 Whoever sheds the blood of *m*,
Dt 8: 3 *m* does not live on bread
1Sa 13:14 a *m* after his own heart
15:29 he is not a *m* that he
16: 7 at the things *m* looks at.
Job 14: 1 *M* born of woman is of few
14:14 If a *m* dies, will he live
Ps 1: 1 Blessed is the *m* who does
8: 4 what is *m* that you are
32: 2 Blessed is the *m* whose sin
40: 4 Blessed is the *m* who makes
84:12 blessed is the *m* who trusts
103: 15 As for *m*, his days are
112: 1 Blessed is the *m* who fears
119: 9 can a young *m* keep his
127: 5 Blessed is the *m* whose quiver
144: 3 what is *m* that you care
Pr 3:13 Blessed is the *m* who finds
9: 9 Instruct a wise *m*
14:12 that seems right to a *m*,
30:19 way of a *m* with a maiden.
Isa 53: 3 a *m* of sorrows,
Jer 17: 5 the one who trusts in *m*,
17: 7 blessed is the *m* who trusts
Eze 22:30 I looked for a *m*
Mt 4: 4 *M* does not live on bread
19: 5 a *m* will leave his father
Mk 8:36 What good is it for a *m*
Lk 4: 4 '*M* does not live on bread
Ro 5:12 entered the world through one *m*
1Co 2:15 spiritual *m* makes judgments
3:12 If any *m* builds on this
7: 1 good for a *m* not to marry.
7: 2 each *m* should have his own
11: 3 head of every *m* is Christ,
11: 3 head of woman is *m*
13:11 When I became a *m*,
15:21 death came through a *m*,
15:45 first *m* Adam became a
15:47 the second *m* from heaven
2Co 12: 2 I know a *m* in Christ
Eph 2:15 create in himself one new *m*
5:31 a *m* will leave his father
Php 2: 8 found in appearance as a *m*,
1Ti 2: 5 the *m* Christ Jesus,
2:11 have authority over a *m*;
2Ti 3:17 that the *m* of God may be
Heb 2: 6 what is *m* that you are
9:27 as *m* is destined to die

MAN'S (MAN)
Pr 20:24 A *m* steps are directed by
Jer 10:23 a *m* life is not his own;
1Co 1:25 is wiser than *m* wisdom,

MAN-MADE (MAKE)
Heb 9:11 perfect tabernacle that is not *m*,
9:24 not enter a *m* sanctuary that was

MANAGE (MANAGER)
Jer 12: 5 how will you *m* in the thickets
1Ti 3: 4 He must *m* his own family well
3:12 one wife and must *m* his children
5:14 to *m* their homes and to give

MANAGER (MANAGE)
Lk 12:42 Who then is the faithful and wise *m*
16: 1 a rich man whose *m* was accused

MANASSEH
1. Firstborn of Joseph (Ge 41:51; 46:20). Blessed by Jacob but not firstborn (Ge 48). Tribe of blessed (Dt 33:17), numbered (Nu 1:35; 26:34), half allotted land east of Jordan (Nu 32; Jos 13:8-33), half west (Jos 17; Eze 48:4), failed to fully possess (Jos 17:12-13; Jdg 1:27), 12,000 from (Rev 7:6).
2. Son of Hezekiah; king of Judah (2Ki 21:1-18; 2Ch 33:1-20). Judah exiled for his detestable sins (2Ki 21:10-15). Repentance (2Ch 33:12-19).

MANDRAKES
Ge 30:14 give me some of your son's *m*."

MANGER
Lk 2:12 in strips of cloth and lying in a *m*."

MANIFESTATION*
1Co 12: 7 to each one the *m* of the Spirit is

MANKIND (MAN)
Ge 6: 7 I will wipe *m*, whom I have created
Ps 33:13 and sees all *m*;
Pr 8:31 and delighting in *m*.
Ecc 7:29 God made *m* upright,
Isa 40: 5 and all *m* together will see it.
45:12 and created *m* upon it.
Jer 32:27 "I am the LORD, the God of all *m*.
Zec 2:13 Be still before the LORD, all *m*,
Lk 3: 6 And all *m* will see God's salvation

MANNA
Ex 16:31 people of Israel called the bread *m*.
Dt 8:16 He gave you *m* to eat in the desert,
Jn 6:49 Your forefathers ate the *m*
Rev 2:17 I will give some of the hidden *m*.

MANNER
1Co 11:27 in an unworthy *m* will be guilty
Php 1:27 conduct yourselves in a *m* worthy

MANSIONS*
Ps 49:14 far from their princely *m*.
Isa 5: 9 the fine *m* left without occupants.
Am 3:15 and the *m* will be demolished,"
5:11 though you have built stone *m*,

MARCH
Jos 6: 4 *m* around the city seven times,
Isa 42:13 LORD will *m* out like a mighty

MARITAL* (MARRY)
Ex 21:10 of her food, clothing and *m* rights.
Mt 5:32 except for *m* unfaithfulness,
19: 9 except for *m* unfaithfulness,
1Co 7: 3 husband should fulfill his *m* duty

MARK (MARKS)
Cousin of Barnabas (Col 4:10; 2Ti 4:11; Phm 24; 1Pe 5:13), see JOHN.
Ge 4:15 Then the LORD put a *m* on Cain
Rev 13:16 to receive a *m* on his right hand

MARKET (MARKETPLACE MARKETPLACES)
Jn 2:16 turn my Father's house into a *m*!"

MARKETPLACE (MARKET)
Lk 7:32 are like children sitting in the *m*

MARKETPLACES (MARKET)
Mt 23: 7 they love to be greeted in the *m*

MARKS (MARK)
Jn 20:25 Unless I see the nail *m* in his hands
Gal 6:17 bear on my body the *m* of Jesus.

MARRED
Isa 52:14 his form *m* beyond human likeness

MARRIAGE (MARRY)
Mt 22:30 neither marry nor be given in *m*;
24:38 marrying and giving in *m*,
Ro 7: 2 she is released from the law of *m*.
Heb 13: 4 by all, and the *m* bed kept pure,

MARRIED (MARRY)
Dt 24: 5 happiness to the wife he has *m*.
Ezr 10:10 you have *m* foreign women,
Pr 30:23 an unloved woman who is *m*,
Mt 1:18 pledged to be *m* to Joseph,
Mk 12:23 since the seven were *m* to her?"
Ro 7: 2 by law a *m* woman is bound
1Co 7:27 Are you *m*? Do not seek a divorce.
7:33 But a *m* man is concerned about
7:36 They should get *m*.

MARRIES (MARRY)
Mt 5:32 anyone who *m* the divorced woman
19: 9 and *m* another woman commits
Lk 16:18 the man who *m* a divorced woman

MARROW
Heb 4:12 joints and *m*; it judges the thoughts

MARRY (INTERMARRY MARITAL MARRIAGE MARRIED MARRIES)
Dt 25: 5 brother shall take her and *m* her
Mt 22:30 resurrection people will neither *m*
1Co 7: 1 It is good for a man not to *m*.
7: 9 control themselves, they should *m*,
7:28 if you do *m*, you have not sinned;
1Ti 4: 3 They forbid people to *m*
5:14 So I counsel younger widows to *m*,

MARTHA*
Sister of Mary and Lazarus (Lk 10:38-42; Jn 11; 12:2).

MARVELED* (MARVELOUS)
Lk 2:33 mother *m* at what was said about
2Th 1:10 and to be *m* at among all those who

MARVELING* (MARVELOUS)
Lk 9:43 While everyone was *m*

MARVELOUS* (MARVELED MARVELING)
1Ch 16:24 his *m* deeds among all peoples.
Job 37: 5 God's voice thunders in *m* ways;
Ps 71:17 to this day I declare your *m* deeds.
72:18 who alone does *m* deeds.
86:10 For you are great and do *m* deeds;
96: 3 his *m* deeds among all peoples.
98: 1 for he has done *m* things;
118: 23 and it is *m* in our eyes.
Isa 25: 1 you have done *m* things,
Zec 8: 6 but will it seem *m* to me?"
8: 6 "It may seem *m* to the remnant
Mt 21:42 and it is *m* in our eyes'?
Mk 12:11 and it is *m* in our eyes'?"
Rev 15: 1 in heaven another great and *m* sign
15: 3 "Great and *m* are your deeds,

MARY
1. Mother of Jesus (Mt 1:16-25; Lk 1:27-56; 2:1-40). With Jesus at temple (Lk 2:41-52), at the wedding in Cana (Jn 2:1-5), questioning his sanity (Mk 3:21), at the cross (Jn 19:25-27). Among disciples after Ascension (Ac 1:14).
2. Magdalene; former demoniac (Lk 8:2). Helped support Jesus' ministry (Lk 8:1-3). At the cross (Mt 27:56; Mk 15:40; Jn 19:25), burial (Mt 27:61; Mk 15:47). Saw angel after resurrection (Mt 28:1-10; Mk 16:1-9; Lk 24:1-12); also Jesus (Jn 20:1-18).
3. Sister of Martha and Lazarus (Jn 11). Washed Jesus' feet (Jn 12:1-8).

MASQUERADES*
2Co 11:14 for Satan himself *m* as an angel

MASTER (MASTER'S MASTERED MASTERS MASTERY)
Ge 4: 7 to have you, but you must *m* it."
Hos 2:16 you will no longer call me 'my *m*.'
Mal 1: 6 If I am a *m*, where is the respect
Mt 10:24 nor a servant above his *m*.
23: 8 for you have only one *M*
24:46 that servant whose *m* finds him
25:21 "His *m* replied, 'Well done,
25:23 "His *m* replied, 'Well done,
Ro 6:14 For sin shall not be your *m*,
14: 4 To his own *m* he stands or falls.
Col 4: 1 you know that you also have a *M*
2Ti 2:21 useful to the *M* and prepared

MASTER'S (MASTER)
Mt 25:21 Come and share your *m* happiness

MASTERED* (MASTER)
1Co 6:12 but I will not be *m* by anything.
2Pe 2:19 a slave to whatever has *m* him.

MASTERS (MASTER)
Pr 25:13 he refreshes the spirit of his *m*.
Mt 6:24 "No one can serve two *m*.
Lk 16:13 "No servant can serve two *m*.
Eph 6: 5 obey your earthly *m* with respect
6: 9 And *m*, treat your slaves
Col 3:22 obey your earthly *m* in everything;
4: 1 *M*, provide your slaves
1Ti 6: 1 should consider their *m* worthy
6: 2 who have believing *m* are not
Tit 2: 9 subject to their *m* in everything,
1Pe 2:18 to your *m* with all respect,

MASTERY* (MASTER)
Ro 6: 9 death no longer has *m* over him.

MAT
Mk 2: 9 'Get up, take your *m* and walk'?
Ac 9:34 Get up and take care of your *m*."

MATCHED*
2Co 8:11 do it may be *m* by your completion

MATTHEW*
Apostle; former tax collector (Mt 9:9-13; 10:3; Mk 3:18; Lk 6:15; Ac 1:13). Also called Levi (Mk 2:14-17; Lk 5:27-32).

MATTHIAS
Ac 1:26 the lot fell to *M*; so he was added

MATURE* (MATURITY)
Lk 8:14 and pleasures, and they do not *m*.
1Co 2: 6 a message of wisdom among the *m*,
Eph 4:13 of the Son of God and become *m*,
Php 3:15 of us who are *m* should take such
Col 4:12 firm in all the will of God, *m*
Heb 5:14 But solid food is for the *m*,
Jas 1: 4 work so that you may be *m*

MATURITY* (MATURE)
Heb 6: 1 about Christ and go on to *m*,

MEAL
Pr 15:17 Better a *m* of vegetables where
1Co 10:27 some unbeliever invites you to a *m*
Heb 12:16 for a single *m* sold his inheritance

MEANING
Ne 8: 8 and giving the *m* so that the people

MEANINGLESS
Ecc 1: 2 "*M*! *M*!" says the Teacher.
1Ti 1: 6 from these and turned to *m* talk.

MEANS
1Co 9:22 by all possible *m* I might save some

MEASURE (MEASURED MEASURES)
Ps 71:15 though I know not its *m*.
Eze 45: 3 In the sacred district, *m*
Zec 2: 2 He answered me, "To *m* Jerusalem
Lk 6:38 A good *m*, pressed
Eph 3:19 to the *m* of all the fullness of God.
4:13 to the whole *m* of the fullness
Rev 11: 1 "Go and *m* the temple of God

MEASURED (MEASURE)
Isa 40:12 Who has *m* the waters
Jer 31:37 if the heavens above can be *m*

MEASURES (MEASURE)
Dt 25:14 Do not have two differing *m*
Pr 20:10 Differing weights and differing *m*

MEAT
Pr 23:20 or gorge themselves on *m*,
Ro 14: 6 He who eats *m*, eats to the Lord,
14:21 It is better not to eat *m*
1Co 8:13 I will never eat *m* again,
10:25 *m* market without raising questions

MEDDLER* (MEDDLES)
1Pe 4:15 kind of criminal, or even as a *m*.

MEDDLES* (MEDDLER)
Pr 26:17 is a passer-by who *m*

MEDIATOR
1Ti 2: 5 and one *m* between God and men,
Heb 8: 6 of which he is *m* is superior
9:15 For this reason Christ is the *m*
12:24 to Jesus the *m* of a new covenant,

MEDICINE*
Pr 17:22 A cheerful heart is good *m*,

MEDITATE* (MEDITATED MEDITATES MEDITATION)
Ge 24:63 out to the field one evening to *m*,
Jos 1: 8 from your mouth; *m* on it day
Ps 48: 9 we *m* on your unfailing love.
77:12 I will *m* on all your works
119: 15 I *m* on your precepts
119: 23 your servant will *m*
119: 27 then I will *m* on your wonders.
119: 48 and I *m* on your decrees.
119: 78 but I will *m* on your precepts.
119: 97 I *m* on it all day long.
119: 99 for I *m* on your statutes.

Ps 119:148 that I may *m* on your promises.
143: 5 I *m* on all your works
145: 5 I will *m* on your wonderful works.

MEDITATED* (MEDITATE)
Ps 39: 3 and as I *m*, the fire burned;

MEDITATES* (MEDITATE)
Ps 1: 2 and on his law he *m* day and night.

MEDITATION* (MEDITATE)
Ps 19:14 of my mouth and the *m* of my heart
104: 34 May my *m* be pleasing to him,

MEDIUM
Lev 20:27 " 'A man or woman who is a *m*

MEEK* (MEEKNESS)
Ps 37:11 But the *m* will inherit the land
Zep 3:12 the *m* and humble,
Mt 5: 5 Blessed are the *m*,

MEEKNESS* (MEEK)
2Co 10: 1 By the *m* and gentleness of Christ,

MEET (MEETING MEETINGS MEETS)
Ps 42: 2 When can I go and *m* with God?
85:10 Love and faithfulness *m* together;
Am 4:12 prepare to *m* your God, O Israel."
1Co 11:34 when you *m* together it may not
1Th 4:17 them in the clouds to *m* the Lord

MEETING (MEET)
Ex 40:34 the cloud covered the Tent of *M*,
Heb 10:25 Let us not give up *m* together,

MEETINGS* (MEET)
1Co 11:17 for your *m* do more harm

MEETS (MEET)
Heb 7:26 Such a high priest *m* our need—

MELCHIZEDEK
Ge 14:18 *M* king of Salem brought out bread
Ps 110: 4 in the order of *M*."
Heb 7:11 in the order of *M*, not in the order

MELT (MELTS)
2Pe 3:12 and the elements will *m* in the heat.

MELTS (MELT)
Am 9: 5 he who touches the earth and it *m*,

MEMBER (MEMBERS)
Ro 12: 5 each *m* belongs to all the others.

MEMBERS (MEMBER)
Mic 7: 6 a man's enemies are the *m*
Mt 10:36 a man's enemies will be the *m*
Ro 7:23 law at work in the *m* of my body,
12: 4 of us has one body with many *m*,
1Co 6:15 not know that your bodies are *m*
12:24 But God has combined the *m*
Eph 3: 6 *m* together of one body,
4:25 for we are all *m* of one body.
5:30 for we are *m* of his body.
Col 3:15 as *m* of one body you were called

MEMORABLE* (MEMORY)
Eze 39:13 day I am glorified will be a *m* day

MEMORIES* (MEMORY)
1Th 3: 6 us that you always have pleasant *m*

MEMORY (MEMORABLE MEMORIES)
Pr 10: 7 *m* of the righteous will be
Mt 26:13 she has done will also be told, in *m*

MEN (MAN)
Ge 6: 2 daughter of *m* were beautiful,
6: 4 heroes of old, *m* of renown
Ps 9:20 nations know they are but *m*.
11: 4 He observes the sons of *m*;
Mt 4:19 will make you fishers of *m*
5:16 your light shine before *m*
6:14 if you forgive *m* when
10:32 acknowledges me before *m*
12:31 blasphemy will be forgiven *m*,
12:36 *m* will have to give account
23: 5 is done for *m* to see:
Mk 7: 7 are but rules taught by *m*.
Lk 6:22 Blessed are you when *m*
6:26 Woe to you when all *m*
Jn 1: 4 life was the light of *m*.
2:24 for he knew all *m*.
3:19 *m* loved darkness instead
12:32 will draw all *m* to myself
13:35 all *m* will know that you
Ac 5:29 obey God rather than *m*!
Ro 1:18 wickedness of *m*
1:27 indecent acts with other *m*,
5:12 death came to all *m*,
1Co 2:11 among *m* knows the thoughts
3: 3 acting like mere *m*?
3:21 no more boasting about *m*!
9:22 all things to all *m*
13: 1 tongues of *m* and of angels
16:13 be *m* of courage;
16:18 Such *m* deserve recognition.
2Co 5:11 we try to persuade *m*.
8:21 but also in the eyes of *m*.
Gal 1: 1 sent not from *m* nor
1:10 to win approval of *m*, or
Eph 4: 8 and gave gifts to *m*.
1Th 2: 4 as *m* approved by God
2:13 not as the word of *m*,
1Ti 2: 4 wants all *m* to be saved
2: 6 as a ransom for all *m*—
4:10 the Savior of all *m*
5: 2 younger *m* as brothers
2Ti 2: 2 entrust to reliable *m*
Tit 2:11 has appeared to all *m*.
Heb 5: 1 is selected from among *m*
7:28 high priests *m* who are weak;
2Pe 1:21 but *m* spoke from God
Rev 21: 3 dwelling of God is with *m*,

MEN'S (MAN)
2Ki 19:18 fashioned by *m* hands.
2Ch 32:19 the work of *m* hands.
1Co 2: 5 not rest on *m* wisdom,

MENAHEM*
King of Israel (2Ki 15:17-22).

MENE
Da 5:25 that was written: *M*, *M*,

MEPHIBOSHETH
Son of Jonathan shown kindness by David (2Sa 4:4; 9; 21:7). Accused of siding with Absalom (2Sa 16:1-4; 19:24-30).

MERCHANT
Pr 31:14 She is like the *m* ships,
Mt 13:45 of heaven is like a *m* looking

MERCIFUL (MERCY)
Dt 4:31 the LORD your God is a *m* God;
Ne 9:31 for you are a gracious and *m* God.
Ps 77: 9 Has God forgotten to be *m*?
78:38 Yet he was *m*;
Jer 3:12 for I am *m*,' declares the LORD,
Da 9: 9 The Lord our God is *m*
Mt 5: 7 Blessed are the *m*,
Lk 1:54 remembering to be *m*
6:36 Be *m*, just as your Father is *m*.
Heb 2:17 in order that he might become a *m*
Jas 2:13 to anyone who has not been *m*.
Jude :22 Be *m* to those who doubt; snatch

MERCY (MERCIFUL)
Ex 33:19 *m* on whom I will have *m*,
2Sa 24:14 of the LORD, for his *m* is great;
1Ch 21:13 for his *m* is very great;
Ne 9:31 But in your great *m* you did not put
Ps 25: 6 O LORD, your great *m* and love,
28: 6 for he has heard my cry for *m*.
57: 1 Have *m* on me, O God, have *m*
Pr 28:13 renounces them finds *m*.
Isa 63: 9 and *m* he redeemed them;
Da 9:18 but because of your great *m*.
Hos 6: 6 For I desire *m*, not sacrifice,
Am 5:15 LORD God Almighty will have *m*
Mic 6: 8 To act justly and to love *m*
7:18 but delight to show *m*.
Hab 3: 2 in wrath remember *m*.
Zec 7: 9 show *m* and compassion
Mt 5: 7 for they will be shown *m*.
9:13 learn what this means: 'I desire *m*,
12: 7 'I desire *m*, not sacrifice,' you
18:33 Shouldn't you have had *m*
23:23 justice, *m* and faithfulness.
Lk 1:50 His *m* extends to those who fear
Ro 9:15 "I will have *m* on whom I have *m*,
9:18 Therefore God has *m*
11:32 so that he may have *m* on them all.
12: 1 brothers, in view of God's *m*,
12: 8 if it is showing *m*, let him do it
Eph 2: 4 who is rich in *m*, made us alive
1Ti 1:13 I was shown *m* because I acted
1:16 for that very reason I was shown *m*
Tit 3: 5 we had done, but because of his *m*.
Heb 4:16 so that we may receive *m*
Jas 2:13 judgment without *m* will be shown
2:13 *M* triumphs over judgment!
3:17 submissive, full of *m* and good fruit
5:11 full of compassion and *m*.
1Pe 1: 3 In his great *m* he has given us new
2:10 once you had not received *m*,
Jude :23 to others show *m*, mixed with fear

MERRY
Lk 12:19 Take life easy; eat, drink and be *m*

MESHACH
Hebrew exiled to Babylon; name changed from Mishael (Da 1:6-7). Refused defilement by food (Da 1:8-20). Refused to worship idol (Da 3:1-18); saved from furnace (Da 3:19-30).

MESSAGE (MESSENGER)
Isa 53: 1 Who has believed our *m*
Jn 12:38 "Lord, who has believed our *m*
Ac 5:20 "and tell the people the full *m*
10:36 You know the *m* God sent
17:11 for they received the *m*
Ro 10:16 who has believed our *m*?"
10:17 faith comes from hearing the *m*,
1Co 1:18 For the *m* of the cross is
2: 4 My *m* and my preaching were not
2Co 5:19 to us the *m* of reconciliation.
2Th 3: 1 pray for us that the *m*
Tit 1: 9 firmly to the trustworthy *m*
Heb 4: 2 the *m* they heard was of no value
1Pe 2: 8 because they disobey the *m*—

MESSENGER (MESSAGE)
Pr 25:13 is a trustworthy *m*
Mal 3: 1 I will send my *m*, who will prepare
Mt 11:10 " 'I will send my *m* ahead of you,
2Co 12: 7 a *m* of Satan, to torment me.

MESSIAH*
Jn 1:41 "We have found the *M*" (that is,
4:25 "I know that *M*" (called Christ) "is

METHUSELAH
Ge 5:27 Altogether, *M* lived 969 years,

MICAH
1. Idolater from Ephraim (Jdg 17-18).
2. Prophet from Moresheth (Jer 26:18-19; Mic 1:1).

MICAIAH
Prophet of the LORD who spoke against Ahab (1Ki 22:1-28; 2Ch 18:1-27).

MICHAEL
Archangel (Jude 9); warrior in angelic realm, protector of Israel (Da 10:13, 21; 12:1; Rev 12:7).

MICHAL
Daughter of Saul, wife of David (1Sa 14:49; 18:20-28). Warned David of Saul's plot (1Sa 19). Saul gave her to Paltiel (1Sa 25:44); David retrieved her (2Sa 3:13-16). Criticized David for dancing before the ark (2Sa 6:16-23); 1Ch 15:29).

MIDIAN
Ex 2:15 Pharaoh and went to live in *M*,
Jdg 7: 2 me to deliver *M* into their hands.

MIDWIVES
Ex 1:17 The *m*, however, feared God

MIGHT (ALMIGHTY MIGHTIER MIGHTY)
Jdg 16:30 Then he pushed with all his *m*,
2Sa 6: 5 with all their *m* before the LORD,
6:14 before the LORD with all his *m*,
2Ch 20: 6 Power and *m* are in your hand,
Ps 21:13 we will sing and praise your *m*.
54: 1 vindicate me by your *m*.
Isa 63:15 Where are your zeal and your *m*?
Mic 3: 8 and with justice and *m*,
Zec 4: 6 'Not by *m* nor by power,
Col 1:11 power according to his glorious *m*
1Ti 6:16 To him be honor and *m* forever.

MIGHTIER (MIGHT)
Ps 93: 4 *M* than the thunder

MIGHTY (MIGHT)
Ge 49:24 of the hand of the *M* One of Jacob,
Ex 6: 1 of my *m* hand he will drive them
13: 3 out of it with a *m* hand.
Dt 5:15 out of there with a *m* hand
7: 8 he brought you out with a *m* hand
10:17 the great God, *m* and awesome,
34:12 one has ever shown the *m* power
2Sa 1:19 How the *m* have fallen!
23: 8 the names of David's *m* men:
Ne 9:32 the great, *m* and awesome God,
Job 36: 5 God is *m*, but does not despise men
Ps 24: 8 The LORD strong and *m*,
45: 3 upon your side, O *m* one;
50: 1 The *M* One, God, the LORD,
62: 7 he is my *m* rock, my refuge.
68:33 who thunders with *m* voice.
71:16 proclaim your *m* acts,
77:12 and consider all your *m* deeds.
77:15 With your *m* arm you redeemed

Ps 89: 8 You are *m*, O LORD,
93: 4 the LORD on high is *m*.
99: 4 The King is *m*, he loves justice—
110: 2 LORD will extend your *m* scepter
118: 15 right hand has done *m* things!
136: 12 with a *m* hand and outstretched
145: 4 they will tell of your *m* acts.
145: 12 all men may know of your *m* acts
147: 5 Great is our Lord and *m* in power;
SS 8: 6 like a *m* flame.
Isa 9: 6 Wonderful Counselor, *M* God,
60:16 your Redeemer, the *M* One
63: 1 *m* to save."
Jer 10: 6 and your name is *m* in power.
20:11 with me like a *m* warrior;
32:19 your purposes and *m* are your
Eze 20:33 I will rule over you with a *m* hand
Zep 3:17 he is *m* to save.
Mt 26:64 at the right hand of the *M* One
Eph 1:19 like the working of his *m* strength,
6:10 in the Lord and in his *m* power.
1Pe 5: 6 therefore, under God's *m* hand,

MILE*
Mt 5:41 If someone forces you to go one *m*,

MILK
Ex 3: 8 a land flowing with *m* and honey—
23:19 a young goat in its mother's *m*.
Pr 30:33 as churning the *m* produces butter,
Isa 55: 1 Come, buy wine and *m*
1Co 3: 2 I gave you *m*, not solid food,
Heb 5:12 You need *m*, not solid food!
1Pe 2: 2 babies, crave pure spiritual *m*,

MILLSTONE (STONE)
Lk 17: 2 sea with a *m* tied around his neck

MIND (DOUBLE-MINDED LIKE-MINDED MINDED MINDFUL MINDS)
Nu 23:19 that he should change his *m*.
Dt 28:65 LORD will give you an anxious *m*,
1Sa 15:29 Israel does not lie or change his *m*;
1Ch 28: 9 devotion and with a willing *m*,
2Ch 30:12 the people to give them unity of *m*
Ps 26: 2 examine my heart and my *m*;
110: 4 and will not change his *m*:
Isa 26: 3 him whose *m* is steadfast,
Jer 17:10 and examine the *m*,
Mt 22:37 all your soul and with all your *m*.'
Mk 12:30 with all your *m* and with all your
Lk 10:27 your strength and with all your *m*';
Ac 4:32 believers were one in heart and *m*.
Ro 1:28 he gave them over to a depraved *m*
7:25 I myself in my *m* am a slave
8: 6 The *m* of sinful man is death,
8: 7 the sinful *m* is hostile to God.
12: 2 by the renewing of your *m*.
14:13 make up your *m* not
1Co 1:10 you may be perfectly united in *m*
2: 9 no *m* has conceived
14:14 spirit prays, but my *m* is unfruitful.
2Co 13:11 be of one *m*, live in peace.
Php 3:19 Their *m* is on earthly things.
Col 2:18 and his unspiritual *m* puffs him up
1Th 4:11 to *m* your own business
Heb 7:21 and will not change his *m*:

MINDED* (MIND)
1Pe 4: 7 be clear *m* and self-controlled

MINDFUL* (MIND)
Ps 8: 4 what is man that you are *m* of him,
Lk 1:48 God my Savior, for he has been *m*
Heb 2: 6 What is man that you are *m* of him,

MINDS (MIND)
Dt 11:18 of mine in your hearts and *m*;
Ps 7: 9 who searches *m* and hearts,
Jer 31:33 "I will put my law in their *m*
Lk 24:38 and why do doubts rise in your *m*?
24:45 Then he opened their *m*
Ro 8: 5 to the sinful nature have their *m* set
2Co 4: 4 god of this age has blinded the *m*
Eph 4:23 new in the attitude of your *m*;
Col 3: 2 Set your *m* on things above,
Heb 8:10 I will put my laws in their *m*
10:16 and I will write them on their *m*."
1Pe 1:13 prepare your *m* for action;
Rev 2:23 I am he who searches hearts and *m*,

MINISTER (MINISTERING MINISTERS MINISTRY)
Ps 101: 6 will *m* to me.
1Ti 4: 6 you will be a good *m*

MINISTERING (MINISTER)
Heb 1:14 Are not all angels *m* spirits sent

MINISTERS (MINISTER)
2Co 3: 6 as *m* of a new covenant—

MINISTRY (MINISTER)
Ac 6: 4 to prayer and the *m* of the word."
Ro 11:13 I make much of my *m*
2Co 4: 1 God's mercy we have this *m*,
5:18 gave us the *m* of reconciliation:
6: 3 so that our *m* will not be
Gal 2: 8 who was at work in the *m* of Peter
2Ti 4: 5 discharge all the duties of your *m*.
Heb 8: 6 But the *m* Jesus has received is

MIRACLE* (MIRACLES MIRACULOUS)
Ex 7: 9 'Perform a *m*,' then say to Aaron,
Mk 9:39 "No one who does a *m*
Lk 23: 8 hoped to see him perform some *m*.
Jn 7:21 "I did one *m*, and you are all
Ac 4:16 they have done an outstanding *m*,

MIRACLES* (MIRACLE)
1Ch 16:12 his *m*, and the judgments he
Ne 9:17 to remember the *m* you performed
Job 5: 9 *m* that cannot be counted.
9:10 *m* that cannot be counted.
Ps 77:11 I will remember your *m* of long ago
77:14 You are the God who performs *m*;
78:12 He did *m* in the sight
105: 5 his *m*, and the judgments he
106: 7 they gave no thought to your *m*;
106: 22 *m* in the land of Ham
Mt 7:22 out demons and perform many *m*?'
11:20 most of his *m* had been performed,
11:21 If the *m* that were performed
11:23 If the *m* that were performed
13:58 And he did not do many *m* there
24:24 and perform great signs and *m*
Mk 6: 2 does *m*! Isn't this the carpenter?
6: 5 He could not do any *m* there,
13:22 and *m* to deceive the elect—
Lk 10:13 For if the *m* that were performed
19:37 for all the *m* they had seen:
Jn 7: 3 disciples may see the *m* you do.
10:25 *m* I do in my Father's name speak
10:32 "I have shown you many great *m*
10:38 do not believe me, believe the *m*,
14:11 the evidence of the *m* themselves.
15:24 But now they have seen these *m*,
Ac 2:22 accredited by God to you by *m*,
8:13 by the great signs and *m* he saw.
19:11 God did extraordinary *m*
Ro 15:19 by the power of signs and *m*,
1Co 12:28 third teachers, then workers of *m*,
12:29 Are all teachers? Do all work *m*?
2Co 12:12 and *m*— were done among you
Gal 3: 5 work *m* among you because you
2Th 2: 9 in all kinds of counterfeit *m*,
Heb 2: 4 it by signs, wonders and various *m*,

MIRACULOUS (MIRACLE)
Dt 13: 1 and announces to you a *m* sign
Mt 12:39 generation asks for a *m* sign!
13:54 this wisdom and these *m* powers?"
Jn 2:11 This, the first of his *m* signs,
2:23 people saw the *m* signs he was
3: 2 could perform the *m* signs you are
4:48 "Unless you people see *m* signs
7:31 will he do more *m* signs
9:16 "How can a sinner do such *m* signs
12:37 Jesus had done all these *m* signs
20:30 Jesus did many other *m* signs
Ac 2:43 *m* signs were done by the apostles.
5:12 apostles performed many *m* signs
1Co 1:22 Jews demand *m* signs and Greeks
12:10 to another *m* powers,

MIRE
Ps 40: 2 out of the mud and *m*;
Isa 57:20 whose waves cast up *m* and mud.

MIRIAM
Sister of Moses and Aaron (Nu 26:59). Led dancing at Red Sea (Ex 15:20-21). Struck with leprosy for criticizing Moses (Nu 12). Death (Nu 20:1).

MIRROR
1Co 13:12 but a poor reflection as in a *m*;
Jas 1:23 a man who looks at his face in a *m*

MISDEEDS*
Ps 99: 8 though you punished their *m*.
Ro 8:13 put to death the *m* of the body,

MISERY
Ex 3: 7 "I have indeed seen the *m*
Jdg 10:16 he could bear Israel's *m* no longer.
Hos 5:15 in their *m* they will earnestly seek
Ro 3:16 ruin and *m* mark their ways,
Jas 5: 1 of the *m* that is coming upon you.

MISFORTUNE
Ob :12 brother in the day of his *m*,

MISLEAD (MISLED)
Isa 47:10 wisdom and knowledge *m* you

MISLED (MISLEAD)
1Co 15:33 Do not be *m*: "Bad company

MISS (MISSES)
Pr 19: 2 nor to be hasty and *m* the way.

MISSES (MISS)
Heb 12:15 See to it that no one *m* the grace

MIST
Hos 6: 4 Your love is like the morning *m*,
Jas 4:14 You are a *m* that appears for a little

MISTREAT (MISTREATED)
Ex 22:21 "Do not *m* an alien or oppress him,
Eze 22:29 and needy and *m* the alien,
Lk 6:28 pray for those who *m* you.

MISTREATED (MISTREAT)
Eze 22: 7 *m* the fatherless and the widow.
Heb 11:25 to be *m* along with the people
11:37 destitute, persecuted and *m*—
13: 3 who are *m* as if you yourselves

MISUSE* (MISUSES)
Ex 20: 7 "You shall not *m* the name
Dt 5:11 "You shall not *m* the name
Ps 139: 20 your adversaries *m* your name.

MISUSES* (MISUSE)
Ex 20: 7 anyone guiltless who *m* his name.
Dt 5:11 anyone guiltless who *m* his name.

MIXED (MIXING)
Da 2:41 even as you saw iron *m* with clay.

MIXING (MIXED)
Isa 5:22 and champions at *m* drinks,

MOAB (MOABITESS)
Ge 19:37 she named him *M*; he is the father
Dt 34: 6 He buried him in *M*, in the valley
Ru 1: 1 live for a while in the country of *M*.
Isa 15: 1 An oracle concerning *M*:
Jer 48:16 "The fall of *M* is at hand;
Am 2: 1 "For three sins of *M*,

MOABITESS (MOAB)
Ru 1:22 accompanied by Ruth the *M*,

MOAN
Ps 90: 9 we finish our years with a *m*.

MOCK (MOCKED MOCKER MOCKERS MOCKING MOCKS)
Ps 22: 7 All who see me *m* me;
119: 51 The arrogant *m* me
Pr 1:26 I will *m* when calamity overtakes
14: 9 Fools *m* at making amends for sin,
Mk 10:34 who will *m* him and spit on him,

MOCKED (MOCK)
Ps 89:51 with which they have *m* every step
Mt 27:29 knelt in front of him and *m* him.
27:41 of the law and the elders *m* him.
Gal 6: 7 not be deceived: God cannot be *m*.

MOCKER (MOCK)
Pr 9: 7 corrects a *m* invites insult;
9:12 if you are a *m*, you alone will suffer
20: 1 Wine is a *m* and beer a brawler;
22:10 Drive out the *m*, and out goes strife

MOCKERS (MOCK)
Ps 1: 1 or sit in the seat of *m*.
Pr 29: 8 *M* stir up a city,

MOCKING (MOCK)
Isa 50: 6 face from *m* and spitting.

MOCKS (MOCK)
Pr 17: 5 He who *m* the poor shows
30:17 "The eye that *m* a father,

MODEL*
Eze 28:12 " 'You were the *m* of perfection,
1Th 1: 7 And so you became a *m*
2Th 3: 9 to make ourselves a *m* for you

MODESTY*
1Co 12:23 are treated with special *m*,

MOLDED*
Job 10: 9 Remember that you *m* me like clay

MOLDY
Jos 9: 5 of their food supply was dry and *m.*

MOLECH
Lev 20: 2 of his children to *M* must be put
1Ki 11:33 and *M* the god of the Ammonites,

MOMENT (MOMENTARY)
Job 20: 5 the joy of the godless lasts but a *m.*
Ps 2:12 for his wrath can flare up in a *m.*
30: 5 For his anger lasts only a *m,*
Pr 12:19 but a lying tongue lasts only a *m.*
Isa 54: 7 "For a brief *m* I abandoned you,
66: 8 or a nation be brought forth in a *m?*
Gal 2: 5 We did not give in to them for a *m,*

MOMENTARY* (MOMENT)
2Co 4:17 and *m* troubles are achieving

MONEY
Pr 13:11 Dishonest *m* dwindles away,
Ecc 5:10 Whoever loves *m* never has *m*
Isa 55: 1 and you who have no *m,*
Mt 6:24 You cannot serve both God and *M.*
27: 5 Judas threw the *m* into the temple
Lk 3:14 "Don't extort *m* and don't accuse
9: 3 no bread, no *m,* no extra tunic.
16:13 You cannot serve both God and *M*
Ac 5: 2 part of the *m* for himself,
1Co 16: 2 set aside a sum of *m* in keeping
1Ti 3: 3 not quarrelsome, not a lover of *m.*
6:10 For the love of *m* is a root
2Ti 3: 2 lovers of *m,* boastful, proud,
Heb 13: 5 free from the love of *m*
1Pe 5: 2 not greedy for *m,* but eager to serve

MONEYLENDER* (LEND)
Ex 22:25 not be like a *m;* charge him no
Lk 7:41 men owed money to a certain *m.*

MONTH (MONTHS)
Ex 12: 2 "This *m* is to be for you the first
Eze 47:12 Every *m* they will bear,
Rev 22: 2 of fruit, yielding its fruit every *m.*

MONTHS (MONTH)
Gal 4:10 and *m* and seasons and years!
Rev 11: 2 trample on the holy city for 42 *m.*
13: 5 his authority for forty-two *m.*

MOON
Jos 10:13 and the *m* stopped,
Ps 8: 3 the *m* and the stars,
74:16 you established the sun and *m.*
89:37 be established forever like the *m,*
104: 19 The *m* marks off the seasons,
121: 6 nor the *m* by night.
136: 9 the *m* and stars to govern the night;
148: 3 Praise him, sun and *m,*
SS 6:10 fair as the *m,* bright as the sun,
Joel 2:31 and the *m* to blood
Hab 3:11 and *m* stood still in the heavens
Mt 24:29 and the *m* will not give its light;
Ac 2:20 and the *m* to blood
1Co 15:41 *m* another and the stars another;
Col 2:16 a New *M* celebration or a Sabbath
Rev 6:12 the whole *m* turned blood red,
21:23 city does not need the sun or the *m*

MORAL*
Jas 1:21 rid of all *m* filth and the evil that is

MORDECAI
Benjamite exile who raised Esther (Est 2:5-15). Exposed plot to kill Xerxes (Est 2:19-23). Refused to honor Haman (Est 3:1-6; 5:9-14). Charged Esther to foil Haman's plot against the Jews (Est 4). Xerxes forced Haman to honor Mordecai (Est 6). Mordecai exalted (Est 8-10). Established Purim (Est 9:18-32).

MORIAH*
Ge 22: 2 and go to the region of *M.*
2Ch 3: 1 LORD in Jerusalem on Mount *M,*

MORNING
Ge 1: 5 and there was *m*— the first day.
Dt 28:67 In the *m* you will say, "If only it
2Sa 23: 4 he is like the light of *m* at sunrise
Ps 5: 3 In the *m,* O LORD,
Pr 27:14 blesses his neighbor early in the *m,*
Isa 14:12 O *m* star, son of the dawn!
La 3:23 They are new every *m;*
2Pe 1:19 and the *m* star rises in your hearts.
Rev 2:28 I will also give him the *m* star.
22:16 of David, and the bright *M* Star."

MORTAL
Ge 6: 3 for he is *m;* his days will be
Job 10: 4 Do you see as a *m* sees?
Ro 8:11 also give life to your *m* bodies
1Co 15:53 and the *m* with immortality.
2Co 5: 4 that what is *m* may be swallowed

MOSES
Levite; brother of Aaron (Ex 6:20; 1Ch 6:3). Put in basket into Nile; discovered and raised by Pharaoh's daughter (Ex 2:1-10). Fled to Midian after killing Egyptian (Ex 2:11-15). Married to Zipporah, fathered Gershom (Ex 2:16-22).

Called by the LORD to deliver Israel (Ex 3-4). Pharaoh's resistance (Ex 5). Ten plagues (Ex 7-11). Passover and Exodus (Ex 12-13). Led Israel through Red Sea (Ex 14). Song of deliverance (Ex 15:1-21). Brought water from rock (Ex 17:1-7). Raised hands to defeat Amalekites (Ex 17:8-16). Delegated judges (Ex 18; Dt 1:9-18).

Received Law at Sinai (Ex 19-23; 25-31; Jn 1:17). Announced Law to Israel (Ex 19:7-8; 24; 35). Broke tablets because of golden calf (Ex 32; Dt 9). Saw glory of the LORD (Ex 33-34). Supervised building of tabernacle (Ex 36-40). Set apart Aaron and priests (Lev 8-9). Numbered tribes (Nu 1-4; 26). Opposed by Aaron and Miriam (Nu 12). Sent spies into Canaan (Nu 13). Announced forty years of wandering for failure to enter land (Nu 14). Opposed by Korah (Nu 16). Forbidden to enter land for striking rock (Nu 20:1-13; Dt 1:37). Lifted bronze snake for healing (Nu 21:4-9; Jn 3:14). Final address to Israel (Dt 1-33). Succeeded by Joshua (Nu 27:12-23; Dt 34). Death (Dt 34:5-12).

"Law of Moses" (1Ki 2:3; Ezr 3:2; Mk 12:26; Lk 24:44). "Book of Moses" (2Ch 25:12; Ne 13:1). "Song of Moses" (Ex 15:1-21; Rev 15:3). "Prayer of Moses" (Ps 90).

MOTH
Mt 6:19 where *m* and rust destroy,

MOTHER (GRANDMOTHER MOTHER-IN-LAW MOTHER'S)
Ge 2:24 and *m* and be united to his wife,
3:20 because she would become the *m*
Ex 20:12 "Honor your father and your *m,*
Lev 20: 9 " 'If anyone curses his father or *m,*
Dt 5:16 "Honor your father and your *m,*
21:18 who does not obey his father and *m*
27:16 who dishonors his father or his *m."*
Jdg 5: 7 arose a *m* in Israel.
1Sa 2:19 Each year his *m* made him a little
Ps 113: 9 as a happy *m* of children.
Pr 10: 1 but a foolish son grief to his *m.*
23:22 do not despise your *m*
23:25 May your father and *m* be glad;
29:15 a child left to himself disgraces his *m.*
30:17 that scorns obedience to a *m,*
31: 1 an oracle his *m* taught him:
Isa 49:15 "Can a *m* forget the baby
66:13 As a *m* comforts her child,
Jer 20:17 with my *m* as my grave,
Mic 7: 6 a daughter rises up against her *m,*
Mt 10:35 a daughter against her *m,*
10:37 or *m* more than me is not worthy
12:48 He replied to him, "Who is my *m,*
15: 4 'Honor your father and *m'*
19: 5 and *m* and be united to his wife,
19:19 honor your father and *m,'*
Mk 7:10 'Honor your father and your *m,'* and,
10:19 honor your father and *m.'* "
Lk 11:27 "Blessed is the *m* who gave you
12:53 daughter and daughter against *m,*
18:20 honor your father and *m.'* "
Jn 19:27 to the disciple, "Here is your *m."*
Gal 4:26 is above is free, and she is our *m.*
Eph 5:31 and *m* and be united to his wife,
6: 2 "Honor your father and *m"*—
1Th 2: 7 like a *m* caring for her little
2Ti 1: 5 and in your *m* Eunice and,

MOTHER-IN-LAW (MOTHER)
Ru 2:19 Ruth told her *m* about the one
Mt 10:35 a daughter-in-law against her *m*—

MOTHER'S (MOTHER)
Job 1:21 "Naked I came from my *m* womb,
Pr 1: 8 and do not forsake your *m* teaching
Ecc 5:15 from his *m* womb,
11: 5 the body is formed in a *m* womb,
Jn 3: 4 time into his *m* womb to be born!"

MOTIVE* (MOTIVES)
1Ch 28: 9 and understands every *m*

MOTIVES* (MOTIVE)
Pr 16: 2 but *m* are weighed by the LORD.
1Co 4: 5 will expose the *m* of men's hearts.
Php 1:18 whether from false *m* or true,
1Th 2: 3 spring from error or impure *m,*
Jas 4: 3 because you ask with wrong *m,*

MOUNT (MOUNTAIN MOUNTAINS MOUNTAINTOPS)
Ps 89: 9 when its waves *m* up, you still them
Isa 14:13 enthroned on the *m* of assembly,
Eze 28:14 You were on the holy *m* of God;
Zec 14: 4 stand on the *M* of Olives,

MOUNTAIN (MOUNT)
Ge 22:14 "On the *m* of the LORD it will be
Ex 24:18 And he stayed on the *m* forty days
Dt 5: 4 face to face out of the fire on the *m.*
Job 14:18 "But as a *m* erodes and crumbles
Ps 48: 1 in the city of our God, his holy *m.*
Isa 40: 4 every *m* and hill made low;
Mic 4: 2 let us go up to the *m* of the LORD,
Mt 4: 8 the devil took him to a very high *m*
17:20 say to this *m,* 'Move from here
Mk 9: 2 with him and led them up a high *m,*
Lk 3: 5 every *m* and hill made low.
Jn 4:21 the Father neither on this *m*
2Pe 1:18 were with him on the sacred *m.*

MOUNTAINS (MOUNT)
Ps 36: 6 righteousness is like the mighty *m,*
46: 2 the *m* fall into the heart of the sea,
90: 2 Before the *m* were born
Isa 52: 7 How beautiful on the *m*
54:10 Though the *m* be shaken
55:12 the *m* and hills
Eze 34: 6 My sheep wandered over all the *m*
Mt 24:16 are in Judea flee to the *m.*
Lk 23:30 they will say to the *m,* "Fall on us!"
1Co 13: 2 if I have a faith that can move *m,*
Rev 6:16 They called to the *m* and the rocks,

MOUNTAINTOPS (MOUNT)
Isa 42:11 let them shout from the *m.*

MOURN (MOURNING MOURNS)
Ecc 3: 4 a time to *m* and a time to dance,
Isa 61: 2 to comfort all who *m,*
Mt 5: 4 Blessed are those who *m,*
Ro 12:15 *m* with those who *m.*

MOURNING (MOURN)
Isa 61: 3 instead of *m,*
Jer 31:13 I will turn their *m* into gladness;
Rev 21: 4 There will be no more death or *m*

MOURNS (MOURN)
Zec 12:10 as one *m* for an only child,

MOUTH (MOUTHS)
Nu 22:38 only what God puts in my *m."*
Dt 8: 3 comes from the *m* of the LORD.
18:18 I will put my words in his *m,*
30:14 it is in your *m* and in your heart
Jos 1: 8 of the Law depart from your *m;*
2Ki 4:34 *m* to *m,* eyes to eyes, hands
Ps 10: 7 His *m* is full of curses and lies
17: 3 resolved that my *m* will not sin.
19:14 May the words of my *m*
37:30 *m* of the righteous man utters
40: 3 He put a new song in my *m,*
71: 8 My *m* is filled with your praise,
119:103 sweeter than honey to my *m!*
141: 3 Set a guard over my *m,* O LORD;
Pr 2: 6 and from his *m* come knowledge
4:24 Put away perversity from your *m;*
10:11 The *m* of the righteous is a fountain
10:31 *m* of the righteous brings forth
16:23 A wise man's heart guides his *m,*
26:28 and a flattering *m* works ruin.
27: 2 praise you, and not your own *m;*
Ecc 5: 2 Do not be quick with your *m,*
SS 1: 2 with the kisses of his *m*—
5:16 His *m* is sweetness itself;
Isa 29:13 come near to me with their *m*
40: 5 For the *m* of the LORD has spoken
45:23 my *m* has uttered in all integrity
51:16 I have put my words in your *m*
53: 7 so he did not open his *m.*
55:11 my word that goes out from my *m:*
59:21 *m* will not depart from your *m,*
Eze 3: 2 So I opened my *m,* and he gave me
Mal 2: 7 and from his *m* men should seek
Mt 4: 4 comes from the *m* of God.' "
12:34 overflow of the heart the *m* speaks.
15:11 into a man's *m* does not make him
15:18 out of the *m* come from the heart,
Lk 6:45 overflow of his heart his *m* speaks.
Ro 10: 9 That if you confess with your *m,*
15: 6 and *m* you may glorify the God
1Pe 2:22 and no deceit was found in his *m."*
Rev 1:16 and out of his *m* came a sharp
2:16 them with the sword of my *m.*
3:16 I am about to spit you out of my *m.*
19:15 Out of his *m* comes a sharp sword

MOUTHS (MOUTH)
Ps 78:36 would flatter him with their *m*,
Eze 33:31 With their *m* they express devotion
Ro 3:14 "Their *m* are full of cursing
Eph 4:29 talk come out of your *m*,
Jas 3: 3 bits into the *m* of horses

MOVE (MOVED MOVES)
Dt 19:14 Do not *m* your neighbor's
Pr 23:10 Do not *m* an ancient boundary
Ac 17:28 and *m* and have our being.'
1Co 13: 2 have a faith that can *m* mountains,
15:58 Let nothing *m* you.

MOVED (MOVE)
Ex 35:21 and whose heart *m* him came
2Ch 36:22 the LORD *m* the heart
Ezr 1: 5 everyone whose heart God had *m*
Ps 93: 1 it cannot be *m*.
Jn 11:33 he was deeply *m* in spirit
Col 1:23 not *m* from the hope held out

MOVES (MOVE)
Dt 23:14 For the LORD your God *m* about

MUD (MUDDIED)
Ps 40: 2 out of the *m* and mire;
Isa 57:20 whose waves cast up mire and *m*.
Jn 9: 6 made some *m* with the saliva,
2Pe 2:22 back to her wallowing in the *m*."

MUDDIED (MUD)
Pr 25:26 Like a *m* spring or a polluted well
Eze 32:13 or *m* by the hoofs of cattle.

MULBERRY*
Lk 17: 6 you can say to this *m* tree,

MULTITUDE (MULTITUDES)
Isa 31: 1 who trust in the *m* of their chariots
Jas 5:20 and cover over a *m* of sins.
1Pe 4: 8 love covers over a *m* of sins.
Rev 7: 9 me was a great *m* that no one could
19: 1 of a great *m* in heaven shouting:

MULTITUDES (MULTITUDE)
Ne 9: 6 and the *m* of heaven worship you.
Da 12: 2 *M* who sleep in the dust
Joel 3:14 *M*, *m* in the valley of decision!

MURDER (MURDERED MURDERER MURDERERS)
Ex 20:13 "You shall not *m*.
Dt 5:17 "You shall not *m*.
Pr 28:17 A man tormented by the guilt of *m*
Mt 5:21 'Do not *m*, and anyone who
15:19 *m*, adultery, sexual immorality,
Ro 1:29 *m*, strife, deceit and malice.
13: 9 "Do not *m*," "Do not steal,"
Jas 2:11 adultery," also said, "Do not *m*."

MURDERED (MURDER)
Mt 23:31 of those who *m* the prophets.
Ac 7:52 now you have betrayed and *m* him
1Jn 3:12 to the evil one and *m* his brother.

MURDERER (MURDER)
Nu 35:16 he is a *m*; the *m* shall be put
Jn 8:44 He was a *m* from the beginning,
1Jn 3:15 who hates his brother is a *m*,

MURDERERS (MURDER)
1Ti 1: 9 for *m*, for adulterers and perverts,
Rev 21: 8 the *m*, the sexually immoral,
22:15 the sexually immoral, the *m*,

MUSIC* (MUSICAL MUSICIAN MUSICIANS)
Ge 31:27 singing to the *m* of tambourines
Jdg 5: 3 I will make *m* to the LORD,
1Ch 6:31 put in charge of the *m* in the house
6:32 They ministered with *m*
25: 6 fathers for the *m* of the temple
25: 7 and skilled in *m* for the LORD—
Ne 12:27 and with the *m* of cymbals,
Job 21:12 They sing to the *m* of tambourine
Ps 27: 6 and make *m* to the LORD.
33: 2 make *m* to him on the ten-stringed
45: 8 the *m* of the strings makes you glad
57: 7 I will sing and make *m*.
81: 2 Begin the *m*, strike the tambourine,
87: 7 As they make *m* they will sing,
92: 1 and make *m* to your name,
92: 3 to the *m* of the ten-stringed lyre
95: 2 and extol him with *m* and song.
98: 4 burst into jubilant song with *m*;
98: 5 make *m* to the LORD
108: 1 make *m* with all my soul.
144: 9 the ten-stringed lyre I will make *m*
147: 7 make *m* to our God on the harp.
149: 3 make *m* to him with tambourine
Isa 30:32 will be to the *m* of tambourines
La 5:14 young men have stopped their *m*.
Eze 26:13 *m* of your harps will be heard no
Da 3: 5 lyre, harp, pipes and all kinds of *m*,
3: 7 and all kinds of *m*, all the peoples,
3:10 and all kinds of *m* must fall down
3:15 lyre, harp, pipes and all kinds of *m*,
Am 5:23 to the *m* of your harps.
Hab 3:19 For the director of *m*.
Lk 15:25 came near the house, he heard *m*
Eph 5:19 make *m* in your heart to the Lord,
Rev 18:22 The *m* of harpists and musicians,

MUSICAL* (MUSIC)
1Ch 15:16 accompanied by *m* instruments:
23: 5 with the *m* instruments I have
2Ch 7: 6 with the LORD's *m* instruments,
23:13 with *m* instruments were leading
34:12 skilled in playing *m* instruments—
Ne 12:36 with *m* instruments prescribed
Am 6: 5 and improvise on *m* instruments.

MUSICIAN* (MUSIC)
1Ch 6:33 Heman, the *m*, the son of Joel,

MUSICIANS* (MUSIC)
1Ki 10:12 to make harps and lyres for the *m*.
1Ch 9:33 Those who were *m*, heads
15:19 The *m* Heman, Asaph
2Ch 5:12 All the Levites who were *m*—
9:11 to make harps and lyres for the *m*.
35:15 The *m*, the descendants of Asaph,
Ps 68:25 are the singers, after them the *m*;
Rev 18:22 The music of harpists and *m*,

MUSTARD
Mt 13:31 kingdom of heaven is like a *m* seed,
17:20 you have faith as small as a *m* seed,
Mk 4:31 It is like a *m* seed, which is

MUTILATORS*
Php 3: 2 those men who do evil, those *m*

MUTUAL* (MUTUALLY)
Ro 14:19 leads to peace and to *m* edification.
1Co 7: 5 by *m* consent and for a time,

MUTUALLY* (MUTUAL)
Ro 1:12 and I may be *m* encouraged

MUZZLE*
Dt 25: 4 Do not *m* an ox while it is treading
Ps 39: 1 I will put a *m* on my mouth
1Co 9: 9 "Do not *m* an ox while it is
1Ti 5:18 "Do not *m* the ox while it is

MYRRH
Ps 45: 8 All your robes are fragrant with *m*
SS 1:13 My lover is to me a sachet of *m*
Mt 2:11 of gold and of incense and of *m*.
Mk 15:23 offered him wine mixed with *m*,
Jn 19:39 Nicodemus brought a mixture of *m*
Rev 18:13 of incense, *m* and frankincense,

MYSTERIES* (MYSTERY)
Job 11: 7 "Can you fathom the *m* of God?
Da 2:28 a God in heaven who reveals *m*.
2:29 of *m* showed you what is going
2:47 Lord of kings and a revealer of *m*,
1Co 13: 2 can fathom all *m* and all knowledge
14: 2 he utters *m* with his spirit.

MYSTERY* (MYSTERIES)
Da 2:18 God of heaven concerning this *m*,
2:19 the night the *m* was revealed
2:27 to the king the *m* he has asked
2:30 this *m* has been revealed to me,
2:47 for you were able to reveal this *m*."
4: 9 and no *m* is too difficult for you.
Ro 11:25 you to be ignorant of this *m*,
16:25 to the revelation of the *m* hidden
1Co 15:51 I tell you a *m*: We will not all sleep,
Eph 1: 9 to us the *m* of his will according
3: 3 the *m* made known to me
3: 4 insight into the *m* of Christ,
3: 6 This *m* is that through the gospel
3: 9 the administration of this *m*,
5:32 This is a profound *m*—
6:19 I will fearlessly make known the *m*
Col 1:26 the *m* that has been kept hidden
1:27 the glorious riches of this *m*,
2: 2 in order that they may know the *m*
4: 3 so that we may proclaim the *m*
1Ti 3:16 the *m* of godliness is great:
Rev 1:20 *m* of the seven stars that you saw
10: 7 the *m* of God will be accomplished,
17: 5 written on her forehead: M
17: 7 explain to you the *m* of the woman

MYTHS*
1Ti 1: 4 nor to devote themselves to *m*
4: 7 Have nothing to do with godless *m*
2Ti 4: 4 from the truth and turn aside to *m*.
Tit 1:14 will pay no attention to Jewish *m*

NAAMAN
Aramean general whose leprosy was cleansed by Elisha (2Ki 5).

NABAL
Wealthy Carmelite the LORD killed for refusing to help David (1Sa 25). David married Abigail, his widow (1Sa 25:39-42).

NABOTH*
Jezreelite killed by Jezebel for his vineyard (1Ki 21). Ahab's family destroyed for this (1Ki 21:17-24; 2Ki 9:21-37).

NADAB
1. Firstborn of Aaron (Ex 6:23); killed with Abihu for offering unauthorized fire (Lev 10; Nu 3:4).
2. Son of Jeroboam I; king of Israel (1Ki 15:25-32).

NAHUM
Prophet against Nineveh (Na 1:1).

NAIL* (NAILING)
Jn 20:25 "Unless I see the *n* marks

NAILING* (NAIL)
Ac 2:23 him to death by *n* him to the cross.
Col 2:14 he took it away, *n* it to the cross.

NAIVE
Ro 16:18 they deceive the minds of *n* people.

NAKED
Ge 2:25 The man and his wife were both *n*,
Job 1:21 *N* I came from my mother's womb,
Isa 58: 7 when you see the *n*, to clothe him,
2Co 5: 3 are clothed, we will not be found *n*.

NAME (NAMES)
Ge 2:19 man to see what he would *n* them;
4:26 to call on the *n* of the LORD.
11: 4 so that we may make a *n*
12: 2 I will make your *n* great,
32:29 Jacob said, "Please tell me your *n*."
Ex 3:15 This is my *n* forever, the *n*
20: 7 "You shall not misuse the *n*
34:14 for the LORD, whose *n* is Jealous,
Lev 24:11 Israelite woman blasphemed the *N*
Dt 5:11 "You shall not misuse the *n*
12:11 choose as a dwelling for his *N*—
18: 5 minister in the LORD's *n* always.
25: 6 carry on the *n* of the dead brother
28:58 this glorious and awesome *n*—
Jos 7: 9 do for your own great *n*?"
Jdg 13:17 "What is your *n*, so that we may
1Sa 12:22 of his great *n* the LORD will not
2Sa 6: 2 which is called by the *N*, the name
7: 9 Now I will make your *n* great,
1Ki 5: 5 will build the temple for my *N*.'
8:29 you said, 'My *N* shall be there,'
1Ch 17: 8 I will make your *n* like the names
2Ch 7:14 my people, who are called by my *n*,
Ne 9:10 You made a *n* for yourself,
Ps 8: 1 how majestic is your *n*
9:10 Those who know your *n* will trust
20: 7 in the *n* of the LORD our God.
29: 2 to the LORD the glory due his *n*;
34: 3 let us exalt his *n* together.
44:20 If we had forgotten the *n*
66: 2 Sing the glory of his *n*;
68: 4 Sing to God, sing praise to his *n*,
79: 9 for the glory of your *n*;
96: 8 to the LORD the glory due his *n*;
103: 1 my inmost being, praise his holy *n*.
115: 1 but to your *n* be the glory,
138: 2 your *n* and your word.
145: 1 I will praise your *n* for ever
147: 4 and calls them each by *n*.
Pr 3: 4 you will win favor and a good *n*
18:10 *n* of the LORD is a strong tower;
22: 1 A good *n* is more desirable
30: 4 What is his *n*, and the *n* of his son?
Ecc 7: 1 A good *n* is better
SS 1: 3 your *n* is like perfume poured out.
Isa 12: 4 thanks to the LORD, call on his *n*;
26: 8 your *n* and renown
40:26 and calls them each by *n*.
42: 8 "I am the LORD; that is my *n*!
56: 5 I will give them an everlasting *n*
57:15 who lives forever, whose *n* is holy:
63:14 to make for yourself a glorious *n*.
Jer 14: 7 do something for the sake of your *n*
15:16 for I bear your *n*,

Eze 20: 9 of my *n* I did what would keep it
20:14 of my *n* I did what would keep it
20:22 of my *n* I did what would keep it
Da 12: 1 everyone whose *n* is found written
Hos 12: 5 the LORD is his *n* of renown!
Joel 2:32 on the *n* of the LORD will be saved
Mic 5: 4 in the majesty of the *n*
Zep 3: 9 call on the *n* of the LORD
Zec 6:12 is the man whose *n* is the Branch,
14: 9 one LORD, and his *n* the only *n*.
Mal 1: 6 O priests, who show contempt for my *n*.
Mt 1:21 and you are to give him the *n* Jesus,
6: 9 hallowed be your *n*,
18:20 or three come together in my *n*,
24: 5 For many will come in my *n*,
28:19 them in the *n* of the Father
Mk 9:41 gives you a cup of water in my *n*
Lk 11: 2 hallowed be your *n*,
Jn 10: 3 He calls his own sheep by *n*
14:13 I will do whatever you ask in my *n*,
16:24 asked for anything in my *n*.
Ac 2:21 on the *n* of the Lord will be saved.'
4:12 for there is no other *n*
Ro 10:13 "Everyone who calls on the *n*
Php 2: 9 him the *n* that is above every *n*,
2:10 at the *n* of Jesus every knee should
Col 3:17 do it all in the *n* of the Lord Jesus,
Heb 1: 4 as the *n* he has inherited is superior
Jas 5:14 him with oil in the *n* of the Lord.
1Jn 5:13 believe in the *n* of the Son of God
Rev 2:17 stone with a new *n* written on it,
3: 5 I will never blot out his *n*
3:12 I will also write on him my new *n*.
19:13 and his *n* is the Word of God.
20:15 If anyone's *n* was not found written

NAMES (NAME)

Ex 28: 9 engrave on them the *n* of the sons
Lk 10:20 but rejoice that your *n* are written
Php 4: 3 whose *n* are in the book of life.
Heb 12:23 whose *n* are written in heaven.
Rev 21:27 but only those whose *n* are written

NAOMI

Wife of Elimelech, mother-in-law of Ruth (Ru 1: 2, 4). Left Bethlehem for Moab during famine (Ru 1:1). Returned a widow, with Ruth (Ru 1:6-22). Advised Ruth to seek marriage with Boaz (Ru 2: 17-3:4). Cared for Ruth's son Obed (Ru 4:13-17).

NAPHTALI

Son of Jacob by Bilhah (Ge 30:8; 35:25; 1Ch 2: 2). Tribe of blessed (Ge 49:21; Dt 33:23), numbered (Nu 1:43; 26:50), allotted land (Jos 19:32-39; Eze 48:3), failed to fully possess (Jdg 1:33), supported Deborah (Jdg 4:10; 5:18), David (1Ch 12: 34), 12,000 from (Rev 7:6).

NARROW

Mt 7:13 "Enter through the *n* gate.
7:14 and *n* the road that leads to life,

NATHAN

Prophet and chronicler of Israel's history (1Ch 29:29; 2Ch 9:29). Announced the Davidic covenant (2Sa 7; 1Ch 17). Denounced David's sin with Bathsheba (2Sa 12). Supported Solomon (1Ki 1).

NATHANAEL*

Apostle (Jn 1:45-49; 21:2). Probably also called Bartholomew (Mt 10:3).

NATION (NATIONS)

Ge 12: 2 "I will make you into a great *n*
Ex 19: 6 a kingdom of priests and a holy *n*.'
Dt 4: 7 What other *n* is so great
Jos 5: 8 And after the whole *n* had been
2Sa 7:23 one *n* on earth that God went out
Ps 33:12 Blessed is the *n* whose God is
Pr 11:14 For lack of guidance a *n* falls,
14:34 Righteousness exalts a *n*,
Isa 2: 4 *N* will not take up sword
26: 2 that the righteous *n* may enter,
60:12 For the *n* or kingdom that will not
65: 1 To a *n* that did not call on my name
66: 8 a *n* be brought forth in a moment?
Mic 4: 3 *N* will not take up sword
Mt 24: 7 *N* will rise against *n*,
Mk 13: 8 *N* will rise against *n*,
1Pe 2: 9 a royal priesthood, a holy *n*,
Rev 5: 9 and language and people and *n*.
7: 9 from every *n*, tribe, people
14: 6 to every *n*, tribe, language

NATIONS (NATION)

Ge 17: 4 You will be the father of many *n*.
18:18 and all *n* on earth will be blessed
Ex 19: 5 of all *n* you will be my treasured
Lev 20:26 apart from the *n* to be my own.
Dt 7: 1 drives out before you many *n*—
15: 6 You will rule over many *n*
Jdg 3: 1 These are the *n* the LORD left
2Ch 20: 6 rule over all the kingdoms of the *n*.
Ne 1: 8 I will scatter you among the *n*,
Ps 2: 1 Why do the *n* conspire
2: 8 I will make the *n* your inheritance,
9: 5 You have rebuked the *n*
22:28 and he rules over the *n*.
46:10 I will be exalted among the *n*,
47: 8 God reigns over the *n*;
66: 7 his eyes watch the *n*—
67: 2 your salvation among all *n*.
68:30 Scatter the *n* who delight in war.
72:17 All *n* will be blessed through him,
96: 3 Declare his glory among the *n*,
99: 2 he is exalted over all the *n*.
106: 35 but they mingled with the *n*
110: 6 He will judge the *n*, heaping up
113: 4 The LORD is exalted over all the *n*
Isa 2: 2 and all *n* will stream to it.
11:10 the *n* will rally to him,
12: 4 among the *n* what he has done,
40:15 Surely the *n* are like a drop
42: 1 and he will bring justice to the *n*.
51: 4 justice will become a light to the *n*.
52:15 so will he sprinkle many *n*,
56: 7 a house of prayer for all *n*."
60: 3 *N* will come to your light,
66:18 and gather all *n* and tongues,
Jer 1: 5 you as a prophet to the *n*."
3:17 and all *n* will gather in Jerusalem
31:10 "Hear the word of the LORD, O *n*;
33: 9 and honor before all *n*
46:28 I completely destroy all the *n*
Eze 22: 4 you an object of scorn to the *n*
34:13 I will bring them out from the *n*
36:23 *n* will know that I am the LORD,
37:22 and they will never again be two *n*
39:21 I will display my glory among the *n*
Hos 7: 8 "Ephraim mixes with the *n*;
Joel 2:17 a byword among the *n*.
3: 2 I will gather all *n*
Am 9:12 and all the *n* that bear my name,"
Zep 3: 8 I have decided to assemble the *n*,
Hag 2: 7 and the desired of all *n* will come,
Zec 8:13 an object of cursing among the *n*,
8:23 *n* will take firm hold of one Jew
9:10 He will proclaim peace to the *n*.
14: 2 I will gather all the *n* to Jerusalem
Mt 12:18 he will proclaim justice to the *n*.
24: 9 and you will be hated by all *n*
24:14 whole world as a testimony to all *n*,
25:32 All the *n* will be gathered
28:19 and make disciples of all *n*,
Mk 11:17 a house of prayer for all *n*'?
Ac 4:25 " 'Why do the *n* rage
Ro 15:12 who will arise to rule over the *n*;
Gal 3: 8 All *n* will be blessed through you."
1Ti 3:16 was preached among the *n*,
Rev 15: 4 All *n* will come
21:24 The *n* will walk by its light,
22: 2 are for the healing of the *n*.

NATURAL (NATURE)

Ro 6:19 you are weak in your *n* selves.
1Co 15:44 If there is a *n* body, there is

NATURE (NATURAL)

Ro 1:20 his eternal power and divine *n*—
7:18 lives in me, that is, in my sinful *n*.
8: 4 do not live according to the sinful *n*
8: 5 to the sinful *n* have their minds set
8: 8 by the sinful *n* cannot please God.
13:14 to gratify the desires of the sinful *n*.
Gal 5:13 freedom to indulge the sinful *n*;
5:19 The acts of the sinful *n* are obvious:
5:24 Jesus have crucified the sinful *n*
Php 2: 6 Who, being in very *n* God,
Col 3: 5 whatever belongs to your earthly *n*
2Pe 1: 4 you may participate in the divine *n*

NAZARENE* (NAZARETH)

Mt 2:23 prophets: "He will be called a *N*."
Mk 14:67 "You also were with that *N*, Jesus,"
16: 6 "You are looking for Jesus the *N*,
Ac 24: 5 He is a ringleader of the *N* sect and

NAZARETH (NAZARENE)

Mt 4:13 Leaving *N*, he went and lived
Lk 4:16 to *N*, where he had been brought
Jn 1:46 "*N*! Can anything good come

NAZIRITE

Nu 6: 2 of separation to the LORD as a *N*,
Jdg 13: 7 because the boy will be a *N* of God

NEBO

Dt 34: 1 Then Moses climbed Mount *N*

NEBUCHADNEZZAR

Babylonian king. Subdued and exiled Judah (2Ki 24-25; 2Ch 36; Jer 39). Dreams interpreted by Daniel (Da 2; 4). Worshiped God (Da 3:28-29; 4:34-37).

NECESSARY*

Ac 1:21 Therefore it is *n* to choose one
Ro 13: 5 it is *n* to submit to the authorities,
2Co 9: 5 I thought it *n* to urge the brothers
Php 1:24 it is more *n* for you that I remain
2:25 But I think it is *n* to send back
Heb 8: 3 and so it was *n* for this one
9:16 it is *n* to prove the death
9:23 It was *n*, then, for the copies

NECK (STIFF-NECKED)

Pr 3:22 an ornament to grace your *n*.
6:21 fasten them around your *n*.
Mt 18: 6 a large millstone hung around his *n*

NECO

Pharaoh who killed Josiah (2Ki 23:29-30; 2Ch 35:20-22), deposed Jehoahaz (2Ki 23:33-35; 2Ch 36:3-4).

NEED (NEEDS NEEDY)

1Ki 8:59 Israel according to each day's *n*,
Ps 79: 8 for we are in desperate *n*.
116: 6 when I was in great *n*, he saved me.
142: 6 for I am in desperate *n*;
Mt 6: 8 for your Father knows what you *n*
Lk 15:14 country, and he began to be in *n*.
Ac 2:45 they gave to anyone as he had *n*.
Ro 12:13 with God's people who are in *n*.
1Co 12:21 say to the hand, "I don't *n* you!"
Eph 4:28 something to share with those in *n*.
1Ti 5: 3 to those widows who are really in *n*
Heb 4:16 grace to help us in our time of *n*.
1Jn 3:17 sees his brother in *n* but has no pity

NEEDLE

Mt 19:24 go through the eye of a *n*

NEEDS (NEED)

Isa 58:11 he will satisfy your *n*
Php 2:25 sent to take care of my *n*.
4:19 God will meet all your *n* according
Jas 2:16 does nothing about his physical *n*,

NEEDY (NEED)

Dt 15:11 toward the poor and *n* in your land.
1Sa 2: 8 and lifts the *n* from the ash heap;
Ps 35:10 and *n* from those who rob them."
69:33 The LORD hears the *n*
72:12 he will deliver the *n* who cry out,
140: 12 and upholds the cause of the *n*.
Pr 14:21 blessed is he who is kind to the *n*.
14:31 to the *n* honors God.
22:22 and do not crush the *n* in court,
31: 9 defend the rights of the poor and *n*
31:20 and extends her hands to the *n*.
Mt 6: 2 "So when you give to the *n*,

NEGLECT* (NEGLECTED)

Dt 12:19 Be careful not to *n* the Levites
14:27 And do not *n* the Levites living
Ezr 4:22 Be careful not to *n* this matter.
Ne 10:39 We will not *n* the house of our God
Est 6:10 Do not *n* anything you have
Ps 119: 16 I will not *n* your word.
Lk 11:42 you *n* justice and the love of God.
Ac 6: 2 for us to *n* the ministry of the word
1Ti 4:14 Do not *n* your gift, which was

NEGLECTED (NEGLECT)

Mt 23:23 But you have *n* the more important

NEHEMIAH

Cupbearer of Artaxerxes (Ne 2:1); governor of Israel (Ne 8:9). Returned to Jerusalem to rebuild walls (Ne 2-6). With Ezra, reestablished worship (Ne 8). Prayer confessing nation's sin (Ne 9). Dedicated wall (Ne 12).

NEIGHBOR (NEIGHBOR'S)

Ex 20:16 give false testimony against your *n*.
20:17 or anything that belongs to your *n*
Lev 19:13 Do not defraud your *n* or rob him.
19:17 Rebuke your *n* frankly
19:18 but love your *n* as yourself.
Ps 15: 3 who does his *n* no wrong
Pr 3:29 Do not plot harm against your *n*,
11:12 who lacks judgment derides his *n*,
14:21 He who despises his *n* sins,
16:29 A violent man entices his *n*
24:28 against your *n* without cause,
25:18 gives false testimony against his *n*.
27:10 better a *n* nearby than a brother far
27:14 If a man loudly blesses his *n*
29: 5 Whoever flatters his *n*

Jer 31:34 No longer will a man teach his *n*,
Zec 8:17 do not plot evil against your *n*,
Mt 5:43 Love your *n* and hate your enemy.'
19:19 and 'love your *n* as yourself.' "
Mk 12:31 The second is this: 'Love your *n*
Lk 10:27 and, 'Love your *n* as yourself.' "
10:29 who is my *n*?" In reply Jesus said:
Ro 13: 9 "Love your *n* as yourself."
13:10 Love does no harm to its *n*.
15: 2 Each of us should please his *n*
Gal 5:14 "Love your *n* as yourself."
Eph 4:25 and speak truthfully to his *n*,
Heb 8:11 No longer will a man teach his *n*,
Jas 2: 8 "Love your *n* as yourself,"

NEIGHBOR'S (NEIGHBOR)
Ex 20:17 You shall not covet your *n* wife,
Dt 5:21 not set your desire on your *n* house
19:14 not move your *n* boundary stone
27:17 who moves his *n* boundary stone."
Pr 25:17 Seldom set foot in your *n* house—

NESTS
Mt 8:20 and birds of the air have *n*,

NET (NETS)
Pr 1:17 How useless to spread a *n*
Hab 1:15 he catches them in his *n*,
Mt 13:47 of heaven is like a *n* that was let
Jn 21: 6 "Throw your *n* on the right side

NETS (NET)
Ps 141: 10 Let the wicked fall into their own *n*
Mt 4:20 At once they left their *n*
Lk 5: 4 and let down the *n* for a catch."

NEVER-FAILING*
Am 5:24 righteousness like a *n* stream!

NEW
Ps 40: 3 He put a *n* song in my mouth,
98: 1 Sing to the LORD a *n* song,
Ecc 1: 9 there is nothing *n* under the sun.
Isa 42: 9 and *n* things I declare;
62: 2 you will be called by a *n* name
65:17 *n* heavens and a *n* earth.
66:22 "As the *n* heavens and the *n* earth
Jer 31:31 "when I will make a *n* covenant
La 3:23 They are *n* every morning;
Eze 11:19 undivided heart and put a *n* spirit
18:31 and get a *n* heart and a *n* spirit.
36:26 give you a *n* heart and put a *n* spirit
Zep 3: 5 and every *n* day he does not fail,
Mt 9:17 Neither do men pour *n* wine
Mk 16:17 they will speak in *n* tongues;
Lk 5:39 after drinking old wine wants the *n*
22:20 "This cup is the *n* covenant
Jn 13:34 "A *n* commandment I give you:
Ac 5:20 the full message of this *n* life."
Ro 6: 4 the Father, we too may live a *n* life.
1Co 5: 7 old yeast that you may be a *n* batch
11:25 "This cup is the *n* covenant
2Co 3: 6 as ministers of a *n* covenant—
5:17 he is a *n* creation; the old has gone,
Gal 6:15 what counts is a *n* creation.
Eph 4:23 to be made *n* in the attitude
4:24 and to put on the *n* self, created
Col 3:10 and have put on the *n* self,
Heb 8: 8 when I will make a *n* covenant
9:15 is the mediator of a *n* covenant,
10:20 by a *n* and living way opened for us
12:24 Jesus the mediator of a *n* covenant,
1Pe 1: 3 great mercy he has given us *n* birth
2Pe 3:13 to a *n* heaven and a *n* earth,
1Jn 2: 8 Yet I am writing you a *n* command;
Rev 2:17 stone with a *n* name written on it,
3:12 the *n* Jerusalem, which is coming
21: 1 I saw a *n* heaven and a *n* earth,

NEWBORN (BEAR)
1Pe 2: 2 Like *n* babies, crave pure spiritual

NEWS
2Ki 7: 9 This is a day of good *n*
Ps 112: 7 He will have no fear of bad *n*;
Pr 15:30 good *n* gives health to the bones.
25:25 is good *n* from a distant land.
Isa 52: 7 the feet of those who bring good *n*,
61: 1 me to preach good *n* to the poor.
Na 1:15 the feet of one who brings good *n*,
Mt 4:23 preaching the good *n*
9:35 preaching the good *n*
11: 5 the good *n* is preached to the poor.
Mk 1:15 Repent and believe the good *n*!"
16:15 preach the good *n* to all creation.
Lk 1:19 and to tell you this good *n*.
2:10 I bring you good *n*
3:18 and preached the good *n* to them.
4:43 "I must preach the good *n*
8: 1 proclaiming the good *n*
Lk 16:16 the good *n* of the kingdom
Ac 5:42 proclaiming the good *n* that Jesus
10:36 telling the good *n* of peace
14: 7 continued to preach the good *n*.
14:21 They preached the good *n*
17:18 preaching the good *n* about Jesus
Ro 10:15 feet of those who bring good *n*!"

NICODEMUS*
Pharisee who visted Jesus at night (Jn 3). Argued fair treatment of Jesus (Jn 7:50-52). With Joseph, prepared Jesus for burial (Jn 19:38-42).

NIGHT (NIGHTS NIGHTTIME)
Ge 1: 5 and the darkness he called "*n*."
1:16 and the lesser light to govern the *n*.
Ex 13:21 and by *n* in a pillar of fire
14:24 During the last watch of the *n*.
Dt 28:66 filled with dread both *n* and day,
Jos 1: 8 and *n*, so that you may be careful
Job 35:10 who gives songs in the *n*,
Ps 1: 2 on his law he meditates day and *n*.
19: 2 *n* after *n* they display knowledge.
42: 8 at *n* his song is with me—
63: 6 of you through the watches of the *n*
77: 6 I remembered my songs in the *n*.
90: 4 or like a watch in the *n*.
91: 5 You will not fear the terror of *n*,
119: 148 through the watches of the *n*,
121: 6 nor the moon by *n*.
136: 9 the moon and stars to govern the *n*;
Pr 31:18 and her lamp does not go out at *n*.
Isa 21:11 Watchman, what is left of the *n*?"
58:10 and your *n* will become like
Jer 33:20 and my covenant with the *n*,
Lk 2: 8 watch over their flocks at *n*.
6:12 and spent the *n* praying to God.
Jn 3: 2 He came to Jesus at *n* and said,
9: 4 *N* is coming, when no one can work
1Th 5: 2 Lord will come like a thief in the *n*.
5: 5 We do not belong to the *n*
Rev 21:25 for there will be no *n* there.

NIGHTS (NIGHT)
Jnh 1:17 the fish three days and three *n*.
Mt 4: 2 After fasting forty days and forty *n*
12:40 three *n* in the belly of a huge fish,
2Co 6: 5 in hard work, sleepless *n*

NIGHTTIME* (NIGHT)
Zec 14: 7 or *n*— a day known to the LORD.

NIMROD
Ge 10: 9 "Like *N*, a mighty hunter

NINEVEH
Jnh 1: 2 "Go to the great city of *N*
Na 1: 1 An oracle concerning *N*.
Mt 12:41 The men of *N* will stand up

NOAH
Righteous man (Eze 14:14, 20) called to build ark (Ge 6-8; Heb 11:7; 1Pe 3:20; 2Pe 2:5). God's covenant with (Ge 9:1-17). Drunkenness of (Ge 9:18-23). Blessed sons, cursed Canaan (Ge 9:24-27).

NOBLE
Ru 3:11 you are a woman of *n* character.
Ps 45: 1 My heart is stirred by a *n* theme
Pr 12: 4 of *n* character is her husband's
31:10 A wife of *n* character who can find?
31:29 "Many women do *n* things,
Isa 32: 8 But the *n* man makes *n* plans,
Lk 8:15 good soil stands for those with a *n*
Ro 9:21 of clay some pottery for *n* purposes
Php 4: 8 whatever is *n*, whatever is right,
2Ti 2:20 some are for *n* purposes

NOSTRILS
Ge 2: 7 and breathed into his *n* the breath
Ex 15: 8 By the blast of your *n*
Ps 18:15 at the blast of breath from your *n*.

NOTE
Ac 4:13 and they took *n* that these men had
Php 3:17 take *n* of those who live according

NOTHING
2Sa 24:24 offerings that cost me *n*."
Ne 9:21 in the desert; they lacked *n*,
Ps 73:25 earth has *n* I desire besides you
Jer 32:17 *N* is too hard for you
Jn 15: 5 apart from me you can do *n*.

NOURISH
Pr 10:21 The lips of the righteous *n* many,

NULLIFY
Mt 15: 6 Thus you *n* the word of God
Ro 3:31 Do we, then, *n* the law by this faith

OATH
Ex 33: 1 up to the land I promised on *o*
Nu 30: 2 or takes an *o* to obligate himself
Dt 6:18 promised on *o* to your forefathers,
7: 8 and kept the *o* he swore
29:12 you this day and sealing with an *o*,
Ps 95:11 So I declared on *o* in my anger,
119: 106 I have taken an *o* and confirmed it,
132: 11 The LORD swore an *o* to David,
Ecc 8: 2 because you took an *o* before God.
Mt 5:33 'Do not break your *o*, but keep
Heb 7:20 And it was not without an *o*!

OBADIAH
1. Believer who sheltered 100 prophets from Jezebel (1Ki 18:1-16).
2. Prophet against Edom (Ob 1).

OBEDIENCE* (OBEY)
Ge 49:10 and the *o* of the nations is his.
Jdg 2:17 of *o* to the LORD's commands.
1Ch 21:19 So David went up in *o*
2Ch 31:21 in *o* to the law and the commands,
Pr 30:17 that scorns *o* to a mother,
Lk 23:56 Sabbath in *o* to the commandment.
Ac 21:24 but that you yourself are living in *o*
Ro 1: 5 to the *o* that comes from faith.
5:19 also through the *o* of the one man
6:16 to *o*, which leads to righteousness?
16:19 Everyone has heard about your *o*,
2Co 9:13 for the *o* that accompanies your
10: 6 once your *o* is complete.
Phm :21 Confident of your *o*, I write to you,
Heb 5: 8 he learned *o* from what he suffered
1Pe 1: 2 for *o* to Jesus Christ and sprinkling
2Jn : 6 that we walk in *o* to his commands.

OBEDIENT* (OBEY)
Dt 30:17 heart turns away and you are not *o*,
Isa 1:19 If you are willing and *o*,
Lk 2:51 with them and was *o* to them.
Ac 6: 7 of priests became *o* to the faith.
2Co 2: 9 if you would stand the test and be *o*
7:15 he remembers that you were all *o*,
10: 5 thought to make it *o* to Christ.
Php 2: 8 and became *o* to death—
Tit 3: 1 to be *o*, to be ready
1Pe 1:14 As *o* children, do not conform

OBEY (OBEDIENCE OBEDIENT OBEYED OBEYING OBEYS)
Ex 12:24 "*O* these instructions as a lasting
19: 5 Now if you *o* me fully and keep my
24: 7 the LORD has said; we will *o*."
Lev 18: 4 You must *o* my laws and be careful
25:18 and be careful to *o* my laws,
Nu 15:40 remember to *o* all my commands
Dt 5:27 We will listen and *o*."
6: 3 careful to *o* so that it may go well
6:24 us to *o* all these decrees
11:13 if you faithfully *o* the commands I
12:28 to *o* all these regulations I am
13: 4 Keep his commands and *o* him;
21:18 son who does not *o* his father
28: 1 If you fully *o* the LORD your God
28:15 if you do not *o* the LORD your
30: 2 and *o* him with all your heart
30:10 if you *o* the LORD your God
30:14 and in your heart so you may *o* it.
32:46 children to *o* carefully all the words
Jos 1: 7 to *o* all the law my servant Moses
22: 5 in all his ways, to *o* his commands,
24:24 the LORD our God and *o* him."
1Sa 15:22 To *o* is better than sacrifice,
1Ki 8:61 by his decrees and *o* his commands
2Ki 17:13 that I commanded your fathers to *o*
2Ch 34:31 and to *o* the words of the covenant
Ne 1: 5 who love him and *o* his commands,
Ps 103: 18 and remember to *o* his precepts.
103: 20 who *o* his word.
119: 17 I will *o* your word.
119: 34 and *o* it with all my heart.
119: 57 I have promised to *o* your words.
119: 67 but now I *o* your word.
119: 100 for I *o* your precepts.
119: 129 therefore I *o* them.
119: 167 I *o* your statutes,
Pr 5:13 I would not *o* my teachers
Jer 7:23 I gave them this command: *O* me,
11: 4 '*O* me and do everything I
11: 7 and again, saying, "*O* me."
42: 6 we will *o* the LORD our God,
Da 9: 4 who love him and *o* his commands,
Mt 8:27 the winds and the waves *o* him!"
19:17 to enter life, *o* the commandments
28:20 to *o* everything I have commanded
Lk 11:28 hear the word of God and *o* it."
Jn 14:15 you will *o* what I command.
14:23 loves me, he will *o* my teaching.

Jn 14:24 not love me will not *o* my teaching.
15:10 If you *o* my commands, you will
Ac 5:29 "We must *o* God rather than men!
5:32 given to those who *o* him."
Ro 2:13 it is those who *o* the law who will
6:12 body so that you *o* its evil desires.
6:16 slaves to the one whom you *o*—
6:16 yourselves to someone to *o* him
15:18 in leading the Gentiles to *o* God
16:26 nations might believe and *o* him—
Gal 5: 3 obligated to *o* the whole law.
Eph 6: 1 *o* your parents in the Lord,
6: 5 *o* your earthly masters with respect
Col 3:20 *o* your parents in everything,
3:22 *o* your earthly masters
2Th 3:14 anyone does not *o* our instruction
1Ti 3: 4 and see that his children *o* him
Heb 5: 9 eternal salvation for all who *o* him
13:17 *O* your leaders and submit
1Pe 4:17 for those who do not *o* the gospel
1Jn 3:24 Those who *o* his commands live
5: 3 love for God: to *o* his commands.
Rev 12:17 those who *o* God's commandments
14:12 the saints who *o* God's

OBEYED (OBEY)
Ge 22:18 blessed, because you have *o* me."
Jos 1:17 we fully *o* Moses, so we will obey
Ps 119: 4 that are to be fully *o*.
Da 9:10 we have not *o* the LORD our God
Jnh 3: 3 Jonah *o* the word of the LORD
Mic 5:15 the nations that have not *o* me."
Jn 15:10 as I have *o* my Father's commands
15:20 If they *o* my teaching, they will
17: 6 and they have *o* your word.
Ac 7:53 through angels but have not *o* it."
Ro 6:17 you wholeheartedly *o* the form
Php 2:12 as you have always *o*— not only
Heb 11: 8 *o* and went, even though he did not
1Pe 3: 6 who *o* Abraham and called him her

OBEYING (OBEY)
1Sa 15:22 as in *o* the voice of the LORD?
Ps 119: 5 steadfast in *o* your decrees!
Gal 5: 7 and kept you from *o* the truth?
1Pe 1:22 purified yourselves by *o* the truth

OBEYS (OBEY)
Lev 18: 5 for the man who *o* them will live
Pr 19:16 He who *o* instructions guards his
Eze 20:11 for the man who *o* them will live
Jn 14:21 has my commands and *o* them,
Ro 2:27 and yet *o* the law will condemn you
1Jn 2: 5 if anyone *o* his word, God's love is

OBLIGATED (OBLIGATION)
Ro 1:14 I am *o* both to Greeks
Gal 5: 3 himself be circumcised that he is *o*

OBLIGATION (OBLIGATED)
Ro 8:12 Therefore, brothers, we have an *o*

OBSCENITY*
Eph 5: 4 Nor should there be *o*, foolish talk

OBSCURES*
Job 42: 3 'Who is this that *o* my counsel

OBSERVE (OBSERVING)
Ex 31:13 'You must *o* my Sabbaths.
Lev 25: 2 the land itself must *o* a sabbath
Dt 4: 6 *O* them carefully, for this will show
5:12 "*O* the Sabbath day
8: 6 *O* the commands of the LORD
11:22 If you carefully *o* all these
26:16 carefully *o* them with all your heart
Ps 37:37 the blameless, *o* the upright;

OBSERVING (OBSERVE)
Ro 3:27 principle? On that of *o* the law?
Gal 2:16 a man is not justified by *o* the law,
3: 2 you receive the Spirit by *o* the law,
3:10 All who rely on *o* the law are

OBSOLETE
Heb 8:13 he has made the first one *o*;

OBSTACLE* (OBSTACLES)
Ro 14:13 or *o* in your brother's way.

OBSTACLES (OBSTACLE)
Ro 16:17 put *o* in your way that are contrary

OBSTINATE
Isa 65: 2 hands to an *o* people,
Ro 10:21 to a disobedient and *o* people."

OBTAIN (OBTAINED OBTAINS)
Ro 11: 7 sought so earnestly it did not *o*,
2Ti 2:10 they too may *o* the salvation that

OBTAINED (OBTAIN)
Ro 9:30 not pursue righteousness, have *o* it,
Php 3:12 Not that I have already *o* all this,
Heb 9:12 having *o* eternal redemption.

OBTAINS* (OBTAIN)
Pr 12: 2 A good man *o* favor

OBVIOUS*
Mt 6:18 so that it will not be *o*
Gal 5:19 The acts of the sinful nature are *o*:
1Ti 5:24 The sins of some men are *o*,
5:25 In the same way, good deeds are *o*,

OCCASIONS
Eph 6:18 in the Spirit on all *o* with all kinds

OFFENDED (OFFENSE)
Pr 18:19 An *o* brother is more unyielding

OFFENDERS* (OFFENSE)
1Co 6: 9 nor homosexual *o* nor thieves

OFFENSE (OFFENDED OFFENDERS OFFENSES OFFENSIVE)
Pr 17: 9 over an *o* promotes love,
19:11 it is to his glory to overlook an *o*.
Gal 5:11 In that case the *o* of the cross has

OFFENSES (OFFENSE)
Isa 44:22 swept away your *o* like a cloud,
59:12 For our *o* are many in your sight,
Eze 18:30 Repent! Turn away from all your *o*;
33:10 "Our *o* and sins weigh us down,

OFFENSIVE (OFFENSE)
Ps 139: 24 See if there is any *o* way in me,

OFFER (OFFERED OFFERING OFFERINGS OFFERS)
Ps 4: 5 *O* right sacrifices
Ro 6:13 Do not *o* the parts of your body
12: 1 to *o* your bodies as living sacrifices,
Heb 9:25 he enter heaven to *o* himself again
13:15 therefore, let us continually *o*

OFFERED (OFFER)
Isa 50: 6 I *o* my back to those who beat me,
1Co 9:13 share in what is *o* on the altar?
10:20 of pagans are *o* to demons,
Heb 7:27 once for all when he *o* himself.
9:14 the eternal Spirit *o* himself
11: 4 By faith Abel *o* God a better
11:17 when God tested him, *o* Isaac
Jas 5:15 prayer *o* in faith will make the sick

OFFERING (OFFER)
Ge 4: 3 of the soil as an *o* to the LORD.
22: 2 a burnt *o* on one of the mountains I
22: 8 provide the lamb for the burnt *o*,
Ex 29:24 before the LORD as a wave *o*.
29:40 quarter of a hin of wine as a drink *o*.
Lev 1: 3 If the *o* is a burnt *o* from the herd,
2: 4 " 'If you bring a grain *o* baked
3: 1 " 'If someone's *o* is a fellowship *o*,
4: 3 a sin *o* for the sin he has committed
5:15 It is a guilt *o*.
7:37 ordination *o* and the fellowship *o*,
9:24 and consumed the burnt *o*
22:18 to fulfill a vow or as a freewill *o*,
22:21 a special vow or as a freewill *o*,
1Sa 13: 9 And Saul offered up the burnt *o*.
1Ch 21:26 from heaven on the altar of burnt *o*.
2Ch 7: 1 and consumed the burnt *o*
Ps 40: 6 Sacrifice and *o* you did not desire,
116: 17 I will sacrifice a thank *o* to you
Isa 53:10 the LORD makes his life a guilt *o*,
Mt 5:23 if you are *o* your gift at the altar
Ro 8: 3 likeness of sinful man to be a sin *o*.
Eph 5: 2 as a fragrant *o* and sacrifice to God.
Php 2:17 I am being poured out like a drink *o*
4:18 are a fragrant *o*, an acceptable
2Ti 4: 6 being poured out like a drink *o*,
Heb 10: 5 "Sacrifice and *o* you did not desire,
1Pe 2: 5 *o* spiritual sacrifices acceptable

OFFERINGS (OFFER)
1Sa 15:22 Does the LORD delight in burnt *o*
2Ch 35: 7 and goats for the Passover *o*,
Isa 1:13 Stop bringing meaningless *o*!
Hos 6: 6 of God rather than burnt *o*.
Mal 3: 8 do we rob you?' "In tithes and *o*.
Mk 12:33 is more important than all burnt *o*
Heb 10: 8 First he said, "Sacrifices and *o*,

OFFERS (OFFER)
Heb 10:11 and again he *o* the same sacrifices,

OFFICER (OFFICIALS)
2Ti 2: 4 wants to please his commanding *o*.

OFFICIALS (OFFICER)
Ex 5:21 a stench to Pharaoh and his *o*.
Pr 17:26 or to flog *o* for their integrity.
29:12 all his *o* become wicked.

OFFSPRING
Ge 3:15 and between your *o* and hers;
12: 7 "To your *o* I will give this land."
13:16 I will make your *o* like the dust
26: 4 and through your *o* all nations
28:14 blessed through you and your *o*.
Ex 13: 2 The first *o* of every womb
Ru 4:12 Through the *o* the LORD gives
Isa 44: 3 I will pour out my Spirit on your *o*,
53:10 he will see his *o* and prolong his
Ac 3:25 'Through your *o* all peoples
17:28 own poets have said, 'We are his *o*.'
17:29 "Therefore since we are God's *o*,
Ro 4:18 said to him, "So shall your *o* be."
9: 8 who are regarded as Abraham's *o*.

OG
Nu 21:33 *O* king of Bashan and his whole
Ps 136: 20 and *O* king of Bashan—

OIL
Ex 29: 7 Take the anointing *o* and anoint
30:25 It will be the sacred anointing *o*.
Dt 14:23 tithe of your grain, new wine and *o*,
1Sa 10: 1 Then Samuel took a flask of *o*
16:13 So Samuel took the horn of *o*
1Ki 17:16 and the jug of *o* did not run dry,
2Ki 4: 6 Then the *o* stopped flowing.
Ps 23: 5 You anoint my head with *o*;
45: 7 by anointing you with the *o* of joy.
104: 15 *o* to make his face shine,
133: 2 It is like precious *o* poured
Pr 21:17 loves wine and *o* will never be
Isa 1: 6 or soothed with *o*.
61: 3 the *o* of gladness
Mt 25: 3 but did not take any *o* with them.
Heb 1: 9 by anointing you with the *o* of joy."

OLIVE (OLIVES)
Ge 8:11 beak was a freshly plucked *o* leaf!
Jdg 9: 8 said to the *o* tree, 'Be our king.'
Jer 11:16 LORD called you a thriving *o* tree
Zec 4: 3 Also there are two *o* trees by it,
Ro 11:17 and you, though a wild *o* shoot,
11:24 of an *o* tree that is wild by nature,
Rev 11: 4 These are the two *o* trees

OLIVES (OLIVE)
Zec 14: 4 stand on the Mount of *O*,
Mt 24: 3 sitting on the Mount of *O*,
Jas 3:12 a fig tree bear *o*, or a grapevine bear

OMEGA*
Rev 1: 8 "I am the Alpha and the *O*,"
21: 6 I am the Alpha and the *O*,
22:13 I am the Alpha and the *O*,

OMIT*
Jer 26: 2 I command you; do not *o* a word.

OMRI
King of Israel (1Ki 16:21-26).

ONESIMUS*
Col 4: 9 He is coming with *O*, our faithful
Phm :10 I appeal to you for my son *O*,

ONESIPHORUS*
2Ti 1:16 mercy to the household of *O*,
4:19 Aquila and the household of *O*.

ONIONS*
Nu 11: 5 melons, leeks, *o* and garlic.

ONYX
Ex 28: 9 "Take two *o* stones and engrave
28:20 in the fourth row a chrysolite, an *o*

OPENHANDED* (HAND)
Dt 15: 8 Rather be *o* and freely lend him
15:11 you to be *o* toward your brothers

OPINIONS*
1Ki 18:21 will you waver between two *o*?
Pr 18: 2 but delights in airing his own *o*.

OPPONENTS (OPPOSE)
Pr 18:18 and keeps strong *o* apart.

OPPORTUNE (OPPORTUNITY)
Lk 4:13 he left him until an *o* time.

OPPORTUNITY* (OPPORTUNE)
1Sa 18:21 "Now you have a second *o*
Jer 46:17 he has missed his *o*.'
Mt 26:16 watched for an *o* to hand him over.

Mk 14:11 So he watched for an o to hand him
Lk 22: 6 and watched for an o to hand Jesus
Ac 25:16 and has had an o to defend himself
Ro 7: 8 seizing the o afforded
7:11 seizing the o afforded
1Co 16:12 but he will go when he has the o.
2Co 5:12 are giving you an o to take pride
11:12 from under those who want an o
Gal 6:10 as we have o, let us do good
Eph 5:16 making the most of every o,
Php 4:10 but you had no o to show it.
Col 4: 5 make the most of every o.
1Ti 5:14 to give the enemy no o for slander.
Heb 11:15 they would have had o to return.

OPPOSE (OPPONENTS OPPOSED OPPOSES OPPOSING OPPOSITION)
Ex 23:22 and will o those who o you.
1Sa 2:10 those who o the LORD will be
Job 23:13 he stands alone, and who can o him
Ac 11:17 I to think that I could o God?"
2Ti 2:25 Those who o him he must gently
Tit 1: 9 doctrine and refute those who o it.
2: 8 so that those who o you may be

OPPOSED (OPPOSE)
Gal 2:11 to Antioch, I o him to his face,
3:21 therefore, o to the promises of God

OPPOSES (OPPOSE)
Jas 4: 6 "God o the proud
1Pe 5: 5 because, "God o the proud

OPPOSING (OPPOSE)
1Ti 6:20 the o ideas of what is falsely called

OPPOSITION (OPPOSE)
Heb 12: 3 Consider him who endured such o

OPPRESS (OPPRESSED OPPRESSES OPPRESSION OPPRESSOR)
Ex 1:11 masters over them to o them
22:21 "Do not mistreat an alien or o him,
Isa 3: 5 People will o each other—
Eze 22:29 they o the poor and needy
Da 7:25 the Most High and o his saints
Am 5:12 You o the righteous and take bribes
Zec 7:10 Do not o the widow
Mal 3: 5 who o the widows

OPPRESSED (OPPRESS)
Jdg 2:18 as they groaned under those who o
Ps 9: 9 The LORD is a refuge for the o,
82: 3 the rights of the poor and o.
146: 7 He upholds the cause of the o
Pr 16:19 in spirit and among the o
31: 5 and deprive all the o of their rights.
Isa 1:17 encourage the o.
53: 7 He was o and afflicted,
58:10 and satisfy the needs of the o,
Zec 10: 2 o for lack of a shepherd.
Lk 4:18 to release the o,

OPPRESSES (OPPRESS)
Pr 14:31 He who o the poor shows contempt
22:16 He who o the poor
Eze 18:12 He o the poor and needy.

OPPRESSION (OPPRESS)
Ps 12: 5 "Because of the o of the weak
72:14 He will rescue them from o
119:134 Redeem me from the o of men,
Isa 53: 8 By o and judgment he was taken
58: 9 "If you do away with the yoke of o,

OPPRESSOR (OPPRESS)
Ps 72: 4 he will crush the o.
Isa 51:13 For where is the wrath of the o?
Jer 22: 3 hand of his o the one who has been

ORDAINED
Ps 8: 2 you have o praise
111: 9 he o his covenant forever—
139: 16 All the days o for me
Eze 28:14 for so I o you.
Hab 1:12 you have o them to punish.
Mt 21:16 you have o praise'?"

ORDER (ORDERLY ORDERS)
Nu 9:23 They obeyed the LORD's o,
Ps 110: 4 in the o of Melchizedek."
Heb 5:10 priest in the o of Melchizedek.
9:10 until the time of the new o.
Rev 21: 4 for the old o of things has passed

ORDERLY (ORDER)
1Co 14:40 done in a fitting and o way.
Col 2: 5 and delight to see how o you are

ORDERS (ORDER)
Mk 1:27 He even gives o to evil spirits
3:12 But he gave them strict o not
9: 9 Jesus gave them o not

ORDINARY
Ac 4:13 that they were unschooled, o men,

ORGIES*
Ro 13:13 not in o and drunkenness,
Gal 5:21 drunkenness, o, and the like.
1Pe 4: 3 o, carousing and detestable

ORIGIN (ORIGINATE ORIGINS)
2Pe 1:21 For prophecy never had its o

ORIGINATE* (ORIGIN)
1Co 14:36 Did the word of God o with you?

ORIGINS* (ORIGIN)
Mic 5: 2 whose o are from of old,

ORNAMENT* (ORNAMENTED)
Pr 3:22 an o to grace your neck.
25:12 of gold or an o of fine gold

ORNAMENTED (ORNAMENT)
Ge 37: 3 and he made a richly o robe for him

ORPHAN* (ORPHANS)
Ex 22:22 advantage of a widow or an o.

ORPHANS (ORPHAN)
Jn 14:18 will not leave you as o; I will come
Jas 1:27 to look after o and widows

OTHNIEL
Nephew of Caleb (Jos 15:15-19; Jdg 1:12-15). Judge who freed Israel from Aram (Jdg 3:7-11).

OUTBURSTS*
2Co 12:20 jealousy, o of anger, factions,

OUTCOME
Heb 13: 7 Consider the o of their way of life
1Pe 4:17 what will the o be for those who do

OUTNUMBER
Ps 139: 18 they would o the grains of sand.

OUTSIDERS*
Col 4: 5 wise in the way you act toward o;
1Th 4:12 daily life may win the respect of o
1Ti 3: 7 also have a good reputation with o,

OUTSTANDING
SS 5:10 o among ten thousand.
Ro 13: 8 no debt remain o,

OUTSTRETCHED
Ex 6: 6 and will redeem you with an o arm
Dt 4:34 by a mighty hand and an o arm,
5:15 with a mighty hand and an o arm.
1Ki 8:42 your mighty hand and your o arm
Ps 136: 12 with a mighty hand and o arm;
Jer 27: 5 and o arm I made the earth
32:17 by your great power and o arm.
Eze 20:33 an o arm and with outpoured wrath

OUTWEIGHS (WEIGH)
2Co 4:17 an eternal glory that far o them all.

OUTWIT*
2Co 2:11 in order that Satan might not o us.

OVERAWED* (AWE)
Ps 49:16 Do not be o when a man grows rich

OVERBEARING*
Tit 1: 7 not o, not quick-tempered,

OVERCAME (OVERCOME)
Rev 3:21 as I o and sat down with my Father
12:11 They o him

OVERCOME (OVERCAME OVERCOMES)
Mt 16:18 and the gates of Hades will not o it.
Mk 9:24 I do believe; help me o my unbelief
Lk 10:19 to o all the power of the enemy;
Jn 16:33 But take heart! I have o the world."
Ro 12:21 Do not be o by evil, but o evil
2Pe 2:20 and are again entangled in it and o,
1Jn 2:13 because you have o the evil one.
4: 4 are from God and have o them,
5: 4 is the victory that has o the world,
Rev 17:14 but the Lamb will o them

OVERCOMES* (OVERCOME)
1Jn 5: 4 born of God o the world.
5: 5 Who is it that o the world?
Rev 2: 7 To him who o, I will give the right
2:11 He who o will not be hurt at all
2:17 To him who o, I will give some
2:26 To him who o and does my will
3: 5 He who o will, like them, be
3:12 Him who o I will make a pillar
3:21 To him who o, I will give the right
21: 7 He who o will inherit all this,

OVERFLOW (OVERFLOWING OVERFLOWS)
Ps 65:11 and your carts o with abundance.
119:171 May my lips o with praise,
La 1:16 and my eyes o with tears.
Mt 12:34 out of the o of the heart the mouth
Lk 6:45 out of the o of his heart his mouth
Ro 5:15 Jesus Christ, o to the many! Again,
15:13 so that you may o with hope
2Co 4:15 to o to the glory of God.
1Th 3:12 o for each other and for everyone

OVERFLOWING (OVERFLOW)
Pr 3:10 then your barns will be filled to o,
2Co 8: 2 their o joy and their extreme
9:12 o in many expressions of thanks
Col 2: 7 as you were taught, and o

OVERFLOWS* (OVERFLOW)
Ps 23: 5 my cup o.
2Co 1: 5 also through Christ our comfort o.

OVERJOYED* (JOY)
Da 6:23 The king was o and gave orders
Mt 2:10 they saw the star, they were o.
Jn 20:20 The disciples were o
Ac 12:14 she was so o she ran back
1Pe 4:13 so that you may be o

OVERLOOK
Pr 19:11 it is to his glory to o an offense.

OVERSEER* (OVERSEERS)
Pr 6: 7 no o or ruler,
1Ti 3: 1 anyone sets his heart on being an o,
3: 2 Now the o must be above reproach,
Tit 1: 7 Since an o is entrusted
1Pe 2:25 returned to the Shepherd and O

OVERSEERS* (OVERSEER)
Ac 20:28 the Holy Spirit has made you o.
Php 1: 1 together with the o and deacons:
1Pe 5: 2 as o—not because you must,

OVERSHADOW* (OVERSHADOWING)
Lk 1:35 power of the Most High will o you.

OVERSHADOWING (OVERSHADOW)
Ex 25:20 wings spread upward, o the cover
Heb 9: 5 the glory, o the atonement cover.

OVERTHROW (OVERTHROWS)
2Th 2: 8 whom the Lord Jesus will o

OVERTHROWS (OVERTHROW)
Pr 13: 6 but wickedness o the sinner.
Isa 44:25 who o the learning of the wise

OVERWHELMED (OVERWHELMING)
2Sa 22: 5 the torrents of destruction o me.
1Ki 10: 5 temple of the LORD, she was o.
Ps 38: 4 My guilt has o me
65: 3 When we were o by sins,
Mt 26:38 "My soul is o with sorrow
Mk 7:37 People were o with amazement.
9:15 they were o with wonder
2Co 2: 7 so that he will not be o

OVERWHELMING (OVERWHELMED)
Pr 27: 4 Anger is cruel and fury o,
Isa 10:22 o and righteous.
28:15 When an o scourge sweeps by,

OWE
Ro 13: 7 If you o taxes, pay taxes; if revenue
Phm :19 to mention that you o me your very

OWNER'S (OWNERSHIP)
Isa 1: 3 the donkey his o manger,

OWNERSHIP* (OWNER'S)
2Co 1:22 He anointed us, set his seal of o

OX (OXEN)
Dt 25: 4 Do not muzzle an o
Isa 11: 7 and the lion will eat straw like the o
Eze 1:10 and on the left the face of an o;
Lk 13:15 of you on the Sabbath untie his o
1Co 9: 9 "Do not muzzle an o
1Ti 5:18 "Do not muzzle the o
Rev 4: 7 second was like an o, the third had

OXEN (OX)
1Ki 19:20 Elisha then left his o and ran
Lk 14:19 'I have just bought five yoke of o,

PAGAN (PAGANS)
Mt 18:17 as you would a p or a tax collector.

Lk 12:30 For the *p* world runs

PAGANS* (PAGAN)
Isa 2: 6 and clasp hands with *p*.
Mt 5:47 Do not even *p* do that? Be perfect,
6: 7 do not keep on babbling like *p*,
6:32 For the *p* run after all these things,
1Co 5: 1 that does not occur even among *p*:
10:20 but the sacrifices of *p* are offered
12: 2 You know that when you were *p*,
1Pe 2:12 such good lives among the *p* that,
4: 3 in the past doing what *p* choose
3Jn : 7 receiving no help from the *p*.

PAID (PAY)
Isa 40: 2 that her sin has been *p* for,
Zec 11:12 So they *p* me thirty pieces of silver.

PAIN (PAINFUL PAINS)
Ge 3:16 with *p* you will give birth
6: 6 and his heart was filled with *p*.
Job 6:10 my joy in unrelenting *p*—
33:19 may be chastened on a bed of *p*
Jer 4:19 I writhe in *p*.
15:18 Why is my *p* unending
Mt 4:24 suffering severe *p*,
Jn 16:21 woman giving birth to a child has *p*
1Pe 2:19 up under the *p* of unjust suffering
Rev 21: 4 or mourning or crying or *p*,

PAINFUL (PAIN)
Ge 3:17 through *p* toil you will eat of it
5:29 and *p* toil of our hands caused
Job 6:25 How *p* are honest words!
Eze 28:24 neighbors who are *p* briers
2Co 2: 1 I would not make another *p* visit
Heb 12:11 seems pleasant at the time, but *p*.
1Pe 4:12 at the *p* trial you are suffering,

PAINS (PAIN)
Ge 3:16 "I will greatly increase your *p*
Mt 24: 8 these are the beginning of birth *p*.
Ro 8:22 as in the *p* of childbirth right up
Gal 4:19 again in the *p* of childbirth
1Th 5: 3 as labor *p* on a pregnant woman,

PAIRS
Ge 7: 8 *P* of clean and unclean animals,

PALACE (PALACES)
2Sa 7: 2 "Here I am, living in a *p* of cedar,
Jer 22: 6 is what the LORD says about the *p*
22:13 "Woe to him who builds his *p*

PALACES (PALACE)
Mt 11: 8 wear fine clothes are in kings' *p*.
Lk 7:25 and indulge in luxury are in *p*.

PALE
Isa 29:22 no longer will their faces grow *p*.
Jer 30: 6 every face turned deathly *p*?
Da 10: 8 my face turned deathly *p*
Rev 6: 8 and there before me was a *p* horse!

PALM (PALMS)
Jn 12:13 They took *p* branches and went out
Rev 7: 9 and were holding *p* branches

PALMS (PALM)
Isa 49:16 you on the *p* of my hands;

PAMPERS*
Pr 29:21 If a man *p* his servant from youth,

PANIC
Dt 20: 3 or give way to *p* before them.
1Sa 14:15 It was a *p* sent by God.
Eze 7: 7 there is *p*, not joy,
Zec 14:13 by the LORD with great *p*.

PANTS
Ps 42: 1 As the deer *p* for streams of water,

PARABLES
See also JESUS: PARABLES
Ps 78: 2 I will open my mouth in *p*,
Mt 13:35 "I will open my mouth in *p*,
Lk 8:10 but to others I speak in *p*, so that,

PARADISE*
Lk 23:43 today you will be with me in *p*."
2Co 12: 4 God knows—was caught up to *p*.
Rev 2: 7 of life, which is in the *p* of God.

PARALYTIC
Mt 9: 2 Some men brought to him a *p*,
Mk 2: 3 bringing to him a *p*, carried by four
Ac 9:33 a *p* who had been bedridden

PARCHED
Ps 143: 6 my soul thirsts for you like a *p* land.

PARCHMENTS*
2Ti 4:13 and my scrolls, especially the *p*.

PARDON* (PARDONED PARDONS)
2Ch 30:18 *p* everyone who sets his heart
Job 7:21 Why do you not *p* my offenses
Isa 55: 7 and to our God, for he will freely *p*.
Joel 3:21 I will *p*."

PARDONED* (PARDON)
Nu 14:19 as you have *p* them from the time
Joel 3:21 bloodguilt, which I have not *p*,

PARDONS* (PARDON)
Mic 7:18 who *p* sin and forgives

PARENTS
Pr 17: 6 and *p* are the pride of their children
19:14 wealth are inherited from *p*,
Mt 10:21 children will rebel against their *p*
Lk 18:29 left home or wife or brothers or *p*
21:16 You will be betrayed even by *p*, brothers,
Jn 9: 3 Neither this man nor his *p* sinned,"
Ro 1:30 they disobey their *p*; they are
2Co 12:14 for their *p*, but *p* for their children.
Eph 6: 1 Children, obey your *p* in the Lord,
Col 3:20 obey your *p* in everything,
1Ti 5: 4 repaying their *p* and grandparents,
2Ti 3: 2 disobedient to their *p*, ungrateful,

PARTAKE*
1Co 10:17 for we all *p* of the one loaf.

PARTIAL* (PARTIALITY)
Pr 18: 5 It is not good to be *p* to the wicked

PARTIALITY (PARTIAL)
Lev 19:15 do not show *p* to the poor
Dt 1:17 Do not show *p* in judging;
10:17 who shows no *p* and accepts no
16:19 Do not pervert justice or show *p*.
2Ch 19: 7 our God there is no injustice or *p*
Job 32:21 I will show *p* to no one,
34:19 who shows no *p* to princes
Pr 24:23 To show *p* in judging is not good:
Mal 2: 9 have shown *p* in matters of the law
Lk 20:21 and that you do not show *p*
1Ti 5:21 keep these instructions without *p*,

PARTICIPANTS (PARTICIPATE)
1Co 10:20 you to be *p* with demons.

PARTICIPATE (PARTICIPANTS PARTICIPATION)
1Pe 4:13 rejoice that you *p* in the sufferings
2Pe 1: 4 that through them you may *p*

PARTICIPATION (PARTICIPATE)
1Co 10:16 is not the bread that we break a *p*

PARTNER (PARTNERS PARTNERSHIP)
Pr 2:17 who has left the *p* of her youth
Mal 2:14 though she is your *p*, the wife
1Pe 3: 7 them with respect as the weaker *p*

PARTNERS (PARTNER)
Eph 5: 7 Therefore do not be *p* with them.

PARTNERSHIP* (PARTNER)
Php 1: 5 because of your *p* in the gospel

PASS (PASSED PASSER-BY PASSING)
Ex 12:13 and when I see the blood, I will *p*
33:19 goodness to *p* in front of you,
1Ki 9: 8 all who *p* by will be appalled
19:11 for the LORD is about to *p* by."
Ps 90:10 for they quickly *p*, and we fly away.
105: 19 till what he foretold came to *p*,
Isa 31: 5 he will '*p* over' it and will rescue it
43: 2 When you *p* through the waters,
62:10 *P* through, *p* through the gates!
Jer 22: 8 "People from many nations will *p*
La 1:12 to you, all you who *p* by?
Da 7:14 dominion that will not *p* away,
Am 5:17 for I will *p* through your midst,"
Mt 24:34 will certainly not *p* away
24:35 Heaven and earth will *p* away,
Mk 13:31 Heaven and earth will *p* away,
Lk 21:33 Heaven and earth will *p* away,
1Co 13: 8 there is knowledge, it will *p* away.
Jas 1:10 he will *p* away like a wild flower.
1Jn 2:17 The world and its desires *p* away,

PASSED (PASS)
Ge 15:17 a blazing torch appeared and *p*
Ex 33:22 you with my hand until I have *p* by.
2Ch 21:20 He *p* away, to no one's regret,
Ps 57: 1 wings until the disaster has *p*.
Lk 10:32 saw him, *p* by on the other side.
1Co 15: 3 For what I received I *p* on to you

Heb 11:29 By faith the people *p*

PASSER-BY* (PASS)
Pr 26:10 is he who hires a fool or any *p*.
26:17 is a *p* who meddles

PASSING (PASS)
1Co 7:31 world in its present form is *p* away.
1Jn 2: 8 because the darkness is *p*

PASSION* (PASSIONATE PASSIONS)
Hos 7: 6 Their *p* smolders all night;
1Co 7: 9 better to marry than to burn with *p*.

PASSIONATE* (PASSION)
1Th 4: 5 not in *p* lust like the heathen,

PASSIONS* (PASSION)
Ro 7: 5 the sinful *p* aroused
Gal 5:24 crucified the sinful nature with its *p*
Tit 2:12 to ungodliness and worldly *p*,
3: 3 and enslaved by all kinds of *p*

PASSOVER
Ex 12:11 Eat it in haste; it is the LORD's *P*.
Nu 9: 2 Have the Israelites celebrate the *P*
Dt 16: 1 celebrate the *P* of the LORD your
Jos 5:10 the Israelites celebrated the *P*.
2Ki 23:21 "Celebrate the *P* to the LORD
Ezr 6:19 the exiles celebrated the *P*.
Mk 14:12 customary to sacrifice the *P* lamb,
Lk 22: 1 called the *P*, was approaching,
1Co 5: 7 our *P* lamb, has been sacrificed.
Heb 11:28 he kept the *P* and the sprinkling

PAST
Isa 43:18 do not dwell on the *p*.
65:16 For the *p* troubles will be forgotten
Ro 15: 4 in the *p* was written to teach us,
16:25 the mystery hidden for long ages *p*,
Eph 3: 9 which for ages *p* was kept hidden
Heb 1: 1 In the *p* God spoke

PASTORS*
Eph 4:11 and some to be *p* and teachers,

PASTURE (PASTURES)
Ps 37: 3 dwell in the land and enjoy safe *p*.
95: 7 and we are the people of his *p*,
100: 3 we are his people, the sheep of his *p*
Jer 50: 7 against the LORD, their true *p*,
Eze 34:13 I will *p* them on the mountains
Zec 11: 4 "*P* the flock marked for slaughter.
Jn 10: 9 come in and go out, and find *p*.

PASTURES (PASTURE)
Ps 23: 2 He makes me lie down in green *p*,

PATCH
Jer 10: 5 Like a scarecrow in a melon *p*,
Mt 9:16 No one sews a *p* of unshrunk cloth

PATH (PATHS)
Ps 16:11 known to me the *p* of life;
27:11 lead me in a straight *p*
119: 32 I run in the *p* of your commands,
119:105 and a light for my *p*.
Pr 2: 9 and fair—every good *p*.
12:28 along that *p* is immortality.
15:10 awaits him who leaves the *p*;
15:19 the *p* of the upright is a highway.
15:24 The *p* of life leads upward
21:16 from the *p* of understanding
Isa 26: 7 The *p* of the righteous is level;
Jer 31: 9 on a level *p* where they will not
Mt 13: 4 fell along the *p*, and the birds came
Lk 1:79 to guide our feet into the *p* of peace
2Co 6: 3 no stumbling block in anyone's *p*,

PATHS (PATH)
Ps 23: 3 He guides me in *p* of righteousness
25: 4 teach me your *p*;
Pr 2:13 who leave the straight *p*
3: 6 and he will make your *p* straight.
4:11 and lead you along straight *p*.
4:26 Make level *p* for your feet
5:21 and he examines all his *p*.
8:20 along the *p* of justice,
22: 5 In the *p* of the wicked lie thorns
Isa 2: 3 so that we may walk in his *p*."
Jer 6:16 ask for the ancient *p*,
Mic 4: 2 so that we may walk in his *p*."
Mt 3: 3 make straight *p* for him.' "
Ac 2:28 to me the *p* of life;
Ro 11:33 and his *p* beyond tracing out!
Heb 12:13 "Make level *p* for your feet,"

PATIENCE* (PATIENT)
Pr 19:11 A man's wisdom gives him *p*;
25:15 Through *p* a ruler can be persuaded
Ecc 7: 8 and *p* is better than pride.

Isa 7:13 Is it not enough to try the p of men?
7:13 Will you try the p of my God also?
Ro 2: 4 and p, not realizing that God's
9:22 bore with great p the objects
2Co 6: 6 understanding, p and kindness;
Gal 5:22 joy, peace, p, kindness, goodness,
Col 1:11 may have great endurance and p,
3:12 humility, gentleness and p.
1Ti 1:16 Jesus might display his unlimited p
2Ti 3:10 my purpose, faith, p, love,
4: 2 with great p and careful instruction
Heb 6:12 p inherit what has been promised.
Jas 5:10 as an example of p in the face
2Pe 3:15 that our Lord's p means salvation,

PATIENT* (PATIENCE PATIENTLY)
Ne 9:30 For many years you were p
Job 6:11 What prospects, that I should be p?
Pr 14:29 A p man has great understanding,
15:18 but a p man calms a quarrel.
16:32 Better a p man than a warrior,
Mt 18:26 'Be p with me,' he begged,
18:29 'Be p with me, and I will pay you
Ro 12:12 Be joyful in hope, p in affliction,
1Co 13: 4 Love is p, love is kind.
2Co 1: 6 produces in you p endurance
Eph 4: 2 humble and gentle; be p,
1Th 5:14 help the weak, be p with everyone.
Jas 5: 7 Be p, then, brothers,
5: 7 and how p he is for the autumn
5: 8 You too, be p and stand firm,
2Pe 3: 9 He is p with you, not wanting
Rev 1: 9 p endurance that are ours in Jesus,
13:10 This calls for p endurance
14:12 This calls for p endurance

PATIENTLY* (PATIENT)
Ps 37: 7 still before the LORD and wait p
40: 1 I waited p for the LORD;
Isa 38:13 I waited p till dawn,
Hab 3:16 Yet I will wait p for the day
Ac 26: 3 I beg you to listen to me p.
Ro 8:25 we do not yet have, we wait for it p.
Heb 6:15 after waiting p, Abraham received
1Pe 3:20 ago when God waited p in the days
Rev 3:10 kept my command to endure p,

PATTERN
Ex 25:40 according to the p shown you
Ro 5:14 who was a p of the one to come.
12: 2 longer to the p of this world,
2Ti 1:13 keep as the p of sound teaching,
Heb 8: 5 according to the p shown you

PAUL
Also called Saul (Ac 13:9). Pharisee from Tarsus (Ac 9:11; Php 3:5). Apostle (Gal 1). At stoning of Stephen (Ac 8:1). Persecuted Church (Ac 9:1-2; Gal 1:13). Vision of Jesus on road to Damascus (Ac 9:4-9; 26:12-18). In Arabia (Gal 1:17). Preached in Damascus; escaped death through the wall in a basket (Ac 9:19-25). In Jerusalem; sent back to Tarsus (Ac 9:26-30).

Brought to Antioch by Barnabas (Ac 11:22-26). First missionary journey to Cyprus and Galatia (Ac 13-14). Stoned at Lystra (Ac 14:19-20). At Jerusalem council (Ac 15). Split with Barnabas over Mark (Ac 15:36-41).

Second missionary journey with Silas (Ac 16-20). Called to Macedonia (Ac 16:6-10). Freed from prison in Philippi (Ac 16:16-40). In Thessalonica (Ac 17:1-9). Speech in Athens (Ac 17:16-33). In Corinth (Ac 18). In Ephesus (Ac 19). Return to Jerusalem (Ac 20). Farewell to Ephesian elders (Ac 20:13-38). Arrival in Jerusalem (Ac 21:1-26). Arrested (Ac 21:27-36). Addressed crowds (Ac 22), Sanhedrin (Ac 23:1-11). Transferred to Caesarea (Ac 23:12-35). Trial before Felix (Ac 24), Festus (Ac 25:1-12). Before Agrippa (Ac 25:13-26:32). Voyage to Rome; shipwreck (Ac 27). Arrival in Rome (Ac 28).

Epistles: Romans, 1 and 2 Corinthians, Galatians, Ephesians, Philippians, Colossians, 1 and 2 Thessalonians, 1 and 2 Timothy, Titus, Philemon.

PAVEMENT
Jn 19:13 as the Stone P (which

PAY (PAID PAYMENT PAYS REPAID REPAY REPAYING)
Lev 26:43 They will p for their sins
Dt 7:12 If you p attention to these laws
Pr 4: 1 p attention and gain understanding
4:20 My son, p attention to what I say;
5: 1 My son, p attention to my wisdom,
6:31 if he is caught, he must p sevenfold,
19:19 man must p the penalty;
22:17 P attention and listen
24:29 I'll p that man back for what he did
Eze 40: 4 and p attention to everything I am
Zec 11:12 give me my p; but if not, keep it."
Mt 20: 2 He agreed to p them a denarius
22:16 you p no attention to who they are.
22:17 Is it right to p taxes to Caesar
Lk 3:14 falsely—be content with your p."
19: 8 I will p back four times the amount
Ro 13: 6 This is also why you p taxes,
2Pe 1:19 you will do well to p attention to it,

PAYMENT (PAY)
Ps 49: 8 no p is ever enough—
Php 4:18 I have received full p and

PAYS (PAY)
Pr 17:13 If a man p back evil for good,
1Th 5:15 sure that nobody p back wrong

PEACE (PEACEABLE PEACEFUL PEACEMAKERS)
Lev 26: 6 " 'I will grant p in the land,
Nu 6:26 and give you p." '
25:12 him I am making my covenant of p
Dt 20:10 make its people an offer of p.
Jdg 3:11 So the land had p for forty years,
3:30 and the land had p for eighty years.
5:31 Then the land had p forty years.
6:24 and called it The LORD is P.
8:28 the land enjoyed p forty years.
1Sa 7:14 And there was p between Israel
2Sa 10:19 they made p with the Israelites
1Ki 2:33 may there be the LORD's p forever
22:44 also at p with the king of Israel.
2Ki 9:17 come in p?' " The horseman rode
1Ch 19:19 they made p with David
22: 9 and I will grant Israel p
2Ch 14: 1 and in his days the country was at p
20:30 kingdom of Jehoshaphat was at p,
Job 3:26 I have no p, no quietness;
22:21 to God and be at p with him;
Ps 29:11 LORD blesses his people with p.
34:14 seek p and pursue it.
37:11 and enjoy great p.
37:37 there is a future for the man of p.
85:10 righteousness and p kiss each other
119:165 Great p have they who love your
120: 7 I am a man of p;
122: 6 Pray for the p of Jerusalem:
147: 14 He grants p to your borders
Pr 12:20 but joy for those who promote p.
14:30 A heart at p gives life to the body,
16: 7 his enemies live at p with him.
17: 1 Better a dry crust with p and quiet
Ecc 3: 8 a time for war and a time for p.
Isa 9: 6 Everlasting Father, Prince of P.
14: 7 All the lands are at rest and at p;
26: 3 You will keep in perfect p
32:17 The fruit of righteousness will be p;
48:18 your p would have been like a river,
48:22 "There is no p," says the LORD,
52: 7 who proclaim p,
53: 5 punishment that brought us p was
54:10 nor my covenant of p be removed,"
55:12 and be led forth in p;
57: 2 enter into p;
57:19 P, p, to those far and near,"
57:21 "There is no p," says my God,
59: 8 The way of p they do not know;
Jer 6:14 'P, p,' they say,
8:11 "P, p," . . . there is no p.
30:10 Jacob will again have p
46:27 Jacob will again have p
Eze 13:10 "P," when there is no p,
34:25 " 'I will make a covenant of p
37:26 I will make a covenant of p
Mic 5: 5 And he will be their p.
Zec 8:19 Therefore love truth and p."
9:10 He will proclaim p to the nations.
Mal 2: 5 a covenant of life and p,
2: 6 He walked with me in p
Mt 10:34 I did not come to bring p,
Mk 9:50 and be at p with each other."
Lk 1:79 to guide our feet into the path of p
2:14 on earth p to men on whom his
19:38 "P in heaven and glory
Jn 14:27 P I leave with you; my p
16:33 so that in me you may have p.
Ro 1: 7 and p to you from God our Father
2:10 and p for everyone who does good:
5: 1 we have p with God
8: 6 by the Spirit is life and p;
12:18 on you, live at p with everyone.
14:19 effort to do what leads to p
1Co 7:15 God has called us to live in p.
14:33 a God of disorder but of p.
2Co 13:11 be of one mind, live in p.
Gal 5:22 joy, p, patience, kindness,
Eph 2:14 he himself is our p, who has made
2:15 thus making p, and in this one body
2:17 and p to those who were near.
6:15 comes from the gospel of p.
Php 4: 7 the p of God, which transcends all
Col 1:20 by making p through his blood,
3:15 Let the p of Christ rule
3:15 of one body you were called to p.
1Th 5: 3 While people are saying, "P
5:13 Live in p with each other.
5:23 the God of p, sanctify you through
2Th 3:16 the Lord of p himself give you p
2Ti 2:22 righteousness, faith, love and p,
Heb 7: 2 "king of Salem" means "king of p."
12:11 p for those who have been trained
12:14 effort to live in p with all men
13:20 May the God of p, who
1Pe 3:11 he must seek p and pursue it.
2Pe 3:14 blameless and at p with him.
Rev 6: 4 power to take p from the earth

PEACEABLE* (PEACE)
Tit 3: 2 to slander no one, to be p

PEACEFUL (PEACE)
1Ti 2: 2 that we may live p and quiet lives

PEACE-LOVING
Jas 3:17 then p, considerate

PEACEMAKERS* (PEACE)
Mt 5: 9 Blessed are the p,
Jas 3:18 P who sow in peace raise a harvest

PEARL* (PEARLS)
Rev 21:21 each gate made of a single p.

PEARLS (PEARL)
Mt 7: 6 do not throw your p to pigs.
13:45 like a merchant looking for fine p.
1Ti 2: 9 or gold or p or expensive clothes,
Rev 21:21 The twelve gates were twelve p,

PEDDLE*
2Co 2:17 we do not p the word of God

PEG
Jdg 4:21 She drove the p through his temple

PEKAH
King of Israel (2Ki 15:25-31; Isa 7:1).

PEKAHIAH*
Son of Menahem; king of Israel (2Ki 15:22-26).

PEN
Ps 45: 1 my tongue is the p
Mt 5:18 letter, not the least stroke of a p,
Jn 10: 1 who does not enter the sheep p

PENETRATES*
Heb 4:12 it p even to dividing soul and spirit,

PENNIES* (PENNY)
Lk 12: 6 not five sparrows sold for two p?

PENNY* (PENNIES)
Mt 5:26 out until you have paid the last p.
10:29 Are not two sparrows sold for a p?
Mk 12:42 worth only a fraction of a p.
Lk 12:59 out until you have paid the last p."

PENTECOST*
Ac 2: 1 of P came, they were all together
20:16 if possible, by the day of P.
1Co 16: 8 I will stay on at Ephesus until P,

PEOPLE (PEOPLES)
Ge 11: 6 as one p speaking the same
Ex 5: 1 Let my p go,
6: 7 take you as my own p,
8:23 between my p and your p.
15:13 the p you have redeemed.
19: 8 The p all responded together,
24: 3 Moses went and told the p
32: 1 When the p saw that Moses
32: 9 they are a stiff-necked p.
33:13 this nation is your p.
Lev 9: 7 for yourself and the p;
16:24 the burnt offering for the p,
26:12 and you will be my p.
Nu 11:11 burden of all these p on
14:11 p treat me with contempt?
14:19 forgive the sin of these p,
22: 5 A p has come out of Egypt
Dt 4: 6 a wise and understanding p.
4:20 the p of his inheritance,
5:28 what this p said to you.
7: 6 a p holy to the LORD
26:18 that you are his p,
31: 7 you must go with this p
31:16 these p will soon prostitute
32: 9 the LORD's portion is his p.

Dt 32:43 atonement for his land and *p*.
33:29 a *p* saved by the LORD?
Jos 1: 6 you will lead this *p*
24:24 the *p* said to Joshua,
Jdg 2: 7 *p* served the LORD throughout
Ru 1:16 Your *p* will be my *p*
1Sa 8: 7 the *p* are saying to you;
12:22 LORD will not reject his *p*
2Sa 5: 2 will shepherd my *p* Israel
7:10 provide a place for my *p*
1Ki 3: 8 among the *p* you have chosen,
8:30 your *p* Israel when they pray
8:56 has given rest to his *p*
18:39 when all the *p* saw this,
2Ki 23: 3 all the *p* pledged themselves
1Ch 17:21 to redeem *p* for himself
29:17 how willingly your *p* who are
2Ch 2:11 Because the LORD loves his *p*,
7: 5 *p* dedicated the temple
7:14 if my *p*, who are called
30: 6 "*P* of Israel, return to
36:16 was aroused against his *p*
Ezr 2: 1 These are the *p* of the
3: 1 *p* assembled as one man
Ne 1:10 your *p*, whom you redeemed
4: 6 *p* worked with all their heart
8: 1 *p* assembled as one man
Est 3: 6 to destroy all Mordecai's *p*,
Job 12: 2 Doubtless you are the *p*,
Ps 29:11 gives strength to his *p*;
33:12 *p* he chose for his inheritance
50: 4 that he may judge his *p*
53: 6 restores the fortunes of his *p*,
81:13 If my *p* would but listen
94:14 LORD will not reject his *p*;
95: 7 we are the *p* of his pasture,
95:10 a *p* whose hearts go astray,
125: 2 the LORD surrounds his *p*
135: 14 LORD will vindicate his *p*
144: 15 *p* whose God is the LORD.
Pr 14:34 sin is a disgrace to any *p*.
29: 2 righteous thrive, the *p* rejoice
29:18 the *p* cast off restraint
Isa 1: 3 my *p* do not understand.
1: 4 a *p* loaded with guilt,
5:13 my *p* will go into exile
6:10 the heart of this *p* calloused;
9: 2 the *p* walking in darkness
12:12 will assemble the scattered *p*
19:25 Blessed be Egypt my *p*,
25: 8 remove the disgrace of his *p*
29:13 These *p* come near to me
40: 1 Comfort, comfort my *p*
40: 7 Surely the *p* are grass.
42: 6 a covenant for the *p*
49:13 the LORD comforts his *p*
51: 4 "Listen to me, my *p*;
52: 6 my *p* will know my name;
53: 8 for the transgression of my *p*
60:21 will all your *p* be righteous
62:12 will be called the Holy *P*,
65:23 they will be a *p* blessed
Jer 2:11 my *p* have exchanged their
2:13 *p* have committed two sins:
2:32 my *p* have forgotten me,
4:22 My *p* are fools;
5:14 Because the *p* have spoken
5:31 my *p* love it this way
7:16 do not pray for this *p*
18:15 my *p* have forgotten me;
25: 7 They will be my *p*,
30: 3 I will bring my *p* Israel
Eze 13:23 I will save my *p* from
36: 8 fruit for my *p* Israel,
36:28 you will be my *p*,
36:38 be filled with flocks of *p*.
37:13 Then you, my *p*, will know
38:14 *p* Israel are living in safety
39: 7 name among my *p* Israel.
Da 7:27 saints, the *p* of the Most High.
8:24 mighty men and the holy *p*
9:19 your *p* bear your name
9:24 are decreed for your *p*
9:26 *p* of the ruler who will come
10:14 will happen to your *p*
11:32 *p* who know their God will
12: 1 prince who protects your *p*.
Hos 1:10 'You are not my *p*,'
2:23 'You are my *p*';
4:14 a *p* without understanding
Joel 2:18 and take pity on his *p*.
3:16 be a refuge for his *p*,
Am 9:14 back my exiled *p* Israel;
Mic 6: 2 a case against his *p*;
7:14 Shepherd your *p* with
Hag 1:12 remnant of the *p* obeyed
Zec 2:11 and will become my *p*.
8: 7 I will save my *p*
13: 9 will say, 'They are my *p*,'
Mk 7: 6 *p* honor me with their lips
8:27 "Who do *p* say I am?"
Lk 1:17 make ready a *p* prepared
1:68 and has redeemed his *p*.
2:10 joy that will be for all the *p*.
21:23 and wrath against this *p*.
Jn 11:50 one man die for the *p*
18:14 if one man died for the *p*.
Ac 15:14 from the Gentiles a *p*.
18:10 have many *p* in this city.
Ro 9:25 will call them 'my *p*.'
11: 1 Did God reject his *p*?
15:10 O Gentiles, with his *p*."
2Co 6:16 and they will be my *p*."
Tit 2:14 a *p* that are his very own,
Heb 2:17 for the sins of the *p*.
4: 9 a Sabbath-rest for the *p*
5: 3 for the sins of the *p*.
10:30 Lord will judge his *p*.
11:25 mistreated along with the *p*
13:12 to make the *p* holy
1Pe 2: 9 you are a chosen *p*,
2:10 Once you were not a *p*,
2:10 you are the *p* of God;
2Pe 2: 1 false prophets among the *p*,
3:11 kind of *p* ought you to be?
Rev 18: 4 "Come out of her, my *p*,
21: 3 They will be his *p*,

PEOPLES (PEOPLE)
Ge 17:16 kings of *p* will come from her
25:23 two *p* from within you will
27:29 and *p* bow down to you
28: 3 become a community of *p*.
48: 4 you a community of *p*.
Dt 14: 2 of all the *p* on the face of
28:10 Then all the *p* on earth
32: 8 set up boundaries for the *p*
Jos 4:24 all the *p* of the earth might
1Ki 8:43 all the *p* of the earth may
2Ch 7:20 of ridicule among all *p*.
Ps 9: 8 he will govern the *p*
67: 5 may all the *p* praise you.
87: 6 in the register of the *p*:
96:10 he will judge the *p*
Isa 2: 4 settle disputes for many *p*.
17:12 Oh, the uproar of the *p*—
25: 6 of rich food for all *p*,
34: 1 pay attention, you *p*!
55: 4 him a witness to the *p*,
Jer 10: 3 customs of the *p* are worthless
Da 7:14 all *p*, nations and men
Mic 4: 1 and *p* will stream to it.
4: 3 will judge between many *p*
5: 7 in the midst of many *p*
Zep 3: 9 purify the lips of the *p*,
3:20 among all the *p* of the
Zec 8:20 Many *p* and the inhabitants
12: 2 all the surrounding *p* reeling.
Rev 10:11 prophesy again about many *p*,
17:15 the prostitute sits, are *p*,

PEOR
Nu 25: 3 joined in worshiping the Baal of *P*.
Dt 4: 3 who followed the Baal of *P*,

PERCEIVE (PERCEIVING)
Ps 139: 2 you *p* my thoughts from afar.
Pr 24:12 not he who weighs the heart *p* it?

PERCEIVING* (PERCEIVE)
Isa 6: 9 be ever seeing, but never *p*.'
Mt 13:14 you will be ever seeing but never *p*.
Mk 4:12 may be ever seeing but never *p*,
Ac 28:26 you will be ever seeing but never *p*

PERFECT* (PERFECTER PERFECTING PERFECTION)
Dt 32: 4 He is the Rock, his works are *p*,
2Sa 22:31 "As for God, his way is *p*;
22:33 and makes my way *p*.
Job 36: 4 one *p* in knowledge is with you.
37:16 of him who is *p* in knowledge?
Ps 18:30 As for God, his way is *p*;
18:32 and makes my way *p*.
19: 7 The law of the LORD is *p*,
50: 2 From Zion, *p* in beauty,
64: 6 "We have devised a *p* plan!"
SS 6: 9 but my dove, my *p* one, is unique,
Isa 25: 1 for in *p* faithfulness
26: 3 You will keep in *p* peace
Eze 16:14 had given you made your beauty *p*,
27: 3 "I am *p* in beauty."
28:12 full of wisdom and *p* in beauty.
Mt 5:48 Do not even pagans do that? Be *p*,
5:48 as your heavenly Father is *p*.
19:21 answered, "If you want to be *p*,
Ro 12: 2 his good, pleasing and *p* will.
2Co 12: 9 for my power is made *p*
Php 3:12 or have already been made *p*,
Col 1:28 so that we may present everyone *p*
3:14 binds them all together in *p* unity.
Heb 2:10 the author of their salvation *p*
5: 9 what he suffered and, once made *p*,
7:19 useless (for the law made nothing *p*
7:28 who has been made *p* forever.
9:11 and more *p* tabernacle that is not
10: 1 make *p* those who draw
10:14 he has made *p* forever those who
11:40 with us would they be made *p*.
12:23 spirits of righteous men made *p*,
Jas 1:17 Every good and *p* gift is from above
1:25 into the *p* law that gives freedom,
3: 2 he is a *p* man, able
1Jn 4:18 But *p* love drives out fear,
4:18 The one who fears is not made *p*

PERFECTER* (PERFECT)
Heb 12: 2 the author and *p* of our faith,

PERFECTING* (PERFECT)
2Co 7: 1 *p* holiness out of reverence for God

PERFECTION* (PERFECT)
Ps 119: 96 To all *p* I see a limit;
La 2:15 the *p* of beauty,
Eze 27: 4 builders brought your beauty to *p*.
27:11 they brought your beauty to *p*.
28:12 " 'You were the model of *p*,
1Co 13:10 but when *p* comes, the imperfect
2Co 13: 9 and our prayer is for your *p*.
13:11 Aim for *p*, listen to my appeal,
Heb 7:11 If *p* could have been attained

PERFORM (PERFORMED PERFORMS)
Ex 3:20 with all the wonders that I will *p*
2Sa 7:23 to *p* great and awesome wonders
Jn 3: 2 no one could *p* the miraculous

PERFORMED (PERFORM)
Mt 11:21 If the miracles that were *p*
Jn 10:41 John never *p* a miraculous

PERFORMS (PERFORM)
Ps 77:14 You are the God who *p* miracles;

PERFUME
Ecc 7: 1 A good name is better than fine *p*,
SS 1: 3 your name is like *p* poured out.
Mk 14: 3 jar of very expensive *p*,

PERIL
2Co 1:10 us from such a deadly *p*,

PERISH (PERISHABLE PERISHED PERISHES PERISHING)
Ge 6:17 Everything on earth will *p*.
Est 4:16 And if I *p*, I *p*."
Ps 1: 6 but the way of the wicked will *p*.
37:20 But the wicked will *p*:
73:27 Those who are far from you will *p*;
102: 26 They will *p*, but you remain;
Pr 11:10 when the wicked *p*, there are
19: 9 and he who pours out lies will *p*.
21:28 A false witness will *p*,
28:28 when the wicked *p*, the righteous
Isa 1:28 who forsake the LORD will *p*.
29:14 the wisdom of the wise will *p*,
60:12 that will not serve you will *p*;
Zec 11: 9 the dying die, and the perishing *p*.
Lk 13: 3 unless you repent, you too will all *p*
13: 5 unless you repent, you too will all *p*
21:18 But not a hair of your head will *p*.
Jn 3:16 whoever believes in him shall not *p*
10:28 eternal life, and they shall never *p*;
Ro 2:12 apart from the law will also *p* apart
Col 2:22 These are all destined to *p* with use,
2Th 2:10 They *p* because they refused
Heb 1:11 They will *p*, but you remain;
1Pe 1: 4 into an inheritance that can never *p*
2Pe 3: 9 not wanting anyone to *p*,

PERISHABLE (PERISH)
1Co 15:42 The body that is sown is *p*,
1Pe 1:18 not with *p* things such
1:23 not of *p* seed, but of imperishable,

PERISHED (PERISH)
Ps 119: 92 I would have *p* in my affliction.

PERISHES (PERISH)
Job 8:13 so *p* the hope of the godless.
1Pe 1: 7 which *p* even though refined by fire

PERISHING (PERISH)
1Co 1:18 foolishness to those who are *p*,
2Co 2:15 being saved and those who are *p*.
4: 3 it is veiled to those who are *p*.

PERJURERS* (PERJURY)
Mal 3: 5 and *p,* against those who defraud
1Ti 1:10 for slave traders and liars and *p*—

PERJURY* (PERJURERS)
Jer 7: 9 murder, commit adultery and *p,*

PERMANENT
Heb 7:24 lives forever, he has a *p* priesthood.

PERMISSIBLE (PERMIT)
1Co 6:12 "Everything is *p* for me"—
10:23 "Everything is *p*"—but not

PERMIT (PERMISSIBLE PERMITTED)
Hos 5: 4 "Their deeds do not *p* them
1Ti 2:12 I do not *p* a woman to teach

PERMITTED (PERMIT)
Mt 19: 8 Moses *p* you to divorce your wives
2Co 12: 4 things that man is not *p* to tell.

PERSECUTE (PERSECUTED PERSECUTION PERSECUTIONS)
Ps119: 86 for men *p* me without cause.
Mt 5:11 *p* you and falsely say all kinds
5:44 and pray for those who *p* you,
Jn 15:20 they persecuted me, they will *p* you
Ac 9: 4 why do you *p* me?" "Who are you,
Ro 12:14 Bless those who *p* you; bless

PERSECUTED (PERSECUTE)
Mt 5:10 Blessed are those who are *p*
5:12 same way they *p* the prophets who
Jn 15:20 If they *p* me, they will persecute
1Co 4:12 when we are *p,* we endure it;
15: 9 because I *p* the church of God.
2Co 4: 9 in despair; *p,* but not abandoned;
1Th 3: 4 kept telling you that we would be *p.*
2Ti 3:12 life in Christ Jesus will be *p,*
Heb 11:37 destitute, *p* and mistreated—

PERSECUTION (PERSECUTE)
Mt 13:21 When trouble or *p* comes
Ro 8:35 or hardship or *p* or famine

PERSECUTIONS (PERSECUTE)
Mk 10:30 and with them, *p*) and in the age
2Co 12:10 in hardships, in *p,* in difficulties.
2Th 1: 4 faith in all the *p* and trials you are
2Ti 3:11 love, endurance, *p,* sufferings—

PERSEVERANCE* (PERSEVERE)
Ro 5: 3 we know that suffering produces *p;*
5: 4 *p,* character; and character, hope.
2Co 12:12 were done among you with great *p.*
2Th 1: 4 churches we boast about your *p*
3: 5 into God's love and Christ's *p.*
Heb 12: 1 run with *p* the race marked out
Jas 1: 3 the testing of your faith develops *p.*
1: 4 *P* must finish its work
5:11 You have heard of Job's *p*
2Pe 1: 6 *p;* and to *p,* godliness;
Rev 2: 2 your hard work and your *p.*
2:19 and faith, your service and *p,*

PERSEVERE* (PERSEVERANCE PERSEVERED PERSEVERES PERSEVERING)
1Ti 4:16 *P* in them, because if you do,
Heb 10:36 You need to *p* so that

PERSEVERED* (PERSEVERE)
Heb 11:27 he *p* because he saw him who is
Jas 5:11 consider blessed those who have *p.*
Rev 2: 3 You have *p* and have endured

PERSEVERES* (PERSEVERE)
1Co 13: 7 trusts, always hopes, always *p.*
Jas 1:12 Blessed is the man who *p*

PERSEVERING* (PERSEVERE)
Lk 8:15 retain it, and by *p* produce a crop.

PERSIANS
Da 6:15 law of the Medes and *P* no decree

PERSISTENCE*
Ro 2: 7 To those who by *p*

PERSUADE (PERSUADED PERSUASIVE)
Ac 18: 4 trying to *p* Jews and Greeks.
2Co 5:11 is to fear the Lord, we try to *p* men.

PERSUADED (PERSUADE)
Ro 4:21 being fully *p* that God had power

PERSUASIVE (PERSUADE)
1Co 2: 4 not with wise and *p* words,

PERVERSION* (PERVERT)
Lev 18:23 sexual relations with it; that is a *p.*
20:12 What they have done is a *p;*
Ro 1:27 the due penalty for their *p.*
Jude : 7 up to sexual immorality and *p.*

PERVERT (PERVERSION PERVERTED PERVERTS)
Ex 23: 2 do not *p* justice by siding
Dt 16:19 Do not *p* justice or show partiality.
Job 34:12 that the Almighty would *p* justice.
Pr 17:23 to *p* the course of justice.
Gal 1: 7 are trying to *p* the gospel of Christ.

PERVERTED (PERVERT)
1Sa 8: 3 and accepted bribes and *p* justice.

PERVERTS* (PERVERT)
1Ti 1:10 for murderers, for adulterers and *p,*

PESTILENCE (PESTILENCES)
Ps 91: 6 nor the *p* that stalks in the darkness

PESTILENCES (PESTILENCE)
Lk 21:11 famines and *p* in various places,

PETER
Apostle, brother of Andrew, also called Simon (Mt 10:2; Mk 3:16; Lk 6:14; Ac 1:13), and Cephas (Jn 1:42). Confession of Christ (Mt 16:13-20; Mk 8:27-30; Lk 9:18-27). At transfiguration (Mt 17:1-8; Mk 9:2-8; Lk 9:28-36; 2Pe 1:16-18). Caught fish with coin (Mt 17:24-27). Denial of Jesus predicted (Mt 26:31-35; Mk 14:27-31; Lk 22:31-34; Jn 13:31-38). Denied Jesus (Mt 26:69-75; Mk 14:66-72; Lk 22:54-62; Jn 18:15-27). Commissioned by Jesus to shepherd his flock (Jn 21:15-23).
Speech at Pentecost (Ac 2). Healed beggar (Ac 3:1-10). Speech at temple (Ac 3:11-26), before Sanhedrin (Ac 4:1-22). In Samaria (Ac 8:14-25). Sent by vision to Cornelius (Ac 10). Announced salvation of Gentiles in Jerusalem (Ac 11; 15). Freed from prison (Ac 12). Inconsistency at Antioch (Gal 2:11-21). At Jerusalem Council (Ac 15).
Epistles: 1-2 Peter.

PETITION (PETITIONS)
1Ch 16: 4 to make *p,* to give thanks,
Php 4: 6 by prayer and *p,* with thanksgiving,

PETITIONS (PETITION)
Heb 5: 7 he offered up prayers and *p*

PHANTOM*
Ps 39: 6 Man is a mere *p* as he goes to

PHARAOH (PHARAOH'S)
Ge 12:15 her to *P,* and she was taken
41:14 So *P* sent for Joseph, and he was
Ex 14: 4 glory for myself through *P*
14:17 And I will gain glory through *P*

PHARAOH'S (PHARAOH)
Ex 7: 3 But I will harden *P* heart, and

PHARISEE (PHARISEES)
Ac 23: 6 brothers, I am a *P,* the son of a *P.*
Php 3: 5 in regard to the law, a *P;* as for zeal,

PHARISEES (PHARISEE)
Mt 5:20 surpasses that of the *P*
16: 6 guard against the yeast of the *P*
23:13 of the law and *P,* you hypocrites!
Jn 3: 1 a man of the *P* named Nicodemus,

PHILADELPHIA
Rev 3: 7 the angel of the church in *P* write:

PHILEMON*
Phm : 1 To *P* our dear friend and fellow

PHILIP
1. Apostle (Mt 10:3; Mk 3:18; Lk 6:14; Jn 1:43-48; 14:8; Ac 1:13).
2. Deacon (Ac 6:1-7); evangelist in Samaria (Ac 8:4-25), to Ethiopian (Ac 8:26-40).

PHILIPPI
Ac 16:12 From there we traveled to *P,*
Php 1: 1 To all the saints in Christ Jesus at *P*

PHILISTINE (PHILISTINES)
Jos 13: 3 of the five *P* rulers in Gaza,
1Sa 14: 1 let's go over to the *P* outpost
17:26 is this uncircumcised *P* that he
17:37 me from the hand of this *P.*"

PHILISTINES (PHILISTINE)
Jdg 10: 7 them into the hands of the *P*
13: 1 the hands of the *P* for forty years.
16: 5 The rulers of the *P* went to her
1Sa 4: 1 at Ebenezer, and the *P* at Aphek.
5: 8 together all the rulers of the *P*
13:23 a detachment of *P* had gone out
17: 1 the *P* gathered their forces for war
23: 1 the *P* are fighting against Keilah
27: 1 is to escape to the land of the *P.*
31: 1 Now the *P* fought against Israel;
2Sa 5:17 When the *P* heard that David had
8: 1 David defeated the *P* and subdued
21:15 there was a battle between the *P*
2Ki 18: 8 he defeated the *P,* as far as Gaza
Am 1: 8 Ekron till the last of the *P* is dead,"

PHILOSOPHER* (PHILOSOPHY)
1Co 1:20 Where is the *p* of this age?

PHILOSOPHY* (PHILOSOPHER)
Col 2: 8 through hollow and deceptive *p,*

PHINEHAS
Nu 25: 7 When *P* son of Eleazar, the son
Ps106: 30 But *P* stood up and intervened,

PHOEBE*
Ro 16: 1 I commend to you our sister *P,*

PHYLACTERIES*
Mt 23: 5 They make their *p* wide

PHYSICAL
Ro 2:28 merely outward and *p.*
Col 1:22 by Christ's *p* body through death
1Ti 4: 8 For *p* training is of some value,
Jas 2:16 but does nothing about his *p* needs,

PICK (PICKED)
Mk 16:18 they will *p* up snakes

PICKED (PICK)
Lk 14: 7 noticed how the guests *p* the places
Jn 5: 9 he *p* up his mat and walked.

PIECE (PIECES)
Jn 19:23 woven in one *p* from top to bottom.

PIECES (PIECE)
Ge 15:17 and passed between the *p.*
Jer 34:18 and then walked between its *p.*
Zec 11:12 So they paid me thirty *p* of silver.
Mt 14:20 of broken *p* that were left over.

PIERCE (PIERCED)
Ex 21: 6 and *p* his ear with an awl.
Pr 12:18 Reckless words *p* like a sword,
Lk 2:35 a sword will *p* your own soul too."

PIERCED (PIERCE)
Ps 22:16 they have *p* my hands and my feet.
40: 6 but my ears you have *p;*
Isa 53: 5 But he was *p* for our transgressions,
Zec 12:10 look on me, the one they have *p,*
Jn 19:37 look on the one they have *p.*"
Rev 1: 7 even those who *p* him;

PIG'S (PIGS)
Pr 11:22 Like a gold ring in a *p* snout

PIGEONS
Lev 5:11 afford two doves or two young *p,*
Lk 2:24 "a pair of doves or two young *p.*"

PIGS (PIG'S)
Mt 7: 6 do not throw your pearls to *p.*
Mk 5:11 A large herd of *p* was feeding on

PILATE
Governor of Judea. Questioned Jesus (Mt 27:1-26; Mk 15:15; Lk 22:66-23:25; Jn 18:28-19:16); sent him to Herod (Lk 23:6-12); consented to his crucifixion when crowds chose Barabbas (Mt 27:15-26; Mk 15:6-15; Lk 23:13-25; Jn 19:1-10).

PILLAR (PILLARS)
Ge 19:26 and she became a *p* of salt.
Ex 13:21 ahead of them in a *p* of cloud
1Ti 3:15 the *p* and foundation of the truth.
Rev 3:12 who overcomes I will make a *p*

PILLARS (PILLAR)
Gal 2: 9 and John, those reputed to be *p,*

PINIONS
Dt 32:11 and carries them on its *p.*

PISGAH
Dt 3:27 Go up to the top of *P* and look west

PIT
Ps 7:15 falls into the *p* he has made.
40: 2 He lifted me out of the slimy *p,*
103: 4 who redeems your life from the *p*
Pr 23:27 for a prostitute is a deep *p*

Pr 26:27 If a man digs a *p*, he will fall into it;
Isa 24:17 Terror and *p* and snare await you,
38:17 me from the *p* of destruction;
Mt 15:14 a blind man, both will fall into a *p*."

PITCH
Ge 6:14 and coat it with *p* inside and out.
Ex 2: 3 and coated it with tar and *p*.

PITIED (PITY)
1Co 15:19 we are to be *p* more than all men.

PITY (PITIED)
Ps 72:13 He will take *p* on the weak
Ecc 4:10 But *p* the man who falls
Lk 10:33 when he saw him, he took *p* on him

PLAGUE (PLAGUED PLAGUES)
2Ch 6:28 "When famine or *p* comes
Ps 91: 6 nor the *p* that destroys at midday.

PLAGUED* (PLAGUE)
Ps 73: 5 they are not *p* by human ills.
73:14 All day long I have been *p*;

PLAGUES (PLAGUE)
Hos 13:14 Where, O death, are your *p*?
Rev 21: 9 full of the seven last *p* came
22:18 to him the *p* described in this book.

PLAIN
Isa 40: 4 the rugged places a *p*.
Ro 1:19 what may be known about God is *p*

PLAN (PLANNED PLANS)
Ex 26:30 according to the *p* shown you
Job 42: 2 no *p* of yours can be thwarted.
Pr 14:22 those who *p* what is good find love
21:30 is no wisdom, no insight, no *p*
Am 3: 7 nothing without revealing his *p*
Eph 1:11 predestined according to the *p*

PLANK
Mt 7: 3 attention to the *p* in your own eye?
Lk 6:41 attention to the *p* in your own eye?

PLANNED (PLAN)
Ps 40: 5 The things you *p* for us
Isa 14:24 "Surely, as I have *p*, so it will be,
23: 9 The LORD Almighty *p* it,
46:11 what I have *p*, that will I do.
Heb 11:40 God had *p* something better for us

PLANS (PLAN)
Ps 20: 4 and make all your *p* succeed.
33:11 *p* of the LORD stand firm forever,
Pr 15:22 *P* fail for lack of counsel,
16: 3 and your *p* will succeed.
19:21 Many are the *p* in a man's heart,
20:18 Make *p* by seeking advice;
Isa 29:15 to hide their *p* from the LORD,
30: 1 those who carry out *p* that are not
32: 8 But the noble man makes noble *p*,
2Co 1:17 Or do I make my *p* in a worldly

PLANT (PLANTED PLANTING PLANTS)
Am 9:15 I will *p* Israel in their own land,
Mt 15:13 "Every *p* that my heavenly Father

PLANTED (PLANT)
Ge 2: 8 the LORD God had *p* a garden
Ps 1: 3 He is like a tree *p* by streams
Jer 17: 8 He will be like a tree *p* by the water
Mt 15:13 Father has not *p* will be pulled
21:33 was a landowner who *p* a vineyard.
Lk 13: 6 "A man had a fig tree, *p*
1Co 3: 6 I *p* the seed, Apollos watered it,
Jas 1:21 humbly accept the word *p* in you,

PLANTING (PLANT)
Isa 61: 3 a *p* of the LORD

PLANTS (PLANT)
Pr 31:16 out of her earnings she *p* a vineyard
1Co 3: 7 So neither he who *p* nor he who
9: 7 Who *p* a vineyard and does not eat

PLATTER
Mk 6:25 head of John the Baptist on a *p*."

PLAY (PLAYED)
1Sa 16:23 David would take his harp and *p*.
Isa 11: 8 The infant will *p* near the hole

PLAYED (PLAY)
Lk 7:32 " 'We *p* the flute for you,
1Co 14: 7 anyone know what tune is being *p*

PLEA (PLEAD PLEADED PLEADS)
1Ki 8:28 to your servant's prayer and his *p*
Ps 102: 17 he will not despise their *p*.
La 3:56 You heard my *p*: "Do not close

PLEAD (PLEA)
Isa 1:17 *p* the case of the widow.

PLEADED (PLEA)
2Co 12: 8 Three times I *p* with the Lord

PLEADS (PLEA)
Job 16:21 on behalf of a man he *p* with God

PLEASANT (PLEASE)
Ge 49:15 and how *p* is his land,
Ps 16: 6 for me in *p* places;
133: 1 How good and *p* it is
135: 3 sing praise to his name, for that is *p*
147: 1 how *p* and fitting to praise him!
Pr 2:10 knowledge will be *p* to your soul.
3:17 Her ways are *p* ways,
16:21 and *p* words promote instruction.
16:24 *P* words are a honeycomb,
Isa 30:10 Tell us *p* things,
1Th 3: 6 that you always have *p* memories
Heb 12:11 No discipline seems *p* at the time,

PLEASANTNESS* (PLEASE)
Pr 27: 9 the *p* of one's friend springs

PLEASE (PLEASANT PLEASANTNESS PLEASED PLEASES PLEASING PLEASURE PLEASURES)
Ps 69:31 This will *p* the LORD more
Pr 20:23 and dishonest scales do not *p* him.
Isa 46:10 and I will do all that I *p*.
Jer 6:20 your sacrifices do not *p* me."
27: 5 and I give it to anyone I *p*.
Jn 5:30 for I seek not to *p* myself
Ro 8: 8 by the sinful nature cannot *p* God.
15: 1 of the weak and not to *p* ourselves.
15: 2 Each of us should *p* his neighbor
1Co 7:32 affairs—how he can *p* the Lord.
10:33 I try to *p* everybody in every way.
2Co 5: 9 So we make it our goal to *p* him,
Gal 1:10 or of God? Or am I trying to *p* men
6: 8 the one who sows to *p* the Spirit,
Col 1:10 and may *p* him in every way:
1Th 2: 4 We are not trying to *p* men
4: 1 how to live in order to *p* God,
2Ti 2: 4 wants to *p* his commanding officer.
Tit 2: 9 to try to *p* them, not to talk back
Heb 11: 6 faith it is impossible to *p* God,

PLEASED (PLEASE)
Dt 28:63 as it *p* the LORD to make you
1Sa 12:22 LORD was *p* to make you his own.
1Ki 3:10 The Lord was *p* that Solomon had
1Ch 29:17 that you test the heart and are *p*
Mic 6: 7 Will the LORD be *p*
Mal 1:10 I am not *p* with you," says
Mt 3:17 whom I love; with him I am well *p*
17: 5 whom I love; with him I am well *p*.
Mk 1:11 whom I love; with you I am well *p*
Lk 3:22 whom I love; with you I am well *p*
1Co 1:21 God was *p* through the foolishness
Col 1:19 For God was *p* to have all his
Heb 10: 6 you were not *p*.
10: 8 nor were you *p* with them"
10:38 I will not be *p* with him."
11: 5 commended as one who *p* God.
13:16 for with such sacrifices God is *p*.
2Pe 1:17 whom I love; with him I am well *p*

PLEASES (PLEASE)
Job 23:13 He does whatever he *p*.
Ps 115: 3 he does whatever *p* him.
135: 6 The LORD does whatever *p* him,
Pr 15: 8 but the prayer of the upright *p* him.
21: 1 it like a watercourse wherever he *p*.
Ecc 2:26 To the man who *p* him, God gives
7:26 man who *p* God will escape her,
Da 4:35 He does as he *p*
Jn 3: 8 The wind blows wherever it *p*.
8:29 for I always do what *p* him."
Eph 5:10 truth) and find out what *p* the Lord
Col 3:20 in everything, for this *p* the Lord.
1Ti 2: 3 This is good, and *p* God our Savior,
1Jn 3:22 his commands and do what *p* him.

PLEASING (PLEASE)
Ge 2: 9 trees that were *p* to the eye
Lev 1: 9 an aroma *p* to the LORD.
Ps 19:14 be *p* in your sight,
104: 34 May my meditation be *p* to him,
Pr 15:26 but those of the pure are *p* to him.
16: 7 When a man's ways are *p*
SS 1: 3 *P* is the fragrance of your perfumes
4:10 How much more *p* is your love
7: 6 How beautiful you are and how *p*,
Ro 12: 1 *p* to God—this is your spiritual
14:18 Christ in this way is *p* to God
Php 4:18 an acceptable sacrifice, *p* to God.

1Ti 5: 4 grandparents, for this is *p* to God.
Heb 13:21 may he work in us what is *p* to him,

PLEASURE (PLEASE)
Ps 5: 4 You are not a God who takes *p*
51:16 you do not take *p* in burnt offerings
147: 10 His *p* is not in the strength
Pr 10:23 A fool finds *p* in evil conduct,
18: 2 A fool finds no *p* in understanding
21:17 He who loves *p* will become poor;
Isa 1:11 I have no *p*
Jer 6:10 they find no *p* in it.
Eze 18:23 Do I take any *p* in the death
18:32 For I take no *p* in the death
33:11 I take no *p* in the death
Lk 10:21 Father, for this was your good *p*.
Eph 1: 5 in accordance with his *p* and will—
1: 9 of his will according to his good *p*,
1Ti 5: 6 the widow who lives for *p* is dead
2Ti 3: 4 lovers of *p* rather than lovers
2Pe 2:13 Their idea of *p* is to carouse

PLEASURES* (PLEASE)
Ps 16:11 with eternal *p* at your right hand.
Lk 8:14 and *p*, and they do not mature.
Tit 3: 3 by all kinds of passions and *p*.
Heb 11:25 rather than to enjoy the *p* of sin
Jas 4: 3 may spend what you get on your *p*.
2Pe 2:13 reveling in their *p* while they feast

PLEDGE
Dt 24:17 take the cloak of the widow as a *p*.
1Pe 3:21 but the *p* of a good conscience

PLEIADES
Job 38:31 "Can you bind the beautiful *P*?
Am 5: 8 (he who made the *P* and Orion,

PLENTIFUL (PLENTY)
Mt 9:37 harvest is *p* but the workers are
Lk 10: 2 harvest is *p*, but the workers are

PLENTY (PLENTIFUL)
2Co 8:14 the present time your *p* will supply
Php 4:12 whether living in *p* or in want.

PLOT (PLOTS)
Est 2:22 Mordecai found out about the *p*
Ps 2: 1 and the peoples *p* in vain?
Pr 3:29 not *p* harm against your neighbor,
Zec 8:17 do not *p* evil against your neighbor,
Ac 4:25 and the peoples *p* in vain?

PLOTS (PLOT)
Pr 6:14 who *p* evil with deceit in his heart

PLOW (PLOWMAN PLOWSHARES)
Lk 9:62 "No one who puts his hand to the *p*

PLOWMAN (PLOW)
1Co 9:10 because when the *p* plows

PLOWSHARES (PLOW)
1Sa 13:20 to the Philistines to have their *p*,
Isa 2: 4 They will beat their swords into *p*
Joel 3:10 Beat your *p* into swords
Mic 4: 3 They will beat their swords into *p*

PLUCK
Mk 9:47 your eye causes you to sin, *p* it out.

PLUNDER (PLUNDERED)
Ex 3:22 And so you will *p* the Egyptians."
Est 3:13 of Adar, and to *p* their goods.
8:11 to *p* the property of their enemies.
9:10 did not lay their hands on the *p*.
Pr 22:23 and will *p* those who *p* them.
Isa 3:14 the *p* from the poor is

PLUNDERED (PLUNDER)
Eze 34: 8 lacks a shepherd and so has been *p*

PLUNGE
1Ti 6: 9 and harmful desires that *p* men
1Pe 4: 4 think it strange that you do not *p*

PODS
Lk 15:16 with the *p* that the pigs were eating,

POINT
Mt 4: 5 on the highest *p* of the temple.
26:38 with sorrow to the *p* of death.
Jas 2:10 yet stumbles at just one *p* is guilty
Rev 2:10 Be faithful, even to the *p* of death,

POISON
Ps 140: 3 the *p* of vipers is on their lips.
Mk 16:18 and when they drink deadly *p*,
Ro 3:13 "The *p* of vipers is on their lips."
Jas 3: 8 It is a restless evil, full of deadly *p*.

POLE (POLES)
Nu 21: 8 "Make a snake and put it up on a *p*;
Dt 16:21 not set up any wooden Asherah *p*

POLES (POLE)
Ex 25:13 Then make *p* of acacia wood

POLISHED
Isa 49: 2 he made me into a *p* arrow

POLLUTE* (POLLUTED POLLUTES)
Nu 35:33 " 'Do not *p* the land where you are.
Jude : 8 these dreamers *p* their own bodies,

POLLUTED* (POLLUTE)
Ezr 9:11 entering to possess is a land *p*
Pr 25:26 Like a muddied spring or a *p* well
Ac 15:20 to abstain from food *p* by idols,
Jas 1:27 oneself from being *p* by the world.

POLLUTES* (POLLUTE)
Nu 35:33 Bloodshed *p* the land,

PONDER (PONDERED)
Ps 64: 9 and *p* what he has done.
119: 95 but I will *p* your statutes.

PONDERED (PONDER)
Ps 111: 2 they are *p* by all who delight
Lk 2:19 up all these things and *p* them

POOR (POVERTY)
Lev 19:10 Leave them for the *p* and the alien.
23:22 Leave them for the *p* and the alien.
27: 8 If anyone making the vow is too *p*
Dt 15: 4 there should be no *p* among you,
15: 7 is a *p* man among your brothers
15:11 There will always be *p* people
24:12 If the man is *p*, do not go to sleep
24:14 advantage of a hired man who is *p*
Job 5:16 So the *p* have hope,
24: 4 force all the *p* of the land
Ps 14: 6 frustrate the plans of the *p*,
34: 6 This *p* man called, and the LORD
35:10 You rescue the *p* from those too
40:17 Yet I am *p* and needy;
68:10 O God, you provided for the *p*.
82: 3 maintain the rights of the *p*
112: 9 scattered abroad his gifts to the *p*,
113: 7 He raises the *p* from the dust
140: 12 the LORD secures justice for the *p*
Pr 10: 4 Lazy hands make a man *p*,
13: 7 to be *p*, yet has great wealth.
14:20 The *p* are shunned
14:31 oppresses the *p* shows contempt
17: 5 who mocks the *p* shows contempt
19: 1 Better a *p* man whose walk is
19:17 to the *p* lends to the LORD,
19:22 better to be *p* than a liar.
20:13 not love sleep or you will grow *p*;
21:13 to the cry of the *p*,
21:17 who loves pleasure will become *p*;
22: 2 Rich and *p* have this in common:
22: 9 for he shares his food with the *p*.
22:22 not exploit the *p* because they are *p*
28: 6 Better a *p* man whose walk is
28:27 to the *p* will lack nothing,
29: 7 care about justice for the *p*,
31: 9 defend the rights of the *p*
31:20 She opens her arms to the *p*
Ecc 4:13 Better a *p* but wise youth
Isa 3:14 the plunder from the *p* is
10: 2 to deprive the *p* of their rights
14:30 of the *p* will find pasture,
25: 4 You have been a refuge for the *p*,
32: 7 schemes to destroy the *p* with lies,
61: 1 me to preach good news to the *p*.
Jer 22:16 He defended the cause of the *p*
Eze 18:12 He oppresses the *p* and needy.
Am 2: 7 They trample on the heads of the *p*
4: 1 you women who oppress the *p*
5:11 You trample on the *p*
Zec 7:10 or the fatherless, the alien or the *p*.
Mt 5: 3 saying: "Blessed are the *p* in spirit,
11: 5 the good news is preached to the *p*.
19:21 your possessions and give to the *p*,
26:11 The *p* you will always have
Mk 12:42 But a *p* widow came and put
14: 7 The *p* you will always have
Lk 4:18 me to preach good news to the *p*.
6:20 "Blessed are you who are *p*,
11:41 is inside the dish, to the *p*,
14:13 invite the *p*, the crippled, the lame,
21: 2 also saw a *p* widow put
Jn 12: 8 You will always have the *p*
Ac 9:36 doing good and helping the *p*.
10: 4 and gifts to the *p* have come up
24:17 to bring my people gifts for the *p*
Ro 15:26 for the *p* among the saints
1Co 13: 3 If I give all I possess to the *p*
2Co 6:10 sorrowful, yet always rejoicing; *p*,
8: 9 yet for your sakes he became *p*,
Gal 2:10 continue to remember the *p*,
Jas 2: 2 and a *p* man in shabby clothes
2: 5 not God chosen those who are *p*
2: 6 But you have insulted the *p*.

POPULATION*
Pr 14:28 A large *p* is a king's glory,

PORTION
Nu 18:29 as the LORD's *p* the best
Dt 32: 9 For the LORD's *p* is his people,
1Sa 1: 5 But to Hannah he gave a double *p*
2Ki 2: 9 "Let me inherit a double *p*
Ps 73:26 and my *p* forever.
119: 57 You are my *p*, O LORD;
Isa 53:12 Therefore I will give him a *p*
Jer 10:16 He who is the *P* of Jacob is not like
La 3:24 to myself, "The LORD is my *p*;
Zec 2:12 LORD will inherit Judah as his *p*

PORTRAIT
Lk 20:24 Whose *p* and inscription are on it?"

PORTRAYED
Gal 3: 1 very eyes Jesus Christ was clearly *p*

POSITION (POSITIONS)
Ro 12:16 to associate with people of low *p*.
Jas 1: 9 ought to take pride in his high *p*.
2Pe 3:17 and fall from your secure *p*.

POSITIONS (POSITION)
2Ch 20:17 Take up your *p*; stand firm
Jude : 6 the angels who did not keep their *p*

POSSESS (POSSESSED POSSESSING POSSESSION POSSESSIONS)
Nu 33:53 for I have given you the land to *p*.
Dt 4:14 you are crossing the Jordan to *p*.
Pr 8:12 I *p* knowledge and discretion.
Jn 5:39 that by them you *p* eternal life.

POSSESSED (POSSESS)
Jn 10:21 the sayings of a man *p* by a demon.

POSSESSING* (POSSESS)
2Co 6:10 nothing, and yet *p* everything.

POSSESSION (POSSESS)
Ge 15: 7 to give you this land to take *p* of it
Ex 6: 8 I will give it to you as a *p*.
19: 5 nations you will be my treasured *p*.
Nu 13:30 "We should go up and take *p*
Dt 7: 6 to be his people, his treasured *p*.
Jos 1:11 take *p* of the land the LORD your
Ps 2: 8 the ends of the earth your *p*.
135: 4 Israel to be his treasured *p*.
Eph 1:14 of those who are God's *p*—

POSSESSIONS (POSSESS)
Mt 19:21 go, sell your *p* and give to the poor,
Lk 11:21 guards his own house, his *p* are safe
12:15 consist in the abundance of his *p*."
19: 8 now I give half of my *p* to the poor,
Ac 4:32 any of his *p* was his own,
2Co 12:14 what I want is not your *p* but you.
Heb 10:34 yourselves had better and lasting *p*.
1Jn 3:17 If anyone has material *p*

POSSIBLE
Mt 19:26 but with God all things are *p*."
26:39 if it is *p*, may this cup be taken
Mk 9:23 "Everything is *p* for him who
10:27 all things are *p* with God."
14:35 prayed that if *p* the hour might pass
Ro 12:18 If it is *p*, as far as it depends on you,
1Co 6: 5 Is it *p* that there is nobody
9:19 to everyone, to win as many as *p*.
9:22 by all *p* means I might save some.

POT (POTSHERD POTTER POTTER'S POTTERY)
2Ki 4:40 there is death in the *p*!"
Jer 18: 4 But the *p* he was shaping

POTIPHAR*
Egyptian who bought Joseph (Ge 37:36), set him over his house (Ge 39:1-6), sent him to prison (Ge 39:7-30).

POTSHERD (POT)
Isa 45: 9 a *p* among the potsherds

POTTER (POT)
Isa 29:16 Can the pot say of the *p*,
45: 9 Does the clay say to the *p*,
64: 8 We are the clay, you are the *p*;
Jer 18: 6 "Like clay in the hand of the *p*,
Zec 11:13 it to the *p*"— the handsome price
Ro 9:21 Does not the *p* have the right

POTTER'S (POT)
Mt 27: 7 to use the money to buy the *p* field

POTTERY (POT)
Ro 9:21 of clay some *p* for noble purposes

POUR (POURED POURS)
Ps 62: 8 *p* out your hearts to him,
Isa 44: 3 I will *p* out my Spirit
Eze 20: 8 So I said I would *p* out my wrath
39:29 for I will *p* out my Spirit
Joel 2:28 I will *p* out my Spirit on all people.
Zec 12:10 I will *p* out on the house of David
Mal 3:10 *p* out so much blessing that you
Ac 2:17 I will *p* out my Spirit on all people.

POURED (POUR)
Ps 22:14 I am *p* out like water,
Isa 32:15 till the Spirit is *p* upon us
Mt 26:28 which is *p* out for many
Lk 22:20 in my blood, which is *p* out for you.
Ac 2:33 and has *p* out what you now see
10:45 of the Holy Spirit had been *p* out
Ro 5: 5 because God has *p* out his love
Php 2:17 even if I am being *p* out like a drink
2Ti 4: 6 I am already being *p* out like
Tit 3: 6 whom he *p* out on us generously
Rev 16: 2 and *p* out his bowl on the land,

POURS (POUR)
Lk 5:37 And no one *p* new wine

POVERTY* (POOR)
Dt 28:48 and thirst, in nakedness and dire *p*,
1Sa 2: 7 The LORD sends *p* and wealth;
Pr 6:11 *p* will come on you like a bandit
10:15 but *p* is the ruin of the poor.
11:24 withholds unduly, but comes to *p*.
13:18 who ignores discipline comes to *p*
14:23 but mere talk leads only to *p*.
21: 5 as surely as haste leads to *p*.
22:16 to the rich—both come to *p*.
24:34 *p* will come on you like a bandit
28:19 fantasies will have his fill of *p*.
28:22 and is unaware that *p* awaits him.
30: 8 give me neither *p* nor riches,
31: 7 let them drink and forget their *p*
Ecc 4:14 born in *p* within his kingdom.
Mk 12:44 out of her *p*, put in everything—
Lk 21: 4 she out of her *p* put in all she had
2Co 8: 2 and their extreme *p* welled up
8: 9 through his *p* might become rich.
Rev 2: 9 I know your afflictions and your *p*

POWER (POWERFUL POWERS)
Ex 15: 6 was majestic in *p*.
32:11 out of Egypt with great *p*
Dt 8:17 "My *p* and the strength
34:12 one has ever shown the mighty *p*
1Sa 10: 6 LORD will come upon you in *p*,
10:10 Spirit of God came upon him in *p*,
11: 6 Spirit of God came upon him in *p*,
16:13 the LORD came upon David in *p*.
1Ch 29:11 LORD, is the greatness and the *p*
2Ch 20: 6 *P* and might are in your hand,
32: 7 for there is a greater *p* with us
Job 9: 4 wisdom is profound, his *p* is vast.
36:22 "God is exalted in his *p*.
37:23 beyond our reach and exalted in *p*;
Ps 20: 6 with the saving *p* of his right hand.
63: 2 and beheld your *p* and your glory.
66: 3 So great is your *p*
68:34 Proclaim the *p* of God,
77:14 you display your *p*
89:13 Your arm is endued with *p*;
145: 6 of the *p* of your awesome works,
147: 5 Great is our Lord and mighty in *p*;
150: 2 Praise him for his acts of *p*;
Pr 3:27 when it is in your *p* to act.
18:21 The tongue has the *p* of life
24: 5 A wise man has great *p*,
Isa 11: 2 the Spirit of counsel and of *p*,
40:10 the Sovereign LORD comes with *p*
40:26 of his great *p* and mighty strength,
63:12 who sent his glorious arm of *p*
Jer 10: 6 and your name is mighty in *p*.
10:12 But God made the earth by his *p*;
27: 5 With my great *p* and outstretched
32:17 and the earth by your great *p*
Hos 13:14 from the *p* of the grave;
Na 1: 3 to anger and great in *p*;
Zec 4: 6 nor by *p*, but by my Spirit,'
Mt 22:29 do not know the Scriptures or the *p*
24:30 on the clouds of the sky, with *p*
Lk 1:35 and the *p* of the Most High will
4:14 to Galilee in the *p* of the Spirit,
9: 1 he gave them *p* and authority
10:19 to overcome all the *p* of the enemy;

Lk 24:49 clothed with *p* from on high."
Ac 1: 8 you will receive *p* when the Holy
4:28 They did what your *p* and will had
4:33 With great *p* the apostles
10:38 with the Holy Spirit and *p*,
26:18 and from the *p* of Satan to God,
Ro 1:16 it is the *p* of God for the salvation
1:20 his eternal *p* and divine nature—
4:21 fully persuaded that God had *p*
9:17 that I might display my *p* in you
15:13 overflow with hope by the *p*
15:19 through the *p* of the Spirit.
1Co 1:17 cross of Christ be emptied of its *p*.
1:18 to us who are being saved it is the *p*
2: 4 a demonstration of the Spirit's *p*,
6:14 By his *p* God raised the Lord
15:24 all dominion, authority and *p*.
15:56 of death is sin, and the *p*
2Co 4: 7 to show that this all-surpassing *p* is
6: 7 in truthful speech and in the *p*
10: 4 they have divine *p*
12: 9 for my *p* is made perfect
13: 4 weakness, yet he lives by God's *p*.
Eph 1:19 and his incomparably great *p*
3:16 you with *p* through his Spirit
3:20 according to his *p* that is at work
6:10 in the Lord and in his mighty *p*.
Php 3:10 and the *p* of his resurrection
3:21 by the *p* that enables him
Col 1:11 strengthened with all *p* according
2:10 who is the head over every *p*
1Th 1: 5 also with *p*, with the Holy Spirit
2Ti 1: 7 but a spirit of *p*, of love
3: 5 form of godliness but denying its *p*.
Heb 2:14 might destroy him who holds the *p*
7:16 of the *p* of an indestructible life.
1Pe 1: 5 by God's *p* until the coming
2Pe 1: 3 His divine *p* has given us
Jude :25 *p* and authority, through Jesus
Rev 4:11 to receive glory and honor and *p*,
5:12 to receive *p* and wealth
11:17 you have taken your great *p*
19: 1 and glory and *p* belong to our God,
20: 6 The second death has no *p*

POWERFUL (POWER)
2Ch 27: 6 Jotham grew *p* because he walked
Est 9: 4 and he became more and more *p*.
Ps 29: 4 The voice of the LORD is *p*;
Jer 32:18 *p* God, whose name is the LORD
Zec 8:22 *p* nations will come to Jerusalem
Mk 1: 7 "After me will come one more *p*
Lk 24:19 *p* in word and deed before God
2Th 1: 7 in blazing fire with his *p* angels.
Heb 1: 3 sustaining all things by his *p* word.
Jas 5:16 The prayer of a righteous man is *p*

POWERLESS
Ro 5: 6 when we were still *p*, Christ died
8: 3 For what the law was *p* to do

POWERS (POWER)
Da 4:35 pleases with the *p* of heaven
Ro 8:38 nor any *p*, neither height nor depth
1Co 12:10 to another miraculous *p*,
Eph 6:12 against the *p* of this dark world
Col 1:16 whether thrones or *p* or rulers
2:15 And having disarmed the *p*
Heb 6: 5 and the *p* of the coming age,
1Pe 3:22 and *p* in submission to him.

PRACTICE (PRACTICED PRACTICES)
Lev 19:26 " 'Do not *p* divination or sorcery.
Ps 119: 56 This has been my *p*:
Eze 33:31 but they do not put them into *p*.
Mt 7:24 into *p* is like a wise man who built
23: 3 for they do not *p* what they preach.
Lk 8:21 hear God's word and put it into *p*."
Ro 12:13 *P* hospitality.
Php 4: 9 or seen in me—put it into *p*.
1Ti 5: 4 to put their religion into *p* by caring

PRACTICED (PRACTICE)
Mt 23:23 You should have *p* the latter,

PRACTICES (PRACTICE)
Ps 101: 7 No one who *p* deceit
Mt 5:19 but whoever *p* and teaches these
Col 3: 9 taken off your old self with its *p*

PRAISE (PRAISED PRAISES PRAISEWORTHY PRAISING)
Ex 15: 2 He is my God, and I will *p* him,
Dt 10:21 He is your *p*; he is your God,
26:19 declared that he will set you in *p*,
32: 3 Oh, *p* the greatness of our God!
Ru 4:14 said to Naomi: "*P* be to the LORD,
2Sa 22: 4 to the LORD, who is worthy of *p*,
22:47 The LORD lives! *P* be to my Rock
1Ch 16:25 is the LORD and most worthy of *p*;
16:35 that we may glory in your *p*."
23: 5 four thousand are to *p* the LORD
29:10 "*P* be to you, O LORD,
2Ch 5:13 they raised their voices in *p*
20:21 and to *p* him for the splendor
29:30 to *p* the LORD with the words
Ezr 3:10 took their places to *p* the LORD,
Ne 9: 5 and *p* the LORD your God,
Ps 8: 2 you have ordained *p*
9: 1 I will *p* you, O LORD,
16: 7 I will *p* the LORD, who counsels
26: 7 proclaiming aloud your *p*
30: 4 *p* his holy name.
33: 1 it is fitting for the upright to *p* him.
34: 1 his *p* will always be on my lips.
40: 3 a hymn of *p* to our God.
42: 5 for I will yet *p* him,
43: 5 for I will yet *p* him,
45:17 the nations will *p* you for ever
47: 7 sing to him a psalm of *p*.
48: 1 the LORD, and most worthy of *p*,
51:15 and my mouth will declare your *p*.
56: 4 In God, whose word I *p*,
57: 9 I will *p* you, O Lord,
63: 4 I will *p* you as long as I live,
65: 1 *P* awaits you, O God, in Zion;
66: 2 make his *p* glorious.
66: 8 *P* our God, O peoples,
68:19 *P* be to the Lord, to God our Savior
68:26 *p* the LORD in the assembly
69:30 I will *p* God's name in song
69:34 Let heaven and earth *p* him,
71: 8 My mouth is filled with your *p*,
71:14 I will *p* you more and more.
71:22 I will *p* you with the harp
74:21 the poor and needy *p* your name.
86:12 I will *p* you, O Lord my God,
89: 5 The heavens *p* your wonders,
92: 1 It is good to *p* the LORD
96: 2 Sing to the LORD, *p* his name;
100: 4 and his courts with *p*;
101: 1 to you, O LORD, I will sing *p*.
102: 18 not yet created may *p* the LORD:
103: 1 *P* the LORD, O my soul;
103: 20 *P* the LORD, you his angels,
104: 1 *P* the LORD, O my soul.
105: 2 Sing to him, sing *p* to him;
106: 1 *P* the LORD.
108: 3 I will *p* you, O LORD,
111: 1 *P* the LORD.
113: 1 *P* the LORD.
117: 1 *P* the LORD, all you nations;
119:175 Let me live that I may *p* you,
135: 1 *P* the LORD.
135: 20 you who fear him, *p* the LORD.
138: 1 I will *p* you, O LORD,
139: 14 I *p* you because I am fearfully
144: 1 *P* be to the LORD my Rock,
145: 3 is the LORD and most worthy of *p*;
145: 10 All you have made will *p* you,
145: 21 Let every creature *p* his holy name
146: 1 *P* the LORD, O my soul.
147: 1 how pleasant and fitting to *p* him!
148: 1 *P* the LORD from the heavens,
148: 13 Let them *p* the name of the LORD,
149: 1 his *p* in the assembly of the saints.
149: 6 May the *p* of God be
149: 9 *P* the LORD.
150: 2 *p* him for his surpassing greatness.
150: 6 that has breath *p* the LORD.
Pr 27: 2 Let another *p* you, and not your
27:21 man is tested by the *p* he receives.
31:31 let her works bring her *p*
SS 1: 4 we will *p* your love more than wine
Isa 12: 1 "I will *p* you, O LORD.
42:10 his *p* from the ends of the earth,
61: 3 and a garment of *p*
Jer 33: 9 *p* and honor before all nations
Da 2:20 "*P* be to the name of God for ever
4:37 *p* and exalt and glorify the King
Mt 5:16 and *p* your Father in heaven.
21:16 you have ordained *p*'?"
Lk 19:37 to *p* God in loud voices
Jn 5:44 effort to obtain the *p* that comes
12:43 for they loved *p* from men more
Ro 2:29 Such a man's *p* is not from men,
15: 7 in order to bring *p* to God.
2Co 1: 3 *P* be to the God and Father
Eph 1: 3 *P* be to the God and Father
1: 6 to the *p* of his glorious grace,
1:12 might be for the *p* of his glory.
1:14 to the *p* of his glory.
1Th 2: 6 We were not looking for *p*
Heb 13:15 offer to God a sacrifice of *p*—
Jas 3: 9 With the tongue we *p* our Lord
5:13 happy? Let him sing songs of *p*.
Rev 5:13 be *p* and honor and glory
7:12 *P* and glory

PRAISED (PRAISE)
1Ch 29:10 David *p* the LORD in the presence
Ne 8: 6 Ezra *p* the LORD, the great God;
Job 1:21 may the name of the LORD be *p*."
Ps 113: 2 Let the name of the LORD be *p*,
Pr 31:30 who fears the LORD is to be *p*.
Isa 63: 7 the deeds for which he is to be *p*,
Da 2:19 Then Daniel *p* the God of heaven
4:34 Then I *p* the Most High; I honored
Lk 18:43 the people saw it, they also *p* God.
23:47 seeing what had happened, *p* God
Ro 9: 5 who is God over all, forever *p*!
Gal 1:24 And they *p* God because of me.
1Pe 4:11 that in all things God may be *p*

PRAISES (PRAISE)
2Sa 22:50 I will sing *p* to your name.
Ps 18:49 I will sing *p* to your name.
47: 6 Sing *p* to God, sing *p*;
147: 1 How good it is to sing *p* to our God,
Pr 31:28 her husband also, and he *p* her:
1Pe 2: 9 that you may declare the *p*

PRAISEWORTHY* (PRAISE)
Ps 78: 4 the *p* deeds of the LORD,
Php 4: 8 if anything is excellent or *p*—

PRAISING (PRAISE)
Lk 2:13 *p* God and saying, "Glory to God
2:20 *p* God for all the things they had
Ac 2:47 *p* God and enjoying the favor
10:46 speaking in tongues and *p* God.
1Co 14:16 If you are *p* God with your spirit,

PRAY (PRAYED PRAYER PRAYERS PRAYING PRAYS)
Dt 4: 7 is near us whenever we *p* to him?
1Sa 12:23 the LORD by failing to *p* for you.
1Ki 8:30 when they *p* toward this place.
2Ch 7:14 will humble themselves and *p*
Ezr 6:10 and *p* for the well-being of the king
Job 42: 8 My servant Job will *p* for you,
Ps 5: 2 for to you I *p*.
32: 6 let everyone who is godly *p*
122: 6 *P* for the peace of Jerusalem:
Jer 29: 7 *P* to the LORD for it,
29:12 upon me and come and *p* to me,
42: 3 *P* that the LORD your God will
Mt 5:44 and *p* for those who persecute you,
6: 5 "And when you *p*, do not be like
6: 9 "This, then, is how you should *p*:
14:23 up on a mountainside by himself to *p*.
19:13 hands on them and *p* for them.
26:36 Sit here while I go over there and *p*
Lk 6:28 *p* for those who mistreat you.
11: 1 us to *p*, just as John taught his
18: 1 them that they should always *p*
22:40 "*P* that you will not fall
Jn 17:20 I *p* also for those who will believe
Ro 8:26 do not know what we ought to *p* for,
1Co 14:13 in a tongue should *p* that he may
Eph 1:18 I *p* also that the eyes
3:16 I *p* that out of his glorious riches he
6:18 And *p* in the Spirit on all occasions
Col 1:10 we *p* this in order that you may live
4: 3 *p* for us, too, that God may open
1Th 5:17 Be joyful always; *p* continually;
2Th 1:11 in mind, we constantly *p* for you,
Jas 5:13 one of you in trouble? He should *p*.
5:16 *p* for each other so that you may be
1Pe 4: 7 self-controlled so that you can *p*.
Jude :20 up in your most holy faith and *p*

PRAYED (PRAY)
1Sa 1:27 I *p* for this child, and the LORD
1Ki 18:36 Elijah stepped forward and *p*:
19: 4 under it and *p* that he might die.
2Ki 6:17 And Elisha *p*, "O LORD,
2Ch 30:18 But Hezekiah *p* for them, saying,
Ne 4: 9 we *p* to our God and posted a guard
Job 42:10 After Job had *p* for his friends,
Da 6:10 got down on his knees and *p*,
9: 4 I *p* to the LORD my God
Jnh 2: 1 From inside the fish Jonah *p*
Mt 26:39 with his face to the ground and *p*,
Mk 1:35 off to a solitary place, where he *p*.
14:35 *p* that if possible the hour might
Lk 22:41 knelt down and *p*, "Father,
Jn 17: 1 he looked toward heaven and *p*:
Ac 4:31 After they *p*, the place where they
6: 6 who *p* and laid their hands on them
8:15 they *p* for them that they might
13: 3 So after they had fasted and *p*,

PRAYER (PRAY)
2Ch 30:27 for their *p* reached heaven,
Ezr 8:23 about this, and he answered our *p*.
Ps 4: 1 be merciful to me and hear my *p*.
6: 9 the LORD accepts my *p*.

Ps 17: 1 Give ear to my *p*—
17: 6 give ear to me and hear my *p*.
65: 2 O you who hear *p*,
66:20 who has not rejected my *p*
86: 6 Hear my *p*, O LORD;
Pr 15: 8 but the *p* of the upright pleases him
15:29 but he hears the *p* of the righteous.
Isa 56: 7 a house of *p* for all nations."
Mt 21:13 house will be called a house of *p*,'
21:22 receive whatever you ask for in *p*."
Mk 9:29 This kind can come out only by *p*."
11:24 whatever you ask for in *p*,
Jn 17:15 My *p* is not that you take them out
Ac 1:14 all joined together constantly in *p*,
2:42 to the breaking of bread and to *p*.
6: 4 and will give our attention to *p*
10:31 has heard your *p* and remembered
16:13 expected to find a place of *p*.
Ro 12:12 patient in affliction, faithful in *p*.
1Co 7: 5 you may devote yourselves to *p*.
2Co 13: 9 and our *p* is for your perfection.
Php 1: 9 this is my *p*: that your love may
4: 6 but in everything, by *p* and petition
Col 4: 2 yourselves to *p*, being watchful
1Ti 2: 8 to lift up holy hands in *p*,
4: 5 by the word of God and *p*.
Jas 5:15 *p* offered in faith will make the sick
1Pe 3:12 and his ears are attentive to their *p*,

PRAYERS (PRAY)
1Ch 5:20 He answered their *p*, because they
Isa 1:15 even if you offer many *p*,
Mk 12:40 and for a show make lengthy *p*.
2Co 1:11 as you help us by your *p*.
Eph 6:18 on all occasions with all kinds of *p*
1Ti 2: 1 then, first of all, that requests, *p*,
1Pe 3: 7 so that nothing will hinder your *p*.
Rev 5: 8 which are the *p* of the saints.
8: 3 with the *p* of all the saints,

PRAYING (PRAY)
Ge 24:45 "Before I finished *p* in my heart,
1Sa 1:12 As she kept on *p* to the LORD,
Mk 11:25 And when you stand *p*,
Lk 3:21 as he was *p*, heaven was opened
6:12 and spent the night *p* to God.
9:29 As he was *p*, the appearance
Jn 17: 9 I am not *p* for the world,
Ac 9:11 from Tarsus named Saul, for he is *p*
16:25 and Silas were *p* and singing hymns
Ro 15:30 in my struggle by *p* to God for me.
Eph 6:18 always keep on *p* for all the saints.

PRAYS (PRAY)
1Co 14:14 my spirit *p*, but my mind is

PREACH (PREACHED PREACHING)
Isa 61: 1 me to *p* good news to the poor.
Mt 10: 7 As you go, *p* this message:
23: 3 they do not practice what they *p*.
Mk 16:15 and *p* the good news to all creation.
Lk 4:18 me to *p* good news to the poor.
Ac 9:20 At once he began to *p*
16:10 us to *p* the gospel to them.
Ro 1:15 am so eager to *p* the gospel
10:15 how can they *p* unless they are sent
15:20 to *p* the gospel where Christ was
1Co 1:17 to *p* the gospel—not with words
1:23 wisdom, but we *p* Christ crucified:
9:14 that those who *p* the gospel should
9:16 Woe to me if I do not *p* the gospel!
2Co 4: 5 For we do not *p* ourselves,
10:16 so that we can *p* the gospel
Gal 1: 8 from heaven should *p* a gospel
2Ti 4: 2 I give you this charge: *P* the Word;

PREACHED (PREACH)
Mt 24:14 gospel of the kingdom will be *p*
Mk 6:12 and *p* that people should repent.
13:10 And the gospel must first be *p*
14: 9 wherever the gospel is *p*
Ac 8: 4 had been scattered *p* the word
28:31 hindrance he *p* the kingdom
1Co 9:27 so that after I have *p* to others,
15: 1 you of the gospel I *p* to you,
2Co 11: 4 other than the Jesus we *p*,
Gal 1: 8 other than the one we *p* to you,
Eph 2:17 *p* peace to you who were far away
Php 1:18 false motives or true, Christ is *p*.
1Ti 3:16 was *p* among the nations,
1Pe 1:25 this is the word that was *p* to you.
3:19 and *p* to the spirits in prison who

PREACHING (PREACH)
Lk 9: 6 *p* the gospel and healing people
Ac 18: 5 devoted himself exclusively to *p*,
Ro 10:14 hear without someone *p* to them?
1Co 2: 4 and my *p* were not with wise
9:18 in *p* the gospel I may offer it free
Gal 1: 9 If anybody is *p* to you a gospel

1Ti 4:13 the public reading of Scripture, to *p*
5:17 especially those whose work is *p*

PRECEDE*
1Th 4:15 will certainly not *p* those who have

PRECEPTS*
Dt 33:10 He teaches your *p* to Jacob
Ps 19: 8 The *p* of the LORD are right,
103: 18 and remember to obey his *p*.
105: 45 that they might keep his *p*
111: 7 all his *p* are trustworthy.
111: 10 who follow his *p* have good
119: 4 You have laid down *p*
119: 15 I meditate on your *p*
119: 27 understand the teaching of your *p*;
119: 40 How I long for your *p*!
119: 45 for I have sought out your *p*.
119: 56 I obey your *p*.
119: 63 to all who follow your *p*.
119: 69 I keep your *p* with all my heart.
119: 78 but I will meditate on your *p*.
119: 87 but I have not forsaken your *p*.
119: 93 I will never forget your *p*,
119: 94 I have sought out your *p*.
119:100 for I obey your *p*.
119:104 I gain understanding from your *p*;
119:110 but I have not strayed from your *p*.
119:128 because I consider all your *p* right,
119:134 that I may obey your *p*.
119:141 I do not forget your *p*.
119:159 See how I love your *p*;
119:168 I obey your *p* and your statutes,
119:173 for I have chosen your *p*.

PRECIOUS
Ps 19:10 They are more *p* than gold,
72:14 for *p* is their blood in his sight.
116: 15 *P* in the sight of the LORD
119: 72 from your mouth is more *p* to me
139: 17 How *p* to me are your thoughts,
Pr 8:11 for wisdom is more *p* than rubies,
Isa 28:16 a *p* cornerstone for a sure
1Pe 1:19 but with the *p* blood of Christ,
2: 4 but chosen by God and *p* to him—
2: 6 a chosen and *p* cornerstone,
2Pe 1: 1 Christ have received a faith as *p*
1: 4 us his very great and *p* promises,

PREDESTINED* (DESTINY)
Ro 8:29 *p* to be conformed to the likeness
8:30 And those he *p*, he also called;
Eph 1: 5 In love he *p* us to be adopted
1:11 having been *p* according

PREDICTED (PREDICTION)
1Sa 28:17 The LORD has done what he *p*
Ac 7:52 killed those who *p* the coming
1Pe 1:11 when he *p* the sufferings of Christ

PREDICTION* (PREDICTED PREDICTIONS)
Jer 28: 9 only if his *p* comes true."

PREDICTIONS (PREDICTION)
Isa 44:26 and fulfills the *p* of his messengers,

PREGNANT
Ex 21:22 who are fighting hit a *p* woman
Mt 24:19 be in those days for *p* women
1Th 5: 3 as labor pains on a *p* woman,

PREPARE (PREPARED)
Ps 23: 5 You *p* a table before me
Isa 25: 6 the LORD Almighty will *p*
40: 3 "In the desert *p*
Am 4:12 *p* to meet your God, O Israel."
Mal 3: 1 who will *p* the way before me.
Mt 3: 3 '*P* the way for the Lord,
Jn 14: 2 there to *p* a place for you.
Eph 4:12 to *p* God's people for works
1Pe 1:13 Therefore, *p* your minds for action;

PREPARED (PREPARE)
Ex 23:20 to bring you to the place I have *p*.
Mt 25:34 the kingdom *p* for you
Ro 9:22 of his wrath—*p* for destruction?
1Co 2: 9 what God has *p* for those who love
Eph 2:10 which God *p* in advance for us
2Ti 2:21 and *p* to do any good work.
4: 2 be *p* in season and out of season;
1Pe 3:15 Always be *p* to give an answer

PRESCRIBED
Ezr 7:23 Whatever the God of heaven has *p*,

PRESENCE (PRESENT)
Ex 25:30 Put the bread of the *P* on this table
33:14 The LORD replied, "My *P* will go
Nu 4: 7 "Over the table of the *P* they are
1Sa 6:20 in the *p* of the LORD, this
21: 6 of the *P* that had been removed

2Sa 22:13 Out of the brightness of his *p*
2Ki 17:23 LORD removed them from his *p*,
23:27 also from my *p* as I removed Israel,
Ezr 9:15 one of us can stand in your *p*."
Ps 16:11 you will fill me with joy in your *p*,
21: 6 with the joy of your *p*.
23: 5 in the *p* of my enemies.
31:20 the shelter of your *p* you hide them
41:12 and set me in your *p* forever.
51:11 Do not cast me from your *p*
52: 9 in the *p* of your saints.
89:15 who walk in the light of your *p*,
90: 8 our secret sins in the light of your *p*
114: 7 O earth, at the *p* of the Lord,
139: 7 Where can I flee from your *p*?
Isa 26:17 so were we in your *p*, O LORD.
Jer 5:22 "Should you not tremble in my *p*?
Eze 38:20 of the earth will tremble at my *p*.
Hos 6: 2 that we may live in his *p*.
Na 1: 5 The earth trembles at his *p*,
Mal 3:16 in his *p* concerning those who
Ac 2:28 you will fill me with joy in your *p*.'
1Th 3: 9 have in the *p* of our God
3:13 and holy in the *p* of our God
2Th 1: 9 and shut out from the *p* of the Lord
Heb 9:24 now to appear for us in God's *p*.
1Jn 3:19 rest in his *p* whenever our hearts
Jude :24 before his glorious *p* without fault

PRESENT (PRESENCE)
1Co 3:22 life or death or the *p* or the future—
7:26 of the *p* crisis, I think that it is good
2Co 11: 2 so that I might *p* you as a pure
Eph 5:27 and to *p* her to himself
1Ti 4: 8 holding promise for both the *p* life
2Ti 2:15 Do your best to *p* yourself to God
Jude :24 and to *p* you before his glorious

PRESERVE
Lk 17:33 and whoever loses his life will *p* it.

PRESERVES
Ps 119:50 Your promise *p* my life.

PRESS (PRESSED PRESSURE)
Php 3:12 but I *p* on to take hold of that
3:14 I *p* on toward the goal

PRESSED (PRESS)
Lk 6:38 *p* down, shaken together

PRESSURE (PRESS)
2Co 1: 8 We were under great *p*, far
11:28 I face daily the *p* of my concern

PRETENDED
1Sa 21:13 So he *p* to be insane

PREVAILS
1Sa 2: 9 "It is not by strength that one *p*;
Pr 19:21 but it is the LORD's purpose that *p*

PRICE (PRICELESS)
Job 28:18 the *p* of wisdom is beyond rubies.
1Co 6:20 your own; you were bought at a *p*.
7:23 bought at a *p*; do not become slaves

PRICELESS* (PRICE)
Ps 36: 7 How *p* is your unfailing love!

PRIDE (PROUD)
Pr 8:13 I hate *p* and arrogance,
11: 2 When *p* comes, then comes
13:10 *P* only breeds quarrels,
16:18 *P* goes before destruction,
29:23 A man's *p* brings him low,
Isa 25:11 God will bring down their *p*
Da 4:37 And those who walk in *p* he is able
Am 8: 7 The LORD has sworn by the *P*
2Co 5:12 giving you an opportunity to take *p*
7: 4 in you; I take great *p* in you.
8:24 and the reason for our *p* in you,
Gal 6: 4 Then he can take *p* in himself,
Jas 1: 9 ought to take *p* in his high position.

PRIEST (PRIESTHOOD PRIESTLY PRIESTS)
Ge 14:18 He was *p* of God Most High,
Nu 5:10 to the *p* will belong to the *p*.'"
2Ch 13: 9 and seven rams may become a *p*
Ps 110: 4 "You are a *p* forever,
Heb 2:17 faithful high *p* in service to God,
3: 1 and high *p* whom we confess.
4:14 have a great high *p* who has gone
4:15 do not have a high *p* who is unable
5: 6 "You are a *p* forever,
6:20 He has become a high *p* forever,
7: 3 Son of God he remains a *p* forever.
7:15 clear if another *p* like Melchizedek
7:26 Such a high *p* meets our need—
8: 1 We do have such a high *p*,
10:11 Day after day every *p* stands

Heb 13:11 The high *p* carries the blood

PRIESTHOOD (PRIEST)
Heb 7:24 lives forever, he has a permanent *p*.
1Pe 2: 5 into a spiritual house to be a holy *p*,
2: 9 you are a chosen people, a royal *p*,

PRIESTLY (PRIEST)
Ro 15:16 to the Gentiles with the *p* duty

PRIESTS (PRIEST)
Ex 19: 6 you will be for me a kingdom of *p*
Lev 21: 1 "Speak to the *p*, the sons of Aaron,
Eze 42:13 where the *p* who approach
46: 2 *p* are to sacrifice his burnt offering
Mal 1: 6 O *p*, who show contempt for my name.
Rev 5:10 to be a kingdom and *p*
20: 6 but they will be *p* of God

PRIME
Isa 38:10 recovery: I said, "In the *p* of my life

PRINCE (PRINCES PRINCESS)
Isa 9: 6 Everlasting Father, *P* of Peace.
Eze 34:24 and my servant David will be *p*
37:25 my servant will be their *p* forever.
Da 8:25 stand against the *P* of princes.
Jn 12:31 now the *p* of this world will be
Ac 5:31 as *P* and Savior that he might give

PRINCES (PRINCE)
Ps 118: 9 than to trust in *p*.
148: 11 you *p* and all rulers on earth,
Isa 40:23 He brings *p* to naught

PRINCESS* (PRINCE)
Ps 45:13 All glorious is the *p*

PRISCILLA*
Wife of Aquila; co-worker with Paul (Ac 18; Ro 16:3; 1Co 16:19; 2Ti 4:19); instructor of Apollos (Ac 18:24-28).

PRISON (PRISONER PRISONERS)
Ps 66:11 You brought us into *p*
142: 7 Set me free from my *p*,
Isa 42: 7 to free captives from *p*
Mt 25:36 I was in *p* and you came to visit me
2Co 11:23 been in *p* more frequently,
Heb 11:36 others were chained and put in *p*.
13: 3 Remember those in *p*
1Pe 3:19 spirits in *p* who disobeyed long ago
Rev 20: 7 Satan will be released from his *p*

PRISONER (PRISON)
Ro 7:23 and making me a *p* of the law of sin
Gal 3:22 declares that the whole world is a *p*
Eph 3: 1 the *p* of Christ Jesus for the sake

PRISONERS (PRISON)
Ps 68: 6 he leads forth the *p* with singing;
79:11 groans of the *p* come before you;
107: 10 *p* suffering in iron chains,
146: 7 The LORD sets *p* free,
Zec 9:12 to your fortress, O *p* of hope;
Lk 4:18 me to proclaim freedom for the *p*
Gal 3:23 we were held *p* by the law,

PRIVILEGE*
2Co 8: 4 pleaded with us for the *p* of sharing

PRIZE*
1Co 9:24 Run in such a way as to get the *p*.
9:24 but only one gets the *p*? Run
9:27 will not be disqualified for the *p*.
Php 3:14 on toward the goal to win the *p*
Col 2:18 of angels disqualify you for the *p*.

PROBE
Job 11: 7 Can you *p* the limits
Ps 17: 3 Though you *p* my heart

PROCEDURE
Ecc 8: 6 For there is a proper time and *p*

PROCESSION
Ps 68:24 Your *p* has come into view, O God,
118: 27 boughs in hand, join in the festal *p*
1Co 4: 9 on display at the end of the *p*,
2Co 2:14 us in triumphal *p* in Christ

PROCLAIM (PROCLAIMED PROCLAIMING PROCLAIMS PROCLAMATION)
Ex 33:19 and I will *p* my name, the LORD,
Lev 25:10 and *p* liberty throughout the land
Dt 30:12 and *p* it to us so we may obey it?"
2Sa 1:20 *p* it not in the streets of Ashkelon,
1Ch 16:23 *p* his salvation day after day.
Ne 8:15 and that they should *p* this word
Ps 2: 7 I will *p* the decree of the LORD:
9:11 *p* among the nations what he has
19: 1 the skies *p* the work of his hands.
22:31 They will *p* his righteousness
40: 9 I *p* righteousness in the great
50: 6 the heavens *p* his righteousness,
64: 9 they will *p* the works of God
68:34 *P* the power of God,
71:16 I will come and *p* your mighty acts,
92: 2 to *p* your love in the morning
96: 2 *p* his salvation day after day.
97: 6 The heavens *p* his righteousness,
106: 2 Who can *p* the mighty acts
118: 17 will *p* what the LORD has done.
145: 6 and I will *p* your great deeds.
Isa 12: 4 and *p* that his name is exalted.
42:12 and *p* his praise in the islands.
52: 7 who *p* salvation,
61: 1 to *p* freedom for the captives
66:19 They will *p* my glory
Jer 7: 2 house and there *p* this message:
50: 2 lift up a banner and *p* it;
Hos 5: 9 I *p* what is certain.
Zec 9:10 He will *p* peace to the nations.
Mt 10:27 in your ear, *p* from the roofs.
12:18 and he will *p* justice to the nations.
Lk 4:18 me to *p* freedom for the prisoners
9:60 you go and *p* the kingdom of God."
Ac 17:23 unknown I am going to *p*
20:27 hesitated to *p* to you the whole will
1Co 11:26 you *p* the Lord's death
Col 1:28 We *p* him, admonishing
4: 4 Pray that I may *p* it clearly,
1Jn 1: 1 this we *p* concerning the Word

PROCLAIMED (PROCLAIM)
Ex 9:16 and that my name might be *p*
34: 5 there with him and *p* his name,
Ps 68:11 was the company of those who *p* it:
Ro 15:19 I have fully *p* the gospel of Christ.
Col 1:23 that has been *p* to every creature
2Ti 4:17 me the message might be fully *p*

PROCLAIMING (PROCLAIM)
Ps 26: 7 *p* aloud your praise
92:15 *p*, "The LORD is upright;
Ac 5:42 and *p* the good news that Jesus is
Ro 10: 8 the word of faith we are *p*:

PROCLAIMS (PROCLAIM)
Dt 18:22 If what a prophet *p* in the name

PROCLAMATION (PROCLAIM)
Isa 62:11 The LORD has made *p*

PRODUCE (PRODUCES)
Mt 3: 8 *P* fruit in keeping with repentance.
3:10 tree that does not *p* good fruit will

PRODUCES (PRODUCE)
Pr 30:33 so stirring up anger *p* strife."
Ro 5: 3 that suffering *p* perseverance;
Heb 12:11 it *p* a harvest of righteousness

PROFANE (PROFANED)
Lev 19:12 and so *p* the name of your God.
22:32 Do not *p* my holy name.
Mal 2:10 Why do we *p* the covenant

PROFANED (PROFANE)
Eze 36:20 the nations they *p* my holy name,

PROFESS*
1Ti 2:10 for women who *p* to worship God.
Heb 4:14 let us hold firmly to the faith we *p*.
10:23 unswervingly to the hope we *p*,

PROFIT (PROFITABLE)
Pr 14:23 All hard work brings a *p*,
21: 5 The plans of the diligent lead to *p*
Isa 44:10 which can *p* him nothing?
2Co 2:17 not peddle the word of God for *p*.
Php 3: 7 was to my *p* I now consider loss

PROFITABLE* (PROFIT)
Pr 3:14 for she is more *p* than silver
31:18 She sees that her trading is *p*,
Tit 3: 8 These things are excellent and *p*

PROFOUND
Job 9: 4 His wisdom is *p*, his power is vast.
Ps 92: 5 how *p* your thoughts!
Eph 5:32 This is a *p* mystery—but I am

PROGRESS
Php 1:25 continue with all of you for your *p*
1Ti 4:15 so that everyone may see your *p*.

PROLONG*
Dt 5:33 *p* your days in the land that you
Ps 85: 5 Will you *p* your anger
Pr 3: 2 for they will *p* your life many years
Isa 53:10 will see his offspring and *p* his days,
La 4:22 he will not *p* your exile.

PROMISE (PROMISED PROMISES)
Nu 23:19 Does he *p* and not fulfill?
Jos 23:14 Every *p* has been fulfilled;
2Sa 7:25 keep forever the *p* you have made
1Ki 8:20 The LORD has kept the *p* he made
8:24 You have kept your *p*
Ne 5:13 man who does not keep this *p*.
9: 8 have kept your *p* because you are
Ps 77: 8 Has his *p* failed for all time?
119: 41 your salvation according to your *p*;
119: 50 Your *p* preserves my life.
119: 58 to me according to your *p*.
119:162 I rejoice in your *p*
Ac 2:39 The *p* is for you and your children
Ro 4:13 offspring received the *p* that he
4:20 unbelief regarding the *p* of God,
Gal 3:14 that by faith we might receive the *p*
Eph 2:12 foreigners to the covenants of the *p*
1Ti 4: 8 holding *p* for both the present life
Heb 6:13 When God made his *p* to Abraham
11:11 him faithful who had made the *p*.
2Pe 3: 9 Lord is not slow in keeping his *p*,
3:13 with his *p* we are looking forward

PROMISED (PROMISE)
Ge 21: 1 did for Sarah what he had *p*.
24: 7 who spoke to me and *p* me on oath,
Ex 3:17 And I have *p* to bring you up out
Nu 10:29 for the LORD has *p* good things
Dt 15: 6 your God will bless you as he has *p*,
26:18 his treasured possession as he *p*,
2Sa 7:28 and you have *p* these good things
1Ki 9: 5 I *p* David your father when I said,
2Ch 6:15 with your mouth you have *p*
Ps 119: 57 I have *p* to obey your words.
Lk 24:49 to send you what my Father has *p*;
Ac 1: 4 but wait for the gift my Father *p*,
13:32 What God *p* our fathers he has
Ro 4:21 power to do what he had *p*.
Tit 1: 2 *p* before the beginning of time,
Heb 10:23 for he who *p* is faithful.
10:36 you will receive what he has *p*.
Jas 1:12 the crown of life that God has *p*
2: 5 the kingdom he *p* those who love
2Pe 3: 4 "Where is this 'coming' he *p*?
1Jn 2:25 And this is what he *p* us—

PROMISES (PROMISE)
Jos 21:45 one of all the LORD's good *p*
23:14 of all the good *p* the LORD your
1Ki 8:56 failed of all the good *p* he gave
1Ch 17:19 and made known all these great *p*.
Ps 85: 8 he *p* peace to his people, his saints
106: 12 Then they believed his *p*
119:140 Your *p* have been thoroughly
119:148 that I may meditate on your *p*.
145: 13 The LORD is faithful to all his *p*
Ro 9: 4 the temple worship and the *p*.
2Co 1:20 matter how many *p* God has made,
7: 1 Since we have these *p*, dear friends,
Heb 8: 6 and it is founded on better *p*.
2Pe 1: 4 us his very great and precious *p*,

PROMOTE (PROMOTES)
Pr 12:20 but joy for those who *p* peace.
16:21 and pleasant words *p* instruction.
1Ti 1: 4 These *p* controversies rather

PROMOTES (PROMOTE)
Pr 17: 9 over an offense *p* love,

PROMPTED
1Th 1: 3 your labor *p* by love, and your
2Th 1:11 and every act *p* by your faith.

PRONOUNCE (PRONOUNCED)
1Ch 23:13 to *p* blessings in his name forever.

PRONOUNCED (PRONOUNCE)
1Ch 16:12 miracles, and the judgments he *p*,

PROOF (PROVE)
Ac 17:31 He has given *p* of this to all men
2Co 8:24 Therefore show these men the *p*

PROPER
Ps 104: 27 give them their food at the *p* time.
145: 15 give them their food at the *p* time.
Ecc 5:18 Then I realized that it is good and *p*
8: 5 the wise heart will know the *p* time
Mt 24:45 give them their food at the *p* time?
Lk 1:20 which will come true at their *p* time
1Co 11:13 Is it *p* for a woman to pray to God
Gal 6: 9 at the *p* time we will reap a harvest
1Ti 2: 6 the testimony given in its *p* time.
1Pe 2:17 Show *p* respect to everyone:

PROPERTY
Heb 10:34 the confiscation of your *p*,

PROPHECIES (PROPHESY)
1Co 13: 8 where there are *p*, they will cease;
1Th 5:20 do not treat *p* with contempt.

PROPHECY (PROPHESY)
Da 9:24 to seal up vision and *p*
1Co 12:10 miraculous powers, to another *p*,
13: 2 of *p* and can fathom all mysteries
14: 1 gifts, especially the gift of *p*.
14: 6 or *p* or word of instruction?
14:22 *p*, however, is for believers,
2Pe 1:20 you must understand that no *p*
Rev 22:18 the words of the *p* of this book:

PROPHESIED (PROPHESY)
Nu 11:25 the Spirit rested on them, they *p*,
1Sa 19:24 and also *p* in Samuel's presence.
Jn 11:51 that year he *p* that Jesus would
Ac 19: 6 and they spoke in tongues and *p*.
21: 9 four unmarried daughters who *p*.

PROPHESIES (PROPHESY)
Jer 28: 9 the prophet who *p* peace will be
Eze 12:27 and he *p* about the distant future.'
1Co 11: 4 *p* with his head covered dishonors
14: 3 But everyone who *p* speaks to men

PROPHESY (PROPHECIES PROPHECY PROPHESIED PROPHESIES PROPHESYING PROPHET PROPHET'S PROPHETESS PROPHETS)
1Sa 10: 6 and you will *p* with them;
Eze 13: 2 Say to those who *p* out
13:17 daughters of your people who *p* out
34: 2 *p* against the shepherds of Israel;
37: 4 "*P* to these bones and say to them,
Joel 2:28 Your sons and daughters will *p*,
Mt 7:22 Lord, did we not *p* in your name,
Ac 2:17 Your sons and daughters will *p*,
1Co 13: 9 know in part and we *p* in part,
14:39 my brothers, be eager to *p*,
Rev 11: 3 and they will *p* for 1,260 days,

PROPHESYING (PROPHESY)
1Ch 25: 1 and Jeduthun for the ministry of *p*,
Ro 12: 6 If a man's gift is *p*, let him use it

PROPHET (PROPHESY)
Ex 7: 1 your brother Aaron will be your *p*.
Nu 12: 6 "When a *p* of the LORD is
Dt 13: 1 If a *p*, or one who foretells
18:18 up for them a *p* like you
18:22 If what a *p* proclaims in the name
1Sa 3:20 that Samuel was attested as a *p*
9: 9 because the *p* of today used
1Ki 1: 8 son of Jehoiada, Nathan the *p*,
18:36 the *p* Elijah stepped forward
2Ki 5: 8 and he will know that there is a *p*
6:12 "but Elisha, the *p* who is in Israel,
20: 1 The *p* Isaiah son of Amoz went
2Ch 35:18 since the days of the *p* Samuel;
36:12 himself before Jeremiah the *p*,
Ezr 5: 1 Haggai the *p* and Zechariah the *p*,
Eze 2: 5 they will know that a *p* has been
33:33 they will know that a *p* has been
Hos 9: 7 the *p* is considered a fool,
Am 7:14 "I was neither a *p* nor a prophet's
Hab 1: 1 that Habakkuk the *p* received.
Hag 1: 1 came through the *p* Haggai
Zec 1: 1 to the *p* Zechariah son of Berekiah,
13: 4 that day every *p* will be ashamed
Mal 4: 5 I will send you the *p* Elijah
Mt 10:41 Anyone who receives a *p*
11: 9 what did you go out to see? A *p*?
12:39 except the sign of the *p* Jonah.
Lk 1:76 will be called a *p* of the Most High;
4:24 "no *p* is accepted in his hometown.
7:16 A great *p* has appeared among us,"
24:19 "He was a *p*, powerful in word
Jn 1:21 "Are you the *P*?" He answered,
Ac 7:37 'God will send you a *p* like me
21:10 a *p* named Agabus came
1Co 14:37 If anybody thinks he is a *p*
Rev 16:13 and out of the mouth of the false *p*.

PROPHET'S (PROPHESY)
2Pe 1:20 about by the *p* own interpretation.

PROPHETESS (PROPHESY)
Ex 15:20 Then Miriam the *p*, Aaron's sister,
Jdg 4: 4 a *p*, the wife of Lappidoth,
Isa 8: 3 I went to the *p*, and she conceived
Lk 2:36 a *p*, Anna, the daughter of Phanuel,

PROPHETS (PROPHESY)
Nu 11:29 that all the LORD's people were *p*
1Sa 10:11 Is Saul also among the *p*?"
1Sa 28: 6 him by dreams or Urim or *p*.
1Ki 19:10 put your *p* to death with the sword.
1Ch 16:22 do my *p* no harm."
Ps 105: 15 do my *p* no harm."
Jer 23: 9 Concerning the *p*:
23:30 "I am against the *p* who steal
Eze 13: 2 prophesy against the *p*
Mt 5:17 come to abolish the Law or the *P*;
7:12 for this sums up the Law and the *P*.
7:15 "Watch out for false *p*.
22:40 and the *P* hang on these two
23:37 you who kill the *p* and stone those
24:24 false Christs and false *p* will appear
26:56 of the *p* might be fulfilled."
Lk 10:24 For I tell you that many *p*
11:49 'I will send them *p* and apostles,
24:25 believe all that the *p* have spoken!
24:44 me in the Law of Moses, the *P*
Ac 3:24 "Indeed, all the *p* from Samuel on,
10:43 All the *p* testify about him that
13: 1 the church at Antioch there were *p*
26:22 nothing beyond what the *p*
28:23 the Law of Moses and from the *P*.
Ro 1: 2 through his *p* in the Holy
3:21 to which the Law and the *P* testify.
11: 3 they have killed your *p*
1Co 12:28 second *p*, third teachers, then
12:29 Are all *p*? Are all teachers?
14:32 The spirits of *p* are subject
Eph 2:20 foundation of the apostles and *p*,
3: 5 Spirit to God's holy apostles and *p*.
4:11 some to be *p*, some
Heb 1: 1 through the *p* at many times
1Pe 1:10 Concerning this salvation, the *p*,
2Pe 1:19 word of the *p* made more certain,
3: 2 spoken in the past by the holy *p*
1Jn 4: 1 because many false *p* have gone out
Rev 11:10 these two *p* had tormented those
18:20 Rejoice, saints and apostles and *p*!

PROPORTION
Dt 16:10 by giving a freewill offering in *p*
16:17 Each of you must bring a gift in *p*

PROPRIETY*
1Ti 2: 9 with decency and *p*,
2:15 in faith, love and holiness with *p*.

PROSPECT*
Pr 10:28 The *p* of the righteous is joy,

PROSPER (PROSPERED PROSPERITY PROSPEROUS PROSPERS)
Dt 5:33 so that you may live and *p*
28:63 pleased the LORD to make you *p*
29: 9 that you may *p* in everything you
1Ki 2: 3 so that you may *p* in all you do
Ezr 6:14 and *p* under the preaching
Pr 11:10 When the righteous *p*, the city
11:25 A generous man will *p*;
17:20 A man of perverse heart does not *p*
28:13 who conceals his sins does not *p*,
28:25 he who trusts in the LORD will *p*.
Isa 53:10 of the LORD will *p* in his hand.
Jer 12: 1 Why does the way of the wicked *p*?

PROSPERED (PROSPER)
Ge 39: 2 was with Joseph and he *p*,
2Ch 14: 7 So they built and *p*.
31:21 And so he *p*.

PROSPERITY (PROSPER)
Dt 28:11 will grant you abundant *p*—
30:15 I set before you today life and *p*,
Job 36:11 will spend the rest of their days in *p*
Ps 73: 3 when I saw the *p* of the wicked.
122: 9 I will seek your *p*.
128: 2 blessings and *p* will be yours.
Pr 3: 2 and bring you *p*.
13:21 but *p* is the reward of the righteous.
21:21 finds life, *p* and honor.
Isa 45: 7 I bring *p* and create disaster;

PROSPEROUS (PROSPER)
Dt 30: 9 your God will make you most *p*
Jos 1: 8 Then you will be *p* and successful.
Job 42:10 the LORD made him *p* again

PROSPERS (PROSPER)
Ps 1: 3 Whatever he does *p*.
Pr 16:20 gives heed to instruction *p*,
19: 8 he who cherishes understanding *p*.

PROSTITUTE (PROSTITUTES PROSTITUTION)
Lev 20: 6 and spiritists to *p* himself
Nu 15:39 and not *p* yourselves by going
Jos 2: 1 the house of a *p* named Rahab
Pr 6:26 for the *p* reduces you to a loaf
7:10 like a *p* and with crafty intent.
Pr 23:27 for a *p* is a deep pit
Eze 16:15 and used your fame to become a *p*.
23: 7 a *p* to all the elite of the Assyrians
Hos 3: 3 you must not be a *p* or be intimate
1Co 6:15 of Christ and unite them with a *p*?
6:16 with a *p* is one with her in body?
Rev 17: 1 you the punishment of the great *p*,

PROSTITUTES (PROSTITUTE)
Pr 29: 3 of *p* squanders his wealth.
Mt 21:31 and the *p* are entering the kingdom
Lk 15:30 property with *p* comes home,
1Co 6: 9 male *p* nor homosexual offenders

PROSTITUTION (PROSTITUTE)
Eze 16:16 where you carried on your *p*.
23: 3 engaging in *p* from their youth.
Hos 4:10 engage in *p* but not increase,

PROSTRATE
Dt 9:18 again I fell *p* before the LORD
1Ki 18:39 they fell *p* and cried, "The LORD

PROTECT (PROTECTED PROTECTION PROTECTS)
Dt 23:14 about in your camp to *p* you
Ps 25:21 integrity and uprightness *p* me,
32: 7 you will *p* me from trouble
40:11 your truth always *p* me.
41: 2 The LORD will *p* him
91:14 I will *p* him, for he acknowledges
140: 1 *p* me from men of violence,
Pr 2:11 Discretion will *p* you,
4: 6 forsake wisdom, and she will *p* you;
Jn 17:11 *p* them by the power of your name
17:15 that you *p* them from the evil one.
2Th 3: 3 and *p* you from the evil one.

PROTECTED (PROTECT)
Jos 24:17 He *p* us on our entire journey
1Sa 30:23 He has *p* us and handed
Ps 37:28 They will be *p* forever,
Jn 17:12 I *p* them and kept them safe

PROTECTION (PROTECT)
Ezr 9: 9 he has given us a wall of *p* in Judah
Ps 5:11 Spread your *p* over them,

PROTECTS (PROTECT)
Ps 116: 6 The LORD *p* the simplehearted;
Pr 2: 8 and *p* the way of his faithful ones.
1Co 13: 7 It always *p*, always trusts,

PROUD (PRIDE)
Ps 31:23 but the *p* he pays back in full.
101: 5 has haughty eyes and a *p* heart,
138: 6 but the *p* he knows from afar.
Pr 3:34 He mocks *p* mockers
16: 5 The LORD detests all the *p*
16:19 than to share plunder with the *p*.
18:12 his downfall a man's heart is *p*,
21: 4 Haughty eyes and a *p* heart,
Isa 2:12 store for all the *p* and lofty,
Ro 12:16 Do not be *p*, but be willing
1Co 13: 4 it does not boast, it is not *p*.
2Ti 3: 2 lovers of money, boastful, *p*,
Jas 4: 6 "God opposes the *p*
1Pe 5: 5 because, "God opposes the *p*

PROVE (PROOF PROVED PROVING)
Pr 29:25 Fear of man will *p* to be a snare,
Jn 8:46 Can any of you *p* me guilty of sin?
Ac 26:20 *p* their repentance by their deeds.
1Co 4: 2 been given a trust must *p* faithful.

PROVED (PROVE)
Ps 51: 4 so that you are *p* right
Mt 11:19 wisdom is *p* right by her actions."
Ro 3: 4 "So that you may be *p* right
1Pe 1: 7 may be *p* genuine and may result

PROVIDE (PROVIDED PROVIDES PROVISION)
Ge 22: 8 "God himself will *p* the lamb
22:14 that place "The LORD will *P*."
Isa 43:20 because I *p* water in the desert
61: 3 and *p* for those who grieve in Zion
1Co 10:13 *p* a way out so that you can stand
1Ti 5: 8 If anyone does not *p*
Tit 3:14 in order that they may *p*

PROVIDED (PROVIDE)
Ps 68:10 O God, you *p* for the poor.
111: 9 He *p* redemption for his people;
Jnh 1:17 But the LORD *p* a great fish
4: 6 Then the LORD God *p* a vine
4: 7 dawn the next day God *p* a worm,
4: 8 God *p* a scorching east wind,
Gal 4:18 to be zealous, *p* the purpose is good
Heb 1: 3 After he had *p* purification for sins,

PROVIDES (PROVIDE)
Ps 111: 5 He *p* food for those who fear him;
Pr 31:15 she *p* food for her family
Eze 18: 7 and *p* clothing for the naked.
1Ti 6:17 who richly *p* us with everything
1Pe 4:11 it with the strength God *p*,

PROVING* (PROVE)
Ac 9:22 by *p* that Jesus is the Christ.
17: 3 and *p* that the Christ had to suffer
18:28 *p* from the Scriptures that Jesus

PROVISION (PROVIDE)
Ro 5:17 who receive God's abundant *p*

PROVOKED
Ecc 7: 9 Do not be quickly *p* in your spirit,
Jer 32:32 Judah have *p* me by all the evil they

PROWLS
1Pe 5: 8 Your enemy the devil *p*

PRUDENCE* (PRUDENT)
Pr 1: 4 for giving *p* to the simple,
8: 5 You who are simple, gain *p*;
8:12 "I, wisdom, dwell together with *p*;
15: 5 whoever heeds correction shows *p*.
19:25 and the simple will learn *p*;

PRUDENT* (PRUDENCE)
Pr 1: 3 acquiring a disciplined and *p* life,
12:16 but a *p* man overlooks an insult.
12:23 A *p* man keeps his knowledge
13:16 Every *p* man acts out of knowledge
14: 8 The wisdom of the *p* is
14:15 a *p* man gives thought to his steps.
14:18 the *p* are crowned with knowledge.
19:14 but a *p* wife is from the LORD.
22: 3 *p* man sees danger and takes
27:12 The *p* see danger and take refuge,
Jer 49: 7 Has counsel perished from the *p*?
Am 5:13 Therefore the *p* man keeps quiet

PRUNES (PRUNING)
Jn 15: 2 that does bear fruit he *p*

PRUNING (PRUNES)
Isa 2: 4 and their spears into *p* hooks.
Joel 3:10 and your *p* hooks into spears.

PSALMS
Eph 5:19 Speak to one another with *p*,
Col 3:16 and as you sing *p*, hymns

PUBLICLY
Ac 20:20 have taught you *p* and from house
1Ti 5:20 Those who sin are to be rebuked *p*,

PUFFS
1Co 8: 1 Knowledge *p* up, but love builds up

PULLING
2Co 10: 8 building you up rather than *p* you

PUNISH (PUNISHED PUNISHES PUNISHMENT)
Ge 15:14 But I will *p* the nation they serve
Ex 32:34 I will *p* them for their sin."
Pr 17:26 It is not good to *p* an innocent man,
23:13 if you *p* him with the rod, he will
Isa 13:11 I will *p* the world for its evil,
Jer 2:19 Your wickedness will *p* you;
21:14 I will *p* you as your deeds deserve,
Zep 1:12 and *p* those who are complacent,
Ac 7: 7 But I will *p* the nation they serve
2Th 1: 8 He will *p* those who do not know
1Pe 2:14 by him to *p* those who do wrong

PUNISHED (PUNISH)
Ezr 9:13 you have *p* us less than our sins
Ps 99: 8 though you *p* their misdeeds.
La 3:39 complain when *p* for his sins?
Mk 12:40 Such men will be *p* most severely."
Lk 23:41 the same sentence? We are *p* justly,
2Th 1: 9 be *p* with everlasting destruction
Heb 10:29 to be *p* who has trampled the Son

PUNISHES (PUNISH)
Heb 12: 6 and he *p* everyone he accepts

PUNISHMENT (PUNISH)
Isa 53: 5 the *p* that brought us peace was
Jer 4:18 This is your *p*.
Mt 25:46 Then they will go away to eternal *p*
Lk 12:48 and does things deserving *p* will be
21:22 For this is the time of *p*
Ro 13: 4 wrath to bring *p* on the wrongdoer.
Heb 2: 2 disobedience received its just *p*,
2Pe 2: 9 while continuing their *p*.

PURCHASED
Ps 74: 2 Remember the people you *p* of old,
Rev 5: 9 with your blood you *p* men for God

PURE (PURIFICATION PURIFIED PURIFIES PURIFY PURITY)
2Sa 22:27 to the *p* you show yourself *p*,
Job 14: 4 Who can bring what is *p*
Ps 19: 9 The fear of the LORD is *p*,
24: 4 who has clean hands and a *p* heart,
51:10 Create in me a *p* heart, O God,
119: 9 can a young man keep his way *p*?
Pr 15:26 those of the *p* are pleasing to him.
20: 9 can say, "I have kept my heart *p*;
Isa 52:11 Come out from it and be *p*,
Hab 1:13 Your eyes are too *p* to look on evil;
Mt 5: 8 Blessed are the *p* in heart,
2Co 11: 2 I might present you as a *p* virgin
Php 4: 8 whatever is *p*, whatever is lovely,
1Ti 1: 5 which comes from a *p* heart
5:22 Keep yourself *p*.
2Ti 2:22 call on the Lord out of a *p* heart.
Tit 1:15 To the *p*, all things are *p*,
2: 5 to be self-controlled and *p*,
Heb 7:26 blameless, *p*, set apart from sinners
13: 4 and the marriage bed kept *p*,
Jas 1:27 that God our Father accepts as *p*
3:17 comes from heaven is first of all *p*;
1Jn 3: 3 him purifies himself, just as he is *p*

PURGE
Pr 20:30 and beatings *p* the inmost being.

PURIFICATION (PURE)
Heb 1: 3 After he had provided *p* for sins,

PURIFIED (PURE)
Ac 15: 9 for he *p* their hearts by faith.
1Pe 1:22 Now that you have *p* yourselves

PURIFIES* (PURE)
1Jn 1: 7 of Jesus, his Son, *p* us from all sin.
3: 3 who has this hope in him *p* himself,

PURIFY (PURE)
Nu 19:12 He must *p* himself with the water
2Co 7: 1 us *p* ourselves from everything that
Tit 2:14 to *p* for himself a people that are
Jas 4: 8 you sinners, and *p* your hearts,
1Jn 1: 9 and *p* us from all unrighteousness.

PURIM
Est 9:26 Therefore these days were called *P*

PURITY* (PURE)
Hos 8: 5 long will they be incapable of *p*?
2Co 6: 6 in *p*, understanding, patience
1Ti 4:12 in life, in love, in faith and in *p*.
5: 2 as sisters, with absolute *p*.
1Pe 3: 2 when they see the *p* and reverence

PURPLE
Pr 31:22 she is clothed in fine linen and *p*.
Mk 15:17 They put a *p* robe on him, then

PURPOSE (PURPOSED PURPOSES)
Ex 9:16 I have raised you up for this very *p*,
Job 36: 5 he is mighty, and firm in his *p*.
Pr 19:21 but it is the LORD's *p* that prevails
Isa 46:10 I say: My *p* will stand,
55:11 and achieve the *p* for which I sent it
Ac 2:23 handed over to you by God's set *p*
Ro 8:28 have been called according to his *p*.
9:11 in order that God's *p*
9:17 "I raised you up for this very *p*,
1Co 3: 8 the man who waters have one *p*,
2Co 5: 5 who has made us for this very *p*
Gal 4:18 be zealous, provided the *p* is good,
Eph 1:11 in conformity with the *p* of his will,
3:11 according to his eternal *p* which he
Php 2: 2 love, being one in spirit and *p*.
2:13 and to act according to his good *p*.
2Ti 1: 9 but because of his own *p* and grace.

PURPOSED (PURPOSE)
Isa 14:24 and as I have *p*, so it will stand.
14:27 For the LORD Almighty has *p*,
Eph 1: 9 which he *p* in Christ, to be put

PURPOSES (PURPOSE)
Ps 33:10 he thwarts the *p* of the peoples.
Jer 23:20 the *p* of his heart.
32:19 great are your *p* and mighty are

PURSE (PURSES)
Hag 1: 6 to put them in a *p* with holes in it."
Lk 10: 4 Do not take a *p* or bag or sandals;
22:36 "But now if you have a *p*, take it,

PURSES (PURSE)
Lk 12:33 Provide *p* for yourselves that will

PURSUE (PURSUES)
Ps 34:14 seek peace and *p* it.
Pr 15: 9 he loves those who *p* righteousness
Ro 9:30 who did not *p* righteousness,
1Ti 6:11 and *p* righteousness, godliness,
2Ti 2:22 and *p* righteousness, faith,
1Pe 3:11 he must seek peace and *p* it.

PURSUES (PURSUE)
Pr 21:21 He who *p* righteousness and love
28: 1 wicked man flees though no one *p*,

QUAIL
Ex 16:13 That evening *q* came and covered
Nu 11:31 and drove *q* in from the sea.

QUALITIES* (QUALITY)
Da 6: 3 by his exceptional *q* that the king
Ro 1:20 of the world God's invisible *q*—
2Pe 1: 8 For if you possess these *q*

QUALITY (QUALITIES)
1Co 3:13 and the fire will test the *q*

QUARREL (QUARRELING QUARRELS QUARRELSOME)
Pr 15:18 but a patient man calms a *q*.
17:14 Starting a *q* is like breaching a dam;
17:19 He who loves a *q* loves sin;
20: 3 but every fool is quick to *q*.
26:17 in a *q* not his own.
26:20 without gossip a *q* dies down.
2Ti 2:24 And the Lord's servant must not *q*;
Jas 4: 2 You *q* and fight.

QUARRELING (QUARREL)
1Co 3: 3 For since there is jealousy and *q*
2Ti 2:14 before God against *q* about words;

QUARRELS (QUARREL)
Pr 13:10 Pride only breeds *q*,
Isa 45: 9 Woe to him who *q* with his Maker,
2Ti 2:23 because you know they produce *q*.
Jas 4: 1 What causes fights and *q*

QUARRELSOME (QUARREL)
Pr 19:13 a *q* wife is like a constant dripping.
21: 9 than share a house with a *q* wife.
26:21 so is a *q* man for kindling strife.
1Ti 3: 3 not violent but gentle, not *q*,

QUEEN
1Ki 10: 1 When the *q* of Sheba heard about
2Ch 9: 1 When the *q* of Sheba heard
Mt 12:42 The *Q* of the South will rise

QUENCH (QUENCHED)
SS 8: 7 Many waters cannot *q* love;

QUENCHED (QUENCH)
Isa 66:24 nor will their fire be *q*,
Mk 9:48 and the fire is not *q*.'

QUICK-TEMPERED* (TEMPER)
Pr 14:17 A *q* man does foolish things,
14:29 but a *q* man displays folly.
Tit 1: 7 not *q*, not given to drunkenness,

QUIET (QUIETNESS)
Ps 23: 2 he leads me beside *q* waters,
Pr 17: Better a dry crust with peace and *q*
Ecc 9:17 The *q* words of the wise are more
Am 5:13 Therefore the prudent man keeps *q*
Zep 3:17 he will *q* you with his love,
Lk 19:40 he replied, "if they keep *q*,
1Th 4:11 it your ambition to lead a *q* life,
1Ti 2: 2 we may live peaceful and *q* lives
1Pe 3: 4 beauty of a gentle and *q* spirit,

QUIETNESS (QUIET)
Isa 30:15 in *q* and trust is your strength,
32:17 the effect of righteousness will be *q*
1Ti 2:11 A woman should learn in *q*

QUIVER
Ps 127: 5 whose *q* is full of them.

RACE
Ecc 9:11 The *r* is not to the swift
Ac 20:24 if only I may finish the *r*
1Co 9:24 that in a *r* all the runners run,
Gal 2: 2 that I was running or had run my *r*
5: 7 You were running a good *r*.
2Ti 4: 7 I have finished the *r*, I have kept
Heb 12: 1 perseverance the *r* marked out

RACHEL
Daughter of Laban (Ge 29:16); wife of Jacob (Ge

29:28); bore two sons (Ge 30:22-24; 35:16-24; 46:19). Stole Laban's gods (Ge 31:19, 32-35). Death (Ge 35:19-20).

RADIANCE (RADIANT)
Eze 1:28 so was the r around him.
Heb 1: 3 The Son is the r of God's glory

RADIANT (RADIANCE)
Ex 34:29 he was not aware that his face was r
Ps 34: 5 Those who look to him are r;
SS 5:10 *Beloved* My lover is r and ruddy,
Isa 60: 5 Then you will look and be r,
Eph 5:27 her to himself as a r church,

RAGE
Ac 4:25 " 'Why do the nations r
Col 3: 8 r, malice, slander, and filthy

RAGS
Isa 64: 6 our righteous acts are like filthy r;

RAHAB
Prostitute of Jericho who hid Israelite spies (Jos 2; 6:22-25; Heb 11:31; Jas 2:25). Mother of Boaz (Mt 1:5).

RAIN (RAINBOW)
Ge 7: 4 from now I will send r on the earth
1Ki 17: 1 nor r in the next few years
18: 1 and I will send r on the land."
Mt 5:45 and sends r on the righteous
Jas 5:17 it did not r on the land for three
Jude :12 They are clouds without r,

RAINBOW (RAIN)
Ge 9:13 I have set my r in the clouds,

RAISE (RISE)
Jn 6:39 but r them up at the last day.
1Co 15:15 he did not r him if in fact the dead

RAISED (RISE)
Isa 52:13 he will be r and lifted up
Mt 17:23 on the third day he will be r to life
Lk 7:22 the deaf hear, the dead are r,
Ac 2:24 But God r him from the dead,
Ro 4:25 was r to life for our justification.
6: 4 as Christ was r from the dead
8:11 And if the Spirit of him who r Jesus
10: 9 in your heart that God r him
1Co 15: 4 that he was r on the third day
15:20 But Christ has indeed been r

RALLY*
Isa 11:10 the nations will r to him,

RAM (RAMS)
Ge 22:13 there in a thicket he saw a r caught
Da 8: 3 before me was a r with two horns,

RAMPART*
Ps 91: 4 will be your shield and r.

RAMS (RAM)
1Sa 15:22 to heed is better than the fat of r.
Mic 6: 7 pleased with thousands of r,

RAN (RUN)
Jnh 1: 3 But Jonah r away from the LORD

RANSOM (RANSOMED)
Isa 50: 2 Was my arm too short to r you?
Hos 13:14 "I will r them from the power
Mt 20:28 and to give his life as a r for many."
Mk 10:45 and to give his life as a r for many."
1Ti 2: 6 who gave himself as a r for all men
Heb 9:15 as a r to set them free

RANSOMED (RANSOM)
Isa 35:10 and the r of the LORD will return.

RARE
Pr 20:15 that speak knowledge are a r jewel.

RAVEN (RAVENS)
Ge 8: 7 made in the ark and sent out a r,
Job 38:41 Who provides food for the r

RAVENS (RAVEN)
1Ki 17: 6 The r brought him bread
Ps 147: 9 and for the young r when they call.
Lk 12:24 Consider the r: They do not sow

READ (READING READS)
Dt 17:19 he is to r it all the days of his life
Jos 8:34 Joshua r all the words of the law—
2Ki 23: 2 He r in their hearing all the words
Ne 8: 8 They r from the Book of the Law
Jer 36: 6 and r to the people from the scroll
2Co 3: 2 known and r by everybody.

READING (READ)
1Ti 4:13 to the public r of Scripture,

READS (READ)
Rev 1: 3 Blessed is the one who r the words

REAFFIRM
2Co 2: 8 therefore, to r your love for him.

REAL* (REALITIES REALITY)
Jn 6:55 is r food and my blood is r drink.
1Jn 2:27 all things and as that anointing is r,

REALITIES* (REAL)
Heb 10: 1 are coming—not the r themselves.

REALITY* (REAL)
Col 2:17 the r, however, is found in Christ.

REALM (REALMS)
Hab 2: 9 "Woe to him who builds his r

REALMS (REALM)
Eph 1: 3 the heavenly r with every spiritual
2: 6 in the heavenly r in Christ Jesus,

REAP (REAPER REAPS)
Job 4: 8 and those who sow trouble r it.
Ps 126: 5 will r with songs of joy.
Hos 8: 7 and r the whirlwind.
10:12 r the fruit of unfailing love,
Jn 4:38 you to r what you have not worked
Ro 6:22 the benefit you r leads to holiness,
2Co 9: 6 generously will also r generously.
Gal 6: 8 from that nature will r destruction;

REAPER (REAP)
Jn 4:36 and the r may be glad together.

REAPS (REAP)
Pr 11:18 who sows righteousness r a sure
22: 8 He who sows wickedness r trouble,
Gal 6: 7 A man r what he sows.

REASON (REASONED)
Ge 2:24 For this r a man will leave his
Isa 1:18 "Come now, let us r together,"
Mt 19: 5 'For this r a man will leave his
Jn 12:27 it was for this very r I came
15:25 'They hated me without r.'
1Pe 3:15 to give the r for the hope that you
2Pe 1: 5 For this very r, make every effort

REASONED (REASON)
1Co 13:11 thought like a child, I r like a child.

REBEKAH
Sister of Laban, secured as bride for Isaac (Ge 24). Mother of Esau and Jacob (Ge 25:19-26). Taken by Abimelech as sister of Isaac; returned (Ge 26:1-11). Encouraged Jacob to trick Isaac out of blessing (Ge 27:1-17).

REBEL (REBELLED REBELLION REBELS)
Nu 14: 9 Only do not r against the LORD.
1Sa 12:14 and do not r against his commands,
Mt 10:21 children will r against their parents

REBELLED (REBEL)
Ps 78:56 and r against the Most High;
Isa 63:10 Yet they r

REBELLION (REBEL)
Ex 34: 7 and forgiving wickedness, r and sin
Nu 14:18 in love and forgiving sin and r.
1Sa 15:23 For r is like the sin of divination,
2Th 2: 3 will not come, until the r occurs

REBELS (REBEL)
Ro 13: 2 he who r against the authority is
1Ti 1: 9 but for lawbreakers and r,

REBIRTH* (BEAR)
Tit 3: 5 us through the washing of r

REBUILD (BUILD)
Ezr 5: 2 set to work to r the house of God
Ne 2:17 let us r the wall of Jerusalem,
Ps 102: 16 For the LORD will r Zion
Da 9:25 and r Jerusalem until the Anointed
Am 9:14 they will r the ruined cities
Ac 15:16 Its ruins I will r,

REBUILT (BUILD)
Zec 1:16 and there my house will be r.

REBUKE (REBUKED REBUKES REBUKING)
Lev 19:17 R your neighbor frankly
Ps 141: 5 let him r me—it is oil on my head.
Pr 3:11 and do not resent his r,
9: 8 r a wise man and he will love you.
15:31 He who listens to a life-giving r
17:10 A r impresses a man
19:25 r a discerning man, and he will gain
25:12 is a wise man's r to a listening ear.
27: 5 Better is open r
30: 6 or he will r you and prove you a liar
Ecc 7: 5 It is better to heed a wise man's r
Isa 54: 9 never to r you again.
Jer 2:19 your backsliding will r you.
Lk 17: 3 "If your brother sins, r him,
1Ti 5: 1 Do not r an older man harshly,
2Ti 4: 2 correct, r and encourage—
Tit 1:13 Therefore, r them sharply,
2:15 Encourage and r with all authority.
Rev 3:19 Those whom I love I r

REBUKED (REBUKE)
Mk 16:14 he r them for their lack of faith
1Ti 5:20 Those who sin are to be r publicly,

REBUKES (REBUKE)
Job 22: 4 "Is it for your piety that he r you
Pr 28:23 He who r a man will
29: 1 remains stiff-necked after many r
Heb 12: 5 do not lose heart when he r you,

REBUKING (REBUKE)
2Ti 3:16 r, correcting and training

RECEIVE (RECEIVED RECEIVES)
Mt 10:41 a righteous man will r a righteous
Mk 10:15 anyone who will not r the kingdom
Jn 20:22 and said, "R the Holy Spirit.
Ac 1: 8 you will r power when the Holy
2:38 you will r the gift of the Holy Spirit
19: 2 "Did you r the Holy Spirit
20:35 'It is more blessed to give than to r
1Co 9:14 the gospel should r their living
2Co 6:17 and I will r you."
1Ti 1:16 believe on him and r eternal life.
Jas 1: 7 should not think he will r anything
2Pe 1:11 and you will r a rich welcome
1Jn 3:22 and r from him anything we ask,
Rev 4:11 to r glory and honor and power,
5:12 to r power and wealth and wisdom

RECEIVED (RECEIVE)
Mt 6: 2 they have r their reward in full.
10: 8 Freely you have r, freely give.
Mk 11:24 believe that you have r it,
Jn 1:12 Yet to all who r him,
1:16 his grace we have all r one blessing
Ac 8:17 and they r the Holy Spirit.
10:47 They have r the Holy Spirit just
Ro 8:15 but you r the Spirit of sonship.
1Co 11:23 For I r from the Lord what I
2Co 1: 4 the comfort we ourselves have r
Col 2: 6 just as you r Christ Jesus as Lord,
1Pe 4:10 should use whatever gift he has r

RECEIVES (RECEIVE)
Pr 18:22 and r favor from the LORD.
27:21 but man is tested by the praise he r.
Mt 7: 8 everyone who asks r; he who seeks
10:40 he who r me r the one who sent me.
10:40 "He who r you r me, and he who
Ac 10:43 believes in him r forgiveness of sins

RECITE
Ps 45: 1 as I r my verses for the king;

RECKLESS
Pr 12:18 R words pierce like a sword,
14:16 but a fool is hotheaded and r.

RECKONING
Isa 10: 3 What will you do on the day of r,
Hos 9: 7 the days of r are at hand.

RECLAIM* (CLAIM)
Isa 11:11 time to r the remnant that is left

RECOGNITION (RECOGNIZE)
1Co 16:18 Such men deserve r.
1Ti 5: 3 Give proper r to those widows who

RECOGNIZE (RECOGNITION RECOGNIZED)
Mt 7:16 By their fruit you will r them.
1Jn 4: 2 This is how you can r the Spirit
4: 6 This is how we r the Spirit of truth

RECOGNIZED (RECOGNIZE)
Mt 12:33 for a tree is r by its fruit.
Ro 7:13 in order that sin might be r as sin,

RECOMPENSE*
Isa 40:10 and his r accompanies him.
62:11 and his r accompanies him.' "

RECONCILE* (RECONCILED RECONCILIATION RECONCILING)
Ac 7:26 He tried to *r* them by saying, 'Men,
Eph 2:16 in this one body to *r* both of them
Col 1:20 him to *r* to himself all things,

RECONCILED* (RECONCILE)
Mt 5:24 First go and be *r* to your brother;
Lk 12:58 try hard to be *r* to him on the way,
Ro 5:10 how much more, having been *r*,
5:10 we were *r* to him through the death
1Co 7:11 or else be *r* to her husband.
2Co 5:18 who *r* us to himself through Christ
5:20 you on Christ's behalf: Be *r* to God.
Col 1:22 he has *r* you by Christ's physical

RECONCILIATION* (RECONCILE)
Ro 5:11 whom we have now received *r*.
11:15 For if their rejection is the *r*
2Co 5:18 and gave us the ministry of *r*:
5:19 committed to us the message of *r*.

RECONCILING* (RECONCILE)
2Co 5:19 that God was *r* the world to himself

RECORD (RECORDED)
Ps 130: 3 If you, O LORD, kept a *r* of sins,
Hos 13:12 his sins are kept on *r*.
1Co 13: 5 is not easily angered, it keeps no *r*

RECORDED (RECORD)
Job 19:23 "Oh, that my words were *r*,
Jn 20:30 which are not *r* in this book.

RECOUNT*
Ps 40: 5 no one can *r* to you;
79:13 we will *r* your praise.
119: 13 With my lips I *r*

RED
Ex 15: 4 are drowned in the *R* Sea.
Ps 106: 9 He rebuked the *R* Sea,
Pr 23:31 Do not gaze at wine when it is *r*,
Isa 1:18 though they are *r* as crimson,

REDEEM (KINSMAN-REDEEMER REDEEMED REDEEMER REDEEMS REDEMPTION)
Ex 6: 6 will *r* you with an outstretched arm
2Sa 7:23 on earth that God went out to *r*
Ps 44:26 *r* us because of your unfailing love.
49: 7 No man can *r* the life of another
49:15 God will *r* my life from the grave;
130: 8 He himself will *r* Israel
Hos 13:14 I will *r* them from death.
Gal 4: 5 under law, to *r* those under law,
Tit 2:14 for us to *r* us from all wickedness

REDEEMED (REDEEM)
Job 33:28 He *r* my soul from going
Ps 71:23 I, whom you have *r*.
107: 2 Let the *r* of the LORD say this—
Isa 35: 9 But only the *r* will walk there,
63: 9 In his love and mercy he *r* them;
Gal 3:13 Christ *r* us from the curse
1Pe 1:18 or gold that you were *r*

REDEEMER (REDEEM)
Job 19:25 I know that my *R* lives,
Ps 19:14 O LORD, my Rock and my *R*.
Isa 44: 6 and *R*, the LORD Almighty:
48:17 your *R*, the Holy One of Israel:
59:20 "The *R* will come to Zion,

REDEEMS (REDEEM)
Ps 34:22 The LORD *r* his servants;
103: 4 he *r* my life from the pit

REDEMPTION (REDEEM)
Ps 130: 7 and with him is full *r*.
Lk 21:28 because your *r* is drawing near."
Ro 3:24 grace through the *r* that came
8:23 as sons, the *r* of our bodies.
1Co 1:30 our righteousness, holiness and *r*.
Eph 1: 7 In him we have *r* through his blood
1:14 until the *r* of those who are God's
4:30 you were sealed for the day of *r*.
Col 1:14 in whom we have *r*, the forgiveness
Heb 9:12 having obtained eternal *r*.

REED
Isa 42: 3 A bruised *r* he will not break,
Mt 12:20 A bruised *r* he will not break,

REFINE*
Jer 9: 7 "See, I will *r* and test them,
Zec 13: 9 I will *r* them like silver
Mal 3: 3 and *r* them like gold and silver.

REFLECT (REFLECTS)
2Co 3:18 unveiled faces all *r* the Lord's

REFLECTS (REFLECT)
Pr 27:19 As water *r* a face,

REFRESH (REFRESHED REFRESHING)
Phm :20 in the Lord; *r* my heart in Christ.

REFRESHED (REFRESH)
Pr 11:25 refreshes others will himself be *r*.

REFRESHING* (REFRESH)
Ac 3:19 that times of *r* may come

REFUGE
Nu 35:11 towns to be your cities of *r*,
Dt 33:27 The eternal God is your *r*,
Jos 20: 2 to designate the cities of *r*,
Ru 2:12 wings you have come to take *r*."
2Sa 22: 3 God is my rock, in whom I take *r*,
22:31 a shield for all who take *r* in him.
Ps 2:12 Blessed are all who take *r* in him.
5:11 But let all who take *r* in you be glad
9: 9 The LORD is a *r* for the oppressed,
16: 1 for in you I take *r*.
17: 7 those who take *r* in you
18: 2 God is my rock, in whom I take *r*.
31: 2 be my rock of *r*,
34: 8 blessed is the man who takes *r*
36: 7 find *r* in the shadow of your wings.
46: 1 God is our *r* and strength,
62: 8 for God is our *r*.
71: 1 In you, O LORD, I have taken *r*;
91: 2 "He is my *r* and my fortress,
144: 2 my shield, in whom I take *r*,
Pr 14:26 and for his children it will be a *r*.
30: 5 a shield to those who take *r* in him.
Na 1: 7 a *r* in times of trouble.

REFUSE (REFUSED)
Jn 5:40 yet you *r* to come to me to have life

REFUSED (REFUSE)
2Th 2:10 because they *r* to love the truth
Rev 16: 9 but they *r* to repent and glorify him

REGARD (REGARDS)
1Th 5:13 Hold them in the highest *r* in love

REGARDS (REGARD)
Ro 14:14 But if anyone *r* something

REGRET
2Co 7:10 leads to salvation and leaves no *r*,

REHOBOAM
Son of Solomon (1Ki 11:43; 1Ch 3:10). Harsh treatment of subjects caused divided kingdom (1Ki 12:1-24; 14:21-31; 2Ch 10-12).

REIGN (REIGNED REIGNS)
Ex 15:18 The LORD will *r*
Ps 68:16 mountain where God chooses to *r*,
Isa 9: 7 He will *r* on David's throne
24:23 for the LORD Almighty will *r*
32: 1 See, a king will *r* in righteousness
Jer 23: 5 a King who will *r* wisely
Lk 1:33 and he will *r* over the house
Ro 6:12 Therefore do not let sin *r*
1Co 15:25 For he must *r* until he has put all
2Ti 2:12 we will also *r* with him.
Rev 11:15 and he will *r* for ever and ever."
20: 6 will *r* with him for a thousand years
22: 5 And they will *r* for ever and ever.

REIGNED (REIGN)
Ro 5:21 so that, just as sin *r* in death,
Rev 20: 4 and *r* with Christ a thousand years.

REIGNS (REIGN)
Ps 9: 7 The LORD *r* forever;
47: 8 God *r* over the nations;
93: 1 The LORD *r*, he is robed
96:10 among the nations, "The LORD *r*."
97: 1 The LORD *r*, let the earth be glad;
99: 1 The LORD *r*, / let the nations tremble;
146: 10 The LORD *r* forever,
Isa 52: 7 "Your God *r*!"
Rev 19: 6 For our Lord God Almighty *r*.

REIN
Jas 1:26 and yet does not keep a tight *r*

REJECT (REJECTED REJECTION REJECTS)
Ps 94:14 For the LORD will not *r* his people
Ro 11: 1 I ask then: Did God *r* his people?

REJECTED (REJECT)
1Sa 8: 7 it is not you they have *r*,
1Ki 19:10 The Israelites have *r* your covenant
2Ki 17:15 They *r* his decrees
Ps 66:20 who has not *r* my prayer
118: 22 The stone the builders *r*
Isa 5:24 for they have *r* the law
41: 9 chosen you and have not *r* you.
53: 3 He was despised and *r* by men,
Jer 8: 9 Since they have *r* the word
Mt 21:42 " 'The stone the builders *r*
1Ti 4: 4 nothing is to be *r* if it is received
1Pe 2: 4 *r* by men but chosen by God
2: 7 "The stone the builders *r*

REJECTION* (REJECT)
Ro 11:15 For if their *r* is the reconciliation

REJECTS (REJECT)
Lk 10:16 but he who *r* me *r* him who sent me
Jn 3:36 whoever *r* the Son will not see life,
1Th 4: 8 he who *r* this instruction does not

REJOICE (JOY)
Dt 12: 7 shall *r* in everything you have put
1Ch 16:10 of those who seek the LORD *r*.
16:31 Let the heavens *r*, let the earth be
Ps 2:11 and *r* with trembling.
5:11 those who love your name may *r*
9:14 and there *r* in your salvation.
34: 2 let the afflicted hear and *r*.
63:11 But the king will *r* in God;
66: 6 come, let us *r* in him.
68: 3 and *r* before God;
105: 3 of those who seek the LORD *r*.
118: 24 let us *r* and be glad in it.
119: 14 I *r* in following your statutes
119:162 I *r* in your promise
149: 2 Let Israel *r* in their Maker;
Pr 5:18 may you *r* in the wife of your youth
23:25 may she who gave you birth *r*!
24:17 stumbles, do not let your heart *r*,
Isa 9: 3 as men *r*
35: 1 the wilderness will *r* and blossom.
61: 7 they will *r* in their inheritance;
62: 5 so will your God *r* over you.
Jer 31:12 they will *r* in the bounty
Zep 3:17 he will *r* over you with singing."
Zec 9: 9 *R* greatly, O Daughter of Zion!
Lk 6:23 "*R* in that day and leap for joy,
10:20 but *r* that your names are written
15: 6 '*R* with me; I have found my lost
15: 9 '*R* with me; I have found my lost
Ro 5: 2 And we *r* in the hope of the glory
12:15 Rejoice with those who *r*; mourn
Php 2:17 I am glad and *r* with all of you.
3: 1 Finally, my brothers, *r* in the Lord!
4: 4 *R* in the Lord always.
1Pe 4:13 But *r* that you participate
Rev 19: 7 Let us *r* and be glad

REJOICES (JOY)
Ps 13: 5 my heart *r* in your salvation.
16: 9 my heart is glad and my tongue *r*;
Isa 61:10 my soul *r* in my God.
62: 5 as a bridegroom *r* over his bride,
Lk 1:47 and my spirit *r* in God my Savior,
Ac 2:26 my heart is glad and my tongue *r*;
1Co 12:26 if one part is honored, every part *r*
13: 6 delight in evil but *r* with the truth.

REJOICING (JOY)
2Sa 6:12 to the City of David with *r*.
Ne 12:43 *r* because God had given them
Ps 30: 5 but *r* comes in the morning.
Lk 15: 7 in the same way there will be more *r*
Ac 5:41 *r* because they had been counted
2Co 6:10 sorrowful, yet always *r*; poor,

RELATIVES
Pr 19: 7 A poor man is shunned by all his *r*
Mk 6: 4 among his *r* and in his own house is
Lk 21:16 betrayed even by parents, brothers, *r*
1Ti 5: 8 If anyone does not provide for his *r*

RELEASE (RELEASED)
Isa 61: 1 and *r* from darkness,
Lk 4:18 to *r* the oppressed,

RELEASED (RELEASE)
Ro 7: 6 we have been *r* from the law
Rev 20: 7 Satan will be *r* from his prison

RELENTED (RELENTS)
Ex 32:14 the LORD *r* and did not bring
Ps 106: 45 and out of his great love he *r*.

RELENTS* (RELENTED)
Joel 2:13 and he *r* from sending calamity.
Jnh 4: 2 a God who *r* from sending calamity

RELIABLE (RELY)
Pr 22:21 teaching you true and *r* words,

Jn 8:26 But he who sent me is *r*,
2Ti 2: 2 witnesses entrust to *r* men who will

RELIANCE* (RELY)
Pr 25:19 is *r* on the unfaithful in times

RELIED (RELY)
2Ch 13:18 were victorious because they *r*
16: 8 Yet when you *r* on the LORD,
Ps 71: 6 From birth I have *r* on you;

RELIEF
Job 35: 9 they plead for *r* from the arm
Ps 94:13 you grant him *r* from days
143: 1 come to my *r*.
La 3:49 without *r*,
3:56 to my cry for *r*."
2Th 1: 7 and give *r* to you who are troubled,

RELIGION* (RELIGIOUS)
Ac 25:19 dispute with him about their own *r*
26: 5 to the strictest sect of our *r*,
1Ti 5: 4 all to put their *r* into practice
Jas 1:26 himself and his *r* is worthless.
1:27 *R* that God our Father accepts

RELIGIOUS (RELIGION)
Jas 1:26 If anyone considers himself *r*

RELY (RELIABLE RELIANCE RELIED)
Isa 50:10 and *r* on his God.
Eze 33:26 you then possess the land? You *r*
2Co 1: 9 this happened that we might not *r*
Gal 3:10 All who *r* on observing the law are
1Jn 4:16 and *r* on the love God has for us.

REMAIN (REMAINS)
Nu 33:55 allow to *r* will become barbs
Ps 102: 27 But you *r* the same,
Jn 1:32 from heaven as a dove and *r* on him
15: 4 *R* in me, and I will *r* in you.
15: 7 If you *r* in me and my words
15: 9 Now *r* in my love.
Ro 13: 8 Let no debt *r* outstanding,
1Co 13:13 And now these three *r*: faith,
2Ti 2:13 he will *r* faithful,
Heb 1:11 They will perish, but you *r*;
1Jn 2:27 just as it has taught you, *r* in him.

REMAINS (REMAIN)
Ps 146: 6 the LORD, who *r* faithful forever.
Heb 7: 3 Son of God he *r* a priest forever.

REMEDY
Isa 3: 7 "I have no *r*.

REMEMBER (REMEMBERED REMEMBERS REMEMBRANCE)
Ge 9:15 I will *r* my covenant between me
Ex 20: 8 "*R* the Sabbath day
33:13 *R* that this nation is your people."
Dt 5:15 *R* that you were slaves in Egypt
1Ch 16:12 *R* the wonders he has done,
Job 36:24 *R* to extol his work,
Ps 25: 6 *R*, O LORD, your great mercy
63: 6 On my bed I *r* you;
74: 2 *R* the people you purchased of old,
77:11 I will *r* the deeds of the LORD;
Ecc 12: 1 *R* your Creator
Isa 46: 8 "*R* this, fix it in mind,
Jer 31:34 and will *r* their sins no more."
Hab 3: 2 in wrath *r* mercy.
Lk 1:72 and to *r* his holy covenant,
Gal 2:10 we should continue to *r* the poor,
Php 1: 3 I thank my God every time I *r* you.
2Ti 2: 8 *R* Jesus Christ, raised
Heb 8:12 and will *r* their sins no more."

REMEMBERED (REMEMBER)
Ex 2:24 he *r* his covenant with Abraham,
3:15 am to be *r* from generation
Ps 98: 3 He has *r* his love
106: 45 for their sake he *r* his covenant
111: 4 He has caused his wonders to be *r*;
136: 23 to the One who *r* us
Isa 65:17 The former things will not be *r*,
Eze 18:22 offenses he has committed will be *r*
33:13 things he has done will be *r*;

REMEMBERS (REMEMBER)
Ps 103: 14 he *r* that we are dust.
111: 5 he *r* his covenant forever.
Isa 43:25 and *r* your sins no more.

REMEMBRANCE (REMEMBER)
Lk 22:19 given for you; do this in *r* of me."
1Co 11:24 which is for you; do this in *r* of me
11:25 whenever you drink it, in *r* of me."

REMIND
Jn 14:26 will *r* you of everything I have said
2Pe 1:12 I will always *r* you of these things,

REMNANT
Ezr 9: 8 has been gracious in leaving us a *r*
Isa 11:11 time to reclaim the *r* that is left
Jer 23: 3 "I myself will gather the *r*
Zec 8:12 inheritance to the *r* of this people.
Ro 11: 5 the present time there is a *r* chosen

REMOVED
Ps 30:11 you *r* my sackcloth and clothed me
103: 12 so far has he *r* our transgressions
Jn 20: 1 and saw that the stone had been *r*

REND
Joel 2:13 *R* your heart

RENEW (RENEWAL RENEWED RENEWING)
Ps 51:10 and *r* a steadfast spirit within me.
Isa 40:31 will *r* their strength.

RENEWAL (RENEW)
Isa 57:10 You found *r* of your strength,
Tit 3: 5 of rebirth and *r* by the Holy Spirit,

RENEWED (RENEW)
Ps 103: 5 that your youth is *r* like the eagle's.
2Co 4:16 yet inwardly we are being *r* day

RENEWING* (RENEW)
Ro 12: 2 transformed by the *r* of your mind.

RENOUNCE (RENOUNCED RENOUNCES)
Da 4:27 *R* your sins by doing what is right,

RENOUNCED (RENOUNCE)
2Co 4: 2 we have *r* secret and shameful

RENOUNCES (RENOUNCE)
Pr 28:13 confesses and *r* them finds

RENOWN*
Ge 6: 4 were the heroes of old, men of *r*.
Ps 102: 12 *r* endures through all generations.
135: 13 *r*, O LORD, through all
Isa 26: 8 your name and *r*
55:13 This will be for the LORD's *r*,
63:12 to gain for himself everlasting *r*,
Jer 13:11 to be my people for my *r* and praise
32:20 have gained the *r* that is still yours.
33: 9 Then this city will bring me *r*, joy,
49:25 the city of *r* not been abandoned,
Eze 26:17 How you are destroyed, O city of *r*,
Hos 12: 5 the LORD is his name of *r*!

REPAID (PAY)
Lk 6:34 to 'sinners,' expecting to be *r* in full
14:14 you will be *r* at the resurrection
Col 3:25 Anyone who does wrong will be *r*

REPAY (PAY)
Dt 7:10 But those who hate him he will *r*
32:35 It is mine to avenge; I will *r*.
Ru 2:12 May the LORD *r* you
Ps 103: 10 or *r* us according to our iniquities.
116: 12 How can I *r* the LORD
Jer 25:14 I will *r* them according
Ro 12:17 Do not *r* anyone evil for evil.
12:19 "It is mine to avenge; I will *r*,"
1Pe 3: 9 Do not *r* evil with evil

REPAYING (PAY)
2Ch 6:23 *r* the guilty by bringing
1Ti 5: 4 so *r* their parents and grandparents

REPEATED
Heb 10: 1 the same sacrifices *r* endlessly year

REPENT (REPENTANCE REPENTED REPENTS)
1Ki 8:47 *r* and plead with you in the land
Job 36:10 commands them to *r* of their evil.
42: 6 and *r* in dust and ashes."
Jer 15:19 "If you *r*, I will restore you
Eze 18:30 *R*! Turn away from all your
18:32 *R* and live! "Take up a lament
Mt 3: 2 "*R*, for the kingdom of heaven is
4:17 "*R*, for the kingdom of heaven is
Mk 6:12 and preached that people should *r*.
Lk 13: 3 unless you *r*, you too will all perish.
Ac 2:38 Peter replied, "*R* and be baptized,
3:19 *R*, then, and turn to God,
17:30 all people everywhere to *r*.
26:20 also, I preached that they should *r*
Rev 2: 5 *R* and do the things you did at first.

REPENTANCE (REPENT)
Isa 30:15 "In *r* and rest is your salvation,
Mt 3: 8 Produce fruit in keeping with *r*.
Mk 1: 4 a baptism of *r* for the forgiveness
Lk 3: 8 Produce fruit in keeping with *r*.
5:32 call the righteous, but sinners to *r*."
24:47 and *r* and forgiveness of sins will be
Ac 20:21 that they must turn to God in *r*
26:20 and prove their *r* by their deeds.
Ro 2: 4 kindness leads you toward *r*?
2Co 7:10 Godly sorrow brings *r* that leads
2Pe 3: 9 but everyone to come to *r*.

REPENTED (REPENT)
Mt 11:21 they would have *r* long ago

REPENTS (REPENT)
Lk 15: 7 in heaven over one sinner who *r*
15:10 of God over one sinner who *r*."
17: 3 rebuke him, and if he *r*, forgive him

REPORTS
Ex 23: 1 "Do not spread false *r*.

REPOSES*
Pr 14:33 Wisdom *r* in the heart

REPRESENTATION*
Heb 1: 3 and the exact *r* of his being,

REPROACH
Job 27: 6 my conscience will not *r* me
Isa 51: 7 Do not fear the *r* of men
1Ti 3: 2 Now the overseer must be above *r*,

REPUTATION
1Ti 3: 7 also have a good *r* with outsiders,

REQUESTS
Ps 20: 5 May the LORD grant all your *r*.
Php 4: 6 with thanksgiving, present your *r*

REQUIRE (REQUIRED REQUIRES)
Mic 6: 8 And what does the LORD *r* of you

REQUIRED (REQUIRE)
1Co 4: 2 it is *r* that those who have been

REQUIRES (REQUIRE)
1Ki 2: 3 what the LORD your God *r*:
Heb 9:22 the law *r* that nearly everything be

RESCUE (RESCUED RESCUES)
Ps 22: 8 let the LORD *r* him.
31: 2 come quickly to my *r*;
69:14 *R* me from the mire,
91:14 says the LORD, "I will *r* him;
143: 9 *R* me from my enemies, O LORD,
Da 6:20 been able to *r* you from the lions?"
Ro 7:24 Who will *r* me from this body
Gal 1: 4 himself for our sins to *r* us
2Pe 2: 9 how to *r* godly men from trials

RESCUED (RESCUE)
Ps 18:17 He *r* me from my powerful enemy,
Pr 11: 8 The righteous man is *r*
Col 1:13 For he has *r* us from the dominion

RESCUES (RESCUE)
Da 6:27 He *r* and he saves;
1Th 1:10 who *r* us from the coming wrath.

RESENT* (RESENTFUL RESENTS)
Pr 3:11 and do not *r* his rebuke,

RESENTFUL* (RESENT)
2Ti 2:24 to everyone, able to teach, not *r*.

RESENTS* (RESENT)
Pr 15:12 A mocker *r* correction;

RESERVE (RESERVED)
1Ki 19:18 Yet I *r* seven thousand in Israel—

RESERVED (RESERVE)
Ro 11: 4 "I have *r* for myself seven

RESIST (RESISTED RESISTS)
Da 11:32 know their God will firmly *r* him.
Mt 5:39 I tell you, Do not *r* an evil person.
Lk 21:15 of your adversaries will be able to *r*
Jas 4: 7 *R* the devil, and he will flee
1Pe 5: 9 *R* him, standing firm in the faith,

RESISTED (RESIST)
Job 9: 4 Who has *r* him and come out

RESISTS* (RESIST)
Ro 9:19 For who *r* his will?" But who are

RESOLVED
Ps 17: 3 I have *r* that my mouth will not sin.
Da 1: 8 But Daniel *r* not to defile himself
1Co 2: 2 For I *r* to know nothing while I was

RESOUNDING*
Ps 150: 5 praise him with *r* cymbals.
1Co 13: 1 I am only a *r* gong or a clanging

RESPECT (RESPECTABLE RESPECTED RESPECTS)
Lev 19: 3 " 'Each of you must *r* his mother
19:32 show *r* for the elderly and revere
Pr 11:16 A kindhearted woman gains *r,*
Mal 1: 6 where is the *r* due me?" says
Eph 5:33 and the wife must *r* her husband.
6: 5 obey your earthly masters with *r*
1Th 4:12 so that your daily life may win the *r*
5:12 to *r* those who work hard
1Ti 3: 4 children obey him with proper *r.*
3: 8 are to be men worthy of *r,* sincere,
3:11 are to be women worthy of *r,*
6: 1 their masters worthy of full *r,*
Tit 2: 2 worthy of *r,* self-controlled,
1Pe 2:17 Show proper *r* to everyone:
3: 7 them with *r* as the weaker partner
3:16 But do this with gentleness and *r,*

RESPECTABLE* (RESPECT)
1Ti 3: 2 self-controlled, *r,* hospitable,

RESPECTED (RESPECT)
Pr 31:23 Her husband is *r* at the city gate,

RESPECTS (RESPECT)
Pr 13:13 he who *r* a command is rewarded.

RESPLENDENT*
Ps 76: 4 You are *r* with light,
132: 18 but the crown on his head will be *r*

RESPOND
Ps 102: 17 He will *r* to the prayer
Hos 2:21 "I will *r* to the skies,

RESPONSIBILITY (RESPONSIBLE)
Ac 18: 6 your own heads! I am clear of my *r.*

RESPONSIBLE (RESPONSIBILITY)
Nu 1:53 The Levites are to be *r* for the care
1Co 7:24 Brothers, each man, as *r* to God,

REST (RESTED RESTS SABBATH-REST)
Ex 31:15 the seventh day is a Sabbath of *r,*
33:14 go with you, and I will give you *r.*"
Lev 25: 5 The land is to have a year of *r.*
Dt 31:16 going to *r* with your fathers,
Jos 14:15 Then the land had *r* from war.
21:44 The LORD gave them *r*
1Ki 5: 4 The LORD my god has given me *r*
1Ch 22: 9 who will be a man of peace and *r,*
Job 3:17 and there the weary are at *r.*
Ps 16: 9 my body also will *r* secure,
33:22 May your unfailing love *r* upon us,
62: 1 My soul finds *r* in God alone;
62: 5 Find *r,* O my soul, in God alone;
90:17 of the Lord our God *r* upon us;
91: 1 will *r* in the shadow
95:11 "They shall never enter my *r.*"
Pr 6:10 a little folding of the hands to *r*—
Isa 11: 2 Spirit of the LORD will *r* on him—
11:10 and his place of *r* will be glorious.
30:15 "In repentance and *r* is your
32:18 in undisturbed places of *r.*
57:20 which cannot *r,*
Jer 6:16 and you will find *r* for your souls.
47: 6 'how long till you *r?*
Mt 11:28 and burdened, and I will give you *r.*
2Co 12: 9 so that Christ's power may *r* on me
Heb 3:11 'They shall never enter my *r.*' "
4: 3 'They shall never enter my *r.*' "
4:10 for anyone who enters God's *r*
Rev 14:13 "they will *r* from their labor,

RESTED (REST)
Ge 2: 2 so on the seventh day he *r*
Heb 4: 4 "And on the seventh day God *r*

RESTITUTION
Ex 22: 3 "A thief must certainly make *r,*
Lev 6: 5 He must make *r* in full, add a fifth
Nu 5: 8 the *r* belongs to the LORD

RESTORE (RESTORES)
Ps 51:12 *R* to me the joy of your salvation
80: 3 *R* us, O God;
126: 4 *R* our fortunes, O LORD,
Jer 31:18 *R* me, and I will return,
La 5:21 *R* us to yourself, O LORD,
Da 9:25 From the issuing of the decree to *r*
Na 2: 2 The LORD will *r* the splendor
Gal 6: 1 are spiritual should *r* him gently.
1Pe 5:10 will himself *r* you and make you

RESTORES (RESTORE)
Ps 23: 3 he *r* my soul.

RESTRAINED (RESTRAINT)
Ps 78:38 Time after time he *r* his anger

RESTRAINING (RESTRAINT)
Pr 27:16 *r* her is like *r* the wind
Col 2:23 value in *r* sensual indulgence.

RESTRAINT (RESTRAINED RESTRAINING)
Pr 17:27 of knowledge uses words with *r,*
23: 4 have the wisdom to show *r.*
29:18 no revelation, the people cast off *r;*

RESTS (REST)
Dt 33:12 and the one the LORD loves *r*
Pr 19:23 one *r* content, untouched
Lk 2:14 to men on whom his favor *r.*"

RESULT
Lk 21:13 This will *r* in your being witnesses
Ro 6:22 to holiness, and the *r* is eternal life.
11:31 as a *r* of God's mercy to you.
2Co 3: 3 from Christ, the *r* of our ministry,
2Th 1: 5 as a *r* you will be counted worthy
1Pe 1: 7 may be proved genuine and may *r*

RESURRECTION*
Mt 22:23 who say there is no *r,* came to him
22:28 at the *r,* whose wife will she be
22:30 At the *r* people will neither marry
22:31 But about the *r* of the dead—
27:53 and after Jesus' *r* they went
Mk 12:18 who say there is no *r,* came to him
12:23 At the *r* whose wife will she be,
Lk 14:14 repaid at the *r* of the righteous."
20:27 who say there is no *r,* came to Jesus
20:33 at the *r* whose wife will she be,
20:35 in the *r* from the dead will neither
20:36 since they are children of the *r.*
Jn 11:24 again in the *r* at the last day."
11:25 Jesus said to her, "I am the *r*
Ac 1:22 become a witness with us of his *r.*"
2:31 he spoke of the *r* of the Christ,
4: 2 in Jesus the *r* of the dead.
4:33 to testify to the *r* of the Lord Jesus,
17:18 good news about Jesus and the *r.*
17:32 When they heard about the *r*
23: 6 of my hope in the *r* of the dead."
23: 8 Sadducees say that there is no *r,*
24:15 that there will be a *r*
24:21 'It is concerning the *r*
Ro 1: 4 Son of God by his *r* from the dead:
6: 5 also be united with him in his *r.*
1Co 15:12 some of you say that there is no *r*
15:13 If there is no *r* of the dead,
15:21 the *r* of the dead comes
15:29 if there is no *r,* what will those do
15:42 So will it be with the *r* of the dead.
Php 3:10 power of his *r* and the fellowship
3:11 to attain to the *r* from the dead.
2Ti 2:18 say that the *r* has already taken
Heb 6: 2 on of hands, the *r* of the dead,
11:35 so that they might gain a better *r.*
1Pe 1: 3 hope through the *r* of Jesus Christ
3:21 It saves you by the *r* of Jesus Christ
Rev 20: 5 This is the first *r.*
20: 6 those who have part in the first *r.*

RETALIATE*
1Pe 2:23 he did not *r;* when he suffered,

RETRIBUTION
Ps 69:22 may it become *r* and a trap.
Jer 51:56 For the LORD is a God of *r;*
Ro 11: 9 a stumbling block and a *r* for them.

RETURN (RETURNED RETURNS)
Ge 3:19 and to dust you will *r.*"
2Sa 12:23 go to him, but he will not *r* to me."
2Ch 30: 9 If you *r* to the LORD, then your
Ne 1: 9 but if you *r* to me and obey my
Job 10:21 joy before I go to the place of no *r,*
16:22 before I go on the journey of no *r.*
22:23 If you *r* to the Almighty, you will
Ps 80:14 *R* to us, O God Almighty!
126: 6 will *r* with songs of joy,
Isa 10:21 A remnant will *r,* a remnant
35:10 the ransomed of the LORD will *r.*
55:11 It will not *r* to me empty,
Jer 24: 7 for they will *r* to me
31: 8 a great throng will *r.*
La 3:40 and let us *r* to the LORD.
Hos 6: 1 "Come, let us *r* to the LORD.
12: 6 But you must *r* to your God;
14: 1 *R,* O Israel, to the LORD your
Joel 2:12 "*r* to me with all your heart,
Zec 1: 3 '*R* to me,' declares the LORD
10: 9 and they will *r.*

RETURNED (RETURN)
Ps 35:13 When my prayers *r*
Am 4: 6 yet you have not *r* to me,"
1Pe 2:25 now you have *r* to the Shepherd

RETURNS (RETURN)
Pr 3:14 and yields better *r* than gold.
Isa 52: 8 When the LORD *r* to Zion,
Mt 24:46 finds him doing so when he *r.*

REUBEN
Firstborn of Jacob by Leah (Ge 29:32; 46:8; 1Ch 2:1). Attempted to rescue Joseph (Ge 37:21-30). Lost birthright for sleeping with Bilhah (Ge 35:22; 49:4). Tribe of blessed (Ge 49:3-4; Dt 33:6), numbered (Nu 1:21; 26:7), allotted land east of Jordan (Nu 32; 34:14; Jos 13:15), west (Eze 48:6), failed to help Deborah (Jdg 5:15-16), supported David (1Ch 12:37), 12,000 from (Rev 7:5).

REVEAL (REVEALED REVEALS REVELATION REVELATIONS)
Mt 11:27 to whom the Son chooses to *r* him.
Gal 1:16 was pleased to *r* his Son in me

REVEALED (REVEAL)
Dt 29:29 but the things *r* belong to us
Isa 40: 5 the glory of the LORD will be *r,*
43:12 I have *r* and saved and proclaimed
53: 1 the arm of the LORD been *r?*
65: 1 I *r* myself to those who did not ask
Mt 11:25 and *r* them to little children.
Jn 12:38 the arm of the Lord been *r?*"
17: 6 "I have *r* you to those whom you
Ro 1:17 a righteousness from God is *r,*
8:18 with the glory that will be *r* in us.
10:20 I *r* myself to those who did not ask
16:26 but now *r* and made known
1Co 2:10 but God has *r* it to us by his Spirit.
2Th 1: 7 happen when the Lord Jesus is *r*
2: 3 and the man of lawlessness is *r,*
1Pe 1: 7 and honor when Jesus Christ is *r.*
1:20 but was *r* in these last times
4:13 overjoyed when his glory is *r.*

REVEALS* (REVEAL)
Nu 23: 3 Whatever he *r* to me I will tell you
Job 12:22 He *r* the deep things of darkness
Da 2:22 He *r* deep and hidden things;
2:28 a God in heaven who *r* mysteries.
Am 4:13 and *r* his thoughts to man,

REVELATION* (REVEAL)
2Sa 7:17 David all the words of this entire *r.*
1Ch 17:15 David all the words of this entire *r.*
Pr 29:18 Where there is no *r,* the people cast
Da 10: 1 a *r* was given to Daniel (who was
Hab 2: 2 "Write down the *r*
2: 3 For the *r* awaits an appointed time;
Lk 2:32 a light for *r* to the Gentiles
Ro 16:25 according to the *r*
1Co 14: 6 I bring you some *r* or knowledge
14:26 a *r,* a tongue or an interpretation.
14:30 And if a *r* comes to someone who is
Gal 1:12 I received it by *r* from Jesus Christ.
2: 2 I went in response to a *r*
Eph 1:17 you the Spirit of wisdom and *r,*
3: 3 mystery made known to me by *r,*
Rev 1: 1 *r* of Jesus Christ, which God gave

REVELATIONS* (REVEAL)
2Co 12: 1 on to visions and *r* from the Lord.
12: 7 of these surpassingly great *r,*

REVELED* (REVELRY)
Ne 9:25 they *r* in your great goodness.

REVELRY (REVELED)
Ex 32: 6 drink and got up to indulge in *r.*
1Co 10: 7 and got up to indulge in pagan *r.*"

REVENGE (VENGEANCE)
Lev 19:18 " 'Do not seek *r* or bear a grudge
Ro 12:19 Do not take *r,* my friends,

REVERE* (REVERENCE REVERENT REVERING)
Lev 19:32 for the elderly and *r* your God.
Dt 4:10 so that they may learn to *r* me
13: 4 must follow, and him you must *r.*
14:23 to *r* the LORD your God always.
17:19 learn to *r* the LORD his God
28:58 and do not *r* this glorious
Job 37:24 Therefore, men *r* him,
Ps 22:23 *R* him, all you descendants
33: 8 let all the people of the world *r* him
102: 15 of the earth will *r* your glory.
Ecc 3:14 God does it so that men will *r* him.
Isa 25: 3 cities of ruthless nations will *r* you.
59:19 of the sun, they will *r* his glory.
63:17 hearts so we do not *r* you?
Jer 10: 7 Who should not *r* you,
Hos 10: 3 because we did not *r* the LORD.
Mal 4: 2 But for you who *r* my name,

REVERENCE (REVERE)
Lev 19:30 and have *r* for my sanctuary.
Ne 5:15 of *r* for God I did not act like that.
Ps 5: 7 in *r* will I bow down
Da 6:26 people must fear and *r* the God
2Co 7: 1 perfecting holiness out of *r* for God
Eph 5:21 to one another out of *r* for Christ.
Col 3:22 of heart and *r* for the Lord.
1Pe 3: 2 when they see the purity and *r*
Rev 11:18 and those who *r* your name,

REVERENT* (REVERE)
Ecc 8:12 with God-fearing men, who are *r*
Tit 2: 3 women to be *r* in the way they live,
Heb 5: 7 because of his *r* submission.
1Pe 1:17 as strangers here in *r* fear.

REVERING* (REVERE)
Dt 8: 6 walking in his ways and *r* him.
Ne 1:11 who delight in *r* your name.

REVERSE*
Isa 43:13 When I act, who can *r* it?"

REVIVE* (REVIVING)
Ps 80:18 *r* us, and we will call on your name.
85: 6 Will you not *r* us again,
Isa 57:15 and to *r* the heart of the contrite.
57:15 to *r* the spirit of the lowly
Hos 6: 2 After two days he will *r* us;

REVIVING* (REVIVE)
Ps 19: 7 *r* the soul.

REVOKED
Isa 45:23 a word that will not be *r*:

REWARD (REWARDED REWARDING REWARDS)
Ge 15: 1 your very great *r*."
1Sa 24:19 May the LORD *r* you well
Ps 19:11 in keeping them there is great *r*.
62:12 Surely you will *r* each person
127: 3 children a *r* from him.
Pr 9:12 are wise, your wisdom will *r* you;
11:18 sows righteousness reaps a sure *r*.
13:21 prosperity is the *r* of the righteous.
19:17 he will *r* him for what he has done.
25:22 and the LORD will *r* you.
31:31 Give her the *r* she has earned,
Isa 40:10 See, his *r* is with him,
49: 4 and my *r* is with my God."
61: 8 In my faithfulness I will *r* them
62:11 See, his *r* is with him,
Jer 17:10 to *r* a man according to his conduct
32:19 you *r* everyone according
Mt 5:12 because great is your *r* in heaven,
6: 1 you will have no *r*
6: 5 they have received their *r* in full.
10:41 a prophet will receive a prophet's *r*,
16:27 and then he will *r* each person
Lk 6:23 because great is your *r* in heaven.
6:35 Then your *r* will be great,
1Co 3:14 built survives, he will receive his *r*.
Eph 6: 8 know that the Lord will *r* everyone
Col 3:24 an inheritance from the Lord as a *r*.
Heb 11:26 he was looking ahead to his *r*.
Rev 22:12 I am coming soon! My *r* is with me

REWARDED (REWARD)
Ru 2:12 May you be richly *r* by the LORD,
2Sa 22:21 of my hands he has *r* me.
2Ch 15: 7 for your work will be *r*."
Ps 18:24 The LORD has *r* me according
Pr 13:13 he who respects a command is *r*.
14:14 and the good man *r* for his.
Jer 31:16 for your work will be *r*,"
1Co 3: 8 and each will be *r* according
Heb 10:35 your confidence; it will be richly *r*.
2Jn : 8 but that you may be *r* fully.

REWARDING* (REWARD)
Rev 11:18 for *r* your servants the prophets

REWARDS (REWARD)
1Sa 26:23 The LORD *r* every man
Pr 12:14 the work of his hands *r* him.
Heb 11: 6 that he *r* those who earnestly seek

RIBS
Ge 2:21 he took one of the man's *r*

RICH (RICHES RICHEST)
Job 34:19 does not favor the *r* over the poor,
Ps 49:16 overawed when a man grows *r*,
145: 8 slow to anger and *r* in love.
Pr 21:17 loves wine and oil will never be *r*.
22: 2 *R* and poor have this in common:
23: 4 Do not wear yourself out to get *r*;
28: 6 than a *r* man whose ways are
Pr 28:20 to get *r* will not go unpunished.
28:22 A stingy man is eager to get *r*
Ecc 5:12 but the abundance of a *r* man
Isa 33: 6 a *r* store of salvation and wisdom
53: 9 and with the *r* in his death,
Jer 9:23 or the *r* man boast of his riches,
Zec 3: 4 and I will put *r* garments on you."
Mt 19:23 it is hard for a *r* man
Lk 1:53 but has sent the *r* away empty.
6:24 "But woe to you who are *r*,
12:21 for himself but is not *r* toward God
16: 1 "There was a *r* man whose
21: 1 Jesus saw the *r* putting their gifts
2Co 6:10 yet making many *r*; having nothing
8: 2 poverty welled up in *r* generosity.
8: 9 he was *r*, yet for your sakes he
9:11 You will be made *r* in every way
Eph 2: 4 love for us, God, who is *r* in mercy,
1Ti 6: 9 want to get *r* fall into temptation
6:17 Command those who are *r*
6:18 to do good, to be *r* in good deeds,
Jas 1:10 the one who is *r* should take pride
2: 5 the eyes of the world to be *r* in faith
5: 1 you *r* people, weep and wail
Rev 2: 9 and your poverty—yet you are *r*!
3:18 you can become *r*; and white

RICHES (RICH)
Job 36:18 that no one entices you by *r*;
Ps 49: 6 and boast of their great *r*?
49:12 despite his *r*, does not endure;
62:10 though your *r* increase,
119: 14 as one rejoices in great *r*.
Pr 3:16 in her left hand are *r* and honor.
11:28 Whoever trusts in his *r* will fall,
22: 1 is more desirable than great *r*;
27:24 for *r* do not endure forever,
30: 8 give me neither poverty nor *r*,
Isa 10: 3 Where will you leave your *r*?
60: 5 to you the *r* of the nations will
Jer 9:23 or the rich man boast of his *r*,
Lk 8:14 *r* and pleasures, and they do not
Ro 9:23 to make the *r* of his glory known
11:33 the depth of the *r* of the wisdom
Eph 2: 7 he might show the incomparable *r*
3: 8 to the Gentiles the unsearchable *r*
Col 1:27 among the Gentiles the glorious *r*
2: 2 so that they may have the full *r*

RICHEST (RICH)
Isa 55: 2 and your soul will delight in the *r*

RID
Ge 21:10 "Get *r* of that slave woman
1Co 5: 7 Get *r* of the old yeast that you may
Gal 4:30 "Get *r* of the slave woman

RIDE (RIDER RIDING)
Ps 45: 4 In your majesty *r* forth victoriously

RIDER (RIDE)
Rev 6: 2 was a white horse! Its *r* held a bow,
19:11 whose *r* is called Faithful and True.

RIDING (RIDE)
Zec 9: 9 gentle and *r* on a donkey,
Mt 21: 5 gentle and *r* on a donkey,

RIGGING
Isa 33:23 Your *r* hangs loose:

RIGHT (RIGHTS)
Ge 4: 7 But if you do not do what is *r*,
18:19 of the LORD by doing what is *r*
18:25 the Judge of all the earth do *r*?"
48:13 on his left toward Israel's *r* hand,
Ex 15: 6 Your *r* hand, O LORD,
15:26 and do what is *r* in his eyes,
Dt 5:32 do not turn aside to the *r*
6:18 Do what is *r* and good
13:18 and doing what is *r* in his eyes.
Jos 1: 7 do not turn from it to the *r*
1Sa 12:23 you the way that is good and *r*.
1Ki 3: 9 to distinguish between *r* and wrong
15: 5 For David had done what was *r*
2Ki 7: 9 to each other, "We're not doing *r*.
Ne 9:13 and laws that are just and *r*,
Ps 16: 8 Because he is at my *r* hand,
16:11 eternal pleasures at your *r* hand.
17: 7 you who save by your *r* hand
18:35 and your *r* hand sustains me;
19: 8 The precepts of the LORD are *r*,
25: 9 He guides the humble in what is *r*
33: 4 For the word of the LORD is *r*
44: 3 it was your *r* hand, your arm,
45: 4 let your *r* hand display awesome
51: 4 so that you are proved *r*
63: 8 your *r* hand upholds me.
73:23 you hold me by my *r* hand.
91: 7 ten thousand at your *r* hand,
Ps 98: 1 his *r* hand and his holy arm
106: 3 who constantly do what is *r*.
110: 1 "Sit at my *r* hand
118: 15 LORD's *r* hand has done mighty
119:144 Your statutes are forever *r*;
137: 5 may my *r* hand forget its skill,
139: 10 your *r* hand will hold me fast.
Pr 1: 3 doing what is *r* and just and fair;
4:27 Do not swerve to the *r* or the left;
14:12 There is a way that seems *r*
18:17 The first to present his case seems *r*
Ecc 7:20 who does what is *r* and never sins.
SS 1: 4 How *r* they are to adore you!
Isa 1:17 learn to do *r*!
7:15 reject the wrong and choose the *r*.
30:10 us no more visions of what is *r*!
30:21 Whether you turn to the *r*
41:10 you with my righteous *r* hand.
41:13 who takes hold of your *r* hand
48:13 my *r* hand spread out the heavens;
64: 5 to the help of those who gladly do *r*
Jer 23: 5 and do what is just and *r* in the land
Eze 18: 5 who does what is just and *r*.
18:21 and does what is just and *r*,
33:14 and does what is just and *r*—
Hos 14: 9 The ways of the LORD are *r*;
Mt 5:29 If your *r* eye causes you to sin,
6: 3 know what your *r* hand is doing,
22:44 "Sit at my *r* hand
25:33 He will put the sheep on his *r*
Jn 1:12 he gave the *r* to become children
Ac 2:34 "Sit at my *r* hand
7:55 Jesus standing at the *r* hand of God
Ro 3: 4 "So that you may be proved *r*
8:34 is at the *r* hand of God and is
9:21 Does not the potter have the *r*
12:17 careful to do what is *r* in the eyes
1Co 9: 4 Don't we have the *r* to food
2Co 8:21 we are taking pains to do what is *r*,
Eph 1:20 and seated him at his *r* hand
6: 1 parents in the Lord, for this is *r*.
Php 4: 8 whatever is *r*, whatever is pure,
2Th 3:13 never tire of doing what is *r*.
Heb 1: 3 down at the *r* hand of the Majesty
Jas 2: 8 as yourself," you are doing *r*.
1Pe 3:14 if you should suffer for what is *r*,
1Jn 2:29 who does what is *r* has been born
Rev 2: 7 I will give the *r* to eat from the tree
3:21 I will give the *r* to sit with me
22:11 let him who does *r* continue to do *r*

RIGHTEOUS (RIGHTEOUSLY RIGHTEOUSNESS)
Ge 6: 9 Noah was a *r* man, blameless
18:23 "Will you sweep away the *r*
Nu 23:10 Let me die the death of the *r*,
Ne 9: 8 your promise because you are *r*.
Job 36: 7 He does not take his eyes off the *r*;
Ps 1: 5 nor sinners in the assembly of the *r*.
5:12 O LORD, you bless the *r*;
11: 7 For the LORD is *r*,
15: 2 and who does what is *r*,
34:15 The eyes of the LORD are on the *r*
37:16 Better the little that the *r* have
37:21 but the *r* give generously;
37:25 yet I have never seen the *r* forsaken
37:30 of the *r* man utters wisdom,
55:22 he will never let the *r* fall.
64:10 Let the *r* rejoice in the LORD
68: 3 But may the *r* be glad
112: 4 compassionate and *r* man.
118: 20 through which the *r* may enter.
119: 7 as I learn your *r* laws.
119:137 *R* are you, O LORD,
140: 13 Surely the *r* will praise your name
143: 2 for no one living is *r* before you.
145: 17 The LORD is *r* in all his ways
Pr 3:33 but he blesses the home of the *r*.
4:18 of the *r* is like the first gleam
10: 7 of the *r* will be a blessing,
10:11 The mouth of the *r* is a fountain
10:16 The wages of the *r* bring them life,
10:20 The tongue of the *r* is choice silver,
10:24 what the *r* desire will be granted.
10:28 The prospect of the *r* is joy,
10:32 of the *r* know what is fitting,
11:23 The desire of the *r* ends only
11:30 The fruit of the *r* is a tree of life,
12:10 A *r* man cares for the needs
12:21 No harm befalls the *r*,
13: 9 The light of the *r* shines brightly,
15:28 of the *r* weighs its answers,
15:29 but he hears the prayer of the *r*.
16:31 it is attained by a *r* life.
18:10 the *r* run to it and are safe.
20: 7 The *r* man leads a blameless life;
21:15 justice is done, it brings joy to the *r*
23:24 The father of a *r* man has great joy;
28: 1 but the *r* are as bold as a lion.

Pr 29: 6 but a r one can sing and be glad.
29: 7 The r care about justice
29:27 The r detest the dishonest;
Ecc 7:20 There is not a r man on earth
Isa 26: 7 The path of the r is level;
41:10 you with my r right hand.
45:21 a r God and a Savior;
53:11 his knowledge my r servant will
64: 6 and all our r acts are like filthy rags
Jer 23: 5 up to David a r Branch,
Eze 3:20 when a r man turns
18: 5 "Suppose there is a r man
18:20 of the r man will be credited
33:12 The r man, if he sins, will not be
Da 9:18 requests of you because we are r,
Hab 2: 4 but the r will live by his faith—
Zec 9: 9 r and having salvation,
Mal 3:18 see the distinction between the r
Mt 5:45 rain on the r and the unrighteous.
9:13 For I have not come to call the r,
10:41 and anyone who receives a r man
13:43 Then the r will shine like the sun
13:49 and separate the wicked from the r
25:37 "Then the r will answer him, 'Lord,
25:46 to eternal punishment, but the r
Ac 24:15 will be a resurrection of both the r
Ro 1:17 as it is written: "The r will live
2: 5 when his r judgment will be
2:13 the law who will be declared r.
3:10 "There is no one r, not even one;
3:20 Therefore no one will be declared r
5:19 one man the many will be made r.
Gal 3:11 because, "The r will live by faith."
1Ti 1: 9 that law is made not for the r
2Ti 4: 8 which the Lord, the r Judge,
Tit 3: 5 because of r things we had done,
Heb 10:38 But my r one will live by faith.
Jas 5:16 The prayer of a r man is powerful
1Pe 3:12 the eyes of the Lord are on the r
3:18 the r for the unrighteous,
4:18 "If it is hard for the r to be saved,
1Jn 2: 1 defense—Jesus Christ, the R One.
3: 7 does what is right is r, just as he is r.
Rev 19: 8 stands for the r acts of the saints.)

RIGHTEOUSLY* (RIGHTEOUS)
Ps 9: 4 on your throne, judging r.
Isa 33:15 He who walks r
Jer 11:20 LORD Almighty, you who judge r

RIGHTEOUSNESS (RIGHTEOUS)
Ge 15: 6 and he credited it to him as r.
Dt 9: 4 of this land because of my r."
1Sa 26:23 LORD rewards every man for his r
1Ki 10: 9 to maintain justice and r."
Job 37:23 great r, he does not oppress.
Ps 7:17 to the LORD because of his r
9: 8 He will judge the world in r;
17:15 And I—in r I will see your face;
23: 3 He guides me in paths of r
33: 5 The LORD loves r and justice;
35:28 My tongue will speak of your r
36: 6 Your r is like the mighty
37: 6 He will make your r shine like
40: 9 I proclaim r in the great assembly;
45: 4 in behalf of truth, humility and r;
45: 7 You love r and hate wickedness;
48:10 your right hand is filled with r.
65: 5 us with awesome deeds of r,
71: 2 Rescue me and deliver me in your r
71:15 My mouth will tell of your r,
71:19 Your r reaches to the skies, O God,
85:10 r and peace kiss each other.
89:14 R and justice are the foundation
96:13 He will judge the world in r
98: 9 He will judge the world in r
103: 6 The LORD works r
103: 17 his r with their children's children
106: 31 This was credited to him as r
111: 3 and his r endures forever.
118: 19 Open for me the gates of r;
132: 9 May your priests be clothed with r;
145: 7 and joyfully sing of your r.
Pr 11: 5 r of the blameless makes a straight
11:18 he who sows r reaps a sure reward.
13: 6 R guards the man of integrity,
14:34 R exalts a nation,
16: 8 Better a little with r
16:12 a throne is established through r.
21:21 He who pursues r and love
Isa 5:16 will show himself holy by his r.
9: 7 it with justice and r
11: 4 but with r he will judge the needy,
16: 5 and speeds the cause of r.
26: 9 the people of the world learn r.
32:17 The fruit of r will be peace;
42: 6 "I, the LORD, have called you in r;
42:21 the LORD for the sake of his r
45: 8 "You heavens above, rain down r;
Isa 51: 1 "Listen to me, you who pursue r,
51: 6 my r will never fail.
51: 8 But my r will last forever,
58: 8 then your r will go before you,
59:17 He put on r as his breastplate,
61:10 and arrayed me in a robe of r,
63: 1 "It is I, speaking in r,
Jer 9:24 justice and r on earth,
23: 6 The LORD Our R.
Eze 3:20 a righteous man turns from his r
14:20 save only themselves by their r.
18:20 The r of the righteous man will be
33:12 r of the righteous man will not save
Da 9:24 to bring in everlasting r,
12: 3 and those who lead many to r,
Hos 10:12 Sow for yourselves r,
Am 5:24 r like a never-failing stream!
Mic 7: 9 I will see his r.
Zep 2: 3 Seek r, seek humility;
Mal 4: 2 the sun of r will rise with healing
Mt 5: 6 those who hunger and thirst for r,
5:10 who are persecuted because of r,
5:20 unless your r surpasses that
6: 1 to do your 'acts of r' before men,
6:33 But seek first his kingdom and his r
Jn 16: 8 world of guilt in regard to sin and r
Ac 24:25 Paul discoursed on r, self-control
Ro 1:17 For in the gospel a r from God is
3: 5 brings out God's r more clearly,
3:22 This r from God comes
4: 3 and it was credited to him as r."
4: 5 wicked, his faith is credited as r.
4: 6 man to whom God credits r apart
4: 9 faith was credited to him as r.
4:13 through the r that comes by faith.
4:22 why "it was credited to him as r."
5:18 of r was justification that brings life
6:13 body to him as instruments of r.
6:16 or to obedience, which leads to r?
6:18 and have become slaves to r.
6:19 in slavery to r leading to holiness.
8:10 yet your spirit is alive because of r.
9:30 did not pursue r, have obtained it,
10: 3 they did not know the r that comes
14:17 but of r, peace and joy
1Co 1:30 our r, holiness and redemption.
2Co 3: 9 is the ministry that brings r!
5:21 that in him we might become the r
6: 7 with weapons of r in the right hand
6:14 For what do r and wickedness have
9: 9 his r endures forever."
Gal 2:21 for if r could be gained
3: 6 and it was credited to him as r."
3:21 then r would certainly have come
Eph 4:24 created to be like God in true r
5: 9 r and truth) and find out what
6:14 with the breastplate of r in place,
Php 1:11 filled with the fruit of r that comes
3: 6 as for legalistic r, faultless.
3: 9 not having a r of my own that
1Ti 6:11 and pursue r, godliness, faith, love,
2Ti 2:22 and pursue r, faith, love and peace,
3:16 correcting and training in r,
4: 8 is in store for me the crown of r,
Heb 1: 8 and r will be the scepter
5:13 with the teaching about r.
7: 2 his name means "king of r";
11: 7 became heir of the r that comes
12:11 it produces a harvest of r
Jas 2:23 and it was credited to him as r,"
3:18 sow in peace raise a harvest of r.
1Pe 2:24 die to sins and live for r;
2Pe 2:21 not to have known the way of r,
3:13 and a new earth, the home of r.

RIGHTS (RIGHT)
Ps 82: 3 maintain the r of the poor
Pr 31: 8 for the r of all who are destitute.
Isa 10: 2 to deprive the poor of their r
La 3:35 to deny a man his r
Gal 4: 5 that we might receive the full r

RING
Pr 11:22 Like a gold r in a pig's snout
Lk 15:22 Put a r on his finger and sandals

RIOTS
2Co 6: 5 imprisonments and r; in hard work,

RIPE
Joel 3:13 for the harvest is r.
Am 8: 1 showed me: a basket of r fruit.
Jn 4:35 at the fields! They are r for harvest.
Rev 14:15 for the harvest of the earth is r."

RISE (RAISE RAISED RISEN ROSE)
Lev 19:32 "'R in the presence of the aged,
Nu 24:17 a scepter will r out of Israel.
Isa 26:19 their bodies will r.
Mal 4: 2 of righteousness will r with healing
Mt 27:63 'After three days I will r again.'
Mk 8:31 and after three days r again.
Lk 18:33 On the third day he will r again."
Jn 5:29 those who have done good will r
20: 9 had to r from the dead.)
Ac 17: 3 had to suffer and r from the dead.
1Th 4:16 and the dead in Christ will r first.

RISEN (RISE)
Mt 28: 6 He is not here; he has r, just
Mk 16: 6 He has r! He is not here.
Lk 24:34 The Lord has r and has appeared

RIVER (RIVERS)
Ps 46: 4 There is a r whose streams make
Isa 66:12 "I will extend peace to her like a r,
Eze 47:12 grow on both banks of the r.
Rev 22: 1 Then the angel showed me the r

RIVERS (RIVER)
Ps 137: 1 By the r of Babylon we sat

ROAD (CROSSROADS ROADS)
Mt 7:13 and broad is the r that leads

ROADS (ROAD)
Lk 3: 5 crooked r shall become straight,

ROARING
1Pe 5: 8 prowls around like a r lion looking

ROB (ROBBERS ROBBERY ROBS)
Mal 3: 8 "Will a man r God? Yet you r me.

ROBBERS (ROB)
Jer 7:11 become a den of r to you?
Mk 15:27 They crucified two r with him,
Lk 19:46 but you have made it 'a den of r.'"
Jn 10: 8 came before me were thieves and r,

ROBBERY (ROB)
Isa 61: 8 I hate r and iniquity.

ROBE (ROBED ROBES)
Ge 37: 3 and he made a richly ornamented r
Isa 6: 1 the train of his r filled the temple.
61:10 arrayed me in a r of righteousness,
Rev 6:11 each of them was given a white r,

ROBED (ROBE)
Ps 93: 1 the LORD is r in majesty
Isa 63: 1 Who is this, r in splendor,

ROBES (ROBE)
Ps 45: 8 All your r are fragrant with myrrh
Rev 7:13 "These in white r—who are they,

ROBS* (ROB)
Pr 19:26 He who r his father and drives out
28:24 He who r his father or mother

ROCK
Ge 49:24 of the Shepherd, the R of Israel,
Ex 17: 6 Strike the r, and water will come
Nu 20: 8 Speak to that r before their eyes
Dt 32: 4 He is the R, his works are perfect,
32:13 him with honey from the r,
2Sa 22: 2 "The LORD is my r, my fortress
Ps 18: 2 The LORD is my r, my fortress
19:14 O LORD, my R and my Redeemer
40: 2 he set my feet on a r
61: 2 lead me to the r that is higher
92:15 he is my R, and there is no
Isa 26: 4 the LORD, is the R eternal.
51: 1 to the r from which you were cut
Da 2:34 you were watching, a r was cut out,
Mt 7:24 man who built his house on the r.
16:18 and on this r I will build my church
Ro 9:33 and a r that makes them fall,
1Co 10: 4 the spiritual r that accompanied
1Pe 2: 8 and a r that makes them fall."

ROD (RODS)
2Sa 7:14 I will punish him with the r of men,
Ps 23: 4 your r and your staff,
Pr 13:24 He who spares the r hates his son,
22:15 the r of discipline will drive it far
23:13 if you punish him with the r,
29:15 r of correction imparts wisdom,
Isa 11: 4 the earth with the r of his mouth;

RODS (ROD)
2Co 11:25 Three times I was beaten with r,

ROLL (ROLLED)
Mk 16: 3 "Who will r the stone away

ROLLED (ROLL)
Lk 24: 2 They found the stone r away

ROMAN
Ac 16:37 even though we are *R* citizens,
22:25 you to flog a *R* citizen who hasn't

ROOF (ROOFS)
Pr 21: 9 Better to live on a corner of the *r*

ROOFS
Mt 10:27 in your ear, proclaim from the *r*.

ROOM (ROOMS)
Mt 6: 6 But when you pray, go into your *r*,
Mk 14:15 He will show you a large upper *r*,
Lk 2: 7 there was no *r* for them in the inn.
Jn 8:37 because you have no *r* for my word
21:25 the whole world would not have *r*
2Co 7: 2 Make *r* for us in your hearts.

ROOMS (ROOM)
Jn 14: 2 In my Father's house are many *r*;

ROOSTER
Mt 26:34 this very night, before the *r* crows,

ROOT (ROOTED ROOTS)
Isa 11:10 In that day the *R* of Jesse will stand
53: 2 and like a *r* out of dry ground.
Mt 3:10 already at the *r* of the trees,
13:21 But since he has no *r*, he lasts only
Ro 11:16 if the *r* is holy, so are the branches.
15:12 "The *R* of Jesse will spring up,
1Ti 6:10 of money is a *r* of all kinds of evil.
Rev 5: 5 the *R* of David, has triumphed.
22:16 I am the *R* and the Offspring

ROOTED (ROOT)
Eph 3:17 being *r* and established in love,

ROOTS (ROOT)
Isa 11: 1 from his *r* a Branch will bear fruit.

ROSE (RISE)
SS 2: 1 I am a *r* of Sharon,
1Th 4:14 believe that Jesus died and *r* again

ROTS
Pr 14:30 but envy *r* the bones.

ROUGH
Isa 42:16 and make the *r* places smooth.
Lk 3: 5 the *r* ways smooth.

ROUND
Ecc 1: 6 *r* and *r* it goes,

ROYAL
Ps 45: 9 at your right hand is the *r* bride
Da 1: 8 not to defile himself with the *r* food
Jas 2: 8 If you really keep the *r* law found
1Pe 2: 9 a *r* priesthood, a holy nation,

RUBBISH*
Php 3: 8 I consider them *r*, that I may gain

RUBIES
Job 28:18 the price of wisdom is beyond *r*.
Pr 3:15 She is more precious than *r*;
8:11 for wisdom is more precious than *r*,
31:10 She is worth far more than *r*.

RUDDER*
Jas 3: 4 by a very small *r* wherever the pilot

RUDDY
1Sa 16:12 He was *r*, with a fine appearance
SS 5:10 *Beloved* My lover is radiant and *r*,

RUDE*
1Co 13: 5 It is not *r*, it is not self-seeking,

RUIN (RUINED RUINING RUINS)
Pr 10: 8 but a chattering fool comes to *r*.
10:10 and a chattering fool comes to *r*.
10:14 but the mouth of a fool invites *r*.
10:29 but it is the *r* of those who do evil.
18:24 many companions may come to *r*,
19:13 A foolish son is his father's *r*,
26:28 and a flattering mouth works *r*.
SS 2:15 that *r* the vineyards,
Eze 21:27 A *r*! A *r*! I will make it a *r*!
1Ti 6: 9 desires that plunge men into *r*

RUINED (RUIN)
Isa 6: 5 "I am *r*! For I am a man
Mt 9:17 and the wineskins will be *r*.
12:25 divided against itself will be *r*,

RUINING* (RUIN)
Tit 1:11 they are *r* whole households

RUINS (RUIN)
Pr 19: 3 A man's own folly *r* his life,
Ecc 4: 5 and *r* himself.
2Ti 2:14 and only *r* those who listen.

RULE (RULER RULERS RULES)
Ge 1:26 let them *r* over the fish of the sea
3:16 and he will *r* over you."
Jdg 8:22 said to Gideon, "*R* over us—
1Sa 12:12 'No, we want a king to *r* over us'—
Ps 2: 9 You will *r* them with an iron
67: 4 for you *r* the peoples justly
119:133 let no sin *r* over me.
Pr 17: 2 A wise servant will *r*
Isa 28:10 *r* on *r*, *r* on *r*;
Eze 20:33 I will *r* over you with a mighty
Zec 6:13 and will sit and *r* on his throne.
9:10 His *r* will extend from sea to sea
Ro 13: 9 are summed up in this one *r*:
15:12 arise to *r* over the nations;
1Co 7:17 This is the *r* I lay down in all
Gal 6:16 and mercy to all who follow this *r*,
Eph 1:21 far above all *r* and authority,
Col 3:15 the peace of Christ *r* in your hearts,
2Th 3:10 we gave you this *r*: "If a man will
Rev 2:27 He will *r* them with an iron scepter;
12: 5 who will *r* all the nations
19:15 He will *r* them with an iron scepter

RULER (RULE)
Ps 8: 6 You made him *r* over the works
Pr 19: 6 Many curry favor with a *r*,
23: 1 When you sit to dine with a *r*,
25:15 Through patience a *r* can be
29:26 Many seek an audience with a *r*,
Isa 60:17 and righteousness your *r*.
Da 9:25 the *r*, comes, there will be seven
Mic 5: 2 one who will be *r* over Israel,
Mt 2: 6 for out of you will come a *r*
Eph 2: 2 of the *r* of the kingdom of the air,
1Ti 6:15 God, the blessed and only *R*,
Rev 1: 5 and the *r* of the kings of the earth.

RULERS (RULE)
Ps 2: 2 and the *r* gather together
119:161 *R* persecute me without cause,
Isa 40:23 reduces the *r* of this world
Da 7:27 and all *r* will worship and obey him
Mt 20:25 "You know that the *r*
Ac 13:27 and their *r* did not recognize Jesus,
Ro 13: 3 For *r* hold no terror
1Co 2: 6 of this age or of the *r* of this age,
Eph 3:10 should be made known to the *r*
6:12 the *r*, against the authorities,
Col 1:16 or powers or *r* or authorities;

RULES (RULE)
Nu 15:15 is to have the same *r* for you
2Sa 23: 3 when he *r* in the fear of God,
Ps 22:28 and he *r* over the nations.
66: 7 He *r* forever by his power,
103: 19 and his kingdom *r* over all.
Isa 29:13 is made up only of *r* taught by men.
40:10 and his arm *r* for him.
Mt 15: 9 their teachings are but *r* taught
Lk 22:26 one who *r* like the one who serves.
2Ti 2: 5 he competes according to the *r*.

RUMORS
Jer 51:46 afraid when *r* are heard in the land;
Mt 24: 6 You will hear of wars and *r* of wars,

RUN (RAN RUNNERS RUNNING RUNS)
Ps 19: 5 champion rejoicing to *r* his course.
Pr 4:12 when you *r*, you will not stumble.
18:10 the righteous *r* to it and are safe.
Isa 10: 3 To whom will you *r* for help?
40:31 they will *r* and not grow weary,
Joel 3:18 ravines of Judah will *r* with water.
Hab 2: 2 so that a herald may *r* with it.
1Co 9:24 *R* in such a way as to get the prize.
Gal 2: 2 that I was running or had *r* my race
Php 2:16 on the day of Christ that I did not *r*
Heb 12: 1 let us *r* with perseverance the race

RUNNERS* (RUN)
1Co 9:24 that in a race all the *r* run,

RUNNING (RUN)
Ps 133: 2 *r* down on Aaron's beard,
Lk 17:23 Do not go *r* off after them.
1Co 9:26 I do not run like a man *r* aimlessly;
Gal 5: 7 You were *r* a good race.

RUNS (RUN)
Jn 10:12 he abandons the sheep and *r* away.

RUSH
Pr 1:16 for their feet *r* into sin,
6:18 feet that are quick to *r* into evil,
Isa 59: 7 Their feet *r* into sin;

RUST
Mt 6:19 where moth and *r* destroy,

RUTH*
Moabitess; widow who went to Bethlehem with mother-in-law Naomi (Ru 1). Gleaned in field of Boaz; shown favor (Ru 2). Proposed marriage to Boaz (Ru 3). Married (Ru 4:1-12); bore Obed, ancestor of David (Ru 4:13-22), Jesus (Mt 1:5).

RUTHLESS
Pr 11:16 but *r* men gain only wealth.
Ro 1:31 are senseless, faithless, heartless, *r*.

SABBATH (SABBATHS)
Ex 20: 8 "Remember the *S* day
31:14 " 'Observe the *S*, because it is holy
Lev 25: 2 the land itself must observe a *s*
Dt 5:12 "Observe the *S* day
Isa 56: 2 keeps the *S* without desecrating it,
56: 6 all who keep the *S*
58:13 if you call the *S* a delight
Jer 17:21 not to carry a load on the *S* day
Mt 12: 1 through the grainfields on the *S*.
Lk 13:10 On a *S* Jesus was teaching in one
Col 2:16 a New Moon celebration or a *S* day

SABBATH-REST* (REST)
Heb 4: 9 then, a *S* for the people of God;

SABBATHS (SABBATH)
2Ch 2: 4 evening and on *S* and New Moons
Eze 20:12 Also I gave them my *S*

SACKCLOTH
Ps 30:11 you removed my *s* and clothed me
Da 9: 3 in fasting, and in *s* and ashes.
Mt 11:21 would have repented long ago in *s*

SACRED
Lev 23: 2 are to proclaim as *s* assemblies.
Mt 7: 6 "Do not give dogs what is *s*;
Ro 14: 5 One man considers one day more *s*
1Co 3:17 for God's temple is *s*, and you are
2Pe 1:18 were with him on the *s* mountain.
2:21 on the *s* command that was

SACRIFICE (SACRIFICED SACRIFICES)
Ge 22: 2 *S* him there as a burnt offering
Ex 12:27 'It is the Passover *s* to the LORD,
1Sa 15:22 To obey is better than *s*,
1Ki 18:38 the LORD fell and burned up the *s*,
1Ch 21:24 or *s* a burnt offering that costs me
Ps 40: 6 *S* and offering you did not desire,
50:14 *S* thank offerings to God,
51:16 You do not delight in *s*,
54: 6 I will *s* a freewill offering to you;
107: 22 Let them *s* thank offerings
141: 2 of my hands be like the evening *s*.
Pr 15: 8 The LORD detests the *s*
21: 3 to the LORD than *s*.
Da 9:27 the 'seven' he will put an end to *s*
12:11 time that the daily *s* is abolished
Hos 6: 6 For I desire mercy, not *s*,
Mt 9:13 this means: 'I desire mercy, not *s*.'
Ro 3:25 God presented him as a *s*
Eph 5: 2 as a fragrant offering and *s* to God.
Php 4:18 an acceptable *s*, pleasing to God.
Heb 9:26 away with sin by the *s* of himself.
10: 5 "*S* and offering you did not desire,
10:10 holy through the *s* of the body
10:14 by one *s* he has made perfect
10:18 there is no longer any *s* for sin.
11: 4 faith Abel offered God a better *s*
13:15 offer to God a *s* of praise—
1Jn 2: 2 He is the atoning *s* for our sins,
4:10 as an atoning *s* for our sins.

SACRIFICED (SACRIFICE)
Ac 15:29 are to abstain from food *s* to idols,
1Co 5: 7 our Passover lamb, has been *s*.
8: 1 Now about food *s* to idols:
Heb 7:27 He *s* for their sins once for all
9:28 so Christ was *s* once

SACRIFICES (SACRIFICE)
Ps 51:17 The *s* of God are a broken spirit;
Mk 12:33 than all burnt offerings and *s*."
Ro 12: 1 to offer your bodies as living *s*,
Heb 9:23 with better *s* than these.
13:16 for with such *s* God is pleased.
1Pe 2: 5 offering spiritual *s* acceptable

SAD
Lk 18:23 he heard this, he became very *s*,

SADDUCEES
Mt 16: 6 the yeast of the Pharisees and *S*."
Mk 12:18 *S*, who say there is no resurrection,
Ac 23: 8 *S* say that there is no resurrection,

SAFE (SAVE)
Ps 27: 5 he will keep me *s* in his dwelling;
37: 3 in the land and enjoy *s* pasture.
Pr 18:10 the righteous run to it and are *s*.
28:26 he who walks in wisdom is kept *s*.
29:25 in the LORD is kept *s*.
Jer 12: 5 If you stumble in *s* country,
Jn 17:12 kept them *s* by that name you gave
1Jn 5:18 born of God keeps him *s*,

SAFETY (SAVE)
Ps 4: 8 make me dwell in *s*.
Hos 2:18 so that all may lie down in *s*.
1Th 5: 3 people are saying, "Peace and *s*,"

SAINTS
1Sa 2: 9 He will guard the feet of his *s*,
Ps 16: 3 As for the *s* who are in the land,
30: 4 Sing to the LORD, you *s* of his;
31:23 Love the LORD, all his *s*!
34: 9 Fear the LORD, you his *s*,
116: 15 is the death of his *s*.
149: 1 his praise in the assembly of the *s*.
149: 5 Let the *s* rejoice in this honor
Da 7:18 the *s* of the Most High will receive
Ro 8:27 intercedes for the *s* in accordance
1Co 6: 2 not know that the *s* will judge
Eph 1:15 Jesus and your love for all the *s*,
1:18 of his glorious inheritance in the *s*,
6:18 always keep on praying for all the *s*
Phm : 7 have refreshed the hearts of the *s*.
Rev 5: 8 which are the prayers of the *s*.
19: 8 for the righteous acts of the *s*.)

SAKE (SAKES)
1Sa 12:22 For the *s* of his great name
Ps 23: 3 righteousness for his name's *s*.
44:22 Yet for your *s* we face death all day
106: 8 Yet he saved them for his name's *s*,
Isa 42:21 for the *s* of his righteousness
43:25 your transgressions, for my own *s*,
48: 9 For my own name's *s* I delay my
48:11 For my own *s*, for my own *s*,
Jer 14: 7 for the *s* of your name.
14:21 For the *s* of your name do not
Eze 20: 9 But for the *s* of my name I did what
20:14 But for the *s* of my name I did what
20:22 and for the *s* of my name I did what
36:22 but for the *s* of my holy name,
Da 9:17 For your *s*, O Lord, look with favor
Mt 10:39 life for my *s* will find it.
19:29 for my *s* will receive a hundred
1Co 9:23 I do all this for the *s* of the gospel,
2Co 12:10 for Christ's *s*, I delight
Php 3: 7 loss for the *s* of Christ.
Heb 11:26 He regarded disgrace for the *s*
1Pe 2:13 for the Lord's *s* to every authority
3Jn : 7 was for the *s* of the Name that they

SAKES* (SAKE)
2Co 8: 9 yet for your *s* he became poor,

SALEM
Ge 14:18 king of *S* brought out bread
Heb 7: 2 "king of *S*" means "king of peace."

SALT
Ge 19:26 and she became a pillar of *s*.
Nu 18:19 covenant of *s* before the LORD
Mt 5:13 "You are the *s* of the earth.
Col 4: 6 with *s*, so that you may know how
Jas 3:11 *s* water flow from the same spring?

SALVATION* (SAVE)
Ex 15: 2 he has become my *s*.
2Sa 22: 3 my shield and the horn of my *s*.
23: 5 Will he not bring to fruition my *s*
1Ch 16:23 proclaim his *s* day after day.
2Ch 6:41 O LORD God, be clothed with *s*,
Ps 9:14 and there rejoice in your *s*.
13: 5 my heart rejoices in your *s*.
14: 7 that *s* for Israel would come out
18: 2 is my shield and the horn of my *s*,
27: 1 The LORD is my light and my *s*—
28: 8 a fortress of *s* for his anointed one.
35: 3 "I am your *s*."
35: 9 and delight in his *s*.
37:39 The *s* of the righteous comes
40:10 I speak of your faithfulness and *s*.
40:16 those who love your *s* always say,
50:23 way so that I may show him the *s*
51:12 Restore to me the joy of your *s*
53: 6 that *s* for Israel would come out
62: 1 my *s* comes from him.
62: 2 He alone is my rock and my *s*;
62: 6 He alone is my rock and my *s*;
62: 7 My *s* and my honor depend
67: 2 your *s* among all nations.
69:13 answer me with your sure *s*.
Ps 69:27 do not let them share in your *s*.
69:29 may your *s*, O God, protect me.
70: 4 those who love your *s* always say,
71:15 of your *s* all day long,
74:12 you bring *s* upon the earth.
85: 7 and grant us your *s*.
85: 9 Surely his *s* is near those who fear
91:16 and show him my *s*."
95: 1 to the Rock of our *s*.
96: 2 proclaim his *s* day after day.
98: 1 have worked *s* for him.
98: 2 The LORD has made his *s* known
98: 3 the *s* of our God.
116: 13 I will lift up the cup of *s*
118: 14 he has become my *s*.
118: 21 you have become my *s*.
119: 41 your *s* according to your promise;
119: 81 with longing for your *s*,
119:123 My eyes fail, looking for your *s*,
119:155 *S* is far from the wicked,
119:166 I wait for your *s*, O LORD,
119:174 I long for your *s*, O LORD,
132: 16 I will clothe her priests with *s*,
149: 4 he crowns the humble with *s*.
Isa 12: 2 Surely God is my *s*;
12: 2 he has become my *s*."
12: 3 from the wells of *s*.
25: 9 let us rejoice and be glad in his *s*."
26: 1 God makes *s*
26:18 We have not brought *s* to the earth;
30:15 "In repentance and rest is your *s*,
33: 2 our *s* in time of distress.
33: 6 a rich store of *s* and wisdom
45: 8 let *s* spring up,
45:17 the LORD with an everlasting *s*;
46:13 I will grant *s* to Zion,
46:13 and my *s* will not be delayed.
49: 6 that you may bring my *s*
49: 8 and in the day of *s* I will help you;
51: 5 my *s* is on the way,
51: 6 But my *s* will last forever,
51: 8 my *s* through all generations."
52: 7 who proclaim *s*,
52:10 the *s* of our God.
56: 1 for my *s* is close at hand
59:16 so his own arm worked *s* for him,
59:17 and the helmet of *s* on his head;
60:18 but you will call your walls *S*
61:10 me with garments of *s*
62: 1 her *s* like a blazing torch.
63: 5 so my own arm worked *s* for me,
Jer 3:23 is the *s* of Israel.
La 3:26 quietly for the *s* of the LORD.
Jnh 2: 9 *S* comes from the LORD."
Zec 9: 9 righteous and having *s*,
Lk 1:69 He has raised up a horn of *s* for us
1:71 of long ago), *s* from our enemies
1:77 give his people the knowledge of *s*
2:30 For my eyes have seen your *s*,
3: 6 And all mankind will see God's *s*
19: 9 "Today *s* has come to this house,
Jn 4:22 for *s* is from the Jews.
Ac 4:12 *S* is found in no one else,
13:26 message of *s* has been sent.
13:47 that you may bring *s* to the ends
28:28 to know that God's *s* has been sent
Ro 1:16 for the *s* of everyone who believes:
11:11 *s* has come to the Gentiles
13:11 because our *s* is nearer now
2Co 1: 6 it is for your comfort and *s*;
6: 2 and in the day of *s* I helped you."
6: 2 of God's favor, now is the day of *s*.
7:10 brings repentance that leads to *s*
Eph 1:13 word of truth, the gospel of your *s*.
6:17 Take the helmet of *s* and the sword
Php 2:12 to work out your *s* with fear
1Th 5: 8 and the hope of *s* as a helmet.
5: 9 to receive *s* through our Lord Jesus
2Ti 2:10 they too may obtain the *s* that is
3:15 wise for *s* through faith
Tit 2:11 of God that brings *s* has appeared
Heb 1:14 to serve those who will inherit *s*?
2: 3 This *s*, which was first announced
2: 3 escape if we ignore such a great *s*?
2:10 of their *s* perfect through suffering.
5: 9 of eternal *s* for all who obey him
6: 9 case—things that accompany *s*.
9:28 to bring *s* to those who are waiting
1Pe 1: 5 the coming of the *s* that is ready
1: 9 of your faith, the *s* of your souls.
1:10 Concerning this *s*, the prophets,
2: 2 by it you may grow up in your *s*,
2Pe 3:15 that our Lord's patience means *s*,
Jude : 3 to write to you about the *s* we share
Rev 7:10 "*S* belongs to our God,
12:10 have come the *s* and the power
19: 1 *S* and glory and power belong

SAMARIA (SAMARITAN)
1Ki 16:24 He bought the hill of *S*
2Ki 17: 6 the king of Assyria captured *S*
Jn 4: 4 Now he had to go through *S*.
4: 5 came to a town in *S* called Sychar,

SAMARITAN (SAMARIA)
Lk 10:33 But a *S*, as he traveled, came where
17:16 and thanked him—and he was a *S*.
Jn 4: 7 When a *S* woman came

SAMSON
Danite judge. Birth promised (Jdg 13). Married to Philistine, but wife given away (Jdg 14). Vengeance on Philistines (Jdg 15). Betrayed by Delilah (Jdg 16:1-22). Death (Jdg 16:23-31). Feats of strength: killed lion (Jdg 14:6), 30 Philistines (Jdg 14:19), 1,000 Philistines with jawbone (Jdg 15: 13-17), carried off gates of Gaza (Jdg 16:3), pushed down temple of Dagon (Jdg 16:25-30).

SAMUEL
Ephraimite judge and prophet (Heb 11:32). Birth prayed for (1Sa 1:10-18). Dedicated to temple by Hannah (1Sa 1:21-28). Raised by Eli (1Sa 2: 11, 18-26). Called as prophet (1Sa 3). Led Israel to victory over Philistines (1Sa 7). Asked by Israel for a king (1Sa 8). Anointed Saul as king (1Sa 9-10). Farewell speech (1Sa 12). Rebuked Saul for sacrifice (1Sa 13). Announced rejection of Saul (1Sa 15). Anointed David as king (1Sa 16). Protected David from Saul (1Sa 19:18-24). Death (1Sa 25:1). Returned from dead to condemn Saul (1Sa 28).

SANBALLAT
Led opposition to Nehemiah's rebuilding of Jerusalem (Ne 2:10, 19; 4; 6).

SANCTIFIED* (SANCTIFY)
Jn 17:19 that they too may be truly *s*.
Ac 20:32 among all those who are *s*.
26:18 among those who are *s* by faith
Ro 15:16 to God, *s* by the Holy Spirit.
1Co 1: 2 to those *s* in Christ Jesus
6:11 But you were washed, you were *s*,
7:14 and the unbelieving wife has been *s*
7:14 the unbelieving husband has been *s*
1Th 4: 3 It is God's will that you should be *s*
Heb 10:29 blood of the covenant that *s* him,

SANCTIFY* (SANCTIFIED SANCTIFYING)
Jn 17:17 *S* them by the truth; your word is
17:19 For them I *s* myself, that they too
1Th 5:23 *s* you through and through.
Heb 9:13 are ceremonially unclean *s* them

SANCTIFYING* (SANCTIFY)
2Th 2:13 through the *s* work of the Spirit
1Pe 1: 2 through the *s* work of the Spirit,

SANCTUARY
Ex 25: 8 "Then have them make a *s* for me,
Lev 19:30 and have reverence for my *s*,
Ps 15: 1 LORD, who may dwell in your *s*?
63: 2 I have seen you in the *s*
68:24 of my God and King into the *s*.
68:35 are awesome, O God, in your *s*;
73:17 me till I entered the *s* of God;
102: 19 looked down from his *s* on high,
134: 2 Lift up your hands in the *s*
150: 1 Praise God in his *s*;
Eze 37:26 I will put my *s* among them forever
41: 1 the man brought me to the outer *s*
Da 9:26 will destroy the city and the *s*.
Heb 6:19 It enters the inner *s*
8: 2 in the *s*, the true tabernacle set up
8: 5 They serve at a *s* that is a copy
9:24 enter a man-made *s* that was only

SAND
Ge 22:17 and as the *s* on the seashore.
Mt 7:26 man who built his house on *s*.

SANDAL (SANDALS)
Ru 4: 7 one party took off his *s*

SANDALS (SANDAL)
Ex 3: 5 off your *s*, for the place where you
Dt 25: 9 take off one of his *s*, spit in his face
Jos 5:15 off your *s*, for the place where you
Mt 3:11 whose *s* I am not fit to carry.

SANG (SING)
Ex 15: 1 and the Israelites *s* this song
15:21 Miriam *s* to them:
Nu 21:17 Then Israel *s* this song:
Jdg 5: 1 Barak son of Abinoam *s* this song:
1Sa 18: 7 As they danced, they *s*:
2Sa 22: 1 David *s* to the LORD the words
2Ch 5:13 in praise to the LORD and *s*:

2Ch 29:30 So they *s* praises with gladness
Ezr 3:11 thanksgiving they *s* to the LORD:
Job 38: 7 while the morning stars *s* together
Ps 106: 12 and *s* his praise.
Rev 5: 9 And they *s* a new song:
5:12 In a loud voice they *s:*
14: 3 they *s* a new song before the throne
15: 3 and *s* the song of Moses the servant

SAP
Ro 11:17 share in the nourishing *s*

SAPPHIRA*
Ac 5: 1 together with his wife *S,*

SARAH
Wife of Abraham, originally named Sarai; barren (Ge 11:29-31; 1Pe 3:6). Taken by Pharaoh as Abraham's sister; returned (Ge 12:10-20). Gave Hagar to Abraham; sent her away in pregnancy (Ge 16). Name changed; Isaac promised (Ge 17:15-21; 18:10-15; Heb 11:11). Taken by Abimelech as Abraham's sister; returned (Ge 20). Isaac born; Hagar and Ishmael sent away (Ge 21:1-21; Gal 4:21-31). Death (Ge 23).

SARDIS
Rev 3: 1 the angel of the church in *S* write:

SASH (SASHES)
Rev 1:13 with a golden *s* around his chest.

SASHES (SASH)
Rev 15: 6 wore golden *s* around their chests.

SAT (SIT)
Ps 137: 1 By the rivers of Babylon we *s*
Mk 16:19 and he *s* at the right hand of God.
Lk 10:39 who *s* at the Lord's feet listening
Heb 1: 3 he *s* down at the right hand
8: 1 who *s* down at the right hand
10:12 he *s* down at the right hand of God.
12: 2 and *s* down at the right hand

SATAN
Job 1: 6 and *S* also came with them.
Zec 3: 2 said to *S,* "The LORD rebuke you,
Mt 12:26 If *S* drives out *S,* he is divided
16:23 *S!* You are a stumbling block to me;
Mk 4:15 *S* comes and takes away the word
Lk 10:18 "I saw *S* fall like lightning
22: 3 *S* entered Judas, called Iscariot,
Ro 16:20 The God of peace will soon crush *S*
1Co 5: 5 is present, hand this man over to *S,*
2Co 11:14 for *S* himself masquerades
12: 7 a messenger of *S,* to torment me.
1Ti 1:20 handed over to *S* to be taught not
Rev 12: 9 serpent called the devil, or *S,*
20: 2 or *S,* and bound him for a thousand
20: 7 *S* will be released from his prison

SATISFIED (SATISFY)
Ps 17:15 I will be *s* with seeing your likeness
22:26 The poor will eat and be *s;*
63: 5 My soul will be *s* as with the richest
104: 28 they are *s* with good things.
105: 40 *s* them with the bread of heaven.
Pr 13: 4 the desires of the diligent are fully *s*
30:15 are three things that are never *s,*
Ecc 5:10 whoever loves wealth is never *s*
Isa 53:11 he will see the light of life, and be *s*
Mt 14:20 They all ate and were *s,*
Lk 6:21 for you will be *s.*

SATISFIES* (SATISFY)
Ps 103: 5 who *s* your desires with good things,
107: 9 for he *s* the thirsty
147: 14 and *s* you with the finest of wheat.

SATISFY (SATISFIED SATISFIES)
Ps 90:14 *S* us in the morning
145: 16 *s* the desires of every living thing.
Pr 5:19 may her breasts *s* you always,
Isa 55: 2 and your labor on what does not *s?*
58:10 and *s* the needs of the oppressed,

SAUL
1. Benjamite; anointed by Samuel as first king of Israel (1Sa 9-10). Defeated Ammonites (1Sa 11). Rebuked for offering sacrifice (1Sa 13:1-15). Defeated Philistines (1Sa 14). Rejected as king for failing to annihilate Amalekites (1Sa 15). Soothed from evil spirit by David (1Sa 16:14-23). Sent David against Goliath (1Sa 17). Jealousy and attempted murder of David (1Sa 18:1-11). Gave David Michal as wife (1Sa 18:12-30). Second attempt to kill David (1Sa 19). Anger at Jonathan (1Sa 20:26-34). Pursued David: killed priests at Nob (1Sa 22), went to Keilah and Ziph (1Sa 23), life spared by David at En Gedi (1Sa 24) and in his tent (1Sa 26). Rebuked by Samuel's spirit for consulting witch at Endor (1Sa 28). Wounded by Philistines; took his own life (1Sa 31; 1Ch 10). Lamented by David (2Sa 1:17-27). Children (1Sa 14:49-51; 1Ch 8).
2. See PAUL

SAVAGE
Ac 20:29 *s* wolves will come in among you

SAVE (SAFE SAFETY SALVATION SAVED SAVES SAVIOR)
Ge 45: 5 to *s* lives that God sent me ahead
1Ch 16:35 Cry out, "*S* us, O God our Savior;
Job 40:14 that your own right hand can *s* you.
Ps 17: 7 you who *s* by your right hand
18:27 You *s* the humble
28: 9 *S* your people and bless your
31:16 *s* me in your unfailing love.
69:35 for God will *s* Zion
71: 2 turn your ear to me and *s* me.
72:13 and *s* the needy from death.
89:48 or *s* himself from the power
91: 3 Surely he will *s* you
109: 31 to *s* his life from those who
146: 3 in mortal men, who cannot *s.*
Pr 2:16 will *s* you also from the adulteress,
Isa 35: 4 he will come to *s* you."
38:20 The LORD will *s* me,
46: 7 it cannot *s* him from his troubles.
59: 1 of the LORD is not too short to *s,*
63: 1 mighty to *s.*"
Jer 17:14 *s* me and I will be saved,
Eze 3:18 ways in order to *s* his life,
7:19 able to *s* them in the day
14:14 they could *s* only themselves
33:12 of the righteous man will not *s* him
34:22 I will *s* my flock, and they will no
Da 3:17 the God we serve is able to *s* us
Hos 1: 7 and I will *s* them—not by bow,
Zep 1:18 will be able to *s* them
3:17 he is mighty to *s.*
Zec 8: 7 "I will *s* my people
Mt 1:21 he will *s* his people from their sins
16:25 wants to *s* his life will lose it,
Lk 19:10 to seek and to *s* what was lost."
Jn 3:17 but to *s* the world through him.
12:47 come to judge the world, but to *s* it.
Ro 11:14 people to envy and *s* some of them.
1Co 7:16 whether you will *s* your husband?
1Ti 1:15 came into the world to *s* sinners—
Heb 7:25 to *s* completely those who come
Jas 5:20 of his way will *s* him from death
Jude :23 others from the fire and *s* them;

SAVED (SAVE)
Ps 22: 5 They cried to you and were *s;*
33:16 No king is *s* by the size of his army;
34: 6 he *s* him out of all his troubles.
106: 21 They forgot the God who *s* them,
116: 6 when I was in great need, he *s* me.
Isa 25: 9 we trusted in him, and he *s* us.
45:22 "Turn to me and be *s,*
64: 5 How then can we be *s?*
Jer 4:14 from your heart and be *s.*
8:20 and we are not *s.*"
Eze 3:19 but you will have *s* yourself.
33: 5 warning, he would have *s* himself.
Joel 2:32 on the name of the LORD will be *s;*
Mt 10:22 firm to the end will be *s.*
24:13 firm to the end will be *s.*
Mk 13:13 firm to the end will be *s.*
16:16 believes and is baptized will be *s,*
Jn 10: 9 enters through me will be *s.*
Ac 2:21 on the name of the Lord will be *s.*'
2:47 daily those who were being *s.*
4:12 to men by which we must be *s.*"
15:11 of our Lord Jesus that we are *s,*
16:30 do to be *s?*" They replied,
Ro 5: 9 how much more shall we be *s*
9:27 only the remnant will be *s.*
10: 1 the Israelites is that they may be *s.*
10: 9 him from the dead, you will be *s.*
10:13 on the name of the Lord will be *s.*"
11:26 so all Israel will be *s,* as it is written:
1Co 1:18 to us who are being *s* it is the power
3:15 will suffer loss; he himself will be *s,*
5: 5 his spirit *s* on the day of the Lord.
10:33 of many, so that they may be *s.*
15: 2 By this gospel you are *s,*
Eph 2: 5 it is by grace you have been *s.*
2: 8 For it is by grace you have been *s,*
2Th 2:13 you to be *s* through the sanctifying
1Ti 2: 4 who wants all men to be *s*
2:15 But women will be *s*
2Ti 1: 9 who has *s* us and called us
Tit 3: 5 He *s* us through the washing
Heb 10:39 but of those who believe and are *s.*

SAVES (SAVE)
Ps 7:10 who *s* the upright in heart.
68:20 Our God is a God who *s;*
145: 19 he hears their cry and *s* them.
1Pe 3:21 It *s* you by the resurrection

SAVIOR* (SAVE)
Dt 32:15 and rejected the Rock his *S.*
2Sa 22: 3 stronghold, my refuge and my *s*—
22:47 Exalted be God, the Rock, my *S!*
1Ch 16:35 Cry out, "Save us, O God our *S;*
Ps 18:46 Exalted be God my *S!*
24: 5 and vindication from God his *S.*
25: 5 for you are God my *S,*
27: 9 O God my *S.*
38:22 O Lord my *S.*
42: 5 my *S* and
42:11 my *S* and my God.
43: 5 my *S* and my God.
65: 5 O God our *S,*
68:19 Praise be to the Lord, to God our *S,*
79: 9 Help us, O God our *S,*
85: 4 Restore us again, O God our *S,*
89:26 my God, the Rock my *S.*'
Isa 17:10 You have forgotten God your *S;*
19:20 he will send them a *s* and defender,
43: 3 the Holy One of Israel, your *S;*
43:11 and apart from me there is no *s.*
45:15 O God and *S* of Israel.
45:21 a righteous God and a *S;*
49:26 that I, the LORD, am your *S,*
60:16 know that I, the LORD, am your *S,*
62:11 'See, your *S* comes!
63: 8 and so he became their *S.*
Jer 14: 8 its *S* in times of distress,
Hos 13: 4 no *S* except me.
Mic 7: 7 I wait for God my *S;*
Hab 3:18 I will be joyful in God my *S.*
Lk 1:47 and my spirit rejoices in God my *S,*
2:11 of David a *S* has been born to you;
Jn 4:42 know that this man really is the *S*
Ac 5:31 *S* that he might give repentance
13:23 God has brought to Israel the *S*
Eph 5:23 his body, of which he is the *S.*
Php 3:20 we eagerly await a *S* from there,
1Ti 1: 1 by the command of God our *S*
2: 3 This is good, and pleases God our *S*
4:10 who is the *S* of all men,
2Ti 1:10 through the appearing of our *S,*
Tit 1: 3 me by the command of God our *S,*
1: 4 the Father and Christ Jesus our *S.*
2:10 about God our *S* attractive.
2:13 appearing of our great God and *S,*
3: 4 and love of God our *S* appeared,
3: 6 through Jesus Christ our *S,*
2Pe 1: 1 *S* Jesus Christ have received a faith
1:11 eternal kingdom of our Lord and *S*
2:20 and *S* Jesus Christ and are again
3: 2 and *S* through your apostles.
3:18 and knowledge of our Lord and *S*
1Jn 4:14 Son to be the *S* of the world.
Jude :25 to the only God our *S* be glory,

SCALE (SCALES)
Ps 18:29 with my God I can *s* a wall.

SCALES (SCALE)
Lev 11: 9 may eat any that have fins and *s.*
19:36 Use honest *s* and honest weights,
Pr 11: 1 The LORD abhors dishonest *s,*
Da 5:27 You have been weighed on the *s*
Rev 6: 5 Its rider was holding a pair of *s*

SCAPEGOAT (GOAT)
Lev 16:10 by sending it into the desert as a *s.*

SCARECROW*
Jer 10: 5 Like a *s* in a melon patch,

SCARLET
Jos 2:21 she tied the *s* cord in the window.
Isa 1:18 "Though your sins are like *s,*
Mt 27:28 They stripped him and put a *s* robe

SCATTER (SCATTERED SCATTERS)
Dt 4:27 The LORD will *s* you
Ne 1: 8 I will *s* you among the nations,
Jer 9:16 I will *s* them among nations that
30:11 the nations among which I *s* you,
Zec 10: 9 I *s* them among the peoples,

SCATTERED (SCATTER)
Isa 11:12 he will assemble the *s* people
Jer 31:10 'He who *s* Israel will gather them
Zec 2: 6 "for I have *s* you to the four winds
13: 7 and the sheep will be *s,*
Mt 26:31 and the sheep of the flock will be *s.*'
Jn 11:52 but also for the *s* children of God,
Ac 8: 4 who had been *s* preached the word
Jas 1: 1 To the twelve tribes *s*

1Pe 1: 1 *s* throughout Pontus, Galatia,

SCATTERS (SCATTER)
Mt 12:30 he who does not gather with me *s*.

SCEPTER
Ge 49:10 The *s* will not depart from Judah,
Nu 24:17 a *s* will rise out of Israel.
Ps 2: 9 You will rule them with an iron *s*;
45: 6 a *s* of justice will be the *s*
Heb 1: 8 and righteousness will be the *s*
Rev 2:27 'He will rule them with an iron *s*;
12: 5 rule all the nations with an iron *s*.
19:15 "He will rule them with an iron *s*."

SCHEMES
Pr 6:18 a heart that devises wicked *s*,
24: 9 The *s* of folly are sin,
2Co 2:11 For we are not unaware of his *s*.
Eph 6:11 stand against the devil's *s*.

SCHOLAR*
1Co 1:20 Where is the *s*? Where is

SCOFFERS
2Pe 3: 3 that in the last days *s* will come,

SCORN (SCORNED SCORNING SCORNS)
Ps 69: 7 For I endure *s* for your sake,
69:20 *S* has broken my heart
89:41 he has become the *s*
109: 25 I am an object of *s* to my accusers;
119: 22 Remove from me *s* and contempt,
Mic 6:16 you will bear the *s* of the nations."

SCORNED (SCORN)
Ps 22: 6 *s* by men and despised

SCORNING (SCORN)
Heb 12: 2 him endured the cross, *s* its shame,

SCORNS (SCORN)
Pr 13:13 He who *s* instruction will pay for it,
30:17 that *s* obedience to a mother,

SCORPION
Lk 11:12 will give him a *s*? If you then,
Rev 9: 5 sting of a *s* when it strikes a man.

SCOUNDREL
Pr 6:12 A *s* and villain,

SCRIPTURE (SCRIPTURES)
Jn 2:22 Then they believed the *S*
7:42 Does not the *S* say that the Christ
10:35 and the *S* cannot be broken—
Ac 8:32 was reading this passage of *S*:
1Ti 4:13 yourself to the public reading of *S*,
2Ti 3:16 All *S* is God-breathed
2Pe 1:20 that no prophecy of *S* came about

SCRIPTURES (SCRIPTURE)
Mt 22:29 because you do not know the *S*
Lk 24:27 said in all the *S* concerning himself.
24:45 so they could understand the *S*.
Jn 5:39 These are the *S* that testify about
Ac 17:11 examined the *S* every day to see
2Ti 3:15 you have known the holy *S*,
2Pe 3:16 as they do the other *S*,

SCROLL
Ps 40: 7 it is written about me in the *s*.
Isa 34: 4 and the sky rolled up like a *s*;
Eze 3: 1 eat what is before you, eat this *s*;
Heb 10: 7 it is written about me in the *s*—
Rev 6:14 The sky receded like a *s*, rolling up,
10: 8 take the *s* that lies open in the hand

SCUM
1Co 4:13 this moment we have become the *s*

SEA (SEASHORE)
Ex 14:16 go through the *s* on dry ground.
Dt 30:13 "Who will cross the *s* to get it
1Ki 7:23 He made the *S* of cast metal,
Job 11: 9 and wider than the *s*.
Ps 93: 4 mightier than the breakers of the *s*
95: 5 The *s* is his, for he made it,
Ecc 1: 7 All streams flow into the *s*,
Isa 57:20 the wicked are like the tossing *s*,
Jnh 1: 4 LORD sent a great wind on the *s*,
Mic 7:19 iniquities into the depths of the *s*.
Hab 2:14 as the waters cover the *s*.
Zec 9:10 His rule will extend from *s* to *s*
Mt 18: 6 drowned in the depths of the *s*.
1Co 10: 1 that they all passed through the *s*.
Jas 1: 6 who doubts is like a wave of the *s*,
Jude :13 They are wild waves of the *s*,
Rev 10: 2 He planted his right foot on the *s*
13: 1 I saw a beast coming out of the *s*.
20:13 The *s* gave up the dead that were

Rev 21: 1 and there was no longer any *s*.

SEAL (SEALED SEALS)
Ps 40: 9 I do not *s* my lips,
SS 8: 6 Place me like a *s* over your heart,
Da 12: 4 and *s* the words of the scroll
Jn 6:27 God the Father has placed his *s*
1Co 9: 2 For you are the *s* of my apostleship
2Co 1:22 set his *s* of ownership on us,
Eph 1:13 you were marked in him with a *s*,
Rev 6: 3 the Lamb opened the second *s*,
6: 5 When the Lamb opened the third *s*,
6: 7 the Lamb opened the fourth *s*,
6: 9 When he opened the fifth *s*,
6:12 I watched as he opened the sixth *s*.
8: 1 When he opened the seventh *s*,
9: 4 people who did not have the *s*
22:10 "Do not *s* up the words

SEALED (SEAL)
Eph 4:30 with whom you were *s* for the day
2Ti 2:19 solid foundation stands firm, *s*
Rev 5: 1 on both sides and *s* with seven seals

SEALS (SEAL)
Rev 5: 2 "Who is worthy to break the *s*
6: 1 opened the first of the seven *s*.

SEAMLESS*
Jn 19:23 This garment was *s*, woven

SEARCH (SEARCHED SEARCHES SEARCHING)
Ps 4: 4 *s* your hearts and be silent.
139: 23 *S* me, O God, and know my heart;
Pr 2: 4 and *s* for it as for hidden treasure,
25: 2 to *s* out a matter is the glory
SS 3: 2 I will *s* for the one my heart loves.
Jer 17:10 "I the LORD *s* the heart
Eze 34:11 I myself will *s* for my sheep
34:16 I will *s* for the lost and bring back
Lk 15: 8 and *s* carefully until she finds it?

SEARCHED (SEARCH)
Ps 139: 1 O LORD, you have *s* me
Ecc 12:10 The Teacher *s* to find just the right
1Pe 1:10 *s* intently and with the greatest

SEARCHES (SEARCH)
1Ch 28: 9 for the LORD *s* every heart
Ps 7: 9 who *s* minds and hearts,
Pr 11:27 but evil comes to him who *s* for it.
20:27 The lamp of the LORD *s* the spirit
Ro 8:27 And he who *s* our hearts knows
1Co 2:10 The Spirit *s* all things,
Rev 2:23 will know that I am he who *s* hearts

SEARCHING (SEARCH)
Jdg 5:15 there was much *s* of heart.
Am 8:12 *s* for the word of the LORD,

SEARED
1Ti 4: 2 whose consciences have been *s*

SEASHORE (SEA)
Jos 11: 4 as numerous as the sand on the *s*.
1Ki 4:29 as measureless as the sand on the *s*.

SEASON (SEASONED SEASONS)
Lev 26: 4 I will send you rain in its *s*,
Ps 1: 3 which yields its fruit in *s*
2Ti 4: 2 be prepared in *s* and out of *s*;

SEASONED* (SEASON)
Col 4: 6 full of grace, *s* with salt,

SEASONS (SEASON)
Ge 1:14 signs to mark *s* and days and years,
Gal 4:10 and months and *s* and years!

SEAT (SEATED SEATS)
Ps 1: 1 or sit in the *s* of mockers.
Pr 31:23 where he takes his *s*
Da 7: 9 and the Ancient of Days took his *s*.
Lk 14: 9 say to you, 'Give this man your *s*.'
2Co 5:10 before the judgment *s* of Christ,

SEATED (SEAT)
Ps 47: 8 God is *s* on his holy throne.
Isa 6: 1 I saw the Lord *s* on a throne,
Lk 22:69 of Man will be *s* at the right hand
Eph 1:20 and *s* him at his right hand
2: 6 and *s* us with him in the heavenly
Col 3: 1 where Christ is *s* at the right hand
Rev 14:14 *s* on the cloud was one "like a son
20:11 white throne and him who was *s*

SEATS (SEAT)
Lk 11:43 you love the most important *s*

SECLUSION*
Lk 1:24 and for five months remained in *s*.

SECRET (SECRETLY SECRETS)
Dt 29:29 The *s* things belong
Jdg 16: 6 Tell me the *s* of your great strength
Ps 90: 8 our *s* sins in the light
139: 15 when I was made in the *s* place.
Pr 11:13 but a trustworthy man keeps a *s*.
21:14 A gift given in *s* soothes anger,
Jer 23:24 Can anyone hide in *s* places
Mt 6: 4 so that your giving may be in *s*.
6:18 who sees what is done in *s*,
Mk 4:11 "The *s* of the kingdom
1Co 2: 7 No, we speak of God's *s* wisdom,
4: 1 entrusted with the *s* things of God.
2Co 4: 2 we have renounced *s* and shameful
Eph 5:12 what the disobedient do in *s*.
Php 4:12 I have learned the *s*

SECRETLY (SECRET)
2Pe 2: 1 They will *s* introduce destructive
Jude : 4 about long ago have *s* slipped

SECRETS (SECRET)
Ps 44:21 since he knows the *s* of the heart?
Ro 2:16 day when God will judge men's *s*
1Co 14:25 the *s* of his heart will be laid bare.
Rev 2:24 Satan's so-called deep *s* (I will not

SECURE (SECURITY)
Dt 33:12 beloved of the LORD rest *s* in him,
Ps 16: 5 you have made my lot *s*.
16: 9 my body also will rest *s*,
112: 8 His heart is *s*, he will have no fear;
Pr 14:26 fears the LORD has a *s* fortress,
Heb 6:19 an anchor for the soul, firm and *s*.
2Pe 3:17 and fall from your *s* position.

SECURITY (SECURE)
Job 31:24 or said to pure gold, 'You are my *s*,'

SEED (SEEDS SEEDTIME)
Ge 1:11 on the land that bear fruit with *s*
Isa 55:10 so that it yields *s* for the sower
Mt 13: 3 "A farmer went out to sow his *s*.
13:31 of heaven is like a mustard *s*,
17:20 have faith as small as a mustard *s*,
Lk 8:11 of the parable: The *s* is the word
1Co 3: 6 I planted the *s*, Apollos watered it,
2Co 9:10 he who supplies *s* to the sower
Gal 3:29 then you are Abraham's *s*,
1Pe 1:23 not of perishable *s*,
1Jn 3: 9 because God's *s* remains in him;

SEEDS (SEED)
Jn 12:24 But if it dies, it produces many *s*.
Gal 3:16 Scripture does not say "and to *s*,"

SEEDTIME* (SEED)
Ge 8:22 *s* and harvest,

SEEK (SEEKING SEEKS SELF-SEEKING SOUGHT)
Lev 19:18 Do not *s* revenge or bear a grudge
Dt 4:29 if from there you *s* the LORD your
1Ki 22: 5 "First *s* the counsel of the LORD."
1Ch 28: 9 If you *s* him, he will be found
2Ch 7:14 themselves and pray and *s* my face
15: 2 If you *s* him, he will be found
Ps 34:10 those who *s* the LORD lack no
105: 3 of those who *s* the LORD rejoice.
105: 4 *s* his face always.
119: 2 and *s* him with all their heart.
119: 10 I *s* you with all my heart;
119:176 *S* your servant,
Pr 8:17 and those who *s* me find me.
18:15 the ears of the wise *s* it out.
25:27 is it honorable to *s* one's own honor
28: 5 those who *s* the LORD understand
Isa 55: 6 *S* the LORD while he may be
65: 1 found by those who did not *s* me.
Jer 29:13 You will *s* me and find me
Hos 10:12 for it is time to *s* the LORD,
Am 5: 4 "*S* me and live;
Zep 2: 3 *S* the LORD, all you humble
Mt 6:33 But *s* first his kingdom
7: 7 and it will be given to you; *s*
Lk 12:31 *s* his kingdom, and these things will
19:10 For the Son of Man came to *s*
Jn 5:30 for I *s* not to please myself
Ro 10:20 found by those who did not *s* me;
1Co 7:27 you married? Do not *s* a divorce.
10:24 Nobody should *s* his own good,
Heb 11: 6 rewards those who earnestly *s* him.
1Pe 3:11 he must *s* peace and pursue it.

SEEKING (SEEK)
2Ch 30:19 who sets his heart on *s* God—
Pr 20:18 Make plans by *s* advice;

Mal 3: 1 the Lord you are *s* will come
Jn 8:50 I am not *s* glory for myself;
1Co 10:33 For I am not *s* my own good

SEEKS (SEEK)
Pr 11:27 He who *s* good finds good will,
Mt 7: 8 he who *s* finds; and to him who
Jn 4:23 the kind of worshipers the Father *s*.
Ro 3:11 no one who *s* God.

SEER
1Sa 9: 9 of today used to be called a *s*.)

SELF-CONTROL* (CONTROL)
Pr 25:28 is a man who lacks *s*.
Ac 24:25 *s* and the judgment to come,
1Co 7: 5 you because of your lack of *s*.
Gal 5:23 faithfulness, gentleness and *s*.
2Ti 3: 3 slanderous, without *s*, brutal,
2Pe 1: 6 and to knowledge, *s*; and to *s*,

SELF-CONTROLLED* (CONTROL)
1Th 5: 6 are asleep, but let us be alert and *s*.
5: 8 let us be *s*, putting on faith and love
1Ti 3: 2 *s*, respectable, hospitable,
Tit 1: 8 who is *s*, upright, holy
2: 2 worthy of respect, *s*, and sound
2: 5 to be *s* and pure, to be busy at home
2: 6 encourage the young men to be *s*.
2:12 to live *s*, upright and godly lives
1Pe 1:13 prepare your minds for action; be *s*;
4: 7 and *s* so that you can pray.
5: 8 Be *s* and alert.

SELF-DISCIPLINE* (DISCIPLINE)
2Ti 1: 7 a spirit of power, of love and of *s*.

SELF-INDULGENCE*
Mt 23:25 inside they are full of greed and *s*.
Jas 5: 5 lived on earth in luxury and *s*.

SELF-SEEKING* (SEEK)
Ro 2: 8 But for those who are *s*
1Co 13: 5 it is not *s*, it is not easily angered,

SELFISH*
Ps 119: 36 and not toward *s* gain.
Pr 18: 1 An unfriendly man pursues *s* ends;
Gal 5:20 fits of rage, *s* ambition, dissensions,
Php 1:17 preach Christ out of *s* ambition,
2: 3 Do nothing out of *s* ambition
Jas 3:14 and *s* ambition in your hearts,
3:16 you have envy and *s* ambition,

SELL (SELLING SELLS SOLD)
Ge 25:31 "First *s* me your birthright."
Mk 10:21 *s* everything you have
Rev 13:17 or *s* unless he had the mark,

SELLING (SELL)
Lk 17:28 buying and *s*, planting and building

SELLS (SELL)
Pr 31:24 makes linen garments and *s* them,

SEND (SENDING SENDS SENT)
Ps 43: 3 *S* forth your light and your truth,
Isa 6: 8 *S* me!" He said, "Go and tell this
Mal 3: 1 "See, I will *s* my messenger,
Mt 9:38 to *s* out workers into his harvest
24:31 And he will *s* his angels
Mk 1: 2 I will *s* my messenger ahead of you,
Lk 20:13 I will *s* my son, whom I love;
Jn 3:17 For God did not *s* his Son
16: 7 but if I go, I will *s* him to you.
1Co 1:17 For Christ did not *s* me to baptize,

SENDING (SEND)
Mt 10:16 I am *s* you out like sheep
Jn 20:21 Father has sent me, I am *s* you."
Ro 8: 3 God did by *s* his own Son

SENDS (SEND)
Ps 57: 3 God *s* his love and his faithfulness.

SENNACHERIB
Assyrian king whose siege of Jerusalem was overthrown by the LORD following prayer of Hezekiah and Isaiah (2Ki 18:13-19:37; 2Ch 32:1-21; Isa 36-37).

SENSES*
Lk 15:17 "When he came to his *s*, he said,
1Co 15:34 Come back to your *s* as you ought,
2Ti 2:26 and that they will come to their *s*

SENSITIVITY*
Eph 4:19 Having lost all *s*, they have given

SENSUAL* (SENSUALITY)
Col 2:23 value in restraining *s* indulgence.
1Ti 5:11 For when their *s* desires overcome

SENSUALITY* (SENSUAL)
Eph 4:19 have given themselves over to *s*

SENT (SEND)
Ex 3:14 to the Israelites: 'I AM has *s* me
Isa 55:11 achieve the purpose for which I *s* it.
61: 1 He has *s* me to bind up
Jer 28: 9 as one truly *s* by the LORD only
Mt 10:40 me receives the one who *s* me.
Mk 6: 7 he *s* them out two by two
Lk 4:18 He has *s* me to proclaim freedom
9: 2 and he *s* them out to preach
10:16 rejects me rejects him who *s* me."
Jn 1: 6 There came a man who was *s*
4:34 "is to do the will of him who *s* me
5:24 believes him who *s* me has eternal
8:16 I stand with the Father, who *s* me.
9: 4 must do the work of him who *s* me.
16: 5 "Now I am going to him who *s* me,
17: 3 and Jesus Christ, whom you have *s*.
17:18 As you *s* me into the world,
20:21 As the Father has *s* me, I am
Ro 10:15 can they preach unless they are *s*?
Gal 4: 4 God *s* his Son, born of a woman,
1Jn 4:10 but that he loved us and *s* his Son

SENTENCE
2Co 1: 9 in our hearts we felt the *s* of death.

SEPARATE (SEPARATED SEPARATES SEPARATION)
Mt 19: 6 has joined together, let man not *s*."
Ro 8:35 Who shall *s* us from the love
1Co 7:10 wife must not *s* from her husband.
2Co 6:17 and be *s*, says the Lord.
Eph 2:12 at that time you were *s* from Christ,

SEPARATED (SEPARATE)
Isa 59: 2 But your iniquities have *s*
Eph 4:18 in their understanding and *s*

SEPARATES (SEPARATE)
Pr 16:28 and a gossip *s* close friends.
17: 9 repeats the matter *s* close friends.
Mt 25:32 as a shepherd *s* the sheep

SEPARATION (SEPARATE)
Nu 6: 2 a vow of *s* to the LORD

SERAPHS*
Isa 6: 2 Above him were *s*, each
6: 6 Then one of the *s* flew to me

SERIOUSNESS*
Tit 2: 7 *s* and soundness of speech that

SERPENT (SERPENT'S)
Ge 3: 1 the *s* was more crafty than any
Isa 27: 1 Leviathan the coiling *s*;
Rev 12: 9 that ancient *s* called the devil
20: 2 that ancient *s*, who is the devil,

SERPENT'S (SERPENT)
2Co 11: 3 Eve was deceived by the *s* cunning,

SERVANT (SERVANTS)
Ex 14:31 trust in him and in Moses his *s*.
21: 2 "If you buy a Hebrew *s*, he is
1Sa 3:10 "Speak, for your *s* is listening."
2Sa 7:19 the future of the house of your *s*.
1Ki 20:40 While your *s* was busy here
Job 1: 8 "Have you considered my *s* Job?
Ps 19:11 By them is your *s* warned;
19:13 Keep your *s* also from willful sins;
31:16 Let your face shine on your *s*;
89: 3 I have sworn to David my *s*,
Pr 14:35 A king delights in a wise *s*,
17: 2 wise *s* will rule over a disgraceful
22: 7 and the borrower is *s* to the lender.
31:15 and portions for her *s* girls.
Isa 41: 8 "But you, O Israel, my *s*,
49: 3 He said to me, "You are my *s*,
53:11 my righteous *s* will justify
Zec 3: 8 going to bring my *s*, the Branch.
Mal 1: 6 his father, and a *s* his master.
Mt 8:13 his *s* was healed at that very hour.
20:26 great among you must be your *s*,
24:45 Who then is the faithful and wise *s*,
25:21 'Well done, good and faithful *s*!
Lk 1:38 I am the Lord's *s*," Mary answered.
16:13 "No *s* can serve two masters.
Jn 12:26 and where I am, my *s* also will be.
Ro 1: 1 a *s* of Christ Jesus, called
13: 4 For he is God's *s* to do you good.
Php 2: 7 taking the very nature of a *s*,
Col 1:23 of which I, Paul, have become a *s*.
2Ti 2:24 And the Lord's *s* must not quarrel;

SERVANTS (SERVANT)
Lev 25:55 for the Israelites belong to me as *s*.
2Ki 17:13 to you through my *s* the prophets."
Ezr 5:11 "We are the *s* of the God of heaven
Ps 34:22 The LORD redeems his *s*;
103: 21 you his *s* who do his will.
104: 4 flames of fire his *s*.
Isa 44:26 who carries out the words of his *s*
65: 8 so will I do in behalf of my *s*;
65:13 my *s* will drink,
Lk 17:10 should say, 'We are unworthy *s*;
Jn 15:15 longer call you *s*, because a servant
Ro 13: 6 for the authorities are God's *s*,
1Co 3: 5 And what is Paul? Only *s*,
Heb 1: 7 his *s* flames of fire."

SERVE (SERVED SERVES SERVICE SERVING)
Dt 10:12 to *s* the LORD your God
11:13 and to *s* him with all your heart
13: 4 *s* him and hold fast to him.
28:47 you did not *s* the LORD your
Jos 22: 5 and to *s* him with all your heart
24:15 this day whom you will *s*,
24:18 We too will *s* the LORD,
1Sa 7: 3 to the LORD and *s* him only,
12:20 but *s* the LORD with all your heart
12:24 *s* him faithfully with all your heart;
2Ch 19: 9 "You must *s* faithfully
Job 36:11 If they obey and *s* him,
Ps 2:11 *S* the LORD with fear
Da 3:17 the God we *s* is able to save us
Mt 4:10 Lord your God, and *s* him only.'"
6:24 "No one can *s* two masters.
20:28 but to *s*, and to give his life
Ro 12: 7 If it is serving, let him *s*;
Gal 5:13 rather, *s* one another in love.
Eph 6: 7 *S* wholeheartedly,
1Ti 6: 2 they are to *s* them even better,
Heb 9:14 so that we may *s* the living God!
1Pe 4:10 gift he has received to *s* others,
5: 2 greedy for money, but eager to *s*;
Rev 5:10 kingdom and priests to *s* our God,

SERVED (SERVE)
Mt 20:28 Son of Man did not come to be *s*,
Jn 12: 2 Martha *s*, while Lazarus was
Ac 17:25 And he is not *s* by human hands,
Ro 1:25 and *s* created things rather
1Ti 3:13 Those who have *s* well gain

SERVES (SERVE)
Lk 22:26 one who rules like the one who *s*.
22:27 But I am among you as one who *s*.
Jn 12:26 Whoever *s* me must follow me;
Ro 14:18 because anyone who *s* Christ
1Pe 4:11 If anyone *s*, he should do it

SERVICE (SERVE)
Lk 9:62 fit for *s* in the kingdom
12:35 "Be dressed ready for *s*
Ro 15:17 in Christ Jesus in my *s* to God.
1Co 12: 5 There are different kinds of *s*,
16:15 themselves to the *s* of the saints.
2Co 9:12 This *s* that you perform is not only
Eph 4:12 God's people for works of *s*,
Rev 2:19 and faith, your *s* and perseverance,

SERVING (SERVE)
Jos 24:15 if *s* the LORD seems undesirable
2Ch 12: 8 learn the difference between *s* me
Ro 12: 7 If it is *s*, let him serve;
12:11 your spiritual fervor, *s* the Lord.
16:18 people are not *s* our Lord Christ,
Eph 6: 7 as if you were *s* the Lord, not men,
Col 3:24 It is the Lord Christ you are *s*.
2Ti 2: 4 No one *s* as a soldier gets involved

SETH
Ge 4:25 birth to a son and named him *S*,

SETTLE
Mt 5:25 "*S* matters quickly
2Th 3:12 in the Lord Jesus Christ to *s* down

SEVEN (SEVENS SEVENTH)
Ge 7: 2 Take with you *s* of every kind
Jos 6: 4 march around the city *s* times,
1Ki 19:18 Yet I reserve *s* thousand in Israel—
Pr 6:16 *s* that are detestable to him:
24:16 a righteous man falls *s* times,
Isa 4: 1 In that day *s* women
Da 9:25 comes, there will be *s* 'sevens,'
Mt 18:21 Up to *s* times?" Jesus answered,
Lk 11:26 takes *s* other spirits more wicked
Ro 11: 4 for myself *s* thousand who have not
Rev 1: 4 To the *s* churches in the province
6: 1 opened the first of the *s* seals.
8: 2 and to them were given *s* trumpets.
10: 4 And when the *s* thunders spoke,
15: 7 to the *s* angels *s* golden bowls filled

SEVENS* (SEVEN)
Da 9:24 "Seventy *'s'* are decreed
9:25 will be seven *'s,'* and sixty-two *'s.'*
9:26 the sixty-two *'s,'* the Anointed

SEVENTH (SEVEN)
Ge 2: 2 By the *s* day God had finished
Ex 20:10 but the *s* day is a Sabbath
23:11 but during the *s* year let the land lie
23:12 but on the *s* day do not work,
Heb 4: 4 "And on the *s* day God rested

SEVERE
2Co 8: 2 Out of the most *s* trial, their
1Th 1: 6 of the Lord; in spite of *s* suffering,

SEWED (SEWS)
Ge 3: 7 so they *s* fig leaves together

SEWS (SEWED)
Mt 9:16 No one *s* a patch of unshrunk cloth

SEXUAL (SEXUALLY)
Ex 22:19 "Anyone who has *s* relations
Lev 18: 6 relative to have *s* relations.
18: 7 father by having *s* relations
18:20 Do not have *s* relations with
Mt 15:19 murder, adultery, *s* immorality,
Ac 15:20 by idols, from *s* immorality,
1Co 5: 1 reported that there is *s* immorality
6:13 body is not meant for *s* immorality,
6:18 Flee from *s* immorality.
10: 8 should not commit *s* immorality,
2Co 12:21 *s* sin and debauchery
Gal 5:19 *s* immorality, impurity
Eph 5: 3 even a hint of *s* immorality,
Col 3: 5 *s* immorality, impurity, lust,
1Th 4: 3 that you should avoid *s* immorality

SEXUALLY (SEXUAL)
1Co 5: 9 to associate with *s* immoral people
6: 9 Neither the *s* immoral nor idolaters
6:18 he who sins *s* sins against his own
Heb 12:16 See that no one is *s* immoral,
13: 4 the adulterer and all the *s* immoral.
Rev 21: 8 the murderers, the *s* immoral,

SHADE
Ps 121: 5 the LORD is your *s*
Isa 25: 4 and a *s* from the heat.

SHADOW
Ps 17: 8 hide me in the *s* of your wings
23: 4 through the valley of the *s* of death,
36: 7 find refuge in the *s* of your wings.
91: 1 will rest in the *s* of the Almighty.
Isa 51:16 covered you with the *s* of my hand
Col 2:17 These are a *s* of the things that
Heb 8: 5 and *s* of what is in heaven.
10: 1 The law is only a *s*

SHADRACH
Hebrew exiled to Babylon; name changed from Hananiah (Da 1:6-7). Refused defilement by food (Da 1:8-20). Refused to worship idol (Da 3:1-18); saved from furnace (Da 3:19-30).

SHAKE (SHAKEN SHAKING)
Ps 64: 8 all who see them will *s* their heads
99: 1 let the earth *s*.
Hag 2: 6 I will once more *s* the heavens
Heb 12:26 "Once more I will *s* not only

SHAKEN (SHAKE)
Ps 16: 8 I will not be *s*.
30: 6 "I will never be *s*."
62: 2 he is my fortress, I will never be *s*.
112: 6 Surely he will never be *s*;
Isa 54:10 Though the mountains be *s*
Mt 24:29 and the heavenly bodies will be *s*.'
Lk 6:38 *s* together and running over,
Ac 2:25 I will not be *s*.
Heb 12:27 that what cannot be *s* may remain.

SHAKING* (SHAKE)
Ps 22: 7 they hurl insults, *s* their heads:
Mt 27:39 insults at him, *s* their heads
Mk 15:29 *s* their heads and saying, "So!

SHALLUM
King of Israel (2Ki 15:10-16).

SHAME (ASHAMED SHAMED SHAMEFUL)
Ps 25: 3 will ever be put to *s*,
34: 5 their faces are never covered with *s*
69: 6 not be put to *s* because of me,
Pr 13:18 discipline comes to poverty and *s*,
18:13 that is his folly and his *s*.
Jer 8: 9 The wise will be put to *s*;
8:12 No, they have no *s* at all;
Ro 9:33 trusts in him will never be put to *s*."
Ro 10:11 trusts in him will never be put to *s*."
1Co 1:27 things of the world to *s* the wise;
Heb 12: 2 endured the cross, scorning its *s*,

SHAMED (SHAME)
Jer 10:14 every goldsmith is *s* by his idols.
Joel 2:26 never again will my people be *s*.

SHAMEFUL (SHAME)
2Co 4: 2 have renounced secret and *s* ways;
2Pe 2: 2 Many will follow their *s* ways
Rev 21:27 nor will anyone who does what is *s*

SHAMGAR
Judge; killed 600 Philistines (Jdg 3:31).

SHAPE (SHAPES SHAPING)
Job 38:14 The earth takes *s* like clay

SHAPES (SHAPE)
Isa 44:10 Who *s* a god and casts an idol,

SHAPING (SHAPE)
Jer 18: 4 the pot he was *s* from the clay was

SHARE (SHARED SHARERS SHARES SHARING)
Ge 21:10 that slave woman's son will never *s*
Lev 19:17 frankly so you will not *s* in his guilt.
Dt 10: 9 That is why the Levites have no *s*
1Sa 30:24 All will *s* alike."
Eze 18:20 The son will not *s* the guilt
Mt 25:21 and *s* your master's happiness!'
Lk 3:11 "The man with two tunics should *s*
Ro 8:17 if indeed we *s* in his sufferings
12:13 *S* with God's people who are
2Co 1: 7 as you *s* in our sufferings,
Gal 4:30 the slave woman's son will never *s*
6: 6 in the word must *s* all good things
Eph 4:28 something to *s* with those in need.
Col 1:12 you to *s* in the inheritance
2Th 2:14 that you might *s* in the glory
1Ti 5:22 and do not *s* in the sins of others.
6:18 and to be generous and willing to *s*.
2Ti 2: 6 the first to receive a *s* of the crops.
Heb 12:10 that we may *s* in his holiness.
13:16 to do good and to *s* with others,
Rev 22:19 from him his *s* in the tree of life

SHARED (SHARE)
Ps 41: 9 he who *s* my bread,
Ac 4:32 but they *s* everything they had.
Heb 2:14 he too *s* in their humanity so that

SHARERS* (SHARE)
Eph 3: 6 and *s* together in the promise

SHARES (SHARE)
Pr 22: 9 for he *s* his food with the poor.
Jn 13:18 'He who *s* my bread has lifted up

SHARING (SHARE)
1Co 9:10 so in the hope of *s* in the harvest.
2Co 9:13 for your generosity in *s* with them
Php 3:10 the fellowship of *s* in his sufferings,
Phm : 6 you may be active in *s* your faith,

SHARON
SS 2: 1 I am a rose of *S*,

SHARP (SHARPENED SHARPENS SHARPER)
Pr 5: 4 *s* as a double-edged sword.
Isa 5:28 Their arrows are *s*,
Rev 1:16 came a *s* double-edged sword.
19:15 Out of his mouth comes a *s* sword

SHARPENED (SHARP)
Eze 21: 9 *s* and polished—

SHARPENS* (SHARP)
Pr 27:17 As iron *s* iron,
27:17 so one man *s* another.

SHARPER* (SHARP)
Heb 4:12 *S* than any double-edged sword,

SHATTER (SHATTERED SHATTERS)
Jer 51:20 with you I *s* nations,

SHATTERED (SHATTER)
1Sa 2:10 who oppose the LORD will be *s*.
Job 16:12 All was well with me, but he *s* me;
17:11 days have passed, my plans are *s*,
Ecc 12: 6 before the pitcher is *s* at the spring,

SHATTERS (SHATTER)
Ps 46: 9 he breaks the bow and *s* the spear,

SHAVED
Jdg 16:17 my head were *s*, my strength would
1Co 11: 5 it is just as though her head were *s*.

SHEAF (SHEAVES)
Lev 23:11 is to wave the *s* before the LORD

SHEARER* (SHEARERS)
Ac 8:32 and as a lamb before the *s* is silent,

SHEARERS (SHEARER)
Isa 53: 7 and as a sheep before her *s* is silent,

SHEAVES (SHEAF)
Ge 37: 7 while your *s* gathered around mine
Ps 126: 6 carrying *s* with him.

SHEBA
1. Benjamite who rebelled against David (2Sa 20).
2. See QUEEN.

SHECHEM
1. Raped Jacob's daughter Dinah; killed by Simeon and Levi (Ge 34).
2. City where Joshua renewed the covenant (Jos 24).

SHED (SHEDDING SHEDS)
Ge 9: 6 by man shall his blood be *s*;
Pr 6:17 hands that *s* innocent blood,
Ro 3:15 "Their feet are swift to *s* blood;
Col 1:20 through his blood, *s* on the cross.

SHEDDING (SHED)
Heb 9:22 without the *s* of blood there is no

SHEDS (SHED)
Ge 9: 6 "Whoever *s* the blood of man,

SHEEP (SHEEP'S SHEEPSKINS)
Nu 27:17 LORD's people will not be like *s*
Dt 17: 1 a *s* that has any defect or flaw in it,
1Sa 15:14 "What then is this bleating of *s*
Ps 44:22 we are considered as *s*
78:52 led them like *s* through the desert.
100: 3 we are his people, the *s*
119:176 I have strayed like a lost *s*.
SS 4: 2 teeth are like a flock of *s* just shorn,
Isa 53: 6 We all, like *s*, have gone astray,
53: 7 as a *s* before her shearers is silent,
Jer 50: 6 "My people have been lost *s*;
Eze 34:11 I myself will search for my *s*
Zec 13: 7 and the *s* will be scattered,
Mt 9:36 helpless, like *s* without a shepherd.
10:16 I am sending you out like *s*
12:11 "If any of you has a *s* and it falls
18:13 he is happier about that one *s*
25:32 as a shepherd separates the *s*
Jn 10: 1 man who does not enter the *s* pen
10: 3 He calls his own *s* by name
10: 7 the truth, I am the gate for the *s*.
10:15 and I lay down my life for the *s*.
10:27 My *s* listen to my voice; I know
21:17 Jesus said, "Feed my *s*.
1Pe 2:25 For you were like *s* going astray,

SHEEP'S* (SHEEP)
Mt 7:15 They come to you in *s* clothing,

SHEEPSKINS* (SHEEP)
Heb 11:37 They went about in *s* and goatskins

SHEKEL
Ex 30:13 This half *s* is an offering

SHELTER
Ps 27: 5 me in the *s* of his tabernacle
31:20 In the *s* of your presence you hide
55: 8 I would hurry to my place of *s*,
61: 4 take refuge in the *s* of your wings.
91: 1 in the *s* of the Most High
Ecc 7:12 Wisdom is a *s*
Isa 4: 6 It will be a *s* and shade
25: 4 a *s* from the storm
32: 2 Each man will be like a *s*
58: 7 the poor wanderer with *s*—

SHEM
Son of Noah (Ge 5:32; 6:10). Blessed (Ge 9:26). Descendants (Ge 10:21-31; 11:10-32).

SHEPHERD (SHEPHERDS)
Ge 48:15 the God who has been my *s*
49:24 because of the *S*, the Rock of Israel
Nu 27:17 will not be like sheep without a *s*."
2Sa 7: 7 commanded to *s* my people Israel,
1Ki 22:17 on the hills like sheep without a *s*,
Ps 23: 1 LORD is my *s*, I shall not be in want.
28: 9 be their *s* and carry them forever.
80: 1 Hear us, O *S* of Israel,
Isa 40:11 He tends his flock like a *s*:
Jer 31:10 will watch over his flock like a *s*.'
Eze 34: 5 scattered because there was no *s*,
34:12 As a *s* looks after his scattered

Zec 11: 9 and said, "I will not be your *s.*
11:17 "Woe to the worthless *s,*
13: 7 "Strike the *s,*
Mt 2: 6 who will be the *s* of my people
9:36 and helpless, like sheep without a *s.*
26:31 " 'I will strike the *s,*
Jn 10:11 The good *s* lays down his life
10:14 "I am the good *s;* I know my sheep
10:16 there shall be one flock and one *s.*
Heb 13:20 that great *S* of the sheep, equip you
1Pe 5: 4 And when the Chief *S* appears,
Rev 7:17 of the throne will be their *s;*

SHEPHERDS (SHEPHERD)
Jer 23: 1 "Woe to the *s* who are destroying
50: 6 their *s* have led them astray
Eze 34: 2 prophesy against the *s* of Israel;
Lk 2: 8 there were *s* living out in the fields
Ac 20:28 Be *s* of the church of God,
1Pe 5: 2 Be *s* of God's flock that is
Jude :12 *s* who feed only themselves.

SHIBBOLETH*
Jdg 12: 6 No," they said, "All right, say '*S.*' "

SHIELD (SHIELDED SHIELDS)
Ge 15: 1 I am your *s,*
2Sa 22: 3 my *s* and the horn of my salvation.
22:36 You give me your *s* of victory;
Ps 3: 3 But you are a *s* around me,
5:12 with your favor as with a *s.*
7:10 My *s* is God Most High,
18: 2 He is my *s* and the horn
28: 7 LORD is my strength and my *s;*
33:20 he is our help and our *s.*
84:11 For the LORD God is a sun and *s;*
91: 4 his faithfulness will be your *s*
115: 9 he is their help and *s.*
119:114 You are my refuge and my *s;*
144: 2 my *s,* in whom I take refuge,
Pr 2: 7 he is a *s* to those whose walk is
30: 5 he is a *s* to those who take refuge
Eph 6:16 to all this, take up the *s* of faith,

SHIELDED (SHIELD)
1Pe 1: 5 through faith are *s* by God's power

SHIELDS (SHIELD)
Dt 33:12 for he *s* him all day long,

SHIFTLESS*
Pr 19:15 and the *s* man goes hungry.

SHIMEI
Cursed David (2Sa 16:5-14); spared (2Sa 19: 16-23). Killed by Solomon (1Ki 2:8-9, 36-46).

SHINE (SHINES SHINING SHONE)
Nu 6:25 the LORD make his face *s*
Job 33:30 that the light of life may *s* on him.
Ps 4: 6 Let the light of your face *s* upon us,
37: 6 make your righteousness *s* like
67: 1 and make his face *s* upon us; *Selah*
80: 1 between the cherubim, *s* forth
118: 27 and he has made his light *s* upon us.
Isa 60: 1 "Arise, *s,* for your light has come,
Da 12: 3 are wise will *s* like the brightness
Mt 5:16 let your light *s* before men,
13:43 the righteous will *s* like the sun
2Co 4: 6 made his light *s* in our hearts
Eph 5:14 and Christ will *s* on you."
Php 2:15 in which you *s* like stars

SHINES (SHINE)
Ps 50: 2 God *s* forth.
Pr 13: 9 The light of the righteous *s* brightly
Jn 1: 5 The light *s* in the darkness,

SHINING (SHINE)
Pr 4:18 *s* ever brighter till the full light
2Pe 1:19 as to a light *s* in a dark place,
Rev 1:16 His face was like the sun *s*

SHIPS
Pr 31:14 She is like the merchant *s,*

SHIPWRECKED*
2Co 11:25 I was stoned, three times I was *s,*
1Ti 1:19 and so have *s* their faith.

SHISHAK
1Ki 14:25 *S* king of Egypt attacked Jerusalem
2Ch 12: 2 *S* king of Egypt attacked Jerusalem

SHOCKING*
Jer 5:30 "A horrible and *s* thing

SHONE (SHINE)
Mt 17: 2 His face *s* like the sun,
Lk 2: 9 glory of the Lord *s* around them,
Rev 21:11 It *s* with the glory of God,

SHOOT
Isa 53: 2 up before him like a tender *s,*
Ro 11:17 and you, though a wild olive *s,*

SHORE
Lk 5: 3 asked him to put out a little from *s.*

SHORT (SHORTENED)
Nu 11:23 "Is the LORD's arm too *s?*
Isa 50: 2 Was my arm too *s* to ransom you?
59: 1 of the LORD is not too *s* to save,
Mt 24:22 If those days had not been cut *s,*
Ro 3:23 and fall *s* of the glory of God,
1Co 7:29 brothers, is that the time is *s.*
Heb 4: 1 of you be found to have fallen *s* of it
Rev 20: 3 he must be set free for a *s* time.

SHORTENED (SHORT)
Mt 24:22 of the elect those days will be *s.*

SHOULDER (SHOULDERS)
Zep 3: 9 and serve him *s* to *s.*

SHOULDERS (SHOULDER)
Dt 33:12 LORD loves rests between his *s.*"
Isa 9: 6 and the government will be on his *s*
Lk 15: 5 he joyfully puts it on his *s*

SHOUT (SHOUTED)
Ps 47: 1 *s* to God with cries of joy.
66: 1 *S* with joy to God, all the earth!
95: 1 let us *s* aloud to the Rock
98: 4 *S* for joy to the LORD, all the earth
100: 1 *S* for joy to the LORD, all the earth
Isa 12: 6 *S* aloud and sing for joy, people
26:19 wake up and *s* for joy.
35: 6 the mute tongue *s* for joy.
40: 9 lift up your voice with a *s,*
42: 2 He will not *s* or cry out,
44:23 *s* aloud, O earth beneath.
54: 1 burst into song, *s* for joy,
Zec 9: 9 *S,* Daughter of Jerusalem!

SHOUTED (SHOUT)
Job 38: 7 and all the angels *s* for joy?

SHOW (SHOWED)
Ex 18:20 and *s* them the way to live
33:18 Moses said, "Now *s* me your glory
2Sa 22:26 the faithful you *s* yourself faithful,
1Ki 2: 2 "So be strong, *s* yourself a man,
Ps 17: 7 *S* the wonder of your great love,
25: 4 *S* me your ways, O LORD,
39: 4 "*S* me, O LORD, my life's end
85: 7 *S* us your unfailing love, O LORD,
143: 8 *S* me the way I should go,
Pr 23: 4 have the wisdom to *s* restraint.
SS 2:14 *s* me your face,
Isa 5:16 the holy God will *s* himself holy
30:18 he rises to *s* you compassion.
Eze 28:25 I will *s* myself holy among them
Joel 2:30 I will *s* wonders in the heavens
Zec 7: 9 *s* mercy and compassion
Ac 2:19 I will *s* wonders in the heaven
10:34 it is that God does not *s* favoritism
1Co 12:31 now I will *s* you the most excellent
Eph 2: 7 ages he might *s* the incomparable
Tit 2: 7 In your teaching *s* integrity,
Jas 2:18 I will *s* you my faith by what I do.
Jude :23 to others *s* mercy, mixed with fear

SHOWED (SHOW)
1Ki 3: 3 Solomon *s* his love for the LORD
Lk 24:40 he *s* them his hands and feet.
1Jn 4: 9 This is how God *s* his love

SHOWERS
Eze 34:26 in season; there will be *s* of blessing
Hos 10:12 and *s* righteousness on you.

SHREWD
2Sa 22:27 to the crooked you show yourself *s.*
Mt 10:16 Therefore be as *s* as snakes and

SHRINK (SHRINKS)
Heb 10:39 But we are not of those who *s* back

SHRINKS* (SHRINK)
Heb 10:38 And if he *s* back,

SHRIVEL
Isa 64: 6 we all *s* up like a leaf,

SHUDDER
Eze 32:10 and their kings will *s* with horror

SHUHITE
Job 2:11 Bildad the *S* and Zophar

SHUN* (SHUNS)
Job 28:28 and to *s* evil is understanding.' "

Pr 3: 7 fear the LORD and *s* evil.

SHUNS (SHUN)
Job 1: 8 a man who fears God and *s* evil."
Pr 14:16 man fears the LORD and *s* evil,

SHUT
Ge 7:16 Then the LORD *s* him in.
Isa 22:22 what he opens no one can *s,*
60:11 they will never be *s,* day or night,
Da 6:22 and he *s* the mouths of the lions.
Heb 11:33 who *s* the mouths of lions,
Rev 3: 7 no one can *s,* and what he shuts
21:25 On no day will its gates ever be *s,*

SICK (SICKNESS)
Pr 13:12 Hope deferred makes the heart *s,*
Eze 34: 4 or healed the *s* or bound up
Mt 9:12 who need a doctor, but the *s.*
10: 8 Heal the *s,* raise the dead, cleanse
25:36 I was *s* and you looked after me,
1Co 11:30 many among you are weak and *s,*
Jas 5:14 of you *s?* He should call the elders

SICKBED* (BED)
Ps 41: 3 LORD will sustain him on his *s*

SICKLE
Joel 3:13 Swing the *s,*
Rev 14:14 gold on his head and a sharp *s*

SICKNESS (SICK)
Mt 4:23 and healing every disease and *s*

SIDE (SIDES)
Ps 91: 7 A thousand may fall at your *s,*
124: 1 If the LORD had not been on our *s*
Jn 18:37 Everyone on the *s* of truth listens
20:20 he showed them his hands and *s.*
2Ti 4:17 But the Lord stood at my *s*
Heb 10:33 at other times you stood *s* by *s*

SIDES (SIDE)
Nu 33:55 in your eyes and thorns in your *s.*

SIFT
Lk 22:31 Satan has asked to *s* you as wheat.

SIGHING
Isa 35:10 and sorrow and *s* will flee away.

SIGHT
Ps 51: 4 and done what is evil in your *s,*
90: 4 For a thousand years in your *s*
116: 15 Precious in the *s* of the LORD
Pr 3: 4 in the *s* of God and man.
Mt 11: 5 The blind receive *s,* the lame walk,
Ac 4:19 right in God's *s* to obey you rather
1Co 3:19 this world is foolishness in God's *s.*
2Co 5: 7 We live by faith, not by *s.*
1Pe 3: 4 which is of great worth in God's *s.*

SIGN (SIGNS)
Ge 9:12 "This is the *s* of the covenant I am
17:11 and it will be the *s* of the covenant
Isa 7:14 the Lord himself will give you a *s:*
55:13 for an everlasting *s,*
Eze 20:12 I gave them my Sabbaths as a *s*
Mt 12:38 to see a miraculous *s* from you."
24: 3 what will be the *s* of your coming
24:30 "At that time the *s* of the Son
Lk 2:12 This will be a *s* to you: You will
11:29 It asks for a miraculous *s,*
Ro 4:11 he received the *s* of circumcision,
1Co 11:10 to have a *s* of authority on her head
14:22 are a *s,* not for believers

SIGNS (SIGN)
Ge 1:14 let them serve as *s* to mark seasons
Ps 78:43 day he displayed his miraculous *s*
105: 27 They performed his miraculous *s*
Da 6:27 he performs *s* and wonders
Mt 24:24 and perform great *s* and miracles
Mk 16:17 these *s* will accompany those who
Jn 3: 2 perform the miraculous *s* you are
20:30 Jesus did many other miraculous *s*
Ac 2:19 and *s* on the earth below,
1Co 1:22 Jews demand miraculous *s*
2Co 12:12 *s,* wonders and miracles—
2Th 2: 9 *s* and wonders, and in every sort

SIHON
Nu 21:21 to say to *S* king of the Amorites:
Ps 136: 19 *S* king of the Amorites

SILAS*
Prophet (Ac 15:22-32); co-worker with Paul on second missionary journey (Ac 16-18; 2Co 1:19). Co-writer with Paul (1Th 1:1; 2Th 1:1); Peter (1Pe 5:12).

SILENCE (SILENCED SILENT)
1Pe 2:15 good you should s the ignorant talk
Rev 8: 1 there was s in heaven

SILENCED (SILENCE)
Ro 3:19 so that every mouth may be s
Tit 1:11 They must be s, because they are

SILENT (SILENCE)
Est 4:14 For if you remain s at this time,
Ps 30:12 to you and not be s.
32: 3 When I kept s,
39: 2 But when I was s and still,
Pr 17:28 a fool is thought wise if he keeps s,
Ecc 3: 7 a time to be s and a time to speak,
Isa 53: 7 as a sheep before her shearers is s,
62: 1 For Zion's sake I will not keep s,
Hab 2:20 let all the earth be s before him."
Ac 8:32 and as a lamb before the shearer is s
1Co 14:34 women should remain s
1Ti 2:12 over a man; she must be s.

SILVER
Ps 12: 6 like s refined in a furnace of clay,
66:10 you refined us like s.
Pr 2: 4 and if you look for it as for s
3:14 for she is more profitable than s
8:10 Choose my instruction instead of s,
22: 1 to be esteemed is better than s
25: 4 Remove the dross from the s,
25:11 is like apples of gold in settings of s.
Isa 48:10 I have refined you, though not as s;
Eze 22:18 They are but the dross of s.
Da 2:32 its chest and arms of s, its belly
Hag 2: 8 'The s is mine and the gold is mine,'
Zec 13: 9 I will refine them like s
Ac 3: 6 Peter said, "S or gold I do not have,
1Co 3:12 s, costly stones, wood, hay or straw
1Pe 1:18 not with perishable things such as s

SILVERSMITH
Ac 19:24 A s named Demetrius, who made

SIMEON
Son of Jacob by Leah (Ge 29:33; 35:23; 1Ch 2:1). With Levi killed Shechem for rape of Dinah (Ge 34:25-29). Held hostage by Joseph in Egypt (Ge 42:24-43:23). Tribe of blessed (Ge 49:5-7), numbered (Nu 1:23; 26:14), allotted land (Jos 19:1-9; Eze 48:24), 12,000 from (Rev 7:7).

SIMON
1. See PETER.
2. Apostle, called the Zealot (Mt 10:4; Mk 3:18; Lk 6:15; Ac 1:13).
3. Samaritan sorcerer (Ac 8:9-24).

SIMPLE
Ps 19: 7 making wise the s.
119:130 it gives understanding to the s.
Pr 8: 5 You who are s, gain prudence;
14:15 A s man believes anything,

SIMPLEHEARTED* (HEART)
Ps 116: 6 The LORD protects the s;

SIN (SINFUL SINNED SINNER SINNERS SINNING SINS)
Ge 4: 7 s is crouching at your door;
Ex 32:32 please forgive their s— but if not,
Nu 5: 7 and must confess the s he has
32:23 be sure that your s will find you
Dt 24:16 each is to die for his own s.
1Sa 12:23 it from me that I should s
15:23 For rebellion is like the s
1Ki 8:46 for there is no one who does not s
2Ch 7:14 and will forgive their s and will heal
Job 1:22 Job did not s by charging God
Ps 4: 4 In your anger do not s;
17: 3 resolved that my mouth will not s.
32: 2 whose s the LORD does not count
32: 5 Then I acknowledged my s to you
36: 2 too much to detect or hate his s.
38:18 I am troubled by my s.
39: 1 and keep my tongue from s;
51: 2 and cleanse me from my s.
66:18 If I had cherished s in my heart,
119: 11 that I might not s against you.
119:133 let no s rule over me.
Pr 5:22 the cords of his s hold him fast.
10:19 words are many, s is not absent,
14: 9 Fools mock at making amends for s
16: 6 faithfulness s is atoned for;
17:19 He who loves a quarrel loves s;
20: 9 I am clean and without s"?
Isa 3: 9 they parade their s like Sodom;
6: 7 is taken away and your s atoned
64: 5 But when we continued to s
Jer 31:30 everyone will die for his own s;
Eze 3:18 that wicked man will die for his s,
18:26 his righteousness and commits s,
33: 8 that wicked man will die for his s,
Am 4: 4 "Go to Bethel and s;
Mic 6: 7 of my body for the s of my soul?
7:18 who pardons s and forgives
Zec 3: 4 "See, I have taken away your s,
Mt 18: 6 little ones who believe in me to s,
Mk 3:29 he is guilty of an eternal s."
9:43 If your hand causes you to s,
Lk 17: 1 people to s are bound to come,
Jn 1:29 who takes away the s of the world!
8: 7 "If any one of you is without s,
8:34 everyone who sins is a slave to s.
8:46 Can any of you prove me guilty of s
Ro 2:12 All who s apart from the law will
5:12 as s entered the world
5:20 where s increased, grace increased
6: 2 By no means! We died to s;
6:11 count yourselves dead to s
6:14 For s shall not be your master,
6:23 For the wages of s is death,
7: 7 I would not have known what s was
7:25 sinful nature a slave to the law of s.
14:23 that does not come from faith is s.
1Co 8:12 When you s against your brothers
15:56 The sting of death is s,
2Co 5:21 God made him who had no s to be s
Gal 6: 1 if someone is caught in a s,
1Ti 5:20 Those who s are to be rebuked
Heb 4:15 just as we are—yet was without s.
9:26 to do away with s by the sacrifice
11:25 the pleasures of s for a short time.
12: 1 and the s that so easily entangles,
Jas 1:15 it gives birth to s; and s,
1Pe 2:22 "He committed no s,
1Jn 1: 7 his Son, purifies us from all s.
1: 8 If we claim to be without s,
2: 1 But if anybody does s, we have one
3: 4 in fact, s is lawlessness.
3: 5 And in him is no s.
3: 6 No one who continues to s has
3: 9 born of God will continue to s,
5:16 There is a s that leads to death.
5:17 All wrongdoing is s, and there is s
5:18 born of God does not continue to s;

SINAI
Ex 19:20 descended to the top of Mount S
31:18 speaking to Moses on Mount S,
Ps 68:17 from S into his sanctuary.

SINCERE* (SINCERITY)
Da 11:34 many who are not s will join them.
Ac 2:46 ate together with glad and s hearts,
Ro 12: 9 Love must be s.
2Co 6: 6 in the Holy Spirit and in s love;
11: 3 somehow be led astray from your s
1Ti 1: 5 a good conscience and a s faith.
3: 8 s, not indulging in much wine,
2Ti 1: 5 have been reminded of your s faith,
Heb 10:22 near to God with a s heart
Jas 3:17 and good fruit, impartial and s.
1Pe 1:22 the truth so that you have s love

SINCERITY* (SINCERE)
1Co 5: 8 bread without yeast, the bread of s
2Co 1:12 in the holiness and s that are
2:17 speak before God with s,
8: 8 but I want to test the s of your love
Eph 6: 5 and with s of heart, just
Col 3:22 but with s of heart and reverence

SINFUL (SIN)
Ps 51: 5 Surely I was s at birth,
51: 5 s from the time my mother
Lk 5: 8 from me, Lord; I am a s man!"
Ro 7: 5 we were controlled by the s nature,
7:18 lives in me, that is, in my s nature.
7:25 but in the s nature a slave to the law
8: 3 Son in the likeness of s man
8: 4 not live according to the s nature
8: 7 the s mind is hostile to God.
8: 8 by the s nature cannot please God.
8: 9 are controlled not by the s nature
8:13 if you live according to the s nature
13:14 to gratify the desires of the s nature
1Co 5: 5 so that the s nature may be
Gal 5:13 freedom to indulge the s nature;
5:16 gratify the desires of the s nature.
5:19 The acts of the s nature are obvious
5:24 Jesus have crucified the s nature
6: 8 sows to please his s nature,
Col 2:11 in the putting off of the s nature,
Heb 3:12 brothers, that none of you has a s,
1Pe 2:11 abstain from s desires, which war
1Jn 3: 8 He who does what is s is

SING (SANG SINGER SINGING SINGS SONG SONGS SUNG)
Ex 15: 1 "I will s to the LORD,
Ps 5:11 let them ever s for joy.
13: 6 I will s to the LORD,
30: 4 S to the LORD, you saints of his;
33: 1 S joyfully to the LORD, you
47: 6 S praises to God, s praises;
57: 7 I will s and make music.
59:16 But I will s of your strength,
63: 7 I s in the shadow of your wings.
66: 2 S to the glory of his name;
89: 1 I will s of the LORD's great love
95: 1 Come, let us s for joy to the LORD
96: 1 S to the LORD a new song;
98: 1 S to the LORD a new song,
101: 1 I will s of your love and justice;
108: 1 I will s and make music
137: 3 "S us one of the songs of Zion!"
147: 1 is to s praises to our God,
149: 1 S to the LORD a new song,
Isa 54: 1 "S, O barren woman,
1Co 14:15 also pray with my mind; I will s
Eph 5:19 S and make music in your heart
Col 3:16 and as you s psalms, hymns
Jas 5:13 Is anyone happy? Let him s songs

SINGER* (SING)
2Sa 23: 1 Israel's s of songs:

SINGING (SING)
Ps 63: 5 with s lips my mouth will praise
68: 6 he leads forth the prisoners with s;
98: 5 with the harp and the sound of s,
Isa 35:10 They will enter Zion with s;
Zep 3:17 he will rejoice over you with s."
Ac 16:25 Silas were praying and s hymns
Rev 5:13 on the sea, and all that is in them, s:

SINGLE
Ex 23:29 I will not drive them out in a s year,
Mt 6:27 you by worrying can add a s hour
Gal 5:14 law is summed up in a s command:

SINGS (SING)
Eze 33:32 more than one who s love songs

SINNED (SIN)
Lev 5: 5 confess in what way he has s
1Sa 15:24 Then Saul said to Samuel, "I have s
2Sa 12:13 "I have s against the LORD."
24:10 I have s greatly in what I have done
2Ch 6:37 'We have s, we have done wrong
Job 1: 5 "Perhaps my children have s
33:27 'I s, and perverted what was right,
Ps 51: 4 Against you, you only, have I s
Jer 2:35 because you say, 'I have not s.'
14:20 we have indeed s against you.
Da 9: 5 we have s and done wrong.
Mic 7: 9 Because I have s against him,
Mt 27: 4 "I have s," he said,
Lk 15:18 I have s against heaven
Ro 3:23 for all have s and fall short
5:12 all s— for before the law was given,
2Pe 2: 4 did not spare angels when they s,
1Jn 1:10 claim we have not s, we make him

SINNER (SIN)
Ecc 9:18 but one s destroys much good.
Lk 15: 7 in heaven over one s who repents
18:13 'God, have mercy on me, a s.'
1Co 14:24 convinced by all that he is a s
Jas 5:20 Whoever turns a s from the error
1Pe 4:18 become of the ungodly and the s?"

SINNERS (SIN)
Ps 1: 1 or stand in the way of s
37:38 But all s will be destroyed;
Pr 1:10 My son, if s entice you,
23:17 Do not let your heart envy s,
Mt 9:13 come to call the righteous, but s."
Ro 5: 8 While we were still s, Christ died
Gal 2:17 evident that we ourselves are s,
1Ti 1:15 came into the world to save s—
Heb 7:26 set apart from s, exalted

SINNING (SIN)
Ex 20:20 be with you to keep you from s."
1Co 15:34 stop s; for there are some who are
Heb 10:26 If we deliberately keep on s
1Jn 3: 6 No one who lives in him keeps on s
3: 9 go on s, because he has been born

SINS (SIN)
Lev 5: 1 " 'If a person s because he does not
16:30 you will be clean from all your s.
26:40 " 'But if they will confess their s
Nu 15:30 " 'But anyone who s defiantly,
1Sa 2:25 If a man s against another man,
2Ki 14: 6 each is to die for his own s."

Ezr 9: 6 our *s* are higher than our heads
9:13 less than our *s* have deserved
Ps 19:13 your servant also from willful *s*;
32: 1 whose *s* are covered.
51: 9 Hide your face from my *s*
79: 9 deliver us and forgive our *s*
85: 2 and covered all their *s*.
103: 3 who forgives all your *s*
103: 10 does not treat us as our *s* deserve
130: 3 O LORD, kept a record of *s*,
Pr 14:21 He who despises his neighbor *s*,
28:13 who conceals his *s* does not
29:22 one commits many *s*.
Ecc 7:20 who does what is right and never *s*.
Isa 1:18 "Though your *s* are like scarlet,
38:17 you have put all my *s*
43:25 and remembers your *s* no more.
59: 2 your *s* have hidden his face
64: 6 like the wind our *s* sweep us away.
Jer 31:34 and will remember their *s* no more
La 3:39 complain when punished for his *s*?
Eze 18: 4 soul who *s* is the one who will die.
33:10 Our offenses and *s* weigh us down,
36:33 day I cleanse you from all your *s*,
Hos 14: 1 Your *s* have been your downfall!
Mt 1:21 he will save his people from their *s*
6:15 if you do not forgive men their *s*,
9: 6 authority on earth to forgive *s* . . . . . . "
18:15 "If your brother *s* against you,
26:28 for many for the forgiveness of *s*.
Lk 5:24 authority on earth to forgive *s* . . . . . . "
11: 4 Forgive us our *s*,
17: 3 "If your brother *s*, rebuke him,
Jn 8:24 you will indeed die in your *s*."
20:23 If you forgive anyone his *s*,
Ac 2:38 for the forgiveness of your *s*.
3:19 so that your *s* may be wiped out,
10:43 forgiveness of *s* through his name."
22:16 be baptized and wash your *s* away,
26:18 they may receive forgiveness of *s*
Ro 4: 7 whose *s* are covered.
4:25 delivered over to death for our *s*
1Co 15: 3 died for our *s* according
2Co 5:19 not counting men's *s* against them.
Gal 1: 4 himself for our *s* to rescue us
Eph 2: 1 dead in your transgressions and *s*,
Col 2:13 us all our *s*, having canceled
1Ti 5:22 and do not share in the *s* of others.
Heb 1: 3 he had provided purification for *s*,
2:17 atonement for the *s* of the people.
7:27 He sacrificed for their *s* once for all
8:12 and will remember their *s* no more
9:28 to take away the *s* of many people;
10: 4 of bulls and goats to take away *s*.
10:12 for all time one sacrifice for *s*,
10:26 of the truth, no sacrifice for *s* is left,
Jas 4:17 ought to do and doesn't do it, *s*.
5:16 Therefore confess your *s*
5:20 and cover over a multitude of *s*.
1Pe 2:24 He himself bore our *s* in his body
3:18 For Christ died for *s* once for all,
4: 8 love covers over a multitude of *s*.
1Jn 1: 9 If we confess our *s*, he is faithful
2: 2 He is the atoning sacrifice for our *s*,
3: 5 so that he might take away our *s*.
4:10 as an atoning sacrifice for our *s*.
Rev 1: 5 has freed us from our *s* by his blood

SISERA
Jdg 4: 2 The commander of his army was *S*,
5:26 She struck *S*, she crushed his head,

SISTER (SISTERS)
Lev 18: 9 have sexual relations with your *s*,
Mk 3:35 does God's will is my brother and *s*

SISTERS (SISTER)
Mt 19:29 or brothers or *s* or father or mother
1Ti 5: 2 as *s*, with absolute purity.

SIT (SAT SITS SITTING)
Dt 6: 7 them when you *s* at home
1Ki 8:25 fail to have a man to *s* before me
Ps 1: 1 or *s* in the seat of mockers.
26: 5 and refuse to *s* with the wicked.
80: 1 you who *s* enthroned
110: 1 "*S* at my right hand
139: 2 You know when I *s* and when I rise
SS 2: 3 I delight to *s* in his shade,
Isa 16: 5 in faithfulness a man will *s* on it—
Mic 4: 4 Every man will *s* under his own
Mt 20:23 to *s* at my right or left is not for me
22:44 "*S* at my right hand
Lk 22:30 in my kingdom and *s* on thrones,
Heb 1:13 "*S* at my right hand
Rev 3:21 right to *s* with me on my throne,

SITS (SIT)
Ps 99: 1 *s* enthroned between the cherubim,
Isa 40:22 He *s* enthroned above the circle
Mt 19:28 of Man *s* on his glorious throne,
Rev 4: 9 thanks to him who *s* on the throne

SITTING (SIT)
Est 2:19 Mordecai was *s* at the king's gate.
Mt 26:64 the Son of Man *s* at the right hand
Rev 4: 2 in heaven with someone *s* on it.

SITUATION (SITUATIONS)
1Co 7:24 remain in the *s* God called him
Php 4:12 of being content in any and every *s*,

SITUATIONS* (SITUATION)
2Ti 4: 5 head in all *s*, endure hardship,

SKIES (SKY)
Ps 19: 1 the *s* proclaim the work
71:19 Your righteousness reaches to the *s*
108: 4 your faithfulness reaches to the *s*.

SKILL (SKILLED SKILLFUL)
Ps 137: 5 may my right hand forget its *s*,
Ecc 10:10 but *s* will bring success.

SKILLED (SKILL)
Pr 22:29 Do you see a man *s* in his work?

SKILLFUL (SKILL)
Ps 45: 1 my tongue is the pen of a *s* writer.
78:72 with *s* hands he led them.

SKIN (SKINS)
Job 19:20 with only the *s* of my teeth.
19:26 And after my *s* has been destroyed,
Jer 13:23 Can the Ethiopian change his *s*

SKINS (SKIN)
Ex 25: 5 ram *s* dyed red and hides
Lk 5:37 the new wine will burst the *s*,

SKULL
Mt 27:33 (which means The Place of the *S*).

SKY (SKIES)
Ge 1: 8 God called the expanse "*s*."
Pr 30:19 the way of an eagle in the *s*,
Isa 34: 4 and the *s* rolled up like a scroll;
Jer 33:22 stars of the *s* and as measureless
Mt 24:29 the stars will fall from the *s*,
24:30 coming on the clouds of the *s*,
Rev 20:11 Earth and *s* fled from his presence,

SLACK*
Pr 18: 9 One who is *s* in his work

SLAIN (SLAY)
1Sa 18: 7 "Saul has *s* his thousands,
Eze 37: 9 into these *s*, that they may live.' "
Rev 5: 6 as if it had been *s*, standing
5:12 "Worthy is the Lamb, who was *s*,
6: 9 the souls of those who had been *s*

SLANDER (SLANDERED SLANDERER SLANDERERS SLANDEROUS)
Lev 19:16 " 'Do not go about spreading *s*
Ps 15: 3 and has no *s* on his tongue,
Pr 10:18 and whoever spreads *s* is a fool.
2Co 12:20 outbursts of anger, factions, *s*,
Eph 4:31 rage and anger, brawling and *s*,
1Ti 5:14 the enemy no opportunity for *s*.
Tit 3: 2 to *s* no one, to be peaceable
1Pe 3:16 in Christ may be ashamed of their *s*
2Pe 2:10 afraid to *s* celestial beings;

SLANDERED (SLANDER)
1Co 4:13 when we are *s*, we answer kindly.

SLANDERER (SLANDER)
1Co 5:11 an idolater or a *s*, a drunkard

SLANDERERS (SLANDER)
Ro 1:30 They are gossips, *s*, God-haters,
1Co 6:10 nor the greedy nor drunkards nor *s*
Tit 2: 3 not to be *s* or addicted

SLANDEROUS (SLANDER)
2Ti 3: 3 unforgiving, *s*, without self-control
2Pe 2:11 do not bring *s* accusations

SLAUGHTER (SLAUGHTERED)
Isa 53: 7 he was led like a lamb to the *s*,
Jer 11:19 been like a gentle lamb led to the *s*;
Ac 8:32 "He was led like a sheep to the *s*,

SLAUGHTERED (SLAUGHTER)
Ps 44:22 we are considered as sheep to be *s*.
Ro 8:36 we are considered as sheep to be *s*

SLAVE (ENSLAVED SLAVERY SLAVES)
Ge 21:10 "Get rid of that *s* woman
Mt 20:27 wants to be first must be your *s*—
Jn 8:34 everyone who sins is a *s* to sin.
Ro 7:14 I am unspiritual, sold as a *s* to sin.
1Co 7:21 Were you a *s* when you were called
12:13 whether Jews or Greeks, *s* or free
Gal 3:28 *s* nor free, male nor female,
4: 7 So you are no longer a *s*, but a son;
4:30 Get rid of the *s* woman and her son
Col 3:11 barbarian, Scythian, *s* or free,
1Ti 1:10 for *s* traders and liars and perjurers
Phm :16 no longer as a *s*, but better than a *s*,
2Pe 2:19 a man is a *s* to whatever has

SLAVERY (SLAVE)
Ex 2:23 The Israelites groaned in their *s*
Ro 6:19 parts of your body in *s* to impurity
Gal 4: 3 were in *s* under the basic principles
1Ti 6: 1 of *s* should consider their masters

SLAVES (SLAVE)
Ps 123: 2 As the eyes of *s* look to the hand
Ecc 10: 7 I have seen *s* on horseback,
Ro 6: 6 that we should no longer be *s* to sin
6:16 you are *s* to sin, which leads
6:22 and have become *s* to God,
Gal 2: 4 in Christ Jesus and to make us *s*.
4: 8 you were *s* to those who
Eph 6: 5 *S*, obey your earthly masters
Col 3:22 *S*, obey your earthly masters
4: 1 provide your *s* with what is right
Tit 2: 9 Teach *s* to be subject

SLAY (SLAIN)
Job 13:15 Though he *s* me, yet will I hope

SLEEP (ASLEEP SLEEPER SLEEPING SLEEPS)
Ge 2:21 the man to fall into a deep *s*;
15:12 Abram fell into a deep *s*,
28:11 it under his head and lay down to *s*.
Ps 4: 8 I will lie down and *s* in peace,
121: 4 will neither slumber nor *s*.
127: 2 for he grants *s* to those he loves.
Pr 6: 9 When will you get up from your *s*?
Ecc 5:12 The *s* of a laborer is sweet,
1Co 15:51 We will not all *s*, but we will all be
1Th 5: 7 For those who *s*, *s* at night,

SLEEPER (SLEEP)
Eph 5:14 "Wake up, O *s*,

SLEEPING (SLEEP)
Mk 13:36 suddenly, do not let him find you *s*.

SLEEPLESS*
2Co 6: 5 in hard work, *s* nights and hunger;

SLEEPS (SLEEP)
Pr 10: 5 he who *s* during harvest is

SLIMY
Ps 40: 2 He lifted me out of the *s* pit,

SLING
1Sa 17:50 over the Philistine with a *s*

SLIP (SLIPPING)
Dt 4: 9 let them *s* from your heart as long
Ps 121: 3 He will not let your foot *s*—

SLIPPING (SLIP)
Ps 66: 9 and kept our feet from *s*.

SLOW
Ex 34: 6 and gracious God, *s* to anger,
Jas 1:19 *s* to speak and *s* to become angry,
2Pe 3: 9 The Lord is not *s* in keeping his

SLUGGARD
Pr 6: 6 Go to the ant, you *s*;
13: 4 The *s* craves and gets nothing,
20: 4 A *s* does not plow in season;
26:15 The *s* buries his hand in the dish;

SLUMBER
Ps 121: 3 he who watches over you will not *s*;
Pr 6:10 A little sleep, a little *s*,
Ro 13:11 for you to wake up from your *s*,

SLUR
Ps 15: 3 and casts no *s* on his fellow man,

SMELL
Ecc 10: 1 As dead flies give perfume a bad *s*,
2Co 2:16 To the one we are the *s* of death;

SMITTEN
Isa 53: 4 *s* by him, and afflicted.

SMOKE
Ex 19:18 Mount Sinai was covered with *s,*
Ps 104: 32 touches the mountains, and they *s.*
Isa 6: 4 and the temple was filled with *s.*
Joel 2:30 blood and fire and billows of *s.*
Ac 2:19 blood and fire and billows of *s.*
Rev 15: 8 filled with *s* from the glory

SMYRNA
Rev 2: 8 the angel of the church in *S* write:

SNAKE (SNAKES)
Nu 21: 8 "Make a *s* and put it up on a pole;
Pr 23:32 In the end it bites like a *s*
Jn 3:14 Moses lifted up the *s* in the desert,

SNAKES (SNAKE)
Mt 10:16 as shrewd as *s* and as innocent
Mk 16:18 they will pick up *s* with their hands;

SNARE (ENSNARE ENSNARED SNARED)
Dt 7:16 for that will be a *s* to you.
Ps 69:22 before them become a *s;*
91: 3 from the fowler's *s*
Pr 29:25 Fear of man will prove to be a *s,*
Ro 11: 9 "May their table become a *s*

SNARED (SNARE)
Pr 3:26 will keep your foot from being *s.*

SNATCH
Jn 10:28 no one can *s* them out of my hand.
Jude :23 *s* others from the fire and save

SNOUT
Pr 11:22 Like a gold ring in a pig's *s*

SNOW
Ps 51: 7 and I will be whiter than *s.*
Isa 1:18 they shall be as white as *s;*

SNUFF (SNUFFED)
Isa 42: 3 a smoldering wick he will not *s* out.
Mt 12:20 a smoldering wick he will not *s* out,

SNUFFED (SNUFF)
Pr 13: 9 but the lamp of the wicked is *s* out.

SOAP
Mal 3: 2 a refiner's fire or a launderer's *s.*

SOAR (SOARED)
Isa 40:31 They will *s* on wings like eagles;

SOARED (SOAR)
2Sa 22:11 he *s* on the wings of the wind.

SOBER
Ro 12: 3 think of yourself with *s* judgment,

SODOM
Ge 13:12 and pitched his tents near *S.*
19:24 rained down burning sulfur on *S*
Isa 1: 9 we would have become like *S,*
Lk 10:12 on that day for *S* than for that town
Ro 9:29 we would have become like *S,*
Rev 11: 8 which is figuratively called *S*

SOIL
Ge 4: 2 kept flocks, and Cain worked the *s.*
Mt 13:23 on good *s* is the man who hears

SOLD (SELL)
1Ki 21:25 who *s* himself to do evil in the eyes
Mt 10:29 Are not two sparrows *s* for a penny
13:44 then in his joy went and *s* all he had
Ro 7:14 I am unspiritual, *s* as a slave to sin.

SOLDIER
1Co 9: 7 as a *s* at his own expense?
2Ti 2: 3 with us like a good *s* of Christ Jesus

SOLE
Dt 28:65 place for the *s* of your foot.
Isa 1: 6 From the *s* of your foot to the top

SOLID
2Ti 2:19 God's *s* foundation stands firm,
Heb 5:12 You need milk, not *s* food!

SOLOMON
Son of David by Bathsheba; king of Judah (2Sa 12:24; 1Ch 3:5, 10). Appointed king by David (1Ki 1); adversaries Adonijah, Joab, Shimei killed by Benaiah (1Ki 2). Asked for wisdom (1Ki 3; 2Ch 1). Judged between two prostitutes (1Ki 3:16-28). Built temple (1Ki 5-7; 2Ch 2-5); prayer of dedication (1Ki 8; 2Ch 6). Visited by Queen of Sheba (1Ki 10; 2Ch 9). Wives turned his heart from God (1Ki 11:1-13). Jeroboam rebelled against (1Ki 11:26-40). Death (1Ki 11:41-43; 2Ch 9:29-31).
Proverbs of (1Ki 4:32; Pr 1:1; 10:1; 25:1); psalms of (Ps 72; 127); song of (SS 1:1).

SON (SONS SONSHIP)
Ge 17:19 your wife Sarah will bear you a *s,*
21:10 rid of that slave woman and her *s,*
22: 2 "Take your *s,* your only *s,* Isaac,
Ex 11: 5 Every firstborn *s* in Egypt will die,
Dt 1:31 father carries his *s,* all the way you
6:20 In the future, when your *s* asks you,
8: 5 as a man disciplines his *s,*
21:18 rebellious *s* who does not obey his
2Sa 7:14 be his father, and he will be my *s.*
1Ki 3:20 and put her dead *s* by my breast.
Ps 2: 7 He said to me, "You are my *S;*
2:12 Kiss the *S,* lest he be angry
8: 4 the *s* of man that you care for him?
Pr 3:12 as a father the *s* he delights in.
6:20 My *s,* keep your father's
10: 1 A wise *s* brings joy to his father,
13:24 He who spares the rod hates his *s,*
29:17 Discipline your *s,* and he will give
Isa 7:14 with child and will give birth to a *s,*
Eze 18:20 The *s* will not share the guilt
Da 3:25 the fourth looks like a *s* of the gods
7:13 before me was one like a *s* of man,
Hos 11: 1 and out of Egypt I called my *s.*
Am 7:14 neither a prophet nor a prophet's *s,*
Mt 1: 1 of Jesus Christ the *s* of David,
1:21 She will give birth to a *s,*
2:15 "Out of Egypt I called my *s.*"
3:17 "This is my *S,* whom I love;
4: 3 "If you are the *S* of God, tell these
8:20 but the *S* of Man has no place
11:27 one knows the *S* except the Father,
12: 8 For the *S* of Man is Lord
12:32 a word against the *S* of Man will be
12:40 so the *S* of Man will be three days
13:41 *S* of Man will send out his angels,
13:55 "Isn't this the carpenter's *s?*
14:33 "Truly you are the *S* of God."
16:16 "You are the Christ, the *S*
16:27 For the *S* of Man is going to come
17: 5 "This is my *S,* whom I love;
19:28 when the *S* of Man sits
20:18 and the *S* of Man will be betrayed
20:28 as the *S* of Man did not come
21: 9 "Hosanna to the *S* of David!"
22:42 Whose *s* is he?" "The *s* of David,"
24:27 so will be the coming of the *S*
24:30 They will see the *S* of Man coming
24:44 the *S* of Man will come at an hour
25:31 "When the *S* of Man comes
26:63 if you are the Christ, the *S* of God."
27:54 "Surely he was the *S* of God!"
28:19 and of the *S* and of the Holy Spirit,
Mk 1:11 "You are my *S,* whom I love;
2:28 So the *S* of Man is Lord
8:38 the *S* of Man will be ashamed
9: 7 "This is my *S,* whom I love.
10:45 even the *S* of Man did not come
13:32 nor the *S,* but only the Father.
14:62 you will see the *S* of Man sitting
Lk 1:32 and will be called the *S*
2: 7 she gave birth to her firstborn, a *s.*
3:22 "You are my *S,* whom I love;
9:35 This is my *S,* whom I have chosen;
9:58 but the *S* of Man has no place
12: 8 the *S* of Man will also acknowledge
15:20 he ran to his *s,* threw his arms
18: 8 when the *S* of Man comes,
18:31 written by the prophets about the *S*
19:10 For the *S* of Man came to seek
Jn 1:34 I testify that this is the *S* of God."
3:14 so the *S* of Man must be lifted up,
3:16 that he gave his one and only *S,*
3:36 believes in the *S* has eternal life,
5:19 the *S* can do nothing by himself;
6:40 is that everyone who looks to the *S*
11: 4 so that God's *S* may be glorified
17: 1 Glorify your *S,* that your *S* may
Ac 7:56 and the *S* of Man standing
13:33 " 'You are my *S;*
Ro 1: 4 with power to be the *S* of God
5:10 to him through the death of his *S,*
8: 3 did by sending his own *S*
8:29 conformed to the likeness of his *S,*
8:32 He who did not spare his own *S,*
1Co 15:28 then the *S* himself will be made
Gal 2:20 I live by faith in the *S* of God,
4: 4 God sent his *S,* born of a woman,
4:30 rid of the slave woman and her *s,*
1Th 1:10 and to wait for his *S* from heaven,
Heb 1: 2 days he has spoken to us by his *S,*
1: 5 "You are my *S;*
2: 6 the *s* of man that you care for him?
4:14 Jesus the *S* of God, let us hold
5: 5 "You are my *S;*
7:28 appointed the *S,* who has been
10:29 punished who has trampled the *S*
Heb 12: 6 everyone he accepts as a *s.*"
2Pe 1:17 saying, "This is my *S,* whom I love;
1Jn 1: 3 is with the Father and with his *S,*
1: 7 his *S,* purifies us from all sin.
2:23 whoever acknowledges the *S* has
3: 8 reason the *S* of God appeared was
4: 9 only *S* into the world that we might
4:14 that the Father has sent his *S*
5: 5 he who believes that Jesus is the *S*
5:11 eternal life, and this life is in his *S.*
Rev 1:13 lampstands was someone "like a *s*
14:14 on the cloud was one "like a *s*

SONG (SING)
Ex 15: 2 LORD is my strength and my *s;*
Ps 40: 3 He put a new *s* in my mouth,
69:30 I will praise God's name in *s*
96: 1 Sing to the LORD a new *s;*
98: 4 burst into jubilant *s* with music;
119: 54 Your decrees are the theme of my *s*
149: 1 Sing to the LORD a new *s,*
Isa 49:13 burst into *s,* O mountains!
55:12 will burst into *s* before you,
Rev 5: 9 And they sang a new *s:*
15: 3 and sang the *s* of Moses the servant

SONGS (SING)
2Sa 23: 1 Israel's singer of *s:*
Job 35:10 who gives *s* in the night,
Ps 100: 2 come before him with joyful *s.*
126: 6 will return with *s* of joy,
137: 3 "Sing us one of the *s* of Zion!"
Eph 5:19 with psalms, hymns and spiritual *s.*
Jas 5:13 Is anyone happy? Let him sing *s*

SONS (SON)
Ge 6: 2 the *s* of God saw that the daughters
10:20 These are the *s* of Ham
Ru 4:15 who is better to you than seven *s,*
Ps 127: 3 *S* are a heritage from the LORD,
132: 12 if your *s* keep my covenant
Hos 1:10 they will be called '*s*
Joel 2:28 Your *s* and daughters will prophesy
Mt 5: 9 for they will be called *s* of God.
Lk 6:35 and you will be *s* of the Most High,
Jn 12:36 so that you may become *s* of light."
Ro 8:14 by the Spirit of God are *s* of God.
9:26 they will be called '*s*
2Co 6:18 and you will be my *s* and daughters
Gal 3:26 You are all *s* of God through faith
4: 5 we might receive the full rights of *s.*
4: 6 Because you are *s,* God sent
Heb 12: 7 discipline; God is treating you as *s.*

SONSHIP* (SON)
Ro 8:15 but you received the Spirit of *s.*

SORCERY
Lev 19:26 " 'Do not practice divination or *s.*

SORROW (SORROWS)
Ps 6: 7 My eyes grow weak with *s;*
116: 3 I was overcome by trouble and *s.*
Isa 60:20 and your days of *s* will end.
Jer 31:12 and they will *s* no more.
Ro 9: 2 I have great *s* and unceasing
2Co 7:10 Godly *s* brings repentance that

SORROWS (SORROW)
Isa 53: 3 a man of *s,* and familiar

SOUGHT (SEEK)
2Ch 26: 5 As long as he *s* the LORD,
31:21 he *s* his God and worked
Ps 34: 4 I *s* the LORD, and he answered me
119: 58 I have *s* your face with all my heart;

SOUL (SOULS)
Dt 6: 5 with all your *s* and with all your
10:12 all your heart and with all your *s,*
30: 6 all your heart and with all your *s,*
Jos 22: 5 with all your heart and all your *s.*"
2Ki 23:25 and with all his *s* and with all his
Ps 23: 3 he restores my *s.*
34: 2 My *s* will boast in the LORD;
42: 1 so my *s* pants for you, O God.
42:11 Why are you downcast, O my *s?*
62: 5 Find rest, O my *s,* in God alone;
63: 8 My *s* clings to you;
94:19 consolation brought joy to my *s.*
103: 1 Praise the LORD, O my *s;*
Pr 13:19 A longing fulfilled is sweet to the *s,*
16:24 sweet to the *s* and healing
22: 5 he who guards his *s* stays far
Isa 55: 2 your *s* will delight in the richest
La 3:20 and my *s* is downcast within me.
Eze 18: 4 For every living *s* belongs to me,
Mt 10:28 kill the body but cannot kill the *s.*
16:26 yet forfeits his *s?* Or what can
22:37 with all your *s* and with all your

Heb 4:12 even to dividing *s* and spirit,
3Jn :2 even as your *s* is getting along well.

SOULS (SOUL)
Pr 11:30 and he who wins *s* is wise.
Jer 6:16 and you will find rest for your *s*.
Mt 11:29 and you will find rest for your *s*.

SOUND (FINE-SOUNDING)
Ge 3: 8 and his wife heard the *s*
Pr 3:21 preserve *s* judgment
Eze 3:12 I heard behind me a loud rumbling *s*
Jn 3: 8 You hear its *s*, but you cannot tell
Ac 2: 2 Suddenly a *s* like the blowing
1Co 14: 8 if the trumpet does not *s* a clear call
15:52 the trumpet will *s*, the dead will
1Ti 1:10 to the *s* doctrine that conforms
2Ti 4: 3 men will not put up with *s* doctrine.
Tit 1: 9 can encourage others by *s* doctrine
2: 1 is in accord with *s* doctrine.

SOUR
Eze 18: 2 " 'The fathers eat *s* grapes,

SOURCE
Heb 5: 9 became the *s* of eternal salvation

SOVEREIGN (SOVEREIGNTY)
Ge 15: 2 But Abram said, "O *S* LORD,
2Sa 7:18 O *S* LORD, and what is my family,
Ps 71:16 your mighty acts, O *S* LORD;
Isa 25: 8 *S* LORD will wipe away the tears
40:10 the *S* LORD comes with power,
50: 4 *S* LORD has given me
61: 1 The Spirit of the *S* LORD is on me,
61:11 so the *S* LORD will make
Jer 32:17 to the LORD: "Ah, *S* LORD,
Eze 12:28 fulfilled, declares the *S* LORD.' "
Da 4:25 that the Most High is *s*
2Pe 2: 1 denying the *s* Lord who bought
Jude :4 and deny Jesus Christ our only *S*

SOVEREIGNTY (SOVEREIGN)
Da 7:27 Then the *s*, power and greatness

SOW (SOWER SOWN SOWS)
Job 4: 8 and those who *s* trouble reap it.
Ps 126: 5 Those who *s* in tears
Hos 8: 7 "They *s* the wind
10:12 *S* for yourselves righteousness,
Mt 6:26 they do not *s* or reap or store away
13: 3 "A farmer went out to *s* his seed.
1Co 15:36 What you *s* does not come to life
Jas 3:18 Peacemakers who *s*
2Pe 2:22 and, "A *s* that is washed goes back

SOWER (SOW)
Isa 55:10 so that it yields seed for the *s*
Mt 13:18 to what the parable of the *s* means:
Jn 4:36 so that the *s* and the reaper may be
2Co 9:10 Now he who supplies seed to the *s*

SOWN (SOW)
Mt 13: 8 sixty or thirty times what was *s*.
Mk 4:15 along the path, where the word is *s*.
1Co 15:42 The body that is *s* is perishable,

SOWS (SOW)
Pr 11:18 he who *s* righteousness reaps a sure
22: 8 He who *s* wickedness reaps trouble
2Co 9: 6 Whoever *s* sparingly will
Gal 6: 7 A man reaps what he *s*.

SPARE (SPARES SPARING)
Est 7: 3 *s* my people—this is my request.
Ro 8:32 He who did not *s* his own Son,
11:21 natural branches, he will not *s* you
2Pe 2: 4 For if God did not *s* angels
2: 5 if he did not *s* the ancient world

SPARES (SPARE)
Pr 13:24 He who *s* the rod hates his son,

SPARING (SPARE)
Pr 21:26 but the righteous give without *s*.

SPARKLE
Zec 9:16 They will *s* in his land

SPARROW (SPARROWS)
Ps 84: 3 Even the *s* has found a home,

SPARROWS (SPARROW)
Mt 10:29 Are not two *s* sold for a penny?

SPEAR (SPEARS)
1Sa 19:10 as Saul drove the *s* into the wall.
Ps 46: 9 breaks the bow and shatters the *s*,

SPEARS (SPEAR)
Isa 2: 4 and their *s* into pruning hooks.
Joel 3:10 and your pruning hooks into *s*.
Mic 4: 3 and their *s* into pruning hooks.

SPECIAL
Jas 2: 3 If you show *s* attention

SPECK
Mt 7: 3 look at the *s* of sawdust

SPECTACLE
1Co 4: 9 We have been made a *s*
Col 2:15 he made a public *s* of them,

SPEECH
Ps 19: 3 There is no *s* or language
Pr 22:11 pure heart and whose *s* is gracious
2Co 8: 7 in faith, in *s*, in knowledge,
1Ti 4:12 set an example for the believers in *s*

SPEND (SPENT)
Pr 31: 3 do not *s* your strength on women,
Isa 55: 2 Why *s* money on what is not bread,
2Co 12:15 So I will very gladly *s*

SPENT (SPEND)
Mk 5:26 many doctors and had *s* all she had,
Lk 6:12 and *s* the night praying to God.
15:14 After he had *s* everything,

SPIN
Mt 6:28 They do not labor or *s*.

SPIRIT (SPIRIT'S SPIRITS SPIRITUAL SPIRITUALLY)
Ge 1: 2 and the *S* of God was hovering
6: 3 "My *S* will not contend
Ex 31: 3 I have filled him with the *S* of God,
Nu 11:25 and put the *S* on the seventy elders.
Dt 34: 9 filled with the *s* of wisdom
Jdg 6:34 Then the *S* of the LORD came
11:29 Then the *S* of the LORD came
13:25 and the *S* of the LORD began
1Sa 10:10 the *S* of God came upon him
16:13 day on the *S* of the LORD came
16:14 the *S* of the LORD had departed
2Sa 23: 2 "The *S* of the LORD spoke
2Ki 2: 9 inherit a double portion of your *s*,"
Ne 9:20 You gave your good *S*
9:30 By your *S* you admonished them
Job 33: 4 The *S* of God has made me;
Ps 31: 5 Into your hands I commit my *s*;
34:18 saves those who are crushed in *s*.
51:10 and renew a steadfast *s* within me.
51:11 or take your Holy *S* from me.
51:17 sacrifices of God are a broken *s*;
106: 33 rebelled against the *S* of God,
139: 7 Where can I go from your *S*?
143: 10 may your good *S*
Isa 11: 2 The *S* of the LORD will rest
30: 1 an alliance, but not by my *S*,
32:15 till the *S* is poured upon us
44: 3 I will pour out my *S*
57:15 him who is contrite and lowly in *s*,
61: 1 The *S* of the Sovereign LORD is
63:10 and grieved his Holy *S*.
Eze 11:19 an undivided heart and put a new *s*
13: 3 prophets who follow their own *s*
36:26 you a new heart and put a new *s*
Da 4: 8 and the *s* of the holy gods is in him
Joel 2:28 I will pour out my *S* on all people.
Zec 4: 6 but by my *S*,' says the LORD
Mt 1:18 to be with child through the Holy *S*
3:11 will baptize you with the Holy *S*
3:16 he saw the *S* of God descending
4: 1 led by the *S* into the desert
5: 3 saying: "Blessed are the poor in *s*,
10:20 but the *S* of your Father speaking
12:31 against the *S* will not be forgiven.
26:41 *s* is willing, but the body is weak."
28:19 and of the Son and of the Holy *S*,
Mk 1: 8 he will baptize you with the Holy *S*
Lk 1:35 "The Holy *S* will come upon you,
1:80 child grew and became strong in *s*;
3:16 will baptize you with the Holy *S*
4:18 "The *S* of the Lord is on me,
11:13 Father in heaven give the Holy *S*
23:46 into your hands I commit my *s*."
Jn 1:33 who will baptize with the Holy *S*.'
3: 5 a man is born of water and the *S*,
4:24 God is *s*, and his worshipers must
6:63 The *S* gives life; the flesh counts
7:39 Up to that time the *S* had not been
14:26 But the Counselor, the Holy *S*,
16:13 But when he, the *S* of truth, comes,
20:22 and said, "Receive the Holy *S*.
Ac 1: 5 will be baptized with the Holy *S*."
1: 8 when the Holy *S* comes on you;
2: 4 of them were filled with the Holy *S*
2:17 I will pour out my *S* on all people.
2:38 will receive the gift of the Holy *S*.
4:31 they were all filled with the Holy *S*
5: 3 that you have lied to the Holy *S*
6: 3 who are known to be full of the *S*
8:15 that they might receive the Holy *S*,
9:17 and be filled with the Holy *S*."
11:16 will be baptized with the Holy *S*.'
13: 2 and fasting, the Holy *S* said,
19: 2 "Did you receive the Holy *S*
Ro 8: 4 nature but according to the *S*.
8: 5 set on what the *S* desires.
8: 9 And if anyone does not have the *S*
8:13 but if by the *S* you put
8:16 The *S* himself testifies
8:23 who have the firstfruits of the *S*,
8:26 the *S* helps us in our weakness.
1Co 2:10 God has revealed it to us by his *S*.
2:14 man without the *S* does not accept
5: 3 present, I am with you in *s*.
6:19 body is a temple of the Holy *S*,
12:13 baptized by one *S* into one body—
2Co 1:22 and put his *S* in our hearts
3: 3 but with the *S* of the living God,
3: 6 the letter kills, but the *S* gives life.
3:17 Now the Lord is the *S*,
5: 5 and has given us the *S* as a deposit,
7: 1 that contaminates body and *s*,
Gal 3: 2 Did you receive the *S*
5:16 by the *S*, and you will not gratify
5:22 But the fruit of the *S* is love, joy,
5:25 let us keep in step with the *S*.
6: 8 from the *S* will reap eternal life.
Eph 1:13 with a seal, the promised Holy *S*,
2:22 in which God lives by his *S*.
4: 4 There is one body and one *S*—
4:30 do not grieve the Holy *S* of God,
5:18 Instead, be filled with the *S*.
6:17 of salvation and the sword of the *S*,
Php 2: 2 being one in *s* and purpose.
1Th 5:23 May your whole *s*, soul
2Th 2:13 the sanctifying work of the *S*
1Ti 3:16 was vindicated by the *S*,
2Ti 1: 7 For God did not give us a *s*
Heb 2: 4 of the Holy *S* distributed according
4:12 even to dividing soul and *s*,
10:29 and who has insulted the *S* of grace
1Pe 3: 4 beauty of a gentle and quiet *s*,
2Pe 1:21 carried along by the Holy *S*.
1Jn 3:24 We know it by the *S* he gave us.
4: 1 Dear friends, do not believe every *s*
4:13 because he has given us of his *S*.
Jude :20 holy faith and pray in the Holy *S*.
Rev 2: 7 let him hear what the *S* says

SPIRIT'S* (SPIRIT)
1Co 2: 4 a demonstration of the *S* power,
1Th 5:19 not put out the *S* fire; do not treat

SPIRITS (SPIRIT)
1Co 12:10 to another distinguishing between *s*,
14:32 The *s* of prophets are subject
1Jn 4: 1 test the *s* to see whether they are

SPIRITUAL (SPIRIT)
Ro 12: 1 to God—this is your *s* act of worship.
12:11 but keep your *s* fervor, serving
1Co 2:13 expressing *s* truths in *s* words.
3: 1 I could not address you as *s* but
12: 1 Now about *s* gifts, brothers,
14: 1 of love and eagerly desire *s* gifts,
15:44 a natural body, it is raised a *s* body.
Gal 6: 1 you who are *s* should restore him
Eph 1: 3 with every *s* blessing in Christ.
5:19 with psalms, hymns and *s* songs.
6:12 and against the *s* forces of evil
1Pe 2: 2 newborn babies, crave pure *s* milk,
2: 5 are being built into a *s* house

SPIRITUALLY (SPIRIT)
1Co 2:14 because they are *s* discerned.

SPIT
Mt 27:30 They *s* on him, and took the staff
Rev 3:16 I am about to *s* you out

SPLENDOR
1Ch 16:29 the LORD in the *s* of his holiness.
29:11 the glory and the majesty and the *s*,
Job 37:22 of the north he comes in golden *s*;
Ps 29: 2 in the *s* of his holiness.
45: 3 clothe yourself with *s* and majesty.
96: 6 *S* and majesty are before him;
96: 9 in the *s* of his holiness;
104: 1 you are clothed with *s* and majesty.
145: 5 of the glorious *s* of your majesty,
145: 12 and the glorious *s* of your kingdom.
148: 13 his *s* is above the earth
Pr 4: 9 and present you with a crown of *s*."
16:31 Gray hair is a crown of *s*;
20:29 gray hair the *s* of the old.
Isa 55: 5 for he has endowed you with *s*."
60:21 for the display of my *s*.

Isa 61: 3 the LORD for the display of his *s*.
63: 1 Who is this, robed in *s*,
Hab 3: 4 His *s* was like the sunrise;
Mt 6:29 in all his *s* was dressed like one
Lk 9:31 appeared in glorious *s*, talking
2Th 2: 8 and destroy by the *s* of his coming.

SPOIL (SPOILS)
Ps 119:162 like one who finds great *s*.

SPOILS (SPOIL)
Isa 53:12 he will divide the *s* with the strong,
Jn 6:27 Do not work for food that *s*,

SPONTANEOUS*
Phm :14 so that any favor you do will be *s*

SPOTLESS
2Pe 3:14 make every effort to be found *s*,

SPOTS (SPOTTED)
Jer 13:23 or the leopard its *s*?

SPOTTED (SPOTS)
Ge 30:32 and every *s* or speckled goat.

SPREAD (SPREADING SPREADS)
Ps 78:19 "Can God *s* a table in the desert?
Ac 6: 7 So the word of God *s*.
12:24 of God continued to increase and *s*.
13:49 of the Lord *s* through the whole
19:20 the word of the Lord *s* widely
2Th 3: 1 message of the Lord may *s* rapidly

SPREADING (SPREAD)
Pr 29: 5 is *s* a net for his feet.
1Th 3: 2 God's fellow worker in *s* the gospel

SPREADS (SPREAD)
Pr 10:18 and whoever *s* slander is a fool.

SPRING (SPRINGS WELLSPRING)
Jer 2:13 the *s* of living water,
Jn 4:14 in him a *s* of water welling up
Jas 3:12 can a salt *s* produce fresh water.

SPRINGS (SPRING)
2Pe 2:17 These men are *s* without water

SPRINKLE (SPRINKLED SPRINKLING)
Lev 16:14 and with his finger *s* it on the front

SPRINKLED (SPRINKLE)
Heb 10:22 having our hearts *s* to cleanse us

SPRINKLING (SPRINKLE)
1Pe 1: 2 to Jesus Christ and *s* by his blood:

SPROUT
Pr 23: 5 for they will surely *s* wings
Jer 33:15 I will make a righteous Branch *s*

SPUR*
Heb 10:24 how we may *s* one another

SPURNS*
Pr 15: 5 A fool *s* his father's discipline,

SPY
Gal 2: 4 ranks to *s* on the freedom we have

SQUANDERED (SQUANDERS)
Lk 15:13 there *s* his wealth in wild living.

SQUANDERS* (SQUANDERED)
Pr 29: 3 of prostitutes *s* his wealth.

SQUARE
Rev 21:16 The city was laid out like a *s*,

STABILITY*
Pr 29: 4 By justice a king gives a country *s*,

STAFF
Ge 49:10 the ruler's *s* from between his feet,
Ex 7:12 Aaron's *s* swallowed up their staffs.
Nu 17: 6 and Aaron's *s* was among them.
Ps 23: 4 your rod and your *s*,

STAIN (STAINED)
Eph 5:27 without *s* or wrinkle or any other

STAINED (STAIN)
Isa 63: 1 with his garments *s* crimson?

STAKES
Isa 54: 2 strengthen your *s*.

STAND (STANDING STANDS STOOD)
Ex 14:13 *S* firm and you will see
Jos 10:12 "O sun, *s* still over Gibeon,
2Ch 20:17 *s* firm and see the deliverance
Job 19:25 in the end he will *s* upon the earth.
Ps 1: 1 or *s* in the way of sinners
1: 5 Therefore the wicked will not *s*
24: 3 Who may *s* in his holy place?
33:11 of the LORD *s* firm forever,
40: 2 and gave me a firm place to *s*.
76: 7 Who can *s* before you
93: 5 Your statutes *s* firm;
119:120 I *s* in awe of your laws.
130: 3 O Lord, who could *s*?
Ecc 5: 7 Therefore *s* in awe of God.
Isa 7: 9 If you do not *s* firm in your faith,
29:23 will *s* in awe of the God of Israel.
Eze 22:30 *s* before me in the gap on behalf
Hab 3: 2 I *s* in awe of your deeds, O LORD.
Zec 14: 4 On that day his feet will *s*
Mal 3: 2 Who can *s* when he appears?
Mt 12:25 divided against itself will not *s*.
Ro 14: 4 for the Lord is able to make him *s*.
14:10 we will all *s* before God's judgment
1Co 10:13 out so that you can *s* up under it.
15:58 Therefore, my dear brothers, *s* firm
16:13 Be on your guard; *s* firm in the faith
Gal 5: 1 *S* firm, then, and do not let
Eph 6:14 *S* firm then, with the belt
2Th 2:15 *s* firm and hold to the teachings we
Jas 5: 8 You too, be patient and *s* firm,
Rev 3:20 Here I am! I *s* at the door

STANDING (STAND)
Ex 3: 5 where you are *s* is holy ground."
Jos 5:15 the place where you are *s* is holy."
Ru 2: 1 a man of *s*, whose name was Boaz.
4:11 May you have *s* in Ephrathah
Lk 21:19 By *s* firm you will gain life.
1Ti 3:13 have served well gain an excellent *s*
1Pe 5: 9 Resist him, *s* firm in the faith,

STANDS (STAND)
Ps 89: 2 that your love *s* firm forever,
119: 89 it *s* firm in the heavens.
Pr 12: 7 the house of the righteous *s* firm.
Isa 40: 8 but the word of our God *s* forever."
Mt 10:22 but he who *s* firm to the end will be
2Ti 2:19 God's solid foundation *s* firm,
1Pe 1:25 but the word of the Lord *s* forever

STAR (STARS)
Nu 24:17 A *s* will come out of Jacob;
Isa 14:12 O morning *s*, son of the dawn!
Mt 2: 2 We saw his *s* in the east
2Pe 1:19 the morning *s* rises in your hearts.
Rev 2:28 I will also give him the morning *s*.
22:16 and the bright Morning *S*."

STARS (STAR)
Ge 1:16 He also made the *s*.
Job 38: 7 while the morning *s* sang together
Da 12: 3 like the *s* for ever and ever.
Php 2:15 in which you shine like *s*

STATURE
1Sa 2:26 boy Samuel continued to grow in *s*
Lk 2:52 And Jesus grew in wisdom and *s*,

STATUTES
Ps 19: 7 *s* of the LORD are trustworthy,
93: 5 Your *s* stand firm;
119: 2 Blessed are they who keep his *s*
119: 14 I rejoice in following your *s*
119: 24 Your *s* are my delight;
119: 36 Turn my heart toward your *s*
119: 99 for I meditate on your *s*.
119:111 Your *s* are my heritage forever;
119:125 that I may understand your *s*.
119:129 Your *s* are wonderful;
119:138 The *s* you have laid
119:152 Long ago I learned from your *s*
119:167 I obey your *s*,

STEADFAST*
Ps 51:10 and renew a *s* spirit within me.
57: 7 My heart is *s*, O God,
57: 7 my heart is *s*;
108: 1 My heart is *s*, O God;
111: 8 They are *s* for ever and ever,
112: 7 his heart is *s*, trusting in the LORD
119: 5 Oh, that my ways were *s*
Isa 26: 3 him whose mind is *s*,
1Pe 5:10 and make you strong, firm and *s*.

STEADY
Isa 35: 3 *s* the knees that give way;

STEAL (STOLEN)
Ex 20:15 "You shall not *s*.
Lev 19:11 " 'Do not *s*.
Dt 5:19 "You shall not *s*.
Mt 19:18 do not *s*, do not give false
Ro 13: 9 "Do not *s*," "Do not covet,"
Eph 4:28 has been stealing must *s* no longer,

STEP (FOOTSTEPS STEPS)
Job 34:21 he sees their every *s*.
Gal 5:25 let us keep in *s* with the Spirit.

STEPHEN
Deacon (Ac 6:5). Arrested (Ac 6:8-15). Speech to Sanhedrin (Ac 7). Stoned (Ac 7:54-60; 22:20).

STEPS (STEP)
Ps 37:23 he makes his *s* firm;
Pr 14:15 prudent man gives thought to his *s*.
16: 9 but the LORD determines his *s*.
20:24 A man's *s* are directed
Jer 10:23 it is not for man to direct his *s*.
1Pe 2:21 that you should follow in his *s*.

STERN (STERNNESS)
Pr 15:10 *S* discipline awaits him who leaves

STERNNESS* (STERN)
Ro 11:22 and *s* of God: *s* to those who fell,

STICKS
Pr 18:24 there is a friend who *s* closer

STIFF-NECKED (NECK)
Ex 34: 9 Although this is a *s* people,
Pr 29: 1 A man who remains *s*

STILL
Jos 10:13 So the sun stood *s*,
Ps 37: 7 Be *s* before the LORD
46:10 "Be *s*, and know that I am God;
89: 9 its waves mount up, you *s* them.
Zec 2:13 Be *s* before the LORD, all mankind
Mk 4:39 said to the waves, "Quiet! Be *s*!"

STIMULATE*
2Pe 3: 1 as reminders to *s* you

STING
1Co 15:55 Where, O death, is your *s*?"

STINGY
Pr 28:22 A *s* man is eager to get rich

STIRRED (STIRS)
Ps 45: 1 My heart is *s* by a noble theme

STIRS (STIRRED)
Pr 6:19 and a man who *s* up dissension
10:12 Hatred *s* up dissension,
15: 1 but a harsh word *s* up anger.
15:18 hot-tempered man *s* up dissension,
16:28 A perverse man *s* up dissension,
28:25 A greedy man *s* up dissension,
29:22 An angry man *s* up dissension,

STOLEN (STEAL)
Lev 6: 4 he must return what he has *s*
SS 4: 9 You have *s* my heart, my sister,

STOMACH
1Co 6:13 Food for the *s* and the *s* for food"—
Php 3:19 their god is their *s*, and their glory

STONE (CAPSTONE CORNERSTONE MILLSTONE STONED STONES)
Ex 24: 4 set up twelve *s* pillars representing
28:10 on one *s* and the remaining six
34: 1 "Chisel out two *s* tablets like
Dt 4:13 then wrote them on two *s* tablets.
19:14 your neighbor's boundary *s* set up
1Sa 17:50 the Philistine with a sling and a *s*;
Ps 91:12 will not strike your foot against a *s*.
118: 22 The *s* the builders rejected
Pr 22:28 not move an ancient boundary *s*
Isa 8:14 a *s* that causes men to stumble
28:16 "See, I lay a *s* in Zion,
Eze 11:19 remove from them their heart of *s*
36:26 remove from you your heart of *s*
Mt 7: 9 will give him a *s*? Or if he asks
21:42 " 'The *s* the builders rejected
24: 2 not one *s* here will be left
Mk 16: 3 "Who will roll the *s* away
Lk 4: 3 tell this *s* to become bread."
Jn 8: 7 the first to throw a *s* at her."
Ac 4:11 " 'the *s* you builders rejected,
Ro 9:32 stumbled over the "stumbling *s*."
2Co 3: 3 not on tablets of *s* but on tablets
1Pe 2: 6 "See, I lay a *s* in Zion,
Rev 2:17 also give him a white *s*

STONED (STONE)
2Co 11:25 once I was *s*, three times I was
Heb 11:37 They were *s*; they were sawed

STONES (STONE)
Ex 28:21 are to be twelve *s*, one for each
Jos 4: 3 to take up twelve *s* from the middle
1Sa 17:40 chose five smooth *s*

Mt 3: 9 out of these *s* God can raise up
1Co 3:12 silver, costly *s*, wood, hay or straw,
1Pe 2: 5 also, like living *s*, are being built

STOOD (STAND)
Jos 10:13 So the sun *s* still,
Lk 22:28 You are those who have *s* by me
2Ti 4:17 But the Lord *s* at my side
Jas 1:12 because when he has *s* the test,

STOOP (STOOPS)
2Sa 22:36 you *s* down to make me great.

STOOPS (STOOP)
Ps 113: 6 who *s* down to look

STOP
Job 37:14 *s* and consider God's wonders.
Isa 1:13 *S* bringing meaningless offerings!
1:16 *S* doing wrong,
2:22 *S* trusting in man,
Jer 32:40 I will never *s* doing good to them,
Mk 9:39 "Do not *s* him," Jesus said.
Jn 6:43 "*S* grumbling among yourselves,"
7:24 *S* judging by mere appearances,
20:27 *S* doubting and believe."
Ro 14:13 Therefore let us *s* passing judgment
1Co 14:20 Brothers, *s* thinking like children.

STORE (STORED)
Pr 2: 1 and *s* up my commands within you,
7: 1 and *s* up my commands within you.
10:14 Wise men *s* up knowledge,
Isa 33: 6 a rich *s* of salvation and wisdom
Mt 6:19 not *s* up for yourselves treasures
6:26 or reap or *s* away in barns,
2Ti 4: 8 Now there is in *s* for me the crown

STORED (STORE)
Lk 6:45 out of the good *s* up in his heart,
Col 1: 5 from the hope that is *s* up for you

STOREHOUSE (HOUSE)
Mal 3:10 Bring the whole tithe into the *s*,

STORIES*
2Pe 1:16 did not follow cleverly invented *s*
2: 3 you with *s* they have made up.

STORM
Job 38: 1 LORD answered Job out of the *s*.
Ps 107: 29 He stilled the *s* to a whisper;
Lk 8:24 the *s* subsided, and all was calm.

STOUTHEARTED* (HEART)
Ps 138: 3 you made me bold and *s*.

STRAIGHT
Ps 27:11 lead me in a *s* path
107: 7 He led them by a *s* way
Pr 2:13 who leave the *s* paths
3: 6 and he will make your paths *s*.
4:11 and lead you along *s* paths.
4:25 Let your eyes look *s* ahead,
11: 5 of the blameless makes a *s* way
15:21 of understanding keeps a *s* course.
Isa 40: 3 make *s* in the wilderness
Mt 3: 3 make *s* paths for him.'"
Jn 1:23 'Make *s* the way for the Lord.'"
2Pe 2:15 They have left the *s* way

STRAIN (STRAINING)
Mt 23:24 You *s* out a gnat but swallow

STRAINING (STRAIN)
Php 3:13 and *s* toward what is ahead,

STRANGE (STRANGER STRANGERS)
Isa 28:11 with foreign lips and *s* tongues
1Co 14:21 "Through men of *s* tongues
1Pe 4: 4 They think it *s* that you do not

STRANGER (STRANGE)
Ps 119: 19 I am a *s* on earth;
Mt 25:35 I was a *s* and you invited me in,
Jn 10: 5 But they will never follow a *s*;

STRANGERS (STRANGE)
Heb 13: 2 Do not forget to entertain *s*,
1Pe 2:11 as aliens and *s* in the world,

STRAW
Isa 11: 7 and the lion will eat *s* like the ox.
1Co 3:12 silver, costly stones, wood, hay or *s*

STRAYED (STRAYS)
Ps 119: 176 I have *s* like a lost sheep.
Jer 31:19 After I *s*,

STRAYS (STRAYED)
Pr 21:16 A man who *s* from the path
Eze 34:16 for the lost and bring back the *s*.

STREAM (STREAMS)
Am 5:24 righteousness like a never-failing *s*!

STREAMS (STREAM)
Ps 1: 3 He is like a tree planted by *s*
46: 4 is a river whose *s* make glad
Ecc 1: 7 All *s* flow into the sea,
Jn 7:38 *s* of living water will flow

STREET
Mt 6: 5 on the *s* corners to be seen by men.
22: 9 Go to the *s* corners and invite
Rev 21:21 The great *s* of the city was of pure gold,

STRENGTH (STRONG)
Ex 15: 2 The LORD is my *s* and my song;
Dt 4:37 by his Presence and his great *s*,
6: 5 all your soul and with all your *s*.
Jdg 16:15 told me the secret of your great *s*."
2Sa 22:33 It is God who arms me with *s*
2Ki 23:25 with all his soul and with all his *s*,
1Ch 16:11 Look to the LORD and his *s*;
16:28 ascribe to the LORD glory and *s*,
29:12 In your hands are *s* and power
Ne 8:10 for the joy of the LORD is your *s*."
Ps 18: 1 I love you, O LORD, my *s*.
21:13 Be exalted, O LORD, in your *s*;
28: 7 The LORD is my *s* and my shield;
29:11 The LORD gives *s* to his people;
33:16 no warrior escapes by his great *s*.
46: 1 God is our refuge and *s*,
59:17 O my *S*, I sing praise to you;
65: 6 having armed yourself with *s*,
73:26 but God is the *s* of my heart
84: 5 Blessed are those whose *s* is in you,
96: 7 ascribe to the LORD glory and *s*.
105: 4 Look to the LORD and his *s*;
118: 14 The LORD is my *s* and my song;
147: 10 not in the *s* of the horse,
Pr 24: 5 a man of knowledge increases *s*;
30:25 Ants are creatures of little *s*,
Isa 12: 2 the LORD, is my *s* and my song;
31: 1 and in the great *s* of their horsemen
40:26 of his great power and mighty *s*,
40:31 will renew their *s*.
63: 1 forward in the greatness of his *s*?
Jer 9:23 or the strong man boast of his *s*
Mic 5: 4 flock in the *s* of the LORD,
Hab 3:19 The Sovereign LORD is my *s*;
Mk 12:30 all your mind and with all your *s*.'
1Co 1:25 of God is stronger than man's *s*.
Eph 1:19 is like the working of his mighty *s*,
Php 4:13 through him who gives me *s*.
Heb 11:34 whose weakness was turned to *s*;
1Pe 4:11 it with the *s* God provides,

STRENGTHEN (STRONG)
2Ch 16: 9 to *s* those whose hearts are fully
Ps 119: 28 *s* me according to your word.
Isa 35: 3 *S* the feeble hands,
41:10 I will *s* you and help you;
Lk 22:32 have turned back, *s* your brothers."
Eph 3:16 of his glorious riches he may *s* you
1Th 3:13 May he *s* your hearts
2Th 2:17 and *s* you in every good deed
Heb 12:12 *s* your feeble arms and weak knees.

STRENGTHENED (STRONG)
Col 1:11 being *s* with all power according
Heb 13: 9 good for our hearts to be *s* by grace,

STRENGTHENING (STRONG)
1Co 14:26 done for the *s* of the church.

STRETCHES
Ps 104: 2 he *s* out the heavens like a tent

STRICKEN (STRIKE)
Isa 53: 8 of my people he was *s*.

STRICT
1Co 9:25 in the games goes into *s* training.

STRIFE (STRIVE)
Pr 17: 1 than a house full of feasting, with *s*.
20: 3 It is to a man's honor to avoid *s*,
22:10 out the mocker, and out goes *s*;
30:33 so stirring up anger produces *s*."
1Ti 6: 4 *s*, malicious talk, evil suspicions

STRIKE (STRIKES STROKE)
Ge 3:15 and you will *s* his heel."
Zec 13: 7 "*S* the shepherd,
Mt 4: 6 so that you will not *s* your foot
26:31 "'I will *s* the shepherd,

STRIKES (STRIKE)
Mt 5:39 If someone *s* you on the right

STRIPS
Lk 2:12 You will find a baby wrapped in *s*
Jn 20: 5 in at the *s* of linen lying there

STRIVE* (STRIFE)
Ac 24:16 I *s* always to keep my conscience
1Ti 4:10 (and for this we labor and *s*),

STROKE (STRIKE)
Mt 5:18 the smallest letter, not the least *s*

STRONG (STRENGTH STRENGTHEN STRENGTHENED STRENGTHENING STRONGER)
Dt 3:24 your greatness and your *s* hand.
31: 6 Be *s* and courageous.
Jos 1: 6 "Be *s* and courageous,
Jdg 5:21 March on, my soul; be *s*!
2Sa 10:12 Be *s* and let us fight bravely
1Ki 2: 2 "So be *s*, show yourself a man,
1Ch 28:20 "Be *s* and courageous,
2Ch 32: 7 them with these words: "Be *s*
Ps 24: 8 The LORD *s* and mighty,
31: 2 a *s* fortress to save me.
62:11 that you, O God, are *s*,
Pr 18:10 The name of the LORD is a *s* tower
31:17 her arms are *s* for her tasks.
Ecc 9:11 or the battle to the *s*,
SS 8: 6 for love is as *s* as death,
Isa 35: 4 "Be *s*, do not fear;
53:12 he will divide the spoils with the *s*,
Jer 9:23 or the *s* man boast of his strength
50:34 Yet their Redeemer is *s*;
Hag 2: 4 Be *s*, all you people of the land,'
Mt 12:29 can anyone enter a *s* man's house
Lk 2:40 And the child grew and became *s*;
Ro 15: 1 We who are *s* ought to bear
1Co 1: 8 He will keep you *s* to the end,
1:27 things of the world to shame the *s*.
16:13 in the faith; be men of courage; be *s*
2Co 12:10 For when I am weak, then I am *s*.
Eph 6:10 be *s* in the Lord and in his mighty
2Ti 2: 1 be *s* in the grace that is
1Pe 5:10 restore you and make you *s*,

STRONGER (STRONG)
Dt 4:38 before you nations greater and *s*
1Co 1:25 of God is *s* than man's strength.

STRONGHOLD (STRONGHOLDS)
2Sa 22: 3 He is my *s*, my refuge and my
Ps 9: 9 a *s* in times of trouble.
18: 2 the horn of my salvation, my *s*.
27: 1 The LORD is the *s* of my life—
144: 2 my *s* and my deliverer,

STRONGHOLDS (STRONGHOLD)
Zep 3: 6 their *s* are demolished.
2Co 10: 4 have divine power to demolish *s*.

STRUGGLE (STRUGGLED STRUGGLING)
Ro 15:30 me in my *s* by praying to God
Eph 6:12 For our *s* is not against flesh
Heb 12: 4 In your *s* against sin, you have not

STRUGGLED (STRUGGLE)
Ge 32:28 because you have *s* with God

STRUGGLING* (STRUGGLE)
Col 1:29 To this end I labor, *s*
2: 1 to know how much I am *s* for you

STUDENT (STUDY)
Mt 10:24 "A *s* is not above his teacher,

STUDY (STUDENT)
Ezr 7:10 Ezra had devoted himself to the *s*
Ecc 12:12 and much *s* wearies the body.
Jn 5:39 You diligently *s* the Scriptures

STUMBLE (STUMBLES STUMBLING)
Ps 37:24 though he *s*, he will not fall,
119: 165 and nothing can make them *s*.
Pr 3:23 and your foot will not *s*;
Isa 8:14 a stone that causes men to *s*
Jer 13:16 before your feet *s*
31: 9 a level path where they will not *s*,
Eze 7:19 for it has made them *s* into sin.
Hos 14: 9 but the rebellious *s* in them.
Mal 2: 8 teaching have caused many to *s*;
Jn 11: 9 A man who walks by day will not *s*,
Ro 9:33 in Zion a stone that causes men to *s*
14:20 that causes someone else to *s*.
1Co 10:32 Do not cause anyone to *s*,
Jas 3: 2 We all *s* in many ways.
1Pe 2: 8 and, "A stone that causes men to *s*
1Jn 2:10 nothing in him to make him *s*.

STUMBLES (STUMBLE)
Pr 24:17 when he *s*, do not let your heart

Jn 11:10 is when he walks by night that he *s*,
Jas 2:10 and yet *s* at just one point is guilty

STUMBLING (STUMBLE)
Lev 19:14 put a *s* block in front of the blind,
Ps 56:13 and my feet from *s*,
Mt 16:23 Satan! You are a *s* block to me;
Ro 9:32 They stumbled over the "*s* stone."
11: 9 a *s* block and a retribution for them
14:13 up your mind not to put any *s* block
1Co 1:23 a *s* block to Jews and foolishness
8: 9 freedom does not become a *s* block
2Co 6: 3 We put no *s* block in anyone's path,

STUMP
Isa 6:13 so the holy seed will be the *s*
11: 1 up from the *s* of Jesse;

STUPID
Pr 12: 1 but he who hates correction is *s*.
2Ti 2:23 to do with foolish and *s* arguments,

STUPOR
Ro 11: 8 "God gave them a spirit of *s*,

SUBDUE (SUBDUED)
Ge 1:28 in number; fill the earth and *s* it.

SUBDUED (SUBDUE)
Jos 10:40 So Joshua *s* the whole region,
Ps 47: 3 He *s* nations under us,

SUBJECT (SUBJECTED)
Mt 5:22 angry with his brother will be *s*
1Co 14:32 of prophets are *s* to the control
15:28 then the Son himself will be made *s*
Tit 2: 5 and to be *s* to their husbands,
2: 9 slaves to be *s* to their masters
3: 1 Remind the people to be *s* to rulers

SUBJECTED (SUBJECT)
Ro 8:20 For the creation was *s*

SUBMISSION (SUBMIT)
1Co 14:34 but must be in *s*, as the Law says.
1Ti 2:11 learn in quietness and full *s*.

SUBMISSIVE (SUBMIT)
Jas 3:17 then peace-loving, considerate, *s*,
1Pe 3: 1 in the same way be *s*
5: 5 in the same way be *s*

SUBMIT (SUBMISSION SUBMISSIVE SUBMITS)
Ro 13: 1 Everyone must *s* himself
13: 5 necessary to *s* to the authorities,
1Co 16:16 to *s* to such as these
Eph 5:21 *S* to one another out of reverence
Col 3:18 Wives, *s* to your husbands,
Heb 12: 9 How much more should we *s*
13:17 Obey your leaders and *s*
Jas 4: 7 *S* yourselves, then, to God.
1Pe 2:18 *s* yourselves to your masters

SUBMITS* (SUBMIT)
Eph 5:24 Now as the church *s* to Christ,

SUBTRACT*
Dt 4: 2 what I command you and do not *s*

SUCCEED (SUCCESS SUCCESSFUL)
Ps 20: 4 and make all your plans *s*.
Pr 15:22 but with many advisers they *s*.
16: 3 and your plans will *s*.
21:30 that can *s* against the LORD.

SUCCESS (SUCCEED)
Ge 39:23 and gave him *s* in whatever he did.
1Sa 18:14 In everything he did he had great *s*,
1Ch 12:18 *S*, *s* to you, and *s*
22:13 you will have *s* if you are careful
2Ch 26: 5 the LORD, God gave him *s*.
Ecc 10:10 but skill will bring *s*.

SUCCESSFUL (SUCCEED)
Jos 1: 7 that you may be *s* wherever you go.
2Ki 18: 7 he was *s* in whatever he undertook.
2Ch 20:20 in his prophets and you will be *s*."

SUFFER (SUFFERED SUFFERING SUFFERINGS SUFFERS)
Job 36:15 those who *s* he delivers
Isa 53:10 to crush him and cause him to *s*,
Mk 8:31 the Son of Man must *s* many things
Lk 24:26 the Christ have to *s* these things
24:46 The Christ will *s* and rise
2Co 1: 6 of the same sufferings we *s*.
Php 1:29 to *s* for him, since you are going
Heb 9:26 would have had to *s* many times
1Pe 3:17 to *s* for doing good
4:16 However, if you *s* as a Christian,

SUFFERED (SUFFER)
Heb 2: 9 and honor because he *s* death,
2:18 Because he himself *s*
1Pe 2:21 Christ *s* for you, leaving you
4: 1 he who has *s* in his body is done

SUFFERING (SUFFER)
Job 36:15 who suffer he delivers in their *s*;
Ps 22:24 the *s* of the afflicted one;
Isa 53: 3 of sorrows, and familiar with *s*.
53:11 After the *s* of his soul,
La 1:12 Is any *s* like my *s*
Ac 5:41 worthy of *s* disgrace for the Name.
Ro 5: 3 know that *s* produces
2Ti 1: 8 But join with me in *s* for the gospel,
Heb 2:10 of their salvation perfect through *s*.
13: 3 as if you yourselves were *s*.
1Pe 4:12 at the painful trial you are *s*,

SUFFERINGS (SUFFER)
Ro 5: 3 but we also rejoice in our *s*,
8:17 share in his *s* in order that we may
8:18 that our present *s* are not worth
2Co 1: 5 as the *s* of Christ flow
Php 3:10 the fellowship of sharing in his *s*,
1Pe 4:13 rejoice that you participate in the *s*
5: 9 are undergoing the same kind of *s*.

SUFFERS (SUFFER)
Pr 13:20 but a companion of fools *s* harm.
1Co 12:26 If one part *s*, every part *s* with it;

SUFFICIENT
2Co 12: 9 said to me, "My grace is *s* for you,

SUITABLE
Ge 2:18 I will make a helper *s* for him."

SUMMED* (SUMS)
Ro 13: 9 there may be, are *s* up
Gal 5:14 The entire law is *s* up

SUMMONS
Ps 50: 1 speaks and *s* the earth
Isa 45: 3 God of Israel, who *s* you by name.

SUMS* (SUMMED)
Mt 7:12 for this *s* up the Law

SUN (SUNRISE)
Jos 10:13 So the *s* stood still,
Jdg 5:31 may they who love you be like the *s*
Ps 84:11 For the LORD God is a *s*
121: 6 the *s* will not harm you by day,
136: 8 the *s* to govern the day,
Ecc 1: 9 there is nothing new under the *s*.
Isa 60:19 The *s* will no more be your light
Mal 4: 2 the *s* of righteousness will rise
Mt 5:45 He causes his *s* to rise on the evil
13:43 the righteous will shine like the *s*
17: 2 His face shone like the *s*,
Lk 23:45 for the *s* stopped shining.
Eph 4:26 Do not let the *s* go
Rev 1:16 His face was like the *s* shining
21:23 The city does not need the *s*

SUNG (SING)
Mt 26:30 When they had *s* a hymn, they

SUNRISE (SUN)
2Sa 23: 4 he is like the light of morning at *s*
Hab 3: 4 His splendor was like the *s*;

SUPERIOR
Heb 1: 4 he became as much *s* to the angels
8: 6 ministry Jesus has received is as *s*

SUPERVISION
Gal 3:25 longer under the *s* of the law.

SUPPER
Lk 22:20 after the *s* he took the cup, saying,
1Co 11:25 after *s* he took the cup,
Rev 19: 9 to the wedding *s* of the Lamb!' "

SUPPLIED (SUPPLY)
Ac 20:34 of mine have *s* my own needs
Php 4:18 and even more; I am amply *s*,

SUPPLY (SUPPLIED SUPPLYING)
2Co 8:14 your plenty will *s* what they need,
1Th 3:10 and *s* what is lacking in your faith.

SUPPLYING* (SUPPLY)
2Co 9:12 you perform is not only *s* the needs

SUPPORT (SUPPORTED SUPPORTING)
Ps 18:18 but the LORD was my *s*.
Ro 11:18 consider this: You do not *s* the root
1Co 9:12 If others have this right of *s*

SUPPORTED (SUPPORT)
Ps 94:18 your love, O LORD, *s* me.
Col 2:19 *s* and held together by its ligaments

SUPPORTING (SUPPORT)
Eph 4:16 held together by every *s* ligament,

SUPPRESS*
Ro 1:18 wickedness of men who *s* the truth

SUPREMACY* (SUPREME)
Col 1:18 in everything he might have the *s*.

SUPREME (SUPREMACY)
Pr 4: 7 Wisdom is *s*; therefore get wisdom.

SURE
Nu 28:31 Be *s* the animals are without defect
32:23 you may be *s* that your sin will find
Dt 6:17 Be *s* to keep the commands
14:22 Be *s* to set aside a tenth
29:18 make *s* there is no root
Jos 23:13 then you may be *s* that the LORD
1Sa 12:24 But be *s* to fear the LORD
Ps 19: 9 The ordinances of the LORD are *s*
132: 11 a *s* oath that he will not revoke:
Pr 27:23 Be *s* you know the condition
Isa 28:16 cornerstone for a *s* foundation;
Eph 5: 5 of this you can be *s*: No immoral,
Heb 11: 1 faith is being *s* of what we hope for
2Pe 1:10 to make your calling and election *s*.

SURFACE
2Co 10: 7 You are looking only on the *s*

SURPASS* (SURPASSED SURPASSES SURPASSING)
Pr 31:29 but you *s* them all."

SURPASSED* (SURPASS)
Jn 1:15 'He who comes after me has *s* me
1:30 man who comes after me has *s* me

SURPASSES* (SURPASS)
Pr 8:19 what I yield *s* choice silver.
Mt 5:20 unless your righteousness *s* that
Eph 3:19 to know this love that *s* knowledge

SURPASSING* (SURPASS)
Ps 150: 2 praise him for his *s* greatness.
2Co 3:10 in comparison with the *s* glory.
9:14 of the *s* grace God has given you.
Php 3: 8 the *s* greatness of knowing Christ

SURPRISE (SURPRISED)
1Th 5: 4 that this day should *s* you like

SURPRISED (SURPRISE)
1Pe 4:12 do not be *s* at the painful trial you
1Jn 3:13 Do not be *s*, my brothers,

SURRENDER
1Co 13: 3 and *s* my body to the flames,

SURROUND (SURROUNDED SURROUNDS)
Ps 5:12 you *s* them with your favor
32: 7 and *s* me with songs of deliverance.
89: 7 awesome than all who *s* him.
125: 2 As the mountains *s* Jerusalem,
Jer 31:22 a woman will *s* a man."

SURROUNDED (SURROUND)
Heb 12: 1 since we are *s* by such a great cloud

SURROUNDS* (SURROUND)
Ps 32:10 *s* the man who trusts in him.
89: 8 and your faithfulness *s* you.
125: 2 so the LORD *s* his people

SUSA
Ezr 4: 9 and Babylon, the Elamites of *S*,
Ne 1: 1 while I was in the citadel of *S*,

SUSPENDS*
Job 26: 7 he *s* the earth over nothing.

SUSPICIONS*
1Ti 6: 4 evil *s* and constant friction

SUSTAIN (SUSTAINING SUSTAINS)
Ps 55:22 and he will *s* you;
Isa 46: 4 I am he, I am he who will *s* you.

SUSTAINING* (SUSTAIN)
Heb 1: 3 *s* all things by his powerful word.

SUSTAINS (SUSTAIN)
Ps 18:35 and your right hand *s* me;
146: 9 and *s* the fatherless and the widow,
147: 6 The LORD *s* the humble
Isa 50: 4 to know the word that *s* the weary.

SWALLOW (SWALLOWED)
Isa 25: 8 he will *s* up death forever.
Jnh 1:17 provided a great fish to *s* Jonah,
Mt 23:24 You strain out a gnat but *s* a camel.

SWALLOWED (SWALLOW)
1Co 15:54 "Death has been *s* up in victory."
2Co 5: 4 so that what is mortal may be *s* up

SWAYED
Mt 11: 7 A reed *s* by the wind? If not,
22:16 You aren't *s* by men, because you
2Ti 3: 6 are *s* by all kinds of evil desires,

SWEAR (SWORE SWORN)
Lev 19:12 " 'Do not *s* falsely by my name
Ps 24: 4 or *s* by what is false.
Isa 45:23 by me every tongue will *s*.
Mt 5:34 Do not *s* at all: either by heaven,
Jas 5:12 Above all, my brothers, do not *s*—

SWEAT*
Ge 3:19 By the *s* of your brow
Lk 22:44 his *s* was like drops of blood falling

SWEET (SWEETER SWEETNESS)
Job 20:12 "Though evil is *s* in his mouth
Ps 119:103 How *s* are your words
Pr 9:17 "Stolen water is *s*;
13:19 A longing fulfilled is *s* to the soul,
16:24 *s* to the soul and healing
20:17 by fraud tastes *s* to a man,
24:14 also that wisdom is *s* to your soul;
Ecc 5:12 The sleep of a laborer is *s*,
Isa 5:20 and *s* for bitter.
Eze 3: 3 it tasted as *s* as honey in my mouth.
Rev 10:10 It tasted as *s* as honey in my mouth

SWEETER (SWEET)
Ps 19:10 they are *s* than honey,
119:103 *s* than honey to my mouth!

SWEETNESS* (SWEET)
SS 4:11 Your lips drop *s* as the honeycomb,
5:16 His mouth is *s* itself;

SWEPT
Mt 12:44 finds the house unoccupied, *s* clean

SWERVE*
Pr 4: 5 do not forget my words or *s*
4:27 Do not *s* to the right or the left;

SWIFT
Pr 1:16 they are *s* to shed blood.
Ecc 9:11 The race is not to the *s*
Isa 59: 7 they are *s* to shed innocent blood.
Ro 3:15 "Their feet are *s* to shed blood;
2Pe 2: 1 bringing *s* destruction

SWINDLER* (SWINDLERS)
1Co 5:11 or a slanderer, a drunkard or a *s*.

SWINDLERS* (SWINDLER)
1Co 5:10 or the greedy and *s*, or idolaters.
6:10 *s* will inherit the kingdom of God.

SWORD (SWORDS)
Ge 3:24 and a flaming *s* flashing back
Dt 32:41 when I sharpen my flashing *s*
Jos 5:13 of him with a drawn *s* in his hand.
1Sa 17:45 "You come against me with *s*
17:47 here will know that it is not by *s*
31: 4 so Saul took his own *s* and fell on it.
2Sa 12:10 therefore, the *s* will never depart
Ps 44: 6 my *s* does not bring me victory;
45: 3 Gird your *s* upon your side,
Pr 12:18 Reckless words pierce like a *s*,
Isa 2: 4 Nation will not take up *s*
Mic 4: 3 Nation will not take up *s*
Mt 10:34 come to bring peace, but a *s*.
26:52 all who draw the *s* will die by the *s*.
Lk 2:35 a *s* will pierce your own soul too."
Ro 13: 4 for he does not bear the *s*
Eph 6:17 of salvation and the *s* of the Spirit,
Heb 4:12 Sharper than any double-edged *s*,
Rev 1:16 came a sharp double-edged *s*.
19:15 Out of his mouth comes a sharp *s*

SWORDS (SWORD)
Ps 64: 3 who sharpen their tongues like *s*
Isa 2: 4 They will beat their *s*
Joel 3:10 Beat your plowshares into *s*

SWORE (SWEAR)
Heb 6:13 for him to swear by, he *s* by himself

SWORN (SWEAR)
Ps 110: 4 The LORD has *s*
Eze 20:42 the land I had *s* with uplifted hand
Heb 7:21 "The Lord has *s*

SYCAMORE-FIG (FIG)
Am 7:14 and I also took care of *s* trees.
Lk 19: 4 and climbed a *s* tree to see him,

SYMBOLIZES*
1Pe 3:21 this water *s* baptism that now saves

SYMPATHETIC* (SYMPATHY)
1Pe 3: 8 in harmony with one another; be *s*,

SYMPATHIZED* (SYMPATHY)
Heb 10:34 You *s* with those in prison

SYMPATHY (SYMPATHETIC SYMPATHIZED)
Ps 69:20 I looked for *s*, but there was none,

SYNAGOGUE
Lk 4:16 the Sabbath day he went into the *s*,
Ac 17: 2 custom was, Paul went into the *s*,

TABERNACLE (TABERNACLES)
Ex 40:34 the glory of the LORD filled the *t*.
Heb 8: 2 the true *t* set up by the Lord,
9:11 and more perfect *t* that is not
9:21 sprinkled with the blood both the *t*
Rev 15: 5 that is, the *t* of the Testimony,

TABERNACLES (TABERNACLE)
Lev 23:34 the LORD's Feast of *T* begins,
Dt 16:16 Feast of Weeks and the Feast of *T*.
Zec 14:16 and to celebrate the Feast of *T*.

TABLE (TABLES)
Ex 25:23 "Make a *t* of acacia wood—
Ps 23: 5 You prepare a *t* before me

TABLES (TABLE)
Jn 2:15 changers and overturned their *t*.
Ac 6: 2 word of God in order to wait on *t*.

TABLET (TABLETS)
Pr 3: 3 write them on the *t* of your heart.
7: 3 write them on the *t* of your heart.

TABLETS (TABLET)
Ex 31:18 he gave him the two *t*
Dt 10: 5 and put the *t* in the ark I had made,
2Co 3: 3 not on *t* of stone but on *t*

TAKE (TAKEN TAKES TAKING TOOK)
Ge 15: 7 land to *t* possession of it."
22:17 Your descendants will *t* possession
Ex 3: 5 "*T* off your sandals,
21:23 you are to *t* life for life, eye for eye,
22:22 "Do not *t* advantage of a widow
Lev 10:17 given to you to *t* away the guilt
25:14 do not *t* advantage of each other.
Nu 13:30 and *t* possession of the land,
Dt 1: 8 and *t* possession of the land that
12:32 do not add to it or *t* away from it.
31:26 "*T* this Book of the Law
1Sa 8:11 He will *t* your sons and make them
1Ch 17:13 I will never *t* my love away
Job 23:10 But he knows the way that I *t*;
Ps 2:12 Blessed are all who *t* refuge in him.
25:18 and *t* away all my sins.
27:14 be strong and *t* heart
31:24 Be strong and *t* heart,
49:17 for he will *t* nothing with him
51:11 or *t* your Holy Spirit from me.
73:24 afterward you will *t* me into glory.
118: 8 It is better to *t* refuge in the LORD
Pr 22:23 for the LORD will *t* up their case
Isa 62: 4 for the LORD will *t* delight in you,
Eze 3:10 and *t* to heart all the words I speak
33:11 I *t* no pleasure in the death
Mt 10:38 anyone who does not *t* his cross
11:29 *T* my yoke upon you and learn
16:24 deny himself and *t* up his cross
26:26 saying, "*T* and eat; this is my body
Mk 14:36 *T* this cup from me.
1Ti 6:12 *T* hold of the eternal life

TAKEN (TAKE)
Ge 2:23 for she was *t* out of man."
Lev 6: 4 must return what he has stolen or *t*
Nu 8:16 I have *t* them as my own in place
19: 3 it is to be *t* outside the camp
Ecc 3:14 added to it and nothing *t* from it.
Isa 6: 7 your guilt is *t* away and your sin
Zec 3: 4 "See, I have *t* away your sin,
Mt 13:12 even what he has will be *t* from him
24:40 one will be *t* and the other left.
26:39 may this cup be *t* from me.
Mk 16:19 he was *t* up into heaven
Ac 1: 9 he was *t* up before their very eyes,
Ro 5:13 But sin is not *t* into account
1Ti 3:16 was *t* up in glory.

TAKES (TAKE)
1Ki 20:11 should not boast like one who *t* it
Ps 5: 4 You are not a God who *t* pleasure
34: 8 blessed is the man who *t* refuge
Lk 6:30 and if anyone *t* what belongs to you
Jn 1:29 who *t* away the sin of the world!
10:18 No one *t* it from me, but I lay it
Rev 22:19 And if anyone *t* words away

TAKING (TAKE)
Ac 15:14 by *t* from the Gentiles a people
Php 2: 7 *t* the very nature of a servant,

TALENT
Mt 25:15 to another one *t*, each according

TALES*
1Ti 4: 7 with godless myths and old wives' *t*

TALL
1Sa 17: 4 He was over nine feet *t*.
1Ch 11:23 who was seven and a half feet *t*.

TAMAR
1. Wife of Judah's sons Er and Onan (Ge 38:1-10). Tricked Judah into fathering children when he refused her his third son (Ge 38:11-30).
2. Daughter of David, raped by Amnon (2Sa 13).

TAMBOURINE
Ps 150: 4 praise him with *t* and dancing,

TAME* (TAMED)
Jas 3: 8 but no man can *t* the tongue.

TAMED* (TAME)
Jas 3: 7 the sea are being *t* and have been *t*

TARSHISH
Jnh 1: 3 from the LORD and headed for *T*.

TARSUS
Ac 9:11 ask for a man from *T* named Saul,

TASK (TASKS)
1Ch 29: 1 The *t* is great, because this palatial
Mk 13:34 each with his assigned *t*,
Ac 20:24 complete the *t* the Lord Jesus has
1Co 3: 5 the Lord has assigned to each his *t*.
2Co 2:16 And who is equal to such a *t*?
1Ti 3: 1 an overseer, he desires a noble *t*.

TASKS (TASK)
Pr 31:17 her arms are strong for her *t*.

TASTE (TASTED TASTY)
Ps 34: 8 *T* and see that the LORD is good;
119:103 sweet are your words to my *t*,
Pr 24:13 from the comb is sweet to your *t*.
SS 2: 3 and his fruit is sweet to my *t*.
Col 2:21 Do not *t*! Do not touch!"?
Heb 2: 9 the grace of God he might *t* death

TASTED (TASTE)
Eze 3: 3 it *t* as sweet as honey in my mouth.
1Pe 2: 3 now that you have *t* that the Lord
Rev 10:10 It *t* as sweet as honey in my mouth,

TASTY (TASTE)
Ge 27: 4 Prepare me the kind of *t* food I like

TATTOO*
Lev 19:28 or put *t* marks on yourselves.

TAUGHT (TEACH)
1Ki 4:33 He also *t* about animals and birds,
2Ki 17:28 *t* them how to worship the LORD.
2Ch 17: 9 They *t* throughout Judah,
Ps 119:102 for you yourself have *t* me.
Pr 4: 4 he *t* me and said,
31: 1 an oracle his mother *t* him:
Isa 29:13 is made up only of rules *t* by men.
50: 4 ear to listen like one being *t*.
Mt 7:29 he *t* as one who had authority,
15: 9 their teachings are but rules *t*
Lk 4:15 He *t* in their synagogues,
Ac 20:20 have *t* you publicly and from house
1Co 2:13 but in words *t* by the Spirit,
Gal 1:12 nor was I *t* it; rather, I received it
1Ti 1:20 to Satan to be *t* not to blaspheme.
1Jn 2:27 just as it has *t* you, remain in him.

TAX (TAXES)
Mt 11:19 a friend of *t* collectors and "sinners
17:24 of the two-drachma *t* came to Peter

TAXES (TAX)
Mt 22:17 Is it right to pay *t* to Caesar or not
Ro 13: 7 If you owe *t*, pay *t*; if revenue,

TEACH (TAUGHT TEACHER TEACHERS TEACHES TEACHING TEACHINGS)
Ex 4:12 and will *t* you what to say."
18:20 *T* them the decrees and laws,
33:13 *t* me your ways so I may know you
Lev 10:11 and you must *t* the Israelites all
Dt 4: 9 *T* them to your children
6: 1 me to *t* you to observe
8: 3 to *t* you that man does not live
11:19 *T* them to your children, talking
1Sa 12:23 I will *t* you the way that is good
1Ki 8:36 *T* them the right way to live,
Job 12: 7 ask the animals, and they will *t* you
Ps 32: 8 *t* you in the way you should go;
34:11 I will *t* you the fear of the LORD.
51:13 I will *t* transgressors your ways,
78: 5 forefathers to *t* their children,
90:12 *T* us to number our days aright,
119: 33 *T* me, O LORD, to follow your
143: 10 *T* me to do your will,
Pr 9: 9 *t* a righteous man and he will add
Jer 31:34 No longer will a man *t* his neighbor
Mic 4: 2 He will *t* us his ways,
Lk 11: 1 said to him, "Lord, *t* us to pray,
12:12 for the Holy Spirit will *t* you
Jn 14:26 will *t* you all things and will remind
Ro 2:21 who *t* others, do you not *t* yourself?
15: 4 in the past was written to *t* us,
1Ti 2:12 I do not permit a woman to *t*
3: 2 respectable, hospitable, able to *t*,
2Ti 2: 2 also be qualified to *t* others.
2:24 kind to everyone, able to *t*,
Tit 2: 1 You must *t* what is in accord
2:15 then, are the things you should *t*.
Heb 8:11 No longer will a man *t* his neighbor
Jas 3: 1 know that we who *t* will be judged
1Jn 2:27 you do not need anyone to *t* you.

TEACHER (TEACH)
Ecc 1: 1 The words of the *T*, son of David,
Mt 10:24 "A student is not above his *t*,
13:52 "Therefore every *t*
23:10 Nor are you to be called '*t*,'
Lk 6:40 A student is not above his *t*,
Jn 3: 2 we know you are a *t* who has come
13:14 and *T*, have washed your feet,

TEACHERS (TEACH)
Ps 119: 99 I have more insight than all my *t*,
Pr 5:13 I would not obey my *t*
Lk 20:46 "Beware of the *t* of the law.
1Co 12:28 third *t*, then workers of miracles,
Eph 4:11 and some to be pastors and *t*,
2Ti 4: 3 around them a great number of *t*
Heb 5:12 by this time you ought to be *t*,
Jas 3: 1 of you should presume to be *t*,
2Pe 2: 1 as there will be false *t* among you.

TEACHES (TEACH)
Ps 25: 9 and *t* them his way.
94:10 Does he who *t* man lack
Pr 15:33 of the LORD *t* a man wisdom,
Isa 48:17 who *t* you what is best for you,
Mt 5:19 *t* these commands will be called
1Ti 6: 3 If anyone *t* false doctrines
Tit 2:12 It *t* us to say "No" to ungodliness
1Jn 2:27 his anointing *t* you about all things

TEACHING (TEACH)
Ezr 7:10 to *t* its decrees and laws in Israel.
Pr 1: 8 and do not forsake your mother's *t*.
3: 1 My son, do not forget my *t*,
6:23 this *t* is a light,
Mt 28:20 *t* them to obey everything I have
Jn 7:17 whether my *t* comes from God or
8:31 to my *t*, you are really my disciples.
14:23 loves me, he will obey my *t*.
Ac 2:42 themselves to the apostles' *t*
Ro 12: 7 let him serve; if it is *t*, let him teach;
Eph 4:14 and there by every wind of *t*
2Th 3: 6 to the *t* you received from us.
1Ti 4:13 of Scripture, to preaching and to *t*.
5:17 whose work is preaching and *t*.
6: 3 Lord Jesus Christ and to godly *t*,
2Ti 3:16 is God-breathed and is useful for *t*,
Tit 1:11 by *t* things they ought not
2: 7 In your *t* show integrity,
Heb 5:13 with the *t* about righteousness.
2Jn 9 and does not continue in the *t*

TEACHINGS (TEACH)
Pr 7: 2 guard my *t* as the apple of your eye.
2Th 2:15 hold to the *t* we passed on to you,
Heb 6: 1 leave the elementary *t* about Christ

TEAR (TEARS)
Rev 7:17 God will wipe away every *t*
21: 4 He will wipe every *t*

TEARS (TEAR)
Ps 126: 5 Those who sow in *t*
Isa 25: 8 LORD will wipe away the *t*
Jer 31:16 and your eyes from *t*,
50: 4 in *t* to seek the LORD their God.
Lk 7:38 she began to wet his feet with her *t*.
2Co 2: 4 anguish of heart and with many *t*,
Php 3:18 and now say again even with *t*,

TEETH (TOOTH)
Job 19:20 with only the skin of my *t*.
Ps 35:16 they gnashed their *t* at me.
Jer 31:29 and the children's *t* are set on edge
Mt 8:12 will be weeping and gnashing of *t*."

TEMPER (EVEN-TEMPERED HOT-TEMPERED ILL-TEMPERED QUICK-TEMPERED)
Pr 16:32 a man who controls his *t*

TEMPERANCE see SELF-CONTROL

TEMPERATE*
1Ti 3: 2 *t*, self-controlled, respectable,
3:11 not malicious talkers but *t*
Tit 2: 2 Teach the older men to be *t*,

TEMPEST
Ps 50: 3 and around him a *t* rages.
55: 8 far from the *t* and storm."

TEMPLE (TEMPLES)
1Ki 6: 1 began to build the *t* of the LORD.
6:38 the *t* was finished in all its details
8:10 the cloud filled the *t* of the LORD.
8:27 How much less this *t* I have built!
2Ch 36:19 They set fire to God's *t*
36:23 me to build a *t* for him at Jerusalem
Ezr 6:14 finished building the *t* according
Ps 27: 4 and to seek him in his *t*.
Isa 6: 1 and the train of his robe filled the *t*.
Eze 10: 4 cloud filled the *t*, and the court was
43: 4 glory of the LORD entered the *t*
Hab 2:20 But the LORD is in his holy *t*;
Mt 12: 6 that one greater than the *t* is here.
26:61 'I am able to destroy the *t* of God
27:51 of the *t* was torn in two from top
Lk 21: 5 about how the *t* was adorned
Jn 2:14 In the *t* courts he found men selling
1Co 3:16 that you yourselves are God's *t*
6:19 you not know that your body is a *t*
2Co 6:16 For we are the *t* of the living God.
Rev 21:22 I did not see a *t* in the city,

TEMPLES (TEMPLE)
Ac 17:24 does not live in *t* built by hands.

TEMPORARY
2Co 4:18 what is seen is *t*, but what is unseen

TEMPT* (TEMPTATION TEMPTED TEMPTER TEMPTING)
1Co 7: 5 again so that Satan will not *t* you
Jas 1:13 does he *t* anyone; but each one is

TEMPTATION* (TEMPT)
Mt 6:13 And lead us not into *t*,
26:41 pray so that you will not fall into *t*.
Mk 14:38 pray so that you will not fall into *t*.
Lk 11: 4 And lead us not into *t*.'"
22:40 "Pray that you will not fall into *t*."
22:46 pray so that you will not fall into *t*
1Co 10:13 No *t* has seized you except what is
1Ti 6: 9 want to get rich fall into *t*

TEMPTED* (TEMPT)
Mt 4: 1 into the desert to be *t* by the devil.
Mk 1:13 was in the desert forty days, being *t*
Lk 4: 2 for forty days he was *t* by the devil.
1Co 10:13 But when you are *t*, he will
10:13 he will not let you be *t*
Gal 6: 1 yourself, or you also may be *t*.
1Th 3: 5 way the tempter might have *t* you
Heb 2:18 able to help those who are being *t*.
2:18 he himself suffered when he was *t*,
4:15 but we have one who has been *t*
Jas 1:13 For God cannot be *t* by evil,
1:13 When *t*, no one should say,
1:14 each one is *t* when, by his own evil

TEMPTER* (TEMPT)
Mt 4: 3 The *t* came to him and said,
1Th 3: 5 some way the *t* might have

TEMPTING* (TEMPT)
Lk 4:13 the devil had finished all this *t*,
Jas 1:13 no one should say, "God is *t* me."

TEN (TENTH TITHE TITHES)
Ex 34:28 covenant—the *T* Commandments.
Lev 26: 8 of you will chase *t* thousand,
Dt 4:13 covenant, the *T* Commandments,
10: 4 The *T* Commandments he had
Ps 91: 7 *t* thousand at your right hand,
Da 7:24 *t* horns are *t* kings who will come
Mt 25: 1 will be like *t* virgins who took
25:28 it to the one who has the *t* talents.
Lk 15: 8 suppose a woman has *t* silver coins
Rev 12: 3 and *t* horns and seven crowns

TENANTS
Mt 21:34 servants to the *t* to collect his fruit.

TEND
Jer 23: 2 to the shepherds who *t* my people:
Eze 34:14 I will *t* them in a good pasture,

TENDERNESS*
Isa 63:15 Your *t* and compassion are
Php 2: 1 fellowship with the Spirit, if any *t*

TENT (TENTMAKER TENTS)
Ex 27:21 In the *T* of Meeting,
40: 2 "Set up the tabernacle, the *T*
Isa 54: 2 "Enlarge the place of your *t*,
2Co 5: 1 that if the earthly *t* we live
2Pe 1:13 as long as I live in the *t* of this body,

TENTH (TEN)
Ge 14:20 Abram gave him a *t* of everything.
Nu 18:26 you must present a *t* of that tithe
Dt 14:22 Be sure to set aside a *t*
1Sa 8:15 He will take a *t* of your grain
Lk 11:42 you give God a *t* of your mint,
18:12 I fast twice a week and give a *t*
Heb 7: 4 patriarch Abraham gave him a *t*

TENTMAKER* (TENT)
Ac 18: 3 and because he was a *t* as they were

TENTS (TENT)
Ge 13:12 and pitched his *t* near Sodom.
Ps 84:10 than dwell in the *t* of the wicked.

TERAH
Ge 11:31 *T* took his son Abram, his

TERRIBLE (TERROR)
2Ti 3: 1 There will be *t* times

TERRIFIED (TERROR)
Dt 7:21 Do not be *t* by them,
20: 3 do not be *t* or give way to panic
Ps 90: 7 and *t* by your indignation.
Mt 14:26 walking on the lake, they were *t*.
17: 6 they fell facedown to the ground, *t*.
27:54 they were *t*, and exclaimed,
Mk 4:41 They were *t* and asked each other,

TERRIFYING (TERROR)
Heb 12:21 The sight was so *t* that Moses said,

TERRITORY
2Co 10:16 done in another man's *t*.

TERROR (TERRIBLE TERRIFIED TERRIFYING)
Dt 2:25 very day I will begin to put the *t*
28:67 of the *t* that will fill your hearts
Job 9:34 so that his *t* would frighten me no
Ps 91: 5 You will not fear the *t* of night,
Pr 21:15 but *t* to evildoers.
Isa 13: 8 *T* will seize them,
24:17 *T* and pit and snare await you,
51:13 live in constant *t* every day
54:14 *T* will be far removed;
Lk 21:26 Men will faint from *t*, apprehensive
Ro 13: 3 For rulers hold no *t*

TEST (TESTED TESTING TESTS)
Dt 6:16 Do not *t* the LORD your God
Jdg 3: 1 to *t* all those Israelites who had not
1Ki 10: 1 came to *t* him with hard questions.
1Ch 29:17 that you *t* the heart and are pleased
Ps 26: 2 *T* me, O LORD, and try me,
78:18 They willfully put God to the *t*
106: 14 wasteland they put God to the *t*.
139: 23 *t* me and know my anxious
Jer 11:20 and *t* the heart and mind,
Lk 4:12 put the Lord your God to the *t*.'"
Ac 5: 9 How could you agree to *t* the Spirit
Ro 12: 2 Then you will be able to *t*
1Co 3:13 and the fire will *t* the quality
10: 9 We should not *t* the Lord,
2Co 13: 5 unless, of course, you fail the *t*?
1Th 5:21 *T* everything.
Jas 1:12 because when he has stood the *t*,
1Jn 4: 1 *t* the spirits to see whether they are

TESTED (TEST)
Ge 22: 1 Some time later God *t* Abraham.
Job 23:10 when he has *t* me, I will come forth
34:36 that Job might be *t* to the utmost
Ps 66:10 For you, O God, *t* us;
Pr 27:21 man is *t* by the praise he receives.
Isa 28:16 a *t* stone,
48:10 I have *t* you in the furnace
1Ti 3:10 They must first be *t*; and then
Heb 11:17 By faith Abraham, when God *t* him

TESTIFIES (TESTIFY)
Jn 5:32 There is another who *t* in my favor,
Ro 8:16 The Spirit himself *t*

TESTIFY (TESTIFIES TESTIMONY)
Pr 24:28 Do not *t* against your neighbor
Jn 1: 7 a witness to *t* concerning that light,
1:34 and I *t* that this is the Son of God."
5:39 are the Scriptures that *t* about me,
7: 7 because I *t* that what it does is evil.
15:26 he will *t* about me. And you
Ac 4:33 continued to *t* to the resurrection
10:43 All the prophets *t* about him that
2Ti 1: 8 ashamed to *t* about our Lord,
1Jn 4:14 *t* that the Father has sent his Son
5: 7 For there are three that *t*: the Spirit

TESTIMONY (TESTIFY)
Ex 20:16 "You shall not give false *t*
31:18 gave him the two tablets of the *T*,
Nu 35:30 only on the *t* of witnesses.
Dt 19:18 giving false *t* against his brother,
Pr 12:17 A truthful witness gives honest *t*,
Isa 8:20 and to the *t*! If they do not speak
Mt 15:19 sexual immorality, theft, false *t*,
24:14 preached in the whole world as a *t*
Lk 18:20 not give false *t*, honor your father
Jn 2:25 He did not need man's *t* about man
21:24 We know that his *t* is true.
1Jn 5: 9 but God's *t* is greater because it is
Rev 12:11 and by the word of their *t*;

TESTING (TEST)
Lk 8:13 but in the time of *t* they fall away.
Heb 3: 8 during the time of *t* in the desert,
Jas 1: 3 because you know that the *t*

TESTS (TEST)
Pr 17: 3 but the LORD *t* the heart.
1Th 2: 4 but God, who *t* our hearts.

THADDAEUS
Apostle (Mt 10:3; Mk 3:18); probably also known as Judas son of James (Lk 6:16; Ac 1:13).

THANK (THANKFUL THANKFULNESS THANKS THANKSGIVING)
Php 1: 3 I *t* my God every time I remember
1Th 3: 9 How can we *t* God enough for you

THANKFUL (THANK)
Col 3:15 And be *t*.
Heb 12:28 let us be *t*, and so worship God

THANKFULNESS (THANK)
1Co 10:30 If I take part in the meal with *t*,
Col 2: 7 taught, and overflowing with *t*.

THANKS (THANK)
1Ch 16: 8 Give *t* to the LORD, call
Ne 12:31 assigned two large choirs to give *t*.
Ps 7:17 I will give *t* to the LORD
28: 7 and I will give *t* to him in song.
30:12 my God, I will give you *t* forever.
35:18 I will give you *t* in the great
75: 1 we give *t*, for your Name is near;
100: 4 give *t* to him and praise his name.
107: 1 Give *t* to the LORD, for he is good;
118: 28 are my God, and I will give you *t*;
136: 1 Give *t* to the LORD, for he is good.
Ro 1:21 as God nor gave *t* to him,
1Co 11:24 when he had given *t*, he broke it
15:57 *t* be to God! He gives us the victory
2Co 2:14 *t* be to God, who always leads us
9:15 *T* be to God for his indescribable
1Th 5:18 give *t* in all circumstances,
Rev 4: 9 and *t* to him who sits on the throne

THANKSGIVING (THANK)
Ps 95: 2 Let us come before him with *t*
100: 4 Enter his gates with *t*
1Co 10:16 cup of *t* for which we give thanks
Php 4: 6 by prayer and petition, with *t*,
1Ti 4: 3 created to be received with *t*

THEFT (THIEF)
Mt 15:19 sexual immorality, *t*, false

THEFTS* (THIEF)
Rev 9:21 their sexual immorality or their *t*.

THEME*
Ps 45: 1 My heart is stirred by a noble *t*
119: 54 Your decrees are the *t* of my song

THIEF (THEFT THEFTS THIEVES)
Ex 22: 3 A *t* must certainly make restitution
Pr 6:30 Men do not despise a *t* if he steals
Lk 12:39 at what hour the *t* was coming,
1Th 5: 2 day of the Lord will come like a *t*
1Pe 4:15 or *t* or any other kind of criminal,
Rev 16:15 I come like a *t*! Blessed is he who

THIEVES (THIEF)
Mt 6:19 and where *t* break in and steal.
Jn 10: 8 who ever came before me were *t*
1Co 6:10 nor homosexual offenders nor *t*

THINK (THINKING THOUGHT THOUGHTS)
Ps 63: 6 I *t* of you through the watches
Isa 44:19 No one stops to *t*,
Mt 22:42 "What do you *t* about the Christ?
Ro 12: 3 Do not *t* of yourself more highly
Php 4: 8 praiseworthy—*t* about such things

THINKING (THINK)
Pr 23: 7 who is always *t* about the cost.
1Co 14:20 Brothers, stop *t* like children.
2Pe 3: 1 to stimulate you to wholesome *t*.

THIRST (THIRSTS THIRSTY)
Ps 69:21 and gave me vinegar for my *t*.
Mt 5: 6 Blessed are those who hunger and *t*
Jn 4:14 the water I give him will never *t*.
2Co 11:27 I have known hunger and *t*
Rev 7:16 never again will they *t*.

THIRSTS (THIRST)
Ps 42: 2 My soul *t* for God,

THIRSTY (THIRST)
Ps 107: 9 for he satisfies the *t*
Pr 25:21 if he is *t*, give him water to drink.
Isa 55: 1 "Come, all you who are *t*,
Mt 25:35 I was *t* and you gave me something
Jn 7:37 "If anyone is *t*, let him come to me
Ro 12:20 if he is *t*, give him something
Rev 21: 6 To him who is *t* I will give to drink
22:17 Whoever is *t*, let him come;

THOMAS
Apostle (Mt 10:3; Mk 3:18; Lk 6:15; Jn 11:16; 14:5; 21:2; Ac 1:13). Doubted resurrection (Jn 20:24-28).

THONGS
Mk 1: 7 *t* of whose sandals I am not worthy

THORN (THORNBUSHES THORNS)
2Co 12: 7 there was given me a *t* in my flesh,

THORNBUSHES (THORN)
Lk 6:44 People do not pick figs from *t*,

THORNS (THORN)
Ge 3:18 It will produce *t* and thistles
Nu 33:55 in your eyes and *t* in your sides.
Mt 13: 7 fell among *t*, which grew up
27:29 and then twisted together a crown of *t*
Heb 6: 8 But land that produces *t*

THOUGHT (THINK)
Pr 14:15 a prudent man gives *t* to his steps.
21:29 an upright man gives *t* to his ways.
1Co 13:11 I talked like a child, I *t* like a child,

THOUGHTS (THINK)
1Ch 28: 9 every motive behind the *t*.
Ps 94:11 The LORD knows the *t* of man;
139: 23 test me and know my anxious *t*.
Isa 55: 8 "For my *t* are not your *t*,
Mt 15:19 For out of the heart come evil *t*,
1Co 2:11 among men knows the *t* of a man
Heb 4:12 it judges the *t* and attitudes

THREE
Ge 6:10 Noah had *t* sons: Shem, Ham
Ex 23:14 "*T* times a year you are
Dt 19:15 the testimony of two or *t* witnesses.
2Sa 23: 8 a Tahkemonite, was chief of the *T*;
Pr 30:15 "There are *t* things that are never
30:18 "There are *t* things that are too
30:21 "Under *t* things the earth trembles,
30:29 "There are *t* things that are stately
Ecc 4:12 of *t* strands is not quickly broken.
Da 3:24 "Weren't there *t* men that we tied up
Am 1: 3 "For *t* sins of Damascus,
Jnh 1:17 inside the fish *t* days and *t* nights.
Mt 12:40 so the Son of Man will be *t* days
12:40 *t* nights in the belly of a huge fish,
12:40 *t* nights in the heart of the earth.
17: 4 I will put up *t* shelters—one
18:20 or *t* come together in my name,
26:34 you will disown me *t* times."
26:75 you will disown me *t* times."
27:63 'After *t* days I will rise again.'
Mk 8:31 and after *t* days rise again.
9: 5 Let us put up *t* shelters—one
14:30 yourself will disown me *t* times."
Jn 2:19 and I will raise it again in *t* days."
1Co 13:13 And now these *t* remain: faith,
14:27 or at the most *t*— should speak,
2Co 13: 1 testimony of two or *t* witnesses."
1Jn 5: 7 For there are *t* that testify:

THRESHER* (THRESHING)
1Co 9:10 plowman plows and the *t* threshes,

THRESHING (THRESHER)
Ru 3: 6 So she went down to the *t* floor
2Sa 24:18 an altar to the LORD on the *t* floor
Lk 3:17 is in his hand to clear his *t* floor

THREW (THROW)
Da 6:16 and *t* him into the lions' den.
Jnh 1:15 took Jonah and *t* him overboard,

THRIVE
Pr 29: 2 When the righteous *t*, the people

THROAT (THROATS)
Ps 5: 9 Their *t* is an open grave;
Pr 23: 2 and put a knife to your *t*

THROATS (THROAT)
Ro 3:13 "Their *t* are open graves;

THROB*
Isa 60: 5 your heart will *t* and swell with joy;

THRONE (ENTHRONED ENTHRONES THRONES)
2Sa 7:16 your *t* will be established forever
1Ch 17:12 and I will establish his *t* forever.
Ps 11: 4 the LORD is on his heavenly *t*.
45: 6 Your *t*, O God, will last for ever
47: 8 God is seated on his holy *t*.
89:14 justice are the foundation of your *t*;
Isa 6: 1 I saw the Lord seated on a *t*,
66: 1 "Heaven is my *t*,
Eze 28: 2 I sit on the *t* of a god
Da 7: 9 His *t* was flaming with fire,
Mt 19:28 Son of Man sits on his glorious *t*,
Ac 7:49 prophet says: " 'Heaven is my *t*,
Heb 1: 8 "Your *t*, O God, will last for ever
4:16 Let us then approach the *t* of grace
12: 2 at the right hand of the *t* of God.
Rev 3:21 sat down with my Father on his *t*.
3:21 the right to sit with me on my *t*,
4: 2 there before me was a *t* in heaven
4:10 They lay their crowns before the *t*
20:11 Then I saw a great white *t*
22: 3 *t* of God and of the Lamb will be

THRONES (THRONE)
Mt 19:28 me will also sit on twelve *t*,
Rev 4: 4 throne were twenty-four other *t*,

THROW (THREW)
Jn 8: 7 the first to *t* a stone at her."
Heb 10:35 So do not *t* away your confidence;
12: 1 let us *t* off everything that hinders

THUNDER (THUNDERS)
Ps 93: 4 Mightier than the *t*
Mk 3:17 which means Sons of *T*); Andrew,

THUNDERS (THUNDER)
Job 37: 5 God's voice *t* in marvelous ways;
Ps 29: 3 the God of glory *t*,
Rev 10: 3 the voices of the seven *t* spoke.

THWART* (THWARTED)
Isa 14:27 has purposed, and who can *t* him?

THWARTED (THWART)
Job 42: 2 no plan of yours can be *t*.

THYATIRA
Rev 2:18 the angel of the church in *T* write:

TIBNI
King of Israel (1Ki 16:21-22).

TIDINGS
Isa 40: 9 You who bring good *t* to Jerusalem
52: 7 who bring good *t*,

TIES
Hos 11: 4 with *t* of love;

Mt 12:29 unless he first *t* up the strong man?

TIGHT*
Jas 1:26 and yet does not keep a *t* rein

TIGHTFISTED*
Dt 15: 7 or *t* toward your poor brother.

TIME (TIMES)
Est 4:14 come to royal position for such a *t*
Ecc 3: 1 There is a *t* for everything,
8: 5 wise heart will know the proper *t*
Da 7:25 to him for a *t*, times and half a *t*.
12: 7 "It will be for a *t*, times and half a *t*.
Hos 10:12 for it is *t* to seek the LORD,
Jn 2: 4 Jesus replied, "My *t* has not yet
17: 1 prayed: "Father, the *t* has come.
Ro 9: 9 "At the appointed *t* I will return,
13:11 understanding the present *t*.
1Co 7:29 brothers, is that the *t* is short.
2Co 6: 2 now is the *t* of God's favor,
2Ti 1: 9 Jesus before the beginning of *t*,
Tit 1: 2 promised before the beginning of *t*,
Heb 9:28 and he will appear a second *t*,
10:12 for all *t* one sacrifice for sins,
1Pe 4:17 For it is *t* for judgment to begin

TIMES (TIME)
Ps 9: 9 a stronghold in *t* of trouble.
31:15 My *t* are in your hands;
62: 8 Trust in him at all *t*, O people;
Pr 17:17 A friend loves at all *t*,
Isa 46:10 from ancient *t*, what is still to come
Am 5:13 for the *t* are evil.
Mt 16: 3 cannot interpret the signs of the *t*.
18:21 how many *t* shall I forgive my
Ac 1: 7 "It is not for you to know the *t*
Rev 12:14 *t* and half a time, out

TIMID (TIMIDITY)
1Th 5:14 encourage the *t*, help the weak,

TIMIDITY* (TIMID)
2Ti 1: 7 For God did not give us a spirit of *t*

TIMOTHY

Believer from Lystra (Ac 16:1). Joined Paul on second missionary journey (Ac 16-20). Sent to settle problems at Corinth (1Co 4:17; 16:10). Led church at Ephesus (1Ti 1:3). Co-writer with Paul (1Th 1:1; 2Th 1:1; Phm 1).

TIP
Job 33: 2 my words are on the *t* of my tongue

TIRE (TIRED)
2Th 3:13 never *t* of doing what is right.

TIRED (TIRE)
Ex 17:12 When Moses' hands grew *t*,
Isa 40:28 He will not grow *t* or weary,

TITHE (TEN)
Lev 27:30 " 'A *t* of everything from the land,
Dt 12:17 eat in your own towns the *t*
Mal 3:10 the whole *t* into the storehouse,

TITHES (TEN)
Nu 18:21 give to the Levites all the *t* in Israel
Mal 3: 8 'How do we rob you?' "In *t*

TITUS*

Gentile co-worker of Paul (Gal 2:1-3; 2Ti 4:10); sent to Corinth (2Co 2:13; 7-8; 12:18), Crete (Tit 1:4-5).

TODAY
Ps 2: 7 *t* I have become your Father.
95: 7 *T*, if you hear his voice,
Mt 6:11 Give us *t* our daily bread.
Lk 2:11 *T* in the town of David a Savior has
23:43 *t* you will be with me in paradise."
Ac 13:33 *t* I have become your Father.'
Heb 1: 5 *t* I have become your Father"?
3: 7 "*T*, if you hear his voice,
3:13 daily, as long as it is called *T*,
5: 5 *t* I have become your Father."
13: 8 Christ is the same yesterday and *t*

TOIL (TOILED TOILING)
Ge 3:17 through painful *t* you will eat of it

TOILED (TOIL)
2Co 11:27 and *t* and have often gone

TOILING (TOIL)
2Th 3: 8 *t* so that we would not be a burden

TOLERANCE* (TOLERATE)
Ro 2: 4 for the riches of his kindness, *t*

TOLERATE (TOLERANCE)
Hab 1:13 you cannot *t* wrong.
Rev 2: 2 that you cannot *t* wicked men,

TOMB
Mt 27:65 make the *t* as secure as you know
Lk 24: 2 the stone rolled away from the *t*,

TOMORROW
Pr 27: 1 Do not boast about *t*,
Isa 22:13 "for *t* we die!"
Mt 6:34 Therefore do not worry about *t*,
1Co 15:32 for *t* we die."
Jas 4:13 "Today or *t* we will go to this

TONGUE (TONGUES)
Ex 4:10 I am slow of speech and *t*."
Job 33: 2 my words are on the tip of my *t*.
Ps 5: 9 with their *t* they speak deceit.
34:13 keep your *t* from evil
37:30 and his *t* speaks what is just.
39: 1 and keep my *t* from sin;
51:14 my *t* will sing of your righteousness
52: 4 O you deceitful *t*!
71:24 My *t* will tell of your righteous acts
119:172 May my *t* sing of your word,
137: 6 May my *t* cling to the roof
139: 4 Before a word is on my *t*
Pr 6:17 a lying *t*,
10:19 but he who holds his *t* is wise.
12:18 but the *t* of the wise brings healing.
15: 4 The *t* that brings healing is a tree
17:20 he whose *t* is deceitful falls
21:23 He who guards his mouth and his *t*
25:15 and a gentle *t* can break a bone.
26:28 A lying *t* hates those it hurts,
28:23 than he who has a flattering *t*.
31:26 and faithful instruction is on her *t*.
SS 4:11 milk and honey are under your *t*.
Isa 32: 4 and the stammering *t* will be fluent
45:23 by me every *t* will swear.
50: 4 has given me an instructed *t*,
59: 3 and your *t* mutters wicked things.
Lk 16:24 of his finger in water and cool my *t*,
Ro 14:11 every *t* will confess to God.'"
1Co 14: 2 speaks in a *t* does not speak to men
14: 4 He who speaks in a *t* edifies himself
14: 9 intelligible words with your *t*,
14:13 in a *t* should pray that he may
14:19 than ten thousand words in a *t*.
14:26 revelation, a *t* or an interpretation.
14:27 If anyone speaks in a *t*, two—
Php 2:11 every *t* confess that Jesus Christ is
Jas 1:26 does not keep a tight rein on his *t*,
3: 5 Likewise the *t* is a small part
3: 8 but no man can tame the *t*.
1Jn 3:18 or *t* but with actions and in truth.

TONGUES (TONGUE)
Ps 12: 4 "We will triumph with our *t*;
126: 2 our *t* with songs of joy.
Isa 28:11 with foreign lips and strange *t*
66:18 and gather all nations and *t*,
Jer 23:31 the prophets who wag their own *t*
Mk 16:17 in new *t*; they will pick up snakes
Ac 2: 3 to be *t* of fire that separated
2: 4 and began to speak in other *t*
10:46 For they heard them speaking in *t*
19: 6 and they spoke in *t* and prophesied
Ro 3:13 their *t* practice deceit."
1Co 12:10 still another the interpretation of *t*.
12:28 speaking in different kinds of *t*.
12:30 Do all speak in *t*? Do all interpret?
13: 1 If I speak in the *t* of men
13: 8 where there are *t*, they will be
14: 5 greater than one who speaks in *t*,
14:18 speak in *t* more than all of you.
14:21 "Through men of strange *t*
14:39 and do not forbid speaking in *t*.

TOOK (TAKE)
Isa 53: 4 Surely he *t* up our infirmities
Mt 8:17 "He *t* up our infirmities
26:26 they were eating, Jesus *t* bread,
26:27 Then he *t* the cup, gave thanks
1Co 11:23 the night he was betrayed, *t* bread,
11:25 after supper he *t* the cup, saying,
Php 3:12 for which Christ Jesus *t* hold of me.

TOOTH (TEETH)
Ex 21:24 eye for eye, *t* for *t*, hand for hand,
Mt 5:38 'Eye for eye, and *t* for *t*.'

TOP
Dt 28:13 you will always be at the *t*,
Isa 1: 6 of your foot to the *t* of your head
Mt 27:51 torn in two from *t* to bottom.

TORMENT (TORMENTED TORMENTORS)
Lk 16:28 also come to this place of *t*.'
2Co 12: 7 a messenger of Satan, to *t* me.

TORMENTED (TORMENT)
Rev 20:10 They will be *t* day and night

TORMENTORS (TORMENT)
Ps 137: 3 our *t* demanded songs of joy;

TORN
Gal 4:15 you would have *t* out your eyes
Php 1:23 I do not know! I am *t*

TORTURED*
Mt 18:34 turned him over to the jailers to be *t*,
Heb 11:35 Others were *t* and refused

TOSSED (TOSSING)
Eph 4:14 *t* back and forth by the waves,
Jas 1: 6 of the sea, blown and *t* by the wind.

TOSSING (TOSSED)
Isa 57:20 But the wicked are like the *t* sea,

TOUCH (TOUCHED TOUCHES)
Ge 3: 3 you must not *t* it, or you will die.'"
Ex 19:12 go up the mountain or *t* the foot
Ps 105: 15 "Do not *t* my anointed ones;
Mt 9:21 If I only *t* his cloak, I will be healed
Lk 18:15 babies to Jesus to have him *t* them.
24:39 It is I myself! *T* me and see;
2Co 6:17 *T* no unclean thing,
Col 2:21 Do not taste! Do not *t*!"?

TOUCHED (TOUCH)
1Sa 10:26 men whose hearts God had *t*.
Isa 6: 7 With it he *t* my mouth and said,
Mt 14:36 and all who *t* him were healed.
Lk 8:45 "Who *t* me?" Jesus asked.
1Jn 1: 1 looked at and our hands have *t*—

TOUCHES (TOUCH)
Ex 19:12 Whoever *t* the mountain shall
Zec 2: 8 for whoever *t* you *t* the apple

TOWER
Ge 11: 4 with a *t* that reaches to the heavens
Pr 18:10 of the LORD is a strong *t*;

TOWN (TOWNS)
Mt 2:23 and lived in a *t* called Nazareth.

TOWNS (TOWN)
Nu 35: 2 to give the Levites *t* to live
35:15 These six *t* will be a place of refuge
Jer 11:13 as many gods as you have *t*,
Mt 9:35 Jesus went through all the *t*

TRACING*
Ro 11:33 and his paths beyond *t* out!

TRACK
Job 14:16 but not keep *t* of my sin.

TRADERS (TRADING)
1Ti 1:10 for slave *t* and liars and perjurers—

TRADING (TRADERS)
1Ki 10:22 The king had a fleet of *t* ships at sea
Pr 31:18 She sees that her *t* is profitable,

TRADITION (TRADITIONS)
Mt 15: 2 "Why do your disciples break the *t*
15: 6 word of God for the sake of your *t*.
Mk 7:13 by your *t* that you have handed
Col 2: 8 which depends on human *t*

TRADITIONS (TRADITION)
Mk 7: 8 are holding on to the *t* of men."
Gal 1:14 zealous for the *t* of my fathers.

TRAIL
1Ti 5:24 the sins of others *t* behind them.

TRAIN* (TRAINED TRAINING)
Ps 68:18 you led captives in your *t*;
Pr 22: 6 *T* a child in the way he should go,
Isa 2: 4 nor will they *t* for war anymore.
6: 1 the *t* of his robe filled the temple.
Mic 4: 3 nor will they *t* for war anymore.
Eph 4: 8 he led captives in his *t*
1Ti 4: 7 rather, *t* yourself to be godly.
Tit 2: 4 they can *t* the younger women

TRAINED (TRAIN)
Lk 6:40 everyone who is fully *t* will be like
Ac 22: 3 Under Gamaliel I was thoroughly *t*
2Co 11: 6 I may not be a *t* speaker,
Heb 5:14 by constant use have *t* themselves
12:11 for those who have been *t* by it.

TRAINING* (TRAIN)
1Co 9:25 in the games goes into strict *t*.
Eph 6: 4 up in the *t* and instruction
1Ti 4: 8 For physical *t* is of some value,
2Ti 3:16 correcting and *t* in righteousness,

TRAITOR (TRAITORS)
Lk 6:16 and Judas Iscariot, who became a *t*.
Jn 18: 5 Judas the *t* was standing there

TRAITORS (TRAITOR)
Ps 59: 5 show no mercy to wicked *t*.

TRAMPLE (TRAMPLED)
Joel 3:13 Come, *t* the grapes,
Am 2: 7 They *t* on the heads of the poor
5:11 You *t* on the poor
8: 4 Hear this, you who *t* the needy
Mt 7: 6 they may *t* them under their feet,
Lk 10:19 I have given you authority to *t*

TRAMPLED (TRAMPLE)
Isa 63: 6 I *t* the nations in my anger;
Lk 21:24 Jerusalem will be *t*
Heb 10:29 to be punished who has *t* the Son
Rev 14:20 They were *t* in the winepress

TRANCE*
Ac 10:10 was being prepared, he fell into a *t*.
11: 5 and in a *t* I saw a vision.
22:17 into a *t* and saw the Lord speaking.

TRANQUILLITY*
Ecc 4: 6 Better one handful with *t*

TRANSACTIONS*
Ru 4: 7 method of legalizing *t* in Israel.)

TRANSCENDS*
Php 4: 7 which *t* all understanding,

TRANSFIGURED*
Mt 17: 2 There he was *t* before them.
Mk 9: 2 There he was *t* before them.

TRANSFORM* (TRANSFORMED)
Php 3:21 will *t* our lowly bodies

TRANSFORMED (TRANSFORM)
Ro 12: 2 be *t* by the renewing of your mind.
2Co 3:18 are being *t* into his likeness

TRANSGRESSED* (TRANSGRESSION)
Da 9:11 All Israel has *t* your law

TRANSGRESSION* (TRANSGRESSED TRANSGRESSIONS TRANSGRESSORS)
Ps 19:13 innocent of great *t*.
Isa 53: 8 for the *t* of my people he was
Da 9:24 and your holy city to finish *t*,
Mic 1: 5 All this is because of Jacob's *t*,
1: 5 What is Jacob's *t*?
3: 8 to declare to Jacob his *t*,
6: 7 Shall I offer my firstborn for my *t*,
7:18 who pardons sin and forgives the *t*
Ro 4:15 where there is no law there is no *t*.
11:11 Rather, because of their *t*,
11:12 if their *t* means riches for the world

TRANSGRESSIONS* (TRANSGRESSION)
Ps 32: 1 whose *t* are forgiven,
32: 5 my *t* to the LORD"—
39: 8 Save me from all my *t*;
51: 1 blot out my *t*.
51: 3 For I know my *t*,
65: 3 you forgave our *t*.
103: 12 so far has he removed our *t* from us
Isa 43:25 your *t*, for my own sake,
50: 1 of your *t* your mother was sent
53: 5 But he was pierced for our *t*,
Mic 1:13 for the *t* of Israel
Ro 4: 7 whose *t* are forgiven,
Gal 3:19 because of *t* until the Seed to whom
Eph 2: 1 you were dead in your *t* and sins,
2: 5 even when we were dead in *t*—

TRANSGRESSORS* (TRANSGRESSION)
Ps 51:13 Then I will teach *t* your ways,
Isa 53:12 and made intercession for the *t*.
53:12 and was numbered with the *t*.
Lk 22:37 'And he was numbered with the *t*';

TRAP (TRAPPED TRAPS)
Ps 69:22 may it become retribution and a *t*.
Pr 20:25 a *t* for a man to dedicate something
28:10 will fall into his own *t*,
Isa 8:14 a *t* and a snare.
Mt 22:15 and laid plans to *t* him in his words.
Lk 21:34 close on you unexpectedly like a *t*.
Ro 11: 9 their table become a snare and a *t*,
1Ti 3: 7 into disgrace and into the devil's *t*.
1Ti 6: 9 and a *t* and into many foolish
2Ti 2:26 and escape from the *t* of the devil,

TRAPPED (TRAP)
Pr 6: 2 if you have been *t* by what you said
12:13 An evil man is *t* by his sinful talk,

TRAPS (TRAP)
Jos 23:13 they will become snares and *t*
La 4:20 was caught in their *t*.

TRAVEL (TRAVELER)
Pr 4:15 Avoid it, do not *t* on it;
Mt 23:15 You *t* over land and sea

TRAVELER (TRAVEL)
Job 31:32 door was always open to the *t*—
Jer 14: 8 like a *t* who stays only a night?

TREACHEROUS (TREACHERY)
Ps 25: 3 who are *t* without excuse.
2Ti 3: 4 not lovers of the good, *t*, rash,

TREACHERY (TREACHEROUS)
Isa 59:13 rebellion and *t* against the LORD,

TREAD (TREADING TREADS)
Ps 91:13 You will *t* upon the lion

TREADING (TREAD)
Dt 25: 4 an ox while it is *t* out the grain.
1Co 9: 9 an ox while it is *t* out the grain."
1Ti 5:18 the ox while it is *t* out the grain,"

TREADS (TREAD)
Rev 19:15 He *t* the winepress of the fury

TREASURE (TREASURED TREASURES TREASURY)
Pr 2: 4 and search for it as for hidden *t*,
Isa 33: 6 of the LORD is the key to this *t*.
Mt 6:21 For where your *t* is, there your
13:44 of heaven is like *t* hidden in a field.
Lk 12:33 a *t* in heaven that will not be
2Co 4: 7 But we have this *t* in jars of clay
1Ti 6:19 In this way they will lay up *t*

TREASURED (TREASURE)
Ex 19: 5 you will be my *t* possession.
Dt 7: 6 to be his people, his *t* possession.
26:18 his *t* possession as he promised,
Job 23:12 I have *t* the words
Mal 3:17 when I make up my *t* possession.
Lk 2:19 But Mary *t* up all these things
2:51 But his mother *t* all these things

TREASURES (TREASURE)
1Ch 29: 3 my God I now give my personal *t*
Pr 10: 2 Ill-gotten *t* are of no value,
Mt 6:19 up for yourselves *t* on earth,
13:52 out of his storeroom new *t*
Col 2: 3 in whom are hidden all the *t*
Heb 11:26 of greater value than the *t* of Egypt,

TREASURY (TREASURE)
Mk 12:43 more into the *t* than all the others.

TREAT (TREATED TREATING TREATMENT)
Lev 22: 2 sons to *t* with respect the sacred
Ps 103: 10 he does not *t* us as our sins deserve
Mt 18:17 *t* him as you would a pagan
18:35 my heavenly Father will *t* each
Eph 6: 9 *t* your slaves in the same way.
1Th 5:20 do not *t* prophecies with contempt.
1Ti 5: 1 *T* younger men as brothers,
1Pe 3: 7 and *t* them with respect

TREATED (TREAT)
Lev 19:34 The alien living with you must be *t*
25:40 He is to be *t* as a hired worker
1Sa 24:17 "You have *t* me well, but I have
Heb 10:29 who has *t* as an unholy thing

TREATING (TREAT)
Ge 18:25 *t* the righteous and the wicked
Heb 12: 7 as discipline; God is *t* you as sons.

TREATMENT (TREAT)
Col 2:23 and their harsh *t* of the body,

TREATY
Ex 34:12 not to make a *t* with those who live
Dt 7: 2 Make no *t* with them, and show
23: 6 Do not seek a *t* of friendship with them

TREE (TREES)
Ge 2: 9 and the *t* of the knowledge of good
2: 9 of the garden were the *t* of life
Dt 21:23 hung on a *t* is under God's curse.
2Sa 18: 9 Absalom's head got caught in the *t*.
1Ki 14:23 and under every spreading *t*.
Ps 1: 3 He is like a *t* planted by streams
52: 8 But I am like an olive *t*
92:12 righteous will flourish like a palm *t*,
Pr 3:18 She is a *t* of life to those who
11:30 of the righteous is a *t* of life,
27:18 He who tends a fig *t* will eat its fruit
Isa 65:22 For as the days of a *t*,
Jer 17: 8 He will be like a *t* planted
Eze 17:24 I the LORD bring down the tall *t*
Da 4:10 before me stood a *t* in the middle
Mic 4: 4 and under his own fig *t*,
Zec 3:10 to sit under his vine and fig *t*,'
Mt 3:10 every *t* that does not produce good
12:33 for a *t* is recognized by its fruit.
Lk 19: 4 climbed a sycamore-fig *t* to see him
Ac 5:30 killed by hanging him on a *t*.
Ro 11:24 be grafted into their own olive *t*!
Gal 3:13 is everyone who is hung on a *t*."
Jas 3:12 My brothers, can a fig *t* bear olives,
1Pe 2:24 sins in his body on the *t*,
Rev 2: 7 the right to eat from the *t* of life,
22: 2 side of the river stood the *t* of life,
22:14 they may have the right to the *t*
22:19 from him his share in the *t* of life

TREES (TREE)
Jdg 9: 8 One day the *t* went out
Ps 96:12 Then all the *t* of the forest will sing
Isa 55:12 and all the *t* of the field
Mt 3:10 The ax is already at the root of the *t*
Mk 8:24 they look like *t* walking around."
Jude :12 autumn *t*, without fruit

TREMBLE (TREMBLED TREMBLES TREMBLING)
Ex 15:14 The nations will hear and *t*;
1Ch 16:30 *T* before him, all the earth!
Ps 114: 7 *T*, O earth, at the presence
Jer 5:22 "Should you not *t* in my presence?
Eze 38:20 of the earth will *t* at my presence.
Joel 2: 1 Let all who live in the land *t*,
Hab 3: 6 he looked, and made the nations *t*.

TREMBLED (TREMBLE)
Ex 19:16 Everyone in the camp *t*.
20:18 in smoke, they *t* with fear.
2Sa 22: 8 "The earth *t* and quaked,
Ac 7:32 Moses *t* with fear and did not dare

TREMBLES (TREMBLE)
Ps 97: 4 the earth sees and *t*.
104: 32 he who looks at the earth, and it *t*,
Isa 66: 2 and *t* at my word.
Jer 10:10 When he is angry, the earth *t*;
Na 1: 5 The earth *t* at his presence,

TREMBLING (TREMBLE)
Ps 2:11 and rejoice with *t*.
Da 10:10 set me *t* on my hands and knees.
Php 2:12 out your salvation with fear and *t*,
Heb 12:21 terrifying that Moses said, "I am *t*

TRESPASS* (TRESPASSES)
Ro 5:15 But the gift is not like the *t*.
5:15 died by the *t* of the one man,
5:17 For if, by the *t* of the one man,
5:18 result of one *t* was condemnation
5:20 added so that the *t* might increase.

TRESPASSES* (TRESPASS)
Ro 5:16 but the gift followed many *t*

TRIAL (TRIALS)
Ps 37:33 condemned when brought to *t*.
Mk 13:11 you are arrested and brought to *t*,
2Co 8: 2 most severe *t*, their overflowing
Jas 1:12 is the man who perseveres under *t*,
1Pe 4:12 at the painful *t* you are suffering,
Rev 3:10 you from the hour of *t* that is going

TRIALS* (TRIAL)
Dt 7:19 saw with your own eyes the great *t*,
29: 3 own eyes you saw those great *t*,
Lk 22:28 who have stood by me in my *t*.
1Th 3: 3 one would be unsettled by these *t*.
2Th 1: 4 the persecutions and *t* you are
Jas 1: 2 whenever you face *t* of many kinds,
1Pe 1: 6 had to suffer grief in all kinds of *t*.
2Pe 2: 9 how to rescue godly men from *t*

TRIBE (HALF-TRIBE TRIBES)
Heb 7:13 no one from that *t* has ever served
Rev 5: 5 See, the Lion of the *t* of Judah,
5: 9 God from every *t* and language
11: 9 men from every people, *t*,
14: 6 to every nation, *t*, language

TRIBES (TRIBE)
Ge 49:28 All these are the twelve *t* of Israel,
Mt 19:28 judging the twelve *t* of Israel.

TRIBULATION*
Rev 7:14 who have come out of the great *t*;

TRICKERY*
Ac 13:10 full of all kinds of deceit and *t*.
2Co 12:16 fellow that I am, I caught you by *t*!

TRIED (TRY)
Ps 73:16 When I *t* to understand all this,
95: 9 where your fathers tested and *t* me,
Heb 3: 9 where your fathers tested and *t* me

TRIES (TRY)
Lk 17:33 Whoever *t* to keep his life will lose

TRIMMED
Mt 25: 7 virgins woke up and *t* their lamps.

TRIUMPH (TRIUMPHAL TRIUMPHED TRIUMPHING TRIUMPHS)
Ps 25: 2 nor let my enemies *t* over me.
54: 7 my eyes have looked in *t*
112: 8 in the end he will look in *t*
118: 7 I will look in *t* on my enemies.
Pr 28:12 When the righteous *t*, there is great
Isa 42:13 and will *t* over his enemies.

TRIUMPHAL* (TRIUMPH)
Isa 60:11 their kings led in *t* procession.
2Co 2:14 us in *t* procession in Christ

TRIUMPHED (TRIUMPH)
Rev 5: 5 of Judah, the Root of David, has *t*.

TRIUMPHING* (TRIUMPH)
Col 2:15 of them, *t* over them by the cross.

TRIUMPHS* (TRIUMPH)
Jas 2:13 Mercy *t* over judgment! What

TROUBLE (TROUBLED TROUBLES)
Ge 41:51 God has made me forget all my *t*
Jos 7:25 Why have you brought this *t* on us?
Job 2:10 good from God, and not *t*?"
5: 7 Yet man is born to *t*
14: 1 is of few days and full of *t*.
42:11 him over all the *t* the LORD had
Ps 7:14 conceives *t* gives birth
7:16 The *t* he causes recoils on himself;
9: 9 a stronghold in times of *t*.
10:14 But you, O God, do see *t* and grief;
22:11 for *t* is near
27: 5 For in the day of *t*
32: 7 you will protect me from *t*
37:39 he is their stronghold in time of *t*.
41: 1 LORD delivers him in times of *t*.
46: 1 an ever-present help in *t*.
50:15 and call upon me in the day of *t*;
59:16 my refuge in times of *t*.
66:14 spoke when I was in *t*.
86: 7 In the day of my *t* I will call to you,
91:15 I will be with him in *t*,
107: 6 to the LORD in their *t*,
107: 13 they cried to the LORD in their *t*,
116: 3 I was overcome by *t* and sorrow.
119:143 *T* and distress have come upon me,
138: 7 Though I walk in the midst of *t*,
143: 11 righteousness, bring me out of *t*.
Pr 11: 8 righteous man is rescued from *t*,
11:17 a cruel man brings *t* on himself
11:29 He who brings *t* on his family will
12:13 but a righteous man escapes *t*.
12:21 but the wicked have their fill of *t*.
15:27 A greedy man brings *t* to his family
19:23 one rests content, untouched by *t*.
22: 8 He who sows wickedness reaps *t*,
24:10 If you falter in times of *t*,
25:19 on the unfaithful in times of *t*.
28:14 he who hardens his heart falls into *t*
Jer 30: 7 It will be a time of *t* for Jacob,
Na 1: 7 a refuge in times of *t*.
Zep 1:15 a day of *t* and ruin,
Mt 6:34 Each day has enough *t* of its own.
13:21 When *t* or persecution comes
Jn 16:33 In this world you will have *t*.
Ro 8:35 Shall *t* or hardship or persecution
2Co 1: 4 those in any *t* with the comfort we
2Th 1: 6 *t* to those who *t* you
Jas 5:13 one of you in *t*? He should pray.

TROUBLED (TROUBLE)
Ps 38:18 I am *t* by my sin.
Isa 38:14 I am *t*; O Lord, come to my aid!"
Mk 14:33 began to be deeply distressed and *t*.
Jn 14: 1 "Do not let your hearts be *t*.
14:27 Do not let your hearts be *t*
2Th 1: 7 and give relief to you who are *t*,

TROUBLES (TROUBLE)
Ps 34: 6 he saved him out of all his *t*.
34:17 he delivers them from all their *t*.
34:19 A righteous man may have many *t*,
40:12 For *t* without number surround me
54: 7 he has delivered me from all my *t*,
1Co 7:28 those who marry will face many *t*
2Co 1: 4 who comforts us in all our *t*,
4:17 and momentary *t* are achieving
6: 4 in *t*, hardships and distresses;
7: 4 in all our *t* my joy knows no bounds
Php 4:14 good of you to share in my *t*.

TRUE (TRUTH)
Nu 11:23 not what I say will come *t* for you."
12: 7 this is not *t* of my servant Moses;
Dt 18:22 does not take place or come *t*,
Jos 23:15 of the LORD your God has come *t*
1Sa 9: 6 and everything he says comes *t*.
1Ki 10: 6 and your wisdom is *t*.
2Ch 6:17 your servant David come *t*.
15: 3 was without the *t* God,
Ps 33: 4 of the LORD is right and *t*;
119:142 and your law is *t*.
119:151 and all your commands are *t*.
119:160 All your words are *t*;
Pr 8: 7 My mouth speaks what is *t*,
22:21 teaching you *t* and reliable words,
Jer 10:10 But the LORD is the *t* God;
28: 9 only if his prediction comes *t*."
Eze 33:33 "When all this comes *t*—
Lk 16:11 who will trust you with *t* riches?
Jn 1: 9 The *t* light that gives light
4:23 when the *t* worshipers will worship
6:32 Father who gives you the *t* bread
7:28 on my own, but he who sent me is *t*
15: 1 "I am the *t* vine, and my Father is
17: 3 the only *t* God, and Jesus Christ,
19:35 testimony, and his testimony is *t*.
21:24 We know that his testimony is *t*.
Ac 10:34 "I now realize how *t* it is that God
11:23 all to remain *t* to the Lord
14:22 them to remain *t* to the faith.
17:11 day to see if what Paul said was *t*.
Ro 3: 4 Let God be *t*, and every man a liar.
Php 4: 8 whatever is *t*, whatever is noble,
1Jn 2: 8 and the *t* light is already shining.
5:20 He is the *t* God and eternal life.
Rev 19: 9 "These are the *t* words of God."
22: 6 These words are trustworthy and *t*.

TRUMPET (TRUMPETS)
Isa 27:13 And in that day a great *t* will sound
Eze 33: 5 Since he heard the sound of the *t*
Zec 9:14 Sovereign LORD will sound the *t*;
Mt 24:31 send his angels with a loud *t* call,
1Co 14: 8 if the *t* does not sound a clear call,
15:52 For the *t* will sound, the dead will
1Th 4:16 and with the *t* call of God,
Rev 8: 7 The first angel sounded his *t*,

TRUMPETS (TRUMPET)
Jdg 7:19 They blew their *t* and broke the jars
Rev 8: 2 and to them were given seven *t*.

TRUST* (ENTRUST ENTRUSTED TRUSTED TRUSTFULLY TRUSTING TRUSTS TRUSTWORTHY)
Ex 14:31 put their *t* in him and in Moses his
19: 9 and will always put their *t* in you."
Nu 20:12 "Because you did not *t*
Dt 1:32 you did not *t* in the LORD your
9:23 You did not *t* him or obey him.
28:52 walls in which you *t* fall down.
Jdg 11:20 did not *t* Israel to pass
2Ki 17:14 who did not *t* in the LORD their
18:30 to *t* in the LORD when he says,
1Ch 9:22 to their positions of *t* by David
Job 4:18 If God places no *t* in his servants,
15:15 If God places no *t* in his holy ones,
31:24 "If I have put my *t* in gold
39:12 Can you *t* him to bring
Ps 4: 5 and *t* in the LORD.
9:10 Those who know your name will *t*
13: 5 But I *t* in your unfailing love;
20: 7 Some *t* in chariots and some
20: 7 we *t* in the name of the LORD our
22: 4 In you our fathers put their *t*;
22: 9 you made me *t* in you
25: 2 I lift up my soul; in you I *t*,
31: 6 I *t* in the LORD.
31:14 But I *t* in you, O LORD;
33:21 for we *t* in his holy name.
37: 3 *T* in the LORD and do good;
37: 5 *t* in him and he will do this:
40: 3 and put their *t* in the LORD.
40: 4 who makes the LORD his *t*,
44: 6 I do not *t* in my bow,
49: 6 those who *t* in their wealth
49:13 of those who *t* in themselves,
52: 8 I *t* in God's unfailing love
55:23 But as for me, I *t* in you.
56: 3 I will *t* in you.
56: 4 in God I *t*; I will not be afraid.
56:11 in God I *t*; I will not be afraid.
62: 8 *T* in him at all times, O people;
62:10 Do not *t* in extortion
78: 7 Then they would put their *t* in God
78:22 or *t* in his deliverance.
91: 2 my God, in whom I *t*."
115: 8 and so will all who *t* in them.
115: 9 O house of Israel, *t* in the LORD—
115: 10 O house of Aaron, *t* in the LORD
115: 11 You who fear him, *t* in the LORD
118: 8 than to *t* in man.
118: 9 than to *t* in princes.
119: 42 for I *t* in your word.
125: 1 Those who *t* in the LORD are like
135: 18 and so will all who *t* in them.
143: 8 for I have put my *t* in you.
146: 3 Do not put your *t* in princes,
Pr 3: 5 *T* in the LORD with all your heart
21:22 the stronghold in which they *t*.
22:19 So that your *t* may be in the LORD
Isa 8:17 I will put my *t* in him.
12: 2 I will *t* and not be afraid.
26: 4 *T* in the LORD forever,
30:15 in quietness and *t* is your strength,
31: 1 who *t* in the multitude
36:15 to *t* in the LORD when he says,
42:17 But those who *t* in idols,
50:10 *t* in the name of the LORD
Jer 2:37 LORD has rejected those you *t*;
5:17 the fortified cities in which you *t*.
7: 4 Do not *t* in deceptive words
7:14 the temple you *t* in, the place I gave
9: 4 do not *t* your brothers.
12: 6 Do not *t* them,
28:15 you have persuaded this nation to *t*
39:18 you *t* in me, declares the LORD.'"
48: 7 Since you *t* in your deeds
49: 4 you *t* in your riches and say,
49:11 Your widows too can *t* in me."
Mic 7: 5 Do not *t* a neighbor;
Na 1: 7 He cares for those who *t* in him,
Zep 3: 2 She does not *t* in the LORD,
3:12 who *t* in the name of the LORD.
Lk 16:11 who will *t* you with true riches?
Jn 12:36 Put your *t* in the light
14: 1 *T* in God; *t* also in me.
Ac 14:23 Lord, in whom they had put their *t*.
Ro 15:13 you with all joy and peace as you *t*
1Co 4: 2 been given a *t* must prove faithful.
9:17 discharging the *t* committed
2Co 13: 6 I *t* that you will discover that we
Heb 2:13 "I will put my *t* in him."

TRUSTED* (TRUST)
1Sa 27:12 Achish *t* David and said to himself,
2Ki 18: 5 Hezekiah *t* in the LORD, the God
1Ch 5:20 their prayers, because they *t*
Job 12:20 He silences the lips of *t* advisers
Ps 5: 9 from their mouth can be *t*;
22: 4 they *t* and you delivered them.
22: 5 in you they *t* and were not
26: 1 I have *t* in the LORD
41: 9 Even my close friend, whom I *t*,
52: 7 but *t* in his great wealth
Isa 20: 5 Those who *t* in Cush and boasted
25: 9 This is the LORD, we *t* in him;
25: 9 we *t* in him, and he saved us.
47:10 You have *t* in your wickedness
Jer 13:25 and *t* in false gods.
38:22 those *t* friends of yours.
48:13 ashamed when they *t* in Bethel.
Eze 16:15 " 'But you *t* in your beauty
Da 3:28 They *t* in him and defied the king's
6:23 because he had *t* in his God.
Lk 11:22 the armor in which the man *t*
16:10 *t* with very little can also be *t*
Ac 12:20 a *t* personal servant of the king,
Tit 2:10 but to show that they can be fully *t*,
3: 8 so that those who have *t*

TRUSTFULLY* (TRUST)
Pr 3:29 who lives *t* near you.

TRUSTING* (TRUST)
Job 15:31 by *t* what is worthless,
Ps 112: 7 his heart is steadfast, *t*
Isa 2:22 Stop *t* in man,
Jer 7: 8 you are *t* in deceptive words that

TRUSTS* (TRUST)
Job 8:14 What he *t* in is fragile;
Ps 21: 7 For the king *t* in the LORD;
22: 8 "He *t* in the LORD;
28: 7 my heart *t* in him, and I am helped.
32:10 surrounds the man who *t* in him.
84:12 blessed is the man who *t* in you.

Ps 86: 2 who *t* in you.
Pr 11:28 Whoever *t* in his riches will fall,
16:20 blessed is he who *t* in the LORD.
28:25 he who *t* in the LORD will prosper.
28:26 He who *t* in himself is a fool,
29:25 whoever *t* in the LORD is kept safe
Isa 26: 3 because he *t* in you.
28:16 one who *t* will never be dismayed.
Jer 17: 5 "Cursed is the one who *t* in man,
17: 7 blessed is the man who *t*
Eze 33:13 but then he *t* in his righteousness
Hab 2:18 For he who makes it *t*
Mt 27:43 He *t* in God.
Ro 4: 5 but *t* God who justifies the wicked,
9:33 one who *t* in him will never be put
10:11 "Anyone who *t* in him will never
1Co 13: 7 always protects, always *t*,
1Pe 2: 6 and the one who *t* in him

TRUSTWORTHY* (TRUST)
Ex 18:21 *t* men who hate dishonest gain—
2Sa 7:28 you are God! Your words are *t*,
Ne 13:13 these men were considered *t*.
Ps 19: 7 The statutes of the LORD are *t*,
111: 7 all his precepts are *t*.
119: 86 All your commands are *t*;
119:138 they are fully *t*.
Pr 11:13 but a *t* man keeps a secret.
13:17 but a *t* envoy brings healing.
25:13 is a *t* messenger to those who send
Da 2:45 and the interpretation is *t*."
6: 4 he was *t* and neither corrupt
Lk 16:11 So if you have not been *t*
16:12 And if you have not been *t*
19:17 'Because you have been *t*
1Co 7:25 one who by the Lord's mercy is *t*.
1Ti 1:15 Here is a *t* saying that deserves full
3: 1 Here is a *t* saying: If anyone sets his
3:11 but temperate and *t* in everything.
4: 9 This is a *t* saying that deserves full
2Ti 2:11 Here is a *t* saying:
Tit 1: 9 must hold firmly to the *t* message
3: 8 This is a *t* saying.
Rev 21: 5 for these words are *t* and true."
22: 6 "These words are *t* and true.

TRUTH* (TRUE TRUTHFUL TRUTHFULNESS TRUTHS)
Ge 42:16 tested to see if you are telling the *t*.
1Ki 17:24 LORD from your mouth is the *t*."
22:16 the *t* in the name of the LORD?"
2Ch 18:15 the *t* in the name of the LORD?"
Ps 15: 2 who speaks the *t* from his heart
25: 5 guide me in your *t* and teach me,
26: 3 and I walk continually in your *t*.
31: 5 redeem me, O LORD, the God of *t*
40:10 do not conceal your love and your *t*
40:11 your *t* always protect me.
43: 3 Send forth your light and your *t*,
45: 4 victoriously in behalf of *t*, humility
51: 6 Surely you desire *t*
52: 3 than speaking the *t*.
86:11 and I will walk in your *t*;
96:13 and the peoples in his *t*.
119: 30 I have chosen the way of *t*;
119: 43 of *t* from my mouth,
145: 18 to all who call on him in *t*.
Pr 16:13 they value a man who speaks the *t*.
23:23 Buy the *t* and do not sell it;
Isa 45:19 I, the LORD, speak the *t*;
48: 1 but not in *t* or righteousness—
59:14 *t* has stumbled in the streets,
59:15 *T* is nowhere to be found,
65:16 will do so by the God of *t*;
65:16 will swear by the God of *t*.
Jer 5: 1 who deals honestly and seeks the *t*,
5: 3 do not your eyes look for *t*?
7:28 *T* has perished; it has vanished
9: 3 it is not by *t*
9: 5 and no one speaks the *t*.
26:15 for in *t* the LORD has sent me
Da 8:12 and *t* was thrown to the ground.
9:13 and giving attention to your *t*.
10:21 what is written in the Book of *T*.
11: 2 "Now then, I tell you the *t*:
Am 5:10 and despise him who tells the *t*.
Zec 8: 3 will be called the City of *T*,
8:16 are to do: Speak the *t* to each other,
8:19 Therefore love *t* and peace."
Mt 5:18 I tell you the *t*, until heaven
5:26 I tell you the *t*, you will not get out
6: 2 I tell you the *t*, they have received
6: 5 I tell you the *t*, they have received
6:16 I tell you the *t*, they have received
8:10 "I tell you the *t*, I have not found
10:15 I tell you the *t*, it will be more
10:23 I tell you the *t*, you will not finish
10:42 I tell you the *t*, he will certainly not
11:11 I tell you the *t*: Among those born
Mt 13:17 For I tell you the *t*, many prophets
16:28 I tell you the *t*, some who are
17:20 I tell you the *t*, if you have faith
18: 3 And he said: "I tell you the *t*,
18:13 And if he finds it, I tell you the *t*,
18:18 "I tell you the *t*, whatever you bind
19:23 to his disciples, "I tell you the *t*,
19:28 "I tell you the *t*, at the renewal
21:21 Jesus replied, "I tell you the *t*,
21:31 Jesus said to them, "I tell you the *t*,
22:16 of God in accordance with the *t*.
23:36 I tell you the *t*, all this will come
24: 2 "I tell you the *t*, not one stone here
24:34 I tell you the *t*, this generation will
24:47 I tell you the *t*, he will put him
25:12 'I tell you the *t*, I don't know you.'
25:40 The King will reply, 'I tell you the *t*
25:45 "He will reply, 'I tell you the *t*,
26:13 tell you the *t*, wherever this gospel
26:21 "I tell you the *t*, one
26:34 "I tell you the *t*," Jesus answered,
Mk 3:28 I tell you the *t*, all the sins
5:33 with fear, told him the whole *t*.
8:12 I tell you the *t*, no sign will be given
9: 1 he said to them, "I tell you the *t*,
9:41 I tell you the *t*, anyone who gives
10:15 I tell you the *t*, anyone who will not
10:29 "I tell you the *t*," Jesus replied,
11:23 "I tell you the *t*, if anyone says
12:14 of God in accordance with the *t*.
12:43 Jesus said, "I tell you the *t*,
13:30 I tell you the *t*, this generation will
14: 9 I tell you the *t*, wherever the gospel
14:18 "I tell you the *t*, one
14:25 "I tell you the *t*, I will not drink
14:30 "I tell you the *t*," Jesus answered,
Lk 4:24 "I tell you the *t*," he continued,
9:27 I tell you the *t*, some who are
12:37 I tell you the *t*, he will dress himself
12:44 I tell you the *t*, he will put him
18:17 I tell you the *t*, anyone who will not
18:29 I tell you the *t*," Jesus said to them,
20:21 of God in accordance with the *t*.
21: 3 "I tell you the *t*," he said, "this
21:32 tell you the *t*, this generation will
23:43 answered him, "I tell you the *t*,
Jn 1:14 from the Father, full of grace and *t*.
1:17 and *t* came through Jesus Christ.
1:51 "I tell you the *t*, you shall see
3: 3 "I tell you the *t*, no one can see
3: 5 Jesus answered, "I tell you the *t*,
3:11 I tell you the *t*, we speak
3:21 But whoever lives by the *t* comes
4:23 worship the Father in spirit and *t*,
4:24 must worship in spirit and in *t*."
5:19 "I tell you the *t*, the Son can do
5:24 "I tell you the *t*, whoever hears my
5:25 I tell you the *t*, a time is coming
5:33 and he has testified to the *t*.
6:26 "I tell you the *t*, you are looking
6:32 Jesus said to them, "I tell you the *t*,
6:47 I tell you the *t*, he who believes has
6:53 Jesus said to them, "I tell you the *t*,
7:18 the one who sent him is a man of *t*;
8:32 Then you will know the *t*,
8:32 and the *t* will set you free."
8:34 Jesus replied, "I tell you the *t*,
8:40 who has told you the *t* that I heard
8:44 to the *t*, for there is no *t* in him.
8:45 I tell the *t*, you do not believe me!
8:46 I am telling the *t*, why don't you
8:51 I tell you the *t*, if anyone keeps my
8:58 "I tell you the *t*," Jesus answered,
10: 1 "I tell you the *t*, the man who does
10: 7 "I tell you the *t*, I am the gate
12:24 I tell you the *t*, unless a kernel
13:16 I tell you the *t*, no servant is greater
13:20 tell you the *t*, whoever accepts
13:21 "I tell you the *t*, one of you is going
13:38 I tell you the *t*, before the rooster
14: 6 I am the way and the *t* and the life.
14:12 I tell you the *t*, anyone who has
14:17 with you forever—the Spirit of *t*.
15:26 the Spirit of *t* who goes out
16: 7 But I tell you the *t*: It is
16:13 But when he, the Spirit of *t*, comes,
16:13 comes, he will guide you into all *t*.
16:20 I tell you the *t*, you will weep
16:23 I tell you the *t*, my Father will give
17:17 them by the *t*; your word is *t*.
18:23 if I spoke the *t*, why did you strike
18:37 into the world, to testify to the *t*.
18:37 on the side of *t* listens to me."
18:38 "What is *t*?" Pilate asked.
19:35 He knows that he tells the *t*,
21:18 I tell you the *t*, when you were
Ac 20:30 and distort the *t* in order
21:24 everybody will know there is no *t*
21:34 commander could not get at the *t*
Ac 24: 8 able to learn the *t* about all these
28:25 "The Holy Spirit spoke the *t*
Ro 1:18 of men who suppress the *t*
1:25 They exchanged the *t* of God
2: 2 who do such things is based on *t*.
2: 8 who reject the *t* and follow evil,
2:20 embodiment of knowledge and *t*—
9: 1 I speak the *t* in Christ—I am not
15: 8 of the Jews on behalf of God's *t*,
1Co 5: 8 the bread of sincerity and *t*.
13: 6 in evil but rejoices with the *t*.
2Co 4: 2 setting forth the *t* plainly we
11:10 As surely as the *t* of Christ is in me,
12: 6 because I would be speaking the *t*.
13: 8 against the *t*, but only for the *t*.
Gal 2: 5 so that the *t* of the gospel might
2:14 in line with the *t* of the gospel,
4:16 enemy by telling you the *t*?
5: 7 and kept you from obeying the *t*?
Eph 1:13 when you heard the word of *t*,
4:15 Instead, speaking the *t* in love,
4:21 him in accordance with the *t* that is
5: 9 and *t*) and find out what pleases
6:14 with the belt of *t* buckled
Col 1: 5 heard about in the word of *t*,
1: 6 understood God's grace in all its *t*.
2Th 2:10 because they refused to love the *t*
2:12 who have not believed the *t*
2:13 and through belief in the *t*.
1Ti 2: 4 to come to a knowledge of the *t*.
2: 7 I am telling the *t*, I am not lying—
3:15 the pillar and foundation of the *t*.
4: 3 who believe and who know the *t*.
6: 5 who have been robbed of the *t*
2Ti 2:15 correctly handles the word of *t*.
2:18 have wandered away from the *t*.
2:25 them to a knowledge of the *t*,
3: 7 never able to acknowledge the *t*.
3: 8 so also these men oppose the *t*—
4: 4 will turn their ears away from the *t*
Tit 1: 1 the knowledge of the *t* that leads
1:14 of those who reject the *t*.
Heb 10:26 received the knowledge of the *t*,
Jas 1:18 birth through the word of *t*,
3:14 do not boast about it or deny the *t*.
5:19 of you should wander from the *t*
1Pe 1:22 by obeying the *t* so that you have
2Pe 1:12 established in the *t* you now have.
2: 2 the way of *t* into disrepute.
1Jn 1: 6 we lie and do not live by the *t*.
1: 8 deceive ourselves and the *t* is not
2: 4 commands is a liar, and the *t* is not
2: 8 its *t* is seen in him and you,
2:20 and all of you know the *t*.
2:21 because no lie comes from the *t*.
2:21 because you do not know the *t*,
3:18 or tongue but with actions and in *t*.
3:19 we know that we belong to the *t*,
4: 6 is how we recognize the Spirit of *t*
5: 6 testifies, because the Spirit is the *t*.
2Jn : 1 whom I love in the *t*—
: 2 who know the *t*—because of the *t*,
: 3 will be with us in *t* and love.
: 4 of your children walking in the *t*,
3Jn : 1 friend Gaius, whom I love in the *t*.
: 3 how you continue to walk in the *t*.
: 3 tell about your faithfulness to the *t*
: 4 my children are walking in the *t*.
: 8 we may work together for the *t*.
:12 everyone—and even by the *t* itself.

TRUTHFUL* (TRUTH)
Pr 12:17 A *t* witness gives honest testimony,
12:19 *T* lips endure forever,
12:22 but he delights in men who are *t*.
14: 5 A *t* witness does not deceive,
14:25 A *t* witness saves lives,
Jer 4: 2 and if in a *t*, just and righteous way
Jn 3:33 it has certified that God is *t*.
2Co 6: 7 in *t* speech and in the power

TRUTHFULNESS* (TRUTH)
Ro 3: 7 "If my falsehood enhances God's *t*

TRUTHS* (TRUTH)
1Co 2:13 expressing spiritual *t*
1Ti 3: 9 hold of the deep *t* of the faith
4: 6 brought up in the *t* of the faith
Heb 5:12 to teach you the elementary *t*

TRY (TRIED TRIES TRYING)
Ps 26: 2 Test me, O LORD, and *t* me,
Isa 7:13 enough to *t* the patience of men?
Lk 12:58 *t* hard to be reconciled to him
13:24 will *t* to enter and will not be able
1Co 10:33 even as I *t* to please everybody
14:12 *t* to excel in gifts that build up
2Co 5:11 is to fear the Lord, we *t*
1Th 5:15 always *t* to be kind to each other

Tit 2: 9 to *t* to please them, not to talk back

TRYING (TRY)
2Co 5:12 We are not *t* to commend ourselves
Gal 1:10 If I were still *t* to please men,
1Th 2: 4 We are not *t* to please men but God
1Pe 1:11 *t* to find out the time
1Jn 2:26 things to you about those who are *t*

TUMORS
1Sa 5: 6 them and afflicted them with *t.*

TUNE
1Co 14: 7 anyone know what *t* is being

TUNIC (TUNICS)
Lk 6:29 do not stop him from taking your *t.*

TUNICS (TUNIC)
Lk 3:11 "The man with two *t* should share

TURMOIL
Ps 65: 7 and the *t* of the nations.
Pr 15:16 than great wealth with *t.*

TURN (TURNED TURNING TURNS)
Ex 32:12 *T* from your fierce anger; relent
Nu 32:15 If you *t* away from following him,
Dt 5:32 do not *t* aside to the right
28:14 Do not *t* aside from any
30:10 and *t* to the LORD your God
Jos 1: 7 do not *t* from it to the right
1Ki 8:58 May he *t* our hearts to him,
2Ch 7:14 and *t* from their wicked ways,
30: 9 He will not *t* his face from you
Job 33:30 to *t* back his soul from the pit,
Ps 28: 1 do not *t* a deaf ear to me.
34:14 *T* from evil and do good;
51:13 and sinners will *t* back to you.
78: 6 they in *t* would tell their children.
119: 36 *T* my heart toward your statutes
119:132 *T* to me and have mercy on me,
Pr 22: 6 when he is old he will not *t* from it.
Isa 17: 7 *t* their eyes to the Holy One
28: 6 to those who *t* back the battle
29:16 You *t* things upside down,
30:21 Whether you *t* to the right
45:22 "*T* to me and be saved,
55: 7 Let him *t* to the LORD,
Jer 31:13 I will *t* their mourning
Eze 33: 9 if you do warn the wicked man to *t*
33:11 *T! T* from your evil ways!
Jnh 3: 9 and with compassion *t*
Mal 4: 6 He will *t* the hearts of the fathers
Mt 5:39 you on the right cheek, *t*
10:35 For I have come to *t*
Lk 1:17 to *t* the hearts of the fathers
Jn 12:40 nor *t*— and I would heal them."
16:20 but your grief will *t* to joy.
Ac 3:19 Repent, then, and *t* to God,
26:18 and *t* them from darkness to light,
1Co 14:31 For you can all prophesy in *t*
15:23 But each in his own *t*: Christ,
1Ti 6:20 *T* away from godless chatter
1Pe 3:11 He must *t* from evil and do good;

TURNED (TURN)
Dt 23: 5 *t* the curse into a blessing for you,
1Ki 11: 4 his wives *t* his heart
2Ch 15: 4 But in their distress they *t*
Est 9: 1 but now the tables were *t*
9:22 when their sorrow was *t* into joy
Ps 14: 3 All have *t* aside,
30:11 You *t* my wailing into dancing;
40: 1 he *t* to me and heard my cry.
Isa 9:12 for all this, his anger is not *t* away,
53: 6 each of us has *t* to his own way;
Hos 7: 8 Ephraim is a flat cake not *t* over.
Joel 2:31 The sun will be *t* to darkness
Lk 22:32 And when you have *t* back,
Ro 3:12 All have *t* away,

TURNING (TURN)
2Ki 21:13 wiping it and *t* it upside down.
Pr 2: 2 *t* your ear to wisdom
14:27 *t* a man from the snares of death.

TURNS (TURN)
2Sa 22:29 the LORD *t* my darkness into light
Pr 15: 1 A gentle answer *t* away wrath,
Isa 44:25 and *t* it into nonsense,
Jas 5:20 Whoever *t* a sinner from the error

TWELVE
Ge 35:22 Jacob had *t* sons: The sons of Leah:
49:28 All these are the *t* tribes of Israel,
Mt 10: 1 He called his *t* disciples to him
Lk 9:17 the disciples picked up *t* basketfuls
Rev 21:12 the names of the *t* tribes of Israel.
21:14 of the *t* apostles of the Lamb.

TWIN (TWINS)
Ge 25:24 there were *t* boys in her womb.

TWINKLING*
1Co 15:52 in a flash, in the *t* of an eye,

TWINS (TWIN)
Ro 9:11 before the *t* were born

TWISTING* (TWISTS)
Pr 30:33 and as *t* the nose produces blood,

TWISTS (TWISTING)
Ex 23: 8 and *t* the words of the righteous.

TYRANNICAL*
Pr 28:16 A *t* ruler lacks judgment,

TYRE
Eze 28:12 a lament concerning the king of *T*
Mt 11:22 it will be more bearable for *T*

UNAPPROACHABLE*
1Ti 6:16 immortal and who lives in *u* light,

UNASHAMED*
1Jn 2:28 and *u* before him at his coming.

UNBELIEF* (UNBELIEVER UNBELIEVERS UNBELIEVING)
Mk 9:24 help me overcome my *u*!"
Ro 4:20 through *u* regarding the promise
11:20 they were broken off because of *u*,
11:23 And if they do not persist in *u*,
1Ti 1:13 because I acted in ignorance and *u*.
Heb 3:19 able to enter, because of their *u*.

UNBELIEVER* (UNBELIEF)
1Co 7:15 But if the *u* leaves, let him do so.
10:27 If some *u* invites you to a meal
14:24 if an *u* or someone who does not
2Co 6:15 have in common with an *u*?
1Ti 5: 8 the faith and is worse than an *u*.

UNBELIEVERS* (UNBELIEF)
Lk 12:46 and assign him a place with the *u*.
Ro 15:31 rescued from the *u* in Judea
1Co 6: 6 another—and this in front of *u*!
14:22 however, is for believers, not for *u*.
14:22 not for believers but for *u*;
14:23 do not understand or some *u* come
2Co 4: 4 this age has blinded the minds of *u*,
6:14 Do not be yoked together with *u*.

UNBELIEVING* (UNBELIEF)
Mt 17:17 "O *u* and perverse generation,"
Mk 9:19 "O *u* generation," Jesus replied,
Lk 9:41 "O *u* and perverse generation,"
1Co 7:14 For the *u* husband has been
7:14 and the *u* wife has been sanctified
Heb 3:12 *u* heart that turns away
Rev 21: 8 But the cowardly, the *u*, the vile,

UNBLEMISHED*
Heb 9:14 the eternal Spirit offered himself *u*

UNCEASING
Ro 9: 2 and *u* anguish in my heart.

UNCERTAIN*
1Ti 6:17 which is so *u*, but to put their hope

UNCHANGEABLE* (UNCHANGING)
Heb 6:18 by two *u* things in which it is

UNCHANGING* (UNCHANGEABLE)
Heb 6:17 wanted to make the *u* nature

UNCIRCUMCISED
Lev 26:41 when their *u* hearts are humbled
1Sa 17:26 Who is this *u* Philistine that he
Jer 9:26 house of Israel is *u* in heart."
Ac 7:51 stiff-necked people, with *u* hearts
Ro 4:11 had by faith while he was still *u*.
1Co 7:18 Was a man *u* when he was called?
Col 3:11 circumcised or *u*, barbarian,

UNCIRCUMCISION
1Co 7:19 is nothing and *u* is nothing.
Gal 5: 6 neither circumcision nor *u* has any

UNCLEAN
Ge 7: 2 and two of every kind of *u* animal,
Lev 10:10 between the *u* and the clean,
11: 4 it is ceremonially *u* for you.
17:15 he will be ceremonially *u* till evening.
Isa 6: 5 ruined! For I am a man of *u* lips,
52:11 Touch no *u* thing!
Mt 15:11 mouth does not make him '*u*,'
Ac 10:14 never eaten anything impure or *u*."
Ro 14:14 fully convinced that no food is *u*
2Co 6:17 Touch no *u* thing,

UNCLOTHED*
2Co 5: 4 because we do not wish to be *u*

UNCONCERNED*
Eze 16:49 were arrogant, overfed and *u*;

UNCOVERED
Ru 3: 7 Ruth approached quietly, *u* his feet
1Co 11: 5 with her head *u* dishonors her head
11:13 to pray to God with her head *u*?
Heb 4:13 Everything is *u* and laid bare

UNDERGOES* (UNDERGOING)
Heb 12: 8 (and everyone *u* discipline),

UNDERGOING* (UNDERGOES)
1Pe 5: 9 the world are *u* the same kind

UNDERSTAND (UNDERSTANDING UNDERSTANDS UNDERSTOOD)
Ne 8: 8 the people could *u* what was being
Job 38: 4 Tell me, if you *u*.
42: 3 Surely I spoke of things I did not *u*,
Ps 14: 2 men to see if there are any who *u*,
73:16 When I tried to *u* all this,
119: 27 Let me *u* the teaching
119:125 that I may *u* your statutes.
Pr 2: 5 then you will *u* the fear
2: 9 Then you will *u* what is right
30:18 four that I do not *u*:
Ecc 7:25 to *u* the stupidity of wickedness
11: 5 so you cannot *u* the work of God,
Isa 6:10 *u* with their hearts,
44:18 know nothing, they *u* nothing;
52:15 they have not heard, they will *u*.
Jer 17: 9 Who can *u* it?
31:19 after I came to *u*,
Da 9:25 and *u* this: From the issuing
Hos 14: 9 Who is discerning? He will *u* them.
Mt 13:15 *u* with their hearts
24:15 Daniel—let the reader *u*—
Lk 24:45 so they could *u* the Scriptures.
Ac 8:30 "Do you *u* what you are reading?"
Ro 7:15 I do not *u* what I do.
15:21 those who have not heard will *u*."
1Co 2:12 that we may *u* what God has freely
2:14 and he cannot *u* them,
14:16 those who do not *u* say "Amen"
Eph 5:17 but *u* what the Lord's will is.
Heb 11: 3 By faith we *u* that the universe was
2Pe 1:20 you must *u* that no prophecy
3: 3 you must *u* that in the last days
3:16 some things that are hard to *u*,

UNDERSTANDING (UNDERSTAND)
1Ki 4:29 and a breadth of *u* as measureless
Job 12:12 Does not long life bring *u*?
28:12 Where does *u* dwell?
28:28 and to shun evil is *u*.'"
32: 8 of the Almighty, that gives him *u*.
36:26 How great is God—beyond our *u*!
37: 5 he does great things beyond our *u*.
Ps 111: 10 follow his precepts have good *u*.
119: 34 Give me *u*, and I will keep your law
119:100 I have more *u* than the elders,
119:104 I gain *u* from your precepts;
119:130 it gives *u* to the simple.
136: 5 who by his *u* made the heavens,
147: 5 his *u* has no limit.
Pr 2: 2 and applying your heart to *u*,
2: 6 his mouth come knowledge and *u*.
3: 5 and lean not on your own *u*;
3:13 the man who gains *u*,
4: 5 Get wisdom, get *u*;
4: 7 Though it cost all you have, get *u*.
7: 4 and call *u* your kinsman;
9:10 knowledge of the Holy One is *u*.
10:23 but a man of *u* delights in wisdom.
11:12 but a man of *u* holds his tongue.
14:29 A patient man has great *u*,
15:21 a man of *u* keeps a straight course.
15:32 whoever heeds correction gains *u*.
16:16 to choose *u* rather than silver!
16:22 *U* is a fountain of life
17:27 and a man of *u* is even-tempered.
18: 2 A fool finds no pleasure in *u*
19: 8 he who cherishes *u* prospers.
20: 5 but a man of *u* draws them out.
23:23 get wisdom, discipline and *u*.
Isa 11: 2 the Spirit of wisdom and of *u*,
40:28 and his *u* no one can fathom.
56:11 They are shepherds who lack *u*;
Jer 3:15 you with knowledge and *u*.
10:12 stretched out the heavens by his *u*.
Da 5:12 a keen mind and knowledge and *u*,
10:12 that you set your mind to gain *u*
Hos 4:11 which take away the *u*
Mk 4:12 and ever hearing but never *u*;
12:33 with all your *u* and with all your

Lk 2:47 who heard him was amazed at his *u*
2Co 6: 6 in purity, *u*, patience and kindness;
Eph 1: 8 on us with all wisdom and *u*.
Php 4: 7 of God, which transcends all *u*,
Col 1: 9 through all spiritual wisdom and *u*.
2: 2 have the full riches of complete *u*,
1Jn 5:20 God has come and has given us *u*,

UNDERSTANDS (UNDERSTAND)
1Ch 28: 9 and *u* every motive
Jer 9:24 that he *u* and knows me,
Mt 13:23 man who hears the word and *u* it.
Ro 3:11 there is no one who *u*,
1Ti 6: 4 he is conceited and *u* nothing.

UNDERSTOOD (UNDERSTAND)
Ne 8:12 they now *u* the words that had
Ps 73:17 then I *u* their final destiny.
Isa 40:13 Who has *u* the mind of the LORD,
40:21 Have you not *u* since the earth was
Jn 1: 5 but the darkness has not *u* it.
Ro 1:20 being *u* from what has been made,

UNDESIRABLE*
Jos 24:15 But if serving the LORD seems *u*

UNDIVIDED*
1Ch 12:33 to help David with *u* loyalty—
Ps 86:11 give me an *u* heart,
Eze 11:19 I will give them an *u* heart
1Co 7:35 way in *u* devotion to the Lord.

UNDOING
Pr 18: 7 A fool's mouth is his *u*,

UNDYING*
Eph 6:24 Lord Jesus Christ with an *u* love.

UNEQUALED*
Mt 24:21 *u* from the beginning of the world
Mk 13:19 of distress *u* from the beginning,

UNFADING*
1Pe 3: 4 the *u* beauty of a gentle

UNFAILING*
Ex 15:13 "In your *u* love you will lead
1Sa 20:14 But show me *u* kindness like that
2Sa 22:51 he shows *u* kindness
Ps 6: 4 save me because of your *u* love.
13: 5 But I trust in your *u* love;
18:50 he shows *u* kindness
21: 7 through the *u* love
31:16 save me in your *u* love.
32:10 but the LORD's *u* love
33: 5 the earth is full of his *u* love.
33:18 those whose hope is in his *u* love,
33:22 May your *u* love rest upon us,
36: 7 How priceless is your *u* love!
44:26 redeem us because of your *u* love.
48: 9 we meditate on your *u* love.
51: 1 according to your *u* love;
52: 8 I trust in God's *u* love
77: 8 Has his *u* love vanished forever?
85: 7 Show us your *u* love, O LORD,
90:14 in the morning with your *u* love,
107: 8 thanks to the LORD for his *u* love
107: 15 thanks to the LORD for his *u* love
107: 21 to the LORD for his *u* love
107: 31 to the LORD for his *u* love
119: 41 May your *u* love come to me,
119: 76 May your *u* love be my comfort,
130: 7 for with the LORD is *u* love
143: 8 bring me word of your *u* love,
143: 12 In your *u* love, silence my enemies;
147: 11 who put their hope in his *u* love.
Pr 19:22 What a man desires is *u* love;
20: 6 Many a man claims to have *u* love,
Isa 54:10 yet my *u* love for you will not be
La 3:32 so great is his *u* love.
Hos 10:12 reap the fruit of *u* love,

UNFAITHFUL (UNFAITHFULNESS)
Lev 6: 2 is *u* to the LORD by deceiving his
Nu 5: 6 and so is *u* to the LORD,
1Ch 10:13 because he was *u* to the LORD;
Pr 11: 6 the *u* are trapped by evil desires.
13: 2 the *u* have a craving for violence.
13:15 but the way of the *u* is hard.
22:12 but he frustrates the words of the *u*.
23:28 and multiplies the *u* among men.
25:19 is reliance on the *u* in times
Jer 3:20 But like a woman *u* to her husband,

UNFAITHFULNESS (UNFAITHFUL)
1Ch 9: 1 to Babylon because of their *u*.
Mt 5:32 except for marital *u*, causes her
19: 9 for marital *u*, and marries another

UNFIT*
Tit 1:16 and *u* for doing anything good.

UNFOLDING
Ps 119: 130 the *u* of your words gives light;

UNFORGIVING*
2Ti 3: 3 unholy, without love, *u*, slanderous

UNFRIENDLY*
Pr 18: 1 An *u* man pursues selfish ends;

UNFRUITFUL
1Co 14:14 my spirit prays, but my mind is *u*.

UNGODLINESS (UNGODLY)
Tit 2:12 It teaches us to say "No" to *u*

UNGODLY (UNGODLINESS)
Ro 5: 6 powerless, Christ died for the *u*.
1Ti 1: 9 the *u* and sinful, the unholy
2Ti 2:16 in it will become more and more *u*.
2Pe 2: 6 of what is going to happen to the *u*;
Jude :15 and to convict all the *u*

UNGRATEFUL*
Lk 6:35 he is kind to the *u* and wicked.
2Ti 3: 2 disobedient to their parents, *u*,

UNHOLY*
1Ti 1: 9 and sinful, the *u* and irreligious;
2Ti 3: 2 ungrateful, *u*, without love,
Heb 10:29 as an *u* thing the blood

UNINTENTIONALLY
Lev 4: 2 'When anyone sins *u* and does
Nu 15:22 " 'Now if you *u* fail to keep any
Dt 4:42 flee if he had *u* killed his neighbor

UNIT
1Co 12:12 body is a *u*, though it is made up

UNITE (UNITED UNITY)
1Co 6:15 and *u* them with a prostitute?

UNITED (UNITE)
Ge 2:24 and mother and be *u* to his wife,
Mt 19: 5 and mother and be *u* to his wife,
Ro 6: 5 If we have been *u* with him like this
Eph 5:31 and mother and be *u* to his wife,
Php 2: 1 from being *u* with Christ,
Col 2: 2 encouraged in heart and *u* in love,

UNITY* (UNITE)
2Ch 30:12 the people to give them *u* of mind
Ps 133: 1 is when brothers live together in *u*!
Jn 17:23 May they be brought to complete *u*
Ro 15: 5 a spirit of *u* among yourselves
Eph 4: 3 effort to keep the *u* of the Spirit
4:13 up until we all reach *u* in the faith
Col 3:14 them all together in perfect *u*.

UNIVERSE*
1Co 4: 9 made a spectacle to the whole *u*,
Eph 4:10 in order to fill the whole *u*.)
Php 2:15 which you shine like stars in the *u*
Heb 1: 2 and through whom he made the *u*.
11: 3 understand that the *u* was formed

UNJUST
Ro 3: 5 That God is *u* in bringing his wrath
9:14 What then shall we say? Is God *u*?
1Pe 2:19 up under the pain of *u* suffering

UNKNOWN
Ac 17:23 TO AN *U* GOD.

UNLEAVENED
Ex 12:17 "Celebrate the Feast of *U* Bread,
Dt 16:16 at the Feast of *U* Bread, the Feast

UNLIMITED*
1Ti 1:16 Jesus might display his *u* patience

UNLOVED
Pr 30:23 an *u* woman who is married,

UNMARRIED
1Co 7: 8 It is good for them to stay *u*,
7:27 Are you *u*? Do not look for a wife.
7:32 An *u* man is concerned about

UNPLOWED
Ex 23:11 the seventh year let the land lie *u*
Hos 10:12 and break up your *u* ground;

UNPRODUCTIVE
Tit 3:14 necessities and not live *u* lives.
2Pe 1: 8 and *u* in your knowledge

UNPROFITABLE
Tit 3: 9 because these are *u* and useless.

UNPUNISHED
Ex 34: 7 Yet he does not leave the guilty *u*;
Pr 6:29 no one who touches her will go *u*.
11:21 of this: The wicked will not go *u*,
19: 5 A false witness will not go *u*,

UNQUENCHABLE
Lk 3:17 he will burn up the chaff with *u* fire

UNREPENTANT*
Ro 2: 5 stubbornness and your *u* heart,

UNRIGHTEOUS*
Zep 3: 5 yet the *u* know no shame.
Mt 5:45 rain on the righteous and the *u*.
1Pe 3:18 the righteous for the *u*, to bring you
2Pe 2: 9 and to hold the *u* for the day

UNSEARCHABLE
Ro 11:33 How *u* his judgments,
Eph 3: 8 preach to the Gentiles the *u* riches

UNSEEN*
Mt 6: 6 and pray to your Father, who is *u*.
6:18 who is *u*; and your Father,
2Co 4:18 on what is seen, but on what is *u*.
4:18 temporary, but what is *u* is eternal.

UNSETTLED*
1Th 3: 3 so that no one would be *u*
2Th 2: 2 not to become easily *u*

UNSHRUNK
Mt 9:16 patch of *u* cloth on an old garment,

UNSPIRITUAL*
Ro 7:14 but I am *u*, sold as a slave to sin.
Col 2:18 and his *u* mind puffs him up
Jas 3:15 down from heaven but is earthly, *u*,

UNSTABLE*
Jas 1: 8 he is a double-minded man, *u*
2Pe 2:14 they seduce the *u*; they are experts
3:16 ignorant and *u* people distort,

UNTHINKABLE*
Job 34:12 It is *u* that God would do wrong,

UNTIE
Mk 1: 7 worthy to stoop down and *u*.
Lk 13:15 each of you on the Sabbath *u* his ox

UNVEILED*
2Co 3:18 with *u* faces all reflect the Lord's

UNWHOLESOME*
Eph 4:29 Do not let any *u* talk come out

UNWISE
Eph 5:15 how you live—not as *u* but as wise,

UNWORTHY*
Ge 32:10 I am *u* of all the kindness
Job 40: 4 "I am *u*— how can I reply to you?
Lk 17:10 should say, 'We are *u* servants;
1Co 11:27 Lord in an *u* manner will be guilty

UPHOLD (UPHOLDS)
Isa 41:10 I will *u* you with my righteous right
Ro 3:31 Not at all! Rather, we *u* the law.

UPHOLDS* (UPHOLD)
Ps 37:17 but the LORD *u* the righteous.
37:24 for the LORD *u* him with his hand.
63: 8 your right hand *u* me.
140: 12 and *u* the cause of the needy.
145: 14 The LORD *u* all those who fall
146: 7 He *u* the cause of the oppressed

UPRIGHT
Dt 32: 4 *u* and just is he.
Job 1: 1 This man was blameless and *u*;
Ps 7:10 who saves the *u* in heart.
11: 7 *u* men will see his face.
25: 8 Good and *u* is the LORD;
33: 1 it is fitting for the *u* to praise him.
64:10 let all the *u* in heart praise him!
92:15 proclaiming, "The LORD is *u*;
97:11 and joy on the *u* in heart.
119: 7 I will praise you with an *u* heart
Pr 2: 7 He holds victory in store for the *u*,
3:32 but takes the *u* into his confidence.
14: 2 whose walk is *u* fears the LORD,
15: 8 but the prayer of the *u* pleases him.
21:29 an *u* man gives thought to his ways.
Isa 26: 7 O *u* One, you make the way
Tit 1: 8 who is self-controlled, *u*, holy
2:12 *u* and godly lives in this present

UPROOTED
Dt 28:63 You will be *u* from the land you are

Jer 31:40 The city will never again be *u*
Jude :12 without fruit and *u*— twice dead.

UPSET
Lk 10:41 are worried and *u* about many

URIAH
Hittite husband of Bathsheba, killed by David's order (2Sa 11).

USEFUL
Eph 4:28 doing something *u*
2Ti 2:21 *u* to the Master and prepared
3:16 Scripture is God-breathed and is *u*
Phm :11 now he has become *u* both to you

USELESS
1Co 15:14 our preaching is *u*
Tit 3: 9 these are unprofitable and *u*.
Phm :11 Formerly he was *u* to you,
Heb 7:18 *u* (for the law made nothing perfect
Jas 2:20 faith without deeds is *u*?

USURY
Ne 5:10 But let the exacting of *u* stop!
Ps 15: 5 who lends his money without *u*

UTMOST
Job 34:36 that Job might be tested to the *u*

UTTER (UTTERS)
Ps 78: 2 I will *u* hidden things, things from of old—
Mt 13:35 I will *u* things hidden

UTTERS (UTTER)
1Co 14: 2 he *u* mysteries with his spirit.

UZZIAH
Son of Amaziah; king of Judah also known as Azariah (2Ki 15:1-7; 1Ch 6:24; 2Ch 26). Struck with leprosy because of pride (2Ch 26:16-23).

VAIN
Ps 33:17 A horse is a *v* hope for deliverance;
73:13 in *v* have I kept my heart pure;
127: 1 its builders labor in *v*.
Isa 65:23 They will not toil in *v*
1Co 15: 2 Otherwise, you have believed in *v*.
15:58 labor in the Lord is not in *v*.
2Co 6: 1 not to receive God's grace in *v*.
Gal 2: 2 running or had run my race in *v*.

VALIANT
1Sa 10:26 by *v* men whose hearts God had

VALID
Jn 8:14 my own behalf, my testimony is *v*,

VALLEY (VALLEYS)
Ps 23: 4 walk through the *v* of the shadow
Isa 40: 4 Every *v* shall be raised up,
Joel 3:14 multitudes in the *v* of decision!

VALLEYS (VALLEY)
SS 2: 1 a lily of the *v*.

VALUABLE (VALUE)
Lk 12:24 And how much more *v* you are

VALUE (VALUABLE VALUED)
Lev 27: 3 set the *v* of a male between the ages
Pr 16:13 they *v* a man who speaks the truth.
31:11 and lacks nothing of *v*.
Mt 13:46 When he found one of great *v*,
1Ti 4: 8 For physical training is of some *v*,
Heb 11:26 as of greater *v* than the treasures

VALUED (VALUE)
Lk 16:15 What is highly *v* among men is

VANISHES
Jas 4:14 appears for a little while and then *v*.

VASHTI*
Queen of Persia replaced by Esther (Est 1-2).

VAST
Ge 2: 1 completed in all their *v* array.
Dt 1:19 of the Amorites through all that *v*
8:15 He led you through the *v*
Ps 139: 17 How *v* is the sum of them!

VEGETABLES
Pr 15:17 of *v* where there is love
Ro 14: 2 whose faith is weak, eats only *v*.

VEIL
Ex 34:33 to them, he put a *v* over his face.
2Co 3:14 for to this day the same *v* remains

VENGEANCE (AVENGE AVENGER AVENGES AVENGING REVENGE)
Nu 31: 3 to carry out the LORD's *v* on them
Isa 34: 8 For the LORD has a day of *v*,
Na 1: 2 The LORD takes *v* on his foes

VERDICT
Jn 3:19 This is the *v*: Light has come

VICTOR'S* (VICTORY)
2Ti 2: 5 he does not receive the *v* crown

VICTORIES* (VICTORY)
2Sa 22:51 He gives his king great *v*;
Ps 18:50 He gives his king great *v*;
21: 1 great is his joy in the *v* you give!
21: 5 Through the *v* you gave, his glory is
44: 4 who decrees *v* for Jacob.

VICTORIOUS (VICTORY)
Ps 20: 5 for joy when you are *v*

VICTORIOUSLY* (VICTORY)
Ps 45: 4 In your majesty ride forth *v*

VICTORY (VICTOR'S VICTORIES VICTORIOUS VICTORIOUSLY)
2Sa 8: 6 gave David *v* wherever he
Ps 44: 6 my sword does not bring me *v*;
60:12 With God we will gain the *v*,
129: 2 they have not gained the *v* over me.
Pr 11:14 but many advisers make *v* sure.
1Co 15:54 "Death has been swallowed up in *v*
15:57 He gives us the *v* through our Lord
1Jn 5: 4 This is the *v* that has overcome

VIEW
Pr 5:21 are in full *v* of the LORD,
2Ti 4: 1 and in *v* of his appearing

VILLAGE
Mk 6: 6 went around teaching from *v* to *v*.

VINDICATED (VINDICATION)
Job 13:18 I know I will be *v*.
1Ti 3:16 was *v* by the Spirit,

VINDICATION (VINDICATED)
Ps 24: 5 and *v* from God his Savior.

VINE (VINEYARD)
Ps 128: 3 Your wife will be like a fruitful *v*
Isa 36:16 one of you will eat from his own *v*
Jnh 4: 6 Jonah was very happy about the *v*.
Jn 15: 1 "I am the true *v*, and my Father is

VINEGAR
Pr 10:26 As *v* to the teeth and smoke
Mk 15:36 filled a sponge with wine *v*,

VINEYARD (VINE)
1Ki 21: 1 an incident involving a *v* belonging
Pr 31:16 out of her earnings she plants a *v*.
SS 1: 6 my own *v* I have neglected.
Isa 5: 1 My loved one had a *v*
1Co 9: 7 Who plants a *v* and does not eat

VIOLATION
Heb 2: 2 every *v* and disobedience received

VIOLENCE (VIOLENT)
Ge 6:11 in God's sight and was full of *v*.
Isa 53: 9 though he had done no *v*,
60:18 No longer will *v* be heard
Eze 45: 9 Give up your *v* and oppression
Joel 3:19 of *v* done to the people of Judah,
Jnh 3: 8 give up their evil ways and their *v*.

VIOLENT (VIOLENCE)
Eze 18:10 "Suppose he has a *v* son, who sheds
1Ti 1:13 and a persecutor and a *v* man,
3: 3 not *v* but gentle, not quarrelsome,
Tit 1: 7 not *v*, not pursuing dishonest gain.

VIPERS
Ps 140: 3 the poison of *v* is on their lips.
Lk 3: 7 "You brood of *v*! Who warned you
Ro 3:13 "The poison of *v* is on their lips."

VIRGIN (VIRGINS)
Dt 22:15 shall bring proof that she was a *v*
Isa 7:14 The *v* will be with child
Mt 1:23 "The *v* will be with child
Lk 1:34 I am a *v*?" The angel answered,
2Co 11: 2 that I might present you as a pure *v*

VIRGINS (VIRGIN)
Mt 25: 1 will be like ten *v* who took their
1Co 7:25 Now about *v*: I have no command

VIRTUES*
Col 3:14 And over all these *v* put on love,

VISIBLE
Eph 5:13 exposed by the light becomes *v*,
Col 1:16 and on earth, *v* and invisible,

VISION (VISIONS)
Da 9:24 to seal up *v* and prophecy
Ac 26:19 disobedient to the *v* from heaven.

VISIONS (VISION)
Nu 12: 6 I reveal myself to him in *v*,
Joel 2:28 your young men will see *v*.
Ac 2:17 your young men will see *v*,

VOICE
Dt 30:20 listen to his *v*, and hold fast to him.
1Sa 15:22 as in obeying the *v* of the LORD?
Job 40: 9 and can your *v* thunder like his?
Ps 19: 4 Their *v* goes out into all the earth,
29: 3 The *v* of the LORD is
66:19 and heard my *v* in prayer.
95: 7 Today, if you hear his *v*,
Pr 8: 1 Does not understanding raise her *v*
Isa 30:21 your ears will hear a *v* behind you,
40: 3 A *v* of one calling:
Mk 1: 3 "a *v* of one calling in the desert,
Jn 5:28 are in their graves will hear his *v*
10: 3 and the sheep listen to his *v*.
Ro 10:18 "Their *v* has gone out
Heb 3: 7 "Today, if you hear his *v*,
Rev 3:20 If anyone hears my *v* and opens

VOMIT
Lev 18:28 it will *v* you out as it vomited out
Pr 26:11 As a dog returns to its *v*,
2Pe 2:22 "A dog returns to its *v*," and,

VOW (VOWS)
Nu 6: 2 a *v* of separation to the LORD
30: 2 When a man makes a *v*
Jdg 11:30 Jephthah made a *v* to the LORD:

VOWS (VOW)
Ps 116: 14 I will fulfill my *v* to the LORD
Pr 20:25 and only later to consider his *v*.

VULTURES
Mt 24:28 is a carcass, there the *v* will gather.

WAGE (WAGES WAGING)
2Co 10: 3 we do not *w* war as the world does.

WAGES (WAGE)
Mal 3: 5 who defraud laborers of their *w*,
Lk 10: 7 for the worker deserves his *w*.
Ro 4: 4 his *w* are not credited to him
6:23 For the *w* of sin is death,
1Ti 5:18 and "The worker deserves his *w*."

WAGING (WAGE)
Ro 7:23 *w* war against the law of my mind

WAILING
Ps 30:11 You turned my *w* into dancing;

WAIST
2Ki 1: 8 and with a leather belt around his *w*."
Mt 3: 4 he had a leather belt around his *w*.

WAIT (AWAITS WAITED WAITING WAITS)
Ps 27:14 *W* for the LORD;
130: 5 I *w* for the LORD, my soul waits,
Isa 30:18 Blessed are all who *w* for him!
Ac 1: 4 *w* for the gift my Father promised,
Ro 8:23 as we *w* eagerly for our adoption
1Th 1:10 and to *w* for his Son from heaven,
Tit 2:13 while we *w* for the blessed hope—

WAITED (WAIT)
Ps 40: 1 I *w* patiently for the LORD;

WAITING (WAIT)
Heb 9:28 to those who are *w* for him.

WAITS (WAIT)
Ro 8:19 creation *w* in eager expectation

WAKE (AWAKE WAKENS)
Eph 5:14 "*W* up, O sleeper,

WAKENS* (WAKE)
Isa 50: 4 He *w* me morning by morning,
50: 4 *w* my ear to listen like one being

WALK (WALKED WALKING WALKS)
Lev 26:12 I will *w* among you and be your
Dt 5:33 *W* in all the way that the LORD
6: 7 and when you *w* along the road,
10:12 to *w* in all his ways, to love him,
11:19 and when you *w* along the road,

Dt 11:22 to *w* in all his ways and to hold fast
26:17 and that you will *w* in his ways,
Jos 22: 5 to *w* in all his ways,
Ps 1: 1 who does not *w* in the counsel
15: 2 He whose *w* is blameless
23: 4 Even though I *w*
84:11 from those whose *w* is blameless.
89:15 who *w* in the light of your presence
119: 45 I will *w* about in freedom,
Pr 4:12 When you *w*, your steps will not be
6:22 When you *w*, they will guide you;
Isa 2: 3 so that we may *w* in his paths."
2: 5 let us *w* in the light of the LORD.
30:21 saying, "This is the way; *w* in it."
40:31 they will *w* and not be faint.
57: 2 Those who *w* uprightly
Jer 6:16 ask where the good way is, and *w*
Da 4:37 And those who *w* in pride he is able
Am 3: 3 Do two *w* together
Mic 4: 5 All the nations may *w*
6: 8 and to *w* humbly with your God.
Mk 2: 9 'Get up, take your mat and *w*'?
Jn 8:12 Whoever follows me will never *w*
1Jn 1: 6 with him yet *w* in the darkness,
1: 7 But if we *w* in the light,
2Jn : 6 his command is that you *w* in love.

WALKED (WALK)
Ge 5:24 Enoch *w* with God; then he was no
Jos 14: 9 which your feet have *w* will be your
Mt 14:29 *w* on the water and came toward Jesus.

WALKING (WALK)
1Ki 3: 3 love for the LORD by *w* according
Da 3:25 I see four men *w* around in the fire,
2Jn : 4 of your children *w* in the truth,

WALKS (WALK)
Pr 10: 9 The man of integrity *w* securely,
13:20 He who *w* with the wise grows wise
Isa 33:15 He who *w* righteously
Jn 11: 9 A man who *w* by day will not

WALL (WALLS)
Jos 6:20 *w* collapsed; so every man charged
Ne 2:17 let us rebuild the *w* of Jerusalem,
Eph 2:14 the dividing *w* of hostility,
Rev 21:12 It had a great, high *w*

WALLOWING
2Pe 2:22 back to her *w* in the mud."

WALLS (WALL)
Isa 58:12 be called Repairer of Broken *W*,
60:18 but you will call your *w* Salvation
Heb 11:30 By faith the *w* of Jericho fell,

WANDER (WANDERED)
Nu 32:13 he made them *w* in the desert forty
Jas 5:19 one of you should *w* from the truth

WANDERED (WANDER)
Eze 34: 6 My sheep *w* over all the mountains
Mt 18:12 go to look for the one that *w* off?
1Ti 6:10 have *w* from the faith and pierced
2Ti 2:18 who have *w* away from the truth.

WANT (WANTED WANTING WANTS)
1Sa 8:19 "We *w* a king over us.
Mt 19:21 Jesus answered, "If you *w*
Lk 19:14 'We don't *w* this man to be our king
Ro 7:15 For what I *w* to do I do not do,
13: 3 Do you *w* to be free from fear
2Co 12:14 what I *w* is not your possessions
Php 3:10 I *w* to know Christ and the power

WANTED (WANT)
1Co 12:18 of them, just as he *w* them to be.
Heb 6:17 Because God *w* to make

WANTING (WANT)
Da 5:27 weighed on the scales and found *w*.
2Pe 3: 9 with you, not *w* anyone to perish,

WANTS (WANT)
Mt 5:42 from the one who *w* to borrow
20:26 whoever *w* to become great
Mk 8:35 For whoever *w* to save his life will
10:43 whoever *w* to become great
Ro 9:18 he hardens whom he *w* to harden.
1Ti 2: 4 who *w* all men to be saved
1Pe 5: 2 you are willing, as God *w* you to be;

WAR (WARRIOR WARS)
Jos 11:23 Then the land had rest from *w*.
1Sa 15:18 make *w* on them until you have
Ps 68:30 the nations who delight in *w*.
120: 7 but when I speak, they are for *w*.
144: 1 who trains my hands for *w*,
Isa 2: 4 nor will they train for *w* anymore.
Da 9:26 *W* will continue until the end,
Ro 7:23 waging *w* against the law
2Co 10: 3 we do not wage *w* as the world does
1Pe 2:11 which *w* against your soul.
Rev 12: 7 And there was *w* in heaven.
19:11 With justice he judges and makes *w*

WARN* (WARNED WARNING WARNINGS)
Ex 19:21 *w* the people so they do not force
Nu 24:14 let me *w* you of what this people
1Sa 8: 9 but *w* them solemnly and let them
1Ki 2:42 swear by the LORD and *w* you,
2Ch 19:10 you are to *w* them not to sin
Ps 81: 8 O my people, and I will *w* you—
Jer 42:19 I *w* you today that you made a fatal
Eze 3:18 and you do not *w* him or speak out
3:19 But if you do *w* the wicked man
3:20 Since you did not *w* him, he will die
3:21 if you do *w* the righteous man not
33: 3 blows the trumpet to *w* the people,
33: 6 blow the trumpet to *w* the people
33: 9 if you do *w* the wicked man to turn
Lk 16:28 Let him *w* them, so that they will
Ac 4:17 we must *w* these men
1Co 4:14 but to *w* you, as my dear children.
Gal 5:21 I *w* you, as I did before, that those
1Th 5:14 brothers, *w* those who are idle,
2Th 3:15 an enemy, but *w* him as a brother.
2Ti 2:14 *W* them before God
Tit 3:10 and then *w* him a second time.
3:10 *W* a divisive person once,
Rev 22:18 I *w* everyone who hears the words

WARNED (WARN)
2Ki 17:13 The LORD *w* Israel and Judah
Ps 19:11 By them is your servant *w*;
Jer 22:21 I *w* you when you felt secure,
Mt 3: 7 Who *w* you to flee
1Th 4: 6 have already told you and *w* you.
Heb 11: 7 when *w* about things not yet seen,
12:25 they refused him who *w* them

WARNING (WARN)
Jer 6: 8 Take *w*, O Jerusalem,
1Ti 5:20 so that the others may take *w*.

WARNINGS (WARN)
1Co 10:11 and were written down as *w* for us,

WARRIOR (WAR)
Ex 15: 3 The LORD is a *w*;
1Ch 28: 3 you are a *w* and have shed blood.'
Pr 16:32 Better a patient man than a *w*,

WARS (WAR)
Ps 46: 9 He makes *w* cease to the ends
Mt 24: 6 You will hear of *w* and rumors of *w*,

WASH (WASHED WASHING)
Ps 51: 7 *w* me, and I will be whiter
Jer 4:14 *w* the evil from your heart
Jn 13: 5 and began to *w* his disciples' feet,
Ac 22:16 be baptized and *w* your sins away,
Jas 4: 8 *W* your hands, you sinners,
Rev 22:14 Blessed are those who *w* their robes

WASHED (WASH)
Ps 73:13 in vain have I *w* my hands
1Co 6:11 you were *w*, you were sanctified,
Heb 10:22 and having our bodies *w*
2Pe 2:22 and, "A sow that is *w* goes back
Rev 7:14 they have *w* their robes

WASHING (WASH)
Eph 5:26 cleansing her by the *w* with water
1Ti 5:10 showing hospitality, *w* the feet
Tit 3: 5 us through the *w* of rebirth

WASTED (WASTING)
Jn 6:12 Let nothing be *w*."

WASTING (WASTED)
2Co 4:16 Though outwardly we are *w* away,

WATCH (WATCHER WATCHES WATCHING WATCHMAN)
Ge 31:49 "May the LORD keep *w*
Ps 90: 4 or like a *w* in the night.
141: 3 keep *w* over the door of my lips.
Pr 4: 6 love her, and she will *w* over you.
6:22 when you sleep, they will *w*
Jer 31:10 will *w* over his flock like a shepherd
Mic 7: 7 I *w* in hope for the LORD,
Mt 24:42 "Therefore keep *w*, because you do
26:41 *W* and pray so that you will not fall
Mk 13:35 "Therefore keep *w* because you do
Lk 2: 8 keeping *w* over their flocks at night
1Ti 4:16 *W* your life and doctrine closely.
Heb 13:17 They keep *w* over you

WATCHER* (WATCH)
Job 7:20 O *w* of men?

WATCHES* (WATCH)
Nu 19: 5 While he *w*, the heifer is
Job 24:15 The eye of the adulterer *w* for dusk;
Ps 1: 6 For the LORD *w* over the way
33:14 from his dwelling place he *w*
63: 6 of you through the *w* of the night.
119:148 through the *w* of the night,
121: 3 he who *w* over you will not slumber
121: 4 indeed, he who *w* over Israel
121: 5 The LORD *w* over you—
127: 1 Unless the LORD *w* over the city,
145: 20 LORD *w* over all who love him,
146: 9 The LORD *w* over the alien
Pr 31:27 She *w* over the affairs
Ecc 11: 4 Whoever *w* the wind will not plant;
La 2:19 as the *w* of the night begin;
4:16 he no longer *w* over them.

WATCHING (WATCH)
Lk 12:37 whose master finds them *w*

WATCHMAN (WATCH)
Eze 3:17 I have made you a *w* for the house
33: 6 but I will hold the *w* accountable

WATER (WATERED WATERING WATERS WELL-WATERED)
Ex 7:20 all the *w* was changed into blood.
17: 1 but there was no *w* for the people
Nu 20: 2 there was no *w* for the community,
Ps 1: 3 like a tree planted by streams of *w*,
22:14 I am poured out like *w*,
42: 1 As the deer pants for streams of *w*,
Pr 25:21 if he is thirsty, give him *w* to drink.
Isa 12: 3 With joy you will draw *w*
30:20 of adversity and the *w* of affliction,
32: 2 like streams of *w* in the desert
49:10 and lead them beside springs of *w*.
Jer 2:13 broken cisterns that cannot hold *w*.
17: 8 will be like a tree planted by the *w*
31: 9 I will lead them beside streams of *w*
Eze 36:25 I will sprinkle clean *w* on you,
Zec 14: 8 On that day living *w* will flow out
Mt 14:29 walked on the *w* and came toward Jesus.
Mk 9:41 anyone who gives you a cup of *w*
Lk 5: 4 to Simon, "Put out into deep *w*,
Jn 3: 5 unless he is born of *w* and the Spirit.
4:10 he would have given you living *w*."
7:38 streams of living *w* will flow
Eph 5:26 washing with *w* through the word,
Heb 10:22 our bodies washed with pure *w*.
1Pe 3:21 this *w* symbolizes baptism that now
2Pe 2:17 These men are springs without *w*
1Jn 5: 6 This is the one who came by *w*
5: 6 come by *w* only, but by *w*
5: 8 the Spirit, the *w* and the blood;
Rev 7:17 to springs of living *w*.
21: 6 cost from the spring of the *w* of life.

WATERED (WATER)
1Co 3: 6 I planted the seed, Apollos *w* it,

WATERING (WATER)
Isa 55:10 it without *w* the earth

WATERS (WATER)
Ps 23: 2 he leads me beside quiet *w*,
Ecc 11: 1 Cast your bread upon the *w*,
SS 8: 7 Many *w* cannot quench love;
Isa 11: 9 as the *w* cover the sea.
43: 2 When you pass through the *w*,
55: 1 come to the *w*;
58:11 like a spring whose *w* never fail.
Hab 2:14 as the *w* cover the sea.
1Co 3: 7 plants nor he who *w* is anything,

WAVE (WAVES)
Lev 23:11 He is to *w* the sheaf
Jas 1: 6 he who doubts is like a *w* of the sea,

WAVER*
1Ki 18:21 "How long will you *w*
Ro 4:20 Yet he did not *w* through unbelief

WAVES (WAVE)
Isa 57:20 whose *w* cast up mire and mud.
Mt 8:27 Even the winds and the *w* obey him
Eph 4:14 tossed back and forth by the *w*,

WAY (WAYS)
Ex 13:21 of cloud to guide them on their *w*
18:20 and show them the *w* to live
Dt 1:33 to show you the *w* you should go.
32: 6 Is this the *w* you repay the LORD,
1Sa 12:23 I will teach you the *w* that is good
2Sa 22:31 "As for God, his *w* is perfect;
1Ki 8:23 wholeheartedly in your *w*.
8:36 Teach them the right *w* to live,
Job 23:10 But he knows the *w* that I take;

Ps 1: 1 or stand in the w of sinners
32: 8 teach you in the w you should go;
37: 5 Commit your w to the LORD;
86:11 Teach me your w, O LORD,
119: 9 can a young man keep his w pure?
139: 24 See if there is any offensive w in me
Pr 4:11 I guide you in the w of wisdom
12:15 The w of a fool seems right to him,
14:12 There is a w that seems right
16:17 he who guards his w guards his life.
19: 2 nor to be hasty and miss the w.
22: 6 Train a child in the w he should go,
30:19 and the w of a man with a maiden.
Isa 30:21 saying, "This is the w; walk in it."
35: 8 it will be called the W of Holiness.
40: 3 the w for the LORD;
48:17 you in the w you should go.
53: 6 each of us has turned to his own w;
55: 7 Let the wicked forsake his w
Jer 5:31 and my people love it this w.
Mal 3: 1 who will prepare the w before me.
Mt 3: 3 'Prepare the w for the Lord,
Lk 7:27 who will prepare your w before you
Jn 14: 6 "I am the w and the truth
Ac 1:11 in the same w you have seen him go
9: 2 any there who belonged to the W,
24:14 of the W, which they call a sect.
1Co 10:13 also provide a w out so that you can
12:31 will show you the most excellent w.
14: 1 Follow the w of love and eagerly
Col 1:10 and may please him in every w:
Tit 2:10 that in every w they will make
Heb 4:15 who has been tempted in every w,
9: 8 was showing by this that the w
10:20 and living w opened for us
13:18 desire to live honorably in every w.

WAYS (WAY)
Ex 33:13 teach me your w so I may know
Dt 10:12 to walk in all his w, to love him,
26:17 and that you will walk in his w,
30:16 in his w, and to keep his commands
32: 4 and all his w are just.
Jos 22: 5 in all his w, to obey his commands,
2Ch 11:17 walking in the w of David
Job 34:21 "His eyes are on the w of men;
Ps 25: 4 Show me your w, O LORD,
25:10 All the w of the LORD are loving
37: 7 fret when men succeed in their w,
51:13 I will teach transgressors your w,
77:13 Your w, O God, are holy.
119: 59 I have considered my w
139: 3 you are familiar with all my w.
145: 17 The LORD is righteous in all his w
Pr 3: 6 in all your w acknowledge him,
4:26 and take only w that are firm.
5:21 For a man's w are in full view
16: 2 All a man's w seem innocent
16: 7 When a man's w are pleasing
Isa 2: 3 He will teach us his w,
55: 8 neither are your w my w,"
Eze 28:15 You were blameless in your w
33: 8 out to dissuade him from his w,
Hos 14: 9 The w of the LORD are right;
Ro 1:30 they invent w of doing evil;
Jas 3: 2 We all stumble in many w.

WEAK (WEAKER WEAKNESS WEAKNESSES)
Ps 41: 1 is he who has regard for the w;
72:13 He will take pity on the w
82: 3 Defend the cause of the w
Eze 34: 4 You have not strengthened the w
Mt 26:41 spirit is willing, but the body is w."
Ac 20:35 of hard work we must help the w,
Ro 14: 1 Accept him whose faith is w,
15: 1 to bear with the failings of the w
1Co 1:27 God chose the w things
8: 9 become a stumbling block to the w.
9:22 To the w I became w, to win the w.
11:30 That is why many among you are w
2Co 12:10 For when I am w, then I am strong.
1Th 5:14 help the w, be patient
Heb 12:12 your feeble arms and w knees.

WEAK-WILLED (WILL)
2Ti 3: 6 and gain control over w women,

WEAKER* (WEAK)
2Sa 3: 1 the house of Saul grew w and w.
1Co 12:22 seem to be w are indispensable,
1Pe 3: 7 them with respect as the w partner

WEAKNESS* (WEAK)
La 1: 6 in w they have fled
Ro 8:26 the Spirit helps us in our w.
1Co 1:25 and the w of God is stronger
2: 3 I came to you in w and fear,
15:43 it is sown in w, it is raised in power;
2Co 11:30 boast of the things that show my w.
12: 9 for my power is made perfect in w
13: 4 he was crucified in w, yet he lives
Heb 5: 2 since he himself is subject to w.
11:34 whose w was turned to strength;

WEAKNESSES* (WEAK)
2Co 12: 5 about myself, except about my w.
12: 9 all the more gladly about my w,
12:10 I delight in w, in insults,
Heb 4:15 unable to sympathize with our w,

WEALTH
Dt 8:18 gives you the ability to produce w,
2Ch 1:11 and you have not asked for w,
Ps 39: 6 he heaps up w, not knowing who
Pr 3: 9 Honor the LORD with your w,
10: 4 but diligent hands bring w.
11: 4 W is worthless in the day of wrath,
13: 7 to be poor, yet has great w.
15:16 than great w with turmoil.
22: 4 bring w and honor and life.
Ecc 5:10 whoever loves w is never satisfied
5:13 w hoarded to the harm of its owner,
SS 8: 7 all the w of his house for love,
Mt 13:22 and the deceitfulness of w choke it,
Mk 10:22 away sad, because he had great w.
12:44 They all gave out of their w; but she
Lk 15:13 and there squandered his w
1Ti 6:17 nor to put their hope in w,
Jas 5: 2 Your w has rotted, and moths have
5: 3 You have hoarded w

WEAPON (WEAPONS)
Ne 4:17 work with one hand and held a w

WEAPONS (WEAPON)
Ecc 9:18 Wisdom is better than w of war,
2Co 6: 7 with w of righteousness
10: 4 The w we fight with are not

WEAR (WEARING)
Dt 8: 4 Your clothes did not w out
22: 5 nor a man w women's clothing,
Ps 102: 26 they will all w out like a garment.
Pr 23: 4 Do not w yourself out to get rich;
Isa 51: 6 the earth will w out like a garment
Heb 1:11 they will all w out like a garment.
Rev 3:18 and white clothes to w,

WEARIES (WEARY)
Ecc 12:12 and much study w the body.

WEARING (WEAR)
Jn 19: 5 When Jesus came out w the crown
Jas 2: 3 attention to the man w fine clothes
1Pe 3: 3 as braided hair and the w
Rev 7: 9 They were w white robes

WEARY (WEARIES)
Isa 40:28 He will not grow tired or w,
40:31 they will run and not grow w,
50: 4 know the word that sustains the w.
Mt 11:28 all you who are w and burdened,
Gal 6: 9 Let us not become w in doing good,
Heb 12: 3 so that you will not grow w
Rev 2: 3 my name, and have not grown w.

WEDDING
Mt 22:11 who was not wearing w clothes.
Rev 19: 7 For the w of the Lamb has come,

WEEDS
Mt 13:25 and sowed w among the wheat,

WEEK
Mt 28: 1 at dawn on the first day of the w,
1Co 16: 2 On the first day of every w,

WEEP (WEEPING WEPT)
Ecc 3: 4 a time to w and a time to laugh,
Lk 6:21 Blessed are you who w now,
23:28 w for yourselves and for your

WEEPING (WEEP)
Ps 30: 5 w may remain for a night,
126: 6 He who goes out w,
Jer 31:15 Rachel w for her children
Mt 2:18 Rachel w for her children
8:12 where there will be w and gnashing

WEIGH (OUTWEIGHS WEIGHED WEIGHS WEIGHTIER WEIGHTS)
1Co 14:29 others should w carefully what is

WEIGHED (WEIGH)
Job 28:15 nor can its price be w in silver.
Da 5:27 You have been w on the scales
Lk 21:34 or your hearts will be w

WEIGHS (WEIGH)
Pr 12:25 An anxious heart w a man down,
15:28 of the righteous w its answers,
21: 2 but the LORD w the heart.
24:12 not he who w the heart perceive

WEIGHTIER* (WEIGH)
Jn 5:36 "I have testimony w than that

WEIGHTS (WEIGH)
Lev 19:36 Use honest scales and honest w,
Dt 25:13 Do not have two differing w
Pr 11: 1 but accurate w are his delight.

WELCOME (WELCOMES)
Mk 9:37 welcomes me does not w me
2Pe 1:11 and you will receive a rich w

WELCOMES (WELCOME)
Mt 18: 5 whoever w a little child like this
2Jn :11 Anyone who w him shares

WELL (WELLED WELLING WELLS)
Mt 15:31 crippled made w, the lame walking
Lk 14: 5 falls into a w on the Sabbath day,
17:19 your faith has made you w."
Jas 5:15 in faith will make the sick person w

WELL-WATERED (WATER)
Isa 58:11 You will be like a w garden,

WELLED* (WELL)
2Co 8: 2 and their extreme poverty w up

WELLING* (WELL)
Jn 4:14 of water w up to eternal life."

WELLS (WELL)
Isa 12: 3 from the w of salvation.

WELLSPRING* (SPRING)
Pr 4:23 for it is the w of life.

WEPT (WEEP)
Ps 137: 1 of Babylon we sat and w
Lk 22:62 And he went outside and w bitterly
Jn 11:35 Jesus w.

WEST
Ps 103: 12 as far as the east is from the w,
107: 3 from east and w, from north

WHEAT
Mt 3:12 gathering his w into the barn
13:25 and sowed weeds among the w,
Lk 22:31 Satan has asked to sift you as w.
Jn 12:24 a kernel of w falls to the ground

WHEELS
Eze 1:16 appearance and structure of the w:

WHIRLWIND (WIND)
2Ki 2: 1 to take Elijah up to heaven in a w,
Hos 8: 7 and reap the w.
Na 1: 3 His way is in the w and the storm,

WHISPER (WHISPERED)
1Ki 19:12 And after the fire came a gentle w.
Job 26:14 how faint the w we hear of him!
Ps 107: 29 He stilled the storm to a w;

WHISPERED (WHISPER)
Mt 10:27 speak in the daylight; what is w

WHITE (WHITER)
Isa 1:18 they shall be as w as snow;
Da 7: 9 His clothing was as w as snow;
7: 9 the hair of his head was w like wool
Mt 28: 3 and his clothes were w as snow.
Rev 1:14 hair were w like wool, as w as snow,
3: 4 dressed in w, for they are worthy.
6: 2 and there before me was a w horse!
7:13 "These in w robes—who are they,
19:11 and there before me was a w horse,
20:11 Then I saw a great w throne

WHITER (WHITE)
Ps 51: 7 and I will be w than snow.

WHOLE
Ge 1:29 plant on the face of the w earth
2: 6 and watered the w surface
11: 1 Now the w world had one language
Ex 12:47 The w community
19: 5 Although the w earth is mine,
Lev 16:17 and the w community of Israel.
Nu 14:21 of the LORD fills the w earth,
32:13 until the w generation
Dt 13:16 w burnt offering to the LORD your
19: 8 gives you the w land he promised
Jos 2: 3 come to spy out the w land."
1Sa 1:28 For his w life he will be given

1Sa 17:46 the *w* world will know that there is
1Ki 10:24 The *w* world sought audience
2Ki 21: 8 and will keep the *w* Law that my
Ps 72:19 may the *w* earth be filled
Pr 4:22 and health to a man's *w* body.
8:31 rejoicing in his *w* world
Ecc 12:13 for this is the *w* duty of man.
Isa 1: 5 Your *w* head is injured,
6: 3 the *w* earth is full of his glory."
14:26 plan determined for the *w* world;
Eze 34: 6 were scattered over the *w* earth,
37:11 these bones are the *w* house
Da 2:35 mountain and filled the *w* earth.
Zep 1:18 the *w* world will be consumed,
Zec 14: 9 will be king over the *w* earth.
Mal 3:10 the *w* tithe into the storehouse,
Mt 5:29 than for your *w* body to be thrown
6:22 your *w* body will be full of light.
16:26 for a man if he gains the *w* world,
24:14 will be preached in the *w* world
Lk 21:35 live on the face of the *w* earth.
Jn 12:19 Look how the *w* world has gone
13:10 to wash his feet; his *w* body is clean
21:25 the *w* world would not have room
Ac 17:26 they should inhabit the *w* earth;
20:27 proclaim to you the *w* will of God.
Ro 1: 9 whom I serve with my *w* heart
3:19 and the *w* world held accountable
8:22 know that the *w* creation has been
1Co 4: 9 made a spectacle to the *w* universe,
12:17 If the *w* body were an ear,
Gal 3:22 declares that the *w* world is
5: 3 obligated to obey the *w* law.
Eph 4:10 in order to fill the *w* universe.)
4:13 attaining to the *w* measure
1Th 5:23 May your *w* spirit, soul
Jas 2:10 For whoever keeps the *w* law
1Jn 2: 2 but also for the sins of the *w* world.
Rev 3:10 going to come upon the *w* world

WHOLEHEARTED* (HEART)
2Ki 20: 3 you faithfully and with *w* devotion
1Ch 28: 9 and serve him with *w* devotion
29:19 my son Solomon the *w* devotion
Isa 38: 3 you faithfully and with *w* devotion

WHOLEHEARTEDLY* (HEART)
Nu 14:24 a different spirit and follows me *w*,
32:11 they have not followed me *w*,
32:12 for they followed the LORD *w*.'
Dt 1:36 because he followed the LORD *w*
Jos 14: 8 followed the LORD my God *w*.
14: 9 followed the LORD my God *w*.'
14:14 the LORD, the God of Israel, *w*.
1Ki 8:23 with your servants who continue *w*
1Ch 29: 9 for they had given freely and *w*
2Ch 6:14 with your servants who continue *w*
15:15 oath because they had sworn it *w*.
19: 9 and *w* in the fear of the LORD.
25: 2 in the eyes of the LORD, but not *w*
31:21 he sought his God and worked *w*.
Ro 6:17 you *w* obeyed the form of teaching
Eph 6: 7 Serve *w*, as if you were serving

WHOLESOME*
2Ki 2:22 And the water has remained *w*
2Pe 3: 1 to stimulate you to *w* thinking.

WICK
Isa 42: 3 a smoldering *w* he will not snuff out
Mt 12:20 a smoldering *w* he will not snuff out

WICKED (WICKEDNESS)
Ge 13:13 Now the men of Sodom were *w*
39: 9 How then could I do such a *w* thing
Ex 23: 1 Do not help a *w* man
Nu 14:35 things to this whole *w* community,
Dt 15: 9 not to harbor this *w* thought:
Jdg 19:22 some of the *w* men
1Sa 2:12 Eli's sons were *w* men; they had no
15:18 completely destroy those *w* people,
25:17 He is such a *w* man that no one can
2Sa 13:12 in Israel! Don't do this *w* thing.
2Ki 17:11 They did *w* things that provoked
2Ch 7:14 and turn from their *w* ways,
19: 2 "Should you help the *w*
Ne 13:17 "What is this *w* thing you are doing
Ps 1: 1 walk in the counsel of the *w*
1: 5 Therefore the *w* will not stand
7: 9 to an end the violence of the *w*
10:13 Why does the *w* man revile God?
11: 5 the *w* and those who love violence
12: 8 The *w* freely strut about
26: 5 and refuse to sit with the *w*.
32:10 Many are the woes of the *w*,
36: 1 concerning the sinfulness of the *w*:
37:13 but the Lord laughs at the *w*,
49: 5 when *w* deceivers surround me—
50:16 But to the *w*, God says:

Ps 58: 3 Even from birth the *w* go astray;
73: 3 when I saw the prosperity of the *w*.
82: 2 and show partiality to the *w*? *Selah*
112: 10 the longings of the *w* will come
119: 61 Though the *w* bind me with ropes,
119:155 Salvation is far from the *w*,
140: 8 do not grant the *w* their desires,
141: 10 Let the *w* fall into their own nets,
146: 9 but he frustrates the ways of the *w*.
Pr 2:12 you from the ways of *w* men,
4:14 Do not set foot on the path of the *w*
6:18 a heart that devises *w* schemes,
9: 7 whoever rebukes a *w* man incurs
10:20 the heart of the *w* is of little value.
10:28 the hopes of the *w* come to nothing
11: 5 *w* are brought down by their own
11:10 when the *w* perish, there are shouts
11:21 The *w* will not go unpunished,
12: 5 but the advice of the *w* is deceitful.
12:10 the kindest acts of the *w* are cruel.
14:19 the *w* at the gates of the righteous.
15: 3 keeping watch on the *w*
15:26 detests the thoughts of the *w*,
21:10 The *w* man craves evil;
21:29 A *w* man puts up a bold front,
28: 1 *w* man flees though no one pursues,
28: 4 who forsake the law praise the *w*,
29: 7 but the *w* have no such concern.
29:16 When the *w* thrive, so does sin,
29:27 the *w* detest the upright.
Isa 11: 4 breath of his lips he will slay the *w*.
13:11 the *w* for their sins.
26:10 Though grace is shown to the *w*,
48:22 says the LORD, "for the *w*."
53: 9 He was assigned a grave with the *w*
55: 7 Let the *w* forsake his way
57:20 But the *w* are like the tossing sea,
Jer 35:15 of you must turn from your *w* ways
Eze 3:18 that *w* man will die for his sin,
13:22 you encouraged the *w* not to turn
14: 7 and puts a *w* stumbling block
18:21 "But if a *w* man turns away
18:23 pleasure in the death of the *w*?
21:25 " 'O profane and *w* prince of Israel,
33: 8 When I say to the *w*, 'O *w* man,
33:11 pleasure in the death of the *w*,
33:14 to the *w* man, 'You will surely die,'
33:19 And if a *w* man turns away
Da 12:10 but the *w* will continue to be *w*.
Mt 12:39 *w* and adulterous generation asks
12:45 be with this *w* generation."
12:45 with it seven other spirits more *w*
Lk 6:35 he is kind to the ungrateful and *w*.
Ac 2:23 and you, with the help of *w* men,
Ro 4: 5 but trusts God who justifies the *w*,
1Co 5:13 "Expel the *w* man from among you
6: 9 not know that the *w* will not inherit
Rev 2: 2 that you cannot tolerate *w* men,

WICKEDNESS (WICKED)
Ge 6: 5 The LORD saw how great man's *w*
Ex 34: 7 and forgiving *w*, rebellion and sin.
Lev 16:21 and confess over it all the *w*
19:29 to prostitution and be filled with *w*.
Dt 9: 4 it is on account of the *w*
Ne 9: 2 and confessed their sins and the *w*
Ps 45: 7 You love righteousness and hate *w*;
92:15 he is my Rock, and there is no *w*
Pr 13: 6 but *w* overthrows the sinner.
Jer 3: 2 land with your prostitution and *w*.
8: 6 No one repents of his *w*,
14:20 O LORD, we acknowledge our *w*
Eze 18:20 the *w* of the wicked will be charged
28:15 created till *w* was found in you.
33:19 wicked man turns away from his *w*
Da 4:27 and your *w* by being kind
9:24 to atone for *w*, to bring
Jnh 1: 2 its *w* has come up before me."
Mt 24:12 Because of the increase of *w*,
Lk 11:39 inside you are full of greed and *w*.
Ac 1:18 (With the reward he got for his *w*,
Ro 1:18 who suppress the truth by their *w*,
1Co 5: 8 the yeast of malice and *w*,
2Co 6:14 what do righteousness and *w* have
2Ti 2:19 of the Lord must turn away from *w*
Tit 2:14 for us to redeem us from all *w*
Heb 1: 9 loved righteousness and hated *w*;
8:12 For I will forgive their *w*
2Pe 2:15 who loved the wages of *w*.

WIDE
Ps 81:10 Open *w* your mouth and I will fill it
Isa 54: 2 stretch your tent curtains *w*,
Mt 7:13 For *w* is the gate and broad is
2Co 6:13 my children—open *w* your hearts
Eph 3:18 to grasp how *w* and long and high

WIDOW (WIDOWS)
Ex 22:22 "Do not take advantage of a *w*

Dt 10:18 cause of the fatherless and the *w*,
Ps 146: 9 sustains the fatherless and the *w*,
Isa 1:17 plead the case of the *w*.
Lk 21: 2 saw a poor *w* put in two very small
1Ti 5: 4 But if a *w* has children

WIDOWS (WIDOW)
Ps 68: 5 to the fatherless, a defender of *w*,
Ac 6: 1 their *w* were being overlooked
1Co 7: 8 to the unmarried and the *w* I say:
1Ti 5: 3 to those *w* who are really
Jas 1:27 look after orphans and *w*

WIFE (WIVES WIVES')
Ge 2:24 and mother and be united to his *w*,
19:26 But Lot's *w* looked back,
24:67 she became his *w*, and he loved her;
Ex 20:17 shall not covet your neighbor's *w*,
Lev 20:10 adultery with another man's *w*—
Dt 5:21 shall not covet your neighbor's *w*.
24: 5 happiness to the *w* he has married.
Ru 4:13 took Ruth and she became his *w*.
Pr 5:18 in the *w* of your youth.
12: 4 *w* of noble character is her
18:22 He who finds a *w* finds what is
19:13 quarrelsome *w* is like a constant
31:10 *w* of noble character who can find?
Hos 1: 2 take to yourself an adulterous *w*
Mal 2:14 the witness between you and the *w*
Mt 1:20 to take Mary home as your *w*,
19: 3 for a man to divorce his *w* for any
Lk 17:32 Remember Lot's *w*! Whoever tries
18:29 or *w* or brothers or parents
1Co 7: 2 each man should have his own *w*,
7:33 how he can please his *w*—
Eph 5:23 the husband is the head of the *w*
5:33 must love his *w* as he loves himself,
1Ti 3: 2 husband of but one *w*, temperate,
Rev 21: 9 I will show you the bride, the *w*

WILD
Ge 1:25 God made the *w* animals according
8: 1 Noah and all the *w* animals
Lk 15:13 squandered his wealth in *w* living.
Ro 11:17 and you, though a *w* olive shoot,

WILL (WEAK-WILLED WILLFUL WILLING WILLINGNESS)
Ps 40: 8 I desire to do your *w*, O my God;
143: 10 Teach me to do your *w*,
Isa 53:10 Yet it was the LORD's *w*
Mt 6:10 your *w* be done
7:21 who does the *w* of my Father
10:29 apart from the *w* of your Father.
12:50 does the *w* of my Father
26:39 Yet not as I *w*, but as you *w*."
26:42 I drink it, may your *w* be done."
Jn 6:38 but to do the *w* of him who sent me.
7:17 If anyone chooses to do God's *w*,
Ac 20:27 to you the whole *w* of God.
Ro 12: 2 and approve what God's *w* is—
1Co 7:37 but has control over his own *w*,
Eph 5:17 understand what the Lord's *w* is.
Php 2:13 for it is God who works in you to *w*
1Th 4: 3 God's *w* that you should be sanctified:
5:18 for this is God's *w* for you
2Ti 2:26 has taken them captive to do his *w*.
Heb 2: 4 distributed according to his *w*.
9:16 In the case of a *w*, it is necessary
10: 7 I have come to do your *w*, O God
13:21 everything good for doing his *w*,
Jas 4:15 "If it is the Lord's *w*,
1Pe 3:17 It is better, if it is God's *w*,
4: 2 but rather for the *w* of God.
2Pe 1:21 never had its origin in the *w*
1Jn 5:14 we ask anything according to his *w*,
Rev 4:11 and by your *w* they were created

WILLFUL (WILL)
Ps 19:13 Keep your servant also from *w* sins;

WILLING (WILL)
1Ch 28: 9 devotion and with a *w* mind,
29: 5 who is *w* to consecrate himself
Ps 51:12 grant me a *w* spirit, to sustain me.
Da 3:28 were *w* to give up their lives rather
Mt 18:14 Father in heaven is not *w* that any
23:37 her wings, but you were not *w*.
26:41 The spirit is *w*, but the body is weak
1Ti 6:18 and to be generous and *w* to share.
1Pe 5: 2 but because you are *w*,

WILLINGNESS* (WILL)
2Co 8:11 so that your eager *w*
8:12 For if the *w* is there, the gift is

WIN (WINS WON)
1Co 9:19 myself a slave to everyone, to *w*
Php 3:14 on toward the goal to *w* the prize
1Th 4:12 your daily life may *w* the respect

WIND (WHIRLWIND WINDS)
Ps 1: 4 that the *w* blows away.
Ecc 2:11 meaningless, a chasing after the *w*;
Hos 8: 7 "They sow the *w*
Mk 4:41 Even the *w* and the waves obey
Jn 3: 8 The *w* blows wherever it pleases.
Eph 4:14 and there by every *w* of teaching
Jas 1: 6 blown and tossed by the *w*.

WINDOW
Jos 2:21 she tied the scarlet cord in the *w*.
Ac 20: 9 in a *w* was a young man named
2Co 11:33 in a basket from a *w* in the wall

WINDS (WIND)
Ps 104: 4 He makes *w* his messengers,
Mt 24:31 gather his elect from the four *w*,
Heb 1: 7 "He makes his angels *w*,

WINE
Ps 104: 15 *w* that gladdens the heart of man,
Pr 20: 1 *W* is a mocker and beer a brawler;
23:20 join those who drink too much *w*
23:31 Do not gaze at *w* when it is red,
31: 6 *w* to those who are in anguish;
SS 1: 2 your love is more delightful than *w*.
Isa 28: 7 And these also stagger from *w*
55: 1 Come, buy *w* and milk
Mt 9:17 Neither do men pour new *w*
Lk 23:36 They offered him *w* vinegar
Jn 2: 3 When the *w* was gone, Jesus'
Ro 14:21 not to eat meat or drink *w*
Eph 5:18 on *w*, which leads to debauchery.
1Ti 5:23 a little *w* because of your stomach
Rev 16:19 with the *w* of the fury of his wrath.

WINEPRESS
Isa 63: 2 like those of one treading the *w*?
Rev 19:15 He treads the *w* of the fury

WINESKINS
Mt 9:17 do men pour new wine into old *w*.

WINGS
Ex 19: 4 and how I carried you on eagles' *w*
Ru 2:12 under whose *w* you have come
Ps 17: 8 hide me in the shadow of your *w*
91: 4 under his *w* you will find refuge;
Isa 6: 2 him were seraphs, each with six *w*:
40:31 They will soar on *w* like eagles;
Eze 1: 6 of them had four faces and four *w*.
Zec 5: 9 in their *w*! They had *w* like those
Mal 4: 2 rise with healing in its *w*.
Lk 13:34 hen gathers her chicks under her *w*,
Rev 4: 8 the four living creatures had six *w*

WINS (WIN)
Pr 11:30 and he who *w* souls is wise.

WINTER
Mk 13:18 that this will not take place in *w*,

WIPE (WIPED)
Isa 25: 8 The Sovereign LORD will *w* away
Rev 7:17 God will *w* away every tear
21: 4 He will *w* every tear

WIPED (WIPE)
Lk 7:38 Then she *w* them with her hair,
Ac 3:19 so that your sins may be *w* out,

WISDOM (WISE)
Ge 3: 6 and also desirable for gaining *w*,
1Ki 4:29 God gave Solomon *w* and very
2Ch 1:10 Give me *w* and knowledge,
Ps 51: 6 you teach me *w* in the inmost place
111: 10 of the LORD is the beginning of *w*;
Pr 2: 6 For the LORD gives *w*,
3:13 Blessed is the man who finds *w*,
4: 7 *W* is supreme; therefore get
8:11 for *w* is more precious than rubies,
11: 2 but with humility comes *w*.
13:10 *w* is found in those who take advice
23:23 get *w*, discipline and understanding
29: 3 A man who loves *w* brings joy
29:15 The rod of correction imparts *w*,
31:26 She speaks with *w*,
Isa 11: 2 Spirit of *w* and of understanding,
28:29 in counsel and magnificent in *w*.
Jer 10:12 he founded the world by his *w*
Mic 6: 9 and to fear your name is *w*—
Mt 11:19 But *w* is proved right by her actions
Lk 2:52 And Jesus grew in *w* and stature,
Ac 6: 3 known to be full of the Spirit and *w*.
Ro 11:33 the depth of the riches of the *w*
1Co 1:17 not with words of human *w*,
1:30 who has become for us *w* from God
12: 8 through the Spirit the message of *w*
Eph 1:17 may give you the Spirit of *w*
Col 2: 3 are hidden all the treasures of *w*
Col 2:23 indeed have an appearance of *w*,
Jas 1: 5 of you lacks *w*, he should ask God,
3:13 in the humility that comes from *w*.
Rev 5:12 and wealth and *w* and strength

WISE (WISDOM WISER)
1Ki 3:12 give you a *w* and discerning heart,
Job 5:13 He catches the *w* in their craftiness
Ps 19: 7 making *w* the simple.
Pr 3: 7 Do not be *w* in your own eyes;
9: 8 rebuke a *w* man and he will love
10: 1 A *w* son brings joy to his father,
11:30 and he who wins souls is *w*.
13: 1 A *w* son heeds his father's
13:20 He who walks with the *w* grows *w*,
16:23 A *w* man's heart guides his mouth,
17:28 Even a fool is thought *w*
Ecc 9:17 The quiet words of the *w* are more
Jer 9:23 "Let not the *w* man boast
Eze 28: 6 " 'Because you think you are *w*,
Da 2:21 He gives wisdom to the *w*
12: 3 Those who are *w* will shine like
Mt 11:25 hidden these things from the *w*
25: 2 them were foolish and five were *w*.
1Co 1:19 I will destroy the wisdom of the *w*;
1:27 things of the world to shame the *w*;
3:19 He catches the *w* in their craftiness
Eph 5:15 but as *w*, making the most
2Ti 3:15 able to make you *w* for salvation
Jas 3:13 Who is *w* and understanding

WISER (WISE)
Pr 9: 9 a wise man and he will be *w* still;
1Co 1:25 of God is *w* than man's wisdom,

WISH (WISHES)
Jn 15: 7 ask whatever you *w*, and it will be
Ro 9: 3 For I could *w* that I myself were
Rev 3:15 I *w* you were either one

WISHES (WISH)
Rev 22:17 let him come; and whoever *w*,

WITCHCRAFT
Dt 18:10 engages in *w*, or casts spells,
Gal 5:20 idolatry and *w*; hatred, discord,

WITHDREW
Lk 5:16 But Jesus often *w* to lonely places

WITHER (WITHERS)
Ps 1: 3 and whose leaf does not *w*.
37:19 In times of disaster they will not *w*;

WITHERS (WITHER)
Isa 40: 7 The grass *w* and the flowers fall,
1Pe 1:24 the grass *w* and the flowers fall,

WITHHELD (WITHHOLD)
Ge 22:12 you have not *w* from me your son,

WITHHOLD (WITHHELD WITHHOLDS)
Ps 84:11 no good thing does he *w*
Pr 23:13 Do not *w* discipline from a child;

WITHHOLDS (WITHHOLD)
Dt 27:19 "Cursed is the man who *w* justice

WITNESS (EYEWITNESSES WITNESSES)
Pr 12:17 truthful *w* gives honest testimony,
19: 9 A false *w* will not go unpunished,
Jn 1: 8 he came only as a *w* to the light.

WITNESSES (WITNESS)
Dt 19:15 by the testimony of two or three *w*.
Mt 18:16 by the testimony of two or three *w*.'
Ac 1: 8 and you will be my *w* in Jerusalem,

WIVES (WIFE)
Eph 5:22 *W*, submit to your husbands
5:25 love your *w*, just as Christ loved
1Pe 3: 1 words by the behavior of their *w*,

WIVES' (WIFE)
1Ti 4: 7 with godless myths and old *w* tales

WOE
Isa 6: 5 "*W* to me!" I cried.
Eze 34: 2 *W* to the shepherds
Mt 18: 7 "*W* to the world
23:13 "*W* to you, teachers of the law
Jude :11 *W* to them! They have taken

WOLF (WOLVES)
Isa 65:25 *w* and the lamb will feed together,

WOLVES (WOLF)
Mt 10:16 you out like sheep among *w*.

WOMAN (MAN)
Ge 2:22 God made a *w* from
2:23 she shall be called '*w*,'
3: 6 *w* saw that the fruit
3:12 The *w* you put here with
3:15 between you and the *w*,
3:16 To the *w* he said,
12:11 a beautiful *w* you are.
20: 3 because of the *w* you have
24: 5 if the *w* is unwilling
Ex 2: 1 married a Levite *w*
3:22 Every *w* is to ask her
21:10 If he marries another *w*
21:22 hit a pregnant *w*
Lev 12: 2 *w* who becomes pregnant
15:19 *w* has her regular flow
15:25 a *w* has a discharge
18:17 sexual relations with both a *w*
20:13 as one lies with a *w*,
Nu 5:29 when a *w* goes astray
30: 3 young *w* still living in
30: 9 by a widow or divorced *w*
30:10 *w* living with her husband
Dt 20: 7 become pledged to a *w*
21:11 the captives a beautiful *w*
22: 5 *w* must not wear men's
22:13 married this *w* but when
Jdg 4: 9 hand Sisera over to a *w*.
13: 6 the *w* went to her husband
14: 2 have seen a Philistine *w*
16: 4 he fell in love with a *w*
20: 4 husband of the murdered *w*
Ru 3:11 a *w* of noble character
1Sa 1:15 a *w* who is deeply troubled
25: 3 intelligent and beautiful *w*,
28: 7 a *w* who is a medium,
2Sa 11: 2 he saw a *w* bathing
13:17 "Get this *w* out of here
14: 2 had a wise *w* brought
20:16 a wise *w* called from
1Ki 3:18 this *w* also had a baby.
17:24 the *w* said to Elijah,
2Ki 4: 8 a well-to-do *w* was there,
8: 1 Elisha had said to the *w*
9:34 "Take care of that cursed *w*,"
Job 14: 1 Man born of *w* is of few
Pr 11:16 A kindhearted *w* gains respect,
11:22 a beautiful *w* who shows no
14: 1 a wise *w* builds her house,
30:23 unloved *w* who is married,
31:30 a *w* who fears the LORD
Isa 54: 1 O barren *w*, you who never
Mt 5:28 looks at a *w* lustfully
9:20 a *w* who had been subject
15:28 *W* you have great faith!
26: 7 a *w* came to him with
Mk 5:25 a *w* was there who had
7:25 a *w* whose little daughter
Lk 7:39 what kind of a *w* she is
10:38 a *w* named Martha opened
13:12 "*W*, you are set free
15: 8 suppose a *w* has ten silver
Jn 2: 4 *w*, why do you involve
4: 7 a Samaritan *w* came
8: 3 a *w* caught in adultery.
19:26 *w*, here is your son,"
20:15 *W*, 'he said, "Why are you crying?
Ac 9:40 Turning toward the dead *w*,
16:14 was a *w* named Lydia,
Ro 7: 2 a married *w* is bound to
1Co 7: 2 each *w* her own husband
7:15 a believing man or *w* is
7:34 an unmarried *w* or virgin
7:39 *w* is bound to her husband
11: 3 the head of the *w* is man,
11: 7 the *w* is the glory of man
11:13 a *w* to pray to God with
Gal 4: 4 his Son, born of a *w*,
4:31 not children of the slave *w*,
1Ti 2:11 A *w* should learn in
5:16 any *w* who is a believer
Rev 2:20 You tolerate that *w* Jezebel,
12: 1 a *w* clothed with the sun
12:13 he pursued the *w* who had
17: 3 a *w* sitting on a scarlet

WOMEN (MAN)
Mt 11:11 among those born of *w*,
28: 5 The angel said to the *w*,
Mk 15:41 Many other *w* who had come
Lk 1:42 Blessed are you among *w*,
8: 2 also some *w* who had been
23:27 *w* who mourned and wailed
24:11 they did not believe the *w*,
Ac 1:14 along with the *w* and Mary
16:13 speak to the *w* who had
17: 4 not a few prominent *w*.
Ro 1:26 *w* exchanged natural relations
1Co 14:34 *w* should remain silent in
Php 4: 3 help these *w* who have
1Ti 2: 9 want *w* to dress modestly
5: 2 older *w* as mothers,

Tit 2: 3 teach the older *w* to be
2: 4 train the younger *w* to love
Heb 11:35 *W* received back their dead
1Pe 3: 5 the holy *w* of the past

WOMB
Job 1:21 Naked I came from my mother's *w*,
Ps 139: 13 in my mother's *w*.
Pr 31: 2 "O my son, O son of my *w*,
Jer 1: 5 you in the *w* I knew you,
Lk 1:44 the baby in my *w* leaped for joy.
Jn 3: 4 into his mother's *w* to be born!"

WON (WIN)
1Pe 3: 1 they may be *w* over without words

WONDER (WONDERFUL WONDERS)
Ps 17: 7 Show the *w* of your great love,
SS 1: 3 No *w* the maidens love you!

WONDERFUL* (WONDER)
2Sa 1:26 Your love for me was *w*,
1:26 more *w* than that of women.
1Ch 16: 9 tell of all his *w* acts.
Job 42: 3 things too *w* for me to know.
Ps 26: 7 and telling of all your *w* deeds.
31:21 for he showed his *w* love to me
75: 1 men tell of your *w* deeds.
105: 2 tell of all his *w* acts.
107: 8 and his *w* deeds for men,
107: 15 and his *w* deeds for men,
107: 21 and his *w* deeds for men.
107: 24 his *w* deeds in the deep.
107: 31 and his *w* deeds for men.
119: 18 *w* things in your law.
119:129 Your statutes are *w*;
131: 1 or things too *w* for me.
139: 6 Such knowledge is too *w* for me,
139: 14 your works are *w*,
145: 5 I will meditate on your *w* works.
Isa 9: 6 *W* Counselor, Mighty God,
28:29 *w* in counsel and magnificent
Mt 21:15 of the law saw the *w* things he did
Lk 13:17 with all the *w* things he was doing.
1Pe 2: 9 out of darkness into his *w* light.

WONDERS (WONDER)
Ex 3:20 with all the *w* that I will perform
Dt 10:21 and awesome *w* you saw
2Sa 7:23 awesome *w* by driving out nations
Job 37:14 stop and consider God's *w*.
Ps 9: 1 I will tell of all your *w*.
89: 5 The heavens praise your *w*,
119: 27 then I will meditate on your *w*.
Joel 2:30 I will show *w* in the heavens
Ac 2:11 we hear them declaring the *w*
2:19 I will show *w* in the heaven above
5:12 many miraculous signs and *w*
2Co 12:12 that mark an apostle—signs, *w*
2Th 2: 9 and *w*, and in every sort
Heb 2: 4 also testified to it by signs, *w*

WOOD
Isa 44:19 Shall I bow down to a block of *w*?"
1Co 3:12 costly stones, *w*, hay or straw,

WOOL
Pr 31:13 She selects *w* and flax
Isa 1:18 they shall be like *w*.
Da 7: 9 hair of his head was white like *w*.
Rev 1:14 and hair were white like *w*,

WORD (BYWORD WORDS)
Nu 30: 2 he must not break his *w*
Dt 8: 3 but on every *w* that comes
2Sa 22:31 the *w* of the LORD is flawless.
Ps 56: 4 In God, whose *w* I praise,
119: 9 By living according to your *w*.
119: 11 I have hidden your *w* in my heart
119:105 Your *w* is a lamp to my feet
Pr 12:25 but a kind *w* cheers him up.
15: 1 but a harsh *w* stirs up anger.
25:11 A *w* aptly spoken
30: 5 "Every *w* of God is flawless;
Isa 55:11 so is my *w* that goes out
Jer 23:29 "Is not my *w* like fire," declares
Mt 4: 4 but on every *w* that comes
12:36 for every careless *w* they have
15: 6 Thus you nullify the *w* of God
Mk 4:14 parable? The farmer sows the *w*.
Jn 1: 1 was the *W*, and the *W* was
1:14 The *W* became flesh and made his
17:17 them by the truth; your *w* is truth.
Ac 6: 4 and the ministry of the *w*."
2Co 2:17 we do not peddle the *w* of God
4: 2 nor do we distort the *w* of God.
Eph 6:17 of the Spirit, which is the *w* of God.
Php 2:16 as you hold out the *w* of life—
Col 3:16 Let the *w* of Christ dwell
2Ti 2:15 and who correctly handles the *w*
Heb 4:12 For the *w* of God is living
Jas 1:22 Do not merely listen to the *w*,
2Pe 1:19 And we have the *w* of the prophets

WORDS (WORD)
Dt 11:18 Fix these *w* of mine in your hearts
Ps 12: 6 the *w* of the LORD are flawless,
119:103 How sweet are your *w* to my taste,
119:130 The unfolding of your *w* gives light;
119:160 All your *w* are true;
Pr 2: 1 My son, if you accept my *w*
10:19 When *w* are many, sin is not absent
16:24 Pleasant *w* are a honeycomb,
30: 6 Do not add to his *w*,
Ecc 12:11 The *w* of the wise are like goads,
Jer 15:16 When your *w* came, I ate them;
Mt 24:35 but my *w* will never pass away.
Lk 6:47 and hears my *w* and puts them
Jn 6:68 You have the *w* of eternal life.
15: 7 in me and my *w* remain in you,
1Co 2:13 but in *w* taught by the Spirit,
14:19 rather speak five intelligible *w*
Rev 22:19 And if anyone takes *w* away

WORK (WORKED WORKER WORKERS WORKING WORKMAN WORKMANSHIP WORKS)
Ge 2: 2 day he rested from all his *w*.
Ex 23:12 "Six days do your *w*,
Nu 8:11 ready to do the *w* of the LORD.
Dt 5:14 On it you shall not do any *w*,
Ps 19: 1 the skies proclaim the *w*
Ecc 5:19 his lot and be happy in his *w*—
Jer 48:10 lax in doing the LORD'S *w*!
Mt 20: 1 to hire men to *w* in his vineyard.
Jn 6:27 Do not *w* for food that spoils,
9: 4 we must do the *w* of him who sent
Ac 13: 2 for the *w* to which I have called
1Co 3:13 test the quality of each man's *w*.
4:12 We *w* hard with our own hands.
Eph 4:16 up in love, as each part does its *w*.
Php 1: 6 that he who began a good *w*
2:12 continue to *w* out your salvation
Col 3:23 Whatever you do, *w* at it
1Th 4:11 and to *w* with your hands,
5:12 to respect those who *w* hard
2Th 3:10 If a man will not *w*, he shall not eat
2Ti 3:17 equipped for every good *w*.
Heb 6:10 he will not forget your *w*
2Jn :11 him shares in his wicked *w*.
3Jn : 8 men so that we may *w* together

WORKED (WORK)
1Co 15:10 No, I *w* harder than all of them—
2Th 3: 8 On the contrary, we *w* night

WORKER (WORK)
Lk 10: 7 for the *w* deserves his wages.
1Ti 5:18 and "The *w* deserves his wages."

WORKERS (WORK)
Mt 9:37 is plentiful but the *w* are few.
1Co 3: 9 For we are God's fellow *w*;

WORKING (WORK)
Col 3:23 as *w* for the Lord, not for men,

WORKMAN (WORK)
2Ti 2:15 a *w* who does not need

WORKMANSHIP* (WORK)
Eph 2:10 For we are God's *w*, created

WORKS (WORK)
Ps 66: 5 how awesome his *w* in man's behalf
145: 6 of the power of your awesome *w*,
Pr 8:22 As the first of his *w*,
31:31 let her *w* bring her praise
Ro 4: 2 in fact, Abraham was justified by *w*
8:28 in all things God *w* for the good
Eph 2: 9 not by *w*, so that no one can boast.
4:12 to prepare God's people for *w*

WORLD (WORLDLY)
Ps 9: 8 He will judge the *w*
50:12 for the *w* is mine, and all that is in it
96:13 He will judge the *w*
Pr 8:23 before the *w* began.
Isa 13:11 I will punish the *w* for its evil,
Zep 1:18 the whole *w* will be consumed,
Mt 5:14 "You are the light of the *w*.
16:26 for a man if he gains the whole *w*,
Mk 16:15 into all the *w* and preach the good
Jn 1:29 who takes away the sin of the *w*!
3:16 so loved the *w* that he gave his one
8:12 he said, "I am the light of the *w*.
15:19 As it is, you do not belong to the *w*,
16:33 In this *w* you will have trouble.
17: 5 had with you before the *w* began.
17:14 not of the *w* any more than I am
18:36 "My kingdom is not of this *w*.
Ac 17:24 "The God who made the *w*
Ro 3:19 and the whole *w* held accountable
10:18 their words to the ends of the *w*."
1Co 1:27 things of the *w* to shame the strong.
3:19 the wisdom of this *w* is foolishness
6: 2 that the saints will judge the *w*?
2Co 5:19 that God was reconciling the *w*
10: 3 For though we live in the *w*,
1Ti 6: 7 For we brought nothing into the *w*,
Heb 11:38 the *w* was not worthy of them.
Jas 2: 5 poor in the eyes of the *w* to be rich
4: 4 with the *w* is hatred toward God?
1Pe 1:20 before the creation of the *w*,
1Jn 2: 2 but also for the sins of the whole *w*.
2:15 not love the *w* or anything in the *w*.
5: 4 born of God overcomes the *w*.
Rev 13: 8 slain from the creation of the *w*.

WORLDLY (WORLD)
1Co 3: 1 address you as spiritual but as *w*—
Tit 2:12 to ungodliness and *w* passions,

WORM
Mk 9:48 " 'their *w* does not die,

WORRY (WORRYING)
Mt 6:25 I tell you, do not *w* about your life,
10:19 do not *w* about what to say

WORRYING (WORRY)
Mt 6:27 of you by *w* can add a single hour

WORSHIP (WORSHIPED WORSHIPS)
Jos 22:27 that we will *w* the LORD
2Ki 17:36 arm, is the one you must *w*.
1Ch 16:29 *w* the LORD in the splendor
Ps 95: 6 Come, let us bow down in *w*,
100: 2 *w* the LORD with gladness;
Zec 14:17 up to Jerusalem to *w* the King,
Mt 2: 2 and have come to *w* him."
4: 9 "if you will bow down and *w* me."
Jn 4:24 and his worshipers must *w* in spirit
Ro 12: 1 to God—this is your spiritual act of *w*.
Heb 10: 1 perfect those who draw near to *w*.

WORSHIPED (WORSHIP)
2Ch 29:30 and bowed their heads and *w*.
Mt 28: 9 clasped his feet and *w* him.

WORSHIPS (WORSHIP)
Isa 44:15 But he also fashions a god and *w* it;

WORTH (WORTHY)
Job 28:13 Man does not comprehend its *w*;
Pr 31:10 She is *w* far more than rubies.
Mt 10:31 are *w* more than many sparrows.
Ro 8:18 sufferings are not *w* comparing
1Pe 1: 7 of greater *w* than gold,
3: 4 which is of great *w* in God's sight.

WORTHLESS
Pr 11: 4 Wealth is *w* in the day of wrath,
Jas 1:26 himself and his religion is *w*.

WORTHY (WORTH)
1Ch 16:25 For great is the LORD and most *w*
Mt 10:37 more than me is not *w* of me;
Lk 15:19 I am no longer *w* to be called your
Eph 4: 1 to live a life *w* of the calling you
Php 1:27 in a manner *w* of the gospel
Col 1:10 in order that you may live a life *w*
1Ti 3: 8 are to be men *w* of respect, sincere,
Heb 3: 3 Jesus has been found *w*
3Jn : 6 on their way in a manner *w* of God.
Rev 5: 2 "Who is *w* to break the seals

WOUND (WOUNDS)
1Co 8:12 and *w* their weak conscience,

WOUNDS (WOUND)
Pr 27: 6 *w* from a friend can be trusted
Isa 53: 5 and by his *w* we are healed.
Zec 13: 6 'What are these *w* on your body?'
1Pe 2:24 by his *w* you have been healed.

WRAPS
Ps 104: 2 He *w* himself in light

WRATH
2Ch 36:16 scoffed at his prophets until the *w*
Ps 2: 5 and terrifies them in his *w*, saying,
76:10 Surely your *w* against men brings
Pr 15: 1 A gentle answer turns away *w*,
Isa 13:13 at the *w* of the LORD Almighty,
51:17 the cup of his *w*,
Jer 25:15 filled with the wine of my *w*
Eze 5:13 my *w* against them will subside,
20: 8 So I said I would pour out my *w*
Am 1: 3 I will not turn back my *w*,
Na 1: 2 maintains his *w* against his enemies

Zep 1:15 That day will be a day of *w*,
Jn 3:36 for God's *w* remains on him."
Ro 1:18 The *w* of God is being revealed
2: 5 you are storing up *w*
5: 9 saved from God's *w* through him!
9:22 choosing to show his *w*
1Th 5: 9 God did not appoint us to suffer *w*
Rev 6:16 and from the *w* of the Lamb!
19:15 the fury of the *w* of God Almighty.

WRESTLED
Ge 32:24 and a man *w* with him till daybreak

WRITE (WRITER WRITING WRITTEN WROTE)
Dt 6: 9 *W* them on the doorframes
10: 2 I will *w* on the tablets the words
Pr 7: 3 *w* them on the tablet of your heart.
Jer 31:33 and *w* it on their hearts.
Heb 8:10 and *w* them on their hearts.
Rev 3:12 I will also *w* on him my new name.

WRITER* (WRITE)
Ps 45: 1 my tongue is the pen of a skillful *w*.

WRITING (WRITE)
1Co 14:37 him acknowledge that what I am *w*

WRITTEN (WRITE)
Dt 28:58 which are *w* in this book,
Jos 1: 8 careful to do everything *w* in it.
23: 6 to obey all that is *w* in the Book
Ps 40: 7 it is *w* about me in the scroll.
Da 12: 1 everyone whose name is found *w*
Mal 3:16 A scroll of remembrance was *w*
Lk 10:20 but rejoice that your names are *w*
24:44 must be fulfilled that is *w* about me
Jn 20:31 these are *w* that you may believe
21:25 for the books that would be *w*.
Ro 2:15 of the law are *w* on their hearts,
1Co 4: 6 "Do not go beyond what is *w*."
10:11 as examples and were *w* down
2Co 3: 3 *w* not with ink but with the Spirit
Col 2:14 having canceled the *w* code,
Heb 10: 7 it is *w* about me in the scroll—
12:23 whose names are *w* in heaven.
Rev 21:27 but only those whose names are *w*

WRONG (WRONGDOING WRONGED WRONGS)
Ex 23: 2 Do not follow the crowd in doing *w*
Nu 5: 7 must make full restitution for his *w*,
Dt 32: 4 A faithful God who does no *w*,
Job 34:12 unthinkable that God would do *w*,
Ps 5: 5 you hate all who do *w*.
Gal 2:11 to his face, because he was clearly in the *w*.
1Th 5:15 that nobody pays back *w* for *w*,

WRONGDOING (WRONG)
Job 1:22 sin by charging God with *w*.
1Jn 5:17 All *w* is sin, and there is sin that

WRONGED (WRONG)
1Co 6: 7 not rather be *w*? Why not rather

WRONGS (WRONG)
Pr 10:12 but love covers over all *w*.
1Co 13: 5 angered, it keeps no record of *w*.

WROTE (WRITE)
Ex 34:28 And he *w* on the tablets the words
Jn 5:46 for he *w* about me.
8: 8 down and *w* on the ground.

XERXES
King of Persia, husband of Esther. Deposed Vashti; replaced her with Esther (Est 1-2). Sealed Haman's edict to annihilate the Jews (Est 3). Received Esther without having called her (Est 5: 1-8). Honored Mordecai (Est 6). Hanged Haman (Est 7). Issued edict allowing Jews to defend themselves (Est 8). Exalted Mordecai (Est 8:1-2, 15; 9: 4; 10).

YEAR (YEARS)
Ex 34:23 Three times a *y* all your men are
Lev 16:34 to be made once a *y* for all the sins
25: 4 But in the seventh *y* the land is
25:11 The fiftieth *y* shall be a jubilee
Heb 10: 1 repeated endlessly *y* after *y*,

YEARS (YEAR)
Ge 1:14 to mark seasons and days and *y*,
Ex 12:40 lived in Egypt was 430 *y*.
16:35 The Israelites ate manna forty *y*,
Job 36:26 of his *y* is past finding out.
Ps 90: 4 For a thousand *y* in your sight
90:10 The length of our days is seventy *y*
Pr 3: 2 they will prolong your life many *y*
Lk 3:23 Jesus himself was about thirty *y* old
2Pe 3: 8 the Lord a day is like a thousand *y*,
Rev 20: 2 and bound him for a thousand *y*.

YEAST
Ex 12:15 are to eat bread made without *y*.
Mt 16: 6 guard against the *y* of the Pharisees
1Co 5: 6 you know that a little *y* works

YESTERDAY
Heb 13: 8 Jesus Christ is the same *y*

YOKE (YOKED)
1Ki 12: 4 and the heavy *y* he put on us,
Mt 11:29 Take my *y* upon you and learn
Gal 5: 1 be burdened again by a *y*

YOKED (YOKE)
2Co 6:14 Do not be *y* together

YOUNG (YOUNGER YOUTH)
2Ch 10:14 he followed the advice of the *y* men
Ps 37:25 I was *y* and now I am old,
119: 9 How can a *y* man keep his way
Pr 20:29 The glory of *y* men is their strength
Isa 40:11 he gently leads those that have *y*.
Joel 2:28 your *y* men will see visions.
Ac 2:17 your *y* men will see visions,
7:58 at the feet of a *y* man named Saul.
1Ti 4:12 down on you because you are *y*,
Tit 2: 6 encourage the *y* men
1Pe 5: 5 *Y* men, in the same way be
1Jn 2:13 I write to you, *y* men,

YOUNGER (YOUNG)
1Ti 5: 1 Treat *y* men as brothers, older
Tit 2: 4 Then they can train the *y* women

YOUTH (YOUNG)
Ps 103: 5 so that your *y* is renewed like
Ecc 12: 1 Creator in the days of your *y*,
2Ti 2:22 Flee the evil desires of *y*,

ZACCHAEUS
Lk 19: 2 A man was there by the name of *Z*;

ZEAL (ZEALOUS)
Ps 69: 9 for *z* for your house consumes me,
Pr 19: 2 to have *z* without knowledge,
Isa 59:17 and wrapped himself in *z*
Jn 2:17 "*Z* for your house will consume me
Ro 10: 2 their *z* is not based on knowledge.
12:11 Never be lacking in *z*,

ZEALOUS (ZEAL)
Nu 25:13 he was *z* for the honor of his God
Pr 23:17 always be *z* for the fear
Eze 39:25 and I will be *z* for my holy name.
Gal 4:18 fine to be *z*, provided the purpose is

ZEBULUN
Son of Jacob by Leah (Ge 30:20; 35:23; 1Ch 2: 1). Tribe of blessed (Ge 49:13; Dt 33:18-19), numbered (Nu 1:31; 26:27), allotted land (Jos 19:10-16; Eze 48:26), failed to fully possess (Jdg 1:30), supported Deborah (Jdg 4:6-10; 5:14, 18), David (1Ch 12:33), 12,000 from (Rev 7:8).

ZECHARIAH
1. Son of Jeroboam II; king of Israel (2Ki 15: 8-12).
2. Post-exilic prophet who encouraged rebuilding of temple (Ezr 5:1; 6:14; Zec 1:1).

ZEDEKIAH
1. False prophet (1Ki 22:11-24; 2Ch 18:10-23).
2. Mattaniah, son of Josiah (1Ch 3:15), made king of Judah by Nebuchadnezzar (2Ki 24:17-25:7; 2Ch 36:10-14; Jer 37-39; 52:1-11).

ZEPHANIAH
Prophet; descendant of Hezekiah (Zep 1:1).

ZERUBBABEL
Descendant of David (1Ch 3:19; Mt 1:3). Led return from exile (Ezr 2:2; Ne 7:7). Governor of Israel; helped rebuild altar and temple (Ezr 3; Hag 1-2; Zec 4).

ZILPAH
Servant of Leah, mother of Jacob's sons Gad and Asher (Ge 30:9-12; 35:26, 46:16-18).

ZIMRI
King of Israel (1Ki 16:9-20).

ZION
2Sa 5: 7 David captured the fortress of *Z*,
Ps 2: 6 King on *Z*, my holy hill."
9:11 to the LORD, enthroned in *Z*;
74: 2 Mount *Z*, where you dwelt.
87: 2 the LORD loves the gates of *Z*
102: 13 and have compassion on *Z*,
Ps 137: 3 "Sing us one of the songs of *Z*!"
Isa 2: 3 The law will go out from *Z*,
28:16 "See, I lay a stone in *Z*,
51:11 They will enter *Z* with singing;
52: 8 When the LORD returns to *Z*,
Jer 50: 5 They will ask the way to *Z*
Joel 3:21 The LORD dwells in *Z*!
Am 6: 1 to you who are complacent in *Z*,
Mic 4: 2 The law will go out from *Z*,
Zec 9: 9 Rejoice greatly, O Daughter of *Z*!
Ro 9:33 I lay in *Z* a stone that causes men
11:26 "The deliverer will come from *Z*;
Heb 12:22 But you have come to Mount *Z*,
Rev 14: 1 standing on Mount *Z*,

ZIPPORAH*
Daughter of Reuel; wife of Moses (Ex 2:21-22; 4:20-26; 18:1-6).

ZOPHAR
One of Job's friends (Job 11; 20).

Index to Color Maps

Map 1: **WORLD OF THE PATRIARCHS**

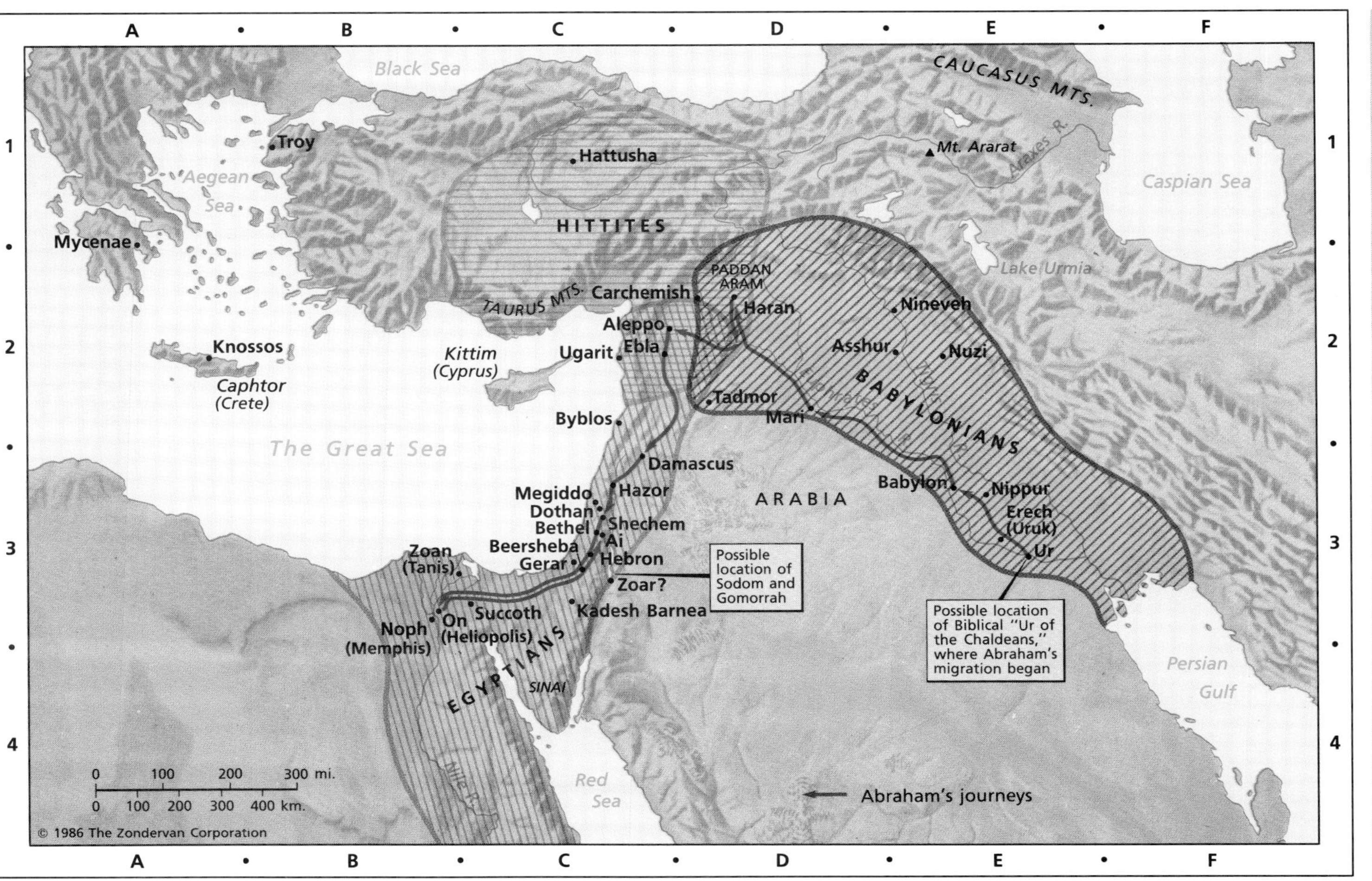

Map 2: PALESTINE AND SINAI

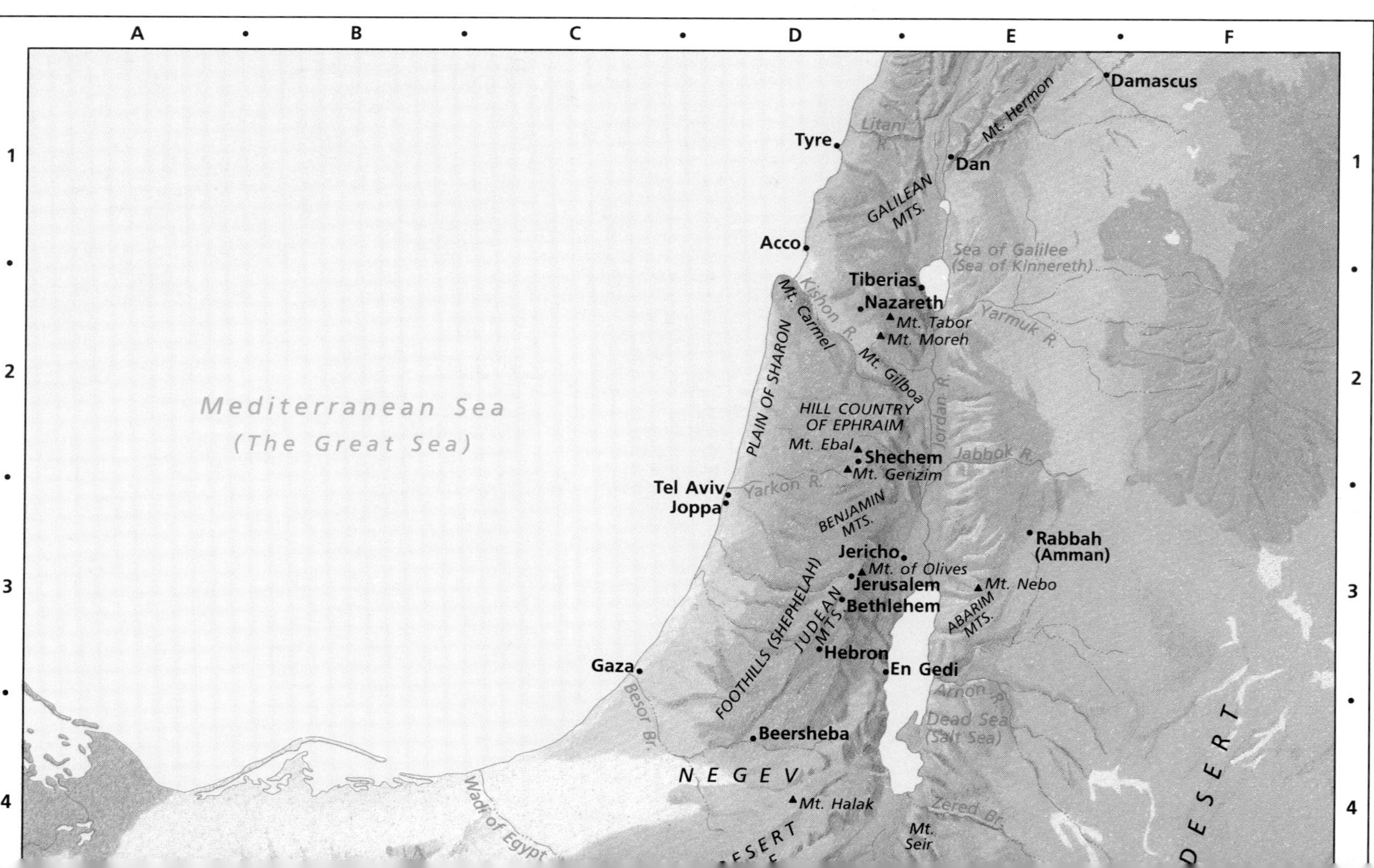

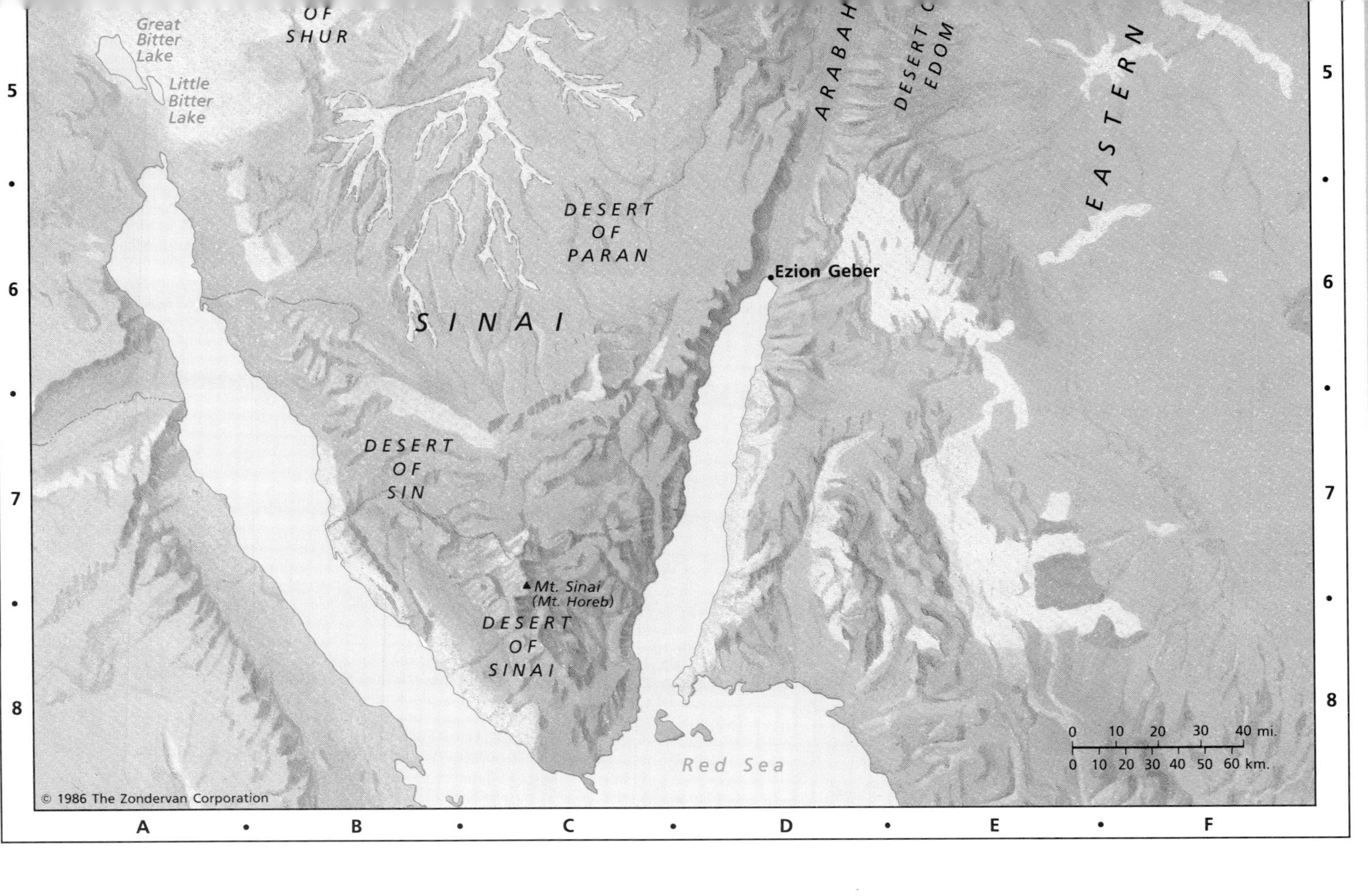

OF SHUR
Great Bitter Lake
Little Bitter Lake
ARABAH
DESERT OF EDOM
EASTERN
DESERT OF PARAN
Ezion Geber
SINAI
DESERT OF SIN
Mt. Sinai (Mt. Horeb)
DESERT OF SINAI
Red Sea
0 10 20 30 40 mi.
0 10 20 30 40 50 60 km.
5
6
7
8
A
B
C
D
E
F

Map 3: EXODUS AND CONQUEST OF CANAAN

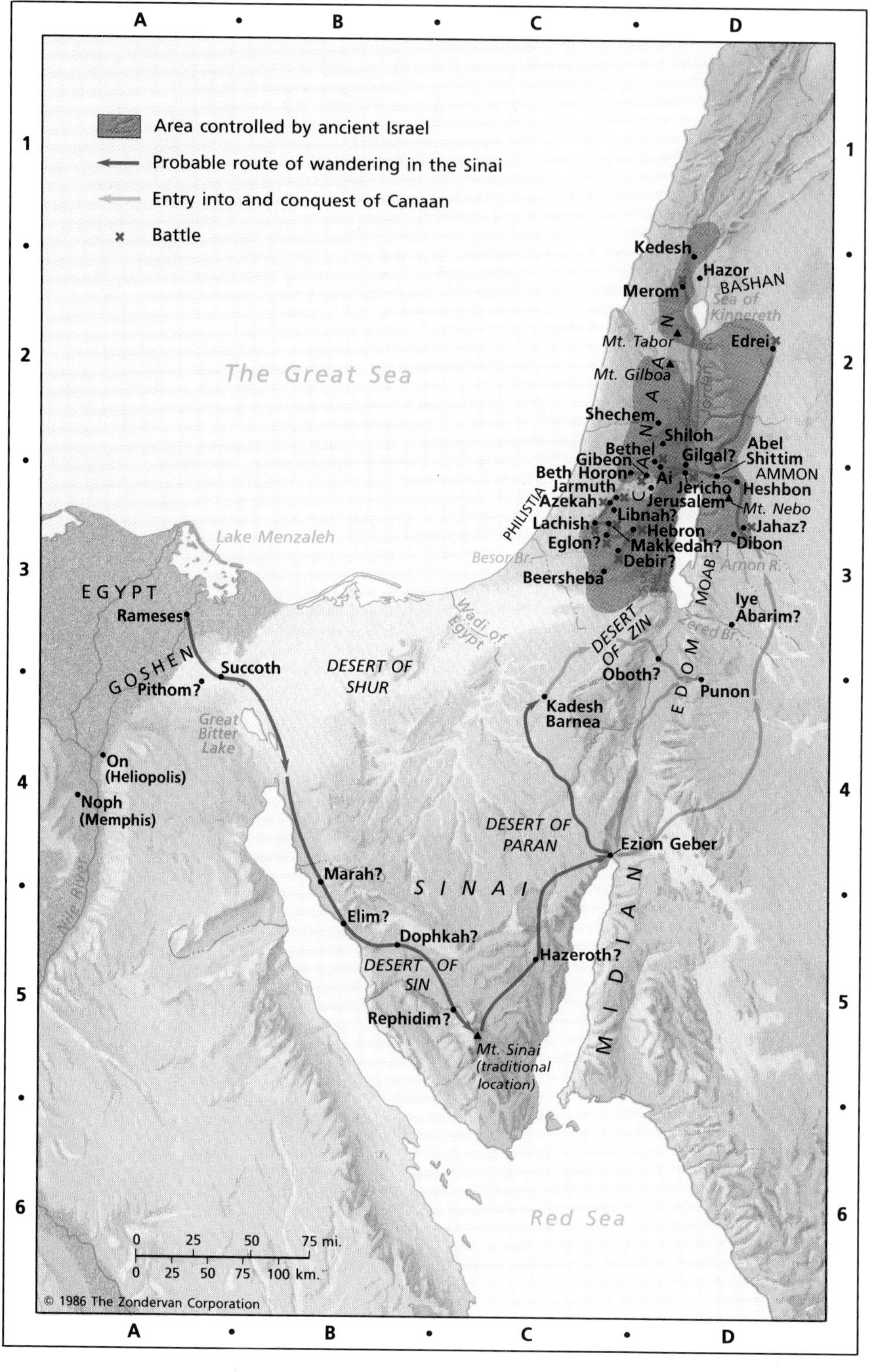
A
B
C
D
1
2
3
4
5
6
Area controlled by ancient Israel
Probable route of wandering in the Sinai
Entry into and conquest of Canaan
Battle
The Great Sea
Kedesh
Hazor
Merom
BASHAN
Sea of Kinnereth
Mt. Tabor
Edrei
Mt. Gilboa
CANAAN
Jordan
Shechem
Shiloh
Bethel
Abel Shittim
Gibeon
Gilgal?
Beth Horon
Ai
AMMON
Jarmuth
Jericho
Heshbon
Azekah
Jerusalem
Mt. Nebo
Libnah?
Jahaz?
PHILISTIA
Lachish
Hebron
Dibon
Eglon?
Makkedah?
Debir?
Arnon R.
Besor Br.
Beersheba
MOAB
Lake Menzaleh
EGYPT
Rameses
Wadi of Egypt
Iye Abarim?
DESERT OF ZIN
Zered Br.
GOSHEN
Succoth
DESERT OF SHUR
Oboth?
EDOM
Pithom?
Punon
Kadesh Barnea
Great Bitter Lake
On (Heliopolis)
Noph (Memphis)
DESERT OF PARAN
Ezion Geber
Marah?
SINAI
Nile River
Elim?
MIDIAN
Dophkah?
Hazeroth?
DESERT OF SIN
Rephidim?
Mt. Sinai (traditional location)
Red Sea
0 25 50 75 mi.
0 25 50 75 100 km.

Map 4: **LAND OF THE TWELVE TRIBES**

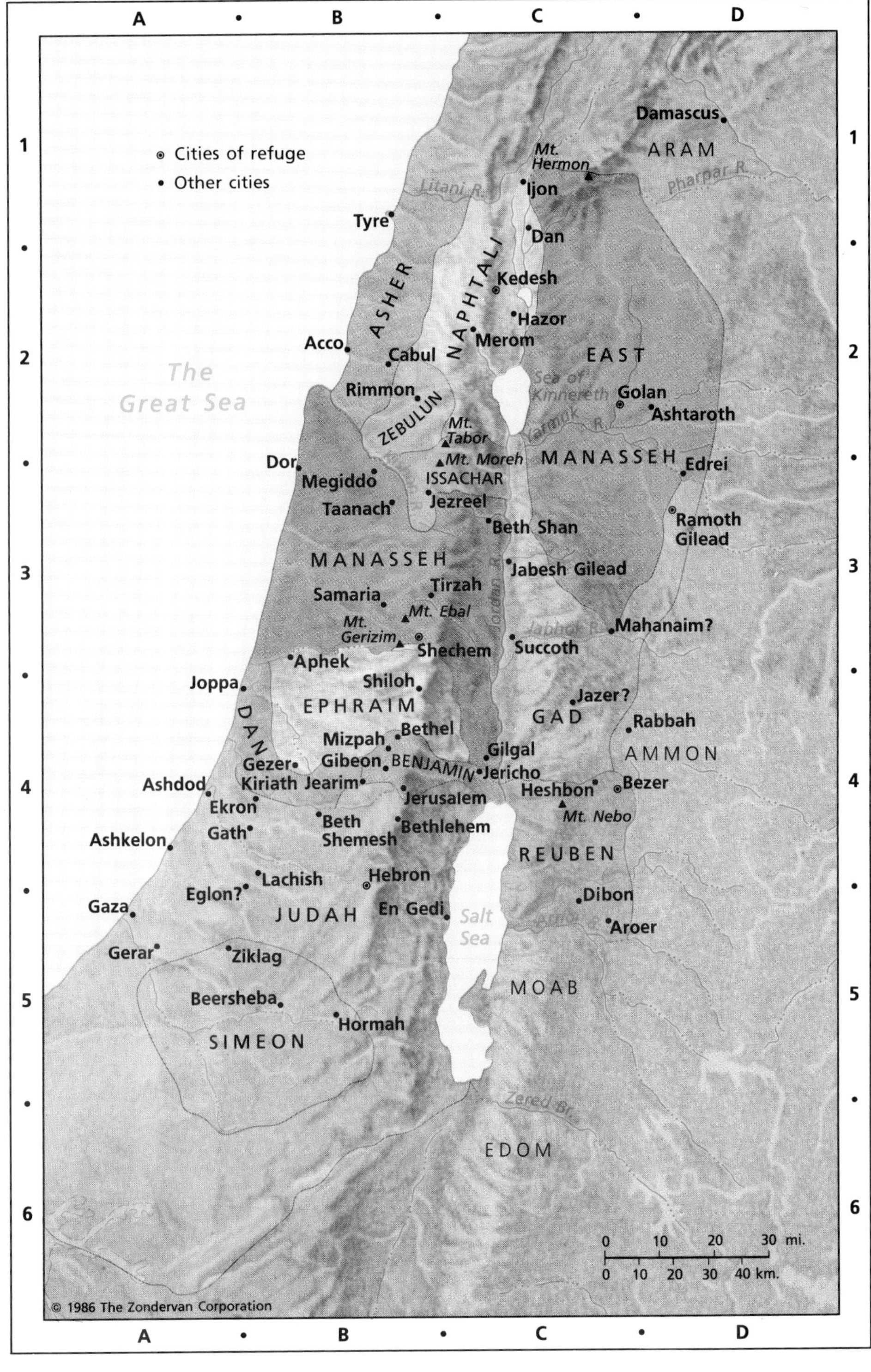
A
B
C
D
1
2
3
4
5
6
Cities of refuge
Other cities
Damascus
ARAM
Mt. Hermon
Pharpar R.
Litani R.
Ijon
Tyre
Dan
ASHER
NAPHTALI
Kedesh
Hazor
Acco
Merom
Cabul
EAST
The Great Sea
Sea of Kinnereth
Golan
Ashtaroth
Rimmon
ZEBULUN
Yarmuk R.
Mt. Tabor
Mt. Moreh
MANASSEH
Edrei
Dor
Megiddo
ISSACHAR
Jezreel
Taanach
Beth Shan
Ramoth Gilead
MANASSEH
Jabesh Gilead
Samaria
Tirzah
Mt. Ebal
Jordan R.
Mt. Gerizim
Shechem
Jabbok R.
Mahanaim?
Succoth
Aphek
Joppa
Shiloh
EPHRAIM
Jazer?
GAD
DAN
Rabbah
Mizpah
Bethel
Gilgal
AMMON
Gezer
Gibeon
BENJAMIN
Jericho
Ashdod
Kiriath Jearim
Heshbon
Bezer
Ekron
Jerusalem
Mt. Nebo
Ashkelon
Gath
Beth Shemesh
Bethlehem
REUBEN
Lachish
Hebron
Dibon
Eglon?
Gaza
JUDAH
En Gedi
Salt Sea
Aroer
Gerar
Ziklag
MOAB
Beersheba
Hormah
SIMEON
Zered Br.
EDOM
0 10 20 30 mi.
0 10 20 30 40 km.

Map 5: **KINGDOM OF DAVID AND SOLOMON**

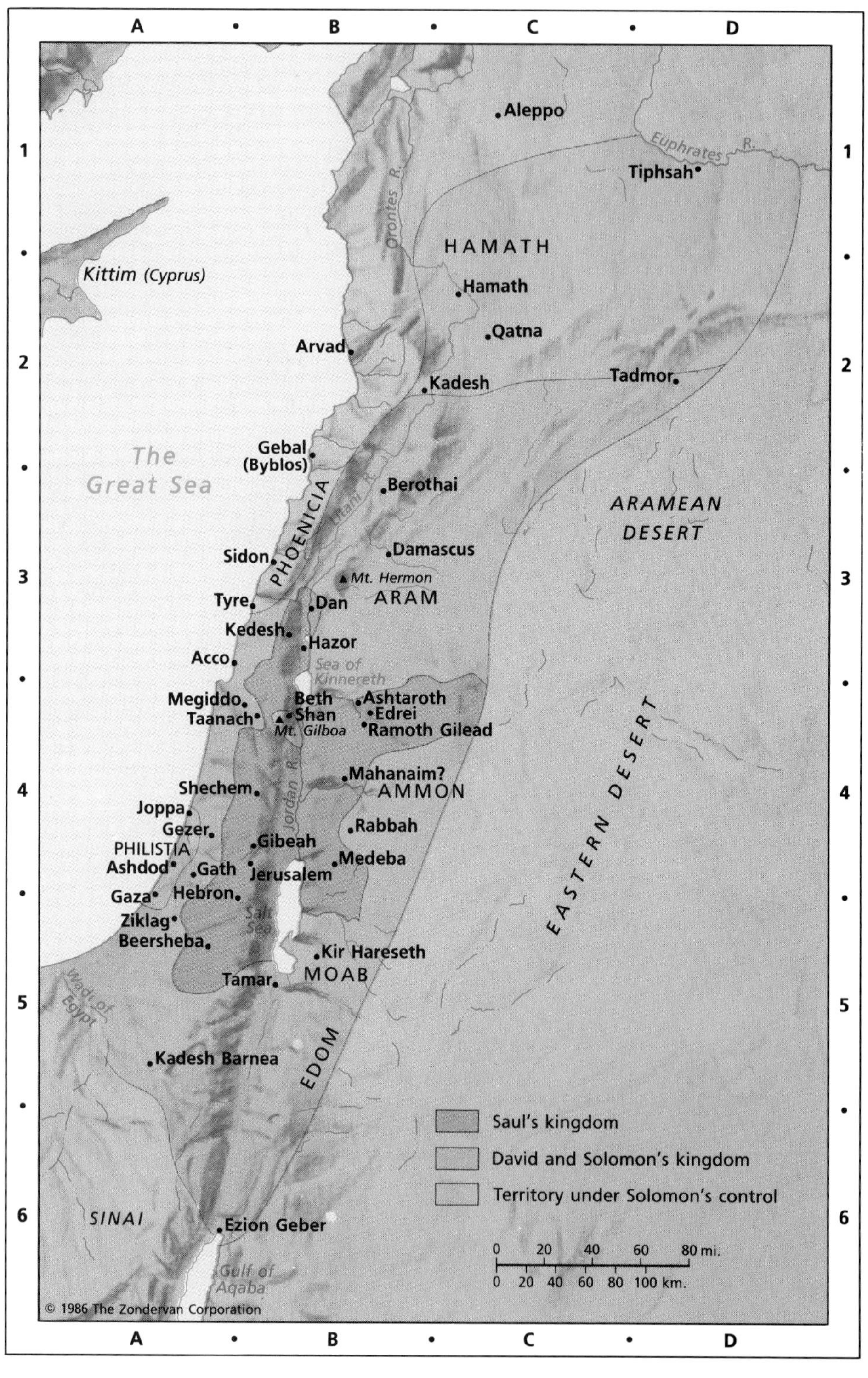

A
B
C
D
1
2
3
4
5
6
Aleppo
Euphrates R.
Tiphsah
Orontes R.
HAMATH
Kittim (Cyprus)
Hamath
Qatna
Arvad
Kadesh
Tadmor
The Great Sea
Gebal (Byblos)
Berothai
PHOENICIA
Litani R.
ARAMEAN DESERT
Sidon
Damascus
Mt. Hermon
Tyre
Dan
ARAM
Kedesh
Hazor
Acco
Sea of Kinnereth
Megiddo
Beth Shan
Ashtaroth
Taanach
Edrei
Mt. Gilboa
Ramoth Gilead
EASTERN DESERT
Jordan R.
Mahanaim?
Shechem
AMMON
Joppa
Gezer
Rabbah
Gibeah
PHILISTIA
Ashdod
Gath
Medeba
Jerusalem
Gaza
Hebron
Salt Sea
Ziklag
Beersheba
Kir Hareseth
MOAB
Tamar
Wadi of Egypt
EDOM
Kadesh Barnea
Saul's kingdom
David and Solomon's kingdom
Territory under Solomon's control
SINAI
Ezion Geber
0 20 40 60 80 mi.
0 20 40 60 80 100 km.
Gulf of Aqaba

Map 6: **PROPHETS IN ISRAEL AND JUDAH**

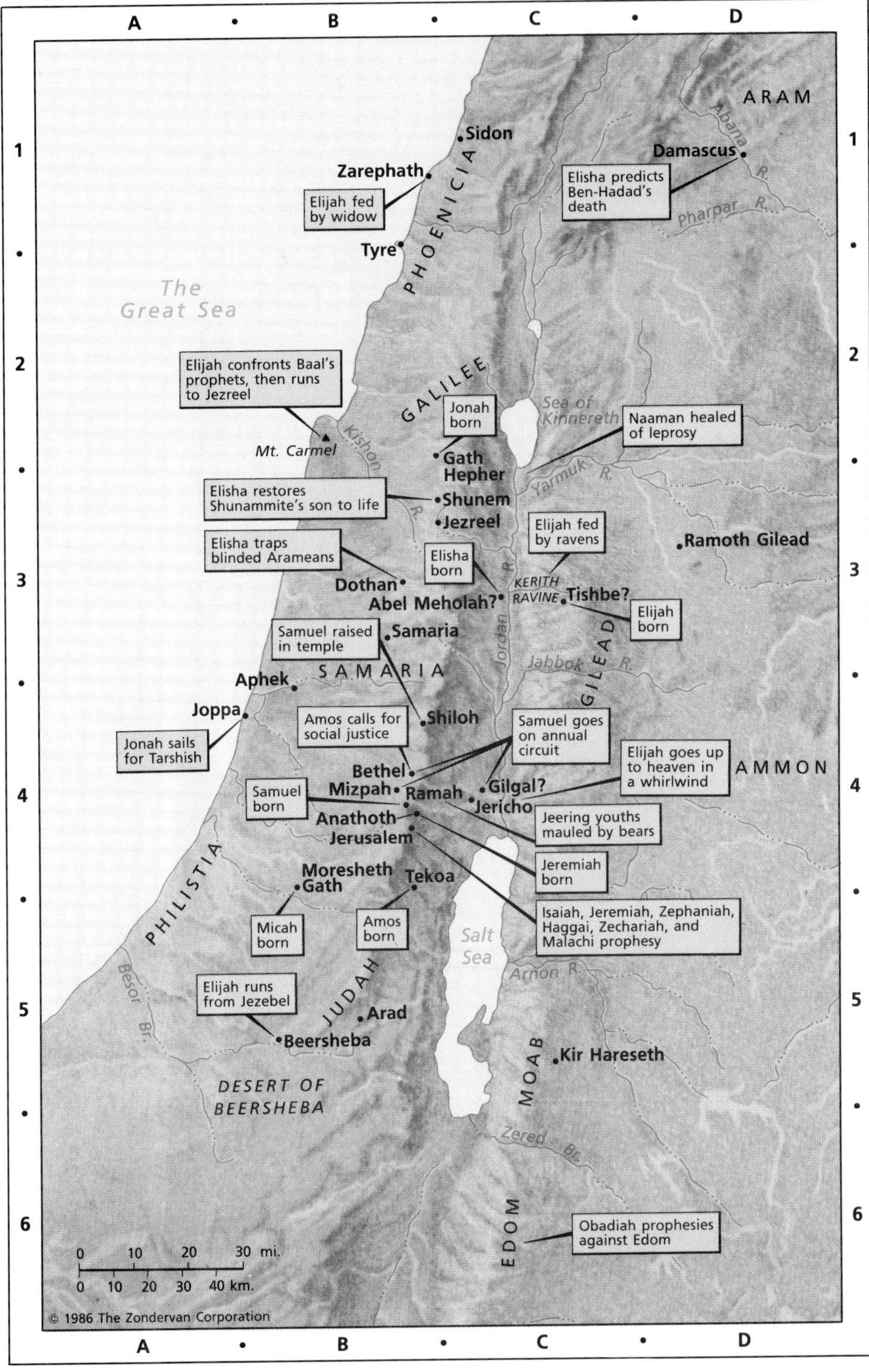

A B C D
1 2 3 4 5 6
ARAM
Abana R.
Pharpar R.
Sidon
Damascus
Zarephath
Elijah fed by widow
Elisha predicts Ben-Hadad's death
PHOENICIA
Tyre
The Great Sea
Elijah confronts Baal's prophets, then runs to Jezreel
GALILEE
Jonah born
Sea of Kinnereth
Naaman healed of leprosy
Mt. Carmel
Kishon R.
Gath Hepher
Yarmuk R.
Elisha restores Shunammite's son to life
Shunem
Jezreel
Elijah fed by ravens
Ramoth Gilead
Elisha traps blinded Arameans
Elisha born
Dothan
KERITH RAVINE
Tishbe?
Abel Meholah?
Elijah born
Samuel raised in temple
Samaria
Jordan R.
GILEAD
SAMARIA
Jabbok R.
Aphek
Joppa
Amos calls for social justice
Shiloh
Samuel goes on annual circuit
Jonah sails for Tarshish
Elijah goes up to heaven in a whirlwind
AMMON
Bethel
Mizpah
Gilgal?
Samuel born
Ramah
Jericho
Anathoth
Jeering youths mauled by bears
Jerusalem
Jeremiah born
Moresheth Gath
Tekoa
PHILISTIA
Isaiah, Jeremiah, Zephaniah, Haggai, Zechariah, and Malachi prophesy
Micah born
Amos born
Salt Sea
Arnon R.
Besor Br.
Elijah runs from Jezebel
JUDAH
Arad
Beersheba
MOAB
Kir Hareseth
DESERT OF BEERSHEBA
Zered Br.
EDOM
Obadiah prophesies against Edom
0 10 20 30 mi.
0 10 20 30 40 km.

Map 7: ASSYRIAN AND BABYLONIAN EMPIRES

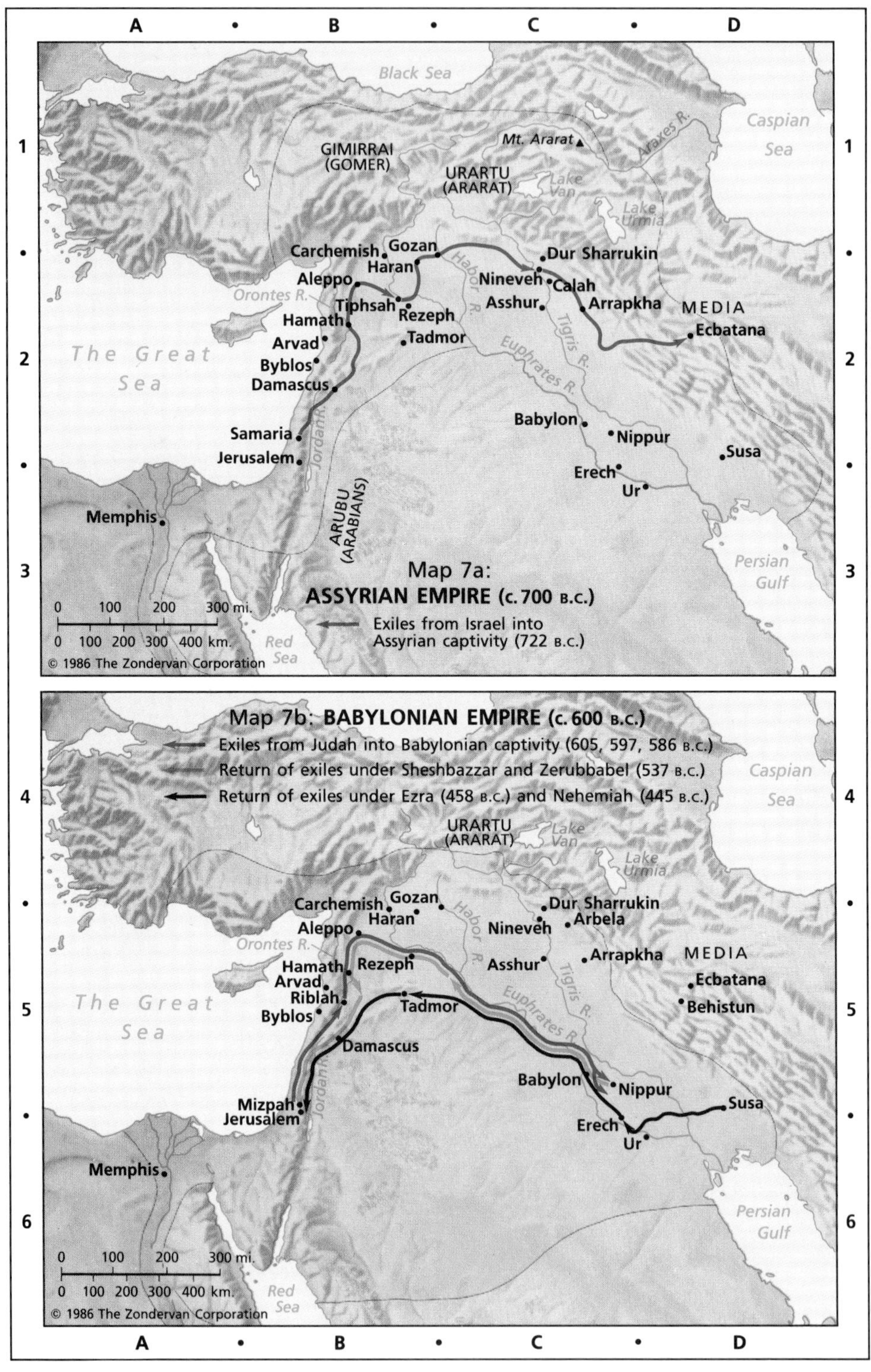

Map 8: **JERUSALEM IN JESUS' TIME**

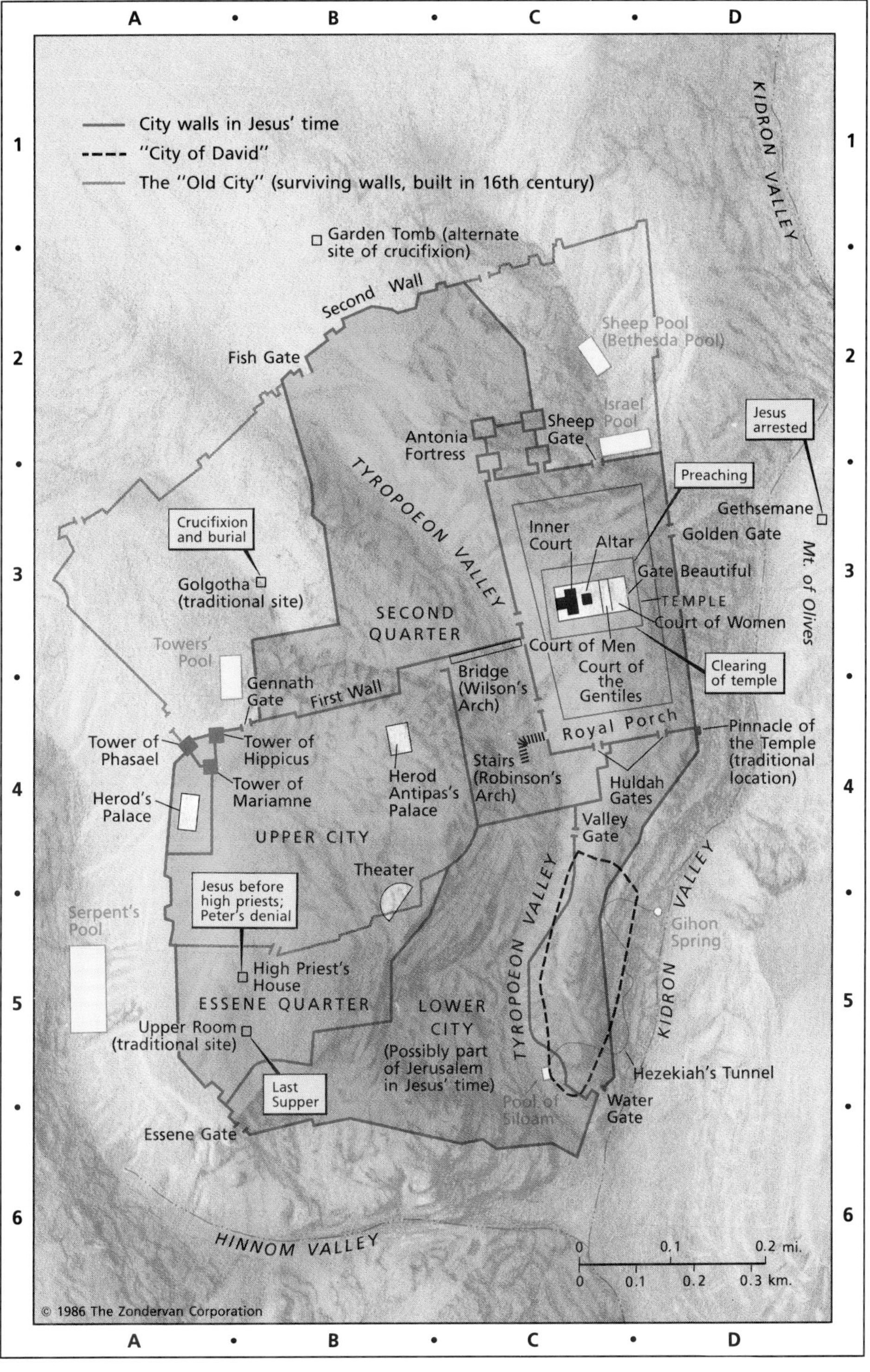

A • B • C • D
City walls in Jesus' time
"City of David"
The "Old City" (surviving walls, built in 16th century)
KIDRON VALLEY
Garden Tomb (alternate site of crucifixion)
Second Wall
Fish Gate
Sheep Pool (Bethesda Pool)
Israel Pool
Antonia Fortress
Sheep Gate
Jesus arrested
Preaching
Gethsemane
TYROPOEON VALLEY
Crucifixion and burial
Inner Court
Altar
Golden Gate
Golgotha (traditional site)
Gate Beautiful
TEMPLE
Mt. of Olives
SECOND QUARTER
Court of Women
Towers' Pool
Court of Men
Court of the Gentiles
Clearing of temple
Gennath Gate
First Wall
Bridge (Wilson's Arch)
Royal Porch
Tower of Phasael
Tower of Hippicus
Pinnacle of the Temple (traditional location)
Tower of Mariamne
Herod Antipas's Palace
Stairs (Robinson's Arch)
Huldah Gates
Herod's Palace
UPPER CITY
Valley Gate
Theater
Jesus before high priests; Peter's denial
Serpent's Pool
Gihon Spring
TYROPOEON VALLEY
KIDRON VALLEY
High Priest's House
ESSENE QUARTER
LOWER CITY
(Possibly part of Jerusalem in Jesus' time)
Upper Room (traditional site)
Last Supper
Hezekiah's Tunnel
Pool of Siloam
Water Gate
Essene Gate
HINNOM VALLEY
0 0.1 0.2 mi.
0 0.1 0.2 0.3 km.
A • B • C • D
1 • 2 • 3 • 4 • 5 • 6

Map 9: **JESUS' MINISTRY**

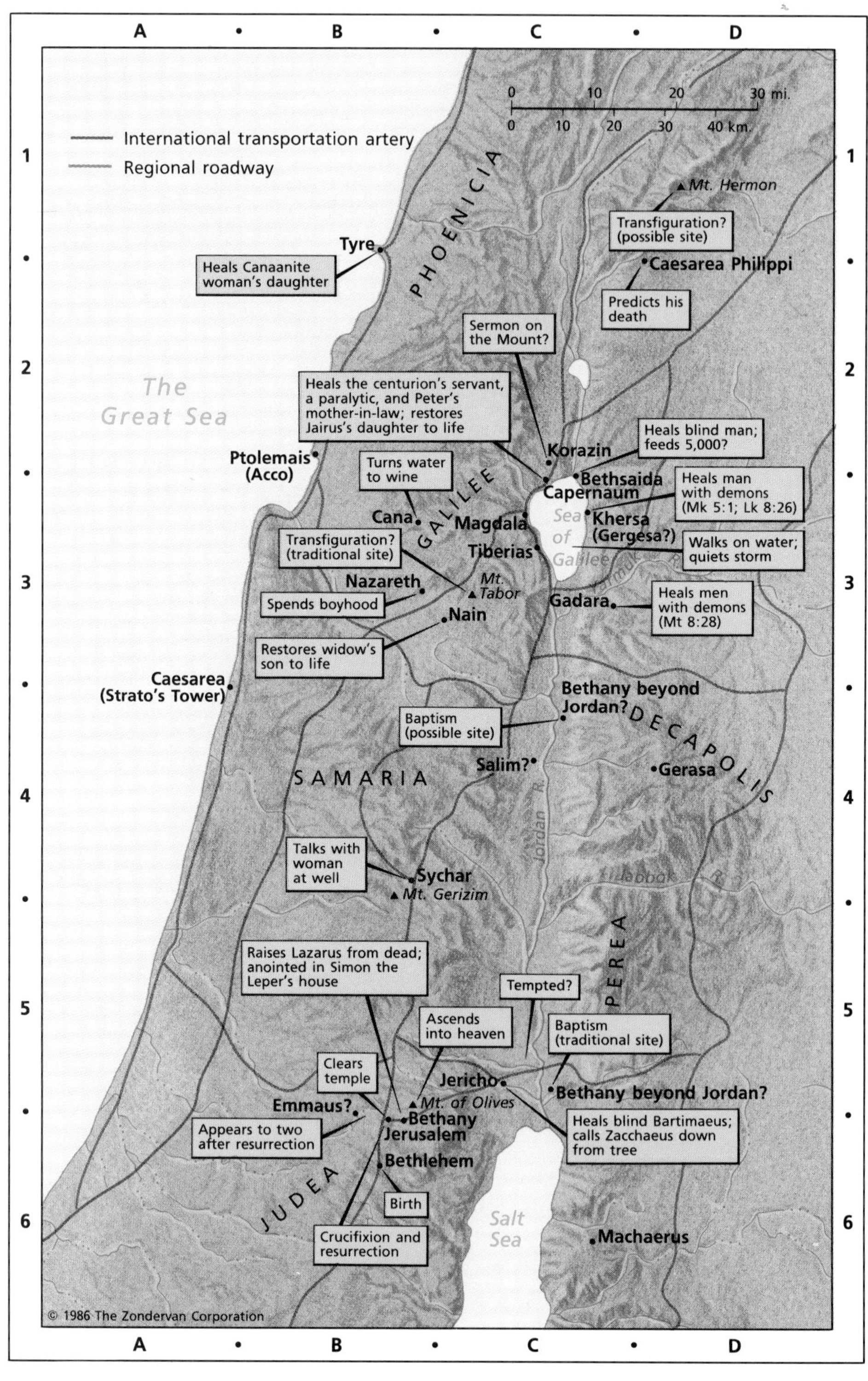

A
B
C
D
1
2
3
4
5
6
0 10 20 30 mi.
0 10 20 30 40 km.
International transportation artery
Regional roadway
PHOENICIA
Mt. Hermon
Transfiguration? (possible site)
Tyre
Heals Canaanite woman's daughter
Caesarea Philippi
Predicts his death
Sermon on the Mount?
The Great Sea
Heals the centurion's servant, a paralytic, and Peter's mother-in-law; restores Jairus's daughter to life
Heals blind man; feeds 5,000?
Korazin
Ptolemais (Acco)
Turns water to wine
GALILEE
Bethsaida
Capernaum
Heals man with demons (Mk 5:1; Lk 8:26)
Cana
Magdala
Sea of Galilee
Khersa (Gergesa?)
Transfiguration? (traditional site)
Tiberias
Walks on water; quiets storm
Yarmuk R.
Nazareth
Mt. Tabor
Gadara
Heals men with demons (Mt 8:28)
Spends boyhood
Nain
Restores widow's son to life
Caesarea (Strato's Tower)
Bethany beyond Jordan?
DECAPOLIS
Baptism (possible site)
Salim?
Gerasa
SAMARIA
Jordan R.
Talks with woman at well
Sychar
Mt. Gerizim
Jabbok R.
PEREA
Raises Lazarus from dead; anointed in Simon the Leper's house
Tempted?
Ascends into heaven
Baptism (traditional site)
Clears temple
Jericho
Bethany beyond Jordan?
Emmaus?
Mt. of Olives
Bethany
Jerusalem
Appears to two after resurrection
Heals blind Bartimaeus; calls Zacchaeus down from tree
Bethlehem
JUDEA
Birth
Salt Sea
Machaerus
Crucifixion and resurrection

Map 10: APOSTLES' EARLY TRAVELS

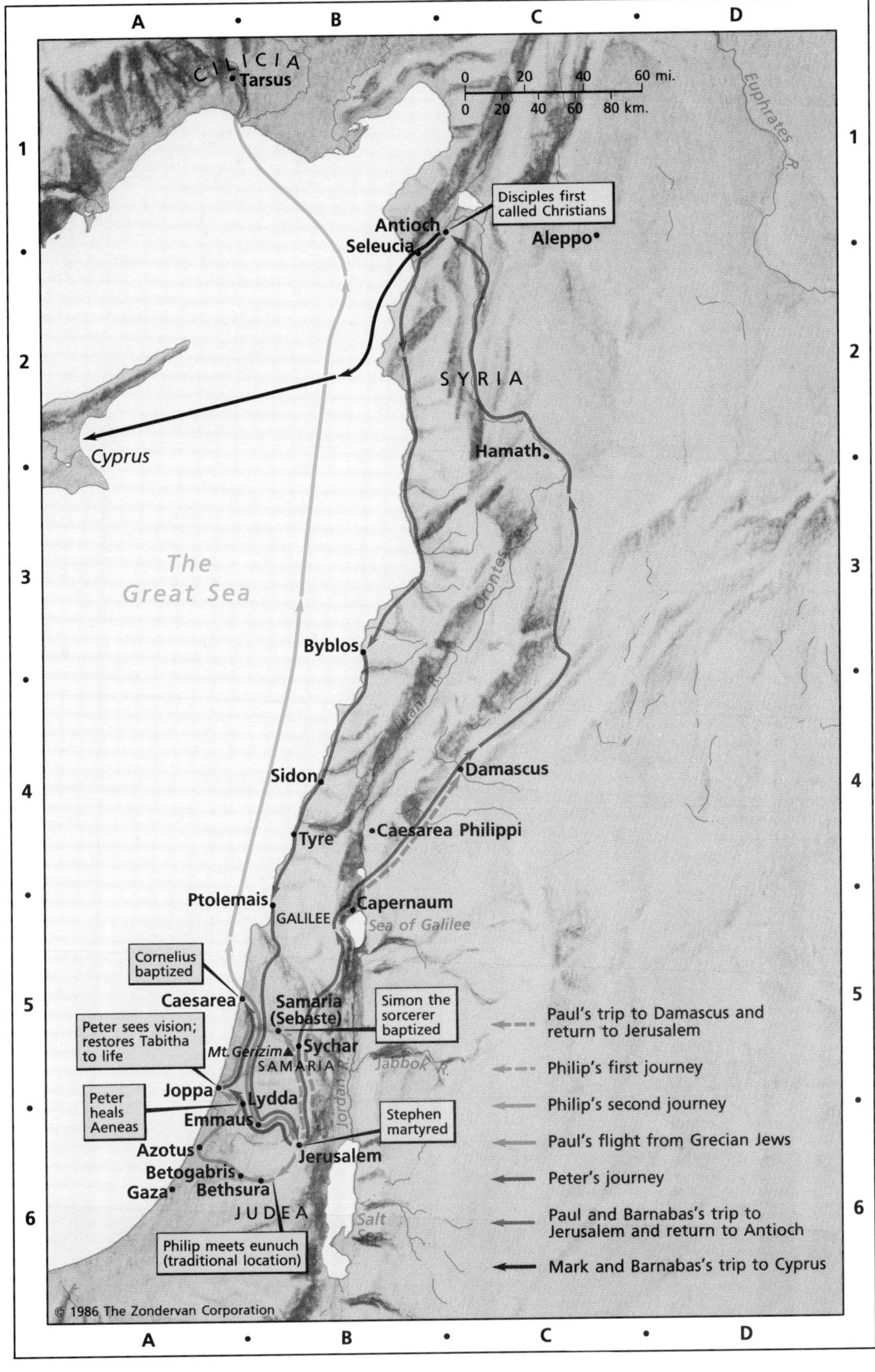

A
B
C
D
1
2
3
4
5
6
CILICIA
Tarsus
0 20 40 60 mi.
0 20 40 60 80 km.
Euphrates R.
Disciples first called Christians
Antioch
Seleucia
Aleppo
SYRIA
Cyprus
Hamath
The Great Sea
Orontes
Byblos
Sidon
Damascus
Tyre
Caesarea Philippi
Ptolemais
Capernaum
GALILEE
Sea of Galilee
Cornelius baptized
Caesarea
Samaria (Sebaste)
Simon the sorcerer baptized
Peter sees vision; restores Tabitha to life
Mt. Gerizim
Sychar
SAMARIA
Jabbok R.
Joppa
Lydda
Peter heals Aeneas
Emmaus
Jordan
Stephen martyred
Azotus
Jerusalem
Betogabris
Gaza
Bethsura
JUDEA
Salt Sea
Philip meets eunuch (traditional location)
Paul's trip to Damascus and return to Jerusalem
Philip's first journey
Philip's second journey
Paul's flight from Grecian Jews
Peter's journey
Paul and Barnabas's trip to Jerusalem and return to Antioch
Mark and Barnabas's trip to Cyprus

Map 11: **PAUL'S MISSIONARY JOURNEYS**

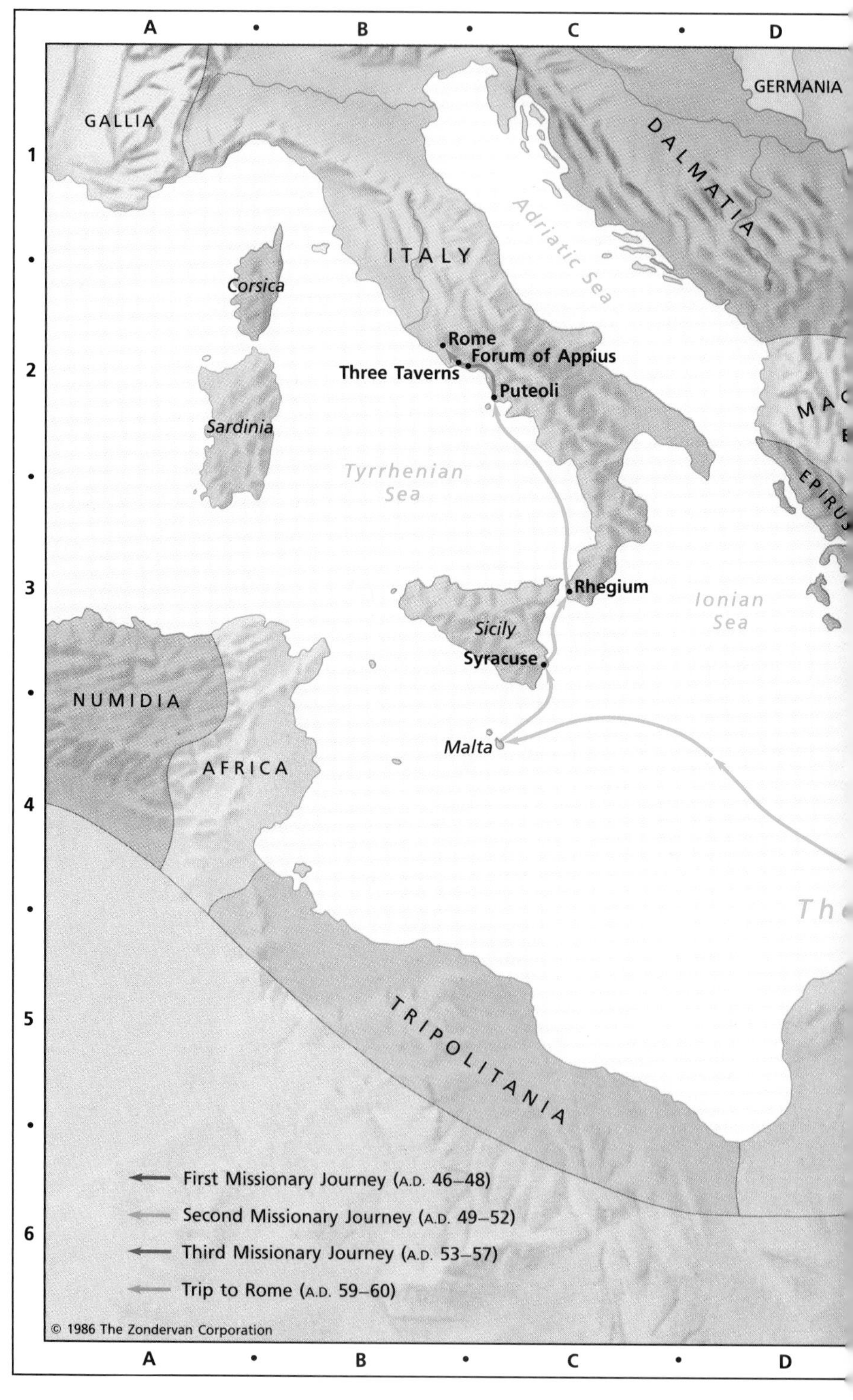

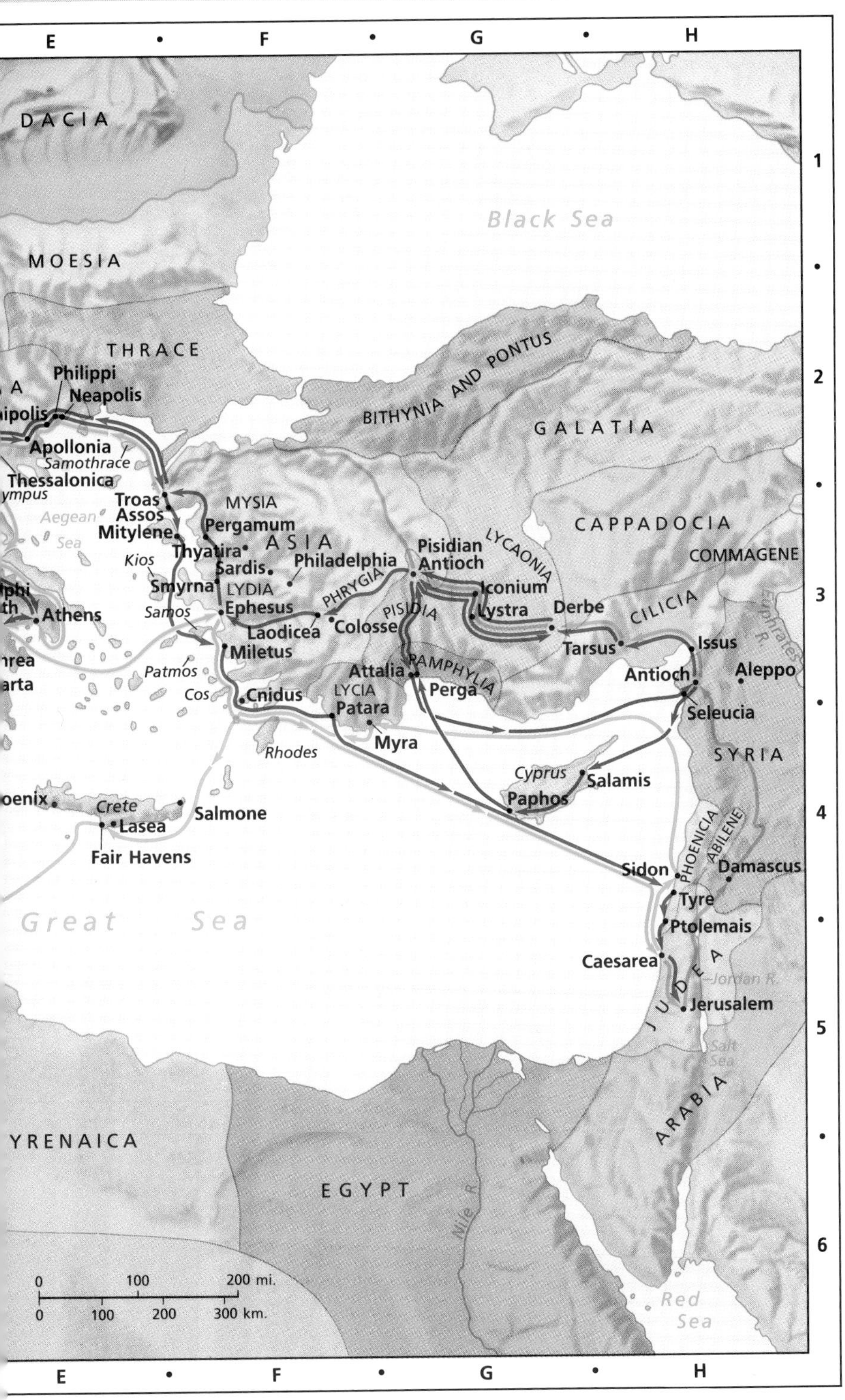
E
F
G
H
1
2
3
4
5
6
DACIA
MOESIA
Black Sea
THRACE
Philippi
Neapolis
Apollonia
Samothrace
Thessalonica
BITHYNIA AND PONTUS
GALATIA
MYSIA
Troas
Assos
Aegean
Sea
Mitylene
Pergamum
ASIA
Thyatira
Sardis
Philadelphia
Kios
Smyrna
LYDIA
Athens
Samos
Ephesus
PHRYGIA
Laodicea
Colosse
Miletus
Patmos
Cos
Cnidus
LYCIA
Patara
Myra
Rhodes
Pisidian
Antioch
LYCAONIA
Iconium
Lystra
Derbe
PISIDIA
PAMPHYLIA
Attalia
Perga
CAPPADOCIA
COMMAGENE
CILICIA
Tarsus
Issus
Euphrates R.
Antioch
Aleppo
Seleucia
SYRIA
Cyprus
Salamis
Paphos
Crete
Lasea
Salmone
Fair Havens
PHOENICIA
ABILENE
Sidon
Damascus
Tyre
Ptolemais
Caesarea
JUDEA
Jordan R.
Jerusalem
Salt
Sea
Great
Sea
ARABIA
EGYPT
Nile R.
Red
Sea
0
100
200 mi.
0
100
200
300 km.

Map 12: THE WORLD TODAY

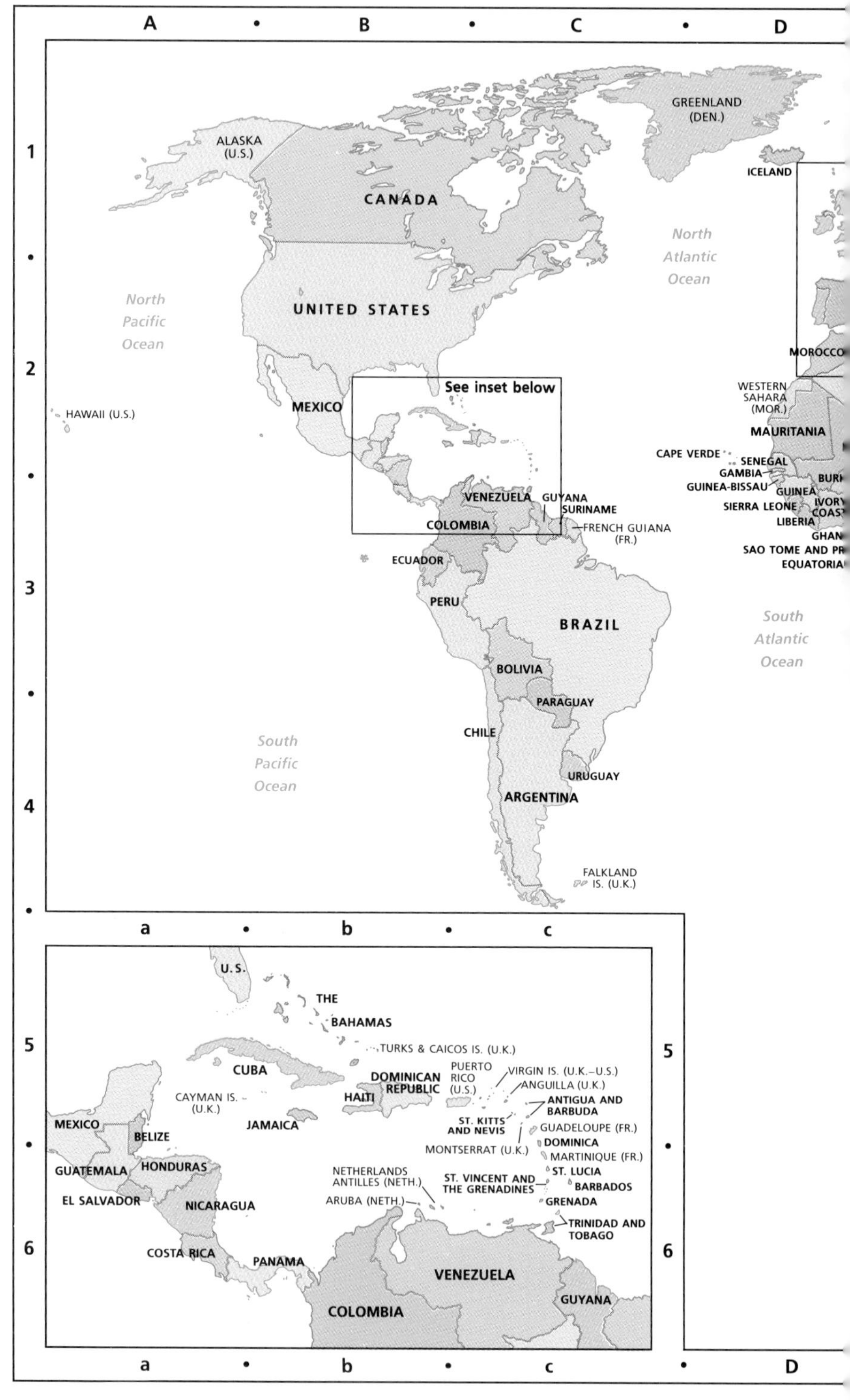
A
B
C
D
1
2
3
4
5
6
a
b
c
GREENLAND
(DEN.)
ALASKA
(U.S.)
ICELAND
CANADA
North
Atlantic
Ocean
North
Pacific
Ocean
UNITED STATES
MOROCCO
See inset below
WESTERN
SAHARA
(MOR.)
HAWAII (U.S.)
MEXICO
MAURITANIA
CAPE VERDE
SENEGAL
GAMBIA
GUINEA-BISSAU
GUINEA
SIERRA LEONE
LIBERIA
VENEZUELA
GUYANA
SURINAME
COLOMBIA
FRENCH GUIANA
(FR.)
SAO TOME AND PR
EQUATORIA
ECUADOR
PERU
BRAZIL
South
Atlantic
Ocean
BOLIVIA
PARAGUAY
CHILE
South
Pacific
Ocean
URUGUAY
ARGENTINA
FALKLAND
IS. (U.K.)
U.S.
THE
BAHAMAS
TURKS & CAICOS IS. (U.K.)
CUBA
DOMINICAN
REPUBLIC
PUERTO
RICO
(U.S.)
VIRGIN IS. (U.K.–U.S.)
ANGUILLA (U.K.)
HAITI
CAYMAN IS.
(U.K.)
ANTIGUA AND
BARBUDA
ST. KITTS
AND NEVIS
JAMAICA
GUADELOUPE (FR.)
MEXICO
BELIZE
DOMINICA
MONTSERRAT (U.K.)
MARTINIQUE (FR.)
GUATEMALA
HONDURAS
NETHERLANDS
ANTILLES (NETH.)
ST. LUCIA
ST. VINCENT AND
THE GRENADINES
BARBADOS
EL SALVADOR
NICARAGUA
ARUBA (NETH.)
GRENADA
TRINIDAD AND
TOBAGO
COSTA RICA
PANAMA
VENEZUELA
GUYANA
COLOMBIA

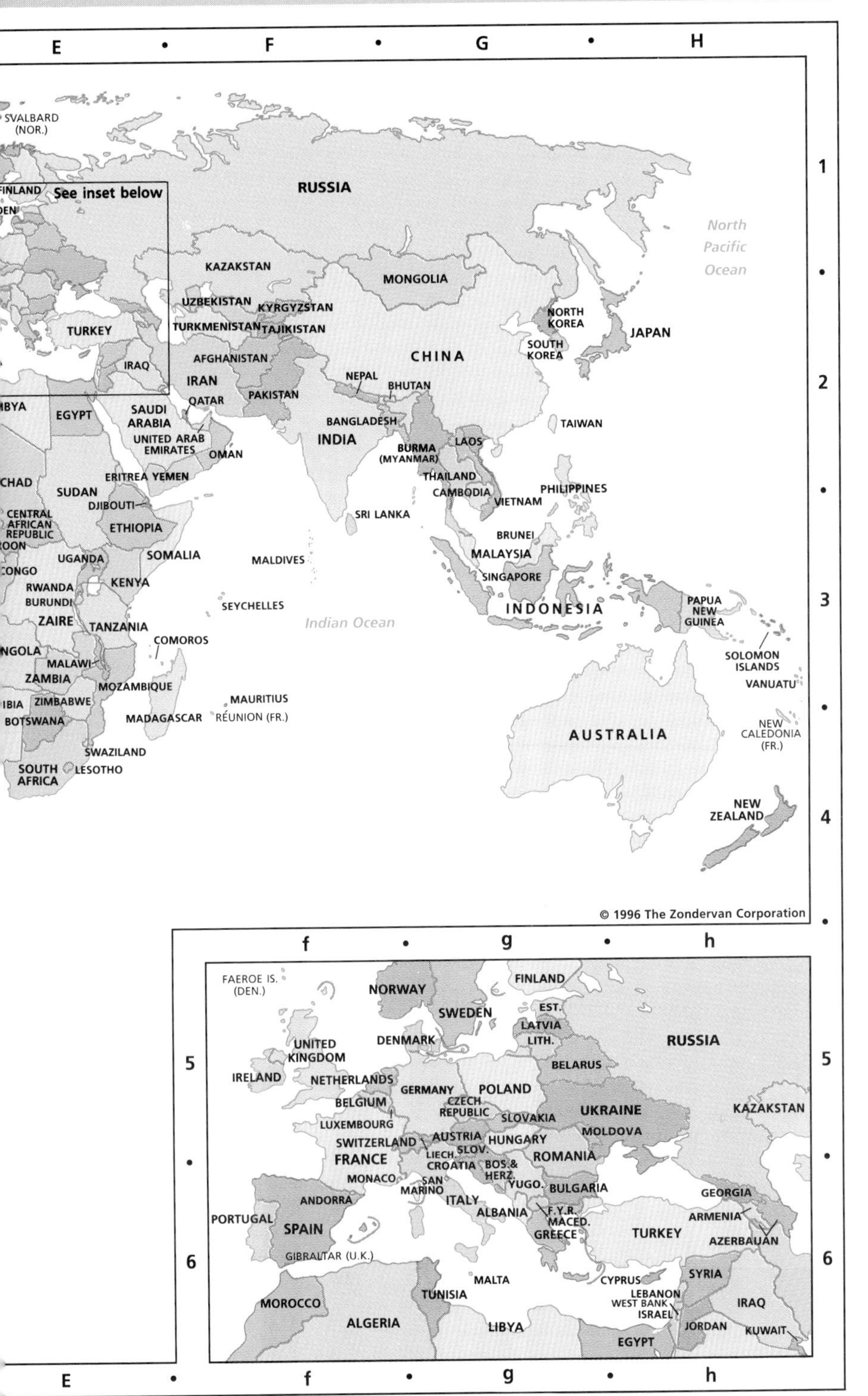

E
F
G
H
1
2
3
4
5
6
SVALBARD (NOR.)
FINLAND
See inset below
RUSSIA
North Pacific Ocean
KAZAKSTAN
MONGOLIA
UZBEKISTAN
KYRGYZSTAN
TURKMENISTAN
TAJIKISTAN
TURKEY
NORTH KOREA
JAPAN
SOUTH KOREA
AFGHANISTAN
CHINA
IRAQ
IRAN
NEPAL
BHUTAN
QATAR
PAKISTAN
EGYPT
SAUDI ARABIA
BANGLADESH
TAIWAN
UNITED ARAB EMIRATES
INDIA
LAOS
OMAN
BURMA (MYANMAR)
CHAD
ERITREA
YEMEN
THAILAND
SUDAN
CAMBODIA
PHILIPPINES
DJIBOUTI
VIETNAM
CENTRAL AFRICAN REPUBLIC
ETHIOPIA
SRI LANKA
BRUNEI
SOMALIA
MALAYSIA
UGANDA
MALDIVES
KENYA
SINGAPORE
RWANDA
BURUNDI
SEYCHELLES
INDONESIA
PAPUA NEW GUINEA
ZAIRE
TANZANIA
Indian Ocean
COMOROS
MALAWI
SOLOMON ISLANDS
ZAMBIA
VANUATU
MOZAMBIQUE
ZIMBABWE
MAURITIUS
BOTSWANA
MADAGASCAR
RÉUNION (FR.)
NEW CALEDONIA (FR.)
AUSTRALIA
SWAZILAND
SOUTH AFRICA
LESOTHO
NEW ZEALAND
f
g
h
FAEROE IS. (DEN.)
NORWAY
FINLAND
SWEDEN
EST.
LATVIA
DENMARK
LITH.
UNITED KINGDOM
RUSSIA
IRELAND
BELARUS
NETHERLANDS
GERMANY
POLAND
BELGIUM
CZECH REPUBLIC
UKRAINE
KAZAKSTAN
LUXEMBOURG
SLOVAKIA
MOLDOVA
AUSTRIA
SWITZERLAND
HUNGARY
SLOV.
LIECH.
ROMANIA
FRANCE
CROATIA
BOS.& HERZ.
MONACO
SAN MARINO
YUGO.
BULGARIA
GEORGIA
ANDORRA
ITALY
ALBANIA
F.Y.R. MACED.
ARMENIA
PORTUGAL
SPAIN
TURKEY
GREECE
AZERBAIJAN
GIBRALTAR (U.K.)
SYRIA
MALTA
CYPRUS
TUNISIA
LEBANON
WEST BANK
IRAQ
MOROCCO
ISRAEL
ALGERIA
LIBYA
JORDAN
KUWAIT
EGYPT

Map 13: **ROMAN EMPIRE**

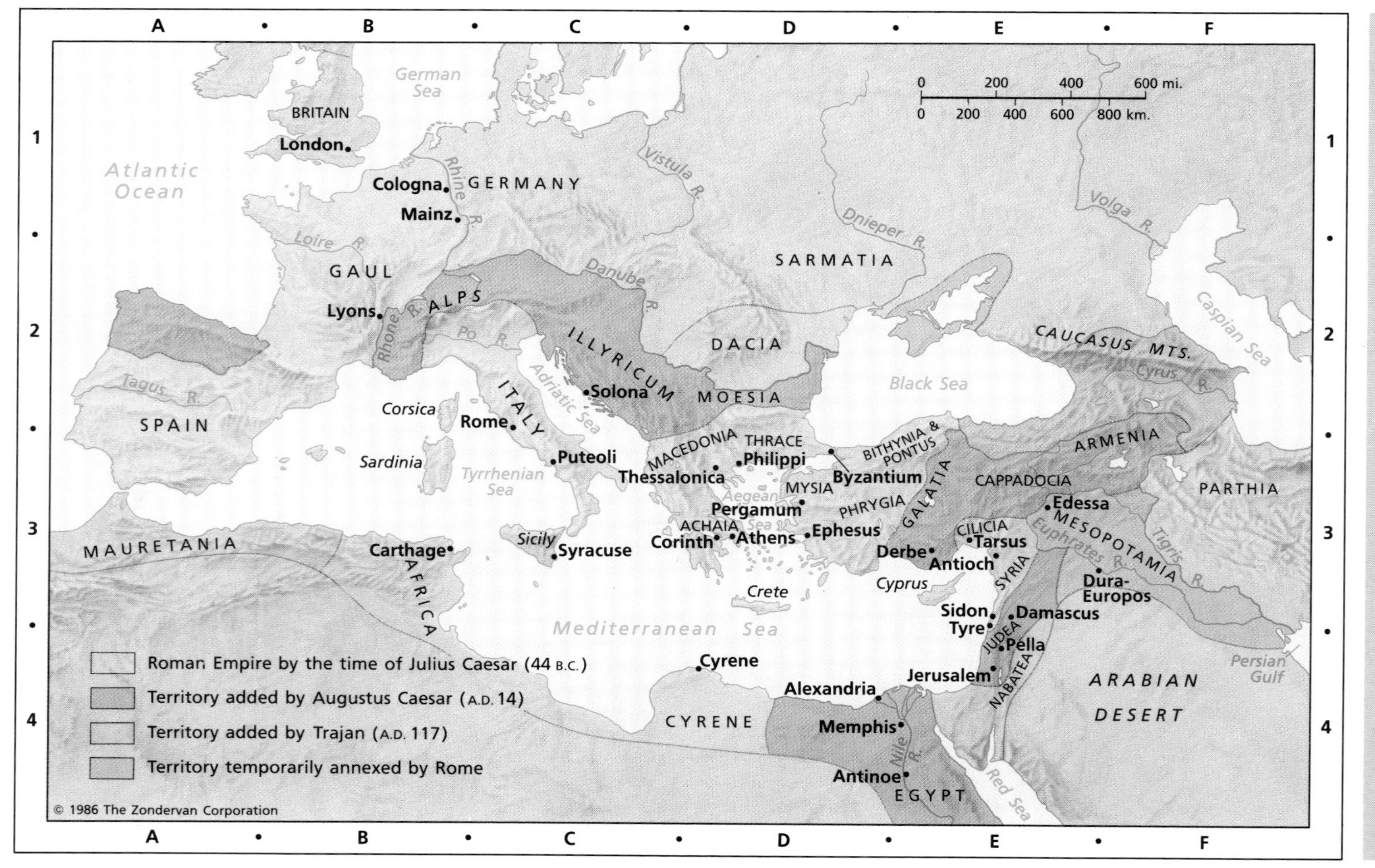